English Clergy Association

Founded 1938

www.clergyassoc.co.uk

Patron: The Rt. Rev'd & Rt. Hon. Sarah Mullally DBE, Bishop of London;
President: Professor Sir Anthony Milnes Coates, Bt., B.Sc., M.D,. F.R.C.P.
Parliamentary Vice-President: The Rt. Hon. The Lord Cormack, F.S.A.
Chairman: Dr. Peter M. Smith, LLB., Ph.D., F.R.Hist.S.

The Association seeks to be a Church of England mutual resource and support for clergy (with Freehold or on Common Tenure) patrons and churchwardens requiring information or insight.

It publishes a magazine; Parson & Parish that is free to memebers. Membership is equally open to men and women; clergy and laity.

The Association administers a charitable *Benefit Fund* that is available to provide holiday grants for clergy (Registered Charity No. 258559). **Donations, legacies, etc. to support the charitable work of the Association are very much appreciated.**

Membership enquiries
to the Revd. Mark Binney
Reverend-mark-binney@hotmail.co.uk

For information concerning the holiday benefit fund
please contact the Revd. Richard Hall
revrichardhall45@gmail.com or at
45 Howard Park, Greystoke CA11 0TU

If you are considering a donation or legacy
please contact the
Revd. Canon Peter Johnson
petrd867@gmail.com or at
4 St John's Road, Windsor, SL4 3QN.

ix

Could you be their Chaplain?

As an RAF chaplain you'll be involved in the lives of our personnel, regardless of their rank or religious background. Your personal sacrifice may be considerable as you'll serve with our people wherever they go, providing vital spiritual, pastoral and ethical support in places of conflict, including on the front-line. Your home-based duties will be equally important, in support of personnel and their families.

A whole new congregation awaits you.

Contact the Branch Recruiting Officer now:
philip.wilson126@mod.gov.uk

The Royal Air Force values every individual's unique contribution, irrespective of race, ethnic origin, religion, gender, sexual orientation or social background.

CROCKFORD'S
CLERICAL DIRECTORY

2020–2021

CROCKFORD'S
CLERICAL DIRECTORY
106TH EDITION

2020–2021

A directory of the clergy
of the Church of England
the Church of Wales
the Scottish Episcopal Church
the Church of Ireland

SINCE 1858

CHURCH HOUSE
PUBLISHING

Crockford's Clerical Directory published December 2019 for The Archbishops' Council by:

Church House Publishing
Church House
Great Smith Street
London SW1P 3AZ

106th edition (2020–2021) © The Archbishops' Council 2019.

Please send any corrections to the Compiler, Crockford (address as above), Tel (020) 7898 1012
E-mail crockford@churchofengland.org

ISBN   978 0 7151 1056 7

Jacket and cover design by Aubrey Design

Typeset by	Printed and bound by
RefineCatch Ltd,	CPI Group (UK) Ltd,
Bungay, Suffolk	Croydon, CR0 4YY

Contents

INTRODUCTION

This, the one hundred and sixth edition of *Crockford's Clerical Directory*, provides details as at 14 August 2019 of all Anglican clergy and deaconesses in the British Isles and overseas who have given their consent under the General Data Protection Regulation (GDPR), including those Michaelmas ordinands of whom we have received advance notice.

First published in 1858, the publication of *Crockford* now spans over one-and-a-half centuries. The Oxford University Press purchased the copyright for *Crockford* in 1921, publishing thirty-six editions before transferring ownership to the Church Commissioners and the Central Board of Finance, on economic grounds, sixty years later. This is the ninth edition under the sole ownership of the Archbishops' Council.

The publishing, design, advertising, selling and distribution of the directory are carried out by Church House Publishing in partnership with the *Crockford* Department, who are responsible for maintaining the data published here and *via* the *Crockford* on-line subscription service (www.crockford.org.uk), first launched in 2004. The information that generates the biographical entries is stored on a database, which is updated daily. The website is also updated after each working day. Much of the information is obtained indirectly from the Church Commissioners' central clergy pay-roll. However, about one-third of the clergy are not on the central pay-roll. These are principally non-stipendiary ministers, those engaged in some form of ministry outside the parochial system (such as hospital, university, prison or service chaplains) and those serving in Wales, Scotland and Ireland. In maintaining the records of these clergy, we continue to rely greatly on the assistance of bishops' secretaries and diocesan offices, and information contained in diocesan directories, year books and the Church Press. We are also grateful for the help provided by the central authorities of the Church in Wales, the Scottish Episcopal Church, the Church of Ireland, the Ministry of Defence, the Hospital Chaplaincies Council, and our various overseas contacts.

A tremendous amount of help has come from the clergy themselves. This is the first print edition of *Crockford* to appear since the introduction of GDPR in 2018, and we have so far received notification from well over 22,000 clergy of their data permissions and preferences. We are grateful for the very high level of response we have seen, and would encourage any clergy who have not been in touch with us since May 2018 to update their data permissions to do so. Full details of our privacy policy can be found via www.crockford.org.uk/privacy.

We are enormously grateful to all those who have provided us with information, and have helped to minimize omissions and errors. We are also grateful to Richard Christmas, Angela Florence, Abigail Clausen, Mark Walsh and James Newhook, who have been responsible for most of the work in compiling this directory.

We are always glad to be informed of amendments to entries, and we particularly appreciate any information about clergy whose addresses are not currently known to us (see list on p. 1168 Information relating to omissions or amendments should be sent to the *Crockford* Department; requests for archival information from earlier editions should be addressed in writing to Lambeth Palace Library; for other information, please consult the Church of England's website at www.churchofengland.org.

Crockford Department
Church House
Great Smith Street
London SW1P 3AZ

The Librarian
Lambeth Palace Library
Lambeth Palace
London SE1 7JU

Telephone (020) 7898 1012
E-mail: crockford@churchofengland.org

Telephone (020) 7898 1400
E-mail: archives@churchofengland.org

JOHN CROCKFORD

John Crockford was the eldest child of a Somerset schoolmaster and his wife, John and Hannah Crockford; and by 1841 he was working as an attorney's clerk in Taunton, Somerset. John Crockford Sr was described in 1869 as Gentleman, of Rowbarton near Taunton. By his early twenties he was in business as a printer and publisher at 29 Essex Street, Strand; and it was from that address that Crockford was first published in 1858. On 6 December of the same year, John Crockford moved to new business premises at 346 Strand and 19 Wellington Street North.

His private address at that time was 16 Oakley Square, Hampstead Road; though by 1865 he had moved to 10 Park Road, Haverstock Hill.

Crockford's business association of more than two decades with Edward William Cox (1809–1879) had begun in 1843, when the *Law Times* first appeared. Both men are claimed as publisher – Crockford by Boase in *Modern English Biography*; Cox by the *Athenaeum* and by *Notes and Queries*. There is similar lack of agreement over other publications, such as the ill-fated *Critic*. "[Crockford] tried to establish a literary paper, the *Critic*. To this he brought all his great ability, but after fifteen years he gave it up in despair" (*Notes and Queries*): whereas the *Dictionary of National Biography* has it that Cox became "proprietor of . . . two other papers called respectively 'The Critic' and 'The Royal Exchange'."

The truth appears to be that the two men, who shared the same business address in Essex Street, were joint founders of a number of projects. Cox – the elder, more established and richer man – was often the financier and named publisher, with Crockford as the manager of the undertaking. Each had his own specialities: Cox, called to the bar in 1843, and successively Recorder of Helston & Falmouth (1857–1868) and of Portsmouth (1868–1879), was no doubt the leader in the establishment of the *Law Times*, to which, in *DNB*'s words, he "thenceforth devoted . . . the larger portion of his time and attention." But the legend which has arisen that Cox, restrained by professional ethics from using his own name, chose, almost at random, the name of one of his clerks to bear the title of his new clerical directory in 1858 – thus, in the words of the first postwar editor (probably Newman) bestowing "a more than tomb-stone meed of remembrance" – cannot be substantiated. As the jubilee account of the *Field* notes, Crockford was an equal partner in the success of the joint enterprises: "It was John Crockford who purchased the paper for Mr Cox. He obtained it from Mr Benjamin Webster for a trifling sum . . . In a short time the net profits amounted to 20,000*l.* a year. The management was placed under Crockford's control. He was a splendid man of business" (*Notes and Queries*).

The first *Clerical Directory* (1858), "A Biographical and Statistical Book of Reference for facts relating to the clergy and the Church", seems to have been assembled in a very haphazard fashion, with names added "as fast as they could be obtained", out of alphabetical order and with an unreliable index. By 1860 the *Directory* had become a very much more useful work of reference; and by 1917, with the absorption of its only serious rival, the *Clergy List*, reigned supreme.

No more than glimpses survive of Crockford's personality, and those mostly from the account of him given by John C. Francis, in the *Field* jubilee article already referred to. "I had occasion to call upon him a short time before his death, when we joined in a hearty laugh over his former furious attacks upon the *Athenaeum*. 'Dilke's Drag' he used to call it, and would accuse it of 'vulgar insolence and coxcombry' and 'the coarsest vulgarity'. As we parted he said, 'You have the *Athenaeum* to be proud of, and we have the *Field*.' "

John Crockford died suddenly at his home on 13 January 1865, at the age of 41. He left a widow, Annie (née Ellam) whom he married on 24 December 1847 at St Pancras Old Church. A daughter, Florence Annie, was born in St Pancras in 1852. (Florence married Arthur Brownlow in 1875 and had a son called Frederick.) His very brief will, proved 6 February 1865 at the Principal Probate Registry, left everything to his widow. His personal effects were valued at less than £1,000, but the family must have lived in some style, since one of the witnesses to the will was the resident coachman. Crockford's widow moved to 4 Upper Eton Place, Tavistock Hill, and died there on 26 July 1868.

BRENDA HOUGH

A request from the *Dictionary of National Biography* for a notice of the life of John Crockford led to the preparation of this article, a shorter version of which appeared in *The Dictionary of National Biography: Missing Persons*, 1993. For the information from the 1841 Census, and the record of Crockford's daughter Florence, we are indebted to Mr Ken Rhoades, of Kent.

A USER'S GUIDE TO *CROCKFORD*

Who is included in Crockford?

Crockford includes details of clergy and deaconesses of the Church of England, the Church in Wales, the Scottish Episcopal Church and the Church of Ireland who have given their consent under GDPR. Clergy currently serving overseas qualify for inclusion if they have trained or have been licensed in this country (see **Overseas clergy**). Clergy who have died since the last edition are listed on p. 1170 Generally, clergy who have resigned their offices (but not their orders) are included unless they are known to have been received into another Church. A small number of clergy are excluded at their own request.

Readers and lay workers are not included: please consult diocesan directories. The *Who's Who* section of *The Church of England Year Book* (published annually by Church House Publishing and covering most aspects of the life and institutions of the Church of England) lists members of General Synod and principal members of staff of the Church's central organizations.

Addresses and telephone numbers

Where more than one land line telephone number is given, the first will normally relate to the address shown.

Addressing the clergy

See p. *12*.

Appointment details in the *Biographies* section

These reflect the legal pastoral situation prevailing at 14 August 2019, the date of the compilation of this edition of *Crockford*. Conventional districts, proprietary chapels and local ecumenical projects are also recorded. Benefice names are only recorded once in a biographical entry when they apply to successive appointments.

Crockford does not record group ministries, informal local arrangements, areas of special responsibility, emeritus appointments (except as reflected in the style of address), licence or permission to officiate when held in conjunction with another appointment from the same diocese, commissary appointments, examining chaplaincies, or secular appointments (except for educational or charitable posts).

Appointments held before ordination are not included (apart from service as a deaconess) unless they straddle the date of ordination.

Archbishops overseas

The presiding (arch-)bishop or metropolitan of each of the provinces of the Anglican Communion is listed in the main *Biographies* section, cross-referenced as appropriate, together with the Moderator of each of the united churches.

Archdeaconries

See *Archdeaconries, deaneries and rural/area deans* on p. 909.

Archdeacons

Look up the place name in *Biographies*: this is cross-referenced to a personal name.

Bishops (diocesan, area, suffragan, and provincial episcopal visitors)

Look up the place name in *Biographies*: this is cross-referenced to a personal name. See also p. 859, which lists the diocesan, area, suffragan and assistant bishops by diocese, as well as provincial episcopal visitors.

Bishops (assistant)

See *Bishops in England, Wales, Scotland and Ireland* on p. 859.

Bishops in the House of Lords

See p. 863.

Bishops overseas
See *Bishops of Anglican dioceses overseas* on p. 1137, and *Bishops of united churches* on p. 1163. Further information about the Anglican Communion can be found in *The Church of England Year Book*.

Bishops and archbishops, former
A list of former archbishops and bishops (diocesan and suffragan) will be found on p. 864.

Boundaries, provincial and diocesan
Maps of England and Wales, Scotland and Ireland, showing provincial and diocesan boundaries and cathedral cities, will be found on pp. 1176–1179.

Cathedral clergy
See *Cathedrals* on p. 902 for full-time cathedral clergy. The list does not include honorary appointments.

Chapel Royal
See *Royal Peculiars* on p. 904.

Christian names
The name by which a person prefers to be known, if not the first Christian name, is underlined (for example, SMITH, David John prefers to be called John). Names 'in religion' or names not part of a person's legal name are shown in parentheses.

Church: how to find the names of clergy responsible for a particular church
Look up the place name in the appropriate *Benefices and churches* section, see p. 917: if the entry is in bold type, the names of all clergy are listed and can be cross-referenced in the *Biographies* section; if the place name is not in bold type, the name of the benefice is given where the names of all clergy will be found.

Church: how to find the names of clergy responsible for a particular church when there is a vacancy
If the benefice is vacant, the telephone number of the clergy house is usually given in the appropriate *Benefices and churches* section to enable contact to be made with a new incumbent or priest-in-charge. The deanery reference (e.g. *Guildf 2*) following the benefice name cross-refers to *Archdeaconries, deaneries and rural deans* on p. 909 by means of which the name of the rural dean responsible for the vacant benefice can be found.

College chaplains
See p. 1132 for chaplains at universities, colleges of further education, colleges of higher education, sixth-form colleges, and schools.

Corrections
Please send notice of any corrections to:
Crockford Compiler, Church House, Great Smith Street, London SW1P 3AZ
T: (020) 7898 1012   E: crockford@churchofengland.org

Crockford
The full title is *Crockford's Clerical Directory*. *Crockford* (not *Crockford's*) is an accepted abbreviation. See also the biography of John Crockford on p. 7.

Deaconesses
See separate section on p. 858.

Deacons
See *Biographies* section.

Deaneries
See rural or area deans below.

Deans

Look up the place name in *Biographies*: this is cross-referenced to a personal name. See also *Cathedrals* on p. 902, and *Royal Peculiars* on p. 904.

Diocesan offices

Details of the diocesan offices in England, Wales, Scotland and Ireland can be found on p. 905

E-mail addresses

These are provided where known. See after the telephone and/or fax number.

Europe, chaplains in

See *Diocese in Europe* on p. 1118.

Fax numbers

The exchange number is only given if different from that of the preceding telephone number.

Hospital chaplains

Whole-time and part-time hospital chaplains are listed under their NHS trusts on p. 1125. Cross-references have been inserted for individual hospitals.

Lay workers

Lay workers are not included in *Crockford*: please consult diocesan directories.

London churches

See English benefices and churches on p. 917. City and Guild churches are listed under LONDON CITY CHURCHES and LONDON GUILD CHURCHES. In other cases, see under church name (e.g. LANGHAM PLACE (All Souls), WESTMINSTER (St Matthew)).

Married or single?

Crockford does not provide information on marital status. However, we have included the form of address Miss, Mrs or Ms where requested. Where there has been a change of surname, a cross-reference may be found from the previous name.

Non-stipendiary clergy

Non-stipendiary clergy are listed in the main *Biographies* section.

Ordination courses

See *Theological colleges and courses* on p. 1135.

Overseas clergy

Clergy who are on the *Crockford* database and who are currently serving overseas qualify for inclusion. Service overseas has in the past been recorded simply by country, though higher office (e.g. as bishop or archdeacon) has also been noted. Other eligible appointments are now being added on request.

Overseas addresses and telephone numbers are given as required by a user in the UK, and include the international access and country codes, as well as the area code. If dialling from within the country concerned, the user will need to omit the international access and country codes, and dial zero immediately before the area code.

Patronage

The patron of each benefice is listed under the benefice name in *English benefices and churches* on p. 917.

Prison chaplains

See p. 1123.

Proprietary chapels

See *English benefices and churches* on p. 917.

Provincial episcopal visitors
Look up the place name in *Biographies*: this is cross-referenced to a personal name. See also p. 859, which lists the diocesan, area, suffragan and assistant bishops and provincial episcopal visitors.

Provosts
Look up the place name in *Biographies*: this is cross-referenced to a personal name. See also *Cathedrals* on p. 902.

Queen's Chaplains
See *Royal Peculiars* on p. 904.

Readers
Readers are not included in *Crockford*: please consult diocesan directories.

Religious orders
For members of religious orders where the Christian name alone is commonly used (e.g. Brother Aidan) a cross-reference is provided to the surname. Names 'in religion' not forming part of a person's legal name will be shown in parentheses. Details of religious communities are provided in *The Church of England Year Book*.

Retired clergy
The description 'rtd' does not imply that ministry has ceased, only that clergy so described are now in receipt of a pension. All eligible appointments are now recorded.

Rural or area deans
See *Archdeaconries, deaneries and rural/area deans* on p. 909. To find who is the rural dean of a particular church, look up the place or benefice name in the appropriate *Benefices* section: the deanery reference (e.g. *Guildf 2*) following the benefice name cross-refers to *Archdeaconries, deaneries and rural deans* on p. 909 where the name of the rural dean responsible can be found.

School chaplains
See p. 1132 for chaplains in schools.

Service chaplains
See p. 1121.

Sixth-form colleges
See p. 1132.

Theological colleges and courses
See p. 1135.

University chaplains
See p. 1132.

HOW TO ADDRESS THE CLERGY

In offering the advice below, we do not intend to imply that other practices are necessarily to be discouraged (for example, the use of Father as in 'Father Smith' or 'Father Alan'). A good deal depends on circumstances, and, where a personal preference is known, it is usually good practice to follow it.

The following notes show acceptable current usage

(a) on an envelope or formal listing
(b) in starting a social letter or in speech, and
(c) when referring to a member of the clergy

Category (a) is not open to much variation, owing to the formality of the context, but categories (b) and (c) will often vary according to circumstances. It is always acceptable to use the appropriate Christian name in place of initials (for example, the Revd Alice Smith). In the absence of any style or title conferred by a post, all deacons and priests are styled 'The Reverend', and all who have been consecrated bishop are styled 'The Right Reverend'.

For abbreviations, see paragraph 13 below.

1 **Deacons and Priests**
(a) The Reverend A B Smith
(b) Mr/Mrs/Miss/Ms Smith (unless it is known that some other style is preferred— the title Vicar or Rector is acceptable only if the person so addressed really is the incumbent of the parish where you live or worship)
(c) The Reverend A B Smith at the first mention, and Mr/Mrs/Miss/Ms Smith thereafter

Notes 1 The form 'Reverend Smith' or 'The Reverend Smith' should never be used this side of the Atlantic. If the Christian name or initials are not known, the correct forms are
(a) The Reverend — Smith, or The Reverend Mr/Mrs/Miss/Ms Smith
(b) Mr/Mrs/Miss/Ms Smith
(c) The Reverend Mr/Mrs/Miss/Ms Smith at the first mention, and Mr/Mrs/Miss/Ms Smith thereafter

2 There is no universally accepted way of addressing an envelope to a married couple of whom both are in holy orders. We recommend the style 'The Reverend A B and the Reverend C D Smith'.
3 Where the husband is in holy orders and the wife is not, the customary style is 'The Reverend A B and Mrs Smith'.
4 Where the wife is in holy orders and the husband is not, we recommend the style 'Mr A B Smith and the Reverend Mrs Smith'.

2 **Prebendaries**
(a) The Reverend Prebendary A B Smith
(b) Prebendary Smith
(c) Prebendary Smith

3 **Canons (both Residentiary and Honorary)**
(a) The Reverend Canon A B Smith
(b) Canon Smith
(c) Canon Smith

4 **Archdeacons**
(a) The Venerable the Archdeacon of X
(b) Archdeacon, or more formally Mr/Madam Archdeacon
(c) The Archdeacon of X at the first mention, and the Archdeacon thereafter

Notes 1 In the case of an archdeacon (or dean/provost, bishop, or archbishop) in office, the style above is to be preferred. The personal name should be used only for the purpose of identification.
2 For an archdeacon emeritus, the correct forms are
(a) The Venerable A B Smith
(b) Archdeacon
(c) Archdeacon Smith

5 **Deans and Provosts**
  (a) The Very Reverend the Dean/Provost of X
  (b) Dean/Provost, *or more formally* Mr/Madam Dean/Provost
  (c) The Dean/Provost of X at the first mention, and the Dean thereafter (see also note 1 to paragraph 4 above)

6 **Bishops, Diocesan and Suffragan**
  (a) The Right Reverend the Bishop of X, *or* The Right Reverend the Lord/Lady Bishop of X
  (b) Bishop, *or more formally* My Lord/Lady
  (c) The Bishop of X at the first mention, and the Bishop thereafter (see also note 1 to paragraph 4 above)

  Notes 1 It is a matter of individual preference whether the title 'Lord/Lady' should be used.
  2 The Bishop of London is a Privy Councillor, and has the style 'The Right Reverend and Right Honourable the Lord Bishop of London'.
  3 The Bishop of Meath and Kildare is styled 'The Most Reverend'.

7 **Assistant and Retired Bishops**
  (a) The Right Reverend A B Smith
  (b) Bishop
  (c) Bishop Smith

8 **Archbishops**
  (a) The Most Reverend the Lord Archbishop of X
  (b) Archbishop, *or more formally* Your Grace
  (c) (His Grace) the Archbishop of X at the first mention, and the Archbishop thereafter (see also note 1 to paragraph 4 above)

  Notes 1 The Archbishops of Canterbury and York, being Privy Councillors, also have 'Right Honourable' included in their style (for example, The Most Reverend and Right Honourable the Lord Archbishop of Canterbury).
  2 The presiding bishop of the Scottish Episcopal Church is the Primus, and the correct forms are
     (a) The Most Reverend the Primus
     (b) Primus
     (c) Primus
  3 A retired archbishop properly reverts to the status of bishop, but may be given as a courtesy the style of an archbishop.

9 **Chaplains to the Armed Services**
  (a) The Reverend A B Smith RN (*or* CF *or* RAF)
  (b) Padre, *or* Padre Smith
  (c) The Padre, *or* Padre Smith

10 **Titled Clerics**
  Where a member of the clergy also holds a temporal title, this is always preceded in writing by the ecclesiastical one.

  Barons (other than retired archbishops)
  (a) The Reverend the Lord Smith of X
  (b) Lord Smith
  (c) The Reverend the Lord Smith at the first mention, and Lord Smith thereafter

  Baronets
  (a) The Reverend Sir Alan Smith Bt
  (b) Sir Alan Smith or Sir Alan
  (c) The Reverend Sir Alan Smith at the first mention, and Sir Alan thereafter

  Knights
  An ordained priest may be appointed to an order of knighthood, but will not normally receive the accolade or title. The appropriate designation will follow the name or ecclesiastical title, e.g. The Right Reverend the Bishop of X, KCVO. If he was knighted *before* he was ordained, he will retain his title, and will be addressed in much the same manner as a baronet.

Dames
(a)   The Reverend Dame Alice Smith
(b)   Dame Alice Smith or Dame Alice
(c)   The Reverend Dame Alice Smith at the first mention, and Dame Alice thereafter

Wives of Barons, Baronets and Knights
(a)   The Reverend Lady Smith (of X)
(b)   Lady Smith
(c)   The Reverend Lady Smith at the first mention, and Lady Smith thereafter

Sons and daughters of peers
(a)   The Reverend the Honourable Jocelyn Smith, *or* The Reverend Lord/Lady Jocelyn Smith (as appropriate)
(b)   Mr/Mrs/Miss/Ms Smith, *or* Lord/Lady Jocelyn Smith
(c)   The Reverend J K Smith at the first mention, and Mr/Mrs/Miss/Ms Smith thereafter; *or* the Reverend Lord/Lady Jocelyn Smith at the first mention, and Lord/Lady Jocelyn thereafter.

11 Ordained Members of Religious Orders
(a)   The Reverend Alan/Alice Smith XYZ; The Reverend Brother Alan/Sister Alice XYZ
(b)   Father, Father Smith, *or* Father Alan; Mother, Mother Smith, *or* Mother Alice; Brother Alan/Sister Alice
(c)   The Reverend Alan/Alice Smith; Father Alan Smith; Mother Alice Smith; Father Smith; Brother Alan/Sister Alice

Notes 1   A name 'in religion', shown in parentheses in the biographical entry, should be used in preference to the baptismal name or initials. Sometimes the surname is not used. In this Directory, however, the entry will be found under the surname, whether it is normally used or not, and, if appropriate, a cross-reference is given under the Christian name.
2   Some orders use 'Brother' and 'Sister' for lay and ordained members without distinction, along with Christian names.
3   It is customary to specify the religious order by giving the appropriate letters after the name.

12 Academics
When a member of the clergy holds more than one title, the ecclesiastical one is normally used.

Professor	(a)	The Reverend Canon A B Smith
also Canon	(b)	Canon Smith, *or* Professor Smith, according to context
	(c)	Canon Smith, *or* Professor Smith, according to context
Canon	(a)	The Reverend Canon A B Smith (degree)
also Doctor	(b)	Canon Smith, *or* Dr Smith, according to context
	(c)	Canon Smith, *or* Dr Smith, according to context

13 Abbreviations
The following abbreviations are in common use

Reverend:	Revd *or* Rev
Father:	Fr
Right Reverend:	Rt Revd *or* Rt Rev
Prebendary:	Preb
Venerable:	Ven

Reverend, Right Reverend, Very Reverend, Most Reverend and Venerable, whether abbreviated or not, should always be preceded by the definite article.

ABBREVIATIONS USED IN
CROCKFORD'S CLERICAL DIRECTORY

A

AAAI	Associate, Institute of Administrative Accountants
AB	Bachelor of Arts (USA)
Ab	(Diocese of) Aberdeen and Orkney
ABEng	Associate Member of the Association of Building Engineers
Aber	Aberdeen
ABIA	Associate, Bankers' Institute of Australasia
ABIPP	Associate, British Institute of Professional Photography
ABIST	Associate, British Institute of Surgical Technology
ABM	Advisory Board of Ministry (now Ministry Division)
Abp	Archbishop
ABPsS	Associate, British Psychological Society (now see AFBPsS)
ABSM	Associate, Birmingham and Midland Institute School of Music
Abth	Aberystwyth
ACA	Associate, Institute of Chartered Accountants
ACABE	Associate, Chartered Association of Building Engineers (formerly ABEng)
ACC	Anglican Consultative Council
ACCA	Associate, Chartered Association of Certified Accountants (formerly AACCA)
ACCM	Advisory Council for the Church's Ministry (now Ministry Division)
ACCS	Associate, Corporation of Secretaries
ACCTS	Association for Christian Conferences, Teaching, and Service
ACE	Associateship of the College of Education
	Member, Association of Conference Executives
ACF	Army Cadet Force
ACIArb	Associate, Chartered Institute of Arbitrators
ACIB	Associate, Chartered Institute of Bankers (formerly AIB)
ACIBS	Associate, Chartered Institute of Bankers in Scotland
ACII	Associate, Chartered Insurance Institute
ACIOB	Associate, Chartered Institute of Building
ACIPA	Associate, Chartered Institute of Patent Agents
ACIPD	Associate, Chartered Institute of Personnel and Development
ACIS	Associate, Institute of Chartered Secretaries and Administrators
ACIT	Associate, Chartered Institute of Transport
ACMA	Associate, Chartered Institute of Management Accountants (formerly ACWA)
ACMI	Associate, Chartered Management Institute (formerly AIMgt)
ACORA	Archbishops' Commission on Rural Areas
ACP	Associate, College of Preceptors
ACS	Additional Curates Society

ACSM	Associate, Camborne School of Mines
ACT	Australian Capital Territory
	Australian College of Theology
ACUPA	Archbishops' Commission on Urban Priority Areas
AD	Area Dean
Ad	Advanced
AdDipEd	Advanced Diploma in Education
Admin	Administration
	Administrative
	Administrator
Adn	Archdeacon
Adnry	Archdeaconry
Adv	Adviser
	Advisory
AEdRD	Associateship in Educational Research and Development
AFAIM	Associate Fellow, Australian Institute of Management
AFBPsS	Associate Fellow, British Psychological Society (formerly ABPsS)
AFC	Air Force Cross
AFIMA	Associate Fellow, Institute of Mathematics and its Applications
AFOM	Associate, Faculty of Occupational Medicine
Agric	Agricultural
	Agriculture
AGSM	Associate, Guildhall School of Music and Drama
AHSM or AHA	Associate, Institute of Health Service Management (formerly Administrators)
AIA	Associate, Institute of Actuaries
AIAS	Associate, Incorporated Association of Architects and Surveyors
AIAT	Associate, Institute of Animal Technicians
Aid	Aidan
	Aidan's
AIDS	Acquired Immunity Deficiency Syndrome
AIFST	Associate, Institute of Food Science and Technology
AIGCM	Associate, Incorporated Guild of Church Musicians
AIIM	Associate, Institute of Investment Management
AIL	Associate, Institute of Linguists
AIMgt	Associate, Institute of Management (now see ACMI)
AIMLS	Associate, Institute of Medical Laboratory Sciences
AIMSW	Associate, Institute of Medical Social Work
AIPM	Associate, Institute of Personnel Management (now see ACIPD)
AITI	Associate, Institute of Taxation in Ireland
AKC	Associate, King's College London
ALA	Associate, Library Association
ALAM	Associate, London Academy of Music
ALBC	Associate, London Bible College
ALCD	Associate, London College of Divinity
ALCM	Associate, London College of Music
ALSM	Associate, Lancashire School of Music
alt	alternate

AM	Albert Medal
	Master of Arts (USA)
AMA	Associate, Museums Association
AMASI	Associate Member of the Architects and Surveyors Institute
AMCST	Associate, Manchester College of Science and Technology
AMCT	Associate, Manchester College of Technology
AMIBF	Associate Member, Institute of British Foundrymen
AMIC	Associate Member, Institute of Counselling
AMICME	Associate Member, Institute of Cast Metal Engineers
AMIDHE	Associate Member, Institute of Domestic Heating Engineers
AMIEHO	Associate Member, Institution of Environmental Health Officers
AMIM	Associate Member, Institute of Metals
AMIMMM	Associate Member, Institute of Materials, Minerals and Mining
AMInstT	Associate Member, Institute of Transport
AMInstTA	Associate Member, Institute of Transport Administration
AMITD	Associate Member, Institute of Training and Development (now see ACIPD)
AMIW	Associate Member, Institute of Welfare (formerly AMIWO)
AMRSH	Associate Member, Royal Society of Health
AMSIA	Associate Member, Society of Investment Analysts
AMusLCM	Associate in Music, London College of Music
AMusTCL	Associate in Music, Trinity College of Music London
ANC	African National Congress
Andr	Andrew
	Andrew's
	Andrews
Angl	Anglican
	Anglicans
Ant	Anthony
	Anthony's
AO	Officer, Order of Australia
APhS	Associate, Philosophical Society of England
Appt	Appointment
ARAM	Associate, Royal Academy of Music
ARCA	Associate, Royal College of Art
ARCIC	Anglican-Roman Catholic International Commission
ARCM	Associate, Royal College of Music
ARCO	Associate, Royal College of Organists
ARCO(CHM)	Associate, Royal College of Organists with Diploma in Choir Training
ARCS	Associate, Royal College of Science
ARCST	Associate, Royal College of Science and Technology (Glasgow)
ARCT	Associate, Royal Conservatory of Music Toronto

ARCUK .... Architects' Registration Council of the United Kingdom
Arg .... (Diocese of) Argyll and The Isles
ARHistS .... Associate, Royal Historical Society
ARIAM .... Associate, Royal Irish Academy of Music
ARICS .... Professional Associate, Royal Institution of Chartered Surveyors (now see MRICS)
Arm .... (Diocese of) Armagh
ARMCM .... Associate, Royal Manchester College of Music
ARPS .... Associate, Royal Photographic Society
ARSCM .... Associate, Royal School of Church Music
ARSM .... Associate, Royal School of Mines
AS .... Associate in Science (USA)
ASCA .... Associate, Society of Company and Commercial Accountants
Assn .... Association
Assoc .... Associate
ASSP .... Society of All Saints Sisters of the Poor
Asst .... Assistant
ASVA .... Associate, Incorporated Society of Valuers and Auctioneers
ATC .... Air Training Corps
ATCL .... Associate, Trinity College of Music London
ATD .... Art Teacher's Diploma
ATh(SA) .... Associate in Theology (South Africa)
ATI .... Associate, Textile Institute
ATII .... Associate Member, Institute of Taxation
ATL .... Association of Teachers and Lecturers
ATV .... Associated Television
Aug .... Augustine
.... Augustine's
Aus .... Australian
Aux .... Auxiliaries
.... Auxiliary
AVCM .... Associate, Victoria College of Music

B

b .... Born
B & W .... (Diocese of) Bath and Wells
B or Bapt .... Baptist
.... Baptist's
BA .... Bachelor of Arts
BA(Econ) .... Bachelor of Arts in Economics
BA(Ed) .... Bachelor of Arts in Education
BA(QTS) .... Bachelor of Arts (Qualified Teacher Status)
BA(Theol) .... Bachelor of Arts in Theology
BA(ThM) .... Bachelor of Arts in Theology in Ministry
BAdmin .... Bachelor of Administration
BAgr .... Bachelor of Agriculture
BAgrSc .... Bachelor of Agricultural Science
BAI .... Bachelor of Engineering (also see BE and BEng)
Ball .... Balliol
Ban .... (Diocese of) Bangor
BAO .... Bachelor of Obstetrics
BAppSc .... Bachelor of Applied Science
BAppSc(Agric) .... Bachelor of Applied Science (Agriculture)
BAppSc(OT) .... Bachelor of Applied Science (Occupational Therapy)
BArch .... Bachelor of Architecture
Barn .... Barnabas
.... Barnabas's
Bart .... Bartholomew
.... Bartholomew's
BASc .... Bachelor of Applied Science
BATM .... Bachelor of Arts in Theology and Ministry
BBA .... Bachelor of Business Administration
BBC .... British Broadcasting Corporation
BBS .... Bachelor of Business Studies

BC .... British Columbia (Canada)
BCA .... Bachelor of Commerce and Administration
BCC .... British Council of Churches (now CTBI)
BCE .... Bachelor of Civil Engineering
BCh or BChir .... Bachelor of Surgery (also see BS and ChB)
BChD .... Bachelor of Dental Surgery
BCL .... Bachelor of Civil Law
BCMS .... Bible Churchmen's Missionary Society (now Crosslinks)
BCom or .... Bachelor of Commerce
BComm
BCombStuds ...... Bachelor of Combined Studies
BCommWelf .... Bachelor of Community Welfare
BD .... Bachelor of Divinity
Bd .... Board
BDA .... Bachelor of Dramatic Art
BDes .... Bachelor of Design
BDiv .... Bachelor of Divinity
BDQ .... Bachelor of Divinity Qualifying Examination
BDS .... Bachelor of Dental Surgery
BDSc .... Bachelor of Dental Science
BE .... Bachelor of Engineering (also see BAI and BEng)
BEc .... Bachelor of Economics (Australia)
BEcon .... Bachelor of Economics (USA)
BEd .... Bachelor of Education
Bedf .... Bedford
BEdSt .... Bachelor of Educational Studies
Belf .... Belfast
BEM .... British Empire Medal
BEng .... Bachelor of Engineering (also see BAI and BE)
BèsL .... Bachelier ès lettres
BFA .... Bachelor of Fine Arts
BFBS .... British and Foreign Bible Society
BHSc .... Bachelor of Health Sciences
Bibl .... Biblical
BIE .... Bachelor of Industrial Engineering (USA)
Birm .... (Diocese of) Birmingham
BL .... Bachelor of Law
Blackb .... (Diocese of) Blackburn
BLib .... Bachelor of Librarianship
BLitt .... Bachelor of Letters
BM .... Bachelor of Medicine (also see MB)
BM, BCh .... Conjoint degree of Bachelor of Medicine, Bachelor of Surgery
BMedSci .... Bachelor of Medical Science
BMet .... Bachelor of Metallurgy
BMin .... Bachelor of Ministry
BMMF .... Bible and Medical Missionary Fellowship (now Interserve)
BMU .... Board for Mission and Unity
BMus .... Bachelor of Music (also see MusB and MusBac)
BMusEd .... Bachelor of Music Education
BN .... Bachelor of Nursing
BNC .... Brasenose College
Bp .... Bishop
BPaed .... Bachelor of Paediatrics
BPh or BPhil .... Bachelor of Philosophy
BPharm .... Bachelor of Pharmacy
BPhil(Ed) .... Bachelor of Philosophy (Education)
BPI .... Bachelor of Planning
BPR&TM .... Bachelor of Parks, Recreation and Tourism Management
BPrimEd .... Bachelor of Primary Education
BProfStud .... Bachelor of Professional Studies
Br .... British
Bradf .... (Diocese of) Bradford
Bre .... (Diocese of) Brechin
BRE .... Bachelor of Religious Education (USA)
BRF .... Bible Reading Fellowship
Brig .... Brigadier
Bris .... (Diocese of) Bristol

BS .... Bachelor of Science (also see BSc)
.... Bachelor of Surgery (also see BCh, BChir and ChB)
BSB .... Brotherhood of St Barnabas
BSc .... Bachelor of Science (also see BS)
BSc(Econ) .... Bachelor of Science in Economics
BSc(Soc) .... Bachelor of Science (Sociology)
BScAgr .... Bachelor of Science in Agriculture
BScEcon .... Bachelor of Science in Economics
BScEng .... Bachelor of Science in Engineering (also see BSE)
BScFor .... Bachelor of Science in Forestry
BScTech .... Bachelor of Technical Science
BSE .... Bachelor of Science in Engineering (also see BScEng)
BSEd .... Bachelor of Science in Education (USA)
BSocAdmin .... Bachelor of Social Administration
BSocSc .... Bachelor of Social Science (also see BSSc)
BSP .... Brotherhood of St Paul
BSS .... Bachelor of Social Studies
BSSc .... Bachelor of Social Science (also see BSocSc)
BST .... Bachelor of Sacred Theology
BSW .... Bachelor of Social Work
BT .... Bachelor of Teaching
Bt .... Baronet
BTech .... Bachelor of Technology
BTh or BTheol ..... Bachelor of Theology (also see STB)
BTS .... Bachelor of Theological Studies
BUniv .... Bachelor of the University
BVetMed .... Bachelor of Veterinary Medicine (also see VetMB)
BVM&S .... Bachelor of Veterinary Medicine and Surgery
BVSc .... Bachelor of Veterinary Science

C

C .... Curate
c .... Consecrated
C & O .... (Diocese of) Cashel and Ossory (united dioceses of Cashel, Waterford, Lismore, Ossory, Ferns and Leighlin)
C of E .... Church of England
C of S .... Church of Scotland
C&G .... City and Guilds
C, C & R .... (Diocese of) Cork, Cloyne and Ross
c/o .... Care of
CA .... Church Army
.... Member, Institute of Chartered Accountants of Scotland
CA(Z) .... Member, Institute of Chartered Accountants of Zimbabwe
CACTM .... Central Advisory Council for the Ministry (now Ministry Division)
Cam .... Cambridge
Can .... Canon
Cand .... Candidate
.... Candidate's
.... Candidates'
CANDL .... Church and Neighbourhood Development in London
Cant .... (Diocese of) Canterbury
Capt .... Captain
CARA .... Care and Resources for people affected by AIDS/HIV
CARE .... Christian Action Research and Education
Carl .... (Diocese of) Carlisle
CASA .... Anglican Church of the Southern Cone of America
Cath .... Catharine/Catherine
.... Catharine's/Catherine's
Cathl .... Cathedral
CB .... Companion, Order of the Bath

CBDTI .... Carlisle and Blackburn Diocesan Training Institute
CBE .... Commander, Order of the British Empire
CBIM .... Companion, British Institute of Management
CBiol .... Chartered Biologist
CCBI .... Council of Churches for Britain and Ireland (now see CTBI)
CCC .... Corpus Christi College
.... Council for the Care of Churches
CCCS .... Commonwealth and Continental Church Society
CChem .... Chartered Chemist
CCWA .... Churches Community Work Alliance
CD .... Canadian Forces Decoration
.... Conventional District (also see ED)
CDir .... Chartered Director
Cdre .... Commodore
CECD .... Church of England Council for the Deaf
CECS .... Church of England Children's Society (now known as the Children's Society)
CEMS .... Church of England Men's Society
Cen .... Centre
.... Center
.... Central
CEng .... Chartered Engineer
CEnv .... Chartered Environmentalist
Cert .... Certificate(e)
CertEd .... Certificate of Education
CertFE .... Certificate of Further Education
CertHE .... Certificate in Higher Education
CETD .... Certificate in the Education of the Deaf
CF .... Chaplain to the Forces
CGA .... Community of the Glorious Ascension
CGeol .... Chartered Geologist
CH .... Companion of Honour
Ch .... Christ
.... Christ's
.... Church
Ch Ch .... Christ Church
Chan .... Chancellor
Chapl .... Chaplain
.... Chaplaincies
.... Chaplaincy
.... Chaplains
Chas .... Charles
.... Charles's
ChB .... Bachelor of Surgery (also see BChir, BChir and BS)
Chelmsf .... (Diocese of) Chelmsford
Chelt .... Cheltenham
Ches .... (Diocese of) Chester
Chich .... (Diocese of) Chichester
Chmn .... Chairman
.... Chairwoman
Chpl .... Chapel
Chr .... Christian
.... Christians
Chris .... Christopher
.... Christopher's
Chrys .... Chrysostom
.... Chrysostom's
Chu .... Churchill
C-in-c .... Curate-in-charge
CIO .... Church Information Office
CIPFA .... Chartered Institute of Public Finance and Accountancy
CITC .... Church of Ireland Theological College
CITP .... Chartered Information Technology Professional
CJGS .... Community of the Companions of Jesus the Good Shepherd
Clem .... Clement
.... Clement's
Cl-in-c .... Cleric-in-charge
Cllr .... Councillor/Counsellor
Clogh .... (Diocese of) Clogher
CMath .... Chartered Mathematician
CMD .... Cambridge Mission to Delhi (now see USPG)

.... Continuing Ministerial Development
CME .... Continuing Ministerial Education
CMG .... Companion, Order of St Michael and St George
CMgr .... Chartered Manager
CMJ .... Church's Ministry among Jewish People
CMP .... Company of Mission Priests
CMS .... Church Mission Society (formerly Church Missionary Society)
CNZM .... Companion, New Zealand Order of Merit
Co .... Company
.... County
.... Counties
Col .... Colonel
Coll .... College
Colleg .... Collegiate
Comdr .... Commander
Comdr OM .... Commander, Order of Merit
(Italy) .... of the Italian Republic
Commn .... Commission
Commr .... Commissioner
Comp .... Comprehensive
Conf .... Confederation
.... Conference
Conn .... (Diocese of) Connor
Co-ord .... Co-ordinator
.... Co-ordinating
COPEC .... Conference on Politics, Economics and Community
CORAT .... Christian Organizations Research and Advisory Trust
CORE .... City Outreach through Renewal Evangelism
Corp .... Corporation
Coun .... Council
Cov .... (Diocese of) Coventry
CP .... Community Priest
CPA .... Chartered Patent Agent (formerly FCIPA)
CPAS .... Church Pastoral Aid Society
CPEng .... Chartered Professional Engineer (of Institution of Engineers of Australia)
CPFA .... Member Chartered Institute of Public Finance and Accountancy (formerly IPFA)
CPhys .... Chartered Physicist of the Institute of Physics
CPM .... Colonial Police Medal
CPsychol .... Chartered Member, British Psychological Society
CQSW .... Certificate of Qualification in Social Work
CR .... Community of the Resurrection (Mirfield)
CSA .... Community of St Andrew
CSC .... Community of the Sisters of the Church
CSci .... Chartered Scientist
CSD .... Community of St Denys
CSF .... Community of St Francis
CSG .... Company of the Servants of God
CSMV .... Community of St Mary the Virgin
CSocSc .... Certificate in Social Science
CSP .... Community of St Peter
CSS .... Certificate in Social Service
CSSM .... Children's Special Service Mission
CStat .... Chartered Statistician
CSWG .... Community of the Servants of the Will of God
CTA .... Chartered Tax Adviser
CTABRSM .... Certificate of Teaching, Associated Board of the Royal Schools of Music
CTBI .... Churches Together in Britain and Ireland (formerly CCBI)
CTE .... Churches Together in England
Cttee .... Committee
CUF .... Church Urban Fund
Cust .... Custodian
.... Custody
Cuth .... Cuthbert
.... Cuthbert's
CVO .... Commander, Royal Victorian Order

CWME .... Commission on World Mission and Evangelism
CY .... Church and Youth
CYCW .... Certificate in Youth and Community Work
CYFA .... Church Youth Fellowships Association
Cypr .... Cyprian
.... Cyprian's

D

d .... Ordained Deacon
D & D .... (Diocese of) Down and Dromore
D & G .... (Diocese of) Dublin and Glendalough
D & R .... (Diocese of) Derry and Raphoe
D&C .... Dean and Chapter
DA .... Doctor of Arts
DACE .... Diploma in Adult and Continuing Education
DAES .... Diploma in Advanced Educational Studies
DAPC .... Diploma in Advanced Psychological Counselling
DArch .... Doctor of Architecture
Darw .... Darwin
DASAE .... Diploma of Advanced Study in Adult Education
DASE .... Diploma in the Advanced Study of Education
DASHE .... Diploma in Advanced Studies in Higher Education
DASS .... Diploma in Applied Social Studies
DASSc .... Diploma in Applied Social Science
Dav .... David
.... David's
DB .... Bachelor of Divinity (USA)
DBA .... Doctor of Business Administration
DBE .... Dame Commander, Order of the British Empire
DBF .... Diocesan Board of Finance
DBP .... Diocesan Board of Patronage
DC .... District of Columbia (USA)
DCC .... Diploma in Crisis Counselling of the Institute of Counselling
DCE .... Diploma of a College of Education
DCL .... Doctor of Civil Law
DCnL .... Doctor of Canon Law
DCR(R) .... Diploma of the College of Radiographers
DCYW .... Diploma in Community and Youth Work
DD .... Doctor of Divinity
DDes .... Doctor of Design
DDS .... Doctor of Dental Surgery
DEd .... Doctor of Education (also see EdD)
DEHC .... Diploma in the Education of Handicapped Children
DEng .... Doctor of Engineering
Dep .... Deputy
Dept .... Department
DèS .... Docteur ès sciences
DèsL .... Docteur ès lettres
Det .... Detention
DFC .... Distinguished Flying Cross
DFM .... Distinguished Flying Medal (Canada)
DHA .... District Health Authority
DHC .... Doctor Honoris Causa
DHL .... Doctor of Humane Letters
DHSc .... Doctor of Health Science
DHumLit .... Doctor of Humane Letters
Dio .... Diocese
Dioc .... Diocesan
Dip .... Diploma
DipAdEd .... Diploma in Advanced Education
DipAE .... Diploma in Adult Education
DipCOT .... Diploma of the College of Occupational Therapists
DipEd .... Diploma in Education
DipHE .... Diploma in Higher Education
DipOT .... Diploma in Occupational Therapy
DipSW .... Diploma in Social Work
Dir .... Director

Distr .... District
Div .... Divinity
Div Test .... Divinity Testimonium
DL .... Deputy Lieutenant
DLC .... Diploma of Loughborough
College
DLitt .... Doctor of Letters (also see
LittD)
DLitt et Phil .... Doctor of Letters and
Philosophy
DLSc .... Doctor of Legal Science
DM .... Doctor of Medicine
DMin .... Doctor of Ministry
DMinTh .... Doctor of Ministry and
Theology
DMus .... Doctor of Music
Dn .... Deacon
Dn-in-c .... Deacon-in-charge
DOE .... Department of the
Environment
Dom .... Domestic
Down .... Downing
DPhil .... Doctor of Philosophy (also
see PhD)
DProf .... Doctor in Professional
Studies
.... Professional Doctorate in
Practical Theology
DPsych .... Doctor of Psychotherapy
DPT .... Doctor of Practical Theology
Dr .... Doctor
Dr rer nat .... Doctor of Natural Science
Dr Théol .... Doctor of Theology (France)
DRCOG .... Diploma of the Royal
College of Obstetricians and
Gynaecologists
DrTheol .... Doctor of Theology
(Germany)
DSc .... Doctor of Science (also see
ScD)
DSC .... Distinguished Service Cross
DSc(Eng) .... Doctor of Science in
Engineering
DSM .... Distinguished Service Medal
DSO .... Companion, Distinguished
Service Order
DSocSc .... Doctor of Social Science
Dss .... Deaconess
dss .... Admitted Deaconess
DST .... Doctor of Sacred Theology
(also see STD)
DSW .... Doctor of Social Work
DTech .... Doctor of Technology
DTh or DTheol ... Doctor of Theology (also see
ThD)
DThM or .... Doctor of Theology and
DThMin .... Ministry
DTI .... Department of Trade and
Industry
Dub .... Dublin
DUniv .... Doctor of the University
DUP .... Docteur de l'Université de
Paris
Dur .... (Diocese of) Durham

E

E .... East
.... Eastern
EAMTC .... East Anglian Ministerial
Training Course
EC .... Emergency Commission
Ecum .... Ecumenical
.... Ecumenics
.... Ecumenism
Ed .... Editor
.... Editorial
ED .... Ecclesiastical District (also
see CD)
.... Efficiency Decoration
EdD .... Doctor of Education (also
see DEd)
Edin .... (Diocese of) Edinburgh
Edm .... Edmund
.... Edmund's
EdM .... Master of Education (USA)
(also see MEd)
Educn .... Education
.... Educational
Edw .... Edward
.... Edward's
Eliz .... Elizabeth
.... Elizabeth's
Em .... Emanuel
.... Emmanuel
Emb .... Embassy

EMMTC .... East Midlands Ministry
Training Course
EN(G) .... Enrolled Nurse (General)
EN(M) .... Enrolled Nurse (Mental)
EngD .... Doctor of Engineering
EngTech .... Engineering Technician
Episc .... Episcopal
.... Episcopalian
ERD .... Emergency Reserve
Decoration
ERMC .... Eastern Region Ministry
Course
ESC .... École Supérieure de
Commerce
ESMI .... Elderly, Sick and Mentally
Infirm
Eur .... (Diocese in) Europe
(formerly Diocese of
Gibraltar in Europe)
.... European
EurIng .... European Engineer
Ev .... Evangelist
.... Evangelist's
.... Evangelists
Evang .... Evangelical
.... Evangelism
Ex .... (Diocese of) Exeter
Exam .... Examining
Exec .... Executive
Exor .... Executor
Ext .... Extension

F

F&HE .... Further and Higher
Education
FAA .... Fellow, Institution of
Administrative Accountants
FACOG .... Fellow, American College of
Obstetricians and
Gynaecologists
FAcSS .... Fellow, Academy of Social
Sciences
FADO .... Fellow, Association of
Dispensing Opticians
FAEB .... Fellow, Academy of
Environmental Biology
(India)
FAIM .... Fellow, Australian Institute
of Management
FAIWCW .... Fellow, Australian Institute
of Welfare and Community
Workers
FASI .... Fellow, Architects' and
Surveyors' Institute
FBA .... Fellow, British Academy
FBCartS .... Fellow, British Cartographic
Society
FBCO .... Fellow, British College of
Ophthalmic Opticians
(Optometrists)
FBCS .... Fellow, British Computer
Society
FBDO .... Fellow, Association of
British Dispensing Opticians
FBEng .... Fellow, Association of
Building Engineers
FBIM .... Fellow, British Institute of
Management (formerly
MBIM)
FBIS .... Fellow, British
Interplanetary Society
FBIST .... Fellow, British Institute of
Surgical Technologists
FBOA .... Fellow, British Optical
Association
FBPICS .... Fellow, British Production
and Inventory Control
Society
FBPsS .... Fellow, British Psychological
Society
FBS .... Fellow, Burgon Society
FCA .... Fellow, Institute of
Chartered Accountants
FCCA .... Fellow, Chartered
Association of Certified
Accountants (formerly
FACCA)
FCFI .... Fellow, Clothing and
Footwear Institute
FCIArb .... Fellow, Chartered Institute
of Arbitrators
FCIB .... Fellow, Chartered Institute
of Bankers
.... Fellow, Corporation of
Insurance Brokers

FCIE .... Fellow, Association of
Charity Independent
Examiners
FCIH .... Fellow, Chartered Institute
of Housing
FCII .... Fellow, Chartered Insurance
Institute
FCILA .... Fellow, Chartered Institute
of Loss Adjusters
FCIM .... Fellow, Chartered Institute
of Marketing (formerly
FInstM)
FCIOB .... Fellow, Chartered Institute
of Building
FCIPD .... Fellow, Chartered Institute
of Personnel and
Development
FCIS .... Fellow, Institute of
Chartered Secretaries and
Administrators
FCIT .... Fellow, Chartered Institute
of Transport
FCMA .... Fellow, Chartered Institute
of Management
Accountants
FCMI .... Fellow, Chartered
Management Institute
(formerly FIMgt)
FCO .... Foreign and
Commonwealth Office
FCollP .... Fellow, College of Preceptors
FCollT .... Fellow, College of Teachers
FCOptom .... Fellow, College of
Optometrists
FCP .... Fellow, College of Preceptors
FCT .... Fellow, Association of
Corporate Treasurers
FDS .... Fellow in Dental Surgery
FDSRCPSGlas ...... Fellow in Dental Surgery,
Royal College of Physicians
and Surgeons of Glasgow
FDSRCS .... Fellow in Dental Surgery,
Royal College of Surgeons of
England
FE .... Further Education
FEI .... Fellow, Energy Institute
Fell .... Fellow
FEPA .... Fellow, Evangelical
Preachers' Association
FETC .... Further Education Teacher's
Certificate
FFA .... Fellow, Institute of Financial
Accountants
FFAEM .... Fellow, Faculty of Accident
and Emergency Medicine
FFARCS .... Fellow, Faculty of
Anaesthetists, Royal College
of Surgeons of England
FFChM .... Fellow, Faculty of Church
Music
FFDRCSI .... Fellow, Faculty of Dentistry,
Royal College of Surgeons in
Ireland
FFHom .... Fellow, the Faculty of
Homoeopathy
FFOM .... Fellow, Faculty of
Occupational Medicine
FFPH .... Fellow, Faculty of Public
Health (formerly FFPHM)
FFPHM .... Fellow, Faculty of Public
Health Medicine (now see
FFPH)
FFPM .... Fellow, Faculty of
Pharmaceutical Medicine
FGA .... Fellow, Gemmalogical
Association
FGMS .... Fellow, Guild of Musicians
and Singers
FGS .... Fellow, Geological Society of
London
FHA .... Fellow, Institute of Hospital
Administrators (now see
FHSM)
.... Fellow, Historical
Association
FHCIMA .... Fellow, Hotel Catering and
Institutional Management
Association
FHEA .... Fellow, Higher Education
Academy
FHSM .... Fellow, Institute of Health
Services Management
FIA .... Fellow, Institute of Actuaries
FIBMS .... Fellow, Institute of
Biomedical Sciences

FICE .... Fellow, Institution of Civil Engineers
FIChemE .... Fellow, Institution of Chemical Engineers
FICM .... Fellow, Institution of Commercial Managers
FICS .... Fellow, International College of Surgeons
FIDiagE .... Fellow, Institute of Diagnostic Engineers
FIED .... Fellow, Institution of Engineering Designers
FIEE .... Fellow, Institution of Electrical Engineers (formerly FIERE)
FIEEE .... Fellow, Institute of Electrical and Electronics Engineers (NY)
FIERE .... Fellow, Institution of Electronic and Radio Engineers (now see FIEE)
FIET .... Fellow, Institution of Engineering and Technology
FIFireE .... Fellow, Institution of Fire Engineers
FIHEEM .... Fellow, Institute of Healthcare Engineering and Estate Management (formerly FIHospE)
FIHT .... Fellow of the Institution of Highways and Transportation
FIIM .... Fellow, Institution of Industrial Managers (formerly FIPlantE)
FIL .... Fellow, Institute of Linguists
FIMA .... Fellow, Institute of Mathematics and its Applications
FIMarEST .... Fellow, Institute of Marine Engineering, Science and Technology
FIMechE .... Fellow, Institution of Mechanical Engineers
FIMI .... Fellow, Institute of the Motor Industry
FIMLS .... Fellow, Institute of Medical Laboratory Sciences
FIMM .... Fellow, Institution of Mining and Metallurgy (now see FIMMM)
FIMMM .... Fellow, Institute of Materials, Minerals and Mining
FIMS .... Fellow, Institute of Management Specialists
FInstAM .... Fellow, Institute of Administrative Management
FInstD .... Fellow, Institute of Directors
FInstE .... Fellow, Institute of Energy
FInstLEx .... Fellow, Institute of Legal Executives
FInstLM .... Fellow, Institute of Leadership and Management
FInstMC .... Fellow, Institute of Measurement and Control
FInstP .... Fellow, Institute of Physics
FInstSMM .... Fellow, Institute of Sales and Marketing Management
FInstTT .... Fellow, Institute of Travel and Tourism
FINucE .... Fellow, Institution of Nuclear Engineers (now see FNucI)
FIOSH .... Fellow, Institute of Occupational Safety and Health
FIPD .... Fellow, Institute of Personnel Development
FIPEM .... Fellow, Institute of Physics and Engineering in Medicine
FIQA .... Fellow, Institute of Quality Assurance
FISM .... Fellow, Institute of Supervisory Management
FIST .... Fellow, Institute of Science and Technology
FIStructE .... Fellow, Institution of Structural Engineers
Fitzw .... Fitzwilliam
FKC .... Fellow, King's College London
FLA .... Fellow, Library Association

FLAME .... Family Life and Marriage Education
FLCM .... Fellow, London College of Music
FLIA .... Fellow, Life Insurance Association
FLS .... Fellow, Linnean Society
FMA .... Fellow, Museums Association
FNI .... Fellow, Nautical Institute
FNMSM .... Fellow, North and Midlands School of Music
FNucI .... Fellow, Nuclear Institute (formerly FINucE)
Foundn .... Foundation
FPhS .... Fellow, Philosophical Society of England
FPS .... Fellow, Pharmaceutical Society of Great Britain
FRACI .... Fellow, Royal Australian Chemical Institute
FRAeS .... Fellow, Royal Aeronautical Society
FRAI .... Fellow, Royal Anthropological Institute
FRAM .... Fellow, Royal Academy of Music
Fran .... Francis
.... Francis's
FRAS .... Fellow, Royal Asiatic Society
.... Fellow, Royal Astronomical Society
FRCA .... Fellow, Royal College of Anaesthetists
FRCGP .... Fellow, Royal College of General Practitioners
FRCM .... Fellow, Royal College of Music
FRCO .... Fellow, Royal College of Organists
FRCOG .... Fellow, Royal College of Obstetricians and Gynaecologists
FRCOphth .... Fellow, Royal College of Ophthalmologists
FRCP .... Fellow, Royal College of Physicians
FRCP(C) .... Fellow, Royal College of Physicians of Canada
FRCPath .... Fellow, Royal College of Pathologists
FRCPCH .... Fellow, Royal College of Paediatrics and Child Health
FRCPEd .... Fellow, Royal College of Physicians Edinburgh
FRCPGlas .... Fellow, Royal College of Physicians and Surgeons, Glasgow (also see FRCSGlas)
FRCPsych .... Fellow, Royal College of Psychiatrists
FRCR .... Fellow, Royal College of Radiologists
FRCS .... Fellow, Royal College of Physicians and Surgeons of England
FRCSE or FRCSEd Fellow, Royal College of Surgeons of Edinburgh
FRCSGlas .... Fellow, Royal College of Physicians and Surgeons, Glasgow (also see FRCPGlas)
FRCSI .... Fellow, Royal College of Surgeons in Ireland
FRCVS .... Fellow, Royal College of Veterinary Surgeons
FREng .... Fellow, Royal Academy of Engineering
FRGS .... Fellow, Royal Geographical Society
FRHistS .... Fellow, Royal Historical Society
FRHS .... Fellow, Royal Horticultural Society
FRIAS .... Fellow, Royal Incorporation of Architects of Scotland
FRIBA .... Fellow, Royal Institute of British Architects
FRICS .... Fellow, Royal Institution of Chartered Surveyors (formerly FLAS and FSI)
FRIN .... Fellow, Royal Institute of Navigation
FRINA .... Fellow, Royal Institution of Naval Architects
FRIPH .... Fellow, Royal Institute of Public Health

FRMetS .... Fellow, Royal Meteorological Society
FRPharmS .... Fellow, Royal Pharmaceutical Society
FRS .... Fellow, Royal Society
FRSA .... Fellow, Royal Society of Arts
FRSAI .... Fellow, Royal Society of Antiquaries of Ireland
FRSB .... Fellow, Royal Society of Biology (formerly FIBiol)
FRSC .... Fellow, Royal Society of Canada
.... Fellow, Royal Society of Chemistry (formerly FRIC)
FRSCM .... Honorary Fellow, Royal School of Church Music
FRSE .... Fellow, Royal Society of Edinburgh
FRSH .... Fellow, Royal Society for Public Health
FRSL .... Fellow, Royal Society of Literature
FRSM .... Fellow, Associated Board of the Royal Schools of Music
FRSocMed .... Fellow, Royal Society of Medicine
FRTPI .... Fellow, Royal Town Planning Institute
FSA .... Fellow, Society of Antiquaries
FSAScot .... Fellow, Royal Society of Antiquaries of Scotland
FSCA .... Fellow, Royal Society of Company and Commercial Accountants
FSJ .... Fellowship of St John the Evangelist
FSR .... Fellowship Diploma of the Society of Radiographers
FSS .... Fellow, Royal Statistical Society
FTC .... Flying Training Command
FTCL .... Fellow, Trinity College of Music London
FTII .... Fellow, Institute of Taxation
FVCM .... Fellow, Victoria College of Music
FWeldI .... Fellow, Institute of Welding

G

G&C .... Gonville and Caius
Gabr .... Gabriel
.... Gabriel's
GB .... Great Britain
GBSM .... Graduate of the Birmingham School of Music
GCMG .... Knight Grand Cross, Order of St Michael and St George
GCVO .... Knight Grand Cross, Royal Victorian Order
Gd .... Good
Gen .... General
Geo .... George
.... George's
GFS .... Girls' Friendly Society
GGSM .... Graduate Diploma of the Guildhall School of Music and Drama
Gib .... Gibraltar
GIBiol .... Graduate of the Institute of Biology
GIFireE .... Graduate of the Institute of Fire Engineers
GIMechE .... Graduate of the Institution of Mechanical Engineers
GInstP .... Graduate of the Institute of Physics
GIPE .... Graduate of the Institution of Production Engineers
Glam .... Glamorgan
Glas .... (Diocese of) Glasgow and Galloway
.... Glasgow
GLCM .... Graduate Diploma of the London College of Music
Glos .... Gloucestershire
Glouc .... (Diocese of) Gloucester
GM .... George Medal
GMus .... Graduate Diploma in Music
GMusRNCM .... Graduate in Music of the Royal Northern College of Music
GNSM .... Graduate of the Northern School of Music

Gov .... Governor
Gp .... Group
Gr .... Grammar
GradCIPD .... Graduate of the Chartered
     Institute of Personnel and
     Development
GradICSA .... Graduate of the Institute of
     Chartered Secretaries and
     Administrators
GradIPM .... Graduate of the Institute of
     Personnel Management
Greg .... Gregory
.... Gregory's
GRIC .... Graduate Membership,
     Royal Institute of Chemistry
GRNCM .... Graduate of the Royal
     Northern College of Music
GRSC .... Graduate of the Royal
     School of Chemistry
GRSM .... Graduate of the Royal
     Schools of Music
GSM .... (Member of) Guildhall
     School of Music and Drama
Gt .... Great
GTCL .... Graduate Diploma of Trinity
     College of Music, London
Gtr .... Greater
Guildf .... (Diocese of) Guildford

H

H .... Holy
H&FE .... Higher and Further
     Education
HA .... Health Authority
Hatf .... Hatfield
HCIMA .... Hotel and Catering
     International Management
     Association
Hd .... Head
HDipEd .... Higher Diploma in
     Education
HE .... Higher Education
Heref .... (Diocese of) Hereford
Hertf .... Hertford
Hist .... Historic
.... Historical
.... History
HIV .... Human Immunodeficiency
     Virus
HM .... Her (or His) Majesty
HMI .... Her (or His) Majesty's
     Inspector (or Inspectorate)
HMS .... Her (or His) Majesty's Ship
Ho .... House
Hon .... Honorary
.... Honourable
Hon GCM .... Honorary Member, Guild of
     Church Musicians
HonDLaws .... Honorary Doctor of Laws
HonFChS .... Honorary Fellow, Society of
     Chiropodists
HonRCM .... Honorary Member, Royal
     College of Music
HonRSCM .... Honorary Member, Royal
     School of Church Music
Hosp .... Hospital
HQ .... Headquarters
HTV .... Harlech Television
HVCert .... Health Visitor's Certificate

I

I .... Incumbent
IAAP .... International Association
     for Analytical Psychology
IBA .... Independent Broadcasting
     Authority
ICF .... Industry Churches Forum
     (formerly Industrial
     Christian Fellowship)
ICM .... Irish Church Missions
ICS .... Intercontinental Church
     Society
IDC .... Inter-Diocesan Certificate
IDWAL .... Inter-Diocesan West Africa
     Link
IEAB .... Igreja Episcopal Anglicana
     do Brasil
IEng .... Incorporated Engineer
     (formerly TEng(CEI))
IFES .... International Fellowship of
     Evangelical Students
ILEA .... Inner London Education
     Authority
IME .... Initial Ministerial Education

IMMM .... Institute of Materials,
     Minerals and Mining
Imp .... Imperial
Inc .... Incorporated
Ind .... Industrial
.... Industry
Info .... Information
INSEAD .... Institut Européen
     d'Administration des
     Affaires
Insp .... Inspector
Inst .... Institut
.... Institute
.... Institution
Intercon .... Intercontinental
Internat .... International
Interpr .... Interpretation
IPFA .... Member, Chartered Institute
     of Public Finance and
     Accountancy
Is .... Island
.... Islands
.... Isle
.... Isles
ISO .... Imperial Service Order
IT .... Information Technology
ITV .... Independent Television
IVF .... Inter-Varsity Fellowship of
     Evangelical Unions (now see
     UCCF)
IVS .... International Voluntary
     Service

J

Jas .... James
.... James's
JCD .... Doctor of Canon Law
JCL .... Licentiate in Canon Law
JD .... Doctor of Jurisprudence
JEM .... Jerusalem and the East
     Mission (now see JMECA)
Jes .... Jesus
JMECA .... Jerusalem and Middle East
     Church Association
     (formerly JEM)
Jo .... John
.... John's
Jos .... Joseph
.... Joseph's
JP .... Justice of the Peace
Jt .... Joint
Jun .... Junior

K

K .... King
.... King's
K, E & A .... (Diocese of) Kilmore, Elphin
     and Ardagh
KA .... Knight of St Andrew, Order
     of Barbados
Kath .... Katharine/Katherine
.... Katharine's/Katherine's
KBE .... Knight Commander, Order
     of the British Empire
KCB .... Knight Commander, Order
     of the Bath
KCMG .... Knight Commander, Order
     of St Michael and St George
KCVO .... Knight Commander, Royal
     Victorian Order
KPM .... King's Police Medal
Kt .... Knight

L

L & K .... (Diocese of) Limerick and
     Killaloe (united dioceses of
     Limerick, Ardfert, Aghadoe,
     Killaloe, Kilfenora, Clonfert,
     Kilmacduagh and Emly)
Lamp .... Lampeter
Lanc .... Lancaster
LASI .... Licentiate, Ambulance
     Service Institute
Laur .... Laurence
.... Laurence's
Lawr .... Lawrence
.... Lawrence's
LBIPP .... Licentiate, British Institute
     of Professional Photography
LCC .... London County Council
LCL .... Licentiate in Canon Law
LCP .... Licentiate, College of
     Preceptors

LCST .... Licentiate, College of
     Speech Therapists
LCTP .... Lancashire and Cumbria
     Theological Partnership
Ld .... Lord
LDiv .... Licentiate in Divinity
Ldr .... Leader
LDS .... Licentiate in Dental Surgery
LEA .... Local Education Authority
Lect .... Lecturer
Leic .... (Diocese of) Leicester
Leon .... Leonard
.... Leonard's
LEP .... Local Ecumenical
     Partnership
LèsL .... Licencié ès lettres
LGCM .... Lesbian and Gay Christian
     Movement
LGSM .... Licentiate, Guildhall School
     of Music and Drama
Lib .... Librarian
.... Library
Lic .... Licence
.... Licensed
.... Licentiate
LICeram .... Licentiate, Institute of
     Ceramics
Lich .... (Diocese of) Lichfield
LicTh .... Licence in Theology
LIMA .... Licentiate, Institute of
     Mathematics and its
     Applications
Linc .... (Diocese of) Lincoln
Lit .... Literature
LittD .... Doctor of Letters (also see
     DLitt)
Liturg .... Liturgical
Liv .... (Diocese of) Liverpool
LLA .... Lady Literate in Arts
LLAM .... Licentiate, London
     Academy of Music and
     Dramatic Art
Llan .... (Diocese of) Llandaff
LLB .... Bachelor of Laws
LLCM .... Licentiate, London College
     of Music
LLCM(TD) .... Licentiate, London College
     of Music (Teachers'
     Diploma)
LLD .... Doctor of Laws
LLM .... Master of Laws
LMH .... Lady Margaret Hall
LMPA .... Licentiate Master,
     Photographers' Association
LNSM .... Local Non-stipendiary
     Minister (or Ministry)
Lon .... (Diocese of) London
LOROS .... Leicestershire Organization
     for the Relief of Suffering
Loughb .... Loughborough
LRAM .... Licentiate, Royal Academy
     of Music
LRCP .... Licentiate, Royal College of
     Physicians
LRCPI .... Licentiate, Royal College of
     Physicians of Ireland
LRCSEng .... Licentiate of the Royal
     College of Surgeons in
     England
LRCSI .... Licentiate, Royal College of
     Surgeons in Ireland
LRPS .... Licentiate, Royal
     Photographic Society
LRSC .... Licentiate, Royal Society of
     Chemistry
LRSM .... Licentiate Diploma of the
     Royal Schools of Music
LSE .... London School of
     Economics and Political
     Science
LSHTM .... London School of Hygiene
     and Tropical Medicine
LSIAD .... Licentiate, Society of
     Industrial Artists and
     Designers
LSocEth .... Licence en Sociologie-
     Ethnologie
Lt .... Lieutenant
.... Little
LTCL .... Licentiate, Trinity College of
     Music London
Ltd .... Limited
LTh .... Licentiate in Theology (also
     see LST)
LtO .... Licence to officiate

LVCM .... Licentiate, Victoria College of Music
LVO .... Lieutenant, Royal Victorian Order
LWCMD .... Licentiate, Welsh College of Music and Drama

M

M & K .... (Diocese of) Meath and Kildare
MA .... Master of Arts
MA(Ed) .... Master of Arts in Education
MA(MM) .... Master of Arts in Mission and Ministry
MA(Theol) .... Master of Arts in Theology
MA(TS) .... Master of Arts in Theological Studies
MAAIS .... Member, Association of Archaeological Illustrators and Surveyors
MAAT .... Member, Association of Accounting Technicians
MACC .... Member, Australian College of Chaplains
MACE .... Member, Australian College of Educators
MACT .... Member, Association of Corporate Treasurers
MAE .... Member, Academy of Experts
Magd .... Magdalen/Magdalene
.... Magdalen's/Magdalene's
MAgrSc .... Master of Agricultural Science
MAJA .... Member, Association of Jungian Analysts
MAMIT .... Member, Associate of Meat Inspectors Trust
Man .... (Diocese of) Manchester
Man Dir .... Managing Director
Mansf .... Mansfield
MAPM .... Member, Association for Project Management
MAPsS .... Member, Australian Psychological Society
MArAd .... Master of Archive Administration
MArch .... Master of Architecture
Marg .... Margaret
.... Margaret's
MASI .... Member, Architects and Surveyors Institute
MAT .... Master of Arts and Teaching (USA)
MATA .... Member, Animal Technicians' Association
MATCA .... Member, Air Traffic Control Association
MATM .... Master of Arts in Theology and Ministry
Matt .... Matthew
.... Matthew's
MB .... Bachelor of Medicine (also see BM)
MB,BS *or* .... Conjoint degree of Bachelor
MB,ChB .... of Medicine, Bachelor of Surgery
MBA .... Master of Business Administration
MBACP .... Member, British Association for Counselling and Psychotherapy
MBAOT .... Member, British Association of Occupational Therapists (formerly MAOT)
MBAP .... Member, British Association of Psychotherapists
MBASW .... Member, British Association of Social Workers
MBATOD .... Member, British Association of Teachers of the Deaf
MBC .... Metropolitan (or Municipal) Borough Council
MBChA .... Member, British Chiropody Association
MBCS .... Member, British Computer Society
MBE .... Member, Order of the British Empire
MBEng .... Member, Association of Building Engineers
MBES .... Member, Biological Engineering Society
MBIM .... Member, British Institute of Management (later MIMgt)

MBiochem .... Master of Biochemstry
MBKSTS .... Member, British Kinematograph, Sound and Television Society
MBM .... Master of Business Management
MBPsS .... Member, British Psychological Society
MC .... Military Cross
MCA .... Member, Institute of Chartered Accountants
MCB .... Master in Clinical Biochemistry
MCCDRCS .... Member in Clinical Community Dentistry, Royal College of Surgeons
MCD .... Master of Civic Design
MCE .... Master of Civil Engineering
MCGI .... Member, City and Guilds of London Institute
MChem .... Master of Chemistry
MChemA .... Master in Chemical Analysis
MChOrth .... Master of Orthopaedic Surgery
MChS .... Member, Society of Chiropodists
MCIArb .... Member, Chartered Institute of Arbitrators
MCIBS .... Member, Chartered Institute of Bankers in Scotland
MCIBSE .... Member, Chartered Institute of Building Service Engineers
MCIEEM .... Member, Chartered Institute of Ecology and Environmental Management (formerly MIEEM)
MCIEH .... Member, Chartered Institute of Environmental Health (formerly MIEH)
MCIH .... Member, Chartered Institute of Housing (formerly MIH)
MCIJ .... Member, Chartered Institute of Journalists
MCIL .... Member, Chartered Institute of Linguists
MCIM .... Member, Chartered Institute of Marketing (formerly MInstM)
MCIMA .... Member, Chartered Institute of Management Accountants
MCIOB .... Member, Chartered Institute of Building
MCIPD .... Member, Chartered Institute of Personnel and Development
MCIPR .... Member, Chartered Institute of Public Relations
MCIPS .... Member, Chartered Institute of Purchasing and Supply
MCIT .... Member, Chartered Institute of Transport
MCIWEM .... Member, Chartered Institution of Water and Enviromental Management
MCL .... Master of Canon Law
MCLIP .... Member, Chartered Institute of Library and Information Professionals
MCMI .... Member, Chartered Management Institute (formerly MBIM and MIMgt)
MCollP .... Member, College of Preceptors
MCom .... Master of Commerce
MCommH .... Master of Community Health
MCS .... Master of Christian Spirituality
.... Master of Christian Studies
MCSD .... Member, Chartered Society of Designers
MCSP .... Member, Chartered Society of Physiotherapy
MCST .... Member, College of Speech Therapists
MCT .... Member, Association of Corporate Treasurers
MD .... Doctor of Medicine
MDA .... Master of Defence Administration
MDefStud .... Master of Defence Studies
MDiv .... Master of Divinity

ME .... Master of Engineering (also see MEng)
MEd .... Master of Education
MEHS .... Member, Ecclesiastical History Society
MEng .... Master of Engineering
Mert .... Merton
MèsL .... Lettres Modernes
Metrop .... Metropolitan
MFA .... Master of Fine Art
MFHom .... Member, Faculty of Homeopathy
MFOM .... Member, Faculty of Occupational Medicine
MGDSRCS .... Membership in General Dental Surgery, Royal College of Surgeons of England
Mgt .... Management
MHCIMA .... Member, Hotel Catering and Institutional Management Association
MHort (RHS) ..... Master of Horticulture, Royal Horticultural Society
MHSc .... Master of Health Science
MHSM .... Member, Institute of Health Services Management
MHums .... Master of Humanities
MIA .... Malawi Institute of Architects
MIAAP .... Member, International Association for Analytical Psychology
MIAAS .... Member, Incorporated Association of Architects and Surveyors
MIAM .... Member, Institute of Administrative Management
MIAP .... Member, Institution of Analysts and Programmers
MIAT .... Member, Institute of Asphalt Technology
MIBC .... Member, Institute of Business Counsellors
MIBCO .... Member, Institution of Building Control Officers
MIBF .... Member, Institute of British Foundrymen
MIBiol .... Member, Institute of Biology
MICA .... Member, International Cartographic Association
MICAS .... Member, Institute of Chartered Accountants of Scotland
MICE .... Member, Institution of Civil Engineers (formerly AMICE)
MICFM .... Member, Institute of Charity Fundraising Managers
MICFor .... Member, Institute of Chartered Foresters
Mich .... Michael
.... Michael's
.... Michael and All Angels
MIChemE .... Member, Institution of Chemical Engineers
MICM .... Member, Institute of Credit Management
MICorrST .... Member, Institution of Corrosion Science and Technology
MICS .... Member, Institute of Chartered Shipbrokers
Midl .... Midlands
MIE .... Member, Institute of Engineers and Technicians
MIEAust .... Member, Institute of Engineers and Technicians Australia
MIED .... Member, Institute of Engineering Designers
MIEE .... Member, Institute of Electrical Engineers (formerly AMIEE & MIERE)
MIEEE .... Member, Institute of Electrical and Electronics Engineers (NY)
MIET .... Member, Institution of Engineering and Technology
MIEx .... Member, Institute of Export
MIHEEM .... Member, Institute of Healthcare Engineering and Estate Management
MIHM .... Member, Institute of Healthcare Management

MIHT .... Member, Institution of Highways and Transportation
MIIExE .... Member, Institute of Incorporated Executive Engineers
MIIM .... Member, Institution of Industrial Managers
MIInfSc .... Member, Institute of Information Scientists
MIL .... Member, Institute of Linguists
Mil .... Military
MILT .... Member, Institute of Logistics and Transport
MIM .... Member, Institute of Metals (formerly Institution of Metallurgists)
MIMA .... Member, Institute of Management Accountants
.... Member, Institute of Mathematics and its Applications
MIMarEST .... Member, Institute of Marine Engineering, Science and Technology
MIMC .... Member, Institute of Management Consultants
MIMechE .... Member, Institution of Mechanical Engineers (formerly AMIMechE)
MIMI .... Member, Institute of the Motor Industry
MIMunE .... Member, Institution of Municipal Engineers
Min .... Minister
.... Ministers
.... Ministries
.... Ministry
.... Minor
Min-in-c .... Minister-in-charge
Minl .... Ministerial
MInstC(Glas) ...... Member, Institute of Counselling (Glasgow)
MInstD .... Member, Institute of Directors
MInstE .... Member, Institute of Energy
MInstGA .... Member, Institute of Group Analysis
MInstP .... Member, Institute of Physics
MInstPI .... Member, Institute of Patentees and Inventors
MInstPkg .... Member, Institute of Packaging
MInstPS .... Corporate Member, Institute of Purchasing and Supply
MInstTA .... Member, Institute of Transport Administration
MINucE .... Member, Institution of Nuclear Engineers
MIOSH .... Member, Institution of Occupational Safety and Health
MIOT .... Member, Institute of Operating Theatre Technicians
MIPI .... Member, Institute of Private Investigators
MIPR .... Member, Institute of Public Relations
MIProdE .... Member, Institution of Production Engineers
MIQA .... Member, Institute of Quality Assurance
MIRSE .... Member, Institution of Railway Signal Engineers
MISE .... Member, Institute of Sales Engineers
MISM .... Member, Institute of Supervisory Management
Miss .... Mission
.... Missions
.... Missionary
Missr .... Missioner
MIStructE .... Member, Institute of Structural Engineers
MISW .... Member, Institute of Social Welfare
MITI .... Member, Institute of Translation and Interpreting
MITMA .... Member, Institute of Trade Mark Agents
MITPA .... Member, International Tax Planning Association
MIW .... Member, Institute of Welfare (formerly MIWO)

ML .... Master of Leadership
MLI .... Member, Landscape Institute
MLib .... Master of Librarianship
MLitt .... Master of Letters
MLL .... Master of Laws
MLS .... Master of Library Studies
MM .... Military Medal
MMath .... Master of Mathematics
MMCET .... Martyrs' Memorial and Church of England Trust
MMedSc .... Master of Medical Science
MMet .... Master of Metallurgy
MMin .... Master of Ministry
MMinTheol .... Master in Ministry and Theology
MMS .... Member, Institute of Management Services
MMus .... Master of Music (also see MusM)
MN .... Master of Nursing
MNI .... Member, Nautical Institute
MOD .... Ministry of Defence
Mon .... (Diocese of) Monmouth
Mor .... (Diocese of) Moray, Ross and Caithness
MPA .... Master of Public Administration
MPerf .... Master of Performance
MPH .... Master of Public Health
MPhil .... Master of Philosophy
MPhilF .... Master of Philosophical Foundations
MPhys .... Master of Physics
MProf .... Master of Professional Studies
MPS .... Master of Professional Studies
MPsychSc .... Master of Psychological Science
MRAC .... Member, Royal Agricultural College
MRAeS .... Member, Royal Aeronautical Society
MRCGP .... Member, Royal College of General Practitioners
MRCO .... Member, Royal College of Organists
MRCOG .... Member, Royal College of Obstetricians and Gynaecologists
MRCP .... Member, Royal College of Physicians
MRCPath .... Member, Royal College of Pathologists
MRCPsych .... Member, Royal College of Psychiatrists
MRCS .... Member, Royal College of Surgeons
MRCSE .... Member, Royal College of Surgeons of Edinburgh
MRCVS .... Member, Royal College of Veterinary Surgeons
MRelSc .... Master of Religious Science
MRes .... Master of Research
MRIA .... Member, Royal Irish Academy
MRICS .... Member, Royal Institution of Chartered Surveyors (formerly ARICS)
MRIN .... Member, Royal Institute of Navigation
MRINA .... Member, Royal Institution of Naval Architects
MRIPHH .... Member, Royal Institute of Public Health and Hygiene
MRPharmS .... Member, Royal Pharmaceutical Society (formerly MPS)
MRSB .... Member, Royal Society of Biologists (formerly MSB)
MRSC .... Member, Royal Society of Chemistry (formerly MRIC)
MRSL .... Member, Order of the Republic of Sierra Leone
MRSPH .... Member, Royal Society for the Promotion of Health
MRST .... Member, Royal Society of Teachers
MRTPI .... Member, Royal Town Planning Institute
MRTvS .... Member, Royal Television Society
MS .... Master of Science (USA)
.... Master of Surgery
MSacMus .... Master of Sacred Music

MSAICE .... Member, South African Institution of Civil Engineers
MSc .... Master of Science
MSc(Econ) .... Master of Science in Economics
MSci .... Master of Natural Sciences
MScRel .... Maitrise es Sciences Religieuses
MSE .... Master of Science in Engineering (USA)
.... Minister (or Ministers) in Secular Employment
MSERT .... Member, Society of Electronic and Radio Technicians
MSHAA .... Member, Society of Hearing Aid Audiologists
MSI .... Member, Securities Institute
MSIAD .... Member, Society of Industrial Artists and Designers
MSLIS .... Master of Science in Library and Information Science
MSNTS .... Member, Society for New Testament Study
MSoc .... Maîtrise en Sociologie
MSocSc .... Master of Social Sciences (also see MSSc)
MSocWork .... Master of Social Work (USA)
MSOSc .... Member, Society of Ordained Scientists
MSOTS .... Member, Society for Old Testament Study
MSR .... Member, Society of Radiographers
MSSc .... Master of Social Science (also see MSocSc)
MSSCh .... Member, School of Surgical Chiropody
MSSTh .... Member, Society for the Study of Theology
MSt .... Master of Studies
MSTSD .... Member, Society of Teachers of Speech and Drama
MSW .... Master of Social Work
Mt .... Mount
MTD .... Master of Transport Design
MTeach .... Master of Teaching
MTech .... Master of Technology
MTh or MTheol .. Master of Theology (also see STM and ThM)
MThSt or MTS .... Master of Theological Studies
MU .... Mothers' Union
MusB or MusBac   Bachelor of Music (also see BMus)
MusD or MusDoc   Doctor of Music
MusM .... Master of Music (also see MMus)
MVO .... Member, Royal Victorian Order

N

N .... North
.... Northern
NACRO .... National Association for the Care and Rehabilitation of Offenders
NASA .... National Aeronautics and Space Administration (USA)
Nat .... National
Nath .... Nathanael/Nathaniel
.... Nathanael's/Nathaniel's
NCEC .... National Christian Education Council
NE .... North East
NEITE .... North East Institute for Theological Education
NEOC .... North East Oecumenical Course (formerly North East Ordination Course)
Newc .... (Diocese of) Newcastle
NHS .... National Health Service
Nic .... Nicholas/Nicolas
.... Nicholas's/Nicolas's
NIDA .... National Institute of Dramatic Art
NJ .... New Jersey
NOC .... Northern Ordination Course
Nor .... (Diocese of) Norwich
Northn .... Northampton
Nottm .... Nottingham
NS .... Nova Scotia (Canada)

NSM .... Non-stipendiary Minister (or Ministry)
NSPCC .... National Society for the Prevention of Cruelty to Children
NSW .... New South Wales (Australia)
NT .... New Testament
NTMTC .... North Thames Ministerial Training Course
Nuff .... Nuffield
NUI .... National University of Ireland
NUU .... New University of Ulster
NW .... North West/Northwestern
NWT .... North West Territories (Canada)
NY .... New York (USA)
NZ .... New Zealand

O

OAM .... Medal of the Order of Australia
OBE .... Officer, Order of the British Empire
OBI .... Order of British India
OCF .... Officiating Chaplain to the Forces
OCM .... Officiating Chaplain to the Military
Offg .... Officiating
Offic .... Officiate
OGS .... Oratory of the Good Shepherd
OH .... Ohio
OHP .... Order of the Holy Paraclete
OLM .... Ordained Local Minister (or Ministry)
OM .... Order of Merit
OM(Ger) .... Order of Merit of Germany
OMF .... Overseas Missionary Fellowship
ONZ .... Order of New Zealand
Ord .... Ordained
.... Ordinands
.... Ordination
Org .... Organization
.... Organizer
.... Organizing
OSB .... Order of St Benedict
OSP .... Order of St Paul
OT .... Old Testament
Ox .... (Diocese of) Oxford

P

P .... Patron(s)
.... Priest
p .... Ordained Priest
P in O .... Priest in Ordinary
Par .... Parish
.... Parishes
Paroch .... Parochial
Past .... Pastoral
Patr .... Patrick
.... Patrick's
.... Patronage
PBS .... Pengeran Bintang Sarawak (Companion of the Order of the Star, Sarawak)
PC .... Perpetual Curate
.... Privy Counsellor
PCC .... Parochial Church Council
Pemb .... Pembroke
Penn .... Pennsylvania (USA)
Perm .... Permission
Pet .... (Diocese of) Peterborough
.... Peter
.... Peter's
Peterho .... Peterhouse
PEV .... Provincial Episcopal Visitor
PGCE .... Postgraduate Certificate in Education
PGDE .... Postgraduate Diploma in Education
PGTC .... Postgraduate Teaching Certificate
PhB .... Bachelor of Philosophy
PhC .... Pharmaceutical Chemist
PhD .... Doctor of Philosophy (also see DPhil)
PhD(Educ) .... Doctor of Philosophy in Education
Phil .... Philip
.... Philip's
PhL .... Licentiate of Philosophy

P-in-c .... Priest-in-charge
plc .... public limited company
PM .... Priest Missioner
PO .... Post Office
Poly .... Polytechnic
Portsm .... (Diocese of) Portsmouth
PPRIBA .... Past President, Royal Institute of British Architects
PQCSW .... Post-Qualifying Certificate in Social Work
Preb .... Prebendary
Prec .... Precentor
Prep .... Preparatory
Pres .... President
Prin .... Principal
Pris .... Prison
.... Prisons
Prof .... Professor
.... Professorial
Progr .... Program
.... Programme
.... Programmes
Prop .... Proprietary
Prov .... Province
.... Provincial
PsychD .... Professional Doctor of Counselling Psychology
Pt .... Point
PtO .... Permission to officiate
PV .... Priest Vicar

Q

QC .... Queen's Counsel
QGM .... Queen's Gallantry Medal
QHC .... Honorary Chaplain to The Queen
Qld .... Queensland
QN .... Queen's Nurse
QPM .... Queen's Police Medal
QSM .... Queen's Service Medal
QSO .... Queen's Service Order of New Zealand
Qu .... Queen
.... Queen's
.... Queens'
QUB .... The Queen's University of Belfast
QVRM .... Queen's Volunteer Reserve Medal

R

R .... Rector
.... Royal
R and D .... Research and Development
R of O .... Reserve of Officers
R&SChTrust .... Rochester and Southwark Church Trust
RAAChD .... Royal Australian Army Chaplains' Department
RAAF .... Royal Australian Air Force
RAChD .... Royal Army Chaplains' Department
RAD or RADD ..... Royal Association in Aid of Deaf People (formerly Deaf and Dumb)
RADA .... Royal Academy of Dramatic Art
RADICLE .... Residential and Drop-in Centre London Enterprises
RAEC .... Royal Army Educational Corps
RAF .... Royal Air Force
RAFVR .... Royal Air Force Volunteer Reserve
RAM .... (Member) Royal Academy of Music
RAN .... Royal Australian Navy
RANSR .... Royal Australian Naval Strategic Reserve
RAuxAF .... Royal Auxiliary Air Force
RC .... Roman Catholic
RCA .... Royal College of Art
RCAF .... Royal Canadian Air Force
RCM .... Royal College of Music
RCN .... Royal Canadian Navy
.... Royal College of Nursing
RCNT .... Registered Clinical Nurse Teacher
RCPS .... Royal College of Physicians and Surgeons
RCS .... Royal College of Surgeons of England

RCSE .... Royal College of Surgeons of Edinburgh
RD .... Royal Navy Reserve Decoration
.... Rural Dean
RE .... Religious Education
Reg .... Registered
Regt .... Regiment
Rehab .... Rehabilitation
Relig .... Religion(s)
.... Religious
Relns .... Relations
Rem .... Remand
Rep .... Representative
Res .... Residence
.... Resident
.... Residential
.... Residentiary
Resp .... Responsibility
Resurr .... Resurrection
Revd .... Reverend
RFN .... Registered Fever Nurse
RGN .... Registered General Nurse
RHV .... Registered Health Visitor
RIA .... Royal Irish Academy
RIBA .... (Member) Royal Institute of British Architects (formerly ARIBA)
Rich .... Richard
.... Richard's
Ripon .... Ripon and Leeds
RLSMD .... Royal London School of Medicine and Dentistry
RM .... Registered Midwife
RMA or RMC ...... Royal Military Academy (formerly College), Sandhurst
RMCM .... Royal Manchester College of Music
RMCS .... Royal Military College of Science, Shrivenham
RMHN .... Registered Mental Health Nurse
RMN .... Registered Mental Nurse
RN .... Registered Nurse (Canada)
.... Royal Navy
RN(MH) .... Registered Nurse (for the mentally handicapped)
RNCM .... Royal Northern College of Music
RNIB .... Royal National Institute for the Blind
RNLI .... Royal National Lifeboat Institution
RNMH .... Registered Nurse for the Mentally Handicapped
RNR .... Royal Naval Reserve
RNT .... Registered Nurse Tutor
RNVR .... Royal Naval Volunteer Reserve
RNZN .... Royal New Zealand Navy
Rob .... Robinson
Roch .... (Diocese of) Rochester
RS .... Religious Studies
RSAMD .... Royal Scottish Academy of Music and Drama
RSCM .... (Member) Royal School of Church Music
RSCN .... Registered Sick Children's Nurse
Rt .... Right
RTCert .... Certified Reality Therapist
Rtd or rtd .... Retired
RTE .... Radio Telefís Éireann
RVC .... Royal Veterinary College
RVO .... Royal Victorian Order

S

S .... South
.... Southern
S & B .... (Diocese of) Swansea and Brecon
S & M .... (Diocese of) Sodor and Man
SA .... Salvation Army
Sacr .... Sacrist
.... Sacristan
SAMS .... South American Mission Society (now see CMS)
SAOMC .... St Albans and Oxford Ministry Course
SAP .... (Member) Society of Analytical Psychologists
Sarum .... (Diocese of) Salisbury
Sav .... Saviour
.... Saviour's

ScD .... Doctor of Science (also see DSc)
Sch .... School
SCM .... State Certified Midwife
.... Student Christian Movement
SCRTP .... South Central Regional Training Partnership
SCTEI .... South Central Theological Education Institution
SE .... South East
Sec .... Secretary
SEITE .... South East Institute for Theological Education
Selw .... Selwyn
Sem .... Seminary
Sen .... Senior
SEN .... State Enrolled Nurse
SFHEA .... Senior Fellow, Higher Education Academy
.... Senior Fellow, Higher Education Academy
SHARE .... Shelter Housing and Renewal Experiment
Sheff .... (Diocese of) Sheffield
Shep .... Shepherd
SM .... Master of Science (USA)
SMF .... Society for the Maintenance of the Faith
SNTS .... Society for New Testament Studies
SNWTP .... Southern North West Training Partnership
So .... Souls
.... Souls'
SOAS .... School of Oriental and African Studies
Soc .... Social
.... Society
SOMA .... Sharing of Ministries Abroad
SOSc .... Society of Ordained Scientists
Southn .... Southampton
SPCK .... Society for Promoting Christian Knowledge
SPG .... Society for the Propagation of the Gospel (now see USPG)
Sqn Ldr .... Squadron Leader
SRCh .... State Registered Chiropodist
SRD .... State Registered Dietician
SRN .... State Registered Nurse
SROT .... State Registered Occupational Therapist
SRP .... State Registered Physiotherapist
SS .... Saints
.... Saints'
.... Sidney Sussex
SSB .... Society of the Sisters of Bethany
SSC .... Solicitor before the Supreme Court (Scotland)
SSEES .... School of Slavonic and East European Studies
SSF .... Society of St Francis
SSJ .... Society of St John of Jerusalem
SSJE .... Society of St John the Evangelist
SSM .... Self-supporting Minister (or Ministry)
.... Society of the Sacred Mission
St .... Saint
St Alb .... (Diocese of) St Albans
.... St Alban
.... St Alban's
St And .... (Diocese of) St Andrews, Dunkeld and Dunblane
St As .... (Diocese of) St Asaph
St D .... (Diocese of) St Davids
St E .... (Diocese of) St Edmundsbury and Ipswich
STB .... Bachelor of Theology (also see BTh)
STD .... Doctor of Sacred Theology (also see DST)

Ste .... Sainte
Steph .... Stephen
.... Stephen's
STETS .... Southern Theological Education and Training Scheme
STh .... Scholar in Theology (also see ThSchol)
.... Student in Theology
STL .... Reader (or Professor) of Sacred Theology
STM .... Master of Theology (also see MTh or MTheol and ThM)
STV .... Scottish Television
Sub .... Substitute
Succ .... Succentor
Suff .... Suffragan
Supt .... Superintendent
SW .... South West
S'wark .... (Diocese of) Southwark
S'well .... (Diocese of) Southwell and Nottingham
.... Southwell
SWJ .... Servants with Jesus
SWMTC .... South West Ministry Training Course
Syn .... Synod

T

T, K & A .... (Diocese of) Tuam, Killala and Achonry
TA .... Territorial Army
Tas .... Tasmania
TAVR .... Territorial and Army Volunteer Reserve
TC .... Technician Certificate
TCD .... Trinity College, Dublin
TCert .... Teacher's Certificate
TD .... Team Deacon
.... Territorial Efficiency Decoration
TDip .... Teacher's Diploma
TEAR .... The Evangelical Alliance Relief
Tech .... Technical
.... Technological
.... Technology
TEM .... Territorial Efficiency Medal
temp .... temporarily
TEng .... Senior Technician Engineer
Th .... Theologian
.... Theological
.... Theology
ThA .... Associate of Theology
ThB .... Bachelor of Theology (USA)
ThD .... Doctor of Theology (also see DTh)
ThL .... Theological Licentiate
ThM .... Master of Theology (also see MTh or MTheol and STM)
Thos .... Thomas
.... Thomas's
ThSchol .... Scholar in Theology (also see STh)
Tim .... Timothy
.... Timothy's
TISEC .... Theological Institute of the Scottish Episcopal Church
TM .... Team Minister (or Ministry)
TP .... Team Priest
TR .... Team Rector
Tr .... Trainer
.... Training
Treas .... Treasurer
.... Treasurer's
Trin .... Trinity
TS .... Training Ship
TSB .... Trustee Savings Bank
TV .... Team Vicar
.... Television
TVS .... Television South

U

UAE .... United Arab Emirates
UCC .... University College, Cork

UCCF .... Universities and Colleges Christian Fellowship of Evangelical Unions (formerly IVF)
UCD .... University College, Dublin
UEA .... University of East Anglia
UED .... University Education Diploma
UK .... United Kingdom
UKRC .... United Kingdom Register of Counsellors
UMCA .... Universities' Mission to Central Africa (now see USPG)
UMIST .... University of Manchester Institute of Science and Technology
UNISA .... University of South Africa
Univ .... University
UPA .... Urban Priority Area (or Areas)
URC .... United Reformed Church
USA or US .... United States (of America)
USCL .... United Society for Christian Literature
USPG .... United Society Partners in the Gospel (formerly SPG, UMCA, and CMD)
UWE .... University of the West of England
UWIC .... University of Wales Institute, Cardiff
UWIST .... University of Wales Institute of Science and Technology

V

V .... Vicar
.... Virgin
.... Virgin's
Ven .... Venerable
VetMB .... Bachelor of Veterinary Medicine (also see BVetMed)
Vic .... Victoria (Australia)
Vin .... Vincent
.... Vincent's
Voc .... Vocation(s)
.... Vocational
VRD .... Royal Naval Volunteer Reserve Officers' Decoration
VRSM .... Volunteer Reserves Service Medal

W

W .... West
.... Western
w .... with
W/Cdr .... Wing Commander
Wadh .... Wadham
Wakef .... (Diocese of) Wakefield
WCC .... World Council of Churches
WEC .... Worldwide Evangelism Crusade
WEMTC .... West of England Ministerial Training Course
Westf .... Westfield
Westmr .... Westminster
Wilts .... Wiltshire
Win .... (Diocese of) Winchester
Wm .... William
WMMTC .... West Midlands Ministerial Training Course
Wolfs .... Wolfson
Wolv .... Wolverhampton
Worc .... (Diocese of) Worcester
WRAF .... Women's Royal Air Force

Y

YMCA .... Young Men's Christian Association
YOI .... Young Offender Institution
YWAM .... Youth with a Mission

A

AAGAARD, Canon Angus Robert. b 64. CQSW 86. Ripon Coll Cuddesdon BTh 93. **d** 93 **p** 94. C Taunton St Andr *B & W* 93–97; TV Southampton (City Cen) *Win* 97–01; TR N Lambeth *S'wark* from 01; Hon Can Asante Mampong Ghana from 15; CF(V) from 15. *St Anselm's Vicarage, 286 Kennington Road, London SE11 5DU* T: (020) 7735 3415 F: 7735 3403 M: 07810-646644 E: angus.aagaard@gmail.com

ABAKUKS, Andris. b 49. Qu Coll Cam BA 70 MA 74 Sussex Univ DPhil 73 CStat 93. K Coll Lon BA 00 MA 03. **p** 02. In Latvian Evang Lutheran Ch from 02; PtO *Guildf* from 16. *4 Richmond Close, Epsom KT18 5EY* T: (01372) 811144 E: abakuks@ntlworld.com

ABAYOMI-COLE, Canon Bimbisara Alfred (Bimbi). b 58. CCC Ox BA 80 MA 85. Trin Coll Bris BA 94. **d** 94 **p** 95. C Deptford St Pet *S'wark* 94–98; V Crofton St Paul *Roch* from 98; Hon Can Roch Cathl from 15. *St Paul's Vicarage, 2 Oakwood Road, Orpington BR6 8JH* T: (01689) 852939 *or* 850697 E: bimbiabayomi_cole@hotmail.com

ABBOTT, Barry Joseph. b 59. Sunderland Univ BA 98 Sarum Coll MA 17 MCIEH. NEOC 89. **d** 92 **p** 93. NSM Bishopwearmouth Ch Ch *Dur* 92–98; NSM Silksworth 98–00; P-in-c Lumley 00–04; AD Chester-le-Street 02–04; P-in-c Whickham 04–08; R from 08. *The Rectory, Church Chare, Whickham, Newcastle upon Tyne NE16 4SH* T: 0191-488 7397 M: 07801-074909

ABBOTT, Christopher Ralph. b 38. Univ of Wales (Lamp) BA 59. Wells Th Coll 59. **d** 61 **p** 62. C Camberwell St Giles *S'wark* 61–67; C Portsea St Mary *Portsm* 67–70; V Portsea St Cuth 70–87; P-in-c Gt Milton *Ox* 87–88; P-in-c Lt Milton 87–88; R Gt w Lt Milton and Gt Haseley 88–93; R Chailey *Chich* 93–00; Chapl Chailey Heritage Hosp Lewes 95–00; rtd 00; PtO *Chich* 01–16; Hon C Purbrook *Portsm* 03–05; PtO 14–16; *Chich* from 17. *23 Ramsay Hall, 9-13 Byron Road, Worthing BN11 3HN* T: (01903) 214135

ABBOTT, Craig Andrew. b 75. St Martin's Coll Lanc BA 96. LCTP 10. **d** 12 **p** 13. C Lancaster St Thos *Blackb* 12–16; V Ellel from 16. *20 Highland Brow, Galgate, Lancaster LA2 0NB* M: 07813-903420

ABBOTT, Canon David John. b 52. CertEd. St Jo Coll Nottm. **d** 87 **p** 88. C Biddulph *Lich* 87–90; C Tunbridge Wells St Jas *Roch* 90–92; TV Tunbridge Wells St Jas w St Phil 92–98; V Sunnyside w Bourne End *St Alb* 98–16; RD Berkhamsted 04–09; Hon Can St Alb 15–16; rtd 16. *11 Stoberry Avenue, Wells BA5 2TF* T: (01749) 572356

ABBOTT, David Robert. b 49. Edin Univ BD 72. Qu Coll Birm 72. **d** 74 **p** 75. C Kirkby *Liv* 74–78; C Ditton St Mich 78–80; R Ashton-in-Makerfield H Trin 80–14; rtd 14; PtO *Liv* from 16. *65 Meadow Brook, Wigan WN5 8ED* T: (01942) 214006

ABBOTT (*née* Bush), **Esther** *Rachma* Hartley. b 66. LMH Ox BA 88 St Jo Coll Dur BA 04. Cranmer Hall Dur 02. **d** 04 **p** 05. C Bethnal Green St Matt w St Jas the Gt *Lon* 04–07; C Staines 07–10; P-in-c Westfield *B & W* 10–15; Chapl Norton Radstock Coll of FE 10–14; P-in-c Woodhill *Sarum* 15–19; C Lyneham w Bradenstoke 15–19; P-in-c 19; R Lyneham and Woodhill from 19. *The Vicarage, Clyffe Pypard, Swindon SN4 7PY* T: (01793) 731134 M: 07854-852806 E: reverendrachma@gmail.com

ABBOTT, Miss Geraldine Mary. b 33. SRN 55 SCM 58 Open Univ BA 77 Lon Univ MTh 85. Oak Hill Th Coll BA 82. **dss** 86 **d** 87 **p** 94. Tutor Oak Hill Th Coll 86–96; St Alb St Paul 86–94; Hon Par Dn 87–94; Hon C from 94. *2 Wheatleys, St Albans AL4 9UE* T: (01727) 860869 E: mary@stpauls-stalbans.org

ABBOTT (*née* ROBERTS), **Ms Judith.** b 55. Collingwood Coll Dur BA 76 Goldsmiths' Coll Lon PGCE 77. SWMTC 00. **d** 03 **p** 04. C Burrington, Chawleigh, Cheldon, Chulmleigh etc *Ex* 03–06; C Axminster, Chardstock, All Saints etc 06–12; PtO *B & W* 13–14; NSM Chaffcombe, Cricket Malherbie etc from 14; Dioc Chapl MU from 16; RD Ilminster *B & W* from 19. *Braytons, Wreath Green, Tatworth, Chard TA20 2SN* T: (01460) 220689 E: judith754@btinternet.com

ABBOTT, Mrs Kathleen Frances. b 60. STETS 96. **d** 99 **p** 00. NSM St Helens and Sea View *Portsm* 99–02; P-in-c Wootton 02–14; AD W Wight 12–14; rtd 15; PtO

Portsm from 16. *48 Fairfield Gardens, Sandown PO36 9EZ* E: abbott.kath@gmail.com

ABBOTT, Canon Nigel Douglas Blayney. b 37. Open Univ BA 87. Bps' Coll Cheshunt 58. **d** 61 **p** 62. C Northampton St Mich *Pet* 61–64; C Wanstead St Mary *Chelmsf* 64–66; Chapl St Jo Sch Tiffield 66–69; V Earls Barton *Pet* 69–73; V Cov H Trin 73–80; Provost St Jo Cathl Oban *Arg* 80–86; R Oban St Jo 80–86; TR Hemel Hempstead *St Alb* 86–96; RD 94–96; R Much Hadham 96–02; Hon Can St Alb 96–02; rtd 02; PtO *Ely* from 03. *1 Cambridge Road, Ely CB7 4HJ* T: (01353) 662256 E: ndba75@icloud.com

ABBOTT, Peter John. b 48. CQSW 86. St Mich Coll Llan 94. **d** 96 **p** 97. C Neath w Llantwit *Llan* 96–98; C Merthyr Tydfil Ch Ch 98–00; P-in-c Llangeinor w Nantymoel and Wyndham 00–02; V Cwm Ogwr 02–03; TV Ebbw Vale *Mon* 03–13; TV Upper Ebbw Valleys 13–14; rtd 14; PtO *Llan* from 15. *19 Pantglas, Llanbradach, Caerphilly CF83 3PD* T: (029) 2086 6434

ABBOTT, Rachma. *See* ABBOTT, Esther Rachma Hartley

ABBOTT, Stephen Anthony. b 43. K Coll Cam BA 65 MA 69 Edin Univ BD 68 Harvard Univ ThM 69. Edin Th Coll 66. **d** 69 **p** 70. C Deal St Leon *Cant* 69–72; Chapl K Coll Cam 72–75; C Cambridge St Matt *Ely* 75–76; Asst Chapl Bris Univ and Hon C Clifton St Paul 77–80; PtO *Bris* 81–04; P-in-c Mangotsfield 04–10; rtd 10; PtO *Bris* 10–17; *Glouc* from 11. *24 Melrose Close, Yate, Bristol BS37 7AY* T: (01454) 315073 E: abbott.steve@btinternet.com

ABBOTT, Stephen John. b 62. Qu Mary Coll Lon LLB 83. Linc Th Coll BTh 92. **d** 92 **p** 93. C E Dereham and Scarning *Nor* 92–95; TV Penistone and Thurlstone *Wakef* 95–97; R Brandon and Santon Downham w Elveden *St E* 97–00; P-in-c Gt Barton 00–04; PtO 04–08; R Bansfield 08–12; rtd 12. *12 Skylark Close, Bury St Edmunds IP32 7GH* M: 07742-396523 E: sj.abbott@lineone.net

ABECASSIS, Canon Joanna Margaret. b 54. Girton Coll Cam BA 75 MA 79 PhD 81. WEMTC 99. **d** 02 **p** 03. C Tavistock and Gulworthy *Ex* 02–07; TV Totnes w Bridgetown, Berry Pomeroy etc 07–10; P-in-c Bradford-on-Avon H Trin *Sarum* 10–13; R Bradford on Avon H Trin, Westwood and Wingfield from 13; Can and Preb Sarum Cathl from 17. *Holy Trinity Vicarage, 18A Woolley Street, Bradford-on-Avon BA15 1AF* T: (01225) 864444 E: joanna.abecassis@cantab.net

ABELL, George Derek. b 31. Selw Coll Cam BA 54 MA 68. Qu Coll Birm 54. **d** 56 **p** 57. C Stoke upon Trent *Lich* 56–60; C Wolverhampton 60–64; R Bridgnorth St Mary *Heref* 64–70; P-in-c Oldbury 64–70; R Atherton N Australia 70–73; R Withington w Westhide and Weston Beggard *Heref* 73–81; R Withington w Westhide 81–83; P-in-c Sutton St Nicholas w Sutton St Michael 76–81; R 81–83; Preb Heref Cathl 82–83; V Basing *Win* 83–88; rtd 88; PtO *Heref* 88–04; *Ox* from 08. *25 Eastfield Court, Church Street, Faringdon SN7 8SL* T: (01367) 240731

ABERDEEN AND ORKNEY, Bishop of. *See* DYER, The Rt Revd Anne Catherine

ABERDEEN AND ORKNEY, Dean of. *Vacant*

✠ABERNETHY, The Rt Revd Alan Francis. b 57. QUB BA 78 BD 89. CITC. **d** 81 **p** 82 **c** 07. C Dundonald *D & D* 81–84; C Lecale Gp 84–86; I Helen's Bay 86–90; I Ballyholme 90–07; Preb Down Cathl 00–07; Cen Dir of Ords 04–07; Bp Conn from 07. *Bishop's House, 3 Upper Malone Road, Belfast BT9 6TD* T: (028) 9066 1942 *or* 9082 8870 E: bishop@connor.anglican.org

ABERNETHY, Cameron Peter. b 75. N Coll of Educn BEd 00 Ox Brookes Univ BA 14. Westcott Ho Cam 16. **d** 18 **p** 19. C Cockerton *Dur* from 18. *175 Brinkburn Road, Darlington DL3 9LD* M: 07725-314995 E: revdcam@gmail.com

ABLETT, Edwin John. b 37. Clifton Th Coll 64. **d** 67 **p** 68. C Sneinton St Chris w St Phil *S'well* 67–70; R High and Gd Easter w Margaret Roding *Chelmsf* 70–73; SAMS Chile 73–75; C Gt Baddow *Chelmsf* 75–78; V Newchapel *Lich* 78–82; V S Westoe *Dur* 82–86; V Tibshelf *Derby* 86–00; rtd 00; PtO *St D* 00–09; *Win* from 10. *Copihue, 18 Sherley Green, Bursledon, Southampton SO31 8FL* T: (023) 8040 6413 E: john.copihue4@gmail.com

ABLETT, Mrs Jennifer Vera. b 46. **d** 00 **p** 01. OLM Claydon and Barham *St E* 00–13; NSM 13–16; rtd 16. *10 Phillipps Road, Barham, Ipswich IP6 0AZ* T: (01473) 830205 E: jenny_and_mick@hotmail.com

ABRAHAM, Brian. b 42. **d** 00 **p** 01. OLM Burscough Bridge *Liv* 00–12; rtd 12; PtO *Liv* from 16. *4 Mere Court, Burscough, Ormskirk L40 0TQ* T: (01704) 892547

ABRAHAM, Canon David Alexander. b 37. AKC 61. **d** 62 **p** 63. C Oswestry St Oswald *Lich* 62–63; C Gt Wyrley 63–65; C Sprowston *Nor* 65–67; V Ormesby w Scratby 67–81; R Oxborough w Foulden and Caldecote 81–87; R Cockley Cley w Gooderstone 81–87; V Didlington 81–87; R Gt and Lt Cressingham w Threxton 81–87; R Hilborough w Bodney 81–87; P-in-c Nor St Giles 87–96; Chapl Asst Norfolk and Nor Hosp 87–91; V Thorpe St Matt *Nor* 96–00; Hon Can Nor Cathl 95–00; rtd 00; PtO *Nor* from 00; Hon PV Nor Cathl from 14. *170 Desmond Drive, Old Catton, Norwich NR6 7JW* T: (01603) 402797 E: dalyn170@yahoo.co.uk

ABRAHAMS, Peter William. b 42. Southn Univ BA 77. Sarum Th Coll 77. **d** 78 **p** 79. C Bitterne Park *Win* 78–82; C Old Brumby *Linc* 82–84; V Mitcham Ascension *S'wark* 84–91; TV Riverside *Ox* 91–06; rtd 06; PtO *Ox* 06–12. *17 Snowberry Close, Wokingham RG41 4AQ* T: 0118-989 3072

ABRAM, Paul Robert Carrington. b 36. Keble Coll Ox BA 62 MA 65. Chich Th Coll 60. **d** 62 **p** 63. C Redcar *York* 62–65; CF 65–89; V Salcombe *Ex* 89–96; Miss to Seafarers from 89; rtd 96; Chapl to The Queen 96–06; Chapl St Pet-ad-Vincula at HM Tower of Lon 96–06; Dep P in O 96–06; PtO *Win* from 09; *Sarum* 16–17. *Paddock End, Kimpton, Andover SP11 8PG* T: (01264) 772349 E: paul.jo@virgin.net *or* abran348@btinternet.com

ABRAM, Steven James. b 50. Lon Univ BD 76. Oak Hill Th Coll 71. **d** 76 **p** 77. C Biddulph *Lich* 76–79; C Heatherlands St Jo *Sarum* 79–83; Libya 83–84; C Stratford-on-Avon w Bishopton *Cov* 84; V Alderholt *Sarum* 84–90; V Daubhill *Man* 90–04; TV Mid Trent *Lich* 04–16; rtd 16; PtO *Eur* from 17. *2 Rue André Malraux, 86400 Civray, France* E: sj@abram.org.uk

ABRAMS, Leonard John. b 54. **d** 14 **p** 15. NSM Purley St Mark *S'wark* 14–17; NSM Merstham, S Merstham and Gatton from 17. *1 Dome Hill, Caterham CR3 6EE* T: (01883) 349665 M: 07941-095086 E: revd.len@gmail.com

ABREY, Mrs Barbara May. b 52. Trin Coll Bris 09. **d** 11 **p** 12. OLM Wroughton and Wichelstowe *Bris* from 11. *17 Edgar Row Close, Wroughton, Swindon SN4 9LR* T: (01793) 633024 E: barbaraabrey@hotmail.com

ABREY, Mark Evans John. b 66. Ripon Coll Cuddesdon BTh 93. **d** 93 **p** 94. C W Derby St Mary *Liv* 93–97; P-in-c Anfield St Mary 97–01; Chapl R Liverpool Children's NHS Trust 95–99; R Chase *Ox* from 01; P-in-c Chadlington and Spelsbury, Ascott under Wychwood 01–05; P-in-c Ascott under Wychwood 05–07. *The Vicarage, Church Road, Chadlington, Chipping Norton OX7 3LY* T: (01608) 676572 E: mark@abreys.com *or* rector@thechasebenefice.org.uk

ABREY, Canon Philip James. b 51. NOC 82. **d** 85 **p** 86. NSM Hindley All SS *Liv* 85–90; C Caversham St Pet and Mapledurham etc *Ox* 90–00; Min Caversham Park LEP 90–00; Co Ecum Officer (Berks) 96–00; PtO *Cov* 00–02; Chapl HM Pris The Mount from 02; Hon Can St Alb from 13. *HM Prison, The Mount, Molyneux Avenue, Bovingdon, Hemel Hempstead HP3 0NZ* T: (01442) 834363 E: philip.abrey@justice.gov.uk

ACHESON, Denise Mary. BTh. **d** 05 **p** 06. C Ballyholme *D & D* 05–08; I Dunmurry *Conn* 08–13; Treas Belf Cathl 13–16; Dean's V 13–16; C Lisburn Ch Ch Cathl *Conn* 16–17; P-in-c Belfast H Trin and St Silas from 18. *45 West Park, Lisburn BT28 2BQ* T: (028) 9260 2400 E: revdacheson@gmail.com

ACHESON, James Malcolm. b 48. BNC Ox BA 70 MA 73. Sarum & Wells Th Coll 83. **d** 85 **p** 86. C Highgate St Mich *Lon* 85–88; TV Tisbury *Sarum* 88–94; R Storrington *Chich* 94–14; rtd 14; PtO *Chich* from 16. *Gilbert Lodge, 1A Gilbert Road, Eastbourne BN22 8JA* T: (01323) 733315

ACKERLEY, Daniel Thomas. b 91. Lindisfarne Regional Tr Partnership 16. **d** 19. NSM Croxdale and Tudhoe *Dur* from 19; NSM Merrington from 19. *41 Kingsley Road, Stockton-on-Tees TS18 5AQ* M: 07720-613301 E: daniel.ackerley@hotmail.com

ACKERLEY, Glyn James. b 57. Kent Univ MA 04 K Coll Lon PhD 13. Cranmer Hall Dur 84. **d** 87 **p** 88. C Tonbridge SS Pet and Paul *Roch* 87–90; R Willingham *Ely* 90–94; R Rampton 90–94; V Chatham St Phil and St Jas *Roch* 94–09; P-in-c Shorne 09–12; V 12–16; Dioc Dir of Ords 09–16; V Bushmead *St Alb* 16–18; rtd 19; PtO *Pet* from 19. *3 Catlin Way, Rushden NN10 9FN* M: 07595-171748 E: g.ackerley@btconnect.com

ACKERMAN, David Michael. b 71. Westmr Coll Ox BTh 95 Brighton Univ PGCE 98 Cardiff Univ LLM 11. Pontificia Institutum Internationale Angelicum Rome STB 01 MA 02. **d** 01 **p** 02. In RC Ch 01–04; C Fairford and Kempsford w Whelford *Glouc* 05–08; P-in-c Sherborne, Windrush, the Barringtons etc 08–12; Dioc Ecum Officer 08–12; V Kensal Green St Jo *Lon* from 13. *St John's Vicarage, Kilburn Lane, London W10 4AA* T: (020) 8969 2615 M: 07826-931399 E: dmackerman@hotmail.com

ACKFORD, Christopher Mark. b 60. Univ Coll Lon BDS 83 K Coll Lon MSc 89. Ripon Coll Cuddesdon 02. **d** 04 **p** 05. C Bracknell *Ox* 04–07; TV Aylesbury 07–14; V Bierton and Hulcott 15–18; P-in-c Stokenchurch and Ibstone 18–19; TR S Chilterns from 19. *The Vicarage, Wycombe Road, Stokenchurch, High Wycombe HP14 3RG* T: (01494) 266891 M: 07780-554032

ACKLAND, Canon John Robert Warwick. b 47. **d** 82 **p** 83. NSM Shooters Hill Ch Ch *S'wark* 82–88; NSM Mottingham St Andr w St Alban 82–94; NSM Woolwich St Thos 94–96; NSM Bellingham St Dunstan 96–03; Hon Chapl *S'wark* Cathl 98–03; P-in-c Perry Hill St Geo w Ch Ch and St Paul 03–04; V 04–12; TR Forest Hill w Lower Sydenham 12–15; Hon Can *S'wark* Cathl 05–15; rtd 15; PtO *S'wark* from 16. *39B Central Hill, London SE19 1BW* M: 07831-516662 E: johnackland100@btinternet.com

ACKROYD, David Andrew. b 66. Coll of Ripon & York St Jo BA 90 St Jo Coll Dur BA 97. Cranmer Hall Dur 94. **d** 97 **p** 98. C Lilleshall and Sheriffhales *Lich* 97–01; Asst Chapl R Wolv Hosps NHS Trust 01–02; C Ogley Hay *Lich* 02–03; PtO 10–11; TR Cheswardine, Childs Ercall, Hales, Hinstock etc 11–17; TR Wrockwardine Deanery from 17; RD Wrockwardine from 17. *The Rectory, Wrockwardine, Telford TF6 5DD* T: (01952) 252078 E: revandy320@btinternet.com

ACKROYD, Dennis. b 36. Cranmer Hall Dur 67. **d** 70 **p** 71. C Newcastle w Butterton *Lich* 70–73; C Horsell *Guildf* 73–77; P-in-c Moreton and Woodsford w Tincleton *Sarum* 77–82; R 82–86; RD Dorchester 79–85; R Ewhurst *Guildf* 86–94; V Cleckheaton St Luke and Whitechapel *Wakef* 94–02; rtd 02; PtO *Sarum* 03–15; *Nor* from 16. *35 Greengate, Swanton Morley, Dereham NR20 4AD* T: (01362) 638078 E: rev.dennis@me.com

ACKROYD, Canon Peter Michael. b 60. Jes Coll Cam BA 82 MA 86 Fontainebleau MBA 87 Edin Univ PhD 02. Wycliffe Hall Ox BA 93 MA 00. **d** 94 **p** 95. C Denton Holme *Carl* 94–97; Sec Proclamation Trust 97–00; V Wootton *St Alb* from 02; Hon Can St Alb from 15. *The Vicarage, Church Road, Wootton, Bedford MK43 9HF* T: (01234) 768391 E: peterackroyd@me.com

ACKROYD, Prof Keith. b 49. St Aid Coll Dur BA 70 Man Univ MPhil 87 Sheff Univ DMinTh 03. **d** 04 **p** 05. NSM Hoole *Ches* 04–15; V Thornton-le-Moors w Ince and Elton 15–19; rtd 19. *Strathmore, Ashby Place, Hoole, Chester CH2 3AG*

ACLAND, Mrs Sophia Caroline Annabel. b 61. Somerville Coll Ox BA 11 MA 11. Ripon Coll Cuddesdon BA 12. **d** 11 **p** 12. NSM Cam w Stinchcombe *Glouc* from 11; NSM All Hallows by the Tower etc *Lon* from 14. *The Mount House, Alderley, Wotton-under-Edge GL12 7QT* T: (01453) 842233 *or* (020) 7481 2928 E: sophia@acland.force9.co.uk *or* sophia@ahbtt.org.uk

ACONLEY, Carole Ann. b 51. Hull Univ BTh 01. NEOC 99. **d** 02 **p** 03. NSM Langtoft w Foxholes, Butterwick, Cottam etc *York* 02–12; PtO from 13. *Hawthorn Farm, Langtoft, Driffield YO25 3BT* T: (01377) 267911 E: caroleaconley@me.com

ACREMAN, John. b 53. Oak Hill Th Coll 86. **d** 88 **p** 89. C Iver *Ox* 88–92; R Hook Norton w Gt Rollright, Swerford etc 92–18; rtd 18. *98 Grange Road, Banbury OX16 9AU* E: acreman@xalt.co.uk *or* john.acreman@btinternet.com

ACWORTH, The Ven Richard Foote. b 36. SS Coll Cam BA 62 MA 65. Cuddesdon Coll 61. **d** 63 **p** 64. C Fulham St Etheldreda *Lon* 63–64; C Langley All SS and Martyrs *Man* 64–66; C Bridgwater St Mary w Chilton Trinity *B & W* 66–69; V Yatton 69–81; V Yatton Moor 81; P-in-c Taunton St Jo 81–84; P-in-c Taunton St Mary 81–85; V 85–93; Preb Wells Cathl 87–93; Adn Wells, Can Res and Preb Wells Cathl 93–03; rtd 03; PtO *B & W* from 04. *Corvedale Cottage, Ganes Terrace, Croscombe, Wells BA5 3QJ* T: (01749) 342242 E: vendick@talktalk.net

ADAIR, Canon William Matthew. b 52. Open Univ BA. CITC 77. **d** 77 **p** 78. C Portadown St Mark *Arm* 77–78; Asst Chapl Miss to Seamen 78–80; C Lisburn Ch Ch Cathl *Conn* 80–84; I Kildress w Altedesert *Arm* 84–92; I Portadown St Columba from 92; Dioc Sec Min of Healing 95–99; Can Arm Cathl from 08. *St Columba's Rectory, 81 Loughgall Road, Portadown, Craigavon BT62 4EG* T: (028) 3833 2746 E: billadair77@btinternet.com

ADAM, Andrew Keith Malcolm. b 57. Bowdoin Coll USA BA 79 Duke Univ (USA) PhD 91. Yale Div Sch MDiv 86 STM 87. **d** 86 **p** 86. Chapl St Thos Day Sch & C New Haven Ch Ch USA 86–87; Chapl Assoc Duke Univ 87–90; Asst Prof Eckerd Coll 90–94; P-in-c Tampa St Jas 91–92; Asst Prof

Princeton Th Sem 94–99; Prof Seabury-Western Th Sem 99–08; P-in-c Evanston St Luke 01–02; Lect Glas Univ 09–13; NSM St Mary's Cathl 10–13; Tutor St Steph Ho Ox from 13; Lect Oriel Coll Ox from 13. *St Stephen's House, 16 Marston Street, Oxford OX4 1JX* T: (01865) 613500 M: 07514-800612 E: akm.adam@gmail.com

ADAM, Canon David. b 36. Kelham Th Coll 54. **d** 59 **p** 60. C Auckland St Helen *Dur* 59–63; C Owton Manor CD 63–67; V Danby *York* 67–90; Can and Preb York Minster 89–90; V Holy Is *Newc* 90–03; rtd 03; PtO *Newc* 03–17. *The Old Granary, Warren Mill, Belford NE70 7EE* T: (01668) 214770

ADAM, Lawrence. b 38. NOC 82. **d** 82 **p** 83. C Thornton-le-Fylde *Blackb* 82–86; Dioc Video Production Co-ord 85–97; P-in-c Scorton 86–91; C W Burnley All SS 91–97; P-in-c Ashton St Jas *Man* 97–99; TV Ashton 00–03; rtd 03; PtO *Ches* from 03. *23 Dryden Avenue, Cheadle SK8 2AW*

ADAM, Lindsay Anne. See YATES, Lindsay Anne

ADAM, Canon Peter James Hedderwick. b 46. Lon Univ BD 73 MTh 76 Dur Univ PhD 81. Ridley Coll Melbourne ThL 69. **d** 70 **p** 71. C Ivanhoe St Jas Australia 70–72; C Rosanna 72; Hon C Holborn St Geo w H Trin and St Bart *Lon* 72–73; C Essendon St Thos Australia 73–74; Tutor Ridley Coll 73–74; Tutor St Jo Coll Dur 75–82; Hon C Dur St Cuth 75–82; P-in-c Carlton St Jude Australia 82–88; V 88–01; Adn Melbourne 88–91; Chapl Melbourne Univ 95–01; Prin Ridley Coll 01–12; rtd 12; Can Melbourne from 96. *PO Box 603, North Carlton VIC 3054, Australia* E: pjhadam@gmail.com

ADAM, William Jonathan. b 69. Man Univ BA 91 Univ of Wales (Cardiff) LLM 03 PhD 09 FRHistS 11. Westcott Ho Cam 92 Bossey Ecum Inst Geneva. **d** 94 **p** 95. C Beaconsfield *Ox* 94–97; C Witney 97–98; TV 98–02; P-in-c Girton *Ely* 02–07; R 07–10; Dioc Ecum Officer 02–10; V Winchmore Hill St Paul *Lon* 10–17; PtO from 17; Abp Cant's Ecum Adv and Ecum Officer Coun for Chr Unity from 17. *Lambeth Palace, Lambeth Palace Road, London SE1 7JU* T: (020) 7898 1474 E: william.adam@lambethpalace.org.uk

ADAMOLEKUN, Abimbola Abolade (Bola). b 72. St Jo Coll Nottm. **d** 14 **p** 15. NSM Shepherd's Bush St Steph w St Thos *Lon* 14–17; Chapl HM Pris Wandsworth from 17; Chapl HM Pris Pentonville from 18. *HM Prison Wandsworth, PO Box 757, Heathfield Road, London SW18 3HS* T: (020) 8588 4000 or 7023 7217 E: abimbola.adamolekun@justice.gov.uk

ADAMS, Canon Alison Mary. b 51. Girton Coll Cam MA 73 Birm Univ BMus 76 CertEd 77 Sheff Univ MPhil 93. EMMTC 94. **d** 97 **p** 98. NSM Burbage w Aston Flamville *Leic* 97–05; Dir Bloxham Project 00–05; Chapl HM YOI Glen Parva 06–13; Dioc and Cathl Soc Resp Enabler *Leic* from 13; Hon Can Leic Cathl 15–16; Can Res Leic Cathl from 16. *29 Leicester Lane, Desford, Leicester LE9 9JJ* T: (01455) 823674 E: alison.adams@leccofe.org

ADAMS, Brian Hugh. b 32. Pemb Coll Ox BA 54 MA 57. Sarum & Wells Th Coll 77. **d** 79 **p** 80. Hon C Crediton *Ex* 79–81; Chapl St Brandon's Sch Clevedon 81–85; C Street w Walton *B & W* 86–88; RD Glastonbury 86–97; V Baltonsborough w Butleigh and W Bradley 88–97; rtd 97; PtO *B & W* 97–18. *18 Hayes End Manor, South Petherton TA13 5BE* M: 07980-605284 E: adamsbj@btinternet.com

ADAMS, Canon Brian Peter. b 47. FInstLD FRSA Avery Hill Coll CertEd 70. S'wark Ord Course 90. **d** 93 **p** 94. NSM Tonbridge SS Pet and Paul *Roch* 93–99; P-in-c Chatham St Mary w St Jo 99–14; Hon Can Roch Cathl 09–14; rtd 14; PtO *Roch* from 15. *3 St Davids Gate, Maidstone ME16 9EP* T: (01622) 728032 M: 07778-777824 E: bpadams@btinternet.com

ADAMS, Mrs Celia. b 39. R Holloway Coll Lon BSc 60 Cam Univ CertEd 61. Sarum & Wells Th Coll 86. **d** 88 **p** 94. NSM Canley *Cov* 88–91; NSM Cov N Deanery 91–92; C Coventry Caludon *Cov* 92–97; Asst to Dioc Dir of Educn 92–93; Asst Chapl Geo Eliot Hosp NHS Trust Nuneaton 97–01; rtd 01; PtO *Ban* from 01; *Cov* from 01. *Cefn-y-Mor, 102 Plas Edwards, Tywyn LL36 0AS* T: (01654) 711604 E: nigeladams864@btinternet.com

ADAMS, Christine Frances. See BULL, Christine Frances

ADAMS, Christopher John. b 40. **d** 98 **p** 99. C Luton St Fran *St Alb* 98–05; rtd 06; PtO *St Alb* from 06. *91 Byron Road, Luton LU4 0HX* T: (01582) 529373 E: chrisandsallyadams@ntlworld.com

ADAMS, David. See ADAMS, John David Andrew

ADAMS, David James. b 58. Trin Coll Bris 95. **d** 97 **p** 98. C Wirksworth *Derby* 97–00; P-in-c Seale and Lullington 00–02; R Seale and Lullington w Coton in the Elms 02–05; CF from 05. *c/o MOD Chaplains (Army)* T: (01264) 383430 F: 381824

ADAMS, Canon David John Anthony. b 46. QUB BSc 70. Bris Sch of Min 81. **d** 84 **p** 85. NSM Sea Mills *Bris* 84–97; C Henbury 97–00; V Longwell Green 00–13; AD Kingswood and S Glos 06–11; Hon Can Bris Cathl 10–13; rtd 13; PtO

Bris 13–19. *31 Elberton Road, Bristol BS9 2PZ* T: 0117-968 4625 M: 07803-330727 E: djaadams@virginmedia.com

ADAMS, Donald John. b 46. St Jo Coll Nottm 86. **d** 88 **p** 89. C Byfleet *Guildf* 88–93; P-in-c E Molesey St Mary 93–03; PtO S'wark 96–03; rtd 03; PtO *Glouc* from 15. *4 Boxbush Close, South Cerney, Cirencester GL7 5XS*

ADAMS, Douglas George. b 39. St Luke's Coll Ex CertEd 69 MEd 87 ALBC 65. SWMTC 86. **d** 89 **p** 90. NSM Bude Haven and Marhamchurch *Truro* 89–93; P-in-c St Mewan 93–04; P-in-c Mevagissey and St Ewe 00–04; Chapl Mt Edgcumbe Hospice 93–96; rtd 04; PtO *Truro* from 05. *9 Arundel Terrace, Bude EX23 8LS* T: (01288) 353842 E: douglas-adams@talktalk.net

ADAMS, Gillian Linda. See WILTON, Gillian Linda

ADAMS, Godfrey Bernard. b 47. **d** 93 **p** 94. OLM Saddleworth *Man* 93–09; PtO from 09. *Shawfields House, Shaws, Uppermill, Oldham OL3 6JX* T: (01457) 875126 M: 07717-222042 E: godfreyadams1@btinternet.com

ADAMS, Hubert Theodore. b 28. FCA. **d** 98 **p** 99. OLM Blurton *Lich* 98–11; OLM Blurton and Dresden 11–13; PtO from 14. *12 Wakefield Road, Stoke-on-Trent ST4 5PT* T: (01782) 415364 E: theoadams@live.co.uk

ADAMS, Ian Robert. b 57. R Holloway Coll Lon BA 79. Ridley Hall Cam 95. **d** 97 **p** 98. C Thame *Ox* 97–04; Ldr mayBe 04–09; Missional Community Developer CMS 09–15; Miss Spirituality Adv from 15; Tutor Ridley Hall Cam from 17; LtO *Ely* from 17. *11 Flagstaff Walk, Plymouth PL1 4SH* M: 07889-906983 E: ian@thestillpoint.org.uk

ADAMS, Canon James Michael. b 49. Man Univ LLB 71 Lon Univ PGCE 79. St Jo Coll Nottm 80. **d** 82 **p** 83. C Luton St Mary *St Alb* 82–85; TV Cove St Jo *Guildf* 85–92; V Chislehurst Ch Ch *Roch* 92–14; Hon Can Roch Cathl 09–14; rtd 14; PtO *Carl* from 15; *Chich* from 18; *Roch* from 18. *20 Piltdown Way, Eastbourne BN23 8LB* T: (01323) 761141 M: 07511-268016 E: michaeladamsjma@gmail.com

ADAMS, Mrs Jayne Maxine. b 57. Westhill Coll Birm CertEd 78. WMMTC 94. **d** 97 **p** 98. NSM Cotteridge *Birm* 97–99; NSM Nechells 99–05; NSM Bournville 05–07; Asst Chapl Dudley Gp NHS Foundn Trust 07–13; NSM Selly Oak St Mary *Birm* from 14. *95 Mavis Road, Birmingham B31 2SB* T: 0121-574 0436 E: jaynevicar@aol.com

ADAMS, John David Andrew. b 37. TCD BA 60 MA 64 BD 69 Div Test 61 Reading Univ MEd 74. **d** 62 **p** 63. C Belfast St Steph *Conn* 62–65; Asst Master Lacunza Academy Spain 65–67; Asst Master Tower Ramparts Sch Ipswich 67–70; Asst Master Robert Haining Sch Surrey 70–74; Hd Master St Paul's Secondary Sch Addlestone 74–82; Hd Master Weydon Secondary Sch Farnham 82–98; NSM Bourne *Guildf* 80–99; NSM The Bourne and Tilford 99–07; Chapl to The Queen 94–07; Consultant to Secondary Schs 98–07; PtO *Guildf* 08–15. *Brookside Farm, Oast House Crescent, Farnham GU9 0NP* T: (01252) 726888

ADAMS, John Frederick. b 82. Univ Coll Ox BA 05. Wycliffe Hall Ox BA 12. **d** 13 **p** 14. C Wimbledon Em Ridgway Prop Chpl *S'wark* from 13. *226 Worple Road, London SW20 8RH* M: 07863-544228 E: johnfredadams@gmail.com or john.adams@emmanuelwimbledon.org.uk

ADAMS, John Mark Arthur. See ADAMS, Mark

ADAMS, John Peter. b 42. Lon Univ BD 69. Oak Hill Th Coll 65. **d** 70 **p** 71. C Whitnash *Cov* 70–73; Hon Asst Chapl Basle *Eur* 73–74; Chapl Davos 74–75; Chapl Düsseldorf 75–76; C Gt Baddow *Chelmsf* 77–80; Miss Eur Chr Miss 80–91; PtO *Chelmsf* 80–91; Hon Asst Vienna w Prague *Eur* 90–91; Asst Chapl Zürich 91–95; P-in-c Harmondsworth *Lon* 95–99; TV Shebbear, Buckland Filleigh, Sheepwash etc *Ex* 99–02; rtd 02; PtO *Ex* 02–18; *Eur* 13–18; *Win* from 18. *21 Florence Court, Andover SP10 5HZ*

ADAMS, Jonathan Henry. b 48. St Andr Univ MA 73. Cranmer Hall Dur 73. **d** 76 **p** 77. C Upperby St Jo *Carl* 76–78; C Sunderland St Chad *Dur* 78–82; Soc Resp Officer 83–91; TV Willington *Newc* 91–96; Local Min Development Officer 91–96; P-in-c Byker St Silas *Newc* 96–01; PtO from 01; *Dur* from 01; rtd 13. *5A Tunstall Vale, Sunderland SR2 7HP* T: 0191-525 1881 M: 07903-911771 E: adams.j@icloud.com

ADAMS, Canon Mark. b 67. Reading Univ BSc 89. St Jo Coll Nottm MA 98 MPhil 07. **d** 99 **p** 00. C Skegby *S'well* 99–02; C Bletchley *Ox* 02–07; P-in-c Mansfield St Jo *S'well* 07–10; P-in-c Ladybrook 09–10; V Mansfield St Jo w St Mary 10–16; AD Mansfield 10–15; V Norwell w Ossington, Cromwell etc from 16; AD Newark and S'well 16–19; Hon Can S'well Minster from 15. *The Vicarage, Main Street, Norwell, Newark NG23 6JT* T: (01636) 636084

ADAMS, Martin Philip. b 57. Open Univ BA 99 K Coll Lon MA 13. Sarum & Wells Th Coll 88. **d** 90 **p** 91. C Sandringham w W Newton *Nor* 90–93; P-in-c Docking w The Birchams and Stanhoe w Barwick 93–95; V Docking, the Birchams,

3

Stanhoe and Sedgeford 95–97; V Orrell *Liv* 97–03; R Aughton St Mich 03–08; Dir Dioc OLM Scheme 03–11; Dir Studies SNWTP 08–11; Dean of Studies All SS Cen for Miss and Min 11–14; Ed ROOTS for Churches Ltd from 15; Hon C Aughton St Mich and Bickerstaffe *Liv* 15–19. *73 Crossdale Street, Northrepps, Cromer NR27 9LB* T: (01263) 512986 M: 07939-396934 E: martin.adams@rootsontheweb.com *or* martin.p.adams@btopenworld.com

ADAMS, Michael. *See* ADAMS, James Michael

ADAMS, Canon Michael John. b 48. St Jo Coll Dur BA 77. Ripon Coll Cuddesdon 77. **d** 79 **p** 80. C Falmouth K Chas *Truro* 79–81; C St Buryan, St Levan and Sennen 81–83; P-in-c Lanlivery w Luxulyan 83–84; V 84–88; V St Agnes 88–99; V Newquay 99–14; RD Powder 90–96; rtd 14; Hon Can Truro Cathl from 03; PtO from 15. *5 Trevemper Road, Newquay TR7 2HR* T: (01637) 853930 E: m.j.adams20@gmail.com

ADAMS, Nicholas Stephen. b 68. K Coll Lon BA 04. Westcott Ho Cam 06. **d** 09 **p** 10. Partnership P E Bris 09–11; C Soundwell 11–13; NSM 13–15; NSM Cotham St Sav w St Mary and Clifton St Paul 15–18; TV Upper Islwyn *Mon* from 18. *The Vicarage, Central Avenue, Oakdale, Blackwood NP12 0JS* E: nickadams100@hotmail.com

ADAMS, Nigel Charles. b 60. St Jo Coll Dur BA 81 Greenwich Univ PGCE 92. Oak Hill Th Coll MA 14. **d** 14 **p** 15. C Barton Seagrave w Warkton *Pet* 14–17; P-in-c Braintree St Mich *Chelmsf* from 17. *St Michael's Vicarage, 10A Marshalls Road, Braintree CM7 2LL* T: (01376) 807662 E: revnigeladams@gmail.com

ADAMS, Nigel David. b 40. Sarum & Wells Th Coll 86. **d** 88 **p** 89. C Tile Hill *Cov* 88–91; C Coventry Caludon 91–92; TV 92–97; Asst Chapl HM YOI Onley 92–95; Sub Chapl HM Pris Birm 95–01; P-in-c Nuneaton St Mary *Cov* 97–01; rtd 01; PtO *Cov* from 01; *Ban* from 01; AD Ystumaner 05–09 and 13–15; AD Synod De Meirionnydd 15–18. *Cefn-y-Mor, 102 Plas Edwards, Tywyn LL36 0AS* T: (01654) 711604 E: nigeladams864@btinternet.com

ADAMS, Olugboyega Adeoye. b 55. Univ of Illinois BSc 81 Univ of Kansas MSc 82 Lon Univ PhD 93 Nottm Univ MA 08 Birm Univ PhD 19. EMMTC 99. **d** 02 **p** 03. C Glenfield *Leic* 02–05; V Peckham St Mary Magd *S'wark* from 05. *St Mary's Vicarage, 22 St Mary's Road, London SE15 2DW* T: (020) 7639 4596 E: oadams.smm@gmail.com

ADAMS, Canon Peter. b 37. K Coll Lon AKC 65 Trin Coll Cam MA 70. St Boniface Warminster 65. **d** 66 **p** 67. C Clapham H Trin *S'wark* 66–70; Chapl Trin Coll Cam 70–75; Warden Trin Coll Cen Camberwell 75–83; V Camberwell St Geo *S'wark* 75–83; RD Camberwell 80–83; P-in-c W Dulwich All SS and Em 83–85; V 85–92; V Addington 92–02; Hon Can S'wark Cathl 99–02; rtd 03; PtO *S'wark* 04–16. *26 Mansfield Road, South Croydon CR2 6HN* T: (020) 8680 3191 E: canon.adams@talk21.com

ADAMS, Canon Raymond William. b 58. Reading Univ BA 79. Oak Hill Th Coll BA 85. **d** 85 **p** 86. C Blackpool St Thos *Blackb* 85–88; C Padiham 88–90; TV Rodbourne Cheney *Bris* 90–02; RD Cricklade 97–99; V Haydon Wick from 02; Hon Can Bris Cathl from 09. *The Vicarage, 54 Furlong Close, Swindon SN25 1QP* T: (01793) 634258 *or* 726000 E: r.adams4@ntlworld.com *or* r.adams3081@gmail.com

ADAMS, Richard John. b 48. Leeds Univ BA 70. SAOMC 94. **d** 97 **p** 98. C N Hinksey and Wytham *Ox* 97–01; V Fence-in-Pendle and Higham *Blackb* 01–11; rtd 11. *Tros y Mor, Llangoed, Beaumaris LL58 8SB* T: (01248) 490770 E: richard@gwyneth.net

ADAMS, Robin Thomas. b 54. QUB BSc 76. Oak Hill Th Coll BA 79. **d** 79 **p** 80. C Magheralin *D & D* 79–82; C Coleraine *Conn* 82–86; I Belfast St Aid 86–89; USA 89–18; V Gainesville Ch of the Word 98–18; Chapl Brittany *Eur* from 18. *La Source, 14 rue Général Dubreton, Ploërmel, 56800 Morbihan, France* T: (0033) 2 97 74 24 82 E: pastor.robin@churchinbrittany.com

ADAMS, Ruth. *See* OATES, Ruth

ADAMS, Ms Ruth Helen. b 73. St Jo Coll Dur BA 94 TCD BTh 97. CITC 94. **d** 97 **p** 98. C Drumragh w Mountfield *D & R* 97–99; Chapl Trin Coll Cam 00–06; P-in-c Bar Hill *Ely* 06–11; V Chesterton St Geo from 12. *St George's Vicarage, 8 Chesterfield Road, Cambridge CB4 1LN* T: (01223) 423374 E: vicar@stgeorgeschesterton.org.uk *or* rev.r.h.adams@gmail.com

ADAMS, Stephen Paul. b 56. Ex Univ BSc 78. Sarum & Wells Th Coll 85. **d** 87 **p** 88. C Swansea St Nic *S & B* 87–88; C Llwynderw 88–91; R Badby w Newham and Charwelton w Fawsley etc *Pet* 91–97; R Abington 97–06; RD Northn 01–06; Dean Min Development St Mich Coll Llan 06–15; TR Cowbridge *Llan* from 15. *The Rectory, 85 Broadway, Llanblethian, Cowbridge CF71 7EY* T: (01446) 771625 E: rector@cowbridgeparish.com

ADAMS (née DABIN), Susan. b 51. NTMTC 96. **d** 00 **p** 01. NSM Hullbridge *Chelmsf* 00–03 and 07–10; NSM Rawreth w Rettendon 07–10; NSM Ashingdon w S Fambridge 03–07; NSM Rettendon and Hullbridge from 10. *49 Crouch Avenue, Hullbridge, Hockley SS5 6BS* T: (01702) 231825 E: susansecretarybird@hotmail.co.uk

ADAMS, Theo. *See* ADAMS, Hubert Theodore

ADAMS, William Thomas. b 47. Ches Coll of HE CertEd 69 Open Univ BA 74 Leic Univ MA 91 FRSA 96. EAMTC 97. **d** 00 **p** 01. NSM Helmdon w Stuchbury and Radstone etc *Pet* 00–03; NSM Astwell Gp 03–05; R 05–12; rtd 12; PtO *Pet* from 12; *Worc* from 14. *Brookdale, Mill Road, Whitfield, Brackley NN13 5TQ* T: (01280) 850683 M: 07787-184510 E: will@adamsbrookdale.com

ADAMSON, Arthur John. b 38. Keble Coll Ox BA 61 MA 65. Tyndale Hall Bris 61. **d** 63 **p** 64. C Redhill H Trin *S'wark* 63–66; Chapl Trent Park Coll of Educn 66–69; C Enfield Ch Ch Trent Park *Lon* 66–70; Ind Chapl and V Battersea St Geo w St Andr *S'wark* 70–74; R Reedham *Nor* 74–80; Min Beighton and Moulton 75–80; P-in-c Cantley w Limpenhoe and Southwood 77–80; R Oulton St Mich 80–90; Chapl Lothingland Hosp 80–90; R Laceby *Linc* 90–98; R Laceby and Ravendale Gp 98–03; rtd 03; PtO *Pet* from 03. *24 Mill Lane, Cottesmore, Oakham LE15 7DL* T: (01572) 812816 E: ajohnadamson@aol.com

ADAMSON, David William Dominic. b 91. Sheff Univ BA 17. Coll of Resurr Mirfield 14. **d** 17 **p** 18. C S'wark St Geo w St Alphege and St Jude from 17; C Bermondsey St Hugh CD from 17; C S'wark Cathl from 17. *54 Balin House, Long Lane, London SE1 1YH* M: 07792-409952 E: daviddominic@stgeorge-themartyr.co.uk

ADAMSON, Graham William. b 76. Robert Gordon Univ Aber BA 98. Trin Coll Bris 12. **d** 14 **p** 15. C Bushey *St Alb* 14–17; V Baswich *Lich* from 17; PtO *Lon* 16–17. *The Vicarage, 97 Baswich Lane, Stafford ST17 0BN* M: 07979-963707 E: frgraham@adamsonweb.com *or* frgrahamadamson@outlook.com

ADAMSON, Mrs Ruth Margaret. b 51. Anglia Poly Univ BSc 95 RGN 89 RHV 95. St Jo Coll Nottm 14 ERMC 15. **d** 16 **p** 17. NSM Aylmerton, Runton, Beeston Regis and Gresham *Nor* from 16. *The White House, Church Close, West Runton, Cromer NR27 9QY* T: (01263) 837668 M: 07980-634826 E: ruth.adamson2@btinternet.com

ADÁN FERNÁNDEZ, Hugo Federico. b 75. San Dámaso Univ Madrid SThB 02 Comillas Pontifical Univ SThM 10 SThD 15. Westcott Ho Cam 13. **d** 03 **p** 04. In RC Ch 03–13; PtO *Ely* 14–17; C Catford St Laur *S'wark* 15–18; P-in-c S'wark H Trin w St Matt 18; R from 18. *The Rectory, Meadow Row, London SE1 6RG* T: (020) 7357 8532 M: 07593-310487 E: hfadan@gmail.com

ADDENBROOKE, Keith Paul. b 67. Warwick Univ BSc 90 MA 05 Lanc Univ MA 03. Qu Coll Birm BA 07. **d** 07 **p** 08. C Upton (Overchurch) *Ches* 07–10; V Tranmere St Paul w St Luke 10–15; V Hale and Ashley 15–18; V Birkenhead St Jas w St Bede from 18. *St James's Vicarage, 56 Tollemache Road, Prenton CH43 8SZ* T: 0151-652 1016 M: 07709-712898 E: k.addenbrooke32@btinternet.com

ADDENBROOKE, Peter Homfray. b 38. Trin Coll Cam BA 59 MA 68 Ex Univ PGCE 60. Lich Th Coll 61. **d** 63 **p** 64. C Bakewell *Derby* 63–67; C Horsham *Chich* 67–73; P-in-c Colgate 73–98; Adv for Past Care and Counselling 73–93; rtd 98; PtO *Chich* from 99. *Ashworth, 10 Collingwood Road, Horsham RH12 2QW* T: (01403) 264818 M: 07970-888107 E: pha2000@wma2005.plus.com

ADDINGTON, David John. b 47. FInstLEx 72 FCIArb 96. St Jo Coll Nottm 88. **d** 01 **p** 03. Asst P Warwick St Mary Bermuda 03–08; Hon C St George St Pet from 08; Chapl Miss to Seafarers from 05. *Eben-Ezer Cottage, 79 New Park, March PE15 8RT* T/F: (01354) 650139 M: 07775-796543 E: fradders@btinternet.com

ADDIS, Rosemary Anne. **d** 14 **p** 15. C Edin Gd Shep 14–18; C Edin St Jo from 18. *Flat 2F1, 8 Marlborough Street, Edinburgh EH15 2BG* T: 0131-669 9231 E: rosieaddis@yahoo.co.uk

ADDISON, David John Frederick. b 37. K Coll Dur BA 60 DipEd 62 Birm Univ MA 79 Bris Univ MLitt 93. Wells Th Coll 64. **d** 66 **p** 71. C Rastrick St Matt *Wakef* 66–67; PtO *Bradf* 67–71; Hon C Manningham St Luke 71–73; PtO *Glouc* 77–79; Hon C Bisley w Oakridge 79–81; V Newland and Redbrook w Clearwell 81–02; Chapl R Forest of Dean Coll 89–02; PtO *Glouc* 02–08; *Mon* 04–08; TV Langtree *Ox* 08–16; Hon C Lon 17–19. *2 Lypiatt Road, Lypiatt Street, Cheltenham GL50 2UA* T: (01242) 238905 M: 07815-806313 E: davidaddison10@btinternet.com

ADDY, William Henry. b 54. SNWTP 09. **d** 12 **p** 13. NSM Fazakerley Em *Liv* 12–14; NSM Mossley Hill 14–17; NSM Liv Our Lady and St Nic from 17. *7 Broadacre Close,*

Liverpool L18 2JW T: 0151-722 3417 M: 07836-225709 E: bill@addyfamily.com

ADELOYE, Emmanuel Olufemi Kehinde. b 60. Ilorin Univ Nigeria BA 85 Ibadan Univ Nigeria MA 95 Crowther Graduate Th Sem Abeokuta PhD 16. Immanuel Coll Ibadan 89. **d** 91 **p** 92. Chapl to Bp Egba Nigeria 91–92; C Egba Cathl 92–95; V Kemta All SS 95–99; Personal Asst to Bp Ibadan S 99–00; Adn Odo-Ona St Paul 00–06; PtO S'wark 07; C Lewisham St Mary 07–08; C Lagos Pentecost Nigeria 09–10; P-in-c 10; Adn Iju-Ishaga St Jo 10–12; V Jakande Estate Our Sav 12–13; Adn Ogunbiyi Memorial Ch 13–18; PtO S'wark 18–19; V Peckham St Jo w St Andr from 19. 10A Meeting House Lane, London SE15 2UN T: (020) 3556 1095 M: 07428-460646 E: rev.eadeloye@yahoo.com

ADEMOLA, Canon Ade. b 62. Goldsmiths' Coll Lon BA 91 N Lon Univ MA 94. NTMTC 95. **d** 98 **p** 99. NSM Lt Ilford St Barn Chelmsf 98–02; V Leyton Em from 02; Can Ibadan from 03. Emmanuel Vicarage, 149 Hitcham Road, London E17 8HL T: (020) 8539 2200 M: 07941-029084 E: orison@ademola.eu

ADENEY, Mrs Susan Margaret Eliza. b 55. **d** 18 **p** 19. NSM Hanley Castle, Hanley Swan and Welland Worc from 18; NSM Upton-on-Severn, Ripple, Earls Croome etc from 18. The Villa, Gilberts End, Hanley Castle, Worcester WR8 0AS

ADENIRAN (née POWIS), Mrs Amy Victoria. b 87. Reading Univ BA 08. Trin Coll Bris BA 14. **d** 14 **p** 15. C Shirley Win 14–18; Min Whiteley CD Portsm from 18. 53 Saffron Way, Whiteley, Fareham PO15 7LG

ADESANYA, The Ven Stephen Adedotun. b 57. Ogun State Univ MEd 97 Ado-Ekiti State Univ PhD 03. Evang Th Faculty Osijek Croatia BTh 91. **d** 91 **p** 92. Nigeria 91–07; Adn Iwade and V Italupe Em 03–07; PtO S'wark 07–09; P-in-c Romaldkirk w Laithkirk Ripon 13; P-in-c Startforth and Bowes and Rokeby w Brignall 09–13; V Burnley St Cuth Blackb from 13; V Brierfield from 13. St Cuthbert's Vicarage, Barbon Street, Burnley BB10 1TS M: 07950-713797 E: dtndsny@yahoo.com

ADETAYO, Mrs Abigail Olufunke. b 47. SRN 74 SCM 75 Greenwich Univ PGCE 07. SEITE 06. **d** 09 **p** 10. NSM Peckham St Mary Magd S'wark 09–17; PtO from 17. 158 Torridon Road, London SE6 1RD T/F: (020) 8695 1713 M: 07746-035727 E: jadetayo@aol.com

ADEY HUISH, Helen Louise. b 59. Bris Univ BA 81 Qu Coll Cam PhD 87. SAOMC 01. **d** 04 **p** 05. NSM Banbury Ox 04–07; Chapl Ox Radcliffe Hosps NHS Trust 07–12; Chapl Ox Univ Hosps NHS Trust 12–13; Chapl Myton Hamlet Hospice 13–19; rtd 19; PtO Ox 09–17; NSM Banbury from 17. Timberhurst, The Green, Shenington, Banbury OX15 6NE T: (01295) 670285 E: louise.adeyhuish@btinternet.com

ADFIELD, Richard Ernest. b 31. Oak Hill Th Coll 62. **d** 64 **p** 65. C Bedworth Cov 64–67; V Whitehall Park St Andr Hornsey Lane Lon 67–77; V Kensington St Helen w H Trin 77–86; V Turnham Green Ch Ch 86–92; rtd 92; PtO Chich from 92; Chapl Brighton and Sussex Univ Hosps NHS Trust 02–03; Chapl Whittington Coll Felbridge 03–11. 363 Hangleton Road, Hove BN3 7LQ T: (01273) 732538 E: ric_the_vic@hotmail.com

ADIDE, Denis. b 86. Brunel Univ BA 11. Trin Coll Bris MA 16. **d** 16 **p** 17. C Turnham Green Ch Ch Lon 16–19; V Shepherd's Bush St Steph w St Thos from 19. St Stephen's Vicarage, 1 Coverdale Road, London W12 8JJ M: 07903-351319

✠**ADIE, The Rt Revd Michael Edgar.** b 29. St Jo Coll Ox BA 52 MA 56 Surrey Univ DUniv 95. Westcott Ho Cam 52. **d** 54 **p** 55 **c** 83. C Pallion Dur 54–57; Abp's Dom Chapl Cant 57–60; V Sheff St Mark Broomhall 60–69; RD Hallam 66–69; R Louth w Welton-le-Wold Linc 69–75; P-in-c N w S Elkington 69–75; TR Louth 75–76; V Morton w Hacconby 76–83; Adn Linc 77–83; Can and Preb Linc Cathl 77–83; Bp Guildf 83–94; rtd 95; PtO Portsm from 95; Hon Asst Bp Portsm 95–14; Hon Asst Bp Chich from 96; LtO Ab from 14. 4 Lochnagar Way, Ballater AB35 5PB T: (01339) 753709 M: 07787-571396 E: michael.adie@btinternet.com

ADKINS, Peter Vincent Alexander (Alex). b 44. Lanc Univ BA 71 Lon Inst of Educn CertEd 78. Kelham Th Coll 63. **d** 69 **p** 70. SSM 64–73; Tutor Kelham Th Coll 71–73; Perm to Offic Jerusalem 73–75; Hon C Cambridge St Giles w St Pet Ely 76–78; Hon C Northolt St Mary Lon 81–83; P-in-c Hanworth St Geo 83–86; R 86–88; Adult Educn Officer 83–86; Burford Priory 89–93; Warden Edw King Ho Linc 93–04; Gen Preacher 93–07; Hon Succ Linc Cathl 99–04; rtd 04. 4 Holly Cottages, Main Street, Horsington, Woodhall Spa LN10 5EX T: (01526) 388448 E: alexad@tiscali.co.uk

ADLAM, David John. b 47. **d** 06 **p** 07. OLM Dickleburgh and The Pulhams Nor from 06. Weggs Farm, Common Road, Dickleburgh, Diss IP21 4PJ T: (01379) 741200 F: 741800 M: 07860-417158 E: john@adlams.net

ADLAM, Keith Richard. b 44. STETS 00. **d** 03 **p** 04. NSM Binstead and Havenstreet St Pet Portsm 03–07; NSM Northwood 07–11; NSM Gurnard 07–11; NSM Cowes St Faith 07–11; P-in-c Wroxall 11–18; rtd 18; PtO Portsm from 18. 71A Arctic Road, Cowes PO31 7PF T: (01983) 296996 M: 07552-793366 E: revkeith@kjr-group.co.uk

ADLEY, Ernest George. b 38. Leeds Univ BA 61. Wells Th Coll 62. **d** 64 **p** 65. C Bideford Ex 64–67; C Yeovil St Mich B & W 67–70; V Taunton Lyngford 70–79; R Skegness and Winthorpe Linc 79–91; R Wantage Downs Ox 91–03; rtd 03; PtO Ox from 04. 13 Pixton Close, Didcot OX11 0BX T: (01235) 210395

ADLEY, Nicholas James Douglas. b 67. Ripon Coll Cuddesdon 11. **d** 13 **p** 14. C Ross w Walford and Brampton Abbotts Heref 13–16; CF from 16. c/o MOD Chaplains (Army) T: (01264) 383430 M: 07877-886740

ADMAN, Fayaz. b 63. Pakistan Adventist Sem Sheikhupura BA 94. St Thos Th Coll Karachi 97. **d** 98 **p** 99. Dn St Jo Cathl Peshawar Pakistan 98–99; P 00–03; Presbyter Peshawar City All SS 99–00; Bp's Chapl 01–03; V Charsada, Shabqadar and Ghalana 00–04; C S Rochdale Man 04–07; P-in-c Bolton St Paul w Em 07–11; P-in-c Daubhill 07–11; TV W Bolton from 11. Emmanuel Vicarage, Edward Street, Bolton BL3 5LQ T: (01204) 393282 or 393282 E: fayaz.a@hotmail.co.uk

ADSHEAD, Adele Elizabeth. b 64. BEd. St Jo Coll Nottm. **d** 14 **p** 15. NSM Ashby-de-la-Zouch and Breedon on the Hill Leic 14–19; V Nanpantan St Mary in Charnwood from 19. 2 Spindle Road, Loughborough LE11 2DL T: (01509) 232262 E: adele.adshead@gmail.com

AECHTNER, Rebecca Barbara. b 83. Calgary Univ BA 04 MA 06 Edin Univ PhD 11. St Mellitus Coll 14. **d** 16 **p** 17. C Lancaster St Mary w St John and St Anne Blackb 16–19; V Scotforth from 19. St Paul's Vicarage, 24 Scotforth Road, Lancaster LA1 4ST M: 07527-102772 E: raechtner@hotmail.com

ÆLRED, Brother. See ARNESEN, Raymond Halfdan

AGAR, George. b 40. Edin Univ BSc 63 Ox Univ PGCE 64. NOC 92. **d** 94 **p** 95. Hd Biddulph High Sch Stoke-on-Trent 94–96; NSM Sandbach Ches 94–99; NSM Hartford from 99. 10 Maes y Ddawns, Llangadfan, Welshpool SY21 0GA T: (01938) 820380 E: georgea@stjohnshartford.org

AGASSIZ, David John Lawrence. b 42. St Pet Hall Ox BA 64 MA 67 Imp Coll Lon PhD 94. Ripon Hall Ox 64. **d** 66 **p** 67. C Southampton St Mary w H Trin Win 66–71; V Enfield St Jas Lon 71–80; P-in-c Grays Thurrock Chelmsf 80–83; P-in-c Grays All SS 81–84; P-in-c Lt Thurrock St Mary 81–84; P-in-c W Thurrock 81–83; P-in-c Grays SS Pet and Paul, S Stifford and W Thurrock 83–84; TR Grays Thurrock 84–90; Hon Can Chelmsf Cathl 90–93; Dioc Development Rep 90–93; PtO 93–94; Kenya 98–00; PtO S'wark 02–07; B & W from 08. The Garden House, Stafford Place, Weston-super-Mare BS23 2QZ T: (01934) 620486 M: 07813-566957 E: david.agassiz@gmail.com

AGBELUSI, Canon Dele Omotayo. b 51. Ahmadu Bello Univ Zaria MSc 81 Oak Hill Th Coll BA 99 Spurgeon's Coll MTh 09. Immanuel Coll Ibadan. **d** 86 **p** 87. Nigeria 86–96; C Edmonton All SS w St Mich Lon 97–99; V Hornsey Ch Ch 99–19; rtd 19; PtO St Alb from 19; Hon Can Akure Nigeria from 08. 9 Cornflower Way, Hatfield AL10 9FY E: agbelusi@aol.com

AGER, Mrs Christabel Ruth. b 51. Bedf Coll Lon BA 73 Gipsy Hill Coll of Educn PGCE 74 MCLIP 98. STETS BA 10. **d** 10 **p** 11. NSM Beercrocombe w Curry Mallet, Hatch Beauchamp etc B & W from 10. 14 Morgans Rise, Bishops Hull, Taunton TA1 5HW T: (01823) 335424 M: 07766-759131 E: crev1951@gmail.com

AGER, David George. b 52. Lon Univ BA 73 Solicitor 77. SWMTC 01. **d** 04 **p** 05. NSM Deane Vale B & W 04–09; NSM Taunton St Jas 09–12; NSM Blackdown 12–16; Bp's Officer for Ord NSM (Taunton Adnry) from 09; PtO 16–19. 14 Morgans Rise, Bishops Hull, Taunton TA1 5HW T: (01823) 335424 M: 07887-893918 E: drev1952@gmail.com

AGNEW, Kevin Raymond Christopher. b 59. Chich Th Coll. **d** 94 **p** 95. C Eastbourne St Mary Chich 94–98; V Roughey 98–14; P-in-c Willingdon 14–19; V from 19. 35A Church Street, Willingdon, Eastbourne BN20 9HR T: (01323) 502079 E: frkevinstmarys@hotmail.com

AGNEW, Stephen Mark. b 54. Univ of Wales (Ban) BSc 76 Southn Univ BTh 81. Sarum & Wells Th Coll 76. **d** 79 **p** 80. C Wilmslow Ches 79–84; V Crewe St Jo 84–90; Chapl Bromsgrove Sch 90–99; V Claines St Jo Worc 99–12; P-in-c Old Swinford Stourbridge 12–18; rtd 18. White Cottage, 53B High Street, Martin, Lincoln LN4 3QY M: 07762-250749 E: revsmagnew@yahoo.com

A'HERNE-SMITH, Mrs Mary Catriona. b 65. Bris Univ BA 86 PGCE 88. Coll of Resurr Mirfield 13. d 14 p 15. C Sutton in Ashfield St Mary *S'well* 14–16; TV Fosse Team *Leic* from 16. *20 Hoby Road, Thrussington, Leicester LE7 4TH* M: 07948-272669 E: mezcat@icloud.com

AIDLEY, Jessica-Jil Stapleton. b 42. Westf Coll Lon BSc 67 UEA PhD 73 PGCE 84. d 99 p 00. OLM High Oak, Hingham and Scoulton w Wood Rising *Nor* 99–04; PtO *Mon* 04–05; NSM Rockfield and Dingestow Gp 05–09; PtO *Chich* 09; NSM Brighton St Nic 09–11; PtO 11–14; NSM New Shoreham and Shoreham Beach from 14. *Myrtle, 2 Riverbank, Shoreham-by-Sea BN43 5YH* T: (01273) 455445 E: j.aidley@btopenworld.com

AIKEN, Canon Nicholas John. b 58. Sheff Univ BA. Wycliffe Hall Ox 80. d 82 p 83. C Ashtead *Guildf* 82–86; Dioc Youth Officer 86–93; R Wisley w Pyrford from 93; RD Woking 03–08; Hon Can Guildf Cathl from 10. *The Rectory, Aviary Road, Woking GU22 8TH* T: (01932) 352914 E: rector@wisleywithpyrford.org

AIKEN, The Very Revd Simon Mark. b 62. St Andr Univ MTheol 85 HonRSCM 15. Ripon Coll Cuddesdon 86. d 88 p 89. C Burnley St Matt w H Trin *Blackb* 88–91; C Heyhouses on Sea 91–94; V Musbury 94–99; V Longridge 99–06; Sub Dean Bloemfontein 06–10; Chapl Free State Univ S Africa 06–10; Adn Maluti 07–09; Dean Kimberley 10–14; Adn Karoo 11–13; Dean Highveld from 13. *19 Mayor Avenue, Benoni, Gauteng 1501, South Africa* T: (0027) (11) 420 3002 E: simonaiken@icloud.com

AIKENHEAD, Mary. *See* CANTACUZENE, Mary

AILWOOD, The Ven Frederick Charles. b 37. Univ of Qld BA 81. St Fran Coll Brisbane. d 63 p 63. C Auchenflower Australia 63–65; C Lutwyche 65–68; V Caboolture 68–74; R Goondiwindi 74–80; R Pittsworth 80–84; R Gympie 84–92; R Caloundra 92–00; R Toowoomba St Jas 00–06; Adn Wide Bay and Burnett 89–93; Adn Wide Bay 93–00; Adn The Downs 00–06; PtO *Eur* from 17. *Tongala, 13 Hickey Street, Toowoomba QLD 4350, Australia* E: fandbailwood@bigpond.com

AINGE, Canon David Stanley. b 47. Ian Ramsey Coll Brasted 68 Oak Hill Th Coll 70. d 73 p 74. C Bitterne *Win* 73–77; C Castle Church *Lich* 77–79; P-in-c Becontree St Alb *Chelmsf* 79–89; P-in-c Becontree St Jo 85–89; TR Becontree S 89–91; RD Barking and Dagenham 86–91; V Leyton St Mary w St Edw 91–96; P-in-c Leyton St Luke 91–96; V Leyton St Mary w St Edw and St Luke 96–03; RD Waltham Forest 94–00; R Gt Dunmow and Barnston 03–13; Hon Can Chelmsf Cathl 97–13; rtd 13; PtO *Chelmsf* from 15. *42 Abels Road, Church End, Halstead CO9 1EW* E: davidainge@btinternet.com

AINSCOUGH, Malcolm Ralph. b 52. Liv Univ BEd 76. St Mich Coll Llan 85. d 87 p 88. C Fleur-de-Lis *Mon* 87–90; C Chepstow 90–91; TV Cwmbran 91–95; V Newport St Steph and H Trin 95–03; rtd 17. *79 Flowery Leys Lane, Alfreton DE55 7HA* E: malcolmainscough@yahoo.com

AINSLIE, John Francis. b 58. Qu Coll Cam BA 79. Ox Min Course 14. d 17 p 18. C The Cookhams *Ox* from 17. *6 Clifton Close, Maidenhead SL6 1DG* T: (01628) 629827 E: revjohnainslie@gmail.com

AINSWORTH, Mrs Janina Helen Margaret. b 50. FCollT 14. Ripon Coll Cuddesdon. d 05 p 06. NSM E Farnworth and Kearsley *Man* 05–07; Chief Educn Officer Abps' Coun 07–14; PtO *Lon* 07–12; Hon C St Geo-in-the-East w St Paul 12–14; rtd 14; NSM Turton Moorland *Man* from 14. *St Maxentius Rectory, Bolton Road, Bolton BL2 3EU* T: (01204) 304240 M: 07825-854945 E: janina.ainsworth@gmail.com

AINSWORTH, Canon Michael Ronald. b 50. K Coll Lon LLB 71 LLM 72 Trin Hall Cam BA 74 MA 79. Westcott Ho Cam 72. d 75 p 76. C Scotforth *Blackb* 75–78; Chapl St Martin's Coll of Educn 78–82; Chapl NOC 82–89; R Withington St Chris *Man* 89–94; TR Worsley 94–07; AD Eccles 00–05; Hon Can Man Cathl from 04; R St Geo-in-the-East w St Paul *Lon* 07–14; rtd 14; PtO *Man* from 15; *Blackb* from 15. *St Maxentius Rectory, Bolton Road, Bolton BL2 3EU* T: (01204) 304240 E: rector.stgite@gmail.com

AINSWORTH-SMITH, Canon Ian Martin. b 41. Selw Coll Cam BA 64 MA 68. Westcott Ho Cam 64. d 66 p 67. C Mill Hill Jo Keble Ch *Lon* 66–69; USA 69–71; C Purley St Mark *S'wark* 71–73; Chapl St Geo Hosp Lon 73–94; Chapl St Geo Healthcare NHS Trust Lon 94–06; Hon Can S'wark Cathl 95–06; rtd 06; PtO *B & W* from 06; Dioc Adv Hosp Chapl from 07. *Knutsford Cottage, North Street, Milverton, Taunton TA4 1LG* T: (01823) 400365 M: 07732-324568 E: jeanianas@btinternet.com

AIRD, Robert Malcolm. b 31. Lon Univ BSc 54. Westcott Ho Cam 75. d 77 p 78. C Burnham *B & W* 77–79; P-in-c Taunton Lyngford 79–84; V 84–87; R Dulverton and

Brushford 87–94; rtd 96. *Arran Cottage, East Street, Chulmleigh EX18 7DD* T: (01769) 581042

AIREY, Mrs Dawn Janine. b 69. Reading Univ MA 02. Ridley Hall Cam 15. d 17 p 18. C Wollaston w Strixton and Bozeat etc *Pet* from 17. *41 The Pyghtles, Wollaston, Wellingborough NN29 7QD* T: (01933) 667481 E: dairey3@gmail.com

AIREY, Simon Christopher. b 60. Trin Coll Bris BA 87. d 87 p 88. C Wilton *B & W* 87–90; Chapl Scargill Ho 90–93; TV Kingswood *Bris* 93–96; Asst P Nether Springs Northumbria Community 96–98 and 02–03; C Bath Abbey w St Jas *B & W* 98–02; C Nailsea Ch Ch w Tickenham 03–09; Chapl Grey Coll Dur 09–11; P-in-c Criftins w Dudleston and Welsh Frankton *Lich* 11–16; V from 16. *The Vicarage, Criftins, Ellesmere SY12 9LN* T: (01691) 690212 M: 07740-799191 E: getthevicar@yahoo.com

AISBITT, Joanne. *See* LISTER, Joanne

AISBITT, Michael. b 60. St Pet Coll Ox BA 81 MA 84. Westcott Ho Cam 81. d 84 p 85. C Norton St Mary *Dur* 84–87; C Kirkleatham *York* 87–90; V S Bank 90–96; R Whitby 96–97; TR Whitby w Aislaby and Ruswarp 97–00; R Attleborough w Besthorpe *Nor* 00–09; RD Thetford and Rockland 03–09. *16 The Acres, Stokesley, Middlesbrough TS9 5QA* E: m_aisbitt@hotmail.com

AISBITT, Osmond John. b 35. St Chad's Coll Dur BA 57. d 61 p 62. C Ashington *Newc* 61–64; C Blyth St Mary 64–68; V Cleckheaton St Jo *Wakef* 68–75; V Horbury 75–78; V Horbury w Horbury Bridge 78–97; rtd 97; PtO *York* 00 and 02–11; P-in-c Nerja and Almuñécar *Eur* 00–02. *8 Stonecross Gardens, Ulverston LA12 7HA* T: (01229) 585622

AITCHISON, Charles Baillie. b 45. New Coll Dur BEd 85 Bede Coll Dur TCert 67 Newc Univ DAES 74 ACP 69. LNSM course 85. d 93 p 98. NSM Peebles *Edin* from 93; NSM Innerleithen from 93. *45 Whitehaugh Park, Peebles EH45 9DB* T: (01721) 729750 or 724008 F: 724008 E: hall100@sky.com

AITKEN, Christopher William Mark. b 53. Dur Univ BA 75. Westcott Ho Cam 76. d 79 p 80. C Finchley St Mary *Lon* 79–82; C Radlett *St Alb* 82–85; V Sprowston *Nor* 85–90; R Beeston St Andr 85–90; R Sprowston w Beeston 90–93; Chapl Sherborne Sch 93–04; Hd Master St Lawr Coll Ramsgate 04–12; Master R Foundn of St Kath in Ratcliffe 13–19; rtd 19. *24 Kilderkin Way, Norwich NR1 1RD* E: cwmaitken@gmail.com

AITKEN, Deborah June. b 65. Qu Foundn (course) 15. d 18 p 19. OLM Hanford *Lich* from 18. *13 Ampthill Place, Stoke-on-Trent ST4 8NP* T: (01782) 644908 M: 07759-072882 E: debhanfordchurch@gmail.com

AITKEN, Janet. b 55. d 16 p 17. NSM Westleigh St Pet *Man* 16–18; NSM Westleigh St Paul 16–18; NSM Westleigh St Pet and St Paul from 18. *9 Browning Street, Leigh WN7 5EF* T: (01942) 740740 M: 07977-661888 E: janetaitken55@hotmail.co.uk

AITKEN, Jonathan William Patrick. b 42. Ch Ch Ox MA 64 Wycliffe Hall Ox BTh 02. d 18 p 19. NSM Westmr St Matt *Lon* from 18; Asst Chapl HM Pris Pentonville from 18. *83 Barkston Gardens, London SW5 0EU* T: (020) 7373 5800 M: 07590-827655 E: jonathanaitken@jwpaitken.co.uk

AITKEN, Valerie Anne. b 46. STETS 01. d 04 p 05. NSM Perivale *Lon* 04–17; P-in-c 14–17; rtd 17; PtO *Lon* from 17. *22 Woodfield Road, London W5 1SH* T: (020) 8997 6819 M: 07968-345992 E: valerie.aitken2@btinternet.com

AITON, Janice Haran. Glas Univ MA 79 Jordanhill Coll Glas PGCE 80 Edin Univ MTh 04. TISEC 98. d 01 p 02. C St Andrews St Andr St Andr 01–04; Chapl NUI 04; R Dumfries Glas from 17. *St John's Rectory, 8 Newall Terrace, Dumfries DG1 1LW* T: (01387) 254126 E: janiceaiton1@gmail.com

AITON, Canon Robert Neilson. b 36. Univ of Wales BA 59 DipEd 60. Chich Th Coll 74. d 76 p 77. C E Grinstead St Swithun *Chich* 76–83; R Lavant 83–90; Chapl St Barn Hospice Worthing 90–95; V Durrington *Chich* 90–01; Can and Preb Chich Cathl from 99; rtd 01; LtO *Chich* from 01. *Fieldings, Joys Croft, Chichester PO19 4NJ* T: (01243) 781728 E: bob.aiton@btopenworld.com

AJAEFOBI, Joseph Obichukwu. b 63. Anambra State Univ of Tech Nigeria BEng 88 Loughb Univ PhD 04. Trin Coll Umuahia 92. d 92 p 93. Chapl Nkpor H Innocents Nigeria 92–00; PtO *Leic* 01–12; Asst Chapl Loughb Univ 05–16; LtO *S'wark* from 16; Chapl Nigerian Congregation *Lon* from 16. *79 Alderney Gardens, Northolt UB5 5BT* M: 07422-465558 E: joeajaefobi@yahoo.com

AJAYI, Timothy Temitope. b 77. Lagos Univ BSc 01 Bedfordshire Univ MSc 08. Ridley Hall Cam 16. d 18 p 19. C Blackheath Park St Mich *S'wark* from 18. *123 Kidbrooke Park Road, London SE3 0DZ* M: 07517-570093 E: ajayitimothy@yahoo.com

AJIBADE, Ms Ijeoma. b 65. Univ of Nigeria LLB 87 S Bank Univ MA 96 Heythrop Coll Lon MA 09. SEITE BA 10.

d 10 **p** 11. NSM Kensington St Mary Abbots w Ch Ch and St Phil *Lon* 10–14; PtO from 14; Hon Min Can S'wark Cathl from 11; Regional Dir Miss to Seafarers from 16; PtO *Eur* from 17. *25 Duffield Drive, London N15 4UH* T: (020) 8376 0598 M: 07757-913318 E: ijeomaajibade@gmail.com

AJUKA, Sampson Chikwere. b 72. Qu Coll Birm BA 08. **d** 08 **p** 09. C Venice w Trieste *Eur* 08–11; Dioc C and P-in-c Devenish w Boho *Clogh* from 12; Chapl to Bp Clogh from 12. *The Rectory, 10 Castletown Road, Monea, Enniskillen BT74 8GG* T: (028) 6634 1672 M: 07908-856207

AKERS, Miss Rachel Leanne. b 81. Ches Univ BA 13 MA 15. St Jo Coll Nottm 13. **d** 15 **p** 16. C Kidderminster E *Worc* 15–18; TV Dudley from 18. *St Augustine's Vicarage, Hallchurch Road, Dudley DY2 0TG* M: 07578-340464 E: rachelakers1@aol.com

AKIBO-BETTS, Hannah Muriel. **d** 18 **p** 19. NSM Bletchley *Ox* from 18. *20 Silicon Court, Shenley Lodge, Milton Keynes MK5 7DL* E: hw2811@tiscali.co.uk

AKKER, Derek Alexander. b 46. Bradf Univ MA 83. NOC 85. **d** 88 **p** 89. C Mossley *Man* 88–90; C Bury St Pet 90–92; V Lever Bridge 92–97; TV Wolstanton *Lich* 97–99; V Hattersley *Ches* 99–09; rtd 09; PtO *Man* from 09; *Ches* from 10; *Eur* 11–16 and from 17. *54 Purbeck Drive, Bury BL8 1JQ* T: 0161-797 0105 M: 07970-646809 E: derekakker@icloud.com

AKRILL, Dean. b 71. York Univ BA 97. Ripon Coll Cuddesdon BTh 00. **d** 00 **p** 01. C Swinton *Sheff* 00–01; C Wath-upon-Dearne 01–04; V Mosborough 04–08; C Sprowston w Beeston *Nor* from 08. *The Newlands, 15 Blue Boar Lane, Norwich NR7 8RX* E: dean@sprowston.org.uk

AKWASI-YEBOAH, Kingsley Nana. b 76. Ridley Hall Cam 14. **d** 16 **p** 18. C Rainham w Wennington *Chelmsf* 16–17; C Forest Gate Em w Upton Cross from 17. *23 Essex Street, London E7 0HL* T: (020) 3583 9100 M: 07982-600092 E: kingsley.akwasi@gmail.com or revking@outlook.com

ALAGOA, Ms Biobelemoye Susan (Belemo). b 56. E Lon Univ LLB 86 Warwick Univ LLM 88. SEITE 10. **d** 13 **p** 14. NSM N Lambeth *S'wark* 13–17; NSM Merton Priory from 17. *32 Lewis Road, Mitcham CR4 3DE* M: 07960-518381 E: belemo.alagoa@gmail.com

ALAN MICHAEL, Brother. *See* PATERSON, Alan Michael

ALASAUKKO-OJA, Tuomas. *See* MÄKIPÄÄ, Tuomas

ALBAN JONES, Canon Timothy Morris. b 64. Warwick Univ BA 85. Ripon Coll Cuddesdon 85. **d** 88 **p** 89. C Tupsley *Heref* 88–93; TV Ross 93–00; P-in-c Soham *Ely* 00–01; P-in-c Wicken 00–01; V Soham and Wicken 02–15; RD Fordham and Quy 10–15; Warden of Readers 12–15; Hon Can Ely Cathl 12–15; Bp's Chapl *Pet* from 15; Can Res Pet Cathl from 15; Vice Dean from 18; Dioc Ecum Officer from 17. *The Bishops' Office, The Palace, Minster Precincts, Peterborough PE1 1YA* T: (01733) 887014 E: tim.albanjones@peterborough-diocese.org.uk

ALBERS, Johannes Reynoud (Joop). b 47. Hogeschool Holland BTh 92 Amsterdam Univ MTh 98. EAMTC 99. **d** 00 **p** 01. C Voorschoten *Eur* 00–02; C Amsterdam w Den Helder and Heiloo 02–04; Asst Chapl 04–12; P-in-c Haarlem 12–15; PtO from 15; Angl Chapl Amsterdam Airport Schiphol from 07. *Dorpsweg 134, 1697 KH Schellinkhout, The Netherlands* T: (0031) (22) 950 1611 *or* (61) 009 8239 E: joopalbers@quicknet.nl

ALBINSON, Thomas Roy. b 79. Ripon Coll Cuddesdon 09. **d** 12 **p** 13. C Littlemore *Ox* 12–16; C Ox St Giles and SS Phil and Jas w St Marg 16–18; C St Louis St Mich USA from 19. *6300 Wydown Boulevard, Clayton, St Louis MO 6315, USA* E: tomalbinson@gmail.com

ALBON, Lionel Frederick Shapland. b 31. CEng MIMechE 60. St Alb Minl Tr Scheme 80. **d** 83 **p** 84. NSM Bromham w Oakley *St Alb* 83–88; NSM Bromham w Oakley and Stagsden 88–89; Ind Chapl 89–96; rtd 96; LtO *St Alb* 96–09; PtO from 09. *38 Glebe Rise, Sharnbrook, Bedford MK44 1JB* T: (01234) 781560 E: lionelalbon@aol.co.uk

ALBONE, Mrs Joy Elizabeth. b 59. Roehampton Inst BA 80 Gwent Coll Newport PGCE 95. Sarum Th Coll 16. **d** 19. NSM Canalside Benefice *Sarum* from 19. *48 Primrose Drive, Melksham SN12 6GB* M: 07931-638524 E: canalsidecurate@gmail.com

ALBY, Harold Oriel. b 45. Witwatersrand Univ BA 68 MA 77. Sarum Th Coll 68. **d** 71 **p** 72. C Germiston St Boniface S Africa 71–74; C Johannesburg Cathl 74–75; R Ermelow w Pet Relief 75–78; R Potchefstroom 78–82; R Boksburg 82–89; P-in-c Forton *Portsm* 89–96; V Milton 96–10; rtd 11; Perm to Offic and Dioc Archivist George S Africa from 11. *7 Plover Road, Heatherlands, George, 6529 South Africa* T: (0027) (44) 873 0797 E: orielalby@hotmail.com

ALCOCK (née TOYNBEE), Mrs Claire Louise. b 65. Reading Univ BA 86 Ox Brookes Univ MA 15 Goldsmiths' Coll Lon PGTC 87. Ox Min Course 07. **d** 10 **p** 11. NSM Langtree *Ox* from 10. *St Mary's House, High Street, Whitchurch on Thames,*

Reading RG8 7DF T: 0118-984 3435 M: 07519-861040 E: claire_alcock@hotmail.com

ALCOCK, Donald. b 52. McGill Univ Montreal BA 74 MA 76 Univ of S California PhD 85. Huron Coll Ontario MDiv 00. **d** 00 **p** 00. Canada 00–10; NSM Gt Amwell w St Margaret's and Stanstead Abbots *St Alb* 10–12; P-in-c Woore and Norton in Hales *Lich* from 12. *The Vicarage, Nantwich Road, Woore, Crewe CW3 9SA* T: (01630) 647911 E: dga952@hotmail.com

ALCOCK, Edwin James. b 31. AKC 57. **d** 58 **p** 59. C Old St Pancras w Bedford New Town St Matt *Lon* 58–62; C Hillingdon St Andr 62–81; V N Acton St Gabr 81–01; rtd 01; PtO *Lon* from 01. *17 Westfields Road, London W3 0AX* T: (020) 8896 2748

ALDCROFT, Malcolm Charles. b 44. Leeds Univ MA 94. NOC 79. **d** 82 **p** 83. NSM Alverthorpe *Wakef* 82–85; NSM Horbury Junction 85–93; Sub Chapl HM Pris and YOI New Hall 94–97; Sub Chapl HM Pris Wakef 96–97; R Cupar and Ladybank *St And* 97–05; Chapl Stratheden Hosp Fife 97–05; Dioc Miss Officer and Min Development Co-ord *Mor* 05–07; Hon C Arpafeelie 05–07; Warden of Readers 06–07; Hon C St Andrews All SS *St And* from 08; TV Edin St Mich and All SS 08–11; LtO from 11. *14 Cherry Lane, Cupar KY15 5DA* T: (01334) 650264 E: m33aldcroft@tiscali.com

ALDEN, Andrew Michael. b 65. Bris Univ BA 88 Ex Univ PGCE 89 Lon Univ MA 98. Wycliffe Hall Ox 01. **d** 03 **p** 04. C Weston-super-Mare St Paul *B & W* 03–07; V from 07. *Somerset House, 20 Addiscombe Road, Weston-super-Mare BS23 4LT* T: (01934) 621120 E: revandrewalden@btinternet.com *or* andrew.alden@stpauls-weston.org.uk

ALDEN, Mrs Pamela Ann (Pat). b 42. St Gabr Coll Lon TCert 67. **d** 02 **p** 03. OLM Camberwell St Giles w St Matt *S'wark* 02–07; NSM Camberwell St Phil and St Mark 07–12; PtO 12–16; *Chich* from 15. *20 Kings Walk, Shoreham-by-Sea BN43 5LG* M: 07710-283710 E: pat@looksouth.net

ALDER, Mrs Alison Kirstine Ruth. b 62. **d** 19. NSM Blyth Valley *St E* from 19. *Address temp unknown* E: alisonalder@hotmail.co.uk

ALDER, Mrs Anne-Louise (Louise). b 63. STETS 99. **d** 02 **p** 03. C Cowes H Trin and St Mary *Portsm* 02–05; C Cowes St Faith 05–06; C Newport St Thos 06–07; P-in-c Shipdham w Bradenham *Nor* 07–14; P-in-c Barnham Broom and Upper Yare 10–12; Dioc Fresh Expressions Asst 13–14; V Hellesdon from 14. *The Vicarage, Broom Avenue, Hellesdon, Norwich NR6 6LG* E: louise.alder@lineone.net *or* louise.alder63@gmail.com

ALDERMAN, Canon John David. b 49. Man Univ BA 71 Selw Coll Cam BA 79 MA 80 Lon Inst of Educn PGCE 72. Ridley Hall Cam 77. **d** 80 **p** 81. C Hartley Wintney, Elvetham, Winchfield etc *Win* 80–83; V Bursledon 83–92; R Dibden 92–05; AD Lyndhurst 04–05; Hon Can Win Cathl 01–05; Patr Sec CPAS 05–11; rtd 11; PtO *Cov* from 05. *32 Stuart Close, Warwick CV34 6AQ* T: (01926) 400743 E: jandgalderman@btinternet.com

ALDERSLEY, Ian. b 42. FIBMS 68. Wycliffe Hall Ox 89. **d** 91 **p** 92. C Allestree *Derby* 91–94; R Brailsford w Shirley and Osmaston w Edlaston 94–06; P-in-c Yeaveley 05–06; P-in-c Ruishton w Thornfalcon *B & W* 06–10; P-in-c Creech St Michael 08–10; rtd 10; Hon C Fenny Bentley, Thorpe, Tissington, Parwich etc *Derby* 11–15; Retirement Chapl 12–15. *5 Clifford Close, Chesterfield S40 3PP* T: (01246) 568448 E: aldersley_ian@yahoo.co.uk

ALDERSON, Mrs Hannah Samantha Joy. b 86. Ex Univ BA 08. Ripon Coll Cuddesdon MTh 13. **d** 13 **p** 14. C Bridgwater H Trin and Durleigh *B & W* 13–16; Dioc Voc Development Officer *Ex* 16–19; Chapl Ex Univ from 16. *3 Spicer Road, Exeter EX1 1SX* M: 07546-397981 E: hannahsjalderson@gmail.com or h.alderson@exeter.ac.uk

ALDERSON, Mrs Maureen. b 40. WMMTC 90. **d** 93 **p** 94. NSM Yardley St Cypr Hay Mill *Birm* 93–96; P-in-c 96–00; V 00–02; P-in-c Gainford and Winston *Dur* 02–07. *5 St Michaels Court, Northallerton DL7 8YX* T: (01609) 779265

ALDERSON, Major Robin Edward Richard. b 44. **d** 04 **p** 05. OLM Alde River *St E* 04–07; NSM Brandeston w Kettleburgh and Easton 07–13; rtd 13; PtO *St E* from 13. *The Cloisters, Sandy Lane, Snape, Saxmundham IP17 1SD* T/F: (01728) 688255 M: 07790-242002 E: robin.alderson@virgin.net *or* robin.alderson@btinternet.com

ALDERSON, Roger James Ambrose. b 47. Lon Univ BD 70 AKC 71 Man Univ 76 Liv Inst of Educn PGCE 93. St Aug Coll Cant. **d** 71 **p** 72. C Lawton Moor *Man* 71–75; C Barton w Peel Green 75–76; R Heaton Norris St Thos 76–85; V Bedford Leigh 85–92; V Cleadon Park *Dur* 99–07; rtd 07. *73 West Drive, Sunderland SR6 7SL* T: 0191-536 1236 M: 07710-722817

ALDERTON, Mary Louise. *See* PRICE, Mary Louise

ALDERTON-FORD, Canon Jonathan Laurence. b 57. St Jo Coll Nottm BTh 85. **d** 85 **p** 86. C Gaywood, Bawsey and Mintlyn *Nor* 85–87; C Herne Bay Ch Ch *Cant* 87–90; Min Bury St Edmunds St Mary *St E* 90–91; Min Moreton Hall Estate CD 91–94; V Bury St Edmunds Ch Ch from 94; Hon Can St E Cathl from 08. *18 Heldhaw Road, Bury St Edmunds IP32 7ER* T: (01284) 769956 *or* 725391 F: 725391 E: worship@ccmh.org.uk *or* revdjonathanford@gmail.com

ALDIS, John Arnold. b 43. Univ of Wales (Cardiff) BA 65 Lon Univ BD 67. Clifton Th Coll 65. **d** 69 **p** 70. C Tonbridge SS Pet and Paul *Roch* 69–72; C St Marylebone All So w SS Pet and Jo *Lon* 72–77; Overseas Service Adv CMS 77–80; C Welling *Roch* 77–80; V Leic H Trin w St Jo 80–89; Hon Can Leic Cathl 88–89; V W Kowloon St Andr Hong Kong 89–99; Sen Chapl Protestant Ch Oman 00–01; V Watford *St Alb* 02–08; rtd 08; PtO *Glouc* from 14. *146 Arrowsmith Drive, Stonehouse GL10 2QR* E: john.aldis@btinternet.com

ALDIS, John Philip. b 83. Keble Coll Ox BA 05 Fitzw Coll Cam BA 11 Peterho Cam MPhil 12 Called to the Bar (Lincoln's Inn) 16. Ridley Hall Cam 09. **d** 12 **p** 13. C Newbury St Nic and Speen *Ox* 12–15; PtO *Worc* from 17. *10 Thetford Avenue, Worcester WR4 0RB* M: 07815-503485 E: johnaldis@gmail.com

ALDIS, Miss Rosemary Helen. b 40. Southn Univ BSc 62 Ox Univ Inst of Educn DipEd 63 Keele Univ MSc 67. All Nations Chr Coll MA 99. **d** 05 **p** 05. NSM Gabalfa *Llan* 05–10; PtO from 11; Hon Tutor St Mich Coll Llan 05–10; Hon Chapl 11–16. *94 Glendower Court, Velindre Road, Cardiff CF14 2TZ* T: (029) 2062 6337 E: aldisrosemary@gmail.com

ALDOUS, Alexander Charles Victor. b 56. Southn Univ BA 81 K Alfred's Coll Win PGCE 83. S Dios Minl Tr Scheme 91. **d** 94 **p** 95. Chapl Oundle Sch 94–97; Chapl Benenden Sch 98–01; Chapl Oakham Sch 02–16; Chapl Shrewsbury Sch from 16; Chapl Prestfelde Sch Shrewsbury from 18; PtO *Lich* from 18. *Shrewsbury School, Kingsland, Shrewsbury SY3 7BA* T: (01743) 280500 E: chaplain@shrewsbury.org.uk

ALDOUS, Benjamin James. b 75. Liv Univ BA 98 Bris Univ MA 02 Redcliffe Coll Glouc MA 12 Stellenbosch Univ PhD 19. **d** 11 **p** 11. C Durban N S Africa 11–13; Min-in-c Wynberg St Jo 13–18; Evang and Miss Officer CTE from 19. *2 Dunstone Cottages, Ashprington, Totnes TQ9 7UW* M: 07547-395382 E: ben.aldous@cte.org.uk

ALDRIDGE, Canon Harold John. b 42. Oak Hill Th Coll 65. **d** 69 **p** 70. C Rawtenstall St Mary *Man* 69–72; CMJ 72–76; C Woodford Wells *Chelmsf* 76–79; TV Washfield, Stoodleigh, Withleigh etc *Ex* 79–86; V Burton Ches 86–90; P-in-c Shotwick 90; V Burton and Shotwick 91–07; Dioc Clergy Widows and Retirement Officer 91–07; RD Wirral S 96–06; Hon Can Ches Cathl 98–07; Chapl Clatterbridge Wirral 86–91; Chapl Wirral Hosp NHS Trust 91–97; Chapl Wirral and W Cheshire Community NHS Trust 97–03; Chapl Cheshire and Wirral Partnerships NHS Trust 03–07; rtd 07; PtO *Ches* from 08. *Tedda Junction, 9 Moorhouse Close, Chester CH2 2HU* T: (01244) 371628

ALDRIDGE, Mark Richard. b 58. Oak Hill Th Coll BA 89. **d** 89 **p** 90. C Combe Down w Monkton Combe and S Stoke *B & W* 89–90; C Woodside Park St Barn *Lon* 90–94; P-in-c Cricklewood St Gabr and St Mich 94–99; V 99–04; Min Oak Tree Angl Fellowship 04–15; Dir New Wine Internat Min from 15; Dir Ch Leadership Development from 17; LtO from 15; PtO *Leic* from 18. *3 Lorne Road, Leicester LE2 1YF* T: 0116-270 3090 M: 07957-204956 E: international@new-wine.org

ALDWINCKLE, Jonathan Frederick. b 62. ERMC 12. **d** 15 **p** 16. C Kettering Ch the King *Pet* 15–18; R Raunds, Hargrave, Ringstead and Stanwick from 18. *The Vicarage, High Street, Raunds, Wellingborough NN9 6HS* E: revjonaldwinckle@btconnect.com *or* revjonaldwinckle@btconnect.com

ALEXANDER, Ann Maria. b 58. Surrey Univ BA 01. Cuddesdon Coll 07. **d** 09 **p** 10. C Chiswick St Nic w St Mary *Lon* 09–13; TV Ifield *Chich* 13–17; V Gossops Green and Bewbush from 17. *St Alban's Vicarage, Gossops Drive, Crawley RH11 8LD* M: 07961-853343 E: anejmi6@gmail.com

ALEXANDER, Christopher Aslan. b 73. Leic Univ BSc 97. St Mellitus Coll 15 Wycliffe Hall Ox BA 17. **d** 17 **p** 18. C Woodside Park St Barn *Lon* from 17. *61 Lullington Garth, London N12 7BB* M: 07462-101242 E: chrisalexander@stbarnabas.co.uk

ALEXANDER, David Graham. b 61. Ridley Hall Cam 87. **d** 89 **p** 90. C New Barnet St Jas *St Alb* 89–93; C Northwood H Trin *Lon* 93–95; V Stopsley St Alb from 95. *The Vicarage, 702 Hitchin Road, Luton LU2 7UJ* T: (01582) 729194 E: stopsley@aol.com

ALEXANDER, James Crighton. b 43. Qu Coll Cam BA 65 MA 69. Cuddesdon Coll 68. **d** 68 **p** 69. C Much Wenlock w

Bourton *Heref* 68–72; V Oakington *Ely* from 72; P-in-c Dry Drayton 85–95. *The Vicarage, 99 Water Lane, Oakington, Cambridge CB24 3AL* T: (01223) 232396

ALEXANDER, Jane Louise. *See* MacLAREN, Jane Louise

ALEXANDER, Canon Loveday Constance Anne. b 47. Somerville Coll Ox BA 69 MA 78 DPhil 78. NOC 98. **d** 99 **p** 00. NSM Alderley Edge *Ches* from 99; Can Th Ches Cathl 03–14; PtO *Sheff* from 00. *5 Nevill Road, Bramhall, Stockport SK7 3ET* T: 0161-439 7946 E: l.c.alexander@sheffield.ac.uk

ALEXANDER, Canon Michael George. b 47. Open Univ BA 90 DipEd 91. Sarum & Wells Th Coll 74. **d** 77 **p** 78. C Wednesfield *Lich* 77–80; C Tettenhall Wood 80–83; Distr Min 83–85; Dioc Adv in Adult and Youth Educn *Derby* 85–89; V Hazlewood 85–89; V Turnditch 85–89; Par Educn Adv (Laity Development) 89–96; Dioc Laity Development Adv 96–00; Dioc Dir Studies Bp's Centres of Learning 96–00; P-in-c Ticknall, Smisby and Stanton-by-Bridge 00–01; P-in-c Barrow-on-Trent w Twyford and Swarkestone 00–01; V Ticknall, Smisby and Stanton by Bridge etc 01–07; RD Melbourne 02–07; P-in-c Loscoe 07–12; C Morley w Smalley and Horsley Woodhouse 07–12; RD Heanor 09–11; Hon Can Derby Cathl 09–12; rtd 12. *79 Allerburn Lea, Alnwick NE66 2NQ*

ALEXANDER, Nancy. b 58. **d** 16 **p** 17. OLM Droylsden St Mary *Man* from 16; Chapl Pennine Acute Hosps NHS Trust from 17. *6 Longcroft Grove, Audenshaw, Manchester M34 5SD* T: 0161-317 9667 M: 07968-688585 E: nancya@milnerb.co.uk

ALEXANDER, Nancy Joan. *See* WALLACE, Nancy Joan

ALEXANDER, Nicholas Edward. b 68. Leic Poly BSc 90. Oak Hill Th Coll BA 06. **d** 06 **p** 07. C Linc Minster Gp 06–12; C Linc St Pet in Eastgate 12–15; C Bury St Edmunds St Mary *St E* from 15. *The Parish Office, St Mary's Church, Honey Hill, Bury St Edmunds IP33 1RT* T: (01284) 754680 E: nickalexander110@hotmail.com

ALEXANDER, Peter John. b 36. CQSW 73. Oak Hill Th Coll 92. **d** 95 **p** 96. NSM Aspenden, Buntingford and Westmill *St Alb* 95–02; rtd 02; PtO *Nor* from 02. *Dell Gate, 4 The Dell, Bodham, Holt NR25 6NG* T: (01263) 588126 E: peter.brenda2@tiscali.co.uk

ALEXANDER, Mrs Rachel Clare. b 57. EAMTC 96. **d** 99 **p** 00. NSM Mattishall w Mattishall Burgh, Welborne etc *Nor* 99–02; PtO 02–03 and NSM Rugby St Matt *Cov* 03–04; NSM Thorpe Acre w Dishley *Leic* 11–15; PtO *Nor* 16–19; C Heacham and Snettisham from 19. *The Rectory, 18 Park Lane, Snettisham, King's Lynn PE31 7NW* E: revrachel.alexander@gmail.com

ALEXANDER, Robert. b 37. Lon Univ LLB 60 St Cath Coll Ox BA 62. St Steph Ho Ox 60. **d** 63 **p** 64. C Kensington St Mary Abbots w St Geo *Lon* 63–68; C Notting Hill 71–74; TV 74–79; Australia from 79; rtd 02. *302/27 Neutral Street, North Sydney NSW 2060, Australia* T/F: (0061) (2) 9954 0543 E: robalexand@bigpond.com

ALEXANDER, Sarah Louise. b 72. Wycliffe Hall Ox 02. **d** 04 **p** 05. C Enfield Ch Ch Trent Park *Lon* 04–08; C Newbury *Ox* 08–14; C Redhill H Trin S'wark from 14. *17 Colman Way, Redhill RH1 2BB* E: sarah@htredhill.com

ALEXANDER, Wilfred Robert Donald. b 35. TCD BA 58 MA 80. **d** 63 **p** 63. C Raheny w Coolock *D & G* 63–67; Min Can St Patr Cathl Dublin 65–67; Hon C Herne Hill St Paul S'wark 68–70; Asst Master Gosforth Gr Sch 71–76; Hon C Long Benton St Mary *Newc* 74–76; Chapl St Mary and St Anne's Sch Abbots Bromley 76–80; V Cauldon *Lich* 80–83; V Waterfall 80–83; P-in-c Calton 80–83; P-in-c Grindon 80–83; V Blackb St Luke w St Phil 83–89; V Rainhill *Liv* 89–92; R Croft w Southworth 92–99; C Croft w Southworth and Newchurch 99–01; rtd 01. *16 Hawkshaw Close, Birchwood, Warrington WA3 7NF* T: (01925) 851472

ALEXANDER-WATTS, Tristan Nathaniel. b 66. SEITE 99. **d** 03 **p** 04. NSM Eltham H Trin S'wark 03–10; Chapl Qu Eliz Hosp NHS Trust 04–11; Chapl Bromley Hosps NHS Trust 05–09; Chapl Oxleas NHS Foundn Trust 05–09; Chapl S Lon Healthcare NHS Trust 09–10; Chapl Barts Health NHS Trust from 12; Chapl Richard Ho Children's Hospice from 12. *The Chaplaincy Office, Whipps Cross Hospital, Whipps Cross Road, London E11 1NR* T: (020) 8535 6988 M: 07974-118104 E: tristan.alexander-watts@nhs.net

ALIDINA (née LINGARD), Jennifer Mary. b 59. Ox Min Course 05. **d** 07 **p** 08. C Chipping Norton *Ox* 07–10; Asst Chapl HM Pris Bullingdon 10–11; P-in-c Ellingham and Harbridge and Hyde w Ibsley *Win* 11–14; PtO *Sarum* 14–19; *Win* 14–16; C W Purbeck *Sarum* from 19. *Iris Hollow, New Road, Stoborough, Wareham BH20 5BB* T: (01929) 505007 E: revjennyalidina@gmail.com *or* jennyalidina@irishollow.co.uk

ALISON, Sister. *See* FRY, Alison Jacquelyn

ALKER, Canon Adrian. b 49. Wadh Coll Ox BA 70 Lanc Univ MA 71. Ripon Coll Cuddesdon 77. **d** 79 **p** 80. C W Derby

St Mary *Liv* 79–83; Dioc Youth Officer *Carl* 83–88; V Sheff St Mark Broomhill 88–08; Dioc Dir of In-Service Tr 90–08; Hon Can Sheff Cathl 05–08; Dir Miss Resourcing *Ripon* 08–14; *Leeds* 14–15; rtd 15; PtO *Sheff* from 16. *23 Meadow Head, Sheffield S8 7UA* T: 0114-274 6266

ALKIRE, Sabina Marie. b 69. Univ of Illinois BA 89 Magd Coll Ox MPhil 94 MSc 95 DPhil 99. **d** 00 **p** 02. NSM Washington St Alb and St Phil USA 00–03; NSM Boston St Steph 03–07; Chapl Assoc Magd Coll Ox from 06; NSM Cowley St Jo *Ox* from 08. *3 Mansfield Road, Oxford OX1 3TB* T: (01865) 271529 F: 281801 M: 07792-505847 E: sabina.alkire@qeh.ox.ac.uk

ALLABY, Simon Arnold Kenworthy. b 65. St Chad's Coll Dur BA 88. Trin Coll Bris 88. **d** 90 **p** 91. C Preston on Tees *Dur* 90–93; C Chester le Street 93–99; R Ardingly *Chich* 99–05. Fenners, *Top Street, Bolney, Haywards Heath RH17 5PP* M: 07837-637113 E: simon@sixnineteen.co.uk

ALLAIN CHAPMAN, The Ven Justine Penelope Heathcote. b 67. K Coll Lon BA 88 AKC 88 PGCE 89 DThMin 11 Nottm Univ MDiv 93. Linc Th Coll 91. **d** 93 **p** 94. C Forest Hill *S'wark* 93–96; TV Clapham Team 96–01; V Clapham St Paul 02–04; Dir Miss and Past Studies SEITE 04–13; Vice Prin 07–13; Adn Boston *Linc* from 13. *Archdeacon's House, Castle Hill, Welbourn, Lincoln LN5 0NF* T: (01400) 273335 M: 07715-077993 E: justine.allainchapman@lincoln.anglican.org *or* archdeacon.boston@lincoln.anglican.org

ALLAN, Andrew John. b 47. Westcott Ho Cam 76. **d** 79 **p** 80. C Whitstable All SS w St Pet *Cant* 79–84; C Whitstable 84–86; P-in-c Littlebourne 86–87; P-in-c Ickham w Wickhambreaux and Stodmarsh 86–87; R Littlebourne and Ickham w Wickhambreaux etc 87–10; rtd 10. *The Moorings, Old Road, Liskeard PL14 6DL* T: (01579) 349074 E: johnallan014@aol.com

ALLAN, Donald James. b 35. Sarum & Wells Th Coll 63. **d** 65 **p** 66. C Royton St Paul *Man* 65–71; V Middleton Junction 71–78; P-in-c Finmere w Mixbury *Ox* 78–83; R Finmere w Mixbury, Cottisford, Hardwick etc 83; Chapl Westcliff Hosp 83–87; V Westcliff St Andr *Chelmsf* 83–87; R Goldhanger w Lt Totham 87–01; rtd 01; P-in-c St Goran w Caerhays *Truro* 01–06; PtO *Sarum* 06–15. *23 Stirrup Close, Wimborne BH21 2UQ* T: (01202) 880645 E: donald.allan2@btinternet.com

ALLAN, Janet Ross. b 57. Ex Univ BA 80 Open Univ MBA 06 MCLIP 88. St Mellitus Coll BA 13. **d** 13 **p** 14. C Thorpe Bay *Chelmsf* 13–17; V Swaffham and Sporle *Nor* from 17. *The Vicarage, White Cross Road, Swaffham PE37 7QY* T: (01760) 622241 M: 07958-534465 E: revdjanetallan@gmail.com

ALLAN, Jeanette Winifred. b 40. ALA 63. St and Dioc Tr Course 79. **dss** 81 **d** 86 **p** 94. NSM Whitfoot's TM St And 81–86; NSM Bridge of Allan *St And* 86–88; NSM Dunblane 88–98; R Glenrothes 98–06; rtd 06; LtO *St And* from 07. *Pernettya, Sinclairs Street, Dunblane FK15 0AH* T: (01786) 821151 E: pernettya@gmail.com

ALLAN, John. See ALLAN, Andrew John

ALLAN, Preb John William. b 58. St Olaf Coll Minnesota BA 80 Birm Univ 86. Trin Lutheran Sem Ohio MDiv 84 Qu Coll Birm 90. **d** 91 **p** 92. In Lutheran Ch (USA) 84–86; C Newport w Longford and Chetwynd *Lich* 91–94; P-in-c Longdon 94–01; Local Min Adv (Wolverhampton) 94–01; V Alrewas from 01; V Wychnor from 01; RD Lich 04–14; Preb Lich Cathl from 11. *The Vicarage, Church Road, Alrewas, Burton-on-Trent DE13 7BT* T: (01283) 790486 E: revdjohnallan@revdjohnallan.plus.com

ALLAN, Kirsty Elizabeth. b 70. York St Jo Coll BEd 92 St Jo Coll Dur BA 18. Cranmer Hall Dur 16. **d** 18 **p** 19. C Wilmslow *Ches* from 18. *53 Park Road, Wilmslow SK9 5BT* E: revkirsty@icloud.com

ALLAN, Peter Burnaby. b 52. Clare Coll Cam BA 74 MA 78 St Jo Coll Dur BA 82. Cranmer Hall Dur 80. **d** 83 **p** 84. C Chaddesden St Mary *Derby* 83–86; C Brampton St Thos 86–89; TV Halesworth w Linstead, Chediston, Holton etc *St E* 89–94; TR Trunch *Nor* 94–03; R Ansley and Arley *Cov* 03–16; RD Nuneaton 06–12; rtd 16; PtO *S'well* from 17. *26 Hazel Grove, Mapperley, Nottingham NG3 6DN* E: peterballan52@gmail.com

ALLAN, Peter George. b 50. Wadh Coll Ox BA 72 MA 76. Coll of Resurr Mirfield 72. **d** 75 **p** 76. C Stevenage St Geo *St Alb* 75–78; Chapl Wadh Coll and C Ox St Mary V w St Cross and St Pet 78–82; CR from 85; Prin Coll of Resurr Mirfield 11–19; C Bicton, Montford w Shrawardine and Fitz *Lich* from 19. *The Vicarage, Baschurch Road, Bomere Heath, Shrewsbury SY4 3PN* E: pallan@mirfield.org.uk

ALLARD, Roderick George. b 44. Lon Univ BA 77 Sheff Poly MSc 88 Loughb Coll of Educn CertEd 96. NOC 97. **d** 99 **p** 00. NSM Charlesworth and Dinting Vale *Derby* 99–13; NSM Glossop and Hadfield 11–13; PtO *Leic* from

14. *37 Sutton Lane, Sutton in the Elms, Broughton Astley, Leicester LE9 6QF* T: (01455) 289356 M: 07976-435160 E: r.allard@sky.com

ALLBERRY, William Alan John. b 49. Ch Coll Cam BA 70 MA 71. Ripon Coll Cuddesdon 84. **d** 86 **p** 87. C Brixton St Matt *S'wark* 86–90; V Wandsworth St Paul 90–98; R Esher *Guildf* 98–12; RD Emly 01–06; rtd 12; Lect Tamilnadu Th Sem Madurai India from 12; PtO *Guildf* from 12; *S'wark* from 12; *St D* from 17. *48 Ditton Road, Surbiton KT6 6RB* T: (020) 8390 2019 E: williamallberry@hotmail.com

ALLBUTT, Mavis Miriam. b 51. **d** 98 **p** 99. OLM Meir *Lich* 98–08; P-in-c 08–13; rtd 13; PtO *Lich* from 13. *9 Bramley Close, Cheadle, Stoke-on-Trent ST10 1PP* T: (01538) 423578 E: mavisall@sky.com

ALLCHIN, Miss Maureen Ann. b 50. Edge Hill Coll of HE CertEd 71 Sussex Univ MA 93. S Dios Minl Tr Scheme 88. **d** 91 **p** 94. Hd Past Faculty Steyning Gr Sch 79–92; NSM Southwick St Mich *Chich* 91–93; C Storrington 93–95; TV Bridport *Sarum* 95–05; LtO 05–06; P-in-c Canalside Benefice 06–08; LtO 08–09 and 10–15; P-in-c Trowbridge H Trin 09–10; rtd 10; P-in-c Seend, Bulkington and Poulshot *Sarum* 15–17; PtO 17–18. *4 Northfields, Bulkington, Devizes SN10 1SE* T: (01380) 828931 E: maureen@mallchin.co.uk

ALLCOCK, Jeremy Robert. b 63. Trin Coll Bris BA 92. **d** 92 **p** 93. C Walthamstow St Luke *Chelmsf* 92–96; V E Ham St Paul 96–05; V Paddington St Steph w St Luke *Lon* 05–18; V Bayswater 12–16; AD Westmr Paddington 11–16; R Birm St Martin w Bordesley St Andr from 18. *37 Barlows Road, Birmingham B15 2PN*

ALLDRIDGE, Dimitri. b 81. Cov Univ BA 03. Gordon-Conwell Th Sem MDiv 13. **d** 13 **p** 14. C Gateshead H Trin S Africa 13–16; C Hartford *Ches* from 16. *The Propagator's House, Greenbank Lane, Hartford, Northwich CW8 1JJ* M: 07706-185297 E: dimitri.alldridge@gmail.com *or* dimitri@christchurchgreenbank.org

ALLDRIT, Nicolas Sebastian Fitz-Ansculf. b 41. St Edm Hall Ox BA 63 MA 69 DPhil 69. Cuddesdon Coll 72. **d** 72 **p** 73. C Limpsfield and Titsey *S'wark* 72–81; Tutor Linc Th Coll 81–96; Sub-Warden 88–96; R Witham Gp *Linc* 97–07; rtd 07; PtO *Pet* 07–12. *104 Orchard Hill, Little Billing, Northampton NN3 9AY* T: (01604) 407115

ALLDRITT, Richard James Lee. b 79. Somerville Coll Ox MEng 01. Oak Hill Th Coll 10. **d** 13 **p** 14. C Cambridge H Sepulchre *Ely* 13–18; V Oakwood St Thos *Lon* from 18. *2 Sheringham Avenue, London N14 4UE* M: 07788-952137 E: rich.alldritt@gmail.com

ALLEN, Andrew Michael. b 84. Ripon Coll Cuddesdon BA 09. **d** 10 **p** 11. C Aston Clinton w Buckland and Drayton Beauchamp *Ox* 10–13; Chapl and Fell Ex Coll Ox from 13; LtO *Ox* from 18. *Exeter College, Turl Street, Oxford OX1 3DP* T: (01865) 279600 E: andrew.allen@exeter.ox.ac.uk

ALLEN, Andrew Stephen. b 55. Nottm Univ BPharm 77 MPS. St Steph Ho Ox 78. **d** 81 **p** 82. C Gt Ilford St Mary *Chelmsf* 81–83; C Luton All SS w St Pet *St Alb* 83–86; TV Chambersbury 86–91; TV Brixham w Churston Ferrers and Kingswear *Ex* 91–01; TR 01–06; P-in-c Upton cum Chalvey *Ox* 06–08; TR from 08. *St Mary's Rectory, 34 Upton Park, Slough SL1 2DE* T/F: (01753) 529988 E: upton.c.chalvey@gmail.com

ALLEN, Beverley Carole. See PINNELL, Beverley Carole

ALLEN, Brian. b 58. Oak Hill NSM Course 90. **d** 93 **p** 94. NSM W Norwood St Luke *S'wark* 93–02; NSM Gipsy Hill Ch Ch 02–08. *76 Bradley Road, London SE19 3NS* T: (020) 8771 4282 *or* 8686 8282 E: lonesomestone@hotmail.co.uk

ALLEN, Brian. See ALLEN, Frank Brian

ALLEN, Mrs Caroline Anne. b 59. ERMC 08. **d** 11 **p** 12. C Kesgrave *St E* 11–14; P-in-c Walton and Trimley 14–17; R 17–18; rtd 18. *Bethany Cottage, Dog Corner, Matlaske Road, Little Barningham, Norwich NR11 7DQ* T: (01263) 570283 M: 07970-737639 E: carolineallen121@gmail.com

ALLEN, Mrs Christine Anne. b 57. Avery Hill Coll CertEd 78 Cant Ch Ch Univ MA 12. St Aug Coll of Th 14. **d** 17 **p** 18. NSM S Gillingham *Roch* from 17. *74 Kingsway, Gillingham ME7 3AU* T: (01634) 853172 E: chrisallen74@hotmail.com *or* revchrisallen74@gmail.com

ALLEN, Christopher Dennis. b 50. Fitzw Coll Cam BA 73 MA 77. Cuddesdon Coll 74. **d** 76 **p** 77. C Kettering St Andr *Pet* 76–79; C Pet H Spirit Bretton 79–82; R Bardney *Linc* 82–87; V Knighton St Mary Magd *Leic* 87–11; V Cosby and Whetstone from 11. *The Vicarage, Church Lane, Whetstone, Leicester LE8 6BA* T: 0116-286 6329 E: rev.c.allen@gmail.com

ALLEN, Christopher Leslie. b 56. Leeds Univ BA 78. St Jo Coll Nottm 79. **d** 80 **p** 81. C Birm St Martin 80–85; Tr and Ed Pathfinders 85–89; Hd 89–92; Midl Youth Dept Co-ord

CPAS 85–89; Hon C Selly Park St Steph and St Wulstan *Birm* 86–92; V Hamstead St Bernard 92–95; NSM Kidderminster St Mary and All SS w Trimpley etc *Worc* 03–11; NSM Ribbesford w Bewdley and Dowles and Wribbenhall 11–17. *The Brambles, Dowles Road, Bewdley DY12 2RD* T: (01299) 409057 M: 07956-303037 E: chris.allen@compass.uk.net

ALLEN, David Edward. b 70. Van Mildert Coll Dur BSc 91. Ripon Coll Cuddesdon BA 94 MA 11. **d** 95 **p** 96. C Grantham *Linc* 95–99; C W Hampstead St Jas *Lon* 99–01; C Kilburn St Mary w All So and W Hampstead St Jas 01–02; V Finsbury St Clem w St Barn and St Matt from 02; Chapl Moorfields Eye Hosp NHS Foundn Trust 04–17. *St Clement's Vicarage, King Square, London EC1V 8DA* T: (020) 7251 0706 E: davideallen@blueyonder.co.uk *or* frdavid@stclementfinsbury.org

ALLEN, Frank Brian. b 47. K Coll Lon BD AKC 71. **d** 71 **p** 72. C Leam Lane *Dur* 71–74; C Tynemouth Ch Ch *Newc* 74–78; Chapl Preston Hosp N Shields 74–78; Chapl Newc Poly 78–84; V Newc St Hilda 84–88; Chapl Nottm Mental Illness and Psychiatric Unit 88–89; Chapl for Mental Health Newc Mental Health Unit 89–94; Chapl Newc City Health NHS Trust 94–96; Chapl Team Leader 96–06; Chapl Team Leader Northumberland, Tyne and Wear NHS Foundn Trust 06–12; Visiting Fell Newc Univ 93–02; rtd 12; PtO *Newc* from 12. *43 Cherryburn Gardens, Newcastle upon Tyne NE4 9UQ* T: 0191-274 9335 E: brian_allen63@hotmail.com

ALLEN, Giles David. b 70. RCM BMus 91 Leeds Univ MA 05. Coll of Resurr Mirfield 92. **d** 95 **p** 96. C Palmers Green St Jo *Lon* 95–99; V Lund *Blackb* 99–12; CF from 12. *c/o MOD Chaplains (Army)* T: (01264) 383430 F: 381824 E: gilesallen@live.co.uk

ALLEN, Hugh Edward. b 47. Bp Otter Coll Chich CertEd 68. Sarum & Wells Th Coll 79. **d** 81 **p** 82. C Frome St Jo *B & W* 81–85; R Old Cleeve, Leighland and Treborough 85–97; RD Exmoor 92–97; P-in-c The Stanleys *Glouc* 97–99; PtO *B & W* 99–05; P-in-c Charlton Musgrove, Cucklington and Stoke Trister 05–10; RD Bruton and Cary 06–10; rtd 10; PtO *B & W* from 11; RD Tone 12–14. *Woodpeckers, Langley Marsh, Wiveliscombe, Taunton TA4 2UL* T: (01984) 624166 E: hallenarkwood@yahoo.co.uk

ALLEN, Jamie. *See* ALLEN, Timothy James

ALLEN, Mrs Jane Rosemary. b 39. Cartrefle Coll of Educn BA 83 PGCE 84. St As & Ban Minl Tr Course 99. **d** 00 **p** 01. C Llandudno *Ban* 00–05; TV 05–09; rtd 09; PtO *St As* from 09. *39 Manor Park, Gloddaeth Avenue, Llandudno LL30 2SE* T: (01492) 860531

ALLEN, Johan. b 49. Lanc Univ CertEd 75 Roehampton Inst BEd 88. S'wark Ord Course 05. **d** 08 **p** 09. NSM W Streatham St Jas *S'wark* 08–12; NSM Furzedown from 12. *54 Leigham Vale, London SW16 2JQ* T: (020) 7564 8588 M: 07743-156786 E: hjohanallen@gmail.com

ALLEN, Jordan. b 94. Trin Coll Bris 16. **d** 19. C Rushden St Pet *Pet* from 19. *43 Melloway Road, Rushden NN10 6XX* E: revjord@hotmail.com

ALLEN, Mrs Kathleen. b 46. Westmr Coll Ox MTh 02. NOC 88. **d** 91 **p** 94. NSM Colne H Trin *Blackb* 91–94; NSM Colne Ch Ch 94–98; NSM Colne and Villages 98–06; rtd 06; PtO *B & W* from 09. *80 Stoddens Road, Burnham-on-Sea TA8 2DB* T: (01278) 793627 E: krabos080@gmail.com

ALLEN, Malcolm. b 60. Open Th Coll BA 00. Trin Coll Bris 94. **d** 96 **p** 97. C Skirbeck H Trin *Linc* 96–00; TV Cheltenham St Mark *Glouc* 00–09; TR Bishop's Cleeve and Woolstone w Gotherington etc from 09; AD Tewkesbury and Winchcombe from 16. *The Rectory, 4 Church Approach, Bishops Cleeve, Cheltenham GL52 8NG* T: (01242) 677851 E: malc.rector@gmail.com

ALLEN, Matthew Frederick James. b 82. Univ of Wales (Cardiff) BSc 03 St Jo Coll Dur BA 09 Dur Univ MA 11. Cranmer Hall Dur 07. **d** 10 **p** 11. C Kendal St Thos *Carl* 10–14; P-in-c Accrington Ch Ch *Blackb* 14–17; Dioc Dir of Studies from 16. *Diocesan Offices, Clayton House, Walker Industrial Estate, Walker Road, Guide, Blackburn BB1 2QE* T: (01254) 824940 M: 07739-465073 E: revmattallen@gmail.com *or* matt.allen@blackburn.anglican.org

ALLEN, Michael Stephen. b 37. Nottm Univ BA 60. Cranmer Hall Dur 60. **d** 62 **p** 63. C Sandal St Helen *Wakef* 62–66; Hon C Tile Cross *Birm* 66–70; V 72–84; Hon C Bletchley *Ox* 70–72; Vice-Prin Aston Tr Scheme 84–91; Hon C Boldmere *Birm* 85–91; P-in-c Easton w Colton and Marlingford *Nor* 91–93; Local Min Officer 91–93; Dioc Adv in Adult Educn *S'well* 93–02; rtd 02; PtO *S'well* from 02. *8 Grenville Rise, Arnold, Nottingham NG5 8EW* T: 0115-967 9515 E: msa1@sky.com

ALLEN, Patricia. *See* LEWER ALLEN, Patricia

ALLEN, Peter Henry. b 34. Nottm Univ BA 66. Kelham Th Coll 58. **d** 66 **p** 67. C Salisbury St Martin *Sarum* 66–70; C Melksham 70–73; C Paignton Ch Ch *Ex* 73–76; P-in-c

W Holloway St Dav *Lon* 76–77; V Barnsbury St Dav w St Clem 77–84; P-in-c Brentford St Faith 84–87; TV Brentford 87–91; TV Catford (Southend) and Downham *S'wark* 91–01; rtd 01; PtO *Roch* 01–13; *S'wark* 14–16. *72 Westmount Road, London SE9 1JE* M: 07962-596398 E: peterbeth46@gmail.com

ALLEN, Peter John. b 34. Leic Coll of Educn CertEd 74 Leic Univ BEd 75 MA 79. EAMTC 89. **d** 92 **p** 93. NSM Ketton w Tinwell *Pet* 92–94; NSM Easton on the Hill, Collyweston w Duddington etc 94–96; Chapl St Pet Viña del Mar Chile 96–99; NSM Culworth w Sulgrave and Thorpe Mandeville etc *Pet* 00–04; rtd 04; PtO *Pet* from 04; *Eur* from 16. *24 Holm Close, Weedon, Northampton NN7 4TJ* T: (01327) 349292 E: peterjallen@tinyworld.co.uk

ALLEN, Peter Richard. b 62. Qu Coll Birm BA 04. **d** 04 **p** 05. C Hackenthorpe *Sheff* 04–07; TV Gleadless 07–08; Chapl for Sport 07–13; TV Halstead Area *Chelmsf* 13–18; P-in-c Hackenthorpe *Sheff* from 19; P-in-c Gleadless from 19; P-in-c Woodhouse St Jas from 19. *S James's Vicarage, 65 Cardwell Avenue, Sheffield S13 7XB* T: 0114-269 0371 M: 07772-926278 E: prallen1962@gmail.com *or* woodhousestjames@gmail.com

ALLEN (née WADEY), Rachel Susan. b 71. Lanc Univ BA 94. St Steph Ho Ox BA 98. **d** 98 **p** 99. C Poulton-le-Fylde *Blackb* 98–01; C Blackpool H Cross 01–03; V Skerton St Chad 03–09; Chapl Prospect Park Hosp Reading 09–15; Chapl E and N Herts NHS Trust 15–18; Chapl Isabel Hospice from 18; PtO *St Alb* from 15. *Isabel Hospice, 61 Bridge Road East, Welwyn Garden City AL7 1JR* T: (01707) 382500 M: 07825-827100 E: rsw904@gmail.com

ALLEN, Richard James. b 46. Wells Th Coll 69. **d** 71 **p** 72. C Upholland *Liv* 71–75; TV 76–79; TV Padgate 79–85; V Weston-super-Mare St Andr Bournville *B & W* 85–93; V Williton 93–10; P-in-c St Decumans 08–10; Chapl Somerset Primary Care Trust 93–10; rtd 10; PtO *B & W* from 10. *26 Causeway Terrace, Watchet TA23 0HP* T: (01984) 248119 M: 07789-242245 E: richzakers@uwclub.net

ALLEN, Richard John. b 57. BA PGCE. SWMTC. **d** 06 **p** 07. NSM Ottery St Mary, Alfington, W Hill, Tipton etc *Ex* from 06; PtO *B & W* from 09; Chapl Ch Coll Brecon from 18; PtO *Eur* from 16. *53 Orchard Stret, Brecon LD3 8AL* M: 07973-463783 E: richard.allen@christcollegebrecon.com

ALLEN, Richard Lee. b 41. Liv Inst of Educn TCert 67. NOC 80. **d** 83 **p** 84. NSM Colne Ch Ch *Blackb* 83–90; P-in-c Trawden 91–98; NSM Colne and Villages 98–06; Chapl Burnley Health Care NHS Trust 99–03; Chapl E Lancs Hosps NHS Trust 03–06; rtd 06; PtO *B & W* from 09. *80 Stoddens Road, Burnham-on-Sea TA8 2DB* T: (01278) 793627 M: 07971-023095 E: krabos@tiscali.co.uk or krabos080@gmail.com

ALLEN, Roy Vernon. b 43. Open Univ BA 81 Birm Univ MA 84. Sarum Th Coll 67. **d** 70 **p** 71. C Hall Green Ascension *Birm* 70–74; V Temple Balsall 74–78; P-in-c Smethwick St Steph 78–81; V Smethwick St Mich 78–81; V Smethwick SS Steph and Mich 81–86; V Marston Green 86–13; rtd 13; PtO *Birm* from 13. *16 Orchard Close, Curdworth, Sutton Coldfield B76 9DX* T: (01675) 470629 E: roy_v_allen@hotmail.com

ALLEN, Rupert. b 63. Worc Coll of HE BA 87 Sussex Univ PGCE 88. Qu Foundn (Course) 15. **d** 17 **p** 18. OLM Chilvers Coton w Astley *Cov* from 17; PtO *Leic* from 17. *24 Park Avenue, Nuneaton CV11 4PQ* T: (024) 7632 5372 E: rupert.allen@leccofe.org *or* rupert@allsaintscoton.org

ALLEN, Canon Steven. b 49. Nottm Univ BA 73. St Jo Coll Nottm 73. **d** 75 **p** 76. C Gt Horton *Bradf* 75–80; V 89–02; V Upper Armley *Ripon* 80–89; RD Bowling and Horton *Bradf* 98–02; Dioc Tr Officer 02–14; *Leeds* 14; Hon Can Bradf Cathl 00–14; rtd 14; PtO *Leeds* from 17. *1 Hawkstone Avenue, Guiseley, Leeds LS20 8ET* T: (01943) 510653

ALLEN, Stuart Philip. b 73. St Cath Coll Ox BA 95. Oak Hill Th Coll BA 02. **d** 02 **p** 03. C Burford w Fulbrook, Taynton, Asthall etc *Ox* 02–06; Lect Proclamation Trust and Hon C Tooting Graveney St Nic *S'wark* 06–10; R S Warks Seven Gp *Cov* from 10. *The Vicarage, Broad Street, Long Compton, Shipston-on-Stour CV36 5JH* T: (01608) 684207 E: rectorsw7@gmail.com

ALLEN, Canon Susan Rosemary. b 47. Warwick Univ BSc 68 Trevelyan Coll Dur PGCE 69. Sarum Th Coll 93. **d** 96 **p** 97. C Goldsworth Park *Guildf* 96–01; TV Hemel Hempstead *St Alb* 01–09; TR 09–13; Hon Can St Alb 11–13; rtd 13; PtO *St Alb* 13–18; *Newc* from 13. *33 Swansfield Park Road, Alnwick NE66 1AT* E: revsue33@gmail.com

ALLEN, Mrs Suzanna Claire. b 75. St Jo Coll Nottm 09. **d** 11 **p** 12. C Wareham *Sarum* 11–15; C Horton, Chalbury, Hinton Martel and Holt St Jas 15; C Witchampton, Stanbridge and Long Crichel etc 15; C Wimborne Minster 15; C Wimborne Minster and the N Villages

10

from 15. *The Rectory, Hinton Martel, Wimborne BH21 7HD* E: suzie-assocpriest@wimborneminster.org.uk

ALLEN, Thomas Henry. b 42. NOC 87. **d** 90 **p** 91. C Upholland *Liv* 90–93; TV Walton-on-the-Hill 93–07; rtd 07; PtO *Eur* 14–17; *Liv* from 16. *13 Crosgrove Road, Liverpool L4 8TE* T: 0151-476 9705

ALLEN, Timothy James. b 71. Warwick Univ BA 93. Ripon Coll Cuddesdon BTh 99. **d** 99 **p** 00. C Nuneaton St Mary *Cov* 99–02; V Seend, Bulkington and Poulshot *Sarum* 02–03; Hon C Winslow w Gt Horwood and Addington *Ox* 03–05; V Gt Cornard *St E* 05–09; V New Plymouth St Mary New Zealand 09–10; Dean Taranaki 10–16. *Taranaki Retreat, 517 Hurford Road, RD4, New Plymouth 4374, New Zealand* E: jamie@taranakiretreat.org.nz

ALLEYNE, Sir John Olpherts Campbell Bt. b 28. Jes Coll Cam BA 50 MA 55. **d** 55 **p** 56. C Southampton St Mary w H Trin *Win* 55–58; Chapl Cov Cathl 58–62; Chapl Clare Hall Cam 62–66; Chapl Bris Cathl 66–68; Area Sec (SW England) Toc H 68–71; V Speke All SS *Liv* 71–73; TR Speke St Aid 73–76; R Win St Matt 76–93; rtd 93; PtO *Guildf* from 93. *2 Ash Grove, Guildford GU2 8UT* T: (01483) 573824 E: jocalleyne@hotmail.com

ALLFORD, Canon Judith Mary. b 55. Sheff Univ BA Lon Univ BD. Trin Coll Bris 77. **dss** 86 **d** 87 **p** 94. Par Dn Deptford St Jo w H Trin *S'wark* 87–91; Asst Chapl Dulwich Hosp 91–93; Asst Chapl King's Healthcare NHS Trust 93–95; Lead Chapl Ashford and St Pet Hosps NHS Foundn Trust 95–15; PtO *Guildf* 15–19; V Englefield Green from 19; Hon Can Guildf Cathl from 15. *The Vicarage, 21 Willow Walk, Englefield Green, Egham TW20 0DQ* T: (01784) 434133 M: 07928-362972 E: jallford@btinternet.com

ALLIES, Lorna Gillian. b 46. UEA BSc 93 Sheff Univ EdD 01. **d** 05 **p** 06. OLM Thurton w Ashby St Mary, Bergh Apton etc *Nor* 05–07; NSM Bunwell, Carleton Rode, Tibenham, Gt Moulton etc 07–09; P-in-c Rackheath and Salhouse 09–14; Dioc Rural Adv 06–09; rtd 14; PtO *Nor* 14–15; Hon C Acle and Bure to Yare 15–19. *426 Unthank Road, Norwich NR4 7QH* M: 07706-482284 E: lorna.allies@gmail.com

ALLIN, Philip Ronald. b 43. Reading Univ MA 96 Birm Univ CQSW. Lich Th Coll 71. **d** 71 **p** 72. C Sutton in Ashfield St Mary *S'well* 71–74; Chapl to Sutton Cen 74–76; LtO *S'well* 74–76; P-in-c Grove 76–77; R Ordsall 76–80; V Mansfield St Mark 81–83; TR Hermitage and Hampstead Norreys, Cold Ash etc *Ox* 83–96; OCM 83–96; Chapl Nine o'clock Service *Sheff* 96–03; rtd 03; Bp's Adv in Past Care and Counselling *Sheff* 03–08; Warden of Spiritual Direction *Dur* 08–10; PtO 14–17. *Hareholme House, New Brancepeth, Durham DH7 7HH* T: 0191-373 9743 E: philip_allin@yahoo.co.uk

ALLINSON, Paul Timothy. b 63. CA Tr Coll 82 Edin Th Coll 89. **d** 91 **p** 92. C Peterlee *Dur* 91–94; C Shadforth and Sherburn w Pittington 94–97; P-in-c Byers Green 97–04; P-in-c Seaton Carew 04–17; P-in-c Greatham 09–17; Dioc Children's Adv 94–09; Chapl Greatham Hosp 09–17; V Ponteland *Newc* from 17. *The Vicarage, Thornhill Road, Ponteland, Newcastle upon Tyne NE20 9PZ* T: (01661) 612533 M: 07888-726535 E: vicar@pontelandstmary.co.uk

ALLISON, Alliandra Bingo. b 86. Keble Coll Ox BA 07 St Jo Coll Dur BA 16. Cranmer Hall Dur 13. **d** 16. C N Wingfield, Clay Cross and Pilsley *Derby* from 16. *15 St Marks Road, Chesterfield S40 1DH* M: 07818-841697

ALLISON, Benjamin John. *See* ALLISON, Alliandra Bingo

ALLISON, Elliott Desmond. b 36. UNISA BA 64 K Coll Lon MTh 74. S Africa Federal Th Coll. **d** 69 **p** 70. PtO *Leeds* 14–16. *Flat 1, 20 Southview Gardens, Worthing BN11 5JA*

ALLISON, Canon James Timothy. b 61. Man Univ BSc 83. Oak Hill Th Coll BA 89. **d** 89 **p** 90. C Walkden Moor *Man* 89–93; Chapl Huddersfield Univ *Wakef* 93–98; V Erringden 98–12; RD Calder Valley 06–12; P-in-c Coley 12–14; *Leeds* from 14; Bp's Rural Adv *Wakef* 14; *Leeds* from 14; C Northowram from 14; Hon Can Wakef Cathl from 10. *Coley Vicarage, 41 Ing Head Terrace, Halifax HX3 7LB* T: (01422) 202292 E: erringden@aol.com

ALLISON, Keith. b 34. Dur Univ BA 59. Ely Th Coll 59. **d** 61 **p** 62. C Sculcoates *York* 61–64; C Stainton-in-Cleveland 64–65; C Leeds St Pet *Ripon* 65–70; V Micklefield *York* 70–74; V Appleton-le-Street w Amotherby 74–78; P-in-c Barton le Street 77–78; P-in-c Salton 77–80; R Amotherby w Appleton and Barton-le-Street 78–82; Chapl Lister Hosp Stevenage 82–90; P-in-c St Ippolyts *St Alb* 82–85; V 85–90; Chapl Hitchin Hosp 86–90; Chapl Shotley Bridge Gen Hosp 90–94; Chapl NW Dur HA 90–94; Sen Chapl N Dur Acute Hosps NHS Trust 94–97; Sen Chapl N Dur Healthcare NHS Trust 94–00; rtd 00; PtO *Dur* from 00. *2 Middlewood Road, Lanchester, Durham DH7 0HL* T: (01207) 529046 M: 07413-298578

ALLISON, Michael John. b 33. Leeds Univ BSc 97 ATI 58. Wilson Carlile Coll 05. **d** 05 **p** 06. NSM Windhill *Brad* 05–08; PtO 08–14; *Leeds* from 14. *33 Busy Lane, Shipley BD18 1DX* T: (01274) 587194 E: m.john.allison@talktalk.net

ALLISON, Rosemary Jean. *See* WHITLEY, Rosemary Jean

ALLISON, Susan Ann. b 61. EMMTC 06. **d** 06 **p** 07. C Gt and Lt Coates w Bradley *Linc* 06–09; P-in-c Fotherby 09–14; R 14–15; P-in-c Somercotes and Grainthorpe w Conisholme 09–14; R 14–15; RD Louthesk 11–15; R Bain Valley Gp from 15. *The Rectory, High Street, Coningsby, Lincoln LN4 4RA* T: (01526) 348505 M: 07920-133329 E: susan.333allison@btinternet.com

ALLISON, Mrs Susan Margaret. b 63. Ridley Hall Cam 18. **d** 19. C Newmarket All SS *St E* from 19. *4 Bunbury Terrace, All Saints Road, Newmarket CB8 8FL* M: 07904-491947 E: susanmallison54@gmail.com

✠**ALLISTER, The Rt Revd Donald Spargo.** b 52. Peterho Cam BA 74 MA 77 Ches Univ Hon DTh 11. Trin Coll Bris 74. **d** 76 **p** 77 **c** 10. C Hyde St Geo *Ches* 76–79; C Sevenoaks St Nic *Roch* 79–83; V Birkenhead Ch Ch *Ches* 83–89; R Cheadle 89–02; RD 99–02; Adn Ches 02–10; Bp Pet from 10. *Bishops Lodging, The Palace, Minster Precincts, Peterborough PE1 1YA* T: (01733) 562492 F: 890077 E: bishop@peterborough-diocese.org.uk

ALLISTER, John Charles. b 77. Ch Coll Cam BA 00 MA 03 MSci 00 St Anne's Coll Ox PGCE 01. Wycliffe Hall Ox BA 08. **d** 09 **p** 10. C Hurdsfield *Ches* 09–12; V Nottingham St Jude *S'well* from 12. *403 Woodborough Road, Nottingham NG3 5HE* T: 0115-960 4102 M: 07092-119317 E: john.allister@cantab.net *or* revjohnallister@gmail.com

ALLMAN, Mrs Susan. b 56. Bris Univ BA 77. WEMTC 93. **d** 96 **p** 97. NSM Henleaze *Bris* 96–99; C Southmead 99–02; V Two Mile Hill St Mich 02–08; Partnership P E Bris 08–10; P-in-c Titchfield *Portsm* from 10; AD Fareham 13–17. *The Vicarage, 24 Frog Lane, Titchfield, Fareham PO14 4DU* T: (01329) 842324 M: 07775-977298 E: susanrev@hotmail.co.uk

ALLMARK, Leslie. b 48. Open Univ BA 90. **d** 01 **p** 02. OLM Halliwell St Luke *Man* 01–08; rtd 08; PtO *Man* from 08. *75 Crosby Road, Bolton BL1 4EJ* T: (01204) 845795 *or* 528491 M: 07582-609735

ALLON-SMITH, Roderick David. b 51. Leic Univ BA PhD Cam Univ MA. Ridley Hall Cam 79. **d** 82 **p** 83. C Kinson *Sarum* 82–86; V Westwood *Cov* 86–96; RD Cov S 92–96; P-in-c Radford Semele 96–04; Dioc Dir Par Development and Evang 01–03; Dioc Missr *Dur* 04–10; AD Dur 08–10; R Lanercost, Walton, Gilsland and Nether Denton *Carl* 10–17; RD Brampton 12–15; rtd 17. *5 Glovers Crescent, Ripon HG4 2TR* T: (01765) 608220 E: allonsmith@btinternet.com

ALLRIGHT, Rebecca Jane. b 72. Aber Univ MA 96 Green Coll Ox MSc 01. St Hild Coll 16. **d** 18 **p** 19. C Carlton and Drax *York* from 18. *The Parsonage, 2 Church Dike Lane, Drax, Selby YO8 8NZ* T: (01904) 733829 M: 07984-742269 E: becky.allright@hotmail.co.uk

ALLS, Mrs Anna Kate. b 78. St Jo Coll Nottm BA 12. **d** 12 **p** 13. C Bestwood Em w St Mark *S'well* 12–14; C Brinsley w Underwood 14–16; C Eastwood 14–16; C Bilsthorpe from 16; C Eakring from 16; C Egmanton from 16; C Kirton from 16; C Kneesall w Laxton and Wellow from 16; C Ollerton w Boughton from 16; C Walesby from 16. *The Rectory, Church Hill, Bilsthorpe, Newark NG22 8RU* T: (01623) 611007 E: growingdisciplespriest@gmail.com *or* reverend.anna.alls@gmail.com

ALLSOP, Anthony James. b 37. AKC 62. **d** 63 **p** 64. C Leytonstone St Marg w St Columba *Chelmsf* 63–68; V Gt Ilford St Alb 68–80; V Gainsborough St Jo *Linc* 80–85; V Hockerill *St Alb* 85–02; Chapl Herts and Essex Hosp Bp's Stortford 85–94; Chapl Essex and Herts Community NHS Trust 95–01; Chapl N Essex Mental Health Partnership NHS Trust 01–02; rtd 02; PtO *Ches* from 03. *63 Longdown Road, Congleton CW12 4QH* T: (01260) 280628

ALLSOP, Mrs Beryl Anne. b 45. EMMTC 94. **d** 97 **p** 98. NSM Clipstone *S'well* 97–00; NSM Blidworth w Rainworth 00–10; rtd 10; PtO *S'well* from 11; *Derby* 14–19. *The Old Post Office, Bottom Row, Pleasley Vale, Mansfield NG19 8RS* T: (01623) 811095 E: beryl@faithfulfish.co.uk

ALLSOP, David. b 50. **d** 10 **p** 11. NSM Musbury *Blackb* from 10; NSM Haslingden w Grane and Stonefold from 10; NSM Laneside from 10. *7 Elizabeth Drive, Haslingden, Rossendale BB4 4JB* T: (01706) 224663 M: 07986-004401 E: davidallsop@hotmail.com

ALLSOP, David George. b 48. Wycliffe Hall Ox. **d** 99 **p** 00. C Chenies and Lt Chalfont, Latimer and Flaunden *Ox* 99–02; P-in-c 02–08; R 08–17; rtd 17; PtO *Ox* from 17. *7 Elizabeth Drive, Haslingden, Rossendale BB4 4JB* T: (01706) 224663 M: 07818-441431 E: cheniesrectory@aol.com

ALLSOP, Peter William. b 33. Kelham Th Coll 58. **d** 58 **p** 59. C Woodford St Barn *Chelmsf* 58–61; C Upholland *Liv* 61–65; V Wigan St Geo 65–71; P-in-c Marham *Ely* 71–72; TV Fincham 72–76; V Trawden *Blackb* 76–90; C Marton 90–92; C S Shore H Trin 92–98; rtd 98; PtO *Blackb* from 98. *33 Grizedale Court, Forest Gate, Blackpool FY3 9AP* E: peter.w.allsop@talktalk.net

ALLSOPP, The Ven Christine. b 47. Aston Univ BSc 68. S Dios Minl Tr Scheme 86. **d** 89 **p** 94. C Caversham St Pet and Mapledurham etc *Ox* 89–94; C Bracknell 94; TV 94–98; P-in-c Bourne Valley *Sarum* 98–00; TR 00–05; RD Alderbury 99–05; Can and Preb Sarum Cathl 02–05; Adn Northn *Pet* 05–13; Can Pet Cathl 05–13; rtd 13; PtO *Ox* from 13. *Mellor Cottage, 2 Walkers Lane, Lambourn, Hungerford RG17 8YE* T: (01488) 674108

ALLSOPP, Mark Dennis. b 66. Cuddesdon Coll 93. **d** 96 **p** 97. C Hedworth *Dur* 96–98; C Gt Aycliffe 98–00; TV Gt Aycliffe and Chilton 00–04; P-in-c Kirklevington and High and Low Worsall *York* 04–08; Chapl HM Pris Kirklevington Grange 04–08; Chapl RN from 08. *Royal Naval Chaplaincy Service, Mail Point 1-2, Leach Building, Whale Island, Portsmouth PO2 8BY* T: (023) 9262 5055 F: 9262 5134

ALLSOPP, Mrs Patricia Ann. b 48. St Mary's Coll Chelt CertEd 69. Qu Coll Birm. **d** 00 **p** 01. C Upton-on-Severn, Ripple, Earls Croome etc *Worc* 00–04; P-in-c Finstall 04–05; V 05–08; RD Bromsgrove 06–08; rtd 08; PtO *Leic* from 15. *18 Stuart Court, High Street, Kibworth Beauchamp, Leicester LE8 0LR* M: 07779-753908 E: pannbeth1@gmail.com

ALLSOPP, Stephen Robert. b 50. BSc 71 MSc 72 PhD 75. Mon Dioc Tr Scheme 81. **d** 84 **p** 85. NSM Trevethin *Mon* 84–88; Asst Chapl K Sch Roch 88–07; Chapl K Prep Sch Roch 99–07; rtd 07; Hon PV Roch Cathl 89–16. *579 Stonegate Road, Leeds LS17 6EJ* E: stephen@allsopps.net

ALLSWORTH, Peter Thomas. b 44. St Mich Coll Llan 93. **d** 93 **p** 94. C Prestatyn *St As* 93–96; V Esclusham 96–06; C Rhyl w St Ann 06–10; P-in-c Bodelwyddan 10–11; P-in-c Rhuddlan and Bodelwyddan 10–11; rtd 11; PtO *St As* from 11. *Subiaco, 10 Tirionfa, Rhuddlan, Rhyl LL18 6LT* T: (01745) 590683 E: peterallsworth@btinternet.com

ALLTON, Canon Paul Irving. b 38. Man Univ BA 60. **d** 63 **p** 64. C Kibworth Beauchamp *Leic* 63–66; C Reading St Mary V *Ox* 66–70; R Caston and V Griston *Nor* 70–75; P-in-c Sturston w Thompson and Tottington 70–75; V Hunstanton St Mary w Lt Ringstead 75–80; V Holme-next-the-Sea 75–80; V Hunstanton St Mary w Ringstead Parva, Holme etc 80–85; RD Heacham and Rising 81–85; Hon Can Nor Cathl 85–93; TR Lowestoft and Kirkley 85–93; TR Keynsham *B & W* 93–96; TR Gaywood *Nor* 96–01; rtd 01; PtO *Nor* from 01; *Roch* from 16. *13 Bromley College, London Road, Bromley BR1 1PE* E: paulallton@btinternet.com

ALLUM, Jeremy Warner. b 32. Wycliffe Hall Ox 60. **d** 62 **p** 63. C Hornchurch St Andr *Chelmsf* 62–67; P-in-c W Derby St Luke *Liv* 67–69; V 69–75; P-in-c Boulton *Derby* 75–90; RD Melbourne 86–90; V Hathersage 90–98; rtd 98; PtO *Derby* from 98. *32 Sandown Avenue, Mickleover, Derby DE3 0QQ* T: (01332) 231253 E: jnmsandown@ntlworld.com

ALLWOOD, Linda Angela Fredrika. b 76. Newc Univ BA 00. Cranmer Hall Dur 01. **d** 03 **p** 04. C Northampton St Giles *Pet* 03–06; PtO *St E* 06–07. *Norrskensgatan 6, 37151 Karlskrona, Sweden* E: linda_allwood@hotmail.com

ALLWOOD, Martin Eardley. b 71. Natal Univ BSc 92. Ripon Coll Cuddesdon 08. **d** 10 **p** 11. C Hundred River *St E* 10–14; R The Street Par *York* from 14. *The Rectory, Church Street, Amotherby, Malton YO17 6TN* T: (01653) 690913 M: 07891-478269 E: meallwood110@gmail.com

ALMOND, Kenneth Alfred. b 36. EMMTC 76 Linc Th Coll 78. **d** 79 **p** 80. C Boston *Linc* 79–82; V Surfleet 82–87; RD Elloe W 86–96; V Spalding St Jo w Deeping St Nicholas 87–98; rtd 98. *18 Century Court, 1 Wilford Lane, West Bridgford, Nottingham NG2 7TU* T: 0115-981 3788 E: ken.hilary@btopenworld.com

ALSBURY, Colin. b 56. Ch Ch Ox BA 77 MA 81. Ripon Coll Cuddesdon 77. **d** 80 **p** 81. C Oxton *Ches* 80–84; V Crewe All SS and St Paul 84–92; Ind Chapl 92–95; V Kettering St Andr *Pet* 95–02; V Frome St Jo *B & W* from 02; V Woodlands from 02; RD Frome 10–17. *St John's Vicarage, Vicarage Close, Frome BA11 1QL* T: (01373) 472853 E: colin.alsbury@btinternet.com

ALSOP, Barbara Lynn. b 48. **d** 11 **p** 12. NSM Epsom St Martin *Guildf* 11–15; PtO from 15. *15 Meadow Way, Bookham, Leatherhead KT23 3NY* T: (01372) 458492 E: revlynnalsop@talktalk.net

ALTY, Mrs Jane Alida. b 55. St Hugh's Coll Ox BA 78 MA 17. St Aug Coll of Th BA 17. **d** 17 **p** 18. NSM Clapton St Jas *Lon* from 17; Chapl St Joseph's Hospice Hackney from 18. *20 Meynell Crescent, London E9 7AS* T: (020) 8986 0601 M: 07710-095404 E: jane.alty3@gmail.com

AMAT-TORREGROSA, Gabriel José. b 42. R Superior Coll of Music Madrid MA 63. Bapt Th Sem Ruschlikon Zürich 64. **d** 71 **p** 72. Spain 71–98; Asst Chapl Zürich *Eur* 98–07; P-in-c Marseille w Aix-en-Provence 08–13; Chapl Agia Napa Cyprus from 15. *10 Tassou Markou, Apart 202, 5281 Paralimni, Cyprus* M: (00357) 9783 9349 E: gjamat@hotmail.com

AMBANI, Stephen Frederick. b 45. Univ of Wales (Lamp) BA 90. St Jo Coll Nottm 86 CA Tr Coll Nairobi 70. **d** 83 **p** 83. Kenya 83–93; C Glan Ely *Llan* 93–95; C Whitchurch 95–97; V Nantymoel w Wyndham 97–99; V Tonyrefail w Gilfach Goch and Llandyfodwg 99–03; V Tonyrefail w Gilfach Goch 04; rtd 05. *68 St Winifred's Road, Bridgend CF31 4PN* T: (01656) 653589

AMBROSE, James Field. b 51. Newc Univ BA 73. Cranmer Hall Dur. **d** 80 **p** 81. C Barrow St Geo w St Luke *Carl* 80–83; C Workington St Jo 83–85; R Montford w Shrawardine and Fitz *Lich* 85–88; Ch Radio Officer BBC Radio Shropshire 85–88; Chapl RAF 88–92; Voc and Min Adv CPAS 92–99; TV Syston *Leic* 99–06; C Leic Martyrs 06–07; V Heald Green St Cath *Ches* 07–17; Chapl St Ann's Hospice Manchester 07–17; rtd 17. *81 Charlecote Road, Poynton, Stockport SK12 1DJ* E: jfambrose@btinternet.com

AMBROSE, John George. b 30. Lon Univ BD Ox Univ PGCE. **d** 74 **p** 75. C Rayleigh *Chelmsf* 74–79; V Hadleigh St Barn 79–95; rtd 95; PtO *Chelmsf* from 95. *9 Fairview Gardens, Leigh-on-Sea SS9 3PD* T: (01702) 474632 E: johng.ambrose@btinternet.com

AMBROSE, Thomas. b 47. Sheff Univ BSc 69 PhD 73 Em Coll Cam BA 77 MA 84. Westcott Ho Cam 75. **d** 78 **p** 79. C Morpeth *Newc* 78–81; C N Gosforth 81–84; R March St Jo *Ely* 84–93; RD March 89–93; P-in-c Witchford w Wentworth 93–99; Dioc Dir of Communications 93–99; Chapl K Sch Ely 94–96; V Trumpington *Ely* 99–08; PtO 14–15; Hon C Cambridge Ascension from 15. *229 Arbury Road, Cambridge CB4 2JJ* M: 07711-263083

AMELIA, Alison. b 67. Hull Univ BA 03 St Jo Coll Dur BA 05. Cranmer Hall Dur 03. **d** 05 **p** 06. C Nunthorpe *York* 05–06; C Hessle 06–09; Chapl United Lincs Hosps NHS Trust from 09. *62 Glengarry Way, Greylees, Sleaford NG34 8XU* E: alison.amelia@ulh.nhs.uk

AMES, Jeremy Peter. b 49. K Coll Lon BD 71 AKC 71. **d** 72 **p** 73. C Kennington St Jo *S'wark* 72–75; Chapl RN 75–04; Chapl RN Engineering Coll 86–89; USA 91–93; Dir of Ords RN 00–04; QHC 02–04; Master St Nic Hosp Salisbury 04–11; PtO *Sarum* from 11. *Springfield, Stratford Road, Stratford sub Castle, Salisbury SP1 3LQ* T: (01722) 322542 E: jeremyames49@gmail.com

AMES-LEWIS, Richard. b 45. Em Coll Cam BA 66 MA 70. Westcott Ho Cam 76. **d** 78 **p** 79. C Bromley St Mark *Roch* 78–81; C Edenbridge 81–84; V 84–91; P-in-c Crockham Hill H Trin 84–91; P-in-c Barnes St Mary *S'wark* 91–97; TR Barnes 97–00; RD Richmond and Barnes 94–00; TR E Dereham and Scarning *Nor* 00–06; P-in-c Swanton Morley w Beetley w E Bilney and Hoe 02–06; TR Dereham and Distr 06–09; RD Dereham in Mitford 03–08; Hon Can Nor Cathl 05–09; rtd 09; PtO *Ely* from 09. *21 Victoria Street, Cambridge CB1 1JP* T: (01223) 300615 E: ameslewis@btinternet.com

AMEY, Graham George. b 44. Lon Univ BD 70. Tyndale Hall Bris 67. **d** 71 **p** 72. C Hornsey Rise St Mary *Lon* 71–74; C St Helens St Helen *Liv* 74–79; V Liv All So Springwood 79–91; V Whiston 91–02; V Aigburth 02–12; rtd 12; PtO *Liv* from 16. *213 Rose Lane, Liverpool L18 5EA* T: 0151-378 4687

AMEY, John Mark. b 59. Ripon Coll Cuddesdon 98. **d** 00 **p** 01. C Winchmore Hill St Paul *Lon* 00–04; V Sutton *Ely* 04–11; R Witcham w Mepal 04–11; V St Ives from 11; Chapl ATC from 03; CF from 18. *The Vicarage, Westwood Road, St Ives PE27 6DH* T: (01480) 384334 M: 07905-122090 E: vicar@stivesparishchurch.org.uk *or* vicar.stives@gmail.com *or* padre.amey@armymail.mod.uk

AMEY, Phillip Mark. b 73. Win Univ BA 11. STETS 03. **d** 06 **p** 07. C Southsea H Spirit *Portsm* 06–09; P-in-c Purbrook 09–12; P-in-c Southsea H Spirit 12–17; C Milton 12–17; Chapl RN from 17. *Royal Naval Chaplaincy Service, Mail Point 1-2, Leach Building, Whale Island, Portsmouth PO2 8BY* T: (023) 9262 5055 E: phillip.amey@sky.com

AMOS, Brother. See YONGE, James Mohun

AMOS, Colin James. b 62. Univ of Wales (Lamp) BA 83 CQSW 85. Ridley Hall Cam 93. **d** 93 **p** 94. C Aberdare *Llan* 93–96; V Port Talbot St Theodore 96–12; AD Margam 08–12; V Kilburn St Aug w St Jo *Lon* from 12. *St Augustine's Vicarage, Kilburn Park Road, London NW6 5XB* T: (020) 7624 1637 E: fr.amos@sky.com

AMOS, Gerald. b 31. St Mich Coll Llan. **d** 58 **p** 62. C Rhosymedre *St As* 58–59; C Peckham St Andr w All SS *S'wark* 62–65; C Walworth 65–72; C S Wimbledon H Trin 72–74; C S Wimbledon H Trin and St Pet 74–75; C Warlingham w

Chelsham and Farleigh 75–78; P-in-c Fazakerley St Nath *Liv* 88–92; TV Walton-on-the-Hill 92–96; rtd 96. *6 Church Walks, Old Colwyn, Colwyn Bay LL29 9RU* T: (01492) 512602

AMYES, Emma Charlotte. b 65. Redcliffe Coll BA 01. Ridley Hall Cam. **d** 04 **p** 05. C Hucclecote *Glouc* 04–10; TV Worle *B & W* from 10. *21 Westmarch Way, Weston-super-Mare BS22 7JY* M: 07866-808635 E: emma.amyes@virgin.net

AMYS, Richard James Rutherford. b 58. Trin Coll Bris BA 90. **d** 90 **p** 91. C Whitnash *Cov* 90–93; P-in-c Gravesend H Family w Ifield *Roch* 93–95; R 95–99; R Eastington, Frocester, Haresfield etc *Glouc* 99–15; rtd 15; PtO *Glouc* from 15. *1 Blossom Court, Bristol Road, Quedgeley, Gloucester GL2 4BT* M: 07796-956050 E: richardjramys@aol.com

ANAN, Gabriel Jaja. b 48. Regents Th Coll BA 92 Univ of E Lon MA 96 PhD 08 Middx Univ BA 03 MCIT 92. NTMTC 00. **d** 03 **p** 04. NSM Victoria Docks St Luke *Chelmsf* 03–07; NSM Forest Gate St Sav w W Ham St Matt 07–09; NSM N Woolwich w Silvertown 09–10; NSM E Ham St Geo 10–18; rtd 18. *67 Bedale Road, Romford RM3 9TU* T: (01708) 349564 M: 07734-707887 E: gabriel58@hotmail.com

ANAND, Jessie Nesam Nallammal. b 54. Madurai Univ BSc 75 BEd 76 Annamalai Univ MA 84. Tamilnadu Th Sem BD 91 New Coll Edin MTh 94 EMMTC 02. **d** 03 **p** 04. NSM Birstall and Wanlip *Leic* 03–05; NSM Emmaus Par Team 05–07; PtO *S'wark* 07–11; C Bermondsey St Hugh CD 11–14; NSM Angell Town St Jo from 15. *All Saints' Vicarage, 100 Prince of Wales Drive, London SW11 4BD* T: (020) 7622 3809 M: 07760-252655 E: jessieanand@yahoo.co.uk

ANAND, The Very Revd Sekar Anand Asir. b 53. Madurai Univ BSc 75 Serampore Univ BD 79 New Coll Edin MTh 93 Annamalai Univ MA 99. **d** 80 **p** 81. C Nayaith St Jo India 80–82; R Tuticorin St Paul 82–84; Sec Tirunelveli Children's Miss 84–91; C Edin St Pet 91–92; Hon C Burmantofts St Steph and St Agnes *Ripon* 92–93; C Edin St Mark 93–95; Provost Palayamcottai Cathl India 95–00; C Leic Resurr 00–07; C Battersea Fields *S'wark* from 07. *All Saints' Vicarage, 100 Prince of Wales Drive, London SW11 4BD* T: (020) 7622 3809 M: 07711-492946 E: anandjessie@yahoo.co.uk

ANDERS, Jonathan Cyril. b 36. Wycliffe Hall Ox 69. **d** 71 **p** 72. C Prescot *Liv* 71–74; C-in-c 74–76; R Wavertree St Mary 76–81; V Aigburth 81–01; rtd 01; PtO *Liv* from 03. *3 Silverleigh, Liverpool L17 5BL* T: 0151-728 9997

ANDERSON, Alice Calder. b 50. Moray Ho Coll of Educn DipEd 76. Local Minl Tr Course 90. **d** 93 **p** 95. NSM Edin St Barn from 93. *20 Pentland Road, Bonnyrigg EH19 2LG* T: 0131-654 0506 E: alicelibby@gmail.com

ANDERSON, Mrs Ann. b 57. Cranmer Hall Dur 01. **d** 03 **p** 04. C Chester le Street *Dur* 03–07; P-in-c Hetton-Lyons w Eppleton 07; R 07–18; TR Gt Aycliffe from 18. *St Clare's Rectory, St Cuthbert's Way, Newton Aycliffe DL5 5NT* T: (01325) 315194 E: a.ann007@btinternet.com

ANDERSON, Preb Brian Arthur. b 42. Sarum Th Coll 75. **d** 78 **p** 79. C Plymouth St Jas Ham *Ex* 78–80; Org Sec CECS B & W, Ex and Truro 80–89; TV Saltash *Truro* 89–94; RD E Wivelshire 91–94; P-in-c St Breoke and Egloshayle 94–96; R 96–02; RD Trigg Minor and Bodmin 95–02; P-in-c Torpoint 02–09; P-in-c Antony w Sheviock 02–09; Preb St Endellion 99; rtd 09; PtO *Truro* from 14. *44 Essa Road, Saltash PL12 4EE* T: (01752) 511271 M: 07710-231219 E: sheriock42@yahoo.co.uk

ANDERSON, David Richard. b 58. Lanc Univ BEd 79. EAMTC 96. **d** 99 **p** 00. C N Walsham w Antingham *Nor* 99–02; R Stalham, E Ruston, Brunstead, Sutton and Ingham 02–06; P-in-c Smallburgh w Dilham w Honing and Crostwight 05–06; TV Wrexham *St As* 06–11; Chapl St Jos High Sch Wrexham 06–11; V Romford St Edw *Chelmsf* 11–14; P-in-c Yeovil St Mich *B & W* 14–15; V from 15. *The Vicarage, 137 St Michael's Avenue, Yeovil BA21 4LW* T: (01935) 474898 M: 07956-267265 E: fr.anderson.yeovil@gmail.com

ANDERSON, Digby Carter. b 44. Reading Univ BA Brunel Univ MPhil 73 PhD 77. **d** 85 **p** 86. NSM Luton St Sav *St Alb* 85–16; PtO from 16. *17 Hardwick Place, Woburn Sands, Milton Keynes MK17 8QQ* T: (01908) 584526

ANDERSON, Donald Whimbey. b 31. Trin Coll Toronto BA 54 MA 58 LTh 57 STB 57 ThD 71. **d** 56 **p** 57. Canada 57–59 and 75–88; and from 96; Japan 59–74; Philippines 74–75; Dir Ecum Affairs ACC 88–96; rtd 96. *Conference on the Religious Life, PO Box 99, Little Britain ON K0M 2C0, Canada* T/F: (001) (705) 786 3330 E: dwa@nexicom.net

ANDERSON, Mrs Elizabeth Anne. b 68. Man Univ BA 90 Lanc Univ PGCE 91. SNWTP 14. **d** 17 **p** 18. C St Helens Town Cen *Liv* from 17. *3 Alexandra Drive, St Helens WA10 3UJ* M: 07736-550818

ANDERSON, Mrs Gillian Ann. b 52. NTMTC 05. **d** 08 **p** 09. NSM Lambourne w Abridge and Stapleford Abbotts *Chelmsf* 08–09; NSM Loughton St Jo 09–11; P-in-c High

Laver w Magdalen Laver and Lt Laver etc 11–17; rtd 17; PtO *St E* from 18. *Virginia Cottage, 25 Church Lane, Worlington, Bury St Edmunds IP28 8SG* M: 07954-429153 E: revgillanderson@gmail.com

ANDERSON, Gordon Stuart. b 49. St Jo Coll Nottm. **d** 82 **p** 83. C Hattersley *Ches* 82–86; C Dagenham *Chelmsf* 86–91; TV Mildenhall *St E* 91–01; V Southminster *Chelmsf* 01–11; P-in-c Steeple 08–11; V Southminster and Steeple 11–14; RD Maldon and Dengie 06–11; rtd 14; PtO *St E* from 14; *Ely* from 14. *11 Yew Tree Close, Mildenhall, Bury St Edmunds IP28 7SJ* T: (01638) 711260 M: 07549-539174 E: gandr42@btinternet.com

ANDERSON, Graeme Edgar. b 59. Poly of Wales BSc 82. St Jo Coll Nottm MTh 02. **d** 02 **p** 03. C Brislington St Luke *Bris* 02–05; C Galleywood Common *Chelmsf* 05–09; P-in-c Radcliffe-on-Trent and Shelford *S'well* 09–11; V 11–17; AD E Bingham 15–16; V Cov H Trin from 17. *Holy Trinity Vicarage, 4 Bishops Walk, Coventry CV5 6RE* T: (024) 7622 0418 M: 07840-926736 E: church.graeme@gmail.com

ANDERSON, Hugh Richard Oswald. b 35. Roch Th Coll 68. **d** 70 **p** 71. C Minehead *B & W* 70–76; C Darley w S Darley *Derby* 76–80; R Hasland 80–94; V Temple Normanton 80–94; rtd 94; PtO *Derby* 94–18. *32 Barry Road, Brimington, Chesterfield S43 1PX* T: (01246) 551020

ANDERSON, James. b 36. Magd Coll Ox BA 59 MA 64 Leeds Univ MA 00. **d** 02 **p** 03. NSM Holme and Seaton Ross Gp *York* 02–08; P-in-c The Beacon from 08. *61 Moor Lane, Carnaby, Bridlington YO16 4UT* T: (01262) 401688

ANDERSON, James Frederick Wale. b 34. G&C Coll Cam BA 58 MA 62. Cuddesdon Coll 60. **d** 62 **p** 63. C Leagrave *St Alb* 62–65; C Eastleigh *Win* 65–70; R Sherfield-on-Loddon 70–86; P-in-c Stratfield Saye w Hartley Wespall 75–86; R Sherfield-on-Loddon and Stratfield Saye etc 86–87; R Newton Valence, Selborne and E Tisted w Colemore 87–99; rtd 99; Chapl Surrey Hants Borders NHS Trust 01–04; Hon C Farnham *Guildf* 01–04; PtO from 07; *Win* from 11. *1 Potter's Gate, Farnham GU9 7EJ* T: (01252) 710728

ANDERSON, Canon James Raffan. b 33. Edin Univ MA 54 FRSA 90. Edin Th Coll 56. **d** 58 **p** 59. Chapl St Andr Cathl *Ab* 58–59; Prec St Andr Cathl 59–62; CF (TA) 59–67; Chapl Aber Univ *Ab* 60–62; Chapl Glas Univ 62–69; Chapl Lucton Sch 69–71; Chapl Barnard Castle Sch 71–74; Asst Dir of Educn *Blackb* 74–78; P-in-c Whitechapel 74–78; Bp's Officer for Min *Cov* 78–87; Hon Can Cov Cathl 83–87; Miss Sec Gen Syn Bd for Miss and Unity 87–92; rtd 92; PtO *Blackb* 98–13. *Bramble Cottage, Lower Quinton, Stratford-upon-Avon CV37 8SG* T: (01789) 721779

ANDERSON, Jane Alison. b 71. **d** 14 **p** 15. NSM Woodhorn w Newbiggin *Newc* 14–17; Chapl Newcastle upon Tyne Hosps NHS Foundn Trust from 17. *52 Castle Way, Pegswood, Morpeth NE61 6XH* E: jalison.anderson@outlook.com

ANDERSON (*née* FLAHERTY), Mrs Jane Venitia. b 68. Oak Hill Th Coll BA 92. **d** 93 **p** 94. C Timperley *Ches* 93–97; C Cheshunt *St Alb* 97–99; P-in-c N Springfield *Chelmsf* 99–18; P-in-c Pleshey 16–17; P-in-c Woldsburn *York* from 19. *The New Rectory, West End, Bainton, Driffield YO25 9NR* E: revjaney@talktalk.net

ANDERSON, Jeffrey. b 56. Cranmer Hall Dur. **d** 07 **p** 08. C Chester le Street *Dur* 07–11; PtO 14–19; TV Gt Aycliffe from 19. *St Clare's Rectory, St Cuthbert's Way, Newton Aycliffe DL5 5NT* T: (01325) 315194 E: jeff.and@btinternet.com

ANDERSON, Jeremy Dudgeon. b 41. Edin Univ BSc 63. Trin Coll Bris 75. **d** 77 **p** 78. C Bitterne *Win* 77–81; TV Wexcombe *Sarum* 81–91; Evang Enabler (Reading Deanery) *Ox* 91–96; V Epsom Common Ch Ch *Guildf* 96–00; C Kinson *Sarum* 00–06; rtd 06; PtO *Chich* 12–17. *The Croft, Church Road, Crowborough TN6 1ED* T: (01892) 655825

ANDERSON, Mrs Joanna Elisabeth. b 53. St Andr Univ MTheol 75. EMMTC 85. **d** 88 **p** 95. Par Dn Crosby *Linc* 88–92; Warden Iona Community *Arg* 92–95; R S Uist Broads *Nor* 95–02; Dir Body, Mind, Spirit Project 02–05; R Stiffkey and Bale *Nor* 05–09; C Hexham *Newc* 09–12; Is Cen Dir Iona Community *Arg* 12–15; TV Dudley *Worc* 15–18; rtd 18. *31 Middleton Road, Pickering YO18 8AN* T: (01751) 623304 M: 07774-446880 E: revjoannacam@gmail.com

ANDERSON, John Robert. b 75. QUB BD 96 TCD MPhil 98. CITC 96. **d** 98 **p** 99. C Magherafelt *Arm* 98–02; C Ballymena w Ballyclug *Conn* 02–05; I Billy w Derrykeighan from 05; Bp's Dom Chapl from 08. *The New Rectory, 231 Castlecat Road, Dervock, Ballymoney BT53 8BL* T: (028) 2074 1241 E: j.e.anderson231@gmail.com

ANDERSON, Julie. b 60. St Jo Coll Nottm 09. **d** 11 **p** 12. C Liv Ch Ch Norris Green 11–14; P-in-c Long Stanton w St Mich *Ely* 14–18; P-in-c Over 14–18; P-in-c Willingham 16–18; P-in-c Lolworth 17–18; P-in-c Swavesey 17–18; P-in-c Newsome and Armitage Bridge and S Crosland *Leeds*

from 18. *The Vicarage, 42 Beaumont Park Road, Huddersfield HD4 5JS* E: julie_anderson51@yahoo.co.uk

ANDERSON, Canon Keith Bernard. b 36. Qu Coll Cam BA 60 MA 64. Tyndale Hall Bris 60. **d** 62 **p** 63. C Bootle St Leon *Liv* 62–65; Lect Can Warner Mem Coll Buye Burundi 66–73; Dir Th Educn by Ext Studies Dio Nakuru Kenya 74–77; Dir Th by Ext Studies Mt Kenya E 78–82; Hon Can Mt Kenya E from 82; P-in-c Newnham and Doddington w Wychling *Cant* 83–88; Chapl Cannes w Grasse *Eur* 88–94; Dir and Chapl Mulberry Ho High Ongar 94–95; TV Horley *S'wark* 96–01; rtd 01; PtO *S'wark* 01–05; *Chich* from 01. *93 Rusper Road, Horsham RH12 4BJ* T: (01403) 262185 E: kb.anderson@virgin.net

ANDERSON, Canon Keith Edward. b 42. Fitzw Coll Cam BA 77 MA 83 MRCS 83. Ridley Hall Cam 74. **d** 77 **p** 78. C Goodmayes All SS *Chelmsf* 77–80; Chapl Coll of SS Mark and Jo Plymouth *Ex* 80–87; RD Plymouth Moorside 83–86; V Northampton H Sepulchre w St Andr and St Lawr *Pet* 87–98; RD Northn 92–98; Adv for Min Willesden *Lon* 98–03; Can Res Win Cathl and Adv for Ord Min Development *Win* 03–08; rtd 08; PtO *Win* from 08. *49 Chaundler Road, Winchester SO23 7HW* T: (01962) 853429 E: keith.anderson20@btinternet.com

ANDERSON, Mark Stuart. b 73. UEA BA 95 Lon Inst of Educn PGCE 05. St Mellitus Coll BA 17. **d** 17 **p** 18. C Oxted *S'wark* from 17. *St Mary's Church Office, Oxted Community Hall, 53 Church Lane, Oxted RH8 9NB* M: 07480-067756 E: oxtedcurate@gmail.com

ANDERSON, Martin Edward. b 73. Humberside Univ BA 95 St Jo Coll Dur BA 02. Cranmer Hall Dur 99. **d** 02 **p** 03. C Gt Aycliffe and Chilton *Dur* 02–05; TV Sunderland 05–07; Chapl Sunderland Minster 07–13; P-in-c Norton St Mary from 13; P-in-c Norton St Mich from 13. *2 Brambling Close, Norton, Stockton-on-Tees TS20 1TX* E: revmartin@outlook.com

ANDERSON, Canon Michael Garland. b 42. Clifton Th Coll 62. **d** 66 **p** 67. C Fareham St Jo *Portsm* 66–69; C Worting *Win* 69–74; V Hordle 74–07; RD Lyndhurst 82–00; Hon Can Win Cathl 92–07; rtd 07; PtO *Win* from 07. *20 Forestlake Avenue, Ringwood BH24 1QU* T: (01425) 471490

ANDERSON, Canon Michael John Austen. b 35. AKC 60. **d** 66 **p** 67. C Southall Ch Redeemer *Lon* 66–69; C Hampstead Garden Suburb 69–73; V S Mimms St Giles 73–80; V The Brents and Davington w Oare and Luddenham *Cant* 80–86; V Margate All SS 86–00; Hon Can Cant Cathl 97–00; rtd 00; PtO *Cant* from 01. *Camwa Ash, Bull Lane, Boughton-under-Blean, Faversham ME13 9AH* T: (01227) 752352 M: 07885-211863 E: camwaash@outlook.com

ANDERSON, Mrs Pearl Ann. b 46. St Andr Univ MA 68 MCIPD 74. Cant Sch of Min 90. **d** 93 **p** 00. Par Dn Epping St Jo *Chelmsf* 93–95; Adv to Coun for Soc Resp Roch and *Cant* 95–02; Asst Chief Exec Ch in Soc Roch and Cant 02–06; PtO *Roch* 95–02; Hon C Biddenden and Smarden *Cant* 00–06; rtd 06; PtO *Cant* from 06. *1 Gibbs Hill, Headcorn, Ashford TN27 9UD* T: (01622) 890043 M: 07811-209448 E: pearlanderson@btinternet.com

ANDERSON, Peter John. b 44. Nottm Univ BA 65 BA 73 Ex Univ CertEd 66. St Jo Coll Nottm. **d** 74 **p** 75. C Otley *Bradf* 74–77; TV Marfleet *York* 77–84; V Greasbrough *Sheff* 84–95; I Clonmel Union *C, C & R* 95–02; I Rathcooney Union 95–02; Chapl Cannes *Eur* 02–09; rtd 09; PtO *Eur* from 17. *100 route de la Colle, 06140 Tourrettes-sur-Loup, France* T: (0033) 9 50 41 68 40 E: pjhmander@yahoo.com

ANDERSON, Philip Gregory. b 80. Keble Coll Ox BA 01. Ripon Coll Cuddesdon BA 04. **d** 05 **p** 06. C Prescot *Liv* 05–09; Chapl Liv Hope Univ 09–12; P-in-c Pemberton St Jo *Liv* 12–15; V from 15; AD Wigan from 17. *St John's Vicarage, 2 Shelley Drive, Orrell, Wigan WN5 8HW* T: (01942) 375209 E: vicarstjohnpemberton@gmail.com

ANDERSON, Canon Roderick Stephen. b 43. Cant Univ (NZ) BSc 63 PhD 67 New Coll Ox BA 72. Wycliffe Hall Ox 70. **d** 73 **p** 74. C Bradf Cathl 73–75; C Allerton 76–78; V Cottingley 78–94; V Heaton St Barn 94–09; C 09–11; RD Airedale 88–95; Chapl Bradf Univ and Bradf Coll 04–11; Hon Can Bradf Cathl 94–11; rtd 11; PtO *Bradf* 11–14; *Leeds* from 14. *40 Low Wood, Wilsden, Bradford BD15 0JS* M: 07900-675350

ANDERSON, Stephen George. b 54. Liv Univ BA 75 ACIB. NOC 05. **d** 08 **p** 09. NSM St Shelford *Ely* 08–12; PtO 12–14; NSM Cambridge St Clem 14–16; PtO 16–17; P-in-c Cambridge St Botolph from 17; PtO *Eur* 12–17 and from 18. *3 Dukes Meadow, Stapleford, Cambridge CB22 5BH* T: (01223) 843859 M: 07889-003588 E: fr.stephen.anderson@gmail.com

ANDERSON, Timothy George. b 59. Ealing Coll of HE BA 82. Wycliffe Hall Ox 83. **d** 86 **p** 87. C Harold Wood *Chelmsf* 86–90; C Whitfield *Derby* 90–93; P-in-c Wolverhampton St Luke *Lich* 95–98; V 98–01; I Dundonald *D & D* from 01. *St Elizabeth's Rectory, 26 Ballyregan Road, Dundonald,*

Belfast *BT16 1HY* T: (028) 9048 3153 *or* 9048 2644 E: t.j.anderson@btinternet.com

ANDERSON-MacKENZIE, Janet Melanie. b 70. Edin Univ BSc 93 PhD 97 Trin Coll Bris MA 07. WEMTC 01. **d** 04 **p** 05. C Woolavington w Cossington and Bawdrip *B & W* 04–05; C Wellington and Distr 05–08; P-in-c Box w Hazlebury and Ditteridge *Bris* from 08; C Colerne w N Wraxall from 11. *The Vicarage, Church Lane, Box, Corsham SN13 8NR* T/F: (01225) 744458 E: janet@anderson-mackenzie.co.uk

ANDERTON, Christopher David. b 86. Hertf Coll Ox MBiochem 09. Oak Hill Th Coll BA 17. **d** 17 **p** 18. C Blackb Redeemer from 17. *1 Whelan Close, Blackburn BB2 4FX* M: 07951-695257 E: christopher.anderton@gmail.com

ANDERTON, David Edward. b 60. Leeds Poly BSc 92. St Jo Coll Nottm 02. **d** 04 **p** 05. C Daybrook *S'well* 04–06; C Hucknall Torkard 06–09; TV Newark w Coddington 09–16; V Collier Row St Jas and Havering-atte-Bower *Chelmsf* from 16. *24 Lower Bedfords Road, Romford RM1 4DG* M: 07751-269412

ANDERTON, Elaine Irene. *See* JONGE, Elaine Irene

ANDERTON, Frederic Michael. b 31. Pemb Coll Cam MA 57 IAAP. Westcott Ho Cam 64. **d** 66 **p** 67. C St John's Wood *Lon* 66–69; C All Hallows by the Tower etc 70–77; C St Giles Cripplegate w St Bart Moor Lane etc 77–82; C Zürich *Eur* 82–86; PtO *Lon* 94–00; rtd 96. *61 Brassey Road, Winchester SO22 6SB* T: (01962) 856326 F: 852851 E: robin.anderton@lineone.net

ANDERTON, Peter. b 45. Sarum & Wells Th Coll 80. **d** 82 **p** 83. C Adel *Ripon* 82–86; P-in-c Dacre w Hartwith 86–90; P-in-c Thornthwaite w Thruscross and Darley 88–90; V Dacre w Hartwith and Darley w Thornthwaite 90–91; V Owton Manor *Dur* 91–02; V Torrisholme *Blackb* 02–03; P-in-c Hunslet St Mary *Ripon* 03; V Hunslet w Cross Green 03–07; rtd 07; PtO *Dur* from 09. *12 School Street, Darlington DL3 0UG* T: (01325) 465841 E: fatherpeteranderton@gmail.com

ANDREW, Brian. b 31. Oak Hill Th Coll 75. **d** 77 **p** 78. C Broadwater St Mary *Chich* 77–81; R Nettlebed w Bix and Highmore *Ox* 81–87; V Shenstone *Lich* 87–96; rtd 96; PtO *Ex* 97–01; *Derby* 01–11; *Chich* from 16. *13 Ramsay Hall, 9-13 Byron Road, Worthing BN11 3HN*

ANDREW, Christopher John. b 61. Cen Lancs Univ BA 87. St Mich Coll Llan 01. **d** 03 **p** 04. C Bingley H Trin *Bradf* 03–07; PtO 07–10; *Derby* 11–18; *Ches* 15–18; C Morton and Stonebroom w Shirland *Derby* 18–19. *The Rectory, Main Road, Shirland, Alfreton DE55 6BB* E: chris.mx@live.co.uk

ANDREW, David Neil. b 62. Down Coll Cam BA 83 MA 87 PhD 88. Ridley Hall Cam 93. **d** 93 **p** 94. C Heatherlands St Jo *Sarum* 93–98; P-in-c White Waltham w Shottesbrooke *Ox* 98–18; P-in-c Waltham St Lawrence 07–11; NSM Maidenhead St Andr and St Mary from 18. *107 Grenfell Road, Maidenhead SL6 1EX*

ANDREW, David Shore. b 39. Liv Univ BA 61 CertEd 62. OLM course 97. **d** 99 **p** 00. NSM Birkenshaw w Hunsworth *Wakef* 99–09; PtO *Leeds* 09–17; *Ches* from 18. *25 Summers Way, Knutsford WA16 9AP* T: (01565) 228921

ANDREW, Donald. b 35. Tyndale Hall Bris 63. **d** 66 **p** 67. C Croydon Ch Ch Broad Green *Cant* 66–69; C Ravenhead *Liv* 69–72; Scripture Union 72–77; V Rushen *S & M* 77–82; TR Heworth H Trin *York* 82–00; rtd 00; PtO *York* 05–15. *60 Viking Road, Bridlington YO16 6TW* T: (01262) 601273

ANDREW, Jeremy Charles Edward. b 68. St Jo Coll Dur BA 01. Cranmer Hall Dur 98. **d** 01. C Newquay *Truro* 01–04; P-in-c Perranzabuloe 04–10; P-in-c Crantock 05–06; C Crantock w Cubert 06–07; P-in-c 07–10; V Perranzabuloe and Crantock w Cubert 10–14; Dioc Dir of Ords 12–14; P-in-c Warmley, Syston and Bitton *Bris* 14–15; R from 15; AD Kingswood and S Glos from 19. *The Vicarage, Church Avenue, Warmley, Bristol BS30 5JJ* T: 0117-967 2724 E: j.andrew.102@btinternet.com

ANDREW, Jonathan William. b 50. Univ Coll Ox MA 78 FCA 80. Ripon Coll Cuddesdon 02. **d** 04 **p** 05. NSM Hersham *Guildf* 04–19; PtO from 19. *Orchard, 6 Westacres, Esher KT10 9JE* T: (01372) 479776 M: 07968-765188 E: jonathanandrew@stpetershersham.com

ANDREW, Paul Roland. b 70. Oak Hill Th Coll BA 06. **d** 06 **p** 07. C Plymouth Em, St Paul Efford and St Aug *Ex* 06–09; Chapl RN from 09. *Royal Naval Chaplaincy Service, Mail Point 1-2, Leach Building, Whale Island, Portsmouth PO2 8BY* T: (023) 9262 5055 F: 9262 5134

ANDREW, The Ven Philip John. b 62. Nottm Univ BSc 84. St Jo Coll Nottm MTh 02. **d** 02 **p** 03. C Reading Greyfriars *Ox* 03–06; V Reigate St Mary *S'wark* 06–17; Hon Can S'wark Cathl 16–17; Adn Cheltenham *Glouc* from 17. *8 Grace Gardens, Cheltenham GL51 6QE* M: 07498-052045 E: archdchelt@glosdioc.org.uk

ANDREW, Sydney William. b 55. Cranmer Hall Dur 82. **d** 85 **p** 86. C Horncastle w Low Toynton *Linc* 85–88; V Worlaby 88–93; V Bonby 88–93; V Elsham 88–93; rtd 93; LtO *Linc* 93–95; Hon C Brocklesby Park 95–04; Hon C Croxton 96–04; Hon C Caistor Gp 04–18; Hon C Caistor from 18. *10 Bentley Lane, Grasby, Barnetby DN38 6AW* T: (01652) 628586 E: bridget.revdoc@clara.co.uk

ANDREW, Canon William Hugh. b 32. Selw Coll Cam BA 56 MA 60. Ridley Hall Cam 56. **d** 58 **p** 59. C Woking St Mary *Guildf* 58–61; C Farnborough 61–64; V Gatten St Paul *Portsm* 64–71; R Weymouth St Mary *Sarum* 71–76; V Heatherlands St Jo 76–82; Can and Preb Sarum Cathl 81–86; R Alderbury and W Grimstead 82–86; PtO *Bris* 86–88; Communications Dir Bible Soc 86–94; Communications Consultant 94–97; Hon C The Lydiards *Bris* 88–94; C W Swindon and the Lydiards 94–96; Hon C 96–98; rtd 96; PtO *Win* 98–19. *Kingfisher Care Home, The Meadows, New Milton BH25 7FJ* T: (01202) 612769

ANDREWES, Nicholas John. b 64. Southn Univ BA 87 La Sainte Union Coll PGCE 88. Cranmer Hall Dur BTh 93. **d** 96 **p** 97. C Dovecot *Liv* 96–00; TV Pendleton *Man* 00–03; P-in-c Lower Crumpsall w Cheetham St Mark 03–10; P-in-c Oldham St Paul 10–14; V Oldham St Paul and Werneth from 14; AD Oldham W from 17. *St Paul's Vicarage, 55 Belgrave Road, Oldham OL8 1LU* T: 0161-624 1068 E: nick.andrewes@phonecoop.coop

ANDREWS, Anthony John. b 35. S'wark Ord Course 75. **d** 80 **p** 81. NSM Cheam *S'wark* 80–83; C Epsom St Martin *Guildf* 83–86; V Barton *Portsm* 86–89; Chapl Northwick Park and St Mark's NHS Trust Harrow 90–98; C Regent's Park St Mark *Lon* 98–00; rtd 00; PtO *Lon* from 00. *112 Albury Drive, Pinner HA5 3RG*

ANDREWS, Benjamin. b 75. St Steph Ho Ox 97. **d** 00 **p** 01. C Whitchurch *Llan* 00–03; C Newton Nottage 03–05; C Cardiff St Mary and St Steph w St Dyfrig etc 05–12; R Cadoxton-juxta-Barry 12–16; TR Barry from 16. *The Rectory, 21 Rectory Road, Barry CF63 3QB* T: (01446) 406690 E: frbenandrews@aol.com

ANDREWS, Canon Brian Keith. b 39. Keble Coll Ox BA 62 MA 69. Coll of Resurr Mirfield 62. **d** 64 **p** 65. C Is of Dogs Ch Ch and St Jo w St Luke *Lon* 64–68; C Hemel Hempstead *St Alb* 68–71; TV 71–79; V Abbots Langley 79–05; RD Watford 88–94; Hon Can St Alb 94–05; rtd 05; PtO *Glouc* from 06. *High Pleck, Littleworth, Amberley, Stroud GL5 5AG* T: (01453) 873068

ANDREWS, Canon Christopher Paul. b 47. Fitzw Coll Cam BA 70 MA 73. Westcott Ho Cam 69. **d** 72 **p** 73. C Croydon St Jo *Cant* 72–75; C Gosforth All SS *Newc* 75–79; TV Newc Epiphany 80–87; RD Newc Cen 82–87; V Alnwick and Chapl Alnwick Infirmary 87–96; R Grantham St Wulfram *Linc* 96–13; P-in-c Grantham, Manthorpe 11–13; RD Grantham 09–11; Can and Preb Linc Cathl 04–13; Chapl United Lincs Hosps NHS Trust 99–01; rtd 13; Chapl to The Queen 09–17; PtO *St E* from 14. *74 Daisy Avenue, Bury St Edmunds IP32 7PH* T: (01284) 723785 E: candrews3007@gmail.com

ANDREWS, Clive Frederick. b 43. St Jo Coll Nottm 81. **d** 83 **p** 84. C Leic St Jas 83–86; Ind Chapl 86–90; Hon TV Melton Gt Framland 89–90; TV Clifton *S'well* 90–92; P-in-c Gamston w Eaton and W Drayton 92–94; R 94–08; P-in-c Elkesley w Bothamsall 92–08; Chapl Bramcote Sch Notts 02–08; PtO *S'well* from 10. *15 Oakwood Grove, Edwinstowe, Mansfield NG21 9JT* E: cliveand@waitrose.com

ANDREWS, Edward Robert. b 33. Brasted Th Coll 60 St Mich Coll Llan 62. **d** 64 **p** 65. C Kingswinford St Mary *Lich* 64–69; Chapl RAF 69–88; R St Just-in-Roseland w Philleigh *Truro* 88–99; rtd 99; PtO *Ex* from 00. *2 Ingleside, Gunsdown Villas, Station Road, South Molton EX36 3EA* T: (01769) 572386

ANDREWS, Mrs Jean. b 48. Leic Univ BSc 70. NTMTC. **d** 10 **p** 11. NSM Downham w S Hanningfield *Chelmsf* 10–11; NSM Downham w S Hanningfield and Ramsden Bellhouse from 11. *3 Sewards End, Wickford SS12 9PB* T: (01268) 733817 E: jean@rjandrews.me.uk

ANDREWS, Preb John Colin. b 47. Open Univ BA 93. Sarum & Wells Th Coll 78. **d** 80 **p** 81. C Burnham *B & W* 80–84; V Williton 84–92; P-in-c Ashwick w Oakhill and Binegar 92–02; Dioc Communications Officer 92–12; TV Yatton Moor 02–12; Preb Wells Cathl 04–12; rtd 12; PtO *B & W* from 12. *Cherry Tree House, Kenn Street, Kenn, Clevedon BS21 6TN* T: (01275) 877806 M: 07971-484061 E: john.andrews150@btinternet.com

ANDREWS, John Elfric. b 35. Ex Coll Ox BA 59 MA 63. Wycliffe Hall Ox 59. **d** 61 **p** 62. C Pittville All SS *Glouc* 61–66; Cand Sec Lon City Miss 66–92; LtO *S'wark* 66–92; R Kingham w Churchill, Daylesford and Sarsden *Ox* 92–99; rtd 99; PtO *St E* from 01. *4 St George's Road, Felixstowe IP11 9PL* T: (01394) 283557 E: jandsandrews@hotmail.co.uk

ANDREWS, John Francis. b 34. Jes Coll Cam BA 58 MA 62. S'wark Ord Course 78. **d** 81 **p** 82. NSM Upper Norwood All SS *S'wark* 81–87; NSM Dulwich St Barn 89–92; NSM S Dulwich St Steph 92–95; PtO 95–01; *Sarum* from 01. *1 Kennington Square, Wareham BH20 4JR* T: (01929) 555311 E: jeca.jfa@btinternet.com

ANDREWS, John George William. b 42. Qu Coll Birm 65. **d** 68 **p** 69. C Smethwick St Matt w St Chad *Birm* 68–71; CF 71–97; Asst Chapl Gen 95–97; QHC 95–97; P-in-c Lyme Regis *Sarum* 97–98; TV Golden Cap Team 98–03; rtd 03. *2 Sparnham Mews, West Street, Ashburton, Newton Abbot TQ13 7DU* T: (01364) 654101

ANDREWS, Judith Marie. b 47. Avery Hill Coll CertEd 68. **d** 00 **p** 01. OLM Wilford Peninsula *St E* 00–08; TV 08–15; rtd 15. *Hillside, Tower Hill, Hollesley, Woodbridge IP12 3QX* T: (01394) 411642 E: judith.andrews@btopenworld.com

ANDREWS, Morey Alisdair Christopher. b 66. Leic Poly BSc 91 MRICS 91. St Jo Coll Nottm MA 99. **d** 99 **p** 00. C Yate New Town *Bris* 99–02; C Downend 02–06; V Eynsham and Cassington *Ox* 06–16; Miss Enabler Sedgemoor Deanery *B & W* from 16. *14 Tundra Walk, Bridgwater TA6 6FH* E: moreyandrews3@gmail.com

ANDREWS, Canon Paul Douglas. b 54. Univ of Wales (Abth) BLib 76 PhD 99. SAOMC. **d** 00 **p** 01. NSM Kempston and Biddenham *St Alb* 00–03; C Leighton Buzzard w Eggington, Hockliffe etc 03–05; TV Billington, Eggington, Hockliffe etc 06–08; P-in-c St Neots *Ely* 08–19; C Eynesbury 12–19; P-in-c Ely St Pet Prop Chpl from 19; Asst Dir of Ords from 14; Hon Can Ely Cathl from 16. *15 Barton Road, Ely CB7 4DB* T: (01353) 656941 E: priest@elystpeterschurch.co.uk

ANDREWS, Peter Douglas. b 52. SEN 72 SRN 78. St Steph Ho Ox 86. **d** 88 **p** 89. C Perry Barr *Birm* 88–92; TV Swindon New Town *Bris* 92–98; V Streatham St Pet *S'wark* 98–19; rtd 19. *Address temp unknown* E: frpeterandrews@aol.com

ANDREWS, Raymond Cyril. b 50. SEITE 00. **d** 03 **p** 04. C E Dulwich St Jo *S'wark* 03–07; P-in-c S'wark St Geo w St Alphege and St Jude 07–13; rtd 13; PtO *S'wark* 13–15; Chapl Greenwich and Bexley Cottage Hospice 13–15; TV Costa Blanca *Eur* 15–18; PtO from 18. *Carrer Sant Antoni 19, 03530 La Nucia, Alicante, Spain* E: revrayandrews@aol.com

ANDREWS, Canon Richard John. b 57. Bris Univ BA 78 CertEd 79. Ripon Coll Cuddesdon 82. **d** 84 **p** 85. C Kidderminster St Mary and All SS, Trimpley etc *Worc* 84–87; Chapl Derbyshire Coll of HE 87–89; Hon C Derby Cathl 87–89; V Chellaston 89–93; V Spondon 93–05; TR Dunstable *St Alb* 05–18; RD 09–14; Hon Can St Alb 17–18; Can for Liturgy Derby Cathl from 18. *Derby Cathedral Centre, 18-19 Iron Gate, Derby DE1 3GP* T: (01332) 341201 E: richard@derbycathedral.org

ANDREWS, Robert. *See* ANDREWS, Edward Robert

ANDREWS, Sharon Elaine. b 59. Qu Foundn Birm 16. **d** 18 **p** 19. NSM Glenfield and Newtown Linford *Leic* from 18. *13 Ainsdale Road, Leicester LE3 0UD* T: 0116-223 9265 E: sharon@stpetersglenfield.org.uk

ANDREWS, Stephen. b 69. **d** 11 **p** 12. OLM Gt Yarmouth *Nor* from 11; Chapl James Paget Univ Hosps NHS Foundn Trust from 17. *19 Forth Close, Caister-on-Sea, Great Yarmouth NR30 5UW* T: (01493) 377897 *or* 452408 M: 07973-468411 E: stephen.andrews@jpaget.nhs.uk *or* revdstephenandrews@gmail.com

ANDREYEV, Michael. b 62. Hatf Coll Dur BA 85. Wycliffe Hall Ox BA 93 MA 03. **d** 96 **p** 97. C Surbiton Hill Ch Ch *S'wark* 96–01; NSM Stapenhill w Cauldwell *Derby* 02–03; P-in-c 03–06; V from 06. *3 Stapenhill Road, Burton-on-Trent DE15 9AF* T: (01283) 530320 E: office@stpetersstapenhill.org.uk *or* andreyevs07@talktalk.net

ANETTS, Roy. b 55. Qu Coll Birm 06. **d** 09 **p** 10. NSM Acocks Green *Birm* 09–12; NSM Yardley St Cypr Hay Mill 12–13; P-in-c 13–17; P-in-c S Yardley St Mich 14–17; R Cupar *St And* from 17; R Ladybank from 17. *The Rectory of St James the Great, 13 Robertson Road, Cupar KY15 5YR* T: (01334) 653141 E: revroy@hotmail.com

ANGEL, Andrew Richard. b 67. St Pet Coll Ox BA 89 Surrey Univ MA 94 Cant Ch Ch Univ MA 06 Lon Inst of Educn PGCE 90. St Jo Coll Nottm PhD 04. **d** 02 **p** 03. C Dartford Ch Ch *Roch* 02–05; Tutor SEITE 05–10; Tutor St Jo Sch of Miss Nottm 10–16; Tutor St Jo Sch Andr *Chich* from 16; PtO *Eur* 11–16. *2 Cants Lane, Burgess Hill RH15 0LG* T: (01444) 232023 M: 07495-310768 E: vicar@standrewsbh.org.uk

ANGELL, Miss Elizabeth Patricia. b 54. Univ of Wales (Ban) BA 72. Trin Coll Bris BA 08. **d** 08 **p** 09. C Fosse Team *Leic* 08–11; TV Bridgnorth, Tasley, Astley Abbotts, etc *Heref* 11–16; R Whitwick, Thringstone and Swannington *Leic* from 16. *The Vicarage, 37 North Street, Whitwick, Coalville LE67 5HB* T: (01530) 589136 E: angell304@btinternet.com

ANGIER, Patrick John Mark. b 61. Leic Univ BSc 83. Trin Coll Bris. d 03 p 04. C Stratford-upon-Avon, Luddington etc *Cov* 03–06; V Prestbury *Ches* from 06. *7 Northmead, Prestbury, Macclesfield SK10 4XD* T: (01625) 829288 M: 07971-923668

ANGLE, John Edwin George. b 42. Lon Bible Coll BD 65 Liv Univ AdDipEd 73 Univ of Wales MEd 75. WEMTC 92. d 94 p 95. NSM Clevedon St Andr and Ch Ch *B & W* 94–97; NSM Worle 97–98; P-in-c Camelot Par 98–01; R 01–06; Warden of Readers Wells Adnry 02–05; rtd 06; PtO *B & W* from 06. *14 Farthing Combe, Axbridge BS26 2DR* T: (01934) 733695 M: 07970-968652 E: johnnangle@btinternet.com

ANGUS, Canon Edward. b 39. Man Univ BA 60. Qu Coll Birm. d 62 p 63. C Chorley St Geo *Blackb* 62–65; C S Shore H Trin 65–68; R Bretherton 68–76; V Altham w Clayton le Moors 76–90; V Preesall 90–04; RD Garstang 96–01; Hon Can Blackb Cathl 98–04; rtd 04; PtO *Blackb* from 04. *14 Lazenby Avenue, Fleetwood FY7 8QH* T: (01253) 686817 E: eandjandgus@hotmail.com

ANGUS, Mrs Sherine Victoria. b 74. Ox Brookes Univ BA 96 BA 12 Univ of W of England BSc 04. St Hild Coll 16. d 19. C Alford Gp *Linc* from 19. *55 South Street, Alford LN13 9AN* T: (01507) 824069 M: 07811-218086 E: sherineangus@yahoo.co.uk

ANI, Joel Osita. b 72. Qu Coll Birm BA 08. d 08 p 10. C Telford Park *S'wark* 08–09; C Clapham Park All SS 09–12. *6 Blenheim Gardens, London SW2 5DB* T: (020) 8674 1889 M: 07903-234444 E: joel_ani123@yahoo.com

ANITA, Sister. *See* COOK, Anita Isabel

ANKER, Malcolm. b 39. Univ of Wales BA 61. Bps' Coll Cheshunt 61. d 63 p 64. C Marfleet *York* 63–66; C Cottingham 66–69; V Skirlaugh w Long Riston 69–74; V Elloughton and Brough w Brantingham 74–84; V Tadcaster 84–86; V Tadcaster w Newton Kyme 86–91; V Oatlands *Guildf* 91–05; rtd 05; PtO *Guildf* 05–13; *Sheff* from 13. *27 Ringstead Avenue, Sheffield S10 5SL* T: 0114-453 4858 E: malcolm.anker@gmail.com

ANKER-PETERSEN, Robert Brian. b 52. Aber Univ MTh 88. Wycliffe Hall Ox BA 79 MA 88. d 93 p 94. C Perth St Ninian *St And* 93–96; Bp's Researcher on Ch's Min of Healing from 93; Dir Bield Retreat and Healing Cen from 93; Dioc Dir of Healing *St And* from 97. *Blackruthven House, Tibbermore, Perth PH1 1PY* T: (01738) 583238

ANKERS, Canon Charles William (**Bill**). b 42. FIMI. NEOC 89. d 93 p 95. NSM York St Luke 93–95; C Kexby w Wilberfoss 95–98; Asst Chapl HM Pris Full Sutton 95–98; V Norton juxta Malton *York* 98–11; Can and Preb York Minster 10–11; rtd 11; PtO *York* from 11. *10 Beechwood Road, Norton, Malton YO17 9EJ* T: (01653) 693930 E: canonbill-norton@hotmail.co.uk

ANKETELL, Jeyarajan. b 41. Lon Univ BSc 62 PhD 67 MInstP. Coll of Resurr Mirfield 69. d 73 p 74. Asst Chapl Newc Univ 73–75; Asst Chapl Lon Univ 75–77; Teacher 78–05; LtO *S'wark* 81–83; Chasetown High Sch 85–05; NSM Lich St Mary w St Mich 86–96; NSM Lich St Mich w St Mary and Wall 96–15; PtO from 15. *7 Wissage Lane, Lichfield WS13 6DQ* T: (01543) 268897 E: jeyan.anketell@ntlworld.com

✠ANNAS, The Rt Revd Geoffrey Peter. b 53. Sarum & Wells Th Coll. d 83 p 84 c 10. C *S'wark* H Trin w St Matt 83–87; TV Walworth 87–94; Warden Pemb Coll Miss Walworth 87–94; V Southampton Thornhill St Chris *Win* 94–10; Hon Can Win Cathl 07–10; Area Bp Stafford *Lich* from 10. *Ash Garth, Broughton Crescent, Barlaston, Stoke-on-Trent ST12 9DD* T: (01782) 373308 F: 373705 E: bishop.stafford@lichfield.anglican.org

ANNE, Sister. *See* PROUDLEY, Anne

ANNIS, Jennifer Mary. b 49. Middx Univ BA 95. Oak Hill Th Coll 92. d 95 p 97. NSM Digswell and Panshanger *St Alb* 95–97; NSM Codicote 97–98 and 99–00; Tanzania 98–99; Chapl ATC from 99; NSM Fishguard w Llanychar and Pontfaen w Morfil etc *St D* 10–18; NSM W Cemaes from 18. *Capel Newydd Dau, Dinas Cross, Newport SA42 0YB* T: (01348) 811121 M: jennie.annis@btinternet.com

ANN-MARIE, Sister. *See* STUART, Ann-Marie Lindsay

ANNS, Pauline Mary. *See* HIGHAM, Pauline Mary

ANSAH, Canon Kwesi Gyebi Ababio (**George**). b 54. Oak Hill Th Coll BTh 97. Simon of Cyrene Th Inst 90. d 93 p 94. C Peckham St Mary Magd *S'wark* 93–96; V W Dulwich Em from 96; Hon Can Kumasi from 04. *Emmanuel Vicarage, 94 Clive Road, London SE21 8BU* T: (020) 8670 2793 M: 07771-783693 E: gkansa@aol.com

ANSCOMBE, John Thomas. b 51. Ex Univ BA 72. Cranmer Hall Dur. d 74 p 75. C Upper Armley *Ripon* 74–77; C Leeds St Geo 78–81; Exec Producer Scripture Union 81–96; Hon C Beckenham Ch Ch *Roch* 82–11; Dir Video Production Unit SA 01–16. *22 Hawthorndene Road, Bromley*

BR2 7DY T/F: (020) 8462 4831 M: 07736-070160 E: john_anscombe@hotmail.com

ANSELL, John Christopher. b 49. Sarum & Wells Th Coll 79. d 81 p 82. C Dartford St Alb *Roch* 81–84; C Leybourne and Larkfield 84–88; TV Mortlake w E Sheen *S'wark* 88–98; V Mitcham SS Pet and Paul 98–14; rtd 14; PtO *Glouc* from 15. *Tankards Spring, High Street, Chalford, Stroud GL6 8DJ* M: 07974-432562 E: jsansell@hotmail.com

ANSELL, Mark Stephen. b 68. Univ of Wales (Abth) BLib 89 Abth Univ PGCE 98. St Mich Coll Llan 12. d 14 p 15. C Henfynyw w Aberaeron and Llanddewi Aberarth etc *St D* 14–16; C Aberystwyth 16–17; TV from 17. *Fenton, Queen's Square, Aberystwyth SY23 2HL* T: (01970) 617849 E: revmarkansell@btinternet.com

ANSELM, Brother. *See* SMYTH, Robert Andrew Laine

ANSLOW, Mrs Patricia Margaret. b 49. Yorks Min Course 08. d 11 p 12. NSM Bramham *York* from 11. *4 Pine Tree Avenue, Boston Spa, Wetherby LS23 6HA* T: (01937) 844789 M: 07903-262880 E: t.anslow@hotmail.co.uk

ANSON (*née* DRAX), Mrs Elizabeth Margaret. b 57. St Jo Coll Nottm 91. d 94 p 95. C Kimberworth *Sheff* 94–95; C Doncaster St Mary 95–97; rtd 97; PtO *Sheff* from 10. *62 School Green Lane, Sheffield S10 4GR* T: 0114-229 5478

ANSTEY, Nigel John. b 55. Cranmer Hall Dur 84. d 87 p 88. C Plumstead St Jo w St Jas and St Paul *S'wark* 87–91; TV Ipswich St Fran *St E* 91–97; TV Walthamstow *Chelmsf* 97–17; C Leyton St Mary w St Edw and St Luke 17–18. *The Vicarage, 17A Greenleaf Road, London E17 6QQ* T: (020) 8520 2885 E: nigel.anstey@btinternet.com

ANSTICE, John Neville. b 39. Lon Univ BSc 63. Cuddesdon Coll 69. d 71 p 72. C Stonebridge St Mich *Lon* 71–74; Chapl Woodbridge Sch 74–76; TV Droitwich *Worc* 76–80; P-in-c Salwarpe 76–79; PtO *Chich* from 80; rtd 99. *5 Ash Grove, Wheathampstead, St Albans AL4 8DF* E: johnanstice@yahoo.com

ANTELL, Roger Howard. b 47. Lon Univ BD 71 Warwick Univ MSc 79 Ox Univ MTh 99. Ripon Coll Cuddesdon 97. d 99 p 00. C Ashchurch *Glouc* 99–03; R Stoke Prior, Wychbold and Upton Warren *Worc* 03–11; rtd 11. *Hafodwen, Dinas Cross, Newport SA42 0SG* T: (01348) 811391 E: roger.antell@btinternet.com

ANTHONY, Canon Ian Charles. b 47. NW Ord Course 76. d 79 p 80. NSM Lt Lever *Man* from 79; Dep Hd St Matt Primary Sch Lt Lever 79–97; Hd 97–07; Chapl St Ann's Hospice Manchester from 07; Hon Can Man Cathl 12–17; Dioc Officer for SSM 12–17. *36 Meadow Close, Little Lever, Bolton BL3 1LG* T: (01204) 791437 E: iancanthony@btinternet.com

ANTHONY, John Thomas. b 49. Trin Coll Carmarthen CertEd 71. d 15 p 16. NSM Cen Swansea *S & B* from 15. *11 Church Close, Neath SA10 7TF* T: (01639) 638434 E: johnanthony1@tiscali.co.uk

ANTHONY, Peter Benedict. b 79. Magd Coll Ox BA 02 MA 05 St Steph Ho Ox MSt 10 DPhil 15. St Steph Ho Ox 03 Ven English Coll Rome 05. d 06 p 07. C Hendon St Mary and Ch Ch *Lon* 06–09; Jun Dean St Steph Ho Ox 09–13; Jun Chapl Mert Coll Ox 10–13; P-in-c Kentish Town *Lon* 13–17; V from 17. *The Church House, Ospringe Road, London NW5 2JB* T: (020) 7284 3728 M: 07949-005550 E: peterbanthony@hotmail.com

ANTHONY, Miss Sheila Margaret. b 52. Wycliffe Hall Ox BTh 04. d 04 p 05. C Bideford, Northam, Westward Ho!, Appledore etc *Ex* 04–08; P-in-c Bluntisham cum Earith w Colne and Woodhurst *Ely* 08–10; P-in-c Holywell w Needingworth 08–10; V Bluntisham cum Earith w Colne and Holywell etc from 10. *The Rectory, 6 Rectory Road, Bluntisham, Huntingdon PE28 3LN* T: (01487) 740456 E: sheila@saintintraining.co.uk

AOKO, Mrs Olushola Ibiwunmi. b 55. SEITE 03. d 06 p 07. C Bermondsey St Mary w St Olave, St Jo etc *S'wark* 06–10; TV St Laur in Thanet *Cant* 10–17; TV Langley Marish *Ox* from 17. *Christ the Worker Vicarage, Parlaunt Road, Slough SL3 8BB* M: 07896-337578 E: shola_aoko@yahoo.co.uk

ap IORWERTH, Geraint. b 50. Univ of Wales (Cardiff) MPhil 90 Open Univ BA 78. Burgess Hall Lamp 69 Westmr Past Foundn 73 St Mich Coll Llan 73. d 74 p 75. C Holyhead w Rhoscolyn w Llanfair-yn-Neubwll *Ban* 74–78; R Pennal w Corris and Esgairgeiliog 78–12; rtd 12. *Oak Tree House, Dranllwyn Lane, Machen, Caerphilly CF83 8QS*

ap ROBERT, Rhun Gwynedd. d 14 p 15. C Aberavon *Llan* 14–17; TV from 17. *St Paul's Centre, Gerald Street, Port Talbot SA12 6DQ* E: rhunaprobert@parishofaberavon.org

ap SION, Tania. b 55. Ex Coll Ox BA 90 MA 96 Univ of Wales (Ban) MA 92 Warwick Univ PhD 10 Univ of Wales (Ban) PGCE 91. d 15 p 16. NSM Bro Tysilio *Ban* from 15. *Gelli*

Wen, Llanfairpwllgwyngyll LL61 6EQ T: (01248) 715131
E: smc.taniaapsion@gmail.com

APARANGA, Herbert Okidi. b 59. Kingston Univ BA 97.
Cranmer Hall Dur 10. **d** 12 **p** 13. C Blackheath St Jo *S'wark*
12–15; P-in-c Plumstead All SS from 15; Chapl Greenwich
and Bexley Cottage Hospice from 15. *All Saints' Vicarage,
106 Herbert Road, London SE18 3PU* M: 07808-300795
E: h.o.okot@gmail.com *or* herbertaparanga@gbch.org.uk

APOKIS, Konstantinos Fotios. b 61. Monash Univ BA 82.
Ridley Coll Melbourne BTh 87 ACT MTh 96. **d** 88 **p** 88. C
Greythorn Australia 88–90; C Port Melbourne 90–91; P-in-c
91–10; Res Asst World Vision 93–95; Chapl Incolink Support
Services Unit 96–99; Manager 96–99; Clergy Tr Officer
S'well 10–12; Dir Educn and Tr CA 12; PtO *Sheff* 12–13;
Roch 13–16; *Cant* 14–16. *1-17 College Crescent, Parkville VIC
3052, Australia* T: (0061) (3) 9349 0500 M: 07500-795477
E: capokis@sky.com

APOKIS, Sally-Ann. b 62. Dip Teaching. Ridley Coll Melbourne
BMin 89. **d** 97. Chapl Camberwell Girls' Gr Sch Australia
97–00; Chapl Shelford Gr Sch 01–07; Chapl Melbourne
Girls' Gr Morris Hall 08; Chapl Galilee Regional Catholic
Sch 09; Asst Dn Port Melbourne H Trin 97–09; Chapl
Sheff Univ 12–13; Hon C Crosspool 12–13; Chapl Medway
Campus Kent, Greenwich and Cant Ch Ch Univ 13–16; Hon
Can Roch Cathl 13–16; Chapl Qu Coll Melbourne Univ
Australia from 16. *1-17 College Crescent, Parkville VIC 3052,
Australia* T: (0061) (3) 9349 0500 M: (0061) 43-979 0480

APPADOO, Aneal Nathan. b 85. Oak Hill Th Coll BA 15. **d** 15
p 16. C Redhill H Trin *S'wark* 15–19; C Surbiton Hill Ch
Ch from 19. *19 Dennan Road, Surbiton KT6 7RY* M: 07834-
665887

APPELBE, Canon Frederick Charles. b 52. CITC 87. **d** 87
p 88. C Waterford w Killea, Drumcannon and Dunhill
C & O 87–90; C Taney *D & G* 90–92; I Rathmichael 92–19;
Can Ch Ch Cathl Dublin 02–19; rtd 19. *Address temp
unknown* M: (00353) 87-248 2410

APPIAH, Kuuku Andrew. b 77. Univ of Benin BSc 00
E Lon Univ MSc 14. Ridley Hall Cam 17. **d** 19. C
Barkingside H Trin *Chelmsf* from 19. *32 Oakhurst Close,
Ilford IG6 2LT* T: (01223) 678323 M: 07853-197937
E: rebuilding.in.christ@gmail.com

APPLEBY, David. b 60. St Jo Coll Dur BA 04. Cranmer Hall
Dur 02. **d** 04 **p** 05. C W Acklam *York* 04–08; R Aylestone
St Andr w St Jas *Leic* 08–14; TV Plymstock and Hooe *Ex* from
14. *The Rectory, 5 Cobb Lane, Plymouth PL9 9BQ* T: (01752)
941844 E: daveappleby2@gmail.com

APPLEBY, Janet Elizabeth. b 58. Bris Univ BSc 80 MSc 81
Newc Poly BA 90. Cranmer Hall Dur 01. **d** 03 **p** 04. C Newc
H Cross 03–06; TV Willington 06–15; Dioc Ecum Officer
12–18; rtd 18; PtO *Newc* from 18. *38 Beech Grove, Whitley Bay
NE26 3PL* E: janeteappleby@yahoo.com

APPLEBY, Ms Jennie. b 58. Southlands Coll Lon CertEd 81.
Cranmer Hall Dur 01. **d** 03 **p** 04. C Marton-in-Cleveland *York*
03–05; C Coatham and Dormanstown 05–08; R Emmaus Par
Team *Leic* 08–14; TV Plymstock and Hooe *Ex* 14–17; TR from
17. *The Rectory, 5 Cobb Lane, Plymouth PL9 9BQ* T: (01752)
941844 E: applebyj5@gmail.com

APPLEBY, Mrs Melanie Jayne. b 65. RGN 86. Ripon
Coll Cuddesdon 01. **d** 03 **p** 04. C Reddish *Man* 03–06;
TV Wythenshawe from 06. *St Richard's Vicarage, 42
Lomond Road, Manchester M22 5JD* T: 0161-215 1181
E: melanieappleby@hotmail.com

APPLEFORD, Kenneth Henry. b 30. Portsm Dioc Tr Course 91.
d 92. NSM Portsea St Mary *Portsm* 92–00; rtd 00. *124 Stride
Avenue, Portsmouth PO3 6HN* T: (023) 9281 4685

APPLEGATE, The Ven John. b 56. Bris Univ BSc 78. Trin
Coll Bris PhD 85. **d** 84 **p** 85. C Collyhurst *Man* 84–87;
Asst Chapl Monsall Hosp 84–87; C Broughton St Jas w
St Clem and St Matthias *Man* 87–94; R Broughton St Jo
94–96; TR Broughton 96–02; AD Salford 97–02; Research
Fell and Lect Man Univ from 00; Bp's Adv for Hosp Chapl
02–08; Adn Bolton 02–08; Prin SNWTP 08–12; Prin All
SS Cen for Miss and Min from 12. *University of Chester,
Crab Lane, Warrington WA2 0DB* T: (01925) 534373
E: john.applegate@allsaintscentre.org

APPLEGATH, Caroline Tracey. b 67. Lon Univ BMus 90
Edin Univ BD 94. Edin Th Coll 91. **d** 94 **p** 95. C Edin
St Martin 94–96; Hon C Edin St Pet 97–99; C 99–01;
Chapl Lothian Univ Hosps NHS Trust 01–18; Hon Can
St Mary's Cathl *Edin* 16–19; PtO from 19; C St Ninian's
Cathl Perth *St And* from 19. *Lauder House, 39 Jeffrey
Street, Edinburgh EH1 1DH* T: 0131-556 3332 *or* 536
0144 M: 07889-981283 E: carrie.applegath@gmail.com *or*
carrie.applegath@nhslothian.scot.nhs.uk

APPLETON, Mrs Bonita. b 55. Man Univ MA 08. St Jo Coll
Nottm 91. **d** 93 **p** 94. C Camberley St Paul *Guildf* 93–96;

Chapl Elmhurst Ballet Sch 95–96; TV Cove St Jo *Guildf*
96–03; Chapl Farnborough Sixth Form Coll 97–00; Dioc Par
Resources Officer *Guildf* 03–10; NSM Knaphill w Brookwood
05–10; TR S Gillingham *Roch* 10–15; RD Gillingham
11–15; PtO from 15; *Cant* from 16. *Egerton House, Egerton
House Road, Egerton, Ashford TN27 9BD* T: (01233) 756354
E: appletonbonnie@gmail.com

APPLETON, John Bearby. b 42. Linc Th Coll 74. **d** 76 **p** 77.
C Selby Abbey *York* 76–79; C Epsom St Barn *Guildf* 79–82;
V Linc All SS 82–94; rtd 02. *33 South End, Osmotherley,
Northallerton DL6 3BN*

APPLETON, Ruth Elizabeth. *See* WALKER, Ruth Elizabeth

APPLIN, David Edward. b 39. Oak Hill Th Coll 63. **d** 65 **p** 66.
C Ox St Clem 65–69; C Felixstowe SS Pet and Paul *St E* 69–71;
LtO *Win* 71–91; Travelling Sec Ruanda Miss 71–74; Home
Sec 74–77; Gen Sec 77–81; Dir Overseas Personnel Dept
TEAR Fund 82–87; Overseas Dir 87–92; Hon C Kempshott
Win 91–92; R Awbridge w Sherfield English 92–97; Exec Dir
Samaritan's Purse Internat from 95. *27 Heath Lodge, Marsh
Road, Pinner HA5 5PB* T: (020) 8429 2332

APPS, Bryan Gerald. b 37. Univ of Wales (Lamp) BA 59
St Cath Coll Ox BA 61 MA 65. Wycliffe Hall Ox 59. **d** 61
p 62. C Southampton St Alb *Win* 61–65; C Andover w
Foxcott 65–69; P-in-c Freemantle 69–72; R 73–78; V
Pokesdown All SS 78–03; rtd 03; PtO *Win* from 03. *14
Bartlett Drive, Bournemouth BH7 7JT* T: (01202) 418360
E: bryanapps@talk21.com

APPS, David Ronald. b 34. Univ of Wales (Lamp) BA 57.
Sarum Th Coll 57. **d** 59 **p** 60. C Southbourne St Chris *Win*
59–62; C Weeke 62–67; V Alton All SS 67–80; V Charlestown
Truro 80–97; Miss to Seamen 80–97; rtd 99. *12 Walnut Close,
Exminster, Exeter EX6 8SZ* T: (01392) 823672

APPS-HUGGINS, Mrs Lorraine Georgina. b 63. Cant Ch
Ch Univ BA 13. Local Minl Tr Course 07. **d** 10 **p** 11. OLM
Deal St Geo *Cant* 10–14; NSM Downsfoot 14; V Shepherds
Lees 14–17; Asst Chapl The Living Well 17–19; Chapl
from 19; Bp's Adv for Healing and Wholeness *Cant* from
19. *Lenham Vicarage, Old Ashford Road, Lenham, Maidstone
ME17 2PX* T: (01304) 842847 E: appshuggins@gmail.com

ARBER, Gerald Kenneth Walter. b 37. Open Univ BA 87. Oak
Hill NSM Course 81. **d** 84 **p** 85. NSM Romford St Edw *Chelmsf*
84–95; NSM Cranham 95–14; PtO *Cant* from 13. *69 Parsonage
Chase, Minster on Sea, Sheerness ME12 3JX* T: (01795) 872186
E: frgerryarber@btinternet.com

ARBUTHNOT, Paul Ian. b 81. TCD BA 03 MA 06 MLitt 07.
CITC BTh 10. **d** 10 **p** 11. C Glenageary *D & G* 10–12; Chan V
St Patr Cathl Dublin 11–12; PV Ch Ch Cathl Dublin *D & G*
11–12; Prec and Min Can St Alb Abbey 12–15; Min Can and
Sacrist Westmr Abbey 15–17; I Cobh and Glanmire *C, C & R*
from 18. *The Rectory, Fota View, Ballycureen, Glounthaune, T45
Y898, Republic of Ireland* T: (00353) (21) 435 5208 M: 83-
896 1465 E: paul.arbuthnot@gmail.com

ARCH, Ian Michael. b 75. Univ Coll Dur MSc 97 Peterho Cam
BA 02. Westcott Ho Cam 00. **d** 03 **p** 04. C Bromborough
Ches 03–05; Chapl Ches Univ 05–11; Dean of Chpl 10–11; V
Marton, Siddington w Capesthorne and Eaton etc 11–18; V
Marton, Siddington w Capesthorne etc from 18. *The Vicarage,
School Lane, Marton, Macclesfield SK11 9HD* T: (01260)
224447 E: revd.arch@gmail.com

ARCHER, David John. b 69. Reading Univ BSc 91 PhD 95 Cam
Univ BTh 05. Ridley Hall Cam 02. **d** 05 **p** 06. C Abingdon
Ox 05–09; R Purley from 09. *The Rectory, 1 Westridge Avenue,
Purley on Thames, Reading RG8 8DE* T: 0118-326 0839
E: david.archer@stmaryspurley.org.uk

ARCHER, Graham John. b 58. Lanc Univ BSc 79. St Jo Coll
Nottm 82. **d** 85 **p** 86. C Ipswich St Matt *St E* 85–89; C Walton
89–95; P-in-c 95–99; Chapl Local Health Partnerships NHS
Trust 96–99; P-in-c Portswood Ch Ch *Win* 99–05; V 05–12;
P-in-c Portswood St Denys 00–02; Hon Can Win Cathl
11–12; Dir Min CPAS from 12; PtO *Cov* 13–15; Acting
Adn Malmesbury *Bris* 18–19. *CPAS, Unit 3, Sir William
Lyons Road, University of Warwick Science Park, Coventry
CV4 7EZ* T: 03001-230780 E: garcher@cpas.org.uk

ARCHER, Keith Malcolm. b 40. Man Univ BA 61 MA 80 Magd
Coll Cam BA 67 MA 72. Ridley Hall Cam 66. **d** 68 **p** 69. C
Newland St Jo *York* 68–72; Hon C Kersal Moor *Man* 72–79;
Ind Chapl 72–93; V Weaste 93–09; TV Pendleton 08–09; TV
Salford All SS 09–10; rtd 10; PtO *Man* from 11. *Flat 2, 86-88
Wellington Road, Eccles, Manchester M30 9GW* M: 07943-
366502 E: keitharcher@hotmail.co.uk

ARCHER, Michael James. b 67. St Jo Coll Dur BA 90 St Edm
Coll Cam PhD 95. Ridley Hall Cam 92. **d** 94 **p** 95. C
Littleover *Derby* 94–97; C Edgware *Lon* 97–98; TV 98–01;
P-in-c Bletchley *Ox* 01–08; R 08–13; P-in-c Portswood Ch Ch
Win from 13; P-in-c Portswood St Denys from 16. *Highfield*

Vicarage, 36 Brookvale Road, Southampton SO17 1QR T: (023) 8122 8151 E: mikearcher101@me.com

ARCHER, Neill John. b 61. UEA BA 82. NTMTC 96. **d** 99 **p** 00. C Ripley *Derby* 99–02; C Forster Tuncurry Australia 02–03; PtO *Lon* 03–04; P-in-c Malmesbury w Westport and Brokenborough *Bris* 04–16; C Gt Somerford, Lt Somerford, Seagry, Corston etc 09–16; V Malmesbury and Upper Avon 16–17; AD N Wilts 09–16; Chapl R United Hosps Bath NHS Foundn Trust 17–18; Chapl Univ Hosps Bris NHS Foundn Trust from 18. *University Hospitals Bristol NHS Foundation Trust, Trust Headquarters, Marlborough Street, Bristol BS1 3NU* T: 0117-923 0000

ARCHER, Nicholas William. b 88. Univ Coll Lon BSc 11. St Steph Ho Ox BA 16. **d** 17 **p** 18. C Eastbourne St Sav and St Pet *Chich* 17–18; C Eastbourne St Mary 18; C St Leonards Ch Ch and St Mary etc from 18. *33 Park Lane Mansions, Eversfield Place, St Leonards-on-Sea TN37 6DD* E: nick@archer.gg

ARCHER, Norman Vivian. b 34. K Coll Lon AKC 57. **d** 60 **p** 61. C Baldock w Bygrave and Clothall *St Alb* 60–62; India 62–77; rtd 99. *29 Westcott Road, London SE17 3QY* T: (020) 7820 1725

ARCHER, Mrs Rachel Louise. b 72. Edin Univ BD 95 Moray Ho Edin PGCE 96. St Mellitus Coll 17. **d** 19. C Biggin Hill *Roch* from 19. *7 Keymer Close, Biggin Hill, Westerham TN16 3DF* M: 07740-368225 E: rachel.vicarintraining@yahoo.com

ARCHER, Sarah Elizabeth. b 66. Charing Cross Hosp Medical Sch MB, BS 89 Heythrop Coll Lon MA 03 MRCGP 95. Ripon Coll Cuddesdon BA 99 MA 07. **d** 00 **p** 01. C Dulwich St Barn *S'wark* 00–03; C Shepherd's Bush St Steph w St Thos *Lon* 03–07; PV Westmr Abbey from 07; PtO *Lon* 07–08; *B & W* 08–11; NSM Bath Abbey w St Jas 11–15; V W Brompton St Mary w St Peter and St Jude *Lon* 15–16; Bp's Dom Chapl *Portsm* 16–17; PtO *Ex* from 17; *Eur* from 18; *B & W* from 19. *Lee Abbey Fellowship, Lee Abbey, Lynton EX35 6JJ*

ARCHER, Simon Antony. b 65. Staffs Poly BA 90. Ripon Coll Cuddesdon 10. **d** 12 **p** 13. C Glouc St Paul and St Steph 12–16; TV Brierley Hill *Worc* 16–19; TV Kidderminster Ismere from 19. *22 Roden Avenue, Kidderminster DY10 2RF* M: 07815-164991 E: revsimonarcher@gmail.com

ARCHER, Simon Frank. b 75. **d** 16 **p** 17. C Erith Ch Ch *Roch* 16–19; P-in-c Belvedere All SS from 19. *All Saints' Vicarage, Nuxley Road, Belvedere DA17 5JE* T: (01322) 432169 M: 07506-464848 E: revsimonfarcher@gmail.com

ARCHIBALD, Peter Ben. b 83. Robert Gordon Univ Aber BSc 04. St Steph Ho Ox BTh 08. **d** 08 **p** 09. C Middlesbrough All SS *York* 08–11; Lead Chapl Middlesbrough Coll 09–11; P-in-c Kettering St Mary *Pet* 11–13; CF from 13. *c/o MOD Chaplains (Army)* T: (01264) 383430 F: 381824 M: 07793-535628 E: peter.archibald100@mod.uk *or* frbenarchibald@gmail.com

ARDAGH-WALTER, Christopher Richard. b 35. Univ of Wales (Lamp) BA 58. Chich Th Coll 58. **d** 60 **p** 61. C Heavitree *Ex* 60–64; C Redcar *York* 64–67; C King's Worthy *Win* 67–69; C-in-c Four Marks 70–73; V 73–76; P-in-c Eling, Testwood and Marchwood 76–78; TR Totton 76–84; R The Sherbornes w Pamber 84–89; V Froyle and Holybourne 88–95; C Verwood *Sarum* 95–97; rtd 97; PtO *Win* 98–14; *Ox* 01–14; *Birm* 14–19. *1 Ashfield Gardens, Ashfield Road, Birmingham B14 7AS* T: 0121-449 9663 E: crawalter@btinternet.com

ARDILL, Robert William Brian. b 40. QUB BSc 63 PhD 67 SOSc. Ox NSM Course 80 St Jo Coll Nottm 84. **d** 83 **p** 85. NSM Sunninghill *Ox* 83–84; Hon Chapl R Holloway Coll *Lon* 83–84; C Lenton *S'well* 85–87; PtO *Leic* 92–95; C Harpenden St Nic *St Alb* 95–00; R N Tawton, Bondleigh, Sampford Courtenay etc *Ex* 00–10; rtd 10. *8 Hanover Gardens, Cullompton EX15 1XA* T: (01884) 798386 E: brian.ardill@gmail.com

ARDING, Richard. b 52. ACIB 84. Oak Hill Th Coll 90. **d** 92 **p** 93. C Bromley Common St Aug *Roch* 92–96; V Wilmington 96–18; RD Dartford 07–13; rtd 18. *15 Mulberry Close, Tunbridge Wells TN4 9XR*

ARDIS, Canon Edward George. b 54. Dur Univ BA 76. CITC 76. **d** 78 **p** 79. C Dublin Drumcondra w N Strand and St Barn *D & G* 78–81; C Dublin St Bart w Leeson Park 81–84; I Ardamine w Kiltennel, Glascarrig etc *C & O* 84–89; Can Tuam Cathl *T, K & A* 89–03; Dean Killala 89–03; I Killala w Dunfeeny, Crossmolina etc 89–93; I Killala w Dunfeeny, Crossmolina, Kilmoremoy etc 94–03; Dir of Ords 95–03; I Dublin Irishtown w Donnybrook *D & G* 03–13; Dean's V Cork Cathl *C, C & R* from 13; Can Ch Ch Cathl Dublin *D & G* from 08; PtO *Eur* 16–17. *9 Dean Street, Cork, Republic of Ireland* T: (00353) (21) 241 6081 M: 87-637 6241 E: tedardis@yahoo.ie

ARDIS, John Kevin. b 06 **p** 07. C Dublin Ch Ch Cathl Gp *D & G* 06–08; Dean's V Cork St Fin Barre's Union *C, C & R* 08–11; Chapl Univ Coll Cork 11–13; I Abbeystrewry Union

from 13; Bp's Dom Chapl from 14. *The Rectory, Coronea Drive, Skibbereen, Co Cork, Republic of Ireland* T: (00353) (28) 21234 M: 87-680 7289 E: abbeystrewryunion@gmail.com

ARDOUIN, Timothy David Peter. Univ of Wales (Lamp) BA 94 Univ of Wales (Cardiff) MTh 08. St Mich Coll Llan. **d** 08 **p** 09. C Gorseinon *S & B* 08–11; P-in-c Llanrhidian w Llanyrnewydd from 11; Interfaith Officer *St D* from 16. *The Vicarage, Llanrhidian, Swansea SA3 1EH* T: (01792) 391353 M: 07871-420089 E: frtimardouin@btinternet.com

ARENS, Johannes. b 69. Heythrop Coll Lon MTh 97. **d** 96 **p** 97. Old Catholic Ch Germany 96–04; TV Harrogate St Wilfrid *Ripon* 04–06; V Manston 06–11; Can Res Leic Cathl 11–19; Faith Adv De Montfort Univ from 19; PtO *Eur* from 16. *The Precentor's House, 23 St Martins, Leicester LE1 5DE* T: 0116-261 5364 E: johannes.arens@leccofe.org

ARGLES, Mrs Christine. b 57. Bris Univ BA 00. Trin Coll Bris 00. **d** 02 **p** 03. C Nailsea Ch Ch w Tickenham *B & W* 02–05; Chapl Weston Area Health NHS Trust 05–07; Chapl Cardiff and Vale NHS Trust 07–08; PtO *B & W* 08–17; Past Care Co-ord St Monica Trust Sandford Station 10–11; NSM Milton and Kewstoke *B & W* 17–18; rtd 18. *21 Hayward Avenue, West Wick, Weston-super-Mare BS24 7FR* T: (01934) 707291 M: 07763-476127 E: chrisargles@aol.com

ARGUILE, Canon Roger Henry William. b 43. Dur Univ LLB 64 Keble Coll Ox BA 70 MA 75. St Steph Ho Ox 69 Ripon Hall Ox 70. **d** 71 **p** 72. C Walsall *Lich* 71–76; TV Blakenall Heath 76–83; TV Stafford 83–95; P-in-c St Neots *Ely* 95–97; V 97–07; Hon Can Ely Cathl 01–07; RD St Neots 02–07; rtd 07; PtO *Nor* from 07. *10 Marsh Lane, Wells-next-the-Sea NR23 1EG* T: (01328) 711788 E: arguile@btinternet.com

ARGYLL AND THE ISLES, Bishop of. See PEARSON, The Rt Revd Kevin

ARGYLL AND THE ISLES, Dean of. Vacant

ARKELL, Canon Kevin Paul. b 53. Preston Poly BTh 86 Leeds Univ MA 95. Sarum & Wells Th Coll 84. **d** 86 **p** 87. C S Petherton w The Seavingtons *B & W* 86–88; P-in-c Gt Harwood St Bart *Blackb* 88–90; V 90–95; TR Darwen St Pet w Hoddlesden 95–03; Acting RD Darwen 97–98; AD Blackb and Darwen 98–03; P-in-c Pokesdown All SS *Win* 03–11; P-in-c Bournemouth St Clem 08–11; V Newport St Thos *Portsm* from 11; V Newport St Jo 11–17; Hon Can Portsm Cathl from 18. *The Vicarage, 72A Medina Avenue, Newport PO30 1HF* T: (01983) 539580 M: 07971-800083 E: kevin@thearkells.co.uk

ARLIDGE, Canon Lucille Monica. b 56. WMMTC 04. **d** 07 **p** 08. NSM Birchfield *Birm* 07–11; PtO *Lich* 11–14 and 15–18; P-in-c Smethwick St Matt w St Chad *Birm* from 14; Hon Can Birm Cathl from 16. *23 Willow Road, Great Barr, Birmingham B43 6LP* T: 0121-358 3321 E: lucyarlidge@yahoo.com

ARMAGH, Archbishop of. See CLARKE, The Most Revd Richard Lionel

ARMAGH, Archdeacon of. See SCOTT, The Ven Terence

ARMAGH, Dean of. See DUNSTAN, The Very Revd Gregory John Orchard

ARMAN, Canon Brian Robert. b 54. St Jo Coll Dur BA 77. Cranmer Hall Dur 74. **d** 78 **p** 79. C Lawrence Weston *Bris* 78–82; C Bishopston 82–88; R Filton 88–15; P-in-c Horfield St Greg 03–05; Hon Can Bris Cathl 01–15; rtd 15. *59 Kenmore Crescent, Bristol BS7 0TP*

✠**ARMES, The Rt Revd John Andrew.** b 55. SS Coll Cam BA 77 MA 81 Man Univ PhD 96. Sarum & Wells Th Coll 77. **d** 79 **p** 80 **c** 12. C Walney Is *Carl* 79–82; Chapl to Agric 82–86; TV Greystoke, Matterdale and Mungrisdale 82–86; TV Watermillock 82–86; TV Man Whitworth 86–88; TR 88–94; Chapl Man Univ 86–94; P-in-c Goodshaw and Crawshawbooth 94–98; AD Rossendale 94–98; R Edin St Jo 98–12; Dean Edin 10–12; Bp Edin from 12. *Bishop's Office, 21A Grosvenor Crescent, Edinburgh EH12 5EL* T: 0131-538 7044 E: bishop@edinburgh.anglican.org

ARMITAGE, Richard Norris. b 51. Birm Univ PhD 10 AKC. St Aug Coll Cant 73. **d** 74 **p** 75. C Chapelthorpe *Wakef* 74–77; C W Bromwich All SS *Lich* 77–82; P-in-c Ketley 82–83; V Oakengates 82–83; V Ketley and Oakengates 83–89; V Evesham *Worc* 89–96; V Evesham w Norton and Lenchwick 96–05; RD Evesham 00–05; Chapl Wilts Constabulary *Bris* 05–16; rtd 16; PtO *Ox* from 17; *Bris* from 17. *6 Witney Road, Long Hanborough, Witney OX29 8BJ*

ARMITAGE, Susan. b 46. Th Ext Educn Coll 91. **d** 92 **p** 95. Pretoria Corpus Christi S Africa 92–97; C Fawley *Win* 97–00; C Chandler's Ford 00–04; rtd 11; PtO *Sarum* from 11. *36 St Margaret's Mead, Marlborough SN8 4BA* T: (01672) 513678 E: sue.armitage@savernake.com

ARMITSTEAD, Margaretha Catharina Maria. b 65. Free Univ of Amsterdam MA 89. SAOMC 00. **d** 03 **p** 04. C Littlemore *Ox* 03–06; P-in-c from 06. *The Vicarage, St Nicholas Road,*

Littlemore, Oxford OX4 4PP T: (01865) 748003 *or* 779885 E: margreetarmitstead@btinternet.com

ARMSTEAD, Canon Paul Richard. b 63. Ox Poly BA 85 ACA 89 FCA 99. St Steph Ho Ox BTh 11. **d** 08 **p** 09. C Northampton St Matt *Pet* 08–12; P-in-c Milton *Portsm* from 12; C Southsea H Spirit from 12; Can Ho Ghana from 18. *St James's Vicarage, 287 Milton Road, Southsea PO4 8PG* T: (023) 9273 2786 E: paularmstead@btinternet.com

ARMSTRONG, Adrian Christopher. b 48. LSE BSc 70 K Coll Lon PhD 80. EAMTC 84. **d** 87 **p** 88. NSM Linton *Ely* 87–95; P-in-c N and S Muskham *S'well* 95–00; P-in-c Averham w Kelham 95–00; PtO *B & W* 01–02; Hon C Wiveliscombe w Chipstable, Huish Champflower etc 02–06; Hon C Lydeard St Lawrence w Brompton Ralph etc 06–09; rtd 10; PtO *B & W* 15–18; *Dur* from 19. *11 The Paddock, Lanchester, Durham DH7 0HW* E: drmudpie@btinternet.com

ARMSTRONG, Alexander Milford. b 57. Local Minl Tr Course. **d** 95 **p** 95. NSM Livingston LEP *Edin* 95–97; C Cleator Moor w Cleator *Carl* 97–98; C Frizington and Arlecdon 97–98; C Crosslacon 98–99; V Westfield St Mary 99–10; P-in-c Aldingham, Dendron, Rampside and Urswick 10–17; rtd 17. *4 Belmont Road, Ayr KA7 2PH* T: (01292) 260471 E: amvarmstrong@hotmail.com

ARMSTRONG, The Very Revd Christopher John. b 47. Nottm Univ BTh 75. Kelham Th Coll 72. **d** 75 **p** 76. C Maidstone All SS w St Phil and H Trin *Cant* 76–79; Chapl St Hild and St Bede Coll *Dur* 79–84; Abp's Dom Chapl and Dir of Ords *York* 85–91; V Scarborough St Martin 91–01; Dean Blackb 01–16; P-in-c Barrowden and Wakerley w S Luffenham etc *Pet* from 16. *The Rectory, 11 Church Lane, Barrowden, Oakham LE15 8ED* E: chris.armstrong@yahoo.com

ARMSTRONG, Christopher John Richard. b 35. Fribourg Univ LTh 60 Ch Coll Cam BA 64 MA 68 PhD 79. Edin Th Coll 74. **d** 59 **p** 59. In RC Ch 59–71; Lect Aber Univ *Ab* 68–74; C Ledbury *Heref* 74–76; P-in-c Bredenbury and Wacton w Grendon Bishop 76–79; P-in-c Edwyn Ralph and Collington w Thornbury 76–79; P-in-c Pencombe w Marston Stannett and Lt Cowarne 76–79; R Cherry Burton *York* 79–80; Tutor Westcott Ho Cam 80–85; V Bottisham *Ely* 85–89; P-in-c Lode and Longmeadow 85–89; P-in-c Cropthorne w Charlton *Worc* 89–93; Dioc Local Min Sec 89–93; R Aberdaron w Rhiw and Llanfaelrhys etc *Ban* 93–99; rtd 99; PtO *Heref* 99–06; *Ban* 99–06; *Bradf* 06–14; *Leeds* from 14. *52 Bradford Road, Burley in Wharfedale, Ilkley LS29 7PU* T: (01943) 864761

ARMSTRONG, David Thomas. b 62. St Mellitus Coll BA 14. **d** 14 **p** 15. C Lexden *Chelmsf* 14–18; P-in-c St Botolph without Bishopgate *Lon* from 18. *42 Gilbert Road, London SE11 4NL* T: (020) 7588 3388 E: david@davidtarmstrong.com

ARMSTRONG, Eileen. **d** 95 **p** 96. NSM Navan w Kentstown, Tara, Slane, Painestown etc *M & K* from 95. *Hennigan, Nobber, Co Meath, Republic of Ireland* T: (00353) (46) 905 2314 E: reveileen2@gmail.com

ARMSTRONG, John Edwin. b 51. Leic Univ CertEd 73 BEd 74. Ridley Hall Cam 91. **d** 93 **p** 94. C Gt Wilbraham *Ely* 93–96; P-in-c Bassingbourn 96–02; V 02–04; P-in-c Whaddon 96–02; V 02–04; P-in-c Southam *Cov* 04–16; P-in-c Ufton 04–16; RD Southam 08–11; C Kenilworth St Jo 16–17; rtd 17; Hon C Kenilworth St Jo *Cov* from 17. *19 Leyes Lane, Kenilworth CV8 2DD* T: (01926) 853942 M: 07513-944468 E: revarmstrong@gmail.com

ARMSTRONG, John Gordon. b 64. Man Poly BSc 86 MSc 91 Man Univ MA 03. Wycliffe Hall Ox 95. **d** 97 **p** 98. C Pennington *Man* 97–01; P-in-c Holcombe and Hawkshaw Lane 01–07; TV Deane 07–18; P-in-c Bolton St Bede 16–18; R Wombwell *Sheff* from 18. *The Rectory, 1 Rectory Close, Wombwell, Barnsley S73 8EY* T: (01226) 891124 E: armstrongfamily@ntlworld.com

ARMSTRONG (formerly READING), Mrs Lesley Jean. b 49. GNSM 70 Trent Park Coll of Educn CertEd 71. NOC 98. **d** 01 **p** 02. NSM Eccles *Man* 01–05; P-in-c Heywood St Jas 05–11; rtd 11; PtO *Man* 12–18; *Lich* from 19. *34 Stafford Road, Newport TF10 7LZ* T: (01952) 273210 M: 07760-202411 E: readinglesley@hotmail.com

ARMSTRONG, Mrs Margaret Betty. b 48. SRN 70 RSCN 71. Westcott Ho Cam 89. **d** 92 **p** 94. NSM Linton *Ely* 92–95; NSM Shudy Camps 92–95; NSM Castle Camps 92–95; NSM Bartlow 92–95; NSM N and S Muskham and Averham w Kelham *S'well* 95–00; P-in-c Lydeard St Lawrence w Brompton Ralph etc *B & W* 01–09; rtd 10; PtO *B & W* 15–18; *Dur* from 19. *11 The Paddock, Lanchester, Durham DH7 0HW*

ARMSTRONG, Canon Maurice Alexander. b 62. Ulster Poly BA 84. CITC 84. **d** 87 **p** 88. C Portadown St Mark *Arm* 87–90; I Sixmilecross w Termonmaguirke 90–95; I Richhill 95–01; I Tempo and Clabby *Clogh* from 01; Can Clogh Cathl from 12. *St Margaret's Rectory, 177 Clabby Road, Clabby, Fivemiletown BT75 0RD* T: (028) 8952 1697

ARMSTRONG, Preb Nicholas Paul. b 58. Bris Univ BSc 79. Trin Coll Bris 91. **d** 93 **p** 94. C Filey *York* 93–97; P-in-c Alveley and Quatt *Heref* 97–98; R 98–15; RD Bridgnorth 13–15; V Tupsley w Hampton Bishop from 15; Preb Heref Cathl from 12. *The Vicarage, 107 Church Road, Hereford HR1 1RT* T: (01432) 353068 E: nicka@inbox.com

ARMSTRONG, Rosemary. See WYNN, Rosemary

ARMSTRONG, Mrs Susan Elizabeth. b 45. **d** 05 **p** 06. OLM Tilstock, Edstaston and Whixall *Lich* 05–09; OLM Edstaston, Fauls, Prees, Tilstock and Whixall 09–15; OLM Whitchurch 13–15; rtd 15; PtO *Lich* from 18. *Tarragon Cottage, Shrewsbury Street, Prees, Whitchurch SY13 2DH* T: (01948) 840039

ARMSTRONG-MacDONNELL, Mrs Vivienne Christine. b 42. Open Univ BA 89 Ex Univ MEd 01 Lambeth MA 05. Ripon Coll Cuddesdon 88. **d** 90 **p** 94. C Crediton and Shobrooke *Ex* 90–93; Dioc Adv in Adult Tr 93–00; rtd 00; PtO *Ex* 00–07 and from 09; Bp's Adv for Spirituality 07–09. *Strand House, Greenway, Woodbury, Exeter EX5 1LU* T/F: (01395) 232790

ARNALL-CULLIFORD, Jane Margaret. See CULLIFORD, Jane Margaret

ARNELL, Andrew. b 65. Hull Univ BA 88. **d** 19. NSM Hampstead Em W End *Lon* from 19. *65 Hale Grove Gardens, London NW7 3LT* E: andyarnell123@aol.com *or* andyarnell123@icloud.com

ARNESEN, Christopher Paul. b 48. Lon Univ BA 70 Sheff Univ MA 02. Sarum & Wells Th Coll 78. **d** 80 **p** 81. C Dalton-in-Furness *Carl* 80–83; C Ranmoor *Sheff* 83–86; R Distington *Carl* 86–93; TV Sheff Manor 93–97; Mental Health Chapl Sheff Care Trust 98–04; PtO *Sheff* from 04; Bp's Adv in Past Care and Counselling 08–13; rtd 13. *39 Greystones Crescent, Sheffield S11 7JN* T: 0114-266 8836 E: paul.arnesen@me.com

ARNESEN, Raymond Halfdan (Brother Ælred). b 25. Qu Coll Cam BA 49 MA 54. Linc Th Coll 50. **d** 52 **p** 53. C Newc St Fran 52–55; SSF 55–66; Cistercian Monk from 66; Ewell Monastery 66–64; rtd 95. *2 Brentmead Close, London W7 3EW* T: (020) 8579 2074 E: aelred@arnesen.co.uk

ARNOLD, Briony Alice. See BOYDE, Briony Alice

ARNOLD, Christine Sabina. b 60. **d** 12 **p** 13. NSM St Peter-in-Thanet *Cant* 12–16; Asst Chapl The Living Well 16–17. *6 East Northdown Close, Margate CT9 3YA* T: (01843) 224449 E: chris.arnold06@btinternet.com

ARNOLD, David Alun. b 78. St Andr Univ MTheol 00 Leeds Univ MA 03. Coll of Resurr Mirfield 01. **d** 03 **p** 04. C Ribbleton *Blackb* 03–05; C Hawes Side and Marton Moss 05–07; Bp's Dom Chapl 07–12; V Adlington from 12; P-in-c Chorley St Geo 17–18; AD Chorley from 17; Asst Dir of Ords from 06. *St Paul's Vicarage, Railway Road, Adlington, Chorley PR6 9QZ* T: (01257) 474025 M: 07786-168261 E: frdavidarnold@gmail.com

ARNOLD, Derek John. b 59. Wycliffe Hall Ox 01. **d** 03 **p** 04. C St Jo in Bedwardine *Worc* 03–06; TV Kidderminster St Jo and H Innocents 06–09; TR 09–14; P-in-c Ombersley w Doverdale 14–16; P-in-c Elmley Lovett w Hampton Lovett and Elmbridge etc 14–16; P-in-c Hartlebury 14–16; R Elmley Lovett w Hampton Lovett and Elmbridge w Rushock and Hartlebury and Ombersley w Doverdale 16–17; TR Appledore, Northam and Westward Ho! *Ex* from 17; RD Hartland from 19. *The Rectory, Fore Street, Northam, Bideford EX39 1AW* T: (01237) 721723 M: 07789-631346 E: darnold.rector@gmail.com

ARNOLD, Elisabeth Anne Truyens. b 44. TCert 66. **d** 91 **p** 94. OLM Ipswich St Thos *St E* 91–00; Chapl Dioc Min Course 00–01; OLM Tutor 01–06; rtd 06; PtO *St E* from 06. *66 Bromeswell Road, Ipswich IP4 3AT* T: (01473) 257406

ARNOLD, Frances Mary. b 64. R Holloway Coll Lon BA 86 Anglia Ruskin Univ MA 07 Dur Univ PGCE 90. Westcott Ho Cam 01. **d** 04 **p** 05. C Biggleswade *St Alb* 04–07; Exec Officer Abps' Coun 07–13; PtO *Lon* 08–13; V Sawbridgeworth *St Alb* 13–19; P-in-c Sutton *S'wark* from 19. *The Rectory, 34 Robin Hood Lane, Sutton SM1 2RG* T: (020) 8642 3499 E: rector.stnicholassutton@gmail.com

ARNOLD, Graham Thomas. b 62. Aston Tr Scheme 87 Ripon Coll Cuddesdon 89. **d** 92 **p** 93. C Margate St Jo *Cant* 92–95; TV Whitstable 95–00; PtO *S'wark* 07–09; NSM N Dulwich St Faith 09–12. *10B Franklin Road, London SE20 8HW* T: (020) 8289 0233 M: 07793-555017 E: grahamt62@btinternet.com

ARNOLD, Jane Elizabeth. b 50. **d** 11 **p** 12. NSM Kingswinford St Mary *Worc* 11–18; rtd 18. *9 Murdoch Drive, Kingswinford DY6 9HG* E: jane.arnold128@btinternet.com

ARNOLD, Sister Janet Rachel. b 64. **d** 14 **p** 15. CA from 88; C Woodchurch *Ches* 14–17; V Newchapel *Lich* from 17. *St James's Vicarage, 32 Pennyfields Road, Newchapel, Stoke-on-Trent ST7 4PN* T: (01782) 782837 E: vicar@stjamesnewchapel.co.uk

ARNOLD, The Very Revd John Robert. b 33. SS Coll Cam BA 57 MA 61 Lambeth DD 99. Westcott Ho Cam 58. **d** 60 **p** 61. C Millhouses H Trin *Sheff* 60–63; Chapl and Lect Southn Univ *Win* 63–72; Gen Sec Gen Syn Bd for Miss and Unity 72–78; Hon Can Win Cathl 74–78; Dean Roch 78–89; Dean Dur 89–02; rtd 03; PtO *Cant* from 02. *26 Hawks Lane, Canterbury CT1 2NU* T: (01227) 764703 E: arnold.jr@btinternet.com

ARNOLD, Jonathan Allen. b 69. St Pet Coll Ox BA 92 MA 99 K Coll Lon PhD 04 LTCL 89 LRAM 94. Ripon Coll Cuddesdon 03. **d** 05 **p** 06. NSM Chalgrove w Berrick Salome *Ox* 05–08; Chapl Worc Coll Ox 08–16; Dean Div and Fell Magd Coll Ox 16–19; Dir Communities and Partnerships Framework *Cant* from 19. *15 The Precincts, Canterbury CT1 2EL* T: (01227) 865228 M: 07939-093085 E: jarnold@diocant.org

✠ARNOLD, The Rt Revd Keith Appleby. b 26. Trin Coll Cam BA 50 MA 55. Westcott Ho Cam 50. **d** 52 **p** 53 **c** 80. C Haltwhistle *Newc* 52–55; C Edin St Jo 55–61; R 61–69; CF (TA) 58–62; V Kirkby Lonsdale w Mansergh *Carl* 69–73; RD Berkhamsted *St Alb* 73–80; TR Hemel Hempstead 73–80; Suff Bp Warw *Cov* 80–90; Hon Can Cov Cathl 80–90; rtd 90; Hon Asst Bp Ox from 97. *9 Dinglederry, Olney MK46 5ES* T: (01234) 713044

ARNOLD, Mark James. b 75. Univ of Wales (Lamp) BA 97. St Mellitus Coll BA 17. **d** 17 **p** 18. NSM Langdale w Standr *Lon* from 17. *108 Whittington Way, Pinner HA5 5JX* T: (020) 8966 9574 E: mjrarnold@hotmail.co.uk

ARNOLD, Mrs Norma. b 48. SNWTP 09. **d** 11 **p** 12. NSM Grassendale *Liv* 11–18; rtd 18. *28 Ambergate Road, Liverpool L19 9AU* T: 0151-427 2320 E: norma.arnold@tesco.net

ARNOLD, Norman. *See* ARNOLD, Victor Norman

ARNOLD, Paul Andrew. b 79. Abth Univ LLB 01 Barrister-at-Law (Gray's Inn). Ridley Hall Cam 15. **d** 18 **p** 19. C Preston-on-Tees and Longnewton *Dur* from 18. *The Vicarage, 65 Bishopton Road, Stockton-on-Tees TS18 4PE* M: 07784-780407 E: curatepaularnold.allsaints@gmail.com

ARNOLD, Canon Roy. b 36. St D Coll Lamp BA 62. **d** 63 **p** 64. C Brislington St Luke *Bris* 63–66; C Ches St Mary 67–70; V Brinnington w Portwood 71–75; V Sale St Paul 75–82; R Dodleston 82–84; V Sheff St Oswald 84–90; Dioc Communications Officer 84–97; Chapl w the Deaf 90–95; Hon Can Sheff Cathl 95–97; rtd 97; PtO *Ches* from 97. *49 Crossfield Road, Bollington, Macclesfield SK10 5EA* T: (01625) 575472

ARNOLD, Victor Norman. b 45. Oak Hill Th Coll 91. **d** 94 **p** 95. NSM Chigwell and Chigwell Row *Chelmsf* 94–98; C W Ham 98–04; C Hornchurch St Andr 04–10; rtd 10; PtO *Chelmsf* from 10. *Spring Cottage, 6 Spring Grove, Loughton IG10 4QA* T: (020) 8508 6572 E: standrews@me.com

ARNOLD-DAVIES, Mrs Elizabeth. Bp Grosseteste Coll TCert 58. St Mich Coll Llan 14. **d** 16. NSM Lampeter w Maestir and Silian and Llangybi and Betws Bledrws *St D* from 16. *3 Queen Street, Aberaeron SA46 0BY* M: 07885-542524

ARNOTT, Preb David. b 44. Em Coll Cam BA 66. Qu Coll Birm 68. **d** 69 **p** 70. C Charlton St Luke w St Paul *S'wark* 69–73; C S Beddington St Mich 73–78; Chapl Liv Poly 78–82; V Bridgwater St Fran *B & W* 86–02; Preb Wells Cathl 00–02; V Yealmpton and Brixton *Ex* 02–09; P-in-c 09–11; RD Ivybridge 03–11; rtd 09. *14 Woodlands Avenue, Exmouth EX8 4QP* E: revdavid.arnott@btinternet.com

ARNOTT, Janine Beverley. b 69. Man Univ BSocSc 02 MRes 03 PhD 07 St Mellitus Coll MA 17 Cam Univ BTh 19. Ridley Hall Cam 17. **d** 19. C Stockport St Geo *Ches* from 19. *40 Beechfield Road, Stockport SK3 8SF* E: jba30@cam.ac.uk

ARRAND, The Ven Geoffrey William. b 44. K Coll Lon BD 66 AKC 66. **d** 67 **p** 68. C Washington *Dur* 67–70; C S Ormsby w Ketsby, Calceby and Driby *Linc* 70–73; TV Gt Grimsby St Mary and St Jas 73–79; TR Halesworth w Linstead and Chediston *St E* 79–80; TR Halesworth w Linstead, Chediston, Holton etc 80–85; R Hadleigh w Layham and Shelley 85–94; Dean Bocking 85–94; RD Hadleigh 86–94; Adn Suffolk 94–09; Hon Can St E Cathl 91–09; rtd 09; PtO *St E* from 09; *Eur* from 10; *Linc* from 17. *86 Broadway, Lincoln LN2 1SR* T: (01522) 826967 E: garrand@virginmedia.com

ARTHUR, Graeme Richard. b 52. Univ of NSW BCom 78 Heythrop Coll Lon MA 09. Linc Th Coll 93. **d** 93 **p** 94. C Witney *Ox* 93–97; R Westcote Barton w Steeple Barton, Duns Tew etc 97–18; rtd 18; PtO *Ox* from 19. *4 Margaret Road, Twyford, Banbury OX17 3JE* T: (01295) 812806 E: graemearthur0@gmail.com

ARTHUR, Canon Ian Willoughby. b 40. Lon Univ BA 63 BA 66 PGCE 64 Lambeth STh 94 Kent Univ MA 98. Ripon Coll Cuddesdon 78. **d** 80 **p** 81. C Kempston Transfiguration *St Alb* 80–83; R Potton w Sutton and Cockayne Hatley 83–96; P-in-c Sharnbrook and Knotting w Souldrop 96–98;

R 98–04; RD Sharnbrook 97–04; Hon Can St Alb 99–04; rtd 04; PtO *St Alb* from 04; *Ox* from 05; *Cov* from 09. *35 London Road, Chipping Norton OX7 5AX* T: (01608) 646839 E: iwarthur@btinternet.com

ARTHUR, Canon Kenneth Paul. b 64. Univ of Wales (Cardiff) BScEcon 86 Roehampton Inst PGCE 87 Cardiff Univ LLM 08. St Steph Ho Ox BTh 05. **d** 00 **p** 01. C Bodmin w Lanhydrock and Lanivet *Truro* 00–02; P-in-c Treverbyn and Boscoppa 02–06; P-in-c St Dennis from 06; RD St Austell 05–10; P-in-c Roche from 17; P-in-c Treverbyn from 17; Warden of Readers 05–10; Deputy Warden of Readers from 10; Dir Minl Formation and Development 06–16; Hon Can Truro Cathl from 13. *The Rectory, 16 Trelavour Road, St Dennis, St Austell PL26 8AH* T: (01726) 822317 E: clayparishes@gmail.com

ARTHY, Canon Nicola Mary. b 64. St Jo Coll Ox BA 85 MA 93. SEITE. **d** 00 **p** 01. C Guildf H Trin w St Mary 00–01; C Farncombe 01–04; P-in-c Toddington, Stanton, Didbrook w Hailes etc *Glouc* 04–05; TV Winchcombe 05–09; AD Tewkesbury and Winchcombe 07–09; P-in-c Glouc St Mary de Lode and St Mary de Crypt etc 09–10; P-in-c Hempsted 09–10; R Glouc City and Hempsted from 10; Can Res Glouc Cathl from 09. *The Rectory, Rectory Lane, Hempsted, Gloucester GL2 5LW* T: (01452) 523808 M: 07944-721835 E: nikkiarthy@btinternet.com

ARTISS, Rebecca Jane. b 72. **d** 18 **p** 19. NSM Four Rivers *St E* from 18. *Address temp unknown* M: 07484-630280

ARTLEY, Miss Pamela Jean. b 47. Worc Coll of Educn CertEd 68 Hull Univ MEd 91 ALCM 73. NEOC 99. **d** 02 **p** 03. NSM Bridlington Priory *York* 02–05; P-in-c Nafferton w Wansford 05–14; rtd 14; PtO *York* from 14. *11 Bempton Drive, Bridlington YO16 7HG* E: revjeanartley@gmail.com

ARTUS, Stephen James. b 60. Man Poly BA 82 W Midl Coll of Educn PGCE 84. St Jo Coll Nottm MA 95. **d** 95 **p** 96. C Altrincham St Geo *Ches* 95–99; P-in-c Norton 99–05; V 05–07; C Wybunbury and Audlem w Doddington 10–12; PtO from 12. *Address withheld by request*

ARUNDEL, Canon Michael. b 36. Qu Coll Ox BA 60 MA 64. Linc Th Coll 60. **d** 62 **p** 63. C Hollinwood *Man* 62–65; C Leesfield 65–69; R Newton Heath All SS 69–80; RD N Man 75–80; P-in-c Eccles St Mary 80–81; TR Eccles 81–91; R Man St Ann 91–01; Hon Can Man Cathl 82–01; rtd 01; PtO *Man* from 01. *20 Kiln Brow, Bromley Cross, Bolton BL7 9NR* T: (01204) 591156 E: m.arundel555@btinternet.com

ARVIDSSON, Canon Carl Fredrik. b 66. Regents Th Coll 88 Chich Th Coll 92. **d** 92 **p** 93. C Southsea H Spirit *Portsm* 92–94; C Botley, Curdridge and Durley 94–96; P-in-c Ringwould w Kingsdown *Cant* 96–97; R 97–01; Sen Chapl K Sch Cant 01–17; Hon Min Can Cant Cathl from 01; Hon C Deal St Andr 13–15; Hon Can Antsiranana from 13; rtd 17; PtO *Cant* from 19. *Monks Hall, 177 Mongeham Road, Great Mongeham, Deal CT14 9LL* T: (01304) 694894 E: carlfredrikarvidsson@gmail.com

ASBRIDGE, Preb John Hawell. b 26. Dur Univ BA 47. Bps' Coll Cheshunt 47. **d** 49 **p** 50. C Barrow St Geo *Carl* 49–52; C Fort William *Arg* 52–54; C Lon Docks St Pet w Wapping St Jo 54–55; C Kilburn St Aug 55–59; V Northolt Park St Barn 59–66; V Shepherd's Bush St Steph w St Thos 66–96; Preb St Paul's Cathl 89–96; rtd 96; PtO *B & W* from 05. *Crystal Glen, The Old Mineral Line, Roadwater, Watchet TA23 0RL* T: (01984) 640211

ASBRIDGE, Nigel Henry. b 58. Bris Univ BA 80. Chich Th Coll 87. **d** 89 **p** 90. C Tottenham St Paul *Lon* 89; C W Hampstead St Jas 89–94; P-in-c Hornsey H Innocents 94–04; P-in-c Stroud Green H Trin 02–04; Nat Chapl-Missr Children's Soc 04–09; NSM Edmonton St Alphege and Ponders End St Matt *Lon* 06–10; P-in-c Edmonton St Mary w St Jo 10–13; V From St Cambridge Road St Jo and St Jas 13–17. *St John's Vicarage, Dysons Road, London N18 2DS* T: (020) 8807 2767 M: 07905-499323 E: nigelasbridge@hotmail.com

ASCOUGH, Mrs Susan Glynis. b 48. STETS 06. **d** 09 **p** 10. NSM Bishop's Cannings, All Cannings etc *Sarum* 09–12; NSM Cannings and Redhorn 12–18; Chapl HM Pris Erlestoke from 09; PtO *Sarum* from 18. *Ashlington, Coate, Devizes SN10 3LA* T: (01380) 860059 E: davide.frenchman@btopenworld.com

ASH, Arthur Edwin. b 44. St Jo Coll Nottm 85. **d** 87 **p** 88. C Attleborough *Cov* 87–91; V Garretts Green *Birm* 91–02; rtd 02; PtO *Birm* 02–12; *Cov* from 04. *1 Margetts Close, Kenilworth CV8 1EN* T: (01926) 853547 E: arthureash@yahoo.co.uk

ASH, Brian John. b 32. ALCD 62. **d** 62 **p** 63. C Plymouth St Andr *Ex* 62–66; Area Sec CMS Cant and Roch 66–73; V Bromley Common St Aug *Roch* 73–97; rtd 97; PtO *Chelmsf* 97–00. *The Vines, 95 Green Lane, Leigh-on-Sea SS9 5QU* T: (01702) 523644 E: brianash2@gmail.com

ASH, Christopher Brian Garton. b 53. Trin Hall Cam MA 76. Wycliffe Hall Ox BA 92. **d** 93 **p** 94. C Cambridge H Sepulchre *Ely* 93–97; P-in-c Lt Shelford 97–02; R 02–04; Dir Cornhill Tr Course 04–15; PtO *Lon* from 15; *Ely* from 17. *23 Fulbrooke Road, Cambridge CB3 9EE* T: (01223) 301165

ASH, David Nicholas. b 61. Southlands Coll Lon BA 82. Wycliffe Hall Ox BTh 03. **d** 03 **p** 04. C Walsall *Lich* 03–06; P-in-c Petton w Cockshutt, Welshampton and Lyneal etc 06–12; C Wellington All SS w Eyton 12–15; Local Par Development Adv Shrewsbury Area 10–15; V Prestatyn *St As* 15–17. *Address temp unknown*

ASH, John Christopher Garton. b 84. St Cuth Soc Dur BA 06. Wycliffe Hall Ox BA 13. **d** 13 **p** 14. C Ches Square St Mich w St Phil *Lon* 13–16; Chapl Dean Close Sch from 16. *Bayley House, Dean Close School, Shelburne Road, Cheltenham GL51 6HE* M: 07886-892995 E: john.ash06@gmail.com

ASH, Canon Nicholas John. b 59. Bath Univ BSc 81 Nottm Univ BTh 88. Linc Th Coll 85. **d** 88 **p** 89. C Hersham *Guildf* 88–93; P-in-c Flookburgh *Carl* 93–97; Dioc Officer for Stewardship 94–97; TV Cartmel Peninsula 97–98; Dir of Ords 97–03; P-in-c Dalston 98–00; P-in-c Wreay 98–00; P-in-c Raughton Head w Gatesgill 98–00; V Dalston w Cumdivock, Raughton Head and Wreay 01–03; Can Res Portsm Cathl 03–09; TR Cartmel Peninsula *Carl* 09–16. *28 Westmorland Rise, Appleby-in-Westmorland CA16 6SJ* E: nickash405@hotmail.com

ASH, Nicholas Martin. b 62. Ch Ch Coll Cant BEd 86. SEITE 06. **d** 09 **p** 10. NSM Faversham *Cant* 09–13; Chapl Medway Secure Tr Cen from 13. *Medway Secure Training Centre, Sir Evelyn Road, Rochester ME1 3YB* T: (01634) 823472 M: 07896-006282 E: nicholas.ash@justice.gov.uk

ASHBRIDGE, Clare Patricia Esther. *See* KAKURU, Clare Patricia Esther

ASHBURNER, David Barrington. b 26. Ch Coll Cam BA 51 MA 55. Wycliffe Hall Ox 51. **d** 53 **p** 54. C Coalville *Leic* 53–56; C Leic H Apostles 56–58; V Bucklebury w Marlston *Ox* 58–70; V Belton *Leic* 70–75; P-in-c Osgathorpe 73–75; R Belton and Osgathorpe 75–79; V Frisby-on-the-Wreake w Kirby Bellars 79–82; V Uffington w Woolstone and Baulking *Ox* 82–91; P-in-c Shellingford 83–91; RD Vale of White Horse 87–91; rtd 91; PtO *Glouc* 91–17; *Ox* 91–13. *7 Stonefern Court, Stow Road, Moreton-in-Marsh GL56 0DW* T: (01608) 650347

✠**ASHBY, The Rt Revd Godfrey William Ernest Candler.** b 30. Lon Univ AKC 54 BD 54 PhD 69. **d** 55 **p** 56 **c** 80. C St Helier *S'wark* 55–57; P-in-c St Mark's Miss Cape Town S Africa 58–60; Sub-Warden St Paul's Th Coll Grahamstown 60–66; R Alice 66–68; Sen Lect Rhodes Univ 68–75; Can Grahamstown Cathl 69–75; Dean and Adm Grahamstown 75–80; Bp St John's 80–85; Prof Div Witwatersrand Univ S Africa 85–88; Asst Bp Johannesburg 85–88; Asst Bp Leic 88–95; P-in-c Newtown Linford 92–95; Hon Can Leic Cathl 93–95; rtd 95; Asst Bp George S Africa 95–08; Hon Asst Bp Portsm 08–11; Hon Asst Bp Ex from 11. *The College of St Barnabas, Blackberry Lane, Lingfield RH7 6NJ* M: 07968-396195 E: godfreyashby@gmail.com

ASHBY, Canon Judith Anne Stuart. b 53. Man Univ BSc 74 MSc 76 Ox Brookes Univ PGCE 99. STETS 96. **d** 99 **p** 00. NSM Swindon Ch Ch *Bris* 99–05; P-in-c Cricklade w Latton 05–12; C Ashton Keynes, Leigh and Minety 07–12; rtd 12; Dean of Women's Min *Bris* 13–15; NSM Swindon Ch Ch 15–17; Adv for Women's Min and Asst Adv for Minl Support from 15; Hon Can Bris Cathl from 14. *57 Greywethers Avenue, Swindon SN3 1QG* T: (01793) 978528 E: judith.ashby@tiscali.co.uk

ASHBY, Mrs Linda. b 48. Dartford Coll of Educn CertEd 70. **d** 03 **p** 04. OLM The Ch in the Woottons *Nor* from 03. *4 Melford Close, South Wootton, King's Lynn PE30 3XH* T: (01553) 672893 E: linda_ashby@tiscali.co.uk

ASHBY, Peter George. b 49. Univ of Wales (Cardiff) BSc(Econ) 70. Linc Th Coll 70. **d** 73 **p** 74. C Bengeo St Alb 73–75; Chapl Hatf Poly 76–79; C Apsley End 80; TV Chambersbury 80–82; Adn N Harare Zimbabwe 82–87; V Eskdale, Irton, Muncaster and Waberthwaite *Carl* 87–93; TR Sedgley All SS *Worc* 93–99; TV Tettenhall Regis *Lich* 99–04; V W Bromwich St Jas w St Paul 04–06; R Bradeley, Church Eaton, Derrington and Haughton 06–11; rtd 11; PtO *B & W* from 12. *24 Bryant Gardens, Clevedon BS21 5HE* T: (01275) 542677 M: 07756-897547 E: peterg.ashby@gmail.com

ASHBY, Philip Charles. b 52. Birm Univ BSc 73 Lon Univ MSc 74 PhD 93. WEMTC 05. **d** 08 **p** 09. NSM Stratton St Margaret w S Marston etc *Bris* 08–11; NSM Garsdon, Lea and Cleverton and Charlton 11–12; NSM N Swindon St Andr from 14; NSM W Swindon and Lydiard Tregoze from 18. *57 Greywethers Avenue, Swindon SN3 1QG* T: (01793) 978528 E: phil.ashby@tiscali.co.uk

✠**ASHCROFT, The Rt Revd Mark David.** b 54. Worc Coll Ox BA 77 MA 82 Fitzw Coll Cam BA 81. Ridley Hall Cam 79.

d 82 **p** 83 **c** 16. C Burnage St Marg *Man* 82–85; Tutor St Paul's Sch of Div Kapsabet Kenya 86–89; Prin St Paul's Th Coll Kapsabet 90–96; R Harpurhey *Man* 96–09; R Harpurhey St Steph 96–06; AD N Man 00–06; Adn Man 09–16; Hon Can Man Cathl 04–09; Suff Bp Bolton from 16; Warden of Readers from 18. *Bishop's Lodge, Walkden Road, Worsley, Manchester M28 2WH* T: 0161-790 8289 M: 07810-272020

ASHDOWN, Andrew William Harvey. b 64. K Coll Lon BD 88 AKC 88 Heythrop Coll Lon MA 15. Sarum & Wells Th Coll 88. **d** 90 **p** 91. C Cranleigh *Guildf* 90–94; V Ryhill *Wakef* 94–98; P-in-c Denmead *Portsm* 98–99; V 99–05; S Asia Regional Officer USPG 05–06; Hon C Tadley S and Silchester *Win* 05–06; P-in-c Knight's Enham and Smannell w Enham Alamein 06–09; TR 09–14; V Knight's Enham 14–15; PtO from 15. *The Vicarage, 33 Crescent Road, North Baddesley, Southampton SO52 9HU* T: (023) 8178 8031 E: andrewashdown@talktalk.net

ASHDOWN, Barry Frederick. b 42. St Pet Coll Ox BA 65 MA 69. Ridley Hall Cam 66. **d** 68 **p** 69. C Shipley St Pet *Bradf* 68–71; C Rushden w Newton Bromswold *Pet* 71–74; R Haworth *Bradf* 74–82; V Ore Ch Ch *Chich* 82–87; C Southwick St Mich 91–93; PtO *Ox* from 17. *9 Bucknell Avenue, Pangbourne, Reading RG8 7JU* T: 0118-984 5129 M: 07888-996763 E: bazzaashdown@hotmail.co.uk

ASHDOWN, Ms Lucyann. b 64. LSE BSc 95 RGN 86 RM 88. NTMTC BA 08. **d** 08 **p** 09. C Stoke Newington St Mary and Brownswood Park *Lon* 08–11; P-in-c Blaenau Irfon *S & B* 11–14; P-in-c Irfon Valley 11–14; Chapl Farleigh Hospice 14–19; Chapl Weldmar Hospice from 19; PtO *St E* from 15. *Weldmar Hospice Care Trust, Hammick House, Bridport Road, Poundbury, Dorchester DT1 3SD* T: (01305) 269898 E: lucyann.ashdown@gmail.com

ASHDOWN, Philip David. b 57. Imp Coll Lon BSc 79 NW Univ Chicago MS 80 Cranfield Inst of Tech PhD 85 ARCS 79. Ripon Coll Cuddesdon 91. **d** 93 **p** 94. C Houghton le Spring *Dur* 93–96; C Stockton and Chapl Stockton Campus Dur Univ 96–02; V Stockton St Pet *Dur* 02–15; P-in-c Elton 09–15; PtO *St D* from 16. *7 Denham Avenue, Llanelli SA15 4DB* T: (01554) 750628 E: pdashdown@aol.com

ASHE, The Ven Francis John. b 53. Sheff Univ BMet 74. Ridley Hall Cam 77. **d** 79 **p** 80. C Ashtead *Guildf* 79–82; S Africa 82–87; R Wisley w Pyrford *Guildf* 87–93; V Godalming 93–01; TR 01–09; RD 96–02; Hon Can Guildf Cathl 03–09; Adn Lynn *Nor* 09–18; Warden of Readers 09–15; rtd 18; PtO *Nor* from 18. *Kirkleigh Farmhouse, Virginstowe, Beaworthy EX21 5DZ*

ASHFORD, Archdeacon of. *See* MILLER, The Ven Darren Noel

ASHFORTH, David Edward. b 37. Lon Univ BSc ARCS 59. Qu Coll Birm. **d** 61 **p** 62. C Scarborough St Columba *York* 61–65; C Northallerton w Kirby Sigston 65–67; V Keyingham 67–73; Chapl Imp Coll *Lon* 73–89; V Balderstone *Blackb* 89–01; Dir Post-Ord Tr 89–01; rtd 01; PtO *Ripon* 02–14; *Leeds* from 14. *Sunnyholme Cottage, Preston under Scar, Leyburn DL8 4AH* T: (01969) 622438 E: d.ashforth@btinternet.com

ASHLEY, Clive Ashley. b 54. Croydon Coll of Art and Design LSIAD 75 Lon Hosp SRN 80 E Ham Coll of Tech TCert 82. Aston Tr Scheme 81 Cranmer Hall Dur 84. **d** 86 **p** 87. C Withington St Paul *Man* 86–89; Asst Chapl Freeman Hosp Newc 89–92; Chapl St Rich and Graylingwell Hosps Chich 92–98; Chapl Sussex Weald and Downs NHS Trust 95–98; Chapl and Bereavement Cllr R W Sussex Trust 98–01; R New Fishbourne *Chich* 01–10; P-in-c Appledram 01–10; P-in-c Lt Baddow *Chelmsf* 10–17; P-in-c Sandon 10–13; P-in-c Danbury 13–17; rtd 17. *3 Glencoyne Drive, Southport PR9 9TS* M: 07939-590628 E: cliveashley@btinternet.com

ASHLEY, Jane Isobel. *See* HULME, Jane Isobel

ASHLEY, Miss Victoria Lesley. St Mich Coll Llan. **d** 08 **p** 09. C Tredegar *Mon* 08–12; P-in-c Pontnewydd 12–16; P-in-c Cwmbran 16–17; TV Cowbridge *Llan* from 17. *The Vicarage, 2 Court Close, Aberthin, Cowbridge CF71 7EH* E: revvla@btinternet.com *or* vicar@cowbridgeparish.com

ASHLEY-ROBERTS, James. b 53. Lon Univ BD 77. Oak Hill Th Coll 75 Wycliffe Hall Ox 79. **d** 80 **p** 81. C Gt Warley Ch Ch *Chelmsf* 80–83; C E Ham St Paul 83–85; TV Holyhead w Rhoscolyn w Llanfair-yn-Neubwll *Ban* 85–88; TR 88–91; V Penrhyndeudraeth w Llanfrothen w Beddgelert 91–97; R Ffestiniog w Blaenau Ffestiniog 97–01; PtO 01–12; P-in-c Llangefni w Tregaean w Llanddyfnan 12–13. *26 Garrabost, Isle of Lewis HS2 0PW* M: 07881-770437 E: revjamesashleyroberts@sky.com

ASHMAN, Paul Andrew. b 70. Wycliffe Hall Ox 05. **d** 07 **p** 08. C Portswood Ch Ch *Win* 07–11; C Auckland St Paul New Zealand 11–14; V Panmure from 14. *5 Thompson Road, Panmure, Auckland 1072, New Zealand* M: (0064) 21-550104 E: ashmanpaul@gmail.com *or* vicar@stmatthias.org.nz

ASHMAN, Peter Michael. b 61. Ex Univ LLB 83 LLM 84 BTh(Min) 12 Called to the Bar (Inner Temple) 85. SWMTC 07. **d** 10 **p** 11. C Ex St Jas 10–13; P-in-c Ipplepen, Torbryan and Denbury 13–14; R Ipplepen w Torbryan, Denbury and Broadhempston w Woodland 14–17; R Weston super Mare St Jo *B & W* from 17. *St John's Rectory, 9D Cecil Road, Weston-super-Mare BS23 2NF* E: revpeterashman@gmail.com

ASHMAN, Mrs Vanessa Mary. b 53. Cant Ch Ch Univ BA 07. **d** 03 **p** 04. NSM Lyminge w Paddlesworth, Stanford w Postling etc *Cant* 03–13; C Bewsborough 13–16; rtd 17. *3 Ocean Heights, Hospital Hill, Hythe CT21 5FB* E: vanessa.ashman@btinternet.com

ASHTON, Anthony Joseph. b 37. Oak Hill Th Coll 62. **d** 65 **p** 66. C Crookes St Thos *Sheff* 65–68; C Heeley 68–73; V Bowling St Steph *Bradf* 73–78; R Chesterfield H Trin *Derby* 78–92; rtd 93; PtO *Derby* 93–00. *19 High Park, Stafford ST16 1BL* T: (01785) 223943

⳨**ASHTON, The Rt Revd Cyril Guy.** b 42. Lanc Univ MA 86. Oak Hill Th Coll 64. **d** 67 **p** 68 **c** 00. C Blackpool St Thos *Blackb* 67–70; Voc Sec CPAS 70–74; Chapl Lee Abbey Dev 74–75; V Lancaster St Thomas *Blackb* 74–91; Lanc Almshouses 76–90; Dioc Dir of Tr *Blackb* 91–00; Hon Can Blackb Cathl 91–00; Suff Bp Doncaster *Sheff* 00–11; rtd 11; Hon Asst Bp Blackb and Liv from 11. *Charis, 17C Quernmore Road, Lancaster LA1 3EB* T: (01524) 848684 M: 07968-371596 E: bpcg.ashton@btinternet.com

ASHTON, David. b 52. Sarum Th Coll 93. **d** 96 **p** 97. NSM St Leonards Ch Ch and St Mary *Chich* 96–98; NSM Upper St Leonards St Jo 98–99; C Uckfield 99–02; V Langney 02–14; rtd 14; PtO *Chich* from 14. *3 Streatfield Road, Uckfield TN22 2BG* T: (01825) 768643 E: frdavidashton@aol.com

ASHTON, Eleanor Jane. *See* RANCE, Eleanor Jane

ASHTON, Grant. *See* ASHTON, William Grant

ASHTON, Hubert Samuel. b 86. Trin Coll Ox BA 08. Oak Hill Th Coll 12. **d** 15 **p** 16. C Chelsea St Jo w St Andr *Lon* 15–18. *The Old Farmhouse, Appledore Road, Tenterden TN30 7DF* M: 07789-870962 E: sam.ashton86@gmail.com

ASHTON, Janet Heather Hephzibah. b 52. Westcott Ho Cam. **d** 07 **p** 08. C Wenlock *Heref* 07–11; TV Kidderminster St Mary and All SS w Trimpley etc *Worc* 11–15; TV Kidderminster Ismere 15–16; rtd 16; PtO *Worc* 16; V Hightown *Liv* from 16. *St Stephen's Vicarage, St Stephen's Road, Hightown, Liverpool L38 0BL* T: 0151-929 3971 M: 07737-916499 E: janhhashton@gmail.com

ASHTON, Miss Joan Elizabeth. b 54. Sheff Hallam Univ BA 10 Eaton Hall Coll of Educn CertEd 76. Cranmer Hall Dur 91. **d** 93 **p** 94. Par Dn Darnall-cum-Attercliffe *Sheff* 93–94; C Hillsborough and Wadsley Bridge 94–96; P-in-c Stainforth 96–98; P-in-c Arksey 98–03; Asst Chapl Doncaster R Infirmary and Montagu Hosp NHS Trust 98–01; Asst Chapl Doncaster and Bassetlaw Hosps NHS Foundn Trust 01–04; Co-ord Chapl Services Rotherham Gen Hosps NHS Trust 04–17; rtd 17. *2 St Albans Court, Wickersley, Rotherham S66 1FG* T: (01709) 544026

ASHTON, Lesley June. b 49. York Univ BA 89. NEOC 00. **d** 04 **p** 05. C Roundhay St Edm *Ripon* 04–08; P-in-c Hawksworth Wood 08–11; TV Abbeylands 11–13; rtd 13; Hon C Fountains Gp *Ripon* 13–14; *Leeds* 14–16; Asst Dir of Ords 10–16; PtO from 17; *York* from 17. *53 The Green, Romanby, Northallerton DL7 8NL* M: 07910-002014 E: lesley493ashton@btinternet.com

ASHTON, Mrs Margaret Lucie. b 40. St Jo Coll Nottm 79. **dss** 83 **d** 87 **p** 94. Billericay and Lt Burstead *Chelmsf* 83–99; NSM 87–99; rtd 99; Hon C Fordingbridge and Breamore and Hale etc *Win* 01–05; PtO from 05. *3 Stephen Martin Gardens, Fordingbridge SP6 1RF* T: (01425) 656205

ASHTON, Mrs Mary Isabel. b 57. Robert Gordon Inst of Tech Aber BSc 78 Open Univ PGCE 96. St Steph Ho Ox 07. **d** 09 **p** 10. C Whitewater *Win* 09–14; V Guildf All SS 13–14; PtO *Blackb* 14–15; C Euxton 15–19; rtd 19; PtO *Blackb* from 19. *Address temp unknown* E: mary.ashton@me.com

ASHTON, Neville Anthony. b 45. Sarum & Wells Th Coll 78. **d** 80 **p** 81. C Hattersley *Ches* 80–82; C Lancaster Ch Ch w St Jo and St Anne *Blackb* 82–84; R Church Kirk 84–15; rtd 15; PtO *Blackb* 16–17. *5 Millbrook Close, Oswaldtwistle, Accrington BB5 3QG* T: (01254) 236946

ASHTON, Nicholas Graham. b 87. Loughb Univ BA 09. Oak Hill Th Coll BA 19. **d** 19. C Mayfair Ch Ch *Lon* from 19. *54 Hamilton Road, London NW10 1NE* M: 07745-622009 E: littleash51@hotmail.com

ASHTON, Canon Peter Donald. b 34. Lon Univ BD 62. ALCD 61. **d** 62 **p** 63. C Walthamstow St Mary *Chelmsf* 62–68; V Girlington *Bradf* 68–73; Dir Past Studies St Jo Coll Nottm 73–80; TR Billericay and Lt Burstead *Chelmsf* 80–99; Chapl Mayflower Hosp Billericay 80–99; Chapl St Andr Hosp Billericay 80–92; Chapl Thameside Community Healthcare NHS Trust 93–99; RD Basildon *Chelmsf* 89–99; Hon Can

Chelmsf Cathl 92–99; rtd 99; Hon C Fordingbridge and Breamore and Hale etc *Win* 01–10; PtO 10–14 and from 17. *3 Stephen Martin Gardens, Fordingbridge SP6 1RF* T: (01425) 656205 E: peterdashton@onetel.com

ASHTON, Samuel. *See* ASHTON, Hubert Samuel

ASHTON, Preb Samuel Rupert. b 42. Sarum & Wells Th Coll. **d** 83 **p** 84. C Ledbury w Eastnor *Heref* 83–86; R St Weonards w Orcop, Garway, Tretire etc 86–98; RD Ross and Archenfield 91–95 and 96–98; P-in-c Cradley w Mathon and Storridge 98–99; R 99–07; Preb Heref Cathl 97–07; rtd 07; PtO *Heref* from 08. *The Old Greyhound, Longtown, Hereford HR2 0LD* T: (01873) 860492

ASHTON (née JONES), Mrs Susan Catherine. b 48. Qu Coll Birm 09. **d** 11 **p** 12. NSM Knowle *Birm* 11–18; PtO from 18. *1467 Warwick Road, Knowle, Solihull B93 9LU* T: (01564) 776895 E: sue.ashton@yahoo.co.uk

ASHTON, Canon William Grant. b 57. St Chad's Coll Dur BA 79. Oak Hill Th Coll BA 85. **d** 85 **p** 86. C Lancaster St Thos *Blackb* 85–89; CF 89–14; Chapl R Memorial Chpl Sandhurst 06–07; QHC 11–14; V Euxton *Blackb* 14–19; Hon Can Blackb Cathl 18–19; rtd 19; PtO *Blackb* from 19. *Address temp unknown* E: wgashton@mac.com

ASHURST, Mrs Judith Anne. b 57. St Aid Coll Dur BA 80 St Jo Coll Dur BA 08 Homerton Coll Cam PGCE 01 ACIB 83. Cranmer Hall Dur 06. **d** 08 **p** 09. C Belmont and Pittington *Dur* 08–11; C Chester le Street 11–16; P-in-c Upper Derwent *Carl* from 17. *Oak Side, Braithwaite, Keswick CA12 5SY* T: (017687) 78092 E: revjudi@icloud.com

ASHWELL, Anthony John. b 42. St Andr Univ BSc 65. Sarum & Wells Th Coll 86. **d** 88 **p** 89. C Plymstock *Ex* 88–91; C Axminster, Chardstock, Combe Pyne and Rousdon 91–92; TV 92–95; C Crediton and Shobrooke 95–97; TV Bride Valley *Sarum* 97–07; P-in-c Symondsbury 05–07; RD Lyme Bay 03–06; rtd 07; PtO *Sarum* 07–11; *Sheff* from 16. *51 Kenbourne Road, Sheffield S7 1NJ* T: 0114-255 0568 E: anthony@vencot.plus.com

ASHWIN, Canon Vincent George. b 42. Worc Coll Ox BA 65. Coll of Resurr Mirfield 65. **d** 67 **p** 68. C Shildon *Dur* 67–70; C Newc St Fran 70–72; R Mhlosheni Swaziland 72–75; R Manzini 75–79; V Shildon *Dur* 79–85; V Fenham St Jas and St Basil *Newc* 85–97; RD Newc W 89–97; V Haydon Bridge and Beltingham w Henshaw 97–04; RD Hexham 97–02; Hon Can Newc Cathl 00–04; rtd 04; PtO *S'well* from 04; *Leic* from 18. *83 Westgate, Southwell NG25 0LS* T: (01636) 813975 E: vincentashwin@tiscali.co.uk

ASHWIN-SIEJKOWSKI, Piotr Jan. b 64. Warsaw Univ PhD 97. Coll of Resurr Mirfield 98. **d** 91 **p** 92. Poland 92–98; C Tile Hill *Cov* 99–01; Chapl and Lect Univ Coll Chich 01–04; TV Richmond St Mary w St Matthias and St Jo *S'wark* 04–13; C Twickenham St Mary *Lon* from 13. *21 Campbell Road, Twickenham TW2 5BY* T: (020) 8894 5102 E: piotrashwin@btinternet.com

ASHWORTH, Canon David. b 40. Nottm Univ BPharm 62. Linc Th Coll 63. **d** 65 **p** 66. C Halliwell St Thos *Man* 65–69; C Heywood St Jas 69–72; C-in-c Heywood St Marg CD 72–78; V Hale *Ches* 78–87; V Hale and Ashley 87–96; V Prestbury 96–05; RD Bowdon 87–95; RD Macclesfield 98–03; Hon Can Ches Cathl 94–05; rtd 05; PtO *Ches* from 05. *12 Lime Close, Sandbach CW11 1BZ* T: (01270) 529187 E: david@davidashworth39.plus.com

ASHWORTH, Canon James Nigel. b 55. York Univ BA 77. Cranmer Hall Dur 93. **d** 93 **p** 94. C Rothwell *Ripon* 93–96; Chapl Campsfield Ho Oxon 96–99; Hon C Akeman *Ox* 96–99; V Kemsing w Woodlands *Roch* 99–08; R Man St Ann from 08; Hon Can Man Cathl from 17. *St Anne's Rectory, 44 George Leigh Street, Manchester M4 5DG* T: 0161-235 5206 or 834 0239 E: rector@stannsmanchester.com

ASHWORTH, John Russell. b 33. Lich Th Coll 57. **d** 60 **p** 61. C Castleford All SS *Wakef* 60–62; C Luton St Sav *St Alb* 63–67; V Clipstone *S'well* 67–70; V Bolton-upon-Dearne *Sheff* 70–82; V Thornhill Lees *Wakef* 82–98; rtd 98; PtO *Wakef* 99–14; *Leeds* from 14. *Walsingham, 2 Vicarage Road, Savile Town, Dewsbury WF12 9PD* T: (01924) 461269

ASHWORTH, Keith Benjamin. b 33. NW Ord Course 76. **d** 79 **p** 80. C Pennington *Man* 79–83; P-in-c Bolton St Bede 83–88; V 88–95; V Hillock 95–01; rtd 01; PtO *Man* 01–06; *Blackb* from 06. *3 Sandpiper Place, Thornton-Cleveleys FY5 3FE* T: (01253) 855793 E: keith_asitworth@sky.com

ASHWORTH, Mark Stephen. b 71. Birm Univ BSocSc 91 Goldsmiths' Coll Lon PGCE 96. Oak Hill Th Coll BA 14. **d** 14 **p** 15. C Crowborough *Chich* from 14; P-in-c High Hurstwood from 17. *1 Mardens, Myrtle Road, Crowborough TN6 1EY* M: 07708-491289 E: mashworth71@gmail.com *or* mark@allsaintscrowborough.org

ASHWORTH, Canon Martin. b 41. AKC 63. **d** 64 **p** 65. C Wythenshawe Wm Temple Ch CD *Man* 64–71; R Haughton

St Anne 71–83; V Prestwich St Marg 83–06; rtd 06; Can Res Bermuda 07–09; PtO *Man* 06–08 and from 15; *Leeds* from 17. *17 Plane Tree Nest Lane, Halifax HX2 7PL*

ASHWORTH, Nigel. *See* ASHWORTH, James Nigel

ASHWORTH, Timothy. b 52. Worc Coll of Educn CertEd 74. Oak Hill Th Coll BA 81. **d** 82 **p** 83. C Tonbridge St Steph *Roch* 82–85; C-in-c Whittle-le-Woods *Blackb* 85–90; Chapl Scargill Ho 90–96; V Ingleton w Chapel le Dale *Bradf* 96–03; TV Yate New Town *Bris* 03–08; NSM Lostock St Thos and St Jo and Bolton St Bede *Man* 09–13; Chapl HM Pris Forest Bank 12–15. *27 Water Lane, West Malling ME19 6HH* T: (01732) 870279 E: timashworth52@tiscali.co.uk *or* timashworth52@gmail.com

ASHWORTH, Mrs Vivien. b 52. Worc Coll of Educn CertEd 73. Trin Coll Bris 79 Oak Hill Th Coll BA 82. **dss** 82 **d** 87 **p** 94. Tonbridge St Steph *Roch* 82–85; Whittle-le-Woods *Blackb* 85–90; Hon Par Dn 87–90; Chapl Scargill Ho 90–96; Hon C Ingleton w Chapel le Dale *Bradf* 96–03; Dioc Youth Adv 96–01; Hon C Yate New Town *Bris* 03–07; TV 07–08; Sub Chapl HM Pris Ashfield 04–09; P-in-c Lostock St Thos and St Jo *Man* 09–15; P-in-c Bolton St Bede 09–15; Guardian Pilsdon at Malling Community from 15. *27 Water Lane, West Malling ME19 6HH* T: (01732) 870279

ASINUGO, Mrs Christiana Chidinma. b 56. NTMTC. **d** 09 **p** 10. C Becontree St Mary *Chelmsf* 09–13; C W Ham St Matt 13–15; P-in-c 15–19; V from 19; C Stratford St Jo w Ch Ch from 15. *St Matthew's Vicarage, 13 Dyson Road, London E15 4JX* T: (020) 8221 0902 E: ccasinugo@yahoo.co.uk

ASIR, Jebamani Sekar Anand. *See* ANAND, Sekar Anand Asir

ASKEW, Miss Alison Jane. b 57. Dur Univ BA 78 PGCE 79 Win Univ MA 12. S Dios Minl Tr Scheme 93. **d** 95 **p** 96. NSM Kingsclere *Win* 95–96; Asst Chapl N Hants Hosps NHS Trust 95–99; Chapl 99–04; Sen Chapl Basingstoke and N Hants NHS Foundn Trust 04–10; P-in-c Kirby-on-the-Moor, Cundall w Norton-le-Clay etc *Ripon* 10–14; *Leeds* 14–15; V from 15. *The Vicarage, 13 The Croft, Kirby Hill, Boroughbridge, York YO51 9YA* T: (01423) 326585

ASKEW, Benjamin Paul. b 79. Sheff Univ BA 01 PGCE 03. St Mellitus Coll BA 13. **d** 13 **p** 14. Pioneer Min *Ripon* 13–14; *Leeds* from 14. *22 Harlow Oval, Harrogate HG2 0DS* T: (01423) 560558 E: askewben@gmail.com *or* ben@kairoschurch.net

ASKEW, Ms Catherine Clasen. b 75. Princeton Th Sem MDiv 01. Cranmer Hall Dur 08. **d** 10 **p** 11. NSM Amble *Newc* 10–12; NSM Bothal and Pegswood w Longhirst 12–15; NSM Chevington 15–17; Asst Dioc Dir of Ords from 17. *1 Lovaine Place, Alnwick NE66 1AQ* E: catherineaskew@gmail.com

ASKEW, Canon Peter Timothy. b 68. Ridley Hall Cam 00. **d** 02 **p** 03. C Bilton *Ripon* 02–06; C Harrogate St Mark and Chapl St Aid Sch Harrogate 06–09; PtO *Newc* 10–11; NSM Felton 11–17; Bp's Chapl from 17; Hon Can Newc Cathl from 18. *1 Lovaine Place, Alnwick NE66 1AQ* M: 07754-046029

ASKEY, John Stuart. b 39. Chich Th Coll 63. **d** 66 **p** 67. C Feltham *Lon* 66–69; C Epsom Common Ch Ch *Guildf* 69–72; C Chesterton Gd Shep *Ely* 72–74; R Stretham w Thetford 74–93; Dioc Spirituality Officer 75–98; Dioc Youth Officer 80–99; P-in-c Brinkley, Burrough Green and Carlton 93–97; P-in-c Westley Waterless 93–97; P-in-c Dullingham 93–97; P-in-c Stetchworth 93–97; R Raddesley Gp 97–99; Chapl Gothenburg w Halmstad, Jönköping etc *Eur* 99–04; rtd 04; PtO *Chich* 11–16. *260 Boulevard, Hull HU3 3ED* T: (01482) 228685 E: johnaskey39@gmail.com

ASKEY, Matthew. b 74. Loughb Coll BA 96 Bretton Hall Coll MA 99 Leeds Univ BA 09 Huddersfield Univ PGCE 06. Coll of Resurr Mirfield 07. **d** 09 **p** 10. C Elland *Wakef* 09–13; Chapl Minster Sch S'well 13–19; Chapl Worksop Coll Notts from 19. *Worksop College, Cuthbert's Avenue, Worksop S80 3AP* T: (01909) 537100 M: 07814-502034 E: frmaskey@btinternet.com

ASKEY, Mrs Susan Mary. b 44. Leeds Univ MA 00. NOC 99. **d** 99 **p** 00. C Golcar *Wakef* 99–02; P-in-c Drighlington 02–12; rtd 12; PtO *Leeds* from 17. *26 Handel Street, Golcar, Huddersfield HD7 4AB* E: susan@smaskey.plus.com

ASKWITH, Angela Catherine. b 58. **d** 18 **p** 19. NSM Frodsham *Ches* from 18. *West Winds, Fingerpost Lane, Norley, Frodsham WA6 8LD* E: a.askwith@sky.com *or* askwith3@me.com

ASKWITH, Mrs Helen Mary. b 57. Thames Valley Univ BSc 00. ERMC 04. **d** 07 **p** 08. NSM Wembley St Jo *Lon* 07–10; NSM Northolt Park St Barn 10–12; V Wembley Park from 12. *St Augustine's Vicarage, 13 Forty Avenue, Wembley HA9 8JL* T: (020) 8908 5995 M: 07711-643220 E: revhelen.askwith@btinternet.com

ASKWITH, Joshua Christian. b 90. Stirling Univ BA 14. Cranmer Hall Dur 14. **d** 17 **p** 18. C Neston *Ches* from 17. *17 Abbots Way, Neston CH64 3SU* M: 07727-187987 E: jcaskwith@gmail.com

ASMELASH, Berhane Tesfamariam. b 56. Addis Ababa Univ MD 89 Lon Bible Coll MPhil 04. SEITE BA 08. **d** 08 **p** 09. C Upper Holloway *Lon* 08–12; NSM Dalston H Trin w St Phil and Haggerston All SS 12–13; C Plumstead Common *S'wark* from 13. *152 Kirkham Street, London SE18 2EN* M: 07838-167198 E: asmelash_b@ymail.com

ASPINALL, Christine Joyce. b 54. SNWTP 14. **d** 17 **p** 18. OLM Old Trafford St Jo *Man* from 17. *382 Kings Road, Stretford, Manchester M32 8GW*

ASPINALL, Philip Norman. b 51. Cam Univ MA ATI. WMMTC 86. **d** 89 **p** 90. NSM Cov E 89–98. *139 Wiltshire Court, Nod Rise, Mount Nod, Coventry CV5 7JP* T: (024) 7646 7509 E: philaspinall@gmail.com

ASQUITH (née SHIPLEY), June Patricia. b 54. Liv Hope BA 00 PGCE 01. SNWTP 08. **d** 10 **p** 11. NSM Walton Breck *Liv* 10–12; C Bootle 12–14; R Wavertree St Mary from 14. *St Mary's Rectory, 1 South Drive, Wavertree, Liverpool L15 8JJ* E: june150@btinternet.com

ASQUITH, Michael John. b 60. St D Coll Lamp BA 82 MPhil 91 Ch Ch Coll Cant PGCE 83. Cant Sch of Min 91. **d** 94 **p** 95. C S Ashford Ch Ch *Cant* 94–98; P-in-c Weldon w Deene *Pet* 98–00; P-in-c Corby Epiphany w St Jo 98–06; Dep Dioc Dir of Educn *Leic* 06–10; R Lowestoft St Marg *Nor* from 11; Jt RD Lothingland from 18. *St Margaret's Rectory, 147 Hollingsworth Road, Lowestoft NR32 4BW* T: (01502) 573046 M: 07503-377360 E: mikeasq@aol.com *or* rector@stmargaretslowestoft.co.uk

ASSON, Geoffrey Ormrod. b 34. Univ of Wales (Ban) BA 54 St Cath Coll Ox BA 56 MA 61. St Steph Ho Ox 54. **d** 57 **p** 58. C Aberdare *Llan* 57–59; C Roath 59–61; R Hagworthingham w Asgarby and Lusby *Linc* 61–65; P-in-c Mavis Enderby w Raithby 62–65; V Friskney 65–69; R S Ormsby w Ketsby, Calceby and Driby 69–74; R Harrington w Brinkhill 69–74; R Oxcombe 69–74; R Ruckland w Farforth and Maidenwell 69–74; R Somersby w Bag Enderby 69–74; R Tetford and Salmonby 69–74; P-in-c Belchford 71–74; P-in-c W Ashby 71–74; V Riverhead w Dunton Green *Roch* 75–80; R Kington w Huntington *Heref* 80–82; RD Kington and Weobley 80–86; P-in-c Almeley 81–82; P-in-c Knill 81–82; P-in-c Old Radnor 81–82; R Kington w Huntington, Old Radnor, Kinnerton etc 82–86; V Mathry w St Edren's and Grandston etc *St D* 86–97; Bp's Rural Adv and Tourist Officer 91–95; rtd 96; PtO *St D* from 97. *Mimulus, Mutton Dingle, New Radnor, Presteigne LD8 2TL* T: (01544) 350358 E: goasson@btinternet.com

ASTBURY, Susan. b 61. St Hugh's Coll Ox BA 82 MA 85 DPhil 85. SWMTC 05. **d** 08 **p** 09. C Teignmouth, Ideford w Luton, Ashcombe etc *Ex* 08–12; PtO from 12. *3 The Strand, Shaldon, Teignmouth TQ14 0DL* T: (01626) 873807 E: sue.ast@btinternet.com

ASTIN, The Ven Moira Anne Elizabeth. b 65. Clare Coll Cam BA 86 MA 90. Wycliffe Hall Ox BA 96. **d** 95 **p** 96. C Newbury *Ox* 95–99; C Thatcham 99–01; TV 01–05; TV Woodley 05–09; V Southlake 09–11; Angl Ecum Officer (Berks) 03–11; Dioc Ecum Officer 10–11; P-in-c Frodingham and New Brumby *Linc* 11–16; Can and Preb Linc Cathl 12–16; Adn Reigate *S'wark* from 16. *Croydon Episcopal Area Office, 6 St Peter's Road, Croydon CR0 1HD* T: (020) 8256 9630 E: moira.astin@southwark.anglican.org

ASTIN, Timothy Robin. b 58. St Edm Hall Ox BA 79 Darw Coll Cam PhD 82 FGS. Ox Min Course 90. **d** 93 **p** 94. NSM Reading St Jo *Ox* 93–95; NSM Newbury 95–99; NSM Beedon and Peasemore w W Ilsley and Farnborough 99–05; NSM Woodley 05–11; NSM Frodingham and New Brumby *Linc* 11–13; P-in-c Bottesford w Ashby 13–16; Public Preacher *S'wark* 16–17; V Tadworth from 17. *The Vicarage, 1 The Avenue, Tadworth KT20 5AS* E: tim.astin@virginmedia.com

ASTLEY, Prof Jeffrey. b 47. Down Coll Cam BA 68 MA 72 Dur Univ PhD 79. Qu Coll Birm 68. **d** 70 **p** 71. C Cannock *Lich* 70–73; Lect and Chapl St Hild Coll Dur 73–75; Sen Lect and Chapl SS Hild and Bede Coll Dur 75–77; Prin Lect and Hd RS Bp Grosseteste Coll Linc 77–81; Dir N of England Inst for Chr Educn 81–13; PtO *Dur* from 81; *Leeds* from 17. *8 Vicarage Court, Heighington Village, Newton Aycliffe DL5 6SD* E: jeff.astley@durham.ac.uk *or* jagdaa71@aol.com

ASTON, Heather Jane. b 54. Cen Lancs Univ MBA 02. SWMTC 10. **d** 13 **p** 14. C Meneage *Truro* 13–17; P-in-c Boscastle and Tintagel Gp from 17; C Week St Mary Circle of Par from 19. *The Rectory, Forrabury, Boscastle PL35 0DJ* T: (01840) 250359 M: 07960-965787 E: heather_solo@msn.com

ASTON, John Bernard. b 34. Leeds Univ BA 55 PGCE 56. Qu Coll Birm 72. **d** 75 **p** 76. NSM Shenstone *Lich* 75–05; NSM Stonnall 00–05; Chapl HM YOI Swinfen Hall 90–99;

PtO *Lich* from 05. *4 Footherley Road, Shenstone, Lichfield WS14 0NJ* T: (01543) 480388 E: bradston@btinternet.com

ASTON, John Leslie. b 47. Open Univ BSc 99 Win Univ MA 07. Oak Hill Th Coll BA 80. **d** 80 **p** 81. C Trentham *Lich* 80–83; C Meir Heath 83–85; V Upper Tean 85–91; CF 91–02; C Andover w Foxcott *Win* 02–05; P-in-c Felixstowe SS Pet and Paul *St E* 05–11; V 11–17; rtd 17. *20 Princes Gardens, Felixstowe IP11 7RH*

ASTON, Michael James. b 48. Loughb Univ BSc 70 MBCS 85. NTMTC 98. **d** 01 **p** 02. NSM Writtle w Highwood *Chelmsf* 01–07; P-in-c W Hanningfield 07–11; rtd 11; PtO *Chelmsf* 11–19; P-in-c Pleshey from 19. *15 Weller Grove, Chelmsford CM1 4YJ* T: (01245) 442547 M: 07957-610235 E: mikaston@globalnet.co.uk

ASTON, Roger. b 52. Ox Poly BEd 83. SAOMC 96. **d** 99 **p** 00. OLM Eynsham and Cassington *Ox* from 99. *9 Bell Close, Cassington, Witney OX29 4EP* T: (01865) 880757 E: rogera52@aol.com

ASTON, Ms Sheelagh Mary. NEOC 02. **d** 05 **p** 06. C Windy Nook St Alb *Dur* 05–10; P-in-c Oxclose 10–16; Dioc Ecum Officer 10–16; P-in-c Blackb St Silas from 16; PtO *Eur* 17–20. *St Silas's Vicarage, Preston New Road, Blackburn BB2 6PS* T: (01254) 664722 E: revsmaston@gmail.com

ASTON, Simon Richard. b 57. SEITE 12. **d** 16 **p** 17. NSM Kidbrooke St Jas *S'wark* from 16. *82A Tyrwhitt Road, London SE4 1QB* T: (020) 8691 7076 E: simonaston@chef.net

ASTON, Archdeacon of. See HEATHFIELD, The Ven Simon David

ASTON, Suffragan Bishop of. See HOLLINGHURST, The Rt Revd Anne Elizabeth

ATACK, Elaine. b 57. Man Univ BA 78. St Mich Coll Llan 09. **d** 12 **p** 13. C St As and Chapl St As Cathl 12–14; R Bala 14–17; C Edstaston, Fauls, Prees, Tilstock and Whixall *Lich* from 17; C Whitchurch from 17. *The Vicarage, Tilstock, Whitchurch SY13 3JL* T: (01948) 880380 M: 07930-443605 E: atacks@hush.com

ATACK, John Philip. b 49. Lanc Univ MA 91. Linc Th Coll 86. **d** 88 **p** 89. C Cleveleys *Blackb* 88–92; V Appley Bridge 92–96; P-in-c Mostyn w Ffynnongroyw *St As* 99–03; P-in-c Colwyn 03–08; R Colwyn and Llanelian 08–14; AD Rhos 09–12; AD Llanrwst and Rhos 12–14; Chapl Conwy and Denbighshire NHS Trust 05–10; Hon Chapl Miss to Seafarers 01–03; rtd 14; PtO *St As* from 15; *Lich* from 17. *The Vicarage, Tilstock, Whitchurch SY13 3JL* T: (01948) 880380 M: 07930-443602 E: atacks@hush.com

ATALLAH, David Alexander. b 74. Ox Univ MPhys 97 Ex Univ MSc 99 PhD 03. Wycliffe Hall Ox 09. **d** 11 **p** 12. C Okehampton, Inwardleigh, Belstone, Sourton etc *Ex* 11–15; C Maidenhead St Andr and St Mary *Ox* 15–18; P-in-c White Waltham w Shottesbrooke from 18; C Maidenhead St Andr and St Mary from 19. *The Vicarage, Waltham Road, White Waltham, Maidenhead SL6 3JD* T: (01628) 822000 E: vicar@atallahfamily.co.uk

ATFIELD, Gladys. b 39. Univ Coll Lon BSc 53. Gilmore Course. **dss** 79 **d** 87 **p** 94. Bexley St Mary *Roch* 79–01; Hon C 87–01; rtd 01; PtO *Roch* 01–16. *6 Clarendon Mews, High Street, Bexley DA5 1JS* T: (01322) 551741

ATFIELD, Graham Roy. b 60. Kent Univ BA 82. SEITE 08. **d** 11 **p** 12. NSM Rye *Chich* 11–15; Chapl E Sussex Healthcare NHS Trust from 15. *104 Elphinstone Road, Hastings TN34 2BS* T: (01424) 717382 M: 07810-554268 E: grahamatfield@hotmail.co.uk

ATFIELD, Tom David. b 80. Bris Univ BA 02 MPhil 10 Inst for Chr Studies Toronto MPhilF 06 Birm Univ ThD 11 PGCE 06. Qu Coll Birm 08. **d** 11 **p** 12. C Bromsgrove *Worc* 11–15; TV Dudley 15–19; V Shrewsbury H Cross *Lich* from 19. *1 Underdale Court, Underdale Road, Shrewsbury SY2 5DD* T: (01743) 245300 E: tomatfield@virginmedia.com *or* vicar@shrewsburyabbey.com

ATHA, Gareth William. b 83. Leeds Univ BSc 05 York St Jo Univ MA 10 Selw Coll Cam BTh 14. Westcott Ho Cam 11. **d** 14 **p** 15. C Beverley Minster *York* 14–17; V Elloe Stone *Linc* from 17. *The Vicarage, 34 Church Lane, Moulton, Spalding PE12 6NP* M: 07779-697383 E: gareth.atha@cantab.net

ATHERFOLD, Mrs Evelyne Sara. b 43. Leeds Inst of Educn CertEd 64. NOC 82. **dss** 85 **d** 92 **p** 94. Kirk Sandall and Edenthorpe *Sheff* 85–87; NSM Fishlake w Sykehouse and Kirk Bramwith etc 87–00; P-in-c 00–03; R 03–11; P-in-c 11–14; Hon C 14–15; Chapl HM YOI Hatfield 96–03; PtO *Sheff* from 15. *Runswick House, Hay Green, Fishlake, Doncaster DN7 5JY* T: (01302) 841396 M: 07980-282270 E: eve.atherfold@virgin.net

ATHERSTONE, Andrew Castell. b 74. Ch Coll Cam BA 95 MA 98 Wycliffe Hall Ox MSt 99 DPhil 01 FRHistS 08. **d** 01 **p** 02. C Abingdon *Ox* 01–05; NSM Eynsham and Cassington from 05; Research Fell Latimer Trust from

05; Tutor Wycliffe Hall Ox from 07. *44 Shakespeare Road, Eynsham, Witney OX29 4PY* T: (01865) 731239 E: andrew.atherstone@wycliffe.ox.ac.uk

ATHERSTONE, Canon Castell Hugh. b 45. Natal Univ BA 67. St Chad's Coll Dur MA 79. **d** 70 **p** 70. C Pietermaritzburg St Alphege S Africa 70–72; C Berea St Thos 72–74; C Kloor 74–77; R Hillcrest 77–80; R Newcastle 80–83; Dioc Stewardship Adv *Ely* 83–87; P-in-c Doddington w Benwick 83–87; R Frant w Eridge *Chich* 87–95; P-in-c Rotherfield w Mark Cross 94–95; RD Rotherfield 90–95; V Seaford w Sutton 95–10; RD Lewes and Seaford 97–07; Can and Preb Chich Cathl 02–10; rtd 10; PtO *Ox* from 10. *9 The Tennis, Cassington, Witney OX29 4EL* T: (01865) 880475 E: hugh@atherstone.net

ATHERTON, Henry Anthony. b 44. Univ of Wales BSc 67 DipEd 68 Fitzw Coll Cam BA 72 MA 75 Heythrop Coll Lon MTh 00 FGS 68. Westcott Ho Cam 70. **d** 72 **p** 73. C Leamington Priors All SS *Cov* 72–75; C Orpington All SS *Roch* 75–78; V Gravesend St Mary 78–87; Chapl St Jas Hosp Gravesend 82–87; V Bromley St Andr *Roch* 87–10; rtd 10; PtO *Roch* from 10; *S'wark* from 12. *20 Laleham Road, London SE6 2HT* T: (020) 8695 0212 E: anthony6atherton@btinternet.com

ATHERTON, Lionel Thomas. b 45. Univ of Wales (Ban) BA 74 St Luke's Coll Ex. St Steph Ho Ox 74. **d** 76 **p** 77. C Chenies and Lt Chalfont *Ox* 76–79; C Fleet *Guildf* 79–84; V S Farnborough 84–89; TR Alston Team *Newc* 89–96; V Chorley St Pet *Blackb* 96–10; Bp's Adv on New Relig Movements 02–10; rtd 10; PtO *Derby* from 14. *36 Windsor Park Road, Buxton SK17 7NP* T: (01298) 74204 E: lionel.atherton@sky.com

ATHERTON, Paul Christopher. b 56. Chich Th Coll. **d** 82 **p** 83. C Orford St Marg *Liv* 82–86; CR 86–88; Chapl Univ of Wales (Cardiff) *Llan* 88–89; TV Walton St Mary *Liv* 89–92; C Westmr St Matt *Lon* 92–96; C Somers Town 96–97; V Bush Hill Park St Mark 97–19; P-in-c Bush Hill Park St Steph 13–19; Chapl N Middx Univ Hosp NHS Trust 97–19; rtd 19. *St Cedd, 41 Spring Road, Brightlingsea, Colchester CO7 0PJ* E: paulc.atherton@gmail.com

ATHERTON, Philip Gordon. b 47. NTMTC BA 07. **d** 07 **p** 08. NSM Hornsey H Innocents *Lon* 07–14; NSM Stroud Green H Trin 07–14; NSM Harringay St Paul 10–14; rtd 14; PtO *Cant* from 18. *12A Beach Court Park, Faversham Road, Seasalter, Whitstable CT5 4FE* M: 07901-555235

ATKINS, Austen Shaun. b 55. St Pet Coll Ox MA 82 Selw Coll Cam MA 85. Ridley Hall Cam 79. **d** 82 **p** 83. C S Mimms Ch Ch *Lon* 82–86; C Fulham St Matt 86–90; P-in-c Fulham St Dionis 91–03; V 03–04; C Ox St Andr 05–09; Chapl Bedford Sch 09–18; rtd 18; Hon C Wootton *St Alb* from 19. *6 The Crescent, Bedford MK40 2RU*

ATKINS, Canon David John. b 43. Kelham Th Coll 64. **d** 68 **p** 69. C Lewisham St Mary *S'wark* 68–72; Min Motspur Park 72–77; P-in-c Mitcham Ascension 77–82; V 82–83; P-in-c Downham w S Hanningfield *Chelmsf* 83–88; R 88–93; P-in-c W Hanningfield 90–93; RD Chelmsf S 93–01; V Maldon All SS w St Pet 01–09; Hon Can Chelmsf Cathl 00–09; rtd 09; PtO *Chelmsf* from 09. *19 The Green, Hadleigh, Ipswich IP7 6AE* T: (01473) 822535 E: atkins.d@hotmail.co.uk

ATKINS, Dean John. b 70. Univ of Wales (Cardiff) BD 93. St Steph Ho Ox 93. **d** 95 **p** 96. C Merthyr Dyfan *Llan* 95–99; V Aberaman and Abercwmboi w Cwmaman 99–01; Dioc Youth Officer 01–12; P-in-c Roath St Sav 08–12; V Cardiff St German w St Sav 12–16; P-in-c Cardiff St Mary from 16. *St Mary's Vicarage, 2 North Church Street, Cardiff CF10 5HB* T: (029) 2048 7777 E: datkins16@btinternet.com

ATKINS, Forrest William (Bill). b 59. Ch Coll Cam MA 85 Lon Univ BD 84. Ridley Hall Cam 83. **d** 86 **p** 87. C Normanton *Derby* 86–90; C Stratford St Jo and Ch Ch w Forest Gate St Jas *Chelmsf* 90–97; Asst Chapl Dubai and Sharjah w N Emirates 97–03; I Mohill w Farnaught, Aughavas, Oughteragh etc *K, E & A* 03–13; Preb Elphin Cathl 08–13; I Eglish w Killylea *Arm* from 13. *154 Killylea Road, Armagh BT60 4LN* T: (028) 3756 8874 E: fwatkins@eircom.net *or* fwatkins123@btinternet.com

ATKINS, Jane Elizabeth. b 51. EMMTC 98. **d** 01 **p** 02. NSM Fenn Lanes Gp *Leic* 01–05; Sub Chapl HM Pris Leic 03–05; P-in-c Ashill w Saham Toney *Nor* 05–07; V Ashill, Carbrooke, Ovington and Saham Toney from 07. *The Rectory, Swaffham Road, Ashill, Thetford IP25 7BT* T: (01760) 441191 E: revd.jane@btinternet.com

ATKINS, Joy Katherine. b 75. Lon Sch of Th BTh 97 Dur Univ PGCE 98. St Jo Coll Nottm MTh 09. **d** 09 **p** 10. C Uxbridge *Lon* 09–12; Chapl Twyford C of E High Sch Acton and Wm Perkin C of E High Sch 12–13; C Reading Greyfriars *Ox* from 13. *93 York Road, Reading RG1 8DU* E: joyatkins@hotmail.com

ATKINS (née HARDING), Ms Lesley Anne. b 58. Westcott Ho Cam 98 SEITE 99. **d** 01 **p** 02. C Walmer *Cant* 01–03; C

Broadstairs 03–04; PtO 05–07; NSM Barkston and Hough Gp *Linc* 07–10; P-in-c Hattersley *Ches* 10–18; V Marton *Blackb* from 18. *St Paul's Vicarage, 55 Vicarage Lane, Blackpool FY4 4EF* E: lesley@revlesleyanne.plus.com

ATKINS, Canon Nicholas Steven. b 60. Oak Hill Th Coll BA 88. **d** 88 **p** 89. C Shepton Mallet w Doulting *B & W* 88–91; C Combe Down w Monkton Combe and S Stoke 91–93; TV N Wingfield, Clay Cross and Pilsley *Derby* 93–98; V Essington *Lich* 98–05; P-in-c Ipswich St Matt *St E* 05–06; R Triangle, St Matt and All SS from 06; AD Ipswich from 17; Hon Can St E Cathl from 17. *St Matthew's Rectory, 3 Portman Road, Ipswich IP1 2ES* T: (01473) 251630 E: rector@smast.org.uk

ATKINS, Canon Paul Henry. b 38. St Mich Coll Llan 62. **d** 65 **p** 66. C Sheringham *Nor* 65–68; V Southtown 68–84; RD Flegg (Gt Yarmouth) 78–84; R Aylmerton w Runton 84–99; P-in-c Beeston Regis 98–99; P-in-c Gresham 98–99; R Aylmerton, Runton, Beeston Regis and Gresham 99–03; RD Repps 86–95; Hon Can Nor Cathl 88–03; rtd 03; PtO *Nor* from 03. *34 Regis Avenue, Beeston Regis, Sheringham NR26 8SW* T: (01263) 820147 E: paulatkins07@btinternet.com *or* paulatkins07@hotmail.co.uk

ATKINS, Robert Brian. b 49. Open Univ BA 94 CIPFA 78. SAOMC 94. **d** 97 **p** 98. NSM Bicester w Bucknell, Caversfield and Launton *Ox* 97–18; PtO *Derby* from 19. *39 Gertrude Road, Chaddesden, Derby DE21 4JQ* T: (01332) 679985 M: 07443-481329 E: bob@frbob.co.uk

ATKINS, Roger Francis. b 30. AKC 54. **d** 55 **p** 56. C Bromley All Hallows *Lon* 55–58; C Eastleigh *Win* 58–62; Missr The Murray Australia 62–65; R Mossman 65–69; Adn Carpentaria 69–71; V Wolverley *Worc* 74–76; V S Hackney St Mich w Haggerston St Paul *Lon* 76–85; TV Gleadless *Sheff* 85–93; rtd 93; PtO *Sheff* from 93. *27 Stannington Glen, Sheffield S6 6NA* T: 0114-234 0543

ATKINS, Mrs Sarah Christine. b 83. Magd Coll Cam MA 09. Ridley Hall Cam 12. **d** 14 **p** 16. C Trumpington *Ely* 14–18; Chapl Magd Coll Cam from 18. *Magdalene College, Cambridge CB3 0AG* T: (01223) 332129 M: 07906-659655 E: sarah.atkins@cantab.net

ATKINS, Mrs Sarah Elizabeth. b 61. Univ Coll Lon LLB 82. St Aug Coll of Th 16. **d** 19. NSM Ham St Rich *S'wark* from 19. *138 Manor Road North, Thames Ditton KT7 0BH* T: (020) 8398 7730 M: 07597-959473 E: sarah.atkins@yahoo.co.uk

ATKINS, Shaun. *See* ATKINS, Austen Shaun

ATKINS, Timothy David. b 45. Ridley Hall Cam 71. **d** 74 **p** 75. C Stoughton *Guildf* 74–79; C Chilwell *S'well* 79–84; R Eastwood 84–91; V Finchley Ch Ch *Lon* 91–10; Chapl Barnet Healthcare NHS Trust 92–01; Chapl Enfield Primary Care Trust 01–10; rtd 10; PtO *Lon* 10–12; Hon C Uxbridge from 12. *75 Belmont Road, Uxbridge UB8 1QU* T: (01895) 231801 M: 07875-747760 E: timanneatkins@gmail.com

ATKINS, Timothy James. b 38. Worc Coll Ox BA 62. Cuddesdon Coll 62. **d** 64 **p** 65. C Stafford St Mary *Lich* 64–67; C Loughborough St Pet *Leic* 67–69; C Usworth *Dur* 69–71; LtO *Newc* 71–76; P-in-c Slaley 76–87; P-in-c Shotley 87–05; Dioc Child Protection Adv 98–06; PtO *Dur* from 06. *5 Railway Terrace, Witton le Wear, Bishop Auckland DL14 0AL* T: (01388) 488626 E: kandtatk@gmail.com

ATKINS, William. *See* ATKINS, Forrest William

ATKINSON, Adam. b 67. Birm Univ BA 89. Wycliffe Hall Ox 05. **d** 07 **p** 08. C Shadwell St Paul w Ratcliffe St Jas *Lon* 07–10; P-in-c Bethnal Green St Pet w St Thos 10–11; V 11–19; Miss Dir Development Two Cities Area from 19. *St Peter's Vicarage, St Peter's Close, London E2 7AE* T: (020) 7229 0550 M: 07780-992112 E: adam.atkinson@london.anglican.org

ATKINSON, Ms Audrey. b 54. Univ of Wales (Lamp) BA 97 Trin Coll Carmarthen PGCE 98. Coll of Resurr Mirfield 06. **d** 08 **p** 09. C Beadnell and N Sunderland *Newc* 08–11; Dep Warden Launde Abbey *Leic* 11; TV Oakham, Ashwell, Braunston, Brooke, Egleton etc *Pet* 11–14; Chapl HM Pris Full Sutton 14–17; rtd 17; PtO *York* 18–19. *Address withheld by request* M: 07833-198968 E: audreyatkinson@hotmail.co.uk

ATKINSON, Brian Colin. b 49. Sarum & Wells Th Coll 85. **d** 87 **p** 88. C Up Hatherley *Glouc* 87–90; R Upper Stour *Sarum* 90–95; TR Trowbridge H Trin 95–04; P-in-c Fairford and Kempsford w Whelford *Glouc* 04–08; TR S Cotswolds 09–14; AD Fairford 04–11; rtd 14; Hon C Minchinhampton w Box and Amberley *Glouc* 14–16; PtO from 17. *54 Lypiatt View, Bussage, Stroud GL6 8DA* E: katki01225@aol.com

ATKINSON, Christopher John. b 57. Man Univ BA 80. Qu Coll Birm 82. **d** 85 **p** 86. C Stalybridge *Man* 85–88; P-in-c Westhall w Brampton and Stoven *St E* 88–89; P-in-c Sotterley, Willingham, Shadingfield, Ellough etc 88–89; P-in-c Hundred River Gp of Par 90–92; R Hundred River 92–97; P-in-c Eye w Braiseworth and Yaxley 97–00; P-in-c Occold 97–00; P-in-c Bedingfield 97–00; R Eye 00–03; RD Hartismere 97–03; V Bourne *Linc* from 03; RD Beltisloe from 13. *Bourne*

Vicarage, Church Walk, Bourne PE10 9UQ T: (01778) 422412 E: chris_atk@yahoo.com

ATKINSON, Canon Christopher Lionel Varley. b 39. K Coll Lon 63. Chich Th Coll 65. **d** 67 **p** 68. C Sowerby Bridge w Norland *Wakef* 67–70; P-in-c Flushing *Truro* 70–73; Dioc Adv in RE 70–73; PtO *Worc* 74–78; TR Halesowen 78–88; RD Dudley 79–87; Hon Can Worc Cathl 83–88; V Cartmel *Carl* 88–97; TV Cartmel Peninsula 97–98; RD Windermere 94–98; Hon Can Carl Cathl 94–98; TR Bensham *Dur* 98–03; AD Gateshead 99–03; rtd 03; Bp's Adv Spiritual Development *Dur* 03–08; Hon Can Dur Cathl 01–03; PtO from 11. *64 Beacon Street, Gateshead NE9 5XN* T: 0191-447 1732 E: chris.atkinson@durham.anglican.org *or* canon.chris.atkinson@gmail.com

ATKINSON, Canon Clive James. b 68. QUB BSc 90. CITC 90. **d** 93 **p** 94. C Belfast H Trin and Ardoyne *Conn* 93–95; C Belfast H Trin and St Silas 96–97; I Belfast Upper Falls 97–02; Chapl Vevey w Château d'Oex *Eur* from 02; Hon Can from 19. *The Parsonage, chemin de Champsavaux 1, 1807 Blonay, Vaud, Switzerland* T: (0041) (21) 943 2239 M: 78-710 1860 E: cliveatkinson@bluewin.ch

ATKINSON, Prof David. b 44. Hull Univ BSc 66 Newc Univ PhD 69 CBiol FIBiol FRSA MIEM. TISEC 03. **d** 05 **p** 06. C Aberdeen St Andr *Ab* 05–07; NSM Bieldside 07–09; NSM Auchindoir from 09; NSM Inverurie from 09; NSM Kemnay from 09. *33 Norman Gray Park, Blackburn, Aberdeen AB21 0ZR* T: (01224) 791163 E: atkinson390@btinternet.com

ATKINSON, Canon David James. b 41. K Coll Lon BD 63 AKC 63 Selw Coll Cam BA 65 MA 72. Linc Th Coll 65. **d** 66 **p** 67. C Linc St Giles 66–70; Asst Chapl Newc Univ 70–73; P-in-c Adbaston *Lich* 73–80; Adult Educn Officer 73–75; Dioc Dir of Educn 75–82; Preb Lich Cathl 79–82; Chapl Hull Univ York 82–87; Dioc Dir of Educn *Linc* 87–94; P-in-c Bishop Norton, Waddingham and Snitterby 94–01; PtO from 01; Can and Preb Linc Cathl 89–06; rtd 06. *4 The Orchards, Middle Rasen, Market Rasen LN8 3TL* T: (01673) 849979

✠**ATKINSON, The Rt Revd David John.** b 43. K Coll Lon BSc 65 AKC 65 PhD 69 Bris Univ MLitt 73 Ox Univ MA 85 MSOSc. Trin Coll Bris and Tyndale Hall Bris 69. **d** 72 **p** 73 **c** 01. C Halliwell St Pet *Man* 72–74; C Harborne Heath *Birm* 74–77; Lib Latimer Ho Ox 77–80; Chapl CCC Ox 80–93; Fell 84–93; Visiting Lect Wycliffe Hall Ox 84–93; Can Res and Chan S'wark Cathl 93–96; Adn Lewisham 96–01; Suff Bp Thetford *Nor* 01–09; rtd 09; Asst Bp S'wark from 09. *6 Bynes Road, South Croydon CR2 0PR* T: (020) 8406 0895 E: davidatkinson43@virginmedia.com

ATKINSON, Donald. b 31. Magd Coll Cam BA 54 MA 57. Chich Th Coll. **d** 56 **p** 57. C Dorking w Ranmore *Guildf* 56–58; C Hillingdon St Andr *Lon* 59–60; Hd Master Friern Barnet Gr Sch 60–96; rtd 96. *9 Maxwell Close, Lichfield WS13 6TY*

ATKINSON, Mrs Heather Dawn. b 69. Leeds Univ BA 02. NOC 03. **d** 05 **p** 06. C Morley *Wakef* 05–08; P-in-c Moldgreen and Rawthorpe *Leeds* 08–16; V New Brighton St Jas w Em *Ches* from 16. *St James's Vicarage, 14 Albion Street, Wallasey CH45 9LF* T: 0151-639 5844 M: 07877-581092 E: revheatheratkinson@gmail.com

ATKINSON, Heather Mary Ann. b 66. Birm Univ BA 89 Nottm Univ PGCE 90. St Mellitus Coll BA 15. **d** 15 **p** 16. NSM S Hackney St Mich w Haggerston St Paul *Lon* 15–16; C 16–18; Chapl The Urswick Sch 14–16; C Bethnal Green St Pet w St Thos *Lon* 18–19; V from 19. *St Peter's Vicarage, St Peter's Close, London E2 7AE* T: (020) 7739 0550 M: 07970-197152 E: heather@stpetersbethnalgreen.org *or* atkinson.heather@gmail.com

ATKINSON, Ian. b 33. BNC Ox BA 58 MA 63. Coll of Resurr Mirfield 56. **d** 58 **p** 59. C Welling *S'wark* 58–62; C Camberwell St Giles 62–63; V Wandsworth Common St Mary 63–67; C Pretoria Cathl S Africa 67–68; C Oxted *S'wark* 68–69; Asst Chapl Ch Hosp Horsham 70–85; NSM Dalmahoy *Edin* 85–91; Asst Master Clifton Hall Sch 85–91; NSM Dunkeld *St And* 92–16; LtO from 16. *2 Pinel Lodge, Druids Park, Murthly, Perth PH1 4ES* T: (01738) 710561

ATKINSON, Jane Louise. b 66. **d** 13 **p** 14. NSM Kirkham *Blackb* 13–17; V Lt Thornton from 17. *St John's Vicarage, 35 Station Road, Thornton-Cleveleys FY5 5HY* T: (01253) 969492 E: revjaneatkinson@sky.com

ATKINSON, Canon Lewis Malcolm. b 34. Cranmer Hall Dur. **d** 82 **p** 83. C Chapeltown *Sheff* 82–85; V Sheff St Barn Ind Chapl 85–99; RD Ecclesfield 90–93; V Oughtibridge 93–99; RD Tankersley 96–99; Hon Can Sheff Cathl 98–99; rtd 99; PtO *Sheff* from 99. *14 Rowan Close, Chapeltown, Sheffield S35 1QE*

ATKINSON, Marianne Rose. b 39. Girton Coll Cam BA 61 CertEd 62 MA 64. Linc Th Coll 86. **d** 88 **p** 94. C S w

N Hayling *Portsm* 88–91; C Rainham *Roch* 91–92; Asst Chapl Salford R Hosps NHS Trust 92–97; Hon C Prestwich St Marg *Man* 94–97; Chapl R United Hosp Bath NHS Trust 97–00; rtd 00; PtO *B & W* 00–03; *St E* from 03. *68 Barons Road, Bury St Edmunds IP33 2LW* T: (01284) 752075 E: torrensatkinson@aol.com

ATKINSON, Michael Hubert. b 33. Qu Coll Ox BA 57 MA 60. Ripon Hall Ox 56. **d** 58 **p** 59. C Attercliffe w Carbrook *Sheff* 58–60; Ind Chapl Sheff 58–66; C Sharrow St Andr 60–66; Ind Chapl *Pet* 66–71; Sen Ind Chapl *Cant* 71–79; Research Officer Gen Syn Bd for Soc Resp 79–87; Representation Sec USPG 88–92; TV High Wycombe *Ox* 92–97; Chapl Bucks Coll of HE 94–97; rtd 97. *7 Birch Court, Old Bridge Rise, Ilkley LS29 9HH* T: (01943) 609891 E: mike.dorothy@gmail.com

ATKINSON, Canon Patricia Anne. b 47. EAMTC 86. **d** 89 **p** 01. NSM Nor St Steph 89–94; LtO 94–17; Chapl Norfolk Primary Care Trust from 00; Chapl Norfolk and Nor Univ Hosps NHS Foundn Trust 01–11; NSM Brundall w Braydeston and Postwick *Nor* 01–02; PtO from 17; Hon Can Nor Cathl from 06. *32 Berryfields, Brundall, Norwich NR13 5QE* T: (01603) 714720 E: patatkinson44@gmail.com

ATKINSON, Paul William. b 64. St Steph Ho Ox 07. **d** 09 **p** 10. C Castleford *Wakef* 09–13; C Smawthorpe 11–12; P-in-c Ravensthorpe and Thornhill Lees w Savile Town 13–14; *Leeds* 14–17; V Cookridge H Trin from 17. *Holy Trinity Vicarage, 53 Green Lane, Cookridge, Leeds LS16 7LW*

ATKINSON, Peter Duncan. b 41. Univ Coll Dur BA 62. Linc Th Coll 63. **d** 65 **p** 66. C Beckenham St Geo *Roch* 65–69; C Caversham *Ox* 69–75; P-in-c Millfield St Mark *Dur* 76–86; V Dedworth *Ox* 86–93; TV Aylesbury 93–05; rtd 05. *24 Grimbald Road, Knaresborough HG5 8HD* T: (01423) 866593 E: pandatkinson@fiscali.co.uk

ATKINSON, The Very Revd Peter Gordon. b 52. St Jo Coll Ox BA 74 MA 78 Worc Univ Hon DLitt 14 FRSA 06. Westcott Ho Cam 77. **d** 79 **p** 80. C Clapham Old Town *S'wark* 79–83; P-in-c Tatsfield 83–90; R Bath H Trin *B & W* 90–91; Prin Chich Th Coll 91–94; Can and Preb Chich Cathl 91–97; R Lavant 94–97; Can Res and Chan Chich Cathl 97–07; Dean Worc from 07; PtO *Eur* from 01. *The Deanery, 10 College Green, Worcester WR1 2LH* T: (01905) 732939 or 732909 F: 732906 E: peteratkinson@worcestercathedral.org.uk

ATKINSON, Philip Stephen. b 58. K Coll Lon BD 80 AKC 80 Dur Univ MA 97. Ridley Hall Cam 81. **d** 83 **p** 84. C Barrow St Matt *Carl* 83–86; C Kirkby Lonsdale 86–89; R Redmarshall *Dur* 89–95; V Bishopton w Gt Stainton 89–95; C Kirkby Lonsdale *Carl* 95–97; Chapl Casterton Sch Lancs 95–09; NSM Kirkby Lonsdale *Carl* 97–09; Chapl Taunton Sch 09–11; R Odd Rode *Ches* from 11. *Odd Rode Rectory, Church Lane, Scholar Green, Stoke-on-Trent ST7 3QN* T: (01270) 882195 E: rector.oddrode@gmail.com

ATKINSON, Richard Timothy Kenneth. b 81. Leic Univ BA 03. Ridley Hall Cam 15. **d** 17 **p** 18. C Onslow Square and S Kensington St Aug *Lon* 17–18; V Aspley S'well from 18; P-in-c Bilborough and Strelley from 19. *319 Aspley Lane, Nottingham NG8 5GA* M: 07736-306568 E: rich@timetorebuild.co.uk

✠ATKINSON, The Rt Revd Richard William Bryant. b 58. Magd Coll Cam MA. Ripon Coll Cuddesdon. **d** 84 **p** 85 **c** 12. C Abingdon w Shippon *Ox* 84–87; TV Sheff Manor 87–91; TR 91–96; Hon Tutor Ripon Coll Cuddesdon 87–92; V Rotherham *Sheff* 96–02; Hon Can Sheff Cathl 98–02; Adn Leic 02–12; Suff Bp Bedford *St Alb* from 12. *Bishop's Lodge, Bedford Road, Cardington, Bedford MK44 3SS* T: (01234) 831432 F: 831484 E: bishopbedford@stalbans.anglican.org

ATKINSON, Miss Ruth Irene. b 58. Worc Coll of Educn BEd 80 Cant Ch Ch Univ MA 08. Qu Coll Birm 06. **d** 09 **p** 10. C Old Swinford Stourbridge *Worc* 09–14; V Bartley Green *Birm* from 14. *96 Romsley Road, Birmingham B32 3PS* T: 0121-476 5287 M: 07432-660538 E: revruthvicarbg@gmail.com

ATKINSON, Simon James. b 71. St Chad's Coll Dur BA 93 Ustinov Coll Dur PGCE 04. St Steph Ho Ox 93. **d** 95 **p** 96. C Norton St Mary *Dur* 95–96; C Hartlepool H Trin 96–99; TV Jarrow 99–01; V Chich St Wilfrid 01–03; PtO *Dur* 03–09; *Lon* 09–18; NSM Old St Pancras 10–17; NSM Colindale St Matthias from 17; Headteacher Hampstead Paroch C of E Primary Sch 10–15; Headteacher St Steph C of E Primary Sch from 15; CMP from 98. *St Stephen's Church of England Primary School, 91 Westbourne Park Road, London W2 5QH* T: (020) 3351 4488 E: head@st-stephensprimary.co.uk

ATKINSON, Mrs Valerie. b 50. **d** 12. NSM Teignmouth, Ideford w Luton, Ashcombe etc *Ex* from 12. *9 Oakley Close, Teignmouth TQ14 8RX* T: (01626) 776771 E: valian09@btinternet.com

ATKINSON, Wendy Sybil. b 53. Man Univ BA 95. NOC 95. **d** 97 **p** 98. NSM Brinnington w Portwood *Ches* 97–99; C 99–01; NSM Werneth from 01. *8 Freshfield Close,*

Marple Bridge, Stockport SK6 5ES T: 0161-427 5612 E: wendyatkinson33@yahoo.co.uk

ATKINSON-JONES, Mrs Susan Florence. b 64. Univ of Wales (Cardiff) BD 93. St Mich Coll Llan 96. **d** 98 **p** 99. C Bargoed and Deri w Brithdir *Llan* 98–05; TV Sanderstead *S'wark* from 05. *35 Audley Drive, Warlingham CR6 9AH* T: (020) 8657 5505 E: susan@sanderstead-parish.org.uk

ATLING, Canon Edwood Brian. b 46. ACIB FCMI. Westcott Ho Cam 00. **d** 02 **p** 03. NSM Godmanchester *Ely* 02–04; P-in-c Abbots Ripton w Wood Walton 04–12; P-in-c Kings Ripton 04–12; P-in-c Houghton w Wyton 04–13; R Hartford and Houghton w Wyton 13–16; P-in-c Fen Drayton 17–18; P-in-c Fenstanton 17–18; P-in-c Fen Drayton w Fenstanton 18–19; RD Huntingdon 06–19; C Hemingford Abbots from 19; C Hemingford Grey from 19; Hon Can Ely Cathl from 10. *Ash Meadow, Meadow Lane, Hemingford Abbots, Huntingdon PE28 9AR* T: (01480) 493975 M: 07775-544679 E: atling@btopenworld.com

ATTLEY, Ronald. b 46. Open Univ BA 87. Brasted Th Coll 66 Chich Th Coll 68. **d** 70 **p** 71. C Heworth St Mary *Dur* 70–73; C Hulme Ascension *Man* 73–75; R Corozal and Orange Walk Belize 76–79; V Leadgate *Dur* 79–84; Chapl HM Rem Cen Ashford 84–87; Chapl HM Pris Ashwell 87–89; Chapl HM Pris Stocken 87–89; Chapl HM Pris Frankland 89–92; Chapl HM YOI Deerbolt 92–96; V Bath St Barn w Englishcombe *B & W* 96–00; Belize 00; V Brinnington w Portwood *Ches* 01–06; P Narrogin Australia 06–12; rtd 12. *103 Clayton Road, Narrogin WA 6312, Australia*

ATTWATER, Mrs Sallyanne. b 48. Westmr Coll Ox MTh 98. S Dios Minl Tr Scheme 86. **d** 94 **p** 95. Chapl Asst Eastbourne Distr Gen Hosp 94–95; Asst Chapl Princess Alice Hospice Esher 94–95; Asst Chapl All SS Eastbourne 94–95; C E Grinstead St Swithun *Chich* 95–98; P-in-c Bishop's Cannings, All Cannings etc *Sarum* 98–10; RD Devizes 07–10; rtd 10; PtO *Chich* from 16. *51 St Kitts Drive, Eastbourne BN23 5TL* T: (01323) 472266 E: sally.attwater@gmail.com

ATTWATER, Canon Stephen Philip. b 47. ALCM 67. Linc Th Coll 85. **d** 87 **p** 88. C Warrington St Elphin *Liv* 87–90; P-in-c Eccleston St Thos 90–94; V 94–99; V Padgate 99–13; AD Warrington 05–12; Hon Can Liv Cathl 05–12; rtd 13; PtO *Ches* from 13. *30 Rowcliffe Avenue, Chester CH4 7PW* M: 07523-492863 E: attwater292@btinternet.com

ATTWOOD, Preb Carl Norman Harry. b 53. Bris Univ BA 74. Cuddesdon Coll BA 76 MA 80. **d** 77 **p** 78. C Tupsley *Heref* 77–82; R Colwall w Upper Colwall and Coddington 82–08; Bp's Voc Officer 83–89; RD Ledbury 90–96; Chapl St Jas Sch Malvern 86–08; Preb Heref Cathl 97–08; rtd 08; PtO *Worc* 82–06; *Heref* from 08. *The Lodge, Old Colwall, Malvern WR13 6HF* T: (01604) 540788 E: carl@attwoods.org

ATTWOOD, David John Edwin. b 51. Dur Univ BA 76 Em Coll Cam BA 73 MA 77. Cranmer Hall Dur 74. **d** 77 **p** 78. C Rodbourne Cheney *Bris* 77–79; C Lydiard Millicent w Lydiard Tregoz 79–85; Dir and Lect Trin Coll Bris 85–97; V Prenton *Ches* 97–02; R Sundridge w Ide Hill and Toys Hill *Roch* 02–13; rtd 13; PtO *Chich* from 17. *65 The Ridge, Hastings TN34 2AB* T: (01424) 440635 E: david.attwood5@btinternet.com

ATTWOOD, Leslie Thomas. b 42. UWE MA 94 Cranfield Univ MBA MCIPD 76. St Steph Ho Ox. **d** 83 **p** 84. C Ascot Heath *Ox* 83–86; Dioc Tr Officer *Truro* 86–88; C Wallasey St Hilary *Ches* 98–00; C Devizes St Pet *Sarum* 00–02; TV Godrevy *Truro* 02–07; TR 07–09; rtd 09; PtO *Truro* from 15. *Chyrempter, Perranuthnoe, Penzance TR20 9NQ* T: (01736) 710449 E: leslie.attwood@gmail.com

ATTWOOD, Peter John. b 44. ACIB 68. SEITE 00. **d** 03 **p** 04. NSM Langton Green *Roch* 03–06; C S Molton w Nymet St George, High Bray etc *Ex* 06–12; RD S Molton 09–12; rtd 12; PtO *B & W* from 12. *Brome Cottage, 86 Castle Hill, Nether Stowey, Bridgwater TA5 1NB* T: (01278) 734588 M: 07714-026402 E: rev@podlea.co.uk

ATTY, Norman Hughes. b 40. Dur Univ BA 62. Cranmer Hall Dur 62. **d** 65 **p** 66. C Blackb St Gabr 65–67; Asst Master Billinge Sch Blackb 67–71; City of Leic Boys' Sch 71–73; P-in-c Elmley Lovett w Hampton Lovett *Worc* 73–78; P-in-c Elmbridge w Rushock 74–78; R Elmley Lovett w Hampton Lovett and Elmbridge etc 78–85; Hon Can Worc Cathl 81–85; rtd 05; PtO *Blackb* from 05. *The Dog Inn, King Street, Whalley, Clitheroe BB7 9SP* T: (01254) 823009 E: attyaoahouse@gmail.com

ATWELL, The Very Revd James Edgar. b 46. Ex Coll Ox BA 68 MA 73 BD 94 Harvard Univ ThM 70. Cuddesdon Coll 68. **d** 70 **p** 71. C E Dulwich St Jo *S'wark* 70–74; C Cambridge Gt St Mary w St Mich *Ely* 74–77; Chapl Jes Coll Cam 77–81; V Towcester w Easton Neston *Pet* 81–95; RD Towcester 83–91; Provost St E 95–00; Dean St E 00–06; Dean Win 06–16; rtd

16; PtO *Bris* from 17; *Ely* from 17. *12 Ventress Farm Court, Cambridge CB1 8HD* E: deanjamesatwell@gmail.com

✠**ATWELL, The Rt Revd Robert Ronald.** b 54. St Jo Coll Dur BA 75 Dur Univ MLitt 79. Westcott Ho Cam 76. **d** 78 **p** 79 **c** 08. C Mill Hill Jo Keble Ch *Lon* 78–81; Chapl Trin Coll Cam 81–87; OSB 87–98; LtO *Ox* 87–97; PtO *Ely* 97–98; V Primrose Hill St Mary w Avenue Road St Paul *Lon* 98–08; Suff Bp Stockport *Ches* 08–14; Bp Ex from 14. *The Palace, Exeter EX1 1HY* T: (01392) 272362 F: 430923 E: bishop.of.exeter@exeter.anglican.org

AUBREY-JONES, Adrian Frederick. b 51. ERMC 04. **d** 07 **p** 08. NSM Dersingham w Anmer and Shernborne *Nor* 07–10; TV Dereham and Distr 10–16; RD Dereham in Mitford 15–16; rtd 16; PtO *Nor* from 17. *23 Tudor Way, Dersingham, King's Lynn PE31 6LX* T: (01485) 542244 M: 07775-514567 E: a335 1adrian@aol.com

AUCHMUTY, Canon John Robert. b 67. ACCA. CITC 89. **d** 92 **p** 93. C Dundela St Mark *D & D* 92–96; I Eglish w Killylea *Arm* 96–01; I Killaney w Carryduff *D & D* 01–07; I Knock from 07; Can Down Cathl from 16. *St Columba's Rectory, 29 King's Road, Knock, Belfast BT5 6JG* T: (028) 9047 1514 E: johnauchmuty@yahoo.com

AUCKEN, Mrs Hazel Margaret. b 61. New Hall Cam BA 83 MA 87 Lon Univ PhD 94. St Hild Coll 17. **d** 19. C Newbold de Verdun, Barlestone and Kirkby Mallory *Leic* from 19; C Peckleton from 19. *36 Main Street, Kirkby Mallory, Leicester LE9 7QB* M: 07976-808959 E: hazel.aucken@outlook.com

AUCKLAND, Mrs Susan Frances. **d** 12 **p** 13. OLM Scole, Brockdish, Billingford, Thorpe Abbots etc *Nor* 12–14; OLM Redenhall w Scole from 14. *Greenbanks, 8 Larch Close, Scole, Diss IP21 4DL* T: (01379) 740325 M: 07825-838403   E: susanauckland@btinternet.com   *or* revsue@7churches.org.uk

AUCKLAND, Archdeacon of. See SIMPSON, The Ven Richard Lee

AUDEN, Lawson <u>Philip</u>. b 45. Qu Coll Birm 73. **d** 78 **p** 81. C Spalding St Mary and St Nic *Linc* 78–81; TV Wordsley *Lich* 81–82; TV Kidderminster St Mary and All SS, Trimpley etc *Worc* 82–87; Ind Chapl 82–87; PtO 87–97; Cov 87–01; *Birm* 90–97; *Lich* 90–97; *Glouc* 94–97; Chapl Wores Community Healthcare NHS Trust 91–97; P-in-c Pebworth w Dorsington and Honeybourne *Glouc* 97–99; Chapl Miss to Seafarers 99–10; Millennium Officer *Glouc* 99–01; PtO 01–16; *B & W* 00–04; rtd 10; PtO *Bris* from 10; *B & W* from 11. *7 Bockenem Close, Thornbury, Bristol BS35 2XH* T: (01454) 412804 M: 07715-553174 E: philipauden@gmail.com

AUDIBERT, Mrs Janice Elizabeth. b 56. **d** 99 **p** 00. OLM Oakdale *Sarum* 99–02; C N Poole Ecum Team 02–06; TV 06–16; P-in-c 16; V Creekmoor from 17. *24 Blackbird Close, Poole BH17 7YA* T/F: (01202) 389751 E: janice.audibert@tesco.net

AUDIBERT, Jean Robert Alain. b 58. Sarum Coll 15. **d** 17 **p** 18. NSM Creekmoor *Sarum* from 17. *24 Blackbird Close, Poole BH17 7YA* T: (01202) 389751

AULD, The Very Revd Jeremy Rodger. b 66. Edin Univ LLB 87 Solicitor 89 Barrister 97. TISEC BD 04. **d** 04 **p** 05. C Edin St Pet 04–06; Hon Chapl Edin Univ 04–06; R Dollar *St And* 06–10; Provost St Paul's Cathl Dundee *Bre* from 10; Hon Chapl Dundee Univ from 10. *4 Richmond Terrace, Dundee DD2 1BQ* T: (01382) 646296 *or* 224486 M: 07828-568002 E: jeremy.auld@btinternet.com *or* provost@saintpaulscathedral.net

AULD, Mrs Sheila Edith. b 38. Newc Poly BA 87 Univ of Northumbria at Newc MA 99. NEOC 91. **d** 94 **p** 95. Project Worker Cedarwood Trust 94–02; rtd 02; PtO *Newc* from 02. *5 Gibson Fields, Hexham NE46 1AS* T: (01434) 602297 E: sheilaauld@ovidian.co.uk

AUSTEN, Canon John. b 46. St Cath Coll Cam BA 69 MA 72. Qu Coll Birm. **d** 71 **p** 72. C Thornaby on Tees *York* 71–74; C Aston St Jas *Birm* 74–82; Chapl Aston Univ 82–88; C Handsworth St Andr 88–11; Hon Can Birm Cathl 06–11; rtd 11; PtO *Birm* from 11. *151 Church Lane, Handsworth, Birmingham B20 2RU* T: 0121-554 8882 E: johnausten151@hotmail.co.uk

AUSTEN, Simon Neil. b 67. Warwick Univ BSc 88. Wycliffe Hall Ox BA 93 MA 97. **d** 94 **p** 95. C Gt Chesham *Ox* 94–98; Chapl Stowe Sch 98–02; V Houghton *Carl* 02–13; R Ex St Leon w H Trin from 13. *St Leonard's Rectory, 27 St Leonard's Road, Exeter EX2 4LA* T: (01392) 286993 E: simon.austen@stleonards.church

AUSTERBERRY, Preb David Naylor. b 35. Birm Univ BA 58. Wells Th Coll 58. **d** 60 **p** 61. C Leek St Edw *Lich* 60–63; Iran 64–70; Chapl CMS Foxbury 70–73; V Walsall Pleck and Bescot *Lich* 73–82; R Brierley Hill 82–88; R Kinnerley w Melverley and Knockin w Maesbrook 88–99; RD Oswestry 92–95; Preb Lich Cathl 96–00; rtd 00; PtO *Heref* from 00;

Lich from 00. *Chad Cottage, Dovaston, Kinnerley, Oswestry SY10 8DT* T: (01691) 682039

AUSTERBERRY, John Maurice. b 62. Birm Univ BA 83 Leeds Univ MA 01. Sarum & Wells Th Coll 84. **d** 86 **p** 87. C Clayton *Lich* 86–89; Asst Chapl Withington Hosp Man 89–95; Chapl Tameside and Glossop NHS Trust 95–99; Chapl Univ Hosp of N Staffs NHS Trust 99–17; Chapl Kath Ho Hospice Stafford from 17; Bp's Adv on Healthcare Chapl *Lich* from 11. *Katharine House Hospice, Weston Road, Stafford ST16 3SB* T: (01785) 254645 E: jausterberry@khhospice.org.uk

AUSTIN (*née* JONES), **Mrs Angela Mary.** b 51. Man Univ BSc 00. WEMTC 10. **d** 13 **p** 14. NSM S Cerney w Cerney Wick, Siddington and Preston *Glouc* 13–17. *April Cottage, Somerford Keynes, Cirencester GL7 6DT* T: (01285) 860692 M: 07776-101253 E: revangiemary@icloud.com

AUSTIN, David Samuel John. b 63. St Jo Coll Dur BATM 11. Cranmer Hall Dur 09. **d** 11 **p** 12. C Addingham *Leeds* 11–15; V New Catton St Luke w St Aug *Nor* 15–18; V Coldhurst and Oldham St Steph *Man* from 18. *Holy Trinity Vicarage, 46 Godson Street, Oldham OL1 2DB* M: 07740-922468 E: dsj.austin@hotmail.com

AUSTIN, Glyn. See AUSTIN, Ronald Glyn

AUSTIN, Miss Jane. b 43. SRN 64 SCM 66. **dss** 81 **d** 87 **p** 94. Tonbridge SS Pet and Paul *Roch* 81–98; C 87–98; Hon Can Roch Cathl 96–98; P-in-c Meltham *Wakef* 98–01; V 01–07; P-in-c Helme 00–01; RD Almondbury 01–06; rtd 07; PtO *Wakef* 08–14; *Leeds* from 14. *177 Bourne View Road, Netherton, Huddersfield HD4 7JS* T: (01484) 664212 E: revjaustin@aol.com

AUSTIN, Leslie Ernest. b 46. Trin Coll Bris 72. **d** 74 **p** 75. C Paddock Wood *Roch* 74–79; C Upper Armley *Ripon* 79–81; V Horton *Bradf* 81–85; V Long Preston w Tosside 85–97; TR Shirwell, Loxhore, Kentisbury, Arlington, etc *Ex* 97–12; RD Shirwell 10–12; rtd 12; PtO *Ches* from 16. *7 Kennedy Close, Chester CH2 2PL* T: (01244) 314723 E: leslie.austin@btinternet.com

AUSTIN, Lucie. b 48. Th Ext Educn Coll. **d** 08 **p** 09. C Sunninghill St Steph S Africa 08–10; PtO *Ox* 11–12; NSM Icknield 12–18; PtO from 18. *20 Raven Road, Stokenchurch, High Wycombe HP14 3QP* T: (01494) 483729 M: 07906-684987 E: luciea48@gmail.com

AUSTIN, Ronald <u>Glyn</u>. b 52. Univ of Wales (Cardiff) BD 90 Univ of Wales MPhil 98. St Mich Coll Llan 88. **d** 90 **p** 91. C Llangynwyd w Maesteg *Llan* 90–91; C Barry All SS 91–93; V Nantymoel w Wyndham 93–97; V Pontyclun w Talygarn 97–02; Tutor St Mich Coll Llan 02–04; V Llansantffraid, Bettws and Aberkenfig *Llan* 04–06; PtO 07–15; Hon C Llangennith w Llanmadoc and Cheriton *S & B* from 15. *The Vicarage, Llangennith, Swansea SA3 1HU* T: (01792) 386782 E: glynaustin52@gmail.com

AUSTIN, Mrs Rosemary Elizabeth. b 68. K Alfred's Coll Win BEd 91 Ex Univ BTh 14. SWMTC 08. **d** 11 **p** 12. C Fremington, Instow and Westleigh *Ex* 11–15; TR Shirwell, Loxhore, Kentisbury, Arlington, etc from 15; RD Shirwell from 18. *The Parsonage, 1 The Glebe, Bratton Fleming, Barnstaple EX31 4RE* T: (01598) 711962 E: rosieaustin@live.co.uk

AUSTIN, Mrs Susan Frances. b 47. Open Univ BA 81. Cant Sch of Min 87. **d** 92 **p** 94. Chapl Ch Ch High Sch Ashford 90–94; C Gt Chart *Cant* 92–94; C Ashford 92–94; C Estover *Ex* 94–96; V Stevenage All SS Pin Green *St Alb* 96–98; P-in-c Bredgar w Bicknor and Frinsted w Wormshill etc *Cant* 00–04; rtd 04; PtO *Cant* 04–13; *B & W* from 14. *Stepping Stones, Park Lane, Carhampton, Minehead TA24 6NL* T: (01643) 822550 M: 07443-948306 E: saraustin@talktalk.net

AVANN, Canon Penelope Joyce. b 46. **dss** 83 **d** 87 **p** 98. Southborough St Pet w Ch Ch and St Matt *Roch* 83–89; Par Dn 87–89; Warden Past Assts 89–10; Par Dn Beckenham St Jo *Roch* 89–94; C 94–02; C Green Street Green and Pratts Bottom 02–16; Hon Can Roch Cathl 94–16; rtd 16; PtO *Chich* from 17. *53 Pilot Road, Hastings TN34 2AP* M: 07745-657557 E: pennyavann@btinternet.com

AVENT, Raymond John. b 28. St D Coll Lamp BA 55 Coll of Resurr Mirfield 55. **d** 57 **p** 58. C Bury H Trin *Man* 57–60; C Holborn St Alb w Saffron Hill St Pet *Lon* 60–66; C Munster Square St Mary Magd 66–67; V Tottenham St Paul 67–77; RD E Haringey 73–77; V Kilburn St Aug w St Jo 77–87; AD Westmr Paddington 79–84; R St Vedast w St Mich-le-Querne etc 87–94; rtd 94; PtO *Lon* 94–00; *Glouc* 00–17. *Maryvale House, Catbrook, Chipping Campden GL55 6DE* T: (01386) 841323 E: raymondavent@btinternet.com

AVERAY, Philip Roger. b 75. **d** 14 **p** 15. C Drybrook, Lydbrook and Ruardean *Glouc* 14–17; V Chepstow *Mon* from 17. *The Vicarage, 25 Mount Way, Chepstow NP16 5NF* T: (01291) 620980 E: revphilipaveray@gmail.com

AVERY, Andrew James. b 58. Open Univ BA 81 Dudley Coll of Educn CertEd 79. St Jo Coll Nottm 06. **d** 08 **p** 09.

C Brundall w Braydeston and Postwick *Nor* 08–11; TV Gt Yarmouth 11–13; P-in-c Greenhithe St Mary *Roch* 13–19; P-in-c Stanground and Farcet *Ely* from 19. *The Vicarage, Main Street, Farcet, Peterborough PE7 3AN* M: 07976-523554 E: revavery@hotmail.co.uk

AVERY, Carol Rosemary. b 58. St Mellitus Coll 14. **d** 16 **p** 17. NSM Stone *Roch* 16–19; C Stanground and Farcet *Ely* from 19. *The Vicarage, Main Street, Farcet, Peterborough PE7 3AN* M: 07976-523555 E: carolavery131@gmail.com

AVERY, Derek Anthony. b 61. Lindisfarne Regional Tr Partnership 16. **d** 19. NSM Newc St Geo and St Hilda from 19. *15 Northumberland Gardens, Jesmond, Newcastle upon Tyne NE2 1HA* E: averyhrd@aol.com

AVERY, Mrs Lydia Dorothy Ann. b 57. Sheff Univ MA 03 Bath Spa Univ Coll PGCE 97. STETS BA 08. **d** 08 **p** 09. C Pilton w Croscombe, N Wootton and Dinder *B & W* 08–11; P-in-c Winscombe and Sandford 11–16; V 16–18; RD Locking 16–18; P-in-c Upper Tas Valley *Nor* from 18. *The Rectory, 16 The Fields, Tacolneston, Norwich NR16 1DG* E: ldavery@btinternet.com

AVERY, Richard Hugh. b 61. All SS Cen for Miss & Min 15. **d** 18 **p** 19. NSM Wallasey St Hilary *Ches* from 18. *90 Dingwall Drive, Wirral CH49 1SQ*

AVERY, Richard Julian. b 52. Keble Coll Ox BA 73. St Jo Coll Nottm 74. **d** 77 **p** 78. C Macclesfield St Mich *Ches* 77–80; Asst P Prince Albert St Dav Canada 82–83; C Becontree St Mary *Chelmsf* 84–87; R Hudson Bay Canada 87–90; R Duncan 90–97; TV Cheltenham St Mark *Glouc* 97–03; PtO 03–06; P-in-c Berkeley w Wick, Breadstone, Newport, Stone etc 06–11; V 11–18; rtd 18. *Timberley, The Ridge, Redlynch, Salisbury SP5 2LN* T: (01725) 238327 E: averys@rjavery.co.uk

AVERY, Robert Edward. b 69. Magd Coll Cam BA 90. Ripon Coll Cuddesdon MPhil 93. **d** 93 **p** 94. C Cen Telford *Lich* 93–96; C Cambridge Gt St Mary w St Mich *Ely* 96–99; V Tamerton Foliot *Ex* 99–03; V Tunbridge Wells K Chas *Roch* 03–15; RD Tunbridge Wells 14–15; R Nor St Pet Mancroft w St Jo Maddermarket 15–17; Nat Adv for Selection Min Division Abps' Coun from 18. *23 Friezland Road, Tunbridge Wells TN4 8LJ* E: robertavery@me.com

AVESON, Ian Henry. b 55. Jes Coll Ox BA 77 MA 81 Univ Coll Dur PGCE 78 Birkbeck Coll Lon MSc 85. St Mich Coll Llan BD 97. **d** 97 **p** 98. C Penarth All SS *Llan* 97–99; TV Aberystwyth *St D* 99–07; V Llandingat w Myddfai 07–19; AD Llandeilo from 12; rtd 19. *18 Chestnut Drive, Abergavenny NP7 5JZ* E: ianaveson@hotmail.com

AVEYARD, Ian. b 46. Liv Univ BSc 68 Sheff Univ MEd 00. ALCD 72 St Jo Coll Nottm 71. **d** 71 **p** 72. C Bradley *Wakef* 71–74; C Knowle *Birm* 74–79; P-in-c Cofton Hackett 79; P-in-c Barnt Green 79; V Cofton Hackett w Barnt Green 80–94; Dioc Dir of Reader Tr 85–94; Warden of Readers 91–94; Course Leader St Jo Coll Nottm 96–99; P-in-c Thanington *Cant* 99–09; Dioc Dir of Ords 99–09; rtd 09; PtO *Glouc* from 16. *19 The Damsells, Tetbury GL8 8JA* T: (01666) 502278 E: ian.aveyard1@btinternet.com

AVIS, Elizabeth Mary. *See* BAXTER, Elizabeth Mary

AVIS, Canon Paul David Loup. b 47. Lon Univ BD 70 PhD 76. Westcott Ho Cam 73. **d** 75 **p** 76. C S Molton, Nymet St George, High Bray etc *Ex* 75–80; V Stoke Canon, Poltimore w Huxham and Rewe etc 80–98; Preb Ex Cathl 93–08; Sub Dean Ex Cathl 97–08; Can Th Ex Cathl 08–13; Hon Prof Ex Univ from 09; Hon Prof Dur Univ from 17; Gen Sec Coun for Chr Unity 98–11; Th Consultant Angl Communion Office 11–12; Chapl to The Queen 08–17; Ed *Ecclesiology* from 04. *Lea Hill, Membury, Axminster EX13 7AQ* T: (01404) 881881 E: reception@leahill.co.uk

AWRE, Canon Richard William Esgar. b 56. Univ of Wales BA 78. Wycliffe Hall Ox 78. **d** 81 **p** 82. C Blackpool St Jo *Blackb* 81–84; Asst Dir of Ords and Voc Adv 84–89; C Altham w Clayton le Moors 84–89; V Longridge 89–99; V Kenilworth St Nic *Cov* 99–15; RD Kenilworth 01–09; Hon Can Cov Cathl 11–15; rtd 15; PtO *Blackb* 16–17. *9 Irwell Mews, Clitheroe BB7 2FR* T: (01200) 424061 E: richard.awre@gmail.com

AXE, Terence Arthur. b 46. **d** 14 **p** 15. NSM Constantine *Truro* 14–16; rtd 16; PtO *Truro* from 16. *Trebarvah Woon, Trebarvah Woon, Constantine, Falmouth TR11 5QJ* T: (01326) 340140 E: tvaxe123@gmail.com

AXELSON, Guy Anton. b 84. Cape Town Univ BCom 07. Wycliffe Hall Ox BTh 16. **d** 16 **p** 17. C Ches Square St Mich w St Phil *Lon* from 16. *24 Sullivan Road, London SE11 4UH* T: (020) 7730 2170 M: 07523-457097 E: guyaxelson@gmail.com *or* guy@stmichaelschurch.org.uk

AXFORD, Mrs Christine Ruth. b 53. Glam Coll of Educn BEd 75. STETS BTh 04. **d** 00 **p** 02. NSM Yeovil w Kingston Pitney *B & W* 00–01; NSM N Hartismere *St E* 02–08; NSM Tyndale *Glouc* 08–18; rtd 18. *12 Cherry Road,*

Chipping Sodbury, Bristol BS37 6HJ T: (01454) 321161 E: chris@robaxford.plus.com

AXFORD, Canon Robert Henry. b 50. Univ of Wales BEng 72 CEng 85. Sarum & Wells Th Coll 89. **d** 91 **p** 92. C Castle Cary w Ansford *B & W* 91–95; P-in-c Queen Camel w W Camel, Corton Denham etc 95–01; R 01–02; R N Hartismere *St E* 02–08; RD Hartismere 04–08; P-in-c Wotton-under-Edge w Ozleworth, N Nibley etc *Glouc* 08–11; V Tyndale 11–18; AD Wotton 09–13; Hon Can Glouc Cathl 13–18; rtd 18. *12 Cherry Road, Chipping Sodbury, Bristol BS37 6HJ* T: (01454) 321161 E: rob@robaxford.plus.com

AXON, Andrew John. b 76. Univ of Wales (Lamp) BTh 97 Univ of Wales (Ban) MTh 09. Trin Coll Bris 99. **d** 01 **p** 02. C Sevenhampton w Charlton Abbots, Hawling etc *Glouc* 01–05; V Ruddington *S'well* 05–10; P-in-c Hucclecote *Glouc* 10–16; P-in-c Lamberhurst and Matfield *Roch* 16–18; V from 18; RD Paddock Wood from 19. *The Vicarage, 29 Hopgarden Close, Lamberhurst, Tunbridge Wells TN3 8DY* E: revandrew@mail.com

AXTELL, Stephen Geoffrey. b 57. Open Univ BSc 96. St Jo Coll Nottm 00. **d** 02 **p** 03. C Coseley Ch Ch *Worc* 02–06; Chapl Rotterdam *Eur* 06–12; Chapl Rotterdam w Schiedam Miss to Seafarers 06–12; V Westfield St Mary *Carl* from 12. *St Mary's Vicarage, Salisbury Street, Workington CA14 3TA*

AYERS, Canon John. b 40. FCollP Bris Univ BEd 75 Newton Park Coll Bath MEd 89 FRSA 94. **d** 77 **p** 78. NSM Corsham *Bris* 77–79; NSM Gtr Corsham 79–88; NSM Ditteridge 88–92; NSM Box w Hazlebury and Ditteridge 93–10; Hon Can Bris Cathl 94–10; rtd 10; PtO *Bris* from 10. *Toad Hall, Middlehill, Box, Corsham SN13 8QP* T: (01225) 742123 E: middlehill@supanet.com

AYERS, Martin John. b 79. Trin Hall Cam MA 03 Solicitor 04. Oak Hill Th Coll 08. **d** 11 **p** 12. C Preston All SS *Blackb* 11–15; R Glas St Silas from 16. *St Silas' Church, 69 Park Road, Glasgow G4 9JE* T: 0141-337 2276 M: 07976-170916 E: martin.ayers@talk21.com

AYERS, The Ven Paul Nicholas. b 61. St Pet Coll Ox BA 82 MA 86. Trin Coll Bris 83. **d** 85 **p** 86. C Clayton *Bradf* 85–88; C Keighley St Andr 88–91; V Wrose 91–97; V Pudsey St Lawr and St Paul 97–17; Adn Leeds from 17; Hon Can Bradf Cathl from 16. *2 Wike Ridge Avenue, Leeds LS17 9NL* T: 0113-269 0594 M: 07837-370678 E: paul.ayers@leeds.anglican.org

AYERST, Gabrielle Mary. b 52. St Luke's Coll Ex BEd 74. SEITE 07. **d** 00 **p** 01. NSM Surbiton St Andr and St Mark *S'wark* 00–08; PtO Newc from 08. *6 Bell Tower Park, Berwick-upon-Tweed TD15 1ND* T: (01289) 302680 E: gadrillea@paff.nsf.org.uk *or* gabrielleayerst@hotmail.co.uk

AYLETT, Miss Barbara Celia. b 46. Open Univ BA 91 SRN 73 SCM 74 Surrey Univ PGCE 83. **d** 14 **p** 15. OLM Harlow Town Cen w Lt Parndon *Chelmsf* 14–18; NSM from 18. *105 Hare Street Springs, Harlow CM19 4AT* T: (01279) 413749 E: b.aylett@btinternet.com

AYLING, Mrs Ann Margaret. b 39. Edge Hill Coll of HE TCert 59. STETS 07. **d** 10 **p** 11. NSM Bridport *Sarum* 10–17; PtO from 17. *4 Manor Farm Court, Walditch, Bridport DT6 4LQ* T: (01308) 424896 E: ann@bridport-team-ministry.org

AYLING, Miss Dallas Jane. b 53. Trin Coll Bris BA 94. **d** 98 **p** 99. C Ellesmere Port *Ches* 98–02; TV Birkenhead Priory 02–06; TR 06–07; R 07–16; RD Birkenhead 11–16; R Dawlish w Holcombe, Cofton and Starcross *Ex* from 16; RD Kenn from 19. *The Vicarage, 13 West Cliff Road, Dawlish EX7 9EB* T: (01626) 867386 E: revddallasayling@yahoo.co.uk

AYO, Ms Margaret Florence Aceng. b 55. Buwalasi Teacher Tr Coll CertEd 75 Lon Metrop Univ MEd 03. St Mellitus Coll BA 15. **d** 15 **p** 16. NSM Notting Dale St Clem w St Mark and St Jas *Lon* 15–19; NSM Earl's Court Road St Phil from 19. *37 Mitchell House, White City Estate, London W12 7PF* T: (020) 8743 0896 M: 07904-045804 E: margaret.ayo@stclementsjames.org

AYODEJI, Olakunle. b 66. Obafemi Awolowo Univ BSc 86. Westcott Ho Cam 12. **d** 14 **p** 15. C Pinner *Lon* 14–17; V Highgate St Mich from 17. *St Michael's Church, South Grove, London N6 6BJ* T: (020) 8340 7279 M: 07790-504812 E: kunleayodeji@yahoo.co.uk *or* office@stmichaelshighgate.org

AYRES, Dean Matthew. b 68. Bris Univ BSc 89. Ridley Hall Cam 00. **d** 02 **p** 03. C Epsom Common Ch Ch *Guildf* 02–06; Chapl W Lon Univ 06–16; C Acton St Mary from 16. *11 Packington Road, London W3 8FB* T: (020) 8992 9384 E: dean.m.ayres@outlook.com

AZER, Ms Helen. b 77. Ch Ch Ox BA 00 MA 03. Wycliffe Hall Ox BTh 04. **d** 04 **p** 05. C Ox St Aldate 04–07; C Cumnor from 07. *St Michael's Church Office, 1 Abingdon Road, Cumnor, Oxford OX2 9QN* T: (01865) 861541 E: helen.azer@heartcry.co.uk

B

BABB, Canon Geoffrey. b 42. Man Univ BSc 64 MA(Theol) 74 Linacre Coll Ox BA 67. Ripon Hall Ox 65. **d** 68 **p** 69. C Heywood St Luke *Man* 68–71; C-in-c Loundsley Green Ascension CD *Derby* 71–76; TV Old Brampton and Loundsley Green 76–77; TV Stafford and Dioc Soc Resp Officer *Lich* 77–88; Preb Lich Cathl 87–88; P-in-c Salford Sacred Trin *Man* 88–99; Dir CME 88–99; TR Wythenshawe 99–06; TV 06–07; Hon Can Man Cathl 89–07; rtd 07; PtO *Man* 07–08 and 13–18; *Newc* 07–10; *Derby* 10–12; *Lich* from 18. *The Vicarage, Clayton Lane, Newcastle ST5 3DW* M: 07751-472632 E: geoffrey-babb@outlook.com

BABB, Mrs Julia Bebbington. b 69. Man Univ BA 98 St Jo Coll Dur MA 00. Cranmer Hall Dur. **d** 00 **p** 01. C Langley and Parkfield *Man* 00–04; V Cowgate *Newc* 04–10; P-in-c Whittington *Derby* 10–11; R 12; Tr Officer CMD and IME 4-7 *Man* 12–18; V Clayton *Lich* from 18. *The Vicarage, Clayton Lane, Newcastle ST5 3DW* E: juliabbabb@icloud.com

BABBINGTON, David Paul Simon. b 66. Newman Univ MA 19. Qu Coll Birm BA 15. **d** 15 **p** 16. C Pelsall *Lich* 15–19; P-in-c Walsall Wood from 19. *The Vicarage, 2 St John's Close, Walsall Wood WS9 9NH* T: (01543) 360558 E: davidbabbington@me.com

BABER, Helen Charlotte. b 67. STETS 10. **d** 13 **p** 14. C Stratton St Margaret w S Marston etc *Bris* 13–17; R Lann Pydar *Truro* from 17. *1 Tippett Meadow, St Columb TR9 6TY* M: 07767-310773 E: helenbaber@me.com

BABINGTON, Canon Peter Gervase. b 69. Aston Univ BSc 91 Birm Univ MPhil 03. Cuddesdon Coll BTh 98. **d** 98 **p** 99. C Salter Street and Shirley *Birm* 98–02; V Bournville from 02; AD Moseley 07–13; Hon Can Birm Cathl from 15. *The Vicarage, 61 Linden Road, Birmingham B30 1JT* T: 0121-472 1209 *or* 472 7215 E: vicar@bournvilleparishchurch.org.uk *or* pgbabington@gmail.com

BACH, Mrs Frances Mary. b 48. Open Univ BA AIL. CITC BTh. **d** 94 **p** 95. NSM Ballynure and Ballyeaston *Conn* 94–96; C Larne and Inver 96–99; C Glynn w Raloo 96–99; I Armoy w Loughguile and Drumtullagh 99–12; rtd 13. *141A Ballinlea Road, Stranocum, Ballymoney BT53 8PX* T: (028) 2075 1081 E: frances.bach@btinternet.com

BACH, John Edward Goulden. b 40. Dur Univ BA 66. Cranmer Hall Dur 66. **d** 69 **p** 70. C Bradf Cathl 69–72; Chapl and Lect NUU 73–84; Chapl and Lect Ulster Univ 84–15; rtd 15. *141A Ballinlea Road, Stranocum, Ballymoney BT53 8PX* T: (028) 2075 1081 E: revjegbach@hotmail.com

BACK, Esther Elaine. *See* McCAFFERTY, Esther Elaine

BACKHOUSE, Alan Eric. b 37. Keble Coll Ox BA 61 MA 67. Tyndale Hall Bris 61. **d** 64 **p** 65. C Burnage St Marg *Man* 64–67; C Cheadle Hulme St Andr *Ches* 67–70; V Buglawton 70–80; V New Ferry 80–87; V Tarvin 87–93; V Knypersley *Lich* 93–99; Patr Sec Ch Soc Trust 99–00; C Watford *St Alb* 99–02; rtd 02; PtO *St As* from 09. *Perelandra, Church Pitch, Llandyssil, Montgomery SY15 6LQ* T: (01686) 669963 E: alanbackhouse@yahoo.com

BACKHOUSE, Miss Carol Louisa. b 86. York Univ BSc 10. Westcott Ho Cam 13. **d** 16 **p** 17. C Northallerton w Kirby Sigston *York* from 16. *1 Ashlands Road, Northallerton DL6 1HA* M: 07720-931415 E: carolbackhouse@yahoo.co.uk

BACKHOUSE, Colin. b 41. Birm Coll of Art & Design BA 67 MCSD 82. Oak Hill Th Coll 85. **d** 87 **p** 88. C Branksome St Clem *Sarum* 87–91; P-in-c Bluntisham cum Earith w Colne and Woodhurst *Ely* 91–92; R 92–07; rtd 07; PtO Cyprus and the Gulf from 09. *2 Spencer Road, Reading RG2 8TR* T: 0118-437 0780 M: 07811-960048 E: colin.backhouse@gmail.com

BACKHOUSE, John. b 30. Univ Coll Southn BA 50. Wycliffe Hall Ox 51. **d** 53 **p** 54. C Eccleston St Luke *Liv* 53–55; C Maghull 55–58; V Lathom 58–64; Area Sec CMS Linc and Ely 64–71; PtO *Leic* 72–78; *Cov* 75–78; V Thorpe Acre w Dishley *Leic* 78–83; R Ab Kettleby Gp 83–89; P-in-c Bitteswell 89–94; RD Guthlaxton II 90–94; rtd 94; PtO *Leic* 94–15. *29 Peashill Close, Sileby, Loughborough LE12 7PT* T: (01509) 812016

BACON, David Gary. b 62. Leic Univ BA 83 Southn Univ BTh 88. Sarum & Wells Th Coll 85. **d** 88 **p** 89. C Bromley St Mark *Roch* 88–92; C Lynton, Brendon, Countisbury, Lynmouth etc *Ex* 92; TV 92–95; P-in-c Lapford, Nymet Rowland and Coldridge 95–99; P-in-c Bramshaw and Landford w Plaitford *Sarum* 99–05; P-in-c Bramshaw and Landford w Plaitford *Sarum* 05–06; TV Forest and Avon from 06; RD Alderbury from 14. *The Rectory, Bramshaw, Lyndhurst SO43 7JF* T: (01794) 390256 E: davidbramrec@aol.com

BACON, Derek Robert Alexander. b 44. Birkbeck Coll Lon BA 92 MSc 94 Ulster Univ PhD 04. TCD Div Sch 69. **d** 71 **p** 72. C Templemore *D & R* 71–73; V Choral Derry Cathl 72–73; C Heeley *Sheff* 74–76; V Sheff St Pet Abbeydale 76–82; Chapl Gt Ormond Street Hosp for Children NHS Trust 82–95; Visiting Fell Ulster Univ 95–97; PtO *Conn* from 04; rtd 09. *19 Ballycairn Road, Coleraine BT51 3HX*

BACON, Janet Ann. b 57. Man Univ LLB 78. NTMTC 95. **d** 98 **p** 99. NSM Stifford *Chelmsf* 98–01; P-in-c Sandbach Heath w Wheelock *Ches* 01–03; V 03–12; V Cheadle Hulme All SS from 12. *All Saints' Vicarage, 27 Church Road, Cheadle Hulme, Cheadle SK8 7JL* T: 0161-485 3455 E: janetbacon23@sky.com

BACON, John Martindale. b 22. St Aid Birkenhead 54. **d** 57 **p** 58. C Bury St Paul *Man* 57–59; C-in-c Clifton Green St Thos CD 59–71; V Astley Bridge 71–87; rtd 87; PtO *Man* 87–00; *Blackb* 87–11. *21 Lichen Close, Charnock Richard, Chorley PR7 5TT* T: (01257) 792535 E: johnandcon.bacon@tiscali.co.uk

BACON, Mrs Julie Sara. b 65. Solicitor. Yorks Min Course. **d** 14 **p** 15. C Shipley St Pet *Leeds* 14–17; P-in-c Kildwick from 17; P-in-c Cononley w Bradley from 17. *2B Nab Lane, Shipley BD18 4HB*

BADEN, Peter Michael. b 35. CCC Cam BA 59 MA 62. Cuddesdon Coll 58. **d** 60 **p** 61. C Hunslet St Mary and Stourton *Ripon* 60–63; Lic to Offic *Wakef* 63–64; C E Grinstead St Swithun *Chich* 65–68; V Brighton St Martin 68–74; TR Brighton Resurr 74–76; R Westbourne and V Stansted 76–84; V Copthorne 84–91; V Clifton and R Dean *Carl* 91–00; P-in-c Mosser 89–00; rtd 00; PtO *Pet* from 00; *Carl* 01–06. *62 Springfield Avenue, Thrapston, Kettering NN14 4TN* T: (01832) 733186 E: pmbaden@gmail.com

BADGER-WATTS, Mrs Lorraine Gwyneth. b 76. De Montfort Univ BSc 99. St Mich Coll Llan BTh 13. **d** 13 **p** 14. C Petryal and Betws yn Rhos *St As* 13–16; V Gorsedd w Brynford, Ysgeifiog and Whitford 16; TV Estuary and Mountain Miss Area 17–19; R Colchester, New Town and The Hythe *Chelmsf* from 19. *The Rectory, 24 New Town Road, Colchester CO1 2EF* M: 07402-429991 E: revbadger.watts@hotmail.com

BADHAM, Prof Paul Brian Leslie. b 42. Jes Coll Ox BA 65 MA 69 Jes Coll Cam BA 68 MA 72 Birm Univ PhD 73. Westcott Ho Cam 66. **d** 68 **p** 69. C Edgbaston St Bart *Birm* 68–69; C Rubery 69–73; LtO *St D* from 73; Lect Th Univ of Wales (Lamp) 73–83; Sen Lect 83-88; Reader 88-91; Prof Th 91–07; rtd 07; Dir Alister Hardy Relig Experience Research Cen from 02. *11 Petherton Mews, Llantrisant Road, Llandaff, Cardiff CF5 2SJ* M: 07968-626902 E: pblbadham@hotmail.com

BAGE, Damon John. b 71. Teesside Univ BA 95. St Steph Ho Ox 01. **d** 03 **p** 04. C Stockton St Jo *Dur* 03–07; P-in-c Norton St Mich 07–13; Chapl John Snow Coll Dur 06–13; V Cockerton from 13. *St Mary's Vicarage, 17 Newton Lane, Darlington DL3 9EX* E: revddamon@icloud.com

BAGG, Marcus Christopher. b 75. Bath Univ BSc 96. Trin Coll Bris BA 07. **d** 07 **p** 08. C Stanmore *Win* 07–11; P-in-c Gatcombe *Portsm* 11–14; R from 14; P-in-c Carisbrooke St Nic 11–14; V from 14; P-in-c Carisbrooke St Mary 11–14; V from 14. *The Vicarage, 56 Castle Road, Carisbrooke, Newport PO30 1DP* T: (01983) 718908 E: marcus.carisbrooke@yahoo.co.uk

BAGGS, Steven. b 70. **d** 09 **p** 10. NSM White Horse *Sarum* 09–12; V Frome Valley *Heref* from 12. *The Vicarage, Bishop's Frome, Worcester WR6 5AP*

BAGNALL, Katherine Janet. b 67. Sunderland Univ BEd 92. NEOC 02. **d** 05 **p** 06. NSM Monkwearmouth *Dur* 05–06; C Darlington St Mark w St Paul 06–10; P-in-c Sunderland St Mary and St Pet from 10. *The Clergy House, Springwell Road, Sunderland SR3 4DY* T: 0191-528 3754 E: katherine.bagnall@ntlworld.com

BAGOTT, Paul Andrew. b 61. Leeds Univ BA 85. Westcott Ho Cam 86. **d** 88 **p** 89. C Chingford SS Pet and Paul *Chelmsf* 88–91; C Pimlico St Sav *Lon* 91–95; P-in-c Clerkenwell H Redeemer and St Mark 95–01; V Clerkenwell H Redeemer 02–13; V Clerkenwell St Mark 02–13; P-in-c Earl's Court St Cuth w St Matthias from 13; PV Westmr Abbey from 08. *St Cuthbert's Clergy House, 50 Philbeach Gardens, London SW5 9EB* T: (020) 7370 3263

BAGSHAW, Paul Stanley. b 55. Selw Coll Cam BA 78 MA 81 CQSW 80. NOC 85. **d** 88 **p** 89. Ind Missr *Sheff* 86–90; C Handsworth Woodhouse 88–90; NSM 91–93; C Newark

S'well 93–96; P-in-c Ordsall 96–08; C Byker St Ant *Newc* 12–14; V Billy Mill from 14; V Marden w Preston Grange from 14. *St Aidan's Vicarage, 29 Billy Mill Lane, North Shields NE29 8BZ* T: 0191-908 4474 E: st.hildamarden@gmail.com

BAGSHAWE, John Allen. b 45. St Jo Coll Dur BA 70. Cranmer Hall Dur 67. **d** 71 **p** 72. C Bridlington Priory *York* 71–75; C N Ferriby 75–79; V Kingston upon Hull St Matt w St Barn 79–10; AD W Hull 00–10; rtd 10; PtO *York* 10–15. *334 Southcoates Lane, Hull HU9 3TR* T: (01482) 702220 E: allen@bagshawe.karoo.co.uk

BAGULEY, Andrew James. b 72. Glas Univ BSc 94 Jordanhill Coll Glas PGCE 97. Ridley Hall Cam 13. **d** 15 **p** 16. C Belper *Derby* 15–19; P-in-c Ilkeston St Jo from 19; P-in-c Ilkeston St Mary from 19. *Address temp unknown* E: andrew.baguley@which.net

BAGULEY, David Mark. b 61. Man Univ BSc 83 MSc 86 Open Univ MBA 94 Wolfs Coll Cam PhD 05. ERMC 09. **d** 11 **p** 12. Visiting Prof Anglia Ruskin Univ *Chelmsf* from 10; NSM Milton *Ely* 11–17; NSM Waterbeach 11–17; NSM Landbeach 11–17; PtO *S'well* 17–18; NSM Sherwood from 18. *St Martin's Vicarage, 12 Trevose Gardens, Nottingham NG5 3FU* T: 0115-840 6454 E: david.baguley@nottingham.ac.uk

BAHADUR, Naeem. b 82. Punjab Univ BA 03 Gujranwala Th Sem MDiv 08. Qu Foundn Birm 15. **d** 17 **p** 18. C Hyson Green and Forest Fields *S'well* from 17. *8 Austen Avenue, Nottingham NG7 6PE* T: 0115-874 0727 M: 07538-129820 E: rev.bahadur@yahoo.com

BAILES, Kenneth. b 35. Dur Univ BA 69 DPhil. **d** 71 **p** 72. C Redcar *York* 71–73; TV Redcar w Kirkleatham 73–74; P-in-c Appleton Roebuck w Acaster Selby 74–80; P-in-c Sutton on the Forest 80–82; R Stamford Bridge Gp 82–90; V Healaugh w Wighill, Bilbrough and Askham Richard 90–95; rtd 95; PtO *York* 98–11. *Lawnwith House, Stuton Grove, Tadcaster LS24 9BD* T: (01937) 831245 M: 07764-614139 E: kb13@btinternet.com

BAILES, Mrs Rachel Jocelyn. b 60. Huddersfield Sch of Music BA 81 Kingston Poly PGCE 83 Leeds Univ MEd 96 BA 07. NOC 04. **d** 07 **p** 08. C Thornes and Lupset *Wakef* 07–11; Chapl Mid Yorks Hosps NHS Trust 11–16; Chapl York Teaching Hosp NHS Foundn Trust from 16. *York Hospitals NHS Foundation Trust, Wigginton Road, York YO31 8HE* T: (01904) 631313 E: rjbailes@tiscali.co.uk *or* rachel.bailes@york.nhs.uk

BAILEY, Preb Adrian Richard. b 57. Cranmer Hall Dur 89. **d** 91 **p** 92. C Oswestry St Oswald *Lich* 91–94; C Shobnall 94–99; C Burton 94–99; Town Cen Chapl 94–99; P-in-c Shobnall 99–01; P-in-c Hengoed w Gobowen 01–08; C Weston Rhyn and Selattyn 05–07; P-in-c Selattyn 07–08; P-in-c Selattyn and Hengoed w Gobowen 08–19; Chapl Robert Jones/Agnes Hunt Orthopaedic and Distr Hosp NHS Trust 01–19; RD Oswestry *Lich* 09–17; Preb Lich Cathl 13–19; rtd 19; PtO *Lich* from 19. *16 Rowlands Close, Morda, Oswestry SY10 9RQ* E: arb2@totalise.co.uk *or* adrian.bailey@rjah.nhs.uk

BAILEY, Alan. *See* BAILEY, Graham Alan

BAILEY, Andrew Henley. b 57. AKC 78. Sarum & Wells Th Coll 79. **d** 80 **p** 81. C Romsey *Win* 80–83; V Bournemouth St Alb 83–93; R Milton from 93. *The Rectory, Church Lane, New Milton BH25 6QN* T/F: (01425) 615150 E: miltonrectory@gmail.com

BAILEY, Andrew John. b 37. Trin Coll Cam BA 61 MA. Ridley Hall Cam 60. **d** 63 **p** 64. C Drypool *York* 63–66; C Melton Mowbray w Thorpe Arnold *Leic* 66–69; C-in-c Skelmersdale Ecum Cen *Liv* 69–79; V Langley Mill *Derby* 79–90; V Gt Faringdon w Lt Coxwell *Ox* 90–02; AD Vale of White Horse 97–01; rtd 02; PtO *Ches* 02–17; *York* from 18. *53 Vyner House, Front Street, Acomb, York YO24 3DW* T: (01904) 914516 E: 58abailey@gmail.com

BAILEY, Canon Angela. b 61. Kent Univ BA 82. Qu Coll Birm 83. **dss** 85 **d** 87 **p** 94. Reculver and Herne Bay St Bart *Cant* 85–88; Par Dn 87–88; Asst Chapl Hull Univ *York* 88–92; Sen Chapl 94–98; PtO 92–94; P-in-c Rowley w Skidby 98–09; R 10–14; V Walkington 10–14; P-in-c Bishop Burton 10–14; RD Beverley 07–12; Chapl E Riding Community Health Trust 98–04; Dioc Ecum Officer *York* 07–09; Dioc Adv for Lay Development from 14; Can and Preb York Minster from 13. *Diocesan House, Aviator Court, Clifton Moor, York YO30 4WJ* T: (01904) 699500 E: angela@petermichael.karoo.co.uk *or* angela.bailey@yorkdiocese.org

BAILEY, Brendan John. b 61. Strathclyde Univ BSc 83 K Coll Lon MA 99. Ripon Coll Cuddesdon BTh 93. **d** 94 **p** 95. C Purley *Ox* 94–99; R Nettlebed w Bix, Highmoor, Pishill etc 99–17; P-in-c Nuffield 06–17; PtO 18–19; C Purley from 19. *St Mary's Church, St Mary's Avenue, Purley on Thames, Reading RG8 8BJ* E: brendan.bailey@stmaryspurley.org.uk

BAILEY, Canon Brian Constable. b 36. K Coll Lon AKC 62. **d** 63 **p** 64. C Mill Hill Jo Keble Ch *Lon* 63–66; C Gt

Stanmore 66–69; C Gt Marlow *Ox* 69–72; R Burghfield 72–81; R Wokingham All SS 81–96; Hon Can Ch Ch 94–96; TV Pinhoe and Broadclyst *Ex* 96–00; rtd 00; V of the Close Sarum Cathl 00–01. *2 Rose Cottages, Maudlin Road, Totnes TQ9 5TG* T: (01803) 865992 E: brianbailey579@btinternet.com

BAILEY, Mrs Carolyn. b 64. Ox Min Course 07. **d** 10 **p** 11. NSM Gt Missenden w Ballinger and Lt Hampden *Ox* 10–17; V Ness Gp *Linc* from 17. *The Vicarage, 10 Church Street, Thurlby, Bourne PE10 0EH* M: 07841-583303 E: carolyn.bailey81@icloud.com

BAILEY, Mrs Christine Ann. b 55. All SS Cen for Miss & Min 11. **d** 14 **p** 15. OLM Urmston *Man* 14–15; OLM Davyhulme Ch Ch and Urmston from 15. *16 Westmorland Road, Urmston, Manchester M41 9HJ* T: 0161-747 5123 E: christine.bailey70@ntlworld.com

BAILEY, The Ven David Charles. b 52. Linc Coll Ox BA 75 MA 78 MSc 77. St Jo Coll Nottm BA 79. **d** 80 **p** 81. C Worksop St Jo *S'well* 80–83; C Edgware *Lon* 83–87; V S Cave and Ellerker w Broomfleet *York* 87–97; RD Howden 91–97; V Beverley Minster 97–08; P-in-c Routh 97–08; Can and Preb York Minster 98–08; Adn Bolton *Man* 08–18; rtd 18. *2 Field View, Clotherholme Road, Ripon HG4 2RH* T: (01765) 607045

BAILEY, David Ross. b 58. UNISA BTh 82. St Bede's Coll Umtata 80. **d** 82 **p** 82. C Somerset West S Africa 82–85; C Elgin 85–87; R Atlantis 87–95; R Salt River 95–08; P-in-c Honicknowle *Ex* 08–14; C Ernesettle 08–14; C Whitleigh 08–14; V Ernesettle, Whitleigh and Honicknowle from 14. *St Francis's Presbytery, 53 Little Dock Lane, Plymouth PL5 2LP* T/F: (01752) 773874 M: 07864-059302 E: fr.david@blueyonder.co.uk

BAILEY, Dennis. b 53. Man Univ BEd 74 BMus 74 TCD MA 06 PhD 11. St Jo Coll Nottm BTh 79. **d** 79 **p** 80. C Netherley Ch Ch CD *Liv* 79–83; S Africa from 83. *PO Box 625, Hilton, 3245 South Africa* T: (0027) 82-275 3641 *or* 33-343 1093 E: dbaileysa@gmail.com

BAILEY, Derek William. b 39. Man Univ BA 96. Cranmer Hall Dur 64. **d** 67 **p** 68. C Sutton *Liv* 67–69; C Chapel-en-le-Frith *Derby* 69–73; V Hadfield 73–90; R Collyhurst *Man* 90–95; V Chaddesden St Mary *Derby* 95–02; rtd 02; PtO *York* from 03. *187 Bishopthorpe Road, York YO23 1PD* T: (01904) 628080 E: derekwbailey@btinternet.co.uk

BAILEY, Edward Peter. b 35. Nottm Univ MA 93. Qu Coll Birm. **d** 62 **p** 63. C Ordsall *S'well* 62–66; C Clifton w Glapton 66–71; V Lady Bay 71–83; Relig Affairs Adv to Radio Trent 83–85; C Gedling 86–89; C Bilborough St Jo 89–00; rtd 00; PtO *York* 00–15. *Cragside Cottage, 18 Egton Road, Aislaby, Whitby YO21 1SU*

BAILEY, Elizabeth. b 47. **d** 03 **p** 04. OLM Bishop's Cannings, All Cannings etc *Sarum* 03–09; rtd 09; PtO *Sarum* from 09. *Lynden, The Street, Bishop's Cannings, Devizes SN10 2LD* T: (01380) 860400 E: liz@iftco.com

BAILEY, Mrs Elizabeth Carmen. b 45. EAMTC 89. **d** 93 **p** 94. NSM Roughton and Felbrigg, Metton, Sustead etc *Nor* 93–95 and 99–02; P-in-c 02–06; NSM Cromer and Gresham 95–99; C Buxton w Oxnead, Lammas and Brampton 06–07; C Bure Valley 07–10; rtd 10; PtO *Nor* from 12. *5 Warren Road, Southrepps, Norwich NR11 8UN* T: (01263) 833785

BAILEY, Graham Alan. b 52. N Staffs Poly BSc 75. **d** 08 **p** 09. NSM Betley *Lich* from 08; NSM Madeley from 11. *10 Ladygates, Betley, Crewe CW3 9AN* T: (01270) 820043 E: alan.bailey@beulahscience.co.uk

BAILEY, Helen Margaret. b 69. Hull Univ BA 92 PGCE 99 SS Coll Cam BA 09 MA 14. Westcott Ho Cam 07. **d** 10 **p** 11. C High Harrogate Ch Ch *Ripon* 10–14; R Minchinhampton w Box and Amberley *Glouc* 14–18; V Broadstone *Sarum* from 18. *St John's Vicarage, Macaulay Road, Broadstone BH18 8AR* E: revdhelenbailey@gmail.com

BAILEY, Canon Ivan John. b 33. Keble Coll Ox BA 57 MA 65. St Steph Ho Ox 57. **d** 59 **p** 60. C Ipswich All Hallows *St E* 59–62; Clerical Sec CEMS 62–66; V Cringleford *Nor* 66–81; RD Humbleyard 73–81; R Colney 80–81; Relig Adv Anglia TV 81–91; P-in-c Kirby Bedon w Bixley and Whitlingham *Nor* 81–92; Hon Can Nor Cathl 84–98; Chapl St Andr Hosp Norwich 92–94; Chapl Mental Health Unit Nor HA 92–94; Chapl Norfolk Mental Health Care NHS Trust 94–98; rtd 98; PtO *Nor* from 98. *21 Cranleigh Rise, Norwich NR4 6PQ* T: (01603) 453565 E: ivanbailey21@gmail.com

BAILEY, Ms Jane Rome. b 50. Univ of Wales (Ban) BA 99 BTh 03. Ban Ord Course 00. **d** 03 **p** 04. C Llifon and Talybolion Deanery *Ban* 03–06; C Trefdraeth w Aberffraw, Llangwaladr etc 06–10; TV Holyhead 10–13; C Bro Cybi from 13. *St Seiriol's House, 25 Gors Avenue, Holyhead LL65 1PB* T: (01407) 764780 E: jane.r.bailey@btinternet.com *or* jane.r.bailey3@gmail.com

BAILEY, Joyce Mary Josephine. *See* OUTEN, Joyce Mary Josephine

BAILEY, Justin Mark. b 55. Birm Univ BA 77 Southn Univ MTh 97 Wolv Poly PGCE 78. Ripon Coll Cuddesdon 90. **d** 92 **p** 93. C Oakdale *Sarum* 92–96; P-in-c Milton Abbas, Hilton w Cheselbourne etc 96–05; P-in-c Piddletrenthide w Plush, Alton Pancras etc 02–05; V Piddle Valley, Hilton, Cheselbourne etc 05–06; P-in-c Bruton and Distr *B & W* 06–17; R Bruton, Brewham, Pitcombe and Shepton Montague from 17. *8 Wellesley Green, Bruton BA10 0DU* T: (01749) 812616 E: frjustin@btinternet.com

BAILEY, Mrs Katharine Ann. b 55. SEITE 14. **d** 16 **p** 17. NSM Horsham *Chich* from 16. *3 Harding Lane, Broadbridge Heath, Horsham RH12 3GS* T: (01403) 276736 E: kate.bailey@stjohnsbbh.org.uk

BAILEY, Mark David. b 62. Ripon Coll Cuddesdon 87. **d** 90 **p** 91. C Leigh Park *Portsm* 90–93; C Fleet *Guildf* 93–95; TV Basingstoke *Win* 95–00; P-in-c Twyford and Owslebury and Morestead 00–08; R Lower Dever from 08. *The Rectory, 6 Green Close, South Wonston, Winchester SO21 3EE* T: (01962) 886883 E: mdbailey066@gmail.com

BAILEY, Martin Tristram. b 57. Oak Hill Th Coll 89. **d** 91 **p** 92. C Brundall w Braydeston and Postwick *Nor* 91–95; TV Plymouth St Andr and Stonehouse *Ex* 95–06; Chapl St Dunstan's Abbey Sch Plymouth 02–05; V Riseley w Bletsoe *St Alb* 06–18; C Harold Hill St Paul *Chelmsf* from 18. *47 Retford Hill, Romford RM3 9NB*

BAILEY, Michael Joseph. b 78. Open Univ BSc 02 City Univ MSc 05 RN 96. St Steph Ho Ox BTh 11. **d** 10 **p** 11. C Holbrooks *Cov* 10–13; Pioneer P *Lon* 13–14; P-in-c Sidley *Chich* 14–18; V from 18; P-in-c Bexhill St Barn from 17. *All Saints' Vicarage, All Saints' Lane, Bexhill-on-Sea TN39 5HA* M: 07713-258429 E: frmichaelbailey@gmail.com

BAILEY, Nicholas Andrew. b 55. Open Univ BA 84 Nottm Univ CertEd 80. Ripon Coll Cuddesdon 88. **d** 90 **p** 91. C Guisborough *York* 90–92; Chapl Repton Prep Sch 92–15; rtd 15; PtO *Leeds* 16. *16 Willow Bridge Lane, Dalton, Thirsk YO7 3QQ* T: (01845) 595925 E: twonickleby@aol.com

BAILEY, Miss Patricia Laura. b 49. Wall Hall Coll Aldenham CertEd 72. NTMTC 95. **d** 98 **p** 99. NSM Hackney Marsh *Lon* 98–01; NSM S Hackney St Jo w Ch Ch 01–04; NSM Cosby and Whetstone *Leic* 04–11; P-in-c Ibstock w Heather 11–16; R 16–19; rtd 19; PtO *Leic* from 19. *Springbank, High Street, Stoke Golding, Nuneaton CV13 6HF*

BAILEY, Peter. *See* BAILEY, Edward Peter

BAILEY, Canon Peter Robin. b 43. St Jo Coll Dur BA 64. Trin Coll Bris 72. **d** 74 **p** 75. C Corby St Columba *Pet* 74–77; C Bishopsworth *Bris* 77–82; V Sea Mills 82–97; RD Westbury and Severnside 91–97; P-in-c Bishopston 97–98; P-in-c Bris St Andr w St Bart 97–98; TR Bishopston and St Andrews 98–09; Hon Can Bris Cathl 97–09; rtd 09; PtO *Bris* from 09; *B & W* from 10. *4 The Croft, Backwell, Bristol BS48 3LY* T: (01275) 790611 M: 07970-180460 E: peterandheather@blueyonder.co.uk

BAILEY, Robert David. b 71. Leeds Metrop Univ BA 95. Cranmer Hall Dur 15. **d** 17 **p** 18. C Elmete Trin *Leeds* from 17. *3 Scholes Lodge Lane, Scholes, Leeds LS15 4BZ* M: 07885-386932 E: rev.bob.bailey@gmail.com

BAILEY, Robert Henry. b 45. FCA 69. NOC 99. **d** 02 **p** 03. NSM Dewsbury *Wakef* 02–05; Sub Chapl HM Pris Leeds 02–05; NSM Felkirk *Wakef* 05–13; rtd 13; PtO *Leeds* from 17. *77 Bennett Lane, Dewsbury WF12 7DZ* E: robertbailey.minster@btinternet.com

BAILEY, Stella. b 76. Westhill Coll Birm BTheol 98. Ripon Coll Cuddesdon 07. **d** 09 **p** 10. C Walsgrave on Sowe *Cov* 09–13; V Cov St Mary 13–16; V Kenilworth St Nic from 16; AD Kenilworth from 18. *The Vicarage, 7 Elmbank Road, Kenilworth CV8 1AL* E: chacethedog@me.com

BAILEY, Stephen. b 39. Leic Univ BA 61. Clifton Th Coll 61. **d** 62 **p** 63. C Wellington w Eyton *Lich* 62–66; C Rainham *Chelmsf* 66–69; V Ercall Magna *Lich* 69–75; V Rowton 69–75; RD Wrockwardine 72–75; V W Bromwich Gd Shep w St Jo 75–83; P-in-c W Bromwich St Phil 80–81; V 81–83; R Chadwell *Chelmsf* 83–96; RD Thurrock 92–96; V Galleywood Common 96–04; rtd 04; PtO *Chelmsf* from 04. *64 Bridport Way, Braintree CM7 9FJ* T: (01376) 619347

BAILEY, Stephen Andrew. b 75. St Jo Coll Nottm 05. **d** 07 **p** 08. C Walton-on-Thames *Guildf* 07–11; TV Oadby *Leic* 11–17; P-in-c 17–19; TR Oadby Gt Glen from 19; Warden of Readers 13–18. *St Paul's House, Hamble Road, Oadby, Leicester LE2 4NX* T: 0116-271 0519 E: vicarstpauloadby@gmail.com

BAILEY, Stephen John. b 57. Sarum & Wells Th Coll 88. **d** 90 **p** 91. C Redhill H Trin *S'wark* 90–95; Chapl E Surrey Coll 91–93; P-in-c Betchworth *S'wark* 95–00; V 00–06; P-in-c Buckland 95–00; R 00–06; R Hamilton H Trin Bermuda 06–13; R Guernsey Ste Marie du Castel *Win* 13–17; V

Guernsey St Matt 13–17; rtd 17. *Brent Cottage, 38 Church Road, East Wittering, Chichester PO20 8PS*

BAILEY, Mrs Susan Mary. b 40. F L Calder Coll Liv CertEd 61. EAMTC 89. **d** 92 **p** 94. NSM Chelmsf Cathl 92–93; NSM Needham Market w Badley *St E* 93–95; NSM Belper *Derby* 96–00; NSM Allestree St Nic and Quarndon 00–05; Chapl Morley Retreat and Conf Ho Derby 00–05; rtd 05; PtO *Glouc* from 14. *28 Burleigh Way, Wickwar, Wotton-under-Edge GL12 8LR* T: (01454) 294112 E: susan.m.bailey@gmail.com

BAILEY, Yvonne Mary. *See* HOBSON, Yvonne Mary

BAILIE, Alison Margaret. b 62. Leeds Univ LLB 83. Trin Coll Bris BA 98. **d** 98 **p** 99. C Halliwell St Pet *Man* 98–05; P-in-c Droylsden St Mary 05–09; R from 09. *St Mary's Rectory, Dunkirk Street, Droylsden, Manchester M43 7FB* T: 0161-370 1569

BAILLIE, Terence John. b 46. New Coll Ox BA 69 MA 78 Man Univ MSc 72 Cardiff Univ MTh 93. St Jo Coll Nottm 74. **d** 77 **p** 78. C Chadwell *Chelmsf* 77–80; C Bickenhill w Elmdon *Birm* 80–84; V Bedminster St Mich *Bris* 84–96; V Clevedon St Andr and Ch Ch *B & W* 96–12; rtd 12; PtO *B & W* from 13; *Bris* from 17. *33 Belgrave Road, Weston-super-Mare BS22 8AJ* T: (01934) 643429 E: tandam.baillie@btinternet.com

BAILY, Linda Rosemary. **d** 06 **p** 07. NSM Llanaber w Caerdeon *Ban* 06–15; NSM Bro Ardudwy from 15. *Address temp unknown* E: lindarbaily@aol.com

BAILY, Mrs Sally. b 65. Kingston Univ MBA 97. Trin Coll Bris MA 14. **d** 13 **p** 14. C Gt Chesham *Ox* 13–16; TV Edgware *Lon* from 16. *2 Savoy Close, Edgware HA8 7QF* M: 07836-251432

BAIN, Alan. b 48. Thames Poly BSc 72. St Jo Coll Nottm. **d** 77 **p** 78. C Wakef St Andr and St Mary 77–81; V Bath Odd Down *B & W* 81–82; P-in-c Combe Hay 81–82; V Bath Odd Down w Combe Hay 82–18; rtd 18; PtO *B & W* from 19. *46 Stonehouse Lane, Bath BA2 5DW*

BAIN, Andrew John. b 55. Newc Poly BA 77 Edin Univ MTh 89. Edin Th Coll 86. **d** 88 **p** 89. Chapl St Mary's Cathl *Edin* 88–91; C Edin St Mary 88–91; R Edin St Jas 91–98; P-in-c Edin St Marg 93–98; R Haddington 98–06; P-in-c Edin St Ninian 06–10; Dioc Dir of Ords 95–98 and 06–07; Chapl Emmaus Ho from 10; R Dunbar *Edin* 13–17; P-in-c Edin St Salvador from 18. *Emmaus House, 14 Gilmore Place, Edinburgh EH3 9NQ* T: 0131-228 1066 M: 07929-047896 E: andrewbain9@hotmail.com

BAIN, Canon John Stuart. b 55. Van Mildert Coll Dur BA 77. Westcott Ho Cam 78. **d** 80 **p** 81. C Washington *Dur* 80–84; C Dunston 84–86; V Shiney Row 86–92; V Herrington 86–92; P-in-c Whitworth w Spennymoor 92–97; P-in-c Merrington 94–97; AD Auckland 96–02; V Spennymoor, Whitworth and Merrington 97–02; Hon Can Dur Cathl 98–02; Adn Sunderland 02–18; P-in-c Hedworth 02–13; P-in-c E Boldon 09–13; P-in-c Boldon 10–13; C The Boldons 13–18; V Sunderland Minster from 18; Can Dur Cathl from 18. *Sunderland Minster, High Street West, Sunderland SR1 3ET* T: 0191-565 4066 E: stuart.bain@sunderlandminster.org

BAIN, Lawrence John Weir. b 60. NTMTC BA 05. **d** 05 **p** 06. C Stoughton *Guildf* 05–09; P-in-c Camberley Heatherside from 09. *30 Yockley Close, Camberley GU15 1QH* T: (01276) 691127 F: 678015 E: revlarrybain@aol.com

BAIN-DOODU, Canon Joseph Justice. b 56. Cape Coast Univ Ghana DipEd 01 MEd 09 Cardiff Univ LLM 11. St Nic Th Coll Ghana LTh 86. **d** 86 **p** 86. Ghana 86–97 and 99–08; Hon C Sheldon *Birm* 97–98; PtO *Portsm* 09–12. *Address temp unknown* M: 07532-104795 E: josephbaindoodu@gmail.com

BAINBRIDGE, Mrs Christine Susan. b 48. St Aid Coll Dur BA 70 K Coll Lon MA 99. SEITE 03. **d** 96 **p** 97. C S'wark H Trin w St Matt 96–99; Asst to Bp Woolwich (Greenwich Area) 99–03; C Lee Gd Shep w St Pet 99–03; P-in-c Deptford St Jo w H Trin 03–06; TR Deptford St Jo w H Trin and Ascension 06–13; rtd 13; PtO *S'wark* 13–14; *Ox* from 14. *16 The Mount, Reading RG1 5HL* T: 0118-931 1587 M: 07939-662980 E: bainbridgerev@gmail.com

BAINBRIDGE, David George. b 42. Wadh Coll Ox BA 63 MA 67 Lon Inst of Educn PGCE 67. Ridley Hall Cam 84. **d** 86 **p** 87. C Downend *Bris* 86–90; TV Yate New Town 90–01; Chapl Lee Abbey Internat Students' Club Kensington 01–07; rtd 07; PtO *Glouc* from 08. *2 Kingsmead, Lechlade GL7 3BW* T: (01367) 250347 E: bainbridge1973@yahoo.co.uk

BAINBRIDGE, Mrs Phyllis Marion. b 58. Aber Univ BSc 81 Ches Univ BA 17. St Jo Coll Nottm 10. **d** 11 **p** 12. NSM Littleover *Derby* 11–12; NSM Mickleover All SS 12–14; NSM Mickleover St Jo 12–14; NSM Mickleover 14–15; NSM Heath 15–16; C Hucknall Torkard *S'well* 18; PtO *Derby* from 16; *S'well* from 18. *357 Duffield Road, Allestree, Derby DE22 2DG* T: (01332) 554700 M: 07776-434792 E: revdphyllisbainbridge@gmail.com

BAINBRIDGE, Richard Densham. b 49. Ch Coll Cam BA 71 MA 75 Edge Hill Coll of HE PGCE 72. S'wark Ord Course 91. **d** 94 **p** 95. C Bermondsey St Jas w Ch Ch *S'wark* 94–99; V Lee Gd Shep w St Pet 99–14; AD E Lewisham 06–13; rtd 14; PtO *Ox* from 14. *16 The Mount, Reading RG1 5HL* T: 0118-931 1587 E: revrdb@yahoo.com

BAINES, Alan William. b 50. S Bank Poly BSc 72. Trin Coll Bris 92. **d** 94 **p** 95. C Chenies and Lt Chalfont, Latimer and Flaunden *Ox* 94–98; V Eye *Pet* 98–05; Post Ord Tr Co-ord 00–05; TV Duston 05–15; rtd 15; PtO *Glouc* from 15. *14 Bittern Avenue, Abbeydale, Gloucester GL4 4WA* E: a.baines93@ntlworld.com

BAINES, Derek Alfred. b 53. MCSP 75. CBDTI 99. **d** 02 **p** 03. NSM Lostock Hall *Blackb* 02–09; NSM Lostock Hall and Farington Moss 09–11; R Hoole 11–18; rtd 18; PtO *Blackb* from 19. *16 Middlefield, Leyland PR26 7AE* T/F: (01772) 641521 M: 07774-200885

BAINES, John Charles. b 68. Ripon Coll Cuddesdon 00. **d** 02 **p** 03. C Morton and Stonebroom w Shirland *Derby* 02–06; P-in-c New Mills 06–12; V 12–18; RD Glossop 10–13; P-in-c Longnor, Quarnford, Sheen etc *Lich* 18; V from 18. *The Vicarage, Longnor, Buxton SK17 0PA* T: (01298) 83411

⊕**BAINES, The Rt Revd Nicholas.** b 57. Bradf Univ BA 80. Trin Coll Bris BA 87. **d** 87 **p** 88 **c** 03. C Kendal St Thos *Carl* 87–91; C Leic H Trin w St Jo 91–92; V Rothley 92–00; RD Goscote 96–00; Adn Lambeth *S'wark* 00–03; Area Bp Croydon 03–11; Bp Bradf 11–14; Bp Leeds from 14; Hon Asst Bp York from 14. *Hollin House, Weetwood Avenue, Leeds LS16 5NG* T: 0113-284 4300 E: bishop.nick@leeds.anglican.org

BAINES, Mrs Sharon June. b 52. Sheff Hallam Univ MSc 05 MCSP 74. LCTP 06. **d** 09 **p** 10. NSM Penwortham St Leon *Blackb* 09–18; rtd 18; PtO *Blackb* from 18. *16 Middlefield, Leyland PR26 7AE* T/F: (01772) 641521

BAIRD, Agnes Murry (Nancy). b 39. Man Univ CertEd 70. EAMTC 93. **d** 96 **p** 97. NSM Bramford *St E* 96–98; NSM Haughley w Wetherden and Stowupland 98–09; rtd 09; PtO *St E* from 09. *1 Burls Yard, Crown Street, Needham Market, Ipswich IP6 8AJ* T: (01449) 720567 E: nancybaird39@gmail.com

BAIRD, Mrs Sally. b 53. St As Minl Tr Course 04. **d** 06. NSM Bistre *St As* 06–16; NSM Borderlands Miss Area from 17. *100 Park Avenue, Bryn-y-Baal, Mold CH7 6TP* T: (01352) 758831 E: sally.baird@btinternet.com

BAISLEY, George. b 45. Sarum & Wells Th Coll 78. **d** 80 **p** 81. C Glouc St Geo w Whaddon 80–83; R Welford w Weston and Clifford Chambers 83–87; Chapl Myton Hamlet Hospice 87–91; Chapl Warw Univ *Cov* 87–91; R Berkswell 91–03; RD Kenilworth 96–01; Chapl Bromley Coll 03–04; P-in-c Doddington, Newnham and Wychling *Cant* 04–07; P-in-c Teynham w Lynsted and Kingsdown 04–07; P-in-c Norton 04–07; rtd 07; PtO *Chelmsf* 07–08; P-in-c Ockendon 08–12; PtO *Roch* from 13. *25 Bromley College, London Road, Bromley BR1 1PE* M: 07974-151056 E: george@baisley45.co.uk

BAKER, Albert George. b 30. Qu Coll Birm. **d** 61 **p** 62. C Merton St Mary *S'wark* 61–64; C Limpsfield and Titsey 64–65; C Chapel-en-le-Frith *Derby* 65–68; R Odd Rode *Ches* 68–76; V Holme Cultram St Mary *Carl* 76–78; R Blofield w Hemblington *Nor* 78–94; rtd 94. *240 Raedwald Drive, Bury St Edmunds IP32 7DN* T: (01284) 701802

BAKER, Alexander David Laing. b 74. **d** 11 **p** 12. C Edin Ch Ch 11–12; NSM Burnley St Matt w H Trin *Blackb* 12–14; PtO 14–16; NSM Gisburn 16–17; V 17; PtO from 17; NSM Halsall, Lydiate and Downholland *Liv* from 18. *Victoria Cottage, Swan Lane, Aughton, Ormskirk L39 6SU* T: 0151-526 2292 E: alexbaker@priests.uk.net

BAKER, Alicia Mary. b 63. Cliff Coll MA 11. Trin Coll Bris BA 03. **d** 03 **p** 04. C E Ham St Paul *Chelmsf* 03–07; P-in-c Abercarn and Cwmcarn *Mon* 07–12; V Dudley Wood and Cradley Heath *Worc* from 12. *St Luke's Vicarage, 29A Upper High Street, Cradley Heath B64 5HX* T: (01384) 591096 E: aliciabakeruk@btinternet.com *or* vicar@stjohnsdudleywood.org

BAKER, Andrew James. b 81. St Mellitus Coll 12. **d** 15 **p** 16. C Maghull and Melling *Liv* 15–16; C Haydock St Mark 16–18; C York St Mich-le-Belfrey from 18. *12 Muncastergate, York YO31 9LA* M: 07972-921587 E: andyjimbaker@gmail.com

BAKER, Angela Mary. b 42. **d** 91. Par Dn Battersea St Sav and St Geo w St Andr *S'wark* 91–94; C 94–96; C Battersea Fields 96–02; rtd 02; PtO *Roch* from 03. *Finches, Ide Hill, Sevenoaks TN14 6JW* T: (01732) 750470 E: angelabaker854@btinternet.com

BAKER, Mrs Ann Christine. b 49. Edin Univ BEd 71. CBDTI 98. **d** 01 **p** 02. NSM St Bees *Carl* 01–04; P-in-c Eskdale, Irton, Muncaster and Waberthwaite 04–09; V 09–12; rtd 12; PtO *Carl* from 13. *Heatherside, Abbey Road, St Bees CA27 0EG* T: (01946) 822498 E: j.h.baker@btinternet.com

BAKER, Anthony Peter. b 38. Hertf Coll Ox BA 59 MA 63. Clifton Th Coll 60. **d** 63 **p** 64. C Ox St Ebbe w St Pet 63–66; C Welling *Roch* 66–70; V Redland *Bris* 70–79; Lect Tyndale Hall Bris 70–71; Lect Trin Coll Bris 71–77; V Beckenham Ch Ch *Roch* 79–94; Chapl Beckenham Hosp 79–94; V Hove Bp Hannington Memorial Ch *Chich* 94–03; rtd 03; PtO *Chich* from 04. *12 Paradise Close, Eastbourne BN20 8BT* T: (01323) 438783

BAKER, Miss Barbara Ann. b 36. Linc Th Coll 85. **d** 87 **p** 94. Par Dn Hornchurch St Andr *Chelmsf* 87–94; C 94–97; rtd 97; PtO *Chelmsf* from 97. *120 Devonshire Road, Hornchurch RM12 4LN* T: (01708) 477759

BAKER, Benjamin Adam. b 89. Nottm Univ BA 12. Wycliffe Hall Ox MTh 18. **d** 18 **p** 19. C Headington St Mary *Ox* from 18. *4 Meadowsweet Way, Oxford OX3 9FW* M: 07981-769797 E: ben.baker68@gmail.com

BAKER, Canon Bernard George Coleman. b 36. Lon Univ BD 61. Oak Hill Th Coll 61. **d** 63 **p** 64. C Broadwater St Mary *Chich* 63–66; BCMS Miss P and Chapl Morogoro Em Ch Tanzania 66–79; V Moshi St Marg 79–84; Hon Can Morogoro from 77; Hon Can Mt Kilimanjaro from 82; C-in-c Ryde St Jas Prop Chpl *Portsm* 84–96; Crosslinks 96–01; Asst P Ruaha Cathl Tanzania 96–01; Teacher Amani Chr Tr Cen 96–01; rtd 01; PtO *Ex* 02–15; *Leic* from 15. *70 Sedgefield Drive, Thurnby, Leicester LE7 9PS* T: 0116-241 9181 E: bernandjenbaker@yahoo.co.uk

BAKER, Miss Carolyn Gay. b 59. All SS Cen for Miss & Min 15. **d** 18 **p** 19. NSM Dronfield w Holmesfield *Derby* from 18. *1 Albion Road, Chesterfield S40 1NB* T: (01246) 297457

BAKER, Prof Christopher James. b 54. St Cath Coll Cam BA 75 MA 78 PhD 78 CEng 83 FICE 96 FIHT 95. EMMTC 85. **d** 88 **p** 89. NSM Matlock Bath *Derby* 88–95; NSM Matlock Bath and Cromford 95; NSM Beeston *S'well* 95–98; PtO *Lich* 98–00; NSM Lich St Mich w St Mary and Wall 00–10; NSM Lich Ch Ch 10–13; PtO from 13. *15 Saddlers Close, Lichfield WS14 9ZW* T: (01543) 256320 *or* 262211 E: cjsmbaker@btinternet.com

BAKER, Christopher Peter. b 64. St Cuth Soc Dur BA 95 Greenwich Univ PGCE 96. SEITE 99. **d** 02 **p** 03. C Kennington St Mark *S'wark* 02–06; Chapl Greenwich Univ 07–13; PtO *Roch* 14–15; *Cant* from 18. *Holy Trinity Vicarage, 241 High Street, Sheerness ME12 1UR*

BAKER, David Ayshford. b 66. St Aid Coll Dur BA 88. Wycliffe Hall Ox BTh 97. **d** 97 **p** 98. C Chadwell Heath *Chelmsf* 97–01; C Surbiton Hill Ch Ch *S'wark* 01–09; R E Dean w Friston and Jevington *Chich* from 09. *The Rectory, Gilberts Drive, East Dean, Eastbourne BN20 0DL* T: (01323) 423266 E: davidbaker1966@gmx.co.uk

BAKER, David Clive. b 47. Sarum & Wells Th Coll 76. **d** 78 **p** 79. C Shirley *Birm* 78–82; R Wainfleet All SS w St Thos *Linc* 82–83; P-in-c Wainfleet St Mary 82–83; P-in-c Croft 82–83; R The Wainfleets and Croft 83–86; V Stirchley *Birm* 86–96; PtO 97–98; V Handsworth St Mich 98–02; Chapl Aston Univ 99–02; C Codsall *Lich* 02–05; P-in-c Coven 04–05; V Bilbrook and Coven 05–12; rtd 12; PtO *Heref* 12–14; P-in-c Rickerscote *Lich* 14–18; V 18. *4 Camrose Close, Oakham LE15 6UW* M: 07958-468819 E: linda.david.baker@gmail.com

BAKER, David John. b 27. LRAM 50 GRSM 51. Ely Th Coll 53. **d** 55 **p** 56. C Swanley St Mary *Roch* 55–58; C Guildf St Nic 58–63; Prec St Alb Abbey 63–67; P-in-c Colney St Pet 67–68; V 68–73; V Tattenham Corner and Burgh Heath *Guildf* 73–84; R Fetcham 84–96; rtd 96; PtO *Guildf* 96–18. *1 Terra Cotta Court, Quennels Hill, Wrecclesham, Farnham GU10 4SL* T: (01252) 734202

BAKER, David Jordan. b 35. Univ of Wales (Lamp) BA 59. Ely Th Coll 59. **d** 61 **p** 62. C Spalding St Mary and St Nic *Linc* 61–66; C Gainsborough All SS 66–69; V Wrawby 69–78; V Melton Ross w New Barnetby 70–78; V Linc St Pet-at-Gowts and St Andr 78–94; rtd 98; PtO *Linc* from 01. *44 Sopwith Road, Eastleigh SO50 5LN*

BAKER, David Peter. b 63. Plymouth Univ CertEd 03. SWMTC 99. **d** 02 **p** 03. NSM Parkham, Alwington, Buckland Brewer etc *Ex* 02–12; C S Molton w Nymet St George, High Bray etc 12–16; C Bishopsnympton, Rose Ash, Mariansleigh etc 12–16; TR Bishopsnympton, Charles, E Anstey, High Bray etc from 16. *The Vicarage, East Street, North Molton, South Molton EX36 3HX* T: (01598) 740325 E: davidbaker.sw@gmail.com

BAKER, Deborah Maureen. b 69. RMN 91. Lindisfarne Regional Tr Partnership 11. **d** 16. NSM Long Benton St Mary *Newc* 16–17; NSM Ulgham from 17; NSM Widdrington from 17. *15 Bradbury Court, New Hartley, Whitley Bay NE25 0SW* M: 07910-087831 E: debbiebaker@gmail.com

BAKER, Dilly. *See* BAKER, Hilary Mary

BAKER, Mrs Elizabeth May Janet Margaret. b 51. Bretton Hall Coll CertEd 73. Ox Min Course 04. **d** 07 **p** 08. NSM Watling Valley *Ox* 07–10; NSM Stantonbury and Willen 10–15; R Pitlochry *St And* from 15; R Strathtay from 15; R Kilmaveonaig from 15; R Kinloch Rannoch from 15. *3 Knockard Place, Pitlochry PH16 5JF* T: (01796) 472005 E: bethmaybaker@yahoo.co.uk

BAKER, Hilary Mary (Dilly). b 61. Man Univ BA 83 Keele Univ MA 09 CQSW 86. Sarum & Wells Th Coll 86. **d** 89 **p** 94. Par Dn E Dulwich St Jo *S'wark* 89–92; Tutor Sarum & Wells Th Coll 92–94; TV Stantonbury and Willen *Ox* 94–01; Warden Scargill Ho 01–08; P-in-c Kirkby-in-Malhamdale w Coniston Cold *Bradf* 08–09; P-in-c Kirkby-in-Malhamdale 09–13; Hon Can Bradf Cathl 12–13; R Stoke Newington St Mary *Lon* from 13. *St Mary's Rectory, Stoke Newington Church Street, London N16 9ES* T: (020) 7254 6072 M: 07773-192888 E: dillybaker@gmail.com

BAKER, Hugh Crispin. b 58. Open Univ BA 92. Linc Th Coll 95. **d** 95 **p** 96. C Birstall and Wanlip *Leic* 95–99; V Middlestown *Wakef* 99–09; P-in-c Mirfield 09–14; V 14; *Leeds* from 14; Dioc Rural Officer *Wakef* 04–14. *The Vicarage, 3 Vicarage Meadow, Mirfield WF14 9JL* T: (01924) 505790 E: hughcbaker@gmail.com

BAKER, Hugh John. b 46. Birm Univ BSocSc 68. Cuddesdon Coll 69. **d** 71 **p** 72. C Binley *Cov* 71–74; C Pemberton St Mark Newtown *Liv* 74–78; TV Sutton 78–90; V Hints *Lich* 90–05; V Fazeley 90–13; V Canwell 05–13; R Drayton Bassett 05–13; rtd 13; PtO *Lich* from 13; Chapl S Staffs and Shropshire Healthcare NHS Foundn Trust 00–10; Chapl Burton Hosps NHS Foundn Trust from 10. *21 Reedmace, Tamworth B77 1BH* E: hughbaker@hughbaker.plus.com

BAKER, Iain. b 70. St D Coll Lamp BA 91. Oak Hill Th Coll BA 99. **d** 99 **p** 00. C Gt Clacton *Chelmsf* 99–03; V Kidsgrove *Lich* from 03. *St Thomas's Vicarage, The Avenue, Kidsgrove, Stoke-on-Trent ST7 1AG* T: (01782) 772895 or 771727

BAKER, Canon James Henry. b 39. Kelham Th Coll 62. **d** 67 **p** 68. C Sheff Arbourthorne 67–70; C Pemberton St Jo *Liv* 70–71; Chapl and Prec St Mary's Cathl *Edin* 71–74; R Lochgelly *St And* 74–84; P-in-c Rosyth and Inverkeithing 76–84; Can St Ninian's Cathl Perth 83–84; TR Whitehaven *Carl* 84–04; RD Calder 96–01; rtd 04; Hon C Eskdale, Irton, Muncaster and Waberthwaite *Carl* 05–12; Hon Can Carl Cathl 96–12; PtO from 13. *Heatherside, Abbey Road, St Bees CA27 0EG* T: (01946) 822498

BAKER, Jenifer Marlene. b 44. Bris Univ BSc 65 Univ of Wales (Swansea) PhD 71 York St Jo Coll BA 05. **d** 05 **p** 06. OLM Ruyton XI Towns w Gt and Lt Ness *Lich* 05–16; rtd 16. *15 Gracey Court, Woodland Road, Broadclyst, Exeter EX5 3GA* T: (01392) 468170

BAKER, Jennifer Elizabeth. *See* ROBINSON, Jennifer Elizabeth

✠**BAKER, The Rt Revd Jonathan Mark Richard.** b 66. St Jo Coll Ox BA 88 MPhil 90. St Steph Ho Ox BA 92. **d** 93 **p** 94 **c** 11. C Ascot Heath *Ox* 93–96; C Reading St Mark 96; P-in-c 96–99; V 99–02; P-in-c Reading H Trin 96–99; V 99–02; Prin Pusey Ho 03–13; Hon C Ox St Thos 08–13; Suff Bp Ebbsfleet (PEV) *Cant* 11–13; Hon Asst Bp Ox 11–13; Asst Bp B & W 11–13; Suff Bp Fulham *Lon* from 13; P-in-c St Dunstan in the West 13–16. *5 St Andrew Street, London EC4A 3AF* T: (020) 7932 1130 E: bishop.fulham@london.anglican.org

BAKER, Canon Jonathan William. b 61. SS Coll Cam MA 85. Wycliffe Hall Ox BA 91. **d** 92 **p** 93. C Sanderstead All SS *S'wark* 92–96; P-in-c Scalby w Ravenscar and Staintondale *York* 96–97; V Scalby 97–04; P-in-c Hackness w Harwood Dale 96–97; V 97–04; P-in-c Scarborough St Luke 03–04; Can Res Pet Cathl 04–17; V Beverley Minster *York* from 17; P-in-c North Ferriby 17. *The Minster Vicarage, Highgate, Beverley HU17 0DN* T: (01482) 881434 or 868540 E: vicar@beverleyminster.org.uk

BAKER, Kate Justine. b 70. Ridley Hall Cam 16. **d** 18 **p** 19. C Hartford and Houghton w Wyton *Ely* from 18. *Bramley House, High Street, Colne, Huntingdon PE28 3ND* M: 07793-554196 E: katejbaker@outlook.com

BAKER, Miss Laura Mary. b 89. St Jo Coll Dur BA 10. Westcott Ho Cam 11. **d** 14 **p** 15. C King's Lynn St Marg w St Nic *Nor* 14–18; P-in-c New Catton Ch Ch from 18. *St Paul's Vicarage, 1 Mill Lane, Norwich NR3 4LD* T: (01603) 620544 E: laurabaker27@tiscali.co.uk

BAKER, Marc Crispin. b 75. Westmr Coll Ox BTh 96. Oak Hill Th Coll 00. **d** 02 **p** 03. C Upton (Overchurch) *Ches* 02–06; TV Cheltenham St Mary, St Matt, St Paul and H Trin *Glouc* 06–07; C Cheltenham St Mary w St Matt 07–12; C Cheltenham St Mary w St Matt and St Luke 12–13; P-in-c Kea *Truro* from 13. *St Kea House, Killiow, Truro TR3 6AE* T: (01872) 260134 E: vicar@stkea.org.uk

BAKER, Margaret. b 55. **d** 08 **p** 09. C Herringthorpe *Sheff* 08–10; C Rivers Team 10–12; TV from 12. *The Vicarage, 24 Highgate, Sheffield S9 1WL* T: 0114-242 1724 E: margaret.baker@sheffield.anglican.org

BAKER, Miles Anthony. b 71. Brunel Univ BA 92. Ridley Hall Cam 99. **d** 02 **p** 03. C Paignton Ch Ch and Preston St Paul *Ex* 02–05; P-in-c Upton 05–08; Dioc Miss Enabler 08–14; Dir Miss *Pet* 14–17; Can Pet Cathl 15–17; R Allesley *Cov* from 17. *The Rectory, Rectory Lane, Coventry CV5 9EQ* E: revmilesbaker@outlook.com

BAKER, Canon Neville Duff. b 35. St Aid Birkenhead 60. **d** 63 **p** 64. C Stranton *Dur* 63–66; C Houghton le Spring 66–68; V Tudhoe Grange 68–07; P-in-c Merrington 84–87 and 91–94; RD Auckland 83–94; Hon Can Dur Cathl 90–07; rtd 07; PtO *Dur* from 09; *Newc* from 10. *2 The Bents, Sunderland SR6 7NX* T: 0191-529 4600

BAKER, Noel Edward Lloyd. b 37. Sarum & Wells Th Coll 73. **d** 75 **p** 76. C Charlton Kings St Mary *Glouc* 75–79; V Clearwell 79–81; R Eastington and Frocester 81–97; RD Stonehouse 90–94; P-in-c Eastington and Frocester 97–98; P-in-c Standish w Haresfield and Moreton Valence etc 97–98; rtd 98; PtO *Glouc* 00–13. *Capel Court, The Burgage, Prestbury, Cheltenham GL52 3EL* T: (01242) 269484 E: noelbaker@greenbee.net

BAKER, Mrs Pamela Daphne. b 53. Ox Min Course. **d** 08. NSM Blackbird Leys *Ox* 08–14. *2 White Lodge, Oak Lane, Sevenoaks TN13 1UA* M: 07717-377516 E: pamelabaker53@gmail.com

BAKER, Paul Anthony. b 64. St Chad's Coll Dur BA 85. St Steph Ho Ox BA 88 MA 98. **d** 89 **p** 90. C Hartlepool St Aid *Dur* 89–93; TV Jarrow 93–98; V Sunderland Pennywell St Thos 98–04; V Darlington St Mark w St Paul from 04. *St Mark's Vicarage, 394 North Road, Darlington DL1 3BH* T: (01325) 382400

BAKER, Peter Colin. b 43. Sarum & Wells Th Coll. **d** 82 **p** 83. C Bridgemary *Portsm* 82–86; V Ash Vale *Guildf* 86–99; P-in-c Earlham St Anne *Nor* 99–08; P-in-c Earlham St Mary 99–08; rtd 08; PtO *Sarum* from 11. *15 Linden Close, Laverstock, Salisbury SP1 1PN* T: (01722) 501305 M: 07710-844243 E: peter.baker854@ntlworld.com

BAKER, Robert James. b 80. Oriel Coll Ox BA 04 MA 08. Wycliffe Hall Ox BA 07. **d** 08 **p** 09. C Chesham Bois *Ox* 08–12; R Stoke H Cross w Dunston, Arminghall etc *Nor* from 12. *15 Basingbourne Road, Fleet GU52 6TE* M: 07855-774384 E: baker_robertj@hotmail.com or bcbaker@sky.com

BAKER, Canon Robert John Kenneth. b 50. Southn Univ BSc 71 MICE 79. Oak Hill Th Coll 88. **d** 90 **p** 91. C Cromer *Nor* 90–94; R Pakefield 94–17; Hon Can Nor Cathl 07–17; rtd 17. *15 Basingbourne Road, Fleet GU52 6TE* E: bcbaker@sky.com

BAKER, Ronald Kenneth. b 43. Open Univ BA 80. St Jo Coll Nottm LTh 87. **d** 87 **p** 88. C Paddock Wood *Roch* 87–90; V Ramsgate St Mark *Cant* 90–95; P-in-c Ewhurst and Bodiam *Chich* 95–98; V 98–03; rtd 03; PtO *Chich* from 03. *49 Coneyburrow Gardens, St Leonards-on-Sea TN38 9RZ* T: (01424) 851870 E: revronbaker@talktalk.net

BAKER, Roy David. b 36. St Aid Birkenhead 59. **d** 62 **p** 63. C Garston *Liv* 62–64; C N Meols 64–68; V Newton-le-Willows 68–73; V Crossens 73–82; V Blundellsands St Nic 82–01; rtd 01; PtO *Liv* from 03. *18 Ennerdale Road, Formby, Liverpool L37 2EA* T: (01704) 830622 E: rdbaker@talktalk.net

BAKER, Sarah Jane. b 59. Lon Univ MB, BS 82 Sheff Univ MPhil 00 Coll of Ripon & York St Jo MA 02. NOC 99. **d** 02 **p** 03. NSM Kinsley w Wragby *Wakef* 02–04; NSM Sandal St Cath 04–07; PtO 07–11; NSM Westbrook St Jas *Liv* 11–14; TR Warrington W from 14. *20 Michigan Place, Great Sankey, Warrington WA5 8DT* T: (01925) 657954 M: 07885-376182 E: sarah.baker17@btinternet.com or sarahbakercouk@gmail.com

BAKER, Preb Simon Nicholas Hartland. b 57. K Coll Lon BD 78. Qu Coll Birm 79. **d** 81 **p** 82. C Tupsley *Heref* 81–85; V Shinfield *Ox* 85–98; Prin Berks Chr Tr Scheme 93–98; Lay Min Adv and Warden of Readers *Win* 98–02; Dir of Min Development 02–07; Dir of Min and Past Planning 07–13; Hon Can Win Cathl 08–13; Adn Lich 13–19; R Lich St Mich w St Mary and Wall from 13; Preb Lich Cathl from 19. *10 Mawgan Drive, Lichfield WS14 9SD* T: (01543) 416232 E: simonbaker57@outlook.com or simon.baker@lichfield.anglican.org

BAKER, Canon William John. b 45. FCII 80. Cranmer Hall Dur 87. **d** 89 **p** 90. C Sale St Anne *Ches* 89–93; V Crewe St Andr w St Jo 93–15; P-in-c Crewe Ch Ch 07–13; RD Nantwich 06–13; Hon Can Ches Cathl 03–15; rtd 15; PtO *Ches* from 16. *16 Lyceum Way, Crewe CW1 3YF* T: (01270) 488063 M: 07768-843654 E: revbaker@sky.com

BAKERE, The Very Revd Ronald Duncan. b 35. TCD BA 58 MA 61 BD 62 Ch Ch Ox MA 66 FRSA 68 FBIM 79. Div Test 59. **d** 59 **p** 60. C Knockbreda *D & D* 59–61; C Dublin Zion Ch *D & G* 61–63; Min Can St Patr Cathl Dublin 62–64;

CF (TA) 65–67; Lect Th Ex Univ Inst Educn 67–72; Prin Kuka Teachers' Coll Nigeria 73–77; Cen Org Red Cross Ex 78–81; PtO *Ex* 82–85; P-in-c Chew Magna w Dundry *B & W* 86–87; Hd RS Sir John Cass Foundn Lon 88–93; Dean Port Moresby Papua New Guinea 93–96; Visiting Prof H Spirit RC Sem 94–96; Hospitaller and Sen Chapl St Barts Hosp Lon 96–97; rtd 97; PtO *Lon* 96–04. *21 Luralda Wharf, 40 Saunders Ness Road, London E14 3BY* M: 07958-061962 E: ronbakere@yahoo.com

BAKEWELL, Jeremy Edgar. b 44. d 12 p 13. OLM Aldridge *Lich* from 12. *37 St Mary's Way, Walsall WS9 0AB* T: (01922) 459345 E: jeremyebakewell@gmail.com

BAKKER (née CAMPBELL), Mrs Jane Judith. b 68. Trin Coll Bris BA 01. d 01 p 02. NSM Lyddington and Wanborough and Bishopstone etc *Bris* 01–03; NSM Stratton St Margaret w S Marston etc 03–08; NSM Sholing *Win* 08–16; NSM Maybush and Southampton St Jude 16–19; P-in-c from 19; AD Southampton 13–19. *The Vicarage, 41 Station Road, Southampton SO19 8FN* T: (023) 8044 8337 E: jjbakker@tiscali.co.uk

BALCHIN, Michael John. b 38. Selw Coll Cam BA 60 MA 64. Wells Th Coll 60. d 62 p 63. C Bournemouth H Epiphany *Win* 62–65; C Bris St Mary Redcliffe w Temple etc 65–69; R Norton sub Hamdon *B & W* 69–70; P-in-c Chiselborough w W Chinnock 69–70; R Norton sub Hamdon w Chiselborough 70–77; P-in-c Chipstable w Huish Champflower and Clatworthy 77–82; R 82–88; PtO *Ban* from 88; rtd 03. *Crogbren, Llandyssil Hill Road, Kerry Road, Trefaldwyn SY15 6PD* T: (01686) 669738 E: balchin844@btinternet.com

BALDING, Christopher Matthew Noel. b 90. Sheff Univ BEng 11 Dur Univ BA 19. Ridley Hall Cam 16. d 19. C Roundhay St Edm *Leeds* from 19. *14 Parkside Green, Leeds LS6 4NY* M: 07746-668140

BALDOCK, Canon Charles William Martin. b 52. Nottm Univ BPharm 73 York St Jo Coll MA 07. St Jo Coll Nottm LTh. d 85 p 86. C Nailsea Ch Ch *B & W* 85–89; V Brampton Bierlow *Sheff* 89–00; RD Wath 95–00; Hon Can Sheff Cathl 98–00; V Dringhouses *York* 00–17; RD City of York 04–12; Chapl St Leon Hospice York 04–05; Can and Preb York Minster 17; rtd 17; PtO *S'well* from 18. *2 Byron Court, Balderton, Newark NG24 3PY* E: ms@msbaldock.plus.com

BALDOCK, Reginald David. b 48. Oak Hill Th Coll 72. d 75 p 76. C Plymouth St Jude *Ex* 75–79; C Ardsley *Sheff* 79–85; V Rawthorpe *Wakef* 85–96; C Salterhebble All SS 96–98; P-in-c Bournemouth St Jo w St Mich *Win* 98–16; rtd 16; PtO *Sarum* from 17. *95 Lulworth Avenue, Poole BH15 4DH* E: r.baldock1@ntlworld.com

BALDWIN, David Frederick Beresford. b 57. Ripon Coll Cuddesdon 93. d 95 p 96. C Uttoxeter w Bramshall *Lich* 95–97; C Uttoxeter Area 97–98; V Tilstock, Edstaston and Whixall 98–08; P-in-c Prees 03–08; P-in-c Fauls 03–08; Rural Chapl (Salop Adnry) 00–08; RD Wem and Whitchurch 06–08; P-in-c The Lulworths, Winfrith Newburgh and Chaldon *Sarum* 08–10; C Wool and E Stoke 09–10; TR Beaminster Area from 10; RD Lyme Bay from 16. *The Rectory, 3 Clay Lane, Beaminster DT8 3BU* T: (01308) 862150 E: revdavidbaldwin@gmail.com

BALDWIN, Mrs Frances Mary. b 49. SRN 71. SEITE 99. d 02 p 03. NSM Caterham *S'wark* 02–10; Asst Chapl E Sussex Healthcare NHS Trust from 11; PtO *Chich* 16–18; NSM Westham from 18. *46 Hawkhurst Way, Bexhill-on-Sea TN39 3SN* T: (01424) 842864 E: francesb@btinternet.com

BALDWIN, John Charles. b 39. Bris Univ BSc 61 Sussex Univ DPhil 65 FBCS CEng. St Steph Ho Ox 82. d 83 p 84. C Llandaff w Capel Llanilltern *Llan* 83–90; V Ewenny w St Brides Major 90–92; LtO from 92; Hon Chapl Llan Cathl from 96; rtd 04. *60 Llantrisant Road, Llandaff, Cardiff CF5 2PX* T: (029) 2055 4457 F: 2038 7835 E: dovemaster@gmail.com

BALDWIN, Canon Jonathan Michael. b 58. Chich Th Coll 92. d 94 p 95. C Crawley *Chich* 94–96; C New Shoreham 96–02; C Old Shoreham 96–02; Chapl Gatwick Airport from 02; C Crawley 02–17; C W Green from 17; Can and Preb Chich Cathl from 17. *18 Aldingbourne Close, Ifield, Crawley RH11 0QJ* T: (01293) 406001 E: jonathan.baldwin@gatwickairport.com

BALDWIN, Julia Clare. b 81. St Chad's Coll Dur BA 02 Darw Coll Cam PGCE 05. Ripon Coll Cuddesdon BA 09 MA 17. d 10 p 11. C Bridge *Cant* 10–13; Chapl to Bp Dover 13–17; Abp's Chapl 13–17; Chapl and Fell BNC Ox from 17. *Brasenose College, Radcliffe Square, Oxford OX1 4AJ* M: 07926-516476 E: revjuliabaldwin@gmail.com

BALDWIN, Mrs Maureen Teresa. b 64. Trin & All SS Coll Leeds BEd 82 Liv Univ MEd 95. All SS Cen for Miss & Min 17. d 19. NSM Chorley St Laur *Blackb* from 19. *The Vicarage, 410 Garstang Road, Broughton, Preston PR3 5JB* T: (01772) 862330 M: 07592-838726 E: mobaldwin@btinternet.com

BALDWIN, Peter Alan. b 48. Bede Coll Dur BA 70. Qu Coll Birm 72. d 73 p 74. C Hartlepool St Oswald *Dur* 73–75; C Darlington H Trin 75–78; OGS from 77; C-in-c Bishop Auckland Woodhouse Close CD *Dur* 78–82; V Ferryhill 82–88; V Pendleton St Thos *Man* 88–89; P-in-c Charlestown 88–89; TR Pendleton St Thos w Charlestown 89–90; TR Newton Aycliffe *Dur* 90–96; TR Gt Aycliffe 96–97; V The Trimdons 97–99; AD Sedgefield 96–99; P-in-c Bramley *Ripon* 99–00; TR 00–02; Hon C Harrogate St Wilfrid 02–03; Hon C Methley w Mickletown 03–04; Dom Chapl to Bp Horsham *Chich* 04–06; P-in-c Ashington, Washington and Wiston w Buncton 05–06; P-in-c Brightlingsea *Chelmsf* 06–11; w Buncton 05–06; P-in-c Brightlingsea *Chelmsf* 06–11; rtd 11; Hon C Halifax *Wakef* 11–13; Hon C Todmorden w Cornholme and Walsden 13–14; *Leeds* 14–15; PtO *Dur* from 15. *61 Hutton Way, Durham DH1 5BW* T: 0191-680 6913 M: 07403-231333 E: peter.baldwin21@yahoo.co.uk

BALDWIN, Shaun. b 64. Man Univ BA 04. Ushaw Coll Dur 82. d 89 p 90. In RC Ch 89–00; NSM Hawes Side and Marton Moss *Blackb* 11–12; P-in-c Waterside Par 12–13; V 13–14; C Stalmine w Pilling 12–13; V 13–14; V Broughton from 14; AD Preston 17–19; P-in-c Ingol 18–19. *The Vicarage, 410 Garstang Road, Broughton, Preston PR3 5JB* T: (01772) 862330 M: 07720-722263 E: shaunbaldwin64@hotmail.com *or* broughtonvicar@gmail.com

BALDWIN, Mrs Vivien Lindsay. b 50. SAOMC 97. d 98 p 99. NSM Westbury w Turweston, Shalstone and Biddlesden Ox 98–00; C W Buckingham 00–02; P-in-c Stoneleigh w Ashow *Cov* 02–07; Rural Life Officer 02–06; Chapl W Midl Police *Birm* 07–09; PtO *Pet* 07–12; Chapl Northants Police 12–19; PtO from 19; *Birm* from 19. *20 Castle Road, Woodford Halse, Daventry NN11 3RS* T: (01327) 264722 M: 07720-811477

BALDWIN, William. b 48. RMN 73 FRSH 83. NW Ord Course 75. d 78 p 79. C Royton St Anne *Man* 78–82; V Halliwell St Thos 82–87; TR Atherton 87–99; TR Atherton and Hindsford 99–02; TV Atherton and Hindsford w Howe Bridge 02–08; AD Leigh 01–08; TV Turton Moorland 08–13; rtd 13; PtO *Man* from 13. *51 Shorefield Mount, Egerton, Bolton BL7 9EW* T: (01204) 302924 M: 07552-931264

BALE, Edward William Carre. b 22. AKC 55. d 55 p 56. C Mansfield SS Pet and Paul *S'well* 55–59; C Corby St Jo *Pet* 59–61; R Corby SS Pet and Andr 61–69; V Wollaston and Strixton 69–87; rtd 88; PtO *Ox* 88–16; *Pet* 89–94. *27 The Crescent, Haversham, Milton Keynes MK19 7AN* T: (01234) 391443 E: tedcarrebale@talktalk.net

BALE, Kenneth John. b 34. Univ of Wales (Lamp) BA 58. Qu Coll Birm. d 60 p 61. C Mitcham St Olave *S'wark* 60–63; C Warlingham w Chelsham and Farleigh 63–67; V Battersea Rise St Mark 67–85; PtO 85–88; Hon C Balham St Mary and St Jo 88–90; V S Wimbledon All SS 90–01; Dioc Adv Min of Healing 91–01; rtd 01; PtO *Sheff* 01–18. *23 Selhurst Crescent, Bessacarr, Doncaster DN4 6EF* T: (01302) 539100 F: 371850 M: 07710-212263

BALE, Mrs Sandra Jane. b 62. SEITE 12. d 15 p 16. NSM Forest Row *Chich* 15–19; NSM Crawley Down All SS from 19. *Borders, Herons Lea, Copthorne, Crawley RH10 3HE* T: (01342) 718303 E: sandra.bale@tesco.net

BALE, Simon John. b 62. Univ of Wales (Cardiff) BSc 84 PhD 88. STETS 10. d 13 p 14. C Highbridge *B & W* 13–17; V Bridgwater St Fran 17–18; Dioc Inter Faith Adv 15–18. *The Vicarage, Saxon Green, Bridgwater TA6 4JA* M: 07970-936325 E: sj_bale@icloud.com

BALE, Canon Susannah. b 67. Univ of Wales (Cardiff) BA 90 BTh 06. St Mich Coll Llan 03. d 06 p 07. C Betws w Ammanford *St D* 06–08; C Bro Teifi Sarn Helen 08–10; P-in-c Llanybydder and Llanwenog w Llanllwni etc 10–18; P-in-c Betws w Ammanford from 18; Can St D Cathl from 18. *The Vicarage, Parc Henry Lane, Ammanford SA18 2EH* T: (01269) 592084 E: suzybale@hotmail.com

BALFOUR, Andrew Crispin Roxburgh. b 49. Coll of Resurr Mirfield 93. d 95 p 96. C S Lafford *Linc* 95–99; P-in-c St Neot and Warleggan *Truro* 99–00; P-in-c Cardynham 99–00; R St Neot and Warleggan w Cardynham 00–14; P-in-c Altarnon w Bolventor, Laneast and St Clether 10–14; rtd 14; PtO *Truro* from 14. *9 Rockfield Close, Teignmouth TQ14 8TS*

BALFOUR, David Ian Bailey. b 33. d 63 p 63. C Ashburton New Zealand 63–66; P-in-c Aranui-Wainoni 66–71; Asst P Christchurch 66–71; V Lyttelton 72–75; V Symonds Street 75–84; P-in-c Kaitaia 85; P-in-c Henderson 85–86; V Rangiora 90–93; V Timaru 93–98; Adn S Canterbury and V Marchwell 94–98; NSM Dumfries *Glas* 05–08; LtO from 08; LtO *Mor* from 08; NSM Keith 09–13. *1 Balleigh Wood, Edderton IV19 1LF* T: (01862) 821645 M: 07527-445156 E: david.loma@baileybalfour.com

BALFOUR, Hugh Rowlatt. b 54. SS Coll Cam BA 76. Ridley Hall Cam 78. d 81 p 82. C Bedford Ch Ch *St Alb* 81–86;

P-in-c Camberwell Ch Ch *S'wark* 86–90; V from 90. *Christ Church Vicarage, 29 Asylum Road, London SE15 2RJ* T: (020) 7639 5662 E: hrbalfours@btinternet.com

BALFOUR, Mark Andrew. b 66. York Univ BA 88 R Holloway Coll Lon PhD 98. Trin Coll Bris BA 01. **d** 02 **p** 03. C Churchdown *Glouc* 02–06; V Furze Platt *Ox* 06–16; CMS Guatemala from 16. *Church Mission Society, Watlington Road, Cowley, Oxford OX4 6BZ*

BALFOUR, Mrs Penelope Mary. b 47. St Andr Univ MA 69 St Jo Coll York DipEd 72. Coates Hall Edin 89 St Jo Coll Nottm 84. **d** 88 **p** 95. C Dundee St Marg *Bre* 88–94; Dioc AIDS Officer 90–94; NSM Invergowrie 94–96; C 00–07; Chapl Abertay Univ 94–97; C Dundee St Marg 96–00; PtO from 08. *10 Strathaird Place, Dundee DD2 4TN* T: (01382) 643114

BALFOUR, Rory John. b 93. Dur Univ BA 14 CCC Cam MPhil 17. Cranmer Hall Dur 17. **d** 19. C Hillside *Dur* from 19. *45 Shotley Gardens, Gateshead NE9 5DP* E: rory.j.balfour@durham.ac.uk

BALKWILL, Canon Michael Robert. b 67. Univ of Wales (Lamp) BD 89 Univ of Wales (Cardiff) MTh 92. St Mich Coll Llan 89 Bp Tucker Coll Mukono 91. **d** 91 **p** 92. C Llanrhos *St As* 91–97; Bp's Visitor from 94; R Llanfyllin and Bwlchycibau 97–11; AD Llanfyllin 05–11; Bp's Chapl and Press Officer from 11; Can Cursal and Can Res St As Cathl from 11. *The Vicarage, 1 Llys Trewithan, St Asaph LL17 0DJ* T: (01745) 583503 E: michaelbalkwill@churchinwales.org.uk

BALL, Alan. b 26. Qu Coll Birm 72. **d** 75 **p** 75. NSM Hamstead St Paul *Birm* 75–93; rtd 93; PtO *Portsm* from 93. *25 Tebourba Drive, Alverstoke, Gosport PO12 2NT* T: (023) 9260 1694 E: alanball72017@gmail.com

BALL, Andrew Thomas. b 54. K Coll Lon BD 75 AKC 75. Sarum & Wells Th Coll 76. **d** 77 **p** 78. C Ribbleton *Blackb* 77–80; C Sedgley All SS *Lich* 80–84; V Pheasey 84–90; Chapl Gd Hope Distr Gen Hosp Sutton Coldfield 90–94; Chapl Gd Hope Hosp NHS Trust Sutton Coldfield 94–06; Chapl Heart of England NHS Foundn Trust 07–18; rtd 18; PtO *Birm* from 18. *42 Falstone Road, Sutton Coldfield B73 6PJ* T: 0121-243 1948 E: andrew.ball7@virgin.net

BALL, Anthony Charles. b 46. Lon Univ BD 71. Chich Th Coll 72. **d** 73 **p** 74. C Heref St Martin 73–76; C Ealing St Pet Mt Park Lon 76–82; V Ruislip Manor St Paul 82–11; rtd 11; PtO *Chich* from 17. *44 Ashdown, Eaton Road, Hove BN3 3AQ*

BALL, Canon Anthony James. b 68. St Chad's Coll Dur BA 89 Heythrop Coll Lon MA 10. NTMTC 97. **d** 00 **p** 01. NSM Madrid *Eur* 00–03; Chapl Damascus 03–05; Apb Cant's Sec for Internat, Ecum and Angl Communion Affairs 05–08; Abp's Sec for Internat and Inter-Relig Relns *Cant* 08–09; Abp's Chapl 09–11; Lic Preacher *Lon* 07–11; Public Preacher *S'wark* 11–16; V Worth, Pound Hill and Maidenbower *Chich* 11–16; Chapl Worth Sch 12–16; Can Westmr Abbey from 16; Hon Can All SS Cathl Cairo from 07; Hon Can Madrid Cathl from 07; Lic Preacher *Lon* from 17. *5 Little Cloister, London SW1P 3PL* T: (020) 7654 4805 E: anthony.ball@westminster-abbey.org

BALL, Anthony Michael. b 46. Kelham Th Coll 66. **d** 70 **p** 71. C Kingswinford St Mary *Lich* 70–74; C W Bromwich All SS 74–76; P-in-c Priorslee 76–80; V 80–82; Asst Chapl HM Pris Lewes 82–83; Chapl 88–95; Chapl HM Pris Lewes 83–88; Featherstone 95-00; The Verne 00–06; PtO *Sarum* from 06; rtd 11. *La Providence, 21 Portland Road, Weymouth DT4 9ES* T: (01305) 787027 E: tonyball2008@hotmail.co.uk

BALL, Ian Raymond. b 45. CertEd Univ of Wales MPhil. Glouc Th Course 81. **d** 85 **p** 87. NSM Churchstoke w Hyssington and Sarn *Heref* 85–15; Lic to Bp Ludlow 87–15; LtO *St As* from 93; PtO *Heref* from 16. *Bachaethlon Cottage, Sarn, Newtown SY16 4HH* T: (01686) 670505 M: 07966-022404 E: ian@pathways.entadsl.com

BALL, Mrs Jane. b 68. Charlotte Mason Coll of Educn BEd 91. St Steph Ho Ox 01. **d** 03 **p** 04. C Bedale and Leeming *Ripon* 03–05; Hon C Devizes St Jo w St Mary *Sarum* 05–07; Chapl Godolphin Sch 07–14; V E Meon *Portsm* from 14; V Langrish from 14; C W Meon and Warnford from 14; AD Petersfield from 16. *The Vicarage, Church Street, East Meon, Petersfield GU32 1NH* T: (01730) 823618 M: 07771-804324 E: jandjball@btinternet.com

BALL, Mrs Jema Mary. b 83. Man Univ BSc 04. Trin Coll Bris BA 12. **d** 12 **p** 13. C Countesthorpe w Foston *Leic* 12–15; C Oundle w Ashton and Benefield w Glapthorn *Pet* from 15; Dioc Young Voc Officer from 16. *41 Hillfield Road, Oundle, Peterborough PE8 4QR* M: 07966-733836

BALL, John Kenneth. b 42. Lon Univ BSc 64 AKC 64. Linc Th Coll 69. **d** 71 **p** 72. C Garston *Liv* 71–74; C Eastham *Ches* 74–75; C Barnston 75–77; V Over St Jo 77–82; V Helsby and Dunham-on-the-Hill 82–94; RD Frodsham 88–94; P-in-c Alvanley 92–94; V Hoylake 94–98; rtd 98; P-in-c Downholme

and Marske *Ripon* 00–05; C Richmond w Hudswell and Downholme and Marske 05–07; PtO *Blackb* from 06. *2 King Street, Longridge, Preston PR3 3RQ* T: (01772) 783172

BALL, John Roy. b 47. Fitzw Coll Cam MA 71. Wycliffe Hall Ox 83. **d** 85 **p** 86. C Stockport St Mary *Ches* 85–88; C Fazeley *Lich* 88–94; Res Min Drayton Bassett 89–94; Chapl Grenoble *Eur* 94–00; P-in-c Lithuania 00–05; Asst Chapl Amsterdam w Den Helder and Heiloo 05–12; rtd 12; PtO *Lich* from 13; *Eur* from 18. *20 Robin Close, Uttoxeter ST14 8TP* T: (01889) 567459 E: royball77@gmail.com

BALL, Mrs Judith Anne. b 48. Nottm Univ BA 70 Liv Univ PGCE 71. NOC 98. **d** 01 **p** 02. C Upholland *Liv* 01–12; rtd 12; PtO *Liv* from 16. *31 Ryder Crescent, Aughton, Ormskirk L39 5EY* T: (01695) 421579

BALL, Kevin Harry. b 55. Linc Th Coll 92. **d** 94 **p** 95. C New Mills *Derby* 94–96; C Walthamstow St Sav *Chelmsf* 96–98; V Stocksbridge *Sheff* 98–00; C Barnsley St Mary *Wakef* 00–01; Chapl Barnsley Coll 00–01; P-in-c Sneinton St Cypr *S'well* 01–05; Chapl Notts Fire and Rescue Service 04–05; Sen Chapl Man Airport 05–11; R Calow and Sutton cum Duckmanton *Derby* from 11; Jt Dioc Ecum Officer from 12. *The Rectory, Top Road, Calow, Chesterfield S44 5AF* T: (01246) 462192 E: k.h.ball@tinyworld.co.uk

BALL, Mrs Marion Elaine. b 68. Hertf Coll Ox BA 90 St Jo Coll Dur BA 99. Cranmer Hall Dur 97. **d** 02 **p** 03. C Kingston upon Hull H Trin *York* 02–11; PtO *Sheff* from 12; Chapl HM Pris Moorland from 19. *10 Downing Street, Doncaster DN1 3BJ* T: (01302) 523000 E: marion.ball001@btinternet.com

BALL, Martin Francis. b 62. Wycliffe Hall Ox 06. **d** 08 **p** 09. C Woking Ch Ch *Guildf* 08–11; V Knutton *Lich* 11–13; V Newcastle St Geo from 11. *St George's Vicarage, 28 Hempstalls Lane, Newcastle ST5 0SS* M: 07816-398459 E: martball@gmail.com

✠**BALL, The Rt Revd Michael Thomas.** b 32. Qu Coll Cam BA 55 MA 59. **d** 71 **p** 71 **c** 80. CGA from 60; Prior Stroud Priory 64–76; C Whiteshill *Glouc* 71–76; LtO 76; P-in-c Stanmer w Falmer *Chich* 76–80; Chapl Sussex Univ 76–80; Suff Bp Jarrow *Dur* 80–90; Angl Adv Tyne Tees TV 84–90; Bp Truro 90–97; rtd 97; PtO *B & W* 01–10 and 15–17. *The Coach House, The Manor, Aller, Langport TA10 0RA*

BALL, Nicholas Edward. b 54. Man Univ BA 75 Ox Univ MA 85. Ripon Coll Cuddesdon 79. **d** 80 **p** 81. C Yardley Wood *Birm* 80–83; C Moseley St Mary 83–86; Chapl Cen 13 83–85; V Bartley Green *Birm* 86–95; P-in-c Hall Green St Pet 95–97; PtO 00–03; Chapl Birm Children's Hosp NHS Trust and Birm Heartlands and Solihull NHS Trust 03–09; rtd 09; Chapl Birm Children's Hosp NHS Foundn Trust 13–16; PtO *Birm* from 16. *12 Apsley Croft, Birmingham B38 0AF* T: 0121-243 1336 E: nicholaseball@hotmail.com

BALL, Norman. b 41. Liv Univ BA 63 Ch Coll Liv CertEd 72. Cuddesdon Coll 65. **d** 68 **p** 69. C Broseley w Benthall *Heref* 68–72; Hd RS Christleton High Sch 72–75; V Plemstall w Guilden Sutton *Ches* 75–79; Hd RS Neston Co High Sch 79–94; NSM Dodleston *Ches* 86–91; NSM Buckley *St As* 91–94; TV Hawarden 94–00; rtd 00; PtO *St As* from 00. *White Cottage, Lower Mountain Road, Penyffordd, Chester CH4 0EX* T: (01244) 661132

BALL, Peter Edwin. b 44. Lon Univ BD 65 DipEd. Wycliffe Hall Ox 75. **d** 77 **p** 78. C Prescot *Liv* 77–80; R Lawford *Chelmsf* 80–99; RD Harwich 91–96; P-in-c Broomfield 99–04; V 04–10; rtd 10; PtO *Chelmsf* from 10; *St E* 11–16. *14 Merriam Close, Brantham, Manningtree CO11 1RY* T: (01206) 393316 E: pebblej@btinternet.com

BALL, Canon Peter William. b 30. Worc Coll Ox BA 53 MA 57. Cuddesdon Coll 53. **d** 55 **p** 56. C Poplar All SS w St Frideswide *Lon* 55–61; V Preston Ascension 61–68; R Shepperton 68–84; RD Staines 72–74; RD Spelthorne 74–83; Preb St Paul's Cathl 76–84; Can Res and Chan St Paul's Cathl 84–90; PtO *Sarum* from 90; rtd 95. *Whittonedge, Whittonditch Road, Ramsbury, Marlborough SN8 2PX* T: (01672) 520259 E: peterball@whittonedge.org.uk

BALL, Philip John. b 52. Bris Univ BEd 75 Ox Univ MTh 98. Ripon Coll Cuddesdon 79. **d** 82 **p** 83. C Norton St Mich *Dur* 82–84; C Greenford H Cross *Lon* 84–88; V Hayes St Edm 88–97; AD Hillingdon 94–97; TR Bicester w Bucknell, Caversfield and Launton *Ox* 97–07; AD Bicester and Islip 00–05; R Abington *Pet* 07–18; Asst Dir Ords 14–18; rtd 18. *Applegrove, 2 Manor Court, Brackley NN13 6EL* T: (01280) 840357 M: 07761-223506 E: phjobal07@gmail.com

BALL, Philip John. b 63. Coll of Ripon & York St Jo BA 91. Cranmer Hall Dur 97. **d** 99 **p** 00. C Linthorpe *York* 99–02; V Kingston upon Hull H Trin 02–07; N Humberside Ind Chapl 08–11; V Airmyn, Hook and Rawcliffe *Sheff* from 11. *The Vicarage, 12 Church Lane, Hook, Goole DN14 5PN* T: (01405) 767721 E: philip.ball@sheffield.anglican.org

BALL, Rita Enid. b 49. Sheff Univ LLB 69. SAOMC 94. **d** 97 **p** 98. NSM Newbury Ox 97–03; R Wantage Downs 03–09; TR Hermitage 09–17; AD Newbury 10–15; Hon Can Ch Ch 12–17; rtd 17; Hon C Newbury St Geo and St Jo Ox 17–19; PtO from 19. *240 Andover Road, Newbury RG14 6PT* T: (01635) 228072 E: ritaball65@gmail.com

BALL, Roy. *See* BALL, John Roy

BALL, Stephen Andrew. b 54. Wycliffe Hall Ox. **d** 05 **p** 06. C Hilperton w Whaddon and Staverton etc *Sarum* 05–07; C Canalside Benefice 07–08; P-in-c 08–12; R 12–15; P-in-c Sherfield-on-Loddon and Stratfield Saye etc *Win* 15–19; R from 19. *The Rectory, 33 Northfield Road, Sherfield-on-Loddon, Hook RG27 0DR* M: 07943-014277 E: vicar.sb54rev@gmail.com

BALL, Susan. b 64. SNWTP 14. **d** 17 **p** 18. OLM Droylsden St Mary *Man* from 17. *72 Graver Lane, Manchester M40 1QW* T: 0161-682 1439

BALL, Canon Timothy William. b 60. Trin Coll Bris 96. **d** 96 **p** 97. C Harlow St Mary and St Hugh w St Jo the Bapt *Chelmsf* 96–99; V Springfield H Trin 99–11; Ind Chapl 00–11; TR Loughrigg *Carl* 11–15; TV Gt Baddow *Chelmsf* from 15; AD Chelmsf S from 17; AD Chelmsf N from 19; Hon Can Chelmsf Cathl from 18. *62 Longmead Avenue, Chelmsford CM2 7EY* T: (01245) 901612 E: timmyball@tesco.net

BALL, Vernon. b 34. Ox Min Course 87. **d** 90 **p** 91. NSM Banbury Ox 90–99; rtd 99; PtO Ox from 06. *20 Springfield Avenue, Banbury OX16 9HT* T: (01295) 265740

BALLANTINE, Canon Peter Sinclair. b 46. Nottm Univ MTh 85. K Coll Lon BA 68 AKC 68 St Jo Coll Nottm 70 Lon Coll of Div ALCD 71 BD 73 LTh 74. **d** 73 **p** 74. C Rainham *Chelmsf* 73–77; C Wennington 73–77; TV Barton Mills *St E* 77–79; TV Barton Mills, Beck Row w Kenny Hill etc 80–82; Chapl Liv Poly 83–86; Tr Officer Rugby Deanery *Cov* 86–97; P-in-c Churchover w Willey 86–97; P-in-c Clifton upon Dunsmore and Newton 86–97; Dir Buckingham Adnry Chr Tr Progr Ox 97–02; TV Stantonbury and Willen 02–15; Hon Can Ch Ch 12–15; rtd 15; PtO Ox from 15. *2 Carroll Close, Newport Pagnell MK16 8QQ* M: 07876-797507 E: pballarev@yahoo.com

BALLANTINE, Roderic Keith. b 44. Chich Th Coll 66. **d** 69 **p** 70. C Nunhead St Antony *S'wark* 69–72; C S Hackney St Jo w Ch Ch *Lon* 72–75; P-in-c Kensal Town St Thos w St Andr and St Phil 75–79; V Stoke Newington St Andr 79–05; rtd 05; PtO *Lon* from 06. *67 Savernake Road, London NW3 2LA* T: (020) 7267 2744

BALLANTYNE, Jane Elizabeth. *See* KENCHINGTON, Jane Elizabeth Ballantyne

BALLARD, The Ven Andrew Edgar. b 44. Dur Univ BA 66. Westcott Ho Cam 66. **d** 68 **p** 69. C St Marylebone St Mary *Lon* 68–72; C Portsea St Mary *Portsm* 72–76; V Haslingden w Haslingden Grane *Blackb* 76–82; V Walkden Moor *Man* 82–93; TR Walkden Moor w Lt Hulton 93–98; AD Farnworth 90–98; Chapl Salford Coll 82–92; P-in-c Rochdale *Man* 98–99; TR 00; Adn Rochdale 00–05; Adn Man 05–09; Hon Can Man Cathl 98–09; rtd 09; PtO *Linc* from 16. *30 Swift Drive, Scawby Brook, Brigg DN20 9FL* T: (01652) 659560 E: ae.ballard@btinternet.com

BALLARD, Miss Anne Christina. b 54. LRAM 76 HonRCM 93 ARAM 94. Wycliffe Hall Ox 82. **dss** 85 **d** 87 **p** 94. Hove Bp Hannington Memorial Ch *Chich* 85–87; Chapl St Mich Sch Burton Park 87–89; Chapl RCM and Imp Coll Lon 89–93; Prec Ch Ch Ox 93–98; P-in-c Ivinghoe w Pitstone and Slapton 98–03; P-in-c Llanbadarn Fawr, Llandegley and Llanfihangel etc *S & B* 03–08; V Alstonfield, Butterton, Ilam etc *Lich* 08–16; V Middle Marches *Heref* from 16. *The Vicarage, Bucknell, Shrewsbury SY7 0AD* T: (01547) 530030 E: revannie.middlemarches@gmail.com

BALLARD, Duncan Charles John. b 65. Sheff Univ BSc 87. St Mich Coll Llan 00. **d** 02 **p** 03. C Worc St Barn w Ch Ch 02–06; TV Worc SE 06–11; P-in-c Hampton in Arden *Birm* 11–12; P-in-c Bickenhill 11–12; R Hampton-in-Arden w Bickenhill 12–17; Chapl Birm Airport 11–17; P-in-c Barston 15–17; AD Solihull 13–17; P-in-c Ashbourne St Oswald w Mapleton *Derby* from 17; P-in-c Ashbourne St Jo from 17; P-in-c Clifton from 17; P-in-c Norbury w Snelston from 17. *The Vicarage, 61 Belle Vue Road, Ashbourne DE6 1AT* T: (01335) 343825 E: duncan.ballard@me.com

BALLARD, Canon Michael Arthur. b 44. Lon Univ BA 66. Westcott Ho Cam 68. **d** 70 **p** 71. C Harrow Weald All SS *Lon* 70–73; C Aylesbury Ox 73–78; V Eastwood *Chelmsf* 78–90; RD Hadleigh 83–90; R Southchurch H Trin 90–13; RD Southend 94–00; Hon Can Chelmsf Cathl 89–13; rtd 13; PtO *Chelmsf* 14–16; Hon C Southend from 16. *159 Kensington Road, Southend-on-Sea SS1 2SZ* T: (01702) 616950 E: michael.ballard473@btinternet.com

BALLARD, Nigel Humphrey. b 48. Linc Th Coll 92. **d** 94 **p** 95. C Old Brumby *Linc* 94; C Bottesford w Ashby 94–97; P-in-c Helpringham w Hale 97–01; rtd 02; PtO *St E* from 14. *37A Alumhurst Road, Bournemouth BH4 8EN*

BALLARD, Steven Peter. b 52. Man Univ BA 73 MA 74 Philipps Univ Marburg DrTheol 98. St Steph Ho Ox 76. **d** 78 **p** 79. C Lancaster St Mary *Blackb* 78–81; C Blackpool St Mich 81–84; V Brierfield 84–94; PtO *Carl* 95–07; Hon C Dumfries *Glas* from 09. *Avalon, Bankend, Dumfries DG1 4RN* T: (01387) 770438 M: 07563-564695 E: revsteven@stjohnsdumfries.org

BALLARD-TREMEER, Mrs Margaret Eileen. b 39. K Alfred's Coll Win TDip 62. Th Ext Educn Coll 86. **d** 90 **p** 94. C St Mary's Cathl Johannesburg S Africa 90–03; C Bramley 03–05; PtO Rochm from 05. *313 Pickhurst Lane, West Wickham BR4 0HW* T: (020) 8777 5694 E: margaret@ecoharmony.org

BALLENTINE, Ian Clarke. b 46. Aston Univ BSc 71 CEng. BTh. **d** 91 **p** 92. C Lurgan St Jo *D & D* 91–95; I Mallusk *Conn* 95–07; Nat Dir (Ireland) SOMA UK 07–17; rtd 17. *12 Gordonville, Coleraine BT52 1EF* T: (028) 7035 8328 M: 07479-544396 E: iancballentine@gmail.com

BALLINGER, Francis James. b 43. AKC 70. **d** 71 **p** 85. C Weston-super-Mare St Sav *B & W* 71–72; Dir Bd Soc Resp *Leic* 85–88; Hon C Bringhurst w Gt Easton 85–88; TV Melksham *Sarum* 88–93; P-in-c Coughton and Spernall, Morton Bagot and Oldberrow *Cov* 93–98; Dioc Rural Adv 93–98; R Kingstone w Clehonger, Eaton Bishop etc *Heref* 98–03; rtd 04; PtO *Sarum* 05–15. *4 Broxburn Road, Warminster BA12 8EX* T: (01985) 300316

BALLISTON THICKE, James. *See* THICKE, James Balliston

BALMER, Richard Ian. b 88. QUB BSc 11. Oak Hill Th Coll BA 16. **d** 18 **p** 19. C Enderby w Lubbesthorpe and Thurlaston *Leic* from 18. *2 Jacques Close, Enderby, Leicester LE19 4RW* M: 07743-574882 E: richbalmer10@gmail.com

BALMER, Walter Owen. b 30. NOC 83. **d** 86 **p** 87. NSM Gateacre *Liv* 86–91; NSM Hale 91–00; PtO from 00. *38 Grangemeadow Road, Liverpool L25 4SU* T: 0151-421 1189

BAMBER, David Beverley. b 51. Univ of Wales (Lamp) BA 75. St Steph Ho Ox 75. **d** 77 **p** 78. C Altrincham St Geo *Ches* 77–80; C Oxton 80–81; PtO *Derby* 85–87; C Staveley and Barrow Hill 87–88; C W Retford *S'well* 89–90; C E Retford 89–90 and 91–92; rtd 12. *10 Marine Park, Wirral CH48 5HW* M: 07984-807663 E: davidbamber2@hotmail.com

BAMBER, Jeremy John. b 56. St Jo Coll Cam MA 82. STETS 06. **d** 09 **p** 10. NSM Southover *Chich* 09–17; NSM Trin in Lewes from 18. *29 Montacute Road, Lewes BN7 1EN* T: (01273) 474923 E: jjbj@bambers.net

BAMBER, Canon Sheila Jane. b 54. Univ of Wales (Lamp) BA 75 Sheff Univ MA 77 Open Univ MBA 94. Ripon Coll Cuddesdon 96. **d** 98 **p** 99. C Dur St Cuth 98–01; C Sacriston and Kimblesworth 01–02; TV Dur N 02–09; Hon C Lanchester 09–10; Dioc Dir of Educn 04–10; Adv for Women's Min 09–10; Hon Can Dur Cathl 06–10; Can Res Newc Cathl 10–12; Can Provost Sunderland Minster *Dur* 12–16; AD Wearmouth 15–16; rtd 17. *23 Strothers Terrace, High Spen, Rowlands Gill NE39 2HL* T: (01207) 544547 M: 07989-542565

BAMBERG, Robert William. b 43. Chu Coll Cam BA 65 PGCE 68. SWMTC 98. **d** 01 **p** 02. NSM Kingsteignton and Teigngrace *Ex* 01–08; PtO 08–10. *Tynyffordd, Ystrad Meurig SY25 6AX* T: (01974) 831725 E: sallybamberg@gmail.com

BAMFORD, Geoffrey Belk. b 35. Lon Univ BA 57 Leic Coll of Educn PGCE 58. **d** 99 **p** 00. OLM Upper Holme Valley *Wakef* 99–14; *Leeds* from 14. *11 Flushouse, Holmbridge, Holmfirth HD9 2QY* T: (01484) 682532 E: jmgbbamford@gmail.com

BAMFORTH, Canon Marvin John. b 48. NOC 78. **d** 81 **p** 82. C Barnoldswick w Bracewell *Bradf* 81–84; V Cullingworth 84–88; V Mornington New Zealand 88–89; V Thornton in Lonsdale w Burton in Lonsdale *Bradf* 89–98; P-in-c Bentham St Jo 93–98; Dioc Chapl MU 91–94; Chapl Paphos Cyprus 98–05; rtd 06; Chapl Miss to Seafarers Limassol Cyprus 06–14; Hon C Ross w Walford and Brampton Abbotts *Heref* 17–18; Hon C NW Hants *Win* from 18; Hon Can Kinkizi from 08. *The Vicarage, 2 Flexford Close, Highclere, Newbury RG20 9PE*

BAMPING, Mrs Susan Janet. b 49. LCTP 08. **d** 11 **p** 12. NSM Cross Fell Gp *Carl* 11–15; PtO *Man* 18–23. *13 Hill End Road, Delph, Oldham OL3 5JA* T: (01768) 879085 E: alan.sue.bamping@btinternet.com

BAMPTON, Edward Thomas William. b 74. Pemb Coll Ox MBiochem 97 WolfsCollOxMSc 98 DPhil 02. QuCollBirm 12. **d** 14 **p** 15. C Shepshed and Oaks in Charnwood *Leic* 14–17; R Groby and Ratby from 17. *23 Ferndale Drive, Ratby, Leicester LE6 0LH* T: 0116-239 6520 E: rector@grobychurch.org.uk *or* revdredbampton@outlook.com

BANBURY, Canon David Paul. b 62. Coll of Ripon & York St Jo BA 84. Ridley Hall Cam 85. **d** 88 **p** 89. C Blackb St Jas 88–90; C Preston St Cuth 90–95; P-in-c Bradf St Clem 95–00; V 00; CPAS Evang 01–08; Dir Miss and Faith Stratford-upon-Avon, Luddington etc *Cov* 08–11; Ldr Par Miss Support *Blackb* 11–18; P-in-c Burscough Bridge *Liv* from 18; Hon Can Blackb Cathl from 17. *St John's Vicarage, 253 Liverpool Road South, Burscough, Ormskirk L40 7RE* M: 07803-184872 E: davidvanbury@icloud.com *or* david.banbury@blackburn.anglican.org

BANBURY, Ruth. *See* GIBBONS, Ruth Banbury

BANCROFT, Barbara Frances. b 57. **d** 16. NSM Bridlington Em and Barmston w Fraisthorpe *York* from 16. *28 Kingsgate, Bridlington YO15 3PU* T: (01262) 603599 E: bfbancroft@btinternet.com

BANCROFT, Mrs Patricia Ann. b 64. Win Univ MA 16. STETS. **d** 10 **p** 11. C Kingsclere and Ashford Hill w Headley *Win* 10–14; R Lynch w Iping Marsh and Milland *Chich* 14–17; P-in-c Stedham w Iping 16–17; R Linch w Iping Marsh, Milland and Rake etc from 17. *St Luke's Rectory, Fernhurst Road, Milland, Liphook GU30 7LU* E: trishbancroft@aol.com

BANDAWE, Mrs Christine. b 57. Liv Univ BTh 06. NOC 01. **d** 04 **p** 05. C Roundhay St Mary *Ripon* 04–08; TV Seacroft 08–18; rtd 18. *30 Fearnville Road, Leeds LS8 3EA* E: christinebandawe@yahoo.co.uk

BANDS, Canon Leonard Michael. b 40. Rhodes Univ BA 64. St Paul's Coll Grahamstown. **d** 69 **p** 70. C Uitenhage S Africa 69–72; R Alexandria 72–75; Chapl Rhodes Univ 75–80; Chapl Dioc Sch for Girls Grahamstown 80–86; Chapl Dioc Coll Cape Town 87–94; Dean Bloemfontein 94–02; C Lockerbie *Glas* 03–11; C Moffat 03–11; rtd 11. *Montagu Cottage, 20 Princes Street, Lochmaben, Lockerbie DG11 1PQ* T: (01387) 811149 M: 07766-341094 E: michael.bands@btinternet.com *or* michael.bands41@gmail.com

BANFIELD, Andrew Henry. b 48. AKC 71. St Aug Coll Cant 72. **d** 73 **p** 74. C Crayford *Roch* 73–76; Youth Chapl *Glouc* 77–89; Soc Services Development Officer Glos Co Coun from 89; PtO *Glouc* from 15. *49 Cleevelands Drive, Cheltenham GL50 4QD*

BANGAY (*formerly* REAST), **Mrs Eileen Joan.** b 40. Open Univ BA 93. EMMTC 81. dss 84 **d** 87 **p** 94. Linc St Mary-le-Wigford w St Benedict etc 80–90; C 87–90; C Stamford All SS w St Jo 90–93; NSM Walesby 93–95; P-in-c Sutton Bridge 95–00; V 00; RD Elloe E 99–00; rtd 01; PtO *Linc* from 01. *15 Heath Court, Grampian Way, Sinfin, Derby DE24 9NG* T: (01332) 989779 E: enj.bangay@btinternet.com

BANGOR, Archdeacon of. *See* STALLARD, The Ven Mary Kathleen Rose

BANGOR, Bishop of. *See* JOHN, The Rt Revd Andrew Thomas Griffith

BANGOR, Dean of. *See* JONES, The Very Revd Kathy Louise

BANHAM, Richard Mark. b 69. Sheff City Poly BSc 92. Trin Coll Bris 04. **d** 06 **p** 07. C Wroughton *Bris* 06–10; P-in-c Wheathampstead *St Alb* 10–12; R from 12; RD from 15. *The Rectory, Old Rectory Gardens, Wheathampstead, St Albans AL4 8AD* T: (01582) 833144 E: richard@banham.org

BANISTER, Desmond Peter. b 52. K Coll Lon BA 75 AKC 75. SAOMC 02. **d** 05 **p** 06. Hd Master Quainton Hall Sch Harrow 98–09; NSM Hatch End St Anselm *Lon* 05–08; NSM Hillingdon All SS 09; V from 09; AD Hillingdon 13–18; PtO *Ox* from 05. *All Saints' Vicarage, Ryefield Avenue, Uxbridge UB10 9BT* T: (01895) 239457 E: ppash@uk2.net

BANISTER, Jane Catherine. b 67. Man Univ BA 90 Em Coll Cam BA 96. Westcott Ho Cam 94. **d** 97 **p** 98. C Addington S'wark 97–00; C Wisley w Pyrford *Guildf* 00–02; PtO *St Alb* 03–08; NSM Tring 08–15; TV from 15. *The Rectory, 2 The Limes, Station Road, Tring HP23 5NW* T: (01442) 822170 E: jane@tringteamparish.org.uk

BANISTER, Canon Martin John. b 39. Worc Coll Ox BA 62 MA 68. Chich Th Coll 62. **d** 64 **p** 65. C Wellingborough All Hallows *Pet* 64–67; C Heene *Chich* 67–70; V Denford w Ringstead *Pet* 70–78; P-in-c Wilshamstead *St Alb* 78–80; P-in-c Houghton Conquest 78–80; V Wilshamstead and Houghton Conquest 80–89; RD Elstow 86–89; V Waltham Cross 89–04; RD Cheshunt 00–04; Hon Can St Alb 03–04; rtd 04; PtO *St Alb* from 04. *35 Cottonmill Lane, St Albans AL1 2BT* T: (01727) 847082 E: martinbanister@hotmail.com

BANKS, Allen James. b 48. CBDTI 98. **d** 01 **p** 02. OLM Kells *Carl* 01–05; NSM from 05; RD Calder from 14. *36 Basket Road, Whitehaven CA28 9AH* T: (01946) 61470 E: allenbanks@btinternet.com

BANKS, Matthew Clayton. b 79. **d** 13 **p** 14. C St Helen Bishopsgate w St Andr Undershaft etc *Lon* 13–16; C Cape Town St Steph S Africa from 16. *c/o David Banks, 37 Riversmead, Hoddesdon EN11 8DP* E: matthewclaytonbanks@gmail.com

BANKS, Canon Michael Thomas Harvey. b 35. Ushaw Coll Dur 58 Open Univ BA 75. **d** 63 **p** 64. C Winlaton *Dur* 69–71; P-in-c Bishopwearmouth Gd Shep 71–75; TV Melton Mowbray w Thorpe Arnold *Leic* 75–80; TR Loughborough Em 80–88; Dir of Ords 83–97; Hon Can Leic Cathl 83–87; Can Res and Chan Leic Cathl 87–03; Assoc P Christianity S 93–95; Hon C Leic H Spirit 01–03; rtd 03; PtO *Glouc* from 04. *Harvard House, 7 Harvard Close, Moreton-in-Marsh GL56 0JT* T: (01608) 650706

✠**BANKS, The Rt Revd Norman.** b 54. Oriel Coll Ox BA 76 MA 80. St Steph Ho Ox 79. **d** 82 **p** 83 **c** 11. C Newc Ch Ch w St Ann 82–87; P-in-c 87–90; V Tynemouth Cullercoats St Paul 90–00; V Walsingham, Houghton and Barsham *Nor* 00–11; P-in-c 11–12; RD Burnham and Walsingham 08–11; Chapl to The Queen 09–11; Suff Bp Richborough (PEV) *Cant* from 11; Hon Asst Bp Guildf from 12; Hon Asst Bp Nor from 12; Hon Asst Bp St E from 12; Hon Asst Bp Ely from 12; Hon Asst Bp St Alb from 13; Hon Asst Bp Linc from 15; PtO *Nor* from 17. *Parkside House, Abbey Mill Lane, St Albans AL3 4HE* T: (01727) 836358 E: bishop@richborough.org.uk

BANKS, Canon Philip Charles. b 61. NE Lon Poly BSc 85 Nottm Univ BTh 93 MRICS 87. Linc Th Coll 90. **d** 93 **p** 94. C Chelmsf Ascension 93–94; C Brentwood St Thos 94–98; P-in-c Elmstead 98–03; V Coggeshall w Markshall 03–12; Bp's Press Officer 97–05; Bp's Dom Chapl 01–04; RD Dedham and Tey 08–11; Can Res St E Cathl from 12. *1 Abbey Precinct, The Great Churchyard, Bury St Edmunds IP33 1RS* T: (01284) 748720 *or* 761982 M: 07798-681886 E: precentor@stedscathedral.org

BANKS, Susan Angela. *See* GRIFFITHS, Susan Angela

BANKS, Mrs Susan June. b 60. NOC 03. **d** 06 **p** 07. C Medlock Head *Man* 06–09; TV Heywood 09–10; P-in-c Heywood St Marg and Heap Bridge 10–18; V from 18. *St Margaret's Vicarage, 27 Heys Lane, Heywood OL10 3RD* T: (01706) 368053 E: sbanks4@sky.com

BANKS, Vivienne Philippa. *See* BRIDGES, Vivienne Philippa

BANNER, John William. b 36. Open Univ BA 78. Tyndale Hall Bris 61. **d** 64 **p** 65. C Bootle St Leon *Liv* 64–66; C Wigan St Jas 66–69; C Stapleton *Bris* 69–70; Gen Sec Scripture Union Australia 70–72; V Liv Ch Ch Norris Green 72–82; V Tunbridge Wells H Trin w Ch Ch *Roch* 82–05; rtd 05. *Dormers, Southview Road, Crowborough TN6 1HG* E: celiabanner@gmail.com

BANNER, Michael Charles. b 61. Ball Coll Ox BA 83 MA 86 DPhil 87. **d** 86 **p** 87. Fell St Pet Coll Ox 85–88; Dean Peterho Cam 88–94; Prof Moral and Soc Th K Coll Lon 94–04; NSM Balsham, Weston Colville, W Wickham etc *Ely* 01–04; Prof Edin Univ 04–06; Dean Trin Coll Cam from 06. *Trinity College, Cambridge CB2 1TQ* T: (01223) 338563 F: 338564 E: chapel@trin.cam.ac.uk

BANNISTER, Preb Anthony Peter. b 40. Ex Univ BA 62. Clifton Th Coll 63. **d** 65 **p** 66. C Uphill *B & W* 65–69; C Hove Bp Hannington Memorial Ch *Chich* 69–74; V Wembdon *B & W* 74–91; Youth Chapl 80–83; RD Bridgwater 80–89; V Taunton St Jas 91–05; Preb Wells Cathl 97–05; rtd 05; PtO *B & W* from 05. *12 Mitre Court, Taunton TA1 3ER* T: (01823) 259110 M: 07576-697889 E: apbannister@talktalk.net

BANNISTER, Clifford John. b 53. Hatf Coll Dur BA 76. Ripon Coll Cuddesdon 84. **d** 86 **p** 87. C Weymouth H Trin *Sarum* 86–89; TV Basingstoke *Win* 89–94; V Hedge End St Jo 94–09; AD Eastleigh 07–09; P-in-c Win St Bart 09–10; R Win St Bart and St Lawr w St Swithun 10–19; rtd 19. *Address withheld by request* E: cliffbannister@hotmail.co.uk

BANNISTER, Gregory Simon. b 80. **d** 14 **p** 15. C Enfield Ch Ch Trent Park *Lon* 14–17; PtO *Chelmsf* from 18. *38 Wallenger Avenue, Romford RM2 6ER* M: 07738-670221 E: gsbannister@gmail.com

BANNISTER, John Leslie. b 55. Lanc Univ MA 99. CBDTI 95. **d** 98 **p** 99. C Flimby and Netherton *Carl* 98–00; C Whitehaven 00–02; TV 02–04; TR 04–13; TV 13–14; Blackb 13–14; V Lund from 14. *Lund Vicarage, Church Lane, Clifton, Preston PR4 0ZE* T: (01772) 683617 M: 07788-562488 E: johnlbannister@gmail.com

BANNISTER, Peter. *See* BANNISTER, Anthony Peter

BANNISTER, Peter Edward. b 38. Leeds Univ BSc 60. Linc Th Coll 72. **d** 74 **p** 75. C Norbury St Steph *Cant* 74–77; C Allington and Maidstone St Pet 77–80; R Temple Ewell w Lydden 80–86; TV Bracknell *Ox* 86–93; P-in-c Swallowfield 93–03; rtd 03; PtO *Bradf* 04–14; *Leeds* from 14. *15 Ryeland Street, Cross Hills, Keighley BD20 8SR* T: (01535) 636036

BANNISTER, Mrs Sophie Claire. b 81. Ch Coll Cam BA 04. Ridley Hall Cam 12 Oak Hill Th Coll 14. **d** 16 **p** 18. C St Sepulchre w Ch Ch Greyfriars etc *Lon* from 16. *38 Wallenger Avenue, Romford RM2 6ER* M: 07813-080075 E: sophiecmaggs@hotmail.com

BANNON, Lyndon Russell. b 73. Ches Coll of HE BA 95 Univ Coll Ches PGCE 96 Leeds Univ MA 06. NOC 04. **d** 06 **p** 07. NSM Leasowe *Ches* 06–10; NSM Willaston from 10; Bp's Officer for SSM from 18. *7 Nelson's Croft, Wirral CH63 3DU* T: 0151-334 9931 E: lyndonbannon123@btinternet.com *or* lyndon.bannon@chester.anglican.org

BANTING, Canon David Percy. b 51. Magd Coll Cam MA 74. Wycliffe Hall Ox MA 79. **d** 80 **p** 81. C Ox St Ebbe w H Trin and St Pet 80–83; Min St Jos Merry Hill CD *Lich* 83–90; V Chadderton Ch Ch *Man* 90–98; V Harold Wood *Chelmsf* 98–18; Hon Can Chelmsf Cathl 09–18; rtd 18; PtO *Chelmsf* from 18. *15 Amersham Close, Romford RM3 9JL*

BANTING, Dawn Ann. b 70. STETS. **d** 13 **p** 14. NSM Portsm Cathl from 13; CF from 13; Chapl Portsm Hosps NHS Trust from 16. *c/o MOD Chaplains (Army)* T: (01264) 383430 E: dawn.banting@portsmouthcathedral.org.uk

BANTING, The Ven Kenneth Mervyn Lancelot Hadfield. b 37. Pemb Coll Cam BA 61 MA 65. Cuddesdon Coll 64. **d** 65 **p** 66. Asst Chapl Win Coll 65–70; C Leigh Park *Portsm* 70–72; TV Hemel Hempstead *St Alb* 73–79; V Goldington 79–88; P-in-c Renhold 80–82; RD Bedford 84–87; V Portsea St Cuth *Portsm* 88–96; RD Portsm 94–96; Adn Is of Wight 96–03; Hon Can Portsm Cathl 95–96; rtd 03; PtO *Portsm* 03–17; *Chich* from 04; RD Westbourne 09–11. *Furzend, 38A Bosham Hoe, Bosham PO18 8ET* T: (01243) 572340 E: furzend@merlinbanting.plus.com

BANTRY WHITE, Robin. *See* WHITE, Robin Edward Bantry

BANYARD, Michael George. b 47. Ch Ch Coll Cant CertEd 69 Birm Univ BPhil 79 Open Univ MA 92. Westcott Ho Cam 01. **d** 03 **p** 04. NSM Chippenham *Ely* 03–08; NSM Fordham St Pet 07–08; NSM Isleham 07–08; NSM Kennett 07–08; NSM Snailwell 07–08; R Three Rivers Gp 08–17; Dioc Spirituality Officer 10–17; RD Fordham and Quy 15–17; rtd 17; PtO *Ely* from 17. *12A Cambridge Road, Ely CB7 4HL* E: banyardmg1@yahoo.co.uk

BARBER, Ms Annabel Ruth. b 58. Leeds Univ BSc 80 Anglia Ruskin Univ MA 10. NEOC 01. **d** 04 **p** 05. C Scawby, Redbourne and Hibaldstow *Linc* 04–07; Chapl N Lincs and Goole NHS Foundn Trust 07–12; Lic Preacher *Linc* 12–14; R Waddington from 14; Discipleship Development Adv from 14; RD Graffoe from 17. *The Rectory, 1 Viking Close, Waddington, Lincoln LN5 9RA* T: (01522) 721306 E: annabel.barber@advancedit.org.uk

BARBER, Anne Louise. *See* STEWART, Anne Louise

BARBER, Canon Christopher Albert. b 33. Ch Coll Cam BA 53 MA 57. Coll of Resurr Mirfield 56. **d** 58 **p** 59. C Cov St Pet 58–61; C Stokenchurch and Cadmore End *Ox* 61–64; V Royton St Paul *Man* 64–70; V Stapleford *Ely* 70–80; RD Shelford 76–80; Hon Can Ely Cathl 88–98; R Cottenham 88–92; RD N Stowe 90–92; V Terrington St John 92–98; V Tilney All Saints 92–98; rtd 98; PtO *Ely* from 98; Asst Rtd Clergy and Clergy Widow(er)s' Officer 00–07; Rtd Clergy Officer from 07; PV Ely Cathl from 03. *20 King Edgar Close, Ely CB6 1DP* T: (01353) 612338 E: chrisbarber2@ntlworld.com

BARBER, Garth Antony. b 48. Southn Univ BSc 69 Lon Univ MSc 79 FRAS MSOSc. St Jo Coll Nottm. **d** 76 **p** 77. C Hounslow H Trin *Lon* 76–79; Chapl City of Lon Poly 79–86; P-in-c Twickenham All Hallows 86–97; Chapl Richmond Coll 87–97; Chapl UEA *Nor* 97–02; P-in-c Kingswood *S'wark* 02–11; V 11–13; AD Reigate 06–12; rtd 13; PtO *Cant* from 14. *11 Jasmine Close, Chartham, Canterbury CT4 7TF* T: (01737) 507293 E: garth.barber@sky.com

BARBER, Canon Hilary John. b 65. Aston Tr Scheme 92 Sarum Th Coll 94. **d** 96 **p** 97. C Moston St Jo *Man* 96–00; R Chorlton-cum-Hardy St Clem 00–07; P-in-c Chorlton-cum-Hardy St Werburgh 05–07; Dioc Music Adv 03–07; V Halifax *Wakef* 07–14; *Leeds* 14–17; P-in-c Siddal *Wakef* 13–14; *Leeds* 14–17; V Halifax w Siddal from 17; Hon Can Wakef Cathl from 11. *The Vicarage, Kensington Road, Halifax HX3 0HN* T: (01422) 365477 E: h.barber@halifaxminster.org

BARBER, John Eric Michael. b 30. Wycliffe Hall Ox 63. **d** 65 **p** 66. C Lupset *Wakef* 65–68; C Halifax St Jo Bapt 68–70; V Dewsbury St Matt and St Jo 70–80; V Perry Common *Birm* 80–95; rtd 95; PtO *Sarum* from 95. *21A Westhill Road, Weymouth DT4 9NB* T: (01305) 786553

BARBER, Miss Marion. b 50. Birkbeck Coll Lon BSc 97 K Coll Lon MSc 03. **d** 07 **p** 08. NSM Lee St Mildred *S'wark* from 07. *12B Beechfield Road, London SE6 4NE* T: (020) 8690 6035 E: marionbarber12@outlook.com

BARBER, Michael. *See* BARBER, John Eric Michael

BARBER, Neil Andrew Austin. b 63. Ealing Coll of Educn BA 85. NTMTC 94. **d** 98 **p** 98. At St Mary's Chr Workers' Trust 95–01; NSM Eastrop *Win* 98–01; V Normanton *Derby* from 01. *St Giles's Vicarage, 16*

Browning Street, Derby DE23 8DN T: (01332) 767483 E: neil.barber@stgiles-derby.org.uk

BARBER, Philip Kenneth. b 43. St Jo Coll Dur BA 65 Sheff Univ DipEd 66. NW Ord Course 74. **d** 76 **p** 77. NSM Burscough Bridge *Liv* 76–84; Asst Master Ormskirk Gr Sch 76–84; P-in-c Brigham *Carl* 84–85; V 85–89; P-in-c Mosser 84–85; V 85–89; P-in-c Borrowdale 89–94; Chapl Keswick Sch 89–94; P-in-c Beetham and Educn Adv *Carl* 94–99; P-in-c Brampton and Farlam and Castle Carrock w Cumrew 99–02; P-in-c Irthington, Crosby-on-Eden and Scaleby 99–02; P-in-c Hayton w Cumwhitton 99–02; TR Eden, Gelt and Irthing 02–04; rtd 04; PtO *Carl* 04–16; *Blackb* from 05. *18 Holbeck Avenue, Morecambe LA4 6NP* T: (01524) 401695 E: philipbarber326@gmail.com

BARBER, Ralph Warwick. b 72. Lon Guildhall Univ BA 94. Ripon Coll Cuddesdon 03. **d** 05 **p** 06. C Newquay *Truro* 05–08; Chapl RN from 08. *Royal Naval Chaplaincy Service, Mail Point 1-2, Leach Building, Whale Island, Portsmouth PO2 8BY* T: (023) 9262 5055 F: 9262 5134 E: ralphwbarber@aol.com

BARBER, Royston Henry. b 38. Univ of Wales (Abth) BD 86. United Th Coll Abth 83. **d** 86 **p** 87. NSM Tywyn w Aberdyfi *Ban* 86–92; NSM Cannington, Otterhampton, Combwich and Stockland *B & W* 93–98; PtO 98–14; Ex 00–13. *30 Carlton Court, Blenheim Road, Minehead TA24 5PL* T: (01643) 708783

BARBOUR, Mrs Jennifer Louise. b 32. St Hugh's Coll Ox BA 54 MA 57 Barrister-at-Law 55. Gilmore Course 80. **dss** 81 **d** 87 **p** 94. Bray and Braywood *Ox* 81–84; Hermitage and Hampstead Norreys, Cold Ash etc 84–87; Chapl Leeds Poly *Ripon* 87–92; Chapl Leeds Metrop Univ 92–95; rtd 95; NSM Shipton Moyne w Westonbirt and Lasborough *Glouc* 95–99; PtO *Bris* 95–04; *Glouc* from 99; *Cov* 00–05; *Worc* 00–12. *1 Newlands Court, Stow on the Wold, Cheltenham GL54 1HN* T: (01451) 798165

BARBOUR, Walter Iain. b 28. Pemb Coll Cam BA 48 MA 53 FICE 65. Ox NSM Course 78. **d** 81 **p** 82. NSM Bray and Braywood *Ox* 81–84; NSM Thatcham 84–87; TV Moor Allerton *Ripon* 87–95; rtd 95; NSM Shipton Moyne w Westonbirt and Lasborough *Glouc* 95–98; PtO *Bris* 95–04; *Glouc* 98–01; *Cov* 00–06; *Worc* 00–12; *Glouc* from 16. *1 Newlands Court, Stow on the Wold, Cheltenham GL54 1HN* T: (01451) 798165

BARBY, Canon Sheana Braidwood. b 38. Bedf Coll Lon BA 59. EMMTC 81. **dss** 84 **d** 87 **p** 94. Derby St Paul 84–87; NSM Derby Cathl 87–03; Dioc Dir of Ords 90–97; Par Educn Adv 93–01; rtd 03; Hon Can Derby Cathl from 96; RD Derby N 00–05; PtO from 05. *2 Margaret Street, Derby DE1 3FE* T: (01332) 383301 E: sheana@talktalk.net

BARCLAY, Adam John. b 61. **d** 18. NSM Stanton *St E* from 18. *Address temp unknown* E: adambarclay86@gmail.com

BARCLAY, Mrs Christine Ann. b 54. TISEC. **d** 07 **p** 08. C St Andrews All SS *St And* 07–10; R Tayport 10–12; R Bathgate *Edin* from 12; R Linlithgow from 12. *The Rectory, 85 Acredales, Linlithgow EH49 6JA* T: (01506) 846069 E: christine.barclay1@btopenworld.com *or* christine.barclay28@gmail.com

BARCLAY, Ian Newton. b 33. Clifton Th Coll 58. **d** 61 **p** 62. C Cullompton *Ex* 61–63; C Ashill w Broadway *B & W* 63–66; V Chatham St Phil and St Jas *Roch* 66–69; C St Helen Bishopsgate w St Martin Outwich *Lon* 70–73; V Prestonville St Luke *Chich* 73–81; LtO 82–93; rtd 93; P-in-c Cannes *Eur* 98–02; PtO *Chich* from 13. *35 Marine Avenue, Hove BN3 4LH*

BARCROFT, The Very Revd Ian David. b 60. UMIST BSc 83 Edin Univ BD 88 Glas Univ MTh 01. Edin Th Coll 85. **d** 88 **p** 89. Prec St Ninian's Cathl Perth *St And* 88–92; Min Perth St Ninian 88–92; P-in-c Aberdeen St Clem *Ab* 92–97; R Hamilton *Glas* from 97; Dean Glas from 10. *The Rectory, 4C Auchingramont Road, Hamilton ML3 6JT* T/F: (01698) 429895 E: dean@glasgow.anglican.org *or* rector@stmaryepiscopalhamilton.co.uk

BARDELL, Alan George. b 44. City Univ BSc. **d** 92 **p** 93. OLM Addlestone *Guildf* 92–06; rtd 06; PtO *Guildf* from 07. *14 Dickens Drive, Addlestone KT15 1AW* T: (01932) 847574 E: alanbardell@aol.com

BARDELL, Terence Richard. b 51. EMMTC 04. **d** 01 **p** 02. OLM Coningsby w Tattershall *Linc* 01–05; C Gt Grimsby St Mary and St Jas 05–06; TV 06–09; P-in-c Chapel St Leonards w Hogsthorpe 09–18; V Chapel St Leonards and Hogsthorpe etc 18–19; rtd 19. *25 De Borg Close, Tetbury GL8 8TW*

BARDER, Joel Alexander Christopher Remilly. b 88. Abth Univ BA 09. Trin Coll Bris 13. **d** 16 **p** 17. C Tenby *St D* 16–19; P-in-c Carew and Cosheston and Nash and Redberth from 19. *9 Sageston Fields, Sageston, Tenby SA70 8TQ* T: (01646) 650114 E: rev.jbarder@zoho.com

BARDWELL, Mrs Elaine Barbara. b 60. K Coll Lon BA 81 AKC 81. St Steph Ho Ox BA 85 MA 90. **dss** 86 **d** 87 **p** 95. Heref H Trin 86–89; C 87–89; Dir Past Studies St Steph

Ho *Ox* 89–96; V New Marston *Ox* from 96; AD Cowley 02–07. *The Vicarage, 8 Jack Straws Lane, Headington, Oxford OX3 0DL* T: (01865) 434340 M: 07779-086231 E: elaine.bardwell@ntlworld.com

BARDWELL, John Edward. b 53. Jes Coll Cam BA 75 MA 79 Ox Univ BA 85 MA 90. St Steph Ho Ox 83. **d** 86 **p** 87. C Heref H Trin 86–89; PtO *Ox* 90–96. *The Vicarage, 8 Jack Straws Lane, Headington, Oxford OX3 0DL* T: (01865) 434340 E: je.bardwell@tiscali.co.uk

BAREHAM, Miss Sylvia Alice. b 36. Hockerill Coll Cam CertEd 59 Open Univ BA 83 Ox Univ DipEd 84. Ox Min Course 86. **d** 89 **p** 94. NSM N Leigh *Ox* 89–93; NSM Bampton w Clanfield 93–95; NSM Kedington *St E* 95–97; NSM Hundon w Barnardiston 95–97; NSM Haverhill w Withersfield, the Wrattings etc 95–97; NSM Stourhead 97–05; NSM Lark Valley 05–07; rtd 07; PtO *Chelmsf* 05–09; *St E* from 07. *Davaar, Old Hall Lane, Fornham St Martin, Bury St Edmunds IP31 1SS* T: (01284) 724899

BARFOOT, John Henry. b 38. **d** 08 **p** 09. NSM Tintagel *Truro* 08–13; rtd 13; PtO *Truro* from 16. *32 Trehannick Close, St Teath, Bodmin PL30 3LF* T: (01208) 851450

BARFORD, Patricia Ann. b 47. Univ of Wales (Cardiff) BSc 68 PhD 73. WMMTC 95. **d** 98 **p** 99. NSM Stoke Prior, Wychbold and Upton Warren *Worc* 98–05; C Redditch H Trin 05–08; TV 08–09; rtd 09; PtO *Worc* from 09. *Greenfields, Church Road, Dodford, Bromsgrove B61 9BY* T: (01527) 871614 E: thebarfords@hotmail.com

BARGE, Preb Ann Marina. b 42. S'wark Ord Course 89. **d** 96 **p** 97. C Ludlow *Heref* 96–12; Preb Heref Cathl 11–12; rtd 12; PtO *Heref* from 12. *8 Old Street, Ludlow SY8 1NP* T: (01584) 877307 E: annbarge123@gmail.com

BARGE, David Robert. b 45. S Dios Minl Tr Scheme 92. **d** 95 **p** 96. NSM Westfield *B & W* 95–00; C Frome St Jo and St Mary 00; V Frome St Mary 01–10; RD Frome 08–10; rtd 10; PtO *B & W* from 10. *26 Charolais Drive, Bridgwater TA6 6EX* T: (01278) 431655 M: 07772-559721 E: dbarge@btinternet.com

BARHAM, Ian Harold. b 40. Clifton Th Coll 64. **d** 66 **p** 67. C Broadwater St Mary *Chich* 66–69 and 72–76; Burundi 71–72; R Beyton and Hessett *St E* 76–79; PtO 79–81; Hon C Bury St Edmunds St Mary 81–84; Chapl St Aubyn's Sch Tiverton 84–96; Chapl Lee Abbey 96–99; rtd 00; PtO *Ex* from 00. *53 Sylvan Road, Exeter EX4 6EY* T: (01392) 251643 E: ian.jacqui@barhams.co.uk

✠**BARHAM, The Rt Revd Kenneth Lawrence.** b 36. Clifton Th Coll BD 63. **d** 63 **p** 64 **c** 93. C Worthing St Geo *Chich* 63–65; C Sevenoaks St Nic *Roch* 65–67; C Cheltenham St Mark *Glouc* 67–70; V Maidstone St Luke *Cant* 70–79; S Area Sec Rwanda Miss 79–84; P-in-c Ashburnham w Penhurst *Chich* 84–01; Asst Bp Cyangugu (Rwanda) 93–96; Bp 96–01; rtd 01; Hon Asst Bp Chich from 05. *Rosewood, Canadia Road, Battle TN33 0LR* T/F: (01424) 773073 E: bishopken@btinternet.com

BARHAM, Peter. b 62. Selw Coll Cam MA 83. Linc Th Coll BTh 94. **d** 94 **p** 95. C Fornham All SS and Fornham St Martin w Timworth *St E* 94–97; P-in-c Cockfield w Bradfield St Clare, Felsham etc 97–01; Min Can St Cathl 98–03; Chapl 01–03; Can Res St E Cathl 03–08; V Ponteland *Newc* 08–16; V Allestree St Edm and Darley Abbey *Derby* from 16; Dioc Ecum Officer from 17. *The Vicarage, King's Croft, Allestree, Derby DE22 2FN* E: revpeterbarham@btinternet.com

BARKER, Adele. b 69. Reading Univ BSc 90 ACA 94. St Mellitus Coll 12 Ridley Hall Cam 14. **d** 16 **p** 17. C Chatham St Phil and St Jas *Roch* from 16. *3A Kit Hill Avenue, Chatham ME5 9ET* T: (01634) 864348 M: 07961-121648 E: adele.barker@cantab.net *or* adele.barker@pipnjims.co.uk

BARKER, Cameron Timothy. b 62. Rhodes Univ BA 83 Nottm Univ MA(TS) 96. St Jo Coll Nottm 94. **d** 96 **p** 97. C W Streatham St Jas *S'wark* 96–00; V Herne Hill 00–17; Chapl R Brompton and Harefield NHS Foundn Trust from 17. *Harefield Hospital, Hill End Road, Harefield, Uxbridge UB9 6JH* T: (01895) 823737 ext 6533 E: c.barker@rbht.nhs.uk

BARKER, Prof Charles Philip Geoffrey. b 50. Lon Univ MB, BS 75 MS 91 FRCS 79 FICS 82. S Dios Minl Tr Scheme 95. **d** 98 **p** 99. NSM Alverstoke *Portsm* 98–02; NSM The Lickey *Birm* 02–06; NSM Empangeni H Cross S Africa 06–10; NSM Maple Ridge St Jo Canada from 10. *36198 Cascade Ridge Drive, Mission BC V2V 7G9, Canada* T/F: (001) (604) 814 2072 E: barkerphilip30@gmail.com

BARKER, David Robert. b 45. Worc Coll Ox BA 67 MA 70. Virginia Th Sem BD 72. **d** 72 **p** 73. C Roehampton H Trin *S'wark* 72–75; Chapl Goldsmiths' Coll Lon 75–79; Min Tr Officer *Cov* 79–85; Selection Sec and Sec for Continuing Minl Educn ACCM 85–90; V Sutton Valence w E Sutton and Chart Sutton *Cant* 90–08; rtd 08. *1 Colletts Close,*

Corfe Castle, Wareham BH20 5HG T: (01929) 481477 E: david_pennybarker@hotmail.com

BARKER, Gordon Frank. b 43. Heriot-Watt Univ MSc 75 Sheff Univ MA 98. S & M Dioc Tr Inst 91. **d** 94 **p** 95. NSM Malew *S & M* 94–00; V Grain w Stoke *Roch* 00–04; Through Faith Miss Ev 00–04; P-in-c Andreas and Jurby *S & M* 04–08; P-in-c Lezayre 04–05; rtd 08; PtO *S & M* from 10; *Eur* from 17. *The Harp Inn, Cross Four Ways, Ballasalla, Isle of Man IM9 3DH* T: (01624) 824116

BARKER, Canon John Howard. b 36. Southn Univ BA 58. Ripon Coll Cuddesdon 80. **d** 82 **p** 83. C W Leigh *Portsm* 82–84; V Cosham 84–88; Bp's Dom Chapl 88–96; Hon Can Portsm Cathl 93–02; V St Helens and Sea View 96–02; rtd 02; PtO *Portsm* from 02. *Coniston Lodge, 3 Coniston Drive, Ryde PO33 3AE* T: (01983) 618674 M: 07802-281797

BARKER, John William. b 53. Newc Univ BSc 75 PhD 80 Qu Coll Ox MSc 76. Ridley Hall Cam 13. **d** 13 **p** 14. Asst Chapl Vienna *Eur* 13–16; R Buxted and Hadlow Down *Chich* 16–19; V Harrow Weald All SS *Lon* from 19. *All Saints' Vicarage, 175 Uxbridge Road, Harrow HA3 6TP* T: (020) 8954 8865 *or* 3669 0022 M: 07391-028956 E: revjohnwbarker@gmail.com

BARKER, Jonathan. b 55. Hull Univ BA 79. Westcott Ho Cam 79. **d** 83 **p** 84. C Sketty *S & B* 83–86; Chapl Sport and Leisure 83–86; C Swansea St Mary w H Trin *S & B* 85–86; Bermuda 86–90; TV Liv Our Lady and St Nic w St Anne 90–93; P-in-c S Shore St Pet *Blackb* 93–98; Chapl Blackpool Victoria Hosp NHS Trust 93–98; V Cleckheaton St Jo *Wakef* 98–08; Chapl St Pancras Internat and K Cross Stations *Lon* 08–14; P-in-c Romaldkirk w Laithkirk *Leeds* 14–17; P-in-c Startforth and Bowes and Rokeby w Brignall 14–17; R Lower Teesdale from 17; P-in-c Eggleston *Dur* from 14; P-in-c Middleton-in-Teesdale w Forest and Frith from 14. *Ashbourne, Cotherstone, Barnard Castle DL12 9PR* T: (01833) 650761 M: 07896-934881 E: jonathanbarker19.jb@gmail.com

BARKER, Ms Joyce. b 46. Nottm Univ BPharm 68. Yorks Min Course 09. **d** 11 **p** 12. NSM Barnby Dun *Sheff* 11–13; NSM Hatfield 13–16; rtd 16; PtO *Sheff* from 16. *52A Harpenden Drive, Dunscroft, Doncaster DN7 4HN* T: (01302) 844970 E: joycebarkertwin@gmail.com

BARKER, Julian Roland Palgrave. b 37. Magd Coll Cam BA 61 MA 65. Westcott Ho Cam 61. **d** 63 **p** 64. C Stafford St Mary *Lich* 63–66; Chapl Clare Hall Cam 66–69; Chapl Clare Coll Cam 66–70; Tutor St Aug Coll Cant 70–71; TV Raveningham *Nor* 71–78; TR 78–82; V Foremark *Derby* 82–02; V Repton 82–02; C Bretby w Newton Solney 01–02; V Foremark and Repton w Newton Solney 02–03; RD Repton 91–95; rtd 03; PtO *St E* from 06. *78 St Barnabas Road, Cambridge CB1 2DE* T: (01223) 501611 E: jrpbarker@gmail.com

BARKER, Canon Mark. b 62. ACIB 90. St Jo Coll Nottm BTh 95. **d** 95 **p** 96. C Barking St Marg w St Patr *Chelmsf* 95–98; C Cranham Park 98–04; V Tonbridge St Steph *Roch* from 04; Hon Can Roch Cathl from 18. *St Stephen's Vicarage, 6 Brook Street, Tonbridge TN9 2PJ* T: (01732) 353079 E: mark.barker@ststephens.org.uk

BARKER, Mrs May Winifred. b 65. Sarum Coll. **d** 16 **p** 17. C Pokesdown All SS *Win* 16–19; P-in-c Hatch Warren and Beggarwood from 19. *Immanuel House, 29 Lapin Lane, Basingstoke RG22 4XH* T: (01256) 330768 M: 07922-516761 E: maybarker@virginmedia.com *or* revmaybarker@gmail.com

BARKER, Miriam Sarah Anne. b 62. Lon Univ MB, BS 86. SEITE 08. **d** 11 **p** 12. C Southborough St Pet w Ch Ch and St Matt etc *Roch* 11–15; Community Chapl Tonbridge Adnry and C Tonbridge St Steph from 15; AD Tonbridge from 18. *St Stephen's Vicarage, 6 Brook Street, Tonbridge TN9 2PJ* T: (01732) 353079 M: 07783-228275 E: miriambarker@live.co.uk

BARKER, Neil Anthony. b 52. St Andr Univ BSc 73. Ridley Hall Cam 74. **d** 77 **p** 78. C Leic H Apostles 77–81; C Camberley St Paul *Guildf* 81–86; R Bradfield *Ox* 86–88; R Bradfield and Stanford Dingley 88–92; R Woodmansterne *S'wark* 92–05; AD Reigate 05; Chapl MU 96–02; TR Modbury, Bigbury, Ringmore, Kingston etc *Ex* 05–15; R Modbury, Bigbury, Ringmore etc 15–17; RD Woodleigh 07–12; rtd 17. *Stonecot, Fore Street, Aveton Gifford, Kingsbridge TQ7 4LB* E: revbarker@btinternet.com

BARKER, The Ven Nicholas John Willoughby. b 49. Oriel Coll Ox BA 73 BA 75 MA 77. Trin Coll Bris 75. **d** 77 **p** 78. C Watford *St Alb* 77–80; TV Didsbury St Jas and Em *Man* 80–86; TR Kidderminster St Geo *Worc* 86–07; RD Kidderminster 01–07; Hon Can Worc Cathl 03–07; Adn Auckland and Can Dur Cathl 07–17; P-in-c Darlington H Trin 07–17; rtd 17; PtO *Dur* from 18. *4 Watson Park, Spennymoor DL16 6NB* T: (01388) 819487 E: nick.barker99@btinternet.com

BARKER, Paul. b 73. Ripon Coll Cuddesdon 14. **d** 16 **p** 18. C Sunderland St Chad *Dur* from 16. *12 Meadow Drive, East Herrington, Sunderland SR3 3RD* M: 07966-208906 E: revpaulbarker@gmail.com

BARKER, Philip. *See* BARKER, Charles Philip Geoffrey

BARKER, Robert Gardiner. b 59. **d** 14 **p** 15. NSM Ellesmere Port *Ches* 14–17; P-in-c Kirby Misperton w Normanby and Salton *York* from 17; P-in-c Middleton, Newton and Sinnington from 17. *St Andrew's House, 15 Middleton Carr Lane, Middleton, Pickering YO18 8PU* E: r.barker@churcharmy.org.uk

BARKER, The Very Revd Timothy Reed. b 56. Qu Coll Cam BA 79 MA 82. Westcott Ho Cam 78. **d** 80 **p** 81. C Nantwich *Ches* 80–83; V Norton 83–88; V Runcorn All SS 88–94; Urban Officer 88–90; Dioc Communications Officer 91–98; Bp's Chapl 94–98; Hon P Asst Ches Cathl 94–98; V Spalding St Mary and St Nic *Linc* 98–09; P-in-c Spalding St Paul 07–09; RD Elloe W 00–09; RD Elloe E 08–09; Adn Linc 09–15; Can and Preb Linc Cathl 03–15; R Guernsey St Andr *Win* from 15; P-in-c Sark from 15; Dean Guernsey from 15; Hon Can Win Cathl from 16. *St Andrew's Rectory, Route de St Andre, St Andrew, Guernsey GY6 8XN* T: (01481) 238568 M: 07781-166095 E: dean@deanery.gg

BARKING, Archdeacon of. *See* BURKE, The Ven Christopher Mark

BARKING, Area Bishop of. *See* HILL, The Rt Revd Peter

BARKS, Jeffrey Stephen. b 45. Cranmer Hall Dur 66. **d** 71 **p** 72. C Wootton *St Alb* 71–74; C Boscombe St Jo *Win* 74–76; C Ringwood 76–80; P-in-c Spaxton w Charlynch *B & W* 80; P-in-c Enmore w Goathurst 80; P-in-c Spaxton w Goathurst, Enmore and Charlynch 80–81; R 81–92; RD Bridgwater 89–94; V Wembdon 92–07; rtd 07. *77 Alfoxton Road, Bridgwater TA6 7NW* T: (01278) 423647 E: stephen.barks@alivecm.org.uk

BARLEY, Ann Christine. b 47. **d** 93 **p** 94. OLM Walton *St E* 93–00; OLM Walton and Trimley 00–08; rtd 08; PtO *St E* from 08. *3 Wolsey Court, Stanley Road, Felixstowe IP11 7DJ* E: carmel.ann@btinternet.com

BARLEY, Canon Christopher James. b 56. St Steph Ho Ox 91. **d** 93 **p** 94. C Upton cum Chalvey *Ox* 93–96; TV High Wycombe 96–01; V Swinton *Sheff* from 01; Dioc Chapl MU from 08; Hon Can Sheff Cathl from 10. *The Vicarage, 50 Golden Smithies Lane, Swinton, Mexborough S64 8DL* T: (01709) 582259 E: chris.barley@sheffield.anglican.org

BARLEY, Gordon Malcolm. b 59. Aston Tr Scheme 94 Oak Hill Th Coll 96. **d** 98 **p** 99. C Walthamstow St Jo *Chelmsf* 98–02; TV Barking St Marg w St Patr 02–12; V Ovenden *Wakef* 12–14; *Leeds* 14–19; rtd 19. *Flat 4, 27 West Street, Scarborough YO11 2QR* E: gordon_barley@ntlworld.com

BARLEY, Ivan William. b 48. Loughb Univ MA 01. **d** 93 **p** 94. OLM Walton *St E* 93–00; OLM Walton and Trimley 00–13; NSM 13–14; Dioc NSM/OLM Officer 02–10; rtd 14; PtO *St E* from 14. *3 Wolsey Court, Stanley Road, Felixstowe IP11 7DJ* E: iwbarley@outlook.com

BARLEY, Canon Lynda Mary. b 53. York Univ BA 74 PGCE 75 Lon Univ MSc 76 Anglia Ruskin Univ DProf 14 FSS 77. S'warp Ord Course 93. **d** 96 **p** 97. NSM Lower Nutfield *S'wark* 96–97; NSM Littleham w Exmouth *Ex* 97–98; NSM Tedburn St Mary, Whitestone, Oldridge etc 98–00; Hd Research and Statistics Abps' Coun 00–11; NSM Cullompton, Willand, Uffculme, Kentisbeare etc *Ex* 03–11; Preb Ex Cathl 09–11; Can Res and Pastor Truro Cathl from 11; C Truro St Mary from 12; P-in-c Tresillian and Lamorran w Merther from 12; P-in-c St Michael Penkevil from 12; RD Powder from 18; PtO *Eur* from 10. *Truro Cathedral, 14 St Mary's Street, Truro TR1 2AF* T: (01872) 245016 F: 277788 E: canonpastor@trurocathedral.org.uk

BARLEY, Victor Laurence. b 41. St Jo Coll Cam MA 66 Ch Ox DPhil 72 FRCSEd 75 FRCR 76. **d** 02 **p** 03. NSM Flax Bourton and Barrow Gurney *B & W* 02–06; NSM Clevedon St Jo 06–09; NSM Chew Stoke w Nempnett Thrubwell 09–16; rtd 16; PtO *Bris* from 13; *B & W* from 16. *Church Farm, Church Lane, Chew Stoke, Bristol BS40 8TU* T: (01275) 331086 M: 07772-559060 E: victor.barley@tiscali.co.uk

BARLING, Michael Keith. b 38. Oak Hill Th Coll 63. **d** 66 **p** 67. C Portman Square St Paul *Lon* 66–70; C Enfield Ch Ch Trent Park 70–74; V Sidcup St Andr *Roch* 74–78; Dir Fountain Trust 78–81; Chapl Bethany Fellowship and Roffey Place 81–88; Hon C Kennington St Mark *S'wark* 88–89; rtd 03. *Address temp unknown* M: 07855-231755

BARLOW, Clive Christopher. b 42. Linc Th Coll 67. **d** 70 **p** 71. C Surbiton St Mark *S'wark* 70–74; C Spring Park *Cant* 74–77; V Ash w Westmarsh 77–92; R Chartham 92–08; RD E Bridge 86–92; RD W Bridge 95–01; rtd 08; PtO *Cant* from 08. *5 Barton Road, Canterbury CT1 1YG* T: (01227) 784779 E: c.barlow@btinternet.com

BARLOW, Canon Darren. b 65. Ridley Hall Cam 96. **d** 98 **p** 99. C Rayleigh *Chelmsf* 98–01; TV Billericay and Lt Burstead 01–06; TR Grays Thurrock from 06; RD Thurrock from 11; Hon Can Chelmsf Cathl from 15. *The Rectory, 10 High View Avenue, Grays RM17 6RU* T: (01375) 377379 or 373215 E: revbarlow@talktalk.net *or* rev.darren@gttm.org

BARLOW, David. b 50. Leeds Univ BA 71 MA 99. Wycliffe Hall Ox 71. **d** 73 **p** 74. C Horninglow *Lich* 73–75; C Wednesfield St Thos 75–77; C Bloxwich 77–78; Chapl RN 78–08; Prin Armed Forces Chapl Cen Amport Ho 05–08; P-in-c Baughurst, Ramsdell, Wolverton w Ewhurst etc *Win* 08–14; R 14–19; rtd 19; QHC from 04. *Address temp unknown* E: barlow857@btinternet.com

BARLOW, Edward Rhys. b 83. Glas Univ MA 05 Heythrop Coll Lon MA 11 St Jo Coll Dur MA 17 York St Jo Univ PGCE 07. Cranmer Hall Dur 14. **d** 16 **p** 17. C Bedford Park *Lon* 16–19; TV Bexley *Roch* from 19. *St John's Vicarage, 29 Parkhill Road, Bexley DA5 1HX* M: 07939-834704 E: fr.edwardbarlow@gmail.com

BARLOW, James Derek. b 64. Ex Univ BA 87. Ripon Coll Cuddesdon 09. **d** 11 **p** 12. C Burnham *Ox* 11–15; C Bracknell 15–18; P-in-c from 18. *1 Old Lands Hill, Bracknell RG12 2QX* T: (01344) 641498

BARLOW, Paul Andrew. b 59. Imp Coll Lon BSc 80 UMIST PhD 84 Bolton Inst of HE PGCE 85. Aston Tr Scheme 89 Chich Th Coll 91. **d** 93 **p** 94. C Hale *Guildf* 93–97; C Christchurch *Win* 97–01; P-in-c Alton All SS 01–09; C Alton 10–11; Chapl Dublin Sandymount *D & G* from 11. *Gealán, Durham Road, Sandymount, Dublin 4, Republic of Ireland* T: (00353) (1) 516 3457 M: 85-284 9564 E: paul.barlow@upcmail.ie

BARLOW, Paul Benson. b 31. Fitzw Coll Cam BA 73 MA 77 FRSA 94. **d** 64 **p** 65. C Bath Abbey w St Jas *B & W* 64–74; Dep Hd Master Leys High Sch Redditch 74–81; Hd Master Jo Kyrle High Sch Ross-on-Wye 82–96; PtO *Heref* 82–85; LtO 85–92; NSM Walford and St John w Bishopswood, Goodrich etc 92–97; PtO from 97. *The Coach House, Hentland, Ross-on-Wye HR9 6LP*

BARLOW, Robert Mark. b 53. St Jo Coll Nottm 84. **d** 86 **p** 87. C Colwich w Gt Haywood *Lich* 86–91; R Crick and Yelvertoft w Clay Coton and Lilbourne *Pet* 91–04; Bp's Rural Officer 98–04; Chapl to Agric and Rural Life *Worc* 04–10; C Worcs W Rural 05–10; P-in-c Teme Valley S 10–17; TR Dudley 17–19. *Oak House, Rhyse Lane, Tenbury Wells WR15 8NH* M: 07947-600627

BARNARD, Canon Anthony Nevin. b 36. St Jo Coll Cam BA 60 MA 64. Wells Th Coll 61. **d** 63 **p** 64. C Cheshunt *St Alb* 63–65; Tutor Wells Th Coll 65–66; Chapl 66–69; Vice-Prin 69–71; Dep Prin Sarum & Wells Th Coll 71–77; Dir S Dios Minl Tr Scheme 74–77; Can Res and Chan Lich Cathl 77–06; Warden of Readers 77–91; Dir of Tr 86–91; rtd 06; PtO *Lich* from 06. *Junction House, 264 Efflinch Lane, Barton under Needwood, Burton-on-Trent DE13 8DF* T: (01283) 711505 E: aandabarnard@tiscali.co.uk

BARNARD, Kevin James. b 52. Keble Coll Ox BA 77 MA 79 Sheff Univ PhD 14. Cranmer Hall Dur 77. **d** 79 **p** 80. C Swinton *Sheff* 79–83; TV Sheff Manor 83–90; V Bolsterstone 90–13; Bp's Adv on Issues Relating to Ageing 94–13; V King Cross *Leeds* from 13; C Southowram and Claremount from 18. *King Cross Vicarage, West Royd Avenue, Halifax HX1 3NU* T: (01422) 352933

BARNARD, Kevin Paul. b 64. Hull Univ BSc 85. Ridley Hall Cam 10. **d** 12 **p** 13. C Warwick *Cov* 12–15; V Westerham *Roch* from 15. *The Vicarage, Borde Hill, Vicarage Hill, Westerham TN16 1TL* T: (01959) 563127 M: 07795-314121 E: rev.kbarnard@gmail.com

BARNARD, Timothy John William. b 53. Magd Coll Cam BA 75 MA 78. **d** 13 **p** 14. OLM Amersham *Ox* from 13. *2A Stanley Hill Avenue, Amersham HP7 9BD* T: (01494) 728478 M: 07971-871667 E: timbar_a@yahoo.co.uk

BARNDEN, Saskia Gail. b 50. Waterloo Univ (Canada) BA 70 Victoria Univ (BC) MA 71 Indiana Univ PhD 88 Westmr Coll Ox CertEd 75. SAOMC 97. **d** 00 **p** 01. Asst Chapl Wycombe Abbey Sch 00–01; Chapl Haberdashers' Monmouth Sch for Girls 01–12; Chapl St Mary's Hospice 13–17; rtd 17; PtO *Birm* from 17. *47 Elvetham Road, Birmingham B15 2LY* T: 0121-440 5677 *or* 472 1191 M: 07813-616574

BARNE, Hugh Nicholas. b 84. Wycliffe Hall Ox 14. **d** 17 **p** 18. C Wargrave w Knowl Hill *Ox* from 17. *46 Fidlers Walk, Wargrave, Reading RG10 8BA*

BARNES, Canon Brian. b 42. Sussex Univ MA 82. Cant Sch of Min 79. **d** 82 **p** 83. NSM Maidstone All SS and St Phil w Tovil *Cant* 82–89; C 89–92; FE Adv Gen Syn Bd of Educn 86–92; R Staplehurst *Cant* 92–02; V Hythe 02–08; RD W Charing 95–99; AD Cranbrook 99–01; Hon Can Cant Cathl 01–08; rtd 08; PtO *Linc* from 16. *9 Egerton Road, Lincoln LN2 4PJ* T: (01522) 569508 E: brian.barnes@virgin.net

BARNES, Brian. b 49. St Mich Coll Llan 93. **d** 93 **p** 94. C Betws w Ammanford *St D* 93–96; V Llanwnda, Goodwick w Manorowen and Llanstinan 96–15; rtd 15; PtO *St D* from 15. *Glan y Don, Penbanc, Fishguard SA65 9BJ* E: revb@hotmail.com

BARNES, Christopher. b 57. d 06 p 07. NSM Bowling St Jo *Bradf* 06–14; *Leeds* from 14. *257 Bowling Hall Road, Bradford BD4 7TJ* T: (01274) 306230 E: chrisbarnes257@hotmail.co.uk

BARNES, David Keith. b 53. Linc Th Coll. d 89 p 90. C E Crompton *Man* 89–93; V Belfield 93–99; V Honley *Wakef* 99–12; P-in-c Bude Haven and Marhamchurch *Truro* 12–16; P-in-c Stratton and Launcells 12–16; R N Kernow 16–19; C from 19; P-in-c Kilkhampton w Morwenstow 16–19; RD Stratton from 18; C Week St Mary Circle of Par from 19. *The Rectory, The Glebe, Week St Mary, Holsworthy EX22 6UY* E: d.barnes645@btinternet.com

BARNES, Mrs Helen Clark. b 61. Worc Coll of Educn BA 82. Ox Min Course 07. d 10 p 11. NSM Haddenham w Cuddington, Kingsey etc *Ox* 10–14; TV Cottesloe from 14. *The Vicarage, 27B Aylesbury Road, Wing, Leighton Buzzard LU7 0PD* E: helen.barnes1503@gmail.com

BARNES, Jennifer. b 45. Leeds Univ MA 96. NOC 94. d 96 p 97. C Thorne *Sheff* 96–99; C Clifton St Jas 99–01; Chapl HM Pris Featherstone 01–04; Chapl HM YOI Swinfen Hall 04–05; P-in-c Barnsley St Luke *Wakef* 07–08; Chapl HM Pris and YOI New Hall 07–08; rtd 08; PtO *Wakef* 07–09; NSM Lundwood 09–11; PtO *Sheff* from 14; *Leeds* from 17. *Carlton House, 71 Woodhead Road, Honley, Holmfirth HD9 6PP* T: (01484) 660876 E: jbjcb@tiscali.co.uk

BARNES, Jeremy Paul Blissard. b 70. Southn Univ BSc 92. Wycliffe Hall Ox BTh 99. d 99 p 00. C Brompton H Trin w Onslow Square St Paul *Lon* 99–05; C Shadwell St Paul w Ratcliffe St Jas 05–09; V E Twickenham St Steph from 09. *17 Claremont Road, Twickenham TW1 2QX*

BARNES, John Christopher. b 43. MA ATI. Linc Th Coll 78. d 80 p 81. C Guiseley *Bradf* 80–83; TV Guiseley w Esholt 83–86; V Rawdon 86–92; R Armthorpe *Sheff* 92–98; TR Maltby 98–01; RD Doncaster 96–98; Hon Can Sheff Cathl 00–01; TR Blakenall Heath *Lich* 01–05; P-in-c Gomersal *Wakef* 05–09; P-in-c Cleckheaton St Jo 08–09; rtd 09; P-in-c Lundwood *Wakef* 09–11; PtO *Leeds* from 17. *Carlton House, 71 Woodhead Road, Honley, Holmfirth HD9 6PP* T: (01485) 660876 E: jbjcb@tiscali.co.uk

BARNES, Josephine Ella. b 39. d 12 p 13. OLM Hope, Castleton and Bradwell *Derby* from 12. *2 Cavedale Cottage, Market Place, Castleton, Hope Valley S33 8WQ* T: (01433) 621443 E: josephine.barnes1@btinternet.com

BARNES, Jules Ann. b 60. St Mary's Coll Dur BA 83 Dur Univ MBA 84 Ox Univ BTh 11 RGN 95. Ripon Coll Cuddesdon 08. d 10 p 11. C Wilton w Netherhampton and Fugglestone *Sarum* 10–14; Bp's Chapl *Bris* 14–16; Min Can Bris Cathl 15–16; P-in-c Warnham *Chich* from 16. *25 Wyvern Place, Warnham, Horsham RH12 3QU* M: 07415-000290

BARNES, Canon Katrina Crawford. b 52. K Coll Lon BA 98 AKC 98. Oak Hill Th Coll 90. d 93 p 94. NSM Bromley H Trin *Roch* 93–98; C Meopham w Nurstead 98–00; Assoc Staff Tutor SEITE 99–03; R Longfield *Roch* 01–06; V Bromley Common St Aug 06–17; P-in-c Bromley Common St Luke 17; V Bromley Common St Aug w St Luke 17–18; Bp's Adv for Ord Women's Min 05–11; AD Bromley 11–15; Hon Can Roch Cathl 05–18; rtd 18. *39 The Fairway, Bromley BR1 2JZ*

BARNES, Lee. b 74. Trin Coll Bris BA 03 MA 09. d 09 p 10. C Malmesbury w Westport and Brokenborough *Bris* 09–12; C Gt Somerford, Lt Somerford, Seagry, Corston etc 09–12; PtO 12–13; LtO 13–14; P-in-c Bris St Steph w St Jas and St Jo w St Mich etc from 14; P-in-c Clifton H Trin, St Andr and St Pet from 14. *Holy Trinity Church, Hotwell Road, Bristol BS8 4ST* T: 0117-907 0804 E: lee@saint-stephens.com

BARNES, Margaret Anne. b 56. d 13 p 14. OLM Oulton Broad *Nor* from 13. *53 Dell Road, Lowestoft NR33 9LA* T: (01502) 538122 E: mooskieanddave09@hotmail.co.uk

BARNES, Mrs Mary Jane. b 48. St Jo Coll Nottm 97. d 99 p 00. C Harefield *Lon* 99–02; TV New Windsor *Ox* 02–10; C 10–15; P-in-c Old Windsor 10–14; V 14–15; rtd 15; PtO *Eur* from 17. *24 rue des Philips, 46220 Prayssac, France* M: 07930-337407 E: rev.mbarnes@gmail.com

BARNES, Canon Matthew John. b 68. Leeds Univ MA 99. St Jo Coll Nottm BA 93. d 96 p 97. C Stanley *Wakef* 96–99; TV N Wingfield, Clay Cross and Pilsley *Derby* 99–08; R Brampton St Thos from 08; RD Chesterfield 11–15; Hon Can Derby Cathl from 13. *The Rectory, 674 Chatsworth Road, Chesterfield S40 3NU* T: (01246) 567634 M: 07977-976348 E: rector@st-thomas-brampton.com

BARNES, Canon Neal Duncan. b 63. Leeds Univ BSc 84 Cranfield Inst of Tech PhD 92. Oak Hill Th Coll 93. d 95 p 96. C Biggleswade *St Alb* 95–99; V Anlaby St Pet *York* 99–10; P-in-c Kingston upon Hull H Trin 10–11; V 11–19; Hon Chapl Ambulance Service Hull 99–19; Can and Preb York Minster 13–19; Can Res Liv Cathl from 19. *4 Cathedral Close, Liverpool L1 7BR* M: 07581-280785 E: neal@anvic.karoo.co.uk

BARNES, Canon Neil. b 42. Kelham Th Coll 61 Bps' Coll Cheshunt 65. d 68 p 69. C Poulton-le-Fylde *Blackb* 68–72; C Ribbleton 72–75; V Knuzden 75–81; Chapl Prestwich Hosp Man 81–88; Chapl Salford Mental Health Services NHS Trust 88–04; Manager Chapl Services 94–04; Hon Can Man Cathl 96–04; rtd 04; PtO *Blackb* from 04; *Man* 04–19. *7 Bouldsworth Road, Burnley BB10 3JT* E: neilbarnes.leads@gmail.com

BARNES, Paul. *See* BYLLAM-BARNES, Paul William Marshall

BARNES, Peter Frank. b 52. St Jo Coll Nottm LTh 81. d 81 p 82. C Colne St Bart *Blackb* 81–83; C Melton Mowbray w Thorpe Arnold *Leic* 83–86; P-in-c Barlestone 86–89; V Broughton and Duddon *Carl* 89–98; V Shrewsbury St Geo w Greenfields *Lich* 98–08; P-in-c Bicton, Montford w Shrawardine and Fitz 98–00; P-in-c Myddle 08–11; P-in-c Broughton 08–11; P-in-c Loppington w Newtown 08–11; R St John's-in-the-Vale, Threlkeld and Wythburn *Carl* 11–17; rtd 17. *10 Stanley Road, Brampton CA8 1DT* E: peterbarnes52@tiscali.co.uk

BARNES, Philip Richard. b 73. Westmr Coll Ox BTh 94 Heythrop Coll Lon MA 99. St Steph Ho Ox 98. d 00 p 01. C Ruislip St Martin *Lon* 00–03; Shrine P Shrine of Our Lady of Walsingham 03–08; V Northwood Hills St Edm *Lon* 08–16; AD Harrow 13–15; P Admin Shrine of Our Lady of Walsingham 16–17; P-in-c S Kensington St Steph *Lon* from 17. *5 Thomas Place, London W8 5UG* M: 07833-132500 E: frphilipbarnes@btinternet.com

BARNES, Roland Peter. b 59. Ban Ord Course 01. d 03 p 04. NSM Bro Ddyfi Uchaf *Ban* 03–05; P-in-c 05–14; P-in-c Bro Cyfeiliog and Mawddwy 14–18; AD Cyfeiliog and Mawddwy 12–15; V Bro Moelwyn from 18. *Y Rheithordy, The Square, Blaenau Ffestiniog LL41 3UW* T: (01766) 831871

BARNES, Stephen. b 46. Hull Univ BA 69. Clifton Th Coll 69. d 72 p 73. C Girlington *Bradf* 72–74; TV Glyncorrwg w Afan Vale and Cymmer Afan *Llan* 74–79; R 79–86; V Aberavon 86–01; V Dulais Valley 01–13; rtd 13. *43 Heol Maes y Dre, Ystradgynlais, Swansea SA9 1HA* T: (01639) 841882 E: stephen.barnes41@btinternet.com

BARNES, Stephen John. b 59. Univ of Wales (Cardiff) BSc 80. Chich Th Coll 83. d 86 p 87. C Neath w Llantwit *Llan* 86–89; C Coity w Nolton 89–95; V Troedyrhiw w Merthyr Vale from 95. *The Vicarage, Nixonville, Merthyr Vale, Merthyr Tydfil CF48 4RF* T: (01443) 690249 E: light2house@btinternet.com

BARNES, Stephen William. b 53. Man Univ BSc. St Jo Coll Nottm. d 83 p 84. C Chadwell Heath *Chelmsf* 83–87; C Becontree St Alb 88–89; Deanery Youth Chapl 88–91; C Becontree S 89–91; TV Worth *Chich* 91–98; Chapl Willen Hospice Milton Keynes 99–18; rtd 18; PtO *Ox* from 18. *90 Bradwell Road, Bradville, Milton Keynes MK13 7AD*

BARNES, Thomas. *See* BARNES, William Thomas

BARNES, Timothy. b 56. Birm Univ BSc 78. Westcott Ho Cam 96. d 98 p 99. C Shrub End *Chelmsf* 98–02; V Leigh-on-Sea St Aid 02–11; P-in-c Bocking St Pet from 11. *The Vicarage, St Peter's in the Fields, Braintree CM7 9AR* T: (01376) 349267 E: timbarnes1@btinternet.com

BARNES, Canon William Thomas. b 39. Dur Univ BA 60. Wycliffe Hall Ox 60. d 62 p 63. C Scotforth *Blackb* 62–66; C Cleveleys 66–67; V Colne Ch 67–74; V Bamber Bridge St Sav 74–04; Hon Can Blackb Cathl 00–04; rtd 04; PtO *Blackb* from 04. *12 Little Close, Farington Moss, Leyland PR26 6QU* T: (01772) 457646 E: tom.beryl.barnes@hotmail.co.uk

BARNES-CLAY, Peter John Granger. b 43. Cam Univ CertEd 69 MCollP. Chich Th Coll 72. d 75 p 82. C Earlham St Anne *Nor* 75–76; Asst Master Hewett Sch Nor 76–83; Chapl Nor Cathl from 80; Hon C Eaton 81–83; C 83–87; R Winterton w E and W Somerton and Horsey 87–92; R Weybourne Gp 92–03; RD Holt 95–02; rtd 03; PtO *Nor* 03–05; C Smallburgh w Dilham w Honing and Crostwight 05–06; P-in-c 06–08; PtO from 08; *St E* 14–18. *Hunters End, 1 Danby Close, Eaton Rise, Norwich NR4 6RH* T: (01603) 501199 E: becketsthree1@aol.com

BARNES-DAVIES, Daniel Simon. b 88. Southn Univ BA 09 Dur Univ BA 17. Westcott Ho Cam 14. d 17 p 18. C Romford St Edw *Chelmsf* from 17. *54 Parkside Avenue, Romford RM1 4ND* M: 07749-778436 E: dan@barnesdavies.co.uk or curate@stedwardsromford.com

BARNET, Carole Ann. b 68. All SS Cen for Miss & Min 17. d 18 p 19. OLM Prestwich St Mary *Man* from 18. *7 Old Hall Road, Whitefield, Manchester M45 7QW*

BARNETT, Dudley Graham. b 36. Ch Ch Ox BA 62 MA 65. St Steph Ho Ox 62. d 64 p 65. C Abbey Hey *Man* 64–68; V Swinton H Rood 68–90; R Old Trafford St Hilda 90–01; R Firswood and Gorse Hill 01–02; rtd 02; PtO *Man* from 02.

6A Gilda Crescent Road, Eccles, Manchester M30 9AG T: 0161-707 9767 E: dudleygbarnett@yahoo.co.uk

BARNETT, Mrs Elizabeth Anne. b 68. Trin Coll Bris 17. **d** 19. C Dulwich St Barn *S'wark* from 19. *41 Woodwarde Road, London SE22 8UN* M: 07765-074102 E: lizbarnett68@gmail.com

BARNETT, Mrs Gillian. b 62. Edge Hill Coll of HE BA 06. All SS Cen for Miss & Min 12. **d** 15 **p** 16. C Walmersley Road, Bury *Man* 15–18; P-in-c Belfield from 18; P-in-c Hamer and Healey from 18. *St Paul's Vicarage, Fir Street, Bury BL9 7QG* E: barnettgill@hotmail.co.uk

BARNETT, Canon John Raymond. b 51. Lon Univ LLB 74 BD 86 Birm Univ MA 98 De Montfort Univ MA 11 Birm Univ DPT 19. Westcott Ho Cam 74. **d** 77 **p** 78. C Northfield *Birm* 77–81; V Hamstead St Bernard 81–91; R The Quinton 91–03; AD Edgbaston 98–03; P-in-c Oldbury 03–07; P-in-c Langley St Jo 03–07; P-in-c Langley St Mich 03–07; P-in-c Londonderry 04–07; V Oldbury, Langley and Londonderry 07–09; Hon Can Birm Cathl 01–09; P-in-c Darlaston All SS *Lich* 09–13; C Moxley 09–13; C Darlaston St Lawr 09–13; P-in-c Pheasey 13–17; Interfaith Officer Wolverhampton Area 09–16; rtd 17; PtO *Birm* from 17; *Worc* from 18. *1 Front Cottages, Withybed Green, Alvechurch, Birmingham B48 7RJ* M: 07967-166931 E: johnbarnett255@gmail.com

BARNETT (née JACKSON), Canon Lisa Helen. b 79. Reading Univ BA(Ed) 01 Cam Univ BA 06. Ridley Hall Cam 04. **d** 07 **p** 08. C Patcham *Chich* 07–11; P-in-c Scaynes Hill 11–15; V from 15; Dep Dir of Ords from 19; Can and Preb Chich Cathl from 18. *The Vicarage, Vicarage Lane, Scaynes Hill, Haywards Heath RH17 7PB* T: (01444) 831827 M: 07989-761575 E: revlisa@btinternet.com

BARNETT, Michael. *See* BARNETT, Raymond Michael

BARNETT, Peter Geoffrey. b 46. AKC 71. St Aug Coll Cant 71. **d** 72 **p** 73. C Wolverhampton *Lich* 72–77; P-in-c Caldmore 77–83; TR Bris St Agnes and St Simon w St Werburgh 83–87; P-in-c Bris St Paul w St Barn 83–87; TR Bris St Paul's 87–94; Warden Pilsdon Community 94–04; PtO *Roch* 04–13; *S & B* from 13. *Catchpool Cottage, Llanmadoc, Swansea SA3 1DE* T: (01792) 386767 E: thebarnettfamily@talktalk.net

BARNETT, Preb Raymond Michael. b 31. Man Univ BA 54. Wells Th Coll 54. **d** 56 **p** 57. C Fallowfield *Man* 56–59; Madagascar 59–60; V Blackrod *Man* 60–67; V Woolavington *B & W* 67–76; RD Bridgwater 72–76; V St Decumans 76–96; RD Quantock 78–86 and 93–95; Preb Wells Cathl 89–96; rtd 96; PtO *B & W* 96–08. *22 Fosbrooke House, Clifton Drive, Lytham St Annes FY8 5RQ*

BARNFATHER, Thomas Fenwick. b 52. Cant Ch Ch Univ BSc 09. Linc Th Coll 86. **d** 88 **p** 89. C Sedgefield *Dur* 88–91; TV E Darlington 91–92; CF 92–96; V Heybridge w Langford *Chelmsf* 96–98; Chapl HM YOI Dover 98–00; Chapl HM Pris Swaleside 00–01; P-in-c Aylesham w Adisham *Cant* 01–04; Asst Dir of Ords 02–05; PtO 04–09; P-in-c Westgate St Sav 09–12; P-in-c Lanzarote *Eur* 12–14; PtO *Leic* 15–16; Hon C Ilkeston H Trin *Derby* from 16; Hon C Long Eaton St Laur from 16. *The Vicarage, 1 Cotmanhay Road, Ilkeston DE7 8HR* M: 07513-060519 E: tombarnfather@gmail.com

BARNSLEY, David Edward. b 75. Ox Brookes Univ BSc 97. Oak Hill Th Coll BA 03. **d** 03 **p** 04. C Kilnhurst *Sheff* 03–06; C Duffield and Lt Eaton *Derby* from 06. *31 Derby Road, Duffield, Belper DE56 4FL* T: (01332) 585190 E: vicar@littleeatonchurch.co.uk

BARNSLEY, Canon Melvyn. b 46. Dur Univ BA 67 Lon Univ CertEd. St Chad's Coll Dur 64. **d** 71 **p** 72. C Cov St Thos 71–74; C Cov St Jo 71–75; V New Bilton 75–82; R Stevenage St Andr and St Geo *St Alb* 82–14; RD Stevenage 99–09; Hon Can St Alb 00–14; rtd 14; PtO *St Alb* from 14; *Ely* from 14. *48 Hogsden Leys, St Neots PE19 6AD* T: (01480) 474498 E: melvynbarnsley@gmail.com

BARNSTAPLE, Archdeacon of. *See* BUTCHERS, The Ven Mark Andrew

BARON, Thomas Michael. b 63. St Steph Ho Ox 85. **d** 88 **p** 89. C Hartlepool St Paul *Dur* 88–92; Chapl Asst Hartlepool Gen Hosp 89–92; Asst Chapl Whittington Hosp NHS Trust 92–95; Chapl Enfield Community Care NHS Trust 95–01; Chapl Chase Farm Hosps NHS Trust 95–99; Chapl Barnet and Chase Farm Hosps NHS Trust 99–14; Chapl Barnet, Enfield and Haringey Mental Health NHS Trust from 01; Chapl Enfield Primary Care Trust from 01. *The Chaplaincy, Chase Farm Hospital, The Ridgeway, Enfield EN2 8JL* T: (020) 8375 1078 *or* 8882 1195 E: frtom.baron@btinternet.com *or* tom.baron@nhs.net

BARON, Mrs Vanessa Lillian. b 57. City Univ BSc 79 Fitzw Coll Cam BA 84 MA 85 Birkbeck Coll Lon MA 06 SRN 79. Ridley Hall Cam 83. **dss** 86 **d** 87 **p** 94. Roxbourne St Andr *Lon* 86–89; Par Dn 87–89; NSM Roxeth 89–95; Lic Preacher 95–17; Asst Chapl Harrow Sch 95–04; Chapl St Paul's Girls'

Sch Hammersmith 04–17; C Lyminster and Wick *Chich* from 17. *Lyminster Vicarage, 3 The Paddock, Lyminster, Littlehampton BN17 7QH*

BARR, Alan. b 59. TCD BTh 07. **d** 07 **p** 08. C Bray *D & G* 07–09; I Sixmilecross w Termonmaguirke *Arm* from 09. *St Michael's Rectory, 104 Cooley Road, Sixmilecross, Omagh BT79 9DH* T: (028) 8075 7097 M: 87-948 4408 E: alnbarr@gmail.com *or* sixmilecross@armagh.anglican.org

BARR, Jacquelime Anne. b 66. **d** 17 **p** 18. C Chinnor, Sydenham, Aston Rowant and Crowell *Ox* from 17. *61 Mill Lane, Chinnor OX39 4QU* E: barrjacqueline@aol.com

BARR, Miss Joanna Margaret Alice. b 93. St Jo Coll Dur BSc 14 Murray Edwards Coll Cam BTh 18. Ridley Hall Cam 16. **d** 19. C Berrow and Breane *B & W* from 19. *17 Links Close, Burnham-on-Sea TA8 2JD* M: 07926-905110 E: joanna.barr123@gmail.com

BARR, John. *See* BARR, Michael John Alexander

BARR (née HAYTER), Mary Elizabeth. b 58. Jes Coll Ox BA 80 CertEd 81 MA 84 Qu Coll Ox DPhil 85. Ridley Hall Cam 84. **dss** 86 **d** 87 **p** 94. Chapl Cam Univ Pastorate 86–91; Cambridge H Trin w St Andr Gt *Ely* 86–87; Par Dn 87–91; PtO 91–92; *Ex* 92–94; NSM Torquay St Luke 94–97; NSM Gt Malvern St Mary *Worc* 97–17; Chapl Worcs Community Healthcare NHS Trust 99–01; Chapl Worcs Community and Mental Health Trust 01–17; TV Melton Mowbray *Leic* from 17. *23 Melton Road, Waltham on the Wolds, Melton Mowbray LE14 4AJ* T: (01664) 464293 E: maryebarr17@gmail.com

BARR, Michael John Alexander. b 60. Qu Coll Ox BA 82 MA 86 Pemb Coll Cam BA 86 MA 90. Ridley Hall Cam 84. **d** 87 **p** 88. C Earley St Pet *Ox* 87–89; C Cambridge Gt St Mary w St Mich *Ely* 89–92; Chapl Girton Coll Cam 90–92; P-in-c Torquay St Luke *Ex* 92–97; Dioc Communications Officer 92–97; P-in-c Gt Malvern St Mary *Worc* 97–99; V 99–17; RD Malvern 01–07; Hon Can Worc Cathl 15–17; R Ironstone Villages *Leic* from 17. *23 Melton Road, Waltham on the Wolds, Melton Mowbray LE14 4AJ* T: (01664) 464265 E: johnbarr2817@gmail.com

BARR, Mrs Ruth. b 63. St Mellitus Coll BA 18. **d** 16 **p** 17. C Stopsley *St Alb* from 16. *221 Old Bedford Road, Luton LU2 7EH* M: 07447-458526 E: ruthbarr77@gmail.com

BARRACLOUGH, Mrs Barbara Amanda Juliet. b 61. Stirling Univ BA 83 Ches Coll of HE MA 00. NOC 97. **d** 00 **p** 01. C Lupset *Wakef* 00–04; V W Ardsley 04–14; Leeds 14–15; R Sprotbrough *Sheff* from 15; AD Adwick 15–18; Dean of Women's Min from 18. The Rectory, 42A Spring Lane, Sprotbrough, Doncaster DN5 7QG* T: (01302) 854836 M: 07890-614579 E: amanda.barraclough1@btinternet.com *or* amanda.barraclough@sheffield.anglican.org

BARRACLOUGH, Mrs Naomi Hannah Shrine. b 88. Lanc Univ BSc 10. Cranmer Hall Dur 12. **d** 15 **p** 16. C Wirksworth *Derby* 15–17; C Carsington 18–19; C Stalmine w Pilling *Blackb* from 19; C Waterside Par from 19. *6 Bluebell Avenue, Hambleton, Poulton-le-Fylde FY6 9FE* M: 07872-056471 E: nhsbarraclough@gmail.com

BARRACLOUGH, Canon Owen Conrad. b 32. Pemb Coll Cam BA 55 MA 59. Westcott Ho Cam 56. **d** 57 **p** 58. C Chippenham St Andr w Tytherton Lucas *Bris* 57–62; V Harringay St Paul *Lon* 62–70; Bp's Chapl for Community Relns *Cov* 70–77; P-in-c Baginton 72–77; V Swindon Ch Ch *Bris* 77–97; Chapl Princess Marg Hosp Swindon 77–89; Hon Can Bris Cathl 87–97; rtd 98; PtO *Bris* 98–02; *Glouc* 98–01; Jt P-in-c Staverton w Boddington and Tredington etc 01–04; Hon C Twigworth, Down Hatherley, Norton, The Leigh etc 04–06; Hon C Leckhampton SS Phil and Jas w Cheltenham St Jas 06–09; Hon C S Cheltenham 10–11; PtO from 17. *Robin Hollow, 10A Church Road, St Marks, Cheltenham GL51 7AN* T: (01242) 230855 E: obarraclough@btinternet.com

BARRATT, Mrs Elizabeth June. b 32. ACP 65. Trin Coll Bris 75. **dss** 78 **d** 87 **p** 94. W Kilburn St Luke w St Simon and St Jude *Lon* 78–87; Par Dn 87–94; C 94–98; rtd 98; Hon C Kensal Rise St Mark and St Martin *Lon* 99–11; Hon C Kensal Rise St Martin from 11. *68A Bathhurst Gardens, London NW10 5HY* T: (020) 8968 5951 M: 07763-474602 E: ejbarratt@hotmail.co.uk

BARRATT, Terrick. b 45. **d** 71 **p** 71. Paraguay 71–73; Argentina 73–80; Chile from 80; rtd 10. *57 Scalwell Park, Seaton EX12 2DB* T: (01297) 21118 E: barratt@vtn.net *or* terrick.barratt@gmail.com

BARRELL (formerly WALLACE), Mrs Julie Michele. b 58. Ox Univ MTh 93 Univ Coll Lon MSc 02. CA Tr Coll 77. **d** 88 **p** 94. Chapl Middx Poly *Lon* 86–90; Voc Adv CA 90-92; Member CA Counselling Service 92–96; Hon C Bellingham St Dunstan *S'wark* 91–96; TV Kidbrooke St Jas 96–99; PtO 99–01; Hon C Croydon Woodside 01–03; PtO *Llan* 09–11;

C Treharris, Trelewis and Bedlinog w Llanfabon 11–12. *1 Ridgeway, Wyesham, Monmouth NP25 3JX* T: (01600) 773283 M: 07960-915047 E: julie.barrell@btinternet.com

BARRETT, Alan. b 48. Southn Univ BA 69. Wycliffe Hall Ox 74. **d** 77 **p** 78. C Conisbrough *Sheff* 77–80; C Lower Homerton St Paul *Lon* 80–81; C-in-c Hounslow Gd Shep Beavers Lane CD 81–87; R Langdon Hills *Chelmsf* 87–97; P-in-c Tamworth *Lich* 97–03; V 03–13; RD 99–04; rtd 13; PtO *Carl* from 14. *Neale House, Neale's Row, Great Urswick, Ulverston LA12 0SX* T: (01229) 582179 E: barrett.alan@btinternet.com

BARRETT, Alastair David. b 75. Fitzw Coll Cam BA 97 MA 01 Birm Univ BD 00. Qu Coll Birm MA 01. **d** 01 **p** 02. C Sutton Coldfield St Chad *Birm* 01–04; C Oldbury, Langley and Londonderry 04–10; P-in-c Hodge Hill 10–13; TR from 13; Jt AD Coleshill from 18. *8 Dreghorn Road, Hodge Hill, Birmingham B36 8LJ* T: 0121-747 6982 E: hodgehillvicar@hotmail.co.uk

BARRETT, Alexandra Mary. b 75. Clare Coll Cam BA 96 MA 99. Westcott Ho Cam 00. **d** 03 **p** 04. C Godmanchester *Ely* 03–07; R Buckden w the Offords 07–14; USA 14–15; Tutor Westcott Ho Cam from 15. *Westcott House, Jesus Lane, Cambridge CB5 8BP* T: (01223) 741000 E: reverendally@gmail.com

BARRETT, Arthur. *See* BARRETT, Kenneth Arthur Lambart.

BARRETT, Mrs Brigid. b 44. RN 90. STETS MA 11. **d** 11 **p** 12. NSM Parkstone St Pet and St Osmund w Branksea *Sarum* 11–15; NSM Wareham 15–17; rtd 17; PtO *Sarum* from 17. *1 Wyatts Lane, Wareham BH20 4NH* T: (01929) 553460

BARRETT, Christopher Paul. b 49. AKC 71 St Aug Coll Cant 71. **d** 72 **p** 73. C Tupsley *Heref* 72–75; C Ex St Thos 75–79; R Atherington and High Bickington 79–83; V Burrington 79–83; Asst Dir of Educn 79–87; P-in-c Sticklepath 83–84; TV Barnstaple 85–90; V Whipton 90–99; TV Ex St Thos and Em 99–05; Chapl Burton Hosps NHS Foundn Trust 05–14; PtO *Derby* 05–16; rtd 14; PtO *Bris* from 17. *51 Barter Close, Kingswood, Bristol BS15 8JN* M: 07557-091747 E: revcpbarrett@aol.com

BARRETT, Clive. b 55. Ox Univ BA 76 MA 80 CertEd 77 Leeds Univ PhD 98. St Steph Ho Ox 80. **d** 83 **p** 84. C Wakef Cathl 83–87; Asst Chapl Leeds Univ *Ripon* 87–97; Dioc Development Rep 89–92; P-in-c Middleton St Cross 98–07; Co Ecum Development Officer W Yorks *Leeds* from 07; Hon C Headingley 08–18; PtO from 18; *Ox* from 18. *81 Becketts Park Drive, Leeds LS6 3PJ* T: 0113-275 5497 M: 07966-540699 E: clivebarrett@wyec.co.uk

BARRETT, John Joseph James. b 38. Lon Univ BD 65. Sarum & Wells Th Coll. **d** 78 **p** 78. C Danbury *Chelmsf* 78–80; Ind Chapl 80–89; C Dovercourt 80–83; TV Dovercourt and Parkeston 83–89; V Rubery *Birm* 89–04; rtd 04; PtO *Sheff* from 04. *4 Arran Hill, Thrybergh, Rotherham S65 4BH* T: (01709) 850288 E: rev.barrett@btinternet.com

BARRETT, Jonathan Murray. b 68. Oak Hill Th Coll BA 98. **d** 98 **p** 99. C Pennycross *Ex* 98–02; TV Plymouth Em, St Paul Efford and St Aug 02–08; V Thurnby w Stoughton *Leic* 08–13; P-in-c Houghton-on-the-Hill, Keyham and Hungarton 11–13; TR Cornerstone Team 13–17; AD Gartree I 16–17; AD Gartree II 16–17; Miss and Communications Enabler from 17. *15 Ruskington Drive, Wigston LE18 1LB* M: 07415-828278 E: jon.barrett@leccofe.org

BARRETT, Canon Kenneth. b 42. Univ of Wales (Lamp) BA 64. St Steph Ho Ox 65. **d** 67 **p** 68. C Poulton-le-Fylde *Blackb* 67–69; C S Shore H Trin 69–72; V Brierfield 72–83; V Chorley St Geo 83–07; Hon Can Blackb Cathl 03–07; rtd 07; PtO *Blackb* from 07. *24 Astley Road, Chorley PR7 1RR* T: (01257) 233421

BARRETT, The Very Revd Kenneth Arthur Lambart. b 60. CITC BTh 94. **d** 97 **p** 98. C Seagoe *D & D* 97–00; I Dublin Booterstown *D & G* 00–04; I Dublin Mt Merrion 00–04; I Boyle and Elphin w Aghanagh, Kilbryan etc *K, E & A* 04–08; I Taunagh w Kilmactranny, Ballysumaghan etc 04–08; I Rossorry *Clogh* 08–14; Dir of Ords 11–14; Can Clogh Cathl 12–14; Dean Raphoe *D & R* from 14; I Raphoe w Raymochy and Clonleigh from 14. *The Deanery, Raphoe, Co Donegal, F93 KT21, Republic of Ireland* T: (00353) (74) 914 5226 E: deanarthur@raphoe.anglican.org

BARRETT, Canon Marion Lily. b 54. Ex Univ BA 01 SRN 75. SWMTC 91. **d** 94 **p** 95. C St Mawgan w St Ervan and St Eval *Truro* 94–97; C St Breoke and Egloshayle 97–98; Asst Chapl R Cornwall Hosps Trust 98–99; Chapl 00–05; R St Mewan w Mevagissey and St Ewe *Truro* from 05; RD St Austell from 10; Convenor Bp's Gp for Min of Healing from 11; Hon Can Truro Cathl from 13. *The Rectory, St Mewan Lane, St Mewan, St Austell PL26 7DP* T: (01726) 72679 E: marionstmewan@btinternet.com

BARRETT, Matthew Edward John. b 73. Ripon Coll Cuddesdon BTh 18. **d** 13 **p** 14. C Guernsey St Michel

du Valle *Win* 13–16; R Guernsey St Peter Port from 16; V Guernsey St Jo from 16. *St John's Vicarage, Les Amballes, St Peter Port, Guernsey GY1 1WY* T: (01481) 720879 E: revmatthewbarrett@gmail.com

BARRETT, Paul. *See* BARRETT, Christopher Paul

BARRETT, Mrs Rachel Jeanne Alexandra. b 56. Ex Univ BA 78 MA 96 PGCE 79. SWMTC 92. **d** 95 **p** 96. NSM Ex St Mark, St Sidwell and St Matt 95–99; Chapl St Margaret's Sch Ex 99–05; Chapl Derby High Sch 05–16; rtd 16; PtO *Bris* from 17. *51 Barter Close, Kingswood, Bristol BS15 8JN* E: raebarrett@aol.com

BARRETT, Robert David. b 48. Linc Sch of Th and Min 08. **d** 11 **p** 12. OLM Alford w Rigsby *Linc* 11–18; OLM Well 11–18; OLM Saleby w Beesby and Maltby 11–18; OLM Bilsby w Farlesthorpe 11–18; OLM Hannah cum Hagnaby w Markby 11–18; OLM Willoughby 13–18. *14 East Street, Alford LN13 9EQ* T: (01507) 462135 E: revd.bob@btinternet.com

BARRETT, Ronald Reginald. b 30. Roch Th Coll 61. **d** 64 **p** 65. C Spring Park *Cant* 64–66; C Thornton Heath St Jude 66–68; V Greengates *Bradf* 68–73; V Shelf 73–79; V Embsay w Eastby 79–87; V Farndon and Coddington *Ches* 87–92; rtd 92; PtO *Bradf* 92–10; *Man* 10–13; *Sheff* from 13. *10 James Smith House, 11 Marlborough Road, Sheffield S10 1DA* T: 0114-266 7206 E: revrb30@gmail.com

BARRETT, Victoria Louise. b 64. Ripon Coll Cuddesdon 15. **d** 17 **p** 18. C Bunbury and Tilstone Fearnall *Ches* 17–19; V Thornton Hough from 19. *54 Neston Road, Thornton Hough, Wirral CH63 1JF* E: revvickybarrett@gmail.com

BARRETT FORD, Mrs Carol Mary. b 67. NUI BA 88 HDipEd 89 Lon Inst of Educn MA 07 St Jo Coll Dur BA 13. Cranmer Hall Dur 11. **d** 13 **p** 14. C Cowgate *Newc* 13–16; Chapl St Jo Coll Cam 16–19; V Kentish Town St Martin w St Andr *Lon* from 19. *St Martin's Vicarage, 26 Vicars Road, London NW5 4NL* E: mthr.carol@gmail.com

BARRIBAL, Richard James Pitt. b 45. Trin Coll Bris. **d** 80 **p** 81. C Northampton St Giles *Pet* 80–82; V Long Buckby w Watford 82–86; PtO 86–00; *Leic* 00–08; P-in-c Welham, Glooston and Cranoe and Stonton Wyville 08–10; PtO from 14. *The Thatched House, 6 Church Bank, Great Easton, Market Harborough LE16 8SN* T: (01536) 772127 E: richard.barribal@btinternet.com

BARRIE, John Arthur. b 38. K Coll Lon 58 Bps' Coll Cheshunt 59. **d** 63 **p** 64. C Southgate St Mich *Lon* 63–66; CF 66–88; Sen CF 88–93; Chapl Guards Chpl Lon 88–92; QHC 91–93; P-in-c Heref H Trin 93–96; P-in-c Breinton 95–96; V St Marylebone St Mark Hamilton Terrace *Lon* 96–10; Ecum Adv Two Cities Area 99–10; rtd 10; PtO *Lon* from 10. *The Vicarage, 4 Beaudesert Mews, West Drayton UB7 7PE* T: (01895) 442194 E: rosybarrie1@btinternet.com *or* john.barrie@london.anglican.org

BARRIE (*née* HEITZMANN), Mrs Pamela. b 58. Open Univ BA 90 Kingston Univ MA 05. STETS 09. **d** 12 **p** 13. NSM Shepperton and Littleton *Lon* from 12. *131A Laleham Road, Staines TW18 2EG* M: 07806-762745 E: pamelabarrie3284@hotmail.co.uk

BARRIE, Mrs Rosemary Joan. b 62. Bris Univ BA 83 PGCE 84. Qu Coll Birm 87 Perkins Sch of Th (USA) 89. **d** 07 **p** 08. NSM W Kilburn St Luke and Kilburn St Mary w All So and W Hampstead St Jas *Lon* 07–08; NSM St Marylebone St Mark Hamilton Terrace 08–10; C Twickenham St Mary 10–13; Chapl St Mary's Sch Twickenham 10–13; V W Drayton *Lon* from 13. *The Vicarage, 4 Beaudesert Mews, West Drayton UB7 7PE* T: (01895) 442194 E: rosybarrie1@btinternet.com

BARRINGTON, The Very Revd Dominic Matthew Jesse. b 62. Hatf Coll Dur BA 84 MSc 85 LTCL. Ripon Coll Cuddesdon BA 94 MA 98 Ch Div Sch of Pacific MTS 95. **d** 95 **p** 96. C Mortlake w E Sheen *S'wark* 95–98; Chapl St Chad's Coll Dur 98–03; P-in-c Kettering SS Pet and Paul 03–10; R 10–15; Dean Chicago USA from 15. *St James Cathedral, 65 East Huron Street, Chicago IL 60611-2728, USA* T: (001) (312) 787 7360 E: dean@saintjamescathedral.org

✠**BARRINGTON-WARD, The Rt Revd Simon.** b 30. Magd Coll Cam BA 53 MA 57. Wycliffe Coll Toronto Hon DD Westcott Ho Cam 54. **d** 56 **p** 57 **c** 85. Chapl Magd Coll Cam 56–60; Nigeria 60–63; Fell and Dean of Chpl Magd Coll Cam 63–69; Prin Crowther Hall CMS Tr Coll Selly Oak 69–74; Gen Sec CMS 75–85; Hon Can Derby Cathl 75–85; Chapl to The Queen 84–85; Bp Cov 85–97; rtd 97; Hon Fell Magd Coll Cam from 87; Hon Asst Chapl from 98; Hon Asst Bp Ely from 97. *c/o 9 Thrifts Walk, Cambridge CB4 1NR*

BARRON, Arthur Henry. b 45. Solicitor 72. SEITE 99. **d** 02 **p** 03. NSM Addiscombe St Mary Magd w St Martin *S'wark* 02–06; Chapl Asst St Mary's NHS Trust Paddington 05–09; Chapl Guy's and St Thos' NHS Foundn Trust 09–12; rtd 12; PtO *S'wark* 06–07 and from 15; NSM Woodmansterne 07–15; Hon Min Can S'wark Cathl from 15; PtO *Lon* 17–18.

23 Little Woodcote Lane, Purley CR8 3PZ T: (020) 8660 1921 M: 07710-275977 E: thebarrons23lwl@hotmail.com
BARRON, John William. b 66. Imp Coll Lon BSc 88. Cranmer Hall Dur 06. **d** 08 **p** 09. C Whickham *Dur* 08–11; V High Spen and Rowlands Gill 11–19; P-in-c Houghton le Spring from 19. *The Rectory, 5 Lingfield, Houghton le Spring DH5 8QA*
BARRON, Leslie Gill. b 44. ACII 69. Lich Th Coll 67. **d** 70 **p** 71. C Bishopwearmouth Ch Ch *Dur* 70–72; C Bishopwearmouth St Mary V w St Pet CD 72–75; C Harton 75–77; V Lumley 77–88; P-in-c Hendon and Sunderland 88–90; R Hendon 90–94; P-in-c Ushaw Moor 94–95; V Bearpark and Ushaw Moor 95–04; PtO from 04; rtd 08. *34 Brecongill Close, Hartlepool TS24 8PH* T: (01429) 291197 E: l.barron7@ntlworld.com
BARRON, Richard Davidson. b 51. Lon Univ BSc 74. Trin Coll Bris 75. **d** 78 **p** 79. C Bradley *Wakef* 78–81; C Heworth H Trin *York* 81–82; TV 82–89; Chapl York Distr Hosp 82–86; R Greenhithe St Mary *Roch* 89–12; R Fairlight and Pett *Chich* from 12. *The Rectory, 15C Battery Hill, Fairlight, Hastings TN35 4AP* T: (01424) 812799 E: rbarron100@yahoo.co.uk
BARRON, Mrs Sonia Patricia. b 55. Lon Univ BEd 80 Nottm Univ MA 00. St Mellitus Coll 08. **d** 11 **p** 12. C Chilwell *S'well* 11–14; R Claypole *Linc* 14–19; RD Loveden 14–19; Dioc Dir of Ords from 19. *55 Lucknow Drive, Nottingham NG3 5EJ* E: rectorclaypole5@gmail.com
BARRON, Ms Sylvia. b 50. Maria Grey Coll Lon CertEd 72. All SS Cen for Miss & Min 11. **d** 14 **p** 15. NSM Spotland and Oakenrod *Man* from 14. *35 Holstein Avenue, Rochdale OL12 6DL* T: (01706) 658766 E: barronsylvia@yahoo.co.uk
BARROW, Christine. *See* BARROW, Margaret Christine
BARROW, Mrs Evelyne. b 68. Yorks Min Course 12. **d** 15 **p** 16. NSM Upper Holme Valley *Leeds* from 15. *17 Windmill Hill Lane, Emley Moor, Huddersfield HD8 9TP* T: (01924) 848070 E: esb44@icloud.com
BARROW, Gillian Stephanie. *See* BARROW-JONES, Gillian Stephanie
BARROW, Jack Alexander. b 81. St Andr Univ BSc 03 MLitt 07 Heythrop Coll Lon MA 18. Ripon Coll Cuddesdon BA 12 MA 17. **d** 13 **p** 14. C Frodingham and New Brumby *Linc* 13–14; C Gt and Lt Coates w Bradley 14–17; TV Mortlake w E Sheen *S'wark* from 17; Dioc Voc Adv from 18. *All Saints' Vicarage, 86 East Sheen Avenue, London SW14 8AU* T: (020) 8876 5801 M: 07971-669587 E: alexbarrow1@gmail.com
BARROW (née DONSON), Mrs Margaret Christine. b 44. Homerton Coll Cam CertEd 65. Westcott Ho Cam 08. **d** 09 **p** 10. NSM Girton *Ely* 09–14; NSM Madingley 12–14; PtO from 14. *2 Cockerton Road, Girton, Cambridge CB3 0QW* T: (01223) 277674 E: mcbarrow@mac.com
BARROW, Paul Beynon. b 48. Liv Univ LLB 69 Man Univ MA 01. St Steph Ho Ox 02. **d** 04 **p** 05. NSM Ches H Trin 04–05; P-in-c Hargrave 05–11; V 11–13; rtd 13; PtO *St As* from 15; *Ches* from 16. *Keepers Cottage, Eyton, Wrexham LL13 0SN* T: (01978) 781534 M: 07592-154388
BARROW-JONES, Mrs Gillian Stephanie. Regent's Park Coll Ox BA 98. Westcott Ho Cam 08. **d** 10 **p** 11. C Gainsborough and Morton *Linc* 10–13; R Wolverton *Ox* from 13. *Holy Trinity House, 28 Harvester Close, Greenleys, Milton Keynes MK12 6LE*
BARRY, Colin Lionel. b 49. Open Univ BSc 94. Bp Attwell Tr Inst 85. **d** 96 **p** 97. NSM Arbory *S & M* 96–13; NSM Arbory and Castletown from 13. *80 Ballanorris Crescent, Ballabeg, Castletown, Isle of Man IM9 4ER* T: (01624) 823080
BARRY, Ms Jacqueline Françoise. Univ of Bordeaux II LSocEth 86 MSoc 87 York Univ PGCE 91. Ridley Hall Cam. **d** 99 **p** 00. C Sydenham H Trin *S'wark* 99–03; C W Kilburn St Luke w St Simon and St Jude *Lon* 03–13; C Paddington Em Harrow Road 03–13; C W Kilburn St Luke and Harrow Road Em from 13. *Emmanuel Vicarage, 44C Fermoy Road, London W9 3NH* T: (020) 8969 0438 E: jackiefbarry@yahoo.co.uk
BARRY, Jonathan Peter Oulton. b 47. TCD BA 70 MA 73 Hull Univ BA 73 QUB PhD 87. Ripon Hall Ox 73. **d** 74 **p** 75. C Dundela St Mark *D & D* 74–79; I Ballyphilip w Ardquin 79–85; Dioc Info Officer 80–90; I Comber 85–18; Preb St Audoen St Patr Cathl Dublin 01–18; rtd 18. *32 Magheraknock Park, Ballynahinch BT24 8FG* M: 07754-508587 E: jpobarry@icloud.com
BARRY, Nicholas Brian Paul. b 62. Leic Univ BA 83. St Steph Ho Ox 84. **d** 87 **p** 88. C St John's Wood *Lon* 87–90; Chapl RAF 90–15; Dep Chapl-in-Chief 09–15; QHC 09–15; V Jersey St Luke w St Jas *Win* from 15. *Longueville Farm, Longueville Road, St Saviour, Jersey JE2 7WG* T: (01534) 851445 E: nbpbarry@hotmail.com
BARRY, Ruth Mary. b 79. Bris Univ BSc 01 Darwin Coll Cam PhD 07. Ridley Hall Cam 17. **d** 19. C Cherry Hinton St Andr *Ely* from 19. *39 Eland Way, Cambridge CB1 9XQ* M: 07808-165121 E: ruth.barry@yahoo.co.uk

BARSLEY, Canon Margaret Ann. b 39. Totley Hall Coll CertEd 60. EMMTC 79. **dss** 83 **d** 87 **p** 94. Kirton in Holland *Linc* 83–89; NSM 87–89; NSM Skirbeck Quarter 89–96; P-in-c Swineshead 96–99; V 99–04; RD Holland W 97–04; Can and Preb Linc Cathl from 00; rtd 04. *44 Sentance Crescent, Kirton, Boston PE20 1XF* T: (01205) 723824
BARTER, The Very Revd Donald. b 34. St Fran Coll Brisbane ThL 69 ACT ThSchol 74. **d** 69 **p** 70. C Townsville Australia 69–72; R Mareeba 72–76; R Ingham 76–81; Adn of the W and R Mt Isa 81–86; Dean Townsville 86–90; Chapl Miss to Seamen 86–90; Appeals Dir SPCK 90–93; LtO *Leic* 90–93; Australia from 93; Asst to Dean St Jas Cathl 94–00. *49 Macrossan Street, South Townsville Qld 4810, Australia* T/F: (0061) (7) 4772 7036 M: 414-989593 E: dba18613@bigpond.net.au
BARTER, Geoffrey Roger. b 41. Bris Univ BSc 63. Clifton Th Coll 65. **d** 67 **p** 68. C Normanton *Derby* 67–70; C Rainham *Chelmsf* 70–75; V Plumstead St Jo w St Jas and St Paul *S'wark* 75–82; V Frogmore St Alb 82–01; rtd 01; PtO *Chich* from 02. *45 West Front Road, Pagham, Bognor Regis PO21 4SZ* T: (01243) 262522 E: geoff.barter@gmail.com
BARTHOLOMEW, David Grant. b 50. Univ of Wales (Lamp) BA 77. Chich Th Coll 91. **d** 93 **p** 94. C Petersfield *Portsm* 93–96; R Etton w Helpston and Maxey *Pet* 96–98; R Burghclere w Newtown and Ecchinswell w Sydmonton *Win* from 98. *The Rectory, Well Street, Burghclere, Newbury RG20 9HS* T: (01635) 278470 E: davidrectory@twang.co.uk
BARTLEM, Gregory John. b 68. Ox Brookes Univ BA 05. Qu Coll Birm 07. **d** 09 **p** 10. NSM Cheylesmore *Cov* 09–11; C Cov Cathl 11–18; R Walton d'Eiville from 18; V Wellesbourne from 18. *St Peter's Vicarage, Church Street, Wellesbourne, Warwick CV35 9LS* M: 07414-675159 E: gregjbartlem@gmail.com
BARTLETT, Aidan Dominic. b 84. Van Mildert Coll Dur BA 07. St Steph Ho Ox BA 18. **d** 18. C Clerkenwell H Redeemer *Lon* from 18; C Clerkenwell St Mark from 18. *24 Exmouth Market, London EC1R 4QE* T: (020) 7837 1861 E: fr.aidan.bartlett@gmail.com
BARTLETT, Canon Alan Bennett. b 58. G&C Coll Cam BA 81 MA 85 Birm Univ PhD 87 St Jo Coll Dur BA 90. Cranmer Hall Dur 88. **d** 91 **p** 92. C Newc H Cross 91–94; C Newburn 94–96; Tutor Cranmer Hall Dur 96–08; V Dur St Giles 08–17; P-in-c Shadforth and Sherburn 08–17; Clergy Development Adv from 17; Hon Can Dur Cathl from 11. *22 Aldin Grange Terrace, Bearpark, Durham DH7 7AN* T: 0191-374 6012 M: 07384-214576 E: alan.bartlett@durham.anglican.org
BARTLETT, Anthony Martin. b 43. Cranmer Hall Dur 74. **d** 77 **p** 78. C Heworth St Mary *Dur* 77–80; V Cleadon 80–84; CF (TA) 81–90; Prec Dur Cathl 85–87; V Harton 87–95; P-in-c Hendon 95–96; R 96–97; V Greenlands *Blackb* 01–12; rtd 12; PtO *Blackb* from 12. *3 Keats Close, Thornton-Cleveleys FY5 2SA* T: (01253) 273471 E: bcressell@aol.com
BARTLETT, David John. b 36. Pemb Coll Ox BA 61. Linc Th Coll 63. **d** 65 **p** 66. C Wollaton *S'well* 65–70; V Woodthorpe 70–83; V Farnsfield 83–01; P-in-c Kirklington w Hockerton 83–01; RD S'well 83–93; Chapl Rodney Sch Kirklington 83–01; rtd 01; PtO *S'well* from 01. *6 De Havilland Way, Farndon Road, Newark NG24 4RF* T: (01636) 651582
BARTLETT, David William. b 59. Trin Coll Bris 89. **d** 91 **p** 92. C Frinton *Chelmsf* 91–95; TV Eston w Normanby *York* 95–96; Assoc P Worksop St Jo *S'well* 96–01; TV Trunch *Nor* 01–14; P-in-c Overstrand, Northrepps, Sidestrand etc 12–14; R Bardney *Linc* from 14. *10 Church Lane, Bardney, Lincoln LN3 5TZ* T: (01526) 397363 E: revdb@btinternet.com
BARTLETT, Ms Jane Louise. b 63. Warwick Univ BA 84 Win Univ MA 10. St Mellitus Coll BA 17. **d** 17 **p** 18. C New Shoreham and Shoreham Beach *Chich* from 17. *19 Buckingham Avenue, Shoreham-by-Sea BN43 5GL* M: 07935-538085 E: bartlett.jane@ntlworld.com
BARTLETT, Prof John Raymond. b 37. BNC Ox BA 59 MA 62 BLitt 62 TCD MA 70 LittD 94. Linc Th Coll 61. **d** 63 **p** 64. C W Bridgford *S'well* 63–66; Lect Div TCD 64–86; Assoc Prof Bibl Studies 86–92; Fell 75–92; Prof Past Th 90–01; Prin CITC 89–01; Treas Ch Ch Cathl Dublin *D & G* 86–88; Prec 88–01; rtd 01. *102 Sorrento Road, Dalkey, Co Dublin, Republic of Ireland* T: (00353) (1) 284 7786 E: jrbartlett@eircom.net
BARTLETT, Kenneth Vincent John. b 36. Oriel Coll Ox BA 61 BTh 63. Ripon Hall Ox 61. **d** 63 **p** 64. C Paddington St Jas *Lon* 63–67; LtO from 67; rtd 01. *25 Tudor Road, Kingston-upon-Thames KT2 6AS* T: (020) 8974 5453 E: ken.bartlett3@btinternet.com
BARTLETT, Michael Fredrick. b 52. Ex Univ BA 74 Liv Univ BPhil 75. Ven English Coll Rome 78 Ripon Coll Cuddesdon BA 79 MA. **d** 79 **p** 80. C Kirkby *Liv* 79–82; C Wordsley *Lich* 82–83; TV 83–88; Chapl Wordsley Hosp 82–88; TV Redditch, The Ridge *Worc* 88–05; TR Redditch Ch the K from 05.

St Peter's House, Littlewoods, Redditch B97 5LB   T: (01527) 545709

BARTLETT, Canon Richard Charles. b 68. St Kath Coll Liv BA 90 Surrey Univ MA 01. Westcott Ho Cam 91. **d** 94 **p** 95. C Wareham *Sarum* 94–98; Assoc V Ealing All SS *Lon* 98–02; Chapl Twyford C of E High Sch Acton 98–02; USPG Brazil 02–05; Hon Can Brasilia Cathl from 05; V Northwood H Trin *Lon* 05–16; AD Harrow 07–13; PtO from 16; *St Alb* from 16; Dir Miss Engagement USPG from 16; Public Preacher *S'wark* from 16. *USPG, Rise House, 5 Trinity Street, London SE1 1DB*   T: (020) 7921 2236   M: 07711-701910 E: richardb@uspg.org.uk

BARTON, Allan Benjamin (Ben). b 77. Univ Coll Lon BA 98 York Univ MA 99 PhD 04 FSA 18. Ripon Coll Cuddesdon 05. **d** 08 **p** 09. C Louth *Linc* 08–09; C Saxilby Gp 09–11; P-in-c Aylmerton, Runton, Beeston Regis and Gresham *Nor* 11–13; PtO from 14; Chapl Univ of Wales (Trin St Dav) *St D* 15–17; R W Wycombe w Bledlow Ridge, Bradenham and Radnage *Ox* from 17. *The Rectory, Church Lane, West Wycombe, High Wycombe HP14 3AH*   T: (01494) 529988 E: benodbarton@gmail.com

BARTON, Andrew Edward. b 53. St Jo Coll Ox MA 77 DPhil 80 Idaho Univ MTh 06 MRSC. Ridley Hall Cam 87. **d** 90 **p** 91. C Ringwood *Win* 90–94; R Baughurst, Ramsdell, Wolverton w Ewhurst etc 95–07; Lect K Alfred's Coll Win 95–98; R Auchterarder and Muthill *St And* 07–14; Chapl N Police Convalescent Homes 07–14; P-in-c Headley All SS *Guildf* 14–18; R from 18; LtO Adelaide Australia from 09. *All Saints' Rectory, High Street, Headley, Bordon GU35 8PP*   T: (01428) 717207   M: 07778-771651   E: james.kessog@gmail.com *or* priest@allsaintsheadley.plus.com

BARTON, Canon Arthur Michael. b 33. CCC Cam BA 57 MA 61. Wycliffe Hall Ox 57. **d** 59 **p** 60. Min Can Bradf Cathl 59–61; C Maltby *Sheff* 61–63; V Silsden *Bradf* 63–70; V Moor Allerton *Ripon* 70–81; TR 81–82; V Wetherby 82–98; Chapl HM YOI Wetherby 82–89; RD Harrogate *Ripon* 88–95; Hon Can Ripon Cathl 89–98; rtd 98; PtO *Ripon* 98–14; *Leeds* from 14. *42 Church Square Mansions, Church Square, Harrogate HG1 4SS*   T: (01423) 520105 E: teambarton@aol.com

BARTON, Benjamin. *See* BARTON, Allan Benjamin

BARTON, The Ven Charles John Greenwood. b 36. ALCD 63. **d** 63 **p** 64. C Cant St Mary Bredin 63–66; V Whitfield w W Langdon 66–75; V S Kensington St Luke *Lon* 75–83; AD Chelsea 80–83; Chief Broadcasting Officer for C of E 83–90; Adn Aston *Birm* 90–03; Can Res Birm Cathl 90–02; P-in-c Bickenhill 02–03; rtd 03; PtO *Cant* from 03; Abp's Communications Adv *York* 05–06; Acting Prin Adv to Abp York 07; Abp's Chapl and Researcher 08. *7 The Spires, Canterbury CT2 8SD*   M: 07743-118544 E: venjohnbarton@gmail.com

BARTON, Dale. b 49. Selw Coll Cam BA 71 MA 76. Linc Th Coll 71. **d** 73 **p** 74. C Gosforth All SS *Newc* 73–77; Lesotho 77–81; Dep Warden CA Hostel Cam 82–83; C Shepton Mallet w Doulting *B & W* 83–88; TV Preston St Steph *Blackb* 88–96; V 96–99; Bp's Adv on Inter-Faith Relns 99–07; P-in-c Bradf St Clem 07–14; *Leeds* 14–16; P-in-c Bradf St Aug Undercliffe 07–14; *Leeds* 14–16; rtd 16; PtO *Leeds* from 16. *84 Park Road, Bingley BD16 4EJ*   M: 07871-992324 E: dale.barton@hotmail.co.uk

BARTON, David Gerald Story. b 38. Selw Coll Cam BA 62 MA 66. Cuddesdon Coll 63. **d** 65 **p** 66. C Cowley St Jas *Ox* 65–67; C Hambleden 67–70; Hon C Hammersmith St Jo *Lon* 72–77; Hon C Paddington St Jas 77–81; Hd Master Soho Par Sch 81–88; Hon C Westmr St Jas *Lon* 81–92; RE Project Officer Lon Dioc Bd for Schs 88–92; Dioc Schs Adv *Ox* 93–99; rtd 00; Hon C Iffley *Ox* 93–06; PtO 06–09 and from 18. *254 Iffley Road, Oxford OX4 1SE*   T: (01865) 240059 E: daviebarton@aol.com *or* davidbarton254@gmail.com

BARTON, Canon Geoffrey. b 27. Oriel Coll Ox BA 48 MA 52. Chich Th Coll 49. **d** 51 **p** 52. C Arnold *S'well* 51–53; C E Retford 53–54; V Mirfield Eastthorpe St Paul *Wakef* 54–60; V Boroughbridge w Roecliffe *Ripon* 60–73; V Aldborough w Boroughbridge and Roecliffe 73; P-in-c Farnham w Scotton and Staveley and Copgrove 73–74; R 74–77; Chapl Roundway Hosp Devizes 77–92; Can and Preb Sarum Cathl 86–92; rtd 92; PtO *Sarum* 01–10. *4B Willow House, Downlands Road, Devizes SN10 5EA*   T: (01380) 725311

BARTON (née CRABB), Helen Maria. b 56. Lon Bible Coll BA 83 St Jo Coll Dur MA 04 St Mary's Coll Strawberry Hill PGCE 98. Cranmer Hall Dur 01. **d** 03 **p** 04. C Wisley w Pyrford *Guildf* 03–04; C Lanchester *Dur* 04–06; C Hexham *Newc* 06–08; V Widdrington 08–15; P-in-c Barlaston *Lich* 15–16; Master St Jo Hosp from 16. *St John's Hospital, St John Street, Lichfield WS13 6PB*   T: (01543) 251884 E: helen@the-bartons.com

BARTON, Canon John. b 25. Keble Coll Ox BA 48 MA 50. Ely Th Coll 48. **d** 50 **p** 51. C Worksop St Anne *S'well* 50–53; C Harrogate St Wilfrid *Ripon* 53–56; V Beeston Hill H Spirit 56–60; Chapl Pinderfields and Stanley Royd Hosp Wakef 60–72; RD Wakef 68–72; Chapl Jo Radcliffe Hosp and Radcliffe Infirmary 72–90; Chapl Chu Hosp Ox 72–89; Hon Can Ch Ch *Ox* 77–94; RD Cowley 89–94; rtd 90; PtO *Ox* 94–01; *Roch* 01–16. *150A Longlands Road, Sidcup DA15 7LF*   T: (020) 8300 7073

BARTON, Prof John. b 48. Keble Coll Ox BA 69 MA 73 Mert Coll Ox DPhil 74 St Cross Coll Ox DLitt 88. **d** 73 **p** 73. Jun Research Fell Mert Coll Ox 73–74; Lect St Cross Coll Ox 74–89; Fell 74–91; Chapl 79–91; Lect Th Ox Univ 74–89; Reader 89–91; Oriel and Laing Prof of Interpr of H Scripture from 91; Fell Oriel Coll Ox from 91; Can Th Win Cathl 91–03; PtO *Ox* from 18. *11 Withington Court, Abingdon OX14 3QA*   T: (01235) 525925 E: john.barton@oriel.ox.ac.uk

BARTON, John. *See* BARTON, Charles John Greenwood

BARTON, John Michael. b 40. TCD BA 62 Div Test. **d** 63 **p** 64. C Coleraine *Conn* 63–68; C Portadown St Mark *Arm* 68–71; I Carnteel and Crilly 71–83; I Derryloran 83–97; Bp's C Acton and Drumbanagher 97–09; Can Arm Cathl 94–09; Treas 98–01; Chan Arm Cathl 01–09; rtd 09. *23 Strand Cottages, Sheskburn Avenue, Ballycastle BT54 6HR*   T: (028) 2076 9673 E: jm7mabarton@talktalk.net

BARTON, Mrs Margaret Ann Edith. b 48. Newc Univ BA 71. EMMTC 95. **d** 98 **p** 99. NSM Castle Bytham w Creeton *Linc* 98–04; P-in-c Corby Glen 04–12; rtd 12; PtO *Linc* from 13. *Blanchland House, 15 Swinstead Road, Corby Glen, Grantham NG33 4NU*   T: (01476) 550763

BARTON, Michael. *See* BARTON, Arthur Michael

BARTON, Michael James. b 78. Sheff Univ MEng 01 Man Univ BSc 06. Wycliffe Hall Ox 11. **d** 13 **p** 14. C Claygate *Guildf* 13–17; V Longridge *Blackb* from 17. *The Vicarage, Church Street, Longridge, Preston PR3 3WA*   M: 07866-508697 E: teambarton@btinternet.com

BARTON, Paul Michael Benson. b 60. **d** 14 **p** 15. NSM Torquay St Matthias, St Mark and H Trin *Ex* from 14. *Rowdale, Ridge Road, Maidencombe, Torquay TQ1 4TD*   T: (01803) 327504 E: revpaulbarton@gmail.com

BARTON (née McVEIGH), Canon Sandra. b 58. Reading Univ BA 80. Cranmer Hall Dur 93. **d** 95 **p** 96. C Stranton *Dur* 95–98; P-in-c Blackhall, Castle Eden and Monkhesleden 98–99; R 99–02; PtO *Blackb* 02–06; *Ely* 06–10; *St E* 08–11; C Mildenhall from 11; Dioc Environment Officer from 17; Hon Can St E Cathl from 15. *The Old Village Stores, 6 The Street, Freckenham, Bury St Edmunds IP28 8HZ*   T: (01638) 720770 E: revsandiebarton@gmail.com

BARTON, Stephen Christian. b 52. Macquarie Univ (NSW) BA 75 DipEd 75 Lanc Univ MA 78 K Coll Lon PhD 92. Cranmer Hall Dur 91. **d** 93 **p** 94. NSM Dur St Jo CD *Dur* 93–00; NSM Dur St Marg and Neville's Cross Jo 00–06; PtO *Newc* 06–15; *Lich* from 15. *St John's Hospital, St John Street, Lichfield WS13 6PB* E: s.c.barton@durham.ac.uk

BARTON, Trevor James. b 50. St Alb Minl Tr Scheme 79. **d** 87 **p** 88. NSM Hemel Hempstead *St Alb* from 87. *Address temp unknown* E: trevorbarton@hotmail.com

BARWELL, Brian Bernard Beale. b 30. Preston Poly CertEd 79. AKC 59 St Boniface Warminster 59. **d** 60 **p** 61. C Heywood St Jas *Man* 60–63; V Smallbridge 63–69; V Farington *Blackb* 69–72; C-in-c Blackb St Luke w St Phil 72–75; C Standish 75–76; LtO 76–92; rtd 92; PtO *Blackb* 92–11. *70 Claytongate, Coppull, Chorley PR7 4PS*   T: (01257) 794251

BARWICK, Lester Mark. b 56. Washington Coll (USA) BA 78. Wesley Th Sem Washington MDiv 89. **d** 09 **p** 10. Belgium 09–17; Chapl Strasbourg *Eur* from 17. *15 rue d'Austerlitz, 67000 Strasbourg, France*   T: (0033) 3 69 57 40 03 E: anglican.chaplaincy.strasbourg@gmail.com *or* mark.barwick@gmail.com

BASH, Anthony. b 52. Bris Univ LLB 73 LLM 76 Glas Univ BD 88 Clare Hall Cam PhD 96. Westcott Ho Cam 94. **d** 96 **p** 97. C Kingston upon Hull H Trin *York* 96–99; V N Ferriby 99–04; Chapl to Legal Profession 97–04; Hon Fell Hull Univ 97–04; Chapl and Fell Univ Coll Dur 05–06; TR Dur N 06–08; Chapl and Tutor Hatf Coll Dur from 08; Hon Research Fell Univ Coll Dur from 08. *Hatfield College, North Bailey, Durham DH1 3RQ*   T: 0191-334 2636 E: anthony.bash@durham.ac.uk

BASHFORD, Robert Thomas. b 49. Ch Coll Cam BA 70 CertEd 72 MA 74 Lon Univ BD 84 MPhil 89. Oak Hill Th Coll 86. **d** 88 **p** 89. C Frinton *Chelmsf* 88–91; C Galleywood Common 91–96; P-in-c Westgate St Jas *Cant* 02–06; V 06–12; rtd 12; PtO *Pet* from 13; *Leic* from 16. *66 Grosvenor Way, Barton Seagrave, Kettering NN15 6TZ*   T: (01536) 723056 E: bashford66@outlook.com

BASHFORTH, Canon Alan George. b 64. Ex Univ MA. Ripon Coll Cuddesdon BTh 96. **d** 96 **p** 97. C Calstock *Truro* 96–98;

C St Ives 98–01; V St Agnes and Mount Hawke w Mithian 01–14; P-in-c St Clement 12–14; RD Powder 04–12; Hon Can Truro Cathl 13–14; Can Res and Chan Truro Cathl from 14; Hon C Truro St Mary from 15. *The Cathedral Office, 14 St Mary's Street, Truro TR1 2AF* T: (01872) 245012 E: alanbashforth@trurocathedral.org.uk

BASINGSTOKE, Suffragan Bishop of. *See* WILLIAMS, The Rt Revd David Grant

BASKERVILLE, John. b 45. Open Univ BA 78. Sarum & Wells Th Coll 92. **d** 93 **p** 94. C Wanstead St Mary w Ch Ch *Chelmsf* 93–96; C Chingford SS Pet and Paul 96–98; V Felkirk w Brierley *Wakef* 98–04; rtd 04. *131 Howard Road, Upminster RM14 2UQ* T: (01708) 641242 M: 07710-209469

BASON, Mrs Carol. b 44. De Montfort Univ BSc 96. **d** 09 **p** 10. OLM S Lawres Gp *Linc* from 09. *Walnut Tree Cottage, 15 Church Lane, Reepham, Lincoln LN3 4DQ* T: (01522) 753282 M: 07749-211397 E: cbason@tiscali.co.uk

BASS, Colin Graham. b 41. Liv Univ BSc 62 Fitzw Ho Cam BA 64 MA 68. Ox NSM Course 84. **d** 87 **p** 88. Dir of Studies Leighton Park Sch Reading 87–97; NSM Earley St Pet *Ox* 87–92; NSM Reading Deanery 92–11; PtO from 11. *9 Bramley Close, Reading RG6 7PL* T: 0118-966 3732 E: colin.bass@cantab.net

BASS, George <u>Michael</u>. b 39. Ely Th Coll 62. **d** 65 **p** 66. C Romaldkirk *Ripon* 65–68; C Kenton Ascension *Newc* 68–71; CF 71–94; Chapl Northumbria Healthcare NHS Trust 95–02; rtd 02; PtO *Newc* from 02. *35 Kelso Drive, North Shields NE29 9NS* T: 0191-258 2514

BASS, Mrs Rosemary <u>Jane</u>. b 38. Linc Th Coll 76. **dss** 79 **d** 87 **p** 94. Bedford All SS *St Alb* 79–84; Leavesden 84–94; Par Dn 87–94; C 94–95; V Luton St Andr 95–01; rtd 01; PtO *St Alb* from 01. *3 Highfield Road, Oakley, Bedford MK43 7TA* T: (01234) 822126 E: roanj@btinternet.com

BASSETT, Mrs Rosemary Louise. b 42. STETS. **d** 00 **p** 01. NSM The Winterbournes and Compton Valence *Sarum* 00–08; P-in-c 03–08; NSM Dorchester 08–14; PtO from 14. *12 Lime Close, Dorchester DT1 2HQ* T: (01305) 262615 E: rosemary.bassett42@gmail.com

BASTABLE, Richard Michael. b 83. Ex Univ BA 04 St Edm Coll Cam MPhil 08. Westcott Ho Cam 06. **d** 08 **p** 09. C Ruislip St Martin *Lon* 08–10; C St Andr Holborn 10–13; V Hammersmith St Luke from 13. *St Luke's Vicarage, 450 Uxbridge Road, London W12 0NS* T: (020) 8749 7523 M: 07816-074597 E: rbastable@gmail.com

BASTEN, Richard Henry. b 40. Codrington Coll Barbados 60. **d** 63 **p** 64. Br Honduras 63–67; Barbados 68–72; C Hartlepool H Trin *Dur* 72–73; Chapl Bedstone Coll 73–88; C Clun w Chapel Lawn *Heref* 73–77; P-in-c Clungunford 77–78; R Clungunford w Clunbury and Clunton, Bedstone etc 78–88; R Rowde and Poulshot *Sarum* 88–95; rtd 95; PtO *Glouc* 95–12. *41 Bewley Way, Churchdown, Gloucester GL3 2DU* T: (01452) 859738

BASTIDE, Derek. b 44. Dur Univ BA 65 Sussex Univ MA 77 Reading Univ DipEd 66. Chich Th Coll 76. **d** 77 **p** 78. Hon C Lewes All SS, St Anne, St Mich and St Thos *Chich* 77–84; Prin Lect Brighton Poly 80–92; Prin Lect Univ Brighton Univ 92–18; P-in-c Hamsey *Chich* 84–18; rtd 18. *42 Mallard Drive, Ridgewood, Uckfield TN22 5PW*

BASTON, Caroline Jane. b 56. Birm Univ BSc 78 CertEd 79. Ripon Coll Cuddesdon 87. **d** 89 **p** 94. Par Dn Southampton Thornhill St Chris *Win* 89–94; C 94–95; R Win All SS w Chilcomb and Chesil 95–06; Dioc Communications Officer 95–98; Dioc Dir of Ords 99–06; Hon Can Win Cathl 00–06; Adn Is of Wight *Portsm* 06–11; P-in-c N Swindon St Andr *Bris* 11–16; Warden CSMV from 13; PtO *Ox* from 13; *Win* 16–19; P-in-c Fawley from 19. *39 Clarendon Road, Southampton SO16 4GB* T: (023) 8051 2272 M: 07780-877895 E: cjbaston17@gmail.com

BATCHELOR, Andrew George. b 59. St Jo Coll Nottm 07. **d** 09 **p** 10. C Ulverston St Mary w H Trin *Carl* 09–13; V Walney Is from 13; P-in-c Barrow St Jo from 18. *St Mary's Vicarage, Promenade, Walney, Barrow-in-Furness LA14 3QU* T: (01229) 227976 M: 07934-483439 E: rev.andyb@gmail.com

BATCHELOR, John Millar. CITC 76. **d** 78 **p** 79. C Belfast All SS *Conn* 78–80; I Eglish w Killylea *Arm* 80–96; I Ballyhalbert w Ardkeen *D & D* 96–01; rtd 01. *Rhone Brae, 102 Eglish Road, Dungannon BT70 1LB* T: (028) 8775 0177 E: jm_batchelor@outlook.com

BATCHELOR, Canon Martin John. b 67. Plymouth Poly BSc 91. St Jo Coll Nottm 94. **d** 95 **p** 96. C Brecon St Mary and Battle w Llanddew *S & B* 95–97; Min Can Brecon Cathl 95–97; C Sketty 97–00; TV Hawarden *St As* 00–05; V Bistre 05–16; I Borderlands Miss Area from 17; AD Hawarden from 10; Can Cursal St As Cathl from 19. *Bistre Vicarage, Mold Road, Buckley CH7 2NH* T: (01244) 550947 E: martinbtchlr@gmail.com

BATCHELOR, Michael Patrick. b 55. Qu Coll Birm 11. **d** 13 **p** 14. OLM Willenhall St Steph *Lich* from 13. *24 Rockland Gardens, Willenhall WV13 3HP* T: (01902) 606615 E: m.batchelor922@btinternet.com

BATCOCK, Neil Gair. b 53. UEA BA 74. Westcott Ho Cam 94. **d** 96 **p** 97. C Barton upon Humber *Linc* 96–99; TV Totnes w Bridgetown, Berry Pomeroy etc *Ex* 99–06; P-in-c Blakeney w Cley, Wiveton, Glandford etc *Nor* 06–10; R 10–13; P-in-c Walpole St Peter w Walpole St Andrew *Ely* 13–15; P-in-c W Walton 13–15; rtd 15; PtO *Nor* from 15. *104 London Road, King's Lynn PE30 5ES* T: (01553) 768547 M: 07584-070123 E: gair2@aol.com

BATE, Dylan Griffin. b 48. Mon Dioc Tr Scheme 91. **d** 94 **p** 95. NSM Fleur-de-Lis *Mon* 94–96; NSM Bedwellty 96–97; C Pontypool 97–99; C Tenby *St D* 99–02; R Begelly w Ludchurch and Crunwere 02–05; C Risca *Mon* 05–13; rtd 13; NSM Lower Islwyn *Mon* 13–18; PtO from 18. *23 Larch Lane, Tredegar NP22 4FA* T: (01495) 718677

BATE, Preb Lawrence <u>Mark</u>. b 40. Univ Coll Ox BA 63. Coll of Resurr Mirfield 65. **d** 67 **p** 68. C Benwell St Jas *Newc* 67–69; C Monkseaton St Pet 69–72; TV Withycombe Raleigh *Ex* 72–84; RD Aylesbeare 81–84; R Alphington 84–00; RD Christianity 95–99; TV Heavitree w Ex St Paul 00–02; TV Heavitree and St Mary Steps 02–05; Preb Ex Cathl 02–10; rtd 05. *Chapple Court, Kenn, Exeter EX6 7UR* T: (01392) 833485 E: morleybate@freeuk.com *or* francisurch70@gmail.com

BATE, Michael Keith. b 42. Lich Th Coll 67. **d** 69 **p** 70. C W Bromwich St Jas 69–73; C Thornhill *Wakef* 73–76; V Wrenthorpe 76–82; V Upper Gornal *Lich* 82–93; V Upper Gornal *Worc* 93–05; TV Gornal and Sedgley 05–08; Chapl Burton Road Hosp Dudley 82–94; Chapl Dudley Gp of Hosps NHS Trust 94–00; rtd 08; PtO *Lich* from 09. *44 Wentworth Road, Wolverhampton WV10 8EF*

BATE, Stephen Donald. b 58. Sheff Univ BSc 79 Cov Univ PhD 92 CEng 97 MIET 97. **d** 05 **p** 06. OLM Whitnash *Cov* 05–12; C Stratford-upon-Avon, Luddington etc 12–16; R Albury, Lt Hadham and Much Hadham *St Alb* from 16. *The Rectory, Hightrees, Station Road, Much Hadham SG10 6AX* M: 07773-583356 E: sbate@aol.com

BATEMAN, Adrian. b 61. **d** 14 **p** 15. C Goole *Sheff* 14–15; C Armthorpe 15–17; V Worsbrough Common w Worsbrough St Thos from 17. *St Thomas's Vicarage, 80 Kingwell Road, Worsbrough, Barnsley S70 4HG* M: 07738-536046 E: adrian.bateman@sheffield.anglican.org

BATEMAN, James Edward. b 44. Univ Coll Lon BSc 65. Trin Coll Bris 71. **d** 74 **p** 75. C Woodlands *Sheff* 74–77; C Rushden w Newton Bromswold *Pet* 77–84; R Vange *Chelmsf* 84–94; V Southminster 94–01; P-in-c Nazeing and Roydon 01–03; Warden Stacklands Retreat Ho W Kingsdown 03–05; C Rainham *Roch* 05–09; rtd 09; PtO *Pet* 11–14. *11 Ryeburn Way, Wellingborough NN8 3AH* T: (01933) 440106 E: lizandjim.bateman@gmail.com

BATEMAN, Nest Wynne. Univ of Wales (Cardiff) BA 71 CQSW 73. Westcott Ho Cam 08. **d** 09 **p** 10. NSM Lich Cathl 09–17; rtd 17; PtO *Lich* from 17. *21 Christchurch Lane, Lichfield WS13 8BA* T: (01543) 257681 M: 07729-256364

BATEMAN, Patrick John. b 64. Ches Univ BA 14. St Jo Coll Nottm 99. **d** 01 **p** 02. C Wallington *S'wark* 01–05; P-in-c Chipstead 05–11; R 11–12; V Ilkley All SS *Bradf* 12–14; *Leeds* 14–18; V Claygate *Guildf* from 18. *The Vicarage, Church Road, Claygate, Esher KT10 0JP* M: 07764-171400

BATEMAN, Richard George. b 46. Cranmer Hall Dur. **d** 82 **p** 83. C Wolviston *Dur* 82–85; C Greenside 85–87; V Newburn *Newc* 87–90; TV Cramlington 00–08; rtd 08; PtO *Dur* from 08. *9 Ripley Road, Stockton-on-Tees TS20 1NX* T: (01642) 356493 E: rgb158@gmail.com

BATEMAN, Rocky. **d** 17 **p** 18. C Estuary and Mountain Miss Area *St As* from 17. *4 Yr Aber, Holywell CH8 7RN* T: (01352) 386604

BATES, Carol. *See* BATES, Trini Mari Carolina

BATES, David Frederick. b 61. Univ Coll Lon BSc 86 K Coll Lon PGCE 87. St Mellitus Coll BA 15. **d** 15 **p** 16. NSM Mardyke *Chelmsf* 15–19; Chapl Basildon & Thurrock Univ Hosps NHS Foundn Trust from 17; PtO *Chelmsf* from 19. *Basildon University Hospital, Nethermayne, Basildon SS16 5NL* T: (01268) 524900 E: david.bates@btuh.nhs.uk

BATES, Canon Elaine Austwick. b 57. Newc Univ BSc 79 MSc 80 Cumbria Univ BA 12 Lanc Univ PGCE 00. LCTP 06. **d** 10 **p** 11. NSM Barrow St Paul *Carl* from 10; Hon Can Carl Cathl from 18. *17 Harrel Lane, Barrow-in-Furness LA13 9LN* T: (01229) 822149 E: elaine.bates@cumbriachristianlearning.org.uk

✠**BATES, The Rt Revd Gordon.** b 34. Kelham Th Coll 54. **d** 58 **p** 59 **c** 83. C New Eltham All SS *S'wark* 58–62; Asst Youth Chapl *Glouc* 62–64; Youth Chapl *Liv* 65–69; Chapl Liv Cathl

65–69; V Huyton St Mich 69–73; Can Res and Prec Liv Cathl 73–83; Dir of Ords 73–83; Suff Bp Whitby *York* 83–99; rtd 99; Hon Asst Bp Carl and Blackb 99–09; NSM Kirkby Lonsdale *Carl* 03–09; Hon Asst Bp York from 12. *19 Fernwood Close, Brompton, Northallerton DL6 2UX* T: (01609) 761586 E: gordonbates606@btinternet.com

BATES, James. b 46. Linc Th Coll 73. **d** 75 **p** 76. C Ewell *Guildf* 75–77; C Farncombe 77–80; V Pet St Mary Boongate 80–92; V Kingston All SS w St Jo *S'wark* 92–05; P-in-c Win St Cross w St Faith and Master St Cross Hosp 05–07; V Offerton *Ches* 07–12; rtd 12. *166 Donaghadee Road, Bangor BT20 4PB* T: (028) 9147 3068 E: bates289@btinternet.com

BATES, James Paul. b 64. QUB BSc PGCE Cranfield Univ MSc MPhil. **d** 06. NSM Bangor Abbey *D & D* 06–07. *16 Craigowen Road, Holywood BT18 0DL* T: (028) 9042 2077 E: paul_tssf@hotmail.com *or* paul-bates@live.co.uk

BATES, Mrs Nichola Jane. b 63. Trin Coll Bris 09. **d** 11 **p** 12. C Freiston, Butterwick w Bennington, and Leverton *Linc* 11–14; C Old Leake w Wrangle 11–14; C Friskney 11–14; C Stamford Ch Ch 14–15; C Stamford St Geo w St Paul 14–15; V Stamford Ch Ch 15–18; V Bestwood Em and St Mark w Rise Park *S'well* from 18. *10 Church View Close, Arnold, Nottingham NG5 9QP* M: 07760-484793

BATES, Robert John. b 50. FRICS 81. EAMTC 99. **d** 02 **p** 03. NSM Pet St Mary Boongate 02–05; C Ketton, Collyweston, Easton-on-the-Hill etc 05–09; Chapl Algarve *Eur* 09–14; Chapl Oporto 14–15; rtd 15; PtO *Eur* from 15; *Heref* from 16. *24 Woodfield Gardens, Belmont, Hereford HR2 9RN* T: (01432) 487485 M: 07751-015391 E: frbobbates@gmail.com

BATES, Stuart Geoffrey. b 61. Univ of Wales (Lamp) BA 82 City Univ MSc 11. St Steph Ho Ox 83. **d** 85 **p** 86. C Bromley St Mark *Roch* 85–88; C Westmr St Matt *Lon* 88–89; C Gt Ilford St Mary *Chelmsf* 89–95; V Crofton Park St Hilda w St Cypr *S'wark* from 95. *St Hilda's Vicarage, 35 Buckthorne Road, London SE4 2DG* T: (020) 8699 1277 E: father.bates@sainthildas.org

BATES, Mrs Susan Rita. b 65. City Univ BSc 89. ERMC 12. **d** 15 **p** 16. C Yoxmere *St E* 15–17; R Debenham and Helmingham from 17. *The Rectory, 6 Raedwald Way, Debenham, Stowmarket IP14 6SN* T: (01728) 860222 M: 07944-159606 E: revsusanbates@icloud.com

BATES, Thomas Henry Robert St John. b 83. Univ of Wales BMus 07 Cardiff Univ BTh 15. St Mich Coll Llan 11. **d** 14 **p** 15. C Merthyr Tydfil St Dav and Abercanaid *Llan* 14–16; C Eglwysilan and Caerphilly 16–17; C Abergavenny H Trin *Mon* from 17; C Abergavenny St Mary w Llanwenarth Citra from 17. *Holy Trinity Vicarage, Baker Street, Abergavenny NP7 5BH* T: (01873) 855889 M: 07540-250720 E: frtombates@gmail.com *or* subprior@stmarys-priory.org

BATES, Trini Mari Carolina (Carol). b 68. Liv Poly BSc 92 Liv Univ PGCE 93. St Aug Coll of Th 17. **d** 19. C E Wickham *S'wark* from 19. *44 Northdown Road, Welling DA16 1NA* M: 07772-394855 E: trinibates@icloud.com

BATES, William Frederic. b 49. St Jo Coll Dur BSc 72 BA 74 MA 97. Cranmer Hall Dur. **d** 75 **p** 76. C Knutsford St Jo and Toft *Ches* 75–78; C Ripley *Derby* 78–80; R Nether and Over Seale 81–93; V Lullington 81–93; V Allestree St Nic 93–16; Bp's Adv on New Relig Movements 99–16; P-in-c Quarndon 00–16; RD Duffield 09–10; rtd 16. *20 Main Avenue, Allestree, Derby DE22 2EG* T: (01332) 603605 E: williamfbates@gmail.com

BATESON, Jack William. b 75. Kent Univ BA 97. St Aug Coll of Th BA 17. **d** 17 **p** 18. C G7 Benefice *Cant* from 17. *8 Glebeland, Egerton, Ashford TN27 9DH* T: (01233) 756731 M: 07523-819190 E: revjackbateson@gmail.com

BATESON, Keith Nigel. b 43. **d** 00 **p** 01. OLM Wonersh w Blackheath *Guildf* 00–13; PtO from 13. *Advent Cottage, Blackheath Lane, Wonersh, Guildford GU5 0PN* T: (01483) 892753 E: keith@batesonfamily.net

BATEY, Caroline Elizabeth. b 52. **d** 08 **p** 09. OLM Warrington H Trin *Liv* 08–14; OLM Warrington H Trin and St Ann from 14. *22 Fairclough Avenue, Warrington WA1 2JS* E: cabethbatey@hotmail.com *or* bstewart1662@gmail.com

BATH, David James William. b 43. Oak Hill NSM Course 87. **d** 89 **p** 90. NSM Henley *Ox* 89–90; Gen Manager Humberside Gd News Trust 90–96; NSM Anlaby St Pet *York* 96–04; P-in-c Anlaby Common St Mark 04–10; rtd 10; PtO *York* from 11. *24 Lawnswood, Hessle HU13 0PT* E: davidjwbath@hotmail.com

BATH AND WELLS, Bishop of. *See* HANCOCK, The Rt Revd Peter

BATH, Archdeacon of. *See* YOUINGS, The Ven Adrian

BATLEY-GLADDEN, Dane Christopher. b 68. St Steph Ho Ox 96. **d** 99 **p** 00. C Hendon St Alphage *Lon* 99–01; C-in-c Grahame Park St Aug CD 01–14; V Swanley St Mary *Roch* from 14. *St Mary's Vicarage, London Road, Swanley BR8 7AQ* T: (01322) 662201 E: vicar@swanleyparish.org.uk

BATSON, Canon Lee Paul. b 77. R Holloway Coll Lon BA 99 MA 00 Selw Coll Cam BA 03 MA 06. Westcott Ho Cam 01. **d** 04 **p** 05. C Saffron Walden w Wendens Ambo, Littlebury etc *Chelmsf* 04–08; P-in-c Boreham 08–17; Co Ecum Officer 08–14; C N Springfield 14–17; P-in-c E Hanningfield 15–17; TR Epping Distr from 17; RD Epping Forest and Ongar from 18; Hon Can Chelmsf Cathl from 19. *The Vicarage, Hartland Road, Epping CM16 4PD* T: (01992) 561517 M: 07526-915645 E: lbatson@chelmsford.anglican.org

BATSON, Paul Leonard. b 47. Southn Univ BTh 79. Sarum & Wells Th Coll 73. **d** 75 **p** 76. C Chesham St Mary *Ox* 75–79; Dioc Youth Adv *Newc* 79–85; V Earley St Pet *Ox* 85–93; PtO *Sarum* 01–08; Hon C N Bradford on Avon and Villages 10–15; PtO from 15. *Maple Cottage, 78 Murhill, Limpley Stoke, Bath BA2 7FB* T: (01225) 722721 E: plbatson@gmail.com

BATSON, William Francis Robert. b 43. St Jo Coll Dur BA 72. Cranmer Hall Dur. **d** 73 **p** 74. C Eastwood *S'well* 73–77; R Long Marton w Dufton and w Milburn *Carl* 77–79; V Flimby 79–85; TR Raveningham *Nor* 85–91; R Kinver and Enville *Lich* 91–00; V Ledsham w Fairburn *York* 00–08; rtd 08; PtO *Carl* 09–19. *8 Langdale Avenue, Carlisle CA2 5QG* T: (01228) 537798 E: wfrbatson@gmail.com

BATSTONE, Bruce. b 70. Bris Univ BA 92. St Steph Ho Ox 98. **d** 00 **p** 01. C Leigh-on-Sea St Marg *Chelmsf* 00–03; C Old St Pancras *Lon* 03–07; TV 07–11; Chapl Camden and Islington NHS Foundn Trust 03–11; R Hornsey St Mary w St Geo *Lon* from 11. *Hornsey Rectory, 140 Cranley Gardens, London N10 3AH* T: (020) 8883 6486 E: fr.bruce@hornseyparishchurch.org

BATT, Canon Joseph William. b 39. Keele Univ BA 62. Ripon Hall Ox 63. **d** 64 **p** 65. C Bushbury *Lich* 64–68; C Walsall 68–71; Tr Officer and Youth Chapl Dio Ibadan Nigeria 71–75; Hon Can Oke-Osun from 94; Area Sec CMS Guildf and Chich 75–84; V Ottershaw *Guildf* 84–04; rtd 04; PtO *Bradf* 07–14; *Leeds* from 14. *8 Parkwood Road, Shipley BD18 4SS* T: (01274) 589775 E: joe@jbatt.force9.co.uk

BATT, Mrs Linda. **d** 14 **p** 15. NSM Magor *Mon* 14–17; NSM Newport Maindee and Lliswerry from 17. *44 Goossens Close, Newport NP19 9JN* T: (01633) 783344

BATTE, Mrs Kathleen. b 47. Homerton Coll Cam TCert 68. NEOC 91. **d** 94 **p** 95. NSM Newc St Gabr 94–96; NSM Wilford Hill *S'well* 96–99; P-in-c Cinderhill 99–05; Bp's Adv for Self-Supporting Min 05–07; Chapl Crowhurst Chr Healing Cen 07–10; Sen Chapl 10–12; rtd 12; PtO *S'well* from 17. *10 Bracey Rise, West Bridgford, Nottingham NG2 7AX* T: 0115-923 4503 E: kath.batte@talk21.com *or* kath.batte@outlook.com

BATTEN, Ms Sibylle. b 62. Sheff Univ BA 88 MA 90 CQSW 90. St Hild Coll 17. **d** 19. NSM Sheff Manor from 19. *Apartment 38, 2 The Dale, Sheffield S8 0PW* T: 0114-258 7150 M: 07966-293303 E: sibylle.batten@manorparish.co.uk

BATTEN, Stuart William. b 73. Univ of Wales (Abth) BD 94 MTh 96. Trin Coll Bris 96. **d** 98 **p** 99. C Northolt St Jos *Lon* 98–01; TV Hucknall Torkard *S'well* 01–06; P-in-c Wickham Bishops w Lt Braxted *Chelmsf* 06–14; P-in-c Barkingside H Trin from 14; P-in-c Barkingside St Fran from 15; Asst Dir of Ords from 06. *Holy Trinity Vicarage, 36 Mossford Green, Ilford IG6 2BJ* T: (020) 8550 2669 E: stuart.batten@btinternet.com

BATTERSBY, David George Sellers. b 32. AKC 57. St Boniface Warminster 57 Lambeth STh 80. **d** 58 **p** 59. C Glas St Marg 58–60; C Burnley St Pet *Blackb* 60–62; V Warton St Paul 62–71; Chapl K Wm's Coll Is of Man 71–91; C Ashchurch *Glouc* 91–97; rtd 97; PtO *Newc* 97–02; *Ox* 03–18; *St E* from 19. *Denehouse, Whatfield Road, Elmsett, Ipswich IP7 6LT* T: (01473) 657467

BATTERSBY, Richard David. b 69. Sheff Univ BA 13 FCCA. Yorks Min Course 10. **d** 13 **p** 14. NSM Brayton *York* 13–16; C Rural Ainsty from 16. *The Old Vicarage, Main Street, Healaugh, Tadcaster LS24 8DB* T: (01937) 918259 M: 07795-302119 E: revdrichardb@gmail.com

BATTERSBY, Simon Charles. *See* CROMPTON-BATTERSBY, Simon Jackson

BATTERSHELL, Mrs Anne Marie. b 33. Ox Poly BEd 83. SAOMC 95. **d** 98 **p** 99. NSM Goring w S Stoke *Ox* 98–01; NSM Brafferton w Pilmoor, Myton-on-Swale etc *York* 01–03; rtd 03; PtO *Wakef* 04–14; *Leeds* from 14; *Man* 07–18. *26 Winterbutlee Grove, Todmorden OL14 7QU* T: (01706) 839848 E: rev.anne@hotmail.co.uk

BATTERSHELL, Rachel Damaris. b 65. RN 88. SNWTP 08. **d** 11 **p** 12. C Coldhurst and Oldham St Steph *Man* 11–14; TV Ashton from 14. *2A Hutton Avenue, Ashton-under-Lyne OL6 6QY* M: 07563-630594 E: rev.rachel@hotmail.co.uk

BATTISON, David John. b 62. ACIB 93. St Jo Coll Nottm 07. **d** 09 **p** 10. C Matlock Bath and Cromford *Derby* 09–11; C Matlock Bank and Tansley from 11. *Blossom House, 4 Ashtree Close, Matlock DE4 3SJ* T: (01629) 581940 M: 07971-506088 E: davidbattison@btinternet.com

BATTLE, Dean of. Qu Coll Cam BA 54 MA 58. Ridley Hall Cam 54. C Bath Abbey w St Jas *B & W* 56–60; V Bermondsey St Anne *S'wark* 60–64; Ind Chapl 60–64; V Heslington *York* 64–69; Chapl York Univ 64–69; V Lawrence Weston *Bris* 69–73; PtO 74–80; P-in-c Wraxall *B & W* 80–82; R 82–84; V Battle *Chich* 84–90; Dean Battle 84–90; RD Battle and Bexhill 86–90; R St Marylebone w H Trin *Lon* 90–96; rtd 96; PtO *Chich* 96–11. *Oak Lodge, 2 Saxonwood Road, Battle TN33 0EY* T: (01424) 772743 E: jlchater@icloud.com

BATTS, Sara Louise. b 72. Nottm Univ BSc 95 City Univ MSc 06 Loughb Univ PhD 13. Westcott Ho Cam 14. d 16 p 17. C Chingford St Edm *Chelmsf* 16–18; C Coggeshall w Markshall from 18; C Cressing w Stisted and Bradwell etc from 18. *5 Shut Lane, Earls Colne, Colchester CO6 2RE* E: rev.dr.batts@gmail.com

BATTY, John Ivan. b 35. Clifton Th Coll 59. d 62 p 63. C Clayton *Bradf* 62–67; V Toxteth Park St Clem *Liv* 67–73; R Darfield *Sheff* 73–90; Chapl Düsseldorf *Eur* 90–95; V The Marshland *Sheff* 95–00; rtd 00; PtO *Sheff* 00–15; *Linc* from 00; *Eur* from 00. *4 St Lawrence Way, Tallington, Stamford PE9 4RH* T/F: (01780) 740151

BATTY, Leslie. b 48. Univ of Wales (Ban) BSc 70 Hull Univ PGCE 71 MSc 93 Univ of Wales MPhil 92. Linc Sch of Th and Min 10. d 14 p 15. OLM Ringstone in Aveland Gp *Linc* 14–16; OLM Grantham, Harrowby w Londonthorpe from 16. *12 Scotney Drive, Grantham NG31 9UA* T: (01476) 578829 M: 07890-010735 E: batty527@btinternet.com

BATTY, Mark Alan. b 56. BSc. Ripon Coll Cuddesdon. d 82 p 83. C Bottesford w Ashby *Linc* 82–86; V Scunthorpe All SS 86–95; P-in-c N Wolds Gp 95–97; V 97–12; rtd 12. *43 Grantham Road, Bracebridge Heath, Lincoln LN4 2LE*

BATTYE, Mrs Alison Jill. b 65. Rob Coll Cam BA 86 Sheff Univ BA 16 PGCE 87. Yorks Min Course 13. d 16 p 17. C Whitkirk *Leeds* 16–19; R Adel from 19. *Adel Rectory, 25 Church Lane, Adel, Leeds LS16 8DQ* M: 07717-564542 E: alison.battye65@btinternet.com *or* alison.battye@leeds.anglican.org

BATTYE, John Noel. b 42. TCD BA 64 MA 73. CITC 66. d 66 p 67. C Drumglass *Arm* 66–69; C Ballynafeigh St Jude *D & D* 70–73; Chapl Pemb Coll Cam 73–78; Bp's C Knocknagoney *D & D* 78–80; I Cregagh 80–08; Preb Castleknock St Patr Cathl Dublin 94–08; rtd 08. *18 Enniscrone Park, Portadown, Craigavon BT63 5DQ* T: (028) 3833 1161 M: 07707-540052 *or* (00353) 86-232 3990 E: noelbattye@outlook.com

BATTYE, Canon Lisa Katherine. b 55. Man Univ BN 78 MA(Theol) 96 Liv Univ MTh 00 Ches Univ MProf 14 RM 79. NOC 96. d 99 p 00. C Clifton *Man* 99–02; R Kersal Moor 02–17; AD Salford 13–17; TV Didsbury St Jas and Em from 17; Hon Can Man Cathl from 16. *453 Parrs Wood Road, Didsbury, Manchester M20 5NE* T: 0161-434 9886 M: 07539-775483 E: lisabattye@stjamesandemmanuel.org

BAUDON, Raymond Jean Grigor. b 78. Glas Univ LLB 03. Ripon Coll Cuddesdon 16. d 18 p 19. C E Dulwich St Jo *S'wark* from 18; Dioc Voc Adv from 19. *St John's Parish Office, Goose Green Community Centre, 62A East Dulwich Road, London SE22 9AT* T: (020) 8693 3897 E: curate@stjohnseastdulwich.org

BAUGHEN, Andrew Jonathan. b 64. Lon Guildhall Univ BA 87. Wycliffe Hall Ox BTh 94. d 94 p 95. C Battersea Rise St Mark *S'wark* 94–97; P-in-c Clerkenwell St Jas and St Jo w St Pet *Lon* 97–00; V 00–18; C from 18. *St James's Church, Clerkenwell Close, London EC1R 0EA* T: (020) 7251 1190 E: andrew@jc-church.org

BAUGHEN, Elizabeth Jane. b 62. Lon Sch of Th BA 08. St Mellitus Coll. d 16 p 17. C Enfield St Andr *Lon* 16–18; C Whetstone St Jo 18–19; PtO from 19. *21 Hyde Close, Barnet EN5 5TJ* T: (020) 8449 6134 M: 07803-008090 E: lizziebaughen@btinternet.com

✠**BAUGHEN, The Rt Revd Michael Alfred.** b 30. Lon Univ BD 55. Oak Hill Th Coll 51. d 56 p 57 c 82. C Hyson Green *S'well* 56–59; C Reigate St Mary *S'wark* 59–61; Org Cand Sec CPAS 61–64; R Rusholme H Trin *Man* 64–70; TV St Marylebone All So w SS Pet and Jo *Lon* 70–75; R 75–82; AD Westmr St Marylebone 78–82; Preb St Paul's Cathl 79–82; Bp Ches 82–96; rtd 96; Hon Asst Bp *Lon* 96–06; Hon Asst Bp Guildf from 06; Hon Asst Bp *Guildf* from 06. *23 The Atrium, Woolsack Way, Godalming GU7 1EN* T: (01483) 808151 M: 07990-275563 E: michaelbaughen23@gmail.com

BAULCOMB, Canon Geoffrey Gordon. b 46. K Coll Lon BD 86. AKC 68. d 69 p 70. C Crofton Park St Hilda w St Cypr *S'wark* 69–74; TV Padgate *Liv* 74–79; R Whitton and Thurleston w Akenham *St E* 79–03; Hon Can St E Cathl 03; rtd 03; PtO *St E* 03–08; *Chich* from 04. *Greenlands, 39 Filching Road, Eastbourne BN20 8SE* T: (01323) 641746 M: 07880-731232 E: geoffreybaulcomb@hotmail.com

BAUN, Jane Ralls. b 60. Yale Univ BA 83 Catholic Univ of America MA 89 Princeton Univ PhD 97. Ripon Coll Cuddesdon 08. d 10 p 11. NSM Abingdon *Ox* 10–18; PtO 18; Lect Ripon Coll Cuddesdon 13–18; Chapl Wadh Coll Ox from 18. *Wadham College, Parks Road, Oxford OX1 3PN* T: (01865) 244559 E: jane.baun@theology.ox.ac.uk

✠**BAVIN, The Rt Revd Timothy John.** b 35. Worc Coll Ox BA 59 MA 61 FRSCM 91. Cuddesdon Coll 59. d 61 p 62 c 74. C Pretoria Cathl S Africa 61–64; Chapl 65–69; C Uckfield *Chich* 69–71; V Brighton Gd Shep Preston 71–73; Dean and Adn Johannesburg 73–74; Bp Johannesburg 74–85; Bp Portsm 85–95; OGS 87–97; OSB from 96; PtO *Win* 96–14; Hon Asst Bp Portsm from 12; Hon Asst Bp Win from 13; Hon Asst Bp Portsm from 16. *Abbey of Our Lady and St John, Abbey Road, Beech, Alton GU34 4AP* T: (01420) 562145 *or* 563575 F: 561691 E: tjbarvin@gmail.com

BAVINGTON, Canon John Eduard. b 68. Loughb Univ BEng 91. Trin Coll Bris BA 99. d 99 p 00. C W Ealing St Jo w St Jas *Lon* 99–02; V Bradf St Clem 02–06; Chapl Giggleswick Sch 06–13; V Gt Horton *Bradf* 13–14; *Leeds* from 14; C Bradf St Wilfrid w St Columba from 17; AD Inner Bradford from 19; Hon Can Bradf Cathl from 17. *St Wilfrid's Vicarage, St Wilfrid's Road, Bradford BD7 2LU* M: 07704-854978 E: john.bavington@leeds.anglican.org *or* revjohnbav@stjohnsgreathorton.org.uk

BAWDEN, Sheila Irene. b 55. d 11 p 12. NSM Bodmin w Lanhydrock and Lanivet *Truro* 11–16; Public Preacher 16–17; NSM Lostwithiel Parishes from 17. *Chimes, 8 Church Lane, Lostwithiel PL22 0EQ* M: 07879-551046 E: sheila.stevens55@btinternet.com

BAWTREE, Andrew James. b 66. Univ of Wales BD 91 Ch Ch Coll Cant PGCE 92. St Jo Coll Nottm MA 95. d 96 p 97. C Hoddesdon *St Alb* 96–99; R S Boston Trin Ch USA 00–07; P-in-c River *Cant* from 07; AD Dover from 17. *The Vicarage, 23 Lewisham Road, Dover CT17 0QG* T: (01304) 822037 E: rockabillyrev@hotmail.com

BAXANDALL, Canon Peter. b 45. Tyndale Hall Bris 67. d 70 p 72. C Kidsgrove *Lich* 70–71; C St Helens St Mark *Liv* 71–75; C Ardsley *Sheff* 75–77; Rep Leprosy Miss E Anglia 77–86; P-in-c March St Wendreda *Ely* 86–87; R 87–11; P-in-c March St Jo 09–11; RD March 93–09; Hon Can Ely Cathl 07–11; rtd 12; PtO *Nor* from 11. *22 Westland Road, Lowestoft NR33 9AB* T: (01502) 583228 E: peterbaxandall@sky.com

BAXENDALE, John Richard. b 48. Cranmer Hall Dur 89. d 91 p 92. C Carl St Jo 91–94; C Dalston 94–95; P-in-c Monton *Man* 95–96; TV Eccles 96–04; V Clifton 04–13; rtd 13; PtO *Carl* from 14. *6 Paddock Way, Storth, Milnthorpe LA7 7JJ* M: 07966-472865 E: baxendale901@btinternet.com

BAXENDALE, Rodney Douglas. b 45. Ex Univ BA 66 Cardiff Univ MTh 10 Leeds Univ PGCE 68. Linc Th Coll 78. d 80 p 81. C Maidstone All SS and St Phil w Tovil *Cant* 80–83; Chapl RN 83–03; Chapl Plymouth Hosps NHS Trust 06–08; Sen Chapl 08–13; rtd 13; Chapl St Luke's Hospice Plymouth 14–15; PtO *Ex* from 13. *17 Valletort Road, Plymouth PL1 5PH* T: (01752) 500573 E: thebaxendales@blueyonder.co.uk

BAXTER, Alexander. b 74. Westcott Ho Cam 10. d 13 p 14. C Eastbourne St Andr *Chich* 13–17; R Clayton w Keymer from 17. *1 The Crescent, Hassocks BN6 8RB* M: 07957-848378 E: alexbaxter66@yahoo.co.uk

BAXTER, Mrs Alison Gilmour. b 70. Nene Coll Northn BSc 93 Cov Univ MSc 02. Ox Min Course 16. d 19. C Kenilworth St Nic *Cov* from 19. *14 The Countess Croft, Coventry CV3 5ET* M: 07910-404475 E: baxter.alison@gmail.com

BAXTER, Anthony. b 54. SEITE 99. d 02 p 08. NSM Romford Ascension Collier Row *Chelmsf* 02–07; NSM Hutton from 07. *44 Prower Close, Billericay CM11 2BU* T: (01277) 655514 M: 07909-984675 E: tony@tonybaxter.co.uk

BAXTER, David. *See* BAXTER, Richard David

BAXTER (*née* AVIS), **Elizabeth Mary.** b 49. Leeds Metrop Univ BA 93 Win Univ MPhil 13 CYCW 77. NOC 81. dss 84 d 87 p 94. Leeds St Marg and All Hallows *Ripon* 84–93; Par Dn 87–93; Chapl Abbey Grange High Sch 85–93; Par Dn Topcliffe *York* 93–94; C 94–96; C Thirsk 96–07; Jt Dir H Rood Ho Cen for Health and Past Care 93–07; Exec Dir from 07; PtO *Ripon* 93–14; *Leeds* 14–16; *Dur* 94–15; *Newc* from 94; *Sheff* 95–12; *Bradf* 95–14; *Wakef* 97–14; *York* 08–17. *5 Glendale Road, Wooler NE71 6DN* T: (01668) 283125 *or* (01845) 522580 E: elizabethbaxter@gmx.co.uk *or* elizabethbaxter@gmail.co.uk

BAXTER, Canon Jane Elizabeth. b 51. EAMTC 98. d 01 p 02. C Clare w Poslingford, Cavendish etc *St E* 01–04; P-in-c Lyddington w Stoke Dry and Seaton etc *Pet* 04–10; C Bulwick, Blatherwycke w Harringworth and Laxton 04–10; V Lyddington, Bisbrooke, Caldecott, Glaston etc from 10; RD Rutland from 18; Can Pet Cathl from 18. *The Rectory,*

4 Windmill Way, Lyddington, Oakham LE15 9LY T: (01572) 822717 E: revjanebaxter@gmail.com

BAXTER, John Richard. b 44. ACII 66. STETS 96. **d** 99 **p** 00. NSM Banstead *Guildf* 99–03; TV Surrey Weald 03–11; rtd 11; PtO *Guildf* from 12. *11 Arundel Avenue, Epsom KT17 2RF* T: (020) 8393 6767 M: 07974-692334 E: revdjohn@virginmedia.com

BAXTER, Canon Richard <u>David</u>. b 33. Kelham Th Coll 53. **d** 57 **p** 58. C Carl St Barn 57–59; C Barrow St Matt 59–64; V Drighlington *Wakef* 64–73; V Penistone 73–80; V Carl St Aid and Ch Ch 80–86; Can Res Wakef Cathl 86–97; Prec from 86; Vice-Provost 92–97; rtd 97; PtO *Carl* from 97; Hon V Choral Carl Cathl 04–14; PtO *York* from 14. *4 Dulverton Hall, Esplanade, Scarborough YO11 2AR* T: (01723) 374106 E: canondavidbaxter@btinternet.com

BAXTER, Stephen Richard. b 63. **d** 14 **p** 15. NSM St Olave Hart Street w All Hallows Staining etc *Lon* 14–18; P-in-c St Steph Walbrook and St Swithun etc from 18; PtO *Chelmsf* from 18. *5 Elm Court, Elmdon, Saffron Walden CB11 4NP* E: priest@ststephenwalbrook.net

BAXTER, Stuart. b 43. Liv Univ BA 65 Nottm Univ PGCE 66. Cuddesdon Coll 66. **d** 70 **p** 71. C Kirkby *Liv* 70–73; C Ainsdale 73–76; CMS 76–77 and 83–84; Sierra Leone 77–83; V Nelson in Lt Marsden *Blackb* 84–92; V Lostock Hall 92–99; P-in-c Hatton *Derby* 99–04; Asst Chapl HM Pris Sudbury 99–03; Asst Chapl HM Pris Foston Hall 03–06; rtd 06; PtO *Derby* from 06. *11 Pingle Crescent, Belper DE56 1DY* T: (01773) 827309

BAXTER, Terence Hugh. b 48. Leeds Poly BSc 74. NOC 89. **d** 92 **p** 93. NSM Guiseley w Esholt *Bradf* 92–04; NSM Weston w Denton 04–08; NSM Leathley w Farnley, Fewston and Blubberhouses 04–08; NSM Washburn and Mid-Wharfe 08–09; PtO *Eur* from 11. *Address temp unknown* M: (0034) 634 300 679

BAYCOCK, Philip <u>Louis</u>. b 33. Wells Th Coll 64. **d** 66 **p** 67. C Kettering SS Pet and Paul 66–68; C St Peter-in-Thanet *Cant* 68–72; V Bobbing w Iwade 72–73; PtO 73–76; V Thanington w Milton 77–84; R Chagford w Gidleigh and Throwleigh *Ex* 84–01; rtd 01; PtO *Ex* from 01. *7 Grove Meadow, Sticklepath, Okehampton EX20 2NE* T: (01837) 840617

BAYES, Frederick <u>Alan</u>. b 60. Imp Coll Lon BSc 81 St Jo Coll Dur BA 92. Cranmer Hall Dur 92. **d** 93 **p** 94. C Talbot Village *Sarum* 93–97; Chapl St Hild and St Bede Coll *Dur* 97–03; Bp's Adv in Interfaith Matters 02–03; V Penllergaer *S & B* 03–16; Chapl Whitgift Sch and Ho Croydon from 16; C Croydon St Jo *S'wark* from 16. *Whitgift School, Haling Park, South Croydon CR2 6YT* T: (020) 8688 9222

✠**BAYES, The Rt Revd Paul.** b 53. Birm Univ BA 75. Qu Coll Birm 76. **d** 79 **p** 80 **c** 10. C Tynemouth Cullercoats St Paul *Newc* 79–82; Chapl Qu Eliz Coll *Lon* 82–87; Chapl Chelsea Coll 85–87; TV High Wycombe *Ox* 87–90; TR 90–94; TR Totton *Win* 95–04; AD Lyndhurst 00–04; Nat Miss and Evang Adv Abps' Coun 04–10; Hon Can Worc Cathl 07–10; Suff Bp Hertford *St Alb* 10–14; Bp Liv from 14. *Bishop's Lodge, Woolton Park, Liverpool L25 6DT* T: 0151-421 0831 F: 428 3055 E: bishopslodge@liverpool.anglican.org

BAYLEY, Anne Christine. b 34. Girton Coll Cam BA 55 MB, ChB 58 FRCS 66 FRCSEd 86. St Steph Ho Ox 90. **d** 91 **p** 94. NSM Wembley Park St Aug *Lon* 91–97; PtO *York* 97–05; *Heref* 05–19. *Address temp unknown*

BAYLEY, Michael John. b 36. CCC Cam BA 60 MA 64 Sheff Univ PhD 73. Linc Th Coll 60. **d** 62 **p** 63. C Leeds Gipton Epiphany *Ripon* 62–66; NSM Sheff St Mark Broomhill 67–93; C Sheff St Mary w Highfield Trin 93–95; C Sheff St Mary Bramall Lane 95–00; rtd 00; PtO *Sheff* from 03. *27 Meadowbank Avenue, Sheffield S7 1PB* T: 0114-258 5248 E: mjbayley@btinternet.com

BAYLEY, Oliver James Drummond. b 49. Mansf Coll Ox MA PGCE. St Jo Coll Nottm 81. **d** 83 **p** 84. C Bath Weston St Jo w Kelston *B & W* 83–88; P-in-c Bathampton 88–93; P-in-c Claverton 92–93; R Bathampton w Claverton 93–96; Chapl Dauntsey's Sch Devizes 96–02; rtd 02; PtO *Win* from 01. *19 Treeside Road, Southampton SO15 5FY* T: (023) 8078 6498 E: ojdb80@hotmail.com

BAYLEY, Canon Raymond. b 46. Keble Coll Ox BA 68 MA 72 Ex Univ PhD 86. St Chad's Coll Dur 68. **d** 69 **p** 70. C Mold *St As* 69–74; Lay Tr Officer 71–74; C Llandaff w Capel Llanilltern *Llan* 74; PV Llan Cathl and Lay Tr Officer 74–77; V Cwmbach 77–80; Dir Past Studies St Mich Coll Llan 80–84; Lect Univ of Wales (Cardiff) *Llan* 80–84; V Ynysddu *Mon* 84–86; V Griffithstown 86–92; Tutor Dioc Minl Tr Course 84–92; V Rhosymedre *St As* 92–96; Warden and R Ruthin w Llanrhydd 96–09; Tutor Dioc Minl Tr Course 92–06; Dir CME 94–01; Warden of Readers 09; Hon Can St As Cathl 04–09; rtd 09; PtO *St As* from 09; *S'wark* from 15. *11 Maes Glanrafon,*

Brook Street, Mold CH7 1RJ T: (01352) 752345 M: 07944-274154 E: raymond.bayley537@btinternet.com

BAYLIS (*née* LOFTS), Mrs Sally Anne. b 55. Kent Univ BA 78 K Coll Lon MA 80 Nottm Univ PGCE 93. St Jo Coll Nottm 01. **d** 03 **p** 04. C Gedling *S'well* 03–07; P-in-c Daybrook 07–11; V from 11. *St Paul's Vicarage, 241 Oxclose Lane, Nottingham NG5 6FB* T: 0115-926 2686 E: sally504@btinternet.com

BAYLISS, Geoffrey Brian Tudor. b 60. R Holloway Coll Lon BSc 83 Univ of Wales (Swansea) PGCE 85 Univ of Wales (Ban) MA 11 Glyndŵr Univ DMin 16. EAMTC 96. **d** 99 **p** 00. NSM Panfield and Rayne *Chelmsf* 99–04; TV Halstead Area 04–10; RD Hinckford 08–10; P-in-c Tolleshunt D'Arcy and Tolleshunt Major 10–11; P-in-c Tollesbury w Salcot Virley 10–11; V N Blackwater 11–15; RD Witham 11–15; Hon Can Chelmsf Cathl 15; TR Cowley St Jas *Ox* from 15; AD Cowley from 18. *Cowley Rectory, 11 Beauchamp Lane, Oxford OX4 3LF* M: 07759-393023 E: g.bayliss41@btinternet.com

BAYLISS, Canon Grant David. b 75. Ex Univ BA 96 Wolfs Coll Ox DPhil 05 Ox Univ MA 05. Ripon Coll Cuddesdon BA 99. **d** 03 **p** 04. C Prestbury and All SS *Glouc* 03–07; Chapl St Jo Coll Cam 07–11; Lect Ripon Coll Cuddesdon 11–17; Can Res and Prec Ch Ch *Ox* from 17. *Cloister House, Christ Church, St Aldates, Oxford OX1 1DP* T: (01865) 276214 E: grant.bayliss@chch.ox.ac.uk

BAYLOR, Canon Nigel Peter. b 58. NUI BA 80 TCD MPhil 88. **d** 84 **p** 86. C Carrickfergus *Conn* 84–87; C Dundela St Mark *D & D* 87–89; I Galloon w Drummully *Clogh* 89–94; Adult Educn Adv 91–94; I Carnmoney *Conn* 94–03; I Jordanstown from 03; Can Belf Cathl from 12. *The Rectory, 120A Circular Road, Jordanstown, Newtownabbey BT37 0RH* T: (028) 9086 2119 E: nigel_stpatricks@outlook.com

BAYLY, Mrs Janet. b 43. **d** 08. OLM Schorne *Ox* 08–15; PtO from 15. *2B Granborough Road, North Marston, Buckingham MK18 3PN* T: (01296) 670245 E: janet.bayly@gmail.com

BAYMAN, Brynn Alton. b 66. Witwatersrand Univ BA 87 PGCE 88. Ripon Coll Cuddesdon 09. **d** 11 **p** 12. OLM Finchampstead and California *Ox* 11–15; Chapl Framlingham Coll from 16. *Framlingham College, College Road, Framlingham, Woodbridge IP13 9EY* E: bbayman@framcollege.co.uk

BAYNE, Canon David William. b 52. St Andr Univ MA 75. Edin Th Coll 88. **d** 90 **p** 91. C Dumfries *Glas* 90–92; P-in-c 92–93; R 93–99; Chapl Dumfries and Galloway Primary Care NHS Trust 92–99; Chapl Crichton R Hosp Dumfries 92–99; Chapl HM Pris Dumfries 96–99; R Castle Douglas *Glas* 99–17; P-in-c Dalbeattie 14–17; Can St Mary's Cathl 99–17; Hon Can St Mary's Cathl *Glas* from 17. *Adrigole, 2 Waterside Close, Askamore, Co Wexford, Republic of Ireland* T: (00353) (53) 941 4543 E: dwbayne@aol.com

BAYNE, Mrs Felicity Meriel. b 47. WEMTC 91. **d** 94 **p** 95. NSM Cheltenham Ch Ch *Glouc* 94–98; NSM Leckhampton St Pet 98–09; Chapl Glenfall Ho 09–13; rtd 13; PtO *Glouc* from 16. *Hamfield House, Ham Road, Charlton Kings, Cheltenham GL52 6NG* T: (01242) 237074 E: felicity.bayne@btinternet.com

BAYNE-JARDINE, Anthea Mary. See GRIGGS, Anthea Mary

BAYNES, Mrs Clare. b 57. Reading Univ BA 79. SAOMC 01. **d** 04 **p** 05. NSM Chambersbury *St Alb* 04–08; NSM St Alb St Steph 08–16; PtO from 16; *Leeds* from 17. *4 Pilgrim Close, Park Street, St Albans AL2 2JD* T: (01727) 875524 E: clarebaynes@gmail.com

BAYNES, Simon Hamilton. b 33. New Coll Ox BA 57 MA 62. Wycliffe Hall Ox 57. **d** 59 **p** 60. C Rodbourne Cheney *Bris* 59–62; Japan 63–80; C Keynsham *B & W* 80–84; P-in-c Winkfield *Ox* 84–85; V Winkfield and Cranbourne 85–99; rtd 99; LtO *Ox* 99–02; Hon C Thame from 02. *23 Moorend Lane, Thame OX9 3BQ* T: (01844) 213673 E: baynes@psa-online.com or baynes@clearmail.net

BAYNES, Timothy Francis de Brissac. b 29. Ely Th Coll 59. **d** 61 **p** 62. C Hockerill *St Alb* 61–65; C Mansfield Woodhouse *S'well* 65–67; Ind Chapl *Man* 67–94; P-in-c Miles Platting St Jo 67–72; rtd 94; PtO *Man* 94–97. *46 Kirkbie Green, Kendal LA9 7AJ* T: (01539) 740605

BAYNES, William Hendrie. b 39. Adelaide Univ BA 60. S'wark Ord Course 77. **d** 79 **p** 80. C Notting Hill All SS w St Columb *Lon* 79–85; PtO 86–87 and 09–10; Hon C Paddington St Sav 88–98; Asst Chapl St Mary's NHS Trust Paddington 94–99; Hon C Paddington St Jas *Lon* 00–10; PtO from 10. *39E Westbourne Gardens, London W2 5NR* T: (020) 7727 9530 E: will.baynes@london.anglican.org

BAYNHAM, Matthew Fred. b 57. BNC Ox BA 78 Birm Univ MPhil 00. Wycliffe Hall Ox 80. **d** 83 **p** 84. C Yardley St Edburgha *Birm* 83–87; TV Bath Twerton-on-Avon *B & W* 87–93; V Reddal Hill St Luke *Worc* 93–00; RD Dudley 98–00; Chapl Bp Grosseteste Coll *Linc* 00–05; Assoc Chapl Liv Univ 05–07; Sen Res Tutor from 07; P-in-c Llanllwchaearn and Llanina *St D* from 11. *Y Ficerdy, Penrhiwgaled Lane,*

Cross Inn, Llandysul SA44 6NS T: (01545) 561878 E: mbaynham@cardigan-bay-churches.org

BAYS, Mrs Helen Margaret. b 48. Kent Univ BA 69 RGN 71 RHV 73. STETS 97. **d** 00 **p** 01. NSM Calne and Blackland *Sarum* 00–02; NSM Dawlish *Ex* 02–12; rtd 12; PtO *Ex* from 12. *14 Stockton Hill, Dawlish EX7 9LP* T: (01626) 862860 E: hbays@talktalk.net

BAZELY, Stephen William. b 80. Ox Brookes Univ BSc 05. Oak Hill Th Coll BA 11. **d** 11 **p** 12. C Deane *Man* 11–14; PtO 14–15; P-in-c Willaston *Ches* from 15. *12 Broadlake, Willaston, Neston CH64 2XB* T: 0151-327 3639 E: cc.willaston@gmail.com

BAZELY, William Francis. b 53. Sheff Univ BEng 75. St Jo Coll Nottm 78. **d** 81 **p** 82. C Huyton St Geo *Liv* 81–84; TV Netherthorpe *Sheff* 84–92; Chapl Lambeth Healthcare NHS Trust 92–98; Chapl Guy's and St Thos' Hosps NHS Trust Lon 98–01; C Rotherham *Sheff* 01–03; Chapl Rotherham Gen Hosps NHS Trust 01–03; Chapl Doncaster and S Humber Healthcare NHS Foundn Trust 01–03; Sen Chapl Norfolk & Waveney Mental Health NHS Foundn Trust 03–11; Sen Chapl Norfolk and Suffolk NHS Foundn Trust 12–14; rtd 14; Hon C Brampton St Thos *Derby* 15–19. *8 Pennywell Drive, Holymoorside, Chesterfield S42 7EY* M: 07702-974680 E: wbazely@gmail.com

✠**BAZLEY, The Rt Revd Colin Frederick.** b 35. St Pet Coll Ox BA 57 MA 61. Tyndale Hall Bris 57. **d** 59 **p** 60 **c** 69. C Bootle St Leon *Liv* 59–62; SAMS Miss Chile 62–00; Adn Cautin and Malleco 67–69; Asst Bp Cautin and Malleco 69–75; Asst Bp Santiago 75–77; Bp Chile 77–00; Primate CASA Chile 77–83; Primate Inglesia Anglicana del Cono Sur 89–95; rtd 00; Hon Asst Bp Ches from 00; Warden of Readers 00–05; RD Wallasey 09–11. *121 Brackenwood Road, Higher Bebington, Wirral CH63 2LU* T: 0151-608 1193 M: 07866-391333 E: cfbazley@gmail.com

BAZLINTON, Stephen Cecil. b 46. Lon Univ BDS RCS LDS. Ridley Hall Cam 78. **d** 85 **p** 86. NSM Stebbing w Lindsell *Chelmsf* 85–04; NSM Stebbing and Lindsell w Gt and Lt Saling 04–08; PtO from 08. *St Helens, High Street, Stebbing, Dunmow CM6 3SE* T: (01371) 856495 E: revbaz@phonecoop.coop

BEACH, Jonathan Mark. b 67. Essex Univ BSc 89. Trin Coll Bris BA 94. **d** 94 **p** 95. C Oulton Broad *Nor* 94–97; Chapl RAF 97–13; Chapl St Mary's Sch Calne from 13. *St Mary's School, 63 Curzon Street, Calne SN11 0DF* T: (01249) 857200 E: jbeach@stmaryscalne.org

BEACH, Mark Howard Francis. b 62. Kent Univ BA 83 Nottm Univ MA 95 K Coll Lon DMin 11. St Steph Ho Ox 85. **d** 87 **p** 88. C Beeston *S'well* 87–90; C Hucknall Torkard 90–93; R Gedling 93–01; R Netherfield 96–01; Bp's Chapl *Wakef* 01–03; TR Rugby *Cov* 03–12; Dean Roch 12–15; Dir Blackfriars Settlement 15–17; Dir of Care The Haven + London from 18. *17 Hickmire, Wollaston, Wellingborough NN29 7SL* M: 07957-584856 E: mark.beach62@gmail.com

BEACHAM, Peter Martyn. b 44. Ex Coll Ox BA 65 MA 70 Lon Univ MPhil 67 FSA 92 MRTPI 69. Sarum Th Coll 70. **d** 73 **p** 74. NSM Ex St Martin, St Steph, St Laur etc 73–74; NSM Cen Ex 74–90; PtO from 99. *Bellever, Barrack Road, Exeter EX2 6AB* T: (01392) 435074 E: peter-beacham1@live.co.uk

BEACON, Canon Ralph Anthony. b 44. St Mich Coll Llan 70. **d** 71 **p** 72. C Neath w Llantwit *Llan* 71–74; TV Holyhead w Rhoscolyn w Llanfair-yn-Neubwll *Ban* 74–78; R Llanenddwyn w Llanddwywe, Llanbedr w Llandanwg 78–99; V Harlech and Llanfair-juxta-Harlech etc 99–11; RD Ardudwy 89–02; AD 02–12; Hon Can Ban Cathl 91–97; Can Cursal Ban Cathl 97–11; Can and Preb Ban Cathl 03–11; rtd 11. *Hen Tyrpeg, Harlech, LL46 2UU* T: (01766) 780031 M: 07713-421858 E: sbeacon@hotmail.co.uk

BEACON, Canon Stephanie Kathleen Nora. b 49. Univ of Wales (Ban) BA 70 PGCE 71. NW Ord Course 94. **d** 96 **p** 97. NSM Llanenddwyn w Llanddwywe, Llanbedr w Llandanwg *Ban* 96–98; C Ardudwy 98–99; P-in-c Llanenddwyn w Llanddwywe, Llanbedr w Llandanwg 99–01; R 01–11; R Bro Ardudwy Uchaf 11–13; Can Cursal Ban Cathl 11–13; rtd 13. *Hen Tyrpeg, Harlech LL46 2UU* T: (01766) 780031 M: 07713-421858 E: sbeacon@hotmail.co.uk

BEADLE, Canon Janet Mary. b 52. Philippa Fawcett Coll CertEd 74. EAMTC 91. **d** 94 **p** 95. C Kingston upon Hull H Trin *York* 94–98; V Ness Gp *Linc* 98–16; Bp's Adv in Women's Min 00–08; Can and Preb Linc Cathl from 03; PtO from 17. *28 Manor Park Road, York YO30 5UD* T: (01904) 903126 E: reverendcanonjanetbeadle@gmail.com

BEADLE, Mrs Lorna. b 40. NEOC 92. **d** 95 **p** 96. NSM Ashington *Newc* 95–10; PtO from 10; Chapl MU from 02. *9 Arundel Square, Ashington NE63 8AW* T: (01670) 816467

BEADLE, Capt Richard Alan. b 68. Wilson Carlile Coll 95 St Jo Coll Nottm 15. **d** 16 **p** 17. Kildallon and Swanlinbar *K, E & A* 16–17; C Cloonclare w Killasnett, Lurganboy and Drumlease

from 17. *309 Lattone Road, Lattone, Belcoo, Enniskillen BT93 5ER* T: (028) 6638 1943 M: 07392-844721 *or* (00353) 86-842 1190 E: rbeadleca@gmail.com

BEAHAN, Alan. b 64. Birm Univ BA 87 St Jo Coll Dur BA 07 York Univ PGCE 89. Cranmer Hall Dur 05. **d** 07 **p** 08. C Warrington St Elphin *Liv* 07–10; P-in-c Hindley All SS 10–16; P-in-c Hindley St Pet 13–15; P-in-c Ormskirk 16–17; C Kirkby 17–18; R Calton, Cauldon, Grindon, Waterfall etc *Lich* from 18. *The Vicarage, Waterfall Lane, Waterhouses, Stoke-on-Trent ST10 3HT* T: (01538) 308506 M: 07908-709405 E: alanbeahan@yahoo.co.uk

BEAKE, The Ven Stuart Alexander. b 49. Em Coll Cam BA 72 MA 76. Cuddesdon Coll 72. **d** 74 **p** 75. C Hitchin St Mary *St Alb* 74–76; C Hitchin 77–79; TV Hemel Hempstead 79–85; Bp's Dom Chapl *S'well* 85–87; V Shottery St Andr *Cov* 87–00; RD Fosse 93–99; Dioc Dir of Ords 96–00; Hon Can Cov Cathl 98–00; Can Res and Sub-Dean Cov Cathl 00–05; Adn Surrey *Guildf* 05–17; Hon Can Guildf Cathl 05–10; Can Res Guildf Cathl 10–17; Warden CSP 08–17; rtd 17. *Hollyhocks Barn, Hollyhocks Cottage, High Street, Bramley, Guildford GU5 0HB* E: sabeake@msn.com

BEAKEN, Robert William Frederick. b 62. SS Paul & Mary Coll Cheltenham BA 83 Lambeth STh 90 MA 01 K Coll Lon PhD 09 FSAScot 01 FRHistS 12. Ripon Coll Cuddesdon 85 Ven English Coll & Pontifical Gregorian Univ Rome 87. **d** 88 **p** 89. C Forton *Portsm* 88–92; C Shepshed *Leic* 92–94; V Colchester St Barn *Chelmsf* 94–02; P-in-c Gt and Lt Bardfield from 02. *The Vicarage, Braintree Road, Great Bardfield, Braintree CM7 4RN* T: (01371) 810267 E: robert@webform.co.uk

BEAL, David Michael. b 61. St Jo Coll Nottm BTh 89. **d** 89 **p** 90. C Marton *Blackb* 89–92; C Darwen St Pet w Hoddlesden 92–93; TV 93–97; R Itchingfield w Slinfold *Chich* 97–09; R W Chiltington 09–16; RD Storrington 11–16; V Billingshurst from 16; RD Horsham from 18. *The Vicarage, East Street, Billingshurst RH14 9PY* T: (01403) 785743 E: beals@tesco.net *or* vicar@stmarysbillingshurst.org

BEALE, Miss Fiona Jane. b 71. Moorlands Coll BA 16. Wycliffe Hall Ox 17. **d** 19. C Beaminster Area *Sarum* from 19. *Orchard Cottage, Mosterton, Beaminster DT8 3HH* M: 07581-233772 E: revfionabeale@gmail.com

BEALES, Canon Christopher Leader Day. b 51. St Jo Coll Dur BA 72. Cranmer Hall Dur 72. **d** 76 **p** 77. C Upper Armley and Ind Chapl *Ripon* 76–79; Ind Chapl *Dur* 79–84; Sen Chapl 82–84; Sec Ind Cttee of Gen Syn Bd for Soc Resp 85–91; Sec Inner Cities Relig Coun (DOE) 92–94; Dir Churches' Regional Commn in the NE Newc and Dur 94–98; Consultant Dir 98; Chief Exec Employment Focus 99–07; C Thamesmead *S'wark* 99–01; PtO 01–10; Chief Exec Afghan Action from 05; P-in-c Woburn Sands *St Alb* 08–12; V 12–17; Hon Can St Alb 14–17; rtd 17; PtO *Eur* from 98; *Dur* from 17. *68 Arncliffe Gardens, Hartlepool TS26 9JF* T: (01429) 861518 M: 07597-135593 E: cbeales@outlook.com

BEALES, John David. b 55. SS Hild & Bede Coll Dur BA 77 Univ of W Aus DipEd 79. St Jo Coll Nottm 81. **d** 83 **p** 84. C Scarborough Australia 83–86; Dioc Youth Chapl Perth 86–89; Dir Educn and Tr Philo Trust 89–90; NSM Nottingham St Nic *S'well* 89–95; Dir Creative Communications Trust 90–95; Dir Evang Melbourne Australia 95–00; PtO *Chelmsf* 99–01; Public Preacher 01–14 and from 18; Pioneer Min 14–18. *52 Wellesley Road, Colchester CO3 3HF* T: (01206) 530934 M: 07791-684699 E: davidbeales@icloud.com

BEAMENT, Canon Owen John. b 41. Bps' Coll Cheshunt 61. **d** 64 **p** 65. C Deptford St Paul *S'wark* 64–68; C Peckham St Jo 69–73; C Vauxhall St Pet 73–74; V Hatcham Park All SS 74–18; Hon Can S'wark Cathl 97–18; rtd 19. *85 Kynaston Road, Orpington BR5 4JY* E: owenbeament@aol.com

BEAMER, Neville David. b 40. Univ of Wales (Lamp) BA 62 Jes Coll Ox BA 65 MA 70. Wycliffe Hall Ox 64. **d** 65 **p** 66. C Hornchurch St Andr *Chelmsf* 65–68; C Warwick St Mary *Cov* 68–72; V Holton-le-Clay *Linc* 72–75; P-in-c Stoneleigh w Ashow *Cov* 75–79; P-in-c Baginton 77–79; V Fletchamstead 79–86; Warden Whatcombe Ho Blandford Forum 86–90; R Jersey St Lawr and V Jersey Millbrook St Matt *Win* 90–95; V Yateley 95–03; P-in-c Eversley 98–03; R Yateley and Eversley 03–05; RD Odiham 95–04; rtd 05; PtO *Cov* from 05. *8 Aintree Road, Stratford-upon-Avon CV37 9FL* T: (01789) 263435 E: ndbeamer@hotmail.com

BEAN, Canon John Victor. b 25. Down Coll Cam BA 47 MA 51. Sarum Th Coll 48. **d** 50 **p** 51. C Milton *Portsm* 50–55; C Fareham SS Pet and Paul 55–59; V St Helens 59–66; V Cowes St Mary 66–91; RD W Wight 68–72; Hon Can Portsm Cathl 70–91; P-in-c Cowes St Faith 77–80; C-in-c Gurnard All SS CD 78–91; Chapl to The Queen 80–95; rtd 91; PtO *Portsm* from 91. *23 Queens Road, Ryde PO33 3BG* T: (01983) 562856 E: johnbean@btinternet.com

BEANE, The Ven Andrew Mark. b 72. St Jo Coll Nottm BA 02. d 02 p 03. C Thorpe St Matt *Nor* 02–05; P-in-c Horsham St Faith, Spixworth and Crostwick 05–06; R 06–12; P-in-c Aylsham 12–17; P-in-c Cawston w Booton and Brandiston etc 12–17; C Lt Barningham, Blickling, Edgefield etc 15–17; P-in-c Bure Valley 16–17; TR Aylsham and Distr 17–19; RD Ingworth 13–18; RD Sparham 17–18; RD Ingworth and Sparham 18–19; Hon Can Nor Cathl 15–19; Adn Ex from 19. *Emmanuel House, Station Road, Ide, Exeter EX2 9RS* T: (01392) 425577 M: 07898-932654 E: andrew.beane@btinternet.com *or* archdeacon.of.exeter@exeter.anglican.org

BEANEY, Canon John. b 47. Trin Coll Bris 77. d 79 p 80. C Bromley Ch Ch *Roch* 79–84; V Broadheath *Ches* 84–08; Chapl Altrincham Gen Hosp 91–94; Chapl Trafford Healthcare NHS Trust 94–98; P-in-c Norton *Ches* 08–14; Ecum Officer (Gtr Man) 02–14; Hon Can Ches Cathl 10–14; rtd 14; PtO *Ches* from 14. *5 Wivern Place, Runcorn WA7 1RZ* T: (01928) 411801 E: jjbea68@gmail.com

BEARCROFT, Bramwell Arthur. b 52. Homerton Coll Cam BEd 82. EAMTC 87. d 90 p 91. Chapl and Hd RS Kimbolton Sch Cambs 88–94; NSM Tilbrook *Ely* 90–94; NSM Covington 90–94; NSM Catworth Magna 90–94; NSM Keyston and Bythorn 90–94; NSM Cary Deanery *B & W* 94–02; Hd Master Hazlegrove Sch 94–02; Asst Chapl Aquitaine *Eur* 10–16; PtO from 16. *1 Lotissement de la Caussade, 33270 Floirac, France* T: (0033) 5 56 40 05 12 E: jenniferbearcroft@hotmail.com

BEARD, Christopher Robert. b 47. Chich Th Coll 81. d 83 p 84. C Chich St Paul and St Pet 83–86; V Haywards Heath St Rich 91–99; P-in-c Donnington 99–12; Chapl St Wilfrid's Hospice Eastbourne 99–12; rtd 12; PtO *Chich* 12–17. *70 Victoria Road, Chichester PO19 7JA* T: (01243) 696034 M: 07845-482779

BEARD, Laurence Philip. b 45. Lon Univ BA 68. Trin Coll Bris 88. d 90 p 91. C Trentham *Lich* 90–94; V Wolverhampton St Matt 94–01; P-in-c Hartshill *Cov* 01–08; rtd 08; PtO *St Alb* 09–18. *14 Beechcroft Avenue, Croxley Green, Rickmansworth WD3 3EQ* T: (01923) 222312 E: lpbeard@talk21.com

BEARDSLEY, Christina. b 51. Sussex Univ BA 73 St Jo Coll Cam PhD 99 Leeds Univ MA 07. Westcott Ho Cam 76. d 78 p 79. C Portsea N End St Mark *Portsm* 78–85; V Catherington and Clanfield 85–00; Chapl Worthing and Southlands Hosps NHS Trust 00–01; Asst Chapl Chelsea and Westmr Hosp NHS Foundn Trust 01–04; Chapl 04–08; Hd Multi-Faith Chapl 08–16; rtd 16; Visiting Lect St Mary's Univ Twickenham *Lon* from 10; PtO from 16. *Flat 7, 81 Belgrave Road, London SW1V 2BG* M: 07904-162312 E: belgravetina@gmail.com

BEARPARK, Canon John Michael. b 36. Ex Coll Ox BA 59 MA 63. Linc Th Coll 59. d 61 p 62. C Bingley H Trin *Bradf* 61–64; C Baildon 64–67; V Fairweather Green 67–77; Chapl Airedale NHS Trust 77–94; V Steeton *Bradf* 77–94; Hon Can Bradf Cathl 89–01; V Bentham St Marg 94–01; P-in-c Bentham St Jo 99–01; RD Ewecross 94–00; rtd 01; PtO *Bradf* 01–14; *Leeds* from 14. *31 Northfields Crescent, Settle BD24 9JP* T: (01729) 822712 E: johnbearpark@gmail.com

BEASLEY, Canon Elizabeth Parish. b 58. Wake Forest Univ USA BA 79 Univ of the S STM 04. Harvard Div Sch MDiv 89. d 98 p 99. V Honolulu St Geo USA 98–01; P-in-c Kapaa All SS 02–05; V Kaneohe St Jo 05–07; Can for Min Development Dio Hawaii 07–11; Can to the Ordinary 11–14; I Adare and Kilmallock w Kilpeacon, Croom etc *L & K* from 14; Chan Can Limerick, Killaloe and Clonfert Cathls from 18. *The Rectory, Adare, Co Limerick, Republic of Ireland* T: (00353) (61) 396227 E: revlizadare@gmail.com

⊞**BEASLEY, The Rt Revd Noel Michael Roy.** b 68. Imp Coll Lon BSc 91 Oriel Coll Ox DPhil 95 St Jo Coll Dur BA 98. Cranmer Hall Dur 96. d 99 p 00 c 15. C Newport w Longford, Chetwynd and Forton *Lich* 99–03; Chapl Westcott Ho Cam 03–07; Vice Prin 07–10; Dioc Dir of Miss *Ox* 10–15; Hon Can Ch Ch 14–15; Suff Bp Hertford *St Alb* from 15. *Bishopswood, 3 Stobarts Close, Knebworth SG3 6ND* T: (01438) 817260 E: bishophertford@stalbans.anglican.org

BEATON, Canon Mark Timothy. b 61. Univ of Wales (Ban) BA 83. Trin Coll Bris 03. d 05 p 06. C Swindon St Jo and St Andr *Bris* 05–08; P-in-c New Radnor and Llanfihangel Nantmelan etc *S & B* 08–11; R from 11; AD Maelienydd 14–15; AD Radnor and Builth from 16; Hon Can Brecon Cathl from 16. *The Rectory, School Lane, New Radnor, Presteigne LD8 2SS* T: (01544) 350342 E: revmarkbeaton@gmail.com

BEATTIE, Angus James. b 65. Northumbria Univ BA 92 PGCE 96. St Mellitus Coll 16. d 19. NSM Ruislip St Mary *Lon* from 19. *69 The Fairway, Ruislip HA4 0SP* T: (020) 8422 7126 M: 07508-482909 E: ajbeattie@hotmail.co.uk

BEATTIE, David George. b 42. MIMechE 76. CITC 01. d 04 p 05. NSM Belfast H Trin and St Silas *Conn* 04–09; NSM Whitehouse 09–10; Chapl Belfast Health and Soc Care Trust 10–16; NSM Ematris w Rockcorry, Aghabog and Aughnamullan *Clogh* 11–16; rtd 16; LtO *Conn* from 16. *6 Blackthorn Way, Newtownabbey BT37 0GW* T: (028) 9086 3406 E: beattie5@talktalk.net

BEATTIE, Margaret. See BREWSTER, Margaret

BEATTIE, Canon Noel Christopher. b 41. TCD BTh 65 Cranfield Inst of Tech MSc 86. d 68 p 69. C Belfast H Trin *Conn* 68–70; C Belfast St Bart 70–73; C Doncaster St Mary *Sheff* 73–77; TV Northampton Em *Pet* 77–88; Ind Chapl 85–88; Ind Chapl *Linc* 88–92; Ind Chapl *Roch* 92–04; Hon Can Roch Cathl 00–04; rtd 04; PtO *Heref* from 05. *6 Oaks Road, Church Stretton SY6 7AX* T: (01694) 725530

BEATTY, Jeremy Sean. b 67. Univ of Cen England in Birm BA 95. All SS Cen for Miss & Min 16. d 19. C Marple All SS *Ches* from 19. *42 Edgeley Road, Stockport SK3 9NQ* T: 0161-718 3493 M: 07914-448760 E: jeremyseanbeatty@gmail.com

BEAUCHAMP, Anthony Hazlerigg Proctor. b 40. Trin Coll Cam BA 62 MA 66 MICE 68. St Jo Coll Nottm 73. d 75 p 76. C New Humberstone *Leic* 75–77; C-in-c Polegate *Chich* 77–80; Chapl Bethany Sch Goudhurst 80–86; Chapl Luckley-Oakfield Sch Wokingham 86–88; Chapl Clayesmore Sch Blandford 89–93; R Kirby-le-Soken w Gt Holland *Chelmsf* 93–00; Asst P Wetheral w Warwick *Carl* 00–01; rtd 01; PtO *Carl* 00–01; *Chich* from 01. *2 Stelvio Cottages, 17 Beachy Head Road, Eastbourne BN20 7QP* T: (01323) 732743 E: tony.beauchamp@askomil.com

BEAUCHAMP, Gerald Charles. b 55. Hull Univ BA 78 K Coll Lon MA 96. Coll of Resurr Mirfield 78. d 80 p 81. C Hatcham St Cath *S'wark* 80–83; S Africa 83–86; C Ealing St Steph Castle Hill *Lon* 86–88; P-in-c Brondesbury St Anne w Kilburn H Trin 88–89; V 89–93; Chapl Kilburn Coll 88–93; C Chelsea St Luke and Ch Ch *Lon* 93–96; V W Brompton St Mary w St Pet 96–04; AD Chelsea 02–04; SSJE 04–07; C St Marylebone All SS *Lon* 07–10; P-in-c St Marylebone St Cypr from 10; P-in-c St Marylebone Annunciation Bryanston Street 10–16; V from 16. *4 Wyndham Place, London W1H 2PS* T: (020) 7258 0031 E: gerald.beauch@btconnect.com

BEAUCHAMP, John Nicholas. b 57. Wycliffe Hall Ox 92. d 94 p 95. C Ipswich St Jo *St E* 94–97; TV Beccles St Mich 97–05; P-in-c Beccles St Mich and St Luke 05–08; R 08–15; V Canonbury St Steph *Lon* from 15. *St Stephen's Vicarage, 9 River Place, London N1 2DE* T: (020) 7226 7526 E: reverendjohnbeauchamp@gmail.com

BEAUCHAMP, Julian Thomas Proctor. b 68. Ex Univ BA 91. Oak Hill Th Coll BA 05. d 05 p 06. C Cheadle *Ches* 05–08; R Waverton w Aldford and Bruera from 08. *The Rectory, Village Road, Waverton, Chester CH3 7QN* T: (01244) 336668 M: 07974-397022 E: jules@stpeterswaverton.org.uk

BEAUMONT, Adam John. b 75. Bris Univ BSc 97 PGCE 01. Trin Coll Bris MA 12. d 12 p 13. C Westbury-on-Trym H Trin *Bris* 12–15; TV Gtr Corsham and Lacock from 15. *The Vicarage, Folly Lane, Lacock, Chippenham SN15 2LL* M: 07903-672067 E: adamjbeaumont@gmail.com

BEAUMONT, Canon Brian Maxwell. b 34. Nottm Univ BA 56. Wells Th Coll 58. d 59 p 60. C Clifton *S'well* 59–62; C E Stoke w Syerston 62; C Edgbaston St Geo *Birm* 62–65; V Smethwick St Alb 65–70; V Blackb H Trin 70–77; Asst Dir RE 70–73; Dir RE 73–92; Hon Can Blackb Cathl 73–77 and 92–99; Can Res Blackb Cathl 77–92; V Goosnargh w Whittingham 92–99; Bp's Adv for Rural Areas 92–99; rtd 99; PtO *Blackb* from 99. *14 Green Drive, Barton, Preston PR3 5AT* T: (01772) 861131

BEAUMONT, Catherine Grace La Touche. See BOND, Catherine Grace La Touche

BEAUMONT, Mrs Jane. b 56. Ches Coll of HE BTh. NOC 01. d 04 p 05. NSM Chadkirk *Ches* 04–08; C Ashton-upon-Mersey St Mary Magd from 08. *23 Rydal Avenue, Sale M33 6WN* T: 0161-282 2207

BEAUMONT, Ms Jennifer Mary. b 76. Man Metrop Univ BA 98. All SS Cen for Miss & Min 15. d 18 p 19. C Davyhulme St Mary *Man* from 18. *76 Whitelake Avenue, Urmston, Manchester M41 5QW* M: 07396-376134 E: jennicarrbeau@gmail.com

BEAUMONT, Canon John Philip. b 32. Leeds Univ BA 55. Coll of Resurr Mirfield 55. d 57 p 58. C Leeds St Marg *Ripon* 57–60; C Wellingborough All Hallows *Pet* 60–64; V Wellingborough St Andr 64–70; Chapl HM Borstal Wellingborough 64–70; V Finedon *Pet* 70–96; Can Pet Cathl 80–96; RD Higham 83–87; rtd 96; PtO *Pet* from 96. *9 Warren Bridge, Oundle, Peterborough PE8 4DQ* T: (01832) 273863 E: john@beaumont.plus.com

BEAUMONT, Stephen Martin. b 51. K Coll Lon BD 73 AKC 74. St Aug Coll Cant 73. d 74 p 75. C Benwell St Jas *Newc* 74–77; Asst Chapl Marlborough Coll 77–81; R Ideford, Luton and Ashcombe *Ex* 81–84; Bp's Dom Chapl 81–84; Chapl Taunton Sch 85–91; Chapl Haileybury Coll 92–00; Second Chapl and Hd Div Tonbridge Sch 00–04; Sen Chapl 04–11; P-in-c Chiddingstone w Chiddingstone Causeway

Roch 11–12; R 12–17; rtd 17; PtO *B & W* from 18. *Hilltop, Butts Way, Milverton, Taunton TA4 1JR*

BEAUMONT, Canon Terence Mayes. b 41. Lon Univ BA 63. Linc Th Coll 68. **d** 71 **p** 72. C Hitchin St Mary *St Alb* 71–74; C Harpenden St Nic 75–79; V Stevenage St Pet Broadwater 79–87; V St Alb St Mich 87–06; Hon Can St Alb 05–06; rtd 06; PtO *St Alb* from 16. *65 Weatherby, Dunstable LU6 1TP* T: (01582) 661333 E: y.beaumont123@btinternet.com

BEAUMONT, Mrs Veronica Jean. b 38. Ox Min Course 90. **d** 93 **p** 94. NSM High Wycombe *Ox* 93–03; NSM W Wycombe w Bledlow Ridge, Bradenham and Radnage from 03; Fundraising Manager (Oxon) Children's Soc from 95. *Edgehill, Upper Stanley Road, High Wycombe HP12 4DB* T: (01494) 523697 E: veronica.beaumont@virgin.net

BEAVAN, Canon Edward Hugh. b 43. Ex Coll Ox BA 70 MA 74 Solicitor 66. Cuddesdon Coll 69. **d** 71 **p** 72. C Ashford St Hilda Lon 71–74; C Newington St Mary *S'wark* 74–76; R Sandon *Chelmsf* 76–86; V Thorpe Bay 86–98; P-in-c Bradwell on Sea 98–05; P-in-c St Lawrence 98–05; V Burnham 05–09; Ind Chapl 98–05; RD Maldon and Dengie 00–05; Hon Can Chelmsf Cathl 02–09; rtd 09; PtO *Chelmsf* from 09. *19 Wordsworth Road, Colchester CO3 4HR* T: (01206) 564577 E: hugh@beavan.go-plus.net

BEAVER, William Carpenter. b 45. Colorado Coll BA Wolfs Coll Ox DPhil 76. Ox NSM Course 79. **d** 82 **p** 83. NSM Kennington St Jo w St Jas *S'wark* 82–95; NSM Avonmouth St Andr *Bris* 96–97; NSM Bris St Mary Redcliffe w Temple etc 95–08; NSM St Andr Holborn *Lon* 01–04; Dir Communications for C of E 97–02; Dir Communications for Br Red Cross 02–04; Speech Writer to the Ld Mayor of Lon 04–10; NSM Iffley *Ox* from 10; Offg Chapl Household Cavalry Mounted Regt 09–15; Chapl Light Cavalry Hon Artillery Co from 15; PtO *Lon* from 16. *Townsend Close, 50 Church Way, Iffley, Oxford OX4 4EF* T: (01865) 778061 E: williambeaver01@gmail.com

BEAVIS, Sandra Kathleen. b 51. Univ Coll Chich BA 01. **d** 98 **p** 07. C Southbourne w W Thorney *Chich* 98–05; C Bedhampton *Portsm* 05–09; PtO 05–10; P-in-c Soberton w Newtown 10–16; OCM 02–16; rtd 16. *1 Princess Gardens, Waterlooville PO8 9PT* E: sandrabeavis@btinternet.com

BEAZLEY, Prof John Milner. b 32. Man Univ MB, ChB 57 MRCOG 62 FRCOG 73 FACOG 89 MD 64. St Deiniol's Hawarden 83. **d** 86 **p** 87. NSM W Kirby St Bridget *Ches* 86–89; NSM Newton 89–92; NSM Hayton w Cumwhitton *Carl* 92–98; rtd 99; PtO *Carl* 99–19; *Ox* from 15. *The Stables, High Street, Great Linford, Milton Keynes MK14 5AX* T: (01908) 665005

BEAZLEY-LONG, Clive. b 77. Greenwich Univ BSc 99. Trin Coll Bris 08. **d** 10 **p** 11. C Chertsey, Lyne and Longcross *Guildf* 10–14; V Erith St Paul *Roch* from 14. *The Vicarage, 44A Colyers Lane, Erith DA8 3NP* E: revclive@hotmail.co.uk

BEBB, Erica Charlotte. b 61. STETS. **d** 09 **p** 10. NSM Sea Mills *Bris* 09–13; NSM Clifton Ch Ch w Em from 13. *21 Bramble Drive, Bristol BS9 1RE* T: 0117-968 2153 E: erica.bebb@ccweb.org.uk

BEBBINGTON, Julia. *See* BABB, Julia Bebbington

BECK, Amanda Ruth. b 68. Liv Univ BA 91 Birm Univ BD 93. Qu Coll Birm 91. **d** 94 **p** 95. C W Derby Gd Shep *Liv* 94–99; Asst Chapl Voorschoten *Eur* 99–02; P-in-c Kingston Vale St Jo *S'wark* 03–12; TV Kingston from 12; Chapl SW Lon and St George's Mental Health NHS Trust from 13. *St John's Vicarage, Robin Hood Lane, London SW15 3PY* T: (020) 8546 4079 E: mandy.beck@alty.org

BECK, Mrs Gillian Margaret. b 50. Sheff Univ CertEd 71 Nottm Univ BTh 78. Linc Th Coll 74. **dss** 78 **d** 87. Gt Grimsby St Mary and St Jas *Linc* 78–83; St Paul's Cathl *Lon* 84–87; Hon Par Dn St Botolph Aldgate w H Trin Minories 87–88; Par Dn Monkwearmouth St Andr *Dur* 88–94; C 94–96; NSM Eppleton and Hetton le Hole 97–04; NSM E Rainton 04–11; NSM W Rainton 04–11; PtO from 13. *3 Ten Fields, Hetton-le-Hole, Houghton le Spring DH5 9NB* T: 0191-526 3886 E: mgtbex@gmail.com

BECK, Ms Karen Maureen. b 53. R Holloway Coll Lon BA 74. St Alb Minl Tr Scheme 88. **d** 92 **p** 94. Par Dn Royston *St Alb* 92–94; C 94–96; TV Chipping Barnet w Arkley 96–02; P-in-c Heddon-on-the-Wall *Newc* 02–07; Chapl Northumbria Police 02–07; P-in-c Didcot All SS *Ox* 07–18; rtd 18. *35 Oulton Lane, Liverpool L36 4QX* E: karen.beck140@gmail.com

BECK, Michael Leonard. b 50. K Coll Lon BD 77 AKC 77 Seabury-Western Th Sem DMin 04. Linc Th Coll 77. **d** 78 **p** 79. C Gt Grimsby St Mary and St Jas *Linc* 78–83; Min Can and Succ St Paul's Cathl *Lon* 83–88; V Monkwearmouth St Andr *Dur* 88–96; TR Monkwearmouth 97; R Eppleton and Hetton le Hole 97–04; AD Houghton 97–04; P-in-c Lyons 00–04; P-in-c W Rainton 04–15; P-in-c E Rainton 04–15; Dir Reader Min 04–09; Tutor Lindisfarne Regional Tr Partnership

09–16; rtd 16; PtO *Dur* from 16. *3 Ten Fields, Hetton-le-Hole, Houghton le Spring DH5 9NB* T: 0191-526 3886 M: 07793-462896 E: mlbparish@gmail.com

BECK, Rachel Gillian. b 80. Bp Grosseteste Coll BA 05 Selw Coll Cam BTh 16. Westcott Ho Cam 14 Yale Div Sch 16. **d** 17 **p** 18. C Linc St Giles from 17. *74 Ruskin Avenue, Lincoln LN2 4BT* E: rgbeck@btinternet.com

BECK, Roger William. b 48. Chich Th Coll 79. **d** 81 **p** 82. C St Marychurch *Ex* 81–85; TV Torre 85–88; V Torquay St Jo and Ellacombe 88–94; C Plympton St Mary 94–16; TV Plympton 16–17; rtd 18. *81 Fore Street, Plympton, Plymouth PL7 1NB* T: (01752) 336393

BECK, Mrs Sandra Veronica. b 52. St Jo Coll Nottm 97. **d** 00 **p** 01. NSM Digswell and Panshanger *St Alb* 00–04; NSM Codicote 04–08; PtO 08–09; Chapl E and N Herts NHS Trust 09–13; PtO *St Alb* 13–16; NSM Welwyn from 16. *4 Grange Rise, Codicote, Hitchin SG4 8YR* T: (01438) 820191 E: csbeck@btinternet.com

BECK, Stephen Andrew. b 70. K Coll Lon BSc 93 Liv Univ PGCE 97. Trin Coll Bris 11. **d** 13 **p** 14. C Woodlands *Sheff* 13–16; R Kirk Sandall and Edenthorpe from 16. *The Rectory, 31 Doncaster Road, Kirk Sandall, Doncaster DN3 1HP* M: 07739-509967 E: revstevebeck@gmail.com *or* stephen.beck@sheffield.anglican.org

BECKERLEG, April Cornelia. b 62. Ox Min Course 15. **d** 17 **p** 18. C Bicester w Bucknell, Caversfield and Launton *Ox* from 17. *Pringle Cottage, Priory Road, Bicester OX26 6BL*

BECKETT, Bonnie. *See* BECKETT, Yvonne Janine

BECKETT *(formerly* MARTIN)*,* Mrs Caroline Evelyn.** b 76. York Univ BA 98 Homerton Coll Cam PGCE 99. St Mellitus Coll BA 15. **d** 15 **p** 16. C Berechurch St Marg w St Mich *Chelmsf* 15–18; V Brightlingsea from 18. *The Vicarage, Richard Avenue, Brightlingsea, Colchester CO7 0LP* T: (01206) 308726 E: revcarolinebeckett@gmail.com

BECKETT, Glynis Joy. b 49. **d** 10 **p** 11. OLM Radley and Sunningwell *Ox* 10–15; OLM Radley, Sunningwell and Kennington from 15. *18 Sadlers Court, Abingdon OX14 2PA* T: (01235) 529505

BECKETT, Graham. b 49. St As Minl Tr Course 95. **d** 99 **p** 00. NSM Hawarden *St As* 99–01; C 01–07; V Gorsedd w Brynford, Ysgeifiog and Whitford 07–14; P-in-c Mostyn 13–14; AD Holywell 11–14; rtd 14; PtO *St As* from 16. *Hillview, Church Lane, Aston Hill, Ewloe, Deeside CH5 3BF* T: (01244) 535269 E: g147beckett@btinternet.com

BECKETT, John Adrian. b 61. Bris Univ BVSc 85. Trin Coll Bris. **d** 00 **p** 01. C Harrogate St Mark *Ripon* 00–04; P-in-c Sevenhampton w Charlton Abbots, Hawling etc *Glouc* 04–14; P-in-c Torquay St Matthias, St Mark and H Trin *Ex* 14–15; R from 15. *The Rectory, Wellswood Avenue, Torquay TQ1 2QE* T: (01803) 293119 M: 07513-346521 E: jandrbeckett@btinternet.com

BECKETT, Michael Shaun. b 55. ACA 79. Oak Hill Th Coll BA 88. **d** 88 **p** 89. C Cambridge St Barn *Ely* 88–93; P-in-c Cambridge St Paul 93–94; V from 94. *St Paul's Vicarage, 15 St Paul's Road, Cambridge CB1 2EZ* T: (01223) 354186 *or* 315832 F: 471792 E: church@centrestpauls.org.uk *or* vicar@stpaulscambridge.org.uk

BECKETT, Mrs Patricia Anne. b 44. **d** 00 **p** 01. NSM Cheddleton *Lich* 00–06; NSM Upper Tean 06–12; PtO from 13. *10 Wallis Way, Stoke-on-Trent ST2 7JQ* T: (01782) 769718

BECKETT, Mrs Yvonne Janine (Bonnie). b 50. Qu Coll Birm 13. **d** 15 **p** 16. C Walsall Pleck and Bescot *Lich* from 15. *1 Newhall Crescent, Cannock WS11 7ZD* T: (01543) 270011 M: 07730-599633 E: bonniebeckett@talktalk.net

BECKINSALE, Mrs Pamela Rachel. b 46. Man Univ BSc 69. Cant Sch of Min 88. **d** 91 **p** 94. NSM Sittingbourne St Mich *Cant* 91–96; Hon Chapl Thames Gateway NHS Trust 96–98; Chapl 98–16; Chapl Kent & Medway NHS and Soc Care Partnership Trust from 16; PtO *Cant* from 16. *8 Glovers Crescent, Bell Road, Sittingbourne ME10 4DU* T: (01795) 471632 E: revpambeckinsale@tiscali.co.uk

BECKLEY, Peter William (Pedr). b 52. Lon Univ BSc 73 CertEd. Trin Coll Bris 76. **d** 79 **p** 80. C Plymouth St Jude *Ex* 79–83; C Ecclesall *Sheff* 83–88; V Greystones 88–18; P-in-c Endcliffe 11–15; rtd 18; PtO *Bris* from 19. *69 Hill View, Henleaze, Bristol BS9 4QF* E: pedrwb@gmail.com

BECKLEY, Simon Richard. b 38. Lon Univ BA 61. Oak Hill Th Coll 58. **d** 63 **p** 64. C Watford St Luke *St Alb* 63–67; C New Ferry *Ches* 67–70; C Chadderton Ch Ch *Man* 70–73; V Friarmere 73–80; V Tranmere St Cath *Ches* 80–03; Chapl Wirral Community Healthcare NHS Trust 80–97; Chapl Wirral and W Cheshire Community NHS Trust 97–03; rtd 03; PtO *Ches* 04–19. *14 Gracey Court, Woodland Road, Broadclyst, Exeter EX5 3GA* T: (01392) 461237

BECKWITH, John James. b 53. UMIST BSc 74 Newc Univ PGCE 88. **d** 02 **p** 03. OLM Bothal and Pegswood w Longhirst

Newc 02–04; C Morpeth 04–07; V Belford and Lucker 07–18; rtd 18; PtO *Newc* from 18. *9 Kenmore Crescent, Greenside, Ryton NE40 4QY* M: 07989-102458 E: john_ang@hotmail.co.uk

BECKWITH, Roger Thomas. b 29. St Edm Hall Ox BA 52 MA 56 BD 85 Lambeth DD 92. Ripon Hall Ox 51 Tyndale Hall Bris 52 Cuddesdon Coll 54. **d** 54 **p** 55. C Harold Wood *Chelmsf* 54–57; C Bedminster St Luke w St Silas *Bris* 57–59; Tutor Tyndale Hall Bris 59–63; Lib Latimer Ho Ox 63–73 and from 94; Warden 73–94; Lect Wycliffe Hall Ox 71–94; Hon C Wytham *Ox* 88–89; Hon C N Hinksey and Wytham 90–96; rtd 94; Hon C Ox St Mich w St Martin and All SS 97–03; PtO 03–18. *310 Woodstock Road, Oxford OX2 7NR* T: (01865) 557340 E: rogerbeckwith@talktalk.net

BEDBOROUGH, Sarah. b 54. **d** 15 **p** 15. Chapl Weldmar Hospice 07–18; C Parkstone St Pet and St Osmund w Branksea *Sarum* from 15. *375 Wimborne Road, Poole BH15 3ED* T: (01202) 245463 E: sarah.bedborough@sky.com

BEDFORD, Christopher John. b 40. CEng 68 MIStructE 68. **d** 05 **p** 06. OLM Chobham w Valley End *Guildf* 05–10; PtO from 10. *23 Swallow Rise, Knaphill, Woking GU21 2LG* T: (01483) 480127 E: ahbedford@hotmail.com

BEDFORD, Michael Anthony. b 38. Reading Univ BSc 59 Heythrop Coll Lon MA 00. **d** 01 **p** 02. NSM Ruislip St Martin *Lon* 01–11; NSM Ruislip St Mary 11–18; PtO from 18. *7 Chandos Road, Eastcote, Pinner HA5 1PR* T: (020) 8866 4332 E: mabedford7cr@waitrose.com

BEDFORD, Miss Susan Frances. b 55. Furzedown Coll of Educn CertEd 77. Yorks Min Course 15. **d** 17 **p** 18. NSM Doncaster St Geo *Sheff* from 17. *16 Granby Crescent, Doncaster DN2 6AN* M: 07503-186929 E: susan.bedford@doncasterminster.org.uk

BEDFORD, Archdeacon of. *See* MIDDLEBROOK, The Ven David John

BEDFORD, Suffragan Bishop of. *See* ATKINSON, The Rt Revd Richard William Bryant

BEE, Mrs Judith Mary. b 52. STETS 03. **d** 06 **p** 07. NSM Hambledon *Portsm* 06–10; NSM Buriton from 10. *St Mary's House, 41 North Lane, Buriton, Petersfield GU31 4RS* T: (01730) 269390 E: judith.bee@clara.co.uk

BEEBEE, Meyrick Richard Legge. b 43. SAOMC 99. **d** 02 **p** 03. NSM Gerrards Cross and Fulmer *Ox* from 02. *Lychgate House, 34 Austenway, Chalfont St Peter, Gerrards Cross SL9 8NW* T: (01753) 424375 M: 07956-435025 E: meyrick.beebee@saintjames.org.uk

BEEBY, Matthew David. b 77. Nottm Univ BA 99. Oak Hill Th Coll BA 11. **d** 11 **p** 12. NSM Mayfair Ch Ch *Lon* 11–19; R Gerrards Cross and Fulmer *Ox* from 19. *St James's Church, Oxford Road, Gerrards Cross SL9 7DJ* T: (01753) 883311 M: 07967-107228 E: matt.beeby@saintjames.org

BEECH, Miss Ailsa. b 44. N Co Coll Newc TDip 65. Trin Coll Bris 78. **dss** 80 **d** 87 **p** 94. Pudsey St Lawr and St Paul *Bradf* 80–88; Par Dn 87–88; C Attleborough *Cov* 88–89; Par Dn Cumnor *Ox* 89–92; Asst Chapl Walsgrave Hosp Cov 92–94; Asst Chapl Walsgrave Hosps NHS Trust 94–96; Chapl 96–00; Chapl Univ Hosps Cov and Warks NHS Trust 00–04; rtd 04; PtO *York* from 04. *Oxenby, Whitby Road, Pickering YO18 7HL* T: (01751) 472689 E: beecha71@gmail.com

BEECH, Preb Charmian Patricia. b 45. RGN 66 RHV 70 TCert 74. St As Minl Tr Course 99. **d** 02 **p** 03. C Connah's Quay *St As* 02–04; P-in-c Hodnet *Lich* 04–14; Dioc Child Protection Officer 04–14; RD Hodnet 11–14; Preb Lich Cathl 13–14; rtd 14; PtO *Heref* from 15; *Lich* from 15. *3 Church Meadow, Ditton Priors, Bridgnorth WV16 6TH* E: salop@charmianbeech14.plus.com or charmianbeech@icloud.com

BEECH, John. b 41. St Jo Coll Nottm. **d** 83 **p** 83. C York St Paul 83–84; P-in-c Bubwith w Ellerton and Aughton 84–85; P-in-c Thorganby w Skipwith and N Duffield 84–85; V Bubwith w Skipwith 85–87; V Acomb H Redeemer 87–00; P-in-c Westleigh St Pet *Man* 00–01; rtd 01; PtO *York* from 04. *6 Water Ark Cottages, Goathland, Whitby YO22 5JZ* E: jobe69@btinternet.com

BEECH, John Thomas. b 38. St Aid Birkenhead 64. **d** 67 **p** 68. C Burton St Paul *Lich* 67–70; Chapl RN 70–85; V Ellingham and Harbridge and Ibsley *Win* 85–94; Chapl Whiteley Village *Guildf* 94–03; rtd 03. *10 Friars Walk, Barton-on-Sea, New Milton BH25 7DA*

BEECH, Peter John. b 34. York St Jo Univ Hon BEd 19. Bps' Coll Cheshunt 58. **d** 61 **p** 62. C Fulham All SS *Lon* 61–64; Prec Kimberley Cathl S Africa 64–68; Dom Chapl to Bp Kimberley and Kuruman 64–68; V S Hackney St Mich *Lon* 68–71; P-in-c Haggerston St Paul 68–71; V S Hackney St Mich w Haggerston St Paul 71–75; V Wanstead H Trin Hermon Hill *Chelmsf* 75–89; V Mary-at-Latton 89–90; V 90–99; rtd 99; PtO *Ely* 99–19. *10 Stuart Court, High Street, Kibworth Beauchamp, Leicester LE8 0LR*

BEECH-GRÜNEBERG, Keith Nigel. b 72. CCC Ox BA 93 MA 96 St Jo Coll Dur BA 97 PhD 02. Cranmer Hall Dur 95. **d** 01 **p** 02. C Pangbourne w Tidmarsh and Sulham *Ox* 01–04; Dir Studies Dioc Bd Stewardship 04–11; Dir Local Min Tr 11–16; IME Pathways Adv Min Division from 16. *Ministry Division, Church House, 27 Great Smith Street, London SW1P 3AZ* T: (020) 7898 1000 M: 07731-894344 E: keith.beech-gruneberg@churchofengland.org

BEECHAM, Mrs Sally-Anne. b 72. Open Univ MA 02. St Hild Coll 16. **d** 19. C Bakewell, Ashford w Sheldon and Rowsley *Derby* from 19; C Chesterfield SS Aug from 19. *161 Old Road, Chesterfield S40 3QL* M: 07849-110495 E: revsalbeecham@gmail.com

BEECROFT, Benjamin Harold. b 77. Trin Coll Bris 98. **d** 00 **p** 01. C Stapleford *S'well* 00–04; C Warfield *Ox* 04–07; V Addlestone *Guildf* from 07. *The Vicarage, 140 Church Road, Addlestone KT15 1SJ* T: (01932) 842879 E: ben.beecroft@btinternet.com

BEECROFT, Mrs Christine Mary. b 62. RGN 85. Trin Coll Bris BA 97 MA 99. **d** 98 **p** 99. C Roxeth *Lon* 98–00; PtO *S'well* 00–02; C Stapleford 02–04; NSM Warfield *Ox* 04–07; C Addlestone *Guildf* from 09. *The Vicarage, 140 Church Road, Addlestone KT15 1SJ* T: (01932) 842879 E: chrisbeecroft@btinternet.com

BEECROFT, Mrs Miriam Joanna. Univ of Wales (Abth) BSc(Soc) 07. St Mich Coll Llan 11. **d** 15 **p** 16. C Bro Ardudwy *Ban* 15–18; V Bro Cyfeiliog and Mawddwy from 18. *16 Pencaemawr, Penegoes, Machynlleth SY20 8PF* T: (01654) 638096 E: miriam@esgobaethbangor.net

BEEDELL, Trevor Francis. b 31. ALCD 65. **d** 65 **p** 66. C Walton *St E* 65–68; R Hartshorne *Derby* 68–79; RD Repton 74–79; V Doveridge 79–86; Chapl HM Det Cen Foston Hall 79–80; Dioc Dir of Chr Stewardship *Derby* 79–97; rtd 97; PtO *Derby* 97–18. *185 High Lane West, West Hallam, Ilkeston DE7 6HP* T: 0115-932 5589

BEEDON, David Kirk. b 59. Birm Univ BA 89 MPhil 93. Qu Coll Birm 86. **d** 89 **p** 90. C Cannock *Lich* 89–92; V Wednesbury St Bart 92–99; R Lich St Mich w St Mary and Wall 99–12; P-in-c Lich Ch Ch 07–09; Chapl HM Pris Ranby 12–18; rtd 18; PtO *S'well* from 18. *Address withheld by request* E: david.beedon59@btinternet.com

BEER, Anthony Mark. St Mich Coll Llan. **d** 09 **p** 10. NSM Caerau w Ely *Llan* 09–11; C Llantwit Major 11–13; TV 13–16; P-in-c Laleston and Merthyr Mawr w Penyfai from 16. *The Vicarage, Rogers Lane, Laleston, Bridgend CF32 0LB* T: (01656) 859487 E: blammp2013@gmail.com

BEER, Ms Deborah Marion. SEITE 12. **d** 15 **p** 16. NSM Hurstpierpoint *Chich* from 15; Dioc Environment Officer from 19. *Address withheld by request* M: 07530-039299 E: revdebbiebeer@gmail.com

BEER, The Ven John Stuart. b 44. Pemb Coll Ox BA 65 MA 70 Fitzw Coll Cam MA 78. Westcott Ho Cam 69. **d** 71 **p** 72. C Knaresborough St Jo *Ripon* 71–74; Chapl Fitzw Coll and New Hall Cam 74–80; Fell Fitzw Coll 77-80; Bye-Fell from 01; P-in-c Toft w Caldecote and Childerley *Ely* 80–83; R 83–87; P-in-c Hardwick 80–83; R 83–87; V Grantchester 87–97; Dir of Ords, Post-Ord Tr and Student Readers from 88; Hon Can Ely Cathl from 89; Adn Huntingdon 97–04; Acting Adn Wisbech 02–04; Adn Cam 04–14; rtd 14. *Fitzwilliam College, Storey's Way, Cambridge CB3 0DG* E: johnbeer1@btinternet.com

BEER, Kevin Lionel Charles. b 74. SWMTC 09. **d** 12 **p** 13. C Parkham, Alwington, Buckland Brewer etc *Ex* 12–14; NSM from 14. *Address withheld by request* M: 07530-039299 *3 Bevil Close, Bideford EX39 5XN* T: (01237) 421823 E: mrkevinlcbeer@btinternet.com

BEER, Kevin Vincent. b 65. Ox Min Course 09. **d** 12. C Beaconsfield *Ox* 12–16; TV Wallingford from 16. *The Vicarage, 34 Thames Mead, Crowmarsh Gifford, Wallingford OX10 8EY* M: 07740-869501 E: kvbeer@gmail.com

BEER, Matthew. b 89. Ridley Hall Cam 13. **d** 16 **p** 17. C Bletchley *Ox* from 16. *14 Hamilton Lane, Bletchley, Milton Keynes MK3 5LU* M: 07891-567518 E: beermatt89@gmail.com

BEER, Nigel David. b 62. Portsm Poly BSc 84. St Jo Coll Nottm MA 93. **d** 93 **p** 94. C Rastrick St Matt *Wakef* 93–96; C Bilton *Ripon* 96–98; TV Moor Allerton 98–99; TV Moor Allerton and Shadwell 09–13; Asst Dir of Ords 05–13; V Stanwix *Carl* from 13; RD Carl from 16. *The Vicarage, Dykes Terrace, Carlisle CA3 9AS* T: (01228) 514600 E: rev.beer@hotmail.co.uk

BEER, William Barclay. b 43. ACT ThA 68 St Steph Ho Ox. **d** 71 **p** 72. C St Marychurch *Ex* 71–76; V Pattishall w Cold Higham *Pet* 76–82; V Northampton St Benedict 82–85; V Chislehurst Annunciation *Roch* 85–12; rtd 12; PtO *Lon* from 14. *St Mary's Vicarage, Lansdowne Road, London N17 9XE* T: (020) 8808 6644 E: williambarclaybeer@gmail.com

BEERE, Adrian Mark. b 69. St Mellitus Coll BA 17. d 19. C Charlton Kings St Mary *Glouc* from 19. *2 Royal Crescent, Cheltenham GL50 3DA* M: 07788-725331 E: adrian.beere@icloud.com

BEESLEY, Aran Paul. b 71. Linc Sch of Th and Min 11 Westcott Ho Cam 14. d 15 p 16. C Stamford All SS w St Jo *Linc* 15–18; R Uffington Gp from 18. *67 Main Road, Uffington, Stamford PE9 4SN* M: 07590-055905 E: aran.beesley@gmail.com

BEESLEY, Daniel Edward. b 76. Man Univ BA 01. Wycliffe Hall Ox 13. d 15 p 16. C Risborough *Ox* 15–19; C Hawridge w Cholesbury and St Leonard 19–20. *7 Churchill Crescent, Thame OX9 3JN* M: 07590-123603 E: revdbeesley@gmail.com

BEESLEY, Mrs Gemma Louise. b 79. Ox Min Course 15. d 18 p 19. C Cowley St Jas *Ox* from 18. *66 East Field Close, Headington, Oxford OX3 7SH* M: 07894-637020 E: curate@cowleyteamministry.co.uk

BEESLEY, John Stanley. b 70. St Martin's Coll Lanc BSc 92. WEMTC 06. d 09 p 10. C Ludlow *Heref* 09–12; R Corvedale Benefice from 12. *St Michael's Rectory, Park Lane, Munslow, Craven Arms SY7 9EU* T: (01584) 841488 E: revjbeesley@gmail.com

BEESLEY, Michael Frederick. b 37. K Coll Cam BA 59. Westcott Ho Cam 60. d 61 p 64. C Eastleigh *Win* 61–69; rtd 02; PtO *Sarum* from 09. *24 Charmouth Grove, Poole BH14 0LP* T: (01202) 773471 E: michaelbeesley97@gmail.com

BEESON, Christopher George. b 48. Man Univ BSc 70. Qu Coll Birm 72. d 75 p 76. C Flixton St Mich *Man* 75–78; C Newton Heath All SS 78–80; R Gorton St Jas 80–90; Dioc Communications Officer *Blackb* 91–92; C Ribbleton 92–93; rtd 93; PtO *Blackb* from 93. *24 Arnold Close, Ribbleton, Preston PR2 6DX* T: (01772) 702675 E: cbeeson@cix.co.uk

BEESON, The Very Revd Trevor Randall. b 26. K Coll Lon MA 76 FKC 87 Southn Univ Hon DLitt 99. d 51 p 52. C Leadgate *Dur* 51–54; C Norton St Mary 54–56; C-in-c Stockton St Chad CD 56–60; V Stockton St Chad 60–65; C St Martin-in-the-Fields *Lon* 65–71; V Ware St Mary *St Alb* 71–76; Can Westmr Abbey 76–87; Treas Westmr Abbey 78–82; R Westmr St Marg 82–87; Chapl to Speaker of Ho of Commons 82–87; Dean Win 87–96; rtd 96; PtO *Win* from 96. *69 Greatbridge Road, Romsey SO51 8FE* T: (01794) 514627 E: alison.beeson@gmail.com

BEESTON, Andrew Bernard. b 41. RMN 64 RGN 67. NEOC 99. d 01 p 02. NSM Cullercoats St Geo *Newc* 01–06; NSM Long Benton 06–09; NSM Earsdon and Backworth 09–11; PtO from 11. *21 Deepdale Road, Cullercoats, North Shields NE30 3AN* T: 0191-259 0431 E: werdnabeeston@btinternet.com

BEET, Duncan Clive. b 65. LLB. Ridley Hall Cam 98. d 01 p 02. C Northampton Em *Pet* 01–04; P-in-c Mears Ashby and Hardwick and Sywell etc 04–17; R Sileby, Cossington and Seagrave *Leic* from 17. *St Mary's Rectory, 11 Mountsorrel Lane, Sileby, Loughborough LE12 7NF* T: (01509) 815640 E: scsparishes@gmail.com

BEETHAM, Anthony. b 32. Lon Univ BSc 53. Ox NSM Course. d 75 p 76. Dir Chr Enquiry Agency 88–97; NSM Ox St Clem 75–02; PtO *Ox* from 03. *44 Rose Hill, Oxford OX4 4HS* T: (01865) 770923

BEEVER, Miss Alison Rosemary. b 59. Man Univ BA 80. Linc Th Coll 88. d 90 p 94. Par Dn Watford Ch Ch *St Alb* 90–94; C 94–96; V Tilehurst St Cath *Ox* 96–01; P-in-c Cen Ex and Dioc Dir of Ords *Ex* 01–04; rtd 04. *7 Langridge Road, Paignton TQ3 3PT* T: (01803) 553645 E: abeever59@icloud.com

BEEVERS, Preb Colin Lionel. b 40. K Coll Lon BSc 62 PhD 66 CEng 70 MIET 70 MBIM 73. Sarum & Wells Th Coll 87. d 89 p 90. C Ledbury w Eastnor *Heref* 89–93; C Lt Marcle 89–93; Asst Dir of Tr 92–96; P-in-c Kimbolton w Hamnish and Middleton-on-the-Hill 93–96; P-in-c Bockleton w Leysters 93–96; P-in-c Ledbury w Eastnor 96–98; P-in-c Much Marcle 96–98; TR Ledbury 98–05; RD 96–02; Preb Heref Cathl 02–05; Chapl Herefordshire Primary Care Trust 96–05; rtd 05; PtO *Worc* from 06; *Heref* from 16. *11 Park View, 33 Abbey Road, Malvern WR14 3HG* T: (01684) 897715 E: colinandann.beevers@btinternet.com

BEGBIE, Prof Jeremy Sutherland. b 57. Edin Univ BA 77 Aber Univ BD 80 PhD 87 LRAM 80 ARCM 77 MSSTh. Ridley Hall Cam 80. d 82 p 83. C Egham *Guildf* 82–85; Chapl Ridley Hall Cam 85–87; Dir Studies 87–92; Vice-Prin 93–00; Assoc Prin 00–09; Hon Reader St Andr Univ 00–09; Research Prof Th Duke Div Sch USA from 09; PtO *Ely* from 15. *Duke University Divinity School, Box 90968, Durham NC 27708, USA* T: (001) (919) 660 3591 E: jeremy.begbie@duke.edu

BEGLEY, Mrs Helen. b 59. Kingston Poly BA 81. NOC 87. d 89 p 94. Par Dn Leeds H Trin *Ripon* 89–93; Chapl to the Deaf 89–96; Par Dn Leeds City 91–94; C 94–96; Chapl to the Deaf (Wilts) *Sarum* 96–06; NSM Upper Wylye Valley 03–11; NSM Melksham from 11. *Beckerley View, 196 The Common, Holt,*

Trowbridge BA14 6QN T: (01225) 783543 M: 07540-314852 E: begleyhelen4@gmail.com

BEGLEY, Peter Ernest Charles. b 55. St Mellitus Coll BA 10. d 10 p 11. C New Thundersley *Chelmsf* 10–15; P-in-c Southminster and Steeple from 15; RD Maldon and Dengie from 19. *The Vicarage, Burnham Road, Southminster CM0 7ES* T: (01621) 772300 E: pf.begley@btinternet.com *or* vicar@stleonardsouthminster.org.uk

BEGLEY, Sally Anne Jane. b 55. St Mellitus Coll 16. d 17 p 18. NSM Waltham H Cross *Chelmsf* from 17. *33 Byron Avenue, London E18 2HH* T: (020) 7421 3854 M: 07572-111387 E: jane.begley@irwinmitchell.com

BEHENNA, Canon Gillian Eve. b 57. CertEd 78 Bris Univ MSc 15. S Dios Minl Tr Scheme 82. dss 85 d 87 p 94. Chapl to the Deaf *Sarum* 85–90; Chapl w Deaf People *Ex* 90–04; Preb Ex Cathl 02–04; Chapl w Deaf Community *Bris* from 05; Nat Deaf Min Adv Abps' Coun from 13; Hon Can Bris Cathl from 11; PtO *B & W* from 16. *1 Saxon Way, Bradley Stoke, Bristol BS32 9AR* T: (01454) 202483 M: 07715-707135 E: gillbehenna@me.com

BEHREND, Michael Christopher. b 60. St Jo Coll Cam BA 82 MA 86 PGCE 83. Oak Hill Th Coll 93. d 97 p 98. C Hensingham *Carl* 97–02; TV Horwich and Rivington *Man* from 02; C Blackrod 11–16. *St Catherine's House, Richmond Street, Horwich, Bolton BL6 5QT* T: (01204) 697162

BELCADE, Joshua Good. BNC Ox BA. S'wark Ord Course 10. d 13 p 14. NSM S Wimbledon All SS *S'wark* from 13; Hon Chapl Epsom Racecourse from 13. *5 Edge Hill, London SW19 4LR* T: (020) 7898 1610 M: 07766-341663

BELCHER, Mrs Catherine Jane Allington. b 53. Charlotte Mason Coll of Educn CertEd 75. EAMTC 02. d 05 p 06. NSM Nor St Mary Magd w St Jas 05–11; PtO 11–13; NSM Nor Lakenham St Jo and All SS and Tuckswood 13–18; PtO from 18. *70 Mill Hill Road, Norwich NR2 3DS* M: 07708-650897 E: revkatebelcher@yahoo.co.uk

BELCHER, David John. b 44. Ch Ch Ox BA 65 MA 69. Cuddesdon Coll 68. d 70 p 71. C Gateshead St Mary *Dur* 70–72; C Stockton St Pet 73–76; LtO *Lich* 76–81; P-in-c W Bromwich Ch Ch 81–85; P-in-c W Bromwich Gd Shep w St Jo 85–89; V 89–95; RD W Bromwich 90–94; R Bratton, Edington and Imber, Erlestoke etc *Sarum* 95–03; rtd 03; Hon C Smestow Vale *Lich* 03–07; PtO 09–14. *81 The Lindens, Newbridge Crescent, Wolverhampton WV6 0LS* T: (01902) 750903

BELCHER, Canon Derek George. b 50. Univ of Wales (Cardiff) MEd 86 LLM 04 Newman Univ BA 15 Open Univ BSc 18 Lon Univ PGCE 82 MRSPH 73 MBIM 82 FRSPH 00. Chich Th Coll 74. d 77 p 78. C Newton Nottage *Llan* 77–81; PV Llan Cathl 81–87; V Margam 87–01; RD 99–01; TR Cowbridge 01–15; AD Vale of Glam 08–11; rtd 15; P-in-c Penmark w Llancarfan w Llantrithyd *Llan* from 15; Can Llan Cathl from 97. *The Rectory, Llancarfan, Barry CF62 3AJ* T: (01446) 750053 M: 07796-170671 E: dgbelc@gmail.com

BELDER, Jacob John. b 83. Redeemer Univ Coll Hamilton BA 06 Reformed Th Sem (USA) MA 10 St Jo Coll Dur DThM 18. Cranmer Hall Dur 14. d 18 p 18. C Selby Abbey *York* from 18. *49 Woodville Terrace, Selby YO8 8AJ* T: (01757) 707154 E: jake.belder@gmail.com

BELDING, Cheryl Pauline. b 54. ERMC 16. d 18. NSM Newmarket St Mary w Exning St Agnes *St E* from 18. *28 Heasman Close, Newmarket CB8 0GR* M: 07801-499179 E: cherylbelding@outlook.com

BELFAST, Archdeacon of. *See* DAVISON, The Ven George Thomas William

BELFAST, Dean of. *See* FORDE, The Very Revd Stephen Bernard

BELHAM, John Edward. b 42. K Coll Lon BSc 65 AKC 65 PhD 70. Oak Hill Th Coll 69. d 72 p 73. C Cheadle Hulme St Andr *Ches* 72–75; C Cheadle 75–83; R Gressenhall w Longham w Wendling etc *Nor* 83–08; P-in-c Mileham 07–08; rtd 08; PtO *Nor* from 08. *6 Brentwood, Norwich NR4 6PW* T: (01603) 456925 E: johnbelham@lords-prayer.co.uk

BELHAM, Michael. b 23. Lon Univ BScEng 50. d 67 p 68. C Northwood Hills St Edm *Lon* 67–69; C Hendon St Mary 69–73; V Tottenham H Trin 73–78; V Hillingdon St Jo 78–85; P-in-c Broughton *Ox* 85; R Broughton w N Newington and Shutford 85–90; Chapl Horton Gen Hosp 85–90; rtd 90; PtO *Pet* 90–01; *Ox* 90–05; Sec DBP 95–01; PtO *B & W* 01–13. *24 Carlton Court, Wells BA5 1SF* T: (01749) 675236

BELITHER, John Roland. b 36. Oak Hill Th Coll 83. d 86 p 87. NSM Bushey Heath *St Alb* 86–91; V Marsh Farm 91–06; rtd 06; PtO *St Alb* 06–18. *43 Mallard Road, Abbots Langley WD5 0GE* T: (01923) 494399

BELL, Adrian Christopher. b 48. AKC 70. St Aug Coll Cant 70. d 71 p 72. C Sheff St Aid w St Luke 71–74; C Willesborough w Hinxhill *Cant* 74–78; P-in-c Bredgar w Bicknor and Frinsted w Wormshill etc 78; P-in-c Hollingbourne w Hucking

78–82; P-in-c Leeds w Broomfield 79–82; V Hollingbourne and Hucking w Leeds and Broomfield 82–84; V Herne Bay Ch Ch 84–91; R Washingborough w Heighington and Canwick *Linc* 91–01; R Fakenham w Alethorpe *Nor* 01–14; rtd 14; PtO *Nor* 14–17; Hon C Caston, Griston, Merton, Thompson etc from 17. *Orchard House, 19 Whitsands Road, Swaffham PE37 7BJ* T: (01760) 627039 M: 07706-480489 E: adrian.bell4@uwclub.net

BELL, Canon Alan John. b 47. Liv Univ BA 68. Ridley Hall Cam 69. **d** 72 **p** 73. C Speke St Aid *Liv* 72–77; P-in-c Halewood 77–81; R Wavertree St Mary 81–88; Chapl Mabel Fletcher Tech Coll and Olive Mt Hosp 81–88; R Fakenham w Alethorpe *Nor* 88–00; RD Burnham and Walsingham 92–00; TR Stockport SW *Ches* 00–07; V Stockport St Geo 07–12; RD Stockport 05–12; Hon Can Ches Cathl 08–12; rtd 12; PtO *Ely* from 13; *Nor* from 14. *24 Hall Road, Clenchwarton, King's Lynn PE34 4AT* T: (01553) 278106 E: vicaralanbell@aol.com

BELL, Anthony Lawson. b 47. AKC 72. St Aug Coll Cant 71. **d** 72 **p** 73. C Peterlee *Dur* 72–77; PtO 77–82; C-in-c Stockton St Jas CD 82–89; P-in-c Byers Green 89–96; Ind Chapl Teesside 89–96; P-in-c Ault Hucknall *Derby* 96–99; V Ault Hucknall and Scarcliffe 99–12; rtd 12; PtO *Roch* from 13; *Eur* from 16. *4 Godfrey Close, Rochester ME2 3QS* T: (01634) 711445 E: glapwell11@btinternet.com

BELL, Arthur James. b 33. Ch Coll Cam BA 57 MA 60. Coll of Resurr Mirfield 57. **d** 59 **p** 60. C New Cleethorpes *Linc* 59–63; C Upperby St Jo *Carl* 63–66; P-in-c Wabasca Canada 67–72; 77–83; PtO *Ely* 73–75; LtO *Carl* 75–76; Warden Retreat of the Visitation Rhandirmwyn 83–99; PtO *Dur* from 00. *Burnside, 22 Rose Terrace, Stanhope, Bishop Auckland DL13 2PE* T: (01388) 526514 E: abell178@btinternet.com

BELL, Barnaby. See BELL, Simon Barnaby

BELL, Bede. See BELL, William Wealands

BELL, Benjamin Lawrence. b 74. K Coll Lon MA 13. Westcott Ho Cam 15. **d** 17 **p** 18. C Poplar *Lon* 17–19; V Hoxton St Anne w St Columba from 19. *St Ann's Vicarage, 37 Hemsworth Street, London N1 5LF* M: 07739-487721 E: revbenbell@gmail.com

BELL, Brian Thomas Benedict. b 64. Newc Poly BA 87 Newc Univ PGCE 88 Univ of Northumbria at Newc MA 93 Leeds Univ BA 97. Coll of Resurr Mirfield. **d** 97 **p** 98. C Tynemouth Cullercoats St Paul *Newc* 97–01; V Horton 01–08; V Horbury w Horbury Bridge *Wakef* 08–14; *Leeds* 14–16; V Monk Bretton from 16. *The Vicarage, Burton Road, Barnsley S71 2HQ* E: fatherbrian@virginmedia.com

BELL, Charles William. b 43. TCD Div Test 66 BA 66 MA 69. CITC 64. **d** 67 **p** 68. C Newtownards *D & D* 67–70; C Larne and Inver *Conn* 70–74; C Ballymena w Ballyclug 74–80; Bp's C Belfast Ardoyne 80–87; Bp's C Belfast Ardoyne w H Redeemer 88; I Eglantine 89–11; S Conn Dioc Info Officer 89–11; Preb Conn Cathl 04–11; rtd 11. *2 Beechwood Crescent, Moira, Craigavon BT67 0LA* T: (028) 9261 9834 E: norma.bell@virgin.net

BELL, Darren Morgan. b 69. Northumbria Univ LLB 01 Newc Univ MPhil 07. Ox Min Course 15. **d** 17 **p** 18. C Seghill *Newc* from 17. *15 Backworth Court, Backworth, Newcastle upon Tyne NE27 0RP* M: 07401-797179 E: revdarrenbell@gmail.com

BELL, David. b 52. **d** 12 **p** 13. NSM Hampton Hill *Lon* 12–15; NSM Kingston *S'wark* from 15; PtO *Lon* from 15; *Truro* from 14. *20 Vicarage Road, Hampton Wick, Kingston upon Thames KT1 4ED* T: (020) 8977 2482 M: 07986-245313 E: davidbell@bell5.co.uk

BELL, David Bain. b 57. Bp Otter Coll BEd 82. Ox Min Course 04. **d** 07 **p** 08. NSM Stantonbury and Willen *Ox* 07–10; TV Watling Valley 10–15; PtO from 15; V Silsoe, Pulloxhill and Flitton *St Alb* 15–19. *The Vicarage, Fir Tree Road, Silsoe, Bedford MK45 4EA* T: (01525) 861163 E: vicar@3churches.uk

BELL, Canon David Owain. b 49. Dur Univ BA 69 Fitzw Coll Cam BA 72 MA 80. Westcott Ho Cam 70. **d** 72 **p** 73. C Houghton le Spring *Dur* 72–76; C Norton St Mary 76–78; P-in-c Worc St Clem 78–84; R 84–85; R Old Swinford Stourbridge 85–97; TR Kidderminster St Mary and All SS w Trimpley etc 97–13; RD Stourbridge 90–96; Hon Can Worc Cathl 96–13; PtO from 13; rtd 14. *60A Main Road, Kempsey WR5 3JF* T: (01905) 820209 E: dowainbell@yahoo.co.uk

BELL, Canon Donald Jon. b 50. Sarum & Wells Th Coll 73. **d** 76 **p** 77. C Jarrow *Dur* 76–80; C Darlington St Cuth w St Hilda 80–83; V Wingate Grange 83–89; V Sherburn w Pittington 89–95; R Shadforth 94–95; P-in-c Dur St Cuth 95–97; V 97–02; R Witton Gilbert 97–02; TR Dur N 02–05; AD Dur 93–05; Chapl Dur and Darlington Fire and Rescue Brigade 95–05; Bp's Sen Chapl and Exec Officer 05–12; P-in-c Kelloe and Coxhoe 12–16; P-in-c Chilton 12–16; Hon Can Dur Cathl 01–16; rtd 16; PtO *Dur* from 16. *20 St Phillips*

Close, Auckland Park, Bishop Auckland DL14 8BD M: 07973-829491 E: jonb22@btinternet.com

BELL, Dorothy Jane. b 53. Teesside Univ BSc 93. Cranmer Hall Dur 01. **d** 03 **p** 04. C Washington *Dur* 03–07; P-in-c Stockton St Jo 07–15; P-in-c Stockton St Jas 07–15; P-in-c Stockton Christchurch 15–17; P-in-c Scarborough St Columba *York* from 17; P-in-c Scarborough St Jas w H Trin from 17. *34 Box Hill, Scarborough YO12 5NG*

BELL, Duncan John. b 83. Sheff Univ MEng 06 PhD 11. Oak Hill Th Coll BA 14. **d** 14 **p** 15. C Woodseats St Chad *Sheff* 14–17; C Leyland St Andr *Blackb* from 17. *11 Stokes Hall Avenue, Leyland PR25 3FA* M: 07833-448014 E: duncan.j.bell@gmail.com

BELL, Evelyn Ruth. b 52. Univ of Wales (Cardiff) BSc(Econ). SAOMC 97. **d** 00 **p** 01. C Waltham Cross *St Alb* 00–03; Chapl HM Pris Edmunds Hill 03–11; Chapl HM Pris Highpoint 11–15; rtd 15. *Address withheld by request* M: 07815-441304 E: evie.bell@icloud.com

BELL, Georgiana Mary. b 48. K Coll Lon BD 81 AKC 81 MTh 93. Westcott Ho Cam 81. **dss** 83 **d** 87 **p** 94. Cobbold Road St Sav w St Mary *Lon* 83–85; St Botolph Aldgate w H Trin Minories 85–87; Par Dn 87; PtO *S'wark* 88–93; Par Dn Kidbrooke St Jas 93–95; Tutor S'wark Ord Course 93–94; Tutor SEITE 94–98; Teacher Eltham Coll 98–02; Asst Chapl Qu Eliz Hosp NHS Trust 03–11; Asst Chapl S Lon Healthcare NHS Trust 11–13; Tutor St Aug Coll of Th 13–17; Hon Chapl S'wark Cathl 95–17; rtd 17; Hon Min Can S'wark Cathl from 17; Public Preacher 12–18; PtO from 18. *4 Roupell Street, London SE1 8SP* T: (020) 7642 1161 M: 07776-122350 E: georgianambell@gmail.com

BELL, Mrs Glynis Mary. b 44. Leeds Univ BA 66. SAOMC 99. **d** 02 **p** 03. OLM Newport Pagnell w Lathbury and Moulsoe *Ox* 02–14; PtO from 14. *6 Kipling Drive, Newport Pagnell MK16 8EB* T: (01908) 612971 E: gmbell@screaming.net

BELL, Godfrey Bryan. b 44. Oak Hill Th Coll 72. **d** 75 **p** 76. C Penn Fields *Lich* 75–79; R Dolton *Ex* 79–89; R Iddesleigh w Dowland 79–89; R Monkokehampton 79–89; R Tollard Royal w Farnham, Gussage St Michael etc *Sarum* 89–96; TV Washfield, Stoodleigh, Withleigh etc *Ex* 96–06; TR 06–09; CF (ACF) 09–87; CF (TA) 87–99; rtd 09. *Bethany, 3 Alstone Road, Tiverton EX16 4JL* T: (01884) 252874 E: bells.bethany@btinternet.com

BELL, Graham Dennis Robert. b 42. K Coll Lon BSc 63 AKC 63 Nottm Univ MTh 73 ALCM 76 Lambeth STh 01. Tyndale Hall Bris 65. **d** 68 **p** 69. C Stapleford *S'well* 68–71; C Barton Seagrave *Pet* 71–73; C Barton Seagrave w Warkton 73–76; PtO *Nor* 76–82; V Wickham Market *St E* 82–86; V Wickham Market w Pettistree and Easton 86–98; R Thrapston *Pet* 98–07; rtd 07; PtO *Pet* from 11. *22 Cottesmore Avenue, Barton Seagrave, Kettering NN15 6QX* T: (01536) 725924 E: bellgood@talktalk.net

BELL, Canon Jack Gorman. b 23. Lon Univ BSc 48. Oak Hill Th Coll 51. **d** 53 **p** 54. C Blackpool Ch Ch *Blackb* 53–55; C Chadderton Ch Ch *Man* 55–59; R Man St Jerome w Ardwick St Silas 59–69; V Mosley Common 69–89; Hon Can Man Cathl 87–89; rtd 89; PtO *Carl* 89–11. *39 The Moorings, Stafford Street, Stone ST15 8QZ* T: (01785) 286126

✠**BELL, The Rt Revd James Harold.** b 50. St Jo Coll Dur BA 72 St Pet Hall Ox BA 74 MA 78. Wycliffe Hall Ox 72. **d** 75 **p** 76 **c** 04. Hon C Ox St Mich w St Martin and All SS 75–76; Chapl and Lect BNC Ox 76–82; R Northolt St Mary *Lon* 82–93; RD Ealing 91–93; Adv for Min Willesden 93–97; Dioc Dir of Min and Tr *Ripon* 97–99; Dioc Dir of Miss 99–04; Can Res Ripon Cathl 97–99; Hon Can from 99; Suff Bp Knaresborough *Ripon* 04–15; Suff Bp Ripon *Leeds* 15–17; rtd 17. *Stone Croft, Bolton, Appleby-in-Westmorland CA16 6AL*

BELL, James Samuel. b 40. RMA 59 St Chad's Coll Dur BA 69. Coll of Resurr Mirfield 71. **d** 72 **p** 73. C Lambeth St Phil *S'wark* 72–73; C N Lambeth 73–74; P-in-c Invergordon St Ninian Mor 74–77; P-in-c Dornoch 74–77; P-in-c Brora 74–77; V Pet H Spirit Bretton 77–83; P-in-c Marholm 82–83; Sen Chapl Tonbridge 83–00; rtd 00. *Clocktower House, Edderton, Tain IV19 1LJ* T: (01862) 821305

BELL, Jane. See BELL, Dorothy Jane

BELL, Canon Jeffrey William. b 37. Buckingham Univ MA 94. Sarum Th Coll 60. **d** 63 **p** 64. C Northampton St Matt *Pet* 63–66; C Portishead *B & W* 66–68; C Digswell *St Alb* 68–72; V Pet St Jude 72–79; V Buckingham *Ox* 79–93; RD 84–88 and 89–90; V Portsea N End St Mark *Portsm* 93–03; Hon Can Portsm Cathl 00–03; rtd 03; Hon C The Bourne and Tilford *Guildf* 03–13; PtO *Portsm* from 13. *164 Northern Parade, Portsmouth PO2 9LT* T: (023) 9265 0033 E: jeffnlinda.bell@btinternet.com

BELL, Jennifer Kathryn. See McWHIRTER, Jennifer Kathryn

BELL, John. See BELL, Donald Jon

BELL, John Holmes. b 50. Sheff City Coll of Educn CertEd 71. Oak Hill Th Coll BA 80. **d** 80 **p** 81. C Leic St Phil 80–83;

C Portswood Ch Ch *Win* 83–86; TV S Molton w Nymet St George, High Bray etc *Ex* 86–01; V Stoke Fleming, Blackawton and Strete 01–15; rtd 15; PtO *Ex* from 15. *40 Balmoral Crescent, Okehampton EX20 1GN* T: (01837) 53084 E: johnbell40@icloud.com

BELL, Jonathan Robert. b 84. Nottm Univ BA 06. Oak Hill Th Coll BA 14. **d** 14 **p** 15. C Stanton-by-Dale w Dale Abbey and Risley *Derby* 14–19; C Grange Park St Pet *Lon* from 19. *2 Firs Lane, London N21 2HU* M: 07736-286861

BELL, Joshua Russell Edmund. b 91. Cliff Coll BA 13. Westcott Ho Cam 15. **d** 18 **p** 19. C S Lynn *Nor* from 18. *29 Sandpiper Way, King's Lynn PE30 5DN* M: 07868-949615 E: frjoshuabell@outlook.com

BELL, Kenneth Murray. b 30. Sarum & Wells Th Coll 75. **d** 74 **p** 76. PtO *Guildf* 74–76; C Hartley Wintney and Elvetham *Win* 76–77; C Hartley Wintney, Elvetham, Winchfield etc 77–80; V Fair Oak 80–95; rtd 96; PtO *Win* from 96. *12 Hill Meadow, Overton, Basingstoke RG25 3JD* T: (01256) 770890 E: k_m_bell@btinternet.com

BELL, Kevin David. b 58. Newc Univ MA 93 Univ of Wales (Lamp) MA 06 FRSA 11. Aston Tr Scheme 78 Sarum & Wells Th Coll 80. **d** 83 **p** 84. C Weoley Castle *Birm* 83–87; C Acocks Green 87–89; CF 89–07; Asst Chapl Gen 07–15; Chapl Guards Chpl Lon 12–14; Dir of Ords 07–11; V Twickenham All Hallows *Lon* from 15. *All Hallows' Vicarage, 138 Chertsey Road, Twickenham TW1 1EW* T: (020) 8892 1322 M: 07764-541364 E: bellscmkd@yahoo.co.uk *or* kevin.bell@allhallowstwick.org.uk

BELL, Mrs Leanne Alix. b 78. Northumbria Univ LLB 02. Ripon Coll Cuddesdon 15. **d** 17 **p** 18. C Monkseaton St Pet *Newc* 17–18. *15 Backworth Court, Backworth, Newcastle upon Tyne NE27 0RP* M: 07411-665195 E: revleannebell@gmail.com

BELL, Canon Nicholas Philip Johnson. b 46. St Jo Coll Dur BSc 69. St Jo Coll Nottm 70. **d** 73 **p** 74. C Chadderton Ch Ch *Man* 73–77; C Frogmore *St Alb* 77–81; V Bricket Wood 81–91; RD Aldenham 87–91; V Luton St Mary 91–12; Hon Can St Alb 01–12; rtd 12; PtO *St Alb* from 12; *Nor* from 14. *6B North Street, Sheringham NR26 8LW* E: revnickbell@gmail.com

BELL, Owain. See BELL, David Owain

BELL, Paul Joseph. b 35. Dur Univ BA 56 DipEd 57. Trin Coll Bris 77. **d** 77 **p** 78. Burundi 77–81; C Highbury Ch Ch w St Jo and St Sav *Lon* 82–85; V Middleton w E Winch *Nor* 85–95; P-in-c Barningham w Matlaske w Baconsthorpe etc 95–99; R 99–02; rtd 02; PtO *Portsm* from 02. *21 Hurst Point View, Totland Bay PO39 0AQ* T: (01983) 756180 E: bell505@btinternet.com

BELL, Mrs Rebecca Mary. b 79. UWE BSc 00. Trin Coll Bris 10. **d** 13 **p** 14. C Charlton Kings H Apostles *Glouc* 13–16; P-in-c St Neot and Warleggan w Cardynham *Truro* 16–17; V St Neot and Warleggan 17–19; P-in-c St Cleer from 16; C St Ive and Pensilva w Quethiock 16–19; P-in-c from 19; P-in-c Menheniot from 19. *Angrouse House, Miners Way, Liskeard PL14 3ET* E: revbeccabell@gmail.com

BELL, Prof Richard Herbert. b 54. Univ Coll Lon BSc 75 PhD 79 Tubingen Univ DrTheol 91. Wycliffe Hall Ox BA 82 MA 87. **d** 83 **p** 84. C Edgware *Lon* 83–86; W Germany 86–90; Lect Th Nottm Univ 90–97; Sen Lect 97–05; Reader 05–08; Prof from 08. *Department of Theology and Religious Studies, University Park, Nottingham NG7 2RD* T: 0115-951 5858 F: 951 5887 E: richard.bell@nottingham.ac.uk

BELL, Robert Mason. b 35. Lon Coll of Div 66. **d** 68 **p** 69. C Burgess Hill St Andr *Chich* 68–78; R Lewes St Jo sub Castro 78–00; rtd 00. *10 Rufus Close, Lewes BN7 1BG* T: (01273) 470561

BELL, Mrs Shena Margaret. b 49. EAMTC. **d** 00 **p** 01. C Earls Barton *Pet* 00–04; P-in-c Raunds 04–07; P-in-c Ringstead and Stanwick w Hargrave 04–07; R Raunds, Hargrave, Ringstead and Stanwick 07–17; rtd 17; PtO *Pet* from 18. *28 High Street, Upton, Northampton NN5 4EH* T: (01604) 586107 E: shena.m.bell@gmail.com

BELL, Simon Barnaby. b 48. Bris Univ CertEd 70. Sarum & Wells Th Coll 87. **d** 89 **p** 90. C Ewyas Harold w Dulas, Kenderchurch etc *Heref* 89–93; P-in-c Clungunford w Clunbury and Clunton, Bedstone etc 93–01; R 01–11; P-in-c Hopesay 02–11; rtd 11; PtO *Heref* from 12. *49 Warden Close, Presteigne LD8 2DH*

BELL, Canon Stuart Rodney. b 46. Ex Univ BA 67. Tyndale Hall Bris 69. **d** 71 **p** 72. C Henfynyw w Aberaeron and Llanddewi Aberarth *St D* 71–74; V 81–88; V Llangeler 74–80; TR Aberystwyth 88–13; Chapl Aberystwyth Univ from 94; Ev St Teilo Trust from 95; AD Llanbadarn Fawr 12–14; Can St D Cathl 01–13; rtd 13; PtO *St D* from 13; *Eur* from 14. *Gwel Enlli, Borth SY24 5NS* E: stuart@prudence45.plus.com

BELL, Mrs Susan. b 62. Lindisfarne Regional Tr Partnership 13. **d** 15 **p** 16. NSM Darlington St Hilda and St Columba *Dur* 15–18; Chapl HM Pris Holme Ho from

18. *HM Prison Holme House, Holme House Road, Stockton-on-Tees TS18 2QU* T: (01642) 744000 M: 07850-675877 E: suebell158@hotmail.co.uk

BELL (née STEWART), Mrs Susan Catherine. b 57. St Martin's Coll Lanc BEd 80. LCTP 08. **d** 10 **p** 11. C Longridge *Blackb* 10–14; I Ballywalter w Inishargie *D & D* from 14. *15 Westland Drive, Ballywalter, Newtownards BT22 2TH* T: (028) 4275 7579 M: 07738-305129 E: bellsue9@gmail.com *or* vicarofballywalter@gmail.com

BELL, Terrance James. b 63. Toronto Univ BA 92. Trin Coll Toronto MDiv 97. **d** 97 **p** 98. C Wedmore w Theale and Blackford *B & W* 97–01; C Hampstead St Jo *Lon* 01–06; Chapl Eden Hall Marie Curie Hospice 01–06; P-in-c King's Walden and Offley w Lilley *St Alb* 06–11; V from 11. *Millstone Corner, Salusbury Lane, Offley, Hitchin SG5 3EG* T: (01462) 768123 E: kwol@btinternet.com

BELL, Timothy John Keeton. b 59. Trin Coll Bris BA 02. **d** 02 **p** 03. C Saltford w Corston and Newton St Loe *B & W* 02–06; Chapl Bath Spa Univ 04–06; P-in-c Wick w Doynton and Dyrham *Bris* from 06. *The Vicarage, 57 High Street, Wick, Bristol BS30 5QQ* T: 0117-937 3581 E: tim.vicar@gmail.com

BELL, Timothy Liam. b 73. Trin Coll Bris 15. **d** 17 **p** 18. C Hastings H Trin *Chich* from 17. *266 Elphinstone Road, Hastings TN34 2AG* E: timbell68@gmail.com

BELL, William. See BELL, Charles William

BELL, William Wealands. b 63. York Univ BA 86 Dur Univ PGCE 87 Leeds Univ BA 99. Coll of Resurr Mirfield 97. **d** 99 **p** 00. C Jarrow *Dur* 99–02; Novice CR 02–04; Chapl Aldenham Sch Herts 04–07; Can Res Lich Cathl 07–14; P-in-c Croydon St Andr *S'wark* 14–15; V 15–17; Chapl St Andr C of E High Sch Croydon 14–17; Chapl Magd Coll Sch Ox from 17. *Magdalen College School, Cowley Place, Oxford OX4 1DZ* T: (01865) 242191 E: wealandsbell@gmail.com

BELL-WINFROW, James Leo. b 89. Cliff Coll BA 10. Ripon Coll Cuddesdon 16. **d** 18 **p** 19. C Aller, High w Low Ham and Huish Episcopi cum Langport *B & W* from 18. *3 Station Court, Langport TA10 9FA* M: 07531-386352 E: curate@gmail.com *or* jamesbellwinfrow@gmail.com

BELLAMY, Canon David Quentin. b 62. Univ of Wales (Cardiff) BMus 84 Univ of Wales (Ban) MA 93. Ripon Coll Cuddesdon 87 Ch Div Sch of the Pacific (USA). **d** 90 **p** 91. C Rhyl w St Ann *St As* 90–94; V Llay 94–04; V Prestatyn 04–15; AD St As 10–15; R Colwyn and Llanelian 15–16; TV Aled Miss Area from 17; Can Cursal St As Cathl from 14. *The Vicarage, 28 Bodelwyddan Avenue, Old Colwyn, Colwyn Bay LL29 9NP* T: (01492) 478659 E: dqbellamy@yahoo.co.uk

BELLAMY, Mrs Janet Mary. b 45. Westf Coll Lon BA 66 Birm Univ BLitt 98 MEd 93 Cam Univ PGCE 67. **d** 09 **p** 10. NSM Hope Bowdler w Eaton-under-Heywood *Heref* 09–13; NSM Apedale Gp 13–15; PtO from 16. *7 The Park, Hereford HR1 1TF* T: (01432) 359308 E: revjanebellamy@gmail.com

BELLAMY, John Stephen. b 55. Jes Coll Ox BA 77 MA 81 Liv Univ PhD 06. St Jo Coll Nottm. **d** 84 **p** 85. C Allerton *Liv* 84–87; C Southport Ch Ch 87–89; Bp's Dom Chapl 89–91; V Birkdale St Jas 91–08; V Dur St Nic 08–16; V Gt Faringdon w Lt Coxwell *Ox* from 16. *The Vicarage, Coach Lane, Faringdon SN7 8AB* T: (01367) 240106 E: revsbellamy@gmail.com

BELLAMY, Mrs Norma Edna. b 44. Birm Univ CertEd 75 Open Univ BA 83. **d** 10 **p** 11. OLM Shareshill *Lich* 10–16; PtO from 16. *10 Meadowlark Close, Hednesford, Cannock WS12 1UE* T: (01543) 876809 M: 07866-431211 E: revnorma.bellamy4@gmail.com

BELLAMY, Peter Charles William. b 38. Birm Univ MA 70 PhD 79 AKC 61. **d** 62 **p** 63. C Allestree *Derby* 62–65; Chapl All SS Hosp Birm 65–73; Chapl St Pet Coll of Educn Saltley 73–78; Chapl and Lect Qu Eliz Hosp Birm 78–90; Lect Past Psychology Birm-Univ 79–92; Manager HIV Services Birm Cen HA 90–92; Commr for Public Health Cen and S Birm HA 92–96; Research Fell Birm Univ 97–02; Local Min Development Adv *Heref* 01–06; Dioc Co-ord for Min of Deliverance 06–19; PtO from 11. *7 The Park, Hereford HR1 1TF* T: (01432) 359308 E: petercbellamy@googlemail.com

BELLAMY, Quentin. See BELLAMY, David Quentin

BELLAMY, Richard William. b 62. SEITE 07. **d** 10 **p** 11. NSM Cheriton St Martin *Cant* 10–11; NSM Cheriton w Newington 11–12; NSM Folkestone Trin 12–17; TV Ashford Town from 17; Chapl Ashford Sch from 17. *Ashford Town Centre Vicarage, Church Yard, Ashford TN23 1QG* M: 07548-021371 E: r.w.bellamy@btinternet.com

BELLAMY, Stephen. See BELLAMY, John Stephen

BELLAMY-KNIGHTS, Peter George. b 41. Leic Univ BSc 63 Man Univ MSc 67 PhD 70 Lon Univ BD 03 CMath 91 FIMA 91 CEng 94 FRAeS 98. Man OLM Scheme 03. **d** 04 **p** 05. NSM Man Cathl 04–11; rtd 11; PtO *Man* from 11. *113*

Old Hall Lane, Manchester M14 6HL T: 0161-224 2702 *or* 833 2220 E: peter.bellamyknights@manchestercathedral.org

BELLENES, Peter Charles. b 49. Thurrock Coll Essex CQSW 72. Linc Th Coll 79. **d** 81 **p** 90. C Penistone *Wakef* 81–82; Hon C Liskeard, St Keyne, St Pinnock, Morval etc *Truro* 89–91; Hon C Menheniot 91–99; P-in-c Marldon *Ex* 99–03; TV Totnes w Bridgetown, Berry Pomeroy etc 03–09; rtd 09; C Duloe, Herodsfoot, Morval and St Pinnock *Truro* 15–17; R Duloe and Herodsfoot 17–18. *Little Grove, Harrow Barrow, Callington PL17 8JN* T: (01822) 833508 E: pbellenes@aol.com

BELLINGER, Richard George. b 47. Univ of Wales (Abth) BSc(Econ) 69. S Dios Minl Tr Scheme 91. **d** 94 **p** 95. NSM Guernsey St Steph *Win* 94–96; NSM Guernsey St Martin 96–09; PtO 09–14 and from 16. *La Maison des Vinaires, Rue des Vinaires, St Pierre du Bois, Guernsey GY7 9EZ* T: (01481) 63203 F: 66989 E: praisethelord@cwgsy.net

BELLIS, Huw. b 72. Univ of Wales (Lamp) BA 94. Westcott Ho Cam 96. **d** 98 **p** 99. C Merrow *Guildf* 98–02; TV Tring *St Alb* 02–08; TR from 08. *The Rectory, 2 The Limes, Station Road, Tring HP23 5NW* T: (01442) 822170 E: huw@tringteamparish.org.uk

BELOE, Mrs Jane. b 46. STETS. **d** 04 **p** 05. NSM Shedfield *Portsm* 04–06; NSM Bishop's Waltham from 06; NSM Upham from 06. *Roughay Cottage, Popes Lane, Upham, Southampton SO32 1JB* T: (01489) 860452 E: jniebeloe@btinternet.com

BELSHAW, Patricia Anne. b 47. **d** 05 **p** 06. OLM Leyland St Jas *Blackb* 05–07; NSM 07–10; NSM Darwen St Pet 10–13; rtd 13; PtO *Blackb* from 13. *9 The Laund, Leyland PR26 7XX* T: (01772) 453624 E: patriciabelshaw@yahoo.co.uk

BEMENT, Peter James. b 43. Univ of Wales (Cardiff) BA 64 PhD 69. Wycliffe Hall Ox 92. **d** 94 **p** 95. C Hubberston *St D* 94–97; V Llandeilo Fawr and Taliaris 97–08; rtd 08; PtO *St D* from 08; *Eur* from 16. *21 Chandler's Yard, Burry Port SA16 0FE* T: (01554) 833905

BENBOW, Susan Catherine. *See* TURNER, Susan Catherine

BENCE, Helen Mary. b 44. Leic Univ BA 65 PGCE 66. EMMTC 93. **d** 97 **p** 98. NSM Humberstone *Leic* 97–02; NSM Thurnby Lodge 01–02; TV Oadby 03–08; NSM Thurnby w Stoughton 08–13; NSM Cornerstone Team from 13. *The Grange, 126 Shanklin Drive, Leicester LE2 3QB* T: 0116-270 7820 E: helenbence@outlook.com

BENDALL, Robin Andrew. b 64. Qu Mary Coll Lon BA 86. SEITE 08. **d** 11 **p** 13. NSM Sandwich and Worth *Cant* from 11. *24 Delfside, Sandwich CT13 9RL* T: (01304) 617458 E: robinbendall@hotmail.com

BENDELL, David James. b 38. ACIB 74. S'wark Ord Course 84. **d** 87 **p** 88. NSM Surbiton Hill Ch Ch *S'wark* 87–03; PtO 10–14; *Guildf* 12–15; *Ely* from 17. *58 North Lodge Park, Milton, Cambridge CB24 6UB* E: bendell@talktalk.net *or* dbendell58@gmail.com

BENDREY (née BRIGNALL), Canon Elizabeth Jane. b 69. St Mary's Coll Twickenham BA 91 Heythrop Coll Lon MA 02 Cam Univ BTh 06. Westcott Ho Cam 04. **d** 06 **p** 07. C Witham *Chelmsf* 06–09; P-in-c Black Notley 09–12; R 12–16; C Panfield and Rayne 15–16; V Black Notley, Gt Notley and Rayne from 16; RD Braintree 13–18; Hon Can Chelmsf Cathl from 15. *The Rectory, 265C London Road, Black Notley, Braintree CM77 8QQ* T: (01376) 567971 M: 07940-516741 E: bethbendrey@hotmail.co.uk

BENEDICT, Brother. *See* WINSPER, Arthur William

BENFIELD, Paul John. b 56. Newc Univ LLB 77 Southn Univ BTh 89 Barrister-at-Law (Lincoln's Inn) 78. Chich Th Coll 86. **d** 89 **p** 90. C Shiremoor *Newc* 89–92; C Hexham 92–93; TV Lewes All SS, St Anne, St Mich and St Thos *Chich* 93–97; R Pulborough 97–00; V Fleetwood St Nic *Blackb* 00–18; C Burnley St Andr w St Marg and St Jas from 18; C Burnley St Mark from 18; Dioc Registrar from 18. *234A Todmorden Road, Burnley BB11 3EZ* T: (01282) 424725 E: benfield@btinternet.com

✠**BENFORD, The Rt Revd Steven Charles.** b 61. Leic Univ MB, ChB 86. NEOC 97. **d** 00 **p** 01 **c** 17. NSM Northallerton w Kirby Sigston *York* 00–04; P-in-c York St Luke 04–14; V Northolt St Jos *Lon* 14–17; Bp Dunedin New Zealand from 17. *1A Howden Street, Green Island, Dunedin 9052, New Zealand* T: (0064) (3) 425 8389 M: 22-074 9923 E: bishop.steven@calledsouth.org.nz

BENISON, Canon Brian. b 41. K Coll Lon 61. Bps' Coll Cheshunt 63. **d** 66 **p** 67. C Tynemouth Ch Ch *Newc* 66–70; C Gosforth All SS 70–72; TV Cullercoats St Geo 73–81; V Denton 81–93; V Blyth St Mary 93–04; RD Bedlington 98–03; Chapl Cheviot and Wansbeck NHS Trust 93–98; Chapl Northumbria Healthcare NHS Trust 98–04; Hon Can Newc Cathl 01–04; rtd 04; PtO *Newc* from 04. *64 Monks Wood, North Shields NE30 2UA* T: 0191-257 1631 E: brian.benison@btinternet.com

BENJAMIN, Adrian Victor. b 42. Wadh Coll Ox BA 66 MA 68. Cuddesdon Coll 66. **d** 68 **p** 69. C Gosforth All SS *Newc* 68–71; C Stepney St Dunstan and All SS *Lon* 71–75; V Friern Barnet All SS 75–12; Relig Ed ITV Oracle 83–92; rtd 12; PtO *Linc* from 14. *Carlton Cottage, 75 Church Lane, Sutton-on-Sea, Mablethorpe LN12 2JA*

✠**BENN, The Rt Revd Wallace Parke.** b 47. UCD BA 69. Trin Coll Bris 69. **d** 72 **p** 73 **c** 97. C New Ferry *Ches* 72–76; C Cheadle 76–82; V Audley *Lich* 82–87; V Harold Wood *Chelmsf* 87–97; Chapl Harold Wood Hosp Chelmsf 87–96; Area Bp Lewes *Chich* 97–12; Can and Preb Chich Cathl 97–12; rtd 12; PtO *Pet* from 13. *10 Glade Close, Burton Latimer, Kettering NN15 5YG* E: twobenns@gmail.com

BENNER, Mrs Joanna Susan. b 76. Leic Univ BA 99. Ripon Coll Cuddesdon 15. **d** 17 **p** 18. C Broughton Astley and Croft w Stoney Stanton *Leic* from 17. *The Rectory, Nock Verges, Stoney Stanton, Leicester LE9 4LR* M: 07723-308142 E: rev.jo.benner@gmail.com

BENNET, Hadley Jane. b 66. **d** 09 **p** 10. NSM Grayshott *Guildf* 09–13; Chapl Alton Coll 13–16; PtO *Guildf* from 18. *Landfall, Three Gates Lane, Haslemere GU27 2ET* T: (01428) 658166 E: hadleybennet@yahoo.co.uk

BENNET, Mark David. b 62. Roch Th Coll 62. SS Coll Cam BA 84 MA 92 Anglia Poly Univ MA 04 ACA 89. Westcott Ho Cam 98. **d** 01 **p** 02. C Chapel Allerton *Ripon* 01–05; TV Gt Parndon *Chelmsf* 05–07; P-in-c 07–09; TR 09–11; TR Thatcham Ox from 11; AD Newbury from 15. *The Rectory, 2 Rectory Gardens, Thatcham RG19 3PR* T: (01635) 867342 E: markbennet@btinternet.com

BENNETT, Alan Robert. b 31. Roch Th Coll 62. **d** 64 **p** 65. C Asterby w Goulceby *Linc* 64–67; C St Alb St Pet 67–70; R Banham *Nor* 70–72; CF 72–77; P-in-c Colchester St Mary Magd *Chelmsf* 77; TV Colchester St Leon, St Mary Magd and St Steph 77–81; R Colne Engaine 81–88; P-in-c Stoke Ferry w Wretton *Ely* 88–89; V 89–96; V Whittington 88–96; rtd 96; Hon C Wimbotsham w Stow Bardolph and Stow Bridge etc *Ely* 96–00; PtO from 00. *34 West Way, Wimbotsham, King's Lynn PE34 3PZ* T: (01366) 385958

BENNETT, Canon Alan William. b 42. Sarum Th Coll 65. **d** 68 **p** 69. C Fareham H Trin *Portsm* 68–71; C Brighton St Matthias *Chich* 71–73; C Stanmer w Falmer and Moulsecoomb 73–75; C Moulsecoomb 76; V Lower Sandown St Jo *Portsm* 76–80; V Soberton w Newtown 80–87; R Aston Clinton w Buckland and Drayton Beauchamp *Ox* 87–07; RD Wendover 94–04; Hon Can Ch Ch 03–07; rtd 07; Asst Chapl Costa Almeria and Costa Calida *Eur* from 10. *2 Chapman Close, Aylesbury HP21 8FY* T: (0034) 678 022 986 E: canonbennett@hotmail.co.uk

BENNETT, Alexander Steven Frederick. b 69. Hull Univ BA 91 Birm Univ BD 95 Cardiff Univ MTh 17. Westcott Ho Cam 93. **d** 95 **p** 96. C Whitton and Thurleston w Akenham *St E* 95–99; OGS from 99; C Oswestry *Lich* 99–01; V Oswestry H Trin 01–04; CF from 04. *c/o MOD Chaplains (Army)* T: (01264) 383430 F: 381824 E: armypadre@hotmail.com

BENNETT, Mrs Alison. b 63. Open Univ BSc 03 DipSW 99. STETS 05. **d** 08 **p** 09. C Bramshott and Liphook *Portsm* 08–12; TV Basingstoke *Win* from 12. *75 Cumberland Avenue, Basingstoke RG22 4BQ*

BENNETT, Ms Anne Yvonne. b 62. Open Univ MSc 95 Imp Coll Lon MBA 00. Cranmer Hall Dur 06. **d** 08 **p** 09. C Harton *Dur* 08–12; C Cleadon Park 09–12; V Borstal *Roch* 12–17; Chapl HM Pris Cookham Wood 12–17; TV Deptford St Jo w H Trin and Ascension *S'wark* from 17. *40 Dartmouth Row, London SE10 8AW* E: timeshift@btinternet.com

BENNETT, Anthony Richard. b 63. Sheff Univ BSc 91 Cranfield Inst of Tech MSc 92 Open Univ MBA 04. St Mellitus Coll 17. **d** 19. C Haworth and Cross Roads cum Lees *Leeds* from 19. *Swallow Barn, Sawood, Oxenhope, Keighley BD22 9SP* T: (01535) 277523 E: anthony.bennett@leeds.anglican.org

BENNETT, Arnold Ernest. b 29. K Coll Lon BD 59 AKC 53. **d** 54 **p** 55. C S w N Hayling *Portsm* 54–59; C Stevenage *St Alb* 59–64; R N w S Wootton *Nor* 64–74; V Hykeham *Linc* 74–85; V Heckfield w Mattingley and Rotherwick *Win* 85–99; rtd 99; PtO *Win* from 99. *24 Cricket Green, Hartley Wintney, Hook RG27 8PP* T: (01252) 843147

BENNETT, Avril Elizabeth Jean. b 63. UCD BEd. **d** 00 **p** 01. NSM Dublin Crumlin w Chapelizod *D & G* 00–03; NSM Tallaght from 03. *17 Ardeevin Court, Lucan, Co Dublin, Republic of Ireland* T: (00353) (1) 628 2353 E: avrilfred@eircom.net

BENNETT, Mrs Christina Mary. b 45. **d** 07 **p** 08. NSM Henfield w Shermanbury and Woodmancote *Chich* 07–18; PtO from 18. *17 Gresham Place, Henfield BN5 9QJ* T: (01273) 492222 E: revd.christina@henfield.org

BENNETT, Christopher Ian. b 75. TCD BA 98 BTh 00. CITC 97. **d** 00 **p** 01. C Larne and Inver *Conn* 00–03; C Holywood

D & D 03–09; Bp's C Belfast Titanic Quarter from 09; P-in-c Belfast St Clem 12–15. *29 Loughview Terrace, Greenisland, Carrickfergus BT38 8RE* T: (028) 9085 2895 M: 07980-885991 E: cands2000@hotmail.com

BENNETT, David Edward. b 35. Fitzw Ho Cam BA 56 MA 60 Lon Univ PGCE. Wells Th Coll 58. d 60 p 61. C Lightcliffe *Wakef* 60–62; NE Area Sec Chr Educn Movement 62–68; Gen Insp RE Nottm Co Coun 68–00; Hon C Holme Pierrepont w Adbolton *S'well* 71–85; NSM Radcliffe-on-Trent and Shelford etc 85–00; rtd 00; PtO *S'well* 04–14. *The Old Farmhouse, 65 Main Street, Gunthorpe, Nottingham NG14 7EY* T: 0115-966 3451

BENNETT, Elizabeth Mary. b 44. d 10 p 11. NSM Broughton Gifford, Gt Chalfield and Holt *Sarum* 10–14; NSM Hordle *Win* 14–19; rtd 19. *Church Cottage, Sway Road, Tiptoe, Lymington SO41 6FR* T: (01425) 627771 E: revelizabeth1@gmail.com

BENNETT, Garry Raymond. b 46. K Coll Lon 66 St Aug Coll Cant 69. d 70 p 71. C Mitcham St Mark *S'wark* 70–73; C Mortlake w E Sheen 73–75; TV 76–78; V Herne Hill St Paul 78–88; P-in-c Ruskin Park St Sav and St Matt 82–88; V Herne Hill 89; Sen Dioc Stewardship Adv *Chelmsf* 89–94; TR Southend 94–98; Dir and Chapl Herne Hill Sch *S'wark* 98–10; PtO *St D* from 00; *Sarum* from 16. *Netherton, Higher Street, Iwerne Minster, Blandford Forum DT11 8LY* T: (01747) 812151 E: phyll.bennett@btinternet.com

BENNETT, Canon Geoffrey Kenneth. b 56. Ex Univ MA 01. Oak Hill Th Coll. d 89 p 90. C Ipswich St Matt *St E* 89–92; R St Ruan w St Grade and Landewednack *Truro* 92–98; V Budock from 98; P-in-c Mawnan 03–13; RD Carnmarth S from 12; Hon Can Truro Cathl from 14. *The Vicarage, Merry Mit Meadow, Budock Water, Falmouth TR11 5DW* T: (01326) 376422 E: g.k.bennett@amserve.net *or* rev.bennett@talk21.com

BENNETT, Canon George Edward. b 51. Univ of Wales (Abth) BA 72. St Steph Ho Ox 73. d 76 p 77. C Clifton All SS w Tyndalls Park *Bris* 76–78; C Clifton All SS w St Jo 78–82; Chapl Newbury and Sandleford Hosps 82–93; TV Newbury *Ox* 82–93; V Llwynderw *S & B* 93–06; V Newton St Pet 06–16; AD Clyne 98–12; Hon Can Brecon Cathl 00–02; Can Res Brecon Cathl 02–16; rtd 16; PtO *S & B* from 16. *20 Dol y Coed, Dunvant, Swansea SA2 7UG* E: bennettgandr@gmail.com

BENNETT, Handel Henry Cecil. b 33. Cant Sch of Min 79. d 82 p 83. NSM St Margarets-at-Cliffe w Westcliffe etc *Cant* 82–85; Dir Holy Land Chr Tours 85–94; Holy Land Consultant F T Tours 95–96; Sen Travel Consultant Raymond Cook Chr Tours from 96; PtO *St Alb* 85–99; *Ex* 99–18. *Camps Bay, 2 Victoria Road, Sidmouth EX10 8TZ* T: (01395) 514211

BENNETT, Helen Anne. *See* EDWARDS, Helen Anne

BENNETT, Herbert Montagu. b 63. Dur Univ BA 17. SEITE 13. d 16 p 17. NSM Kemp Town St Mary *Chich* from 16. *6 Southover Manor House, Southover High Street, Lewes BN7 1HT* T: (01273) 470341 E: revherbert.bennett@gmail.com

BENNETT, Ivan. b 64. Qu Coll Birm 17. d 19. NSM Emmaus Par Team *Leic* from 19. *102 Dumbleton Avenue, Leicester LE3 2EH* T: 0116-223 9730 E: ivanbennettsaysgodlovesyou@gmail.com

BENNETT, James Duncan. b 58. St Aug Coll of Th BA 17. d 17 p 18. NSM Slade Green *Roch* 17–19; C 19; P-in-c from 19. *59 Hillingdon Road, Bexleyheath DA7 6LN* T: (01322) 553421 M: 07787-292094 E: jdbbarnehurst@aol.com

BENNETT, John David. b 58. Ox Univ BA 79 MA 83. Westcott Ho Cam 81. d 83 p 84. C Taunton St Andr *B & W* 83–86; Chapl Trowbridge Coll *Sarum* 86–90; Asst P Studley 86–90; V Yeovil H Trin *B & W* 90–95; R Yeovil H Trin w Barwick 95–02; R Sprowston w Beeston *Nor* 02–10; RD Nor N 05–10; V Spalding St Mary and St Nic *Linc* from 10; P-in-c Spalding St Paul from 10. *The Parsonage, 1 Halmer Gate, Spalding PE11 2DR* T: (01775) 719668 E: jdbennett@gmail.com

BENNETT, John Dudley. b 44. Open Univ BA 87 Lanc Univ MA 92 Huddersfield Univ PGCE 04. Coll of Resurr Mirfield 08. d 09 p 09. NSM Bolton Abbey *Bradf* 09–14; rtd 14; PtO *Leeds* from 15; *Eur* from 15. *Honeysuckle Cottage, The Green, Linton, Skipton BD23 5HJ* T: (01756) 753763 E: brj.linton@virgin.net

BENNETT, John Seccombe. b 59. Wye Coll Lon BSc 81 Leic Poly CertEd 84. Trin Coll Bris. d 00 p 01. C Llanrhian w Llanhywel and Carnhedryn etc *St D* 00–01; C Dewisland 01–02; TV 02–11; V Cardigan w Mwnt and Y Ferwig w Llangoedmor 11–18; V Bro Teifi from 18; Min Can St D Cathl from 00; AD Cemais and Sub-Aeron from 14. *The Vicarage, Maesydderwen, Cardigan SA43 1PE* T: (01239) 615466 E: jsbkbennett@btinternet.com

BENNETT, Mark Ian. b 61. K Coll Cam BA 83 MA 86. Trin Coll Bris BA 94. d 94 p 95. C Selly Park St Steph and St Wulstan *Birm* 94–97; C Harrow Trin St Mich *Lon* 97–99; Hon C Redland *Bris* 99–00; TV Drypool *York* 00–06; V Gee Cross

Ches 06–16; V Shenley Green *Birm* from 16. *49 Shenley Green, Birmingham B29 4HH* E: mark@thebennetts.org.uk

BENNETT, Mark Stephen. b 66. Cant Univ (NZ) MusB 89 Cant Ch Ch Univ BA 14. SEITE 07. d 10 p 11. NSM Staplehurst *Cant* 10–12; Chapl Dulwich Prep Sch Cranbrook 10–12; Chapl St Edm Sch Cant from 13; Hon Min Can Cant Cathl 11–12 and from 18; Min Can 13–18. *2 The Close, St Thomas' Hill, Canterbury CT2 8HS* M: 07709-376668 E: chaplain@stedmunds.org.uk

BENNETT, Michael John. b 43. AKC 66. St Boniface Warminster 66. d 67 p 68. C Chester le Street *Dur* 67–71; C Portland All SS w St Pet *Sarum* 71–74; V Portland St Jo 74–85; Chapl Portland Hosp Weymouth 74–85; R Alveley and Quatt *Heref* 85–92; Dep Chapl HM YOI Glen Parva 93–95; TV Wrexham *St As* 95–99; V Llansantffraid-ym-Mechain and Llanfechain 99–05; C Rhyl w St Ann 05–09; rtd 09; Hon C Redmarley D'Abitot, Bromesberrow, Pauntley etc *Glouc* 09–12; PtO from 15. *65 Robert Raikes Avenue, Tuffley, Gloucester GL4 0HL* T: (01452) 301337 E: sheilabennett@btinternet.com

BENNETT, Nigel John. b 47. Oak Hill Th Coll 66. d 71 p 72. C Tonbridge St Steph *Roch* 71–75; C Heatherlands St Jo *Sarum* 75–79; P-in-c Kingham w Churchill, Daylesford and Sarsden *Ox* 79; R 80–85; Chapl Blue Coat Sch Reading 85–08; rtd 08; PtO *Ox* 08–09; Hon C Southsea St Jude *Portsm* 09–14; PtO from 14. *19 Ashburton Road, Southsea PO5 3JS* T: (023) 9242 1463 E: nigelbennett@virginmedia.com

BENNETT, Paul. b 55. Southn Univ BTh 94. St Steph Ho Ox 95. d 97 p 98. C Willingdon *Chich* 97–00; C Hangleton 00–04; R Letchworth *St Alb* 04–18; rtd 18; PtO *Ely* from 19. *162 Cavalry Park, March PE15 9DL* E: revpaulbennett@ntlworld.com

BENNETT, Paul William. b 61. Linc Th Coll 95. d 95 p 96. C Thornton-le-Fylde *Blackb* 95–00; V Wesham 00–03; P-in-c Treales 00–03; V Wesham and Treales 03–08; Chapl Dunkirk Miss to Seafarers *Eur* 08–14; P-in-c Meir *Lich* 14–17; P-in-c Longton 14–17; R Longton and Meir from 17. *The Rectory, Rutland Road, Stoke-on-Trent ST3 1EH* T: (01782) 595098 E: mowbreck@aol.com

BENNETT, Miss Rachel Elizabeth. b 56. W Sussex Inst of HE CertEd 79. d 04. NSM Littlehampton and Wick *Chich* 04–05; C Durrington 05–07; Chapl Worthing and Southlands Hosps NHS Trust 08–09; Chapl W Sussex Hosps NHS Foundn Trust from 09. *Worthing Hospital, Lyndhurst Road, Worthing BN11 2DH* T: (01903) 205111 M: 07810-350098 E: rachel.bennett3@tesco.net *or* rachel.bennett@wsht.nhs.uk

BENNETT, Robert Geoffrey. b 43. FCA. d 05 p 06. OLM Woking St Jo *Guildf* 05–13; PtO from 13. *10 Barricane, Woking GU21 7RB* T: (01483) 722832 E: robgbennett@tiscali.co.uk

BENNETT, Roger Sherwood. b 35. Nottm Univ BA 56. Wells Th Coll 58. d 59 p 60. C Mansfield Woodhouse *S'well* 59–60; C Spalding St Mary and St Nic *Linc* 60–63; V Gedney 63–69; Chapl RNR 65–68; Chapl RN 69–90; V Amport, Grateley, Monxton and Quarley *Win* 90–95; rtd 96; PtO *Win* 96–12 and 16–19. *5 Ashlawn Gardens, Winchester Road, Andover SP10 2EU* T: (01264) 351137

BENNETT, Sarah Grace. b 91. Ches Univ BTh 13. Qu Foundn Birm MA 19. d 19. C Glascote and Stonydelph *Lich* from 19. *9 Friars Walk, Tamworth B77 2FH*

BENNETT, Stephen. *See* BENNETT, Mark Stephen

BENNETT, Ms Toni Elizabeth. b 56. Worc Coll of Educn BA 81 Sheff Poly 87. St Jo Coll Nottm MA 94. d 96 p 97. C Heanor *Derby* 96–00; TV Bedworth *Cov* 00–08; R Montgomery and Forden and Llandyssil *St As* 08–17; P-in-c Pool Miss Area 18; AD Pool 10–15; rtd 18. *3A Runnings Park, Croft Bank, Malvern WR14 4DU* E: tonibrev@gmail.com

BENNETT, William Leslie. b 52. TCD Div Sch. d 90 p 91. C Carrickfergus *Conn* 90–93; I Lisnaskea *Clogh* 93–00; I Newcastle w Newtownmountkennedy and Calary *D & G* from 00. *The Rectory, Church Lane, Newcastle, Greystones, Co Wicklow, Republic of Ireland* T: (00353) (1) 281 9300 M: 87-948 0317 E: bennettwilliam1@gmail.com

BENNETT-SHAW, Miss Anne Elizabeth. b 38. d 02 p 03. OLM Upper Wylye Valley *Sarum* 02–08; rtd 08; PtO *Sarum* from 08. *5 Hospital of St John, Heytesbury, Warminster BA12 0HW* T: (01985) 840339 E: revannebennettshaw@btinternet.com

BENNETTS, Ms Rachel Mary. b 69. Homerton Coll Cam BEd 91. Trin Coll Bris BA 01. d 02 p 03. C Wroughton *Bris* 02–06; TV N Farnborough *Guildf* 06–17; Chapl Farnborough Sixth Form Coll 07–17; Prior Community of the Tree of Life from 17. *The Community of the Tree of Life, St Martin's House, 7 Peacock Lane, Leicester LE1 5PZ* M: 07749-045449 E: rachelmbennetts@gmail.com *or* rob@leicestertreeoflife.org

BENNIE, Stanley James Gordon. b 43. Edin Univ MA 65. Coll of Resurr Mirfield 66. d 68 p 69. C Ashington *Newc* 68–70;

Prec St Andr Cathl Inverness *Mor* 70–74; Itinerant Priest 74–81; R Portsoy *Ab* 81–84; R Buckie 81–84; R Stornoway *Arg* 84–10; R Eoropaidh 84–95; rtd 10. *St Lennan, 13A Scotland Street, Stornoway HS1 2JN* T: (01851) 703259 M: 07768-660612 E: gm4ptq@btinternet.com

BENNISON, Andrew Mark Kinsey. b 92. Trin Coll Ox BA 13 MA 17 Lon Inst of Educn PGCE 14. Ripon Coll Cuddesdon BA 18. **d** 19. C Burnage St Nic *Man* from 19. *16 Francis Road, Manchester M20 4XP* M: 07852-864627 E: andrew.mk.bennison@gmail.com

BENNISON, Philip Owen. b 42. Dur Univ BA 64. Coll of Resurr Mirfield 64. **d** 66 **p** 67. C Guisborough *York* 66–67; C S Bank 67–71; C Thornaby on Tees St Paul 71–72; TV Thornaby on Tees 72–74; R Skelton in Cleveland 74–78; R Upleatham 75–78; Chapl Freeman Hosp Newc 78–84; V Ashington *Newc* 84–93; Chapl N Tees Health NHS Trust Stockton-on-Tees 93–98; Chapl N Tees and Hartlepool NHS Trust 99–02; P-in-c Newton Flowery Field *Ches* 02–10; P-in-c Hyde St Thos 02–10; rtd 10; PtO *York* from 10; *Dur* from 12. *62 Glaisdale Road, Yarm TS15 9RP* T: (01642) 646624 M: 07740-852832 E: philip_bennison@hotmail.com

BENOY, Canon Stephen Michael. b 66. Clare Coll Cam BA 87 MA 90. Trin Coll Bris BA 93. **d** 96 **p** 97. C New Malden and Coombe *S'wark* 96–02; Kingston Borough Youth Project 00–02; V Kettering Ch the King *Pet* 02–11; Dir of Ords and Voc from 11; Dir Voc and Formation from 17; Can Pet Cathl from 13. *Diocese of Peterborough, Bouverie Court, 6 The Lakes, Bedford Road, Northampton NN4 7YD* T: (01604) 887047 E: steve.benoy@peterborough-diocese.org.uk

BENSKIN, David Peter. b 53. Qu Coll Birm 11. **d** 13 **p** 14. C Heart of England *Cov* 13–17; P-in-c Aston Cantlow and Wilmcote w Billesley from 17; Asst Chapl Rainsbrook Secure Tr Cen 13–15; Chapl 15–18. *The Vicarage, Church Road, Wilmcote, Stratford-upon-Avon CV37 9XD* T: (01789) 263216 E: thebenskins@gmail.com

BENSON, Ashley Dawn. *See* ROSS, Ashley Dawn

BENSON, Christopher Hugh. b 53. Bath Academy of Art BA 75 Keble Coll Ox BA 78 MA 87. Chich Th Coll 78. **d** 80 **p** 81. C Heavitree w Ex St Paul 80–83; P-in-c Broadclyst 83–85; TV Pinhoe and Broadclyst 85–90; V Kingsteignton and Teigngrace 90–08; Chapl Plymouth Univ 92–95; RD Newton Abbot and Ipplepen 01–07; C Baslow w Curbar and Stoney Middleton *Derby* 08–11; C Ashford w Sheldon and Longstone 08–11; V Longstone, Curbar and Stony Middleton 11–14; rtd 14. *1 Leighon Cottages, Manaton, Newton Abbot TQ13 9UP* T: (01629) 640257 E: chbfiftythree@gmail.com

BENSON, David. *See* BENSON, John David

BENSON, Gareth Neil. b 47. Jordan Hill Coll Glas TCert 80. St And NSM Tr Scheme 77. **d** 81 **p** 82. NSM Glenrothes *St And* 81–88; NSM Kirkcaldy 88–04; P-in-c 04–12; NSM Kinghorn 88–04; P-in-c 04–12; rtd 12; PtO *St And* from 12. *129 Waverley Drive, Glenrothes KY6 2LZ* T: (01592) 769869 E: fathergareth@btinternet.com

BENSON, The Ven George Patrick (Paddy). b 49. Ch Ch Ox BA 70 Lon Univ BD 77 Open Univ MPhil 94. All Nations Chr Coll 78 St Jo Coll Nottm 89. **d** 91 **p** 92. C Upton (Overchurch) *Ches* 91–95; V Barnston 95–11; RD Wirral N 98–08; Hon Can Ches Cathl 09–11; Adn Heref 11–18; rtd 18. *26 West Park Drive, Leeds LS16 5BL* T: 0113-450 7856 E: muhunjia@aol.com

BENSON, Mrs Hilary Christine. b 51. Man Univ BA 72 Hughes Hall Cam PGCE 73. Trin Coll Bris 81. dss 84 **d** 87 **p** 94. Starbeck *Ripon* 84–86; Birm St Martin w Bordesley St Andr 86–91; NSM 87–91; NSM Brandwood 91–97; Chapl Birm Univ 92–97; Chapl St Edw Birm 00–07; Chapl Qu Anne's Sch Caversham 00–13; rtd 14; PtO *Derby* from 14. *31 Dale Road, Buxton SK17 6LN* T: (01298) 213519 E: hilarybenson@icloud.com

BENSON, John David. b 36. St Aid Birkenhead 58. **d** 61 **p** 62. C Kingston upon Hull St Martin *York* 61–65; C Marfleet 65–68; V Ingleby Greenhow 68–72; P-in-c Kildale 68–72; Asst Youth Chapl 68–72; Dioc Youth Chapl *Sheff* 72–78; V Thorne 78–91; V Totley 91–98; rtd 98; PtO *Sheff* from 98. *14 Ash Hill Crescent, Hatfield, Doncaster DN7 6HY* T: (01302) 846359 E: david7.benson@homecall.co.uk

BENSON, Canon John Patrick. b 52. Ch Coll Cam BA 73 MA 76 PhD 76. Trin Coll Bris 78. **d** 81 **p** 82. C Walmley Birm 81–84; C Chadkirk *Ches* 84–86; V St Geo Singapore 87–95; Dir of Tr 95–01; V Chpl of Resurr 01–07; Hon Can Singapore 96–07; Dean Cambodia 93–05; Dean Laos 98–00; rtd 07; PtO *Ches* from 09. *Cherry Trees, Queens Park Road, Chester CH4 7AD* T: (01244) 671170 E: johnpbenson@gmail.com

BENSON, John Patrick. b 51. Univ of Wales (Ban) BSc 72. Trin Coll Bris 83. **d** 85 **p** 86. C Stoke Damerel *Ex* 85–88; P-in-c Petrockstowe, Petersmarland, Merton and Huish 88; TV Shebbear, Buckland Filleigh, Sheepwash etc 89–94;

RD Torrington 93–94; P-in-c Newport, Bishops Tawton and Tawstock 94–97; TV Barnstaple 97–07; R Knockholt w Halstead *Roch* 07–16; rtd 16; PtO *Heref* from 17. *The Mill House, Monkland, Leominster HR6 9DB* T: (01568) 720035 M: 07982-627206 E: john.benson3@btinternet.com

BENSON, Nicholas Henry. b 53. Man Univ BSc 75 Leeds Univ MSc 77. Trin Coll Bris 81. **d** 84 **p** 85. C Starbeck *Ripon* 84–86; C Birm St Martin w Bordesley St Andr 86–91; Chapl to the Markets 86–91; V Brandwood 91–97; PtO *Ox* 99–01; NSM Reading St Jo 01–14; PtO *Derby* from 14. *31 Dale Road, Buxton SK17 6LN* T: (01298) 213519

BENSON, Nigel Anthony Stewart. b 58. St Hild Coll 18. **d** 19. NSM Haxby and Wigginton *York* from 19. *28 Oaken Grove, Haxby, York YO32 3QZ* E: revnas@btinternet.com

BENSON, Patrick. *See* BENSON, George Patrick

BENSON, Philip Richard. b 85. QUB BTh 06 MTh 09 TCD MTh 15. **d** 14 **p** 15. Finaghy *Conn* 14–15; C Larne and Inver 15–18; P-in-c Kilwaughter and Cairncastle w Craigy Hill from 18. *9 Oakdene, Larne BT40 2FD* M: 07850-345156

BENSON, Philip Steven. b 59. Ulster Univ BSc 81 LLCM 80. S Dios Minl Tr Scheme 88. **d** 92 **p** 93. Producer Relig Broadcasting Dept BBC 91–94; NSM W Ealing St Jo w St Jas *Lon* 92–94; Relig Progr Producer BBC Man from 94. *6 Sudlow Barns, Sudlow Lane, Tabley, Knutsford WA16 0TN* T: (01565) 652513 F: 641695 E: steven@benson5.co.uk

BENSON, Mrs Rachel Candia. b 43. TCD MA 66 Lon Univ PGCE 67. S'wark Ord Course 84. **d** 87 **p** 94. NSM Putney St Marg *S'wark* 87–97; NSM Sand Hutton and Whitwell w Crambe, Flaxton and Foston *York* 97–07; PtO from 07. *Grange Farm, Westow, York YO60 7NJ* T: (01653) 658296 F: 658456 E: rachelbenson43@gmail.com

BENSON, Richard John. b 55. Birm Coll of Educn CertEd 78. Ripon Coll Cuddesdon 92. **d** 94 **p** 95. C Alford w Rigsby *Linc* 94–97; R Partney Gp 97–12; V Taddington, Chelmorton and Monyash etc *Derby* from 12. *The Vicarage, Church Street, Monyash, Bakewell DE45 1JH* T: (01629) 812234 E: parson_benson@yahoo.co.uk

BENSON, Steven. *See* BENSON, Philip Steven

BENT, David Michael. b 55. Leeds Univ BSc 77. Trin Coll Bris BA 94. **d** 96 **p** 97. C Gorleston St Andr *Nor* 96–00; TR Brinsworth w Catcliffe and Treeton *Sheff* 00–03; TR Rivers Team 03–19; P-in-c Walgrave w Hannington and Wold and Scaldwell *Pet* from 19. *The Rectory, Lower Green, Walgrave, Northampton NN6 9QF* E: davidbent99@btinternet.com

BENT, Helen Margaret. b 56. Sheff Univ BMus 77 Trent Poly PGCE 78 Suffolk Poly BA 00. EAMTC 97. **d** 98 **p** 99. C Gorleston St Mary *Nor* 98–00; C Brightside w Wincobank *Sheff* 00–04; Bp's Adv in Music and Worship 05–15; Hd Minl Tr RSCM from 15; C Rivers Team *Sheff* 15–19; Hon Can Sheff Cathl 15–19; C Walgrave w Hannington and Wold and Scaldwell *Pet* from 19. *The Rectory, Lower Green, Walgrave, Northampton NN6 9QF* E: helen@thebents.co.uk

BENT, The Very Revd Michael Charles. b 31. Kelham Th Coll 51. **d** 55 **p** 56. C Wellingborough St Mary *Pet* 55–60; New Zealand 60–85; Adn Taranaki 76–85; Dean H Trin Cathl Suva Fiji 85–89; Can St Pet Cathl Hamilton New Zealand 90–94; Papua New Guinea 94–96; New Zealand from 96. *34 Brooklands Road, New Plymouth 4310, New Zealand* T: (0064) (6) 753 5507 E: miro@clear.net.nz

BENTALL, Canon Jill Margaret. b 44. MCSP 66. S Dios Minl Tr Scheme 91. **d** 94 **p** 95. NSM Knights Enham *Win* 94–02; C Andover w Foxcott 02–09; P-in-c Pastrow 09–14; RD Andover 06–10; Hon Can Win Cathl 11–14; rtd 14; PtO *Win* from 14; *Sarum* from 15. *2 Lodge Close, Andover SP10 3EY*

BENTHAM, Philip John (Ben). b 55. Hull Univ BA 83 PGCE 85. Trin Coll Bris MA 96. **d** 96 **p** 97. C Wrockwardine Deanery *Lich* 96–00; P-in-c Chipinge and Chimanimani Zimbabwe 00–03; Chapl Viña del Mar St Pet Chile 03–07; Chapl Bethany Sch Goudhurst 08–13; Chapl Dur Sch 13–14; C Stockton Country Par *Dur* 15–16; V Wye Brooks Benefice *Heref* from 17. *The Vicarage, Llangrove, Ross-on-Wye HR9 6EZ* T: (01989) 770454 M: 07437-447054 E: benbentham@yahoo.co.uk

✠**BENTLEY, The Rt Revd David Edward.** b 35. Leeds Univ BA 56. Westcott Ho Cam 58. **d** 60 **p** 61 **c** 86. C Bris St Ambrose Whitehall 60–62; C Guildf H Trin w St Mary 62–66; R Headley All SS 66–73; R Esher 73–86; RD Emly 77–82; Hon Can Guildf Cathl 80–86; Chmn Dioc Coun Soc Resp 80–86; Suff Bp Lynn *Nor* 86–93; Chmn Cand Cttee ACCM 87–91; ABM 91–93; Bp Glouc 93–03; rtd 04; Hon Asst Bp Lich from 04; PtO *Cov* 04–08. *19 Gable Croft, Lichfield WS14 9RY* T: (01543) 419376 E: dandebentley@talktalk.net

BENTLEY, Frances Rymer. *See* COCKER, Frances Rymer

BENTLEY, The Ven Frank William Henry. b 34. AKC 57. **d** 58 **p** 59. C Shepton Mallet *B & W* 58–62; R Kingsdon w Podymore-Milton 62–66; P-in-c Yeovilton 62–66; P-in-c

Babcary 64–66; V Wiveliscombe 66–76; RD Tone 73–76; V St Jo in Bedwardine *Worc* 76–84; P-in-c Worc St Mich 82–84; RD Martley and Worc W 80–84; Hon Can Worc Cathl 81–84; Adn Worc and Can Res Worc Cathl 84–99; rtd 99; PtO *Worc* from 04; Chapl to The Queen 94–04. *Willow Cottage, Station Road, Fladbury, Pershore WR10 2QW* T: (01386) 861847 E: f.bentley123@btinternet.com

BENTLEY, The Ven Ian Robert. b 55. Sheff Univ BA 76 Sheff City Poly PGCE 78. Cranmer Hall Dur 93. **d** 95 **p** 96. C Mattishall w Mattishall Burgh, Welborne etc *Nor* 95–98; R Ditchingham, Hedenham, Broome, Earsham etc 98–06; V Oulton Broad 06–17; RD Lothingland 10–14; R Nor St Pet Mancroft w St Jo Maddermarket 17–18; Adn Lynn from 18; Hon Can Nor Cathl 10–16; Chapter Can from 16. *Holly Tree House, Whitwell Road, Sparham, Norwich NR9 5PN* T: (01362) 688032 E: archdeacon.lynn@dioceseofnorwich.org

BENTLEY, Ian Ronald. b 51. BA 79. Oak Hill Th Coll 76. **d** 79 **p** 80. C Northwood Em *Lon* 79–85; C St Marylebone All So w SS Pet and Jo 85–88; C Langham Place All So 88–91; V Eynsham and Cassington *Ox* 91–05; V Chineham *Win* 05–17; rtd 17; PtO *Glouc* from 18. *22 Fosseway Avenue, Moreton-in-Marsh GL56 0EA* E: ibentley4@googlemail.com

BENTLEY, Lesley. b 55. Univ of Wales (Lamp) BA 76 RMN 80. St Jo Coll Nottm MTh 82. **dss** 82 **d** 87 **p** 94. Mickleover St Jo *Derby* 82–84; Thornton *Liv* 84–89; Par Dn 87–89; Dir Diaconal Mins 89–92; Par Dn Farnworth 92–94; C 94–95; V Westbrook St Phil 95–01; Hon Can Liv Cathl 99–01; V Bilton *Ripon* 01–03; TR 03–09; Initial Minl Educn Officer 03–09; Dir Min Development *Lich* 09–10; Dir Min from 10. *The Vicarage, Salt Lane, Salt, Stafford ST18 0BW* T: (01889) 508066 E: lesley_bentley@btinternet.com

BENTLEY, Canon Paul. b 48. Sarum & Wells Th Coll. **d** 93 **p** 94. C Ex St Dav 93–96; P-in-c Marlpool *Derby* 96–01; V 01–02; Chapl Derbyshire Community Health Services 96–00; Chapl Amber Valley Primary Care Trust 00–02; Chapl Mansfield Distr Primary Care Trust 02–13; P-in-c Mansfield St Lawr *S'well* 13–17; Hon Can S'well Minster 11–17; rtd 17; PtO *S'well* from 18. *27 Sandringham Road, Mansfield Woodhouse, Mansfield NG19 9HN* E: revpaulb@aol.com

BENTLEY, Paul Nicholas. b 80. Man Univ BA 03. St Jo Coll Nottm MTh 14. **d** 14 **p** 15. C Frankby w Greasby *Ches* 14–17; R Birkenhead Priory from 17. *10 Cavendish Road, Birkenhead CH41 8AX* M: 07967-672778 E: paulnbentley@gmail.com

BENTON-EVANS, Martin James William. b 69. K Coll Lon BA 90 Anglia Poly Univ PGCE 97. Ripon Coll Cuddesdon BTh 03. **d** 03 **p** 04. C Ivybridge w Harford *Ex* 03–06; P-in-c St Teath *Truro* 06–12; P-in-c Lanteglos by Camelford w Advent 06–12; Chapl Sir Jas Smith's Community Sch Camelford 10–12; R Peebles *Edin* 12–18; R Innerleithen 12–18; P-in-c Glas E End from 18. *38 Old Gartloch Road, Gartcosh, Glasgow G69 8ET* M: 07702-842727 E: jimbentonevans@gmail.com

BENWELL, Michael Patrick. b 55. Jes Coll Cam BA 77 Glas Univ PhD 90. Sarum & Wells Th Coll BTh 92. **d** 92 **p** 93. C Eastleigh *Win* 92–95; Chapl Leeds Metrop Univ *Ripon* 95–99; TV Seacroft 99–06; TR 06–14; *Leeds* from 14; AD Whitkirk *Ripon* 09–14; *Leeds* 14–16. *St Luke's Vicarage, Stanks Lane North, Leeds LS14 5AS* T: 0113-273 1302 E: benwell@ndirect.co.uk

BENYON, Oliver William Yates. b 80. Ox Brookes Univ BA 02. Wycliffe Hall Ox 13. **d** 15 **p** 16. C Cambridge H Trin *Ely* from 15. *42 Pretoria Road, Cambridge CB4 1HE* M: 07739-710947 E: olibenyon@me.com

BENYON, Thomas Yates. b 74. Edin Univ MA 98 Lon Inst of Educn PGCE 99. Trin Coll Bris. **d** 15 **p** 16. C Peasedown St John w Wellow and Foxcote etc *B & W* 15–19; C Stoke Gifford *Bris* from 19. *21 Hermitage Wood Road, Bristol BS16 1BF* M: 07725-037435 E: tybenyon@mac.com

BENZIES, Neil Graham. b 43. Bede Coll Dur. Cranmer Hall Dur 93. **d** 95 **p** 96. NSM Stockton St Pet *Dur* 95–08; PtO from 15. *62 Fairwell Road, Stockton-on-Tees TS19 7HX* T: (01642) 582322

BERDINNER, Clifford. b 24. SS Mark & Jo Univ Coll Plymouth BA 88 Ex Univ MPhil 95. **d** 64 **p** 65. C Leic St Pet 64–67; R Heather 67–72; NSM Totnes and Berry Pomeroy *Ex* 86–91; NSM Totnes, Bridgetown and Berry Pomeroy etc 91–94; rtd 89; PtO *Ex* 89–09. *Little Croft, 30 Droridge, Dartington, Totnes TQ9 6JQ* T: (01803) 732518

BERESFORD, Charles Edward. b 45. St Jo Coll Nottm. **d** 86 **p** 87. C Bushbury *Lich* 86–90; TV Glascote and Stonydelph 90–98; TR N Wingfield, Clay Cross and Pilsley *Derby* 98–11; rtd 11. *8 Spring Close, Belper DE56 2TY* T: (01773) 826519 E: charles.belper@uwclub.net

BERESFORD, David Charles. b 56. Leeds Univ BA 09 ACIB 93. Coll of Resurr Mirfield 07. **d** 09 **p** 10. C Lancing w Coombes *Chich* 09–11; C Bury w Houghton and Coldwaltham and Hardham 11–13; P-in-c Marsh Farm *St Alb* 13–16; Hon

C Wilmington Ch Ch USA from 16. *507 East Buck Road, Wilmington DE 19807, USA* E: davidberesford@gmail.com

BERESFORD, Patrick Larner. b 53. Lon Bible Coll BA 77. **d** 10 **p** 11. NSM Weston super Mare St Jo *B & W* 10–12; TV Horsham *Chich* 12–18; rtd 18; PtO *Guildf* from 18. *128 Cranleigh Mead, Cranleigh GU7 6JX* E: paddyjfj04@btinternet.com

BERESFORD, Peter Marcus de la Poer. b 49. Cranmer Hall Dur 74. **d** 77 **p** 78. C Walney Is *Carl* 77–80; C Netherton 80–83; TV Wednesfield *Lich* 83–88; TV Rugby *Cov* 88–97; Chapl Rugby Hosps 88–97; R Barby w Kilsby *Pet* 97–14; rtd 14; PtO *Cov* from 15. *The Barn, 41C School Street, Long Lawford, Rugby CV23 9AT* T: (01788) 570229 E: petermberesford@hotmail.co.uk

BERESFORD-PEIRSE, Mark de la Poer. b 45. Qu Coll Birm 73. **d** 76 **p** 77. C Garforth *Ripon* 76–79; C Beeston 79–83; V Barton and Manfield w Cleasby 83–90; V Pannal w Beckwithshaw 90–01; Dioc Chapl MU 91–98; R W Tanfield and Well w Snape and N Stainley 01–09; rtd 09; PtO *Leeds* from 17. *15 Eastfield Avenue, Richmond DL10 4NH* T: (01748) 826649 E: b_peirse@hotmail.com

BERESFORD-WEBB, Miss Petra May Elizabeth Broomé. b 66. Cardiff Univ BTh 14 NE Wales Inst of HE CertEd 01. St Mich Coll Llan 09. **d** 12 **p** 13. C E Radnor *S & B* 12–14; C Blaenau Irfon 14–15; P-in-c from 16; C Irfon Valley 14–15; P-in-c from 16; P-in-c Upper Wye from 16; Bp's Officer for Min to Children and Families from 14. *9 Cae Nant, Newbridge-on-Wye, Llandrindod Wells LD1 6LQ* T: (01597) 860842 M: 07966-799546 E: petra.beresfordwebb@yahoo.com

BERG, John Russell. b 36. Sarum Th Coll 57. **d** 60 **p** 61. C Ipswich St Aug *St E* 60–64; C Whitton and Thurleston w Akenham 64–65; Miss to Seafarers 65–04; Hong Kong 65–68; Japan 68–04; rtd 01; PtO *St E* from 04. *23 Old Maltings Court, Old Maltings Approach, Melton, Woodbridge IP12 1AE* T: (01394) 383748 E: johnberg270@gmail.com

BERGQUIST, Anders Karim. b 58. Peterho Cam BA 79 MA 83 PhD 90. St Steph Ho Ox BA 85 MA 90. **d** 86 **p** 87. C Abbots Langley *St Alb* 86–89; Hon C Cambridge St Mary Less *Ely* 89–97; Tutor Westcott Ho Cam 89–95; Vice-Prin 95–97; Can Res St Alb 97–02; Minl Development Officer 97–02; V St John's Wood *Lon* from 02. *St John's House, St John's Wood High Street, London NW8 7NE* T: (020) 7722 4378 or 7586 3864 E: vicar.stjohnswood@london.anglican.org

BERK, Dennis Bryan Alban. b 65. Wheaton Coll Illinois BA 86 Toronto Univ MDiv 90. Lanc Th Sem Penn DMin 98. **d** 90 **p** 91. C Brockville St Pet Canada 90–92; C Tamworth 92–94; NSM Reading St Mary USA 94–96; R 96–01; Zambia 03–06; USA 06–09; R Ellon *Ab* from 18; R Cruden Bay from 18; CR 09–18. *The Rectory, 1 South Side, Ellon AB41 9NP* T: (01358) 720366 M: 07717-804481 E: rector@stmarystjames.org.uk

BERKSHIRE, Archdeacon of. *Vacant*

BERMUDA, Archdeacon of. *See* DOUGHTY, The Ven Andrew William

BERMUDA, Bishop of. *See* DILL, The Rt Revd Nicholas Bayard Botolf

BERNARDI, Frederick John. b 33. Chich Th Coll 55. **d** 58 **p** 59. C Blackb St Luke 58–60; C Ribbleton 60–63; V Brinsley w Underwood *S'well* 63–66; V St Leon Barbados 67–71; V Sparkbrook St Agatha *Birm* 71–77; P-in-c Sparkbrook Ch Ch 73–75; V Haywards Heath St Wilfrid *Chich* 77–80; TR 80–87; Chapl Madrid *Eur* 87–90; NSM Tooting All SS *S'wark* 90–91; V Hanger Hill Ascension and W Twyford St Mary *Lon* 91–95; rtd 95; PtO *Chich* from 95. *42 Woodlands Way, Southwater, Horsham RH13 9HZ* T: (01403) 733335 E: stella@knights-templar.org.uk

BERNERS-WILSON, Preb Angela Veronica Isabel. b 54. St Andr Univ MTheol 76. Cranmer Hall Dur 77. **dss** 79 **d** 87 **p** 94. Southgate Ch Ch *Lon* 79–82; St Marylebone Ch Ch 82–84; Ind Chapl 82–84; Chapl Thames Poly *S'wark* 84–91; Chapl Bris Univ 91–95; C Bris St Mich and St Paul 94–95; P-in-c Colerne w N Wraxall 95–01; R 01–04; Chapl Bath Univ *B & W* 04–16; R Quantock Towers from 16; Preb Wells Cathl from 09. *The Rectory, 11 Trendle Lane, Bicknoller, Taunton TA4 4EG* T: (01984) 656067 E: a.bernerswilson@btinternet.com

BERNHARD, Peter James. b 55. Magd Coll Ox BA 76 MA 80. SAOMC 03. **d** 06 **p** 07. NSM Homerton St Luke *Lon* 06–08; Hon Chapl Homerton Univ Hosp NHS Foundn Trust *Lon* 07–08; PtO *Ox* 08–10; *Lon* 09–15; NSM Clerkenwell H Redeemer 15–17; Dir of Ords 15–19; rtd 19. *16 Doves Yard, London N1 0HQ* M: 07970-855354 E: souldernspring@tiscali.co.uk

BERRETT, Michael Vincent. b 56. St Chad's Coll Dur BA 78. Ox Min Course 06. **d** 09 **p** 10. NSM Wantage *Ox* 09–17; NSM Stokenham, Slapton, Charleton w Buckland etc *Ex* from 17. *The Vicarage, Stokenham, Kingsbridge TQ7 2ST* T: (01548) 580908 E: mvberrett@gmail.com

BERRIDGE, Grahame Richard. b 38. S'wark Ord Course 71. d 72 p 73. NSM S Beddington St Mich *S'wark* 72–75; NSM Merton St Jas 75–81; PtO from 81. *11 Cedar Walk, Kingswood, Tadworth KT20 6HW* T: (01737) 358882

BERRIMAN, Brinley John. b 50. Univ Coll Lon BSc 71. SWMTC 95. d 98 p 99. NSM St Ives and Halsetown *Truro* 98–00; P-in-c Lanteglos by Camelford w Advent 00–05; P-in-c St Buryan, St Levan and Sennen 05–12; rtd 12; PtO *Truro* from 15. *Bosorne House, Bosorne, St Just, Penzance TR19 7NR* T: (01736) 787322 E: brin@dreckly.net

BERRIMAN, Gavin Anthony. b 60. S'wark Ord Course 87. d 90 p 91. C Greenwich St Alfege w St Pet and St Paul *S'wark* 90–94; V Lee St Aug from 94. *St Augustine's Vicarage, 336 Baring Road, London SE12 0DU* T: (020) 8857 4941 E: gavin.staug@hotmail.co.uk

BERRY, Canon Adrian Charles. b 50. Mert Coll Ox BA 71 MA 74. Cuddesdon Coll 72. d 75 p 76. C Prestbury *Glouc* 75–79; C Cirencester 79–83; V Cam w Stinchcombe 83–88; Dioc Ecum Officer 83–95; P-in-c Twyning 88–95; R Leckhampton St Pet 95–02; Dioc Min Development Officer *Llan* 02–14; P-in-c Wenvoe and St Lythans 02–09; R Barry All SS 09–14; Can Llan Cathl 02–14; rtd 14. *70 Meek Road, Newent GL18 1DX* T: (01531) 820981

BERRY, Anthony Nigel. b 53. Lon Bible Coll BA 80. Sarum & Wells Th Coll 84. d 87 p 88. NSM Howell Hill *Guildf* 87–90; C 90; C Farnham 90–93; R Abinger cum Coldharbour 93–14; R Abinger and Coldharbour and Wotton and Holmbury St Mary from 15; Tr Officer for Past Assts from 94. *The Rectory, Abinger Lane, Abinger Common, Dorking RH5 6HZ* T: (01306) 730746 E: revanberry@aol.com

BERRY, David Llewellyn Edward. b 39. St Jo Coll Cam BA 61 MA 65. Wells Th Coll 64. d 66 p 67. C Poplar All SS w St Frideswide *Lon* 66–69; C Ellesmere Port *Ches* 69–73; V Brafferton w Pilmoor and Myton-on-Swale *York* 73–79; P-in-c Thormanby 78–79; R Skelton w Upleatham 79–87; Chapl Barrow St Aid *Carl* 87–97; Rotterdam *Eur* 97–99; rtd 99; PtO *Carl* from 04. *22 Pele Court, Friargate, Penrith CA11 7XT* T: (01768) 867150 E: dandjberry3944@btinternet.com

BERRY, David Nicholas. b 77. York Univ BA 00 St Jo Coll Dur BA 10. Cranmer Hall Dur 08. d 10 p 11. C Mansfield St Jo w St Mary *S'well* 10–14; V Bentley *Sheff* from 14. *Bentley Vicarage, 3A High Street, Bentley, Doncaster DN5 0AA* T: (01302) 876272 M: 07733-127698 E: dave.b@stpetersbentley.org

BERRY, Mrs Diane Jayne. b 62. York Sch of Min 14. d 19. NSM S Holderness Coast *York* from 19. *Berry House, 96A Queen Street, Withernsea HU19 2HB* T: (01964) 613212 M: 07709-000556 E: dianejayneberry@hotmail.com

BERRY, Prof Frank John. b 47. Lon Univ BSc 72 PhD 75 DSc 88 FRSC 84. Qu Coll Birm 96. d 99 p 00. Prof Inorganic Chemistry Open Univ from 91; Hon Prof Chemistry Birm Univ from 07; NSM Rednal 99–04; NSM Birm St Martin w Bordesley St Andr 04–07; NSM Moseley St Mary and St Anne 07–17; PtO from 17. *44 Middle Park Road, Selly Oak, Birmingham B29 4BJ* T: 0121-475 2718 E: frank_berry44@hotmail.com

BERRY, Miss Heather Evelyn. b 45. Lon Univ BA 67 Ex Univ PGCE 68. d 00 p 01. OLM Gaywood *Nor* 00–14; C Gt w Lt Massingham, Harpley, Rougham etc 14–15; R Rougham, Weasenham and Wellingham 15–16; rtd 16; PtO *Nor* from 16. *12 Kent Road, King's Lynn PE30 4AF* T: (01553) 764098 E: heberry@talktalk.net

BERRY, Canon Ian Thomas Henry. b 73. QUB BSc 94. CITC BTh 98. d 98 p 99. C Bangor Abbey *D & D* 98–02; I Monaghan w Tydavnet and Kilmore *Clogh* from 02; Preb Clogh Cathl from 11; Chan from 19. *The Rectory, Clones Road, Monaghan, Republic of Ireland* T: (00353) (47) 81136 E: monaghan@clogher.anglican.org

BERRY, John. b 41. Dur Univ BA 62. Oak Hill Th Coll 63. d 65 p 66. C Burnage St Marg *Man* 65–68; C Middleton 68–70; Travelling Sec IVF 70–73; V Derby St Pet 73–76; P-in-c Derby St Pet and Ch Ch w H Trin 73–76; V 76–81; Bp's Officer for Evang *Carl* 81–86; P-in-c Bampton w Mardale 81–86; Evang Sec N Wingfield, Pilsley and Tupton *Derby* 86–89; Evang Alliance 89–92; V Guernsey H Trin *Win* 92–98; TR Broadwater *Chich* 98–07; rtd 07; PtO *Ox* from 08. *27 Blythe Close, Newport Pagnell MK16 9DN* T: (01908) 217631 E: reverendjohn@sky.com

BERRY, Paul Edward. b 56. NOC 91. d 94 p 95. C Halliwell St Luke *Man* 94–98; TV Horwich and Rivington 98–08; TV Edgware *Lon* 08–16; TR 16–18; AD W Barnet 16–18; Chapl Trin Hospice in the Fylde from 18. *Trinity Hospice, Low Moor Road, Blackpool FY2 0BG* T: (01253) 358881 E: paul.berry@trinityhospice.co.uk

BERRY, Mrs Philippa Raines. b 51. Man Univ BA 72 Univ of Wales (Cardiff) CertEd 73. St Jo Coll Nottm 82. d 95

p 96. NSM Leic H Apostles 95–04; P-in-c 04–17; rtd 17; PtO *Leic* from 17. *37 The Glade, Leicester LE3 2WB* E: pipberry@hotmail.com

BERRY, Simon David. b 86. G&C Coll Cam BA 09 MPhil 10. Wycliffe Hall Ox 13. d 17 p 18. C Pet St Mark from 17. *45 Huntly Grove, Peterborough PE1 2QW* E: curate@stmarkspeterborough.org.uk

BERRY, Sister Susan Patricia (Sister Sue). b 49. Bris Univ BA 70 Hughes Hall Cam PGCE 72. Qu Coll Birm 77. dss 86 d 87 p 94. Chapl Barn Fellowship Whatcombe Ho 86–89; Chapl Lee Abbey 89–91; NSM Thatcham *Ox* 93–95; CSF from 95; PtO *B & W* 96–97 and 98–10; Chapl Guy's and St Thos' Hosps NHS Trust Lon 97–98; PtO *S'wark* 97–98 and from 10; Hon Min Can S'wark Cathl from 12. *St Alphege Clergy House, Pocock Street, London SE1 0BJ* T: (020) 7928 8910 E: suecsf@franciscans.org.uk

BERRY, Timothy Hugh. b 50. Reading Univ BA 72. Oak Hill NSM Course 81. d 84 p 85. NSM Swanley St Paul *Roch* 84–88; C Gorleston St Andr *Nor* 88–93; V Grain w Stoke *Roch* 93–95; rtd 95; PtO *Roch* 01–15; *Leeds* from 17. *2 De Lacy Road, Northallerton DL7 8WD* M: 07932-182981 E: timberry@bigfoot.com

BERRY-DAVIES, Charles William Keith. b 48. MIOT 71. Linc Th Coll. d 83 p 84. C Hythe *Cant* 83–86; Chapl RAF 86–09; rtd 09; PtO *B & W* from 09. *11 Stafford Place, Weston-super-Mare BS23 2QZ* T: (01934) 621344 E: keith.vicarage@btinternet.com

BERSWEDEN, Judith Anne. b 63. St Jo Coll Dur BA 84. Ripon Coll Cuddesdon BA 91. d 92 p 94. Par Dn Mirfield *Wakef* 92–94; NSM Robert Town 94–97; NSM Roberttown w Hartshead 97–00; NSM Alderbury Deanery *Sarum* 00–18; Chapl Bp Wordsworth's Sch Salisbury 01–18; NSM Merton St Mary *S'wark* from 18. *3 Arthur Road, London SW19 7DL* T: (020) 3665 8746 E: judith.bersweden@dsl.pipex.com

BERSWEDEN, Nils Herry Stephen. b 57. Newc Univ BSc 78. Ripon Coll Cuddesdon 88. d 90 p 91. C Mirfield *Wakef* 90–93; P-in-c Purlwell 93–94; P-in-c Robert Town 94–97; V Roberttown w Hartshead 97–00; P-in-c Winterslow *Sarum* 00–01; TV Clarendon 01–08; TR 08–18; Hon C Wimbledon *S'wark* from 18. *3 Arthur Road, London SW19 7DL* T: (020) 3665 8746

BESSANT, Brian Keith. b 32. Roch Th Coll 65. d 67 p 68. C Chatham St Wm *Roch* 67–70; C Cove St Jo *Guildf* 71–74; V Frimley Green 74–97; rtd 97; PtO *Guildf* 97–12. *14 Tay Close, Farnborough GU14 9NB* T: (01252) 376530

BESSANT, Christopher Dixon. b 69. Nottm Univ MA 14. Ridley Hall Cam 07. d 09 p 10. C Gt Bookham *Guildf* 09–13; V Chobham w Valley End from 13; Tutor Local Min Progr from 14. *Chobham Vicarage, Bagshot Road, Chobham, Woking GU24 8BY* T: (01276) 858197 M: 07800-719405 E: c_bessant@hotmail.com

BESSANT, Canon Idwal Brian. b 39. Cardiff Coll of Art ATD 62. St Mich Coll Llan 65. d 68 p 69. C Llantwit Major and St Donat's *Llan* 68–73; R Llangammarch w Garth, Llanlleonfel etc *S & B* 73–77; V Crickhowell 77–78; CMS Miss 78–83; Cyprus 80–83; V Crickhowell w Cwmdu and Tretower *S & B* 83–91; RD Crickhowell 86–91; V Llanwrtyd w Llanddulas in Tir Abad etc 91–04; Can Res Brecon Cathl 98–04; RD Builth 02–04; rtd 04. *10 Bronant, Bronllys Road, Talgarth, Brecon LD3 0HF* T: (01874) 712380

BESSANT, Canon Simon David. b 56. Sheff Univ BMus 77 MA 00. St Jo Coll Nottm. d 81 p 82. C Litherland St Jo and St Jas *Liv* 81–84; C Holloway Em w Hornsey Road St Barn *Lon* 84–86; C Holloway St Mark w Em 86–91; V Blackb Redeemer 91–98; Acting RD Blackb 97–98; Dir Miss and Evang 98–07; Dir CME 02–07; Hon Can Blackb Cathl 06–07; V Ecclesall *Sheff* 07–12; V Mortomley St Sav High Green 12–19; P-in-c Grenoside 14–19; Miss Development Officer from 19. *68 Kennedy Avenue, Macclesfield SK10 3DE*

BESSANT, Stephen Michael. b 53. St Seiriol Cen 13. d 14 p 15. NSM Llanstadwel St D 14–16; NSM Burton and Rosemarket 14–16; NSM Llanstadwel and Burton and Rosemarket from 16. *28 Greenhall Park, Johnston, Haverfordwest SA62 3PT* T: (01437) 890701 E: smbessant@btinternet.com

BESSENT, Preb Stephen Lyn. b 53. Bris Univ BA 75. Wycliffe Hall Ox 75. d 77 p 78. C Patchway *Bris* 77–80; TV Swindon St Jo and St Andr 80–83; TV Eston w Normanby *York* 83–90; V Cogges *Ox* 90–94; P-in-c S Leigh 90–94; V Cogges and S Leigh 94–01; P-in-c Alphington, Shillingford St George and Ide *Ex* 01–12; R 12–17; RD Christianity 06–17; Preb Ex Cathl 09–17; rtd 17; PtO *Ox* from 17. *25 Lancaster Place, Carterton OX18 3ET* E: stephenbessent@btinternet.com

BEST, Gary John. b 62. SEITE 13. d 16 p 17. C Bexley *Roch* 16–19; V Shortlands from 19. *St Mary's Church,*

Kingswood Road, Bromley BR2 0HG M: 07493-072695
E: revgarybest@gmail.com

BEST, Canon Raymond. b 42. Sarum & Wells Th Coll 71. **d** 74 **p** 75. C Whorlton Newc 74–78; C Seaton Hirst 78–83; C Benwell St Jas 83–85; TV Benwell 85–89; V Walker 89–00; P-in-c Byker St Martin 96–99; V Haltwhistle and Greenhead 00–10; Hon Can Newc Cathl 97–10; AD Hexham 02–06; rtd 10; PtO Newc from 10. The Annexe, 3 Admiral Close, Swarland, Morpeth NE65 9GZ T: (01670) 783434 E: canonbest@aol.com

BESTELINK, Canon William Meindert Croft. b 48. Hull Univ BA 70 FRSA 78. Cuddesdon Coll 71. **d** 73 **p** 74. C Holt Nor 73–74; C E Dereham w Hoe 74–76; C Thorpe St Andr 76–80; R Colby w Banningham and Tuttington 80–90; R Felmingham 80–90; R Suffield 80–90; P-in-c Roydon St Remigius 90–04; P-in-c Scole, Brockdish, Billingford, Thorpe Abbots etc 02–04; P-in-c Gillingham w Geldeston, Stockton, Ellingham etc 04–09; RD Redenhall 00–03; Dioc Rural Officer 99–09; Hon Can Nor Cathl 02–09; rtd 09; PtO Nor from 09. 4 Francis Close, Cromer NR27 0HR T: (01263) 514045 M: 07909-690073 E: wmcbestelink@hotmail.co.uk

BESTLEY, Peter Mark. b 60. Qu Coll Cam MA Univ of Wales (Cardiff) MPhil 92. St Mich Coll Llan 89. **d** 92 **p** 93. C Hampton All SS Lon 92–95; Chapl W Middx Univ Hosp NHS Trust 95–99; Hon C Bracknell Ox 04–06; C Easthampstead 06–17; rtd 17; PtO Ox from 17. 40 Parkway, Crowthorne RG45 6EW M: 07792-928624 E: peter.bestley@gmail.com

BESWETHERICK, Andrew Michael. b 55. Ex Univ BEd 80. S'wark Ord Course 87. **d** 90 **p** 91. Dep Hd Maze Hill Sch Greenwich 88–98; NSM Blackheath St Jo S'wark from 90; Hd Sixth Form Rosemary Sch Islington from 98. 112 Charlton Road, London SE7 7EY T: (020) 8853 0853 E: andrewbmh@gmail.com

BESWICK, Canon Gary Lancelot. b 38. ALCD 63. **d** 63 **p** 64. C Walthamstow St Mary Chelmsf 63–67; C Laisterdyke Bradf 67–70; V Idle 70–78; Area Sec (NW England) SAMS 78–92; Area Sec (N Thames) 92–97; Hon Can N Argentina from 87; R Gt Smeaton w Appleton Wiske and Birkby etc Ripon 97–03; rtd 03. 14 Bolton Way, Boston Spa, Wetherby LS23 6PT

BESWICK, Jane. See VOST, Jane

BESWICK, Jonathan Warwick. b 67. Jes Coll Cam BA 95. Westcott Ho Cam 91. **d** 95 **p** 96. C Dudley St Fran Worc 95–96; C Brookfield St Mary and Brookfield St Anne, Highgate Rise Lon 96–99; C St John's Wood 99–02; R Catsfield and Crowhurst Chich 02–08; P-in-c Ox St Barn and St Paul 08–15; P-in-c Ox St Thos 11–15; V Ox St Barn and St Paul w St Thos 15–18; R Lon Docks St Pet w Wapping St Jo from 18. St Peter's Clergy House, Wapping Lane, London E1W 2RW T: (020) 7481 2985

BESWICK PALLISTER, John Jorge. b 81. Coimbra Univ (Portugal) BA 05. Ridley Hall Cam 16. **d** 18 **p** 19. C Betley Lich from 18; C Madeley from 18. St John's Vicarage, High Street, Alsagers Bank, Stoke-on-Trent ST7 8BQ M: 07923-135787 E: longobedience@gmail.com

BETSON, Christopher James. b 81. Writtle Agric Coll BSc 03 St Jo Coll Dur BA 09. Cranmer Hall Dur 06. **d** 09 **p** 10. C Anston Sheff 09–12; V Tickhill w Stainton 12–17. The Vicarage, 9 Sutton Park Road, Kidderminster DY11 6LB E: chrisbetson@outlook.com

BETSON (née BIDDINGTON), Mrs Laura Claire. b 84. Trin Coll Cam BA 05 St Jo Coll Dur MA 08. Cranmer Hall Dur 06. **d** 08 **p** 09. C Aston cum Aughton w Swallownest and Ulley Sheff 08–12; PtO 12–17; TV Kidderminster St Jo and H Innocents Worc from 17. The Vicarage, 9 Sutton Park Road, Kidderminster DY11 6LB T: (01562) 228712 M: 07984-960749 E: laura.betson@yahoo.co.uk

BETSON, Mark John. b 77. Univ Coll Lon BSc 99 Birkbeck Coll Lon PhD Cam Univ BA 06. Westcott Ho Cam 04. **d** 07 **p** 08. C Southwick Chich 07–10; P-in-c Lower Beeding 10–15; V 15–19; Nat Rural Officer Miss and Public Affairs from 19. Church House, Great Smith Street, London SW1P 3AZ T: (020) 7898 1000 M: 07801-273074 E: m.betson@hotmail.co.uk

BETSON, Stephen. b 53. Sarum & Wells Th Coll 89. **d** 91 **p** 92. C Sittingbourne St Mich Cant 91–95; V Fairweather Green Bradf 95–01; R Hockwold w Wilton Ely 01–06; R Weeting 01–06; P-in-c Stanground 06–12; P-in-c St Mary Cray and St Paul's Cray Roch 12–14; rtd 14; PtO Chich from 15. 1 Purbeck Close, Eastbourne BN23 8EX E: stephenbetson@hotmail.co.uk

BETTELEY, John Richard. b 46. Sarum & Wells Th Coll 81. **d** 83 **p** 84. C Auchterarder St And 83–85; C Dunblane 83–85; Chapl RAF 85–89; R Callander St And 89–94; P-in-c Aberfoyle 89–94; P-in-c Doune 89–94; R Ballachulish Arg 94–04; R Glencoe 94–04; R Onich 94–04; Dioc Youth Officer 94–01; Syn Clerk 99–04; Can St Jo Cathl Oban 99–04; Can Cumbrae 99–04; R Aboyne Ab 04–06; R Ballater 04–06; R Braemar 04–06; PtO Mor from 12. Camusfearna, 3 School Street,

Fearn, Tain IV20 1SX T: (01862) 832774 M: 07713-914602 E: camus.jrb@tesco.net

BETTERIDGE, Kelly Anne. b 69. Roehampton Inst BA 92. Qu Coll Birm 08. **d** 10 **p** 11. C Nuneaton St Nic Cov 10–14; V from 14; P-in-c Weddington and Caldecote from 14. 61 Ambleside Way, Nuneaton CV11 6AU T: (024) 7634 6900 or 7634 4553 E: revkells@gmail.com

BETTERIDGE, Simon Frank. b 66. St Jo Coll Nottm. **d** 00 **p** 01. C Studley Cov 00–02; C Leamington Priors St Paul 02–04; Chapl Univ Hosps Cov and Warks NHS Trust from 04. 61 Ambleside Way, Nuneaton CV11 6AU M: 07743-870601 E: simon.betty@yahoo.com or simon.betteridge@uhcw.nhs.uk

BETTINSON, Philip Keith. b 79. Univ of Wales (Abth) BEng 01. St Mich Coll Llan BTh 11. **d** 11 **p** 12. C Cilcain, Gwernaffield, Llanferres etc St As 11–14; C Wrexham 14–17; TV Offa Miss Area from 17. The Vicarage, Wrexham Road, Johnstown, Wrexham LL14 1PE T: (01978) 846204 E: rev@jara23.co.uk

BETTIS, Canon Margaret Jean. b 42. Gilmore Ho 72. **dss** 77 **d** 87 **p** 94. Kenya 77–79; Tutor Crowther Hall CMS Tr Coll Selly Oak 79–82; Hodge Hill Birm 82–87; Par Dn 87; Par Dn Flitwick St Alb 87–93; P-in-c Westoning w Tingrith 93–94; V 94–04; Hon Can St Alb 97–04; rtd 04; PtO St Alb 04–05; Glouc 05–06; Hon C Cirencester from 06. 58 Aldsworth Close, Fairford GL7 4LB T: (01285) 238992 E: canmjb42@talktalk.net

BETTRIDGE, Canon Graham Winston. b 39. Kelham Th Coll 60. **d** 65 **p** 66. C Burley in Wharfedale Bradf 65–67; C Baildon 67–70; V Harden and Wilsden 70–81; TR Kirkby Lonsdale Carl 81–06; Hon Can Carl Cathl 89–06; rtd 06; Chapl Cumbria Constabulary Carl 96–09; PtO Bradf 06–14; Leeds from 14; Carl from 09; Blackb from 14. Moorgate Cottage, Maypole Green, Long Preston, Skipton BD23 4PJ T: (01729) 841113 E: canongraham@mintegrity.co.uk

BETTS, Alan John. b 55. Portsm Poly BSc 77 St Martin's Coll Lanc PGCE 81. St Jo Coll Nottm 93. **d** 93 **p** 94. C Cannock Lich 93–01; P-in-c Endon w Stanley 01–04; V Bagnall w Endon from 04; P-in-c Brown Edge from 15. St Luke's Vicarage, Leek Road, Endon, Stoke-on-Trent ST9 9BH T: (01782) 502166

BETTS, David John. b 38. Lon Univ BSc 61. Oak Hill Th Coll 63. **d** 65 **p** 66. C Slough Ox 65–70; C Welling Roch 70–75; V Swanley St Paul 75–93; R Nottingham St Nic S'well 93–98; TV Canford Magna Sarum 98–04; rtd 04; PtO Sarum from 05. 290 Rempstone Road, Wimborne BH21 1SZ T: (01202) 840537 E: davidbetts@tesco.net

BETTS, Edmund John. b 51. St Chad's Coll Dur BA 72 Lanc Univ MA 81 Ches Univ DProf 15. Qu Coll Birm 73. **d** 76 **p** 77. C Leagrave St Alb 76–79; Asst Chapl R Albert Hosp Lanc 79–81; Chapl Lea Castle Hosp Kidderminster 81–86; Chapl Kidderminster Gen Hosp 81–86; Prov Officer Educn for Min Ch in Wales 86–88; Exec Sec for Min 88–90; TR Haverhill w Withersfield, the Wrattings etc St E 90–97; V Haverhill w Withersfield 97–06; RD Clare 91–06; Hon Can St E Cathl 02–06; CUF Link Officer 02–06; V Altrincham St Geo Ches 06–16; P-in-c Altrincham St Jo 07–16; V Altrincham from 17. St George's Vicarage, Townfield Road, Altrincham WA14 4DS T: 0161-928 1279 E: edmund.betts1@btinternet.com

BETTS, Ivan Ringland. b 38. TCD BA 61 MA 67. **d** 62 **p** 63. C Ballyholme D & D 62–65; C Dundela St Mark 65–69; Miss to Seamen 69–73; Sudan 69–71; Trinidad and Tobago 71–73; C Drumglass Arm 73–81; I Augher w Newtownsaville and Eskrahoole Clogh 81–86; Bp's C Ballymacarrett St Martin D & D 86–02; rtd 02. 56 Norwood Drive, Belfast BT4 2EB T: (028) 9065 0723 E: ivanbetts@btinternet.com

BETTS, Mrs Patricia Joyce. b 43. St Kath Coll Lon CertEd 64 FRSA 96. S Dios Minl Tr Scheme 90. **d** 96 **p** 97. NSM Bath Widcombe B & W 96–00; P-in-c 00–05; PtO from 05. Hunter's Lodge, North Road, Bath BA2 6HP T: (01225) 464918 M: 07545-350565 E: candpbetts@talktalk.net

BETTS, The Ven Steven James. b 64. York Univ BSc 86. Ripon Coll Cuddesdon 87. **d** 90 **p** 91. C Bearsted w Thurnham Cant 90–94; Bp's Chapl Nor 94–97; V Old Catton 97–05; RD Nor N 01–05; Bp's Officer for Ord and Initial Tr 05–12; Adn Norfolk from 12; Hon Can Nor Cathl from 08. 8 Boulton Road, Thorpe St Andrew, Norwich NR7 0DF T: (01603) 559199 E: archdeacon.norfolk@dioceseofnorwich.org

BEURKLIAN-CARTER, Mrs Santou. b 70. McMaster Univ Ontario BA 92 Toronto Univ MDiv 02. St Mellitus Coll 10. **d** 12 **p** 13. C Gt Ilford St Jo Chelmsf 12–14; C Woodford St Mary w St Phil and St Jas 14–17; Chapl Guy's and St Thos' NHS Foundn Trust from 18; Chapl Forest Healthcare NHS Trust Lon from 18. 116 Blythswood Road, Ilford IG3 8SG T: (020) 8599 0399 M: 07939-876045 E: sbcarter@btinternet.com

BEVAN, Andrew Paul. b 68. ERMC 16. **d** 19. OLM Stalham, E Ruston, Brunstead, Sutton and Ingham *Nor* from 19; OLM Smallburgh w Dilham w Honing and Crostwight from 19. *The Saplings, New Road, Catfield, Great Yarmouth NR29 5BQ* T: (01692) 582358 E: apbevan@btinternet.com

BEVAN, Christopher Jeremy. Lon Inst BA 89 Lon Guildhall Univ MA 97 Cardiff Univ BA 11. **d** 11 **p** 12. C Llanelli *S & B* 11–15; P-in-c from 16. *Llanelly Rectory, Abergavenny Road, Gilwern, Abergavenny NP7 0AD* T: (01873) 830280 E: christopher.bevan@btinternet.com

BEVAN, David Graham. b 34. Univ of Wales (Lamp) BA 54 LTh 56. Gen Th Sem (NY) MDiv 57. **d** 57 **p** 58. C Llanelli *St D* 57–60; CF 60–76; rtd 99. *148 Bromley Heath Road, Bristol BS16 6JJ* T: 0117-956 0946

BEVAN, Janet Mary. *See* MOORE, Janet Mary

BEVAN, Judith Anne. *See* EGAR, Judith Anne

BEVAN, Paul John. b 49. Bris Sch of Min 84. **d** 87. NSM Bishopsworth *Bris* 87–96. *10 Brookdale Road, Headley Park, Bristol BS13 7PZ* T: 0117-964 6330

BEVAN, Peter John. b 54. K Coll Lon BA 76 AKC 76. St Steph Ho Ox BA 79 MA 86. **d** 80 **p** 81. C Brighouse *Wakef* 80–83; C Chapelthorpe 83–86; V Scholes 86–95; V Potters Bar *St Alb* 95–15; V Gt and Lt Torrington and Frithelstock *Ex* from 15. *The Vicarage, Calf Street, Torrington EX38 8EA* T: (01805) 622166 E: peter.bevan900@gmail.com

BEVAN, Philip Frank. b 41. Brasted Th Coll 63 Chich Th Coll 65. **d** 67 **p** 68. C Walton St Mary *Liv* 67–71; P-in-c Long Is SS Pet and Paul Bahamas 71–73; R Nassau St Matt 73–78; PtO *S'wark* 00–17; *Ox* from 16; *Lon* from 17. *32 Collingwood House, 103 New Cavendish Street, London W1W 6XH* T: (020) 7436 8010 M: 07970-961539 E: fr.philip@btinternet.com

BEVAN, Mrs Rebecca Anne. b 64. Reading Univ BA 86. Ox Min Course 04. **d** 07 **p** 08. NSM Thatcham *Ox* 07–10; R Aldermaston and Woolhampton 10–17; V Newbury St Geo and St Jo from 17. *The Vicarage, 206 Andover Road, Newbury RG14 6NU* E: bbevan.awb@gmail.com

BEVAN, Rodney. b 57. Leeds Univ BA 80 Keele Univ PGCE 81 Open Univ MA 99. Cranmer Hall Dur 97. **d** 99 **p** 00. C Ogley Hay *Lich* 99–03; TV Rossendale Middle Valley *Man* 03–04; TR 04–17; V Edgeside from 17; AD Rossendale from 18. *St Anne's Vicarage, Ashworth Road, Rossendale BB4 9JE* T: (01706) 221889 M: 07837-608637 E: revrodbev@hotmail.com

BEVER, Canon Michael Charles Stephen. b 44. Selw Coll Cam BA 66 MA 70. Cuddesdon Coll 67. **d** 69 **p** 70. C Steeton *Bradf* 69–72; C Northampton St Mary *Pet* 72–74; Niger 75–79; P-in-c Elmstead *Chelmsf* 80–83; V 83–85; V Bocking St Pet 85–96; P-in-c Odiham *Win* 96–07; rtd 07; Hon Can Awka from 93; PtO *Portsm* from 08; *Win* 07–14. *68A Drift Road, Waterlooville PO8 0NX* T/F: (023) 9259 6895 E: mcsb@ozala.plus.com

BEVERIDGE, Mrs Freda Joy. b 38. Qu Mary Coll Lon BA 59 Lon Inst of Educn PGCE 60. Ripon Coll Cuddesdon 83. **dss** 85 **d** 87 **p** 94. Ox St Giles and SS Phil and Jas w St Marg 85–88; Par Dn 87–88; Par Dn Woughton 88–94; C 94–95; TR 95–97; C Woodham *Guildf* 97–00; rtd 00; PtO *Sarum* from 01. *Moonraker Cottage, 27 New Road, Chiseldon, Swindon SN4 0LY* T: (01793) 741064 E: freda.27@btinternet.com

BEVERLEY, Anne Ruth. b 56. Cen Lancs Univ BA 97 Cumbria Univ BA 14. LCTP 11. **d** 14 **p** 15. NSM S Shore H Trin *Blackb* 14–18; NSM S Shore St Pet 14–18; V Wesham from 18. *Christ Church Parish Office, Garstang Road North, Wesham, Preston PR4 3DE* M: 07841-742022 E: anne.beverley@btinternet.com

BEVERLEY, David John. b 46. Univ of Wales (Lamp) BA 68. Linc Th Coll 71. **d** 73 **p** 74. C Cov E 73–76; C Immingham *Linc* 76–84; V Bracebridge Heath 84–86; Ind Chapl 86–97; P-in-c Scunthorpe Resurr 97–01; V 01–02; R Trentside E 02–11; rtd 11; PtO *Linc* from 16. *73 Peveril Avenue, Scunthorpe DN17 1BG* T: (01724) 279914

BEVERLEY, Sister. *See* DAVIES, Beverley

BEVERLEY, Suffragan Bishop of (Provincial Episcopal Visitor). *See* WEBSTER, The Rt Revd Glyn Hamilton

BEVERLY, Mrs Sue. b 53. Cardiff Univ BTh 08. St Mich Coll Llan 05. **d** 07 **p** 08. NSM Coity, Nolton and Brackla *Llan* 07–12; Asst Dir of Min 10; AD Bridgend 11–12; R Broseley w Benthall, Jackfield, Linley etc *Heref* 12–16; NSM Malvern Link w Cowleigh *Worc* from 16. *4 Dairy Close, Malvern WR14 2FB* T: (01684) 568208 E: revdsue@mlwc.church

BEVINGTON, David John. b 51. Ch Coll Cam BA 72 MA 76. Trin Coll Bris 73. **d** 76 **p** 77. C Tulse Hill H Trin *S'wark* 76–79; C Galleywood Common *Chelmsf* 79–82; TV Hanley H Ev *Lich* 82–90; TV Hemel Hempstead *St Alb* 90–99; V Calbourne w Newtown *Portsm* 99–16; V Shalfleet 99–16; rtd 16; PtO *Ox* from 17. *35 Gainsborough Green, Abingdon OX14 5JH* T: (01235) 521133 E: dbevington@lineone.net

BEWES, Anthony Charles Neill. b 71. Birm Univ BA 93. Wycliffe Hall Ox 96. **d** 99 **p** 00. C Sevenoaks St Nic *Roch* 99–05; Team Ldr Titus Trust from 05. *45 Lonsdale Road, Oxford OX2 7ES* T: (01865) 553625 E: anthony@bewes.com

BEWES, Helen Catherine. *See* SCAMMAN, Helen Catherine

BEWICK, Lisa Marie. b 83. Ex Univ BA 05 Surrey Univ PGCE 06. Sarum Coll 15. **d** 18 **p** 19. NSM Waterloo St Jo w St Andr *S'wark* from 18. *21 Windmill House, Windmill Walk, London SE1 8LX* E: lisa@stjohnswaterloo.org

BEWLEY, Robin John. b 63. St Jo Coll Ox BA 86 MA 95 Fitzw Coll Cam BA 99 PhD 05. Ridley Hall Cam. **d** 00 **p** 01. NSM Histon and Impington *Ely* 00–04; C Harborne Heath *Birm* 04–11; V Kettering Ch the King *Pet* from 11. *The Vicarage, Deeble Road, Kettering NN15 7AA* T: (01536) 512828 M: 07733-346631 E: rob@thebewleys.co.uk *or* vicar@ctk.org.uk

BEXON, Valerie Joan. *See* THORNE, Valerie Joan

BEYNON, Malcolm. b 36. Univ of Wales (Lamp) BA 56 Univ of Wales (Cardiff) PGCE 71. St Mich Coll Llan 56. **d** 59 **p** 60. C Aberavon *Llan* 59–62; C Whitchurch 63–68; V Llanwynno 68–73; Chapl Old Hall Sch Wellington Shropshire 74–75; Chapl Nevill Holt Sch Market Harborough 75–82; Chapl Denstone Coll Prep Sch Uttoxeter 82–93; V Dale and St Brides w Marloes *St D* 93–01; rtd 01. *22 Ostrey Bank, St Clears, Carmarthen SA33 4AH* T: (01994) 231872

BEYNON, Paul John. b 66. SWMTC 09. **d** 12 **p** 13. C Boscastle w Davidstow *Truro* 12–15; C Boscastle and Tintagel Gp 15–16; P-in-c Lostwithiel Parishes from 16. *The Rectory, 3 Springfield Close, Lostwithiel PL22 0RW* T: (01208) 623577 M: 07730-037113 E: p-beynon@sky.com

BEYNON, Canon Vincent Wyn. b 54. Anglia Poly Univ MA 04 Hockerill Coll Cam CertEd 76 Lambeth STh 97. St Mich Coll Llan. **d** 81 **p** 82. C Llantrisant *Llan* 81–83; C Caerphilly 84–85; R Gelligaer 85–88; TV Gtr Corsham *Bris* 88–97; R Potton w Sutton and Cockayne Hatley *St Alb* 97–08; RD Biggleswade 01–06; P-in-c Stoke Prior, Wychbold and Upton Warren *Worc* from 12; NSM Bowbrook N from 14; NSM Bowbrook S from 14; RD Droitwich from 18; Hon Can Worc Cathl from 19. *The Rectory, Fish House Lane, Stoke Prior, Bromsgrove B60 4JT* T: (01527) 832501 E: wynbeynon@gmail.com

BHATTI, Javed. b 51. 16. **d** 71 **p** 08. Pakistan 71–00; PtO *Leic* from 16. *59 Ravenhouse Road, Dewsbury WF13 3QW* T: (01924) 467466 M: 07966-885643 E: javedbhatti_4540@yahoo.co.uk

BHUTTA, Mrs Patricia Frances Mary. b 52. Kent Univ BA 74. Ox Min Course 08. **d** 10 **p** 11. NSM Cumnor *Ox* 10–13; NSM Aldermaston and Woolhampton 13–19; rtd 19; PtO *Ox* from 19. *2 The Garth, Oxford OX2 9AL* M: 07968-089566 E: pat@patbhutta.co.uk *or* pbhutta.awb@gmail.com

BIANCHI, Matthew Robert. b 87. Dur Univ BA 19. Wycliffe Hall Ox 16. **d** 19. C Hartley Wintney, Elvetham, Winchfield etc *Win* from 19. *40 Pool Road, Hartley Wintney, Hook RG27 8RD* T: (01252) 492129 E: thebianchis@ymail.com

BICK, David Jim. b 33. ALCD 59 LTh 74. **d** 59 **p** 60. C Glouc St Cath 59–61; C Coleford w Staunton 61–63; R Blaisdon w Flaxley 63–72; V Coaley 72–83; P-in-c Arlingham 80–83; P-in-c Frampton on Severn 80–83; Hon C Saul w Fretherne and Framilode 83–84; rtd 98. *St Joseph's, Prinknash Park, Cranham, Stroud GL4 8EU* T: (01452) 812973

BICK (*née* GRIFFITHS), Mrs Sarah. b 75. Ex Univ BA 96 Homerton Coll Cam PGCE 99. Qu Coll Birm 07. **d** 09 **p** 10. C Coleford, Staunton, Newland, Redbrook etc *Glouc* 09–13; V from 13. *40 Boxbush Road, Coleford GL16 8DN* T: (01594) 835476 M: 07773-651893 E: sarah@thebickerage.org.uk

BICKERSTAFF, Denise Mary. *See* ACHESON, Denise Mary

BICKERSTETH, David Craufurd. b 50. Wycliffe Hall Ox 71. **d** 75 **p** 76. C Beverley Minster *York* 75–79; C Farnborough *Guildf* 79–81; P-in-c Dearham *Carl* 81–85; V 85–86; R Gosforth w Nether Wasdale and Wasdale Head 86–93; P-in-c Harraby 93–97; V Maryport 98–04; TR Maryport, Netherton and Flimby 04–06; Dioc Chapl MU 94–97; R Brayton-le-Moors w Forsbrook *Lich* 06–15; P-in-c Upper Tean 08–14; rtd 15. *Sunnybrae, Greenodd, Ulverston LA12 7RG* T: (01229) 861184 E: david.bickersteth@btinternet.com

BICKERSTETH, Edward Piers. b 56. MRICS 80. Wycliffe Hall Ox 89. **d** 91 **p** 92. NSM Bebington *Ches* 91–92; C 92–94; Proclamation Trust 94–98; P-in-c Arborfield w Barkham *Ox* 98–02; R from 02. *The Rectory, Church Lane, Arborfield, Reading RG2 9HZ* T: 0118-976 0285

BICKERSTETH, Simon Craufurd. b 77. St Jo Coll Dur BA 98. Wycliffe Hall Ox 99. **d** 01 **p** 02. C Windermere *Carl* 01–05; TV Walsall St Matt *Lich* 05–11; V Walsall St Martin 11–16; P-in-c Denton Holme *Carl* from 16. *St James's Vicarage, Goschen Road, Carlisle CA2 5PF* M: 07752-853148 E: simon.bickersteth@talktalk.net

BICKLEY, Mrs Alice Elizabeth Ann. b 60. Qu Coll Birm 06. **d** 09 **p** 10. C Leagrave *St Alb* 09–13; P-in-c Hexagon *Leic* 13–16; R from 16. *The Rectory, Honeypot Lane, Husbands Bosworth, Lutterworth LE17 6LY* T: (01858) 880351 M: 07977-601437 E: lizbickley@btinternet.com

BICKLEY, Mrs Pamela. b 59. Birm Univ BPhil 99. WEMTC 06. **d** 09 **p** 10. NSM Minsterley *Heref* 09–13; NSM Habberley 09–13; NSM Minsterley, Habberley and Hope w Shelve 13–19; Dioc Voc Adv 12–14; rtd 19; PtO *Heref* from 19. *High Ridge, Gorsty Bank, Snailbeach, Shrewsbury SY5 0LX* T: (01743) 792824

BICKNELL (née RIDING), Mrs Pauline Alison. b 61. SEN 82. Oak Hill Th Coll BA 90. **d** 90 **p** 96. Par Dn Moor Allerton *Ripon* 90–93; Par Dn Leeds St Aid 93–94; C 94–96; C Rothwell 96–99; TV Drypool *York* 99–05; P-in-c Slyne w Hest *Blackb* 05–06; R Slyne w Hest and Halton w Aughton 06–17; P-in-c Ormskirk *Liv* from 17. *18 Chestnut Grange, Ormskirk L39 4YG* E: pauline.bicknell@outlook.com

BIDDINGTON, Laura Claire. *See* BETSON, Laura Claire

BIDDINGTON, Terence Eric. b 56. Hull Univ BA 77 Trin & All SS Coll Leeds PGCE 78 Leeds Univ PhD 86 Nottm Univ BTh 88 Man Univ MA(Theol) 96 MCollP 83 FRSA 15. Linc Th Coll 85. **d** 88 **p** 89. C Harpenden St Jo *St Alb* 88–90; Chapl Keele Univ *Lich* 90–93; Freelance Th Educator and Asst Lect Keele Univ 94–99; Assoc Min Betley and Keele *Lich* 90–93; Asst Dir Cornerstone St Aug Man 95–96; Mental Health Advocate Stockport 96–98; Dir and Sen Advocate Stockport MIND 99–16; PtO *Man* 99–01; P-in-c Heaton Norris Ch w All SS 01–02; C Heatons 02–03; Asst Chapl Man Mental Health and Soc Care Trust 01–03; Chapl Man Univ 03–16; Chapl Man Metrop Univ 03–16; Chapl RNCM 03–16; Dean of Spiritual Life Win Univ from 17. *Theology Department, The University of Winchester, Sparkford Road, Winchester SO22 4NR* T: (01962) 827063 E: terry.biddington@winchester.ac.uk

BIDDINGTON, Mrs Wendy Elizabeth. b 51. Cov Univ BSc 93 SRN 73 SCM 74. Qu Coll Birm 07. **d** 09 **p** 10. OLM Wellesbourne *Cov* 09–12; NSM from 12; PtO *Ox* from 17. *72 Mountford Close, Wellesbourne, Warwick CV35 9QQ* T: (01789) 840953 E: w.nbiddington701@btinternet.com

BIDDLE, Joanna Elizabeth. *See* JEPSON, Joanna Elizabeth

BIDDLE, Nicholas Lawrence. *See* JEPSON-BIDDLE, Nicholas Lawrence

BIDDLECOMBE, Francis William. b 30. St Mich Coll Llan 57. **d** 59 **p** 60. C Llangynwyd w Maesteg *Llan* 59–62; C Roath 62–65; V Llanddewi Rhondda w Bryn Eirw 65–71; V Berse and Southsea *St As* 71–79; P-in-c Teme Valley S *Worc* 79–85; rtd 92; PtO *Heref* 92–13; *Worc* 92–09. *Four Winds, New Road, Highley, Bridgnorth WV16 6NN* T: (01746) 861746 E: fwbiddlecombe@hotmail.com

BIDDLESTONE, Simon Christopher. b 77. York Univ BA 99 Coll of Ripon & York St Jo PGCE 00. Cranmer Hall Dur 15. **d** 17 **p** 18. C Tadcaster *York* from 17. *The Vicarage, Church Street, Church Fenton, Tadcaster LS24 9RD* T: (01937) 558172 M: 07738-975927

BIDDULPH, John Whitmore. b 66. Lon Univ BPharm 87 MSc 91. St Mellitus Coll 16. **d** 19. NSM Doddinghurst *Chelmsf* from 19; NSM Bentley Common, Kelvedon Hatch and Navestock from 19. *100 Longfields, Ongar CM5 9DE* T: (01277) 364927 E: johnwbiddulph@btinternet.com

BIDE, Mary Elizabeth. b 53. St Anne's Coll Ox BA 74 MA 78. S Dios Minl Tr Scheme 91. **d** 94 **p** 95. C Gt Bookham *Guildf* 94–98; P-in-c Frimley Green 98–01; V Frimley Green and Mytchett 02–03; Year Tutor Dioc Min Course 96–03; Prec Ch Ch *Ox* 03–07; TR Wimbledon *S'wark* 07–16; rtd 16; Chapl to The Queen from 13; PtO *B & W* from 16. *Roselands, Weston Lane, Christon, Axbridge BS26 2XT* T: (01934) 827705 E: mary.bide@gmail.com

BIDEN, Neville Douglas. b 31. S'wark Ord Course 76. **d** 79 **p** 80. C Ash *Guildf* 79–82; NSM Surbiton St Andr and St Mark *S'wark* 87–91; Chapl Asst Long Grove Hosp Epsom 90–91; PtO *Guildf* 90–91 and 97–06; C Coulsdon St Jo *S'wark* 91–96; rtd 96; PtO *Heref* 95–97; *Win* from 01. *5 Taylor Drive, Bramley, Tadley RG26 5XB* T: (01256) 880459 E: rev.biden@gmail.com

BIDGOOD, Julian Paul. b 71. Sussex Univ BA 92. Oak Hill Th Coll BA 03. **d** 03 **p** 04. C Ox St Ebbe w H Trin and St Pet 03–08; C Arborfield w Barkham from 08. *5 Somerville Close, Wokingham RG41 4SW* M: 07779-296511 E: julian@abch.org.uk

BIELBY, Canon Elaine Elizabeth. b 57. Surrey Univ MSc 83. Ripon Coll Cuddesdon 96. **d** 98 **p** 99. C Marton-in-Cleveland *York* 98–01; P-in-c Welton w Melton 01–12; V from 12; Tr Officer E Riding from 01; Dean of Women's Min from 08; Can and Preb York Minster from 10. *St Helen's Vicarage, Cowgate, Welton, Brough HU15 1ND* T: (01482) 666677 E: ebielby@ebielby.karoo.co.uk

BIENFAIT, Alexander. b 61. Hatf Poly BSc 86. Sarum & Wells Th Coll BTh 94. **d** 94 **p** 95. C Battersea St Luke *S'wark* 94–96; C Clapham Team 96–99; TV Whitstable *Cant* 99–07; P-in-c Biddenden and Smarden from 07; AD Romney and Tenterden from 19. *The Rectory, High Street, Biddenden, Ashford TN27 8AH* T: (01580) 291454 E: rector@sbcofe.org

BIERBAUM, Ms Ruth Anne. b 67. RN 89. Trin Coll Bris BA 98. **d** 99 **p** 00. C Filey *York* 99–02; C Coxheath, E Farleigh, Hunton, Linton etc *Roch* 02–08; Lead Mental Health Chapl Kent & Medway NHS and Soc Care Partnership Trust from 08; PtO *Roch* from 08; *Cant* from 08. *Room 314, Priority House, Hermitage Lane, Maidstone ME16 9PH* T: (01622) 722180 E: ruth.bierbaum@kmpt.nhs.uk

BIGG, Andrew John. Jes Coll Ox MPhys 05 Leeds Univ BA 10 Sheff Univ MA 11. Coll of Resurr Mirfield. **d** 11 **p** 12. C Cottingham *York* 11–14; Asst Chapl Paris St Geo *Eur* 14–17; Chapl and Dean of Chpl CCC Cam from 17; PtO *Ox* from 19; *Eur* from 19; *Chich* from 19. *Address withheld by request*

BIGG, Howard Clive. b 40. Fitzw Coll Cam BA 68 MA 72. Ridley Hall Cam 73. **d** 74 **p** 75. C Worksop St Jo *S'well* 74–76; Min Can St Alb 76–77; PtO *Ches* 78–82; *Ely* 82–99; Vice-Prin Romsey Ho Cam 86–89; NSM Cambridge St Benedict *Ely* 99–01; rtd 05; PtO *Ely* 08–13 and from 15. *4 Pershore Road, Hardwick, Cambridge CB23 7XQ* T: (01954) 211673 E: hcbigg40@gmail.com

BIGG, Michael David. b 81. Dur Univ BA 07 Wolfs Coll Cam MPhil 08 PGCE 09 Dur Univ MA 17. Ridley Hall Cam 15. **d** 17 **p** 18. C E Leightonstone *Ely* from 17. *2 Bell Field, Brampton, Huntingdon PE28 4PT* M: 07380-809377 E: revmichaelbigg@gmail.com

BIGGAR, Prof Nigel John. b 55. Worc Coll Ox BA 76 MA 88 Chicago Univ AM 80 PhD 86 Regent Coll Vancouver MCS 81. **d** 90 **p** 91. Lib Latimer Ho Ox 85–91; Asst Lect Chr Ethics Wycliffe Hall Ox 87–94; Chapl Oriel Coll Ox 90–99; Prof Th Leeds Univ *Ripon* 99–04; Prof Th TCD 04–07; Can Ch Ch Cathl Dublin *D & G* 05–07; Regius Prof Moral and Past Th Ox Univ from 07; Can Res Ch Ch *Ox* from 07. *Christ Church, Oxford OX1 1DP* T: (01865) 276219 E: nigel.biggar@chch.ox.ac.uk

BIGGS, David James. b 55. St Jo Coll Auckland LTh 82. **d** 81 **p** 82. New Zealand 81–86; C Stevenage St Andr and St Geo *St Alb* 86–89; TV Moulsecoomb *Chich* 89–99; C Brighton St Pet w Chpl Royal 99–02; P-in-c 02–09; V Brighton Chpl Royal from 09; Chapl St Mary's Hall Brighton 03–09. *The Chapel Royal, 164 North Street, Brighton BN1 1EA* T: (01273) 774492 or 328767 E: frbiggs@gmail.com

BIGGS, David James. b 93. Teesside Univ BSc 15. Ridley Hall Cam 15. **d** 18 **p** 19. C Thirsk *York* from 18. *3 Herriot Way, Thirsk YO7 1FL* M: 07857-143881 E: david.biggs@hotmail.com

BIGGS, Philip John. b 51. Ripon Hall Ox 74. **d** 77 **p** 78. C Maidstone All SS w St Phil and H Trin *Cant* 77–80; Dioc Youth Officer Truro 80–84; Chapl St Hilda's Angl Sch Australia 84–87; R Bicton 87–91; R Mosman Park 92–10; 98–04; Hon Chapl Miss to Seafarers 84–10; Can Res and Chan Blackb Cathl 10–11; Poland 11–12; P-in-c Lytham St Cuth *Blackb* 12–15; Hon C St Neot and Warleggan w Cardynham Truro 15–17; Hon C St Neot and Warleggan from 17; Hon C St Cleer from 17. *The Vicarage, St Neot, Liskeard PL14 6NG* T: (01579) 320472 M: 07521-282876

BIGNELL, Alan Guy. b 39. Lon Univ BA 64. Ox NSM Course 78. **d** 81 **p** 82. NSM Upton cum Chalvey *Ox* 81–90; NSM Burnham and Slough Deanery 90–10; PtO from 10. *Little Gidding, 2 Turners Road, Slough SL3 7AN* T: (01753) 523005 E: abignell@waitrose.com

BILES, David George. b 35. AKC 58 Open Univ BA 75 Lambeth STh 91 Leeds Univ MA 96. **d** 59 **p** 60. C Cockerton *Dur* 59–62; C Winlaton 62–67; P-in-c Dipton 67–74; R Wolviston 74–89; P-in-c Thirkleby w Kilburn and Bagby *York* 89–90; V 90–00; RD Thirsk 90–91; RD Mowbray 91–00; rtd 00; PtO *York* from 00; *Sheff* 11–13. *10 King Rudding Close, Riccall, York YO19 6RY* T/F: (01757) 248829 E: biles.cofferwood10@gmail.com

BILES, Mrs Kathleen Anne. b 52. Bradf Univ BA 74. St Jo Coll Nottm 98. **d** 04 **p** 06. C Ch Ch Cathl Stanley Falkland Is from 04. *PO Box 166, 14 Kent Road, Stanley FIQQ 1ZZ, Falkland Islands* T/F: (00500) 21897 E: kbiles@horizon.co.fk

BILES, Canon Timothy Mark Frowde. b 35. St Mich Coll Llan 60. **d** 64 **p** 66. C Middleton St Cross *Ripon* 64–66; Chapl Chapl St Fran Sch Hooke 66–72; P-in-c Toller Porcorum w Hooke *Sarum* 72–79; P-in-c Melplash w Mapperton 74–79; P-in-c Beaminster 77–79; TR Beaminster Area 79–00; Can and Preb Sarum Cathl 83–00; RD Beaminster 84–89; rtd 00; PtO *Sarum* from 01. *36 Hound Street, Sherborne DT9 3AA* T: (01935) 816247 E: timbiles35@gmail.com

BILINDA, Mrs Lesley Anne. b 59. Aber Univ MA 81 All Nations Chr Coll BA 98. Ripon Coll Cuddesdon MA 13. **d** 13 **p** 14. C

Fulham St Andr *Lon* 13–16; V from 16; Dean of Women's Min Kensington Area from 17. *St Andrew's Vicarage, 10 St Andrew's Road, London W14 9SX* T: (020) 7385 5023 M: 07956-587176 E: vicar@standrewsfulham.com

BILL, Alan. b 29. K Coll Lon BD 66 AKC 66. d 67 p 68. C Gt Burstead *Chelmsf* 67–70; TV Thornaby on Tees *York* 71–76; R E Gilling 76–81; V Ormesby 81–91; rtd 91; PtO *Newc* from 91. *13 Wilmington Close, Tudor Grange, Newcastle upon Tyne NE3 2SF* T: 0191-242 4467 E: alanbill_uk@yahoo.co.uk

BILL, Canon Thomas Andrew Graham. b 47. Dur Univ BA 76. Cranmer Hall Dur. d 77 p 78. C Penwortham St Mary *Blackb* 77–80; C Torrisholme 80–82; P-in-c Accrington St Pet 82–89; P-in-c Haslingden St Jo Stonefold 82–89; V Skerton St Chad 89–03; R Burnley St Pet 03–11; P-in-c Burnley St Steph 08–11; R Burnley St Pet and St Steph 11–13; Hon Can Blackb Cathl 03–13; rtd 13; PtO *Blackb* from 13. *26 Thornton Road, Morecambe LA4 5PE* T: (01524) 417117 E: tom@tombill.entadsl.com

BILLETT, Canon Anthony Charles. b 56. Bris Univ BEd. Wycliffe Hall Ox 82. d 85 p 86. C Waltham Abbey *Chelmsf* 85–88; C Nor St Pet Mancroft w St Jo Maddermarket 88–91; V Stalham and E Ruston w Brunstead 91–00; R Stalham, E Ruston, Brunstead, Sutton and Ingham 00–01; R Diss 01–14; TR from 14; RD Redenhall 06–15; Hon Can Nor Cathl from 10. *The Rectory, 26 Mount Street, Diss IP22 4QG* T: (01379) 642072 E: disschurch2@btconnect.com

BILLETT (née RANDALL), Mrs Elizabeth Nicola. b 55. RGN 75 SCM 81. EAMTC 94. d 97 p 98. C Loddon, Sisland w Hales and Heckingham *Nor* 97–98; C Loddon, Sisland, Chedgrave, Hardley and Langley 98–01; TV Hempnall from 02. *The Flat, George's House, The Street, Woodton, Bungay NR35 1LZ* T: (01508) 482366

BILLETT, Mrs Justine Elizabeth Stearman. b 82. Reading Univ BSc 06. Ripon Coll Cuddesdon BA 15. d 15 p 17. C Banwell *B & W* 15–17; C Congresbury w Puxton and Hewish St Ann 15–17; C Backwell w Chelvey and Brockley 17–19. *15 Marsh Farm Road, Twickenham TW2 6SH* M: 07778-049265 E: rev.j.billett@gmail.com

BILLIN, David Robert. b 55. S Bank Poly BSc 77 CEng 82 MIET 82 MIRSE 86 EurIng 89. d 06 p 07. NSM Carshalton *S'wark* 06–19; NSM Sutton from 19. *33 Beeches Avenue, Carshalton SM5 3LJ* T: (020) 8647 5046 M: 07946-609387 E: davidbillin1955@btinternet.com *or* davidbillin@outlook.com

BILLIN, Mrs Susan Lynn. b 59. S Bank Univ BSc 99 Greenwich Univ CertEd 99. SEITE 02. d 05 p 06. NSM S Beddington and Roundshaw *S'wark* 05–16; P-in-c Hackbridge and Beddington Corner 16–19; V from 19. *33 Beeches Avenue, Carshalton SM5 3LJ* M: 07816-140385 E: lynnbillin234@hotmail.co.uk

BILLINGHURST, Richard George. b 48. St Jo Coll Cam BA 70 MA 74 FIA 76. Ridley Hall Cam 76. d 79 p 80. C Caverswall *Lich* 79–81; C Cullompton *Ex* 81–84; R Redgrave cum Botesdale w Rickinghall *St E* 84–92; R Skellingthorpe w Doddington *Linc* 92–17; RD Graffoe 94–02 and 14–17; rtd 17; PtO *Linc* from 18. *12 Chiltern Road, Lincoln LN5 8SD* M: 07971-590378 E: acorns@clara.co.uk

BILLINGS, Canon Alan Roy. b 42. Em Coll Cam BA 65 MA 69 Bris Univ PGCE 66 Leic Univ MEd 75 NY Th Sem DMin 87. Linc Th Coll 66. d 68 p 69. C Knighton St Mary Magd *Leic* 68–72; P-in-c Sheff Gillcar St Silas 72–76; V Beighton 76–77; Hd RE Broadway Sch Barnsley 77–81; PtO *Sheff* 77–81; V Walkley 81–86; Dir Ox Inst for Ch and Soc 86–92; PtO *Ox* 86–92; Vice-Prin Ripon Coll Cuddesdon 88–92; Prin WMMTC 92–94; V Kendal St Geo *Carl* 94–07; C Grayrigg 06–07; Warden of Readers 96–03; Dir Cen for Ethics and Relig Lanc Univ 00–07; Hon Can Carl Cathl 05–07; rtd 07; PtO *Sheff* from 07. *43 Northfield Court, Sheffield S10 1QR* T: 0114-267 6549 E: alanbillingsuk@yahoo.co.uk

BILLINGS, Roger Key. b 41. ACIB. Oak Hill Th Coll BA 80. d 80 p 81. C Tunbridge Wells St Jas *Roch* 80–84; V Thatcham St Paul w All SS 84–95; V Carterton *Ox* 95–03; TR Brize Norton and Carterton 03–07; AD Witney 03–07; rtd 07; PtO *Nor* from 07. *Maudville, Norwich Road, Cromer NR27 9JU* T: (01263) 519055 E: rogerbillings@btinternet.com

BILLINGS, Mrs Valerie Ann. b 52. Nottm Trent Univ CertEd 02. EMMTC 07. d 09 p 10. NSM Ockbrook *Derby* 09–14; PtO from 15. *14 Conway Avenue, Borrowash, Derby DE72 3GT* T: (01332) 726285 E: valbillings1@gmail.com

BILLINGTON, George. b 45. St Jo Coll Nottm 92. d 94 p 95. C Accrington St Jo w Huncoat *Blackb* 94–98; C Whittle-le-Woods 98–00; V Stalmine w Pilling 00–10; rtd 10. *Brookvale, Sterridge Valley, Berrynarbor, Ilfracombe EX34 9TB* T: (01271) 883546

BILLSON, Jennifer Ann Margaret. b 46. d 16 p 17. NSM Crowland *Linc* from 16. *2 Ambury Gardens, Crowland, Peterborough PE6 0ET* E: annie@maildaemon.co.uk

BILLSON, Kevin Michael. b 58. Lon Univ BD 81. Qu Coll Birm 10. d 11 p 12. C Brereton and Rugeley *Lich* 11–15; R Blofield *Nor* from 15; PtO *Eur* from 16. *The Rectory, 10 Oak Wood, Blofield, Norwich NR13 4JQ* T: (01603) 712299 M: 07941-341911 E: kevin.billson@eraith.net

BILTON, Canon Paul Michael. b 52. AKC 74. St Aug Coll Cant 74. d 75 p 76. C Skipton Ch Ch *Bradf* 75–79; Ind Chapl *Worc* 79–81; V Greetland and W Vale *Wakef* 81–88; R Mablethorpe w Trusthorpe *Linc* 88–91; V Bradf St Wilfrid Lidget Green 91–04; P-in-c Bradf St Columba w St Andr 00–04; V Bradf St Wilfrid w St Columba 04–14; *Leeds* 14–17; RD Bowling and Horton *Bradf* 02–14; AD *Leeds* 14; Hon Can Bradf Cathl 04–17; rtd 17. *7 Middle Burn End, Stonehaugh, Hexham NE48 3DY* E: paulmichaelbiltonbb@gmail.com

BIMSON, Sara Margaret. b 56. St Jo Coll Nottm BA. d 03 p 04. C Maidstone St Martin *Cant* 03–08; rtd 08; Voc Officer *Cant* 08–10; PtO from 08; Hon Min Can Cant Cathl from 12. *166 Westwood Drive, Canterbury CT2 7US* T: (01227) 760655 E: sara.bimson@canterbury-cathedral.org

BINDING, Ms Frances Mary. b 59. York Univ BA 81 Newc Poly PGCE 82. WEMTC 98. d 02 p 03. C Bromyard *Heref* 02–07; TV Worc SE 07–13; P-in-c Wraxall *B & W* 13–15; R from 15. *41 Vowles Close, Wraxall, Bristol BS48 1PP* E: franmbinding@gmail.com

BINDOFF, Ms Anna. b 70. Leeds Univ BA 94. Ripon Coll Cuddesdon BA 97. d 98 p 99. Asst Chapl New Coll Ox 98–01; Hon C Blackbird Leys *Ox* 98–01; C 01–04. *23 Brook Street, Watlington OX49 5JH* T: (01491) 613327 E: abindoff@btinternet.com

BING, Canon Alan Charles. b 56. St Edm Hall Ox BA 78 MA 91 Ex Univ MA 96. Oak Hill Th Coll 89. d 91 p 92. C Fremington *Ex* 91–94; C-in-c Roundswell CD 94–97; TV Barnstaple 97–99; Chapl N Devon Coll Barnstaple 96–99; P-in-c Ulverston St Mary w H Trin *Carl* 99–04; R from 04; RD Furness 01–19; Hon Can Carl Cathl from 09. *The Rectory, 15 Ford Park Crescent, Ulverston LA12 7JR* T/F: (01229) 584331 E: alanbing@live.co.uk *or* rector@ulverstonparishchurch.org

BINGHAM, Norman James Frederick. b 26. Lon Univ BSc 51. Tyndale Hall Bris 61. d 63 p 64. C Chell *Lich* 63–67; C Macclesfield St Mich *Ches* 67–71; P-in-c Macclesfield St Pet 71–73; V Leyton St Mary w St Edw *Chelmsf* 73–91; RD Waltham Forest 81–86; P-in-c Leyton St Luke 82–91; rtd 91; PtO *St Alb* from 91. *97 Monks Walk, Buntingford SG9 9DP* T: (01763) 272275

BINKS, Robert Peter. b 73. Trin Coll Bris 08. d 10 p 11. C Basildon St Andr w H Cross *Chelmsf* 10–14; P-in-c Warley Ch Ch and Gt Warley St Mary 14–18. *Address temp unknown* E: rob.binks@me.com

BINKS, Susan Jane. b 59. Edin Univ MA 81. Yorks Min Course 13. d 15 p 16. NSM Kirkdale w Harome, Nunnington and Pockley *York* 15–18; V from 18. *Helleborus Cottage, Main Street, Harome, York YO62 5JF* T: (01439) 770523 M: 07908-747796 E: binksharome@btinternet.com

BINLEY, Miss Teresa Mary. b 37. Dalton Ho Bris 61. d 87 p 94. Par Dn Ashton-upon-Mersey St Mary Magd *Ches* 87–92; Bp's Officer for Women in Min 87–92; C Chaddesden St Mary *Derby* 92–98; rtd 98; PtO *Derby* from 98. *27 Hindscarth Crescent, Mickleover, Derby DE3 9NN* T: (01332) 511146

BINNEY, Mark James Gurney. b 58. K Coll Lon BD 80. Qu Coll Birm 84. d 86 p 87. C Hornchurch St Andr *Chelmsf* 86–89; C Hutton 89–91; V Pheasey *Lich* 91–96; TV Wombourne w Trysull and Bobbington 96–99; V Wilnecote 99–08; P-in-c Hampton w Sedgeberrow and Hinton-on-the-Green *Worc* 08–18; P-in-c Bengeworth 12–18; R Bengeworth and Hampton etc from 18. *St Andrew's Vicarage, 54 Pershore Road, Evesham WR11 2PQ* T: (01386) 446381 E: reverend-mark-binney@hotmail.co.uk

BINNS, Miss Elizabeth Ann. b 55. Man Metrop Univ BA 87 RGN 77. d 05 p 06. OLM Bury St Jo w St Mark *Man* 05–10; OLM Walmersley Road, Bury 10–14; NSM Radcliffe from 14; TV from 17. *36 Raymond Avenue, Bury BL9 6NN* T: 0161-764 5071 M: 07976-818157 E: e.binns@bury.gov.uk

BINNS, Mrs Janet Victoria. b 57. ACIB 96. Ox Min Course 04. d 07 p 08. C Slough *Ox* 07–10; C Eton w Eton Wick, Boveney and Dorney 10–11; Olympics Co-ord 11–12; PtO 13; R Hedsor and Bourne End from 13. *34 Fieldhead Gardens, Bourne End SL8 5RN* T: (01628) 523046 E: revjanetbinns@btinternet.com

BINNS, Canon John Richard Elliott. b 51. St Jo Coll Cam MA 76 K Coll Lon PhD 89. Coll of Resurr Mirfield 74. d 76 p 77. C Clapham Old Town *S'wark* 76–80; TV Mortlake w E Sheen 80–87; V Upper Tooting H Trin 87–94; V Cambridge

Gt St Mary w St Mich *Ely* 94–17; RD Cambridge N 07–11; Hon Can Ely Cathl 07–17; rtd 17; PtO *Lich* from 17. *Laburnum Cottage, 197 Chase Road, Burntwood WS7 0EB* T: (01543) 670217 E: johnrbinns@gmail.com

BINNS, Peter Rodney. b 44. St Andr Univ MA 66. Ox NSM Course 72. **d** 75 **p** 76. NSM Amersham on the Hill *Ox* 75–90; NSM Wingrave w Rowsham, Aston Abbotts and Cublington 90–97; NSM Hawridge w Cholesbury and St Leonard 90–97; NSM Amersham on the Hill from 97. *16 Turnfurlong Row, Turnfurlong Lane, Aylesbury HP21 7FF* T: (01296) 330836 F: 337965 E: peter.binns166@btinternet.com

BINNY, Canon John Wallace. b 46. Univ of Wales (Lamp) BA 70. St Mich Coll Llan 69. **d** 71 **p** 72. C Llantrisant *Llan* 71–77; V Troedyrhiw w Merthyr Vale 77–82; R Eglwysbrewis w St Athan, Flemingston, Gileston 82–95; R Eglwysbrewis w St Athan w Gileston 95–03; V Pentyrch w Capel Llanilltterne 03–11; rtd 11; PtO *Llan* from 11; Hon Can St Helena from 18. *Oakdene, 27 Porthamal Road, Cardiff CF14 6AQ* T: (029) 2062 0360 E: johnbinny@live.co.uk

BINSLEY, Michael Robert. b 44. **d** 09 **p** 10. OLM Yoxall *Lich* 09–18; OLM Kings Bromley, The Ridwares and Yoxall 18–19; PtO from 19. *83 Lightwood Road, Yoxall, Burton-on-Trent DE13 8QE* T: (01543) 472761

BIRBECK, Anthony Leng. b 33. Linc Coll Ox BA 59 MA 61. Linc Th Coll 58. **d** 60 **p** 61. C Redcar *York* 60–73; C Redcar w Kirkleatham 73–74; Chapl Teesside Ind Miss 62–74; Can Res and Treas Wells Cathl *B & W* 74–78; NSM Wells St Thos w Horrington 89–98; rtd 98; PtO *B & W* from 98; RD Shepton Mallet 07–11. *Beeches, Cannards Grave Road, Shepton Mallet BA4 4LX* T: (01749) 330382 M: 07802-725024 E: tony-birbeck@msn.com

BIRBECK, John Trevor. b 49. ACIB 77. St Jo Coll Nottm 86. **d** 88 **p** 89. C Eccleshill *Bradf* 88–92; V Hurst Green and Mitton 92–03; R Rawmarsh w Parkgate *Sheff* 03–16; C Greasbrough 10–16; C Kimberworth and Kimberworth Park 10–16; rtd 16; PtO *Guildf* from 17; *Blackb* from 18. *3 Winston Avenue, Lytham St Annes FY8 3NS* T: (01253) 985986 E: susan4john@gmail.com

BIRCH, Barry. b 46. Sheff Univ CertEd 69 Lon Univ BA 74 MIL 84 MCollP 85. **d** 06 **p** 07. NSM Cantley *Sheff* 06–08; P-in-c Eastchurch w Leysdown and Harty *Cant* 08–12; Hon C W Sheppey 12; rtd 12; PtO *Eur* 13–18. *Richard Holstraat 133, 2551 HR Gravenhage, The Netherlands* T: (0031) (70) 213 4042 E: barrybirch@hotmail.com

BIRCH, Graham James. b 62. NOC BTh 94. **d** 97 **p** 98. C Southport St Phil and St Paul *Liv* 97–01; P-in-c Wigan St Cath 01–07; V Ainsdale 07–19; V Gt Harwood *Blackb* from 19. *The Vicarage, Church Lane, Great Harwood, Blackburn BB6 7PU*

BIRCH, Mark Russell. b 70. Bris Univ BVSc 93 Em Coll Cam BA 99. Westcott Ho Cam 97. **d** 00 **p** 01. C Cirencester *Glouc* 00–03; Chapl and Fell Ex Coll Ox 03–06; Chapl Helen and Douglas Ho Ox 06–10; Chapl Treloar Coll Alton 10–12; P-in-c Win St Cross w St Faith 12–14; Chapl St Cross Hosp 12–14; Min Can and Chapl Westmr Abbey from 14. *The Chapter Office, 20 Dean's Yard, London SW1P 3PA* T: (020) 7654 4968 E: mark.birch@me.com *or* mark.birch@westminster-abbey.org

BIRCH, Richard Arthur. b 51. Brighton Poly BSc 73 Chelsea Coll Lon MSc 76. SEITE 98. **d** 01 **p** 02. NSM Folkestone St Jo *Cant* 01–04; NSM Hawkinge w Acrise and Swingfield 04–07; NSM Hythe 07–08; NSM Doddington, Newnham and Wychling 08–14; NSM Kingsdown and Creekside 14–19; rtd 19. *42 Robins Close, Lenham, Maidstone ME17 2LD* E: richard.a.birch@gmail.com

BIRCH, Thomas David Keith. b 81. Glas Univ MA 03 Edin Univ MSc 06. Ripon Coll Cuddesdon BA 14. **d** 14 **p** 15. C Gosforth St Nic *Newc* 14–17; P-in-c Wylam 17–18; P-in-c Ovingham 17–18; V Ovingham and Wylam from 18. *The Vicarage, Church Road, Wylam NE41 8AT* T: (01661) 853254 M: 07976-047707 E: revdtombirch@gmail.com

BIRCHALL, John Dearman. b 70. St Andr Univ MA 93. Wycliffe Hall Ox BTh 99. **d** 99 **p** 00. C Purley Ch Ch *S'wark* 99–02; C Fisherton Anger *Sarum* 02–08; V Surbiton Hill Ch Ch *S'wark* from 08. *Christ Church Vicarage, 7 Christ Church Road, Surbiton KT5 8JJ* T: (020) 8399 3733 *or* 8390 7215 E: john.birchall@ccsurbiton.org

BIRCHALL, Robert Gary. b 59. Sheff Univ BA 81. St Jo Coll Nottm 85. **d** 88 **p** 89. C Manston *Ripon* 88–91; C Leic Martyrs 91–94; C New Humberstone 94–95; V Burnopfield *Dur* 95–14; V Burnopfield and Dipton 14; AD Lanchester 06–14; V Boldmere *Birm* from 14. *209 Station Road, Sutton Coldfield B73 5LE* T: 0121-354 4501 E: garybirchall1@gmail.com

BIRCHARD, Canon Thaddeus Jude. b 45. Louisiana State Univ BA 66. Kelham Th Coll 66. **d** 70 **p** 71. C Devonport St Mark Ford *Ex* 70–73; C Southend St Jo w St Mark, All SS w St Fran etc *Chelmsf* 73–76; TV Poplar *Lon* 76–80; V Paddington St Jo

w St Mich 80–01; Hon Can Louisiana from 90; rtd 01; PtO *Lon* 02–13 and from 18. *142 Dibdin House, Maida Vale, London W9 1QG* T: (020) 7328 2380 E: thaddeus@birchard.co.uk

BIRD, The Very Revd David John. b 46. St D Coll Lamp BA 70 Duquesne Univ PhD 87. Gen Th Sem (NY) STM 74. **d** 70 **p** 71. C Kidderminster St Geo *Worc* 70–72; Chapl Trin Sch New York USA 72–78; V Rochdale Ch Ch 78–79; R New Kensington St Andr 79–89; R Washington Grace Ch 89–03; Dean Trin Cathl San Jose from 03. *Trinity Cathedral, 81 North 2nd Street, San Jose, CA 95113-1205, USA* T: (001) (408) 293 7953 F: 293 4993 E: david3933@aol.com

BIRD, Canon David Ronald. b 55. York Univ BA 76. St Jo Coll Nottm 83. **d** 86 **p** 87. C Kinson *Sarum* 86–90; R Thrapston *Pet* 90–97; P-in-c Islip 94–95; RD Higham 94–97; V Northampton St Giles 97–12; Can Pet Cathl 01–12; P-in-c Tollington *Lon* 12–14; TR 14–19; rtd 19. *5C Kidbrooke Park Road, London SE3 0LR* E: drbirdis@gmail.com

BIRD, Douglas Norman. b 38. **d** 92 **p** 93. OLM New Bury *Man* 92–06; PtO *Blackb* 06–14; *Man* from 06. *10 Hawthorne Avenue, Horwich, Bolton BL6 6JD* T: (01204) 695916 M: 07737-136306 E: aviary1712@outlook.com

BIRD, Canon Frederick Hinton. b 38. St Edm Hall Ox BA 62 MA 66 Univ of Wales MEd 81 PhD 86. St D Coll Lamp BD 65. **d** 65 **p** 66. C Mynyddislwyn *Mon* 65–67; Min Can St Woolos Cathl 67–70; Chapl Anglo-American Coll Farringdon 70–71; PtO *Ox* 70–78; Cant 72–78; *Mon* 76–82; V Rushen *S & M* 82–03; Can St German's Cathl 93–03; rtd 03; PtO *S & M* from 04. *Conrhenny, 56 Selborne Drive, Douglas, Isle of Man IM2 3NL* T: (01624) 621624 E: hinton.bird@gmail.com

BIRD, Geoffrey. b 44. Dioc OLM tr scheme 97. **d** 99 **p** 00. Asst Chapl HM YOI and Remand Cen Brinsford 99; Sen Chapl 99–04; Chapl HM Pris Shepton Mallet 04–09; rtd 09. *2 Hosey Road, Sturminster Newton DT10 1QP* T: (01258) 472904 E: revgeoffbird@gmail.com

BIRD, Henry John Joseph. b 37. ARCO 58 Qu Coll Cam BA 59 MA 63. Linc Th Coll 62. **d** 64 **p** 65. C Harbledown *Cant* 64–68; C Skipton H Trin *Bradf* 68–70; V Oakworth 70–81; Chapl Abingdon Sch 81–82; P-in-c Doncaster St Geo *Sheff* 82–85; V 85–02; rtd 02; PtO *Sheff* from 05; *Wakef* 14; *Leeds* from 14. *332 Thorne Road, Doncaster DN2 5AL* T: (01302) 365589 E: hbird588@btinternet.com

BIRD, Hinton. *See* BIRD, Frederick Hinton

BIRD, Ian Nicholas. b 62. Qu Eliz Coll Lon BSc 83 Newc Univ PhD 87 Heythrop Coll Lon MA 10. SAOMC 03. **d** 06 **p** 07. C Chandler's Ford *Win* 06–10; V from 10. *The Vicarage, 30 Hursley Road, Chandler's Ford, Eastleigh SO53 2FT* T: (023) 8025 4739 M: 07733-213535 E: ianbird@parishofchandlersford.org.uk

BIRD, Jeremy Paul. b 56. Ex Univ BSc 77 Hull Univ MA 88. Sarum Th Coll 78. **d** 80 **p** 81. C Tavistock and Gulworthy *Ex* 80–83; Chapl Teesside Poly *York* 83–88; R Chipstable w Huish Champflower and Clatworthy *B & W* 88–93; Rural Affairs Officer 88–93; V Uffculme *Ex* 93–01; P-in-c Dawlish 01–09; P-in-c Exwick from 09. *The Vicarage, Exwick Hill, Exeter EX4 2AQ* T: (01392) 255500

BIRD, Joel Timothy. b 88. St Mellitus Coll BA 18. **d** 18 **p** 19. C Dronfield w Holmesfield *Derby* from 18. *43 Firthwood Road, Coal Aston, Dronfield S18 3BW* M: 07888-657529 E: joeltbird88@gmail.com *or* joel.bird@dwhparish.org.uk

BIRD, John. *See* BIRD, Henry John Joseph

BIRD, Mrs Margaret Kathleen. b 48. SAOMC 04. **d** 06 **p** 07. NSM Cox Green *Ox* 06–10; NSM New Windsor 10–18; AD Maidenhead and Windsor 14–17; rtd 18; PtO *Win* from 18. *47 Boundary Road, Bournemouth BH10 4HH* T: (01202) 251896 M: 07881-712611 E: margretkbird@gmail.com

BIRD, Nicholas William Randle. b 70. Univ of Cen England in Birm BSc 99 RGN 92. NEOC 02. **d** 05 **p** 06. C Thirsk *York* 05–09; P-in-c Dunnington 09–12; P-in-c Stockton-on-the-Forest w Holtby and Warthill 09–12; R Rural E York from 12; RD Derwent from 16. *The Rectory, 30 Church Street, Dunnington, York YO19 5PW* T: (01904) 489349 E: revnickbird@gmail.com

BIRD, Patricia Moira. b 53. RGN 75. **d** 19. NSM Charlbury w Shorthampton *Ox* from 19. *4 Elm Crescent, Charlbury, Chipping Norton OX7 3PZ* E: tish@stmaryscharlbury.org.uk

BIRD, Canon Peter Andrew. b 40. Wadh Coll Ox BA 62 MA 68. Ridley Hall Cam 63. **d** 65 **p** 66. C Keynsham w Queen Charlton *B & W* 65–68; C Strood St Nic *Roch* 68–72; TV Strood 72–79; V S Gillingham 79–89; V Westerham 89–02; Hon Can Roch Cathl 01–02; PtO 02–05; *Derby* 05–18. *Iona, Prospect Terrace, Stanedge Road, Bakewell DE45 1DG* T: (01629) 813087 E: pabird@googlemail.com

BIRDSEYE, Miss Jacqueline Ann. b 55. Sussex Univ BEd 78 Southn Univ BTh 88 K Coll Lon MTh 93. Sarum & Wells Th Coll 85. **d** 88 **p** 94. C Egham Hythe *Guildf* 88–91; C Fleet 91–92; C Shottermill 92–95; C Leavesden *St Alb* 95–98; R

Ashwell w Hinxworth and Newnham 98–05; R Moreton, Woodsford and Crossways w Tincleton *Sarum* from 05. *The Rectory, 17 Warmwell Road, Crossways, Dorchester DT2 8BS* T: (01305) 854046 E: j.birdseye@btinternet.com

BIRKENHEAD, Suffragan Bishop of. *See* SINCLAIR, The Rt Revd Gordon Keith

BIRKETT, Christine Joy. b 53. Univ of Wales (Cardiff) BTheol 99 PGCE 01. Trin Coll Bris 07. **d** 08 **p** 09. NSM Berkeley w Wick, Breadstone, Newport, Stone etc *Glouc* 08–10; NSM Cainscross w Selsley 10–12; NSM Rodborough and The Stanleys w Selsley 12–13; P-in-c Upton St Leonards 13–16; rtd 16; PtO *Glouc* from 16. *7 Ann Edwards Mews, Abbeydale, Gloucester GL4 4FG* E: cjoyb1953@yahoo.co.uk

BIRKETT, Mrs Joyce. b 38. WMMTC 84. **d** 87 **p** 94. Par Dn Hill *Birm* 87–91; Asst Chapl Highcroft Hosp Birm 87–91; Par Dn Rowley Regis *Birm* 91–94; C 94–96; V Londonderry 96–01; rtd 01; PtO *Birm* from 01. *83 Callowbrook Lane, Rubery, Rednal, Birmingham B45 9HP* T: 0121-457 9759

BIRKETT, Mrs Julie Anne. b 56. SWMTC. **d** 10 **p** 11. NSM Hutton and Locking *B & W* 10–13; NSM Weston super Mare St Jo from 13. *19 Stanhope Road, Weston-super-Mare BS23 4LP* T: (01934) 625587 M: 07763-335481 E: rebelrevd@gmail.com

BIRKETT, Neil Warren. b 45. Lanc Univ BEd 74 Southn Univ MA 84. Kelham Th Coll 65. **d** 77 **p** 77. NSM Win St Matt 77–15; PtO from 15. *Corrymeela, 132 Teg Down Meads, Winchester SO22 5NS* T: (01962) 864910

BIRKIN, Mrs Angela Elizabeth. b 58. New Hall Cam BA 79 MB, BChir 82 MRCGP 86. Yorks Min Course 15. **d** 17 **p** 18. NSM Headingley *Leeds* from 17. *2 Lakeside View, Rawdon, Leeds LS19 6RN* T: 0113-414 6835 M: 07506-056185 E: ange.birkin1@sky.com

BIRKIN, Mrs Elspeth Joyce (Joy). b 36. CertEd 58. WMMTC 95. **d** 96 **p** 97. NSM Hanley Castle, Hanley Swan and Welland *Worc* 96–01; NSM Berrow w Pendock, Eldersfield, Hollybush etc 01–04; PtO 04–13; *Llan* from 13. *11 Spitzkop, Llantwit Major CF61 1RD* E: revjoy@uwclub.net

BIRKIN, Ms Julie. b 65. Qu Foundn (Course) 16. **d** 19. NSM Stoke-upon-Trent and Fenton *Lich* from 19. *87 Constance Avenue, Stoke-on-Trent ST4 8TE* T: (01782) 924728 M: 07748-856180 E: juliebirkin519@sky.com

BIRKINSHAW, Ian George. b 58. Pemb Coll Ox BA 81 Leeds Univ MA 97 Sheff Univ PGCE 82. NOC 93. **d** 96 **p** 97. NSM Chapeltown *Sheff* 96–97; C Normanton *Wakef* 98–01; C York St Mich-le-Belfrey 01–08; TR Huntington 08–10; R from 10. *The Rectory, Chestnut Court, Huntington, York YO32 9RD* T: (01904) 766550 *or* 768006 E: ian.birkinshaw@huntingtonparish.org.uk

BIRKS, Andrew Graham James. b 75. Dur Univ BA 17. SEITE 11. **d** 16 **p** 17. NSM Portslade St Nic and St Andr and Mile Oak *Chich* 16–19; C Bexhill St Barn from 19; C Sidley from 19. *The Vicarage, Cantelupe Road, Bexhill-on-Sea TN40 1JG* M: 07795-117270 E: agb.75@hotmail.com

BIRMINGHAM, Archdeacon of. *See* TOMLINSON, The Ven Jennifer Clare

BIRMINGHAM, Bishop of. *See* URQUHART, The Rt Revd David Andrew

BIRMINGHAM, Dean of. *See* THOMPSON, The Very Revd Matthew

BIRNIE, Ms Ruth Burdett. b 41. Glas Univ MA 64 Jordanhill Coll Glas PGCE 65 Leeds Univ MA 73. NEOC 02. **d** 04 **p** 05. NSM Gosforth All SS *Newc* 04–11; PtO from 11. *27 Delaval Terrace, Newcastle upon Tyne NE3 4RT* T: 0191-284 1393 E: ruthbirnie27@gmail.com

BIRON-SCOTT, Laura Rebecca. b 83. Qu Coll Cam BA 06 MPhil 08 PhD 10. SEITE 16. **d** 16 **p** 17. C Kidlington w Hampton Poyle *Ox* 16–19; V Headington Quarry from 19. *The Vicarage, 46 Quarry Road, Headington, Oxford OX3 8NU* E: laura.biron@gmail.com

BIRT, Herbert Michael. b 56. ERMC 14. **d** 17 **p** 18. NSM Woolpit w Drinkstone *St E* from 17. *7 Meadowlands, Woolpit, Bury St Edmunds IP30 9SE* E: mikebirt856@btinternet.com

BIRT, Richard Arthur. b 43. Ch Ch Ox BA 66 MA 69. Cuddesdon Coll 67. **d** 69 **p** 70. C Sutton St Mich *York* 69–71; C Wollaton *S'well* 71–75; R Kirkby in Ashfield 75–80; P-in-c Duxford *Ely* 80–87; R 87–88; P-in-c Hinxton 80–87; V 87–88; P-in-c Ickleton 80–87; V 87–88; V Weobley w Sarnesfield and Norton Canon *Heref* 88–00; P-in-c Letton w Staunton, Byford, Mansel Gamage etc 88–00; rtd 00; PtO *Heref* from 00. *8 Queens Hill Gardens, Hereford HR4 0EZ*

BIRTWISTLE, Canon James. b 33. FCA 66. Ely Th Coll 57. **d** 59 **p** 60. C Southport St Luke *Liv* 59–63; V Cleator Moor w Cleator *Carl* 63–70; R Letchworth *St Alb* 70–73; P-in-c Wareside 73–80; Dep Dir of Educn 77–80; Dioc Dir of Educn 80–98; Hon Can St Alb 85–98; P-in-c Hertingfordbury 88–98; rtd 98; PtO *Ex* from 99. *9 Stoneborough Lane, Budleigh Salterton EX9 6HL* T: (01395) 442517

BIRTWISTLE, Lesley Sutherland. b 44. LLB. EMMTC 00. **d** 00 **p** 01. NSM Appleby Gp *Leic* 00–07; NSM Measham 07–08; NSM Packington w Normanton-le-Heath 07–08; NSM Donisthorpe and Moira w Stretton-en-le-Field 07–08; NSM Woodfield 08–16; PtO from 16. *14 Nethercroft Drive, Packington, Ashby-de-la-Zouch LE65 1WT* T: (01530) 413309

BISCOE, Mrs Erika Jayne. b 66. Ox Min Course 12. **d** 15 **p** 16. C Bicester w Bucknell, Caversfield and Launton *Ox* from 15. *8 Pippin Close, Bicester OX27 8AX* T: (01869) 369473 M: 07867-515900 E: erika.biscoe@mail.com

BISCOE, Ian Rowland. b 68. Ox Min Course 06. **d** 07 **p** 08. C Cherwell Valley *Ox* 07–12; TV Bicester w Bucknell, Caversfield and Launton from 12. *8 Pippin Close, Bicester OX27 8AX* M: 07971-519234 E: ian.biscoe@googlemail.com

BISH, Jonathan James Peter. b 88. Ball Coll Ox BA 09 Peterho Cam BA 12. Westcott Ho Cam 10. **d** 13 **p** 14. C Halifax *Leeds* 13–17; C Outwood 17; C Outwood, Stanley and Wrenthorpe from 17. *The Vicarage, 121 Wrenthorpe Road, Wrenthorpe, Wakefield WF2 0JS* T: (01924) 373758 M: 07772-601259 E: frjonathanbish@gmail.com

BISHOP, Andrew Scott. b 70. Leeds Univ BA 93 Heythrop Coll Lon MTh 02 K Coll Lon DThMin 14. St Steph Ho Ox BTh 93. **d** 96 **p** 97. C Westmr St Steph w St Jo *Lon* 96–99; C Kensington St Mary Abbots w St Geo 99–03; V Old Basing and Lychpit *Win* 03–11; AD Basingstoke 08–11; Can Res Guildf Cathl 11–18; Chapl Surrey Univ 11–18; P-in-c Croydon St Jo *S'wark* from 18; P-in-c Croydon St Andr from 18. *84 Higher Drive, Purley CR8 2HJ*

BISHOP, Canon Anthony John. b 43. G&C Coll Cam BA 66 MA 69 Lon Univ MTh 69. ALCD 67. **d** 69 **p** 70. C Eccleston St Luke *Liv* 69–73; C Gt Baddow *Chelmsf* 73–77; CMS Nigeria 77–84; Lect Lon Bible Coll 84–85; TV Chigwell *Chelmsf* 85–93; P-in-c Walthamstow St Jo 93–98; V 98–09; rtd 09; Hon Can Kano from 00; PtO *Chelmsf* from 12. *7 High Meadows, Chigwell IG7 5JY* T: (020) 8501 4998 E: tony_bishop@talktalk.net

BISHOP, Canon Christopher. b 48. St Aug Coll Cant 71. **d** 72 **p** 73. C Gt Ilford St Mary *Chelmsf* 72–75; C Upminster 75–78; Adn's Youth Chapl 77–80; Dioc Youth Officer 80–86; Chapl Stansted Airport 86–13; P-in-c Manuden w Berden 86–03; P-in-c Manuden w Berden and Quendon w Rickling 03–13; RD Newport and Stansted 89–05; Hon Can Chelmsf Cathl 99–13; rtd 13; PtO *Chelmsf* from 14. *2 St Mary's View, Saffron Walden CB10 2GF* T: (01799) 523722 E: chrismitre@hotmail.com

BISHOP, Craig. *See* BISHOP, Stephen Craig

BISHOP, David. b 65. St Jo Coll Nottm 01. **d** 03 **p** 04. C Boulton *Derby* 03–07; V Ogley Hay *Lich* 07–19; TV Stroudwater Team *Glouc* from 19. *The Vicarage, Elm Road, Stonehouse GL10 2NP* T: (01453) 822332

BISHOP, Donald. b 22. Lon Univ BSc 48. Qu Coll Birm 56. **d** 57 **p** 58. C Trowbridge H Trin *Sarum* 57–60; CF (TA) 58–68; V Bodicote *Ox* 60–87; P-in-c Broughton 71–85; rtd 87; PtO *Cov* 87–01; *Wakef* 01–14; *Leeds* 14–16. *17 Westminster Road, Halifax HX3 8DH* T: (01422) 200844

BISHOP, Mrs Evelyn Joy. b 43. **d** 01 **p** 02. NSM Penkridge *Lich* 01–04; NSM Baswich 04–18; PtO from 18. *21 Farmdown Road, Stafford ST17 0AP* T: (01785) 603074

BISHOP, Huw Daniel. b 49. Univ of Wales (Lamp) BA 71. Bp Burgess Hall Lamp 71. **d** 73 **p** 74. C Carmarthen St Pet *St D* 73–77; Prov Youth Chapl Wales 77–79; V Llanybydder and Llanwenog w Llanwnnen *St D* 79–80; Youth and Community Officer 80–81; Hd RS Carre's Gr Sch Sleaford 81–85; Hd RS K Sch Pet 85–91; Assoc Hd Teacher St Pet Colleg Sch Wolv 91–98; Hd Teacher St Teilo's High Sch Cardiff 98–01; Prin St Pet Colleg Sch Wolv 01–10; Asst Dioc Dir of Educn *Lich* 10–13; PtO from 11; *St D* 13–14; CF (TA) from 85. *Ger y Bryn, 217 Waterloo Road, Penygroes, Llanelli SA14 7RB*

BISHOP, The Ven Ian Gregory. b 62. Portsm Poly BSc 84 MRICS 87. Oak Hill Th Coll BA 91. **d** 91 **p** 92. C Purley Ch Ch *S'wark* 91–95; P-in-c Saxlingham Nethergate and Shotesham *Nor* 95–97; TR Newton Flotman, Swainsthorpe, Tasburgh, etc 98–01; V Middlewich w Byley *Ches* 01–11; RD Middlewich 05–10; Adn Macclesfield from 11. *57A Sandbach Road, Congleton CW12 4LH* T: (01260) 272875 M: 07715-102519 E: ian.bishop@chester.anglican.org

BISHOP, Jeremy Simon. b 54. Nottm Univ BSc 75 Yonsei Univ S Korea 84. All Nations Chr Coll 82 Wycliffe Hall Ox 89. **d** 91 **p** 92. C Macclesfield Team *Ches* 91–98; R Carlton Colville w Mutford and Rushmere *Nor* 98–99; V Carlton Colville and Mutford 99–19; RD Lothingland 14–18; rtd 19. *Corner Cottage, 14 Church Street, Trimingham, Norwich NR11 8AL* E: jeremybishop532@gmail.com

BISHOP, John Charles Simeon. b 46. Chich Th Coll 77. **d** 79 **p** 79. SSF 66–86; P-in-c Edin St Dav 82–86; Chapl to the Deaf *Birm* 86–99; C Portsea N End St Mark *Portsm* 99–01; Chapl to the Deaf *Linc* 01–11; rtd 11; PtO *Dur* from 11; *Newc* from 14. *66 York Crescent, Durham DH1 5PU* T: 0191-384 8838 E: jcsbishop@btinternet.com

BISHOP, Joy. *See* BISHOP, Evelyn Joy

BISHOP, Kathleen Rachel. b 51. Open Univ BA 88 Saffron Walden Coll CertEd 76. ERMC 05. **d** 08 **p** 09. NSM Raddesley Gp *Ely* 08–12; NSM Balsham, Weston Colville, W Wickham etc 12–18; NSM Gt w Lt Abington 12–18; NSM Hildersham 12–18; NSM Granta Vale Gp from 18. *14 Granta Vale, Linton, Cambridge CB21 4LB* T: (01223) 892288 E: revkathy@hotmail.co.uk *or* michael.bishop@virgin.net

BISHOP, Mrs Louise Suzanne. b 64. St Aug Coll of Th 16. **d** 19. C Weybridge *Guildf* from 19. *87 Greenlands Road, Weybridge KT13 8PS* M: 07974-018160 E: louisebshp@aol.com

BISHOP, Mandy Louise. b 61. Univ of E Lon BA 00. NTMTC BA 09. **d** 09 **p** 10. C Moulsham St Luke *Chelmsf* 09–13; V Ormesby St Marg w Scratby, Ormesby St Mich etc *Nor* 13–19; R Kessingland, Gisleham and Rushmere from 19. *The Rectory, 1 Wash Lane, Kessingland, Lowestoft NR33 7QZ* M: 07854-790234 E: revdmandy@btinternet.com

BISHOP, His Honour Judge Mark Andrew. b 58. Down Coll Cam BA 80 MA 83 Barrister 81. EAMTC 99. **d** 02 **p** 03. Dep Chan *Roch* from 01; NSM Cambridge St Mary Less *Ely* from 02; Chan *Linc* from 07. *Inner London Crown Court, Sessions House, Newington Causeway, London SE1 6AZ* T: (01223) 264527 *or* (020) 7234 3100

BISHOP, Mark Christopher. b 81. Sheff Hallam Univ BA 03. **d** 08 **p** 09. C Oak Tree Angl Fellowship *Lon* 08–11; LtO 11–14; Pioneer Min from 14. *19 Larch Avenue, London W3 7LH* M: 07779-585105 E: revmarkbishop@gmail.com

BISHOP, Philip Michael. b 47. Lon Univ BD 69 AKC 69. St Aug Coll Cant 70. **d** 71 **p** 72. C Mansfield Woodhouse *S'well* 71–76; C Liscard St Mary w St Columba *Ches* 76–78; V Thornton-le-Moors w Ince and Elton 78–90; V Sutton w Carlton and Normanton upon Trent etc *S'well* 90–96; P-in-c Ch Broughton w Barton Blount, Boylestone etc *Derby* 96–98; P-in-c Longford, Long Lane, Dalbury and Radbourne 96–98; R Boylestone, Church Broughton, Dalbury, etc 98–17; rtd 17; PtO *S'well* from 18. *17 Beech Avenue, Keyworth, Nottingham NG12 5DE* T: 0115-937 5637 E: rev@michael.bishop.name

BISHOP, Phillip Leslie. b 44. K Coll Lon BD 66 AKC 66. **d** 67 **p** 68. C Albrighton *Lich* 67–70; C St Geo-in-the-East St Mary *Lon* 70–71; C Middlesbrough Ascension *York* 71–73; P-in-c Witherwick 73–77; Ind Chapl 73–82; V Gt Ayton w Easby and Newton-in-Cleveland 82–89; RD Stokesley 85–89; R Guisborough 89–08; Chapl S Tees Community and Mental NHS Trust 90–99; Chapl Tees and NE Yorks NHS Trust 99–08; Chapl Langbaurgh Primary Care Trust 02–08; rtd 08; PtO *York* 08–18; *Dur* from 13. *2 Sunny Side Grove, Stockton-on-Tees TS18 5DH* T: (01642) 582281 E: 317bishop@gmail.com

BISHOP, Roger John. b 49. SEITE 06. **d** 09 **p** 10. NSM Lamberhurst and Matfield *Roch* 09–19; rtd 19. *Brambletye, Maidstone Road, Five Oak Green, Tonbridge TN12 6QR* T: (01892) 833232 E: rogerjbishop@hotmail.com

BISHOP, Simeon. *See* BISHOP, John Charles Simeon

BISHOP, Stephen Craig. b 68. Wye Coll Lon BSc 90 Man Univ MA 92 Ex Univ MPhil 97 Glos Univ PGCE 98. Wycliffe Hall Ox 03. **d** 05 **p** 06. C Thornbury and Oldbury-on-Severn w Shepperdine *Glouc* 05–09; TV S Cotswolds 09–14; TR Vale and Cotswold Edge from 14. *The Vicarage, Church Street, Chipping Campden GL55 6JG* T: (01386) 840677 E: scriagbishop@hotmail.com

BISHOP, Stephen Patrick. b 60. Dioc OLM tr scheme 99. **d** 02 **p** 03. OLM Purley Ch Ch *S'wark* from 02. *Elmwood, 117 Mitchley Avenue, South Croydon CR2 9HP* T: (020) 8651 2840 E: bishopelmwood@aol.com

BISHOP, Mrs Susan Linda. b 66. Trin Coll Bris 12. **d** 15 **p** 16. NSM Filton *Bris* 15–17; NSM Warmley, Syston and Bitton from 17. *100 North Road, Stoke Gifford, Bristol BS34 8PE* T: 0117-979 8371 E: susiebishop.uk@gmail.com

BISSET, Michael Davidson. b 55. NTMTC 96. **d** 99 **p** 00. C Ickenham *Lon* 99–03; P-in-c Penn *Ox* 03–04; P-in-c Tyler's Green 03–04; V Penn and Tylers Green from 04. *The Vicarage, Church Road, Penn, High Wycombe HP10 8NU* T: (01494) 816700 E: vicar@holytrinityandstmargarets.co.uk

BISSETT, William Campbell. b 68. Westmr Coll Lon BA 89 PGCE 90 Cliff Coll MA 98 GradICSA 04. STETS 10. **d** 12 **p** 13. NSM Virginia Water *Guildf* from 12. *Cedar Cottage, Mount Lee, Egham TW20 9PD* T: (01784) 434873 M: 07900-227748 E: w.bissett@ntlworld.com

BISSEX, Mrs Janet Christine Margaret. b 50. Westhill Coll Birm CertEd 72. Trin Coll Bris 76. **dss** 86 **d** 87 **p** 94. Toxteth Park St Bede *Liv* 86–93; Par Dn 87–93; Dn-in-c Kirkdale

St Mary and St Athanasius 93–94; P-in-c 94–03; C Litherland St Andr 03; TV Bootle 04–12; rtd 12; PtO *Liv* from 16. *4 Garth Court, Haigh Road, Liverpool L22 3XL* T: 0151-538 4767 E: revjanetb@yahoo.co.uk

BISSON, Joyce Elaine. b 52. Liv Univ BTh 98 Nottm Coll of Educn TCert 73. NOC 06. **d** 08 **p** 09. NSM Gt Meols *Ches* 08–11; NSM Bromborough 11–16; PtO from 17. *14 Howbeck Drive, Prenton CH43 6UY* T: 0151-652 7888 E: elainebisson@yahoo.co.uk

BISTRAN, Petrica. b 85. Pentecostal Inst Bucharest BA 08 St Jo Coll Dur BA 15 MATM 16. Cranmer Hall Dur 13. **d** 16 **p** 17. C Silksworth *Dur* 16–18; C Sunderland St Matt and St Wilfrid from 18. *12 Bordeaux Close, Sunderland SR3 2SR* M: 07772-028520 E: petricabistran@yahoo.com

BJARNASON, Bjarni Thor. b 62. Univ of Iceland MSc 10. **p** 91. Iceland 91–97 and from 01; C Brumby *Linc* 99–01; PtO *Eur* 07–13; P-in-c Angl Congregation Iceland from 13. *Fannafold 87, 112 Reykjavík, Iceland* T: (00354) 565 8290 M: (00354) 899 6979 E: srbjarni@seltjarnarneskirkja.is

BLACK, Canon Alexander Stevenson. b 28. Glas Univ MA 53. Edin Th Coll 53. **d** 55 **p** 56. C Dumfries *Glas* 55–58; Chapl Glas Univ 58–61; C Glas St Mary 58–61; P-in-c E Kilbride 61–69; R Edin St Columba 69–79; TV Edin St Jo 79–83; R Haddington 83–93; R Dunbar 83–93; rtd 93; Can St Mary's Cathl *Edin* 88–00; Hon Can St Mary's Cathl from 00. *3 Bass Rock View, Canty Bay, North Berwick EH39 5PJ* T: (01620) 894771 E: alexander3black@btinternet.com

BLACK, David Roger. b 46. **d** 12 **p** 13. NSM Tattenhall w Burwardsley and Handley *Ches* 12–14; NSM Tilston and Shocklach 14–16; rtd 16; PtO *Ches* from 16. *Woodcroft, Church Road, Tilston, Malpas SY14 7HB* T: (01829) 250615 E: revdavidblack@mail.com

BLACK, Dominic Paul. b 70. S Bank Univ BSc 95 St Jo Coll Dur BA 98 MA 11. Cranmer Hall Dur 95. **d** 98 **p** 99. C N Hull St Mich *York* 98–04; V N Ormesby from 04; RD Middlesbrough from 11. *The Vicarage, James Street, North Ormesby, Middlesbrough TS3 6LD* T: (01642) 271814 M: 07445-395806 E: dominic.black@trinitycentre.org

BLACK, Canon Ian Christopher. b 62. Kent Univ BA 85 Nottm Univ MDiv 93. Linc Th Coll 91. **d** 93 **p** 94. C Maidstone All SS and St Phil w Tovil *Cant* 93–96; P-in-c The Brents and Davington w Oare and Luddenham 96–02; Hon Min Can Cant Cathl 97–02; Asst Dir Post-Ord Tr 98–02; V Whitkirk *Ripon* 02–12; Capitular Can Ripon Cathl 08–12; Can Res Pet Cathl from 12; V Pet St Jo from 12; RD Pet from 15. *26 Minster Precincts, Peterborough PE1 1XZ* T: (01733) 873064 E: canonianblack@btinternet.com

BLACK, Miss Imogen Nadine Laura. b 79. Trin Coll Ox BA 02 MA 05 MSt 03. St Steph Ho Ox 08. **d** 11 **p** 12. C Belper Ch Ch w Turnditch *Derby* 11–15; P-in-c Somercotes from 15; C Alfreton from 15. *St Thomas's Vicarage, 114 Nottingham Road, Somercotes, Alfreton DE55 4LY* T: (01773) 603793 E: imogen.black@trinity-oxford.com

BLACK (formerly NAPIER), Jennifer Beryl. b 39. S Dios Minl Tr Scheme 89. **d** 93 **p** 96. NSM Itchen Valley *Win* 93–01; PtO from 02; Hon C Cupar *St And* from 05. *Forresters Cottage, Edenwood, Cupar KY15 5NX* T: (01334) 653159 *or* (01962) 771702 E: jenniblackedenwood@yahoo.co.uk

BLACK, Canon Neville. b 36. Oak Hill Th Coll 61. **d** 64 **p** 65. C Everton St Ambrose w St Tim *Liv* 64–69; P-in-c Everton St Geo 69–71; V 71–81; P-in-c Everton St Benedict 70–72; P-in-c Everton St Chad w Ch Ch 70–72; Nat Project Officer Evang Urban Tr Project 74–81; TR St Luke in the City *Liv* 81–04; Chapl Liv Women's Hosp NHS Trust 82–04; Tutor NOC 82–89; Dir Gp for Urban Min and Leadership *Liv* 84–95; Hon Can Liv Cathl 87–04; P-in-c Edgehill St Dunstan 98–02; rtd 05; PtO *Liv* from 16. *19 Montfort Drive, Liverpool L19 3RJ* T: 0151-427 9803 M: 07970-235817 E: nevilleblack55a@me.com

BLACK, Samuel James. b 38. CITC. **d** 68 **p** 69. C Cloughfern *Conn* 68–72; C Lisburn St Paul 72–78; I Rasharkin w Finvoy 78–82; I Belfast Upper Malone (Epiphany) 82–95; I Ballymore *Arm* 95–05; rtd 05. *Toberhewny Hall, 22 Toberhewny Lane, Lurgan, Craigavon BT66 8JZ* T: (028) 3834 3267 E: sblack381@btinternet.com

BLACK, William Henry. St Deiniol's Hawarden. **d** 88 **p** 89. NSM Malahide w Balgriffin *D & G* 88–89; NSM Dublin St Ann and St Steph 89–94; C 94–00; Hon Asst Chapl Miss to Seamen 89–00; I Dublin Drumcondra w N Strand *D & G* 00–07; rtd 07. *27 Greendale Avenue, Dublin 5, Republic of Ireland* T: (00353) (1) 832 3141 M: 86-150 3747 E: willieblack@eircom.net

BLACKALL, Mrs Ivy Margaret. b 38. St Kath Coll Lon CertEd 58. EAMTC 82. **dss** 86 **d** 87 **p** 94. NSM Wickham Market w Pettistree and Easton *St E* 86–88; Par Dn Leiston 88–92; Par Dn Gt and Lt Glemham, Blaxhall etc 92–94; P-in-c 94–96; R 96–02; P-in-c Sternfield w Benhall and

Snape 98–02; rtd 03; PtO *St E* from 03. *6 Orchard Place, Wickham Market, Woodbridge IP13 0RU* T: (01728) 747326 M: 07850-632900 E: mgtblack@globalnet.co.uk *or* margaret@mgtblack.plus.com

BLACKALL, Robin Jeremy McRae. b 35. Ridley Hall Cam 67. **d** 69 **p** 70. C Stowmarket *St E* 69–72; R Stanstead w Shimplingthorne and Alpheton 72–77; R Bradwell on Sea *Chelmsf* 77–79; R St Lawrence 77–79; Warden Bede Ho Staplehurst 79–81; Chapl HM Det Cen Blantyre Ho 81–82; R Edith Weston w N Luffenham and Lyndon w Manton *Pet* 86–95; P-in-c Upwell St Pet *Ely* 95–99; P-in-c Outwell 95–99; Dioc Rural Miss Officer 95–01; P-in-c Barton Bendish w Beachamwell and Shingham 99–01; P-in-c Boughton 99–01; P-in-c Wereham 99–01; rtd 01; PtO *Ely* from 01; *Nor* from 02. *The Pightle House, Eastmoor Road, Eastmoor, King's Lynn PE33 9PZ* T: (01366) 328663 F: 328163 E: r.jmb@btinternet.com

BLACKALL, Susan Elizabeth. b 52. Qu Univ Kingston Ontario BA 74 MA 75 CCC Ox DPhil 82. SEITE 00. **d** 03 **p** 04. NSM Eltham St Barn *S'wark* 03–12; NSM Greenwich St Alfege 12–16; Asst Chapl Greenwich Univ 12–16; Asst Chapl RN Coll Greenwich 12–16; PtO *S'wark* from 17; Dir Ords Woolwich Area 13–16. *8 Park Place House, Park Vista, London SE10 9ND* T: (020) 8853 3302 *or* 7656 5000 E: sblackall@btinternet.com

BLACKBURN, Anne Dorothy. *See* WOOD, Anne Dorothy

BLACKBURN, David James. b 45. Hull Univ BA 67. Trin Coll Bris 85. **d** 87 **p** 88. C Bromsgrove St Jo *Worc* 87–90; V Cradley 90–01; R Kinver and Enville *Lich* 01–12; rtd 12; PtO *Worc* from 12. *39 Milestone Drive, Hagley, Stourbridge DY9 0LW* T: (01562) 720389 E: davidblackburn43@gmail.com

BLACKBURN, Helen Claire. b 55. Leeds Univ BA 76 MA 99 PGCE 78 ARCM 75. NOC 96. **d** 99 **p** 00. C Sheff Cathl 99–01; Asst Chapl Cen Sheff Univ Hosps NHS Trust 01–04; Chapl Sheff Teaching Hosps NHS Trust 04–06; C Ranmoor *Sheff* 06–07; P-in-c Abbeydale St Jo 07–09; Lead Chapl Willowbrook Hospice 10–13; TR E Widnes *Liv* 13–17; rtd 17. *9 Ventnor Place, Sheffield S7 1LA* M: 07714-329638 E: helen_blackburn@hotmail.co.uk

BLACKBURN, Jane Elizabeth. *See* PROUDFOOT, Jane Elizabeth

BLACKBURN, Jay Johnson. b 54. Univ of Wales BA 06 N Staffs Poly BA 76. Lindisfarne Regional Tr Partnership 19. **d** 19. *34 Troon Avenue, Darlington DL1 3HY* T: (01325) 460151 M: 07900-984302 E: paddlerjay@aol.com

BLACKBURN, The Ven John. b 47. Open Univ BA 88. St Mich Coll Llan 66. **d** 71 **p** 72. C Risca *Mon* 71–76; CF (TA) 73–76; CF 76–99; Dep Chapl Gen 99–00; Chapl Gen 00–04; Adn for the Army 99–04; QHC from 96; Hon Can Ripon Cathl 01–04; V Risca *Mon* 04–13; V Lower Islwyn 13; rtd 13; PtO *Mon* from 14. *St Hilary, 11 Gelli Avenue, Risca, Newport NP11 6QF* E: venblackburn@aol.com

BLACKBURN, Sister Judith Elizabeth. b 58. SEITE 99. **d** 02 **p** 03. NSM Old Ford St Paul and St Mark *Lon* 02–05; P-in-c Bethnal Green St Pet w St Thos 05–11; NSM Bethnal Green St Matt w St Jas the Gt from 11. *St Saviour's Priory, 18 Queensbridge Road, London E2 8NX* T: (020) 7739 9976 M: 07855-510393 E: judithblackburn@aol.com

✠**BLACKBURN, The Rt Revd Richard Finn.** b 52. St Jo Coll Dur BA 74 Hull Univ MA 97. Westcott Ho Cam 81. **d** 83 **p** 84 **c** 09. C Stepney St Dunstan and All SS *Lon* 83–87; P-in-c Isleworth St Jo 87–92; V Mosborough *Sheff* 92–99; RD Attercliffe 96–99; Hon Can Sheff Cathl 98–99; Adn Sheff and Rotherham 99–09; Can Res Sheff Cathl 99–05; Suff Bp Warrington *Liv* 09–18; rtd 18; PtO *Sheff* from 18; Hon Asst Bp Sheff from 19. *9 Ventnor Place, Sheffield S7 1LA* E: bishoprichard.blackburn@hotmail.com

BLACKBURN, Archdeacon of. *See* IRELAND, The Ven Mark Campbell

BLACKBURN, Bishop of. *See* HENDERSON, The Rt Revd Julian Tudor

BLACKBURN, Dean of. *See* HOWELL JONES, The Very Revd Peter

BLACKDEN, Mrs Diane Janice. b 40. **d** 06. NSM Buxted and Hadlow Down *Chich* 06–18; rtd 18; PtO *Chich* from 18. *Oak Hill, Five Ashes, Mayfield TN20 6HL* T: (01435) 872082

BLACKER, Herbert John. b 36. Bris Univ BSc 59. Cranmer Hall Dur. **d** 61 **p** 62. C Wednesbury St Bart *Lich* 61–63; C Chasetown 63–65; C Chigwell *Chelmsf* 65–69; TV Barnham Broom w Kimberley, Bixton etc *Nor* 69–76; R Burgh Parva w Briston 76–92; P-in-c Melton Constable w Swanton Novers 86–92; R Briston w Burgh Parva and Melton Constable 92–01; rtd 01; PtO *Nor* from 01; *St E* 04–10. *Webdor, Olney Road, Dereham NR19 2BZ*

BLACKETT, James Gilbert. b 27. Tyndale Hall Bris 52. **d** 55 **p** 56. C Heworth H Trin *York* 55–57; C Newburn *Newc* 57–58; C Newc St Barn and St Jude 58–61; V Broomfleet

York 61–67; V Ledsham 67–74; V Burton All SS *Lich* 74–82; V Burton All SS w Ch Ch 82–92; rtd 92; PtO *Ox* 92–11; *Pet* from 92. *103 Milford Avenue, Stony Stratford, Milton Keynes MK11 1EZ* T: (01908) 265149 E: jjgblackett@gmail.com

BLACKETT, Robert Peter. b 63. Dur Univ BSc 85 Open Univ BSc 07. Ripon Coll Cuddesdon BTh 95. **d** 95 **p** 96. C Wigton *Carl* 95–00; R Bowness-on-Solway, Kirkbride and Newton Arlosh 00–19; PtO *York* from 19. *Lyngreen, Moor Lane, Cloughton, Scarborough YO13 0AH*

BLACKFORD, Barry Douglas. b 52. Southn Inst BSc 96 MCMI 00 MBCS 04. STETS 05. **d** 08 **p** 09. C N Poole Ecum Team *Sarum* 08–12; TV Melksham 12–14; TR from 14. *The Rectory, Canon Square, Melksham SN12 6LX* T: (01225) 709083 M: 07866-430428 E: revbor@hotmail.co.uk

BLACKLEDGE, David John. b 51. Oak Hill Th Coll 89. **d** 92 **p** 93. NSM Woodford Wells *Chelmsf* from 92. *Hornbeam, 143 Monkhams Lane, Woodford Green IG8 0NW* T: (020) 8262 7690 E: davidjblackledge@aol.com

BLACKLEY, Miles. b 69. Wycliffe Hall Ox. **d** 05 **p** 06. C Ches Square St Mich w St Phil *Lon* 05–08; C St Olave Hart Street w All Hallows Staining etc 08–10; C St Kath Cree 08–10; PtO *S'wark* from 11. *22 Assembly Apartments, 24 York Grove, London SE15 2NZ* E: milesblackley@gmail.com

BLACKMAN, Clive John. b 51. Hull Univ BSc 73 MSc 74. Qu Coll Birm 76. **d** 78 **p** 79. C Folkestone St Sav *Cant* 78–81; Chapl Birm Univ 81–86; V Thorpe St Matt *Nor* 86–94; R Cringleford w Colney and Bawburgh 94–98; Asst Dir Lay and Reader Tr 98–03; Dir Reader Tr 03–11; Chapl Nor City Coll of F&HE 03–15; rtd 15. *13 Norvic Drive, Norwich NR4 7NN* T: (01603) 505776

BLACKMAN, Michael Orville. b 46. Univ of W Ontario BMin 80. Codrington Coll Barbados 67. **d** 71 **p** 71. C St Jo Cathl Antigua 71–73; R H Innocents w St Sav Barbados 73–78; Hon C Westminster St Jas Canada 78–80; P-in-c St Patr Barbados 80–86; TV E Ham w Upton Park and Forest Gate *Chelmsf* 86–91; R St Pet Barbados 91–97; V Dalton *Sheff* 97–03; P-in-c Raynes Park St Sav *S'wark* 03–10; P-in-c S Wimbledon All SS 03–10; V Raynes Park St Sav and S Wimbledon All SS 10–16; rtd 16; PtO *S'wark* from 16. *2 Glenbuck Road, Surbiton KT6 6BS* T: (020) 3726 6731 E: michaelblackman1@sky.com

BLACKMORE, Miss Eunice Sheila. b 57. Bris Univ BSc 79. All SS Cen for Miss & Min 12. **d** 16 **p** 17. NSM Higher Bebington *Ches* from 16. *4 Elms Park, Thingwall, Wirral CH61 9PJ* T: 0151-648 5343 M: 07763-890840 E: euniceblackmore@talktalk.net

BLACKMORE, Robert Ivor. b 37. Univ of Wales (Lamp) 59 Open Univ BA 78 Univ of Wales MTh 94. **d** 62 **p** 63. C Llangynwyd w Maesteg *Llan* 62–65; C Dowlais 65–67; C Neath w Llantwit 67–71; V Fochriw w Deri 71–73; V Troedrhiwgarth 73–80; V Seven Sisters 80–00; rtd 02. *28 Hen Parc Lane, Upper Killay, Swansea SA2 7EY*

BLACKSHAW, Brian Martin. b 43. Lanc Univ MA 74 Ch Ch Ox BA 95 MA 96. Ox NSM Course 87. **d** 90 **p** 91. NSM Amersham *Ox* 90–93; C Hatch End St Anselm *Lon* 93–95; V Cheshunt St Alb 96–07; rtd 07; PtO *St Alb* from 13; *Lon* from 13. *Holly Bush, Flaunden Lane, Flaunden, Hemel Hempstead HP3 0PQ* T: (01442) 832254 E: brianblackshaw@f2s.com

BLACKWALL, David d'Arcy Russell. b 35. Southn Univ BSc 60. Wycliffe Hall Ox 63. **d** 65 **p** 66. C Southampton Thornhill St Chris *Win* 65–68; V Long Sutton 69–72; Chapl Lord Wandsworth Coll Hook 69–74; Hon C Odiham w S Warnborough *Win* 72–75; Chapl St Lawr Coll Ramsgate 75–95; Hd Lan Sch 95–97; rtd 97; PtO *Sarum* from 98; *Eur* from 09. *3 Constable Way, Salisbury SP2 8LN* T: (01722) 335695 E: dandmblackwall@btopenworld.com

BLACKWELL-SMYTH, Charles Peter Bernard. b 42. TCD BA 64 MA 71 MB 73. Gen Th Sem (NY) MDiv 65. **d** 65 **p** 66. C Bangor Abbey *D & D* 65–67; C Dublin Ch Ch Leeson Park *D & G* 67–69; P-in-c Carbury *M & K* 73–75; Hon C St Stephen in Brannel *Truro* 87–94; PtO from 94. *Parcgwyn, Rectory Road, St Stephen, St Austell PL26 7RL* T: (01726) 822465 E: blackwellsmyth@gmail.com

BLACOE, Brian Thomas. b 36. Open Univ BA. Oak Hill Th Coll 63. **d** 66 **p** 67. C Dundonald *D & D* 66–69; C Drumcree *Arm* 69–74; I Ardtrea w Desertcreat 74–78; I Annalong *D & D* 78–95; I Knocknamuckley 95–08; Can Dromore Cathl 93–08; Prec 02–08; rtd 08. *91 Richmond Drive, Tandragee, Craigavon BT62 2GW* T: (028) 3884 2029 M: 07745-564056 E: briantblacoe@icloud.com

BLADE, Mrs Susan Joan. b 58. SEITE 97. **d** 00 **p** 01. NSM Wateringbury and Teston *Roch* 00–02; Asst Chapl Maidstone and Tunbridge Wells NHS Trust 02–06; Sen Chapl 02–06; Chapl Cant Ch Ch Univ 07–10; P-in-c Sampford Peverell, Uplowman, Holcombe Rogus etc *Ex* 10–11; TR 11–17. *The*

Molehole, South Pool, Kingsbridge TQ7 2RW M: 07960-104173 E: sue.blade@gmail.com

BLADEN, Mrs Catherine Robin. b 64. ERMC 12. **d** 15 **p** 16. C Sancroft *St E* 15–18; R Hepworth, Hinderclay, Wattisfield and Thelnetham 18; R Stanton, Hopton, Market Weston, Barningham etc 18; R Stanton from 18. *The Rectory, 1 Old Rectory Gardens, Stanton, Bury St Edmunds IP31 2JH* T: (01359) 250239 E: revcathybladen@gmail.com

BLAGDEN, Ms Susan. b 64. Ox Min Course 89 Ripon Coll Cuddesdon 97. **d** 99 **p** 00. C Grantham St Wulfram *Linc* 99–03; Asst Chapl Stoke Mandeville Hosp NHS Trust 03–10; R Bangor Monachorum, Worthenbury and Marchwiel *St As* 10–12; R Bro Enlli *Ban* 12–14; Tr and Voc Officer 14–15; C Dwylan 14–15; Tutor St Padarn's Inst from 15. *Address withheld by request* E: blagdensm@gmail.com

BLAINE, Alastair John Park. b 79. Westmr Coll of Educn BEd 03. Ripon Coll Cuddesdon 11. **d** 13 **p** 14. C Witney *Ox* 13–17; Chapl RN from 17. *Royal Naval Chaplaincy Service, Mail Point 1-2, Leach Building, Whale Island, Portsmouth PO2 8BY* T: (023) 9262 5055 E: rev.alastair.blaine@gmail.com

BLAINE (née King), Helen Sarah Elizabeth. b 81. Middx Univ BSc 04. Ripon Coll Cuddesdon BA 15. **d** 15 **p** 16. C Aldenham, Radlett and Shenley *St Alb* 15–18; P-in-c Ashreigney *Ex* from 18; P-in-c Broadwoodkelly from 18; P-in-c Brushford from 18; P-in-c Winkleigh from 18. *The Vicarage, Torrington Road, Winkleigh EX19 8HR* T: (01837) 83710 E: revhelenking@outlook.com

BLAIR, Catherine Jill. b 62. Nottm Univ BA 84 BArch 87 RIBA 88. St Jo Coll Nottm MA 02. **d** 02 **p** 03. C Goldsworth Park *Guildf* 02–06; C Woking St Paul 06–16; RD Woking 10–16; Jt V Walton-on-Thames from 16. *The Vicarage, 27 Bowes Road, Walton-on-Thames KT12 3HT* T: (01932) 917736 E: cathy@waltonparish.org.uk

BLAIR, Henry. *See* BLAIR, William Henry

BLAIR, John Wallace. b 48. Lon Univ BSc 70. Qu Coll Birm 79. **d** 81 **p** 82. C Chorlton-cum-Hardy St Werburgh *Man* 81–83; CF 83–97; I Faughanvale *D & R* 97–13; Can Derry Cathl 09–13; rtd 13; Chapl Madeira *Eur* 14–17; PtO *Ox* from 18. *82 Albert Road, Caversham, Reading RG4 7PL* E: revjwblair@gmail.com

BLAIR, Jonathan Lewis. Nottm Univ BA 84 ACA 88. St Jo Coll Nottm. **d** 02 **p** 03. C Goldsworth Park *Guildf* 02–06; P-in-c Woking St Paul 06–16; Jt V Walton-on-Thames from 16. *The Vicarage, 27 Bowes Road, Walton-on-Thames KT12 3HT* T: (01932) 917736 E: jonny@waltonparish.org.uk *or* jonny.blair@tiscali.co.uk

BLAIR, William Henry. b 66. QUB BAgr 89 TCD BTh 04. CITC 01. **d** 04 **p** 05. C Monaghan w Tydavnet and Kilmore *Clogh* 04–06; C Magheraculmoney 06–11; I 11–19; Can Clogh Cathl 15–19; I Tullaniskin w Clonoe *Arm* from 19. *Address temp unknown* E: henry@ardess.org

BLAIR-CHAPPELL, Mrs Elcineide. b 47. Sao Paulo Univ Brazil 74 Birm Poly PGCE 88. WMMTC 00. **d** 03 **p** 04. NSM Erdington *Birm* 03–08; NSM Birm St Martin w Bordesley St Andr from 08; Hon Chapl Birm Children's Hosp NHS Foundn Trust from 07. *18 Kempson Avenue, Sutton Coldfield B72 1HJ* T: 0121-682 5340

BLAKE, Ian Martyn. b 57. Oak Hill Th Coll BA 79. **d** 80 **p** 81. C Widford *Chelmsf* 80–84; C Barton Seagrave w Warkton *Pet* 84–90; V Sneinton St Chris w St Phil *S'well* 90–01; C Howell Hill w Burgh Heath *Guildf* 01–06; PtO 06–12; *S'wark* 08–12; P-in-c Thornton Heath St Paul 12–15; V Skirbeck H Trin *Linc* 15–18. *42 Bartlemere, Barnard Castle DL12 8LR* M: 07904-340783

BLAKE, Mrs Margaret. b 48. Open Univ BA 87. S'wark Ord Course 92. **d** 95 **p** 96. C Farnham *Guildf* 95–01; P-in-c Farncombe 01–05; R 05–09; rtd 09. *Tan-y-Llan, Llanfihangel-Nant-Bran, Brecon LD3 9NA* T: (01874) 636390 E: tanyllan2@gmail.com

BLAKE, Stephen. b 59. Ch Coll Cam MA 85 Wadh Coll Ox BM, BCh 84 MRCGP 88. Ox Min Course 07. **d** 10 **p** 11. NSM Burford w Fulbrook, Taynton, Asthall etc *Ox* 10–13; NSM Chipping Norton 13–15; NSM Broadwell, Evenlode, Oddington, Adlestrop etc *Glouc* from 15; Chapl HM Pris Long Lartin from 15. *HM Prison Long Lartin, South Littleton, Evesham WR11 8TZ* T: (01386) 295100 E: sb@evenlodevalechurches.org

BLAKELEY, John Michael. b 77. Lanc Univ BA 99 PGCE 00. St Mellitus Coll 17. **d** 19. C Nottingham St Nic *S'well* from 19. *26 Ridgeway Close, West Bridgford, Nottingham NG2 6HL* T: 0115-923   2790   M: 07722-713450 E: jmblakeley1998@gmail.com

BLAKELEY, Julian Graham. b 60. Oak Hill Th Coll BA 88. **d** 88 **p** 89. C Bedworth *Cov* 88–91; C Harlow St Mary and St Hugh w St Jo the Bapt *Chelmsf* 91–95; R Darfield *Sheff* 95–03; TR Eston w Normanby *York* from 03. *429*

Normanby Road, Middlesbrough TS6 0ED T: (01642) 206264 E: julianblakeley@hotmail.co.uk

BLAKELY, Denise Irene. *See* CADDOO, Denise Irene

BLAKELY, Mark Francis James. b 75. Wolv Univ LLB 98 Lon Metrop Univ MA 09 Solicitor 01. St Mellitus Coll BA 15. **d** 15 **p** 16. C Becontree S *Chelmsf* 15–18; Bp's Chapl 18–19; V Lamorbey H Trin *Roch* from 19. *Holy Trinity Vicarage, 1 Hurst Road, Sidcup DA15 9AE* T: (020) 8300 8231 M: 07979-863409 E: mfjblakely@gmail.com *or* vicar@holytrinitylamorbey.org

BLAKEMAN, Mrs Janet Mary. b 36. Man Univ BA 57 CertEd 58. Carl Dioc Tr Course 87. **d** 90 **p** 97. NSM Wetheral w Warwick *Carl* 90–97; NSM Thornthwaite cum Braithwaite, Newlands etc 97–01; rtd 01; PtO *Carl* 01–14; *Leeds* 17. *1 The Coach House, Romaldkirk, Barnard Castle DL12 9ED* T: (01833) 650143

BLAKESLEY, John. b 50. Keble Coll Ox BA 72 MA 76. St Steph Ho Ox 72. **d** 74 **p** 75. C Egremont *Carl* 74–77; C Doncaster Ch Ch *Sheff* 77–79; V Auckland St Helen *Dur* 79–94; Chapl Tindale Crescent Hosp Dur 90–94; Tutor St Chad's Coll Dur 95–00; C Ch the King *Newc* 00–03; V Cambois and Sleekburn 03–12; rtd 12; PtO *York* from 12; Lect Th Dur Univ from 91. *11 Clarence Road, Nunthorpe, Middlesbrough TS7 0DA* T: (01642) 318995 E: jblakesley@btinternet.com

BLAKEY, Cedric Lambert. b 54. Fitzw Coll Cam BA 76 MA 80. St Jo Coll Nottm 77. **d** 79 **p** 80. C Cotmanhay *Derby* 79–83; C-in-c Blagreaves St Andr CD 83–89; P-in-c Sinfin Moor 84–89; V Heanor 89–97; RD 94–97; Bp's Dom Chapl 97–05; NSM Derby Cathl 05–10; Hon Can Derby Cathl 02–10; Vice Provost St Mary's Cathl *Glas* 10–18; Dioc Interfaith Adv 14–18; Can St Mary's Cathl *Glas* 17–18; rtd 18; PtO *Edin* from 19. *11 Glenbenna, Walkerburn EH43 6DD* E: revcanclb@gmail.com

BLAKEY, William George. b 51. Southn Univ BSc 72 PGCE 73. Oak Hill Th Coll BA 82. **d** 82 **p** 83. C Cheltenham St Mark *Glouc* 82–85; P-in-c Parkham, Alwington, Buckland Brewer etc *Ex* 85–86; R 86–94; TR 94–01; P-in-c Lundy Is 92–01; RD Hartland 89–96; TR Wareham *Sarum* 01–07; TR Brize Norton and Carterton *Ox* 07–18; AD Witney 08–13; rtd 18. *7 Chiltern Avenue, Bishops Cleeve, Cheltenham GL52 8XP* T: (01242) 678305 M: 07905-757920 E: bill@theblakeys.co.uk

BLAKEY WILLIAMS, Mrs Diane Patricia. b 53. Dur Univ CertEd 74 Lanc Univ MA 84. Cranmer Hall Dur 84. **dss** 86 **d** 87 **p** 94. Clubmoor *Liv* 86–90; Par Dn 87–90; Dioc Lay Tr Officer 90–96; Par Dn Everton St Geo 90–94; Assoc P 94–96; Chapl Lanc Univ *Blackb* 96–00; Chapl Edin Univ 00–10; Ldr Still Paths 11–16; PtO *Leeds* from 17. *Meadowcroft, Kettlewell, Skipton BD23 5RL* T: (01242) 678305 E: diwilliams.labyrinth@gmail.com

BLAMEY, Mark Kendall. b 62. Bris Poly BSc 84 MRICS 86. Ripon Coll Cuddesdon 99. **d** 01 **p** 02. C Cowley St Jo *Ox* 01–04; P-in-c Goring w S Stoke 04–07; V Goring and Streatley w S Stoke 07–13; PtO *Win* 14–18; Manager Jersey Alzheimer's Assn from 14; PtO *Cant* from 19. *6 Gros Puits, Fountain Lane, St Saviour, Jersey JE2 7RL* T: (01534) 631875 E: mkblamey@gmail.com

BLAMIRE, Jean. *See* PROSSER, Jean

BLAMIRE, Philip Gray. b 50. St Pet Coll Birm CertEd 71 Wall Hall Coll Aldenham BEd 76 UEA MA 91. EAMTC 00. **d** 03 **p** 04. C Swaffham *Nor* 03–07; P-in-c Weybourne Gp 07–10; R 10–19; RD Holt 17–19; rtd 20. *Address temp unknown*

BLANCH, Michael Dennis. b 46. Birm Univ BSocSc 69 PhD 75 DipEd 70. Yorks Min Course 07. **d** 09 **p** 10. NSM Askrigg w Stallingbusk *Ripon* 09–12; NSM Hawes and Hardraw 09–12; NSM Eastbourne St Mich *Chich* 12–13; P-in-c Hampden Park and The Hydnye 13–17; PtO 17–18; Hon C Isfield from 18. *The Parsonage, Station Road, Isfield, Uckfield TN22 5EY* M: 07792-240684 E: isfield.vicar@gmail.com

BLANCH, Paul Frederick. b 56. St Cuth Soc Dur BA 97. Chich Th Coll 83. **d** 86 **p** 87. C Chaddesden St Phil *Derby* 86–88; C Auckland St Andr and St Anne *Dur* 88–91; P-in-c Hunwick 91–94; Chapl HM Pris Edin 98–02; P-in-c Edin St Salvador 98–00; R 00–02; P-in-c Wester Hailes St Luke 00–02; P-in-c Melton *St E* 02–03; P-in-c Ufford w Bredfield and Hasketon 02–03; R Melton and Ufford 03–05; V Meir Heath and Normacot *Lich* 05–09; R Schenectady St Geo USA 09–14; R Redding All SS 14–17; V Kirton in Holland w Algarkirk and Fosdyke *Linc* from 17. *The Vicarage, Penny Gardens, Kirton, Boston PE20 1HN* E: ppkirtalgardyke@gmail.com

BLANCHARD, Canon Christopher John. b 46. Univ of Wales (Lamp) BA 70. St Mich Coll Llan 86. **d** 79 **p** 80. NSM Chepstow *Mon* 79–81; NSM Itton and St Arvans w Penterry and Kilgwrrwg etc 81–86; TV Ebbw Vale 87–89; R Llangenni and Llanbedr Ystrad Yw w Patricio *S & B* 89–97; V Chepstow *Mon* 98–17; Hon Can St Woolos Cathl 14–17; rtd 17; Hon C Ross w Walford and Brampton Abbotts *Heref* from 17.

The Vicarage, Walford, Ross-on-Wye HR9 5QP T: (01989) 762368 M: 07711-961237 E: frchris2@icloud.com

BLANCHARD, Frank Hugh. b 30. St Jo Coll Dur BA 54 MA 62. **d** 55 **p** 56. C Bottesford *Linc* 55–58; CMS 58–65; C Kirby Grindalythe *York* 65–67; V 67–71; C N Grimston w Wharram Percy and Wharram-le-Street 65–67; V 67–71; P-in-c Thorpe Bassett 67–71; P-in-c Settrington 67–68; V Scarborough St Jas 71–79; P-in-c Scarborough H Trin 78–79; V Scarborough St Jas and H Trin 79–86; R Stockton-on-the-Forest w Holtby and Warthill 87–94; rtd 94; P-in-c Rothesay *Arg* 94–96; PtO *York* 00–16. *23 Front Street, Sowerby, Thirsk YO7 1JG* T: (01845) 574446

BLANCHARD, Canon Lawrence Gordon. b 36. Edin Univ MA 60. Linc Th Coll 63. **d** 65 **p** 66. C Woodhouse *Wakef* 65–67; C Cannock *Lich* 67–70; Chapl Waterford Sch Mbabane Swaziland 70–72; R Mbabane All SS 72–75; Lic to Offic 75–76; TV Raveningham *Nor* 76–80; V Ancaster *Linc* 80–87; Dir LNSM 80–87; Can and Preb Linc Cathl 85–88; Dir of Tr CA 88–93; V Roxton w Gt Barford *St Alb* 93–98; rtd 98; PtO *St E* 99–09; *Ely* from 09. *7A Barton Road, Ely CB7 4HZ* T: (01353) 654133

BLANCHARDE, Hilary Mary. b 61. STETS. **d** 09 **p** 10. NSM Horfield H Trin *Bris* 09–18; PtO from 18. *149 Abbey Road, Bristol BS9 3QH* E: hilaryblancharde@talktalk.net

BLAND, Mrs Elizabeth Anne. b 63. Collingwood Coll Dur BA 85. SAOMC 01. **d** 04 **p** 05. C N Shields *Newc* 04–08; V Ashington 08–15; TV Gt Aycliffe *Dur* 15–19; TV Upper Skerne from 19. *St Alban's Vicarage, Trimdon Grange, Trimdon Station TS29 6EX* M: 07497-434304 E: elizabeth.a.bland@gmail.com

BLAND, Jean Elspeth. b 42. K Coll Lon BA 63. Glouc Sch of Min 87. **d** 90 **p** 94. Par Dn Cen Telford *Lich* 90–94; Asst Chapl HM Pris Shrewsbury 92–94; Chapl HM Pris and YOI Doncaster 94–98; C Goole *Sheff* 99; P-in-c Purleigh, Cold Norton and Stow Maries *Chelmsf* 99–08; rtd 08; PtO *Chelmsf* from 11. *33 Seagers, Great Totham, Maldon CM9 8PB* T: (01621) 829646 E: ebland@prowselyon.plus.com

BLAND, Mrs Lesley Nicole. b 57. Ch Ch Coll Cant BEd 78. ERMC 10. **d** 13 **p** 14. NSM Kym Valley *Ely* 13–16; NSM S Leightonstone 17; Chapl Kimbolton Sch 13–17; V The Staughtons w Hail Weston *Ely* from 17. *The Vicarage, Causeway, Great Staughton, St Neots PE19 5BF* M: 07805-078992 E: revlesnicki@gmail.com

BLANDFORD-BAKER, Canon Neil James. b 64. Dundee Univ BSc 86. St Jo Coll Nottm BTh 92. **d** 93 **p** 94. C The Quinton *Birm* 93–96; V E Acton St Dunstan w St Thos *Lon* 96–06; Dir of Ords Willesden Area 02–06; V Histon *Ely* from 06; P-in-c Impington 06–17; V from 17; RD N Stowe from 07; RD Bourn 16–17; Hon Can Ely Cathl from 16. *The Vicarage, 9A Church Street, Histon, Cambridge CB24 9EP* T: (01223) 320425 *or* 320420 E: jamesbb@me.com

BLANEY, Laurence. b 41. Open Univ BA 85 Essex Univ MA 88 PhD 95. Oak Hill Th Coll 66. **d** 69 **p** 70. C Leyton St Mary w St Edw *Chelmsf* 69–73; P-in-c Wimbish w Thunderley 73–77; P-in-c Mayland 77–82; P-in-c Steeple 77–82; R Pitsea 82–95; R Pitsea w Nevendon 95–96; P-in-c Mayland 96–06; P-in-c Steeple 96–06; rtd 06; PtO *Chelmsf* 06–12; P-in-c Purleigh 12–15. *14 Piercys, Basildon SS13 3HN* T: (01268) 552254 E: laurie@blaney.info

BLATCHLEY, Ms Elizabeth. b 62. Wycliffe Hall Ox 01. **d** 03 **p** 04. C Northolt St Jos *Lon* 03–06; C Telford Park *S'wark* 06–11; V Homerton St Luke *Lon* 11–18; C Battersea Fields *S'wark* from 18. *11 Cupar Road, London SW11 4JW* E: betsy.blatchley@southwark.anglican.org

BLATCHLY, Owen Ronald Maxwell. b 30. Bps' Coll Cheshunt 62. **d** 64 **p** 65. C Boxmoor St Jo *St Alb* 64–67; C Boreham Wood All SS 67–69; C Frimley *Guildf* 69–77; V Manaccan w St Anthony-in-Meneage *Truro* 77–82; R Binfield *Ox* 82–97; rtd 97; PtO *Truro* from 97. *1 Rose Cottages, East Road, Stithians, Truro TR3 7BD* T: (01209) 860845

BLAY, Canon Ian. b 65. Man Univ BA 88. Westcott Ho Cam 89. **d** 91 **p** 92. C Withington St Paul *Man* 91–94; C Elton All SS 94–96; R Droylsden St Andr 96–05; Dioc Ecum Officer 98–05; R Mobberley *Ches* from 05; RD Knutsford from 16; Hon Can Asante Mampong Ghana from 15. *The Rectory, Church Lane, Mobberley, Knutsford WA16 7RA* T: (01565) 873218 M: 07776-195176 E: ianblay@btinternet.com

BLAY, Linda Jean. Warwick Univ DipEd 89 Essex Coll of Educn CertEd. Trin Coll Bris 98. **d** 00 **p** 01. C Foleshill St Paul *Cov* 00–04; C Bilton 04–08; R Fenn Lanes Gp *Leic* from 08. *The Vicarage, High Street, Stoke Golding, Nuneaton CV13 6HE* T: (01455) 213988 E: lindablay@hotmail.com

BLEAKLEY, Melvyn Thomas. b 43. K Coll Lon BD 66 AKC 66 Reading Univ TCert 78. **d** 67 **p** 68. C Cross Heath *Lich* 67–70; TV High Wycombe *Ox* 70–77; PtO 77–00; NSM Chalfont St Giles 00–15; NSM Chalfont St Giles, Seer Green

and Jordans from 15. *294 Hughenden Road, High Wycombe HP13 5PE* T: (01494) 529315 E: melvynbleakley@gmail.com

BLEASE, Oliver Robert. b 86. Leic Univ LLB 10. Ripon Coll Cuddesdon BA 18. **d** 18 **p** 19. C R Wootton Bassett *Sarum* from 18. *2 Swallows Mead, Royal Wootton Bassett, Swindon SN4 8QA* M: 07469-706657

BLEAZARD, John George. b 57. Univ of Wales (Abth) BA 79 Qu Coll Birm MA 06. Ripon Coll Cuddesdon 06. **d** 08 **p** 09. C Gt Cornard *St E* 08–11; R W Kirby St Bridget *Ches* 11–20; rtd 20. *40 Village Road, West Kirby, Wirral CH48 7HE* T: 0151-625 1052 E: johnbleazard@hotmail.com

BLEWETT, Martin Arthur. b 60. Keele Univ BA 82 Glos Univ MA 04. Trin Coll Bris 07. **d** 09 **p** 10. C Seaford w Sutton *Chich* 09–13; P-in-c Timsbury w Priston, Camerton and Dunkerton *B & W* from 13. *The Rectory, South Road, Timsbury, Bath BA2 0EJ* T: (01761) 472448 M: 07854-273489 E: martinblewett@gmail.com

BLEWETT, Timothy John. b 67. Surrey Univ BA 88 Cam Univ MA 92 MA 92 Coll of Ripon & York St Jo MA 96 Buckingham Univ MA 11. Westcott Ho Cam 89. **d** 92 **p** 93. C Knaresborough *Ripon* 92–95; V Hanmer, Bronington, Bettisfield, Tallarn Green *St As* 95–98; Can Res and Can Cursal St As Cathl 98–03; Asst Dioc Dir of Ords 98–00; 00–03; Dioc Officer for Min and Adv for CME 98–03; CF 03–04; P-in-c Loddington *Leic* 04–12; Warden Launde Abbey 04–12; Dir and Chapl Ark Trust from 12. *Sycamore House, New Road, Burton Lazars, Melton Mowbray LE14 2UU* M: 07971-528915

BLICK, John Harold Leslie. b 36. Univ of Wales (Lamp) BA 61. Bps' Coll Cheshunt 61. **d** 63 **p** 64. C Radlett *St Alb* 63–66; Min St Cem Miss Labrador Canada 66–71; Min Marsh Farm CD *St Alb* 71–76; R Shaw cum Donnington *Ox* 76–89; rtd 96; PtO *Mon* from 99. *Springwood, Cleddon, Trelleck NP25 4PN* T: (01600) 860094 F: 869045

BLIGH, Philip Hamilton. b 36. Lon Univ BSc 57 PhD 61 MEd 79 St Cath Coll Ox BA 63 MInstP 75. S'wark Ord Course 86. **d** 88 **p** 89. C Abington *Pet* 88–90; V Bozeat w Easton Maudit 90–99; R Hackett Australia 99–01; rtd 01; PtO *Nor* from 02. *49 Norwich Road, Cromer NR27 0EX* T: (01263) 511385 E: philipbligh752@btinternet.com

BLISS, Canon David Charles. b 52. Aston Univ BSc 75 Cranfield Inst of Tech MSc 82. St Jo Coll Nottm 87. **d** 89 **p** 90. C Burntwood *Lich* 89–93; Chapl St Matt Hosp Burntwood 89–93; TV Aston cum Aughton w Swallownest, Todwick etc *Sheff* 93–02; R Todwick 02–08; AD Laughton 03–08; Chapl among Deaf People 97–08; V Rotherham 08–17; AD 08–11; Hon Can Sheff Cathl 06–17; rtd 17. *5 Hanging Bank Court, North Anston, Sheffield S25 4DG* T: (01909) 566551 E: bliss.david@me.com

BLISS, John Derek Clegg. b 40. Sarum Th Coll. **d** 68 **p** 69. C Wymondham *Nor* 68–73; V Easton 73–80; R Colton 73–80; R Madera H Trin USA 80–89; Human Outreach Agency Hayward 92–96; rtd 01; C Coconut Grove St Steph USA from 01. *4 Edgewater Hillside, Westport CT 06880-6101, USA* T: (001) (203) 222 1879 E: jb106600@aol.com

BLISS, Mrs Lyn Elizabeth. b 54. SS Mark & Jo Univ Coll Plymouth CertEd 76. Ox Min Course 06. **d** 09 **p** 10. NSM Bradfield and Stanford Dingley *Ox* from 09; NSM Bucklebury w Marlston from 09. *Holly Hedges, 2 Broad Lane, Upper Bucklebury, Reading RG7 6QJ* T: (01635) 862281 M: 07824-741225 E: toccata1428@gmail.com

BLISSARD-BARNES, Christopher John. b 36. ARCO 55 Linc Coll Ox BA 61 MA 64. Ridley Hall Cam 61. **d** 63 **p** 64. C Woking St Paul *Guildf* 63–67; C Orpington Ch Ch *Roch* 67–71; P-in-c Heref St Jas 71–78; Chapl Heref Gen Hosp 71–78; R Hampreston *Sarum* 78–88; TR 88–89; RD Wimborne 80–85; P-in-c Hambledon *Guildf* 89–94; R Newdigate 94–01; Warden of Readers 93–99; rtd 01; PtO *Win* from 02. *148 Olivers Battery Road South, Winchester SO22 4LF* T/F: (01962) 862082 E: chrisandfreda@virginmedia.com

BLOCKLEY, Christopher John Hamilton. b 72. UWE LLB 96 Rob Coll Cam BTh 04 Barrister-at-Law (Gray's Inn) 98. Ridley Hall Cam 01. **d** 04 **p** 05. C Kingswood *Bris* 04–07; Chapl Bps' Coll Glouc 07–15; PtO *Glouc* from 15. *29 Wellesley Street, Gloucester GL1 4QP* T: (01452) 539956 M: 07984-072630 E: chrisjhblockley@outlook.com

BLODWELL, Ms Christine Maria. b 46. Open Univ BA Jo Dalton Coll Man CertEd 71. NOC 04. **d** 05 **p** 06. NSM Marple All SS *Ches* 05–15; rtd 16; PtO *Leic* from 17. *5 White Hart Close, Billesdon, Leicester LE7 9AU* T: 0116-259 9606 M: 07931-714130 E: revchrisb@hotmail.com

BLOGG, Kevin Derek. b 55. Ch Ch Coll Cant BSc 82 PGCE 87. Franciscan Ho of Studies. **d** 84 **p** 85. NSM Eythorne and Elvington w Waldershare etc *Cant* 89–92; Orchard Sch Cant 89–90; Harbour Sch Dover 92–93; NSM Colkirk w Oxwick w Pattesley, Whissonsett etc *Nor* 95–02; NSM Gressenhall w Longham w Wendling etc 02–18; NSM Launditch and the

Upper Nar from 18; Sidestrand Hall Sch Nor from 94. *Mill House, The Street, Mileham, King's Lynn PE32 2RB* T: (01328) 701124 E: bloggbarn@aol.com

BLOKLAND, Janneke Hendrika. b 82. Radboud Univ Nijmegen MSc 06 PhD 10 Utrecht Univ BA 10 Nottm Univ MA 14. Westcott Ho Cam 12. **d** 14 **p** 15. C Marlborough *Sarum* 14–17; Asst Chapl Marlborough Coll from 17. *New Court RHT, Marlborough College, Marlborough SN8 1PA* M: 07554-486575 E: jblokland@gmail.com

BLOOD, David John. b 36. G&C Coll Cam BA 60 MA 64. Westcott Ho Cam 60. **d** 62 **p** 63. C Rushmere *St E* 62–66; C Harringay St Paul *Lon* 66–70; LtO 71–81; rtd 01. *42 Churston Gardens, London N11 2NL*

BLOOD, Canon Michael William. b 44. AKC 67. **d** 69 **p** 70. C Moseley St Agnes *Birm* 69–75; V Cotteridge 75–09; Relig Progr Producer BBC Radio W Midl 76–06; Hon Can Birm Cathl 97–09; rtd 09; PtO *Birm* 09–18. *19 Nursery Drive, Birmingham B30 1DR* T: 0121-458 2815 E: michaelblood@blueyonder.co.uk

BLOOM, Mrs Lara Susan. b 67. Ripon Coll Cuddesdon 13. **d** 15 **p** 16. C Redmarley D'Abitot, Bromesberrow, Pauntley etc *Glouc* 15–17; C Abenhall w Mitcheldean 17–18; P-in-c Huntley and Longhope, Churcham and Bulley from 18. *56 Byfords Road, Huntley, Gloucester GL19 3EL* M: 07901-003575 E: rev.larabloom@gmail.com

BLOOMER, Ms Sherry Lesley. b 50. Liv Jo Moores Univ BA 91 Wolv Poly CertEd 83 RN 73 RM 74 RHV 78. Westcott Ho Cam 95. **d** 97 **p** 98. C Llangollen w Trevor and Llantysilio *St As* 97–00; R Cilcain and Nannerch and Rhydymwyn 00–04; V Worc St Clem and Lower Broadheath 04–12; Chapl Worc Univ 04–12; rtd 12; PtO *St As* from 14. *13 Furrocks Lane, Ness, Neston CH64 4EH* T: 0151-336 1686 E: sherrybloomer@btinternet.com

BLOOMFIELD, Mrs Brenda Elizabeth. b 41. Gipsy Hill Coll of Educn TCert 63. **d** 07 **p** 08. NSM Upper Weardale *Dur* 07–11; rtd 11; PtO *Dur* from 11. *1 Broadwood View, Frosterley, Bishop Auckland DL13 2RT* T: (01388) 527980

BLOOMFIELD, John Michael. b 35. Univ of Wales (Lamp) BA 57. Sarum Th Coll 59. **d** 61 **p** 62. C Fordington *Sarum* 61–64; C Branksome St Aldhelm 64–66; Youth Chapl *Win* 66–69; R Win All SS w Chilcomb and Chesil 71–79; P-in-c Corsley *Sarum* 79–81; P-in-c Swanage and Studland 83–86; Chapl HM Pris Dorchester 87–89; C Dorchester *Sarum* 87–89; Chapl HM Pris The Verne 89–00; rtd 00; PtO *Sarum* 01–17; *Win* 16–19. *15 Provost Street, Fordingbridge SP6 1AY* T: (01425) 837735 E: swanbeck3@gmail.com

BLOOMFIELD, John Stephen. b 56. Chich Th Coll 83. **d** 86 **p** 87. C Chich St Paul and St Pet 86–89; TV Littlehampton and Wick 89–98; V Hunstanton St Edm w Ringstead *Nor* 98–19; P-in-c Flegg Coastal Benefice from 19. *The Rectory, Somerton Road, Winterton-on-Sea, Great Yarmouth NR29 4AW* T: (01493) 393628 E: jonstefanfield@btinternet.com

BLOOR, Amanda Elaine. b 62. Leic Univ BA 83 York Univ MA 02 K Coll Lon PhD 12 Open Univ PGCE 96. Ripon Coll Cuddesdon 02. **d** 04 **p** 05. C Hambleden Valley *Ox* 04–07; Bp's Dom Chapl 07–13; Dioc Adv for Women's Min and Dir of Ords (Berks) 13–15; P-in-c Bembridge *Portsm* from 15; Assoc Dir of Ords from 15. *The Vicarage, Church Road, Bembridge PO35 5NA* T: (01983) 717053 E: amandaebloor@googlemail.com

BLOOR, Preb Terence Bernard. b 62. Liv Univ BTh 02. NOC 99. **d** 02 **p** 03. C Hadley *Lich* 02–06; Chapl N Staffs Combined Healthcare NHS Trust 06–13; P-in-c Basford *Lich* from 06; P-in-c Wolstanton from 16; RD Newcastle from 11; Preb Lich Cathl from 15. *211 Basford Park Road, Newcastle ST5 0PG* T: (01782) 619045 M: 07890-980749 E: terry.bloor@btinternet.com

BLORE, Canon John Francis. b 49. Jes Coll Ox BA 72 MA 76. Wycliffe Hall Ox 73. **d** 75 **p** 76. C Waltham Abbey *Chelmsf* 75–78; C E Ham St Geo 78–81; R Colchester St Mich Myland 81–00; Chapl Oxley Parker Sch Colchester 81–00; P-in-c Halstead St Andr w H Trin and Greenstead Green *Chelmsf* 00–04; TR Halstead Area 04–15; RD Hinckford 03–08; Hon Can Chelmsf Cathl 09–15; rtd 15; PtO *Nor* from 15. *Alden Cottage, Lexham Road, Litcham, King's Lynn PE32 2QQ* T: (01328) 701242 E: jf.blore@btinternet.com

BLOUNT, Robin George. b 38. Lon Coll of Div 61 Wycliffe Hall Ox 67. **d** 68 **p** 69. C Bletchley *Ox* 68–71; C Washington *Dur* 71–74; TV Chelmsley Wood *Birm* 74–76; Ind Chapl *Worc* 76–89; Asst P Dudley St Jo 76–88; Asst P Dudley St Thos and St Luke 88–89; Ind Chapl (Eurotunnel Development) *Cant* 89–03; rtd 03; PtO *Cant* from 03. *82 Mabledon Avenue, Ashford TN24 8BN* E: robin.blount38@gmail.com

BLOWEY, Mrs Judith Ann. b 55. SWMTC 14. **d** 17 **p** 18. C Tavistock, Gulworthy and Brent Tor *Ex* from 17.

Higher Woodley Farm, Sydenham Damerel, Tavistock PL19 8QU T: (01822) 832374 E: jablowey@gmail.com

BLUNDELL, Peter Grahame. b 61. Ealing Coll of Educn BA 83. Oak Hill NSM Course 91. **d** 94 **p** 95. NSM Kensington St Barn *Lon* 94–97; Zimbabwe 97–99; Assoc Min Romford Gd Shep *Chelmsf* 99–04; I Richmond Hill St Jo Canada from 04. *19 Waldron Crescent, Richmond Hill ON L4E 4A3, Canada* T: (001) (289) 809 1450 E: peter@ecclesiact.com

BLUNDEN, Jacqueline Ann. *See* MILLER, Jacqueline Ann

BLUNDEN, Canon Jeremy Augustine. b 61. BSc CEng 88 MIStructE 88. SEITE 99. **d** 99 **p** 00. NSM Sydenham St Bart *S'wark* 99–01; C 01–03; V Clapham H Spirit 03–12; TR Warlingham w Chelsham and Farleigh 12–16; R Beckenham St Geo *Roch* 16–18; R Beckenham St Geo and St Barn from 18; Bp's Adv for Black, Asian and Minority Ethnic Affairs from 18; Hon Can Roch Cathl from 18. *The Rectory, 14 The Knoll, Beckenham BR3 5JW* T: (020) 8650 0983 E: jeremy.blunden@btinternet.com

BLUNSUM, Charles Michael. b 28. ACIB 51 MBIM 86. **d** 74 **p** 75. C Stoke Bishop *Bris* 74–79; Chapl Brunel Manor Chr Cen Torquay 79–94; rtd 94; PtO *Ex* from 94. *16A Hollywater Close, Torquay TQ1 3TN* T: (01803) 214371

BLUNT, Christopher John Scawen. b 73. Rob Coll Cam MA 97 MEng 97. St Jo Coll Nottm MTh 13. **d** 13 **p** 14. C Ches St Paul w St Luke 13–17; V from 17. *St Luke's Vicarage, 14 Celandine Close, Huntington, Chester CH3 6DT* T: (01244) 460058 M: 07503-706906 E: chrisblunt.jas@gmail.com

BLUNT, Jeremy William. b 49. Birm Univ MEd 85 GRNCM 73. **d** 07 **p** 08. OLM Streetly *Lich* 07–15; PtO from 16. *63 Lindrosa Road, Sutton Coldfield B74 3LB* T: 0121-353 9712 M: 07849-689180

BLYDE, Ian Hay. b 52. Liv Univ BSc 74 Edin Univ BD 80. Edin Th Coll 77. **d** 80 **p** 81. C Ainsdale *Liv* 80–83; Chapl Birkenhead Sch 83–90; V Over St Chad *Ches* 90–93; Chapl Ex Sch and St Marg Sch 93–98; NSM Littleham w Exmouth *Ex* 03–06; TV Brixham w Churston Ferrers and Kingswear 06–13; TR 13–19; rtd 19. *2 Hulham Road, Exmouth EX8 3HR*

BLYTH, Florence Anne. b 56. ERMC 16. **d** 19. NSM Nor Colegate and Tombland from 19. *2 Willow Lane, Norwich NR2 1EU* M: 07904-188948 E: rev.annie.blyth@gmail.com

BLYTH, Graham. *See* BLYTH, Michael Graham

BLYTH, Kenneth Henry. b 35. Oak Hill Th Coll 58. **d** 61 **p** 62. C St Alb St Paul 61–65; P-in-c Aspenden and Layston w Buntingford 65–66; R 66–72; R Washfield, Stoodleigh, Withleigh etc *Ex* 72–82; P-in-c Cruwys Morchard 72–74; RD Tiverton 76–82; V Eastbourne H Trin *Chich* 82–00; rtd 00; PtO *Ex* from 00. *Hamslade House, Bampton, Tiverton EX16 9JA* T: (01398) 351461

BLYTH, Canon Michael Graham. b 53. Jes Coll Ox BA 75 MA 78 Dur Univ PhD 79. Qu Coll Birm 82. **d** 84 **p** 85. C Nantwich *Ches* 84–86; C Coppenhall 86–88; TV Southend *Chelmsf* 88–95; P-in-c Danbury 95–11; R 11–12; RD Chelmsf S 01–07; Hon Can Chelmsf Cathl 07–12; rtd 12; PtO *Chelmsf* from 14. *Selkirk House, 8 Rennie Walk, Heybridge, Maldon CM9 4QH* T: (01621) 854068 E: michaelg@canongate.org.uk

BOAG, David. b 46. Edin Th Coll 69. **d** 72 **p** 73. C Edin Old St Paul 72–75; P-in-c Edin St Andr and St Aid 75–88; LtO from 88. *13 Fleming Place, Fountainhall, Galashiels TD1 2TA* T: (01578) 760606 E: daviebfree@gmail.com

BOAG, Michael John. b 61. Leeds Univ BA 00. Coll of Resurr Mirfield 98. **d** 00 **p** 01. C Howden *York* 00–03; Min Can and Succ Windsor 03–11; Chapl St Geo Sch Windsor 03–06; Dean's V 06–11; R Upper Coquetdale *Newc* 11–17; R Worth, Pound Hill and Maidenbower *Chich* from 17. *Worth Rectory, Church Road, Worth, Crawley RH10 7RT* T: (01293) 882229 E: rector@worthparish.org

BOAK, Canon Donald Kenneth. b 30. MBAOT 53. S'wark Ord Course 82. **d** 85 **p** 86. C Tulse Hill H Trin and St Matthias *S'wark* 85–88; C Surbiton St Matt 88–91; Intercon Ch Soc, SAMS and Miss to Seamen 91–95; Peru 91–95; Dean Lima 93–95; rtd 95; Hon Can Peru from 95; Hon C Bournemouth St Andr *Win* 96–99; PtO *Sarum* 98–01; *Win* 99–14. *3 Hymans Way, Totton, Southampton SO40 3DL* T: (023) 8086 8265

BOAKES, Canon Norman. b 50. Univ of Wales (Swansea) BA 71 Univ of Wales (Lamp) LTh 73 Ox Univ MTh 96. Bp Burgess Hall Lamp 71. **d** 73 **p** 74. C Swansea St Mary w H Trin *S & B* 73–78; Chapl Univ of Wales (Swansea) 76–78; Chapl K Alfred Coll *Win* 78–82; V Colbury 82–91; Chapl Ashurst Hosp 82–91; Chapl Mental Handicap Services Unit 82–91; V Southampton Maybush St Pet *Win* 91–06; P-in-c Southampton St Jude 04–06; V Maybush and Southampton St Jude 06–07; Bp's Adv for Hosp Chapl 87–00; AD Southampton 02–07; CMD Officer 07–11; Can Win Cathl 11–14; PtO 14–19; Archdeacons' Nat Exec Officer 14–19; Hon C N Stoneham and Bassett *Win* from 19. *21*

Redcourt, Chetwynd Road, Southampton SO16 3TX   T: (023) 8076 7735 E: norman.boakes@btinternet.com

BOARDMAN, Frederick Henry. b 25. Liv Univ BSc 46 St Cath Soc Ox BA 49 MA 54 Birm Univ MEd 71 PhD 77 Lon Univ PGCE 68. Wycliffe Hall Ox 47. **d** 50 **p** 51. C Bootle Ch Ch *Liv* 50–52; C-in-c Netherton CD 52–57; V Stechford *Birm* 57–63; LtO 63–69; LtO *Liv* 71–89; Hon C Sutton 76–89; Hon C Burtonwood 89–02; rtd 90; PtO *Liv* from 92. *Woodside, Burtonwood Road, Great Sankey, Warrington* WA5 3AN   T: (01925) 635079

BOARDMAN, Jonathan Thomas. b 63. Magd Coll Cam BA 89 Magd Coll Ox MA 90. Westcott Ho Cam 87. **d** 90 **p** 91. C W Derby St Mary *Liv* 90–93; Prec St Alb Abbey 93–96; TR Catford (Southend) and Downham *S'wark* 96–99; RD E Lewisham 99; Chapl Rome *Eur* 99–18; Sen Tutor Angl Cen Rome 01–14; Can Gib Cathl *Eur* 07–18; Adn Italy and Malta 09–16; P-in-c Padova 13–18; V Clapham St Paul *S'wark* from 18; PtO *Eur* from 18. *St Paul's Vicarage, 6A Rectory Grove, London* SW4 0DZ   T: (020) 7207 9546   M: 07946-085977 E: vicar@stpaulsclapham.org

BOARDMAN, Miss Kathryn Louise. b 72. Hull Univ BA 94 MA 95 Cam Univ BTh 12 FHEA 07. Westcott Ho Cam 10. **d** 12 **p** 13. C Heworth St Mary *Dur* 12–16; P-in-c Harton from 16; P-in-c Cleadon Park from 16. *3 Page Avenue, South Shields* NE34 0SY   T: 0191-455 4682 E: kate.boardman@durham.anglican.org

BOARDMAN, Philippa Jane. b 63. Jes Coll Cam BA 85 MA 89. Ridley Hall Cam 87. **d** 90 **p** 94. Par Dn Walthamstow St Mary w St Steph *Chelmsf* 90–93; C Hackney Wick St Mary of Eton w St Aug *Lon* 93–96; P-in-c Old Ford St Paul and St Mark 96–03; V 03–13; Dean of Women's Min Stepney Area 94–02; Preb St Paul's Cathl 02–13; Can Res and Treas St Paul's Cathl 13–17; P-in-c Wandsworth Common St Mary *S'wark* 17–19; V from 19. *The Vicarage, 291 Burntwood Lane, London* SW17 0AP

BOCKING (Essex), Dean of. *Vacant*

BOCKING (Suffolk), Dean of. *Vacant*

BODDAM-WHETHAM, Paul Nathaniel. b 52. Em Coll Cam BA 73. ERMC 09. **d** 12 **p** 13. NSM St Alb Ch Ch 12–16; R Ducklington *Ox* from 16. *The Rectory, 6 Standlake Road, Ducklington, Witney* OX29 7XG   T: (01993) 776625   M: 07713-069876 E: paulbw32@icloud.com

BODDAM-WHETHAM, Tudor Alexander. b 76. St Aid Coll Dur BA 97. Wycliffe Hall Ox 06. **d** 08 **p** 09. C Houghton *Carl* 08–11; P-in-c Barony of Burgh from 11. *The Rectory, Burgh-by-Sands, Carlisle* CA5 6AW   T: (01228) 576324 E: vicartudor@gmail.com

BODDINGTON, Canon Alan Charles Peter. b 37. Oak Hill Th Coll 63. **d** 66 **p** 67. C Bedworth *Cov* 66–69; Bp's Officer for Min 69–75; Bp's Chapl for Miss 69–73; P-in-c Wroxall and Honiley 72–75; V Westwood 75–85; Asst Chapl Warw Univ 78–85; TR N Farnborough *Guildf* 85–02; RD Aldershot 88–93; Hon Can Guildf Cathl 92–02; rtd 02; PtO *Cov* from 02. *Tremar, Hathaway Lane, Stratford-upon-Avon* CV37 9BJ   T: (01789) 263643   M: 07866-909092 E: bodds4@btinternet.com

BODDY, Alan Richard. b 47. Ripon Coll Cuddesdon. **d** 84 **p** 85. C Eastcote St Lawr *Lon* 84–87; C Kensington St Mary Abbots w St Geo 87–90; Chapl HM Pris Brixton 90–91; Chapl HM Pris Send 91–92; Chapl HM Pris Downview 91–92; Chapl HM Pris High Down 92–98; Chapl HM Pris Wormwood Scrubs 98–02; rtd 02; PtO *Lon* from 02; Ox 02–04; *S'wark* 02–13; PV Westmr Abbey from 02. *105 Valiant House, Vicarage Crescent, London* SW11 3LX   E: arboddy@btinternet.com

BODDY, David. b 57. Linc Th Coll 92. **d** 92 **p** 93. C Peterlee *Dur* 92–95; C Penshaw 95–97; P-in-c Shiney Row 95–98; P-in-c Herrington 95–98; TV S Shields All SS 98–04; V Haswell, Shotton and Thornley 04–13; P-in-c Somerleyton, Ashby, Fritton, Herringfleet etc *Nor* 13–16; rtd 16. *455 Felixstowe Road, Ipswich* IP3 9DQ   T: (01473) 720196   M: 07971-304622 E: davidboddy1@gmail.com

BODEKER, Brian Mark. b 60. Cant Univ (NZ) BCom 82. Ox Min Course 09. **d** 12 **p** 13. NSM Didcot All SS *Ox* 12–14; C from 14. *1 Holly Lane, Harwell, Didcot* OX11 6DA   T: (01235) 816501   M: 07970-111110 E: markbodeker@btinternet.com

BODLE, Richard Talbot. b 70. Southn Univ LLB 91. Wycliffe Hall Ox BTh 98. **d** 98 **p** 99. C S Mimms Ch Ch *Lon* 98–02; TV Edgware 02–08; V Churt and Hindhead *Guildf* from 08. *St Alban's Vicarage, Wood Road, Hindhead* GU26 6PX   T: (01428) 605305 E: richard@bodle.plus.com *or* vicar@stalbanshindhead.org.uk

BODMIN, Archdeacon of. *See* ELKINGTON, The Ven Audrey Anne

BODY, Andrew. b 46. Pemb Coll Cam BA 68 MA 71. Ridley Hall Cam 68. **d** 70 **p** 71. C New Bury *Man* 70–73; TV Droylsden St Mary 73–78; V Low Harrogate St Mary *Ripon* 78–92; TR Redhorn *Sarum* 92–97; V Chobham w Valley End

Guildf 97–12; RD Surrey Heath 06–11; rtd 12; PtO *Heref* from 12. *Holyrood, 17 Temeside Estate, Ludlow* SY8 1LD   T: (01584) 877465 E: corpora12@btinternet.com

BODY, Mrs Shuna Jane. b 67. SEITE 98. **d** 01 **p** 02. NSM Brookland, Fairfield, Brenzett w Snargate etc *Cant* from 01. *Hope Farm, Snargate, Romney Marsh* TN29 9UQ   T: (01797) 343977   M: 07977-981990 E: shunabody@hotmail.com

BODYCOMBE, Stephen John. b 58. Lanchester Poly Cov BA. St Mich Coll Llan. **d** 83 **p** 84. C Cardiff St Jo *Llan* 83–86; V Dinas and Penygraig w Williamstown 86–00; V Dyffryn from 00. *The Vicarage, Dyffryn, Neath* SA10 7AZ   T: (01792) 814237

BOGGUST, Mrs Patricia Anne. b 42. Portsm Dioc Tr Course. **d** 90 **p** 98. NSM Hook w Warsash *Portsm* 90–94; NSM Locks Heath 94–09; Chapl Univ Hosp Southn NHS Foundn Trust from 01. *21 Beverley Close, Park Gate, Southampton* SO31 6QU   T: (01489) 573586 E: annieb.boggust@btinternet.com

BOGLE, Ms Elizabeth. b 47. York Univ BA 68 Leeds Univ PGCE 69. S'wark Ord Course 93. **d** 96 **p** 97. NSM E Greenwich *S'wark* 96–00; NSM Hatcham St Jas 00–06; NSM Newington St Paul 06–14; PtO from 14. *96 Grierson Road, London* SE23 1NX   T: (020) 8699 9996 E: elizabethbogle@hotmail.com

BOGLE, James Main Lindam Linton. b 33. Peterho Cam BA 56 MA 60. Wells Th Coll 59. **d** 61 **p** 62. C Bermondsey St Anne *S'wark* 61–65; Chapl York Univ 65–72; V Brayton 72–76; V Forest Hill St Aug *S'wark* 76–83; C Hatcham St Cath 83–85; Hon C 91–03; C Herne Hill St Paul 86–87; rtd 87; PtO *S'wark* 94–16. *96 Grierson Road, London* SE23 1NX   T: (020) 8699 9996 E: jamesmllbogle@hotmail.com

BOGLE, The Very Revd Paul David. b 57. CITC BTh 10. **d** 10 **p** 11. C Dunboyne and Rathmolyon *M & K* 10–13; I Trim and Athboy Gp from 13; Dean Clonmacnoise from 14. *St Patrick's Deanery, St Loman's Street, Trim, Co Meath, Republic of Ireland*   T: (00353) (46) 943 6698 E: pdbogle@gmail.com

BOHAN, Kimberly. b 72. St Andr Univ MA 93 Smith Coll (USA) MAT 94 St Andr Univ BD 99 Edin Univ MTh 03. **d** 03 **p** 04. C Glas St Ninian 03–06; R Dunoon *Arg* 06–09; P-in-c Rothesay 06–09; P-in-c Tighnabruaich 06–09; R Dunblane *St And* 09–12; P-in-c Waltham *Linc* 13–14; P-in-c Barnoldby le Beck 13–14; P-in-c New Waltham 13–14; C Laceby and Ravendale Gp 13–14; R Waltham Gp from 14. *The Rectory, 95 High Street, Waltham, Grimsby* DN37 0PN   E: kimberly@walthamgroupchurches.co.uk

BOL, Ann Kathleen Ruth. b 60. **d** 16 **p** 17. NSM Shingay Gp *Ely* from 16. *36 Hillfield, Foxton, Cambridge* CB22 6RZ   T: (01223) 871058   M: 07733-468436 E: ann.bol@btinternet.com

BOLAND, Christopher Paul. b 75. Hertf Coll Ox MPhys 97. Ridley Hall Cam BTh 01. **d** 01 **p** 02. C Skirbeck H Trin *Linc* 01–05; P-in-c Grantham, Harrowby w Londonthorpe 05–18; RD Grantham 12–18; P-in-c Fulwood Ch Ch *Blackb* from 18. *Christ Church Vicarage, 19 Vicarage Close, Fulwood, Preston* PR2 8EG   M: 07791-702537 E: cpboland@outlook.com

BOLAND, Geoffrey. b 56. Open Univ BA 03. Oak Hill Th Coll 87. **d** 89 **p** 90. C Ormskirk *Liv* 89–94; C Woodside Park St Barn *Lon* 94–99; TV Canford Magna *Sarum* from 99; PtO *Eur* from 17. *11 Plantagenet Crescent, Bournemouth* BH11 9PL   T: (01200) 573872 E: brevgeoff@ntlworld.com

BOLD, Peter Edward. b 64. Sheff Univ BEng 86 PhD 90. Cranmer Hall Dur BA 94. **d** 95 **p** 96. C Grenoside *Sheff* 95–97; C Rotherham and Dioc Communications Officer 97–01; P-in-c Brampton Bierlow 01–05; V 05–11; TR Dronfield w Holmesfield *Derby* from 11. *The Rectory, 24 Church Street, Dronfield* S18 1QB   T: (01246) 411531 E: pebold@talk21.com

BOLDING, Alan Frederick. b 40. NTMTC. **d** 07 **p** 07. NSM Woodford Bridge *Chelmsf* 07–13; PtO from 13. *21 Portman Drive, Woodford Green* IG8 8QN   T: (020) 8550 2070   M: 07932-797983 E: apbolding@onetel.com

BOLE, Malcolm Dennis. b 30. Oak Hill Th Coll 65. **d** 67 **p** 68. C Bridlington Priory *York* 67–70; Lect Stanley Smith Th Coll Gahini Rwanda 71; Prin 71–72; Lect École de Théologie Butare 72–73; P-in-c Combe Hay *B & W* 74–81; V Bath Odd Down 74–81; P-in-c Taunton St Jas 81–84; V 84–90; R Bicknoller w Crowcombe and Sampford Brett 90–98; rtd 98; PtO *B & W* from 01. *7 Putsham Mead, Kilve, Bridgwater* TA5 1DZ   T: (01278) 741297 E: mjbole@btinternet.com

BOLEN, Mrs Susan Melanie. INSEAD MBA 91 K Coll Lon MA 11. ERMC 12. **d** 15 **p** 16. C Frimley *Guildf* 15–19; P-in-c Wandsworth St Paul *S'wark* from 19. *97 Alexandra Road, London* SW19 7LE   M: 07799-656615 E: s.bolen@mac.com

BOLLARD, Canon Richard George. b 43. Fitzw Ho Cam BA 61 MA 65 K Coll Lon BD 63 AKC 63. **d** 64 **p** 65. C Southampton Maybush St Pet *Win* 64–68; Chapl Aston Univ *Birm* 68–74; TR Chelmsley Wood 74–82; V Coleshill and Maxstoke 82–04; RD Coleshill 82–92; Hon Can Birm Cathl

85–04; Dioc Ecum Officer 97–02; rtd 04; PtO *Heref* 05–19. *15 Riverdale Gardens, Otley LS21 2SX* T: (01432) 267414

BOLLEY, Michael Francis. b 55. St Cath Coll Ox BA 76 MSc 77 MA 92. Ripon Coll Cuddesdon 90. **d** 92 **p** 93. C Pinner *Lon* 92–95; C Eastcote St Lawr 95–99; P-in-c Southall H Trin 99–06; V from 06. *Holy Trinity Vicarage, Park View Road, Southall UB1 3HJ* T: (020) 8571 7329 E: vicar.htsouthall@gmail.com

BOLSTER, Christopher David. b 77. St Mary's Coll Twickenham BA99. STETS MA 11. **d** 11 **p** 12. C Stanwix *Carl* 11–15; V Clifton *Man* 15–19; V Barking St Patr *Chelmsf* from 19. *St Patrick's Vicarage, 79 Sparsholt Road, Barking IG11 7YG* T: (020) 8507 7487 M: 07970-943244 E: cdbolster2000@tiscali.co.uk or chrisdbolster@virginmedia.com

BOLSTER, David Richard. b 50. BA. St Jo Coll Nottm. **d** 84 **p** 85. C Luton Lewsey St Hugh *St Alb* 84–87; V Woodside w E Hyde 87–01; V Edmonton St Aldhelm *Lon* 01–10; PtO *Blackb* from 15. *3 Arnside Crescent, Morecambe LA4 5PP* T: (01524) 923861 E: davidbolster50@gmail.com

BOLSTER (née NICHOLSON), Mrs Lucy Clare. b 74. Sheff Univ BMedSci 97. St Jo Coll Nottm 12. **d** 15 **p** 16. NSM Sheffield Vine *Sheff* 15–19; LtO *Sarum* from 19. *38 Links Road, Poole BH14 9QS* M: 07948-403155

BOLT, George Henry. b 34. Lon Univ BSc 60 Bath Univ MSc 75 CPhys 75 MInstP 75. S Dios Minl Tr Scheme 85. **d** 88 **p** 89. NSM Oldbury *Sarum* 88–89; Chapl Chippenham Tech Coll 89–90; C Kington St Michael *Bris* 90–92; P-in-c Aldenham *St Alb* 92–98; rtd 98; PtO *Ban* 98–17. *Ty Capel Ffrwd, Llanfachreth, Dolgellau LL40 2NR* T: (01341) 422006 E: georgebolt34@gmail.com

BOLT, Mrs Mary Veronica. b 36. S Dios Minl Tr Scheme 90. **d** 93 **p** 94. NSM Aldenham *St Alb* 93–98; Sub-Chapl HM Pris The Mount 93–98; rtd 98; PtO *Ban* 98–99; P-in-c Maentwrog w Trawsfynydd 99–03. *Ty Capel Ffrwd, Llanfachreth, Dolgellau LL40 2NR* T: (01341) 422006 E: maryboltminstrel@gmail.com

BOLTON, Canon Jane Elizabeth. b 53. Leic Univ BA 75. Ripon Coll Cuddesdon 95. **d** 97 **p** 98. C Sheff St Mark Broomhill 97–02; P-in-c Dinnington 02–04; P-in-c Laughton w Throapham 03–04; P-in-c Dinnington w Laughton and Throapham 04–05; R 05–11; AD Laughton 08–11; P-in-c Ravenfield, Hooton Roberts and Braithwell 11–16; SSM Officer 11–16; Hon Can Sheff Cathl 10–16; rtd 16; PtO *Sheff* 16–18; *York* from 16. *3 Stakesby Manor, Manor Close, Whitby YO21 1HG* E: mail@janebolton.co.uk

BOLTON, John. b 43. SS Paul & Mary Coll Cheltenham DipEd 64. Trin Coll Bris 83. **d** 85 **p** 86. C Minehead *B & W* 85–89; R Winford w Felton Common Hill 89–98; C-in-c Locking Castle CD 98–06; rtd 06; PtO *B & W* from 06. *The Poppies, 13 Cornlands, Sampford Peverell, Tiverton EX16 7UA* T: (01884) 821445 E: johnbolton455@btinternet.com

BOLTON, Mrs Judith Ann. b 48. ERMC 12. **d** 13 **p** 14. NSM Hemingford Abbots *Ely* 13–18; NSM Hemingford Grey 13–18; rtd 18; PtO *Ely* from 18. *10 Westmeare, Hemingford Grey, Huntingdon PE28 9BZ* T: (01480) 370036 E: judithbolton10@gmail.com

BOLTON, Kelvin. b 53. Wilson Carlile Coll 88 Trin Coll Bris BA 98. **d** 98 **p** 99. C Walton Breck Ch Ch *Liv* 98–01; V Goose Green 01–08; P-in-c Walton Breck 08–17; rtd 17. *4 Woodland Drive, Ashton-in-Makerfield, Wigan WN4 8LX* T: (01942) 583273

BOLTON, Paul Edward. b 71. St Jo Coll Ox BA 94 MA 98 Peterho Cam BA 97. Ridley Hall Cam 95. **d** 98 **p** 99. C Lowestoft Ch Ch *Nor* 98–01; Titus Trust from 01; LtO *Ox* from 05. *33 Wharton Road, Headington, Oxford OX3 8AL* T: (01865) 756334 E: paulbolton1971@gmail.com

BOLTON, Peter Richard Shawcross. b 58. Warwick Univ BA 79. Sarum & Wells Th Coll 80. **d** 83 **p** 84. C Beckenham St Jas *Roch* 83–86; C Bedford Leigh *Man* 86–88; V Royton St Paul 88–94; AD Tandle 93–94; P-in-c Lower Broughton Ascension 95–01; P-in-c Salford Ordsall St Clem 98–01; P-in-c Ardwick St Benedict 99–01; V Leavesden St Alb 01–07; V Weston super Mare All SS and St Sav *B & W* 07–10; rtd 10; PtO *Ches* 12–14; Hon C Ilkeston H Trin *Derby* 14–15; Hon C Long Eaton St Laur 14–15; PtO *Man* 15–17 and from 18; CMP 99–10 and from 13. *Address withheld by request*

BOLTON, Richard David Edward. b 52. MA. St Steph Ho Ox 79. **d** 81 **p** 82. C Rawmarsh w Parkgate *Sheff* 81–84; Chapl Wellingborough Sch 85–92; Chapl Merchant Taylors' Sch Northwood 91–11; P-in-c Winchmore Hill H Trin *Lon* from 12; P in O from 96. *Holy Trinity Vicarage, 6 King's Avenue, London N21 3NA* T: (020) 8364 1583 E: rdeb2010@btinternet.com

BOLTON-DEBBAGE, Grant William Vivian. b 86. St Aid Coll Dur BA 08. Ripon Coll Cuddesdon 12. **d** 14 **p** 15. C Gt

Yarmouth *Nor* 14–18; C Upper Chelsea H Trin and St Sav *Lon* from 18. *First Floor Flat, 15-17 Pont Street, London SW1X 9EH* E: gboltondebbage@gmail.com

BOLTON, Archdeacon of. *See* BURGESS, The Ven Jean Ann

BOLTON, Suffragan Bishop of. *See* ASHCROFT, The Rt Revd Mark David

BOMFORD, Canon Rodney William George. b 43. BNC Ox BA 64 MA 68. Coll of Resurr Mirfield 67 Union Th Sem (NY) STM 69. **d** 69 **p** 70. C Deptford St Paul *S'wark* 69–77; V Camberwell St Giles w St Matt 77–01; RD Camberwell 87–97; Hon Can S'wark Cathl 93–01; rtd 01. *The Manor House, Modbury, Ivybridge PL21 0RA* T: (01548) 831277 E: rodney@bomford.eclipse.co.uk

BOMYER, Julian Richard Nicholas Jeffrey. b 55. AKC 78 Sarum & Wells Th Coll 78. **d** 79 **p** 80. C Rugby *Cov* 79–84; TV 85–88; P-in-c Clifton upon Dunsmore w Brownsover 84–85; Prec Ch Ch *Ox* 88–93; V Hampton *Worc* 93–01; P-in-c Sedgeberrow w Hinton-on-the-Green 00–01; R Hampton w Sedgeberrow and Hinton-on-the-Green 01–06; rtd 06; PtO *Worc* from 15. *52 Elmside, Evesham WR11 3DZ* T: (01386) 421559 M: 07900-824264 E: julian@bomyer.co.uk

BOND, Andrew James Douglas. b 81. Ridley Hall Cam 11. **d** 14 **p** 15. C Penge Lane H Trin *Roch* 14–17; C Derby St Alkmund and St Werburgh from 17. *St Paul's Vicarage, 6 Old Chester Road, Derby DE1 3SA* M: 07939-051990 E: andy.bond@stwderby.org

BOND, Andrew Thomas. b 50. Leeds Univ BA 74 Solicitor 79. Ox Min Course 09. **d** 12 **p** 13. NSM Pangbourne w Tidmarsh and Sulham *Ox* 12–16; NSM Reading St Mary the Virgin from 16. *Heron Lodge, 32 The Moors, Pangbourne, Reading RG8 7LP* T: 0118-984 5297 M: 07917-623444 E: at.bond@btinternet.com

BOND, Anne. *See* BOND, Sybilla Anne

BOND, Catherine Grace La Touche. b 60. SS Coll Cam MA 83 Darw Coll Cam PGCE 83 Solicitor 87. **d** 09 **p** 10. OLM Clopton w Otley, Swilland and Ashbocking *St E* 09–13; OLM Carlford 13–17. *230 Ferry Road, Felixstowe IP11 9RU* M: 07801-342336 E: catherine.beaumont@otleyhall.co.uk

BOND, David. b 36. Oak Hill Th Coll 72. **d** 74 **p** 75. C Leyton St Mary w St Edw *Chelmsf* 74–78; C Slough *Ox* 78–80; V Selby St Jas *York* 80–93; P-in-c Wistow 80–82; V 82–93; RD Selby 89–93; P-in-c Northiam *Chich* 93–94; R 94–99; rtd 99; PtO *Chich* from 00. *24 The Sackville, De La Warr Parade, Bexhill-on-Sea TN40 1LS*

BOND, David Hugh Tremayne. b 64. Ripon Coll Cuddesdon 13. **d** 15 **p** 16. C Kingsbridge, Dodbrooke, and W Alvington *Ex* 15–19; R Queen Thorne *Sarum* from 19. *The Rectory, Trent, Sherborne DT9 4SL* T: (01935) 850201 M: 07875-781709 E: trentrectory@gmail.com

BOND, David Matthew. b 38. Leic Univ BA 59 Leeds Univ PGCE 67 Nottm Univ MA 85. Sarum Th Coll 59. **d** 61 **p** 62. C Leic St Anne 61–64; E England Sec SCM 64–66; Hon C Nor St Pet Mancroft 64–67; Lect and Hd of Section Pet Regional Coll 67–96; Lect Pet Coll of Adult Educn from 96; Hon C Stamford All SS w St Pet *Linc* 74–81; Hon C Stamford All SS w St Jo from 81; PtO *Pet* 85–07 and 12–17. *2 The Courtyard, Cotterstock, Peterborough PE8 5HD* T: (01832) 226255 E: david@dbond.me.uk

BOND, David Warner. b 32. MA BSc(Econ). Cant Sch of Min 79. **d** 82 **p** 83. NSM Otham w Langley *Cant* 82–10; PtO from 11. *6 Denton Close, Maidstone ME15 8ER* T: (01622) 202239 F: 205149 E: dwbond@blueyonder.co.uk or dwbond@bigfoot.com

BOND, David William. b 46. New Coll Edin BD 99. **d** 18 **p** 18. NSM S Hetton *Dur* from 18. *23 Pinedale Drive, South Hetton, Durham DH6 2XG* T: 0191-526 9604 E: david.radian53@outlook.com

BOND, Mrs Gita Deborah. b 57. N Lon Poly BSc 80 Chelsea Coll Lon PGCE 81. Ridley Hall Cam 06. **d** 08 **p** 09. C The Ramseys and Upwood *Ely* 08–16; NSM W Green Ch Ch w St Pet *Lon* from 16. *Christ Church Vicarage, Waldeck Road, London N15 3EP* M: 07977-555895 E: gitabond@hotmail.com

BOND, Gordon. b 44. Chich Th Coll 68. **d** 71 **p** 72. C Wisbech St Aug *Ely* 71–74; C Wembley Park St Aug *Lon* 74–77; C York Town St Mich *Guildf* 77–80; TV Haywards Heath St Wilfrid *Chich* 80–82; V Lower Beeding 82–86; V E Grinstead St Mary 86–06; RD E Grinstead 98–04; rtd 06; PtO *Chich* 12–17; *Eur* from 16. *6 St Andrew's Close, Reigate RH2 7JF* T: (01737) 340193 E: frgordon@hotmail.co.uk

BOND, Mrs Hilary Rowenna. b 65. W Lon Inst of HE BA 86 Sussex Univ PGCE 87. Sarum Coll BA 17. **d** 17 **p** 18. NSM The Lytchetts and Upton *Sarum* from 17. *Holme Priory, East Holme, Wareham BH20 6AG* T: (01929) 551219 M: 07766-228189 E: hilary.bond@mac.com

BOND, Mrs Jill Margaret. b 45. Newton Park Coll Bath TCert 67. WEMTC 04. **d** 06 **p** 07. OLM Redmarley D'Abitot, Bromesberrow, Pauntley etc *Glouc* 06–11; NSM from 11. *Southfield, Hawcross, Redmarley, Gloucester GL19 3JQ* T: (01452) 840202 E: rev.jbond@googlemail.com

BOND, The Very Revd John Frederick Augustus. b 45. Open Univ BA 75. CITC 64. **d** 67 **p** 69. C Lisburn St Paul *Conn* 67–70; C Finaghy 70–77; I Ballynure and Ballyeaston 77–99; I Skerry w Rathcavan and Newtowncrommelin 99–16; Can Conn Cathl 96–98; Prec 98–01; Dean Conn 01–16; rtd 16; Dioc C *Conn* from 19. *3 Rectory Green, Broughshane, Ballymena BT42 4LH* T: (028) 2586 1415 M: 07711-285728 E: jfa.bond@btinternet.com

BOND, Lawrence. b 53. ACIB 77. Sarum & Wells Th Coll 92. **d** 92 **p** 93. C Saffron Walden w Wendens Ambo and Littlebury *Chelmsf* 92–95; TV 96–00; P-in-c Takeley w Lt Canfield 00–04; R 04–09; RD Dunmow and Stansted 02–09; P-in-c Sible Hedingham w Castle Hedingham 09–15; RD Hinckford 10–15; rtd 15; PtO *Chelmsf* from 15. *34 Cedar Close, Walton on the Naze CO14 8NJ* T: (01255) 484741 E: revlbond@hotmail.com

BOND, Linda. b 52. Nottm Univ BEd 80 Lon Inst of Educn MA 89. EAMTC 96. **d** 99 **p** 00. C Brackley St Pet w St Jas *Pet* 99–03; C Skegness Gp *Linc* 03–09; P-in-c Bromham w Oakley and Stagsden *St Alb* 09–17; rtd 17; PtO *Pet* from 18. *Address withheld by request* E: revdlinda@talktalk.net

BOND, Mrs Marian Nancy Hamlyn. b 49. Univ of Wales (Cardiff) BSc(Econ) 71 Westmr Coll Ox PGCE 72 Ex Univ MEd 77. SEITE BA 06. **d** 06 **p** 07. NSM Marden *Cant* 06–09; NSM Len Valley 09–11; NSM Tunstall and Bredgar 11–16; Asst Dir of Ords 09–16; rtd 16; PtO *Nor* from 16; *Truro* from 16. *Coach House 2, Manor Court, Attleborough Road, Hingham, Norwich NR9 4HP* T: (01953) 852576 M: 07966-442181 E: mnhbond@gmail.com

BOND, Mark Francis Wilson. b 53. Sarum & Wells Th Coll 89. **d** 91 **p** 92. C Taunton Lyngford *B & W* 91–95; V Highbridge 95–02; R Jersey St Brelade *Win* from 02. *The Rectory, La Marquanderie Hill, St Brelade, Jersey JE3 8EP* T: (01534) 742302 F: 490878 E: rector@stbreladeschurch.com

BOND, Norman. b 23. Wycliffe Hall Ox. **d** 70 **p** 71. C Warrington St Ann *Liv* 70–73; P-in-c 73–77; P-in-c Warrington St Pet 73–77; V Wigan St Cath 77–88; rtd 88; PtO *Carl* 88–01; *Liv* 88–98; *S & M* 01–09. *Longs Croft, Gate Lane, Freshwater PO40 9QD* T: (01983) 760799

BOND, Paul Maxwell. b 36. Glos Univ BA 00 ACIB 56. Oak Hill Th Coll 76. **d** 79 **p** 80. NSM Wisley w Pyrford *Guildf* 79–91; Org Children's Soc SW Lon 88–91; C Egham *Guildf* 91–93; C Horsell 93–94; V Rockfield and St Maughen's w Llangattock etc *Mon* 94–99; rtd 99; Hon C Islip w Charlton on Otmoor, Oddington, Noke etc *Ox* 99–01; Hon C Ray Valley 01–04; Nat Liaison Officer Ch Tourism Assn 99–04; PtO *Glouc* from 05; *Guildf* 08–13. *Fosters, Pyrford Heath, Pyrford, Woking GU22 8SS* T: (01932) 351137 E: paul_bond@bigfoot.com

BOND, Mrs Susan Fraser. b 55. SS Hild & Bede Coll Dur BEd 78 Leeds Univ MA 00. NOC 96. **d** 99 **p** 00. C Tickhill w Stainton *Sheff* 99–02; R Warmsworth 02–10; AD W Doncaster 06–07; V Ampleforth w Oswaldkirk, Gilling E etc *York* 10–16; rtd 16; PtO *York* from 17. *South View, Wrelton, Pickering YO18 8PF* T: (01751) 475885 E: sfbond007@gmail.com

BOND, Mrs Sybilla Anne. b 44. **d** 12 **p** 13. NSM Corfe Castle, Church Knowle, Kimmeridge etc *Sarum* 12–17; NSM Swanage and Studland 12–17; rtd 17; PtO *Sarum* from 17. *51 West Street, Corfe Castle, Wareham BH20 5HA* T: (01929) 480249

BONE, David Hugh. b 39. Worc Coll Ox BA 63 MA 67. **d** 06 **p** 07. OLM Almondsbury and Olveston *Bris* from 06. *3 Hardy Lane, Tockington, Bristol BS32 4LJ* T: (01454) 614601 M: 07958-414729 E: david.bone10@btinternet.com

BONE, Janet Mary. **d** 05 **p** 06. NSM Trellech and Penallt *Mon* 05–09; NSM Monmouth w Overmonnow etc from 09. *Ty Ffynnon, The Narth, Monmouth NP25 4QJ* T: (01600) 860466 E: revjanetbone@gmail.com

BONE, Canon Simon Adrian. b 78. Ripon Coll Cuddesdon BA 09. **d** 09 **p** 10. C Newquay *Truro* 09–11; C Chacewater w St Day and Carharrack 11–14; P-in-c from 14; C Devoran 11–14; P-in-c from 14; C Feock 11–14; P-in-c from 14; C St Stythians w Perranarworthal and Gwennap 11–14; P-in-c from 14; Asst Rural Link Officer from 13; Hon Can Truro Cathl from 18. *The Rectory, Church Street, St Day, Redruth TR16 5LD* T: (01209) 822862 M: 07971-270615 E: fathersimon@btinternet.com

BONHAM, Mrs Valerie. b 47. ALA 94. SAOMC 94. **d** 97 **p** 98. NSM Newbury *Ox* 97–98; C Cookham 98–02; P-in-c Coleford w Holcombe *B & W* 02–14; rtd 14; PtO *B & W* from 15. *89 Balch Road, Wells BA5 2BX* T: (01749) 676326 E: valerie.bonham@zen.co.uk

BONIFACE, Lionel Ernest George. b 36. Lon Coll of Div BD 64 ALCD 63. **d** 64 **p** 65. C Attenborough w Chilwell *S'well* 64–69; C Farndon 69–71; C Thorpe 69–71; P-in-c Mansfield St Aug 71–77; V Oughtibridge *Sheff* 77–92; Ind Chapl 79–81; P-in-c Treeton 92–93; TV Brinsworth w Catcliffe and Treeton 93–98; rtd 98; PtO *Sheff* 99–13. *1 Green Oak Grove, Sheffield S17 4GG* T: 0114-235 0415

BONIFACE, Timothy Roger. b 82. Ex Univ BA 05 Nottm Univ MA 12 St Chad's Coll Dur PhD 17. Westcott Ho Cam 12. **d** 16 **p** 17. C Chislehurst St Nic *Roch* from 16. *Southbeech, Old Perry Street, Chislehurst BR7 6PP* E: tim.r.boniface@gmail.com

BONNEY, The Very Revd Mark Philip John. b 57. St Cath Coll Cam BA 78 MA 82. St Steph Ho Ox BA 84 MA 89. **d** 85 **p** 86. C Stockton St Pet *Dur* 85–88; Chapl St Alb Abbey 88–90; Prec 90–92; V Eaton Bray w Edlesborough 92–96; R Gt Berkhamsted 96–04; RD Berkhamsted 02–04; Can Res and Treas Sarum Cathl 04–12; Dean Ely from 12. *The Deanery, The College, Ely CB7 4DN* T: (01353) 660316 E: m.bonney@elycathedral.org

BONNEYWELL, Miss Christine Mary. b 57. Univ of Wales (Lamp) BA 78 LTh 80. Sarum & Wells Th Coll 81 **p** 94. C Swansea St Pet *S & B* 81–84; C Llangyfelach 84–86; Chapl Univ of Wales (Lamp) *St D* 86–90; Educn Officer Wells Cathl *B & W* 90–95; C Yeovil H Trin w Barwick 95–97; Chapl Yeovil Distr Hosp 95–97; Chapl Pilgrim Health NHS Trust Boston 97–01; Chapl United Lincs Hosps NHS Trust from 01. *The Chaplaincy, Pilgrim Hospital, Sibsey Road, Boston PE21 9QT* T: (01205) 364801 ext 2243 F: 354395

BONSEY, Hugh Richmond Lowry. b 49. Win Univ MA 12. Sarum & Wells Th Coll 74. **d** 76 **p** 77. C Bris St Mary Redcliffe w Temple etc 76–80; TV Sutton *Liv* 80–88; P-in-c Yatton Keynell *Bris* 88–89; P-in-c Biddestone w Slaughterford 88–89; P-in-c Castle Combe 88–89; P-in-c W Kington 88–89; P-in-c Nettleton w Littleton Drew 88–89; C Westbury-on-Trym H Trin 89–90; V Peasedown St John w Wellow *B & W* 90–04; rtd 18; C Sherborne w Castleton, Lillington and Longburton *Sarum* from 18. *67 Acreman Street, Sherborne DT9 3PH* E: hughbonsey@gmail.com

BOOKER, Canon Alison Susan Wray. b 74. Worc Coll of Educn BA 95 York St Jo Coll MA 04. Westcott Ho Cam 06. **d** 08 **p** 09. C Countesthorpe w Foston *Leic* 08–11; C Church Langton cum Tur Langton etc 11–13; C Houghton-on-the-Hill, Keyham and Hungarton 11–13; V Coplow from 13; Warden Past Assts 14–17; AD Launde from 17; AD Gartree from 17; Hon Can Leic Cathl from 18. *The Vicarage, Gaulby Road, Billesdon, Leicester LE7 9AG* T: 0116-259 6321 E: alisonbooker@btinternet.com

BOOKER, Gerald Dennis. b 30. St Pet Coll Ox BA 52 MA 56. Ridley Hall Cam 53 Oak Hill Th Coll 80. **d** 81 **p** 82. Hon C Hertford All SS *St Alb* 81–83; R Bramfield w Stapleford and Waterford 83–96; Chapl Herts Univ 90–96; rtd 96; PtO *St Alb* from 96. *The Garden House, Churchfields, Hertford SG13 8AE* E: gerald.brooker@ntlworld.com

BOOKER, Michael Charles. b 36. LLCM 57 ARCO 58. Lon Coll of Div LTh 63. **d** 63 **p** 64. C Royston *St Alb* 63–66; C Mildenhall *St E* 66–68; Min Can St E Cathl 68–83; Prec 70–83; Chapl Framlingham Coll 84–99; rtd 99; PtO *St E* 99–16. *29 The Mowbrays, Framlingham, Woodbridge IP13 9DL* T: (01728) 723122 E: mail@michaelbooker.plus.com

BOOKER, Canon Michael Paul Montague. b 57. Jes Coll Ox BA 79 Bris Univ PGCE 80. Trin Coll Bris BA 87. **d** 87 **p** 88. C Cant St Mary Bredin 87–91; V Leamington Priors St Mary *Cov* 91–96; Dir Miss and Past Studies Ridley Hall Cam 96–05; P-in-c Comberton *Ely* 05–10; P-in-c Toft w Caldecote and Childerley 05–10; TR Lordsbridge 10–16; RD Bourn 13–16; Bp's Change Officer w Resp for Market Towns from 16; Hon Can Ely Cathl from 15. *6 Common Lane, Hemingford Abbots, Huntingdon PE28 9AN* E: mike.booker@elydiocese.org

BOOKLESS, Andrew Pitcairn. b 63. Sheff Univ BA 85. St Jo Coll Nottm 90. **d** 92 **p** 93. C Llantrisant *Llan* 92–95; C Llangynwyd w Maesteg 95–97; V Bargoed and Deri w Brithdir 97–12; R Hubberston *St D* 12–14; I Hubberston and Herbrandston from 15. *The Rectory, 35 Westaway Drive, Hakin, Milford Haven SA73 3EQ* T: (01646) 696914 E: ahbookless@googlemail.com

BOOKLESS, Mrs Anne Karen. b 68. St Mellitus Coll 16. **d** 19. C Norwood St Mary *Lon* from 19. *The Rectory, 26A Tentelow Lane, Southall UB2 4LE* E: revdannebookless@gmail.com

BOOKLESS, David John Charles. b 62. Jes Coll Cam MA 83 PGCE. Trin Coll Bris MA 91. **d** 91 **p** 92. C Southall St Jo *Lon* 91–99; P-in-c Southall St Geo 99–01; Nat Dir A Rocha UK 01–11; Dir Th A Rocha Internat from 11; Hon C Southall Green St Jo Lon 03–18; P-in-c Norwood St Mary from 18. *The Rectory, 26A Tentelow Lane, Southall UB2 4LE* M: 07974-212713 E: dave.bookless@arocha.org

BOOKLESS, Mrs Rosemary. b 26. Westf Coll Lon BA 47 DipEd 49 Serampore Univ BD 72. St Mich Ho Ox 56. **dss** 80 **d** 91 **p** 94. Willoughby-on-the-Wolds w Wysall and Widmerpool *S'well* 80–85; rtd 85; PtO *Leic* 85–89; Loughborough Em 89–91; NSM 91–95; NSM Loughborough Em and St Mary in Charnwood 95–97; PtO 97–03; *Glouc* 16–17. *19 Capel Court, The Burgage, Prestbury, Cheltenham GL52 3EL* T: (01242) 236937 E: rosemary.bookless926@btinternet.com

BOON, Mrs Linda Margaret Claire. b 57. Buckingham Univ BA 79 Birm Univ PGCE 80 MEd 91. Yorks Min Course 09. **d** 12 **p** 13. NSM Ripon Cathl 12–14; *Leeds* 14–17; NSM Bishop Thornton, Burnt Yates, Markington etc from 17; Tutor St Hild Coll from 17. *Cowgate Manor Barn, Shaw Mills, Harrogate HG3 3HP* T: (01423) 779179 M: 07961-893163 E: lindaboon@dsl.pipex.com

BOON, Marion. *See* SIMMONS, Marion

BOON, Stephen David. b 81. Em Coll Cam MA 04. Wycliffe Hall Ox BA 10. **d** 12 **p** 13. NSM Tunbridge Wells St Jo *Roch* 12–16; Tutor Cornhill Tr Course from 16. *10 Dunstan Grove, Tunbridge Wells TN4 9ND* T: (01892) 528451 E: stephen.boon@cantab.net

BOON, William John. b 54. Glouc Sch of Min 84. **d** 88 **p** 89. NSM Matson *Glouc* 88–91; C Gt Witcombe 91–95; C Brockworth 91–96; P-in-c Sharpness w Purton and Brookend 96–99; P-in-c Slimbridge 97–99; R Sharpness, Purton, Brookend and Slimbridge from 00; AD Dursley 02–07. *The Vicarage, Sanigar Lane, Newtown, Berkeley GL13 9NF* T: (01453) 811360 E: bill.boon@btinternet.com

BOOT, Felicity Olivia. b 43. TCert 64. STETS 94. **d** 97 **p** 98. NSM Lyndhurst and Emery Down and Minstead *Win* 97–04; Chapl Southn Univ Hosps NHS Trust 04–09; rtd 09; PtO *Win* from 09. *The Firs, Pikes Hill, Lyndhurst SO43 7AY* T: (023) 8028 2616 E: felicityboot@hotmail.com *or* felicityboot@yahoo.com

BOOTH, Charles. *See* BOOTH, Ewart Charles

BOOTH, David. b 44. Coll of Resurr Mirfield 72. **d** 74 **p** 75. C Osmondthorpe St Phil *Ripon* 74–77; C Armley w New Wortley 77–79; V Leeds St Wilfrid 79–95; V Royton St Paul *Man* 95–09; rtd 09. *13 Lyon Street, Shaw, Oldham OL2 7RU* T: (01706) 661172 E: davidbooth6@live.co.uk

BOOTH, Derek. b 36. LTCL ALCM AKC 61. **d** 62 **p** 63. C Woodchurch *Ches* 62–65; C Penrith St Andr *Carl* 65–67; C Tranmere St Paul *Ches* 67–70; C Wilmslow 70–72; V Micklehurst 73–97; C Staveley and Barrow Hill *Derby* 97–01; rtd 01; PtO *Derby* from 01. *9 Ilam Close, Inkersall, Chesterfield S43 3EW* T: (01246) 475421 E: delbooth@talktalk.net

BOOTH, Eric James. b 43. Open Univ BA 84. NOC 86. **d** 89 **p** 90. NSM Nelson St Phil *Blackb* 89–93; NSM Fence and Newchurch-in-Pendle 93–97; NSM Padiham w Hapton and Padiham Green 97–03; rtd 03; PtO *Blackb* from 04. *5 Round Hill Place, Cliviger, Burnley BB10 4UA* T: (01282) 450708 E: ericjbooth1@yahoo.co.uk

BOOTH, Ewart Charles. b 67. LTCL 85 K Coll Lon LLB 88. Sarum & Wells Th Coll BTh 93. **d** 93 **p** 95. NSM Tadley St Pet *Win* 93–95; C Highcliffe w Hinton Admiral 95–00; R W Parley *Sarum* from 00. *The Rectory, 250 New Road, West Parley, Ferndown BH22 8EW* T: (01202) 873561

BOOTH, Graham Richard. b 55. Birm Univ BSocSc 75. St Jo Coll Nottm 89. **d** 91 **p** 92. C Woodthorpe *S'well* 91–96; P-in-c Trowell 96–02; P-in-c Awsworth w Cossall 00–02; R Trowell, Awsworth and Cossall 02–05; Warden Open Gate Retreat Ho 05–15; Guardian Community of Aid and Hilda from 12; NSM Burravoe *Ab* from 19; NSM Lerwick from 19. *The Glebe, Fetlar, Shetland ZE2 9DJ* T: (01957) 733380

BOOTH, Ian George. b 64. Chich Th Coll 85 Linc Th Coll 87. **d** 88 **p** 89. C Pet St Mary Boongate 88–90; C Hawley H Trin *Guildf* 90–94; V Willesden St Mary *Lon* 94–03; P-in-c Gosport H Trin *Portsm* 03–05; V Gosport Ch Ch 05–06; RD Gosport 03–06; V Leigh-on-Sea St Marg *Chelmsf* 09–17; TR Wood Green St Mich w Bounds Green St Gabr etc *Lon* from 17; AD E Haringey from 17. *The Rectory, 1A Selborne Road, London N22 7TL* E: frianbooth@gmail.com

BOOTH, Martin Allison. b 54. K Coll Lon MA 06. SEITE. **d** 09 **p** 10. C Wimbledon *S'wark* 09–12; V Riverhead w Dunton Green *Roch* 12–19; RD Sevenoaks 16–19; rtd 19. *2 Russet Grove, Cranleigh GU6 7FT*

BOOTH, Paul Harris. b 49. St Jo Coll Nottm. **d** 79 **p** 80. C Thorpe Edge *Bradf* 79–82; P-in-c Frizinghall 82–83; TV Shipley St Paul and Frizinghall 83–97; rtd 97; PtO *Bradf* 97–14; *Leeds* from 14; Hon Chapl Bradf Cathl from 11. *11 Derwent Avenue, Wilsden, Bradford BD15 0LY* T: (01535) 958939

BOOTHBY, Mrs Julia. b 64. St Andr Univ MTheol 87. SAOMC 02. **d** 04 **p** 05. C Welwyn *St Alb* 04–08; TV Ouzel Valley 08–11; TV Bp's Hatfield, Lemsford and N Mymms

11–18; P-in-c Dingwall *Mor* from 18; P-in-c Strathpeffer from 18; P-in-c Invergordon St Ninian from 18. *4 Castle Street, Dingwall IV15 9HU* M: 07952-514228 E: juliabby@sky.com *or* julia.boothby@btinternet.com

BOOTHROYD, Callum. b 69. All SS Cen for Miss & Min 17. **d** 19. C Hyde St Geo w St Thos *Ches* from 19. *72 Market Street, Mottram, Hyde SK14 6JG* M: 07881-026594 E: revcallum@outlook.com

BOOYS, Canon Susan Elizabeth. b 56. Bris Univ BA 78 LMH Ox PGCE 79. SAOMC 92. **d** 95 **p** 96. C Kidlington w Hampton Poyle *Ox* 95–99; TV Dorchester 99–05; TR from 05; TV Warborough 99–05; TR from 05; AD Aston and Cuddesdon 07–12; Hon Can Ch Ch from 08. *The Rectory, Manor Farm Road, Dorchester-on-Thames, Wallingford OX10 7HZ* T/F: (01865) 340007 E: rector@dorchester-abbey.org.uk

BOREHAM, Harold Leslie. b 37. S'wark Ord Course. **d** 72 **p** 73. C Whitton and Thurleston w Akenham *St E* 72–77; R Saxmundham 77–85; V Felixstowe SS Pet and Paul 85–96; Chapl Felixstowe Hosp 85–96; Chapl Bartlet Hosp Felixstowe 95–96; P-in-c Ramsgate St Mark *Cant* 96–01; V 01–03; Chapl E Kent NHS and Soc Care Partnership Trust 98–03; rtd 03; PtO *St E* from 03; *Chelmsf* from 05. *313 St John's Road, Colchester CO4 0JR* T: (01206) 853769 E: harrylboreham@googlemail.com

BORLEY, Mark Letchford. b 61. Lon Univ BSc 83 PhD 87. St Jo Coll Nottm MTh 03. **d** 04 **p** 05. C W Swindon and the Lydiards *Bris* 04–05; C Swindon St Aug and Swindon All SS w St Barn 05–07; C Cricklade w Latton 07–09; P-in-c Allington and Maidstone St Pet *Cant* 09–12; PtO 12–14; C W Sheppey 14–15; V Ewell St Fran *Guildf* 15–18; P-in-c Stoneleigh from 18. *The Minister's House, 71 Ruxley Lane, Epsom KT19 9FF* T: (020) 8397 2208 M: 07811-124237 E: rev.mark@borley.org.uk

BORMAN, Alexander John. b 88. Linc Sch of Th and Min 17. **d** 19. NSM Branston w Nocton and Potterhanworth *Linc* from 19. *2 Bottesford Close, Lincoln LN6 3YR* T: (01522) 688496 E: aborman3.142@gmail.com

BORROWDALE, Geoffrey Nigel. b 61. Southn Univ BSc 83 W Sussex Inst of HE PGCE 94. Chich Th Coll 87. **d** 90 **p** 99. C Tilehurst St Mich *Ox* 90–91; PtO *Chich* 93–97; NSM Sunninghill *Ox* 98–99; C Bracknell 99–01; P-in-c Theale and Englefield 01–11; C The Churn 11–13; V Hayes St Anselm *Lon* 13–19; R Hasland *Derby* from 19; V Temple Normanton from 19. *The Rectory, 49 Church Side, Hasland, Chesterfield S41 0JX* T: (01246) 232486 E: frgeoffrey@stpaulshasland.com

BORTHWICK, Anne Christine. *See* ROWLEY, Anne Christine

BOSHER, Philip Ross. b 61. Greenwich Univ CertEd 03 Univ of Wales MTh 07. Sarum & Wells Th Coll 84. **d** 87 **p** 88. C Warminster St Denys *Sarum* 87–88; C Warminster St Denys, Upton Scudamore etc 88–90; P-in-c Farley w Pitton and W Dean w E Grimstead 90–91; TV Alderbury Team 91–96; CF 96–16; P-in-c Winshill *Derby* from 16; C Hartshorne and Bretby from 16. *The Vicarage, 54 Mill Hill Lane, Burton-on-Trent DE15 0BB* M: 07906-956883 E: prbosher@gmail.com

BOSS, Mrs Ann. b 42. Cen Lancs Univ BA 93. CBDTI 99. **d** 02 **p** 03. NSM Scorton and Barnacre and Calder Vale *Blackb* 02–05; P-in-c Hanmer Springs New Zealand 05–10; PtO *Blackb* from 10. *School House Barn, Inglewhite Road, Inglewhite, Preston PR3 2LD* T: (01995) 643146 E: ann.boss227@btinternet.com

BOSSWARD, Eric Paul. b 63. CQSW 90. Trin Coll Bris BA 99. **d** 99 **p** 00. C Ecclesall *Sheff* 99–01; C Netherthorpe St Steph 01–04; Co-ord Chapl HM YOI Castington 04–12; V Preston St Cuth *Blackb* 12–16; V Headington St Mary *Ox* from 16. *St Mary's Vicarage, Bayswater Road, Headington, Oxford OX3 9EY* M: 07982-264424 E: eric.bossward@talktalk.net

BOSTON, Jonathan Bertram. b 40. Ely Th Coll 61. **d** 64 **p** 65. C Eaton *Nor* 64–70; Sen Chapl ACF Norfolk 66–05; Chapl Norfolk Constabulary *Nor* 94–16; V Horsham St Faith w Newton St Faith 70–90; V Horsford 71–90; V Horsford and Horsham w Newton St Faith 90–97; P-in-c Litcham w Kempston, E and W Lexham, Mileham etc 97–06; rtd 06; PtO *Nor* 06–17. *Bevan House, Front Street, Litcham, King's Lynn PE32 2QG* T: (01328) 701200

BOSTON, Archdeacon of. *See* ALLAIN CHAPMAN, The Ven Justine Penelope Heathcote

BOSWELL, Canon Colin John Luke. b 47. Sarum & Wells Th Coll 72. **d** 74 **p** 75. C Upper Tooting H Trin *S'wark* 74–78; C Sydenham St Phil 78–79; C St Helier 80–83; P-in-c Caterham 83–95; P-in-c Chaldon 85–95; RD Caterham 85–95; V Croydon St Jo 95–16; RD Croydon Cen 00–06; rtd 16; Chapl St Dunstan's Coll Catford from 16; Hon C Sydenham H Trin and St Aug *S'wark* 16–19; P-in-c Honor Oak Park St Aug from 19; Hon Can S'wark Cathl from 99. *129A Honor Oak Park,*

London SE23 3LD   T: (020) 8699 4469   M: 07854-265277 E: colinlukeboswell@outlook.com

BOSWELL, Stephen James. b 84. Oak Hill Th Coll 15. d 18 p 19. C Normanton *Derby* from 18. *23 Nevinson Drive, Sunnyhill, Derby DE23 1GX* E: steve.boswell@stgiles-derby.org.uk

BOTHAM, Arthur. b 53. St Jo Coll Nottm. d 00 p 01. C Hartley Wintney, Elvetham, Winchfield etc *Win* 00–04; TV Basingstoke 04–14; V Popley w Limes Park and Rooksdown from 14; AD Basingstoke 11–15. *The Vicarage, 25 Tewkesbury Close, Popley, Basingstoke RG24 9DU*   T: (01256) 324734 E: arthur.botham@btinternet.com

BOTT, Graham Paul. b 49. Staffs Univ MBA 95. NOC 00. d 03 p 04. NSM Rickerscote *Lich* 03–13; P-in-c Hoar Cross w Newchurch from 13; Chapl Abbots Bromley Sch from 14. *Church Cottage, Maker Lane, Hoar Cross, Burton-on-Trent DE13 8QR*   T: (01283) 576058 E: graham.pbott@btopenworld.com

BOTTERILL, David Darrell. b 45. Open Univ BA. Sarum & Wells Th Coll. d 83 p 84. C Blandford Forum and Langton Long etc *Sarum* 83–86; TV Shaston 86–00; Chapl HM YOI Guys Marsh 89–91; P-in-c Portland St Jo *Sarum* 00–09; Asst Chapl N Dorset Primary Care Trust 01–09; rtd 09; Hon Chapl Miss to Seafarers from 02; PtO *Sarum* from 10. *41 Hawthorn Avenue, Gillingham SP8 4ST*   T: (01747) 821017   E: david.botterill45@btinternet.com   *or* ddbotterill@gmail.com

BOTTING, Paul Lloyd. b 43. Brasted Th Coll 67 St Mich Coll Llan 69. d 71 p 72. C Hucknall Torkard *S'well* 71–74; C Cen Torquay *Ex* 74–76; P-in-c Sutton in Ashfield St Mich *S'well* 76; V 77–88; Chapl King's Mill Hosp Sutton-in-Ashfield 85–88; NSM Vale of Belvoir *Leic* 95–97; C High Framland Par 97–01; C Waltham on the Wolds, Stonesby, Saxby etc 97–01; C Wymondham w Edmondthorpe, Buckminster etc 97–01; P-in-c High Framland Par 01–10; rtd 10; PtO *Leic* from 10; *S'well* from 11. *9 Orchard Close, Radcliffe-on-Trent, Nottingham NG12 2BN*   T: 0115-933 2591   M: 07770-853762 E: plbpixie@gmail.com

BOTTLEY, Mrs Kate. b 75. Trin & All SS Coll Leeds BA 97 Open Univ MTh 08. St Jo Coll Nottm LTh 08. d 08 p 09. C Skegby w Teversal *S'well* 08–11; P-in-c Blyth and Scrooby w Ranskill 11–13; V 13–16; Chapl N Notts Coll of FE 11–16; NSM Retford Area from 17. *Address withheld by request*

BOTTOMER, Sally Ann. b 68. d 14 p 15. C Aston Clinton w Buckland and Drayton Beauchamp *Ox* 14–18; R from 18. *The Rectory, 23 New Road, Aston Clinton, Aylesbury HP22 5BB*   M: 07967-208181 E: revsally.bottomer@btinternet.com

BOTWRIGHT, Adrian Paul. b 55. St Jo Coll Ox MA PGCE. Westcott Ho Cam 80. d 82 p 83. C Chapel Allerton *Ripon* 82–85; Chapl Chapel Allerton Hosp 82–85; C Bourne *Guildf* 85–88; V Weston 88–94; R Skipton H Trin *Bradf* 94–13; P-in-c Embsay w Eastby 05–13; Hon Can Bradf Cathl 02–13; PtO *York* from 14; *Leeds* from 17. *24 Ripon Way, Carlton Miniott, Thirsk YO7 4LR*   T: (01845) 523491 E: adrianbotwright@gmail.com

BOUCHER, Geoffrey John. b 61. Warwick Univ BA 82 K Coll Lon 94 ACA 87. Ridley Hall Cam 94. d 96 p 97. C Tavistock and Gulworthy *Ex* 96–01; P-in-c W Monkton *B & W* 01–11; R W Monkton w Kingston St Mary, Broomfield etc 11–15; RD Taunton 10–15; R Hartford and Houghton w Wyton *Ely* from 16. *The Rectory, 3 Rectory Lane, Wyton, Huntingdon PE28 2AQ*   T: (01480) 461846 E: geoffboucher@btinternet.com

BOUDIER, Rosemary. *See* TALLOWIN, Rosemary

BOUGHTON, Mrs Elisabeth Mary Victoria. b 66. St Anne's Coll Ox BA 87 MA 93. Ridley Hall Cam 89. d 91 p 94. C Guildf Ch 91–95; Chapl St Cath Sch Bramley 92–97; NSM Fetcham *Guildf* 97–14; Chapl Guildf YMCA 04–14; Tutor CME *Guildf* 08–14; PtO *Ox* from 14. *91 Marlborough Road, Oxford OX1 4LX*

BOUGHTON, Canon Michael John. b 37. Kelham Th Coll 57. d 62 p 63. C Grantham St Wulfram *Linc* 62–66; C Kingsthorpe *Pet* 66–68; C Linc St Nic w St Jo Newport 68–72; V Scunthorpe All SS 72–79; V Crowle 79–89; TR Bottesford w Ashby 89–02; Can and Preb Linc Cathl from 00; rtd 02; PtO *Linc* from 02. *45 Albion Crescent, Lincoln LN1 1EB*   T: (01552) 569653 E: mboughton@aol.com

BOUGHTON, Miss Ruth Frances. b 52. Ox Brookes Univ BA 10. Birm Bible Inst 71. d 07 p 08. OLM Chenies and Lt Chalfont, Latimer and Flaunden *Ox* 07–10; NSM from 10. *17 Bell Lane, Amersham HP7 9PF*   T: (01494) 764221 E: revboughton@live.co.uk

BOULLIER, Canon Kenneth John. b 51. Trin Coll Bris 82. d 84 p 85. C Heref St Pet w St Owen and St Jas 84–87; V Nutley *Chich* 88–93; R Maresfield 88–93; New Zealand 93–97; R Nailsea H Trin *B & W* 97–08; P-in-c St Just-in-Roseland and St Mawes *Truro* 08–18; RD Powder 13–17; Hon Can Truro Cathl 15–18; rtd 18. *7 Carnjewey Way, St Austell PL25 4FU* E: revkjb@hotmail.co.uk

BOULT, David Ronald. b 51. Bris Univ BSc 73. St Mich Coll Llan 04. d 07 p 08. NSM Llantwit Major *Llan* 07–10; NSM Cowbridge 11–16; PtO from 16. *52 The Verlands, Cowbridge CF71 7BY*   T/F: (01446) 772166   M: 07767-818257 E: daveboult@hotmail.co.uk

BOULT, Geoffrey Michael. b 56. Southn Univ BTh 88 Bris Univ MA 92 Birm Univ MSc 96 PGCE 98. Sarum & Wells Th Coll 77. d 80 p 81. C Newark w Hawton, Cotham and Shelton *S'well* 80–83; TV Melksham *Sarum* 83–90; P-in-c Charminster and Stinsford 90–95; PtO *Birm* 95–96; *Sarum* 95–98; Hon C Bradford Peverell, Stratton, Frampton etc 09–14; P-in-c Arlesey w Astwick *St Alb* 14–17; V from 17. *The Rectory, 77 Church Lane, Arlesey SG15 6UX*   T: (01462) 731227   M: 07970-371757 E: vicar@arlesey.org.uk

BOULTER, Adam Charles. b 71. Bath Coll of HE BA 93 Kingston Univ MA 04 Fitzw Coll Cam BA 07 MA 11. Westcott Ho Cam 05. d 08 p 09. C Battersea St Mary *S'wark* 08–12; Port Chapl Aqaba Jordan 12–16; PtO *S'wark* 16–17; P-in-c Poitou-Charentes *Eur* 16–19. *8 avenue Armand Blanc, 16700 Ruffec, France*   T: (0033) 5 45 30 64 01 E: adamboulter@cantab.net

BOULTER, Michael Geoffrey. b 32. Lon Univ BD 56. Tyndale Hall Bris 53. d 57 p 58. C Tranmere St Cath *Ches* 57–60; R Cheetham Hill *Man* 60–65; R Tollard Royal w Farnham *Sarum* 65–66; Chapl Alderney Hosp Poole 66–96; V Branksome St Clem *Sarum* 66–96; rtd 96. *7 Temple Trees, 13 Portarlington Road, Bournemouth BH4 8BU*   T: (01202) 768718

BOULTER, Paul Roger. b 81. St Jo Coll Dur BA 03. Ridley Hall Cam 12. d 15 p 16. C Bedford Ch Ch *St Alb* 15–18; V Caton w Littledale *Blackb* from 18; V Over Kellet from 18. *The Vicarage, 153 Brookhouse Road, Brookhouse, Lancaster LA2 9NX*   T: (01524) 770300 E: revpaulboulter@gmail.com

BOULTON, Mrs Alison Peta. b 55. St Mich Coll Sarum CertEd 76. All SS Cen for Miss & Min 16. d 18 p 19. NSM Middlewich w Byley *Ches* from 18. *21 Main Road, Moulton, Northwich CW9 8NU*   T: (01606) 591559   M: 07879-681827 E: alisonb_b@yahoo.co.uk

BOULTON, Christopher David. b 50. Keble Coll Ox BA 71 MA 80. Cuddesdon Coll 71. d 74 p 75. C St Mary-at-Latton *Chelmsf* 74–77; C Shrub End 77–80; P-in-c Gt Bentley 80–83; V 83–89; V Cherry Hinton St Andr *Ely* 89–04; P-in-c Teversham 90–04; P-in-c Much Hadham *St Alb* 04–05; TR Albury, Braughing, Furneux Pelham, Lt Hadham etc 06–12; RD Bishop's Stortford 07–12; Chapl Pendine Park Coll 12–19; rtd 19. *7 Stamford Drive, Coalville LE67 4TA*   T: (01530) 451001   M: 07580-137977 E: boultonc50@gmail.com

BOULTON, Kingsley Garth. b 50. Sheff Univ BA 72 MA 74 MCLIP 74. d 18. NSM York St Lawr w St Nic from 18; NSM York All SS Pavement w St Crux and St Mich from 18; NSM York St Denys from 18; NSM York St Helen w St Martin from 18; NSM York St Olave w St Giles from 18; NSM York H Trin Micklegate from 18. *15 Blakeney Place, York YO10 3HZ*   T: (01904) 411535 E: kingsley.boulton@gmail.com

BOULTON, Ms Louise Jane. b 72. Goldsmiths' Coll Lon BA 93 Heythrop Coll Lon MA 98. SEITE 02. d 05 p 06. NSM Wandsworth St Anne *S'wark* 05–08; NSM Wandsworth St Anne w St Faith 08–10; PtO from 12. *17 Somers Road, London SW2 2AE*   T: (020) 7096 1646   M: 07989-333016 E: louise@trespassersw.net

BOULTON, Wallace Dawson. b 31. MCIJ 86. Lon Coll of Div 65. d 67 p 68. C Bramcote *S'well* 67–71; Dioc Public Relns Officer 69–71; Hon C St Bride Fleet Street w Bridewell etc *Lon* 71–86; Guild Chapl from 86; Publicity Sec CMS 71-79; Media Sec 79–86; Ed C of E Newspaper 86–88; LtO *Chich* 84–94; PtO 94–96; rtd 96; Hon C St Leonards St Leon *Chich* 96–01 and 04–09; P-in-c 01–03; Hon C St Leonards St Ethelburga and St Leon from 09. *44 Winterbourne Close, Hastings TN34 1XQ*   T: (01424) 713743 E: revw.boulton@talktalk.net *or* wallace@revwboulton.plus.com

BOULTON-LEA, Peter John. b 46. St Jo Coll Dur BA 68. Westcott Ho Cam 69. d 71 p 72. C Farlington *Portsm* 72–75; C Darlington St Jo *Dur* 75–77; R E and W Horndon w Lt Warley *Chelmsf* 77–82; V Hersham *Guildf* 82–91; R Kirk Sandall and Edenthorpe *Sheff* 91–96; RD Doncaster 95–96; V Campsall 96–97; R Burghwallis and Campsall 97–98; V Tattenham Corner and Burgh Heath *Guildf* 98–03; V Thorne *Sheff* 03–08; rtd 08; PtO *Ox* from 08. *25 Larkfields, Headington, Oxford OX3 8PF*   T: (01865) 744302

BOULTON-REYNOLDS, Mrs Jean. b 49. Sarum Th Coll 93. d 96 p 97. C Harnham *Sarum* 96–99; C Salisbury St Mark 99–01; TV Westborough *Guildf* 01–05; TV Barnes *S'wark* 05–11; rtd 11; PtO *Sarum* from 12; *Bris* from 15. *17 Springfield*

Crescent, Royal Wootton Bassett, Swindon SN4 7AP T: (01793) 854259 E: jeanboultonreynolds@gmail.com

BOUMENJEL, Nejib. b 73. St Jo Coll Nottm. **d** 14 **p** 15. C Birm St Geo 14–18; V Hall Green Ascension from 18. The Vicarage, 592 Fox Hollies Road, Hall Green, Birmingham B28 9DX M: 07769-624598 E: b_nejib2002@yahoo.co.uk

BOUNDY, Canon Gerald Neville. b 36. BA. Linc Th Coll. **d** 65 **p** 66. C Bris St Mary Redcliffe w Temple etc 65–70; P-in-c Southmead 70–72; V 72–81; V Cotham St Sav w St Mary 81–99; Hon Can Bris Cathl 96–99; rtd 99; PtO Bris from 99. 10 Morley Road, Southville, Bristol BS3 1DT T: 0117-966 3337

BOURDEAUX, Canon Michael Alan. b 34. St Edm Hall Ox BA 57 MA 61 Lambeth DD 96. Wycliffe Hall Ox BA 59. **d** 60 **p** 61. C Enfield St Andr Lon 60–64; P-in-c Charlton St Luke w St Paul S'wark 64–65; LtO Roch 65–91; LtO Ox 91–04; Visiting Prof St Bernard's Sem Rochester USA 69; Gen Dir Keston Inst 69–99; Hon Can Roch Cathl 90–99; rtd 99; PtO Ox 04–18. 101 Church Way, Iffley, Oxford OX4 4EG T: (01865) 777276 E: mbourdeaux@yahoo.co.uk

✠**BOURKE, The Rt Revd Michael Gay.** b 41. CCC Cam BA 63 MA 67. Cuddesdon Coll 65. **d** 67 **p** 68 **c** 93. C Gt Grimsby St Jas Linc 67–71; C Digswell St Alb 71–73; C-in-c Panshanger CD 73–78; Course Dir St Alb Minl Tr Scheme 75–87; V Southill St Alb 78–86; Adn Bedford 86–93; Area Bp Wolverhampton Lich 93–06; rtd 07; PtO Heref 07–08; Hon Asst Bp Heref from 08. The Maltings, Little Stretton, Church Stretton SY6 6AP T: (01694) 722910

BOURKE, Canon Ronald Samuel James. b 50. MA HDipEd. **d** 79 **p** 80. C Portadown St Mark Arm 79–83; I Carnteel and Crilly 83–90; I Mountmellick w Coolbanagher, Rosenallis etc M & K 90–97; I Kingscourt w Syddan 97–09; Chan Kildare Cathl 00–09; Can Meath 00–09; I Boyle and Elphin w Aghanagh, Kilbryan etc K, E & A 09–16; Preb Tipper St Patr Cathl Dublin 00–16; Can Elphin Cathl K, E & A 12–16; rtd 16. Mullaghnabreena, Collooney, Co Sligo, Republic of Ireland T: (00353) (71) 916 7596 M: 89-458 1920 E: rsjbourke@hotmail.com

BOURKE, Stanley Gordon. b 48. CITC 78. **d** 78 **p** 79. C Dundonald D & D 78–80; C Lurgan Ch the Redeemer 81–82; I Dungiven w Bovevagh D & R 82–89; I Lurgan St Jo D & D 89–03; I Inishmacsaint Clogh 03–14; Preb Clogh Cathl 06–14; Chan Clogh Cathl 11–14; rtd 14. 63 Church Avenue, Bangor BT20 3EG M: 07975-993213 E: sgbourke@hotmail.co.uk

BOURNE, Anne Clare. b 63. Univ of Wales (Cardiff) BEd 85. SEITE 08. **d** 11 **p** 12. NSM Sevenoaks St Luke Roch 11–18; C from 18. Charein, 27 St James's Road, Sevenoaks TN13 3NQ T: (01732) 456788 M: 07512-734224 E: rev.annebourne@gmail.com

BOURNE, Mrs Carole Sylvia. b 47. York Univ BA 68 LSE MSc 79 PhD 85. SEITE 99. **d** 02 **p** 03. C Epsom St Martin Guildf 02–05; NSM E Molesey 05–12; RD Emly 10–12; PtO 13–16 and from 18; S'wark from 14. Flat 21, 9 St Mary's Road, Surbiton KT6 4JG M: 07957-295864 E: cbeezles@me.com

BOURNE, Colin Douglas. b 56. Culham Coll of Educn CertEd 77. Oak Hill Th Coll BA 04. **d** 04 **p** 05. C Wellington All SS w Eyton Lich 04–08; P-in-c Toton S'well 08–11; V from 11. 95 Stapleford Lane, Beeston, Nottingham NG9 6FZ T: 0115-973 1138 M: 07821-967879 E: revcolinbourne@googlemail.com

BOURNE, David James. b 54. Reading Univ BA 76. Trin Coll Bris 77. **d** 79 **p** 80. C W Bromwich Gd Shep w St Jo Lich 79–84; V Riseley w Bletsoe St Alb 84–05; V Hailsham Chich from 05. St Mary's Vicarage, Vicarage Road, Hailsham BN27 1BL T: (01323) 842381 E: davidjbourne@googlemail.com

BOURNE, Canon Dennis John. b 32. Ridley Hall Cam 58. **d** 60 **p** 61. C Gorleston St Andr Nor 60–64; Min Gorleston St Mary CD 64–79; V Costessey 79–86; R Hingham w Wood Rising w Scoulton 86–97; RD Hingham and Mitford 90–95; Hon Can Nor Cathl 93–97; rtd 97; PtO Nor 97–06. Amron, Star Lane, Long Stratton, Norwich NR15 2XH T: (01508) 530863 E: johnbourne@onetel.com

BOURNE, Mrs Diana Mary. b 46. St Jo Coll York BEd 68. S Dios Minl Tr Scheme 92. **d** 95 **p** 96. C Pinner Lon 95–00; V Lamberhurst and Matfield Roch 00–06; rtd 07; PtO Roch 07–17; Cant from 07. The Pump House, Angley Road, Cranbrook TN17 2PN T: (01580) 712005 E: revdbourne@hotmail.com

BOURNE, Hugh Edward. b 86. Sussex Univ BSc 08. Oak Hill Th Coll BA 15. **d** 15 **p** 16. C Lindfield Chich from 15. 2 Church Close, Francis Road, Lindfield, Haywards Heath RH16 2JB T: (01444) 483945 M: 07879-620322 E: revhughbo@gmail.com

BOURNE, The Ven Ian Grant. b 32. Univ of NZ BA 55 Otago Univ BD 75. **d** 56 **p** 57. New Zealand 56–65 and from 67; Adn Wellington 78–86 and 90–95; C Epsom St Martin Guildf

65–67. 19 Nelson Street, Riccarton, Christchurch 8011, New Zealand T: (0064) (4) 233 0466 E: ian.marg@bourne.co.nz

BOURNE, John. See BOURNE, Dennis John

BOURNE, Nigel Irvine. b 60. St Jo Coll Ox BA 82 MA 86 Open Univ MBA 09. Trin Coll Bris BA 92. **d** 92 **p** 93. C Bedhampton Portsm 92–94; C Newport St Jo 94–98; V Chalk Roch from 98; RD Gravesend from 18. The Vicarage, 2A Vicarage Lane, Gravesend DA12 4TF T: (01474) 567906 F: 745147 E: vicarofchalk@hotmail.com

BOURNE, Canon Philip John. b 61. Sussex Univ BEd 83 Aber Univ MLitt 86 Ex Univ MEd 96 FRSA 97. Cranmer Hall Dur 85. **d** 87 **p** 88. C Gildersome Wakef 87–89; Chapl Ex Univ 89–93; Assoc Chapl The Hague and Voorschoten Eur 94 and 95; Chapl Voorschoten 96–06; Can Brussels Cathl 04–06; Dir of Ords Chich 07–14; TR Sidmouth, Woolbrook, Salcombe Regis, Sidbury etc Ex 14–18; Chapl Oporto Eur from 18. St James, Largo de Maternidade Júlio Dinis, 4050 Porto, Portugal E: philipbourne@btinternet.com

BOURNE, Mrs Sarah Madeleine. b 66. New Hall Cam BA 88 PGCE 89 MA 92. Wycliffe Hall Ox 12. **d** 15 **p** 16. Asst Chapl Tudor Hall Sch from 12; PtO Ox 15–19; C Shipston-on-Stour w Honington and Idlicote Cov 15–18; C Cov Cathl 17–18; NSM Banbury Ox from 19. 2 Home Farm, Willington, Shipston-on-Stour CV36 5AS T: (01608) 661249 E: revsarahbourne@gmail.com

BOURNEMOUTH, Archdeacon of. See ROUCH, The Ven Peter Bradford

BOURNER, Paul. b 48. CA Tr Coll. **d** 90 **p** 91. CA from 79; C Ipswich St Mary at Stoke w St Pet St E 90–93; R Ufford w Bredfield and Hasketon 93–01; V Ipswich St Thos 01–14; rtd 14; PtO St E from 15. 62 Dereham Avenue, Ipswich IP3 0QF E: paul.bourner@ntlworld.com

BOUSFIELD, Andrew Michael. b 70. Middx Univ BA 92. Oak Hill Th Coll BA 00. **d** 00 **p** 01. C Beckenham Ch Ch Roch 00–03; C Surbiton Hill Ch Ch S'wark 03–07; C Patcham Chich 07–18; V Salisbury St Mark and Laverstock Sarum from 18. St Mark's Vicarage, 62 Barrington Road, Salisbury SP1 3JD M: 07866-434117 E: andybousfield@outlook.co.uk

BOUSKILL, David Walter. b 72. Westcott Ho Cam 95. **d** 98 **p** 99. C Henley w Remenham Ox 98–02; TV Bicester w Bucknell, Caversfield and Launton 02–08; TV Horsham Chich from 08. Holy Trinity House, Blunts Way, Horsham RH12 2BL T: (01403) 265401 E: fr.david@bouskill.co.uk

BOUTLE, David Francis. b 44. Leeds Univ BSc 67. Cuddesdon Coll 69. **d** 72 **p** 73. C Boston Linc 72–77; C Waltham 77–80; P-in-c Morton 80–81; V 81–94; Chapl W Lindsey NHS Trust 80–94; Local Mental Health Chapl 88–94; P-in-c Heckington Gp Linc 94–10; rtd 10; PtO Linc from 17. 3 Hengist Close, Quarrington, Sleaford NG34 8WU T: (01529) 415384 E: boutle.heck@btinternet.com

BOUTLE, Toby Jefferson. b 79. Magd Coll Ox BA 00 MA 11 Barrister 04. St Steph Ho Ox BA 15. **d** 16 **p** 17. C Whyke w Rumboldswhyke and Portfield Chich from 16. 36 Victoria Road, Chichester PO19 7HY M: 07773-377503 E: toby_boutle@yahoo.co.uk

BOVEY, Denis Philip. b 29. Ely Th Coll 50. **d** 53 **p** 54. C Southwick St Columba Dur 53–57; PtO Ox 57–59; LtO Chich 62–64; C W Hartlepool St Aid Dur 64–66; R Aberdeen St Jas Ab 66–74; R Old Deer 74–89; R Longside 74–89; R Strichen 74–89; Can St Andr Cathl 75–88; Syn Clerk 78–83; Dean Ab 83–88; R Alford 89–94; R Auchindoir 89–94; R Inverurie 89–94; P-in-c Dufftown 89–94; P-in-c Kemnay 89–94; rtd 94. 15 Loskin Drive, Glasgow G22 7QW T: 0141-574 3603

BOVILL, Francis William. b 34. St Aid Birkenhead 55. **d** 58 **p** 59. C Bispham Blackb 58–61; C Crosthwaite Keswick Carl 61–64; V Radcliffe St Andr Man 64–68; P-in-c Woodside St Steph Glouc 68; V 69–73; V Scotby Carl 73–96; P-in-c Cotehill and Cumwhinton 94–96; rtd 96; PtO Carl from 96. Crosthwaite, West Road, Wigton CA7 9RG T: (016973) 43410

BOWDEN, Andrew. See BOWDEN, Robert Andrew

BOWDEN, Andrew David. b 59. Newc Univ BA 80 BArch 83. Cranmer Hall Dur 95. **d** 97 **p** 98. C Monkseaton St Pet Newc 97–01; V Whorlton 01–09; PtO York 10–11; P-in-c Weaverthorpe w Helperthorpe, Luttons Ambo etc 11–19; V from 19; C Malton and Old Malton 11–19. Chapel House, Back Lane, West Lutton, Malton YO17 8TF M: 07544-705064 E: andy@woldsvalley.plus.com

BOWDEN, Andrew John. b 77. Nottm Trent Univ BSc 99. Wycliffe Hall Ox 09. **d** 11 **p** 12. C Laleham Lon 11–15; Chapl All SS Academy Plymouth from 15. Oaklands Cottage, Pridham Lane, Plymouth PL2 3PH T: (01752) 208182

BOWDEN, John-Henry David. b 47. Magd Coll Cam BA 69 MA 73 MIL 78. S Dios Minl Tr Scheme 81. **d** 84 **p** 85. NSM Redlynch and Morgan's Vale Sarum 84–88; NSM Cuckfield Chich 88–92; NSM St Mary le Bow w St Pancras Soper Lane etc Lon 92–98; NSM Chailey Chich 98–04; P-in-c Venice w

BOWDEN, Lynne. b 53. Bris Univ BA 77 Heythrop Coll Lon MA 12 Ban Univ BTh 12 Bris Univ PGCE 78. **d** 06 **p** 07. NSM Oatlands *Guildf* 06–15; PtO *Ches* 16–17; NSM High Lane 17–18; PtO from 18; *Derby* from 18. *Sitch House Farm, Taxal, Whaley Bridge, High Peak SK23 7EA* T: (01663) 732097 E: a.curate@btinternet.com

BOWDEN, Mrs Mary Eiluned. **d** 07 **p** 08. NSM Gipsy Hill Ch Ch *S'wark* 07–09; C W Dulwich All SS 09–11; P-in-c Haslemere and Grayswood *Guildf* 11–16; R 16–19; rtd 19. *Address temp unknown* M: 07921-315894 E: revmarybowden@btconnect.com

BOWDEN, Canon Robert Andrew. b 38. Worc Coll Ox BA 62 MA 67 BDQ 68. Cuddesdon Coll 63. **d** 65 **p** 66. C Wolverhampton St Geo *Lich* 65–69; C Duston *Pet* 69–72; R Byfield 72–79; Chapl R Agric Coll Cirencester 79–93; R Coates, Rodmarton and Sapperton etc *Glouc* 79–04; Bp's Adv on Rural Soc 81–93; Local Min Officer 84–04; rtd 04; Hon C Kemble, Poole Keynes, Somerford Keynes etc *Glouc* 04–08; Chapl to The Queen 92–08; Hon Can Glouc Cathl 90–08; PtO from 08. *Washbrook Cottage, Caudle Green, Cheltenham GL53 9PW* T: (01285) 821067 E: bowdencoates@btinternet.com

BOWDEN-PICKSTOCK, Mrs Susan Mary. b 63. Bp Otter Coll BA 85 RGN 88. Ridley Hall Cam 09. **d** 11 **p** 12. C Bluntisham cum Earith w Colne and Holywell etc *Ely* 11–14; P-in-c Hunstanton St Mary w Ringstead Parva etc *Nor* 14–19; C Harston w Hauxton and Newton *Ely* from 19. *The Vicarage, Church Street, Harston, Cambridge CB22 7NP* M: 07912-293905 E: revroses@gmail.com

BOWEN, Daniel Joseph George. b 51. St Mich Coll Llan 96. **d** 98 **p** 99. C Gorseinon *S & B* 98–00; C Cen Swansea 00–01; TV 01–02; V Birchfield *Birm* 02–07; rtd 07. *Dryslwyn, 41 Station Road, Ystradgynlais, Swansea SA9 1NX* T: (01639) 843020 E: dejagebe@gmail.com

BOWEN, David Gregory. b 47. Lanchester Poly Cov BSc 69. Cuddesdon Coll 69. **d** 74 **p** 75. C Rugby St Andr *Cov* 74–77; C Charlton St Luke w H Trin *S'wark* 78–80; TV Stantonbury *Ox* 80–82; PtO *B & W* 82–07; Ab from 08. *Erraid Station House, Stronsay, Orkney KW17 2AS* T: (01857) 616435 M: 07762-569920 E: dbowenuk@btinternet.com

BOWEN, Ms Delyth. b 54. St D Coll Lamp BA 90. St Mich Coll Llan. **d** 91 **p** 97. C Llandybie *St D* 91–95; Dn-in-c Llanllwni 95–97; V Llanybydder and Llanwenog w Llanllwni 97–02; V Betws w Ammanford 02–11; V Cynwyl Gaeo w Llansawel and Talley etc 11–12; rtd 12. *6 Roderick Close, Townhill, Swansea SA1 6AJ* T: (01792) 920081

BOWEN, Canon Jennifer Ethel. b 46. Liv Univ BSc 68 CertEd 69. NOC 80. dss 83 **d** 87 **p** 94. Blundellsands St Nic *Liv* 83–86; W Derby St Mary 86–94; Par Dn 87–94; C 94–08; AD W Derby 01–08; Hon Can Liv Cathl 03–08; rtd 08; PtO *Liv* from 16. *6 Springhill Court, Liverpool L15 9EJ* T: 0151-291 0845

BOWEN, John Roger. b 34. St Jo Coll Ox BA 59 MA 62. Tyndale Hall Bris 59. **d** 61 **p** 62. C Cambridge St Paul *Ely* 61–65; Tanzania 65–76; Kenya 76–80; Dir Past Studies St Jo Coll Nottm 80–85; Tutor 85–95; Gen Sec Crosslinks 96–00; rtd 99; PtO *Ely* from 01; Asst Rtd Clergy Officer from 09. *26 Lingholme Close, Cambridge CB4 3HW* T: (01223) 352592 E: bowenrw@onetel.com

BOWEN, Julie Elizabeth. b 64. S Glam Inst HE BEd 86. SEITE 09. **d** 12 **p** 13. C Bexley *Roch* 12–16; V Bromley St Andr from 16; Chapl St Olave's Gr Sch Orpington from 15. *St Martin's Vicarage, 93 Pelham Road, Bexleyheath DA7 4LY* T: (01322) 523344 M: 07775-674503 E: julie@bowen.to

BOWEN, Mark Franklin. b 61. Coll of H Cross (USA) BA 79 Univ of S Florida MA 89. **d** 93. Asst Chapl Univ of S Florida USA 93–96; C Tampa St Andr 96–97; PtO *S'wark* 07–09; Co-ord Inclusive Ch *Eur* from 09; Teacher Internat Sch of Basel from 09. *309 Guterstrasse, Basel 4053, Switzerland* T: (0041) (61) 331 0961 E: markfbowen@hotmail.com

BOWEN, Roger. See BOWEN, John Roger

BOWEN, Canon Stephen Allan. b 51. Leic Univ BA 72. Glouc Sch of Min 88. **d** 91 **p** 92. NSM Bream *Glouc* 91–92; NSM Tidenham w Beachley and Lancaut 91–94; C Glouc St Jas and All SS 94–97; P-in-c Woodchester and Brimscombe 97–00; R 00–11; AD Stonehouse 07–08; AD Stroud 08–11; TR Cheltenham St Mark 11–16; Hon Can Glouc Cathl 09–16; Community Can Glouc Cathl 16–17; rtd 17. *1 Clifford Villas, Scotts Lane, Wellington TA21 8PH* E: sabowen75@gmail.com

BOWER, Allen Cleeve. b 71. Trin Coll Bris 10. **d** 12 **p** 13. C Kensal Rise St Mark *Lon* 12–15; V Tipton St Matt *Lich* 15–18; V Tipton St Matt w St Martin and St Paul from 19. *St Matthew's Vicarage, 107A Dudley Road, Tipton DY4 8DJ* T: 0121-522 2555 E: revallenb@gmail.com

BOWERMAN, Mrs Lynn Joan. b 56. STETS 12. **d** 15 **p** 16. C Branksome St Clem *Sarum* from 15. *6 Tree Hamlets, Poole BH16 5SA*

BOWERS, Canon David. b 56. Man Univ BA 79. Wycliffe Hall Ox 82. **d** 84 **p** 85. C Lawton Moor *Man* 84–87; C Walmsley 87–93; V Milnrow 93–98; P-in-c Deerhurst and Apperley w Forthampton etc *Glouc* 98–04; V 04–08; Assoc Dir of Ords 98–08; V S Cerney w Cerney Wick, Siddington and Preston *Glouc* 08–16; R Sodbury Vale from 16; Hon Can Glouc Cathl from 12. *The Vicarage, Horseshoe Lane, Chipping Sodbury, Bristol BS37 6ET* T: (01454) 313159 or 325160 E: dbowers@btinternet.com or office@svbcofe.org.uk

BOWERS, Denise Frances. See BROWN, Denise Frances

BOWERS, Canon Francis Malcolm. b 44. Chan Sch Truro 79. **d** 82 **p** 83. NSM Penzance St Mary w St Paul *Truro* 82–83; C 86–88; NSM Madron 83–86; TV Redruth w Lanner and Treleigh 88–91; V St Blazey 91–15; P-in-c Lanlivery w Luxulyan 01–08; P-in-c Luxulyan 08–15; P-in-c Tywardreath w Tregaminion 02–15; RD St Austell 96–05; Hon Can Truro Cathl 01–15; rtd 15; PtO *Truro* from 15. *10 The Green, St Austell PL25 4TB* T: (01276) 624901 M: 07974-818631 E: canonmalcolm@gmail.com

BOWERS, Canon John Edward William. b 32. St Aid Birkenhead 60. **d** 63 **p** 64. C Bromborough *Ches* 63–68; Ind Chapl 68–74; P-in-c Crewe St Pet 69–71; V Crewe St Mich 71–74; TR Ellesmere Port 74–79; V Hattersley 79–91; Hon Can Ches Cathl 80–02; RD Mottram 88–91; V Bunbury and Tilstone Fearnall 91–98; P-in-c Leasowe 98–02; rtd 02; PtO *Ches* from 02. *2 Shalford Grove, Wirral CH48 9XY* T: 0151-625 4831

BOWERS, Canon Julian Michael. b 48. Middx Univ BA 97 Goldsmiths' Coll Lon MA 00. Edin Th Coll 69. **d** 72 **p** 73. C Chippenham St Andr w Tytherton Lucas *Bris* 72–74; C Henbury 74–77; Chapl Kandy H Trin Sri Lanka 77–82; P-in-c Evercreech w Chesterblade and Milton Clevedon *B & W* 82–83; V 83–89; V Enfield St Jas *Lon* 89–04; Chapl St Andr Hosp Northn 04–12; Can Pet Cathl 10–12; rtd 12; Past Care and Counselling Adv *Pet* 13–18; Hon C Brigstock w Stanion and Lowick and Sudborough 13–17; PtO from 17. *41 Kipling Road, Kettering NN16 9JZ* T: (01536) 525520 E: revjbowers@gmail.com

BOWERS, Preb Peter. b 47. Linc Th Coll 72. **d** 76 **p** 77. C Mackworth St Fran *Derby* 76–78; C Maidstone St Martin *Cant* 78–83; V Elmton *Derby* 83–89; R Swimbridge w W Buckland and Landkey *Ex* 89–10; RD Shirwell 01–10; Preb Ex Cathl 07–10; rtd 10; PtO *York* from 11. *Endellion, 30 Kingsgate, Bridlington YO15 3PU* T: (01262) 676096 E: pbowers62@btinternet.com or pebo@live.co.uk or endellion47@icloud.com

BOWERS, Mrs Rosemary Christine. b 49. Ripon Coll Cuddesdon 99. **d** 01 **p** 02. C Rossendale Middle Valley *Man* 01–04; P-in-c Micklehurst *Ches* 04–09; P-in-c Kinnerley w Melverley and Knockin w Maesbrook *Lich* 09–12; P-in-c Maesbury 11–12; rtd 12; Hon C Ripponden *Wakef* 12–14; Hon C Barkisland w W Scammonden 12–14; TV Rossendale Middle Valley *Man* 14–15; PtO from 15. *7 Bowler Way, Greenfield, Oldham OL3 7FQ* T: (01457) 514172 E: revrosie86@sky.com

BOWES, Mrs Beryl Sylvia. b 48. Hull Univ BTh 89 Leeds Univ MA 06 SRN 70 RSCN 71. NEOC 89. **d** 91 **p** 94. NSM Kirk Ella *York* 91–99; Chapl R Hull Hosps NHS Trust 93–99; P-in-c Kexby w Wilberfoss *York* 99–04; R The Street Par 04–12; rtd 12; PtO *York* from 12. *Apartment 1, 33 Great Pulteney Street, Bath BA2 4BX* T: (01225) 462490 M: 07410-627223 E: bsbowes@gmail.com

BOWES, Canon John Anthony Hugh. b 39. Ch Ch Ox BA 62 MA 65. Westcott Ho Cam 63. **d** 65 **p** 66. C Langley All SS and Martyrs *Man* 65–68; Asst Chapl Bris Univ 68–73; TV Cramlington *Newc* 73–76; P-in-c Oldland *Bris* 76–80; TR 80–84; V Westbury-on-Trym St Alb 84–05; Hon Can Bris Cathl 02–05; rtd 05; PtO *Bris* from 05. *4 Royal Albert Road, Bristol BS6 7NY* T: 0117-973 5844

BOWES, Peter Hugh. b 48. Hull Univ LLB 69 Dur Univ MA 05 DThM 12 Solicitor 72. Cranmer Hall Dur 02. **d** 03 **p** 04. NSM Pocklington and Owsthorpe and Kilnwick Percy etc *York* 03–04; NSM The Street Par 04–07; NSM New Malton 06–07; P-in-c 07–13; C Old Malton 10–13; C Weaverthorpe w Helperthorpe, Luttons Ambo etc 11–13; Assoc Dir of Ords 05–10; RD S Ryedale 11–13; rtd 13; PtO *York* from 13. *Apartment 1, 33 Great Pulteney Street, Bath BA2 4BX* T: (01225) 462490 M: 07775-757723 E: peter.bowes@123mail.org

BOWES-SMITH, Canon Edward Michael Crispin. b 67. K Coll Lon LLB 89 AKC 89 Solicitor 90 Selw Coll Cam BA 96. Ridley

Hall Cam 94. **d** 97 **p** 98. C Combe Down w Monkton Combe and S Stoke *B & W* 97–00; C Enfield Ch Ch Trent Park *Lon* 00–03; P-in-c Linc Minster Gp 03–12; V Linc St Pet in Eastgate from 12; V Linc St Pet in Carlton from 17; Can and Preb Linc Cathl from 18. *St Peter's Vicarage, Lee Road, Lincoln LN2 4BH* T: (01522) 568529 E: bowessmith@btinternet.com *or* edward@stpeterineastgate.org.uk

BOWETT, Canon Richard Julnes. b 45. EAMTC 86. **d** 89 **p** 90. C Hunstanton St Mary w Ringstead Parva, Holme etc *Nor* 89–93; C King's Lynn St Marg w St Nic 93–95; V Watton w Carbrooke and Ovington 95–02; RD Breckland 99–02; P-in-c Ashill w Saham Toney 00–01; Dioc Sec 02–09; rtd 09; Hon Can Nor Cathl 05–13; PtO from 13. *The Red House, 9 Acorn Drive, Gayton, King's Lynn PE32 1XG* T: (01553) 636020 E: richard.bowett@sky.com

BOWIE, Michael Nicholas Roderick. b 59. Sydney Univ BA 78 CCC Ox DPhil 90. St Steph Ho Ox MA 90. **d** 91 **p** 92. C Swanley St Mary *Roch* 91–93; C Penarth w Lavernock *Llan* 93–96; Australia 96–00; R Norton *Sheff* 00–05; TR Gt Berkhamsted, Gt and Lt Gaddesden etc *St Alb* 05–14; RD Berkhamsted 09–14; C St Marylebone All SS *Lon* from 14. *6 Margaret Street, London W1W 8RQ* T: (020) 7636 1788 M: 07581-180963 E: mnrbowie@gmail.com

BOWIE, Sara. b 53. Open Univ BA 83 Surrey Univ BA 02. STETS 99. **d** 02 **p** 03. NSM Camberley St Mich Yorktown *Guildf* 02–07; C Coity, Nolton and Brackla *Llan* 07–10; P-in-c Essington *Lich* 10–18; P-in-c Shareshill 10–18; rtd 18; PtO *Cov* from 19. *2 Parkfield Road, Rugby CV21 1EN*

BOWKER, Prof John Westerdale. b 35. Worc Coll Ox BA 58. Ripon Hall Ox. **d** 61 **p** 62. C Endcliffe *Sheff* 61–62; Fell Lect and Dir of Studies CCC Cam 62–74; Lect Div Cam Univ 70–74; Prof RS Lanc Univ 74–86; Hon Prov Can Cant Cathl 85–03; Dean of Chpl Trin Coll Cam 86–91; rtd 91; LtO *Cant* 91–94; PtO *Ely* 94–00. *14 Bowers Croft, Cambridge CB1 8RP*

BOWKETT, Graham Philip. b 67. Open Univ BSc 99. NEOC 06. **d** 09 **p** 10. C Thirsk *York* 09–12; P-in-c Upper Itchen *Win* 12–15; R 15–18; RD Alresford 16–18; V Charlton Kings St Mary *Glouc* from 18. *St Mary's Vicarage, 63 Church Street, Charlton Kings, Cheltenham GL53 8AT* E: po@stmarysck.org.uk *or* vicar@stmarysck.org.uk

✠**BOWLBY, The Rt Revd Ronald Oliver.** b 26. Trin Coll Ox BA 50 MA 54. Westcott Ho Cam 50. **d** 52 **p** 53 **c** 73. C Pallion *Dur* 52–56; C Billingham St Cuth 56–57; C-in-c Billingham St Aid CD 57–60; V Billingham St Aid 60–66; V Croydon St Jo *Cant* 66–73; Hon Can Cant Cathl 70–73; Bp Newc 73–80; Bp S'wark 80–91; rtd 91; Hon Asst Bp Lich 91–10; PtO 10–14. *Swan Hill House, 6 Swan Hill, Shrewsbury SY1 1NQ* E: ronnie.bowlby@gmail.com

BOWLER, Christopher William. *See* JAGE-BOWLER, Christopher William

BOWLER, David Edward. b 53. Northumbria Univ BA 04 RMN 80. NEOC 05. **d** 08 **p** 09. NSM Cramlington *Newc* 08–13; Chapl Northgate and Prudhoe NHS Trust 10–13; Chapl Northumberland, Tyne and Wear NHS Foundn Trust 10–13; V Delaval *Newc* from 13. *The Vicarage, The Avenue, Seaton Sluice, Whitley Bay NE26 4QW* T: 0191-237 1982 E: djbowler@sky.com

BOWLER, David Henderson. b 54. Kent Univ BA 75. St Jo Coll Nottm 75. **d** 78 **p** 79. C Bramcote *S'well* 78–82; TV Kirby Muxloe *Leic* 82–88; V Quorndon from 88. *27 Mansfield Avenue, Quorn, Loughborough LE12 8BD* E: dhb300154@aol.com

BOWLER, Preb Kenneth Neville. b 37. K Coll Lon 57. **d** 61 **p** 62. C Buxton *Derby* 61–67; R Sandiacre 67–75; V E Bedfont *Lon* 75–87; AD Hounslow 82–87; V Fulham All SS 87–02; Preb St Paul's Cathl 85–02; rtd 02; PtO *St Alb* from 03; *Sheff* from 06. *The Coach House, 22 Brincliffe Crescent, Sheffield S11 9AW* T: 0114-250 0043 E: kenneth@kandsbowler.plus.com

BOWLER, Canon Neil. b 70. Nottm Trent Univ LLB 92 Leeds Univ BA 05 Solicitor 93. Coll of Resurr Mirfield 03. **d** 05 **p** 06. C Doncaster St Jude *Sheff* 05–09; R Whiston 09–13; AD Rotherham 11–13; V Ranmoor 13–17; Bp's Adv in Spirituality from 16; Hon C Bramley from 17; Hon C Ravenfield, Hooton Roberts and Braithwell from 17; Hon C Thrybergh from 17; Hon C Wickersley from 17; Hon Can Sheff Cathl from 15. *14 Manor Farm Court, Thrybergh, Rotherham S65 4NZ* E: nbowler34@gmail.com

BOWLES, David Gordon Desmond. **d** 13 **p** 15. Taney *D & G* 13–15; C Douglas Union w Frankfield *C, C & R* from 15. *64 Willowbank, Church Road, Blackrock, Cork, Republic of Ireland* M: (00353) 89-236 4969 E: dgd_bowles@yahoo.co.uk

BOWLES, Peter John. b 39. Lon Univ BA 60. Linc Th Coll 71. **d** 73 **p** 74. C Clay Cross *Derby* 73–76; C Boulton 76–79; R Brailsford w Shirley 79–85; P-in-c Osmaston w Edlaston 81–85; R Brailsford w Shirley and Osmaston w Edlaston 85–89; TR Old Brampton and Loundsley Green 89–98; V

Hope, Castleton and Bradwell 98–04; rtd 04; PtO *Nor* from 04. *3 Blackhorse Yard, Wells-next-the-Sea NR23 1BN* T: (01328) 711119 E: peterbowles23@gmail.com

BOWMAN, Canon Alison Valentine. b 57. St Andr Univ MA 79. St Steph Ho Ox 86. **d** 89 **p** 94. Par Dn Peacehaven Chich 89–94; C 94–95; Chapl to Bp Lewes 93–95; TV Rye 95–03; P-in-c Preston St Jo w Brighton St Aug and St Sav 03–09; V from 09; Can and Preb Chich Cathl from 15. *St John's Vicarage, 33 Preston Drove, Brighton BN1 6LA* T: (01273) 555033

BOWMAN, Clifford William. b 57. St Jo Coll Dur BA 78 Nottm Univ MA 96. Ridley Hall Cam 80. **d** 82 **p** 83. C Sawley *Derby* 82–85; C Hucknall Torkard *S'well* 85–89; R Warsop 89–00; Dioc Chapl amongst Deaf People 00–06; TV Uxbridge *Lon* 06–17; rtd 17; PtO *Leeds* from 17. *10 Mallorie Park Drive, Ripon HG4 2QD* E: cliff.bowman@btinternet.com

BOWMAN, Canon Ivelaw Alexander. b 46. **d** 97 **p** 98. OLM Stockwell Green St Andr *S'wark* 97–03; OLM Stockwell St Andr and St Mich 03–16; Chapl S Lon and Maudsley NHS Foundn Trust 03–07; Hon Can S'wark Cathl 05–16; PtO from 16. *16 Horsford Road, London SW2 5BN* T: (020) 7733 2309 E: ivelawbowman@hotmail.co.uk

BOWMAN-EADIE, Preb Russell Ian. b 45. K Coll Lon BD 71 AKC 71 ACP 68 FCP. St Aug Coll Cant 71. **d** 72 **p** 73. C Hammersmith St Pet *Lon* 72–74; V Leic St Nic 74–81; Chapl Leic Univ 74–81; Adult Educn Adv *Dur* 81–84; Dir of Tr *B & W* 84–09; Preb Wells Cathl 90–09; Can Res and Treas Wells Cathl 02–09; rtd 10. *8 Shaftesbury Place, Rustington, Littlehampton BN16 2GA* T: (01903) 774580 E: russell.bowmaneadie@googlemail.com

BOWN, Nicola Jenny. b 62. N Lon Poly BA 90 Sussex Univ MA 91 DPhil 96. ERMC 13. **d** 16 **p** 17. C Linton *Ely* from 16. *5 Keene Fields, Linton, Cambridge CB21 4AA* M: 07414-595160 E: nicolabown@icloud.com

BOWNASS (née FRYER), Alison Jane. b 56. Univ Coll of Swansea BSc 78 Birm Poly PGCE 90. Qu Coll Birm 05. **d** 07 **p** 08. C The Quinton *Birm* 07–10; PtO 10–11; C Hill 11–14; PtO from 14. *41 Silvermead Road, Sutton Coldfield B73 5SR* T: 0121-321 1600 M: 07958-911378 E: alison@bownass.co.uk

BOWRON, Hugh Mark. b 52. Cant Univ (NZ) BA 74 MA 76 Otago Univ MTh 16. Coll of Resurr Mirfield 76. **d** 79 **p** 80. C Northampton St Mary *Pet* 79–82; V Ellesmere New Zealand 82–86; V Addington St Mary 86–95; V Wellington St Pet 95–05; V Avonside H Trin 05–12; V Caversham St Pet from 12. *57 Baker Street, Caversham, Dunedin 9012, New Zealand* T: (0064) (3) 455 3961 *or* 27-755 5831 E: hugh.bowron@xtra.co.nz

BOWRY, Nicholas John. b 60. FCIPD. TISEC. **d** 16 **p** 17. C Aberdeen St Clem *Ab* from 16. *St Clement's Episcopal Church House, Mastrick Drive, Aberdeen AB16 6UF* T: (01224) 789560 M: 07950-607574 E: nick.bowry@yahoo.co.uk

BOWSER, Alan. b 35. Univ of Wales (Lamp) BA 60. **d** 63 **p** 64. C Gateshead St Chad Bensham *Dur* 63–67; C Owton Manor CD 67–72; V Horden 72–02; rtd 02. *Kengarth House, Coast Road, Blackhall Colliery, Hartlepool TS27 4HF* T: 0191-586 1753

BOWSHER, Andrew Peter. b 59. Reading Univ BA 81. St Jo Coll Nottm 83. **d** 86 **p** 87. C Grenoside *Sheff* 86–89; C Darfield 89–91; P-in-c Haley Hill *Wakef* 91–96; V Bradf St Aug Undercliffe 96–99; Chapl Bradf Univ and Bradf Coll 99–04; PtO *Dur* from 04; Tutor St Jo Coll Nottm 07–11; Chapl Northumbria Univ *Newc* from 11. *52 Fern Avenue, Jesmond, Newcastle upon Tyne NE2 2QX* T: 0191-209 9705 M: 07876-401339 E: andii.bowsher@northumbria.ac.uk

BOWSKILL, Mrs Amanda. b 49. STETS 96. **d** 99 **p** 00. NSM Winklebury *Win* 99–03; NSM Tadley S and Silchester 03–04; NSM Kempshott 05–10; PtO from 10. *10 Portway Place, Basingstoke RG23 8DT* T: (01256) 327301 E: mandy.bowskill@cwcom.net

BOWSKILL, Robert Preston. b 48. S Dios Minl Tr Scheme 88. **d** 91 **p** 92. NSM Eastrop *Win* 91–94; NSM Winklebury 94–05; NSM Kempshott 05–10; PtO from 10. *10 Portway Place, Basingstoke RG23 8DT* T: (01256) 327301 E: bob.bowskill@cwcom.net

BOWTELL, Paul William. b 47. Lon Univ BSc 68. St Jo Coll Nottm 80. **d** 82 **p** 83. C Gorleston St Andr *Nor* 82–85; TV Forest Gate St Sav w W Ham St Matt *Chelmsf* 85–91; R Spitalfields Ch Ch w All SS *Lon* 91–02; Co-ord Transform Newham 02–06; Chapl to Bp Barking *Chelmsf* 06–14; C Leyton St Cath and St Paul 07–14; rtd 14; PtO *Chelmsf* from 15. *14 Chapel Street, Rowhedge, Colchester CO5 7JS* T: (01206) 729073 E: pbowtell@chelmsford.anglican.org *or* paul.bowtell@gmail.com

BOWYER, Andrew Derek. b 83. R Melbourne Inst of Tech BBA 04 Chas Sturt Univ NSW BTh 09 Sydney Univ MA 13

Edin Univ PhD 16. **d** 08 **p** 09. C Sapphire Coast Australia 08–10; C Sydney St Jas 10–12; Hon C Edin Old St Paul 12–15; Chapl Trin Coll Cam 15–19; Tutor Westcott Ho Cam 17–19; Chapl Dean of Div and Chapl Magd Coll Ox from 19. *Magdalen College, High Street, Oxford OX1 4AU* M: 07833-762626 E: andrew.bowyer@gmail.com *or* andrew.bowyer@magd.ox.ac.uk

BOWYER, Arthur Gustavus Frederick. b 36. **d** 00 **p** 01. NSM Kingswood *S'wark* 00–09; PtO from 09; *Guildf* from 17. *41 Tattenham Grove, Epsom KT18 5QT* T: (01737) 357913 M: 07939-533506 E: arthurbowyer578@btinternet.com

BOWYER, Geoffrey Charles. b 54. ACA 79 ATII 82 Lanc Univ BA 76. St Jo Coll Nottm 85. **d** 87 **p** 88. C Walton *St E* 87–89; C Macclesfield Team 89–91; V Cinderford St Steph w Littledean *Glouc* 91–95; V Brockenhurst *Win* 95–98; Hon C Trull w Angersleigh *B & W* 00–15; PtO from 15. *36 Bakers Close, Bishops Hull, Taunton TA1 5HD* T: (01823) 335289 M: 07709-268431 E: geoff@gella.co.uk

BOWYER, Gerry. b 60. Cliff Th Coll MA 10. **d** 10 **p** 10. C Aberdeen St Ninian *Ab* 10; Bp's Ev for Fresh Expressions and Ch Planting from 11. *2 Buckie Road, Bridge of Don, Aberdeen AB22 8DG* T: (01224) 706916 M: 07956-098566 E: gerry.caf4e@outlook.com *or* gerry.bowyer@live.com

BOX, Mrs Patricia Jane. b 54. ERMC 12. **d** 15 **p** 16. NSM Bures w Assington and Lt Cornard *St E* from 15. *Water House, 4 Croftside, Bures CO8 5LL* T: (01787) 227528 E: triciajbox@gmail.com

BOXALL, Canon Martin Alleyne. b 37. Wells Th Coll 65. **d** 67 **p** 68. C Crowthorne *Ox* 67–70; C Tilehurst St Mich 70–76; V Tilehurst St Cath 76–78; V Padstow *Truro* 78–00; Miss to Seafarers from 78; RD Pydar *Truro* 93; Hon Can Truro Cathl from 93; rtd 01; Dioc Officer for Unity *Truro* from 01; PtO from 16. *Goonhilland Farmhouse, Burnthouse, St Gluvias, Penryn TR10 9AS* T: (01872) 863241 E: martinboxall@aol.com

BOXALL, Simon Roger. b 55. St Jo Coll Cam BA 76 MA 80. Ridley Hall Cam 77. **d** 79 **p** 80. C Eaton *Nor* 79–82; SAMS Brazil 82–04; P-in-c Belo Horizonte St Pet 84–88; P-in-c Santiago St Tim 88–91; P-in-c Horizontina H Spirit 88–91; C Bagé Crucifixion 93–94; R Jaguarao Ch Ch 94–98; English Chapl Rio de Janeiro 99–04; TV Thamesmead *S'wark* 05–14; V Chesterton *Lich* from 14. *The Vicarage, Church Street, Chesterton, Newcastle ST5 7HJ* T: (01782) 562479

BOXER, Caroline Victoria. *See* SKELTON, Caroline Victoria

BOXLEY, Christopher. b 45. K Coll Lon BD 68 AKC 68 Southn Univ CertEd 73 Reading Univ MA 84. **d** 69 **p** 70. C Bitterne Park *Win* 69–73; Hd RS Midhurst Gr Sch from 73; Dir Midhurst and Petworth RS Cen from 78; PtO *Chich* 73–78; P-in-c Heyshott 78–15; PtO from 16. *1 Pinewood Court, Church Road, West Lavington, Midhurst GU29 0EH* E: boxley@talktalk.net

BOYCE, Christopher Allan. b 44. ARIBA 69. S Dios Minl Tr Scheme 84. **d** 87 **p** 88. NSM Eastbourne All SS *Chich* 87–93; C Upton (Overchurch) *Ches* 93–96; V New Brighton St Jas w Em 96–02; P-in-c New Brighton All SS 98–02; TV Bicester w Bucknell, Caversfield and Launton *Ox* 02–11; rtd 11. *4 Freshwaters, 92/94 Sturgeon Street, Ormiston QLD 4160, Australia* E: christopher.boyce468@gmail.com

BOYCE, Joy. b 46. **d** 05 **p** 06. NSM Streatham Ch Ch w St Marg *S'wark* 05–09; NSM Southfields St Barn from 09. *60 Westover Road, London SW18 2RH* T: (020) 8874 1905 M: 07867-830273 E: joy@redzonecommunications.com

BOYCE, Ms Susan. b 59. Ch Ch Coll Cant MA 00 Birm Univ BPhil 06. Ripon Coll Cuddesdon 05. **d** 06 **p** 07. NSM Rushall *Lich* 06–11; PtO 11–16; C Blakenall Heath 16–18; PtO from 18. *c/o the Lord Bishop of Lichfield, 22 The Close, Lichfield WS13 7LG* M: 07941-927245 E: sueboyceca@hotmail.com

BOYCE-TILLMAN, Prof June Barbara. b 43. St Hugh's Coll Ox BA 65 Lon Inst of Educn PGCE 66 PhD 87 LRAM 74. Dioc OLM tr scheme. **d** 06 **p** 07. NSM Streatham St Paul *S'wark* 06–10; PtO from 10; *Win* from 10. *108 Nimrod Road, London SW16 6TQ* F: (020) 8677 8752 M: 07850-208721 E: junebt@globalnet.co.uk

BOYD, Alan McLean. b 50. St Jo Coll Nottm BTh 79. **d** 79 **p** 80. C Bishop's Waltham *Portsm* 79–83; Chapl Reading Univ *Ox* 83–88; Chapl E Birm Hosp 88–94; Chapl Birm Heartlands and Solihull NHS Trust 94–14; rtd 14. *38 Rodborough Road, Dorridge, Solihull B93 8EF* T: (01564) 730115

BOYD, Canon Alexander Jamieson. b 46. St Chad's Coll Dur BSc 68 Nottm Univ PGCE 69 MRSB FSAScot. Coll of Resurr Mirfield 69. **d** 79 **p** 80. NSM Musselburgh *Edin* 79–83; CF 83–00; P-in-c Loddington *Leic* 00–03; Warden Launde Abbey 00–03; P-in-c Mareham-le-Fen and Revesby *Linc* 03–06; P-in-c Hameringham w Scrafield and Winceby 03–06; P-in-c Mareham on the Hill 03–06; R Fen and Hill Gp 06–14; P-in-c Bain Valley Gp 12–14; RD Horncastle 06–11; Can and Preb

Linc Cathl 09–14; rtd 14; PtO *Arg* from 16. *Springfield, 14B Bute Terrace, Millport, Isle of Cumbrae KA28 0BA* T: (01475) 530151 E: canonalec@btinternet.com

BOYD, Allan Gray. b 41. St Jo Coll Nottm 84. **d** 87 **p** 88. Hon Chapl Miss to Seafarers from 87; NSM Glas St Gabr 87–93; NSM Greenock 93–96; NSM Paisley St Barn 96–00; NSM Paisley H Trin 96–00; NSM Alexandria 00–01; NSM Clydebank 02–08; rtd 09; LtO *Glas* from 09. *47 Holms Crescent, Erskine PA8 6DJ* T: 0141-812 2754

BOYD, Canon David Anthony. b 42. Sarum & Wells Th Coll 72. **d** 75 **p** 76. C Ches H Trin 75–79; R 85–93; V Congleton St Jas 79–85; V Farndon and Coddington 93–07; RD Malpas 97–04; Hon Can Ches Cathl 02–07; rtd 07; PtO *Ches* from 08. *68 St James Avenue, Upton, Chester CH2 1NL* T: (01244) 348800 E: tony.boyd42@googlemail.com

BOYD, David George. b 37. Cant Univ (NZ) BSc 62 LTh 64. St Aug Coll Cant. **d** 63 **p** 64. New Zealand 63–66; St Aug Coll Cant 66–67; Chapl RAF 67–71; New Zealand from 71; Adn Mid-Canterbury 92–96. *Flat 4, 100 Park Terrace, Christchurch Central, Christchurch 8013, New Zealand* T: (0064) (3) 974 0826 E: daboyd@slingshot.co.nz

BOYD, Mrs Hannah Ruth. b 81. St Martin's Coll Lanc BA 05. St Mellitus Coll BA 15 MA 16. **d** 16 **p** 17. C Layton and Staining *Blackb* from 16. *18 Burwood Drive, Blackpool FY3 8NS* T: (01253) 825932 E: hannahboyd@talktalk.net

BOYD, Mrs Julie Marie. b 67. Ox Poly BSc 89. ERMC 09. **d** 12 **p** 13. C Dersingham w Anmer and Shernborne *Nor* 12–15; C Dersingham, Anmer, Ingoldisthorpe etc 15–16; TR Gaywood from 16. *The Rectory, Gayton Road, Gaywood, King's Lynn PE30 4DZ* M: 07923-473103 E: rector@stfaithsgaywoodlep.org.uk

BOYD, Samuel Robert Thomas. b 62. **d** 90 **p** 91. NSM Derryloran *Arm* 90–95; C 95–97; I Woodschapel w Gracefield 97–05; I Killyman 05–17; Can Arm Cathl 13–17; I Glendermott *D & R* from 17. *Glendermott Rectory, 11 Church Brae, Altnagelvin, Londonderry BT47 2LS* T: (028) 7134 3001 E: robert449@btinternet.com

BOYD-WILLIAMS, Anthony Robert. b 46. St Mich Coll Llan 86. **d** 88 **p** 89. C Tonyrefail w Gilfach Goch *Llan* 88–91; V Treharris w Bedlinog 91–96; V Ocker Hill *Lich* 96–05; RD Wednesbury 03–05; rtd 05; PtO *Cov* 05–15; *Cant* from 17. *1 Sir John Killick Road, Ashford TN23 3SL* M: 07393-902646 E: stratters@btinternet.com

BOYDE (née Arnold), Briony Alice (Bee). b 79. Univ of E Lon BA 01. BA 14. **d** 14 **p** 15. C Cov St Fran N Radford 14–17; R Cov St Pet from 17. *129A London Road, Coventry CV1 2JQ* M: 07872-326008 E: revbeeboyde@gmail.com

BOYDEN, Peter Frederick. b 41. Lon Univ BSc 62 AKC 62 Em Coll Cam BA 64 MA 68 MLitt 69. Ridley Hall Cam 63. **d** 66 **p** 67. C Chesterton St Andr *Ely* 66–68; C Wimbledon *S'wark* 68–72; Chapl K Coll Cam 72–89; Asst Chapl Radley Coll 89–02; rtd 02; PtO *Derby* 02–17; *Birm* from 17. *1 Longdon Croft, Warwick Road, Knowle, Solihull B93 9LJ* E: pandjboyden@aol.com

BOYES, Matthew John. b 70. Roehampton Inst BA 91. Wycliffe Hall Ox BTh 99. **d** 99 **p** 00. C Bury St Edmunds Ch Ch *St E* 99–02; P-in-c Penn Street Ox 02–06; V Turnham Green Ch Ch *Lon* 06–11; Chapl HM YOI Feltham from 11. *HM Young Offender Institution, Bedfont Road, Feltham TW13 4ND* T: (020) 8844 5000 F: 8844 5001 E: matt_boyz@dsl.pipex.com *or* matt.boyes@justice.gov.uk

BOYLAND, David Henry. b 58. TCD BA 79 BAI 79. TCD Div Sch BTh 91. **d** 91 **p** 92. C Seapatrick *D & D* 91–94; I Celbridge w Straffan and Newcastle-Lyons *D & G* 94–98; I Kilmakee Conn from 98. *Kilmakee Rectory, 60 Killeaton Park, Dunmurry, Belfast BT17 9HE* T: (028) 9061 0505 *or* 9061 1024

BOYLAND, Peter James. b 68. TCD BA 92 MA 07. St Steph Ho Ox 07. **d** 09 **p** 10. C Towcester w Caldecote and Easton Neston etc *Pet* 09–11; R Claremont Australia from 11. *The Rectory, 2 Queenslea Drive, Claremont WA 6010, Australia* T: (0061) (8) 9384 9244 M: 40-680 3152 E: frboyland@gmail.com

BOYLE, Charles Robert. b 69. Edin Univ MA 92. Ridley Hall Cam 08. **d** 10 **p** 11. C Kea *Truro* 10–13; V Branksome Park All SS *Sarum* from 13. *The Vicarage, 28 Western Road, Poole BH13 7BP* T: (01202) 041147 M: 07979-857200 E: vicarallsaints@gmail.com

✠**BOYLE, The Rt Revd Christopher John.** b 51. AKC 75. St Aug Coll Cant 75. **d** 76 **p** 77 **c** 01. C Wylde Green *Birm* 76–80; Bp's Dom Chapl 80–83; R Castle Bromwich SS Mary and Marg 83–01; AD Coleshill 92–99; P-in-c Shard End 96–97; Hon Can Birm Cathl 96–01; Bp N Malawi 01–09; Asst Bp Leic 09–17; rtd 17; Hon Asst Bp Leic from 17. *5 The Pastures, Anstey, Leicester LE7 7QR* T: 0116-234 1473 E: bishopboyle@gmail.com

BOYLE, Robert Leslie. b 52. EMMTC 97. **d** 00 **p** 01. NSM Derby St Anne and St Jo 00–08; C Paignton St Jo *Ex*

08–13; P-in-c Douglas St Matt *S & M* 13–14; V 14–17; Assoc P Dartmouth and Dittisham *Ex* from 17. *16 South Ford Road, Dartmouth TQ6 9QS* T: (01803) 361379 E: robert.boyle7@btinternet.com

BOYLES, Peter John. b 59. Univ of Wales (Lamp) BA 84. Sarum & Wells Th Coll 86. **d** 88 **p** 89. C Ches St Mary 88–91; C Neston 91–95; R Lavendon w Cold Brayfield, Clifton Reynes etc *Ox* 95–99; V Dent w Cowgill *Bradf* 99–12; V Dent w Cowgill *Carl* 12–17; C Heart of Eden from 17. *The Vicarage, Appleby-in-Westmorland CA16 6QW* T: (01768) 354161

BOYLING, The Very Revd Mark Christopher. b 52. Keble Coll Ox BA 74 MA 78. Cuddesdon Coll BA 76. **d** 77 **p** 78. C Kirkby *Liv* 77–79; P-in-c 79–80; TV 80–85; Bp's Dom Chapl 85–89; V Formby St Pet 89–94; Can Res and Prec Liv Cathl 94–04; Dean Carl from 04. *The Deanery, The Abbey, Carlisle CA3 8TZ* T: (01228) 523335 F: 548151 E: dean@carlislecathedral.org.uk

BOYNS, Martin Laurence Harley. b 26. St Jo Coll Cam BA 49 MA 51. Ridley Hall Cam 50. **d** 52 **p** 53. C Woodmansterne *S'wark* 52–55; C Folkestone H Trin w Ch Ch *Cant* 55–58; V Duffield *Derby* 58–71; V Rawdon *Bradf* 71–76; Chapl Woodlands Hosp Rawdon 71–76; R Melton *St E* 76–85; R Gerrans w St Anthony in Roseland *Truro* 85–92; Miss to Seamen 85–92; rtd 92; PtO *Truro* from 92. *Bojunda, Boscaswell Village, Pendeen, Penzance TR19 7EP* T: (01736) 788390

BOYNS, Timothy Martin Harley. b 58. Warwick Univ BA 80 Nottm Univ BCombStuds 84. Linc Th Coll 81. **d** 84 **p** 85. C Oxhey St Matt *St Alb* 84–87; TV Solihull *Birm* 87–94; V Lillington *Cov* 94–06; RD Warwick and Leamington 99–06; V Hessle *York* 06–18; AD W Hull 10–17; RD Hull 11–18; PtO *Lich* from 19. *11 Alamein Way, Lichfield WS14 0GG* T: (01543) 257329 E: timboyns@timboyns.karoo.co.uk

BOYSE, Felix Vivian Allan. b 17. CCC Cam BA 39 MA 42. Cuddesdon Coll 39. **d** 40 **p** 41. C New Mills *Derby* 40–43; P-in-c 43–45; Vice-Prin Cuddesdon Coll 46–51; V Kingswood *S'wark* 51–58; V St Mary Abchurch *Lon* 58–61; Prin St Geo Coll Jerusalem 61–64; Chapl Chpl Royal Hampton Court Palace 65–82; Preacher Lincoln's Inn 82–93; rtd 93; PtO *Chich* from 83. *Rose Cottage, Rookwood Road, West Wittering, Chichester PO20 8LT* T: (01243) 514320

BRABIN-SMITH, Ms Lorna Daphne. b 54. Leeds Univ BSc 75. Westcott Ho Cam 03. **d** 05 **p** 06. C Emmaus Par Team *Leic* 05–08; TV Fosse Team 08–16; R Branston w Nocton and Potterhanworth *Linc* from 16. *The Rectory, Abel Smith Gardens, Branston, Lincoln LN4 1NN*

BRABY (née QUINTON), Rosemary Ruth. b 53. Univ Coll Lon BA 75 Lon Inst of Educn PGCE 79. **d** 06 **p** 07. OLM Old Catton *Nor* 06–09; PtO 09–10; NSM Trowse 10–19; P-in-c from 19. *49 Woodland Drive, Norwich NR6 7AZ* T: (01603) 427165 F: 479556 E: rosemary.braby@ntlworld.com

BRACE, Alistair Andrew. b 53. Newc Univ MB, BS 76. WMMTC 90. **d** 94. NSM Broseley w Benthall, Jackfield, Linley etc *Heref* 94–98. *58 Spout Lane, Benthall, Broseley TF12 1QY* T: (01952) 884031 E: braceali@aol.com

BRACEGIRDLE, Canon Christopher Andrew. b 56. Dur Univ BEd 79 St Edm Ho Cam BA 84 MA 89 Cov Univ PhD 05. Ridley Hall Cam 82. **d** 85 **p** 86. C Livesey *Blackb* 85–88; TV E Farnworth and Kearsley *Man* 88–92; V Astley and Chapl Wigan and Leigh Health Services NHS Trust 92–98; P-in-c Walkden Moor w Lt Hulton *Man* 98–99; TR Walkden and Lt Hulton 99–03; V Heaton Ch Ch 03–10; Tutor Dioc OLM and Reader Course 97–06; AD Bolton 05–10; Bp's Sen Chapl 10–14; TR Daisy Hill, Westhoughton and Wingates 14–16; TR Blackrod, Daisy Hill, Westhoughton and Wingates 16–18; Warden of Readers 08–18; V Bolton St Pet w St Phil from 18; Borough Dean Bolton from 18; Hon Can Man Cathl from 07. *130 Green Lane, Bolton BL3 2HX* T: (01204) 396298 E: vicar@boltonparishchurch.co.uk

BRACEGIRDLE, Canon Cynthia Wendy Mary. b 52. LMH Ox BA 73 MA 77 Liv Univ DipAE 82. NOC. **d** 87 **p** 94. Chapl Asst Man R Infirmary 85–88; Dir Dioc OLM Scheme *Man* 89–02; Hon Can Man Cathl 98–02; rtd 03; PtO *Carl* from 03. *Drigg Hall, Drigg, Holmrook CA19 1XG* T: (019467) 24366 E: cwmb@sky.com

BRACEGIRDLE, Robert Kevin Stewart. b 47. Univ Coll Ox BA 69 MA 73. St Steph Ho Ox 70. **d** 73 **p** 74. C Dorchester *Sarum* 73–75; C Woodchurch *Ches* 75–78; V Bidston 78–82; P-in-c Salford St Ignatius *Man* 82–86; R Salford St Ignatius and Stowell Memorial 86–02; P-in-c Salford Ordsall St Clem 99–02; P-in-c Millom *Carl* 02–06; V 06–13; rtd 13; PtO *Carl* from 13. *Drigg Hall, Drigg, Holmrook CA19 1XG* T: (019467) 24366 E: cwmb@sky.com

BRACEWELL, Canon David John. b 44. Leeds Univ BA 66 Man Univ MA 82. Tyndale Hall Bris 67. **d** 69 **p** 70. C Tonbridge St Steph *Roch* 69–72; C Shipley St Pet *Bradf* 72–75; V Halliwell St Paul *Man* 75–84; R Guildf St Sav 84–10; Hon Can

Guildf Cathl 05–10; rtd 10; PtO *Guildf* 12–18. *350 Kedleston Road, Derby DE22 2TE*

BRACEWELL, Howard Waring. b 35. FRGS 73. Tyndale Hall Bris. **d** 63 **p** 63. Canada 63–72; Travel Missr World Radio Miss Fellowship 72–77; P-in-c Ashill *Nor* 72–74; Hon C Bris St Phil and St Jacob w Em 77–84; PtO *St Alb* 84–86; R Odell 86–88; V Pavenham 86–88; LtO *Man* 88–93; Assoc Min St Andrew's Street Bapt Ch Cambridge 94–99; Assoc Min Halliwell St Luke *Man* 99–01; rtd 01; PtO *Man* 01–14. *16 Avon Road, Melksham SN12 8AY* T: (01225) 353692

BRACEWELL, Mrs Norma Lesley. b 47. SEITE 08. **d** 10 **p** 11. OLM Cant All SS 10–12; NSM 12–13; PtO *Derby* 13–15; C Derby St Andr w St Osmund 15–16; C Allenton and Shelton Lock 15–16; PtO from 16. *33 Sinfin Avenue, Derby DE24 9JA* T: (01332) 704195 E: norma@bracewell.org

BRACEY, David Harold. b 36. AKC 63. **d** 64 **p** 65. C Westleigh St Pet *Man* 64–67; C Dunstable *St Alb* 67–70; V Benchill *Man* 70–76; V Elton St Steph 76–87; V Howe Bridge 87–00; rtd 00; PtO *Ban* from 06. *Rhiw Awel, Sarn, Pwllheli LL53 8EY* T: (01758) 730381

BRACEY, Dexter Lee. b 70. Lanc Univ BA 92. St Steph Ho Ox BTh 11. **d** 09 **p** 10. C St Marychurch *Ex* 09–13; P-in-c Swindon New Town *Bris* 13–17; R Cov St Jo from 17. *St John's Rectory, 9 Davenport Road, Coventry CV5 6QA* E: dexter_bracey@yahoo.co.uk

BRACHER, Paul Martin. b 59. Solicitor 84 Ex Univ LLB 80. Trin Coll Bris BA 90. **d** 90 **p** 91. C Sparkhill w Greet and Sparkbrook *Birm* 90–93; Chapl Birm Women's Hosp 92–93; P-in-c Lea Hall *Birm* 93–98; V 98–18; V Garretts Green and Lea Hall from 18. *St Richard's Vicarage, Hallmoor Road, Birmingham B33 9QY* T: 0121-783 2319 E: richard1552@aol.com

BRACKENBURY, The Ven Michael Palmer. b 30. Linc Th Coll 64. **d** 66 **p** 67. C S Ormsby w Ketsby, Calceby and Driby *Linc* 66–69; V Scothern w Sudbrooke 69–77; RD Lawres 73–78; Bp's Personal Asst 77–88; Dioc Dir of Ords 77–87; Can and Preb Linc Cathl 79–95; Dioc Lay Min Adv 86–87; Adn Linc 88–95; rtd 95. *18 Lea View, Ryhall, Stamford PE9 4HZ* T: (01780) 752415

✠**BRACKLEY, The Rt Revd Ian James.** b 47. Keble Coll Ox BA 69 MA 73. Cuddesdon Coll 69. **d** 71 **p** 72 **c** 96. C Bris Lockleaze St Mary Magd w St Fran 71–74; Asst Chapl Bryanston Sch 74–77; Chapl 77–80; V E Preston w Kingston *Chich* 80–88; RD Arundel and Bognor 82–87; TR Haywards Heath St Wilfrid 88–96; RD Cuckfield 89–95; Suff Bp Dorking *Guildf* 96–15; Hon Can Guildf Cathl 96–15; rtd 15; Hon Asst Bp Portsm from 16; PtO *Chich* from 16; *Portsm* from 16. *1 Bepton Down, Petersfield GU31 4PR* T: (01730) 266465 E: ijbrackley@gmail.com

BRADBERRY, Canon John Stephen. b 47. Hull Univ BSc 70 Leeds Univ CertEd 71 MEd 86 Bradf Univ PhD 91. NW Ord Course 76. **d** 79 **p** 80. NSM Warley *Wakef* 79–14; Leeds 14–16; Chapl H Trin Sch Holmfield 91–06; Chapl Rishworth Sch Ripponden from 16; Bp's Officer for NSMs *Wakef* 95–04; RD Halifax 07–14; AD *Leeds* 14–17; NSM Warley and Halifax St Hilda 16–17; Hon Can Wakef Cathl 13–17; PtO *York* from 19. *7 Chestnut Avenue, Hemingbrough, Selby YO8 6UG* T: (01757) 335221 E: sbradberry@tiscali.co.uk

BRADBROOK, Mrs Averyl. b 46. Girton Coll Cam BA 67 MA 88 Man Univ PGCE 69 MA(Theol) 96. NOC 90. **d** 93 **p** 94. C Heaton Ch Ch *Man* 93–96; P-in-c Elton St Steph 96–02; Bp's Adv on Women in Min 01–02; V Moseley St Mary *Birm* 02–05; P-in-c Moseley St Anne 04–05; TR Eden, Gelt and Irthing *Carl* 05–10; rtd 10; PtO *Carl* from 11. *2 Ellerbank, Cowan Head, Burneside, Kendal LA8 9HX* T: (01539) 724262 M: 07808-290817 E: abradbrook@btinternet.com

BRADBROOK, Peter David. b 33. Kelham Th Coll 54. **d** 60 **p** 61. C Ches St Oswald St Thos 60–63; C Fulham St Etheldreda *Lon* 64–65; V Congleton St Jas *Ches* 65–79; V Wheelock 79–92; V Crewe All SS and St Paul 92–98; rtd 98; PtO *Ches* from 00. *136 Pickmere, Rose Terrace, Crewe CW1 3ET*

BRADBURY, Mrs Jane. b 58. Liv Univ BA 80 Wolfs Coll Cam BTh 13. Westcott Ho Cam 11. **d** 13 **p** 14. C Helston and Wendron *Truro* 13–16; P-in-c S Weald *Chelmsf* from 16. *The Vicarage, Wigley Bush Lane, South Weald, Brentwood CM14 5QP* T: (01277) 212054 E: janebradbury1@gmail.com

BRADBURY, Julian Nicholas Anstey. b 49. BNC Ox BA 71 MA 75 Birm Univ MA 84 Cardiff Univ PhD 07. Cuddesdon Coll 71. **d** 73 **p** 74. C S'wark H Trin 73–74; C S'wark H Trin w St Matt 74–76; USA 76–79; V Tottenham H Trin *Lon* 79–85; Dir Past Th Sarum & Wells Th Coll 85–90; P-in-c Yatton Keynell *Bris* 90–97; P-in-c Biddestone w Slaughterford 90–97; P-in-c Castle Combe 90–97; P-in-c W Kington 90–97; P-in-c Nettleton w Littleton Drew 90–97; R Horfield H Trin 97–02; Fell K Fund 02–07; Sen Fell 07–12; Dir Nursing and Cross-

Sector Leadership Development NHS Leadership Academy from 13; PtO *Ox* 02–09; Hon C Ox St Giles and SS Phil and Jas w St Marg 09–16; PtO from 16. *8 Osberton Road, Oxford OX2 7NU* T: (01865) 580823 M: 07900-607099 E: nicholas@nicholasbradbury.co.uk

BRADBURY, Justin Robert Grant. b 66. St Andr Univ MA 92. Wycliffe Hall Ox 06. **d** 08 **p** 09. C Southbroom *Sarum* 08–12; CF from 12. *c/o MOD Chaplains (Army)* T: (01264) 383430 F: 381464

BRADBURY, Canon Matthew Laurence. b 58. Kent Univ BA 79 Solicitor 83. EAMTC 00. **d** 03 **p** 04. NSM Sutton and Witcham w Mepal *Ely* 03–06; NSM Haddenham and Wilburton 06–08; V Wisbech St Mary and Guyhirn w Ring's End etc 08–16; P-in-c Wisbech SS Pet and Paul from 16; RD Wisbech Lynn Marshland 11–19; Hon Can Ely Cathl from 12. *The Vicarage, Love Lane, Wisbech PE13 1HP* M: 07704-139898

BRADBURY, Nicholas. *See* BRADBURY, Julian Nicholas Anstey

BRADBURY, Paul. b 72. St Cath Coll Cam BA 93 N Lon Univ MA 99. Trin Coll Bris BA 04. **d** 04 **p** 05. C Bitterne Park *Win* 04–08; Pioneer Min Poole Old Town *Sarum* from 08. *43 Green Road, Poole BH15 1QH* E: bradsare@btinternet.com

BRADBURY, Robert Douglas. b 50. Ripon Coll Cuddesdon 75. **d** 76 **p** 77. C Hawarden *Lich* 76–81; V Ruyton 81–88; P-in-c Gt w Lt Ness 84–88; V Ruyton XI Towns w Gt and Lt Ness 88–99. *Fairview, Holyhead Road, Froncysyllte, Llangollen LL20 7PU* T: (01691) 777898

BRADDOCK, Canon Andrew Jonathan. b 71. SS Coll Cam BA 92 MA 96 PhD 13. Ridley Hall Cam 95. **d** 98 **p** 99. C Ranworth w Panxworth, Woodbastwick etc *Nor* 98–01; R Cringleford and Colney 01–08; RD Humbleyard 04–08; Miss and Evang Officer *Glouc* 08–13; Hon Can Glouc Cathl 11–13; Dir Miss and Min from 13; Can Res Glouc Cathl from 13. *Church House, College Green, Gloucester GL1 2LY* T: (01452) 835549 E: abraddock@glosdioc.org.uk

BRADDY, Andrew Richard. b 67. Birm Univ BA 88 City Univ MA 89 Goldsmiths' Coll Lon PhD 99 ABSM 88. SEITE BA 10. **d** 10 **p** 11. C Whitstable *Cant* 10–14; V Wantsum Gp from 14; Jt AD Thanet from 18. *The Vicarage, St Mildred's Road, Minster, Ramsgate CT12 4DE* T: (01843) 821250 M: 07813-384972 E: arichard.braddy@gmail.com

BRADFORD, John. b 34. Lon Univ BA 60 Birm Univ MEd 81 FRSA FRGS. Oak Hill Th Coll 55. **d** 60 **p** 61. C Walcot *B & W* 60–64; Asst Master Wendover C of E Primary Sch 64–65; Hd RE Dr Challoner's High Sch Lt Chalfont 65–69; PtO *Ox* 66–70; Lect St Pet Coll of Educn Saltley 70–77; PtO *Birm* 70–71 and from 05; LtO 71–03; PtO *Cov* from 77; Nat Chapl-Miss Children's Soc 77–99; PtO Ch in Wales from 89; rtd 99. *27 Marsh Lane, Solihull B91 2PG* T: 0121-704 9895 E: revjohnbradford@btinternet.com

BRADFORD, Mark James. b 78. York Univ BA 00. St Jo Coll Nottm 10. **d** 13 **p** 14. C Ripon H Trin 13–14; Leeds 14–16; V Preston St Cuth *Blackb* from 16. *66 Kings Drive, Fulwood, Preston PR2 3HQ* M: 07967-740536 E: markjamesbradford@googlemail.com *or* mark.bradford@stcuthbertschurch.net

BRADFORD, Phillip James. b 81. York Univ BA 02 MA 04 PhD 08. Westcott Ho Cam 07. **d** 10 **p** 11. C Worc SE 10–13; C St Jo in Bedwardine 13–15; P-in-c Worc Dines Green St Mich and Crown E, Rushwick from 15; P-in-c St Jo in Bedwardine from 18. *The Rectory, 124 Laugherne Road, Worcester WR2 5LT*

BRADFORD, Simon. b 77. **d** 12 **p** 13. NSM Milton *Ely* from 12; NSM Waterbeach from 12; NSM Landbeach from 12. *22 Heron Walk, Waterbeach, Cambridge CB25 9BZ* E: sd_bradford@hotmail.com

BRADFORD, Archdeacon of. *See* JOLLEY, The Ven Andrew John

BRADFORD, Dean of. *See* LEPINE, The Very Revd Jeremy John

BRADFORD, Suffragan Bishop of. *See* HOWARTH, The Rt Revd Toby Matthew

BRADING, Christopher. b 58. St Steph Ho Ox 12. **d** 14 **p** 15. C Swinton *Sheff* 14–17; V Haywards Heath St Rich *Chich* from 17. *St Richard's Vicarage, Queens Road, Haywards Heath RH16 1EB* T: (01444) 413621

BRADING, Jeremy Clive. b 74. Birm Univ BA 95 MPhil 98. Westcott Ho Cam 00. **d** 02 **p** 03. C Man Clayton St Cross w St Paul 02–05; TV Pendleton 05–07; P-in-c Daisy Hill 07–12; C Westhoughton and Wingates 11–12; R Chickerell w Fleet *Sarum* from 12; P-in-c Abbotsbury, Portesham and Langton Herring from 12. *The Rectory, East Street, Chickerell, Weymouth DT3 4DS* T: (01305) 784915 M: 07786-567140 E: jeremybrading@gmail.com

BRADISH, Christopher James. b 85. Birm Univ LLB 07 Solicitor 10. Ripon Coll Cuddesdon BA 15. **d** 16 **p** 17. C Alton *Win* 16–18; C Onslow Square and S Kensington St Aug *Lon* 18–19; P-in-c Andover *Win* 19; V from 19. *The Vicarage,*

1 Church Close, Andover SP10 1DP T: (01264) 366373 E: chris.bradish@stmarysandover.org

BRADISH, Paul Edward. b 61. Reading Univ LLB 83. Ripon Coll Cuddesdon MA 07. **d** 07 **p** 08. C Wokingham St Sebastian *Ox* 07–08; C Upper Kennet *Sarum* 08–10; R Shiplake w Dunsden and Harpsden *Ox* 10–15; P-in-c Headbourne Worthy *Win* 15–19; R from 19; P-in-c King's Worthy 15–19; R from 19; P-in-c Upper Dever 16–19. *The Rectory, 4 Campion Way, Kings Worthy, Winchester SO23 7QP* T: (01962) 882166 M: 07469-392397 E: worthysrev@gmail.com

BRADLEY, Andrew Robert. b 65. Clare Coll Cam BA 88. St Jo Coll Nottm MA 94. **d** 94 **p** 95. C Burnage St Marg *Man* 94–98; TV Didsbury St Jas and Em 98–04; Nat Co-ord Acorn Chr Foundn 04–11; Chapl Christie NHS Foundn Trust Man from 11; P-in-c Northenden *Man* from 16. *Northenden Rectory, Ford Lane, Northenden, Manchester M22 4NQ* T: 0161-998 2615 M: 07342-230797 E: stwilfridspic@gmail.com

BRADLEY, Anthony Edward. b 39. Perth Bible Coll 93. **d** 89 **p** 96. Dn-in-c Ravensthorpe Australia 95–96; P-in-c 96–99; C Wotton St Mary *Glouc* 00–04; rtd 04. *PO Box 1083, Bridgetown WA 6255, Australia* T: (0061) (8) 9761 2917 E: tonychris@westnet.com.au

BRADLEY, Colin John. b 46. Edin Univ MA 69. Sarum & Wells Th Coll 72. **d** 75 **p** 76. C Easthampstead *Ox* 75–79; V Shawbury *Lich* 79–90; R Moreton Corbet 80–90; P-in-c Stanton on Hine Heath 81–90; Can Res Portsm Cathl and Dir of Ords *Portsm* 90–98; C Chich 98–00; C Chich St Paul and Westhampnett 00–01; P-in-c Cocking, Bepton and W Lavington 01–14; rtd 14. *26 Kenwyn Street, Truro TR1 3BU* E: zen101842@zen.co.uk

BRADLEY (née DRAPER), Mrs Elizabeth Ann. b 38. Nottm Univ BTh 75. Linc Th Coll 71. **dss** 84 **d** 87 **p** 94. Ind Chapl *Linc* 84–91; Bracebridge 84–91; Hon C 87–91; GFS Ind Chapl *Lon* 91–96; Hon Chapl GFS 96–98; Riverside Chapl *S'wark* 96; C Leighton Buzzard w Eggington, Hockliffe etc *St Alb* 98–01; PtO 01–02; Chapl Luton and Dunstable Univ Hosp NHS Foundn Trust from 02; PtO *St Alb* from 10. *14 Wren Terrace, Wixams, Bedford MK42 6BP* E: elizabeth.bradley@ldh-tr.anglox.nhs.uk

BRADLEY, Gary Scott. b 53. Lon Univ LLB 75. Ripon Coll Cuddesdon 75. **d** 78 **p** 79. C St John's Wood *Lon* 78–83; V Paddington St Sav 83–11; P-in-c Paddington St Mary 95–11; P-in-c Paddington St Mary Magd 98–03; V Lt Venice from 11. *24 Formosa Street, London W9 2QA* T: (020) 7723 1968 *or* 7262 3787 F: 7724 5332 M: 07957-140371 E: vicar@parishoflittlevenice.com

BRADLEY, Joy Elizabeth. *See* COUSANS, Joy Elizabeth

BRADLEY, Mrs Julie Caroline. b 59. Ex Univ BSc 80. WEMTC 00. **d** 03 **p** 04. NSM Stoke Gifford *Bris* from 03. *113 North Road, Stoke Gifford, Bristol BS34 8PE* T: 0117-979 3418 E: cjcbradley@deltats.co.uk

BRADLEY, Mrs Mary. **d** 12 **p** 13. NSM Meanwood *Ripon* 12–14; Leeds from 14. *3 Dale Park Close, Leeds LS16 7PR*

BRADLEY, Canon Michael Frederick John. b 44. Qu Coll Birm 76. **d** 77 **p** 78. C Sheff St Cuth 77–78; C Alford w Rigsby *Linc* 78–83; V Bracebridge 83–90; V Flitwick *St Alb* 90–14; RD Ampthill and Shefford 08–13; Hon Can St Alb 10–14; rtd 14; PtO *St Alb* from 14. *14 Wren Terrace, Wixams, Bedford MK42 6BP* E: revmichael@virginmedia.com

BRADLEY, Michael Louis. b 54. Dartington Coll of Arts BA 77 K Coll Lon MMus 84. ERMC. **d** 11 **p** 12. NSM Loughton St Jo *Chelmsf* 11–15; NSM Barkingside St Fran from 15. *144 Fencepiece Road, Ilford IG6 2LA* T: (020) 8500 2970 E: mikebradley03@yahoo.co.uk *or* frmichael@stfrancisbarkingside.com

BRADLEY, The Ven Peter David Douglas. b 49. Nottm Univ BTh 79. Ian Ramsey Coll Brasted 74 Linc Th Coll 75. **d** 79 **p** 80. C Upholland *Liv* 79–83; TR 94–01; V Dovecot 83–94; Dir CME 89–02; Hon Can Liv Cathl 00–15; Adn St Helens and Warrington 01–15; TR Upholland 01–11; rtd 15; PtO *Liv* from 17. *30 Sandbrook Road, Orrell, Wigan WN5 8UD* T: (01695) 624131 E: peterddbradley@gmail.com

BRADLEY, The Very Revd Peter Edward. b 64. Trin Hall Cam BA 86 MA 90 FRSA 02. Ripon Coll Cuddesdon 86. **d** 88 **p** 89. C Northampton St Mich w St Edm *Pet* 88–91; Chapl G&C Coll Cam 91–95; TV Abingdon *Ox* 95–98; TV High Wycombe 98–03; TR 03; Dean Sheff from 03. *Sheffield Cathedral, Church Street, Sheffield S1 1HA* T: 0114-263 6063 F: 263 6075 E: dean@sheffield-cathedral.org.uk

BRADLEY, Philip John Paul. b 64. Birm Univ BSc 85. Trin Coll Bris 09. **d** 11 **p** 12. C Oldland *Bris* 11–14; C Longwell Green 13–14; P-in-c Cricklade w Latton 14–16; V Upper Thames from 16. *14 Bath Road, Cricklade, Swindon SN6 6EY* T: (01793) 226350 M: 07947-030808 E: philipjpbradley@me.com

BRADLEY, Mrs Susan Kathleen. b 47. Hull Coll of Educn TCert 68 Open Univ BA 84 MA 96. **d** 05 **p** 06. OLM S Lawres Gp *Linc* from 05. *17 Holly Close, Cherry Willingham, Lincoln LN3 4BH* T: (01522) 750292 E: rev.s.bradley@gmail.com

BRADLEY, Miss Wendy Jayne. b 66. All SS Cen for Miss & Min 12. **d** 15 **p** 16. NSM Aspley *S'well* 15–18; C from 18. *10 Norwood Road, Nottingham NG7 3FJ* M: 07971-770836 E: wendyjayne.bradley@gmail.com

BRADNUM, Canon Ella Margaret. b 41. CertEd 64 St Hugh's Coll Ox MA 65. **dss** 69 **d** 87 **p** 94. Illingworth *Wakef* 69–72; Batley All SS 72–73; Lay Tr Officer 77–82; Min Tr Officer 82–88; Sec Dioc Bd of Min *Wakef* 88–06; Warden of Readers 88–02; Co-ord Lay Tr 88–02; Hon Can Wakef Cathl 94–06; Prin Wakef Min Scheme 97–06; rtd 06. *4 Southlands Drive, Huddersfield HD2 2LT* T: (01484) 420721

BRADNUM, Richard James. b 39. Pemb Coll Ox BA 62 MA 67. Ridley Hall Cam 62. **d** 64 **p** 65. C Birm St Martin 64–68; C Sutton St Jas *York* 68–69; PtO *Wakef* 71–72; C Batley All SS 72–74; V Gawthorpe and Chickenley Heath 74–86; V Mixenden 86–97; rtd 97; PtO *Wakef* 97–99; Hon Retirement Officer 99–12. *4 Southlands Drive, Huddersfield HD2 2LT* T: (01484) 420721

BRADSHAW, Benjamin James. b 86. Sheff Univ BA 12. Coll of Resurr Mirfield 09. **d** 13. C Braunton *Ex* 13–15; Bp's Chapl *S & M* from 17; PtO *Man* 17–18. *Thie yn Aspick, 4 The Falls, Douglas, Isle of Man IM4 4PZ* T: (01624) 622108 M: 07535-187713 E: brother_ben@btinternet.com *or* chaplain@sodorandman.im

BRADSHAW, Charles Anthony. b 44. Qu Coll Birm MA 76. **d** 75 **p** 76. C Whickham *Dur* 75–78; C Bilton *Cov* 78–81; TV Coventry Caludon 81–89; V Birstall and Wanlip *Leic* 89–99; TR Vale of Belvoir 00–04; TV Caterham *S'wark* 04–12; rtd 12; PtO *S'wark* from 13. *39 Mill Lane, Hurst Green, Oxted RH8 9DF* T: (01883) 724742 E: charles@bradshaw39.plus.com

BRADSHAW, Denis Matthew. b 52. Chich Th Coll 77. **d** 80 **p** 81. C Ruislip St Martin *Lon* 80–84; V Northolt St Jos 86–01; P-in-c Hayes St Nic CD 94–00; V Kennington St Jo w St Jas *S'wark* 01–09; V Burgess Hill St Edw *Chich* 09–19; rtd 19; PtO *Chich* from 19. *4 Lily Gardens, Worthing BN13 2FB* E: denis.bradshaw1@btinternet.com

BRADSHAW, Graham. b 58. Edin Univ BD 86. Edin Th Coll 83. **d** 86 **p** 87. C Thornton-le-Fylde *Blackb* 86–89; C Kirkby Lonsdale *Carl* 89–91; V Langford *St Alb* 91–97; Papua New Guinea 97–99; R Aspley Guise w Husborne Crawley and Ridgmont *St Alb* from 00. *The Rectory, Church Street, Aspley Guise, Milton Keynes MK17 8HN* T: (01908) 583169 E: gbradshaw@tinyworld.co.uk

BRADSHAW (née DAY), Mrs Jennifer Ann. b 67. Aber Univ BSc 89. Wycliffe Hall Ox BTh 95. **d** 95 **p** 96. C Whitburn *Dur* 95–98; C Monkwearmouth 98–99; TV 99–01; NSM Silksworth 02–12; TV N Wearside from 12. *The Rectory, 2A Park Avenue, Sunderland SR6 9PU* T: 0191-548 6607 M: 07443-228077 E: jenniferabradshaw@btinternet.com

BRADSHAW, Julia Dawn. b 60. ERMC 16. **d** 19. NSM Gtr Athens *Eur* from 19. *PO Box 32, Kalyves, 73003 Chania, Crete, Greece* T: (0030) (2825) 022733 E: juliaworld21@yahoo.co.uk

BRADSHAW, Canon Paul Frederick. b 45. Clare Coll Cam BA 66 MA 70 K Coll Lon PhD 71 Ox Univ DD 94 FRHistS 91. Westcott Ho Cam 67. **d** 69 **p** 70. C W Wickham St Jo *Cant* 69–71; C Cant St Martin and St Paul 71–73; Tutor Chich Th Coll 73–78; V Flamstead *St Alb* 78–82; Dir of Minl Tr Scheme 78–82; Vice-Prin Ripon Coll Cuddesdon 83–85; USA 85–95; Prof Th Notre Dame Univ 85–13; Hon Can N Indiana from 90; PV Westmr Abbey 95–13; PtO *Guildf* 96–13; Dioc Liturg Officer *Eur* from 07; rtd 10. *367 Pine Valley Drive, Fairview TX 75069, USA* T: (001) (214) 856 0799 E: bradshaw.1@nd.edu

BRADSHAW, Philip Hugh. b 39. Qu Coll Ox BA 64 MA 67. S'wark Ord Course 88. **d** 91 **p** 92. NSM Bletchingley *S'wark* 91–98; Ldr Community of Celebration 91–98; NSM Redhill St Jo *S'wark* 98–10; PtO from 10. *35 Cavendish Road, Redhill RH1 4AL* T: (01737) 778760 E: bradshaws@ccct.co.uk

BRADSHAW, Richard Gordon Edward. b 66. Southn Univ LLB 90. Wycliffe Hall Ox BTh 94. **d** 97 **p** 98. C Bishopwearmouth St Gabr *Dur* 97–00; C Silksworth 00–01; P-in-c 01–03; V 03–12; TR Monkwearmouth from 12; AD Wearmouth 08–15. *The Rectory, 2A Park Avenue, Sunderland SR6 9PU* T: 0191-548 6607

BRADSHAW, Roy John. b 49. Sarum & Wells Th Coll 85. **d** 87 **p** 88. C Gainsborough All SS *Linc* 87–90; V New Waltham 90–94; R Killamarsh *Derby* 94–06; C Barlborough and Renishaw 05–06; rtd 06; PtO *Derby* from 07. *22 St Peter's Close, Duckmanton, Chesterfield S44 5JJ* T: (01246) 822280 E: rbradshaw@hotmail.co.uk

BRADSHAW, Timothy. b 50. Keble Coll Ox BA 72 MA 78 PhD. St Jo Coll Nottm BA 75. **d** 76 **p** 77. C Clapton Park All So *Lon* 76–79; Lect Trin Coll Bris 80–91; Hon C Sea Mills *Bris* 83–91; Tutor Regent's Park Coll Ox from 91; NSM Ox St Aldate w St Matt 91–94; NSM Ox St Matt 95–18; rtd 18. *54 St Giles, Oxford OX1 3LU* T: (01865) 288147 E: timothy.bradshaw@regents.ox.ac.uk

BRADSHAW, Veronica. *See* CAROLAN, Veronica

BRADWELL, Area Bishop of. *See* PERUMBALATH, The Rt Revd John

BRADY, Benjamin Eric. b 88. Leeds Univ BA 10 St Jo Coll Dur BA 16. Cranmer Hall Dur 14. **d** 17 **p** 18. C Ashton Ch Ch *Man* from 17. *2 Ryecroft Street, Ashton-under-Lyne OL7 0BL* M: 07792-052783 E: benjamin.e.brady@gmail.com

BRADY, Ian. b 59. Ridley Hall Cam. **d** 01 **p** 02. C Cromer *Nor* 01–04; V Belmont *Lon* 04–09; P-in-c Douglas St Thos *S & M* 09–14; V 14–16; Can St German's Cathl 14–16; R Doddington w Benwick and Wimblington *Ely* from 16; P-in-c Christchurch and Manea and Welney from 16. *The Rectory, 8 Church Street, Wimblington, March PE15 0QS* T: (01354) 740627 E: revianbrady@btinternet.com

BRADY, Karen. b 62. Newc Univ BSc 85 Open Univ MBA 97 MA 08. All SS Cen for Miss & Min 10. **d** 17 **p** 18. C Macclesfield Team *Ches* from 17. *1 Rochester House, Pavilion Way, Macclesfield SK10 3LX* T: 07419-820864 E: revkarenbrady@gmail.com

BRADY, Mrs Lynda. b 60. SRN 83. SA Internat Tr Coll 87 Oak Hill Th Coll 07. **d** 07 **p** 08. NSM Belmont *Lon* 07–09; NSM Douglas St Thos *S & M* 09–16; Chapl Hospice Is of Man 09–16; NSM Christchurch and Manea and Welney *Ely* from 16. *The Rectory, 8 Church Street, Wimblington, March PE15 0QS* T: (01354) 740627 M: 07974-995561 E: revbrady@btinternet.com

BRADY, Mrs Natasha Dawn. b 71. St Mellitus Coll BA 15. **d** 15 **p** 16. C Rushden St Mary w Newton Bromswold *Pet* 15–18; V Stoke Poges *Ox* from 18. *The Rectory, Victoria Road, Farnham Common, Slough SL2 3NJ* M: 07539-424821 E: natasha_brady@btinternet.com

BRAGG, Annette Frances. *See* STICKLEY, Annette Frances

BRAGG, The Hon Marie-Elsa Beatrice Roche. UEA MA 16. Ripon Coll Cuddesdon 06. **d** 07 **p** 09. NSM St Marylebone St Paul *Lon* 07–08; NSM Kilburn St Mary w All So and W Hampstead St Jas 08–14; PtO 14–18. *Address withheld by request* E: marieelsabragg@gmail.com

BRAGG, Mrs Rosemary Eileen. b 41. MRPharmS 64. St Steph Ho Ox 99. **d** 00 **p** 01. NSM Boyne Hill *Ox* 00–06; NSM Golden Cap Team *Sarum* 06–11; rtd 11; PtO *Sarum* from 11. *Dove Inn Cottage, 48 Silver Street, Lyme Regis DT7 3HR* T: (01297) 442403 E: rosie@bragg.eu

BRAID, Simon. b 54. SS Coll Cam MA 76 FCA 79. SEITE 06. **d** 09 **p** 10. NSM Hildenborough *Roch* from 09. *Petresfield, Fordcombe Road, Penshurst, Tonbridge TN11 8DL* T: (01892) 871453 M: 07802-809849 E: simonbraid@uwclub.net

BRAILSFORD, Matthew Charles. b 64. Newc Univ BSc 86 St Jo Coll Dur BA 95. Cranmer Hall Dur 92. **d** 95 **p** 96. C Hull St Jo Newland *York* 95–06; P-in-c N Ferriby 06–14; V from 14; AD W Hull from 17. *The Vicarage, 20 Aston Hall Drive, North Ferriby HU14 3EB* T: (01482) 631306 E: matthew.brailsford@ukgateway.net

BRAIN, Michael Charles. b 39. Culham Coll Ox TCert 61 ACP 65. Lich Th Coll 68. **d** 70 **p** 71. C Stone St Mich *Lich* 70–73; C Harlescott 73–76; C Longton St Jas 76–77; P-in-c Dudley St Edm *Worc* 77–79; V 79–04; Chapl Dudley Coll of Tech 77–04; rtd 04; PtO *Worc* from 04. *33 Dibdale Road, Dudley DY1 2RX* T: (01384) 232774

BRAITHWAITE, Catherine Anne. *See* HALE-HEIGHWAY, Catherine Anne

BRAITHWAITE, Canon Michael Royce. b 34. Linc Th Coll 71. **d** 73 **p** 74. C Barrow St Geo w St Luke *Carl* 73–77; V Kells 77–88; RD Calder 84–88; V Lorton and Loweswater w Buttermere 88–99; Ldr Rural Life and Agric Team 93–96; Member Rural Life and Agric Team 96–99; RD Derwent 94–98; Hon Can Carl Cathl 94–99; rtd 99; PtO *Carl* from 00. *High Green Farm, Bothel, Carlisle CA7 2JA* T: (016973) 23429

BRAITHWAITE, Canon Roy. b 34. Dur Univ BA 56. Ridley Hall Cam 58. **d** 60 **p** 61. C Blackb St Gabr 60–63; C Burnley St Pet 63–66; V Accrington St Andr 66–74; V Blackb St Jas 74–95; RD Blackb 86–91; Hon Can Blackb Cathl 93–98; V Garstang St Helen Churchtown 95–98; Dioc Ecum Officer 95–98; rtd 98; PtO *Blackb* from 98. *9 Barker Lane, Mellor, Blackburn BB2 7ED* T: (01254) 240724

BRALESFORD, Nicholas Robert. b 53. St Jo Coll Nottm LTh 79 BTh 79. **d** 79 **p** 80. C Leic St Chris 79–82; C Heeley

Sheff 82–85; TV Kings Norton *Birm* 85–90; V Chapel-en-le-Frith *Derby* 90–13; rtd 13; PtO *Blackb* from 13. *Flat 4, Anselm Court, Pembroke Avenue, Blackpool FY2 9QD* T: (01253) 500474 M: 07505-338853 E: nrb24601@hotmail.co.uk

BRALEY, Robert James. *See* RILEY-BRALEY, Robert James

BRAMHALL, Eric. b 39. St Cath Coll Cam BA 61 MA 65. Tyndale Hall Bris 61. **d** 63 **p** 64. C Eccleston St Luke *Liv* 63–66; C Bolton Em *Man* 66–69; PtO *Ches* 70–74; V Aughton Ch Ch *Liv* 75–92; Chapl Ormskirk Children's Hosp 75–92; V Childwall All SS *Liv* 92–04; rtd 04; PtO *St As* from 09. *Henfaes, Prior Street, Ruthin LL15 1LT* T: (01824) 702757

BRAMHALL, John. b 52. **d** 08. NSM Greenham *Ox* from 08. *56 Greyberry Copse Road, Thatcham RG19 8XB* T: (01635) 42348 E: johnbramuk@yahoo.co.uk

BRAMLEY, Mrs Elizabeth. b 46. Bedf Coll Lon BA 68 Lon Inst of Educn PGCE 70. St Mich Coll Llan 11. **d** 15 **p** 16. OLM The Beacons *S & B* from 15; OLM Llyn Safaddan from 15. *Weatheroak, Llanhamlach, Brecon LD3 7YB* T: (01874) 665267 E: liz.bramley@icloud.com

BRAMLEY, Thomas Antony. b 44. BSc PhD. TISEC 95. **d** 96 **p** 97. NSM Penicuik *Edin* 96–12; NSM W Linton 96–12; LtO 12–15; PtO from 15. *70 The Links, Hyde SK14 4GR* E: tbramley44@sky.com

BRAMMER, David John. b 62. **d** 99 **p** 00. C Acton St Mary *Lon* 99–02; C Ealing All SS and Chapl Twyford C of E High Sch Acton 02–09; R Acton St Mary *Lon* 09–14; Chapl Twyford C of E High Sch Acton from 17; Chapl Wm Perkin C of E High Sch from 17. *Twyford C of E Academies Trust Ealing, Twyford C of E High School, Twyford Crescent, London W3 9PP* T: (020) 8752 0141 E: rev.d.brammer@btinternet.com *or* dbrammer@twyfordacademies.org.uk

BRAMPTON, Canon Fiona Elizabeth Gordon. b 56. St Jo Coll Dur BA 78 BA 83. Cranmer Hall Dur 81. **dss** 84 **d** 87 **p** 94. Bris St Andr Hartcliffe 84–90; Par Dn 87–90; C Orton Waterville *Ely* 90–96; C-in-c Orton Goldhay CD 90–96; TV The Ortons, Alwalton and Chesterton 96–00; V Haddenham from 00; V Wilburton from 00; P-in-c Witchford w Wentworth from 08; RD Ely 03–09; Hon Can Ely Cathl from 05. *The Vicarage, Church Lane, Haddenham, Ely CB6 3TB* T: (01353) 740309

BRAMPTON, Timothy John Gordon. b 59. Coll of SS Mark and Jo Plymouth BA 01 Sheff Univ BA 12. Coll of Resurr Mirfield 10. **d** 12 **p** 13. C Standish *Blackb* 12–15; P-in-c Marks Gate *Chelmsf* 15–18; V 18–19; P-in-c Basildon St Martin from 19. *The Rectory, St Martin's Square, Basildon SS14 1DX* M: 07450-962688 E: timbrampton@btinternet.com

BRANCHE, Caren Teresa. *See* TOPLEY, Caren Teresa

BRAND, Peter John. b 52. Edin Dioc NSM Course 75. **d** 83 **p** 84. NSM Edin St Jo from 83. *24 Drum Brae Park, Edinburgh EH12 8TF* T: 0131-339 4406

BRAND, The Ven Richard Harold Guthrie. b 65. Univ Coll Dur BA 87 St Jo Coll Dur MA 16. Ripon Coll Cuddesdon 87. **d** 89 **p** 90. C N Lynn w St Marg and St Nic *Nor* 89–92; C King's Lynn St Marg w St Nic 92–93; C Croydon St Jo *S'wark* 93–96; TV Fendalton New Zealand 96–98; P-in-c Hambleton *Portsm* 98–06; Dir of Ords 98–06; P-in-c Market Harborough and The Transfiguration etc *Leic* 06–08; TR 08–13; AD Gartree I 13–16; AD Gartree II 13–16; Hon Can Leic Cathl 16; Adn Win from 16. *22 St John's Street, Winchester SO23 0HF* T: (01962) 710960 E: richard.brand@winchester.anglican.org

BRANDES, Simon Frank. b 62. Univ of Wales (Ban) BA 83. Edin Th Coll 83. **d** 85 **p** 86. C Barton w Peel Green *Man* 85–88; C Longsight St Jo w St Cypr 88–90; R 90–94; Asst Dioc Youth Officer 88–94; V Lt Lever 94–02; P-in-c Lydgate w Friezland 02–03; TR Saddleworth 03–07; V Chiswick St Nic w St Mary *Lon* from 07. *Chiswick Vicarage, Chiswick Mall, London W4 2PJ* T: (020) 8995 4717 M: 07775-526285

BRANDIE, Canon Beaumont Lauder. b 40. K Coll Lon AKC 64 BD 66. **d** 65 **p** 66. C Whitton St Aug *Lon* 65–71; C Portsea St Mary *Portsm* 71–77; TR Brighton Resurr *Chich* 77–09; V Brighton St Martin w St Wilfrid and St Alban 09–11; RD Brighton 97; Can and Preb Chich Cathl 87–11; rtd 11; PtO *Chich* from 11. *48 A'Becket Gardens, Worthing BN13 2BN* T: (01903) 264471 M: 07789-044476 E: beaumont.brandie@btinternet.com

BRANDON, Helen Beatrice. b 55. Heythrop Coll Lon MA 02 Lambeth DD 12. SAOMC 03. **d** 06 **p** 07. NSM Burton Latimer *Pet* 06–07; NSM Earls Barton 07–09; Abps' Adv for Healing Min from 07; PtO *Lon* 07–13; *Pet* 09–19; *Carl* from 13; *Linc* from 13; Abp's Adv and Adv to Bps for Deliverance and Healing Ch in Wales from 16; NSM Aldwincle, Clopton, Pilton, Stoke Doyle etc *Pet* from 19. *Clopton Manor, Clopton, Kettering NN14 3DZ* T: (01832) 720346 E: beatrice@healingministry.org.uk

BRANDSMA, Michael John. b 55. Trin Coll Bris 12. **d** 14 **p** 15. C Hartshill and Galley Common *Cov* 14–17; P-in-c

Atherstone 17–18; V from 18. *40 Holte Road, Atherstone CV9 1HN* T: (01827) 437292 M: 07979-680213 E: visionhope@live.co.uk

BRANFORD, Jack Oliver. b 89. Sheff Univ BA 11 Trin Coll Cam BA 15. Westcott Ho Cam 13. **d** 16 **p** 17. C Aylsham *Nor* 16–17; C Aylsham and Distr from 17. *95 Holman Road, Aylsham, Norwich NR11 6BT* M: 07855-759024 E: jackbranford1@hotmail.com

BRANSCOMBE, Michael Peter. b 65. St Jo Coll Cur BA 95 Trin Episc Sch for Min DMin 08. Cranmer Hall Dur 92. **d** 95 **p** 96. C Ogley Hay *Lich* 95–01; Dioc Voc Officer 98–01; Asst R Palm Harbor USA 01–03; Assoc R Clearwater Ascension 03–15; C Birm St Martin 15–18; P-in-c Cobham and Stoke D'Abernon *Guildf* 18–19; V Cobham from 19. *The Vicarage, St Andrew's Walk, Cobham KT11 3EQ* M: 07481-726762 E: mike@branscombe.us

BRANSON, Robert David. b 46. Linc Th Coll 74. **d** 77 **p** 78. C Kempston Transfiguration *St Alb* 77–80; C Goldington 80–82; V Marsh Farm 82–91; V Aylsham *Nor* 91–11; RD Ingworth 00–10; Chapl Norfolk Primary Care Trust 99–11; rtd 11; PtO *Nor* from 11. *28 Alford Grove, Norwich NR7 8XB* T: (01603) 418177 E: rdlbransons@gmail.com

BRANSTON, Ms Anna Louise. b 63. WEMTC 12. **d** 15 **p** 16. C Heref S Wye 15–18; R Pembridge w Moor Court, Shobdon, Staunton etc from 18. *The Rectory, Manley Crescent, Pembridge, Leominster HR6 9EB* M: 07777-692458 E: abranston2@gmail.com

BRANT, Jonathan David. b 70. K Coll Lon MA 02 Trin Coll Ox MPhil 06 DPhil 09. St Mellitus Coll 09. **d** 11 **p** 12. Chapl Ox Pastorate from 11; NSM Ox St Clem 11–15; PtO 15. *33 Jack Straw's Lane, Headington, Oxford OX3 0DL* T: (01865) 426778 M: 07854-771041 E: jonathan.brant@oxfordpastorate.org

BRASCHI, Lawrence. b 77. Bris Univ BSc 98 SOAS Lon MA 04. Wycliffe Hall Ox 12. **d** 14 **p** 15. C Plymouth St Andr and Stonehouse Ex 14–18; V Pennycross from 19. *St Pancras' Vicarage, 66 Glentor Road, Plymouth PL3 5TR* M: 07773-429467 E: lawrence.braschi@stps.org.uk

BRASIER, Ralph Henry (Jim). b 30. Cant Sch of Min 82. **d** 85 **p** 86. C S Ashford Ch Ch *Cant* 85–89; V Pembury *Roch* 89–95; rtd 95; PtO *Win* 95–14; *Portsm* from 95. *72 Jenkyns Close, Botley, Southampton SO30 2UU* T: (01489) 788332

BRASIER (née Rudge), Mrs Susannah Mary. b 84. Trin Coll Ox BA 05 MA 10 Jes Coll Cam MPhil 10. Westcott Ho Cam 08. **d** 10 **p** 11. C Bournville *Birm* 10–15; R Upminster *Chelmsf* from 15. *The Rectory, 4 Gridiron Place, Upminster RM14 2BE* T: (01708) 220174 E: susannah.brasier@gmail.com

BRASSIL, Seán Adrian. b 56. Westf Coll Lon BSc 79. STETS 97. **d** 00 **p** 01. NSM Westborough *Guildf* 00–04; NSM Woking St Jo 04–05; C Addlestone 05–10; P-in-c Whitchurch *Ex* from 10. *The Vicarage, 204 Whitchurch Road, Tavistock PL19 9DQ* T: (01822) 612936 E: priest.incharge@standrewandjames.org

BRASSIL, Thomas James. b 83. Ex Univ BSc 05. Wycliffe Hall Ox 11. **d** 14 **p** 15. C Elburton *Ex* from 14. *3 Vinery Lane, Plymouth PL9 8DD* T: (01752) 547492 M: 07729-466942 E: tom.brassil@gmail.com

BRATLEY, David Frederick. b 42. Linc Th Coll 80. **d** 82 **p** 83. C Holbeach *Linc* 82–85; R Fleet w Gedney 85–07; RD Elloe E 01–05; rtd 07; PtO *Linc* from 17. *1 Setts Green, Bourne PE10 0FZ* T: (01778) 392567

BRATTON, Mark Quinn. b 62. Lon Univ BA 84 K Coll Lon MA 98 Warwick Univ PhD 12 Barrister-at-Law (Middle Temple) 87. Pontifical Gregorian Univ 93 Wycliffe Hall Ox BA 94. **d** 94 **p** 95. C W Ealing St Jo w St Jas *Lon* 94–98; Chapl Warw Univ *Cov* 98–09; AD Cov S 02–09; P-in-c Berkswell 09–14; R from 14; AD Kenilworth 13–18. *The Rectory, Meriden Road, Berkswell, Coventry CV7 7BE* T: (01676) 533766 *or* 533605 M: 07540-604225 E: markbratton@berkswellchurch.org.uk

BRAVERY, Christine Louise. *See* WILSON, Christine Louise

BRAVINER, William Edward. b 66. Leic Poly BSc 88 St Jo Coll Dur BA 94 MA 10 ACA 91 FCA 11. Cranmer Hall Dur 92. **d** 95 **p** 96. C Royton St Anne *Man* 95–99; R Lansallos *Truro* 99–03; V Talland 99–03; P-in-c Duloe, Herodsfoot, Morval and St Pinnock 01–03; TR Jarrow *Dur* 03–14; P-in-c S Shields St Simon 09–13; AD Jarrow 05–14; TV Billingham 14–17; P-in-c Stockton St Pet from 17; P-in-c Elton from 17. *11 Lorne Court, Stockton-on-Tees TS18 3UB* M: 07875-385982 E: bill@braviner.com *or* bill.braviner@durham.anglican.org

BRAVINGTON, Timothy Frederick Desmond. b 34. Trin Coll Cam BA 56 MA 70. Cuddesdon Coll 56. **d** 58 **p** 59. C Caledon S Africa 58–61; Asst Chapl St Andr Coll Grahamstown 61–64; R Namaqualand 64–71; R Bellville Transfiguration 71–76; R Durban N St Martin-in-the-Fields

76–83; R Stellenbosch St Mary 84–88; R Elgin St Mich 88–98; rtd 98; PtO *Eur* 06–09 and from 15; *Ox* from 08. *63 Cutteslowe House, Park Close, Oxford OX2 8NP* T: (01865) 511416 E: timbrav@gmail.com

BRAY, Christopher Laurence. b 53. Leeds Univ BSc 74 Qu Univ Kingston Ontario MSc 76. St Jo Coll Nottm 78. d 81 p 82. C Aughton Ch Ch *Liv* 81–84; Hon C Scarborough St Mary w Ch Ch and H Apostles *York* 84–88; Chapl Scarborough Coll 84–88; V St Helens St Matt Thatto Heath *Liv* 88–98; V Southport All SS and All So 98–02; rtd 02; PtO *Liv* from 03; *Ches* from 12. *6 Ford Close, Wirral CH49 9AR* E: clb53@mac.com

BRAY, Gerald Lewis. b 48. McGill Univ Montreal BA 69 Sorbonne Univ Paris LittD 73. Ridley Hall Cam 76. d 78 p 79. C Canning Town St Cedd *Chelmsf* 78–80; Tutor Oak Hill Th Coll 80–92; Ed *Churchman* from 83; Angl Prof Div Beeson Div Sch Samford Univ Alabama 93–06; Research Prof Div from 06. *16 Manor Court, Cambridge CB3 9BE* T: (01223) 311804 *or* (001) (205) 726 2585 F: (01223) 566608 *or* (001) (205) 726 2234 E: glbray@samford.edu

BRAY, Jason Stephen. b 69. SS Hild & Bede Coll Dur BA 90 MA 91 Fitzw Coll Cam PhD 96 MSOTS 97. Westcott Ho Cam 95. d 97 p 98. C Abergavenny St Mary w Llanwenarth Citra *Mon* 97–99; Min Can St Woolos Cathl 99–02; V Blaenavon w Capel Newydd 02–15; P-in-c Abersychan and Garndiffaith 09–11; TV Wrexham *St As* from 15. *The Rectory, 7 Westminster Drive, Wrexham LL12 7AT* T: (01978) 350971 E: jasonbray@aol.com

BRAY, Jeremy Grainger. b 40. Man Univ BA 62. Wells Th Coll 62. d 64 p 65. C Bris St Andr w St Bart 64–67; C Bris H Cross Inns Court 67–71; C-in-c Stockwood CD 71–73; V Bris Ch the Servant Stockwood 73–83; RD Brislington 79–83; P-in-c Chippenham St Pet 83–88; V 88–93; V Fishponds St Jo 93–04; rtd 04; PtO *Bris* from 04. *46 Charter Road, Chippenham SN15 2RA* T: (01249) 655661 E: jg.bray@btinternet.com

BRAY, Mrs Madeline Mary Elizabeth. b 54. SWMTC 10. d 13 p 14. NSM Bideford, Northam, Westward Ho!, Appledore etc *Ex* 13–17; NSM Bideford, Landcross, Littleham etc 17–18; TV Parkham, Alwington, Buckland Brewer etc from 18. *The Vicarage, 5 Manor Court, Parkham, Bideford EX39 5PG* M: 07812-957971 E: revmadelinebray@gmail.com

BRAY, Richard Antony. b 77. CCC Ox MA 05. Oak Hill Th Coll BA 09. d 09 p 10. C St Botolph without Aldersgate *Lon* 09–14; R Limehouse from 14. *Limehouse Rectory, 5 Newell Street, London E14 7HP* T: (020) 7987 1502 M: 07798-940554 E: brayra2001@yahoo.co.uk

BRAY, Simon Lee. b 77. Birm Univ BMus 00 St Jo Coll Dur BA 15. Cranmer Hall Dur 13. d 15 p 16. C Beverley St Nic *York* 15–18; Abp's Dom Chapl from 18. *Bishopthorpe Palace, Bishopthorpe, York YO23 2GE* T: (01904) 707021 M: 07912-240854 E: simon.bray@archbishopofyork.org

BRAY, Mrs Wendy Gillian. b 60. UEA BEd 83 Bris Univ MA 14. Trin Coll Bris 12. d 14 p 15. C Pennycross *Ex* 14–17; C Clifton All SS w St Jo Bris from 18. *1 Ardern Close, Bristol BS9 2QT* M: 07887-987159 E: wendyebray@hotmail.co.uk

BRAYBROOKE, Marcus Christopher Rossi. b 38. Magd Coll Cam BA 62 MA 65 Lon Univ MPhil 68 Lambeth DD 04. Wells Th Coll 63. d 64 p 65. C Highgate St Mich *Lon* 64–67; C Frindsbury w Upnor *Roch* 67–72; TV 72–73; P-in-c Swainswick w Langridge and Woolley *B & W* 73–76; R 76–79; Dir of Tr 79–84; Hon C Bath Ch Ch Prop Chpl 84–91; Exec Dir Coun of Chrs and Jews 84–87; rtd 88; PtO *Bris* 88–93; Preb Wells Cathl *B & W* 90–93; Chapl Bath St Mary Magd Holloway 92–93; Hon C Dorchester *Ox* 93–05; PtO from 07. *17 Courtiers Green, Clifton Hampden, Abingdon OX14 3EN* T: (01865) 407566

BRAZELL, Denis Illtyd Anthony. b 42. Trin Coll Cam BA 64 MA 68. Wycliffe Hall Ox 78. d 80 p 81. C Cheltenham Ch Ch *Glouc* 80–84; V Reading St Agnes w St Paul *Ox* 84–96; PtO *Guildf* 96–97; Warden and Chapl Acorn Chr Healing Trust 97–99; rtd 99; Co-Dir Word for Life Trust from 99; PtO *Glouc* 02–09; Lead Chapl St Andr Healthcare 09–15; rtd 16. *129 Balden Road, Harborne, Birmingham B32 2EL* T: 0121-427 2934 M: 07980-813159 E: denisbrazell@mac.com

BRAZIER, Annette Michaela. *See* HAWKINS, Annette Michaela

BRAZIER, Catharine Honor. b 67. ERMC 09. d 12 p 13. NSM Thrapston, Denford and Islip *Pet* 12–13; NSM Aldwincle, Clopton, Pilton, Stoke Doyle etc 13–16; R Barnwell, Hemington, Luddington in the Brook etc from 16. *Beechcroft, Barnwell, Peterborough PE8 5PU* E: cathy.h.brazier@btopenworld.com

BRAZIER, Eric James Arthur. b 37. Qu Coll Birm 84. d 86 p 87. C Lighthorne *Cov* 86–89; P-in-c 89–92; P-in-c Chesterton 89–92; P-in-c Newbold Pacey w Moreton Morrell 89–92; R Astbury and Smallwood *Ches* 92–99; rtd 99; PtO *Ches* 99–14;

Lich 00–11; *Heref* from 00; *St As* 12–18. *Wolf's Head Cottage, Chirbury, Montgomery SY15 6BP* T: (01938) 561450

BRAZIER, Canon Raymond Venner. b 40. Wells Th Coll 68. d 71 p 72. C Horfield St Greg *Bris* 71–75; P-in-c Bris St Matt and St Nath 75–79; V 79–05; RD Horfield 85–91; P-in-c Bishopston 93–97; Hon Can Bris Cathl 94–05; rtd 05; PtO *Bris* from 05; Chapl to The Queen 98–10. *51 Chalks Road, Bristol BS5 9EP* T: 0117-329 4611 E: rayvb@tiscali.co.uk

BRAZIER, Thomas Ian. b 72. Natal Univ BSc 95 MSc 97. Cranmer Hall Dur 10. d 12 p 13. C Washington *Dur* 12–16; V Greenside from 16; AD Gateshead W from 18. *St John's Vicarage, Greenside, Ryton NE40 4AA* M: 07799-217775 E: tom_coe@firstsolo.net *or* greensidevicar@firstsolo.net

BRAZIER-GIBBS, Samantha Elizabeth. b 78. Ridley Hall Cam 03. d 06 p 08. C Grays Thurrock *Chelmsf* 06–09; NSM Harlow St Mary and St Hugh w St Jo the Bapt 10–12; NSM Church Langley 10–12; C Fyfield, Moreton w Bobbingworth etc 12–15; C Chipping Ongar w Shelley 12–15; V Blackmore and Stondon Massey from 15. *The Vicarage, Church Street, Blackmore, Ingatestone CM4 0RN* T: (01277) 821464 M: 07894-948867 E: revsbg@mac.com

BREADEN, Robert William. b 37. Edin Th Coll 58. d 61 p 62. C Broughty Ferry *Bre* 61–65; R 72–07; R Carnoustie 65–72; Can St Paul's Cathl Dundee 77–07; Dean *Bre* 84–07; rtd 07; P-in-c Portree *Arg* 07–12; PtO *Mor* from 13. *6 Chapel Road, Evanton, Dingwall IV16 9XT*

BREADMORE, The Ven Martin Christopher. b 67. Lon Univ LLB 89. Wycliffe Hall Ox BTh 93. d 93 p 94. C Herne Bay Ch Ch *Cant* 93–97; C Camberley St Paul *Guildf* 97–01; Chapl Elmhurst Ballet Sch 97–98; C Wallington *S'wark* 01–10; Dir Lic Min Kensington Area *Lon* 10–19; Adn Dorking *Guildf* from 19. *Address temp unknown*

BREALEY, Mrs Frances Elizabeth. b 56. Univ of Wales (Lamp) BA 77 Univ of Wales (Trin St Dav) MA 14 Dur Univ PGCE 79. Sarum Coll 17. d 18 p 19. NSM Lawrence Weston and Avonmouth *Bris* from 18. *123 Sylvan Way, Bristol BS9 2LX* T: 0117-968 5479 M: 07948-676581 E: fran.brealey@btinternet.com

BREARLEY, Mrs Heather Gay. b 66. Sarum Coll 16. d 18 p 19. C Amesbury *Sarum* from 18. *26 Harvard Way, Amesbury, Salisbury SP4 7XE* M: 07760-386677 E: heatherbrearey@gmail.com

BREBNER, Martin James. b 47. Imp Coll Lon BSc 68 ARCS 68. St Alb Minl Tr Scheme 87. d 90 p 91. Hon C Letchworth St Paul w Willian *St Alb* 90–94; Hon C St Ippolyts 95–01; PtO 01–02; *Linc* from 02. *Willowcroft, Greatford, Stamford PE9 4QA* T: (01778) 561145 F: 561157 E: martinbrebner@yahoo.com

BRECHIN, Bishop of. *See* SWIFT, The Rt Revd Andrew Christopher

BRECHIN, Dean of. *See* BRIDGER, The Very Revd Francis William

BRECKLES, Robert Wynford. b 48. St Edm Hall Ox BA 72 MA 74 CertEd. Cranmer Hall Dur. d 79 p 80. C Bulwell St Mary *S'well* 79–84; V Lady Bay 84–05; V Lady Bay w Holme Pierrepont and Adbolton 06–12; rtd 12; PtO *S'well* from 13. *25 Goodwood Road, Nottingham NG8 2FT* T: 0115-854 3795

BRECKNELL, David Jackson. b 32. Keble Coll Ox BA 53 MA 57. St Steph Ho Ox 56. d 58 p 59. C Streatham St Pet *S'wark* 58–62; C Sneinton St Steph w St Alb *S'well* 62–64; C Solihull *Birm* 64–68; V Streatham St Paul *S'wark* 68–75; R Rumboldswyke *Chich* 75–81; P-in-c Portfield 79–81; R Whyke w Rumboldswhyke and Portfield 81–95; rtd 95; PtO *Chich* from 95; P-in-c Boxgrove 98–99. *8 Priory Close, Boxgrove, Chichester PO18 0EA* T: (01243) 784841 E: davidjbrecknell@gmail.com

BRECON, Archdeacon of. *See* JEVONS, The Ven Alan Neil

BRECON, Dean of. *See* SHACKERLEY, The Very Revd Albert Paul

BREED, Canon Verena. b 69. d 02 p 02. NSM Prestbury *Ches* 02–04; V Bosley and N Rode w Wincle and Wildboarclough 04–14; RD Macclesfield 12–14; TR Bicester w Bucknell, Caversfield and Launton *Ox* from 14; Hon Can Ch Ch from 19. *The Rectory, 6 Tinkers Lane, Bicester OX26 6ES* T: (01869) 240744 E: verenabreed@talktalk.net

BREEDS, Christopher Roger. b 51. Lon Univ CertEd 73 LGSM 83. Chich Th Coll 84. d 87 p 88. C E Grinstead St Swithun *Chich* 87–90; TV Aldrington 90–92; P-in-c Hove St Andr Old Ch 92–93; TV Hove 93–99; V Wivelsfield 99–16; RD Cuckfield 06–11; rtd 16; PtO *Chich* from 16; *Eur* from 17. *67 South Undercliff, Rye TN31 7HN* T: (01797) 224765 E: christopher.breeds@icloud.com

BREEN, Alan Terence. d 14 p 15. Greystones *D & G* 14–15; C 15–17; I Kill from 17. *The Rectory, Kill Lane, Deansgrange, Blackrock, Co Dublin, Republic of Ireland* M: (00353) 86-805 4818 E: alanwfc@me.com

BREENE, Timothy Patrick Brownell. b 59. Kent Univ BA 81 CCC Cam BA 89 MA 90. Ridley Hall Cam 87. **d** 90 **p** 93. C Hadleigh w Layham and Shelley *St E* 90–95; C Martlesham w Brightwell 95–03; rtd 03. *85 Cliff Road, Felixstowe IP11 9SQ* T: (01394) 283718

BREFFITT, Geoffrey Michael. b 46. CChem MRIC 72 Trent Poly CertEd 77. Qu Coll Birm 87. **d** 89 **p** 90. C Prenton *Ches* 89–92; V Frankby w Greasby 92–01; Dioc Ecum Officer 00–01; V German St Jo *S & M* 01–08; V Foxdale 01–08; V Patrick 01–08; RD Castletown and Peel 04–08; P-in-c Weston *Ches* 08–13; rtd 13. *181 Marion Road, Prestatyn LL19 7DG* E: geoff.breffitt@sky.com

BRENCHER, Lucy Jane. b 71. Ex Univ BA 94. St Hild Coll 15. **d** 18 **p** 19. NSM Rural Ainsty *York* 18–19; C from 19. *3 Fairfax Close, Bolton Percy, York YO23 7AY* T: (01904) 744281 M: 07940-514492 E: ruralainstycurate@gmail.com

BRENNAND (née PUNSHON), Ms Carol Mary. b 59. Liv Inst of Educn BEd 83. Ridley Hall Cam 92. **d** 94 **p** 95. C Bushey *St Alb* 94–97; C Watford Ch Ch 97–00; P-in-c Ash Vale *Guildf* 00–06; V 06–07; P-in-c Claybrooke cum Wibtoft and Frolesworth *Leic* 07–08; P-in-c Leire w Ashby Parva and Dunton Bassett 07–08; C Upper Soar 08–09; R 09–18; P-in-c W Leightonstone *Ely* from 18. *Brington Rectory, Church Lane, Brington, Huntingdon PE28 5AE* E: carolbrennand@btinternet.com

BRENNAND, Ian Peter. b 55. Univ of Wales (Trin St Dav) BA 12. STETS 01. **d** 04 **p** 05. C Frimley *Guildf* 04–07; Chapl Univ Hosps Leic NHS Trust 08–18; rtd 18; PtO *Leic* 18; *Ely* from 18; RD Huntingdon from 19. *Brington Rectory, Church Lane, Brington, Huntingdon PE28 5AE* E: ianbrennan@btinternet.com

BRENTFORD, Philip Bernard. b 73. UWE LLB 95 Coll of Eur Bruges LLM 97. Oak Hill Th Coll BA 15. **d** 15 **p** 16. C St Botolph without Aldersgate *Lon* from 15. *St Botolph-without-Aldersgate, Aldersgate Street, London EC1A 4EU* T: (020) 7606 0684 M: 07966-522099 E: philipbrentford@yahoo.co.uk *or* philip.brentford@thealdersgatetalks.org

BRERETON, Catherine Louise. *See* WILLIAMS, Catherine Louise

BRETHERTON, Canon Anthony Atkinson. b 51. Cant Univ (NZ) BA 74 Waikato Univ (NZ) MMS 97. St Jo Th Coll (NZ) LTh 74 STh 76. **d** 75 **p** 76. Asst C Ashburton New Zealand 75–78; Asst P St Geo-in-the-East w St Paul *Lon* 79–80; V Te Kauwhata New Zealand 80–85; V Cam 85–91; Can St Pet Cathl Waikato 88–90; Offg Min Waikato 91–01; Lic *L & K* 02–07; PtO *B & W* 07–10. *18 Vicars Close, Wells BA5 2UJ* M: 07738-993809 E: tonybretherton@hotmail.com

BRETT, Dennis Roy Anthony. b 46. Sarum & Wells Th Coll 86. **d** 88 **p** 89. C Bradford-on-Avon H Trin *Sarum* 88–92; P-in-c Bishopstrow and Boreham 92–01; R 01–15; Chapl Warminster Hosp 92–14; rtd 16; PtO *Sarum* from 16. *50 Gipsy Lane, Warminster BA12 9LR* T: (01985) 301366 M: 07742-059704 E: revdb@yahoo.co.uk

BRETT, Canon Paul Gadsby. b 41. St Edm Hall Ox BA 62 MA 66. Wycliffe Hall Ox 64. **d** 65 **p** 66. C Bury St Pet *Man* 65–68; Asst Ind Chapl 68–72; Ind Chapl *Worc* 72–76; Sec Ind Cttee of Gen Syn Bd for Soc Resp 76–84; Dir Soc Resp *Chelmsf* 85–94; Can Res Chelmsf Cathl 85–94; R Shenfield 94–08; rtd 08. *23 Stothert Avenue, Bath BA2 3FF* T: (01225) 312678 E: paul.brett@btinternet.com

BRETT, Canon Peter Graham Cecil. b 35. Em Coll Cam BA 59 MA 63. Cuddesdon Coll 59. **d** 61 **p** 62. C Tewkesbury w Walton Cardiff *Glouc* 61–64; C Bournemouth St Pet *Win* 64–66; Chapl Dur Univ 66–72; R Houghton le Spring 72–83; RD Houghton 80–83; Can Res Cant Cathl 83–01; rtd 01; PtO *Cant* from 01. *3 Appledore Road, Tenterden TN30 7AY* T: (01580) 761794 E: pandgbrett@btinternet.com

BRETT, Steven Anthony. Univ of Wales (Lamp) BA 98 Cardiff Univ BTh 16. St Mich Coll Llan. **d** 16 **p** 17. C Llantrisant *Llan* from 16. *23 Park View, Llantrisant, Pontyclun CF72 8DL* E: revstevebrett@gmail.com

BREUSS, Mrs Kristin Lynn. b 68. Univ of N Carolina BA 90 Columbia Univ MBA 98. St Mellitus Coll BA 14. **d** 14 **p** 15. C W Hampstead Trin *Lon* from 14. *29 Netherhall Gardens, London NW3 5RL* T: (020) 7435 0083 M: 07932-770239 E: kristinbreuss@gmail.com

BREW, Canon William Kevin Maddock. b 49. **d** 78 **p** 79. C Raheny w Coolock *D & G* 78–80; Bp's C Dublin Finglas 80–83; I Mountmellick w Coolbanagher, Rosenallis etc *M & K* 83–89; I Ahoghill w Portglenone *Conn* 89–05; I Howth *D & G* from 05; Can Ch Ch Cathl Dublin from 17. *The Rectory, 94 Howth Road, Howth, Co Dublin, Republic of Ireland* (00353) (1) 832 3019 E: howth@dublin.anglican.org

BREW, William Philip. b 43. Derby Coll of Educn CertEd 64 FCollP 84. NOC 84. **d** 87 **p** 88. In Independent Methodist Ch 70–90; Hd Master Birtenshaw Sch 78–90; NSM

Holcombe *Man* 87–90; TV Horwich 91–93; TV Horwich and Rivington 93–97; V Lostock St Thos and St Jo 97–08; P-in-c Bolton St Bede 04–08; AD Deane 98–05; rtd 08; PtO *Wakef* 08–14; *Leeds* from 14; *Eur* 12–18. *22 Deganwy Drive, Kirkheaton, Huddersfield HD5 0NG* T: (01484) 301295 E: brewsp@gmail.com

BREWER, Barry James. b 44. Oak Hill Th Coll 72. **d** 75 **p** 76. C Hove Bp Hannington Memorial Ch *Chich* 75–78; C Church Stretton *Heref* 78–81; TV Bishopsnympton, Rose Ash, Mariansleigh etc *Ex* 81–87; R Swynnerton and Tittensor *Lich* 87–07; RD Stone 01–07; rtd 07; PtO *Lich* 14–15. *2 Hazel Close, Seaton EX12 2UG* T: (01297) 24880 E: barrybrewer29@gmail.com

BREWER, Canon Susan Comport. b 55. LMH Ox MA 76 Cant Ch Ch Univ MA 10. SEITE 99. **d** 02 **p** 03. C Dartford St Edm *Roch* 02–07; V Milton next Gravesend Ch Ch 07–18; RD Gravesend 13–18; P-in-c Borstal from 18; Can Res Roch Cathl from 18. *37 Love Lane, Rochester ME1 1JD* M: 07930-492323 E: suec@brewer86.plus.com

BREWER-LENNON, Oliver Thomas. b 75. Kentucky Univ BMus 97 Roch Univ NY MMus 00. Scottish Episc Inst 13. **d** 16. C Edin St Pet 16–18; C Edin St Ninian from 18. *St Ninian's Church, 40 Comely Bank, Edinburgh EH4 1AG* M: 07954-314374 E: oliver@oliverb.nu

BREWERTON, Andrew Robert. b 70. Oak Hill Th Coll BA 05. **d** 05 **p** 06. C Gt Clacton *Chelmsf* 05–09; V Kilnhurst *Sheff* from 09; AD Wath from 12. *The Vicarage, Highthorn Road, Kilnhurst, Mexborough S64 5TX* T: (01709) 589674 E: andy@brewerton.org

BREWIN, David Frederick. b 39. Leic Poly BSc PhD. Lich Th Coll 63. **d** 66 **p** 67. C Shrewsbury H Cross *Lich* 66–69; C Birstall *Leic* 69–73; V Eyres Monsell 73–79; V E Goscote 79–82; V E Goscote w Ratcliffe and Rearsby 82–90; R Thurcaston 90–91; R Thurcaston w Cropston 92–05; rtd 05; PtO *Leic* 05–16; *Pet* 06–17. *28 Welland Way, Oakham LE15 6SL* T: (01572) 720073

BREWIN, Canon Donald Stewart. b 41. Ch Coll Cam BA 62 MA 66. Ridley Hall Cam 68. **d** 71 **p** 72. C Ecclesall *Sheff* 71–75; V Anston 75–81; V Walton H Trin Ox 81–89; TR 89–94; RD Aylesbury 90–94; Nat Dir SOMA UK 94–07; PtO *St Alb* from 94; rtd 07; Hon Can Boga from 17. *Wickham Cottage, Gaddesden Turn, Great Billington, Leighton Buzzard LU7 9BW* T: (01525) 373644 M: 07816-362797 E: donsbrewin@gmail.com

BREWIN, Karan Rosemary. b 42. CA Tr Coll 77 Glas NSM Course 80. **dss** 84 **d** 85 **p** 15. Clarkston *Glas* 84–89; Hon C 86–89 and 91–97; OHP 89 and 98–02 and from 11; PtO *York* 01–02 and from 13; PtO Johannesburg S Africa 03–05; PtO Swaziland 06–11. *1A Minster Court, York YO1 7JJ* T: (01904) 557276 E: karanohp@gmail.com

BREWIN, Wilfred Michael. b 45. Nottm Univ BA 69. Cuddesdon Coll 69. **d** 70 **p** 71. C Walker *Newc* 70–73; C Alnwick St Paul 73–74; C Alnwick w Edlingham and Bolton Chpl 74–77; Fell Sheff Univ 77–79; C Greenhill *Sheff* 79; P-in-c Eggleston *Dur* 79–81; V Norton St Mich 81–87; V Headington Ox 87–10; rtd 10; PtO *Newc* from 14; *Eur* from 18. *Rose Cottage, New Road, Chatton, Alnwick NE66 5PU* T: (01668) 215319 E: michael.brewin@hotmail.co.uk

BREWIS, Mrs Kalantha Katherine. b 67. Em Coll Cam BA 89 MA 94. WEMTC 13. **d** 16 **p** 17. C Worc St Barn w Ch Ch from 16. *70 Gregory's Bank, Worcester WR3 8AQ* T: (01905) 26715 M: 07808-295457 E: revk@brewis.net

BREWIS, Robert David. b 81. Lanc Univ BSc 03. Oak Hill Th Coll MTh 11. **d** 11 **p** 12. C Washfield, Stoodleigh, Withleigh etc *Ex* 11–14; NSM Chadderton Ch Ch *Man* from 14. *58 Oakbank Avenue, Chadderton, Oldham OL9 0PP* E: rbrewis02@hotmail.com

BREWSTER, Christine Elaine. b 45. Newc Univ BA 67 CertEd 68 Lon Univ MA 84 DipEd 92 Univ of Wales (Ban) PhD 07 ALCM 76 LTCL 78. SAOMC 95. **d** 98 **p** 99. NSM Aylesbury *Ox* 98–00; NSM Dacre w Hartwith and Darley w Thornthwaite *Ripon* 00–01; C Wetherby 01–04; PtO 04–08; P-in-c Llanwnnog and Caersws w Carno *Ban* 08–12; rtd 12; PtO *Ban* 12–16; *Heref* from 13; Visiting Research Fell Glyndŵr Univ from 11. *Michaelmas Cottage, Lingen, Bucknell SY7 0DY* T: (01544) 267338 E: cbmichaelmas@gmail.com

BREWSTER, David Thomas. b 68. GLCM 90 ALCM 89. Cranmer Hall Dur 89. **d** 99 **p** 00. C Bidston *Ches* 99–03; TV Stockport SW 03–07; V Edgeley and Cheadle Heath from 07; RD Stockport from 17. *St Mark's Vicarage, 66 Berlin Road, Stockport SK3 9QF* T: 0161-480 5896 E: dtbrewster@talktalk.net

BREWSTER, Canon Jonathan David. b 67. Bucks Coll of Educn BA 89 Bris Univ BA 94 K Coll Lon MA 01. Trin Coll Bris 91. **d** 94 **p** 95. C Gt Horton *Bradf* 94–98; Chapl Univ of Westmr *Lon* 98–03; V Highbury Ch Ch w St Jo and St Sav 03–17; AD Islington 14–17; Can Res and Treas St Paul's Cathl from 17. *St Paul's Cathedral, The Chapter House, St Paul's Churchyard, London EC4M 8AD* M: 07977-127244   E: treasurer@stpaulscathedral.org.uk   *or* jbrewster@stpaulscathedral.org

BREWSTER, Mrs Lucinda Anne Morrine. b 68. GLCM 90. St Mellitus Coll 17. **d** 19. C Partington and Carrington *Ches* from 19. *66 Berlin Road, Stockport SK3 9QF* T: 0161-480 5896 M: 07436-017841 E: lucybrewster@talktalk.net

BREWSTER (*née* **BEATTIE**), **Margaret.** b 43. S'wark Ord Course 90. **d** 93 **p** 94. NSM S'wark H Trin w St Matt 93–97; NSM Newington St Paul 97–04; NSM Dunstable *St Alb* 04–07; rtd 07; PtO *Linc* from 07. *39 Glen Drive, Boston PE21 7QB* T: (01205) 351298 E: m.brewster789@btinternet.com

BREWSTER, Samuel Paul William. b 86. Selw Coll Cam MA 11. Wycliffe Hall Ox MTh 13. **d** 13 **p** 14. C Maidenhead St Andr and St Mary *Ox* 13–18; C Henley H Trin from 18. *9 Hobbs End, Henley-on-Thames RG9 1RT* M: 07899-843461 E: sam@thebrewsters.org.uk

BRIAN, Stephen Frederick. b 54. Sussex Univ BEd 77 Open Univ MA 90 Lanc Univ MPhil 97 Surrey Univ PhD 03. Qu Coll Birm 82. **d** 85 **p** 86. C Scotforth *Blackb* 85–88; V Freckleton 88–97; V Bagshot *Guildf* 97–06; Chapl Heathfield St Mary's Sch Wantage 06–07; P-in-c Mid Loes *St E* 07–08; R from 08; RD Loes 13–14. *The Rectory, Church Lane, Earl Soham, Woodbridge IP13 7SD* T: (01728) 685308 E: sfb4510@aol.com

BRICE, Christopher John. b 48. St Edm Ho Cam MA 80. Wycliffe Hall Ox 82. **d** 82 **p** 83. C N Hinksey *Ox* 82–86; Chapl Nuff Coll Ox 84–86; V S Hackney St Mich w Haggerston St Paul *Lon* 86–93; Dir Dioc Bd for Soc Resp 93–00; Adv for Soc Justice 01–08; Hon C De Beauvoir Town St Pet 93–08; P-in-c Kentish Town St Martin w St Andr 08–13; V 13–18; rtd 18; PtO *Lon* from 18. *9 Beresford Road, London N5 2HS* T: (020) 7226 3834 M: 07913-733669

BRICE, Derek William Fred. b 39. Poly Cen Lon MA 87 MCIM 89 FCMI 82. **d** 02 **p** 03. OLM Cheam *S'wark* 02–09; PtO from 09. *Mallow, Parkside, Cheam, Sutton SM3 8BS* T: (020) 8642 0241 *or* 8693 4324 E: derekbrice@blueyonder.co.uk

BRICE, Jonathan Andrew William. b 61. **d** 92 **p** 93. C Buckhurst Hill *Chelmsf* 92–96; C Victoria Docks Ascension 96; P-in-c 96–98; V 98–06; Chapl Felsted Sch 06–11; R Aspen Ch Ch USA from 11. *536 West North Street, Aspen CO 81611-1253, USA* T: (001) (970) 987 1524 E: rev@christchurchaspen.org

BRICE, Neil Alan. b 59. Man Univ BA 81 Hughes Hall Cam CertEd 87. Westcott Ho Cam 82. **d** 84 **p** 85. C Longton *Lich* 84–86; Hd of Relig Studies Coleridge Community Coll Cam 87–89; NSM Cherry Hinton St Andr *Ely* 88–89; C Fulbourn 89–92; C Gt Wilbraham 89–92; C Lt Wilbraham 89–92; V Arrington 92–00; R Orwell 92–00; R Wimpole 92–00; R Croydon w Clopton 92–00; P-in-c Barrington 98–00; R Orwell Gp 00–09; R Lerwick *Ab* from 10; P-in-c Burravoe from 10. *St Magnus' Rectory, Greenfield Place, Lerwick, Shetland ZE1 0AQ* T: (01595) 693862 M: 07713-259262 E: revnab@btinternet.com

BRICE, Paul Earl Philip. b 54. Bath Univ BSc 77. Wycliffe Hall Ox 83. **d** 86 **p** 87. C Gt Baddow *Chelmsf* 86–89; Chapl Imp Coll Lon and St Mary's Hosp Med Sch 89–95; Chapl R Coll of Art 90–95; Sec HE/Chapl C of E Bd of Educn 95–02; Hon C S Kensington St Jude *Lon* 95–02; R Hartfield w Coleman's Hatch *Chich* 02–12; Chapl Zürich *Eur* from 15. *St Andrew, Promenadengasse 9, 8001 Zürich, Switzerland* T: (0041) (44) 261 2241 *or* 252 6024 E: zurich@anglican.ch

BRICKMAN, Mark. b 60. Jes Coll Cam MA 81. Trin Coll Bris 10. **d** 12 **p** 13. C Ox St Aldate 12–16; NSM from 16. *25 Norreys Avenue, Oxford OX1 4ST* T: (01865) 254800 E: mark.brickman@staldates.org.uk

BRIDEWELL, Mrs Alison Clare. b 66. Win Univ BA 11. STETS 11. **d** 14 **p** 15. C Bemerton *Sarum* 14–17; P-in-c Potterne w Worton and Marston 17–18; R Wellsprings from 18. *The Rectory, 9 Coxhill Lane, Potterne, Devizes SN10 5PH* M: 07847-952868

BRIDGE, Mrs Sheila Margaret. b 62. St Jo Coll Nottm. **d** 11 **p** 12. C Rugby W *Cov* 11–13; Min Rugby St Pet and St Jo CD 13–19; V Rugby St Pet and St Jo from 19. *St Peter's Vicarage, 63A Lower Hillmorton Road, Rugby CV21 3TQ*

BRIDGE, Siobhan Claire. b 80. K Alfred's Coll Win BA 02. Qu Foundn Birm 14. **d** 16 **p** 17. C Erdington St Barn *Birm* from 16. *17 Greenhill Road, Sutton Coldfield B72 1DS* T: 0121-294 7590 M: 07403-843585 E: revdsiobhanbridge@gmail.com

BRIDGE, Susan. BA LLB MBA BTh Regent's Park Coll Ox MPhil. **d** 09 **p** 10. C Canberra Australia 10–15; PtO *Ox* 16–18; Asst Chapl New Coll Ox from 17; PtO *Ox* from 16.

New College, Holywell Street, Oxford OX1 3BN M: 07402-123473 E: susan.bridge@theology.ox.ac.uk

BRIDGEN, John William. b 40. K Coll Cam BA 62 MA 66. Ripon Hall Ox 66. **d** 70 **p** 72. C Headstone St Geo *Lon* 70–71; C Hanwell St Mary 71–75; C Tolladine *Worc* 75; TV Worc St Barn w Ch Ch 76; R Barrow *St E* 76–83; V Denham St Mary 76–83; PtO *Ely* 84–88 and 91–16; rtd 88; PtO *Glas* 89–91. *57 St Philip's Road, Cambridge CB1 3DA* T: (01223) 571748 E: j.bridgen@ntlworld.com

BRIDGEN, Mark Stephen. b 63. K Coll Lon BD 85. Cranmer Hall Dur 86. **d** 88 **p** 89. C Kidderminster St Jo and H Innocents *Worc* 88–92; C Nor St Pet Mancroft w St Jo Maddermarket 92–94; V Longbridge *Birm* 94–00; V Wednesbury St Bart *Lich* 00–07; P-in-c Gnosall and Moreton 08–10; R Adbaston, High Offley, Knightley, Norbury etc 10–15; R Paston *Pet* from 15. *The Rectory, 236 Fulbridge Road, Peterborough PE4 6SN* T: (01733) 579778 E: mark.bridgen@btinternet.com

BRIDGER, The Very Revd Francis William. b 51. Pemb Coll Ox BA 73 MA 78 Bris Univ PhD 81. Trin Coll Bris 74. **d** 78 **p** 79. C Islington St Jude Mildmay Park *Lon* 78–82; Lect St Jo Coll Nottm 82–90; V Woodthorpe *S'well* 90–99; Prin Trin Coll Bris 99–05; Prof Fuller Th Sem USA 05–08; PtO *Nor* 11–12; R Broughty Ferry *Bre* from 12; Dean Bre from 13; P-in-c Dundee St Jo from 16; P-in-c Dundee St Martin from 16. *3 Wyvis Place, Broughty Ferry, Dundee DD5 3SX* T: (01382) 739035 M: 07507-885476 E: fbridger@yahoo.ie

BRIDGER, Canon Gordon Frederick. b 32. Selw Coll Cam BA 53 MA 58. Ridley Hall Cam 54. **d** 56 **p** 57. C Islington St Mary *Lon* 56–60; C Cambridge Se Sepulchre *Ely* 60–62; V Fulham St Mary N End *Lon* 62–69; C Edin St Thos 69–76; R Heigham H Trin *Nor* 76–87; RD Nor S 79–86; Hon Can Nor Cathl 84–87; Prin Oak Hill Th Coll 87–96; rtd 96; PtO *Nor* from 96. *The Elms, 4 Common Lane, Sheringham NR26 8PL* T: (01263) 823522 E: gordonbridger123@btinternet.com

BRIDGER, Mrs Helen Ruth. b 68. Bradf Univ BA 91. Trin Coll Bris BA 06. **d** 05 **p** 06. C Altadena USA 05–06; C Arcadia Transfiguration 06–08; C Nuthall and Kimberley *S'well* 08–10; Chapl Qu Eliz Hosp King's Lynn NHS Foundn Trust 10–12; C Broughty Ferry *Bre* from 12; C Dundee St Jo from 16; C Dundee St Martin from 16. *3 Wyvis Place, Broughty Ferry, Dundee DD5 3SX* T: (01382) 739035 E: helenbridger@yahoo.com

BRIDGES, John Malham. b 57. Goldsmiths' Coll Lon BSc 80. Ridley Hall Cam 03. **d** 05 **p** 06. C Cranleigh *Guildf* 05–08; Chapl RN 08–18; rtd 18; Chapl RNR from 18; PtO *Lon* 18–19; NSM Northwood H Trin from 19. *50 Moor Lane, Rickmansworth WD3 1LG* T: (01923) 775306 E: revdjohnbridges@gmail.com

BRIDGES, Simon Patrick (Sid). b 73. Ox Brookes Univ BA 04. Ridley Hall Cam 13. **d** 14 **p** 15. C Orton Longueville w Bottlebridge *Ely* 14; C The Ortons 14–18; PtO from 19. *The Rectory, 67 Church Drive, Orton Waterville, Peterborough PE2 5HE* T: (01733) 233402 M: 07851-609020 E: sidbridges@live.co.uk

BRIDGES (*née* **BANKS**), **Mrs Vivienne Philippa.** b 46. Somerville Coll Ox BA 69. SAOMC 02. **d** 05 **p** 06. NSM Wolvercote *Ox* 05–10; NSM Wolvercote and Wytham 10–16; PtO from 16. *6 Haslemere Gardens, Oxford OX2 8EL* T: (01865) 558705

BRIDGEWATER, Guy Stevenson. b 60. Ch Ch Ox BA 83. Trin Coll Bris BA 87. **d** 87 **p** 88. C Radipole and Melcombe Regis *Sarum* 87–90; Chapl Lee Abbey 90–93; V Cranbrook *Cant* 93–98; Dioc Officer for Par Resources (Miss and Lay Tr) *Glouc* 98–07; Dioc Can Res Glouc Cathl 02–07; TR Horsham *Chich* 07–18; RD 09–18; R Bath Abbey w St Jas *B & W* from 18. *12 Cleveland Walk, Bath BA2 6JX* T: (01225) 422462 E: rector@bathabbey.org

BRIDGEWATER, Robert. b 69. Sheff Hallam Univ BEd 92 MSc 97. Oak Hill Th Coll BA 15. **d** 15 **p** 16. C Chapeltown *Sheff* 15–18; LtO from 18. *7 Haugh Lane, Sheffield S11 9SA* M: 07595-938138 E: rob@bridgewaterfamily.me.uk *or* robert.bridgewater@sheffield.anglican.org

BRIDGEWOOD, Bruce William. b 41. K Coll Lon BA 02 Heythrop Coll Lon MA 06. St Paul's Coll Grahamstown LTh 67. **d** 67 **p** 68. C Plumstead S Africa 67–69; C Somerset W 70–71; Hon C Salvator w Falmer *Chich* 81–86; Hon C Westmr St Matt *Lon* 90–93; Hon C Alexandra Park 93–04; P-in-c Friern Barnet St Pet le Poer 04–13; rtd 13; PtO *Ox* 13–16; *Cant* from 16. *Flat 2, 54 Bouverie West, Folkestone CT20 2RL* T: (01303) 680432 E: brucebridgewood@gmail.com

BRIDGMAN, Canon Gerald Bernard. b 22. St Cath Coll Cam BA 50 MA 55. Bible Churchmen's Coll Bris 46 Wycliffe Hall Ox 50. **d** 51 **p** 52. C Broadwater St Mary *Chich* 51–54; C Ox St Aldate 54–56; C-in-c Southgate CD *Chich* 56–59; V Southgate 59–67; V Kingston upon Hull

H Trin *York* 67–87; Chapl Hull R Infirmary 67–87; AD Cen and N Hull *York* 81–86; Can and Preb York Minster 83–87; rtd 87; PtO *Chich* from 87. *129 The Welkin, Lindfield, Haywards Heath RH16 2PL* T: (01444) 484563 E: ggbridgman@btinternet.com

BRIDGMAN, James William. b 85. Man Univ BA 06. Trin Coll Bris BA 09 MA 10. **d** 10 **p** 11. C Heswall *Ches* 10–13; V Timperley from 13. *The Vicarage, 12 Thorley Lane, Timperley, Altrincham WA15 7AZ* T: 0161-980 4330 E: revjimb1017@gmail.com

BRIDGMAN (née JOYCE), Mrs Jennifer Claire. b 84. Man Univ BA 06. Trin Coll Bris BA 08 MPhil 10. **d** 10 **p** 11. C Heswall *Ches* 10–13; Young Voc Adv 11–13; C Broadheath 13–14; C Timperley from 14; Asst Dioc Dir of Ords from 16. *The Vicarage, 12 Thorley Lane, Timperley, Altrincham WA15 7AZ* T: 0161-980 4330 M: 07709-471494 E: revjb99@gmail.com

BRIDGWATER, Philip Dudley. b 31. St Alb Minl Tr Scheme 88. **d** 91 **p** 92. NSM Buxton w Burbage and King Sterndale *Derby* 91–94 and 98–01; NSM Fairfield 91–98. *Millstone, 9 College Road, Buxton SK17 9DZ* T: (01298) 72876

BRIDLE, Canon Geoffrey Peter. b 52. CITC 87. **d** 87 **p** 88. C Lurgan Ch the Redeemer *D & D* 87–91; I Carnteel and Crilly *Arm* 91–99; I Cleenish w Mullaghdun *Clogh* from 99; Can Clogh Cathl from 15. *Cleenish Rectory, Bellanaleck, Enniskillen BT92 2BA* T: (028) 6634 8259 F: 6634 8620 E: geoffreypbridle@email.com *or* geoffreypeterbridle@me.com

BRIDSON, Canon Raymond Stephen. b 58. Southn Univ BTh 82. Chich Th Coll. **d** 82 **p** 83. C St Luke in the City *Liv* 82–86; TV Ditton St Mich 86–98; V Anfield St Columba 98–19; AD Walton 02–13; Hon Can Liv Cathl 03–19; rtd 19. *St Columba's Vicarage, Pinehurst Avenue, Liverpool L4 2TZ* T: 0151-474 7231 E: frray@blueyonder.co.uk

BRIDSTRUP, Juergen Walter. b 44. St Alb Minl Tr Scheme 84. **d** 87 **p** 88. C Leagrave *St Alb* 87–90; V Goff's Oak St Jas 90–08; TV Cheshunt 08–09; rtd 09; PtO *Heref* from 09. *4 The Vineyard, Lower Broad Street, Ludlow SY8 1PH* T: (01584) 876992 E: juergen.bridstrup@btinternet.com

BRIEN, John Richard. b 57. Kingston Poly BSc 80. EAMTC 98. **d** 01 **p** 02. NSM Mistley w Manningtree and Bradfield *Chelmsf* from 01. *2 Elmdale Drive, Manningtree CO11 2HP* T: (01206) 397549 E: brienfamily@btinternet.com

BRIERLEY, John Michael. b 32. Lon Univ BD 71. Lich Th Coll 57. **d** 60 **p** 61. C Lower Mitton *Worc* 60–62; C-in-c Dines Green St Mich CD 62–68; V Worc St Mich 69–71; R Eastham w Rochford 71–79; P-in-c Knighton-on-Teme 76–79; P-in-c Teme Valley N 79; P-in-c Reddal Hill St Luke 79–81; V 81–92; rtd 92; PtO *Worc* from 92. *10 Woodhouse Way, Cradley Heath, Warley B64 5EL* T: (01384) 633527

BRIERLEY, Canon Michael William. b 73. CCC Cam BA 94 MA 98 Birm Univ PhD 07. Ripon Coll Cuddesdon BA 98. **d** 98 **p** 99. C Marnhull *Sarum* 98–01; C Okeford 98–01; Bp's Dom Chapl *Ox* 01–07; P-in-c Tavistock and Gulworthy *Ex* 07–14; Can Res and Prec Worc Cathl from 14. *15A College Green, Worcester WR1 2LH* T: (01905) 732940 E: michaelbrierley@worcestercathedral.org.uk

BRIERLEY, Philip. b 49. Salford Univ BSc 74. OLM Stalybridge *Man* 92–13; P-in-c 13–16; V 16–19; rtd 19. *30 Cranworth Street, Stalybridge SK15 2NW* T: 0161-338 2368 E: philip.brierley@yahoo.co.uk

BRIGGS, Christopher Ronald. b 58. K Coll Lon BD 79 AKC 79 PGCE 80. Sarum & Wells Th Coll 87. **d** 89 **p** 90. C Horsell *Guildf* 89–93; Hong Kong 93–97; V Norton *St Alb* 97–00; Sen Chapl Haileybury Coll 00–19; Chapl Shiplake Coll Henley from 19. *Shiplake College, Shiplake Court, Shiplake, Henley-on-Thames RG9 4BW* T: 0118-940 5258 E: cbriggs@shiplake.org.uk

BRIGGS, Enid. b 50. CBDTI 03. **d** 06 **p** 07. NSM Walton-le-Dale St Leon w Samlesbury St Leon *Blackb* 06–13; NSM Walton-le-Dale St Leon 12–14; NSM Bamber Bridge St Aid 11–14; LtO from 14. *Ground Floor Flat, 169 Manchester Road, Burnley BB11 4HR* E: enid_briggs@hotmail.com

BRIGGS, George William. b 76. Wadh Coll Ox BA 98 Fitzw Coll Cam BA 02. Ridley Hall Cam 00. **d** 03 **p** 04. C Old Trafford St Bride *Man* 03–06; P-in-c Clapham Park All SS *S'wark* 06–11; V 11–14; P-in-c St Thos *Carl* from 14; P-in-c Crook from 14. *St Thomas's Vicarage, South View Lane, Kendal LA9 4QN* T: (015395) 83058 E: georgebriggs.work@gmail.com

BRIGGS, Gordon John. b 39. CIPFA. SAOMC 95. **d** 98 **p** 99. OLM Farnham Royal w Hedgerley *Ox* 98–11; PtO from 11. *52 Freemans Close, Stoke Poges, Slough SL2 4ER* T: (01753) 662536 E: revgordon@hotmail.co.uk

BRIGGS, Canon John. b 39. Edin Univ MA 61. Ridley Hall Cam 61. **d** 63 **p** 64. C Jesmond Clayton Memorial *Newc*

63–66; Schs Sec Scripture Union 66–79; Tutor St Jo Coll Dur 67–74; LtO *Dur* 67–74; LtO *Edin* 74–79; V Chadkirk *Ches* 79–88; RD 85–88; TR Macclesfield Team 88–04; Hon Can Ches Cathl 96–04; Chapl W Park Hosp Macclesfield 90–99; rtd 04; PtO *Ches* from 04. *16 Lostock Hall Road, Poynton, Stockport SK12 1DP* T: (01625) 267228 E: briggsjohn63@gmail.com

BRIGGS, Richard Stephen. b 66. Hertf Coll Ox BA 88 MA 95 Lon Bible Coll MA 95 Nottm Univ PhD 00. Yorks Min Course 14. **d** 15 **p** 16. NSM Dur St Giles from 15; NSM Shadforth and Sherburn from 15. *St Catherine's House, Front Street, Broompark, Durham DH7 7QX* T: 0191-386 9506 M: 07810-880133 E: richard.briggs@durham.anglican.org

BRIGGS, William James. b 75. Univ of Tasmania BE 97. Ridley Coll Melbourne BMin 03. **d** 02 **p** 03. C Burnie Australia 02–08; P-in-c 10–11; P-in-c Wynyard 05–07; Project P Somerset Project 09–13; C Hobart Cathl 11–15; C Newbury St Nic and Speen *Ox* 15–18; V Sheffield Vine *Sheff* from 18. *The Vicarage, 115 Upperthorpe Road, Sheffield S6 3EA* T: 0114-275 1480 M: 07548-050745 E: will.briggs@gmail.com

BRIGHT, George Frank. b 50. Peterho Cam BA 71 MA 75 LSE MSc 83 SAP 99. Coll of Resurr Mirfield 71. **d** 74 **p** 75. C Notting Hill *Lon* 74–77; PtO 77–84; P-in-c Kentish Town St Benet and All SS 84–89; P-in-c Kensington St Jo 89–93; V 93–06. *The Vicarage, 176 Holland Road, London W14 8AH* T: (020) 7602 4655 E: gfb@dircon.co.uk

BRIGHTMAN, Peter Arthur. b 30. ALCD 61 LTh 74. **d** 64 **p** 65. C Westgate St Jas *Cant* 64–67; C Lydd 67–70; C Lt Coates *Linc* 70; C Heaton Ch Ch *Man* 71–72; V Bolton SS Simon and Jude 72–77; R Bath St Sav *B & W* 77–85; R Farmborough, Marksbury and Stanton Prior 85–90; C Coney Hill *Glouc* 90–93; C Hardwicke, Quedgeley and Elmore w Longney 93–95; rtd 95; PtO *B & W* 95–18. *172 The Hollow, Bath BA2 1NG* T: (01225) 315076 M: 07528-891148

BRIGHTON, Terrence William. b 43. SWMTC 85. **d** 88 **p** 89. C Dawlish *Ex* 88–92; P-in-c Newton Poppleford w Harpford 92–94; V Newton Poppleford, Harpford and Colaton Raleigh 94–98; RD Ottery 96–98; P-in-c W Lavington and the Cheverells *Sarum* 98–02; Rural Officer (Ramsbury Area) 98–02; P-in-c Charleton w Buckland Tout Saints etc *Ex* 02–05; R 05–08; RD Woodleigh 03–07; rtd 08. *30 Millway, Chudleigh, Newton Abbot TQ13 0JN* M: 07974-294044 E: twb@madasafish.com

BRIGHTWELL, Miss Elaine. b 57. STETS 09. **d** 12 **p** 13. NSM Pilton w Croscombe, N Wootton and Dinder *B & W* 12–17; TV Nadder Valley *Sarum* from 17. *The Vicarage, 11A Tyndales Meadow, Dinton, Salisbury SP3 5HU* M: 07986-639230 E: elainebri57@gmail.com

BRIGHTWELL, Johanna Clare. See CLARE, Johanna Howard

BRIGNALL, Elizabeth Jane. See BENDREY, Elizabeth Jane

BRIGNALL, Simon Francis Lyon. b 54. St Jo Coll Dur BA 78. Wycliffe Hall Ox 80. **d** 83 **p** 84. C Colne St Bart *Blackb* 83–86; SAMS Peru 86–96; P-in-c Tetsworth, Adwell w S Weston, Lewknor etc *Ox* 96–98; TV Thame 98–09; P-in-c Wriggle Valley *Sarum* 09–13; TV Three Valleys 13–15; Chapl St Pet Viña del Mar Chile from 15. *c/o The Hope, Ampney St Peter, Cirencester GL7 5SH* M: 07718-627674 E: sflbrignall@gmail.com

BRIMACOMBE, Keith John. b 59. Open Univ BA 92 Westmr Coll Ox MTh 00. SWMTC 99. **d** 01 **p** 03. NSM Ottery St Mary, Alfington, W Hill, Tipton etc *Ex* 01–07; Trinidad and Tobago 07–09; Perm to Offic Cyprus and the Gulf 09–10; Chapl Ahmadi St Paul Kuwait 11–13; C Fremington, Instow and Westleigh *Ex* from 13. *61 Hanson Park, Northam, Bideford EX39 3SB* E: brimacombe.keith@gmail.com

BRIMICOMBE, Mark. b 44. Nottm Univ BA 66 CertEd. SWMTC 83. **d** 85 **p** 86. NSM Plympton St Mary *Ex* 85–14; PtO from 14. *4 David Close, Stoggy Lane, Plympton, Plymouth PL7 3BQ* T: (01752) 338454 E: mark@thebrambles.eclipse.co.uk

BRIMSON, Dawn Diana. b 44. Ex Univ BTh 08. SWMTC 02. **d** 05 **p** 06. NSM Quantoxhead *B & W* 05–07; NSM Quantock Coast 07–14; PtO from 14. *Ridges, Holford, Bridgwater TA5 1DU* T: (01278) 741413 E: ddbrimson70@btinternet.com

BRINDLE, Peter John. b 47. MIStructE 72 FLS 05. NOC 78. **d** 81 **p** 82. NSM Bingley All SS *Bradf* 81–84; NSM Bingley H Trin 84–86; V Keighley All SS 86–91; V Kirkstall *Ripon* 91–96; V Beeston 96–02; TR 02–04; TR Leic Presentation 04–09; P-in-c Leic St Chad 04–07; P-in-c N Evington 07–09; rtd 09; PtO *York* 14–18. *5 Showfield Close, Sherburn in Elmet, Leeds LS25 6LW* T: (01977) 680026 M: 07860-157363 E: peter.brindle23@gmail.com

BRINDLEY, Angela Mary. See SPEEDY, Angela Mary

BRINDLEY, The Very Revd David Charles. b 53. K Coll Lon BD 75 AKC 75 MTh 76 MPhil 81 Open Univ MA 16. St Aug Coll Cant 75. **d** 76 **p** 77. C Epping St Jo *Chelmsf* 76–79; Lect

Coll of SS Paul and Mary Cheltenham 79–82; Dioc Dir of Tr *Leic* 82–86; V Quorndon 82–86; Prin WEMTC *Glouc* 87–92 and 92–94; Dir of Minl Tr 87–94; Dioc Officer for NSM 88–94; Hon Can Glouc Cathl 92–94; TR Warwick *Cov* 94–02; Dean Portsm 02–18; rtd 18. *8 Rookwood Gardens, Fordingbridge SP6 1TA* T: (01425) 650090 E: davidbrindley3@gmail.com

BRINKLEY, Mrs Penelope Heather. b 57. ERMC 13. **d** 16 **p** 17. NSM Felixstowe St Jo *St E* from 16. *70 Leopold Road, Felixstowe IP11 7NR* M: 07901-950768 E: rev.pennybrinkley@yahoo.com

BRINKWORTH, Canon Christopher Michael Gibbs. b 41. Lanc Univ BA 70. Kelham Th Coll 62. **d** 67 **p** 68. C Lancaster St Mary *Blackb* 67–70; C Milton *Portsm* 70–74; V Ault Hucknall *Derby* 74–84; V Derby St Anne and St Jo 84–06; Hon Can Derby Cathl 00–06; rtd 06; PtO *Derby* from 06. *3 Westfield Grove, Derby DE22 3SG* T: (01332) 208478 E: michaelbrinkworth@btinternet.com *or* michaelbrinkworth@icloud.com

BRION, Martin Philip. b 33. Ex Univ BA 55. Ridley Hall Cam 57. **d** 59 **p** 60. C Balderstone *Man* 59–62; C Morden *S'wark* 62–66; V Low Elswick *Newc* 66–73; P-in-c Giggleswick *Bradf* 73–77; V 77–80; V Camerton H Trin W Seaton *Carl* 80–86; V Dearham 86–95; rtd 95; PtO *Carl* 95–19. *7 Falcon Place, Moresby Parks, Whitehaven CA28 8YF* T: (01946) 691912

BRISCOE, Allen. b 42. Liv Univ BSc 64 CertEd 65. Coll of Resurr Mirfield 90. **d** 92 **p** 93. C Shiremoor *Newc* 92–95; V Barnsley St Pet and St Jo *Wakef* 95–10; Asst Dioc Ecum Officer 01–03; Bp's Adv for Ecum Affairs 03–06; RD Barnsley 04–09; rtd 10; Hon C Goldthorpe w Hickleton *Sheff* from 11; PtO *Leeds* from 17. *37 Holly Grove, Goldthorpe, Rotherham S63 9LA* T: (01709) 896739 E: abriscoe@talk21.com

BRISCOE, Canon Frances Amelia. b 35. Univ of Wales CertEd 55 Man Univ BA 71 MA 74. Gilmore Course 74. **dss** 77 **d** 87 **p** 94. Gt Crosby St Luke *Liv* 77–81; Dioc Lay Min Adv 81–87; Chapl Liv Cathl 81–89; Dir Diaconal Mins 87–89; Lect St Deiniol's Minl Tr Scheme 88–00; Hon Can Liv Cathl 88–00; AD Sefton 89–00; Dir of Reader Studies 89–00; Dn-in-c Hightown *Liv* 92–94; P-in-c 94–00; rtd 00; PtO *Liv* from 01. *5 Derwent Avenue, Formby, Liverpool L37 2JT* T: (01704) 830075

BRISCOE, Mark. b 71. Coll of Ripon & York St Jo BA 95. Ripon Coll Cuddesdon 05. **d** 07 **p** 08. C Saxilby Gp *Linc* 07–10; P-in-c Corringham and Blyton Gp 10–14; P-in-c Glentworth Gp 10–14; V Trentcliffe Gp from 14. *The Vicarage, Church Lane, Blyton, Gainsborough DN21 3JZ* T: (01427) 629105 E: markbriscoe71@gmail.com

BRISON, The Ven William Stanley. b 29. Alfred Univ NY BSc 51 Connecticut Univ MDiv 57 STM 71. Berkeley Div Sch. **d** 57 **p** 57. USA 57–72; V Davyhulme Ch Ch *Man* 72–81; R Newton Heath All SS 81–85; AD N Man 81–85; Hon Can Man Cathl 82–85; Adn Bolton 85–92; TV E Farnworth and Kearsley 85–89; C Bolton St Thos 89–92; CMS 92–94; Nigeria 92–94; P-in-c Pendleton St Thos w Charlestown *Man* 94–95; TR Pendleton 95–98; rtd 98; PtO *Man* 99–17. *2 Scott Avenue, Bury BL9 9RS* T: 0161-764 3998

BRISTOL, Archdeacon of. *See* WARWICK, The Ven Neil Michael

BRISTOL, Bishop of. *See* FAULL, The Rt Revd Vivienne Frances

BRISTOL, Dean of. *Vacant*

BRISTOW, Keith Raymond Martin. b 56. Ex Univ BA 78. Chich Th Coll 87. **d** 89 **p** 90. C Kirkby *Liv* 89–93; C Portsea St Mary *Portsm* 93–03; R Ash *Guildf* from 03. *The Rectory, Ash Church Road, Ash, Aldershot GU12 6LU* T: (01252) 321517

BRISTOW, Malcolm William. b 49. SNWTP 11. **d** 12 **p** 13. OLM Bolton St Bede *Man* 12–19; rtd 19. *8 Winton Grove, Bolton BL3 4UX* T: (01204) 659816 M: 07702-519007 E: malcolm.bristow@ntlworld.com

BRISTOW, Canon Peter Edmund. b 49. Pontificium Institutum Internationale Angelicum Rome JCL 77 St Jos Coll Upholland 67. **d** 72 **p** 73. In RC Ch 72–87; C Poplar *Lon* 89–92; Lay Tr Officer 89–90; TV Droitwich Spa *Worc* 92–94; TR 94–00; V Boston Spa *York* 00–11; P-in-c Bramham 09–11; P-in-c Thorp Arch w Walton 00–11; V Bramham 11–17; RD New Ainsty 06–11; Can Asante Mampong Ghana from 14; rtd 17; PtO *York* from 18. *Craiglea, 8 Church Lane, Ormesby, Middlesbrough TS7 9AH* E: pebristow49@gmail.com

BRISTOW, Roger. b 60. Aston Tr Scheme 81 Ridley Hall Cam 83. **d** 86 **p** 87. C Leyton St Mary w St Edw *Chelmsf* 86–90; TV Kings Norton *Birm* 90–98; V Bromley H Trin *Roch* from 98. *Holy Trinity Vicarage, Church Lane, Bromley BR2 8LB* T/F: (020) 8462 1280 M: 07778-397224 E: vicar@htc-bc.org.uk

BRITT, Eric Stanley. b 47. St Jo Coll Nottm BTh 75. **d** 74 **p** 75. C Chorleywood Ch Ch *St Alb* 74–78; C Frimley *Guildf* 78–80; P-in-c Alresford *Chelmsf* 80–88; R Takeley w Lt Canfield 88–93; Asst Chapl R Free Hosp Lon 93–96; Chapl Mid-Essex Hosp Services NHS Trust 96–00; Chapl Algarve *Eur* 01–06; rtd 06; PtO *Ely* from 16. *5 De Lisle Close, Papworth Everard, Cambridge CB23 3UT* E: e.britt@btinternet.com

BRITT, Thomas Allen. b 90. Leeds Univ BA 12. Ripon Coll Cuddesdon BA 18. **d** 18 **p** 19. C Wanstead St Mary w Ch Ch *Chelmsf* from 18. *17 St David's Court, Grosvenor Road, London E11 2HH* E: tomallenbritt@gmail.com

BRITT, William Thomas. b 60. Westmr Coll Fulton (USA) BA 82. St Mellitus Coll BA 11. **d** 11 **p** 12. C Kempston Transfiguration *St Alb* 11–15; V Stotfold and Radwell from 15. *The Vicarage, 61 Church Road, Stotfold, Hitchin SG5 4NE* E: revd.bill.britt@gmail.com

BRITTON, Christine Mary. *See* BEECROFT, Christine Mary

BRITTON, David Robert. b 80. Leeds Univ BA 03 Fitzw Coll Cam BA 09. Ridley Hall Cam 07. **d** 10 **p** 11. C W Streatham St Jas *S'wark* 10–12; C Furzedown 12–14; V Leytonstone St Jo *Chelmsf* from 14. *St John's Vicarage, 44 Hartley Road, London E11 3BL* T: (020) 8279 7738 M: 07732-135178 E: rev.britton@gmail.com

BRITTON, John Timothy Hugh. b 50. Dundee Univ BSc 73. Trin Coll Bris 73. **d** 76 **p** 77. C Cromer *Nor* 76–79; P-in-c Freethorpe w Wickhampton 79–82; P-in-c Beighton and Moulton 79–82; P-in-c Halvergate w Tunstall 79–82; CMS 82–89; Uganda 83–89; R Allesley *Cov* 89–02; P-in-c Offchurch 02–15; P-in-c Long Itchington and Marton 02–15; P-in-c Wappenbury w Weston under Wetherley 02–15; P-in-c Hunningham 02–15; rtd 15; PtO *Nor* from 16; *Chelmsf* from 16. *49 Clifton Park, Cromer NR27 9BG* T: (01263) 512776 E: tim@brittonfamily.org.uk

BRITTON, Neil Bryan. b 35. Em Coll Cam BA 59 MA 63. Clifton Th Coll 61. **d** 63 **p** 64. C Eastbourne All SS *Chich* 63–67; C Ashtead *Guildf* 67–70; Chapl Scargill Ho 70–74; Chapl Aiglon Coll and Asst Chapl Villars *Eur* 74–78; In Reformed Ch of Switzerland 78–98; rtd 00; USA 01–05; PtO *Win* from 10. *Rose Cottage, 7 Newbury Road, Kingsclere, Newbury RG20 5SP* T: (01635) 297687 M: 07903-120368 E: britton.neil@googlemail.com

BRITTON, Canon Paul Anthony. b 29. SS Coll Cam BA 52 MA 57. Linc Th Coll 52. **d** 54 **p** 55. C Upper Norwood St Jo *Cant* 54–57; C Wantage Ox 57–61; V Stanmore *Win* 61–70; V Bitterne Park 70–80; Can Res Win Cathl 80–94; Lib Win Cathl *Worc* 81–85; Can Res and Treas Win Cathl 85–94; rtd 94; PtO *Sarum* from 94. *Pemberton, High Street, Hindon, Salisbury SP3 6DR* T: (01747) 820406 E: paul.britton02@virgin.net

BRITTON, Robert. b 37. Oak Hill Th Coll 78. **d** 79 **p** 80. C St Helens St Helen *Liv* 79–83; V Lowton St Mary 83–02; AD Winwick 89–01; rtd 02; PtO *Man* 03–14; *Liv* from 03. *15 Balmoral Avenue, Lowton, Warrington WA3 2ER* T: (01942) 711135

BRITTON, Ronald George Adrian Michael (Robert). b 24. Univ of State of NY BSc 78 Lambeth STh 82. St D Coll Lamp 63. **d** 82 **p** 82. Arabia 82–85; Chapl Alassio *Eur* 85–90; 92–93; Chapl San Remo 86; Hon C Southbourne St Kath *Win* 90–92; rtd 96; PtO *Bris* from 97. *2 Cherry Tree Road, Bristol BS16 4EY* T: 0117-965 5734 E: nonalienum@talktalk.net

BRITTON, Stephen Paul. b 55. Trin Coll Bris. **d** 12 **p** 13. OLM Longwell Green *Bris* from 12. *15 Central Avenue, Bristol BS15 3PG* T: 0117-961 4796 E: s.britton@btinternet.com *or* revds.britton@gmx.com

BRITTON, Timothy. *See* BRITTON, John Timothy Hugh

BRIXTON, Miss Corinne Jayne. b 63. Ex Univ BSc 84. Wycliffe Hall Ox BTh 95. **d** 95. C Leytonstone St Jo *Chelmsf* 95–00; C Buckhurst Hill 00–15; PtO *Win* from 16; C Hampstead St Jo Downshire Hill Prop Chpl *Lon* from 19. *2A Camfield Close, Basingstoke RG21 3AQ* T: (01256) 327840 E: cbrixton@aol.com

BRIXWORTH, Suffragan Bishop of. *See* HOLBROOK, The Rt Revd John Edward

BROAD, Mrs Christine Jane. b 63. Leeds Univ BSc 86 BA 06. NOC 03. **d** 06 **p** 07. C Newchapel *Lich* 06–09; TV Hanley H Ev 09–13; TR 13–16; C Oxton *Ches* 16–19; R Woodchurch from 19; Dean of Women in Min from 19. *Woodchurch Rectory, 1 Church Lane, Upton, Wirral CH49 7LS* E: christinejanebroad@virginmedia.com

BROAD, Canon Hugh Duncan. b 37. Lich Th Coll 64. **d** 67 **p** 68. C Heref H Trin 67–72; Asst Master Bp's Sch Heref 72–73; C Fareham SS Pet and Paul *Portsm* 74–76; V Heref All SS 76–90; R Matson *Glouc* 90–97; V Glouc St Geo w Whaddon 97–03; Hon Can Glouc Cathl 02–03; rtd 03; P-in-c Costa Almeria and Costa Calida *Eur* 03–13; Hon Can Gib Cathl 13. *44 Vensfield Road, Quedgeley, Gloucester GL2 4FX* E: hugh.broad@yahoo.co.uk

BROAD, Canon William Ernest Lionel. b 40. Ridley Hall Cam 64. **d** 66 **p** 67. C Ecclesfield *Sheff* 66–69; Chapl HM Pris Wormwood Scrubs 69; Chapl HM Pris Albany 70–74;

Chapl HM Rem Cen Risley 74–76; V Ditton St Mich *Liv* 76–81; TR 82–83; P-in-c Mayland and Steeple *Chelmsf* 83–91; V Blackhall *Dur* 91–97; TR Gt Aycliffe 97–03; P-in-c Chilton 03; TV Gt Aycliffe and Chilton 03–04; Hon Can Dur Cathl 02–04; rtd 04; PtO *Dur* from 04. *Moorcote, Thornley, Tow Law, Bishop Auckland DL13 4NU* T: (01388) 731350 E: broad054@gmail.com

BROADBENT, Mrs Doreen. b 36. d 94 p 95. OLM Stalybridge *Man* 94–02; PtO 02–14. *37 Ladysmith Road, Ashton-under-Lyne OL6 9DJ* T: 0161-330 9085 E: doreen261@btinternet.com

BROADBENT, Gerald. b 44. LRAM 64. Westcott Ho Cam 66. d 68 p 69. C Tilbury Docks *Chelmsf* 68–71; C Woodford St Mary w St Phil and St Jas 71–74; rtd 09. *7 West Terrace, Richmond DL10 4EQ* T: (01748) 824047 E: gerrybroad@aol.com

BROADBENT, Hugh Patrick Colin. b 53. Selw Coll Cam BA 75 MA. d 78 p 79. C Chatham St Steph *Roch* 78–82; C Shortlands 82–84; C Edenbridge 84–87; C Crockham Hill H Trin 84–87; V Bromley H Trin 87–97; V Bromley St Jo 97–09; Chapl St Olave's Gr Sch Orpington 95–09; R Snodland All SS w Ch Ch *Roch* 09–18; RD Cobham 11–13; rtd 18. *Mayfield, Pinesfield Lane, Trottiscliffe, West Malling ME19 5EL*

BROADBENT, Neil Seton. b 53. Qu Coll Birm. d 81 p 82. C Knaresborough *Ripon* 81–84; C Leeds Gipton Epiphany 84–87; Lic to Offic 87–89; Chapl Minstead Community *Derby* 89; PtO from 89; Dir Sozein from 93. *The Old Vicarage, Church Lane, Horsley Woodhouse, Ilkeston DE7 6BB* T: (01332) 780598 E: neil.broadbent@sozein.org.uk

BROADBENT, Paul John. b 41. Oak Hill Th Coll 83. d 85 p 86. C Duston *Pet* 85–88; TV Ross w Brampton Abbotts, Bridstow and Peterstow *Heref* 88–91; R Pattishall w Cold Higham and Gayton w Tiffield *Pet* 91–10; rtd 10; P-in-c Fairwarp *Chich* 10–16; PtO from 16; *S'wark* from 17; *Guildf* from 18. *1 Glebe Cottages, Village Street, Newdigate, Dorking RH5 5AA* T: (01306) 631687 M: 07786-865015 E: pj.broadbent1@btinternet.com

✠**BROADBENT, The Rt Revd Peter Alan.** b 52. Jes Coll Cam BA 74 MA 78. St Jo Coll Nottm 74. d 77 p 78 c 01. C Dur St Nic 77–80; C Holloway Em w Hornsey Road St Barn *Lon* 80–83; Chapl N Lon Poly 83–89; Hon C Islington St Mary 83–89; V Harrow Trin St Mich 89–94; Adn Harrow 94; Adn Northolt 95–01; P-in-c Southall H Trin 98–99; Area Bp Willesden from 01. *173 Willesden Lane, London NW6 7YN* T: (020) 8451 0189 F: 8451 4606 M: 07957-144674 E: bishop.willesden@btinternet.com

BROADBENT, Ralph Andrew. b 55. K Coll Lon BD 76 AKC 76 Birm Univ PhD 04. Chich Th Coll 77. d 78 p 79. C Prestwich St Mary *Man* 78–82; R Man Miles Platting 82–84; CF 84–87; TV Wordsley *Lich* 88–93; Chapl Wordsley Hosp 88–93; Chapl Ridge Hill Hosp 88–93; V Wollescote *Worc* 93–15; rtd 15. *273 route des Corbières, 16100 Boutiers-Saint-Trojan, France* E: ralphbroadbent1@icloud.com

BROADBENT, Thomas William. b 45. Chu Coll Cam BA 66 MA 70 PhD 70. Ridley Hall Cam 75. d 78 p 79. C Allington and Maidstone St Pet *Cant* 78–82; Chapl Mid Kent Coll of H&FE 80–82; C Kings Heath *Birm* 82–84; Hon C Pendleton St Thos *Man* 84–89; TV Pendleton St Thos w Charlestown 89–92; Chapl Salford Univ 84–92; P-in-c Claydon and Barham *St E* 92–08; P-in-c Coddenham w Gosbeck and Hemingstone w Henley 99–08; P-in-c Gt and Lt Blakenham w Baylham and Nettlestead 02–08; Chapl Suffolk Coll 92–00; P-in-c Witham Gp *Linc* 08–14; rtd 14; PtO *Linc* 15–18. *8 Abbey Road, Bardney, Lincoln LN3 5XA* T: (01526) 397101 E: broadbentevans@btinternet.com

BROADHEAD, Mrs Lynn. b 59. Yorks Min Course 08. d 11 p 12. NSM Thorpe Hesley *Sheff* 11–13; NSM Greasbrough 13–15; V Thorpe Hesley from 15. *The Vicarage, 30 Barnsley Road, Thorpe Hesley, Rotherham S61 2RR* T: 0114-246 3487 M: 07811-336183 E: revd.lynn.broadhead@sky.com

BROADHURST, Dorothy Bronwyn. b 48. Lon Univ LLB 70 MPhil 76. d 19. NSM Pocklington Wold *York* from 19; NSM Londesborough Wold from 19. *21 Pinewood Road, Pocklington, York YO42 2UZ* T: (01759) 307479 M: 07950-049891 E: bronnie.broadhurst@hotmail.com

BROADHURST, Jonathan Robin. b 58. Univ Coll Ox BA 81 MA 86. Wycliffe Hall Ox 85. d 88 p 89. C Hull St Jo Newland *York* 88–91; P-in-c Burton Fleming w Fordon, Grindale etc 91–92; V 92–98; C Kingston upon Hull H Trin 98–01; P-in-c Rastrick St Jo *Wakef* 01–06; rtd 06; PtO *Leeds* from 17. *1 Moravian Terrace, Halifax HX3 8AL* T: (01422) 209549 M: 07790-899195

BROADIE, Stephen Kim. b 76. Leeds Univ BA 99 Bris Univ PGCE 03. Ridley Hall Cam 10. d 12 p 13. C Welling *Roch* 12–16; C Farnborough from 16. *Church House, Leamington Avenue, Orpington BR6 9QB* M: 07722-428553 E: sjwcurate@gmail.com

BRODIE, Michael John. b 66. Roehampton Inst BA 87. Trin Coll Bris 89. d 96 p 97. C Egham *Guildf* 96–01; TV Horsham *Chich* 01–10; P-in-c Loughborough Em and St Mary in Charnwood *Leic* 10–14; P-in-c Loughborough Em from 15. *Emmanuel Rectory, 47 Forest Road, Loughborough LE11 3NW* T: (01509) 263264 E: broadley@bigfoot.com

BROADWAY, Mark Philip. b 87. Glam Univ LLB 09 Cardiff Univ MTh 14. St Mich Coll Llan 14. d 17 p 18. C Coity, Nolton and Brackla w Coychurch *Llan* from 17. *1 Cae Rhedyn, Coity, Bridgend CF35 6AQ* T: (01656) 652788 E: mark@cnb-parish.org.uk

BROCK, Michael John. b 52. Birm Univ BSc 74. St Jo Coll Nottm BA 77. d 78 p 79. C Stapleford *S'well* 78–82; C Bestwood St Matt 82–86; TV Bestwood 86–90; R Epperstone 90–05; R Gonalston 90–05; V Oxton 90–05; P-in-c Woodborough 02–05; RD S'well 93–96; Dioc Adv in Rural Affairs 97–02; R Dersingham w Anmer and Shernborne *Nor* 05–15; RD Heacham and Rising 07–11; C Snettisham w Ingoldisthorpe and Fring 14–15; rtd 15; P-in-c Sutton Bonington w Normanton-on-Soar *S'well* 15–19. *133 Ashby Road, Loughborough LE11 3AB* E: mjb65@btinternet.com

BROCKBANK, Arthur Ross. b 51. NOC 87. d 90 p 91. C Haughton St Mary *Man* 90–93; V Bircle 93–12; C Walmersley 04; Chapl Bury Healthcare NHS Trust 93–02; Chapl Co-ord Pennine Acute Hosps NHS Trust 02–03; rtd 12; Chapl Jospice from 14; Chapl Alder Hey Children's NHS Foundn Trust from 14; PtO *Liv* from 14. *12 Dickinson Road, Liverpool L37 4BX* T: (01704) 461346

BROCKBANK, Donald Philip. b 56. Univ of Wales (Ban) BD 78. Sarum & Wells Th Coll 79. d 81 p 82. C Prenton *Ches* 81–85; TV Birkenhead Priory 85–91; V Altrincham St Jo 91–96; Urban Officer 91–96; Dioc Ecum Officer *Lich* 96–98; C Lich St Mich w St Mary and Wall 96–98; V Acton and Worleston, Church Minshull etc *Ches* 98–06; rtd 07; Dioc Adv in Spirituality *Ches* 07–12; PtO from 12. *1 Plover Avenue, Winsford CW7 1LA* T: (01606) 593651 E: brockbankrev@gmail.com

BROCKBANK, John Keith. b 44. Dur Univ BA 65. Wells Th Coll 66. d 68 p 69. C Preston St Matt *Blackb* 68–71; C Lancaster St Mary 71–73; V Habergham All SS 73–83; P-in-c Gannow 81–83; V W Burnley All SS 83–86; Dioc Stewardship Adv 86–92; P-in-c Shireshead 86–92; V Kirkham 92–09; rtd 09; PtO *Blackb* from 09. *44 Esthwaite Gardens, Lancaster LA1 3RG* T: (01524) 847520 E: revjkb@talktalk.net

BROCKBANK, John Stanley. b 41. CBDTI 97. d 00 p 01. OLM Arnside *Carl* 00–11; rtd 11; PtO *Carl* from 11. *Hough Close, 5 Ash Meadow Road, Arnside, Carnforth LA5 0AE* T: (01524) 761634

BROCKHOUSE, Canon Grant Lindley. b 47. Adelaide Univ BA 71 Ex Univ MA 81. St Barn Coll Adelaide 70. d 73 p 74. C Edwardstown w Ascot Park Australia 73–74; Tutor St Barn Coll Belair 74–78; C Ex St Jas 78–80; Asst Chapl Ex Univ 80–83; V Marldon 83–98; Dep PV Ex Cathl 81–98; RD Torbay 95–98; V Higham Ferrers w Chelveston *Pet* 98–13; RD Higham 03–11; Can Pet Cathl 07–13; rtd 13; PtO *Pet* from 14. *71 Bishops Road, Peterborough PE1 5AS* T: (01733) 753339 E: grantbrockhouse@gmail.com

BROCKIE, Canon William James Thomson. b 36. Pemb Coll Ox BA 58 MA 62. Linc Th Coll 58. d 60 p 61. C Lin St Jo Bapt CD *Linc* 60–63; V Gt Staughton *Ely* 63–68; Chapl HM Borstal Gaynes Hall 63–68; TV Edin St Jo 68–76; Chapl Edin Univ 71–76; USA 76; R Edin St Martin 76–01; P-in-c Wester Hailes St Luke 79–90; Hon Can St Mary's Cathl from 98; rtd 00; Hon C Edin St Hilda and Edin St Fillan 02–03. *31 Holly Bank, Edinburgh EH11 1SP* T: 0131-337 6482 E: billjennybrockie@hotmail.com

BROCKLEHURST, Ian Christopher. b 62. Nottm Univ BMedSci 83 BM, BS 85 FRCA 93. All SS Cen for Miss & Min 12. d 15 p 16. NSM Coldhurst and Oldham St Steph *Man* 15–18; NSM Mossley from 18; NSM Roughtown from 18. *4 Higher Lydgate Park, Grasscroft, Oldham OL4 4EF* T: (01457) 877731 E: iancb53@btinternet.com

BROCKLEHURST, Simon. b 63. Cranmer Hall Dur 86. d 89 p 90. C Clifton *S'well* 89–93; TV 93–96; P-in-c Mabe *Truro* 96–99; Miss to Seamen 96–99; V Ham St Andr *S'wark* 99–16; P-in-c Southwick w Boarhunt *Portsm* from 16; Inland Hon Chapl Miss to Seafarers from 00. *White House, 13 High Street, Southwick, Fareham PO17 6EB* T: (023) 9238 0802 E: revsimonb@btinternet.com

BRODIE, Miss Ann. b 55. Ex Univ BA 76 PGCE 77. St Jo Coll Nottm 03. d 05 p 06. C Putney St Marg *S'wark* 05–09; P-in-c 09–12; V 12–17; PtO from 18. *1 Alfriston Road, London SW11 6NS*

BRODIE, Frederick. b 40. Leic Teacher Tr Coll TCert 61. St Jo Coll Nottm 90. d 92 p 93. C Lutterworth w Cotesbach *Leic* 92–95; P-in-c Mountsorrel Ch Ch and St Pet 95–97; V

97–03; rtd 03; PtO *Leic* from 03. *25 Stuart Court, High Street, Kibworth Beauchamp, Leicester LE8 0LR* M: 07710-461865 E: fesbrodie@btinternet.com

BROGGIO, Bernice Muriel Croager. b 35. Bedf Coll Lon BA 57 K Coll Lon BD 66 Glas Univ DASS 72. **dss** 84 **d** 87 **p** 94. Bris St Paul w St Barn 84–87; Hon Par Dn Bris St Paul's 87–88; C Charlton St Luke w H Trin *S'wark* 88–95; V Upper Tooting H Trin 95–03; Hon Can *S'wark* Cathl 95–03; RD Tooting 96–02; TV Bensham *Dur* 03–05; PtO 05–06; Hon C Bensham 06–07; Hon C Birtley from 07; PtO *Eur* from 10; rtd 06. *86 Woodburn, Gateshead NE10 8LY* T: 0191-495 0959 M: 07900-327316 E: b.broggio@btinternet.com

BROKENSHIRE, Phillip Laurence. b 87. Ex Univ BSc 10. Wycliffe Hall Ox BTh 16. **d** 16. C Ex H Trin from 16. *48 Mulligan Drive, Exeter EX2 7SJ* M: 07401-867876 E: phillipbrokenshire@yahoo.co.uk

BROMFIELD, Michael. b 32. Kelham Th Coll 54 Lich Th Coll 59. **d** 62 **p** 63. C Sedgley All SS *Lich* 62–64; C Tunstall Ch Ch 64–67; P-in-c Grindon 67–70; R 70–80; P-in-c Butterton 67–70; V 70–80; R Hope Bowdler w Eaton-under-Heywood *Heref* 80–97; R Rushbury 80–97; V Cardington 80–97; rtd 98; PtO *Lich* from 98. *11 Walklate Avenue, Newcastle ST5 0PR* T: (01782) 630716 E: pbromfield@btinternet.com

BROMFIELD, Nicholas Robert. b 60. St Jo Coll Cam MA 82. WEMTC 98. **d** 02 **p** 03. C Tidenham w Beachley and Lancaut *Glouc* 02–07; C St Briavels w Hewelsfield 05–07; R Drybrook, Lydbrook and Ruardean 07–16; TR N Cheltenham from 16. *The Rectory, Tatchley Lane, Prestbury, Cheltenham GL52 3DQ* E: bromfields@email.msn.com or revbromfield@btinternet.com

BROMFIELD, Richard Allan. b 47. Sussex Univ MA 96 LVCM 85. Chich Th Coll 86. **d** 88 **p** 89. C Durrington *Chich* 88–95; V Woodingdean 95–12; Chapl Nuffield Hosp Brighton 96–12; rtd 12; PtO *Chich* 12–17. *34 Rowan Way, Angmering, Littlehampton BN16 4FW* E: r.a.bromfield@btinternet.com

BROMILEY, Philip Arthur. b 73. Westmr Coll Ox BTh 94 St Jo Coll Dur MA 98. Cranmer Hall Dur 95. **d** 98 **p** 99. C Marton *Blackb* 98–01; Assoc P Calne and Blackland *Sarum* 01–06; P-in-c Oldbury 06–08; R 08–17; TR Avon River from 17. *The Rectory, Church Street, Durrington, Salisbury SP4 8AL* T: (01980) 258549 E: philbromiley@gmail.com

BROMLEY, Deborah Joan. *See* SCOTT-BROMLEY, Deborah Joan

BROMLEY, Richard. b 60. Birm Chr Coll MA 02. Qu Foundn Birm 08. **d** 08 **p** 09. NSM Binley *Cov* 08–11; PtO from 11; Miss Dir ICS from 13; PtO *Eur* from 16. *Intercontinental Church Society, Unit 11, Ensign Business Centre, Westwood Way, Westwood Business Park, Coventry CV4 8JA* T: (024) 7646 3940 M: 07772-496029 E: rbromley@ics-uk.org

BROMLEY, Mrs Tracy Le Couteur. STETS 06. **d** 09 **p** 10. NSM Jersey St Clem *Win* from 09; Chapl Jersey Gp of Hosps from 10. *11 Oakland Vineries, Rue du Presbytere, St Clement, Jersey JE2 6RB* T: (01534) 857693 E: tracylecouteur@hotmail.com

BROMLEY AND BEXLEY, Archdeacon of. *See* WRIGHT, The Ven Paul

BRONNERT, Preb David Llewellyn Edward. b 36. Ch Coll Cam BA 57 MA 61 PhD 61 Lon Univ BD 62. Tyndale Hall Bris 60. **d** 63 **p** 64. C Cheadle Hulme St Andr *Ches* 63–67; C Islington St Mary *Lon* 67–69; Chapl N Lon Poly 69–75; V Southall Green St Jo 75–01; Preb St Paul's Cathl 89–01; P-in-c Southall St Geo 92–99; AD Ealing W 84–90; rtd 01; PtO *Ox* from 04. *101 Walton Way, Aylesbury HP21 7JP* T: (01296) 484048 E: david.bronnert@talk21.com

BRONNERT, John. b 33. Man Univ MA(Theol) 84 Univ of Wales (Lamp) PhD 98 ACA 57 FCA 68. Tyndale Hall Bris 65. **d** 68 **p** 69. C Hoole *Ches* 68–71; P-in-c Parr *Liv* 71–73; TV 73–85; V Runcorn St Jo Weston *Ches* 85–98; rtd 98; PtO *Liv* 85–04; *Man* 98–14. *Tyndale, 15 Craig Avenue, Flixton, Urmston, Manchester M41 5RS* T: 0161-748 7061

BROOK, David Thomas. b 46. **d** 11 **p** 12. OLM Lt Aston *Lich* 11–15; OLM Burntwood, Chase Terrace etc 15–16; rtd 16; PtO *Lich* from 16. *16 Brentnall Drive, Sutton Coldfield B75 5BB* T: 0121-353 6106 E: dtbrook9@gmail.com

BROOK, John Brendan Paul. b 79. CCC Ox MEng 01. Oak Hill Th Coll BA 06. **d** 06 **p** 07. C Hailsham *Chich* 06–10; Min The Haven CD from 10; C Eastbourne H Trin from 15. *1 Columbus Drive, Eastbourne BN23 6RR* T: (01323) 325989 E: revjbrook@bfol.org

BROOK, Neville. *See* BROOK, William Neville

BROOK, Priestly. b 42. CBDTI 04. **d** 07 **p** 08. NSM Colne and Villages *Blackb* 07–12; rtd 12; PtO *Blackb* from 12; *Bradf* 13–14; *Leeds* from 14. *The Coach House, Foulds Road, Trawden, Colne BB8 8NT* T: (01282) 869876 E: priestlybrook1@btinternet.com

BROOK, Stephen Edward. b 44. Univ of Wales (Abth) BSc 64 DipEd 66. Wycliffe Hall Ox 71 All Nations Chr Coll 85.

d 74 **p** 75. C Heworth H Trin *York* 74–77; C Linthorpe 77–80; TV Deane *Man* 80–85; Crosslinks 86–96; Portugal 88–96; P-in-c Bacup St Sav *Man* 96–03; P-in-c Tunstead 99–03; V Blackpool St Mark *Blackb* 03–12; P-in-c Blackpool St Mich 10–12; V Layton and Staining 12; rtd 12; PtO *Leic* from 13. *35 Oakham Grove, Ashby-de-la-Zouche LE65 2QP* E: revstephenbrook@gmail.com

BROOK, William Neville. b 31. S'wark Ord Course 66. **d** 69 **p** 70. C Maidstone St Martin *Cant* 69–75; V Hartlip w Stockbury 75–80; R Willesborough w Hinxhill 80–87; R Willesborough 87–89; V Gt Staughton and Hail Weston *Ely* 89–96; rtd 96; PtO *Chich* from 96. *73 Drummond Grove, Willesborough, Ashford TN24 0US* T: (01233) 632765

BROOKE, Ailsa Rosanne. b 47. Yorks Min Course 10. **d** 12 **p** 13. NSM Upper Holme Valley *Wakef* 12–14; *Leeds* from 14. *20 Fulstone Hall Lane, New Mill, Holmfirth HD9 7DW* T: (01484) 681155 E: ailsabrooke@tinyworld.co.uk

BROOKE, Miss Bridget Cecilia. b 31. Coll of Resurr Mirfield 88. **d** 89 **p** 94. Hon Par Dn Ranmoor *Sheff* 89–94; Hon C 94–04; Bp's Adv for NSMs 94–01; PtO from 04. *3 Magnolia Court, Storth Lane, Sheffield S10 3HN* T: 0114-230 2147 E: revbridgetbrooke@gmail.com

BROOKE, David Fewsdale. b 43. St Paul's Coll Grahamstown 80. **d** 90 **p** 90. Asst Chapl Dioc Coll Cape Town S Africa 90–92; NSM Crawford St Jo 93–97; NSM Sea Point St Jas 98–99; PtO *Newc* 00; C Norham and Duddo 01–04; C Cornhill w Carham 01–04; C Branxton 01–04; R Dunkeld *St And* 04–13; R Strathtay 04–13. *43 Innewan Gardens, Bankfoot, Perth PH1 4AZ* M: 07840-183707

BROOKE, David Martin. b 58. Selw Coll Cam BA 80 MA 83 Lon Inst of Educn PGCE 81. SAOMC 96. **d** 99 **p** 00. C Luton Lewsey St Hugh *St Alb* 99–00; NSM Sunnyside w Bourne End 00–02; C 02–04; V Bishopton w Gt Stainton *Dur* 04–13; R Redmarshall 04–13; R Grindon and Stillington 04–13; R Stockton Country Par 14–16; P-in-c Billingham St Mary 10–13; AD Stockton 07–16; NSM Stockton St Thos 16–18; Lead Miss Support Partner 16–18; Hon Can Dur Cathl 16–18; TR Chapelfields *Liv* from 18. *10 St Nathaniel's Close, Platt Bridge, Wigan WN2 3FT* M: 07967-326085 E: revdbrooke@gmail.com

BROOKE, Katherine Margaret. b 58. GRSM 79 LRAM 80 ARCM 80. SAOMC 01. **d** 04 **p** 05. C Auckland St Andr and St Anne *Dur* 04–07; C Stranton 07–11; Chapl HM Pris Holme Ho 11–18; Managing Chapl from 18. *HM Prison Holme House, Holme House Road, Stockton-on-Tees TS18 2QU* T: (01642) 744000 M: 07973-539729 E: katherine.brooke@justice.gov.uk

BROOKE, Canon Robert. b 44. Qu Coll Birm 70. **d** 73 **p** 74. C Man Resurr 73–76; C Bournville *Birm* 76–77; Chapl Qu Eliz Coll *Lon* 77–82; C Bramley *Ripon* 82–85; TV 85–86; V Hunslet Moor St Pet and St Cuth 86–93; Chapl People w Learning Disabilities 86–14; *Leeds* from 14; TV Seacroft *Ripon* 93–03; TV Beeston 03–10; Chapl Leeds Mental Health Teaching NHS Trust 94–03; Hon Can Ripon Cathl 01–10; rtd 10. *103 Crossgates Road, Leeds LS15 7PA* E: bob.brooke@another.com or bob.brooke@hotmail.co.uk

BROOKE, Canon Rosemary Jane. b 53. Newnham Coll Cam BEd 75 Open Univ BA 84. NOC 86. **d** 89 **p** 94. NSM Poynton *Ches* 89–05; Bp's Adv for Women in Min 96–05; P-in-c Werneth 05–10; Can Res Ches Cathl from 10. *3 Bridge Place, Chester CH1 1SA* T: (01244) 351432 E: scrolls2@btinternet.com

BROOKE, Timothy Cyril. b 38. Jes Coll Cam BA 60 MA 70 Middx Poly CQSW 76. Ripon Coll Cuddesdon 84. **d** 86 **p** 87. C Hillmorton *Cov* 86–90; V Earlsdon 90–98; V Cov St Fran N Radford 98–05; rtd 05; PtO *Cov* from 05; *Leic* from 15; *Eur* from 05. *80 Broadway, Coventry CV5 6NU* T: (024) 7667 9126 E: brooke@care4free.net

BROOKE, Vernon. b 41. St Aid Birkenhead 62. **d** 65 **p** 66. C Crofton Park St Hilda w St Cypr *S'wark* 65–68; C Eccleshill *Bradf* 68–70; Ind Chapl *Linc* 70–84; *Derby* 84–97; Chich 97–06; rtd 06; PtO *Pet* from 06. *5 Blakesley Close, Northampton NN2 8PA* T: (01604) 845585 E: vernonbrooke@yahoo.co.uk

BROOKE-TAYLOR, John Drury Arthur. b 48. Cam Univ BA 69 MA 73 Solicitor 72. Trin Coll Bris 11. **d** 13 **p** 14. OLM Clifton H Trin, St Andr and St Pet *Bris* from 13; OLM Bris St Steph w St Jas and St Jo w St Mich etc from 14. *2 Oldfield Road, Bristol BS8 4QQ* T: 0117-926 5517 E: drbrooketaylor@outlook.com

BROOKER, Mrs Anna Lesley. b 56. York Univ BA 78 MA 79 Homerton Coll Cam PGCE 80. SAOMC 01. **d** 03 **p** 04. C Brentford *Lon* 03–06; P-in-c Isleworth All SS 06–11; V 11–15; Dean of Women's Min Kensington Area

12–15; P-in-c Haswell and Shotton *Dur* 15–19; P-in-c S Hetton 18–19; P-in-c Brancepeth from 19; Chapl St Jo Coll Dur from 19. *The Rectory, Brancepeth, Durham DH7 8EL* E: albrooker@email.com *or* anna.brooker@durham.ac.uk

BROOKES, Colin Stuart. b 70. Lon Bible Coll BA 93. Ridley Hall Cam 00. **d** 02 **p** 03. C Cambridge St Barn *Ely* 02–06; C Woodside Park St Barn *Lon* 06–19; C Oseney Crescent St Luke from 19. *St Barnabas' Vicarage, 68 Westbury Road, London N12 7PD* T: (020) 8343 6144 M: 07973-840340

BROOKES, David Charles. b 45. St Mich Coll Llan 84. **d** 86 **p** 87. C Llanishen and Lisvane *Llan* 86–88; TV Brighouse St Martin *Wakef* 89–92; TV Brighouse and Clifton 92–94; V Hollingbourne and Hucking w Leeds and Broomfield *Cant* 94–03; rtd 03. *19 Orchards Rise, Richards Castle, Ludlow SY8 4EZ* T: (01584) 831276

BROOKES, Edwin William. b 39. St Mark & St Jo Coll Lon TCert 63 Birm Univ BPhil(Ed) 85 Open Univ BA 73 BA 93. OLM course 95. **d** 98 **p** 99. OLM Cen Wolverhampton *Lich* 98–19; PtO 19. *104 Napier Road, Wolverhampton WV2 3DX* T: (01902) 654979 F: 562616 E: ed.brookes@blueyonder.co.uk

BROOKES, Laurence. b 33. **d** 02 **p** 03. OLM Flockton cum Denby Grange *Wakef* 02–06; OLM Emley 02–06; PtO 06–14; *Leeds* from 14. *Treetops, 6 Chessington Drive, Flockton, Wakefield WF4 4TJ* T: (01924) 848238 E: lauriemarybrookes@supanet.com

BROOKES, Steven David. b 60. Lanc Univ BA 81. Ripon Coll Cuddesdon 82. **d** 85 **p** 86. C Stanley *Liv* 85–88; C W Derby St Mary 88–90; Chapl RN 90–94; R Weybridge *Guildf* 94–03; P-in-c Liv Our Lady and St Nic w St Anne 03–07; R Liv Our Lady and St Nic 07–13; Chapl R Hosp Chelsea from 13; Dep P in O from 19. *15 College Court, Royal Hospital Chelsea, Royal Hospital Road, London SW3 4SR* T: (020) 7881 5238 *or* 7881 5234 M: 07930-855146 E: chaplain@chelsea-pensioners.org.uk

BROOKFIELD, Patricia Anne. *See* HARDACRE, Patricia Anne

BROOKS, Mrs Christine Anne. b 62. STETS. **d** 09 **p** 10. C N Poole Ecum Team *Sarum* 09–13; C Kinson and W Howe 13–14; TV from 14. *41 Moore Avenue, Bournemouth BH11 8AT* T: (01202) 581135 *or* 911962 E: christine.brooks3@uwclub.net

BROOKS, Mrs Christine Ellen. b 43. Sheff Univ BA 65 Lon Univ BD 81 Lambeth STh 81. EAMTC 86. **d** 88 **p** 94. NSM Palgrave w Wortham and Burgate *St E* 88–89; Par Dn Thorndon w Rishangles, Stoke Ash, Thwaite etc 89–94; P-in-c Aldringham w Thorpe, Knodishall w Buxlow etc 94–04; R Whinlands 04–13; Asst P Sternfield w Benhall and Snape 98–03; P-in-c Alde River 03–06; rtd 13; PtO *St E* from 13. *Far End Cottage, Low Road, Friston, Saxmundham IP17 1PW* T: (01728) 688972 M: 07752-652833 E: cebwhinlands@btinternet.com

BROOKS, David Edward. b 73. **d** 09 **p** 10. OLM Middleton and Thornham *Man* from 09. *St Michael's Vicarage, 184 Kirkway, Manchester M24 1LN* T: 0161-643 4477 M: 07904-520906 E: dave@thelaunch.org.uk *or* revdavidbrooks@middletonparishchurch.org.uk

BROOKS, Dorothy Anne. *See* MOORE BROOKS, Dorothy Anne

BROOKS, Glen. b 62. Ripon Coll Cuddesdon 12. **d** 14 **p** 15. C Northampton H Trin and St Paul *Pet* 14–17; P-in-c Somerleyton, Ashby, Fritton, Herringfleet etc *Nor* 17–18; R from 18; CF (ACF) from 16. *The Rectory, The Street, Somerleyton, Lowestoft NR32 5PT* T: (01502) 732420 E: frglen@outlook.com

BROOKS, Hannah Victoria. *See* HIGGINSON, Hannah Victoria

BROOKS, Jeremy Paul. b 67. Leic Univ LLB 88 Clare Coll Cam BA 96 MA 01 K Coll Lon MA 00 DMin 12. Ridley Hall Cam 94. **d** 97 **p** 98. C Highgate St Mich *Lon* 97–01; P-in-c Hoddesdon *St Alb* 01–07; V 07–10; TR Beaconsfield *Ox* from 10. *The Rectory, Wycombe End, Beaconsfield HP9 1NB* T: (01494) 730876 E: rector@stmarysbeaconsfield.org.uk

BROOKS, Malcolm David. b 45. **d** 71 **p** 72. C Pontlottyn w Fochriw *Llan* 71–72; C Caerphilly 72–78; V Ferndale w Maerdy 78–81; C Port Talbot St Theodore 82–84; V Ystrad Mynach 84–85; V Ystrad Mynach w Llanbradach 85–06. *33 Heol y Gors, Whitchurch, Cardiff CF14 1HF*

BROOKS (née LEWIS), Mrs Marjorie Ann. b 47. Liv Univ BA 68 Man Univ CertEd 69. WEMTC 07. **d** 13 **p** 14. OLM Bridgnorth, Tasley, Astley Abbotts, etc *Heref* 13–16; NSM Bridgnorth and Morville Par from 16. *2 The Hawthorns, Bridgnorth WV16 5JG* T: (01746) 761942 M: 07751-553736 E: marjorie.brooks47@googlemail.com

BROOKS, Michael. b 57. K Coll Lon BSc 78 MB, BS 81 AKC 81. SEITE 05. **d** 08 **p** 09. NSM Sydenham H Trin and St Aug *S'wark* 08–19; NSM Honor Oak Park St Aug from 19; AD

W Lewisham from 17. *Holy Trinity Church, 4 Trinity Path, Sydenham SE26 4EA* T: (020) 7771 3541 M: 07730-885187 E: michael@mybroadbandmail.com

BROOKS, Patrick John. b 27. Man Univ BA 49 DipEd. Oak Hill Th Coll 78. **d** 77 **p** 79. Burundi 77–80; PtO *Ex* 80–83; P-in-c Phillack w Gwithian and Gwinear *Truro* 83–88; R 88–93; rtd 93; PtO *Chich* from 93. *Abbots, Claigmar Road, Rustington, Littlehampton BN16 2NL* T: (01903) 784660 E: pbrooks08@googlemail.com

BROOKS, Paul John. b 59. Loughb Univ BSc 81. St Jo Coll Nottm 87. **d** 90 **p** 91. C Long Eaton St Jo *Derby* 90–94; Min Jersey St Paul Prop Chpl *Win* from 94. *5 Claremont Avenue, St Saviour, Jersey JE2 7SF* T: (01534) 880393

BROOKS, Canon Peter. b 55. St Mich Coll Llan 97. **d** 99 **p** 00. C Morriston *S & B* 99–01; P-in-c Rhayader and Nantmel 01–02; P-in-c Cwmdauddwr w St Harmon and Llanwrthwl 02–05; P-in-c Llanwrthwl w St Harmon, Rhayader, Nantmel etc 05–08; P-in-c Gwastedyn 08–11; V Three Cliffs from 11; AD Gower 14–15; AD Gtr Gower from 16; Can Res Brecon Cathl from 15. *The Vicarage, 88 Pennard Road, Pennard, Swansea SA3 2AD* T: (01792) 232928 E: peter.brooks256@btinternet.com

BROOKS, Philip. b 82. Reading Univ BA 03 MA 04 K Coll Lon MA 10. Ridley Hall Cam 10. **d** 13 **p** 14. C Oxted *S'wark* 13–16; TV Sutton from 16. *Christchurch Vicarage, 14C Christchurch Park, Sutton SM2 5TN* M: 07969-066906 E: phil_brooks1982@hotmail.com

BROOKS, Philip David. b 52. MA Cam Univ MTh. St Jo Coll Nottm 80. **d** 83 **p** 84. C Ipsley *Worc* 83–87; V Fulford w Hilderstone *Lich* 87–95; Chapl Stallington Hosp 87–95; P-in-c Crich *Derby* 95–01; V Crich and S Wingfield 01–17; Dioc Adv Past Care and Counselling 03–09; RD Alfreton 09–16; rtd 17; PtO *Dur* from 18. *10 Bedale Close, Durham DH1 2BB* E: philipdbro@aol.com

BROOKS, Mrs Susan Vera. b 51. NOC 87. **d** 90 **p** 94. Par Dn Carleton and E Hardwick *Wakef* 90–93; TV Almondbury w Farnley Tyas 93–98; Chapl Huddersfield NHS Trust 98–01; Chapl Calderdale and Huddersfield NHS Trust 01–03; Lead Chapl 03–12; NSM Crosland Moor and Linthwaite *Wakef* 12–14; *Leeds* from 14. *5 Miry Lane, Thongsbridge, Holmfirth HD9 7SA* T: (01484) 538778

BROOKS, Mrs Vivien June. b 47. Univ of Wales (Ban) BA 68 Southn Univ MA 70. Ridley Hall Cam 87. **d** 89 **p** 95. C Exning St Martin w Landwade *St E* 89–92; Par Dn Hermitage and Hampstead Norreys, Cold Ash etc *Ox* 92–94; C 94–95; P-in-c Cox Green 95–03; Co Ecum Officer (Berks) 00–03; P-in-c Earls Colne w White Colne and Colne Engaine *Chelmsf* 03–04; TV Halstead Area 04–12; rtd 12; PtO *St E* 13–18; *Chelmsf* 14–18; *Sarum* from 18. *104 Castleview Road, Chiseldon, Swindon SN4 0NT* T: (01793) 741286 E: vivienbrooks@gmail.com

BROOKS, Vivienne Christine. *See* ARMSTRONG-MacDONNELL, Vivienne Christine

BROOKSBANK, Alan Watson. b 43. Univ of Wales (Lamp) BA 64 Edin Univ MEd 76. Edin Th Coll 64. **d** 66 **p** 67. C Cleator Moor w Cleator *Carl* 66–70; V Dalston 70–80; P-in-c Greystoke, Matterdale and Mungrisdale 80–81; R 81–83; R Watermillock 80–83; R Hagley *Worc* 83–95; Bp's Officer for NSM 88–95; V Claines St Jo 95–98; rtd 98. *169 Northfields Lane, Brixham TQ5 8RD* E: awbrooksbank@gmail.com

BROOKSHAW, Miss Janice Chitty. b 48. Anglia Ruskin Univ MA 12 MCIPD 90. Ripon Coll Cuddesdon 96. **d** 98 **p** 99. C Beaconsfield *Ox* 98–02; P-in-c The Stodden Churches *St Alb* 02–03; R 03–14; rtd 14; PtO *Win* 14–16; C Upper Itchen from 16. *3 The Old Dairy, Easton, Winchester SO21 1EU* T: (01962) 779988 E: revjanb@gmail.com

BROOM, The Ven Andrew Clifford. b 65. Keele Univ BSocSc 86. Trin Coll Bris BA 92. **d** 92 **p** 93. C Wellington All SS w Eyton *Lich* 92–96; C Brampton St Thos *Derby* 96–00; V Walton St Jo 00–09; Dir of Miss and Min 09–14; Hon Can Derby Cathl 11–14; Adn E Riding *York* from 14. *Brimley Lodge, 27 Molescroft Road, Beverley HU17 7DX* T: (01482) 881659 E: ader@yorkdiocese.org

BROOME, Mildred Dorothy. b 43. **d** 00 **p** 01. NSM Malden St Jo *S'wark* 00–13; PtO from 13. *124 The Manor Drive, Worcester Park KT4 7LW* T: (020) 8337 1572 E: m.broome@hotmail.co.uk

BROOMFIELD, Iain Jonathan. b 57. Univ Coll Ox MA 87. Wycliffe Hall Ox 80. **d** 83 **p** 84. C Beckenham Ch Ch *Roch* 83–87; Sen Schs Worker Titus Trust 87–00; V Bromley Ch Ch *Roch* from 00. *Christ Church Vicarage, 18 Highland Road, Bromley BR1 4AD* T: (020) 8313 9882 *or* 8464 1898 F: 8464 5846 E: iain.broomfield@christchurchbromley.org

BROOMHEAD, Mark Roger. b 71. Nottm Univ BSc 00. St Jo Coll Nottm 06. **d** 08 **p** 09. C N Wingfield, Clay Cross and Pilsley *Derby* 08–10; C Brampton St Thos from 10; C Chesterfield St Mary and All SS from 11; C Chesterfield H Trin and Ch Ch from 11; C Chesterfield SS Aug 11–15; P-in-c 15–16. *35 Whitecotes Park, Chesterfield S40 3RT* T: (01246) 555988 E: mark@theorderoftheblacksheep.com

BROSNAN, Mark. b 61. St Martin's Coll Lanc BA 83 RMN 88 Otley Agric Coll. EAMTC 92. **d** 95 **p** 96. C Rushmere *St E* 95–98; PtO *Chelmsf* 01–05; Hon C W w E Mersea 05–08; Hon C Peldon w Gt and Lt Wigborough 05–08; P-in-c Hadleigh St Barn 08–12; P-in-c Kirkbymoorside w Gillamoor, Farndale etc *York* 12; V from 12; C Kirby Misperton w Normanby and Salton from 12. *The Vicarage, Church Street, Kirkbymoorside, York YO62 6AZ* T: (01751) 431452 E: gohiking@hotmail.co.uk

BROSTER, Godfrey David. b 52. Ealing Tech Coll BA 75. Ripon Coll Cuddesdon 78. **d** 81 **p** 82. C Crayford *Roch* 81–82; C Brighton Resurr *Chich* 82–86; C-in-c The Hydneye CD 86–91; R Plumpton w E Chiltington 91–93; R Plumpton w E Chiltington cum Novington from 93. *The Rectory, Station Road, Plumpton Green, Lewes BN7 3BU* T: (01273) 890570

BROTHERSTON, Miss Isabel Mary. b 42. Cranmer Hall Dur 81. **dss** 83 **d** 87 **p** 94. Coleshill *Birm* 83–87; Par Dn Duddeston w Nechells 87–92; Par Dn Harlescott *Lich* 92–94; C 94–04; R Llanddulas and Llysfaen *St As* 04–08; rtd 08; PtO *St As* from 08. *3 Marlow Terrace, Mold CH7 1HH* T: (01352) 756011 E: mbrother@live.co.uk

BROTHERTON, The Ven John Michael. b 35. St Jo Coll Cam BA 59 MA 63. Cuddesdon Coll 59. **d** 61 **p** 62. C Chiswick St Nic w St Mary *Lon* 61–65; Chapl Trin Coll Port of Spain Trinidad and Tobago 65–69; R Diego Martin 69–75; V Cowley St Jo *Ox* 76–81; Chapl St Hilda's Coll Ox 76–81; RD Cowley *Ox* 78–81; V Portsea St Mary *Portsm* 81–91; Hon Can Kobe Japan from 86; Adn Chich 91–02; rtd 02; PtO *Lon* from 03; *Chich* from 03. *Flat 2, 23 Gledhow Gardens, London SW5 0AZ* T: (020) 7373 5147 E: jmbrotherton@yahoo.co.uk

BROTHERTON, Michael. b 56. Univ of Wales (Abth) BD 80. Wycliffe Hall Ox 80. **d** 81 **p** 82. Hon Chapl Miss to Seamen 81–84; C Pembroke Dock *St D* 81–84; Chapl RN 84–11; rtd 11; PtO *St D* from 13. *North Studdock Farm House, Angle, Pembroke SA71 5AZ* T: (01646) 641438 M: 07887-534666 E: entopan007@gmail.com

BROTHWELL, Paul David. b 37. Lich Th Coll 62. **d** 65 **p** 66. C Honley *Wakef* 65–68; Min Can Wakef Cathl 68–71; V Whittington St Giles *Lich* 71–83; P-in-c Weeford 78–83; V Whittington w Weeford 83–92; Chapl Kidderminster Gen Hosp 92–94; Chapl Kidderminster Health Care NHS Trust 94–99; Chapl Worcs Acute Hosps NHS Trust 00–01; Chapl Worcs Community and Mental Health Trust 01–02; Hon Can Antananarivo 02; rtd 02; PtO *Worc* from 02. *8 Hillside Close, Stourport-on-Severn DY13 0JW* T: (01299) 823495 or (01562) 823424 ext 3306 E: paul.brothwell@btopenworld.com

BROTHWELL, Ruth. b 60. **d** 10 **p** 12. NSM Merrow *Guildf* 10–13; NSM Worplesdon 13–15; PtO 15–17; NSM Worplesdon from 17. *Foxgrove, Burnt Common Lane, Ripley, Woking GU23 6HD* T: (01483) 223571 E: ruth@worplesdonparish.com

BROUGH (*née* CROWLE), Mrs Sarah Ann. b 65. Ripon Coll Cuddesdon BTh 99. **d** 99 **p** 00. C Godalming *Guildf* 99–03; Chapl Godalming Coll 01–03; R Chiddingfold *Guildf* 03–18; PtO from 18. *Robinlea, Friday Street, Ockley, Dorking RH5 5TE* M: 07747-031524 E: sarahbrough@btinternet.com

BROUGHTON, James Roger. b 48. Leeds Univ BA 71 Liv Univ MEd 00 Nottm Univ CertEd 72. Wycliffe Hall Ox 87. **d** 89 **p** 90. C Stoneycroft All SS *Liv* 89–92; P-in-c Carr Mill 92–94; V 94–96; Chapl Duke of York's R Mil Sch Dover 96–08; rtd 08; PtO *Cant* from 08. *Woodstock, St Vincent Road, St Margarets-at-Cliffe, Dover CT15 6ET* T: (01304) 853840 M: 07934-560557 E: james@broughtonfamily.co.uk

BROUGHTON, Lynne Mary. b 46. Melbourne Univ BA 67 PhD 79. EAMTC 99. **d** 00 **p** 01. NSM Wood Ditton w Saxon Street *Ely* 00–07; NSM Kirtling 00–07; NSM Cheveley 00–07; NSM Ashley w Silverley 00–07; PtO from 07. *85 Richmond Road, Cambridge CB4 3PS* T: (01223) 322014 E: lmb27@hermes.cam.ac.uk *or* lmb27@cam.ac.uk

BROUGHTON, Matthew David. b 88. Sheff Univ BA 10 Trin Hall Cam BTh 17. Ridley Hall Cam 15. **d** 18 **p** 19. C Ireland Wood *Leeds* from 18. *11 Bedford View, Leeds LS16 6DL* M: 07982-197632 E: mbroughton1088@gmail.com

BROUGHTON, Canon Stuart Roger. b 36. Wilson Carlile Coll 59 St Mich Coll Llan 61. **d** 64 **p** 65. C Bromley Ch Ch *Roch* 64–67; SAMS 67–79 and 86–95; Miss Paraguayan Chaco Paraguay 67–70; R Salvador Gd Shep Brazil 70–79; V Stoke sub Hamdon *B & W* 79–83; Hon CF 82–86; V Blackb Ch Ch w St Matt 83–86; R Alcacer do Sal Portugal 86–91; Chapl Rio de Janeiro Brazil 91–95; rtd 96; Chapl Agia Napa Cyprus 96; Chapl Ch Ch Cathl Falkland Is 97–98; P-in-c Corfu *Eur*

98–01; Hon C Jersey St Paul Prop Chpl *Win* 01–03; Chapl to Abp Congo 03–05; Hon Can Bukavu from 04; LtO Sydney Australia 06–11; PtO *St Alb* 12–13; *Liv* 13–19; *Ches* from 18. *34 Fosbrooke House, 8 Clifton Drive, Lytham St Annes FY8 5RQ* T: (01253) 667005 E: stuartrbroughtonsouthport@gmail.com

BROWELL (*née* SHILLINGTON), Mrs Maureen Lesley. b 57. MIH 89. NEOC 02. **d** 05 **p** 06. Soc Resp Officer *Ripon* 99–08; NSM Hoylandswaine and Silkstone w Stainborough *Wakef* 05–08; TV Almondbury w Farnley Tyas 08–12; Dioc Coord for Soc Resp 08–10; V Hoylandswaine and Silkstone w Stainborough 12–14; *Leeds* 14–16; V W Barnsley from 16; Dean of Women's Min Wakef Area from 17. *The Vicarage, 12 High Street, Silkstone, Barnsley S75 4JN* T: (01226) 492294 M: 07930-194421 E: maureenbrowell@talktalk.net

BROWN, Mrs Ailsa Elizabeth. b 64. Hull Univ BA 94 Nottm Univ MA 10. EMMTC 07. **d** 10 **p** 11. NSM Barton upon Humber *Linc* 10–18; C Barrow and Goxhill from 18; Asst Dioc Dir of Ords from 13. *21 Ferriby Road, Barton-upon-Humber DN18 5LE* T: (01652) 634855 M: 07805-694614 E: brown5le@btinternet.com

BROWN, Canon Alan. b 37. Tyndale Hall Bris 59. **d** 63 **p** 64. C Braintree *Chelmsf* 63–66; C Tooting Graveney St Nic *S'wark* 66–68; C Chesham St Mary *Ox* 68–70; V Hornsey Rise St Mary *Lon* 70–75; V Sidcup Ch Ch *Roch* 75–88; V Newport St Jo *Portsm* 88–01; P-in-c Newport St Thos 96–99; V 99–01; RD W Wight 91–96; Hon Can Portsm Cathl 95–01; rtd 01. *65 Sherbourne Avenue, Ryde PO33 3PW* T: (01983) 566956

BROWN, Alan George. b 51. Bradf Univ BSc 84 Leeds Univ CertEd 81 MBA 92 SRN 72 RMN 75 RNT 81. NOC 92. **d** 95 **p** 96. NSM Ilkley St Marg *Bradf* 95–10; Hd of Division Applied Health Studies Leeds Univ 98–07; Bp's Adv for Hosp Chapl *Bradf* 03–14; Lic to Offic 10–14; Bp's Inspector for Minl Tr *Wakef* 10–14; *Leeds* from 14; PtO *York* from 14. *Argyll Lodge, High Street, Scalby, Scarborough YO13 0PT* T: (01723) 503122 E: brown.alan.george@gmail.com

BROWN, Alec George. b 53. Univ of Zimbabwe DipSW 80 Univ of Wales (Cardiff) MSc(Econ) 87. St Deiniol's Hawarden 88 NOC 90. **d** 93 **p** 94. C Stockton Heath *Ches* 93–96; C Thelwall 96–97; V 97–01; V Gt Budworth from 01; P-in-c Antrobus from 13; RD Gt Budworth from 10. *The Vicarage, High Street, Great Budworth, Northwich CW9 6HF* T: (01606) 891324 E: alecgbrown@gmail.com

BROWN, Allan James. b 47. K Coll Lon BD 69 AKC 69 MTh 70. St Aug Coll Cant 69. **d** 73 **p** 74. Chapl St Geo Sch Jerusalem 73–74; Chapl St Marg Sch Nazareth 74–75; C Clifton *S'well* 75–77; CF 77–99; Asst Chapl Gen 99–00; V Ilkeston St Mary *Derby* 00–10; P-in-c Ilkeston St Jo 05–10; rtd 10; PtO *S'well* from 10. *63 Highfield Road, Nottingham NG2 6DR*

BROWN, The Ven Andrew. b 55. St Pet Coll Ox BA 80 MA 82. Ridley Hall Cam 79. **d** 80 **p** 81. C Burnley St Pet *Blackb* 80–82; C Elton All SS *Man* 82–86; P-in-c Ashton St Pet 86–93; V 94–96; V Halliwell St Luke 96–03; Can Th Derby Cathl and Dioc CME Adv *Derby* 03–11; Adn of Man *S & M* from 11; V Douglas St Geo 11–14; V Douglas St Geo and All SS from 15. *St George's Vicarage, 16 Devonshire Road, Douglas, Isle of Man IM2 3RB* T: (01624) 675430 E: archdeacon@sodorandman.im

BROWN, Andrew (Bod). b 66. Man Univ BSc 87. Oak Hill Th Coll BA 02. **d** 03 **p** 04. C Hyde St Geo *Ches* 03–06; V Weaverham 06–18; V Shevington *Blackb* from 18. *St Ann's Vicarage, Gathurst Lane, Shevington, Wigan WN6 8HW* T: (01257) 252136

BROWN, Andrew James. b 60. Univ of Wales (Ban) BA 81. Ripon Coll Cuddesdon 07. **d** 09 **p** 10. C Castle Bromwich SS Mary and Marg *Birm* 09–13; P-in-c Eccleston *Blackb* 13–19; P-in-c Charnock Richard 13–19; R Eccleston and Charnock Richard from 19. *The Rectory, 30 Lawrence Lane, Eccleston, Chorley PR7 5SJ* T: (01257) 452777 E: rector@ecclestonstmaryschurch.org

BROWN, Andrew Robert James. b 90. Cant Ch Ch Univ BA 13. Ripon Coll Cuddesdon 16. **d** 18 **p** 19. C Ashford Town *Cant* from 18. *The Vicarage, 66 Church Road, Willesborough, Ashford TN24 0JG* E: rev.arjbrown@gmail.com

BROWN, Mrs Angela. b 58. SWMTC 11. **d** 14 **p** 15. C Redruth w Lanner and Treleigh *Truro* 14–18; Public Preacher from 18. *22 Trescobeas Road, Falmouth TR11 2JE* M: 07729-118696 E: angelabythesea@icloud.com

BROWN, Canon Anne Elizabeth. b 61. SWMTC 06. **d** 09 **p** 10. C Probus, Ladock and Grampound w Creed and St Erme *Truro* 09–12; P-in-c Three Rivers 12–16; P-in-c St Agnes and Mount Hawke w Mithian from 16; P-in-c Perranzabuloe and Crantock w Cubert from 16; Hon Can Truro Cathl from 15. *The Vicarage, Cox Hill, Cocks, Perranporth TR6 0AT* T: (01872) 572654

BROWN, Anthony Frank Palmer. b 31. Fitzw Ho Cam BA 56 Fitzw Coll Cam MA 84. Cuddesdon Coll 56. **d** 58 **p** 59. C Aldershot St Mich *Guildf* 58–61; C Chiswick St Nic w St Mary *Lon* 61–66; Asst Chapl Lon Univ 65–70; LtO 70–72; C-in-c Hammersmith SS Mich and Geo White City Estate CD 72–74; P-in-c Upper Sunbury St Sav 74–80; V 80–01; rtd 01; PtO *Chich* 02–18. *6 Church Lane, Ditchling, Hassocks BN6 8TB* T: (01273) 843847

BROWN, Preb Anthony Paul. b 55. Reading Univ BSc 75 MRICS 87. Qu Coll Birm 77. **d** 80 **p** 81. C Pelsall *Lich* 80–83; C Leighton Buzzard w Eggington, Hockliffe etc *St Alb* 83–87; TV Langley Marish *Ox* 87–93; V Pet St Mary Boongate 93–98; TR Wombourne w Trysull and Bobbington *Lich* 98–02; TR Smestow Vale from 02; Preb Lich Cathl from 09. *The Vicarage, School Road, Wombourne, Wolverhampton WV5 9ED* T: (01902) 892234 *or* 897700 E: revpbrown@aol.com

BROWN, Arthur William Stawell. b 26. St Jo Coll Ox BA 50 MA 51. Cuddesdon Coll 63. **d** 65 **p** 66. C Edin St Jo 65–66; C Petersfield w Sheet *Portsm* 67–75; V Portsea St Alb 75–79; R Smithfield St Bart Gt *Lon* 79–91; R St Sepulchre w Ch Ch Greyfriars etc 81–91; Chapl Madeira *Eur* 90–93; rtd 91; PtO *Ex* 93–09. *Clare Park, Crondall, Farnham GU10 5DT* T: (01252) 851200

BROWN, Barry Ronald. b 48. Ridley Coll Melbourne ThL 72. **d** 73 **p** 74. Australia 73–77 and 82–95; C Richmond St Mary w St Matthias *S'wark* 78–79; C Richmond St Mary w St Matthias and St Jo 79; C Edin Old St Paul 79–80; Chapl Belgrade w Zagreb *Eur* 81–82; Canada from 95. *52 Queen Street, Belleville ON K8N 1T7, Canada* T: (001) (613) 968 9873 E: bbrownhome@hotmail.com

BROWN, Bill Charles Balfour. b 44. Linc Th Coll 87. **d** 89 **p** 90. C Moulsham St Luke *Chelmsf* 89–91; C Prittlewell 91–94; V Worksop St Paul *S'well* 95–12; rtd 12. *46 Holding, Worksop S81 0TD* E: fatherbill@btopenworld.com

BROWN, Bod. *See* BROWN, Andrew

BROWN (née BRYCE), Mrs Brenda Dorothy. b 48. **d** 11 **p** 13. NSM Trowell, Awsworth and Cossall *S'well* 11–18; rtd 18; PtO *S'well* from 18. *41 Park Hill, Awsworth, Nottingham NG16 2RD* T: 0115-932 9328 E: brenda.brown1408@outlook.com

BROWN, Brian Ernest. b 36. ALA 64. Oak Hill NSM Course 82. **d** 85 **p** 86. NSM Wallington *S'wark* 85–91; C 91–00; rtd 00; PtO *Nor* from 00. *6 Burnside, Necton, Swaffham PE37 8ER* T: (01760) 721292 E: briansylviabrown@aol.com

BROWN, Caryll Diane. b 50. **d** 13 **p** 14. OLM E w W Harling, Bridgham w Roudham, Larling etc *Nor* from 13. *Carrick House, 7 West Harling Road, East Harling, Norwich NR16 2SL* T: (01953) 717451 E: c@rrickhouse.com

BROWN, Charles Henry. b 48. Tulane Univ (USA) BA 70 Ch Coll Cam BA 75 MA 81. Westcott Ho Cam. **d** 00 **p** 01. C Boston *Linc* 00–03; Lect 03–05; Lic Preacher 05–06; P-in-c Crowland from 06. *The Abbey Rectory, East Street, Crowland, Peterborough PE6 0EN* T: (01733) 211763

BROWN, Mrs Christine Ann. b 42. Keele Univ CertEd 72. LCTP 10. **d** 11 **p** 12. NSM Dent w Cowgill *Bradf* 11–12; NSM Dent w Cowgill *Carl* 12–19; rtd 19; PtO *Carl* from 19. *Dale View, Laning, Dent, Sedbergh LA10 5QJ* T: (015396) 25418 E: christinelucy2014@gmail.com

BROWN, Canon Christine Lilian. b 54. Ex Univ BA 75 Newc Univ MA 93. NEOC 01. **d** 04 **p** 05. NSM Ponteland *Newc* from 04; Chapl St Oswald's Hospice Newc from 08; AD Newc W from 17; Hon Can Newc Cathl from 17. *4 Woodlands, Ponteland, Newcastle upon Tyne NE20 9EU* T: (01661) 824196

BROWN, Christopher. b 43. Linc Th Coll 79. **d** 81 **p** 82. C Stafford St Jo *Lich* 81–85; V Alton w Bradley-le-Moors and Oakamoor w Cotton 85–94; Chapl Asst Nottm City Hosp NHS Trust 94–05; Sen Chapl 05–06; rtd 06. *3 Kingsbury Drive, Nottingham NG8 3EP* T: 0115-929 4821 E: christopher.brown20@sky.com

BROWN, Christopher. b 38. AKC 62 CQSW 68. St Boniface Warminster 62. **d** 63 **p** 64. C Crofton Park St Hilda w St Cypr *S'wark* 63–64; C S Beddington St Mich 64–67; C Herne Hill St Paul 67–68; LtO 68–72; *Lich* 72–76; *Worc* 76–79; *Ox* 79–86; PtO *Birm* 74–76; *Chelmsf* from 86; Dir and Chief Exec NSPCC 89–95. *7 Baronia Croft, Colchester CO4 9EE* T: (01206) 852904 E: chribrow@yahoo.co.uk

BROWN, Christopher. *See* BROWN, Paul David Christopher

BROWN, Christopher Charles. b 58. Univ of Wales (Cardiff) LLB 79 Solicitor 82. Westcott Ho Cam 87. **d** 90 **p** 91. C Taunton St Mary *B & W* 90–94; R Timsbury and Priston 94–00; P-in-c Urmston *Man* 00–10; AD Stretford 05–10; TR Radcliffe 10–14; V Fishguard w Llanychar and Pontfaen w Morfil etc *St D* 14–18; P-in-c W Cemaes from 18; AD Dewisland and Fishguard from 15. *The Vicarage,*

High Street, Fishguard SA65 9AU T: (01348) 875536 E: revchrisbrown4@gmail.com

BROWN, Christopher David. b 49. Birm Univ BEd 72. St Mich Coll Llan 92. **d** 94 **p** 95. C Swansea St Thos and Kilvey *S & B* 94–96; C Swansea St Jas 96–98; St Helena 99–01; Chapl and Hd RS Epsom Coll 01–03; Chapl Ellesmere Coll 03–05. *Flat 1, 13 Worcester Road, Malvern WR14 4QY* E: kristophdavid@hotmail.com

BROWN, Christopher Edgar Newall. b 31. Oak Hill Th Coll 51. **d** 55 **p** 56. C Surbiton Hill Ch Ch *S'wark* 55–57; C Gipsy Hill Ch Ch 57–61; V Plumstead All SS 61–70; V Sissinghurst *Cant* 70–73; P-in-c Frittenden 72–73; R Sissinghurst w Frittenden 73–76; PtO *S & M* 84–91 and 96–10; Bp's Dom Chapl 91–95; rtd 96. *21 College Green, Castletown, Isle of Man IM9 1BE* T: (01624) 822364

BROWN, Christopher Howard. b 49. **d** 03 **p** 04. OLM Uttoxeter Area *Lich* from 03. *21 Carter Street, Uttoxeter ST14 8EY* T: (01889) 567492 E: revchrishbrown@aol.co.uk

BROWN, Daniel James. b 83. Sheff Univ BA 06 MA 13. Yorks Min Course 10. **d** 13 **p** 14. C Philadelphia St Thos *Sheff* 13–15; C Wadsley 15–17; P-in-c from 17. *The Vicarage, 91 Airedale Road, Sheffield S6 4AW* E: dan.brown@sheffield.anglican.org *or* danbrown@wadsleychurch.com

BROWN, David Andrew. b 72. York Univ BA 93. Wycliffe Hall Ox BTh 04. **d** 04 **p** 05. C Rugby St Matt *Cov* 04–07; C Rugby W 08; P-in-c Budbrooke 08–14; V from 14. *23 Robins Grove, Warwick CV34 6RF* T: (01926) 497298

BROWN, David Charles Girdlestone. b 42. Solicitor 67. S'wark Ord Course 87. **d** 90 **p** 91. NSM Milford *Guildf* 90–92; NSM Haslemere 92–01; PtO *Chich* 02–04 and from 14; LtO 04–08; P-in-c Barlavington, Burton w Coates, Sutton and Bignor 08–14; rtd 14. *The Orchard, Rogate, Petersfield GU31 5HU* T: (01730) 821867 E: dbrown501@btinternet.com

BROWN, David George. b 55. Lon Univ BD 75 Sussex Univ MSc 06 MInstLM 03. Lon Bible Coll 72. **d** 15 **p** 15. OLM Woodside Park St Barn *Lon* 15–17; PtO 17–18; *Portsm* 17–18; C Warfield *Ox* from 19. *2 Dorset Vale, Warfield, Bracknell RG42 3JL* M: 07490-089255 E: davidgbrown@outlook.com

BROWN, Canon David Lloyd. b 44. TCD BTh 90. **d** 86 **p** 87. C Cregagh *D & D* 86–91; Bp's C Knocknagoney 91–12; I from 12; Can Down Cathl from 07. *The Aslan Centre, 13A Knocknagoney Road, Belfast BT4 2NR* T/F: (028) 9076 3343 *or* 9076 0420 E: davidlloydbrown@googlemail.com

BROWN, David Mark. b 67. Bp Grosseteste Coll BSc 93. Oak Hill Th Coll 05. **d** 07. C Sidmouth, Woolbrook, Salcombe Regis, Sidbury etc *Ex* 07–11; P-in-c Stevenage St Nic and Graveley *St Alb* 11–15; V from 15. *St Nicholas' House, 2A North Road, Stevenage SG1 4AT* T: (01438) 354355 M: 07814-911937 E: rector@saintnicholaschurch.org.uk

BROWN, David Victor Arthur. b 44. Em Coll Cam BA 66 MA 70 CertEd. Linc Th Coll 72. **d** 74 **p** 75. C Bourne *Linc* 74–77; Chapl St Steph Coll Broadstairs 77–79; Chapl Asst N Gen Hosp Sheff 81–84; C Sheff St Cuth 81–84; Chapl Ridge Lea Hosp Lanc 84–92; Chapl Lanc Moor Hosp 84–92; Chapl Lanc R Infirmary 87–92; Chapl Lanc Priority Services NHS Trust and Lanc Acute Hosps NHS Trust 92–98; Chapl Morecambe Bay Hosps NHS Trust and Morecambe Bay Primary Care Trust 98–09; Hon C Scorton and Barnacre and Calder Vale *Blackb* 06–09; P-in-c 09–12; V 12–14; P-in-c Warsaw *Eur* from 14. *ul Dorotowska 7/5, Warsaw 02-347, Poland* E: dlgbrown@aol.com

BROWN, Prof David William. b 48. Edin Univ MA 70 Oriel Coll Ox BA 72 Clare Coll Cam PhD 76 FBA 02. Westcott Ho Cam 75. **d** 76 **p** 77. Chapl, Fell and Tutor Oriel Coll Ox 76–90; Van Mildert Prof Div Dur Univ 90–07; Can Res Dur Cathl 90–07; Wardlaw Prof St Andr Univ *St And* 07–15; LtO from 09. *Mansfield, 1A Grey Street, Tayport DD6 9JF* T: (01382) 550063

BROWN (née BOWERS), Lady (Denise Frances). b 50. City Univ BSc 72. SAOMC 99. **d** 02 **p** 03. NSM Beedon and Peasemore w W Ilsley and Farnborough *Ox* 02–10; NSM Brightwalton w Catmore, Leckhampstead etc 05–10; NSM E Downland 10–17; rtd 17; PtO *Ox* from 17. *Bridleway Cottage, Stanmore, Beedon, Newbury RG20 8SR* T/F: (01635) 281825 M: 07901-914975 E: denisefbrown@gmail.com

BROWN, Derek. b 42. Lindisfarne Regional Tr Partnership 10. **d** 10 **p** 11. NSM Gateshead St Helen *Dur* 10–15; PtO from 15. *29 Heathfield Road, Gateshead NE9 5HH* T: 0191-487 5922 M: 07985-512766 E: derekderekb@aol.com

BROWN, Derek Henry Pridgeon. b 46. Cam Coll of Art and Tech BA 67 Leeds Univ PGCE 71. St Steph Ho Ox 90. **d** 92 **p** 93. C Finchley St Mary *Lon* 92–95; C W Hampstead St Jas 95–99; V Eyres Monsell *Leic* 99–08; TV Leic Presentation 08–09; Min Leic St Barn CD 09–13; rtd 13; PtO *Leic* from

13. *38 Gainsborough Road, Leicester LE2 3DE* T: 0116-270 9750 M: 07526-124023 E: dbrown@leicester.anglican.org

BROWN, Canon Donald Fryer. b 31. St Jo Coll Dur BA 56. Cranmer Hall Dur 60. **d** 61 **p** 62. Min Can Bradf Cathl 61–64; C Bingley All SS 64–66; V Low Moor H Trin 66–97; Hon Can Bradf Cathl 85–97; RD Bowling and Horton 87–95; rtd 97; PtO *Bradf* 97–14; *Leeds* from 14. *3 Northfield Gardens, Wibsey, Bradford BD6 1LQ* T: (01274) 671869 E: donaldandiris@hotmail.co.uk

BROWN, Douglas Adrian Spencer. b 29. Univ of W Aus BA 50 MA 71 K Coll Lon MTh 90. St Mich Th Coll Crafers 50. **d** 53 **p** 54. SSM 54–00; Chapl St Mich Th Coll Crafers Australia 54–60; Chapl Kelham Th Coll 60–66; Chapl Univ of W Aus Australia 66–71; P-in-c Canberra St Alb 71–75; Warden St Mich Th Coll Crafers 75–82; P-in-c Adelaide St Jo 78–82; Academic Dean Adelaide Coll of Div 79–81; Visiting Scholar Union Th Sem NY 82; President Adelaide Coll of Div 88; PtO *Lon* 88–90; Chapl Bucharest w Sofia *Eur* 90–91; Dir Angl Cen Rome 91–95; Chapl Palermo w Taormina *Eur* 95–96; Lect Newton Th Coll Papua New Guinea 97; PtO *Dur* 97–00; *S'wark* 99–00; Dir Nor Cathl Inst 00–02; Hon PV Nor Cathl 00–02; PtO 01–02. *6 Gilmour Road, Roleystone WA 6111, Australia* E: brown.douglas75@gmail.com

BROWN, Mrs Elizabeth Alexandra Mary Gordon. b 67. Westcott Ho Cam 06. **d** 08 **p** 09. C Merrow *Guildf* 08–11; NSM Bedlington *Newc* 12–18; PtO from 18; Chapl Northumbria Healthcare NHS Foundn Trust from 17. *68 Shields Road, Morpeth NE61 2RZ* T: (01670) 515556 M: 07768-075803 E: lizzieegg@hotmail.co.uk

BROWN, Ms Elizabeth Ann. b 43. **d** 00 **p** 01. OLM W Bromwich All SS *Lich* 01–08; OLM Wednesbury St Paul Wood Green 08–10; rtd 10; PtO *Lich* from 11. *307 Beaconview Road, West Bromwich B71 3PS* T: 0121-588 7530 E: elizabethbrown630@gmail.com

BROWN, Mrs Elizabeth Mary Godwin. b 48. St Matthias Coll Bris CertEd 69. WEMTC 07. **d** 10 **p** 11. NSM Leominster *Heref* 10–18; PtO from 18. *14 Fairleigh House, Hereford Terrace, Leominster HR6 8JP* T: (01568) 613636 M: 07971-917141 E: elizabethmgbrown@hotmail.com

BROWN, Eric. b 28. Leeds Univ BA 98. NW Ord Course 73. **d** 76 **p** 77. NSM S Kirkby *Wakef* 76–83; NSM Knottingley 83–94; NSM Kellington w Whitley 89–94; Sub Chapl HM Pris Lindholme 90–94; PtO *Wakef* 94–14; *Leeds* from 14. *8 Ashfield House, Southmoor Road, Hemsworth, Pontefract WF9 4SQ* T: (01977) 618987 E: josephinehunter42@gmail.com

BROWN, Geoffrey Alan. b 34. **d** 99 **p** 00. OLM Bury St Edmunds St Mary *St E* 99–07; rtd 07; PtO *St E* from 07. *Rodenkirchen, 12A Sharp Road, Bury St Edmunds IP33 2NB* T: (01284) 769725

BROWN, Geoffrey Gilbert. b 38. Dur Univ BA 62 DipEd 63 Fitzw Coll Cam BA 69 MA 73 FBIS. Westcott Ho Cam 67. **d** 70 **p** 71. C Gosforth All SS *Newc* 70–73; Chapl Dauntsey's Sch Devizes 73–76; Chapl St Paul's Colleg Sch Hamilton New Zealand 76–78; V Barrow St Aid *Carl* 79–86; Chapl Ch Ch Canterbury New Zealand 86–90; C Digswell and Panshanger *St Alb* 91–93; Chapl E Herts Hospice Care 94–07; rtd 07. *32 Uplands, Welwyn Garden City AL8 7EW* T: (01707) 327565

BROWN, Mrs Harriet Nina. b 37. Open Univ BA 77 Lon Univ CertEd 57. Gilmore Course 80 Oak Hill Th Coll 83. **dss** 83 **d** 87 **p** 94. Greenstead *Chelmsf* 83–90; Par Dn 87–90; Asst Chapl R Hosp Sch Holbrook 90–93; PtO *Chelmsf* from 93; *St E* 93–96; P-in-c Gt and Lt Blakenham w Baylham and Nettlestead 96–01; rtd 01; PtO *Chelmsf* 18–19. *22 Gainsborough Road, Colchester CO3 4QN* T: (01206) 523072 E: adhnbrown@tiscali.co.uk

BROWN, Ian Barry. See KING-BROWN, Ian Barry

BROWN, Ian David. b 53. UEA BA 76. Wycliffe Hall Ox BA 80. **d** 81 **p** 82. C Southsea St Jude *Portsm* 81–84; Chapl Coll of SS Paul and Mary Cheltenham 84–89; V Lt Heath *St Alb* 89–05; V Frindsbury w Upnor and Chattenden *Roch* 05–14; P-in-c Chalfont St Giles Ox 14–15; P-in-c Seer Green and Jordans 14–15; R Chalfont St Giles, Seer Green and Jordans from 15. *The Rectory, 2 Deanway, Chalfont St Giles HP8 4JH* T: (01494) 872097 E: ianandjuliebrown@gmail.com *or* rectorcsg@stgileschurch2.plus.com

BROWN, Canon Jack Robin. b 44. Linc Th Coll 67. **d** 69 **p** 70. C Canning Town St Cedd *Chelmsf* 69–72; C Dunstable *St Alb* 72–78; V Luton St Andr 78–85; V Kempston Transfiguration 85–00; RD Bedford 92–98; Hon Can St Alb 97–09; Dioc Officer for Local Min 00–09; rtd 10. P-in-c Mill End and Heronsgate w W Hyde *St Alb* 10–11; Asst Dir of Ords from 11. *9 Westmead, Princes Risborough HP27 9HP* T: (01844) 347178 E: randvbrown4@btinternet.com

BROWN, Mrs Jacqueline Kay. b 43. Saffron Walden Coll CertEd 65. **d** 08 **p** 09. OLM Newton Longville, Mursley,

Swanbourne etc *Ox* from 08. *5 Berry Way, Newton Longville, Milton Keynes MK17 0AS* T: (01908) 270159 E: jackie.br@tiscali.co.uk

BROWN, James Christie. b 86. Van Mildert Coll Dur BSc 07 Peterho Cam BA 14. Ridley Hall Cam 12. **d** 17 **p** 18. C Harpenden St Jo *St Alb* from 17. *2 Lindwood Road, Harpenden AL5 1RR* T: (01582) 933358 M: 07813-464643 E: james@stjohnsharpenden.org.uk

BROWN, Mrs Jane Catherine Deborah. b 65. York Univ BA 89. Cranmer Hall Dur 13. **d** 15 **p** 16. C Bramham *York* 15–18; R Garforth *Leeds* from 18. *The Rectory, Croft Foulds Court, Garforth, Leeds LS25 1NQ* T: 0113-286 3737 M: 07981-310373 E: janebrown160@live.com *or* jane.brown@leeds.anglican.org

BROWN, Jane Madeline. See SHARP, Jane Madeline

BROWN, Mrs Janice Elizabeth. b 65. Univ of Wales (Ban) BTh 04. **d** 04 **p** 05. C Botwnnog w Bryncroes w Llangwnnadl w Penllech *Ban* 04–05; C Llyn and Eifionydd 05–07; P-in-c Denio w Abererch 07–09; V 09–12; V Dwylan from 12. *The Vicarage, Church Road, Penmaenmawr LL34 6BN* T: (01492) 339781 M: 07969-655497

BROWN, Mrs Jean Louise. b 49. WEMTC 05. **d** 08 **p** 09. NSM Lechlade *Glouc* 08; NSM S Cotswolds 09–17; TV 11–17; Chapl Gt Western Hosps NHS Foundn Trust 16–17; rtd 17. *5 Manor Gardens, Lechlade GL7 3EQ*

BROWN, Mrs Jennifer Elizabeth. b 70. Geo Mason Univ Virginia BSc 91 Heythrop Coll Lon MA 09. SAOMC 02. **d** 05 **p** 06. C Ox St Clem 05–08; Chapl Jes Coll Ox 09; LtO *Ox* 09–16; NSM Kidlington w Hampton Poyle 12–14; NSM The Churn 14–19; NSM Abingdon from 19; Tutor Ripon Coll Cuddesdon from 10. *St John's Cottage, 45 Little Wittenham Road, Long Wittenham, Abingdon OX14 4QT* T: (01865) 407167 *or* 877455 E: science.missioner@churchchurches.co.uk *or* jen.brown@rcc.ac.uk

BROWN, Canon John Bruce. b 42. Nottm Univ BA 64 MA 68. Cuddesdon Coll 64. **d** 66 **p** 67. C Warwick St Nic *Cov* 66–71; C Bp's Hatfield *St Alb* 71–78; V Watford St Mich 78–08; RD Watford 94–99; Hon Can St Alb 02–08; rtd 08; PtO *St Alb* 08–18; *Ox* from 09. *Broomfield Cottage, Poffley End, Hailey, Witney OX29 9US* T: (01993) 703029 E: patandjohnb@yahoo.co.uk

BROWN, Canon John Duncan. b 43. St Pet Coll Ox BA 64 BA 66 MA 68 Lon Univ BSc. Wycliffe Hall Ox 65. **d** 67 **p** 68. C Kingston upon Hull H Trin *York* 67–69; C St Leonards St Leon *Chich* 69–72; Hon C Norbiton *S'wark* 72–75; C Kirkcaldy *St And* 75–78; Prec and Chapl Chelmsf Cathl 78–86; P-in-c Kelvedon Hatch 86–92; P-in-c Navestock 86–92; P-in-c Fryerning w Margaretting 92–99; Bp's ACORA Officer 92–99; Hon Can Chelmsf Cathl 93–03; rtd 99; PtO *Chelmsf* from 09. *556 Galleywood Road, Chelmsford CM2 8BX* T: (01245) 358185 E: canonjbrown@mac.com

BROWN, Jonathan. b 60. Univ Coll Dur BA 83 MA 85 Ex Univ CertEd 86. Ripon Coll Cuddesdon 86 Ch Div Sch of the Pacific (USA) 88. **d** 89 **p** 90. C Esher *Guildf* 89–97; TV Crawley *Chich* 97–04; Chapl St Cath Hospice Crawley 97–04; V Earlsfield St Andr *S'wark* from 04. *22 St Andrew's Court, Waynflete Street, London SW18 3QF* T: (020) 8946 4214

BROWN, Prof Judith Margaret. b 44. Girton Coll Cam MA 69 PhD 68 Natal Univ Hon DSocSc 01. Ripon Coll Cuddesdon 09. **d** 09 **p** 10. NSM Osney *Ox* 09–10; Past Assoc to Chapl Ball Coll Ox from 09; Chapl BNC Ox 17; PtO *Ox* from 14. *97 Victoria Road, Oxford OX2 7QG* T: (01865) 514486 E: judith.brown@history.ox.ac.uk

BROWN, Mrs Kathleen Margaret. b 40. QUB BD BTh. **d** 88 **p** 90. C Carrickfergus *Conn* 88–92; I Belfast St Paul w St Barn *Conn* 92–97; Can Belf Cathl 00–07; rtd 07. *3 The Avenue, Carrickfergus BT38 8LT* T: (028) 9336 6787 E: kbrown117@btinternet.com

BROWN, Keith Michael. b 42. **d** 07 **p** 08. OLM Earlham *Nor* 07–12; rtd 12; PtO *Nor* from 12. *115 Colman Road, Norwich NR4 7HF* T: (01603) 464707 E: keith.brown93@ntlworld.com

BROWN, Kenneth Roger. b 48. St Chad's Coll Dur BA 69. Liturg Inst Trier 72. **d** 73 **p** 74. C Patchway *Bris* 73–77; C Fishponds St Jo 77–79; Chapl RAF 79–95; Chapl HM Pris Pentonville 95–96; Chapl HM Pris Wellingborough 96–98; PtO *B&W* 99–00; P-in-c Crook Peak 00–11; R 11–14; rtd 14; PtO *B&W* from 15. *7 Peelers Court, Moorland Street, Axbridge BS26 2BB* T: (01934) 733805 E: kenandyvonne@hotmail.co.uk

BROWN, Kim. b 68. Ox Min Course 12. **d** 15 **p** 16. C Tetbury, Beverston, Long Newnton etc *Glouc* 15–18; LtO from 18. *10A Bowling Green Avenue, Cirencester GL7 2HB* T: (01285) 642661 E: revkimbrown10a@gmail.com

BROWN, Canon Malcolm Arthur. b 54. Oriel Coll Ox BA 76 MA 82 Man Univ PhD 00. Westcott Ho Cam 77. **d** 79 **p** 80.

C Riverhead w Dunton Green *Roch* 79–83; TV Southampton (City Cen) *Win* 83–91; Assoc Dir Wm Temple Foundn 91-93; Exec Sec 93–00; Hon C Heaton Moor *Man* 95–00; Prin EAMTC *Ely* 00–05; Prin ERMC 05–07; Dir Miss and Public Affairs Abps' Coun from 07; Hon Can Ely Cathl from 14; Hon Can Man Cathl from 15. *Church House, Great Smith Street, London SW1P 3AZ* T: (020) 7898 1000 E: malcolm.brown@churchofengland.org

BROWN, Marcus Clement. b 51. SEITE 08. **d** 10 **p** 11. NSM Iford w Kingston and Rodmell *Chich* 10–13; NSM Iford w Kingston and Rodmell and Southease from 13. *Abergavenny House, Mill Lane, Rodmell, Lewes BN7 3HS* T: (01273) 473939 M: 07815-157756 E: marcusandjennyrodmell@gmail.com

BROWN (née PATTERSON), Preb Marjorie Jean. b 54. Wooster Coll USA BA 76 K Coll Lon MA 04. S Dios Minl Tr Scheme 92. **d** 95 **p** 96. C Poplar *Lon* 95–99; P-in-c Stamford Hill St Thos 99–02; V 02–09; P-in-c Upper Clapton St Matt 06–08; Dean of Women's Min Stepney Area 02–07; V Primrose Hill St Mary w Avenue Road St Paul from 09; Asst Dir of Ords Edmonton Area 14–16; Dir Ords from 16; Preb St Paul's Cathl from 17. *St Mary's Vicarage, 44 King Henry's Road, London NW3 3RP* T: (020) 7722 3062 E: vicar@smvph.org.uk

BROWN, Canon Mark Edward. b 61. Southn Univ BSc 83 Cam Univ PGCE 84 Brunel Univ MTh 98. Trin Coll Bris BA 88. **d** 88 **p** 89. C Egham *Guildf* 88–92; C Northwood Em *Lon* 92–96; Assoc V 96–02; Bp's Officer for Evang 96–02; Can Missr *S'well* 02–07; Hon Can S'well Minster 02–07; P-in-c Tonbridge SS Pet and Paul *Roch* 07–10; V from 10; AD Tonbridge 10–18; Hon Can Roch Cathl from 16. *The Vicarage, Church Street, Tonbridge TN9 1HD* T: (01732) 770962 E: mark@tonbridgeparishchurch.org.uk

BROWN, Michael Brian. b 56. Trin Coll Bris BA 97 Coll of Resurr Mirfield 98. **d** 99 **p** 00. C Trowbridge St Jas *Sarum* 99–02; C Bruton and Distr *B & W* 02–09; C Bickleigh and Shaugh Prior *Ex* 09–12; Chapl Plymouth Hosps NHS Trust 09–12; P-in-c St John w Millbrook *Truro* 12–18; P-in-c Maker w Rame 12–18; R Rame Peninsula 18–19; R Maker w Rame, Millbrook, St John and Torpoint from 19; C Torpoint 12–15. *The Vicarage, Newport Street, Millbrook, Torpoint PL10 1BW* T: (01752) 822264 E: fr.michaelbrown1662@gmail.com

BROWN, Murray. See BROWN, Phillip Murray

BROWN, Nerys Ann. b 62. Univ of Wales (Abth) BA 83 PhD 87. TISEC 06. **d** 15 **p** 16. C Perth St Jo *St And* 14–18; R Dunblane from 18. *St Mary's Rectory, Smithy Loan, Dunblane FK15 0HQ* T: (01786) 824225 E: rector@stmarysdunblane.org

BROWN, Nicholas James Watson. b 76. R Holloway Coll Lon BMus 98 Dur Univ MA 17 FTCL 08 Lon Inst of Educn PGCE 99. Ripon Coll Cuddesdon BTh 11. **d** 09 **p** 10. C Warminster St Denys and Upton Scudamore *Sarum* 09–13; P-in-c Louth *Linc* 13; TR from 13; RD Louthesk from 17. *The Rectory, Westgate, Louth LN11 9YE* T: (01507) 605360 M: 07901-852198 E: nick.brown@teamparishoflouth.org.uk

BROWN, Nina. See BROWN, Harriet Nina

BROWN, Canon Norman Charles Harry. b 27. Univ of Wales BSc 46. St Mich Coll Llan 48. **d** 50 **p** 51. C Canton St Jo *Llan* 50–57; C Llanishen and Lisvane 58–63; V Miskin 63–97; RD Aberdare 82–97; Can Llan Cathl 86–97; rtd 97; PtO *Llan* from 04. *33 Bron y Deri, Mountain Ash CF45 4LL* T: (01443) 476631 E: normanbrown234@btinternet.com

BROWN, Canon Norman John. b 34. Thames Poly MA 90. Ripon Hall Ox 72. **d** 74 **p** 75. C High Wycombe *Ox* 74–78; V Tilehurst St Cath 78–82; V Boyne Hill 82–90; Chapl Windsor and Maidenhead Coll 87–89; Hon Can Ch Ch *Ox* 03–04; rtd 04; PtO *Ox* from 04. *Bosbury, 1 St James Close, Pangbourne, Reading RG8 7AP* T: 0118-984 5823 E: revbrown@waitrose.com

BROWN, Patricia Valerie. b 37. CertEd 58. STETS BTh 95. **d** 98 **p** 99. NSM Tadley St Pet *Win* 98–02; NSM Tadley S and Silchester 02–07; rtd 07; PtO *Win* 10–16 and from 17. *58 Bowmonts Road, Tadley, Basingstoke RG26 3SB* T: 0118-981 4860 E: pvbrown@tinyonline.co.uk

BROWN, Paul. See BROWN, Anthony Paul

BROWN, Paul David Christopher. b 50. Lon Univ LLB 71. EMMTC 81. **d** 84 **p** 85. NSM Wollaton *S'well* 84–13; PtO *Chelmsf* 13–14; NSM Thaxted 14–17; NSM Thaxted, The Sampfords, Radwinter and Hempstead from 17. *6 Bellrope Meadow, Sampford Road, Thaxted, Dunmow CM6 2FE* T: (01371) 831515 M: 07734-605921 E: pdchrisbrown@yahoo.co.uk

BROWN, Canon Penelope Jane. b 57. St Steph Ho Ox 94. **d** 96 **p** 97. C Croydon St Jo *S'wark* 96–99; V Croydon St Matt 99–09; AD Croydon Cen 07–09; P-in-c Limpsfield and Titsey

09–10; TR Limpsfield and Tatsfield 10–12; Hon Can S'wark Cathl 08–12; PtO *Lon* 12–15; *St E* 13–13; Hon C Woodbridge St Mary 13–14; PtO 14–16; Hon C Melton and Ufford from 16. *Vale House, 71 Ipswich Road, Woodbridge IP12 4BT* T: (01394) 388472 M: 07710-883787 E: canpennyb@btinternet.com

BROWN, Peter. b 38. Leeds Univ BSc 62 PhD 65. Nashotah Ho 85. **d** 87 **p** 88. R Minneapolis St Andr USA 87–89; C Sprowston w Beeston *Nor* 89–92; P-in-c W Winch w Setchey and N Runcton 92–98; P-in-c Middleton w E Winch 96–98; P-in-c Nor St Andr and Nor St Geo Colegate 98–99; Chapl Norfolk and Nor Health Care NHS Trust 98–99; rtd 00; PtO *Leic* 00–12. *41 Main Street, Cosby, Leicester LE9 1UW* T: 0116-286 6184 E: peterbrown@tesco.net *or* peter@pbrownrev.plus.com

BROWN, Canon Peter. b 47. RMN 69. Kelham Th Coll 69. **d** 74 **p** 75. CMP from 75; C Hendon *Dur* 74–80; C Byker St Ant *Newc* 80–90; C Brandon and Ushaw Moor *Dur* 90–05; V 05–12; Hon Can Dur Cathl 01–12; rtd 12; PtO *Dur* from 12. *29 Willow Green, Sunderland SR2 7NL* T: 0191-903 1863 M: 07719-545522 E: 47peterbrown@btinternet.com

BROWN, Peter Russell. b 43. Oak Hill Th Coll. **d** 71 **p** 72. C Gt Faringdon w Lt Coxwell *Ox* 71–73; C Reading Greyfriars 73–74; V Forty Hill Jes Ch *Lon* 74–81; V Laleham 81–09; rtd 09; PtO *Cant* from 10. *42A Tothill Street, Minster, Ramsgate CT12 4AJ* T: (01843) 822294 E: revprb43@yahoo.com

BROWN, Philip Anthony. b 54. Oak Hill Th Coll Bris BA 91 **p** 92. C Rock Ferry *Ches* 91–95; V Hattersley 95–98; V Harold Hill St Geo *Chelmsf* 98–09; P-in-c Chartham *Cant* 09–14; P-in-c Stone Street Gp 11–14; V Chartham and Upper Hardres w Stelling from 14; Asst Dir of Ords from 09. *The Rectory, The Green, Chartham, Canterbury CT4 7JW* T: (01227) 730141 E: filbrown@ymail.com

BROWN, Phillip John. b 75. Univ of Wales (Lamp) BTh 10 Nottm Univ MA 14. WEMTC 05. **d** 08 **p** 09. C Heref S Wye 08–13; TV 13–18; P-in-c Burghill from 18; P-in-c Pipe-cum-Lyde and Moreton-on-Lugg from 18; P-in-c Stretton Sugwas from 18. *The Vicarage, Burghill, Hereford HR4 7SG* E: pbrown777@aol.com *or* burghillchurch@gmail.com

BROWN, Phillip Murray. b 59. Keele Univ BSc 80. Trin Coll Bris. **d** 87 **p** 88. C Greasbrough *Sheff* 87–91; Ind Chapl 87–93; V Thorne 91–99; V Norton Lees St Paul from 99; C Norton from 17; C Greenhill from 17; C Woodseats St Chad from 17. *St Paul's Vicarage, 6 Angerford Avenue, Sheffield S8 9BG* T: 0114-255 1945 E: murray.stpauls@btinternet.com

BROWN, Raymond John. b 49. Ox Univ BEd 71. Wycliffe Hall Ox 72. **d** 75 **p** 76. C Barking St Marg w St Patr *Chelmsf* 75–78; C Walton H Trin *Ox* 78–82; V Enfield St Mich *Lon* 82–91; Chapl St Mich Hosp Enfield 82–91; R Springfield All SS *Chelmsf* 91–14; rtd 14; PtO *York* from 15. *18 Sidney Road, Rugby CV22 5LB* E: raymondjohnbrown@talktalk.net

BROWN, Richard Alexander Hamilton. b 74. **d** 13 **p** 14. NSM N Thornaby *York* 13–14; NSM Middlesbrough Ascension 14–17; NSM Grangetown 17–18; P-in-c Marsh Farm *St Alb* from 18. *Holy Cross Vicarage, Buckle Close, Luton LU3 3RT* T: (01582) 512228 M: 07867-494688 E: fr.richard.brown@gmail.com

BROWN, Robert. b 47. Man Univ BSc 72 Open Univ BA 86 Dur Univ MA 87. NEOC 95. **d** 98 **p** 99. C Yarm *York* 98–01; V Ormesby 01–12; rtd 12. *The Old Stone House, 7 High Street, Bishopton, Stockton-on-Tees TS21 1EZ* E: robert.cuthbert@gmail.com

BROWN, Robert Peter Cameron. b 63. K Coll Lon BSc 84 Imp Coll Lon MSc 87 Lon Bible Coll BA 97 Dur Univ PhD 13. Cranmer Hall Dur 01. **d** 03 **p** 04. C Upper Weardale *Dur* 03–08; PtO *Cant* 09–13; NSM Bewcastle, Stapleton and Kirklinton etc 13–18; P-in-c from 18. *Greenholme, Bewcastle, Carlisle CA6 6PW* T: (016977) 48438 E: rob@bewcastlehouseofprayer.org.uk

BROWN, Robin. b 38. Leeds Univ BA 60 MPhil 69. Qu Coll Birm 89. **d** 91 **p** 92. C Far Headingley St Chad *Ripon* 91–94; V Hawksworth Wood 94–00; rtd 00; PtO *Ripon* 00–14; *Leeds* from 14. *Dale Edge, 2A Harbour View, Bedale DL8 2DQ* T/F: (01677) 425483 M: 07960-277495 E: robin.stel1@btinternet.com

BROWN, Robin. See BROWN, Jack Robin

BROWN, Capt Roger George. b 37. CQSW. CA Tr Coll SEITE 92. **d** 95 **p** 96. C Maidstone St Martin *Cant* 95–97; C Oakham, Hambleton, Egleton, Braunston and Brooke *Pet* 97–04; Chapl Leics and Rutland Healthcare NHS Trust 97–04; rtd 04; Asst Chapl Kettering Gen Hosp NHS Foundn Trust 04–12; Chapl from 12. *5 Valley Walk, Kettering NN16 0LY* T: (01536) 524954 E: chaplaincy@kgh.nhs.uk

BROWN, Canon Roger Lee. b 42. Univ of Wales (Lamp) BA 63 Univ Coll Lon MA 73 Univ of Wales (Ban) DLitt 08 FSA 01. Wycliffe Hall Ox 66. **d** 68 **p** 69. C Dinas and Penygraig w Williamstown *Llan* 68–70; C Bargoed and Deri w Brithdir

70–72; TV Glyncorrwg w Afan Vale and Cymmer Afan 72–74; R 74–79; V Tongwynlais 79–93; R Welshpool w Castle Caereinion *St As* 93–07; AD Pool 01–07; Can Cursal St As Cathl 02–07; rtd 07; PtO *St As* from 09. *14 Berriew Road, Welshpool SY21 7SS* T: (01938) 552161

BROWN, Canon Rosalind. b 53. Lon Univ BA 74. Yale Div Sch MDiv 97. **d** 97 **p** 97. V Canonsburg St Thos USA 97–99; Vice-Prin OLM Scheme *Sarum* 99–05; Tutor STETS 99–05; Can Res Dur Cathl 05–18; rtd 18; PtO *Dur* from 19. *Birdsong, Hillcrest, Durham DH1 1RB* T: 0191-384 9200 E: rosalindbrown.durham@googlemail.com

BROWN, Preb Rosémia. b 53. Ripon Coll Cuddesdon 97. **d** 99 **p** 00. C Shoreditch St Leon and Hoxton St Jo *Lon* 99–00; C Shoreditch St Leon w St Mich 00–02; TV Hackney 02–03; V Clapton St Jas from 03; AD Hackney from 15; Preb St Paul's Cathl from 13. *St James's Vicarage, 105 Mayola Road, London E5 0RG* T: (020) 7686 3861 or 8985 1750 M: 07896-964693 E: office@stjamesclapton.co.uk *or* rosemia.brown@sky.com

BROWN, Canon Sarah Romilly Denner. b 65. Nottm Univ BA 86. ERMC 05. **d** 08 **p** 09. NSM Welford w Sibbertoft and Marston Trussell *Pet* 08–11; TV Daventry, Ashby St Ledgers, Braunston etc 11–16; TV Daventry 16–18; RD 13–18; Can Pet Cathl 15–18; Can Res Pet Cathl from 18; Adv in Women's Min from 18. *Peterborough Cathedral, Cathedral Office, Minster Precincts, Peterborough PE1 1XS* T: (01733) 355360 M: 07803-902864 E: sarah@talkingdirect.co.uk

BROWN, Sharon Lesley. b 63. Leeds Univ BA 86 Sheff Univ BA 14 MA 17 Bretton Hall Coll PGCE 88. Yorks Min Course 11. **d** 14 **p** 15. C Abbeylands *Leeds* 14–18; P-in-c Brotherton from 18; P-in-c Ferrybridge from 18. *St Andrew's Vicarage, 5 Pontefract Road, Ferrybridge, Knottingley WF11 8PN* M: 07951-708937 E: sharondrums@sky.com *or* sharon.brown@leeds.anglican.org

BROWN, Canon Simon Nicolas Danton. b 37. Clare Coll Cam BA 61 MA 65. S'wark Ord Course 61 Linc Th Coll 63. **d** 64 **p** 65. C Lambeth St Mary the Less *S'wark* 64–66; Chapl and Warden LMH Settlement 66–72; P-in-c Southampton St Mary w H Trin *Win* 72–73; V Southampton (City Cen) 73–79; R Gt Brickhill w Bow Brickhill and Lt Brickhill *Ox* 79–84; TR Burnham w Dropmore, Hitcham and Taplow 84–04; RD Burnham and Slough 87–02; Hon Can Ch Ch 94–04; Dioc Consultant for Deanery Development 97–04; Sen Exec Asst to Bp Buckingham 02–04; rtd 04; PtO *St E* from 04. *Seagulls, Pin Mill Road, Chelmondiston, Ipswich IP9 1JN* T: (01473) 780051 E: sandrseagulls@btinternet.com

BROWN, Sonya Helen Joan. See WRATTEN, Sonya Helen Joan

BROWN, Stephen Charles. b 60. Leeds Univ BA 83 BA 89 Reading Univ PGCE 89. Coll of Resurr Mirfield 87. **d** 90 **p** 91. C Whitkirk *Ripon* 90–93; Asst Youth Chapl 92–95; C Chapel Allerton 93–95; R Stanningley St Thos 95–01; Chapl MU 98–01; V Laneside *Blackb* from 01; Hon Chapl ATC 03–07. *St Peter's Vicarage, Helmshore Road, Haslingden, Rossendale BB4 4BG* T: (01706) 213838 E: highlow@talktalk.net

BROWN, Stephen George. b 54. STETS 13. **d** 15 **p** 16. NSM Kilburn St Aug w St Jo *Lon* 15–17; NSM Hayes St Mary 17–19; P-in-c Edmonton St Alphege from 19; P-in-c Ponders End St Matt from 19; PtO *Man* 15–19. *St Alphage Vicarage, Rossdale Drive, London N9 7LG* T: 07966-427213 *or* (020) 8374 8205 E: frstephenb@outlook.com

BROWN, Stephen James. b 44. Bradf Univ BSc 69. Westcott Ho Cam 71. **d** 72 **p** 73. C Seaton Hirst *Newc* 72–75; C Marton-in-Cleveland *York* 75–77; Dioc Youth Adv *Dur* 77–82; V Thorner *Ripon* 82–92; Dioc Officer for Local Min 90–01; P-in-c Ripley w Burnt Yates 92–09; Chapl Yorkshire TV 89–09; rtd 09; PtO *York* from 10. *88 Prince Rupert Drive, Tockwith, York YO26 7QS* T: (01423) 359142 M: 07521-705350 E: stephenbrown83@hotmail.co.uk

BROWN, Susan Gertrude. b 48. Univ of Wales (Swansea) BA 71 Roehampton Inst PGCE 72. St Mich Coll Llan 98. **d** 02 **p** 03. NSM Gelligaer *Llan* 02–04; NSM Eglwysilan 04–07; LtO 07–08; NSM Caerphilly 08–13; Dioc Adv for NSM 10–13; rtd 14; PtO *Llan* from 14. *2 Caerleon Court, Caerphilly CF83 2UF* T: (029) 2140 3773 E: suebrown27_uk@yahoo.com

BROWN, Terence George Albert. b 49. SS Mark & Jo Univ Coll Plymouth BEd 75. ERMC 04. **d** 06 **p** 09. NSM Langdon Hills *Chelmsf* 06–09; NSM Gt Wakering w Foulness 09–13; NSM Barling w Lt Wakering 09–13; P-in-c Sandon 13–17; R from 17; P-in-c E Hanningfield from 17. *The Vicarage, 1 Glebe Meadow, Great Waltham, Chelmsford CM3 1EX* T: (01245) 698988 M: 07944-444675 E: tgabrown@hotmail.com

BROWN, Terry Frederick. b 51. **d** 16 **p** 17. OLM Canvey Is *Chelmsf* from 16. *59 Lionel Road, Canvey Island SS8 9DJ* E: terry.f.brown@blueyonder.co.uk

BROWN, Thomas Andrew. b 86. Essex Univ BA 08. Oak Hill Th Coll BA 18. **d** 18 **p** 19. C Kilnhurst *Sheff* from 18. *20 Canalside View, Kilnhurst, Mexborough S64 5SD* M: 07825-913286 E: tom.brown371@gmail.com

BROWN, Thomas Edward. b 86. Clare Coll Cam MSci 09. Oak Hill Th Coll 15. **d** 18 **p** 19. C Lutterworth w Cotesbach and Bitteswell *Leic* from 18. *The Vicarage, Lutterworth Road, Bitteswell, Lutterworth LE17 4RX* M: 07818-404287 E: tebrown39@gmail.com

BROWN, Mrs Verity Joy. b 68. Qu Mary Coll Lon BA 89. Ripon Coll Cuddesdon BTh 93. **d** 93 **p** 94. C Barnard Castle w Whorlton *Dur* 93–95; C Bensham 95–97; PtO 97–10; NSM Hartlepool St Hilda 10–16; P-in-c from 16. *The Rectory, Church Close, Hartlepool TS24 0PW* T: (01429) 423186 M: 07846-064456 E: veritybrwn@gmail.com

BROWN, Victor Charles. b 31. S'wark Ord Course 67. **d** 71 **p** 72. C Pinhoe *Ex* 71–73; C Egg Buckland 73–74; C Oakdale St Geo *Sarum* 74–77; R Old Trafford St Hilda *Man* 77–83; R Chigwell Row *Chelmsf* 83–92; R Fenny Bentley, Kniveton, Thorpe and Tissington *Derby* 92–96; rtd 96; PtO *Sarum* 96–08. *5 Gracey Court, Woodland Road, Broadclyst, Exeter EX5 3GA* T: (01392) 462799

BROWN, Wendy Anne. See WALE, Wendy Anne

BROWNE, Arnold Samuel. b 52. St Jo Coll Ox BA 73 MA 77 SS Coll Cam PhD 87 Surrey Univ MSc 89 MBPsS 92. Westcott Ho Cam 76. **d** 78 **p** 79. C Esher *Guildf* 78–81; C Worplesdon 81–86; Chapl R Holloway and Bedf New Coll 86–92; Fell and Dean of Chpl Trin Coll Cam 92–06; PtO *Nor* from 06. *18 Riverside Road, Norwich NR1 1SN* T: (01603) 629362 E: arnoldbrowne@btinternet.com

BROWNE, Daniel Michael. b 67. Leic Poly MA 90. Trin Coll Bris MA 17. **d** 17 **p** 18. C Newent and Gorsley w Cliffords Mesne *Glouc* from 17. *22 Drovers Way, Newent GL18 1ET* M: 07734-906281 E: d.browne@btinternet.com

BROWNE, Ian Cameron. b 51. St Cath Coll Ox BA 74 MA 78 Fitzw Coll Cam BA 76 MA 80. Ridley Hall Cam 74. **d** 77 **p** 78. C Cheltenham Ch Ch *Glouc* 77–80; Hon C Shrewsbury St Chad *Lich* 80–83; Asst Chapl Shrewsbury Sch 80–83; Chapl Bedford Sch 83–96; Sen Chapl Oundle Sch 97–11; rtd 11; PtO *Pet* from 12. *46C North Street, Oundle, Peterborough PE8 4AL* T: (01832) 273541 E: the.revb@virgin.net

BROWNE, Leonard Joseph. b 58. St Cath Coll Cam BA 81 MA 84. Trin Coll Bris 87. **d** 89 **p** 90. C Reading Greyfriars *Ox* 89–92; V Cambridge St Barn *Ely* 92–00; Sen Chapl Dean Close Sch 00–04; Hd Master Dean Close Prep Sch 04–14; Asst Chapl Dean Close Sch 14–16; V Harborne Heath *Birm* from 16. *99 Wentworth Road, Birmingham B17 9ST* T: 0121-427 4601 M: 07584-680910 E: leonardbrowne@stjohns-church.co.uk

BROWNE, Peter Clifford. b 59. Bris Univ BA 80 SRN 82. Ripon Coll Cuddesdon 88. **d** 90 **p** 91. C Southgate Ch Ch *Lon* 90–92; NSM Kemp Town St Mary *Chich* 93–95; Chapl United Bris Healthcare NHS Trust 96–98; NSM Southmead *Bris* 98–02; Chapl HM Pris Preston 02–10; Chapl HM Pris Shepton Mallet 10–13; Chapl HM Pris and YOI Guys Marsh from 13. *HM Prison Guys Marsh, Shaftesbury SP7 0AH* T: (01747) 856400 E: peter.browne@justice.gov.uk

BROWNHILL, Mrs Diane. b 56. Dioc OLM tr scheme 03. **d** 06 **p** 07. C Man Apostles w Miles Platting 06–09; TV Heatons from 09. *St Thomas' Rectory, 6 Heaton Moor Road, Stockport SK4 4NS* T: 0161-432 1912 M: 07505-781530 E: gldbrownhill@aol.com

BROWNING, Derek. See BROWNING, Robert Derek

BROWNING, Edward Barrington Lee (Barry). b 42. St Pet Coll Saltley TCert 65. Ripon Coll Cuddesdon 90. **d** 92 **p** 93. C Falmouth K Chas *Truro* 92–96; R Roche and Withiel 96–01; P-in-c Manaccan w St Anthony-in-Meneage and St Martin 01–06; P-in-c Cury and Gunwalloe w Mawgan 01–06; rtd 06; PtO *Truro* 06–10; P-in-c St Goran w Caerhays 10–13; PtO from 14. *73 Park Way, St Austell PL25 4HR* T: (01726) 65194 E: barry.browning@btinternet.com

✠**BROWNING, The Rt Revd George Victor.** b 42. Chas Sturt Univ NSW DLitt 07. St Jo Coll Morpeth Th 66. **d** 66 **p** 67 **c** 85. C Inverell Australia 66–68; C Armidale 68–69; V Warialda 69–73; Vice Prin St Jo Coll Morpeth 73–76; R Singleton and Adn Upper Hunter 76–84; R Woy Woy and Adn Cen Coast 84–85; Asst Bp Brisbane 85–93; Prin St Fran Th Coll 88–91; Bp Canberra and Goulburn 93–08; Dir Aus Cen Christianity and Culture 96–08; P-in-c Wriggle Valley *Sarum* 08–09; rtd 09. *24 Henry Place, Long Beach NSW 2536, Australia* T: (0061) (2) 4472 7470 E: gandmbrowning@bigpond.com

BROWNING, Canon Jacqueline Ann. b 44. Sarum Th Coll 93. **d** 96 **p** 97. NSM New Alresford w Ovington and Itchen Stoke *Win* 96–02; Past Asst Win Cathl 02–12; Min Can Win Cathl 06–09; Hon Can Win Cathl 09–12; rtd 13; PtO *Win* from 16. *1 Paddock Way, Alresford SO24 9PN* T: (01962) 734372 *or* 857237 E: alresfordjackie@gmail.com

BROWNING, Julian. b 51. St Jo Coll Cam BA 72 MA 76. Ripon Coll Cuddesdon 77. **d** 80 **p** 81. C Notting Hill *Lon* 80–81; C W Brompton St Mary w St Pet 81–84; PtO 84–91; NSM Paddington St Sav 99–06; NSM St Marylebone St Cypr 06–14; NSM St Marylebone All SS from 14. *82 Ashworth Mansions, Grantully Road, London W9 1LN* T: (020) 7286 6034 E: julian.browning@yahoo.co.uk

BROWNING, Kevin John. b 56. Ridley Hall Cam 96. **d** 98 **p** 99. C Northampton Em *Pet* 98–01; P-in-c Hardwick *Ely* 01–09; C Cranham Park *Chelmsf* 10–18; V S Hornchurch St Jo and St Matt from 18. *St John's Vicarage, South End Road, Rainham RM13 7XT* T: (01708) 555260 E: rev.kevinbrowning@stjohnsparishchurch.org

BROWNING, Miss Rachel. b 69. Oak Hill Th Coll BA 08. **d** 09. NSM Hastings Em and St Mary in the Castle *Chich* from 09; PtO *Ely* from 15. *11A Emmanuel Road, Hastings TN34 3LB* T: (01424) 430980 M: 07939-126955 E: rach.browning@gmail.com *or* rach@emmanuelhastings.org.uk

BROWNING, Robert Derek. b 42. Guildf Dioc Min Course 98. **d** 01 **p** 02. OLM Lightwater *Guildf* 01–12; PtO from 12. *16 Guildford Road, Lightwater GU18 5SN* T: (01276) 474345 E: derekandcarol.b@tiscali.co.uk

BROWNING, Mrs Rosheen Elizabeth. b 76. Middx Univ BA 98 Cant Ch Ch Univ PGCE 03. Ridley Hall Cam 13. **d** 15 **p** 16. C Paddock Wood *Roch* 15–19; P-in-c Camborne, Tuckingmill and Penponds *Truro* from 19; P-in-c Crowan and Treslothan from 19. *The Vicarage, 37 Trethannas Gardens, Praze, Camborne TR14 0LL* T: (01209) 831175 M: 07701-085736 E: rev.rosh@icloud.com

BROWNLIE, Miss Caroline Heddon. b 47. CQSW 75. Qu Coll Birm IDC 81. **d** 87 **p** 94. Asst Chapl Fairfield Hosp Hitchin 87–91; NSM Ashwell w Hinxworth and Newnham *St Alb* 92–98; Chapl HM Rem Cen Low Newton 99–01; PtO *St Alb* 04–05; P-in-c Gilling and Kirkby Ravensworth *Ripon* 05–07; rtd 07; PtO *Ely* from 07. *13 Vicarage Close, Melbourn, Royston SG8 6DY* T: (01763) 263375 E: carolineatno9@john-lewis.com

BROWNSELL, Preb John Kenneth. b 48. Hertf Coll Ox BA 69 BA 72 MA 89. Cuddesdon Coll 70. **d** 73 **p** 74. C Notting Hill All SS w St Columb *Lon* 73–74; C Notting Hill 74–76; TV 76–82; V Notting Hill All SS w St Columb 82–18; AD Kensington 84–92; Dir of Ords 95–12; Preb St Paul's Cathl 92–18; rtd 18. *2 Morley College, Market Street, Winchester SO23 9LF* T: (01962) 867315 E: jkb194805@gmail.com

BROXHAM, Ms Ann. b 47. York St Jo Coll BA 03. Westcott Ho Cam 10. **d** 10. NSM Littleport *Ely* 10–13; NSM Crosland Moor and Linthwaite *Leeds* 13–18; rtd 18. *45 Edale Avenue, Newsome, Huddersfield HD4 6LN* T: (01484) 420365 E: annbroxham@yahoo.co.uk

BRUCE, Adam. See BRUCE, Henry Adam Francis

BRUCE, Canon Amanda Jane. b 67. Liv Univ BSc 87 Southn Univ PGCE 89 Chelt & Glouc Coll of HE AdDipEd 01. Wycliffe Hall Ox 06. **d** 08 **p** 09. C Haydock St Mark *Liv* 08–12; TR Sutton 12–16; V Gt Crosby St Luke from 16; Hon Can Liv Cathl from 19. *St Luke's Vicarage, 71 Liverpool Road, Crosby, Liverpool L23 5SE* T: 0151-932 9253 E: revamandabruce@gmail.com

BRUCE, David Crosby. b 72. SS Coll Cam MA 94 PGCE 95 Bris Univ MEd 05. Trin Coll Bris 10. **d** 12 **p** 13. C Meole Brace *Lich* 12–16; TR Malvern Chase *Worc* from 16. *48 Longridge Road, Malvern WR14 3JB* E: davecbruce@gmail.com *or* dave.bruce@chaseteam.org

BRUCE, The Hon Henry Adam Francis. b 62. Trin Coll Ox MA 89. **d** 17 **p** 18. NSM Llan-llwch w Llangain and Llangynog and Llansteffan etc *St D* 17–18; NSM Bro Sancler from 18. *St Davids Court, Llanboidy Road, Meidrim, Carmarthen SA33 5QF* T: (01994) 231470 M: 07976-829111 E: hafbruce@hotmail.com

BRUCE, James Hamilton. b 57. Dur Univ BSc 78 Newc Univ MSc 79 St Andr Univ PhD 99. Trin Coll Bris 81. **d** 84 **p** 85. C Walmley *Birm* 84–86; PtO *Carl* 87–95; W Cumbria Sch Worker N Schs Chr Union 87–93; Nat Development Officer Wales Scripture Union 93–94; Chapl Turi St Andr Kenya 95–96; NSM St Andrews St Andr *St And* 96–99; R Penicuik and W Linton *Edin* 99–03; PtO *Win* 03–06; V Lyndhurst and Emery Down and Minstead 06–17; P-in-c Cartmel Peninsula *Carl* from 18. *Applebeck, Glebe Road, Bowness-on-Windermere, Windermere LA23 3HB* E: bruces@talktalk.net

BRUCE, John Cyril. b 41. EMMTC 95. **d** 98 **p** 99. NSM Spalding St Mary and St Nic *Linc* 98–05; P-in-c Grantham, Manthorpe 05–08; rtd 09; PtO *Linc* from 16. *5 Welwyn Close, Grantham NG31 7JU* T: (01476) 561546 M: 07947-156933 E: jcb.churchmail@gmail.com

BRUCE, Kathrine Sarah. b 68. Leeds Univ BA 89 St Jo Coll Dur BA 01 MATM 07 Dur Univ PhD 14 Trin & All SS Coll Leeds PGCE 91. Cranmer Hall Dur 98. **d** 01 **p** 02. C Ripon H Trin 01–04; Chapl Trevelyan Coll *Dur* 04–08; Chapl Van Mildert Coll 04–08; NSM Dur St Oswald 04–06; NSM Dur St Oswald and Shincliffe 06–08; Chapl St Jo Coll Dur 08–13; Dep Warden and Tutor 13–18; Chapl RAF from 18. *Chaplaincy Services (RAF), HQ Air Command, RAF High Wycombe HP14 4UE* T: (01494) 496800 E: katebruce971@gmail.com

BRUCE, Mrs Susan Elizabeth. b 52. **d** 08 **p** 09. OLM Haughton le Skerne *Dur* 08–14; NSM Middleton St George 14–16; rtd 16; PtO *Dur* from 16. *14 Haughton Green, Darlington DL1 2DF* T: (01325) 281567 M: 07810-720490 E: sue.bruce.014@gmail.com

BRUECK, Ms Jutta. b 61. LSE MSc 89 Heythrop Coll Lon MA 92 Fitzw Coll Cam BA 96 MA 00. Westcott Ho Cam 94. **d** 97 **p** 98. C Is of Dogs Ch Ch and St Jo w St Luke *Lon* 97–01; Chapl Guildhall Sch of Music and Drama 01–06; Chapl Fitzw Coll Cam 06–08; P-in-c Cambridge St Jas *Ely* 08–15; P-in-c Ipswich St Thos *St E* from 15. *St Thomas's Vicarage, 102 Cromer Road, Ipswich IP1 5EP* M: 07958-360564 E: jutta.brueck@cofesuffolk.org

BRUMWELL, Suzanne. **d** 16 **p** 17. C Cowbridge *Llan* from 16. *3 Leoline Close, Cowbridge CF71 7BU* T: (01446) 771515 E: curate@cowbridgeparish.com

BRUNNING, Canon David George. b 32. St D Coll Lamp BA 53. St Mich Coll Llan 53. **d** 55 **p** 56. C Llantwit Major and St Donat's *Llan* 55–59; C Usk and Monkswood w Glascoed Chpl and Gwehelog *Mon* 59–62; V Abercarn 62–71; V Pontnewydd 71–89; RD Pontypool 89–97; R Panteg 90–98; Can St Woolos Cathl from 94; rtd 98; LtO *Mon* from 98; PtO *Llan* from 98. *6 Spitzkop, Llantwit Major CF61 1RD* T: (01446) 792124

BRUNO, Canon Allan David. b 34. AKC 59. St Boniface Warminster 59. **d** 60 **p** 61. C Darlington H Trin *Dur* 60–64; C Kimberley Cathl and Chapl Bp's Hostel S Africa 64–65; Asst Chapl Peterhouse Dioc Boys' Sch Rhodesia 65–70; Overseas Chapl Scottish Episc Ch 70–75; C Edin Old St Paul 75–76; Dir of Miss Prov of S Africa 76–80; Namibia 80–86; Dean Windhoek 81–86; R Falkirk *Edin* 86–95; Hon Can Kinkizi from 95; Bp's Dom Chapl *Bradf* 96–99; Bp's Past Asst 99–01; rtd 01; PtO *Bradf* 01–14; *Leeds* from 14; *Blackb* 02–14; Bp's Officer for Rtd Clergy and Widows Craven Adnry *Bradf* 10–14; *Leeds* from 14. *Pond House, 5 Twine Walk, Burton in Lonsdale, Carnforth LA6 3LR* T: (015242) 61616 E: davidmaggiebruno@gmail.com

BRUNSWICK, Canon Robert John. b 38. St Aid Birkenhead 60. **d** 63 **p** 64. C Neston *Ches* 63–66; CF (TA - R of O) 65–96; C Warrington St Paul *Liv* 66–68; V Liv St Paul Stoneycroft 68–78; V Southport St Luke 78–87; R Croston *Blackb* 87–01; R Croston and Bretherton 01–05; Chapl Bp Rawstorne Sch Preston 88–05; Hon Can Koforidua from 94; rtd 05. *60 St Clements Avenue, Farington, Leyland PR25 4QU* T: (01772) 426094

BRUNT, Alison. b 60. Nottm Univ BSc 82 K Coll Lon MA 01 SS Coll Cam BTh 12. Westcott Ho Cam 10. **d** 12 **p** 13. C S Croydon St Pet and St Aug *S'wark* 12–15; V Norbury St Oswald from 15. *The Vicarage, 2B St Oswald's Road, London SW16 3SB* T: (020) 8764 2853 E: rev.alison@outlook.com

BRUNT, Prof Peter William. b 36. Liv Univ MB 59 MD 67 Lon Univ FRCP 74 FRCPEd. Ab Dioc Tr Course. **d** 96 **p** 97. NSM Bieldside *Ab* 96–07; PtO *Carl* from 08; *Ab* from 11. *81 Wansdyke, Morpeth NE61 3QY*

BRUNT, Canon Philippa Ann. b 53. Leeds Univ BA 74 Leeds and Carnegie Coll PGCE 75. WEMTC 95. **d** 98 **p** 99. C Cinderford St Steph w Littledean *Glouc* 98–01; V Parkend and Viney Hill 01–17; AD Forest S 09–15; Hon Can Glouc Cathl 10–17; rtd 17. *Address temp unknown* E: pabrunt@btinternet.com

BRUSH, Canon Sally. b 47. Lon Univ BD 75 Univ of Wales MPhil 96. Trin Coll Bris 73. **dss** 76 **d** 80 **p** 97. Flint *St As* 76–83; C 80–83; C Cefn 83–87; C St As and Tremeirchion 83–87; Chapl St As Cathl 83–87; Dn-in-c Cerrigydrudion w Llanfihangel Glyn Myfyr etc 87–97; V 97–07; RD Edeirnion 98–04; Hon Can St As Cathl 01–07; rtd 07; PtO *St As* from 09; *Ban* 10–17. *Persondy, 1 Tyddyn Terrace, Cerrigydrudion, Corwen LL21 9TN* T: (01490) 420048

BRUSH (née HAMILTON), Sarah Louise. b 74. Reading Univ BA 97 MA 98 PhD 01. Qu Coll Birm MA 14. **d** 14 **p** 15. C Halas *Worc* 14–18; Lect Ripon Coll Cuddesdon from 18. *3 Church Close, Cuddesdon, Oxford OX44 9HD* E: sarahbrush@hotmail.co.uk *or* sarah.brush@rcc.ac.uk

BRYAN, Angela Edwina. b 82. York Univ BA 03 York St Jo Coll PGCE 04. St Jo Coll Nottm 07. **d** 10 **p** 11. C Tipton St Matt *Lich* 10–14; P-in-c Kirkholt *Man* 14–18; C Saddleworth from

18. *15 Grotton Hollow, Grotton, Oldham OL4 4LN* M: 07522-316952 E: revangbryan@icloud.com

BRYAN, The Ven Christopher Paul. b 75. Univ Coll Ox BA 96 St Jo Coll Dur BA 99. Cranmer Hall Dur 97. **d** 00 **p** 01. C Old Swinford Stourbridge *Worc* 00–04; P-in-c Lechlade *Glouc* 04–08; TV Fairford Deanery 09–10; P-in-c Sherston Magna, Easton Grey, Luckington etc *Bris* 10–16; P-in-c Hullavington, Norton and Stanton St Quintin 10–16; R Gauzebrook 16–19; AD N Wilts 17–19; Adn Malmesbury from 19. *The Rectory, 1 Rectory Close, Stanton St Quintin, Chippenham SN14 6DT* T: 0117-906 0100 M: 07906-175331 E: christopher.bryan123@btinternet.com

BRYAN, David John. b 56. Liv Univ BSc 77 Hull Univ BTh 85 Qu Coll Ox DPhil 89. Ox Min Course 89. **d** 90 **p** 91. C Abingdon *Ox* 90–93; Tutor Qu Coll Birm 93–01; Dean of Studies 95–01; R Haughton le Skerne *Dur* 01–11; Dir Studies Lindisfarne Reg Tr Partnership 11–17; Dean Lindisfarne Coll of Th from 17. *2 Kingfisher Close, Esh Winning, Durham DH7 9AN* T: 0191-373 9698 *or* 270 4150 E: davidbryan@lindisfarnect.org

BRYAN, Helen Ann. b 68. NTMTC BA 07. **d** 07 **p** 08. NSM Laindon w Dunton *Chelmsf* 07–13; P-in-c E and W Horndon w Lt Warley and Childerditch 13–18; V 18–19; TV Cheshunt *St Alb* from 19. *Address temp unknown* M: 07747-397973 E: hbryan@talktalk.net

BRYAN, Judith Claire. See STEPHENSON, Judith Claire

BRYAN, Patrick Joseph. b 41. St Jo Coll Cam BA 63 MA 67. St Steph Ho Ox 73. **d** 75 **p** 76. C Rushall *Lich* 75–78; C Brierley Hill 78–80; P-in-c Walsall St Mary and All SS Palfrey 80–87; PtO from 13. *12 Derwent Road, Wolverhampton WV6 9ES* T: (01902) 689550 E: pjjmbryan@blueyonder.co.uk

BRYAN, Canon Sherry Lee. b 49. Open Univ BA 12. WMMTC 88. **d** 91 **p** 94. Par Dn St Columb Minor and St Colan *Truro* 91–94; C 94–95; P-in-c St Teath 95–05; P-in-c Blisland w St Breward 05–15; P-in-c Helland 05–15; R Blisland w Temple, St Breward and Helland 15–17; P-in-c St Tudy w St Mabyn and Michaelstow 16–17; Adv for Women's Min 92–99; Chapl Cornwall Fire Brigade 93–95; Chapl Cornwall Healthcare NHS Trust 99–02; RD Trigg Minor and Bodmin *Truro* 02–13; Hon Can Truro Cathl 03–17; rtd 17. *Address withheld by request*

BRYAN, Canon Timothy Andrew. b 56. St Edm Hall Ox MA 80. S'wark Ord Course 93. **d** 96 **p** 97. NSM Morden S'wark 96–99; NSM Carshalton Beeches 99–05; NSM Sutton 05–08; Resettlement Chapl HM Pris Wandsworth 07–08; Co-ord Chapl 08–17; Chapl Adv HM Pris and Probation Service (Midl, Yorks and NE) from 17; Hon Can S'wark Cathl from 15; PtO *Heref* from 17. *Sycamores, Carding Mill Valley, Church Stretton SY6 6JF* T: (01694) 723192 M: 07974-366810 E: timbryan57@gmail.com *or* timothy.bryan@justice.gov.uk

BRYAN, Canon Andrew Watts. b 57. St Jo Coll Dur BA 78 Birm Univ MA 81. Qu Coll Birm 80. **d** 83 **p** 84. C Pelsall *Lich* 83–87; NSM 91–94; PtO 87–92; NSM Streetly 94–96; NSM Beckbury, Badger, Kemberton, Ryton, Stockton etc 96–99; R Worplesdon *Guildf* 99–09; Chapl Merrist Wood Coll of Agric and Horticulture 95–09; TR Portishead *B & W* 09–15; Can Res Nor Cathl from 15; P-in-c Nor St Mary in the Marsh 15–16. *52 The Close, Norwich NR1 4EG* T: (01603) 218331 E: canon.missionandpastoral@cathedral.org.uk

BRYANT, Benjamin Mark. b 82. RCM BMus 05. St Mellitus Coll BA 16. **d** 16 **p** 17. C Portsea St Alb *Portsm* 16–18; C Onslow Square and S Kensington St Aug *Lon* from 18. *23 Pooles Lane, London SW10 0RH* M: 07887-868445 E: ben.bryant@htb.org

BRYANT, Canon Christopher. b 32. K Coll Lon AKC 60. **d** 61 **p** 62. C Fareham H Trin *Portsm* 61–65; C Yatton Keynell *Bris* 65–71; C Biddestone w Slaughterford 65–71; C Castle Combe 65–71; V Chirton, Marden and Patney *Sarum* 71–76; V Chirton, Marden, Patney, Charlton and Wilsford 76–78; P-in-c Devizes St Jo w St Mary 78–79; R 79–97; RD Devizes 83–93; Can and Preb Sarum Cathl 87–04; rtd 97; Master St Nic Hosp Salisbury 97–04; PtO *Sarum* from 06. *34 Mill Road, Salisbury SP2 7RZ* T: (01722) 502336

BRYANT, Donald Thomas. b 29. SE Essex Coll BSc 56 Birkbeck Coll Lon BSc 58 FSS 59. S'wark Ord Course 85. **d** 88 **p** 89. NSM Redhill St Matt *S'wark* 88–99; PtO 99–04 and 05–17; NSM Salfords 00–05. *3 Mulberry Walk, Ditchling Common, Burgess Hill RH15 0SZ* T: (01444) 254167   E: frdonaldtbryant@hotmail.co.uk   *or* donbry87@outlook.com

BRYANT, Canon Edward Francis Paterson. b 43. S'wark Ord Course 75. **d** 78 **p** 79. NSM Hadlow *Roch* 78–84; C Dartford St Alb 84–87; R Hollington St Leon *Chich* 87–93; V Bexhill St Aug 93–99; TR Bexhill St Pet 99–12; P-in-c Sedlescombe w Whatlington 02–05; rtd 12; RD Battle and Bexhill *Chich* 98–04 and 10–13; Can and Preb Chich

Cathl from 00. *14 Highwater View, St Leonards-on-Sea TN38 8EL* T: (01424) 853687 F: 07970-991268 M: 07824-859044 E: invenietis@gmx.com

BRYANT, Graham Trevor. b 41. Keble Coll Ox BA 63 MA 67. Chich Th Coll 64. **d** 66 **p** 67. C Leeds St Wilfrid *Ripon* 66–69; C Haywards Heath St Wilfrid *Chich* 69–74; V Crawley Down All SS 74–79; V Bexhill St Aug 79–85; V Charlton Kings St Mary *Glouc* 85–02; rtd 02; PtO *Glouc* from 03. *6 The Close, Cheltenham GL53 0PQ* T: (01242) 520313

✠**BRYANT, The Rt Revd Mark Watts.** b 49. St Jo Coll Dur BA 72. Cuddesdon Coll 72. **d** 75 **p** 76 **c** 07. C Addlestone *Guildf* 75–79; C Studley *Sarum* 79–83; V 83–88; Chapl Trowbridge Coll 79–83; Voc Development Adv and Dioc Dir of Ords *Cov* 88–96; Hon Can Cov Cathl 93–01; TR Coventry Caludon 96–01; AD Cov E 99–01; Adn Cov 01–07; Can Res Cov Cathl 06–07; Suff Bp Jarrow *Dur* 07–18; rtd 18; PtO *Newc* from 18. *59 Eastfield Avenue, Whitley Bay NE25 8NQ* T: 0191-252 2429 E: markbryant@dunelm.org.uk

BRYANT, Patricia Ann. b 36. Qu Mary Coll Lon BA 58. St Mich Coll Llan 94. **d** 91 **p** 97. NSM Llanbadoc *Mon* 91–93; NSM Llangybi and Coedypaen w Llanbadoc 93–94; C 94–98; Asst Chapl Gwent Tertiary Coll 94–98; V Merthyr Cynog and Dyffryn Honddu etc *S & B* 98–02; rtd 03. *5 Trebarried Court, Llandefalle, Brecon LD3 0NB* T: (01874) 754087 E: email@peterpatbryant.plus.com

BRYANT, Canon Richard Kirk. b 47. Ch Coll Cam BA 68 MA 72. Cuddesdon Coll 70. **d** 72 **p** 73. C Newc St Gabr 72–75; C Morpeth 75–78; C Benwell St Jas 78–82; V Earsdon and Backworth 82–93; V Wylam 93–97; Prin Local Min Scheme 97–11; Prin Reader Tr 97–11; Hon Can Newc Cathl 97–11; rtd 11; PtO *Newc* from 11. *10 Highworth Drive, Newcastle upon Tyne NE7 7FB* T: 0191-240 1510 E: rk.bryant@virginmedia.com

BRYANT, Richard Maurice. b 46. MAAIS 80. WMMTC 90. **d** 93 **p** 94. NSM The Stanleys *Glouc* 93–98; NSM Glouc St Geo w Whaddon 98–04; NSM Twigworth, Down Hatherley, Norton, The Leigh etc 04–08; NSM Bisley, Chalford, France Lynch, and Oakridge 08–11; rtd 11; PtO *Glouc* from 11. *6 Church Street, Kings Stanley, Stonehouse GL10 3HW* T: (01453) 823172

BRYANT, Sarah Elizabeth. See WOOD-ROE, Sarah Elizabeth

BRYANT-SCOTT, Canon David Bruce. b 62. Trin Coll Toronto BA 84 MDiv 88 Harvard Div Sch ThM 03. **d** 88 **p** 89. C Welland St Dav Canada 88–90; C St Catharine St Geo 90–95; R Gulf Is Pender and Saturna 95–04; Dioc Adn BC 04–12; R Victoria St Matthias 14–17; P-in-c Cobble Hill St Jo 17; P-in-c Victoria St Dunstan 17–18; Asst Chapl Gtr Athens *Eur* from 18. *Box 421, Gavalohori, Chania 73008, Crete, Greece* T: (0030) (2825) 023270 M: (0030) 6947-600686 E: bbryantscott@gmail.com

BRYARS, Peter John. b 54. BA MEd PhD. St Jo Coll Nottm. **d** 84 **p** 85. C Hull St Martin w Transfiguration *York* 84–87; TV Drypool 87–90; TV Glendale Gp *Newc* 90–94; P-in-c Heddon-on-the-Wall 94–01; Adult Educn Adv 94–01; V Delaval 01–11; AD Bedlington 03–09; Dioc Chapl MU 02–07; rtd 12; PtO *Newc* from 12; Bp's Adv for Healing Min from 06. *36 Newlands Road, Blyth NE24 2QJ* E: pjbryars@btinternet.com

BRYCE, Brenda Dorothy. See BROWN, Brenda Dorothy

BRYCE, Michael Adrian Gilpin. b 47. TCD BA 71 MA 95. CITC 74. **d** 77 **p** 78. C Clondalkin w Tallaght *D & G* 77–79; C Ch Ch Cathl and Chapl Univ Coll Dub 79–82; I Ardamine w Kiltennel, Glascarrig etc *C & O* 82–84; CF 84–00; I Lisbellaw *Clogh* 00–05; R Bolam w Whalton and Hartburn w Meldon *Newc* 05–16; V Nether Witton 05–16; Chapl Kirkley Hall Coll 05–16; rtd 16; PtO *Newc* from 19. *5 Church View, Longhorsley, Morpeth NE65 8UH*

BRYDON, Michael Andrew. b 73. St Chad's Coll Dur BA 95 MA 96 PhD 00. St Steph Ho Ox BA 01. **d** 02 **p** 03. C Bexhill St Pet *Chich* 02–06; C Brighton St Paul 06–08; Dioc Adv for Educn and Tr of Adults 06–08; R Catsfield and Crowhurst from 08. *The Rectory, Church Lane, Catsfield, Battle TN33 9DR* T: (01424) 892988

BRYER, Anthony Colin. b 51. Qu Eliz Coll Lon BSc 72. Trin Coll Bris 72. **d** 75 **p** 76. C Preston St Cuth *Blackb* 75–78; C Becontree St Mary *Chelmsf* 78–81; TV Loughton St Mary and St Mich 81–88; C Clifton St Paul *Bris* 88–91; P-in-c 91–94; R Bris St Mich and St Paul 94–96; In C of S and LtO *Edin* 96–04; P-in-c Towcester w Caldecote and Easton Neston *Pet* 04–07; C Greens Norton w Bradden and Lichborough 06–07; V Towcester w Caldecote and Easton Neston 11–15; Ind Chapl *Edin* 11–16; rtd 16; LtO *Edin* from 16. *4 Yewlands Gardens, Edinburgh EH16 6TA* T: 0131-672 2232 M: 07814-832004 E: tony.bryer51@gmail.com

BRYER, The Ven Paul Donald. b 58. Sussex Univ BEd 80 Nottm Univ MA 96. St Jo Coll Nottm. **d** 90 **p** 91. C Tonbridge St Steph *Roch* 90–94; TV Camberley St Paul

Guildf 94–99; V Camberley St Mary 99–01; V Dorking St Paul 01–14; RD Dorking 09–14; Adn Dorking 14–19; Hon Can Guildf Cathl 14–19; Adn Cornwall *Truro* from 19. *The Vicarage, 2 Devoran Lane, Devoran, Truro TR3 6PA* E: paul.bryer@truro.anglican.org

BRYSON, James Ferguson. b 55. NE Lon Poly BSc 79 Glas Univ DipArch 89 RIBA 93. SEITE 04. **d** 07 **p** 08. C Old Ford St Paul and St Mark *Lon* 07–10; P-in-c Eltham St Jo *S'wark* from 11. *The Vicarage, Sowerby Close, London SE9 6HB* E: fergusonbryson@btinternet.com

BRYSON, Neil Dominic. b 50. Open Univ BA 76 Lon Inst of Educn MA 84 St Matthias Coll Bris CertEd 71. Ox Min Course 10. **d** 12 **p** 13. NSM Boyne Hill *Ox* 12–16; PtO 16–17; C Maidstone St Mich *Cant* from 17. *The Vicarage, 416 Tonbridge Road, Maidstone ME16 9LW* M: 07553-091225 E: frneil@ymail.com

BRYSON, Philip Neil William. b 82. Man Metrop Univ BA 05. St Jo Coll Nottm 12. **d** 15 **p** 16. C Bedford St Paul *St Alb* 15–18; Lay Min Officer from 18. *St John's Rectory, 36 St John's Street, Bedford MK42 0DH* E: fr.phil.bryson@outlook.com

BRYSON (née O'NEILL), Victoria Elaine. b 82. Lanc Univ BA 05. St Jo Coll Nottm 12. **d** 15 **p** 16. C Kempston Transfiguration *St Alb* 15–18; R Bedford St Jo and St Leon from 18. *St John's Rectory, 36 St John's Street, Bedford MK42 0DH* E: rev.vicki.bryson@outlook.com

BRYZAK, Nicholas. d 16. OLM Stratford St Jo w Ch Ch *Chelmsf* from 16. *4 Caledonian Wharf, London E14 3EW* T: (020) 7987 5106 E: nicholas.citred.96@gmail.com

BUBBERS, Richard David. b 55. Keble Coll Ox BA 78 MA 93 Solicitor 81. St Jo Coll Nottm 10. **d** 12 **p** 13. C Ipsley *Worc* 12–15; P-in-c Alvechurch 15–19; R from 19; Ind Chapl from 15. *The Rectory, School Lane, Alvechurch, Birmingham B48 7SB* M: 07968-507078 E: rdb9999@hotmail.com

BUCHAN, Ms Janet Elizabeth Forbes. b 56. Ex Univ BA 79 K Coll Lon MSc 90 Surrey Univ PGCE 93. SEITE 08. **d** 11 **p** 12. C W Hackney *Lon* 11–14; P-in-c Goodmayes St Paul *Chelmsf* 14–19; V from 19. *St Paul's Vicarage, 20 Eastwood Road, Ilford IG3 8XA* T: (020) 8590 6596 M: 07749-104870 E: janetbuchan@gmail.com

BUCHAN, Canon Matthew Alexander John. b 69. St Andr Univ MA 92. Wycliffe Hall Ox BTh 95. **d** 98 **p** 99. C Horninglow *Lich* 98–01; TV Moulsecoomb *Chich* 01–04; Bp's Chapl *Glouc* 04–06; P-in-c Leybourne *Roch* 06–14; R from 14; RD Malling 14–19; Hon Can Roch Cathl from 18; Chapl RAuxAF from 11. *The Rectory, 73 Rectory Lane North, Leybourne, West Malling ME19 5HD* T: (01732) 842187 E: leybournepriest@hotmail.com

BUCHANAN, Andrew Derek. b 64. Stirling Univ BA 90. Wycliffe Hall Ox 98. **d** 01 **p** 02. C Plas Newton *Ches* 01–03; C Ches Ch Ch 03–06; C Plas Newton w Ches Ch Ch 07–11; Asst Chapl Ches Univ 03–11; V Ruddington *S'well* from 11. *The Vicarage, Wilford Road, Ruddington, Nottingham NG11 6EL* T: 0115-921 4522 E: rev_buchanan@hotmail.com

⊕**BUCHANAN, The Rt Revd Colin Ogilvie.** b 34. Linc Coll Ox BA MA Lambeth DD 93. Tyndale Hall Bris 59. **d** 61 **p** 62 **c** 85. C Cheadle *Ches* 61–64; Tutor St Jo Coll Nottm 64–85; Lib 64–69; Registrar 69–74; Dir of Studies 74–75; Vice-Prin 75–78; Prin 79–85; Hon Can S'well Minster 81–85; Suff Bp Aston *Birm* 85–89; Asst Bp Roch 89–96; Asst Bp S'wark 90–91; V Gillingham St Mark *Roch* 91–96; Area Bp Woolwich *S'wark* 96–04; rtd 04; Hon Asst Bp Bradf 04–14; Ripon 05–14; Leeds from 14. *21 The Drive, Alwoodley, Leeds LS17 7QB* T: 0113-267 7721 E: cobdleeds@btinternet.com

BUCHANAN, Eoin George. b 59. Glyndŵr Univ MA 11. Qu Coll Birm 98. **d** 00 **p** 01. C Dovercourt and Parkeston w Harwich *Chelmsf* 00–04; C Ramsey w Lt Oakley 02–04; TR N Hinckford 04–12; R Flegg Coastal Benefice *Nor* 12–13; P-in-c Kirkley St Pet and St Jo 16; R 16–19; rtd 19. *Low Allers Cottage, 5 Low Allers, Cowshill, Bishop Auckland DL13 1DF* M: 07740-051812 E: okyan12@icloud.com

BUCHANAN, Stephanie Joan. b 65. Linc Coll Ox BA 88 MA 02 Selw Coll Cam BA 01 Goldsmiths' Coll Lon PGCE 93. Ridley Hall Cam 99. **d** 02 **p** 03. C Mirfield *Wakef* 02–06; TV Em TM 06–12; V Wakef St Jo 12–14; Leeds from 14. *St John's Vicarage, 65 Bradford Road, Wakefield WF1 2AA* T: (01924) 371029 E: stephanie.buchanan@leeds.anglican.org

BUCK, Mrs Jacqueline Rosemary. b 66. ERMC 06. **d** 09 **p** 10. NSM Cople, Moggerhanger and Willington *St Alb* 09–12; NSM Goldington 12–16; R Gt Doddington and Wilby and Ecton *Pet* from 16. *The Rectory, 72 High Street, Great Doddington, Wellingborough NN29 7TH* T: (01933) 631232 E: jackiebuck@hotmail.co.uk

BUCK (née JONES), Kathryn Mary. b 59. Birm Univ BA 81 MEd 91 Sheff Univ PGCE 82. Ripon Coll Cuddesdon. **d** 99

p 00. C Uttoxeter Area *Lich* 99–00; C Scotforth *Blackb* 00–03; TV Cannock *Lich* 03–09; TV Cannock and Huntington 09–10; C Hednesford 05–10; V Lightcliffe and Hove Edge *Wakef* 11–14; Leeds from 14. *The Vicarage, Wakefield Road, Lightcliffe, Halifax HX3 8TH* T: (01422) 202424

BUCK, Canon Nicholas John. b 57. Leic Univ BScEng 79. Ridley Hall Cam 81. **d** 84 **p** 85. C Oakwood St Thos *Lon* 84–87; C Darnall and Attercliffe *Sheff* 87–90; V Kimberworth 90–96; Chapl Scargill Ho 96–01; P-in-c Bassingham Gp *Linc* 01–06; R 06–15; P-in-c Branston w Nocton and Potterhanworth 12–15; P-in-c Metheringham w Blankney and Dunston 12–15; RD Graffoe 09–14; V Linc St Giles from 15; Can and Preb Linc Cathl from 10. *The Vicarage, 25 Shelley Drive, Lincoln LN2 4BY* E: stgileslincoln@gmail.com

BUCKINGHAM, The Ven Hugh Fletcher. b 32. Hertf Coll Ox BA 57 MA 60. Westcott Ho Cam 55. **d** 57 **p** 58. C Halliwell St Thos *Man* 57–60; C Sheff Gillcar St Silas 60–65; V Hindolveston *Nor* 65–70; V Guestwick 65–70; R Fakenham w Alethorpe 70–88; Chmn Dioc Bd Soc Resp 81–88; RD Burnham and Walsingham *Nor* 81–87; Hon Can Nor Cathl 85–88; Adn E Riding *York* 88–98; Can and Preb York Minster 88–01; rtd 98; PtO *York* from 01. *Orchard Cottage, Rectory Corner, Brandsby, York YO61 4RJ* T: (01347) 888202

BUCKINGHAM, Richard Arthur John. b 49. Univ of Wales (Cardiff) BA 71 PGCE 72. Chich Th Coll 73. **d** 76 **p** 77. C Llantwit Major *Llan* 76–80; C Leigh-on-Sea St Marg *Chelmsf* 80–84; C Westmr St Matt *Lon* 84–87; R Stock Harvard *Chelmsf* 87–02; PtO *Lon* from 02. *3 Priory Close, London N3 1BB* T: (020) 8371 0178 E: rbuckingham@waitrose.com

BUCKINGHAM, Terence John. b 52. Aston Univ BSc 73 MSc 75 PhD 78 FCOptom 74. Coll of Resurr Mirfield 01. **d** 03 **p** 04. NSM Harrogate St Wilfrid *Ripon* 03–09; P-in-c Nidd 09–10; NSM Leeds St Wilfrid 10–14 and from 14. *Woodstock, Thorpe Lane, Guiseley, Leeds LS20 8LE* T: (01943) 876066 M: 07815-994017 E: terry.j.buckingham@btopenworld.com

BUCKINGHAM, Archdeacon of. See ELSMORE, The Ven Guy Charles

BUCKINGHAM, Area Bishop of. See WILSON, The Rt Revd Alan Thomas Lawrence

BUCKLE, Graham Charles. b 59. ERMC 08. **d** 11 **p** 12. NSM Silverstone and Abthorpe w Slapton etc *Pet* 11–16; P-in-c Castle Bytham w Creeton *Linc* 16–18; C Witham Gp 16–18; P-in-c Riversmeet *St Alb* from 18. *The Rectory, Park Lane, Blunham, Bedford MK44 3NJ* T: (01767) 640412 M: 07901-660593 E: dovecote10@btinternet.com

BUCKLE, Graham Martin. b 62. Southn Univ BTh 89 Sheff Univ MMinTheol 04. Sarum & Wells Th Coll 85. **d** 89 **p** 90. C Paddington St Jas *Lon* 89–94; P-in-c Paddington St Pet 94–00; R St Marylebone St Paul 00–14; Dir of Ords Two Cities Area 99–08; V Westmr St Steph w St Jo from 14. *21 Vincent Square, London SW1P 2NA* T: (020) 7834 1300 E: vicar@sswsj.org

BUCKLER, Andrew Jonathan Heslington. b 68. Trin Coll Ox BA 89 MA 96 Protestant Inst Th France MTh 02. Wycliffe Hall Ox BTh 93. **d** 96 **p** 97. C Ox St Aldate 96–00; Crosslinks France 00–17; V Kensington St Barn *Lon* from 17. *23 Addison Road, London W14 8LH* T: (020) 7471 7000 E: andy@stbk.org.uk

BUCKLER, Canon Guy Ernest Warr. b 46. ACA 69 FCA 79. Linc Th Coll 71. **d** 74 **p** 75. C Dunstable *St Alb* 74–77; C Houghton Regis 77–86; TV Willington *Newc* 86–88; TR 88–95; Chapl N Tyneside Coll of FE 88–95; R Bedford St Pet w St Cuth *St Alb* 95–05; R Bushey 05–11; RD Aldenham 08–11; Hon Can St Alb 10–11; rtd 11; PtO *St Alb* from 11. *18 Deans Close, Abbots Langley WD5 0HL* T: (01923) 269975 E: gbuckler@hotmail.com

BUCKLER, Miss Jennifer Anne. b 82. Reading Univ BA 06. Trin Coll Bris 15. **d** 17 **p** 18. C Bath Widcombe *B & W* from 17. *13A Fox Hill, Bath BA2 5QL* T: (01225) 612244 M: 07753-785930 E: curate@widcombe.church

BUCKLER, Kenneth Arthur. b 50. S Bank Univ MSc 94. NTMTC 95. **d** 98 **p** 99. C Welwyn w Ayot St Peter *St Alb* 98–01; P-in-c Kimpton w Ayot St Lawrence 01–05; Asst Chapl E Herts NHS Trust 99–00; Asst Chapl E and N Herts NHS Trust 00–04; Chapl Team Ldr 04–05; V Hounslow W Gd Shep *Lon* 05–12; rtd 12; PtO *Lon* from 12. *104 Royal Lane, Uxbridge UB8 3QY* M: 07909-970545 E: kenbuckler@ymail.com

BUCKLER, The Very Revd Philip John Warr. b 49. St Pet Coll Ox BA 70 MA 74 Bp Grosseteste Univ Hon DUniv 15. Cuddesdon Coll 70. **d** 72 **p** 73. C Bushey Heath *St Alb* 72–75; Chapl Trin Coll Cam 75–81; Min Can and Sacr St Paul's Cathl *Lon* 81–87; V Hampstead St Jo 87–99; AD N Camden 93–98; Can Res St Paul's Cathl 99–07; Treas 00–07; Dean Linc 07–16; rtd 16; PtO *St E* from 17. *Green Acre, Whelp*

Street, Preston St Mary, Sudbury CO10 9NL T: (01787) 249760 E: pjwb@hotmail.co.uk

BUCKLEY, Alexander Christopher Nolan. b 67. Univ of Wales (Abth) BD 89 Man Univ MA 06. St Mich Coll Llan. **d** 91 **p** 94. C Llandudno *Ban* 91–92; C Ynyscynhaearn w Penmorfa and Porthmadog 92–93 and 94–96; Jesuit Volunteer Community Manchester 93–94; C Caerau w Ely *Llan* 96–01; V Trowbridge Mawr *Mon* 01–03; Chapl ATC 96–03; PtO *Mon* 03–09; *Man* 04–09; R Llanllyfni *Ban* 09–12; P-in-c Leeds Belle Is St Jo and St Barn *Ripon* 12–14 and 14–18; C Hunslet w Cross Green *Ripon* 12–14; *Leeds* 14–18; V Belle Isle and Hunslet from 18; CMP from 02. *The Vicarage, 30 Low Grange View, Leeds LS10 3DT* E: father-chris@ssjbchurchleeds.org.uk *or* chris.buckley@leeds.anglican.org

BUCKLEY, Anthony Graham. b 63. Keble Coll Ox BA 84 MA 90 Cant Ch Ch Univ Coll MA 03 Keble Coll Ox PGCE 85. Wycliffe Hall Ox 96. **d** 98 **p** 99. C Folkestone St Jo *Cant* 98–00; V 00–08; AD Elham 05–08; Hon Can Cant Cathl 08; Chapl Alleyn's Sch Dulwich 08–19; Hon C Dulwich St Barn *S'wark* 08–19; Dir of IME Woolwich Area 09–19; V Ox St Mich w St Martin and All SS from 19. *37 Lonsdale Road, Oxford OX2 7ES* M: 07841-800609 E: antmon64@hotmail.com

BUCKLEY, Mrs Catherine Anne. d 17 **p** 18. OLM Hartshorne and Bretby *Derby* from 17; OLM Seale and Lullington w Coton in the Elms from 17; OLM Stapenhill Immanuel from 17; OLM Swadlincote from 17; OLM Walton-on-Trent w Croxall, Rosliston etc from 17. *22 Ordish Street, Burton-on-Trent DE14 3SA* T: (01283) 531257 M: 07753-751882 E: katebuckley9@gmail.com

BUCKLEY, Christine Judith. d 15 **p** 16. NSM Poynton *Ches* from 15. *74 Vernon Road, Poynton, Stockport SK12 1YR* M: 07709-032435 E: bcklyc@aol.com

BUCKLEY, Christopher Ivor. b 48. Chich Th Coll 84. **d** 86 **p** 87. C Felpham w Middleton *Chich* 86–89; C Jersey St Brelade *Win* 89–93; V Jersey St Mark 93–06; Chapl Jersey Airport 00–06; V E Radnor *S & B* 06–10; rtd 10; PtO *Win* from 10. *A Cappella, 15 Byron Road, St Helier, Jersey JE2 4LQ* T: (01534) 738265 M: 07797-714595 E: revcbuckley@gmail.com

BUCKLEY, David Rex. b 47. Ripon Coll Cuddesdon 75. **d** 77 **p** 78. C Witton *Ches* 77–81; V Backford 81–85; Youth Chapl 81–85; V Barnton 85–93; P-in-c Bickerton w Bickley 93–97; P-in-c Harthill and Burwardsley 93–97; V Bickerton, Bickley, Harthill and Burwardsley 97–01; P-in-c Sandbach 01–03; V 03–07; rtd 08; Chapl Cheshire Constabulary *Ches* 08–12; PtO from 15; *Ely* from 18. *39 The Croft, Fulbourn, Cambridge CB21 5DR* T: (01223) 882338 M: 07810-791417 E: rex.buckley.308@btinternet.com

BUCKLEY, Ms Debra. b 59. Birm Poly BA 81. Qu Coll Birm 08. **d** 10 **p** 11. C Balsall Heath and Edgbaston SS Mary and Ambrose *Birm* 10–14; V Smethwick from 14; AD Warley from 17. *The Vicarage, 93A Church Road, Smethwick B67 6EE* T: 0121-558 1763 E: debbuckley@phonecoop.coop

BUCKLEY, Ernest Fairbank. b 25. Jes Coll Cam BA 49 MA 50 Jes Coll Ox BLitt 53. Westcott Ho Cam 55. **d** 55 **p** 56. C Rochdale *Man* 55–58; V Hey 58–64; V Baguley 64–79; V Clun w Chapel Lawn, Bettws-y-Crwyn and Newcastle *Heref* 79–87; RD Clun Forest 82–87; rtd 88. *The Old Barn, Brassington, Matlock DE4 4HL* T: (01629) 540821 E: buckley@w3z.co.uk

BUCKLEY, Michael. b 49. Cranmer Hall Dur 77. **d** 79 **p** 80. C Birkdale St Jo *Liv* 79–82; TV Maghull 82–88; V Earlestown 88–98; V Gt Sankey 98–14; TR Warrington W 14; rtd 14; PtO *Blackb* from 14. *7 College Close, Longridge, Preston PR3 3AX* T: (01772) 386634 E: m3uckley@gmail.com

BUCKLEY, Rex. *See* BUCKLEY, David Rex

BUCKLEY, Richard Francis. b 44. FRSA. Ripon Hall Ox 69. **d** 72 **p** 73. C Portsea St Cuth *Portsm* 72–75; C Portsea All SS w St Jo Rudmore 75–79; Chapl RN 79–00; PtO *B & W* 00–15; *Glouc* from 13. *2 Nourse Close, Cheltenham GL53 0NQ* T: (01242) 220805 M: 07990-836802 E: r.f.buckley@me.com

BUCKLEY, Richard Simon Fildes. b 63. WMMTC 97. **d** 00 **p** 01. NSM Moseley St Mary *Birm* 00–04; NSM Soho St Anne w St Thos and St Pet *Lon* 05–09 and 12–13; P-in-c from 13; PtO 09–12. *St Anne's Rectory, 55 Dean Street, London W1D 6AF* T: (020) 7437 1012 M: 07976-290351 E: simon@simonbuckley.co.uk

BUCKLEY, Canon Stephen Richard. b 45. Cranmer Hall Dur 82. **d** 84 **p** 85. C Iffley Ox 84–88; TV Halesowen *Worc* 88–00; TR Sedgley All SS 00–05; TR Gornal and Sedgley 05–15; P-in-c Sedgley St Mary 10–15; Hon Can Worc Cathl 12–15; rtd 15; PtO from 15; Hon Warden Abbey from 17. *70 Blenheim Road, Worcester WR2 5NG* T: (01905) 428802 M: 07746-206905

BUCKLEY, Timothy Denys. b 57. BA. St Jo Coll Nottm. **d** 83 **p** 84. C S Westoe *Dur* 83–85; C Paddington Em Harrow Road *Lon* 85–88; C Binley *Cov* 88–98; Min Binley Woods

LEP 88–98; V Belton Gp *Linc* 98–13; P-in-c Crowle Gp 09–12; PtO *Chich* from 14. *34 Outerwyke Road, Bognor Regis PO22 8HX* T: (01243) 278731 E: revtimbuckley@gmail.com

BUCKLEY, Timothy John. b 67. Jes Coll Cam BA 90 MA 94 Lambeth MA 11. Wycliffe Hall Ox BTh 99. **d** 99 **p** 00. C Langdon Hills *Chelmsf* 99–02; P-in-c Devonport St Mich and St Barn *Ex* 02–15; V 15–19; V Devonport St Mich and St Barn w St Aubyn from 19. *St Barnabas' Vicarage, 10 De la Hay Avenue, Plymouth PL3 4HU* T: (01752) 666544 E: rev.tim@virgin.net

BUCKLEY, Timothy Simon. b 72. St Mellitus Coll. **d** 11 **p** 12. C Combe Down w Monkton Combe and S Stoke *B & W* 11–14; C Bath Widcombe 11–14; P-in-c 14–16; V from 16. *The Orchard, Forefield Rise, Bath BA2 4PL* E: tim@timbuck2.co.uk

BUCKMAN, Stephen Leslie. b 55. Open Univ BA 99 Sussex Univ PGCE 01. SEITE 09. **d** 12 **p** 13. NSM Roughey *Chich* 12–15; P-in-c Corby Glen *Linc* from 15. *The Rectory, 14 Mussons Close, Corby Glen, Grantham NG33 4NY* T: (01476) 550884 M: 07768-116563 E: revstephen@btinternet.com

BUCKNALL, Allan. b 35. St Matthias Coll Bris CertEd 73. ALCD 62. **d** 62 **p** 63. C Harlow New Town w Lt Parndon *Chelmsf* 62–69; Chapl W Somerset Miss to Deaf 69–71; PtO *Bris* 71–77; P-in-c Wisborough Green *Chich* 77–79; R Tillington 78–86; R Duncton 82–86; R Upwaltham 82–86; C Henfield w Shermanbury and Woodmancote 86–89; Asst Chapl Princess Marg Hosp Swindon 89–96; Angl Chapl Swindon and Marlborough NHS Trust 96–00; rtd 00; PtO *Bris* from 00. *5 The Willows, Highworth, Swindon SN6 7PG* T: (01793) 762721

BUCKNALL, Miss Ann Gordon. b 32. K Coll Lon BSc 53 Hughes Hall Cam DipEd 54. Qu Coll Birm 80. **dss** 81 **d** 87 **p** 94. Birm St Aid Small Heath 81–85; Balsall Heath St Paul 85–92; Par Dn 87–92; C Handsworth St Jas 92–95; rtd 95; PtO *Lich* from 95. *29 The Oaks, St John's Hospital, St John Street, Lichfield WS13 6PB* T: (01543) 257382 E: bucknall20ann@talktalk.net

BUDD, Philip John. b 40. St Jo Coll Dur BA 63 MLitt 71 Bris Univ PhD 78. Cranmer Hall Dur. **d** 66 **p** 67. C Attenborough w Chilwell *S'well* 66–69; Lect Clifton Th Coll 69–71; Lect Trin Coll Bris 72–80; Tutor Ripon Coll Cuddesdon 80–88; Asst Chapl and Tutor Westmr Coll Ox 80–00; Lect 88–00; Asst Chapl and Tutor Ox Brookes Univ 00–03; Lect 00–03; Hon C N Hinksey and Wytham 03–06; PtO from 06. *4 Clover Close, Oxford OX2 9JH* T: (01865) 863682 E: budds@talk21.com

BUDD, Robert John. b 77. Nottm Univ BA 99 Warwick Univ PGCE 05. Trin Coll Bris 11. **d** 13 **p** 14. C Cov H Trin 13–16; C Warwick 16–17; C Whitnash 17–18; V Heathcote from 18. *72 Banquo Approach, Heathcote, Warwick CV34 6GB* T: (01926) 335367 M: 07811-945647 E: revrobbudd@gmail.com

BUDDEN, Alexander Mark. b 60. UEA BA 84. SEITE 01. **d** 04 **p** 05. NSM Mitcham St Barn *S'wark* 04–08; PtO 09–11; NSM Wimbledon 11–17; NSM Merton St Jas from 17. *29 Dane Road, London SW19 2NB* T: (020) 8542 0622 M: 07738-290534 E: amarksw19@yahoo.co.uk

BUDDEN, Carl James. b 57. SWMTC 12. **d** 15 **p** 16. C Egg Buckland *Ex* 15–17; C Eggbuckland w Estover 17–19; TV Plymstock and Hooe from 19. *Merrivale, Woodside, Plymouth PL4 8QE* M: 07525-210645 E: carljamesbudden@gmail.com

BUDGELL, Mrs Anne Margaret. b 44. RGN 66. STETS 07. **d** 10 **p** 11. NSM Vale of White Hart Sarum 10–13; NSM Three Valleys 13–18; PtO from 18. *7 Fox's Close, Holwell, Sherborne DT9 5LH* T: (01963) 23428 E: budgells@hotmail.co.uk

BUDGELL, Peter Charles. b 50. Lon Univ BD 74. **d** 83 **p** 84. C Goodmayes All SS *Chelmsf* 83–86; C Chipping Barnet w Arkley *St Alb* 86–88; V Luton St Anne 86–06; V Luton St Anne w St Chris 06–16; rtd 17; PtO *Ex* from 17. *5 Vicarage Road, Sidmouth EX10 8TS* T: (01395) 513770 E: pcbudgell@aol.com

BUDGETT, Preb Anthony Thomas. b 26. Oriel Coll Ox BA 50 MA 57. Wells Th Coll 57. **d** 59 **p** 60. C Hendford *B & W* 59–63; PC Lopen 63–68; R Seavington St Mich w St Mary 63–68; V Somerton 68–80; RD Ilchester 72–81; P-in-c Compton Dundon 76–80; R Somerton w Compton Dundon 80–81; R Somerton w Compton Dundon, the Charltons etc 81–84; Preb Wells Cathl 83–90; P-in-c Bruton w Lamyatt, Wyke and Redlynch 84–85; P-in-c Batcombe w Upton Noble 84–85; P-in-c S w N Brewham 84–85; TR Bruton and Distr 85–90; rtd 90; PtO *Ex* 90–09; *B & W* from 94. *Cornerways, White Ball, Wellington TA21 0LS* T: (01823) 672321

BUIKE, Desmond Mainwaring. b 32. Ex Coll Ox BA 55 MA 69 Leeds Univ CertEd 72. **d** 57 **p** 58. C Man St Aid 57–60; C Ox SS Phil and Jas 60–63; V Queensbury *Bradf* 63–71; PtO 71–85; V Glaisdale *York* 85–93; rtd 93; PtO *York* from 93. *2 Pentland Grove, Wakefield WF2 8JX*

BULL, Andrew David. b 70. Hull Univ BSc 91 Sheff Univ PGCE 92. Regents Th Coll BA 99. **d** 07 **p** 08. C Macclesfield

Team *Ches* 07–10; P-in-c Bredbury St Mark from 10. *St Mark's Vicarage, 61 George Lane, Bredbury, Stockport SK6 1AT* T: 0161-406 6552 E: ukbulls@aol.com

BULL, Mrs Christine. b 45. Bedf Coll Lon BA 67. NOC 91. d 94 p 95. NSM High Lane *Ches* 94–98; NSM Stockport SW 98–99; PtO *Derby* 98–04; *Ches* 99–04; Man 00–06; C Hale and Ashley *Ches* 04–07; NSM Wormhill, Peak Forest w Peak Dale and Dove Holes *Derby* 07–08; P Pastor Ches Cathl 08–13; rtd 13; PtO *Ches* from 07; *Derby* 09–18. *2 River Sett Cottages, Hyde Bank Road, New Mills, High Peak SK22 4BF* T: (01663) 740847 E: revchristinebull@yahoo.co.uk

BULL (*née* ADAMS), Canon Christine Frances. b 53. Cam Inst of Educn CertEd 74. NEOC 97. d 00 p 01. NSM St Oswald in Lee w Bingfield *Newc* from 00; P-in-c 07–19; NSM Chollerton w Birtley and Thockrington *Newc* from 19; Hon Can Newc Cathl from 17. *East Side Lodge, Bingfield, Newcastle upon Tyne NE19 2LE* T: (01434) 672303 E: bull.christine4@gmail.com

BULL, Christopher Bertram. b 45. Lon Bible Coll BA 87. Wycliffe Hall Ox 88. d 90 p 91. C Leominster *Heref* 90–95; P-in-c Westbury 95–02; R 02–10; P-in-c Yockleton 95–02; R 02–10; P-in-c Gt Wollaston 95–02; V 02–07; P-in-c Worthen 07–10; rtd 10; PtO *Lich* 12–14 and from 18. *12 Aldersley Way, Ruyton XI Towns, Shrewsbury SY4 1NE* T: (01939) 260059 E: cbbull@live.co.uk

BULL, Canon Christopher David. b 59. Univ of Wales MA 08. St Jo Coll Nottm 89. d 91 p 92. C Bowbrook S *Worc* 91–95; P-in-c Flackwell Heath *Ox* 95–00; V from 00; RD Wycombe 97–05; Hon Can Ch Ch from 19. *The Vicarage, 9 Chapel Road, Flackwell Heath, High Wycombe HP10 9AA* T: (01628) 522795 *or* 533004 E: vicar@ccfh.org.uk *or* christopherbull@oxford.anglican.org

BULL, David. b 72. Worc Coll Ox BA 94. Wycliffe Hall Ox BA 07. d 08 p 09. C Reigate St Mary *S'wark* 08–12; TR Gt Marlow w Marlow Bottom, Lt Marlow and Bisham *Ox* from 12; AD Wycombe from 16. *The Rectory, The Causeway, Marlow SL7 2AA* T: (01628) 471650 E: davebull@marlowanglican.org

BULL, John. *See* BULL, Michael John.

BULL, Malcolm George. b 35. Portsm Dioc Tr Course 87. d 87 p 98. NSM Farlington *Portsm* 87–90; NSM Widley w Wymering 92–93; NSM S Hayling 93–97; NSM Hayling Is St Andr 97–00; Bp's Adv for Cults and New Relig Movements 99–00; rtd 00; PtO *Portsm* 00–01 and from 04; P-in-c Greatworth and Marston St Lawrence etc *Pet* 01–04. *20 Charleston Close, Hayling Island PO11 0JY* T: (023) 9246 2025

BULL, Malcolm Harold. b 44. BDS. St Alb Minl Tr Scheme. d 83 p 84. NSM Bedford St Paul *St Alb* 83–93. *27 Cardington Road, Bedford MK42 0BN* T: (01234) 368163

BULL, Martin Wells. b 37. Worc Coll Ox BA 61 MA 68. Ripon Hall Ox 61. d 63 p 64. C Blackley St Andr *Man* 63–67; C Horton *Bradf* 67–68; V Ingrow w Hainworth 68–78; RD S Craven 74–77; V Bingley All SS 78–80; TR 80–92; P-in-c Gargrave 92–02; rtd 02; PtO *Ripon* 03–14; *Leeds* from 14. *21 Magdalen's Close, Ripon HG4 1HH* T: (01765) 601422 M: 07870-138386

BULL, Michael John. b 35. Roch Th Coll 65. d 67 p 68. C N Wingfield *Derby* 67–69; C Skegness *Linc* 69–72; R Ingoldmells w Addlethorpe 72–79; Area Sec USPG *S'wark* 79–85; Area Org RNLI (Lon) 86–88; C Croydon St Jo *S'wark* 89–93; P-in-c Mitcham Ch 93–97; V Colliers Wood Ch Ch 97–00; rtd 00; PtO *Nor* 00–04; Hon C Guiltcross 04–08; P-in-c 08–13. *21 Buckshorn Lane, Eye IP23 7AZ* T: (01379) 871509 E: mjbull@waitrose.com

BULL, Canon Robert David. b 51. Westmr Coll Ox MTh 03 Ches Univ DProf 16. Ripon Coll Cuddesdon 74. d 77 p 78. C Worsley *Man* 77–80; C Peel 80–81; TV 81–86; P-in-c Wisbech St Aug *Ely* 86–88; V 88–02; RD Wisbech 92–02; R Lich St Chad 02–11; P-in-c Longdon 08–10; Can Res Bris Cathl 11–17; rtd 18. *1 Myford Cottages, Myford, Horsehay, Telford TF4 3BU* T: (01952) 507414 E: robertdb8083@gmail.com

BULL, Mrs Ruth Lois Clare. b 54. Univ of Wales (Lamp) BA 76 W Midl Coll of Educn PGCE 77. Qu Coll Birm 08. d 11 p 12. NSM Burntwood *Lich* 11–12; NSM Lich St Mich w St Mary and Wall from 12. *36 Broadlands Rise, Lichfield WS14 9SF* T: (01543) 319296 E: dkbrlcb@hotmail.com

BULL, Stephen Andrew. b 58. St Jo Coll Nottm 91. d 93 p 94. C Wroughton *Bris* 93–96; P-in-c Eyemouth *Edin* 96–98; LtO from 98. *12 Craigs Court, Torphichen, Bathgate EH48 4NU* T: (01506) 650070 E: stvbull@btinternet.com

BULL, Miss Susan Helen. b 58. Qu Mary Coll Lon BSc 79 All Hallows Coll Dublin MA 11 ACIS 84. STETS BTh 98. d 98 p 99. NSM Epsom St Barn *Guildf* 98–04; Chapl Surrey and Borders Partnership NHS Foundn Trust 04–18; Chapl Epsom and St Helier Univ Hosps NHS Trust 18; PtO *S'wark* from 06; *Guildf* from 18. *41 Stamford Green Road, Epsom KT18 7SR* T: (01372) 742703 E: shbull@btinternet.com

BULL, Canon Timothy Martin. b 65. Worc Coll Ox BA 87 MA 93 Dur Univ PhD 94 Fitzw Coll Cam BA 98 MA 07 K Coll Lon PhD 11 FRSA 96 CEng 96 MBCS 96. Ridley Hall Cam 96. d 99 p 00. C Bath Walcot *B & W* 99–03; P-in-c Langham w Boxted *Chelmsf* 03–13; Colchester Area CME Adv 03–13; Dir Min and Min Development Officer *St Alb* from 13; Can Res St Alb from 13. *43 Holywell Hill, St Albans AL1 1HD* T: (01727) 818151 E: dom@stalbans.anglican.org *or* canondrtim@gmail.com

BULL, Mrs Wendy Jane. b 63. Birm Chr Coll MA 08. Ripon Coll Cuddesdon 11. d 13 p 14. C Gt Marlow w Marlow Bottom, Lt Marlow and Bisham *Ox* 13–16; C High Wycombe 16; TV from 16. *9 Chapel Road, Flackwell Heath, High Wycombe HP10 9AA* T: (01628) 522795 E: wendy@revbull.co.uk *or* revwbull@gmail.com

BULLAMORE, John Richard. b 41. Linc Coll Ox BA 69 MA 69. Wycliffe Hall Ox 74. d 95 p 95. NSM Eoropaidh *Arg* 95–98; NSM Bath St Sav w Swainswick and Woolley *B & W* 98–08; NSM Knaresborough *Ripon* 08–12; rtd 12; PtO *Ripon* 12–14; *Leeds* 14–17. *21 Hornbeam Way, Leeds LS14 2HP* T: 0113-318 9756 E: john.bullamore@hotmail.co.uk

BULLEN, Mrs Jacqueline. b 61. Westcott Ho Cam 11. d 13 p 14. C Fosse Team *Leic* 13–17; V Longthorpe *Pet* from 17. *Longthorpe Vicarage, 315 Thorpe Road, Peterborough PE3 6LU* T: (01733) 263016 M: 07729-706157 E: jacqbullen@aol.com

BULLEN, Marilyn Patricia. *See* MARTIN, Marilyn Patricia

BULLEN, Neil Geoffrey Osbourne. b 64. Qu Coll Birm 13. d 15 p 16. C Knighton *Leic* 15–18; R Ringstone in Aveland Gp *Linc* from 18. *The Vicarage, 46A High Street, Morton, Bourne PE10 0NR* M: 07729-004642 E: revdneil@yahoo.com

BULLIMORE, Canon Christine Elizabeth. b 46. Nottm Univ BA 67. St Jo Coll Nottm 96. d 96 p 97. Bp's Adv Past Care and Counselling *Wakef* 92–99 and 01–14; *Leeds* from 14; NSM S Ossett *Wakef* 96–99; P-in-c Emley and Flockton cum Denby Grange 99–11; RD Kirkburton 05–11; Hon Can Wakef Cathl 08–11; rtd 11. *5 Snowgate Head, New Mill, Holmfirth, Huddersfield HD9 7DH* T: (01484) 521025 M: 07921-588276 E: chrisbullimore@sky.com

BULLIMORE, Matthew James. b 77. Em Coll Cam BA 99 MA 03 PhD 07 Man Univ MPhil 02. Harvard Div Sch 99 Westcott Ho Cam 01. d 05 p 06. C Robertstown w Hartshead *Wakef* 05–07; Bp's Dom Chapl 07–11; V Royston 11–14; *Leeds* 14–16; P-in-c Felkirk *Wakef* 13–14; *Leeds* 14–16; V Royston and Felkirk 16–17; Widening Participation Officer Chu Coll Cam from 18. *Churchill College, Cambridge CB3 0DS* T: (01223) 336248 E: mjb56@cantab.net

BULLIVANT, Ronald. b 32. CertEd. St Mich Coll Llan. d 59 p 60. C Roath St German *Llan* 59–61; P-in-c Bradf H Trin 61–66; V Horbury *Wakef* 66–69; Lic to Offic *Ripon* 78; PtO *Nor* 78–81; LtO 81–98; PtO *Man* 99–11. *14 St Albans Terrace, Manchester M8 8BZ* T: 0161-832 0824

BULLOCK, Andrew Belfrage. b 50. Univ of Wales (Ban) BSc 73 MEd 81 Westmr Coll Ox PGCE 79. Wycliffe Hall Ox 94. d 97 p 98. C Sandhurst *Ox* 97–02; P-in-c Alfrick, Lulsley, Suckley, Leigh and Bransford *Worc* 02–08; TV Worcs W Rural 09–14; rtd 15; PtO *Heref* from 18. *Gladstone House, Whitbourne, Worcester WR6 5SP* M: 07958-654331 E: ochse@waitrose.com

BULLOCK, Andrew Timothy. b 56. Southn Univ BTh 91. Sarum & Wells Th Coll 89. d 91 p 92. C Erdington St Barn *Birm* 91–94; TV Solihull 94–03; P-in-c Acocks Green 03–08; V from 08; AD Yardley and Bordesley from 12. *The Vicarage, 34 Dudley Park Road, Acocks Green, Birmingham B27 6QR* T/F: 0121-706 9764 E: andrewbullock2@blueyonder.co.uk

BULLOCK, Gary Kenneth. b 64. Staffs Univ BA 87 Wycliffe Hall Ox 06. d 16 p 17. NSM Heapey and Withnell *Blackb* from 16. *2 Richmond Close, Brinscall, Chorley PR6 8PY* T: (01254) 830575 E: gary@bowdenash.net

BULLOCK, Ian. b 74. York St Jo Univ BA 11. Cranmer Hall Dur. d 08 p 09. C Pontefract St Giles *Wakef* 08–11; P-in-c Heckmondwike 11–12; P-in-c Liversedge w Hightown 11–12; V Heckmondwike (w Norristhorpe) and Liversedge 12–15; V Littleborough *Man* from 15. *The Vicarage, 4 Stansfield Hall, Littleborough OL15 9RH* T: (01706) 375322 E: rev.ian@btinternet.com

BULLOCK, Jude Ross. b 58. Heythrop Coll Lon BD 89. Allen Hall 84. d 89 p 90. In RC Ch 89–97; C Lt Ilford St Mich *Chelmsf* 01–05; V Chingford St Anne from 05. *St Anne's Vicarage, 200A Larkshall Road, London E4 6NP* T: (020) 8529 4740 M: 07976-395732 E: juderbullock1@yahoo.co.uk

BULLOCK, Canon Michael. b 49. Hatf Coll Dur BA 71. Coll of Resurr Mirfield 72. d 75 p 76. C Pet St Jo 75–79; Zambia 79–86; V Longthorpe *Pet* 86–91; Chapl Naples w Sorrento, Capri and Bari *Eur* 91–99; OGS from 93; P-in-c Liguria *Eur*

99–00; Chapl Gtr Lisbon 00–12; Can Malta Cathl 98–12; rtd 12; PtO *Eur* 12–17; Chapl Bonn w Cologne from 17; PtO *Linc* from 13. *22 Georgian Court, Spalding PE11 2QT* T: (01775) 714454 E: bullock583@btinternet.com

BULLOCK, Philip Mark. b 59. Qu Coll Birm 05. **d** 08 **p** 09. C Cov E 08–10; TV 10–13; P-in-c S Shields St Aid and St Steph *Dur* 13–19; P-in-c Rekendyke 13–19; P-in-c Greatham from 19; P-in-c Seaton Carew from 19. *12 Dauntless Close, Hartlepool TS25 1EX* M: 07831-147822 E: rev.philip@virginmedia.com

BULLOCK, Miss Rosemary Joy. b 59. Portsm Poly BA 81 Southn Univ BTh 94. Sarum & Wells Th Coll 89. **d** 91 **p** 94. Par Dn Warblington w Emsworth *Portsm* 91–94; C 94–95; C Gt Parndon *Chelmsf* 95–98; TV Beaminster Area *Sarum* 98–03; P-in-c Ridgeway 03–04. *82 Green Lane, Shanklin PO37 7HD* T: (01983) 863345

✠**BULLOCK (née WHEALE), The Rt Revd Sarah Ruth.** b 64. Surrey Univ BA 86 St Jo Coll Dur BA 93. Cranmer Hall Dur 90. **d** 93 **p** 94 **c** 19. C Kersal Moor *Man* 93–98; P-in-c Whalley Range St Edm 98–04; P-in-c Moss Side St Jas w St Clem 99–04; R Whalley Range St Edm and Moss Side etc 04–13; Dioc Voc Adv 98–05; Chapl MU 00–06; Bp's Adv for Women's Min *Man* 09–13; Borough Dean Man 10–12; AD Hulme 12–13; Hon Can Man Cathl 07–13; Adn York 13–19; Area Bp Shrewsbury *Lich* from 19. *Athlone House, 68 London Road, Shrewsbury SY2 6PG* T: (01743) 235867

BULLOCK, Stephanie Clair. b 46. St Mary's Hosp Medical Sch Lon MB, BS 70. Ripon Coll Cuddesdon 90. **d** 92 **p** 94. Par Dn Cuddesdon *Ox* 92–94; Tutor Ripon Coll Cuddesdon 92–94; Asst Chapl Ox Radcliffe Hosp NHS Trust 94–97; Chapl Ox Radcliffe Hosps NHS Trust 97–02; Hon C Headington St Mary *Ox* 03–09; PtO from 09. *Church Farm, Church Lane, Old Marston, Oxford OX3 0PT* T: (01865) 722926 E: stephaniebullock9@gmail.com

BULLOCK, Canon Victor James Allen. b 67. Southn Univ BTh 90 St Mary's Coll Twickenham PGCE 91. St Steph Ho Ox 92. **d** 94 **p** 95. C Cowley St Jas *Ox* 94–95; C Reading St Giles 95–99; V Fenny Stratford from 99; Canon Ruvuma Tanzania from 13. *The Vicarage, Manor Road, Milton Keynes MK2 2HW* T: (01908) 372825 E: saintmartinschurch@hotmail.com *or* victorbullock@talktalk.net

BULLWORTHY, Rita Irene. b 48. Glos Univ BA 09. SWMTC 09. **d** 11. NSM N Tawton, Bondleigh, Sampford Courtenay etc *Ex* 11–13; NSM Chagford, Gidleigh, Throwleigh etc from 13. *Rivendell House, Sampford Courtenay, Okehampton EX20 2TF* T: (01837) 89168 E: ritabullworthy@yahoo.co.uk

BUNCE, Christopher Edward. b 82. Westcott Ho Cam. **d** 12 **p** 13. C Hammersmith St Pet *Lon* 12–15; R Stevenage St Andr and St Geo *St Alb* from 15; RD Stevenage from 16. *The Rectory, Cuttys Lane, Stevenage SG1 1UP* E: cebunce@gmail.com

BUNCH, Canon Andrew William Havard. b 53. Selw Coll Cam BA 74 MA 78 PhD 79. Ox NSM Course 84. **d** 87 **p** 88. NSM Wantage *Ox* 87–91; C New Windsor 91–93; TV 93–97; V Ox St Giles and SS Phil and Jas w St Marg from 97; Hon Can Ch Ch from 09. *The Vicarage, Church Walk, Oxford OX2 6LY* T: (01865) 510460 E: vicar@churchwalk.eclipse.co.uk

BUNDAY, Mrs Janet Lesley. b 56. Nottm Univ BA 78 Univ of Wales (Lamp) MA 08. Ridley Hall Cam 08. **d** 10 **p** 11. NSM Potton w Sutton and Cockayne Hatley *St Alb* 10–12; C Blyth Valley *St E* 12–13; TV 13–19. *Address withheld by request* E: jan@bunday.co.uk

BUNDAY, Canon Paul. b 30. Wadh Coll Ox BA 54 MA 58. ALCD 56. **d** 56 **p** 57. C Woking St Jo *Guildf* 56–60; Chapl Reed's Sch Cobham 60–66; R Landford w Plaitford *Sarum* 66–77; RD Alderbury 73–77; TR Radipole and Melcombe Regis 77–86; RD Weymouth 82–85; Can and Preb Sarum Cathl 83–95; TV Whitton 86–91; TV 91–95; Chapl Duchess of Somerset Hosp Froxfield 86–94; rtd 95; PtO *Sarum* 95–10. *4 Springfield Park, Tisbury, Salisbury SP3 6QN* T: (01747) 871530

BUNDAY, Richard William. b 76. Lanc Univ BA 98 MA 04. Cranmer Hall Dur 98. **d** 00 **p** 01. C Redcar *York* 00–01; C Marton *Blackb* 01–04; P-in-c Ashton-on-Ribble St Mich w Preston St Mark 04–06; TR W Preston 06–10; P-in-c Kirkham 10–11; V from 11; AD 15–17. *The Vicarage, Church Street, Kirkham, Preston PR4 2SE* T: (01772) 687076 E: vicarofkirkham@outlook.com

BUNDOCK, Canon Anthony Francis. b 49. Qu Coll Birm 81. **d** 83 **p** 84. C Stansted Mountfitchet *Chelmsf* 83–86; TV Borehamwood *St Alb* 86–94; TR Seacroft *Ripon* 94–05; AD Whitkirk 00–05; TR Leeds City 05–14; rtd 14; TV Risborough *Ox* from 14. *The Vicarage, 1 Church Lane, Lacey Green, Princes Risborough HP27 0QX* T: 0113-278 6237 E: tony.pat.bundock@virgin.net

BUNDOCK, Edward Leigh. b 52. Keble Coll Ox BA 73 Open Univ PhD 94 MAAT. St Steph Ho Ox 74. **d** 76 **p** 77. C Malvern Link w Cowleigh *Worc* 76–80; C-in-c Portslade Gd Shep CD *Chich* 80–88; V Wisborough Green 88–94; PtO *Guildf* 96–97; P-in-c E and W Rudham, Houghton-next-Harpley etc *Nor* 97–99; R E w W Rudham, Helhoughton etc from 99. *The Rectory, South Raynham Road, West Raynham, Fakenham NR21 7HH* T: (01328) 838385

BUNDOCK, Canon John Nicholas Edward. b 45. Wells Th Coll 66. **d** 70 **p** 71. C Chingford SS Pet and Paul *Chelmsf* 70–74; P-in-c Gt Grimsby St Matt Fairfield CD *Linc* 74–81; V Hindhead *Guildf* 81–99; RD Farnham 91–96; V Bramley and Grafham 99–15; RD Cranleigh 04–12; Chapl Gosden Ho Sch 99–15; Hon Can Guildf Cathl 09–15; rtd 15; PtO *Guildf* from 15; *Chich* from 15. *18 Hall Hurst Close, Loxwood, Billingshurst RH14 0BE* M: 07789-487695 E: jnebundock@gmail.com

BUNDOCK, Nicholas John. b 73. Sheff Univ BSc 94 PhD 98 Fitzw Coll Cam BA 01. Ridley Hall Cam 99. **d** 02 **p** 03. C Mortomley St Sav High Green *Sheff* 02–05; TV Didsbury St Jas and Em *Man* 05–10; TR from 10. *St James's Rectory, 9 Didsbury Park, Manchester M20 5LH* T: 0161-434 6518 *or* 446 4150 E: nickbundock@stjamesandemmanuel.org

BUNDOCK, Ronald Michael. b 44. Leeds Univ BSc 65. Ox NSM Course 87. **d** 90 **p** 91. NSM Buckingham *Ox* 90–98; NSM Stowe 98–14; P-in-c 03–14; PtO from 14; AD Buckingham 11–17. *1 Holton Road, Buckingham MK18 1PQ* T: (01280) 813887

BUNGARD, Mrs Rosemary Felicity. GTCL 72. TISEC 12. **d** 15 **p** 16. C Portree *Arg* from 15. *Ceòl na Mara, West Suisnish, Isle of Raasay, Kyle IV40 8NX* T: (01478) 660248 M: 07719-585732 E: ceolmara@waitrose.com

BUNKER (née HARDING), Mrs Elizabeth. b 45. Chelsea Coll Lon BSc 67 MSc 69. SAOMC 04. **d** 06 **p** 07. NSM Baldock w Bygrave and Weston *St Alb* 06–10; NSM St Paul's Walden 10–16; NSM Hitchin and St Paul's Walden 16–18; rtd 18; PtO *St Alb* from 18. *Arana, 6 Hitchin Road, Letchworth Garden City SG6 3LL* T: (01462) 686808 F: 679276 M: 07850-413724 E: elizabethbunker@hotmail.com

BUNN, Mrs Rosemary Joan. b 60. EAMTC 94. **d** 97 **p** 98. NSM Sprowston w Beeston *Nor* 97–01; R Stoke H Cross w Dunston, Arminghall etc 01–11; R Belton and Burgh Castle from 11. *The Rectory, Beccles Road, Belton, Great Yarmouth NR31 9JQ* T: (01493) 780210

BUNNELL, Adrian. b 49. Univ of Wales (Abth) BSc 72. St Mich Coll Llan 74. **d** 75 **p** 76. C Wrexham *St As* 75–78; C Rhyl w St Ann 78–79; CF 79–95; R Aberfoyle and Callander *St And* 95–03; R Newport-on-Tay 03–06; rtd 06. *4 Williamsburgh Cottages, Forneth, Blairgowrie PH10 6SP* T: (01350) 724317

BUNTER, Andrew Stuart. b 84. Univ of Wales (Abth) LLB 05. St Mellitus Coll BA 19. **d** 19. C Sprowston w Beeston *Nor* from 19. *4 Mallard Way, Sprowston, Norwich NR7 8DD* T: (01603) 400751 M: 07425-154454 E: andybunter@sprowston.org.uk

BUNTING, Canon Ian David. b 33. Ex Coll Ox BA 58 MA 61. Tyndale Hall Bris 57 Princeton Th Sem ThM 60. **d** 60 **p** 61. C Bootle St Leon *Liv* 60–63; V Waterloo St Jo 64–71; Dir Past Studies St Jo Coll Dur 71–78; R Chester le Street *Dur* 78–87; RD Chester-le-Street 79–84; Kingham Hill Fellow 87–89; Dioc Dir of Ords *S'well* 90–99; C Lenton 90–97; Hon Can S'well Minster 93–99; Bp's Research Officer 97–00; rtd 00; PtO S'well from 00. *8 Crafts Way, Southwell NG25 0BL* T: (01636) 813868 E: ibunting@waitrose.com

BUNTING (née SIMPSON), Mrs Rachel Victoria. b 89. Ban Univ BD 11 Cardiff Univ MTh 14. St Mich Coll Llan 11. **d** 13 **p** 14. C Llantwit Major *Llan* 13–16; Bp's Officer for Family Min *S & B* from 16; PtO from 16. *The Vicarage, Lewis Street, St Thomas, Swansea SA1 8BP* T: (01792) 652891 E: revrachelbunting@hotmail.co.uk

BUNYAN, David Richard. b 48. Edin Th Coll 93. **d** 96 **p** 97. NSM Musselburgh *Edin* 96–98; NSM Prestonpans 96–98; C Edin St Dav 98–00; R Grangemouth 00–13; P-in-c Bo'ness 00–13; rtd 13; LtO *Edin* from 14. *14 Clerwood Bank, Edinburgh EH12 8PZ* T: 0131-476 6586 E: bunyandr@gmail.com

BUQUÉ, Mrs Helena Margareta. b 55. Chich Inst of HE BEd 95. SEITE 09. **d** 12 **p** 13. NSM Findon w Clapham and Patching *Chich* 12–15; P-in-c from 15; RD Worthing from 17. *The Rectory, School Hill, Findon, Worthing BN14 0TR* T: (01903) 873601 M: 07504-333853 E: findon.rectory@btinternet.com

BURBERRY, The Very Revd Frances Sheila. b 60. ACII 83. TISEC 03. **d** 06 **p** 07. C Edin St Pet 06–11; R Edin St Ninian from 11; Chapl Edin Univ from 06; Syn Clerk 16–17; Can St Mary's Cathl from 16; Dean Edin from 17. *163 Craigleith Road, Edinburgh EH4 2EB* T: 0131-315 0404 E: frances.burberry@ed.ac.uk *or* dean@dioceseofedinburgh.org

BURBIDGE, Barry Desmond. b 52. STETS 94. **d** 97 **p** 98. NSM Fleet *Guildf* 97–03; NSM Crondall and Ewshot 03–11; Chapl Frimley Park Hosp NHS Foundn Trust 06–14; Chapl Frimley Health NHS Foundn Trust from 14. *Frimley Park Hospital, Portsmouth Road, Frimley, Camberley GU16 7UJ* T: (01276) 604604   E: barry.burbidge@fph-tr.nhs.uk   *or* padrebarry@hotmail.com

BURBIDGE, Richard John. b 77. Lon Guildhall Univ BSc 00. Oak Hill Th Coll BTh 11. **d** 11 **p** 12. C Lowestoft Ch Ch *Nor* 11–14; C Moulton *Pet* 14–16; R Billing from 16. *25 Church Walk, Great Billing, Northampton NN3 9ED* M: 07973-801254 E: richburbidge@googlemail.com

BURBRIDGE, The Very Revd John Paul. b 32. K Coll Cam BA 54 MA 58 New Coll Ox BA 54 MA 58 FSA 89. Wells Th Coll 58. **d** 59 **p** 60. C Eastbourne St Mary *Chich* 59–62; V Choral York Minster 62–66; Can Res and Prec York Minster 66–76; Adn Richmond *Ripon* 76–83; Can Res Ripon Cathl 76–83; Dean Nor 83–95; rtd 95; PtO *Ripon* 95–06; LtO *Glas* from 08. *The Clachan Bothy, Newtonairds, Dumfries DG2 0JL* T: (01387) 820403 E: fremington124@yahoo.co.uk *or* revpaul@stjohnsdumfries.org

BURBRIDGE, Richard James. b 47. Univ of Wales (Ban) BSc 68. Oak Hill Th Coll 68. **d** 72 **p** 73. C Rodbourne Cheney *Bris* 72–75; C Downend 75–78; P-in-c Bris H Cross Inns Court 78–83; P-in-c Fishponds All SS 83–86; V 86–97; RD Stapleton 89–95; C Bishopston 97–98; C Bris St Andr w St Bart 97–98; TV Bishopston and St Andrews 98–12; rtd 12; PtO *Bris* from 12. *10 Scandrett Close, Bristol BS10 7SS* T: 0117-950 4945 E: burbridge466@btinternet.com

BURBURY, Canon Janet. b 56. Sunderland Univ CertEd 02. Cranmer Hall Dur 05. **d** 07 **p** 08. C Hart w Elwick Hall *Dur* 07–11; P-in-c from 11; AD Hartlepool from 13; Hon Can Dur Cathl from 16. *The Vicarage, Hart, Hartlepool TS27 3AP* T: (01429) 262340 M: 07958-131271 E: janetb_231@hotmail.co.uk

BURCH, Charles Edward. b 57. Trin Coll Cam MA 80 Lon Business Sch MBA 87. ERMC 05. **d** 07 **p** 08. NSM Harpenden St Jo *St Alb* 07–11; V Bovingdon from 11; Dioc Voc Officer from 11. *10 Church Street, Bovingdon, Hemel Hempstead HP3 0LU* E: charlesburch57@hotmail.com

BURCH, Canon Peter John. b 36. ACA 60 FCA 71. Ripon Hall Ox 62. **d** 64 **p** 65. C Brixton St Matt *S'wark* 64–67; Chapl Freetown St Aug Sierra Leone 68–72; P-in-c Chich St Pet 72–76; V Broadwater Down 76–85; V Steyning 85–94; R Ashurst 85–94; Hon Can Bauchi from 93; V Broadway *Worc* 94–96; V Broadway w Wickhamford 96–02; rtd 02; PtO *Glouc* from 03; *Worc* from 04. *6 Jordan's Close, Willersey, Broadway WR12 7QD* T: (01386) 853837 E: pj_pjburch@hotmail.com

BURCH, Stephen Roy. b 59. St Jo Coll Nottm 82. **d** 85 **p** 86. C Ipswich St Aug *St E* 85–89; Youth Chapl *Cov* 89–94; P-in-c Kinwarton w Gt Alne and Haselor 89–99; R 99–04; P-in-c Coughton 02–04; RD Alcester 99–04; V Fletchamstead from 04; AD Cov S 10–18; AD Kenilworth 10–13. *St James's Vicarage, 395 Tile Hill Lane, Coventry CV4 9DP* T: (024) 7646 6262 E: vicar@stjamesfletch.org.uk

BURCHELL, Mrs Elizabeth Susan. b 53. Sheff Univ BSc 74. SAOMC 04. **d** 07 **p** 08. NSM Banbury St Leon *Ox* 07–10; P-in-c 10–13; V from 13. *St Leonard's Vicarage, 46A Middleton Road, Banbury OX16 4RG* T: (01295) 271008 M: 07709-754914 E: revsueb@btinternet.com

BURDEN, Derek Ronald. b 37. Sarum Th Coll 59. **d** 62 **p** 63. C Cuddington *Guildf* 62–64; C Leamington Priors All SS *Cov* 64–66; C Stamford All SS w St Pet *Linc* 66–74; C-in-c Stamford Ch Ch CD 71–74; P-in-c Ashbury w Compton Beauchamp *Ox* 74–77; V 77–81; V Ashbury, Compton Beauchamp and Longcot w Fernham 81–84; V Wokingham St Sebastian 84–97; P-in-c Wooburn 97–02; rtd 02; PtO *Sarum* 03–05; *Win* from 06. *5 Cranford Park Drive, Yateley GU46 6JR* T: (01252) 890657

BURDEN, Lucy Angela Margaret. Cumbria Univ BA. CITI. **d** 16 **p** 17. Mt Merrion *D & D* 16–17; C Portadown St Mark *Arm* from 17. *9 Willow Drive, Portadown, Craigavon BT62 3SD* M: 07541-953148

BURDEN, Paul. b 62. Rob Coll Cam BA 84 MA 88 AMIMechE 87. Wycliffe Hall Ox BA 91. **d** 92 **p** 93. C Clevedon St Andr and Ch Ch *B & W* 92–96; R Bathampton w Claverton 96–14; Warden of Readers Bath Adnry 06–14; Tutor STETS 14–15; Dir Contextual Learning Sarum Coll from 15; PtO *B & W* from 15. *Sarum College, 19 The Close, Salisbury SP1 2EE* T: (01722) 424816 E: pburden@sarum.ac.uk

BURDEN, Robert John. b 55. Imp Coll Lon BSc 76 ARCS 76. ERMC 11. **d** 13 **p** 14. OLM Cressing w Stisted and Bradwell etc *Chelmsf* 13–17; NSM from 17; NSM Coggeshall w Markshall from 17. *Broadview, Ferry Road, Fingringhoe, Colchester CO5 7BY* T: (01206) 729248 M: 07808-516349 E: robeburd@gmail.com

BURDETT, Canon Stephen Martin. b 49. AKC 72. St Aug Coll Cant 73. **d** 74 **p** 75. C Walworth St Pet *S'wark* 74–75; C Walworth 75–77; C Benhilton 77–80; P-in-c Earlsfield St Jo 80–83; V 83–89; V N Dulwich St Faith 89–99; Ldr Post Ord Tr Woolwich Area 96–99; TR Southend *Chelmsf* 99–15; Hon Can Chelmsf Cathl 09–15; RD Southend 10–15; rtd 15; PtO *Chelmsf* from 15. *51 Admirals Walk, Shoeburyness, Southend-on-Sea SS3 9HR* T: (01702) 294454 E: revstephenburdett@gmail.com

BURDON, Anthony James. b 46. Ex Univ LLB 67 Lon Univ BD 73. Oak Hill Th Coll 71. **d** 73 **p** 74. C Ox St Ebbe w St Pet 73–76; C Church Stretton *Heref* 76–78; Voc Sec CPAS and Hon C Bromley Ch Ch *Roch* 78–81; V Filkins w Broadwell, Broughton, Kelmscot etc *Ox* 81–84; R Broughton Poggs w Filkins, Broadwell etc 84–85; V Reading St Jo 85–96; C California and Adv for Spirituality (Berks) 96–98; Warden and P-in-c Cumbrae (or Millport) *Arg* 98–04; V Burstwick w Thorngumbald *York* 04–11; P-in-c Roos and Garton w Tunstall, Grimston and Hilston 08–11; RD S Holderness 06–09; rtd 11; PtO *York* from 11. *22 Wheatlands Close, Pocklington, York YO42 2UT* T: (01759) 304290 E: pamandtonyburdon@btinternet.com

BURDON, Canon Christopher John. b 48. Jes Coll Cam BA 70 MA 74 Glas Univ PhD 95. Coll of Resurr Mirfield 71. **d** 74 **p** 75. C Chelmsf All SS 74–78; TV High Wycombe *Ox* 78–84; P-in-c Olney w Emberton 84–90; R 90–92; LtO *Glas* 92–94; Lay Tr Officer *Chelmsf* 94–99; Prin NOC 00–07; Can Th and CME Adv *St E* 07–13; rtd 13; PtO *Chelmsf* 14–16; *Sarum* from 17. *24 Newman Road, Devizes SN10 5LE* E: cjburdon@btinternet.com

BURDON, Mrs Pamela Muriel. b 46. Ex Univ BA 68 Reading Univ DipEd 69. Wycliffe Hall Ox 88. **d** 90 **p** 94. Par Dn Reading St Jo *Ox* 90–94; C 94–96; P-in-c California 96–98; NSM Cumbrae (or Millport) *Arg* 98–04; NSM Burstwick w Thorngumbald *York* 04–11; C Preston and Sproatley in Holderness 05–06; P-in-c 06–11; C Roos and Garton w Tunstall, Grimston and Hilston 08–11; rtd 11; PtO *York* from 12. *22 Wheatlands Close, Pocklington, York YO42 2UT* T: (01759) 304290

BURFORD, Anthony Francis. b 55. Oak Hill Th Coll BA 98. **d** 98 **p** 99. C Cov H Trin 98–02; P-in-c Rye Park St Cuth *St Alb* 02–07; V 07–11; V S Hornchurch St Jo and St Matt *Chelmsf* 11–16; rtd 16; PtO *Chelmsf* 17–18; Hon C Grays Thurrock from 18. *14 Chelmer Drive, South Ockendon RM15 6EE* M: 07500-007479 E: revdtonyburford@gmail.com

BURGE, Edward Charles Richard. b 70. Liv Univ BA 92. Ridley Hall Cam 93. **d** 96 **p** 97. C Cayton w Eastfield *York* 96–99; P-in-c Lythe w Ugthorpe 99–03; Children's Officer (Cleveland Adnry) 99–03; Hon Chapl Miss to Seafarers 02–03; Dioc Youth and Children's Work Co-ord *Wakef* 04–10; P-in-c Roberttown w Hartshead 10–12; P-in-c Scholes 10–12; V Hartshead, Hightown, Roberttown and Scholes 12–14; *Leeds* 14–19; TR Harden and Wilsden, Cullingworth and Denholme from 19. *The Vicarage, Wilsden Old Road, Harden, Bingley BD16 1JD* T: (01535) 273758 E: richard.burge@talktalk.net *or* richard.burge@leeds.anglican.org

BURGE, Stephen Russell. b 81. St Andr Univ MA 03 Edin Univ MSc 04 PhD 09 FRSA 10 FHEA 16. ERMC 16. **d** 18 **p** 19. NSM Eaton Bray w Edlesborough *St Alb* from 18. *67 Grasmere Road, Leighton Buzzard LU7 2QL* T: (020) 7756 2766 E: sburge@iis.ac.uk

BURGE-THOMAS, Mrs Ruth Anne. b 66. **d** 04 **p** 05. C Clapham H Spirit *S'wark* 04–14; V from 14; Chapl St Mark's C of E Academy Mitcham from 10. *The Vicarage, 15 Elms Road, London SW4 9ER* E: ruth@burgethomas.com *or* office@holyspirit-clapham.org.uk

BURGESS, Alan James. b 51. Ridley Hall Cam 87. **d** 89 **p** 90. C Glenfield *Leic* 89–92; V Donisthorpe and Moira w Stretton-en-le-Field 92–06; RD Akeley W 00–06; RD Akeley S 05–06; C Ravenstone and Swannington 06–09; P-in-c Thringstone St Andr 06–09; P-in-c Whitwick St Jo the Bapt 07–09; R Whitwick, Thringstone and Swannington 09–15; rtd 15. *242 Hearthcote Road, Swadlincote DE11 9DU* T: (01283) 213251 E: sylvanus06@gmail.com

BURGESS, Andrew Graham. b 84. Middx Univ BA 08. Wycliffe Hall Ox BA 19. **d** 19. C Bushey *St Alb* from 19. *2 University Close, Bushey WD23 3AL* M: 07811-314911 E: andy.burgess@icloud.com

BURGESS, Charles Anthony Robert. b 58. STETS. **d** 11 **p** 12. NSM Bath Weston All SS w N Stoke and Langridge *B & W* 11–15; NSM Bathford 15–16; PtO 16–18; Hon C Corfe Mullen *Sarum* from 17. *The Rectory, 32 Wareham Road, Corfe Mullen, Wimborne BH21 3LE* T: (01202) 699319 M: 07895-860399 E: burgesscj@gmail.com

BURGESS, Preb David John. b 39. Trin Hall Cam BA 62 MA 66 Univ Coll Ox MA 66 FRSA 91. Cuddesdon Coll 62. **d** 65 **p** 66. C Maidstone All SS w St Phil *Cant* 65; Asst Chapl Univ Coll Ox 66–70; Chapl 70–78; Can and Treas Windsor 78–87; V St Lawr Jewry *Lon* 87–08; Preb St Paul's Cathl 02–08; Chapl to The Queen 87–09; rtd 08. *62 Orbel Street, London SW11 3NZ* T: (020) 7585 1572

BURGESS, Mrs Denise. b 49. **d** 00 **p** 01. OLM Glascote and Stonydelph *Lich* 00–06; NSM 06–07; NSM Elford 07–15; NSM Mease Valley 15; rtd 16; PtO *Cov* from 16. *37 Greendale Road, Nuneaton CV11 6RH* M: 07818-890184 E: burgess.denise@virgin.net

BURGESS, Canon Edwin Michael. b 47. Ch Coll Cam BA 69 MA 73. Coll of Resurr Mirfield 70. **d** 72 **p** 73. C Beamish *Dur* 72–77; C Par *Truro* 77–80; P-in-c Duloe w Herodsfoot 80–83; R 83–86; Jt Dir SWMTC 80–86; Subwarden St Deiniol's Lib Hawarden 86–91; R Oughtrington *Ches* 91–05; P-in-c Warburton 95; R Oughtrington and Warburton from 05; CME Officer 99–03; Asst Chapl (Warrington) Ches Univ from 03; Dioc Chapl MU from 02; Hon Can Ches Cathl from 10. *The Rectory, Stage Lane, Lymm WA13 9JB* T: (01925) 752388 E: m.burgess154@btinternet.com

BURGESS, Mrs Geraldine Mary. b 54. Ox Univ BA 75 Southn Univ PGCE 76. SEITE 12. **d** 15 **p** 16. NSM Ifield *Chich* 15–17; NSM Gossops Green and Bewbush 17–18; P-in-c Amberley w N Stoke and Parham, Wiggonholt etc from 18. *Amberley New Vicarage, School Road, Amberley, Arundel BN18 9NA* E: revgerryburgess@gmail.com

BURGESS, Hugh Nigel. b 55. Edin Univ BSc 76 Aber Univ MA 79. St As Minl Tr Course. **d** 06 **p** 07. NSM Halkyn w Caerfallwch w Rhesycae *St As* 06–16; P-in-c 07–16; TV Estuary and Mountain Miss Area from 17. *The Chimneys, 7 Leete Park, Rhydymwyn, Mold CH7 5JJ* T: (01352) 741646

BURGESS, Jane Ellen. b 63. Chelsea Coll Lon BSc 85. STETS BA 10. **d** 07 **p** 08. C Frome H Trin *B & W* 07–10; P-in-c Bathford 10–16; Asst RD Bath 15–17; R Corfe Mullen *Sarum* from 17. *The Rectory, 32 Wareham Road, Corfe Mullen, Wimborne BH21 3LE* T: (01202) 699319 E: revjaneb@gmail.com

BURGESS, The Ven Jean Ann. b 62. Nottm Univ MA 03. EMMTC 00. **d** 03 **p** 04. C Gresley *Derby* 03–09; C Derby St Alkmund and St Werburgh 09–13; P-in-c 13–18; Hon Can Derby Cathl 16–18; Adn Bolton *Man* from 18. *The Vicarage, 14 Springside Road, Bury BL9 5JE* T: 0161-761 6117 E: archbolton@manchester.anglican.org

BURGESS, John David. b 51. Ex Univ BSc 73 Sussex Univ PGCE 94. Trin Coll Bris 07. **d** 08 **p** 09. NSM Westfield and Guestling *Chich* 08–15; NSM Brede w Udimore and Beckley and Peasmarsh 15–17; rtd 17. *25 Fairlight Gardens, Fairlight, Hastings TN35 4AY* E: revd.john.burgess@gmail.com

BURGESS, John Michael. b 36. ALCD 61. **d** 61 **p** 62. C Eccleston St Luke *Liv* 61–64; C Avondale St Mary Magd Rhodesia 64–68; R Marlborough 68–74; V Nottingham St Andr *S'well* 74–79; Bp's Adv on Community Relns 77–79; V Earlestown *Liv* 79–87; RD Warrington 82–87; TR Halewood 87–94; V Southport St Phil and St Paul 94–01; AD N Meols 95–00; rtd 01; PtO *Liv* from 03. *38 Brunlees Court, 19-23 Cambridge Road, Southport PR9 9DH*

BURGESS, John Mulholland. b 32. Cranmer Hall Dur 58. **d** 61 **p** 62. C Frimley *Guildf* 61–67; C Cheltenham St Luke and St Jo *Glouc* 67–69; P-in-c Withington w Compton Abdale 69–74; R Woolstone w Gotherington and Oxenton 74–75; Chapl Rotterdam w Schiedam etc *Eur* 75–78; Chapl Sliema 78–80; C Nottingham All SS *S'well* 80; C Rolleston w Morton 80–83; C Rolleston w Fiskerton, Morton and Upton 83–84; V Mansfield St Aug 84–99; Asst RD Mansfield 88–92; RD 92–98; rtd 99; PtO *S'well* from 03. *278 Westfield Lane, Mansfield NG19 6NQ* T: (01623) 421163

BURGESS, Kate Lamorna. b 64. Man Poly BA 86 Leeds Univ MA 97. NEOC 99. **d** 02 **p** 03. OHP 92–03; C Hessle *York* 02–06; TV Howden 06–10; P-in-c Stretford St Matt *Man* 10–18; R from 18. *St Matthew's Rectory, 39 Sandy Lane, Stretford, Manchester M32 9DB* T: 0161-865 2535 E: kburgess1@tiscali.co.uk

BURGESS, Laura Jane. See JØRGENSEN, Laura Jane

BURGESS, Michael. See BURGESS, Edwin Michael

BURGESS, Canon Michael James. b 42. Coll of Resurr Mirfield 74. **d** 76 **p** 77. C Leigh-on-Sea St Marg *Chelmsf* 76–79; C St Peter-in-Thanet *Cant* 79–82; Chapl Royal St Geo Coll Toronto Canada 82–89; R Toronto Epiphany and St Mark 89–04; R Toronto Transfiguration from 04; Can Toronto from 01. *318W-118 Montgomery Avenue, Toronto ON M4R 1E3, Canada* T: (001) (416) 482 2462 *or* (416) 489 7798 F: 489 3272 E: michaelburgess@sympatico.ca

BURGESS, Canon Neil. b 53. Univ of Wales (Lamp) BA 75 Nottm Univ MTh 87 PhD 93. St Mich Coll Llan 75. **d** 77

p 78. C Cheadle *Lich* 77–79; C Longton 79–82; TV Hanley H Ev 82–86; C Uttoxeter w Bramshall 86–87; Lect Linc Th Coll 87–95; Hon C Linc Minster Gp 88–95; Dioc Dir of Clergy Tr *S'well* 95–00; C Newark 97–00; PtO *Linc* 00–06; Hon C Linc St Pet-at-Gowts and St Andr from 06; Hon C Linc St Botolph from 06; Hon C Linc St Mary-le-Wigford w St Benedict etc from 06; Hon C Linc St Faith and St Martin w St Pet 06–15; Hon C Linc St Swithin from 06; Min Team Ldr from 13; Can and Preb Linc Cathl from 18. *Edward King House, The Old Palace, Lincoln LN2 1PU* T: (01522) 539408 E: neil.burgess@lincoln.anglican.org

BURGESS, Prof Paul Christopher James. b 41. Qu Coll Cam BA 63 MA 67. Lon Coll of Div 66. **d** 68 **p** 69. C Islington St Mary *Lon* 68–72; C Church Stretton *Heref* 73–74; Lect Gujranwala Th Sem Pakistan 74–83; Warden Carberry Tower (Ch of Scotland) 84–86; Progr Co-ord 86–88; TV Livingston LEP *Edin* 88–92; Prof and Lib Gujranwala Th Sem 94–08; rtd 08. *Springvale, Halket Road, Lugton, Kilmarnock KA3 4EE* T: (01505) 850254 E: paulandcathie@gmail.com

BURGESS, Peter Alan. b 40. St Edm Ho Cam BA 86 MA 89 MPhil 86 St Jo Coll York MA 99. Cranmer Hall Dur 02. **d** 03 **p** 04. NSM Wheldrake w Thorganby *York* 03–08; NSM Derwent Ings 08–14; PtO from 14. *2 Derwent Drive, Wheldrake, York YO19 6AL* T: (01904) 448309 E: burgesspr@btinternet.com

BURGESS, Roy. b 32. S Dios Minl Tr Scheme 80. **d** 83 **p** 84. NSM Bentworth and Shalden and Lasham *Win* 83–89; R Ingoldsby *Linc* 89–97; RD Beltisloe 93–97; rtd 97; PtO *Nor* from 98. *28 Stuart Court, High Street, Kibworth Beauchamp, Leicester LE8 0LR*

BURGESS, Roy Graham. b 47. Birm Univ CertCYW 72. Ox Min Course 91. **d** 94 **p** 95. C Easthampstead *Ox* 94–99; C Wokingham St Paul 99–04; P-in-c Owlsmoor 04–09; V 09–14; rtd 15; PtO *Ox* from 15. *Strathpeffer, 4 Appletree Place, Bracknell RG42 1YN* T: (01344) 304993 E: revroy@btinternet.com

BURGESS, Mrs Tina. b 61. Yorks Min Course 14. **d** 17 **p** 18. NSM Ormesby *York* 17–18; NSM Redcar from 18. *Park House, Rosehill, Great Ayton, Middlesbrough TS9 6BH*

BURGHALL, Kenneth Miles. b 34. Selw Coll Cam BA 57 MA 61. Qu Coll Birm 57. **d** 59 **p** 60. C Macclesfield St Mich *Ches* 59–63; CF 63–67; P-in-c Birkenhead Priory *Ches* 67–71; V Macclesfield St Paul 71–87; V Lower Peover 87–04; P-in-c Over Peover 92–04; rtd 04; PtO *Ches* from 04. *12 Linksway, Congleton CW12 3BS* T: (01260) 289277

BURGON, Canon George Irvine. b 41. Open Univ BA 92. Edin Th Coll 62 Univ of the S (USA) 63. **d** 65 **p** 66. C Dundee St Mary Magd *Bre* 65–68; C Wellingborough All Hallows *Pet* 68–71; P-in-c Norton 71–73; TV Daventry w Norton 73–75; V Northampton St Mary 75–98; R Rothwell w Orton, Rushton w Glendon and Pipewell 98–08; Can Pet Cathl 95–08; rtd 08; PtO *Pet* 09–13. *47 Woodlands Avenue, Barton Seagrave, Kettering NN15 6QS* T: (01536) 722193 E: georgeburgon@yahoo.co.uk

BURGON, Mrs Lynne. b 58. RGN 80 RM 83. SWMTC 03. **d** 06 **p** 07. NSM Fremington *Ex* 06–07; C Okehampton w Inwardleigh, Bratton Clovelly etc 07–11; V Bampton, Morebath, Clayhanger, Petton etc 11–14; PtO from 14. *2 Barton Cottages, Monkleigh, Bideford EX39 5JX* E: lynneburgon@live.co.uk

BURKE, The Ven Christopher Mark. b 65. Cov Poly LLB 87 Heythrop Coll Lon MA 06. Ripon Coll Cuddesdon 89. **d** 92 **p** 93. C Nunthorpe *York* 92–96; V S Bank 96–02; R Stepney St Dunstan and All SS *Lon* 02–10; Can Res Sheff Cathl 10–13; Can Res and Prec Sheff Cathl 13–19; Vice Dean 14–19; Adn Barking *Chelmsf* from 19. *11 Bridgefields Close, Hornchurch RM11 1GQ* T: (01708) 474951 M: 07950-434333 E: a.barking@chelmsford.anglican.org

BURKE, Colin Douglas. b 41. Bp Otter Coll CertEd 64. **d** 92 **p** 93. OLM Fressingfield, Mendham, Metfield, Weybread etc *St E* 92–99; P-in-c Oare w Culbone *B & W* 99–19; rtd 19. *Victoria Church Cottage, Parson's Street, Porlock, Minehead TA24 8QJ* M: 07810-563529 E: colin.barbara.burke@googlemail.com

BURKE, Elisabeth Ann. b 44. St Matthias Coll Bris CertEd 66. **d** 05 **p** 06. OLM E Horsley and Ockham w Hatchford and Downside *Guildf* 05–14; PtO from 14. *39 Copse Road, Cobham KT11 2TW* T: (01932) 863886 E: elisabethb@ntlworld.com

BURKE, Mrs Elizabeth Mary Ann. b 72. Liv Univ BA 95 Surrey Univ MBA 06. Westcott Ho Cam 12. **d** 13 **p** 14. C Bickleigh and Shaugh Prior *Ex* 13–14; C Plymouth Crownhill Ascension 14–17; P-in-c Holsworthy, Hollacombe, Pyworthy etc from 17. *The Rectory, Bodmin Street, Holsworthy EX22 6BH* T: (01409)   255490   M: 07990-978485 E: elizabethmaburke@icloud.com

BURKE, Jonathan. b 53. Lon Univ BEd. Westcott Ho Cam 79. **d** 82 **p** 83. C Weymouth H Trin *Sarum* 82–85; R Bere Regis and Affpuddle w Turnerspuddle 85–92; NSM Talbot Village 04–08; TR White Horse 08–15; RD Heytesbury 13–15; rtd 15; PtO *Sarum* from 15. *10 Graycot Close, Bournemouth BH10 7BU* E: jonathan_burke2003@yahoo.co.uk

BURKE, Kelvin Stephen. b 56. Man Univ BA 77 FCA 81. Cranmer Hall Dur. **d** 99 **p** 00. C Stanley *Wakef* 99–02; P-in-c Wakef St Andr and St Mary 02–06; Asst Chapl Leeds Teaching Hosps NHS Trust 06–10; PtO *Portsm* 11–14; Chapl Isle of Wight NHS Trust from 12. *7 Steephill Court Road, Ventnor PO38 1UH* T: (01983) 854261 M: 07793-979907

BURKE, Michael Robert. b 61. Leeds Univ BA 83. Trin Coll Bris BA 89. **d** 89 **p** 90. C Anston *Sheff* 89–92; V Crosspool 92–00; V Hucclecote *Glouc* 00–09; PtO 09–15; TV Keynsham *B & W* from 15. *9 Chelmer Grove, Keynsham, Bristol BS31 1QA* T: 0117-909 9425 M: 07432-530153 E: mikburke1@outlook.com *or* mikeburke@keynshamparish.org.uk

BURKE, Canon William Spencer Dwerryhouse. b 46. Ripon Coll Cuddesdon 90. **d** 92 **p** 93. C Watford St Mich *St Alb* 92–95; R Castor w Sutton and Upton w Marholm *Pet* 95–15; Can Pet Cathl 07–15; rtd 15; PtO *Ely* 12–16; *Pet* from 15; *Sarum* 15–17; RD Fincham and Feltwell *Ely* from 17. *The Rectory, High Street, Fincham, King's Lynn PE33 9EL* E: wsdburke@outlook.com

BURKETT, Canon Christopher Paul. b 52. Warwick Univ BA 75 Westmr Coll Ox MTh 93 Liv Univ PhD 10. Qu Coll Birm 75. **d** 78 **p** 79. C Streetly *Lich* 78–81; C Harlescott 81–83; TV Leek and Meerbrook 83–89; Chapl Leek Morlands Hosp 83–89; Area Sec USPG Ches 89–92; V Whitegate w Lt Budworth *Ches* 92–00; Asst CME Officer 93–00; Can Res Ches Cathl 00–10; Hon Can Ches Cathl from 11; Bp's Chapl 00–10; Dioc Dir of Min from 10; C Ches H Trin from 10. *36 Abbots Park, Chester CH1 4AN* T: (01244) 399941 *or* 681973 ext 256 M: 07921-040153 E: christopher.burkett@chester.anglican.org

BURKILL, Mark Edward. b 56. MA PhD. Trin Coll Bris. **d** 84 **p** 85. C Cheadle *Ches* 84–88; C Harold Wood *Chelmsf* 88–91; V Leyton Ch Ch from 91. *The Vicarage, 52 Elm Road, London E11 4DW* T: (020) 8539 4980 E: m.burkill@ntlworld.com

BURKITT, Paul Adrian. b 49. RMN 75 SRN 77. St Steph Ho Ox 84. **d** 86 **p** 87. C Whitby *York* 86–90; V Egton w Grosmont 90–93; V Newington w Dairycoates 93–96; P-in-c Kingston upon Hull St Mary 96–07; P-in-c Sculcoates 04–07; rtd 07; PtO *York* 07–14; P-in-c Kingston upon Hull St Mary 14–16; PtO from 16. *2 Plane Tree Way, Filey YO14 9PA* E: paul2planetrees@gmail.com

BURKITT-GRAY, Mrs Joan Katherine. b 47. Portsm Poly BSc 68 Southn Univ MPhil 74. SEITE 00. **d** 04 **p** 05. NSM Lee St Marg *S'wark* 04–17; Hon Asst Chapl St Chris Hospice Lon 08–09; PtO *S'wark* from 17. *7 Foxes Dale, London SE3 9BD* T: (020) 8463 0365 *or* 8768 4500

BURLAND, Clive Beresford. b 37. Sarum & Wells Th Coll 81. **d** 85 **p** 86. C Warblington w Emsworth *Portsm* 85–87; C Cowes St Mary 87–92; V Gurnard 92–98; R Northwood 93–98; rtd 98; PtO *Portsm* from 98. *5A Orchard Close, Freshwater PO40 9BQ* T: (01983) 753949 E: clive.burland@talktalk.net

BURLEIGH, David John. b 42. FCII 69. St Deiniol's Hawarden 84. **d** 87 **p** 88. NSM Lache cum Saltney *Ches* 87–88; NSM Eastham 89–92; C Birkenhead Priory 92–95; P-in-c Duloe w Herodsfoot *Truro* 95–99; TV Liskeard, St Keyne, St Pinnock, Morval etc 95–99; R Duloe, Herodsfoot, Morval and St Pinnock 99–01; V Bath St Barn w Englishcombe *B & W* 01–10; rtd 10; PtO *B & W* 11–18. *1 Vine Gardens, Frome BA11 2LX* T: (01373) 300820 E: david.burleigh@hotmail.com

BURLEIGH, Walter Coleridge. b 41. WMMTC 89. **d** 89 **p** 90. NSM N Evington *Leic* 90–96; PtO from 96. *20 Border Drive, Leicester LE4 2JH* T: 0116-235 9230

BURLES, Robert John. b 54. Bris Univ BSc 75. St Jo Coll Nottm LTh 86. **d** 88 **p** 89. C Mansfield SS Pet and Paul *S'well* 88–91; C The Lydiards *Bris* 91–92; TV W Swindon and the Lydiards 92–97; TR Swindon St Jo and St Andr 97–11; AD Swindon 06–11; Hon Can Bris Cathl 04–11; P-in-c Takeley w Lt Canfield *Chelmsf* from 11. *The Rectory, Parsonage Road, Takeley, Bishop's Stortford CM22 6QX* T: (01279) 870214 M: 07946-496418 E: rob@burles.org.uk

BURLEY, John Roland James. b 46. St Jo Coll Cam BA 67 MA 70. Trin Episc Sch for Min Ambridge Penn MDiv 88. **d** 81 **p** 82. SAMS Chile 81–90; TV Southgate *Chich* 90–99; R Alfold and Loxwood *Guildf* 99–07; P-in-c 08–11; rtd 11; PtO *Heref* from 11. *72 Dahn Drive, Ludlow SY8 1XZ* T: (01584) 873155 E: john@burleys.co.uk

BURLEY, Michael. b 58. Ridley Hall Cam 86. **d** 89 **p** 90. C Scarborough St Mary w Ch Ch and H Apostles *York* 89–92; C Drypool 93; TV Drypool 93–97; V Sutton St Mich 97–03; V Burley in Wharfedale *Bradf* 03–13; Assoc Dioc Dir of Ords 07–13; P-in-c Staines *Lon* 13–18; V Staines St Mary and St Peter

18–19; V Staines Ch Ch from 19. *The Vicarage, 44 Kenilworth Gardens, Staines-upon-Thames TW18 1DR* T: (01784) 455457 E: michael.burley@btinternet.com

BURLEY, Richard Alexander. b 80. Warwick Univ BA 01 Fitzw Coll Cam BA 07. Ridley Hall Cam 05. **d** 08 **p** 09. C Bilton *Cov* 08–12; V Wythall *Birm* 12–17. *The Rectory, Church Lane, Lapworth, Solihull B94 5NX* M: 07875-123867 E: richburley80@gmail.com

BURLTON, Aelred Harry. b 49. Sarum & Wells Th Coll 75. **d** 78 **p** 79. C Feltham *Lon* 78–82; Chapl Heathrow Airport 83–94; P-in-c Harmondsworth 92–94; R St Buryan, St Levan and Sennen *Truro* 94–05; rtd 05; PtO *Truro* from 14. *Farway Barn, Hellangove Farm, Gulval, Penzance TR20 8XD* T: (01736) 330426 E: zoeb.sing@hotmail.co.uk

BURMAN, Philip Harvey. b 47. Kelham Th Coll 66. **d** 70 **p** 71. C Huyton St Mich *Liv* 70–75; C Farnworth 75–77; TV Kirkby 77–83; V Hindley All SS 83–93; V Middlesbrough St Martin *York* 93–97; V Middlesbrough St Martin w St Cuth 97–99; P-in-c Eccleston St Thos *Liv* 99–08; V Liv St Chris Norris Green 08–16; rtd 16; PtO *York* from 17; Hon C Heaton Ch Ch w Halliwell St Marg *Man* from 17. *1 Somerset Road, Bolton BL1 4NE* E: philip.h.burman@googlemail.com

BURMESTER, Stephen John. b 66. Leeds Univ BSc 87. Wycliffe Hall Ox 96. **d** 98 **p** 99. C Lenton *S'well* 98–02; C Bebington *Ches* 02–08; V Handforth from 08. *The Vicarage, 36 Sagars Road, Handforth, Wilmslow SK9 3EE* T: (01625) 250559 *or* 532145

BURN, Geoffrey Livingston. b 60. Sydney Univ BSc 83 Imp Coll Lon PhD 87 St Jo Coll Dur BA 95. Cranmer Hall Dur 93. **d** 96 **p** 97. C St Austell *Truro* 96–03; PtO *Cant* 03–06; P Forest S Deanery *Glouc* 06–11; Hon C Cinderford St Jo 06–10; Hon C Cinderford w Littledean 10–11; Chapl Glos Primary Care Trust 06–11; Chapl HM YOI Roch 11–17; Chapl HM Pris Maidstone from 17. *HM Prison, 36 County Road, Maidstone ME14 1UZ* T: (01622) 775300 E: geoffrey.burn@justice.gov.uk

BURN, Mrs Helen Mary. b 64. Down Coll Cam BA 86 New Coll Ox PGCE 88 Ex Univ MA 02 PhD 11. SWMTC 00. **d** 03 **p** 04. C Eythorne and Elvington w Waldershare etc *Cant* 03–06; Dir of Studies Local Min Tr Scheme 03–06; Dir Reader Tr *Glouc* 06–11; Tutor WEMTC 06–12; Dir of Studies Ripon Coll Cuddesdon 11–12; Sen Lect Glos Univ *Glouc* 09–12; V Roch St Justus from 12; AD Roch from 17. *St Justus's Vicarage, 1 Binnacle Road, Rochester ME1 2XR* T: (01634) 841183 M: 07818-492553 E: helenmburn@gmail.com

BURN, Leonard Louis. b 44. K Coll Lon BD 67 AKC 67. **d** 68 **p** 69. C Kingswinford St Mary *Lich* 68–70; C S Ascot *Ox* 70–72; C Caversham 72–76; Chapl Selly Oak Hosp Birm 76–81; Chapl Bris City Hosp 81–82; P-in-c Bris St Mich 81–83; R Peopleton and White Ladies Aston w Churchill etc *Worc* 83–88; V Bengeworth 88–97; Chapl St Richard's Hospice Worc 88–97; Chapl Evesham Coll 90–97; rtd 97; PtO *Glouc* from 97; *Worc* 97–98; Chapl Worcs Community and Mental Health Trust from 98. *Beckford Rise, Beckford, Tewkesbury GL20 7AN* T/F: (01386) 881160 M: 07734-505663 E: leonard.burn@btinternet.com

BURN, Michael Campbell. b 46. City of Leeds Coll of Educn CertEd 68 Open Univ MA 88 Univ of Wales (Trin St Dav) LTh 12. Yorks Min Course 12. **d** 12 **p** 13. NSM Rotherham *Sheff* 12–14; NSM Wath-upon-Dearne 14–16; rtd 16; PtO *Sheff* from 16; *Leeds* from 17. *6 Greenway, Honley, Holmfirth HD9 6NQ* M: 07712-620303 E: michaelcburn@btinternet.com

BURN, Richard James Southerden. b 34. Pemb Coll Cam BA 56. Wells Th Coll 56. **d** 58 **p** 59. C Cheshunt *St Alb* 58–62; C Leighton Buzzard 65–66; C Glastonbury St Jo *B & W* 66–68; P-in-c Prestonpans *Edin* 68–71; P-in-c Stokesay *Heref* 71–75; P-in-c Dorrington 75–81; P-in-c Stapleton 75–81; P-in-c Leebotwood w Longnor 75–81; P-in-c Smethcott w Woolstaston 81; TR Melbury *Sarum* 81–87; P-in-c Quendon w Rickling and Wicken Bonhunt *Chelmsf* 87–92; R Quendon w Rickling and Wicken Bonhunt etc 92–95; rtd 95; V Isleworth St Fran *Lon* 95–00; Hon C S Warks Seven Gp *Cov* 06–09; PtO *Heref* from 12. *The Old School House, 29 Lydbury North, Craven Arms SY7 8AU* T: (01588) 680465 E: richard.burn58@yahoo.co.uk

BURN, Robert Pemberton. b 34. Peterho Cam BA 56 MA 60 Lon Univ PhD 68. CMS Tr Coll Chislehurst 60. **d** 63 **p** 81. India 63–71; PtO *Ely* 71–81; P-in-c Foxton 81–88; PtO *Ex* from 89. *Sunnyside, Barrack Road, Exeter EX2 6AB* T: (01392) 430028

BURNAGE, Arthur Gavin. b 63. Ulster Univ BA 85 Cam Univ MA 05. Wycliffe Hall Ox 05. **d** 07 **p** 08. C Aldridge *Lich* 07–12; C Walsall St Pet 12–13; P-in-c 13–18; V from 18. *2 Brewer Street, Walsall WS2 8BH* T: (01922) 640955 E: gav.burnage@gmail.com

BURNE, Sambrooke Roger. b 47. Lon Univ MB, BS 70 MRCGP 74. SAOMC 03. **d** 06 **p** 07. NSM Blackbird Leys *Ox* 06–14; PtO *Pet* from 14. *43 Glebe Rise, Kings Sutton, Banbury OX17 3PH* T: (01295) 811936 M: 07901-882957 E: rogerburne@gmail.com

BURNETT (formerly DRURY), Mrs Caroline Norah. b 60. SAOMC 00. **d** 03 **p** 04. C Leavesden *St Alb* 03–09; C Bushey 09–13; P-in-c Compton w Shackleford and Peper Harow *Guildf* 13–19. *Address temp unknown* E: caroline_burnett@btinternet.com

BURNETT, Susan Mary. b 50. Lon Univ BEd 73. Cranmer Hall Dur 76. **dss** 78 **d** 87 **p** 94. Welling *S'wark* 78–83; C Greenwich Ch Ch w St Andr and St Mich 83–91; Par Dn 87–91; Par Dn Sydenham All SS 91–94; C 94–95; C Lower Sydenham St Mich 91–95; V 95–09; rtd 09; PtO *Chich* from 19. *9 Grove Park, Chichester PO19 3HY* T: (01243) 532748 E: sueburnett.s@mgial.com

BURNETT-HALL, Mrs Karen. b 46. Bp Grosseteste Coll CertEd 68 Lon Univ BD 82. Oak Hill Th Coll 86. **d** 89 **p** 94. Par Dn Norbury *Ches* 89–92; NSM York St Paul 93–95; NSM York St Barn 95–99; P-in-c 00–09; P-in-c Wimbotsham w Stow Bardolph and Stow Bridge etc *Ely* 11–17; PtO from 16. *8 The Vineyards, Ely CB7 4QG* T: (01353) 665249 E: karen.bh@btinternet.com

BURNHAM, Adam Henry. b 83. Moody Bible Inst Chicago BSc 09 Sheff Univ BA 16. Westcott Ho Cam 13 Coll of Resurr Mirfield 14. **d** 16 **p** 17. C Taunton H Trin *B & W* from 16. *The Curatage, 5 Redlake Drive, Taunton TA1 2RU* T: (01823) 974544 E: fatherburnham@gmail.com

BURNIE, Judith. *See* SWEETMAN, Judith

BURNINGHAM, Richard Anthony. b 47. Keele Univ BA 70 Aber Univ CQSW 77 Roehampton Inst PGCE 85. All Nations Chr Coll 82 Oak Hill Th Coll 94. **d** 96 **p** 97. C Reigate St Mary *S'wark* 96–00; V Weston *Win* 00–12; rtd 12; PtO *Win* 12–19; Hon C Somborne w Ashley from 19. *The New Vicarage, Romsey Road, King's Somborne, Stockbridge SO20 6PR* E: burninghamr@btinternet.com

BURNISTON, Aubrey John. b 53. St Jo Coll Dur BA 92 Leeds Univ MA 03. Cranmer Hall Dur 79. **d** 83 **p** 84. C Owton Manor *Dur* 83–86; TV Rugby *Cov* 86–93; V Heaton St Martin *Bradf* 93–09; Bp's Adv in Liturgy 00–09; V Islington St Jas w St Pet *Lon* from 09. *St James's Vicarage, 1A Arlington Square, London N1 7DS* T: (020) 7226 4108 E: vicar@stjamesislington.org

BURNLEY, Suffragan Bishop of. *See* NORTH, The Rt Revd Philip John

BURNS, Arthur. *See* BURNS, Williams Arthur

BURNS, Canon Edward Joseph. b 38. Liv Univ BSc 58 St Cath Soc Ox BA 61 MA 64. Wycliffe Hall Ox 58. **d** 61 **p** 62. C Leyland St Andr *Blackb* 61–64; C Burnley St Pet 64–67; V Chorley St Jas 67–75; V Fulwood Ch Ch 75–03; RD Preston 79–86; Chapl Sharoe Green Hosp Preston 81–94; Hon Can Blackb Cathl 86–03; Bp's Adv on Hosp Chapls 89–94; rtd 03; PtO *Blackb* from 03. *2 Brook Croft, Ingol, Preston PR2 3TW* T: (01772) 725528 E: ejburns3tw@btinternet.com

BURNS, Canon James Denis. b 43. Lich Th Coll 69. **d** 72 **p** 73. C Gt Wyrley *Lich* 72–75; C Atherton *Man* 75–76; Asst Chapl Sheff Ind Miss 76–79; C-in-c Masborough St Paul w St Jo 76–78; C-in-c Northfield St Mich 76–78; V Rotherham St Paul, St Mich and St Jo Ferham Park 78–79; V Lancaster Ch Ch *Blackb* 79–81; V Lancaster Ch Ch w St Jo and St Anne 81–86; V Chorley St Pet 86–96; R Rufford 96–07; Warden Past Assts 96–06; C Croston and Bretherton 06–07; rtd 07; Hon C Hesketh w Becconsall *Blackb* 07–09; Hon Can Blackb Cathl 99–09; PtO from 09; *Man* from 09. *81 Church Road, Uppermill, Oldham OL3 6DY* M: 07940-850982 E: jimdburns@sky.com

BURNS, Mrs Jane Elizabeth. b 64. ERMC 15. **d** 18 **p** 19. NSM Finedon *Pet* from 18. *51 Broadway, Kettering NN15 6DE* T: (01536) 524936 E: janeburns2211@gmail.com

BURNS, Mark John. b 64. York St Jo Coll MA 00. Yorks Min Course 15. **d** 17 **p** 18. NSM Barnsley St Mary *Leeds* 17–18; NSM Cen Barnsley from 18. *30 Monument Drive, Brierley, Barnsley S72 9LU* T: (01226) 717608 E: mark-burns1@sky.com

BURNS, Matthew. b 79. Leeds Univ BA. Coll of Resurr Mirfield. **d** 05 **p** 06. C Wrexham *St As* 05–08; V Towyn 08–10; P-in-c 10–11; TV Wrexham 11–15; V Leominster *Heref* from 15. *118 Buckfield Road, Leominster HR6 8SQ* E: matthew@jmburns.co.uk

BURNS, Michael John. b 53. AKC 76. Chich Th Coll 76. **d** 77 **p** 78. C Broseley w Benthall *Heref* 77–81; C Stevenage All SS Pin Green *St Alb* 81–84; V Tattenham Corner and Burgh Heath *Guildf* 84–92; C and Chapl Younger People Milton Keynes *Ox* 92–00; P-in-c Potters Bar K Chas *St Alb* 00–12; V 12–17; AD Barnet 11–16; Hon Can St Alb 13–17; P-in-c W Wimbledon Ch Ch *S'wark* 17–18; V from 18.

46 Pepys Road, London SW20 8PF T: (020) 8946 5954 E: ccww.vicar@gmail.com

BURNS, Canon Stuart Keith. b 66. Bp Grosseteste Coll BEd 88 Lon Univ BD 94 Leeds Univ MA 95 PhD 99. St Jo Coll Nottm. **d** 03 **p** 04. C Gt Bowden w Welham, Glooston and Cranoe etc *Leic* 03–06; Hd Sch for Min 06–16; Dir Miss and Min Dept from 16; Hon Can Leic Cathl from 17. *The Rectory, 3 Stonton Road, Church Langton, Market Harborough LE16 7SZ* T: (01858) 540202 E: stuart.burns@leccofe.org

BURNS, The Rt Revd Stuart Maitland. b 46. Leeds Univ BA 67. Coll of Resurr Mirfield 67. **d** 69 **p** 70. C Wyther *Ripon* 69–73; Asst Chapl Leeds Univ and Leeds Poly 73–77; P-in-c Thornthwaite w Thruscross and Darley 77–84; V Leeds Gipton Epiphany 84–89; OSB from 89; Prior Burford Priory 96–01; Abbot 01–17; LtO *Ox* 89–08; PtO *Worc* from 10. *Mucknell Abbey, Mucknell Farm Lane, Stoulton, Worcester WR7 4RB* T: (01905) 345900 E: stuart@mucknellabbey.org.uk

BURNS, Stuart Sandeman. b 62. Natal Univ BA 85 Ball Coll Ox BA 89 MA 94. St Paul's Coll Grahamstown. **d** 89 **p** 90. C Stanger S Africa 90–91; Dir Scripture Union Ind Schs 92–94; R Drakensberg 95–97; Chapl W Prov Prep Sch 98–99; I Kinneigh Union *C, C & R* 99–02; TV Bourne Valley *Sarum* 02–08; I Down H Trin w Hollymount *D & D* 08–16; Min Can Down Cathl 10–16; R Cheddar, Draycott and Rodney Stoke *B & W* from 16. *The Vicarage, Station Road, Cheddar BS27 3AH* T: (01934) 743649 M: 07796-493174 E: stuart.burns01@gmail.com *or* cheddardraycottandrodneystoke@gmail.com

BURNS, William Arthur. b 51. CITC 08. **d** 11 **p** 12. NSM Glendermott *D & R* from 11. *33 Sevenoaks, Londonderry BT47 6AL* T: (028) 7134 4354 M: 07917-358317 E: arthurburns33@hotmail.co.uk

BURR, Mrs Ann Pamela. b 39. S Dios Minl Tr Scheme 83. **dss** 86 **d** 87 **p** 94. Fareham H Trin *Portsm* 86–06; Hon C 87–06; Hon Asst Chapl Knowle Hosp Fareham 86–90; Asst Chapl Qu Alexandra Hosp Portsm 90–92; Chapl Portsm Hosps NHS Trust 92–00; rtd 06; PtO *Portsm* from 06. *3 Bruce Close, Fareham PO16 7QJ* T: (01329) 281375 E: ann.burr@hotmail.co.uk

BURR, Mrs Anna Victoria. b 58. Southn Univ BA 80 Leeds Univ MA 07. NOC 04. **d** 07 **p** 08. NSM Fulford *York* 07–11; P-in-c Haddlesey w Hambleton and Birkin from 11; P-in-c Carlton and Drax from 18. *The Rectory, Millfield Road, Chapel Haddlesey, Selby YO8 8QF* T: (01757) 270325 E: burrannav@gmail.com

BURR, Christopher Edward. b 68. Univ of Wales (Cardiff) BTh 01. St Mich Coll Llan 98. **d** 01 **p** 02. C Llantrisant *Llan* 01–04; P-in-c Pwllgwaun and Llanddewi Rhondda 04–10; V Lisvane from 10. *The Vicarage, Green Gables, 2 Llwyn y Pia Road, Lisvane, Cardiff CF14 0SY* T: (029) 2075 3338 E: office@stdenyschurch.org.uk

BURR, Paul David. b 62. Birm Univ LLB 83. St Jo Coll Nottm MA 99. **d** 99 **p** 00. C Newark *S'well* 99–02; C Eaton *Nor* 02–05; P-in-c Swardeston w E Carleton, Intwood, Keswick etc 05–09; R from 09; RD Humbleyard 15–18. *The Vicarage, The Common, Swardeston, Norwich NR14 8EB* T: (01508) 570550 E: pburr100@gmail.com

BURR, Raymond Leslie. b 43. NEOC 82 Edin Th Coll 84. **d** 85 **p** 86. C Hartlepool St Paul *Dur* 85–87; C Sherburn w Pittington 87–89; R Lyons 89–95; RD Houghton 94–96; V S Shields St Hilda w St Thos 95–08; rtd 08. *57 Pierremont Road, Darlington DL3 6DN* T: (01325) 463666 E: ray@burr.org.uk

BURRELL, David Philip. b 56. Southn Univ BTh 90. Sarum & Wells Th Coll 85. **d** 88 **p** 89. C Ixworth and Bardwell *St E* 88–91; P-in-c Haughley w Wetherden 91–96; P-in-c Culford, W Stow and Wordwell w Flempton etc 96–98; R Lark Valley 98–14; R Four Rivers from 14. *The Vicarage, 15 Noyes Avenue, Laxfield, Woodbridge IP13 8EB* T: (01986) 798136 E: theparsnips@gmail.com

BURRELL, Martin John. b 51. Cant Ch Ch Univ Coll MA 00 ARCM 71. Trin Coll Bris BA 95. **d** 95 **p** 96. C Cant St Mary Bredin 95–99; V Cranbrook 99–09; Asst Dir of Ords 06–09; P-in-c Bushmead *St Alb* 09–14; V 14–15; Chapl to Gypsies, Travellers and Roma 15–18; rtd 18. *5 Woodbury Hill, Luton LU2 7JP* M: 07791-536713 E: mburrell51@googlemail.com

BURRELL, Timothy Graham. b 43. St Steph Ho Ox 69. **d** 72 **p** 07. C Haltwhistle *Newc* 72–73; NSM Harrogate St Wilfrid *Ripon* 06–13; rtd 13; PtO *Ripon* 13–14; *Leeds* from 14; Chapl to Suff Bp Beverley (PEV) *York* from 10. *8 St Hilda's Road, Harrogate HG2 8JY* T: (01423) 883832 M: 07885-681379 E: tim.burrell@virgin.net

BURRIDGE, Matthew Guy. b 73. Univ Coll Lon BSc 94 MB, BS 97. NTMTC BA 08. **d** 08 **p** 09. NSM Kentish Town St Silas and H Trin w St Barn *Lon* 08–14; NSM Tottenham St Benet Fink from 14; NSM Tottenham St Phil from 14. *Health E1 Homeless*

Medical Centre, 9-11 Brick Lane, London E1 6PU T: (020) 7247 0090 E: fr.matthewburridge@googlemail.com

BURRIDGE, Canon Richard Alan. b 55. Univ Coll Ox BA 77 MA 81 Nottm Univ CertEd 78 PhD 89. St Jo Coll Nottm 82. **d** 85 **p** 86. C Bromley SS Pet and Paul *Roch* 85–87; Chapl Ex Univ 87–94; Dean K Coll Lon from 94; Lic Preacher *Lon* from 94; PtO *S'wark* from 98; *Chelmsf* from 05; Can Th Sarum Cathl from 13; NSM St Mary le Strand w St Clem Danes *Lon* from 17. *King's College, Strand, London WC2R 2LS* T: (020) 7848 2333 F: 7848 2344 E: dean@kcl.ac.uk

BURRIDGE-BUTLER, Paul David. *See* BUTLER, Paul David

BURROW, Miss Alison Sarah. b 59. Homerton Coll Cam BEd 82. Westcott Ho Cam 84. **d** 87 **p** 03. Par Dn Hebden Bridge *Wakef* 87–88; Par Dn Prestwood and Gt Hampden *Ox* 88–90; Par Dn Olney w Emberton 90–92; rtd 92; Hon C Bedford St Pet w St Cuth *St Alb* 02–07; P-in-c Renhold 07–16; PtO from 16; *Ox* from 16. *Flat D, 7 Merton Road, Bedford MK40 3AF* E: sarahburrow1313@gmail.com

BURROW, Canon Margaret Anne. b 46. Open Univ BA 82 Leeds Univ MSc 85 Lon Univ TCert 68. Coll of Resurr Mirfield 06. **d** 07 **p** 08. NSM Douglas St Ninian *S & M* 07–08; NSM St German's Cathl 08–13; Bp's Chapl 14–17; Can St German's Cathl 14–16; rtd 17; PtO *S & M* from 18. *Balley Beg, 24A Derby Road, Peel, Isle of Man IM5 1HW* T: (01624) 662173 M: 07624-235711 E: burrow.margaret@gmail.com

BURROW, Ronald. b 31. Univ Coll Dur BA 55. St Steph Ho Ox 83. **d** 85 **p** 86. C Dawlish *Ex* 85–87; TV Ottery St Mary, Alfington, W Hill, Tipton etc 87–91; P-in-c Pyworthy, Pancrasweek and Bridgerule 91–95; rtd 95; PtO *Ex* from 95. *Abbeyfield Society, Apartment 1, Marjorie Baker House, Vicarage Street, Colyton EX24 6LJ* T/F: (01297) 553882

BURROW, Stephen Paul. b 62. Univ Coll Dur BA 84. Trin Coll Bris 09. **d** 11 **p** 12. C Chilcompton w Downside and Stratton on the Fosse *B & W* 11–15; R Heyford w Stowe Nine Churches and Flore etc *Pet* from 15. *The Rectory, Church Lane, Nether Heyford, Northampton NN7 3LQ* M: 07511-544375 E: s_p_burrow@yahoo.co.uk

BURROWS, Clive Robert. b 60. Bath Coll of HE BEd 82 Ches Coll of HE BA 04. NOC 01. **d** 04 **p** 05. C N Wingfield, Clay Cross and Pilsley *Derby* 04–09; P-in-c Hyson Green and Forest Fields *S'well* 09–11; V from 11. *St Stephen's Vicarage, 18 Russell Road, Nottingham NG7 6HB* T: 0115-978 4480 E: clive@revburrows.plus.com

BURROWS, Canon David. b 62. Leeds Univ BA 85 MA 03. Linc Th Coll 86. **d** 88 **p** 89. C Kippax w Allerton Bywater *Ripon* 88–91; C Manston 91–95; Chapl Killingbeck Hosp 94; V Halifax St Anne Southowram w Charlestown 95–00; P-in-c Charlestown 95–00; V Southowram and Claremount 00–02; Chapl Overgate Hospice from 02; TV Elland *Wakef* 02–05; TR 05–12; R 12–14; *Leeds* from 14; C Greetland and W Vale *Wakef* 08–14; *Leeds* from 14; C Stainland w Outlane *Wakef* 06–14; Stainland and Outlane *Leeds* from 14; RD Brighouse and Elland *Wakef* 08–14; AD *Leeds* 14–16; Hon Can Wakef Cathl from 10. *All Saints' Vicarage, Charles Street, Elland HX5 0JF* T: (01422) 373184 M: 07932-694555 E: rectorofelland@btinternet.com

BURROWS, David MacPherson. b 43. NOC. **d** 82 **p** 83. NSM Newburgh *Liv* 82–93; NSM Newburgh w Westhead 93–12; Dioc Adv NSM 03–11; rtd 12; PtO *Liv* from 12. *34 Woodrow Drive, Newburgh, Wigan WN8 7LB* T: (01257) 462948

BURROWS, Diane. b 48. **d** 05 **p** 06. NSM Saltash *Truro* 05–18. *20 Andrews Way, Hatt, Saltash PL12 6PE* T: (01752) 842540 E: revdburrows@gmail.com

BURROWS, Graham Charles. b 47. Leeds Univ CertEd 69 Open Univ BA 81. NOC 87. **d** 90 **p** 91. C Chorlton-cum-Hardy St Clem *Man* 90–93; TV Horwich 93; TV Horwich and Rivington 93–94. *20 Glazebury Drive, Westhoughton, Bolton BL5 3JZ* T: (01942) 550404

BURROWS, Graham John. b 63. Jes Coll Cam BA 84 MA 88 Goldsmiths' Coll Lon PGCE 94. Oak Hill Th Coll 07. **d** 09 **p** 10. C Polegate *Chich* 09–13; P-in-c Burton and Holme *Carl* 13–19; V from 19. *The Vicarage, Glebe Close, Burton, Carnforth LA6 1PL* T: (01524) 781210 M: 07740-622962 E: vicarburtonholme@btinternet.com

BURROWS, Jean. b 54. CertEd 75. Trin Coll Bris 89. **d** 91 **p** 94. C Allesley *Cov* 91–95; C Thorley *St Alb* 95–99; P-in-c Harrold and Carlton w Chellington 99–06; R 06–07; P-in-c Boughton under Blean w Dunkirk and Hernhill *Cant* 07–16; P-in-c Goodnestone w Graveney 15–16; V Boughton-under-Blean w Dunkirk etc from 16. *The Vicarage, 101 The Street, Boughton-under-Blean, Faversham ME13 9BG* T: (01227) 751410 E: jeanburrows@jeanius.me.uk

BURROWS, Canon John Edward. b 36. Leeds Univ BA 60 PGCE 63. Coll of Resurr Mirfield. **d** 63 **p** 65. C Much Hadham *St Alb* 63–65; Hon C Haggerston St Mary w St Chad

Lon 65–73; P-in-c Finsbury St Clem w St Barn and St Matt 73–76; Chapl Woodbridge Sch 76–83; V Ipswich St Bart *St E* 83–03; Hon Can St E Cathl 01–03; rtd 03; PtO *St E* from 03; *Chelmsf* 14–16. *Flat 518, 1 Coprolite Street, Ipswich IP3 0BN* T: (01473) 216629

✠**BURROWS, The Rt Revd Michael Andrew James.** b 61. TCD BA 82 MA 85 MLitt 86. **d** 87 **p** 88 **c** 06. C Douglas Union w Frankfield *C, C & R* 87–91; Dean of Res TCD 91–94; Min Can St Patr Cathl Dublin 91–94; I Bandon Union *C, C & R* 94–02; Can Cork and Cloyne Cathls 96–02; Dean Cork and I Cork St Fin Barre's Union 02–06; Bp C & R from 06. *Bishop's House, Troysgate, Kilkenny, Republic of Ireland* T: (00353) (56) 778 6633 E: cfobishop@gmail.com

BURROWS, Canon Paul Anthony. b 55. Nottm Univ BA 77 Gen Th Sem NY STM 88. St Steph Ho Ox 77. **d** 79 **p** 80. C Camberwell St Giles *S'wark* 79–81; C St Helier 81–83; C Fareham SS Pet and Paul *Portsm* 83–85; V Union St Luke and All SS New Jersey USA 85–90; R Temple Hills St Barn Maryland 90–95; P-in-c Des Moines St Mark Iowa 95–01; Can Des Moines Cathl 98–01; R San Francisco Advent of Ch the K 01–15; rtd 15. *51 Learmonth Grove, Edinburgh EH4 1BX* M: 07746-827791 E: paulburrows1@mac.com

BURROWS, Philip Geoffrey. b 59. Birm Univ BSc 80. Oak Hill Th Coll 90. **d** 92 **p** 93. C Poynton *Ches* 92–96; Min Cheadle Hulme Em CD 96–03; V Mottram in Longdendale 03–11; CF from 11. *c/o MOD Chaplains (Army)* T: (01264) 383430 M: 07817-314979 E: philipburrows@man4god.co.uk

BURROWS, Samuel Reginald. b 30. AKC 57. **d** 58 **p** 59. C Shildon *Dur* 58–62; C Heworth St Mary 62–67; C-in-c Leam Lane CD 67–72; C-in-c Bishopwearmouth St Mary V w St Pet CD 72–77; R Bewcastle and Stapleton *Carl* 77–82; R Harrington 82–90; P-in-c Millom 90; V 90–95; rtd 95. *40 Lindisfarne Road, Durham DH1 5YQ*

BURROWS, Victoria Elizabeth. b 61. STETS 01. **d** 04 **p** 05. C The Bourne and Tilford *Guildf* 04–07; R Long Ditton 07–14; P-in-c R Wootton Bassett *Sarum* 14–15; V 15–16; RD Calne 14–16; V Bramley and Grafham *Guildf* 16–18; C Pendoylan w Welsh St Donats *Llan* 18–19; C Peterston-super-Ely w St Brides-super-Ely 18–19; P-in-c Radyr from 19. *The Rectory, Rectory Close, Radyr, Cardiff CF15 8EW* M: 07515-965781 E: vicki.burrows@me.com

BURSELL, Michael Hingston McLaughlin. b 70. K Coll Cam MA 96 Open Univ MBA 02. ERMC 05. **d** 08 **p** 09. NSM Halstead Area *Chelmsf* 08–16; NSM Upper Colne 16–17; NSM Sible Hedingham w Castle Hedingham 16–17; NSM The Hedinghams and Upper Colne from 17. *Bowyer's, North Road, Great Yeldham, Halstead CO9 4QD* T: (01787) 237486 F: 08700-517360 M: 07971-926937 E: mike.bursell@anglicanpriest.org

BURSELL, His Honour the Revd Canon Rupert David Hingston. b 42. Ex Univ LLB 63 St Edm Hall Ox BA 67 MA 72 DPhil 72. St Steph Ho Ox 67. **d** 68 **p** 69. NSM St Marylebone w H Trin *Lon* 68–69; NSM Almondsbury *Bris* 69–71; NSM Bedminster St Fran 71–75; NSM Bedminster 75–82; NSM Bris Ch Ch w St Ewen and All SS 83–88; NSM City of Bris 83–08; LtO 88–95; LtO *B & W* 72–92; Chan *Dur* 89–17; Chan *B & W* 92; Chan *St Alb* 92–02; Hon Can St Alb 96–02; NSM Cheddar *B & W* 93–11; Dep Chan *York* 94–02; Hon CF 96–01; Chan *Ox* 02–13; Hon Can Ch Ch from 11; LtO from 11; rtd 17. *Pear Tree Cottage, Hatchet Leys Lane, Thornborough, Buckingham MK18 2BU*

BURSON-THOMAS, Canon Michael Edwin. b 52. Sarum & Wells Th Coll 84. **d** 86 **p** 87. C Bitterne Park *Win* 86–89; V Lockerley and E Dean w E and W Tytherley 89–95; P-in-c Fotherby *Linc* 95–99; Asst Local Min Officer 95–99; V Horncastle w Low Toynton 99–06; R Greetham w Ashby Puerorum 99–06; V High Toynton 99–06; R Horncastle Gp 06–07; RD Horncastle 01–06; P-in-c Scotter w E Ferry 07–14; P-in-c Scotton w Northorpe 07–14; RD Manlake and Is of Axholme 11; rtd 14; Gen Preacher *Linc* from 14; Can and Preb Linc Cathl from 12. *The Rectory, Church Road, Waddingham, Gainsborough DN21 4ST* T: (01673) 818974 E: mbursonthomas@btinternet.com

BURSTON, Canon Robert Benjamin Stuart. b 45. St Chad's Coll Dur BA 68. **d** 70 **p** 71. C Whorlton *Newc* 70–77; V Alwinton w Holystone and Alnham 77–83; TR Glendale Gp 83–15; Hon Can Newc Cathl 95–15; rtd 15; PtO *Newc* from 16. *Woodbine Cottage, Holystone, Morpeth NE65 7AJ*

BURT, David Alan. b 44. Southn Univ BTh 98. STETS 95. **d** 98 **p** 99. C Goring-by-Sea *Chich* 98–06; P-in-c Lyminster 06–10; rtd 10; PtO *Chich* from 15. *15 Fernhurst Drive, Goring-by-Sea, Worthing BN12 5AH*

BURT, Canon Paul Andrew. b 52. Leeds Univ BA 74 K Coll Lon MA 02 Univ of Wales (Ban) PhD 09. Ridley Hall Cam 82. **d** 84 **p** 85. C Edin St Thos 84–88; CMS Bahrain 88–90; R

Melrose *Edin* 91–00; Chapl Borders Gen Hosp NHS Trust 93–98; Ho Master Win Coll 00–04; Hd RS Pilgrims' Sch 00–04; Chapl and Hd RE K Coll Sch Cam 04–06; Sen Chapl Win Coll 06–12; Sen Chapl Miss to Seafarers Dubai 12–18; Regional Dir Gulf and S Asia Miss to Seafarers 14–18; Hon Can St Paul's Cathl Nicosia from 18. *The Angel Appeal, The Mission to Seafarers, Dubai, United Arab Emirates* M: (00971) 50-552 6044 E: paul.burt.mts@gmail.com

BURT, Roger Malcolm. b 45. St Jo Coll Auckland. **d** 73 **p** 74. V Tinui New Zealand 73–80; P-in-c Colton *Nor* 80; P-in-c Easton 80; V Easton w Colton and Marlingford 80–88; CF 88–01; P-in-c E Coker w Sutton Bingham and Closworth *B & W* 01–10; rtd 10; PtO *B & W* 15–16; Chapl Yeovil Distr Hosp NHS Foundn Trust from 16; PtO *Sarum* 16–18. *Hugh Sexey's Hospital, Bruton BA10 0AS* E: rogermburt@gmail.com

BURTON, Andrew John. b 63. St Kath Coll Liv BA 84. Cranmer Hall Dur 86. **d** 88 **p** 89. C Harlescott *Lich* 88–91; C Ches H Trin 91–94; P-in-c Congleton St Jas 94–01; R Calton, Cauldon, Grindon, Waterfall etc *Lich* 01–08; RD Alstonfield 03–08; V Bushey Heath *St Alb* from 08. *St Peter's Vicarage, 19 High Road, Bushey Heath, Bushey WD23 1EA* T: (020) 8950 1424 E: fr.burton@btinternet.com

BURTON, Miss Barbara Louise. b 57. Leic Univ LLB 81 Solicitor 84. ERMC 03. **d** 06 **p** 07. NSM March St Jo *Ely* 06–10; P-in-c Barton Bendish w Beachamwell and Shingham 10–16; P-in-c Wereham 10–16; P-in-c Fincham 10–16; P-in-c Shouldham 10–16; P-in-c Shouldham Thorpe 10–16; P-in-c Boughton 10–16; P-in-c Marham 10–16; P-in-c Watlington 14–16; P-in-c Holme Runcton w S Runcton and Wallington 14–16; P-in-c Tottenhill w Wormegay 14–16; RD Fincham and Feltwell 12–16; P-in-c W Walton 16–18; R from 18; P-in-c Walpole St Peter w Walpole St Andrew 16–18; R from 18. *The Rectory, Church Road, Walpole St Peter, Wisbech PE14 7NS* E: barbaraburton@btinternet.com

BURTON, Charles Edmund. b 71. Newc Univ BSc 95. St Hild Coll 16. **d** 19. C Wath-upon-Dearne *Sheff* from 19. *The Vicarage, Church Drive, Wentworth, Rotherham S62 7TW* T: (01226) 102729 M: 07803-219746 E: charlesburton@uk2.net

BURTON, Christopher Paul. b 38. FCA 75 Bris Univ PhD 00. Clifton Th Coll 67. **d** 69 **p** 70. C Wandsworth All SS *S'wark* 69–72; C York St Paul 72–75; V Castle Vale *Birm* 75–82; R Gt Parndon *Chelmsf* 82–99; TR 99–03; rtd 03; PtO *St E* 04–07. *Damson Cottage, 69B London Road North, Poynton, Stockport SK12 1AG* T: (01625) 875266 E: damson.cottage@talktalk.net

BURTON, Canon Daniel John Ashworth. b 63. Regent's Park Coll Ox BA 88 MA 93 Heythrop Coll Lon MTh 93. St Mich Coll Llan 93. **d** 94 **p** 95. C Mountain Ash *Llan* 94–97; R St Brides Minor w Bettws 97–02; R St Brides Minor w Bettws w Aberkenfig 02–03; P-in-c Cheetham *Man* 03–12; AD N Man 10–12; TR Salford All SS from 12; AD Salford from 17; Hon Can Man Cathl from 13. *The Rectory, 92 Fitzwarren Street, Salford M6 5RS* T: 0161-745 7608 E: ashworthburton@hotmail.com

BURTON, David Alan. b 53. St Jo Coll Dur BA 75. Westcott Ho Cam 81. **d** 84 **p** 85. C Bedford St Andr *St Alb* 84–87; C Leighton Buzzard w Eggington, Hockliffe etc 87–91; V Kingsbury Episcopi w E Lambrook *B & W* 91–94; V Kingsbury Episcopi w E Lambrook, Hambridge etc 94–95; R Bishops Lydeard w Bagborough and Cothelstone 95–03; rtd 04; C Dawlish and Kenton, Mamhead, Powderham, Cofton and Starcross *Ex* 06–11; P-in-c Hemyock w Culm Davy, Clayhidon and Culmstock 11–18. *5 Clay Court, Uffculme, Cullompton EX15 3FE* E: david_burton@dsl.pipex.com *or* dave.burton@mac.com

BURTON, Desmond Jack. b 49. Sarum & Wells Th Coll 70. **d** 73 **p** 74. C Lakenham St Jo *Nor* 73–77; C Gt Yarmouth 77–80; R Tidworth *Sarum* 80–83; Chapl HM Pris Pentonville 83–84; Chapl HM Pris Standford Hill 84–88; Chapl HM Pris Swaleside 88–93; Chapl HM Pris Roch 93–99; Chapl HM Pris Whitemoor 99–05; Chapl HM Pris Whatton 05–09; P-in-c Balcombe *Chich* 09–17; rtd 17. *6 Goldring Avenue, Hellingly, Hailsham BN27 4BX*

BURTON, Graham John. b 45. Bris Univ BA 69. Tyndale Hall Bris 69. **d** 71 **p** 72. C Leic St Chris 71–75; C Southall Green St Jo *Lon* 75–79; CMS Pakistan 80–92; P-in-c Basford w Hyson Green *S'well* 92–98; P-in-c Hyson Green and Forest Fields 98–01; Assoc P 01–02; V Cheetham Project 01–07; rtd 07; PtO *S'well* from 07. *6 Meadow Brown Road, Nottingham NG7 5PH* E: burlongraham2@gmail.com

BURTON, Hugh Anthony. b 56. Edin Univ BD 79. Cranmer Hall Dur 81. **d** 83 **p** 84. C Coalville and Bardon Hill *Leic* 83–87; P-in-c Packington w Normanton-le-Heath 87–92; V 92–96; TV Kidderminster St Geo *Worc* 96–08; P-in-c 08–12;

TR Kidderminster E 12–19; RD Kidderminster 13–19; TR Dudley from 19. *50 Laurel Road, Dudley DY1 3ER*

BURTON, Karen. b 68. Graduate Soc Dur MA 92 PhD 98. ERMC 13. **d** 16 **p** 17. NSM Bury St Edmunds All SS w St Jo and St Geo *St E* 16–19; NSM Lark Valley 16–19; TR Blackbourne from 19. *The Vicarage, Commister Lane, Ixworth, Bury St Edmunds IP31 2HE* E: revkarenburton@outlook.com

BURTON, Michael John. b 55. Leeds Univ BSc 76 Leeds Poly BSc 80. St Jo Coll Nottm 86. **d** 88 **p** 89. C Charles w Plymouth St Matthias *Ex* 88–92; V Paignton St Paul Preston 92–99; TV Almondbury w Farnley Tyas *Wakef* 99–02; V Roade and Ashton w Hartwell *Pet* 02–11; C Collingtree w Courteenhall and Milton Malsor 09–11; V Salcey from 11; RD Towcester 03–09. *The Vicarage, 18 Hartwell Road, Roade, Northampton NN7 2NT* T: (01604) 862284 E: michaelburton5@aol.com

BURTON, Nicholas Guy. b 69. Bris Univ BSc 91 ACCA 00. Ridley Hall Cam 03. **d** 05 **p** 06. C Ore St Helen and St Barn *Chich* 05–09; C Bexhill St Steph 09–11. *6 Hilbert Close, Tunbridge Wells TN2 3SN* M: 07851-742049 E: ngb.cofe@tiscali.co.uk

BURTON, Nicholas John. b 52. St Steph Ho Ox 77. **d** 80 **p** 81. C Leic St Matt and St Geo 80–82; C Leic Resurr 82–83; TV 83–88; C Narborough and Huncote 88–90; R 90–10; rtd 10. *Address withheld by request* E: mrnjb@talktalk.net

BURTON, Richard Peter. b 56. Nottm Univ BA 80. Cranmer Hall Dur 80. **d** 82 **p** 83. C Linthorpe *York* 82–85; R Bishop Burton w Walkington 85–91; V Tadcaster w Newton Kyme 91–06; RD New Ainsty 01–06; Par Miss Development Officer *Ches* 06–11; C East Mary 06–11; PtO *Lich* 11–16; C Whittington and W Felton w Haughton 16–19. *8 Parc Bronhyddon, Llansantffraid SY22 6DZ* M: 07443-910608

BURTON, Mrs Sarah Elizabeth. b 59. Nottm Univ BMedSci 80 Dur Univ PGCE 82. NOC 05. **d** 08 **p** 09. C Eastham *Ches* 08–11; R Whittington and W Felton w Haughton *Lich* 11–19; P-in-c Vyrnwy Miss Area *St As* from 19. *8 Parc Bronhyddon, Llansantffraid SY22 6DZ*

BURTON, Mrs Virginia Ann. b 55. St As Minl Tr Course 00. **d** 03 **p** 04. C Llanrhos *St As* 03–08; C Colwyn Bay w Brynymaen 08–12; P-in-c Towyn 12–15; C Llanddulas and Llysfaen 12–15; C Abergele and St George 12–15; rtd 15; Hon C Llanrwst, Llanddoged w Capel Garmon etc *St As* 15–16; Hon C Aberconwy Miss Area 17; PtO from 17. *Siabod, Ffordd Trwyn Swch, Llanddoged, Llanrwst LL26 0DZ* T: (01492) 642778 E: ginnyburton@hotmail.co.uk

BURTON EVANS, David. *See* EVANS, David Burton

✠**BURTON-JONES, The Rt Revd Simon David.** b 62. Em Coll Cam BA 84 MA 88. St Jo Coll Nottm BTh 92 MA 93. **d** 93 **p** 94 **c** 18. C Darwen St Pet w Hoddlesden *Blackb* 93–96; C Biggin Hill Roch 96–98; P-in-c Plaistow St Mary 98–00; V 00–05; R Chislehurst St Nic 05–10; AD Bromley 01–06; Adn Roch 10–18; Can Res Roch Cathl 10–18; Suff Bp Tonbridge from 18. *Bishop's Lodge, 25 Shoesmith Lne, Kings Hill, West Malling ME19 4FF* E: bishop.tonbridge@rochester.anglican.org

BURTT, Andrew Keith. b 50. Massey Univ (NZ) BA 72 MA 74 DipEd 76. St Jo Coll (NZ) LTh 82. **d** 81 **p** 82. New Zealand 81–83; CF 84–92; Sen Chapl Brighton Coll 93–03; Chapl Portsm Gr Sch 03–16; Par P Paphos Cyprus and the Gulf from 16. *PO Box 61083, Kato Paphos, 8130 Paphos, Cyprus* T: (00357) (26) 953373 E: chaplain.acp@cytanet.com.cy

BURTWELL, Stanley Peter. b 32. Leeds Univ BA 55. Coll of Resurr Mirfield 55. **d** 57 **p** 58. C Leeds St Hilda *Ripon* 57–61; S Africa 61–72; P-in-c Gt Hanwood *Heref* 72–78; R 78–83; RD Pontesbury 80–83; V Upper Norwood St Jo *Cant* 83–84; V Upper Norwood St Jo *S'wark* 85–90; RD Croydon N 85–90; TR Bourne Valley *Sarum* 90–97; rtd 97; PtO *Sarum* from 97. *Splinters, 116 High Street, Swanage BN19 2NY* T: (01929) 421785 E: pburtwell@yahoo.co.uk

BURY, Dennis Richard. b 43. Man Univ BA 66. Andover Newton Th Coll MA 71 Sarum Th Coll 66. **d** 69 **p** 71. C Southport H Trin *Liv* 69–71; C Gt Crosby St Faith 71–72; PtO *Lon* 92–98 and from 03; Hon C Belsize Park 02–03; rtd 08. *47 Mayfield Road, London N8 9LL* T: (020) 8348 9181 E: d.bury@rhul.ac.uk *or* dennisscience@hotmail.com

BURY, Miss Dorothy Jane. b 53. Lanc Univ BA 96 MA 98 St Hild Coll Dur CertEd 75. Ripon Coll Cuddesdon 00. **d** 02 **p** 03. C Thornton-le-Fylde *Blackb* 02–06; P-in-c Wigan St Anne *Liv* 06–12; Chapl Deanery C of E High Sch Wigan 06–12; V Fence-in-Pendle and Higham *Blackb* 12–18; rtd 18; PtO *Blackb* from 18. *1 Feilden's Farm Lane, Mellor Brook, Blackburn BB2 7PD* T: (01254) 659526 M: 07715-560031 E: tillybury@btinternet.com

BURY, The Very Revd Nicholas Ayles Stillingfleet. b 43. Qu Coll Cam BA 65 MA 69 Ch Ch Ox MA 71. Cuddesdon Coll. **d** 68 **p** 69. C Liv Our Lady and St Nic 68–71; Chapl Ch Ch Ox 71–75; V Stevenage St Mary Shephall *St Alb* 75–84; V

St Peter-in-Thanet *Cant* 84–97; RD Thanet 93–97; Hon Can Cant Cathl 94–97; Dean Glouc 97–10; rtd 10; PtO *Heref* from 11. *122 The Homend, Ledbury HR8 1BZ* T: (01531) 636075 E: n.bury95@btinternet.com

BUSBY, John. b 38. St Cath Coll Cam MA 60 CEng. **d** 93 **p** 94. OLM Worplesdon *Guildf* 93–02; OLM Pirbright 02–04; PtO from 06. *Iona, Fox Corner, Worplesdon, Guildford GU3 3PP* T: (01483) 234562 E: john.busby@ionafoxcorner.plus.com

BUSBY, Nicola Jane. b 68. Qu Foundn (Course) 15. **d** 18 **p** 19. OLM Mease Valley *Lich* from 18. *Bramble Cottage, Church Lane, Chilcote, Swadlincote DE12 8DL* T: (01827) 373390 M: 07740-822095 E: busbynicola@gmail.com

BUSFIELD, Miss Lynn Maria. b 60. Trin Coll Bris BA 99. **d** 99 **p** 00. C Scartho *Linc* 99–03; TV Marlborough *Sarum* 03–05; Chapl Mt Edgcumbe Hospice 05–08; P-in-c Fladbury, Hill and Moor, Wyre Piddle etc *Worc* 09–11; P-in-c Peopleton and White Ladies Aston w Churchill etc 11–13; C Fladbury, Hill and Moor etc and Abberton, The Flyfords, Naunton Beauchamp etc 11–13; Chapl Heart of England NHS Foundn Trust from 13. *60 Horrell Road, Birmingham B26 2PD* T: 0121-742 2895 E: lynnbusfield@btinternet.com

BUSH, Caspar James Barnard. b 68. Newc Univ BSc 90. SWMTC 09. **d** 12 **p** 13. C Perranzabuloe and Crantock w Cubert *Truro* 12–15; TR Redruth w Lanner and Treleigh from 15; RD Carnmarth N from 17. *1 Wheal Uny, Trewirgie Road, Redruth TR15 2TD* T: (01209) 216958 E: casparbush@gmail.com

BUSH, George Raymond. b 57. St Jo Coll Cam BA 81 MA 84 Univ of Wales LLM 95. Ripon Coll Cuddesdon BA 84 MA 88. **d** 85 **p** 86. C Leeds St Aid *Ripon* 85–89; Chapl St Jo Coll Cam 89–94; V Hoxton St Anne w St Columba *Lon* 94–02; R St Mary le Bow w St Pancras Soper Lane etc from 02. *The Rector's Lodgings, Cheapside, London EC2V 6AU* T: (020) 7248 5139 F: 7248 0509 E: grbush@london.anglican.org

BUSH, Kieran John Christopher. b 80. Ch Coll Cam BA 01 MA 05. Oak Hill Th Coll MTh 11. **d** 11 **p** 12. C Dagenham *Chelmsf* 11–15; V Walthamstow St Jo from 15. *The Vicarage, 18 Brookscroft Road, London E17 4LH* M: 07709-119325 E: kieranbush@hotmail.com

BUSH, Rachma. *See* ABBOTT, Esther Rachma Hartley

BUSH, The Very Revd Roger Charles. b 56. K Coll Lon BA 78 Leeds Univ BA 85. Coll of Resurr Mirfield 83. **d** 86 **p** 87. C Newbold w Dunston *Derby* 86–90; TV Leic Resurr 90–94; TR Redruth w Lanner and Treleigh *Truro* 94–03; Hon Can Truro Cathl 03–04; Can Res Truro Cathl 04–12; Adn Cornwall 06–12; Dean Truro from 12. *Westwood House, Tremorvah Crescent, Truro TR1 1NL* T: (01872) 225630 E: dean@trurocathedral.org.uk

BUSH, Lt Col Walter Patrick Anthony. b 39. **d** 07 **p** 08. OLM Watercombe *Sarum* 07–11; NSM 11–17; PtO from 17. *Holworth Farmhouse, Holworth, Dorchester DT2 8NH* T: (01305) 852242 E: bushinarcadia@yahoo.co.uk

BUSHAU, Reginald Francis. b 49. Shimer Coll Illinois AB 71. St Steph Ho Ox BA 73 MA 98. **d** 74 **p** 75. C Deptford St Paul *S'wark* 74–77; C Willesden St Andr and Gladstone Park St Fran *Lon* 77–82; P-in-c Brondesbury St Anne w Kilburn H Trin 83–88; V Paddington St Mary Magd 88–97; AD Westmr Paddington 92–97; P-in-c S Kensington St Steph 96–98; V 98–16; rtd 16; PtO *Lon* from 16; *Chelmsf* from 17. *236 Prospect Road, Woodford Green IG8 7NQ* E: bushrf@aol.com

BUSHBY, Michael Reginald. b 42. LSE BSc 70 Leeds Univ MA 97. **d** 02 **p** 03. NSM S Cave and Ellerker w Broomfleet *York* 02–05; P-in-c Newbald from 05. *The Vicarage, 7 Dot Hill Close, North Newbald, York YO43 4TS* T: (01430) 801068 M: 07976-493359 E: michaelbushby@btinternet.com

BUSHELL, Anthony Colin. b 59. Pemb Coll Ox MA 82 Barrister 83. S'wark Ord Course 93. **d** 96 **p** 97. NSM Felsted and Lt Dunmow *Chelmsf* 96–98; NSM Stanway 98–06; NSM Greenstead w Colchester St Anne 06–14; P-in-c Stanway from 14. *Pump Hall, Middle Green, Wakes Colne, Colchester CO6 2BJ* T: (01787) 222361 M: 07484-265258 E: vicar@stalbrights.org

BUSHELL, Mrs Linda Mary. b 52. Bradf and Ilkley Coll BEd 91. STETS 06. **d** 09 **p** 10. NSM Bembridge *Portsm* 09–16; rtd 16; NSM Brighstone and Brooke w Mottistone *Portsm* 16–19; NSM Shorwell w Kingston 16–19; NSM Calbourne w Newtown 19; NSM Freshwater 19; NSM Shalfleet 19; NSM Thorley 19; NSM Totland Bay 19; NSM Yarmouth 19; NSM W Wight from 19. *5 Northcourt Close, Newport PO30 3LD* E: linda.bushell1@btinternet.com

BUSK, David Westly. b 60. Magd Coll Cam BA 83 St Jo Coll Dur BA 88. Cranmer Hall Dur 86. **d** 89 **p** 90. C Old Swinford Stourbridge *Worc* 89–93; USPG Japan 94–95; C Fukuoka Cathl 95–96; P-in-c Nagasaki H Trin 96–06; P-in-c Godmanchester *Ely* 06–13; P-in-c Hilton 11–13; V Godmanchester

and Hilton from 13. *The Vicarage, 59 Post Street, Godmanchester, Huntingdon PE29 2AQ* T: (01480) 436400 or T/F: 453354 M: 07765-851757 E: dwbusk@hotmail.com

BUSK, Horace. b 34. Clifton Th Coll 56. **d** 60 **p** 61. C Burton All SS *Lich* 60–63; Paraguay 63–66; C Silverhill St Matt *Chich* 66–67; LtO *Sarum* 67–69; C W Kilburn St Luke w St Simon and St Jude *Lon* 69–74; TV Ashwellthorpe w Wreningham *Nor* 74–81; P-in-c Meysey Hampton w Marston Meysey and Castle Eaton *Glouc* 81–82; R 82–04; rtd 04; PtO *Glouc* from 04. *23 Eastcote Road, Cirencester GL7 2DB* T: (01285) 650884

BUSSELL, Canon Ian Paul. b 62. Reading Univ BA 84 Kingston Poly PGCE 85. Qu Coll Birm MA 98. **d** 98 **p** 99. C Twickenham St Mary *Lon* 98–01; TV Godalming *Guildf* 01–07; P-in-c Leckhampton SS Phil and Jas w Cheltenham St Jas *Glouc* 07–09; TV S Cheltenham 10–11; Dioc Dir of Ords 11–19; Hd Minl Development from 19; Hon Can Glouc Cathl from 18. *4 College Green, Gloucester GL1 2LR* T: (01452) 835545 E: ianbussell@gmail.com *or* ibussell@glosdioc.org.uk

BUSSELL, Ronald William. b 34. CA Tr Coll 57 St Deiniol's Hawarden 81. **d** 83 **p** 84. C Claughton cum Grange *Ches* 83–85; P-in-c Preston St Oswald *Blackb* 85–87; V Fleetwood St Nic 87–93; Dioc Chapl MU 91–95; R Tarleton 93–95; rtd 95; PtO *Blackb* from 95. *4 Willoughby Avenue, Thornton-Cleveleys FY5 2BW* T: (01253) 820067 E: ron.bussell@talk21.com

BUSSEY, Diane Jean. b 57. **d** 07 **p** 08. OLM Clifton w Newton and Brownsover *Cov* 07–16; NSM Newbold on Avon from 16; Chapl Rainsbrook Secure Tr Cen from 09. *2 Teasel Close, Rugby CV23 0TJ* T: (01788) 339278 E: diane.bussey1@ntlworld.com

BUSTIN, Canon Peter Ernest. b 32. Qu Coll Cam BA 56 MA 60. Tyndale Hall Bris 56. **d** 57 **p** 58. C Welling *Roch* 57–60; C Farnborough *Guildf* 60–62; V Hornsey Rise St Mary *Lon* 62–70; R Barnwell *Pet* 70–78; RD Oundle 76–84; P-in-c Luddington w Hemington and Thurning 77–78; R Barnwell w Thurning and Luddington 78–84; V Southwold *St E* 84–97; RD Halesworth 90–95; Hon Can St E Cathl 91–97; rtd 97; PtO *St E* from 97. *55 College Street, Bury St Edmunds IP33 1NH* T: (01284) 767708 E: bush@saintedmunds.vispa.com

BUTCHER, Andrew John. b 43. Trin Coll Cam BA 66 MA 69. Cuddesdon Coll 66. **d** 68 **p** 69. C Sheff St Mark Broomhall 68–70; P-in-c Louth H Trin *Linc* 70–72; Chapl RAF 72–87; LtO *Ox* 85–87; TR Cove St Jo *Guildf* 87–91; V Egham Hythe 91–98; V Docking, the Birchams, Stanhoe and Sedgeford *Nor* 98–08; rtd 08; PtO *Nor* from 08. *67 The Street, Hindringham, Fakenham NR21 0PR* T: (01328) 878526 M: 07887-506876 E: andrewj.butcher2@btinternet.com

BUTCHER, Mrs Caroline. b 56. **d** 19. NSM Mildenhall *St E* from 19. *9 Courier Close, Mildenhall, Bury St Edmunds IP28 7SB* T: (01638) 515665 M: 07879-857015 E: caroline@butchermail.com

BUTCHER, David Alan. b 58. **d** 18 **p** 19. NSM Mildenhall *St E* from 18. *9 Courier Close, Mildenhall, Bury St Edmunds IP28 7SB* T: (01638) 718939 E: revdavidbutcher@gmail.com

BUTCHER (née POTTS), Canon Heather Dawn. b 52. **d** 98 **p** 99. C Attleborough w Besthorpe *Nor* 98–01; R Bunwell, Carleton Rode, Tibenham, Gt Moulton etc 01–09; RD Depwade 03–09; R Cringleford and Colney 09–16; P-in-c Litcham w Kempston, E and W Lexham, Mileham etc 16–18; P-in-c Gressenhall w Longham w Wendling etc 16–18; P-in-c Wellingham 17–18; TR Launditch and the Upper Nar *Nor* from 18; Bp's Adv for Women's Min from 11; Hon Can Nor Cathl from 13. *The Rectory, Pound Lane, Litcham, King's Lynn PE32 2QR* T: (01328) 700071 E: canonhdb@gmail.com

BUTCHER, Philip Ian Christopher. b 77. Seale-Hayne Agric Coll BSc 01. Ripon Coll Cuddesdon 11. **d** 13 **p** 14. C Honiton, Gittisham, Combe Raleigh, Monkton etc *Ex* 13–17; V Chaffcombe, Cricket Malherbie etc *B & W* from 17. *3 Home Farm, Tatworth, Chard TA20 2SH* M: 07775-762376 E: twoshiresrector@gmail.com

BUTCHER, Philip Warren. b 46. Trin Coll Cam BA 68 MA 70. Cuddesdon Coll 68. **d** 70 **p** 71. C Bris St Mary Redcliffe w Temple etc 70–73; Hon C W Wickham St Fran *Cant* 73–78; Chapl Abingdon Sch 78–85; Chapl Nor Sch 85–98; V Horsford and Horsham w Newton St Faith *Nor* 98–04; rtd 04; P-in-c Barningham w Matlaske w Baconsthorpe etc *Nor* 05–09; PtO from 09. *The Rectory, Pound Lane, Litcham, King's Lynn PE32 2QR* T: (01328) 700071 E: pw.butcher@btinternet.com

BUTCHER, Roger John. b 71. St Steph Ho Ox 10. **d** 12 **p** 13. C Wyke Regis *Sarum* 12–16; V Piddle Valley, Hilton and Ansty, Cheselbourne etc from 16. *The Vicarage, Church Lane, Piddletrenthide, Dorchester DT2 7QY* T: (01300) 348211 M: 07502-118210 E: roger_butcher@hotmail.com

BUTCHER, Mrs Sallie Eleanor. b 58. Open Univ MBA 99. WEMTC 14. **d** 16 **p** 17. NSM Teme Valley N *Worc* 16–17;

NSM Shrawley, Witley, Astley and Abberley 16–17; NSM Mamble w Bayton, Rock w Heightington etc 17–18; C from 18. *Summerhill, The Village, Abberley, Worcester WR6 6BN* T: (01299) 896837 M: 07850-062911 E: revsallie@4rivers.church *or* vicar@wyreforestwest.org.uk

BUTCHERS, The Ven Mark Andrew. b 59. Trin Coll Cam BA 81 K Coll Lon MTh 90 PhD 06. Chich Th Coll BTh 87. **d** 87 **p** 88. C Chelsea St Luke and Ch Ch *Lon* 87–90; C Mitcham SS Pet and Paul *S'wark* 90–93; R N Tawton, Bondleigh, Sampford Courtenay etc *Ex* 93–99; Chapl and Fell Keble Coll Ox 99–05; C Wolvercote w Summertown *Ox* 05–07; P-in-c Wolvercote 07–10; V Wolvercote and Wytham 10–15; AD Ox 12–15; Adn Barnstaple *Ex* from 15. *Stage Cross, Sanders Lane, Bishops Tawton, Barnstaple EX32 0BE* T: (01271) 375475 E: archdeacon.of.barnstaple@exeter.anglican.org

BUTCHER-TUSET, Richard James. b 69. Westcott Ho Cam 15. **d** 17 **p** 18. C Sidley *Chich* 17–19; C Bexhill St Barn 17–19; C Brighton St Mich and St Paul from 19. *18 Titian Road, Hove BN3 5QS*

BUTLAND, Canon Cameron James. b 58. UEA BA 79 Open Univ MA 12. Ripon Coll Cuddesdon BA 84. **d** 84 **p** 85. C Tettenhall Regis *Lich* 84–88; V Bodicote *Ox* 88–95; TR Witney 95–04; RD 97–02; R Grasmere *Carl* 04–15; V Rydal 04–15; Chapl Rydal Hall 04–15; Dioc Ecum Officer 11–14; Bp's Dom Chapl from 15; Hon Can Carl Cathl from 14. *The Rectory, Clifton, Penrith CA10 2EA* T: (01768) 201027 E: cdsa03@gmail.com

BUTLAND, Canon Godfrey John. b 51. Grey Coll Dur BA 72. Wycliffe Hall Ox 73. **d** 75 **p** 76. C Much Woolton *Liv* 75–78; Bp's Dom Chapl 78–81; V Everton St Geo 81–94; AD Liv N 89–94; V Allerton 94–05; P-in-c Mossley Hill St Barn 04–05; TV Mossley Hill 05–06; TR 06–15; AD Liv S 00–06; Hon Can Liv Cathl 03–06; TR Cockermouth Area *Carl* from 15. *The Vicarage, Little Broughton, Cockermouth CA13 0YG* T: (01900) 825763 E: gof15@btinternet.com

BUTLER, Canon Alan. b 53. Carl Dioc Tr Inst 89. **d** 89 **p** 90. NSM Flookburgh *Carl* 89–93; C Maryport 93–96; C Flimby 93–96; P-in-c 96–98; TV Saltash *Truro* 98–09; TR 09–15; P-in-c Landrake w St Erney and Botus Fleming 12–15; C St Germans 12–15; Hon Can Truro Cathl 10–15; rtd 15; PtO *Sarum* from 16. *Ashways, 3 Ashurst Road, West Moors, Ferndown BH22 0LR* T: (01202) 874641 M: 07890-717136

BUTLER, Angela Marie. b 47. Oak Hill NSM Course 87. **d** 90 **p** 94. Hon Par Dn Chipperfield St Paul *St Alb* 90–93; Dn-in-c 93–94; P-in-c 94–01; Staff Oak Hill Th Coll 93–97; Springboard Missr 97–01; P-in-c Hempsted and Dioc Springboard Missr *Glouc* 01–07; rtd 07; PtO *Truro* from 14. *22 Esplanade Road, Newquay TR7 1QB* T: (01637) 859238 E: angelambutler@btinternet.com

BUTLER, Catherine Elizabeth. b 46. **d** 06 **p** 07. NSM Waltham Gp *Linc* 06–16; PtO from 16. *8 Danesfield Avenue, Waltham, Grimsby DN37 0QE* T: (01472) 587692 E: elsiebutlerdane@msn.com

BUTLER, Cecil Anthony. b 37. Sarum Th Coll 65. **d** 68 **p** 69. C Gillingham *Sarum* 68–70; CF 70–74; R Whittington St Jo *Lich* 74–83; rtd 02; PtO *S & M* from 10. *The Mines House, The Mines Yard, Laxey, Isle of Man IM4 7NJ* T: (01624) 860085 M: 07967-497721 E: dorsetoak@gmail.com

BUTLER, Charles Hugh. b 87. Fitzw Coll Cam BA 08 MA 13. Oak Hill Th Coll BA 18 MA 19. **d** 19. C Edgbaston St Bart *Birm* from 19. *31 Vicarage Road, Harborne, Birmingham B17 0SN* M: 07388-685561 E: charlie.butler@edgbastonoldchurch.org.uk

BUTLER, Christine Jane. b 66. Cranmer Hall Dur. **d** 10 **p** 11. C Cheddar, Draycott and Rodney Stoke *B & W* 10–14; P-in-c Pilton w Croscombe, N Wootton and Dinder 14–18; R from 18. *The Rectory, Pilton, Shepton Mallet BA4 4DX* M: 07910-479145 E: butlerchristine19@gmail.com

BUTLER, Christopher. b 67. St Jo Coll Nottm 99. **d** 01 **p** 02. C Retford *S'well* 01–05; P-in-c Holbeck *Ripon* 05–12; C Beeston Hill and Hunslet Moor 11–12; V Ripon H Trin 12–14; *Leeds* from 14. *Holy Trinity Vicarage, 3 College Road, Ripon HG4 2AE* T: (01765) 605865 E: crbutler@bigfoot.com

BUTLER, Christopher John. b 25. Leeds Univ BA 50. Chich Th Coll 50. **d** 52 **p** 53. C Kensington St Mary Abbots w St Geo *Lon* 52–57; Australia 57–59; V Blackmoor *Portsm* 60–70; V Wellingborough St Andr *Pet* 70–79; P-in-c Garsington *Ox* 79–83; R Garsington and Horspath 83–95; rtd 95; PtO *Portsm* from 95; *Chich* from 95; *Guildf* from 95; *Win* from 95. *33 Oak Tree Road, Whitehill, Bordon GU35 9DF* T: (01420) 475311

BUTLER, Colin Sydney. b 59. Bradf Univ BSc 81 Cardiff Univ MTh 09 PhD 17. Wycliffe Hall Ox 81. **d** 84 **p** 85. C Farsley *Bradf* 84–87; C Bradf St Aug Undercliffe 87–89; P-in-c Darlaston All SS *Lich* 89–95; Ind Missr 89–95; TR Chell 95–99; CF 99–15; PtO *Birm* from 14; P-in-c Ankara

Eur 16–17; V Worc St Martin w St Swithun and St Paul from 18. *33 Cotton Lane, Birmingham B13 9SB* M: 07808-476982 E: revcsb@btopenworld.com

BUTLER, Derek John. b 53. Aston Univ BSc 74 St Jo Coll York PGCE 75. Cranmer Hall Dur 79. **d** 82 **p** 83. C Bramcote *S'well* 82–86; Lon and SE Co-ord CPAS 86–88; NSM Bromley Ch Ch *Roch* 88–91; NSM Chesham Bois *Ox* 92–10; PtO from 10. *121 Woodside Road, Amersham HP6 6AL* T: (01494) 724577 M: 07801-662110 E: derek@derekbutler.tv

BUTLER, Edward Daniel. b 42. Rhodes Univ BA 65 MA 70. Qu Coll Birm. **d** 68 **p** 69. C Edgbaston St Bart *Birm* 68–72; PtO 72–73; *Chich* 74–99. *Address temp unknown*

BUTLER, George James. b 53. AKC 74 Kent Univ MA 95. St Aug Coll Cant 75. **d** 76 **p** 77. C Ellesmere Port *Ches* 76–79; C Eastham 79–81; Chapl RAF 81–83; C W Kirby St Bridget *Ches* 83–84; V Newton 84–86; CF 86–91; V Folkestone St Sav *Cant* 91–99; P-in-c Wool and E Stoke *Sarum* 99–04; P-in-c Mansfield St Mark *S'well* 04–10; AD Mansfield 06–10; V Goring-by-Sea *Chich* 10–18; rtd 18. *1 Redcotts, St Botolphs Road, Worthing BN11 4JW* E: revgjb@btinternet.com

BUTLER, George William. b 52. CITC. **d** 90 **p** 91. C Drung w Castleterra, Larah and Lavey etc *K, E & A* 90–93; I 93–95; I Castlemacadam w Ballinaclash, Aughrim etc *D & G* 95–18; Can Ch Ch Cathl Dublin 03–18; rtd 18. *Dunamon, Fiddler's Lane, Ballinabarney, Redcross, Co Wicklow, A67 YC99, Republic of Ireland* M: (00353) 87-679 5625 E: gwb2@hotmail.com

BUTLER, Mrs Helen Carole. b 66. Bath Coll of HE BEd 87. Dioc OLM tr scheme 02. **d** 04 **p** 05. NSM Mirfield *Wakef* 04–14; *Leeds* from 14. *19 Woodbottom, Mirfield WF14 8HG* M: 07495-181509 E: revhelenb@gmail.com

BUTLER, Huw. b 63. Univ of Wales (Ban) BSc 84. St Mich Coll Llan BTh 95. **d** 95 **p** 96. C Llantwit Fardre *Llan* 95–00; R Llangynhafal w Llanbedr DC and Llanychan *St As* 00–02; R Llanbedr DC w Llangynhafal, Llanychan etc 02–10; P-in-c Llanynys 10; AD Dyffryn Clwyd 10; TR Llantwit Major *Llan* 10–16; V Llay, Rossett and Isycoed *St As* 16; TV Alyn Miss Area from 17. *The New Vicarage, First Avenue, Llay, Wrexham LL12 0TN* T: (01446) 794670 E: huwbutler63@gmail.com

BUTLER, Jane. *See* BUTLER, Linda Jane

BUTLER, John Frederick. b 53. Yorks Min Course. **d** 14 **p** 15. NSM Heaton St Barn *Leeds* 14–17; NSM Heaton St Martin 14–17; NSM Manningham 16–18; NSM Shipley St Paul from 18. *48 Toller Grove, Bradford BD9 5NP* T: (01274) 887498 M: 07785-624117 E: revdjohnbutler@icloud.com

BUTLER, John Philip. b 47. Leeds Univ BA 70. Coll of Resurr Mirfield 70. **d** 72 **p** 73. C Elton All SS *Man* 72–75; C Bolton St Pet 75–78; Chapl Bolton Colls of H&FE 75–78; Asst Chapl Bris Univ 78–81; Hon C Clifton St Paul 78–81; V Llansawel w Briton Ferry *Llan* 81–84; Warden Bp Mascall Cen *Heref* 84–88; Vice-Prin Glouc Sch for Min 85–88; Chapl Univ of Wales (Ban) 88–07; rtd 07; PtO *Ban* 11–17. *Cefn Engan, Llangybi, Pwllheli LL53 6LZ* T: (01766) 810046 E: johnbutler@phonecoop.coop

BUTLER, Mrs Lesley Ann. b 52. Cov Univ BSc 75 Nottm Univ MA 05. EMMTC 08. **d** 10 **p** 12. NSM Loughborough Em and St Mary in Charnwood *Leic* 10–11; NSM Kegworth, Hathern, Long Whatton, Diseworth etc 11–17; rtd 17; PtO *Man* from 18; *Leic* from 18. *1 Cheriborough Road, Castle Donington, Derby DE74 2RY* T: (01332) 391780 M: 07505-384527

BUTLER, Mrs Linda. b 51. Liv Univ CertEd 72. Cranmer Hall Dur 01. **d** 03 **p** 04. C Middlewich w Byley *Ches* 03–06; R Ditchingham, Hedenham, Broome, Earsham etc *Nor* 06–12; P-in-c Hartlepool St Luke *Dur* 12–17; rtd 17; PtO *Newc* from 18. *6 Gresham Close, Cramlington NE23 6EJ* T: (01670) 735371 E: revlbutler@gmail.com

BUTLER, Canon Linda Jane. b 56. SRN 77. St Jo Coll Nottm 85. **d** 88 **p** 94. C Burbage w Aston Flamville *Leic* 88–91; Asst Chapl Leic R Infirmary 91–93; Asst Chapl Towers Hosp Humberstone 93–95; Chapl 95–97; Chapl Leics and Rutland Healthcare NHS Trust 97–03; Chapl amongst Deaf People *Pet* 03–10; P-in-c Kingsthorpe 10–14; TR from 14; Can Pet Cathl from 14. *The Rectory, 16 Green End, Kingsthorpe, Northampton NN2 6RD* T: (01604) 717133 M: 07773-018260 E: revjane94@me.com

BUTLER, Mrs Louise Gail Nesta. b 53. **d** 04 **p** 05. OLM Blewbury, Hagbourne and Upton *Ox* 04–06; OLM S w N Moreton, Aston Tirrold and Aston Upthorpe 05–06; OLM The Churn from 06. *Penridge, Church Road, Blewbury, Didcot OX11 9PY* T: (01235) 851011 E: revlouiseb@aol.com

BUTLER, Malcolm. b 40. Linc Th Coll 76. **d** 78 **p** 79. C Whickham *Dur* 78–82; V Leam Lane 82–87; R Penshaw 87–90; rtd 90; PtO *Dur* from 90. *Lincoln Lodge, Front Street, Castleside, Consett DH8 9AR* T: (01207) 507672

BUTLER, Canon Michael. b 41. St Mich Coll Llan 62 St Deiniol's Hawarden 63. **d** 64 **p** 65. C Welshpool *St As* 64; C Welshpool w Castle Caereinion 65–73; TV Aberystwyth

St D 73–80; Chapl Univ of Wales (Abth) 73–80; V St Issell's and Amroth 80–09; V St Issell's and Amroth w Crunwere 09–12; V St Issell's and Amroth w Crunwere and Marros 12–13; AD Narberth 94–09; AD Pembroke 10–13; Can St D Cathl 01–13; rtd 13; PtO *St D* from 13. *Roxborough, 45 Whitlow, Saundersfoot SA69 9AE* T: (01834) 810475

BUTLER, Canon Michael Weeden. b 38. Clare Coll Cam BA 60 MA 65. Westcott Ho Cam 63. d 65 p 66. C Bermondsey St Mary w St Olave, St Jo etc *S'wark* 65–68; Ind Chapl 68–72; Sierra Leone 73–77; Ind Chapl and R Gt Chart *Cant* 77–86; RD E Charing 81–86; V Glouc St Jas and All SS 86–04; RD Glouc City 94–99; Hon Can Glouc Cathl 96–04; rtd 04; Dioc Clergy Retirement Officer *Glouc* 05–17. *121 London Road, Gloucester GL2 0RR* T: (01452) 421563 M: 07761-586588 E: butlermichael121@gmail.com

BUTLER, Ms Pamela. b 53. Nottm Univ BTh 86 CertEd 74. Linc Th Coll 83. dss 86 d 87 p 94. Rotherhithe H Trin *S'wark* 86–87; Par Dn 87–88; Par Dn Old Trafford St Jo *Man* 88–89; Par Dn Claremont H Angels 90–94; C 94–95; C Pendleton 95–97; Chapl Asst S Man Univ Hosps NHS Trust 96–00; rtd 00. *St Mary's Vicarage, 18 Rushcroft Road, Shaw, Oldham OL2 7PP* T: (01706) 847455

BUTLER, Patrick. b 61. All Nations Chr Coll 89. d 07 p 07. V Asunción St Andr Paraguay 07–09; C Stoughton *Guildf* 09–13; Min Elvetham Heath LEP from 13. *1 Dunley Drive, Fleet GU51 1BH* T: (01252) 695067 M: 07847-121092 E: patrickbutler61@hotmail.com

BUTLER, Paul David. b 67. Sheff Univ BA 88. Linc Th Coll 92. d 92 p 93. C Handsworth Woodhouse *Sheff* 92–96; V Bellingham St Dunstan *S'wark* 96–06; AD E Lewisham 99–06; R Deptford St Paul from 06; AD Deptford 13–16. *St Paul's Rectory, Mary Ann Gardens, London SE8 3DP* T: (020) 8692 7449 E: paulredbutler@btinternet.com

BUTLER, Paul Harnett. b 58. Perkins Sch of Th (USA) MTS 94 Girton Coll Cam MPhil 99. Ridley Hall Cam 05. d 07 p 08. C Histon and Impington *Ely* 07–11; C Landbeach from 12; C Waterbeach from 12. *The Vicarage, 8 Chapel Street, Waterbeach, Cambridge CB25 9HR* T: (01223) 860353 M: 07903-904599 E: revpbutler@gmail.com

✠**BUTLER, The Rt Revd Paul Roger.** b 55. Nottm Univ BA 77. Wycliffe Hall Ox BA 82. d 83 p 85 c 04. C Wandsworth All SS *S'wark* 83–87; Inner Lon Ev Scripture Union 87–92; Dep Hd of Miss 92–94; NSM E Ham St Paul *Chelmsf* 87–94; P-in-c Walthamstow St Mary w St Steph 94–97; P-in-c Walthamstow St Luke 94–97; TR Walthamstow 97–04; AD Waltham Forest 00–04; Suff Bp Southampton *Win* 04–09; Bp S'well and Nottm 09–14; Bp Dur from 14; Hon Can Byumba from 01. *Auckland Castle, Bishop Auckland DL14 7NR* T: (01388) 602576 F: 605264 E: bishop.of.durham@durham.anglican.org

BUTLER, Perry Andrew. b 49. York Univ BA 70 Lon Univ PGCE 75 Jes Coll Ox DPhil 78 FRHistS. Linc Th Coll 78 Ven English Coll & Pontifical Gregorian Univ Rome 79. d 80 p 81. C Chiswick St Nic w St Mary *Lon* 80–83; C S Kensington St Steph 83–87; V Bedford Park 87–95; Angl Adv Lon Weekend TV 87–99; P-in-c Bloomsbury St Geo w Woburn Square Ch Ch *Lon* 95–02; R 02–09; Dioc Dir of Ords 96–09; rtd 09; PtO *Cant* from 10; Hon Fell Kent Univ from 13. *6 Mikyle Court, 39 South Canterbury Road, Canterbury CT1 3LH* T: (01227) 767692 E: holmado@aol.com

BUTLER, Canon Robert Edwin. b 37. Ely Th Coll 60. d 62 p 63. C Lewisham St Jo Southend *S'wark* 62–65; C Eastbourne St Elisabeth *Chich* 65–69; V Langney 69–86; TR 86–96; Can and Preb Chich Cathl 94–97; rtd 96; PtO *Chich* from 97. *10 Langdale Close, Langney, Eastbourne BN23 8HS* T: (01323) 461135

BUTLER, Sandra. *See* BARTON, Sandra

BUTLER, Canon Simon. b 64. UEA BSc 86 RN Coll Dartmouth 86. St Jo Coll Nottm MA 92. d 92 p 93. C Chandler's Ford *Win* 92–94; C Northolt St Jos *Lon* 94–97; V Streatham Immanuel and St Andr *S'wark* 97–04; RD Streatham 01–04; Lambeth Adnry Ecum Officer 99–02; P-in-c Sanderstead All SS 04–05; TR Sanderstead 05–11; V Battersea St Mary from 11; Hon Can S'wark Cathl from 06. *St Mary's Vicarage, 32 Vicarage Crescent, London SW11 3LD* T: (020) 7228 8141 M: 07941-552407 E: simon.butler7@gmail.com

BUTLER, Simon Richard. b 80. Oak Hill Th Coll BA 03 Ripon Coll Cuddesdon MTh 06. d 06 p 07. C W Bridgford *S'well* 06–10; C Ashtead *Guildf* 10–16; R N Hants Downs *Win* from 16. *The Vicarage, Church Street, Upton Grey, Basingstoke RG25 2RB* M: 07803-909284 E: nhdbrector@gmail.com *or* simon@fairtradeclergyshirts.co.uk

BUTLER, Mrs Susan Jane. b 60. Anglia Ruskin Univ BA 99. Ridley Hall Cam 08. d 11 p 12. C Cambridge St Phil *Ely* 11–14; Pioneer Min from 11. *The Vicarage, 8 Chapel Street, Waterbeach, Cambridge CB25 9HR* T: (01223) 635316 M: 07985-406371 E: susybu@gmail.com

✠**BUTLER, The Rt Revd Thomas Frederick.** b 40. Leeds Univ BSc 61 MSc 62 PhD 72. Coll of Resurr Mirfield 62. d 64 p 65 c 85. C Wisbech St Aug *Ely* 64–66; C Folkestone St Sav *Cant* 66–67; Lect Univ of Zambia 68–73; Chapl Kent Univ *Cant* 73–80; Six Preacher Cant Cathl 79–84; Adn Northolt *Lon* 80–85; Area Bp Willesden 85–91; Bp Leic 91–98; Bp S'wark 98–10; rtd 10; Hon Asst Bp Wakef 10–14; Asst Bp Leeds from 14. *Overtown Grange Cottage, The Balk, Walton, Wakefield WF2 6JX* E: tom.butler5340@gmail.com

BUTLER, Valerie Joyce. *See* WHITE, Valerie Joyce

BUTLER GALLIE, Fergus Bruce. b 91. St Jo Coll Ox BA 14 MA 18 Em Coll Cam BA 17. Westcott Ho Cam 15. d 18 p 19. C Liv Our Lady and St Nic from 18. *Liverpool Parish Church, Old Churchyard, Liverpool L2 8TZ* M: 07557-683727 E: butlergalliefb@gmail.com

BUTLIN, David Francis Grenville. b 55. Bris Univ BA 77 Ox Univ CertEd 78. Sarum & Wells Th Coll 85. d 87 p 88. C Bedford St Andr *St Alb* 87–90; C Milton *Portsm* 90–92; V Hurst Green *S'wark* 92–12; RD Godstone 04–08; Chapl Heart of Kent Hospice 12–17; Chapl R Marsden NHS Foundn Trust 14–15; PtO *S'wark* from 13. *10 Florence Road, South Croydon CR2 0PP*

BUTLIN, Timothy Greer. b 53. St Jo Coll Dur BA 75 Ox Univ CertEd 76 Spurgeon's Coll MTh 05. Wycliffe Hall Ox 85. d 87 p 88. C Eynsham and Cassington *Ox* 87–91; V Loudwater 91–18; rtd 18. *149 South Road, Taunton TA1 3ED* T: (01823) 353874

BUTT, Adrian. b 37. d 71 p 72. C Umtata Cathl S Africa 71–76; C Ilkeston St Mary *Derby* 76–79; R N and S Wheatley w W Burton *S'well* 79–84; P-in-c Bole w Saundby 79–84; P-in-c Sturton w Littleborough 79–84; R N Wheatley, W Burton, Bole, Saundby, Sturton etc 84–85; R Kirkby in Ashfield 85–05; rtd 05; PtO *Derby* 14–18; *S'well* from 19. *25 Searby Road, Sutton-in-Ashfield NG17 5JQ* T: (01623) 555650

BUTT, Mrs Catherine. b 76. St Hilda's Coll Ox BA 99 MA 02 St Jo Coll Dur BA 02. Cranmer Hall Dur 00. d 03 p 04. C Bletchley *Ox* 03–17; P-in-c Water Eaton from 17. *38 Mill Road, Bletchley, Milton Keynes MK2 2LD* T: (01908) 630599 M: 07878-411584 E: revcatherinebutt@yahoo.co.uk *or* mkcatherinebutt@gmail.com

BUTT, The Very Revd Christopher Martin. b 52. St Pet Coll Ox BA 74 Fitzw Coll Cam BA 77. Ridley Hall Cam 75. d 79 p 80. C Cambridge St Barn *Ely* 79–82; Hong Kong 82–89; P-in-c Windermere *Carl* 89–98; TR S Gillingham *Roch* 98–09; Dean St Chris Cathl Bahrain from 09. *St Christopher's Cathedral, PO Box 36, Manama, Bahrain* T: (00973) 1725 3866 F: 1724 6436 E: revbutt@ymail.com

BUTT, Martin James. b 52. Sheff Univ LLB 75. Trin Coll Bris 75. d 78 p 79. C Aldridge *Lich* 78–84; C Walsall 84–87; TV 87–94; P-in-c Farewell *Lich* 92–12; P-in-c Gentleshaw 94–12; C Hammerwich 96–03; P-in-c 03–12; rtd 12; PtO *Cov* from 15. *36 Buttermere Avenue, Nuneaton CV11 6ET* T: (024) 7767 6068

BUTT, Nicola Mary. b 60. Sarum Coll 15. d 17 p 18. NSM Exmoor *B & W* from 17. *Little Hawkwell, Wheddon Cross, Minehead TA24 7EF* E: rev.nicola@icloud.com

BUTT, William Arthur. b 44. Kelham Th Coll 70 Linc Th Coll 71. d 71 p 72. C Mackworth St Fran *Derby* 71–75; C Aston cum Aughton *Sheff* 76–79; V Dalton 79–88; TR Staveley and Barrow Hill *Derby* 88–11; rtd 12. *17 Ramsey Avenue, Chesterfield S40 3EF* T: (01246) 239131

BUTTANSHAW, Graham Charles. b 59. TCD BA(Econ) 80 BA 85. St Jo Coll Nottm 88. d 91 p 92. C Toxteth St Cypr w Ch Ch *Liv* 91–94; CMS 94–99; Uganda 95–99; V Otley *Bradf* 99–14; Leeds from 14. *The Vicarage, Vicarage Gardens, Otley LS21 3PD* T: (01943) 462240 E: graham.buttanshaw@leeds.anglican.org

BUTTERFIELD, Amanda Helen. *See* DIGMAN, Amanda Helen

BUTTERFIELD, David John. b 52. Lon Univ BMus 73. St Jo Coll Nottm. d 77 p 78. C Southport Ch Ch *Liv* 77–81; Min Aldridge St Thos CD *Lich* 81–91; V Lilleshall, Muxton and Sheriffhales 91–07; RD Edgmond 97–00; RD Shifnal 99–00; RD Edgmond and Shifnal 01–06; Adn E Riding *York* 07–14; Can and Preb York Minster 07–14; Adn for Generous Giving and Can Res York Minster 14–17; rtd 17. *18 Kirkby Drive, Ripon HG4 2DP* T: (01765) 609394 E: david@justanote.co.uk

BUTTERFIELD, Mrs Katharine Mary. Aston Univ BSc 78 FCOptom 79. LCTP 13. d 15 p 16. NSM Morland, Thrimby, Gt Strickland and Cliburn *Carl* 15–17; NSM N Westmorland 17–18; R Kirkoswald, Renwick w Croglin, Gt Salkeld etc from 18; C Cross Fell Gp from 18. *The Vicarage, Kirkoswald, Penrith CA10 1DQ* M: 07867-533131 E: kmbutterfield@btinternet.com

BUTTERFIELD, Peter Graham. b 60. Lanc Univ BSc 82 Trent Poly PGCE 83 CPhys 90 MInstP 90. SWMTC 11. **d** 13 **p** 14. NSM Gulval and Madron *Truro* from 13. *Stable Cottage, St Buryan, Penzance TR19 6DJ* T: (01736) 810528 M: 07812-959460 E: peter.butterfield@physics.org

BUTTERWORTH, Canon Antony James. b 51. Hull Univ BSc 73. Trin Coll Bris 73. **d** 76 **p** 77. C Halliwell St Pet *Man* 76–81; V Werneth 81–90; V Tonge Fold 90–06; V Pennington 06–16; Hon Can Man Cathl 11–16; rtd 16; PtO *Man* from 16. *28 Marlborough Road, Atherton, Manchester M46 9LT* T: (01942) 790612 M: 07960-794291

BUTTERWORTH, David Frederick. b 48. Oak Hill Th Coll BA 88. **d** 88 **p** 89. R Telegraph Creek Canada 88–92; R Barrhead and Westlock 92–94; R Yellowknife 94–98; V Hanmer, Bronington, Bettisfield, Tallarn Green *St As* 98–04; PtO from 09. *Bettisfield Hall, Bettisfield, Whitchurch SY13 2LB* T: (01948) 710525 E: butterworthdavef@aol.com

BUTTERWORTH, George John. b 58. Liv Univ BA 85. Chich Th Coll 92. **d** 92 **p** 93. C Mayfield *Chich* 92–93; C Hastings St Clem and All SS 93–96; TV Brighton Resurr 96–02; P-in-c Saltdean 02–09; V 09–14; rtd 15; PtO *Chich* from 16. *2 Harlech Close, Worthing BN13 3QS* E: george.butterworth1@ntlworld.com

BUTTERWORTH, Canon George Michael. b 41. Man Univ BSc 63 Lon Univ BD 67 PhD 89 Nottm Univ MPhil 71. Tyndale Hall Bris. **d** 67 **p** 68. C S Normanton *Derby* 67–71; India 72–79; Lect United Th Coll Bangalore 72–77; Lect Oak Hill Th Coll 80–96; Prin SAOMC *Ox* 97–05; Prin Ox Min Course 05–06; Prin ERMC 05–06; Hon Can St Alb 02–06; PtO from 80; *Ox* from 11; Hon C Walton H Trin 06–09; Hon C Broughton 09–11. *3 Horseshoe Close, Cheddington, Leighton Buzzard LU7 0SB* T: (01296) 661903 M: 07870-242250 E: mikebutterworth@waitrose.com

BUTTERWORTH, Ian Eric. b 44. Aber Univ MA 67 MTh 79. Edin Th Coll 67. **d** 69 **p** 70. C Langley All SS and Martyrs *Man* 69–71; Prec St Andr Cathl *Ab* 71–75; V Bolton St Matt w St Barn *Man* 75–85; C-in-c Lostock CD 85–92; Laity Development Officer (Bolton Adnry) 85–92; Teacher Fairfield High Sch Droylsden 92–99; PtO *Man* 96–99; Hon C Sudden St Aidan 00–05; P-in-c Castleton Moor 00–05; V 05–10; AD Heywood and Middleton 07–10; rtd 10; PtO *Man* from 10. *7 Bruce Street, Rochdale OL11 3NH* T: (01706) 522264 E: ianbutterworth70@gmail.com

BUTTERWORTH, James Kent. b 49. Southn Univ BTh 79 PGCE 12. Chich Th Coll 75. **d** 79 **p** 80. C Heckmondwike *Wakef* 79–83; V Wrenthorpe 83–95; V Staincross 95–14; CF (TA) 82–86; rtd 14; PtO *Leeds* from 14. *Address withheld by request* E: jim@radiouk.com

BUTTERWORTH, Mrs Janet Mary. b 49. Bris Univ CertEd 70. SNWTP 09. **d** 12 **p** 13. OLM Heatons *Man* 12–19; rtd 19; PtO *Man* from 19. *71 Berwick Avenue, Stockport SK4 3AA* T: 0161-431 3851 E: janetmbutterworth@gmail.com

BUTTERWORTH, Canon Julia Kay. b 42. Edin Univ MA 64 Bris Univ CertEd 66. Linc Th Coll 73. **dss** 77 **d** 87 **p** 94. Cov E 77–79; Cant Cathl 79–84; Dioc Adv in Women's Min 82–92; Faversham 84–92; Par Dn 87–92; Team Dn Whitstable 92–94; TV 94–97; P-in-c Tenterden St Mich 97–07; Dioc Adv in Spirituality 97–07; Hon Can Cant Cathl 96–07; rtd 07; PtO *Cant* from 07. *14 Cobham Close, Canterbury CT1 1YL* T: (01227) 472806 E: jkbutterworth@btinternet.com

BUTTERWORTH, Michael. See BUTTERWORTH, George Michael

BUTTERWORTH, Mrs Nicola Jane. b 70. All SS Cen for Miss & Min 16. **d** 19. NSM Horwich and Rivington *Man* from 19. *57 Arlington Drive, Leigh WN7 3QP* T: (01942) 680032 M: 07706-979393 E: n.butterworth@outlook.com

BUTTERWORTH, Roderick. b 35. K Coll Lon 58. **d** 59 **p** 60. C Castleford All SS *Wakef* 59–63; V Sowerby St Geo 63–67; V Sowerby St Mary 67; V Mytholm Royd 67–75; rtd 97. *27 Fensway, Hutton, Preston PR4 5SX* T: (01772) 611703

BUTTERY, Bernard. b 36. Culham Coll *Ox* CertEd 58 LCP 75. OLM course 96. **d** 99 **p** 00. OLM Stafford *Lich* 99–11; PtO from 12. *7 Dearnsdale Close, Tillington, Stafford ST16 1SD* T: (01785) 244771 E: bb.ngb@talktalk.net

BUTTERY, Canon Graeme. b 62. York Univ BA 84. St Steph Ho Ox 85. **d** 88 **p** 89. C Peterlee *Dur* 88–91; C Sunderland 91–92; TV 92–94; V Horsley Hill St Lawr 94–05; AD Jarrow 01–05; V Hartlepool St Oswald from 05; Hon Can Dur Cathl from 10. *St Oswald's Clergy House, Brougham Terrace, Hartlepool TS24 8EY* T: (01429) 273201 E: g_buttery@sky.com

BUTTERY, Nathan James. b 72. Em Coll Cam BA 94 MA 97. Wycliffe Hall Ox BA 98. **d** 00 **p** 01. C Hull St Jo Newland *York* 00–08; C Cambridge H Sepulchre *Ely* 09–17; V Preston All SS *Blackb* from 17. *All Saints' Vicarage, 94 Watling Street Road, Fulwood, Preston PR2 8BP* E: nathan.buttery@gmail.com

BUTTIMER, Mrs Cynthia Margaret. b 45. STETS 07. **d** 08 **p** 09. OLM Clarendon *Sarum* 08–12; NSM 12–15; rtd 15; PtO *Sarum* from 15. *Willow Cottage, Gunville Road, Winterslow, Salisbury SP5 1PP* T: (01980) 862017 E: cynthiabuttimer@hotmail.com

BUTTLE, Leslie Albert. b 32. Open Univ BA 89. Edin Th Coll 61. **d** 64 **p** 65. C Sowerby Bridge w Norland *Wakef* 64–66; C Plymstock *Ex* 66–69; C Ilfracombe H Trin 69–71; V Woolfardisworthy and Buck Mills 71–76; C Sticklepath 76–77; Asst Chapl HM Pris Leeds 77–80; Lic to Offic *Ripon* 77–80; Chapl HM Youth Cust Cen Hindley 80–84; PtO *Ex* 86–93; Hon C Braunton from 93; rtd 97. *63 Caen View, Braunton EX33 1FE* T: (01271) 817022

BUTTON, Daniel Christopher. b 65. Bethel Univ BA 89 Univ of Minnesota BA 89 Columbia Internat Univ MDiv 98. **d** 04 **p** 06. Uganda 04–11; PtO *Glouc* 12–17 and from 18; NSM Churchdown St Jo and Innsworth 17–18. *113 Denmark Road, Gloucester GL1 3JW* T: (01452) 549271 M: 07580-571274 E: danielbutton2011@gmail.com

BUTTRESS, Andrew Kevin. b 63. Lon Sch of Th MA 16. Cranmer Hall Dur 17. **d** 18 **p** 19. C Triangle, St Matt and All SS *St E* from 18. *19 Dales View Road, Ipswich IP1 4HJ* E: curate@smast.org.uk

BUXTON, Francis Edmund. b 42. Trin Coll Cam MA 68 Sheff Univ MA 93. Linc Th Coll 65. **d** 67 **p** 68. C Wanstead St Mary *Chelmsf* 67–70; C Cambridge Gt St Mary w St Mich *Ely* 70–73; C Barking St Marg w St Patr *Chelmsf* 74–75; Chapl Vellore Hosp S India 75–79; Chapl Bath Univ *B & W* 79–89; TR Willenhall H Trin *Lich* 89–96; Chapl Team Leader Univ Hosp Birm NHS Foundn Trust 96–07; rtd 07; Hon C St Briavels w Hewelsfield *Glouc* 08–12. *Bridge Cottage, Mill Lane, Govilon, Abergavenny NP7 9SA* T: (01873) 831424 M: 07899-673096 E: fjbuxton@yahoo.co.uk

BUXTON, James Andrew Denis. b 64. Newc Univ BA 86 CCC Cam MA 11. Westcott Ho Cam 95. **d** 97 **p** 98. C Portsea St Mary *Portsm* 97–01; Succ S'wark Cathl 01–07; Chapl Guy's Campus K Coll Lon 01–07; Fell CCC Cam 07–17; Chapl 07–11; Dean of Chpl 11–17; Tutor Westcott Ho Cam 08–15; Chapl Izmir (Smyrna) w Bornova *Eur* from 17. *1458 Sokak 32 Daire 6, Alsancak, 38210 Izmir, Turkey* M: (0090) 537-772 1964 E: james.buxton@mtsmail.org

BUXTON, Nicholas Alexander Vavasseur. b 66. Wolfs Coll Cam BA 02 Trin Hall Cam MPhil 03 PhD 07. St Steph Ho Ox MTh 08. **d** 08 **p** 09. C and Hon Min Can Ripon Cathl 08–12; P-in-c Newc St Jo 12–18; Dioc Ch and Soc Adv 12–18; Dir St Ant Priory Dur from 18; PtO *Newc* from 18. *St Antony's Priory, 74 Claypath, Durham DH1 1QT* T: 0191-384 3747 E: buxton.nicholas@gmail.com

BUXTON, Richard Fowler. b 40. Lon Univ BScEng 62 Linacre Coll Ox BA 67 MA 71 Ex Univ PhD 73 Surrey Univ Hon BUniv 11. St Steph Ho Ox 65. **d** 68 **p** 69. C Whitley Ch Ch *Ox* 68–70; C Pinhoe *Ex* 70–71; Asst Chapl Ex Univ 71–73; Tutor Sarum & Wells Th Coll 73–77; Vice-Prin 77; PtO *Ches* 77–97; Lect Liturgy Man Univ 80–94; PtO *Man* 81–94; Squamish St Deiniol's Lib Hawarden 94–97; PtO *Ban* from 96; *St As* 97–10; *Ely* 13–18. *Golygfa'r Orsaf, 6 Garth Terrace, Porthmadog LL49 9BE* T: (01766) 514782 E: cynhaearn@gmail.com

BUXTON, Canon Trevor George. b 57. Ex Univ BEd 78. Chich Th Coll 81. **d** 83 **p** 84. C Hove All SS *Chich* 83–87; C Burgess Hill St Jo 87–91; V Brighton St Aug and St Sav 91–03; P-in-c Sidley 02–04; V 04–11; V Brighton St Martin w St Wilfrid and St Alban from 11; Can and Preb Chich Cathl from 01. *St Martin's Vicarage, Upper Wellington Road, Brighton BN2 3AN* T: (01273) 604687 M: 07885-942901 E: hojoe@waitrose.com

BUYERS, Stanley. b 39. Leeds Univ CertEd 71 Sunderland Poly BEd 78 Newc Univ MEd 90. NEOC 97. **d** 00 **p** 01. NSM E Boldon *Dur* 00–03; P-in-c Boldon 03–09; rtd 09; PtO *Dur* from 09. *37 Tarragon Way, South Shields NE34 8TB* T: 0191-536 5452 M: 07979-693153 E: stanbuyers@btinternet.com

BYARD, Nigel Gordon. b 65. Leic Poly BEng 88 CEng MIMechE. Ox Min Course 06. **d** 09 **p** 10. NSM Sunningdale *Ox* 09–11; TV Penrith w Newton Reigny and Plumpton Wall *Carl* 11–14; P-in-c Droitwich Spa *Worc* from 14; P-in-c Salwarpe and Hindlip w Martin Hussingtree from 14. *The Rectory, Salwarpe, Droitwich WR9 0AH* T: (01905) 778265 E: nigelbyard@btinternet.com

BYATT, John William. b 55. St Jo Coll Nottm 99. **d** 01 **p** 02. C Heanor *Derby* 01–05; C Ilkeston St Jo 05–07; P-in-c Whipton *Ex* from 07. *The Vicarage, 9 Summer Lane, Exeter EX4 8BY* T: (01392) 462206 M: 07773-906919 E: john.byatt1@btinternet.com

BYE, Paul Andrew. b 82. Nottm Univ BSc 04. Wycliffe Hall Ox BTh 12. **d** 12 **p** 13. C Blackb Ch Ch w St Matt 12–16;

V Fairhaven from 16. *The Vicarage, 83 Clifton Drive, Lytham St Annes FY8 1BZ* M: 07923-552339 E: p_bye@hotmail.com

BYE, Canon Peter John. b 39. Lon Univ BD 65. Clifton Th Coll 62. **d** 67 **p** 68. C Hyson Green *S'well* 67–70; C Dur St Nic 70–73; V Lowestoft Ch Ch *Nor* 73–80; V Carl St Jo 80–04; Hon Can Carl Cathl 98–04; RD Carl 00–04; Chapl Carl Hosps NHS Trust 80–94 and 94–98; rtd 04; PtO *Carl* 08–18. *21 McIlmoyle Way, Carlisle CA2 5GY* T: (01228) 596256 E: peterbye@mcilmoyleway.plus.com

BYFORD, The Ven Edwin Charles. b 47. Aus Nat Univ BSc 70 Melbourne Coll of Div BD 73 Univ of Chicago MA 76 Man Univ PhD 85. Trin Coll Melbourne 70. **d** 73 **p** 73. C Qeanbeyan Ch Ch Australia 73–75; Chapl Univ of Chicago USA 75–76; Hon C Chorlton-cum-Hardy St Werburgh *Man* 76–79; Australia from 79; Chapl Woden Valley Hosp 80–83; Asst P Wagga Wagga 83–84; Asst P Ainslie All SS 84–87; Chapl Aus Nat Univ 87–91; R Binda 91–95; R Broken Hill St Pet and Adn The Darling from 95. *PO Box 185, Broken Hill NSW 2880, Australia* T/F: (0061) (8) 8087 3221 M: 409-467981 E: e-byford-4@alumni.uchicago.edu

BYLLAM-BARNES, Preb Paul William Marshall. b 38. Birm Univ BCom Lon Univ MSc. Sarum & Wells Th Coll. **d** 84 **p** 85. C Gt Bookham *Guildf* 84–87; R Cusop w Blakemere, Bredwardine w Brobury etc *Heref* 87–03; RD Abbeydore 96–00; Preb Heref Cathl 99–03; rtd 03. *90 Granger Avenue, Maldon CM9 6AN* T: (01621) 858978

BYNON, William. b 43. St Aid Birkenhead 63. **d** 66 **p** 67. C Huyton St Mich *Liv* 66–69; C Maghull 69–72; TV 72–75; V Highfield 75–82; V Southport All SS 82–88; P-in-c Southport All So 86–88; V Newton in Makerfield St Pet 88–94; V Caerhun w Llangelynin w Llanbedr-y-Cennin *Ban* 94–06; rtd 06. *Swn-y-Don, Maes Hyfryd, Moelfre LL72 8LR* T: (01248) 410749 E: williambynon@btinternet.com

BYRNE, David Patrick. b 48. PGCE 96. St Jo Coll Nottm 74. **d** 77 **p** 78. C Bordesley Green *Birm* 77–79; C Weoley Castle 79–82; TV Kings Norton 82–92; TV Hodge Hill 92–94; PtO 94–97; Chapl Asst Birm Heartlands and Solihull NHS Trust 96–98; Chapl NW Lon Hosp NHS Trust 98–13; Chapl Harrow and Hillingdon Healthcare NHS Trust 98–13; rtd 13; Hon C Greenhill St Jo Lon from 11. *214 Currie Court, Harrow HA1 3GX* E: dave.byrne7@gmail.com

BYRNE, David Rodney. b 47. St Jo Coll Cam BA 70 MA 73. Cranmer Hall Dur 71. **d** 73 **p** 74. C Maidstone St Luke *Cant* 73–77; C Patcham *Chich* 77–83; TV Stantonbury *Ox* 83–87; TV Stantonbury and Willen 87–92; TV Woodley 92–02; V Patchway *Bris* 02–10; rtd 11; PtO *Ex* from 11. *4 Pound Lane, Topsham, Exeter EX3 0NA* T: (01392) 758557 E: dbyrne@talktalk.net

BYRNE, Canon Georgina Ann. b 72. Trin Coll Ox BA 92 MA 96 CCC Cam MPhil 98. Westcott Ho Cam. **d** 97 **p** 98. NSM W Bromwich All SS *Lich* 97–98; C 98–01; Hon Asst Chapl CCC Cam 97–98; Chapl to Bp Kensington *Lon* 01–04; Hon C Twickenham St Mary 01–04; TV Halas *Worc* 04–09; Can Res Worc Cathl from 09; Dir of Ords 09–15; Convenor for Women's Min 05–16; Chapl to The Queen from 17. *15B College Green, Worcester WR1 2LH* T: (01905) 732938 M: 07740-706448 E: georginabyrne@worcestercathedral.org.uk

BYRNE, Ian Barclay. b 53. Ripon Coll Cuddesdon 01. **d** 03 **p** 04. C Blyth Valley *St E* 03–06; P-in-c Bungay H Trin w St Mary 06–13; C Wainford 06–13; V Bungay from 13; C The Saints from 14. *The Vicarage, 3 Trinity Gardens, Bungay NR35 1HH* T: (01986) 892553 E: rev.ib@btinternet.com

BYRNE, Canon John Victor. b 47. FCA. St Jo Coll Nottm LTh 73. **d** 73 **p** 74. C Gillingham St Mark *Roch* 73–76; C Cranham Park *Chelmsf* 76–80; V Balderstone *Man* 80–87; V Southsea St Jude *Portsm* 87–95; P-in-c Southsea St Pet 95–03; Hon Can Portsm Cathl 97–06; RD Portsm 01–06; V Branksome Park All SS *Sarum* 06–12; rtd 12; Chapl to The Queen 03–17; PtO *Portsm* from 13. *4 St Georges Terrace, Southwick Road, Denmead, Waterlooville PO7 6FR* T: (023) 9225 3621 E: byrne.jv@gmail.com

BYROM, Alan. b 51. Magd Coll Ox BA 72 Bris Univ MA 85 Man Univ MPhil 99 Leeds Univ PGCE 73. NOC 97. **d** 99 **p** 00. C Leyland St Andr *Blackb* 99–03; TV Solway Plain *Carl* 03–10; P-in-c Blackpool Ch Ch w All SS *Blackb* 10–13; V 13–19; rtd 19; PtO *Blackb* from 19. *5 Beech Avenue, Warton, Preston PR4 1BY* T: (01772) 633559

BYROM, Catherine Mary. b 66. Nottm Univ BA 88 MA 04. St Jo Coll Nottm 11. **d** 13 **p** 14. C Skegby w Teversal *S'well* 13–18; V Ravenshead from 18. *St Peter's Vicarage, 55 Sheepwalk Lane, Ravenshead, Nottingham NG15 9FD* M: 07527-548644 E: katebyrom@hotmail.co.uk

BYRON, Terence Sherwood. b 26. Keble Coll Ox BA 50 MA 54. Linc Th Coll 50. **d** 52 **p** 53. C Melton Mowbray w Burton Lazars, Freeby etc *Leic* 52–55; C Whitwick St Jo the Bapt 55–60; India 60–76; C-in-c Beaumont Leys (Extra-paroch Distr) *Leic* 76–85; V Beaumont Leys 85–86; RD Christianity N 86–92; P-in-c Leic St Phil 86–88; V 88–92; rtd 93; PtO *Leic* 93–15. *84 Flax Road, Leicester LE4 6QD* T: 0116-266 1922

BYSOUTH, Paul Graham. b 55. Oak Hill Th Coll. **d** 84 **p** 85. C Gorleston St Andr *Nor* 84–87; C Ripley *Derby* 87–91; TV N Wingfield, Clay Cross and Pilsley 91–00; V Blagreaves 00–17; TV Newton Tracey, Horwood, Alverdiscott etc *Ex* from 17. *The Rectory, Newton Tracey, Barnstaple EX31 3PL* T: (01271) 858888 E: paemlu@gmail.com

BYWORTH, Mrs Ruth Angela. b 49. Cranmer Hall Dur BA 82. **dss** 83 **d** 92 **p** 94. Kirkby *Liv* 83–89; Aintree St Pet 89–97; Dn-in-c 92–94; P-in-c 94–97; P-in-c St Helens St Mark 97–98; C Sutton 98–03; TV 03–04; rtd 04; PtO *Liv* from 16. *11 Oakleigh, Skelmersdale WN8 9QU* T: (01744) 886481

C

CABLE, Kevin John. b 74. Ripon Coll Cuddesdon BA 08. **d** 08 **p** 09. C Bromley Common St Aug *Roch* 08–11; NSM Brenchley 12–14; C Perry Street 14–16; TV Northfleet and Rosherville 14–16; P-in-c Southbourne St Kath *Win* 16–19; V from 19. *St Katherine's Vicarage, 7 Wollaston Road, Bournemouth BH6 4AR* T: (01202) 460005 M: 07739-539448 E: fr.kevin@btopenworld.com

CABLE, Patrick John. b 50. AKC 72. **d** 74 **p** 75. C Herne *Cant* 74–78; CF 78–05; Rtd Officer Chapl RAChD from 05; PtO *St Alb* from 16. *c/o MOD Chaplains (Army)* T: (01799) 550466 E: paddycable@gmail.com

CACKETT, Janice Susan. b 39. Goldsmiths' Coll Lon BA 76 Surrey Univ MSc 83. SWMTC 99. **d** 99 **p** 00. NSM Clyst St Mary, Clyst St George etc *Ex* 99–03; P-in-c E Budleigh w Bicton and Otterton 03–10; rtd 10. *27 Elm Grove Road, Topsham, Exeter EX3 0EJ* T: (01392) 877468

CACOURIS, Alexander Xenophon. b 71. St Mellitus Coll. **d** 13 **p** 14. C Twickenham St Steph *Lon* 13–16; Chapl Rio de Janeiro Ch Ch Brazil 16–19; C Dorking St Paul *Guildf* from 19. *Address temp unknown* E: acacouris@hotmail.co.uk

CADDELL, Richard Allen. b 54. Auburn Univ Alabama BIE 77. Trin Coll Bris BA 88. **d** 88 **p** 89. C Uphill *B & W* 88–94; PtO 94–96; TV Beaconsfield *Ox* 96–07; P-in-c Lamp 07–09; R from 09; AD Newport 13–15. *The Rectory, High Street, Haversham, Milton Keynes MK19 7DT* T: (01908) 312136 E: caddells@holtspur.plus.com

CADDEN, Brian Stuart. b 58. BSc BTh TCD. **d** 89 **p** 90. C Lecale Gp *D & D* 89–92; C Killowen *D & R* 92–95; I Muckamore *Conn* 95–06; I Castlewellan w Kilcoo *D & D* from 06. *5 Cedar Heights, Bryansford, Newcastle BT33 0PJ* T: (028) 4372 3198 E: castlewellan@dromore.anglican.org

CADDEN, Canon Terence John. b 60. TCD BTh 89. CITC 86. **d** 89 **p** 90. C Coleraine *Conn* 89–92; C Lurgan Ch the Redeemer *D & D* 92–93; Past Dir 93–01; I Gilford 01–06; I Seagoe from 06; Bp's C Ardmore w Craigavon from 16; Can Dromore Cathl from 10. *Seagoe Rectory, 8 Upper Church Lane, Portadown, Craigavon BT63 5JE* T: (028) 3833 2538 *or* 3835 0583 F: 3833 0773 M: 07894-987702 E: cadden@talktalk.net *or* seagoechurch@btinternet.com

CADDICK, Jeremy Lloyd. b 60. St Jo Coll Cam BA 82 MA 86 K Coll Lon MA 93. Ripon Coll Cuddesdon BA 86 MA 91. **d** 87 **p** 88. C Kennington St Jo w St Jas *S'wark* 87–90; Chapl Lon Univ 90–94; Chapl R Free Medical Sch 90–94; Chapl R Veterinary Coll Lon 90–94; PV Westmr Abbey 92–94; Dean Em Coll Cam from 94. *Emmanuel College, Cambridge CB2 3AP* T: (01223) 334264 *or* 330195 F: 334426 E: jlc24@cam.ac.uk

CADDOO (née **BLAKELY**), **Mrs Denise Irene**. b 69. QUB BD 91 PGCE 92. CITC 93. **d** 95 **p** 96. C Holywood *D & D* 95–99; C Portadown St Columba *Arm* 99–00; I Carrowdore w Millisle *D & D* 00–04; C Holywood 04–06; I Gilford from 06. *The Vicarage, 18 Scarva Road, Gilford, Craigavon BT63 6BG* T: (028) 3883 1130

CADDY, Canon Michael George Bruce Courtenay. b 45. K Coll Lon. **d** 71 **p** 72. C Walton St Mary *Liv* 71–76; C Solihull *Birm* 76–79; TV 79–81; V Shard End 81–87; TR Shirley 87–00; P-in-c Tanworth St Patr Salter Street 97–00; TR Salter Street and Shirley 00–13; AD Shirley 97–02; Hon Can Birm Cathl 99–13; Dioc Chapl MU 07–11; rtd 13; Bps' Dom Chapl *B & W* 13–15; PtO from 15. *12 Dial Hill Road, Clevedon BS21 7HJ* T: (01275) 219059 E: anncaddy60@gmail.com

CADDY, Ms Susan. b 50. Westcott Ho Cam 99. **d** 01 **p** 02. C Sutton in Ashfield St Mary *S'well* 01–05; P-in-c Shelton and Oxon *Lich* 05–10; TV Retford Area *S'well* from 10. *The Rectory, Hine Close, Retford DN22 7ZH* T: (01777) 703322 E: suecee123@btinternet.com

CADE, Simon Peter Vincent. b 69. Univ of Wales BA 90. Westcott Ho Cam 92. **d** 94 **p** 95. C Calne and Blackland *Sarum* 94–98; Chapl St Mary's Sch Calne 94–97; TV Basingstoke *Win* 98–05; TR Redruth w Lanner and Treleigh *Truro* 05–14; P-in-c 14; Dioc Dir of Educn and Discipleship from 14; Public Preacher from 14. *Church House, Woodlands Court, Truro Business Park, Threemilestone, Truro TR4 9NH* T: (01872) 247214 E: simon.cade@truro.anglican.org

CADMORE, Albert Thomas. b 47. Open Univ BA 81 UEA MA 94 Lon Inst of Educn CertEd 68. EAMTC 85. **d** 88 **p** 89. NSM Gorleston St Andr *Nor* 88–96; NSM Winterton w E and W Somerton and Horsey 94–96; NSM Flegg Coastal Benefice 96–12; rtd 12; PtO *Nor* from 12. *10 Upper Cliff Road, Gorleston, Great Yarmouth NR31 6AL* T: (01493) 668762 E: acadmore@ntlworld.com

CADOGAN, Paul Anthony Cleveland. b 47. AKC 74. **d** 75 **p** 76. C Fishponds St Jo *Bris* 75–79; C Swindon New Town 79–81; P-in-c Swindon All SS 81–82; V 82–90; R Lower Windrush *Ox* 90–94. *2 Malthouse Close, Ashbury, Swindon SN6 8PB* T: (01793) 710488 E: paul-anthony@hotmail.com

CADOGAN, Percil Lavine. b 41. WMMTC. **d** 01 **p** 02. NSM Bournville *Birm* 01–05; NSM Bordesley St Benedict 05–14; P-in-c 12–14; rtd 14; PtO *Birm* from 14. *76 Highbury Road, Birmingham B14 7QW* T: 0121-680 9595 E: percil.cadogan@gmail.com

CADWALLADER, Michael Godfrey. b 56. Bris Univ BEd 79 St Jo Coll Dur BA 06. Cranmer Hall Dur 05. **d** 07 **p** 08. C Kingston upon Hull St Aid Southcoates *York* 07–11; P-in-c Burton Dassett *Cov* 11–16; P-in-c Avon Dassett w Farnborough and Fenny Compton 11–16; P-in-c Gaydon w Chadshunt 11–16; TV Mid Trent *Lich* from 16. *2 Vicarage Way, Hixon, Stafford ST18 0FT* E: cadwalladermg@waitrose.com *or* cadwalladermg@gmail.com

CADY, Mrs Susan Janet. b 68. Wycliffe Hall Ox 15. **d** 17 **p** 18. C Reading St Agnes w St Paul and St Barn *Ox* from 17. *19 Gweal Avenue, Reading RG2 0PF* M: 07977-219305 E: sjcady@sky.com *or* rev.sue.cady@gmail.com

CAFFREY (formerly **McNEIL**), **Mrs Ann**. b 41. **d** 89 **p** 94. NSM Henfield w Shermanbury and Woodmancote *Chich* 89–99; PtO from 00. *6 Holbrook Close, Eastbourne BN20 7JT* T: (01323) 736018 E: ann@annmcneil.com

CAFFYN, Douglas John Morris. b 36. Peterho Cam MA 60 Nairobi Univ MSc 69 Westmr Coll *Ox* DipEd 61 ACIS 77. S Dios Minl Tr Scheme 87. **d** 90 **p** 91. NSM Hampden Park *Chich* 90–94; Chapl among Deaf People 94–97; Jt Sec Cttee for Min among Deaf People 95–97; PtO *Chich* from 97; rtd 01. *34 St Lawrence Forstal, Canterbury CT1 3PA*

CAGE, Doreen Anne. b 51. **d** 13 **p** 14. Asst Chapl Málaga *Eur* from 13. *Buzón 40, La Parrilla, 21930 Villanueva de Algaidas, (Málaga), Spain* T: (0034) 952 745 028 E: jmnct123@gmail.com

CAHILL, Canon Nigel. b 59. St Mich Coll Llan. **d** 82 **p** 83. C Whitchurch *Llan* 82–86; V Tonypandy w Clydach Vale 86–96; RD Rhondda 93–96; V Fairwater 96–03; V Caerau w Ely 03–08; AD Llan 06–08; TR Aberavon from 08; Can Llan Cathl from 09. *The Rectory, Forge Road, Port Talbot SA13 1US* T: (01639) 883630 E: rector@parishofaberavon.org

CAHUSAC, Henry William James. b 73. Wycliffe Hall Ox BTh 06. **d** 06 **p** 07. C Tollington *Lon* 06–10; C Onslow Square and S Kensington St Aug 10–15; PtO from 15; *Guildf* from 15. *12 Rowly Lane, Cranleigh GU6 8PU* T: (01483) 613068 E: bill.cahusac@emmausrd.com

CAIN, Andrew David. *See* FORESHEW-CAIN, Andrew David

CAIN, Andrew Paul. b 76. St Jo Coll Nottm. **d** 08 **p** 09. C Hinckley H Trin *Leic* 08–11; C Bosworth and Sheepy Gp 11–12; V Cuddington *Guildf* 12–16; PtO *Leic* from 17. *Address withheld by request*

CAIN, Frank Robert. b 56. Liv Univ MA 97. Oak Hill Th Coll BA 88. **d** 88 **p** 89. C Aughton Ch Ch *Liv* 88–91; P-in-c Toxteth Park St Clem 91–99; V Toxteth St Bede w St Clem 99–04; AD Toxteth and Wavertree 01–04; Hon Can Liv Cathl 03–04; Chapl N Mersey Community NHS Trust 96–04; V New Brighton St Jas w Em *Ches* 04–15; RD Wallasey 07–09; TR Halewood and Hunts Cross *Liv* 15–17; V Walton St Luke from 17. *65 Fazakerley Road, Liverpool L9 2AJ* E: vicarfrank@btinternet.com *or* frankcain100@btinternet.com

CAIN, Jonathan Michael Field. b 69. Nottm Univ BEng 90 Bradf Univ MBA 03. Yorks Min Course 13. **d** 15 **p** 16. C Bolton Abbey *Leeds* 15–18; V Woodside from 18. *55 Bridgland Avenue, Menston, Ilkley LS29 6PD* T: (01943) 871149 M: 07957-713387 E: jonathan.cain@leeds.anglican.org

CAIN, Michael Christopher. b 68. St Jo Coll Dur BA 90 K Coll Lon MA 92 Selw Coll Cam BA 94. Ridley Hall Cam 92. **d** 95 **p** 96. C Wimbledon Em Ridgway Prop Chpl *S'wark* 95–99; Asst Chapl Leipzig *Eur* 99–02; C Clifton Ch Ch w Em *Bris* 02–10; Pioneer Min Clifton Em from 11. *35 Walsingham Road, Bristol BS6 5BU* T: 0117-942 7385 E: mike@emmanuelbristol.org.uk

CAINE, Diane Audrey. b 56. Ex Univ BTh 12. SWMTC 09. **d** 12 **p** 13. NSM Dawlish *Ex* 12–15; NSM Dawlish, Cofton and Starcross 15–17; C Yelverton, Meavy, Sheepstor, Walkhampton, Sampford Spiney and Horrabridge from 17. *The Vicarage, 1 Manor Farm, Dousland, Yelverton PL20 6NR* M: 07415-897502 E: rev.dicaine@outlook.com

CAINE, Mrs Helen. b 71. Open Univ BA 98. WEMTC 14. **d** 16 **p** 17. NSM S Cotswolds *Glouc* from 16. *17 Links View, Cirencester GL7 2NF* M: 07958-686621 E: hel.caine@btinternet.com

CAINES, Julia Clare. *See* CHARD, Julia Clare

CAIRNS, Dorothy Elizabeth. b 66. Wilson Carlile Coll 87 CITC 07. **d** 09 **p** 10. CA from 90; C Portadown St Columba *Arm* 09–11; I 11–13; I Mullavilly from 13. *The Rectory, 89 Mullavilly Road, Tandragee, Craigavon BT62 2LX* T: (028) 3884 0221 M: 07719-857187 E: revecairns@gmail.com

CAISSIE, Mrs Elizabeth Anne. b 40. CBDTI 07. **d** 08 **p** 09. NSM Keighley St Andr *Bradf* 08–13; PtO 13–14; *Leeds* 13–16; York from 14. *2A Turmer Avenue, Bridlington YO15 2HJ* T: (01262) 229763

CAITHNESS, Mrs Joyce Marigold. b 45. **d** 06 **p** 07. OLM Bris St Matt and St Nath 06–13; OLM Southmead 13–18; rtd 18. *383 Southmead Road, Westbury-on-Trym, Bristol BS10 5LT* T: 0117-983 3755 E: jm.caithness@blueyonder.co.uk

CAKE, Nichola Carla. *See* CHATER, Nichola Carla

CAKE, Simon Charles Eagle. b 61. Wilson Carlile Coll 91 Cranmer Hall Dur 08. **d** 10 **p** 11. C Hebburn St Jo *Dur* 10–14; TV Egremont and Haile *Carl* 14–19; Chapl N Cumbria Univ Hosps NHS Trust 14–19; C Galashiels *Edin* from 19; C Hawick from 19; C Selkirk from 19. *1 Parsonage Road, Galashiels TD1 3HS* M: 07710-523856 E: cakekands@btinternet.com

CALDER, Canon Ian Fraser. b 47. York Univ BA 68 CertEd 69. Glouc Sch of Min 84. **d** 87 **p** 88. NSM Lydney w Aylburton *Glouc* 87–91; C Cirencester 91–95; V Coney Hill 95–01; RD Glouc City 99–01; R Bishop's Cleeve 01–08; AD Tewkesbury and Winchcombe 02–07; Hon Can Glouc Cathl 03–08; rtd 08; PtO *Glouc* from 15. *11 Riversley Road, Elmbridge, Gloucester GL2 0QU* T: (01452) 537845 E: revian@blueyonder.co.uk

CALDERBANK, Martin Nicholas. St Aug Coll of Th 16. **d** 19. NSM Barnes *S'wark* from 19. *St Michael and All Angels Church, Elm Bank Gardens, London SW13 0NX* E: curate@stmichaelbarnes.org

CALDERWOOD, Emma Louise. *See* WILLIAMS, Emma Louise

CALDWELL, Jacob Wilson (Jim). b 84. St Andr Univ MA 07 AVCM 04. TCD Div Sch MTh 09. **d** 11 **p** 12. Intern Dn Magherafelt *Arm* 11–12; C Larne and Inver *Conn* 12–15; CF from 15. *c/o MOD Chaplains (Army)* T: (01264) 383430 F: 381824 M: 07564-418252 E: caldwelj@tcd.ie

CALDWELL, Miss Janet Elizabeth. b 56. Hull Univ BA 78 PGCE 79. **d** 19. NSM Ormesby *York* from 19. *11 Normanby Road, Ormesby, Middlesbrough TS7 9NU* T: (01642) 454790 M: 07809-041169 E: janet925@btinternet.com

CALDWELL, Mrs Jill. b 47. Lon Univ BPharm 69 MRPharmS 70. S Dios Minl Tr Scheme 89. **d** 92 **p** 94. NSM Yiewsley *Lon* 92–97; NSM St Marylebone w H Trin 97–02; Chapl St Marylebone Girls' Sch Lon 97–98; Chapl R Academy of Music 97–98; Chapl Lon Sch of Pharmacy 97–98; Chapl Liv Cathl 03–04; PtO *Derby* 04–05; NSM Darley Abbey 05–10; NSM Allestree St Edm and Darley Abbey 10–13; PtO Ox 14–17. *1 Pheasants Ridge, Marlow SL7 3QT* E: jill-caldwell@talk21.com

CALDWELL, Sarah Louise. *See* HARE, Sarah Louise

CALE, Canon Clifford Roy Fenton. b 38. St Mich Coll Llan 65. **d** 67 **p** 68. C Griffithstown *Mon* 67–72; V Cwm 72–73; V Abersychan 73–79; V Abersychan and Garndiffaith 79–82; R Goetre w Llanover and Llanfair Kilgeddin 82–84; R Goetre w Llanover 85–01; RD Raglan-Usk 90–01; Can St Wooloos Cathl 98–01; rtd 01; PtO *Mon* from 17. *3 Trelawny Close, Usk NP15 1SP* T: (01291) 672252 E: canonroycale@btinternet.com

CALE, Mrs Heather. b 68. Ches Coll of HE BEd 90. St Mich Coll Llan 12. **d** 14 **p** 15. NSM Haverfordwest *St D* 14–18. *Greenway Cottage, 79 Hill Mountain, Houghton, Milford Haven SA73 1NB* E: heather.cale@btinternet.com

CALEY, Clare Yvonne. **d** 17. C Inverness St Jo *Mor* from 17; C Inverness St Mich from 17. *12 Fasaich, Strath, Gairloch IV21 2DH* T: (01445) 712775

CALLADINE, Matthew Robert Michael. b 65. St Jo Coll Dur BSc 87 BA 95 Reading Univ MSc 89. Cranmer Hall Dur 93. **d** 96 **p** 97. C Blurton *Lich* 96–01; P-in-c Moston St Mary *Man* 01–16; R Burnage St Marg from 16. *St Margaret's Rectory, 250 Burnage Lane, Manchester M19 1FL* T: 0161-432 1844 E: matt.calladine@ntlworld.com

CALLAGHAN, Martin Peter. b 57. Edin Th Coll 91. **d** 93 **p** 94. C Ayr *Glas* 93–96; C Girvan 93–96; C Maybole 93–96; P-in-c Gretna from 96; P-in-c Eastriggs from 96; P-in-c Annan from 97; P-in-c Lockerbie from 97; P-in-c Moffat from 97; Clergy Ldr Annandale Gp from 03. *South Annandale Rectory, 28 Northfield Park, Annan DG12 5EZ* T: (01461) 202924 E: martinpcallaghan@btinternet.com

CALLAGHAN, Michael James. b 63. Clare Coll Cam BA 85. SEITE 94. **d** 97 **p** 98. NSM Blackheath Park St Mich *S'wark* 97–08; PtO *Guildf* 12–14; NSM Egham from 14; PtO *Lon* from 15. *3 College Avenue, Egham TW20 8NR* T: (01784) 435678

CALLAGHAN, Robert Paul. b 59. K Coll Lon BD 81 Kent Univ MA 04. Linc Th Coll 81. **d** 83 **p** 85. C Winchmore Hill St Paul *Lon* 83–85; C Paddington St Jo w St Mich 85–91; V Dartford St Edm *Roch* 91–11; Nat Co-ordinator Inclusive Ch 11–17; PtO *Glouc* from 14. *4 Ferney, Dursley GL11 5AB* T: (01453) 549955 M: 07989-178558 E: bcall@hotmail.co.uk

CALLAGHAN, Yvonne Susan. b 58. St Jo Coll Nottm 06. **d** 08 **p** 09. C Middleham w Coverdale and E Witton etc *Ripon* 08–13; V Easby w Skeeby and Brompton on Swale etc *Leeds* from 13; AD Richmond from 17. *The Vicarage, St Paul's Drive, Brompton on Swale, Richmond DL10 7HQ* T: (01748) 811748 E: revyvonnecallaghan@esbb.co.uk

CALLARD, Canon David Kingsley. b 37. St Pet Coll Ox BA 61 MA 65. Westcott Ho Cam 61. **d** 63 **p** 64. C Leamington Priors H Trin *Cov* 63–66; C Wyken 66–68; C Bp's Hatfield *St Alb* 68–73; R Bilton *Cov* 73–83; TR Swanage and Studland *Sarum* 83–93; TR Oakdale 93–02; Can and Preb Sarum Cathl 95–02; rtd 02; PtO *Sarum* from 04; *B & W* 05–15. *Woodlands, 29 Folkestone Road, Salisbury SP2 8JP* T: (01722) 501200 E: katcallard@ntlworld.com

CALLEN, Nicola Geraldine. b 48. Open Univ BA 85. Trin Coll Bris 09. **d** 11 **p** 12. OLM Fishponds St Jo *Bris* from 11; OLM Bristol St Aid w St Geo from 15; OLM Two Mile Hill St Mich from 15. *164 Ridgeway Road, Bristol BS16 3EG*

CALLIS, Gillian Ruth. See TURNER-CALLIS, Gillian Ruth

CALLON, Andrew McMillan. b 56. Chich Th Coll 77. **d** 80 **p** 81. C Wigan All SS *Liv* 80–85; V Abram 85–90; V Bickershaw 89–90; Chapl RN 90–12; rtd 12; PtO *B & W* from 13. *Kings Living, Prigg Lane, South Petherton TA13 5BX* T: (01460) 242537 M: 07777-670319 E: a.mcallon@btinternet.com

CALLWAY, Peter Stanley. b 55. SEITE 06. **d** 09 **p** 10. C Paddock Wood *Roch* 09–13; R Coxheath, E Farleigh, Hunton, Linton etc from 13. *The Rectory, 144 Heath Road, Coxheath, Maidstone ME17 4PL* T: (01622) 747570 E: peter@callways.co.uk

CALOW, Jacqueline. b 60. SNWTP. **d** 11 **p** 12. C Langley *Man* 11–14; NSM Saddleworth 14–16; P-in-c Tonge w Alkrington 16–18; C Rhodes 16–18; V Tonge, Rhodes and Alkrington from 18. *The New Vicarage, Boardman Lane, Middleton, Manchester M24 4TU* T: 0161-655 1816 E: jackie.2026309@gmail.com

CALOW, Timothy. b 58. **d** 10 **p** 11. NSM Sutton w Cowling and Lothersdale *Bradf* 10–14; *Leeds* 14–16; NSM Embsay w Eastby from 16. *3 Laurel Close, Embsay, Skipton BD23 6PS* T: (01756) 799517 E: tim@calows.me.uk

CALVELEY, Mrs Susan. b 47. **d** 02 **p** 03. OLM Birkdale St Pet *Liv* 02–06; NSM 06–11; rtd 11; PtO *Liv* from 16. *22 Warren Court, Southport PR8 2DE* E: revd.sue@gmail.com

CALVER, Canon Gillian Margaret. b 47. Qu Eliz Coll Lon BSc 68. Cant Sch of Min 89. **d** 92 **p** 94. NSM Folkestone H Trin w Ch Ch *Cant* 92–95; P-in-c Alkham w Capel le Ferne and Hougham 95–01; V 01–02; Chapl Dover Coll 95–99; R Staplehurst *Cant* 02–11; AD Weald 06–10; Hon Can Cant Cathl 08–11; rtd 11; PtO *Cant* from 12; Chapl to The Queen

08–17. *6 Grand Court, Grand Parade, Littlestone, New Romney TN28 8NT* T: (01797) 366082 E: gill.calver@btinternet.com

CALVER, Nicholas James. b 58. Nottm Univ BTh 83 Dur Univ MA 90. Cranmer Hall Dur 86. **d** 88 **p** 89. C Forest Hill Ch Ch *S'wark* 88–91; C Forest Hill 91–92; P-in-c Mottingham St Edw 92–95; V 95–97; Voc Advr Lewisham Adnry 94–97; V Redhill St Jo *S'wark* 97–14; P-in-c Burstow w Horne 14–15; C S Nutfield w Outwood 14–15; R The Windmill from 15. *The Rectory, 5 The Acorns, Redehall Road, Smallfield, Horley RH6 9QJ* T: (01342) 842224 E: nicholas.calver@btinternet.com

CALVERLEY, Mrs Denise Marie. b 66. Trin Coll Bris 10. **d** 12 **p** 13. C Saltford w Corston and Newton St Loe *B & W* 12–14; C Keynsham 14–16; P-in-c Publow w Pensford, Compton Dando and Chelwood from 16. *The Rectory, Old Road, Pensford, Bristol BS39 4BB* M: 07849-821588 E: dmcalverley@icloud.com

CALVERT, Geoffrey Richard. b 58. Edin Univ BSc 79 PhD 84 Leeds Univ BA 86. Coll of Resurr Mirfield 84. **d** 87 **p** 88. C Curdworth w Castle Vale *Birm* 87–90; C Barnsley St Mary *Wakef* 90–92; TV Halifax 92–94; V Halifax H Trin 95–99; V Luton St Aug Limbury *St Alb* 99–09; P-in-c Watford St Mich 09–12; V from 12. *St Michael's Vicarage, 5 Mildred Avenue, Watford WD18 7DY* T: (01923) 232460 E: geoffreycalvert@virginmedia.com

CALVERT, Canon Jean. b 34. Lightfoot Ho Dur IDC 63. **dss** 78 **d** 87 **p** 94. S Bank *York* 78–84; Chapl Asst Rampton Hosp Retford 84–88; Dn-in-c Dunham w Darlton, Ragnall, Fledborough etc *S'well* 88–94; P-in-c 94–04; Hon Can S'well Minster 93–04; rtd 04; PtO *S'well* from 16. *The Rafters, Lincoln Road, Darlton, Newark NG22 0TF* T: (01777) 228758

CALVERT, John Raymond. b 42. Lon Coll of Div 64. **d** 67 **p** 68. C Kennington St Mark *S'wark* 67–70; C Southborough St Pet w Ch Ch and St Matt *Roch* 70–72; C Barton Seagrave *Pet* 72–73; C Barton Seagrave w Warkton 73–75; Asst Master Shaftesbury High Sch 78–79; Dioc Children's Officer *Glouc* 79–87; P-in-c S Cerney w Cerney Wick and Down Ampney 87–89; V 89–07; P-in-c Siddington w Preston 02–07; rtd 07. *46 Penn Lane, Brixham TQ5 9NR* E: jrcalvertuk@googlemail.com

CALVERT, Mrs Judith. b 50. NOC 04. **d** 07 **p** 08. NSM Woodchurch *Ches* 07–12; NSM Neston from 12. *33 Centurion Drive, Wirral CH47 7AL* T: 0151-632 4729 E: rev.judithcalvert@btinternet.com

CALVERT, Canon Peter Noel. b 41. Ch Coll Cam BA 63 MA 67. Cuddesdon Coll 64. **d** 66 **p** 67. C Brighouse *Wakef* 66–71; V Heptonstall 71–82; V Todmorden 82–07; P-in-c Cross Stone 83–93; RD Calder Valley 84–06; Hon Can Wakef Cathl 92–07; rtd 07; P-in-c Leven Valley *Carl* 07–11; TV Cartmel Peninsula 12–15; Chapl to The Queen 98–11; PtO *Blackb* 16–17. *26 Stonemere Avenue, Todmorden OL14 5RW* T: (01706) 817166 E: pncalvert@btinternet.com

CALVERT, Philip. b 62. St Steph Ho Ox 00. **d** 02 **p** 03. C Holbrooks *Cov* 02–06; P-in-c Kingstanding St Mark *Birm* 06–10; V from 10; AD Handsworth 14–19; Jt AD Handsworth and Central from 19. *St Mark's Clergy House, Bandywood Crescent, Birmingham B44 9JX* T: 0121-360 7288 M: 07969-362577 E: frphilipcalvert@outlook.com

CALVIN-THOMAS, David Nigel. b 43. Univ of Wales (Cardiff) BSc 64 Lon Univ BD 77. St Mich Coll Llan 77. **d** 78 **p** 79. C Pontypridd St Cath *Llan* 78–80; Malawi 81–84; V Rastrick St Matt *Wakef* 84–88; V Birchencliffe 88–93; Chapl Huddersfield R Infirmary 88–93; R Aberdeen St Pet *Ab* 93–01; P-in-c Cove Bay 93–01; TV Glenrothes *St And* 01–07; R 07–09; R Leven and Lochgelly 07–09; rtd 09. *2 Ruthin Way, Tonteg, Pontypridd CF38 1TF* T: (01443) 203633 E: davidcalvinthomas@btinternet.com

CAM, Julian Howard. b 48. York Univ BA 69 Man Univ MA 99. Qu Coll Birm 73. **d** 75 **p** 76. C St Ives *Truro* 75–80; C Lelant 78–80; V Flookburgh *Carl* 80–82; V St Stephen by Saltash *Truro* 82–83; V Low Marple *Ches* 83–08; rtd 08; PtO *Ches* from 08; *Derby* from 08; *Man* from 15. *14 High Lea Road, New Mills, High Peak SK22 3DP* T: (01663) 744065 E: julian.angela.cam08@btinternet.com

CAMAIONI, Orazio. b 83. Chieti Univ BA 08 MA 11 Reading Univ PhD 15. St Steph Ho Ox 14. **d** 16 **p** 17. C Wantage *Ox* 16–19; R Wantage Downs from 19. *The Rectory, Church Street, East Hendred, Wantage OX12 8LA* M: 07449-968816 E: ocamaioni@gmail.com

CAMBER, Mrs Victoria Clare. b 69. Man Univ BA 91 Leeds Univ BA 10. Yorks Min Course 07. **d** 10 **p** 11. C Wales *Sheff* 10–12; C Todwick 12–13; P-in-c from 13. *The Rectory, 15 Rectory Gardens, Todwick, Sheffield S26 1JU* T: (01909) 771101 E: vicky_camber@yahoo.co.uk

CAMBRIDGE, Benedict Howard. b 73. Westmr Coll Ox BTh 95. Cranmer Hall Dur 99. **d** 01 **p** 02. C Chilwell *S'well* 01–05; Sen Chapl Staffs Univ *Lich* 05–12; TV Littleham w Exmouth *Ex* 12–13; C Lympstone and Woodbury w Exton 12–13; TV Littleham-cum-Exmouth w Lympstone from 13. *The Vicarage, 96 Littleham Road, Exmouth EX8 2RD* M: 07535-480077 E: rev.benedict@btinternet.com

CAMBRIDGE, Archdeacon of. See HUGHES, The Ven Alexander James

✠**CAMERON, The Rt Revd Andrew** Bruce. b 41. Edin Th Coll 61. **d** 64 **p** 65 **c** 92. C Helensburgh *Glas* 64–67; C Edin H Cross 67–71; Prov and Dioc Youth Chapl 69–75; Chapl St Mary's Cathl *Edin* 71–75; R Dalmahoy 75–82; Chapl Heriot-Watt Univ 75–82; TV Livingston LEP 82–88; R Perth St Jo *St And* 88–92; Convener Prov Miss Bd 88–92; Bp Ab 92–06; Primus 00–06; rtd 06; LtO *St And* from 07; PtO *Ab* from 19. *21/1 Barossa Place, Perth PH1 5HH* M: 07715-323119 E: bruce2541@gmail.com

CAMERON, David Alan. b 59. Glas Univ MA 81 DipEd 82 PGCE 82. Ripon Coll Cuddesdon 88. **d** 91 **p** 92. C Farncombe *Guildf* 91–93; C Guildf H Trin w St Mary 93–96; V Fenton *Lich* 96–15; R Forfar *St And* 15–17; R Lunan Head 15–17. *Flat 1/1, 14 Darnley Road, Glasgow G41 4NB* M: 07931-644143

CAMERON, David Alexander. b 42. Reading Univ BA 63 MRTPI. St And Dioc Tr Course 80. **d** 90 **p** 93. NSM Blairgowrie *St And* from 90; NSM Coupar Angus from 90; NSM Alyth from 90. *Firgrove, Golf Course Road, Blairgowrie PH10 6LF* T: (01250) 873272 *or* 874583 E: dacameron@talk21.com

✠**CAMERON, The Rt Revd Douglas MacLean.** b 35. Edin Th Coll 59. **d** 62 **p** 63 **c** 93. C Falkirk *Edin* 62–65; Miss P Eiwo Papua New Guinea 66–67; Miss P Movi 67–72; R Goroka and Adn New Guinea Mainland 72–74; P-in-c Edin St Fillan 74–78; R 78–88; R Edin St Hilda 77–88; R Dalkeith 88–92; R Lasswade 88–92; Can St Mary's Cathl 90–91; Syn Clerk 90–91; Dean Edin 91–92; Bp Arg 93–03; rtd 03; LtO *Edin* from 04. *23 Craigs Way, Rumford, Falkirk FK2 0EU* T: (01324) 714137 E: dcamera@tiscali.co.uk

✠**CAMERON, The Rt Revd Gregory Kenneth.** b 59. Linc Coll Ox BA 80 MA 84 Down Coll Cam BA 82 MA 85 Univ of Wales (Cardiff) MPhil 92 LLM 95. St Mich Coll Llan 82. **d** 83 **p** 84 **c** 09. C Newport St Paul *Mon* 83–86; Tutor St Mich Coll Llan 86–89; C Llanmartin *Mon* 86–87; TV 87–88; Chapl Wycliffe Coll Glos 88–94; Dir Bloxham Project 94–00; Research Fell Cardiff Univ Cen for Law and Relig 98–00; Chapl to Abp Wales 00–03; Dir Ecum Relns ACC 03–04; Dep Sec 04–09; Hon Can St Woolos Cathl *Mon* 03–09; Bp St As from 09. *Esgobty, St Asaph LL17 0TW* T: (01745) 583503 E: bishop.stasaph@churchinwales.org.uk *or* bishop.stasaph@cinw.org.uk

CAMERON, Mrs Janice Irene. b 43. Reading Univ BA. TISEC 93. **d** 96 **p** 96. C Blairgowrie *St And* 96–98; C Coupar Angus 96–98; C Alyth 96–98; Can Blackburn 99–08; Can St Ninian's Cathl Perth 05–08; rtd 08; LtO *St And* from 08. *Firgrove, Golf Course Road, Blairgowrie PH10 6LF* T: (01250) 873272 E: janicecameron@freeola.net

CAMERON, Mrs Laura Bluebell. b 55. SRN 77. STETS 10. **d** 13 **p** 14. NSM Shedfield and Wickham *Portsm* 13–16; NSM Fareham H Trin 16; NSM Portsdown from 19; NSM Purbrook from 19. *Wentworth, Heath Road, Wickham, Fareham PO17 6LA* T: (01329) 830145 M: 07562-217104 E: revdlauracameron@gmail.com

CAMERON, Preb Margaret Mary. b 48. Qu Mary Coll Lon BA 69 Ex Univ MA 95. SWMTC 87. **d** 90 **p** 94. NSM Budleigh Salterton *Ex* 90–95; C Whipton 95–97; R Hemyock w Culm Davy, Clayhidon and Culmstock 97–03; RD Cullompton 99–03; V Plympton St Mary 03–13; Preb Ex Cathl 05–13; rtd 13. *Belair, 9 Cyprus Road, Exmouth EX8 2DZ* T: (01395) 223395 E: margaretcameron271@btinternet.com

CAMERON, Michael John. b 41. Linc Th Coll 91. **d** 92 **p** 93. C Dinnington *Sheff* 92–96; V Beighton 96–06; AD Attercliffe 99–02; rtd 07; PtO *Sheff* 09–18. *17 Western Street, Barnsley S70 2BP* T: (01226) 249573 E: michaelcameron851@btinternet.com

CAMERON, Monica Eunice. b 58. Newc Univ BA 82 Solicitor 01. Westcott Ho Cam 12. **d** 15 **p** 16. C Gt Shelford *Ely* 15–18; V Erith Ch Ch *Roch* from 18. *Christ Church Vicarage, Victoria Road, Erith DA8 3AN* M: 07985-304860 E: mothermonicachristchurch@gmail.com

CAMERON, Ms Sheila. b 34. TCert 54. Gilmore Ho 65. **d** 98 **p** 99. NSM Catford St Laur *S'wark* 98–02; PtO from 02. *49 Keedonwood Road, Bromley BR1 4QJ* T: (020) 8695 5521 E: sheilacameron@rocketmail.com

CAMERON, Sheila Helen MacLeod. b 46. St Andr Univ MA 68 MLitt 15 Anglia Ruskin Univ MA 06. ERMC 04. **d** 06 **p** 07. NSM Cherry Hinton St Andr *Ely* 06–07; NSM Chesterton St Geo 07–09; P-in-c Dunbar *Edin* 09–12; NSM Lasswade and Dalkeith 12–13; NSM N Tyne and Redesdale *Newc* 13–16; rtd 16; PtO *Newc* from 16; *Edin* from 18. *1 Elderberry*

Cottages, Otterburn, Newcastle upon Tyne NE19 1LJ T: (01830) 520071 M: 07432-504308 E: shmcameron@btinternet.com

CAMERON, Thomas Edward. b 46. **d** 06. NSM St Paul's Cathl *Lon* 06–11; NSM Clayton w Keymer *Chich* from 11. *11 The Spinney, Hassocks BN6 8EJ* T: (01273) 846274 E: tom.cameron2@aol.com

CAMMIDGE, Jacqueline Ann. b 57. **d** 15 **p** 16. NSM Hampton Hill *Lon* from 15. *32 Uxbridge Road, Hampton TW12 3AD* E: cammidgeclan@blueyonder.co.uk

CAMP, Lin. b 47. Loughb Univ MA 07. SNWTP 07. **d** 10 **p** 11. OLM Ormskirk *Liv* 10–17; rtd 17; PtO *Liv* from 17. *9 Whiterails Drive, Ormskirk L39 3BE* T: (01695) 574152 E: lin.camp@mypostoffice.co.uk

CAMP, Michael Maurice. b 52. Southn Univ BTh 83 K Coll Lon MA 99 Brentwood Coll of Educn CertEd 73. Sarum & Wells Th Coll 78. **d** 81 **p** 82. C Loughton St Jo *Chelmsf* 81–84; C Chingford SS Pet and Paul 84–87; V Northfleet *Roch* 87–94; V Hadlow 94–01; RD Paddock Wood 99–01; V Bromley SS Pet and Paul 01–12; AD Bromley 06–11; Hon Can Roch Cathl 11–13; Abp's Chapl *Cant* 12–13; Hon C Stockwell St Andr and St Mich *S'wark* 12–13; R Parkstone St Pet and St Osmund w Branksea *Sarum* 13–19; rtd 19. *24 Berkshire Road, Salisbury SP2 8NY* M: 07734-424996

CAMPBELL, Andrew Philip. b 82. QUB BA MTh. **d** 12 **p** 13. C Belfast St Anne *Conn* 12–13; C Bangor Abbey *D & D* 13–16; I Skerry w Rathcavan and Newtowncrommelin *Conn* from 16. *The Rectory, 49 Rectory Gardens, Broughshane, Ballymena BT42 4LF* T: (028) 2586 1215 E: acampbell31@qub.ac.uk

CAMPBELL, Mrs Brenda. b 52. St Jo Coll Nottm 92. **d** 94 **p** 95. C Rothley *Leic* 94–97; C Market Bosworth, Cadeby w Sutton Cheney etc 97–00; TV Bosworth and Sheepy Gp 00–07; rtd 07; PtO *Derby* 09–18; *Leic* from 13. *28 Ashfield Drive, Moira, Swadlincote DE12 6HQ* T: (01530) 413534 E: brendajones101@sky.com *or* brendajones101@tiscali.co.uk

CAMPBELL, Christine Emily. b 78. Imp Coll Lon BSc 00. Westcott Ho Cam 16. **d** 18 **p** 19. C Cherry Hinton St Jo *Ely* from 18. *22 Levitt Lane, Waterbeach, Cambridge CB25 9AZ* T: (01223) 440014 M: 07383-512636 E: chris@revcc.uk

CAMPBELL, Miss Elizabeth Hume. b 53. Glas Univ MA 74 Hamilton Coll of Educn TCert 75. St Jo Coll Nottm 01. **d** 02 **p** 03. NSM Alstonfield, Butterton, Ilam etc *Lich* 02–08; NSM Stonehaven and Catterline *Bre* 08–10; P-in-c Dundee St Luke 10–12; Chapl Grampian Univ Hosp NHS Trust 12–13; NSM Muchalls, Stonehaven and Catterline *Bre* 12–15; P-in-c S Shields St Simon *Dur* 15–18; C Jarrow 15–18; rtd 18; PtO *Dur* from 19. *74 Hexham Avenue, Hebburn NE31 2JQ* M: 07809-830556 E: lizziecampbell@o2.co.uk *or* lizziecampbell18@gmail.com

CAMPBELL, George St Clair. b 32. Lon Univ BSc 53. Clifton Th Coll 58. **d** 60 **p** 61. C Tunbridge Wells St Pet *Roch* 60–64; C Clitheroe St Jas *Blackb* 64–70; V Tibshelf *Derby* 70–86; V W Bromwich H Trin *Lich* 86–97; Chapl Heath Lane Hosp 87–97; rtd 97; PtO *Guildf* 98–15. *1 Green Drive, Fulwood, Preston PR2 9SA*

CAMPBELL, Mrs Hilary Anne. b 58. UMIST BSc 80. SAOMC. **d** 01 **p** 02. C Goring w S Stoke *Ox* 01–05; TV Kidlington w Hampton Poyle 05–13; V Shires' Edge from 13. *The Vicarage, High Street, Cropredy, Banbury OX17 1NG* T: (01295) 750385 E: vicar@thecampbells.demon.co.uk

CAMPBELL, Ian George. b 47. FRICS 74 FBEng 93. SEITE 96. **d** 99 **p** 00. NSM Chilham w Challock and Molash *Cant* 99–01; P-in-c Crundale w Godmersham 01–12; NSM King's Wood 12–14; C A20 Benefice 14–17; rtd 17; PtO *Cant* from 18. *19 Quarry House, Calleywell Lane, Aldington, Ashford TN25 7FZ* T: (01233) 721445 E: campbellkent66@gmail.com

CAMPBELL, James Duncan. b 55. Qu Eliz Coll Lon BSc 77 Oak Hill Th Coll MA 00. Cranmer Hall Dur 85. **d** 87 **p** 88. C Hendon St Paul Mill Hill *Lon* 87–92; V Stevenage St Hugh and St Jo *St Alb* 92–13; RD Stevenage 11–13; V Watford Ch Ch from 13. *Christ Church Vicarage, Leggatts Way, Watford WD24 5NQ* T: (01923) 674142 E: vicarccwatford@gmail.com

CAMPBELL, James Larry. b 46. Indiana Univ BSc 69 E Kentucky Univ MA 73 Hull Univ MA 91. Linc Th Coll 86. **d** 88 **p** 89. C N Hull St Mich *York* 88–92; C Hessle 92–95; V Burton Pidsea and Humbleton w Elsternwick 95–12; rtd 12; PtO *Linc* 15–18. *The Mullburys, Bardney Road, Wragby, Market Rasen LN8 5QZ* T: (01673) 857646 E: campbell822@aol.com

CAMPBELL, James Malcolm. b 55. MRICS 81. Wycliffe Hall Ox 89. **d** 91 **p** 92. C Scole, Brockdish, Billingford, Thorpe Abbots etc *Nor* 91–95; R Bentley and Binsted *Win* 95–08; RD Alton 02–08; Hon Can Win Cathl 08; R The Lavingtons, Cheverells, and Easterton *Sarum* 08–16; P-in-c Withyham St Mich *Chich* 16–17; R from 17. *The*

CAMPBELL, James Norman Thompson. b 49. BTh MA. **d** 86 **p** 87. C Arm St Mark w Aghavilly 86–89; I Belfast H Trin and Ardoyne *Conn* 89–95; I Dundela St Mark *D & D* 95–01; I Portadown St Mark *Arm* 01–15; Can Arm Cathl 09–15; rtd 15. *41 Cavanacaw Manor, Armagh BT60 2FH* T: (028) 3731 0696 M: 07784-556026 E: jim.campbell149@sky.com

CAMPBELL, Jane Judith. *See* BAKKER, Jane Judith

CAMPBELL, Kenneth Scott. b 47. BA 82. Oak Hill Th Coll. **d** 82 **p** 83. C Aughton St Mich *Liv* 82–85; V Brough w Stainmore *Carl* 85–90; R Brough w Stainmore, Musgrave and Warcop 90–92; rtd 92. *4 Quarry Close, Kirkby Stephen CA17 4SS* T: (01768) 372390

CAMPBELL, Kenneth William. b 66. Oak Hill Th Coll. **d** 10 **p** 11. C Leyland St Andr *Blackb* 10–13; PtO *Ox* 13–16; P-in-c Appleton 16–18; R from 18; P-in-c Besselsleigh 16–18; R from 18. *The Rectory, Oakesmere, Appleton, Abingdon OX13 5JS* T: (01865) 655737 E: kencampbell66@gmail.com

CAMPBELL, Lerys William. b 85. Win Univ BA 06. Trin Coll Bris MA 14. **d** 14 **p** 15. C Ringwood *Win* 14–17; P-in-c Darby Green and Eversley from 17. *St Barnabas House, Green Lane, Frogmore, Camberley GU17 0NU* M: 07952-303970 E: revlerys@gmail.com *or* vicar@stmaryseversley.org.uk

CAMPBELL, The Very Revd Margaret Ruth. b 62. Trin Coll Bris BA 02. **d** 02 **p** 03. C Yeovil w Kingston Pitney *B & W* 02–06; TV Wellington and Distr 06–11; R Backwell w Chelvey and Brockley 11–18; RD Portishead 17–18; Provost St Jo Cathl Oban *Arg* from 18; R Ardbrecknish from 18. *The Rectory, Ardconnel Terrace, Oban PA34 5DJ* E: jmbt2001@hotmail.com *or* provostoban@argyll.anican.org

CAMPBELL, Patrick Alistair. b 36. Qu Coll Birm 64. **d** 67 **p** 68. C Paston *Pet* 67–71; C Stockton Heath *Ches* 71–73; V Egremont St Jo 73–78; V Bredbury St Mark 78–85; R Astbury and Smallwood 85–91; V Wybunbury w Doddington 91–97; rtd 97; PtO *Ches* 97–01; Warden Coll of St Barn Lingfield 01–07; PtO *Chich* 12–17. *8 Brookside, Crawley Down, Crawley RH10 4UU* T: (01342) 713667

CAMPBELL, Roger Stewart. b 40. Birm Univ BSc 61 PhD 65. St Jo Coll Dur BA 71. Cranmer Hall Dur 68. **d** 71 **p** 72. C Jesmond Clayton Memorial *Newc* 71–77; V St Jo and St Marg Singapore 78–85; C Nottingham St Nic *S'well* 86–90; V Holloway St Mark w Em *Lon* 90–97; TR Tollington 92–97; Chapl Leeds Teaching Hosps NHS Trust 97–04; rtd 04; PtO *Carl* from 05. *Redesdale Cottage, Lazonby, Penrith CA10 1AJ* T: (01768) 870695 E: rogercampbell456@btinternet.com

CAMPBELL, Stephen Lloyd. b 46. St Andr Univ LLB 67 Solicitor 72. SEITE 95. **d** 98 **p** 99. NSM Quantoxhead *B & W* 98–07; NSM Quantock Coast 07–16; RD Quantock 06–12; PtO from 16. *Hodderscombe Lodge, Holford, Bridgwater TA5 1SA* T/F: (01278) 741329 M: 07523-350145 E: campbell1sa@btinternet.com

CAMPBELL-SMYTH, Jonathan David. QUB BSc. St Jo Coll Nottm MTh 11. **d** 11 **p** 12. C Coleraine *Conn* 11–13; C Jordanstown 13–17; I Ballynure and Ballyeaston from 17. *Ballynure Rectory, 11 Church Road, Ballynure, Ballyclare BT39 9UF* M: 07808-479649 E: jonathan@campbellsmyth.co.uk

CAMPBELL-TAYLOR, William Goodacre. b 65. Ox Univ BA 87 Cam Univ BA 93 MA 95 Princeton Th Sem DMin 11. Westcott Ho Cam 90. **d** 94 **p** 95. C Chingford SS Pet and Paul *Chelmsf* 94–97; Chapl Lon Guildhall Univ 97–02; Chapl Lon Metrop Univ 02–04; Research Fell St Ethelburga's Cen for Reconciliation and Peace 05–08; Hon C Hoxton St Anne w St Columba *Lon* 05–09; V Stamford Hill St Thos from 09; P-in-c Upper Clapton St Matt from 14; Hon C Stoke Newington Common St Mich from 16. *The Vicarage, 1 Clapton Terrace, London E5 9BW* T: (020) 8806 1463 E: fatherwilliamtaylor@hotmail.com

CAMPBELL-WILSON, Allan. b 43. Dur Univ BEd 74. NEOC 79. **d** 82 **p** 83. NSM Boosbeck w Moorsholm *York* 82–85; R Easington w Skeffling, Kilnsea and Holmpton 85–87; P-in-c Middlesbrough St Jo the Ev 89–95; V 95–99; V Cayton w Eastfield 99–12; rtd 12; PtO *York* from 12. *51 Oak Road, Scarborough YO12 4AP* T: (01723) 362426 E: campbellwilson165@btinternet.com

CAMPEN, William Geoffrey. b 50. Liv Univ CertEd 71 Southn Univ BTh 81 Lon Univ MA 08. Sarum & Wells Th Coll 76. **d** 79 **p** 80. C Peckham St Jo w St Andr *S'wark* 79–83; P-in-c Mottingham St Edw 83–92; R Charlwood 92–15; R Sidlow Bridge 92–15; rtd 15; PtO *Cant* from 18. *41 Old Park Avenue, Canterbury CT1 1DN* T: (01227) 764340 E: campenwg@googlemail.com

CAMPION (*formerly* HOUSEMAN), **Mrs Patricia Adele.** b 39. St Mich Coll Llan. **d** 93 **p** 97. C St Issell's and Amroth *St D* 93–95; C Llanegryn w Aberdyfi w Tywyn *Ban* 95–97; rtd 97;

PtO *St D* from 99. *3 Mariners Reach, The Strand, Saundersfoot SA69 9EX* T: (01834) 811047

CAMPION, Canon Peter Robert. b 64. Bp's Univ Canada BA 87 TCD BTh 90 MA 93 MPhil 97 Homerton Coll Cam PGCE 94. **d** 90 **p** 91. C Belfast H Trin and Ardoyne *Conn* 90–93; C Taney *D & G* 94–00; Dean's V St Patr Cathl Dublin 96–00; Chapl Netherwood Sch Rothesday Canada 00–05; Chapl K Hosp Sch Dub from 05; Treas V St Patr Cathl Dublin 05–11; Prec Ch Ch Cathl Dublin *D & G* from 08; Prec St Patr Cathl Dublin from 15. *The King's Hospital, Palmerstown, Dublin 20, Republic of Ireland* T: (00353) (1) 626 5933 F: 623 0349 E: chaplain@thekingshospital.ie

CAMPION-SPALL, Ms Kathryn May. b 79. York Univ BA 02 Fitzw Coll Cam BA 09. Westcott Ho Cam 07. **d** 10 **p** 11. C Merton St Mary *S'wark* 10–14; C Bris St Mary Redcliffe w Temple etc from 14. *2 Colston Parade, Bristol BS1 6RA* T: 0117-929 1519 *or* 929 1605 M: 07960-588015 E: kat.campion-spall@stmaryredcliffe.co.uk

CAMPLING, Camilla Anne. *See* CAMPLING-DENTON, Camilla Anne

CAMPLING, The Very Revd Christopher Russell. b 25. St Edm Hall Ox BA 50 MA 54. Cuddesdon Coll 50. **d** 51 **p** 52. C Basingstoke *Win* 51–55; Chapl K Sch and Min Can Ely Cathl 55–60; Chapl Lancing Coll 60–68; P-in-c Birlingham w Nafford *Worc* 68–75; V Pershore w Wick 68–75; V Pershore w Pinvin, Wick and Birlingham 75–76; RD Pershore 70–76; Hon Can Worc Cathl 74–84; Dioc Dir of Educn 76–84; Adn Dudley 76–84; P-in-c Dodderhill 76–84; Dean Ripon 84–95; Chmn CCC 88–94; rtd 95; PtO *Chich* from 95. *Pebble Ridge, Aglaia Road, Worthing BN11 5SW* T: (01903) 246598 E: campling238@btinternet.com

CAMPLING, Michael. b 27. Trin Coll Cam BA 50 MA 61. Wells Th Coll 51. **d** 53 **p** 54. C Calne *Sarum* 53–57; C Roehampton H Trin *S'wark* 57–61; V Crowthorne *Ox* 61–75; P-in-c Foleshill St Laur *Cov* 75–81; V 81–83; R Old Alresford and Bighton *Win* 83–92; rtd 92; Chapl St Marg Convent E Grinstead 92–99; Hon C Bexhill St Pet *Chich* 99–05; PtO *Ox* from 05. *9 Orchard Grove, Bloxham, Banbury OX15 4NZ* T: (01295) 721599

CAMPLING-DENTON, Camilla Anne. b 76. St Andr Univ MA 98 Jes Coll Cam MPhil 04. Westcott Ho Cam 02. **d** 05 **p** 06. C Fountains Gp *Ripon* 05–07; C Caerleon w Llanhennock *Mon* 07–09; C Caerleon and Llanfrechfa 09–10; Hon C Washburn and Mid-Wharfe *Bradf* 10–14; R Walkingham Hill *Leeds* 14–17; P-in-c Forcett and Aldbrough and Melsonby 17–18; R from 18. *The Rectory, 1 Appleby Close, Aldbrough St John, Richmond DL11 7TT* T: (01325) 374634 M: 07817-386070 E: camilla.cd@cantab.net *or* milly@c-d.eclipse.co.uk

CAMPOS DE SANTANA, Levy Henrique. b 85. **d** 13 **p** 14. C High Wycombe *Ox* 13–17; CMS from 17. *Rua El Greco, Qd 31, Lt 06, Casa 03, Setor Gentil Meireles, Goiania, GO 74575-140, Brazil* M: 07950-212347 E: levysantana@me.com

CANDLIN, David James. b 68. St Cath Coll Cam BA 89 Imp Coll Lon MBA 00. Ripon Coll Cuddesdon 16. **d** 18 **p** 19. C Epsom St Martin *Guildf* from 18. *12 Worple Road, Epsom KT18 5EE* E: revcandlin@gmail.com

CANDY, Julia Elaine. b 80. K Coll Cam BA 01 QUB PhD 06 Jes Coll Cam BA 09. Westcott Ho Cam 07. **d** 10 **p** 11. C Dur St Giles 10–13; C Shadforth and Sherburn 10–13; P-in-c Aberdeen St Jas *Ab* 13; P-in-c Aberdeen St Clem 13; Asst Chapl Univ Coll Lon Hosps NHS Foundn Trust 14–17; V W Hendon St Jo and Cricklewood St Pet *Lon* from 17. *St John's Vicarage, Vicarage Road, London NW4 3PX* E: jec1492@hotmail.com

CANE, The Very Revd Anthony William Nicholas Strephon. b 61. Cape Town Univ BA 81 Birm Univ MPhil 93 PhD 03. Westcott Ho Cam 87. **d** 90 **p** 91. C Kings Heath *Birm* 90–93; Chapl Brighton Univ *Chich* 93–99; P-in-c Torquay St Luke *Ex* 99–01; Dioc Adv in Adult Tr 99–01; C Ringmer and Dioc Adv for Educn and Tr of Adults *Chich* 01–07; Can Res and Chan Chich Cathl 07–19; Dean Portsm from 19. *The Deanery, 13 Pembroke Road, Portsmouth PO1 2NS* T: (023) 9282 4400 E: anthony.cane@portsmouthcathedral.org

CANESSA, Jonathan. b 70. Ox Brookes Univ BA 02. Westcott Ho Cam 11. **d** 13 **p** 14. C Cambridge St Paul *Ely* from 13; Bp's Officer for Homelessness from 16. *25 Days Meadow, Oakington, Cambridge CB24 3GS* E: joncanessa@gmail.com *or* jon@stpaulscambridge.org.uk

CANEY, Canon Robert Swinbank. b 37. St Jo Coll Cam 57. Lich Th Coll 58. **d** 61 **p** 62. C Kingswinford H Trin *Lich* 61–64; C Castle Church 64–67; V Bradwell *Derby* 67–73; V Fairfield 73–84; RD Buxton 78–84; P-in-c Peak Forest and Wormhill 79–83; R Wirksworth w Alderwasley, Carsington etc 84–92; TR Wirksworth 92–02; Hon Can Derby Cathl 93–02; rtd 02;

PtO *Derby* 02–18. *2 Erica Drive, South Normanton, Alfreton DE55 2ET* T: (01773) 581106 E: randjcaney@gmail.com

CANHAM, Frances Elizabeth. b 55. MCIPD 93. St Mich Coll Llan 05. **d** 07 **p** 08. NSM Thanington *Cant* 07–10; Asst Chapl Salisbury NHS Foundn Trust 10–13; Chapl from 13. *Chaplain's Office, Salisbury District Hospital, Salisbury SP2 8BJ* T: (01258) 489331

CANNAM, Martin Stafford John. b 68. Jes Coll Ox BA 90 MA 95. Wycliffe Hall Ox 93. **d** 96 **p** 97. C Childwall All SS *Liv* 96–00; V Biddulph *Lich* 00–15; RD Leek 13–15; R Heswall *Ches* from 15. *The Rectory, Village Road, Heswall, Wirral CH60 0DZ* T: 0151-342 3471 M: 07999-594373

CANNELL, Anthea Marjorie. b 45. UEA MA 85. EAMTC 01. **d** 02 **p** 03. NSM Theydon Bois *Chelmsf* 02–10; P-in-c Roydon 10–15; rtd 15; PtO *Chelmsf* from 15. *118 High Street, Roydon, Harlow CM19 5EF* T: (01279) 792543 E: amcannell@btinternet.com

CANNING, Canon Arthur James. b 45. St Jo Coll Dur BA 66 Linacre Coll Ox BA 70 MA 74 Lambeth STh 90. Ripon Hall Ox 67. **d** 71 **p** 72. C Coleshill *Birm* 71–74; C Frome St Jo *B & W* 75–76; V Frizington and Arlecdon *Carl* 76–80; P-in-c Foleshill St Paul *Cov* 80–81; V 81–12; Hon Can Cov Cathl 00–12; rtd 12; PtO *Cov* from 12. *13 Broadlands Close, Coventry CV5 7AJ* T: (024) 7671 3220 E: jcxwx@aol.com

CANNING, Peter Christopher. b 52. Birm Poly CQSW. St Jo Coll Nottm 87. **d** 89 **p** 90. C Cov St Mary 89–93; V Hartshill 93–96; rtd 96. *Address withheld by request*

CANNINGS, Karen Rachel. *See* SKIDMORE, Karen Rachel

CANNON, Elizabeth Mary. b 50. EAMTC 94. **d** 97 **p** 98. NSM New Catton Ch Ch *Nor* 97–00; P-in-c Cross Roads cum Lees *Bradf* 00–06; TV Blyth Valley *St E* 06–15; rtd 15; PtO *Nor* from 16; *St E* from 17. *88 Colney Lane, Cringleford, Norwich NR4 7RG* T: (01603) 452767

CANNON, Mark Harrison. b 60. Keble Coll Ox BA 82. Cranmer Hall Dur 83. **d** 85 **p** 86. C Skipton Ch Ch *Bradf* 85–88; Dioc Youth Officer 88–92; C Baildon 88–92; P-in-c Church Coniston *Carl* 92–00; P-in-c Torver 92–00; P-in-c Brindle *Blackb* 00–10; Dioc Voc Adv 00–05; NSM E Lonsdale 10–11; P-in-c 11–16; V from 16. *The Vicarage, Home Farm Close, Wray, Lancaster LA2 8RG* T: (01524) 221030 E: markhcannon1@gmail.com

CANNON, Ms Rebekah Lindsey. b 77. Man Metrop Univ BA 99 Middx Univ MA 06 PGCE 06 SS Coll Cam BTh 09. Westcott Ho Cam 07. **d** 10 **p** 11. C Whyke w Rumboldswhyke and Portfield *Chich* 10–14; Chapl RAF from 14. *Chaplaincy Services (RAF), HQ Air Command, RAF High Wycombe HP14 4UE* T: (01494) 496800 E: rebecca.cannon103@mod.gov.uk

CANNON, Tony Arthur. b 57. Oak Hill Th Coll 94. **d** 96 **p** 97. C Church Stretton *Heref* 96–00; P-in-c Kingham w Churchill, Daylesford and Sarsden *Ox* 00–01; TV Chipping Norton 01–10; V Woking St Jo *Guildf* 11–17; rtd 17. *42 Coach Barn Lane, Hailsham BN27 3YR* T: (01323) 398539

CANSDALE, George Graham. b 38. Mert Coll Ox BA 60 MA 64 DipEd 61. Clifton Th Coll 62. **d** 64 **p** 65. C Heatherlands St Jo *Sarum* 64–67; BCMS Kenya 68–76; P-in-c Clapham *St Alb* 76–80; V 80–89; Asst Chapl Bedford Sch 89–97; LtO *St Alb* 93–01; PtO *Wakef* 01–14; *Leeds* from 14; rtd 03. *Serendipity, 4 Brier Hey Lane, Mytholmroyd, Hebden Bridge HX7 5PJ* T: (01422) 706761 E: graham.cansdale@virgin.net

CANSDALE, Canon Michael Cranmer. b 70. Bradf Univ BA 93 St Jo Coll Dur BA 06. Cranmer Hall Dur 04. **d** 06 **p** 07. C Silsden *Bradf* 06–09; P-in-c Morton St Luke 09–15; P-in-c Riddlesden 09–15; V Morton and Riddlesden *Leeds* 15–16; TR Keighley from 16; Hon Can Bradf Cathl from 19. *St Mark's Vicarage, 64 Green Head Road, Keighley BD20 6ED* T: (01535) 607003 M: 07545-566898

CANSDALE, Philip John. b 73. Keble Coll Ox BA 95 MA 99. Trin Coll Bris BA 98 MA 99. **d** 99 **p** 00. C Cant St Mary Bredin 99–03; C Penn Fields *Lich* 03–09; V Meole Brace from 09; RD Shrewsbury from 18. *The Vicarage, Vicarage Road, Shrewsbury SY3 9EZ* T: (01743) 231744

CANSDALE, Simon James Lee. b 68. Keble Coll Ox BA 90. Wycliffe Hall Ox 93. **d** 95 **p** 96. C Bletchley *Ox* 95–98; C Cambridge H Trin *Ely* 98–01; R W Bridgford *S'well* 01–08; TR Gt Chesham *Ox* 08–19; V Win Ch Ch from 19. *Christchurch Vicarage, Sleepers Hill, Winchester SO22 4ND*

CANT, Anthony David. b 59. Middx Univ BA 04. NTMTC 01. **d** 04 **p** 05. C Walthamstow *Chelmsf* 04–07; TV 07–10; Chapl Anglia Ruskin Univ 10–19; rtd 19. *5 Knoll Road, Tamborine Mountain QLD 4272, Australia* E: revtonyc@gmail.com

CANT, Christopher Somerset Travers. b 51. Keble Coll Ox BA 72 MA 76 Ex Univ PGCE 77. All Nations Chr Coll 80 Wycliffe Hall Ox 93. **d** 87 **p** 90. C Tando Muhammad Khan Pakistan 87–90; P-in-c Badin 90–92; LtO *Cov* 92–93; Warden St Clem Family Cen Ox 93–95; C Gt Ilford St Andr *Chelmsf*

95–98; V Hainault 98–10; C Aylesbeare, Clyst St George, Clyst St Mary etc *Ex* 11–16. *15 Stoneborough Lane, Budleigh Salterton EX9 6HL* T: (01395) 488178 E: chriscant@tiscali.co.uk

CANT, Joseph Clifford. b 72. UEA BA 94 MA 98 DipSW 98 Cam Univ BTh 08. Westcott Ho Cam 06. **d** 08 **p** 09. C Hilton w Marston-on-Dove *Derby* 08–11; TV Uttoxeter Area *Lich* from 11. *The Parish Office, St Mary's Church, Bridge Street, Uttoxeter ST14 8AW* M: 07952-798649 E: joecant214@gmail.com

CANT, Miss Sheila Phyllis. b 59. All SS Cen for Miss & Min 13. **d** 15 **p** 16. OLM Denton St Lawr *Man* from 15. *3 Ashlands Drive, Audenshaw, Manchester M34 5EL* T: 0161-336 1566 E: sheila.cant@btinternet.com

CANTACUZENE, Mrs Mary. b 52. **d** 05 **p** 06. OLM Bures w Assington and Lt Cornard *St E* 05–13; NSM from 13. *Peartree Barn, Peartree Hill, Mount Bures, Bures CO8 5BA* T: (01787) 227616 F: 227220 M: 07932-033019 E: mary.cantacuzene@gmail.com

CANTERBURY, Archbishop of. *See* WELBY, The Most Revd and Rt Hon Justin Portal

CANTERBURY, Archdeacon of. *Vacant*

CANTERBURY, Dean of. *See* WILLIS, The Very Revd Robert Andrew

CANTLOW, Tony Loram. b 61. St Hild Coll 17. **d** 18. NSM Skipton Ch Ch w Carleton *Leeds* from 18. *3 Spences Court, Main Street, Carleton, Skipton BD23 3BY* E: tony.cantlow@leeds.anglican.org

CANTRILL, Mark James. b 67. Lanc Univ BEd 89. St Jo Coll Nottm 00. **d** 02 **p** 03. C Warsop *S'well* 02–07; TV Retford Area from 07. *Clarborough Vicarage, Church Lane, Clarborough, Retford DN22 9NA* T: (01777) 711530 M: 07985-160694 E: revmark.cantrill@btinternet.com

CANTY, Canon Katherine Anne. b 52. York Univ BA 74 Coll of Ripon & York St Jo PGCE 75. NOC 05. **d** 07 **p** 08. Asst Chapl HM Pris Altcourse 04–07; Chapl 07–16; NSM Gateacre *Liv* from 07; Dean Sector Min from 18; Hon Can Liv Cathl from 19. *c/o Crockford, Church House, Great Smith Street, London SW1P 3AZ* E: katy.canty@liverpool.anglican.org

CAPEL, Luke Thomas. *See* IRVINE-CAPEL, Luke Thomas

CAPEL-EDWARDS, Maureen. b 36. Southn Univ BSc 60 Reading Univ PhD 69. St Alb Minl Tr Scheme 84. **d** 87 **p** 94. NSM Ware St Mary *St Alb* 87–90; Chapl Hertf Regional Coll of FE 87–00; NSM Hertford All SS *St Alb* 90–94; NSM Aspenden and Layston w Buntingford 94–95; NSM Aspenden, Buntingford and Westmill 95–00; P-in-c Ardeley and Cottered w Broadfield and Throcking 00–05; rtd 05; PtO *Portsm* from 05. *Capeland, High Street, Soberton, Southampton SO32 3PN* T: (01489) 878192 E: capeland@waitrose.com

CAPERON, John Philip. b 44. Bris Univ BA 66 Open Univ MPhil 80 Ox Univ MSc 83 Kent Univ MA 99 Anglia Ruskin Univ DProf 13. Ox Univ Course 80. **d** 83 **p** 84. NSM Hook Norton w Gt Rollright, Swerford etc *Ox* 83–86; NSM Knaresborough *Ripon* 86–92; Dep Hd St Aid Sch Harrogate 86–92; Hd and Chapl Bennett Memorial Dioc Sch Tunbridge Wells 92–04; rtd 04; PtO *Chich* 98–03 and 11–17; Hon C Mayfield 03–11; P-in-c Fairwarp from 17; Dir Bloxham Project 06–11; PtO *Roch* from 15; *Cant* from 17. *Sarum, 5 Twyfords, Beacon Road, Crowborough TN6 1YE* T: (01892) 667207 E: johncaperon@btinternet.com

CAPES, Dennis Robert. b 34. Handsworth Coll Birm 55 Linc Th Coll 65. **d** 64 **p** 65. In Methodist Ch (Sarawak) 59–63; C Lt Coates *Linc* 64–66; R Miri Malaysia 66–69; V Gosberton Clough *Linc* 69–71; V Kirton in Holland 71–80; Area Sec USPG Cov, Heref and Worc 80–87; Chapl Copenhagen w Aarhus *Eur* 87–93; TV Liv Our Lady and St Nic w St Anne 93–99; rtd 99. *35 Hardwick Avenue, Newark NG24 4AW* T: (01636) 672874 E: dennis@capes.plus.com

CAPIE, Fergus Bernard. b 47. Auckland Univ BA 68 MA 71. Wycliffe Hall Ox BA 77. **d** 77 **p** 78. C Ox St Mich w St Martin and All SS 77–80; Chapl Summer Fields Sch Ox 80–91; Hon C Wolvercote w Summertown *Ox* 87–91; PtO *St E* 91; TV E Ham w Upton Park and Forest Gate *Chelmsf* 91–95; P-in-c Brondesbury St Anne w Kilburn H Trin *Lon* 95–01; V 01–12; Chapl NW Lon Coll 95–12; rtd 12. *27 Olympus Way, Richmond 7020, Nelson, New Zealand* E: ferguscapie@yahoo.co.uk

CAPITANCHIK, Sophie Rebecca. *See* JELLEY, Sophie Rebecca

CAPLE, Stephen Malcolm. b 55. Chich Th Coll 86. **d** 88 **p** 89. C Newington St Mary *S'wark* 88–92; V Eltham St Sav 92–97; V Salfords 97–07; P-in-c S Kensington St Aug *Lon* 07–10; V Whitton St Aug 10–19; Dir Evang Kensington Area 07–19; rtd 19. *Address temp unknown* E: stephen.caple@hotmail.co.uk

CAPON, The Very Revd Gerwyn Huw. b 65. Liv Jo Moores Univ BSc 92. St Steph Ho Ox 01. **d** 03 **p** 04. C W Derby St Mary *Liv* 03–07; Chapl to Abp Wales and Dir of Ords *Llan* 07–09; P-in-c Bolton-le-Sands *Blackb* 09–12; Chapl to Abp Wales *Llan* 12–14; Dean Llan from 14; V Llandaff from 14.

The Deanery, The Cathedral Green, Cardiff CF5 2YF T: (029) 2056 1545 E: thedean@llandaffcathedral.org.uk

CAPORN, David Richard. b 78. St Jo Coll Cam BA 00 MA 04 ACA 03. Trin Coll Bris MA 13. **d** 13 **p** 14. C Highworth w Sevenhampton and Inglesham etc *Bris* 13–17; C Broad Blunsdon 13–17; TV Sidmouth, Woolbrook, Salcombe Regis, Sidbury etc *Ex* 17–19; TR from 19. *All Saints' Vicarage, All Saints Road, Sidmouth EX10 8ES* T: (01395) 515963 M: 07900-55390 E: david.caporn@sidvalley.org.uk

CAPPER, Alan. *See* CAPPER, William Alan

CAPPER, Mrs Katherine Frances. b 64. Warwick Univ BA 86. SEITE 07. **d** 10 **p** 11. NSM Horley *S'wark* 10–14; NSM Betchworth and Buckland 14–15; C Reigate St Mary from 15. *12 Beaufort Close, Reigate RH2 9DG* T: (01737) 217191 M: 07710-813177 E: revkate@thecappers.co.uk *or* kate.capper@stmaryreigate.org

CAPPER, Lorraine Alberta. Ulster Univ BTh. **d** 10 **p** 11. C Drumragh w Mountfield *D & R* 10–15; C Donagh w Tyholland and Errigal Truagh *Clogh* from 18. *The Rectory, 3 Castlebalfour Road, Lisnaskea, Enniskillen BT92 0LT* T: (028) 6772 2413 E: lorraine.capper@gmail.com

CAPPER, Canon Richard. b 49. Leeds Univ BSc 70 Fitzw Coll Cam BA 72 MA 79. Westcott Ho Cam 70. **d** 73 **p** 74. C Wavertree H Trin *Liv* 73–76; P-in-c Ince St Mary 76–79; V 79–83; V Gt Crosby St Faith 83–97; AD Bootle 89–97; Can Res Wakef Cathl 97–05; Can Res Nor Cathl 05–14; P-in-c Nor St Mary in the Marsh 05–14; rtd 15; PtO *Nor* from 15; *S'wark* from 16; *Eur* from 17. *3 Kingfisher Walk, Loddon, Norwich NR14 6FB* T: (01508) 520046 E: richardcapper49@gmail.com

CAPPER, Canon Robert Melville. b 52. Chu Coll Cam BA 74 MA 80. Wycliffe Hall Ox 74. **d** 77 **p** 78. C Maindee Newport *Mon* 77–80; TV Aberystwyth *St D* 80–87; Chapl Univ of Wales (Abth) 80–87; V Malpas *Mon* 87–00; V Gabalfa *Llan* 00–17; P-in-c Tremorfa St Phil CD 05–17; AD Cardiff 13–17; Hon Can Llan Cathl 14–17; rtd 17. *Cleddau View, Haven View, Neyland, Milford Haven SA73 1LS* T: (01646) 562804

CAPPER, William Alan. QUB BTh. **d** 88 **p** 89. C Dundonald *D & D* 88–91; C Lisburn Ch Ch *Conn* 91–94; I Tamlaght O'Crilly Upper w Lower *D & R* 94–96; I Lack *Clogh* 03–09; I Lisnaskea from 09. *The Rectory, 3 Castlebalfour Road, Lisnaskea, Enniskillen BT92 0LT* T: (028) 6772 2413 *or* 6772 3977 E: lisnaskea@clogher.anglican.org

CAPPLEMAN, Graham Robert (Sam). b 56. Chelsea Coll Lon BSc 79 Sheff Univ PhD 83. SAOMC 94. **d** 97 **p** 98. NSM Bedf St Mark *St Alb* 97–19; Bp's Dom Chapl from 19. *107 Dover Crescent, Bedford MK41 8QR* T: (01234) 266952 M: 07836-784051 E: sam_cappleman@hotmail.com

CAPPLEMAN, Mrs Jennifer Margaret. b 53. C F Mott Coll of Educn CertEd 74. SAOMC 97. **d** 00 **p** 01. NSM Bedford St Pet w St Cuth *St Alb* 00–03; C Goldington 03–07; TV Ouzel Valley 07–13; rtd 13; PtO *St Alb* 13–14; NSM Keysoe w Bolnhurst and Lt Staughton 14–15; PtO from 17. *107 Dover Crescent, Bedford MK41 8QR* T: (01234) 266952 M: 07714-701008 E: jennie.cappleman@yahoo.co.uk

CAPRON, Canon David Cooper. b 45. Open Univ BA 80. Sarum & Wells Th Coll 71. **d** 75 **p** 76. C Cov St Mary 75–79; V Shottery St Andr 79–86; TV Stratford-on-Avon w Bishopton 79–86; V Shottery St Andr 86; V Newton Aycliffe *Dur* 86–89; TR 89–90; P-in-c Alcester and Arrow w Oversley and Weethley *Cov* 90–95; R 95–12; P-in-c Kinwarton w Gt Alne and Haselor 06–12; P-in-c Coughton 06–12; Hon Can Cov Cathl 07–12; Chapl Warks Fire and Rescue Service 93–09; rtd 13; PtO *Cov* from 13; *Worc* from 13. *19 Holbrook Road, Stratford-upon-Avon CV37 9DZ* T: (01789) 762904 M: 07780-707521 E: canon@caprons.co.uk

CAPRON, Mark Andrew. b 80. Staffs Univ BA 02. Ridley Hall Cam 09. **d** 12 **p** 13. C Pakefield *Nor* 12–16; C Carlton Colville and Mutford 12–16; R Dersingham, Anmer, Ingoldisthorpe etc from 16. *The Vicarage, Shernborne Road, Dersingham, King's Lynn PE31 6JA* E: revmarkcapron@gmail.com

CAPSTICK, Mrs Jean Rose. b 44. **d** 09 **p** 10. NSM Sodbury Vale *Glouc* 09–11; NSM Winterbourne *Bris* 12–13; NSM Frenchay and Winterbourne Down 12–13; NSM Frampton Cotterell and Iron Acton 12–13; NSM Coalpit Heath 12–13; PtO from 13; *Glouc* from 14. *Lerryn, Wotton Road, Rangeworthy, Bristol BS37 7LZ* T: (01454) 228236 E: jean.capstick@homecall.co.uk *or* jean@lescapstick.plus.com

CARBERRY, Leon Carter. b 54. Penn State Univ BSc 76. St Steph Ho Ox 81. **d** 84 **p** 85. C Peterlee *Dur* 84–87; C Newton Aycliffe 87–89; V Choral York Minster 89–94; Chapl St Pet Sch York 94–95; V Flyingdales and Hawsker cum Stainsacre *York* 95–01; Chapl Burrswood Chr Cen *Roch* 01–03; V Beckenham St Jas 03–16; P-in-c Beckenham St Mich w St Aug 15–16; V Beckenham St Jas w St Mich and

St Aug from 16; AD Beckenham 12–15. *The Vicarage, 15 St James' Avenue, Beckenham BR3 4HF* T/F: (020) 8650 0420 E: leoncarberry@gmail.com

CARBY, Stuart Graeme. b 51. Man Univ BSc 73 Open Univ MA 96 Leeds Univ PGCE 74 CBiol 77 MRSB 77 LRSC 78. St Jo Coll Nottm 92. **d** 92 **p** 93. C Magor w Redwick and Undy *Mon* 92–96; TV Cyncoed 96–18; rtd 18. *10 Rectory Drive, Huddersfield HD5 0JT*

CARD-REYNOLDS, Charles Leonard. b 67. Lon Univ BD 92 Hughes Hall Cam BA 94 MA 98 FRSA 13. St Steph Ho Ox 96. **d** 98 **p** 99. C Reading H Trin *Ox* 98–06; C Reading St Mark 98–06; V Stamford Hill St Bart *Lon* from 06. *The Vicarage, 31 Craven Park Road, London N15 6AA* T: (020) 8800 1554 E: c.cardreynolds@me.com

CARDALE, Edward Charles. b 50. CCC Ox BA 72 MA 73. Cuddesdon Coll 72 Union Th Sem (NY) STM 74. **d** 74 **p** 75. C E Dulwich St Jo *S'wark* 74–77; Asst P Bainbridge Is USA 77–80; V Ponders End St Matt *Lon* 80–84; V Lytchett Minster *Sarum* 84–98; Dir Past Studies Coll of the Resurr Mirfield 98–02; P-in-c Lemsford *St Alb* 02–05; TV Bp's Hatfield, Lemsford and N Mymms 05–14; Tutor SAOMC 02–05; Dir Past Studies ERMC 05–14; rtd 14; PtO *St Alb* from 14. *28 Warren Way, Welwyn AL6 0DH* E: edward.cardale@btopenworld.com

CARDELL-OLIVER, John Anthony. b 43. Em Coll Cam BA 67 MA 72 Univ of W Aus BEd 75 MEd 85 Murdoch Univ Aus PhD 15. Westcott Ho Cam 86. **d** 86 **p** 88. C Subiaco w Leederville Australia 86–88; PtO *Ely* 88–89; C Stansted Mountfitchet *Chelmsf* 89–92; R Langham w Boxted 92–02; rtd 02. *40 Halesworth Road, Jolimont, Perth WA 6014, Australia* T: (0061) (0) 432 298 111 E: john.cardell-oliver@cantab.net

CARDEN, Edwin William. b 54. Cranmer Hall Dur 85. **d** 87 **p** 88. C Thundersley *Chelmsf* 87–91; CUF 91–93; NSM Poplar *Lon* 91–93; Chapl Pathfinder Mental Health Services NHS Trust 93–99; Chapl SW Lon and St George's Mental Health NHS Trust 99–00; Selection Sec Min Division 00–05; NSM Maldon St Mary w Mundon *Chelmsf* 00–02; Dioc Dep Chief Exec 03–08; PtO from 08; Chief Exec WHCM from 08. *21 Plume Avenue, Maldon CM9 6LB* T: (01621) 854908 E: mudmonkeys4@btinternet.com *or* eddie@renew-us.org

CARDIGAN, Archdeacon of. *See* DAVIES, The Ven Rachel Hannah Eileen

CARDINAL, Preb Ian Ralph. b 57. Qu Coll Birm 81. **d** 84 **p** 85. C Whitkirk *Ripon* 84–87; C Knaresborough 87–89; R Ancaster Wilsford Gp *Linc* 89–94; P-in-c Wigginton *Lich* 94–07; Warden of Readers 96–03; P-in-c Stone St Mich and St Wulfad w Aston St Sav 07–08; R from 08; RD Stone from 16; RD Eccleshall 17–18; Preb Lich Cathl from 18. *11 Farrier Close, Stone ST15 8XP* T: (01785) 812747 M: 07778-055993 E: rector@stmichaelschurchstone.co.uk

CARDWELL, Edward Anthony Colin. b 42. Trin Coll Cam BA 63 MA 68. St Jo Coll Nottm 73. **d** 75 **p** 76. C Stapenhill w Cauldwell *Derby* 75–78; C Bramcote *S'well* 78–81; V S'well H Trin 81–92; R Eastwood 92–07; rtd 07; PtO *S'well* from 08. *49 Bramcote Road, Beeston, Nottingham NG9 1DW* T: 0115-925 5866

CARDWELL, Joseph Robin. b 47. Qu Coll Cam BA 68 MA 77. Trin Coll Bris 73. **d** 76 **p** 77. C Bromley Ch Ch *Roch* 76–79; C Shirley *Win* 79–82; V Somborne w Ashley 82–90; V Derry Hill *Sarum* 90–94; V Derry Hill w Bremhill and Foxham 94–00; Community Affairs Chapl 90–94; V Lyddington and Wanborough and Bishopstone etc *Bris* 00–12; rtd 12; PtO *Ox* from 13. *Winter's Tale, 18 Stainswick Lane, Shrivenham, Swindon SN6 8DX* T: (01793) 783822

CARE, Benjamin Lewis. b 78. Warwick Univ BA 99 Lon Sch of Th MA 09. Wycliffe Hall Ox MTh 17. **d** 17 **p** 18. C Burton St Chad *Lich* from 17; C Stretton w Claymills from 17. *St Mary's Vicarage, Church Road, Stretton, Burton-on-Trent DE13 0HD* T: (01283) 565795 M: 07504-579953 E: curate@stchadstmary.org.uk

CAREW, Richard Clayton. b 72. York Univ BA 94 PGCE 96 St Jo Coll Dur BA 04. Cranmer Hall Dur 02. **d** 05 **p** 06. C Beverley Minster *York* 05–10; Abp's Dom Chapl 10–18; V Dringhouses from 18. *St Edward's Vicarage, Tadcaster Road, Dringhouses, York YO24 1QG* T: (01904) 709111 M: 07725-239072 E: dringhousesvicar@hotmail.com

CAREY, Alan Lawrence. b 29. K Coll Lon AKC 53. **d** 54 **p** 55. C Radford *Cov* 54–57; C Burnham *Ox* 57–65; C-in-c Cippenham CD 65–77; rtd 94. *12 Ormsby Street, Reading RG1 7YR* T: 0118-961 2309

CAREY, Charles John. b 29. K Coll Lon BD 53 AKC 53. St Aug Coll Cant 71. **d** 72 **p** 73. C Spring Park *Cant* 72–74; C Ifield *Chich* 74–78; C Burgess Hill St Jo 78–80; Chapl Rush Green Hosp Romford 80–94; Chapl Oldchurch Hosp Romford 80–94; rtd 94. *Address withheld by request*

CAREY, Christopher Lawrence John. b 38. St Andr Univ BSc 61 Lon Univ BD 64. Clifton Th Coll 61. **d** 64 **p** 65. C Battersea Park St Sav *S'wark* 64–67; P-in-c Ukia Kenya 68–71; Warden Trin Coll Nairobi 72–76; CMS Rep Kenya 76–79; Overseas Regional Sec for E and Cen Africa CMS 79–98; NSM Chislehurst Ch Ch *Roch* 79–98; R Stickney Gp *Linc* 99–04; RD Bolingbroke 02–03; rtd 04; PtO *Mon* from 04. *83 Wentwood View, Caldicot NP26 4QH* T: (01291) 425010 E: crcandkili@tiscali.co.uk

CAREY, Donald Leslie. b 50. ACII 78. CBDTI 01. **d** 04 **p** 05. OLM Ashton-on-Ribble St Mich w Preston St Mark *Blackb* 04–06; OLM W Preston 06–07; NSM 07–08; P-in-c Fairhaven 08–11; V 11–15; rtd 15; PtO *Blackb* from 15. *31 Roman Way, Kirkham, Preston PR4 2YG* E: frdonaldcarey@gmail.com

CAREY, Mark Jonathan. b 65. St Jo Coll Nottm BTh 94. **d** 94 **p** 95. C S Ossett *Wakef* 94–97; C Chapeltown *Sheff* 97–99; V Grenoside 99–07; P-in-c Low Harrogate St Mary *Ripon* 07–13; Pioneer Min 13–14; *Leeds* 14–17; P-in-c Bessingby York 17–18; P-in-c Bridlington Quay Ch Ch 17–18; V Bridlington Ch Ch w Bessingby and Ulrome from 18. *Christ Church Vicarage, 21 Kingston Road, Bridlington YO15 3NF* E: mpjcarey@aol.com or mcarey@christchurchbrid.co.uk

CAREY, Philip John. d 15 **p** 16. NSM Rhosllanerchrugog and Penycae *St As* 15–16; NSM Offa Mission Area 17–18; NSM Valle Crucis Miss Area from 18. *146 Stockwell Grove, Wrexham LL13 7HJ* T: (01978) 312604 E: carey711@btinternet.com

CAREY, Mrs Wendy Marion. b 45. St Jo Coll Nottm BA 66 Lon Inst of Educn CertEd 67. WMMTC 90. **d** 93 **p** 94. NSM Milton Keynes *Ox* 93–96; Sub Chapl HM Pris Woodhill 93–96; Chapl HM Pris Bullingdon 96–00; Ecum Tr Officer HM Pris Service Chapl 00–06; rtd 06; PtO *Ox* from 00. *46 Parklands, Great Linford, Milton Keynes MK14 5DZ* T: (01908) 605997

✠**CAREY OF CLIFTON, The Rt Revd and Rt Hon Lord (George Leonard).** b 35. Lon Univ BD 62 MTh 65 PhD 71 Dur Univ Hon DD 93 Open Univ Hon DD 95 FRSA 91 FKC 93. ALCD 61. **d** 62 **p** 63 **c** 87. C Islington St Mary *Lon* 62–66; Lect Oak Hill Th Coll 66–70; Lect St Jo Coll Nottm 70–75; V Dur St Nic 75–82; Chapl HM Rem Cen Low Newton 77–81; Prin Trin Coll Bris 82–87; Hon Can Bris Cathl 84–87; Bp B & W 87–91; Abp Cant 91–02; rtd 02. *16 Badsworth Gardens, Newbury RG14 6PH* E: carey.george01@gmail.com

CAREY-SLATER, Paul John. b 73. St Jo Coll Nottm 10. **d** 12 **p** 13. C Skirbeck H Trin *Linc* 12–17; Min Grange Park LEP *Pet* from 17. *10 Foxglove Close, Grange Park, Northampton NN4 5DD* T: (01604) 709302 M: 07863-164134 E: paul.slaterclan@sky.com

CARGILL, Christine Elizabeth. b 68. Chas Sturt Univ NSW BA(Ed) 91 New England Univ NSW MLitt 99 Sydney Univ MA 03. NTMTC 07. **d** 10 **p** 11. C Kilburn St Mary w All So and W Hampstead St Jas *Lon* 10–13; V Brondesbury St Anne w Kilburn H Trin from 13. *125 Salusbury Road, London NW6 6RG* T: (020) 7624 5306 M: 07906-067569 E: motherchristinenw6@gmail.co.uk

CARGILL THOMPSON, Edmund Alwyn James. b 72. St Jo Coll Ox BA 94. Cranmer Hall Dur 98. **d** 00 **p** 01. C St Jo on Bethnal Green *Lon* 00–03; V Barkingside H Trin *Chelmsf* 03–13; V Pimlico St Pet w Westmr Ch Ch *Lon* 13–14; V Northolt Park St Barn from 14. *The Vicarage, Raglan Way, Northolt UB5 4SX* T: (020) 8422 3775 M: 07908-949166

CARHART, John Richards. b 29. Bris Univ BA 50 Salford Univ MSc 77 Liv Univ MTh 99 FRSA. St Deiniol's Hawarden 63. **d** 65 **p** 66. C Ches St Oswald w Lt St Jo 65–72; Lect Ches Coll of HE 63–72; Prin Lect from 72; Dean Academic Studies 88–94; C Ches 72; Lect Ches 73–85; Hon C Ches St Mary 85–00; rtd 00; PtO *Ches* from 00. *29 Abbot's Grange, Chester CH2 1AJ* T: (01244) 380923 E: jcarhart@nepc.co.uk

CARLILL, Adam Jonathan. b 66. Keble Coll Ox BA 88. Linc Th Coll 88. **d** 90 **p** 91. C Romford St Edw *Chelmsf* 90–94; C Uckfield *Chich* 94–98; V Tilehurst St Geo *Ox* 98–12; P-in-c Tilehurst St Mary 02–12; V Tilehurst St Geo and St Mary from 12. *St George's Vicarage, 98 Grovelands Road, Reading RG3 2PD* T: 0118-958 8354 E: adamcarlill@me.com

CARLILL, Richard Edward. b 38. Westcott Ho Cam 77. **d** 79 **p** 80. C Prittlewell *Chelmsf* 79–83; TV Saffron Walden w Wendens Ambo and Littlebury 83–89; V Langtoft w Foxholes, Butterwick, Cottam etc *York* 89–94; V Gt and Lt Driffield 94–03; RD Harthill 99–02; rtd 03; PtO *Newc* from 03. *31 Riverdene, Tweedmouth, Berwick-upon-Tweed TD15 2JH* T: (01289) 303701

CARLIN, William Patrick Bruce. b 53. St Steph Ho Ox 75. **d** 78 **p** 79. C Penistone *Wakef* 78–81; C Barnsley St Mary 81–83; V Stockton St Chad *Dur* 83–93; V Hedworth 93–01; TR Kippax w Allerton Bywater *Ripon* 01–11; V Bury, Roch Valley *Man* 11–13; rtd 13; PtO *Leeds* from 17. *44 Frank Lane, Dewsbury WF12 0JJ* T: (01924) 511066 E: brucecarlin@cooptel.net

CARLISLE, Matthew David. b 74. Man Univ BA 96. Westcott Ho Cam 99. **d** 02 **p** 03. C E Crompton *Man* 02–06; TV Heywood 06–11; V Heywood St Jo and St Luke 11–15; V Gatley *Ches* from 15. *St James's Vicarage, 14 Elm Road, Gatley SK8 4LY* M: 07870-760746 E: matthewcarlisle@aol.com

CARLISLE, Archdeacon of. See TOWNEND, The Ven Lee Stuart

CARLISLE, Bishop of. See NEWCOME, The Rt Revd James William Scobie

CARLISLE, Dean of. See BOYLING, The Very Revd Mark Christopher

CARLSON, Blair Truett. b 52. Wheaton Coll Illinois BA 74. Cranmer Hall Dur 00. **d** 02 **p** 03. C Hailsham *Chich* 02–05; USA from 05. *4619 Arden Avenue, Edina MN 55424, USA* T: (001) (952) 924 9062 E: btcarlson@gmail.com

CARLSON, Joshua Alan. b 79. St Jo Coll Cur BA 18. Cranmer Hall Dur 16. **d** 18 **p** 19. C Heswall *Ches* from 18. *5 St Peter's Close, Wirral CH60 0DU* M: 07736-370806 E: josh.carlson@mac.com or josh@heswallparish.co.uk

CARLSSON, Canon Susanne Fredrika. b 71. BA 96 MA 96. **d** 97 **p** 98. Sweden 98–99; C Whitstable *Cant* 99–01; PtO *Roch* from 08; Hon Can Roch Cathl from 15. *65 Maidstone Road, Chatham ME4 6DP* M: 07795-167603 E: susanne.carlsson@rochester.anglican.org

CARLTON, Preb Roger John. b 51. **d** 80 **p** 81. NSM Downend *Bris* 80–83; NSM Heavitree w Ex St Paul 83–87; Chapl Ex Sch and St Marg Sch 83–87; TV Bickleigh (Plymouth) *Ex* 87–91; TR 91–93; TR Bickleigh and Shaugh Prior 94–10; RD Ivybridge 93–98; V Paignton St Jo from 10; RD Torbay from 16; Preb Ex Cathl from 06. *The Vicarage, Palace Place, Paignton TQ3 3AQ* T: (01803) 551866 E: roger.carlton@btinternet.com

CARLYON, Miss Catherine Rachel. b 67. RN 89. Ripon Coll Cuddesdon BTh 06. **d** 02 **p** 03. C Launceston *Truro* 02–06; C Crediton, Shobrooke and Sandford etc *Ex* 06–14; Chapl w Deaf People 06–14; Chapl among Deaf and Deafblind People Lon from 14; PtO *Chelmsf* from 16; *S'wark* from 16. *2 Anatola Road, London N19 5HN* T: (020) 7272 1292 M: 07918-567435 E: catherine.carlyon@btinternet.com or catherine.carlyon@london.anglican.org

CARMAN, Philip Gordon. b 80. York St Jo Coll BA 01 St Jo Coll Dur BA 07. Cranmer Hall Dur 04. **d** 07 **p** 08. C Acomb St Steph and St Aid *York* 07–10; C Huntington 10–16; V Starbeck *Leeds* from 16. *51 Bogs Lane, Harrogate HG1 4EB* M: 07954-895731 E: philcarman3@gmail.com

CARMARTHEN, Archdeacon of. See DAVIES, The Ven Dorrien Paul

CARMICHAEL (née Edwards), Mrs Anthea Mirenda. b 78. N Lon Univ BSc 01. St Mellitus Coll 16. **d** 19. C Kensal Rise St Mark *Lon* from 19. *82 Herbert Gardens, London NW10 3BU* T: (020) 8960 3929 E: anthea@stmkr.org

CARMICHAEL, Elizabeth Dorothea Harriet. b 46. LMH Ox MA 73 BM 73 BCh 73 Worc Coll Ox BA 83 Ox Univ DPhil 91. **d** 91 **p** 92. S Africa 91–96; Chapl and Tutor St Jo Coll Ox 96–11; rtd 11; Research Fell from 11; LtO *Ox* 15–18. *St John's College, Oxford OX1 3JP* T: (01865) 277351 F: 277435 E: liz.carmichael@sjc.ox.ac.uk

CARMICHAEL-DAVIS, Ms Caitlin Louise. b 88. Ball Coll Ox BA 11 Sheff Hallam Univ PGCE 12. Ripon Coll Cuddesdon BA 16 MSt 17. **d** 17 **p** 18. C Ripon Cathl *Leeds* from 17. *24 High St Agnesgate, Ripon HG4 1QR* E: reverendcaitlin@riponcathedral.org.uk

CARMODY, Canon Dermot Patrick Roy. b 41. CITC 77. **d** 77 **p** 78. C Dublin Zion Ch *D & G* 77–79; I Dunganstown w Redcross 79–84; TV Dublin Ch Ch Cathl Gp 84–93; Can Ch Ch Cathl Dublin 84–92; Preb Ch Ch Cathl Dublin 92–93; I Mullingar, Portnashangan, Moyliscar, Kilbixy etc *M & K* 93–08; Dir of Ords (Meath) 97–08; Can Meath 98–08; Can Kildare Cathl 98–08; Treas Kildare Cathl 00–08; P-in-c Rathmolyon w Castlerickard, Rathcore and Agher 00–07; rtd 08. *32 The Mageough, Cowper Road, Rathmines, Dublin 6, DO6 W6V4, Republic of Ireland* M: (00353) 86-829 0183 E: patkcarmody@gmail.com

CARMYLLIE, Mrs Kathryn Ruth. b 61. Cov Poly BA 84 CQSW 84 Univ Coll Ches BTh 04. NOC 01. **d** 04 **p** 05. C Leigh St Mary *Man* 04–07; TV Worsley 07–12; TR Atherton and Hindsford w Howe Bridge 12–14; PtO from 15; *Blackb* from 15; Chapl Pennine Acute Hosps NHS Trust from 17. *The Vicarage, 40 The Sands, Whalley, Clitheroe BB7 9TL* T: (01254) 824679 E: k.carmyllie@btinternet.com

CARMYLLIE, Robert Jonathan. b 63. Cov Poly BSc 85. Cranmer Hall Dur 85. **d** 88 **p** 89. C Horwich *Man* 88–92; P-in-c Edgeside 92–99; P-in-c Astley 99–06; TR Astley, Tyldesley and Mosley Common 06–15; AD Leigh 12–15; V W Pendleside *Blackb* from 15; AD Whalley from 18. *The*

Vicarage, 40 The Sands, Whalley, Clitheroe BB7 9TL T: (01254) 824679 E: j.carmyllie@btinternet.com

CARNALL, Mrs Nicola Jane. b 66. St Jo Coll Nottm 99. **d** 01 **p** 02. C Edwinstowe *S'well* 01–05; P-in-c Sowerby *York* 05–12; V 12–19; P-in-c Sessay 05–12; R 12–19; V Thirkleby w Kilburn and Bagby 12–19; V Mansfield Woodhouse *S'well* from 19. *The Vicarage, 7 Butt Lane, Mansfield Woodhouse, Mansfield NG19 9JS* E: revnjcarnall@gmail.com

CARNEGIE, Ms Rachel Clare. b 62. New Hall Cam BA 84 Sussex Univ MA 94. SEITE 01. **d** 04 **p** 05. NSM Richmond St Mary w St Matthias and St Jo *S'wark* 04–09; Abp's Sec for Internat Development *Cant* 09–13; Co-Dir Angl Alliance from 13; PtO *Ox* from 17. *Anglican Communion Office, 16 Tavistock Crescent, London W11 1AP* T: (020) 7313 3922 E: rachel.carnegie@aco.org

CARNELLEY, The Ven Desmond. b 29. Open Univ BA 77 Leeds Univ CertEd. Ripon Hall Ox 59. **d** 60 **p** 61. C Aston cum Aughton *Sheff* 60–63; C-in-c Ecclesfield St Paul CD 63–67; V Balby w Hexthorpe 67–73; P-in-c Mosborough 73–74; V 74–85; RD Attercliffe 79–84; Adn Doncaster 85–94; Dioc Dir of Educn 91–94; rtd 94; PtO *Sheff* from 94; *Derby* from 94. *11 Fairways, Wickersley, Rotherham S66 1AE* T: (01709) 544927

CARNELLEY, Ms Elizabeth Amy. b 64. St Aid Coll Dur BA 85 Selw Coll Cam MPhil 87. Ripon Coll Cuddesdon 88. **d** 90 **p** 94. Par Dn Sharrow St Andr *Sheff* 90–93; Par Dn Is of Dogs Ch Ch and St Jo w St Luke *Lon* 93–94; C 94–95; P-in-c Woolfold *Man* 95–99; TV Man Whitworth 99–02; Chapl Man Univ and Man Metrop Univ 99–02; Policy Officer Chs' Regional Commn for Yorks and the Humber 02–06; Chief Exec 06–11; Near Neighbours Progr Dir CUF from 11; PtO *S'well* from 17. T: (01777) 248869 M: 07812-984818 E: elizabeth.carnelley@cuf.org.uk

CARNEY, David Anthony. b 42. Salford Univ BSc 77. Linc Th Coll 77. **d** 79 **p** 80. C Wythenshawe St Martin *Man* 79–81; CF 81–84; Chapl Canadian Armed Forces Canada 84–87; R Burford H Trin Ontario 87–91; P-in-c Whaplode *Linc* 91–97; V 97–02; P-in-c Holbeach Fen 91–97; V 97–02; R Colsterworth Gp 02–05; P-in-c Kirton in Holland 05–09; rtd 09; PtO *Linc* from 17. *6 South Road, Bourne PE10 9JD* T: (01778) 426061

CARNEY, Mrs Mary Patricia. b 42. Univ of Wales (Ban) BSc 62. Wycliffe Hall Ox. **d** 90 **p** 94. Par Dn Carterton *Ox* 90–93; Par Dn Harwell w Chilton 93–94; C 94–01; P-in-c Ray Valley 01–07; rtd 07; PtO *Ox* from 07. *104 Pensclose, Witney OX28 2EQ* T: (01993) 358139

CARNEY, The Ven Richard Wayne. b 52. Lon Teachers' Coll Ontario TCert 73 Toronto Univ BA 79. Trin Coll Toronto MDiv 84. **d** 84 **p** 85. C Scarborough St Andr Canada 84–86; I Roche's Pt 86–91; P Asst Newmarket St Paul 91–93; Assoc P 93–95; I Clonfert Gp *L & K* 95–03; I Birr w Lorrha, Dorrha and Lockeen from 03; Adn Killaloe, Kilfenora, Clonfert etc from 02; Preb Taney St Patr Cathl Dublin from 12. *The Rectory, Birr, Co Offaly, Republic of Ireland* T: (00353) (57) 912 0021 M: 87-786 5234 E: mapleire@eircom.net *or* archdeacon@killaloe.anglican.org

CAROLAN (née STUART-BLACK), Mrs Veronica. b 52. St Jo Coll Dur BA 75. Cranmer Hall Dur. **dss** 82 **d** 87 **p** 08. Borehamwood *St Alb* 82–84; Watford Ch Ch 84–85; Stevenage St Mary Shephall 85–86; Stevenage St Mary Shephall w Aston 86–87; Par Dn 87–88; Hon C 08–14; PtO 98–08; V Lower Esk *York* 14–19. *2 Marlborough Avenue, Whitby YO21 3JE*

CAROLIN CLARE, Sister. See CLAPPERTON, Carolin Beryl

CARPENTER, Canon Bruce Leonard Henry. b 32. Lon Univ BA 54. St Chad's Coll Dur. **d** 59 **p** 60. C Portsea N End St Mark *Portsm* 59–63; C Fareham SS Pet and Paul 63–67; V Locks Heath 67–74; TR Fareham H Trin 74–84; RD Alverstoke 71–76; Hon Can Portsm Cathl 79–84; V Richmond St Mary w St Matthias and St Jo *S'wark* 84–91; Chapl Ch Ch High Sch Ashford 91–93; P-in-c S Ashford Ch Ch *Cant* 94–97; rtd 97; Chapl Huggens Coll Northfleet 97–02; PtO *Portsm* from 02; Hon Chapl MU from 03. *48 Summerson Lodge, 94 Alverstone Road, Southsea PO4 8GS* T: (023) 9307 6722 E: angelbru@btinternet.com

CARPENTER, David James. b 52. Trin Coll Carmarthen CertEd 74. St Steph Ho Ox 74. **d** 76 **p** 77. C Newport St Julian *Mon* 76–77; C Pontypool 77–79; C Ebbw Vale 79–81; TV 81–85; V Pontnewynydd 85–88; V Bedwellty 88–00; Chapl Aberbargoed Hosp 88–99; V Staincliffe and Carlinghow *Wakef* 00–05; Chapl Yorks Ambulance Service 05–11; PtO *Wakef* 10–11; P-in-c Birkby and Woodhouse 11–14; *Leeds* 14–15; V 15–19; rtd 19; Hon C Halifax w Siddal *Leeds* from 19. *48A Stratton Road, Brighouse HD6 3TA* E: carpenterdj@aol.com

CARPENTER, Canon Derek George Edwin. b 40. K Coll Lon BD 62 AKC 62. **d** 63 **p** 64. C Friern Barnet All SS *Lon* 63–66; C Chingford SS Pet and Paul *Chelmsf* 66–70; V Dartford

St Alb *Roch* 70–79; R Crayford 79–90; RD Erith 82–90; R Beckenham St Geo 90–02; Hon Can Roch Cathl 97–02; rtd 02; PtO *Roch* from 04. *39 Chatfield Way, East Malling, West Malling ME19 6QD* T: (01732) 874420

CARPENTER, Donald Arthur. b 35. Roch Th Coll 65. **d** 67 **p** 68. C Thornton Heath St Jude *Cant* 67–73; V Earby *Bradf* 73–78; V Skipton Ch Ch 78–88; V Baildon 88–91; P-in-c Perivale *Lon* 91–96; rtd 96; PtO *Lon* 96–05. *1 Bootham Green, Newborough Street, York YO30 7EJ* T: (01904) 280623 M: 07516-304390 E: donarth610@gmail.com

CARPENTER, Giles Michael Gerard. b 67. Trin Coll Bris BA 10. **d** 10 **p** 11. C Shottermill *Guildf* 10–14; V Eastbourne St Jo *Chich* from 14. *9 Buxton Road, Eastbourne BN20 7LL* T: (01323) 721105 M: 07710-498906 E: giles.rev@gmail.com

CARPENTER, Canon Judith Margaret. b 47. Bris Univ BA 68 CertEd 69. Trin Coll Bris BA 95. **d** 95 **p** 96. C Warmley, Syston and Bitton *Bris* 95–99; V Withywood 99–12; Hon Can Bris Cathl 06–12; rtd 12; PtO *Glouc* from 16. *Dawes Orchard, Latchen, Longhope GL17 0QB*

CARPENTER, Leonard Richard. b 32. EMMTC 82. **d** 85 **p** 86. NSM Leic H Apostles 85–90; P-in-c Barlestone 90–98; rtd 98; PtO *Leic* from 98; *Derby* from 98. *10 Main Street, Albert Village, Swadlincote DE11 8EW* T: (01283) 229335

CARPENTER, Thomas David Leonard. b 88. Mansf Coll Ox BA 09 MA 15 Keble Coll Ox MSt 10 DPhil 16. Coll of Resurr Mirfield 14. **d** 16 **p** 17. C Goldthorpe w Hickleton *Sheff* 16–18; C Sheff St Cath Richmond Road 18–19; V Southport H Trin *Liv* from 19; P-in-c Southport All SS from 19. *Holy Trinity Vicarage, 24 Roe Lane, Southport PR9 9DX* M: 07140-395154 E: thomasdcarpenter@gmail.com

CARR, Alan Cobban. b 49. Nottm Univ BTh 88. Linc Th Coll 85. **d** 88 **p** 89. C Rustington *Chich* 88–92; V Highbrook and W Hoathly 92–10; C St Giles-in-the-Fields *Lon* 10–15; R from 15. *15A Gower Street, London WC1E 6HW* T: (020) 7274 0407 E: alancarr17@gmail.com

CARR, Canon Amanda Helen. b 70. Univ of Wales (Cardiff) BA 91 Kent Univ MA 97. SEITE 01. **d** 04 **p** 05. C Meopham w Nurstead *Roch* 04–07; P-in-c Lamberhurst and Matfield 07–09; V 09–15; RD Paddock Wood 12–13; V Sevenoaks Weald from 15; Bp's Adv for Ord Women's Min from 18; Hon Can Roch Cathl from 18. *St George's Vicarage, Church Road, Weald, Sevenoaks TN14 6LT* T: (01732) 463291 M: 07866-675015 E: mandy@carrfamilyonline.co.uk

CARR, David Scott. b 72. Derby Univ BA 97 MCIM 05. NEOC 06. **d** 09 **p** 10. NSM Horden *Dur* 09–14. *Glen View, 26 Station Avenue, Brandon, Durham DH7 8QQ* T: 0191-378 0126 M: 07990-775054 E: david.s.carr@btinternet.com

CARR, Derrick Charles. b 43. MCIPD. SAOMC 99. **d** 02 **p** 03. NSM Amersham *Ox* 02–13; AD 09–12; PtO from 13. *52 Warren Wood Drive, High Wycombe HP11 1EA* T/F: (01494) 452389 M: 07768-507391 E: carrd@btopenworld.com

CARR, Mrs Elaine Susan. b 46. LTCL 82. SAOMC 99. **d** 02 **p** 03. NSM High Wycombe *Ox* 02–09; Bp's NSM Officer (Bucks) from 09. *52 Warren Wood Drive, High Wycombe HP11 1EA* T/F: (01494) 452389 M: 07500-140935 E: revcarr@btinternet.com

CARR, Miss Eveline. b 45. Cranmer Hall Dur 91. **d** 93 **p** 95. NSM Eighton Banks *Dur* 93–98; NSM Gateshead 98–12; rtd 12; PtO *Dur* from 12. *10 Lanchester Avenue, Gateshead NE9 7AJ* T: 0191-482 1157 E: eveline.c@blueyonder.co.uk

CARR, Jeremy Barnardo Quintin. b 75. Wycliffe Hall Ox 13. **d** 15 **p** 16. C St Margaret's-on-Thames *Lon* 15–18. *The Spinney, The Green, Cuddington, Aylesbury HP18 0AN*

CARR, Canon John Bernard. b 53. Lindisfarne Regional Tr Partnership 11. **d** 13 **p** 14. NSM Jesmond H Trin *Newc* 13–17; NSM Cornhill w Carham from 17; NSM Branxton from 17; Hon Can Newc Cathl from 18. *The Old School House, Branxton, Cornhill-on-Tweed TD12 4SW* E: jbcarr@btinternet.com

CARR, Canon John Henry Percy. b 52. NTMTC 95. **d** 98 **p** 99. C Hackney Wick St Mary of Eton w St Aug *Lon* 98–01; R Walesby *Linc* 01–17; Can and Preb Linc Cathl 15–17; rtd 17; PtO *Nor* from 17. *19 Wades Way, Trunch, North Walsham NR28 0PW* E: carr.ide@btinternet.com

CARR, John Robert. b 40. ACII 62. Oak Hill Th Coll 63. **d** 66 **p** 67. C Tonbridge St Steph *Roch* 66–70; C Cheadle Hulme St Andr *Ches* 70–79; R Widford *Chelmsf* 79–87; TV Becontree W 87–93; V Basildon St Andr w H Cross 93–05; rtd 05; PtO *Chelmsf* from 06. *3 Windsor Way, Rayleigh SS6 8PE* T: (01268) 741065 E: johnandwendycarr3@hotmail.com

CARR, Mandy. See CARR, Amanda Helen

CARR, Paul Anthony. b 62. Univ of Wales MA 13. Aston Tr Scheme 93 Oak Hill Th Coll 95. **d** 97 **p** 98. C Handforth *Ches* 97–01; V Chadwell Heath *Chelmsf* 01–08; TR Billericay and Lt Burstead from 08. *The Rectory, 40*

Laindon Road, Billericay CM12 9LD T: (01277) 658055
E: revpaulcarr@btinternet.com

CARR, Mrs Wendy Dawn. b 70. Ridley Hall Cam 15.
d 17 **p** 18. C Tonbridge SS Pet and Paul *Roch* from 17. *14
Salisbury Road, Tonbridge TN10 4PB* M: 07971-048416
E: wdcarr6@gmail.com

CARRINGTON, Mrs Elizabeth Ashby. b 46. Open Univ BA 02.
EMMTC 86. **d** 90 **p** 94. NSM Nottingham St Ann w Em *S'well*
90–91; C Basford w Hyson Green 92–97; Lect Nottingham
St Mary and St Cath 97–00; LtO W Bingham Deanery 00; PtO
00–01; Chapl Woodford Ho Sch New Zealand 01–10; NSM
Napier Cathl 03–06; rtd 11. T: 0115-914 2504 M: 07900-
417275 E: ea.carrington@yahoo.co.nz

CARRINGTON, Margaret Elizabeth. b 44. **d** 09.
NSM York St Luke 09–19; PtO from 19. *202
Boroughbridge Road, York YO26 6BD* T: (01904) 798916
E: carringtone@btinternet.com

CARRINGTON, Philip John. b 48. **d** 85 **p** 86. C W Acklam *York*
85–88; V Middlesbrough St Agnes 88–92; Chapl S Cleveland
Hosp 88–92; Trust Chapl S Tees Hosps NHS Foundn Trust
92–06; V Guernsey St Steph *Win* 06–13; Hd Chapl Services
States of Guernsey Health and Soc Care 07–13; rtd 13;
PtO *Ripon* 13–14; *Leeds* from 14. *Stonecroft, Hackforth
Road, Little Crakehall, Bedale DL8 1HY* T: (01677) 425077
E: philipjcarrington@gmail.com

CARRIVICK, Derek Roy. b 45. Birm Univ BSc 66. Ripon
Hall Ox 71. **d** 74 **p** 75. C Enfield St Jas *Lon* 74–78; C-in-c
Woodgate Valley CD *Birm* 78–83; TR Chelmsley Wood
83–92; Dioc Ecum Officer 86–96; R Baxterley w Hurley
and Wood End and Merevale etc 92–99; AD Polesworth
96–99; P-in-c Helland *Truro* 99–04; P-in-c Blisland w
St Breward 99–04; Bp's Dom Chapl 04–09; rtd 09; P-in-c
Devoran *Truro* 04–11; Hon C 11–12; Hon C Chacewater w
St Day and Carharrack 11–12; Hon C Feock 11–12; Hon C
St Stythians w Perranarworthal and Gwennap 11–12; PtO
from 15. *30 Par Green, Par PL24 2AF* T: (01726) 813566
E: pjc87@tutor.open.ac.uk *or* derek.carrivick@gmail.com

CARROLL, Anthony Joseph. b 65. **d** 16. NSM Folkestone
St Mary, St Eanswythe and St Sav *Cant* 16–19; Dean Past
Studies Coll of the Resurr Mirfield from 19. *The College of the
Resurrection, Stocks Bank Road, Mirfield WF14 0BW* T: (01924)
490441

CARROLL, John Hugh. b 31. Bris Univ BA 57. Tyndale Hall
Bris 54. **d** 58 **p** 59. C Slough *Ox* 58–61; V S Lambeth St Steph
S'wark 61–72; V Norwood St Luke 72–81; P-in-c Purley
Ch Ch 81–85; V 85–93; rtd 93; PtO *S'wark* 93–13; *Guildf*
12–17. *11 Manormead, Tilford Road, Hindhead GU26 6RA*
E: jonthelc@gmail.com

CARROLL, Ruth Ellen. b 68. **d** 14 **p** 15. C Boston *Linc* 14–15;
C Alford w Rigsby 15–18; C Bilsby w Farlesthorpe 15–18; C
Hannah cum Hagnaby w Markby 15–18; C Saleby w Beesby
and Maltby 15–18; C Well 15–18; C Willoughby 15–18; V
Stevenage H Trin *St Alb* from 18. *Holy Trinity Vicarage, 18
Letchmore Road, Stevenage SG1 3JD* T: (01438) 353229
E: vicar@holytrinity-stevenage.org.uk

CARROLL WALLIS, Ms Joy Ann. b 59. SS Mark & Jo Univ Coll
Plymouth BEd 82. Cranmer Hall Dur 85. **d** 88 **p** 94. Par Dn
Hatcham St Jas *S'wark* 88–93; Par Dn Streatham Immanuel
and St Andr 93–94; C 94–97; USA from 97. *1305 Fairmont
Street NW, Washington DC 20009, USA* T: (001) (202) 483
0119 E: joycwallis@aol.com

CARRUTHERS, John Alexander. b 69. Natal Univ BA 91
Bond Univ Aus MBA 06. Ripon Coll Cuddesdon 15.
d 17 **p** 18. C Newington St Paul *S'wark* from 17. *89
Ambergate Street, London SE17 3RZ* M: 07814-948325
E: john.carruthers1@gmail.com

CARSON, Claire. b 76. St Martin's Coll Lanc BA 98 Birm Univ
MA 99. Qu Coll Birm 00. **d** 03 **p** 04. C Stretly *Lich* 03–04; C
Stafford 04–05; C Lich St Mich w St Mary and Wall 05–07;
Chapl R Free Hampstead NHS Trust 07–10; Chapl Imp Coll
Healthcare NHS Trust 10–11; Chapl St Geo Healthcare NHS
Trust Lon 11–18; Hd Spiritual Care 15–18; Hd Spiritual Care
R Free London NHS Foundn Trust from 18. *Royal Free London
NHS Foundation Trust, Royal Free Hospital, Pond Street, London
NW3 2QG* T: (020) 7830 2742 E: clairecarson@nhs.net

CARSON, Canon James Irvine. b 59. TCD BA MTh. **d** 84
p 85. C Willowfield *D & D* 84–87; C Lecale Gp 87–89;
I Devenish w Boho *Clogh* 89–95; Dioc Youth Adv 91–95;
Dioc Communications Officer 93–95; I Belfast Upper
Malone (Epiphany) *Conn* 95–99; I Lisburn St Paul 99–16;
P-in-c Belfast St Steph w St Luke from 16; Preb Conn Cathl
from 11. *92 Lansdowne Road, Belfast BT15 4AB* T: (028) 9077
3964 E: jamescarson203@btinternet.com

CARSON, Tom Patrick. b 83. Regent's Park Coll Ox MA 09
Heythrop Coll Lon MA 10 K Coll Lon PGCE 06. Ripon
Coll Cuddesdon MTh 12. **d** 12 **p** 13. C Mortlake w E Sheen

S'wark 12–15; Chapl Ex Sch from 15; PtO *Truro* from 15.
Exeter School, Victoria Park Road, Exeter EX2 4NS T: (01392)
258712 M: 07974-080946 E: tompcarson@gmail.com

CARSON-FEATHAM, Canon Lawrence William. b 53. AKC.
d 78 **p** 79. SSM from 77; C Walton St Mary *Liv* 78–82; Chapl
Bolton Colls of H&FE 82–87; C Bolton St Pet *Man* 82–87;
TV Oldham 87–92; V Ashton St Jas 92–95; PtO *Liv* 95–97; C
Leeds Belle Is St Jo and St Barn *Ripon* 97–01; TV Accrington
Ch the King *Blackb* 01–13; V Accrington St Andr, St Mary
and St Pet 13–16; R Accrington St Andr, St Mary and St Pet
and Church Kirk 16–19; Hon Can Blackb Cathl 18–19; rtd
19. *Address temp unknown* E: carsonfeatham@btinternet.com

CARTER, Ashley Stuart Bourn. b 79. Lanc Univ BA 00.
Oak Hill Th Coll MTheol 14. **d** 14 **p** 15. C Mayfair Ch
Ch *Lon* 14–18; R Kirk Ella and Willerby *York* from 18. *The
Rectory, 2 School Lane, Kirk Ella, Hull HU10 7NR* T: (01482)
653040 M: 07908-779325 E: revdashcarter@gmail.com

CARTER, Barry Graham. b 54. K Coll Lon BD 76 AKC 76.
St Steph Ho Ox 76. **d** 77 **p** 78. C Evesham *Worc* 77–81; C
Amblecote 81–84; TV Ovingdean w Rottingdean and
Woodingdean *Chich* 84–85; V Woodingdean 85–95; V
Lancing St Mich 95–16; rtd 16; PtO *Chich* from 16. *Flat 2, 15
Parkhurst Road, Bexhill-on-Sea TN40 1DE* T: (01424) 211395
E: fatherbarrycarter@gmail.com

CARTER, Benjamin Huw. b 77. Ex Univ BA 99 St Cath
Coll Cam MPhil 00 Middx Univ PhD 04. Cranmer Hall
Dur 08. **d** 10 **p** 11. C Monkseaton St Mary *Newc* 10–14; V
Haydon Bridge and Beltingham w Henshaw from 14. *The
Vicarage, Haydon Bridge, Hexham NE47 6LL* T: (01434)
684307 M: 07985-412542 E: benj_carter@yahoo.co.uk

CARTER, Carl. b 56. LCTP 11. **d** 14 **p** 15. NSM Millom
Carl from 14. *13 Pepper Hall Walk, Haverigg, Millom
LA18 4HT* T: (01229) 774427 M: 07738-618350

CARTER, Celia. b 38. Glouc Sch of Min 86. **d** 89 **p** 94. NSM
Avening w Cherington *Glouc* 89–13; P-in-c 95–13; Asst
Chapl Severn NHS Trust 89–05; Asst Chapl Glos Primary
Care Trust 05–13; rtd 13; PtO *Glouc* from 16. *Avening Park,
West End, Avening, Tetbury GL8 8NE* T: (01453) 836390
E: rev.celiacarter@gmail.com

CARTER (née SMITH), Mrs Christine Lydia. b 43. SRN 64
SCM 67. Trin Coll Bris 89. **d** 91 **p** 94. Par Dn Penkridge *Lich*
91–94; C 94–96; PtO *Blackb* 96–97; NSM Blackb Sav 97–01;
Chapl Asst St Helens and Knowsley Hosps NHS Trust 97–01;
NSM Elmdon St Nic *Birm* 01–11; PtO *Lich* from 12. *Elmdon,
4 Goods Station Lane, Penkridge, Stafford ST19 5AU* T: (01785)
710809 E: chris@tworevs.co.uk

CARTER, Christopher Franklin. b 37. Wadh Coll Ox BA 59
MA 63. Wycliffe Hall Ox 60. **d** 64 **p** 65. C Clifton St Jas *Sheff*
64–67; C Handsworth 67–70; C Clun w Chapel Lawn *Heref*
70–74; LtO 74–76; P-in-c Ironbridge 76–78; C Coalbrookdale,
Iron-Bridge and Lt Wenlock 78–80; V Llansilin w
Llangadwaladr and Llangedwyn *St As* 80–05; RD Llanfyllin
88–05; rtd 05; PtO *St As* from 09. *Ysgubor Goch, Cefn Coch,
Llanrhaeadr-ym-Mochnant, Oswestry SY10 0BQ* T: (01691)
860577 M: 07792-858584 E: revkitcarter@gmail.com

CARTER, Christopher Paul. b 43. CCC Cam BA 64.
SAOMC 02. **d** 05 **p** 06. NSM W Buckingham *Ox*
05–13; rtd 13; PtO *Ox* 13–18. *The Mount, Upper Street,
Tingewick, Buckingham MK18 4QN* T/F: (01280) 848291
E: rev.c.carter@btinternet.com *or* r.c.carter@btinternet.com

CARTER, Colin John. b 56. Fitzw Coll Cam BA 77 MB, BChir 80
MA 81 FRCS 86 FRCOphth 89. Trin Coll Bris BA 93. **d** 93
p 94. C Ripley *Derby* 93–97; TV Horsham *Chich* 97–00. *48
Swindon Road, Horsham RH12 2HD* T: (01403) 252146

CARTER, Canon Edward John. b 67. Ex Univ BA 88. Ripon
Coll Cuddesdon BA 96 MA 01. **d** 97 **p** 98. C Thorpe
St Matt *Nor* 97–00; Min Can and Dean's V Windsor 00–04;
P-in-c Didcot St Pet *Ox* 04–12; AD Wallingford 07–12;
Can Th Chelmsf Cathl 12–18; R Nor St Pet Mancroft w
St Jo Maddermarket from 18. *37 Unthank Road, Norwich
NR2 2PB* T: (01603) 610443 E: revedwardcarter@gmail.com
or vicar@stpetermancroft.org.uk

CARTER, Grayson Leigh. b 53. Univ of S California BSc 76 Ch
Ch Ox DPhil 90. Fuller Th Sem California MA 84 Wycliffe
Hall Ox 89. **d** 90 **p** 91. C Bungay H Trin w St Mary *St E* 90–92;
Chapl BNC Ox 92–96; Hon C Ox St Mary V w St Cross and
St Pet 93–96; USA from 96; Assoc Prof Methodist Coll
Fayetteville 96–03; Asst R Fayetteville H Trin 96–03; Assoc
Prof Fuller Th Sem from 03. *1602 Palmcroft Drive SW,
Phoenix AZ 85007-1738, USA* T: (001) (602) 252 5582 *or*
(602) 220 0400 F: 220 0444 E: gcarter10@yahoo.com *or*
gcarter@fuller.edu

CARTER, Hazel June. b 48. Doncaster Coll of Educn CertEd 72.
Carl Dioc Tr Inst 89. **d** 92 **p** 94. C Wreay *Carl* 92–98; C
Dalston and Raughton Head w Gatesgill 92–98; TV Carl H

Trin and St Barn 98–02; TR 02–07; rtd 07; PtO *Carl* from 08. *4 Wandales Lane, Natland, Kendal LA9 7QY* T: (015395) 60429

CARTER, Heather Ruth. b 62. Trin Coll Bris 85. **d** 02 **p** 04. Dn Montevideo Cathl Uruguay 02–04; Chapl among Deaf People 02–04; NSM Dalston w Cumdivock, Raughton Head and Wreay *Carl* 04–10; Chapl to the Deaf and Hard of Hearing 05–10; Chapl N Cumbria Acute Hosps NHS Trust 05–10; V Blackbird Leys *Ox* from 12. *Church House, 1 Cuddesdon Way, Oxford OX4 6JH* T: (01865) 778728 E: revhev2@gmail.com

CARTER, Ian Sutherland. b 51. Trin Coll Ox BA 73 MA 77 DPhil 77 Leeds Univ BA 80 Man Univ MA 05. Coll of Resurr Mirfield 78. **d** 81 **p** 82. C Shildon *Dur* 81–84; C Darlington H Trin 84–87; Chapl Liv Univ 87–93; V Hindley St Pet 93–98; Chapl Oldham NHS Trust 98–02; Chapl Pennine Acute Hosps NHS Trust 02–03; Chapl Salford R NHS Foundn Trust 03–14; P-in-c Hamer *Man* 14–15; P-in-c Healey 14–15; V Hamer and Healey 15–17; rtd 17. *Awel y Mor, 29 Lon Ceredigion, Pwllheli LL53 5PP* T: (01758) 701535 E: ianscarter@aol.com

CARTER, Mrs Jacqueline Ann. b 50. St Mich Coll Llan 01. **d** 03 **p** 04. C Ebbw Vale *Mon* 03–06; TV 06–11; V Rhosllannerchrugog *St As* 11; V Rhosllanerchrugog and Penycae 11–16; rtd 16; PtO *Llan* from 16. *50 Fox Hollows, Brackla, Bridgend CF31 2NG* T: (01656) 668303 E: jackiecarter16@hotmail.com

CARTER, Canon John Howard Gregory. b 55. York Univ BA 76 Leeds Univ CertEd 77 Nottm Univ MA 96. St Jo Coll Nottm LTh 87. **d** 87 **p** 88. C Nailsea H Trin *B & W* 87–91; TV Camberley St Paul *Guildf* 91–97; Chapl Elmhurst Ballet Sch 91–97; Bp's Press Officer *Ripon* 00–14; Dioc Communications Officer 97–14; *Leeds* from 14; Hon Can Ripon Cathl from 10. *7 Blenheim Court, Harrogate HG2 9DT* T: (01423) 530369 F: 08717-333778 M: 07798-652707 E: jhgcarter@aol.com

CARTER, Jonathan James. b 88. Nottm Univ BA 11. St Mellitus Coll BA 19. **d** 19. C Pentonville St Silas w All SS and St Jas *Lon* from 19. *136 Bunning Way, London N7 9UW* T: (020) 3432 5396 E: jon.carter@kxc.org.uk

CARTER, Jonathan Mark. b 77. Imp Coll Lon MSci 99 PhD 04 Cam Univ MPhil 12 Edin Univ PhD 17. **d** 17 **p** 18. C Lowestoft Ch Ch *Nor* from 17. *10 Station Road, Lowestoft NR32 4QF* M: 07771-614836 E: jon@christ-church.info

CARTER, Katherine Elizabeth. b 71. Ripon Coll Cuddesdon 16. **d** 19. C Hoddesdon *St Alb* from 19. *134 Plomer Avenue, Hoddesdon EN11 9FS*

CARTER, Lewis. *See* CARTER, Stephen Lewis

CARTER, Mrs Linda Susan. b 61. STETS 11. **d** 14 **p** 15. C Broadstone *Sarum* 14–17; TV Marden Vale from 17. *The Vicarage, Church Road, Derry Hill, Calne SN11 9NN* E: lscarter@btinternet.com

CARTER, Marian. b 40. Whitelands Coll Lon TCert 61 Lon Univ BD 67 Nottm Univ MPhil 79 Man Univ MA 84 Ex Univ PhD 05. N Bapt Coll 81. **d** 92 **p** 94. Par Dn Kempshott *Win* 92–93; Tutor SWMTC 92–96; Tutor Coll of SS Mark and Jo Plymouth 93–00; NSM Plymstock and Hooe *Ex* 94–98; NSM Widecombe-in-the-Moor, Leusdon, Princetown etc 98–00; Chapl St Eliz Hospice Ipswich 00–05; rtd 05; PtO *St E* from 06. *Shalom, 80 Woodlands, Chelmondiston, Ipswich IP9 1DU* T: (01473) 780259 E: marian.carter@btinternet.com

CARTER, Melissa Jane. b 80. **d** 16 **p** 17. C N Downs *Cant* 16–19; TV Dover Town from 19. *Address temp unknown* M: 07825-910116 E: melissa.j.carter@btinternet.com

CARTER, Canon Michael John. b 32. St Alb Minl Tr Scheme 81. **d** 84 **p** 85. NSM Radlett *St Alb* 84–88; Chapl SW Herts HA 88–94; Chapl Watford Gen Hosp 88–94; LtO *St Alb* 88–99; Chapl Mt Vernon and Watford Hosps NHS Trust 94–99; Bp's Adv for Hosp Chapl *St Alb* 95–99; Hon Can St Alb 96–99; rtd 99; PtO *St Alb* from 99; Hon Chapl Peace Hospice Watford from 99. *4 Field View Rise, Bricket Wood, St Albans AL2 3RT* T: (01923) 279870 E: mail@mjcarter.com

CARTER, Nicholas Adrian. b 47. Ripon Hall Ox 71. **d** 74 **p** 75. C Sowerby *Wakef* 74–79; V Hanging Heaton 79–83; CF 83–86; V Elton All SS *Man* 86–90; C Milton *Win* 90–94; P-in-c Boscombe St Andr 94–00; V 00–09; rtd 09; TV Winchcombe *Glouc* 09–17. *The Warren, Velindre, Brecon LD3 0TE* T: (01497) 842736 E: cdevildodger@aol.com

CARTER, Noel William. b 53. Birm Univ BSc 75 Bris Univ CertEd 76 Nottm Univ BSc 83. Linc Th Coll. **d** 83 **p** 84. C Penrith w Newton Reigny and Plumpton Wall *Carl* 83–86; C Barrow St Matt 86–87; V Netherton 87–91; TR Penrith w Newton Reigny and Plumpton Wall 91–97; P-in-c Jersey St Brelade *Win* 97–98; R 98–01; Vice-Dean Jersey 00–01; P-in-c Brymbo and Southsea *St As* 05–07; P-in-c Brymbo, Southsea and Tanyfron 07–14; AD Minera 08–12; TR Rhos-Cystennin 14–16; I Aberconwy Miss Area from 17; AD

Llanrwst and Rhos from 15; PtO *Ban* from 15. *8 Llys Helyg, Deganwy, Conwy LL31 9BN* T: (01492) 339521

CARTER, Paul Joseph. b 67. St Chad's Coll Dur BA 88. St Steph Ho Ox 89. **d** 91 **p** 92. C Ipswich All Hallows *St E* 91; C Newmarket St Mary w Exning St Agnes 91–94; V Thorpe-le-Soken *Chelmsf* 94–04; V Ipswich St Bart *St E* from 04. *St Bartholomew's Vicarage, Newton Road, Ipswich IP3 8HQ* T: (01473) 727441 E: frpaulcarter@hotmail.com

CARTER, Paul Rowley. b 45. Lon Univ BD 69 Lon Bible Coll ALBC 69 Southn Univ PGCE 70. Trin Coll Bris. **d** 91 **p** 92. C Penkridge *Lich* 91–96; V Blackb Sav 96–01; R Elmdon St Nic *Birm* 01–11; rtd 11; PtO *Birm* 11; *Lich* 12–18. *Elmdon, 4 Goods Station Lane, Penkridge, Stafford ST19 5AU* T: (01785) 710809 E: paul@tworevs.co.uk

CARTER, Richard Anthony. b 59. Univ of Wales (Abth) BA 80 Melbourne Coll of Div BD 94 Leeds Univ MA 02 Lon Inst of Educn PGCE 87. Bp Patteson Th Coll (Solomon Is) 90. **d** 91 **p** 92. Lect Bp Patteson Th Coll 91–00; Miss and Tr Co-ord Melanesian Brotherhood 00–05; Chapl 94-00 and 02–05; PtO *Lon* 00–06; C St Martin-in-the-Fields from 06. *Flat 1, 6 St Martin's Place, London WC2N 4JJ* T: (020) 7766 1100 F: 7839 5163 E: richard.carter@smitf.org

CARTER, Richard William. b 75. Newc Univ BSc 96. Westcott Ho Cam 04. **d** 07 **p** 08. C Llanbedr DC w Llangynhafal, Llanychan etc *St As* 07–10; P-in-c 10; P-in-c Clocaenog and Gyffylliog 10–16; P-in-c Llanfair DC, Derwen, Llanelidan and Efenechtyd 10–16; TV Dyffryn Clwyd Miss Area from 17. *The Vicarage, Bron y Clwyd, Llanfair Dyffryn Clwyd, Ruthin LL15 2SB* T: (01824) 703867 M: 07769-727985 E: reverendcarter@gmail.com

CARTER, Robert Desmond. b 35. Cranmer Hall Dur 62. **d** 65 **p** 66. C Otley *Bradf* 65–69; C Keighley 69–73; V Cowling 73–00; rtd 00; PtO *Bradf* 00–14; *Leeds* 14–16. *1 Quincy Close, Eccleshill, Bradford BD2 2EP* T: (01274) 638385

CARTER, Robert Edward. b 44. Univ of Wales (Ban) BSc 66. St Jo Coll Nottm 79. **d** 81 **p** 82. C Caverswall *Lich* 81–86; V Biddulph 86–94; V Wolverhampton St Jude 94–10; rtd 11; PtO *Lich* from 11; NSM Penn Fields 12–18. *17 The Spinney, Wolverhampton WV3 9HE* E: gear.carter@gmail.com

CARTER, Robin. b 46. Cam Univ MSt 02. Chich Th Coll 71. **d** 74 **p** 75. C Wortley-de-Leeds *Ripon* 74–76; C Hutton *Chelmsf* 76–78; C Wickford 78–81; TV Wickford and Runwell 81–83; Chapl HM Pris Leeds 83–85; Chapl HM Pris Reading 85–89; Chapl HM YOI Huntercombe and Finnamore 85–89; Chapl HM YOI Finnamore Wood Camp 86–89; Gov 5, Hd of Operations, HM Pris Channings Wood 89–94; Gov 4, Hd of Operations/Régime and Throughcare, HM Pris Woodhill 94–99; Gov HM Pris E Sutton Park 99–05; Sen Operational Pris Service Manager 05–08; Chapl Costa Blanca *Eur* 08–12; rtd 12; PtO *Ox* from 13. *1 Symington Court, Shenley Lodge, Milton Keynes MK5 7AN* E: robincarter@yahoo.com

CARTER, Ronald George. b 31. Leeds Univ BA 58. Coll of Resurr Mirfield 58. **d** 60 **p** 61. C Wigan St Anne *Liv* 60–63; Prec Wakef Cathl 63–66; V Woodhall *Bradf* 66–77; Chapl Qu Marg Sch Escrick Park 77–83; Min Can, Prec and Sacr Pet Cathl 83–88; R Upper St Leonards St Jo *Chich* 88–94; rtd 94; PtO *York* from 95. *5 Greenwich Close, York YO30 5WN* T: (01904) 610237

CARTER, Russell James Wigney. b 29. Chich Th Coll 80. **d** 82 **p** 83. C Aldwick *Chich* 82–86; R Buxted and Hadlow Down 86–90; rtd 90; PtO *Chich* from 90. *1 Bishopsgate Walk, Chichester PO19 6FG* T: (01243) 931900

CARTER, Samuel Nicholas Cato. b 83. Mert Coll Ox BA 05 Trin Coll Cam BA 16 MPhil 17. Ridley Hall Cam 14. **d** 17 **p** 18. C Eastbourne All So *Chich* from 17. *Wellesley House, Longstone Road, Eastbourne BN21 3SL* M: 07810-744528 E: snccarter@yahoo.co.uk

CARTER, Sarah Helen Buchanan. *See* GORTON, Sarah Helen Buchanan

CARTER, Stanley Reginald. b 24. St Jo Coll Dur BA 49. **d** 50 **p** 51. C Stoughton *Guildf* 50–53; C Bucknall and Bagnall *Lich* 53–56; R Salford St Matthias w St Simon *Man* 56–62; V Highbury New Park St Aug *Lon* 62–69; V Sneinton St Chris w St Phil *S'well* 69–89; rtd 89; PtO *S'well* 89–18. *31 Pateley Road, Nottingham NG3 5QF* T: 0115-953 2122 E: stan.carter@dunelm.org.uk

CARTER, Canon Stephen. b 56. Univ of Wales (Lamp) BA 77 Southn Univ BTh 81. Sarum & Wells Th Coll 78. **d** 81 **p** 82. C Halstead St Andr w H Trin and Greenstead Green *Chelmsf* 81–84; C Loughton St Jo 84–89; V N Shoebury 89–95; R Lexden 95–09; RD Colchester 01–06; V Maldon All SS w St Pet from 09; P-in-c Woodham Mortimer w Hazeleigh 16–19; P-in-c Woodham Walter 16–19; Hon Can Chelmsf Cathl from 07. *All Saints' Vicarage, Church Walk, Maldon CM9 4PY* T: (01621) 854179 E: revscarter@gmail.com

CARTER, Stephen Howard. b 47. City Univ BSc 72. St Jo Coll Nottm 83. **d** 85 **p** 86. C Hellesdon *Nor* 85–88; Chapl Birm Children's Hosp 88–91; Chapl Birm Maternity Hosp 88–91; TV Tettenhall Wood *Lich* 91–98; Chapl Compton Hospice 91–98; P-in-c Coalbrookdale, Iron-Bridge and Lt Wenlock *Heref* 98–00; R 00–07; Asst Dioc Co-ord for Evang 00–01; P-in-c Darby End *Worc* 07–08; V 08–12; P-in-c Netherton St Andr 07–08; V 08–12; V Darby End and Netherton 12–14; RD Dudley 10–13; rtd 14; PtO *Cov* from 15. *33 Manse Close, Exhall, Coventry CV7 9NT* T: (024) 7631 2831 M: 07811-222020 E: stevecarter@fastmail.net

CARTER, Stephen Lewis. b 86. Lon Sch of Th BA 09 Homerton Coll Cam MEd 12 PGCE 10. Trin Coll Bris 14. **d** 16 **p** 17. C Cant St Mary Bredin from 16. *38 Nunnery Road, Canterbury CT1 3LS* M: 07950-969633 E: stephenlewiscarter@gmail.com

CARTER, Stephen Paul. b 55. Cartrefle Coll of Educn CertEd 76. Trin Coll Bris BA 88. **d** 98 **p** 99. Dn-in-c Montevideo H Spirit Uruguay 98–99; P-in-c 00–04; V Dalston w Cumdivock, Raughton Head and Wreay *Carl* 04–19; rtd 19; PtO *Carl* from 19. *14 Crookburn Close, Carlisle CA3 0PZ*

CARTER, Stuart Conway. b 58. Lon Bible Coll 81 St Jo Coll Nottm 90. **d** 92 **p** 93. C Birm St Luke 92–96; C The Quinton 96–10; V Castle Bromwich St Clem from 10; AD Coleshill 13–18. *The Vicarage, Lanchester Way, Castle Bromwich, Birmingham B36 9JG* T: 0121-218 6118 E: vicar@stclementschurchcb.com

CARTER, Terence John. b 31. K Coll Lon BD 57 AKC 57 Lon Univ BA 68 PGCE 69. **d** 58 **p** 59. C Winchmore Hill H Trin *Lon* 58–60; PV S'wark Cathl 60–63; Sacr S'wark Cathl 60–61; Succ S'wark Cathl 61–63; R Ockham w Hatchford *Guildf* 63–69; LtO S'wark 69–78; LtO *Portsm* 78–82; PtO 82–15; rtd 91. *15 Balliol Road, Portsmouth PO2 7PP* T: (023) 9269 9167 M: 07811-474020 E: terence.carter1@ntlworld.com

CARTER, Mrs Wendy Elise Grace. b 46. Battersea Coll of Educn TCert 67. Qu Coll Birm 01. **d** 04 **p** 05. C Kingshurst *Birm* 04–07; P-in-c High Wych and Gilston w Eastwick *St Alb* 07–10; rtd 10; PtO *St Alb* 11–16; P-in-c Hunsdon w Salter Street and Shirley 14–16; PtO from 16; P-in-c High Wych and Gilston w Eastwick *St Alb* from 18. *The Rectory, 1 Dovedale, High Wych, Sawbridgeworth CM21 0DT* T: (01279) 726476 E: revwendy@sky.com

CARTLEDGE, Margery. *See* TÖLLER, Elizabeth Margery

CARTMELL, Canon Richard Peter Watkinson. b 43. Cranmer Hall Dur 77. **d** 79 **p** 80. C Whittle-le-Woods *Blackb* 79–85; V Lower Darwen St Jas 85–03; RD Darwen 91–96; P-in-c S Shore H Trin 03–08; Hon Can Blackb Cathl 98–08; rtd 08; PtO *Blackb* from 08. *4 Salwick Avenue, Blackpool FY2 9BT* T: (01253) 590083

CARTMILL, Canon Ralph Arthur. b 40. St Jo Coll Dur BA 62 Em Coll Cam MA 64. Ridley Hall Cam 63. **d** 65 **p** 66. C Dukinfield St Jo *Ches* 65–68; C Wilmslow 68–69; Warden Walton Youth Cen Liv 69–70; Asst Master Aylesbury Gr Sch 70–74; PtO *Ox* 72–74; V Terriers 74–85; P-in-c Chinnor w Emmington and Sydenham 85–86; R Chinnor w Emmington and Sydenham 86–98; Hon Can Ch Ch 97–98; rtd 98; PtO *Nor* from 00. *1 Stuart Court, High Street, Kibworth Beauchamp, Leicester LE8 0LR* T: 0116-279 3614 E: r.cartmill58@btinternet.com

CARTMILL, Mrs Amanda Jane. b 58. St Jo Coll Nottm 00. **d** 02 **p** 03. C Beeston *S'well* 02–07; P-in-c Bilborough St Jo 07–13; V 13–15; P-in-c Bilborough w Strelley 07–13; R 13–15; R Bilborough and Strelley 15–16; V E Trent from 16. *The Rectory, 1 Vicarage Close, Collingham, Newark NG23 7PQ* E: revdmand@hotmail.com

CARTWRIGHT, Hannah Rosina. b 88. Ripon Coll Cuddesdon 14. **d** 18 **p** 19. C Littlemore *Ox* from 18. *20 Vicarage Close, Oxford OX4 4PL* E: hannahrosinacartwright@gmail.com

CARTWRIGHT, Julia Ann. b 58. Nottm Univ BA 80. Linc Th Coll 84. **dss** 86 **d** 87 **p** 94. Asst Chapl HM Pris Morton Hall 85–90; Linc St Jo 86–88; Hon C 87–88; Hon C Bardney 88–97; Chapl Linc Co Hosp 90–93; Chapl St Geo Hosp Linc 90–93; Chapl Linc Distr Health Services and Hosps NHS Trust 93–97; Chapl S Bucks NHS Trust 97–04; LtO *Ox* 97–04; Chapl S Warks Combined Care NHS Trust 04–12; Chapl N Devon Healthcare NHS Trust from 12. *North Devon District Hospital, Raleigh Park, Barnstaple EX31 4JB* T: (01271) 322362 E: juliecartwright1@nhs.net

CARTWRIGHT, Michael. *See* CARTWRIGHT, William Michael

CARTWRIGHT, Michael John. b 42. Qu Coll Birm 67. **d** 70 **p** 71. C Astwood Bank w Crabbs Cross *Worc* 70–75; P-in-c Worc St Mich 75–77; V Stockton St Paul *Dur* 77–87; V Market Rasen *Linc* 87–12; R Linwood 87–12; V Legsby 87–12; V Wickenby Gp 95–00; V Lissington 00–12; RD W Wold 89–01; rtd 12; PtO *Linc* from 16. *The Coach House,*

Main Road, Welbourn, Lincoln LN5 0PA T: (01400) 279062 E: pontiac57@hotmail.com *or* rostigcs7@outlook.com

CARTWRIGHT, Canon Paul. b 71. Leeds Metrop Univ BA 99 Leeds Univ BA 08 MA 13 Huddersfield Univ PGCE 06. Coll of Resurr Mirfield 06. **d** 08 **p** 09. C Athersley *Wakef* 08–11; C Carlton 10–11; P-in-c Barnsley St Pet and St Jo 11–14; *Leeds* 14–16; V 16–19; P-in-c Grimethorpe w Brierley from 19; P-in-c Ryhill from 19; P-in-c S Kirkby from 19; Hon Can Wakef Cathl from 17. *The Vicarage, 20 School Lane, Ryhill, Wakefield WF4 2DW* M: 07852-174303 E: fr.paul.cartwright@gmail.com

CARTWRIGHT, Ms Ruth. b 59. St Mellitus Coll BA 14. **d** 14 **p** 15. C Grays Thurrock *Chelmsf* 14–17; P-in-c Hadleigh St Barn from 17; P-in-c Hadleigh St Jas from 17. *The Rectory, 50 Rectory Road, Benfleet SS7 2ND* M: 07432-599404 E: ruth@cartmann.eclipse.co.uk

CARTWRIGHT, Samuel. b 27. Cuddesdon Coll 71. **d** 72 **p** 72. C Rochdale *Man* 72–76; V Roundthorn 76–83; V Ashton Ch Ch 83–93; rtd 93; PtO *Derby* 93–13. *8 Wentworth Avenue, Walton, Chesterfield S40 3JB* T: (01246) 232252 E: elsieandsam@yahoo.co.uk

CARTWRIGHT, Simon John. b 71. R Holloway Coll Lon BA 93 Sheff Univ MA 95. St Jo Coll Nottm MTh 05. **d** 06 **p** 07. C Ward End w Bordesley Green *Birm* 06–11; TV Walbrook Epiphany *Derby* from 11. *The Vicarage, 81 Palmerston Street, Derby DE23 6PF* T: (01332) 762573 M: 07720-769631 E: revscartwright@gmail.com

CARTWRIGHT, William Michael. b 44. Birm Univ CertEd 67. Coll of Resurr Mirfield 83. **d** 83 **p** 84. Hd Master Chacombe Sch 83–85; Hon C Middleton Cheney w Chacombe *Pet* 83–85; Hd Master Chacombe Sch Banbury 83–85; C Kettering SS Pet and Paul 85–86; PtO 86–88; Chapl Northaw Prep Sch Win 89–92; P-in-c Altarnon w Bolventor, Laneast and St Clether *Truro* 92–97; V Treverbyn 97–01; V Bempton w Flamborough, Reighton w Speeton *York* 01–03; V Ampleforth w Oswaldkirk, Gilling E etc 03–09; rtd 09; P-in-c Barningham w Matlaske w Baconsthorpe etc *Nor* 09–14; PtO 14–16; Chapl Beeston Hall Sch 16–17; P-in-c Matlaske *Nor* 17–18; TV Heart of Norfolk from 18. *The Rectory, 1 Guist Road, Foulsham, Dereham NR20 5RZ*

CARUANA, Mrs Rosemary Anne. b 38. St Alb Minl Tr Scheme 81. **dss** 84 **d** 87 **p** 94. Hertford St Andr *St Alb* 84–87; Par Dn Hertingfordbury 87–94; C 94–98; P-in-c 98–05; rtd 05; PtO *St Alb* from 05. *36 Holly Croft, Hertford SG14 2DR* T: (01992) 306427 M: 07769-658756 E: rosemarycaruana2@sky.com

CARVER, Miss Elizabeth Ann. b 36. Bp Otter Coll BA 00 Chich Univ MA 09 ACIB 73. **d** 99. NSM Littlehampton and Wick *Chich* 99–15; rtd 15; PtO *Chich* 15–17. *13 Hearnfield Road, Littlehampton BN17 7PR* T: (01903) 713169 E: deaconelizabethann@gmail.com

CARVETH, Mrs Marlene. b 51. Ex Univ BA 07. SWMTC 04. **d** 07 **p** 08. NSM Camborne *Truro* 07–13; NSM St Illogan from 14 and from 15. *Trelowarren, 5 Rosevale Crescent, Camborne TR14 7LU* T: (01209) 713175 E: roseyvale@tiscali.co.uk

CARVOSSO, John Charles. b 45. ACA 71 FCA 79. Oak Hill Th Coll 75. **d** 78 **p** 79. C Chelsea St Jo w St Andr *Lon* 78–81; Chapl RAF 81–84; P-in-c Tawstock *Ex* 84–85; TV Newport, Bishops Tawton and Tawstock 85–96; TV Newton Tracey, Horwood, Alverdiscott etc 96–11; RD Torrington 97–02; rtd 11. *45 Trafalgar Drive, Torrington EX38 7AD* M: 07507-369127 E: revjcc@gmail.com

CASE, Preb Catherine Margaret. b 44. Ripon Coll Cuddesdon 86. **d** 88 **p** 94. C Blurton *Lich* 88–92; TD Hanley H Ev and Min to Hanley Care Agencies 92–94; P-in-c Wrockwardine Wood *Lich* 95–98; R 98–00; V Gnosall 00–06; V Gnosall and Moreton 06–07; Preb Lich Cathl 02–07; rtd 07; PtO *Lich* 07–14 and from 17; C Barlaston 14–16. *2 Fulmar Place, Stoke-on-Trent ST3 7QF* T: (01782) 399291 E: preb.case@gmail.com

CASE, Clive Anthony. b 70. St Andr Univ MTheol 93 Surrey Univ BA 05 St Jo Coll Dur PGCE 94. STETS 02. **d** 05 **p** 06. NSM Epsom St Martin *Guildf* 05–11; Asst Chapl Epsom Coll 05–07; Chapl St Jo Sch Leatherhead 08–11; Sen Chapl Charterhouse Sch Godalming from 11. *Charterhouse School, Brook Hall, Charterhouse, Godalming GU2 2DX* T: (01483) 291741 M: 07801-288943 E: cac@charterhouse.org.uk

CASEBOW, Ronald Philip. b 31. Roch Th Coll 59. **d** 61 **p** 62. C Southgate Ch Ch *Lon* 61–64; C Oseney Crescent St Luke w Camden Square St Paul 64–70; Warden St Paul's Ho Student Hostel 64–70; V Colchester St Steph *Chelmsf* 70–74; V Burnham 74–89; rtd 89; PtO *Nor* from 95. *The Priory, Priory Road, Palgrave, Diss IP22 1AJ* T: (01379) 651804

CASH, Simon Andrew. b 62. St Jo Coll Nottm 99. **d** 01 **p** 02. C Aston cum Aughton w Swallownest and Ulley *Sheff* 01–04; P-in-c Worksop St Anne *S'well* 04–16; P-in-c Norton Cuckney

05–16; AD Bassetlaw and Bawtry 14–16; TR Dewsbury *Leeds* from 16; AD from 16; AD Birstall from 18. *The Rectory, Oxford Road, Dewsbury WF13 4JT* T: (01909) 472069 E: simon_cash@sky.com

CASHEL, Dean of. *See* FIELD, The Very Revd Gerald Gordon

CASHEL, WATERFORD AND LISMORE, Archdeacon of. *See* GRAY, The Ven Robert James

CASHEL, WATERFORD, LISMORE, OSSORY, FERNS AND LEIGHLIN, Bishop of. *See* BURROWS, The Rt Revd Michael Andrew James

CASHMORE, Matthew James. b 80. Dur Univ BA 17. Ripon Coll Cuddesdon 14. **d** 17 **p** 18. C W Heref 17–19; C Kenton *Lon* from 19. *344 Kenton Lane, Harrow HA3 8RG* T: (020) 3882 0553 E: father@matthewcashmore.com

CASSAM, Victor Reginald. b 33. Chich Univ BA 05. Chich Th Coll 59. **d** 62 **p** 63. C Portsea St Jo Rudmore *Portsm* 62–64; C W Leigh CD 64–66; C Torquay St Martin Barton *Ex* 66–69; C Stanmer w Falmer and Moulsecoomb *Chich* 69–73; P-in-c Catsfield 73–76; R Catsfield and Crowhurst 76–81; R Selsey 81–01; RD Chich 96–01; rtd 01; PtO *Chich* from 01; *Portsm* 01–15. *195 Oving Road, Chichester PO19 7ER* T/F: (01243) 783998 M: 07976-757451 E: frvictor@gmail.com

CASSELTON, John Charles. b 43. Univ of Wales (Swansea) MA 95. Oak Hill Th Coll 64. **d** 68 **p** 69. C Upton *Ex* 68–73; C Braintree *Chelmsf* 73–80; V Ipswich St Jo *St E* 80–92; RD Ipswich 86–92; Chapl St Clem Hosp Ipswich 92–98; Chapl St Eliz Hospice Ipswich 92–00; Dir Inspire Chr Counselling 00–05; rtd 05; PtO *St E* from 00. *54C Westerfield Road, Ipswich IP4 2UT* M: 07421-143167 E: johnandmidge@hotmail.co.uk

✠**CASSIDY, The Rt Revd George Henry.** b 42. QUB BSc 65 Lon Univ MPhil 67. Oak Hill Th Coll 70. **d** 72 **p** 73 **c** 99. C Clifton Ch ch w Em *Bris* 72–75; V Sea Mills 75–82; V Portman Square St Paul *Lon* 82–87; Adn Lon and Can Res St Paul's Cathl 87–99; Hon C St Ethelburga Bishopgate 89–91; Bp S'well and Nottm 99–09; rtd 09; Hon Asst Bp B & W from 10; Hon Asst Bp Bris from 10. *Darch House, 17 St Andrew's Road, Stogursey, Bridgwater TA5 1TE* T: (01278) 732625 E: georgecassidy123@btinternet.com

CASSON, David Christopher. b 41. Qu Coll Cam BA 64 MA 68. Ridley Hall Cam 65. **d** 67 **p** 68. C Bury St Martin 67–72; C Luton St Mary *St Alb* 72–77; P-in-c Luton St Fran 77; V 77–84; V Richmond H Trin and Ch Ch *S'wark* 84–97; R Acle w Fishley, N Burlingham, Beighton w Moulton *Nor* 97–04; rtd 04; PtO *Nor* from 04. *70 The Street, Brundall, Norwich NR13 5LH* T: (01603) 712092

CASSWELL, Canon David Oriel. b 52. Loughb Coll of Educn DipEd 74 CQSW 79. Oak Hill Th Coll 85. **d** 87 **p** 88. C Acomb St Steph and St Aid *York* 87–91; Dep Chapl HM Pris Leeds 91–92; Chapl HM Pris Everthorpe 92; Chapl HM Pris Wolds 92–98; V Clifton *York* 98–17; Can and Preb York Minster 13–17; rtd 17; PtO *York* from 18. *68 Seebohm Mews, York YO31 0SJ*

CASTER, John Forristall. b 71. Texas A&M Univ BA 93. St Steph Ho Ox BTh 05. **d** 05 **p** 06. C Hendon St Alphage *Lon* 05–09; TV Old St Pancras 09–12; P-in-c Tunbridge Wells St Barn *Roch* 12–17; V from 17. *The Clergy House, 114 Upper Grosvenor Road, Tunbridge Wells TN1 2EX* T: (01892) 525656 E: john.caster@ssho.oxon.org

CASTILLO-BURLEY, Jassica Geraldine. b 67. Greenwich Univ BSc 96. Ridley Hall Cam 15. **d** 17 **p** 18. C Whittington and W Felton w Haughton *Lich* from 17. *The Rectory, West Felton, Oswestry SY11 4LE* T: (01691) 611749 M: 07850-543446 E: princessjassica1@gmail.com

✠**CASTLE, The Rt Revd Brian Colin.** b 49. Lon Univ BA 72 Ox Univ BA 77 MA 80 Birm Univ PhD 89. Cuddesdon Coll 74. **d** 77 **p** 78 **c** 02. C Limpsfield and Titsey *S'wark* 77–81; USPG Zambia 81–84; Lect Ecum Inst WCC Geneva 84–85; V N Petherton w Northmoor Green *B & W* 85–92; Dir Past Studies and Vice-Prin Cuddesdon Coll 92–01; Suff Bp Tonbridge *Roch* 02–15; Hon Can Roch Cathl 02–15; rtd 15; Hon Asst Bp B & W from 16. *Pound Cottage, Wootton Courtenay, Minehead TA24 8RH* T: (01643) 841062 E: brianc@briancastle.org

CASTLE, Canon Brian Stanley. b 47. Oak Hill Th Coll 70. **d** 73 **p** 74. C Barnsbury St Andr w St Thos and St Matthias *Lon* 73–76; C Lower Homerton St Paul 76–79; P-in-c Bethnal Green St Jas Less 79–82; V Tile Cross *Birm* 98–08; P-in-c Garretts Green 03–08; V Garretts Green and Tile Cross 08–17; P-in-c Sheldon 12–16; AD Coleshill 06–13; Hon Can Birm Cathl 16–17; rtd 17; PtO *Birm* from 17. *Hafan, Penisarwaun, Caernarfon LL55 3BS* T: (01286) 871705 M: 07710-251790 E: revbcastle@me.com

CASTLE, John Arthur. b 61. G&C Coll Cam BA 83 St Jo Coll Dur BA 95. Aston Tr Scheme 90 Cranmer Hall Dur 92. **d** 95 **p** 96. C Southborough St Pet w Ch Ch and St Matt *Roch* 95–99; Miss Partner CMS 99–04; P-in-c Sandhurst *Ox* 04–10; R from 10.

The Rectory, 155 High Street, Sandhurst GU47 8HR T: (01252) 872168 E: rector@stmichaels-sandhurst.org.uk

CASTLE, Martin Roger. b 69. Leic Univ BA 92 Liv Univ MCD 95 St Edm Coll Cam BTh 09. Ridley Hall Cam. **d** 09 **p** 10. C Leic Martyrs 09–12; P-in-c Earl Shilton w Elmesthorpe from 12. *The Vicarage, Maughan Street, Earl Shilton, Leicester LE9 7BA* T: (01455) 843961

CASTLE, Michael David. b 38. Wells Th Coll 69. **d** 71 **p** 72. C Acocks Green *Birm* 71–75; C Weoley Castle 76–78; V 78–08; rtd 08. *339 Bournville Gardens, 49 Bristol Road South, Birmingham B31 2FS*

CASTLE, Phillip Stanley. b 43. **d** 97 **p** 98. OLM E Farnworth and Kearsley *Man* 97–09; OLM Farnworth, Kearsley and Stoneclough 10–13; rtd 13; PtO *Man* from 13. *73 Bradford Street, Farnworth, Bolton BL4 9JY* T: (01204) 571439 E: phillip.castle43@gmail.com

CASTLE, Roger James. b 39. St Jo Coll Cam BA 62 MA 66. Clifton Th Coll 63. **d** 65 **p** 66. C Rushden w Newton Bromswold *Pet* 65–68; C Stapenhill w Cauldwell *Derby* 68–72; V Hayfield 72–89; R Coxheath, E Farleigh, Hunton, Linton etc *Roch* 89–04; Chapl Invicta Community Care NHS Trust 91–04; rtd 04; PtO *Bris* from 04. *10 College Park Drive, Bristol BS10 7AN* T: 0117-950 7028

CASTLETON, Mark Peter. b 82. Bath Spa Univ BA 04 Cam Univ BTh 09. Ridley Hall Cam 06. **d** 09 **p** 10. C Salisbury St Mark *Sarum* 09–13; C Aldridge *Lich* 13–19; C Woodford Wells *Chelmsf* from 19. *3 Inmans Road, Woodford Green IG8 0NH* E: markcastleton@ymail.com

CASWELL, Roger John. b 47. St Chad's Coll Dur BA 70. St Steph Ho Ox 75. **d** 77 **p** 78. C Brighton Resurr *Chich* 77–83; TV Crawley 83–90; TR Littlehampton 90–18; Chapl Worthing Priority Care NHS Trust 90–18; rtd 18. *5 Magnolia Close, Worthing BN13 3PT*

CATALLO, Leon Peter. b 84. Down Coll Cam MSci 06. Wycliffe Hall Ox BA 14. **d** 15 **p** 16. C Plymouth St Andr *Ex* 15–18; C Ox St Ebbe w H Trin and St Pet from 18. *43 Ash Grove, Headington, Oxford OX3 9JN* E: leoncatallo@googlemail.com

CATER, Lois May. b 37. S Dios Minl Tr Scheme 81. **dss** 84 **d** 87 **p** 94. Calne and Blackland *Sarum* 84–89; Hon Par Dn 87–89; Hon Par Dn Devizes St Jo w St Mary 89–94; Hon C 94–96; Hon TV Alderbury Team 96–01; Hon TV Clarendon 01–07; PtO from 06. *18 St Margaret's Close, Calne SN11 0UQ* T: (01249) 819432 E: lois.cater@tiscali.co.uk

CATERER, James Albert Leslie Blower. b 44. New Coll Ox BA 67 MA 81. Sarum & Wells Th Coll 79. **d** 81 **p** 82. C Cheltenham St Luke and St Jo *Glouc* 81–85; V Standish w Haresfield and Moreton Valence etc 85–96; P-in-c Glouc St Steph 96–09; rtd 09. *Copelands, 180 Stroud Road, Gloucester GL1 5JX* T/F: (01452) 524694 E: jimscaterer@googlemail.com

CATHERALL, Mark Leslie. b 64. Chich Th Coll BTh 93. **d** 93 **p** 94. C Lancing w Coombes *Chich* 93–95; C Selsey 95–98; Chapl RN 98–04; V S Thornaby *York* 04–19; V Up Hatherley *Glouc* from 19. *The Vicarage, 336 Hatherley Road, Cheltenham GL51 6HX* T: (01242) 210673 E: frmark.catherall@ntlworld.com

CATHIE, Sean Bewley. b 43. Dur Univ BA 67 Birkbeck Coll Lon MSc 03 K Coll Lon DThMin 15. Cuddesdon Coll 67. **d** 69 **p** 70. C Kensal Rise St Martin *Lon* 69–73; C Paddington H Trin w St Paul 73–75; P-in-c Bridstow w Peterstow *Heref* 76–79; Hon C Westmr St Jas *Lon* 85–97; Hon C St Marylebone w H Trin 99–06; Hon C St Marylebone St Cypr 99–06; rtd 06; PtO *Heref* from 09. *The Vicarage, Mount Way, St Weonards, Hereford HR2 8NN* T: (01981) 580137 E: scathie@waitrose.com

CATLEY, John Howard. b 35. AKC 60. K Coll Lon 57 St Boniface Warminster 60. **d** 61 **p** 62. C Sowerby Bridge w Norland *Wakef* 61–64; C Almondbury 64–67; V Earl's Heaton 67–75; V Brownhill 75–86; V Morley St Pet w Churwell 86–92; V St Annes St Marg *Blackb* 92–98; RD Kirkham 94–98; rtd 98; PtO *Blackb* from 98. *Flat 6, Herne Hill Lodge, 598 Lytham Road, Blackpool FY4 1RB* T: (01253) 408129

CATLEY, Marc. b 59. Liv Univ BA 82 Lon Bible Coll BA 85 Man Poly PGCE 90. St Jo Coll Nottm MTh 06. **d** 07 **p** 08. C E Claydon *Cov* 07–11; V Packwood w Hockley Heath *Birm* from 11. *The Vicarage, Nuthurst Lane, Hockley Heath, Solihull B94 5RP* T: (01564) 783121 M: 07952-456846 E: marc.catley@yahoo.co.uk

CATLING, Michael David. b 56. Goldsmiths' Coll Lon CertEd 77 DipEd 84 Newc Univ MLitt 06. Cranmer Hall Dur 88. **d** 90 **p** 91. C Cullercoats St Geo *Newc* 90–94; TV Glendale Gp 94–01; V Whittingham and Edlingham w Bolton Chapel 01–09; R Wigmore Abbey *Heref* from 09. *The Rectory, Dark Lane, Leintwardine, Craven Arms SY7 0LJ* T: (01547) 540235 E: mikecat7@btinternet.com

CATON, Philip Cooper. b 47. Oak Hill Th Coll 79. **d** 81 **p** 82. C Much Woolton *Liv* 81–85; TV Parr 85–98; V Birkdale

St Jo 98–11; rtd 11; PtO *Liv* from 16. *Cooper's Cottage, 23 Alma Road, Southport PR8 4AN* T: (01704) 565785 E: p.caton@sky.com

CATTELL, Angela Kathleen. b 48. Trin Coll Bris. d 12 p 13. OLM Stoke Bishop *Bris* from 12. *9 Eastmead Lane, Bristol BS9 1HW* T: 0117-968 3069 E: angela.cattell@blueyonder.co.uk

CATTELL, Mrs Rosemary Ann. b 51. Open Univ BA 87 Univ Coll Chich BA 04 Chich Univ MA 09. SEITE 10. d 12 p 13. NSM Warnham *Chich* 12–16; NSM Itchingfield w Slinfold from 16. *Whitegates, Salisbury Road, Horsham RH13 0AL* T: (01403) 264396 E: r.a.cattell@btinternet.com

CATTERALL, David Arnold. b 53. Lon Univ BSc 74 ARCS 74. Cranmer Hall Dur. d 78 p 79. C Swinton St Pet *Man* 78–81; C Wythenshawe St Martin 81–83; R Heaton Norris Ch w All SS 83–88; I Fanlobbus Union *C, C & R* 88–95; Can Cork and Ross Cathls 93–95; Warden Ch's Min of Healing in Ireland 95–02; I Templemichael w Clongish, Clooncumber etc *K, E & A* 02–19; Can Elphin Cathl 08–19. *28 St Albans, Battery Road, Longford, Co Longford, N39 R2T6, Republic of Ireland* T: (00353) (43) 334 9285 E: djcatt@eircom.net

CATTERALL, Canon Janet Margaret. b 53. Univ of Wales (Ban) BA 74. Cranmer Hall Dur 77. dss 81 d 87 p 90. Wythenshawe St Martin *Man* 81–83; Heaton Norris Ch w All SS 83–88; Par Dn 87–88; C Bandon Union *C, C & R* 88–89; Dioc Youth Adviser (Cork) 89–94; Dioc Youth Chapl 94–95; I Drung w Castleterra, Larah and Lavey etc *K, E & A* 95–02; P-in-c Mostrim w Granard, Clonbroney, Killoe etc 02–16; Preb Mulhuddart St Patr Cathl Dublin 05–16; rtd 16. *28 St Albans, Battery Road, Longford, Co Longford, N39 R2T6, Republic of Ireland* T: (00353) (43) 334 9285 E: djcatt@eircom.net

CATTERICK, Matthew John. b 68. W Sussex Inst of HE BA 90 Heythrop Coll Lon MA 11. St Steph Ho Ox BTh 95. d 95 p 96. C Colchester St Jas and St Paul w All SS etc *Chelmsf* 95–98; C Leic Resurr 98–99; TV 99–04; TR Wembley Park *Lon* 04–11; V Pimlico St Sav from 11. *59 Aylesford Street, London SW1V 3RY* T: (020) 7592 9733 E: vicar@stsp.org.uk

CATTERMOLE, Elke Brunhilde Emma. b 52. Anglia Ruskin Univ MSc 11 RGN 74 RM 76. Westcott Ho Cam 16. d 17 p 18. NSM Lavenham w Preston *St E* from 17. *Over Hall, Bures CO8 5BN* T: (01787) 227058 M: 07957-419055 E: ecattermole@hotmail.com

CATTLE, David James. b 75. ACCA 00 FCCA 05. Trin Coll Bris BA 06 MA 07. d 07 p 08. C Firswood and Gorse Hill *Man* 07–10; TV Digswell and Panshanger *St Alb* 11–16; PtO *Nor* 16–18; V Galleywood Common *Chelmsf* from 18; C Widford from 18; C Moulsham St Luke from 18; C Moulsham St Jo from 18. *The Vicarage, 450 Beehive Lane, Chelmsford CM2 8RN* M: 07891-148884 E: revdcattle@gmail.com

CATTLE, Canon Richard John. b 40. WMMTC 88. d 90 p 91. NSM Brixworth Deanery *Pet* 90–91; NSM Welford w Sibbertoft and Marston Trussell 91–92; V 92–97; Bp's Dioc Chapl 97–00; Dioc Sec 98–00; Can Pet Cathl 98–02; rtd 01; PtO *Pet* from 02; Dean's Asst 05–16. *Cedar Hay Farm, 3 School Lane, Yelvertoft, Northampton NN6 6LH* E: richardcattle1874@gmail.com

CATTLEY, Richard Melville. b 49. Trin Coll Bris. d 73 p 74. C Kendal St Thos *Carl* 73–77; Nat Sec Pathfinders CPAS 77–82; Exec Sec 82–85; V Dalton-in-Furness *Carl* 85–90; V Dulwich St Barn *S'wark* 90–99; Chapl Alleyn's Foundn Dulwich 90–99; V Milton Keynes *Ox* 99–05; AD 01–05; V Dorking w Ranmore *Guildf* 05–10; rtd 11; PtO *Ox* from 13. *9 St Margaret's Road, Maidenhead SL6 5DZ*

CATTON, Canon Cedric Trevor. b 36. Lambeth STh 94. Wells Th Coll 70. d 72 p 73. C Solihull *Birm* 72–74; R Hawstead and Nowton w Whepstead and Brockley *St E* 74–75; R Hawstead and Nowton w Stanningfield etc 74–79; Dioc Stewardship Adv 77–83; R Cockfield 79–83; V Exning St Martin w Landwade 83–99; Chapl Mid Anglia Community Health NHS Trust 85–99; Dioc Par Resources and Stewardship Officer *St E* 99–02; Asst Can Past *St E* Cathl 02; Hon Can St E Cathl 90–02; rtd 02; Dioc Clergy Retirement Officer *St E* 02–10; Acting Can Past St E Cathl 03–05; Aux P from 05. *24 Manson Gardens, Northgate Street, Bury St Edmunds IP33 1HR*

CATTON, Stanley Charles. b 44. d 99 p 00. NSM Bermondsey St Jas w Ch Ch and St Crispin *S'wark* 99–13; NSM Bermondsey St Jas and St Anne 13–14; PtO from 14. *44 Old Farm Avenue, Sidcup DA15 8AF* E: scatton4@btinternet.com

CAUDWELL, Juliet Lesley. *See* STRAW, Juliet Lesley

CAUDWELL, Lynn Fraser. b 62. Lon Univ BSc 83 Redcliffe Coll Glouc MA 13. Cranmer Hall Dur 18. d 19. C Corbridge w Halton and Newton Hall *Newc* from 19. *6 St Cuthbert's Terrace, Hexham NE46 2EL* M: 07824-558350 E: lynn.caudwell9@gmail.com

CAUNT, Mrs Margaret. b 55. Coll of Ripon & York St Jo MA 97. NOC 93. d 97 p 98. NSM Brightside w Wincobank *Sheff* 97–00; C Ecclesfield 00–02; TV Gleadless 02–07; V Anston 07–16; AD Laughton 15–16; V Arnold *S'well* from 16. *St Mary's Vicarage, 6 Church Lane, Arnold, Nottingham NG5 8HJ* M: 07543-563099 E: caunt@sky.com

CAVAGHAN, Dennis Edgar. b 45. Ex Univ MA 99. St Jo Coll Nottm BTh 74. d 74 p 75. C Hartford *Ches* 74–77; C Plymouth St Andr w St Paul and St Geo *Ex* 77–80; V Cofton w Starcross 80–88; P-in-c W Exe 88–93; PtO *B & W* 94–02; Hon C Taunton St Mary 02–14; Hon C Taunton St Mary and St Jo 14–16; PtO from 16. *Combe House, Corfe, Taunton TA3 7BU* T: (01823) 421013 M: 07810-796025 E: revdencav@gmail.com

CAVALCANTI, Canon Joabe Gomes. b 69. Federal Univ of Pernambuco BA 97 Trin Coll Bris MA 00. Nordeste Th Sem BA 91. d 98 p 98. PtO *Bris* 99; *S'wark* 01–05; Chapl St Sav and St Olave's Sch Newington 05–08; C Bermondsey St Hugh CD 05–08; V Mitcham St Barn from 08; Hon Can Rio de Janeiro from 15. *St Barnabas' Vicarage, 46 Thirsk Road, Mitcham CR4 2BD* T: (020) 8648 2571 M: 07940-444241 E: joabec@gmail.com

CAVALIER, Mrs Sandra Jane. b 48. Guildf Dioc Min Course 98. d 00 p 01. OLM Guildf Ch Ch w St Martha-on-the-Hill 00–04; NSM Westborough 04–08; NSM Wrecclesham 08–18; PtO from 18. *17 Marston Road, Farnham GU9 7BN* T: (01252) 591068 M: 07761-833786 E: revcav@gmail.com

CAVAN, Lawrence Noel. b 38. Trin Coll Bris 72. d 75 p 76. C Lurgan Ch the Redeemer *D & D* 75–78; C Chorleywood Ch Ch *St Alb* 78–82; I Kilmocomogue w Snave, Durrus and Rooska *C, C & R* 82–85; I Portarlington w Cloneyhurke and Lea *M & K* 85–90; TV Eston w Normanby *York* 90–03; rtd 03; PtO *Derby* 05–13; *Sheff* 11–15. *22 Wentworth Road, Dronfield Woodhouse, Dronfield S18 8ZU* T: (01246) 418814 E: thecavans@hotmail.com

CAVANAGH, Anthony James. b 49. Ushaw Coll Dur 72. d 79 p 80. In RC Ch 79–95; C Goole *Sheff* 99–01; TV Cullercoats St Geo *Newc* 01–06; V Billy Mill 06–09; V Marden w Preston Grange 06–09; P-in-c Shilbottle 09–11; P-in-c Gosforth St Hugh 11–14; rtd 14; PtO *Newc* from 14; *Dur* from 15. *7 Westfield Drive, Crook DL15 9NX* T: (01388) 762064 E: a.cavanagh258@btinternet.com

CAVANAGH, Lorraine Marie. b 46. Lucy Cavendish Coll Cam BA 97 MA 01 PhD 03. Ridley Hall Cam 00. d 01 p 02. PtO *Ely* 01–03; Chapl Fitzw Coll Cam 03; Chapl Cardiff Univ *Llan* 04–09; rtd 09. *Cae Hedd, Talycoed Lane, Llantilio Crossenny, Abergavenny NP7 8TL* T: (01600) 780244 E: lorraine@lorrainecavanagh.net

CAVANAGH, Canon Peter Bernard. b 49. Sarum & Wells Th Coll 71. d 73 p 74. C Gt Crosby St Faith *Liv* 73–76; C Stanley 76–79; V Anfield St Columba 79–97; V Lancaster St Mary w St John and St Anne *Blackb* 97–09; P-in-c Scorton and Barnacre and Calder Vale 06–09; Hon Can Blackb Cathl 00–09; rtd 09; PtO *Blackb* from 09; *Eur* from 16. *6 Lunesdale Court, Derwent Road, Lancaster LA1 3ET* T: (01524) 62786 E: manderley552@btinternet.com

CAVE, Bill. *See* CAVE-BROWNE-CAVE, Bernard James William

CAVE, Mrs Margaret. b 62. Van Mildert Coll Dur BSc 84 Cant Ch Ch Univ MA 15. SEITE 07. d 10 p 11. C Kidbrooke St Jas *S'wark* 10–13; TR E Greenwich from 13. *3 Hardy Road, London SE3 7NS* T: (020) 8853 3235 M: 07740-859958 E: vicar@christchurchgreenwich.org.uk

CAVE-BROWNE-CAVE, Canon Bernard James William (Bill). b 54. Trin Hall Cam BA 76 MA 80 Bradf Univ MA 90 Open Univ LLB 14 LLM 18. Westcott Ho Cam 77. d 79 p 80. C Chesterton Gd Shep *Ely* 79–83; Chapl Lanc Univ *Blackb* 83–95; Chapl HM Pris Service 95–14; Chapl Wilts Police from 17; Dioc Inter-Faith Adv *Sarum* from 18; Can and Preb Sarum Cathl from 15. *Address withheld by request*

CAVELL-NORTHAM, Canon Cavell Herbert James. b 32. St Steph Ho Ox 53. d 56 p 57. C W Wycombe *Ox* 56–61; CF (TA) 60–63; V Lane End *Ox* 61–68; V Stony Stratford 68–97; P-in-c Calverton 69–72; R 72–97; Hon Can Ch H 91–97; rtd 97; LtO *Ox* 97–04; PtO from 04. *The Glebe House, Finings Road, Lane End, High Wycombe HP14 3EU* T: (01494) 881552

CAW (née FINLAY), Alison Mary. b 40. Natal Univ BA 62 Ox Univ PGCE 64. Ox Min Course 90. d 93 p 94. NSM Beaconsfield *Ox* 93–04; NSM Penn and Tylers Green 04–08; PtO 08–16; *Chelmsf* from 16. *13 King Harold Lodge, Broomstick Hall Road, Waltham Abbey EN9 1LN* T: (01992) 700232 E: matopos@waitrose.com

CAW, Hannah Mary. *See* JEFFERY, Hannah Mary

CAWDELL, Dominic Austin. b 95. CCC Cam BA 16. St Padarn's Inst 16. d 18 p 19. OGS from 17; C Alyn Miss Area *St As* from 18. *9 Fairoaks Crescent, Llay, Wrexham*

LL12 0NQ   T: (01978)   852729   M: 07538-974020
E: dominicaustin.ogs@outlook.com

CAWDELL, Mrs Sarah Helen Louise. b 65. St Hugh's Coll Ox BA 88 MA 91 Trin Coll Cam BA 94 MA 99 K Coll Lon MA 99. Ridley Hall Cam 92. **d** 95 **p** 96. C Belmont *S'wark* 95–98; PtO *Heref* 98–00; Hon C Claverley w Tuckhill 00–10; CME Officer 06–09; Public Preacher 06–17; TV Bridgnorth and Morville Par from 17; PtO *Worc* 15–17; *Lich* from 15; *S'well* 16–17. *The Rectory, 16 East Castle Street, Bridgnorth WV16 4AL*   T: (01746) 761573 E: sarah.h.l.cawdell@btinternet.com

CAWDELL, Preb Simon Howard. b 65. Univ Coll Dur BA 86 K Coll Lon MA 99. Ridley Hall Cam 91. **d** 94 **p** 95. C Cheam Common St Phil *S'wark* 94–98; V Claverley w Tuckhill *Heref* 98–10; TR Bridgnorth, Tasley, Astley Abbotts, etc 10–16; V Morville w Aston Eyre 10–16; TR Bridgnorth and Morville Par from 16; RD Bridgnorth 09–13; Preb Heref Cathl from 15; PtO *Worc* from 17. *The Rectory, 16 East Castle Street, Bridgnorth WV16 4AL*   T: (01746) 761573 E: s.h.cawdell@btinternet.com

CAWLEY, David Lewis. b 44. AKC 71 FSA 81. St Aug Coll Cant 71. **d** 72 **p** 73. C Sprowston *Nor* 72–75; Chapl HM Pris Nor 74–75; C Wymondham *Nor* 75–77; C Buckland in Dover w Buckland Valley *Cant* 77–83; V Eastville St Anne w St Mark and St Thos *Bris* 83–95; V Leic St Mary 95–09; TV Leic H Spirit 97–02; Chapl Trin Hosp Leic 96–09; rtd 09; C Margate All SS *Cant* 09–16; PtO from 17. *2B St John's Hospital, Northgate, Canterbury CT1 1BG*   T: (01227) 479871 E: davidl.cawley@btinternet.com

CAWRSE, Christopher William. b 60. Birkbeck Coll Lon BA 97 Qu Mary and Westf Coll Lon MA 00. Westcott Ho Cam 82. **d** 84 **p** 85. C Stoke Newington St Mary *Lon* 84–86; Chapl St Mark's Hosp Lon 86–90; C Islington St Jas w St Pet *Lon* 86–90; Chapl Asst Charing Cross Hosp Lon 90–93; PtO *Lon* 93–06; P-in-c St Pancras H Cross w St Jude and St Pet from 06. *Holy Cross Vicarage, 47 Argyle Square, London WC1H 8AL*   T: (020) 7278 6263 E: chriscawrse@blueyonder.co.uk

CAWTE, Martin Charles. b 51. Jes Coll Ox BA 73 MA 77 IPFA 76. SEITE 97. **d** 00 **p** 01. NSM Sanderstead All SS *S'wark* 00–03; NSM Greenham *Ox* 03–06; NSM Hermitage 06–12; P-in-c Lambourn 12–13; P-in-c Eastbury and E Garston 12–13; V Lambourn Valley 13–18; rtd 18; PtO *Ox* from 19. *9 Night Owls, Greenham, Thatcham RG19 8SB*   T: (01635) 36736 E: martin_cawte@hotmail.com

CAWTHORNE, Paul Howarth. b 66. St Hild Coll Dur BA 88. Cuddesdon Coll 98. **d** 98 **p** 99. C Cen Telford *Lich* 98–01; TV Wrockwardine Deanery 01–13; TV Dorchester *Ox* 13–18; P-in-c Astley, Clive, Grinshill and Hadnall *Lich* from 18. *The Vicarage, Shrewsbury Road, Hadnall, Shrewsbury SY4 4AG*   M: 07981-345820 E: paulcawthorne@tiscali.co.uk

CECIL, John Richard. b 75. Univ of Wales (Lamp) BA 97 Univ of Wales (Abth) PGCE 98. St Mich Coll Llan 11. **d** 13 **p** 14. NSM Hubberston *St D* 13–14; NSM Hubberston and Herbrandston 15; NSM Steynton 15–18; P-in-c from 18; Dioc Dir of Educn from 18. *The Vicarage, Steynton, Milford Haven SA73 1AW* E: revjohncecil@btinternet.com

CECILE, Sister. See HARRISON, Cécile

CERMAKOVA, Ms Helena Maria Alija. b 43. **d** 88 **p** 95. NSM Roath *Llan* 88–91; Asst Chapl Univ Hosp of Wales NHS Trust 92–95; Chapl United Bris Healthcare NHS Trust 95–99; Lead Chapl Jersey Gp of Hosps 99–06; Tutor St Mich Coll Llan 06–12. *9 Orchard View, Wear Farm, Newton Road, Bishopsteignton, Teignmouth TQ14 9PU* E: revhelena@icloud.com

CERRATTI, Christa Elisabeth. See PUMFREY, Christa Elisabeth

CHABALA, Patches. b 78. St Jo Coll Nottm BA 11. **d** 11 **p** 12. C Plas Newton *Ches* 11–15; TV Hampreston *Sarum* from 15. *The Vicarage, 44 Albert Road, Ferndown BH22 9HE*   T: (01202) 895099   M: 07791-250300

CHADD, Jeremy Denis. b 55. Jes Coll Cam BA 77 MA 81. Coll of Resurr Mirfield 78. **d** 81 **p** 82. C Seaton Hirst *Newc* 81–84; C N Gosforth 84–88; V Sunderland St Chad *Dur* from 88. *St Chad's Vicarage, Charter Drive, Sunderland SR3 3PG*   T: 0191-528 2397 E: jeremy.chadd@durham.anglican.org

CHADDER, Philip Thomas James. b 66. Ex Univ BA 88. Oak Hill Th Coll 01. **d** 03 **p** 04. C Gt Chesham *Ox* 03–07; Chapl HM Pris Brixton 07–15; Chapl Tr and Development Officer HM Pris Service from 15; PtO *St Alb* from 16. *Chaplaincy HQ, Post Point 8.34, 8th Floor Blue Zone, Ministry of Justice, 102 Petty France, London SW1H 9AJ*   M: 07885-239812 E: phil.chadder@noms.gsi.gov.uk

CHADWICK, Canon Alan Michael. b 61. St Cath Coll Cam BA 83 MA 87. Wycliffe Hall Ox 96. **d** 98 **p** 99. C Hubberston *St D* 98–01; R 01–11; P-in-c Llanstadwell 11–16; P-in-c Llanstadwel and Burton and Rosemarket from 16; AD Roose from 10; Hon Can St D Cathl from 15. *The Vicarage, 68 Church Road, Llanstadwell, Milford Haven SA73 1EB*   T: (01646) 600227 E: alanandmarychadwick@btinternet.com

CHADWICK, Arnold. See CHADWICK, Francis Arnold Edwin

CHADWICK, Carolyn Ann. b 52. Westhill Coll Birm CertEd 73 Birm Univ BMus 93 ABSM 78. WMMTC 04. **d** 07 **p** 08. NSM Pontesbury I and II *Heref* 07–08; NSM Minsterley 08–13; NSM Minsterley, Habberley and Hope w Shelve 13–17; PtO from 17. *The Hermitage, Asterley, Minsterley, Shrewsbury SY5 0AW*   T/F: (01743)   792421   M: 07766-832547 E: carolyn.chadwick@gmail.com

CHADWICK, Charles John Peter. b 59. Birm Univ BA 81 Southn Univ BTh 90. Sarum & Wells Th Coll 85. **d** 88 **p** 89. C Chalfont St Peter *Ox* 88–91; C Gt Marlow 91–93; TV Gt Marlow w Marlow Bottom, Lt Marlow and Bisham 93–95; P-in-c Stokenchurch and Ibstone 95–01; Asst Dir Chiltern Ch Tr Course 95–01; V Bridgwater St Mary and Chilton Trinity *B & W* 01–14; Preb Wells Cathl 11–14; Par Development Adv *Ox* from 14. *Church House Oxford, Langford Locks, Kidlington OX5 1GF*   T: (01865) 208200 E: charles.chadwick@oxford.anglican.org

CHADWICK, David Emmerson. b 73. Lincs & Humberside Univ BA 96. Ridley Hall Cam BTh 00. **d** 00 **p** 01. C Whickham *Dur* 00–06; V Ryhope from 06. *St Paul's Vicarage, Ryhope Street North, Sunderland SR2 0HH*   T: 0191-523 7884

CHADWICK, David Guy Evelyn St Just. b 36. Bps' Coll Cheshunt 61. **d** 68 **p** 69. C Edmonton All SS *Lon* 68–71; C Edmonton St Mary w St Jo 71–72; C Greenhill St Jo 72–74; Bp's Dom Chapl *Truro* 74–79; Chapl Community of the Epiphany Truro 77–78; P-in-c Crantock *Truro* 79–83; R Clydebank *Glas* 83–87; R Renfrew 87–94; rtd 94. *Alverna, 1 Nithsdale Crescent, Bearsden, Glasgow G61 4DF*

CHADWICK, Francis Arnold Edwin. b 30. AKC 54. **d** 55 **p** 56. C Chapel Allerton *Ripon* 55–58; C Hayes *Roch* 58–61; V Arreton *Portsm* 61–67; V Newchurch 61–67; V Kingshurst *Birm* 67–73; V York Town St Mich *Guildf* 73–83; P-in-c Long Sutton w Long Load *B & W* 83–87; R Stockbridge and Longstock and Leckford *Win* 87–93; rtd 93; Chapl Helsinki w Tallinn *Eur* 95–98; PtO *B & W* 98–03; *Sarum* from 02. *Hillway, Wickfield, Devizes SN10 5DU*   T: (01380) 721489 E: fachadwick@tiscali.co.uk

CHADWICK, Helen Jane. See MARSHALL, Helen Jane

CHADWICK, Mark William Armstrong. b 67. Coll of Resurr Mirfield. **d** 05 **p** 06. C Colwyn Bay w Brynymaen *St As* 05–08; V Kerry, Llanmerewig, Dolfor and Mochdre 08–13; V Shrewsbury St Chad, St Mary and St Alkmund *Lich* 13–18; CF(V) 15–18; CF from 18. *c/o MOD Chaplains (Army)*   T: (01264) 383430

CHAFFEY, Jane Frances. b 59. Somerville Coll Ox BA 80 MA 84 St Jo Coll Dur BA 86. Cranmer Hall Dur 84. **d** 88 **p** 94. Par Dn Roby *Liv* 88–90; NSM Finningley w Auckley *S'well* 95–96; PtO *Pet* 96–99; *Linc* 98–01; Chapl Wycombe Abbey Sch 08–18; PtO *Ox* from 18. *Stone Cottage, 133 Main Road, Naphill, High Wycombe HP14 4SA*

CHAFFEY, The Ven Jonathan Paul Michael. b 62. St Chad's Coll Dur BA 83. Cranmer Hall Dur 84. **d** 87 **p** 88. C Gateacre *Liv* 87–90; Chapl RAF 90–14; Chapl-in-Chief RAF 14–18; Adn RAF 14–18; Can and Preb Linc Cathl 14–18; PtO *Ox* from 18. *Stone Cottage, 133 Main Road, Naphill, High Wycombe HP14 4SA*

CHAFFEY, Michael Prosser. b 30. Lon Univ BA 51. St Steph Ho Ox 53. **d** 55 **p** 56. C Victoria Docks Ascension *Chelmsf* 55–59; C Leytonstone H Trin and St Aug Harrow Green 59–62; V Walthamstow St Mich 62–69; R Cov St Jo 69–85; P-in-c Cov St Thos 69–74; Hon C Bideford *Ex* 85; P-in-c Charlestown *Man* 85–88; V Sutton St Mich *York* 88–96; rtd 96; PtO *York* from 96. *17 Highcliffe Court, St Annes Road, Bridlington YO15 2JZ*   T: (01262) 602758

CHALCRAFT, Mrs Sharon Anita. b 62. Ex Univ BTh 09. SWMTC 05. **d** 08 **p** 09. NSM Carbis Bay w Lelant, Towednack and Zennor *Truro* 08–09; NSM Breage w Godolphin and Germoe 09–14; Public Preacher from 14; NSM Godrevy from 15. *Summerhill Cottage, Nancledra, Penzance TR20 8AY*   T: (01736) 350779   M: 07889-406326 E: mrschalc@gmail.com

CHALKLEY, Andrew William Guy. b 64. Aston Tr Scheme 90 St Jo Coll Nottm BTh 92. **d** 95 **p** 96. C Liskeard, St Keyne, St Pinnock, Morval etc *Truro* 95–99; TV Uphill *B & W* 99–07; P-in-c Beckington w Standerwick, Berkley, Rodden etc 07–10; R 10–18. *Address temp unknown*

CHALLEN (née O'DONNELL), Paula Ella. b 72. ERMC 11. **d** 14 **p** 16. C Towcester w Caldecote and Easton Neston etc *Pet* 14–19; V from 99. *The Vicarage, Chantry Lane, Towcester NN12 6YY* E: revpaula@btinternet.com

CHALLEN, Canon Peter Bernard. b 31. Clare Coll Cam BA 56 MA 60 FRSA 94. Westcott Ho Cam 56. **d** 58 **p** 59. C Goole *Sheff* 58–61; V Dalton 61–67; Sen Ind Chapl *S'wark* 67–96; R

S'wark Ch Ch 67–96; Hon Can S'wark Cathl 74–96; rtd 96; PtO S'wark 96–16. *Flat 12, Manormead, Tilford Road, Hindhead GU26 6RA* T: (01428) 601512 E: peterchallen@gmail.com

CHALLENDER, John Clifford. b 32. CITC 67. d 67 p 68. C Belfast St Luke *Conn* 67–70; Bp's V and Lib Kilkenny Cathl and C Kilkenny w Aghour and Odagh *C & O* 70–71; I Fenagh w Myshall and Kiltennel 71–76; I Fenagh w Myshall, Aghade and Ardoyne 76–79; I Crosspatrick Gp 79–95; Preb Ferns Cathl 85–88; Dioc Glebes Sec (Ferns) 86–91; Treas Ferns Cathl 88–91; Chan Ferns Cathl 91–95; I Killeshin w Cloydagh and Killabban 95–02; Can Ossory and Leighlin Cathls 00–02; rtd 02. *3 Adare Close, Killincarrig, Greystones, Co Wicklow, Republic of Ireland* T: (00353) (1) 201 7268 *or* 287 6359 M: 86-243 3678 E: challen1@eircom.net

CHALLENGER, Peter Nelson. b 33. St Jo Coll Cam BA 57 MA 61. Ripon Hall Ox 57. d 59 p 60. C Bushbury *Lich* 59–62; V Horsley Woodhouse *Derby* 62–67; V Derby St Barn 67–75; Brazil 75–80; TV New Windsor *Ox* 80–89; V Wootton (Boars Hill) 89–98; rtd 99; PtO *Ox* from 06. *39 Moorland Road, Witney OX28 6LS* T: (01993) 774630 E: peterleni@tiscali.co.uk

CHALLIS, Terence Peter. b 40. St Aid Birkenhead 65. d 68 p 69. C Billericay St Mary *Chelmsf* 68–71; Admin Sec Dio Maseno S Kenya 72–75; Bp's Chapl 72–74; P-in-c Sparkbrook Ch Ch *Birm* 76–80; V Enfield St Jas *Lon* 80–89; V Astley Bridge *Man* 89–98; P-in-c Leigh St Mary and Leigh St Jo 99–02; rtd 02; PtO *Blackb* from 03. *48 Wilson Square, Thornton-Cleveleys FY5 1RF* T: (01253) 864534

CHALLIS, William George. b 52. Keble Coll Ox BA 73 K Coll Lon MTh 75. Oak Hill Th Coll 73. d 75 p 76. C Islington St Mary *Lon* 75–79; Lect Trin Coll Bris 79–81; C Stoke Bishop *Bris* 79–81; Lect Oak Hill Th Coll 82; Burundi 82–85; P-in-c Bishopston *Bris* 86–89; TR 89–92; Vice-Prin Wycliffe Hall Ox 93–98; V Bitterne *Win* 98–03; Dir of Ords *Guildf* 03–19; Hon Can Guildf Cathl 13–19; rtd 19. *80 York Road, Woking GU22 7XR* T: (01483) 769759

CHALMERS, Canon Brian. b 42. Oriel Coll Ox BA 64 MA 68 DPhil 70 BA 71. Wycliffe Hall Ox 71. d 72 p 73. C Luton St Mary *St Alb* 72–76; Chapl Cranfield Inst of Tech 76–81; Chapl Kent Univ *Cant* 81–89; Six Preacher Cant Cathl 85–96; V Charing w Charing Heath and Lt Chart 89–05; AD Ashford 98–03; Hon Can Cant Cathl 97–05; rtd 05; PtO *Cant* 05–08. *The Chantry, Pilgrims Lane, Chilham, Canterbury CT4 8AB* T: (01227) 730669 E: brian.chalmers@tesco.net

CHALMERS, Malcolm McMahon. b 65. Witwatersrand Univ BPrimEd 88 BEd 97 MA 08 ARSCM 13. d 10 p 11. C Germiston S Africa 10–19; C Bracknell *Ox* from 19. *2 Buckhurst Hill, The Warren, Bracknell RG12 9YP* T: (01344) 249259 E: chantry.music@gmail.com

CHAMBERLAIN, Elizabeth Ann. b 58. St Jo Coll Nottm 08. d 10 p 11. C Walsall St Matt *Lich* 10–14; V Shenstone and Stonnall from 14. *The Vicarage, St John's Hill, Shenstone, Lichfield WS14 0JB* T: (01543) 480286 E: lizchamberlainuk@yahoo.co.uk

CHAMBERLAIN, Helen. b 66. d 09 p 10. NSM Farnham Royal w Hedgerley *Ox* 09–14; C The Cookhams from 14. *St John's House, Spring Lane, Cookham, Maidenhead SL6 9PN* T: (01628) 486744 E: revhec@zoho.com

CHAMBERLAIN, Jane Louise. b 62. Bedf Coll Lon BSc 84. WEMTC 04. d 07 p 08. NSM Blagdon w Compton Martin and Ubley *B & W* 07–11; R 11–17; RD Chew Magna 14–17. *Grove House, The Street, Compton Martin, Bristol BS40 6JF* T: (01761) 220070 M: 07949-037548 E: revjanechamberlain@gmail.com

CHAMBERLAIN, The Ven Malcolm Leslie. b 69. York Univ BA 92 Liv Hope Univ MPhil 11. Wycliffe Hall Ox BTh 96. d 96 p 97. C Walsall Pleck and Bescot *Lich* 96–99; C Mossley Hill St Matt and St Jas *Liv* 99–02; Asst Chapl Liv Univ 99–02; Chapl Liv Univ and Dioc 18–30s Officer 02–08; P-in-c Wavertree St Mary 08–11; R 11–14; AD Toxteth and Wavertree 12–14; Adn Sheff and Rotherham from 14. *34 Wilson Road, Sheffield S11 8RN* T: 0114-418 3917 *or* (01709) 309110 E: malcolm.chamberlain@sheffield.anglican.org

✠**CHAMBERLAIN, The Rt Revd Nicholas Alan.** b 63. St Chad's Coll Dur BA 85 PhD 91 New Coll Edin BD 91. Edin Th Coll 88. d 91 p 92 c 15. C Cockerton *Dur* 91–94; C Newton Aycliffe 94–95; TV 95–96; TV Gt Aycliffe 96–98; P-in-c Burnmoor 98–06; Bp's Adv for CME 98–06; V Newc St Geo and St Hilda 06–15; Can and Preb Linc Cathl from 15; Suff Bp Grantham from 15. *The Bishops' Office, The Old Palace, Lincoln LN2 1PU* E: bishop.grantham@lincoln.anglican.org

CHAMBERLAIN, Paul Martin. b 74. Southn Univ MChem 97 Bris Univ PhD 02. Ripon Coll Cuddesdon 08. d 10 p 11. C Thame *Ox* 10–14; P-in-c Lee-on-the-Solent *Portsm* 14–18; V from 18. *8 Victoria Square, Lee-on-the-Solent PO13 9NF* T: (023) 9200 6184 E: revdr.paulchamberlain@gmail.com

CHAMBERLAIN, Roger Edward. b 53. Culham Coll of Educn BEd 75. Trin Coll Bris BA 87. d 87 p 88. C Plymouth Em w Efford *Ex* 87–90; C Selly Park St Steph and St Wulstan *Birm* 90–94; V Yardley St Cypr Hay Mill 94–96; PtO 96–10; P-in-c Baddesley Ensor w Grendon 10–14; V 14–19; rtd 19; PtO *Birm* from 19. *22 Hanbury Croft, Birmingham B27 6RX* M: 07749-266863 E: revrog@hotmail.co.uk

CHAMBERLAIN, Roy Herbert. b 44. Oak Hill Th Coll 91 NOC 95. d 96 p 97. C Gee Cross *Ches* 96–98; PtO *Blackb* 01–06. *125 Lancaster Road, Morecambe LA4 5QJ* T: (01524) 409070 E: rhchamberlain@btinternet.com

CHAMBERLAIN, Russell Charles. b 51. Univ of Wales (Cardiff) LLM 00. Oak Hill Th Coll 76. d 78 p 79. C Harold Hill St Geo *Chelmsf* 78–80; C Uckfield *Chich* 80–83; R Balcombe 83–90; V Okehampton w Inwardleigh *Ex* 90–94; TR Okehampton w Inwardleigh, Bratton Clovelly etc 94–01; RD Okehampton 93–98; R Wolborough and Ogwell 01–15; rtd 15; St Jo Hosp Heytesbury from 15. *96 The Butts, Westbury BA13 3EZ* M: 07770-270019 E: russell.chamberlain70@gmail.com

CHAMBERLIN, David John. b 56. St Jo Coll Nottm. d 94 p 95. C Chatham St Phil and St Jas *Roch* 94–97; R Swardeston w E Carleton, Intwood, Keswick etc *Nor* 97–04; RD Humbleyard 03–04; R Milton *Ely* from 04; P-in-c Landbeach from 12; P-in-c Waterbeach from 12. *The Rectory, 24 Church Lane, Milton, Cambridge CB24 6AB* T: (01223) 861511 M: 07805-083300 E: rector@allsaintsmilton.org.uk

CHAMBERLIN, John Malcolm. b 38. MRSC. Carl Dioc Tr Course 84. d 87 p 88. NSM Cockermouth w Embleton and Wythop *Carl* 87–97; Master St Mary Magd and H Jes Trust 97–05; Hon C Newc St Jo 98–05; rtd 05; PtO *Newc* from 05. *45 Wansbeck Avenue, North Shields NE30 3DU* T: 0191-253 0022 E: johnchamberlin@btinternet.com

CHAMBERLIN, Mrs Julia Joanne. b 61. UEA BA 02 PGCE 03. St Mellitus Coll BA 15. d 15 p 16. C Bluntisham cum Earith w Colne and Holywell etc *Ely* 15–16; C Ely 16–17; Chapl NW Anglia NHS Foundn Trust from 17. *24 Church Lane, Milton, Cambridge CB24 6AB* T: (01223) 861511 *or* (01480) 847474 E: julia.chamberlin@nhs.net *or* julia@chamberlin.org.uk

CHAMBERLIN, Peter John. b 86. St Cath Coll Cam BA 09 MSci 09 MA 12. Oak Hill Th Coll BA 17. d 17 p 18. C New Ferry *Ches* from 17; C Rock Ferry from 17. *98 Highfield Road, Birkenhead CH42 2DA* T: 0151-201 8399 M: 07914-524278 E: peter.chamberlin@gmail.com

CHAMBERS, Canon Anthony Frederick John. b 40. ACII 69. Sarum Th Coll 69. d 71 p 72. C Hall Green St Pet *Birm* 71–74; C Holdenhurst *Win* 74–77; P-in-c Ropley w W Tisted 77–79; R Bishop's Sutton and Ropley and W Tisted 79–83; V Pokesdown St Jas 83–99; RD Bournemouth 95–99; P-in-c Heckfield w Mattingley and Rotherwick 99–02; V 02–04; Chapl N Foreland Lodge Sch Basingstoke 99–04; Hon Can Win Cathl 03–04; rtd 05; PtO *Ex* from 05. *4 J H Taylor Drive, Northam, Bideford EX39 1TU* T: (01237) 421306 E: anthony.chambers1@virgin.net

CHAMBERS, Miss Barbara Ada. b 51. d 98 p 99. OLM Gt Crosby St Luke *Liv* 98–15; rtd 15; PtO *Liv* from 17. *12 Vale Road, Crosby, Liverpool L23 5RZ* T: 0151-924 5851

CHAMBERS, Mrs Barbara Mary Sinnott. b 43. SRN 65 RM 67 HVCert 75 Keele Univ TCert 77. WMMTC 87. d 93 p 94. Par Dn Blurton *Lich* 93–94; C 94–96; Chapl Asst Qu Medical Cen Nottm Univ Hosp NHS Trust 96–03; Chapl 03–07; Chapl United Lincs Hosps NHS Trust from 07; PtO *Linc* from 17. *51 Mill Lane, Woodhall Spa LN10 6QZ* T: (01526) 354872 E: barbara.chambers@ulh.nhs.uk

CHAMBERS, Carl Michael. b 68. Pemb Coll Cam BA 90 Oak Hill Th Coll BA 00 MA 02. d 01 p 02. C Hove Bp Hannington Memorial Ch *Chich* 01–05; C Preston St Jo w Brighton St Aug and St Sav 05–10; LtO 10–16; V Wilmington *Roch* from 19. *The Vicarage, 1 Curate's Walk, Dartford DA2 7BJ* E: vicar.wilmington@gmail.com

CHAMBERS, Canon John Richard. b 50. EMMTC 01. d 04 p 05. C Farnsfield *S'well* 04–07; C Kirklington w Hockerton 04–07; C Bilsthorpe 04–07; C Eakring 04–07; C Maplebeck 04–07; C Winkburn 04–07; P-in-c E Bridgford and Kneeton 07–10; P-in-c Flintham 08–10; P-in-c Car Colston w Screveton 08–10; R Richmond w Hudswell and Downholme and Marske *Leeds* 10–17; AD Richmond 15–16; Hon Can Ripon Cathl 16–17; rtd 17; PtO *S'well* from 18. *27 Fairway, Newark NG24 4RN* M: 07875-348245 E: j_echambers@btinternet.com

CHAMBERS, Marion Patricia. See HINKS, Marion Patricia

CHAMBERS, Canon Peter Lewis. b 43. Imp Coll Lon BScEng 64. St Steph Ho Ox 64. d 66 p 67. C Llandaff w Capel Llanilltern *Llan* 66–70; Chapl Ch in Wales Youth Coun 70–73; Youth Chapl *Bris* 73–78; V Bedminster St Mich 78–84; RD Bedminster 81–84; Adv Ho of Bps Marriage Educn

Panel Gen Syn 84–88; Dir Dioc Coun for Soc Resp *Guildf* 88–94; Hon Can Guildf Cathl 89–94; Dir Tr *Sheff* 95–00; P-in-c Harthill and Thorpe Salvin 00–07; Dioc Min Teams Officer 00–04; Hon Can Sheff Cathl 96–07; rtd 07; PtO *Bris* from 08. *5 Henley Grove, Bristol BS9 4EQ* T: 0117-307 9427

CHAMBERS, Rachel Jill. *See* GANNEY, Rachel Jill

CHAMBERS, Simon Paul. b 65. Liv Univ BEng 87 PhD 91. Ripon Coll Cuddesdon 00. **d** 02 **p** 03. C Parkstone St Pet and St Osmund w Branksea *Sarum* 02–05; P-in-c Ashwell w Hinxworth and Newnham *St Alb* 05–10; TV Shaftesbury *Sarum* 10–19; RD Blackmore Vale 17–19; TR Clarendon from 19. *The Rectory, West Winterslow, Salisbury SP5 1RE*

CHAMBERS, Timothy John Essex. b 69. St Jo Coll Cam MA 95. St Mellitus Coll BA 16. **d** 16 **p** 17. C W Bridgford *S'well* from 16. *St Giles' Church, Church Drive, West Bridgford, Nottingham NT2 6AY* M: 07946-526569 E: curate@stgilesparish.com

CHAMP, Darren David. b 60. Kent Univ BA 93. Linc Th Coll MA 95. **d** 95 **p** 96. C Ashford *Cant* 95–97; PtO 02–03. *154 Beaver Road, Ashford TN23 7SS* T: (01233) 663090 E: daz@dazchamp.co.uk

CHAMPION, Arthur. b 51. Loughb Univ BSc 76 Aston Univ MSc 77 CEng 88 MIMechE 88 FIOSH 88. WEMTC 03. **d** 08 **p** 09. NSM Badgeworth, Shurdington and Witcombe w Bentham *Glouc* 08–13; NSM Bourton-on-the-Water w Clapton etc 13–14; Environmental Officer from 14; Public Preacher from 14; NSM Churn Valley from 15. *The New Rectory, Cowley, Cheltenham GL53 9NJ* T: (01242) 870402 M: 07768-658723 E: championarthur@gmail.com

CHAMPNEYS, Michael Harold. b 46. LRAM 66 GRSM 67 ARCO 67. Linc Th Coll 69. **d** 72 **p** 73. C Poplar *Lon* 72–73; C Bow w Bromley St Leon 73–75; P-in-c Bethnal Green St Barn 75–76; C Hawkesbury w Walton Cardiff *Glouc* 76–78; V Bedford Park *Lon* 78–83; V Shepshed *Leic* 84–87; Community Educn Tutor Bolsover 88–93; PtO *Derby* 90–92; NSM Bolsover 92–93; V Potterspury, Furtho, Yardley Gobion and Cosgrove *Pet* 93–98; RD Towcester 94–98; V Shap w Swindale and Bampton w Mardale *Carl* 98–01; R Calow and Sutton cum Duckmanton *Derby* 01–10; rtd 10; P-in-c Wentworth *Sheff* 15–18. *1 New Road, Holymoorside, Chesterfield S42 7EW* T: (01246) 566172 E: michaelchampneys@yahoo.co.uk

CHANCE, David Newton. b 44. Univ of Wales (Lamp) BA 68. St Steph Ho Ox 68. **d** 70 **p** 71. C Selsdon St Jo w St Fran *Cant* 70–73; C Plymstock *Ex* 73–77; P-in-c Northam 77–79; TR Northam w Westward Ho! and Appledore 79–93; V Banstead *Guildf* 93–10; rtd 10; PtO *Cant* from 11. *3 Norman Road, Westgate-on-Sea CT8 8RR* T: (01843) 836882 E: andrea3david@yahoo.co.uk

CHAND, Richard. b 62. SAOMC 02. **d** 05 **p** 06. NSM Headington St Mary *Ox* 05–09; NSM Cowley St Jas from 09. *94 Bayswater Road, Headington, Oxford OX3 9NZ* M: 07590-431903 E: richardwchand@outlook.com

CHANDLER, Anthony. b 43. Lon Inst of Educn CertEd 65. EAMTC 94. **d** 97 **p** 98. Dioc Youth Officer *Ely* 96–00; NSM March St Mary 97–00; R 00–12; P-in-c 12–15; NSM March St Pet 97–00; R 00–12; P-in-c 12–15; rtd 12; PtO *Ely* from 15. *17 St Peter's Road, March PE15 9NA* T/F: (01354) 652894 E: anthonychandler@btinternet.com

CHANDLER, Barbara Janet. b 58. Newc Univ BMedSci 79 MB, BS 82 MD 93 FRCP 00. NEOC 04. **d** 07 **p** 08. NSM Ponteland *Newc* 07–11; PtO *Mor* from 11. *Highfield House, Lentran, Inverness IV3 8RN* T: (01463) 704393 E: chandlernorth@gmail.com

CHANDLER, Derek Edward. b 67. Southn Univ BTh 91 Nottm Univ MDiv 93. Linc Th Coll 91. **d** 93 **p** 94. C Bitterne Park *Win* 93–97; C Sholing 97–00; R Emmer Green w Caversham Park *Ox* from 00. *20 St Barnabas Road, Emmer Green, Reading RG4 8RA* T: 0118-947 8239 E: rev.derek.chandler@virgin.net

CHANDLER, John. b 49. ACIB 73. NTMTC 05. **d** 07 **p** 08. NSM Colchester St Mich Myland *Chelmsf* 07–19; P-in-c Wormingford, Mt Bures and Lt Horkesley 14–19; NSM Colchester St Luke 18–19; NSM Langham w Boxted 18–19; NSM W Bergholt and Gt Horkesley 18–19; rtd 19. *4 Longdryve, Wavell Avenue, Colchester CO2 7HH* T: (01206) 366930 M: 07951-160558 E: john@mylandchurch.org.uk

CHANDLER, John Charles. b 46. Solicitor. Oak Hill Th Coll 91. **d** 94 **p** 95. C Tonbridge St Steph *Roch* 94–98; V Felsted and Lt Dunmow *Chelmsf* 98–05; V Hildenborough *Roch* 05–13; rtd 13; PtO *Nor* from 13. *1 Beach Close, Overstrand, Cromer NR27 0PJ* T: (01263) 576970 E: chandlerjandm@gmail.com

CHANDLER, The Very Revd Michael John. b 45. Lambeth STh 80 K Coll Lon PhD 87. Linc Th Coll 70. **d** 72 **p** 73. C Cant St Dunstan w H Cross 72–75; C Margate St Jo 75–78; V Newington w Bobbing and Iwade 78–83; P-in-c Hartlip w Stockbury 80–83; V Newington w Hartlip and Stockbury 83–88; RD Sittingbourne 84–88; R Hackington 88–95; RD

Cant 94–95; Can Res Cant Cathl 95–03; Dean Ely 03–11; rtd 11; PtO *Cant* from 12; Prior St Jo Hosp Cant from 16. *218 Tankerton Road, Whitstable CT5 2AT* T: (01227) 262937 E: deanemeritus@gmail.com

CHANDLER, Canon Quentin David. b 62. Anglia Ruskin Univ MA 08 DProf 15. Aston Tr Scheme 87 Trin Coll Bris BA 92. **d** 92 **p** 93. C Goldington *St Alb* 92–96; TV Rushden w Newton Bromswold *Pet* 96–00; V Rushden St Pet 00–03; Dir Tr for Past Assts 03–08; Dir Studies Dioc Lay Min Course 08–11; R Burton Latimer 03–11; CME Officer and Lic Lay Min Officer 11–16; C Gt w Lt Harrowden and Orlingbury and Isham etc 12–16; Dir of Ords *St Alb* from 16; P-in-c Marston Morteyne w Lidlington 16–18; R from 18; Hon Can St Alb from 18. *The Vicarage, High Street, Lidlington, Bedford MK43 0RN* T: (01525) 840477 M: 07909-542060 E: ddo@stalbans.anglican.org

CHANDLER, Stephen Michael. b 54. NTMTC. **d** 09 **p** 10. NSM Victoria Docks St Luke *Chelmsf* 09–12; NSM W Ham 12–18. *3 Charnock Close, Kirby Cross, Frinton-on-Sea CO13 0RT* E: rev.stephen@hotmail.co.uk

CHANDLER, Mrs Susan May. b 54. Newman Univ BA 15. WMMTC 06. **d** 09 **p** 10. NSM Olton *Birm* from 09. *14 Hollyberry Avenue, Solihull B91 3UA* T: 0121-709 1512 M: 07970-791288 E: j14chand@sky.com

CHANDRA, Kevin Douglas Naresh. b 65. Lon Bible Coll BA 91. Qu Coll Birm 94. **d** 96 **p** 97. C Walmley *Birm* 96–00; P-in-c Erdington St Chad 00–02; TV Erdington 02–05; Chapl St Pet Sch Ex 06–15; V Bampton, Morebath, Clayhanger, Petton etc *Ex* from 15. *The New Vicarage, Station Road, Bampton, Tiverton EX16 9NG* T: (01398) 332885 E: hukeleymissioncommunity@yahoo.co.uk

CHANNER, Christopher Kendall. b 42. K Coll Lon BD 64 AKC 64. St Boniface Warminster 64. **d** 65 **p** 66. C Norbury St Steph *Cant* 65–68; C S Elmsall *Wakef* 68–70; V Dartford St Edm *Roch* 70–75; Chapl Joyce Green Hosp Dartford 73–75; V Bromley St Andr *Roch* 75–81; V Langton Green 81–94; Chapl Holmewood Ho Sch Tunbridge Wells 94–98; P-in-c Lewes All SS, St Anne, St Mich and St Thos *Chich* 98–00; R Lewes St Mich and St Thos at Cliffe w All SS 00–08; rtd 08; PtO *Chich* from 16. *Abbots Croft, Lower Lake, Battle TN33 0BE* T: (01424) 777396

CHANT, Harry. b 40. Oak Hill Th Coll. **d** 78 **p** 79. C Heatherlands St Jo *Sarum* 78–81; P-in-c Bramshaw 81–83; P-in-c Landford w Plaitford 81–83; R Bramshaw and Landford w Plaitford 83–87; V Fareham St Jo *Portsm* 87–00; rtd 00; PtO *Truro* from 00. *141 Pendeen Park, Helston TR13 0SL* T/F: (01326) 561916 E: tellharrychant@aol.com

CHANTER, Canon Anthony Roy. b 37. ACP 60 Open Univ BA 72 Lon Univ MA 75. Sarum Th Coll 64. **d** 66 **p** 67. C W Tarring *Chich* 66–69; Chapl St Andr Sch Worthing 69–70; Hd Master Bp King Sch Linc 70–73; Hon PV Linc Cathl 70–73; Hd Master Grey Court Comp Sch Richmond 73–76; Hon C Kingston All SS *S'wark* 73–76; Hd Master Bp Reindorp Sch Guildf 77–84; Dir of Educn *Guildf* 84–01; Hon Can Guildf Cathl 84–01; rtd 02; PtO *Chich* from 02. *14 Broadmark Beach, Broadmark Lane, Rustington, Littlehampton BN16 2JF* T: (01903) 411891 E: tonychanter@hotmail.com

CHANTREY, Preb David Frank. b 48. K Coll Cam BA 70 PhD 73 MA 74. Westcott Ho Cam 83. **d** 86 **p** 87. C Wordsley *Lich* 86–89; C Beckbury 89–90; P-in-c 90–93; C Badger 89–90; P-in-c 90–93; C Kemberton, Sutton Maddock and Stockton 89–90; P-in-c 90–93; C Ryton 89–90; P-in-c 90–93; R Beckbury, Badger, Kemberton, Ryton, Stockton etc 93–08; TR Wrockwardine Deanery 08–16; RD Wrockwardine 08–16; Preb Lich Cathl 99–16; rtd 16; Preb *Lich* from 18; *Heref* from 18. *85 Victoria Road, Bridgnorth WV16 4LD* T: (01746) 218892 M: 07785-524495 E: david01wdtm@talktalk.net

CHANTRY, Canon Helen Fiona. b 59. Bradf Univ BSc 82 Leeds Univ CertEd 83. Trin Coll Bris BA 89. **d** 89 **p** 94. NSM Hyde St Geo *Ches* 89–92; Dioc Youth Officer 92–00; NSM Barrow 94–99; C Acton and Worleston, Church Minshull etc 00–04; P-in-c Audlem 04–11; Bp's Adv for Women in Min 05–09; V Wybunbury and Audlem w Doddington from 11; RD Nantwich from 13; Hon Can Ches Cathl from 10. *St James's Vicarage, 66 Heathfield Road, Audlem, Crewe CW3 0HG* T: (01270) 811543 E: helenchantry@btopenworld.com

CHANTRY, Peter Thomas. b 62. Bradf Univ BSc 83. Trin Coll Bris BA 89. **d** 89 **p** 90. C Hyde St Geo *Ches* 89–92; Dioc Youth Officer 91–99; P-in-c Barrow 94–99; R Nantwich 99–12; PtO from 12; Hon C Edstaston, Fauls, Prees, Tilstock and Whixall *Lich* 13; V Betley from 13; V Madeley from 13. *St James's Vicarage, 66 Heathfield Road, Audlem, Crewe CW3 0HG* T: (01270) 811543 E: peterchantry@hotmail.com

CHAPLIN, Colin. b 33. Edin Dioc NSM Course 74. **d** 76 **p** 77. NSM Penicuik *Edin* 76–91; P-in-c Peebles 89–90;

NSM Bathgate 91–95; rtd 95; Asst P Edin St Mark 97–00; Asst P Innerleithen from 00; Asst P Peebles from 00; P-in-c Galashiels 02–03. *26 Broomhill Road, Penicuik, Edinburgh EH26 9EE* T: (01968) 672050

CHAPLIN, Canon Douglas Archibald. b 59. Em Coll Cam BA 81 MA 91 Birm Univ MPhil 98. St Jo Coll Nottm. **d** 86 **p** 87. C Glouc St Geo w Whaddon 86–89; C Lydney w Aylburton 89–93; R Worc St Clem 93–01; TV Droitwich Spa 01–13; Dioc Miss Development Officer from 13; Dir Reader Tr from 04; Hon Can Worc Cathl from 19. *The Old Palace, Deansway, Worcester WR1 2JE* T: (01905) 20537 M: 07858-501120 E: doug.chaplin@cofe-worcester.org.uk

CHAPLIN, Paul. b 57. Hull Univ BA 80 PGCE 81 K Coll Lon MA 89. St Steph Ho Ox 85. **d** 87 **p** 88. C Ex St Jas 87–90; C Wokingham St Paul *Ox* 90–98; V Stratfield Mortimer and Mortimer W End etc from 98. *The Vicarage, 10 The Avenue, Mortimer, Reading RG7 3QY* T: 0118-933 1718 *or* 933 3704 E: admin@mortimerbenefice.co.uk

CHAPMAN, Andrew John. b 81. Leeds Univ BA 03 St Jo Coll Dur BA 09. Cranmer Hall Dur 06. **d** 09 **p** 10. C Hykeham *Linc* 09–12; Chapl RAF from 12. *Chaplaincy Services (RAF), HQ Air Command, RAF High Wycombe HP14 4UE* T: (01494) 496800 E: a.j.chapman@live.co.uk

CHAPMAN, Barry Frank. b 48. Trin Coll Bris 83. **d** 82 **p** 83. NSM Bradford-on-Avon Ch Ch *Sarum* 82–11; NSM N Bradford on Avon and Villages 11–18; Assoc Chapl Bath Univ *B & W* 83–18; rtd 18. *16 Church Acre, Bradford-on-Avon BA15 1RL* T: (01225) 866861 E: ann.barry.chapman@btinternet.com

CHAPMAN, Mrs Celia. b 32. Whitelands Coll Lon TCert 53 Open Univ BA 82. WMMTC 84. **d** 87 **p** 94. NSM Bilston *Lich* 87–93; Chapl St Pet Colleg Sch Wolv and Ind Chapl Black Country Urban Ind Miss 93–98; rtd 99; PtO *Glouc* 99–16; *Worc* 99–16. *Flat 10, Manormead Supported Housing, Tilford Road, Hindhead GU26 6RA*

CHAPMAN, Canon Christopher Robin. b 37. Ripon Hall Ox 72. **d** 73 **p** 74. C Kidbrooke St Jas *S'wark* 73–77; V Corton *Nor* 77–80; V Hopton 77–80; V Hopton w Corton 80–92; RD Lothingland 80–86; P-in-c Loddon w Sisland 92–93; P-in-c Loddon, Sisland w Hales and Heckingham 93–98; P-in-c Chedgrave w Hardley and Langley 97–98; V Loddon, Sisland, Chedgrave, Hardley and Langley 98–03; RD Loddon 95–98; Hon Can Nor Cathl 96–03; Chapl Langley Sch Nor 00–03; rtd 04; PtO *Chelmsf* 04–06; *St E* from 06. *Preveli, 16 Riley Close, Ipswich IP1 5QD* T: (01473) 462109 E: canons.chapman@btinternet.com

CHAPMAN, Colin Gilbert. b 38. St Andr Univ MA 60 Lon Univ BD 62 Birm Univ MPhil 94. Ridley Hall Cam 62. **d** 64 **p** 65. C Edin St Jas 64–67; Asst Chapl Cairo Cathl Egypt 68–73; Tutor Crowther Hall CMS Tr Coll Selly Oak 73–75; Prin 90–97; Lebanon 75–82; Chapl Limassol St Barn 82–83; Lect Trin Coll Bris 83–90; Dir Faith to Faith Consultancy 97–99; Lect Near E Sch of Th Lebanon 99–03; rtd 04; PtO *Ely* from 07. *12 Daniels Park, Milton, Cambridge CB24 6UD* T: (01223) 860317 E: beirutchapman@hotmail.com

CHAPMAN, Mrs Elizabeth Ann. b 55. SEITE 05. **d** 09 **p** 10. NSM Gillingham St Mary *Roch* 09–11; Chapl Pilgrims Hospice Cant 11–13; NSM Cant St Pet w St Alphege and St Marg etc 11–13; PtO 13–15. *93 Hempstead Road, Hempstead, Gillingham ME7 3RH* T: (01634) 233477 M: 07961-337083 E: l.chapman431@btinternet.com

CHAPMAN, Preb Gorran. b 55. Dur Univ BA. Westcott Ho Cam 78. **d** 80 **p** 81. C Par *Truro* 80–82; C Kenwyn 82–84; P-in-c Penwerris 84–89; V 89–92; V Torquay St Martin Barton *Ex* from 92; Preb Ex Cathl from 07. *St Martin's Vicarage, Beechfield Avenue, Barton, Torquay TQ2 8HU* T: (01803) 327223

CHAPMAN, Guy Godfrey. b 33. Southn Univ BSc 57. Clifton Th Coll 60. **d** 62 **p** 63. C Chadderton Ch Ch *Man* 62–67; V Edgeside 67–70; P-in-c Shipton Bellinger *Win* 70–72; V 72–83; RD Andover 75–85; Hon Can Win Cathl 79–91; R Over Wallop w Nether Wallop 83–91; V Ambrosden w Merton and Piddington *Ox* 91–00; RD Bicester and Islip 95–00; rtd 00; PtO *Sarum* 01–16; *Win* 01–15. *65 St Ann Place, Salisbury SP1 2SU* T: (01722) 335339

CHAPMAN, Henry Davison. b 31. Bris Univ BA 55. Tyndale Hall Bris 52. **d** 56 **p** 57. C St Helens St Mark *Liv* 56–60; R Clitheroe St Jas *Blackb* 60–67; V Tipton St Martin *Lich* 67–68; SW Area Sec CPAS 68–72; V Eccleston St Luke *Liv* 72–78; P-in-c Ringshall w Battisford, Barking w Darmsden etc *St E* 78–80; R 80–93; RD Bosmere 87–91; rtd 93; PtO *Sarum* 93–10. *Daracombe, 4 The Clays, Market Lavington, Devizes SN10 4AY* T: (01380) 813774

CHAPMAN (née CRAVEN), Canon Janet Elizabeth. b 58. St Jo Coll Dur BSc 80 MA 92. Cranmer Hall Dur 84. **d** 87 **p** 95. Par Dn Darlington St Cuth *Dur* 87–92; NSM Edin Gd Shep 93–95;

NSM Long Marston and Rufforth w Moor Monkton and Hessay *York* 95–98; Chapl Qu Ethelburga's Coll York 97–99; Chapl Harrogate Ladies' Coll 00; P-in-c Banbury *Ox* 01–08; Can Res Birm Cathl 08–16; R Northfield from 16; Hon Can Birm Cathl from 16. *The Rectory, Rectory Road, Birmingham B31 2NA* T: 0121-475 1518 E: stlaurence@btconnect.com

CHAPMAN, John Brown. b 54. Strathclyde Univ BSc 76 Lon Bible Coll BA 80. NTMTC 00. **d** 02 **p** 03. C W Ealing St Jo w St Jas *Lon* 02–05; C Northolt St Mary 05–08; Chapl for Internat Chs 08–13; Chapl Sharjah and Asst Chapl Dubai UAE 13–14; Chapl Barcelona *Eur* from 14. *St George, Horacio 38, 08022 Barcelona, Spain* T: (0034) 934 178 867 F: 932 128 433 E: info@st-georges-church.com

CHAPMAN (née WHITFIELD), Mrs Joy Verity. b 46. SRN 67 SCM 71. Trin Coll Bris BA 88. **d** 88 **p** 94. C Littleover *Derby* 88–92; Par Dn Bucknall and Bagnall *Lich* 92–94; TV 94–97; Chapl LOROS Hospice 97–03; rtd 03; PtO *Leic* from 03. *15 Templar Way, Rothley, Leicester LE7 7RB* T: 0116-230 1994

CHAPMAN, Mrs Lesley. b 61. NEOC 02. **d** 05 **p** 06. C Fenham St Jas and St Basil *Newc* 05–09; P-in-c Kenton Ascension 09–16; P-in-c Riding Mill from 16; Bp's Adv for Spirituality and Spiritual Direction from 16; AD Corbridge from 17. *The Vicarage, Riding Mill NE44 6AT* T: (01434) 682120 E: lesley.chapman414@btopenworld.com

CHAPMAN, Mrs Linda. b 46. Lon Univ BSc 67 Lon Inst of Educn PGCE 68. Guildf Dioc Min Course 98. **d** 00 **p** 01. NSM Ewell St Fran *Guildf* 00–04; NSM Cheswardine, Childs Ercall, Hales, Hinstock etc *Lich* 04–14; TV 11–14; rtd 14; PtO *Newc* from 15. *Dalrigh, 12 Lords Mount, Berwick upon Tweed TD15 1LY* T: (01289) 307466 M: 07956-429116 E: rev.linda@btinternet.com

CHAPMAN, Linda Rosa. *See* HILLIER, Linda Rosa

CHAPMAN, Miss Lynn Marie. b 71. Coll of Ripon & York St Jo BEd 93 Cant Ch Ch Univ MA 98. ERMC 08. **d** 11 **p** 12. C Sheringham *Nor* 11–14; P-in-c Brooke, Kirstead, Mundham w Seething and Thwaite from 14; Asst Dioc Dir of Ords from 18; PtO *St E* from 19. *The Vicarage, 105 The Street, Brooke, Norwich NR15 1JU* T: (01508) 558479 E: chapman.lynn@btinternet.com

CHAPMAN, Margaret. *See* FLINTOFT-CHAPMAN, Margaret

CHAPMAN, Prof Mark David. b 60. Trin Coll Ox MA 83 DPhil 89. Ox Min Course 93. **d** 94 **p** 95. Lect Ripon Coll Cuddesdon from 92; Vice-Prin from 02; Prof Hist of Modern Th Ox Univ from 15; NSM Dorchester *Ox* 94–99; NSM Wheatley 99–14; NSM Garsington, Cuddesdon and Horspath from 14; Can Th Truro Cathl from 16. *Ripon College, Cuddesdon, Oxford OX44 9EX* T: (01865) 877405 E: mark.chapman@rcc.ac.uk

CHAPMAN, Nigel Leonard. b 58. York St Jo Coll MA 02. Cranmer Hall Dur 04. **d** 05 **p** 06. Dioc Youth Officer *York* 00–16; NSM Coxwold and Husthwaite 05–16; V Filey from 16. *5 Belle Vue Crescent, Filey YO14 9AD* T: (01723) 512645 M: 07877-793179 E: fileyvicar@gmail.com

CHAPMAN, Peter Harold White. b 40. AKC 64. **d** 65 **p** 66. C Havant *Portsm* 65–69; C Stanmer w Falmer and Moulsecoomb *Chich* 69–73; Chapl RN 73–86; Chapl Chigwell Sch Essex 86–90; P-in-c Stapleford Tawney w Theydon Mt *Chelmsf* 87–01. *Unit F, 33/F, Block 6, Tung Chung Crescent, 2 Mei Tung Street, Lantau, Hong Kong, China* E: phwchapman@aol.com

CHAPMAN, Peter John. b 50. ERMC 05. **d** 08 **p** 09. NSM Lt Barningham, Blickling, Edgefield etc *Nor* 08–11; NSM Trunch 11–12; NSM Roughton and Felbrigg, Metton, Sustead etc 12–17; NSM Aylsham and Distr 17–19; Chapl Qu Eliz Hosp King's Lynn NHS Foundn Trust 12–14; PtO *Nor* from 19. *Pump Cottage, The Street, Bessingham, Norwich NR11 7JR* T: (01263) 577782 E: mail@peterminachapman.plus.com

CHAPMAN, Peter John. b 33. Dur Univ BA 56. Cranmer Hall Dur. **d** 59 **p** 60. C Boulton *Derby* 59–62; Uganda 63–70; P-in-c Southampton St Matt *Win* 71–73; TV Southampton (City Cen) 73–78; V Bilston St Leon *Lich* 78–79; P-in-c Bilston St Mary 79–79; TR Bilston 80–98; RD Wolverhampton 89–98; rtd 99; PtO *Glouc* 99–16; *Worc* 99–16. *Flat 10, Manormead Supported Housing, Tilford Road, Hindhead GU26 6RA*

CHAPMAN, Raymond. b 41. Linc Th Coll 68. **d** 71 **p** 72. C Dronfield *Derby* 71–74; C Delaval *Newc* 75–76; TV Whorlton 76–79; V Newc St Hilda 79–83; V Blyth St Cuth 83–89; Hon C Fareham SS Pet and Paul *Portsm* 95–98; PtO 98–00 and from 05; C Purbrook 00–05. *Address withheld by request*

CHAPMAN, Canon Rex Anthony. b 38. Univ Coll Lon BA 62 St Edm Hall Ox BA 64 MA 68. Wells Th Coll 64. **d** 65 **p** 66. C Stourbridge St Thos *Worc* 65–68; Chapl Aber Univ *Ab* 68–78; Can St Andr Cathl 76–78; Bp's Adv for Educn *Carl* 78–85; Dir of Educn 85–04; Can Res Carl Cathl 78–04; rtd 04; LtO *Ab* from 06; Chapl to The Queen 97–08. *Myreside Cottage, Finzean, Banchory AB31 6NB* T: (01330) 850485 E: rex.chapman@btinternet.com

CHAPMAN, Robert Bertram. b 68. St Jo Coll Nottm BA 00 Lambeth PhD 15. **d** 00 **p** 01. C Daybrook *S'well* 00–03; P-in-c Colwick and Netherfield 03–11; V Hanwell St Thos *Lon* from 11. *St Thomas's Vicarage, 182 Boston Road, London W7 2AD* T: (020) 3302 1040 E: fatherrobert@thomashanwell.org.uk

CHAPMAN, Rodney Andrew. b 53. AKC 75. St Aug Coll Cant 75. **d** 76 **p** 77. C Hartlepool St Aid *Dur* 76–81; LtO 81–83; C Owton Manor 83–87; P-in-c Kelloe 87–92; V Sharlston *Wakef* 92–01; V Stainland w Outlane 01–14; Stainland and Outlane *Leeds* from 14; C Elland *Wakef* 06–14; *Leeds* from 14. *The Vicarage, 345 Stainland Road, Stainland, Halifax HX4 9HF* T: (01422) 311848 E: stainlandvicarage@btinternet.com

CHAPMAN, Roger. b 60. Leic Univ BSc 82 Anglia Ruskin Univ BA 09. Westcott Ho Cam 04 Seabury-Western Th Sem 05. **d** 06 **p** 07. C Norton *St Alb* 06–09; P-in-c Eaton Bray w Edlesborough 09–10; rtd 10; PtO *St Alb* 11–18; Hon C Cheshunt 18–19. *13 The Pastures, Hatfield AL10 8PB* T: (01707) 882509 M: 07905-391890 E: revrogerchapman@gmail.com *or* rchapman27@virginmedia.com

CHAPMAN, Roger John. b 34. AKC 58. **d** 59 **p** 60. C Guildf Ch Ch 59–61; Kenya 61–67; R S Milford *York* 68–77; RD Selby 72–77; V Beverley St Mary 77–88; RD Beverley 85–88; V Desborough *Pet* 88–95; R Brampton Ash w Dingley and Braybrooke 88–95; rtd 95; PtO *York* 95–15. *14 Scrubwood Lane, Beverley HU17 7BE* T: (01482) 881267

CHAPMAN, Ruth Elizabeth. b 84. St Jo Coll Dur BA 13. Cranmer Hall Dur 10. **d** 13 **p** 14. C Queen Thorne *Sarum* 13–17; PtO 17–18; C Preston Plucknett *B & W* from 19. *1 Old School Close, Yeovil BA21 3UB* M: 07739-161120 E: revruth@mail.com

CHAPMAN, Canon Sarah Jean. b 55. Lon Univ DipCOT 77. Sarum & Wells Th Coll 86. **d** 89 **p** 94. NSM Rogate w Terwick and Trotton w Chithurst *Chich* 89–94; NSM Easebourne 94–96; PtO *Portsm* 96–97; V Sheet 97–02; V Bitterne Park *Win* 02–12; Chapl The Living Well and Dioc Adv for Healing and Wholeness *Cant* 12–19; Hon Can Cant Cathl 16–19; rtd 19. *2 Wyndham Mews, Porsmouth PO1 2NY* T: (023) 9204 4542 E: revsarah@sargil.co.uk

CHAPMAN, Stephen Gerard. b 61. Man Univ BSc 83 Sheff Univ BA 15. Yorks Min Course 13. **d** 15 **p** 16. C Sheff Manor 15–18; V Worsbrough w Elsecar from 18. *The Vicarage, Wath Road, Elsecar, Barnsley S74 8HJ* T: (01226) 744953 M: 07980-065236 E: steve.chapman2015@gmail.com

CHAPMAN, Thomas Graham. b 33. Trin Coll Bris 73. **d** 75 **p** 76. C Branksome St Clem *Sarum* 75–81; V Quarry Bank *Lich* 81–93; V Quarry Bank *Worc* 93–99; rtd 99; PtO *Worc* from 99. *8 Somerset Drive, Wollaston, Stourbridge DY8 4RH* T: (01384) 373921 E: thomas.chapman1@btinternet.com

CHAPMAN, Timothy Mark. b 69. Clare Coll Cam BA 91. Oak Hill Th Coll BA 02. **d** 02 **p** 03. C Lt Shelford *Ely* 02–13. *6 Wakelin Avenue, Sawston, Cambridge CB22 3DS* T: (01223) 830169 *or* 820116 M: 07815-686072 E: timandlucy@gmail.com

CHAPMAN, Tristan David. b 79. K Alfred's Coll Win BA 01. Ripon Coll Cuddesdon BTh 07. **d** 07 **p** 08. C Bocking St Mary *Chelmsf* 07–10; TV Chipping Barnet St Alb from 10. *St Mark's Vicarage, 56 Potters Road, Barnet EN5 5HY* T: (020) 8440 7490 E: fr.tristan@googlemail.com

CHAPMAN, Miss Yvonne Hazel. b 50. Serampore Th Coll BRE 63 Brighton Coll of Educn CertEd 55. EAMTC 95. **d** 96 **p** 97. NSM Duston *Pet* 96–02; NSM Officer 99–02; rtd 02; PtO *Pet* from 02. *St Christopher's Home, Abington Park Crescent, Northampton NN3 3AD* E: rev.yhc@btinternet.com

CHAPPELL, Frank Arnold. b 37. Dur Univ BA 58. Bps' Coll Cheshunt. **d** 60 **p** 61. C Headingley *Ripon* 60–65; V Beeston Hill St Luke 65–73; R Garforth 73–91; V Dacre w Hartwith and Darley w Thornthwaite 91–02; rtd 02; PtO *York* from 02; *Ripon* 02–14; *Leeds* from 14. *14 Nelsons Lane, York YO24 1HD* T: (01904) 709566 E: frankngail.chappell@sky.com

CHARD, Mrs Julia Clare. b 54. Trin Coll Bris 09. **d** 11 **p** 12. OLM Soundwell *Bris* 11–16; OLM Fromeside from 17. *8 Glenside Close, Bristol BS16 2QY* T: 0117-902 1774 E: chardjulia7@gmail.com

CHARD, Reginald Jeffrey. b 40. Univ of Wales (Lamp) BA 62 CQSW 75. Coll of Resurr Mirfield 62. **d** 64 **p** 65. C Ystrad Mynach *Llan* 64–67; C Aberdare St Fagan 67–71; V Hirwaun 71–74; Hon C Stechford *Birm* 74–78; TV Banbury *Ox* 78–86; Ind Chapl 86–09; P-in-c Claydon w Mollington 86–96; R Ironstone 96–09; rtd 09. *15 The Glen, Yarmouth PO41 0PZ* T: (01983) 760554 E: jeffreychard@btinternet.com

CHARING CROSS, Archdeacon of. *Vacant*

CHARKHAM, Rupert Anthony. b 59. Ex Univ BA 81. Wycliffe Hall Ox 83. **d** 89 **p** 89. C Ox St Aldate w St Matt 89–92; P-in-c Fisherton Anger *Sarum* 92–99; R 99–03; V Cambridge H Trin *Ely* from 03; Chapl to The Queen from 16. *Holy Trinity Vicarage, 1 Selwyn Gardens, Cambridge CB3 9AX* T: (01223) 354774 *or* 355397 E: rupert.charkham@htcambridge.org.uk

CHARLES, Ms Beverley Maria. b 65. FCCA 92. Trin Coll Bris 13. **d** 15 **p** 16. C Yate *Bris* 15–18; TR Kingswood from 18; V Hanham from 18. *Holy Trinity Vicarage, 18 High Street, Kingswood, Bristol BS15 4AB* M: 07801-056553 E: beverleycharles@blueyonder.co.uk

CHARLES, David Gordon. b 79. Ex Coll Ox BA 01 MA 04 CCC Cam BA 05 MA 09. Westcott Ho Cam 03. **d** 06 **p** 07. C Willingdon *Chich* 06–10; P-in-c Waldron 10–12; V Eastbourne Ch Ch and St Phil from 12; Chapl to Bp Lewes from 10. *Christ Church Vicarage, 18 Addingham Road, Eastbourne BN22 7DY* T: (01323) 728522 E: davidgcharles@hotmail.com *or* vicar@ccwithsp.org

CHARLES, James Richard. b 67. St Edm Hall Ox BA 90 CertEd 91. Oak Hill Th Coll BA 03. **d** 03 **p** 04. C Throop *Win* 03–07; P-in-c Bexleyheath St Pet *Roch* 07–11; V from 11. *St Peter's Vicarage, 50 Bristow Road, Bexleyheath DA7 4QA* T: (020) 8303 8713 E: jimrcharles@mac.com

CHARLES, Canon Jonathan. b 42. St Luke's Coll Ex CertEd 64. Ripon Hall Ox 72 Ripon Coll Cuddesdon 78. **d** 79 **p** 80. C Leagrave *St Alb* 79–82; Chapl Denstone Coll Uttoxeter 82–86; Chapl Malvern Girls' Coll 86–89; Chapl K Sch Worc 89–95; Min Can Worc Cathl 89–95; R Burnham Gp of Par *Nor* 95–09; RD Burnham and Walsingham 00–08; Hon Can Nor Cathl 05–09; rtd 09; PtO *Nor* from 09. *Michaelmas Cottage, 99 Burnham Road, North Creake, Fakenham NR21 9LB* T: (01328) 738249 E: revj.charles@virgin.net

CHARLES, Kevin. b 58. EMMTC 08. **d** 11 **p** 12. NSM Annesley w Newstead *S'well* 11–15; Chapl E Midl Ambulance Service from 15; NSM Kirkby in Ashfield St Thos *S'well* from 15. *6 Boughton Close, Sutton-in-Ashfield NG17 4NJ* T: (01623) 514294 E: kevin.charles1@btinternet.com

CHARLES, Meedperdas Edward. b 28. Fitzw Ho Cam BA 60 MA 64. Bangalore Th Coll BD 54. **d** 54 **p** 55. C Malacca Malaya 54–55; P-in-c Singapore St Paul and St Pet Singapore 55–58; PtO *Ely* 58–60; V Sheff St Bart Langsett Road 60–64; Chapl Univ of Singapore 64–66; V Gravelly Hill *Birm* 66–78; V Endcliffe *Sheff* 79–90; rtd 91; PtO *Sheff* from 91. *60 Ringinglow Road, Sheffield S11 7PQ* T: 0114-266 4980

CHARLES, Nathan John. b 80. Wycliffe Hall Ox. **d** 13 **p** 14. C Broadwell, Evenlode, Oddington, Adlestrop etc *Glouc* 13–16; C Hoxton St Anne w St Columba *Lon* from 16. *19 Pelter Street, London E2 7PE* M: 07968-975236 E: njcharles@gmail.com

CHARLES, Robert Sidney James. b 40. Lon Univ CertEd 77 Open Univ BA 79 Univ of Wales LLM 97. St Mich Coll Llan. **d** 65 **p** 66. C Merthyr Tydfil *Llan* 65–68; C Shotton *St As* 68–70; R Stock and Lydlinch *Sarum* 70–74; R Hubberston *St D* 74–76; PtO *Chelmsf* 81–83; V Crossens *Liv* 83–97; V Budleigh Salterton *Ex* 97–10; rtd 10; PtO *Ex* from 11. *8 Old Bystock Drive, Exmouth EX8 5RB* T: (01395) 223419 E: r.charles@btinternet.com

CHARLES, Mrs Susan Jane. b 67. Cant Ch Ch Univ BA 12. SEITE 05. **d** 08 **p** 09. NSM Eltham H Trin *S'wark* 08–13; NSM Mottingham St Edw 13–16; PtO from 16. *Address withheld by request* M: 07909-037690 E: susanjcharles@aol.com

CHARLES-EDWARDS, David Mervyn. b 38. Trin Coll Cam BA 61. Linc Th Coll 62. **d** 64 **p** 89. C Putney St Mary *S'wark* 64–65; Chief Exec Officer Br Assn for Counselling 82–87; Gen Manager Lon Lighthouse AIDS Project 87–88; Consultant in leadership and team building from 88; NSM Rugby *Cov* 89–99; P-in-c Clifton upon Dunsmore and Newton 99–03; PtO from 03. *3 Pudding Bag Lane, Thurlaston, Rugby CV23 9JZ* T: (01788) 815395 E: adce@btinternet.com

CHARLESWORTH, Eric Charlesworth. b 29. Kelham Th Coll 49. **d** 54 **p** 56. C Woodbridge St Mary *St E* 54–57; Asst Chapl Oslo St Edm *Eur* 57–59; Canada 60–66; R Huntingfield w Cookley *St E* 66–70; R Slimbridge *Glouc* 70–96; rtd 96; PtO *Glouc* 96–16; *Ox* 04–12. *37 Pavilion Walk, South Street, Letcombe Regis, Wantage OX12 9SQ*

CHARLESWORTH, Ian Peter. b 65. Lanc Univ BA 87. St Mich Coll Llan 91. **d** 93 **p** 94. C Caereithin *S & B* 93–95; C Oystermouth 95–97; R Llandefalle and Llyswen w Boughrood etc from 97. *The Rectory, Church Lane, Llyswen, Brecon LD3 0UU* T: (01874) 754255 E: ian.charlesworth@btinternet.com

CHARLESWORTH, Philip. b 55. Sheff City Poly BSc 85 Anglia Poly MSc 92. **d** 07 **p** 08. OLM Sprowston w Beeston *Nor* 07–13; NSM Taverham 13–16; NSM Taverham w Ringland from 16. *63 Wroxham Road, Norwich NR7 8TN* T: (01603) 411316 M: 07545-968435 E: revdphilcharlesworth@gmail.com

CHARLTON, Mrs Elizabeth Anne. b 55. STETS BA 08. d 08 p 09. C W Moors *Sarum* 08–11; C Budleigh Salterton *Ex* 11–12; P-in-c 12–13; C E Budleigh w Bicton and Otterton 11–12; P-in-c 12–13; V Budleigh Salterton, E Budleigh w Bicton etc 13–17; P-in-c St Goran w Caerhays *Truro* 17–18. *11 Sid Park Road, Sidmouth EX10 9BW* M: 07807-827781 E: eacharlton@btinternet.com

CHARLTON, Dr Fraser Graham. b 67. Newc Univ BMedSci 88 MB, BS 91 PhD 97. Lindisfarne Regional Tr Partnership 12. d 15 p 17. NSM Wallsend St Jo *Newc* 15–16; NSM Newc St Gabr from 16. *17 Northumberland Avenue, Forest Hall, Newcastle upon Tyne NE12 9NR* T: 0191-292 1033 M: 07783-402007 E: fraser.charlton@ncl.ac.uk

CHARLTON, Thomas David. b 53. York St Jo Univ BA 12 IEng MIET 80. Cranmer Hall Dur 12. d 13 p 14. NSM Whorlton w Carlton and Faceby *York* 13–15; NSM Eston w Normanby 15–16; NSM Ingleby Barwick from 16. *28 Brougham Close, Ingleby Barwick, Stockton-on-Tees TS17 5GH* T: (01642) 767176 M: 07805-388165 E: td.charlton@btinternet.com

CHARMAN, Canon Jane Ellen Elizabeth. b 60. St Jo Coll Dur BA 81 Selw Coll Cam BA 84 MA 88. Westcott Ho Cam 82. d 87 p 94. C Glouc St Geo w Whaddon 87–90; Chapl and Fell Clare Coll Cam 90–95; R Duxford *Ely* 95–04; V Hinxton 95–04; V Ickleton 95–04; RD Shelford 03–04; Dir of Min *Sarum* 04–07; Dir of Learning for Discipleship and Min from 07; Can and Preb Sarum Cathl from 07. *4 The Sidings, Downton, Salisbury SP5 3QZ* T: (01722) 411944 M: 07867-146524 E: jane.charman@salisbury.anglican.org

CHARMAN, Mrs Karen. b 71. Birm Univ BA 97 Newc Univ PGCE 98. Ripon Coll Cuddesdon 14. d 16 p 17. C Delaval *Newc* from 16. *103 Holyfields, West Allotment, Newcastle upon Tyne NE27 0EU* M: 07535-943805 E: marlowecharman@googlemail.com

CHARMLEY, Mrs Tracy-Belinda. b 72. Ex Univ BA 93 St Luke's Coll Ex PGCE 95 Birm Univ MEd. Ripon Coll Cuddesdon 07. d 10 p 11. NSM Guernsey St Martin *Win* 10–14; NSM Guernsey W Par 14–16; NSM Guernsey St Philippe de Torteval from 16; NSM Guernsey St Sav from 16. *The Rectory, Le Neuf Chemin Road, St Saviour, Guernsey GY7 9FQ* T: (01481) 263045 E: charmley@cwgsy.net

CHARNLEY, Anthony Keith. b 49. Dur Univ BSc 71 PhD 76 FHEA 07. STETS. d 12 p 13. NSM N Bradford on Avon and Villages *Sarum* from 12; Visiting Prof Chongqing Univ China from 08. *41 Leigh Park Road, Bradford-on-Avon BA15 1TF* T: (01225) 866515 E: akeithcharnley@gmail.com

CHARNOCK, Deryck Ian. b 47. Oak Hill Th Coll 78. d 80 p 81. C Rowner *Portsm* 80–84; TV Southgate *Chich* 84–90; V Penge St Paul *Roch* 90–98; V Whitwick St Jo the Bapt *Leic* 98–06; R Hollington St Leon *Chich* 06–15; rtd 15; PtO *Roch* from 16. *10 Faraday Ride, Tonbridge TN10 4RL* T: (01732) 365617 E: deryckc@btinternet.com

CHARNOCK, Ms Tracy. b 75. Leeds Univ BA 97 BA 08. Coll of Resurr Mirfield 06. d 08 p 09. C Man Victoria Park 08–11; P-in-c S Shore H Trin *Blackb* 11–13; V from 13; P-in-c S Shore St Pet 11–13; V from 13. *92 Watson Road, Blackpool FY4 2DE* T: (01253) 344773 M: 07778-163920 E: tracy.charnock@hotmail.co.uk

CHARTERS, Alan Charles. b 35. Trin Hall Cam BA 60 MA 63 FCollP 88. Linc Th Coll 60. d 62 p 63. C Gt Grimsby St Mary and St Jas *Linc* 62–65; Chapl and Hd RE Eliz Coll Guernsey 65–70; P-in-c Guernsey St Jas the Less 65–70; Dep Hd Master Park Sen High Sch Swindon 70–73; Chapl St Jo Sch Leatherhead 73–83; Dep Hd Master 76; Visiting Lect and Tutor Lon Univ Inst of Ed 76–80; Headmaster The K Sch Glouc 83–92; V Aberedw w Llandeilo Graban and Llanbadarn etc *S & B* 92–00; Bp's Visitor to Schs 92–00; rtd 00; PtO *Eur* 00–03; P-in-c Dinard 03–06. *Crescent House, Church Street, Talgarth, Brecon LD3 0BL* T: (01874) 711135 E: ac.charters@btinternet.com

✠**CHARTRES, The Rt Revd and Rt Hon Lord (Richard John Carew).** b 47. Trin Coll Cam BA 68 MA 73 Lambeth BD 83 Hon DLitt 98 Hon DD 99 FSA 99 Hon FGCM 97. Cuddesdon Coll 69 Linc Th Coll 72. d 73 p 74 c 92. C Bedford St Andr *St Alb* 73–75; Bp's Dom Chapl 75–80; Abp's Chapl *Cant* 80–84; P-in-c Westmr St Steph w St Jo *Lon* 84–85; V 86–92; Dir of Ords 85–92; Prof Div Gresham Coll 86–92; Six Preacher Cant Cathl 91–97; Area Bp Stepney *Lon* 92–95; Bp Lon 95–17; rtd 17; Dean of Hm Chpls Royal from 95; Hon Asst Bp Eur from 17; PtO *Sarum* from 19. *House of Lords, Houses of Parliament, London SW1A 0PW*

CHASE, Mrs Elisabeth. b 49. Wycliffe Hall Ox. d 09 p 10. NSM Headbourne Worthy *Win* from 09; NSM King's Worthy from 09. *The Vicarage, Sloe Lane, Micheldever, Winchester SO21 3DA* E: lis.chase@gmail.com

CHATER, John Augustus. b 43. SEITE 99. d 04 p 05. NSM St Peter-in-Thanet *Cant* 04–07; Ramsgate Town Cen Missr 07–13; rtd 13; PtO *Cant* from 13. *125 High Street, Ramsgate CT11 9UA* T: (01843) 596175 E: john.chater@gmail.com

CHATER, John Leathley. b 29. Qu Coll Cam BA 54 MA 58. Ridley Hall Cam 54. d 56 p 57. C Bath Abbey w St Jas *B & W* 56–60; V Bermondsey St Anne *S'wark* 60–64; Ind Chapl 60–64; V Heslington *York* 64–69; Chapl York Univ 64–69; V Lawrence Weston *Bris* 69–73; PtO 74–80; P-in-c Wraxall *B & W* 80–82; R 82–84; V Battle *Chich* 84–90; Dean Battle 84–90; RD Battle and Bexhill 86–90; R St Marylebone w H Trin *Lon* 90–96; rtd 96; PtO *Chich* 96–11. *Oak Lodge, 2 Saxonwood Road, Battle TN33 0EY* T: (01424) 772743 E: jlchater@icloud.com

CHATER (née CAKE), Nichola Carla. b 58. Liv Univ BSc 79 MB, ChB 85 MRCGP FRCP 08. Cranmer Hall Dur 05. d 07 p 08. NSM Dur St Marg and Neville's Cross St Jo from 07. *37 Hill Meadows, High Shincliffe, Durham DH1 2PE* T: 0191-383 1869 E: nicky_chater@yahoo.co.uk

CHATFIELD, Adrian Francis. b 49. Leeds Univ BA 71 MA 72 MPhil 89 PhD 97. Coll of Resurr Mirfield 71. d 72 p 73. Trinidad and Tobago 72–83; TV Barnstaple, Goodleigh and Landkey *Ex* 83–84; TV Barnstaple 85; TR 85–88; Lect St Jo Coll Nottm 88–98; S Africa 99–05; Tutor Wycliffe Hall Ox 05–07; Hon C Wallingford *Ox* 05–07; Co-ord Mixed Mode Tr Ridley Hall Cam 07–15; Tutor 15–16; Dir Simeon Cen 07–16; rtd 16; PtO *S'well* from 17. *63 Wesley Street, Ilkeston DE7 8QW* T: 0115-930 1065 E: adrian.chatfield@btinternet.com

CHATFIELD, Mrs Gillian. b 50. Leeds Univ BA 71 PGCE 72. St Jo Coll Nottm MA 94. d 94 p 95. C Greasley *S'well* 94–98; Miss Partner Th Coll by Ext S Africa 99–05; TV Wallingford *Ox* 05–07; Past Tutor Ridley Hall Cam 07–13; Hon C Lordsbridge *Ely* 13–15; PtO 15–16; *S'well* from 17. *63 Wesley Street, Ilkeston DE7 8QW* T: 0115-930 1065 M: 07758-591430 E: jill.chatfield@btinternet.com

CHATFIELD, Michael Francis. b 75. York Univ BSc 96 Fitzw Coll Cam BA 99 MA 03. Ridley Hall Cam. d 00 p 01. C Attenborough *S'well* 00–03; P-in-c Chaguanas St Thos Trinidad and Tobago 04–09; Chapl RAF from 09. *Chaplaincy Services (RAF), HQ Air Command, RAF High Wycombe HP14 4UE* T: (01494) 496800 M: 07540-848758 E: thechatalots@hotmail.com

CHATFIELD, Canon Norman. b 37. Fitzw Ho Cam BA 59 MA 68. Ripon Hall Ox 60. d 62 p 63. C Burgess Hill St Jo *Chich* 62–65; C Uckfield 65–69; V Lower Sandown St Jo *Portsm* 69–76; V Locks Heath 76–83; R Alverstoke 83–91; Hon Can Portsm Cathl 85–91; Can Res Glouc Cathl 91–02; rtd 02; PtO *Portsm* from 03. *Ellwood, Garfield Road, Bishop's Waltham SO32 1AT* T: (01489) 891995 E: chat.field@btinternet.com

CHATTELL, David Malcolm. b 63. St Luke's Coll Ex BEd 93. Wycliffe Hall Ox 03. d 05 p 06. C Bucklebury w Marlston *Ox* 05–11; R Farleigh, Candover and Wield *Win* from 11; RD Alresford from 19. *The Rectory, Alresford Road, Preston Candover, Basingstoke RG25 2EE* T: (01256) 389474 E: davidchattell172@btinternet.com

CHATTEN, Mrs Sophie. b 79. d 15 p 16. C Stoughton *Guildf* from 15. *12 Grange Close, Guildford GU2 9QJ* M: 07969-604514 E: sophiebish@gmail.com

CHATTERLEY, Mrs Marion Frances. b 55. Edin Th Coll 95. d 98 p 99. C Edin Gd Shep 98–00; C Edin Ch Ch 00–05; Hon C Edin St Mich and All SS 07–11; Chapl Edin Napier Univ 99–12; Dioc Dir of Ords from 06. *102 Relugas Road, Edinburgh EH9 2LZ* T: 0131-667 6847 M: 07771-982163 E: marion.chatterley@blueyonder.co.uk

CHATTERTON, Mrs Nicola Mary. b 63. Qu Coll Birm BA 15. d 14 p 15. NSM Stratford-upon-Avon, Luddington etc *Cov* 14–17; C Avon Dassett w Farnborough and Fenny Compton 17–18; P-in-c from 18; C Burton Dassett 17–18; P-in-c from 18; C Gaydon w Chadshunt 17–18; P-in-c from 18. *Burton Dassett Vicarage, Bottom Street, Northend, Southam CV47 2TH* M: 07769-871237 E: chat2rev.nicki@gmail.com

CHATWIN, Ronald Ernest. b 34. St Aid Birkenhead 58. d 60 p 61. C Selsdon *Cant* 60–64; C Crawley *Chich* 64–68; V Coldwaltham 68–74; TV Ovingdean w Rottingdean and Woodingdean 74–83; V Saltdean 83–91; V Hellingly and Upper Dicker 91–02; rtd 02; PtO *Chich* from 03. *Cold Waltham, 29A New Road, Hellingly, Hailsham BN27 4EW* T: (01323) 843346 E: ronaldchatwin@hotmail.com

CHAUDHARY, Jaisher Masih. b 56. Qu Coll Birm. d 08 p 09. NSM Handsworth St Mich *Birm* from 08; NSM Handsworth Good News Asian Ch from 12. *29 George Street, Handsworth, Birmingham B21 0EG* T: 0121-551 6279 E: jaisher@hotmail.com

CHAVE, Preb Brian Philip. b 51. Open Univ BA. Trin Coll Bris. d 84 p 85. C Cullompton *Ex* 84–87; TV Bishopsnympton, Rose Ash, Mariansleigh etc 87–93; Chapl for Agric *Heref* 93–96; Communications Adv and Bp's Staff Officer

97–01; Bp's Dom Chapl 97–01; TV W Heref 01–15; Bp's Dom Chapl from 15; RD Heref City 04–07; Preb Heref Cathl from 97; Can Heref Cathl 97–01. *The Bishop's Office, The Palace, Hereford HR4 9BN* T: (01432) 271355 E: b.chave@hereford.anglican.org

CHAVE-COX, Guy. b 56. St Andr Univ BSc 79. Wycliffe Hall Ox 83. **d** 86 **p** 87. C Wigmore Abbey *Heref* 86–88; C Bideford *Ex* 88–91; TV Barnstaple 91–17; V Sticklepath w Roundswell from 17. *St Paul's Vicarage, Old Sticklepath Hill, Barnstaple EX31 2BG* T: (01271) 344400 E: vicar@barnstaple-st-paul.org.uk

CHAVNER, Robert. b 59. ALCM 82 AGSM 85 FGMS 00 FRSA 05. Linc Th Coll 90. **d** 92 **p** 93. C Beckenham St Geo *Roch* 92–96; V Sevenoaks St Luke 96–06; P-in-c Brighton St Nic *Chich* 06–11; V 11–16; rtd 16; PtO *Ex* from 17; *Eur* from 18. *The Old School, Whittingham, Alnwick NE66 4UP* M: 07714-653264 E: robertchavner@outlook.com

CHEATLE, Adèle Patricia. b 46. York Univ BA 73. Trin Coll Bris 76. **d** 87 **p** 98. Par Dn Harborne Heath *Birm* 87; NSM 92–93; PtO *Heref* 96–97; NSM Burghill and Stretton Sugwas 97–99; NSM Heref St Pet w St Owen and St Jas 99–04; NSM Ches Square St Mich w St Phil *Lon* 04–07; PtO *Birm* from 11. *26 Oakham Road, Harborne, Birmingham B17 9DG* T: 0121-427 5362 E: thecheatles@googlemail.com

CHEDZEY, The Ven Derek Christopher. b 67. Univ of Wales MA 12. Trin Coll Bris BA 93. **d** 93 **p** 94. C Bedgrove *Ox* 93–95; C Haddenham w Cuddington, Kingsey etc 95–98; TV High Wycombe 98–01; Deanery Tr Officer and C Washfield, Stoodleigh, Withleigh etc *Ex* 01–04; P-in-c Frenchay and Winterbourne Down *Bris* 04–06; Dioc Dir Lay Min 04–08; Adv for Initial Minl Educn 08–15; Warden of Readers 04–15; Hon C Yate 09–15; Asst Adn 13–15; Hon Can Bris Cathl 11–15; Hd of Min Development 15–18; Can Res Bris Cathl 15–18; Dioc Dir of Ords 15–18; Adn Heref from 18. *The Diocesan Office, The Palace, Hereford HR4 9BL* T: (01432) 373316 M: 07811-878774 E: archdeacon@hereford.anglican.org

CHEESEMAN (*née* DUNHAM), **Mrs Angela Mary.** b 40. New Hall Cam MB, BChir 66 MRCOG 74 FRCSEd 75 FRCOG 96. **d** 05 **p** 06. OLM Eastling w Ospringe and Stalisfield w Otterden *Cant* 05–10; PtO 11–17. *New House Farm, Otterden Road, Eastling, Faversham ME13 0BN* T: (01795) 890629

CHEESEMAN, Colin Henry. b 47. Reading Univ BA 69 Kent Univ PhD 00. Sarum & Wells Th Coll 82. **d** 84 **p** 85. C Cranleigh *Guildf* 84–87; C Godalming 87–89; V Cuddington 89–96; Chapl HM Pris Wealstun 96–97; P-in-c Tockwith and Bilton w Bickerton *York* 97–01; RD New Ainsty 99–01; P-in-c Roundhay St Jo *Ripon* 01–14; Dioc Ecum Adv 09–14; rtd 14; PtO *York* from 16. *Scatwell House, Church Fenton Lane, Ulleskelf, Tadcaster LS24 9DW* E: colin.cheeseman3@gmail.com

CHEESEMAN, Janet. See GOODAIR, Jan

CHEESEMAN, Trevor Percival. b 38. Auckland Univ PhD 64 Lon Univ BD 67. K Coll Lon and St Boniface Warminster AKC 67. **d** 68 **p** 69. C Warmsworth *Sheff* 68–71; C Manurewa New Zealand 71–73; P-in-c Birkdale-Beach Haven 73–77; V Meadowbank 77–85; Chapl K Coll Auckland 86–99; P-in-c Whitford 00–03; rtd 03; PtO New Zealand from 03. *Apartment 803, Betty Pyatt Building, 101 Shaftesbury Avenue, Selwyn Village, Point Chevalier, Auckland 1022, New Zealand* T: (0064) (9) 849 9303 M: (0064) 27-610 3768 E: tpandhmc@middleearth.net.nz

CHEESMAN, Peter. b 43. ACA 65 FCA 76 MCMI. Ridley Hall Cam 66. **d** 69 **p** 70. C Herne Bay Ch Ch *Cant* 69–74; TV Lowestoft St Marg *Nor* 75–78; TV Lowestoft and Kirkley 79–81; Ind Chapl *Glouc* 81–84; P-in-c Saul w Fretherne and Framilode 84–85; V Frampton on Severn, Arlingham, Saul etc 85–08; rtd 08; PtO *Glouc* from 15. *Frampton Court, The Green, Frampton on Severn, Gloucester GL2 7EX* T: (01452) 740533 E: peter@the-cheesman.net

CHEETHAM, David Andrew. b 69. **d** 12 **p** 13. NSM Kenilworth St Jo *Cov* 12–13; NSM Olton *Birm* 13–16; NSM Birm Cathl from 16. *75 Solihull Road, Shirley, Solihull B90 3HJ* T: 0121-744 4407 E: d.cheetham@bham.ac.uk

CHEETHAM (*née* MUMFORD), **Mrs Lesley Anne.** b 51. Man Univ BA 73. NOC 01. **d** 04 **p** 05. C Halifax *Wakef* 04–08; V Easby w Skeeby and Brompton on Swale etc *Ripon* 08–12; Chapl Overgate Hospice 12–19; P-in-c Greetland and W Vale *Leeds* 15–19; rtd 19. *Mokes Barn, Wainstalls Lane, Halifax HX2 7TR* M: 07963-620391 E: lesley_cheetham@btinternet.com

✠**CHEETHAM, The Rt Revd Richard Ian.** b 55. CCC Ox BA 77 CertEd 78 MA 82 Lon Univ PhD 99. Ripon Coll Cuddesdon 85. **d** 87 **p** 88 **c** 02. C Newc H Cross 87–90; V Luton St Aug Limbury *St Alb* 90–99; RD Luton 95–98; Adn St Alb 99–02; Area Bp Kingston *S'wark* from 02. *Kingston Episcopal Area Office, 620 Kingston Road, London*

SW20 8DN T: (020) 8545 2440 *or* 8789 3218 F: 8545 2441 E: bishop.richard@southwark.anglican.org

CHEGWIN HALL, Elaine. See HALL, Elaine Chegwin

CHELASHAW, Godfrey Kiprotich (Kip). b 76. Oak Hill Th Coll BA 08 MA 10. **d** 10 **p** 11. C Audley *Lich* 10–15; C Talke 14–15; C Alsagers Bank 14–15; C Alsagers Bank, Audley and Talke 15; C E Dean w Friston and Jevington *Chich* 15–17; Kenya from 17. *PO Box 42383-00100, GPO Nairobi, Kenya* E: kchelashaw@yahoo.com

CHELMSFORD, Bishop of. See COTTRELL, The Rt Revd Stephen Geoffrey

CHELMSFORD, Dean of. See HENSHALL, The Very Revd Nicholas James

CHELTENHAM, Archdeacon of. See ANDREW, The Ven Philip John

CHERRY, David. b 30. Roch Th Coll 59. **d** 61 **p** 62. C Seacroft *Ripon* 61–67; R Bamford *Derby* 67–75; Chapl Málaga w Almuñécar *Eur* 83–91; rtd 91; NSM Waltham St Lawrence *Ox* 97–01; PtO *Leic* from 01. *2 Church Lane, Rearsby, Leicester LE7 4YE* T: (01664) 424099

CHERRY, David Warwick. b 61. Cape Town Univ BMus 86 Leeds Univ BA 91. Coll of Resurr Mirfield 92. **d** 92 **p** 93. C Hammersmith SS Mich and Geo White City Estate CD *Lon* 92–01; C Hammersmith St Luke 94–01; Chapl Greenwich Univ *S'wark* 01–03; Chapl Univ of Westmr *Lon* 03–10; Hon C St Marylebone St Cypr 06–08; V Pimlico St Mary Bourne Street 10–15; V Pimlico St Barn 10–15; PtO 15–16; NSM Kilburn St Aug w St Jo 16–18; PtO 18. *The Curate's Flat, St Paul's Vicarage, 60 Park Lane, London N17 0JR* T: (020) 7624 1637 M: 07939-553547 E: davidcherry@onetel.com

CHERRY, Stephen Arthur. b 58. St Chad's Coll Dur BSc 79 Fitzw Coll Cam BA 85 MA 90 K Coll Lon PhD 95. Westcott Ho Cam 83. **d** 86 **p** 87. C Baguley and Asst Chapl Wythenshawe Hosp Man 86–89; Chapl K Coll Cam 89–94; R Loughborough All SS w H Trin *Leic* 94–06; RD Akeley E 96–99; Hon Can Leic Cathl 04–06; Dir Min and Tr *Dur* 06–14; Can Res Dur Cathl 06–14; Dean K Coll Cam from 14. *King's College, Cambridge CB2 1ST* T: (01223) 331419 E: sacherry@btinternet.com *or* dean@kings.cam.ac.uk

CHESHIRE, Mrs Charlotte Amy. b 77. St Jo Coll Nottm 11. **d** 14 **p** 15. C Shifnal and Sheriffhales *Lich* 14–16; C Tong 14–16; C Shifnal, Sheriffhales and Tong 16–17; C Wellington All SS w Eyton 17–18; P-in-c Moldgreen and Rawthorpe *Leeds* from 18; Chapl Huddersfield Univ from 18. *The Vicarage, 35 Church Lane, Moldgreen, Huddersfield HD5 9DL* M: 07553-432657 E: rev.charlottecheshire@gmail.com

CHESHIRE, James Wilson. b 73. Univ of Florida BA 05. Gordon-Conwell Th Sem MDiv 00 CITC 13. **d** 14 **p** 15. Bangor Abbey *D & D* 14–15; C 15–18; I Ballybeen from 18. *1 Grahams Bridge Road, Dundonald, Belfast BT16 2DB* T: (028) 9058 6939 M: 07751-576954 E: revjimcheshire@gmail.com

CHESNEY, David Vince. b 69. UMIST BSc 99. NTMTC BA 08. **d** 08 **p** 09. C Springfield H Trin *Chelmsf* 08–12; V Victoria Docks Ascension from 12. *75 Baxter Road, London E16 3HJ* E: dave.chesney@btinternet.com

✠**CHESSUN, The Rt Revd Christopher Thomas James.** b 56. Univ Coll Ox BA 78 MA 82 Trin Hall Cam BA 82. Westcott Ho Cam. **d** 83 **p** 84 **c** 05. C Sandhurst *Ox* 83–87; C Portsea St Mary *Portsm* 87–89; Min Can and Chapl St Paul's Cathl *Lon* 89–93; Voc Adv 90–05; R Stepney St Dunstan and All SS 93–01; AD Tower Hamlets 97–01; Adn Northolt 01–05; Area Bp Woolwich *S'wark* 05–11; Bp *S'wark* from 11. *Bishop's House, 38 Tooting Bec Gardens, London SW16 1QZ* T: (020) 8769 3256 *or* 7939 9420 F: 8769 4126 E: bishop.christopher@southwark.anglican.org

CHESTER, David Kenneth. b 50. Dur Univ BA 73 Aber Univ PhD 78 CGeol 92 FGS 88. NOC 93. **d** 96 **p** 97. NSM Hoylake *Ches* 96–04; NSM W Kirby St Bridget from 04; PtO *Liv* from 16. *Yenda, Grange Old Road, West Kirby, Wirral CH48 4ET* T: 0151-625 8004 E: jg54@liv.ac.uk

CHESTER, Irene Mary. See GREENNAM, Irene Mary

CHESTER, Letitia Irene. b 46. Yorks Min Course 08. **d** 10 **p** 11. NSM Clifton *York* 10–13; NSM Dringhouses 13–17; rtd 17; PtO *York* from 17. *6 Woodland Chase, York YO30 6RE* T: (01904) 692652 E: letitiachester@btinternet.com

CHESTER, Mark. b 55. Lanc Univ BA 79. Wycliffe Hall Ox 86. **d** 88 **p** 89. C Plymouth St Andr w St Paul and St Geo *Ex* 88–94; V Burney Lane *Birm* 94–99; V Camberley St Paul *Guildf* 99–15; Sen Chapl Waterways from 15; PtO *Guildf* from 15; Public Preacher *St Alb* from 15; CF (TA) from 89. *Berisay, Guildford Road, Frimley Green GU16 6NS* E: markwith29@gmail.com

CHESTER, Maureen Olga. b 47. Univ of Wales (Swansea) BA 70. NEOC 94. **d** 97 **p** 98. NSM Morpeth *Newc* 97–11; rtd 11; PtO *Newc* from 11. *10 Leland Place, Morpeth NE61 2AN* T: (01670) 514569 E: mochester2001@yahoo.co.uk

CHESTER, Philip Anthony Edwin. b 55. Birm Univ LLB 76. Cranmer Hall Dur 77. **d** 80 **p** 81. C Shrewsbury St Chad *Lich* 80–85; C St Martin-in-the-Fields *Lon* 85–88; Chapl K Coll Lon 88–95; P-in-c Westmr St Matt *Lon* 95–03; V from 03; P-in-c St Mary le Strand w St Clem Danes from 14; AD Westmr St Marg from 05; PV Westmr Abbey from 90. *St Matthew's House, 20 Great Peter Street, London SW1P 2BU* T: (020) 7222 3704 F: 7233 0255 E: paec@stmw.org

CHESTER, Archdeacon of. *See* GILBERTSON, The Ven Michael Robert

CHESTER, Bishop of. *See* FORSTER, The Rt Revd Peter Robert

CHESTER, Dean of. *See* STRATFORD, The Very Revd Timothy Richard

CHESTERFIELD, Archdeacon of. *See* COSLETT, The Ven Carol Ann

CHESTERFIELD-TERRY, John Darcy Francis Malcolm. b 82. Kingston Univ BEng 05. Ripon Coll Cuddesdon 12. **d** 15 **p** 16. C Portsea St Mary *Portsm* 15–19; V Colnbrook and Datchet *Ox* from 19. *St Mary's Vicarage, London Road, Datchet, Slough SL3 9JW* M: 07442-197723 E: vicar@colnbrookanddatchet.co.uk

CHESTERMAN, Canon George Anthony (Tony). b 38. Man Univ BSc 62 DipAdEd Nottm Univ PhD 89. Coll of Resurr Mirfield 62. **d** 64 **p** 65. C Newbold w Dunston *Derby* 64–68; C Derby St Thos 68–70; Adult Educn Officer 70–79; R Mugginton and Kedleston 70–89; Vice-Prin EMMTC 79–86; Can Res Derby Cathl and Dioc Clergy In-Service Tr Adv *Derby* 89–03; rtd 03; Chapl to The Queen 98–08; PtO *Newc* from 04. *7 Hillside, Lesbury, Alnwick NE66 3NR* T: (01665) 833124 E: teve-a@tiscali.co.uk

⌖**CHESTERS, The Rt Revd Alan David.** b 37. St Chad's Coll Dur BA 59 St Cath Soc Ox BA 61 MA 65 Ches Univ Hon DTheol 10. St Steph Ho Ox 59. **d** 62 **p** 63 **c** 89. C Wandsworth St Anne *S'wark* 62–66; Hon C 66–68; Chapl Tiffin Sch Kingston 66–72; Hon C Ham St Rich *S'wark* 68–72; Dioc Dir of Educn *Dur* 72–85; R Brancepeth 72–85; Hon Can Dur Cathl 75–85; Adn Halifax *Wakef* 85–89; Bp Blackb 89–03; rtd 03; Hon Asst Bp Ches 03–10; Eur 05–09; St As 09–10; S'wark 11–14; Chich from 11. *14 Pegasus Court, Deanery Close, Chichester PO19 1EA* T: (01243) 788053 M: 07768-955534 E: achesters1937@gmail.com

CHESTERS, Simon. b 66. Rob Coll Cam BA 87 MA 91. Wycliffe Hall Ox BA 94. **d** 95 **p** 96. C Bidston *Ches* 95–99; P-in-c Runcorn St Jo Weston 99–03; Dioc Min Development Officer 03–09; Hon C Lache cum Saltney from 03; Dir Reader Tr 99–09; Regional Leadership Development Adv (NW) CPAS 10–11; Dir Studies Dioc Lifelong Learning *Liv* from 11; Lic Preacher *Man* from 10. *25 Marlston Avenue, Chester CH4 8HE* T: (01244) 679311 E: chesters.simon@gmail.com *or* simon.chesters@liverpool.anglican.org

CHESWORTH (née NAYLOR), Mrs Alison Louise. b 68. St Andr Univ MTheol 97 New Coll Edin MTh 99. TISEC 98. **d** 00 **p** 01. C Ayr, Girvan and Maybole *Glas* 00–03; R Glas All SS and P-in-c Glas H Cross 03–10; TV Ipswich St Mary at Stoke w St Pet and St Fran *St E* 10–17; P-in-c Penhill *Bris* from 17; P-in-c Upper Stratton from 17. *St Philip's Vicarage, 67 Beechcroft Road, Swindon SN2 7RE* T: (01793) 723095 *or* 721921 E: revd.alicesworth@gmail.com

CHESWORTH, John Martin. b 44. Leeds Univ BSc 67 PhD 71 FRSC 80. S Dios Minl Tr Scheme 90. **d** 92 **p** 93. Oman 92–95; PtO *Ab* 96–98; *Ches* 98–03; C Egremont St Jo 03–04; V Tranmere St Paul w St Luke 04–09; rtd 09; PtO *Lich* from 10. *21 Oerley Way, Oswestry SY11 1TD* T: (01691) 653922 E: chez.ches@talktalk.net

CHEVERTON, Miss Jill. b 48. Cranmer Hall Dur 93. **d** 93 **p** 94. Par Dn Bilton *Ripon* 93–94; C 94–96; V Burmantofts St Steph and St Agnes 96–03; Min Binley Woods LEP *Cov* 03–13; rtd 13; PtO *York* from 14. *51 Fairway, Selby YO8 9AF* T: (01757) 428876 E: jillcheverton@gmail.com

CHEVILL, Elizabeth Jane. *See* PITKETHLY, Elizabeth Jane

CHEW, Philip Vivian Frederick. b 62. St Martin's Coll Lanc BA 96. Qu Coll Birm 96. **d** 98 **p** 99. C Chorley St Laur *Blackb* 98–02; V Burnley St Steph 02–08; P-in-c Blackb St Fran and St Aid 08–10; R Llanbedr DC, Llangynhafal, Llanychan etc. *St As* 10–16; I Dyffryn Clwyd Miss Area from 17; AD Dyffryn Clwyd from 10. *The Rectory, Llanbedr Dyffryn Clwyd, Ruthin LL15 1UP* T: (01824) 705755 E: revpchew@gmail.com

CHICHESTER, Caroline Margaret. b 57. STETS. **d** 09 **p** 10. NSM Winterborne Valley and Milton Abbas *Sarum* 09–16; NSM Red Post from 16. *Kingston Farmhouse, West Street, Winterborne Kingston, Blandford Forum DT11 9AX* E: cmchichester@tiscali.co.uk

CHICHESTER, Archdeacon of. *See* IRVINE CAPEL, The Ven Luke Thomas

CHICHESTER, Bishop of. *See* WARNER, The Rt Revd Martin Clive

CHICHESTER, Dean of. *See* WAINE, The Very Revd Stephen John

CHIDLAW, Richard Paul. b 49. St Cath Coll Cam BA 71 MA. Ripon Hall Ox 72. **d** 74 **p** 81. C Ribbesford w Bewdley *Worc* 74–76; NSM Coaley *Glouc* 81–83; NSM Frampton on Severn 81–83; NSM Arlingham 81–83; NSM Saul w Fretherne and Framilode 83–84; NSM Cam w Stinchcombe 85–90; PtO 90–91; NSM Berkeley w Wick, Breadstone, Newport, Stone etc 91–19; rtd 19. *38 May Lane, Dursley GL11 4HU* T: (01453) 547838

CHIDLOW, Ian Luke. b 90. Sheff Univ BA 11. Oak Hill Th Coll BA 19. **d** 19. C Cheadle *Ches* from 19. *39 Oakfield Avenue, Cheadle SK8 1EF* M: 07475-004360 E: ilchidlow@gmail.com

CHIDWICK, Alan Robert. b 49. MA MIL. Oak Hill NSM Course. **d** 84 **p** 85. NSM Pimlico St Pet w Westmr Ch Ch *Lon* 84–06; rtd 06; PtO *Nor* from 06; *Lon* from 14. *85 Claremont House, 14 Aerodrome Road, London NW9 5NW* T: (020) 8032 5402 E: deslannw9@gmail.com

CHIKE, Mrs Obaka Echenim. b 70. Westmr Univ BSc 98 City Univ BSc 10. St Mellitus Coll 15. **d** 18 **p** 19. C E Ham St Paul *Chelmsf* from 18. *Emmanuel Vicarage, 2B Margery Park Road, London E7 9JY* T: (020) 8534 6796 M: 07981-435711 E: chikeobaka@yahoo.co.uk

CHILCOTT, Mark David. b 62. Ch Coll Cam BA 83 MA 87 PhD 88. Ripon Coll Cuddesdon BA 92. **d** 93 **p** 94. C Warrington St Elphin *Liv* 93–99; P-in-c Westbrook St Jas 99–01; V 01–02. *Estates Branch, Sedgley Park Centre, Sedgley Park Road, Prestwich, Manchester M25 0JT* T: 0161-856 0505 F: 856 0506

CHILD, Corin James. b 73. Man Univ BA 95. Trin Coll Bris BA 02 MA 03. **d** 03 **p** 04. C Sanderstead *S'wark* 03–07; V King's Lynn St Jo the Ev *Nor* 07–14; Chapl Coll of W Anglia 07–14; Chapl Nor Sch from 14; Hon PV Nor Cathl from 14. *The Chaplain's Office, Norwich School, 70 The Close, Norwich NR1 4DD* T: (01603) 728450 E: corin.child@sky.com *or* cchild@norwich-school.org.uk

CHILD, Canon David Francis. b 44. Birm Univ MB, ChB 67 FRCP 88. St As Minl Tr Course 02. **d** 04 **p** 05. NSM Gresford *St As* 04–07; NSM Bangor Isycoed Deanery 08–12; P-in-c Overton and Erbistock *St As* 12–16; TV Maelor Miss Area 17–18; AD Dee Valley 12–14; Hon Can St As Cathl 13–18; rtd 18. *11 Maelor Court, Overton, Wrexham LL13 0HE* E: d_f_child@yahoo.co.uk

CHILD, James John. b 79. St Jo Coll Ox BA 00. Oak Hill Th Coll BTh 10. **d** 10 **p** 11. C St Helen Bishopsgate w St Andr Undershaft etc *Lon* from 10; PtO *Chelmsf* from 16. *4 Merrick Square, London SE1 4JB* E: jamiejchild@hotmail.com

CHILD, Margaret Mary. *See* MASLEN, Margaret Mary

CHILDS, Adam Raymond. b 90. Ridley Hall Cam 14. **d** 17 **p** 18. C Walthamstow *Chelmsf* from 17. *19 Barrett Road, London E17 9ES* T: (020) 8923 0224 M: 07807-908034 E: mr.a.childs@gmail.com

CHILDS, Christopher. b 59. **d** 05 **p** 06. NSM Gt Finborough w Onehouse, Harleston, Buxhall etc *St E* 05–11; P-in-c 11–18; P-in-c Combs and Lt Finborough 13–18; R Combs and Finborough from 18. *The Rectory, 135 Poplar Hill, Stowmarket IP14 2AY* T: (01449) 673280 E: revcchilds@aol.com

CHILDS, David Robert. b 64. Univ Coll Lon BSc 86 Regent's Park Coll Ox MA 95. Ripon Coll Cuddesdon 99. **d** 99 **p** 00. C Bloxham w Milcombe and S Newington *Ox* 99–02; TV Witney 02–06; TR 06–08; P-in-c Hadleigh St Jas *Chelmsf* 08–16; P-in-c Hadleigh St Barn 12–16; Chapl Southend Univ Hosp NHS Foundn Trust from 16. *Southend University Hospital NHS Foundation Trust, Prittlewell Chase, Westcliff-on-Sea SS0 0RY* T: (01702) 435555 E: dekm@sky.com *or* david.childs@southend.nhs.uk

CHILDS, Emma Jane. *See* WESTERMANN-CHILDS, Emma Jane

CHILDS, Ernest Edmund. b 23. Lich Th Coll 63. **d** 65 **p** 66. C Billesley Common *Birm* 65–68; C Elland *Wakef* 68–69; Clerical Org Sec CECS Pet, Leic and Ely 69–72; V Staverton w Helidon and Catesby *Pet* 72–76; rtd 77; PtO *Nor* 77–91; Hon C W Lynn *Ely* 92–94; P-in-c 94–95; PtO 95–00; *Nor* from 96. *4 Fieldview Court, Fakenham NR21 8PB* T: (01328) 856595

CHILDS, Mrs Frances Mary. b 54. MIOSH 98 GIFireE 09. Wycliffe Hall Ox 02 Ripon Coll Cuddesdon 15. **d** 16 **p** 17. OLM Didcot St Pet *Ox* from 16. *3 South Park Avenue, Didcot OX11 8NB* T: (01235) 816166 M: 07798-643962 E: fran.childs@btinternet.com

CHILDS, Michael Thomas. b 79. Hull Univ BA 01. St Steph Ho Ox BTh 10. **d** 10 **p** 11. C Swinton *Sheff* 10–13; C Edmonton St Alphege *Lon* 13–17; P-in-c 17–18; C Ponders End St Matt 13–17; P-in-c 17–18; V Morecambe St Barn *Blackb* from 18. *St Barnabas' Vicarage, 101 Regent Road, Morecambe LA3 1AG* T: (01524) 951521 E: westendpriest@gmail.com

✠**CHILLINGWORTH, The Rt Revd David Robert.** b 51. TCD BA 73 Oriel Coll Ox BA 75 MA 81. Ripon Coll Cuddesdon 75. **d** 76 **p** 77 **c** 05. C Belfast H Trin *Conn* 76–79; Ch of Ireland Youth Officer 79–83; C Bangor Abbey *D & D* 83–86; I Seagoe 86–05; Dean Dromore 95–02; Adn Dromore 02–05; Bp St And 05–17; Primus 09–17; rtd 17; PtO *Edin* from 18. *9 Almondhill Steading, Kirkliston EH29 9LA* T: 0131-333 2038 E: david@chillingworth.org.uk

CHILTON, Janice Marguerite. b 43. **d** 08. NSM Wallingford *Ox* 08–13; rtd 13; PtO *Ox* from 13. *2 Fairthorne Memorial, West End, Brightwell-cum-Sotwell, Wallingford OX10 0RY* T: (01491) 836661 E: jchilton894@btinternet.com

CHINDABATA, Miss Unesu Audrey. b 74. Birkbeck Coll Lon BSc 06 K Coll Lon BA 13 AKC 13 Anglia Ruskin Univ MA 15. Westcott Ho Cam 13. **d** 15 **p** 16. C Is of Dogs Ch Ch and St Jo w St Luke *Lon* 15–18; V Thames View *Chelmsf* from 18. *Christ Church Vicarage, Bastable Avenue, Barking IG11 0NG* T: (020) 8594 1976 M: 07534-582578 E: rev@christchurch-thamesview.org.uk

CHIPLIN, Christopher Gerald. b 53. Lon Univ BSc 75. St Steph Ho Ox BA 77 MA 81. **d** 78 **p** 79. C Chesterfield St Mary and All SS *Derby* 78–80; C Thorpe St Andr *Nor* 80–84; V Highbridge *B & W* 84–94; V Midsomer Norton w Clandown from 94. *The Vicarage, 42 Priory Close, Midsomer Norton, Radstock BA3 2HZ* T: (01761) 412118 E: cchi759070@aol.com

CHIPLIN, Howard Alan. b 43. Sarum & Wells Th Coll 84. **d** 86 **p** 87. C Caerleon *Mon* 86–89; V Ferndale w Maerdy *Llan* 89–91; V Ysbyty Cynfyn w Llantrisant and Eglwys Newydd *St D* 91–95; R Narberth w Mounton w Robeston Wathen and Crinow 95–02; V Grwp Bro Ystwyth a Mynach 02–08; rtd 08; PtO *St D* from 08; *Ban* 08–14; AD Arwystli 11–15; PtO from 15. *Minffordd, 15 Hafren Terrace, Llanidloes SY18 6AT* T: (01686) 413619

CHIPLIN, Malcolm Leonard. b 42. St Mich Coll Llan 86. **d** 88 **p** 89. C Newton Nottage *Llan* 88–91; V Pwllgwaun w Llanddewi Rhondda 91–03; V Mountain Ash and Miskin 03–08; rtd 08; PtO *Llan* from 08. *3 Maes y Ffynon Grove, Aberaman, Aberdare CF44 6PJ* T: (01685) 874720 E: malcolmchiplin@aol.com

CHIPPENDALE, Peter David. b 34. Dur Univ BA 55. Linc Th Coll 57. **d** 59 **p** 60. C Claines St Jo *Worc* 59–63; V Defford w Besford 63–73; P-in-c Eckington 66–69; V 69–73; V Kidderminster St Geo 73–76; V The Lickey *Birm* 76–96; rtd 96. *1 Fairways, Pershore WR10 1HA* T: (01386) 553478

CHISHOLM, Canon Ian Keith. b 36. AKC 62. **d** 63 **p** 64. C Lich St Chad 63–66; C Sedgley All SS 66–69; V Rough Hills 69–77; V Harrow Weald All SS *Lon* 77–88; V W Moors *Sarum* 88–01; Can and Preb Sarum Cathl 00–01; rtd 01; PtO *Sarum* from 02. *33 Meadway, Shrewton, Salisbury SP3 4HE* T: (01980) 620579 E: ian.chisholm250@btinternet.com

CHISHOLM, Ian Stuart. b 37. ALCD 63. **d** 63 **p** 64. C Worksop St Jo *S'well* 63–66; Succ Sheff Cathl 66–68; Bp's Chapl for Soc Resp 68–72; C Ox St Andr 72–76; Tutor Wycliffe Hall Ox 72–76; V Conisbrough *Sheff* 76–94; Chapl Conisbrough Hosp 76–94; RD W Doncaster *Sheff* 82–87 and 93–94; V Chilwell *S'well* 94–99; rtd 99; PtO *Sheff* 94–10; *Linc* from 00; *S'well* from 03. *72 Broadbank, Louth LN11 0EW* T: (01605) 605970 E: ianchisholm700@btinternet.com

CHISLETT, David Edward. b 52. **d** 79 **p** 80. C Sydney St Laur Australia 79–80; C Warnambool 80–82; R Skipton 82–85; R Horsham 85–93; P-in-c S Ballarat 93–95; R Brisbane All SS 95–05; PtO The Murray 07–15; PtO *S'wark* 15–18; V Benhilton from 18. *All Saints' Vicarage, All Saints' Road, Sutton SM1 3DA* E: david@fministry.com

CHISLETT, David Norman Hilton. b 61. Kingston Poly BSc 83 UEA PGCE 84. Ridley Hall Cam 00. **d** 02 **p** 03. C Highley w Billingsley, Glazeley etc *Heref* 02–05; TV Eston w Normanby *York* 05–09; C Bridlington Quay Ch Ch 09–14; C Bessingby 09–14; rtd 14. E: dave.chislett@me.com

CHITHAM, Ernest John. b 57. LSE BSc 79 Leeds Univ PGCE 80 Dur Univ MA 84. NEOC 88. **d** 91 **p** 92. C Swanborough *Sarum* 91–94; CMS 94–99; R Beirut All SS Lebanon 95–98; TV Worthing Ch the King *Chich* 99–05; P-in-c 05–08; V Worthing St Matt 08–16; Bp's Dom Chapl *Blackb* 16–19; R Standon and The Mundens w Sacombe *St Alb* from 19. *The Vicarage, Kents Lane, Standon, Ware SG11 1PJ* M: 07940-498549 E: chitham.john@gmail.com *or* rector@ubsms.org

CHITHAM-MOSLEY, Conan Martin Maximillian. b 68. **d** 16 **p** 17. NSM Moseley St Mary and St Anne *Birm* 16–19; NSM Birm St Paul from 19. *Buritt's House, 11 Victoria Road, Harborne, Birmingham B17 0AG* M: 07775-833884 E: revconan@burritt.co.uk *or* conanchitham@gmail.com

CHITTY, Lynne. b 64. **d** 06. NSM Glouc Cathl 06–08. *Rocknell Manor Farm, Westleigh, Tiverton EX16 7ES* T: (01884) 829000 E: lynnechittyso@gmail.com

CHIUMBU, Esther Tamisa. *See* PRIOR, Esther Tamisa

CHIVERS, Canon Christopher Mark. b 67. Magd Coll Ox BA 88 MA 92 Selw Coll Cam BA 96 MA 00. Westcott Ho Cam 94. **d** 97 **p** 98. C Friern Barnet St Jas *Lon* 97–99; Can Prec St Geo Cathl Cape Town S Africa 99–01; Min Can and Prec Westmr Abbey 01–05; Can Res and Chan Blackb Cathl 05–10; V Mill Hill Jo Keble Ch *Lon* 10–15; C Mill Hill St Mich 11–15; AD W Barnet 14–15; PV Westmr Abbey from 12; Hon Can Saldhana Bay S Africa from 14; Prin Westcott Ho Cam from 15. *Westcott House, Jesus Lane, Cambridge CB5 8BP* T: (01223) 741000

CHIVERS, Royston George. b 34. Glouc Th Course. **d** 83 **p** 84. NSM Gorsley w Cliffords Mesne *Glouc* 83–85; NSM Newent and Gorsley w Cliffords Mesne from 85. *Mayfield, Gorsley, Ross-on-Wye HR9 7SJ* T: (01989) 720492 E: gillian.orpin@talktalk.net

CHO, Paul Hang-Sik. b 61. Kent Univ MA 96 PhD 04. Chr Th Sem & Div Sch of Korea BTh 93. **d** 00 **p** 01. C Munster Square Ch Ch and St Mary Magd *Lon* 00–07; Chapl Angl Korean Community 00–07; Consultant for Institutional Advancement Ox Cen for Miss Studies 08–11; Prof St Andr Th Sem Philippines 10–15; PtO *Birm* 15–19; P-in-c W Heath from 19. *54A Lilley Lane, Birmingham B31 3JT* T: 0121-251 0123 M: 07445-985165 E: frpaulcho@gmail.com

CHOI, Soon-Han. b 64. Bapt Sem Seoul BA 94 Surrey Univ MA 99. **d** 10. NSM St Marylebone Annunciation Bryanston Street *Lon* 10–14; PtO from 14; Chapl Qu Mary Univ of Lon 16–17; Chapl W Lon Univ 17; PtO *Eur* from 18. *Flat 8, 33 Lexham Gardens, London W8 5JR* T: (020) 7373 5025 M: 07808-081179 E: soonpray@gmail.com

CHOLDCROFT, Graham Charles. b 49. Ripon Coll Cuddesdon 07. **d** 10 **p** 11. NSM Thame *Ox* from 10; Chapl Thames Valley Police from 10. *100 Aylesbury Road, Thame OX9 3AY* T: (01844) 216979 M: 07851-191842 E: graham-choldcroft@supanet.com

CHORLTON, Christopher James Woodard. b 73. Westmr Coll Ox BTh 94 Leeds Univ PGCE 98. **d** 10 **p** 12. C Cairo Cathl Egypt 10–16; C Maadi 14–16; C Manningham *Leeds* 16–18; C Heaton St Barn 16–18; C Girlington, Heaton and Manningham 18–19; R from 19. *The Vicarage, 130 Haworth Road, Bradford BD9 6LL* E: chris.chorlton@leeds.anglican.org

CHORLTON, John Samuel Woodard. b 45. Newc Univ BSc 67. Wycliffe Hall Ox 89. **d** 89 **p** 91. Jerusalem 79–92; C Ox St Aldate 92–04; AD Ox 99–04; TV W Slough 04–08; V Britwell 08–14; Voc Adv 98–14; rtd 14; PtO *Ox* from 14. *6 Martin Close, Botley, Oxford OX2 9GU* M: 07517-454433 E: jsw@chorlton.org

CHOW, Suie Suie Roy. b 46. Brasted Th Coll 68 Sarum & Wells Th Coll 70. **d** 72 **p** 73. C Weaste *Man* 72–74; C Swinton St Pet 74–78; R Blackley St Paul 78–85; Sec SPCK (Dio Man) from 80; R Burnage St Nic *Man* 85–95; P-in-c Man Gd Shep 95–97; P-in-c Openshaw 95–97; R Manchester Gd Shep and St Barn 97–13; rtd 13; PtO *Man* from 13. *66 Bluestone Road, Manchester M40 9HY* T: 0161-681 6215 M: 07855-182990

CHOWN, William Richard Bartlett. b 27. AKC 54. **d** 55 **p** 56. C Egremont *Carl* 55–58; C Upminster *Chelmsf* 58–61; R Romford St Andr 61–78; R Newton Longville w Stoke Hammond, Whaddon etc Ox 78–83; P-in-c Kidmore End 83–85; V 85–90; rtd 90; NSM Harpsden Ox 93–94; PtO 94–03; Hon C Shiplake w Dunsden and Harpsden 03–05; PtO *Guildf* from 07. *3 Coniston Court, Weybridge KT13 9YR* T: (01932) 821936

CHRICH, Andrew James. b 70. Girton Coll Cam BA 92 MA 96. Cranmer Hall Dur BA 96. **d** 96 **p** 97. C Gerrards Cross and Fulmer *Ox* 96–99; Chapl Trin Coll Cam 99–04; R Linton in Craven *Bradf* 04–09; P-in-c Burnsall w Rylstone 04–09; V Trumpington *Ely* 09–18; V Highbury Ch Ch w St Jo and St Sav *Lon* from 18. *Christ Church Vicarage, 155 Highbury Grove, London N5 1SA* T: (020) 7226 2201 *or* 7354 0741 E: andychrich@virginmedia.com *or* vicar@christchurchhighbury.com

CHRISTENSEN, Mrs Carole Glenda. b 45. Qu Coll Birm 07. **d** 09 **p** 10. NSM Blackheath *Birm* 09–15; rtd 15; PtO *Man* from 15; *Birm* from 15. *73 John Street, Rowley Regis B65 0EN* T: 0121-561 5761 E: christensen_250@hotmail.com *or* carolechristensen250@gmail.com

CHRISTENSEN, Nikolaj. b 86. Aarhus Univ BTh 11 MTh 13 Birm Univ PhD 17. Ripon Coll Cuddesdon 18. **d** 19. C Iffley Ox from 19. *Church House, The Oval, Oxford OX4 4SE* M: 07741-087877 E: nikolajchr@gmail.com

CHRISTENSEN, Canon Norman Peter. b 37. St D Coll Lamp BA 63. Ridley Hall Cam 63. **d** 65 **p** 66. C Barnston *Ches* 65–70; V Over St Jo 70–77; R Bromborough 77–92; RD Wirral S 86–92; Hon Can Ches Cathl 90–02; Chapl Arrowe Park Hosp Wirral 92–96; V Higher Bebington *Ches*

96–02; rtd 02; PtO *Ches* from 02. *13 Howbeck Close, Prenton CH43 6TH* T: 0151-652 9869 E: canonpc@uwclub.net

CHRISTIAN, Canon Alison Jean. b 51. S Dios Minl Tr Scheme 88. **d** 91 **p** 94. Par Dn Uxbridge *Lon* 91–94; C 94–95; Chapl Uxbridge Coll 91–95; V Sudbury St Andr *Lon* 95–02; R Gt Stanmore 02–12; Warden Launde Abbey *Leic* 12–16; P-in-c Loddington 12–16; Hon Can Leic Cathl 15–16; rtd 17; Adv and Advocate for Spiritual Direction Lon Cen for Spiritual Direction 17–19; PtO from 19. *3 Crown Street, Harrow HA2 0HT* T: (020) 8423 7970 E: alijchristian@gmail.com

CHRISTIAN, Daniel Chung. b 85. St Jo Coll Dur BA 07. Wycliffe Hall Ox MSt 10. **d** 12 **p** 13. C Chester le Street *Dur* 12–16; C Ecclesall *Sheff* from 16. *162 Knowle Lane, Sheffield S11 9SJ* M: 07841-835711 E: dan.christian@dunelm.org.uk *or* dan.christian@allsaintsecclesall.org.uk

CHRISTIAN, Helen. *See* HORNBY, Helen

CHRISTIAN, Mark Robert. b 58. Linc Th Coll 95. **d** 95 **p** 96. C Stockport SW *Ches* 95–98; CF 98–08; Sen CF 08–11; Dep Asst Chapl Gen 11–15; Hon C Whitchurch w Tufton and Litchfield *Win* from 15; Asst Chapl Naomi Ho Hospice from 17. *Red House Bungalow, Litchfield, Whitchurch RG28 7PT* T: (01256) 8969888 M: 07702-516518

CHRISTIAN, Paul. b 49. Cant Sch of Min 84. **d** 87 **p** 88. C Folkestone St Sav *Cant* 87–91; R Temple Ewell w Lydden 91–17; rtd 17. *The Sanctuary, 29 The Boulevard, Pevensey Bay, Pevensey BN24 6RP*

CHRISTIAN, Richard. b 37. Nottm Univ DipEd 74 Ox Univ MA 81. AKC 62. **d** 63 **p** 65. C Camberwell St Mich w All So w Em *S'wark* 63–66; C Woolwich St Mary w H Trin 66–70; Chapl and Lect Bp Lonsdale Coll Derby 70–74; P-in-c Hurley *Ox* 76–79; Chapl Lancing Coll 79–81; Chapl Harrow Sch 82–89; Chapl R W Sussex Hosp Chich 89–91; P-in-c Cowley *Lon* 91–95; Chapl Hillingdon Hosp NHS Trust 91–11; PtO *Leic* 12–16; *Pet* 12–17; *Lon* from 17. *3 Crown Street, Harrow HA2 0HT* T: (020) 8423 7970 E: r.christian10@gmail.com

CHRISTIAN-EDWARDS, Canon Michael Thomas. b 36. Down Coll Cam BA 60 MA 64. Clifton Th Coll 60. **d** 62 **p** 63. C Ex St Leon w H Trin 62–67; V Trowbridge St Thos *Sarum* 67–75; R Wingfield w Rowley 67–75; P-in-c Fisherton Anger 75–81; R 81–92; Ind Chapl 85–92; RD Salisbury 85–90; Can and Preb Sarum Cathl 87–92; V Crofton *Portsm* 92–00; rtd 00; PtO *Win* from 02. *Rivendell, Westbeams Road, Sway, Lymington SO41 6AE* T: (01590) 682353 E: mmce@ukpiglet.com *or* michaelchristianedwards@gmail.com

CHRISTIAN-IWUAGWU, Canon Amatu Onundu. b 73. Port Harcourt Univ Nigeria BEng 93. **d** 00 **p** 01. NSM Stonebridge St Mich *Lon* 00–03; PtO *St Alb* 02–19; NSM Welwyn 04–05; Can Ideato from 03; NSM Stonebridge St Mich *Lon* 05–07; V Harmondsworth from 07. *St Mary's Vicarage, High Street, Harmondsworth, West Drayton UB7 0AQ* T: (020) 8897 2385 M: 07429-863280 E: iwuagwuoa@yahoo.co.uk

CHRISTIANSON, Canon Rodney John (Bill). b 47. St Paul's Coll Grahamstown. **d** 72 **p** 73. C St Sav Cathl Pietermaritzburg S Africa 72–76; Miss to Seafarers 76–09; Min Sec Miss to Seamen 93–00; Sec Gen Miss to Seafarers 00–09; R Richard's Bay S Africa 82–91; Chapl Hull Miss to Seamen 91–93; LtO *Lon* 94–97; V St Mich Paternoster Royal 00–09; rtd 09; PtO *Lon* from 09; Hon Can Bloemfontein Cathl from 93. *45 Wimbledon Park Court, Wimbledon Park Road, London SW19 6NN* T: (020) 7251 1554 E: bill.christianson@btinternet.com

CHRISTIE, Alexander Robert. b 58. Qu Coll Cam BA 79 LLM 80. Oak Hill Th Coll 92. **d** 94 **p** 95. C W Norwood St Luke *S'wark* 94–98; C Wandsworth All SS 98–03; V Blackheath Park St Mich from 03. *St Michael's Vicarage, 2 Pond Road, London SE3 9JL* T: (020) 8852 5287 E: ar.christie@outlook.com

CHRISTIE (née MOUK), Mae Elizabeth. b 83. **d** 14 **p** 15. C Walworth St Chris *S'wark* 14–17; P-in-c Tooting All SS 17–19; V from 19. *84 Franciscan Road, London SW17 8DQ* T: (020) 8767 7705 M: 07500-309540 E: mae.mouk@icloud.com

CHRISTODOULOU, Kostakis. b 53. Southn Univ CertEd 76 BEd 76. St Mellitus Coll BA 10. **d** 10 **p** 11. NSM Edgware *Lon* from 10. *226 East End Road, London N2 8AX* T: (020) 8883 9971 E: kostakis_christodoulou2002@yahoo.co.uk

CHRISTOPHER, Miss Barbara. b 58. Univ of Wales (Swansea) BA 80. **d** 09 **p** 10. OLM Saddleworth *Man* from 09. *2 St Mary's Crest, Greenfield, Oldham OL3 7DS* T: (01457) 876802 E: barbara.christopher@outlook.com

CHRISTOU, Sotirios. b 51. St Jo Coll Nottm 84. **d** 88 **p** 92. C Berechurch St Marg w St Mich *Chelmsf* 88–89; C Goodmayes All SS 89–90; NSM Harston w Hauxton *Ely* 92–94; LtO 94–95; C Burgess Hill St Andr *Chich* 95–98; PtO *Ely* from 98. *18 Bullen Close, Cambridge CB1 8YU* T: (01223) 977764 E: christousotirios@hotmail.co.uk

CHRYSOSTOMOU, Stefan. b 87. R Holloway Coll Lon BA 08 SS Coll Cam BA 11. Westcott Ho Cam 09. **d** 12 **p** 13. C Finchley St Mary *Lon* 12–16; V Potters Bar *St Alb* from 16. *The Vicarage, 15 The Walk, Potters Bar EN6 1QN* E: revstef@me.com

CHUDLEY, Cyril Raymond. b 29. Lon Univ BA 53 DipEd. Wells Th Coll 70. **d** 72 **p** 73. C Newark St Mary *S'well* 72–75; C Egg Buckland *Ex* 75–77; P-in-c Plymouth St Aug 77–80; V 80–83; V Milton Abbot, Dunterton, Lamerton etc 83–91; TV Wickford and Runwell *Chelmsf* 91–95; rtd 95; PtO *Truro* from 95. *Ten Acres, Coxpark, Gunnislake PL18 9BB* T: (01822) 832345

CHUKUKA, Ifeanyi Emmanuel Chukwunonso. b 76. **d** 09 **p** 10. PtO *Chelmsf* 12–15; NSM Victoria Docks St Luke 15–17; Chapl Barts Health NHS Trust 16–17; TV Forest Hill w Lower Sydenham *S'wark* from 17. *St Michael's Vicarage, Champion Crescent, London SE26 4HH* T: (020) 3601 7026 M: 07930-614660 E: ifeanchuks@yahoo.com

CHUMBLEY, Lore Elinor Jane. b 59. **d** 12 **p** 13. NSM Stockton Heath *Ches* 12–16; P-in-c Bath Ch Ch Prop Chpl *B & W* from 16. *8 St James's Street, Bath BA1 2TW* E: lore.chumbley@talktalk.net

CHUMU MUTUKU, Norbert. b 68. Urbanian Univ Rome BA 89 St Jo Fisher Coll USA MSc 00. St Mathias Mulumba Sem Kenya 89. **d** 93 **p** 94. In RC Ch 93–02; C Milton *Portsm* 03–06; C Pitsea w Nevendon *Chelmsf* 06–11; TV Wickford and Runwell 11–18; NSM Risborough *Ox* from 18. *The Rectory, Church End, Bledlow, Princes Risborough HP27 9PD* T: (01844) 344762 E: nchumu@yahoo.com

CHURCH, Mrs Annette Marie. b 56. **d** 09 **p** 10. C Caldicot *Mon* 09–14; P-in-c Shaldon, Stokeinteignhead, Combeinteignhead etc *Ex* 14–15; R from 15. *The Rectory, Torquay Road, Shaldon, Teignmouth TQ14 0AX* T: (01626) 873173 M: 07789-778312 E: anniechurch@hotmail.com *or* revannie@hotmail.co.uk

CHURCH, Canon Linda Ann. b 51. MCSP 73. EMMTC 88. **d** 91 **p** 94. NSM Kirkby in Ashfield St Thos *S'well* 91–95; NSM Skegby and Teversal 95–98; P-in-c Annesley w Newstead 98–03; TR Hucknall Torkard 03–09; Hon Can *S'well* Minster 07–09; R Fowlmere, Foxton, Shepreth and Thriplow *Ely* 09–13; RD Shingay 13; Dir Min from 14; Hon Can *Ely* Cathl from 14; PtO 14–18. *Diocesan Office, Bishop Woodford House, Barton Road, Ely CB7 4DX* T: (01353) 652701 E: canonlinda.church@btinternet.com

CHURCH, Robert Hugh. b 89. K Coll Lon BA 11. Ripon Coll Cuddesdon BA 16. **d** 17 **p** 18. C Tetbury, Beverston, Long Newnton etc *Glouc* from 17. *Hollyridge, Longtree Close, Tetbury GL8 8LN* M: 07854-656547 E: robert-church@hotmail.co.uk

CHURCH, William John. b 41. Qu Coll Cam MA 62 Solicitor. SAOMC 96. **d** 99 **p** 00. NSM Bengeo *St Alb* 99–01; NSM Gt Amwell w St Margaret's and Stanstead Abbots 01–05; NSM Hertford 05–18; PtO from 18. *115 Queen's Road, Hertford SG13 8BJ* T: (01992) 410469 F: 583079 E: bill.church@hertscc.gov.uk *or* churchwj@hotmail.com

CHURCHER, Ms Mandy. b 54. Brunel Univ MEd 92 Surrey Univ PGCE 87 RN 75 RM 77. NTMTC 96. **d** 99 **p** 00. C Wolverhampton St Matt *Lich* 99–02; Assoc Chapl Plymouth Hosps NHS Trust 02–06; Chapl S Devon Healthcare NHS Foundn Trust 06–11; NSM Malmesbury w Westport and Brokenborough *Bris* 11–16; NSM Malmesbury and Upper Avon from 16. *The Old Squash Court, Holloway, Malmesbury SN16 9BA* T: (01666) 826666 E: mandy@malmesburyabbey.com

CHURCHER, Peter. b 87. Cardiff Univ BA 08. St Jo Coll Nottm 14. **d** 16 **p** 17. C W Wickham St Jo *S'wark* 16–19; R Ilfracombe SS Phil and Jas, Combe Martin and Berrynarbor *Ex* from 19. *St James's Vicarage, Kingsley Avenue, Ilfracombe EX34 8ET* M: 07584-302071 E: revchurcher@gmail.com

CHYNCHEN, John Howard. b 38. FRICS 72. Sarum & Wells Th Coll 88. **d** 89 **p** 90. Bp's Dom Chapl *Sarum* from 89; Hon Chapl Hong Kong Cathl 90–07; Chapl 07–14; Hon Chapl from 14; PtO *Eur* from 10. *St John's Cathedral, 4-8 Garden Road, Hong Kong* T: (00852) 2523 4157 F: 3487 6404 E: chynchen@stjohnscathedral.org.hk

CICILY ANTONY, Dioynisious. b 66. Urban Univ Rome BPh 88 BTh 94 Indira Gandhi Nat Open Univ MA 07 MBA 09. **p** 93. NSM Uxbridge *Lon* 17–19; NSM Hillingdon All SS from 19; PtO *Chelmsf* from 18. *10 Queens Road, Uxbridge UB8 2NN* T: (01895) 473942 M: 07775-503510 E: dinysca@yahoo.com

CIECHANOWICZ, Edward Leigh Bundock. *See* BUNDOCK, Edward Leigh

CINNAMOND, Andrew Victor. b 71. St Andr Univ MA 94 Lon Sch of Th PhD 12. Wycliffe Hall Ox BA 00. **d** 01 **p** 02. C Clapham H Trin and St Pet *S'wark* 01–05; C Wandsworth

All SS 05–11; TV S Cotswolds *Glouc* from 11. *The Vicarage, Sherborne Street, Lechlade GL7 3AH* T: (01367) 253651 E: andrew_cinnamond@hotmail.com

CLACEY, Derek Phillip. St Jo Coll Nottm 76. **d** 79 **p** 80. C Gt Parndon *Chelmsf* 79–82; C Walton H Trin *Ox* 82–88; R Bramshaw and Landford w Plaitford *Sarum* 88–04; P-in-c Redlynch and Morgan's Vale 03–04; TV E Greenwich *S'wark* 04–13; rtd 13; PtO *Bris* from 15. *111 Forest Road, Fishponds, Bristol BS16 3ST* E: derekclacey@aol.com

CLACK (*née* **JERWOOD), Mrs Eleanor Alice Jerwood.** b 80. Bath Univ BSc 03. St Jo Coll Nottm MTh 09. **d** 08 **p** 09. C New Milverton *Cov* 08–11; PtO 11–18; LtO from 18; Dioc Communications Officer 13–15; Dioc Voc Adv from 15; Dioc Dir of Ords from 18. *198 Rugby Road, Leamington Spa CV32 6DU* T: (024) 7652 1374 M: 07802-657768 E: ellie.clack@covcofe.org

CLACK, Robert John Edmund. b 63. Lanc Univ BA 85 Ches Univ MA 14. Coll of Resurr Mirfield 89. **d** 92 **p** 93. C Bury St Pet *Man* 92–95; Chapl Bury Colls of FE 93–95; TV New Bury *Man* 95–97; R Ashton-upon-Mersey St Martin *Ches* 97–11; V Ches St Oswald and St Thos 11–16; Chapl Ches Univ 14–19; PtO *Liv* 17–19; R Wavertree H Trin from 19. *The Rectory, Hunters Lane, Liverpool L15 8HL* T: 0151-733 2172

CLAMMER, Thomas Edward. b 80. Sussex Univ BA 01 CCC Cam BA 04 MA 09 Win Univ PhD 17. Westcott Ho Cam 02. **d** 05 **p** 06. C Wotton St Mary *Glouc* 05–08; P-in-c Deerhurst and Apperley w Forthampton etc 08–12; Dioc Worship Officer 08–12; C Tewkesbury w Walton Cardiff and Twyning 10–12; Can Res Sarum Cathl 12–19; PtO from 19; *Glouc* from 19. *6 Lime Kiln Way, Salisbury SP2 8RN* M: 07811-639741 E: tomclammer@gmail.com

CLAPHAM, Christopher Charles. b 69. Man Univ BA 91 St Jo Coll Dur BA 96 Man Univ PhD 04. Cranmer Hall Dur 94 Union Th Sem (NY) STM 98. **d** 99 **p** 00. NSM Withington St Chris *Man* 99–01; C Didsbury Ch Ch 01–03; P-in-c Swinton H Rood 03–08; Chapl Keele Univ *Lich* 08–12; TV Wolstanton 12–14; V 14–15; V Hammersmith St Pet *Lon* from 15. *17 Ravenscourt Road, London W6 0UH* M: 07979-093418 E: charles.clapham@sky.com

CLAPHAM, John. b 47. Open Univ BA 76. Sarum & Wells Th Coll 77. **d** 80 **p** 81. Dep PV Ex Cathl 80–09; C Lympstone 85–87; P-in-c 87–99; P-in-c Woodbury 97–99; RD Aylesbeare 96–01; R Lympstone and Woodbury w Exton 99–09; rtd 09. *375 Topsham Road, Exeter EX2 6HB* T: (01392) 873345 E: johnclaphamuk@btinternet.com

CLAPHAM, Kenneth. b 47. Trin Coll Bris 76. **d** 78 **p** 79. C Pemberton St Mark Newtown *Liv* 78–81; C Darfield *Sheff* 81–83; P-in-c Over Kellet *Blackb* 83–88; V 88–16; rtd 16; PtO *Blackb* 16–17. *38 Fairhope Avenue, Morecambe LA4 6JZ* T: (01524) 415069 E: ukvicar@gmail.com

CLAPHAM, Stephen James. b 61. Portsm Poly BSc 84 Ches Coll of HE BTh 04. NOC 01. **d** 04 **p** 05. C Nantwich *Ches* 04–06; V Crewe All SS and St Paul w St Pet 07–15; P-in-c Church Lawton from 15; Dioc Ecum Officer from 15; RD Congleton from 18. *Alphabet House, Liverpool Road West, Church Lawton, Stoke-on-Trent ST7 3DZ* T: (01270) 876604 E: steveclapham@outlook.com

CLAPPERTON, Carolin Beryl (Sister Carolin Clare). b 43. Westcott Ho Cam 04. **d** 05 **p** 06. NSM Faversham *Cant* 05–08; NSM The Brents and Davington w Oare and Luddenham 08–11; rtd 11; PtO *Cant* 12–13; *Ox* 13–15 and from 19; OSC from 16. *St Mary's Convent, Wroslyn Road, Freeland, Witney OX29 8AJ* T: (01993) 881227 E: carolin@oscfreeland.co.uk

CLAPSON, Clive Henry. b 55. Leeds Univ BA 76. Trin Coll Toronto MDiv 79. **d** 79 **p** 80. C Belleville St Thos Canada 79–80; R Loughborough 80–83; V Alpine Ch the K USA 83–88; C Hawley H Trin *Guildf* 88–90; R Invergordon St Ninian *Mor* 90–00; Prin Moray Ord and Lay Tr Course 90–94; Can St Andr Cathl Inverness 97–00; R Aberdeen St Mary *Ab* 00–05; R Dundee St Salvador *Bre* from 05. *St Salvador's Rectory, 9 Minard Crescent, Dundee DD3 6LH* T: (01382) 221785 E: father.clive@blueyonder.co.uk

CLAPTON, Timothy. b 59. Westmr Coll Ox MTh 92. Westcott Ho Cam 96. **d** 98 **p** 99. C Wimborne Minster *Sarum* 98–02; Ecum Chapl Milton Keynes Gen NHS Trust 02–05; Milton Keynes Miss Partnership Development Chapl *Ox* 05–10; PtO *S'wark* 11–15; *Lon* 14–15; Hon C St Geo-in-the-East w St Paul from 15; PtO *S'wark* from 16; Chapl HM Pris Wandsworth from 17. *HM Prison Wandsworth, PO Box 757, London SW18 3HS* T: (020) 8588 4249 E: timothy.clapton@justice.gov.uk

CLARE, Christopher. b 52. Sheff Univ BSc 73 Nottm Univ PGCE 74. Ox Min Course 89. **d** 92 **p** 93. NSM Chesham Bois *Ox* from 92. *5 Lime Tree Walk, Amersham HP7 9HY* T: (01494) 766513 E: cc@challoners.com

CLARE, Ms Johanna Howard. b 64. Bris Univ BSc 86 Heythrop Coll Lon MA 98. Ridley Hall Cam 97. **d** 99 **p** 00. C Coulsdon St Jo *S'wark* 99–02; TV Morden 02–09; Dioc Continuing Professional Development Officer 09–14; PtO 14; *Truro* 14–18; P-in-c Mawnan from 18. *Trelowen, 16 Forth An Cos, Ponsanooth, Truro TR3 7RJ* T: (01872) 864129 M: 07919-186307 E: rev.johanna.clare@gmail.com

CLARE, Mrs Sarah Catherine Jane. b 57. Reading Univ BA 79. St Mellitus Coll BA 11. **d** 11 **p** 12. C St Helier's Bay New Zealand 11–17; PtO *Chelmsf* from 17. *Mellwick, 5 Monks Walk, Tollesbury, Maldon CM9 8XP* T: (01621) 868819 M: 07762-840905 E: sarahclare9@gmail.com

CLARE, Sister. See LOCKHART, Clare Patricia Anne

CLARIDGE, Antony Arthur John. b 37. Hull Univ MA LRAM. Bris & Glouc Tr Course. **d** 84 **p** 85. NSM Keynsham *B & W* 84–97; Bp's Officer for NSMs 90–10; Min Bath Ch Ch Prop Chpl 97–10; rtd 10; PtO *B & W* from 11. *62 Cranwells Park, Bath BA1 2YE* T: (01225) 427462 M: 07988-745721 E: antony.claridge@btinternet.com

CLARIDGE, Michael John. b 61. MCIEH. Qu Coll Birm 89 Bossey Ecum Inst Geneva 91. **d** 92 **p** 93. C Harlescott *Lich* 92–95; P-in-c Wellington Ch Ch 95–97; V 97–03; V W Bromwich St Andr w Ch Ch 03–17; RD W Bromwich 15–17; P-in-c Cotteridge *Birm* from 17; Bp's Ecum Adv from 18. *118 Northfield Road, Kings Norton, Birmingham B30 1DX* T: 0121-433 5176 E: mjclaridge@me.com *or* mike.claridge@thecotteridgechurch.org.uk

CLARINGBULL (*née* **DAVID), Canon Faith Caroline.** b 55. St Aid Coll Dur BA 77. Ripon Coll Cuddesdon 87. **d** 89 **p** 94. Par Dn Is of Dogs Ch Ch and St Jo w St Luke *Lon* 89–93; Asst Chapl R Lon Hosps NHS Trust 93–98; NSM Wheatley *Ox* 98–00; Asst Dioc Dir of Ords *Worc* 00–04; Dioc CME Officer 02–04; Dioc Dir of Ords *Birm* 04–17; Dean of Women's Min 04–17; Hon Can Birm Cathl 05–17; PtO *Lich* from 18. *3 King George Street, Stoke-on-Trent ST1 2DZ* M: 07539-217072 E: faithclaringbull@hotmail.co.uk

CLARINGBULL, Keith. b 49. Ripon Coll Cuddesdon 98. **d** 00 **p** 01. SSF 69–89; C Droitwich Spa *Worc* 00–04; P-in-c Hampton in Arden *Birm* 04–10; P-in-c Bickenhill 04–10; Chapl Univ Hosp Birm NHS Foundn Trust 13–14; PtO *Birm* 14–17. *3 King George Street, Stoke-on-Trent ST1 2DZ* T: (01782) 857380 M: 07946-150919 E: keithclaringbull@hotmail.com

CLARK, Andrew. b 76. Anglia Poly Univ BA 97. Oak Hill Th Coll BA 08. **d** 08 **p** 09. C Heref St Pet w St Owen and St Jas 08–11; C Barton Seagrave w Warkton *Pet* from 11. *Rectory Cottage, St Botolph's Road, Barton Seagrave, Kettering NN15 6SR* T: (01536) 660363 E: lurpak@aol.com *or* andy@stbots.church

CLARK, Antony. b 61. York Univ BA 83 St Andr Univ PhD. Wycliffe Hall Ox 84. **d** 88 **p** 89. C Ashton-upon-Mersey St Mary Magd *Ches* 88–92; Chapl Lee Abbey 92–95; LtO *Ex* 92–95; Chapl Univ of Westmr *Lon* 95–98; C Bletchley *Ox* 98–00; Chapl Fettes Coll Edin from 12. *Fettes College, Carrington Road, Edinburgh EH4 1QX* T: 0131-332 2281 E: a.clark@fettes.com

CLARK, Bernard Charles. b 34. Open Univ BA 81. S'wark Ord Course 65. **d** 68 **p** 69. C Pemberton St Jo *Liv* 68–71; C Winwick 71–73; P-in-c Warrington St Barn 74–76; V 76–78; V Hindley All SS 78–83; PtO 86–94; R Glazebury w Hollinfare 94–99; rtd 99; PtO *Man* 00–08 and 11–18. *31 Linkfield Drive, Worsley, Manchester M28 1JU* T: 0161-799 7998

CLARK, Canon Caroline Robbins (Robbin). b 45. Mt Holyoke Coll USA BA 67 Columbia Univ BS 70 Univ of California MS 74. Ch Div Sch of Pacific MDiv 81 Ripon Coll Cuddesdon 79. **d** 81 **p** 82. C Upland St Mark USA 81–84; R Santa Fé St Bede 85–93; R Berkeley St Mark 93–10; Dean of Women Clergy *Glouc* 11–16; Hon Can Glouc Cathl 12–16; rtd 16. *Address temp unknown* T: (001) (510) 410 9998

CLARK, Cecil. b 44. Sarum Th Coll. **d** 98 **p** 99. OLM Canford Magna *Sarum* 98–15; PtO from 15. *Fermain Cottage, 133 Magna Road, Bearwood, Bournemouth BH11 9NE* T: (01202) 577898 *or* 663275 E: fermain133@btinternet.com

CLARK, Mrs Christine Margaret. b 44. SAOMC 01. **d** 01 **p** 02. NSM Croxley Green St Oswald *St Alb* 01–06; P-in-c Odell 06–14; rtd 14; PtO *St Alb* from 14. *99 High Street, Clapham, Bedford MK41 6AQ* T: (01234) 918985 M: 07812-524992

CLARK, Christopher Austin. b 52. Liv Univ BSc 73 Chich Univ BA 13. STETS 08. **d** 10 **p** 11. NSM Worthing St Geo *Chich* 10–11; NSM Rustington 11–14; P-in-c Westham 14–19; rtd 19. *2 Hardham Close, Rustington, Littlehampton BN16 2SB*

CLARK, Daniel Alastair. b 74. St Jo Coll Dur BA 96. Wycliffe Hall Ox BA 99. **d** 00 **p** 01. C Rusholme H Trin *Man* 00–06; NSM 04–06; C Clifton Ch Ch w Em *Bris* 06–12; P-in-c Shirley Win from 12. *The Vicarage, 2B Wordsworth Road, Southampton SO15 5LX*

CLARK, David. b 60. Coll of SS Mark and Jo Plymouth BEd 82. Qu Foundn (Course) 17. **d** 19. NSM Baswich *Lich* from 19. *140 Rickerscote Road, Stafford ST17 4HE* T: (01785) 253111 M: 07999-596590 E: david.clark@berkswich.org.uk

CLARK, Canon David George Neville. b 25. Linc Coll Ox BA 49 MA 59. Wells Th Coll 49. **d** 51 **p** 52. C Sanderstead All SS *S'wark* 51–54; C Lewisham St Jo Southend 54–59; V Sutton New Town St Barn 59–72; R Charlwood 72–90; P-in-c Sidlow Bridge 76–77; R 77–90; P-in-c Buckland 85–87; P-in-c Leigh 87–90; Hon Can S'wark Cathl 88–90; rtd 90; PtO *Cov* from 90. *12 Marlborough Road, Coventry CV2 4EP* T: (024) 7644 2400 E: david@revdgnc.plus.com

CLARK, David Humphrey. b 39. G&C Coll Cam BA 60. Wells Th Coll 62. **d** 64 **p** 65. C Leigh St Mary *Man* 64–68; Min Can and Prec Man Cathl 68–70; Ind Chapl *Nor* 70–85; P-in-c Nor St Clem and St Geo 70–76; P-in-c Nor St Sav w St Paul 70–76; V Norwich-over-the-Water Colegate St Geo 76–79; Hon Asst P Nor St Pet Mancroft 79–85; TR Oadby *Leic* 85–98; C Leic St Jas 98–04; rtd 04; PtO *Leic* from 04. *46 St James Road, Leicester LE2 1HQ* T: 0116-255 8988 E: dhclark2@btinternet.com

CLARK, David John. b 61. Bretton Hall Coll BA 82 MA 06 PGCE 83 Sheff Univ BA 13. Yorks Min Course 10. **d** 13 **p** 14. C Gildersome *Wakef* 13–14; *Leeds* 14–16; C Drighlington *Wakef* 13–14; *Leeds* 14–16; V Upper Wensleydale from 16. *The Vicarage, Burtersett Road, Hawes DL8 3NP* T: (01969) 667553 M: 07891-329614 E: davejclark61@gmail.com

CLARK, David John. b 40. Surrey Univ MPhil 75 CEng MIStructE. Ridley Hall Cam 81. **d** 83 **p** 84. C Combe Down w Monkton Combe and S Stoke *B & W* 83–89; Voc Adv Bath Adnry 89–96; R Freshford, Limpley Stoke and Hinton Charterhouse *B & W* 89–05; rtd 05; PtO *B & W* from 05. *14 Barn Close, Frome BA11 4ER* T: (01373) 461073 M: 07710-507327 E: david@astrorev.co.uk

CLARK, Diane Catherine. See FITZGERALD CLARK, Diane Catherine

CLARK, Edward Robert. b 39. Ex Coll Ox BA 61 MA 65. St Steph Ho Ox 61. **d** 63 **p** 64. C Solihull *Birm* 63–67; PtO *Bris* 67–69; *Leic* 69–71; *Ox* 71–80; *St Alb* 80–84; *Cant* from 84; rtd 04. *3 Hunters Bank, Old Road, Elham, Canterbury CT4 6SS* T: (01303) 840134 E: edward.clark.elham@gmail.com

CLARK, Ms Erin Marie. b 87. Houghton Coll USA BA 09 Lon Sch of Th MA 13. Westcott Ho Cam 13. **d** 16 **p** 17. C Bethnal Green St Matt w St Jas the Gt *Lon* 16–19; R from 19. *The Rectory, Hereford Street, London E2 6EX* M: 07974-010157 E: erin.clark@london.anglican.org

CLARK, Graham John. b 62. Westf Coll Lon BA 85 Brighton Poly PGCE 86. ERMC 16. **d** 19. NSM Stotfold and Radwell *St Alb* from 19. *17 Heathermere, Letchworth Garden City SG6 4QH* T: (01462) 625270 M: 07842-215560 E: graham.clark@ntlworld.com

CLARK, Ian Duncan Lindsay. b 35. K Coll Cam BA 59 MA 63 PhD 64. Ripon Hall Ox 62. **d** 64 **p** 65. C Willington *Newc* 64–66; India 66–76; Lect Bp's Coll Calcutta 66; Vice-Prin 69–74; Chapl St Cath Coll Cam 76; Fell 77–85; Tutor 78–85; Dean of Chpl and Lect 80–85; Select Preacher Cam Univ 82; Hon Asst P Kelso *Edin* 85–06. *4 Yewtree Lane, Yetholm, Kelso TD5 8RZ* T: (01573) 420323 E: revbirdbath@gmail.com

CLARK, Jacqueline Mary. b 58. **d** 08 **p** 09. OLM Canalside Benefice *Sarum* 08–12; NSM Devizes St Jo w St Mary from 12. *3 Stonelea, Trowbridge Road, Hilperton, Trowbridge BA14 7QQ* T: (01225) 769940 M: 07948-089865 E: revjclark@hotmail.co.uk

CLARK, Miss Janet Elizabeth. b 44. Derby Coll of Educn CertEd 65 Open Univ BA 75. Oak Hill Th Coll BA 92. **d** 92 **p** 94. Par Dn Edmonton All SS w St Mich *Lon* 92–94; C 94–96; V Ealing St Steph Castle Hill 96–08; rtd 08; PtO *Ox* from 09. *55 Cranwells Lane, Farnham Common, Slough SL2 3GW* T: (01753) 646546

CLARK, Mrs Jean Robinson. b 32. K Coll Lon AKC BD 79. dss 85 **d** 87 **p** 94. Cov E 85–88; C 87–88; NSM Upper Mole Valley Gp *S'wark* 89–90; Hon Par Dn Charlwood 89–90; LtO *Cov* 90–92; rtd 92; PtO *Cov* from 92. *12 Marlborough Road, Coventry CV2 4EP* T: (024) 7644 2400 E: david@revdgnc.plus.com

CLARK, John David Stanley. b 36. Dur Univ BA 64. Ridley Hall Cam 64. **d** 66 **p** 67. C Benchill *Man* 66–69; C Beverley Minster *York* 69–74; P-in-c S'well 74–76; LtO 76–77; Miss to Seamen 77–80; PtO *York* 80–83; V Egton w Grosmont 83–89; R Thornton Dale w Ellerburne and Wilton 89–01; R Thornton Dale w Allerston, Ebberston etc 01–05; rtd 05; PtO *York* from 05. *22 Swainsea Lane, Pickering YO18 8AP* T: (01751) 476118 E: jdsclark@btinternet.com

CLARK, John Edward Goodband. b 49. Leeds Univ MA 01. Chich Th Coll 70. **d** 73 **p** 74. C Thorpe St Andr *Nor* 73–76; C Earlham St Anne 76–78; Chapl RN 78–82; P-in-c Tittleshall w Godwick, Wellingham and Weasenham *Nor* 82–85; P-in-c Helhoughton w Raynham 82–85; R S Raynham, E w W Raynham, Helhoughton, etc 85–90; R Taverham w Ringland 90–96; V Eggleston and R Middleton-in-Teesdale w Forest and Frith *Dur* 96–03; AD Barnard Castle 00–03; R Caston, Griston, Merton, Thompson etc *Nor* 03–05; PtO from 07. *Old Orchards, Gateley Road, Brisley, Dereham NR20 5LR* T: (01362) 667879

CLARK, John Patrick Hedley. b 37. St Cath Coll Cam BA 61 MA 65 Worc Coll Ox BA 63 MA 72 BD 74 Lambeth Hon DD 89. St Steph Ho Ox 61. **d** 64 **p** 65. C Highters Heath *Birm* 64–67; C Eglingham *Newc* 67–72; P-in-c Newc St Anne 72–77; V Longframlington w Brinkburn 77–95; V Chevington 95–02; rtd 02; PtO *Dur* from 02. *6 The Cottage, West Row, Greatham, Hartlepool TS25 2HW* T: (01429) 870203

CLARK, Canon John Ronald Lyons. b 47. TCD BA 69 MA 72. Div Hostel Dub 67. **d** 70 **p** 71. C Dundela St Mark *D & D* 70–72; CF 72–75; C Belfast St Aid *Conn* 75–76; I Stranorlar w Meenglas and Kilteevogue *D & R* 76–81; Chapl Wythenshawe Hosp Man 81–95; I Kilgariffe Union C, C & R 95–96; Chapl Blackb, Hyndburn and Ribble Valley NHS Trust 96–03; Chapl Co-ord E Lancs Hosps NHS Trust 03–09; Chapl E Lancs Hospice 96–05; Hon Can Blackb Cathl 06–09; rtd 09. *25 Castle Meadow Drive, Cloughey, Newtownards BT22 1RT* T: (028) 4277 2431 M: 07823-380179 E: rcronnieclark@googlemail.com

✠**CLARK, The Rt Revd Jonathan Dunnett.** b 61. Ex Univ BA 83 Bris Univ MLitt 90 Southn Univ MA 96. Trin Coll Bris 84. **d** 88 **p** 89 **c** 12. C Stanwix *Carl* 88–92; Chapl Bris Univ 92–93; Dir of Studies STETS 94–97; Chapl Lon Metrop Univ 97–03; AD Islington 99–03; R Stoke Newington St Mary 03–12; P-in-c Brownswood Park 04–11; Area Bp Croydon *S'wark* from 12. *Croydon Episcopal Area Office, 6 St Peter's Road, Croydon CR0 1HD* T: (020) 8256 9630 F: 8256 9631 M: 07968-845698 E: bishop.jonathan@southwark.anglican.org

CLARK, Jonathan Giles. b 72. **d** 14 **p** 16. C Stroud Team *Glouc* 14–15; C S Cotswolds 15–18; V Chineham Win from 18. *1 Hartswood, Chineham, Basingstoke RG24 8SJ* M: 07989-055147 E: jonathan@christchurchchineham.org.uk

CLARK, Judith Alison. b 88. Man Univ BA 13 MA 14. Ripon Coll Cuddesdon 16. **d** 19. C Leeds City from 19. *Flat 5, 41 The Calls, Leeds LS2 7EY* M: 07968-730544 E: judith.clark@leedsminster.org

CLARK, Julia Ann. b 62. Linc Sch of Th and Min 10. **d** 13 **p** 14. NSM Brumby *Linc* from 13. *13 Rivelin Crescent, Scunthorpe DN16 2AL* T: (01724) 862273 E: julia.clark23@virginmedia.com

CLARK, Kenneth William. b 69. R Holloway Coll Lon BA 92 Trin Coll Cam BA 99 MA 04. Westcott Ho Cam 97. **d** 00 **p** 01. C Pimlico St Gabr *Lon* 15–17; C Kentish Town 17–18; RD Dartford 13–19. *The Rectory, Church Road, Greenhithe DA9 9BE* T: (01322) 382076 E: kenofkent@outlook.com

CLARK, Lance Edgar Dennis. b 52. Linc Th Coll 74. **d** 77 **p** 78. C Arnold *S'well* 77–82; V Brinsley w Underwood 82–87; Chapl RAF 87–02; Chapl Cardiff and Vale NHS Trust 02–10; rtd 10. *Hafod, Gileston, Vale of Glamorgan CF62 4HX* T: (01446) 751077 E: lanceedclark@aol.co.uk

CLARK, Lee Robert. b 82. St Steph Ho Ox BTh 15. **d** 15 **p** 16. C Pimlico St Gabr *Lon* 15–17; C Kentish Town 17–18; P-in-c Tottenham St Phil from 18. *226 Philip Lane, London N15 4HH* M: 07908-675619 E: lee.clark82@gmail.com

CLARK, Lynn. See PURVIS-LEE, Lynn

CLARK, Canon Martin Hudson. b 46. K Coll Lon BD 68 AKC 68 MTh 91 Birm Univ PGCE 89. **d** 71 **p** 72. C S'wark H Trin 71–74; C Parkstone St Pet w Branksea and St Osmund *Sarum* 74–77; V E Wickham *S'wark* 77–86; V Wandsworth St Anne 86–98; RD Wandsworth 90–95; V Angell Town St Jo 98–07; RD Brixton 01–05; Hon Can S'wark Cathl 05–07; rtd 07; PtO *Cant* 07–08 and from 11; Hon C Deal St Leon w St Rich and Sholden etc 08–10. *27 Century Walk, Deal CT14 6AL* T: (01304) 366586 E: eveandmartin@hotmail.com

CLARK, Michael Arthur. b 46. S Dios Minl Tr Scheme. **d** 83 **p** 84. NSM Monkton Farleigh, S Wraxall and Winsley *Sarum* 83–05; PtO *Chich* from 05. *5 Park West, Southdowns Park, Haywards Heath RH16 4SG* T: (01444) 440831 E: mike_clark55@hotmail.com

CLARK, Michael David. b 45. Ox Univ MA 68. Trin Coll Bris. **d** 72 **p** 73. C Cheadle *Ches* 72–76; Brazil 77–86; Bolivia 86–88; C Wilton *B & W* 89–90; TV 90–99; C Tollington *Lon* 99–01; TR Edgware 01–15; rtd 15; Hon C Bisley, Chalford, France Lynch, and Oakridge etc *Glouc*

15–18. *4 Coates Road, Exeter EX2 5RH* T: (01392) 795406 E: mikeclark@wayfarer99.go-plus.net

CLARK, Michael James. b 71. Univ of Wales (Cardiff) BSc 92. Trin Coll Bris BA 02. **d** 02 **p** 03. C Tiverton St Geo and St Paul *Ex* 02–07; TV Newton Tracey, Horwood, Alverdiscott etc 07–16; TR 16–19; Miss Community Development Adv from 19. *Address temp unknown* M: 07889-570159 E: mike.clark@exeter.anglican.org

CLARK, Miss Patricia Mary. b 36. Liv Univ BSc. **d** 88 **p** 94. Par Dn Leasowe *Ches* 88–92; Bp's Officer for Women in Min 89–97; Par Dn Davenham 92–94; C 94–97; rtd 97; PtO *Ches* 97–12; *Blackb* from 12. *7 Fosbrooke House, 8 Clifton Drive, Lytham St Annes FY8 5RQ* T: (01253) 667052

CLARK, Peter. b 47. DipCOT 92. ERMC 04. **d** 07 **p** 08. NSM Vange *Chelmsf* 07–11; Public Preacher 11–13; NSM Thundersley 13–15; PtO from 15. *283 Church Road, Basildon SS14 2NE* T: (01268) 527570 M: 07828-642518 E: frpeterclark@hotmail.com

CLARK, Canon Peter. b 39. Ch Coll Cam BA 61 MA 65. Chich Th Coll 61. **d** 63 **p** 64. C Huddersfield SS Pet and Paul *Wakef* 63–67; C Notting Hill St Jo *Lon* 67–74; Grenada 75–79; C Hove All SS *Chich* 79; P-in-c Hove St Patr 79–82; V Hove St Patr w Ch Ch and St Andr 82–83; V Battersea Ch Ch and St Steph *S'wark* 83–08; RD Battersea 90–01; Hon Can S'wark Cathl 96–08; rtd 08; PtO *S'wark* from 08. *46 Havil Street, London SE5 7RS* T: 020-7708 8915 M: 07824-198889 E: peterclark263@btinternet.com

CLARK, Peter. b 45. Sarum & Wells Th Coll 87. **d** 89 **p** 90. C Portsea St Cuth *Portsm* 89–92; TV Rye *Chich* 92–96 and 04–08; P-in-c Chiddingly w E Hoathly 96–98; R 98–04; rtd 08; PtO *Chich* from 14. *44 Ingrams Way, Hailsham BN27 3NP* T: (01323) 841809 E: clucksville@tiscali.co.uk

CLARK, Peter Rodney. b 58. Oriel Coll Ox BA 81 MCIH 93. NOC 97. **d** 00 **p** 01. C Stone St Mich and St Wulfad w Aston St Sav *Lich* 00–03; TV Hanley H Ev 03–12; RD Stoke N 08–12; R Lich St Chad from 12. *St Chad's Rectory, The Windings, Lichfield WS13 7EX*

CLARK, Mrs Prudence Anne. b 44. Man Coll of Educn CertEd 78. NOC 89. **d** 92 **p** 94. NSM Royton St Anne *Man* 92–94; Hon C 94–95; NSM Haughton St Anne 95–09; PtO from 09. *1 Hereford Way, Stalybridge SK15 2TD* T: 0161-338 5275 E: prueclark1@btinternet.com

CLARK, Miss Rebekah Amy. b 91. UEA BA 12. Ridley Hall Cam 12. **d** 15 **p** 16. C Weston super Mare Ch Ch and Em *B & W* from 15. *3 The Drive, Weston-super-Mare BS23 2SR* T: (01934) 628641 M: 07749-162996 E: rebekah.clark36@gmail.com

CLARK, Richard Martin. b 60. Ch Coll Cam MA 81 Nottm Univ MA 99. Trin Coll Bris BA 86. **d** 86 **p** 87. C Orpington Ch Ch *Roch* 86–89; C Marple All SS *Ches* 89–92; V Nottingham St Andr *S'well* 92–13; AD Nottingham Cen 08–13; TR Redditch H Trin *Worc* from 13; V Tardebigge from 15. *The Vicarage, 20 Church Road, Webheath, Redditch B97 5PG* M: 07970-823462

CLARK, Rodney. *See* CLARK, Peter Rodney

CLARK, Ronald. *See* CLARK, John Ronald Lyons

✠**CLARK, The Rt Revd Sarah Elizabeth.** b 65. Loughb Univ BA 86 Keele Univ MBA 94. St Jo Coll Nottm MA 97. **d** 98 **p** 99 **c** 19. C Porchester *S'well* 98–02; R Carlton-in-Lindrick and Langold w Oldcotes 02–09; AD Worksop 06–09; TR Clifton 09–14; Dean of Women's Min 10–14; Hon Can S'well Minster 10–14; Adn Nottingham 14–19; Suff Bp Jarrow *Dur* from 19. *Bishop's House, 25 Ivy Lane, Gateshead NE9 6QD* T: 0191-491 0917 E: bishop.of.jarrow@durham.anglican.org

CLARK, Canon Stephen Kenneth. b 52. Bris Univ BEd 74. Wycliffe Hall Ox 80. **d** 83 **p** 84. C Pitsea *Chelmsf* 83–86; Chapl Scargill Ho 86–89; R Elmley Castle w Bricklehampton and Combertons *Worc* 89–96; Chapl Burrswood Chr Cen *Roch* 96–01; Chapl Team Ldr 01–07; I Annagh w Drumaloor, Cloverhill and Drumlane *K, E & A* 07–12; Can Kilmore Cathl 10–12; Dep Chapl Crowhurst Chr Healing Cen 12–17; rtd 17; PtO *Ely* from 18. *4 Tennyson Place, Ely CB6 3WE* E: skclar@googlemail.com

CLARK, Terence Paul. b 62. Leeds Univ BSc 85 PGCE 94 St Jo Coll Ox DPhil 91. Wycliffe Hall Ox 98. **d** 00 **p** 01. C Whitfield *Derby* 00–10; TR Deane *Man* from 10; P-in-c Lostock St Thos and St Jo from 16; AD Deane 12–19. *Deane Rectory, 234 Wigan Road, Bolton BL3 5QE* T: (01204) 61819 E: deanechurchoffice@btinternet.com *or* rectordeane@btinternet.com

CLARK MAXWELL, James Michael Gilchrist. b 75. Edin Univ BSc 98 MSc 99 Imp Coll Lon MB, BS 04. TISEC 06 St Jo Coll Nottm 06. **d** 11 **p** 18. NSM Dumfries *Glas* from 11. *Speddoch, Dumfries DG2 9UB* T: (01556) 610355 M: 07720-455253 E: james@speddoch.com

CLARKE, Adrian Melvin. b 68. Middx Univ MA 02. St Mellitus Coll 16. **d** 19. C Woodside Park St Barn *Lon* from 19. *124 Gammons Lane, Watford WD24 5HY* M: 07976-373381

CLARKE, Alan John. b 55. St Jo Coll Dur BA 77 MA 85 PGCE. Westcott Ho Cam 78. **d** 80 **p** 81. C Heworth St Mary *Dur* 80–83; C Darlington St Jo 83–87; Asst Chapl Bryanston Sch 87–91; Chapl St Pet High Sch Ex 93–99; Chapl and Hd RS Reed's Sch Cobham 99–15; rtd 15; PtO *Dur* from 16. *Bear's Den, 22 Blackcliffe Way, Bearpark, Durham DH7 7TJ* T: 0191-659 9114 E: alanbearsden@gmail.com

CLARKE, Alexandra Naomi Mary. b 75. Trin Coll Cam BA 96 MA 99 MPhil 97 SS Hild & Bede Coll Dur PhD 02 Anglia Poly Univ BA 04. Westcott Ho Cam 02. **d** 05 **p** 06. C Papworth *Ely* 05–09; R Upper Itchen *Win* 09–11; TV Papworth *Ely* 11–16; Chapl St Bede's Inter-Church School, Birdwood Road, Cambridge CB1 3TD* T: (01223) 568816 E: alexandra.clarke@elydiocese.org *or* aclarke@stbedes.cambs.sch.uk

CLARKE, Miss Alison Clare. b 33. MCST 54 Open Univ BA 85. EAMTC 90. **d** 93 **p** 94. NSM Lt Ilford St Mich *Chelmsf* 93–98; Asst Chapl Newham Healthcare NHS Trust Lon 93–98; PtO *Lon* 94–98; NSM Woodford St Mary w St Phil and St Jas *Chelmsf* 98–03; rtd 03; PtO *Chelmsf* 03–04 and from 07. *20 Manor Court Lodge, 175 High Road, London E18 2PD* T: (020) 8504 5106

CLARKE, Andrew John. b 58. New Coll Edin BD 82 Graduate Soc Dur PGCE 89. Linc Th Coll 84. **d** 86 **p** 87. C High Harrogate Ch Ch *Ripon* 86–88; RE Teacher Royds Hall High Sch Huddersfield 89–91; C Thornbury *Bradf* 91–93; P-in-c Bingley H Trin 93–99; V 99–14; Leeds from 14; RD Airedale *Bradf* 00–05. *6 Woodvale Crescent, Bingley BD16 4AL* T: (01274) 562278 E: andrew.clarke@leeds.anglican.org

CLARKE, Ann. *See* CLARKE, Geraldine Ann

CLARKE, Anne. b 51. **d** 04 **p** 05. OLM E Dulwich St Jo *S'wark* from 04. *62 Oakhurst Grove, London SE22 9AQ* T: (020) 8693 1276 M: 07788-766783 E: anne@oakhurstgrove.com

CLARKE, Canon Barbara. b 51. Bradf Univ BA 87 Leeds Univ PGCE 89 MA 07. NOC 04. **d** 07 **p** 08. NSM Addingham *Bradf* 07–14; Admin and Tutor Yorks Min Course 07–15; Hon Can Bradf Cathl *Leeds* from 13. *3 Radley Court, Mirfield WF14 9FD* T: (01924) 506575 E: bclarke3@virginmedia.com

CLARKE, Bernard Ronald. b 53. Nottm Univ MA 97 FRGS. Ridley Hall Cam 74. **d** 77 **p** 78. C Leigh Park *Portsm* 77–78; C Petersfield w Sheet 78–81; Chapl RN 81–13; Dir of Ords RN 93–03; Chapl RNR from 13; QHC from 08. *Royal Naval Chaplaincy Service, Mail Point 1-2, Leach Building, Whale Island, Portsmouth PO2 8BY* T: (023) 9262 5055 F: 9262 5134

CLARKE, Mrs Caroline Anne. b 49. Girton Coll Cam BA 75 MA 79 K Coll Lon PGCE 76. SEITE 97. **d** 00 **p** 01. NSM Clapham H Trin *S'wark* from 00; Chapl Trin Hospice Lon 03–11; AD Lambeth N *S'wark* from 17. *42 The Chase, London SW4 0NH* T: (020) 7622 0765 M: 07808-858674 E: clarkecaroline@hotmail.com *or* caroline.clarke@holytrinityclapham.org

CLARKE, Canon Christopher George. b 43. Sarum Th Coll 67. **d** 68 **p** 69. C Sprowston *Nor* 68–72; V Hemsby 72–77; V Sutton Courtenay w Appleford *Ox* 77–84; TR Bracknell 84–97; RD 90–96; Hon Can Ch 95–08; P-in-c Sonning 97–98; V 98–08; rtd 08; PtO *Worc* from 08. *Oak Lodge, Upton Snodsbury, Worcester WR7 4NH* T: (01905) 381146 E: cgandcgclarke@googlemail.com

CLARKE, Canon David James. b 55. Univ of Wales (Abth) BSc(Econ) 77 Keele Univ MA 78 PhD 83. Trin Coll Bris. **d** 84 **p** 85. C Cardigan w Mwnt and Y Ferwig *St D* 84–87; P-in-c Llansantffraed and Llanbadarn Trefeglwys etc 87–88; V 88–91; Chapl Coll of SS Mark and Jo Plymouth 91–96; V Lindfield *Chich* from 96; Can and Preb Chich Cathl from 06. *The Vicarage, High Street, Lindfield, Haywards Heath RH16 2HR* T: (01444) 482386 E: tavyd@aol.com

CLARKE, Duncan James Edward. b 54. Wycliffe Hall Ox 75. **d** 78 **p** 79. C Newport St Andr *Mon* 78–80; C Griffithstown 80–82; Trinidad and Tobago 82–84 and 95–99; NSM Fleckney and Kilby *Leic* 92–95; USPG 95–99; C Wednesfield *Lich* 99; TV 99–01; Asst Chapl HM Pris Wormwood Scrubs 01–02; Chapl HM Pris Haverigg 02–07; Chapl HM Pris Garth 07–09; P-in-c Leyland St Ambrose *Blackb* 09–11; V from 11. *St Ambrose Vicarage, 85 Moss Lane, Leyland, Preston PR25 4XA* T: (01772) 623426 M: 07946-668786 E: namabiah@msn.com

CLARKE, Mrs Elizabeth Hazel. b 55. Ridley Hall Cam 02. **d** 04 **p** 05. C Frankby w Greasby *Ches* 04–09; P-in-c Dodleston 09–11; R from 11. *St Mary's Rectory, Pulford Lane, Dodleston, Chester CH4 9NN* T: (01244) 660257 E: hazelclarke@jcscomputers.co.uk

CLARKE (*née* **GILMARTIN**), **Mrs Frances.** b 53. Reading Univ BSc 75 PGCE 92. **d** 11 **p** 12. OLM Skellingthorpe w Doddington *Linc* from 11. *12 Shaftesbury Avenue, Lincoln LN6 0QN* T: (01522) 685487 E: frances_clarke@hotmail.co.uk

CLARKE, Francis Alfred. b 46. MCLIP 67 MCMI 82. **d** 08 **p** 09. OLM Weybourne Gp *Nor* 08–16; rtd 16; PtO *Nor* from 16. *7 Alexandra Road, Sheringham NR26 8HU* T: (01263) 825677 E: f.clarke46@btinternet.com

CLARKE, Geraldine Ann. b 46. Hockerill Coll of Educn CertEd 68 ACP 81. NTMTC 93. **d** 96 **p** 97. NSM Aldersbrook *Chelmsf* 96–01; TR Becontree S 01–09; P-in-c N Bersted *Chich* 09–17; Can and Preb Chich Cathl 14–17; Hon C Wanstead St Mary w Ch Ch *Chelmsf* from 17. *13 Wanstead Place, London E11 2SW* E: annclarke@talktalk.net

CLARKE, Hazel. See CLARKE, Elizabeth Hazel

CLARKE, James. See CLARKE, David James

CLARKE, Jennifer Anna. b 78. Edge Hill Coll of HE BA 99. Ripon Coll Cuddesdon 16. **d** 18 **p** 19. C Bradshaw and Holmfield *Leeds* from 18. *3 Burnholme, Denhholme, Bradford BD13 4NJ* E: rev.jen@outlook.com

CLARKE, John Charles. b 31. St Jo Coll Nottm 91. **d** 92 **p** 93. NSM Winshill *Derby* 92–95; P-in-c Stanley 95–98; rtd 98; PtO *Win* from 98. *4 Campion Drive, Romsey SO51 7RD* T: (01794) 523945

CLARKE, The Very Revd John Martin. b 52. Edin Univ BD 76 Hertf Coll Ox BA 89 MA 89. Edin Th Coll 73. **d** 76 **p** 77. C Kenton Ascension *Newc* 76–79; Prec St Ninian's Cathl Perth *St And* 79–82; Info Officer to Gen Syn of Scottish Episc Ch 82–87; Greece 87–88; V Battersea St Mary *S'wark* 89–96; Prin Ripon Coll Cuddesdon 97–04; Can and Preb Linc Cathl 00–04; Dean Wells *B & W* 04–15; rtd 16; PtO *Bris* from 16. *1 Blackbridge Road, Chippenham SN15 3LS* T: (01249) 709246

CLARKE, John Patrick Hatherley. b 46. Pemb Coll Ox BA 68 Man Univ MBA 73. St Jo Coll Nottm. **d** 83 **p** 84. C Leic H Trin w St Jo 83–87; C Selly Park St Steph and St Wulstan *Birm* 87–92; Hon C Woking St Mary *Guildf* 92–94; V Greenham *Ox* 94–14; rtd 14; Hon C The Churn *Ox* from 14. *The Rectory, Church Lane, South Moreton, Didcot OX11 9AF* T: (01235) 512987 E: jphclarke@gmail.com

CLARKE, Mrs Joy Irene. b 44. **d** 98 **p** 02. OLM Ditton St Mich w St Thos *Liv* 98–10; rtd 10; PtO *Ches* from 12. *55 Spinney Avenue, Widnes WA8 8LB* T: 0151-424 8747 E: jiclarke1144@gmail.com

CLARKE, Judith Irene. b 46. SRN 67 SCM 69. EAMTC 97. **d** 00 **p** 01. NSM Shingay Gp *Ely* 00–02; P-in-c Gt Staughton 02–05; P-in-c Hail Weston and Southoe 04–05; R Gt Staughton w Hail Weston w Southoe 05–15; V The Staughtons w Hail Weston 15–16; rtd 16; PtO *Ely* from 16; *St Alb* from 14. *8 Munkman Close, Potton, Sandy SG19 5BY* E: judi195@btinternet.com

CLARKE (*née* **PULLIN**), **Kathleen Jean Rebecca.** b 58. Qu Coll Birm BA 07. **d** 07 **p** 08. C Kings Norton *Birm* 07–11; V Highters Heath 11–17; TR N Meols *Liv* from 17. *20 Moss Lane, Churchtown, Southport PR9 7QR* E: rebeccapullin@hotmail.com

✠**CLARKE, The Rt Revd Kenneth Herbert.** b 49. TCD BA 71. **d** 72 **p** 73 **c** 01. C Magheralin *D & D* 72–75; C Dundonald 75–78; Chile 78–81; I Crinken *D & G* 82–86; I Coleraine *Conn* 86–01; Chmn SAMS (Ireland) from 94; Can Conn Cathl 96–98; Adn Dalriada 98–01; Bp K, E & A 01–12; Miss Dir SAMS (Ireland) from 13. *Address temp unknown*

CLARKE, Miss Kirsty Ann. b 81. Chich Univ BA 03. Qu Foundn Birm BA 15. **d** 15 **p** 16. C Leominster *Heref* 15–19; TV Shaftesbury *Sarum* from 19. *Address temp unknown* M: 07720-323916 E: kclarke1981@yahoo.co.uk

CLARKE, Mrs Lynnette Jean. b 46. Qu Coll Birm 05. **d** 08 **p** 09. OLM Allesley Park and Whoberley *Cov* 08–13; OLM Cov E 13–16; PtO from 16. *14 High Park Close, Coventry CV5 7BE* T: (024) 7646 7097 M: 07890-048210 E: lynnette@mountnod.co.uk

CLARKE, Martin Howard. b 47. AKC 70. St Aug Coll Cant 70. **d** 71 **p** 72. C Saffron Walden w Wendens Ambo *Chelmsf* 71–74; C Ely 74–78; V Messing w Inworth *Chelmsf* 78–90; V Layer de la Haye 90–96; R Layer de la Haye and Layer Breton w Birch etc 96–12; rtd 12; PtO *Chelmsf* from 14. *Saddlers, 2 Stable Close, West Mersea, Colchester CO5 8HP* T: (01206) 383952 E: martinandangela2@btinternet.com

CLARKE, Ms Mary Margaret. b 65. K Coll Lon BD 86 AKC 86. Linc Th Coll 89. **d** 89 **p** 94. Par Dn Northampton St Jas *Pet* 89–93; Chapl Nene Coll of HE Northn 92–93; Team Dn Coventry Caludon *Cov* 93–94; TV 94–01; PtO *Lon* 01–08; C Notting Dale St Clem w St Mark and St Jas 12–19. *1 Porchester Gardens, London W2 3LA* T: (020) 7229 6359 E: revdmaryclarke@gmail.com

CLARKE, Maurice Harold. b 30. K Alfred's Coll Win CertEd 56 Sussex Univ MA 79 LCP 69. Cuddesdon Coll 65. **d** 67 **p** 68. Hd Master Co Sec Sch Cowplain (Lower Sch) 67–72; Dep Hd Master Thamesview High Sch 72–80; Hd Master Eltham Green Comp Sch 80–83; Hon C Waterlooville *Portsm* 67–70; Hon C Fareham SS Pet and Paul 70–72; Hon C Higham and Merston *Roch* 72–83; V Hamble le Rice *Win* 83–90; rtd 91; PtO *Win* 91–14; *Chich* from 92. *10 Worcester Road, Chichester PO19 8DJ* T: (01243) 775646

CLARKE, Canon Neil Malcolm. b 53. Solicitor 79. WMMTC 89. **d** 92 **p** 93. NSM Desborough, Brampton Ash, Dingley and Braybrooke *Pet* from 92; Can Pet Cathl from 04. *53 Breakleys Road, Desborough, Kettering NN14 2PT* T: (01536) 760667 E: revnclarke@aol.com

CLARKE, Nicholas John. b 57. Sarum Coll 14. **d** 17 **p** 18. NSM Merriott w Hinton, Dinnington and Lopen *B & W* from 17. *Grovely Farm, Hewish Lane, Crewkerne TA18 8RE* T: (01460) 72838 E: nickclarke504y@hotmail.co.uk

CLARKE, Nicholas John. b 57. Lon Univ BA 78 Lon Inst of Educn PGCE 80 St Andr Univ MLitt 09. Ridley Hall Cam 95. **d** 97 **p** 98. C Attleborough *Cov* 97–00; V Fillongley and Corley 00–07; Chapl Chantilly *Eur* 07–16; TR Radipole and Melcombe Regis *Sarum* from 16; RD Weymouth and Portland from 17. *39 Icen Road, Weymouth DT3 5JL* T: (01305) 520163 M: 07514-119314 E: teamrector@staldhelmstann.co.uk

CLARKE, Norman. b 28. Keble Coll Ox BA 52 MA 58. St Steph Ho Ox 52. **d** 54 **p** 55. C Ellesmere Port *Ches* 54–57; C Kettering St Mary *Pet* 57–60; Chapl and Tutor St Monica Mampong Ghana 60–62; C Friern Barnet All Ss *Lon* 62–63; LtO *Leic* 63–74; C Knighton St Mary Magd 74–81; Dioc Communications Officer *St E* 81–88; P-in-c Sproughton w Burstall 81–88; P-in-c Dunsford and Doddiscombsleigh *Ex* 88–95; P-in-c Cheriton Bishop 88–95; rtd 95; PtO *Ex* 95–08; RD Ottery 02–03; Perm to Offic St Helena from 96. *78 Malden Road, Sidmouth EX10 9NA* T: (01395) 515849

CLARKE, Paul Ian. b 72. W Suffolk Coll BA 09. Trin Coll Bris BA 11. **d** 11 **p** 12. C Haughley w Wetherden and Stowupland *St E* 11–14; P-in-c Coxley w Godney, Henton and Wookey *B & W* 14–18; V from 18. *The Vicarage, Vicarage Lane, Wookey, Wells BA5 1JT* M: 07456-936475 E: revpaulclarke@me.com *or* vicar@chwchurches.co.uk

CLARKE, Rachel Frances. See HARTLAND, Rachel Frances

✠**CLARKE, The Most Revd Richard Lionel.** b 49. TCD BA 71 MA 79 PhD 90 K Coll Lon BD 75 AKC 75. **d** 75 **p** 76 **c** 96. C Holywood *D & D* 75–77; C Dublin St Bart w Leeson Park *D & G* 77–79; Dean of Residence TCD 79–84; I Bandon Union C, *C & R* 84–93; Dir of Ords 85–93; Cen Dir of Ords 82–97; Can Cork and Ross Cathls *C, C & R* 91–93; Dean Cork 93–96; I Cork St Fin Barre's Union 93–96; Chapl Univ Coll Cork 93–96; Bp M & K 96–12; Abp Arm from 12; Hon Can St Ninian's Cathl Perth *St And* from 04. *Church House, 46 Abbey Street, Armagh BT61 7DZ* T: (028) 3752 7144 E: archbishop@armagh.anglican.org

CLARKE, Robert Graham. b 28. S Dios Minl Tr Scheme 78. **d** 81 **p** 82. NSM Woolston *Win* 81–89; NSM Portswood St Denys 89–93; Chapl Torrevieja *Eur* 93–95; PtO *Win* 95–17; *Eur* from 95. *10 River Green, Hamble, Southampton SO31 4JA* T: (023) 8045 4230

CLARKE, Robert Michael. b 45. Oak Hill Th Coll BD 71 Sarum & Wells Th Coll 78. **d** 78 **p** 79. Hon C Glastonbury St Jo w Godney *B & W* 78–81; Asst Hd Master Edington Sch 78–81; Chapl Felsted Sch 81–84; Asst Chapl and Ho Master 85–92; Hd Master Brocksford Hall 92–94; Hd Master The Park Sch Bath 94–96; Chapl Seaford Coll Petworth 96–99; Hd Master Bredon Sch 99–00; PtO *Lich* from 01; Hon Chapl ATC from 07. *1 Long Croft, Weston Rhyn, Oswestry SY10 7JP* T: (01691) 581571 E: revbclarke@hotmail.co.uk

CLARKE, Robert Sydney. b 35. K Coll Lon AKC 64 MA 65. **d** 65 **p** 66. C Hendon St Mary *Lon* 65–69; C Langley Marish *Ox* 69–70; Chapl New Cross Hosp Wolv 70–74; Chapl Dorchester Hosps 74–79; Sen Chapl Chelsea and Westmr Hosp Lon 80–85; Sen Chapl Win Hosps 88–94; Sen Chapl Win and Eastleigh Healthcare NHS Trust 94–00; Chapl to The Queen 87–05; Sec and Dir Tr Gen Syn Hosp Chapl Coun 94–00; PtO *S'wark* 95–05; *Lon* 95–00; rtd 00; PtO *Eur* 00–19; *Win* from 05. *3 Brook Court, Middlebridge Street, Romsey SO51 8HR* T: (01794) 524215 E: robertsclarke@tiscali.co.uk

CLARKE, Canon Robert William. b 56. CITC. **d** 83 **p** 84. C Cloughfern *Conn* 83–85; C Drumragh w Mountfield *D & R* 85–87; I Edenderry w Clanabogan from 87; Can Derry Cathl from 05. *Edenderry Rectory, 91 Crevenagh Road, Omagh BT79 0EZ* T: (028) 8224 5525 E: rw.clarke@btinternet.com

CLARKE, Roger Anthony. b 69. **d** 16 **p** 17. OLM Romford St Edw *Chelmsf* from 16. *65 Birch Close, Romford RM7 8ES*

CLARKE, Canon Roger David. b 58. Man Univ BA Ox Univ MA. Ripon Coll Cuddesdon 80. **d** 83 **p** 84. C Frodsham *Ches* 83–86; C Wilmslow 86–88; V High Lane 88–93; V Heald Green St Cath 93–99; R W Kirby St Bridget 99–10; V Hale Barns w Ringway 10–15; R Eccleston and Pulford from 15; Bp's Chapl from 15; Hon Can Ches Cathl from 15. *The Rectory, Church Road, Eccleston, Chester CH4 9HT* T: (01244) 679969 E: yfficerdy@btopenworld.com

CLARKE, Sandra Lea. b 62. N Illinois Univ BSc 84. St Mellitus Coll BA 19. **d** 19. C The Bourne and Tilford *Guildf* from 19. *4 Priory Court, 1 Frensham Road, Farnham GU9 8HA* M: 07806-624560 E: sandy.clarke@hotmail.com

CLARKE, Sheelagh Alison. b 56. Bulmershe Coll of HE BEd 79 Open Univ MA(Ed) 90. Gen Th Sem NY MDiv 05. **d** 05 **p** 06. C Gladstone St Luke USA 05–07; C Westfield St Paul 07–09; C Monmouth Junction St Barn 09–11; C Millburn St Steph 11–17; Co-ord Young Adult and Youth Min Newark 17–19; PtO *St Alb* from 19. *20 Browns Way, Aspley Guise, Milton Keynes MK17 8JA* M: 07835-514363 E: sheelaghclarke@hotmail.com

CLARKE, Stephen Robert. b 77. Southn Univ BA 99. Trin Coll Bris BA 10. **d** 10 **p** 11. C Pioneer Min Glouc City 10–14; V Whitehall Park *Lon* from 14. *St Andrew's Vicarage, 43 Dresden Road, London N19 3BG* T: (020) 3712 6501 E: steve@standrewsn19.org *or* steveclarkey@gmail.com

CLARKE, Steven David. b 54. All SS Cen for Miss & Min 17. **d** 19. NSM Chapelfields *Wigan* from 19. *120 Camberwell Crescent, Wigan WN2 1AT* T: (01942) 498861 M: 07958-077549 E: steven.clarke1@tiscali.co.uk

CLARKE (*formerly* GARDNER), **Mrs Susan Carol.** b 54. SRN 75. St Jo Coll Nottm 02. **d** 04 **p** 05. C Abington *Pet* 04–07; P-in-c Woodhouse *Wakef* 07–08; V Birkby and Woodhouse 08–10; P-in-c Thornhill and Whitley Lower 10–14; R *Leeds* 14–17; rtd 17; PtO *Leeds* from 17; *York* from 19. *Heselwood House, 199 Woodhead Road, Holmbridge, Holmfirth HD9 2NW* M: 07896-464417 E: sue.clarke@btinternet.com

CLARKE (*née* DAVIS), **Canon Susan Elizabeth Mary.** b 50. St Thos Hosp Lon MB, BS 74 Univ Coll Lon MSc 81 FRCP 84 FRCR 03. SEITE 03. **d** 06 **p** 07. NSM W Streatham St Jas *S'wark* 06–12; NSM Streatham St Paul 10–12; Hon TV Furzedown from 12; AD Tooting from 16; Hon Can S'wark Cathl from 15. *26 Abbotsleigh Road, London SW16 1SP* T: (020) 8769 5117 M: 07710-744006 E: sue.clarke@kcl.ac.uk *or* semclarke@btinternet.com

CLARKE, Timothy John. b 69. Jes Coll Cam BA 91 MA 95 Barrister 92. WMMTC 00. **d** 03 **p** 04. NSM Birm Cathl 03–16; NSM Worc St Martin w St Swithun and St Paul from 16; PtO 10–16; *Birm* from 16; Dep Chan Derby from 15. *15B College Green, Worcester WR1 2LH* T: (01905) 732938 E: timclarke@waitrose.com

CLARKE, Ms Valerie Diane. b 45. St Jo Coll Nottm BA 00. NOC 91. **d** 95 **p** 96. C Sherburn in Elmet w Saxton *York* 95–97; C Brayton 97–99; Chapl Scargill Ho 00–03; P-in-c Barnburgh w Melton on the Hill etc *Sheff* 03–09; rtd 09; PtO *Wakef* 09–12; *Sheff* 11–12; *Leeds* from 17; Hon C Beverley Minster *York* 12–16. *1 Arrunden Court, Holmfirth HD9 2AP* T: (01484) 688609 M: 07974-698458 E: valclarke@googlemail.com

CLARKE, Mrs Yvonne Veronica. b 58. CA Tr Coll. **dss** 86 **d** 87 **p** 94. Nunhead St Silas *S'wark* 86–90; Par Dn 87–90; Par Dn Nunhead St Antony w St Silas 90–91; Par Dn Mottingham St Andr w St Alban 91–94; C 94–98; V Spring Park All SS from 98. *All Saints' Vicarage, 1 Farm Drive, Croydon CR0 8HX* T: (020) 8777 2775 F: 8777 5228

CLARKE-MOISLEY, Lisselle Roseanne Sarah. b 88. Trin Coll Bris 17. **d** 19. C Harwich Peninsula *Chelmsf* from 19. *19 Beacon Hill Avenue, Harwich CO12 3NR* E: lissellecm@gmail.com

CLARKSON, The Ven Alan Geoffrey. b 34. Ch Coll Cam BA 57 MA 61. Wycliffe Hall Ox 57. **d** 59 **p** 60. C Penn *Lich* 59–60; C Oswestry St Oswald 60–63; C Wrington *B & W* 63–65; V Chewton Mendip w Emborough 65–74; Dioc Ecum Officer 65–75; V Glastonbury St Jo w Godney 74–84; P-in-c W Pennard 80–84; P-in-c Meare 81–84; P-in-c Glastonbury St Benedict 82–84; V Glastonbury w Meare, W Pennard and Godney 84; Hon Can Win Cathl 84–99; Adn Win 84–99; V Burley Ville 84–99; rtd 99; PtO *Chelmsf* from 99; *Ely* from 99; *St E* 99–18. *Cantilena, 4 Harefield Rise, Linton, Cambridge CB21 4LS* T: (01223) 892988 E: agclarkson@hotmail.com *or* a.clarkson@talktalk.net

CLARKSON, Geoffrey. b 35. AKC 61. **d** 62 **p** 63. C Shildon *Dur* 62–65; Asst Chapl HM Pris Liv 65–66; Chapl HM Borstal Feltham 66–71; Development Officer Br Assn of Settlements 71–74; Dir Community Projects Foundn 74–87; Chapl HM Rem Cen Ashford 88–90; Chapl HM Pris Coldingley 90–99; Chapl HM Pris Send 92–94; rtd 00; Hon C Hampton St Mary *Lon* 71–05; PtO from 05. *109*

Cambridge Road, Teddington TW11 8DF T: (020) 8977 1434 E: geoffreyclarkson@virginmedia.com

CLARKSON, Mrs Julie Marie. b 60. York St Jo Univ BA 13. Yorks Min Course 13. **d** 16 **p** 17. C Barnoldswick w Bracewell *Leeds* from 16. *33 Chapman Court, Barnoldswick BB18 5EE* T: (01282) 851724 M: 07764-976431 E: julie.clarkson@btinternet.com

CLARKSON, Michael. *See* CLARKSON, Richard Michael

CLARKSON, Canon Richard. b 33. Man Univ BSc 54 Ball Coll Ox DPhil 57. Oak Hill Th Coll 89. **d** 91 **p** 92. NSM Sunnyside w Bourne End *St Alb* 91–03; RD Berkhamsted 97–02; Hon Can St Alb 02–03; rtd 03; PtO *St Alb* from 09. *Kingsmead, Gravel Path, Berkhamsted HP4 2PH* T: (01442) 873014 E: r.sclarkson@btopenworld.com

CLARKSON, Richard Anthony. b 85. Nottm Univ BSc 06. Trin Coll Bris BA 14. **d** 14 **p** 15. C Whitchurch *Lich* 14–17; C Edstaston, Fauls, Prees, Tilstock and Whixall 14–17; R Adderley, Ash, Calverhall, Ightfield etc from 17. *The Rectory, Moreton Say, Market Drayton TF9 3RS* M: 07763-909110 E: revrichclarkson@gmail.com

CLARKSON, Richard Michael. b 38. St Jo Coll Dur BA 60 Lanc Univ PGCE 68. Cranmer Hall Dur 60. **d** 62 **p** 63. C Heyhouses on Sea *Blackb* 62–66; C Lancaster St Mary 66–68; Asst Master Kirkham Gr Sch 68–90; Asst Master Hurstpierpoint Coll 90–91; Asst Master St Mary's Hall Brighton 92–98; Chapl 96–98; rtd 93; PtO *Chich* from 93. *121 College Lane, Hurstpierpoint, Hassocks BN6 9AF* T: (01273) 834117

CLARKSON, Robert Christopher. b 32. Dur Univ BA 53 DipEd 54. S Dios Minl Tr Scheme 85. **d** 87 **p** 88. NSM Lower Dever Valley *Win* 87–03; PtO from 03. *27 Wrights Way, South Wonston, Winchester SO21 3HE* T: (01962) 881692

CLARRIDGE, Mrs Ann. b 44. Bournemouth Univ BSc 89 S Bank Univ MSc 94. SEITE 01. **d** 04 **p** 05. NSM Shepherd's Bush St Steph w St Thos *Lon* 04–07; NSM Whitton St Aug 07–11; NSM Northwood H Trin 11–18; NSM Cowley from 18. *18 Elgar Close, Ickenham, Uxbridge UB10 8HN* T: (01895) 349005 E: annclarridge@hotmail.co.uk

CLARRIDGE, Donald Michael. b 41. DipOT 86. Oak Hill Th Coll 63. **d** 66 **p** 67. C Newc St Barn and St Jude 66–70; C Pennycross *Ex* 70–76; R Clayhanger 76–83; R Petton 76–83; R Huntsham 76–83; V Bampton 76–83. *Winkley, Broad Road, Hambrook, Chichester PO18 8RF* T: (01243) 576535 E: donjanwinkley@btinternet.com

CLASBY, Michael Francis Theodore. b 37. Univ Coll Lon BA 59. Chich Th Coll 59. **d** 61 **p** 62. C Leigh-on-Sea St Marg *Chelmsf* 61–64; C Forest Gate St Edm 64–69; V Walthamstow St Mich 69–70; Chapl Community of Sisters of the Love of God 87–89; PtO *St Alb* 87–89; NSM Hemel Hempstead 90–93; PtO 93–98; rtd 02. *2 Heritage Close, High Street, St Albans AL3 4EB* T: (01727) 869818 M: 07506-785442 E: michael.clasby@gmail.com

CLATWORTHY, Jonathan Richard. b 48. Univ of Wales BA 70. Sarum & Wells Th Coll 71. **d** 76 **p** 77. C Man Resurr 76–78; C Bolton St Pet 78–81; V Ashton St Pet 81–85; Chapl Sheff Univ 85–91; V Denstone w Ellastone and Stanton *Lich* 91–98; Chapl Liv Univ 98–02; rtd 02; PtO *Liv* from 04. *9 Westward View, Aigburth, Liverpool L17 7EE* T: 0151-727 6291 E: jonathan@clatworthy.org

CLAVIER, Canon Mark Forbes Moreton. b 70. Coll of Wm & Mary (USA) AB 93 Duke Univ (USA) MTS 95 St Chad's Coll Dur PhD 11. **d** 09 **p** 09. C Langley Park, Hamsteels, Esh and Waterhouses *Dur* 09–10; P-in-c Steeple Aston w N Aston and Tackley *Ox* 11–13; Dean of Res Tr St Mich Coll Llan 13–16; Vice-Prin St Steph Ho Ox 16–17; Can Res Brecon Cathl *S & B* from 17. *The Cathedral Office, Cathedral Close, Brecon LD3 9DP* M: 07531-856943 E: mark.clavier@gmail.com *or* rescanon@breconcathedral.org.uk

CLAXTON, Mrs Claire Marie. b 58. R Academy of Music BMus 79 LRAM 78 K Alfred's Coll Win PGCE 80. STETS 12. **d** 14 **p** 15. C Guernsey St Martin *Win* 14–17; C Guernsey St Marguerite de la Foret 17–18; R from 18. *Carillon, Rue des Bailleuls, St Andrew, Guernsey GY6 8XB* T: (01481) 238815 M: 07781-433225 E: carillon@cwgsy.net

CLAY, Geoffrey. b 51. CertEd. Ridley Hall Cam. **d** 86 **p** 87. C Birstall *Wakef* 86–90; V Lupset 90–03; P-in-c Marsden 03–10; P-in-c Kirkburton 10–14; *Leeds* 14–15; P-in-c Cumberworth, Denby and Denby Dale *Wakef* 10–14; *Leeds* 14–15; Min Development Officer *Wakef* 03–14; *Leeds* 14–15; rtd 15. *3 The Chase, Coldwell End, Youlgrave, Bakewell DE45 1UY* E: geoff@ejclay.demon.co.uk *or* geoffclay@me.com

CLAYDEN, David Edward. b 42. Oak Hill Th Coll 74. **d** 76 **p** 77. C Worksop St Jo *S'well* 76–79; V Clarborough w Hayton 79–84; C Bloxwich *Lich* 87–90; TV 90–93; TV Tollington *Lon* 93–99; P-in-c Thorndon w Rishangles, Stoke Ash, Thwaite etc *St E* 99–00; P-in-c Thornhams Magna and Parva, Gislingham and Mellis 99–00; R S Hartismere 00–06; rtd 06; PtO *S'well* from 06. *151 Southview Road, Carlton, Nottingham NG4 3QT* T: 0115-987 2690

CLAYDON, Preb Graham Leonard. b 43. K Coll Lon BA 65. Clifton Th Coll 66. **d** 68 **p** 69. C Walthamstow St Mary w St Steph *Chelmsf* 68–71; C St Marylebone All So w SS Pet and Jo *Lon* 71–73; Hon C 73–81; Warden All So Clubhouse 71–81; V Islington St Mary *Lon* 81–99; Dioc Ev (Stepney) and C Highbury Ch Ch w St Jo and St Sav 99–03; TV Hackney Marsh 03–06; Preb St Paul's Cathl 92–06; rtd 07; PtO *Chich* 12–17. *Acre End, Tangmere Road, Tangmere, Chichester PO20 2HW* T: (01243) 536789

CLAYDON, Mrs Marilyn Pamela. b 53. Middx Univ MA 04 RGN 74 HVCert 76. St Mellitus Coll 17. **d** 19. OLM Chingford SS Pet and Paul *Chelmsf* from 19. *25 Whitehall Gardens, London E4 6EH* T: (020) 8524 9173 M: 07931-967167 E: marilyn.claydon@ntlworld.com

CLAYTON, Adam Jonathan Barnett. b 56. **d** 06 **p** 07. OLM Icknield *Ox* 06–12; P-in-c Myddle *Lich* 12–18; R from 18; P-in-c Broughton 12–18; V from 18; P-in-c Loppington w Newtown from 12; RD Wem and Whitchurch from 15. *The Rectory, Myddle, Shrewsbury SY4 3RX* T: (01939) 291801 E: revajbelayton@gmail.com

CLAYTON, Benjamin Theo. b 90. Nottm Univ BA 11. Wycliffe Hall Ox 13. **d** 15 **p** 16. C Nottingham St Jude *S'well* 15–18; C Retford Area from 18. *St Saviour's Vicarage, 31 Richmond Road, Retford DN22 6SJ*

CLAYTON, Christopher Charles. b 81. Ripon Coll Cuddesdon BA 18. **d** 18 **p** 19. C High Harrogate St Pet *Leeds* from 18. *23 Azerley Grove, Harrogate HG3 2SY* M: 07407-258733 E: christopher.charles.clayton@gmail.com

CLAYTON, Geoffrey Buckroyd. b 26. Newc Univ BA 67. Roch Th Coll 62. **d** 64 **p** 65. C Newc St Geo 64–67; C Byker St Ant 67–68; Chapl Salonika *Eur* 68–69; C Cheddleton *Lich* 69–72; V Arbory *S & M* 72–97; RD Castletown 82–97; V Santan 88–97; rtd 97; PtO *St D* from 97. *The Cottage, Hendre Mynach Caravan Park, Llanaber Road, Barmouth LL42 1YR* T: (01341) 280409 E: revgbclayton@hotmail.co.uk

CLAYTON, Matthew Anthony. b 89. St Mellitus Coll BA 16. **d** 16 **p** 17. C Bournemouth Town Cen *Win* from 16. *2A St Anthony's Road, Bournemouth BH2 6PD* T: (01202) 241077 M: 07763-115512 E: matt@stswithuns.me

CLAYTON, Paul. b 47. Cranmer Hall Dur 03. **d** 04 **p** 05. NSM Elton and Preston-on-Tees and Longnewton *Dur* 04–06; NSM Bishopton w Gt Stainton 06–13; NSM Redmarshall 06–13; NSM Grindon, Stillington and Wolviston 06–13; NSM Billingham St Mary 09–13; rtd 13. PtO *Dur* from 13. *144 Darlington Lane, Stockton-on-Tees TS19 0NG* T: (01642) 607233 E: gandpclayton@btinternet.com

CLAYTON, Ross. b 47. EMMTC 82. **d** 85 **p** 86. C Cotmanhay *Derby* 85–89; TV Eckington w Handley and Ridgeway 89–90; PtO from 08; Spiritual Dir Derby Angl Cursillo from 18. *69 Beresford Road, Long Eaton, Nottingham NG10 3EF* T: 0115-946 0084 E: mosesclayton@sky.com

CLAYTON, William Terence. b 42. Lon Univ BSc 71 MSc 73. AKC 66. **d** 67 **p** 68. C Rotherhithe St Mary w All SS *S'wark* 67–71; Hon C Camberwell St Mich w All So w Em 71–76; Hon C Newington St Paul 71–76; Hon C Winterslow *Sarum* 76–77; rtd 07. *Dungarth, Middleton Road, Winterslow, Salisbury SP5 1QL* T: (01980) 862286 E: wtclayton@btinternet.com

CLEALL, Mary Jane Anne. *See* LINDSAY, Mary Jane Anne

CLEALL-HILL, Malcolm John. b 51. Salford Univ Man Metrop Univ. **d** 01 **p** 02. OLM Chorlton-cum-Hardy St Werburgh *Man* 01–11; rtd 11; PtO *Man* from 11. *62 Buckingham Road, Chorlton cum Hardy, Manchester M21 0RP* T: 0161-881 7024 *or* 242 5288 E: m.cleall-hill@mmu.ac.uk *or* malcalnoll@tiscali.co.uk

CLEATON, Mrs Nancy Thomas. b 45. Lon Bible Coll BD 67. WEMTC 05. **d** 07 **p** 08. NSM Church Stretton *Heref* 07–12; P-in-c Hope Bowdler w Eaton-under-Heywood 12–13; P-in-c Rushbury 12–13; P-in-c Cardington 12–13; R Apedale Gp from 13. *The Rectory, Hope Bowdler, Church Stretton SY6 7DD* T: (01694) 328132 E: nancy.cleaton@tiscali.co.uk

CLEATON, Sheena Faith. b 74. Colchester Inst BA 97 R Holloway Coll Lon MMus 02 PhD 07. Ripon Coll Cuddesdon BTh 14. **d** 11 **p** 12. C Bourne *Linc* 11–16; R Scartho from 16. *St Matthew's House, 8 Thirlmere Avenue, Grimsby DN33 3EA* E: sheena_cleaton@hotmail.com

CLEAVER, John Martin. b 42. K Coll Lon BD 64 AKC 64. St Boniface Warminster 61. **d** 65 **p** 66. C Bexley St Mary *Roch* 65–69; C Ealing St Steph Castle Hill *Lon* 69–71; P-in-c Bostall Heath *Roch* 71–76; V Green Street Green 76–85; Primary Adv Lon Dioc Bd for Schs 85–92; V Teddington St Mary w St Alb 92–08; rtd 08; PtO *Chich* from 13; *Lon* from 14. *5*

Oaklands, Westham, Pevensey BN24 5AW T: (01323) 769964 E: cleaverjohn@hotmail.com

CLEAVER, Stuart Douglas. b 46. ACIS. Oak Hill Th Coll. **d** 83 **p** 84. C Portsdown *Portsm* 83–86; C Blendworth w Chalton w Idsworth etc 86–88; P-in-c Whippingham w E Cowes 88–98; R 98–01; rtd 01. *The Crest, Soake Road, Waterlooville PO7 6HY* T: (023) 9226 2277 E: eandscleaver@gmail.com

CLEE, Mrs Norma. b 53. Lindisfarne Regional Tr Partnership 13. **d** 15 **p** 16. NSM Eighton Banks *Dur* from 15. *19 Cromarty, Outston, Chester le Street DH2 1LA* T: 0191-492 0293 M: 07964-029986 E: normaclee@icloud.com

CLEEVE, Martin. b 43. Bp Otter Coll TCert 65 ACP 67 Open Univ BA 80. Oak Hill Th Coll 69. **d** 72 **p** 73. C Margate H Trin *Cant* 72–76; V Southminster *Chelmsf* 76–86; Teacher Castle View Sch Canvey Is 86–91; Hd RE Bromfords Sch Wickford 91–94; Hd RE Deanes Sch Thundersley 94–98; P-in-c Gt Mongeham w Ripple and Sutton by Dover *Cant* 99–04; rtd 04; PtO *Cant* from 04; Chapl Kent & Medway NHS and Soc Care Partnership Trust from 08. *Euphony, Waldershare Road, Ashley, Dover CT15 5JA*

CLEEVES, Canon David John. b 56. Univ of Wales (Lamp) BA Fitzw Coll Cam MA 85. Westcott Ho Cam. **d** 82 **p** 83. C Cuddington *Guildf* 82–85; C Dorking w Ranmore 85–87; V Ewell St Fran 87–94; P-in-c Rotherfield w Mark Cross *Chich* 94–01; V Masham and Healey *Ripon* 01–14; *Leeds* from 14; Jt AD Ripon 04–05; AD 05–09; Hon Can Ripon Cathl *Leeds* from 19. *The Vicarage, Rodney Terrace, Masham, Ripon HG4 4JA* T: (01765) 689255 E: cleevesmasham@onetel.com

CLEGG, Canon John Anthony Holroyd. b 44. Kelham Th Coll 65. **d** 70 **p** 71. C Heyhouses on Sea *Blackb* 70–74; C Lancaster St Mary 74–76; V Lower Darwen St Jas 76–80; TV Shaston *Sarum* 80–86; Chapl HM Youth Cust Cen Guys Marsh 80–86; R Poulton-le-Sands w Morecambe St Laur *Blackb* 86–97; RD Lancaster 89–94; TR Cartmel Peninsula *Carl* 97–04; RD Windermere 01–04; P-in-c Appleby 04–08; P-in-c Ormside 04–08; TR Heart of Eden 08–09; RD Appleby 04–09; Hon Can Carl Cathl 01–09; rtd 09; PtO *Carl* 09–19; *Blackb* from 10; *Sarum* from 16. *10 Townsend Road, Swanage BH19 2PT* T: (01929) 425301 M: 07855-740928 E: anthonyhclegg@gmail.com

CLEGG, John Lovell. b 48. Qu Coll Ox BA 70 MA 74. Trin Coll Bris. **d** 75 **p** 76. C Barrow St Mark *Carl* 75–79; R S Levenshulme *Man* 79–98; P-in-c Blackley St Paul 98–10; rtd 10; PtO *Man* from 11. *5 Mough Lane, Chadderton, Oldham OL9 9NT* T: 0161-684 1226 E: jclegg12@btinternet.com

CLEGG, Patricia Ann. b 45. STETS 96. **d** 99 **p** 00. NSM Harnham *Sarum* 99–03; PtO 03–05; NSM Bemerton 05–07; NSM Arle Valley *Win* 07–11; rtd 11; PtO *Sarum* from 11. *23 Richards Way, Salisbury SP2 8NT* T: (01722) 333573 E: pat.clegg@btinternet.com

CLEGG, Roger Alan. b 46. St Jo Coll Dur BA 68 Nottm Univ CertEd 69. St Jo Coll Nottm 75. **d** 78 **p** 79. C Harwood *Man* 78–81; TV Sutton St Jas and Wawne *York* 81–87; V Kirk Fenton w Kirkby Wharfe and Ulleskelfe 87–09; Chapl HM Pris Askham Grange 95–12; PtO from 09. *8 Wolsey Grange, Cawood, Selby YO8 3SB* T: (01757) 268060 M: 07957-474030 E: rogclegg@dunelm.org.uk

CLEGHORN, Mrs Catherine Grace. b 79. Grey Coll Dur BA 02 Dur Univ MA 08. St Mellitus Coll 15. **d** 18 **p** 19. C Crewe St Andr w St Jo *Ches* from 18; C Crewe All SS and St Paul w St Pet from 18. *413 Alton Street, Crewe CW2 7RX* M: 07813-117385 E: catherinegracesmith@hotmail.co.uk

CLELAND, Miss Lucy Eleanor. b 74. Aston Univ BSc 97 Cam Univ BTh 05. Ridley Hall Cam 02. **d** 05 **p** 06. C Yaxley and Holme w Conington *Ely* 05–08; P-in-c Landbeach and Waterbeach 08–11; Bp's Dom Chapl *S'well* 11–17; Chapl Scargill Ho from 17. *Scargill House, Kettlewell, Skipton BD23 5HU* T: (01756) 760500 E: lecleland@hotmail.com

CLELAND, Trevor. b 66. QUB BTh 94 TCD MPhil 97. CITC 94. **d** 96 **p** 97. C Lisburn Ch Ch *Conn* 96–99; C Carrickfergus 99–03; I Belfast Upper Falls 03–12; I Ballinderry from 12. *Ballinderry Rectory, 124 Ballinderry Road, Ballinderry Upper, Lisburn BT28 2NL* T: (028) 9265 0134 M: 07875-361682 E: tcleland@btinternet.com

CLEMAS, Preb Nigel Antony. b 53. Wycliffe Hall Ox. **d** 83 **p** 84. C Bootle St Mary w St Paul *Liv* 83–87; V Kirkdale St Mary and St Athanasius 87–91; TV Netherthorpe *Sheff* 91–93; V Netherthorpe St Steph 93–98; R Chapel Chorlton, Maer and Whitmore *Lich* from 98; RD Eccleshall 00–16; Preb Lich Cathl from 13. *The Rectory, Snape Hall Road, Whitmore, Newcastle ST5 5HS* T: (01782) 680258 E: nclemas@hotmail.com

CLEMENCE, Paul Robert Fraser. b 50. St Edm Hall Ox MA 90 MRTPI 82. Wycliffe Hall Ox 88. **d** 90 **p** 91. C Lancaster

St Mary *Blackb* 90–94; Chapl HM Pris Lanc Castle 90–94; V Lt Thornton *Blackb* 94–16; AD Poulton 00–09; rtd 16; PtO *Blackb* 16–17. *94 Victoria Road East, Thornton-Cleveleys FY5 5HH* E: p.clemence@tiscali.co.uk *or* p.clemence61@gmail.com

CLEMENT, Geoffrey Paul. b 64. **d** 94 **p** 96. Jardines del Hipódromo St Aug Uruguay 94–96; Colón St Jas Miss 95–97; Barrio Fátima Salto St Luke w H Spirit 97–01; TV Wilford Peninsula *St E* 01–07; R Holbrook, Stutton, Freston, Woolverstone etc 07–18; V Wychwood *Ox* from 18. *The Vicarage, Church Street, Shipton-under-Wychwood, Chipping Norton OX7 6BP* T: (01993) 832467 M: 07955-721332 E: revgclement@btinternet.com

CLEMENT, Paskal. b 63. Punjab Univ BA 92 Univ of Wales MA 08. Nat Catholic Inst of Th Karachi 82. **d** 88 **p** 88. Pakistan 88–01; NSM Hounslow H Trin w St Paul and St Mary *Lon* 04–08; C Oadby *Leic* 08–13; P-in-c *Leic* Resurr from 13. *St Alban's House, Weymouth Street, Leicester LE4 6FN* M: 07727-286905 E: paskalm@yahoo.com

CLEMENT, Canon Peter James. b 64. UMIST BSc 88 Man Univ MA 98. Qu Coll Birm 89. **d** 92 **p** 93. C Grange St Andr *Ches* 92–95; C Man Apostles w Miles Platting 95–97; TV Uggeshall w Sotherton, Wangford and Henham *St E* 97–99; TV Sole Bay 99–00; Dioc Youth Officer 01–02; V Fairweather Green *Bradf* 02–07; Assoc Dioc Dir of Ords 04–07; Dioc Dir of Ords *Ripon* 07–14; Dir of Ords *Leeds* 14–15; Voc Development Officer and Dir of Ords *Carl* from 15; Can Res Carl Cathl from 17. *Church House, West Walls, Carlisle CA3 8UE* T: (01228) 522573 E: peter.clement@carlislediocese.org.uk

CLEMENT, Richard Percy. b 63. Bris Univ BA 85. ERMC 04. **d** 06 **p** 08. C Framlingham w Saxtead *St E* 06–09; Chapl RAF from 09. *Chaplaincy Services (RAF), HQ Air Command, RAF High Wycombe HP14 4UE* T: (01494) 496800 E: richardclement98@yahoo.co.uk

CLEMENT, Thomas Gwyn. b 51. Lon Univ BMus 73 Goldsmiths' Coll Lon PGCE 74 LRAM 73 LTCL 74. St Steph Ho Ox. **d** 93 **p** 94. C Friern Barnet St Jas *Lon* 93–96; V Edmonton St Alphege 96–04; P-in-c Ponders End St Matt 02–04; AD Enfield 01–04; V Hendon St Mary and Ch Ch 04–18; Warden of Readers Edmonton Area 08–17; AD W Barnet 09–14; rtd 18; PtO *Lon* from 18. *46 Princes Avenue, London N3 2DB* T: (020) 8346 1119 E: fr.gwyn@btinternet.com

CLEMENT, Canon Timothy Gordon. b 54. Trin Coll Bris 92. **d** 94 **p** 95. C Chepstow *Mon* 94–97; R Bettws Newydd w Trostrey etc 97–14; R Raglan Gp from 14; Rural Min Adv from 02; AD Raglan-Usk from 05; Can St Woolos Cathl from 08. *The Rectory, Bettws Newydd, Usk NP15 1JN* T: (01873) 880258 E: timtherec@icloud.com

CLEMENTS, Alan Austin. b 39. Newc Univ MA 93 ACIB 66 FCIE 05. Linc Th Coll 74. **d** 76 **p** 77. C Woodley St Jo the Ev *Ox* 76–79; C Wokingham All SS 79–83; V Felton *Newc* 83–95; P-in-c Wallsend St Pet 95–01; rtd 01; PtO *Newc* from 01; *Blackb* from 07; *Man* from 09. *15 Carleton Road, Chorley PR6 8TQ* T/F: (01257) 271782 E: fr_alan@btinternet.com

CLEMENTS, Andrew. b 48. K Coll Lon BD 72 AKC 72 Leeds Univ MA 02. St Aug Coll Cant 72. **d** 73 **p** 74. C Langley All SS and Martyrs *Man* 73–76; C Westhoughton 76–81; R Thornton Dale w Ellerburne and Wilton *York* 81–89; Prec Leic Cathl 89–91; V Market Weighton *York* 91–97; R Goodmanham 91–97; V Osbaldwick w Murton 97–19; RD Derwent 11–16; rtd 19. *Address temp unknown* E: andrewrev73@gmail.com

CLEMENTS, Miss Christine Hilda. b 49. Ex Univ BTh 04. SWMTC 99. **d** 02 **p** 03. C Halsetown *Truro* 02–05; Zambia 05–07; PtO *Nor* 07; TR Thamesmead *S'wark* 07–13; rtd 13; PtO *Truro* from 16. *3 Torwood House, Old Torwood Road, Torquay TQ1 1PN* T: (01803) 295469 E: revdchrisclements@gmail.com

CLEMENTS, Canon Doris Thomasina Sara. b 46. TCD BA 68 MA 90. CITC 92. **d** 95 **p** 96. NSM Killala w Dunfeeny, Crossmolina, Kilmoremoy etc *T, K & A* 95–14; Dioc C from 14; Can Achonry Cathl 05–11 and from 13; Can Tuam Cathl from 11. *Doobeg House, Bunninadden, Ballymote, Co Sligo, Republic of Ireland* T: (00353) (71) 918 5425 F: 918 5255 M: 86-249 7806 E: doristsclements@gmail.com

CLEMENTS, Miss Mary Holmes. b 43. Bedf Coll Lon BA 64 Lon Inst of Educn PGCE 69. Ox Min Course 92. **d** 94 **p** 95. NSM High Wycombe *Ox* 94–01; C N Petherton w Northmoor Green and N Newton w St Michaelchurch, Thurloxton etc *B & W* 01–03; C Alfred Jewel 03–10; rtd 10; PtO *B & W* from 12. *18 Meadway, Woolavington, Bridgwater TA7 8HA* T: (01278) 683099 E: kharaclements@btinternet.com

CLEMENTS, Philip Christian. b 38. K Coll Lon BD 64 AKC 64. **d** 65 **p** 66. C S Norwood St Mark *Cant* 65–68; Chapl R Russell Sch Croydon 68–75; Asst Chapl Denstone Coll Uttoxeter 75–76; Chapl 76–81; Chapl Lancing Coll 82–90; R Ninfield *Chich* 90–99; V Hooe 90–99; rtd 99; PtO

Cant 95–15; Chapl St Bart Hosp Sandwich 04–07; Hon Chapl Northbourne Park Sch 12–14. *Hopehaven, Roman Road, Maydensole, Dover CT15 5HP* M: 07546-077775 E: philipclements660@gmail.com

CLEMENTS, Philip John Charles. b 42. Nottm Univ CertEd 64 Loughb Univ Hon BA 09. Ridley Hall Cam. **d** 85 **p** 86. C Aylestone St Andr w St Jas *Leic* 85–87; P-in-c Swinford w Catthorpe, Shawell and Stanford 87–91; V 91–99; Dioc Rural Officer 91–96; RD Guthlaxton II 94–99; P-in-c N w S Kilworth and Misterton 96–99; P-in-c Barrowden and Wakerley w S Luffenham *Pet* 99–02; R Barrowden and Wakerley w S Luffenham etc 02–06; RD Barnack 00–06; rtd 06; PtO *Pet* from 06; *Leic* from 07. *Clementine Cottage, 51 Laughton Road, Lubenham, Market Harborough LE16 9TE* T/F: (01858) 432548 E: clements.philip@sky.com

CLEMENTS, Canon Roy Adrian. b 44. St Chad's Coll Dur BA 68 MA 74. **d** 69 **p** 70. C Royston *Wakef* 69–73; V Clifton 73–77; V Rastrick St Matt 77–84; Dioc Communications Officer 84–98; V Horbury Junction 84–92; Bp's Chapl 92–00; V Battyeford 00–08; Hon Can Wakef Cathl 94–08; rtd 08; PtO *Wakef* 08–14; *Leeds* from 14. *12 Castle Crescent, Sandal, Wakefield WF2 7HX* T: (01924) 251834 E: royaclements@tiscali.co.uk

CLEMENTS, Mrs Virginia. b 47. Weymouth Coll of Educn CertEd 68. **d** 13 **p** 14. OLM Apedale Gp *Heref* from 13. *Rock Edge, 3 Windle Hill, Church Stretton SY6 7AP* T: (01694) 724078 E: virginia_clements@me.com

CLEMETT, Peter Thomas. b 33. Univ of Wales (Lamp) BA 60. Sarum Th Coll 59. **d** 61 **p** 62. C Tredegar St Geo *Mon* 61–63; Chapl St Woolos Cathl 63–66; CF 66–99; Chapl R Memorial Chpl Sandhurst 84–88; rtd 88; OCM Hound from 99; PtO *Win* from 01. *Silver Birches, Gardeners Lane, East Wellow, Romsey SO51 6AD* T: (023) 8081 4261

CLEMINSON, Lee James. b 84. Sheff Univ BA 16. Coll of Resurr Mirfield 13. **d** 16 **p** 17. C Bothal and Pegswood w Longhirst *Newc* 16–18; C Balkwell from 19; C Tynemouth St Jo from 19. *St John's Vicarage, 36 St John's Terrace, North Shields NE29 6HS* M: 07976-296733 E: revleecleminson@gmail.com

CLEMOW (*née* WINDER), Cynthia Frances. b 48. SWMTC 02. **d** 05 **p** 06. NSM Bodmin w Lanhydrock and Lanivet *Truro* 05–17; TV Bodmin from 17. *Denton, 2 Boxwell Park, Bodmin PL31 2BB* T: (01208) 73306

CLEPHANE, Alexander Honeyman. b 48. **d** 97 **p** 98. OLM Flixton St Mich *Man* 97–11; NSM from 11; AD Stretford 15–19; Dioc Officer for SSM from 17. *306 Church Road, Urmston, Manchester M41 6JJ* T: 0161-747 8816 M: 07443-902511 E: alexclephane@btinternet.com

CLEUGH, David Robert. b 80. New Coll Ox MA 07. Ripon Coll Cuddesdon BTh 09. **d** 09 **p** 10. C Dorchester *Ox* 09–13; P-in-c Leadgate *Dur* 13–17; P-in-c Ebchester 14–17; P-in-c Medomsley 14–17; R Three Rivers Gp *Ely* from 17. *The Vicarage, 24 Mildenhall Road, Fordham, Ely CB7 5NR* M: 07805-332979 E: davidrcleugh@gmail.com

CLEUGH, Hannah Felicity. b 81. Worc Coll Ox MA 08 MSt 04 DPhil 07. Ripon Coll Cuddesdon 07. **d** 09 **p** 10. C Dorchester *Ox* 09–12; Chapl Univ Coll Dur 13–17; Bp's Sen Chapl *Ely* from 17. *The Bishop's House, The College, Ely CB7 4DW* T: (01353) 662749 F: 669477 E: hannah.cleugh@elydiocese.org

CLEVELAND, Michael Robin. b 52. Warwick Univ BA 73. St Jo Coll Nottm 86 Serampore Th Coll BD 88. **d** 88 **p** 89. C Bushbury *Lich* 88–92; V Foleshill St Laur *Cov* 92–17; rtd 17. *88 Victoria Street, Exeter EX4 6JG*

CLEVELAND, Archdeacon of. See RUSHTON, The Ven Samantha Jayne

CLEVERLEY, Michael Frank. b 36. Man Univ BScTech 57. Wells Th Coll 61. **d** 63 **p** 64. C Halifax St Aug *Wakef* 63; C Huddersfield St Jo 63–66; C Brighouse 66–69; V Gomersal 69–83; P-in-c Clayton W w High Hoyland 83–89; P-in-c Scissett St Aug 83–89; R High Hoyland, Scissett and Clayton W 89–96; rtd 96; Hon C Leathley w Farnley, Fewston and Blubberhouses *Bradf* 96–04; PtO 04–14; *Leeds* from 14. *86 Riverside Park, Otley LS21 2RW*

CLEWS, Nicholas. b 57. SS Coll Cam BA 80 MA 84 Leeds Univ BA 87 CIPFA 85. Coll of Resurr Mirfield 85. **d** 88 **p** 89. C S Elmsall *Wakef* 88–91; V Featherstone 91–07; P-in-c Purston cum S Featherstone 04–07; P-in-c Thornbury *Bradf* 07–14; *Leeds* 14–17; P-in-c Woodhall 07–17; V Thornbury, Woodhall and Waterloo from 17; Prayer and Spirituality Co-ord Bradf Area from 17. *St James's Vicarage, Galloway Lane, Pudsey LS28 8JR* T: (01274) 662735 M: 07985-091748 E: n.clews@sky.com

CLIFF, Frank William. b 51. ERMC. **d** 14 **p** 15. NSM Gt Yarmouth *Nor* from 14. *2 Barrack Road, Great Yarmouth NR30 3DR* T: (01493) 851097 E: fwc1234@gmail.com

CLIFF, Julian Arnold. b 41. Univ Coll Ches BEd 86. Cranmer Hall Dur 63. **d** 66 **p** 67. C Bowdon *Ches* 66–69; C Poynton 69–73; P-in-c Crewe St Barn 73–74; V 74–79; Hon C Higher Bebington 98–00; PtO 06–17. *24 Coombe Road, Wirral CH61 4UR* E: ja.cliff.cottage@gmail.com

CLIFF, Mrs Sarah Jane. b 66. St Jo Coll Dur BA 18. Cranmer Hall Dur 17. **d** 19. C Barnard Castle w Whorlton *Dur* from 19. *17 Mayfield, Barnard Castle DL12 8EA* E: revsarahcliff@gmail.com

CLIFFE, Canon Christopher George. b 47. CITC 94. **d** 97 **p** 98. C Fiddown w Clonegam, Guilcagh and Kilmeaden *C & O* 97–00; I 00–13; Bp's Dom Chapl 97–13; Can Ossory Cathl 07–13; rtd 13. *Hawthorn, 51 Fan Glas, Kilmeaden, Waterford, X91 E8N3, Republic of Ireland* T: (00353) (51) 399699 M: 87-236 8682 E: cgc2@eircom.net *or* georgecliffe47@gmail.com

CLIFFORD, Bruce Douglas. b 52. Birm Univ BA 73 Southn Univ MSocSc 76. Trin Coll Bris 09. **d** 11 **p** 12. NSM Glouc St Cath 11–15; NSM Glouc St Geo w Whaddon 15; V from 15. *St George's Vicarage, Grange Road, Tuffley, Gloucester GL4 0PE* T: (01452) 520851 M: 07855-228943 E: vicar-bruce@outlook.com

CLIFFORD, Paula Margaret. b 45. **d** 11 **p** 12. NSM Ox St Giles and SS Phil and Jas w St Marg 11–13; NSM Akeman 13–14; P-in-c Minster Lovell 14–17; Deanery Miss Enabler 14–16; rtd 17; PtO *Ox* from 17; Chapl Puerto de la Cruz Tenerife *Eur* from 18. *3 Pound Close, Kirtlington, Kidlington OX5 3JR* T: (01869) 350806 E: paulaclifford4@gmail.com

CLIFTON, Daphne Sheila. b 59. St Aug Coll of Th 14. **d** 17 **p** 18. NSM Lee St Mildred *S'wark* from 17. *54 Shearman Road, London SE3 9HX* T: (020) 8318 3857 E: daphne@cliftonconsulting.com

CLIFTON, Canon Robert Walter. b 39. Solicitor. Westcott Ho Cam 82. **d** 84 **p** 85. C Bury St Edmunds St Geo *St E* 84–87; P-in-c Culford, W Stow and Wordwell 87–88; R Culford, W Stow and Wordwell w Flempton etc 88–95; P-in-c Fornham All SS and Fornham St Martin w Timworth 93–95; RD Thingoe 93–95; P-in-c Orford w Sudbourne, Chillesford, Butley and Iken 95–00; P-in-c Eyke w Bromeswell, Rendlesham, Tunstall etc 98–99; TR Wilford Peninsula 00–05; RD Woodbridge 96–04; Hon Can St E Cathl 00–05; rtd 05; PtO *Nor* from 05; *St E* 05–16. *12 Stan Petersen Close, Norwich NR1 4QJ* T: (01603) 631758 M: 07713-237754 E: cliftonrobert@sky.com

CLIFTON, Canon Roger Gerald. b 45. ACA 70 FCA. Sarum & Wells Th Coll 70. **d** 73 **p** 74. C Winterbourne *Bris* 73–76; P-in-c Brislington St Cuth 76–83; P-in-c Colerne w N Wraxall 83–95; RD Chippenham 88–94; Hon Can Bris Cathl 94–09; TR Gtr Corsham 95–01; TR Gtr Corsham and Lacock 01–09; rtd 09; PtO *Bris* from 10; *B & W* from 11. *20 Southcot Place, Bath BA2 4PE* T: (01225) 330211 M: 07762-324596 E: rogerclifton@btinternet.com

CLIFTON-SMITH, Canon Gregory James. b 52. Goldsmiths' Coll Lon BMus 82 GGSM 73 Lon Univ TCert 74 Leeds Univ MA 02 Ches Univ DProf 13. Sarum & Wells Th Coll 87. **d** 89 **p** 90. C Welling *S'wark* 89–93; V Tattenham Corner and Burgh Heath *Guildf* 93–97; Asst Chapl R Berks and Battle Hosps NHS Trust 97–99; Chapl Isle of Wight NHS Primary Care Trust 99–12; Close V Win Cathl 12–17; Min Can Win Cathl 12–16; Hon Can Win Cathl 16–17; rtd 17; PtO *Portsm* from 12; *Win* from 17. *46 Gills Cliff Road, Ventnor PO38 1LH* M: 07790-089989

CLINCH, Christopher James. b 60. Nottm Univ BEd 82 BTh 89. Linc Th Coll 86. **d** 89 **p** 90. C Newc St Geo 89–92; C Seaton Hirst 92–94; TV Ch the King 94–00; V Newc St Fran 00–09; Chapl K Sch Tynemouth 09–15; PtO *Newc* 15–16; Chapl Northumbria Healthcare NHS Foundn Trust from 16. *Chaplains' Office, North Tyneside General Hospital, Rake Lane, North Shields NE29 8NH* T: 03448-118111

CLINES, Emma Christine. See LOUIS, Emma Christine

CLINES, Jeremy Mark Sebastian. b 68. Birm Univ PhD 11. Cranmer Hall Dur. **d** 97 **p** 98. C Birm St Martin w Bordesley St Andr 97–99; Chapl York St Jo Univ 99–10; Chapl Sheff Univ from 10. *Flat 1, 5 Ranmoor Park Road, Sheffield S10 3GX* E: jeremyclines@gmail.com *or* j.clines@sheffield.ac.uk

CLITHEROW, Canon Andrew. b 50. St Chad's Coll Dur BA 72 Ex Univ MPhil 87. Sarum & Wells Th Coll 78. **d** 79 **p** 80. Hon C Bedford Ch *St Alb* 79–84; Asst Chapl Bedford Sch 79–84; Chapl Caldicott Sch Farnham Royal 84–85; C Penkridge w Stretton *Lich* 85–88; Min Acton Trussell w Bednall 85–88; Chapl Rossall Sch Fleetwood 89–94; V Scotforth *Blackb* 94–00; Dioc Dir of Tr and Can Res Blackb Cathl 00–07; Hon Can Blackb Cathl from 07; P-in-c Lytham St Cuth 07–12; P-in-c Lytham St Jo 08–12; Chapl Cen Lancs Univ from 12; Chapl to The Queen from 08. *Address temp unknown* E: candrew@uclan.ac.uk

CLOAKE, David Michael. b 72. Ox Brookes Univ BA 15. Ripon Coll Cuddesdon 07. **d** 08 **p** 09. C Aylesbury *Ox* 08–11; V Whitton SS Phil and Jas *Lon* from 11; CF (ACF) from 10. *The Vicarage, 205 Kneller Road, Twickenham TW2 7DY* T: (020) 8894 1932 M: 07758-289702 E: vicar@whittonchurch.com

CLOCKSIN (née HOYLE), Mrs Pamela Margaret. b 61. Nottm Univ BA 82. St Jo Coll Nottm 84. **d** 87 **p** 94. Par Dn Bulwell St Jo *S'well* 87–91; Cam Pastorate Chapl 91–95; C Cambridge H Trin *Ely* 91–95; PtO 95–01. *26 York Avenue, Oxford OX3 8NS* T: (01865) 766263 E: ella@clocksin.com

CLOCKSIN, Prof William Frederick. b 55. BA 76 St Cross Coll Ox MA 81 Trin Hall Cam MA 87 PhD 93. EAMTC 91. **d** 94 **p** 95. Asst Chapl Trin Hall Cam 94–01; Acting Dean 00–01; PtO *St Alb* from 17. *101 Park Meadow, Hatfield AL9 5HE* M: 07515-336540 E: wfc@me.com

CLOETE, Richard James. b 47. AKC 71. St Aug Coll Cant 72. **d** 72 **p** 73. C Redhill St Matt *S'wark* 72–76; V Streatham St Paul 76–84; P-in-c W Coker w Hardington Mandeville, E Chinnock etc *B & W* 84–88; R 88; R Wincanton and Pen Selwood 88–97; Sec and Treas Dioc Hosp Chapl Fellowship 91–97; PtO *Lon* 97–98; *Ex* 99–02; C Sampford Peverell, Uplowman, Holcombe Rogus etc 02–11; rtd 11; PtO *B & W* from 12. *19 Mount Nebo, Taunton TA1 4HG* T: (01823) 338428 M: 07455-493868 E: r.j.cloete@btinternet.com

CLOGHER, Archdeacon of. See HARPER, The Ven Brian John

CLOGHER, Bishop of. See MACDOWELL, The Rt Revd Francis John

CLOGHER, Dean of. See HALL, The Very Revd Kenneth Robert James

CLONMACNOISE, Dean of. See BOGLE, The Very Revd Paul David

CLOSE (née HITCHEN), Mrs Carol Ann. b 47. St Mary's Coll Ban CertEd 69 St Martin's Coll Lanc DipEd 91 Ches Coll of HE BTh 02. NOC 99. **d** 02 **p** 03. NSM Hindley St Pet *Liv* 02–07; PtO *Man* 08–18; NSM Hindley Green *Liv* 11–14; NSM Newton from 15. *271 Warrington Road, Abram, Wigan WN2 5RQ* T: (01942) 861670 E: revclose@blueyonder.co.uk *or* revcarolclose@gmail.com

CLOSE, Mrs Jane. b 48. WMMTC 00. **d** 03 **p** 04. NSM Fillongley and Corley *Cov* 03–06; P-in-c Leam Valley 06–17; PtO *Leic* from 18. *129 Ashby Road, Hinckley LE10 1SH* T: (01455) 619843 M: 07958-685423 E: closejane35@gmail.com

CLOVER, Brendan David. b 58. G&C Coll Cam BA 79 MA 83 LTCL 74. Ripon Coll Cuddesdon 79. **d** 82 **p** 83. C Friern Barnet St Jas *Lon* 82–85; C W Hampstead St Jas 85–87; Chapl Em Coll Cam 87–92; Dean 92–94; P-in-c St Pancras w St Jas and Ch Ch *Lon* 94–99; P-in-c St Pancras H Cross w St Jude and St Pet 96–99; Can Res Bris Cathl 99–06; Sen Provost Woodard Corp from 06; PtO *Lich* from 06; *B & W* from 16; Llan 17–18. *The Woodard Corporation, High Street, Abbots Bromley, Rugeley WS15 3BW* T: (01283) 840670 *or* 840120 E: brendanclover@woodard.co.uk

CLOW, Laurie Stephen. b 65. Man Univ BA 86 MA 88. Wycliffe Hall Ox 96. **d** 98 **p** 99. C Trentham *Lich* 98–01; TV Hampreston *Sarum* 01–15; R Chesham Bois *Ox* from 15. *The Rectory, 1 Glebe Way, Amersham HP6 5ND* T: (01494) 728318 M: 07825-135616 E: rector@stleonardscb.org.uk

CLOWES, John. b 45. AKC 67. **d** 68 **p** 69. C Corby St Columba *Pet* 68–71; R Itchenstoke w Ovington and Abbotstone *Win* 71–73; R New Alresford w Ovington and Itchen Stoke 73–74; V Acton w Gt and Lt Waldingfield *St E* 74–80; Asst Dioc Chr Stewardship Adv 75–80; TV Southend St Jo w St Mark, All SS w St Fran etc *Chelmsf* 80–82; TV Southend 82–85; Ind Chapl 80–85; R Ashwick w Oakhill and Binegar *B & W* 85–91; P-in-c Brompton Regis w Upton and Skilgate 91–97; rtd 98. *The Tythings, Tythings Court, Minehead TA24 5NT* M: 07964-022682

CLOYNE, Dean of. See GREEN, The Very Revd Susan Denise

CLUCAS, Anthony John. b 56. Portsm Poly BA 77. WMMTC 96. **d** 99 **p** 00. NSM Erdington *Birm* 99–04; NSM Nechells 04–05; P-in-c Shard End 05–12; V from 12. *Apartment 1, 11 York Crescent, Birmingham B34 7NS* T: 0121-747 3299 E: clucas@btinternet.com

CLUES, David Charles. b 66. K Coll Lon BD 87 Lon Univ PGCE 95. St Steph Ho Ox 88. **d** 90 **p** 91. C Notting Hill All SS w St Columb *Lon* 90–94; NSM 94–96; NSM Notting Hill St Mich and Ch Ch 96–98; Asst Chapl HM Pris Wormwood Scrubs 97–98; C Paddington St Mary Magd *Lon* 98–03; C Paddington St Mary 98–03; C Paddington St Sav 98–03; V Willesden St Mary 03–11; P-in-c Brighton St Bart *Chich* 11–16; Chapl Heathfield Sch Ascot from 16; PtO *Ox* from 16. *Heathfield School, London Road, Ascot SL5 8BQ* T: (01344) 898343 E: dcclues@btinternet.com

CLUETT, Preb Michael Charles. b 53. Kingston Poly BSc 78. St Steph Ho Ox 84. **d** 86 **p** 87. C Pontesbury I and II *Heref* 86–90; TV Wenlock 90–99; P-in-c Canon Pyon w Kings Pyon and Birley 99–04; V Canon Pyon w King's Pyon, Birley and Wellington 04–17; RD Leominster 08–14; Preb Heref Cathl 10–17; rtd 17; PtO *Heref* from 18. *1 Scholars Walk, Hereford HR4 0GH* E: m.charles802@btinternet.com

CLUNE, David Julian. b 60. Open Univ BSc 03. Wilson Carlile Coll 99 St Jo Coll Nottm LTh 07. **d** 07 **p** 08. C Spalding St Mary and St Nic *Linc* 07–11; TV Sutton St Jas and Wawne *York* 11–12; V Sutton St Jas 12–15; NSM Digby Gp *Linc* 16–17. *3 High Street, Howden le Wear, Crook DL15 8EZ* M: 07891-912450 E: me@davidclune.com

CLUTTERBUCK, Ms Elizabeth Lesieli. b 81. LSE BA 02 K Coll Lon MA 04. St Mellitus Coll BA 14 MA 15. **d** 15 **p** 16. C Highbury Ch Ch w St Jo and St Sav *Lon* 15–18; C Tollington 18–19; TR from 19. *Emmanuel Vicarage, 145 Hornsey Road, London N7 6DU* M: 07763-852258 E: liz.clutterbuck@gmail.com

CLUTTERBUCK, Marion Isobel. b 56. Oak Hill Th Coll BA 91. **d** 92 **p** 94. C Lindfield *Chich* 92–96; TV Alderbury Team *Sarum* 96–01; TV Clarendon 01–05; PtO *Win* 13–16 and from 17; P-in-c Six Pilgrims *B & W* from 19. *Jessamine Cottage, South Barrow, Yeovil BA22 7LN* T: (01963) 441604 E: mcdeanridge@icloud.com

CLUTTON, Canon Barbara Carol. b 47. WMMTC 00. **d** 04 **p** 05. NSM Draycote Gp *Cov* 04–14; P-in-c 08–14; Rural Life Officer 07–14; Hon Can Cov Cathl 11–14; rtd 14. *Church Cottage, Main Street, Grandborough, Rugby CV23 8DQ* T: (01788) 810172 M: 07808-137550 E: barbaraclutton@gilberthouse.co.uk

COAD, Dominic John. b 82. Ex Univ BA 02 MA 06 PhD 10. Westcott Ho Cam 10. **d** 12 **p** 13. C Oakham, Ashwell, Braunston, Brooke, Egleton etc *Pet* 12–16; TV Benwell and Scotswood *Newc* from 16. *5 Lynnwood Avenue, Newcastle upon Tyne NE4 6XB* T: 0191-256 7020 M: 07713-165193

COAKLEY (*née* FURBER), **Prof Sarah Anne.** b 51. New Hall Cam BA 73 PhD 82. Harvard Div Sch ThM 75. **d** 00 **p** 01. Edw Mallinckrodt Jr Prof Div Harvard Div Sch 95–07; Visiting Prof 07–08; Hon C Waban The Gd Shep 00–08; Hon C Littlemore *Ox* 00–07; Norris-Hulse Prof Div Cam Univ from 07; LtO *Ely* 08–18; PtO from 18; Hon Can Ely Cathl 11–18. *Faculty of Divinity, West Road, Cambridge CB3 9BS* T: (01223) 763002 E: sc545@cam.ac.uk

COATES, Andrew Peter Richard. b 86. Warwick Univ BA 07 Down Coll Cam BTh 17. Westcott Ho Cam 15. **d** 18 **p** 19. C Wood Green St Mich w Bounds Green St Gabr etc *Lon* from 18. *1B Selbourne Road, London N22 7TL* M: 07870-864699 E: revdandrewcoates@gmail.com

COATES, Archie. *See* COATES, Richard Michael

COATES, Canon Christopher Ian. b 59. Qu Coll Birm 81. **d** 84 **p** 85. C Cottingham *York* 84–87; TV Howden 87–91; V Sherburn in Elmet 91–94; V Sherburn in Elmet w Saxton 94–02; V Bishopthorpe from 02; V Acaster Malbis from 02; P-in-c Appleton Roebuck w Acaster Selby 07–12; V from 12; RD New Ainsty 11–16; Hon Can Ho from 10. *The Vicarage, 48 Church Lane, Bishopthorpe, York YO23 2QG* T: (01904) 707840 E: chriscoates@hotmail.col.ca

COATES, Mrs Clare Louise Gye. b 72. Trin Call Cam BA 94 Trin Coll Cam MA 98. Ridley Hall Cam 17. **d** 19. C Stapleford *Ely* from 19. *16 Cranmer Road, Cambridge CB3 9BL* T: (01223) 359747 M: 07917-845968 E: claregyecoates@btinternet.com

COATES, David Martin. b 57. Sheff Univ BSc 78 Reading Univ MSc 80 Birm Univ PhD 83. STETS 04. **d** 07 **p** 08. NSM Salisbury St Mark *Sarum* 07–10; NSM Bourne Valley from 10. *2 St Matthew's Close, Bishopdown, Salisbury SP1 3FJ* T: (01722) 325944 E: dmcoates@hotmail.co.uk

COATES, Jean. b 55. Linc Univ BA 10. OLM Bolingbroke Deanery *Linc* from 13. *The Vicarage, Church Street, Spilsby PE23 5EF* T: (01790) 752526 E: coatesjean@yahoo.co.uk

COATES, Canon Jean Margaret. b 47. Sussex Univ BSc 68 Reading Univ PhD 72 CBiol MRSB. SAOMC 93. **d** 96 **p** 97. C Wallingford *Ox* 96–99; P-in-c Watercombe *Sarum* 99–02; R 02–13; Rural Officer (Dorset) 99–13; Can and Preb Sarum Cathl 05–13; rtd 13; PtO *Sarum* from 15. *Three Gables, Colesbrook, Gillingham SP8 4HH* T: (01747) 229168 E: jeanmcoates@gmail.com

COATES, Maxwell Gordon. b 49. Lon Univ CertEd 70 Open Univ BA 83 UEA MA 86. Trin Coll Bris. **d** 77 **p** 78. C Blackheath Park St Mich *S'wark* 77–79; Chapl Greenwich Distr Hosp Lon 77–79; Asst Teacher Saintbridge Sch Glouc 79–81; Teacher Gaywood Park High Sch King's Lynn 81–85; NSM Lynn St Jo *Nor* 81–85; Dep Hd Teacher Winton Comp Sch Bournemouth 85–90; Hd Teacher St Mark's Comp Sch Bath 90–97; NSM Canford Magna *Sarum* 85–90 and 90–05; NSM Stoke Gifford *Bris* 93–96; PtO *B & W* 91–96; rtd 97.

3 Oakley Road, Wimborne BH21 1QJ T: (01202) 883162 E: maxgcoates@gmail.com

COATES, Canon Nigel John. b 51. Reading Univ BSc MA. Trin Coll Bris. **d** 83 **p** 84. C Epsom St Martin *Guildf* 83–86; C Portswood Ch Ch *Win* 86–88; Chapl Southn Univ 89–97; Chapl Southn Inst of HE 89–95; P-in-c Freemantle 97–00; R 00–05; Can Res S'well Minster 05–19; rtd 19. *Address temp unknown*

COATES, Canon Peter Frederick. b 50. K Coll Lon BD 79 AKC 79. St Steph Ho *Ox* 79. **d** 80 **p** 81. C Woodford St Barn *Chelmsf* 80–83; C E and W Keal *Linc* 83–86; R The Wainfleets and Croft 86–94; R The Wainfleet Gp 94–03; RD Calcewaithe and Candleshoe 92–03; P-in-c Spilsby Gp 03–13; TR Bolingbroke Deanery from 14; RD Bolingbroke from 03; Can and Preb Linc Cathl from 02. *The Vicarage, Church Street, Spilsby PE23 5DU* T: (01790) 752526 E: peter.coates50@yahoo.com

COATES, Canon Richard Michael (Archie). b 70. Birm Univ BA 92. Wycliffe Hall Ox BA 99. **d** 00 **p** 01. C Ashtead *Guildf* 00–03; C Brompton H Trin w Onslow Square St Paul *Lon* 03–09; V Brighton St Pet *Chich* from 09; P-in-c Whitehawk from 13; Can and Preb Chich Cathl from 15. *10 West Drive, Brighton BN2 0GD* T: (01273) 695064 M: 07887-522402 E: archie@stpetersbrighton.org

COATES, Robert. b 63. St Steph Ho *Ox* 89. **d** 92 **p** 93. C Heavitree w Ex St Paul 92–95; Chapl RN 95–00; V Bexhill St Aug *Chich* from 00. *St Augustine's Vicarage, St Augustine's Close, Bexhill-on-Sea TN39 3AZ* T/F: (01424) 210785 E: robert.coates24@gmail.com

COATES, Robert Charles. b 44. Open Univ BA 76. Cant Sch of Min 83. **d** 86 **p** 87. C Deal St Leon and St Rich and Sholden *Cant* 86–89; V Loose 89–00; V Barnwood *Glouc* 00–06; rtd 06; PtO *B & W* from 06. *4 The Poplars, Weston-super-Mare BS22 6RB* T: (01934) 249387 M: 07874-202318 E: robert.coates@hotmail.co.uk

COATES, Stuart Murray. b 49. Lon Univ BA 70 Edin Univ MTh 91. Wycliffe Hall Ox 72. **d** 75 **p** 76. C Rainford *Liv* 75–78; C Orrell 78–79; V 79–86; Chapl Strathcarron Hospice Denny from 86; Hon C Stirling *Edin* 86–90; NSM Aberfoyle St And 89–94; NSM Doune 89–12; R 12–14; rtd 14. *Westwood Smithy, Chalmerston Road, Stirling FK9 4AG* T: (01786) 860531 *or* (01324) 826222 E: revsmc1@gmail.com

COATSWORTH, Mrs Deborah Margaret. b 58. **d** 13 **p** 14. NSM Baschurch and Weston Lullingfield w Hordley *Lich* from 13. *Oakmere House, 69 Hill Park, Dudleston Heath, Ellesmere SY12 9LB* T: (01691) 690261 E: deborahcoatsworth@btinternet.com

COATSWORTH, Nigel George. b 39. Trin Hall Cam BA 61 MA. Cuddesdon Coll 61. **d** 63 **p** 64. C Hellesdon *Nor* 63–66; Ewell Monastery 66–80; TV Folkestone H Trin and St Geo w Ch Ch *Cant* 83–85; C Walton next Sittingbourne 85–86; P-in-c Selattyn *Lich* 86–91; P-in-c Weston Rhyn 88–91; R Weston Rhyn and Selattyn 91–05; rtd 05; PtO *Lich* 05–09 and from 16. *Oakmere House, 69 Hill Park, Dudleston Heath, Ellesmere SY12 9LB* T: (01691) 690261 E: rev.coatsworth@btinternet.com

COBB, George Reginald. b 50. Oak Hill Th Coll BA 81. **d** 81 **p** 82. C Ware Ch Ch *St Alb* 81–84; C Uphill *B & W* 84–89; R Alresford *Chelmsf* 89–99; Chapl Mt Vernon and Watford Hosps NHS Trust 99–00; Chapl E and N Herts NHS Trust 00–15; rtd 15; PtO *St Alb* from 15. *25 Church Meadows, St Neots PE19 1PR* M: 07890-091973 E: george.cobb@cobbweb.co.uk

COBB, Canon John Philip Andrew. b 43. Man Univ BSc 65 New Coll Ox BA 67 MA 71. Wycliffe Hall Ox 66. **d** 68 **p** 69. C Reading St Jo *Ox* 68–71; C Romford Gd Shep *Chelmsf* 71–73; SAMS Chile 74–08; Can from 99; Dioc Ecum Officer 00–06; rtd 08; Lic to Offic Chile from 08. *Casilla 330, Correo Paine, Paine, Región Metropolitana, Chile* T: (0056) (2) 259 4099 E: jn.cobb@yahoo.co.uk

COBB, Mark Robert. b 64. Lanc Univ BSc 86 Keele Univ MA 99 Liv Univ PhD 13. Ripon Coll Cuddesdon 88. **d** 91 **p** 92. C Hampstead St Jo *Lon* 91–94; Asst Chapl Derbyshire R Infirmary NHS Trust 94–96; Palliative & Health Care Chapl Derbyshire R Infirmary NHS Trust 96–98; Chapl Manager Cen Sheff Univ Hosps NHS Trust 98–02; Sen Chapl 98–04; Sen Chapl Sheff Teaching Hosps NHS Foundn Trust from 04. *Chaplaincy Services, Royal Hallamshire Hospital, Glossop Road, Sheffield S10 2JF* T: 0114-271 3327 E: mark.cobb@sth.nhs.uk

COBB, Peter Graham. b 27. St Jo Coll Cam BA 48 MA 52. Ridley Hall Cam 66. **d** 68 **p** 69. C Porthkerry *Llan* 68–71; P-in-c Penmark 71–72; V Penmark w Porthkerry 97–00; V Magor w Redwick and Undy *Mon* 82–95; rtd 95. *2 Talycoed Court, Talycoed, Monmouth NP25 5HR* T: (01600) 780309 E: petercobb@waitrose.com

COBBOLD, Richard Nevill. b 55. Bris Univ BScEng 76. Local Minl Tr Course. **d** 11 **p** 12. NSM N Farnborough *Guildf*

11–17; NSM Farnborough St Pet from 17. *4 Penns Wood, Farnborough GU14 6RB* T: (01252) 515547 M: 07776-352240 E: richard@cobbold.plus.com

COBLEY, Mrs Irene Patricia Mary. b 51. Ox Min Course 16. **d** 18 **p** 19. NSM Cogenhoe and Gt and Lt Houghton w Brafield *Pet* from 18. *1 Donovan Court, Northampton NN3 3DD* T: (01604) 402543 E: irene.cobley@sky.com

COBURN, Mrs Sharron Dawn. b 73. Trin Coll Bris BA 12 MA 13. **d** 13 **p** 14. C Stanton, Hopton, Market Weston, Barningham etc *St E* 13–16; C Brandon and Santon Downham w Elveden etc 16–17; V Brandon from 17; Asst Dioc Dir of Ords from 17. *215 London Road, Brandon IP27 0LR* T: (01359) 221946 M: 07739-250135 E: sha.coburn@me.com

COCHRANE, Mrs Anthea Mary. b 38. **d** 02 **p** 03. OLM Clarendon *Sarum* 02–07; PtO 07–08 and from 14. *1 Home Farm Dairy, Shute End, Alderbury, Salisbury SP5 3DJ* T: (01722) 710503 E: a.cochrane03@btinternet.com

COCHRANE, Philip Andrew. b 70. Reading Univ BA 92 FRSA 17. Trin Coll Bris BA 07. **d** 07 **p** 08. C Fareham H Trin *Portsm* 07–09; TV 09–12; V Win St Barn 12–15; P-in-c Caerleon and Llanfrechfa *Mon* 15–16; R Banbury *Ox* 16–19; AD Deddington 17–19; R Vancouver St Paul Canada from 19. *1205-2020 Hard Street, Vancouver BC VG6 1J3, Canada* M: (001) (604) 685 6832

COCKAYNE, Canon Mark Gary. b 61. UEA LLB 82. St Jo Coll Nottm BTh 92 MA 93. **d** 93 **p** 94. C Armthorpe *Sheff* 93–96; V Malin Bridge 96–05; AD Hallam 02–05; C Haydock St Mark *Liv* 05–08; V 08–14; AD St Helens 06–14; Hon Can Liv Cathl 06–14; Dir Par Support Team *Sheff* from 14; Hon Can Sheff Cathl from 15. *16 Ormsby Close, Thurgoland, Sheffield S35 7BN* E: mark.cockayne@sheffield.anglican.org

COCKBILL, Douglas John. b 53. Chicago Univ BA 75. Gen Th Sem (NY) MDiv 78. **d** 78 **p** 79. Virgin Is 79–80; Bahamas 80–83; USA 84–90; P-in-c Roxbourne St Andr *Lon* 90–92; V 92–04; USA 05–06; Chapl Larnaca St Helena Cyprus 06–09; USA from 09. *428 King Street, Wenatchee WA 98801-2846, USA* E: dcockbill22@yahoo.com

COCKBURN, Kathleen. b 50. NEOC 04. **d** 07 **p** 08. NSM Walker *Newc* 07–10; NSM N Shields 10–15; rtd 16; PtO *Newc* from 16. *92 Paignton Avenue, Whitley Bay NE25 8SZ* T: 0191-252 0710 E: kath.co@blueyonder.co.uk

COCKELL, Ms Helen Frances. b 69. Trin Hall Cam BA 90 MA 94. Qu Coll Birm BD 94. **d** 95. C Bracknell *Ox* 95–98; PtO *Cov* from 00; Chapl S Warks Gen Hosps NHS Trust from 09. *The New Rectory, Pool Close, Rugby CV22 7RN* T: (01788) 812613 E: nfchub-nellwork@yahoo.co.uk

COCKELL, Timothy David. b 66. Qu Coll Birm BTheol 95. **d** 95 **p** 96. C Bracknell *Ox* 95–98; C Rugby *Cov* 98–99; TV 99–04; P-in-c Bilton 04–08; R from 08; AD Rugby from 17. *The New Rectory, Pool Close, Rugby CV22 7RN* T: (01788) 812613   E: tim.cockell@btopenworld.com   *or* rectorbilton@icloud.com

COCKER (née BENTLEY), Mrs Frances Rymer (Sister Frances Anne). b 22. Man Univ BSc 48 TDip 49 PGCE 49. **d** 95 **p** 95. Mother Superior CSD 87–00; PtO *Sarum* 95–15. *Braemar Lodge, 18-20 Stratford Road, Salisbury SP1 3JH* M: 07702-659609

COCKERELL, David John. b 47. Univ of Wales (Cardiff) BA 71 Univ of Wales (Swansea) MA 74 Qu Coll Cam BA 75. Westcott Ho Cam 73. **d** 76 **p** 77. C Chapel Allerton *Ripon* 76–79; C Farnley 79–81; TV Hitchin *St Alb* 81–89; TV Dorchester *Ox* 89–92; Adult Educn and Tr Officer *Ely* 92–00; R Raddesley Gp 00–06; rtd 06. *44 Humberley Close, Eynesbury, St Neots PE19 2SE* T: (01480) 218225 E: david@cockerell.co.uk

COCKETT, The Ven Elwin Wesley. b 59. Aston Tr Scheme 86 Oak Hill Th Coll BA 91. **d** 91 **p** 92. C Chadwell Heath *Chelmsf* 91–94; Chapl W Ham United Football Club 92–12; C Harold Hill St Paul *Chelmsf* 94–95; P-in-c 95–97; V 97–00; TR Billericay and Lt Burstead 00–07; RD Basildon 04–07; Adn W Ham from 07; PtO *B & W* from 19. *86 Aldersbrook Road, London E12 5DH* T: (020) 8989 8557 E: a.westham@chelmsford.anglican.org

COCKFIELD, Mrs Myrtle Jacqueline. b 51. S Bank Univ BSc 96. SEITE 05. **d** 08 **p** 09. NSM Mitcham SS Pet and Paul *S'wark* from 08. *28 Garden Avenue, Mitcham CR4 2EA* T: (020) 8646 2333 M: 07722-568604 E: jackiecockfield@yahoo.co.uk

COCKING, Ann Louisa. b 44. **d** 03 **p** 04. OLM The Lavingtons, Cheverells, and Easterton *Sarum* 03–12; rtd 12; PtO *Sarum* from 12. *High Acre, Eastcott, Devizes SN10 4PH* T: (01380) 812763 E: alc.highacre@btinternet.com

COCKING, Mrs Anne Frances Patricia. b 60. SEITE 12. **d** 15 **p** 16. NSM Clapham Common St Barn *S'wark* from 15. *St Barnabas Church Office, Clapham Common North Side, London SW4 9SW* T: (020) 7223 6750 M: 07956-342540

COCKING, Keith. b 59. Ripon Coll Cuddesdon 08. **d** 09 **p** 10. C Newbold w Dunston *Derby* 09–13; TV Buxton w Burbage and King Sterndale from 13. *The Vicarage, 2A New Market Street, Buxton SK17 6LP* T: (01298) 213212 M: 07903-736791 E: keithcocking@live.co.uk

COCKING, Martyn Royston. b 53. Trin Coll Bris 83. **d** 85 **p** 86. C Weston-super-Mare Cen Par *B & W* 85–88; C Kingswood *Bris* 88–89; TV 89–93; V Pill w Easton in Gordano and Portbury *B & W* 93–96; PtO *Man* 12–13. *39 Down Green Road, Bolton BL2 3QD*

COCKS, Canon Howard Alan Stewart. b 46. St Barn Coll Adelaide 78. **d** 80 **p** 81. C Portland Australia 80–82; C Prestbury *Glouc* 82–87; P-in-c Stratton w Baunton 87–94; P-in-c N Cerney w Bagendon 91–94; R Stratton, N Cerney, Baunton and Bagendon 95–98; V Leic St Aid 98–04; RD Christianity S 01–04; R Winchelsea and Icklesham *Chich* 04–12; rtd 12; PtO *Lon* 13–19; *S'wark* 15–19; Can The Murray from 06; PtO Sydney from 19. *50 Cook Terrace, Mona Vale, Sydney NSW 2103, Australia* T: (0061) (2) 9997 1604 E: hascocks@gmail.com

COCKS, Michael Dearden Somers. b 28. Univ of NZ MA 50 St Cath Coll Ox BA 53 MA 57. Ripon Hall Ox. **d** 53 **p** 54. C Merivale New Zealand 53–56; V Geraldine 56–58; V Ross and S Westland 58–60; V Hinds 60–63; V St Martins 63–70; V Barrington Street w Speydon St Nic 70–79; V Hororata 79–93; Chapl Gothenburg w Halmstad, Jönköping etc *Eur* 93–98; rtd 98. *23 Fairfield Avenue, Addington, Christchurch 8024, New Zealand* T: (0064) (3) 981 7057 E: michaelandgertrud@gmail.com

COCKSEDGE, Simon Hugh. b 56. Univ Coll Lon BSc 78 New Coll Ox BM, BCh 81 Man Univ MD 03 FRCGP 96. NOC 05. **d** 07 **p** 08. NSM Hayfield and Chinley w Buxworth *Derby* 07–11; P-in-c Edale from 11; Chapl Blythe Ho Hospice from 13. *Glen Thorne, Barber Booth, Edale, Hope Valley S33 7ZL* E: cocksedge@doctors.org.uk

COCKSEDGE, Stuart John. b 78. Ex Univ BA 99 Univ Coll Lon MSc 07. St Jo Coll Nottm 11. **d** 13 **p** 14. C Hinckley St Jo *Leic* 13–17; TV Wareham *Sarum* from 17. *9 Keysworth Drive, Wareham BH20 7BD* M: 07779-345852 E: stuart.cocksedge@gmail.com

⊕**COCKSWORTH, The Rt Revd Christopher John.** b 59. Man Univ BA 80 PhD 89 PGCE 81. St Jo Coll Nottm 84. **d** 88 **p** 89. C 08. C Epsom Common Ch Ch *Guildf* 88–92; Chapl R Holloway and Bedf New Coll 92–97; Dir STETS 97–01; Hon Can Guildf Cathl 99–01; Prin Ridley Hall Cam 01–08; Bp Cov from 08. *The Bishop's House, 23 Davenport Road, Coventry CV5 6PW* T: (024) 7667 2244 F: 7671 3271 E: bishop@bishop-coventry.org

CODRINGTON-MARSHALL, Louise. b 64. Westcott Ho Cam 06. **d** 08 **p** 09. C Mortlake w E Sheen *S'wark* 08–11; P-in-c Deptford St Nic and St Luke 11–14; V from 14. *11 Evelyn Street, London SE8 5RQ* T: (020) 8876 7162 *or* 8692 2749 E: stnicholaschurchdeptford@gmail.com

CODY (née TAYLOR), Julia Mary. b 73. Reading Univ LLB 94. Ridley Hall Cam 06. **d** 08 **p** 09. C Penkridge *Lich* 08–12; TV Tettenhall Wood and Perton from 12; RD Trysull from 19. *Church House, 23 Portrush Road, Perton, Wolverhampton WV6 7YZ* T: (01902) 750232 M: 07990-976859 E: jules.m.taylor@googlemail.com

CODY, Paul James Luke. b 73. Westcott Ho Cam. **d** 08 **p** 09. C Cen Wolverhampton *Lich* 08–12; Chapl St Pet Colleg Sch Wolv 12–17; Chapl Kemp Hospice Kidderminster from 17; PtO *Lich* from 18. *Church House, 23 Portrush Road, Perton, Wolverhampton WV6 7YZ* T: (01902) 750232 M: 07834-345269 E: paulcody@hotmail.co.uk

COE, Andrew Derek John. b 58. Nottm Univ BTh 86. St Jo Coll Nottm 83. **d** 86 **p** 87. C Pype Hayes *Birm* 86–88; C Erdington St Barn 88–91; C Birm St Martin w Bordesley St Andr 91–96; P-in-c Hamstead St Bernard 96; V 96–02; P-in-c Newdigate *Guildf* 02–03; TR Surrey Weald from 03; RD Dorking 04–09. *St Peter's Rectory, Church Lane, Newdigate, Dorking RH5 5DL* T: (01306) 631469 E: revdandrewdj.coe@btinternet.com

COE, David. b 45. **d** 69 **p** 70. C Belfast St Matt *Conn* 69–72; C Belfast St Donard *D & D* 72–75; I Tullylish 75–81; I Lurgan St Jo 81–89; I Ballymacarrett St Patr 89–02; I Richhill *Arm* 02–11; rtd 11. *49 Toberhewny Lodge, Lurgan, Craigavon BT66 7FL* T: (028) 3834 2579 M: 07794-356030 E: davidcoe144@aol.com

COE, Michael Stephen. b 63. Bath Univ BSc 85. Wycliffe Hall Ox. **d** 00 **p** 01. C Moulton *Pet* 00–03; P-in-c Silverhill St Matt *Chich* 03–05; R 05–18; P-in-c St Leonards St Ethelburga and St Leon 17–18; RD Hastings 13–18; V Ilkley All SS *Leeds* from 18. *58 Curly Hill, Ilkley LS29 0BA* E: vlear@ilkleyallsaints.org.uk

COE, Noelle Elizabeth. b 60. Anglia Ruskin Univ BA 10. **d** 08 **p** 09. NSM N Holmwood *Guildf* 08–10; NSM Westcott 10–12; NSM Surrey Weald from 12. *St Peter's Rectory, Church*

Lane, Newdigate, Dorking RH5 5DL T: (01306) 631469
E: noellecoe@btinternet.com

COE, Stephen David. b 49. Ch Coll Cam MA 72 Oak Hill Th Coll MA 99. Ox Min Course 90. **d** 93 **p** 94. NSM Abingdon *Ox* 93–97; Assoc Min Ox St Andr 97–05; V Wallington H Trin *S'wark* 05–17; rtd 17; PtO *Ox* from 17. *Stile House, 53A Wootton Village, Boars Hill, Oxford OX1 5HP* E: sdcoe@btinternet.com

COEKIN, Philip James. b 64. Wye Coll Lon BScAgr 87. Oak Hill Th Coll BA 93. **d** 96 **p** 97. C Eastbourne All SS *Chich* 96–00; V Hastings Em and St Mary in the Castle 00–11; V Eastbourne H Trin from 11. *Holy Trinity Vicarage, 2 Hartington Place, Eastbourne BN21 3BE* T: (01323) 325421 E: pcoekin@gmail.com

COEKIN, Richard John. b 61. Solicitor 86 Jes Coll Cam BA 83 MA 87. Wycliffe Hall Ox 89. **d** 91 **p** 92. C Cheadle *Ches* 91–95; NSM Wimbledon Em Ridgway Prop Chpl *S'wark* 95–15; PtO *Lon* from 02; *S'wark* from 15. *264 Worple Road, London SW20 8RG* T: (020) 8545 2734 E: richard.coekin@dundonald.org

COFFEY, Helen Theresa. b 63. Salford Univ BA 08 Sheff Univ BA 12. Coll of Resurr Mirfield 10. **d** 12 **p** 13. C Ashton-in-Makerfield St Thos *Liv* 12–16; P-in-c Ashton-in-Makerfield H Trin 16–18; TR Eccleston Team from 18. *St James's Vicarage, 159A St Helen's Road, Eccleston Park, Prescot L34 2QB* M: 07742-590672 E: helentcoffey@gmail.com

COFFEY (formerly COOMBS), **Patrick Michael Joseph.** b 65. Sheff Univ MA 00 Brighton Univ MBA 04 Plymouth Univ MA 11. St Steph Ho Ox BTh 94. **d** 94 **p** 95. C Torquay St Martin Barton *Ex* 94–95; C Goodrington 95–98; V Sheff St Cuth 98–99. *Thornbury Manor, Thornbury, Holsworthy EX22 7DD* M: 07393-207977 E: coffey@coffey.cc or admin@pmjcoffey.com

COFFIN, Pamela. See PENNELL, Pamela

COGGINS, Glenn. b 60. Warwick Univ BA 81. Cranmer Hall Dur 93. **d** 95 **p** 96. C Cley Hill Warminster *Sarum* 95–99; R Doddington w Benwick and Wimblington *Ely* 99–06; V E Ardsley *Wakef* 06–14; *Leeds* 14–19; V Outwood, Stanley and Wrenthorpe from 19; P-in-c Alverthorpe from 19; Bp's Adv for Ecum Affairs *Wakef* 07–14; *Leeds* from 14. *St Paul's Vicarage, St Paul's Drive, Wakefield WF2 0BT* M: 07951-651952 E: cogginsglenn@gmail.com

COGHLAN, Jennifer Mary. See WILTSHIRE, Jennifer Mary

COGHLAN, Canon Patrick John. b 47. Down Coll Cam BA 69. St Jo Coll Nottm MA 73. **d** 73 **p** 74. C Crookes St Thos *Sheff* 73–78; Brazil 78–92; V Anston *Sheff* 92–06; V Malin Bridge 06–13; Hon Can Sheff Cathl 07–13; rtd 13; PtO *Sheff* from 13. *1 Bradway Road, Sheffield S17 4QQ* T: 0114-236 9483 E: patrick.coghlan@sheffield.anglican.org

COHEN, Grant Geoffrey. b 71. Regents Th Coll BA 08. Ridley Hall Cam 09. **d** 11 **p** 12. C Sale St Anne *Ches* 11–14; TV Sanderstead *S'wark* 14–18; V Sanderstead St Mary from 18; P-in-c Riddlesdown from 16. *St Mary's Vicarage, 85 Purley Oaks Road, South Croydon CR2 0NY* M: 07717-170358 E: grant_cohen@hotmail.co.uk

COHEN, Canon Ian Geoffrey Holland. b 51. Nottm Univ BA 74. Ripon Coll Cuddesdon 77. **d** 79 **p** 80. C Sprowston *Nor* 79–83; TV Wallingford w Crowmarsh Gifford etc *Ox* 83–88; V Chalgrove w Berrick Salome 88–18; Hon Can Ch Ch 11–18; rtd 18. *19 Nun Street, St Davids, Haverfordwest SA62 6NS* E: ianghcohen@hotmail.com

COHEN, Janet Elizabeth. See GASPER, Janet Elizabeth

COHEN, Malcolm Arthur. b 38. Canberra Coll of Min. **d** 78 **p** 79. C Moruya, Bega and Cootamundra Australia 79–80; R Braidwood 82–83; R Stifford *Chelmsf* 84–92; Chapl Asst Thurrock Community Hosp Grays 84–86; Hon Chapl ATC from 86; P-in-c Mayland and Steeple *Chelmsf* 92–95; C Prittlewell 95–99; C Greenstead 99–00; TV Greenstead w Colchester St Anne 00–03; rtd 03; PtO *Chelmsf* from 08. *177 Straight Road, Colchester CO3 5DG* T: (01206) 573231 E: lynnpcohen@googlemail.com

COLAM (née TAVERNER), **Mrs Lorraine Dawn.** b 61. SRN 82 RSCN 86. **d** 07 **p** 08. OLM Tilehurst St Cath and Calcot *Ox* 07–18; Chapl R Berks NHS Foundn Trust 14–18; NSM Burghfield *Ox* from 18. *120 Chapel Hill, Tilehurst, Reading RG31 5DH* T: 0118-943 2001 M: 07790-076450 E: lorraine.colam@virginmedia.com

COLBROOK, Mrs Andrea Dorothy. b 70. Reading Univ BA 96 RGN 92. Ripon Coll Cuddesdon 17. **d** 19. C Ridgeway *Ox* from 19. *Fawler Paddock, Fawler, Wantage OX12 9QJ* T: (01367) 820553 M: 07749-865052 E: revd.acolbrook@gmail.com

COLBY, Mrs Ruth Mary. b 61. ERMC 13. **d** 16 **p** 17. C Rothwell w Orton, Rushton w Glendon and Pipewell *Pet* 16–18; C Broughton w Loddington and Cransley etc 16–18; C Rothwell w Orton and Rushton w Glendon etc 18–19; P-in-c Car Colston w Screveton *S'well* from 19; P-in-c E

Bridgford and Kneeton from 19; P-in-c Flintham from 19. *The Vicarage, Woods Lane, Flintham, Newark NG23 5LR* E: ruthcolby2@gmail.com

COLCHESTER, Archdeacon of. *See* PATTEN, The Ven Ruth Janet

COLCHESTER, Area Bishop of. *See* MORRIS, The Rt Revd Roger Anthony Brett

✠**COLCLOUGH, The Rt Revd Michael John.** b 44. Leeds Univ BA 69. Cuddesdon Coll 69. **d** 71 **p** 72 **c** 96. C Bilston St Werburgh *Lich* 71–75; C Ruislip St Mary *Lon* 75–79; P-in-c Hayes St Anselm 79–85; V 85–86; AD Hillingdon 85–92; P-in-c Uxbridge St Marg 86–88; P-in-c Uxbridge St Andr w St Jo 86–88; TR Uxbridge 88–92; Adn Northolt 92–94; P-in-c St Vedast w St Mich-le-Querne etc 94–96; P-in-c St Magnus the Martyr w St Marg New Fish Street 95–96; Bp's Sen Chapl 94–96; Dean of Univ Chapls 94–96; Dep P in O 95–96; Area Bp Kensington *Lon* 96–08; Can Res St Paul's Cathl 08–13; rtd 13; Hon Asst Bp Lon from 13; Hon Asst Bp Eur from 13; PtO from 18. *12 Grosvenor Court, 99 Sloane Street, London SW1X 9PF* T: (020) 3612 3135 E: michaeljcolclough@gmail.com

COLDICOTT, Richard Spencer. b 69. Leeds Univ BSc 90 PhD 93 PGCE 94. Trin Coll Bris 06. **d** 08 **p** 09. C Aspley *S'well* 08–11; TV Horsham *Chich* 11–16; V Holbrook from 16. *St Mark's House, North Heath Lane, Horsham RH12 4PJ* T: (01403) 260435 M: 07742-014444 E: vicar@stmarksholbrook.org.uk

COLDWELL, Canon John Philip. b 62. Trin Coll Bris 04. **d** 06 **p** 07. C Inglewood Gp *Carl* 06–09; P-in-c Douglas St Ninian *S & M* 09–13; V from 13; Dioc Communications Officer from 10; Hon Can St German's Cathl 15–16; Can St German's Cathl from 16. *St Ninian's Vicarage, 58 Ballanard Road, Douglas, Isle of Man IM2 5HE* T: (01624) 621694 M: 07624-203395 E: media@sodorandman.im

COLDWELL, Rosemary Anne. b 52. Bretton Hall Coll CertEd 75 Open Univ BA 82 LTCL 74 LLCM 74. STETS 04. **d** 07 **p** 08. NSM Blandford Forum and Langton Long *Sarum* 07–12; PtO *Bradf* 12–13; *Sarum* from 16. *12 Stileham Bank, Milborne St Andrew, Blandford Forum DT11 0LE* M: 07929-090948 E: rosemarycoldwell@btinternet.com

COLE, Canon Alan John. b 35. Bps' Coll Cheshunt 63. **d** 66 **p** 67. C Boreham Wood All SS *St Alb* 66–69; C St Alb St Mich 69–72; V Redbourn 72–80; R Thorley w Bishop's Stortford H Trin 80–87; Chapl St Edw K and Martyr Cam *Ely* 87–94; Chapl Arthur Rank Hospice Cam 87–94; P-in-c Gamlingay w Hatley St George and E Hatley *Ely* 94–99; Hon Can Ely Cathl 96–00; P-in-c Everton w Tetworth 98–99; R Gamlingay and Everton 99–00; rtd 01; PtO *St E* 01–15; *Ely* from 01. *73 Finchams Close, Linton, Cambridge CB21 4ND* E: alan703cole@btinternet.com

COLE, Alan Michael. b 40. Melbourne Univ DipEd 74 BA 74. ACT. **d** 66 **p** 67. Australia 66–75 and 90–97; Chapl Bp Otter Coll *Chich* 76–77; Chapl Ardingly Coll 77–82; Chapl Bonn w Cologne *Eur* 82–86; Chapl Helsinki w Moscow 86–90; P-in-c Ilkeston H Trin *Derby* 97–01; V 02–10; rtd 10; PtO *Pet* from 10; *Leic* from 10; *Eur* from 10. *30 St Mary's Paddock, Wellingborough NN8 1HJ* T: (01933) 274650

COLE, Mrs Alice Alexandra Judith. b 87. St Andr Univ MMath 09 Lanc Univ MSc 10 PhD 15. St Mellitus Coll BA 17. **d** 17 **p** 18. C Lower Darwen St Jas *Blackb* from 17; C Over Darwen St Jas and Hoddlesden from 17. *81 Delphinium Way, Lower Darwen, Darwen BB3 0SX* T: (01254) 671229 M: 07793-712757

COLE, Guy Spenser. b 63. Univ of Wales (Ban) BA 84 Jes Coll Cam BA 88 MA 91. Westcott Ho Cam 85. **d** 88 **p** 89. C Eastville St Anne w St Mark and St Thos *Bris* 88–92; P-in-c Penhill 92–95; V 95–01; R Easthampstead *Ox* from 01; AD Bracknell from 19. *The Rectory, Crowthorne Road, Easthampstead, Bracknell RG12 7ER* T: (01344) 423253 or 425205 E: guy.s.cole@btinternet.com

COLE, Jennifer Ann. b 52. Open Univ MBA 04. STETS 07. **d** 09 **p** 10. NSM Kilmersdon w Babington and Radstock w Writhlington *B & W* 09–13; PtO 13–14; NSM Wells St Cuth w Wookey Hole 14–19; PtO from 19. *8 The Grange, Easton Hill, Easton, Wells BA5 1DU* M: 07749-079276 E: jennifer.cole@bathwells.anglican.org

COLE, John Spensley. b 39. Clare Coll Cam BA 62 MA 66 FCA 65. Linc Th Coll 78. **d** 80 **p** 81. C Cowes St Mary *Portsm* 80–83; C Portchester 83–87; V Modbury *Ex* 87–95; R Aveton Gifford 87–95; TR Modbury, Bigbury, Ringmore w Kingston etc 95–98; P-in-c Alne and Brafferton w Pilmoor, Myton-on-Swale etc *York* 98–05; rtd 05; PtO *S'well* from 14. *11 Long Meadow, Farnsfield, Newark NG22 8DR* T: (01623) 883595 E: johncole@phonecoop.coop

COLE, Canon Michael John. b 34. St Pet Hall Ox BA 56 MA 60. Ridley Hall Cam 56. **d** 58 **p** 59. C Finchley Ch Ch *Lon* 58; C Leeds St Geo *Ripon* 58–61; Travelling Sec IVF 61–64; V Crookes St Thos *Sheff* 64–71; R Rusholme H Trin *Man* 71–75;

V Woodford Wells *Chelmsf* 75–00; Chapl Leytonstone Ho Hosp 85–00; Hon Can Chelmsf Cathl 89–00; RD Redbridge 95–00; rtd 00; PtO *Chelmsf* 00–06; *Chich* from 13. *1 Paradise Drive, Eastbourne BN20 7SX* T: (01323) 723425 E: canoncole@yahoo.com

COLE, Canon Peter George Lamont. b 27. Pemb Coll Cam BA 49 MA 52. Cuddesdon Coll 50. **d** 52 **p** 53. C Aldershot St Mich *Guildf* 52–55; C St Jo Cathl Bulawayo S Rhodesia 55–59; P-in-c Riverside All SS 55–59; R 59–62; Chapl St Steph Coll Balla Balla 63–65; V Bromley St Andr *Roch* 65–72; V Folkestone St Mary and St Eanswythe *Cant* 72–87; Hon Can Cant Cathl 80–87; V E and W Worldham, Hartley Mauditt w Kingsley etc *Win* 87–92; RD Alton 89–92; rtd 92; RD Petworth *Chich* 94–95; PtO from 95. *29 Swan View, Pulborough RH20 2BF* T: (01798) 873238 E: petergcole@outlook.com

COLE, Mrs Vanessa Anne. b 73. K Alfred's Coll Win BA 94. Trin Coll Bris BA 03. **d** 04 **p** 05. C Congresbury w Puxton and Hewish St Ann *B & W* 04–09; TV Portway and Danebury *Win* from 09. *The Rectory, Over Wallop, Stockbridge SO20 8HT* T: (01264) 782615 E: vanessa@cole.org.uk

COLE, William. b 45. Oak Hill Th Coll BA 96. **d** 96 **p** 97. NSM St Keverne *Truro* 96–99; P-in-c St Ruan w St Grade and Landewednack 99–10; rtd 10; PtO *Carl* 11–16; C Combe Martin, Berrynarbor, Lynton, Brendon etc *Ex* 16–18; C Ilfracombe SS Phil and Jas, Combe Martin and Berrynarbor from 18. *The Rectory, Rectory Road, Combe Martin, Ilfracombe EX34 0NS* M: 07792-932559 E: billcole124@btinternet.com

COLE-BAKER, Peter Massey. b 58. New Univ of Ulster BSc 80 TCD BTh 98. CITC 95. **d** 98 **p** 99. C Ballywillan *Conn* 98–01; I Templemore w Thurles and Kilfithmone *C & O* 01–14; Can Ossory Cathl 12–14; rtd 14. *The Bungalow, Springfield, Clonard Road, Wexford, Y35 X2R1, Republic of Ireland* E: pcolebaker@eircom.net

COLEBROOK, Canon Christopher John. b 36. Qu Mary Coll Lon BA 60 BD 69. St D Coll Lamp 60. **d** 62 **p** 63. C Llandeilo Tal-y-bont *S & B* 62–66; C Llansamlet 66–71; V Nantmel w St Harmon's and Llanwrthwl 71–76; V Glantawe 76–85; V Gowerton 85–01; RD Llwchwr 93–00; Hon Can Brecon Cathl 97–01; Prec 00–01; rtd 01. *79 Vivian Road, Sketty, Swansea SA2 0UN* T: (01792) 521966

COLEBROOK, Peter Acland. b 29. Coates Hall Edin 52. **d** 55 **p** 56. C Northfield *Birm* 55–62; C Bideford *Ex* 62–66; Teacher Duchy Manor Middle Sch 72–89; rtd 89; PtO *B & W* 70–74; *Sarum* 86–16. *Danes Lee, Ham Lane, Marnhull, Sturminster Newton DT10 1JN* T: (01258) 820242

COLEBROOKE, Andrew. b 50. Imp Coll Lon BSc 71 MSc 72 PhD 75. Ridley Hall Cam 92. **d** 94 **p** 95. C Shrub End *Chelmsf* 94–98; R Mistley w Manningtree and Bradfield 98–09; RD Harwich 04–09; R Icknield Way Villages 09–16; rtd 16; PtO *Chelmsf* 17–19. *42 Crabtrees, Saffron Walden CB11 3BH* T: (01799) 732970 E: andy.colebrooke@gmail.com

COLEBY, Andrew Mark. b 59. Linc Coll Ox MA 85 DPhil 85 Dur Univ BA 90 FRHistS 88. Cranmer Hall Dur 88. **d** 91 **p** 92. C Heeley *Sheff* 91–93; TV Gleadless 94–97; Chapl Ox Brookes Univ 97–01; P-in-c Didcot All SS 01–06; Dioc FE Officer and Chapl Abingdon and Witney Coll 06–09; Soc Resp Adv *St Alb* 09–13; R Shipston-on-Stour w Honington and Idlicote *Cov* 13–17; PtO *Ox* from 11; Min Tr Officer *Pet* from 17. *Silver Birches, Picklers Hill, Abingdon OX14 2BA* T: (01235) 528374 E: am.coleby@btopenworld.com

COLEMAN, Andrew David. b 78. Monash Univ BA 00. Melbourne Coll of Div MDiv 08. **d** 07 **p** 08. C Kilmore Australia 07–09; C Port Elliot w Goolwa 09–11; V Longford *Cov* 13–19; P-in-c Radford from 19; P-in-c Ansty and Shilton from 13. *The Vicarage, 65 Hurst Road, Longford, Coventry CV6 6EL* T: (024) 7636 6635 M: 07517-373587 E: andrewdavidcoleman@hotmail.com

COLEMAN, Mrs Ann Valerie. b 51. K Coll Lon BD 72 Heythrop Coll Lon MA 03. St Aug Coll Cant. **dss** 80 **d** 87 **p** 94. Hampstead Garden Suburb *Lon* 80–84; Golders Green 85–87; Selection Sec and Voc Adv ACCM 87–91; Teacher Bp Ramsey Sch 92–93; Chapl 93–99; Dir of Ords Willesden Area *Lon* 96–99; Course Leader NTMTC 99–04; Hon C Eastcote St Lawr *Lon* 93–04; Dir Wydale Hall *York* 04–08; Dioc Moderator Reader Tr 05–08; Tutor St Mellitus Coll *Lon* 08–12; Asst Dean St Mellitus Coll and Dir NTMTC 12–15; Hon C Doddinghurst *Chelmsf* 14–19; NSM Bentley Common, Kelvedon Hatch and Navestock from 14; Hon C 15–19. *The Rectory, Church Lane, Doddinghurst, Brentwood CM15 0NJ* T: (01277) 821366 E: annvcol@gmail.com

COLEMAN, Brian James. b 36. K Coll Cam BA 58 MA 61. Ripon Hall Ox 58. **d** 60 **p** 61. C Allestree *Derby* 60–65; V Allestree St Nic 65–69; Chapl and Lect St Mich Coll Salisbury 69–77; P-in-c Matlock Bank *Derby* 77–86; R Frimley *Guildf*

86–92; V Guildf All SS 92–02; rtd 02; PtO *Sarum* 03–15. *6 Kingfisher Close, Salisbury SP2 8JE* T: (01722) 410034

COLEMAN, Preb David. b 49. K Coll Lon BD 72 AKC 72. St Aug Coll Cant 72. **d** 73 **p** 74. C Is of Dogs Ch Ch and St Jo w St Luke *Lon* 73–77; C Greenford H Cross 77–80; V Cricklewood St Pet 80–85; V Golders Green 85–90; V Eastcote St Lawr 90–04; P-in-c Upper Ryedale and CME Officer Cleveland Adnry *York* 04–08; V Heston *Lon* 08–15; Preb St Paul's Cathl 13–15; rtd 15; PtO *Chelmsf* from 15. *The Rectory, Church Lane, Doddinghurst, Brentwood CM15 0NJ* T: (01227) 821366 E: frdavid.coleman@tiscali.co.uk

COLEMAN, David. b 61. **d** 14 **p** 15. C Horley *S'wark* 14–16; C S Nutfield 16–18; R W Chiltington *Chich* 18–19; V Steeton *Leeds* from 19. *The Vicarage, 2 Halsteads Way, Steeton, Keighley BD20 6SN* M: 07958-997455 E: davidmcoleman61@gmail.com

COLEMAN, David Kenneth. b 60. Ex Univ BTh 10. SWMTC 06. **d** 09 **p** 10. NSM Bickleigh and Shaugh Prior *Ex* 09–14; NSM Whitchurch 14–16; NSM Peter Tavy and Mary Tavy 14–16; TV S Molton w Nymet St George, Chittlehamholt etc from 16. *The Vicarage, Chittlehampton, Umberleigh EX37 9QL* E: revd.davecoleman@gmail.com

COLEMAN, Frank. b 58. Hull Univ BA 79. St Steph Ho Ox BA 83 MA 87. **d** 83 **p** 84. C Brandon *Dur* 83–85; C Newton Aycliffe 85–88; V Denford w Ringstead *Pet* 88–00; P-in-c Islip 95–00; V Caldecote, Northill and Old Warden *St Alb* from 00. *The Vicarage, 2A Biggleswade Road, Upper Caldecote, Biggleswade SG18 9BL* T: (01767) 315578 F: 317988 M: 07738-357458 E: frankcoleman@ntlworld.com

COLEMAN, Jonathon Mark. b 59. Kent Univ BA 81. Qu Coll Birm MA 99. **d** 99 **p** 00. C Warrington St Elphin *Liv* 99–02; P-in-c Liv St Chris Norris Green 02–07; Area Dean W Derby and Hon Can Liv Cathl 06–07; P-in-c W Derby St Mary 07–09; P-in-c W Derby St Jas 07–09; V W Derby St Mary and St Jas 09–14; R Rochdale *Man* from 14; AD 15–17; Borough Dean Rochdale from 16. *St Edmund's Vicarage, 89 Clement Royds Street, Rochdale OL12 6PL* T: (01706) 632809 M: 07795-202955 E: hellomarkcoleman@gmail.com

COLEMAN, Neil Geoffrey. b 77. Trin Coll Bris BA 11. **d** 11 **p** 12. C N Mundham w Hunston and Merston *Chich* 11–15; V St Paul's Cray St Barn *Roch* from 15. *The Vicarage, Rushet Road, Orpington BR5 2PU* M: 07826-850273 E: n-coleman@hotmail.co.uk

COLEMAN, Ms Nicola Jane. b 63. Goldsmiths' Coll Lon BA 86. Ripon Coll Cuddesdon 99. **d** 01 **p** 02. C Croydon St Jo *S'wark* 01–05; P-in-c S Norwood H Innocents 05–12; P-in-c The Lulworths, Winfrith Newburgh and Chaldon *Sarum* 12–16; P-in-c Barton Hill St Luke w Ch Ch and Moorfields *Bris* from 17; P-in-c E Bris St Ambrose and St Leon from 17. *St Luke's Vicarage, 60 Barton Hill Road, Bristol BS5 0AW* T: 0117-955 6678 M: 07985-659667 E: revncoleman@gmail.com

COLEMAN, Patrick Francis. b 58. Pontifical Univ Rome PhB 79 STB 82 STL 84. Ven English Coll Rome 77. **d** 82 **p** 83. In RC Ch 82–92; NSM Abergavenny St Mary w Llanwenarth Citra *Mon* 96–99; Asst Chapl Milan w Genoa and Varese *Eur* 99–01; R Goetre w Llanover *Mon* 01–06; Dir CME 01–06; P-in-c Abertillery w Cwmtillery 06–10; V Abertillery w Cwmtillery w Llanhilleth etc 10–14; V Chesterfield St Mary and All SS *Derby* from 14. *The Vicarage, 28 Cromwell Road, Chesterfield S40 4TH* T: (01246) 462866 E: abervicar@me.com

COLEMAN, Canon Peter Nicholas. b 42. St Mich Coll Llan 83. **d** 85 **p** 86. C Skewen *Llan* 85–88; R Ystradyfodwg 88–07; P-in-c Treorchy and Treherbert 04–07; RD Rhondda 96–04; Can Llan Cathl 04–07; rtd 07; PtO *Llan* from 07. *15 Pant Hendre, Pencoed, Bridgend CF35 6LN*

COLEMAN, Richard Ian. b 70. Open Univ BSc 00. Wycliffe Hall Ox 05. **d** 07 **p** 08. C Peterlee *Dur* 07–11; P-in-c Barton in Fabis *S'well* 11–19; P-in-c Gotham 11–19; P-in-c Kingston and Ratcliffe-on-Soar 11–19; P-in-c Thrumpton 11–19; R A453 churches of S Notts from 19. *The New Rectory, 39 Leake Road, Gotham, Nottingham NG11 0HW* T: 0115-983 0608 E: coleman@orpheusmail.co.uk

COLEMAN, Stephen Paul Losack. b 80. St Benet's Hall Ox BA 02 MSt 03 Cardiff Univ LLM 17. Westcott Ho Cam 12. **d** 14 **p** 15. C Winchmore Hill St Paul *Lon* 14–17; V Grange Park St Pet from 17. *The Vicarage, Langham Gardens, London N21 1DN* T: (020) 8360 2294 E: stephenplcoleman@hotmail.com

COLEMAN, Timothy. b 57. Southn Univ BSc 79 MBACP. Ridley Hall Cam 87. **d** 89 **p** 90. C Bisley and W End *Guildf* 89–93; C Hollington St Jo *Chich* 93–97; V Aldborough Hatch *Chelmsf* 97–02; Chapl Princess Alexandra Hosp NHS Trust 02–04; Chapl Barking Havering and Redbridge Hosps NHS Trust from 04. *The Chaplain's Office, Queen's Hospital, Rom Valley Way, Romford RM7 0AG* T: (01708) 503201 E: tim.coleman@bhrhospitals.nhs.uk

COLERIDGE, William Paul Hugh. b 76. Newc Univ LLB 98 Solicitor 01. Wycliffe Hall Ox 07. **d** 09 **p** 10. C Ches Square St Mich w St Phil *Lon* 09–12; C Paddington St Steph w St Luke 12–16; C Bayswater 12–16; V from 16. *The Vicarage, 27 St Petersburgh Place, London W2 4LA* T: (020) 7229 2192 E: will@stmatthewsbayswater.com

COLES, Canon Alasdair Charles. b 67. St Andr Univ BSc 90 Homerton Coll Cam PGCE 91 Heythrop Coll Lon PhD 03. Ripon Coll Cuddesdon 96. **d** 96 **p** 97. C Wymondham *Nor* 96–99; Min Can and Sacr St Paul's Cathl *Lon* 99–04; P-in-c Pimlico St Mary Bourne Street 04–07; V 07–09; P-in-c Pimlico St Barn 04–07; V 07–09; Asst Vice Prin and Chapl All SS Academy Dunstable 09–15; PV Westmr Abbey 04–15; R St Andrews All SS *St And* from 15; Hon Can Mampong Ghana from 14. *All Saints' Rectory, 39 North Street, St Andrews KY16 9AQ* T: (01334) 473153 M: 07729-962723 E: rector@allsaints-standrews.com

COLES, Alasdair John. b 66. Pemb Coll Ox BA 87 Green Coll Ox BM, BCh 90 CCC Cam PhD 98 MRCP 94. ERMC 05. **d** 08 **p** 09. NSM Chesterton St Andr *Ely* from 08. *Department of Neurology, Box 165, Addenbrooke's Hospital, Cambridge CB2 2QQ* T: (01223) 216751 F: 336941 E: ajc1020@medschl.cam.ac.uk

COLES, Preb Alison Elizabeth. b 60. St Mary's Coll Dur BA 81. Ripon Coll Cuddesdon 95. **d** 97 **p** 98. C Leckhampton SS Phil and Jas w Cheltenham St Jas *Glouc* 97–00; Asst Chapl Dudley Gp of Hosps NHS Trust 00–04; Chapl Walsall Healthcare NHS Trust from 04; Bp's Adv on Healthcare Chapl *Lich* from 19; Preb Lich Cathl from 15. *Walsall Hospitals NHS Trust, Manor Hospital, Moat Road, Walsall WS2 9PS* T: (01922) 656216 E: chaplaincy@walsallhospitals.nhs.uk

✠**COLES, The Rt Revd David John.** b 43. Auckland Univ MA 67 Otago Univ BD 69 MTh 71 Man Univ PhD 74. St Jo Coll Auckland 66. **d** 68 **p** 69 **c** 90. C Remuera New Zealand 68–70; Chapl Selwyn Coll Dunedin 70–71; Hon C Fallowfield *Man* 72–74; Chapl Hulme Gr Sch Oldham 73–74; V Glenfield New Zealand 74–76; V Takapuna 76–80; Dean Napier 80–84; Dean Christchurch 84–90; Bp Christchurch 90–08; V Wakatipu New Zealand 08–14; Chapl Denmark *Eur* 14–15; V Heathcote Mt Pleasant New Zealand from 15. *88 Canon Street, St Albans, Christchurch 8014, New Zealand* T: (0064) (3) 366 0359 M: (0064) 27-306 9961 E: vicar@heathcote-mtpleasant.org.nz *or* dandjcoles@gmail.com

COLES, Preb Francis Herbert. b 35. Selw Coll Cam BA 59 MA 63. Coll of Resurr Mirfield 59. **d** 61 **p** 62. C Wolvercote *Ox* 61–65; C Farnham Royal 65–69; V Lynton and Brendon *Ex* 69–73; V Countisbury 70; V Lynton, Brendon, Countisbury and Lynmouth 70–73; TR Lynton, Brendon, Countisbury, Lynmouth etc 73–76; P-in-c Iffley *Ox* 76–88; V Ivybridge w Harford *Ex* 88–00; Preb Ex Cathl from 87; rtd 00; PtO *Ex* from 00. *8 Glenthorne Road, Exeter EX4 4QU* T: (01392) 420238

COLES, Graham Robert. b 60. Qu Coll Birm 07. **d** 09 **p** 10. C Lillington and Old Milverton *Cov* 09–12; C Leamington Spa H Trin 09–12; P-in-c Cubbington 12–14; V from 14. *St Mary's Vicarage, 15 Pinehurst, Cubbington, Leamington Spa CV32 7XA* T: (01926) 330596

COLES, Preb John Spencer Halstaff. b 50. Hertf Coll Ox BA 72 MA 76. Wycliffe Hall Ox 72. **d** 75 **p** 76. C Reading Greyfriars *Ox* 75–79; C Clifton Ch Ch w Em *Bris* 79–82; V Woodside Park St Barn *Lon* 82–06; C 06–11; Dir New Wine Internat Min 11–15; LtO from 13; Preb St Paul's Cathl from 11. *33 Arnos Road, London N11 1AP* T: (020) 3441 5264 M: 07779-016930

COLES, Mrs Olivia Mary Kana. b 64. Cen Sch Speech & Drama BEd 87. ERMC 12. **d** 15 **p** 16. NSM Histon *Ely* 15–18; NSM Impington 15–18; NSM Whittlesford from 18; Baptism Co-ord from 17. *The Vicarage, 22A North Road, Whittlesford, Cambridge CB22 4NZ* M: 07720-985889 E: revolivia@gmail.com

COLES, Mrs Pamela. b 39. Nottm Univ CertEd 59. NOC 04. **d** 05 **p** 06. NSM Clayton *Bradf* 05–09; PtO 09–14; *Leeds* from 14. *4 Ferndale Avenue, Clayton, Bradford BD14 6PG* T: (01274) 427956 E: pamcolesclayton@yahoo.com

COLES, Richard Keith Robert. b 62. K Coll Lon BA 94 AKC 94 Leeds Univ MA 05 Northn Univ Hon PhD 12 FRSA 12. Coll of Resurr Mirfield 03. **d** 05 **p** 06. C Boston *Linc* 05–07; C Wilton Place St Paul *Lon* 07–11; Chapl R Academy of Music 07–08; P-in-c Finedon *Pet* 11–15; V from 15. *St Mary's Vicarage, Church Hill, Finedon, Wellingborough NN9 5NR* T: (01933) 681786 E: revdrichardcoles@yahoo.co.uk

COLES, Canon Robert Reginald. b 47. Surrey Univ BSc 69. Cant Sch of Min 82. **d** 85 **p** 86. NSM Sittingbourne St Mich *Cant* 85–87; C St Laur in Thanet 87–93; P-in-c St Nicholas at Wade w Sarre and Chislet w Hoath 93–13; P-in-c Minster

w Monkton 96–13; Hon Can Cant Cathl 09–13; rtd 13; PtO *Cant* from 14. *4 Millfield, St Margaret-at-Cliffe, Dover CT15 6JL* T: (01304) 852091

COLES, Preb Stephen Richard. b 49. Univ Coll Ox BA 70 MA 74 Leeds Univ BA 80. Coll of Resurr Mirfield 78. **d** 81 **p** 82. C Stoke Newington St Mary *Lon* 81–84; Chapl K Coll Cam 84–89; V Finsbury Park St Thos *Lon* from 89; Preb St Paul's Cathl from 13. *25 Romilly Road, London N4 2QY* T: (020) 7359 5741 E: cardinal.jeoffry@btconnect.com

COLES, Mrs Sylvia Margaret. b 48. ERMC 04. **d** 07 **p** 08. NSM Northampton St Benedict *Pet* 07–10; NSM Duston 10–14; NSM Dallington 14–17; NSM Northampton St Jas 14–17; NSM Dallington and St James 17–18; rtd 18. *37 Delapre Crescent Road, Northampton NN4 8NG* T: (01604) 767305

COLEY (née JOHNSON), Mrs Emma Louise. b 76. Ex Univ BA 97 PGCE 98. Wycliffe Hall Ox BTh 04. **d** 04 **p** 05. C Wendover and Halton *Ox* 04–09; C Kennington and Radley and Sunningwell 09–12; P-in-c Sandridge *St Alb* 12–14; V 14–19; Asst Dir of Ords 12–19; Young Voc Officer Min Division Abps' Coun from 19. *Church House, Great Smith Street, London SW1P 3AZ* T: (020) 7898 1554 E: emcoley@me.com *or* em.coley@churchofengland.org

COLEY, Peter Leonard. b 45. Bath Univ BSc 67 City Univ MSc 84 CEng MIMechE. Oak Hill Th Coll 85. **d** 87 **p** 88. C Mile Cross *Nor* 87–92; R Stratton St Mary w Stratton St Michael etc 92–01; R Kirby-le-Soken w Gt Holland *Chelmsf* 01–10; rtd 10; PtO *Portsm* from 11. *6 Forest Rise, Liss GU33 7AU* T: (01730) 300659 M: 07706-037108 E: rev.petercoley@googlemail.com

COLLEDGE, Ms Anthea June. b 78. St Jo Coll Ox BA 00 Imp Coll Lon MSc 06 MPhil 09 St Jo Coll Dur BA 10. Cranmer Hall Dur 08. **d** 10 **p** 11. C Wortley-de-Leeds *Ripon* 10–13; C Wortley and Farnley 13–14; Chapl Sheff Univ 14–17; PtO *Leeds* from 17; Chapl Leeds Univ from 19. *University of Leeds, Woodhouse Lane, Leeds LS2 9JT* M: 07518-319475 E: a.j.colledge@gmail.com

COLLETT, Reginald Martin Vizor. b 50. Thames Poly CertEd 87. Sarum Coll 17. **d** 19. NSM Dulverton w Brushford, Brompton Regis etc *B & W* from 19. *5 Musgraves, Dulverton TA22 9EB* T: (01398) 324211 E: colletts36@btinternet.com

COLLETT-WHITE, Thomas Charles. b 36. Trin Coll Cam BA 61 MA 86. Ridley Hall Cam 60. **d** 62 **p** 63. C Gillingham St Mark *Roch* 62–66; V 79–90; C Normanton *Wakef* 66–69; V Highbury New Park St Aug *Lon* 69–76; R Huntingdon w Ormston Canada 76–79; Chapl Medway Hosp Gillingham 79–85; P-in-c Clerkenwell St Jas and St Jo w St Pet *Lon* 90–96; rtd 01; PtO *Cant* from 06. *77 The Street, Boughton-under-Blean, Faversham ME13 9BE* T: (01227) 750770 E: tcollettwhite@yahoo.co.uk

COLLEY, Elizabeth Jane. b 51. Open Univ BA 89 DipSW 96. **d** 13 **p** 14. NSM Crewe All SS and St Paul w St Pet *Ches* 13–16; P-in-c 16–19; rtd 19. *8 Tatton Drive, Sandbach CW11 1DR* T: (01270) 748669 M: 07404-778831 E: ejmmcc@aol.com

COLLEY, Graham Albert. b 46. Auckland Teachers' Coll TCert 68. St Jo Th Coll (NZ) LTh 71. **d** 70 **p** 71. C Papakura New Zealand 70–73; P-in-c 73; V Waimate N 73–83; P-in-c Ynysddu *Mon* 78; V Thames St Geo New Zealand 81–16; Adn Hunua 89–00; PtO 16–17; C Birchington w Acol and Minnis Bay *Cant* 17–18; rtd 18; P-in-c Bucklands Beach New Zealand from 18. *Bay Tree House, 103 Victoria Street, Thames 3500, New Zealand* E: gandj.colley@gmail.com

COLLEY, Mrs Karen. b 68. Sheff Hallam Univ BA 96 Leeds Metrop Univ MSc 01. Yorks Min Course 11. **d** 13 **p** 14. NSM Sheff Manor from 13. *4 Bramley Hall Road, Handsworth, Sheffield S13 8TX* E: revdkaren@btinternet.com *or* karen.colley@manorparish.co.uk

COLLEY, Leonard Noel. b 51. Qu Coll Birm 12. **d** 15 **p** 16. NSM Nanpantan St Mary in Charnwood *Leic* 15–19; NSM Groby and Ratby from 19. *The Vicarage, 58 Pymm Ley Lane, Groby, Leicester LE6 0GZ*

COLLICUTT McGRATH, Canon Joanna Ruth. b 54. LMH Ox BA 76 MA 85 Lon Univ MPhil 78 Ox Brookes Univ PhD 98 K Coll Lon MA 17. Wycliffe Hall Ox 00 Ripon Coll Cuddesdon 05. **d** 06 **p** 07. NSM Witney *Ox* from 06; Tutor Ripon Coll Cuddesdon from 07; Lect from 10; Dioc Adv for Spiritual Care for Older People *Ox* from 10; Hon Can Ch Ch from 16. *Ripon College, Cuddesdon, Oxford OX44 9EX* T: (01865) 877404 E: jcollicutt@aol.com *or* joanna.collicutt@hmc.ox.ac.uk

COLLIER, Anthony Charles. b 45. Peterho Cam BA 68 MA 72 Whitelands Coll Lon PGCE 76. Cuddesdon Coll 68. **d** 71 **p** 72. C N Holmwood *Guildf* 71–75; PtO *S'wark* 75–79; Chapl Colfe's Sch Lon 80–10; rtd 10; Hon C Shirley St Jo *Cant* 80–84; Hon C Shirley St Jo *S'wark* 85–13; PtO from

13. *56 Bennetts Way, Croydon CR0 8AB* T: (020) 8777 6456 E: accollier@hotmail.com

COLLIER, Capt David Leslie. b 60. Wilson Carlile Coll 02 Qu Coll Birm 12. **d** 14 **p** 15. C Birkdale St Pet *Liv* 14–18; V Branston and Burton All SS w Ch Ch *Lich* from 18. *The Vicarage, Church Road, Branston, Burton-on-Trent DE14 3ER* E: davecollier3@gmail.com

COLLIER, Janice Margaret. b 57. MCSP 79. Cam Th Federation 99. **d** 01 **p** 02. C Formby H Trin *Liv* 01–05; P-in-c Hale 05–10; TR S Widnes 10–18; AD Widnes 13–18; Hon Can Liv Cathl 13–18; V Bampton w Clanfield *Ox* from 18. *The Vicarage, 5 Deanery Court, Broad Street, Brampton OX18 2LY*

COLLIER, John Alfred. **d** 13 **p** 13. NSM Mamhilad w Monkswood and Glascoed Chapel *Mon* 13–14; R from 14; R Goetre w Llanover from 14. *The Rectory, Nantyderry, Abergavenny NP7 9DW* T: (01873) 880378 E: collierjohn1@aol.com

COLLIER, Richard John Millard. b 45. FRSA 92. EAMTC 78. **d** 81 **p** 82. NSM Nor St Pet Mancroft w St Jo Maddermarket 81–97; NSM Thurton w Ashby St Mary, Bergh Apton etc 99–09; NSM Rockland St Mary w Hellington, Bramerton etc 09–12; PtO 12–14; NSM Docking, the Birchams, Stanhoe and Sedgeford 14–15; NSM Docking, The Birchams, Fring etc from 15. *The Old Buck, Church Lane, Sedgeford, Hunstanton PE36 5NA* T: (01485) 579091 E: rjsjc@yahoo.com

COLLIER, Stephen John. b 46. St Pet Coll Ox MA 68 Univ of Wales (Cardiff) DipSW 74. Qu Coll Birm 92. **d** 94 **p** 95. C Thorpe St Andr *Nor* 94–98; C Nor St Pet Mancroft w St Jo Maddermarket 98–01; R Kessingland, Gisleham and Rushmere 01–05; rtd 05; Hon C N Greenford All Hallows *Lon* 06–16; PtO from 16. *9 Drew Gardens, Greenford UB6 7QF* T: (020) 8903 9697

COLLIER, Steven Philip. Roehampton Univ BA 07. Wycliffe Hall Ox BTh 12. **d** 12 **p** 13. C Upper Sunbury St Sav *Lon* 12–13; C Isleworth All SS 13–15; TV Broadwater *Chich* 15–18; C 18–19; C Westcliff St Mich *Chelmsf* from 19. *62 Leigh Road, Leigh-on-Sea SS9 1LF* T: (01702) 480736 E: steve@stmichaelswestcliff.org

COLLIER, Susan Margaret. b 47. Cam Univ MB, BChir 73. NOC 95. **d** 98 **p** 99. NSM Dringhouses *York* 98–12; PtO from 12. *12 St Helen's Road, York YO24 1HP* T: (01904) 706064 F: 708052 E: susan.collier@me.com

COLLIN, Mrs Fiona Maria. b 62. RGN 83. Cranmer Hall Dur 11. **d** 13 **p** 14. C Sunderland Minster *Dur* 13–16; TV Dur N from 16. *1 Aykley Court, Durham DH1 4NW* T: 0191-697 0320 M: 07743-589429 E: fionamariacollin@gmail.com

COLLIN, Terry. b 39. St Aid Birkenhead 65. **d** 67 **p** 68. C Bolton St Jas w St Chrys *Bradf* 67–71; C Keighley 71–74; V Greengates 74–04; rtd 04; PtO *Bradf* 05–11. *275 Leeds Road, Eccleshill, Bradford BD2 3LD* T: (01274) 200855

COLLING, Terence John. b 47. Linc Th Coll 84. **d** 86 **p** 87. C Wood End *Cov* 86–90; V Willenhall 90–02; V Wolvey w Burton Hastings, Copston Magna etc 02–14; rtd 14; PtO *Cov* from 14; *Leic* from 14. *2 Roman Close, Claybrooke Magna, Lutterworth LE17 5DU* T: (01455) 209712 E: terencecolling@btinternet.com

COLLINGBOURNE, David Edward. b 42. St D Coll Lamp. **d** 01. Treas Dioc Coun of Educn *Mon* from 94; NSM Bishton 01–06; NSM Newport Ch Ch 06–08; NSM Bedwas w Machen w Rudry 08–12; P-in-c Marshfield w St Bride's Wentloog from 12. *The Gables, Llanwern, Newport NP18 2DS* T: (01633) 411883 E: davidcollingbourne42@tiscali.co.uk

COLLINGBOURNE, Mrs Susan Lynne. b 48. Caerleon Coll of Educn TCert 75 Univ of Wales (Cardiff) BEd 82 MEd 94. **d** 09 **p** 10. NSM Maesglas and Duffryn *Mon* 09–12; P-in-c Marshfield w St Bride's Wentloog from 12; Dioc Child Protection Officer from 98. *The Gables, Llanwern, Newport NP18 2DS* T: (01633) 411883 E: susan.collingbourne@tinyworld.co.uk

COLLINGE, Mrs Christine Elizabeth. b 47. Doncaster Coll of Educn CertEd 68. SAOMC 95. **d** 98 **p** 99. NSM W Slough *Ox* 98–04; TV Stantonbury and Willen 04–12; rtd 12; PtO *Ox* from 13. *26 Bell Close, Slough SL2 5UQ* T: (01753) 575332 E: chriscollinge@hotmail.com

COLLINGRIDGE, Graham Ian. b 58. Pemb Coll Ox BA 80 MA 84 Bedf Coll Lon MSc 84 Anglia Ruskin Univ MA 10. Ridley Hall Cam 07. **d** 09 **p** 10. C Bitterne Park *Win* 09–13; V Long Buckby w Watford and W Haddon w Winwick *Pet* from 13. *The Vicarage, 10 Hall Drive, Long Buckby, Northampton NN6 7QU* T: (01327) 842204 E: vicar.longbuckby@btinternet.com

COLLINGRIDGE, Susan Rachel. b 61. St Mary's Coll Dur BA 83. Cranmer Hall Dur 85. **d** 88 **p** 94. Par Dn Luton St Mary *St Alb* 88–93; PtO *St Alb* 93–94; NSM Parkham, Alwington, Buckland Brewer etc 94–98; TV Cove St Jo *Guildf* 98–03; V Guildf Ch Ch w St Martha-on-the-Hill 03–11; PtO *Ches* 11–14; NSM Antrobus 14–16; PtO *Portsm*

17–18; NSM Steep and Froxfield w Privett from 18. *18 Silent Garden Road, Liphook GU30 7GU* M: 07734-879224 E: susie.collingridge@gmail.com

COLLINGS, Ms Helen Mary. b 67. Warwick Univ BA 88 St Jo Coll Dur BA 06 Jes Coll Ox PGCE 90. Cranmer Hall Dur 04. **d** 06 **p** 07. C Ossett and Gawthorpe *Wakef* 06–09; P-in-c Sandal St Cath 09–14; *Leeds* 14–15; V Sutton w Cowling and Lothersdale from 15. *The Vicarage, Main Street, Sutton-in-Craven, Keighley BD20 7JS* T: (01535) 636679 M: 07708-066063 E: revd.helen.collings@gmail.com

COLLINGTON, Cameron James. b 68. Wycliffe Hall Ox BTh 01. **d** 01 **p** 02. C Ealing St Paul *Lon* 01–05; V Hammersmith St Simon from 05. *153 Blythe Road, London W14 0HL* T: (020) 7602 1043 E: cameron@stsimons.co.uk

COLLINGWOOD, Canon Christopher Paul. b 54. Birm Univ BMus 76 PGCE 77 Ox Univ BA 82 MA 87 K Coll Lon MA 01 PhD 07 LRSM 04. Ripon Coll Cuddesdon 80. **d** 83 **p** 84. C Tupsley *Heref* 83–86; Prec St Alb Abbey 86–90; V Bedford St Paul 90–97; Can Res and Prec Guildf Cathl 97–99; Hon C Loughton St Jo *Chelmsf* 99–09; Chapl Chigwell Sch Essex 99–09; Sen Tutor 01–09; R Minchinhampton w Box and Amberley *Glouc* 09–13; AD Stroud 11–13; Can Res and Chan York Minster from 13. *3 Minster Court, York YO1 7JJ* T: (01904) 557267 or 557204 E: christopherc@yorkminster.org

COLLINGWOOD, Deryck Laurence. b 50. St Jo Coll Cam BA 72. Edin Th Coll BD 85. **d** 85 **p** 85. Chapl Napier Poly *Edin* 85–88; C Edin Ch Ch 85–88; TV 88–89; Tutor Edin Th Coll 89–94; Asst P Edin St Hilda and Edin St Fillan 94–03; Chapl Edin Napier Univ 95–03; P-in-c Dalmahoy 03–06; R 06–16; rtd 16; LtO *Edin* from 18. *40 Hunter Avenue, Loanhead EH20 9SN* T: 0131-448 0240 E: dcollingwood131@btinternet.com

COLLINGWOOD, Graham Lewis. b 63. Open Univ BA 92 Ex Univ MA 98. St Steph Ho Ox 92. **d** 95 **p** 96. C Heavitree w Ex St Paul 95–97; CF 97–99; C St Marychurch *Ex* 99–00; C Cottingham *York* 00–02; Chapl RAF 02–11; V New Rossington *Sheff* 11–13; CF from 13. *c/o MOD Chaplains (Army)* T: (01264) 383430 F: 381824 E: rafglc@hotmail.co.uk

COLLINGWOOD, John Jeremy Raynham. b 37. Barrister 64 CCC Cam BA 60 MA 68 Lon Univ BD 78. Trin Coll Bris 75. **d** 78 **p** 79. C Henleaze *Bris* 78–80; P-in-c Clifton H Trin, St Andr and St Pet 80–81; V 81–91; RD Clifton 84–87; Bp's Officer for Miss and Evang 87–91; V Guildf Ch Ch 91–98; V Guildf Ch Ch w St Martha-on-the-Hill 98–02; RD Guildf 95–00; rtd 02; PtO *Chelmsf* from 08; *Eur* from 15. *The Old Manse, 55 Audley Road, Saffron Walden CB11 3HD* T: (01799) 529055 E: mporokoso@aol.com

COLLINS, Mrs Ann Maureen. b 62. St Pet Coll Ox BA 83 Cam Univ PGCE 84. St Jo Coll Nottm MA 13. **d** 13 **p** 14. C Wilford *S'well* 13–17; V Nottingham St Ann w Em from 18. *The Vicarage, 17 Robin Hood Chase, Nottingham NG3 4EY* M: 07988-079224 E: revmaureen@live.com

COLLINS, Barry Douglas. b 47. Kelham Th Coll 66. **d** 70 **p** 71. C Peel Green *Man* 70–73; C Salford St Phil w St Steph 73–75; R Blackley H Trin 75–79; PtO *Ripon* 80–82; *Pet* 83–93; *Cov* 85–93; *Ox* 93–97; P-in-c Bengeworth *Worc* 98–99; V 99–11; rtd 11. *9 Holbrook Avenue, Rugby CV21 2QG* T: (01788) 878993 E: barry2047@btinternet.com

COLLINS, Canon Cheryl Anne. b 62. Rob Coll Cam BA 85 MA 89 MCA 90. Ripon Coll Cuddesdon 91. **d** 93 **p** 94. C Sharrow St Andr *Sheff* 93–95; Chapl Sheff Univ 95–01; Hon C Endcliffe 96–01; P-in-c Barton *Ely* 01–10; P-in-c Coton 01–10; P-in-c Dry Drayton 01–10; RD Bourn 03–10; Miss P Red Lodge *St E* 10–12; P-in-c Chevington w Hargrave, Chedburgh w Depden etc 12–15; R 15–16; Acting RD Clare 14–16; P-in-c Sudbury and Chilton from 16; Hon Can St E Cathl from 15. *The Rectory, Christopher Lane, Sudbury CO10 2AS* E: cheryl62collins@btinternet.com

COLLINS, Christopher. b 46. K Coll Lon BSc 67 AKC 67 Pemb Coll Ox BA 70. St Steph Ho Ox 68. **d** 71 **p** 72. C Pennywell St Thos and Grindon St Oswald *CD Dur* 71–74; C Pallion, Millfield St Mary and Bishopwearmouth Gd Shep 74–76; C Harton Colliery 76–78; TV Winlaton 78–85; V Grangetown 85–11; rtd 12; PtO *Dur* from 15. *15 Linthorpe Avenue, Seaham SR7 7JW* T: 0191-581 7186 E: christopher_collins@lineone.net

COLLINS, Canon Christopher David. b 43. Sheff Univ BA(Econ) 64. Tyndale Hall Bris 65. **d** 68 **p** 69. C Rusholme H Trin *Man* 68–71; C Bushbury *Lich* 71–74; V Fairfield *Liv* 74–81; V Tunbridge Wells St Jo *Roch* 81–92; R Luton Ch Ch and Chapl Thames Gateway NHS Trust 92–05; Chapl Medway NHS Trust 92–99; RD Roch 94–00; P-in-c Cobham w Luddesdowne and Dode 05–08; Hon Can Roch Cathl 98–08; rtd 08. *2 Courtenay*

Gardens, Alphington, Exeter EX2 8UH T: (01392) 203975
E: canonchris@blueyonder.co.uk

COLLINS, Darren Victor. b 69. NTMTC. **d** 05 **p** 06. C Chingford SS Pet and Paul *Chelmsf* 05–07; Min Can St Alb Abbey 07–11; P-in-c Norton 11–13; V 13–16; TR Bp's Hatfield, Lemsford and N Mymms from 16. *The Rectory, 1 Fore Street, Hatfield AL9 5AN* T: (01707) 256638 M: 07453-624061 E: frdarren@yahoo.co.uk

COLLINS, Donard Michael. b 55. Oak Hill Th Coll BA 83. **d** 83 **p** 84. C Lurgan Ch the Redeemer *D & D* 83–87; I Ardmore w Craigavon 87–98; I Killowen *D & R* from 98. *St John's Rectory, 4 Laurel Hill, Coleraine BT51 3AT* T: (028) 7034 2629 E: revdonard@yahoo.co.uk

COLLINS, Earl Martin. b 60. QUB BA 82 PhD 90. **d** 94 **p** 95. Chapl Westcott Ho Cam 17–18; C Chesterton St Andr *Ely* 18–19; P-in-c Hove St Jo *Chich* from 19; CMD Officer from 19. *The Rectory, 119 Holland Road, Hove BN3 1JS* T: (01273) 725811 M: 07810-576853 E: earlcollins@hotmail.com

COLLINS, Elaine Judith. b 56. **d** 12 **p** 13. NSM The Bourne and Tilford *Guildf* from 12. *49 Carlton Road, Headley Down, Bordon GU35 8JT* T: (01428) 714385 E: elainecollins25@btinternet.com

COLLINS, Gary Steven. b 69. Ripon Coll Cuddesdon 14. **d** 16 **p** 17. C Reading St Jo *Ox* from 16. *69B Chapel Street, Thatcham RG18 4JS* T: (01635) 827526 M: 07986-901879

COLLINS, The Ven Gavin Andrew. b 66. Trin Hall Cam BA 89 MA 93. Trin Coll Bris BA 96 MA 97. **d** 97 **p** 98. C Cambridge St Barn *Ely* 97–02; V Chorleywood Ch Ch *St Alb* 02–11; RD Rickmansworth 06–11; Hon Can St Alb 09–11; Adn The Meon *Portsm* from 11; Warden of Readers from 14. *Victoria Lodge, 36 Osborn Road, Fareham PO16 7DS* T: (01329) 608895 E: gavin-collins@supanet.com *or* admeon@portsmouth.anglican.org

COLLINS, Mrs Helen Marie. b 83. Magd Coll Ox BA 04 K Coll Lon MA 08. Trin Coll Bris 10. **d** 12 **p** 13. C Bris Ch the Servant Stockwood 12–15; Dioc Dir of Ords 15–17; Warden of Readers 15–17; NSM Hengrove 16–17; Tutor Trin Coll Bris from 17. *Trinity College, Stoke Hill, Bristol BS9 1JP* T: 0117-968 2803 E: h.collins@trinitycollegebristol.ac.uk

COLLINS, Canon Ian Geoffrey. b 37. Hull Univ BA 60 CertEd. Sarum Th Coll 60. **d** 62 **p** 63. C Gainsborough All SS *Linc* 62–65; Min Can Windsor 65–81; Succ Windsor 67–81; R Kirkby in Ashfield *S'well* 81–85; Can Res *S'well* Minster 85–02; P-in-c Edingley w Halam 91–00; rtd 02. *2 Marston Moor Road, Newark NG24 2GN* T: (01636) 702866 E: iancollins1908@outlook.com

COLLINS, John Gilbert. b 32. S'wark Ord Course 67. **d** 71 **p** 72. C Coulsdon St Jo *S'wark* 71–75; Chapl St Fran Hosp Haywards Heath 75–84; Chapl Hurstwood Park Hosp Haywards Heath 75–84; R Stedham w Iping, Elsted and Treyford-cum-Didling *Chich* 84–92; rtd 92; PtO *Chich* 94–00. *Kings Lodge Nursing Home, Main Road, Bosham, Chichester PO18 8PN* M: 07421-388541

COLLINS, Preb John Theodore Cameron Bucke. b 25. Clare Coll Cam BA 49 MA 52. Ridley Hall Cam 49. **d** 51 **p** 52. C St Marylebone All So w SS Pet and Jo *Lon* 51–57; V Gillingham St Mark *Roch* 57–71; Chapl Medway Hosp Gillingham 70–71; V Canford Magna *Sarum* 71–80; RD Wimborne 79–80; V Brompton H Trin w Onslow Square St Paul *Lon* 80–85; C 85–89; AD Chelsea 84–88; Preb St Paul's Cathl 85–89; rtd 89; PtO *Lon* 89–90; *Win* 89–97. *3 Laundry Cottages, Adlestrop Park, Adlestrop, Moreton-in-Marsh GL56 0YN* T: (01608) 658605 E: jtcbcollins@gmail.com

COLLINS, John William Michael. b 54. Bp Otter Coll 95. **d** 98 **p** 07. NSM S Patcham *Chich* 98–06; NSM Moulsecoomb from 06. *2 Buxted Rise, Brighton BN1 8FG* T: (01273) 509388

COLLINS, Mrs Joy Christina. b 53. K Coll Lon MA. STETS. **d** 14 **p** 15. NSM Westfield and Guestling *Chich* from 14. *23 Croft Road, Hastings TN34 3HP* T: (01424) 447643

COLLINS, Ms Linda Kathleen. b 56. Girton Coll Cam BA 77 MA 80. Bris Univ PGCE 78. WMMTC 99. **d** 02 **p** 03. C Harborne St Pet *Birm* 02–05; C Cen Wolverhampton *Lich* 05–09; TV 09–10; Chapl K Sch Wolv and St Pet Colleg Sch Wolv 05–10; C Lich St Mich w St Mary and Wall 10–19; rtd 19. *17 Leyfields, Lichfield WS13 7NJ* M: 07985-033476 E: lindacollins@hotmail.co.uk

COLLINS, Mrs Lindsay Rosemary Faith. b 70. K Coll Lon BD 91 AKC 91 PGCE 92. Ripon Coll Cuddesdon MTh 95. **d** 97 **p** 98. C Witney *Ox* 97–99; NSM 00–01; Chapl Cokethorpe Sch Witney 00–01; Chapl and Hd RE St Paul's Girls' Sch Hammersmith 01–04; Chapl K Coll Sch Wimbledon 04–10; Hon C Barnes *S'wark* 04–10; Chapl Sherborne Sch 10–17; PtO *B & W* 13–18; Chapl K Sch Cant from 17. *The King's School, 25 The Precincts, Canterbury CT1 2ES* T: (01227) 595501 E: lrfcollins@gmail.com

COLLINS, Martin. *See* COLLINS, William Francis Martin

COLLINS, Maureen. *See* COLLINS, Ann Maureen

COLLINS, Canon Norman Hilary. b 33. Mert Coll Ox BA 55 MA 58. Wells Th Coll 58. **d** 60 **p** 61. C Ystrad Mynach *Llan* 60–62; C Gelligaer 62–67; V Maerdy 67–77; R Penarth w Lavernock 77–98; RD Penarth and Barry 87–98; Can Llan Cathl 92–98; rtd 98; PtO *Llan* from 04. *4 Llys Steffan, Llantwit Major CF61 2UF* T: (01446) 794976

COLLINS, Paul Michael. b 71. St Jo Coll Nottm 06. **d** 08 **p** 09. C Chenies and Lt Chalfont, Latimer and Flaunden *Ox* 08–10; Chapl RAF 11–14; C Warfield *Ox* 14–17; C Chich St Pancras and St Jo from 17. *12 Palmers Field Avenue, Chichester PO19 6UW* M: 07973-838003 E: pmcollins2@yahoo.co.uk *or* paul@immanuelchichester.com

COLLINS, Peter Graham. b 60. Anglia Ruskin Univ MA 07. EMMTC 99 Westcott Ho Cam 05. **d** 07 **p** 08. C S Lawres Gp *Linc* 07–11; P-in-c Upper Wreake *Leic* 11–14; R Hykeham *Linc* from 14. *The Rectory, Mill Lane, North Hykeham, Lincoln LN6 9PA* M: 07896-066302 E: revdpeter@msn.com

COLLINS, Canon Philip Howard Norton. b 50. AKC 73. St Aug Coll Cant 73. **d** 74 **p** 75. C Stamford Hill St Thos *Lon* 74–78; C Upwood w Gt and Lt Raveley *Ely* 78–81; C Ramsey 78–81; R Leverington 81–92; P-in-c Wisbech St Mary 89–92; RD Wisbech 90–92; TR Whittlesey and Pondersbridge 92–95; TR Whittlesey, Pondersbridge and Coates 95–02; R New Alresford w Ovington and Itchen Stoke *Win* 02–07; R Arle Valley 07–16; RD Alresford 09–16; Hon Can Win Cathl 14–16; rtd 16; PtO *Win* from 17. *9 River Close, Four Marks, Alton GU34 5XB* T: (01420) 563489 E: philcollinsrector@yahoo.co.uk

COLLINS, Roger Richardson. b 48. Birm Univ BPhil 88. WMMTC 78. **d** 81 **p** 82. NSM Cotteridge *Birm* from 81. *6 Chesterfield Court, Middleton Hall Road, Birmingham B30 1AF* T: 0121-459 4009

COLLINS, Prof Ross Nicoll Ferguson. b 64. Edin Univ MA 87 Ven English Coll Rome 91 Pontifical Gregorian Univ 91. Ripon Coll Cuddesdon BA 91 MA 13. **d** 92 **p** 93. C Goring w S Stoke *Ox* 92–96; P-in-c N Leigh 96–01; TR Barnes *S'wark* 01–10; NSM Sherborne w Castleton, Lillington and Longburton *Sarum* 10–17; Prof Nat Univ Asunción Paraguay from 18. *Le Paraguayen 4D, Profesor Manuel Riquelme, Asunción, Paraguay* M: (00595) 9-8133 2732 E: rossnfcollins@btinternet.com

COLLINS, Thomas Daniel. b 82. Ox Univ MEng 05 Surrey Univ MSc 07. Trin Coll Bris 16. **d** 18 **p** 19. C Balham Hill Ascension *S'wark* from 18. *124 Alderbrook Road, London SW12 8AA* M: 07947-270785 E: who2tom@hotmail.com

COLLINS, Timothy Paul. b 58. Open Univ BA 92. SWMTC 15. **d** 18. C Dawlish w Holcombe, Cofton and Starcross *Ex* from 18. *14 Shillingate Close, Dawlish EX7 9SQ* T: (01626) 862383 E: revtimpaul@btinternet.com

COLLINS, Canon William Francis Martin. b 43. St Cath Coll Cam BA 66 MA 70. Cuddesdon Coll 68. **d** 70 **p** 71. C Man Victoria Park 70–73; P-in-c Ancoats 73–78; Chapl Abraham Moss Cen 78–91; Hon C Cheetham Hill 81–84; Chs' FE Officer for Gtr Man 84–91; V Norbury *Ches* 91–98; Hon Can Ches Cathl 05–08; rtd 08. *9 Milldale Avenue, Buxton SK17 9BE* T: (01298) 74906 M: 07866-505589 E: martin.collins1@o2.co.uk

COLLINS, Winfield St Clair. b 41. Univ of W Indies BA 83 Man Univ BA 88 MEd 91. Codrington Coll Barbados. **d** 76 **p** 76. Asst Chapl HM Pris Wakef 76; C St Jo Barbados 76; P-in-c St Mark and St Cath 77–84; Asst Chapl HM Pris Wandsworth 85; Chapl HM YOI Thorn Cross 85–91; Chapl HM Pris Pentonville 91–01; Can Res Barbados 01–02; rtd 02; PtO *Lon* 09–18. *92 Barclay Road, London N18 1EQ* T: (020) 8245 4145

COLLINSON, Mrs Amanda. b 74. Luton Univ BA 96. Ripon Coll Cuddesdon 07. **d** 09 **p** 10. C Catherington and Clanfield *Portsm* 09–13; P-in-c Gurnard 13–14; P-in-c Cowes St Faith 13–14; V Gurnard w Cowes St Faith from 14; P-in-c Northwood 13–14; R from 14; AD Is of Wight from 19. *The Rectory, Chawton Lane, Cowes PO31 8PR* T: (01983) 294913 E: amandacollinson01@gmail.com

COLLINSON, Canon Mark Peter Charles. b 68. City Univ BSc 90 Fitzw Coll Cam BA 97 MA 01 Vrije Univ Amsterdam MA 10. Ridley Hall Cam 95. **d** 98 **p** 99. C Ashton-upon-Mersey St Mary Magd *Ches* 98–01; Chapl Amsterdam w Den Helder and Heiloo *Eur* 01–15; Hon Can 12–15; Can Res Win Cathl from 15; Prin Win Sch of Miss from 15; PtO *Eur* from 18. T: (01962) 710970 M: 07469-859517 E: mark.collinson@winchester.anglican.org

COLLISON, Roger Alfred. b 36. St Jo Coll Dur BA 58. Cranmer Hall Dur 60. **d** 63 **p** 97. C Liv St Mich 63–64; NSM Ormside *Carl* 97–06; NSM Appleby 97–06; PtO from 06. *1 Caesar's View, Appleby-in-Westmorland CA16 6SH* T: (017683) 52886

COLLIS, Janet Mary. b 57. Plymouth Poly BA 78 PhD 83 SS Mark & Jo Univ Coll Plymouth MA 03. SWMTC 08. **d** 10 **p** 11. NSM Plympton St Mary *Ex* 10–12; Chapl Plymouth Community Healthcare Trust from 12; Chapl Plymouth Hosps NHS Trust from 13. *Department of Pastoral and Spiritual Care, Level 7, Derriford Hospital, Derriford Road, Derriford, Plymouth PL6 8DH* T: (01752) 792313 E: j.collis@nhs.net

COLLIS, Canon Jonathan. b 69. Selw Coll Cam BA 91 MA 94. Aston Tr Scheme 96 Westcott Ho Cam 97. **d** 99 **p** 00. C St Neots *Ely* 99–02; Chapl Jes Coll Cam 02–09; V Thorpe Bay *Chelmsf* from 09; P-in-c N Shoebury 16–17; RD Southend from 15; Hon Can Chelmsf Cathl from 15. *The Vicarage, 88 Tyrone Road, Southend-on-Sea SS1 3HB* T: (01702) 587597 E: jonathan.collis@cantab.net

COLLIS, Canon Stephen Thomas. b 47. MHCIMA 94. Cranmer Hall Dur 80. **d** 82 **p** 83. C Crewe All SS and St Paul *Ches* 82–84; C Wilmslow 84–86 and 95–98; Chapl RAF 86–95; P-in-c Barthomley *Ches* 98–00; S Cheshire Ind Chapl 98–00; Chapl Abu Dhabi UAE 00–02; Dean St Paul's Cathl and Chapl Nicosia 02–09; Adn Cyprus 06–09; Hon Can Cyprus and the Gulf from 09; R Montrose and Inverbervie *Bre* 09–12; rtd 12; PtO *Bre* 12–16; *Eur* from 12. *27 Townfoot Park, Brampton CA8 1RZ* T: (01697) 508158 M: 07791-618320 E: collis.steve@btinternet.com *or* angushasinview@me.com

COLLISHAW, Ashley Stuart. b 66. Wycliffe Hall Ox 03. **d** 05 **p** 06. C Worc City 05–09; Hon C Cheltenham H Trin and St Paul *Glouc* 09–15; 1c12 15–19; V Charlton Kings H Apostles from 19; P-in-c Cheltenham St Mich from 19. *7 Cirencester Road, Charlton Kings, Cheltenham GL53 8EP* T: (01242) 237882 M: 07932-045598 E: ashley.collishaw@holyapostles.org.uk

COLLISON, Christopher John. b 48. Oak Hill Th Coll 68. **d** 72 **p** 73. C Cromer *Nor* 72–75; C Costessey 76–78; V 87–95; C Heckmondwike *Wakef* 78–79; P-in-c Shepley and Dioc Communications Officer 79–83; Chapl Flushing Miss to Seamen *Eur* 83–85; Asst Min Sec Miss to Seamen 85–87; C St Mich Paternoster Royal *Lon* 85–87; P-in-c Swainsthorpe w Newton Flotman *Nor* 95–97; TV Newton Flotman, Swainsthorpe, Tasburgh, etc 98–02; R Henfield w Shermanbury and Woodmancote *Chich* 02–09; Dioc Evang Officer *Nor* 95–01; RD Hurst *Chich* 04–09; P-in-c Hartlepool St Hilda *Dur* 09–15; AD Hartlepool 10–13; Chapl Miss to Seafarers 09–15; rtd 15; PtO *Dur* 17–18. *17 Blatchington Road, Seaford BN25 2AB* M: 07931-646745 E: cjc72@btinternet.com

COLLISON, Ms Elizabeth. b 38. Man Univ CertEd 58. NOC 85. **d** 88 **p** 94. C Huyton St Mich *Liv* 88–94; C Rainhill 94–05; rtd 05; PtO *Liv* from 16. *25 Lowther Drive, Rainhill, Prescot L35 0NG* T: 0151-426 3853 E: liz_collison@yahoo.co.uk

COLLYER, David John. b 38. Keble Coll Ox BA 61 MA 86. Westcott Ho Cam 61. **d** 63 **p** 64. C Perry Beeches *Birm* 63–65; P-in-c Deritend 66–70; Bp's Chapl for Special Youth Work 65–70; Bp's Youth Chapl and Dioc Youth Officer 70–73; R Northfield 73–78; Hon Chapl Birm Cathl 78–81; Hon C Birm St Geo 81–86; V Handsworth St Andr 86–97; Dioc Development Officer 97–01; Hon Can Birm Cathl 95–06; PtO from 01. *19 Birch Close, Bournville, Birmingham B30 1NA*

COLLYER, Leon John. b 72. SS Hild & Bede Coll Dur BSc 95 Leeds Univ BA 00. Coll of Resurr Mirfield 98. **d** 01 **p** 02. C Airedale w Fryston *Wakef* 01–04; P-in-c Crofton and Warmfield 04–10; C Reading St Agnes w St Paul and St Barn *Ox* 10–19; NSM The Saints *St E* from 19. *Parsonage House, Low Street, Ilketshall St Margaret, Bungay NR35 1QZ* M: 07714-986462 E: leoncollyer@gmail.com

COLMAN, Susan. b 59. **d** 12 **p** 13. NSM Onslow Square and S Kensington St Aug *Lon* from 12; PtO *Win* from 14. *Address temp unknown* E: sue.colman@htb.org

COLMER, Andrew John. b 68. De Montfort Univ Leic BSc 90. St Jo Coll Nottm MA 96 LTh 97. **d** 97 **p** 98. C Roby *Liv* 97–01; C Litherland St Andr 01–02; P-in-c Liv All So Springwood 02–10; Chapl Enterprise S Liv Academy 10–19; V Childwall All SS *Liv* from 19. *All Saints' Vicarage, Childwall Abbey Road, Liverpool L16 0JW* E: andrewcolmer@hotmail.co.uk

COLMER, The Ven Malcolm John. b 45. Sussex Univ MSc 67. St Jo Coll Nottm BA 73. **d** 73 **p** 74. C Egham *Guildf* 73–76; C Chadwell *Chelmsf* 76–79; V S Malling *Chich* 79–85; V Hornsey Rise St Mary w St Steph *Lon* 85–87; TR Hornsey Rise Whitehall Park Team 87–96; AD Islington 90–94; Adn Middx 96–05; Adn Heref 05–10; Can Res Heref Cathl 05–10; rtd 10; PtO *St D* 12–15. *59 Station Road, Pershore WR10 1PE* T: (01386) 556583

COLPUS (née EDWARDS), Mrs Anita Carolyn. b 71. Trin Coll Bris 01. **d** 03 **p** 04. C Notting Hill St Pet *Lon* 03–06; NSM Sittingbourne St Mary and St Mich *Cant* 07–10; P-in-c Reigate St Luke *S'wark* 10–17; V from 17; AD Reigate from 19; Jt Dir of IME Croydon Area from 13. *St Luke's Church,*

5 Church Road, Reigate RH2 8HY T: (01737) 243846 E: anitacolpus@tesco.net

COLSTON, Canon John Edward. b 43. Open Univ BA 91 Leeds Univ MA 94. Lich Th Coll 65. **d** 68 **p** 69. C Bromsgrove All SS *Worc* 68–71; C Tettenhall Wood *Lich* 71–74; V Alrewas 74–88; V Wychnor 74–88; R Ainderby Steeple w Yafforth and Kirby Wiske etc *Ripon* 88–95; V High Harrogate Ch Ch 95–07; Warden of Readers 90–96; AD Harrogate 01–05; Hon Can Ripon Cathl 06–07; rtd 08; PtO *Leeds* from 14. *15 Sycamore Road, Ripon HG4 2LR* T: (01765) 600747 E: john.colston@yahoo.co.uk

COLTON, Mrs Christine Ann. b 56. Univ of Wales (Cardiff) BA 00. St Mich Coll Llan 01. **d** 06 **p** 07. NSM Cen Cardiff *Llan* 06–07; NSM Radyr 07–13; PtO *S'wark* 14; P-in-c Kingswood from 14. *St Mark's Vicarage, 8 Alma Road, Reigate RH2 0DA* T: (01737) 241161 M: 07941-011337 E: chriscolton@ntlworld.com

COLTON, Christopher Francis. b 52. **d** 12 **p** 14. NSM Holme-in-Cliviger w Worsthorne *Blackb* 12–13; NSM Oswaldtwistle 13–16; PtO 16–17. *357 Newbrook Road, Atherton, Manchester M46 9HN* E: fr.chriscolton@gmail.com

COLTON, Martin Philip. b 67. Sheff Univ BMus 89 MMus 92 FRCO 92 Open Univ PGCE 97. St Mich Coll Llan BA 03. **d** 03 **p** 04. C Whitchurch *Llan* 03–06; TV Canton Cardiff 06–14; V Reigate St Mark *S'wark* from 14. *St Mark's Vicarage, 8 Alma Road, Reigate RH2 0DA* T: (01737) 241161 E: martin.colton@ntlworld.com

✠**COLTON, The Rt Revd William Paul.** b 60. NUI BCL 81 TCD MPhil 87 Univ of Wales (Cardiff) LLM 06 Cardiff Univ PhD 13. **d** 84 **p** 85 **c** 99. C Lisburn St Paul *Conn* 84–87; Bp's Dom Chapl 85–90; V Choral Belf Cathl 87–90; Min Can Belf Cathl 89–90; PV, Registrar and Chapter Clerk Ch Ch Cathl Dub *D & G* 90–95; I Castleknock and Mulhuddart w Clonsilla 90–99; Co-ord Protestant Relig Progr RTE 93–99; Hon Chapl Actors' Ch Union 94–96; Area Chapl (Ireland) Actors' Ch Union 96–97; Can Ch Ch Cathl Dublin *D & G* 97–99; Bp C, C & R from 99. *St Nicholas' House, 14 Cove Street, Cork, Republic of Ireland* T: (00353) (21) 500 5080 F: 432 0960 E: bishop@corkchurchofireland.com

COLVER, Mrs Sarah Marianne. b 63. RGN 85. Westcott Ho Cam. **d** 13 **p** 14. C Aston cum Aughton w Swallownest and Ulley *Sheff* 13–16; C Sheff St Mark Broomhill from 16. *9 Betjeman Gardens, Sheffield S10 3FW* M: 07975-689403 E: smcolver@hotmail.com *or* sarah.colver@sheffield.anglican.org

COLWELL, Ms Katherine Elizabeth. b 57. Man Univ BA 78 Nottm Univ MA 08 Man Poly PGCE 79. EMMTC 05. **d** 08 **p** 09. C Barton upon Humber *Linc* 08–11; P-in-c Kirton in Lindsey w Manton from 11; P-in-c Bishop Norton, Waddingham and Snitterby from 11; P-in-c Grayingham from 11. *The Vicarage, 28 South Cliff Road, Kirton Lindsey, Gainsborough DN21 4NR* T: (01652) 640552 E: katherine.colwell@btinternet.com

COLWILL, Canon James Patrick (Jay). b 68. Man Poly BA 91. St Jo Coll Nottm BTh 93 MA 94. **d** 94 **p** 95. C Reading St Agnes w St Paul *Ox* 94–97; C Easthampstead 97–03; V Orpington Ch Ch *Roch* 03–18; AD Orpington 10–14; Dir Miss and Can Res S'wark Cathl from 18. *483A Southwark Park Road, London SE16 2JP* M: 07952-988312 E: jay.colwill@southwark.anglican.org

COLYER, Kevin Peter. b 70. CMS 16. **d** 18 **p** 19. C Furze Platt *Ox* from 18. *150 Kingfisher Drive, Woodley, Reading RG5 3LQ* M: 07967-105273 E: kevin@thecolyers.net

COMBE, Edward Charles. b 40. Man Univ MSc PhD QUB DSc. NOC. **d** 89 **p** 90. NSM Broadheath *Ches* 89–94; USA from 94. *1760 Southwind Lane, Maplewood MN 55109, USA* T: (001) (651) 773 3066 E: combe001@gold.tc.umn.edu

COMBE, The Very Revd John Charles. b 33. TCD BA 53 MA 56 BD 57 MLitt 65 PhD 70. **d** 56 **p** 57. C Cork St Luke w St Ann *C, C & R* 56–58; C Ballynafeigh St Jude *D & D* 58–61; I Crinken *D & G* 61–66; Hon Clerical V Ch Ch Cathl Dublin 63–66; C Belfast St Bart *Conn* 66–70; I Belfast St Barn 70–74; I Portadown St Mark *Arm* 74–84; I Arm St Mark w Aghavilly 84–90; Can Arm Cathl 85–90; Dean Kilmore *K, E & A* 90–96; I Kilmore w Ballintemple, Kildallan etc 90–96; rtd 96. *24 Kensington Park, Maxwell Road, Bangor BT20 3RF* T: (028) 9146 6123

COMBER, The Ven Anthony James. b 27. Leeds Univ BSc 49 MSc 52. St Chad's Coll Dur 53. **d** 56 **p** 57. C Manston *Ripon* 56–60; V Oulton 60–69; V Hunslet St Mary 69–77; RD Armley 72–75 and 79–81; R Farnley 77–82; Hon Can Ripon Cathl 80–92; Adn Leeds 82–92; rtd 92; PtO *Bradf* 93–99; *Ripon* 92–14; *Leeds* from 14. *28 Blayds Garth, Woodlesford, Leeds LS26 8WN* T: 0113-288 0489 M: 07840-763818 E: tony.comber@btinternet.com *or* tonycomber20@gmail.com

COMBES, The Ven Roger Matthew. b 47. K Coll Lon LLB 69. Ridley Hall Cam 72. **d** 74 **p** 75. C Onslow Square St Paul *Lon* 74–77; C Brompton H Trin 76–77; C Cambridge H Sepulchre w All SS *Ely* 77–86; R Silverhill St Matt *Chich* 86–03; RD Hastings 98–02; Adn Horsham 03–14; rtd 14; PtO *Chich* from 14. *3 Aldingbourne Close, Ifield, Crawley RH11 0QJ* T: (01293) 538161 E: rogercombes@gmail.com

COMER, Michael John. b 30. St Mich Coll Llan 79. **d** 81 **p** 82. C Bistre *St As* 81–84; R Llanfyllin and Bwlchycibau 84–91; V Hattersley *Ches* 91–94; rtd 94; PtO *St As* from 09. *8 Cae Camlas, Newtown SY16 2HT* T: (01686) 624557 E: michaelcomer@btinternet.com

COMERFORD, Canon Patrick. b 52. Pontifical Univ Maynooth BD 87 FRSAI 87. CITC 99. **d** 00 **p** 01. NSM Dublin Whitechurch *D & G* 00–17; Dir Spiritual Formation CITC 06–11; Lect 11–17; Can Ch Ch Cathl Dublin *D & G* 07–17; Dir CME and P-in-c Rathkeale w Askeaton, Kilcornan and Kilnaughtin *L & K* from 17; Can Limerick Cathl from 17. *75 Glenvara Park, Knocklyon, Dublin 16, D16 RR29, Republic of Ireland* T: (00353) (1) 495 0934 M: 87-663 5116 E: revpatrickcomerford@gmail.com

COMFORT, Alan. b 64. Ridley Hall Cam 91. **d** 94 **p** 95. C Chadwell Heath *Chelmsf* 94–97; C Buckhurst Hill 97–98; TV 98–03; V Loughton St Mary 03–09; TR Gt Baddow 09–10; V Walthamstow St Jo 10–14; R Standon and The Mundens w Sacombe *St Alb* 14–18; V Upper Holloway *Lon* from 18. *St John's Vicarage, 51 Tytherton Road, London N19 4PZ* E: alancomfort11@gmail.com

COMLEY, Thomas Hedges. b 36. Leeds Univ BA 62. Coll of Resurr Mirfield 62. **d** 64 **p** 65. C Leadgate *Dur* 64–67; C Shirley *Birm* 67–71; V Smethwick St Alb 71–76; PtO 76–82; V N Wembley St Cuth *Lon* 82–92; V Taddington, Chelmorton and Flagg, and Monyash *Derby* 92–01; rtd 01; PtO *Derby* from 01. *19 Wentworth Avenue, Walton, Chesterfield S40 3JB* T: (01246) 270911

COMMIN, Robert William. b 47. Cape Town Univ BA 79. St Paul's Coll Grahamstown. **d** 70 **p** 71. S Africa 70–80 and from 89; Chapl Loretto Sch Musselburgh 80–84; TV Thetford *Nor* 84–89. *42 Earl Street, Woodstock, 7925 South Africa* M: (0027) 82-202 5303 E: bcommin@netactive.co.za

COMPTON, Barry Charles Chittenden. b 33. Linc Th Coll 60. **d** 62 **p** 63. C Beddington *S'wark* 62–65; C Limpsfield and Titsey 66–68; Hon C 71–94; rtd 94; R Ridley *Roch* 69–70; R Ash 69–70; PtO *S'wark* 70–16; *Roch* from 11. *14 Hallsland Way, Oxted RH8 9AL* T: (01883) 714896 F: 722842 E: bcccompton@aol.com

CONALTY, The Ven Julie Anne. b 63. SEITE. **d** 99 **p** 00. NSM E Wickham *S'wark* 99–04; NSM Charlton 04–10; C Plumstead Common 10–12; V Erith Ch Ch *Roch* 12–17; AD Erith 14–17; Bp's Adv for Ord Women's Min 13–17; Hon Can Roch Cathl 16–17; Adn Tonbridge from 17. *The Archdeaconry, 8 Mill Stream Rise, Leigh, Tonbridge TN11 9FD* T: (01732) 833840 M: 07511-900265 E: archdeacon.tonbridge@rochester.anglican.org

CONANT, Alan Richard. b 67. Kent Univ BSc 89 PhD 92. St Jo Coll Nottm 09. **d** 11 **p** 12. C Maghull and Melling *Liv* 11–14; V Rainhill from 14. *The Vicarage, 1 View Road, Rainhill, Prescot L35 0LE* T: 0151-426 4666 E: revd_al@btinternet.com

CONANT, Fane Charles. b 46. Oak Hill Th Coll 83. **d** 85 **p** 86. C Hoole *Ches* 85–89; V Kelsall 89–01; P-in-c Seer Green and Jordans *Ox* 01–06; rtd 06; PtO *Heref* from 06; Partner Evang Luis Palau Evang Assn from 06. *1 Spring Bank, Shrewsbury Road, Church Stretton SY6 6HA* T: (01694) 722610 E: fanesue@aol.com

CONANT (née PARR), Mrs Vanessa Caroline. b 78. Lanc Univ BA 00. Trin Coll Bris BA 07. **d** 08 **p** 09. C Hoddesdon *St Alb* 08–11; C Edin St Paul and St Geo 11–15; TR Walthamstow *Chelmsf* from 15. *The Rectory, 117 Church Hill, London E17 3BD* T: (020) 3722 2041 M: 07811-444435 E: vcconant@gmail.com

CONAWAY, Barry Raymond. b 41. CertEd 69 Nottm Univ BEd 70. Sarum & Wells Th Coll 86. **d** 88 **p** 89. C Ross w Brampton Abbotts, Bridstow and Peterstow *Heref* 88–91; R Bishop's Frome w Castle Frome and Fromes Hill 91–96; P-in-c Acton Beauchamp and Evesbatch w Stanford Bishop 91–96; P-in-c Charminster and Stinsford *Sarum* 96–01; rtd 01; PtO *Glouc* 01–02; *Sarum* 03–11. *9 Constable Way, West Harnham, Salisbury SP2 8LN* T: (01722) 334870 E: mcbonaway@gmail.com

CONDER, Paul Collingwood Nelson. b 33. St Jo Coll Cam BA 56 MA 60. Ridley Hall Cam 56. **d** 58 **p** 59. C Grassendale *Liv* 58–61; Tutor St Jo Coll Dur 61–67; R Sutton *Liv* 67–74; TR 74–75; V Thames Ditton *Guildf* 75–86; RD Emly 82–86; V Blundellsands St Mich *Liv* 86–99; rtd 99; PtO *York* 00–15; *Ches* from 14. *21 Bowling Green Court, Brook Street, Chester CH1 3DP* T: (01244) 460151 E: pconder787@gmail.com

✠**CONDRY, The Rt Revd Edward Francis.** b 53. UEA BA 74 Ex Coll Ox BLitt 77 DPhil 80 Open Univ MBA 02. Linc Th Coll 80. **d** 82 **p** 83 **c** 12. C Weston Favell *Pet* 82–85; V Bloxham w Milcombe and S Newington *Ox* 85–93; TR Rugby *Cov* 93–02; Can Res Cant Cathl 02–12; Dir Post-Ord Tr 02–06; Treas and Dir of Educn 06–12; Area Bp Ramsbury *Sarum* 12–18; Can and Preb Sarum Cathl 12–18; rtd 18; Hon Asst Bp Pet from 18. *The Meadow, 16 Westhorpe Lane, Byfield, Daventry NN11 6XB* T: (01327) 438729

CONEY, Joanna Margery. b 39. Culham Coll of Educn CertEd 75 Open Univ BA 83. Ox Min Course 90. **d** 93 **p** 94. C Wolvercote w Summertown *Ox* 93–97; Hon C New Marston 97–06; Hon C Wolvercote w Summertown 06–07; Hon C Wolvercote 07–10; OLM Tr Officer (Ox Adnry) 97–00; Dioc Portfolio Officer 00–04; rtd 04; Dioc Adv to Lic Lay Min *Ox* 02–09; NSM Voc Adv from 09; Min Prov (Eur) Third Order SSF 09–12; Hon C Wolvercote and Wytham *Ox* 10–17; PtO from 17. *4 Rowland Close, Wolvercote, Oxford OX2 8PW* T/F: (01865) 556456 E: joanna.coney@gmail.com

CONEYS, Canon Stephen John. b 61. Sheff Univ LLB 82. St Jo Coll Nottm 87. **d** 90 **p** 91. C Plymouth Em w Efford *Ex* 90–92; C Plymouth Em, Efford and Laira 93–94; TV Whitstable *Cant* 94–02; TR 02–17; Jt AD Reculver 12–17; Dioc Miss and Growth Adv from 17; Hon Can Cant Cathl from 08. *Diocesan House, Lady Wootton's Green, Canterbury CT1 1NQ* T: (01227) 459401 E: steveconeys@btinternet.com

CONEYS, Mrs Victoria Susan. b 60. St Mary's Coll Dur BA 83. St Aug Coll of Th 14. **d** 17 **p** 18. C Wantsum Gp *Cant* from 17. *1 Warwick Drive, Ramsgate CT11 0JP* M: 07583-684338 E: vickysconeys@hotmail.com

CONGDON, John Jameson. b 30. St Edm Hall Ox BA 53 MA 57. Wycliffe Hall Ox 53. **d** 55 **p** 56. C Aspley *S'well* 55–58; C-in-c Woodthorpe CD 58–63; V Woodthorpe 63–69; V Spring Grove St Mary *Lon* 70–84; V Woodley St Jo the Ev *Ox* 84–89; Chapl W Middx Univ Hosp Isleworth 95–99; rtd 95; PtO *Lon* from 95; *Ox* 06–09. *23 Pates Manor Drive, Feltham TW14 8JJ* T: (020) 8893 1823 E: john.congdon@btinternet.com

CONLIN, Tiffany Jane Kate. b 71. K Coll Lon BA 93 MA 94 PhD 00 AKC 93. Westcott Ho Cam 03. **d** 05 **p** 06. C Wisbech St Aug and Wisbech SS Pet and Paul *Ely* 05–08; Chapl Fitzw Coll Cam 08–11; Dir Past Studies Westcott Ho Cam 11–14; Chapl HM Pris Wakef 15–18; Chapl HM Pris Northd from 18. *HM Prison Northumberland, Acklington, Morpeth NE65 9XG* T: (01670) 762300

CONLON, Shaun. b 69. Birm Univ BA 90. Ripon Coll Cuddesdon 91. **d** 93 **p** 94. C Castle Bromwich SS Mary and Marg *Birm* 93–97; C Hockerill *St Alb* 97–00; St Mary-at-Latton *Chelmsf* 00–07; V Prittlewell 07–14; P-in-c Ashton-upon-Mersey St Martin *Ches* from 14. *St Martin's Rectory, 367 Glebelands Road, Sale M33 5GG* T: 0161-973 4204

CONN, Alistair Aberdein. b 37. Down Coll Cam BA 60 MA 64. Linc Th Coll 60. **d** 62 **p** 63. C W Hartlepool St Paul *Dur* 62–65; Uganda 65–66; Chapl Shrewsbury Sch 66–73; R Coupar Angus *St And* 73–78; V Ravenshead *S'well* 78–93; RD Newstead 90–93; R Collingham w S Scarle and Besthorpe and Girton 93–02; RD Newark 95–02; rtd 02; PtO *S'well* 02–17. *17 Beacon Heights, Newark NG24 2JS* T: (01636) 706291

CONN, Christopher Kenneth. b 83. Dur Univ BSc 05. Oak Hill Th Coll BA 15. **d** 15 **p** 16. C Laleham *Lon* 15–18; C Fulwood Ch Ch *Sheff* from 18. *Christ Church Fulwood, Canterbury Avenue, Sheffield S10 3RT* T: 0114-230 1911 M: 07917-191303 E: c.conn@hotmail.co.uk

CONNELL, Anthony. **d** 12. NSM Dolton *Ex* 12–15; NSM Iddesleigh w Dowland 12–15; NSM Monkokehampton 12–15; NSM Dolton, Dowland, Iddesleigh etc from 15. *Long Parks, Coldridge, Crediton EX17 6BA* E: tonyandjeanconnell@gmail.com

CONNELL, Clare. *See* CONNELL, Penelope Clare

CONNELL, John Richard. b 63. K Coll Lon BD 84. St Mich Coll Llan 92. **d** 94 **p** 96. C Caldicot *Mon* 94–97; C Risca 97–00; V Llantilio Pertholey w Bettws Chpl etc 00–05; P-in-c Wokingham St Paul *Ox* 05–11; Chapl R Berks NHS Foundn Trust 11–12; R Chingford SS Pet and Paul *Chelmsf* 12–15; P-in-c Rumney *Mon* from 15; AD Bassaleg from 17. *St Augustine's Vicarage, 702 Newport Road, Rumney, Cardiff CF3 4FF* T: (029) 2241 5848 E: frjohnrconnell@gmail.com

CONNELL, Julie. b 58. **d** 08 **p** 09. NSM Brixton Road Ch Ch *S'wark* 08–12; NSM Furzedown from 12. *8 Helix Road, London SW2 2JS* T: (020) 8671 0481 *or* 7587 0375 F: 7582 7421 E: julieconnell@gmail.com

CONNELL, Mrs Penelope Clare. b 44. EMMTC. **d** 03 **p** 04. NSM Whatton w Aslockton, Hawksworth, Scarrington etc *S'well* 03–06; NSM Nottingham St Nic 06–07; NSM Ironstone Villages *Leic* 07–12; rtd 12; PtO *Leic* from 12; *S'well* from 14. *Colston Bassett House, Church Gate, Colston Bassett,*

Nottingham NG12 3FE T: (01949) 81424 M: 07866-495720 E: clare2connell@icloud.com

CONNELL, Sister Sharon Margaret. b 65. Cardiff Univ MTh 11. Wilson Carlile Coll 86 St Jo Coll Nottm BA 03. **d** 03 **p** 04. C S Hackney St Jo w Ch Ch *Lon* 03–06; C Stepney St Dunstan and All SS 06–08; Ecum Chapl Chelsea and Westmr Hosp NHS Foundn Trust 08–13; Dep Hd Multi-Faith Chapl 13–15; Chapl St Nic Hospice Care Bury St Edmunds from 15; PtO *St E* from 09; Bp's Adv for Healthcare Chapl from 16. *St Nicholas Hospice Care, Macmillan Way, Hardwick Lane, Bury St Edmunds IP33 2QY* T: (01284) 715551 E: sharon.connell@stnh.org.uk

CONNER, Mrs Cathryn. b 42. Birm Univ BSc 64. NEOC 91. **d** 94 **p** 95. NSM Bainton w N Dalton, Middleton-on-the-Wolds etc *York* 94–98; NSM Woldsburn 98–04; rtd 04; PtO *York* from 04. *Deepdale, Main Street, North Dalton, Driffield YO25 9XA* T: (01377) 217430 E: cathrynconner@hotmail.co.uk

✠**CONNER, The Rt Revd David John.** b 47. Ex Coll Ox BA 69 MA 77. St Steph Ho Ox 69. **d** 71 **p** 72 **c** 94. Asst Chapl St Edw Sch Ox 71–73; Chapl 73–80; Hon C Summertown *Ox* 71–76; TV Wolvercote w Summertown 76–80; Chapl Win Coll 80–87; V Cambridge Gt St Mary w St Mich *Ely* 87–94; RD Cambridge 89–94; Suff Bp Lynn *Nor* 94–98; Dean Windsor and Dom Chapl to The Queen from 98; Bp HM Forces 01–09. *The Deanery, Windsor Castle, Windsor SL4 1NJ* T: (01753) 865561 F: 819002 E: david.conner@stgeorges-windsor.org

CONNING, Dowell Paul. b 64. Univ of Wales (Cardiff) MTh 12. Ripon Coll Cuddesdon BTh 00. **d** 00 **p** 01. C Leckhampton St Pet *Glouc* 00–03; CF from 03; Hon Min Can Ripon Cathl 05–14; *Leeds* from 14; Chapl Guards Chpl Lon 14–16. *c/o MOD Chaplains (Army)* T: (01264) 383430 F: 381824 E: dowell.conning199@mod.gov.uk *or* dconning@gmail.com

CONNOLL, Miss Helen Dorothy. b 45. Oak Hill Th Coll BA 86. **dss** 86 **d** 87 **p** 94. Leytonstone St Jo *Chelmsf* 86–90; Par Dn 87–90; Asst Chapl Grimsby Distr Gen Hosp 90–93; Chapl Kent and Cant Hosp 93–94; Chapl Kent and Cant Hosps NHS Trust 94–99; Chapl E Kent Hosps NHS Trust 99–01; Hon C Aylesham w Adisham and Nonington w Wymynswold and Goodnestone etc *Cant* 01–09; rtd 09; PtO *Cant* from 09; Chapl St Jo Hosp Cant from 16. *1 St John's House, 40 Northgate, Canterbury CT1 1BE* E: helen.therev@virgin.net

CONNOLLY, Catherine Hannah Victoria. b 90. Anglia Ruskin Univ BA 13. Ripon Coll Cuddesdon BA 17. **d** 18 **p** 19. C Ipswich St Thos *St E* from 18. *95 Tuddenham Road, Ipswich IP4 2SY* T: (01473) 422528 E: revcatconnolly@gmail.com

CONNOLLY, Daniel. b 51. BEng. St Jo Coll Nottm 82. **d** 84 **p** 85. C Bedgrove *Ox* 84–87; C-in-c Crookhorn Ch Cen CD *Portsm* 87–88; V Crookhorn 88–97; R Sutton Coldfield H Trin *Birm* 97–98; V Reigate St Mary *S'wark* 98–05; RD Reigate 03–05; P-in-c Kenilworth St Jo *Cov* 05–08; Adnry Miss Enabler 08–09; P-in-c Blackpool St Jo *Blackb* 09–13; V 13–16; rtd 16; PtO *Man* from 16. *26 Ashley Drive, Leigh WN7 5HP* E: dan@famcon.co.uk

CONNOLLY, Canon Lynne. b 53. Aston Tr Scheme 88 Linc Th Coll 92. **d** 92 **p** 94. Par Dn Hurst *Man* 92–94; C 94–96; R Burnage St Nic 96–02; V Spotland 02–10; P-in-c E Crompton 10–14; V 14–15; Hon Can Man Cathl 15; rtd 15; PtO *Man* from 15; *Leeds* from 17. *5 Cross Bank, Skipton BD23 6AH* T: (01756) 796657 E: tyc@clara.co.uk

CONNOLLY, Canon Sydney Herbert. b 40. Leeds Univ BA 66. Coll of Resurr Mirfield 66. **d** 68 **p** 69. C W Derby St Mary *Liv* 68–71; C Prescot 71–74; V Burtonwood 74–80; V Walker *Newc* 80–89; TR Whorlton 89–96; V Chapel House 96–99; TR N Shields 99–06; Hon Can Newc Cathl 04–06; rtd 06; PtO *Newc* from 06. *222 Brunton Walk, Newcastle upon Tyne NE3 2TL* T: 0191-271 1473 E: sydandpat@kingstonpark.plus.com

CONNOP PRICE, Martin Randall. *See* PRICE, Martin Randall Connop

CONNOR, Canon Geoffrey. b 46. K Coll Lon BD 73 AKC 73. St Aug Coll Cant. **d** 74 **p** 75. C Cockerton *Dur* 74–79; Dioc Recruitment Officer 79–87; Chapl St Chad's Coll 84–87; R Edin St Mary and Vice Provost St Mary's Cathl *Edin* 87–90; Dioc Dir of Ords Edin and Arg 87–90; V Whitechapel w Admarsh-in-Bleasdale *Blackb* 90–00; Dir of Ords 90–00; TR Epping Distr *Chelmsf* 00–16; RD Epping Forest 04–10; Hon Can Chelmsf Cathl 12–16; rtd 16; PtO *Chelmsf* from 16. *18 Milestone Road, Newhall, Harlow CM17 9NW* M: 07787-568529 E: geoffrey_connor@priest.com

CONNOR, Archdeacon of. *See* MACBRIDE, The Ven Stephen Richard

CONNOR, Bishop of. *See* ABERNETHY, The Rt Revd Alan Francis

CONNOR, Dean of. *See* WRIGHT, The Very Revd William Samuel

CONRAD, Canon Paul Derick. b 54. Worc Coll Ox BA 76 MA 82. St Steph Ho Ox 78. **d** 80 **p** 81. C Wanstead St Mary *Chelmsf* 80–83; C Somers Town *Lon* 83–85; P-in-c Kentish Town St Martin w St Andr 85–91; V 91–95; P-in-c Hampstead Ch Ch 95–97; V from 97; Chapl R Free London NHS Foundn Trust from 95; Can Wiawso Ghana from 09. *Christ Church Vicarage, 10 Cannon Place, London NW3 1EJ* T/F: (020) 7435 6784 E: paulconrad@btinternet.com

CONROY, Kevin Paul. b 14 **p** 16. Stillorgan w Blackrock *D & G* 14–16; NSM Dalkey St Patr from 16. *St Patrick's, Harbour Road, Dalkey, Co Dublin, Republic of Ireland* T: (00353) (1) 284 5941 M: 86-040 6256 E: revkvn@gmail.com

CONSTABLE, Douglas Brian. b 40. Lon Univ BA 62 Southn Univ MPhil 05. Linc Th Coll 63. **d** 65 **p** 66. C Stockwood CD *Bris* 65–70; Asst Chapl Bris Univ 70–72; Hon C Clifton St Paul 70–72; Chapl Lee Abbey 72–77; V Derby St Thos 77–85; TV Southampton (City Cen) *Win* 85–92; rtd 92; PtO *Win* 92–05; *St D* from 05. *Y Bwthyn, 9 Church Street, Llandeilo SA19 6BH* T: (01558) 823518 E: douglasconstable@btinternet.com

CONSTABLE, Mrs Sharon Joanne. b 57. STETS 95. **d** 98 **p** 99. NSM Hutton *B & W* 98–01; Bp's Officer for NSMs 01–04; C E Clevedon w Clapton in Gordano etc 01–04; Chapl St Jo Cathl Hong Kong 04–10; TV Melton Mowbray *Leic* 10–15; Bp's Adv for Women's Min 10–14; P-in-c Broughton Astley and Croft w Stoney Stanton 15–18; R from 18; RD Guthlaxton from 18. *The Rectory, St Marys Close, Broughton Astley, Leicester LE9 6ES* T: (01455) 644779 E: sharonconstable@msn.com

CONVERY, Canon Arthur Malcolm. b 42. Sheff Univ BSc 63 DipEd 64. NOC 79. **d** 82 **p** 83. NSM Parr *Liv* 82–87; V Marown *S & M* 87–04; V Onchan 04–10; Can St German's Cathl 99–10; rtd 10; P-in-c German St Jo *S & M* 10–12; C Michael 10–12. *50 Faaie ny Cabbal, Kirk Michael, Isle of Man IM6 2HU* T: (01624) 878855

CONWAY, Canon Glyn Haydn. b 38. St Mich Coll Llan. **d** 65 **p** 66. C Wrexham *St As* 65–71; TV 71–77; V Holywell 77–83; V Upton Ascension *Ches* 83–05; rtd 05; Hon Can Accra from 03; PtO *Ches* from 05; *St As* from 07; *St D* from 10. *18 Salmon Leap, Chester CH4 7JJ* T: (01244) 678298

CONWAY, The Very Revd John Arthur. b 67. Leeds Univ BEng 90 Edin Univ BD 97. Linc Th Coll 94 TISEC 95. **d** 97 **p** 98. C Edin St Mary 97–01; R Edin St Martin 01–17; Dioc IME Co-ord 04–07 and from 09; Chapl Edin Sick Children's NHS Trust 98–99; Chapl Lothian Univ Hosps NHS Trust 99–01; Provost St Mary's Cathl *Edin* from 17; R Edin St Mary from 17. *8 Lansdowne Crescent, Edinburgh EH12 5EQ* T: 0131-225 2978 *or* 225 6293 E: provost@cathedral.net

CONWAY, Philip James. b 66. Liv Inst of Educn BA 91. St Steph Ho Ox 92. **d** 95 **p** 96. C High Harrogate Ch Ch *Ripon* 95–99; P-in-c Menheniot *Truro* 99–08; C St Ive and Pensilva w Quethiock 02–08; P-in-c Lostwithiel, St Winnow w St Nectan's Chpl etc 08–15; P-in-c Lanlivery 08–15; C Lanreath, Pelynt and Bradoc 08–15; Public Preacher 15–18; PtO *Lich* 16; Chapl Abbots Bromley Sch from 16. *Abbots Bromley School, High Street, Abbots Bromley, Rugeley WS15 3BW*

CONWAY, Robert. b 51. Bris Poly MBA 90. Trin Coll Bris 09. **d** 12 **p** 13. OLM Filton *Bris* 12–17; OLM Fromeside from 17; Chapl N Bris NHS Trust from 17. *71 Juniper Way, Bradley Stoke, Bristol BS32 0BR* T: (01454) 612661 M: 07733-228878 E: bob.conway1@btinternet.com

CONWAY, Mrs Sandra Coralie. b 45. Bris Univ BA 66. S'wark Ord Course 89. **d** 92 **p** 00. NSM Kenley *S'wark* 92–05; PtO 06–07; *Guildf* 07–09; NSM E Horsley and Ockham w Hatchford and Downside 09–15; rtd 15; PtO *Guildf* from 15. *Rowan Tree Cottage, Norrels Drive, East Horsley, Leatherhead KT24 5DR* T: (01483) 281497 E: sandyconwayrtc@btinternet.com

✠**CONWAY, The Rt Revd Stephen David.** b 57. Keble Coll Ox BA 80 MA 84 CertEd 81 Selw Coll Cam BA 85. Westcott Ho Cam 83. **d** 86 **p** 87 **c** 06. C Heworth St Mary *Dur* 86–89; C Bishopwearmouth St Mich w St Hilda 89–90; Dir of Ords and Hon C Dur St Marg 90–94; P-in-c Cockerton 94–96; V 96–98; Bp's Sen Chapl and Communications Officer 98–02; Adn Dur and Can Res Dur Cathl 02–06; Area Bp Ramsbury *Sarum* 06–10; Bp Ely from 10. *The Bishop's House, The College, Ely CB7 4DW* T: (01353) 662749 F: 669477 E: bishop@elydiocese.org

COOGAN, The Ven Robert Arthur William. b 29. Univ of Tasmania BA 51. St Jo Coll Dur 51. **d** 53 **p** 54. C Plaistow St Andr *Chelmsf* 53–56; R Bothwell Australia 56–62; V N Woolwich *Chelmsf* 62–73; P-in-c W Silvertown St Barn 62–73; V Hampstead St Steph *Lon* 73–77; P-in-c N St Pancras All Hallows 74–77; RD S Camden 75–81; P-in-c Old St Pancras w

Bedford New Town St Matt 76–80; V Hampstead St Steph w All Hallows 77–85; P-in-c Kentish Town St Martin w St Andr 78–81; AD N Camden 78–83; Preb St Paul's Cathl 82–85; Adn Hampstead 85–94; rtd 94; PtO *Chich* 94–00. *Salters Hall West, Stour Street, Sudbury CO10 2AX* T: (01787) 370026

COOK, Alan. b 27. St Deiniol's Hawarden 79. **d** 80 **p** 81. Hon C Gatley *Ches* 80–83; Chapl Man R Eye Hosp 83–86; Chapl Asst Man R Infirmary 80–83 and 86–88; V Congleton St Jas *Ches* 89–93; rtd 93; PtO *Ches* 93–09. *15 Buttermere Road, Gatley, Cheadle SK8 4RQ* T: 0161-428 4350

COOK, Alan James. b 61. Univ Coll Ox BA 83. Wycliffe Hall Ox 86. **d** 00 **p** 01. C Fonthill Canada 00–02; R St Catharine's 02–06; Chapl St Monica Trust Westbury Fields from 16. *Gate Lodge, Cote Lane, Bristol BS9 3UN* T: 0117-962 8372 M: 07397-150680 E: alancook61@hotmail.com

COOK, Mrs Alison Mary. b 63. Leeds Univ BEd 85. St Hild Coll 17. **d** 19. NSM Stannington *Sheff* from 19. *20 Hanmoor Road, Stannington, Sheffield S6 6BL* T: 0114-234 3463 M: 07951-470911 E: alison42cook@hotmail.co.uk

COOK, Sister Anita Isabel. b 44. Whitelands Coll Lon CertEd 66 Toronto Univ BA 93. **d** 06 **p** 07. CSC from 67; PtO *S'wark* 10–15; Hon C E Clevedon w Clapton in Gordano etc *B & W* from 10. *St Gabriel's, 27A Dial Hill Road, Clevedon BS21 7HL* T: (01275) 544471 M: 07588-684380 E: anita@sistersofthechurch.org.uk

COOK, Benjamin William. b 85. St Mellitus Coll 14. **d** 17 **p** 18. C Walmley *Birm* from 17. *90 Walmley Ash Road, Sutton Coldfield B76 1JB* M: 07545-309018 E: bencookw@gmail.com

COOK, Canon Brian Edwin. b 36. Sarum & Wells Th Coll 78. **d** 80 **p** 81. C E Wickham *S'wark* 80–83; C Petersfield w Sheet *Portsm* 83–86; R Liss 86–01; RD Petersfield 91–96; Acting RD 99; Hon Can Portsm Cathl 96–01; rtd 01; PtO *Chich* from 01. *Daubeney Cottage, Bersted Street, South Bersted, Bognor Regis PO22 9QE* T: (01243) 828379 E: pconder787@gmail.com

COOK, Celia Jane. b 66. Anglia Ruskin Univ BA 88 BA 13 DipCOT 94. ERMC 07. **d** 10 **p** 11. C Aldeburgh w Hazlewood *St E* 10–14; TV Thurstable and Winstree *Chelmsf* 14–15; P-in-c Gt and Lt Bealings w Playford and Culpho *St E* 15–18; Chapl E Suffolk and N Essex NHS Foundn Trust from 18; PtO *Chelmsf* from 19. *26 St Edmunds Road, Ipswich IP1 3RD* T: (01473) 878104 M: 07857-823617 E: thecooksonline@hotmail.co.uk

COOK, Christopher. *See* COOK, James Christopher Donald

COOK, Christopher Charles Holland. b 56. K Coll Lon BSc 77 MB, BS 81 MD 95 MRCPsych 87. SEITE 97. **d** 00 **p** 01. Prof Psychiatry Alcohol Misuse Kent Inst of Medicine and Health Science 97–03; NSM Otham w Langley *Cant* 00–03; Chapl and Prof Fell St Chad's Coll Dur 03–05; Prof Research Fell Dur Univ from 05; Tutor and Lect Cranmer Hall Dur 08–13; Hon Min Can Dur Cathl from 13. *Department of Theology and Religion, Abbey House, Palace Green, Durham DH1 3RS* T: 0191-334 3885 E: c.c.h.cook@durham.ac.uk

COOK, David. b 46. Hertf Coll Ox BA MA 72. Wycliffe Hall Ox 69. **d** 73 **p** 74. C Stranton *Dur* 74–75; Lect Qu Coll Birm 75–81; Chapl Cranbrook Sch Kent 81–11; rtd 11; PtO *Cant* from 11. *33 Oatfield Drive, Cranbrook TN17 3LA* T: (01580) 713310 E: senor_aardvark@hotmail.com

COOK, Canon David Charles Murray. b 41. MA. Wycliffe Hall Ox 65. **d** 67 **p** 68. C Chatham St Phil and St Jas *Roch* 67–71; S Africa 71–89; TR Newbury *Ox* 89–02; RD 98–02; Hon Can Ch Ch 02; P-in-c Chipping Campden w Ebrington *Glouc* 02–13; rtd 13; PtO *Glouc* from 17. *Laverton Cottage, Lansdowne, Bourton-on-the-Water, Cheltenham GL54 2AR*

COOK, David Smith. b 47. Hull Univ BTh 88 MA 93. Lich Th Coll 68. **d** 71 **p** 72. C Tudhoe Grange *Dur* 71–75; C Bishopwearmouth St Mary V w St Pet CD 75–77; V Copley *Wakef* 77–80; V Birstall 80–83; V Holme upon Spalding Moor *York* 83–98; R Holme and Seaton Ross Gp 98–01; RD S Wold 96–01; V Copmanthorpe 01–07; P-in-c Askham Bryan 01–07; Chapl Askham Bryan Coll 01–04; P-in-c Eskdaleside w Ugglebarnby and Sneaton *York* 07–09; V Lower Esk 09–13; RD Whitby 08–13; rtd 13; PtO *York* from 13. *15 Farndale Drive, Guisborough TS14 8JD* T: (01287) 619296 E: farndalecook@gmail.com

COOK, Elspeth Jean. b 34. Edin Univ BSc 56 PhD 66. S Dios Minl Tr Scheme 85. **d** 88 **p** 94. C Yateley *Win* 88–91; Assoc Chapl Ld Mayor Treloar Hosp Alton 91–93; NSM Dunfermline *St And* 93–99; P-in-c Aberdour 99–01; rtd 01. *12 River View, Dalgety Bay, Dunfermline KY11 9YE* T: (01383) 825222 E: andrewandjean.cook@btinternet.com

COOK, Helen Jane. b 63. SEITE 13. **d** 16 **p** 17. NSM Redhill St Matt *S'wark* from 16. *15 Hilltop Road, Whyteleafe CR3 0DE* T: (01883) 627716 M: 07530-609511 E: hjwcook@yahoo.co.uk

COOK, Ian. b 63. Trin Coll Bris. **d** 09 **p** 10. C Plymouth St Jude *Ex* 09–13; R Wellington St Mark New Zealand from 13. *5 Birdwood Street, Karori, Wellington, New Zealand* E: ianruthcook@aol.com

COOK, Ian Bell. b 38. NW Ord Course 70. **d** 73 **p** 74. C Oldham St Paul *Man* 73–75; Ind Chapl 76–79; P-in-c Newton Heath St Wilfrid and St Anne 76–79; V Middleton Junction 79–08; rtd 08; PtO *Man* from 09. *109 Hollin Lane, Middleton, Manchester M24 5LA* T: 0161-654 7724 E: reviancook@gmail.com

COOK, Preb Ian Brian. b 38. Aston Univ MSc 72 Birm Univ MA 76 MBIM 73. Kelham Th Coll 58. **d** 63 **p** 64. C Langley Marish *Ox* 63–66; C Stokenchurch and Cadmore End 66–68; V Lane End 68–72; P-in-c Ibstone w Fingest 68–72; Tutor W Bromwich Coll of Comm and Tech 72–74; Sen Tutor 74–80; NSM W Bromwich St Pet *Lich* 77–80; R Wednesbury St Jas and St Jo 80–03; Dir St Jas Tr Inst 81–03; RD Wednesbury *Lich* 88–03; Preb Lich Cathl 94–03; rtd 03; PtO *Lich* from 03; RD Penkridge 06–11; P-in-c Tipton St Martin and St Paul 17–18. *4 Orams Lane, Brewood, Stafford ST19 9EA* T: (01902) 850960

COOK, Canon James Christopher Donald. b 49. Ch Ch Ox BA 70 MA 74. St Steph Ho Ox 79. **d** 80 **p** 81. C Witney *Ox* 80–83; CF 83–04; P-in-c Toxteth Park St Agnes and St Pancras *Liv* 04–06; V 06–16; Can Wiawso Ghana from 09; rtd 16; PtO *Liv* from 17. *St Agnes's Vicarage, 1 Buckingham Avenue, Liverpool L17 3BA* T/F: 0151-733 1742 E: leoclericus@aol.com

COOK, James Robert. b 45. ACCA 68 FCCA 73. Ox Min Course 05. **d** 08 **p** 09. NSM Newbury *Ox* 08–10; NSM W Woodhay w Enborne, Hampstead Marshall etc 10–11; NSM Kintbury w Avington 10–11; NSM Walbury Beacon 11–13; P-in-c Totland Bay *Portsm* 13–18; rtd 18. *St Blasius Rectory, Rectory Road, Shanklin PO37 6NX* T: (01983) 867887 E: jamesrobertcook@aol.com

COOK, Jean. *See* COOK, Elspeth Jean

COOK, Mrs Joan Lindsay. b 46. SRN 70. Cranmer Hall Dur 86. **d** 88 **p** 94. Par Dn Hartlepool St Hilda *Dur* 88–93; Dn-in-c 93–94; P-in-c 94–96; rtd 96. *10 Peakston Close, Hartlepool TS26 0PN* T: (01429) 231778 E: joancook14@gmail.com

COOK, John. b 32. Linc Th Coll 87. **d** 89 **p** 90. C Bourne *Linc* 89–92; R Colsterworth Gp 92–02; rtd 02; PtO *Linc* from 17. *24 Portrush Drive, Grantham NG31 9GD* T: (01476) 569063

COOK, John Edward. b 35. AKC 61. **d** 62 **p** 63. C York Town St Mich *Guildf* 62–67; Singapore 67–77; P-in-c Beoley *Worc* 78–83; V 83–89; V Bromsgrove All SS 89–01; rtd 01; PtO *Cov* from 02. *61 Newport Drive, Alcester B49 5BJ* T: (01789) 762553 F: 400040 E: jcook120@btinternet.com

COOK, John Michael. b 48. Coll of Resurr Mirfield 72. **d** 74 **p** 75. C Weymouth H Trin *Sarum* 74–76; C Felixstowe St Jo *St E* 76–79; P-in-c Gt and Lt Whelnetham 79–84; P-in-c Cockfield 84–85; P-in-c Bradfield St George w Bradfield St Clare etc 84–85; R Cockfield w Bradfield St Clare, Felsham etc 85–87; V Workington St Jo *Carl* 87–14; rtd 14; PtO *Carl* from 14. *28 Braeside, Seaton, Workington CA14 1EH* T: (01900) 267031

COOK, John Richard Millward. b 61. St Jo Coll Dur BA. Wycliffe Hall Ox 83. **d** 85 **p** 86. C Brampton St Thos *Derby* 85–89; C Farnborough *Guildf* 89–92; C Langham Place All So *Lon* 92–98; V Chelsea St Jo w St Andr 98–08; V Wargrave w Knowl Hill *Ox* from 08; PtO *Lon* from 19. *The Vicarage, Station Road, Wargrave, Reading RG10 8EU* T: 0118-940 2202 E: johnrmcook@btconnect.com

COOK, Kenneth Hugh. b 30. ALAM. AKC 55. **d** 56 **p** 57. C Netherfield *S'well* 56–59; C Newark w Coddington 59–61; V Basford St Aid 61–67; V Gargrave *Bradf* 67–77; Dir of Ords 77–89; Can Res Bradf Cathl 77–95; rtd 95; PtO *Ripon* 95–14; *Leeds* from 14. *25 Hollins Close, Hampsthwaite, Harrogate HG3 2EH* T: (01423) 772521

COOK (née McCLEAN), Mrs Lydia Margaret Sheelagh. b 72. Ball Coll Ox BA 94 MA 98. Cuddesdon Coll 94. **d** 96 **p** 97. C Brackley St Pet w St Jas *Pet* 96–99; Chapl Cranford Ho Sch Ox 99–02; NSM Wallingford *Ox* 99–01; NSM Wallingford Deanery 01–04; NSM Sandford-on-Thames 04–06; NSM Sturminster Newton, Hinton St Mary and Lydlinch *Sarum* 06–15; R Okeford from 15; RD Blackmore Vale from 19. *The Rectory, Church Road, Shillingstone, Blandford Forum DT11 0SL* T: (01258) 863774 M: 07725-046700 E: lydia@revrock.net

COOK, Marcus John Wyeth. b 41. Chich Th Coll 67. **d** 70 **p** 71. C Friern Barnet St Jas *Lon* 70–73; Hon C St Geo-in-the-East w St Paul 73–00. *3 Hugh Platt House, Patriot Square, London E2 9NS* M: 07890-207726

COOK, Mrs Myrtle Bridget Weigela. b 47. BA LLM. EMMTC. **d** 04 **p** 05. NSM Kibworth and Smeeton Westerby and Saddington *Leic* 04–08; NSM Church Langton cum Tur Langton etc 08–13; P-in-c 11–13; P-in-c Thundridge *St Alb*

13–17; P-in-c High Cross 13–17; rtd 17; PtO *Leic* from 18. *1 Highcroft, Husbands Bosworth, Lutterworth LE17 6LF* E: mchighcroft@aol.com

COOK, Nicholas Leonard. b 59. Nottm Univ BCombStuds 84 Greenwich Univ PGCE 01 MCGI 12. Linc Th Coll 81. **d** 84 **p** 85. C Leic St Pet 84–85; C Knighton St Mich 85–86; Chapl Asst Towers Hosp Humberstone 86–89; Chapl Leics Mental Health Service Unit 89–91; Chapl Quainton Hall Sch Harrow 91–94; CF(V) 88–94; CF 94–14; Chapl Duke of York's R Mil Sch Dover 14–16; Chapl Woodbridge Sch 16–18; Chapl RAuxAF from 14; PtO *Chelmsf* from 14. *Chaplaincy Services (RAF), HQ Air Command, RAF High Wycombe HP14 4UE* T: (01494) 496800 F: 496343 E: nick.cook324@mod.gov.uk

COOK, Paul Raymond. *See* McLAREN-COOK, Paul Raymond

COOK, Peter John. b 57. Ridley Hall Cam 93. **d** 95 **p** 96. C Romford Gd Shep *Chelmsf* 95–98; C Colchester St Jo 98–06; V Bangkok Ch Ch Thailand 06–15; Miss P Singapore from 15. *11 St Andrew's Road, Singapore, S178959* T: (0065) (9) 335 5520 E: peterjcook@gmail.com

COOK, Peter Ralph. b 69. Portsm Univ BA 92 Kent Univ BA 06. SEITE 03. **d** 06 **p** 07. C Hadlow *Roch* 06–09; V Docking, the Birchams, Stanhoe and Sedgeford *Nor* 09–15; P-in-c Fring 14–15; R Docking, The Birchams, Fring etc from 15; RD Heacham and Rising from 19. *The Vicarage, Sedgeford Road, Docking, King's Lynn PE31 8PN* T: (01485) 517157 E: t2andnor@supanet.com

COOK, Canon Richard John Noel. b 49. Univ Coll Ox BA 70 MA 74 PGCE 72. Wycliffe Hall Ox MA 77. **d** 78 **p** 79. C Fulwood *Sheff* 78–80; C Bolton St Paul w Em *Man* 81–86; TV 86–93; V Goldsworth Park *Guildf* 93–14; RD Woking 99–03; Hon Can Guildf Cathl 10–14; rtd 14; PtO *Ox* from 15. *7 Rye Close, Banbury OX16 1XG* T: (01295) 367944 E: cookingwok@gmail.com

COOK, Mrs Ruth Anna Margaret. b 52. Bedf Coll of Educn CertEd 74. **d** 08 **p** 09. OLM Smestow Vale *Lich* 08–12. *Le Havre, 315 rue Johé Gormand, Toury, 71250 Cortambert, France* T: (0033) 3 85 36 11 70 E: ruthfromstourbridge@gmail.com

COOK, Simon David James. b 74. St Cath Coll Ox BA 97 St Jo Coll Dur BA 08. Cranmer Hall Dur 06. **d** 08 **p** 09. C Broughton *Man* 08–11; V Kirklees Valley from 11; Borough Dean Bury 12–17; AD Bury from 16. *All Saints' Vicarage, 10 Kirkburn View, Bury BL8 1DL* T: 0161-797 1595 M: 07745-232662 E: simondjcook@aol.com

COOK, Stephen. b 62. Brunel Univ BSc(Econ) 84 Open Univ LLB 12. S'wark Ord Course 89. **d** 92 **p** 93. Hon C Forest Hill St Aug *S'wark* 92–98; P-in-c Eltham St Barn 98–10; V from 11; CF (TA) 00–03; Lead Chapl Greenwich Univ *S'wark* from 14. *St Barnabas' Vicarage, 449 Rochester Way, London SE9 6PH* T: (020) 8856 8294 E: cooksca@aol.com

COOK, Stephen William. b 57. Bris Univ BA 80 Lambeth STh 86. Trin Coll Bris 82. **d** 85 **p** 86. C Heref St Pet w St Owen and St Jas 85–89; TV Keynsham *B & W* 89–95; V Hanham *Bris* 95–02; RD Bitton 98–99; AD Kingswood and S Glos 99–02; TR Okehampton w Inwardleigh, Bratton Clovelly etc *Ex* 02–11; TR Okehampton, Inwardleigh, Belstone, Sourton etc from 12; Chapl R Devon and Ex NHS Foundn Trust from 09. *The Rectory, 1 Church Path, Okehampton EX20 1LW* T: (01837) 659297 E: scook9673@aol.com

COOK, Tom Adrian. b 86. Glos Univ BA 12. Trin Coll Bris MA 19. **d** 19. C W Cheltenham *Glouc* from 19. *50 Robert Burns Avenue, Cheltenham GL51 6NT* M: 07538-048647 E: revtomcook@gmail.com

COOK, Trevor Vivian. b 43. Sarum Th Coll 67. **d** 69 **p** 70. C Lambeth St Phil *S'wark* 69–73; C St Buryan, St Levan and Sennen *Truro* 73–75; V The Ilketshalls *St E* 75–79; P-in-c Rumburgh w S Elmham 75–79; R Rumburgh w S Elmham w the Ilketshalls 79–84; TR Langport Area *B & W* 84–96; P-in-c Rode Major 96–02; C Hardington Vale 02–04; rtd 04; PtO *B & W* from 04. *Hedge End, 5 Queen Street, Keinton Mandeville, Somerton TA11 6EH* T: (01458) 224448 E: sandracook838@btinternet.com *or* sandracook838@outlook.com

COOK, Alan. b 50. Nottm Univ BTh 74 Lanc Univ PGCE 75. Kelham Th Coll 69. **d** 75 **p** 76. C Tyldesley w Shakerley *Man* 75–78; C Langley All SS and Martyrs 80–82; TV Langley and Parkfield 82–83; P-in-c Chadderton St Mark 83–85; V 85–14; rtd 14; PtO *Man* 14–17. *6 Hallet Court, Hughes Hallet Street, Sliema SLM 3142, Malta GC* T: (00356) 2783 6339 E: theplookes@gmail.com

COOK, Angela Elizabeth. b 42. SRN 65 SCM 67. St Jo Coll Nottm 85. **d** 87 **p** 94. Par Dn Walton H Trin *Ox* 87–92; Par Dn Bexleyheath Ch Ch *Roch* 92–94; C 94–97; V St Mary Cray and St Paul's Cray 97–05; rtd 05; PtO *Chich* from 15. *7 Maytree Gardens, Bexhill-on-Sea TN40 2PE* T: (01424) 213268

COOKE, Christopher Stephen. b 54. Lon Univ BA 76 MA 77 Ox Univ BA 81 MA 88. Ripon Coll Cuddesdon 79. **d** 82 **p** 83. C Cen Telford *Lich* 82–86; R Uffington, Upton Magna and Withington 86–95; RD Wrockwardine 92–01; TR Wrockwardine Deanery 95–01; P-in-c Wem and Lee Brockhurst 01–13; P-in-c Loppington w Newtown 01–02; rtd 13; PtO *Heref* from 14. *Broomfield, Station Road, Pontesbury, Shrewsbury SY5 0QY* E: christophercooke@mscsolutions.co.uk

COOKE, Claire. b 80. St Mellitus Coll 14. **d** 17 **p** 18. C Lancaster St Thos *Blackb* from 17. *97 Barton Road, Lancaster LA1 4EN*

COOKE, David John. b 31. Linc Th Coll 60. **d** 62 **p** 63. C Brighton Gd Shep Preston *Chich* 62–65; C Clayton w Keymer 65–70; R Stone w Hartwell w Bishopstone *Ox* 70–77; R Stone w Dinton and Hartwell 77–07; rtd 07; PtO *Ox* from 08. *5 Astronomy Way, Aylesbury HP19 7WD* T: (01296) 392296 E: david.j.cooke@btinternet.com

COOKE, David Michael Randle. b 68. Newc Univ BA 90. Wycliffe Hall Ox 05. **d** 07 **p** 08. C Richmond H Trin and Ch Ch *S'wark* 07–12; TV Barnes from 12. *162 Castelnau, London SW13 9ET* T: (020) 8741 7330 M: 07766-900267 E: davidcooke2003@hotmail.com *or* david@htbarnes.org

COOKE, Ms Gillian Freda. b 39. Lon Univ BD 73 Leeds Univ MA 87. Linc Th Coll 74. **dss** 78 **d** 87 **p** 94. Cricklewood St Pet CD *Lon* 78–80; Chapl Middx Poly 78–80; Chapl Leeds Poly *Ripon* 80–87; N Humberside Ind Chapl *York* 87–90; Asst Chapl HM Pris Hull 90–94; Chapl Keele Univ *Lich* 94–97; Assoc Min Betley and Keele 94–97; Chapl Rampton Hosp Retford 97–99; rtd 99; PtO *York* 00–12; Chapl HM Pris Wolds 05–12. *7 Northfield, Swanland, North Ferriby HU14 3RG* T: (01482) 633971

COOKE, Heather Ann. QUB BEd. **d** 17. Belfast St Steph w St Luke Conn from 17. *23 Westmount Avenue, Carrickfergus BT38 3DQ* T: (028) 9336 0370 M: 07745-688605 E: hcooke84@hotmail.com *or* cookehe@tcd.ie

COOKE (née MORRALL), Mrs Heather Lynne. b 55. LMH Ox BA 76 MA 80 MIPR 88. Dioc OLM tr scheme 96. **d** 99 **p** 00. OLM Martlesham w Brightwell *St E* 99–12; PtO from 12. *9 Swan Close, Martlesham Heath, Ipswich IP5 3SD* T: (01473) 623770 M: 07703-568051 E: hcookema@aol.com

COOKE, James Martin. b 46. Trin Coll Ox BA 67 Ox Univ DipEd 68. **d** 07 **p** 08. OLM Wonersh w Blackheath *Guildf* 07–16; PtO from 16. *7 Durnsford Way, Cranleigh GU6 7LN* T: (01483) 276049 E: james.cooke2015@gmail.com

COOKE, John Stephen. b 35. K Coll Lon BD 58 AKC 58. **d** 59 **p** 60. C W Bromwich St Fran *Lich* 59–62; C Chalfont St Peter *Ox* 62–66; V Cross Heath *Lich* 66–72; R Haughton 72–86; P-in-c Ellenhall w Ranton 72–80; V Eccleshall 86–00; Sub Chapl HM Pris Drake Hall 89–95; rtd 00; PtO *Lich* from 00. *34 Stone Road, Eccleshall, Stafford ST21 6DL* T: (01785) 850189 E: jstephencooke@btinternet.com

COOKE, Mrs Katherine Mary. b 69. Univ of Wales (Lamp) BA 92. Ox Min Course 08. **d** 12 **p** 13. C Eynsham and Cassington *Ox* 12–16; C N Abingdon from 16. *33 Foster Road, Abingdon OX14 1YN* M: 07540-568055 E: revkathcooke@gmail.com

COOKE, Canon Kenneth John. b 29. Linc Coll Ox BA 53 MA 57. Ely Th Coll 53. **d** 55 **p** 56. C Nuneaton St Mary *Cov* 55–58; C Cov St Thos 58–61; V Willenhall 61–66; V Meriden 66–76; V Cov St Geo 76–84; V Leamington Spa H Trin and Old Milverton 84–94; Hon Can Cov Cathl 92–94; rtd 94; PtO *Cov* 94–13. *2 Chantry Crescent, Alcester B49 5BT* T: (01789) 763460

COOKE, Lesley Elizabeth. b 49. **d** 12 **p** 13. NSM Hawarden *St As* 12–15; PtO *Ches* from 14; *St As* from 15. *University of Chester, Parkgate Road, Chester CH1 4BJ* T: (01244) 511136 E: l.cooke@chester.ac.uk

COOKE, Lorraine Mary. b 48. **d** 12 **p** 13. OLM Droylsden St Martin *Man* 12–14; NSM Audenshaw St Steph 14–16; NSM Denton Ch Ch 14–16; NSM Denton St Lawr 14–16; NSM Haughton St Anne 14–16; PtO from 16. *Address withheld by request* E: revlmcooke@gmail.com

COOKE, Michael David. b 46. New Coll Ox BA 68 MA 71 DPhil 71. Ox NSM Course 75. **d** 78 **p** 79. NSM Newport Pagnell *Ox* 78–79; NSM Newport Pagnell w Lathbury 79–85; NSM Newport Pagnell w Lathbury and Moulsoe 85–88; NSM Beckenham Ch Ch *Roch* 90–96; P-in-c Seal St Lawr 96–10; P-in-c Underriver 96–10; rtd 10; PtO *Cant* from 11. *92 Dumpton Park Drive, Broadstairs CT10 1RL* T: (01843) 863293 E: mcooke.92@btinternet.com

COOKE, Michael John. b 39. Ab Dioc Tr Course 78. **d** 80 **p** 81. NSM St Andr Cathl *Ab* 80–81; Chapl Miss to Seamen 81–88; Miss to Seamen Tilbury 88–91; Hon C Immingham *Linc* 81–88; Ind Chapl Teesside *Dur* 91–97; V Kelloe and Coxhoe 97–06; rtd 06. *36 Nuneaton Drive, Hemlington, Middlesbrough TS8 9PR* E: mikecooke8@yahoo.co.uk

COOKE, Patrick Arthur. b 45. d 12. NSM Winterton Gp *Linc* from 12. *10 West Street, Winterton, Scunthorpe DN15 9QQ* T: (01724) 734885

COOKE, Philip George. b 66. Plymouth Univ BSc 88 Univ of Wales (Lamp) PhD 96. Lon Bible Coll 99 Ox Min Course 10. d 12 p 13. NSM Hanborough and Freeland *Ox* 12–16; PtO 16–17; NSM N Abingdon from 17; Dir Local Min Tr from 16. *33 Foster Road, Abingdon OX14 1YN* T: (01865) 881366 M: 07857-822053 E: revphilcooke@gmail.com *or* phil.cooke@oxford.anglican.org

COOKE, Raymond. b 34. Liv Univ BSc 56. Wells Th Coll 58. d 60 p 61. C Newton Heath All SS *Man* 60–64; C-in-c Failsworth H Family CD 64–75; R Failsworth H Family 75–83; P-in-c Man Gd Shep 83–88; V Westleigh St Pet 88–99; rtd 99; PtO *Man* from 99. *136 Victoria Avenue East, Manchester M9 6HF* T: 0161-740 0664

COOKE, Richard James. b 60. Pemb Coll Ox BA 82 MA 88 Bris Univ PhD 96. Trin Coll Bris 85. d 88 p 89. C Rugby St Matt *Cov* 88–92; V Fletchamstead 92–04; Dir Initial Tr for Readers 97–02; CME Lay Development and Local Min Adv *Cov* 04–07 and 07–08; Dir of Discipleship Development from 09; C Warmington w Shotteswell and Radway w Ratley 07–14; C Kineton 07–14; C Combroke w Compton Verney 07–14; C Edgehill Churches from 14; Gen LtO from 18. *Diocesan Office, 1 Hill Top, Coventry CV1 5AB* T: (024) 7652 1200 E: richard.cooke@covcofe.org

COOKE, Roger. b 68. Heriot-Watt Univ BA 90 BArch 91 Edin Univ MTh 02. TISEC 98. d 99 p 00. C Prestonpans *Edin* 99–02; R 02–09; C Musselburgh 99–02; R 02–09; I Coleraine *Conn* from 09. *St Patrick's Rectory, 28 Mountsandel Road, Coleraine BT52 1JE* T: (028) 7034 3429 E: carrington20@aol.com

COOKE, Stephen. *See* COOKE, John Stephen

COOKE, Miss Susan Marilyn. b 76. K Coll Lon BA 97 MA 02 AKC 97 PGCE 98. Ridley Hall Cam 10. d 12 p 13. C Sunningdale *Ox* 12–16; V W Ewell *Guildf* from 16. *All Saints' Vicarage, 7 Church Road, West Ewell, Epsom KT19 9QY* M: 07780-606124 E: revsuecooke@gmail.com

COOKE, Mrs Susan Patricia. b 63. Ox Brookes Univ MA 99. WEMTC 10. d 13 p 14. C Barnwood *Glouc* 13–17; R Badgeworth, Shurdington and Witcombe w Bentham from 17. *The Vicarage, School Lane, Shurdington, Cheltenham GL51 4TF* M: 07736-770797 E: revsusancooke@gmail.com

COOKE, Mrs Suzanne. b 65. Westmr Coll Ox BTh 96 Anglia Ruskin Univ MA 13. Westcott Ho Cam 08. d 10 p 11. C Watton *Nor* 10–13; P-in-c Upper Tas Valley 13–16; V 16–17; V Doddington, Ilderton, Kirknewton and Wooler *Newc* from 17. *2 Queens Road, Wooler NE71 6DR* E: suzanne@cookehouse.co.uk

COOKSEY, Miss Diane Marie. b 75. Univ of Cen England in Birm BA 97. St Jo Coll Nottm 09. d 11 p 12. C Churchill-in-Halfshire w Blakedown and Broome *Worc* 11–14; C Warndon St Nic from 14; RD Worc E from 18. *4 Daty Croft, Home Meadow, Worcester WR4 0JB* M: 07974-556514 E: diane_cooksey@hotmail.com

COOKSEY, Mrs Emma. b 80. Qu Foundn (Course) 15. d 18 p 19. C Lichfield and Longdon *Lich* from 18. *The Vicarage, Longdon, Rugeley WS15 4PS* T: (01543) 322742 E: emma.cooksey@sky.com

COOKSON, Canon Diane Veronica. b 51. NOC 81. dss 84 d 87 p 94. Gt Sutton *Ches* 84–86; Neston 86–87; Par Dn 87–94; C 94–96; V Stockport St Sav from 96; Ecum Adv (Gtr Man) 00–02; RD Stockport 12–17; Hon Can Ches Cathl from 04. *St Saviour's Vicarage, 22 St Saviour's Road, Great Moor, Stockport SK2 7QE* T: 0161-483 2633 E: st.saviours@virgin.net

COOKSON, Canon Graham Leslie. b 37. Bernard Gilpin Soc Dur 63 Sarum Th Coll 64. d 67 p 68. C Upton Ascension *Ches* 67–69; C Timperley 69–75; V Godley cum Newton Green 75–83; R Tarporley 83–07; Hon Can Ches Cathl 04–07; rtd 07; PtO *Ches* from 08. *15 Dolphin Court, Chester CH4 8JX* T: (01244) 671044 E: g.cookson532@btinternet.com

COOKSON, Canon William. b 61. d 98 p 99. C Haydock St Mark *Liv* 98–02; Min Wallington Springfield Ch *S'wark* 02–17; Public Preacher from 17; Dioc Dean of Fresh Expressions from 15; Hon Can S'wark Cathl from 15. *Christ Church Vicarage, 52 Earlswood Road, London SE10 9ES* T: (020) 7939 9414 E: willcookson@blueyonder.co.uk

COOLING (née YOUNG), Mrs Margaret Dorothy. b 37. K Coll Lon BA 59 AKC Lon Univ BD 69 PGCE 70 MSc 10 Univ of Wales (Cardiff) MEd 81. Mon Dioc Tr Scheme 89. d 90 p 95. NSM Bettws *Mon* 90–95; NSM Purleigh, Cold Norton and Stow Maries *Chelmsf* 95–98; rtd 98; PtO *Mon* from 98; *Glouc* from 01. *St Thomas Cottage, The Fence, St Briavels, Lydney GL15 6QG* T: (01594) 530926 E: maggieandderrick@outlook.com

COOMBER, Ian Gladstone. b 47. Southn Univ BTh 79 Ch Ch Coll Cant CertEd 68. Sarum & Wells Th Coll 73. d 76 p 77. C Weeke *Win* 76–79; TV Saffron Walden w Wendens Ambo and Littlebury *Chelmsf* 79–82; V Weston *Win* 82–90; R Bedhampton *Portsm* 90–96; R Botley and Durley 96–05; V Curdridge 96–05; RD Bishop's Waltham 98–03; TR Cartmel Peninsula *Carl* 05–09; rtd 09; PtO *B & W* 09–19; *Win* from 19. *28 Hebron Court, 35 Hill Lane, Southampton SO15 5WE* T: (023) 8071 5128 E: iancoomber747@outlook.com

COOMBS, Christopher. b 48. UWIC MSc 05. Trin Coll Bris 10. d 12 p 13. OLM Rodbourne Cheney *Bris* 12–19. *230 Cheney Manor Road, Swindon SN2 2NZ* T: (01793) 643465 M: 07789-514310 E: chris.coombs8@gmail.com

COOMBS, John Allen. b 46. Portsm Poly BSc 70. Oak Hill Th Coll 86 Sarum & Wells Th Coll 89. d 89 p 90. C Leverington and Wisbech St Mary *Ely* 89–93; P-in-c Emneth 93–96; V Emneth and Marshland St James 96–99; P-in-c Papworth Everard 99–00; TV Papworth 00–02; Chapl Papworth Hosp NHS Foundn Trust 99–06; P-in-c Roche *Truro* 06–12; rtd 12; PtO *Ex* 13–14; *Portsm* from 14. *The Little Haven, Castle Road, Ventnor PO38 1LG* T: (01983) 854290 E: john.coombs.7@gmail.com

COOMBS, John Kendall. b 47. Culham Coll Ox BEd 73. Sarum & Wells Th Coll 75. d 77 p 78. C Fareham H Trin *Portsm* 77–80; C Petersfield w Sheet 80–83; TV Beaminster Area *Sarum* 83–87; TR Preston w Sutton Poyntz, Littlemoor etc 87–97; TR Hermitage *Ox* 97–05; P-in-c Hurst 05–11; rtd 11; PtO *Ox* from 11. *65 Rosedale Gardens, Thatcham RG19 3LF*

COOMBS, Martin. *See* COOMBS, Walter James Martin

COOMBS, Matthew Robert. b 90. Heythrop Coll Lon BA 11. St Mellitus Coll 15. d 18 p 19. C Bryanston Square St Mary w St Marylebone St Mark *Lon* from 18. *St Mary's Church Office, 255 Old Marylebone Road, London NW1 5QT* T: (020) 7258 5040 M: 07889-793536 E: matt@stmaryslondon.com

COOMBS, Patrick Michael Joseph. *See* COFFEY, Patrick Michael Joseph

COOMBS, The Ven Peter Bertram. b 28. Bris Univ BA 58 MA 61. Clifton Th Coll 55. d 60 p 61. C Beckenham Ch Ch *Roch* 60–63; R Nottingham St Nic *S'well* 63–68; V New Malden and Coombe *S'wark* 68–75; RD Kingston 71–75; Adn Wandsworth 75–88; Adn Reigate 88–95; rtd 95; PtO *Portsm* from 97. *92 Locks Heath Park Road, Locks Heath, Southampton SO31 6LZ* T: (01489) 577288

COOMBS, Richard Murray. b 63. St Chad's Coll Dur BSc 85 Rob Coll Cam BA 89 MA 90. Ridley Hall Cam 87. d 90 p 91. C Enfield Ch Ch Trent Park *Lon* 90–94; C St Helen Bishopsgate w St Andr Undershaft etc 94–98; P-in-c St Pet Cornhill 95–98; V Burford w Fulbrook, Taynton, Asthall etc *Ox* 98–18; R Cheltenham St Mary w St Matt and St Luke *Glouc* from 18. *38 Sydenham Villas Road, Cheltenham GL52 6DZ* T: (01242) 703154 E: rmcoombs@btinternet.com

COOMBS, Canon Walter James Martin. b 33. Keble Coll Ox BA 57 MA 61. Cuddesdon Coll 59. d 61 p 62. C Kennington St Jo *S'wark* 61–64; Chapl Em Coll Cam 64–68; Bp's Dom Chapl *S'wark* 68–70; V E Dulwich St Jo 70–77; V Pershore w Pinvin, Wick and Birlingham *Worc* 77–92; Hon Can Worc Cathl 84–92; RD Pershore 85–91; TV Dorchester *Ox* 92–98; rtd 98; PtO *Ox* from 01. *54 Divinity Road, Oxford OX4 1LJ* T: (01865) 243865

COONEY, Canon Michael Patrick. b 55. City of Lon Poly BA 77. Ripon Coll Cuddesdon 77. d 80 p 81. C Cov E 80–83; C Old Brumby *Linc* 83–85; V Linc St Jo 85–90; V Frodingham 90–05; RD Manlake 99–10; RD Is of Axholme 05–10; Ind Chapl 05–19; P-in-c Gainsborough and Morton 12–19; Can and Preb Linc Cathl 04–19; rtd 19. *Address withheld by request* E: mccooney593@gmail.com

COONEY, William Barry. b 47. K Coll Lon 69. d 70 p 71. C W Bromwich All SS *Lich* 70–73; C Wolverhampton St Pet 73–75; C Rugeley 75–78; V Sneyd Green 78–87; R Sandiacre *Derby* 87–11; rtd 11; PtO *S'well* from 11. *15 Newthorpe Common, Newthorpe, Nottingham NG16 2BX* T: (01773) 711549 E: rosemary.c@talk21.com

COOPER, Alexander James Goodenough. b 47. Bath Univ BSc 69. WEMTC 04. d 06 p 07. NSM Soundwell *Bris* from 06. *1 Deerhurst, Bristol BS15 1XH* T: 0117-973 9441 E: linsand@blueyonder.co.uk

COOPER, Mrs Alison Beryl. b 51. Ripon Coll Cuddesdon 03. d 04 p 05. NSM Ascot Heath *Ox* 04–07; NSM Sunninghill and S Ascot 07–10; NSM Limpsfield and Tatsfield *S'wark* 10–13; PtO 13–16; *Roch* from 15. *Rosemary Cottage, Oakdale Lane, Crockham Hill, Edenbridge TN8 6RL* T: (01732) 669447 M: 07747-682139 E: alison8@talktalk.net

COOPER, Andrew John. b 62. W Sussex Inst of HE BA 87 Greenwich Univ PGCE 03 FRSA 14. St Steph Ho Ox 88. d 91 p 92. C Rawmarsh w Parkgate *Sheff* 91–93; C Mosborough

93–95; P-in-c Donnington Wood *Lich* 95–96; CF 96–14; PtO *Bris* from 10; *Sarum* from 18. *Address withheld by request* E: revajcooper@btinternet.com

COOPER, Andrew Richard James. b 81. Lon Metrop Univ BSc 04. Ridley Hall Cam 07. **d** 10 **p** 11. C S Harrow St Paul *Lon* 10–13; Chapl HM YOI Feltham 13–17; PtO *Lon* 17–18 and from 19; Chapl R Brompton and Harefield NHS Foundn Trust 18–19. *106 Acton Lane, London NW10 8TX* M: 07947-722277 E: arjcooper@aim.com

COOPER, Miss Angela Jean. b 56. SWMTC 09. **d** 12 **p** 13. C St Just-in-Roseland and St Mawes *Truro* 12–16; P-in-c Lanteglos by Camelford w Advent 16–19; P-in-c St Teath 16–19; R Camel-Allen from 19. *Fairway View, Helstone, Camelford PL32 9RL* T: (01840) 212468 M: 07753-517304 E: angelajeancooper@hotmail.com

COOPER, Anne. *See* COOPER, Margaret Anne

COOPER, The Ven Annette Joy. b 53. Open Univ BA 80 Dur Univ MA 13 CQSW 84. S'wark Ord Course 85. **d** 88 **p** 94. NSM Pembury *Roch* 88; Chapl Asst Kent and Sussex Hosp Tunbridge Wells 88–91; Chapl Asst Leybourne Grange Hosp W Malling 88–91; Chapl Bassetlaw Hosp and Community Services NHS Trust 91–96; P-in-c Edwinstowe *S'well* 96–04; Chapl Center Parcs Holiday Village 96–01; AD Worksop 99–04; Hon Can S'well Minster 02–04; Adn Colchester *Chelmsf* 04–19; rtd 19. *1 Fox Hill, Hollesley, Woodbridge IP12 3RD*

COOPER, Arthur. b 47. **d** 15 **p** 15. C Stoneycroft All SS *Liv* 15–16; P-in-c 16–18; rtd 18; Hon C Glazebury w Hollinfare *Liv* from 18. *The Vicarage, 468 Manchester Road, Rixton, Warrington WA3 6HY* T: 0161-775 8368 E: akc@f2s.com *or* sthelenhollinfare@gmail.com

COOPER, Canon Bede Robert. b 42. Ex Univ BA 63. Coll of Resurr Mirfield 69. **d** 71 **p** 72. C Weymouth H Trin *Sarum* 71–74; P-in-c Broad Town 74–79; V Wootton Bassett 74–86; R Wilton w Netherhampton and Fugglestone 86–07; Can and Preb Sarum Cathl 88–07; rtd 07; PtO *B & W* 09–19; *Win* 11–14; *Sarum* 13–18. *205 High Street, Milborne Port, Sherborne DT9 5AG* T: (01963) 250503 E: b.cooper789@btinternet.com

COOPER, Benedict Christopher. b 68. K Coll Cam BA 90 Wolfs Coll Ox MPhil 94 DPhil 97 W Sydney Univ PhD 10. Oak Hill Th Coll BA 03. **d** 03 **p** 04. C St Helen Bishopsgate w St Andr Undershaft etc *Lon* 03–07; Australia 07–10; C Fulwood *Sheff* from 10. *1 Silver Birch Avenue, Sheffield S10 3TA* T: 0114-230 4444 *or* 229 5567 M: 07402-065857 E: bencooper@fulwoodchurch.co.uk *or* ben.cooper@sheffield.anglican.org

COOPER, Clive Anthony Charles. b 38. Lon Univ BEd 74. ALCD 62. **d** 62 **p** 63. C Morden *S'wark* 62–65; SAMS Argentina 65–71; Asst Master St Nic Sch Cranleigh 74–92; Hon C Cranleigh *Guildf* 78–79; Hon C Ewhurst 80–82; Hon Chapl Duke of Kent Sch Ewhurst 83–92; Chapl Felixstowe Coll 92–93; PtO *Ex* 94–95; Chapl Puerto Pollensa *Eur* 95–02; P-in-c Instow and Westleigh *Ex* 03–07; rtd 08; PtO *Eur* 08–12; *Ex* 09–12. *64 Benfer Road, Victoria Point QLD 4165, Australia* E: clivecooper141@yahoo.com.au

COOPER, Colin. b 55. Open Univ BA. St Jo Coll Nottm 83. **d** 86 **p** 87. C Cheadle Hulme St Andr *Ches* 86–89; C Tunbridge Wells St Jo *Roch* 89–93; V Whitfield *Derby* 93–11; TR N Wingfield, Clay Cross and Pilsley from 11. *The Rectory, St Lawrence Road, North Wingfield, Chesterfield S42 5HX* T: (01246) 851181 E: revccooper@gmail.com

COOPER, Colin Charles. b 40. Middx Univ BA 94. Oak Hill Th Coll 62. **d** 66 **p** 67. C Islington St Andr w St Thos and St Matthias *Lon* 66–69; Bermuda 69–76; V Gorleston St Andr *Nor* 77–94; R Emporia Ch Ch w Purdy Grace USA 94–12; rtd 12. *2608 South Anchor Lane, Nags Head NC 27959, USA* T: (001) (434) 430 0107 E: colincooper9540@gmail.com

COOPER, Mrs Corynne Elizabeth. b 54. Kent Univ BA 76 PGCE 77 Nottm Univ MA 98. EMMTC 95. **d** 98 **p** 99. NSM Kneesall w Laxton and Wellow *S'well* 98–01; C Widecombe-in-the-Moor, Leusdon, Princetown etc *Ex* 01–05; TV Ashburton, Bickington, Buckland in the Moor etc 05–15. *15 Amberley Close, Ashburton, Newton Abbot TQ13 7JE* T: (01364) 653812

COOPER, David. b 44. AKC 69. **d** 69 **p** 70. C Wortley-de-Leeds *Ripon* 69–73; CF 73–83; LtO *Ox* 84–04; Chapl Eton Coll 85–04; rtd 09; PtO *Ox* from 11. *Old Shute, Dulverton TA22 9RJ* T: (01398) 323624 E: godshot@btinternet.com

COOPER, David Philip. b 65. York Univ BA 86. Qu Coll Birm BTheol 94. **d** 94 **p** 95. C Burslem *Lich* 94–98; TV Cen Wolverhampton and Dioc Inter-Faith Officer 98–05; P-in-c Arnside *Carl* 05–19; Dioc Ecum Officer 14–19; TR Walkden and Lt Hulton *Man* from 19. *St John's Vicarage, Algernon Road, Worsley, Manchester M28 3RD* E: revdavidcooper@btinternet.com

COOPER, Derek Edward. b 30. Bps' Coll Cheshunt 61. **d** 62 **p** 63. C Bishop's Stortford St Mich *St Alb* 62–66; V Westcliff St Cedd *Chelmsf* 66–89; R Camerton w Dunkerton, Foxcote and Shoscombe *B & W* 89–95; rtd 95; PtO *Win* 95–14. *6 Caerleon Drive, Andover SP10 4DE* T: (01264) 362807

COOPER, Frances. b 57. Lindisfarne Regional Tr Partnership 15. **d** 17 **p** 18. NSM Gainford *Dur* 17–18; NSM Winston 17–18; NSM Bishop Auckland from 18. *4 Riverside, South Church, Bishop Auckland DL14 6XT*

COOPER, Gavin Ashley. b 85. Chich Univ BA 06. St Steph Ho Ox BA 10 MA 15. **d** 11 **p** 12. C Old St Pancras *Lon* 11–14; C Stamford St Mary and St Martin *Linc* 14–16; R from 16. *St Martin's Rectory, 6 Pinfold Lane, Stamford PE9 2LS* T: (01780) 753356 E: frgavincooper@gmail.com

COOPER, Gordon William. b 54. Aston Tr Scheme 93 Ripon Coll Cuddesdon 95. **d** 97 **p** 98. C Kippax w Allerton Bywater *Ripon* 97–01; V Wyther 01–08; P-in-c Garforth 08–12; R 12–14; *Leeds* 14–17; rtd 17; PtO *Leeds* from 17. *18 Neville Grove, Swillington, Leeds LS26 8QN* M: 07896-329055 E: gordon.cooper1954@gmail.com

COOPER, Graham Denbigh. b 48. Nottm Univ BTh 75. St Jo Coll Nottm LTh 75. **d** 75 **p** 76. C Collyhurst *Man* 75–78; C Stambermill *Worc* 78–80; V The Lye and Stambermill 80–90; P-in-c Frome H Trin *B & W* 90; V 91–95; Appeals Organiser Children's Soc 95–97; Area Manager Save the Children Fund from 97. *9 Maxwell Road, Shepton Mallet BA4 5RF* T: (01749) 938156

COOPER, Mrs Gwenda. d 11 **p** 12. NSM Colwyn and Llanelian *St As* 11–16; NSM Aled Miss Area 17–18; P-in-c from 18. *Bron Digain, Llangernyw, Abergele LL22 8PP* T: (01745) 860349 E: brondigain@googlemail.com

COOPER, Ian. b 57. St Jo Coll Nottm 00. **d** 02 **p** 03. C Mildenhall *St E* 02–05; TV 05–06; V Blacklands Hastings Ch Ch and St Andr *Chich* 06–10; P-in-c Peacehaven and Telscombe Cliffs 10–13; P-in-c Piddinghoe 10–13; P-in-c Telscombe Village 10–13; V Peacehaven and Telscombe Cliffs w Piddinghoe etc 13–14; Chapl HM Pris Wayland 15–16; Chapl HM Pris Bure from 16. *HM Prison Bure, Jaguar Drive, Badersfield, Norwich NR10 5GB* T: (01603) 326180 E: ian@rpmo.co.uk *or* ian.cooper5@justice.gov.uk

COOPER, Ian Clive. b 48. Ex Univ BA 76 K Coll Lon MTh 94 FCA. Linc Th Coll 76. **d** 78 **p** 79. C Sunbury *Lon* 78–81; P-in-c Astwood Bank *Worc* 81–85; P-in-c Feckenham w Bradley 82–85; TV Hemel Hempstead *St Alb* 85–95; R Bushey 95–04; TR Witney *Ox* 04–06; TV Marlborough *Sarum* 06–13; rtd 13; Learning for Discipleship Support Officer *Sarum* 13–15; PtO *Glouc* from 17. *73 Bowbridge Lane, Stroud GL5 2JL* T: (01453) 298364 E: iancoopermth@talktalk.net

COOPER, James Peter. b 61. Westf Coll Lon BSc 82 Portsm Univ BA 04 Heythrop Coll Lon MA 12. Sarum & Wells Th Coll 82. **d** 85 **p** 86. C Durrington *Chich* 85–88; C Clayton w Keymer 88–95; TV Chich and Chapl Chich Coll of Tech 95–01; Chapl R W Sussex NHS Trust 01–11; R Cessnock Australia 11–15; P-in-c Donnington *Chich* 15–17; V from 17; Chapl St Wilfrid's Hospice Chich from 15. *The Vicarage, 34 Graydon Avenue, Chichester PO19 8RF* T: (01243) 788321 E: lizandjimcooper@gmail.com

COOPER, Mrs Jennifer Ann Lisbeth. b 45. MCSP 67. **d** 04 **p** 05. OLM Ashwellthorpe, Forncett, Fundenhall, Hapton etc *Nor* 04–13; rtd 13; PtO *Nor* 13–16. *Address temp unknown*

COOPER, Jennifer Elaine. b 62. Toronto Univ BA 83 Ottawa Univ MA 90 Keble Coll Ox DPhil 05. Ripon Coll Cuddesdon 05. **d** 06 **p** 07. C Cotham St Sav w St Mary and Clifton St Paul *Bris* 06–09; Lect and Tutor Coll of Resurr Mirfield 09–18; Visiting Lect Leeds Univ 09–18; Dir IME Newc from 19. *Church House, St John's Terrace, North Shields NE29 6HS* T: 0191-270 4100

COOPER, Jeremy Llewellyn John. b 51. Lanc Univ BA 73 Sussex Univ PGCE 74 York Univ MSc 87. **d** 07 **p** 08. OLM Morpeth *Newc* 07–11; Chapl Northumbria Healthcare NHS Foundn Trust from 11. *Southdown, 13 Curlew Hill, Morpeth NE61 3SH* E: jeremylcooper@aol.com

COOPER, Jill Mary. b 49. Qu Foundn (Course) 14. **d** 17 **p** 18. OLM Milton *Lich* from 17. *117 Hanley Road, Stoke-on-Trent ST1 6BG* E: jillcooper777@hotmail.com

COOPER, John. b 47. Sarum & Wells Th Coll 71. **d** 74 **p** 75. C Spring Grove St Mary *Lon* 74–77; C Shepherd's Bush St Steph w St Thos 77–82; V Paddington St Pet 82–89; V Darwen St Cuth w Tockholes St Steph *Blackb* 89–96; V Northampton St Mich w St Edm *Pet* 96–99; PtO *St Alb* from 99; *Lon* 02–15. *The Charterhouse, Charterhouse Square, London EC1M 6AN* T: (020) 3560 1336 M: 07749-502929 E: buster6913@yahoo.co.uk

COOPER, Canon John Leslie. b 33. Lon Univ BD 65 MPhil 78. Chich Th Coll 59. **d** 62 **p** 63. C Kings Heath *Birm* 62–65; Asst Chapl HM Pris Wandsworth 65–66; Chapl HM Borstal

Portland 66–68; Chapl HM Pris Bris 68–72; P-in-c Balsall Heath St Paul *Birm* 73–81; V 81–82; Adn Aston and Can Res Birm Cathl 82–90; Adn Coleshill 90–93; C Sutton Coldfield H Trin 93–97; Hon Can Birm Cathl 93–97; rtd 97; PtO *Derby* from 98. *9 Ramsay Hall, 9-13 Byron Road, Worthing BN11 3HN* T: (01903) 207939 E: jl612cooper@gmail.com

COOPER, John Northcott. b 44. Ox Min Course 89. **d** 92 **p** 93. NSM Burghfield *Ox* 92–99; P-in-c Wootton (Boars Hill) 99–00; V Wootton and Dry Sandford 00–10; AD Abingdon 02–07; rtd 10; PtO *Sarum* from 14. *Dinosaur Footprints, 21 Townend Road, Swanage BH19 2PU* T: (01929) 423591 E: dinofoot@hotmail.co.uk *or* aandcedwards@talk21.com

COOPER, Jonathan Charles. b 91. Fitzw Coll Cam BA 13 MEng 13 MA 17. Coll of Resurr Mirfield BA 16. **d** 17 **p** 18. C Newc St Fran from 17. *48 Freeman Road, South Gosforth, Newcastle upon Tyne NE3 1ST* E: revjoncooper@gmail.com

COOPER, Jonathan Mark Eric. b 62. Man Univ BSc 83 Edin Univ BD 88. Edin Th Coll 85. **d** 88 **p** 89. C Stainton-in-Cleveland *York* 88–91; C W Bromwich All SS *Lich* 91–93; P-in-c Ingleby Barwick CD *York* 93–98; P-in-c Hinderwell w Roxby 98–03; R Kirby Misperton w Normanby, Edston and Salton 03–10; V Brompton w Deighton from 10; R Rounton w Welbury from 10. *The Vicarage, Northallerton Road, Brompton, Northallerton DL6 2QA* T: (01609) 772436 E: j.m.e.c@btinternet.com

COOPER, Joseph Edward. b 87. St Hild Coll 15. **d** 18 **p** 19. C Stannington *Sheff* from 18. *10 Clark Grove, Stannington, Sheffield S6 6AY* M: 07748-648492 E: revjoecooper@gmail.com

COOPER, Judith Mary. b 52. Leeds Univ BA 09. NOC 06. **d** 09 **p** 10. C Prestwich St Mary *Man* 09–12; P-in-c Westleigh St Pet 12–15; V 15–18; P-in-c Westleigh St Paul 12–18; V Westleigh St Pet and St Paul from 18. *St Peter's and St Paul's Vicarage, 6 Malham Close, Leigh WN7 4SD* T: (01942) 673626 M: 07752-676007 E: judith.cooper5@virginmedia.com

COOPER, Ms Louise Helena. b 68. Leeds Univ BA 90. Qu Coll Birm. **d** 93 **p** 94. Par Dn Dovecot *Liv* 93–94; C 94–96; Dep Chapl HM YOI Glen Parva 96–01; Chapl HM Pris Styal 01–02; Chapl HM Pris Man 02–09; Chapl HM Pris Nottm 09–11; Chapl HM Pris Dartmoor from 11. *The Chaplaincy, HM Prison Dartmoor, Princetown, Yelverton PL20 6RR* T: (01822) 322000

COOPER, Malcolm Tydeman. b 37. Pemb Coll Ox BA 61 MA 64. Linc Th Coll 63. **d** 63 **p** 64. C Spennithorne *Ripon* 63–66; C Caversham *Ox* 66–71; Hon C Blackbird Leys CD 71–75; LtO *Sarum* 75–78; LtO *B & W* 78–82; NSM Sutton and Witcham w Mepal *Ely* 82–97; P-in-c Coveney 97–06. *8 The Coppice, Merrington, Bomere Heath, Shrewsbury SY4 3QE* E: mtcm4@waitrose.com

COOPER, Marc Ashley Rex. b 62. Leeds Univ BA 85 MA 95. Linc Th Coll 92. **d** 92 **p** 93. C Bolton St Jas w St Chrys *Bradf* 92–96; P-in-c Fishtoft *Linc* 96–97; R from 97; RD Holland E 03–09. *The Rectory, Rectory Close, Fishtoft, Boston PE21 0RZ* T/F: (01205) 363216 E: rector@fishtoftchurch.org.uk

COOPER, Mrs Margaret Anne. b 54. SRN 76. STETS 11. **d** 14 **p** 15. NSM Guildf St Nic 14–18; PtO from 18. *68 Horseshoe Lane East, Guildford GU1 2TW* T: (01483) 825191 E: anne.cooper9@btinternet.com

COOPER, Canon Michael Leonard. b 30. St Jo Coll Cam BA 53 MA 58. Cuddesdon Coll 53. **d** 55 **p** 56. C Croydon St Jo *Cant* 55–61; V Spring Park 61–71; V Boxley 71–82; RD Sutton 74–80; V Cranbrook 82–92; Hon Chapl to Bp Dover 93–97; Asst Chapl Kent and Cant Hosps NHS Trust 94–97; Hon Can Cant Cathl 76–97; PtO *Roch* 97–06; rtd 00. *The Rectory, Bellingham, Hexham NE48 2JS* T: (01434) 220019

COOPER, Canon Michael Sydney. b 41. Univ of Wales (Lamp) BA 63. Westcott Ho Cam 63. **d** 65 **p** 66. C Farlington *Portsm* 65–69; Pakistan 70–71; Mauritius 71–73; C-in-c Hayling St Pet CD *Portsm* 74–81; V Carisbrooke St Mary 81–92; V Carisbrooke St Nic 81–92; V Hartplain 92–98; V Portchester 98–06; RD Fareham 99–04; Hon Can Portsm Cathl 02–06; rtd 06; PtO *Portsm* from 06. *122 Paxton Road, Fareham PO14 1AE* T: (01329) 822152

COOPER, Nicholas John. Wycliffe Hall Ox. **d** 06 **p** 07. C Tenterden St Mildred w Smallhythe *Cant* 06–09; C Tenterden St Mich 07–09; P-in-c Saltwood 09–13; C Aldington w Bonnington and Bilsington etc 10–13; R Lympne and Saltwood 13–15; V Frindsbury w Upnor and Chattenden *Roch* from 15. *Frindsbury Vicarage, 4 Parsonage Lane, Rochester ME2 4UR* T: (01634) 717580 E: vicar@allsaintsfrindsbury.org.uk

COOPER, Canon Nigel Scott. b 53. Qu Coll Cam BA 75 MA 79 PGCE 76 CEnv MCIEEM FRSB FLS. Ripon Coll Cuddesdon BA 83 MA 88. **d** 83 **p** 84. C Moulsham St Jo *Chelmsf* 83–88; R Rivenhall 88–05; Chapl Anglia Ruskin Univ *Ely* from 05; Bp's Adv on Further Educn from 08; Hon Can Ely Cathl from 13. *The Chaplaincy Office, Anglia Ruskin University, East Road, Cambridge CB1 1PT* T: 08451-962398 *or* (01223) 698398 E: nigel.cooper@anglia.ac.uk

COOPER, Canon Peter David. b 48. Sarum & Wells Th Coll 70. **d** 73 **p** 74. C Yateley *Win* 73–78; C Christchurch 78–81; P-in-c Southampton St Mark 81–83; V 83–98; P-in-c Tadley St Pet 98–02; R Tadley S and Silchester 02–13; rtd 13; PtO *Win* from 13; Hon Can Ife Nigeria from 00. *42 Tuckton Road, Bournemouth BH6 3HS* T: (01202) 986894 E: peter.clairecooper@gmail.com

COOPER, Canon Richard Thomas. b 46. Leeds Univ BA 69. Coll of Resurr Mirfield 69. **d** 71 **p** 72. C Rothwell *Ripon* 71–75; C Adel 75–78; C Knaresborough 78–81; P-in-c Croft 81–90; P-in-c Eryholme 81–90; P-in-c Middleton Tyas and Melsonby 81–90; RD Richmond 86–90; V Aldborough w Boroughbridge and Roecliffe 90–98; RD Ripon 93–96; R Richmond w Hudswell 98–05; R Richmond w Hudswell and Downholme and Marske 05–09; Hon Can Ripon Cathl 97–09; rtd 09; Chapl to The Queen 03–16; PtO *Leeds* from 17. *13 Ash Bank Road, Ripon HG4 2EQ* E: richard@hargill.plus.com

COOPER, The Ven Robert Gerard. b 68. Univ of Wales (Abth) BD 91. Linc Th Coll 93. **d** 93 **p** 94. C Whitkirk *Ripon* 93–96; C Leeds Richmond Hill 96–97; Chapl Agnes Stewart C of E High Sch Leeds 96–97; Chapl Chigwell Sch Essex 97–98; V Lightcliffe *Wakef* 98–05; V Pontefract St Giles 05–14; *Leeds* 14–18; RD Pontefract *Wakef* 06–14; AD *Leeds* 14–18; Hon Can Wakef Cathl 08–18; Adn Sunderland *Dur* from 18; Can Mara Tanzania from 17. *St Nicholas' Vicarage, Hedworth Lane, Boldon Colliery NE35 9JA* M: 07384-510731 E: robert_cooper@msn.com *or* archdeacon.of.sunderland@durham.anglican.org

COOPER, Robert James. b 52. Bris Univ BA 75. Ridley Hall Cam 76. **d** 78 **p** 79. C Street w Walton *B & W* 78–82; C Batheaston w St Cath 82–86; P-in-c Sadberge *Dur* 86–03; Asst Chapl Arts and Recreation 86–05; Chapl 05–08; Lic to AD Stockton 08–18; Chapl N Tees and Hartlepool NHS Foundn Trust 14–18; rtd 18. *12 Hutton Close, Fishburn, Stockton-on-Tees TS21 4HE* T: (01740) 622788 E: cooperphoto@btinternet.com

COOPER, Canon Roger Charles. b 48. GRSM ARMCM 69 PGCE 70. Coll of Resurr Mirfield 79. **d** 81 **p** 82. C Monkseaton St Mary *Newc* 81–85; C Morpeth 83–87; Min Can and Prec Man Cathl 87–90; V Blackrod 90–15; AD Deane 05–12; C Horwich and Rivington 11–15; Hon Can Man Cathl 11–15; rtd 15; PtO *Man* from 15. *62 Belmont Road, Adlington, Chorley PR6 9PU* T: (01257) 434373 E: revrog17@gmail.com

COOPER, Sarah Fiona Louise. b 69. Coll of SS Mark and Jo Plymouth BEd 92. Qu Foundn Birm 15. **d** 17 **p** 18. C Perry Barr *Birm* from 17. *37 Hillside Drive, Great Barr, Birmingham B42 1NY* E: curate@sjpb.org.uk

COOPER, Canon Seth William. b 62. Westcott Ho Cam 94. **d** 96 **p** 97. C Golders Green *Lon* 96–00; TV Uxbridge 00–05; V Walmer *Cant* 05–18; R Walmer and Cornilo from 18; AD Sandwich from 10; Hon Can Cant Cathl from 17. *Elizabeth House, 32 St Mary's Road, Walmer, Deal CT14 7QA* T: (01304) 366605 E: sethandjen@tinyworld.co.uk *or* vicar@walmerparishchurches.org

COOPER, Stephen. b 54. Bernard Gilpin Soc Dur 73 Chich Th Coll 74. **d** 77 **p** 78. C Horbury *Wakef* 77–78; C Horbury w Horbury Bridge 78–81; C Barnsley St Mary 81–84; TV Elland 84–91; Hon C Huddersfield St Thos 93–94; P-in-c Middlesbrough St Columba w St Paul *York* 94–08; V from 09; P-in-c Middlesbrough St Jo the Ev 05–08; V from 09; Chapl S Tees Hosps NHS Foundn Trust 94–18. *St Columba's Vicarage, 115 Cambridge Road, Middlesbrough TS5 5HF* T: (01642) 824779 E: fr_s_cooper@hotmail.com

COOPER, Stephen Paul Crossley. b 58. Trin Coll Bris 91. **d** 93 **p** 94. C Blackb Redeemer 93–95; C Altham w Clayton le Moors 95–98; V Langho Billington 98–03; Chapl Rossall Sch Fleetwood 03–09; TV Fellside Team *Blackb* 09–15; TR from 15. *The Vicarage, Goosnargh Lane, Goosnargh, Preston PR3 2BN* T: (01722) 865274 E: revscooper@gmail.com

COOPER, Mrs Susan Elizabeth Courtenay. b 50. Open Univ BA 94 LLAM 70. **d** 10 **p** 12. New Zealand 01–13; NSM Rotherfield Peppard and Kidmore End etc *Ox* 14–16; P-in-c Purleigh *Chelmsf* 16–18; rtd 18; Hon C W Rotorua New Zealand from 18. *43/15 Hodgkins Street, Pukehangi, Rotorua 3015, New Zealand* E: revdsusancooper@gmail.com

COOPER, Mrs Susan Mary. b 45. Westcott Ho Cam 01. **d** 03 **p** 04. C Syston *Leic* 03–06; R Chipping Ongar w Shelley *Chelmsf* 06–14; rtd 14; PtO *Leic* 14–16; NSM Market Harborough and The Transfiguration etc from 16. *89 Scotland Road, Market Harborough LE16 8AY* E: scoople@btinternet.com

COOPER, Susan Mira. *See* RAMSARAN, Susan Mira

COOPER, Mrs Suzanne Tracey. b 62. Ripon Coll Cuddesdon 13. **d** 15 **p** 16. C Blisworth, Alderton, Grafton Regis etc *Pet* 15–19; R Aynho and Croughton w Evenley etc from 19. *The Rectory, Croughton Road, Aynho, Banbury OX17 3BD* T: (01869) 810903 E: revsue.cooper@gmail.com

COOPER, Thomas Joseph Gerard Strickland. b 46. Lanc Univ PhD 85. Ven English Coll & Pontifical Gregorian Univ Rome PhB 66 PhL 67 STB 69 STL 71. **d** 70 **p** 70. In RC Ch 70–92; Chapl St Woolos Cathl *Mon* 93–95; V Llandaff N *Llan* 95–08; rtd 08; PtO *St D* from 08. *Arwel, Cwmdegwel, St Dogmaels, Cardigan SA43 3JH* T: (01239) 614156 E: teilo@woolos.supanet.com *or* woolos@gmail.com

COOPER, Ms Wendy. b 58. **d** 12 **p** 14. NSM Salisbury St Thos and St Edm *Sarum* 12–15; PtO from 16. *Parish Office, St Thomas's House, St Thomas's Square, Salisbury SP1 1BA* E: mukinge.minstead@yahoo.co.uk

COOPER, William Douglas. b 42. Open Univ BA 83 BSc 11 St Andr Univ MA 08 Aber Univ MA 09. St Jo Coll Nottm 88 Qu Coll Birm 93. **d** 94 **p** 95. NSM Melbourne *Derby* 94–97; C Penwortham St Mary *Blackb* 97–00; P-in-c Smeeth w Monks Horton and Stowting and Brabourne *Cant* 00–04; rtd 04. *18A Market Street, St Andrews KY16 9NS* T: (01334) 460678

COORE, Jonathan. b 71. LTCL GTCL 94 Lon Inst of Educn PGCE 97. Trin Coll Bris 05. **d** 07 **p** 08. C Heref St Pet w St Owen and St Jas 07–12; Bp's Dom Chapl 08–12; Min Can and Succ St Paul's Cathl *Lon* 12–14; R S'wark Ch Ch 14–19; PV Westmr Abbey 16–19; Hon Min Can S'wark Cathl 14–19; Min Can and Succ Windsor from 19; Chapl St Geo Sch Windsor from 19. *St George's School, Windsor Castle, Windsor SL4 1QF* T: (01753) 865553 M: 07786-431451 E: jonathancoore@gmail.com

COOTE, Bernard Albert Ernest. b 28. Lon Univ BD 53. Chich Th Coll 54. **d** 55 **p** 56. C Addiscombe St Mary *Cant* 55–57; C Hawkhurst 57–59; C Sanderstead All SS *S'wark* 59–63; Chapl HM Borstal E Sutton Park 63–74; V Sutton Valence w E Sutton *Cant* 63–76; P-in-c Chart next Sutton Valence 71–76; P-in-c Sutton Valence w E Sutton and Chart Sutton 76; Chapl and Dir R Sch for the Blind Leatherhead 76–91; rtd 91; PtO *Chich* from 91; *Guildf* 91–05. *25 Raphael Road, Hove BN3 5QP* T: (01273) 640732

COPE, Elizabeth Ruth. b 80. Ch Coll Cam BA 04 MSci 04 MA 07 PhD 10. Ridley Hall Cam 14. **d** 16 **p** 17. C Lordsbridge *Ely* 16–18; C Long Stanton w St Mich from 18; C Over from 18; C Swavesey from 18; C Willingham from 18. *6 Woodpecker Close, Northstowe, Cambridge CB24 1AW* E: beth.cope@northstowe.church

COPE, James Brian Andrew. b 58. Chich Th Coll 80. **d** 83 **p** 84. C Poulton-le-Fylde *Blackb* 83–86; C Fleetwood St Pet 86–87; V Fleetwood St Dav 87–94; P-in-c Somercotes *Derby* 94–99; V Watford St Jo *St Alb* 99–07; V Castle Vale w Minworth *Birm* from 07. *St Cuthbert's Vicarage, St Cuthbert's Place, Birmingham B35 7PL* T: 0121-747 4041 E: fr.jamescopessc@sky.com

COPE, Judith Diane. b 50. St Hilda's Coll Ox BA 72 Lon Univ MB, BS 75 MRCGP 80. SAOMC 00. **d** 03 **p** 04. NSM Lt Berkhamsted and Bayford, Essendon etc *St Alb* 03–13; rtd 13; PtO *St Alb* 13–18. *23 Gresley Court, Hawkshead Road, Potters Bar EN6 1LF* T: (01707) 644391 E: m_cope@btinternet.com

COPE, Canon Melia Lambrianos. b 53. Cape Town Univ BSocSc 73. St Jo Coll Nottm 80 WMMTC 83. **dss** 86 **d** 93 **p** 94. W Bromwich All SS *Lich* 86–93; NSM 93–94; NSM W Bromwich St Mary Magd CD 93–94; TV Cen Telford 94–02; Chapl HM Pris Shrewsbury 95–98; P-in-c Stokesay *Heref* 02–12; P-in-c Halford w Sibdon Carwood 02–12; P-in-c Acton Scott 02–12; P-in-c Wistanstow 06–12; V E Radnor *S & B* from 12; Can Res Brecon Cathl from 17. *The Vicarage, Church Street, Knighton LD7 1AG* T: (01547) 528566 E: revdmeliacope@gmail.com

COPE, Miss Olive Rosemary. b 29. Gilmore Ho 63. **dss** 69 **d** 87 **p** 94. Kentish Town St Martin w St Andr *Lon* 69–72; Enfield St Andr 73–99; Par Dn 87–89; Hon Par Dn 89–94; Hon C 94–99; PtO 99–18. *7 Calder Close, Enfield EN1 3TS* T: (020) 8363 8221 E: oliveclose2003@yahoo.co.uk

COPE, Mrs Patricia Millicent. b 51. Man Univ BEd 73 MEd 88. SNWTP 10. **d** 12 **p** 13. NSM Knutsford St Cross *Ches* 12–15; NSM Rostherne w Bollington from 15; NSM High Legh from 15; NSM Over Tabley from 15. *23 North Drive, High Legh, Knutsford WA16 6LX* T: (01925) 754787 M: 07703-470101 E: trishcope2012@btinternet.com

COPE, Peter John. b 42. Mert Coll Ox BA 64 MA 67 Lon Univ MSc 74 Man Univ PhD 91. Cuddesdon Coll 64. **d** 66 **p** 67. C Chapel Allerton *Ripon* 66–69; Ind Chapl *Lon* 69–76; Ind Chapl *Worc* 76–85; Min Can Worc Cathl 76–85; P-in-c Worc St Mark 76–81; Ind Chapl W Bromwich and Men W Bromwich St Mary Magd CD *Lich* 85–94; Telford Town Cen Chapl 94–07; W Midl FE Field Officer 94–97; Churches Ind

Officer 97–07; rtd 07; PtO *Heref* 96–14; *Lich* 07–10; *S & B* from 12. *The Vicarage, Church Street, Knighton LD7 1AG* T: (01547) 528566 E: peter.cope123@btinternet.com

COPE, Canon Stephen Victor. b 60. St Jo Coll Ox BA 81 MA 87. Chich Th Coll 86. **d** 89 **p** 90. C Newmarket St Mary w Exning St Agnes *St E* 89–92; C Northampton St Matt *Pet* 92–94; V Rudston w Boynton and Kilham *York* 94–98; V Rudston w Boynton, Carnaby and Kilham 98–06; P-in-c Burton Fleming w Fordon, Grindale etc 00–06; RD Bridlington 98–03; P-in-c Owthorne and Rimswell w Withernsea 06–07; P-in-c Easington w Skeffling, Kilnsea and Holmpton 06–07; R Withernsea w Owthorne and Easington etc 07–14; P-in-c Roos and Garton w Tunstall, Grimston and Hilston 12–14; V Withernsea w Owthorne, Garton-in-Holderness etc 14; RD S Holderness 09–14; R Holme and Seaton Ross Gp from 14; Can and Preb York Minster from 10. *The Vicarage, Market Weighton Road, Holme-on-Spalding-Moor, York YO43 4AG* T: (01964) 611462 E: stephenvcope@tiscali.co.uk

COPELAND, Annabel Susan Mary. b 64. Roehampton Inst BEd 87. Wycliffe Hall Ox 03. **d** 05 **p** 06. C Billericay and Lt Burstead *Chelmsf* 05–08; TV Gt Baddow 08–14; P-in-c Tidworth *Sarum* 14–17; Chapl Wellington Academy 14–17; Chapl Bluecoat Sch Nottm 17–18; LtO *Lon* from 18. *141 Brunswick Park Road, London N11 1EG* E: copeland321@btinternet.com

COPELAND, Christopher Paul. b 38. AKC 64. **d** 65 **p** 66. C Luton St Andr *St Alb* 65–67; C Droitwich St Nic w St Pet *Worc* 67–71; C Kings Norton *Birm* 71–72; TV 73–78; V Tyseley 78–88; P-in-c Grimley w Holt *Worc* 88–96; Dioc Stewardship Missr 88–96; P-in-c Forest of Dean Ch Ch w English Bicknor *Glouc* 96–03; rtd 03; PtO *Worc* from 03. *24 Players Avenue, Malvern WR14 1DU* T: (01684) 563323 E: chriscopeland@mypostoffice.co.uk

COPELAND, Derek Norman. b 38. Worc Coll Ox BA 62 MA 68. Westcott Ho Cam 63. **d** 64 **p** 65. C Portsea St Mary *Portsm* 64–71; P-in-c Avonmouth St Andr *Bris* 71–77; P-in-c Chippenham St Paul w Langley Burrell 78–79; Ind Chapl from 78; TR Chippenham St Paul w Hardenhuish etc 79–89; V Kington St Michael 79–89; PtO from 89; *B & W* 89–06; *Sarum* from 89; rtd 03. *51B Lowden, Chippenham SN15 2BG* T: (01249) 443879

COPESTAKE, Mrs Sharon Louise. b 70. Cov Univ BA 94 Cant Ch Ch Univ BA 12. SEITE 09. **d** 12 **p** 13. C Chatham St Phil and St Jas *Roch* 12–15; V Strood St Fran from 15; RD Strood from 17. *The Vicarage, Galahad Avenue, Rochester ME2 2YS* T: (01634) 717162 E: vicar.stfrancisstrood@gmail.com

COPLEY, Paul. b 58. NEOC 97. **d** 99 **p** 00. C Hessle *York* 99–02; TV Sutton St Jas and Wawne 02–07; P-in-c Kingston upon Hull St Nic 07–14; V from 14; P-in-c Newington w Dairycoates 07–10. *St Nicholas' Vicarage, 898 Hessle High Road, Hull HU4 6SA* T: (01482) 504088 E: copleypaul@hotmail.com

COPPEN, Colin William. b 53. BCombStuds 85. Linc Th Coll. **d** 85 **p** 86. C Tokyngton St Mich *Lon* 85–88; C Somers Town 88–90; P-in-c Edmonton St Alphege 90–92; V 92–95; P-in-c W Hampstead St Jas 95–97; C Kilburn St Mary w All So 95–97; TR Wood Green St Mich w Bounds Green St Gabr etc 97–16; C Munster Square Ch Ch and St Mary Magd 16–18; rtd 18; PtO *Birm* from 19; *Lich* from 19. *20 Wood Street, Tipton DY4 9BQ*

COPPEN, George. See COPPEN, Robert George

COPPEN, Canon Martin Alan. b 48. Ex Univ BA 69. St Jo Coll Nottm 83. **d** 85 **p** 86. C Bitterne *Win* 85–88; V St Mary Bourne and Woodcott 88–99; V Hurstbourne Priors, Longparish etc 00–13; RD Whitchurch 98–03; Hon Can Win Cathl 04–13; rtd 13; PtO *Win* from 14. *5 Acre Path, Andover SP10 1HJ*

COPPEN, Robert George. b 39. Cape Town Univ BA 66. Cranmer Hall Dur 79. **d** 81 **p** 82. C Douglas St Geo and St Barn *S & M* 81–84; TV Kidlington w Hampton Poyle *Ox* 84–05; Chapl HM Detention Cen Campsfield Ho 84–91; rtd 05; LtO *Mor* from 05. *Taobh Mol, Kildary, Invergordon IV18 0NJ* T: (01862) 842381 E: coppen@dunelm.org.uk

COPPING, Canon Adrian Walter Alexander. b 52. Ridley Hall Cam. **d** 00 **p** 01. C Royston *St Alb* 00–04; R Bangor Monachorum, Worthenbury and Marchwiel *St As* 04–09; AD Bangor Isycoed 05–09; R Cilcain, Gwernaffield, Llanferres etc 09–16; AD Mold 11–16; Can St As Cathl 14–16; rtd 16; PtO *St E* from 17. *57 Briar Hill, Woolpit, Bury St Edmunds IP30 9SD* E: adriancopping@hotmail.com

COPPING, Mary Catriona. b 50. STETS. **d** 12 **p** 13. NSM Win St Matt from 12. *2 Churchill Close, King's Worthy, Winchester SO23 7PD* T: (01962) 881321 E: marycopping@btinternet.com

COPPING, Raymond. b 36. St Mark & St Jo Coll Lon TCert 59. Wycliffe Hall Ox 72. **d** 74 **p** 75. C High Wycombe *Ox* 74–77; TV 77–87; TV Digswell and Panshanger *St Alb* 87–95; P-in-c Charlton Kings H Apostles *Glouc* 95–00; rtd 00; Hon C Thame *Ox* from 04. *20 Friars Furlong, Long Crendon, Aylesbury HP18 9DQ* T: (01844) 208509

COPSEY, Nigel John. b 52. K Coll Lon BD 75 AKC 75 Surrey Univ MSc 88 Middx Univ DProf 01. St Aug Coll Cant 72. **d** 76 **p** 77. C Barkingside St Fran *Chelmsf* 76–78; C Canning Town St Cedd 78–80; P-in-c Victoria Docks Ascension 80–87; Chapl E Surrey Mental Health Unit 87–90; Hd Past and Spiritual Care E Surrey Priority Care NHS Trust from 90; Co-ord Past Care Surrey Oaklands NHS Trust 99–05; Hd Past and Spiritual Care Surrey and Borders Partnership NHS Foundn Trust from 08; Co-ord Relig Care Newham Community Health Services NHS Trust 99–01; Co-ord Relig Care Newham Primary Care Trust from 01; Team Ldr Spiritual, Relig & Cultural Care E Lon NHS Foundation Trust from 08. *Newham Centre for Mental Health, Glen Road, London E13 8SP* T: (020) 7540 4380 F: 7540 2970 E: nigel.copsey@eastlondon.nhs.uk

COPUS, Brian George. b 36. AKC 59. **d** 60 **p** 61. C Croydon St Mich *Cant* 60–63; C Swindon New Town *Bris* 63–69; V Colebrooke *Ex* 69–73; P-in-c Hittisleigh 69–73; R Perivale *Lon* 73–82; V Ruislip St Mary 82–01; rtd 01; PtO *Win* 02–11. *Le Bec, 84 Carbery Avenue, Bournemouth BH6 3LQ* T: (01202) 428943

COPUS, John Cecil. b 38. TCert 64 Maria Grey Coll Lon DipEd 71 Open Univ BA 78. Cant Sch of Min. **d** 83 **p** 84. Hon C Folkestone H Trin and St Geo w Ch Ch *Cant* 83–85; Hon C Midsomer Norton w Clandown *B & W* 85–91; Dioc Adv for Children's Work *Ex* 91–98; Hon C Aylesbeare, Rockbeare, Farringdon etc 95–98; P-in-c 98–01; rtd 01; PtO *Ex* 01–17; Clergy Widow(er)s Officer from 02; C N Creedy 08–10. *The Sidings, Park Road, Lapford, Crediton EX17 6QJ* T: (01363) 83408

COPUS, Jonathan Hugh Lambert. b 44. BNC Ox BA 66 MA 71 LGSM 66 MInstPI 94. S'wark Ord Course 68. **d** 71 **p** 72. C Horsell *Guildf* 71–73; Producer Relig Progr BBC Radio Solent 73–87; V Maenclochog and New Moat etc *St D* 06–07; V Martletwy w Lawrenny and Minwear etc 07; PtO 07–11; rtd 10; P-in-c Crymych Gp *St D* from 11. *Llys Myrddin, Efailwen, Clynderwen SA66 7XG* T: (01994) 438414 M: 07828-510283 E: revjc@dentron.co.uk

CORBETT, The Very Revd Ian Deighton. b 42. St Cath Coll Cam BA 64 MA 67 Cam Univ PGCE 65. Westcott Ho Cam 67. **d** 69 **p** 70. C New Bury *Man* 69–72; C Bolton St Pet 72–75; Chapl Bolton Colls of H&FE 72–75; R Man Victoria Park 75–80; Chapl Salford Univ 80–83; Dioc FE Officer 74–83; R Salford Sacred Trin 83–87; Dir CME and Hon Can Man Cathl 83–87; Warden Lelapa la Jesu Sem Lesotho 88–91; Can Missr Harare Zimbabwe 92–93; Can Missr Botswana 93–95; R Kuruman St Mary S Africa 95–97; Dean Tuam and I Tuam w Cong and Aasleagh *T, K & A* 97–99; R Whitesands Canada 99–01; V Utah Region USA 01–08; Hon C E Clevedon w Clapton in Gordano etc *B & W* 09–13; PtO *Worc* from 13. *6 The Quadrangle, Newland, Malvern WR13 5AX* T: (01684) 574091 E: iancorbett123@btinternet.com

CORBETT, Philip Peter. b 80. St Andr Univ MTheol 03 Yale Univ STM 04 Keble Coll Ox MPhil 06. Coll of Resurr Mirfield 06. **d** 08 **p** 09. C Worksop Priory *S'well* 08–11; P Lib and Chapl Pusey Ho 11–13; P-in-c Lewisham St Steph and St Mark *S'wark* 13–16; V 16–19; P-in-c Notting Hill All SS w St Columb *Lon* from 19; P-in-c Notting Hill St Mich and Ch Ch from 19. *All Saints' Vicarage, Clydesdale Road, London W11 1JE* M: 07929-750054 E: philippetercorbett@gmail.com

CORBETT, Miss Phyllis. b 34. Cranmer Hall Dur 76. **dss** 80 **d** 87 **p** 94. Walsall Wood *Lich* 80–87; Par Dn Baswich 87–94; C 94–95; rtd 95; PtO *Lich* 95–13. *45 Alrewych Court, 220 Northgate, Aldridge, Walsall WS9 8AF* T: (01922) 456663

CORBYN, Canon John. b 58. Man Univ BA 79 Ven English Coll & Pontifical Gregorian Univ Rome 83. Wycliffe Hall Ox BA 83 MA 87. **d** 84 **p** 85. C Deane *Man* 84–87; C Lancaster St Mary *Blackb* 87–90; Sub-Chapl HM Pris Lanc 89–90; V Blackb St Gabr 90–01; V Bearsted w Thurnham *Cant* 01–16; TR N Downs from 16; AD from 18; Hon Can Cant Cathl from 16. *The Vicarage, Church Lane, Bearsted, Maidstone ME14 4EF* T: (01622) 737135 E: vicar@holycrosschurch.co.uk

CORCORAN, Daniel Chad. b 71. Man Metrop Univ BA 93. St Jo Coll Nottm 04. **d** 06 **p** 07. C Stapleford *S'well* 06–10; C Bilborough w Strelley 10–15; C Broxtowe 14–17; C Bilborough and Strelley 15–17; PtO *Cant* 17–19; C Faversham from 19. *83 St Peter's Lane, Canterbury CT1 2BP* M: 07963-332221

CORCORAN, Jennifer Miriam. b 78. Lanc Univ BA 01. St Jo Coll Nottm MA(MM) 07. **d** 07 **p** 08. C Chilwell *S'well* 07–10; NSM Chilwell and Lenton Abbey 10–13; Tutor St Jo Coll Nottm 13–17; Chapl to Bp Dover *Cant* from 17; Abp's Chapl from 17. *The Bishop of Dover's Office, The Old Palace, The Precincts, Canterbury CT1 2EE* T: (01227) 459382 E: jenny.corcoran@bishcant.org

CORCORAN, Michael Patrick. b 65. Man Univ BSocSc 86. St Jo Coll Nottm MTh 17. **d** 14 **p** 15. C Brunswick *Man* 14–17; Chapl Man Univ NHS Foundn Trust from 17; C Withington St Paul *Man* from 19. *34 Mauldeth Road, Manchester M20 4WD* T: 0161-445 1178 M: 07825-153455 E: corkie@sky.com

CORCORAN, Mrs Valerie A'Court. b 46. UEA BA 68 Lon Inst of Educn PGCE 69. STETS 99. **d** 02 **p** 03. NSM Boyatt Wood *Win* 02–10; rtd 10; PtO *Win* from 13. *Ashley, Finches Lane, Twyford, Winchester SO21 1QB* T: (01962) 712951 F: 715770 M: 07736-459500 E: v.corcoran@btinternet.com

CORDELL, Derek Harold. b 34. Chich Th Coll 57. **d** 60 **p** 61. C Whitstable All SS *Cant* 60–63; C Moulsecoomb *Chich* 63–69; Chapl Bucharest *Eur* 69–71; V Brighton St Wilfrid *Chich* 71–74; Chapl HM Borstal Roch 74–80; Asst Chapl HM Pris Man 80–81; Chapl HM Pris The Verne 81–89; Chapl HM Pris Channings Wood 89–90; Chapl Milan w Genoa and Varese *Eur* 90–91; Chapl Mojácar 91–94; PtO 95–14; rtd 97; PtO *B & W* from 15. *27 Scalwell Mead, Seaton EX12 2DW* T: (01297) 624182

CORFE, David Robert. b 35. Pemb Coll Cam BA 58 MA 60 Lambeth STh 70. Cuddesdon Coll 58. **d** 60 **p** 61. C Wigan All SS *Liv* 60–63; SPG Miss India 63–68; V Lucknow Ch Ch w All SS and St Pet 70–75; C Northwood Em *Lon* 75; V Westwell and Eastwell w Boughton Aluph *Cant* 75–80; V Hildenborough *Roch* 80–91; Lic Preacher Stretford St Bride *Man* 91–98; Interserve 98–00; rtd 00; PtO *Win* from 03; *Birm* from 18. *1 Hartley Court, 12 Winn Road, Southampton SO17 1EN* T: (023) 8058 5557 E: davidrobertcorfe@gmail.com

CORIO, Alec Stephen. b 82. Qu Coll Cam BA 09 MA 09 MPhil 07 Open Univ PhD 14. Westcott Ho Cam 13. **d** 16 **p** 17. C Stockport St Geo *Ches* 16–19; R E Barnet *St Alb* from 19. *1 Spring Close, Barnet EN5 2UR* M: 07871-576021 E: alec.corio@gmail.com *or* rector.stmaryeastbarnet@gmail.com

CORK, CLOYNE AND ROSS, Archdeacon of. See WILKINSON, The Ven Adrian Mark

CORK, CLOYNE AND ROSS, Bishop of. See COLTON, The Rt Revd William Paul

CORK, Dean of. See DUNNE, The Very Revd Nigel Kenneth

CORKE, Andrew John. b 55. Bris Univ LLB 77. **d** 98 **p** 99. NSM Canford Magna *Sarum* 98–10; TV Swanage and Studland from 10. *The Vicarage, 5 Redcliffe Road, Swanage BH19 1LZ* T: (01929) 421836 M: 07711-898723 E: vicar@allsaints-swanage.org

CORKE, Colin John. b 59. St Pet Coll Ox BA 81. Cranmer Hall Dur 83. **d** 85 **p** 86. C Chapel Allerton *Ripon* 85–88; C Burmantofts St Steph and St Agnes 88–91; P-in-c Tatsfield *S'wark* 91–01; Reigate Adnry Ecum Officer 92–01; V Longbridge *Birm* from 01; Dioc Ecum Officer 02–05; AD Kings Norton 06–12; Ind Chapl from 08. *St John's Vicarage, 220 Longbridge Lane, Birmingham B31 4JT* T: 0121-475 3484 E: colincorke@gmail.com

CORKE, Francis Bonny. See RODRIGUEZ-VEGLIO, Francis Bonny

CORKE, Canon Louise Dorothy. b 59. Southn Univ BSc 80 PGCE 81. Trin Coll Bris BA 97. **d** 97 **p** 98. C Ipsley *Worc* 97–01; TV Bradgate Team *Leic* 01–15; C Groby and Ratby 15–17; TV Kegworth, Hathern, Long Whatton, Diseworth etc from 17; Bp's NSM Officer from 13; Hon Can Leic Cathl from 18. *The Vicarage, Presents Lane, Belton, Loughborough LE12 9UN* T: (01530) 588868

CORKE, Roderick Geoffrey. b 58. UEA BEd 79 Open Univ MA 96. St Jo Coll Nottm 90. **d** 92 **p** 93. C Trimley *St E* 92–95; C Walton 95–00; TR Walton and Trimley 00–05; P-in-c Taunton St Mary *B & W* 05–08; V 08–14; V Taunton St Mary and St Jo 14–18; V Gt Malvern St Mary *Worc* from 18. *Priory Vicarage, 7 Clarence Road, Malvern WR14 3EN* E: rodcorke@tiscali.co.uk

CORKER, Mrs Elizabeth Jane. b 42. **d** 99 **p** 00. OLM Martlesham w Brightwell *St E* 99–10; OLM Felixstowe St Jo 10–12; rtd 12. *12 Fairfield Avenue, Felixstowe IP11 9JN* T: (01394) 210793 E: e.corker@ntlworld.com

CORKER, John Anthony. b 37. AKC 63 ACIB 75. K Coll Lon 1960 St Boniface Warminster 63. **d** 64 **p** 65. C Lindley *Wakef* 64–68; V Brotherton 68–72; PtO 72–82; CF (TA) 80–93; Hon C Askham Bryan *York* 82–91; TV York All SS Pavement w St Crux and St Martin etc 91–96; Chapl York Health Services

NHS Trust 91–96; Chapl Dudley Gp of Hosps NHS Trust 96–99; Asst P Amblecote *Worc* 96–01; Asst P Dudley St Barn 01–02; rtd 02; PtO *Worc* from 02. *15 Holly Grove, Stourbridge DY8 1UF* T: (01384) 897378 E: the.corkers@talktalk.net

CORLETT, Daniel James. b 77. Birm Univ MEng 00. Wycliffe Hall Ox 17. **d** 19. C Arden Marches *Cov* from 19. *6 Lansdowne Road, Studley B80 7RB* M: 07543-370637 E: curate@ardenmarches.co.uk

CORLEY, Claire Marie. b 76. St Mary's Coll Dur BA 98. St Hild Coll 14. **d** 17 **p** 18. C Roundhay St Edm *Leeds* from 17. *2A Ryder Gardens, Leeds LS8 1JS* T: 0113-268 0260 M: 07811-151027

CORLEY, Canon Samuel Jon Clint. b 76. St Aid Coll Dur BA 97 MA 98 Hughes Hall Cam PGCE 99. St Jo Coll Nottm MA 04. **d** 04 **p** 05. C Lancaster St Thos *Blackb* 04–08; Asst Dioc Missr 08–11; P-in-c Ellel w Shireshead 08–11; Can Res Bradf Cathl *Leeds* 11–15; Chapl Bradf Univ 11–15; P-in-c Leeds City 15–17; R from 17; Hon Can Ripon Cathl from 15. *2A Ryder Gardens, Leeds LS8 1JS* T: 0113-268 0260 M: 07966-524683 E: sam.corley76@gmail.com

CORMACK, Donald Stuart. b 45. Brock Univ Ontario TCert 67 McMaster Univ Ontario BA 71. Regent Coll Vancouver MTh 85. **d** 92 **p** 93. C St Geo Singapore 92–93; P-in-c Phnom Penh Cambodia 93–96; PtO *Glouc* 06–15; *Chich* from 15. *Address withheld by request* E: doncormack@outlook.com

CORNE, Ronald Andrew. b 51. Sarum & Wells Th Coll 87. **d** 89 **p** 90. C Bitterne Park *Win* 89–93; R Headbourne Worthy and King's Worthy 93–01; P-in-c Broughton, Bossington, Houghton and Mottisfont 01–03; R 03–17; RD Romsey 06–13; rtd 17; PtO *Win* from 17; Clergy Retirement Officer from 18; PtO *Eur* from 17. *5 Morley College, Market Street, Winchester SO23 9LF* E: cronandrew@aol.com

CORNELL, Nicholas Simon. b 78. Trin Hall Cam BA 00 MA 03. Oak Hill Th Coll MTh 08. **d** 08 **p** 09. C Eastbourne All SS *Chich* 08–12; R Maresfield 12–18; V Nutley 12–18; C Southborough St Pet w Ch Ch and St Matt etc *Roch* 18–19; R Southborough Ch Ch from 19. *The Rectory, 86 Prospect Road, Southborough, Tunbridge Wells TN4 0EG* T: (01825) 769004 M: 07946-220638 E: nscornell@gmail.com or revnickcornell@gmail.com

CORNES, Canon Andrew Charles Julian. b 49. CCC Ox BA 70 MA 74. Wycliffe Hall Ox 70 Cranmer Hall Dur 72. **d** 73 **p** 74. C York St Mich-le-Belfrey 73–76; C St Marylebone All So w SS Pet and Jo *Lon* 76–85; R Pittsburgh Ascension USA 85–88; V Crowborough *Chich* 89–15; RD Rotherfield 97–03; Can and Preb Chich Cathl 00–15; Chapl Eastbourne and Co Healthcare NHS Trust 89–02; Chapl Sussex Downs and Weald Primary Care Trust 02–15; rtd 15; PtO *Chich* 15–17. *20 Gorringe Road, Eastbourne BN22 8XL* T: (01323) 732561

CORNESS, Andrew Stuart. b 69. Bp Otter Coll Chich BA 91 Westmr Coll Ox PGCE 93. Wycliffe Hall Ox BA 00 MA 05. **d** 01 **p** 02. C Ewood *Blackb* 01–04; Chapl RN from 04. *Royal Naval Chaplaincy Service, Mail Point 1-2, Leach Building, Whale Island, Portsmouth PO2 8BY* T: (023) 9262 5055 F: 9262 5134 E: andrewcorness@hotmail.com

CORNFIELD, Richard James. b 67. St Jo Coll Nottm BA 96. **d** 96 **p** 97. C Cheltenham Ch Ch *Glouc* 96–00; C Aldridge *Lich* 00–03; R 03–11; C Edin St Paul and St Geo 11–17; Dioc Dir of Ords from 12; Pioneer P Mustard Seed Edinburgh from 17. *24 North Fort Street, Edinburgh EH6 4HD* M: 07966-165043 E: rich.cornfield@gmail.com

CORNISH, Gillian Lesley. b 45. ACIB 77. **d** 96 **p** 97. OLM Moston St Mary *Man* 96–08; OLM Blackley St Pet 08–10; rtd 10; PtO *Man* from 10. *11 Rishworth Drive, New Moston, Manchester M40 3PS* T: 0161-681 2839 E: revd.gillian@talktalk.net

CORNISH, Graham Peter. b 42. Dur Univ BA 67 FLA. NEOC 82. **d** 84 **p** 85. NSM Harrogate St Wilfrid and St Luke *Ripon* 84–96; PtO *York* from 84; NSM Bilton *Ripon* 96–09; PtO *Leeds* from 17. *33 Mayfield Grove, Harrogate HG1 5HD* T: (01423) 562747 F: 529928

CORNISH, Ivor. b 40. Reading Univ BSc 61 DipEd 62. Ox Min Course 86. **d** 89 **p** 90. NSM Aston Clinton w Buckland and Drayton Beauchamp *Ox* 89–97; NSM The Lee and Hawridge w Cholesbury and St Leonard 97–10; PtO from 10; *St Alb* from 11. *79 Weston Road, Aston Clinton, Aylesbury HP22 5EP* T: (01296) 630345 E: rev.ivor@btinternet.com

CORNISH, Peter Andrew. b 55. Ch Ch Ox BA 77 MA 80 Ex Univ CertEd 78. St Jo Coll Nottm 84. **d** 87 **p** 88. C Sanderstead All SS *S'wark* 87–92; TV Cen Telford *Lich* 92–98; R Sturry w Fordwich and Westbere w Hersden *Cant* from 98; Jt AD Cant 11–14. *The Rectory, 2 The Hamels, Sturry, Canterbury CT2 0BL* T: (01227) 490520 E: rector@sturrychurch.org.uk

CORNISH, Mrs Rachel. b 54. **d** 14 **p** 15. NSM Felixstowe St Jo *St E* 14–15; NSM Combs and Lt Finborough 15–17; NSM Gt Finborough w Onehouse, Harleston, Buxhall etc

15–17; P-in-c Alde River 17–18; R from 18. *The Rectory, Great Glemham Road, Stratford St Andrew, Saxmundham IP17 1LJ* T: (01728) 768136 E: rev.rachelcornish@gmail.com

CORNWALL, Valerie Cecilia. See SAUNDERS, Valerie Cecilia

CORNWALL, Archdeacon of. See BRYER, The Ven Paul Donald

CORNWELL, Christopher Richard. b 43. Dur Univ BA 67. Cuddesdon Coll 67. **d** 69 **p** 70. C Cannock *Lich* 69–75; P-in-c Hadley 75–80; V 80–81; Bp's Dom Chapl 81–86; Subchanter Lich Cathl 81–86; V Ellesmere 86–89; V Welsh Frankton 86–89; V Ellesmere and Welsh Frankton 89–92; TV Leeds City *Ripon* 92–00; AD Allerton 94–97; V Ireland Wood 00–08; AD Headingley 01–07; Hon C Bishop Monkton and Burton Leonard 08–13; Hon Min Can Ripon Cathl *Leeds* from 08; PtO from 14. *41 Skelldale Close, Ripon HG4 1UH* T: (01765) 602837 E: cr.cornwell43@btinternet.com

CORNWELL, Lisa Michele. b 70. Lon Bible Coll BA 94 Westmr Coll Ox PGCE 95 K Coll Lon MA 99 PhD 18. Ridley Hall Cam 00. **d** 02 **p** 03. C Newport Pagnell w Lathbury and Moulsoe *Ox* 02–06; V Crowthorne from 06. *The Vicarage, 56 Duke's Ride, Crowthorne RG45 6NY* T: (01344) 772413 E: revlisacornwell@aol.com

CORP, Ronald Geoffrey. b 51. Ch Ch Ox MA 77. STETS. **d** 98 **p** 99. NSM Kilburn St Mary w All So and W Hampstead St Jas *Lon* 98–02; NSM Hendon St Mary and Ch Ch 02–07; NSM Holborn St Alb w Saffron Hill St Pet from 07. *The Clergy House, 18 Brooke Street, London EC1N 7RD* M: 07956-847792 E: ronald.corp@btconnect.com

CORRIE, John. b 48. Imp Coll Lon BScEng 69 MSc 70 PhD 73 Nottm Univ MTh 86. Trin Coll Bris 74. **d** 77 **p** 78. C Kendal St Thos *Carl* 77–80; C Attenborough *S'well* 80–86; ICS Peru 86–91; Tutor and Lect All Nations Chr Coll Ware 91–02; Lect/ Development Officer Cen for Angl Communion Studies Selly Oak 02–05; Abp's Internat Project Officer *Cant* 05–06; Tutor Trin Coll Bris 07–17; PtO *Birm* 03–17; rtd 17. *Brambles, Higher Batson, Salcombe TQ8 8NF* E: revjohncorrie@gmail.com

CORRIE, Paul Allen. b 43. St Jo Coll Nottm 77. **d** 79 **p** 80. C Beverley Minster *York* 79–82; V Derby St Werburgh 82–84; V Derby St Alkmund and St Werburgh 84–95; Singapore 95–99; R Hawkwell *Chelmsf* 00–05; rtd 06; PtO *Bradf* 06–14; *Leeds* from 14. *5 Airedale Ings, Cononley, Keighley BD20 8LF*

CORSIE, Andrew Russell. b 57. Middx Univ BA 97 Birkbeck Coll Lon MSc 11. Trin Coll Bris 91. **d** 93 **p** 94. C Northolt Park St Barn *Lon* 93–97; C Perivale 97–01; P-in-c 01–06; R 06–14; AD Ealing 03–10; Dir Tr and Development Willesden Area from 14. *37 Ridding Lane, Greenford UB6 0JX* T: (020) 8991 9571 M: 07940-722184 E: andrew.corsie@london.anglican.org

CORY, Valerie Ann. See DAWSON, Valerie Ann

COSGRAVE-HANLEY, Máirt Joseph. See HANLEY, Máirt Joseph

COSH, Canon Roderick John. b 56. Lon Univ BSc 78 Heythrop Coll Lon MA 03. St Steph Ho Ox 78. **d** 81 **p** 82. C Swindon New Town *Bris* 81–86; Chapl Asst R Marsden Hosp 86–91; V Whitton St Aug *Lon* 91–00; P-in-c Staines St Mary and St Pet 00–05; P-in-c Staines Ch Ch 04–05; V Staines 06–13; AD Spelthorne 04–10; AD Burnham and Slough *Ox* from 13; C Colnbrook and Datchet from 13; Hon Can Ch Ch from 16. *The New Vicarage, Mill Street, Colnbrook, Slough SL3 0JJ* T: (01753) 681432 M: 07771-527141 E: rod@tommiez.com

COSLETT, Anthony Allan. b 49. Cuddesdon Coll. **d** 84 **p** 85. C Notting Hill St Clem and St Mark *Lon* 84–85; C Brentford 85–87; C-in-c Hounslow Gd Shep Beavers Lane CD 87–90; V Hounslow W Gd Shep 90–92; CF 92–08; TR Leic Resurr 08–12; C Broughton Astley and Croft w Stoney Stanton 12–17; rtd 17. *Ty am Byth, 62 Strathmore Road, Hinckley LE10 0LR* T: (01455) 611896

COSLETT (*née* SLATER), **The Ven Carol Ann.** b 63. Univ of Wales (Ban) BD 85 Jes Coll Cam PGCE 86 Lon Inst of Educn MA 92. Ripon Coll Cuddesdon 01. **d** 03 **p** 04. C Horsell *Guildf* 03–07; R Betchworth and Buckland *S'wark* 07–18; P-in-c Merstham, S Merstham and Gatton 13–15; Hon Can S'wark Cathl 16–18; Adn Chesterfield *Derby* from 18. *4 Woodnook Close, Ashgate, Chesterfield S42 7JB* T: (01246) 569764 or (01332) 388658 M: 07503-447830 E: ccoslett@btinternet.com or archchesterfield@derby.anglican.org

COSS, Oliver James. b 82. Hull Univ BSc 04 Leeds Univ BA 06 MA 09. Coll of Resurr Mirfield 04. **d** 07 **p** 08. C Cottingham *York* 07–11; V Small Heath *Birm* 11–16; R Northampton All SS w St Kath and St Pet *Pet* from 16. *7 Towpath Avenue, Northampton NN4 9DW* T: (01604) 632845 E: oliver.coss@gmail.com

COSSAR, David Vyvyan. b 34. Lon Univ BA 63. Chich Th Coll 63. **d** 65 **p** 66. C Upper Clapton St Matt *Lon* 65–68; C Withycombe Raleigh *Ex* 68–72; V Honiknowle 72–78; V Brixham w Churston Ferrers 78–86; P-in-c Kingswear

85–86; TR Brixham w Churston Ferrers and Kingswear 86–90; V Lamorbey H Trin *Roch* 90–03; rtd 03; PtO *Roch* from 03. *7 Broadbridge Close, London SE3 7AD*   T: (020) 3730 9003   M: 07741-406407 E: davidanddianec4@talktalk.net

COSSINS, John Charles. b 43. Hull Univ BSc 65. Oak Hill Th Coll 65. **d** 67 **p** 68. C Kenilworth St Jo *Cov* 67–70; C Huyton St Geo *Liv* 70–73; TV Maghull 73–79; Chapl Oakwood Hosp Maidstone 79–85; Maidstone Hosp 85–88; Chapl Park Lane Hosp Maghull 88–03; Chapl Moss Side Hosp Liv 88–03; Chapl Ashworth Hosp Maghull 88–03; rtd 03; PtO *Liv* 03–16; Guildf from 17. *68 Brookwood Farm Drive, Knaphill, Woking GU21 2FW*   T: (01483) 480570 E: jcossins@gmail.com

COSSINS, Roger Stanton. b 40. K Coll Lon BD 67 AKC 67. **d** 68 **p** 69. C Bramley *Ripon* 68–71; C W End *Win* 71–76; V Bramley 76–91; P-in-c Bournemouth H Epiphany 91–94; V 94–00; rtd 00. *5 Allen Court, Trumpington, Cambridge CB2 9LU*   T: (01223) 841571

COSTER, Canon Catherine Anne. b 47. Bris Poly BEd 85. WEMTC 97. **d** 00 **p** 01. NSM Yate New Town *Bris* 00–04; NSM Warmley, Syston and Bitton 04–17; Hon Min Can Bris Cathl 04–13; Hon Can 13–17; rtd 17; PtO *Bris* from 17. *31 Vayre Close, Chipping Sodbury, Bristol BS37 6NT*   T: (01454) 329377   M: 07762-349691 E: catherinecoster3@gmail.com

COSTERTON, Alan Stewart. b 40. Bris Univ BA 67. Clifton Th Coll 67. **d** 69 **p** 70. C Peckham St Mary Magd *S'wark* 69–73; C Forest Gate St Sav w W Ham St Matt *Chelmsf* 73–76; TV 76–79; V Thornton cum Bagworth *Leic* 79–85; V Thornton, Bagworth and Stanton 85–95; TR Sileby, Cossington and Seagrave 95–04; R 04–05; rtd 05; PtO *Leic* from 14. *71 Fowke Street, Leicester LE7 7PJ*   T: 0116-234 1026 E: alan.costerton@gmail.com

COSTIGAN, Esther Rose. *See* FOSS, Esther Rose

COSTIN, Pamela Lindsay. *See* REEVES, Pamela Lindsay

COSTIN, Richard George Charles. b 38. Liv Univ CertEd 59 Anglia Poly BEd 85 ACP 67 FCollP 82. Coll of Resurr Mirfield 04. **d** 05 **p** 06. NSM Scarborough St Martin *York* 05–16; PtO from 16; *Chelmsf* from 18. *64 Dame Mary Walk, Halstead CO9 2FF*   T: (01787) 829118   M: 07768-856175 E: rcos38@hotmail.com

COTMAN, John Sell Granville (Jan). b 44. St Jo Coll Dur BA 69. Wells Th Coll 70. **d** 73 **p** 74. C Leigh St Mary *Man* 73–76; P-in-c Coldhurst 76–78; TV Oldham 78–82; TV E Ham w Upton Park and Forest Gate *Chelmsf* 82–85; C Hove All SS *Chich* 88–93; TV Hove 93–00; TV W Slough *Ox* 01–08; V Manor Park and Whitby Road 08–13; rtd 13. *6 Riley Close, Aylesbury HP20 2TH*

COTTEE, Christopher Paul. b 54. Newc Univ BSc 75. Wycliffe Hall *Ox* 77. **d** 80 **p** 81. C Much Woolton *Liv* 80–84; C Prescot 84–88; NSM Parr 89–91; V Watford St Pet *St Alb* 91–19; rtd 19. *98 Linaker Street, Southport PR8 5DG* E: chris.cottee@ntlworld.com

COTTEE, Mary Jane. b 43. Open Univ BA 81 CertEd 64. Oak Hill Th Coll 87. **d** 90 **p** 94. NSM Gt Baddow *Chelmsf* 90–95; P-in-c Woodham Ferrers and Bicknacre 95–11; rtd 11; PtO *Chelmsf* from 11. *20 Elm Road, South Woodham Ferrers, Chelmsford CM3 5QE*   M: 07735-975423 E: marycottee@gmail.com

COTTELL, Avril Jane. *See* GAUNT, Avril Jane

COTTER, Preb Graham Michael. b 54. Univ of Wales (Ban) BA 72. Ridley Hall Cam 75. **d** 78 **p** 79. C Headley All SS *Guildf* 78–81; C Plymouth St Andr w St Paul and St Geo *Ex* 81–84; V Buckland Monachorum 84–18; RD Tavistock 93–98; Preb Ex Cathl 16–18; rtd 18. *9 Lakes Down, Upton Pyne, Exeter EX5 5BD* E: cotters@onetel.com

COTTER, Robert Edmund. d 05 **p** 06. NSM Mossley *Conn* 05–09; NSM Skerry w Rathcavan and Newtowncrommelin 09–13; Aux Min Belfast St Mary Magd from 13. *33 Deerfin Road, Ballymena BT42 4HP*   T: (028) 2563 1303 E: bobcotter56@icloud.com

COTTERELL, Michael Clifford. b 54. Oak Hill Th Coll 81. **d** 84 **p** 85. C Lutterworth w Cotesbach *Leic* 84–87; C Belper *Derby* 87–91; V Locking *B & W* 91–98; V Slough *Ox* 98–19; PtO *Lich* from 19; rtd 19. *5 Sycamore Drive, Whitchurch Road, Wem, Shrewsbury SY4 5AQ* E: mikeccotterell@gmail.com

COTTERILL, Joseph Charles. b 17. AMCT 38 Lon Univ BD California Coll Peking MA 46. Ox Min Course 92. **d** 93 **p** 94. NSM Marcham w Garford *Ox* 93–98; PtO from 98. *8 Draycott Road, Southmoor, Abingdon OX13 5BY*   T: (01865) 820436

COTTERILL, Steven Derek. b 64. **d** 16 **p** 17. NSM Annesley w Newstead and Kirkby Woodhouse *S'well* from 16. *1 Bracken Close, Kirkby-in-Ashfield, Nottingham NG17 8NU* E: stevencotterill@hotmail.co.uk

COTTON, Charles Anthony. b 50. Linc Coll Ox BA 72 MA 77 PGCE 73. Ridley Hall Cam 89. **d** 91 **p** 92. C Hendon St Paul Mill Hill *Lon* 91–96; C Wandsworth All SS *S'wark* 96–97; V Clapham St Jas 97–08; rtd 08; PtO *S'wark* from 08. *9*

Woodcote Avenue, Wallington SM6 0QR   T: (020) 8669 1143 E: revdcharlie@btinternet.com

COTTON, David John. b 65. Linc Sch of Th and Min 12. **d** 14 **p** 16. OLM Lea Gp *Linc* from 14. *42 Meadow Rise, Saxilby, Lincoln LN1 2HW*   T: (01522) 702634   M: 07944-669166 E: david.cotton500@ntlworld.com

COTTON, John Horace Brazel. b 28. MIMechE St Jo Coll Cam BA 50 MA 76. St Alb Minl Tr Scheme 78. **d** 81 **p** 82. NSM Lt Berkhamsted and Bayford, Essendon etc *St Alb* 81–87; P-in-c 87–96; rtd 96; PtO *St Alb* from 96. *49 Sherrardspark Road, Welwyn Garden City AL8 7LD*   T: (01707) 321815 E: cottons49@tiscali.co.uk

COTTON, John William. b 53. Oak Hill Th Coll 86. **d** 86 **p** 87. C New Clee *Linc* 86–89; Chapl St Andr Hospice Grimsby 88–89; R Middle Rasen Gp *Linc* 89–95; P-in-c Broughton 95–97; R 97–10; Chapl Humberside Airport 99–00; rtd 11; PtO *Linc* 11–18; Chapl United Lincs Hosps NHS Trust 11–12. *Address withheld by request* E: coulingwill@yahoo.com

COTTON, Mrs Margaret Elizabeth. b 30. Newnham Coll Cam BA 53 MA 66. St Alb Minl Tr Scheme 78. **dss** 82 **d** 87 **p** 94. Lt Berkhamsted and Bayford, Essendon etc *St Alb* 82–87; Hon Par Dn 87–94; Hon C 94–96; rtd 96; PtO *St Alb* from 96. *49 Sherrardspark Road, Welwyn Garden City AL8 7LD*   T: (01707) 321815

COTTON, Miss Michelle Susan. b 77. Ox Brookes Univ BA 13. Ripon Coll Cuddesdon 09. **d** 11 **p** 12. C Weston Favell *Pet* 11–15; P-in-c Wellingborough St Andr 15–16; V 16–18; V Wellingborough St Andr and St Barn from 18. *St Andrew's Vicarage, Berrymoor Road, Wellingborough NN8 2HU*   T: (01933) 222634   M: 07817-905423 E: michelle.cotton123@btinternet.com

COTTON, Miss Patricia Constance. b 32. Gilmore Ho 54. **dss** 60 **d** 87 **p** 94. Forest Gate St Edm *Chelmsf* 60–64; Reading St Giles *Ox* 64–65; Basildon St Martin w H Cross and Laindon *Chelmsf* 65–79; Gt Burstead 79–87; Par Dn Maldon All SS w St Pet 87–91; rtd 92; NSM Holland-on-Sea *Chelmsf* 94–96; PtO from 96. *29 Alexander Mews, Sandon, Chelmsford CM2 7TT*   T: (01245) 473983

COTTON, Patrick Arthur William. b 46. Essex Univ BA 67 Down Coll Cam MA 73 Homerton Coll Cam PGCE 96. Linc Th Coll 68. **d** 71 **p** 72. C Earlham St Anne *Nor* 71–73; Chapl Down Coll Cam 73–78; V Eaton Socon *St Alb* 78–84; TR Newc Epiphany 84–90; V Tunstall w Melling and Leck *Blackb* 90–95; Chapl Pet High Sch 01–05; P-in-c Debenham and Helmingham *St E* 06–16; rtd 16; PtO *Ely* from 16. *4 Brook Lane, Coton, Cambridge CB23 7PY*   T: (01954) 210285

COTTON, Peter John. b 45. BNC Ox BA 66 CQSW 76. Cuddesdon Coll 67. **d** 69 **p** 70. C Salford St Phil w St Steph *Man* 69–73; Asst Educn Officer *St Alb* 73–75; C Bris St Geo 75; C-in-c Portsea St Geo CD *Portsm* 76–80; Soc Resp Adv 78–88; Can Res Portsm Cathl 84–88; V St Laur in Thanet *Cant* 88–93; TR 93–97; Hon Min Can Cant Cathl 93–97; TR Hemel Hempstead *St Alb* 97–09; RD 03–08; Hon Can St Alb 08–09; rtd 09; PtO *Portsm* from 09. *7 Armory Lane, Portsmouth PO1 2PE*   T: (023) 9281 6075 E: petercotton172@btinternet.com

COTTON, Canon Robert Lloyd. b 58. Mert Coll Ox MA 79. Westcott Ho Cam 81. **d** 83 **p** 84. C Plaistow St Mary *Roch* 83–86; C Bisley and W End *Guildf* 87–89; P-in-c E Molesey St Paul 89–96; Dir of Reader Tr from 90; R Guildf H Trin w St Mary from 96; Hon Can Highveld S Africa from 06; Hon Can Guildf Cathl from 10. *Holy Trinity Rectory, 9 Eastgate Gardens, Guildford GU1 4AZ*   T: (01483) 575489 E: rector@holytrinityguildford.org.uk

COTTON-BETTERIDGE, Mrs Fiona Jane Marson. b 56. Nottm Univ MA 05. EMMTC 02. **d** 05 **p** 06. NSM Burton Joyce w Bulcote and Stoke Bardolph *S'well* 05–08; P-in-c Old Leake w Wrangle *Linc* from 08; P-in-c Friskney from 08. *The Vicarage, Yawling Gate Road, Friskney, Boston PE22 8QF*   T: (01754) 820104 E: fionacb@aol.com

COTTRELL, Matthew Brian. b 80. Ban Univ BTh 09. Ripon Coll Cuddesdon 11. **d** 14 **p** 16. C Thornbury and Oldbury-on-Severn w Shepperdine *Glouc* 14–17; C Glouc St Paul and St Steph 17–19. *11 Hackett Close, Swindon SN2 7UB*   M: 07491-951538 E: revmattcottrell@gmail.com

✠**COTTRELL, The Rt Revd Stephen Geoffrey.** b 58. Poly Cen Lon BA 79. St Steph Ho Ox 81. **d** 84 **p** 85 **c** 04. C Forest Hill Ch Ch *S'wark* 84–88; P-in-c Parklands St Wilfrid CD *Chich* 88–93; Asst Dir Past Studies Chich Th Coll 88–93; Dioc Missr *Wakef* 93–98; Bp's Chapl for Evang 93–98; Springboard Missr and Consultant in Evang 98–01; Can Res Pet Cathl 01–04; Area Bp Reading *Ox* 04–10; Bp Chelmsf from 10. *Bishopscourt, Main Road, Margaretting, Ingatestone CM4 0HD*   T: (01277) 352001   F: 355374 E: bishopscourt@chelmsford.anglican.org

COTTRILL, Derek John. b 43. MA. Qu Coll Birm. **d** 82 **p** 83. C Southampton Maybush St Pet *Win* 82–85; V Barton Stacey and Bullington etc 85–92; R Bishopstoke 92–06; Asst Chapl Win and Eastleigh Healthcare NHS Trust 92–06; rtd 06; PtO *Sarum* from 14. *7 The Old Green, Sherborne DT9 3JY* T: (01935) 816746 E: revdc@live.co.uk

COTTRILL, Mrs Sarah. b 64. **d** 14 **p** 15. C St Jo in Bedwardine *Worc* 14–18; C Worc St Clem and Lower Broadheath from 18. *7 Manor Road, Worcester WR2 4PD* E: salocot@gmail.com

COUCH, Ms Felicity Anne. b 59. CQSW 85. SEITE 00. **d** 03 **p** 04. NSM Stockwell St Andr and St Mich *S'wark* 03–08; P-in-c Ulceby Gp, Croxton and Brocklesby Park *Linc* 08–11; R Orwell Gp *Ely* from 11; RD Shingay from 15. *The Rectory, Fishers Lane, Orwell, Royston SG8 5QX* T: (01223) 207212 M: 07745-905417 E: fcouch@btinternet.com

COUCH, John. b 46. Trin Coll Carmarthen BEd 85. **d** 14 **p** 15. NSM Llansadwrn w Llanwrda and Manordeilo *St D* 14–18; PtO from 18. *Capel Seion, Llansadwrn, Llanwrda SA19 8HL* T: (01550) 779062 E: john@wales123.plus.com

COUCHMAN, Anthony Denis. b 37. Sarum Th Coll 66. **d** 69 **p** 70. C Barkingside St Fran *Chelmsf* 69–71; C Chingford SS Pet and Paul 71–76; P-in-c Walthamstow St Barn and St Jas Gt 76–80; V 80–07; rtd 07; PtO *Nor* from 08. *Friarscot, Church Street, King's Lynn PE30 5EB* T: (01553) 766643 E: anthonycouchman@yahoo.co.uk

COUCHMAN, Kathryn. b 60. Open Univ BA 92 Coll of Ripon & York St Jo MA 00 MBPsS. NOC 02. **d** 06 **p** 07. C Wetherby *Ripon* 06–08; C Collingham w Harewood 08–10; C Spofforth w Kirk Deighton 08–10; Chapl HM YOI Wetherby 08–11; NSM Bishop Thornton, Burnt Yates, Markington etc *Ripon* 11–12; R Middleham w Coverdale and E Witton etc 12–15; Chapl St Mich Hospice Harrogate from 15. *St Michael's Hospice, Crimple House, Hornbeam Park Avenue, Harrogate HG2 8QL* T: (01423) 879687 E: kathycouchman1@gmail.com

COUGHTREY, Miss Sheila Frances. b 48. RSCN 73 SRN 73 S Bank Poly BSc 79. Qu Coll Birm 79. **dss** 81 **d** 87 **p** 94. Sydenham St Bart *S'wark* 81–85; Roehampton H Trin 85–91; Par Dn 87–91; Par Dn Brixton Hill St Sav 91–94; P-in-c 94–01; Min King's Acre LEP 91–01; RD Brixton *S'wark* 99–01; P-in-c Pleshey *Chelmsf* 01–15; Warden Dioc Retreat Ho 01–15; rtd 15. *7 Hereward Way, Wethersfield, Braintree CM7 4EG* T: (01371) 580378

COULDRIDGE, Janice Evelyn. See FOX, Janice Evelyn

COULING, Canon David Charles. b 36. Open Univ BA 89. Qu Coll Birm 61. **d** 63 **p** 64. C Harborne St Faith and St Laur *Birm* 63–66; C E Grinstead St Mary *Chich* 66–70; V Copthorne 70–75; V Eastbourne St Mich 75–82; V Brighton St Matthias 82–83; C-in-c Harton St Lawr CD *Dur* 84–90; V Horsley Hill St Lawr 91–94; P-in-c Greatham 94–97; V 97–01; AD Hartlepool 95–01; Master Greatham Hosp 94–00; Hon Can Dur Cathl 99–01; rtd 01; P-in-c Brancepeth *Dur* 01–04; Chapl Dur Cathl 04–18. *6 Ferens House, Sherburn Hospital, Durham DH1 2SE* T: 0191-597 3088 E: davidanncouling@talktalk.net

COULSON, Kenneth. b 51. **d** 15 **p** 16. NSM Windy Nook St Alb *Dur* from 15; NSM Gateshead Fell from 18. *13 Beaconsfield Avenue, Low Fell, Gateshead NE9 5XT* T: 0191-487 1544

COULSON, Renée Yvonne. b 45. **d** 03 **p** 04. OLM Potterne w Worton and Marston *Sarum* 03–09; P-in-c Seend, Bulkington and Poulshot 09–15; rtd 15; PtO *Sarum* from 15. *40 Highlands, Potterne, Devizes SN10 5N* T: (01380) 725208 E: renee.coulson.2@googlemail.com *or* revren.d@btinternet.com *or* rycoulson40@gmail.com

COULSON, Canon Stephen Hugh. b 60. St Edm Hall Ox BA 82 MA 88 Lon Univ CertEd 83. Wycliffe Hall Ox 85. **d** 88 **p** 89. C Summerfield *Birm* 88–91; PtO 91–92; CMS Uganda 92–01; Asst V Namirembe 92–96; Can from 96; Prin Uganda Martyrs Sem Namugongo 96–01; V Mitcham St Mark *S'wark* 01–12; AD Merton 09–12; V Kennington St Mark from 12. *St Mark's Vicarage, 56 Kennington Oval, London SE11 5SW* T: (020) 7735 1801 E: vicar@stmarkskennington.org

COULSON, Tony Erik Frank. b 32. St Edm Hall Ox BA 55 MA 59. Wycliffe Hall Ox 55. **d** 57 **p** 58. C Walthamstow St Mary *Chelmsf* 57–60; C Reading St Jo *Ox* 60–63; V Iver 63–86; R White Waltham w Shottesbrooke 86–97; rtd 97; PtO *Ox* from 98. *30 Ravensbourne Drive, Reading RG5 4LH* T: 0118-969 3556 E: tefcoulson@gmail.com

COULTER, Edmond James. b 60. QUB BSc 82 BD 96. **d** 87 **p** 88. C Ballymena w Ballyclug *Conn* 87–90; C Knockbreda *D & D* 90–92; I Belfast Upper Falls *Conn* 92–97; I Milltown *Arm* 97–03; Supt Dublin Irish Ch Miss *D & G* 03–16; I Lambeg *Conn* from 16. *Lambeg Rectory, 58 Belfast Road, Lisburn BT27 4AT*

COULTER, Ian Herbert Young. b 54. TCD BA 77 HDipEd 78. **d** 99 **p** 00. LtO Cashel, Waterford and Lismore *C & O*

99–10; NSM Castlecomer w Colliery Ch, Mothel and Bilboa 10–13; NSM Templemore w Thurles and Kilfithmone 13–16; NSM Clonenagh w Offerlane, Borris-in-Ossory etc from 16. *22 Rose Hill Court, Kilkenny, Co Kilkenny, Republic of Ireland* T/F: (00353) (56) 776 2675 M: 86-813 0290 E: ianhycoulter@gmail.com

COULTER (née REEVES), Mrs Maria Elizabeth Ann. b 72. Leeds Univ BA 95 Heythrop Coll Lon MTh 03 Buckingham Univ PGCE 18. St Steph Ho Ox 96. **d** 98 **p** 99. C Newington St Mary *S'wark* 98–02; V Dulwich St Clem w St Pet 02–17; Asst Chapl Oundle Sch from 17. *2 Cricketers Way, Oundle, Peterborough PE8 4JU* E: meareeves@hotmail.com

COULTER, Miss Marilyn Judith. b 48. City of Birm Coll BEd 70 Qu Coll Birm BA 05. WMMTC 02. **d** 05 **p** 06. NSM Brewood *Lich* 05–19; NSM Bishopswood 05–19; Chapl Mid Staffs NHS Foundn Trust 08–14; PtO *Lich* from 19. *14 St Chad's Close, Brewood, Stafford ST19 9DA* T: (01902) 851168 E: coulter14@aol.com

COULTHARD, Miss Nina Marion. b 50. CertEd 71 Bp Lonsdale Coll BEd 72. Trin Coll Bris 89. **d** 91 **p** 94. Par Dn Cant St Mary Bredin 91–94; C 94–95; C Bath Abbey w St Jas *B & W* 95–99; Chapl R Nat Hosp for Rheumatic Diseases NHS Trust 95–99; C Northwood Em *Lon* 99–06; V Loughton St Mich *Chelmsf* 06–18; rtd 18; PtO *Cant* from 19. *22 Grays Way, Canterbury CT1 3XY* M: 07956-513615 E: revninac@gmail.com

COULTHURST, Jeffrey Evans. b 38. Man Univ BA 61 Leeds Univ PGCE 62. **d** 84 **p** 85. OLM Ancaster *Linc* 84–89; OLM Ancaster Wilsford Gp 89–05. *152 Cirencester Road, Charlton Kings, Cheltenham GL53 8DY* E: jeff.coulthurst38@gmail.com

COULTON, David John. b 45. St Jo Coll Cam BA 69 MA 71 Glos Univ MA 04 CertEd 69. WEMTC 07. **d** 09 **p** 10. NSM Tewkesbury w Walton Cardiff and Twyning *Glouc* 09–18; NSM Deerhurst and Apperley w Forthampton etc 12–16; rtd 18. *4 Conigree Lane, Abbots Road, Tewkesbury GL20 5TF* T: (01684) 293523 E: davidcoulton@btinternet.com

COULTON, David Stephen. b 41. Bernard Gilpin Soc Dur 63 Sarum Th Coll 64. **d** 67 **p** 68. C Guildf H Trin w St Mary 67–70; Asst Chapl St Luke's Hosp Guildf 67–70; Asst Chapl Radley Coll 70–83; Sen Chapl 83–01; Chapl Eton Coll 01–04; rtd 04; PtO *Sarum* from 06. *Address withheld by request*

COULTON, The Very Revd Nicholas Guy. b 40. Lon Univ BD 72 Ox Univ MA 07. Cuddesdon Coll 65. **d** 67 **p** 68. C Pershore w Wick *Worc* 67–70; Bp's Dom Chapl *St Alb* 71–75; P-in-c Bedford St Paul 75–79; V 79–90; Hon Can St Alb 89–90; Provost Newc 90–01; Dean Newc 01–03; Can Res and Sub-Dean Ch Ch *Ox* 03–08; rtd 08. *123 Merewood Avenue, Headington, Oxford OX3 8EQ* T: (01865) 763790 E: ngc@proscenia.co.uk

COULTON, Philip Ernest. b 31. St Cath Coll Cam BA 54 MA 58 TCD BD 68 Open Univ BA 84. Ely Th Coll 55. **d** 57 **p** 58. Asst Master Perse Sch Cam 54–55; Asst Master Bradf Gr Sch 57; C Newark w Coddington *S'well* 57–61; Min Can and Sacr Cant Cathl 61–63; Min Can Ripon Cathl 63–68; Hd of RE Ashton-under-Lyne Gr Sch 69–84; V Ulceby Gp *Linc* 85–89; P-in-c Ingatestone w Buttsbury *Chelmsf* 89–99; P-in-c Fryerning w Margaretting 89–92; rtd 99; PtO *Sarum* from 01; *B & W* 02–06. *90 Boreham Road, Warminster BA12 9JW* T: (01985) 219353 E: pecoulton@talktalk.net

COUPAR, Thomas. b 50. BA 71 ACE 80 Edin Univ MTh 15. Edin Dioc NSM Course 77. **d** 80 **p** 81. NSM Dunbar *Edin* 80–86; NSM Haddington 80–86; Hd Master Pencaitland Primary Sch E Lothian 80–81; Hd Master K Meadow Sch E Lothian 81–87; Asst Dioc Supernumerary *Edin* 87–89; Primary Educn Adv Fife Coun 88–06; Dioc Supernumerary *Edin* 90–96 and 13–15; rtd 19; LtO *Edin* from 19. *21/9 Rennie's Isle, Edinburgh EH6 6QB* M: 07765-431321 E: tcoupar@hotmail.com

COUPE, Christopher John. b 57. Cumbria Univ BA 15. LCTP 10. **d** 12 **p** 13. NSM Lower Darwen St Jas *Blackb* 12–16; V Chell *Lich* from 16. *The Rectory, 203 St Michael's Road, Stoke-on-Trent ST6 6JT*

COUPER (née WOOD), Mrs Audrey Elizabeth. b 54. Edin Univ BSc 75 Westmr Coll of Educn PGCE 76. ERMC 05. **d** 08 **p** 09. NSM Digswell and Panshanger *St Alb* 08–13; NSM Luton St Fran 13–14; PtO *Edin* from 15. *2 St Ninian's Way, Linlithgow EH49 7BU* E: audreycouper@gmail.com

COUPER, Jonathan George. b 51. St Jo Coll Dur BA 73. Wycliffe Hall Ox 73. **d** 75 **p** 76. C Clifton *York* 75–78; C Darfield *Sheff* 78–81; V Bridlington Quay Ch Ch *York* 81–95; P-in-c Bessingby 99–12; V 12–16; rtd 16; PtO *York* from 18. *3 Tudor Close, Bridlington YO15 3TA* E: joncouper@yahoo.co.uk

COUPLAND, Robert Lee. b 92. Dur Univ BA 16. Westcott Ho Cam 13. **d** 16 **p** 17. C Brighton St Mich and St Paul *Chich* 16–19; Min Can and Sacr St Paul's Cathl *Lon* from 19. *St Paul's Cathedral, The Chapter House, St Paul's Churchyard, London EC4M 8AD* M: 07528-806902 E: robertleecoupland@yahoo.com

COUPLAND, Simon Charles. b 59. St Jo Coll Cam BA 82 MA 85 PhD 87 Dur Univ PGCE 83. Ridley Hall Cam 88. **d** 91 **p** 92. C Bath St Luke *B & W* 91–95; TV Broadwater *Chich* 95–04; V Kingston Hill St Paul *S'wark* 04–18; AD Kingston 12–16; P-in-c Ham St Rich from 18. *28 Dysart Avenue, Kingston upon Thames KT2 5RB* T: (020) 8546 1438 E: strichardsvicar@btinternet.com

✠**COURT, The Rt Revd David Eric.** b 58. Southn Univ BSc 80 PhD 83 PGCE 84. Oak Hill Th Coll BA 91. **d** 91 **p** 92 **c** 14. C Barton Seagrave w Warkton *Pet* 91–94; C Kinson *Sarum* 94–97; P-in-c Mile Cross *Nor* 97–99; V 99–03; V Cromer 03–14; RD Repps 10–14; Hon Can Nor Cathl 10–14; Suff Bp Grimsby *Linc* from 14. *The Bishops' Office, The Old Palace, Lincoln LN2 1PU* E: revdavidcourt@btinternet.com *or* bishop.grimsby@lincoln.anglican.org

COURT, Canon Kenneth Reginald. b 36. AKC 60. **d** 61 **p** 62. C Garforth *Ripon* 61–63; C Harrogate St Wilfrid 63–65; V Thornbury *Bradf* 65–73; Prec Leic Cathl 73–76; V Douglas St Matt *S & M* 76–84; V Syston *Leic* 84–93; TR 93–98; RD Goscote 90–95; Hon Can Leic Cathl 92–98; rtd 98; PtO *Leic* 99–12; *Linc* 01–03; *Pet* 03–08. *12 Lord Burghley's Hospital, Station Road, Stamford PE9 2LD* T: (01780) 754372 E: kenneth.court554@gmail.com

COURT, Martin Jeremy. b 61. GRNCM 84 Nottm Univ BTh 89. Linc Th Coll 86. **d** 89 **p** 90. C Thurmaston *Leic* 89–92; C Leic St Jas 92–93; TV Leic Resurr 93–98; V Scraptoft from 98; P-in-c Leic St Chad from 08; Dioc Info Tech Co-ord from 96. *All Saints' Vicarage, 331 Scraptoft Lane, Scraptoft, Leicester LE5 2HU* T: 0116-241 3205 M: 07798-876837 E: mcourt@leicester.anglican.org

COURT, Canon Martin John. b 64. Ridley Hall Cam 03. **d** 05 **p** 06. C Blandford Forum and Langton Long *Sarum* 05–09; V Chadwell Heath *Chelmsf* from 09; AD Barking and Dagenham from 17; Hon Can Chelmsf Cathl from 18. *The Vicarage, 7 Chadwell Heath Lane, Romford RM6 4LS* T: (020) 8590 2391 M: 07905-612542 E: martin_stchads@live.co.uk

COURT, Canon Nicholas James Keble. b 56. Chich Th Coll 86. **d** 88 **p** 89. C Golders Green *Lon* 88–91; C Westbury-on-Trym H Trin *Bris* 91–94; PV Llan Cathl 94–96; V Graig 96–02; P-in-c Cilfynydd 96–01; Miss P *Mor* 09–11; Can St Andr Cathl Inverness from 13. *Cair Paravel, Ardmuir, Ullapool IV26 2TN* T: (01854) 612506 E: nicholas.court@btinternet.com

COURT, Richard Leonard. b 54. Univ of Wales (Ban) BTh 04. EAMTC 94. **d** 97 **p** 98. NSM Framlingham w Saxtead *St E* 97–05; V Badsey w Aldington and Offenham and Bretforton *Worc* 05–15; P-in-c Evesham 10–15; rtd 15. *Brookside, Green Lane, Redlingfield, Eye IP23 7QT* T: (01379) 678772 M: 07751-775917 E: richard.court@btinternet.com

COURTIE, John Malcolm. b 42. BNC Ox BA 65 DPhil 72 St Jo Coll Dur BA 76. Cranmer Hall Dur 74. **d** 77 **p** 78. C Mossley Hill St Matt and St Jas *Liv* 77–80; V Litherland St Paul Hatton Hill 80–84; Wellingborough Sch 84–89; Hon C Wollaston and Strixton *Pet* 84–89; V Woodford Halse w Eydon 89–99; R Blisworth and Stoke Bruerne w Grafton Regis etc 99–02; rtd 02; Hon C NW Hants *Win* 09–10; PtO *Ex* from 11. *Brooksong, Longmeadow Road, Lympstone, Exmouth EX8 5LF* T: (01395) 260242 E: thecourties@hotmail.com

COURTNEY, Canon Brian Joseph. b 44. BD 92 MA 97. CITC 70. **d** 73 **p** 74. C Willowfield *D & D* 73–75; P-in-c Knocknagoney 75–78; I Aghavea *Clogh* 78–83; I Carrickfergus *Conn* 83–95; I Enniskillen *Clogh* 95–09; Prec Clogh Cathl 95–09; rtd 09. *10 Berkeley Road, Carrickfergus BT38 9DS* T: (028) 9335 5139 E: briancourtney09@googlemail.com

COURTNEY, Miss Louise Anita Hodd. b 48. Ex Univ BTh 04. SWMTC 99. **d** 02 **p** 03. C St Keverne *Truro* 02–05; P-in-c Lanteglos by Fowey 05–15; P-in-c Lansallos 05–15; P-in-c Talland 10–15; C Lanreath, Pelynt and Bradoc 13–15; rtd 15. *Le Pinet, 24500 Razac-d'Eymet, France* E: louiseanitacourtney@gmail.com

COURTNEY, Martin Horace. b 34. SAOMC 95. **d** 98 **p** 99. OLM Flackwell Heath *Ox* from 98. *1 Green Crescent, Flackwell Heath, High Wycombe HP10 9JQ* T: (01628) 526354 E: martin@ccfh.org.uk

COUSANS (née BRADLEY), Mrs Joy Elizabeth. b 63. Sheff Univ MA 85 Fitzw Coll Cam BA 91 MA 95. Ridley Hall Cam 89. **d** 92 **p** 94. Par Dn Wadsley *Sheff* 92–94; C 94–96; C Mosborough 96–97; V Hillsborough and Wadsley Bridge 97–06; P-in-c High Hoyland, Scissett and Clayton W *Wakef* 06–14; *Leeds* 14–17; Asst Dir of Ords 08–17; V Eaton Bray w Edlesborough *St Alb* from 17. *The Vicarage, 11 High Street, Eaton Bray, Dunstable LU6 2DN* T: (01525) 220261 E: vicar@stmaryseatonbray.org.uk

COUSINS, Mrs Deborah Ann. b 52. LCST 74. ERMC 06. **d** 09 **p** 10. C Earlham *Nor* 09–13; C Bure Valley 13–17; TV

Aylsham and Distr 17–19; rtd 19; PtO *Nor* from 19. *c/o Mrs Forkes, Greenways, Sandpit Lane, Thorpe Market, Norwich NR11 8TJ* M: 07814-282307 E: debstherev@gmail.com

COUSINS, Canon Graham John. b 55. Oak Hill Th Coll BA 91. **d** 91 **p** 92. C Birkenhead St Jas w St Bede *Ches* 91–95; C Bebington 95–01; R Moreton from 01; RD Wallasey 11–18; Hon Can Ches Cathl from 12. *The Rectory, Dawpool Drive, Moreton, Wirral CH46 0PH* T: 0151-641 0303 *or* 604 0049 E: rector@christchurchmoreton.org.uk

COUSINS, Canon Philip John. b 35. K Coll Cam BA 58 MA 62. Cuddesdon Coll 59. **d** 61 **p** 62. C Marton *Blackb* 61–63; PV Truro Cathl 63–67; USPG Ethiopia 67–75; V Henleaze *Bris* 75–84; RD Clifton 79–84; Provost All SS Cathl Cairo 84–89; Chan Malta Cathl *Eur* 89–95; Chapl Valletta w Gozo 89–95; R Llandudno *Ban* 95–04; rtd 04; PtO *York* from 04; *Eur* from 05. *17 Chalfonts, York YO24 1EX* T: (01904) 700316 E: janet.philip1@gmail.com

COUSINS, Stephen Michael. b 53. SAOMC 98. **d** 01 **p** 02. OLM Caversham St Jo *Ox* 01–03; PtO 03–04; NSM Shiplake w Dunsden and Harpsden 04–11; Chapl Shiplake Coll Henley 09–19; NSM Benson w Ewelme *Ox* from 19. *101 The Street, Ewelme, Wallingford OX10 6HQ* M: 07753-166687 E: scousins@shiplake.org.uk

COUSSENS, Mervyn Haigh Wingfield. b 47. St Jo Coll Nottm BTh 74. **d** 74 **p** 75. C Clifton Ch Ch w Em *Bris* 74–77; C Morden *S'wark* 77–83; V Patchway *Bris* 83–91; R Lutterworth w Cotesbach *Leic* 91–98; P-in-c Bitteswell 95–98; R Lutterworth w Cotesbach and Bitteswell 99–12; RD Guthlaxton II 01–05; rtd 12. *8 Chestnut Avenue, Lutterworth LE17 4TJ* T: (01455) 556279

COUTTS, Diana Angela. *See* COUTTS-PAULING, Diana Angela

COUTTS, James Allan. b 58. Fitzw Coll Cam MA. St Jo Coll Nottm MTh 84. **d** 84 **p** 85. C Thorpe Acre w Dishley *Leic* 84–88; TV Kirby Muxloe 88–99; P-in-c Trowbridge St Thos and W Ashton *Sarum* 99–07; V from 07; Chapl Wilts and Swindon Healthcare NHS Trust 99–08; Chapl Gt Western Hosps NHS Foundn Trust from 08. *St Thomas's Vicarage, York Buildings, Trowbridge BA14 8PT* T: (01225) 754826 E: allan@stthomastrowbridge.org

COUTTS, Canon Mandy Rosalind. b 65. Ox Poly BSc 87 St Jo Coll Dur BA 06 Leeds Univ MA 11 Bath Univ PGCE 88. Cranmer Hall Dur 04. **d** 06 **p** 07. C Chapel Allerton *Ripon* 06–10; TV Bramley 10–14; Can Res Bradf Cathl *Leeds* from 15. *2 Cathedral Close, Bradford BD1 4EG* T: (01274) 777728 E: mandy.coutts@virgin.net

COUTTS, Canon Robin Iain Philip. b 52. Portsm Univ MA 00. Sarum & Wells Th Coll 80. **d** 83 **p** 84. C Alverstoke *Portsm* 83–86; Min Leigh Park St Clare CD 86–88; V Warren Park 89–91; V Purbrook 91–04; RD Havant 00–04; P-in-c Blendworth w Chalton w Idsworth 04–06; P-in-c Hambledon 06–17; Dioc Dir NSM 04–17; Dioc Dir of Ords 06–16; Hon Can Portsm Cathl 06–17; rtd 17; PtO *Portsm* from 18; *Sarum* from 18. *3 Oakwood Grove, Alderbury, Salisbury SP5 3BN* E: robin.rocket@btinternet.com

COUTTS-PAULING, Diana Angela. Cant Ch Ch Univ BA 11. **d** 07 **p** 08. Chapl Qu Mary's Sidcup NHS Trust 07–08; Chapl S Lon Healthcare NHS Trust 09–13; rtd 13; PtO *Roch* from 14. *16 Darwin Close, Orpington BR6 7EP* T: (01689) 853122 E: revdacp@gmail.com

COUTURE (née MAWBEY), Mrs Diane. b 55. Birm Univ MMedSc 97. Cranmer Hall Dur. **d** 89 **p** 94. Par Dn Menston w Woodhead *Bradf* 89–92; C Barnoldswick w Bracewell 92–93; Chapl Asst Birm Children's Hosp 93–96; Chapl Asst Birm Maternity Hosp 93–96; Chapl Birm Women's Healthcare NHS Trust 96–98; R The Whitacres, Lea Marston, and Shustoke *Birm* 98–15; rtd 15; PtO *Birm* from 15. *14 Atherstone Road, Hurley, Atherstone CV9 2HU* T: (01827) 873223 M: 07710-281648 E: diane.couture@btinternet.com

COUVELA, Ms Stephanie Joy. b 68. Sheff City Poly BA 89. Ridley Hall Cam 95. **d** 98 **p** 99. C Upper Holloway *Lon* 98–01; TV 01–04; C Busbridge and Hambledon *Guildf* 04–10; Chapl Scargill Ho 10–15; Chapl Keele Univ *Lich* from 15. *51 Quarry Bank Road, Keele, Newcastle ST5 5AG* T: (01782) 734919 E: s.couvela@keele.ac.uk

COUZENS (formerly WATERS), Brenda Mary. b 51. Bp Otter Coll. **d** 99. NSM Whyke w Rumboldswhyke and Portfield *Chich* 99–04; NSM Chich Cathl 05–14; PtO 14–18; Chapl St Wilfrid's Hospice Chich 01–18; NSM Chich St Paul and Westhampnett from 18. *12 Peacock Close, Chichester PO19 6YD* E: brendacouzens51@gmail.com

COUZENS, Mrs Carolyn Mary. b 67. St Mellitus Coll 13. **d** 15 **p** 16. C Lilliput *Sarum* 15–19; P-in-c Bridge Par from 19. *61 Felton Road, Poole BH14 0QR* T: (01202) 743819 E: revcarolyncouzens@gmail.com

COVENTRY, Archdeacon of. *See* FIELD, The Ven Susan Elizabeth

COVENTRY, Bishop of. *See* COCKSWORTH, The Rt Revd Christopher John

COVENTRY, Dean of. *See* WITCOMBE, The Very Revd John Julian

COVERLEY, Mrs Cheryl Joy. b 62. SS Hild & Bede Coll Dur BA 83 PGCE 84. St Jo Coll Nottm MA 07. **d** 05 **p** 06. C Birkenhead St Jas w St Bede *Ches* 05–07; V Newton from 07; Asst Warden of Readers from 08. *St Michael's Vicarage, 56 Queensbury, Wirral CH48 6EP* T: 0151-625 8517 E: cheryl.coverley@tiscali.co.uk

COVINGTON, Canon Michael William Rock. b 38. Open Univ BA 78. Sarum Th Coll 60. **d** 63 **p** 64. C Daventry *Pet* 63–66; C Woolwich St Mary w H Trin *S'wark* 66–68; C Northampton All SS w St Kath *Pet* 68–71; V Longthorpe 71–86; Hon Min Can Pet Cathl 75–86; V Warmington, Tansor, Cotterstock and Fotheringhay 86–95; Warden of Readers 87–95; RD Oundle 89–95; V Oakham, Hambleton, Egleton, Braunston and Brooke 95–03; P-in-c Langham 97–03; RD Rutland 02–03; Can Pet Cathl 86–03; rtd 03; PtO *Leic* 05–06 and 10–13 and from 16; C Burrough Hill Pars 07–10; P-in-c S Framland 13–16. *Hall Farm House, Burrough Road, Little Dalby, Melton Mowbray LE14 2UG* T: (01664) 454015

COWAN, David John. b 47. Selw Coll Cam BA 69 MA 73. SEITE 06. **d** 09 **p** 10. NSM Dorking w Ranmore *Guildf* 09–17; PtO from 17. *25 Falkland Road, Dorking RH4 3AB* T: (01306) 885341 E: mave@uwclub.net

COWAN, Helen Jane. b 42. **d** 00 **p** 01. OLM Redhill H Trin *S'wark* 00–12; PtO from 12. *15 Westway Gardens, Redhill RH1 2JA* T: (01737) 762543 E: cowan@clara.co.uk

COWAN, John Conway. b 71. Liv Univ BA 93 Liv Inst of HE PGCE 94. Trin Coll Bris BA 03. **d** 03 **p** 04. C Redcar *York* 03–07; V Hull St Cuth from 07; Chapl Hull Univ from 10; AD Cen and N Hull from 17; AD Hull from 18. *The Vicarage, 112 Marlborough Avenue, Hull HU5 3JX* T: (01482) 342848 E: cowanjohnc@yahoo.com

COWAN, Mrs Lynda Barbette. b 55. ALAM 77. Ban Ord Course 02. **d** 05 **p** 06. C Arwystli Deanery Ban 05–08; P-in-c Llandinam w Trefeglwys w Penstrowed *Ban* 08–10; V 10–14; V Bro Arwystli from 14. *The Coach House, Old Hall Road, Llanidloes SY18 6PQ* T: (01686) 413099 E: lyndacowan@pc-q.net

COWAN, Malcolm. b 45. CBDTI. **d** 00 **p** 01. NSM Keswick St Jo *Carl* 00–05; TV Whitehaven 05–07; P-in-c Kirkby Ireleth 07–15; C Dalton-in-Furness and Ireleth-with-Askam 07–15; rtd 15; PtO *Carl* from 16. *The Spinney, Bridekirk, Cockermouth CA13 0PF* E: malcolm-cowan@o2.co.uk

COWAN, Malcolm. b 60. Ches Coll of HE BTh 04. NOC 01. **d** 04 **p** 05. C W Kirby St Bridget *Ches* 04–07; V Witton 07–11; R Christleton 11–18; Chapl Wirral Univ Teaching Hosp NHS Foundn Trust from 18. *44 Westbourne Road, West Kirby, Wirral CH48 4DH* E: jandmcowan@gmail.com

COWAN, Paul Hudson. b 69. Ripon Coll Cuddesdon BTh 05. **d** 02 **p** 03. C Wokingham All SS *Ox* 02–05; C Kimberley Cathl S Africa 05–06; TV Newbury *Ox* 06–15; V Newbury St Geo and St Jo 15–17; Bp's Dom Chapl from 17. *Church House Oxford, Langford Locks, Kidlington OX5 1GF* T: (01865) 208221 E: paul.cowan@oxford.anglican.org

COWAN, Shirley. b 64. **d** 12 **p** 13. C Gateacre *Liv* 12–16; V Warrington H Trin and St Ann from 16. *St Ann's Vicarage, 1A Fitzherbert Street, Warrington WA2 7QE* T: (01925) 631781

COWAN, Sophie Valentine. b 87. Wycliffe Hall Ox BA 18. **d** 19. C Desborough, Brampton Ash, Dingley and Braybrooke *Pet* from 19. *134 Pioneer Avenue, Desborough, Kettering NN14 2PB* M: 07800-909768 E: cowansophie@icloud.com

COWARD, Colin Charles Malcolm. b 45. Kingston Poly DArch 72. Westcott Ho Cam 75. **d** 78 **p** 79. C Camberwell St Geo *S'wark* 78–82; P-in-c Wandsworth St Faith 82–90; V 90–96; Chapl Richmond, Twickenham and Roehampton NHS Trust 96–97; Co-ord Changing Attitude 97–03; Dir 03–15; PtO *Sarum* 07–10; rtd 15. *6 Norney Bridge, Mill Road, Worton, Devizes SN10 5SF* T: (01380) 724908 E: ccmcoward@aol.com

COWARD, Raymond. b 41. NW Ord Course 79. **d** 82 **p** 83. C Turton *Man* 82–84; C Heaton Ch Ch 84–86; V Rochdale St Geo w St Alb 86–92; V Daisy Hill 92–06; rtd 06; PtO *Man* from 06. *433 Hough Fold Way, Bolton BL2 3PY* T: (01204) 789253 E: raymond.coward@sky.com

COWELL, Anthony. *See* COWELL, Neil Anthony

COWELL, Irene Christine. b 58. RGN 80. Ridley Hall Cam 92. **d** 94 **p** 95. C Litherland St Phil *Liv* 94–98; R Sefton and Thornton 98–11; P-in-c Southport Em 11–17; Dioc Adv on HIV/AIDS and Sexual Health 97–06; Dioc Dir CME 02–17; Dir Leadership and Management Tr 05–17; V Arbory and Castletown *S & M* from 17; Dioc Dir CME

from 17. *The Vicarage, Arbory Road, Castletown, Isle of Man IM9 1ND* T: (01624) 823509 E: irene.cowell@btinternet.com

COWELL, Neil Anthony. b 61. **d** 98 **p** 99. OLM New Bury *Man* 98–06; OLM New Bury w Gt Lever from 06. *16 Castle Mews, Farnworth, Bolton BL4 9JX* T: (01204) 706957 E: revtonycowell@yahoo.co.uk

COWEN, Canon Brian. b 45. Nottm Univ BTh 77. Linc Th Coll 73. **d** 77 **p** 78. C Hexham *Newc* 77–80; C Ledbury w Eastnor *Heref* 80–81; TV Glendale Gp *Newc* 81–90; V Lesbury w Alnmouth 90–08; V Longhoughton w Howick 98–08; AD Alnwick 93–05; Hon Can Newc Cathl 01–08; rtd 08; PtO *Newc* from 08; *Edin* from 14. *13 Fenton Grange, Wooler NE71 6AW* T: (01668) 281991 E: rev.cowen@btopenworld.com

COWGILL, Canon Michael. b 48. Linc Th Coll 84. **d** 86 **p** 87. C Bolton St Jas w St Chrys *Bradf* 86–89; V Buttershaw St Paul 89–93; P-in-c Cullingworth 93–97; Dir Dioc Foundn Course 93–97; V Sutton 97–07; V Sutton w Cowling and Lotherdale 07–14; *Leeds* 14; rtd 14; PtO *Leeds* from 17. *2 Garforth Avenue, Steeton, Keighley BD20 6SP* T: (01535) 652363 E: michael@cowgill.force9.co.uk

COWIE, Andrew Cameron. b 66. Wycliffe Hall Ox. **d** 11 **p** 12. C Woking St Paul *Guildf* 11–15; V Thames Ditton from 15; AD Emly from 18. *The Vicarage, Summer Road, Thames Ditton KT7 0QQ* T: (020) 8398 9641 E: stnicparishoffice@btinternet.com

COWIE, David James. b 87. Ches Univ BEd 09. Ripon Coll Cuddesdon BTh 14. **d** 14 **p** 15. C Ches H Trin 14–16; C Ches St Mary 16–17; P-in-c High Framland Par *Leic* from 17; P-in-c S Framland from 17. *The Rectory, 7 Sycamore Lane, Wymondham, Melton Mowbray LE14 2AZ* M: 07377-873837 E: revd.david.cowie@gmail.com

COWIE, Derek Edward. b 33. S'wark Ord Course 70. **d** 73 **p** 74. C Maldon All SS w St Pet *Chelmsf* 73–76; R Bowers Gifford w N Benfleet 76–79; V Chelmsf Ascension 79–84; V Shrub End 84–95; P-in-c Gosfield 95–03; RD Hinckford 01–03; rtd 03; PtO *Nor* from 03. *Bruar Cottage, 68 Wash Lane, Kessingland, Lowestoft NR33 7QY* T: (01502) 740989 M: 07788-662211 E: revcowie73@outlook.com

COWIE, Margaret Harriet. *See* KING, Margaret Harriet

COWLES, Richard Martin. b 53. Birm Univ BSc 74. Ripon Coll Cuddesdon 91. **d** 93 **p** 94. C Iffley *Ox* 93–96; TV Wheatley 96–08; V Bray and Braywood 08–17; rtd 17; PtO *Llan* from 17. *The Dower House, Gwern-y-Domen Farm Lane, Caerphilly CF83 3RN*

COWLEY, Anne. *See* COWLEY, Judith Anne

COWLEY, Mrs Elizabeth Mary. b 47. Bris Univ PQCSW 84. WMMTC 89. **d** 92 **p** 94. NSM Wolston and Church Lawford *Cov* 92–97; Soc Resp Officer 97–02; P-in-c Churchover w Willey 97–02; TV Daventry, Ashby St Ledgers, Braunston etc *Pet* 02–13; Adv for Healing Min (Northn Adnry) 06–13; rtd 13; PtO *Pet* from 14; *Cov* from 15. *57 Daventry Road, Barby, Rugby CV23 8TP* T: (01788) 891411 E: liz.cowley@btinternet.com

COWLEY, Ian Michael. b 51. Natal Univ BCom 72 BA 75 Sheff Univ MA 83. Wycliffe Hall Ox 75. **d** 78 **p** 79. C Scottsville S Africa 78–81; C Norton Woodseats St Chad *Sheff* 81–83; R Hilton S Africa 83–94; R Milton *Ely* 94–03; RD Quy 00–02; V Yaxley and Holme w Conington 03–08; Co-ord of Voc and Spirituality *Sarum* 08–16; Hon C Clarendon 15–16; rtd 16; PtO *Ely* from 17. *12 Stockwell Avenue, Stamford PE9 2WH* T: (01780) 755612 E: iancowley3@outlook.com

COWLEY, Jean Louie Cameron. *See* HERRICK, Jean Louie Cameron

COWLEY, Mrs Judith Anne. b 59. Nottm Univ BSc 80. Ox Min Course. **d** 08 **p** 09. NSM Shepherd's Bush St Steph w St Thos *Lon* 08–18; NSM Fulham St Andr from 18. *10 Barlby Road, London W10 6AR* T: (020) 8960 9587 M: 07824-511029 E: anne.cowley@btinternet.com or anne@standrewsfulham.com

COWLEY, Paul William. b 55. Middx Univ BA 02. NTMTC 99. **d** 02 **p** 03. C Brompton H Trin w Onslow Square St Paul *Lon* 02–11; C Onslow Square and S Kensington St Aug from 11. *72 Archel Road, London W14 9QP* T: (020) 7386 5140 or 08456-447544 M: 07860-146552 E: paul.cowley@htb.org

COWLEY, Peter. b 53. NOC 06. **d** 08 **p** 09. NSM Prescot *Liv* 08–12; NSM Knowsley 12–14; NSM Stockbridge Village 12–14; NSM Huyton St Geo 12–14; NSM W Derby St Luke 12–14; NSM 4Saints Team 14–15; NSM Prescot from 15. *17 Kingsway, Prescot L35 5BG* T: 0151-426 5441 E: petercowley@blueyonder.co.uk

COWLEY, Samuel Henry. b 44. St Jo Coll Nottm 85. **d** 87 **p** 88. C Hadleigh w Layham and Shelley *St E* 87–91; P-in-c Ipswich St Mich 91–99; P-in-c Westerfield and Tuddenham w Witnesham 99–10; rtd 10; PtO *St E* from 10. *44 Hunters End, Trimley St Mary, Felixstowe IP11 0XH* T: (01394) 200462

COWLIN, Clare Margaret. b 54. d 13 p 14. NSM Wells St Thos w Horrington *B & W* 13–17; NSM Chewton Mendip w Ston Easton, Litton etc 13–17; PtO 17–18; NSM Wells St Cuth w Wookey Hole from 18. *Garden Cottage, The Liberty, Wells BA5 2SU* T: (01749) 678022 E: clare.cowlin@outlook.com

COWLING, Felicity Gabrielle. b 87. SOAS Lon BA 10 Chu Coll Cam BTh 16. Ridley Hall Cam 14. d 17 p 18. C Ashton-in-Makerfield St Thos *Liv* from 17. *79 Greenfields Crescent, Ashton-in-Makerfield, Wigan WN4 8QY* M: 07906-866650 E: felicity.cowling@gmail.com

COWLING, The Very Revd Simon Charles. b 59. G&C Coll Cam BA 80 MA 88 K Coll Lon PGCE 82. Linc Th Coll BTh 91. d 91 p 92. C Potternewton *Ripon* 91–94; C Far Headingley St Chad 94–96; V Roundhay St Edm 96–07; AD Allerton 04–07; Can Res and Prec Sheff Cathl 07–13; R Bolton Abbey *Bradf* 13–14; *Leeds* 14–18; Hon Can Ripon Cathl 15–18; Dean Wakef from 18. *The Deanery, 1 Cathedral Close, Wakefield WF1 2DP* T: (01924) 373923 E: dean@wakefield-cathedral.org.uk

COWPER, Christopher Herbert. b 44. Open Univ BA 76. AKC 67. d 68 p 69. C Pitsmoor *Sheff* 68–71; C Ulverston St Mary w H Trin *Carl* 71–74; R Kirklinton w Hethersgill and Scaleby 74–83; V Bridekirk and Chapl Dovenby Hall Hosp Cockermouth 83–94; P-in-c Wetheral w Warwick *Carl* 94–98; R Barningham w Hutton Magna and Wycliffe *Ripon* 98–09; rtd 09; PtO *Leeds* from 17. *6 Darnborough Gate, Ripon HG4 2TF* T: (01765) 692221 E: chrisjchrish@gmail.com

COWPER, Peter James. *See* SELLICK, Peter James

COX, Alan John. b 34. Lon Coll of Div ALCD 65 LTh. d 65 p 66. C Kirkheaton *Wakef* 65–67; C Keynsham w Queen Charlton *B & W* 67–71; R Chipstable w Huish Champflower and Clatworthy 71–76; TV Strood *Roch* 76–80; V Strood St Fran 80–83; R Keston 83–95; rtd 95; PtO *Roch* from 00. *12 Beech Court, 46 Copers Cope Road, Beckenham BR3 1LD* T: (020) 8639 0082

COX, Alison Hilda. b 57. Coll of Ripon & York St Jo BEd 79 Nottm Univ MA 02. EMMTC 99. d 02 p 03. NSM Bakewell *Derby* 02–04; NSM Walton St Jo 04–05; TV Buxton w Burbage and King Sterndale 05–07; Lay Tr Officer *S'well* 07–17; PtO *Derby* from 16. *The Cruck Barn, 191 Old Road, Chesterfield S40 3QH* T: (01246) 211179 E: alison.cox@southwell.anglican.org *or* alison.cox@totalise.co.uk

COX, Canon Anthony James Stuart. b 46. BNC Ox BA 68 MA 74. Qu Coll Birm 69. d 71 p 72. C Smethwick St Matt w St Chad *Birm* 71–74; Chapl Liv Univ 74; Chapl Malosa Secondary Sch Malawi 75–79; Hd Master 80–87; Hon Can S Malawi from 80; Chapl Loughborough Gr Sch 87–09; rtd 09; PtO *Leic* from 87; *S'well* from 97. *Orchard House, 169 Main Street, Willoughby on the Wolds, Loughborough LE12 6SY* T: (01509) 880861 E: tonycox14@gmail.com

COX, Brian Leslie. b 49. S Dios Minl Tr Scheme 91. d 94 p 95. C Southampton Maybush St Pet *Win* 94–98; P-in-c Knights Enham 98–05; R Knight's Enham and Smannell w Enham Alamein 05–06; P-in-c Freemantle 06–09; R 09–14; rtd 14; PtO *Win* 14–19; *Portsm* from 14. *2 Arden Close, Gosport PO12 3RS* M: 07796-070850 E: brianandlys@icloud.com

COX, Colin John. b 57. Open Univ BSc 97 Dur Univ BA 18. St Aug Coll of Th 14. d 17 p 18. NSM Findon w Clapham and Patching *Chich* from 17. *40 Hide Gardens, Rustington, Littlehampton BN16 3NP* T: (01903) 771981 M: 07716-117905 E: colin@cjcox.name

COX, David John. b 51. Lon Univ BD 97 Man Univ MA 04. Qu Coll Birm 76. d 79 p 80. C Brampton Bierlow *Sheff* 79–82; Miss Partner CMS 82–88; V N Perak W Malaysia 83–88; V Friarmere *Man* 88–96; P-in-c Denton Ch Ch 96–06; rtd 06; PtO *Carl* from 07. *5 Main Street, St Bees CA27 0DE* T: (01946) 821601 E: davidj.cox@hotmail.co.uk

COX (née FRANKLIN), Mrs Dianne Mary. b 48. UEA BA 69 Univ Coll of Swansea PGCE 70. NEOC 03. d 06 p 07. NSM Osbaldwick w Murton *York* 06–09; Chapl Aiglon Coll Switzerland 09–10; NSM Berne *Eur* 11–13; rtd 13; Chapl York Teaching Hosp NHS Foundn Trust from 14; PtO *York* from 14; *Eur* from 14. *101 Old Orchard, Haxby, York YO32 3DS* T: (01904) 421556 E: diannecoxuk@yahoo.co.uk

COX, Elizabeth Anne. b 55. SEITE 01. d 04 p 05. NSM Newington w Hartlip and Stockbury *Cant* 04–11; Chapl HM Pris Standford Hill 11–13; Chapl HM Pris Swaleside from 13. *HM Prison Swaleside, Church Road, Eastchurch, Sheerness ME12 4AX* T: (01795) 804100 M: 07789-510499

COX, Canon Eric William. b 30. Dur Univ BA 54. Wells Th Coll 54. d 56 p 57. C Sutton in Ashfield St Mary *S'well* 56–59; Asst Chapl Brussels *Eur* 59–62; V Winnington *Ches* 62–71; V Middlewich 71–76; Chapl Mid Cheshire Hosps Trust 73–95; P-in-c Biley *Ches* 73–76; V Middlewich w Byley 76–95; RD Middlewich 80–94; Hon Can Ches Cathl 84–95;

rtd 95; PtO *Ches* 95–09; *Lich* 96–14. *Lovel Hollow, Church Road, Baschurch, Shrewsbury SY4 2EE* T: (01939) 261258 E: ewcox@hotmail.co.uk

COX, Geoffrey Sidney Randel. b 33. Mert Coll Ox BA 56 MA 60. Tyndale Hall Bris. d 58 p 59. C St Paul's Cray St Barn CD *Roch* 58–61; C Bromley Ch Ch 61–64; V Gorsley w Cliffords Mesne *Glouc* 64–79; V Hucclecote 79–89; V Wollaston and Strixton *Pet* 89–96; rtd 96; PtO *Glouc* from 96. *32 Murvagh Close, Cheltenham GL53 7QY* T: (01242) 251604 E: g.cox25@btinternet.com

COX, Hugh Teversham. b 42. Keble Coll Ox BA 76 MA 82 Trin Evang Div Sch (USA) DMin 99. Moore Th Coll Sydney. d 69 p 70. C Manuka St Paul Australia 70–71; P-in-c Kameruka 71–74; PtO *Ox* 75–76; P-in-c Canberra Ch Ch Australia 76–82; Tutor and Lect St Mark's Nat Th Cen 77–87; R Lane Cove 82–87; R Castle Hill St Paul 87–01; Tervuren *Eur* 01–06; R E Sydney Australia 06–10; Asst to Bp S Sydney 10–16; rtd 16; PtO *Eur* from 13. *Weemalah, 201 Mt Lindsay Road, Barraba NSW 2347, Australia* T: (0061) (2) 6783 1406 M: (0061) 42-389 5810 E: htevershamcox@hotmail.com

COX, James David Robert. b 65. Lanc Univ BA 88. Qu Coll Birm BD 92. d 93 p 94. C Harborne St Pet *Birm* 93–96; C Chelmsley Wood 96–97; TV 97–00; V Smethwick Resurr 00–07; V Taunton St Andr *B & W* 07–09; V Selly Oak St Mary *Birm* 09–18; C S Quantock *B & W* from 18. *55 Batt Drive, Cheddon Fitzpaine, Taunton TA2 8FY* E: jimcox11@googlemail.com

COX, Janet. b 48. CBDTI 04. d 05 p 06. NSM Long Marton w Dufton and w Milburn *Carl* 05–08; NSM Heart of Eden 08–13; rtd 13; PtO *Carl* from 13. *86 Ainsty Road, Wetherby LS22 7FY* E: peter_janet_cox@hotmail.com

COX, John Anthony. b 45. Hull Univ BA 67. Qu Coll Birm 71. d 73 p 74. C Buckingham *Ox* 73–76; C Whitley Ch Ch 76–81; V Reading St Agnes w St Paul 81–83; V Chaddesley Corbett and Stone *Worc* 83–10; rtd 10; PtO *Worc* from 11. *7 Burlington Close, Kidderminster DY10 3DQ* T: (01562) 637966 E: jacm.cox@ukgateway.net

COX, The Ven John Stuart. b 40. Fitzw Ho Cam BA 62 MA 66 Linacre Coll Ox BA 67. Wycliffe Hall Ox 64. d 68 p 69. C Prescot *Liv* 68–71; C Birm St Geo 71–73; R 73–78; Selection Sec ACCM 78–83; Hon C Orpington All SS *Roch* 78–83; Dioc Dir of Ords *S'wark* 83–91; Can Res and Treas S'wark Cathl 83–91; V Roehampton H Trin 91–95; Adn Sudbury *St E* 95–06; rtd 06; PtO *St E* from 06; Dioc Dir of Educn from 07. *2 Bullen Close, Bury St Edmunds IP33 3JP* T/F: (01284) 766796 E: archdeacon.john@stedmundsbury.anglican.org

COX, Julie Margaret. b 55. SAOMC. d 00 p 01. NSM Luton St Chris Round Green *St Alb* 00–06; NSM Luton St Anne w St Chris 06–08; PtO from 08. *29 Maple Close, Pulloxhill, Bedford MK45 5EF* T: (01525) 717002 E: revjuliecox@hotmail.com

COX, Mrs Linda Jayne. b 66. RGN 88. Qu Coll Birm 10. d 12 p 13. C Woodfield *Leic* 12–16; R Baschurch and Weston Lullingfield w Hordley *Lich* from 16; RD Ellesmere from 17. *The Rectory, Nobold, Baschurch, Shrewsbury SY4 2EB* T: (01939) 260305 E: lindac40@btinternet.com

COX, Martin Brian. b 64. Keele Univ BA 91 CQSW 91. St Jo Coll Nottm 01. d 03 p 04. C Sale St Anne *Ches* 03–05; V Sandiway 05–10; P-in-c Chorley St Laur *Blackb* 10–11; R 11–16; TR Astley, Tyldesley and Mosley Common *Man* from 16; AD Leigh from 19. *The Rectory, 7 Holbeck, Astley, Tyldesley, Manchester M29 7DU* T: (01942) 883313

COX, Martin Lloyd. b 57. Wilson Carlile Coll and Sarum & Wells Th Coll. d 88 p 89. C Risca *Mon* 88–91; TV Pontypool 91–96; V Monkton *St D* 96–04; TR 04–10; V Gorseinon *S & B* 10–16; AD Llwchwr 13–15; P-in-c Narberth w Mounton w Robeston Wathen etc *St D* from 16. *New Rectory, Adams Drive, Narberth SA67 7AE* T: (01834) 861192 E: martinlloydcox@btinternet.com

COX, Noel Stanley Bertie. b 65. Auckland Univ LLB 88 LLM 95 PhD 01 MTheol Lambeth MA 05 Univ of Wales (Lamp) LTh 07 FRHistS 04. St Mich Coll Llan 10. d 12 p 13. Prof Law Aberystwyth Univ *St D* 10–14; NSM Llanbadarn Fawr and Elerch and Penrhyncoch etc 12–15. *16 William Blofield Avenue, Mount Roskill, Auckland 1041, New Zealand* E: noel.cox34@gmail.com

COX, Ms Patricia Jean. b 44. WEMTC. d 00 p 01. NSM Coleford, Staunton, Newland, Redbrook etc *Glouc* 00–07; NSM Lydney 07–13; rtd 14; PtO *Glouc* from 14. *67 Primrose Hill, Lydney GL15 5SW* T: (01594) 843852

COX, Canon Peter Allard. b 55. Univ of Wales (Lamp) BA 76. Wycliffe Hall Ox 77. d 79 p 80. C Penarth All SS *Llan* 79–82; V Aberpergwm and Blaengwrach 82–86; V Bargoed and Deri w Brithdir 86–97; V Penarth All SS from 97; AD Penarth and Barry 11–16; Can Llan Cathl from 15. *All Saints' Vicarage, 2 Lower Cwrt-y-Vil Road, Penarth CF64 3HQ* T: (029) 2070 8952 E: peterallard.cox@ntlworld.com

COX, Miss Rosemary Jennifer. b 54. St Aid Coll Dur BA 75 Lon Bible Coll BTh 97 Trin Coll Bris MA 99. Cranmer Hall Dur 01. **d** 03 **p** 04. C Leeds All SS w Osmondthorpe *Ripon* 03–05; C Ireland Wood 05–07; PtO *Dur* from 05. *7 The Paddock, Waterhouses, Durham DH7 9AW* T: 0191-373 1539 E: rosemaryjcox@aol.com

COX, Canon Sheila Margaret. b 54. Nottm Univ BA 76 Reading Univ PGCE 77 Win Univ MA 15. SEITE 00. **d** 03 **p** 04. NSM Cranbrook *Cant* 03–08; NSM Mersham w Hinxhill and Sellindge 08–12; NSM Smeeth w Monks Horton and Stowting and Brabourne 08–12; R G7 Benefice 12–19; Asst Dir of Ords 08–19; Bp's Adv for Women's Min 13–19; Hon Can Cant Cathl 14–19; rtd 19. *Address temp unknown* M: 07985-003095 E: sheila.m.cox@btopenworld.com

COX, Mrs Sheila Stuart. b 41. Aber Coll of Educn CertEd 63. Edin Dioc NSM Course 85. **d** 88 **p** 94. NSM Livingston LEP *Edin* 88–93; Asst Chapl St Jo and Bangour Hosps W Lothian 89–93; Chapl 96–98; Hon C Edin St Mark 93–96; Missr Edin St Andr and St Aid 95–96; NSM Eyemouth 98–05; rtd 05; LtO *Edin* 06–17. *5 Northfield Farm Cottages, St Abbs, Eyemouth TD14 5QF* T: (01890) 771764

COX, Canon Simon John. b 53. Qu Mary Coll Lon BSc 74 Liv Univ PhD 81 Selw Coll Cam BA 81 MA 85 Lanc Univ MA 87 CBiol 79 MRSB 79. Ridley Hall Cam 79. **d** 82 **p** 83. C Livesey *Blackb* 82–85; C Cheadle Hulme St Andr *Ches* 85–89; V Disley 89–94; R Bispham *Blackb* from 94; P-in-c S Shore St Pet 05–07; AD Blackpool 04–19; P-in-c Copp w Inskip from 19; Hon Can Blackb Cathl from 07. *16 Wolverton Avenue, Bispham, Blackpool FY2 9NT* M: 07703-475586 E: drsjcox@yahoo.co.uk

COX, Stephen John Wormleighton. b 54. New Coll Ox MA 79 Fitzw Coll Cam BA 79. Ridley Hall Cam 77. **d** 80 **p** 81. C Clapton Park All So *Lon* 80–85; TV Hackney Marsh 85–87; V Holloway St Mary w St Jas 87–88; P-in-c Barnsbury St Dav w St Clem 87–88; V Holloway St Mary Magd 88–97; AD Islington 93–99; TR Upper Holloway 97–10; Preb St Paul's Cathl 07–10; Local Miss Adv *Guildf* 10–18; rtd 18; PtO *Guildf* from 19. *17 Glenmount Road, Mytchett, Camberley GU16 6AY* T: (01483) 790330 E: stephenj.cox@virgin.net

COXALL, Mrs Jayne. b 66. Open Univ BSc 09. All SS Cen for Miss & Min 14. **d** 17 **p** 18. C Bredbury St Mark *Ches* 17–19; P-in-c Aber-Morfa Miss Area *St As* from 19. *18 Tirionfa, Rhuddlan, Rhyl LL18 6LT* M: 07896-652261 E: jaynecoxall@aol.com

COYNE, Deborah Margaret. b 88. Cranmer Hall Dur 12. **d** 15 **p** 16. C Rural E York 15–18; C Tadcaster 18–19; P-in-c Alne from 19; P-in-c Brafferton w Pilmoor, Myton-on-Swale etc from 19; C Coxwold and Husthwaite from 19; C Crayke w Brandsby and Yearsley from 19; C Easingwold w Raskelf and Newton on Ouse from 19; C Strensall from 19. *1 Hollygarth, Brafferton, York YO61 2NZ* M: 07704-855759 E: rev.deborah.coyne@gmail.com

COYNE, John Edward. b 55. Sheff Univ MA 98. Oak Hill Th Coll BA 79. **d** 79 **p** 80. C Cheadle Hulme St Andr *Ches* 79–81; C Macclesfield St Mich 81–83; V Stalybridge H Trin and Ch Ch 83–88; Chapl RAF 88–03; Command Chapl RAF 03–05; RAF Adv in Evangelism 93–98; Hon C Hemingford Grey *Ely* 96–98; Dean of Coll St Jo Coll Nottm 05–09; Dir Local and Regional Delivery CPAS 09–12; R Aldridge *Lich* 12–17; Patr Leadership Specialist CPAS from 17. *Windrush House, London Road, Moreton-in-Marsh GL56 0HB* T: (01608) 652159 E: j2scoyne@hotmail.com

COZENS (née FULLER), Mrs Alison Jane. b 61. St Andr Univ MTheol 84. Edin Th Coll 85. **d** 87 **p** 94. C Selkirk *Edin* 87–89; C Melrose 87–89; C Galashiels 87–89; C Edin H Cross 89–92; Dn-in-c Edin St Columba 92–94; R 94–10; Chapl Edin Univ 96–00; P-in-c Leic Presentation 10–15; R Dunfermline *St And* 15–18; P-in-c Birm St Geo from 18; P-in-c Lozells St Paul and St Silas from 18. *St James's Vicarage, 21 Austin Road, Birmingham B21 8NU* T: 0121-551 3470 E: revalisonjanecozens18@gmail.com

COZENS, Daniel Harry. b 44. Oak Hill Th Coll. **d** 71 **p** 72. C St Paul's Cray St Barn *Roch* 71–74; C Deptford St Nic w Ch Ch *S'wark* 74–76; C Deptford St Nic and St Luke 76–78; Rees Missr *Ely* 78–09; PtO *Ely* from 09; Six Preacher Cant Cathl 94–04. *Walnut Top, High Street, Bury, Ramsey, Huntingdon PE26 2NR* T: (01487) 814533

COZENS, Canon Michael Graeme. b 59. Chich Th Coll 91. **d** 93 **p** 94. C Emscote *Cov* 93–96; C Prestbury *Glouc* 96–03; TV Prestbury and All SS 03–06; P-in-c 06–08; TR N Cheltenham 08–14; P-in-c Dursley 14–18; R Dursley, Uley, Owlpen etc from 18; Hon Can Glouc Cathl from 10. *The Rectory, Broadwell, Dursley GL11 4JE* T: (01453) 542035

CRABB, Helen Maria. See BARTON, Helen Maria

CRABB, Paul Anthony. b 58. St Chad's Coll Dur BSc 79 Leeds Univ PGCE 80. Qu Coll Birm 90. **d** 91 **p** 92. C Gomersal *Wakef* 91–95; V Drighlington 95–01; TV Dewsbury 01–09; P-in-c Hanging Heaton 09–12; P-in-c Batley St Thos 09–12; P-in-c Bramley *Ripon* 14; Leeds 14–17; R from 17. *The Vicarage, 8 Hough Lane, Leeds LS13 3NE* T: 0113-257 8590 *or* 225 8562 M: 07946-530415 E: paulthepriest.pc@gmail.com

CRABTREE, Hazel. b 40. SRN 82 Yorks & Humberside Assn for F&HE TCert 89. **d** 07 **p** 08. OLM Went Valley *Wakef* 07–10; PtO 10–14; Leeds 14–16. *11 Hillcroft Close, Darrington, Pontefract WF8 3BD* T: (01977) 793268 E: hazel@darringtonchurch.com *or* rev.hcrabtree@gmail.com

CRABTREE, Martine Charmaine. b 74. Glas Bible Coll BA 96 St Jo Coll Nottm MTh 02. **d** 02 **p** 03. C Kippax w Allerton Bywater *Ripon* 02–06; P-in-c Sowerby *Wakef* 06–12; P-in-c Norland 09–12; P-in-c Lupset 12–14; *Leeds* from 14; P-in-c Thornes *Wakef* 12–14; *Leeds* from 14; Adv on Urban Issues from 12. *Lupset Vicarage, 23C Broadway, Wakefield WF2 8AA* T: (01422) 832830 E: martinecrabtree@aol.com

CRACKNELL, Heather Louise. b 76. UEA BSc 97. ERMC 08. **d** 11 **p** 12. C Cringleford and Colney *Nor* 11–17; V Nor Heartsease St Fran 17–19. *Address temp unknown* E: heather.cracknell@gmail.com

CRADDOCK, Mrs Lesley-Ann. b 58. Ridley Hall Cam 10. **d** 12 **p** 13. C Hatfield Hyde *St Alb* 12–15; P-in-c Glas St Oswald 15–18. *12 Mary Slessor Wynd, Rutherglen, Glasgow G73 5RJ* T: 0141-391 4050 M: 07903-020509 E: lesley.craddock@btinternet.com

CRADDUCK, Stuart William. b 74. Bp Otter Coll Chich BA 97. Ripon Coll Cuddesdon BTh 00. **d** 00 **p** 01. C W Leigh *Portsm* 00–03; Min Can St Alb Abbey 03–07; R Whyke w Rumboldswhyke and Portfield *Chich* 07–14; P-in-c Grantham, Manthorpe from 14. *The Rectory, Church Street, Grantham NG31 6RR* T: (01476) 569582 E: rector@stwulframs.com

CRAFER, Mrs Jeanette Angela. b 48. Keswick Hall Coll CertEd 78. EAMTC 99. **d** 01 **p** 02. C Ashmanhaugh, Barton Turf etc *Nor* 01–05; P-in-c Martham and Repps w Bastwick, Thurne etc 05–07; V 07–13; rtd 13; PtO *Nor* from 14. *Whispers, Chapel Road, Sea Palling, Norwich NR12 0UQ* T: (01692) 598590 E: jeanette.crafer@tiscali.co.uk *or* rev.jeanette@btinternet.com

CRAFT, William Newham. b 46. Lon Univ BSc 68 MCIPD 70. Oak Hill Th Coll 87. **d** 89 **p** 90. C Werrington *Pet* 90–93; C-in-c Norfolk Park St Leonard CD *Sheff* 93–02; P-in-c Sheff St Jo 99–02; V 02–03; V Stapleford *S'well* 03–09; AD Beeston 07–09; rtd 09; PtO *Sheff* from 09. *435 Redmires Road, Sheffield S10 4LF* T: 0114-230 2718 E: billncraft@gmail.com

CRAGG, Edward William Adrian. b 55. St Cath Coll Cam BA 77 MA 81. Cranmer Hall Dur 97. **d** 99 **p** 00. C Clifton *York* 99–02; R Skelton w Shipton and Newton on Ouse 02–09; Chapl York Hosps NHS Foundn Trust 02–09; R Bridlington Priory *York* 09–12; V Wyke *Bradf* 12–14; *Leeds* 14–18; rtd 18. *6 Ward Street, Skipton BD23 2EY* E: adrian@cragg.myzen.co.uk

CRAGG, Mrs Sandra Anne. b 45. St Hugh's Coll Ox BA 67. SEITE 94. **d** 97 **p** 98. NSM Kingston All SS w St Jo *S'wark* 97–12; NSM Kingston 12–15; PtO from 15. *10 Lingfield Avenue, Kingston upon Thames KT1 2TN* T: (020) 8546 1997 F: 8541 5281 E: sandy@toadstool.co.uk *or* sandycragg26@gmail.com

CRAGGS, Michael Alfred. b 43. Open Univ BA 79. St Mich Coll Llan 66. **d** 69 **p** 70. C Clee *Linc* 69–72; C Old Brumby 72–76; TV Kingsthorpe w Northampton St Dav *Pet* 76–83; P-in-c Gt w Lt Addington 83–89; RD Higham 88–89; TR Corby SS Pet and Andr w Gt and Lt Oakley 89–02; V Corby SS Pet and Andr 02–08; RD Corby 90–95; rtd 08. *1 Johnson Drive, Scotter, Gainsborough DN21 3HA* T: (01724) 764200 E: mikeccorb@aol.com

CRAGO, Geoffrey Norman. b 44. Linc Th Coll 67. **d** 70 **p** 71. C Matson *Glouc* 70–75; V Dean Forest H Trin 75–80; Relig Progr Producer Radio Severn Sound 80–85; P-in-c Huntley *Glouc* 80–82; PtO 82–90; Dioc Communications Officer 84; Gen Syn Broadcasting Dept 85–88; Hon C Highnam, Lassington, Rudford, Tibberton etc *Glouc* 90–08; Relig Progr Producer BBC Radio Gloucestershire 94–03; Bp's Press Officer and Dioc Communications Officer *Glouc* 97–01; rtd 09; PtO *Glouc* from 16. *Milestones, 2 Two Mile Lane, Highnam, Gloucester GL2 8DW* T: (01452) 750575 F: 08700-940404 E: g.crago@btinternet.com

CRAIG, Canon Alan Stuart. b 38. Leeds Univ BA 59. Cranmer Hall Dur. **d** 61 **p** 62. C Newcastle w Butterton *Lich* 61–65; C Scarborough St Mary w Ch Ch, St Paul and St Thos *York* 65–67; V Werrington *Lich* 67–72; Asst Chapl HM Pris Man 72–73; Chapl HM Borstal Hindley 73–78; Chapl HM Pris

Acklington 78–84; V Longhirst *Newc* 84–90; R Morpeth 90–99; RD 84–95; Dir of Ords and Bp's Chapl 99–02; Hon Can Newc Cathl 90–02; Chapl Northd Mental Health NHS Trust 90–99; Chapl to The Queen 95–08; rtd 02; PtO *Newc* from 02. *5 Springfield Meadows, Alnwick NE66 2NY* T: (01665) 602806 M: 07779-519040

CRAIG, Andrew John. b 54. Selw Coll Cam BA 76 MA 80 PhD 80 Dur Univ MBA 92. NEOC 00. **d** 03 **p** 04. NSM Stranton *Dur* 03–19; rtd 19. *25 Egerton Road, Hartlepool TS26 0BW* T: (01429) 422461 E: revdrandrewcraig@gmail.com

CRAIG, Gillean Weston. b 49. York Univ BA 72 Qu Coll Cam BA 76 MA 80. Westcott Ho Cam 76. **d** 77 **p** 78. C St Marylebone Ch Ch *Lon* 77–82; C Ealing St Barn 82–88; P-in-c St Geo-in-the-East w St Paul 88–89; R 89–02; V Kensington St Mary Abbots w St Geo 02–06; V Kensington St Mary Abbots 06–18; Preb St Paul's Cathl 16–18; rtd 18; PtO *Cant* from 19. *Address temp unknown* E: vicar@smaw8.org

CRAIG, James Owen Maxwell. b 72. Open Univ BA 98. Cranmer Hall Dur 99. **d** 02 **p** 03. C Ch the K *Dur* 02–05; Gateshead and Bensham Community Chapl to Arts 05–16; TV Gateshead 11–16; Chapl Guy's Campus K Coll Lon *Lon* 16–17; C S'wark St Geo w St Alphege and St Jude *S'wark* 16–17; NSM St Mary le Strand w St Clem Danes *Lon* from 17. *11 Wilkinson Street, London SW8 1DD* M: 07918-659088 E: rev.jim@btopenworld.com *or* jim.craig@kcl.ac.uk

CRAIG, Canon John Newcome. b 39. Selw Coll Cam BA 63 MA 67. Linc Th Coll 63. **d** 65 **p** 66. C Cannock *Lich* 65–71; V Gt Wyrley 71–79; TR Wednesfield 79–91; Prec Leic Cathl 91–03; Hon Can Leic Cathl 93–03; Can Res Leic Cathl 03–04; rtd 04; PtO *Birm* from 04; *Lich* from 19. *231 Beacon Park Village, Lower Sandford Street, Lichfield WS13 6JZ* E: john.olivia.craig@lineone.net

CRAIG, Judy Howard. *See* CRAIG PECK, Judy Howard

CRAIG, Julie Elizabeth. *See* EATON, Julie Elizabeth

CRAIG, Richard Harvey. b 31. Em Coll Cam BA 58. Linc Th Coll. **d** 60 **p** 61. C Bottesford *Linc* 60–65; Bp's Ind Chapl 65–69; Dioc Adv on Laity Tr *Bris* 69–74; V Whitchurch 74–86; TV N Lambeth *S'wark* 86–96; Bp's Ecum Adv 88–96; Ecum Officer 90–96; rtd 96; PtO *St Alb* 96–99; *S'wark* 01. *18 Holst Court, Westminster Bridge Road, London SE1 7JQ* T: (020) 7928 0495

CRAIG, Robin Joseph. b 43. TCD BA 65 Div Test 66 Birm Univ CertEd 70. **d** 66 **p** 67. C Carrickfergus *Conn* 66–69; Chapl Lord Wandsworth Coll Hook 75–85; Vice Prin and Chapl K Sch Macclesfield 85–01; LtO *Ches* 85–01; rtd 01. *5 Winston Court, Lavant Road, Chichester PO19 5RG* T: (01243) 778636

CRAIG PECK, Judy Howard. b 57. Lon Univ MB, BS 81 MRCGP 86. WMMTC 97. **d** 00 **p** 01. NSM Billing *Pet* 00–07; NSM Yardley Hastings, Denton and Grendon etc 07–15; NSM Officer 03–10; C Guilsborough and Hollowell and Cold Ashby etc from 15. *The Vicarage, 15 Church Mount, Guilsborough, Northampton NN6 8QA* T: (01604) 743734 E: judy@revpeck.co.uk

CRAIGHEAD, Mrs Patricia Anne. b 60. Northumbria Univ BSc 02. NEOC 05. **d** 08 **p** 09. C Monkseaton St Pet *Newc* 08–12; V Long Benton St Mary from 12. *St Mary's Vicarage, Blackfriars Way, Newcastle upon Tyne NE12 8ST* T: 0191-266 2326 M: 07967-316615 E: patcraighead@hotmail.co.uk

CRAMERI, Mrs Mary Barbara. b 44. K Coll Lon BD 65 AKC 91 Lon Inst of Educn PGCE 66. S Dios Minl Tr Scheme 86. **d** 88 **p** 94. C Whitton SS Phil and Jas *Lon* 88–91; Tutor STETS 91–97; Vice-Prin 93-96; Acting Prin 96–97; Dep Dir and Minl Formation Officer 97–98; Par Dn Bemerton *Sarum* 91–92; TV Pewsey and Swanborough 98–00; TR Whitton 00–01; rtd 01; PtO *Sarum* 02–05; *Ox* 10–12; *Cov* 10–19; Hon C Chase *Ox* 05–10. *6 Browning Close, Stratford-upon-Avon CV37 7PF* T: (01789) 296650 E: mary.crameri@btinternet.com

CRAMPTON, John Leslie. b 41. CITC 64. **d** 67 **p** 68. C Lurgan Ch the Redeemer *D & D* 67–71; C Dundela St Mark 71–73; C Umtali Rhodesia 73–76; R Fort Victoria 73–76; I Killanne w Killegney, Rossdroit and Templeshanbo *C & O* 82–88; Preb Ferns Cathl 85–88; Chapl Wilson's Hosp Sch Multyfarnham *M & K* 88–91; C Mullingar, Portnashangan, Moyliscar, Kilbixy etc 89–91; I Athy w Kilberry, Fontstown and Kilkea *D & G* 91–01; Can Ch Ch Cathl Dublin 95–01; I Geashill w Killeigh and Ballycommon *M & K* 01–06; rtd 06. *41 Beech Avenue, The Paddock, Enniscorthy, Co Wexford, Y21 Y6H9, Republic of Ireland* T: (00353) (53) 923 2589 M: 87-907 7981 E: cramptonjl41@gmail.com

CRANE, Mrs Judith. b 53. Matlock Coll of Educn BCombStuds 81. Cranmer Hall Dur 94. **d** 96 **p** 97. C Tadcaster w Newton Kyme *York* 96–99; TV Brayton 99–02; V Blackwell w Tibshelf *Derby* 02–08; Asst Dir of Ords 06–09;

PtO 09–18; rtd 18. *27 Highfield Road, Little Eaton, Derby DE21 5AG* T: (01332) 833872 E: judithcrane@yahoo.co.uk

CRANFIELD, Charlotte Clare. b 60. **d** 16. NSM Easingwold w Raskelf *York* from 16; NSM Alne from 17; NSM Brafferton w Pilmoor, Myton-on-Swale etc from 17; NSM Coxwold and Husthwaite from 17; NSM Crayke w Brandsby and Yearsley from 17; NSM Skelton w Shipton and Newton on Ouse from 17; NSM Stensall from 17; NSM Forest of Galtres from 17. *12 Penny Lane, Easingwold, York YO61 3RR* T: (01347) 824399

CRANFIELD, Canon Nicholas William Stewart. b 56. Mert Coll Ox BA 77 MA 81 DPhil 88 Leeds Univ BA 81 Selw Coll Cam PhD 95 FSA 07. Coll of Resurr Mirfield 79 Union Th Sem (NY) STM 84. **d** 86 **p** 87. C Ascot Heath *Ox* 86–89; Prin Berks Chr Tr Scheme 89–92; Hon C Reading St Mary the Virgin 89–92; Chapl and Fell Selw Coll Cam 92–99; Dean of Chpl 94–99; Chapl Newnham Coll Cam 92–99; V Blackheath All SS *S'wark* from 99; Chapl St Dunstan's Coll Catford 00–05; Hon Can S'wark Cathl from 17. *All Saints' Vicarage, 10 Duke Humphrey Road, London SE3 0TY* T: (020) 8852 4280 E: vicar@allsaintsblackheath.org

CRANKSHAW, Ronald. b 41. Coll of Resurr Mirfield 74. **d** 76 **p** 77. C Orford St Andr *Liv* 76; C N Meols 76–79; V Abram 79–85; V Wigan St Anne 85–99; AD Wigan W 94–99; V Heston *Lon* 99–07; rtd 07; PtO *Carl* 09–16; *Liv* from 16. *Orchard House, Westlinton, Carlisle CA6 6AA* T: (01228) 791434 E: roncrankshaw@sky.com

CRANMER, Ms Elaine. b 56. Hockerill Coll Cam CertEd 77. SEITE 97. **d** 00 **p** 01. C Charlton *S'wark* 00–03; P-in-c Eltham Park St Luke 03–10; V 11–14; AD Eltham and Mottingham 06–13; TR S Chatham H Trin *Roch* from 14. *The Rectory, 18 Marion Close, Chatham ME5 9QA* T: (01634) 685556 E: rev.elaine@virgin.net

CRANSHAW, Trevor Raymond. b 58. Trin Coll Bris 00. **d** 03 **p** 04. C Westbury-on-Trym H Trin *Bris* 03–07; P-in-c Wheathill Priory Gp *B & W* 07–14; P-in-c Clevedon St Andr and Ch Ch 14–18; V Clevedon St Andr and St Pet from 18; Warden of Readers Bath Adnry from 17. *The Vicarage, 10B Coleridge Road, Clevedon BS21 7TB* T: (01275) 871458 *or* 872982 M: 07753-397404 E: trevcranshaw@hotmail.com *or* vicar@standrews-clevedon.org.uk

CRANSTON, Andrew David. b 79. Ex Univ MEng 02 PGCE 04 Cam Univ BTh 11. Ridley Hall Cam 08. **d** 11 **p** 12. C Stone Ch Ch and Oulton *Lich* 11–14; Chapl Oswestry Sch from 14. *Oswestry School, Upper Brook Street, Oswestry SY11 2TL* T: (01691) 655711 E: ac@oswestryschool.org.uk

CRANSTON, Miss Margaret Elizabeth. b 56. Newnham Coll Cam BEd 78 Ex Univ BTh 10. SWMTC 04. **d** 07 **p** 08. NSM Heanton Punchardon w Marwood *Ex* 07–13; NSM Isle Valley *B & W* 13–16; rtd 16. *55 Adams Meadow, Ilminster TA19 9DB* E: mecranston@btinternet.com

CRANWELL, Brian Robert. b 32. Sheff Poly MSc Sheff Hallam Univ MPhil 06. Cranmer Hall Dur. **d** 84 **p** 85. C Ecclesfield *Sheff* 84–86; V Handsworth Woodhouse 86–99; rtd 99; PtO *Sheff* from 99; *Derby* from 00. *9 Westview Close, Totley, Sheffield S17 3LT* T: 0114-262 1499 E: brian_cranwell@lineone.net

CRASKE, Leslie Gordon Hamilton. b 29. AKC 54 Lambeth STh 80. St Boniface Warminster 54. **d** 55 **p** 56. C Malden St Jo *S'wark* 55–58; C Streatham St Leon 58–60; SPG S Rhodesia 60–65; SPG Rhodesia 65–66; V Upper Norwood St Jo *Cant* 67–83; R Guernsey St Sav *Win* 83–97; rtd 97; PtO *Win* from 97. *La Gruterie, 3 Mount Row, St Peter Port, Guernsey GY1 1NS* T: (01481) 716027

CRASTON (*née* FULLALOVE), Mrs Brenda Hurst. b 33. Open Univ BA 75 Man Univ MPhil 86. St Mich Ho Ox 58. **dss** 80 **d** 87 **p** 94. Bolton St Paul w Em *Man* 80–93; Par Dn 87–93; rtd 93; PtO *Man* from 94. *12 Lever Park Avenue, Horwich, Bolton BL6 7LE* T: (01204) 699972 E: colbrencraston@gmail.com

CRAVEN, Colin Peter. b 48. Dartmouth RN Coll. St Steph Ho Ox 83. **d** 85 **p** 86. C Holbeach *Linc* 85–88; Chapl Fleet Hosp 86–97; TV Grantham *Linc* 88–97; P-in-c Fairfield *Derby* 97–03; OCM 88–03; CF 03–06; Rtd Officer Chapl RAChD 06–14; rtd 14. *154 Mudeford Lane, Christchurch BH23 3HS* E: revcp@hotmail.com

CRAVEN, David Alex. b 80. Univ of Wales (Ban) BA 01. Wycliffe Hall Ox BTh 06. **d** 06 **p** 07. C Holme Eden and Wetheral w Warwick *Carl* 06–09; R 09–17; C Croglin 06–09; P-in-c 09–12; R Rufford and Tarleton *Blackb* 17–19; C Preston St Jo and St Geo from 19. *97 Garstang Road, Preston PR1 1LD* E: dacraven@hotmail.com

CRAVEN, Janet Elizabeth. *See* CHAPMAN, Janet Elizabeth

CRAVEN, Mrs Janet Mary. b 43. Bp Otter Coll TCert 64. **d** 06 **p** 07. OLM Shelley and Shepley *Wakef* 06–14; *Leeds* 14–16; OLM Kirkburton and Shelley from 16. *70 Jenkyn Lane, Shepley, Huddersfield HD8 8AW* T: (01484) 604107

CRAVEN, Rebecca Clare. b 58. Bris Univ BDS 80 Glas Univ MPH 90 Man Univ PhD 97 RCPS FDS 97. **d** 01 **p** 02. OLM Reddish *Man* 01–06; NSM 06–07; NSM Salford Sacred Trin and St Phil 07–16; NSM Salford Sacred Trin from 16. *201 Thornton Road, Fallowfield, Manchester M14 7NS* T: 0161-225 7336 E: rebecca.c.craven@manchester.ac.uk

CRAW, Jane Mary. b 53. Stockwell Coll of Educn CertEd 76 Lon Inst of Educn BEd 77. STETS BA 13. **d** 10 **p** 11. NSM Sherborne w Castleton, Lillington and Longburton *Sarum* 10–16; TV from 16. *Jubilee Cottage, Lower Kingsbury, Milborne Port, Sherborne DT9 5ED* T: (01963) 251527 E: jane@jubileecottage.plus.com

CRAWFORD, Alexander Ian George. b 88. Univ Coll Dur BA 11 Sheff Univ MA 18. Coll of Resurr Mirfield 16. **d** 18 **p** 19. C Bensham and Teams *Dur* from 18; C Gateshead St Helen from 18. *St Columba House, Peterborough Close, Gateshead NE8 1NL* M: 07840-123198 E: revd.crawford@outlook.com *or* aigc88@hotmail.com

CRAWFORD, Mrs Anne Elizabeth. b 59. SAOMC 01. **d** 04 **p** 05. C Billington, Egginton, Hockliffe etc *St Alb* 04–08; R Toddington and Chalgrave 08–16; TV Richmond St Mary w St Matthias and St Jo *S'wark* from 16. *St Matthias' House, 22 Cambrian Road, Richmond TW10 6JQ* T: (020) 8948 7217 E: annie.anselm@btinternet.com

CRAWFORD, Canon Ivy Elizabeth. b 50. Trin Coll Bris 83. **dss** 85 **d** 87 **p** 94. Collier Row St Jas *Chelmsf* 85; Collier Row St Jas and Havering-atte-Bower 86–89; Par Dn 87–89; Par Dn Harlow New Town w Lt Parndon 89–94; C Harlow Town Cen w Lt Parndon 94–95; V Blackmore and Stondon Massey 95–09; RD Ongar 06–09; P-in-c Broxted w Chickney and Tilty etc 09–16; CME Adv 09–16; Hon Can Chelmsf Cathl 98–16; rtd 16. *118B Holden Road, London N12 7EA* T: (020) 3560 1299 E: ivycrawford@btinternet.com

CRAWFORD, James Robert Harry. b 55. Cumbria Univ BA 08. CBDTI 00. **d** 03 **p** 04. NSM Lower Darwen St Jas *Blackb* 03–10; C Colne and Villages 10–14; C Pendle Deanery 14–16; C Bispham *Blackb* from 16. *89 Ashfield Road, Blackpool FY2 0EN* T: (01253) 592166 E: jayjay644@btinternet.com *or* jrcrawford645@gmail.com

CRAWFORD, Kenneth Ian. b 48. Melbourne Univ BMus 77 Columbia Univ MA 79 MEd 80 MACE 84. Trin Coll Melbourne BD 86. **d** 87 **p** 87. C Ringwood St Paul Australia 87–89; C Cheltenham St Matt 89–90; Prec Melbourne Cathl 93–97; P-in-c Warndon St Nic *Worc* 97–03; V Pershore w Pinvin, Wick and Birlingham 03–14; P-in-c Darlington St Jas *Dur* from 14. *The Vicarage, 30 Smithfield Road, Darlington DL1 4DD* T: (01325) 240183 E: kenneth.priest@stjamesdarlington.org

CRAWFORD, Louise Dorothy Anita. *See* CRAWFORD-McCAFFERTY, Louise Dorothy Anita

CRAWFORD, Michael Davis. b 45. Oak Hill Th Coll BA 97 K Coll Lon PGCE 98. **d** 00 **p** 01. NSM New Barnet St Jas *St Alb* 00–04; C Limassol St Barn Cyprus 04–08; Chapl SE Cyprus 08–11; PtO *Eur* from 11; Cyprus and the Gulf from 11; PtO *Nor* from 18. *3 Brewers Green Lane, Diss IP22 4QP* T: (01379) 650365 M: 07527-480921 E: rev.michaelcrawford@gmail.com

CRAWFORD-McCAFFERTY, Louise Dorothy Anita. b 60. Oak Hill Th Coll BA 91 Princeton Th Sem MDiv 00. Irish Sch of Ecum MPhil 02. **d** 02 **p** 03. C Drumragh w Mountfield *D & R* 02–05; I Aghadowey w Kilrea 05–17; I Aghadowey from 17. *40 Brone Road, Garvagh, Coleraine BT51 4EQ* T: (028) 7086 9277 M: 07890-745359 E: louisecrawfordmccafferty@yahoo.com

CRAWLEY, Alan John. b 58. Trin Coll Cam MA 83. SAOMC 04. **d** 07 **p** 08. NSM Gt Marlow w Marlow Bottom, Lt Marlow and Bisham *Ox* 07–08; C Amersham on the Hill 08–11; P-in-c Badshot Lea and Hale *Guildf* 11–15; NSM from 15. *The Rectory, 25 Upper Hale Road, Farnham GU9 0NX* T: (01252) 820537 E: reverend.alan@gmail.com

CRAWLEY, Canon David. b 47. St Steph Ho Ox 75. **d** 78 **p** 79. C Solihull *Birm* 78–81; TV Newbury *Ox* 81–84; LtO 84–95; Chapl Stoke Mandeville Hosp Aylesbury 84–95; Distr Chapl 88–95; Hd Chapl Services W Suffolk Hosps NHS Trust 95–11; Bp's Adv on Hosp Chapl *St E* 00–11; Hon Can St E Cathl 05–17; Chapl 11–17; PtO from 18. *22 Westbury Avenue, Bury St Edmunds IP33 3QE* T: (01284) 750526 E: davidandrew@davidandrew.plus.com

CRAWLEY (née FELLOWS), Lesley June. b 70. Salford Univ BEng 91 New Coll Ox DPhil 01. Ox Min Course 04. **d** 07 **p** 08. C Bernwode *Ox* 07–11; NSM Badshot Lea and Hale *Guildf* 12–15; R from 15. *The Rectory, 25 Upper Hale Road, Farnham GU9 0NX* T: (01252) 820537 E: revdlesley@gmail.com

CRAWLEY, Nicholas Simon. b 58. Southn Univ BSc 79 ACIB 82 AIIM 85. Wycliffe Hall Ox 85. **d** 88 **p** 89. C E Twickenham St Steph *Lon* 88–93; R Avondale Zimbabwe

93–99; P-in-c Netherthorpe St Steph *Sheff* 99–04; Network Miss P (Bris Adnry) *Bris* from 04; P-in-c Clifton H Trin, St Andr and St Pet 10–12; NSM Redland from 17. *27 Carnarvon Road, Bristol BS6 7DU* T: 0117-944 1980 E: nick.crawley@blueyonder.co.uk

✠**CRAY, The Rt Revd Graham Alan.** b 47. Leeds Univ BA 68. St Jo Coll Nottm 69. **d** 71 **p** 72 **c** 01. C Gillingham St Mark *Roch* 71–75; N Area Co-ord CPAS Youth Dept 75–78; C York St Mich-le-Belfrey 78–82; V 82–92; Prin Ridley Hall Cam 92–01; Six Preacher Cant Cathl 97–01; Suff Bp Maidstone 01–09; Abps' Missr and Team Ldr Fresh Expressions 09–14; rtd 14; Hon Asst Bp Cant 09–14; Hon Asst Bp York from 09; Hon Asst Bp Roch from 11. *The Dovecote, Main Street, Kirby Misperton, Malton YO17 6XL* T: (01653) 669365 E: grahamcray@me.com

CRAY, Mrs Jacqueline. b 49. Glos Coll of Educn CertEd 70. SEITE 01. **d** 04 **p** 05. NSM Gt Chart Cant 04–08; P-in-c Maidstone St Faith 08–14; Asst Dir of Ords 09–14; rtd 14; PtO *York* from 14. *The Dovecote, Main Street, Kirby Misperton, Malton YO17 6XL* T: (01653) 669365 M: 07889-742973 E: jackiecray@hotmail.co.uk

CREAN, Patrick John Eugene. b 38. TCD BA 81 MA 84. Edin Th Coll 82. **d** 84 **p** 85. C Perth St Jo *St And* 84–86; P-in-c Liv St Phil w St Dav 86–87; V 87–90; R Cupar and Ladybank *St And* 90–92; P-in-c Sefton *Liv* 92–97; Dioc Children's Officer 92–03; V Aintree St Giles 97–98; V Aintree St Giles w St Pet 98–03; rtd 03; PtO *Liv* from 03. *36 Lingfield Close, Netherton, Bootle L30 1BB* T: 0151-525 8838 E: paddycream@hotmail.co.uk

CREASER, Canon David Edward. b 35. St Cath Coll Cam BA 58 MA 62. Clifton Th Coll 59. **d** 61 **p** 62. C Cheadle *Ches* 61–67; V Weston *Bradf* 67–69; P-in-c Denton 67–69; V Weston w Denton 69–74 and 82–02; Dir Educn 73–96; V Frizinghall 74–82; Hon Can Bradf Cathl 80–02; P-in-c Leathley w Farnley, Fewston and Blubberhouses 96–02; rtd 02; PtO *Bradf* 03–14; *Leeds* from 14. *Rose Cottage, Pant Lane, Austwick, Lancaster LA2 8BH* T: (01542) 51536 E: david@creaser.com

CREASEY, Mrs Alison Frances. b 72. Yorks Min Course 12. **d** 15 **p** 16. NSM Dore *Sheff* from 15; NSM Totley from 18. *142 Meadowhead, Sheffield S8 7UF* M: 07496-451687 E: alison.creasey@sheffield.anglican.org

CREASEY, Graham. *See* GOLDSTONE-CREASEY, Graham

CREBER, Preb Arthur Frederick. b 45. NOC 84. **d** 87 **p** 88. C Rickerscote *Lich* 87–91; V Gt Wyrley 91–99; RD Rugeley 94–98; P-in-c Newcastle w Butterton 99–07; R 07–08; Preb Lich Cathl 04–08; rtd 08; PtO *St As* from 09. *22 Malvern Rise, Rhos-on-Sea, Colwyn Bay LL28 4RX* T: (01492) 547761 E: arthur.creber@btinternet.com

CREDITON, Suffragan Bishop of. *See* SEARLE, The Rt Revd Jacqueline Ann

CREE, John Richard. b 44. Open Univ BA 74 Lanc Univ MA 92. Coll of Resurr Mirfield. **d** 83 **p** 84. C Blackb St Jas 83–86; V Feniscowles 86–01; Chapl Blackb Coll 86–01; R Chorley St Laur *Blackb* 01–09; rtd 09; PtO *Bre* from 86; *Blackb* from 09. *5 Bromley Green, Chorley PR6 8TX* T: (01257) 263398 E: john.cree@tiscali.co.uk

CREEDON, Mrs Anna Clare. b 90. Cardiff Univ BA 12 K Coll Lon MA 15 Southn Univ PGCE 13. Trin Coll Bris 16. **d** 19. C Camelot Par *B & W* from 19. *Fourposts, Long Street, Galhampton, Yeovil BA22 7AZ* E: annaclarecreedon@gmail.com

CREER, Irene. *See* SHAW, Irene

CREES, David Paul. b 68. Southn Univ BSc 89. Trin Coll Bris BA 99 MA 00. **d** 00 **p** 01. C Patcham *Chich* 00–04; CF 04–17; Sen CF from 17; Chapl R Memorial Chpl Sandhurst from 17. *c/o MOD Chaplains (Army)* T: (01276) 686540 E: rmcrmas@gmail.com

CREES, Geoffrey William. b 35. Open Univ BA 85. Cranmer Hall Dur 65. **d** 67 **p** 68. C Hoddesdon *St Alb* 67–70; C Harwell and Chilton All SS *Ox* 70–73; V Greenham 73–82; TR Marfleet and AD E Hull *York* 82–88; TR Rodbourne Cheney *Bris* 88–99; rtd 99; PtO *Glouc* from 99. *The Thatch, New Road, Popes Hill, Newnham GL14 1JT* T: (01452) 760843 M: 07551-201617 E: creesjean@gmail.com

CREGAN, Mark. b 59. Lon Bible Coll BA 91. Wycliffe Hall Ox 95. **d** 97 **p** 98. C Chippenham St Pet *Bris* 97–01; P-in-c Stapleton 01–05; Asst Chapl Colston's Sch Bris 01–03; Chapl 03–05; Chapl Stanley Bay All SS Egypt 05–07; P-in-c Casablanca *Eur* 07–12; PtO *B & W* 13; R Clutton w Cameley, Bishop Sutton and Stowey from 13. *Cameley Rectory, Main Road, Temple Cloud, Bristol BS39 5DA* T: (01761) 451315 M: 07770-295461 E: r.cregan59@gmail.com

CREGEEN, Canon Gary Marshall. b 62. Oak Hill Th Coll BA 00. **d** 00 **p** 01. C Carl St Jo 00–03; P-in-c Scotby and Cotehill w Cumwhinton 03–05; V 06–12; N Area Chapl Cumbria Constabulary 04–12; RD Brampton 09–12; TR S Barrow 12–19; RD Barrow 12–19; TV Penrith w Newton Reigny and

Plumpton Wall from 19; Hon Can Carl Cathl from 14. *7 Park Close, Penrith CA11 8ND* E: gary@gandjcregeen.co.uk

CREIGHTON, Frederick David. b 50. TCD BTh 88 QUB MSSc 00 ACII 74. **d** 88 **p** 89. C Lisburn Ch Ch *Conn* 88–91; I Drumclamph w Lower and Upper Langfield *D & R* 91–00; I Glendermott 00–16; Can Derry Cathl 08–16; rtd 16. *22 Greenmount Drive, Coleraine BT51 3QE* T: (028) 7035 7275

CREIGHTON, Mrs Judith. b 36. Reading Univ BSc 57. Trin Coll Bris 80 Edin Th Coll 81. **dss** 83 **d** 87 **p** 94. Greenock *Glas* 83–85; Lawrence Weston *Bris* 85–87; Par Dn Kingswood 87–90; Chapl Stoke Park and Purdown Hosps Stapleton 90–91; Chapl Phoenix NHS Trust 92–93; Hon C Marshfield w Cold Ashton and Tormarton etc *Bris* 93–97; rtd 96; PtO *Bris* 97–15. *Rose Cottage, West Littleton, Marshfield, Chippenham SN14 8JE* T: (01225) 891021

CREIGHTON, Ms Rachel Margaret Maxwell. b 64. Br Is Nazarene Coll BTh 86 BD 87 Lon Bible Coll MA 89 Man Univ MA. Cranmer Hall Dur 92. **d** 94 **p** 95. C Basford w Hyson Green *S'well* 94–96; C Nottingham All SS 96–98; P-in-c Broxtowe 98–02; Chapl HM Pris Bedf 02–04; Chapl HM Pris Wellingborough 04–09; I Belfast H Trin and St Silas *Conn* 09–18; R Hollington St Leon *Chich* from 18; RD Hastings from 18. *Hollington Rectory, Tilebarn Road, St Leonards-on-Sea TN38 9PA* T: (01424) 854535 M: 07748-063770 E: rachelcreighton16@yahoo.com

CRELLIN, Gary Paul. b 67. Kingston Poly BSc 88 Aston Business Sch MBA 06. WEMTC 11. **d** 14 **p** 15. NSM Stoke Prior, Wychbold and Upton Warren *Worc* 14–16; C 16–18; R Powick and Guarlford and Madresfield w Newland from 18. *The Vicarage, 31 The Greenway, Powick, Worcester WR2 4RZ* M: 07708-488705 E: revgarycrellin@gmail.com

CREMIN (née LAKE), Mrs Eileen Veronica. b 58. Aston Tr Scheme 83 Sarum & Wells Th Coll 85. **d** 88 **p** 94. Par Dn Islington St Mary *Lon* 88–92; Asst Chapl Homerton Hosp Lon 92–94; Asst Chapl Hackney Hosp Gp Lon 92–94; P-in-c Brondesbury Ch Ch and St Laur *Lon* 94–01; C Douglas Union w Frankfield *C, C & R* 01–06; I Fermoy Union 06–18; rtd 18. *2 Bearna Deara, Limerick Road, Kildorrery, Co Cork, P67 YR91, Republic of Ireland* T: (00353) (22) 40919 M: 86-333 0206 E: evcremin@eircom.net *or* ecremin@hotmail.com *or* ecremin23@gmail.com

CRESSEY, Canon Roger Wilson. b 35. Chich Th Coll 72. **d** 74 **p** 75. C Pontefract St Giles *Wakef* 74–77; Hon C Dewsbury All SS 77–80; Chapl Pinderfields Gen Hosp Wakef 80–94; Chapl Carr Gate Hosp Wakef 80–94; Chapl Fieldhead Hosp Wakef 80–94; Chapl Pinderfields and Pontefract Hosps NHS Trust 94–00; Hon Can Wakef Cathl 98–00; rtd 00. *1 Wellhead Mews, Chapelthorpe, Wakefield WF4 3JG* T: (01924) 258972 E: roger-cressey@supanet.com *or* rwcressey@gmail.com

CRESSWELL, Howard Rex. b 31. Ely Th Coll 56. **d** 59 **p** 60. C Dovercourt *Chelmsf* 59–61; C Victoria Docks Ascension 61–64; V 64–71; R E w W Harling *Nor* 71–72; TV Quidenham w Eccles and Snetterton 72–75; V Arminghall 75–82; R Caistor w Markshall 75–82; V Trowse 75–82; V Heigham St Barn w St Bart 82–91; rtd 91; PtO *Nor* from 91. *61 Field Acre Way, Long Stratton, Norwich NR15 2WE* E: enesp11@gmail.com

CRESSWELL, Jane Stella. b 62. Bris Univ BA 84. SEITE 04. **d** 07 **p** 08. C Sutton *S'wark* 07–11; P-in-c Nork *Guildf* 11–17; V Taplow and Dropmore *Ox* from 17. *The Rectory, Rectory Road, Taplow, Maidenhead SL6 0ET* T: (01628) 661182 E: janecresswell523@gmail.com

CRESSWELL, Canon Jeremy Peter. b 49. St Jo Coll Ox BA 72 MA 78 K Coll Lon MA 83. Ridley Hall Cam 73. **d** 75 **p** 76. C Wisley w Pyrford *Guildf* 75–78; C Weybridge 78–82; P-in-c E Clandon 82–83; P-in-c W Clandon 82–83; R E and W Clandon 83–90; V Oxshott 90–15; RD Leatherhead 03–08; Hon Can Owerri from 01; Hon Can Guildf Cathl 10–15; rtd 15; PtO *Sarum* from 16; *Bris* from 17; *B & W* from 18. *Grant's House, 13A Castle Street, Calne SN11 0DX* T: (01249) 814350 E: jeremy.cresswell@outlook.com

CRESSWELL, Mark Charles Stewart. b 63. **d** 18 **p** 19. NSM Carlford *St E* from 18. *15 Gurdon Road, Grundisburgh, Woodbridge IP13 6XA* T: (01473) 738313

CRESSWELL, Richard James. b 78. Liv Univ BDS 01. St Jo Coll Nottm 13. **d** 15 **p** 16. C Lilleshall and Muxton *Lich* 15–18; P-in-c Moreton Corbet 18–19; R from 19; P-in-c Shawbury 18–19; V from 19; P-in-c Stanton on Hine Heath 18–19; V from 19. *36 Millbrook Drive, Shawbury, Shrewsbury SY4 4PQ* M: 07974-157862 E: revrichcresswell@gmail.com

CRETNEY, Mrs Antonia Lois. b 48. York Univ BA 69 Bris Univ BA 87 PGCE 89. S Dios Minl Tr Scheme 92. **d** 94 **p** 95. NSM Bedminster *Bris* 94–96; C 96–97; P-in-c Beedon and Peasemore w W Ilsley and Farnborough *Ox* 97–99; R 99–04; Deanery P Wantage from 04; Bp's Adv for Women in Ord Min *Ox* from 05; PtO from 14. *8 Elm Farm Close, Grove, Wantage OX12 9FD* T: (01235) 763192 E: antcret@aol.com

CREW, Ruan John. b 70. Bris Univ BSc 92 PGCE 93 All Nations Chr Coll BA 99 Anglia Ruskin Univ MA 10. ERMC 07. **d** 10 **p** 11. C Almondsbury and Olveston *Bris* 10–13; C Pilning w Compton Greenfield 10–13; Chapl Voorschoten *Eur* from 13. *Chopinlaan 17, 2253 BS Voorschoten, Netherlands* T: (0031) (71) 561 3020 E: ruancrew@gmail.com

CREWES, Jennifer Ruth. b 86. Glas Univ MA 08 MTh 09. Qu Foundn Birm MA 17. **d** 17 **p** 18. C Hodge Hill *Birm* from 17. *1 Ayala Croft, Birmingham B36 8SN* M: 07377-363915 E: revjennicrewes@gmail.com

CRIBB, Mrs Karen Elisabeth. b 63. Liv Univ BA 85 Leeds Univ BA 10. Yorks Min Course 97. **d** 10 **p** 11. NSM Sheff St Mary Bramall Lane from 10; Bp's Adv for SSM from 14. *40 Whirlow Lane, Sheffield S11 9QF* T: 0114-262 1876 E: revkaren@stmarys-church.co.uk

CRICK, Peter. b 39. Lon Univ BD 68 NY Univ DMin 84. Wells Th Coll 66. **d** 67 **p** 68. C Horsham *Chich* 67–71; Asst Dioc Youth Officer *Ox* 71–75; R Denham 75–88; Bp's Adv for CME *Dur* 88–97; P-in-c Coniscliffe 88–97; Hon Can Dur Cathl 93–97; R City of Bris 97–04; rtd 04; PtO *Win* from 06; *Portsm* from 16. *7 Westfield Common, Hamble, Southampton SO31 4LB* T: (023) 8045 7025

CRICK, Philip Benjamin Denton (Ben). b 33. Bris Univ BA 63. Clifton Th Coll 60. **d** 64 **p** 65. C Clerkenwell St Jas and St Jo w St Pet *Lon* 64–67; CF 67–72; C Southall Green St Jo *Lon* 72–75; P-in-c Southall H Trin 75–83; P-in-c Kidbrooke St Jas *S'wark* 83–85; TV 85–92; C E Acton St Dunstan w St Thos *Lon* 92–95; Sub-Chapl HM Pris Wormwood Scrubs 92–95; rtd 95; PtO *Cant* 95–17; Sub-Chapl HM Pris Cant 97–06. *232 Canterbury Road, Birchington CT7 9TD* T: (01843) 846049 M: 07818-040651 E: ben.crick@ormail.co.uk

CRIDDLE, Richard Benjamin. b 86. Imp Coll Lon MEng 09. Oak Hill Th Coll BA 18. **d** 19. C Rusholme H Trin *Man* from 19. *1 Aldwych Avenue, Manchester M14 5NL* M: 07963-428932 E: richard@plattchurch.org

CRIDLAND, Clarissa Rosemary Dorothea. b 55. STETS 03. **d** 06 **p** 07. NSM Coleford w Holcombe *B & W* from 06. *The Vicarage, Church Street, Coleford, Radstock BA3 5NG* T: (01373) 812705 M: 07800-578967 E: clarissacridland@hotmail.co.uk

CRINKS, Kevin David. b 63. Aston Tr Scheme 86 Sarum & Wells Th Coll BTh 91. **d** 93 **p** 94. C Aylesford *Roch* 93–96; C Hessle *York* 96–97; TV Upholland *Liv* 97–00; V Platt Bridge 00–09; P-in-c Leigh St Mary *Man* 09–12; V from 12; Borough Dean Wigan 10–13. *St Mary's Vicarage, 34 Vicarage Square, Leigh WN7 1YD* T: (01942) 603603 E: kcrinks@btinternet.com

CRIPPS, Martyn Cyril Rowland. b 46. Birm Univ LLB 68 Solicitor 71. Wycliffe Hall Ox 80. **d** 82 **p** 83. C Canford Magna *Sarum* 82–86; V Preston St Cuth *Blackb* 87–94; Warden Les Cotils *Win* 94–96; V Gipsy Hill Ch Ch *S'wark* 96–00; R Ashmanhaugh, Barton Turf etc *Nor* 00–04; P-in-c Davenham *Ches* 04–06; R 06–14; rtd 14; PtO *Blackb* from 14. *11 Lancaster Road, Pilling, Preston PR3 6AU* E: mandmc2@btopenworld.com

CRIPPS, Michael Frank Douglas. b 28. Ch Ch Ox BA 50 MA 53. Ridley Hall Cam 58. **d** 59 **p** 60. C Cambridge Gt St Mary w St Mich *Ely* 59–62; Ceylon 62–66; C-in-c Swindon Covingham CD *Bris* 66–72; V Swindon St Paul 72–73; P-in-c Aldbourne and Baydon *Sarum* 73; TV Whitton 73–81; C Marlborough 81–94; rtd 94; Chapl Pau *Eur* 94–96; PtO *Sarum* 96–15. *1 Irving Way, Marlborough SN8 1UE* T: (01672) 512748 E: mkcripps@btinternet.com

CRISPIN, Mrs Mavis Avril. b 46. Stranmillis Coll TCert 69 Open Univ BA 75 Lon Sch of Th BA 03. **d** 06 **p** 09. Peru 06–09; NSM Finchley St Paul and St Luke *Lon* from 09. *47 Etchingham Park Road, London N3 2EB* T: (020) 8346 8698 E: mavecrispin@yahoo.co.uk

CRITCHELL, Denise Eileen. b 49. SAOMC 96. **d** 99 **p** 00. C Flackwell Heath *Ox* 99–03; TV Risborough 03–13; rtd 13; PtO *Cant* 14–18. *3 Somerset Close, Whitstable CT5 4RA* T: (01227) 771885 E: denisecritchell@btconnect.com

CRITCHLEY, Colin. b 41. Dur Univ BA 63 Liv Univ MA 69 AFBPsS 94. NW Ord Course 75. **d** 78 **p** 79. NSM Halewood *Liv* 78–06; Dioc Child Protection Adv 96–06; rtd 06; PtO *Liv* from 16. *53 Elwyn Drive, Halewood, Liverpool L26 0UX* T: 0151-487 5710 F: 280 4937

CRITCHLEY, Mrs Patsy Eva. b 49. Reading Univ CertEd 70. ERMC 04. **d** 07 **p** 08. NSM Meppershall and Shefford *St Alb* 07–10; NSM Henlow and Langford 10–15; rtd 15; PtO *St Alb* from 15. *39 Rooktree Way, Haynes, Bedford MK45 3PT* T: (01234) 381510 E: patsy@critchley04.plus.com

CRITCHLOW, Mrs Anne-Louise. b 51. Westf Coll Lon BA 73 Qu Mary Coll Lon MA 75 Leeds Univ MA 05 Grenoble Univ MèsL 74 Cam Univ PGCE 76. NOC 03. **d** 05 **p** 06. C Eccles *Man* 05–08; TV 08–17; SW Chapl Abbeyfield from 17;

PtO *Bris* from 18. *25 Meg Thatcher's Green, Bristol BS5 8ND* E: malcritch@gmail.com

CRITCHLOW, Melville Mark. b 54. SS Coll Cam BA 77 MA 81 Sheff Univ PhD 15 PGCE 82. Trin Coll Bris 17. **d** 18. NSM Bristol St Aid w St Geo *Bris* from 18; NSM Fishponds St Jo from 18; NSM Two Mile Hill St Mich from 18. *25 Meg Thatchers Green, Bristol BS5 8ND* M: 07745-033144 E: mmcritchlow@btinternet.com

CRITCHLOW (née KHARITONOVA), Mrs Natalia (Tasha). b 74. St Petersburg State Univ MA 98 Dallas Th Sem MTh 04. Westcott Ho Cam 07. **d** 09 **p** 10. C Brondesbury Ch Ch and St Laur *Lon* 09–12; PtO from 12; Chapl Barts Health NHS Trust from 16. *St Dunstan's Rectory, Rectory Square, London E1 3NQ* T: (020) 7791 3545 M: 07540-588860 E: tasha.critchlow@googlemail.com

CRITCHLOW, Trevor Francis. b 61. Lanc Univ BA 83 K Coll Lon MA 96. Westcott Ho Cam 88. **d** 90 **p** 91. C Croydon St Jo *S'wark* 90–92; C Lewisham St Mary 92–94; PtO *Ely* 94–05; Development Dir Westmr St Matt *Lon* 95–99; TV Wembley Park *Lon* 05–11; CME Officer Willesden Area 06–10; R Stepney St Dunstan and All SS from 11. *St Dunstan's Rectory, Rectory Square, London E1 3NQ* T: (020) 7790 1920 F: 07092-868327 M: 07850-578193 E: trevor.critchlow@googlemail.com

CRITTALL, Richard Simon. b 47. Sussex Univ BA 69 Linacre Coll Ox BA 71. St Steph Ho Ox 69. **d** 72 **p** 73. C Oswestry H Trin *Lich* 72–75; C E Grinstead St Mary *Chich* 75–78; TV Brighton Resurr 78–83; R E Blatchington 83–95; V Heathfield St Rich 95–07; Dioc Ecum Officer *Ex* 07–12; P-in-c Broadhembury, Payhembury and Plymtree 07–12; rtd 12; PtO *Sarum* 12–16; *Ex* 13–18; *Derby* from 16; S'well from 18. *7 Laurel Grove, Broadmeadows, South Normanton, Alfreton DE55 3LT*

CROAD, Arthur Robert. b 35. Down Coll Cam BA 58 MA 61. Clifton Th Coll 58. **d** 61 **p** 62. C Sneinton St Chris w St Phil *S'well* 61–64; C Kinson *Sarum* 64–72; R Sherfield English *Win* 72–74; R Awbridge w Sherfield English 74–92; P-in-c Hinton Ampner w Bramdean and Kilmeston 92–01; rtd 01; PtO *Win* from 10. *2 Nursery House, 26 Hursley Road, Chandler's Ford, Eastleigh SO53 2RQ* T: (023) 8184 8646

CROAD, David Richard. b 31. Reading Univ BSc 55. Clifton Th Coll. **d** 57 **p** 58. C Iver *Ox* 57–60; C Rushden *Pet* 60–63; V Loudwater *Ox* 63–72; SW Area Sec CPAS 72–78; V Bovingdon *St Alb* 78–91; Min Hampstead St Jo Downshire Hill Prop Chpl *Lon* 91–94; rtd 94; PtO *Guildf* 97–07; *Win* from 97. *8 Compass Court, 42 Winn Road, Southampton SO17 1EZ* T: (023) 8058 2022

CROCKER, Mrs Fiona Jane. b 64. Southn Univ BN 87 Univ of Wales (Lamp) BA 14 RGN 87. St Jo Coll Nottm. **d** 14 **p** 15. C Brailsford w Shirley, Osmaston w Edlaston etc *Derby* 14–17; V Cam w Stinchcombe *Glouc* from 17. *The Vicarage, Church Road, Cam, Dursley GL11 5PQ* M: 07817-021196 E: fionacrocker@aol.com

CROCKER, The Very Revd Jeremy Robert. b 67. S Bank Univ MA 94 Heythrop Coll Lon MA 98 MCIM 92. Westcott Ho Cam 94 CITC 96. **d** 97 **p** 98. C Stevenage H Trin *St Alb* 97–00; TV Bp's Hatfield 00–04; TR Elstow 04–15; PtO 15; Dean St Paul's Cathl and Chapl Nicosia from 15; PtO *St Alb* from 15. *St Paul's Cathedral, PO Box 22014, 1516 Nicosia, Cyprus* T: (00357) (22) 677897 E: jeremy.crocker@live.co.uk

CROCKER, Richard Campbell. b 54. Nottm Univ BSc 76. Wycliffe Hall Ox BA 81 MA 85. **d** 82 **p** 83. C Summerfield *Birm* 82–84; Chapl K Edw Sch Birm 84–91; R Council Bluffs USA 91–99; C Truro Ch Fairfax 99–08; R Newport Beach St Jas 08–17; Gen Sec Evang Fellowship in the Angl Communion 18–19. *10229 Shiloh Street, Fairfax VA 22030, USA* T: (001) (949) 873 3101 E: revcrocker@icloud.com

CROCKFORD, James Robert William. b 86. Nottm Univ BA 07 Trin Hall Cam BA 13 MA 18 MPhil 15 FRSM. Ridley Hall Cam 11. **d** 14 **p** 15. C Crayford *Roch* 14–17; C Ox St Mary V w St Cross and St Pet from 17; Chapl Magd Coll Ox from 18. *22 Stratford Street, Oxford OX4 1SW* T: (01865) 604383 E: james.crockford@universitychurch.ox.ac.uk

CROFT, James Stuart. b 57. K Coll Lon BD 80 Leeds Univ MA 95. Ripon Coll Cuddesdon 83. **d** 85 **p** 86. C Friern Barnet St Jas *Lon* 85–88; R Lea *Linc* 88–93; V Knaith 88–93; V Upton 88–93; R Gate Burton 88–93; R Lea Gp 93–97; Chapl N Lincs Coll 90–93; V Froyle and Holybourne *Win* 97–10; P-in-c Chesterfield SS Aug *Derby* 10–15; P-in-c Brampton St Mark 10–15; V Longstone, Curbar and Stony Middleton from 15. *The Vicarage, Church Lane, Great Longstone, Bakewell DE45 1TB* T: (01629) 640257

CROFT, Michael Peter. b 60. GradIPM MCIPD 95 FCIPD 08. Trin Coll Bris BA 88. **d** 88 **p** 89. C Drypool *York* 88–91; P-in-c Sandal St Cath *Wakef* 91–95; V 95–07; PtO 07–14; *Leeds* from 14. *5 College Terrace, Ackworth, Pontefract*

WF7 7LB T: (01977) 611251 M: 078139-59066 E: michael@innovationpeople.co.uk

CROFT, Ronald. b 30. St Aid Birkenhead 61. **d** 63 **p** 64. C Lawton Moor *Man* 63–65; C Withington St Crispin 65–66; R 74–86; C Prestwich St Marg 66–67; V Oldham St Ambrose 67–71; P-in-c Oldham St Jas 67–68; V 68–71; V Prestwich St Hilda 71–74; P-in-c 96–00; R Heaton Norris St Thos 86–96; rtd 00; PtO *Man* from 00. *St Hilda's Vicarage, 55 Whittaker Lane, Prestwich, Manchester M25 1ET* T: 0161-773 1642

CROFT, Simon Edward Owen. b 51. Ch Ch Coll Cant CertEd 73. St Steph Ho Ox 75. **d** 78 **p** 79. C Heavitree w Ex St Paul 78–83; V Seaton 83–93; P-in-c Ex St Marks 93–96; P-in-c Ex St Sidwell and St Matt 96; R Ex St Mark, St Sidwell and St Matt 96–09; C Dawlish 09–10; P-in-c 10–15; R Dawlish, Cofton and Starcross 15; rtd 15; Hon C Ashburton, Bickington, Buckland in the Moor etc *Ex* 17. *16 Madison Avenue, Exeter EX1 3AH* T: (01392) 667877 E: simoncdevon@yahoo.co.uk

✠**CROFT, The Rt Revd Steven John Lindsey.** b 57. Worc Coll Ox BA 80 MA 83 St Jo Coll Dur PhD 84. Cranmer Hall Dur 80. **d** 83 **p** 84 **c** 09. C Enfield St Andr *Lon* 83–87; V Ovenden *Wakef* 87–96; Dioc Miss Consultant 94–96; Warden Cranmer Hall Dur 96–04; Abps' Missr and Team Ldr Fresh Expressions 04–09; Bp Sheff 09–16; Bp Ox from 16. *Bishop's Office, Church House Oxford, Langford Locks, Kidlington OX5 1GF* T: (01865) 208222 E: bishop.oxford@oxford.anglican.org

CROFT, Canon William Stuart. b 53. Trin Hall Cam BA 76 MA 79 K Coll Lon MTh 88. Ripon Coll Cuddesdon BA 80. **d** 80 **p** 81. C Friern Barnet St Jas *Lon* 80–83; Tutor Chich Th Coll 83–92; Vice-Prin 88–92; V Fernhurst *Chich* 92–98; Dir of Ords *Pet* 98–03; Prec and Min Can Pet Cathl 98–01; Can Res and Prec 01–04; Liturg Officer 03–04; Non-res Can from 04; P-in-c Longthorpe *Pet* 04–16; P-in-c Pet H Spirit Bretton from 11. *The Vicarage, 23 Westhawe, Bretton, Peterborough PE3 8BA* T: (01733) 330349 E: williamsbill_croft@hotmail.com

CROFTON, Edwin Alan. b 46. Univ Coll Ox BA 68 MA 72. Cranmer Hall Dur. **d** 73 **p** 74. C Hull St Jo Newland *York* 73–77; C Worksop St Jo *S'well* 77–81; Chapl Kilton Hosp Worksop 80–81; V Scarborough St Mary w Ch Ch and H Apostles *York* 81–91; Miss to Seamen 81–91; Chapl St Mary's Hosp Scarborough 82–91; V Cheltenham Ch Ch *Glouc* 91–02; RD Cheltenham 95–00; Hon Can Glouc Cathl 01–02; TR Eccles *Man* 02–11; P-in-c Hope St Jas 07–09; AD Eccles 05–11; rtd 11; PtO *Worc* from 12. *177 Leigh Sinton Road, Malvern WR14 1LB* T: (01886) 833376 E: ea_crofton@msn.com

CROFTON, Robert Edwin. b 75. UEA BSc 98. Ridley Hall Cam 03. **d** 06 **p** 07. C Churchdown *Glouc* 06–09; TV Cheltenham St Mark 09–18; V Barnwood from 18. *The Vicarage, 27A Barnwood Avenue, Gloucester GL4 3AB* T: (01452) 668761 M: 07810-338542 E: rob.crofton@tiscali.co.uk

CROFTS, David Thomas. b 47. Cheshire Coll of Educn CertEd 68 Open Univ BA 76. **d** 99 **p** 00. OLM Bury St Edmunds St Mary *St E* 99–13; NSM 13–17; PtO from 19. *8 Linton Gardens, Bury St Edmunds IP33 2DZ* T: (01284) 761801 F: 765501 E: dtc01@icloud.com

CROFTS, Ian Hamilton. b 55. BSc. St Jo Coll Nottm 79. **d** 82 **p** 83. C Leamington Priors St Paul *Cov* 82–86; C Oadby *Leic* 86; TV 86–91; V Maidstone St Faith *Cant* 91–07; V Forty Hill Jes Ch *Lon* from 07. *The Vicarage, Forty Hill, Enfield EN2 9EU* T: (020) 8363 1935 E: ian.crofts@gmail.com

CROFTS, Mrs Sharon Lucy. b 65. Qu Foundn (Course) 15. **d** 18 **p** 19. C Hartshill and Galley Common *Cov* from 18. *4 Burton Close, Allesley, Coventry CV5 9EG* M: 07855-551004

CROFTS, Stephen Andrew. b 76. Ch Ch Coll Cant BA 98 Ox Brookes Univ MA 09. Ripon Coll Cuddesdon 07. **d** 09 **p** 10. C Birstall and Wanlip *Leic* 09–14; C Setagaya and St Andr Cathl Shibakoen Japan from 14; PtO *Leic* 14–16. *154-0023 Tokyo, Setagaya-ku, Wakabayashi 4-18-8, Japan* E: crofts.stephen@icloud.com

CROISDALE-APPLEBY, Mrs Carolynn Elizabeth. b 46. Ch Ch Coll Cant CertEd 68. SAOMC 01. **d** 04 **p** 05. NSM Amersham and Gt Coxwell w Buscot, Coleshill etc *Ox* 04–07; NSM Beaconsfield 07–16; PtO from 16. *Abbotsholme, Hervines Road, Amersham HP6 5HS* T: (01494) 725194 F: 725474 E: revcarolynn@aol.com

CROMARTY, Andrew Robert McKean. b 63. Newc Univ MB, BS 86 Homerton Coll Cam PGCE 89 St Jo Coll Dur BA 04. Cranmer Hall Dur 02. **d** 06 **p** 07. NSM Crook *Dur* 06–10; C Upper Weardale 10–14; V Hipswell *Leeds* from 14. *The Vicarage, 7 Forest Drive, Colburn, Catterick Garrison DL9 4PN* E: andrew.cromarty63@btinternet.com

CROMBIE, Calum Dugald Ferguson. b 81. Nazarene Th Coll *Man* BA 05 Keele Univ MA 13. LCTP 12. **d** 13 **p** 14. NSM Leyland St Ambrose *Blackb* from 13;

Chapl HM Pris Preston 13–15; Chapl HM Pris Wymott from 15. *Chaplaincy Office, HM Prison Wymott, Ulnes Walton Lane, Leyland PR26 8LW* T: (01772) 442000 E: calum.crombie@justice.gov.uk

CROMPTON, Mrs Christine Mary. b 39. Newnham Coll Cam BA 61 MA York Univ MA 86 Lon Inst of Educn PGCE 62. **d** 06 **p** 07. OLM Newc St Geo and St Hilda 06–18; PtO from 18. *11 South Bend, Newcastle upon Tyne NE3 5TR* T: 0191-236 3679

CROMPTON, Gillian Kay. *See* STANNING, Gillian Kay

CROMPTON, Canon Roger Martyn Francis. b 47. Sheff Univ BA 69 PGCE 73 St Jo Coll Dur BA 84. Cranmer Hall Dur 82. **d** 85 **p** 86. C Woodford Wells *Chelmsf* 85–89; V Golcar *Wakef* 89–12; P-in-c Longwood 10–12; RD Huddersfield 99–09; Hon Can Wakef Cathl 06–12; rtd 12. *16 Colders Green, Meltham, Holmfirth HD9 5JH* T: (01484) 859320

CROMPTON-BATTERSBY, Holly Jo. b 74. Bath Coll of HE BA 95. Wycliffe Hall Ox BTh 01. **d** 01 **p** 02. C Luton Lewsey St Hugh *St Alb* 01–04; Chapl Bennett Memorial Dioc Sch Tunbridge Wells 04–07; Chapl Bedgebury Sch Kent 05–06; Chapl St Bede's Sch Cam 09–15; Chapl Ipswich Sch from 15. *Ipswich School, 25 Henley Road, Ipswich IP1 3SG* T: (01473) 408300 ext 338 M: 07447-913109 E: hollycrompton@hotmail.com *or* hcb@ipswich.suffolk.sch.uk

CROMPTON-THOMAS, Lionel Edrich. b 47. **d** 12. NSM Walthamstow St Barn and St Jas *Gt Chelmsf* 13–19; PtO *Birm* from 18; *Chelmsf* from 19. *81 Caversham Road, Birmingham B44 0TH*

CROMPTON-BATTERSBY, Simon Jackson. b 64. Wycliffe Hall Ox BTh 01. **d** 01 **p** 02. C Askern *Sheff* 01–03; Chapl Bethany Sch Goudhurst 03–07; Chapl Culford Sch Bury St Edmunds 08–18; P-in-c Elmsett w Aldham, Hintlesham, Chattisham etc *St E* from 18. *The Rectory, Hadleigh Road, Elmsett, Ipswich IP7 6ND* M: 07894-488315 E: rev@kind.church

CRONIN, Alan. **d** 18 **p** 19. NSM Borderlands Miss Area *St As* from 18. *8 Little Meadows, Bradley, Wrexham LL11 4AR* T: (01978) 750440 E: 794alan@gmail.com

CRONIN, Mrs Linda Nancy. b 61. NTMTC BA 08. **d** 08 **p** 09. C Barrow St Mark *Carl* 08–10; C S Barrow 10–11; TV 11–13; Chapl All SS Academy Cheltenham 13–14; NSM Cheltenham St Mark *Glouc* 13–14; P-in-c Madeley *Heref* from 14. *The Vicarage, Park Lane, Madeley, Telford TF7 5HN* M: 07817-678775 E: linda@thecronins.org.uk *or* linda.cronin@tf7.org.uk

CROOK, Colin. b 44. Lon Univ BSc(Econ) 74 ALA 67 FLA 93. S'wark Ord Course 87. **d** 90 **p** 91. NSM Dartford Ch Ch *Roch* 90–97; P-in-c Crockenhill All So 97–05; Dioc Ecum Officer 96–04; rtd 05; Chapl Crowhurst Chr Healing Cen from 05; PtO *Chich* from 06. *57 Martello Court, 3-15 Jevington Gardens, Eastbourne BN21 4SD*

CROOK, David Creighton. b 37. Trin Coll Cam BA 61 MA 68. Cuddesdon Coll 61. **d** 63 **p** 64. C Workington St Mich *Carl* 63–66; C Penrith St Andr 66–68; V Barrow St Jas 70–78; V Maryport 78–81; TV Greystoke, Matterdale and Mungrisdale 81–87; TV Watermillock 84–87; V Hesket-in-the-Forest and Armathwaite 87–98; rtd 98; PtO *Carl* 01–14. *11 Lowther Street, Penrith CA11 7UW* T: (01768) 866773

CROOK, David Robert. b 64. Liv Univ BA 85 PGCE 86 Univ of Wales (Swansea) PhD 07. Westcott Ho Cam 13. **d** 15 **p** 16. C Easebourne, Lodsworth and Selham *Chich* 15–19; P-in-c Stopham and Fittleworth from 19. *The Rectory, Church Lane, Fittleworth, Pulborough RH20 1HL* M: 07902-485877 E: david.crook15@btinternet.com

CROOK, Dennis Eric. b 40. AKC 65. **d** 66 **p** 67. C Penwortham St Mary *Blackb* 66–69; C Kirkham 69–71; V Accrington St Jo 72–89; RD Accrington 82–90; P-in-c Huncoat 86–89; Hon Can Blackb Cathl 89–96; V Accrington St Jo w Huncoat 89–96; rtd 00; PtO *Blackb* from 13. *224 Pleckgate Road, Blackburn BB1 8QW* T: (01254) 248720

CROOK, Mrs Diana Elizabeth. b 47. Hull Univ BA 73 Open Univ BSc 93 City Univ MSc 97 Middx Univ BA 03 RGN 70 CPsychol. NTMTC 00. **d** 03 **p** 04. NSM Waltham H Cross *Chelmsf* 03–07; P-in-c Uley w Owlpen and Nympsfield *Glouc* 07–17; rtd 17. *Upper Redlap, Redlap, Dartmouth TQ6 0JR* E: revdiana@dianacrook.org

CROOK, Graham Leslie. b 49. Chich Th Coll 74. **d** 76 **p** 77. C Withington St Crispin *Man* 76–79; C Prestwich St Marg 79–82; V Nelson St Bede *Blackb* 82–92; Chapl Southend Health Care NHS Trust 92–15; Bp's Adv for Hosp Chapl (Bradwell Area) *Chelmsf* 98–04; LtO 92–09; PtO from 09. *Ebenezer, 249 Woodgrange Drive, Southend-on-Sea SS1 2SQ* T: (01702) 613429

✠**CROOK, The Rt Revd John Michael.** b 40. Univ of Wales (Lamp) BA 62. Coll of Resurr Mirfield 62. **d** 64 **p** 65 **c** 99. C Horninglow *Lich* 64–66; C Bloxwich 66–70; R Inverness St Mich *Mor* 70–78; R Inverness St Jo 74–78; Dioc Youth

Chapl *St And* 78–86; R Aberfoyle 78–87; R Doune 78–87; R Callander 78–87; Can St Ninian's Cathl Perth 85–99; R Bridge of Allan 87–99; Syn Clerk 97–99; Bp Mor 99–06; rtd 06; LtO *St And* from 07. *163 Lothian Crescent, Stirling FK9 5SG* E: johnmcrook99@gmail.com

CROOK, Malcolm Geoffrey. b 53. St Steph Ho Ox 88. **d** 90 **p** 91. C Pet St Jude 90–93; C Barrow St Matt *Carl* 93–96; TV Langley and Parkfield *Man* 96–97; R Man Apostles w Miles Platting 97–03; P-in-c Sneinton St Steph w St Alb *S'well* 03–04; P-in-c Sneinton St Matthias 03–04; V Sneinton St Steph w St Matthias 04–11; P-in-c Sculcoates *York* 11–16; P-in-c Hull St Mary Sculcoates 15–16; TR Glas E End 16–17; LtO from 17. *228 Myreside Street, Glasgow G32 6DX* T: 0141-554 5398 E: malccrook@hotmail.com

CROOK, Rowland William. b 39. Tyndale Hall Bris 61. **d** 64 **p** 65. C Penn Fields *Lich* 64–68; C Lower Broughton St Clem w St Matthias *Man* 68–70; C Bucknall and Bagnall *Lich* 70–76; V New Shildon *Dur* 76–86; V Northwich St Luke and H Trin *Ches* 86–99; P-in-c Helsby and Dunham-on-the-Hill 99–04; rtd 04; PtO *Ches* from 04. *14 Bollington Avenue, Northwich CW9 8SB* T: (01606) 45177 E: rowland.crook@talktalk.net

CROOK, Simon Charles. b 72. Imp Coll Lon BSc 95 Ox Brookes Univ PGCE 97 Sheff Univ BA 14. Coll of Resurr Mirfield 12. **d** 14 **p** 15. C Huddersfield St Pet *Leeds* 14–18; V Golcar and Longwood from 18. *The Vicarage, Church Street, Golcar, Huddersfield HD7 4PX* M: 07742-177610 E: vicar@stjohnschurchgolcar.org

CROOK, Timothy Mark. b 68. Oak Hill Th Coll BA 00. **d** 00 **p** 01. C Charles w Plymouth St Matthias *Ex* 00–03; C Harold Wood *Chelmsf* 03–09; V S w N Bersted *Chich* from 09. *121 Victoria Drive, Bognor Regis PO21 2EH* T: (01243) 862018 E: timothycrook@hotmail.com

CROOKS, Canon Christopher John (Kip). b 53. St Bede's Coll Dur CertEd 75. Trin Coll Bris BA 90. **d** 90 **p** 91. C The Quinton *Birm* 90–93; V Ince Ch Ch *Liv* 93–03; R Much Woolton from 03; AD Liv S 06–14; Hon Can Liv Cathl from 06. *The Rectory, 67 Church Road, Woolton, Liverpool L25 6DA* T: 0151-428 1853

CROOKS, Canon David William Talbot. b 52. TCD BA 75 MA 78 BD 83. **d** 77 **p** 78. C Glendermott *D & R* 77–81; C Edin Old St Paul 81–84; I Taughboyne, Craigadooish, Newtowncunningham etc *D & R* from 84; Bp's Dom Chapl 88–07; Can Raphoe Cathl from 91; Can St Patr Cathl Dublin from 17. *Taughboyne Rectory, Churchtown, Carrigans, Lifford, Co Donegal, Republic of Ireland* T: (00353) (74) 914 0135 M: 86-212 5670 E: dcrooks@eircom.net

CROOKS, Mrs Jayne Barbara. b 52. Birm Univ BSc 73 Avery Hill Coll PGCE 74. WMMTC 01. **d** 04 **p** 05. NSM Kings Norton *Birm* 04–08; C 08–11; TV 11–15; rtd 15; PtO *Birm* from 15. *15 Chalgrove Avenue, Birmingham B38 8YP* T: 0121-459 3733 E: jayne.crooks@blueyonder.co.uk

CROOKS, Kenneth Robert. b 36. CEng FIEE FCMI FCIM. S'wark Ord Course 80. **d** 83 **p** 84. NSM Wisley w Pyrford *Guildf* 83–92; PtO *Ex* from 98. *1 Glenside, Manor Road, Sidmouth EX10 8FG* T: (01395) 489254 E: revken.sidmouth@talktalk.net

CROOKS, Kip. *See* CROOKS, Christopher John

CROOKS, Peter James. b 50. St Jo Coll Cam BA 72. Cranmer Hall Dur. **d** 76 **p** 77. C Onslow Square St Paul *Lon* 76–77; C Brompton H Trin w Onslow Square St Paul 77–79; C Wembley St Jo 79–82; CMS 82–92; Lebanon 83–89; Syria 85–89; Dean Jerusalem 89–92; P-in-c Hunningham and Wappenbury w Weston under Wetherley *Cov* 92–01; P-in-c Offchurch 96–01; V Long Itchington and Marton 96–01; CMS Iran 01–02; TV Dolgellau w Llanfachreth and Brithdir etc *Ban* 02–04; Chapl Aden Ch Ch Yemen 04–09; Dir Ras Morbat Clinics 04–09; rtd 09; P-in-c Arthog w Fairbourne w Llangelynnin w Rhoslefain *Ban* 09–10; PtO 10–16; *Ox* from 14. *25 Radstock Road, Reading RG1 3PS* T: 0118-375 3103 M: 07866-276562 E: petercrooks781@btinternet.com *or* crookspeter300@gmail.com

CROOS, Sebastian John Princely. b 59. Madurai Univ BA 82. Oak Hill Th Coll BA 04. **d** 04 **p** 05. C Becontree St Mary *Chelmsf* 04–07; C E Ham St Paul 07–08; Chapl Lon City Miss 08–11; NSM Forest Gate St Mark *Chelmsf* 11–13; P-in-c N Woolwich w Silvertown 13–19; rtd 19. *Address temp unknown* M: 07449-043579 E: sprincecroos@hotmail.com

CROSBIE, Andrew. b 62. St Steph Ho Ox 96. **d** 98 **p** 99. C St Paul's Cathl St Helena 98–00; CF 00–03; PtO *Blackb* 03–11; Chantry P Shrine of Our Lady of Haddington from 08. *The Parish Office, 92 Whitesands, Dumfries DG1 2RX* M: 07791-540535 E: dumfriesanglican@gmail.com

CROSBIE, Timothy John. b 44. ACMA 72. **d** 00 **p** 01. OLM Shotley *St E* 00–08; OLM Shoreline 08–13; NSM 13–14; rtd 14; PtO *St E* from 15. *5 Mill Rise, Holbrook, Ipswich IP9 2QH* T: (01473) 328297 E: txb44@btinternet.com

CROSBY, Mrs Anne Denise. b 58. Dur Univ BA 14 De Montfort Univ CertEd 02. Linc Sch of Th and Min 11. **d** 14 **p** 15. NSM Birstall and Wanlip *Leic* 14–17; V Luton St Anne w St Chris *St Alb* from 17. *St Christopher's Vicarage, 33 Felix Avenue, Luton LU2 7LE* M: 07946-178087 E: anne@crosbytextiles.co.uk

CROSBY, Bernard Edward. b 47. Oak Hill Th Coll 86. **d** 88 **p** 89. C Springfield H Trin *Chelmsf* 88–91; C Penn Fields *Lich* 91–94; V St Leonards St Ethelburga *Chich* 94–02; R Fairlight, Guestling and Pett 02–10; rtd 10; PtO *Chich* from 15. *4 Willowbed Walk, Hastings TN34 2QL* T: (01424) 435800 E: bernardcrosby@supanet.com

CROSBY, David Edward. b 48. SAOMC 96. **d** 99 **p** 00. NSM Newbury *Ox* 99–01; C The Bourne and Tilford *Guildf* 01–04; P-in-c Hurst Green and Mitton *Bradf* 04. *7 Murfitt Way, Gamlingay, Sandy SG19 3EW* T: (01767) 651787 M: 07936-703541 E: davidec@live.co.uk

CROSLAND, Sarah Rosita. *See* WILLIAMS, Sarah Rosita

CROSS, Canon Alan. b 43. Chich Th Coll 68. **d** 70 **p** 71. C Bordesley St Oswald *Birm* 70; C S Yardley St Mich 70–73; C Colchester St Jas, All SS, St Nic and St Runwald *Chelmsf* 73–77; V Leigh-on-Sea St Jas 77–89; V Woodford St Barn 89–09; Hon Can Chelmsf Cathl 97–09; rtd 09; PtO *Chelmsf* from 09. *11 Grayling Drive, Colchester CO4 3EN* T: (01206) 790984

CROSS, Preb Elizabeth Mary. b 46. Leeds Univ BA 69 CertEd 70. Sarum Th Coll 80. **dss** 83 **d** 87 **p** 94. Wootton Bassett *Sarum* 83–86; Westbury 86–87; Par Dn 87–89; C Glastonbury w Meare, W Pennard and Godney *B & W* 89–95; Asst Dir of Ords 89–95; Preb Wells Cathl 93–07; V Wedmore w Theale and Blackford 95–07; rtd 07; PtO *Sarum* from 08. *10 Manor Farm Court, Martinstown, Dorchester DT2 9JN* T: (01305) 889194 E: lizmcross@btinternet.com

CROSS, Canon Greville Shelly. b 49. Sarum & Wells Th Coll 73. **d** 76 **p** 77. C Kidderminster St Mary *Worc* 76–80; P-in-c Worc St Mark 80–81; TV Worc St Martin w St Pet, St Mark etc 81–85; R Inkberrow w Cookhill and Kington w Dormston 85–98; RD Evesham 93–97; R Old Swinford Stourbridge 98–11; RD Stourbridge 01–04; rtd 11; NSM Upton-on-Severn, Ripple, Earls Croome etc *Worc* 11–14; NSM Hanley Castle, Hanley Swan and Welland 11–14; Hon Can Worc Cathl from 05. *4 Oakland Close, Upton-upon-Severn, Worcester WR8 0ES* T: (01905) 29438 E: greville.cross@outlook.com

CROSS, James Stuart. b 36. Magd Coll Ox BA 65 MA 71. Ripon Hall Ox 62. **d** 65 **p** 66. C Leckhampton SS Phil and Jas *Glouc* 65–66; CF 66–92; QHC 89–92; R Stretford St Pet *Man* 92–00; rtd 00; PtO *Heref* 11–16. *St Davids, Redbrook Road, Monmouth NP25 3LY* T/F: (01600) 715977 E: jimcross1@aol.com

CROSS, Jeremy Burkitt. b 45. St Pet Coll Ox BA 68 MA 71. Wycliffe Hall Ox 67. **d** 69 **p** 70. C Mildenhall *St E* 69–72; C Lindfield *Chich* 72–77; V Framfield 77–89; R St Leonards St Leon 89–01; R Birling, Addington, Ryarsh and Trottiscliffe *Roch* 01–10; rtd 10; PtO *Roch* 10–14. *Les Sapins Verts, Branla, 56140 Réminiac, France* T: (0033) 2 97 93 25 63 E: jandscross@aol.com

CROSS, Katie Louise. b 70. Ox Brookes Univ BA 08. St Jo Coll Nottm 11. **d** 13 **p** 14. C Newton Tracey, Horwood, Alverdiscott etc *Ex* 13–16; R Brampford Speke, Cadbury, Newton St Cyres etc from 16. *The Rectory, School Lane, Thorverton, Exeter EX5 5NR* M: 07976-263514 E: katie.cross@gmx.com

CROSS, Kenneth James. b 69. Trin Coll Bris BA 09. **d** 09 **p** 10. C Alcombe *B & W* 09–12; R Old Cleeve, Leighland and Treborough 12–18; V Alcombe from 18. *The Vicarage, 34 Manor Road, Minehead TA24 6EJ* M: 07951-568703 E: kennethjcross@gmail.com

CROSS, Mrs Linda Ann. b 57. St Jo Coll Dur BA 79 Wye Coll Lon MSc 80. **d** 10 **p** 11. OLM Wye w Brook and Hastingleigh etc *Cant* 10–14; OLM Wye from 14. *Yew Tree House, The Street, Brook, Ashford TN25 5PF* T: (01233) 813360 E: jandlcross@btinternet.com

CROSS, Max David. b 68. **d** 14 **p** 15. C Sheet *Portsm* 14–18; R Bedhampton from 18. *The Rectory, Bidbury Lane, Havant PO9 3JG* M: 07590-608766 E: max@maxcross.com

CROSS, Canon Michael Anthony. b 45. Leeds Univ BA 67 BA 69. Coll of Resurr Mirfield 68. **d** 70 **p** 71. C Bloemfontein Cathl S Africa 70–73; C Adel *Ripon* 74–76; Chapl Birm Univ 76–81; V Chapel Allerton *Ripon* 81–92; V Headingley 92–04; AD 96–01; P-in-c Wetherby 04–11; Hon Can Ripon Cathl 06–10; rtd 11; PtO *York* from 11. *1 Angram Close, York YO30 5ZN* T: (01904) 347051 E: mikeanthonycross@gmail.com

CROSS, Mrs Rachel Beth. b 73. Ox Brookes Univ BA 95. STETS 06. **d** 09 **p** 11. C Ponteland *Newc* 09–12; C Benwell 10–13; NSM Kenton Ascension 14; TV Thame *Ox* from 14. *22 Stuart Way, Thames OX9 3WP* T: (01844) 212344 M: 07795-292280 E: rachel@thecrosses.f9.co.uk

CROSS, Stephanie (Stevie). b 53. Essex Univ BSc 74 Loughb Univ MSc 76 Bris Univ BA 01 Reading Univ PGCE 93. Trin Coll Bris 99. **d** 01 **p** 02. C Lytchett Minster *Sarum* 01–05; TV Wheatley *Ox* 05–11; R Aston-le-Walls, Byfield, Boddington, Eydon etc *Pet* from 11. *The Rectory, 55 Church Street, Byfield, Daventry NN11 6XN* T: (01327) 260783 E: crossstevie@hotmail.com

CROSSLEY, Dennis Thomas. b 23. AKC 52 St Boniface Warminster. **d** 53 **p** 54. C Crofton Park St Hilda *S'wark* 53–56; C Beddington 56–59; C Talbot Village *Sarum* 59–62; R Finchampstead *Ox* 62–97; rtd 97; PtO *Ox* from 97. *1 Larkswood Close, Sandhurst, Camberley GU47 8QJ* T: (01344) 751456 E: dtcrossley@web-hq.com

CROSSLEY, George John. b 57. Bradf Univ BA 81 PhD 84. NOC 91. **d** 94 **p** 95. C Balderstone *Man* 94–98; V Branston w Tatenhill *Lich* 98–02; RD Tutbury 00–02; Chapl Burton Hosps NHS Foundn Trust 04–16; P-in-c Burton St Chad *Lich* from 09; P-in-c Stretton w Claymills from 16. *St Chad's Vicarage, 113 Hunter Street, Burton-on-Trent DE14 2SS* T: (01283) 564044 M: 07976-979755 E: vicar@stchadsburton.org.uk

CROSSLEY, Jeremy. *See* CROSSLEY, William Jeremy Hugh

CROSSLEY, John Eric. b 51. St Martin's Coll Lanc BA 92. Carl Dioc Tr Inst 92. **d** 94 **p** 95. C Westfield St Mary *Carl* 94–97; P-in-c Penrith w Newton Reigny and Plumpton Wall 97–02; Chapl Newton Rigg Coll of H&FE 97–02; TV Cartmel Peninsula *Carl* 02–09; rtd 09; PtO *Carl* from 10. *The Vicarage, Market Place, Dalton-in-Furness LA15 8AZ* E: rjoncros@aol.com

CROSSLEY, Kenneth Ernest. b 38. NEOC 01. **d** 03 **p** 04. NSM Ripon Cathl 03–14; Leeds from 14. *11 Station Drive, Ripon HG4 1JA* T: (01765) 692499 E: kennethecrossley@aol.com

CROSSLEY, Reuben Verity. b 74. Man Univ BSc 96 Leic Univ MSc 10. St Mellitus Coll BA 18. **d** 18. C Charles w Plymouth St Matthias *Ex* from 18. *St Gabriel's Vicarage, 1 Peverell Terrace, Plymouth PL3 4JJ* M: 07879-416233 E: reubencrossley@outlook.com

CROSSLEY, Canon Robert Scott. b 36. Lon Univ BSc 61 BD 68 PhD 75. ALCD 64. **d** 64 **p** 65. C Beckenham St Jo *Roch* 64–68; C Morden *S'wark* 68–72; Chapl Ridley Hall Cam 72–75; V Camberley St Paul *Guildf* 75–83; TR 83–98; RD Surrey Heath 81–84; Hon Can Guildf Cathl 89–98; rtd 98; PtO *Guildf* 98–01 and from 07; Hon C Camberley St Mich Yorktown 01–07. *20 Highbury Crescent, Camberley GU15 1JZ* T: (01276) 500036 E: robertcrossley@ntlworld.com

CROSSLEY, Canon Ruth Joy. b 54. Cranmer Hall Dur 00. **d** 02 **p** 03. C Cartmel Peninsula *Carl* 02–06; P-in-c Levens 06–17; Bp's Adv for CME 06–11; P-in-c Dalton-in-Furness and Ireleth-with-Askam from 17; RD Furness from 19; Hon Can Carl Cathl from 13. *The Vicarage, Market Place, Dalton-in-Furness LA15 8AZ* E: vicar@daltonparish.co.uk

CROSSLEY, Preb William Jeremy Hugh. b 55. St Jo Coll Dur BA 76. Cranmer Hall Dur 81. **d** 84 **p** 85. C Gillingham St Mark *Roch* 84–87; C Ches Square St Mich w St Phil *Lon* 87–94; V Westminster St Jas the Less 94–00; R St Marg Lothbury and St Steph Coleman Street etc from 00; P-in-c St Edm the King and St Mary Woolnoth etc 11–17; AD The City 06–09; Dir Post-Ord Tr from 06; Dir of Ords Two Cities Area from 08; Preb St Paul's Cathl from 11. *74 Antill Road, London E3 5BP* T: (020) 7726 4878 M: 07963-441212 E: the.rector@stml.org.uk

CROSSMAN, Maria Antoinette (Manette). b 64. ERMC 09. **d** 12 **p** 13. C Haverhill w Withersfield *St E* 12–15; C Haughley w Wetherden and Stowupland 15; V Gt Barton and Thurston from 15. *The Vicarage, Church Road, Great Barton, Bury St Edmunds IP31 2QR* M: 07947-737789 E: revmcrossman@gmail.com

CROSSMAN, Sharon Margaret Joan. b 65. DipCOT 87. Linc Th Coll BTh 93. **d** 93 **p** 94. Par Dn Chippenham St Andr w Tytherton Lucas *Bris* 93–94; C 94–96; Chapl UWE 96–02; Hon C Almondsbury 97–98; Hon C Almondsbury and Olveston 98–02; Chapl Würzburg Univ Germany 02–03; TV Portishead *B & W* 03–10; V Highbridge 10–19; C The Huntspills and Mark 13–19; RD Axbridge 15–19; Chapl MU 05–19; Preb Wells Cathl *B & W* 17–19; Dioc Voc Co-ord *Sarum* from 19. *Church House, Crane Street, Salisbury SP1 2QB* T: (01722) 411922 E: sharon.crossman@btopenworld.com

CROSTHWAITE, Howard Wellesley. b 37. St Cuth Soc Dur BA 59. St Steph Ho Ox 59. **d** 61 **p** 62. C Workington St Mich *Carl* 61–63; Grenada 63–64; C Barnsley St Mary *Wakef* 64–68; V Milnsbridge 68–70; V Thurgoland 70–79; rtd 99; PtO *Sheff* from 19. *26 Lower Malton Road, Scawsby, Doncaster DN5 8SF* T: (01302) 811164 E: howard@yogadon.co.uk

CROTON, John Barry. b 43. **d** 09 **p** 10. NSM Reading Ch Ch *Ox* 09–13; PtO from 13. *35 Vine Crescent, Reading*

RG30 3LT T: 0118-954 3134 M: 07704-858928
E: revjohnc@virginmedia.com

CROUCH, Daniel David. b 82. Ox Brookes Univ BA 09 Glos Univ MA 15. Trin Coll Bris 16. **d** 18 **p** 19. C Highbridge *B & W* from 18. *26 Hamley Close, Burnham-on-Sea TA8 1DS* M: 07890-569534 E: revdancrouch@gmail.com

CROUCH, Keith Matheson. Whitelands Coll Lon CertEd 71 Westhill Coll Birm BPhil 00. K Coll Lon AKC 70. **d** 72 **p** 73. C Hill *Birm* 72–75; C-in-c Woodgate Valley CD 75–77; V Bishop's Castle w Mainstone *Heref* 91–98; Vice-Prin WEMTC 98–04; TV Tenbury Wells 98–02; Public Preacher 02–04; Chapl Dorothy House Hospice Winsley 05–10; rtd 10; PtO *B & W* 05–11; *Heref* 12–15. *3 Julian Road, Ludlow SY8 1HA* T: (01584) 875567 E: keithandjoy@btinternet.com

CROUCHER, James Christopher William. b 84. Univ Coll Ox MChem 06. Oak Hill Th Coll BA 12. **d** 12 **p** 13. C Harold Wood *Chelmsf* 12–16; V Elburton *Ex* from 16. *The Vicarage, 3 Sherford Road, Plymouth PL9 8DQ* T: (01752) 547534 M: 07902-076783 E: james_croucher@yahoo.com

CROUCHER, Jonathan Edward. b 68. Trin Coll Cam BA 90 MA 93. SEITE 01. **d** 04 **p** 05. NSM Lee Gd Shep w St Pet *S'wark* 04–08; C Blackheath Park St Mich 08–12; P-in-c Gipsy Hill Ch Ch 12–13; V from 13; AD Lambeth S from 18. *Christ Church Vicarage, 1 Highland Road, London SE19 1DP* T: (020) 8670 0799 M: 07766-072750 E: revjec@hotmail.co.uk

CROUCHER, Mrs Susan Rosemary. b 47. **d** 16 **p** 17. OLM Thundersley *Chelmsf* from 16. *10 Douglas Road, Benfleet SS7 2HN* T: (01702) 555543 M: 07902-463829 E: scroucher@live.co.uk

CROUCHMAN, Eric Richard. b 30. Bps' Coll Cheshunt 64. **d** 66 **p** 67. C Ipswich H Trin *St E* 66–69; C Ipswich All Hallows 69–72; R Crowfield w Stonham Aspal and Mickfield 72–81; R Combs 81–90; RD Stowmarket 84–90; P-in-c Lydgate w Ousden and Cowlinge 90–95; R Wickhambrook w Lydgate, Ousden and Cowlinge 95–96; rtd 96; PtO *St E* from 97. *6 Mitre Close, Woolpit, Bury St Edmunds IP30 9SJ* T/F: (01359) 240070 E: ericthecleric@lineone.net

CROW, Michael John. b 35. AKC 63. **d** 64 **p** 65. C Welwyn Garden City *St Alb* 64–67; C Sawbridgeworth 67–68; C Biscot 69–71; V Luton St Aug Limbury 71–79; TR Borehamwood 79–87; V Markyate Street 87–00; P-in-c Flamstead 98–00; rtd 00; PtO *Ex* from 00. *216 Pinhoe Road, Exeter EX4 7HH* T: (01392) 424804 E: mickeviv@talktalk.net

CROWDER, George Timothy. b 74. Liv Univ MEng 96. Oak Hill Th Coll MTh 07. **d** 07 **p** 08. C Hartford *Ches* 07–11; V Over St Jo from 11. *St John's Vicarage, Delamere Street, Winsford CW7 2LY* T: (01606) 594651 E: george@stjohnover.org.uk

CROWE, Anthony Murray. b 34. St Edm Hall Ox BA 58 MA 61. Westcott Ho Cam 57. **d** 59 **p** 60. C Stockingford *Cov* 59–62; C New Eltham All SS *S'wark* 62–66; V Clapham St Jo 66–73; R Charlton St Luke w H Trin 73–94; rtd 94; Sub-Chapl HM Pris Elmley 94–97; Sub-Chapl HM Pris Swaleside 94–99; PtO *Cant* 94–19. *4 South Lodge Close, Whitstable CT5 2AD* T: (01227) 273046 E: tonycrowe34@btinternet.com

CROWE, Brian John. b 57. Trin Hall Cam BA 78. LCTP 08. **d** 10 **p** 11. NSM Kendal St Thos *Carl* 10–15; NSM Crook 10–15; NSM Crosthwaite Kendal 10–15; NSM Cartmel Fell 10–15; NSM Winster 10–15; NSM Witherslack 10–15; NSM Helsington 10–15; P-in-c 15; NSM Underbarrow 10–15; P-in-c 15; P-in-c Underbarrow w Helsington 15–17; rtd 17. *Middle Blakebank, Underbarrow, Kendal LA8 8HP* T: (015395) 68959 M: 07711-919572 E: brian.crowe@ymail.com

CROWE, Grant Norman. b 74. Keele Univ LLB 96. Cranmer Hall Dur 00. **d** 03 **p** 04. C Burton All SS w Ch Ch *Lich* 03–07; TV Cen Telford 07–15; Asst Chapl Utrecht w Zwolle *Eur* from 15. *Muiderslot 11, 3813 RR Amersfoort, The Netherlands* M: (0031) (06) 2997 2303 E: grantcrowe@ziggo.nl

CROWE, Canon John Yeomans. b 39. Keble Coll Ox BA 62 MA 66. Linc Th Coll 62. **d** 64 **p** 65. C Tettenhall Regis *Lich* 64–67; C Caversham *Ox* 67–71; V Hampton *Worc* 72–76; P-in-c Leek St Edw *Lich* 76–79; TR Leek 79–83; TR Leek and Meerbrook 83–87; RD Leek 82–87; TR Dorchester and V Warborough *Ox* 87–04; RD Aston and Cuddesdon 93–02; Hon Can Ch Ch 94–04; rtd 04; PtO *Heref* 08–16; *B & W* from 17. *16 Alexandra House, Midland Road, Bath BA2 3GD* T: (01225) 336839 E: johncrowemessages@gmail.com

CROWE, Canon Philip Anthony. b 36. Selw Coll Cam BA 60 MA 64. Ridley Hall Cam 60. **d** 62 **p** 63. Tutor Oak Hill Th Coll 62–67; C Enfield Ch Ch Trent Park *Lon* 62–65; Ed C of E Newspaper 67–71; Lect Birm St Martin 71–76; R Breadsall *Derby* 77–88; Prin and Tutor Sarum & Wells Th Coll 88–95; Can and Preb Sarum Cathl 91–95; R Overton and Erbistock and Penley *St As* 95–97; Dir St As and Ban Minl Tr from 96; rtd 97; PtO *Lich* 01–14; *St As* 09–16. *Alder Lea, Babbinswood, Whittington, Oswestry SY11 4PQ* T: (01691) 671698

CROWE, Rebecca Helena. *See* ROBERTS, Rebecca Helena

CROWE, Toby Nicholas. b 70. Oriel Coll Ox BA 94 Univ of Wales (Swansea) PGCE 97 Cam Univ BTh 09. Ridley Hall Cam 07. **d** 09 **p** 10. C Alperton *Lon* 09–12; R Elmdon St Nic *Birm* from 12; AD Solihull from 17. *Elmdon Rectory, 86 Tanhouse Farm Road, Solihull B92 9EY* T: 0121-743 6336 E: rector@elmdonchurch.org

CROWHURST, Preb David Brian. b 40. Qu Coll Birm 77. **d** 80 **p** 81. NSM Ribbesford w Bewdley *Worc* 80–82; Hon Chapl Birm Cathl 81–82; C Kidderminster St Jo *Worc* 82–83; C-in-c Wribbenhall 83–84; P-in-c 84–87; V Oswestry St Oswald *Lich* 87–94; P-in-c Oswestry H Trin 93–94; V Oswestry 98–04; P-in-c Rhydycroesau 90–91; R 91–08; RD Oswestry 95–01; Preb Lich Cathl 00–08; rtd 08; PtO *Heref* from 08; *Lich* from 08. *The Old Hall Coach House, Main Road, Dorrington, Shrewsbury SY5 7JD* T: (01743) 718049 M: 07885-021878 E: d.crowhurst@btinternet.com

CROWIE, Hermon John. b 41. Kelham Th Coll 61. **d** 69 **p** 73. C Sneinton St Cypr *S'well* 69; C Balderton 72–75; V Basford St Aid 75–78; R Everton and Mattersey w Clayworth 78–84; St Helena 84–89; Chapl HM Pris Nor 89–91; Chapl HM Pris Cant 91–02; Bulgaria from 02; PtO *Nor* from 15. *Nova Mahala 6191, Municipality Nikolaevo, Stara Zagora, Bulgaria* E: hermon.jc@hotmail.com

CROWLE, Sarah Ann. *See* BROUGH, Sarah Ann

CROWLEY, Mrs Jennifer Eileen. b 55. CITC 00. **d** 03 **p** 04. NSM Waterford w Killea, Drumcannon and Dunhill *C & O* 03–07; NSM New w Old Ross, Whitechurch, Fethard etc 07–10; Chapl Waterford Regional Hosp 10–17; rtd 17. *Glen, Stradbally, Kilmacthomas, Co Waterford, Republic of Ireland* T: (00353) (51) 293143 M: 87-780 0257 E: jcrowleyglen@gmail.com

CROWLEY, Melanie. b 55. **d** 10 **p** 11. NSM St Alb St Mich 10–13; TV Hitchin 13–16; TV Hitchin and St Paul's Walden from 16. *St Faith's Vicarage, 31 Meadowbank, Hitchin SG4 0HY* E: melanie.crowley@btinternet.com

CROWLEY, Thomas Philip Valentine. b 90. Wadh Coll Ox BA 12 LSE MSc 14. St Steph Ho Ox BA 18. **d** 19. C Eastbourne St Sav and St Pet *Chich* from 19. *4 Courland, 19 Grange Road, Eastbourne BN21 4HA* M: 07807-610034 E: father.thomas@yahoo.com

CROWTHER, Mrs Sheila Ann. b 52. Homerton Coll Cam CertEd 74. Ripon Coll Cuddesdon 12. **d** 15 **p** 16. NSM Osney *Ox* 15–18; NSM Wolvercote and Wytham from 18. *15 Bullingdon Road, Oxford OX4 1QQ* T: (01865) 430704 M: 07774-254440 E: sacrowther@hotmail.com

CROWTHER-ALWYN, Benedict Mark. b 53. Kent Univ BA 74. Qu Coll Birm 74. **d** 77 **p** 78. C Fenny Stratford and Water Eaton *Ox* 77–80; C Moulsecoomb *Chich* 80–81; TV 81–83; R Glas St Serf and Baillieston *Glas* 83–87; R Bassingham *Linc* 87–90; V Aubourn w Haddington 87–90; V Carlton-le-Moorland w Stapleford 87–90; R Thurlby w Norton Disney 87–90; V Elmton *Derby* 90–03; P-in-c Matlock 03–05; R 05–14; R Matlock, Dethick, Lea and Holloway from 14. *The Rectory, 116 Church Street, Matlock DE4 3BZ* T: (01629) 582199 E: mcrowther-alwyn@tiscali.co.uk

CROYDON, Archdeacon of. *See* SKILTON, The Ven Christopher John

CROYDON, Area Bishop of. *See* CLARK, The Rt Revd Jonathan Dunnett

CRUMPLER, Peter George. b 56. ERMC. **d** 13 **p** 14. NSM Sandridge *St Alb* 13–18; SSMs' Officer St Alb Adnry from 17; Public Preacher from 18. *4 Belsize Close, St Albans AL4 9YD* T: (01727) 847760 E: sandridgepeter900@gmail.com

CRUMPTON, Colin. b 38. AKC 61 Sheff Univ Dip Leadership, Renewal & Miss Studies 97. **d** 64 **p** 65. C Billingham St Cuth *Dur* 64–66; C Shirley *Birm* 66–69; V Mossley *Ches* 69–75; Miss to Seamen 75–77; V Burslem St Paul *Lich* 77–82; V Edensor 82–97; V Llanrhaeadr-ym-Mochnant etc *St As* 97–00; Dir Accra Retreat Cen Ghana 00–01; rtd 02; Hon C Redmarley D'Abitot, Bromesberrow, Pauntley etc *Glouc* 02–03; PtO *Lich* 03–17; *Ches* from 04; *Blackb* from 18. *5 Fosbrooke House, 8 Clifton Drive, Lytham St Annes FY8 5RQ* T: (01253) 667015 M: 07799-183971 E: colin.crumpton@virgin.net

CRUSE, John Jeremy. b 58. Univ of Wales (Lamp) BA 79 Hughes Hall Cam CertEd 87. Sarum & Wells Th Coll 81. **d** 82 **p** 83. C Newton St Pet *S & B* 82–84; P-in-c Newbridge-on-Wye and Llanfihangel Brynpabuan 84–86; PtO *Heref* 88–89; C Waltham H Cross *Chelmsf* 89–91; TV Yatton Moor *B & W* 91–00; V Shalford *Guildf* 00–18; TV Diss *Nor* from 18. *61 Roydon Road, Diss IP22 4LW* M: 07889-919928

CRUSE, Mrs Susan Elizabeth. b 51. Middx Univ BA 04. NTMTC 01. **d** 04 **p** 05. NSM Ingatestone w Fryerning *Chelmsf* 04–11; TV Halstead Area 11–16; rtd 16; PtO *Chelmsf* 16–17; Hon C Two Rivers from 17. *Goston Mount, Pottery*

Lane, Castle Hedingham, Halstead CO9 3EU   T: (01787) 462062   M: 07885-909837 E: sue.cruse@sky.com

CRUST, Mrs Erica Doreen. b 51. **d** 10 **p** 11. NSM Moulton Linc 10–14; NSM Mid Elloe Gp from 14. 3 St Guthlac's Close, Crowland, Peterborough PE6 0ES   T: (01733) 321077   M: 07751-323584 E: erica.crust@gmail.com

CRUTCHLEY, John Hamilton. b 62. Kingston Poly LLB 85 K Coll Lon MA 13. Trin Coll Bris 99. **d** 01 **p** 02. C Barnstaple Ex 01–06; R Ardingly Chich from 06. The Rectory, Church Lane, Ardingly, Haywards Heath RH17 6UR   T: (01444) 892332 E: crutchley631@btinternet.com

CRYER, Gordon David. b 34. St D Coll Lamp BA 63. **d** 64 **p** 65. C Mortlake w E Sheen S'wark 64–67; C Godstone 67–70; Chapl St Dunstan's Abbey Sch Plymouth 71–02; R Stoke Damerel Ex 71–02; P-in-c Devonport St Aubyn 88–02; rtd 02; PtO Truro from 02. 9 St Stephens Road, Saltash PL12 4BG   T: (01752) 510436 E: gandvcryer@blueyonder.co.uk

CUBITT, Canon Paul. b 64. Sheff Univ BA 86. Cranmer Hall Dur 95. **d** 97 **p** 98. C Bromyard Heref 97–01; V Elloughton and Brough w Brantingham York 01–07; R Blofield w Hemblington Nor 07–14; RD Blofield 08–14; V N Walsham and Edingthorpe 14–18; V N Walsham, Edingthorpe, Worstead and Westwick from 18; Hon Can Nor Cathl from 18. The Vicarage, 28A Yarmouth Road, North Walsham NR28 9AT   T: (01692) 406380 E: revpcubitt@btinternet.com

CUFF, Gregor John. b 61. Keele Univ BSc 82 Liv Hope Univ MA 12 LTCL 07. Ridley Hall Cam 93. **d** 95 **p** 96. C Stanley Liv 95–99; V Waterloo Ch Ch and St Jo from 99; Hon Chapl Mersey Miss to Seafarers from 06. The Vicarage, 22 Crosby Road South, Liverpool L22 1RQ   T/F: 0151-920 7791 E: gregor.cuff@btinternet.com

CUFF, Preb Pamela. b 47. MCSP 68. S Dios Minl Tr Scheme 89. **d** 92 **p** 94. NSM Nether Stowey w Over Stowey B & W 92–93; NSM Quantoxhead 93–07; NSM Quantock Coast 07–12; Asst Chapl Taunton Hosps 93–94; Asst Chapl Taunton and Somerset NHS Trust 94–05; Bp's Officer for Ord NSM (Taunton Adnry) B & W 06–09; PtO from 12; Preb Wells Cathl from 08. Millands, Kilve, Bridgwater TA5 1EA   T: (01278) 741229 E: pam.cuff@hotmail.co.uk

CUFF, Simon Lloyd. b 88. Keble Coll Ox BA 09 MSt 10 DPhil 14. Ox Min Course 10. **d** 13 **p** 14. C Ealing Ch the Sav Lon 13–17; Tutor St Mellitus Coll from 17. Flat 5, 38 Nottingham Place, London W1U 5NU   T: (020) 7052 0573 E: frsimon@ymail.com or simon.cuff@stmellitus.ac.uk

CULL, John. b 31. Oak Hill Th Coll 56. **d** 59 **p** 60. C Radipole Sarum 59–66; Chapl Mariners' Ch Glouc 66–70; R Woodchester Glouc 70–90; RD Stonehouse 85–89; V Walton St E 90–94; rtd 94; PtO Glouc from 94. Hillgrove Stables, Bear Hill, Woodchester, Stroud GL5 5DH   T: (01453) 872145

CULLEN, Canon John Austin. b 43. Auckland Univ BA 67 Otago Univ BD 76 Keble Coll Ox DPhil 86 FRSA 89. St Jo Coll Auckland 66. **d** 69 **p** 70. C Papatoetoe New Zealand 69–73; Assoc P Mt Albert St Luke 73–75; P-in-c 74; Hon C Remuera St Aiden 75–78; Asst Chapl Keble Coll Ox 79–82; PtO Lon 82–84; Chapl and Lect Worc Coll Ox 84–86; C St Botolph Aldgate w H Trin Minories Lon 86–87; Dir Inst of Chr Studies 87–91; Hon C St Marylebone All SS 87–91; Dir of Min Development Win 91–97 and 97–01; Hon Can Win Cathl 96–02; Sen Asst to Bp Lon 02–04; P-in-c St Geo-in-the-East w St Paul 03–04; V Palmers Green St Jo 05–12; rtd 12; PtO Lon from 14. 73 Stanley Road, London N11 2LB   T: (020) 8350 5616 E: john.cullen1@virgin.net

CULLEN, Samantha Anne. b 72. NUI BA 93 Keele Univ MSc 96 Northumbria Univ PhD 04. Ox Min Course 14. **d** 17 **p** 18. C Petersfield Portsm from 17; C Buriton from 17. 38 Larcombe Road, Petersfield GU32 3LS E: revsamcullen@gmail.com

CULLENS, Lynne Susan. b 64. Man Univ BA 86. SNWTP 09. **d** 12 **p** 13. C Congleton Ches 12–15; NSM Sandbach Heath w Wheelock 15–16; P-in-c Crewe St Andr w St Jo 16–19; R Stockport and Brinnington from 19. St Mary's Rectory, Gorsey Mount Street, Stockport SK1 4DU   M: 07544-350692 E: lynne.cullens@gmail.com

CULLIFORD, Jane Margaret. b 48. Lon Univ MB, BS 73. STETS 03. **d** 06 **p** 07. NSM Dorchester Sarum 06–14; NSM Dorchester and the Winterbournes from 14; Bp's Adv for Wholeness and Healing from 10. 8 Grosvenor Road, Dorchester DT1 2BB   T: (01305) 264360 E: janeculliford@aol.com

CULLIMORE, Jeremy Stuart. b 53. Westcott Ho Cam. **d** 06 **p** 07. C New Sleaford Linc 06–10; P-in-c Linc St Pet-at-Gowts and St Andr from 10; P-in-c Linc St Botolph from 10; P-in-c Linc St Mary-le-Wigford w St Benedict etc from 10. St Peter-at-Gowts Vicarage, 1 Sibthorpe Street, Lincoln LN5 7SP   T: (01522) 530256   M: 07733-114280 E: jscullimore@btinternet.com

CULLING, Elizabeth Ann. See HOARE, Elizabeth Ann

CULLINGWORTH, Anthony Robert. b 42. BSc. Ox NSM Course. **d** 83 **p** 84. NSM Slough Ox 83–99; NSM Denham

99–02; NSM Morton St Luke Bradf 02–04; PtO 04–14; Leeds from 14. 2 Thurleston Court, East Morton, Keighley BD20 5RG   T: (01535) 601187 E: thecullies@aol.com

CULLIS, Andrew Stanley Weldon. b 48. Hertf Coll Ox BA 69 LTh. St Jo Coll Nottm 70. **d** 73 **p** 74. C Reigate St Mary S'wark 73–78; C Yateley Win 78–82; V Dorking St Paul Guildf 82–00; RD Dorking 94–99; P-in-c Chilwell S'well 00–04; R Fisherton Anger Sarum 04–13; rtd 13; PtO Sarum from 15. 76 Fernside Road, Poole BH15 2JL

CULLWICK, Christopher John. b 53. Hull Univ BA 75. Wycliffe Hall Ox BA 80 MA 85. **d** 81 **p** 82. C Nottingham St Jude S'well 81–84; C York St Mich-le-Belfrey 84–87; TV Huntington 87–03; Ind Chapl 02–10; Ldr York Community Chapl 10–13; rtd 13; PtO York from 13. 11 Mulberry Court, Huntington, York YO32 9TU   T: (01904) 764608   M: 07792-565805 E: chriscullwick@gmail.com

CULLY, Miss Elizabeth Faith. b 46. SRN 67 SCM 69 RGN 72. Trin Coll Bris BA 88. **d** 88 **p** 94. Par Dn Filton Bris 88–92; Par Dn Fishponds St Jo 92–94; C 94–95; P-in-c Brinsley w Underwood S'well 95–98; V 98–02; P-in-c Farnsfield 02–08; P-in-c Kirklington w Hockerton 02–08; P-in-c Bilsthorpe 02–08; P-in-c Eakring 02–08; P-in-c Maplebeck 02–08; P-in-c Winkburn 02–08; rtd 08; Hon C Salcombe and Malborough w S Huish Ex 08–16; PtO D & D from 17. 20 Seahaven Crescent, Groomsport, Bangor BT19 6PR   T: (028) 9146 6791   M: 07802-494260 E: e.faith.cully@gmail.com

CUMBERLAND, The Very Revd Barry John. b 44. Birm Univ BA 67 Worc Coll Ox DipEd 68. Trin Coll Singapore MDiv 88. **d** 88 **p** 89. NSM Westmr St Matt Lon 88–90; PtO 90–96; Philippines 90–96, 98-01 and from 03; Dean Manila 93–96; Chapl Stockholm w Gävle and Västerås Eur 96–98; P-in-c Las Palmas 01–03; rtd 09. 85A Aurora Pijuan Street, BFRV, Las Pinas City 1740, Metro Manila, Philippines   T: (0063) (2) 875 3528 E: barrycumberland@yahoo.co.uk

CUMBERLAND, John Allan. b 51. Chu Coll Cam BA 73 MA 78. WEMTC 07. **d** 10 **p** 11. NSM Wenlock Heref from 10. Priory Cottage, 5 The Bull Ring, Much Wenlock TF13 6HS   T: (01952) 727386 E: jacumberland@btinternet.com

CUMBERLEGE, Francis Richard. b 41. AKC 65. **d** 66 **p** 67. C Leigh Park St Fran CD Portsm 66–71; P-in-c Gona Papua New Guinea 71–75; R Popondetta 79–81; Adn N Papua 74–81; R Hastings St Clem and All SS Chich 81–86; V Broadwater Down 86–91; V Tunbridge Wells St Mark Roch 91–99; RD Tunbridge Wells 96–99; P-in-c Brockenhurst Win 99–03; V 03–06; rtd 06; P-in-c Ashburnham w Penhurst Chich 09–12; PtO 12–17; Win from 14. Kairos, 10 Forward Drive, Pennington, Lymington SO41 8GA   T: (01590) 719421 E: cumberlege@littleoaks.net

CUMBERLIDGE, Anthony Wynne. b 49. ACIB 75. Sarum & Wells Th Coll 79. **d** 82 **p** 83. C Llanrhos St As 82–85; R Llanfair Talhaearn and Llansannan etc 85–87; CF 87–04; P-in-c Lambourn and Eastbury and E Garston Ox 04–11; rtd 12. 17 Juniper Close, Bilsthorpe, Newark NG22 8UN   T: (01623) 871883

CUMBRAE, Provost of. See PEARSON, The Rt Revd Kevin

CUMINGS, Llewellyn Frank Beadnell. b 29. Natal Univ BA 50 St Cath Coll Cam CertEd 53. Ridley Hall Cam 65. **d** 67 **p** 68. C Leamington Priors St Mary Cov 67–70; V Lobley Hill Dur 70–74; R Denver Ely 74–82; V Ryston w Roxham 74–82; R St Leonards St Leon Chich 82–88; V Billinghay Linc 88–93; rtd 93; PtO St As from 09. Y Bwthyn, Coedllan, Llanfyllin SY22 5BP   T: (01691) 648013

CUMMING, Miss Catriona Mary. b 82. York Univ BA 04 MA 05. Westcott Ho Cam 11. **d** 14 **p** 15. C Melton Mowbray Leic 14–17; Succ York Minster from 17. Church House, 10-14 Ogleforth, York YO1 7JN   T: (01904) 559546   M: 07843-339982 E: succentor@yorkminster.org

CUMMING, Canon Nigel Patrick. b 42. St Jo Coll Nottm 73. **d** 75 **p** 76. C Castle Hall Ches 75–77; C Stalybridge H Trin and Ch Ch 77–78; C Tadley St Pet Win 78–82; R Overton w Laverstoke and Freefolk 82–07; RD Whitchurch 89–98; Hon Can Win Cathl 99–07; rtd 07; PtO Win from 08; Sarum from 09. Pasture House, Whitsbury, Fordingbridge SP6 3QB   T: (01725) 518248 E: nigel.cumming@btinternet.com

CUMMING, Paul James. b 79. Cliff Coll BA 00. St Jo Coll Nottm 09. **d** 11 **p** 12. C Poynton Ches 11–14; V Cheadle All Hallows from 14. All Hallows' Vicarage, 222 Councillor Lane, Cheadle SK8 2JG   T: 0161-478 8789 E: cumming-no-s@hotmail.co.uk or revpaul@live.co.uk

CUMMING, Susan Margaret. See FORSHAW, Susan Margaret

CUMMING-LATTEY, Mrs Susan Mary Ruth. b 47. Open Univ BA 77 SRN 69. STETS 00. **d** 03 **p** 04. NSM Ash Vale Guildf 03–07; NSM Crondall and Ewshot from 07; Chapl Phyllis Tuckwell Hospice Farnham from 12. 38A Elms Road, Fleet GU51 3EQ   T: (01252) 621295   F: 815882   M: 07761-126354 E: suelattey@btinternet.com

CUMMINGS, Mrs Elizabeth. b 45. St Jo Coll Dur BA 84. NEOC 85. **d** 87 **p** 94. NSM Dur St Giles 87–89; Chapl HM Pris Dur 89–90; Chapl HM Rem Cen Low Newton 90–95; Chapl HM Pris Stocken 95–96; Chapl HM Pris Frankland 96–05; rtd 05; PtO *Dur* from 05. *8 Bridgemere Drive, Framwellgate Moor, Durham DH1 5FG* T: 0191-383 0832

CUMMINGS, Canon William Alexander Vickery. b 38. Ch Ch Ox BA 62 MA 64. Wycliffe Hall Ox 61. **d** 64 **p** 65. C Leytonstone St Jo *Chelmsf* 64–67; C Writtle 67–71; R Stratton St Mary w Stratton St Michael *Nor* 71–73; R Wacton Magna w Parva 71–73; R Stratton St Mary w Stratton St Michael etc 73–91; RD Depwade 81–91; Hon Can Nor Cathl 90–91; V Battle *Chich* 91–04; Dean Battle 91–04; rtd 04; PtO *Win* from 13. *80 Samber Close, Lymington SO41 9LF* T: (01590) 610426

CUMMINS, Ashley Wighton. b 56. St Andr Univ BD 83. Coates Hall Edin 82. **d** 84 **p** 85. C Broughty Ferry *Bre* 84–87; P-in-c Dundee St Ninian 87–92; P-in-c Invergowrie from 92; Chapl Angl Students Dundee Univ 92–07. *27 Errol Road, Invergowrie, Dundee DD2 5AG* T: (01382) 562525 E: ashleycummins@outlook.com

CUMMINS, Daphne Mary. *See* GREEN, Daphne Mary

CUMMINS, Nicholas Marshall. b 36. CITC 65. **d** 67 **p** 68. C Ballymena w Ballyclug *Conn* 67–70; C Belfast St Nic 70–73; I Buttevant Union *C, C & R* 73–78; I Mallow Union 78–83; I Kilmoe Union 83–96; Can Cork Cathl 90–96; Treas Cork Cathl 95–96; Preb Tymothan St Patr Cathl Dublin 95–01; Dean Killaloe and Clonfert *L & K* 96–01; Dean Kilfenora and Provost Kilmacduagh 96–01; I Killaloe w Stradbally 96–01; rtd 01; PtO *Chich* from 15. *13 Borough Hill, Petersfield GU32 3LQ* T: (01730) 269742

CUNLIFFE, Anne. b 48. CBDTI 01. **d** 04 **p** 05. OLM Poulton-le-Sands w Morecambe St Laur *Blackb* 04–07; NSM 04–14; rtd 14; PtO *Blackb* from 14. *14 Coniston Road, Morecambe LA4 5PS* T: (01524) 422509 E: revanne@gmail.com

CUNLIFFE, The Ven Christopher John. b 55. Ch Ch Ox BA 77 MA 81 DPhil 81 Trin Coll Cam BA 82 MA 86 ARHistS 94. Westcott Ho Cam 80. **d** 83 **p** 84. C Chesterfield St Mary and All SS *Derby* 83–85; Chapl Linc Coll Ox 85–89; Chapl City Univ and Guildhall Sch of Music and Drama *Lon* 89–91; Voc Officer and Selection Sec ABM 91–97; Dir Professional Min *Lon* 97–03; Chapl to Bp Bradwell *Chelmsf* 04–06; Adn Derby from 06; Can Res Derby Cathl 06–08. *1 Thatch Close, Derby DE22 1EA* T: (01332) 553455 *or* 382233 F: 552322 *or* 292969 E: archderby@derby.anglican.org

CUNLIFFE, Harold. b 28. St Aid Birkenhead 57. **d** 60 **p** 61. C Hindley All SS *Liv* 60–64; V Everton St Chad w Ch Ch 64–69; R Golborne 70–93; rtd 93; PtO *Liv* from 93. *51 Greenfields Crescent, Ashton-in-Makerfield, Wigan WN4 8QY* T: (01942) 202956 E: haroldcunliffe@sky.com

CUNLIFFE, The Ven Helen Margaret. b 54. St Hilda's Coll Ox BA 77 MA 78. Westcott Ho Cam 81. **dss** 83 **d** 87 **p** 94. Chesterfield St Mary and All SS *Derby* 83–85; Ox St Mary V w St Cross and St Pet 86–89; Par Dn 87–89; Chapl Nuff Coll Ox 86–89; Team Dn Clapham Team *S'wark* 89–94; TV 94–96; Can Res S'wark Cathl 96–03; Chapl Welcare 96–03; Adn St Alb 03–07; rtd 08. *1 Thatch Close, Derby DE22 1EA* T: (01332) 553455

CUNLIFFE, Mrs Katherine Helen. b 79. Man Univ BMus 00 St Martin's Coll Lanc PGCE 07. Coll of Resurr Mirfield BA 15. **d** 15 **p** 16. C Manchester Gd Shep and St Barn *Man* 15–18; V Shaw from 18. *Holy Trinity Vicarage, 13 Church Road, Shaw, Oldham OL2 7AT* M: 07548-295229 E: revkatycunliffe@gmail.com

CUNLIFFE, Peter Henry. b 54. Univ of Wales MA 93 SRN 77 RSCN 79 RCNT 83. Trin Coll Bris 92. **d** 94 **p** 95. C Carshalton Beeches *S'wark* 94–95; C Reigate St Mary 95–02; P-in-c Hemingford Grey *Ely* 02–04; V from 04; P-in-c Hemingford Abbots from 04. *The Vicarage, 6 Braggs Lane, Hemingford Grey, Huntingdon PE28 9BW* T: (01480) 394378 E: vicar@churchbytheriver.org.uk

CUNNINGHAM, Brian James. b 65. York Univ BA 88. Ripon Coll Cuddesdon BA 91. **d** 92 **p** 93. C Merrow *Guildf* 92–96; C Kennington St Jo w St Jas *S'wark* 96–99; Chapl Pangbourne Coll 99–11; Chapl Oundle Sch from 11. *Oundle School, New Street, Oundle, Peterborough PE8 4GH* T: (01832) 277122 E: bjc@oundleschool.org.uk

CUNNINGHAM, Canon Philip John. b 52. St Jo Coll Dur BA 74 PGCE 75 MA 85. NOC 93. **d** 95 **p** 96. NSM York St Luke 95–97; NSM York St Olave w St Giles 97–99; TV Haxby w Wigginton 99–02; V Gosforth St Nic *Newc* 02–18; AD Newc Cen 05–13; Hon Can Newc Cathl 11–18; rtd 18; PtO *Newc* from 18. *8 Prior Terrace, Hexham NE46 3EU* T: (01434) 601589 E: philipcunningham@hotmail.com

CUNNINGHAM, Wendy. b 42. SAOMC 01. **d** 04 **p** 05. NSM Hook Norton w Gt Rollright, Swerford etc *Ox* from 04.

Dewlands, Church End, Great Rollright, Chipping Norton OX7 5RX T: (01608) 737135 E: wendy@dewlands.me.uk

CUNNINGTON, Canon Andrew Thomas. b 56. Southn Univ BTh 86. Sarum & Wells Th Coll 82. **d** 85 **p** 86. C Ifield *Chich* 85–89; TV Haywards Heath St Wilfrid 89–94; V Midhurst 94–06; R Woolbeding 94–06; RD Midhurst 03–06; V Redhill St Matt *S'wark* from 06; Jt Dir of IME Croydon Area 09–13; AD Reigate 13–18; Hon Can S'wark Cathl from 15. *St Matthew's Vicarage, 27 Ridgeway Road, Redhill RH1 6PQ* T: (01737) 761568 E: andrew@stmatthews-redhill.org.uk

CUNNINGTON, Miss Averil. b 41. St Mary's Coll Chelt CertEd 61 Man Univ BA 68 MEd 73. NOC 93. **d** 95 **p** 96. Hd Mistress Counthill Sch Oldham 84–96; NSM Milnrow *Man* 95–98; NSM Hey 98–02; Lic Preacher 02–05; Tutor NOC 98–05; PtO *Newc* 05–10; *Man* from 10. *6 Summerhill View, Denshaw, Oldham OL3 5TB* E: averil.cunnington@zen.co.uk

CUNNINGTON, Howard James. b 56. Southn Univ BA 77 St Jo Coll Dur PGCE 78. Trin Coll Bris 90. **d** 92 **p** 93. C Ex St Leon w H Trin 92–96; V Sandown Ch Ch and Lower Sandown St Jo *Portsm* 96–04; PtO from 04. *5 The Mall, Lake Hill, Sandown PO36 9ED* E: howard@cunnington.org.uk

CUNNOLD, David Allen. b 36. St Boniface Warminster AKC 62. **d** 63 **p** 64. C Gillingham St Barn *Roch* 63–66; C Chilvers Coton w Astley *Cov* 66–69; C Banbury *Ox* 69–71; rtd 01. *14 Kirton Grove, Tettenhall, Wolverhampton WV6 8RX* T: (01902) 756008

CUPITT, Don. b 34. Trin Hall Cam BA 55 MA 58 Bris Univ Hon DLitt 84. Westcott Ho Cam 57. **d** 59 **p** 60. C Salford St Phil w St Steph *Man* 59–62; Vice-Prin Westcott Ho Cam 62–66; Dean Em Coll Cam 66–91; Asst Lect Div Cam Univ 68–73; Lect 73–96; rtd 96; Life Fell Em Coll Cam from 96. *Emmanuel College, Cambridge CB2 3AP* T: (01223) 334200

CURD, Preb Christine Veronica. b 51. Bris Univ BA Leic Univ MSc 05. Oak Hill Th Coll 84 WMMTC 88. **d** 89 **p** 94. NSM Widecombe-in-the-Moor, Leusdon, Princetown etc *Ex* 89–93; NSM Bovey Tracey SS Pet, Paul and Thos w Hennock 94–97; Asst Chapl HM Pris Channings Wood 92–01; Chapl HM Pris Ex 01–10; Bp's Officer for Pris *Ex* 10–13; NSM Dawlish w Holcombe, Cofton and Starcross from 13; Preb Ex Cathl from 05. *St George's, Holcombe Village, Dawlish EX7 0JT* M: 07710-159751 E: stgeorgesholcombe@live.co.uk

CURD, Clifford John Letsom. b 45. SRN RNT. Oak Hill Th Coll 84. **d** 86 **p** 87. C Stone Ch Ch *Lich* 86–89; TV Widecombe-in-the-Moor, Leusdon, Princetown etc *Ex* 89–93; P-in-c Ilsington 93–04; rtd 05. *Address withheld by request* M: 07881-442031

CURL, Roger William. b 50. BA BD DPhil. Oak Hill Th Coll. **d** 82 **p** 83. C Cromer *Nor* 82–86; C Sevenoaks St Nic *Roch* 86–88; V Fulham St Mary N End *Lon* from 88. *St Mary's Vicarage, 2 Edith Road, London W14 9BA* T: (020) 7602 1996 E: stmarys.westken@london.anglican.org

CURNEW, Brian Leslie. b 48. Qu Coll Ox BA 69 DPhil 77 MA 77. Ripon Coll Cuddesdon 77. **d** 79 **p** 80. C Sandhurst *Ox* 79–82; Tutor St Steph Ho Ox 82–87; V Fishponds St Mary *Bris* 87–94; TR Ludlow *Heref* 94–09; P-in-c Bitterley w Middleton, Stoke St Milborough etc 09; Preb Heref Cathl 02–09; P-in-c Headcorn *Cant* 09–11; P-in-c Sutton Valence w E Sutton and Chart Sutton 09–11; V Headcorn and The Suttons 11–14; rtd 14; PtO *Lon* from 15. *16 Richmond Road, London N11 2QR* M: 07540-441271 E: briancurnew@gmail.com

CURNOCK, Canon Karen Susan. b 50. Nottm Univ BTh 78. Linc Th Coll 74. **d** 95 **p** 97. NSM Graffoe Gp *Linc* 95–96; Dioc Sec *Sarum* 96–03; NSM Chalke Valley 96–03; V Buckland Newton, Cerne Abbas, Godmanstone etc 03–10; Can and Preb Sarum Cathl 02–10; RD Dorchester 06–09; rtd 10. *Stoneacre, Castle Hill, Seaton EX12 2QP* T: (01297) 24266 E: karen.curnock@gmail.com

CURNOW, Bronwyn Ellen. Ex Univ BA 05. St Padarn's Inst 16. **d** 17 **p** 18. C Glan Ithon *S & B* from 17. *16 Holcombe Drive, Llandrindod Wells LD1 6DN* T: (01597) 829133 M: 07719-854768 E: revbroncurnow@gmail.com

CURNOW, Terence Peter. b 37. Univ of Wales (Lamp) BA 62. **d** 63 **p** 64. C Llanishen and Lisvane *Llan* 63–71; Youth Chapl 67–71; Asst Chapl K Coll Taunton 71–74; Chapl Taunton Sch 74–84; Ho Master 84–98; PtO *B & W* 84–18; rtd 02. *19 Stonegallows, Taunton TA1 5JW* T: (01823) 330003 E: mai.curnow@googlemail.com

CURRAH, Michael Ewart. b 31. Down Coll Cam BA 54 MA 58. Sarum Th Coll 54. **d** 56 **p** 57. C Calne *Sarum* 56–60; V Southbroom 60–69; PtO 70–88; Asst Master Woodroffe Sch Lyme Regis 71–85; Hon C Taunton H Trin *B & W* 88–96; rtd 96; PtO *B & W* 96–06; *Leic* from 06. *19 Avon House, Welland Place, St Mary's Road, Market Harborough LE16 7GD* T: (01858) 288948 E: mecandmec@talktalk.net

CURRALL, James Edward Patrick. b 55. Man Univ BSc 76 Aber Univ PhD 81. TISEC 09. **d** 12 **p** 13. C Largs *Glas* 12–15; LtO

15; LtO *Mor* from 15; P-in-c Tain from 17; P-in-c Dornoch from 17; P-in-c Lairg from 17; C Ardgay and Crask from 17. *Kennic Cottage, Spinningdale, Ardgay IV24 3AD* T: (01862) 881737 M: 07989-383439 E: jcurrall@talktalk.net

CURRAM, Deborah Ann. b 62. Ripon Coll Cuddesdon 14. d 16 p 17. NSM Minchinhampton w Box and Amberley *Glouc* 16–18; NSM Rodborough, Woodchester and Brimscombe 18–19; C Hayling Is St Andr *Portsm* from 19. *29 Selsmore Road, Hayling Island PO11 9JZ* T: (023) 9246 2379 E: revdeborah01@gmail.com

CURRAN, John Henry. b 77. Nottm Univ BA 00. Wycliffe Hall Ox 00. d 02 p 03. C W Bridgford *S'well* 02–05; PtO 05–07; P-in-c Wollaton Park 07–11; V from 11; Chapl Nottm Univ 07–11. *St Mary's Vicarage, Wollaton Hall Drive, Nottingham NG8 1AF* T: 0115-978 4914 E: henry@stmaryswollatonpark.co.uk

CURRAN, The Ven Patrick Martin Stanley. b 56. K Coll (NS) BA 80 Southn Univ BTh 84. Chich Th Coll 80. d 84 p 85. C Heavitree w Ex St Paul 84–87; Bp's Chapl to Students *Bradf* 87–93; Chapl Bonn w Cologne *Eur* 93–00; Chapl Vienna from 00; Can Malta Cathl from 00; Adn E Adnry 02–15. *The British Embassy, Jaurèsgasse 12, A-1030 Vienna, Austria* T: (0043) (1) 714 8900 *or* 718 5902 E: office@christchurchvienna.org

CURRELL, Linda Anne. *See* SCOTT, Linda Anne

CURRER, Caroline Mary. b 49. Keele Univ BA 71 Warwick Univ PhD 86 Anglia Ruskin Univ MA 09 CQSW 71. EAMTC 02. d 04 p 05. NSM Stansted Mountfitchet w Birchanger and Farnham *Chelmsf* 04–09; P-in-c Poynings w Edburton, Newtimber and Pyecombe *Chich* 09–17; rtd 17. *28 West Road, Saffron Walden CB11 3DS* E: c.currer@btinternet.com

CURREY, Pauline Carol. *See* REES, Pauline Carol

CURRIE, Daniel Robert. b 71. Trin Coll Bris 07. d 09 p 10. C Gorleston St Andr *Nor* 09–12; C Marple All SS *Ches* 12–16; V from 16. *155 Church Lane, Marple, Stockport SK6 7LD* T: 0161-292 9305 E: revdcurrie@gmail.com

CURRIE, John Stuart. b 47. SEITE 94. d 97 p 98. C S Chatham H Trin *Roch* 97–01; TV 01–13; Dioc Ecum Officer 09–13; rtd 13; PtO *Roch* from 13; *Cant* from 14. *Pilgrim's House, Oxenden Street, Herne Bay CT6 8TD* T: (01227) 364842 M: 07814-670051 E: revjsc@gmail.com

CURRIE, Mrs Katherine Barbara. b 55. Huddersfield Univ BSc 01 York St Jo Univ BA 13 SRN 78. Yorks Min Course 12. d 14 p 15. NSM High Hoyland, Scissett and Clayton W *Leeds* from 14. *158 Blacker Lane, Netherton, Wakefield WF4 4EZ* T: (01924) 279295 M: 07949-850460 E: kate.currie158@yahoo.co.uk

CURRIE, Lesley Sarah. b 70. Nene Coll Northn BA 95 Herts Univ PGCE 97. All SS Cen for Miss & Min 11. d 14 p 15. NSM Marple All SS *Ches* from 14; RD Chadkirk from 19. *155 Church Lane, Marple, Stockport SK6 7LD* T: 0161-292 9305 E: dalcurrie5@gmail.com

CURRIE, Canon Stuart William. b 53. Hertf Coll Ox MA 79 Fitzw Coll Cam MA 85 Univ Coll Dur CertEd K Coll Lon PhD 11. Westcott Ho Cam 82. d 85 p 86. C Whitley Ch Ch *Ox* 85–89; TV Banbury 89–94; V Barbourne *Worc* 94–16; Hon Can Worc Cathl from 09; Bp's Chapl from 16. *The Old Palace, Deansway, Worcester WR1 2JE* T: (01905) 731599 E: bishopschaplain@cofe-worcester.org.uk

CURRIN, John. b 56. Keele Univ CertEd 78. St Jo Coll Nottm MA 93. d 93 p 94. C Eastwood *S'well* 93–97; P-in-c Matlock Bath and Cromford *Derby* 97–02; V 02–06; R Dibden *Win* 06–18; rtd 18; PtO *Win* from 19. *8 Velsheda Court, Hythe Marina Village, Hythe, Southampton SO45 6DW*

CURRY, Canon Bruce. b 33. Wells Th Coll 61. d 63 p 64. C Shepton Mallet *B & W* 63–67; C Cheam *S'wark* 67–71; R W Walton *Ely* 71–78; V St Neots 78–94; P-in-c Everton w Tetworth 94–98; P-in-c Abbotsley 94–99; P-in-c Waresley 94–99; P-in-c Gt w Lt Gransden 98–99; R Gt Gransden and Abbotsley and Lt Gransden etc 99–04; RD St Neots 90–02; Hon Can Ely Cathl 98–04; rtd 04; PtO *Ely* from 05. *10 Ravens Court, Ely CB6 3ED* T: (01353) 661494 E: brucecurry10@gmail.com *or* janeandbruce@waitrose.com

CURRY, George Robert. b 51. Bede Coll Dur BA 72 Newc Univ MA 97. Cranmer Hall Dur Oak Hill Th Coll. d 76 p 77. C Denton Holme *Carl* 76–81; V Low Elswick *Newc* 81–06; P-in-c High Elswick St Paul 97–06; V Elswick from 06. *St Stephen's Vicarage, Clumber Street, Newcastle upon Tyne NE4 7ST* T: 0191-273 4680 E: g.r.curry@btinternet.com

CURRY, James Sebastian. b 63. Hatf Coll Dur BA 84. Ripon Coll Cuddesdon BTh 93. d 93 p 94. C Four Oaks *Birm* 93–96; C Erdington St Barn 96–99; TV Jarrow *Dur* 99–06; R Aboyne, Ballater and Braemar *Ab* 06–13; P-in-c Golcar *Wakef* 13–14; *Leeds* 14–17; P-in-c Longwood *Wakef* 13–14; *Leeds* 14–17; C Mansfield St Mark *S'well* from 17; C Mansfield SS Pet and Paul from 17. *The*

Vicarage, 112 Nottingham Road, Mansfield NG18 1BP E: revjamescurry@btinternet.com

CURTIS, Anthony Gordon. b 74. Selw Coll Cam BTh 10. Westcott Ho Cam 07. d 10 p 11. C Morpeth *Newc* 10–13; V Shiremoor from 13. *St Mark's Vicarage, Brenkley Avenue, Shiremoor, Newcastle upon Tyne NE27 0PP* T: 0191-253 7020 M: 07969-737763 E: tony_curtis@europe.com

CURTIS, Colin. b 47. Open Univ BA 80 ALA 69. St Jo Coll Nottm 83. d 93 p 94. NSM Clarkston *Glas* 93–10; LtO from 12. *78 Auldhouse Road, Glasgow G43 1UR* T: 0141-569 4206 E: colin.curtis540@ntlworld.com

CURTIS, Canon Geoffrey John. b 35. Dur Univ BA 57. Ripon Hall Ox 59. d 61 p 62. C Gosport Ch Ch *Portsm* 61–65; C Bedhampton 65–68; Producer Schs Broadcasting Dept BBC Lon 68–75; Dioc Communications Adv *Guildf* 75–00; P-in-c Grayswood 75–91; Dir Grayswood Studio 84–00; Hon Can Guildf Cathl 87–00; rtd 00; PtO *Guildf* from 00. *1 Clairville, Woodside Road, Chiddingfold, Godalming GU8 4QY* T: (01428) 685943

CURTIS, Mrs Jacqueline Elaine. b 60. Sarum & Wells Th Coll 87. d 90 p 94. Par Dn Bridport *Sarum* 90–94; C 94–95; TV Melbury 95–00; TV Maltby *Sheff* 00–02; TR 02–08; TR Crosslacon *Carl* 08–16; TR Chellington *St Alb* from 16. *The Rectory, 3 The Moor, Carlton, Bedford MK43 7JR* T: (01234) 720961 E: jecurtisx3@gmail.com *or* chellingtonteam@gmail.com

CURTIS, Jane Darwent. b 64. Leic Univ BA 86. Linc Th Coll BTh 93. d 93 p 94. Par Dn Oadby *Leic* 93–94; C 94–96; Chapl De Montfort Univ 96–03; C Leic H Spirit 96–97; TV 97–03; TV Gilmorton, Peatling Parva, Kimcote etc 03–09; Bp's Adv for Women's Min 04–09; V Whatborough Gp 09–17; Officer for IME 4-7 09–17; Bp's Adv for Women's Min 15–16; Hon Can Leic Cathl 06–17; V R Wootton Bassett *Sarum* from 17; RD Calne from 17. *St Bartholomew's Vicarage, Glebe Road, Royal Wootton Bassett, Swindon SN4 7DU* E: jane@chelmsworth.com

CURTIS, John Durston. b 43. Lich Th Coll 65. d 68 p 69. C Coseley Ch Ch *Lich* 68–71; C Sedgley All SS 71–74; CF 74–79; P-in-c Newton Valence *Win* 79–82; P-in-c Selborne 79–82; R Newton Valence, Selborne and E Tisted w Colemore 82–87; R Marchwood 87–09; AD Lyndhurst 05–08; rtd 09; PtO *Nor* from 09. *7 Pearce Road, Diss IP22 4YF* T: (01379) 640036 E: linda.john7@btinternet.com

CURTIS, Mrs Julia. b 67. Warwick Univ BSc 89 Anglia Ruskin Univ BA 13 MA 15 ACA 92. Westcott Ho Cam 13. d 15 p 16. C Creech St Michael and Ruishton w Thornfalcon *B & W* 15–18; C Teme Valley S *Worc* from 18. *The Rectory, Broadheath, Tenbury Wells WR15 8QW* T: (01886) 853286 M: 07908-925693 E: revjuliacurtis@gmail.com

CURTIS, Layton Richard. b 61. Leic Univ BSc 84 PGCE 85. Linc Th Coll BTh 93. d 93 p 94. C Knighton St Mary Magd *Leic* 93–96; C Leic St Phil 96–01; P-in-c Wigston Magna 01–12; P-in-c Hallaton and Allexton, w Horninghold, Tugby etc 12–17; TR Cannings and Redhorn *Sarum* from 17. *St Bartholomew's Vicarage, Glebe Road, Royal Wootton Bassett, Swindon SN4 7DU* M: 07855-746041

CURTIS, Mrs Marian Ruth. b 54. Nottm Univ BA 75 CQSW 80. Trin Coll Bris 03. d 05 p 06. C Blackheath Park St Mich *S'wark* 05–08; Asst Chapl Salisbury NHS Foundn Trust 08–09; P-in-c Slindon, Eartham and Madehurst *Chich* 09–15; rtd 15; PtO *Sarum* from 16. *Short Street Farm, 160 Short Street, Chapmanslade, Westbury BA13 4AA* T: (01373) 832654 E: mariancurtis@btinternet.com

CURTIS, Ronald Victor. b 47. SAOMC 98. d 01 p 02. NSM Shipton-under-Wychwood w Milton, Fifield etc *Ox* 01–05; P-in-c Stourbridge St Thos *Worc* 05–12; rtd 12; PtO *Ox* from 13; *Eur* from 19. *12 Waites Close, Aston, Bampton OX18 2ES* E: rev.ron@btinternet.com

CURTIS, Mrs Susan Anne. b 51. Birm Univ CertEd 72 Open Univ BA 79. d 07 p 08. OLM Epsom Common Ch Ch *Guildf* 07–12; NSM from 12. *The Rye, 38C Woodlands Road, Epsom KT18 7HW* E: sacsac@ntlworld.com

CURTIS, Susannah Ruth. b 83. Jes Coll Cam BA 05 MA 09. Wycliffe Hall Ox MTh 10. d 08 p 09. C Preston-on-Tees and Longnewton *Dur* 08–12; C Stockton 08–12; C Billingham 12–13; P-in-c Doxford St Wilfrid 13–18; Chapl St Jo Coll Dur 13–18; PtO *Derby* 18–19; C Derby St Alkmund and St Werburgh from 19. *17 Roman Road, Derby DE1 3RX*

CURTIS, Thomas John. b 32. Pemb Coll Ox BA 55 MA 59 Lon Univ BD 58. Clifton Th Coll 55. d 58 p 59. C Wandsworth All SS *S'wark* 58–61; Chile 61–71; R Saxmundham *St E* 71–77; V Cheltenham St Mark *Glouc* 77–84; TR 84–86; V Chipping Norton *Ox* 86–95; rtd 95; Hon Dioc Rep SAMS St E 95–01; PtO *St E* 95–01; *Glouc* from 01; *Worc* 01–10. *60 Courtney Close, Tewkesbury GL20 5FB* T: (01684) 295298 E: curtistomjon@aol.com

CUSHING, Mrs Barbara Anne. b 51. Doncaster Coll of Educn CertEd 72 Sheff Univ BEd 73. Yorks Min Course 12. **d** 13 **p** 14. NSM Anston *Sheff* from 13. *17 Lindale Close, North Anston, Sheffield S25 4FD* T: (01909) 564905 M: 07854-728444 E: barbara_cush@hotmail.com

CUSHING, Gregory Douglas. b 84. Plymouth Univ BA 05 Cam Univ BTh 12. Ridley Hall Cam 09. **d** 12 **p** 13. C Wandsworth All SS *S'wark* 12–16; P-in-c Alfold and Loxwood *Guildf* from 16. *The Rectory, Vicarage Hill, Loxwood, Billingshurst RH14 0RG* T: (01403) 753821 *or* 752320 M: 07746-721504 E: gregory_cushing@hotmail.com

CUTCLIFFE, Canon Neil Robert. b 50. NUU BA 72 TCD BA 72. **d** 75 **p** 76. C Belfast St Mary *Conn* 75–78; C Lurgan Ch the Redeemer *D & D* 78–80; I Garrison w Slavin and Belleek *Clogh* 80–86; I Mossley *Conn* 86–16; Can Belf Cathl 07–16; rtd 16. *6 Ballymontenagh Road, Gracehill, Ballymena BT42 2QG* T: (028) 2587 8779 E: rathdune@hotmail.com

CUTHBERT, Canon John. b 52. Edin Univ BSc 76 PhD 80. Coates Hall Edin BD 92. **d** 92 **p** 93. Chapl St Mary's Cathl *Edin* 92–98; C Edin St Mary 92–98; P-in-c Forres *Mor* 98–03; R Arbroath *Bre* 04–14; R Auchmithie 04–14; Can St Paul's Cathl Dundee 09–14; P-in-c Inverness St Jo *Mor* from 14; P-in-c Inverness St Mich from 14. *St Michael's Rectory, 28 Abban Street, Inverness IV3 8HH* T: (01463) 223218 *or* 233797 E: john2cuthbert@gmail.com

CUTHBERT, Mrs Penelope Jane. b 65. Collingwood Coll Dur BA 87 Ox Brookes Univ BA 12. Ox Min Course 09. **d** 12 **p** 13. C Reading St Agnes w St Paul and St Barn *Ox* 12–16; C Caversham Thameside and Mapledurham from 16. *St John's Vicarage, St John's Road, Caversham, Reading RG4 5AN* M: 07825-331810 E: penny_cuthbert@btinternet.com

CUTHBERT, Vernon John. Trin Coll Bris 02. **d** 04 **p** 05. C Alvaston *Derby* 04–08; P-in-c Cleadon *Dur* from 08; AD Jarrow from 15. *The Vicarage, 5 Sunderland Road, Cleadon, Sunderland SR6 7UR* T: 0191-536 7147

CUTHBERT, Victor. b 46. **d** 01 **p** 02. OLM Surbiton St Matt *S'wark* 01–11; PtO from 11. *4 St Thomas Close, Surbiton KT6 7TU* T: (020) 8399 8722 E: victorcuthbert@btinternet.com

CUTHBERTSON, Canon Amanda. b 54. K Coll Lon BD 92 AKC 92 Open Univ PGCE 98 Loughb Univ MA 00 ALCM 85 LLCM 87. EAMTC 98. **d** 00 **p** 01. C Northampton St Benedict *Pet* 00–03; V Wellingborough St Mark 03–17; Dioc Chapl MU 04–16; Can Pet Cathl 15–17; rtd 17; Bp's Adv for Healing Min *Pet* from 17; P-in-c Northampton Ch Ch from 17. *25 Glebe Road, Roade, Northampton NN7 2QH* T: (01604) 863488 M: 07525-257547 E: amandacuthbertson123@gmail.com

CUTLER, Robert Francis. b 37. Lon Univ BSc 57. Clifton Th Coll 62. **d** 64 **p** 65. C Peckham St Mary Magd *S'wark* 64–68; C Redhill H Trin 68–70; Travel Sec Inter-Coll Chr Fellowship of IVF 70–74; Hon C Selly Hill St Steph *Birm* 70–74; Interserve Internat Bangladesh 74–93; Internat Fellowship Evang Students 74–85; Bible Students Fellowship of Bangladesh 85–93; V Rochdale Deeplish St Luke *Man* 94–99; TV S Rochdale 00–02; rtd 02; PtO *St Alb* 03–19; *Pet* from 11. *10 Troon Crescent, Wellingborough NN8 5WG* T: (01933) 676322 E: robertcutler@btinternet.com

CUTLER, Roger Charles. b 49. Liv Univ BSc 70 Glas Univ MPhil 98. Coll of Resurr Mirfield 86. **d** 88 **p** 89. C Walney Is *Carl* 88–91; Chapl RN 91–98; PtO *Glas* 91–95; Hon C Challoch w Newton Stewart 95–98; V Gosforth St Nic *Newc* 98–01; P-in-c St John Lee 01–04; R 05–08; P-in-c Warden w Newbrough 01–04; V 05–08; R Kirkcudbright *Glas* 08–14; R Gatehouse of Fleet 08–14; rtd 14. *14 St John Street, Creetown, Newton Stewart DG8 7JF* T: (01671) 820832 E: rogercutler49@gmail.com

CUTTER, John Douglas. b 31. Lon Univ BD 61. Chich Th Coll 56. **d** 59 **p** 60. C Blyth St Mary *Newc* 59–62; C Rugeley *Lich* 62–65; V Rocester 65–73; V Shrewsbury St Giles 73–83; R Yoxall and Dean's V Lich Cathl 83–91; rtd 91; PtO *Win* from 91; Hon Chapl Win Cathl from 98. *3 Morley College, Market Street, Winchester SO23 9LF* T: (01962) 852203

CUTTING, The Ven Alastair Murray. b 60. Westhill Coll Birm BEd 83 Heythrop Coll Lon MA 03. St Jo Coll Nottm 84. **d** 87 **p** 88. C Woodlands *Sheff* 87–88; C Wadsley 89–91; C Uxbridge *Lon* 91–96; Chapl to the Nave and Uxbridge Town Cen 91–96; V Copthorne *Chich* 96–10; R Henfield w Shermanbury and Woodmancote 10–13; Adn Lewisham and Greenwich *S'wark* from 13; P-in-c Sydenham H Trin and St Aug 15–19. *1 Sydenham Park Road, London SE26 4DY* M: 07736-676106 E: alastair.cutting@southwark.anglican.org

CUTTS, Canon David. b 52. Van Mildert Coll Dur BSc 73. St Jo Coll Nottm BA 79. **d** 80 **p** 81. C Ipswich St Matt *St E* 80–82; Bp's Dom Chapl 82–85; R Coddenham w Gosbeck and Hemingstone w Henley 85–94; RD Bosmere 92–94; V Ipswich St Marg from 94; RD Ipswich 96–01; Hon Can St E Cathl from 00. *St Margaret's Vicarage, 32 Constable Road, Ipswich IP4 2UW* T: (01473) 253906 M: 07733-406552 E: david.cutts3@ntlworld.com

CUTTS, Elizabeth Joan Gabrielle. See STRICKLAND, Elizabeth Joan Gabrielle

CYPRUS, Archdeacon of. See HOLDSWORTH, John Ivor

CYPRUS, Archdeacon of. See FUTCHER, Christopher David

CYRUS, Keyvan Dominic. b 74. Univ of Sistan & Baluchestan BSc 98 Lon Sch of Th MA 11. Westcott Ho Cam 12. **d** 15 **p** 16. C Tividale *Lich* 15–18; Vice-Prin SWMTC from 18. *25 Eton Walk, Exeter EX4 1FD* T: (01392) 264404 E: fr.dominiccyrus@gmail.com

CZERNIAWSKA EDGCUMBE, Preb Irena Christine. b 59. Trin Coll Ox BA 82. Oak Hill Th Coll 93. **d** 95 **p** 96. NSM De Beauvoir Town St Pet *Lon* 95–99; Chapl Raines Foundn Sch Tower Hamlets 99–04; NSM Bow Common 00–04; P-in-c Hoxton St Anne w St Columba 04–12; Min Development Adv Stepney Area 04–07; Dean of Women's Min Stepney Area 07–12; Dir Tr and Development Stepney Area from 12; Preb St Paul's Cathl from 16. *24 Calabria Road, London N5 1JA* T: (020) 7033 3446 *or* 3837 5238 E: irenaczerniawskaedgcumbe@hotmail.com

D

DABIN, Susan. See ADAMS, Susan

DABORN, Mark Henry. b 55. Magd Coll Cam BA 76 MA 80 Glos Univ BA 11 MRICS 82 QTS 01. WEMTC 99. **d** 05 **p** 06. NSM Cleobury Mortimer w Hopton Wafers etc *Heref* 05–15; P-in-c Stottesdon w Farlow, Cleeton St Mary etc 15–17; R from 17; RD Bridgnorth from 17; Asst Dir of Ords from 19. *The Rectory, Stottesdon, Kidderminster DY14 8UE* T: (01746) 718127 M: 07857-514909 E: mark.daborn@hotmail.co.uk

DABORN, Robert Francis. b 53. Keble Coll Ox BA 74 MA 78 Fitzw Coll Cam BA 77. Ridley Hall Cam 75. **d** 78 **p** 79. C Mortlake w E Sheen *S'wark* 78–81; Chapl Collingwood and Grey Coll *Dur* 82–83; V Lapley w Wheaton Aston *Lich* 86–91; P-in-c Blymhill w Weston-under-Lizard 89–91; P-in-c Tibberton w Bolas Magna and Waters Upton 91–99; Shropshire Local Min Adv 91–99; P-in-c Childs Ercall and Stoke upon Tern 92–95; Dir Local Min Development 99–05; Dir Past Studies WEMTC 05–14; Vice-Prin 09–14; Preb Heref Cathl 14; R Newcastle w Butterton *Lich* 14–18; rtd 18; PtO *Lich* 19. *20 Whiteway Drive, Bratton, Telford TF5 0DR* E: robert.daborn@btinternet.com

DACK, Mrs Karen Ann. b 61. Univ of Otago MMin 13. **d** 08 **p** 09. New Zealand 08–15; PtO *Win* 15–17; P-in-c Guernsey St Matt 17–18; P-in-c Guernsey Ste Marie du Castel 17–18. *48 Hokianga Road, Dargaville, Northland 0310, New Zealand* M: 07839-247143 E: karenann.nz@gmail.com

DACK, Timothy William. b 59. Didsbury Coll Man BTh 87 Newc Univ PGCE 93. **d** 05 **p** 05. V Tirau Co-operating New Zealand 05–12; PtO 11–15; R Guernsey St Sampson *Win* 15–18. *48 Hokianga Road, Dargaville, Northland 0310, New Zealand* E: reverendtimothydack@gmail.com

DADD, Alan Edward. b 50. St Jo Coll Nottm 77. **d** 78 **p** 79. C Bishopsworth *Bris* 78–81; V Springfield *Birm* 81–85; Chapl Poly Cen Lon 85–86; V Hanger Lane St Ann 86–93; rtd 93; PtO *Bris* 96–98; *Win* from 10. *C14 Elizabeth Court, Grove Road, Bournemouth BH1 3DU* E: al.e.dd@btinternet.com

DADD, Canon Peter Wallace. b 38. Sheff Univ BA 59. Qu Coll Birm 59. **d** 61 **p** 62. C Grays Thurrock *Chelmsf* 61–65; C Grantham St Wulfram *Linc* 65–70; C Grantham w Manthorpe 70–72; TV 72–73; V Haxey 73–90; RD Is of Axholme 82–90; V Gainsborough All SS 90–98; Can and Preb Linc Cathl 91–08; P-in-c Flixborough w Burton upon Stather 98–00; V 00–08; rtd 08; PtO *S'well* from 08; *Cant* 16–19. *11 Manor Farm Rise, North Leverton, Retford DN22 0BH* T: (01427) 884191 E: peterdadd@tiscali.co.uk

DADSWELL, David Ian. b 58. New Coll Ox BA 80 MA 83 Brunel Univ MPhil 97. Westcott Ho Cam 80. **d** 83 **p** 84. C W Derby St Mary *Liv* 83–87; Chapl Brunel Univ *Lon* 87–96; PtO 96–04; *Ox* 98–04; Hon C New Windsor 04–17; Strategic Implementation Adv to Bp Linc 17–18; Dioc Sec *Linc* from 18. *1 St Giles Avenue, Lincoln LN2 4PE* M: 07773-800731 E: d.dadswell@me.com

DADY (formerly MARTIN), Elizabeth Anne. b 60. Sheff Univ BMedSci 82. ERMC 05. **d** 09 **p** 10. C Gaywood *Nor* 09–14; R Blakeney w Cley, Wiveton, Glandford etc 14–18; rtd 18; PtO *Nor* from 19. *3 The Sheltons, Barsham Road, Great Snoring, Fakenham NR21 0HP* M: 07503-747484 E: reverend.libby@yahoo.co.uk

D'AETH, Mrs Emma Louise Alice. b 63. Portsm Univ BA 03. STETS 04. **d** 07. NSM Portsea St Mary *Portsm* 07–11; PtO from 11; *Chich* from 19. *52 Belmont Street, Southsea PO5 1ND* T: (023) 9286 2108 E: emmadaeth@yahoo.co.uk

DAFFERN, Canon Adrian Mark. b 68. St Jo Coll Dur BA 89 MA 06 Ox Univ MTh 15 FRCO 98 FRSA 99. St Steph Ho Ox 90. **d** 92 **p** 93. C Lich St Chad 92–95; TV Stafford 95–00; V Walsall Wood 00–03; Treas V Lich Cathl 97–03; Can Res and Prec Cov Cathl 03–10; TR Blenheim *Ox* 10–17; V Woodstock and Bladon 17–18; Asst Adn Dorchester 16–18; AD Woodstock 17–18; V Cambridge Gt St Mary w St Mich *Ely* from 18. *Great St Mary's Church, St Mary's Passage, Cambridge CB2 3PQ* T: (01223) 747273 E: office@gsm.cam.ac.uk *or* vicar@gsm.cam.ac.uk

DAFFERN, Mrs Megan Isobel Jane. b 80. Ex Coll Ox BA 02 MA 06 DPhil 14 SS Coll Cam BA 05 MA 09. Westcott Ho Cam 03. **d** 06 **p** 07. C Rugby *Cov* 06–09; Chapl Jes Coll Ox 09–19; LtO *Ox* 09–19; Dir Ord and Voc *Ely* from 19. *Ely Diocesan Office, Bishop Woodford House, Barton Road, Ely CB7 4DX* T: (01353) 652710 E: megan.daffern@elydiocese.org

DAGGER, Ms Rose-Mary Anne. **d** 14 **p** 15. OLM Llandogo w Whitebrook Chpl and Tintern Parva *Mon* from 14. *Fox Cottage, Llandogo, Monmouth NP25 4TA* T: (01594) 530700 E: rm.a.dagger@icloud.com

DAGLISH, John David. b 44. RMCS BSc 70. Cranmer Hall Dur 74. **d** 77 **p** 78. C Ormesby *York* 77–79; C Kirk Ella 79–82; V Hull St Cuth 82–97; NSM Beverley St Mary 00–01; P-in-c Thorpe Edge *Bradf* 01–05; V Gt Marsden w Nelson St Phil *Blackb* 05–09; rtd 09. *13 St Barnabas Close, Gloucester GL1 5LH*

DAGNALL, Canon Bernard. b 44. K Coll Lon BSc 65 AKC 65 Ox Univ BA 75 MA 78 CChem MRSC MSOSc 88 CSci 04. St Steph Ho Ox 72. **d** 75 **p** 76. C Stanningley St Thos *Ripon* 75–76; C Lightbowne Man 76–78; C-in-c Grahame Park St Aug CD *Lon* 78–84; V Earley St Nic *Ox* 84–91; Ind Chapl 85–91; TR N Huddersfield *Wakef* 91–93; TV Newbury *Ox* 93–09; Chapl W Berks Priority Care Services NHS Trust 93–01; Chapl Newbury and Community Primary Care Trust 01–06; Chapl Berks W Primary Care Trust 06–09; Superior Soc of Retreat Conductors 00–05; rtd 09; PtO *Ox* from 10; *Lon* from 15; Hon Can Ho Ghana from 04. *10 Windsor Street, Headington, Oxford OX3 7AP* T: (01865) 751854 E: bernarddagnall@btinternet.com

DAHL, Madeleine Sara Martina. b 77. Skövde Univ MA 02 Uppsala Univ MTh 06. Past Inst Uppsala 06. **p** 07. C Vårgårda Sweden 07–09; C Österstund 09–15; C Chatham St Mary w St Jo *Roch* 15–19; C Chatham St Paul w All SS 15–19; C Vårgårda Sweden from 19. *Ornunga, Östergården 2b, 44793 Vårgårda, Sweden* M: 07469-246443 E: madeleine.dahl@outlook.com *or* madeleine.dahl@svenskakyrkan.se

DAINTREE, Canon Geoffrey Thomas. b 54. Bris Univ BSc 77. Trin Coll Bris 78. **d** 81 **p** 82. C Old Hill H Trin *Worc* 81–85; C Tunbridge Wells St Jo *Roch* 85–89; V Framfield *Chich* 89–00; RD Uckfield 96–00; V Eastbourne St Jo 00–09; Chs Relns Manager Chr Aid 09–17; rtd 17; PtO *Chich* from 09; Hon Can Cyangugu (Rwanda) from 97. *Wellstead, Caneheath, Polegate BN26 6SJ* T: (01323) 488110 M: 07921-722403 E: geoff.daintree@gmail.com

DAKIN (née HOLLETT), Mrs Catherine Elaine. b 53. Qu Eliz Coll Lon BSc 74. St Jo Coll Nottm 88. **d** 90 **p** 05. Par Dn Horley *S'wark* 90–93; NSM Heydon, Gt and Lt Chishill, Chrishall etc *Chelmsf* 93–97; NSM Gt and Lt Maplestead w Gestingthorpe 97–99; NSM Knights and Hospitallers Par 99–01; NSM Fulford w Hilderstone *Lich* 01–18. *29 The Flashes, Gnosall, Stafford ST20 0HL* T: (01785) 824340 M: 07971-101259 E: cathy.dakin@mha.org.uk

DAKIN, Preb Peter David. b 52. Wye Coll Lon BSc 79. St Jo Coll Nottm 91. **d** 91 **p** 92. NSM Southgate *Chich* 91–93; C Heydon, Gt and Lt Chishill, Chrishall etc *Chelmsf* 93–97; P-in-c Gt and Lt Maplestead w Gestingthorpe 97–99; P-in-c Alphamstone w Lamarsh and Pebmarsh 99; V Knights and Hospitallers Par 99–01; P-in-c Fulford w Hilderstone *Lich* 01–15; V 15–16; Rural Officer for Staffs 01–16; RD Stone

07–16; Preb Lich Cathl 16; rtd 16; PtO *Lich* from 17. *29 The Flashes, Gnosall, Stafford ST20 0HL* T: (01785) 824340

DAKIN, Mrs Sally. b 58. SRN 79 SCM 82 RHV 85 K Coll Lon MSc 89 TCert 92. SAOMC 02. **d** 04 **p** 05. NSM Ruscombe and Twyford *Ox* 04–12; PtO *Win* from 12. *Wolvesey, Winchester SO23 9ND* T: (01962) 854050 F: 897088 E: sally.dakin@btinternet.com

✠**DAKIN, The Rt Revd Timothy John.** b 58. SS Mark & Jo Univ Coll Plymouth BA 86 K Coll Lon MTh 87. **d** 93 **p** 94 **c** 12. Prin Carlile Coll Kenya 93–00; C Nairobi Cathl 94–00; Gen Sec CMS 00–12; Gen Sec SAMS 09–12; Hon C Ruscombe and Twyford *Ox* 00–12; Can Th Cov Cathl 01–12; Bp Win from 11. *Wolvesey, Winchester SO23 9ND* T: (01962) 854050 F: 897088 E: bishop.tim@winchester.anglican.org

DALAIS, Duncan John. b 56. St Paul's Coll Grahamstown. **d** 83 **p** 84. C Pinetown S Africa 83–87; C Chingford SS Pet and Paul *Chelmsf* 87–92; V Aldersbrook 92–02; P-in-c Leytonstone St Andr 02–14; V 14; P-in-c Leytonstone H Trin and St Aug Harrow Green 11–14; Asst Chapl Forest Healthcare NHS Trust Lon 02–09; rtd 14; PtO *Ely* from 15. *The Cedars, 60 Mount Street, Diss IP22 4QQ* M: 07983-560245 E: duncan.dalais@virgin.net

DALE, Charles William. b 49. **d** 02 **p** 03. OLM Uttoxeter Area *Lich* from 02. *Manor Court, Kingstone, Uttoxeter ST14 8QH* T: (01889) 500428 E: charles.dale@tesco.net

DALE, Canon Christine. b 62. Trin Coll Bris BA 94. **d** 94 **p** 95. C Thatcham *Ox* 94–98; TV Bracknell 98–02; R E Woodhay and Woolton Hill *Win* 02–09; R NW Hants from 09; RD Whitchurch 08–14; Hon Can Win Cathl from 17. *The Rectory, The Mount, Highclere, Newbury RG20 9QZ* T: (01635) 253323 E: cdale001@btinternet.com

DALE, John Anthony. b 42. Open Univ BSc 00. Qu Coll Birm 72. **d** 75 **p** 76. C Elmley Castle w Bricklehampton and Combertons *Worc* 75–81; P-in-c 81–83; R 83–88; Hon Can Worc Cathl 87–92; V Hallow 88–92; Dioc Registrar 92; P-in-c Michaelston-y-Fedw *Mon* 03–08; rtd 08; PtO *Ban* 08–15; C Willand, Uffculme, Kentisbeare etc *Ex* from 15. *3 Bonds Cottages, High Street, Honiton EX14 1JU* E: jadale@onetel.com *or* revjohndale@googlemail.com

DALE, Mrs Joy. b 57. **d** 13 **p** 14. NSM Penn Fields *Lich* from 13. *17 Haden Hill, Wolverhampton WV3 9PT* T: (01902) 772239 E: steveandjoydale@blueyonder.co.uk

DALE, Martin Nicholas. b 55. Chelsea Coll Lon BSc 76 CPA 83. Wycliffe Hall Ox 99. **d** 01 **p** 02. C Stiffkey and Cockthorpe w Morston, Langham etc *Nor* 01–03; C Stiffkey and Bale 03–04; C Brinton, Briningham, Hunworth, Stody etc 01–04; P-in-c New Romney w Old Romney and Midley *Cant* 04–07; P-in-c St Mary's Bay w St Mary-in-the-Marsh etc 04–07; P-in-c Dymchurch w Burmarsh and Newchurch 05–07; P-in-c Upper Wreake *Leic* 07–10; P-in-c S Croxton Gp 07–10; P-in-c Burrough Hill Pars 07–10; V E Marshland *Ely* from 10; PtO *Eur* from 17. *The Vicarage, 37 Church Road, Tilney St Lawrence, King's Lynn PE34 4QQ* T: (01945) 880259 M: 07887-554761 E: fcbasle@aol.com

DALE (née LIVESEY), Mrs Rachel Elizabeth. b 67. Univ of Wales (Cardiff) BSc 89 MBA 96 Homerton Coll Cam BTh 09 Huddersfield Univ PGCE 99. Ridley Hall Cam 07. **d** 09 **p** 10. C Streetly *Lich* 09–12; R Watershed from 12. *The Rectory, Pinfold Lane, Wheaton Aston, Stafford ST19 9PD* T: (01785) 840395 M: 07977-310049 E: revracheldale@gmail.com *or* rachel.livesey@gmail.com

DALEY, David Michael. b 50. Oak Hill Th Coll BA 90. **d** 92 **p** 92. C Enfield Ch Ch Trent Park *Lon* 92–94; V Chitts Hill St Cuth 94–14; rtd 14. *65 Victoria Road, Bude EX23 8RH* T: (01288) 488546 E: ddaley24@btinternet.com

DALEY, Judith Hilda. b 54. Sheff Univ BA 94 Leeds Univ PhD 03. NOC 03. **d** 04 **p** 05. NSM Sheff St Leon Norwood from 04; Chapl Sheff Teaching Hosps NHS Foundn Trust from 02. *112 Broad Inge Crescent, Chapeltown, Sheffield S35 1RU* T: 0114-246 2882 *or* 271 1900 E: judith.daley@sth.nhs.uk *or* judith.daley@sheffield.anglican.org

DALGLISH, David John. b 45. Heriot-Watt Univ BSc 70 Open Univ BA 94 Edin Univ MBA 97. TISEC 07. **d** 08. NSM Melrose *Edin* 08–10; R Jedburgh 10–15; rtd 15; LtO *Edin* from 16. *Kirkbrae House, The Woll, Askirk, Selkirk TD7 4NY* T: (01750) 32293 M: 07858-140200 E: david_dalglish@btinternet.com

DALLAS, Lucy Joanne Clair. b 73. Kent Univ BA 95 Herts Univ PGCE 98. Ripon Coll Cuddesdon BA 11. **d** 12 **p** 13. C Welwyn *St Alb* 12–15; TV Elstree and Borehamwood 15–18; PtO from 18. *12 Crofts Path, Hemel Hempstead HP3 8HB* E: ljcdallas@gmail.com

DALLEN, Julia Anne. b 58. Matlock Coll of Educn TCert 79 Ex Univ BTh 10. SWMTC 07. **d** 10 **p** 11. NSM Brampford Speke, Cadbury, Newton St Cyres etc *Ex* 10–14; NSM Sark *Win* 14–17; NSM Brampford Speke, Cadbury, Newton St Cyres etc *Ex* from 19. *5 Prispen House, Prispen Drive, Silverton, Exeter EX5 4DR* M: 07936-282078 E: juliadallen@btinternet.com

DALLEY, Mrs Gail Margaret. b 53. Cranmer Hall Dur 05. **d** 07 **p** 08. NSM Pocklington Wold *York* 07–10; V Barmby Moor Gp 10–13; rtd 13; PtO *York* from 14. *63 Algarth Rise, Pocklington, York YO42 2HX* T: (01759) 301920 E: gaildalley@outlook.com

DALLEY, Neil Michael. b 71. Reading Univ BA 92. Coll of Resurr Mirfield MA 16. **d** 16 **p** 17. C Leigh St Clem *Chelmsf* from 16. *12 Leigh Cliff Road, Leigh-on-Sea SS9 1DJ* M: 07947-363043 E: fr.neil.dalley@icloud.com

DALLISTON, The Very Revd Christopher Charles. b 56. Ox Univ BA Cam Univ MA. St Steph Ho Ox 81. **d** 84 **p** 85. C Halstead St Andr w H Trin and Greenstead Green *Chelmsf* 84–87; Bp's Dom Chapl 87–91; V Forest Gate St Edm 91–95; P-in-c Boston *Linc* 95–97; V 97–03; RD Holland E 97–03; Dean Newc 03–18; Dean Pet from 18. *The Deanery, 14 Minster Precincts, Peterborough PE1 1XX*

DALLISTON, Mrs Michelle Aleysha Caron. b 67. Qu Mary Coll Lon BSc 89 St Jo Coll Dur 10. Cranmer Hall Dur 08. **d** 10 **p** 11. C Gosforth St Nic *Newc* 10–13; C Newc St Gabr 13–14; C Hexham 14–15; TR Cha the King 15–18; C Higham Ferrers w Chelveston *Pet* from 19. *The Deanery, 14 Minster Precincts, Peterborough PE1 1XX* E: michelleacd@hotmail.co.uk

DALLOW, Gillian Margaret. b 45. Univ of Wales (Ban) BA 66 DipEd 67 Bris Univ MEd 87. Oak Hill Th Coll 93. **d** 96 **p** 97. NSM w Ealing St Jo w St Jas *Lon* 96–99; P-in-c Barlestone and Dioc Children's Min Adv *Leic* 99–08; rtd 08; PtO *Lon* 08–09; NSM Gabalfa *Llan* 09–15; PtO from 15. *26 Baron's Court Road, Penylan, Cardiff CF23 9DF* T: (029) 2046 3754 M: 07801-650187 E: g.dallow@btinternet.com

DALLY, Keith Richard. b 47. FCCA 77. St Jo Coll Nottm 80. **d** 82 **p** 83. C Southend St Sav Westcliff *Chelmsf* 82–85; Ind Chapl 85–93; C Southend 85–86; TV 86–92; C Harold Hill St Geo 92–93; Cen Co-ord Langham Place All So Clubhouse *Lon* 97–02; PtO *Ox* 02–05; *Pet* 05–11; Hon C Northampton Em 11–13; P-in-c King's Beck *Nor* 13–18; R from 18. *The Rectory, Aylsham Road, Felmingham, North Walsham NR28 0LD* T: (01692) 406045 E: keithdally@aol.com

DALRIADA, Archdeacon of. See DUNDAS, The Ven Edward Paul

DALRYMPLE, Wendy Margaret. b 75. Coll of Resurr Mirfield. **d** 07 **p** 08. C Mirfield *Wakef* 07–10; Chapl Sir Robert Woodard Academy Lancing 10–12; P-in-c Alfold and Loxwood *Guildf* 12–15; R Loughborough All SS w H Trin *Leic* from 15; AD Akeley E from 16. *The Rectory, 69 Westfield Drive, Loughborough LE11 3QL* T: (01509) 217029 E: priestwendy@btinternet.com

DALTON, Bertram Jeremy (Tod). b 32. ACIB 64. Sarum & Wells Th Coll 81. **d** 83 **p** 84. C Ringwood *Win* 83–86; R Norton sub Hamdon, W Chinnock, Chiselborough etc *B & W* 86–97; rtd 97; PtO *B & W* from 97. *Meadow Cottage, 8 Woodbarton, Milverton, Taunton TA4 1LU* T: (01823) 400302

DALTON, Darren Dean. b 78. Ripon Coll Cuddesdon 16. **d** 18 **p** 19. C Kinson and W Howe *Sarum* from 18. *1 Graycot Close, Bournemouth BH10 7BU* M: 07899-666561 E: ddalton103@googlemail.com

DALTON, Tod. See DALTON, Bertram Jeremy

DALTRY, Paul Richard. b 56. St Jo Coll Nottm 90. **d** 92 **p** 93. C Ipswich St Matt *St E* 92–96; P-in-c Needham Market w Badley 96–05; RD Bosmere 01–05; R Ipswich St Helen, H Trin, and St Luke 05–09; Min for Ch and Community Engagement 09–17; Hon Can St E Cathl 10–17; P-in-c N Blackwater *Chelmsf* 17–19; rtd 19. *Brooklands, Chapels, Kirkby-in-Furness LA17 7XY* E: paul@daltry.co.uk

DALY, Ms Bernadette Theresa. b 45. TCD BTh 94. **d** 97 **p** 98. C Taney *D & G* 97–00 and 05–06; Dir Past Studies CITC 00–04; rtd 06. *27 Southmede, Balinteer Road, Dublin 16, D16 NK69, Republic of Ireland* T: (00353) (1) 294 8815 M: 86-241 9009 E: berdaly@live.com

DALY, Gary James. b 63. Wycliffe Hall Ox 07. **d** 09 **p** 10. C Muswell Hill St Jas w St Matt *Lon* 09–16; TR Broadwater *Chich* from 16. *8 Sompting Avenue, Worthing BN14 8HN* M: 07889-630207

DALY, Jeffrey. b 50. Bris Univ BA 73 Jes Coll Cam PGCE 74 Fitzw Coll Cam BA 82 MA 86 Westmr Coll Ox MTh 03 Win Univ MTh 16. Ridley Hall Cam 80. **d** 83 **p** 84. C Tilehurst St Mich *Ox* 83–89; P-in-c Steventon w Milton 89–92; Asst Chapl Sherborne Sch 92–96; Chapl St Pet Sch York 96–11; rtd 11; PtO *Eur* from 07; *York* from 11. *3 Shotel Close, York YO30 5FY* T: (01904) 630142 E: fatherj.daly@cantab.net

DALY, Martin Jonathan. b 48. Woolwich Poly BSc 69. **d** 05 **p** 06. C Upton (Overchurch) *Ches* 05–13; rtd 13; PtO *Ches* from 13. *Fairfield Lodge, 1 Columbia Road, Prenton CH43 6TU* T: 0151-670 1461 *or* 677 1186 M: 07710-242241 E: martindaly1948@gmail.com

DANCE, Peter Patrick. b 31. Em Coll Saskatoon 66. **d** 69 **p** 69. R Mannville Canada 69–71; C Hednesford *Lich* 71–75; P-in-c Westcote Barton and Steeple Barton *Ox* 76–77; P-in-c Sandford St Martin 76–77; R Westcote Barton w Steeple Barton, Duns Tew etc 77–89; R Castle Douglas *Glas* 89–97; rtd 97. *Mannville, High Street, Adderbury, Banbury OX17 3NA* T: (01295) 811989

DANDO, Ms Elaine Vera. b 53. Coll of Resurr Mirfield 94 NOC 98. **d** 00 **p** 01. C Luddenden w Luddenden Foot *Wakef* 00–03; C Halifax 03–04; Lic to Offic 04–05; Chapl Univ Coll *Lon* 05–08; C St Pancras w St Jas and Ch Ch 05–08; C Northwood H Trin 08–10; rtd 10; PtO *Lon* 11–13; *Chich* from 13. *37 Wilderness Road, Hurstpierpoint, Hassocks BN6 9XD* T: (01273) 835277 E: evd.macrina@btinternet.com

DANDO, Stephen. b 49. Goldsmiths' Coll Lon TCert 70. Coll of Resurr Mirfield 81. **d** 83 **p** 84. C Wandsworth St Anne *S'wark* 83–87; V Stainland *Wakef* 87–99; V Illingworth 99–05; V Eastcote St Lawr *Lon* 05–13; rtd 13; PtO *Chich* from 14. *37 Wilderness Road, Hurstpierpoint, Hassocks BN6 9XD* T: (01273) 835277 E: revstephendando@hotmail.co.uk

DANE, John William. b 52. St Jo Coll Nottm 04. **d** 06 **p** 07. C Deddington w Barford, Clifton and Hempton *Ox* 06–09; Chapl Chich Univ 09–17; C Chich St Paul and Westhampnett 12–15; rtd 17. *15 Salthill Road, Chichester PO19 3QL* E: john@ausome.co.uk

DANES, Charles William. b 28. Chich Th Coll 54. **d** 56 **p** 57. C N Greenford All Hallows *Lon* 56–59; C Caversham *Ox* 59–63; V Walsgrave on Sowe *Cov* 63–65; P-in-c Hanworth All SS *Lon* 65–67; V 68–76; P-in-c Wick *Chich* 76–78; V Littlehampton St Jas 76–78; P-in-c Littlehampton St Mary 76–78; V W Worthing St Jo 78–87; Chapl Monte Carlo *Eur* 87–93; rtd 93; PtO *Chelmsf* from 93; *Eur* from 93. *31 Oakley Road, Braintree CM7 5QS* T: (01376) 324586

DANGERFIELD, Canon Andrew Keith. b 63. Univ of Wales (Ban) BD 87. St Steph Ho Ox 87. **d** 89 **p** 90. C St Marychurch *Ex* 89–93; C-in-c Grahame Park St Aug CD *Lon* 93–96; V Tottenham St Paul 96–06; P-in-c Edmonton St Mary w St Jo 98–04; AD E Haringey 00–05; V Kensal Green St Jo 06–12; Miss to Seafarers Yokohama Japan from 12; Hon Can Cape Coast from 04. *235 Yamate-cho, Naka-ku, Yokohama 231-0862, Japan* T: (0081) (80) 4929 2763 E: andrew.dangerfield@mtsmail.org

DANGERFIELD, Miss Sarah Ann. b 66. Ripon Coll Cuddesdon 09. **d** 11 **p** 12. C Badgeworth, Shurdington and Witcombe w Bentham *Glouc* 11–15; P-in-c Fladbury, Hill and Moor, Wyre Piddle etc *Worc* from 15; C Abberton, The Flyfords, Naunton Beauchamp etc from 15; C Peopleton and White Ladies Aston w Churchill etc from 15; C Stoulton w Drake's Broughton and Pirton etc from 17; RD Pershore from 18. *The Rectory, Station Road, Fladbury, Pershore WR10 2QW* T: (01386) 861669 E: s.dangerfield150@btinternet.com

DANIEL, Canon Herrick Haynes. b 38. Open Univ BA 81. Trin Coll Bris 73. **d** 75 **p** 76. C Harlesden St Mark *Lon* 75–78; C Livesey *Blackb* 78–81; V Blackb St Barn 81–08; Hon Can Blackb Cathl 98–08; rtd 08; PtO *Blackb* from 08; *Eur* from 16. *40 Appletree Drive, Lancaster LA1 4QY* T: (01524) 389764 E: herrickdaniel@hotmail.co.uk

DANIEL, Mrs Joy. b 44. Gilmore Course 81 Oak Hill Th Coll 81. **dss** 84 **d** 87 **p** 94. Luton St Fran *St Alb* 84–02; Par Dn 87–94; C 94–02; P-in-c Woodside 02–10; rtd 10; PtO *St Alb* 10–17; Hon C Luton St Paul 17–18; PtO from 18. *22 Rowelfield, Luton LU2 9HN* E: joy.daniel@virginmedia.com

DANIEL, Pamela Olive. b 52. Middx Poly BEd 86 Brunel Univ MA 87 K Coll Lon MA 94 Westmr Coll Ox BTh 98 Cardiff Univ LLM 13. Wycliffe Hall Ox 04. **d** 06 **p** 07. C Kennington St Mark *S'wark* 06–10; P-in-c W Bromwich St Phil *Lich* 10–18. *54 Lytton Road, Oxford OX4 3PA* M: 07771-633035 E: p.daniel001@btinternet.com

DANIEL, Philip Sharman. b 62. Man Univ BA 83 Rob Coll Cam CertEd 84. Wycliffe Hall Ox 84. **d** 86 **p** 87. C Macclesfield Team *Ches* 86–89; C Cheadle 89–94; V Disley 94–07; TR Mid Trent *Lich* 07–18; RD Stafford 15–18; V Lt Aston from 18. *The Vicarage, 3 Walsall Road, Little Aston, Sutton Coldfield B74 3BD*

DANIEL, Rajinder Kumar. b 34. St Steph Coll Delhi 55 Westcott Ho Cam 61. **d** 63 **p** 64. C Purley St Barn *S'wark* 63–66; C Battersea St Pet 66–67; C N Harrow St Alb *Lon* 67–72; TV Beaconsfield *Ox* 72–75; V Smethwick St Matt w St Chad *Birm* 75–87; Dioc Adv on Black Min 87–92; Chapl Birm Gen Hosp 91–92; TR Braunstone *Leic* 92–01; rtd 01; USPG and R Arima St Jude Trinidad and Tobago 03–04. *508 Chester Road, Kingshurst, Birmingham B36 0LG* T: 0121-770 1066

DANIELL, Robert. b 37. d 87 p 88. C Camberwell St Giles w St Matt *S'wark* 90–92; V Lewisham St Swithun 92–07; rtd 07; PtO *S'wark* 10–16; *Roch* 12–18. *4 Glenhouse Road, London SE9 1JQ* T: (020) 8850 4594 E: r.daniell@btinternet.com

DANIELS, Ian Geoffrey. b 72. Univ of Wales (Ban) BEng 93. ERMC 09. d 12 p 13. NSM Ipswich St Aug *St E* from 12. *44 Lindbergh Road, Ipswich IP3 9QX* T: (01473) 719089 M: 07777-698353 E: iandaniels@btinternet.com

DANIELS, Preb John Wyn. b 60. Southn Univ BSc 82 PhD 87. Trin Coll Bris MA 92. d 92 p 93. C Roundhay St Edm *Ripon* 92–95; India 96; C Ambleside w Brathay *Carl* 97–01; Chapl St Martin's Coll Lanc 97–01; Res Can Ban Cathl 01–05; Min Development Officer *Bradf* 05–10; C Embsay w Eastby and Skipton H Trin 05–10; Local Min Officer *Heref* from 10; Warden of Readers from 13; Preb Heref Cathl from 16. *Diocese of Hereford, Unit 8-9, The Business Quarter, Eco Park Road, Ludlow SY8 1FD* T: (01584) 871084 E: j.daniels@hereford.anglican.org *or* jd001@supanet.com

DANIELS, Lee Martin. b 61. Coll of Resurr Mirfield 99. d 01 p 02. C Toxteth Park St Agnes and St Pancras *Liv* 01–05; TV Staveley and Barrow Hill *Derby* 05–10; P-in-c Blackb St Thos w St Jude 10–13; P-in-c Blackb St Mich w St Jo and H Trin 10–13; V N and E Blackb 13–17; V Hawes Side and Marton Moss from 17. *The Vicarage, Hawes Side Lane, Blackpool FY4 5AH* E: martindvvic@gmail.com

DANIELS, Philip John. b 70. Southn Univ BA 92 Reading Univ MA 93 PGCE 96. Ox Min Course 09. d 12 p 13. C Hullavington, Norton and Stanton St Quintin *Bris* 12–15; C Sherston Magna, Easton Grey, Luckington etc 12–15; P-in-c Ashley, Crudwell, Hankerton and Oaksey 15–16; R Braydon Brook 16–18. *Dyers Farm, Nethercott, Braunton EX33 1HT* M: 07896-742233 E: philjdaniels@talktalk.net

DANKS, Alan Adam. b 41. Essex Univ MA 01. Edin Th Coll 61. d 64 p 65. C Dumfries *Glas* 64–67; C Earl's Court St Cuth w St Matthias *Lon* 68–71; C St Steph Walbrook and St Swithun etc 71–74; C Brookfield St Mary 75–76; C Hendon St Mary 76–85. *327 Hanworth Road, Hampton TW12 3EJ* T: (020) 8941 6055 E: luccas@btinternet.com

DANKS, Mark James. b 71. Qu Coll Birm. d 12 p 13. C Blakenall Heath *Lich* 12–16; Chapl HM Pris Brinsford 16–18; R Wednesbury St Bart, St Jas and St John *Lich* from 18. *The Vicarage, 4 Little Hill, Wednesbury WS10 9DE*

DANKS-FLOWER, Marilyn Clare. b 42. d 08 p 11. Chapl Barts and The Lon NHS Trust 08–10; NSM Egremont and Haile *Carl* 11–15; Chapl N Cumbria Univ Hosps NHS Trust from 11; PtO *Carl* from 15. *18 Lamb Lane, Egremont CA22 2AH* T: (01946) 822913 M: 07967-369103 E: kajori1@gmail.com

DAPLYN, Timothy James. b 52. Ripon Coll Cuddesdon 92. d 94 p 95. C Southmead *Bris* 94–97; P-in-c Abbots Leigh w Leigh Woods 97–99; Dioc Communications Officer 97–99; R Clutton w Cameley *B & W* 99–04; RD Chew Magna 03–04; P-in-c E w W Harptree and Hinton Blewett 04–08; LtO *Mor* 09–10; R Poolewe 10–13; R Kishorn 10–13; P-in-c Lochalsh 10–13; rtd 13. *Coillegillie, Applecross, Strathcarron IV54 8LZ* M: 07747-464833 E: coillegillie@hotmail.com

DARBY, George. b 48. SWMTC 06. d 09 p 10. NSM Egloskerry, N Petherwin, Tremaine and Tresmere *Truro* 09–10; NSM Egloskerry, N Petherwin, Tremaine, Tresmere etc 10–12; NSM Lezant w Lawhitton and S Petherwin w Trewen 09–10; NSM Altarnon w Bolventor, Laneast and St Clether 10–11; P-in-c Slaidburn *Bradf* 12–14; *Leeds* 14–15; P-in-c Long Preston w Tosside 14–15; P-in-c Long Preston w Tosside *Bradf* 12–14; rtd 15; PtO *Truro* from 15. *7 Edymead Court, Tavistock Road, Launceston PL15 9EZ* T: (01566) 770850 E: gdandpd@btinternet.com

DARBY, Canon Nicholas Peter. b 50. Kent Univ BA 82 Surrey Univ MSc 02. Sarum & Wells Th Coll 71. d 74 p 75. C Walton-on-Thames *Guildf* 74–78; C Horsell 78–80; USA 82–84; Chapl Lon Univ 84–89; Chapl R Lon Hosp (Whitechapel) 90–91; V Kew St Phil and All SS w St Luke *S'wark* 91–04; Dean Gaborone Botswana 04–07; V Fenham St Jas and St Basil *Newc* 09–17; AD Newc W 11–17; Hon Can Newc Cathl 12–17; rtd 17; PtO *Newc* from 17; *S'wark* from 18. *45 Gloucester Court, Kew Road, Richmond TW9 3EA* T: (020) 8940 6494

DARBY, Preb Philip William. b 44. Bede Coll Dur TCert 66. Qu Coll Birm. d 70 p 71. C Kidderminster St Geo *Worc* 70–74; P-in-c Dudley St Jo 74–79; V 79–80; P-in-c Catshill 80–81; P-in-c Catshill and Dodford 81–82; V 82–88; V Ipplepen w Torbryan *Ex* 88–00; V Ipplepen, Torbryan and Denbury 01–02; RD Newton Abbot and Ipplepen 93–01; V Ashburton w Buckland in the Moor and Bickington 02–05; P-in-c Widecombe-in-the-Moor, Leusdon, Princetown etc 04–05; TR Ashburton, Bickington, Buckland in the Moor etc 05–10; Preb Ex Cathl 02–10; rtd 10. *3 Kellett Close, Ashburton,*

Newton Abbot TQ13 7FB T: (01364) 652844 M: 07814-272198 E: pwdarby@supanet.com

DARBYSHIRE, Brian. b 48. Oak Hill Th Coll BA 83. d 83 p 84. C Enfield St Jas *Lon* 83–86; R Slaidburn *Bradf* 86–92; V Gt Harwood St Jo *Blackb* 92–02; V Douglas St Ninian *S & M* 02–08; CF (TA) 90–04; V Bingara Australia 08–13; rtd 13; PtO Brisbane from 13. *27/91 Dorset Drive, Rochedale South QLD 4123, Australia* T: (0061) (7) 3423 2529 E: brian.darbyshire@bigpond.com

DARBYSHIRE, Paul. b 50. City Univ BSc 77 Sheff Univ MA 80 N Lon Univ DipSW 97. Linc Sch of Th and Min 11. d 14 p 16. NSM Quarrington w Old Sleaford *Linc* 14; NSM Kesgrave *St E* 15–19; rtd 19. *5 Park Avenue, Felixstowe IP11 9JP* T: (01394) 671349 M: 07938-861643 E: pd@darbyshirehouse.co.uk

DARCH, John Henry. b 52. Univ of Wales (Lamp) BA 73 PhD 97 Lon Univ PGCE 74 MA 77 FRHistS 09 FHEA 04. Trin Coll Bris 80. d 82 p 83. C Meole Brace *Lich* 82–85; C Hoole *Ches* 85–88; V Hyde St Geo 88–99; P-in-c Godley cum Newton Green 89–93; RD Mottram 91–99; Lect St Jo Coll Nottm 99–06; Chapl 03–06; Public Preacher *S'well* 99–06; PtO *Derby* 03–06; Dir of Ords and Dir IME 4-7 *Blackb* 06–18; Hon C Mellor 11–13; rtd 18; PtO *Lich* from 18; *St As* from 18. *41 Swan Hill, Ellesmere SY12 0LZ* T: (01691) 624726 M: 07917-723972 E: j.darch248@btinternet.com *or* johnhdarch@gmail.com

DARK, Nicholas John. b 62. Leic Univ BA 83 ACIB 92. CITC BTh 98. d 98 p 99. C Ballyholme *D & D* 98–05; I Magheragall *Conn* from 05. *Magheragall Rectory, 70 Ballinderry Road, Lisburn BT28 2QS* T: (028) 9262 1273 E: magheragall@aol.com

DARKINS, Mrs Judith Rosemary. b 45. d 10 p 11. OLM Biddenden and Smarden *Cant* 10–12; NSM Wittersham w Stone and Ebony 12–13; C Rother and Oxney 13–16; C Tenterden and Smallhythe 13–16; TV Tenterden, Rother and Oxney from 16. *The Rectory, The Street, Wittersham, Tenterden TN30 7EA* T: (01797) 270418 E: judy.darkins@btinternet.com

DARLEY, Canon Shaun Arthur Neilson. b 36. Dur Univ BA 61 Reading Univ Hall Dur 61. d 63 p 64. C Luton w E Hyde *St Alb* 63–67; Chapl Bris Tech Coll 67–69; Chapl Bris Poly 69–92; Sen Chapl UWE 92–01; Lect 69–75; Sen Lect 75–01; Dir Cen for Performing Arts 85–02; Bp's Cathl Chapl *Bris* 69–76; Hon Can Bris Cathl 89–01; PtO *B & W* from 98; rtd 01; PtO *Bris* 02–06. *Church Paddock, Winscombe Hill, Bristol BS25 1DE* T: (01934) 843633 E: san.darley@btinternet.com

DARLING, Colin Patrick. QUB BA. St Jo Coll Nottm MTh. d 12 p 13. C Saintfield *D & D* 12–13; C Cregagh 13–16; I Killyleagh from 16. *34 Inishbeg, Killyleagh, Downpatrick BT30 9TR* M: 07925-672340 E: colin.darling@talktalk.net

DARLING, David Francis. b 55. K Coll Lon BSc 09 Heythrop Coll Lon MA 13. TISEC 93. d 96 p 97. SSF 88–05; Novice Guardian 99–05; NSM Edin St Ninian 96–98; Chapl W Gen Hosps NHS 96–98; Chapl Edin Sick Children's NHS Trust 96–98; Lic Preacher *Lon* 03–05; PtO from 15; Tutor Lon Cen for Spiritual Direction 16–19; PtO *Roch* from 19. *33 Sheppard's College, London Road, Bromley BR1 1PF* M: 07811-405835 E: davidfrancis.darling@gmail.com

✠**DARLING, The Rt Revd Edward Flewett.** b 33. TCD BA 55 MA 58. CITC. d 56 p 57 c 85. C Belfast St Luke *Conn* 56–59; C Orangefield *D & D* 59–62; C-in-c Carnalea 62–72; Chapl Ban Hosp 63–72; I Belfast Malone St Jo *Conn* 72–85; Min Can Belf Cathl 78–85; Chapl Ulster Independent Clinic 81–85; Bp L & K 85–00; rtd 00. *17 Queensfort Court, Carryduff, Belfast BT8 8NF* T: (028) 9081 7949 E: edwarddarling@hotmail.com

DARLING, John. b 47. Sarum & Wells Th Coll 76. d 79 p 80. NSM Trowbridge St Thos *Sarum* 79–82; NSM Trowbridge St Thos and W Ashton 82–92; NSM Atworth w Shaw and Whitley 07–13; NSM Melksham 01–13; NSM Broughton Gifford, Gt Chalfield and Holt 07–13; PtO 13–15. *43 Horse Road, Hilperton Marsh, Trowbridge BA14 7PF* T: (01225) 777803 E: revjohndarling@yahoo.co.uk

DARLINGTON, Paul Trevor. b 71. Imp Coll Lon BSc 92 K Coll Lon PGCE 93. Oak Hill Th Coll BA 99 MPhil 00. d 00 p 01. C Bispham *Blackb* 00–05; P-in-c Oswestry H Trin *Lich* 05–10; V from 10; RD Oswestry from 18. *Holy Trinity Vicarage, 29 Balmoral Crescent, Oswestry SY11 2XQ* T: (01691) 652184 E: paultrevordarlington@gmail.com

DARLISON, Geoffrey Stuart. b 49. MRTPI 80. St Jo Coll Nottm 89. d 91 p 92. C Horncastle w Low Toynton *Linc* 91–95; P-in-c Welton and Dunholme w Scothern 95–97; V 97–08; RD Lawres 07–08; P-in-c Thorpe Edge *Bradf* 08–14; P-in-c Greengates 08–14; rtd 14; PtO *Sheff* from 19. *3 Chestnut Road, Swallownest, Sheffield S26 4SJ*

DARMODY, Canon Richard Arthur. b 52. Lon Univ BD 90. Linc Th Coll MDiv 94. d 94 p 95. C Cherry Hinton St Jo *Ely* 94–97; I Belfast St Aid *Conn* 97–99; TR The Ramseys and

Upwood *Ely* 99–10; R from 10; RD St Ives 02–06; Asst Dir of Ords from 16; Hon Can Ely Cathl from 08. *The Rectory, 16 Hollow Lane, Ramsey, Huntingdon PE26 1DE* T: (01487) 813271 E: darmodyrichard@hotmail.com

DARRALL, Charles Geoffrey. b 32. Nottm Univ BA 55 MA 57. Qu Coll Birm 56. **d** 57 **p** 58. C Cockermouth All SS w Ch Ch *Carl* 57–63; Chapl Dioc Youth Cen 63–95; V St John's in the Vale w Wythburn 63–95; P-in-c Threlkeld 85–95; rtd 96; PtO *Carl* 98–07. *Piper House, Naddle, Keswick CA12 4TF* T: (017687) 74500 E: geoff.darrall@btinternet.com

DARRALL, John Norman. b 34. Nottm Univ BA 57. Ripon Hall Ox 57. **d** 60 **p** 61. C Nottingham St Mary *S'well* 60–65; Chapl Nottm Children's Hosp 64–65; V Bole w Saundby and Sturton w Littleborough *S'well* 65–66; Chapl Oakham Sch 84–99; rtd 99; PtO *Leic* 01–13; *Pet* from 05. *Grange Cottage, 69 Main Street, Cottesmore, Oakham LE15 7DH* T: (01572) 812443 E: johndarrall@googlemail.com

DARRANT, Louis Peter. b 77. Aber Univ BD 00 Leeds Univ MA 03. Coll of Resurr Mirfield 01. **d** 03 **p** 04. C Kennington St Jo w St Jas *S'wark* 03–07; R Maldon St Mary w Mundon *Chelmsf* 07–15; C Wilton Place St Paul *Lon* 15–18; PtO *Chelmsf* from 15; *S'wark* 15–16; Chapl Costa Azahar *Eur* from 18. *Calle Llantia 20-5, 12500 Vinaros, (Castellon), Spain* M: 07779-103826 E: louis.darrant@gmail.com

DART, Miss Andrea Elizabeth. b 47. Northd Coll of Educn TCert 68. Lindisfarne Regional Tr Partnership 12. **d** 14 **p** 15. NSM Stanley and S Moor *Dur* 14–17; rtd 17; PtO *Dur* from 17. *13 Tweed Terrace, Stanley DH9 6JQ* T: (01207) 237214 E: andrea.dart@gmail.com

DART, John Peter. b 40. St Jo Coll Ox BA 62. Cuddesdon Coll 62. **d** 64 **p** 65. C W Hartlepool St Aid *Dur* 64–67; C Alverthorpe *Wakef* 67–70; Lic to Offic 70–79; rtd 05. *3 Springhill Avenue, Crofton, Wakefield WF4 1HA* T: (01924) 860374 E: mail@dart.eclipse.co.uk

DARVILL, Canon Christopher Mark. b 61. Ox Univ BA 83. St Steph Ho Ox 84. **d** 86 **p** 87. C Tottenham St Paul *Lon* 86–88; C Oystermouth *S & B* 88–90; Chapl Univ of Wales (Swansea) 90–94; Asst Dioc Warden of Ords from 92; V Llansamlet 94–17; V Newton St Pet from 17; Hon Can Brecon Cathl from 16. *The Vicarage, Mary Twill Lane, Mumbles, Swansea SA3 4RB* T: (01792) 219156

DARVILL, Canon George Collins. b 36. Kelham Th Coll 56. **d** 61 **p** 62. C Middlesbrough St Chad *York* 61–64; C Manston *Ripon* 64–66; V Kippax 66–79; V Catterick 79–88; RD Richmond 80–86; P-in-c Adel 88–89; R 89–01; RD Headingley 91–96; Hon Can Ripon Cathl 91–01; rtd 01; PtO *Ripon* 01–14; *Bradf* 01–14; *Leeds* 14–16. *39 Woodlea Lane, Meanwood, Leeds LS6 4SX* T: 0113-275 7973

✠**DARWENT, The Rt Revd Frederick Charles.** b 27. ACIB. Wells Th Coll 61. **d** 63 **p** 64 **c** 78. C Pemberton St Jo *Liv* 63–65; R Strichen *Ab* 65–71; R New Pitsligo 65–71; R Fraserburgh w New Pitsligo 71–78; Can St Andr Cathl 71–78; Dean Ab 73–78; Bp Ab 78–92; rtd 92; LtO *Ab* from 92. *107 Osborne Place, Aberdeen AB25 2DD* T: (01224) 646497

DARWENT, Thomas James. b 74. Wycliffe Hall Ox. **d** 07 **p** 08. C Claygate *Guildf* 07–11; C Guildf St Sav 11–16; V Camberley St Paul from 16. *The Vicarage, Sandy Lane, Camberley GU15 2AG* T: (01276) 700210

DASH, Mrs Janet Eleanor Gillian. b 47. SRN 69. Cant Sch of Min 89. **d** 93 **p** 94. C Morden *S'wark* 93–96; C S Croydon Em 96–98; P-in-c Borstal and Chapl HM Pris Cookham Wood 98–05; P-in-c Darenth *Roch* 05–10; rtd 10; PtO *Cant* 11–17; *York* from 17. *9 Horseman Avenue, York YO23 3UF* T: (01904) 289788 M: 07853-844509 E: jandash@hotmail.co.uk

DATTA, Adrian. b 66. STETS. **d** 13 **p** 14. NSM Guernsey W Par *Win* 13–16; PtO *Win* from 17. *The Rectory, Rue de l'Eglise, St Pierre du Bois, Guernsey GY7 9SB* E: adriandatta@icloud.com

DAULMAN, John Henry. b 33. Lich Th Coll 60. **d** 62 **p** 63. C Monkseaton St Mary *Newc* 62–65; Min Can Newc Cathl 65–67; Chapl Crumpsall and Springfield Hosp 67–73; V Tyldesley w Shakerley *Man* 73–81; V Turton 81–00; rtd 00; PtO *Blackb* 01–14; *Man* 13–14. *17 Higher Bank Street, Withnell, Chorley PR6 8SF* T: (01254) 832597

DAUNTON-FEAR, Andrew. b 45. Univ of Tasmania BSc 64 Qu Coll Cam BA 67 MA 72 St Andr Univ BPhil 76 K Coll Lon PhD 00. Ridley Hall Cam 66. **d** 68 **p** 70. Lect Ridley Coll Melbourne Australia 68–70; C Epping w Thomastown 68–71; P-in-c Islington H Trin Cloudesley Square *Lon* 71–75; Hon C Islington St Mary 71–75; C Stoke Bishop *Bris* 76–79; R Thrapston *Pet* 79–89; R Barming *Roch* 89–03; Lect St Andr Th Sem Philippines 03–15; rtd 15; PtO *Bris* from 16. *17 Keys Avenue, Bristol BS7 0HQ* T: 0117-307 0082 M: 07532-154421 E: fear.no.evil70@gmail.com

DAVAGE, William Ernest Peter. b 50. MA 94. St Steph Ho Ox 89. **d** 91 **p** 92. C Eyres Monsell *Leic* 91–94; P Lib Pusey Ho 94–11; rtd 11; PtO *Lon* from 14. *7 Hampstead Square, London NW3 1AB* T: (020) 7209 5375 E: william.davage@stx.ox.ac.uk

DAVENPORT, Canon Ian Arthan. b 54. Linc Th Coll 85. **d** 87 **p** 88. C Ches H Trin 87–91; V Newton 91–97; V Oxton 97–10; RD Birkenhead 05–10; R Malpas and Threapwood 10–11; R Malpas and Threapwood and Bickerton from 11; RD Malpas from 14; Hon Can Ches Cathl from 06; Chapl to The Queen from 15. *The Rectory, Church Street, Malpas SY14 8PP* T: (01948) 860922

DAVENPORT, Ms Sally Elizabeth. b 59. Lon Bible Coll BA 99. Ripon Coll Cuddesdon 99. **d** 01 **p** 02. C Bishop's Stortford St Mich *St Alb* 01–05; TV Bp's Hatfield, Lemsford and N Mymms 05–10; P-in-c Fareham H Trin *Portsm* 11–15; TR from 15. *Bishopsgrove, 26 Osborn Road, Fareham PO16 7DQ* T: (01329) 232688 M: 07500-775926 E: sally.davenport@portsmouth.anglican.org

DAVENPORT, Susan Jane. *See* MILLINCHIP, Susan Jane

DAVEY, Andrew John. b 57. Magd Coll Ox BA 78 MA 83. Wycliffe Hall Ox 80. **d** 83 **p** 84. C Bermondsey St Jas w Ch Ch *S'wark* 83–87; Chapl Trin Coll Cam 87–92; Pilsdon Community 94–04. *Kingswood, North Street, Axminster EX13 5QF* T: (01297) 33534

DAVEY, Andrew John. b 53. St Mich Coll Llan. **d** 77 **p** 78. C Gt Stanmore *Lon* 77–79; NSM Watford St Jo *St Alb* 87–92; C Potters Bar 92–95; P-in-c Clenchwarton *Ely* 95–96; P-in-c W Lynn 95–96; R Clenchwarton and W Lynn 96–19; rtd 19; PtO *Nor* from 19. *Address temp unknown* E: postmaster@andrewdavey.plus.com

DAVEY, Andrew Paul. b 61. Southn Univ BA 82 Sheff Univ DMinTh 98. Tamilnadu Th Sem 84 Westcott Ho Cam 85. **d** 87 **p** 88. C S'wark H Trin w St Matt 87–91; V Camberwell St Luke 91–96; Min Development Officer Woolwich Area Miss Team 96–98; Ho of Bps' Officer for UPAs 96–98; Asst Sec Abps' Coun Bd for Soc Resp 98–03; Nat Adv on Community and Urban Affairs 03–12; V Upper Tooting H Trin w St Aug *S'wark* from 12; Hon Chapl S'wark Cathl from 01. *Holy Trinity Vicarage, 14 Upper Tooting Park, London SW17 7SW* T: (020) 8672 4790 E: vicar@uppertooting.net

DAVEY, Canon Christopher Mark. b 64. EN(G) 84 RGN 89. St Steph Ho Ox 92. **d** 95 **p** 96. C Leeds Belle Is St Jo and St Barn *Ripon* 95–97; C-in-c Grahame Park St Aug CD *Lon* 97–01; V St Alb St Mary Marshalswick 01–08; P-in-c Leavesden 08–12; V 12–13; P-in-c Coggeshall w Markshall *Chelmsf* from 13; P-in-c Cressing w Stisted and Bradwell etc from 15; RD Braintree from 18; Hon Can Chelmsf Cathl from 19. *The Vicarage, 4 Church Green, Coggeshall, Colchester CO6 1UD* T: (01376) 561234 E: vicarcoggeshall@btinternet.com

DAVEY, Mrs Hilary Margaret. b 49. Bris Univ BSc 70. EAMTC 98. **d** 01 **p** 02. NSM Saffron Walden w Wendens Ambo, Littlebury etc *Chelmsf* 01–07; P-in-c Debden and Wimbish w Thunderley 07–11; TV Saffron Walden and Villages 12–17; rtd 17; PtO *Chelmsf* from 17. *Barltrops, High Street, Debden, Saffron Walden CB11 3LE* T: (01799) 522616 E: hilarydavey@btopenworld.com

DAVEY, Julian Warwick. b 45. LRCPI 70 LRCSI 70. Qu Coll Birm 78. **d** 81 **p** 82. NSM Ipsley *Worc* 81–05; PtO *Cov* from 05; *Worc* from 05. *The Field House, Allimore Lane, Alcester B49 5PR* T: (01789) 764640 E: julianw.davey@yahoo.com *or* affgan1@yahoo.com

DAVEY, Kenneth William. b 41. Qu Coll Birm 84. **d** 86 **p** 87. C Baswich *Lich* 86–90; V Lostock Gralam *Ches* 90–96; P-in-c Thornton-le-Moors w Ince and Elton 96–07; rtd 07; PtO *Ches* from 08. *4 Firbank, Elton, Chester CH2 4LY* T: (01928) 726166 M: 07977-361059

DAVEY, Mark Sydney Henry. b 80. Wycliffe Hall Ox 10. **d** 13 **p** 14. C Herne Bay Ch Ch *Cant* 13–17; TV Morden *S'wark* from 17. *49 Camborne Road, Morden SM4 4JL*

DAVEY, Peter Francis. b 40. Trin Coll Cam BA 63 MA 68. Cuddesdon Coll 63. **d** 65 **p** 66. C Atherton *Man* 65–69; C Leesfield 69–72; V High Crompton 72–79; V Blackrod 79–89; P-in-c Ringley 89–91; V Ringley w Prestolee 91–95; P-in-c Dearnley 95–05; rtd 05; PtO *Man* 06–14. *73 Trimingham Drive, Bury BL8 1EP* T: 0161-964 9267 M: 07530-502228

DAVEY, Peter James. b 59. Bris Univ BSc 81 Loughb Univ MBA 91. Trin Coll Bris BA 00. **d** 00 **p** 01. C Long Eaton St Jo *Derby* 00–04; V Cotmanhay from 04; RD Erewash 13–18. *The Vicarage, 197 Heanor Road, Ilkeston DE7 8TA* T: 0115-932 5670 E: revpete@outlook.com

DAVEY, Richard Henry. b 66. Man Univ BA 88 Nottm Univ PhD 06. Linc Th Coll BTh 93. **d** 93 **p** 94. C Parkstone St Pet w Branksea and St Osmund *Sarum* 93–96; Chapl and Min Can St E Cathl 96–99; Can Res S'well Minster 99–04;

Chapl Nottm Trent Univ from 04; C Clifton from 04; C Nottingham St Pet and All SS from 10. *All Saints Vicarage, 16 All Saints Street, Nottingham NG7 4DP* T: 0115-808 4149 E: rdavey1175@aol.com

DAVID, Brother. *See* JARDINE, David John

DAVID, Faith Caroline. *See* CLARINGBULL, Faith Caroline

DAVID, Gilbert. b 56. Karachi Univ BA 76. Ripon Coll Cuddesdon 08. **d** 11 **p** 12. C New Bury w Gt Lever *Man* 11–15; TV Darlaston and Moxley *Lich* from 15. *Moxley Vicarage, 5 Sutton Road, Wednesbury WS10 8SG* M: 07880-710122 E: gildavid2u@hotmail.com

DAVID, Kaushal. b 65. **d** 15 **p** 16. C Nantwich *Ches* 15–17; P-in-c Totternhoe, Stanbridge and Tilsworth *St Alb* 17–19; V from 19. *The Vicarage, Mill Road, Stanbridge, Leighton Buzzard LU7 9HX* T: (01525) 211864 *or* (01582) 662778 M: 07824-603592 E: kaushaldavid@hotmail.com

DAVID, Canon Kenith Andrew. b 39. Natal Univ BA(Theol) 64. Coll of Resurr Mirfield 64. **d** 66 **p** 67. C Harpenden St Nic *St Alb* 66–69; R Chatsworth Epiphany S Africa 69–71; P-in-c Southwick St Mich *Chich* 71–72; Th Educn Sec Chr Aid 72–75; Project Officer India and Bangladesh 76–81; Hon C Kingston All SS *S'wark* 72–76; Hon C Kingston All SS w St Jo 76–81; Lic to Offic Botswana 81–83; Hon C Geneva *Eur* 83–95; Co-ord Urban Rural Miss WCC 83–94; Can Lundi Zimbabwe from 93; V Hessle *York* 95–05; rtd 05; PtO *Cant* 05–11. *5 Randolph Close, Canterbury CT1 3AZ* T/F: (01227) 452009

DAVID, William John. b 57. Ban Univ BTh 07. **d** 04 **p** 05. OLM Eltham St Barn *S'wark* 04–07; NSM 07–09 and 11–15; C Toowoomba St Luke Australia 09–11; Chapl Lewisham and Greenwich NHS Trust from 14. *12 Tarnwood Park, London SE9 5NY* T: (020) 8333 6338 M: 07929-644503 E: williamdavid10@aol.com

DAVID FRANCIS, Brother. *See* DARLING, David Francis

DAVIDGE-SMITH, Mrs Margaret Kathleen. b 53. CQSW 77. STETS 99. **d** 02 **p** 03. NSM E Acton St Dunstan w St Thos *Lon* 02–06; Asst Chapl Ealing Hosp NHS Trust 04–06; Asst Chapl Meadow House Hospice 04–06; Asst Chapl W Middx Univ Hosp NHS Trust 05–06; Asst Chapl W Lon Mental Health NHS Trust 05–06; Chapl Ealing Hosp NHS Trust 06–16; rtd 16; PtO *Lon* from 16. *36 Newburgh Road, London W3 6DQ* M: 07790-354464 E: mdavidge_s@hotmail.com *or* maggie.davidge-smith@london.anglican.org

DAVIDSON, Canon Charles Hilary. b 29. St Edm Hall Ox BA 52 MA 56 Leic Univ MPhil 89. Lich Th Coll 52. **d** 54 **p** 55. C Abington *Pet* 54–59; C Pet St Jo 59–60; R Sywell w Overstone 60–66; P-in-c Lamport w Faxton 66–76; R Maidwell w Draughton and Scaldwell 67–76; R Maidwell w Draughton, Scaldwell, Lamport etc 77–80; RD Brixworth 77–79; V Roade 80–87; V Roade and Ashton w Hartwell 87–94; RD Towcester 91–94; Can Pet Cathl 79–94; rtd 94; PtO *Pet* from 94. *Croftside, Butlins Lane, Roade, Northampton NN7 2PU* T: (01604) 863016

DAVIDSON, Christopher John. b 45. St Luke's Coll Ex CertEd 67 St Martin's Coll Lanc BEd 74. EAMTC. **d** 91 **p** 92. NSM Taverham w Ringland *Nor* 91–93; Dir of Educn 87–93; P-in-c Whixley w Green Hammerton *Ripon* 93–96; RE Adv 93–96; Dioc Dir of Educn *Ex* 97–01; Assoc P Exminster and Kenn 97–01; R Quidenham Gp *Nor* 01–08; P-in-c Guiltcross 04–08; rtd 08; P-in-c Pyworthy, Pancrasweek and Bridgerule *Ex* 08–11; PtO *Nor* from 11; *St E* from 16. *2 The Old School, Hinderclay Road, Rickinghall, Diss IP22 1HD* T: (01379) 890465 E: chris.davidson@btinternet.com

DAVIDSON, Mrs Dawn Margaret. b 59. **d** 09 **p** 10. OLM Mulbarton w Bracon Ash, Hethel and Flordon *Nor* 09–14; TV Newton Flotman, Swainsthorpe, Tasburgh, etc 14–18; TR from 18. *The Rectory, The Street, Saxlingham Nethergate, Norwich NR15 1AJ* T: (01508) 498924 M: 07784-003432 E: dawndavidson@btinternet.com

DAVIDSON, Donald. b 52. TISEC 00. **d** 05 **p** 06. C W Highland Region *Arg* 05–15; rtd 15. *4 Kearan Road, Kinlochleven, Argyll PH50 4QU* T: (01855) 831444 E: donaldd@btinternet.com

DAVIDSON, Hilary. *See* DAVIDSON, Charles Hilary

DAVIDSON, Trevor John. b 49. CertEd. Oak Hill Th Coll 80. **d** 85 **p** 86. C Drypool *York* 85–88; V Bessingby 88–97; V Carnaby 88–97; Chapl Bridlington and Distr Gen Hosp 88–94; Chapl E Yorks Community Healthcare NHS Trust 94–97; V Felling *Dur* 97–14; CUF Projects Officer 97–14; rtd 14; PtO *Dur* from 15. *10 Alder Grove, Seaham SR7 7RT* T: 0191-435 5685 M: 07447-772070 E: revtjd@gmail.com

DAVIE (*née* JONES), Canon Alyson Elizabeth. b 58. Ex Univ BA 86. Wycliffe Hall Ox 86. **d** 88 **p** 94. Par Dn Ipswich St Fran *St E* 88–92; PtO *Ox* 92–93; St Alb 93–94; NSM E Barnet 94–97; Asst Chapl Oak Hill Th Coll 94–96; P-in-c The Mundens w Sacombe *St Alb* 97–06; V St Paul's Cray St Barn *Roch* 06–14; P-in-c Meopham w Nurstead 14–19; R from 19; RD Cobham

from 18; Hon Can Roch Cathl from 18. *The Rectory, Shipley Hills Road, Meopham, Gravesend DA13 0AD* T: (01474) 812068 E: alyson@stjohnsmeopham.co.uk

DAVIE, Peter Edward Sidney. b 36. LSE BSc 57 Birm Univ MA 73 K Coll Lon MPhil 78 Kent Univ PhD 90. Coll of Resurr Mirfield 57. **d** 60 **p** 61. C De Beauvoir Town St Pet *Lon* 60–63; C-in-c Godshill CD *Portsm* 63–67; R Upton St Leonards *Glouc* 67–73; Sen Lect Ch Ch Coll of HE Cant 73–98; Prin Lect Cant Ch Ch Univ Coll 98–01; rtd 01; Hon C Cant St Pet w St Alphege and St Marg etc 79–10; PtO 10–16; *Leeds* from 17. *Middle Cottage, Manor Heath Road, Halifax HX3 0EB* T: (01422) 751873 E: pedavie@dircon.co.uk *or* peteresdavie@talktalk.net

DAVIE, Canon Stephen Peter. b 52. S Bank Poly BA 75 Spurgeon's Coll PhD 03 MRTPI 77. Oak Hill Th Coll BA 93. **d** 93 **p** 94. C Luton Ch Ch *Roch* 93–97; R Cobham w Luddesdowne and Dode 97–04; P-in-c Horley *S'wark* 04–08; TR 08–12; P-in-c Tong *Bradf* 12–14; *Leeds* 14; AD N Bradford 14; Dir Bradf Sch of Min 14–18; Hon Can Bradf Cathl 13–14; *Leeds* 14–18; rtd 18; PtO *Sheff* from 18. *93 The Village, Holme, Holmfirth HD9 2QG* T: (01484) 684973 M: 07918-654956

DAVIES, Adrian. *See* DAVIES, Glanmor Adrian

DAVIES, Adrian Paul. b 43. K Coll Lon. **d** 69 **p** 70. C Nottingham St Mary *S'well* 69–74; C Gt w Lt Billing *Pet* 74–75; P-in-c Marholm 75–82; R Castor 75; R Castor w Sutton and Upton 76–82; V Byker St Mich w St Lawr *Newc* 82–94; rtd 95. *27 Clougha Avenue, Halton, Lancaster LA2 6NR* T: (01524) 811141

DAVIES, Alan. *See* DAVIES, James Alan

DAVIES, Alan Douglas. b 49. ERMC 08. **d** 10 **p** 11. NSM Downham Market and Crimplesham w Stradsett *Ely* 10–19; NSM Downham Market and Stradsett from 19. *The Lodge, Wallington Hall, Runcton Holme, King's Lynn PE33 0EP* T: (01553) 810675 E: fralandavies@hotmail.co.uk

DAVIES, Alastair John. b 56. Nottm Univ BA MTh. Westcott Ho Cam. **d** 84 **p** 85. C Eltham St Jo *S'wark* 84–87; C Dulwich St Barn 87–89; Chapl RAF 89–07; P-in-c Lyneham w Bradenstoke *Sarum* 01–03; Sen Chapl R United Hosps Bath NHS Foundn Trust 07–17; rtd 17; PtO *Bris* from 17; *Eur* from 17; Spiritual Dir Cursillo *Bris* from 17. *8 Blicks Close, Hullavington, Chippenham SN14 6HQ* E: alastair.davies@icloud.com

DAVIES, Mrs Alison Margaret. b 57. Nottm Univ BA 78. STETS 96. **d** 99 **p** 00. NSM Win St Barn 99–04; PtO 04–07; *Nor* 07–10 and 13; Chapl S Lon Healthcare NHS Trust 10–13; PtO *St Alb* from 16. *Broadgate, Hillside Road, Leighton Buzzard LU7 3BU*

DAVIES, Mrs Allison Claire. b 65. Qu Coll Birm 12. **d** 15 **p** 16. NSM Redditch H Trin *Worc* 15–17; C 17–19; V Eckington from 19. *The Vicarage, Drakes Bridge Road, Eckington, Pershore WR10 3BN*

DAVIES, Andrew John. *See* GRACE, Andrew John

DAVIES, Anthony. *See* DAVIES, David Anthony

DAVIES, Anthony. *See* DAVIES, Vincent Anthony

DAVIES, Anthony Paul. b 56. Univ of Wales (Swansea) BSc 76 CEng 85. St Mich Coll Llan 03. **d** 06 **p** 07. NSM Penllergaer *S & B* 06–07; NSM Gorseinon 07–12; PtO from 12; *B & W* from 16. *The Gate House, 1 Westend Court, Frome BA11 1ET* T: (01373) 473668 M: 07855-237866 E: anthonypdavies@yahoo.com

DAVIES, Barry Lewis. b 46. Boro Road Teacher Tr Coll CertEd 69 Lon Inst of Educn DipEd 84 MA 86. STETS 02. **d** 05 **p** 06. NSM Hardington Vale *B & W* 05–08; rtd 08; PtO *B & W* 09–13; *Bris* 10–15; Chapl Avon and Somerset Constabulary *B & W* from 10; Chapl Partis Coll Bath 10–13; NSM Mells w Buckland Dinham, Elm, Whatley etc *B & W* from 13. *3 The Lays, Goose Street, Beckington, Frome BA11 6RS* T: (01373) 831344 E: bandkdavies@msn.com

DAVIES, Beth. *See* DAVIES, Elizabeth

DAVIES, Sister Beverley. b 55. **d** 11 **p** 12. NSM Leic Presentation 11–14; PtO from 14; Chapl LOROS Hospice from 15; Chapl Qu Th Foundn Birm from 15. *St Matthew's House, 25 Kamloops Crescent, Leicester LE1 2HX* T: 0116-253 9158

DAVIES, Catharine Mary. *See* FURLONG, Catharine Mary

DAVIES, Mrs Catherine Olive Sarah Skeel. b 61. Univ of Wales (Cardiff) BA 84. WMMTC 03. **d** 06 **p** 07. NSM Wootton Wawen and Claverdon w Preston Bagot *Cov* 06–09; NSM Barford w Wasperton and Sherbourne and Hampton Lucy w Charlecote and Loxley 09–13; PtO 13–15; NSM Launde Abbey *Leic* from 15; PtO *Pet* from 15. *Launde Abbey, Launde Road, Launde, Leicester LE7 9XB* T: (01572) 717254 E: revcathydavies@aol.com

DAVIES, Ceri John. b 61. Univ of Wales (Lamp) BA 91 Univ of Wales (Abth) PGCE 92 Univ of Wales (Cardiff)

BTh 00. St Mich Coll Llan 97. **d** 00 **p** 01. C Carmarthen St Dav *St D* 00–03; TV Llanelli 03–11; C Cynwyl Elfed w Newchurch and Trelech a'r Betws 11–14; PtO from 14. *79-80 Priory Street, Carmarthen SA31 1NU* T: (01267) 233976 E: cdavies465@btinternet.com

DAVIES, Chris. *See* DAVIES, David Christopher

DAVIES, Christopher Edward. b 72. **d** 03 **p** 04. OLM Bilston *Lich* 03–18; TV Bloxwich from 18. *6 Cresswell Crescent, Walsall WS3 2UW* M: 07952-196204

DAVIES, Christopher John. b 55. St Alb Minl Tr Scheme 83. **d** 86 **p** 87. C Tooting All SS *S'wark* 86–90; V Malden St Jas 90–96; RD Kingston 92–96; TR Wimbledon 96–06; RD Humbleyard 08–15; rtd 16; C Foulsham, Guestwick, Stibbard, Themelthorpe etc *Nor* 17; C N Elmham, Billingford, Bintree, Guist etc 17; TV Heart of Norfolk from 17. *The Old Rectory, Deopham Road, Morley St Botolph, Wymondham NR18 9DB* M: 07702-865412 E: cjdoldirectory@gmail.com

DAVIES, Christopher Mark. b 76. Essex Univ BA 97 Sheff Univ BA 13 Southn Inst DipSW 02. Coll of Resurr Mirfield 11. **d** 13 **p** 14. C Gt Grimsby St Mary and St Jas *Linc* 13–16; R Loughton St Jo *Chelmsf* from 16. *St John's Rectory, Church Lane, Loughton IG10 1PD* E: cmdavies76@yahoo.co.uk

DAVIES, David Anthony. b 57. Thames Poly BSc 81 MRICS 84. Coll of Resurr Mirfield 85. **d** 88 **p** 89. C Stalybridge *Man* 88–91; C Swinton and Pendlebury 91–92 and 01–02; TV 92–01; V Tonge Moor from 02. *St Augustine's Vicarage, Redthorpe Close, Bolton BL2 2PQ* T/F: (01204) 523899 M: 07866-359864 E: tony@davieses.co.uk

DAVIES, David Berwyn. b 42. St Mich Coll Llan 95. **d** 96 **p** 97. C Llanelli *St D* 96–98; I Llanerch Aeron w Ciliau Aeron and Dihewyd etc 98–07; rtd 07; PtO *St D* from 07. *56 Tyisha Road, Llanelli SA15 1RW* T: (01554) 774391 E: taddavid@aol.com

DAVIES, Canon David Christopher. b 52. Lon Univ BSc 73 UWE MSc 11. Coll of Resurr Mirfield 73. **d** 76 **p** 77. C Bethnal Green St Jo w St Simon *Lon* 76–78; C Bethnal Green St Jo w St Bart 78–80; C-in-c Portsea St Geo CD *Portsm* 80–81; V Portsea St Geo 81–87; Relig Affairs Producer Radio Victory 81–86; Chapl Ham Green Hosp Bris 87–94; Chapl Southmead Hosp Bris 87–94; Chapl Southmead Health Services NHS Trust 94–99; Chapl N Bris NHS Trust 99–05; Hd Spiritual and Past Care 05–13; Hd Spiritual and Past Care Univ Hosps Bris NHS Foundn Trust 05–13; PtO *B & W* 94–13; Hon Can Bris Cathl 99–13; rtd 13; PtO *Bris* from 13. *28 Hortham Lane, Almondsbury, Bristol BS32 4JL* T: (01454) 616608 E: chris.davies1958@talktalk.net

DAVIES, Canon David Jeremy Christopher. b 46. CCC Cam BA 68 MA 72. Westcott Ho Cam 68. **d** 71 **p** 72. C Stepney St Dunstan and All SS *Lon* 71–74; Chapl Qu Mary Coll 74–78; Chapl Univ of Wales (Cardiff) *Llan* 78–85; Can Res Sarum Cathl 85–12; rtd 12; PtO *Sarum* from 13. *The Old Chapel, The Street, Farley, Salisbury SP5 1AB* T: (01722) 712879 E: jeremy@theoldchapelfarley.co.uk *or* jeremy.davies1000@gmail.com

DAVIES, Canon David Michael Cole. b 44. St D Coll Lamp. **d** 68 **p** 69. C Carmarthen St Pet *St D* 68–72; R Dinas 72–77; V Ty-Croes w Saron 77–79; V Llanedi w Tycroes and Saron 80–90; RD Dyffryn Aman 85–90; V Dafen and Llwynhendy 90–94; V Dafen 94–08; Hon Can St D Cathl 00–08; rtd 08; PtO *St D* from 09. *30 Bro'r Dderwen, Clynderwen SA66 7NR* E: dcmcd@aol.com *or* revdmcd@btinternet.com

DAVIES, David Peter. b 47. **d** 13 **p** 14. NSM Worc City 13–14; NSM Worc St Nic and All SS w St Helen 14–15; NSM Claines St Jo from 15; NSM Worc St Geo w St Mary Magd from 15. *44 Battenhall Rise, Worcester WR5 2DE* T: (01905) 356714 E: peterdaviesworcs@waitrose.com

DAVIES, Canon Dewi Gwynfor. b 56. Univ of Wales (Abth) BD 92 MTh 98 RIBA 81. **d** 98 **p** 99. C Llangunnor w Cwmffrwd *St D* 98–99; P-in-c Elerch w Penrhyncoch w Capel Bangor and Goginan 99–00; P-in-c Cil-y-Cwm and Ystrad-ffin w Rhandir-mwyn etc 00–01; V 01–03; V Llanedi w Tycroes and Saron 03–09; V Pen-bre from 09; AD Cydweli 15–18; Hon Can St D Cathl from 18. *The Vicarage, Ar-y-bryn, Pembrey, Burry Port SA16 0AJ* T: (01554) 833766 E: frdewivicarage@btinternet.com

DAVIES, The Ven Dorrien Paul. b 64. Univ of Wales (Lamp) BA 95. Llan Dioc Tr Scheme 86. **d** 88 **p** 89. C Llanelli *St D* 88–91; V Llanfihangel Ystrad and Cilcennin w Trefilan etc 91–99; V St Dogmael's w Moylgrove and Monington w Meline 99–10; TV Dewisland 10–17; Adn Carmarthen from 17; P-in-c St Clears w Llangynin and Llanddowror etc 18. *The New Vicarage, St Clears, Carmarthen SA33 4ED* T: (01994) 231611 M: 07384-631292 E: archdeacon.carmarthen@churchinwales.org.uk

DAVIES, Prof Douglas James. b 47. St Jo Coll Dur BA 69 St Pet Coll Ox MLitt 72 Nottm Univ PhD 80 DLitt 04 Uppsala Univ Hon DTh 98. Cranmer Hall Dur 71. **d** 75 **p** 76. Lect Nottm Univ 75–97; Sen Lect 90–97; Hon C Wollaton *S'well* 75–83; Hon C Attenborough 83–85; Hon C E Leake 85–91; Hon C Daybrook 91–97; Prof RS Nottm Univ 93–97; Prin SS Hild and Bede Coll Dur 97–00; Prof Th Dur Univ from 97; Prof Study of Relig Dur Univ from 00; PtO *Dur* from 13. *Department of Theology and Religion, Abbey House, Palace Green, Durham DH1 3RS* T: 0191-375 7697 E: douglas.davies@durham.ac.uk

DAVIES, Canon Douglas Tudor. b 20. Univ of Wales (Ban) BA 44. Coll of Resurr Mirfield 44. **d** 46 **p** 47. C Swansea Ch Ch *S & B* 46–52; C Oystermouth 52–57; R Llangynllo and Bleddfa 57–63; C-in-c Treboeth CD 63–65; V Treboeth 65–90; RD Penderi 78–90; Hon Can Brecon Cathl 82–83; Can Brecon Cathl 83–90; rtd 90. *245A Swansea Road, Waunarlwydd, Swansea SA5 4SN* T: (01792) 879587

DAVIES, Edna Nansi Margaret. b 37. **d** 97 **p** 98. NSM Netherwent *Mon* 97–01; NSM Caerwent w Dinham and Llanfair Discoed etc 01–13; NSM Caerwent w Dinham and Llanvair Discoed etc 13–14; NSM Wentwood 14–17; rtd 17; PtO *Mon* from 17. *Junipers, Court House Road, LLanfair Discoed, Chepstow NP16 6LW* T: (01633) 400519 E: enm.davies@icloud.com

DAVIES, Edward Earl. b 40. Llan Dioc Tr Scheme 88. **d** 90 **p** 91. C Pontypridd St Cath w St Matt *Llan* 90–93; V Ferndale w Maerdy 93–00; V Cardiff Ch Ch Roath Park 00–09; rtd 09; PtO *Llan* from 10. *4 St Augustine Road, Heath, Cardiff CF14 4BD* T: (029) 2061 0054 E: eeandsidavies@outlook.com

DAVIES, Edward Trevor. b 37. MRSC 62 MInstE 74 CEng 78. NOC 92. **d** 95 **p** 96. Hon Asst Chapl Countess of Chester Hosp NHS Foundn Trust 95–02; Chapl 02–05; NSM Waverton *Ches* 95–99; NSM Hargrave 99–00; C Bunbury and Tilstone Fearnall 00–02; NSM 02–03; PtO 05–10 and from 11; C Waverton w Aldford and Bruera 10–11; rtd 11. *Athergreen, 5 Allansford Avenue, Waverton, Chester CH3 7QH* T: (01244) 332106 E: etdavies1@btinternet.com

DAVIES, Canon Edward William Llewellyn. b 51. St Jo Coll Nottm BTh 77. **d** 78 **p** 79. C Southsea St Jude *Portsm* 78–81; C Alverstoke 81–84; R Abbas and Templecombe w Horsington *B & W* 84–89; PtO *Ches* 89–99; V Sutton St Jas 99–13; RD Macclesfield 05–12; Warden Foxhill Retreat and Conf Cen 13–15; Asst Warden of Readers 02–15; Hon Can Ches Cathl 10–15; rtd 15; PtO *Ches* from 15. *37 Minor Avenue, Lyme Green, Macclesfield SK11 0LQ* T: (01260) 253671 E: taffy@parishpump.co.uk

DAVIES, Eileen. *See* DAVIES, Rachel Hannah Eileen

DAVIES, Elizabeth. b 60. Trin Coll Carmarthen BA 04 PGCE 06. **d** 16 **p** 17. NSM Llandysul w Bangor Teifi and Llanfairollwyn etc *St D* from 16. *Tynewydd, Gorrig Road, Llandysul SA44 4JP* T: (01559) 362850 M: 07901-716957 E: bethan@cd1340.f9.co.uk

DAVIES, Mrs Elizabeth Jean. b 39. Lon Univ MB, BS 63 MRCS 63 LRCP 63. Chich Th Coll 86. **d** 89 **p** 95. Par Dn Southwick St Mich *Chich* 89–91; Par Dn Littlehampton and Wick 91–95; C Seaford w Sutton 95–97; NSM E Preston w Kingston 97–04; rtd 99; P-in-c Everton and Mattersey w Clayworth *S'well* 04–05; PtO from 06. *16 Blackstope Lane, Retford DN22 6NF* T: (01777) 711513

DAVIES, Canon Emma Louise. b 67. St Andr Univ MA 89. Ripon Coll Cuddesdon 05. **d** 07 **p** 08. C Market Harborough and The Transfiguration etc *Leic* 07–10; TV Avon-Swift from 10; Hon Can Leic Cathl from 18. *The Rectory, Church Lane, Gilmorton, Lutterworth LE17 5LU* T: (01455) 553475 E: emma.davies4@sky.com

DAVIES, Mrs Felicity Ann. b 58. Wycliffe Hall Ox. **d** 11 **p** 12. C Wadhurst *Chich* 11–14; C Stonegate 11–14; C Tidebrook 11–14; R Ickenham *Lon* from 14. *St Giles's Rectory, 38 Swakeleys Road, Ickenham, Uxbridge UB10 8BE* T: (01895) 622970 E: fadavies58@gmail.com

DAVIES, Frances Elizabeth. b 38. BA CertEd. Moray Ord Course. **d** 95. Hon C Thurso *Mor* 95–12; Hon C Wick 95–12; PtO from 12. *22 Granville Crescent, Thurso, Caithness KW14 7NP* T: (01847) 892386 E: reallyfed@yahoo.co.uk

DAVIES, Gareth Clement. b 61. LSE BSc(Econ) 83 Open Univ LLB 03. Westcott Ho Cam 14. **d** 16 **p** 17. C Mortlake w E Sheen *S'wark* 16–18; C W Dulwich All SS from 18. *27 Maitland Road, London SE26 5NN* T: (020) 8676 0184 *or* 8676 4550 E: revd.gareth.davies@icloud.com

DAVIES, Gareth Rhys. b 51. Oak Hill Th Coll. **d** 83 **p** 84. C Gt Warley Ch Ch *Chelmsf* 83–86; C Oxhey All SS *St Alb* 86–90; C Aldridge *Lich* 90–99; V Colney Heath St Mark *St Alb* 99–00; V Sneyd Green *Lich* 00–16; Bp's Adv on Healing 09–15; rtd 16. *10 Durness Street, Thurso KW14 8BQ*

DAVIES, George William. b 51. Open Univ BA 74 MPhil 89 MCIPD. Sarum & Wells Th Coll 83. **d** 85 **p** 86.

C Mansfield SS Pet and Paul *S'well* 85–89; Chapl Cen Notts HA 86–89; P-in-c Fobbing and Ind Chapl *Chelmsf* 89–96; Chapl Thurrock Lakeside Shopping Cen 93–96; R Mottingham St Andr w St Alban *S'wark* 96–04; V Lamorbey H Trin *Roch* 04–12; Chapl Rose Bruford Coll 04–12; rtd 12; PtO *S'well* 16–17. *106 Kirklington Road, Rufford Grange, Rainworth NG21 0JX* T: (01623) 490653 E: georgeandkatedavies@btinternet.com

DAVIES, Glanmor Adrian. b 51. St D Coll Lamp. **d** 73 **p** 75. C Llanstadwel *St D* 73–78; R Dinas w Llanllawer and Pontfaen w Morfil etc 78–84; V Lamphey w Hodgeston 84–85; V Lamphey w Hodgeston and Carew 85–03; V Borth and Eglwys-fach w Llangynfelyn 03–06; PtO from 16. *4 Somerset Place, Park Road, Tenby SA70 7NF* T: (01834) 843316 E: judymcg@hotmail.co.uk

✠**DAVIES, The Most Revd Glenn Naunton.** b 50. Sydney Univ BSc 72 Sheff Univ PhD 88. Westmr Th Sem (USA) BD 78 ThM 79. **d** 81 **p** 81 **c** 01. Australia 81–85; Hon C Fulwood *Sheff* 85–87; Hon C Lodge Moor St Luke 86–87; Lect Moore Th Coll Australia 87–95; R Miranda 95–01; Bp N Sydney 01–13; Abp from 13. *PO Box Q190, Queen Victoria Building, Sydney NSW 1230, Australia* T: (0061) (2) 9265 1555 F: 9261 1170 E: registry@sydney.anglican.asn.au

DAVIES, Glyndwr George. b 36. Glouc Sch of Min 88. **d** 91 **p** 92. NSM Clodock and Longtown w Craswall, Llanveynoe etc *Heref* 91–02; rtd 02; PtO *Heref* 02–12. *White House Farm, Llanfihangel Crucorney, Abergavenny NP7 8HW* T: (01873) 890251

DAVIES, The Ven Graham James. b 35. Univ of Wales BD 72 St D Coll Lamp BA 56. St Mich Coll Llan 56 Episc Th Sch Cam Mass 58. **d** 59 **p** 60. C Johnston w Steynton *St D* 59–62; C Llangathen w Llanfihangel Cilfargen 62–64; Min Can St D Cathl 64–66; R Burton 66–71; R Hubberston 71–74; Hon C Lenham w Boughton Malherbe *Cant* 74–80; V Cwmdauddwr w St Harmon and Llanwrthwl *S & B* 80–86; V Cydweli and Llandyfaelog *St D* 86–97; Can St D Cathl 92–02; Adn St D 96–02; V Steynton 97–02; rtd 02. *16 Freshwater East Road, Lamphey, Pembroke SA71 5JX* T: (01646) 672272

DAVIES, Huw. *See* DAVIES, Peter Huw

DAVIES, Hywel John. b 45. Univ of Wales (Abth) BA 67 Univ of Wales (Ban) DipEd 68 Univ of Wales (Cardiff) MA 90 Univ of Wales (Ban) BTh 99. St Mich Coll Llan 94 Qu Coll Birm 96. **d** 97 **p** 98. Min Can Ban Cathl 97–98; C Llandudno 98–99; LtO *Llan* 99–03; NSM Canton Cardiff 03–04; P-in-c Llanarthne and Llanddarog *St D* 04–07; Chapl Coleg Sir Gâr 04–07; rtd 07; P-in-c Cardiff Dewi Sant *Llan* 08–10; PtO from 10; *Eur* from 17. *68 Glas y Gors, Cwmbach, Aberdare CF44 0BQ* T: (01685) 378457 E: hywel33@btinternet.com

DAVIES, Canon Ian. b 54. Sheff Hallam Univ BA 80 Univ of Wales (Cardiff) MSc(Econ) 86 MBA 92 Bris Univ PhD 01 CQSW 80. Wycliffe Hall Ox 02. **d** 04 **p** 05. C Swansea St Pet *S & B* 04–06; C Waunarllwydd 06–07; P-in-c 07–10; V from 10; Hon Can Brecon Cathl from 12; Bp's Officer for Formation from 18. *The New Vicarage, 59A Victoria Road, Waunarlwydd, Swansea SA5 4SY* T: (01792) 874286 M: 07779-145267 E: iandavies12@hotmail.com

DAVIES, Ian. b 45. Man Coll of Educn TCert 74 Open Univ BA 79. Carl Dioc Tr Inst 88. **d** 91 **p** 92. NSM Harraby *Carl* 91–95; C Barrow St Jo 95–96; P-in-c 96–00; P-in-c Beetham and Youth and Sch Support Officer 00–05; V Marown *S & M* 05–11; rtd 11; PtO *Dur* from 12. *10 Capulet Terrace, Sunderland SR2 8JL* T: 0191-514 3055 E: reviand@manx.net

DAVIES, Canon Ian Elliott. b 64. Univ of Wales (Ban) BD 85. Ridley Hall Cam 86. **d** 88 **p** 89. C Baglan *Llan* 88–90; C Skewen 90–96; C St Marylebone All SS *Lon* 96–01; R Hollywood St Thos USA from 02; Can Los Angeles from 14. *St Thomas's Church, 7501 Hollywood Boulevard, Hollywood CA 90046, USA* T: (001) (323) 876 2102 F: 876 7738 E: frdavies@saintthomashollywood.org

DAVIES, Mrs Jacqueline Ann. b 42. Bris Univ BA 64 CertEd 65 Univ of Wales (Lamp) MA 99. EMMTC 84 St As MinI Tr Course 97. **d** 98 **p** 99. NSM Llanfair DC, Derwen, Llanelidan and Efenechtyd *St As* 98–00; PtO 00–14; *Chich* 12–17; *B & W* from 16. *2 Delphinium Drive, Langport TA10 9TN* T: (01458) 259300

DAVIES, James Alan. b 38. Lambeth STh 95. St Jo Coll Nottm. **d** 83 **p** 84. C Fletchamstead *Cov* 83–87; P-in-c Hartshill 87–89; V 89–93; V E Green 93–03; rtd 03; Hon C Mickleton, Willersey, Saintbury etc *Glouc* 04–05; PtO *Cov* from 05. *5 Margetts Close, Kenilworth CV8 1EN* T: (01926) 854337 E: a.davies861@btinternet.com

DAVIES, James William. b 51. Trin Hall Cam BA 72 MA 76 St Jo Coll Dur BA 79. Cranmer Hall Dur 77. **d** 80 **p** 81. C Croydon Ch Ch Broad Green *Cant* 80–83; CMS 83–86; Chapl Bethany Sch Goudhurst 86–90; P-in-c Parkstone St Luke *Sarum* 90–00;

Hon C Bournemouth St Andr *Win* from 05; PtO *Sarum* from 05. *8 Newton Road, Swanage BH19 2DZ* T: (01929) 475770

DAVIES, Preb Jane Ann. b 58. Coll of Ripon & York St Jo MA 97. Aston Tr Scheme 91 WMMTC 93 NOC 94. **d** 96 **p** 97. NSM Heref S Wye 96–97; C 97–00; P-in-c Bishop's Frome w Castle Frome and Fromes Hill 00–08; P-in-c Acton Beauchamp and Evesbatch w Stanford Bishop 00–08; P-in-c Stoke Lacy, Moreton Jeffries w Much Cowarne etc 00–08; V Frome Valley 09–12; P-in-c Lugwardine w Bartestree, Weston Beggard etc 12; P-in-c Withington w Westhide 12; R Bartestree Cross 12–18; V Canon Pyon w King's Pyon, Birley and Wellington from 18; Preb Heref Cathl from 10. *The Vicarage, Brookside, Canon Pyon, Hereford HR4 8NY* T: (01432) 830581 E: trendy.rev2@btinternet.com

DAVIES, Jeffrey William. b 45. St Cath Coll Cam BA 66 MA 69 LLM 67 Liv Univ MTh 07 Solicitor 69. NOC 01. **d** 04 **p** 05. NSM Ramsbottom and Edenfield *Man* 04–11; NSM Heaton Ch Ch w Halliwell St Marg 11–14; rtd 14; PtO *Man* from 14. *44 Higher Dunscar, Egerton, Bolton BL7 9TF* T/F: (01204) 412503 E: jeffdavies1@ntlworld.com

DAVIES, Jeremy. *See* DAVIES, David Jeremy Christopher

DAVIES, Joanna. b 65. St Mellitus Coll. **d** 10 **p** 11. C Onslow Square and S Kensington St Aug *Lon* 10–18; Chapl HM Pris Pentonville from 18; PtO *Lon* from 18. *HM Prison Pentonville, Caledonian Road, London N7 8TT* T: (020) 7023 7217 E: jo.davies@justice.gov.uk

DAVIES, John. b 62. Univ of Wales (Cardiff) BA 88. Ridley Hall Cam 98. **d** 00 **p** 01. C Wavertree H Trin *Liv* 00–04; P-in-c W Derby Gd Shep 04–09; V 09–10; TV Okehampton w Inwardleigh, Bratton Clovelly etc *Ex* 10–11; TV Okehampton, Inwardleigh, Belstone, Sourton etc 12–13; V Whitegate w Lt Budworth *Ches* 13–14; R Cam Vale *B & W* 14–18; P-in-c Clapham-with-Keasden and Austwick *Leeds* from 18. *The Vicarage, Clapham Road, Austwick, Lancaster LA2 8BE* T: (01524) 805928 E: john.davies@leeds.anglican.org

DAVIES, John. *See* PAGE DAVIES, David John

DAVIES, John. *See* DAVIES, Kenneth John

✠**DAVIES, The Most Revd John David Edward.** b 53. Southn Univ LLB 74 Univ of Wales (Cardiff) LLM 95. St Mich Coll Llan 82. **d** 84 **p** 85 **c** 08. C Chepstow *Mon* 84–86; C-in-c Michaelston-y-Fedw and Rudry 86–89; R Bedwas and Rudry 89–95; V Maindee Newport 95–00; Dean Brecon and V Brecon St Mary w Llanddew *S & B* 00–08; P-in-c Cynog Honddu 05–08; Bp *S & B* from 08; Abp Wales from 17. *Ely Tower, Castle Square, Brecon LD3 9DJ* T: (01874) 622008 E: bishop.swanbrec@churchinwales.org.uk

✠**DAVIES, The Rt Revd John Dudley.** b 27. Trin Coll Cam BA 51 MA 63. Linc Th Coll 52. **d** 53 **p** 54 **c** 87. C Leeds Halton St Wilfrid *Ripon* 53–56; C Yeoville S Africa 57; R Evander 57–61; R Empangeni 61–63; Chapl Witwatersrand Univ 63–71; Sec Chapls in HE Gen Syn Bd of Educn 71–74; P-in-c Keele *Lich* 74–76; Chapl Keele Univ 74–76; Prin USPG Coll of the Ascension Selly Oak 76–81; Preb Lich Cathl 76–87; Can Res, Preb and Sacr St As Cathl 82–85; Dioc Missr 82–87; V Llanrhaeadr-ym-Mochnant, Llanarmon, Pennant etc 85–87; Suff Bp Shrewsbury *Lich* 87–92; rtd 94; PtO *Lich* 05–14; *St As* from 09. *Nyddfa, By-Pass Road, Gobowen, Oswestry SY11 3NG* T/F: (01691) 653434 E: davies.johnd@btinternet.com

DAVIES, John Gwylim. b 27. Ripon Hall Ox 67. **d** 70 **p** 71. C Ox St Mich 70–71; C Ox St Mich w St Martin and All SS 71–72; TV New Windsor 73–77; R Hagley *Worc* 77–83; TV Littleham w Exmouth *Ex* 83–92; Asst Dioc Stewardship Adv 83–92; rtd 92; PtO *Ex* from 92. *Harding House, 101 Salterton Road, Exmouth EX8 2NG* E: daviesjg70@gmail.com

DAVIES, The Very Revd John Harverd. b 57. Keble Coll Ox BA 80 MA 84 CCC Cam MPhil 82 Lanc Univ PhD. Westcott Ho Cam 82. **d** 84 **p** 85. C Liv Our Lady and St Nic w St Anne 84–87; C Pet St Jo 87–90; Min Can Pet Cathl 88–90; V Anfield St Marg *Liv* 90–94; Chapl, Fell and Lect Keble Coll Ox 94–99; V Melbourne *Derby* 99–10; P-in-c Ticknall, Smisby and Stanton by Bridge etc 07–10; V Melbourne, Ticknall, Smisby and Stanton 10; Dioc Dir of Ords 00–09; Hon Can Derby Cathl 10; Dean Derby 10–16; Dean Wells *B & W* from 16. *The Dean's Lodging, 25 The Liberty, Wells BA5 2SZ* T: (01749) 670278 E: thedeanofwells@gmail.com

DAVIES, Canon John Howard. b 29. St Jo Coll Cam BA 50 MA 54 Nottm Univ BD 62. Westcott Ho Cam 54. **d** 55 **p** 56. Succ Derby Cathl 55–58; Chapl Westcott Ho Cam 58–63; Lect Th Southn Univ 63–81; LtO *Win* 63–81; Sen Lect 74–81; Dir Th and RS Southn Univ 81–94; Can Th Win Cathl 81–91; Hon C Southampton St Alb 88–91; Hon C Swaythling 91–94; rtd 94. *13 Glen Eyre Road, Southampton SO16 3GA* T: (023) 8067 9359

DAVIES, John Hugh Conwy. b 42. Bris Univ BSc 64 PhD 67 CEng 72 MICE 72. Linc Th Coll 84. **d** 86 **p** 87. C Limber Magna w Brocklesby *Linc* 86–89; R Wickenby Gp 89–94; R Denbigh *St As* 94–00; V Llanrhaeadr-ym-Mochnant etc 01–07; rtd 07; PtO *St As* 09–14; from 16. *2 Delphinium Drive, Langport TA10 9TN* T: (01458) 259300 E: jackiejohnlla@gmail.com

DAVIES, Canon John Hywel Morgan. b 45. St D Coll Lamp BA 71 LTh 73. **d** 73 **p** 74. C Milford Haven *St D* 73–77; V 89–11; R Castlemartin w Warren and Angle etc 77–82; R Walton W w Talbenny and Haroldston W 82–89; Can St D Cathl 03–11; rtd 11; PtO *St D* from 11. *6 Waterloo Road, Hakin, Milford Haven SA73 3PB* T: (01646) 692766 E: johnmorgandavies@talk21.com

DAVIES, John Keith. b 33. St Mich Coll Llan 80. **d** 82 **p** 83. C Llanbadarn Fawr w Capel Bangor and Goginan *St D* 82–84; V Llandygwydd and Cenarth w Cilrhedyn etc 84–89; V Abergwili w Llanfihangel-uwch-Gwili etc 89–98; RD Carmarthen 93–98; rtd 98. *Tanyfron, 81 Hafod Cwnin, Carmarthen SA31 2AS* T: (01267) 223931 E: j50ked@yahoo.co.uk

✠**DAVIES, The Rt Revd John Stewart.** b 43. Univ of Wales BA 72 Qu Coll Cam MLitt 74. Westcott Ho Cam 72. **d** 74 **p** 75 **c** 99. C Hawarden *St As* 74–78; Tutor St Deiniol's Lib Hawarden 76–83; V Rhosymedre *St As* 78–87; Dir Dioc Minl Tr Course 83–93; Warden of Ords *St As* 83–91; Hon Can St As Cathl 86–91; V Mold 87–92; Adn St As 91–99; R Llandyrnog and Llangwyfan 92–99; Bp St As 99–08; rtd 09; PtO *St As* from 09. *17 Pont y Bedol, Llanrhaeadr, Denbigh LL16 4NF* T: (01745) 890899 E: johnstewartdavies@gmail.com

DAVIES, The Ven Jonathan Byron. b 69. Univ of Wales (Cardiff) BTh 95. St Mich Coll Llan 94. **d** 96 **p** 97. C Betws w Ammanford *St D* 96–99; Dioc Youth Chapl 96–99; C Newton St Pet *S & B* 99–00; P-in-c Swansea St Luke 03–05; V Manselton and Cwmbwrla 05–15; AD Penderi 12–15; Chapl Mid and W Wales Fire and Rescue Service 05–16; Can Res Brecon Cathl *S & B* from 15; V Llwynderw from 15; Adn Gower from 16. *The Vicarage, Fairwood Road, West Cross, Swansea SA3 5JP* T: (01792) 512747 E: archdeacon.gower@churchinwales.org.uk

DAVIES, Judith. b 54. Man Univ BA 75. WEMTC 97. **d** 00 **p** 01. C Harlescott *Lich* 00–04; Chapl Shrewsbury and Telford NHS Trust 04–05; Asst Chapl Severn Hospice Shrewsbury 05–06; PtO *Heref* 05–15; TV Wenlock 06–14; rtd 14; PtO *Lich* from 15. *3 Carnforth Close, Shrewsbury SY3 9QW* E: judydaviesrev@gmail.com

DAVIES, Prof Julia Mary. b 44. Ex Univ BA 65 FCIPD 00. **d** 04 **p** 05. OLM Deane *Man* 04–14; Hon Assoc Dioc Dir of Ords from 10; PtO from 15. *15 Newland Drive, Bolton BL5 1DS* T: (01204) 660260 M: 07966-528877

DAVIES, Justin Wyn. Cam Coll of Art & Tech BA 82. **d** 16 **p** 17. NSM Bishopston *S & B* 16–18; C SW Gower from 18. *The Rectory, Knelston, Reynoldston, Swansea SA3 1AR* M: 07881-501292 E: justindavies26@gmail.com

DAVIES, Mrs Karen Elizabeth. b 44. Univ of Wales (Abth) BA 66 Univ of Wales (Ban) MEd 85. **d** 11 **p** 12. OLM Criftins w Dudleston and Welsh Frankton *Lich* 11–16; rtd 16; PtO *Lich* from 16; RD Ellesmere 15–17. *Horseshoe Cottage, Horseshoe Lane, Eastwick, Ellesmere SY12 9JT* T: (01691) 690346 M: 07787-324953 E: karendavies2000@btinternet.com *or* karendavies2000@gmail.com

DAVIES, Keith. *See* BERRY-DAVIES, Charles William Keith
DAVIES, Keith. *See* DAVIES, John Keith
DAVIES, Kenneth John. b 42. Ripon Coll Cuddesdon 79. **d** 80 **p** 81. C Buckingham *Ox* 80–83; V Birstall *Wakef* 83–91; TV Crookes St Thos *Sheff* 91–94; TR Huntington *York* 94–07; rtd 07; PtO *York* from 14. *18 Hall Rise, Haxby, York YO32 3LP* T: (01904) 768211

DAVIES, Canon Kevin Godfrey. b 62. Univ Coll Ox BA 84 MA 87. Trin Coll Bris BA 93. **d** 93 **p** 94. C Otley *Bradf* 93–97; P-in-c Scotby *Carl* 97–00; P-in-c Scotby and Cotehill w Cumwhinton 00–02; TR Langtree *Ox* from 02; P-in-c Whitchurch St Mary 02–03; AD Henley 11–16; Hon Can Ch Ch from 17. *The Rectory, Checkendon, Reading RG8 0SR* T: (01491) 680252

DAVIES, Lee. b 76. St Jo Coll Nottm 12. **d** 14 **p** 15. C Andover *Win* 14–17; P-in-c Knight's Enham from 17. *2 Red Cottages, East Anton, Andover SP11 6AA* T: (01264) 333474 M: 07809-682085 E: revlee@daviestribe.co.uk

DAVIES, Leonard Hamblyn Kenneth. b 57. Birm Univ MA 03 Dur Univ MA 06. Sierra Leone Bible Coll 84. **d** 93 **p** 94. C St Geo Cathl Freetown Sierra Leone 93–96; C Freetown St Jo 96–98; P-in-c Freetown H Spirit 98–01; PtO *Worc* 01–02; *Birm* 02–03; *Chelmsf* 03–08; LtO 08–15; Asst Chapl E Lon Univ 08–09; Asst Chapl YMCA 09–10; C Forest

Gate All SS *Chelmsf* 10–15; PtO from 15. *28B High Street, London SW19 2AB* T: (020) 8542 7957 M: 07834-971467 E: kendavies90@hotmail.com

DAVIES, The Ven Lorys Martin. b 36. Univ of Wales (Lamp) BA 57 ALCM 52. Wells Th Coll 57. **d** 59 **p** 60. C Tenby w Gumfreston *St D* 59–62; Asst Chapl Brentwood Sch 62–66; Chapl Solihull Sch 66–68; V Moseley St Mary *Birm* 68–81; Can Res Birm Cathl 81–92; Dioc Dir of Ords 82–90; Adn Bolton *Man* 92–01; Bp's Adv for Hosp Chapl 92–01; Warden of Readers 94–01; rtd 02; PtO *Birm* 04–13; *Worc* from 04. *18 Bilberry Place, Recreation Road, Bromsgrove B61 8DT* T: (01527) 577337

DAVIES, Lynda. b 64. Cov Univ BA 87 CQSW 87 Leic Univ MA 09. ERMC 10. **d** 13 **p** 14. C Oundle w Ashton and Benefield w Glapthorn *Pet* 13–16; C Long Stanton w St Mich *Ely* 16–17; C Over 16–17; C Willingham 16–17; C Fen Drayton w Conington and Lolworth etc 16–17; P-in-c Cottenham 17–18; P-in-c Rampton 17–18; R Cottenham w Rampton from 18. *The Rectory, 6 High Street, Cottenham, Cambridge CB24 8SA* M: 07598-927416 E: revlyndadavies559@gmail.com

DAVIES, Mrs Margaret Adelaide. b 45. Weymouth Coll of Educn CertEd 67. S Dios Minl Tr Scheme 92. **d** 95 **p** 96. NSM Westbury *Sarum* 95–02; NSM White Horse 02–11; TV 07–11; rtd 11; PtO *Sarum* from 12. *20 The Knoll, Westbury BA13 3UB* T: (01373) 228671

✠**DAVIES, The Rt Revd Mark.** b 62. Leeds Univ BA 85. Coll of Resurr Mirfield 86. **d** 89 **p** 90 **c** 08. C Barnsley St Mary *Wakef* 89–95; R Hemsworth 95–96; Dioc Vocations Adv and Asst Dir of Ords 98–06; RD Pontefract 00–06; Hon Can Wakef Cathl 02–06; Adn Rochdale *Man* 06–08; Suff Bp Middleton from 08. *The Hollies, Manchester Road, Rochdale OL11 3QY* T: (01706) 358550 F: 354851 E: bishopmark@manchester.anglican.org

DAVIES, Martin. *See* DAVIES, William Martin
DAVIES, Canon Martyn John. b 60. Chich Th Coll 82. **d** 85 **p** 86. C Llantrisant *Llan* 85–87; C Whitchurch 87–90; V Porth w Trealaw 90–01; R Merthyr Tydfil St Dav 01–10; R Merthyr Tydfil St Dav and Abercanaid 10–12; AD Merthyr Tydfil 04–12; R Peterston-super-Ely w St Brides-super-Ely from 12; P-in-c St Nicholas w Bonvilston and St George-super-Ely from 12; C Pendoylan w Welsh St Donats from 12; AD Vale of Glam from 12; Hon Can Llan Cathl from 16. *The Rectory, Peterston-super-Ely, Cardiff CF5 6LH* T: (01446) 760498 E: fr.martyn@sky.com

DAVIES, Michael. *See* DAVIES, David Michael Cole
DAVIES, Miss Moira Kathleen. b 41. Cant Sch of Min. **d** 88 **p** 94. Par Dn Walmer *Cant* 88–94; C 94–96; P-in-c Somercotes and Grainthorpe w Conisholme *Linc* 96–99; R 99–06; rtd 06; PtO *Linc* 15–18. *9 Amanda Drive, Louth LN11 0AZ* T: (01507) 609960 E: revmoirak@btinternet.com

DAVIES, Canon Mostyn David. b 37. AKC 64. **d** 65 **p** 66. C Corby St Columba *Pet* 65–69; Ind Chapl 69–03; P-in-c Pet St Barn 80–03; Can Pet Cathl 95–03; rtd 03; PtO *Pet* from 03; *Linc* from 17. *92 West End, Langtoft, Peterborough PE6 9LU* T: (01778) 342838 E: mostyn@mostyn.myzen.co.uk

DAVIES, Canon Myles Cooper. b 50. Sarum & Wells Th Coll 71. **d** 74 **p** 75. C W Derby St Mary *Liv* 74–77; C Seaforth 77–80; V 80–84; V Stanley 84–07; P-in-c Liv St Paul Stoneycroft 05–07; V Stanley w Stoneycroft St Paul 07–11; Chapl Rathbone Hosp Liv 84–92; Chapl N Mersey Community NHS Trust 92–05; Dioc Voc Adv *Liv* 94–05; Hon Can Liv Cathl 01–05; Can Res Liv Cathl from 06; Prec from 08. *2 Cathedral Close, Liverpool L1 7BZ* T: 0151-702 7203 E: myles.davies@liverpoolcathedral.org

DAVIES, Nicholas Duff. b 67. Sheff Univ BA 88 Edin Univ MTh 89 Anglia Ruskin Univ MA 09 FRSA 01. Westcott Ho Cam 06. **d** 08 **p** 09. C S Dulwich St Steph *S'wark* 08–12; TV S Cheltenham *Glouc* 12–16; TR from 16; Asst Chapl Glos Univ from 16; AD Cheltenham 17–18. *The Rectory, 80 Painswick Road, Cheltenham GL50 2EU* T: (01242) 321268 M: 07801-336144 E: nickduffdavies@gmail.com

DAVIES, Nicola Louise. b 69. STETS. **d** 14 **p** 15. NSM Fordingbridge and Hyde and Breamore etc *Win* from 14. *Godshill Wood Cottage, Woodgreen, Fordingbridge SP6 2QU* T: (01725) 512306 E: daviesnicky@live.co.uk

DAVIES, Canon Nigel Lawrence. b 55. Lanc Univ BEd 77. Sarum & Wells Th Coll 84. **d** 87 **p** 88. C Heywood St Luke w All So *Man* 87–91; V Burneside *Carl* 91–07; P-in-c Crosscrake 04–06; P-in-c Skelsmergh w Selside and Longsleddale 06–07; TR Beacon from 07; RD Kendal 03–08; Hon Can Carl Cathl from 06. *St Oswald's Vicarage, The Main Road, Burneside, Kendal LA9 6QX* T: (01539) 722015 *or* 795419 F: 07974-448370 E: canon.nigel@beaconteam.org

DAVIES, Noel Paul. b 47. Chich Th Coll 83. **d** 85 **p** 86. C Milford Haven *St D* 85–89; R Jeffreyston w Reynoldston and E Williamston etc 89–09; R Jeffreyston w Reynoldston and

Loveston etc 09–12; rtd 12; PtO *St D* from 12. *Hungerford Farm, Loveston, Kilgetty SA68 0NY*

DAVIES, Mrs Pamela Elizabeth. b 55. Oak Hill Th Coll 09. **d** 11 **p** 12. C Berechurch St Marg w St Mich *Chelmsf* 11–15; R Sundridge w Ide Hill and Toys Hill *Roch* from 15. *Sundridge Rectory, Chevening Road, Sundridge, Sevenoaks TN14 6AB* T: (01959) 467223

DAVIES, Canon Patricia Elizabeth. b 36. Westf Coll Lon BA 58 Hughes Hall Cam CertEd 59 Leeds Univ MA 74. NEOC 83. **dss** 86 **d** 87 **p** 94. Killingworth *Newc* 86–90; Hon C 87–90; Hon C Newc H Cross 91–96; NSM Newc Epiphany 96–99; NSM Gosforth St Hugh 99–00; P-in-c 00–01; Hon Can Newc Cathl 00–01; rtd 01; PtO *York* from 01. *Applegarth, Middlewood Lane, Fylingthorpe, Whitby YO22 4TT* T: (01947) 881175

DAVIES, Patrick Charles Steven. b 59. Leeds Univ BA 99 Man Univ MA 13 RGN 86 RMN 92 RHV 94. Coll of Resurr Mirfield 97. **d** 99 **p** 00. C Reddish *Man* 99–04; P-in-c Withington St Crispin 04–18; R from 18. *296 Wilbraham Road, Manchester M21 0UU* T: 0161-282 8514 M: 07967-385357 E: fr.patrick@ntlworld.com

DAVIES, Paul. b 80. City Univ BSc 05. SEITE BA 16. **d** 16 **p** 17. C Bexleyheath Ch Ch *Roch* 16–18; C Barnehurst 18–19; NSM from 19. *36 Horsham Road, Bexleyheath DA6 7HP* M: 07582-914056 E: revpauldavies@outlook.com

DAVIES, Paul. See DAVIES, Richard Paul

DAVIES, Paul Lloyd. b 46. Bris Univ LLB 68 Solicitor 71. Trin Coll Carmarthen 84. **d** 87 **p** 88. NSM Newport w Cilgwyn and Dinas w Llanllawer *St D* 87–97; P-in-c Mathry w St Edren's and Grandston etc 97–01; V 01–08; rtd 08; PtO *St D* from 09. *Treetops, Osborn Park, Neyland, Milford Haven SA73 1SX* T: (01646) 602919 E: revpaullloyddavies@gmail.com

DAVIES, Paul Martin. b 35. Lon Univ BD 75. Sarum & Wells Th Coll 75. **d** 75 **p** 76. C Walthamstow St Mary w St Steph *Chelmsf* 75–79; Kenya 79–86; R Leven w Catwick *York* 86–95; RD N Holderness 90–95; rtd 95; PtO *York* from 95. *48 All Saints Court, Market Weighton, York YO43 3NT*

DAVIES, Paul Scott. b 59. Cranmer Hall Dur 85. **d** 88 **p** 89. C New Addington *S'wark* 88–91; C Croydon H Sav 91–94; P-in-c Norton in the Moors *Lich* 94–99; R 99–03; V Sunbury *Lon* 03–15; Sen P Doha Epiphany Qatar 15–19; P-in-c Bedford All SS *St Alb* from 19. *All Saints' Vicarage, 1 Cutcliffe Place, Bedford MK40 4DF* E: paul@zippor.com

DAVIES, Paul Trevor. b 85. Oak Hill Th Coll 16. **d** 19. C Whittle-le-Woods *Blackb* from 19. *16 Carr Meadow, Bamber Bridge, Preston PR5 8HS* M: 07934-112146 E: revptd@gmail.com

DAVIES, Peter Huw. b 57. Crewe & Alsager Coll BEd 79. Wycliffe Hall Ox 87. **d** 89 **p** 90. C Moreton *Ches* 89–93; V Weston-super-Mare St Paul *B & W* 93–05; P-in-c Chesham Bois *Ox* 05–08; R 08–13; R Sandy *St Alb* from 13. *The Rectory, 34 High Street, Sandy SG19 1AQ* T: (01767) 680512

DAVIES, Preb Peter Timothy William. b 50. Leeds Univ BSc 74. Oak Hill Th Coll 75. **d** 78 **p** 79. C Kingston Hill St Paul *S'wark* 78–81; C Hove Bp Hannington Memorial Ch *Chich* 81–88; V Audley *Lich* 88–15; P-in-c Alsagers Bank 06–15; P-in-c Talke 13–15; Preb Lich Cathl 13–15; rtd 15; PtO *Lich* from 16. *174 Cheadle Road, Cheddleton, Leek ST13 7BD* T: (01538) 528349

DAVIES, Canon Philip James. b 58. UEA BA 79 Keswick Hall Coll PGCE 80 K Coll Lon MA 92. Ridley Hall Cam 86. **d** 89 **p** 90. C Rainham *Roch* 89–90; C Gravesend St Geo and Rosherville 90–95; V 95–98; Dioc Schs Development Officer *Pet* 98–13; P-in-c King's Cliffe 98–10; C Bulwick, Blatherwycke w Harringworth and Laxton 07–10; R King's Cliffe, Bulwick and Blatherwycke etc 10–17; C Ketton, Collyweston, Easton-on-the-Hill and Tinwell 13–17; V King's Cliffe, Bulwick and Blatherwycke, Collyweston etc from 17; Can Pet Cathl from 18. *The Rectory, 3 Hall Yard, King's Cliffe, Peterborough PE8 6XQ* T: (01780) 470314 E: p.j.davies@tesco.net

DAVIES, Philip Simon. b 65. Trin Coll Ox BA 87 MA 91. Aston Tr Scheme 93 Ridley Hall Cam 95. **d** 97 **p** 98. C Burntwood *Lich* 97–00; TV Cheswardine, Childs Ercall, Hales, Hinstock etc 00–03; TR 03–04; P-in-c Olney *Ox* 04–08; P-in-c Banbury St Hugh 08–12; PtO from 12. *5 Kedlestone Rise, Banbury OX16 9TX* T: (01295) 255744 E: revdavies@btinternet.com

DAVIES, Canon Philip Wyn. b 50. Univ of Wales BA 72 MA 82 BD 96. St D Dioc Tr Course 93 St Mich Coll Llan 94. **d** 96 **p** 97. C Llandysul *St D* 96–98; V Tregaron w Ystrad Meurig and Strata Florida 98–14; P-in-c Blaenpennal 01–07; V 07–14; V Tregaron Gp from 14; Dioc Archivist from 04; AD Lampeter and Ultra-Aeron from 11; Can St D Cathl from 12. *The Vicarage, Tregaron SY25 6HL* T: (01974) 299010 E: philipwyn@btinternet.com

DAVIES, The Ven Rachel Hannah Eileen. b 64. Ban Univ BTh 08. St Mich Coll Llan 01. **d** 04 **p** 05. NSM Lampeter and Llanddewibrefi Gp *St D* 04–06; NSM Bro Teifi Sarn Helen 06–08; P-in-c Llanerch Aeron w Ciliau Aeron and Dihewyd etc 08–19; Dioc Adv on Rural Matters 05–19; Hon Can St D Cathl 12–14; Can St D Cathl 14–19; Adn Cardigan from 19. *The Vicarage, Llanllwni, Pencader SA39 9DR* T: (01559) 395775 M: 07814-272998 E: eileengwndwn@yahoo.co.uk *or* archdeacon.cardigan@churchinwales.org.uk

DAVIES, Reginald Charles. b 33. Hull Univ MA 93 Birm Univ MPh 09. Tyndale Hall Bris 58. **d** 64 **p** 65. C Heywood St Jas *Man* 64–66; C Drypool St Columba w St Andr and St Pet *York* 66–69; V Denaby Main *Sheff* from 69. *The Vicarage, Church Road, Denaby Main, Doncaster DN12 4AD* T: (01709) 862297 E: ailsa.reg@hotmail.co.uk

DAVIES, Rhiannon Mary Morgan. See JOHNSON, Rhiannon Mary Morgan

DAVIES, The Ven Richard Paul. b 73. Univ of Wales (Lamp) BA 94 Ox Univ MTh 98. Ripon Coll Cuddesdon 94. **d** 97 **p** 98. Min Can St D Cathl 97–01; Succ 01–06; TV Dewisland *St D* 01–06; V Burry Port and Pwll 06–12; Dioc Ecum Officer 02–06; OCM 05–07; Dioc Warden Ords *St D* 11–12; Adn Ban 12–17; R Llanfair Mathafarn Eithaf w Llanbedrgoch etc 12–14; Adn Surrey *Guildf* from 17; PtO *Ox* from 17; *Ban* from 17. *Archdeacon's House, Lime Grove, West Clandon, Guildford GU4 7UT* T: (01483) 212663 or 790350 or 211924 E: archdeacon.surrey@cofeguildford.org.uk

DAVIES, Richard Paul. b 48. Wycliffe Hall Ox 72. **d** 75 **p** 76. C Everton St Sav w St Cuth *Liv* 75–78; Chapl Asst Basingstoke Distr Hosp 78–80; TV Basingstoke *Win* 80–85; V Southampton Thornhill St Chris 85–94; V Eastleigh 94–13; rtd 13; PtO *Win* from 14; *Sarum* from 14. *1 Woodcock Gardens, Warminster BA12 9JH* T: (01985) 300606 E: rp.davies@yahoo.co.uk

DAVIES, Robert Emlyn. b 56. N Staffs Poly BA 79. Coll of Resurr Mirfield 83. **d** 86 **p** 87. C Cardiff St Jo *Llan* 86–90; V Aberdare from 97; AD Cynon Valley 02–08. *13 Tan y Bryn Gardens, Llwydcoed, Aberdare CF44 0TQ* T: (01685) 884769

DAVIES, Roger Charles. b 46. Univ of Wales BD 72. St Mich Coll Llan 67. **d** 73 **p** 74. C Llanfabon *Llan* 73–75; C Llanblethian w Cowbridge and Llandough etc 75–78; CF 78–84; TV Halesworth w Linstead, Chediston, Holton etc *St E* 84–87; R Claydon and Barham 87–91; R Lavant and Chapl Lavant Ho Sch 91–94; TV Gt Aycliffe and Chilton *Dur* 04–08; P-in-c Wheatley Hill and Wingate w Hutton Henry 08–13; rtd 13; PtO *Dur* 13–17; Hon C Blackhall, Castle Eden and Monkhesleden from 17. *19 Taylor Grove, Wingate TS28 5PA* M: 07866-649300 E: r876davies@btinternet.com

DAVIES, Mrs Sally Jane. b 63. Linc Coll Ox BA 86. Trin Coll Bris BA 92. **d** 92 **p** 94. C E Molesey St Paul *Guildf* 92–96; C Chalfont St Peter *Ox* 96–99; Chapl RN Coll Greenwich and Trin Coll of Music 99–06; Hon C Greenwich St Alfege *S'wark* 99–06; P-in-c Shamley Green *Guildf* 06–11; V from 11. *The Vicarage, Church Hill, Shamley Green, Guildford GU5 0UD* T: (01483) 892030 E: vicar@shamleygreen.net

DAVIES (née Goddard), Mrs Sara Jayne. b 65. Liv Univ BSc 87 Sheff Univ MMedSc 92. Linc Coll of Th and Min 17. **d** 19. NSM Graffoe Gp *Linc* from 19. *31 Priory Road, Ruskington, Sleaford NG34 9DJ* T: (01526) 834490 M: 07768-706952 E: saraj65@btinternet.com

DAVIES, Canon Sarah Isabella. b 39. Llan Dioc Tr Scheme 87. **d** 91 **p** 97. NSM Pontypridd St Cath w St Matt *Llan* 91–93; C Ferndale w Maerdy 93–00; Chapl Univ Hosp of Wales and Llandough NHS Trust 98–00; Chapl Pontypridd and Rhondda NHS Trust 98–00; C Cardiff Ch Ch Roath Park *Llan* 00–09; Dioc Child Protection Officer 02–09; Hon Can Llan Cathl 06–09; rtd 09; PtO *Llan* from 10. *4 St Augustine Road, Heath, Cardiff CF14 4BD* T: (029) 2061 0054 E: sallydavies@outlook.com

DAVIES, Scott Lee. b 73. St Jo Coll Nottm. **d** 06 **p** 07. C Childwall All SS *Liv* 06–10; V Carr Mill from 10. *St David's Vicarage, 27 Eskdale Avenue, St Helens WA11 7EN* T: (01744) 732330 E: vicar.stdavids@uwclub.net

DAVIES, Stephen. b 56. Nottm Univ BSc 77. Wycliffe Hall Ox 01. **d** 03 **p** 04. C Crawley and Littleton and Sparsholt w Lainston *Win* 03–07; V Heacham *Nor* 07–13; RD Heacham and Rising 11–13; Min Abbeydale Ch Ch LEP *Glouc* 13–18; rtd 18; PtO *St Alb* from 19. *Broadgate, Hillside Road, Leighton Buzzard LU7 3BU* E: revdstevedavies@gmail.com

DAVIES, Stephen John. b 55. Bp Otter Coll Chich BA 01 IEng 77 CEng 82. St Steph Ho Ox 96. **d** 98 **p** 99. C Leigh Park and Warren Park *Portsm* 98–02; C Durrington *Chich* 02–05; P-in-c Earnley and E Wittering 05–08; R from 08; Chapl Chich Cathl 02–19; Chapl W Sussex Police from 00. *The Rectory,*

190

Church Road, East Wittering, Chichester PO20 8PS T: (01243) 672260 M: 07899-948493 E: frsteve@btinternet.com

DAVIES, Mrs Susan Anne. b 48. N Co Coll Newc CertEd 69. St Mich Coll Llan 98. **d** 01 **p** 02. NSM Monmouth w Overmonnow etc *Mon* 01–05; NSM Goetre w Llanover 05; TV Rossendale Middle Valley *Man* 05–13; Dioc Rural Officer 07–13; AD Rossendale 08–13; rtd 13; PtO *Sheff* from 13. *10 Grange Mews, Wickersley, Rotherham S66 1YA* T: (01709) 207098 E: susanannedavies@aol.com

DAVIES, Taffy. *See* DAVIES, Edward William Llewellyn

DAVIES, Canon Timothy Robert. b 64. Bradf Univ BSc 87. Wycliffe Hall Ox BTh 93. **d** 93 **p** 94. C Eynsham and Cassington *Ox* 93–97; C Fulwood *Sheff* 97–03; Crosslinks Assoc Ch Ch Cen from 03; Hon Can Nairobi Cathl from 08. *Egerton Hall, Fitzwilliam Street, Sheffield S1 4JR* T: 0114-273 9750 E: tim.davies@christchurchcentral.co.uk

DAVIES, Trevor. *See* DAVIES, Edward Trevor

DAVIES, The Ven Vincent Anthony (Tony). b 46. Brasted Th Coll 69 St Mich Coll Llan 71. **d** 73 **p** 74. C Owton Manor CD *Dur* 73–76; C Wandsworth St Faith *S'wark* 76–78; P-in-c 78–81; V Walworth St Jo 81–94; RD S'wark and Newington 88–93; Adn Croydon 94–11; Bp's Adv for Hosp Chapl 00–11; P-in-c Sutton New Town St Barn 04–06; rtd 11; PtO *S'wark* from 11; *Chich* from 12. *1 High Beeches, Worthing BN11 4TJ* M: 07946-640288 E: v.a.davies@hotmail.com

DAVIES, William Martin. b 56. Univ of Wales (Cardiff) BSc 78. Wycliffe Hall Ox 78. **d** 81 **p** 82. C Gabalfa *Llan* 81–84; P-in-c Beguildy and Heyope *S & B* 84–85; V 85–87; V Swansea St Thos and Kilvey 87–93; V Belmont *Lon* 93–03; Asst Chapl Miss to Seafarers 87–03; Area Co-ord Leprosy Miss for Wales 04–07; Area Co-ord Lon and Essex 07–11; V Harefield *Lon* from 11. *The Vicarage, 28 Countess Close, Harefield, Uxbridge UB9 6DL* T: (01895) 825960 M: 07050-042586 E: office@stmarys-harefield.org.uk *or* martin@stmarys-harefield.org.uk

DAVIES-COLE, Charles Sylester. b 38. New Coll Dur BA BD. Edin Th Coll 66. **d** 66. Hon C Edin Old St Paul 66–13; Prin Teacher Jas Gillespie's High Sch 82–03; LtO *Edin* from 14. *121 Mayburn Avenue, Loanhead EH20 9ER* T: 0131-440 4190

DAVIES-HANNEN, Robert John. b 65. W Glam Inst of HE BEd 89. St Mich Coll Llan BTh 92. **d** 92 **p** 93. C Gorseinon *S & B* 92–95; P-in-c Swansea St Luke 95–02; V Llangyfelach 02–17; V Sketty from 17. *The Vicarage, De La Beche Road, Sketty, Swansea SA2 9AR* T: (01792) 774120 E: rdhannen@gmail.com

DAVIES-JAMES, Mrs Roxana Ruth de la Tour. b 56. **d** 05 **p** 06. OLM Cusop w Blakemere, Bredwardine w Brobury etc *Heref* 05–11; P-in-c Magnis Gp from 11. *8 Hillside View, Credenhill, Hereford HR4 7FD* T: (01432) 760443 M: 07870-929040 E: rana.james@virgin.net

DAVILL, Robin William. b 51. SS Paul & Mary Coll Cheltenham CertEd 73 BEd 74 Leic Univ MA 79. Westcott Ho Cam 86. **d** 88 **p** 89. C Broughton *Blackb* 88–91; C Howden *York* 91–93; NSM Crayke w Brandsby and Yearsley 93–97; P-in-c 97–03; P-in-c Thirkleby w Kilburn and Bagby 03–09; P-in-c Topcliffe, Baldersby w Dishforth, Dalton etc 09–12; rtd 12; PtO *York* from 12. *Leyland House, 44 Uppleby, Easingwold, York YO61 3BB* T: (01347) 823472 E: robin@davill.eclipse.co.uk

DAVIS, Alan. b 34. Birm Univ BSc 56. Ox NSM Course. **d** 75 **p** 76. NSM Chesham St Mary *Ox* 75–80; NSM Gt Chesham 80–00; rtd 00; PtO *Ox* from 00. *18 Cheyne Walk, Chesham HP5 1AY* T: (01494) 782124

DAVIS, Alan John. b 33. St Alb Minl Tr Scheme 77. **d** 80 **p** 81. NSM Goddington *St Alb* 80–84; C Benchill *Man* 84–86; R Gt Chart *Cant* 86–02; rtd 02; PtO *Cant* from 02. *8 Roberts Road, Greatstone, New Romney TN28 8RL* T: (01797) 361917 E: alanandpat.davis@yahoo.com

DAVIS, The Ven Alan Norman. b 38. Open Univ BA 75. Lich Th Coll 63. **d** 65 **p** 66. C Kingstanding St Luke *Birm* 65–68; C-in-c Ecclesfield St Paul CD *Sheff* 68–73; V Sheff St Paul 73–75; V Shiregreen St Jas and St Chris 75–80; R Maltby 80–81; TR 81–89; Abp's Officer for UPA 90–92; P-in-c Carl St Cuth w St Mary 92–96; Dioc Communications Officer 92–96; Adn W Cumberland and Hon Can Carl Cathl 96–04; RD Solway 98–99; rtd 04; PtO *Cov* from 05; *Leic* from 05; RD Sparkenhoe W 07–08. *71 North Street, Atherstone CV9 1JW* T: (01827) 718210 E: alanfran1944@gmail.com

DAVIS, Preb Andrew Fisher. b 46. St Chad's Coll Dur BA 67 K Coll Lon MA 99 MPhil 06. St Steph Ho Ox 68. **d** 70 **p** 71. C Beckenham St Jas *Roch* 70–74; C Kensington St Mary Abbots w St Geo *Lon* 74–80; V Sudbury St Andr 80–90; AD Brent 85–90; V Ealing Ch the Sav 90–16; Preb St Paul's Cathl 07–16; rtd 16. *The End House, 17 Weavering Close, Rochester ME2 4RQ* T: (01634) 921542 M: 07973-176445 E: fr.a@btopenworld.com

DAVIS, Andrew George. b 63. Bath Univ BSc Edin Univ BD. Edin Th Coll. **d** 89 **p** 90. C Alverstoke *Portsm* 89–92; C Portsea N End St Mark 92–96; Bp's Dom Chapl 96–98; R Bishop's Waltham and Upham 98–07; V Gosport H Trin from 07; V Gosport Ch Ch from 07; AD Gosport 14–15. *Holy Trinity House, 9 Britannia Way, Gosport PO12 4FZ* T: (023) 9258 0173 E: fr.andydavis@gmail.com

DAVIS, Anne. *See* DAVIS, Maureen Anne

DAVIS, Canon Bernard Rex. b 33. Sydney Univ BA 55 Gen Th Sem (NY) MDiv 60 Newc Univ MA 67 FRSA 87. Coll of Resurr Mirfield 55. **d** 57 **p** 58. C Guildf St Nic 57–59; USA 59–61; R Wickham Australia 62–66; Studies Sec ACC 66–68; Exec Sec Unit 3 WCC Geneva 68–77; Warden Edw K Ho 77–03; Can Res and Subdean Linc Cathl 77–03; PtO *S'well* 01–03; rtd 03; PtO *Lon* from 06; *Eur* from 06. *425 Bromyard House, Bromyard Avenue, London W3 7BY* T: (020) 8743 0181 E: subdean@aol.com

DAVIS, Canon Brian. b 40. AKC 69 BD 69. St Aug Coll Cant 69. **d** 70 **p** 71. C Humberstone *Leic* 70–73; C Kirby Muxloe 73–74; V Countesthorpe w Foston 74–91; RD Guthlaxton I 90–91; V Hinckley St Mary 91–10; RD Sparkenhoe W 92–02; Hon Can Leic Cathl 94–10; Bp's Adv for Wholeness and Healing 04–10; rtd 10; PtO *Leic* 10–13; P-in-c Gaulby from 13. *62 Lubenham Hill, Market Harborough LE16 9DQ* T: (01858) 431843 E: revbdavis@aol.com

DAVIS, Mrs Bryony Elizabeth. b 64. Ban Univ BTh 09 DipCOT 86. EAMTC 99. **d** 02 **p** 03. C Beccles St Mich *St E* 02–05; P-in-c Ottershaw *Guildf* 05–08; rtd 08; Chapl HM Pris Bronzefield 10–18; Methodist Min from 10; PtO *Guildf* 11–18; Chapl HM Pris Leyhill from 18. *HM Prison Leyhill, Wootton-under-Edge, Gloucester GL12 8BT* T: (01454) 264000 E: bryony@tiscali.co.uk

DAVIS, Christopher James. b 63. Worc Coll Ox BA 85. Cranmer Hall Dur 88. **d** 91 **p** 92. C Margate H Trin *Cant* 91–94; C Cambridge H Sepulchre *Ely* 94–00; C Wimbledon Em Ridgway Prop Chpl *S'wark* 00–04; R Tooting Graveney St Nic from 04. *The Rectory, 20A Rectory Lane, London SW17 9QJ* T: (020) 8672 7691

DAVIS, Clinton Ernest Newman. b 46. Solicitor 71. Wycliffe Hall Ox 78. **d** 80 **p** 81. C Margate H Trin *Cant* 80–84; C St Laur in Thanet 84–87; V Sandgate St Paul 87–92; P-in-c Folkestone St Geo 92; V Sandgate St Paul w Folkestone St Geo 92–97; Chapl HM Pris Standford Hill 97–08; rtd 08; PtO *Cant* from 08. *Springfield, 39 Ashford Road, Maidstone ME14 5DP* T: (01622) 682330 E: clintonendavis@btinternet.com

DAVIS, Colin Anthony John. b 65. St Jo Coll Nottm. **d** 99 **p** 00. C Bletchley *Ox* 99–02; C S Molton w Nymet St George, High Bray etc *Ex* 02–03; TV 03–10; I Carrowdore w Millisle D & D from 10. *15 Kilbright Road, Carrowdore, Newtownards BT22 2HQ* T: (028) 9186 1802 M: 07768-781357 E: revcol23@btinternet.com

DAVIS, Canon Edward Gabriel Anastasius. b 75. R Holloway Coll Lon BA 97. Trin Coll Bris BA 02. **d** 03 **p** 04. C Boldmere *Birm* 03–06; Chapl Aston Univ 06; Chapl Bris Univ from 07; NSM Inner Ring Partnership from 07; Hon Can Bris Cathl from 17. *47 Waverley Road, Bristol BS6 6ET* T: 0117-942 5390 E: ed.davis@bris.ac.uk

DAVIS, Mrs Elizabeth Jane. b 42. S'wark Ord Course 91. **d** 94 **p** 95. NSM Plaistow St Mary *Roch* 94–99; NSM Bromley St Andr from 99. *11 Park Avenue, Bromley BR1 4EF* T: (020) 8460 4672 E: elizabeth.irwin.davis@gmail.com

DAVIS (née GENT), Emily Louise. b 88. Cant Ch Ch Univ BA 10. St Steph Ho Ox BA 13. **d** 14 **p** 15. C Bishop's Stortford St Mich *St Alb* 14–17; C Easthampstead *Ox* from 17. *16 Blackcap Lane, Bracknell RG12 8AA* T: (01344) 360306 E: jennettsparkpriest@gmail.com

DAVIS, Felicity Ann. *See* SMITH, Felicity Ann

DAVIS, Geoffrey. *See* DAVIS, Ronald Geoffrey

DAVIS, George Shaun. b 75. Middx Univ BA 01 Lon Inst of Educn PGCE 02 Leeds Univ BA 10. Coll of Resurr Mirfield 08. **d** 10 **p** 11. C W Bromwich All SS *Lich* 10–14; TV Worc SE 14–18; TV N Cheltenham *Glouc* from 18. *The Rectory, Rectory Lane, Swindon Village, Cheltenham GL51 9RD* E: fr.georgedavis@hotmail.com

DAVIS, Canon Herbert Roger. b 36. Kelham Th Coll 60. **d** 65 **p** 66. C Barkingside St Fran *Chelmsf* 65–69; C Harpenden St Nic *St Alb* 69–73; P-in-c Eaton Bray 73–75; P-in-c Eaton Bray w Edlesborough 75; V 75–81; RD Dunstable 77–81; R Gt Berkhamsted 81–95; Hon Can St Alb 93–95; rtd 99. *6 St Thomas Terrace, St Thomas Street, Wells BA5 2XG* T: (01749) 677195

DAVIS, Mrs Jacqueline. b 47. Cant Ch Ch Univ Coll BA 01. **d** 05 **p** 06. OLM Upchurch w Lower Halstow *Cant* 05–13; NSM The Six 13–14. *Mill House, The Street,*

Lower Halstow, Sittingbourne ME9 7DY T: (01795) 842557
E: revjackytd@gmail.com
DAVIS, Jennifer Anne Stanway. b 38. SWMTC 04. **d** 05 **p** 06.
NSM Cullompton, Willand, Uffculme, Kentisbeare etc *Ex*
06–08; rtd 08; PtO *B & W* from 09; *Sarum* from 11. *36 Church
Acre, Bradford-on-Avon BA15 1RL* T: (01225) 866479
DAVIS, Mrs Jessica Hazel. b 80. St Mellitus Coll BA 18. **d** 18
p 19. C Brunswick *Man* from 18. *13 Mawson Road, Manchester
M13 9HG* E: revjessdavis@gmail.com
DAVIS, Mrs Joanna Helen. b 82. Ex Univ BA 04 K Coll Lon
PGCE 05. St Jo Coll Nottm MTh 10. **d** 10 **p** 11. C Inglewood
Gp *Carl* 10–14; Chapl Milton Abbey Sch Dorset from 14. *Nether
Fen, Milton Abbas, Blandford Forum DT11 0DA* T: (01258)
880484   E: joannahelendavis@hotmail.com   *or*
joanna.davis@miltonabbey.co.uk
DAVIS, John George. b 65. Roehampton Inst BSc 87 S Glam
Inst HE PGCE 88. St Steph Ho Ox BTh 96. **d** 96 **p** 97. C
Newton Nottage *Llan* 96–00; V Tredegar *Mon* 00–18; TR
Whitchurch *Llan* from 18. *The Rectory, 6 Penlline Road,
Cardiff CF14 2AD* T: (029) 2062 6072 E: stgandj@gmail.com
DAVIS, John James. b 48. Keele Univ MA 93 Staffs Univ
PGCE 98. Qu Coll Birm BA 05. **d** 05 **p** 06. NSM Baswich
Lich 05–08; NSM Bradeley, Church Eaton, Derrington and
Haughton 08–09; NSM Stafford 09–13; NSM Stafford St Mary
and Marston 13–18; NSM Stafford St Chad 13–18; RD
Stafford 11–15; CF (ACF) 06–09; Chapl Abbots Bromley Sch
13; PtO *Lich* from 18. *Stockton Croft, 87 Weeping Cross, Stafford
ST17 0DQ* T: (01785) 661382 E: john_davis19@sky.com
DAVIS, Miss Judith Alison. b 88. Cam Univ BTh 11 Sheff
Univ MA 14. Ridley Hall Cam 08. **d** 11 **p** 12. C Doncaster
St Geo *Sheff* 11–14; P-in-c Hathersage w Bamford and
Derwent and Grindleford *Derby* 14–17; R 17–19; Adv for
Women in Min 18–19. *24 Roe Lane, Southport PR9 9DX*
E: jude.a.davis@cantab.net
DAVIS, Mrs Kathleen Mary. b 37. Derby Coll of Educn
TCert 58. **d** 07 **p** 08. OLM Morley *Wakef* 07–14; *Leeds* from
14. *13 New Park Street, Morley, Leeds LS27 0PT* T: 0113-253
4521
DAVIS, Lloyd Martin. b 88. Cant Ch Ch Univ BA 11.
Ridley Hall Cam 17. **d** 19. C Huntingdon *Ely* from 19. *1
The Walks East, Huntingdon PE29 3AP* M: 07910-123111
E: lloydmdavis@live.com
DAVIS, Mrs Lucy Frances. b 72. Keble Coll Ox BA 93
Lon Inst of Educn PGCE 94. ERMC 09. **d** 12 **p** 13. NSM
Redbourn *St Alb* 12–15; V Flitwick from 15. *The Vicarage,
26 Dew Pond Road, Flitwick, Bedford MK45 1RT* T: (01525)
712369 M: 07803-357891 E: lucy@flitwickchurch.org
DAVIS, Margaret Ann. b 59. Kingston Poly BA 81 Liv
Univ MSc 93 RGN 85. Westcott Ho Cam 06. **d** 08 **p** 09. C
Abbots Langley *St Alb* 08–11; P-in-c Clavering and Langley
w Arkesden etc *Chelmsf* 11–13; V Clavering w Langley,
Arkesden etc from 13. *The Vicarage, 54 Pelham Road,
Clavering, Saffron Walden CB11 4PQ* T: (01799) 550703
E: m.davis.sasha@gmail.com
DAVIS, Martin John. b 59. Van Mildert Coll Dur BSc 80 K
Coll Lon MA 11. Ox Min Course 07. **d** 09 **p** 10. C Colnbrook
and Datchet *Ox* 09–13; PtO 14–15; TV Kidlington w
Hampton Poyle from 15. *St John's Vicarage, 16 Broadway,
Kidlington OX5 1EF* T: (01865) 421316 M: 07909-976637
E: martindavis26@tiscali.co.uk
DAVIS, Matthew William. b 82. **d** 16. C Toxteth St Philemon
w St Gabr and St Cleopas *Liv* 16–17; C Aigburth from 17.
16 Ashfield Road, Liverpool L17 0BZ M: 07989-846871
E: m.w.davis@cantab.net
DAVIS, Maureen Anne. b 59. St Hilda's Coll Ox BA 80 MA 84.
NOC 96. **d** 99 **p** 00. NSM Plemstall w Guilden Sutton *Ches*
99–01; C Ches St Mary 01–03; R Woodchurch 03–16; Hon
Can Ches Cathl 11–16; V Northampton St Benedict *Pet*
from 16. *St Benedict's Vicarage, 16 Sentinel Road, Northampton
NN4 9UF* M: 07974-816390 E: marianne2june@gmail.com
DAVIS, Nicholas Anthony Wylie. b 56. Univ of Wales
(Lamp) BA 80. Chich Th Coll 82. **d** 84 **p** 85. C N Lambeth
S'wark 84–88; TV Catford (Southend) and Downham
88–94; V Camberwell St Phil and St Mark 94–04;
V Shrub End *Chelmsf* 04–19. *Address temp unknown*
E: nicholasdavis676@btinternet.com
DAVIS, Nicholas Edward. b 75. Univ of Wales (Ban)
BD 96. Coll of Resurr Mirfield 98. **d** 00 **p** 01. C Darwen
St Cuth w Tockholes St Steph *Blackb* 00–05; P-in-c
Tarleton 05–11; P-in-c Rufford 07–11; P-in-c Rufford and
Tarleton 11–12; R 12–16; P-in-c Hesketh w Becconsall
07–16; P-in-c Darwen St Cuth w Tockholes St Steph
from 16. *St Cuthbert's Vicarage, 21 The Meadows, Darwen
BB3 0PF* T: (01254) 701360 E: httarleton@hotmail.com *or*
darwen.tockholes.priest@gmail.com

DAVIS, Canon Norman. b 38. FCII 66. Oak Hill Th Coll 77.
d 79 **p** 80. C Walton *St E* 79–82; P-in-c Grundisburgh w
Burgh 82–91; P-in-c Bredfield w Boulge 86–91; R Boulge w
Burgh and Grundisburgh 91–03; P-in-c Ufford w Bredfield
and Hasketon 01–03; R Boulge w Burgh, Grundisburgh
and Hasketon 03–04; RD Woodbridge 90–96; Hon Can
St E Cathl 01–04; rtd 04; PtO *St E* from 04. *The Randalls,
Front Street, Orford, Woodbridge IP12 2LN* T: (01394) 459449
E: n.l.davis@btinternet.com
DAVIS, Peter Thomas. b 61. Flinders Univ Aus BTh 87
MThSt 02. St Barn Coll Adelaide 83. **d** 87 **p** 87. C Modbury
and Dioc Youth Chapl Adelaide Australia 87–89; C Port
Lincoln 89–91; TV Gt and Lt Coates w Bradley *Linc* 91–92;
Dioc Youth Officer Adelaide Australia 92–94; P-in-c Parafield
Gardens St Barbara 94–98; R Elizabeth H Cross 98–01; Chapl
Anglicare S 98–01; V Satley, Stanley and Tow Law *Dur* 01–04. *5
Mercury Court, 4 Eversholt Street, London NW1 1BR* M: 07795-
417337 E: montedog2000@yahoo.co.uk
DAVIS, Rex. *See* DAVIS, Bernard Rex
DAVIS, Roger. *See* DAVIS, Herbert Roger
DAVIS, Ronald Geoffrey. b 47. St Jo Coll Nottm 79. **d** 81
p 81. C Maidstone St Luke *Cant* 81–84; P-in-c Lostwithiel
Truro 84–86; P-in-c Lanhydrock 84–86; Asst Dioc Youth
Officer 84–86; P-in-c Boughton Monchelsea *Cant* 86–88;
V 88–15; Six Preacher Cant Cathl 94–99; C-in-c Parkwood
CD 95–98; AD N Downs 99–02; rtd 15; PtO Cant from 15;
Truro from 16. *3 The Links, Falmouth TR11 5UJ* T: (01326)
619468 M: 07802-422991
DAVIS, Royston Grandfield. b 33. Sarum & Wells Th
Coll 86. **d** 88 **p** 89. C Cainscross w Selsley *Glouc* 88–90;
TV Hugglescote w Donington, Ellistown and Snibston *Leic*
90–93; P-in-c Gilmorton w Peatling Parva and Kimcote etc
93–95; R Ogwell and Denbury *Ex* 95–99; rtd 00; OSB from
00. *22 Lock House, Keeper Close, Taunton TA1 1AX* T: (01823)
974467 E: royston.davis@prcdtr.org.uk
DAVIS, Ruth Elizabeth. *See* TAIT, Ruth Elizabeth
DAVIS, Simon Charles. b 63. Plymouth Poly BSc 86 Univ
of Wales (Lamp) MTh 08 MIET. Trin Coll Bris BA 92. **d** 92
p 93. C Bollington St Jo *Ches* 92–96; P-in-c Abbots Bromley
w Blithfield *Lich* 96–10; P-in-c Colton, Colwich and Gt
Haywood 05–10; R Abbots Bromley, Blithfield, Colton,
Colwich etc from 11; RD Rugeley from 15. *The Vicarage,
Market Place, Abbots Bromley, Rugeley WS15 3BP* T: (01283)
840242
DAVIS, Susan Elizabeth Mary. *See* CLARKE, Susan Elizabeth
Mary
DAVIS, Terence Lionel. b 46. FCA 72. **d** 16 **p** 17. NSM Llanilar
w Rhostie and Llangwyryfon etc *St D* from 16. *Felinpontfaen,
Llangwyryfon, Aberystwyth SY23 4HA* T: (01974) 241653
E: terryd147@hotmail.co.uk
DAVIS, Thomas Henry. b 60. OLM course 97 Coll of Resurr
Mirfield 05. **d** 99 **p** 00. OLM Sudbury and Chilton *St E* 99–03;
NSM Preston St Jo and St Geo *Blackb* 03–05; C Torrisholme
05–08; C Blackpool St Steph 08–09; PtO 09–10; C
Morecambe St Barn 10–12; V 12–17; V Douglas St Matt *S & M*
from 17. *St Matthew's Vicarage, Alexander Drive, Douglas, Isle
of Man IM2 3QN* T: (01624) 676310 M: 07854-770360
E: father.tom@live.co.uk *or* priest@stmatthewsiom.org
DAVIS, Timothy Alwyn. b 74. Trin Coll Bris BTh. **d** 01 **p** 02.
C Crich and S Wingfield *Derby* 01–05; V Leyton St Mary
w St Edw and St Luke *Chelmsf* 05–10; V Clifton w Newton
and Brownsover *Cov* 10–18; TV Dunstable *St Alb* from 18;
Chapl All SS Academy Dunstable from 18; Chapl Manshead
Academy Luton from 18. *St Fremund's Vicarage, 20 Friars
Walk, Dunstable LU6 3JA* E: revd.timdavis@yahoo.co.uk
DAVIS, Mrs Yvonne Annie. b 30. CQSW 75. **d** 96 **p** 97. OLM
Purley St Barn *S'wark* 96–00; PtO from 00. *8 Meadow Hill, Purley
CR8 3HL* T: (020) 3441 9348 E: yvonnea.davis@talktalk.net
DAVISON, Canon Andrew Paul. b 74. Mert Coll Ox BA 96
MA 99 DPhil 00 CCC Cam BA 02 MA 08 PhD 13. Westcott
Ho Cam 00 Ven English Coll Rome 02. **d** 03 **p** 04. C
Bellingham St Dunstan *S'wark* 03–06; Tutor and Fell St Steph
Ho Ox 06–10; Jun Chapl Mert Coll Ox 06–10; Tutor Westcott
Ho Cam 10–14; Lect Div Cam Univ from 14; Fell CCC Cam
from 14; Dean of Chpl from 19; Hon Can St Alb from 15.
Faculty of Divinity, West Road, Cambridge CB3 9BS T: (01223)
763027 E: apd31@cam.ac.uk
DAVISON, Deborah Karin Mary. b 56. Ex Univ BA 79 SRN 83
RHV 85. Ripon Coll Cuddesdon 09. **d** 11 **p** 12. C Boyne Hill
Ox 11–13; V Wokingham St Paul 13–15; C Newbury St Geo
and St Jo 15–19; R Paisley H Trin and St Barn *Glas* from 19.
31 Westfield Drive, Glasgow G52 2SG M: 07833-935901
DAVISON, The Ven George Thomas William. b 65. St Andr
Univ BD 88. Oak Hill Th Coll 88 CITC BTh 92. **d** 92 **p** 93. C
Portadown St Mark *Arm* 92–95; I Kinawley w H Trin *K, E & A*
95–09; Dir of Ords 97–09; Preb Kilmore Cathl 02–09; Adn

Kilmore 04–09; I Carrickfergus *Conn* from 09; Adn Belfast from 13. *The Rectory, 12 Harwood Gardens, Carrickfergus BT38 7US* T: (028) 9336 3244 *or* 9336 0061 F: 9336 3244 M: 07771-812844 E: geordie1965@icloud.com

DAVISON, Philip Anthony. b 66. Magd Coll Cam BA 88 MA 93. Cuddesdon Coll BA 98. **d** 98 **p** 99. C Lancaster St Mary w St John and St Anne *Blackb* 98–02; P-in-c Feniscowles 02–08; R Finchley St Mary *Lon* from 08; Warden of Readers Edmonton Area from 17. *St Mary's Rectory, Rectory Close, London N3 1TS* T: (020) 8346 4600 *or* 8248 3818 F: 8248 3818 E: rector@stmaryatfinchley.org.uk

DAVISON, Canon Richard Ireland. b 42. St Chad's Coll Dur BSc 63. Linc Th Coll 64. **d** 66 **p** 67. C Cockerton *Dur* 66–70; C Houghton le Spring 70–73; V Heworth St Alb 73–80; Ascension Is 80–82; V Dunston *Dur* 82–85; V Bishopwearmouth Ch Ch 85–98; AD Wearmouth 94–99; P-in-c Dur St Giles 99–00; V 00–08; P-in-c Shadforth and Sherburn 03–08; Hon Can Dur Cathl 97–08; AD Dur 06–08; rtd 08; PtO *Dur* from 08. *16 Loraine Crescent, Darlington DL1 5TF* T: (01325) 486999 E: ridavison@hotmail.co.uk

DAVY, Mrs Helen Mary. b 44. **d** 05 **p** 06. OLM Kirton w Falkenham *St E* 05–06; OLM Nacton and Levington w Bucklesham etc 06–13; NSM 13–15; PtO from 15. *9 Roman Way, Felixstowe IP11 9NJ* T: (01394) 270703

DAVY, Martin Edward. b 82. Hull Univ LLB 03 Nottm Trent Univ LLM 05. Oak Hill Th Coll BA 16. **d** 16 **p** 17. C Morden *S'wark* 16–19; V Theale *Ox* from 19. *The Rectory, Englefield Road, Theale, Reading RG7 5AS* M: 07825-408926 E: mdavy82@gmail.com *or* martindavy@holytrinitytheale.org.uk

DAVY, Peter Geoffrey. b 31. St Pet Coll Saltley TCert 54. SWMTC 93. **d** 94 **p** 94. NSM St Columb Minor and St Colan *Truro* 94–99; rtd 99; PtO *Truro* from 00. *9 Tredour Road, Newquay TR7 2EY* T: (01637) 872241 E: gdavy9@googlemail.com

DAVYS, Mark Andrew. b 66. St Cath Coll Ox BA 87 MA 97 Keele Univ MA 01 Qu Coll Birm BA 04 Solicitor 90. WMMTC 01. **d** 04 **p** 05. NSM Colton, Colwich and Gt Haywood *Lich* 04–10; NSM Abbots Bromley, Blithfield, Colton, Colwich etc from 11. *Deer's Leap, Meadow Lane, Little Haywood, Stafford ST18 0TT* T: (01889) 882855 E: revmdavys@deersleap.org.uk

DAW, Geoffrey Martin. b 57. Oak Hill Th Coll 81. **d** 84 **p** 85. C Hollington St Leon *Chich* 84–87; C Seaford w Sutton 87–90; V Iford w Kingston and Rodmell 90–13; V Iford w Kingston and Rodmell and Southease from 13; RD Lewes and Seaford 08–17. *The Rectory, 14 Lockitt Way, Kingston, Lewes BN7 3LG* T: (01273) 473665 E: geoffrey.daw@btinternet.com

DAW, Nicholas William. b 69. **d** 13 **p** 14. NSM Worc SE 13–16; NSM Worc St Wulstan 16–17. *21 Oak Avenue, Worcester WR4 9UG* T: (01905) 745645 E: revdnickdaw@gmail.com

DAWES, Mrs Helen Elizabeth. b 74. Trin Coll Cam BA 96 MA 00. Westcott Ho Cam 99. **d** 02 **p** 03. C Chesterton St Andr *Ely* 02–05; P-in-c Sandon, Wallington and Rushden w Clothall *St Alb* 05–09; Dep Public Affairs Sec to Abp Cant 09–13; Abp's Soc and Public Affairs Adv 13–15; TR Shaftesbury *Sarum* from 15; Dean of Women's Min from 16. *10 Heathfields Way, Shaftesbury, Dorset SP7 9JZ* T: (01747) 853060 E: helen@shaftesburycofe.org.uk

DAWES, Hugh William. b 48. Univ Coll Ox BA 71 MA 76. Cuddesdon Coll 71. **d** 74 **p** 75. C Purley St Mark *S'wark* 74–77; Chapl G&C Coll Cam 77–82; Chapl Em Coll Cam 82–87; V Cambridge St Jas *Ely* 87–00; Dir Focus Chr Inst Cambridge 87–00; V N Dulwich St Faith *S'wark* 00–10; rtd 10; PtO *S'wark* from 10; *Guildf* from 11. *8 The Wells, Lower Street, Haslemere GU27 2PA* T: (01428) 652466 E: hugh@hughdawes.com

DAWKES, Peter. b 31. Roch Th Coll 64. **d** 66 **p** 67. C Newbold w Dunston *Derby* 66–69; C Buxton 69–72; V Somercotes 72–93; rtd 93; Hon C Kenton, Mamhead, Powderham, Cofton and Starcross *Ex* 93–15; Hon C Exminster, Kenn, Kenton w Mamhead, and Powderham from 15. *115 Exeter Road, Dawlish EX7 0AN* T: (01626) 862593

DAWKIN, Peter William. b 60. Nottm Univ BTh 88 Open Univ BA 91. St Jo Coll Nottm 85. **d** 88 **p** 89. C Birkdale St Jo *Liv* 88–91; C Netherton 91–93; V Liv Ch Ch Norris Green 93–03; Assoc Min Wigan Deaneries 03–06; V Hough Green St Basil and All SS from 06. *339 Ditchfield Road, Widnes WA8 8XR* T: 0151-420 4963 M: 07852-484802 E: peter.dawkin@btinternet.com

DAWKINS (née LEWIS-MORRIS), Mrs Catherine Mary. b 76. St Hilda's Coll Ox MA 98 Qu Mary Coll Lon MSc 01 Peterho Cam BA 08. Ridley Hall Cam 06. **d** 10 **p** 11. C Aden Yemen 10–11; C Dubai UAE 11–12; PtO *S'wark* 12–15; LtO from 15; PtO *Chich* from 17; Hon Min Can

S'wark Cathl 15–17. *41 Harestone Hill, Caterham CR3 6SG* E: catherinemarydawkins@gmail.com

DAWKINS, Ms Jennifer Claire. b 76. Nottm Univ BA 97 SOAS Lon MSc 05 Wolfs Coll Cam BTh 13. Ridley Hall Cam 11. **d** 13 **p** 14. C Peckham All SS *S'wark* from 13. *18 Martock Court, Consort Road, London SE15 2PL* M: 07773-963198 E: jennydawkins@hotmail.com *or* jenny.dawkins@allsaintspeckham.org.uk

DAWKINS, John Haswell. b 47. MBIM 81. NEOC 98. **d** 01 **p** 02. NSM Barmby Moor Gp *York* 01–11; PtO from 17. *Norton Grove Lodge, Scarborough Road, Norton, Malton YO17 8AE*

DAWKINS, Michael Howard. b 44. Bris Univ BTh 68 Man Univ MA 96. Tyndale Hall Bris 67. **d** 69 **p** 69. C Drypool St Columba w St Andr and St Pet *York* 69–73; CF 74–80; P-in-c Bulford *Sarum* 80–81; P-in-c Figheldean w Milston 80–81; R Meriden *Cov* 85–09; rtd 09. *60 Wassell Road, Wollescote, Stourbridge DY9 9DB* T: (01384) 893299 M: 07854-833460 E: mhdawkins@aol.com

DAWKINS, Nigel Jonathan. b 72. St Jo Coll Ox BA 94 MA 97 Univ Coll Lon MSc 97 Peterho Cam BA 05 MA 07. Westcott Ho Cam 03. **d** 06 **p** 07. C Caterham *S'wark* 06–09; Chapl Aden Ch Ch and Yemen 09–11; Chapl Miss to Seafarers Dubai and UAE 11–12; PtO *S'wark* 12–13; Min Can and Sacr St Paul's Cathl *Lon* 13–14; PtO *S'wark* 15–16; NSM Caterham 16–17. *41 Harestone Hill, Caterham CR3 6SG* E: nigeldawkins@gmail.com

DAWKINS, Staffan Anthony. b 69. SEITE 12. **d** 15 **p** 16. C Stanground and Farcet *Ely* 15–17; C Whittlesey, Pondersbridge and Coates 17–18; V Tottenham St Paul *Lon* from 18. *St Paul's Vicarage, 60 Park Lane, London N17 0JR* M: 07481-861817 E: staffan.dawkins@gmail.com

DAWN, Maggi Eleanor. b 59. Fitzw Coll Cam MA 96 Selw Coll Cam PhD 02. Ridley Hall Cam 96. **d** 99 **p** 00. C Ely 99–01; Chapl K Coll Cam 01–03; Chapl Rob Coll Cam 03–11; Assoc Dean and Prof Yale Div Sch USA from 11. *Yale Divinity School, 409 Prospect Street, New Haven CT 06511, USA* T: (001) (203) 432 5766 E: maggi.dawn@yale.edu

DAWSON, Alan David Hough. b 67. St Jo Coll Dur BA 09 ACIB 92. Cranmer Hall Dur 07. **d** 09 **p** 10. C Hale and Ashley *Ches* 09–13; V Neston from 13. *The Vicarage, High Street, Neston CH64 9TZ* T: 0151-353 1000 M: 07919-278104 E: alan.dawson21@btinternet.com

DAWSON, Andrew. *See* DAWSON, William James Andrew

DAWSON, Andrew. *See* DAWSON, Francis Andrew Oliver Duff

DAWSON, Miss Anne. b 54. Nottm Univ BA 76 Hull Coll of Educn PGCE 77. NEOC 03. **d** 06 **p** 07. NSM Market Weighton *York* 06–09; P-in-c Sigglesthorne w Nunkeeling and Bewholme 10–11; rtd 11; PtO *York* from 11. *23 Sloe Lane, Beverley HU17 8ND* T: (01482) 862940 E: andaw@andaw.karoo.co.uk

DAWSON, Barry. b 38. Oak Hill Th Coll 63. **d** 66 **p** 67. C Fulham St Mary N End *Lon* 66–69; C St Marylebone All So w SS Pet and Jo 69–73; Bp's Chapl *Nor* 73–76; Gen Sec CEMS 76–81; V Rye Park St Cuth *St Alb* 81–89; V Attenborough *S'well* 89–98; rtd 98; PtO *S'well* 98–14. *27 Orlando Drive, Carlton, Nottingham NG4 3FN*

DAWSON, Canon Brian. b 33. Leeds Univ BA 54 Man Univ MA 84 Newc Univ MPhil 01. Coll of Resurr Mirfield 56. **d** 58 **p** 59. C Hollinwood *Man* 58–62; C Rawmarsh w Parkgate *Sheff* 62–63; V Royton St Anne *Man* 63–75; V Urswick *Carl* 75–86; V Bardsea 75–86; R Skelton and Hutton-in-the-Forest w Ivegill 86–98; RD Penrith 91–96; Hon Can Carl Cathl 94–98; rtd 98; PtO *Carl* from 98. *Apple Croft, High Hesket, Carlisle CA4 0HS* T: (016974) 73069 E: b.dawson324@btinternet.com

DAWSON, Miss Claire Louise. b 68. Nottm Poly BA 92 CQSW 92 Nottm Univ MA 04. EMMTC 01. **d** 04 **p** 05. C Mansfield Woodhouse *S'well* 04–05; C Sutton in Ashfield St Mary 05–08; C Orrell Hey St Jo and St Jas *Liv* 08–11; P-in-c 11–17; P-in-c Litherland St Phil 15–17; V Sheff St Mary Bramall Lane from 17; P-in-c Endcliffe from 17. *St Mary's Vicarage, 42 Charlotte Road, Sheffield S1 4TL* T: 0114-272 4987 E: cdawson@blueyonder.co.uk

DAWSON, Canon Cyril. b 34. St Chad's Coll Dur BA 58. **d** 59 **p** 60. C Honicknowle *Ex* 59–63; C Paignton St Jo 63–66; V Heptonstall *Wakef* 66–71; V Todmorden 71–82; RD Calder Valley 75–82; Can Res Wakef Cathl 82–92; Vice-Provost Wakef Cathl 86–92; Hon Can Wakef Cathl 92–99; V Darrington 92–99; rtd 99; PtO *York* 00–15; *Wakef* 00–14; *Leeds* 14–16. *24 Beacon Road, Bridlington YO16 6UX* T: (01262) 672911

DAWSON, David. b 57. TISEC 99. **d** 99 **p** 00. NSM Kirkwall *Ab* from 99; P-in-c 05–10; R from 10. *St Olaf's Rectory, Dundas Crescent, Kirkwall, Orkney KW15 1JQ* T: (01856) 872024 M: 07881-932657 E: ddawson572@gmail.com

DAWSON, Francis Andrew Oliver Duff. b 48. Keble Coll Ox BA 70 MA 74. St Jo Coll Nottm 74. **d** 76 **p** 77. C Billericay St Mary *Chelmsf* 76–77; C Billericay and Lt Burstead 77–80; C Childwall All SS *Liv* 80–84; Chapl St Kath Coll 80–84; V Shevington *Blackb* 84–97; Internat Officer and Team Ldr for Evang Affairs *Man* 97–03; P-in-c Werneth 03–14; rtd 14; PtO *Ches* from 14; *Man* from 14. *3 Woodside Drive, Hyde SK14 5QB* T: 0161-368 2129 E: andrewdawson51@hotmail.com

DAWSON, The Ven Hilary Joan. b 64. Univ of Wales (Lamp) BA 85 UWE PGCE 89 Ex Univ MA 08. SWMTC 05. **d** 08 **p** 09. C Thorverton, Cadbury, Upton Pyne etc *Ex* 08–10; C Brampford Speke, Cadbury, Newton St Cyres etc 10–11; P-in-c Colyton, Musbury, Southleigh and Branscombe 11–15; R 15–19; Preb Ex Cathl 17–19; Adn Glouc from 19; Can Res Glouc Cathl from 19. *9 College Green, Gloucester GL1 2LX* T: (01452) 835555 E: hilary.dawson2@btinternet.com or archdglos@glosdioc.org.uk

DAWSON, John William Arthur. b 43. EMMTC. **d** 95 **p** 96. NSM Breedon cum Isley Walton and Worthington *Leic* 95–05; NSM Ashby-de-la-Zouch and Breedon on the Hill 05–16; PtO 16–17; Chapl E Midl Airport from 17. *Orchard House, 2 Manor Drive, Worthington, Ashby-de-la-Zouch LE65 1RN* T: (01530) 222673 E: johndawson@benefice.org.uk

DAWSON, Miss Mary. b 51. Loughb Coll ALA 73. EMMTC 85. **d** 90 **p** 94. Par Dn Braunstone *Leic* 90–92; Par Dn Shrewsbury H Cross *Lich* 92–94; C 94–95; P-in-c Glentworth Gp *Linc* 95–97; V 97–10; rtd 10; PtO *Linc* from 11. *20 Newbolt Close, Caistor, Market Rasen LN7 6NY* T: (01472) 859802 E: fenellacoughdrop@btinternet.com

DAWSON, Neil. b 49. Ripon Hall Ox 71. **d** 74 **p** 75. C Putney St Mary *S'wark* 74–78; C Camberwell St Giles 78–80; TV N Lambeth 84–86; V E Dulwich St Clem 86; V Dulwich St Clem w St Pet 86–89; Hon C Wilton Place St Paul *Lon* 92–06; P-in-c Madeira *Eur* 06–14; rtd 14; PtO *S'wark* from 15; *Eur* from 15. *18 The High, Streatham High Road, London SW16 1HE* T: (020) 8769 9408 E: neildawson1949@gmail.com

DAWSON, Nicholas Anthony. b 52. St Jo Coll Nottm 88. **d** 90 **p** 91. C Mortomley St Sav High Green *Sheff* 90–95; V Owlerton from 95; P-in-c Hillsborough and Wadsley Bridge 06–09. *Owlerton Vicarage, Forbes Road, Sheffield S6 2NW* T: 0114-234 3560 E: nick.dawson@sheffield.anglican.org

DAWSON, Canon Norman William. b 41. K Coll Lon BD 63 AKC 63. **d** 65 **p** 66. C Salford St Phil w St Steph *Man* 65–68; C Heaton Ch Ch 68–70; R Longsight St Jo 70–75; R Longsight St Jo w St Cypr 75–82; R Withington St Paul 82–99; Chapl Christie Hosp Man 81–91; AD Withington *Man* 91–99; P-in-c Davyhulme St Mary 99–04; Hon Can Man Cathl 98–04; rtd 04; PtO *Blackb* from 04; *Man* 04–12. *Well House, Lowgill, Lancaster LA2 8RA* T: (01524) 262936 E: ann@hindburn.com

DAWSON, Canon Paul Christopher Owen. b 61. Leeds Univ BA 82. Ripon Coll Cuddesdon 83. **d** 85 **p** 86. C Dovecot *Liv* 85–89; V Westbrook St Phil 89–94; Bp's Dom Chapl 94–98; V Witton *Ches* 98–06; R Ches St Mary 06–19; RD Ches 14–18; V Whitegate w Lt Budworth from 19; Hon Can Ches Cathl from 11. *The Vicarage, Cinderhill, Whitegate, Northwich CW8 2BH* T: (01606) 301563 E: paulcodawson@outlook.com

DAWSON, Paul Richard. b 67. Bris Univ BSc 89. Oak Hill Th Coll 99. **d** 01 **p** 02. C Wimbledon Em Ridgway Prop Chpl *S'wark* 01–09; V Chelsea St Jo w St Andr *Lon* from 09. *The Vicarage, 43 Park Walk, London SW10 0AU* T: (020) 7352 1675 E: paul@standrewschelsea.org

DAWSON, Peter John. b 44. Local Minl Tr Course. **d** 06 **p** 07. NSM Heckmondwike *Wakef* 06–12; NSM Liversedge w Hightown 06–12; NSM Roberttown w Hartshead 06–12; NSM Heckmondwike (w Norristhorpe) and Liversedge 12–14; NSM Hartshead, Hightown, Robertown and Scholes 12–14; rtd 14; PtO *Wakef* 14; *Leeds* from 14. *10 Meadow Drive, Liversedge WF15 7QF* T: (01924) 404311 E: manxpeter@yahoo.co.uk

DAWSON, Ruth Adelaide. b 44. **d** 15 **p** 16. NSM Heighington and Darlington St Matt and St Luke *Dur* from 15. *27 Wilton Court, Greenfields, Newton Aycliffe DL5 7PU* T: (01325) 321729 M: 07786-154638

DAWSON, Ms Sarah. b 70. **d** 15 **p** 16. C Mitcham St Barn *S'wark* 15–19; P-in-c Camberwell St Geo from 19. *138 Friary Road, London SE15 5UW* M: 07421-136431 E: vicar.stgeorgescamberwell@outlook.com

DAWSON, Stephen Charles. b 62. LCTP 08. **d** 10 **p** 11. C Bentham *Bradf* 10–13; P-in-c Langcliffe w Stainforth and Horton 13–14; *Leeds* from 14; C Settle *Bradf* 13–14; *Leeds* from 14; C Giggleswick and Rathmell w Wigglesworth *Bradf*

13–14; *Leeds* from 14; AD Bowland and Ewecross from 17; PtO *Blackb* 12–14. *The Vicarage, Bankwell Road, Giggleswick, Settle BD24 0AP* E: scudawson@hotmail.com

DAWSON (formerly CORY), Mrs Valerie Ann. b 44. CertEd 65 Nottm Univ BEd 85. EMMTC 85. **d** 88 **p** 94. Area Sec CMS Linc and Pet 87–91; NSM Grantham *Linc* 88–91; Par Dn Ealing St Mary *Lon* 91–94; Chapl NW Lon Poly 91–92; Chapl Thames Valley Univ 92–96; C Ealing St Mary 94–96; Chapl Birm Cathl 96–99; C Surbiton St Andr and St Mark *S'wark* 99–08; rtd 08. *15A Greengate Close, Chesterfield S40 3SJ* T: (01246) 550445

DAWSON, Canon William James Andrew. b 48. TCD MA 72. CITC 88. **d** 88 **p** 89. NSM Killyman *Arm* 88–91; NSM Pomeroy 91–13; NSM Derryloran from 14; Can Arm Cathl from 98; Preb 98–01. *Tamlaght House, 29 Bridgend Road, Cookstown BT80 0AB* T: (028) 8673 7151 or 8676 2227 F: 8676 2227 E: wjadawson@gmail.com

DAWSON-CAMPBELL, Olive Sheila. b 37. ACIB 70. WEMTC 99. **d** 00 **p** 01. OLM Longden and Annscroft w Pulverbatch *Heref* 00–13; OLM Gt Hanwood and Longden and Annscroft etc from 13. *Braeburn, Castle Pulverbatch, Pulverbatch, Shrewsbury SY5 8DS* T: (01743) 719001

DAWSON-JONES, Garry Alan. b 66. Cliff Coll MA 02. Yorks Min Course 11. **d** 12 **p** 13. C Hackenthorpe *Sheff* 12–15; R Warboys w Broughton and Bury w Wistow *Ely* from 15. *The Rectory, 1 Oaklands, Warboys, Huntingdon PE28 2XH* T: (01487) 824612 M: 07976-382681 E: garrydawsonjones@yahoo.com

DAWSWELL, Jonathan Andrew. b 65. Jes Coll Cam BA 86. Wycliffe Hall Ox BA 91. **d** 92 **p** 93. C Childwall All SS *Liv* 92–96; C Leyland St Andr *Blackb* 96–99; V Knypersley *Lich* 99–09; P-in-c Biddulph Moor 05–09; R Biddulph Moor and Knypersley 09–11; V Westlands St Andr from 11. *St Andrew's Vicarage, 50 Kingsway West, Newcastle ST5 3PU* T: (01782) 619594 E: ja.dawswell@gmail.com

DAWTRY, The Ven Anne Frances. b 57. Westf Coll Lon BA 79 PhD 85. Ripon Coll Cuddesdon 91. **d** 93 **p** 94. C Corfe Mullen *Sarum* 93–96; C Parkstone St Pet w Branksea and St Osmund 96–97; Chapl Bournemouth Univ and Bournemouth and Poole Coll of FE 97–99; Prin OLM and Integrated Tr 99–03; Dir Tr and Prin Dioc OLM Scheme *Man* 03–06; Course Dir SNWTP 06–08; C Chorlton-cum-Hardy St Werburgh 06–08; P-in-c 08–09; R 09–11; Hon Can Man Cathl 06–11; Adn Halifax *Wakef* 11–14; *Leeds* from 14; Warden of Readers *Wakef* 12–14; *Leeds* from 14; Hon Can Wakef Cathl from 11; Hon Can Bradf Cathl from 15; Hon Can Ripon Cathl from 15. *2 Vicarage Gardens, Brighouse HD6 3HD* T: (01484) 714553 M: 07980-751902 E: archdeacon.halifax@leeds.anglican.org

DAY, Canon Charles Ian. b 48. Univ of Wales (Ban) BA 72. St Mich Coll Llan 73. **d** 75 **p** 76. C Llanrhos *St As* 75–79; V Mochdre 79–83; CF 80–91; V Minera *St As* 83–92; Dioc Soc Resp Officer 89–94; V Mold 92–11; AD 03–11; V Rhuddlan and Bodelwyddan 11–16; I Aber-Morfa Miss Area 17–18; AD St As 15–18; Hon Can St As Cathl 14–18; rtd 18; PtO *St As* from 18. *2 Ffordd Craiglun, Kinmel Bay, Rhyl LL18 5JL* T: (01745) 339050 M: 07977-001692 E: revian@spamex.com

DAY, Christine Audrey. b 63. K Alfred's Coll Win BTh 01 Univ of Wales (Lamp) MA(Theol) 06. STETS 02. **d** 04 **p** 05. NSM N Stoneham *Win* 04–08; NSM Swaythling 08–14; Chapl Southn Univ 11–14; Chapl Win Univ from 14. *The University of Winchester, Sparkford Road, Winchester SO22 4NR* T: (01962) 827246 M: 07580-968215 E: revchrisday@gmail.com or chaplaincy@winchester.ac.uk

DAY, Canon Colin Michael. b 40. Lon Univ BSc 62 AKC 62 Em Coll Cam BA 66 MA 71. Ridley Hall Cam 65. **d** 67 **p** 68. C Heworth w Peasholme St Cuth *York* 67–70; C Ox St Clem 70–76; V Kidsgrove *Lich* 76–86; Exec Officer Angl Evang Assembly and C of E Coun 86–90; Adv on Miss and Evang *Sarum* 90–95; P-in-c Branksome Park All SS 95–01; V 01–05; Can and Preb Sarum Cathl 94–05; Dioc Tr in Evang 95–05; rtd 05; PtO *Win* from 13. *113 Archery Grove, Southampton SO19 9ET* T: (023) 8043 9854 E: colin@ncd-uk.com

DAY, David John. b 44. CEng 72 MICE 72. Trin Coll Bris. **d** 90 **p** 91. C Stratton St Margaret w S Marston etc *Bris* 90–94; PtO from 95; Manager SA Addictions Rehab Cen Highworth 98–09; rtd 09. *62 Eastern Avenue, Swindon SN3 1AD* T: (01793) 524766 E: davidjday1@hotmail.com

DAY, David Vivian. b 36. Lon Univ BA 57 Nottm Univ MEd 73 MTh 77. **d** 99 **p** 00. NSM Dur St Nic 99–07; rtd 07; PtO *Dur* from 07. *35 Orchard Drive, Durham DH1 1LA* T: 0191-386 6909

DAY, Canon David William. b 37. St Andr Univ MA 58 BD 61 CertEd 73. St And Dioc Tr Course 74. **d** 76 **p** 77. C St Andrews All SS *St And* 76–77; P-in-c Dundee St Ninian *Bre* 77–84; Itinerant Priest *Arg* 84–02; R Duror *Arg* 84–02; P-in-c

Gruline 84–02; P-in-c Kentallen 84–02; P-in-c Kinlochleven 84–02; P-in-c Kinlochmoidart 84–96; P-in-c Lochbuie 84–96; P-in-c Portnacrois 84–96; P-in-c Strontian 84–96; Can St Jo Cathl Oban 99–02; rtd 02; Hon Can Cumbrae *Arg* from 02; LtO from 02; Hon C St Andrews All SS *St And* from 03. *10 Doocot Road, St Andrews KY16 8QP* T: (01334) 476991 E: arkvillewest@gmail.com

DAY, George Chester. b 45. Ex Univ BA 66 Lon Univ BD 70. Clifton Th Coll 67. **d** 71 **p** 72. C Reading St Jo *Ox* 71–75; C Morden *S'wark* 75–81; Sec for Voc and Min CPAS 81–86; Hon C Bromley Ch Ch *Roch* 83–86; V St Paul's Cray St Barn 86–05; RD Orpington 01–05; V Joydens Wood St Barn 05–10; rtd 10. *5 Abbey Grange Close, Buckfast, Buckfastleigh TQ11 0EU* T: (01364) 643912

DAY, Jennifer Ann. See BRADSHAW, Jennifer Ann

DAY, John Kenneth. b 58. Hull Univ BA 85. Cranmer Hall Dur 85. **d** 87 **p** 88. C Thornbury *Bradf* 87–90; V 90–96; V Whitkirk *Ripon* 96–01; V Fendalton New Zealand 01–15; Miss Strategy Development Officer *York* from 16; Asst Chapl to Abp from 16; P-in-c York St Chad from 16. *St Chad's Vicarage, 36 Campleshon Road, York YO23 1EY* T: (01904) 689634

DAY, Mrs Judith Mollie. b 43. Warwick Univ BPhil 95 SRN 64 Lady Spencer Chu Coll of Educn CertEd 74. **d** 15 **p** 16. NSM Brecon St Mary *S & B* from 15. *Maes yr Haf, Pentrefelin, Sennybridge, Brecon LD3 8TT* T: (01874) 638307 E: judyday.jd@gmail.com

DAY, Martyn John. b 69. Univ Coll Lon BSc 90. St Jo Coll Nottm 07. **d** 09 **p** 10. C Horwich and Rivington *Man* 09–12; C Blackrod 11–12; V Epsom St Geo New Zealand 12–15; P Asst to Bp Auckland 15–16; C Blockhouse Bay from 17. *24A Liverpool Street, Epsom, Auckland 1023, New Zealand* T: (0064) (9) 520 5652 or 948 7427 E: martyn.day9@gmail.com

DAY, Canon Mary Elizabeth. b 57. Leic Poly BEd 79. St Jo Coll Nottm 93. **d** 93 **p** 94. C Newbarns w Hawcoat *Carl* 93–98; P-in-c Allonby 98–03; P-in-c Cross Canonby 98–03; P-in-c Dearham 02–03; V Allonby, Cross Canonby and Dearham from 03; Adv for Women in Min from 07; RD Solway 08–11; Hon Can Carl Cathl from 08. *The Vicarage, Crosscanonby, Maryport CA15 6SJ* T: (01900) 814192 E: vicarmary@talktalk.net

DAY, Paul Geoffrey. b 56. St Pet Coll Ox BA 77. St Jo Coll Nottm 87. **d** 89 **p** 90. C Mildmay Grove St Jude and St Paul *Lon* 89–92; C Loughborough Em *Leic* 92–95; TV Loughborough Em and St Mary in Charnwood 95–98; PtO *Birm* 15–17; C Shirley from 17. *18 Widney Lane, Solihull B91 3LS* M: 07545-615924 E: pgday@hotmail.co.uk

DAY, Paul Geoffrey. b 51. Dur Univ BEd 75. Trin Coll Bris 76. **d** 78 **p** 79. C Roxeth Ch Ch *Lon* 78–82; TV Barking St Marg w St Patr *Chelmsf* 82–87; V Barrow St Mark *Carl* 87–00; V Eccleston St Luke *Liv* 00–07; TV Eccleston Team 07–13; rtd 13. *2 St Paul's Villas, King Street, Acrefair, Wrexham LL14 3RW* E: paulgday@btinternet.com

DAY, Peter. b 50. BPharm 71. Coll of Resurr Mirfield 85. **d** 87 **p** 88. C Eastcote St Lawr *Lon* 87–91; C Wembley Park St Aug 91–94; V Glen Parva and S Wigston *Leic* 94–14; C Wigston 14–15; rtd 15; PtO *Nor* from 16. *2A Eastfields Close, Gaywood, King's Lynn PE30 4HQ* T: (01553) 676158 E: peterday260@gmail.com

DAY, Peter Andrew. b 67. Westmr Coll Ox BTh 98 Bris Univ PhD 03. Ripon Coll Cuddesdon 07. **d** 10 **p** 11. C Wokingham St Paul *Ox* 10–13; P-in-c Reading Ch Ch 13–15; V from 15. *Christ Church Vicarage, Vicarage Road, Reading RG2 7AJ* T: 0118-931 3468 M: 07702-043857 E: fr.peterday@virginmedia.com

DAY, Roy Frederick. b 24. S'wark Ord Course 63. **d** 67 **p** 68. C Newington St Paul *S'wark* 67–70; C Radlett *St Alb* 70–72; P-in-c Ponsbourne 72–76; R Campton 76–82; V Shefford 76–82; R Shenley 82–89; rtd 89; PtO *St Alb* 89–14. *11 Hill End Lane, St Albans AL4 0TX* T: (01727) 845782

DAY, Miss Sally Ann. b 43. **d** 07 **p** 08. OLM Shifnal and Sheriffhales *Lich* 07–16; OLM Shifnal, Sheriffhales and Tong 16–18; PtO from 18. *11 Cherry Tree Hill, Coalbrookdale, Telford TF8 7EF* T/F: (01952) 433213 M: 07831-101361 E: sallyannday@hotmail.com

DAY, Stephen Michael. b 60. Down Coll Cam BA 82 MA 85 Open Univ BA 00. Ridley Hall Cam 02. **d** 05 **p** 06. C Waltham H Cross *Chelmsf* 05–09; TV Papworth *Ely* from 09. *The Rectory, 32 High Street, Bourn, Cambridge CB23 2SQ* T: (01954) 264226 E: revdsmday@cantab.net *or* stephen.day@elydiocese.org

DAY, Timothy Robert. b 63. WMMTC 07. **d** 10 **p** 11. NSM Leic H Apostles 10–14; TV Fosse Team from 14. *St Michael's Vicarage, 828 Melton Road, Thurmaston, Leicester LE4 8BE* T: 0116-348 6896 M: 07976-186546 E: revtimday.fosseteam@gmail.com

DAY, Trevor Martin. b 51. STETS 09. **d** 12 **p** 13. NSM Highworth w Sevenhampton and Inglesham etc *Bris* 12–15; NSM Broad Blunsdon 12–15; NSM W Swindon and the Lydiards 15–18; NSM W Swindon and Lydiard Tregoze from 18; Min Can Bris Cathl from 15. *23 Melfort Close, Sparcells, Swindon SN5 5FG* T: (01793) 875373 M: 07918-125826 E: trevor.day@btinternet.com

DAY, William Charles. b 47. Portsm Poly BEd 86. Ripon Coll Cuddesdon 88. **d** 90 **p** 91. C Bishop's Waltham *Portsm* 90–93; P-in-c Greatham w Empshott and Hawkley w Prior's Dean 93–95; R 95–98; V Titchfield 98–09; RD Fareham 04–08; C-in-c Whiteley CD 08–09; rtd 09; PtO *Portsm* from 09. *19 Peter's Road, Locks Heath, Southampton SO31 6EB* T: (01489) 564035 E: revbillday@btinternet.com

DAY, William George. b 45. SNWTP 14. **d** 14 **p** 15. OLM Derby St Barn 14–18; PtO from 18. *2 Whenby Close, Mickleover, Derby DE3 0RQ* T: (01332) 518449 E: wwgday@btinternet.com

DAYKIN, Timothy Elwin. b 54. R Holloway Coll Lon BSc 75 St Jo Coll Dur MA 81 K Coll Lon MPhil 93 MEHS 89. Cranmer Hall Dur 75. **d** 78 **p** 79. C Bourne *Guildf* 78–81; Chapl K Alfred Coll *Win* 82–87; C-in-c Valley Park CD 87–91; V Valley Park 91–92; P-in-c Fordingbridge 92–98; V 98–01; P-in-c Hale w S Charford 94–01; P-in-c Breamore 99–01; TR Fordingbridge and Breamore and Hale etc 01–05; TV Southampton (City Cen) 05–14; PtO from 14; *Nor* from 16; *Sarum* from 19; Producer/Presenter Relig Progr BBC Radio Solent from 05. *Address withheld by request* E: tim.daykin@bbc.co.uk

DAYNES, Andrew John. b 47. Jes Coll Cam BA 69 MA 73. Westcott Ho Cam 69. **d** 72 **p** 73. C Radlett *St Alb* 72–76; Chapl St Alb Abbey 76–80; Chapl Bryanston Sch 80–08; rtd 08; PtO *B & W* from 09. *Romneya, Claycastle, Haselbury Plucknett, Crewkerne TA18 7PE* T: (01460) 78971 M: 07580-003822 E: hilandandy@gmail.com

DAZELEY, Mrs Lorna. b 31. CertEd 53 New Hall Cam BA 82 MA 86. EAMTC 82. **dss** 84 **d** 87 **p** 94. Chesterton St Andr *Ely* 84–97; C 87–97; rtd 97; PtO *Ely* from 01. *Chesterton House, Church Street, Chesterton, Cambridge CB4 1DT* T: (01223) 356243 E: lorna.dazeley@gmail.com

DE ALMEIDA FEITAL, Peterson. b 75. Cliff Coll BA 05 MA 09. Ridley Hall Cam 09. **d** 11 **p** 12. C Muswell Hill St Jas w St Matt *Lon* 11–14; Licensed Preacher Under Seal Stepney Area from 15; Missr to the Arts from 15; PtO *Ox* from 15. *4 Dollings Yard, 3 Bellingdon Road, Chesham HP5 2HA* M: 07889-463333 E: petersonfeital@hotmail.com *or* peterson.feital@london.anglican.org

DE ANDRADE LIMA, Luiz Henrique. b 80. Trin Coll Bris BA 14. **d** 14 **p** 15. C Worksop St Anne *S'well* 14–17; C Norton Cuckney 14–17; V Worksop St Cuth and Shireoaks from 17. *34 Boscombe Road, Worksop S81 7SB* T: (01909) 530127 M: 07899-674364 E: revluizlima@outlook.com

DE BERRY, Robert Delatour. b 42. Qu Coll Cam BA 64 MA 68. Ridley Hall Cam 65. **d** 67 **p** 68. C Bradf Cathl 67–70; Youth Worker CMS Uganda 71–75; V Attercliffe *Sheff* 75–83; V W Kilburn St Luke w St Simon and St Jude *Lon* 83–97; Gen Sec Mid-Africa Min (CMS) 97–99; P-in-c Kennington St Mark *S'wark* 99–01; V 01–08; rtd 08; PtO *Sarum* from 10. *27 Cossor Road, Pewsey SN9 5HX* T: (01672) 562907 E: robertdeberry@btinternet.com *or* robertdeberry42@gmail.com

de BOURCIER, Miss Katherine Elizabeth. b 71. Clare Coll Cam BA 92. St Mellitus Coll BA 12. **d** 12 **p** 13. C Gt Baddow *Chelmsf* 12–15; P-in-c Halstead Area from 15. *The Rectory, Parsonage Street, Halstead CO9 2LD* T: (01787) 472171 E: halsteadrector@gmail.com

DE CHAIR LADD, Anne. See LADD, Anne de Chair

de GARIS, Canon Jean Helier Thomson. b 60. K Alfred's Coll Win BA 82 PGCE 83. Sarum & Wells Th Coll BTh 93. **d** 93 **p** 94. C Chandler's Ford *Win* 93–98; P-in-c Lytchett Minster *Sarum* 98–10; TR The Lytchetts and Upton 10–19; RD Poole and N Bournemouth 09–16; Can and Preb Sarum Cathl from 14. *The Vicarage, 52 Park Lane, Salisbury SP1 3NP* T: (01722) 334214 M: 07760-224424 E: jeandegaris@st-francischurch.org.uk

DE GARIS, Juliette Elizabeth Charmaine. See ROBILLIARD, Juliette Elizabeth Charmaine

de GRUCHY, Heidi-Maria. Cardiff Univ BTh 12. St Mich Coll Llan 08. **d** 10 **p** 11. C Bedwellty w New Tredegar *Mon* 10–12; C Bassaleg 12–14; C Tredegar 14–16; P-in-c Goodna Australia 16–18; C St Ishmael's w Llan-saint and Ferryside *St D* from 18. *The Vicarage, Water Street, Ferryside SA17 5RT* T: (01267) 267559 E: heididegruchy@hotmail.co.uk

DE GRUYTHER, Mrs Heather Louise. b 79. Glos Univ BA 04. Ripon Coll Cuddesdon BA 19. **d** 19. C Glouc St Paul and

St Steph from 19. *126 Fieldcourt Gardens, Quedgeley, Gloucester GL2 4TZ* T: (01452) 535970 E: revheatherdg@gmail.com

de JONGE, Elaine Irene. b 73. Sussex Univ BA 96. WMMTC 06. **d** 09 **p** 10. C Smestow Vale *Lich* 09–13; C Tettenhall Wood and Perton 13; Spiritual Care Co-ord and Chapl Compton Care from 13. *Compton Care, Compton Hall, 4 Compton Road West, Wolverhampton WV3 9DH* T: (01902) 774554 E: spiritualcare@comptoncare.org.uk

de la HOYDE, Canon Denys Ralph Hart. b 33. G&C Coll Cam BA 57 MA 61. Westcott Ho Cam 57. **d** 59 **p** 60. C Moss Side Ch Ch *Man* 59–60; Chapl G&C Coll Cam 60–64; P-in-c Naini Tal etc India 64–68; C Eltham H Trin *S'wark* 68–69; Chapl Bromsgrove Sch 69–71; Asst Master Harrogate High Sch 71–78; Lic to Offic *Ripon* 71–78; V Pool w Arthington 86–98; Dioc Dir of Ords 86–98; Hon Can Ripon Cathl 92–98; rtd 98; PtO *Ripon* 00–14; *Leeds* from 14. *36 Hookstone Chase, Harrogate HG2 7HS* T: (01423) 548146 E: denys.delahoyde@ntlworld.com

de la MOUETTE, Norman Harry. b 39. Southn Univ BEd 73 MA 98. Sarum & Wells Th Coll 76. **d** 79 **p** 80. NSM Win St Lawr and St Maurice w St Swithun 79–99; Deputation Appeals Org CECS Win and Portsm 83–96; Chapl St Jo Win Charity 96–99; NSM Win St Lawr and St Maurice w St Swithun 99–04; rtd 04; PtO *Win* from 04. *146 Greenhill Road, Winchester SO22 5DR* T: (01962) 853191 E: norman.delamouette@yahoo.co.uk

DE LYON, Hilary Barbara. b 56. **d** 13 **p** 14. NSM Swaffham and Sporle *Nor* from 13. *Woodford Lodge, Tittleshall, King's Lynn PE32 2PF* T: (01328) 700066 E: hilary@delyon.plus.com

de MATTOS, Dominic James. b 63. St Aug Coll of Th 16. **d** 19. C Southborough St Thos *Roch* from 19. *19 Streamside, Tonbridge TN10 3PU* M: 07851-095264 E: revdomdem@gmail.com

de MELLO, Bridget Dorothea. *See* DEUCHAR de MELLO, Bridget Dorothea

de POMERAI, David Ian Morcamp. b 50. Edin Univ BSc 72 Univ Coll Lon PhD 75. EMMTC 90. **d** 93 **p** 94. NSM Sutton in Ashfield St Mary *S'well* 93–96; NSM Clifton 96–02; NSM Walton-on-Trent w Croxall, Rosliston etc *Derby* 02–13; LtO 13–15; rtd 15; LtO *Edin* from 16. *141/1 Comely Bank Road, Edinburgh EH4 1BH* T: 0131-332 4743

de QUIDT, Mrs Fiona Margaret Munro. b 53. St Andr Univ MTheol 76. NTMTC 97. **d** 00 **p** 01. NSM Kingston Hill St Paul *S'wark* from 00. *10 Norbiton Avenue, Kingston-upon-Thames KT1 3QS* T: (020) 8541 4700 E: revfiona.dequidt@btopenworld.com

de QUIDT, Marion Elizabeth. b 59. Girton Coll Cam MPhil 83 MA 85 PhD 86. STETS 09. **d** 11 **p** 12. C Fetcham *Guildf* 11–15; P-in-c Whitewater *Win* 15–19; R from 19; AD Odiham from 17. *The Vicarage, London Road, Hook RG27 9EG* T: (01256) 760169 M: 07866-304516 E: mariondequidt@whitewaterchurches.co.uk or marion.dequidt@gmail.com

DE ROBECK, Fiona Caroline. *See* GIBBS, Fiona Caroline

DE SALIS, Mary. *See* FANE DE SALIS, Mary

DE SAUSMAREZ, Canon John Havilland Russell. b 26. Lambeth MA 81 Wells Th Coll 54. **d** 56 **p** 57. C N Lynn w St Marg and St Nic *Nor* 56–58; C Hythe *Cant* 58–61; V Maidstone St Martin 61–68; V St Peter-in-Thanet 68–81; RD Thanet 74–81; Hon Can Cant Cathl 78–81; Can Res Cant Cathl 81–94; rtd 94; PtO *Cant* 94–12. *6 Chantry Court, St Radigunds Street, Canterbury CT1 2AD* T: (01227) 458868

DE SILVA, David Ebenezer Sunil. b 48. **d** 72 **p** 73. Sri Lanka 72–84; C Elm Park St Nic Hornchurch *Chelmsf* 84–87; R Mistley w Manningtree and Bradfield 87–90; TR Stanground and Farcet *Ely* 90–01; V Stanground 01–05; rtd 05. *10 Anson House, Cottesmore Close, Peterborough PE3 9ET* E: desdesilva84@gmail.com

DE SMET, Andrew Charles. b 58. Ex Univ BSc 79 Southn Univ BTh 88. Sarum & Wells Th Coll 85. **d** 88 **p** 89. C Portsea St Mary *Portsm* 88–93; R Shipston-on-Stour w Honington and Idlicote *Cov* 93–00; Warden Offa Retreat Ho and Dioc Spirituality Adv 00–07; P-in-c Kirkdale w Harome, Nunnington and Pockley *York* 07–14; V 14–17; Abp's Adv and Co-ord of Past Care from 07. *Egrons, Tower Street, Flamborough, Bridlington YO15 1PD* M: 07583-279459 E: andrewdesmet@btinternet.com

de VIAL, Raymond Michael. b 39. Oak Hill Th Coll 77. **d** 80 **p** 81. NSM Beckenham St Jo *Roch* 80–84; C Morden *S'wark* 84–88; TV 88–94; V Kingston Hill St Paul 94–04; rtd 04; PtO *S'wark* 04–05; *Carl* from 05. *39 Helme Drive, Kendal LA9 7JB* T: (01539) 729396 E: revray@btinternet.com

de WAAL, Victor Alexander. b 29. Pemb Coll Cam BA 49 MA 53 Nottm Univ Hon DD 83. Ely Th Coll 50. **d** 52 **p** 53. C Isleworth St Mary *Lon* 52–56; Chapl Ely Th Coll 56–59; Chapl K Coll Cam 59–63; Hon C Nottingham St Mary *S'well* 63–69; Chapl Nottm Univ 63–69; Can Res and Chan

Linc Cathl 69–76; Dean Cant 76–86; PtO *Heref* 88–99; rtd 90; Chapl Soc of Sacred Cross Tymawr 90–00; LtO *Mon* 90–02; PtO from 02. *6 St James Close, Bishop Street, London N1 8PH* T: (020) 7354 2741

DEACON, Mrs Selina Frances. b 52. SRN 74. Ripon Coll Cuddesdon 01. **d** 03 **p** 04. C White Horse *Sarum* 03–07; P-in-c Studley 07–12; V 12–17; rtd 17; PtO *Sarum* 18–19; Hon C Salisbury St Thos and St Edm from 19. *51 St Mark's Road, Salisbury SP1 3AY* M: 07867-521909 E: selinadeacon@gmail.com

DEACON, Susan. b 47. **d** 14 **p** 15. OLM Spring Line Gp *Linc* from 14; OLM Owmby Gp from 14. *Parsonage Lodge, High Street, Scampton, Lincoln LN1 2SE* T: (01522) 730167 E: susan.deacon3@btinternet.com

DEADMAN, Hugo Charles. b 67. Wadh Coll Ox BA 89 Birkbeck Coll Lon MA 94. Ripon Coll Cuddesdon 16. **d** 19. C Milton *Portsm* from 19. *102B Copnor Road, Portsmouth PO3 5AL* M: 07947-127349 E: hugo@hdeadman.myzen.co.uk

DEADMAN, Richard George Spencer. b 63. Ex Univ BA 85. Coll of Resurr Mirfield 86. **d** 88 **p** 89. C Grangetown York 88–91; P-in-c 91–93; V 93–96; V Wallsend St Luke *Newc* 96–01; V Newc St Phil and St Aug and St Matt w St Mary from 01. *St Matthew's Vicarage, 10 Winchester Terrace, Newcastle upon Tyne NE4 6EH* T: 0191-232 9039 E: richardgsd@aol.com

DEAKIN, Caroline Sarah Ann. b 73. Trin Coll Bris 16. **d** 18 **p** 19. C Bath St Mich Without *B & W* from 18. *6 The Linleys, Bath BA1 2XE* M: 07951-132629 E: caroline.sa.deakin@gmail.com

DEAKIN, Christopher Harold. b 49. ARMCM 72. Qu Coll Birm 02. **d** 04 **p** 05. C Wrockwardine Deanery *Lich* 04–07; P-in-c Bicton, Montford w Shrawardine and Fitz 07–14; P-in-c Leaton and Albrighton w Battlefield 07–14; rtd 14; P-in-c Hargrave *Ches* 14–19; V from 19. *The Vicarage, Church Lane, Hargrave, Chester CH3 7RN* T: (01829) 781378 E: revdeakin@gmail.com

DEAKIN, John David. b 58. Qu Coll Birm BA 03. **d** 03 **p** 04. C Blakenall Heath *Lich* 03–07; TV Willenhall H Trin 07–11; TV Bentley Em and Willenhall H Trin 11–15; TR from 15. *129 Essington Road, Willenhall WV12 5DT* T: (01922) 409460 M: 07784-001503

DEAKIN, Kirsty Hayley. b 86. Qu Foundn Birm BA 15. **d** 16 **p** 17. C Blackrod, Daisy Hill, Westhoughton and Wingates *Man* from 16. *The Vicarage, 91 Chorley Road, Westhoughton, Bolton BL5 3PG* M: 07786-578776 E: revkirstyscreeton@gmail.com

DEAKIN, Paul David. b 62. Sheff Univ BA 13. Coll of Resurr Mirfield 11. **d** 13 **p** 14. C Bramhall *Ches* 13–14; C Hale and Ashley 14–16; V Knutsford St Cross from 16. *St Cross Vicarage, Mobberley Road, Knutsford WA16 8EL* T: (01565) 640702 M: 07813-368845 E: revdpauldeakin@gmail.com

DEAMER, Mrs Carylle. b 40. SAOMC 96. **d** 99 **p** 00. OLM Riverside *Ox* 99–05; rtd 05; PtO *Ox* 05–08; *B & W* from 09. *7 Coombe Close, Castle Cary BA7 7HJ* T: (01963) 359243 E: rev.carylle@deamer.me.uk

DEAN, Antonia Jane. *See* LYNN, Antonia Jane

DEAN, Benjamin Timothy Frederic. b 70. Lon Bible Coll BA 93 K Coll Lon MA 94 Selw Coll Cam MPhil 02 PhD 06. Ridley Hall Cam 04. **d** 07. C Georgeham *Ex* 07–08; Lect Geo Whitefield Coll S Africa from 08. *George Whitefield College, PO Box 64, Muizenberg, 7950 South Africa* T: (0027) (21) 788 1652 E: btfd@mac.com

DEAN, Hazel Michaela. b 48. **d** 14 **p** 15. OLM Long Sutton w Lutton etc *Linc* from 14. *Milldean Cottage, Broadgate, Sutton St James, Spalding PE12 0EL* T: (01945) 440341 E: hazel-makaila.dean@sky.com

DEAN, Jonathan Charles. b 57. St Cath Coll Cam MA 83. NEOC 04. **d** 07 **p** 08. NSM Gt Ayton w Easby and Newton under Roseberry *York* from 07. *The White House, 2 Dikes Lane, Great Ayton, Middlesbrough TS9 6HJ* T: (01642) 722649 E: jondean@cantab.net

DEAN, Kathryn Ann. b 54. **d** 19. NSM Middlesbrough St Oswald and St Chad *York* from 19. *7 North Wood, Middlesbrough TS5 7LL* E: kath.dean@hotmail.com

DEAN, Mrs Linda Louise. b 39. **d** 04 **p** 05. NSM Primrose Hill St Mary w Avenue Road St Paul *Lon* 04–13. *52 Lanchester Road, London N6 4TA* T: (020) 8883 5417

DEAN, Lucas John William. b 57. St Jo Coll Nottm 05. **d** 07 **p** 08. C St Laur in Thanet *Cant* 07–11; V Hollington St Jo *Chich* from 11. *The Vicarage, 94 Lower Glen Road, St Leonards-on-Sea TN37 7AR* T: (01424) 751103 M: 07712-834472 E: ljwdean@hotmail.com

DEAN, Malcolm. b 34. Tyndale Hall Bris 67. **d** 69 **p** 70. C Daubhill *Man* 69–73; P-in-c Constable Lee 73–74; V 74–79; P-in-c Everton St Sav w St Cuth *Liv* 79–86; P-in-c Anfield SS Simon and Jude 81–86; V Walton Breck Ch Ch 86–89; rtd

89; PtO *Man* 89–17. *40 Grasmere Road, Haslingden, Rossendale BB4 4EB* T: (01706) 215953 E: mac.dean@btopenworld.com

DEAN, Canon Margaret Heath. b 50. Newton Park Coll Bris BEd 72. STETS 05. **d** 07 **p** 08. C Farncombe *Guildf* 07–11; R Reepham, Hackford w Whitwell, Kerdiston etc *Nor* 11–17; P-in-c Wensum Benefice 16–17; Hon Can Nor Cathl 16–17; rtd 17; PtO *Guildf* from 18. *10 Henchley Dene, Guildford GU4 7BH* T: (01483) 562776 E: margaretdean@cnet.org

DEAN, Mark William John. b 58. **d** 10 **p** 11. NSM N Greenford All Hallows *Lon* 10–13; Chapl Univ of the Arts from 13; PtO *S'wark* from 13. *Chaplaincy, University of the Arts London, 272 High Holborn, London WC1V 7EY* M: 07843-329587 E: m.w.dean@arts.ac.uk

DEAN, Simon Christopher. b 82. Dur Univ BA 18. St Mellitus Coll 17. **d** 19. C Bottesford w Ashby *Linc* from 19. *10 Old School Lane, Bottesford, Scunthorpe DN16 3RD* E: revdsimondean@gmail.com

DEAN, Timothy Charles Painter. b 50. STETS MA 08. **d** 07 **p** 08. NSM Godalming *Guildf* 07–11; CMD Officer *Nor* 11–15; NSM Reepham, Hackford w Whitwell, Kerdiston etc 11–17; NSM Wensum Benefice 16–17; NSM Lyng, Sparham, Elsing, Bylaugh, Bawdeswell etc 16–17; RD Sparham 14–17; rtd 17; PtO *Guildf* from 18. *10 Henchley Dene, Guildford GU4 7BH* T: (01483) 562776 E: timdean@cnet.org

DEAN, Trevor Stephen. b 58. Lon Hosp MB, BS 81. Trin Coll Bris BA 03. **d** 10 **p** 11. NSM Nailsea H Trin *B & W* from 10. *3 Ilminster Close, Nailsea, Bristol BS48 4YU* T: (01275) 851218 M: 07905-757649 E: trevor.dean@blueyonder.co.uk

DEAN-REVILL, David Frank. b 68. Univ Coll Ches BA 06. NOC 03. **d** 06 **p** 07. C Dinnington w Laughton and Throapham *Sheff* 06–09; P-in-c Shiregreen from 09. *The Vicarage, 510 Bellhouse Road, Sheffield S5 0RG* T: 0114-245 6526 E: daviddeanrevill@hotmail.com

DEANE, Nicholas Talbot Bryan. b 46. Bris Univ BA 69. Clifton Th Coll 70. **d** 72 **p** 73. C Accrington Ch Ch *Blackb* 72–75; OMF Korea 75–89; P-in-c Newburgh *Liv* 90–93; P-in-c Westhead 90–93; V Newburgh w Westhead 93–97; R Chadwell *Chelmsf* 97–11; rtd 11; C Waverton w Aldford and Bruera *Ches* 11–15; PtO *S'well* from 16. *1 Patient Close, Chilwell, Beeston, Nottingham NG9 4HA* T: 0115-922 2926 M: 07712-153882 E: nicholasdeane7@gmail.com

DEANE, Robert William. b 52. CITC. **d** 85 **p** 86. C Raheny w Coolock *D & G* 85–88; I Clonsast w Rathangan, Thomastown etc *M & K* 88–00; Can Kildare Cathl 97–00; Can Meath Cathl 98–00; I Swords w Donabate and Kilsallaghan *D & G* 00–18; Can Ch Ch Cathl Dublin 08–18; rtd 18. *209 St Werburghs, Malahide Road, Swords, Co Dublin, K67 VR64, Republic of Ireland* T: (00353) (1) 840 4282 M: 87-346 1342 E: rwdeane@eircom.net

DEANE, Stuart William. b 45. Sarum & Wells Th Coll 86. **d** 88 **p** 89. C Bromyard *Heref* 88–92; V Astley, Clive, Grinshill and Hadnall *Lich* 92–98; TV Cen Telford 98–00; TR 00–05; rtd 05; PtO *Heref* from 07. *38 Crest Court, Hereford HR4 9QD* T: (01432) 351937

DEANS, Bruce Gibson. b 64. MCIBS 86. Wycliffe Hall Ox 02. **d** 04 **p** 05. C Hartley Wintney, Elvetham, Winchfield etc *Win* 04–08; R Shedfield and Wickham *Portsm* 08–15; P-in-c Fareham St Jo 15–18; V from 18. *3A Upper St Michael's Grove, Fareham PO14 1DN* T: (01329) 281544

DEANS, Robert. b 58. Stirling Univ BA 82 Edin Univ MSc 83 Anglia Ruskin Univ MA 12. ERMC 09. **d** 12 **p** 13. NSM Pet St Jo 12–17; Chapl HM Pris Peterborough 17; PtO *York* from 19. *Hill View, Egton, Whitby YO21 1UT* E: robdeans@outlook.com

DEAR, Graham Frederick. b 44. St Luke's Coll Ex CertEd 66. Wycliffe Hall Ox 67. **d** 70 **p** 71. C Chigwell *Chelmsf* 70–73; C Chingford SS Pet and Paul 73–75; V Southchurch Ch Ch 75–82; CF 82–89; P-in-c The Cowtons *Ripon* 89–94; RE Adv 89–94; V Startforth and Bowes and Rokeby w Brignall 94–97; Chapl HM Pris Garth 97–01; rtd 09; PtO *Ripon* 01–14; *Leeds* from 14. *1 The Old Wynd, Bellerby, Leyburn DL8 5QJ* T: (01969) 623960

DEAR, Neil Douglas Gauntlett. b 35. Linc Th Coll 87. **d** 89 **p** 90. C Framlingham w Saxtead *St E* 89–92; P-in-c Eyke w Bromeswell, Rendlesham, Tunstall etc 92–98; Chapl Local Health Partnerships NHS Trust 98–02; Chapl Cen Suffolk Primary Care Trust 02–05; P-in-c Worlingworth, Southolt, Tannington, Bedfield etc *St E* 02–05; rtd 05; PtO *St E* from 05. *Peacehaven, Duke Street, Stanton, Bury St Edmunds IP31 2AB* T: (01359) 252001

DEAR, Virginia Anne. b 65. Westcott Ho Cam. **d** 13 **p** 14. C Hertford *St Alb* 13–16; R St Ippolyts w Gt and Lt Wymondley from 16. *The Vicarage, Stevenage Road, St Ippolyts, Hitchin SG4 7PE* T: (01462) 237032 E: revginni@gmail.com

DEARDEN, Geoffrey. b 36. Salford Univ MSc 74. CBDTI 05. **d** 06 **p** 07. NSM Hurst Green and Mitton *Bradf* 06–10;

PtO 10–14; *Leeds* 14–16; *Blackb* from 15. *14 Church Close, Waddington, Clitheroe BB7 3HX* T: (01200) 427380 E: geoffandann@btinternet.com

DEARDEN, Canon Philip Harold. b 43. AKC 65. **d** 66 **p** 67. C Haslingden w Haslingden Grane *Blackb* 66–69; C Burnley St Pet 69–71; V Langho Billington 71–78; TR Darwen St Pet w Hoddlesden 78–91; RD Darwen 86–91; V Altham w Clayton le Moors 91–97; RD Accrington 95–97; V Clitheroe St Mary 97–08; Hon Can Blackb Cathl 96–08; rtd 08; PtO *Blackb* 08–14; *Carl* 11–16. *20 South Park, Lincoln LN5 8EP* T: (01522) 533210

DEARMER, Juliet. See WOOLLCOMBE, Juliet

DEARNLEY, Ms Helen Elizabeth Booker. b 77. De Montfort Univ LLB 98 Cam Univ BTh 02 MSt 19 York St Jo Univ MA 09. Westcott Ho Cam 99. **d** 02 **p** 03. C Knighton St Mary Magd *Leic* 02–06; Co-ord Chapl HM Pris Leic 06–13; Adv Prison Chapl HQ 13–18; Angl Adv from 19. *HMPPS Chaplaincy HQ, Post Points 8.34-8.37, Ministry of Justice, 102 Petty France, London SW1H 9AJ* T: 03000-476790 M: 07891-121388 E: helen.dearnley@justice.gov.uk

DEARNLEY, Mark Christopher. b 59. Cranmer Hall Dur 84. **d** 87 **p** 88. C Purley Ch Ch *S'wark* 87–91; C Addiscombe St Mary 91–93; C Addiscombe St Mary Magd w St Martin 93–94; V Hook 94–02; R Wendover and Halton *Ox* 02–16; AD Wendover 04–16; Hon Can Ch Ch 14–16; V St Alb St Pet from 16. *The Vicarage, 35 Hall Place Gardens, St Albans AL1 3SB* T: (01727) 851464 M: 07769-960447 E: mark.dearnley@btinternet.com

DEARNLEY, Preb Patrick Walter. b 34. Nottm Univ BA 55 LTh 75. ALCD 64. **d** 64 **p** 65. C New Malden and Coombe *S'wark* 64–68; C Portswood Ch Ch *Win* 68–71; C Leeds St Geo *Ripon* 71–74; Hon C Nottingham St Nic *S'well* 74–77; P-in-c Holloway Em w Hornsey Road St Barn *Lon* 77–85; AD Islington 80–85; Abp's Officer for UPA 85–90; Preb St Paul's Cathl *Lon* 86–91; P-in-c Waterloo St Jo *Liv* 91–99; rtd 99; PtO *Bradf* 00–14; *Leeds* from 14. *14 Beanlands Parade, Ilkley LS29 8EW* T: (01943) 603927 E: gilrea@blueyonder.co.uk

DEAS, Leonard Stephen. b 52. New Coll Ox BA 75 CertEd 76 MA 78. St Mich Coll Llan 80. **d** 82 **p** 83. C Dowlais *Llan* 82–84; Chapl St Mich Coll Llan 84–85; Chapl Univ of Wales (Cardiff) *Llan* 85–86; V Newbridge *Mon* 86–93; Can Res St Woolos Cathl 92–96; Master Charterhouse Hull 96–17; rtd 17. *98 Walkergate, Beverley HU17 9BT* T: (01482) 861399 E: dysgamyser@hotmail.co.uk

DEAVES, Mrs Hannah Claire. b 73. York Univ BSc 94 Bp Grosseteste Coll PGCE 95 Univ of Wales (Ban) BTh 06. **d** 11 **p** 12. OLM Triangle, St Matt and All SS *St E* 11–15; PtO from 15. *2 Exeter Road, Ipswich IP3 8JL* T: (01473) 399635 M: 07906-372733 E: hannahdeaves@yahoo.co.uk

DEAVES, Peter. b 76. Sheff Univ BA 97. Ridley Hall Cam 14. **d** 16 **p** 17. C Rudgwick *Chich* from 16. *1 Orchard Hill, Rudgwick, Horsham RH12 3EQ* M: 07900-185591 E: peterevd@gmail.com or curate@rudgwickchurch.org.uk

DEBNEY, Nicholas Johnathan. b 72. SWMTC 10. **d** 13 **p** 14. C Dartmouth and Dittisham *Ex* 13–17; TV Newton Abbot from 17; P-in-c Bovey Tracey St Jo w Heathfield from 19. *St Luke's Vicarage, 10 Laburnum Road, Newton Abbot TQ12 4LQ* T: (01626) 334357 E: fr.debney@hotmail.co.uk

DEBOO, Canon Alan John. b 45. Qu Coll Cam BA 73 MA 77. Westcott Ho Cam 72. **d** 74 **p** 75. C Brackley St Pet w St Jas Pet 74–77; PtO *Sarum* 85–94; NSM Wexcombe 94–02; NSM Savernake 02–09 and 13–15; PtO from 15; Bp's Officer for NSMs 03–09; Bp's Adv for Assoc Min from 09; Can and Preb Sarum Cathl from 05. *Mayzells Cottage, Collingbourne Kingston, Marlborough SN8 3SD* T: (01264) 850683 E: alandeboo@aol.com

DEBOYS, David Gordon. b 54. QUB BD 76 Wolfs Coll Ox MLitt. Ridley Hall Cam 90. **d** 92 **p** 93. C Ipswich St Aug *St E* 92–93; C Whitton and Thurleston w Akenham 93–95; R Hardwick *Ely* 95–00; R Toft w Caldecote and Childerley 95–00; V Cambridge St Jas 00–07; Dir Focus Chr Inst Cambridge 00–07; V Ealing St Barn *Lon* 07–12; C Tewkesbury w Walton Cardiff and Twyning *Glouc* 12–15; Dioc Worship Officer 12–15; TV Southampton (City Cen) *Win* 15–18; V Southampton St Mich from 18. *St Michael's Vicarage, 55 Bugle Street, Southampton SO14 2AG* T: (023) 8194 3684 M: 07773-613172 E: daviddeboys@btconnect.com

DEDMAN, Canon Roger James. b 45. Oak Hill Th Coll 68. **d** 71 **p** 72. C Gresley *Derby* 71–74; C Ipswich St Fran *St E* 74–79; P-in-c Bildeston w Wattisham 79–92; P-in-c Bramford 92–10; P-in-c Somersham w Flowton and Offton w Willisham 94–02; P-in-c Gt and Lt Blakenham w Baylham and Nettlestead 02–10; RD Bosmere 96–01 and 05–07; Hon Can St E Cathl 01–10; rtd 10; PtO *Bradf* 10–14; *Leeds* from 14; *St E* 10–17. *10 St Martin's Field, Otley LS21 2FN* E: roger.dedman@talktalk.net

DEEDES, Ms Rosemary Anne. b 66. Birm Univ BA 87 City Univ 90. Westcott Ho Cam 94. **d** 96 **p** 97. C St Botolph Aldgate w H Trin Minories *Lon* 96–99; Asst Chapl HM Pris Holloway 99–02; Chapl HM Pris Downview 02–10; Chapl HM Pris Is of Wight 10–15; Chapl Cov Univ 15–17; Chapl Earl Mountbatten Hospice from 17. *Earl Mountbatten Hospice, Halberry Lane, Newport PO30 2ER* T: (01983) 529511

DEEGAN, Arthur Charles. b 49. CertEd 71 Birm Univ BEd 86. Qu Coll Birm 86. **d** 88 **p** 89. C Leic St Jas 88–91; C Melton Gt Framland 91–92; TV 92–93; TV Melton Mowbray 93–96; R Barwell w Potters Marston and Stapleton 96–08; P-in-c Braunstone Town w Thorpe Astley 08–15; TR 15–18; CF (TA) 95–15; rtd 18; PtO *Leic* from 19. *58 Amy Street, Leicester LE3 2FB* T: 0116-224 8346 E: ac.deegan@ntlworld.com

DEEGAN, Michael Joseph. b 54. Ripon Coll Cuddesdon. **d** 09 **p** 10. Dir Soc Justice and C Sarum Cathl 09–12; Warden Pilsdon Community 12–19; rtd 19. *Pilsdon Manor, Pilsdon, Bridport DT6 5NZ* T: (01308) 868308 F: 868161 M: 07502-216607 E: mdeegan01@aol.com

DEEMING, Paul Leyland. b 44. CA Tr Coll 65 CMS Tr Coll Selly Oak 70. **d** 80 **p** 80. CMS Pakistan 71–82; R E and W Horndon w Lt Warley *Chelmsf* 83–89; V Gt Ilford St Andr 89–01; Co-ord Chapl Heatherwood & Wexham Park Hosps NHS Foundn Trust 01–09; rtd 09. *10 Glenthorn Road, Bexhill-on-Sea TN39 3QH* T: (01424) 222287

DEETH, William Stanley. b 38. St Pet Coll Ox BA 59 MA 67. St Steph Ho Ox 66. **d** 68 **p** 69. C Eastbourne St Mary *Chich* 68–71; C Benwell St Jas *Newc* 71–75; C-in-c Byker St Martin CD 75–76; P-in-c Byker St Martin 76; V 76–89; P-in-c Bothal 89–91; R Bothal and Pegswood w Longhirst 91–94; rtd 94; PtO *Newc* 94–08; *Leeds* from 17. *2 All Saints Square, Ripon HG4 1FN* T: (01765) 690366 E: w.deeth@talktalk.net

DEGG, Miss Jennifer Margaret. b 39. Open Univ BA 85 Rolle Coll CertEd 64. NOC. **d** 06 **p** 07. NSM Saddleworth *Man* 06–09; PtO from 09. *2 Lowerfields, Dobcross, Oldham OL3 5NW* E: jennydegg@talktalk.net

DEHOOP, Brother Thomas Anthony. b 38. Bp's Univ Lennox BA 63 LTh 63. **d** 68 **p** 69. C Fort George w Painthills Canada 68–70; I Mistassini 70–72; R La Tuque 72–75; Assoc P Pierrefonds 75–79; SSF from 79; PtO *Sarum* 79–80; Hon C Toxteth St Marg *Liv* 80–85; Chapl Newsham Gen Hosp Liv 82–85; P-in-c Cambridge St Benedict *Ely* 85–88; V 88–92; PtO *Liv* 92–94; *Ely* 92–96; *Eur* from 94. *43 Balaam Street, London E13 8AQ* E: glasshamptonssf@franciscans.org.uk *or* thomasanthonyssf@franciscans.org.uk

DEIGHTON, Gary. b 61. Dundee Univ MA 83 Nottm Univ MA 89 Heythrop Coll Lon MA 11 PGCE 84. SWMTC 10. **d** 12 **p** 13. C Paignton St Jo *Ex* 12–16; V Goodrington and Collaton St Mary from 16. *The Vicarage, 17 Seafields, Paignton TQ4 6NY* T: (01803) 843038 E: fr.gary@outlook.com

DEJA, Jonathan Joseph. b 87. Clare Coll Cam BA 08. Oak Hill Th Coll BA 16. **d** 16 **p** 17. C Harold Wood *Chelmsf* 16–19; C Moulton *Pet* from 19. *8 Cubleigh Close, Moulton, Northampton NN3 7BG* M: 07743-250432 E: jonniedeja@gmail.com *or* associatevicar@moultonchurch.co.uk

DEKKER, Denise Rosemary Irene. b 43. Th Ext Educn Coll 90. **d** 95 **p** 96. C Stutterheim S Africa 95–99; P-in-c 99–04; P-in-c Kokstad 04–09; PtO *Win* 09–11; P-in-c Guernsey St Andr 11–15; NSM Coventry Caludon *Cov* 15–18; rtd 18. *64 Waun Sidan, Pembrey, Burry Port SA16 0JY* M: 07850-995716 E: dekkerd1@hotmail.com

DEL PINO, Mrs Helena Mary Elizabeth. b 62. K Coll Lon LLB 85. Ox Min Course 13. **d** 16 **p** 18. NSM Pet H Spirit Bretton from 16. *17 Alexandra Road, Peterborough PE1 3DB* T: (01733) 310795 M: 07715-857970 E: revhelenadelpino@gmail.com

DELAFORCE, Stephen Robert. b 52. Middx Poly BSc 80 Cranfield Inst of Tech MSc 88 Nottm Univ MA 03 CEng MIMechE 83. EMMTC 04. **d** 07 **p** 08. NSM Woodhouse, Woodhouse Eaves and Swithland *Leic* 07–10; C Beaumont Leys 10–15; V Stocking Farm and Beaumont Leys from 15. *The Vicarage, 97 Halifax Drive, Leicester LE4 2DR* T: 0116-319 8177 E: steve.delaforce@gmail.com

DELAMERE, Isaac George. b 71. CITC BTh 02. **d** 02 **p** 03. C Newtownards *D & D* 02–05; I Narraghmore and Timolin w Castledermot etc *D & G* 05–14; I Tullamore w Durrow, Newtownfertullagh, Rahan etc *M & K* from 14; Can Meath from 18; Can Kildare Cathl from 18. *St Catherine's Rectory, Church Avenue, Tullamore, Co Offaly, Republic of Ireland* T: (00353) (57) 932 1731 M: 86-060 9241 E: revisaacdelamere@eircom.net *or* tullamore@meath.anglican.org

DELANEY, Anthony. b 65. St Jo Coll Nottm BTh 95. **d** 95 **p** 96. C Cullompton *Ex* 95–98; C Maidstone St Luke *Cant* 98–01; P-in-c W Horsley *Guildf* 01–03; R 03–08; PtO *Man* from 09. *99*

Barlow Moor Road, Didsbury, Manchester M20 2GP T: 0161-445 0446 M: 07881-902966 E: anthony@ivychurch.org

DELANEY, Janet. b 50. STETS. **d** 07 **p** 08. C Wootton Bassett *Sarum* 07–11; R Askerswell, Loders, Powerstock and Symondsbury 11–17; RD Lyme Bay 14–16; rtd 17; PtO *Win* from 17. *10 Doe Copse Way, New Milton BH25 5GB* T: (01425) 837746 E: jan.delaney@talktalk.net

DELANEY, The Ven Peter Anthony. b 39. AKC 65. **d** 66 **p** 67. C St Marylebone w H Trin *Lon* 66–70; Chapl Nat Heart Hosp Lon 66–70; Res Chapl Univ Ch Ch the K *Lon* 70–73; Can Res and Prec S'wark Cathl 73–77; V All Hallows by the Tower etc *Lon* 77–04; P-in-c St Kath Cree 98–02; Can Cyprus and the Gulf from 88; Preb St Paul's Cathl *Lon* 95–99; Adn Lon 99–09; P-in-c St Steph Walbrook and St Swithun etc 04–14; rtd from 14. *29 Portland Square, London E1W 2QR* T: (020) 7481 1786 E: padelaney@btinternet.com

DELAP, Ms Dana Lurkse. b 65. St Jo Coll Dur BA 87 MA 93 MATM 11. Cranmer Hall Dur 09. **d** 11 **p** 12. C Fenham St Jas and St Basil *Newc* 11–14; TV Vale and Cotswold Edge *Glouc* from 14. *The Vicarage, High Street, Blockley, Moreton-in-Marsh GL56 9ES* T: (01386) 700676 M: 07952-096789 E: dana@delap.org.uk

DELFGOU, Jonathan Hawke. b 63. Aston Tr Scheme 89 Linc Th Coll BTh 94. **d** 94 **p** 95. C Greenstead *Chelmsf* 94–98; TV Wickford and Runwell 98–18; Chapl Southend Community Care Services NHS Trust 98–99; Chapl S Essex Mental Health & Community Care NHS Trust 00–06; Chapl S Essex Partnership Univ NHS Foundn Trust 06–17; Chapl Essex Partnership Univ NHS Foundn Trust 17–18; V Hadleigh, Layham and Shelley *St E* from 18. *The Deanery, Church Street, Hadleigh, Ipswich IP7 5DT* E: delfgou@live.co.uk

DELINGER, Ian Michael. b 70. Truman State Univ (USA) BSc 92 SS Coll Cam BTh 04. Westcott Ho Cam 01. **d** 04 **p** 05. C Chorlton-cum-Hardy St Clem *Man* 04–07; Chapl Ches Univ 08–16; R San Luis Obispo USA from 16. *St Stephen's Episcopal Church, 1344 Nipomo Street, San Luis Obispo CA 93401-3935 , USA* T: (001) (805) 543 7212 F: 543 0744 E: fatherimd@aol.com

DELMEGE, Canon Andrew Mark. b 68. Essex Univ BA 91 Southn Univ MTh 98. SWMTC 94. **d** 97 **p** 98. C Kings Heath *Birm* 97–01; V Brandwood from 01; Chapl to Deaf People 01–10; P-in-c Weoley Castle 10–14; Hon Can Birm Cathl from 18. *The Vicarage, 77 Doversley Road, Birmingham B14 6NN* T: 0121-693 0217 or 456 1535 or 246 6100 F: 246 6125 E: andydelmege@hotmail.com

DELVE, Eric David. b 42. Trin Coll Bris. **d** 89 **p** 90. NSM Bris St Matt and St Nath 89–92; P-in-c Kirkdale St Lawr *Liv* 93–96; V Maidstone St Luke *Cant* 96–12; AD Maidstone 99–03; Six Preacher Cant Cathl 99–09; rtd 13; PtO *Roch* 13–17; *B & W* from 19. *35 Manor Road, Weston-super-Mare BS23 2SU*

DELVES, Canon Anthony James. b 47. Birm Univ BSocSc 70 Hull Univ PhD 94. St Steph Ho Ox 83. **d** 85 **p** 86. C Cantley *Sheff* 85–90; V Goldthorpe w Hickleton 90–07; Hon Can Sheff Cathl 98–07; AD Wath 00–06; rtd 07; PtO *Sheff* from 07; *Wakef* 07–14; *Leeds* from 14. *3 Pelham Cottages, Pelmham Yard, Seaford BN25 1PQ* T: (01323) 893695 E: ajd@delwood.plus.com *or* creesjean@gmail.com

DELVES (formerly MANHOOD), Canon Phyllis. b 32. Aston Tr Scheme 78 Qu Coll Birm 79. **dss** 82 **d** 87 **p** 94. Harwich *Chelmsf* 82–83; Dovercourt and Parkeston 83–85; Fawley *Win* 85–87; Par Dn 87–92; P-in-c Bournemouth St Aug 92–99; Hon Can Win Cathl 96–99; rtd 99; PtO *Win* from 01. *11 Rhyme Hall Mews, Fawley, Southampton SO45 1FX* T: (023) 8089 4450 E: phyllis.delves@sky.com

DELVES BROUGHTON, Simon Brian Hugo. b 33. Ex Coll Ox BA 56 MA 64. Kelham Th Coll 56. **d** 59 **p** 60. Ox Miss to Calcutta India 60–64; C Skirbeck St Nic *Linc* 64–67; Chapl Chittagong E Pakistan/Bangladesh 67–69; V St Thos Cathl Dhaka 69–74; V Northampton Ch Ch *Pet* 74–95; Chapl Northn Gen Hosp 77–87; rtd 95; PtO *Ox* 95–00. *71A Observatory Street, Oxford OX2 6EP* T: (01865) 515463

DEMAIN, Peter James. b 64. Salford Univ BA 85. SNWTP 07. **d** 10 **p** 11. OLM Middleton and Thornham *Man* from 10. *3 St Gabriel's Close, Rochdale OL11 2TG* T: (01706) 522985 M: 07747-398012 E: peterdemain@tiscali.co.uk

DEMERY, Rupert Edward Rodier. b 72. Trin Hall Cam BA 94 MA 01 BTh 01. Ridley Hall Cam 98. **d** 01 **p** 02. C New Borough and Leigh *Sarum* 01–05; Lower Chapl Eton Coll from 05. *Burnham Thorpe, Eton Wick Road, Eton College, Windsor SL4 6ET* T: (01753) 441629 M: 07801-825671 E: r.demery@etoncollege.org.uk

DEMPSTER, Adrian. b 49. Newc Univ BSc 70. EMMTC 05. **d** 08 **p** 09. NSM Kirkby in Ashfield *S'well* 08–12; NSM Skegby w Teversal 12–17; NSM Selston from 17. *105 Nottingham Road, Selston, Nottingham NG16 6BU* T: (01773) 811846 T: 0115-950 4646 M: 07971-142829

DENBY, Canon Paul. b 47. NW Ord Course 73. **d** 76 **p** 77. C Stretford All SS *Man* 76–80; V Stalybridge 80–87; Chapl Tameside Gen Hosp 82–87; Dir of Ords *Man* 87–95; LNSM Officer 91–95; Hon Can Man Cathl 92–95; Bp's Dom Chapl 94–95; Can Admin and Prec Man Cathl 95–07; rtd 07; PtO *Man* 07–08 and from 12. *14 Cranberry Drive, Bolton BL3 3TB* T: (01204) 655157 *or* 0161-834 0490 E: paul@thedenbys.co.uk

DENCH, Canon Christopher David. b 62. RGN 83. Aston Tr Scheme 86 Sarum & Wells Th Coll 88. **d** 91 **p** 92. C Crayford *Roch* 91–94; P-in-c Leybourne 94–98; R 98–05; Dioc Lay Tr Adv 01–05; Tr Officer for CME 03–10; Min Development Officer 05–10; Bp's Officer for Min and Tr from 10; Hon Can Roch Cathl 11–18; Can Res Roch Cathl from 18. *Easter Garth, The Precinct, Rochester ME1 1SX* T: (01634) 560000 *or* (01732) 220245 M: 07961-433545 E: chris.dench@rochester.anglican.org

DENERLEY, John Keith Christopher. b 34. Qu Coll Ox BA 58 MA 61. St Steph Ho Ox 58. **d** 61 **p** 62. C Airedale w Fryston *Wakef* 61–64; Chapl Sarum Th Coll 64–68; Min Can Cov Cathl 68–76; Chapl Lanchester Poly 70–76; Chapl The Dorothy Kerin Trust Burrswood 76–85; V Trellech and Cwmcarvan *Mon* 85–86; V Penallt 85–86; V Penallt and Trellech 87–99; Chapl Ty Mawr Convent (Wales) 85–90; RD Monmouth *Mon* 93–99; rtd 99; PtO *Glouc* from 00. *1 The Pales, English Bicknor, Coleford GL16 7PQ* T: (01594) 860028 E: janeandkeith@mypostoffice.co.uk

DENGATE, Richard Henry. b 39. Cant Sch of Min 82. **d** 85 **p** 86. NSM Wittersham w Stone and Ebony *Cant* 85; R Sandhurst w Newenden 90–01; rtd 01; PtO *Cant* from 01; *Chich* from 15. *Apuldram, Main Street, Peasemarsh, Rye TN31 6UL* T: (01797) 230980 E: rhdengate@btinternet.com

DENHAM, Anthony Christopher. b 43. Keble Coll Ox BA 65 MA 70. Oak Hill Th Coll 91. **d** 93 **p** 94. C Hythe *Cant* 93–97; V Haddenham w Cuddington, Kingsey etc *Ox* 97–08; rtd 08; PtO *Guildf* from 08. *3 The Larches, Woking GU21 4RE* T: (01483) 823310 E: a.chris.denham@gmail.com

DENHAM, Nicholas Philip. b 50. Salford Univ BSc 72 Dur Univ MA 10 Birm Univ CertEd 74. Wycliffe Hall Ox 87. **d** 89 **p** 90. C Bishopwearmouth St Gabr *Dur* 89–90; C Chester le Street 90–92; TV Rushden w Newton Bromswold *Pet* 92–95; R Teigh w Whissendine and Market Overton 95–02; P-in-c Greetham and Thistleton w Stretton and Clipsham 01–02; RD Rutland 01–02; TR Bedworth *Cov* 02–05; V Escomb *Dur* 05–08; R Etherley 05–08; V Witton Park 05–08; V Hamsterley and Witton-le-Wear 05–08; rtd 08; PtO *Ox* 09–14; *Ely* 14–19; *Derby* from 19. *8 Hardwick Avenue, Allestree, Derby DE22 2LL*

DENHOLM, Robert Jack. b 31. Edin Th Coll 53. **d** 56 **p** 57. C Dundee St Mary Magd *Bre* 56–59; C Edin St Pet 59–61; R Bridge of Allan *St And* 61–69; Chapl Stirling Univ 67–69; R N Berwick *Edin* 69–80; R Gullane 76–80; R Edin St Mark 80–90; Can St Mary's Cathl 88–90; rtd 90. *20 St Vincent Court, 131 St Vincent Street, Broughty Ferry, Dundee DD5 2DA* T: (01382) 525400 E: jackdenholm@googlemail.com

DENIS LE SÈVE, Hilary. See LE SÈVE, Jane Hilary

DENISON, Canon Keith Malcolm. b 45. Down Coll Cam BA 67 MA 71 PhD 70. Westcott Ho Cam 70. **d** 71 **p** 72. C Chepstow *Mon* 71–72; C Bassaleg 72–75; Post-Ord Tr Officer 75–85; V Mathern and Mounton 75–80; V Mathern and Mounton w St Pierre 80–85; RD Chepstow 82–85; V Risca 85–91; V Goldcliffe and Whitson and Nash 91–96; Dioc Dir of Educn Monmouth 91–11; Hon Can St Woolos Cathl 91–94; Can St Woolos Cathl 94–11; Can Res St Woolos Cathl 96–11; rtd 11; PtO *Pet* from 12; *Linc* from 18. *21 Melbourne Road, Stamford PE9 1UD* T: (01780) 751571 E: keith_denison@hotmail.com

DENISON, Philip. b 55. York Univ BA 77 CertEd. St Jo Coll Nottm 83. **d** 86 **p** 87. C Barnoldswick w Bracewell *Bradf* 86–88; P-in-c Basford St Leodegarius *S'well* 88–91; C Basford w Hyson Green 91–94; V Nether Stowey w Over Stowey *B & W* 94–04; R Aisholt, Enmore, Goathurst, Nether Stowey etc 05; RD Quantock 01–05; PtO 06–10; C Alfred Jewel 10–16; V Isle Valley from 16. *The Rectory, Broadway, Ilminster TA19 9RE* T: (01460) 259155 E: denisonphil15@hotmail.com

DENLEY, Adam Spencer. b 81. New Coll Dur BSc 06. Oak Hill Th Coll 14. **d** 16 **p** 17. C Southsea St Jude *Portsm* from 16. *92 Marmion Road, Southsea PO5 2BB* M: 07990-020445 E: adam.denley@gmail.com

DENLEY, Trevor Maurice. b 47. **d** 06 **p** 07. Partnership P E Bris from 06; OLM Bristol St Aid w St Geo from 06. *31 Dundridge Gardens, Bristol BS5 8SZ* T: 0117-961 4468 M: 07960-329127

DENNEN, Lyle. b 42. Harvard Univ LLB 67 Trin Coll Cam BA 70 MA 75. Cuddesdon Coll 70. **d** 72 **p** 73. C S Lambeth St Ann *S'wark* 72–75; C Richmond St Mary w St Matthias

75–78; P-in-c Kennington St Jo 78–79; V Kennington St Jo w St Jas 79–99; P-in-c Brixton Road Ch Ch 81–89; RD Brixton 90–99; Hon Can S'wark Cathl 99; Adn Hackney *Lon* 99–10; V St Andr Holborn 99–14; rtd 14; PtO *Lon* from 14. *1 Victoria Wharf, 46 Narrow Street, London E14 8DD* T: (020) 7353 3544 F: 7583 2750 E: lyle.dennen@hotmail.com

DENNER-BROWN, Sarah. See BROWN, Sarah Romilly Denner

DENNESS, Mrs Linda Christine. b 51. Portsm Dioc Tr Course 88. **d** 89 **p** 01. NSM Milton *Portsm* 89–93; Chapl Asst Portsm Hosps NHS Trust 89–91; NSM Portsea St Mary *Portsm* 93–96; NSM Wymering 96–06; P-in-c Cosham 06–09; P-in-c Wymering 07–09; PtO 09–10 and from 13; NSM Portsea N End St Mark 10–13. *19 Fourth Avenue, Cosham, Portsmouth PO6 3HX* T: (023) 9232 6885

DENNIS, Barbara Christine. See HUME, Barbara Christine

DENNIS, David Alan. b 46. St Luke's Coll Ex BSc 90. **d** 05 **p** 06. OLM Alderholt *Sarum* 05–16; PtO from 16. *18 Oak Road, Alderholt, Fordingbridge SP6 3BL* T: (01425) 655230 E: davidalan.dennis@btinternet.com

DENNIS, Miss Drucilla Lyn. b 49. Ox Univ BEd 71 Southn Univ MA(Ed) 82 Win Univ MA 10. S Dios Minl Tr Scheme 92. **d** 95 **p** 96. NSM Cowes H Trin and St Mary *Portsm* 95–01; TV Dorchester *Sarum* 01–08; Hon C Chale, Shorwell w Kingston and Brighstone and Brooke w Mottistone *Portsm* 08–11; Chapl Earl Mountbatten Hospice and Isle of Wight NHS Primary Care Trust 09–11; P-in-c Brading w Yaverland *Portsm* 11–16; rtd 16; PtO *Portsm* from 16. *40 Park Road, Cowes PO31 7LT* T: (01983) 297002 E: drucilladennis@hotmail.com

✠**DENNIS, The Rt Revd John.** b 31. St Cath Coll Cam BA 54 MA 59. Cuddesdon Coll 54. **d** 56 **p** 57 **c** 79. C Armley St Bart *Ripon* 56–60; C Kettering SS Pet and Paul 60–62; V Is of Dogs Ch Ch and St Jo w St Luke *Lon* 62–71; V Mill Hill Jo Keble Ch 71–79; RD W Barnet 73–79; Preb St Paul's Cathl 77–79; Suff Bp Knaresborough *Ripon* 79–86; Dioc Dir of Ords 80–86; Bp St E 86–96; rtd 96; PtO *St E* from 96; Hon Asst Bp Win from 99. *7 Conifer Close, Winchester SO22 6SH* T: (01962) 868881 E: 7johndennis@gmail.com

DENNIS, Canon Robert Franklin. b 51. St Paul's Coll Grahamstown 91. **d** 94 **p** 94. C Kuils River S Africa 94–96; C Matroosfontein 96–99; R Maitland 99–03; TR Bredasdorp 03–05; P-in-c Crumpsall *Man* 06–09; Min Can St Woolos Cathl *Mon* 09–11; P-in-c Llantilio Pertholey w Bettws Chpl etc 11–14; V Connah's Quay *St As* 14–16; TV Borderlands Miss Area 17; rtd 17; Chapl Pau *Eur* from 17; PtO *St As* from 17; Hon Can Saldanha Bay S Africa from 14; PtO *Eur* from 17. *3 bis rue Pasteur, 64000 Pau, France* T: (0033) 5 59 30 91 84 E: rfd.stmark2@gmail.com

DENNIS, Samuel James. b 85. Peterho Cam BA 07. Westcott Ho Cam 08. **d** 11 **p** 12. C Catford (Southend) and Downham *S'wark* 11–16; P-in-c Croydon Woodside 16–18; V from 18. *St Luke's Vicarage, Portland Road, London SE25 4RB* T: (020) 8654 9841 M: 07940-576397 E: fr.sam.dennis@gmail.com

DENNIS, Timothy William. b 81. Southn Univ BSc 02. Wycliffe Hall Ox BA 19. **d** 19. C Winklebury and Worting *Win* from 19. *77 Camrose Way, Basingstoke RG21 3AW* M: 07734-663313 E: timwdennis@icloud.com

DENNIS, Canon Trevor John. b 45. St Jo Coll Cam BA 68 MA 71 PhD 74. Westcott Ho Cam 71. **d** 72 **p** 73. C Newport Pagnell *Ox* 72–74; Chapl Eton Coll 75–82; Tutor Sarum & Wells Th Coll 82–94; Vice-Prin 89–94; Can Res Ches Cathl 94–10; rtd 10; PtO *Ches* from 11. *11 Anne's Way, Chester CH4 7BA* T: (01244) 638441 E: trevordennis11@gmail.com

DENNISON, Philip Ian. b 52. Nottm Univ BTh 81. St Jo Coll Nottm 77. **d** 81 **p** 82. C Stalybridge H Trin and Ch Ch *Ches* 81–84; C Heswall 84–91; TV Bushbury *Lich* 91–04; V Shevington *Blackb* 04–17; rtd 17; PtO *York* from 18. *1 Algarth Rise, York YO31 1HD* E: joycecdphilipid@gmail.com

DENNISS, Mrs Amanda Jane. b 57. Univ Coll Lon LLB 78. Oak Hill Th Coll 98 NTMTC 00. **d** 03 **p** 04. C Turnham Green Ch Ch *Lon* 03–06; PtO 06–08; C Westwood *Cov* 08–11; R Itchen Valley *Win* 15–18; PtO *Lon* from 13; *Win* from 18. *3C Longridge Road, London SW5 9SB* E: amandadenniss@gmail.com

DENNISTON, Jennifer. b 58. Edin Univ BA 79. St Mellitus Coll 15. **d** 18 **p** 19. NSM Worcs W Rural *Worc* from 18. *Sapey Court Cottage, Clifton-on-Teme, Worcester WR6 6HE* T: (01886) 853280 M: 07783-432017 E: jendenniston@gmail.com

DENNO, Basil. b 52. Dundee Univ BSc 74. Oak Hill Th Coll BA 81. **d** 81 **p** 83. C Chaddesden St Mary *Derby* 81–83; Hon C 83–84; PtO from 08. *24 Macclesfield Old Road, Buxton SK17 6TY* T: (01298) 22193 E: lizziedenno@talk21.com

DENNY, Annita. b 46. **d** 13 **p** 15. NSM Budleigh Salterton, E Budleigh w Bicton etc *Ex* 13–17; NSM Sidmouth, Woolbrook, Salcombe Regis, Sidbury etc from 17. *119 Cotmaton Road, Sidmouth EX10 8XN* T: (01395) 512735

DENNY, Lorne Robert. b 58. Pemb Coll Ox MA 84 Lon Inst of Educn PGCE 84. SAOMC 98. **d** 01 **p** 02. NSM Ox St Barn and St Paul 01–04; NSM Cowley St Jas 04–07; P-in-c Milton next Sittingbourne *Cant* 07–12; TV Cheam *S'wark* 12–15; R Holkham w Egmere w Warham etc *Nor* 15–17; PtO *Eur* from 17; *Ox* from 19. *Address withheld by request* E: lrdenny@btinternet.com

DENNY, Michael Thomas. b 47. Kelham Th Coll 68 St Jo Coll Nottm 71. **d** 73 **p** 74. C Gospel Lane St Mich *Birm* 73–77; P-in-c Frankley 77–82; R 82–07; rtd 07; PtO *Birm* 07–13; *Heref* from 08. *Orchard Cottage, Green Lane, Yarpole, Leominster HR6 0BE* T: (01568) 780874 E: revdenny1@btinternet.com

DENSMORE, Robert McCutchen. b 78. Amherst Coll (USA) BA 00 K Coll Lon MA 07. Duke Div Sch MDiv 16. **d** 16. C Upton *Ex* from 16. *Silverhill Lodge, Meadfoot Road, Torquay TQ1 2JP* T: (01803) 394805 M: 07852-335515 E: robert.densmore@gmail.com

DENT, Canon Christopher Mattinson. b 46. K Coll Lon BA 68 AKC 68 MTh 69 Jes Coll Cam BA 72 MA 76 New Coll Ox MA 76 DPhil 80. Westcott Ho Cam 70. **d** 72 **p** 73. C Chelsea St Luke *Lon* 72–76; Asst Chapl New Coll Ox 76–79; Fell Chapl and Dean Div 79–84; V Hollingbourne and Hucking w Leeds and Broomfield *Cant* 84–93; V Bedford St Andr *St Alb* 93–12; Hon Can St Alb 11–12; RD Bedford 05–10; rtd 12; PtO *Cant* from 13. *20 Ardent Avenue, Walmer, Deal CT14 7UE* T: (01304) 361624 E: cmdent@btinternet.com

DENT, Joseph Michael. b 73. Jes Coll Cam BA 94 MA 98. Wycliffe Hall Ox BTh 99. **d** 99 **p** 00. C Plymouth St Andr and Stonehouse *Ex* 99–03; C Sevenoaks St Nic *Roch* 03–13; TR Plymouth St Andr and Stonehouse *Ex* from 13. *St Andrew's Rectory, 13 Bainbridge Avenue, Plymouth PL3 5QZ* T: (01752) 211241 E: josephdent@gmail.com

DENT, Marie Penelope. b 46. K Coll Lon BA 88. Westcott Ho Cam 02. **d** 04 **p** 05. C N Walsham and Edingthorpe *Nor* 04–08; TV Redditch H Trin *Worc* 08–10; rtd 10; PtO *Nor* from 10. *1 Stirling Road, Mundesley, Norwich NR6 6GE* T: (01603) 487938 M: 07799-220357 E: mpd46@outlook.com

DENT, Michael Leslie. b 54. Leeds Univ BEd 76. St Steph Ho Ox 93. **d** 95 **p** 96. C Cockerton *Dur* 95–98; V Escomb 98–03; R Etherley 98–03; V Witton Park 98–03; Chapl Dur Constabulary 02–03; TR E Darlington 03–12; V Darlington St Jo 12–13; V Warkworth and Acklington *Newc* 13–17; rtd 17. *16 Dorchester Court, Marlborough Drive, Darlington DL1 5YD* E: mikedent54@gmail.com

DENT, Raymond William. b 47. Open Univ BA 84 Birm Coll of Educn CertEd 68. Ridley Hall Cam 70. **d** 73 **p** 74. C Hyde St Geo *Ches* 73–76; C Eastham 76–79; TV E Runcorn w Halton 79–80; V Hallwood 80–83; V New Brighton Em 83–94; V Willaston 94–13; rtd 13; PtO *Ches* from 14. *32 Proctor Road, Wirral CH47 4BB* T: 0151-792 2022 E: raymondwdent@gmail.com

DENT, Stephen Edward. b 55. STETS 12. **d** 15 **p** 19. NSM Lee-on-the-Solent *Portsm* from 15. *St Faith's Church, Victoria Square, Lee-on-the-Solent PO13 9NF* M: 07722-902344 E: steve.e.dent@btinternet.com

DENTON, Peter Brian. b 37. Kelham Th Coll 57. **d** 62 **p** 63. C Ellesmere Port *Ches* 62–66; Chapl HM Borstal Hollesley Bay 66–69; CF 69–89; Warden Bridge Cen and C Hounslow H Trin w St Paul *Lon* 89–92; V Northolt Park St Barn 92–04; P-in-c Perivale 97–01; P-in-c N Greenford All Hallows 00–04; rtd 04; PtO *Ely* 05–10; *Pet* 05–10; P-in-c Pet All SS 10–13. *52 Lornas Field, Hampton Hargate, Peterborough PE7 8AY* T: (01733) 552353 E: revddenton@aol.com

DENTON, Robert Gary. b 76. Leeds Univ BEng 99 PGCE 00. Trin Coll Bris BA 18. **d** 18 **p** 19. C Halton and Osmondthorpe *Leeds* from 18. *St Philip's Vicarage, Osmondthorpe Lane, Leeds LS9 9EF* M: 07402-052527 E: denton.robg@gmail.com

DENYER, Alan Frederick. b 31. Wycliffe Hall Ox 80. **d** 82 **p** 83. C Rodbourne Cheney *Bris* 82–84; P-in-c Garsdon w Lea and Cleverton 84–87; R Garsdon, Lea and Cleverton and Charlton 87–91; V Lydbury N w Hopesay and Edgton *Heref* 91–97; Asst Dioc Soc Resp Officer 91–97; rtd 97; Hon C Long Preston w Tosside *Bradf* 97–02; PtO *Ripon* 03–14; *Leeds* from 14. *1 Old Deanery Close, St Marygate, Ripon HG4 1LZ* T: (01765) 602397 E: denyer1955@btinternet.com

DENYER, Christopher Richard Terence. b 79. Kent Univ BA 01 Cant Ch Ch Univ MA 05 PGCE 02. SEITE 13. **d** 15 **p** 16. C Bethersden w High Halden and Woodchurch *Cant* 15–18; P-in-c Stour Downs from 18. *The Rectory, Church Road, Smeeth, Ashford TN25 6SA* M: 07702-584260 E: chrisdenyer1@sky.com

DENYER, Canon Paul Hugh. b 46. Lon Univ BA 68. Ripon Coll Cuddesdon 74. **d** 77 **p** 78. C Horfield H Trin *Bris* 77–82; TV Yate New Town 82–88; V Bris Lockleaze St Mary Magd w St Fran 88–95; Dioc Dir of Ords 95–02; R Warmley, Syston and Bitton 02–13; Hon Can Bris Cathl 99–13; rtd 13; PtO *Bris* from

13. *21 Westfield Close, Hanham, Bristol BS15 3SB* M: 07539-356222 E: paul.joanne4647@btinternet.com

DENYER, Samuel. b 74. Ripon Coll Cuddesdon 07. **d** 09 **p** 10. C Lostwithiel, St Winnow w St Nectan's Chpl etc *Truro* 09–12; C Lanreath, Pelynt and Bradoc 09–12; C Lanlivery 09–12; R Winnersh *Ox* 12–17; V Wells St Cuth w Wookey Hole *B & W* from 17. *3 Orchard Lea, Wells BA5 2LZ* T: (01749) 674613 M: 07443-418598 E: denyer.samuel@gmail.com

DEO, Paul Ernest. b 60. Coll of Ripon & York St Jo CertEd 81. St Jo Coll Nottm 95. **d** 97 **p** 98. C Tong *Bradf* 97–00; P-in-c Laisterdyke 00–02; V 02–07; C Baildon 07–12; V Heworth Ch *Ch York* from 12. *Christ Church Vicarage, 13 Lawnway, York YO31 1JD* T: (01904) 269054 E: pauldeo@sky.com

DERBY, Archdeacon of. See CUNLIFFE, The Ven Christopher John

DERBY, Bishop of. See LANE, The Rt Revd Elizabeth Jane Holden

DERBY, Dean of. See HANCE, The Very Revd Stephen John

DERBYSHIRE, Philip Damien. b 50. Leic Poly LLB 71. Sarum & Wells Th Coll 80. **d** 82 **p** 83. C Chatham St Wm *Roch* 82–86; R Melfort Zimbabwe 86–88; TV Burnham w Dropmore, Hitcham and Taplow *Ox* 88–92; Chapl HM Pris Reading 92–97; Chapl HM Pris Holloway 97–00; Chapl HM Pris Bullingdon 00–04; C Buckingham *Ox* 04–11; AD 10–11; P-in-c Stewkley w Soulbury 11–12; TR Cottesloe from 12. *The Vicarage, High Street North, Stewkley, Leighton Buzzard LU7 0HH* T: (01525) 240287 E: revphil16@gmail.com

DERLÉN, Mrs Eva Teresia Birgitta Andersdotter. b 75. Lund Univ Sweden MTheol 02. Westcott Ho Cam 02. **p** 03. Sweden 03–11; Hon C Prestwood and Gt Hampden *Ox* 12–19; NSM Swedish Ch from 19. *6-11 Harcourt Street, London W1H 4AG* E: chaplain@swedishchurch.com

DEROSAIRE, Leslie John. b 50. Univ of Wales BA 85 Univ of Wales Coll Newport MA 03. St Mich Coll Llan 01. **d** 04 **p** 05. NSM Govilon w Llanfoist w Llanelen *Mon* 04–07; NSM Llanddewi Rhydderch w Llangattock-juxta-Usk etc 07–09; P-in-c 09–11. *Elmgrove, Hereford Road, Mardy, Abergavenny NP7 6HU* T: (01873) 857256 E: derosaire@tiscali.co.uk

DeROY-JONES, Philip Antony. b 49. St Mich Coll Llan 92. **d** 92 **p** 93. C Neath w Llantwit *Llan* 92–95; V Caerau St Cynfelin 95–98; V Pontlottyn w Fochriw 98–14; rtd 14; PtO *Llan* from 14; *S & B* from 17. *Nyth Clyd, 36 Hoo Street, Neath SA11 2PA* T: (01639) 415304 E: fathertony@outlook.com

DERRICK, David John. b 46. S'wark Ord Course. **d** 84 **p** 85. NSM Angell Town St Jo *S'wark* 84–98; NSM St Mary le Strand w St Clem Danes *Lon* 86–93; PtO *Chelmsf* from 12. *Station View, Black Boy Lane, Wrabness, Manningtree CO11 2TL* T: (01255) 880125 E: davidderrick3@btinternet.com

DERRICK, Mrs Dorothy Margaret. b 41. St Mary's Coll Chelt CertEd 63. Ox Min Course 89. **d** 92 **p** 94. NSM Gt Missenden w Ballinger and Lt Hampden *Ox* 92–98; P-in-c Drayton St Pet (Abingdon) 98–04; rtd 04; PtO *Carl* from 05. *Croft Cottage, 6 Milton Lane, Burgh-by-Sands, Carlisle CA5 6BG* T: (01228) 576860 E: dorothyderrick@btinternet.com

DERRIMAN, Canon Graham Scott. b 39. Bps' Coll Cheshunt 63. **d** 66 **p** 67. C Wandsworth St Mich *S'wark* 66–70; C Merton St Mary 70–74; P-in-c Earlsfield St Andr 74–79; V 79–81; V Camberwell St Luke 81–90; V Croydon St Aug 90–04; Voc Adv Croydon Adnry 93–04; RD Croydon Cen *S'wark* 95–04; Hon Can S'wark Cathl 01–04; rtd 04; PtO *S'wark* from 05. *15 Goodwood Close, Morden SM4 5AW* T: (020) 8648 1550 M: 07952-471515 E: gsd.24@virginmedia.com

DERRY AND RAPHOE, Bishop of. *Vacant*

DERRY, Archdeacon of. See MILLER, The Ven Robert Stephen

DERRY, Dean of. See STEWART, The Very Revd Raymond John

DESBOROUGH, Mrs Margaret Maureen. b 63. S Bank Univ BSc 96 Goldsmiths' Coll Lon MA 00 PGCE 97. Yorks Min Course 13. **d** 15 **p** 16. NSM Skirlaugh, Catwick, Long Riston, Rise, Swine w Ellerby *York* from 15; NSM Sigglesthorne w Nunkeeling and Bewholme from 15; NSM Aldbrough, Mappleton w Goxhill and Withernwick from 18; NSM Beeford w Frodingham and Foston from 18; NSM Brandesburton and Leven from 18; NSM Hornsea, Atwick and Skipsea from 18. *The New Rectory, 105 Main Street, Brandesburton, Driffield YO25 8RG* M: 07941-494731 E: mo.desborough@gmail.com

DESBOROUGH, Paul. b 63. Regents Th Coll BA 99. Qu Foundn (Course) 15. **d** 17 **p** 18. C Boulton *Derby* from 17. *The Beehive, 1B Grange Road, Alvaston, Derby DE24 0JW* T: (01332) 756336 M: 07958-618507 E: revpaulcofe@gmail.com

DESCOMBES, Raymond Patrick Claude. b 51. Birkbeck Coll Lon BA 01. St Mellitus Coll 14. **d** 15 **p** 16. OLM Becontree S *Chelmsf* from 15. *129 Ballards Road, Dagenham RM10 9AR* M: 07918-050491 E: revraydescombes@gmail.com

DESERT, Thomas Denis. b 31. Bps' Coll Cheshunt 54. **d** 56 **p** 57. C Goldington *St Alb* 56–60; C-in-c Luton St Hugh Lewsey CD 60–63; C St Alb St Sav 63–65; C Cheshunt 65–68; V Bedford All SS 68–89; R Northill w Moggerhanger 89–96; rtd 96; PtO *St Alb* 96–13. *2 Phillpotts Avenue, Bedford MK40 3UJ* T: (01234) 211413 E: denisdesert@ntlworld.com

DESHPANDE, Lakshmi Anant. *See* JEFFREYS, Lakshmi Anant

DESROSIERS, Jacques Thomas Maurice. b 55. Qu Univ Kingston Ontario BCom 77. S'wark Ord Course 91. **d** 94 **p** 95. NSM Benenden *Cant* 94–97; C Maidstone All SS and St Phil w Tovil 97–01; TV Pewsey and Swanborough *Sarum* 01–04; P-in-c Rolvenden *Cant* 04–10; P-in-c Newenden and Rolvenden 10–13; R Rother and Oxney 13–14; AD Tenterden 07–11; AD Romney and Tenterden 11–13; P-in-c Warminster St Denys and Upton Scudamore *Sarum* 14–17; R River Were from 17. *The Rectory, 5 Church Street, Warminster BA12 8PG* T: (01985) 213456 E: jtmdesrosiers@gmail.com

d'ESTERRE, Mrs Jennifer Ann. b 48. Coll of St Matthias Bris BEd 77. WEMTC 01. **d** 04 **p** 05. NSM Sharpness, Purton, Brookend and Slimbridge *Glouc* 04–11; C Cromhall, Tortworth, Tytherington, Falfield etc 11–15; rtd 15; NSM Matson *Glouc* 15–17. *Gossington Cottage, Gossington, Slimbridge, Gloucester GL2 7DN* T: (01453) 890384 M: 077877-959439 E: revdjenny@gmail.com

DETTMER, The Ven Douglas James. b 64. Univ of Kansas BA 86 Yale Univ MDiv 90. Berkeley Div Sch 90. **d** 90 **p** 91. C Ilfracombe, Lee, Woolacombe, Bittadon etc *Ex* 90–94; Bp's Dom Chapl 94–98; P-in-c Thorverton, Cadbury, Upton Pyne etc 98–10; P-in-c Stoke Canon, Poltimore w Huxham and Rewe etc 06–10; R Brampford Speke, Cadbury, Newton St Cyres etc 10–15; Adn Totnes from 15; Preb Ex Cathl from 12. *Blue Hills, Bradley Road, Bovey Tracey, Newton Abbot TQ13 9EU* T: (01626) 832064 E: archdeacon.of.totnes@exeter.anglican.org

DEUCHAR de MELLO, Bridget Dorothea. b 55. Sussex Univ BA 77 Leic Univ PGCE 78. SEITE BA 08. **d** 08 **p** 09. NSM Gt Ilford St Luke *Chelmsf* 08–13; C Leytonstone H Trin and St Aug Harrow Green 13–19. *Address temp unknown* E: demellobridget@gmail.com

DEVADASON, Jacob. b 61. Madras Bible Sem BTh Serampore Univ BTh Annamalai Univ MA United Th Coll Bangalore MTh. Tamilnadu Th Sem BD NOC. **d** 06 **p** 07. C Man Clayton St Cross w St Paul 06–09; TV Wythenshawe 09–13; P-in-c Croydon Ch Ch *S'wark* 13–18; V 18; Interfaith Adv Croydon Area 13–18; V Heald Green St Cath *Ches* from 18. *The Vicarage, 217 Outwood Road, Heald Green, Cheadle SK8 3JS* M: 07814-845053 E: 2revjacob@gmail.com

DEVADASON, Mrs Jasmine. b 67. Kakatiya Univ India BA 91 Tamilnadu Th Sem BD 96 United Th Coll Bangalore MTh 99. SNWTP. **d** 08 **p** 09. C W Didsbury and Withington St Chris *Man* 08–11; PtO 12–14. *The Vicarage, 217 Outwood Road, Heald Green, Cheadle SK8 3JS* M: 07515-726923 E: jasdevadason@yahoo.co.uk

DEVAL, Mrs Joan Margaret. b 38. Southlands Coll Lon TDip 58. SAOMC 95. **d** 98 **p** 99. OLM Chinnor, Sydenham, Aston Rowant and Crowell *Ox* 98–10; PtO from 10. *3 Orchard Way, Chinnor OX39 4UD* T: (01844) 353404

DEVALL, Elizabeth Jane. b 70. SNWTP. **d** 10 **p** 11. C Royton St Anne *Man* 10–13; C Heyside 12–13; P-in-c Hurst 13–18; V from 18. *St John's Vicarage, 155 Kings Road, Ashton-under-Lyne OL6 8EZ* T: 0161-330 1935 M: 07725-739506 E: lizdevall@btinternet.com

DEVAS, Thomas Christopher. b 86. Nottm Univ BSc 09. Wycliffe Hall Ox BTh 15. **d** 15 **p** 16. C Wollaton Park *S'well* 15–19; C Cornerstone Team *Leic* from 19. *16 Wadkins Way, Bushby, Leicester LE7 9NA* M: 07817-435483

DEVENISH, Nicholas Edward. b 64. Ridley Hall Cam 02. **d** 04 **p** 05. C Huntingdon *Ely* 04–07; C Farcet Hampton 07–12; TV Cartmel Peninsula *Carl* from 12. *The Vicarage, Priest Lane, Cartmel, Grange-over-Sands LA11 6PU* T: (015395) 36261 E: nickdevenish@mac.com *or* vicar.cartmel@virgin.net

DEVENNEY, Raymond Robert Wilmont. b 47. TCD BA 69 MA 73. CITC 70. **d** 70 **p** 71. C Ballymena w Ballyclug *Conn* 70–75; C Ballyholme *D & D* 75–81; I Killinchy w Kilmood and Tullynakill 81–00; I Drumbeg 00–12; rtd 12; PtO *Newc* from 18. *21 Thirlington Close, Newcastle upon Tyne NE5 4BN* T: 0191-271 2036 E: raydev@hotmail.com

DEVER, Paul. b 71. BSc. Wycliffe Hall Ox. **d** 06 **p** 07. C Fair Oak *Win* 06–10; TV Horwich and Rivington *Man* 10–12; Dioc Young Adults Missr 10–12; C Blackrod 11–12; C Howell Hill *Guildf* from 12. *18 Nonsuch Walk, Cheam SM2 7NG* T: (020) 8224 9838 M: 07726-302862 E: revpaul@gmail.com

DEVERAJ, Jacob Devadason. *See* DEVADASON, Jacob

DEVERELL, Clive Dennis. b 61. Anglia Ruskin Univ BA 09. CA Tr Coll 83 ERMC 04. **d** 07 **p** 08. C Paston *Pet* 07–10; TV W Swindon and the Lydiards *Bris* 10–18; V W Swindon and Lydiard Tregoze from 18; AD Swindon from 17. *26 The Bramptons, Shaw, Swindon SN5 5SL* T: (01793) 877111 E: clive.deverell@btinternet.com

DEVERELL, Canon William Robert Henry. b 61. CITC 88 St Jo Coll Nottm 90. **d** 92 **p** 93. C Agherton *Conn* 92–95; I Sixmilecross w Termonmaguirke *Arm* 95–99; I Tallaght *D & G* 99; Can Ch Ch Cathl Dublin from 14. *St Maelruain's Rectory, 6 Sally Park, Firhouse Road, Tallaght, Dublin 24, Republic of Ireland* (00353) (1) 462 1044 *or* 462 6006 F: 462 1044 M: 86-803 0239 E: tallaghtparish@gmail.com

DEVEREUX, Canon John Swinnerton. b 32. Lon Univ BSc 53. Wells Th Coll. **d** 58 **p** 59. C Wigan St Mich *Liv* 58–60; C Goring-by-Sea *Chich* 60–69; Ind Chapl 69–97; Can and Preb Chich Cathl 90–97; rtd 97; PtO *Chich* from 97. *4 Pony Farm, Findon, Worthing BN14 0RS* T: (01903) 873638

DEVINE, Margaret Rose. b 50. Sunderland Poly BEd 76. NEOC 00. **d** 03 **p** 04. NSM E Boldon *Dur* 03–12; rtd 12; PtO *Dur* from 12; Hon Min Can Dur Cathl from 15. *13 Coniston Close, Belmont, Durham DH1 2UQ* M: 07708-222634 E: devinemargaret@gmail.com

DEVONISH, Clive Wayne. b 51. Ridley Hall Cam. **d** 96 **p** 97. C Meole Brace *Lich* 96–05; V Greenside *Dur* 05–15; rtd 15; Hon C Shrewsbury H Trin w St Julian *Lich* 16–18; P-in-c from 19; PtO *Heref* from 17. *Maranatha, 3 Dorricotts Place, Yockleton, Shrewsbury SY5 9PH* E: revclivedevo@gmail.com

DEW, Canon Lindsay Charles. b 52. Wilson Carlile Coll 76 Cranmer Hall Dur 85. **d** 86 **p** 86. C Knottingley *Wakef* 86–89; V Batley St Thos 89–97; R Thornhill and Whitley Lower 97–09; RD Dewsbury 96–06; Hon Can Wakef Cathl 05–09; P-in-c Dunton w Wrestlingworth and Eyeworth *St Alb* 09–14; R 14–18; RD Biggleswade 11–18; Hon Can St Alb 16–18; rtd 18; PtO *St Alb* from 18. *22 Angell's Meadow, Ashwell, Baldock SG7 5QS* T: (01462) 742165 M: 07545-878082 E: canon.lindsaydew@gmail.com

DEW, Martin John. b 49. CBDTI 00. **d** 04 **p** 05. NSM Natland *Carl* 04–09; NSM Shap w Swindale and Bampton w Mardale 09–13; rtd 13; PtO *Carl* from 13. *9 Burton Park, Burton, Carnforth LA6 1JB* T: (01524) 781645 E: martindew23@live.co.uk

DEW, Maureen. b 51. Univ of Wales (Newport) MA 00. Qu Coll Birm BA 99. **d** 99 **p** 00. C Inkberrow w Cookhill and Kington w Dormston *Worc* 99–02; C Redditch, The Ridge 02–05; TV Redditch Ch the K 05–12; rtd 12; PtO *Worc* from 13; *Birm* from 18. *21 Ashmead Drive, Cofton Hackett, Birmingham B45 8AA* E: revmodew@btinternet.com

DEW, Robert David John. b 42. St Pet Coll Ox BA 63. St Steph Ho Ox 63. **d** 65 **p** 66. C Abington *Pet* 65–69; Chapl Tiffield Sch Northants 69–71; Ind Chapl *Pet* 71–79; Ind Chapl *Liv* 79–87; Sen Ind Missr 88–91; V Skelsmergh w Selside and Longsleddale *Carl* 91–06; Bp's Adv for CME 95–06; rtd 06; PtO *Carl* from 07. *Tither Crag Barn, Crook, Kendal LA8 8LE* T: (015395) 68680 E: bobdew68@gmail.com

DEWAR, Ian John James. b 61. Kingston Poly BA 83. Cranmer Hall Dur 89. **d** 92 **p** 93. C Blackb St Gabr 92–95; C Darwen St Cuth w Tockholes St Steph 95–97; V Appley Bridge 97–05; Chapl St Cath Hospice Preston 05–14; Chapl Univ Hosps of Morecambe Bay NHS Foundn Trust from 14. *Chaplain's Office, Royal Lancaster Infirmary, Ashton Road, Lancaster LA1 4RP* T: (01524) 65944 E: ijjdewar@hotmail.com *or* ian.dewar@mbht.nhs.uk

DEWAR, John. b 32. Chich Th Coll 58. **d** 61 **p** 62. C Leeds St Hilda *Ripon* 61–63; C Cross Green St Sav and St Hilda 63–65; C Cullercoats St Geo *Newc* 65–69; V Newsham 69–76; V Kenton Ascension 76–86; R Wallsend St Pet 86–92; V Longhorsley and Hebron 92–96; rtd 96; PtO *S'well* from 96. *51 Bonner Lane, Calverton, Nottingham NG14 6FU* T: 0115-965 2599 E: jandmdewar@ntlworld.com

DEWES, Canon Deborah Mary. b 59. Homerton Coll Cam BEd 81 St Jo Coll Dur BA 90 MA 93. Cranmer Hall Dur 88. **d** 92 **p** 94. C Stockton St Pet *Dur* 92–96; C Knowle *Birm* 96–03; C Bath Abbey w St Jas *B & W* 03–08; Chapl R United Hosp Bath NHS Trust 03–08; P-in-c Brislington St Luke *Bris* 08–14; V from 14; Hon Can Bris Cathl from 17. *The Vicarage, 9 St Luke's Gardens, Bristol BS4 4NW* T: 0117-977 7633 E: vicar@stlukesbrislington.org.uk

DEWEY, David Malcolm. b 45. Lon Univ BA 72 LSE MSc 87 Fitzw Coll Cam MPhil 94. Westcott Ho Cam 76. **d** 78 **p** 79. Sen Lect Middx Poly 72–92; Sen Lect Middx Univ 92–01; Hon C Enfield St Mich *Lon* 78–79; Hon C Bush Hill Park St Steph 79–84; Hon C Palmers Green St Jo 84–90; PtO 90–95; *St Alb* 95–98; Hon C Hertford All SS 98–01; P-in-c St Paul's Walden 01–08; rtd 08; PtO *St Alb* from 09. *9 Bowling Road, Ware SG12 7EH* T: (01920) 467287 M: 07813-439463 E: daviddewey8566@gmail.com

DEWEY, Peter Lewis. b 38. Wycliffe Hall Ox 69. **d** 71 **p** 72. C Hammersmith St Sav *Lon* 71–73; Chapl to Bp Kensington 73–75; C Isleworth All SS 75–81; TV Dorchester *Ox* 81–91; CF (TA) 86–91; Chapl Gordonstoun Sch 92–97; TR St Laur in Thanet *Cant* 97–03; rtd 03; P-in-c Sulhamstead Abbots and Bannister w Ufton Nervet *Ox* 03–10; Hon C 10–12; AD Bradfield 10–11; Chapl Allnutt's Hosp Goring Heath from 12. *Old School Cottage, Goring Heath, Reading RG8 7RR* T: (01491) 680261 M: 07784-912935 E: revpeterdewey@yahoo.co.uk

DEWEY, Sanford Dayton. b 44. Syracuse Univ AB 67 MA 72. Gen Th Sem (NY) MDiv 79. **d** 79 **p** 80. Assoc Chapl Roosevelt Hosp New York USA 80–81; Assoc Dir Relig Services 81–86; C St Mary le Bow w St Pancras Soper Lane etc *Lon* 87–92; C Hampstead St Steph w All Hallows 92–94; Co-Dir Hampstead Counselling Service 94–00; Dir from 00; NSM Hampstead Ch Ch *Lon* 94–96; Hon C Grosvenor Chpl from 96; Prov Past Consultant URC from 96; PtO *Lon* from 97. *B908 New Providence Wharf, 1 Fairmont Avenue, London E14 9PJ* E: daytondewey@gmail.com

DEWHIRST, Janice. b 50. EMMTC 99. **d** 02 **p** 03. NSM Forest Town *S'well* 02–09; NSM Mansfield SS Pet and Paul 04–06; P-in-c Ladybrook 06–09; rtd 09; PtO *S'well* from 18. *26 King Street, Mansfield Woodhouse, Mansfield NG19 9AU* T: (01623) 454471 E: revd.jan@dmntlworld.com

DEWHURST, Russell James Edward. b 77. Magd Coll Ox MPhys 99 Selw Coll Cam BTh 03 Cardiff Univ LLM 10. Westcott Ho Cam 00. **d** 03 **p** 04. C Blewbury, Hagbourne and Upton *Ox* 03–05; P-in-c Ox St Frideswide w Binsey 05–09; Web Pastor i-church 05–07; Asst Chapl Ex Coll Ox 06–09; V Ewell *Guildf* from 09. *St Mary's Vicarage, 14 Church Street, Ewell, Epsom KT17 2AQ* T: (020) 8393 2643 E: rdewhurst@mac.com *or* vicar@stmarysewell.com

DEWING, Robert Mark Eastwood. b 68. Bris Univ BA 90 PGCE 91. Ridley Hall Cam BA 98. **d** 99 **p** 00. C Alverstoke *Portsm* 99–03; V Sheet 03–11; AD Petersfield 09–11; Past Dir Lee Abbey 11–16; TR Portishead *B & W* from 16. *2 Brambling Lane, Portishead, Bristol BS20 7NN* T: (01275) 846592 M: 07923-484297 E: robdewing@gmail.com *or* rector@portisheadparish.co.uk

DEWING, William Arthur. b 52. NEOC 99. **d** 02 **p** 03. NSM Middlesbrough St Oswald *York* 02–06; NSM Stainton w Hilton 06–17; NSM Brookfield 14–17; NSM Osmotherley w Harlsey and Ingleby Arncliffe from 17; NSM Cowesby from 17; NSM Felixkirk w Boltby from 17; NSM Kirkby Knowle from 17; NSM Leake w Over and Nether Silton and Kepwick from 17. *Orchard House, Ingleby Arncliffe, Northallerton DL6 3LN* T: (01609) 882233 M: 07966-191640 E: bill@revd.me.uk

DEXTER, Canon Frank Robert. b 40. Cuddesdon Coll 66. **d** 68 **p** 69. C Newc H Cross 68–71; C Whorlton 71–73; V Pet Ch Carpenter 73–80; V High Elswick St Phil *Newc* 80–85; RD Newc W 81–85; V Newc St Geo 85–05; Hon Can Newc Cathl 94–05; P-in-c Newc St Hilda 95–98; rtd 05; PtO *Newc* from 05. *8 Tynedale Terrace, Hexham NE46 3JE* T: (01434) 601759 E: frank.dexter@talk21.com

DEY, Canon Charles Gordon Norman. b 46. Lon Coll of Div. **d** 71 **p** 72. C Almondbury *Wakef* 71–76; V Mixenden 76–85; TR Tong *Bradf* 85–11; C Laisterdyke 08–11; Hon Can Bradf Cathl 00–11; rtd 11. *23 St Abbs Walk, Bradford BD6 1EP* E: gordondey1@gmail.com

DI CASTIGLIONE, James Alexander. b 81. St Jo Coll Nottm. **d** 08 **p** 09. C Mid-Sussex Network Ch *Chich* 08–12; Chapl Sir Robert Woodard Academy Lancing 12–13; R Chanctonbury *Chich* from 13. *The Rectory, Mill Lane, Ashington, Pulborough RH20 3BX* T: (01903) 893878 M: 07796-945662 E: jamesdicastiglione@me.com *or* james.dicas@chanctonbury.org.uk

DI CASTIGLIONE, Nigel Austin. b 57. St Jo Coll Dur BA 78. St Jo Coll Nottm MA 94. **d** 94 **p** 95. C Tamworth *Lich* 94–97; P-in-c Trentham 97–01; V 02–10; V Hanford 02–10; V Harborne Heath *Birm* 10–15; TR Papworth *Ely* from 15; P-in-c Conington 17–18; P-in-c Lolworth 18. *Elsworth Rectory, The Drift, Elsworth, Cambridge CB23 4JN* T: (01954) 267241 M: 07770-697240 E: nigel.dicastiglione@gmail.com

DI CHIARA, Miss Alessandra Maddalena. b 59. Univ of Wales (Swansea) BA 80. Wycliffe Hall Ox 00. **d** 02 **p** 03. C Hooton *Ches* 02–05; P-in-c Millbrook 05–15; P-in-c Micklehurst 14–15; C Douglas St Geo and All SS *S & M* from 15. *62 Ballabrooie Way, Douglas, Isle of Man IM1 4HB* T: (01624) 679274

DI LEO, Paolo. b 62. ERMC. **d** 16 **p** 17. NSM Streatley *St Alb* from 16. *Woodlands, 27 Old Road, Barton-le-Clay, Bedford MK45 4LB* M: 07968-606377 E: pdileo@fidelioexec.com

DIAKIESE, Guy. See MATUMONA, Guy Diakiese

DIAMOND, Canon Michael Lawrence. b 37. St Jo Coll Dur BA 60 MA 74 Sussex Univ DPhil 84. ALCD 62. **d** 62 **p** 63. C Wandsworth St Mich *S'wark* 62–64; C Patcham *Chich* 64–69; R Hamsey 70–75; P-in-c Cambridge St Andr Less *Ely* 75–86; V 86–04; Hon Can Ely Cathl 94–04; RD Cambridge 96–04; rtd 04; PtO *S'well* 04–17; *Ely* from 17. *58 Desborough Road, Hartford, Huntingdon PE29 1SW*

DIAMOND, Capt Richard Geoffrey Colin. b 49. CA Tr Coll. **d** 93 **p** 93. Miss to Seafarers Kenya 90–01; rtd 01; PtO *Win* from 02. *209A Priory Road, Southampton SO17 2LR* T: (023) 8067 8558 E: rgcdiamond@ic24.net

DIANA, Sister. See MORRISON, Diana Mary

DIBB SMITH, John. b 29. Ex & Truro NSM Scheme 78. **d** 81 **p** 82. NSM Carbis Bay *Truro* 81–82; NSM Carbis Bay w Lelant 82–84; Warden Trelowarren Fellowship Helston 84–89; Chapl 89–91; NSM Halsetown *Truro* 91–97; rtd 98; PtO *Truro* 00–15. *Maple Cottage, Penstraze, Chacewater, Truro TR4 8GB* T: (01872) 560134

DIBBENS, Canon Hugh Richard. b 39. Lon Univ BA 63 MTh 67 St Pet Coll Ox BA 65 MA 74. Oak Hill Th Coll 60. **d** 67 **p** 68. C Holborn St Geo w H Trin and St Bart *Lon* 67–72; CMS 73–74; Japan 74–77; TR Chigwell *Chelmsf* 78–92; V Hornchurch St Andr 92–06; RD Havering 98–04; Hon Can Chelmsf Cathl 01–06; rtd 06; PtO *Chelmsf* from 07. *9 Stonehill Road, Roxwell, Chelmsford CM1 4PF* T: (01245) 248173 E: hrdibbens@gmail.com

DIBDEN, Alan Cyril. b 49. Hull Univ LLB 70 Fitzw Coll Cam BA 72 MA 76. Westcott Ho Cam 70 Virginia Th Sem 73. **d** 73 **p** 74. C Camberwell St Luke *S'wark* 73–77; TV Walworth 77–79; TV Langley Marish *Ox* 79–84; C Chalfont St Peter 84–90; TV Burnham w Dropmore, Hitcham and Taplow 90–08; V Taplow and Dropmore 08–15; rtd 15; PtO *Ox* from 15. *Russett Cottage, 228 Windsor Lane, Burnham SL1 7HN* M: 07900-824528 E: alan.dibden13@gmail.com

DICK, Canon Angela. b 62. Sheff Univ BA 92. St Jo Coll Nottm MA 94. **d** 96 **p** 97. C Mixenden *Wakef* 96–97; C Mount Pellon 97–99; P-in-c Bradshaw 99–00; P-in-c Holmfield 99–00; V Bradshaw and Holmfield 00–10; P-in-c Sowerby Bridge 10–11; V 11–14; *Leeds* from 14; Asst Dioc Dir of Ords *Wakef* 13–14; Asst Dir of Ords *Leeds* from 14; Hon Can Wakef Cathl from 10. *The Vicarage, 62 Park Road, Sowerby Bridge HX6 2BJ* T: (01422) 831253 E: angedix110@talktalk.net

DICK, Canon Caroline Ann. b 61. Nottm Univ BTh 88. Linc Th Coll 85. **d** 88 **p** 94. Par Dn Houghton le Spring *Dur* 88–93; Par Dn Hetton le Hole 93–94; C 94–96; Asst Chapl Sunderland Univ 94–98; C Harton 96–09; Development Officer Dioc Bd of Soc Resp 98–09; Adv for Women's Min 02–09; TV Dur N 09–16; TR from 16; Hon Can Dur Cathl from 03. *The Vicarage, 1A Church Parade, Sacriston, Durham DH7 6AD* M: 07947-741517 E: carolinedick@btinternet.com

DICK, Cecil Bates. b 42. Selw Coll Cam BA 68 MA 72. EMMTC 73. **d** 76 **p** 78. NSM Cinderhill *S'well* 76–79; Chapl Dame Allan's Schs Newc 79–85; CF (TA) 84–99; C Gosforth All SS *Newc* 85–87; Chapl HM Pris Dur 88–89; Chapl HM Pris Hull 89–04; rtd 04; PtO *Newc* from 01; *York* from 04. *11 Juniper Chase, Beverley HU17 8GD* T: (01482) 862985

DICK, Malcolm Gordon (Mac). b 40. SWMTC 10. **d** 11 **p** 12. NSM Ottery St Mary, Alfington, W Hill, Tipton etc *Ex* from 11. *27 Beech Park, West Hill, Ottery St Mary EX11 1UJ* E: macdick1@aol.com

DICK, Canon Raymond Owen. b 53. Edin Univ BD 77. Edin Th Coll 73. **d** 77 **p** 78. C Glas St Mary 77–84; PtO *Ox* Glas 84–85; P-in-c Edin St Paul and St Geo 85; Edin St Phil 85–86; P-in-c Edin St Marg 85–87; TV Edin Old St Paul 87–88; R Hetton le Hole *Dur* 88–96; V Harton 96–13; P-in-c Cleadon Park 09–13; R The Boldons 13–19; AD Jarrow 14–15; Hon Can Dur Cathl 11–19; rtd 19. *The Vicarage, 1A Church Parade, Sacriston, Durham DH7 6AD* E: raymonddick53@gmail.com

DICKENS, Adam Paul. b 65. Man Univ BA 89 Nottm Univ MDiv 93. Linc Th Coll 91. **d** 93 **p** 94. C Pershore w Pinvin, Wick and Birlingham *Worc* 93–98; C Portsea St Mary *Portsm* 98–04; Pilsdon Community 04–12; Chapl Derby Univ from 14; Chapl Derby Cathl from 14. *1 Flamsteed Court, Kedleston Old Road, Derby DE22 1GA* T: (01332) 591878 E: adampdickens@hotmail.co.uk *or* a.dickens@derby.ac.uk

DICKENS, John Franklin. b 50. Birm Univ BEd 72 Leeds Univ MEd 82. St Mellitus Coll 12. **d** 13 **p** 14. OLM Maldon St Mary w Mundon *Chelmsf* 13–16; P-in-c from 16. *7 Viking Road, Maldon CM9 6JN* T: (01621) 858136 M: 07582-423219 E: johndickens129@btinternet.com

DICKENS, Timothy Richard John. b 45. Leeds Univ BSc 68. Westcott Ho Cam 68. **d** 71 **p** 72. C Meole Brace *Lich* 71–74; C-in-c Stamford Ch Ch CD *Linc* 74–80; V Anlaby St Pet *York* 80–91; V Egg Buckland *Ex* 91–10; P-in-c Estover 04–10; RD Plymouth Moorside 03–09; rtd 10. *52 Budshead Road, Plymouth PL5 2RA* T: (01752) 298570

DICKENSON, Charles Gordon. b 29. Bps' Coll Cheshunt 53. **d** 56 **p** 57. C Ellesmere Port *Ches* 56–61; R Egremont St Columba 61–68; V Latchford Ch Ch 68–74; P-in-c Hargrave 74–79; Bp's Chapl 75–79; V Birkenhead St Jas w St Bede 79–83; R Tilston and Shocklach 83–94; rtd 94; PtO *Ches* 94–14. *58 Kingsway, Crewe CW2 7ND* T: (01270) 560722

DICKENSON, Canon Robin Christopher Wildish. b 44. Lon Univ CertEd 67 Ex Univ BPhil 81 MA 98. SWMTC 94. **d** 97 **p** 98. NSM Week St Mary w Poundstock and Whitstone *Truro* 97–98; P-in-c 98–06; P-in-c St Gennys, Jacobstow w Warbstow and Treneglos 02–06; R Week St Mary Circle of Par 06–13; RD Stratton 05–11; Hon Can Truro Cathl 07–13; rtd 13; PtO *Truro* from 16. *Ranelagh, Week St Mary, Holsworthy EX22 6XA* T: (01288) 341016

DICKER, Jane Elizabeth Marie. b 64. Whitelands Coll Lon BA 87 Anglia Ruskin Univ MA 08 Greenwich Univ PGCE 11. Linc Th Coll 87. **d** 89 **p** 94. Par Dn Merton St Jas *S'wark* 89–93; C Littleham w Exmouth *Ex* 93–97; Chapl Plymouth Univ 93–97; Ecum Chapl for F&HE Grimsby *Linc* 97–02; Chapl Univ of Greenwich *Roch* 02–05; Chapl Kent Inst of Art and Design 02–04; Chapl Univ Coll for the Creative Arts *Roch* 05; Hon PV Roch Cathl 03–05; P-in-c Waltham Cross *St Alb* 05–08; TV Cheshunt 08–16; V W Bromwich All SS *Lich* from 16. *7 Hopkins Drive, West Bromwich B71 3RR* T: 0121-525 5673 M: 07843-667971 E: mthr_jane@btinternet.com

DICKER, Mary Elizabeth. b 45. Girton Coll Cam BA 66 MA 70 Sheff Univ MSc 78. Cranmer Hall Dur 83. **dss** 85 **d** 87 **p** 94. Mortlake w E Sheen *S'wark* 85–88; Par Dn 87–88; Par Dn Irlam *Man* 88–92; Par Dn Ashton Ch Ch 92–94; C 94–97; P-in-c Hopwood 97–98; TV Heywood 98–05; rtd 05; PtO *Man* from 05. *33 Waltham House, St John Street, Wirksworth, Matlock DE4 4DT* T: (01629) 820234

DICKIE, James Graham Wallace. b 50. Worc Coll Ox BA 72 MA BLitt 77. Westcott Ho Cam 78. **d** 81 **p** 82. C Bracknell *Ox* 81–84; LtO *Ely* 84–89; Chapl Trin Coll Cam 84–89; Chapl Clifton Coll Bris 89–96; Sen Chapl Marlborough Coll 96–10; rtd 10; PtO *Sarum* from 10. *Grey Gables, Easton Royal, Pewsey SN9 5LY* T: (01672) 810961

DICKIN, Patricia Margarita. See LENTON de DICKIN, Patricia Margarita

DICKINSON, Canon Anthony William. b 48. New Coll Ox BA 71 MA 74. Linc Th Coll 80. **d** 82 **p** 83. C Leavesden *St Alb* 82–86; TV Upton cum Chalvey *Ox* 86–94; P-in-c Terriers 94–99; V 99–18; Chapl Bucks New Univ 03–18; Hon Can Ch Ch *Ox* 15–18; Chapl Genova *Eur* from 18. *Via Goito 18/a, 16122 Genova, Italy* T: (0039) (10) 889 268 E: canontonyd@gmail.com

DICKINSON, David Charles. b 58. BA 79 Lanc Univ MA 97. CBDTI. **d** 99 **p** 00. NSM Ewood *Blackb* 99–04; NSM Blackb Redeemer 04–05; P-in-c Hoghton 05–12; V 12–13; PtO 13–15; NSM Hesketh w Becconsall from 16; R from 17. *1 Silverdale, Hesketh Bank, Preston PR4 6RZ* M: 07805-598256 E: dickinsonrev@aol.com

DICKINSON, Dyllis Annie. b 52. **d** 01 **p** 02. OLM Stalmine w Pilling *Blackb* 01–07; NSM 07–17; rtd 17; PtO *Blackb* from 18. *Springfield, Moss Side Lane, Stalmine, Poulton-le-Fylde FY6 0JP* T: (01253) 700011

DICKINSON, Gareth Lee. b 69. Ridley Hall Cam 06. **d** 08 **p** 09. C Bryanston Square St Mary w St Marylebone St Mark *Lon* 08–10; NSM Cheltenham H Trin and St Paul *Glouc* from 10. *Trinity Cheltenham, 100-102 Winchcombe Street, Cheltenham GL52 2NW* T: (01242) 808780 M: 07788-742700 E: garethdickinson@me.com

DICKINSON, The Very Revd the Hon Hugh Geoffrey. b 29. Trin Coll Ox BA 53 MA 56. Cuddesdon Coll 54. **d** 56 **p** 57. C Melksham *Sarum* 56–58; Chapl Trin Coll Cam 58–63; Chapl Win Coll 63–69; P-in-c Milverton *Cov* 69–77; V St Alb St Mich 77–86; Dean Sarum 86–96; rtd 96; PtO *Glouc* from 96. *5 St Peter's Road, Cirencester GL7 1RE* T: (01285) 657710

DICKINSON, Paul John. b 66. Leic Univ BSc 88 Nottm Univ MA 89 Univ Coll Lon MSc 93 St Jo Coll Dur BA 18. Cranmer Hall Dur 15. **d** 18 **p** 19. C Brumby *Linc* from 18. *2A Town Hill Drive, Broughton, Brigg DN20 0HF* T: (01652) 659125 M: 07730-385045

DICKINSON, Canon Robert Edward. b 47. Nottm Univ BTh 74. St Jo Coll Nottm 70. **d** 74 **p** 75. C Birm St Martin 74–78; P-in-c Liv St Bride w St Sav 78–81; TV St Luke in the City 81–86; Chapl Liv Poly 86–92; Chapl Liv Jo Moores Univ 92–08; Hon Can Liv Cathl 03–08; rtd 08. *3 Wightman Avenue, Newton-le-Willows WA12 0LS* T: (01925) 271124 E: bobdicko@blueyonder.co.uk

DICKINSON, Stephen Paul. b 54. SRN 75. NOC 85. **d** 88 **p** 89. NSM Purston cum S Featherstone *Wakef* 88–91; C Goldthorpe w Hickleton *Sheff* 91–94; V New Bentley 94–05; P-in-c Arksey

04–05; V New Bentley w Arksey from 05. *The Vicarage, Victoria Road, Bentley, Doncaster DN5 0EZ* T: (01302) 875266

DICKSON, Anthony Edward. b 59. Nottm Univ BTh 88. Linc Th Coll 85. **d** 88 **p** 89. C Portsea St Alb *Portsm* 88–91; C Cleobury Mortimer w Hopton Wafers *Heref* 91–94; R Fownhope w Mordiford, Brockhampton etc 94–99; PtO *B & W* 09–11; P-in-c Leigh upon Mendip w Stoke St Michael from 11; P-in-c Nunney and Witham Friary, Marston Bigot etc from 11. *The Rectory, High Street, Nunney, Frome BA11 4LZ* T: (01373) 837337 E: nunney.rectory@gmail.com

DICKSON (née TURPIN), Christine Lesley. b 63. Westcott Ho Cam. **d** 09 **p** 10. C Bredon w Bredon's Norton *Worc* 09–12; P-in-c Worc St Wulstan 12–14; Sen Chapl Dorothy House Hospice Winsley 15–16; Asst Chapl R United Hosps Bath NHS Foundn Trust from 18; PtO *B & W* from 15; *Sarum* from 15. *The Rectory, High Street, Nunney, Frome BA11 4LZ* T: (01373) 837337 M: 07511-522581 E: c.dickson22@icloud.com

DICKSON, Colin James. b 74. St Andr Univ MA 96 MPhil 00 Leeds Univ BA 01. Coll of Resurr Mirfield 99. **d** 02 **p** 03. C Tottenham St Paul *Lon* 02–05; C Croydon St Mich w St Jas *S'wark* 05–10; SSF from 10; PtO *Newc* from 15. *The Friary of St Francis, Alnmouth, Alnwick NE66 3NJ* E: josephemmanuelssf@franciscans.org.uk

DICKSON, Colin Patrick Gavin. b 56. **d** 96 **p** 97. C Grays Thurrock *Chelmsf* 96–00; V Glantawe *S & B* 00–16. *73 Webster Street, Treharris CF46 5HW* E: cdickson1@sky.com

DICKSON, Samuel Mervyn James. b 41. CITC. **d** 66 **p** 67. C Ballyholme *D & D* 66–70; C Knockbreda 70–75; I Clonallon w Warrenpoint 75–84; I Down H Trin w Hollymount 84–06; Bp's C Rathmullan 00–05; Bp's C Tyrella 00–06; Bp's C Loughinisland 01–06; Can Down Cathl 91–06; Treas Down Cathl 98–00; Prec Down Cathl 00–01; Chan Down Cathl 01–06; rtd 06. *Apartment 1, 40A Main Street, Dundrum, Newcastle BT33 0LY* T: (028) 4375 1112

DIDUK, Sergiy. b 74. Ukranian Nat Academy BA 08. St Jo Coll Nottm MA 11. **d** 11 **p** 12. C Hucknall Torkard *S'well* 11–15; C Hanworth All SS *Lon* from 15; C Hanworth St Rich from 15. *All Saints' Vicarage, Uxbridge Road, Feltham TW13 5EE* T: (020) 8894 9330 M: 07525-216850 E: sergius_nd99@hotmail.co.uk

DIETZ, Matthew Paul Richard. b 70. Magd Coll Cam MA 95. Wycliffe Hall Ox 05. **d** 07 **p** 08. C Win Ch Ch 07–08; C Throop 08–11; Chapl Monkton Combe Sch Bath 11–14; Chapl Taunton Sch 14–18. *Address temp unknown* M: 07751-454993 E: matthew.dietz@btinternet.com

DIFFEY, Margaret Elsie. b 39. MCSP. **d** 02 **p** 03. OLM Nor St Geo Tombland 02–10; rtd 10; PtO *Nor* from 10. *45 Welsford Road, Norwich NR4 6QB* T/F: (01603) 457248 E: maggiediffey@tiscali.co.uk

DIFFIN, Rosemary Gwendoline. MTh. St Jo Coll Nottm. **d** 12 **p** 13. C Drumglass w Moygashel *Arm* 12–13; C Seapatrick *D & D* 13–15; P-in-c Knockbreda St Aid w St Sav *Arm* 15–16; I from 16. *The Rectory, 38 Vicarage Road, Portadown, Craigavon BT62 4HF* T: (028) 3839 8721 M: 07714-887977 E: rosie.diffin@tesco.net *or* rosemarydiffin@gmail.com

DIGGLE, Judith Margaret. See BROWN, Judith Margaret

DIGGLE, Richard James. b 47. Lon Inst BA 69 Man Poly CertEd 73. **d** 01 **p** 02. OLM Chorlton-cum-Hardy St Werburgh *Man* 01–05; NSM Bickerton, Bickley, Harthill and Burwardsley *Ches* 05–08; V Antrobus, Aston by Sutton, Lt Leigh etc 08–12; P-in-c Bickley from 12. *Ebnal House, Ebnal Lane, Malpas SY14 8DL* T: (01948) 820885 M: 07749-849783 E: diggle163@btinternet.com *or* rdiggle50@gmail.com

DIGGORY, Mrs Susan Jane. b 51. SEITE BA 09. **d** 09 **p** 10. NSM Tunbridge Wells St Mark *Roch* 09–14; V Crockham Hill H Trin from 14. *The Vicarage, Oakdale Lane, Crockham Hill, Edenbridge TN8 6RL* T: (01732) 446466 M: 07799-892583 E: sue.diggory@outlook.com

DIGMAN (née BUTTERFIELD), Mrs Amanda Helen. b 73. Derby Univ BA 96 Ches Univ MTh 15. St Jo Coll Nottm 07. **d** 09 **p** 10. C Sutton in Ashfield St Mary *S'well* 09–12; C Huthwaite 09–10; P-in-c Carlton from 12; P-in-c Colwick from 12. *The Vicarage, 261 Oakdale Road, Carlton, Nottingham NG4 1BP* M: 07803-625049 E: revamandadigman@me.com

DIGNUM, Keith Anthony. **d** 08 **p** 09. OLM Coltishall w Gt Hautbois, Frettenham etc *Nor* from 08. *Mill House, 4 Newton Road, Hainford, Norwich NR10 3LZ* T: (01603) 710397 E: kdignum@googlemail.com

DILKES, Nigel Bruce. b 58. Univ of Wales (Ban) BSc 97 Lanc Univ PhD 01. Ridley Hall Cam 03. **d** 05 **p** 06. C Llandudno *Ban* 05–07; C Holyhead 07–09; TV Barnstaple *Ex* 09–17; V Pilton w Ashford from 17. *The Rectory, 4 Northfield Lane, Barnstaple EX31 1QB* T: (01271) 343225 E: nigeldilkes@aol.com

✠DILL, The Rt Revd Nicholas Bayard Botolf. b 63. Toronto Univ BA 86 Lon Univ LLB 89 Barrister 91. Wycliffe Hall Ox 96. d 98 p 99 c 13. C Lindfield *Chich* 98–05; R Pembroke St Jo Bermuda 05–13; Bp Bermuda from 13. *Diocesan Office, PO Box HM 769, Hamilton HM CX, Bermuda* T: (001) (441) 292 6987 F: 292 5421 E: bishop@anglican.bm

DILL, Peter Winston. b 41. ACP 66 K Coll Lon BD 72 AKC 72. St Aug Coll Cant 72. d 73 p 74. C Warsop *S'well* 73–75; C Rhyl w St Ann *St As* 75–77; C Oxton *Ches* 77–78; V Newton in Mottram 78–82; P-in-c Shelton and Oxon *Lich* 82–84; V 84–87; Chapl Clifton Coll Bris 87–00; C Thorverton, Cadbury, Upton Pyne etc *Ex* 00–01; PtO *Bris* 02–03; Past Co-ord St Monica Trust Westbury Fields 03–06; rtd 06; PtO *Bris* from 07. *85B Pembroke Road, Clifton, Bristol BS8 3EB* T: 0117-973 9769

DILLON, Gerard Francis. d 14 p 15. C Glenrothes *St And* from 14. *18 Sappi Road, Glenrothes KY7 6ZJ* T: (01592) 612602 E: gerryd74@gmail.com

DILNOT, Canon John William. b 36. Selw Coll Cam BA 60 MA 64. Cuddesdon Coll 60. d 62 p 63. C Stafford St Mary *Lich* 62–66; C Stoke upon Trent 66–67; V Leek All SS 67–74; V Leeds w Broomfield *Cant* 74–79; P-in-c Aldington 79–81; P-in-c Bonnington w Bilsington 79–81; P-in-c Fawkenhurst 79–81; R Aldington w Bonnington and Bilsington 81–87; RD N Lympne 82–87; Hon Can Cant Cathl 85–99; V Folkestone St Mary and St Eanswythe 87–99; rtd 99; PtO *Cant* from 99. *2 St Elizabeth House, St John's Hospital, Northgate, Canterbury CT1 1AY* T: (01227) 788115

DILWORTH, Anthony. b 41. St Deiniol's Hawarden 87. d 90 p 91. NSM Gt Saughall *Ches* 90–93; P-in-c Cwmcarn *Mon* 93–95; V 95–98; V Abercarn and Cwmcarn 99–01; TV Upholland *Liv* 01–06; rtd 06; PtO *St As* 09–10 and from 12; P-in-c Llansilin w Llangadwaladr and Llangedwyn 10–12. *4 Maes Owain, Glyndyfrdwy, Corwen LL21 9HF* T: (01490) 430586 M: 07773-389179 E: anthonydilworth536@btinternet.com

DIMES, Stuart Christopher Laurence. b 60. Warwick Univ BSc 81. St Jo Coll Nottm 99. d 01 p 02. C Branksome St Clem *Sarum* 01–05; P-in-c W Heath *Birm* 05–10; V 10–17; R Hampton-in-Arden w Bickenhill from 17; P-in-c Barston from 17. *The Vicarage, High Street, Hampton-in-Arden, Solihull B92 0AE* T: (01675) 442339 E: revsdimes@live.com

DIMOND, Canon Mark James. b 68. Kent Univ BA 90 St Ant Coll Ox MPhil 93 Univ of Wales (Swansea) PhD 04 Cardiff Univ DipEd 06. d 11 p 12. C Penarth All SS *Llan* 11–14; Chapl to Abp Wales 14–17; Can Res St Woolos Cathl *Mon* from 17. *Canon's House, Stow Hill, Newport NP20 4EA* T: (01633) 376977 E: markdimond@churchinwales.org.uk

DIN, Munawar. b 67. Punjab Univ MSc 92 Azad Jammu and Kashmir Univ MBA 96. Cranmer Hall Dur 15. d 17 p 18. C Blackb Ch Ch w St Matt from 17. *31 Britten Close, Blackburn BB2 3TD* T: (01254) 388254 M: 07728-373209 E: dinmunawar@gmail.com

DINELEY, Margaret Anne. b 44. d 15 p 15. NSM Lochgelly *St And* from 15. *2 Dreghorn Park, Edinburgh EH13 9PH* E: margaret.dineley@gmail.com

DINES, Miss Rachael Irene Elizabeth. b 68. St Paul's Coll Chelt BEd 92. Cranmer Hall Dur 14. d 16 p 17. C N Walsham and Edingthorpe *Nor* 16–18; C N Walsham, Edingthorpe, Worstead and Westwick from 18. *8 Plumbly Close, North Walsham NR28 9YB* T: (01692) 405363 M: 07763-211901 E: rachaeldines@hotmail.com

DINGWALL-JONES, Christopher Lawrence. b 88. St Hugh's Coll Ox BA 11 Edin Univ MSc 11 Kent Univ PhD 15. St Steph Ho Ox BA 17. d 18 p 19. C Fleetwood St Pet and St Dav *Blackb* from 18. *211 Broadway, Fleetwood FY7 8AZ* M: 07914-829793 E: fr.chrisdj@gmail.com

DINNEN, John Frederick. b 42. TCD BA 65 BD 72 QUB MTh 91. CITC. d 66 p 67. C Belfast All SS *Conn* 66–68; ICM Dub 69–71; C Carnmoney *Conn* 71–73; Asst Dean of Residences QUB 73-74; Dean 74–84; I Hillsborough *D & D* 84–07; Preb Down Cathl 93–96; Dir of Ords 96–98; Dean Down 96–06; rtd 08; PtO *Eur* from 18. *74 Demesne Road, Ballynahinch BT24 8NS* T: (028) 4481 1148 E: jdinnen@btinternet.com

DINNEN, Mrs Judith Margaret. b 48. Open Univ BA 87 Univ of Wales (Cardiff) MA 00 Goldsmiths' Coll Lon TCert 71. WEMTC 01. d 05 p 06. NSM Madley w Tyberton, Peterchurch, Vowchurch etc *Heref* 05–19; PtO from 19. *The Hawthorns, Madley, Hereford HR2 9LU* T: (01981) 251866 E: judy@dinnen.plus.com

DINSMORE, Stephen Ralph. b 56. Wye Coll Lon BSc 78 Man Univ MA 06. Cranmer Hall Dur 82. d 85 p 86. C Haughton le Skerne *Dur* 85–88; C Edgware *Lon* 88–93; V Plymouth St Jude *Ex* 93–05; RD Plymouth Sutton 96–01; Dioc Adv for Miss and Par Development *Chelmsf* 05–07; Hon C Cranham Park 05–07; Nat Dir SOMA UK from 07.

SOMA UK, PO Box 69, Merriott TA18 9AP T: (01460) 279737 E: stephen.dinsmore@somauk.org

DINWIDDY SMITH, Emma Ruth. b 67. St Hugh's Coll Ox BA 89 MA 10 Ox Brookes Univ MA 10. Ripon Coll Cuddesdon 08. d 10 p 11. C Hampstead St Jo *Lon* 10–13; C Chelsea St Luke and Ch Ch 13–19; AD Chelsea 17–19; V Kensington St Mary Abbots from 19. *St Mary Abbots Parish Office, Vicarage Gate, London W8 4HN* T: (020) 7937 2419

DIPLOCK, Susan Elizabeth. b 47. Birm Univ BA 69 Lon Inst of Educn MA 99. St Mellitus Coll 16. d 17 p 18. NSM Walthamstow St Pet *Chelmsf* from 17. *8 Ravenswood Road, London E17 9LY* T: (020) 8923 4455 M: 07710-211176 E: diplock@diplock.demon.co.uk

DISLEY, Mrs Edith Jennifer. b 51. Sheff Univ BSc 72 Man Univ BD 79. NOC 99. d 01 p 02. NSM Man Victoria Park 01–10; NSM Withington St Paul 02–10; NSM Wythenshawe 10–12; P-in-c Leesfield 12–15; V from 15. *St Thomas's Vicarage, 2 Wild Street, Lees, Oldham OL4 5AD* T: 0161-624 3731 E: edithdisley@hotmail.com

DITCH, David John. b 45. St Cath Coll Cam BA 67 MA 70 Leeds Univ PGCE 68. WMMTC 88. d 91 p 92. C Biddulph *Lich* 91–94; V Hednesford 94–02; V Chasetown 02–08; rtd 09; PtO *Derby* from 09. *6 Redwing Croft, Derby DE23 1WT* T: (01332) 271767

DITCHBURN, Hazel. b 44. NEOC 82. dss 84 d 87 p 94. Scotswood *Newc* 84–86; Ind Chapl *Dur* 86–95; TV Gateshead 95–98; AD 92–98; P-in-c Stella 98–04; P-in-c Swalwell 01–04; R Blaydon and Swalwell 04–06; AD Gateshead W 98–00; Hon Can Dur Cathl 94–06; rtd 06; P-in-c Freshwater Australia 06–09; PtO *Newc* from 09. *2 Woburn Way, Westerhope, Newcastle upon Tyne NE5 5JD* T: 0191-286 0553

DITCHFIELD, Timothy Frederick. b 61. CCC Cam BA 83. Cranmer Hall Dur 85. d 88 p 89. C Accrington St Jo *Blackb* 88–89; C Accrington St Jo w Huncoat 89–91; C Whittle-le-Woods 91–95; Chapl K Coll Lon from 95; NSM St Mary le Strand w St Clem Danes *Lon* from 17. *King's College, Strand, London WC2R 2LS* T: (020) 7848 2373 F: 7848 2344 E: tim.ditchfield@kcl.ac.uk

DIX, Edward Joseph. b 77. Goldsmiths' Coll Lon BMus 00. Wycliffe Hall Ox BTh 09. d 09 p 10. C Shadwell St Paul w Ratcliffe St Jas *Lon* 09–13; C Is of Dogs Ch Ch and St Jo w St Luke from 13. *170 Wheat Sheaf Close, London E14 9UZ* T: (020) 7515 5772 M: 07899-075935 E: edjdix@gmail.com *or* ed@stlukesmillwall.org

DIXON, Ms Anne Elizabeth. b 56. Leeds Univ LLB 77 Solicitor 80. Westcott Ho Cam. d 01 p 02. C Guildf H Trin w St Mary 01–05; Chapl HM Pris Bullwood Hall 06–09; PtO *Guildf* from 05; *Blackb* from 10; *S'wark* 14–17; *Ox* from 15. *2 Highcroft Court, Bookham, Leatherhead KT23 3QU* T: (01372) 450643 M: 07973-542467

DIXON, Bruce Richard. b 42. Lon Univ BScEng 63. Sarum Th Coll 66. d 68 p 69. C Walton St Mary *Liv* 68–70; C Harnham *Sarum* 70–73; C Streatham St Leon *S'wark* 73–77; R Thurcaston *Leic* 77–83; R Cranborne w Boveridge, Edmondsham etc *Sarum* 83–02; rtd 07; PtO *Sarum* from 16. *20 Cypress Road, Charlton Down, Dorchester DT2 9FF* E: bandk2d@hotmail.com

DIXON, Bryan Stanley. b 61. St Jo Coll Nottm BTh 93. d 93 p 94. C Beverley Minster *York* 93–96; C Kingston upon Hull St Aid Southcoates 96–97; Asst Chapl HM Pris *Dur* 97–98; R Mid Marsh Gp *Linc* 98–03; R Brandesburton and Leven w Catwick *York* 03–10; P-in-c Patrick Brompton and Hunton *Ripon* 10–14; *Leeds* 14–16; P-in-c Crakehall *Ripon* 10–14; *Leeds* 14–16; P-in-c Hornby *Ripon* 10–14; *Leeds* 14–16; AD Wensley *Ripon* 11–13; P-in-c Spennithorne w Finghall and Hauxwell 12–14; *Leeds* 14–16; R Middle Rasen Gp *Linc* from 16. *The Vicarage, North Street, Middle Rasen, Market Rasen LN8 3TS* T: (01673) 842759 E: rev.bryan@icloud.com

DIXON, Campbell Boyd. Ulster Univ MA. d 07 p 08. NSM Jordanstown *Conn* 07–11; C Belf Cathl 11–16; P-in-c Belfast St Mark *Conn* from 16. *10 Meadowbank, Newtownabbey BT37 0UP* T: (028) 9059 9880 M: 07879-427980 E: campbelldixon@hotmail.co.uk

DIXON, Charles William. b 41. NW Ord Course 78. d 81 p 82. C Almondbury *Wakef* 81–82; C Almondbury w Farnley Tyas 82–84; P-in-c Shelley 84–88; P-in-c Shepley 84–88; V Shelley and Shepley 88–89; V Ripponden 89–94; V Barkisland w W Scammonden 89–94; P-in-c Thornes 94–98; Chapl among Deaf People *Chelmsf* 98–06; rtd 06; Chapl among Deaf People *Ely* 06–10; PtO from 10. *9 The Paddock, Huntingdon PE29 1BY* T: (01480) 451109 M: 07749-702924 E: c.dixon41@btinternet.com

DIXON, David Hugh. b 40. Chich Th Coll 90. d 92 p 93. C Launceston *Truro* 92–95; TV Probus, Ladock and Grampound w Creed and St Erme 95–06; rtd 06. *1 Rectory Close, Old Village, Willand, Cullompton EX15 2RH* T: (01884) 839984

DIXON, David Michael. b 58. Preston Poly BA 82 Barrister 83. Coll of Resurr Mirfield BA 98. **d** 98 **p** 99. C Goldthorpe w Hickleton *Sheff* 98–01; P-in-c W Kirby St Andr *Ches* 01–07; V 07–10; P-in-c Scarborough St Martin *York* 10–12; V from 12; P-in-c Scarborough St Sav w All SS 10–12; V from 12. *St Martin's Vicarage, Craven Street, Scarborough YO11 2BY* T: (01723) 363828 E: frdavidstmart@gmail.com

DIXON, Edward Michael. b 42. St Chad's Coll Dur BA 64 Newc Univ MA 93. **d** 66 **p** 67. C Hartlepool H Trin *Dur* 66–70; C Howden *York* 70–73; Chapl HM Pris Liv 73; Chapl HM Pris Onley 74–82; Chapl HM Pris Frankland 82–87; Chapl HM Pris Dur 87–97; Chapl HM Pris Acklington 97–98; Asst Chapl 98–02; P-in-c Shilbottle *Newc* 98–07; P-in-c Chevington 03–07; rtd 07; PtO *Dur* from 07; *Newc* from 18. *2 Crowley Place, Newton Aycliffe DL5 4JH* T: (01325) 312872 E: dixon4474@gmail.com

DIXON, John Kenneth. b 40. Linc Th Coll 79. **d** 81 **p** 82. C Goldington *St Alb* 81–85; V Cardington 85–94; RD Elstow 89–94; R Clifton 94–95; P-in-c Southill 94–95; R Clifton and Southill 95–05; RD Shefford 95–01; rtd 05. *7 Milton Fields, Brixham TQ5 0BH* T: (01803) 854396

DIXON, John Scarth. b 69. Aber Univ MA 92. Westcott Ho Cam 95. **d** 98 **p** 99. C Walney Is *Carl* 98–01; R Harrington 01–06; V Hawkshead and Low Wray w Sawrey and Rusland etc from 06. *The Vicarage, Vicarage Lane, Hawkshead, Ambleside LA22 0PD* T: (015394) 36301 E: jjcedixon@btinternet.com

DIXON, Kenneth. *See* DIXON, John Kenneth

DIXON, Canon Kerry John. b 59. Wilson Carlile Coll 84. **d** 13 **p** 14. LtO *Bre* 13–14; P Missr from 14; P-in-c Dundee St Luke from 14; Can St Paul's Cathl Dundee from 17. *6 Dudhope Street, Dundee DD1 1JU* T: (01382) 523911 M: 07711-410017 E: kerry.dixon@churcharmy.org

DIXON, Lorraine. b 65. Leeds Univ BA 96. Qu Coll Birm BD 98. **d** 98 **p** 99. C Potternewton *Ripon* 98–01; Chapl Ches Univ 01–05; Min Can Ches Cathl 04–05; Deanery Missr to Young Adults Yardley & Bordsley *Birm* 05–12; PtO from 13. E: l.dixon65@btopenworld.com

DIXON, Margaret Innes Goodwin. b 58. Reading Univ BA 01. Ox Min Course 08. **d** 11 **p** 12. NSM Ellesborough, The Kimbles and Stoke Mandeville *Ox* 11–14; C N Leigh 14–17; V from 17; C Cogges and S Leigh from 14. *The Vicarage, New Yatt Road, North Leigh, Witney OX29 6TT* T: (01993) 880095 M: 07773-017636 E: rev.margaret.dixon@btinternet.com

DIXON, Michael. *See* DIXON, Edward Michael

DIXON, Canon Peter. b 36. Qu Coll Ox BA 58 MA 62 Birm Univ BD 65 PhD 75. Qu Coll Birm. **d** 60 **p** 61. C Mountain Ash *Llan* 60–63; C Penrhiwceiber w Matthewstown and Ynysboeth 63–68; P-in-c 68–70; V Bronllys w Llanfilo *S & B* 70–02; Bp's Chapl for Readers 80–02; Bp's Chapl for Th Educn 83–02; Warden of Readers 92–02; RD Hay 90–02; Can Res Brecon Cathl 98–02; rtd 02. *22 The Caerpound, Hay-on-Wye, Hereford HR3 5DU* T: (01497) 820775

DIXON, Peter. b 70. Ex Univ BTh 08. SWMTC 04. **d** 07 **p** 08. C Redruth w Lanner and Treleigh *Truro* 07–10; V Wisborough Green *Chich* 10–13; P-in-c Lanteglos by Camelford w Advent *Truro* 13–15; P-in-c St Teath 13–15; CF from 15. *c/o MOD Chaplains (Army)* T: (01264) 383430 F: 381824

DIXON, Peter David. b 48. Edin Univ BSc 71 MIMechE. Edin Dioc NSM Course 75. **d** 79 **p** 80. NSM Prestonpans *Edin* 79–89; NSM Musselburgh 79–89; NSM Wester Hailes St Luke 90; P-in-c Edin St Barn from 91. *8 Oswald Terrace, Prestonpans EH32 9EG* T: (01875) 812985

DIXON, Philip. b 48. Leeds Univ BSc 69 Open Univ BA 91. St Jo Coll Nottm 77. **d** 80 **p** 81. C Soundwell *Bris* 80–82; C Stoke Bishop 82–84; TV Hemel Hempstead *St Alb* 84–85; Chapl Westonbirt Sch 85–11; rtd 11; PtO *Bris* from 86. *27 Downfield Lodge, Downfield Road, Bristol BS8 2TQ* T: 0117-373 8528 E: pdnovenoe@yahoo.com

DIXON, Philip Roger. b 54. CCC Ox BA 77 MA 80. Oak Hill Th Coll BA 80. **d** 80 **p** 81. C Droylsden St Mary *Man* 80–84; TV Rochdale 84–91; V Audenshaw St Steph from 91; C Denton Ch Ch from 13; C Denton St Lawr from 13; C Haughton St Anne from 13; AD Ashton-under-Lyne 03–08 and from 16. *St Stephen's Vicarage, 176 Stamford Road, Audenshaw, Manchester M34 5WW* T: 0161-370 1863 E: revrogerdixon@outlook.com

DIXON, Robert. b 50. Univ of Wales (Lamp) BA 80 Sussex Univ MA 04. Chich Th Coll 80. **d** 81 **p** 82. C Maidstone St Martin *Cant* 81–84; Chapl HM Youth Cust Cen Dover 84–88; C All Hallows by the Tower etc *Lon* 88–90; P-in-c Southwick H Trin *Dur* 90–97; R 97; R Etchingham *Chich* 97–10; V Hurst Green 97–10; V Bedford Leigh *Man* 10–19; rtd 19. *65 Church Lane,*

South Bersted, Bognor Regis PO22 9QA* M: 07779-121169 E: lancsrob@aol.com

DIXON, Stephen. b 65. York St Jo Univ MA 07. Lindisfarne Regional Tr Partnership 13. **d** 15 **p** 16. C Gosforth All SS *Newc* 15–18; V Tynemouth Priory from 18. *1 Crossway, North Shields NE30 2LB* E: s.c.dixon@hotmail.co.uk

DIXON, Stephen William. b 53. Nottm Univ BA 75 Liv Univ MTh 00 Ches Univ DProf 12 Man Metrop Univ PGCE 88. NOC 96. **d** 99 **p** 00. NSM Meltham *Wakef* 99–02; Upper Holme Valley *Leeds* from 02; Children's Officer *Man* 01–15. *83 Totties, Holmfirth HD9 1UJ* T: (01484) 687376 E: familymasondixon@uwclub.net

DIXON, Mrs Teresa Mary. b 61. Southn Univ BSc 82 Ball Coll Ox PGCE 83. EAMTC 99. **d** 02 **p** 03. NSM Sutton and Witcham w Mepal *Ely* 02–04; C Littleport 04–06; NSM Witchford w Wentworth 06–19; PtO from 19. *Ash Tree Farm, Furlong Drove, Little Downham, Ely CB6 2EW* T: (01353) 699552 E: revteresa@aol.com

DIXON, Tina Ann. b 51. Liv Univ MB, ChB 74 MRCP 79 FRCP 97. St Mellitus Coll 17. **d** 18 **p** 19. NSM Oxton *Ches* from 18. *48 Birch Road, Prenton CH43 5UA* T: 0151-653 3256 E: dixon.tina51@gmail.com *or* tina.dixon@oxtonstsaviour.co.uk

DNISTRIANSKYJ, Stefan Mykola. b 61. Leic Univ BSc 82 Ches Coll of HE BTh 02. NOC 99. **d** 02 **p** 03. C Halliwell St Luke *Man* 02–06; TV New Bury w Gt Lever 06–09; P-in-c Anchorsholme *Blackb* 09–12; V 12–18; V Wrightington from 18. *The Vicarage, 92 Church Lane, Wrightington, Wigan WN6 9SP* M: 07931-785598 E: dnists@gmail.com

DOBBIE, Charles William Granville. b 49. Wycliffe Hall Ox 94. **d** 96 **p** 97. C Morriston *S & B* 96–00; Asst Chapl Morriston Hosp/Ysbyty Treforys NHS Trust 97–98; Asst Chapl Swansea NHS Trust 99–00; V Lyonsdown H Trin *St Alb* from 00. *Holy Trinity Vicarage, 18 Lyonsdown Road, Barnet EN5 1JE* T: (020) 8216 3786 E: charles@holytrinitylyonsdown.org.uk

DOBBIN, Canon Charles Philip. b 51. Jes Coll Cam BA 73 MA 77 Oriel Coll Ox BA 75 MA 88 Birm Univ MPhil 04. St Steph Ho Ox 74. **d** 76 **p** 77. C New Addington *Cant* 76–79; C Melton Mowbray w Thorpe Arnold *Leic* 79–83; V Loughb Gd Shep 83–89; RD Akeley W 93–00; Hon Can Leic Cathl 94–00; TR Moor Allerton *Ripon* 00–09; TR Moor Allerton and Shadwell 09–16; Dioc Interfaith Relns Officer 09–15; rtd 16; PtO *Leic* from 17. *3 Outwoods Avenue, Loughborough LE11 3LP* E: cdobbin@aol.com

DOBBIN, Harold John. b 47. Liv Univ BSc 69. St Steph Ho Ox 70. **d** 73 **p** 74. C Newbold w Dunston *Derby* 73–77; C Leckhampton SS Phil and Jas w Cheltenham St Jas *Glouc* 77–80; V Hebburn St Cuth *Dur* 80–86; R Barlborough *Derby* 86–95; P-in-c Alfreton 95–00; V 00–04; RD 02–04; P-in-c Clifton 04–08; P-in-c Norbury w Snelston 04–08; rtd 08. *21 Dale Close, Fritchley, Belper DE56 2HZ* T: (01773) 857002 E: harolddobbin@yahoo.co.uk

DOBBINS, Lorraine Sharon. b 72. Ripon Coll Cuddesdon BTh 01. **d** 01 **p** 02. C Talbot Village *Sarum* 01–05; TV Preston w Sutton Poyntz, Littlemoor etc 05–15; TV Weymouth Ridgeway 15–19; V Warminster Ch Ch from 19; Asst Dioc Dir of Ords from 13. *Address temp unknown* E: vicarlorraine@gmail.com

DOBBS, Michael John. b 48. Linc Th Coll 74. **d** 77 **p** 78. C Warsop *S'well* 77–82; V Worksop St Paul 82–89; P-in-c Mansfield St Mark 89–03; V Kirk Hallam *Derby* 03–05; rtd 05; PtO *S'well* from 06; *Derby* 13–18. *Address withheld by request* E: mjdmjd@ntlworld.com

DOBELL (née PRICE), Mrs Alison Jane. b 63. Open Univ BA 98. Aston Tr Scheme 91 Westcott Ho Cam 93. **d** 95 **p** 96. C Upper Norwood All SS *S'wark* 95–99; V Mitcham St Barn 99–07; Chapl St Jo Win Charity from 11. *74 Radway Road, Southampton SO15 7PJ* T: (023) 8077 3631 E: alisonjane.price@btinternet.com

DOBLE, Dominic Julian Anderson. b 71. Wye Coll Lon BSc 92 Univ of Wales (Ban) MSc 99 Leeds Univ BA 10. Coll of Resurr Mirfield 08. **d** 10 **p** 11. C Crediton, Shobrooke and Sandford etc *Ex* 10–14; R Watercombe *Sarum* from 14. *The Rectory, Main Street, Broadmayne, Dorchester DT2 8EB* T: (01305) 852435 M: 07743-554955 E: office@watercombe.org.uk *or* dominic.doble@phonecoop.coop

DOBLE, Mrs Maureen Mary Thompson. b 44. RGN 65. S Dios Minl Tr Scheme 90. **d** 93 **p** 94. NSM Kingston St Mary w Broomfield etc *B & W* 93–07; Chapl Taunton and Somerset NHS Foundn Trust 03–07; rtd 07; PtO *B & W* from 07. *Rosebank, Lyngford Lane, Taunton TA2 7LL* T: (01823) 286772 E: rosebank@maureendoble.co.uk

DOBLE, Peter. b 29. Univ of Wales (Cardiff) BA 51 Fitzw Coll Cam BA 54 MA 58 St Edm Hall Ox MA 68 Leeds Univ PhD 92. Wesley Ho Cam 52. **d** 55 **p** 58. In Ch of S India 55–60;

In Methodist Ch 60–64; Hd of RE Qu Mary Sch Lytham St Annes *Blackb* 64–67; Lect RS Culham Coll Abingdon *Ox* 67–69; Sen Lect 69-74; Prin Lect and Hd Relig Studies 74–80; PtO *York* 80–17; Dir York RE Cen 80–94; Sen Fell Th and RS Leeds Univ *Ripon* 95–98; Hon Lect from 98. *6 Witham Drive, Huntington, York YO32 9YD* T: (01904) 761288 E: peter.doble@btinternet.com

DOBRZYNSKI, Adam Andrzej. b 75. Catholic Univ of Lublin MPhil 01 Ivan Franko Nat Univ Lviv PhD 18. Pontifical Academy of Th Krakow MTS 06 LTh 07. **d** 07 **p** 07. C Ealing St Pet Mt Park *Lon* from 19. *St Peter's Church, Mount Park Road, London W5 2RU* T: (020) 8997 3655 M: 07453-619591 E: a.a.dobrzynski@gmail.com

DOBSON, Catherine Heather. b 71. ERMC. **d** 09 **p** 10. NSM Broughton w Loddington and Cransley etc *Pet* 09–11; C 11–14; C Rothwell w Orton, Rushton w Glendon and Pipewell 11–14; R Bacton, Happisburgh, Hempstead w Eccles etc *Nor* from 14; RD St Benet from 19. *The Rectory, The Hill, Happisburgh, Norwich NR12 0PW* T: (01692) 650359 E: revcdobson@live.com

DOBSON, Christopher John. b 62. Univ of Wales (Abth) BA 83. Wycliffe Hall Ox BA 88. **d** 89 **p** 90. C Biggin Hill *Roch* 89–92; C Tunbridge Wells St Jas w St Phil 92–95; USPG Zimbabwe 95–99; V Paddock Wood *Roch* 00–08; Dioc Ecum Officer *Bris* from 08; Hon C Downend from 09; Dioc Chapl MU from 19. *23 Ducie Road, Staple Hill, Bristol BS16 5JZ* M: 07904-831829 E: chris.j.dobson@gmail.com or chris.dobson@bristoldiocese.org

DOBSON, Mrs Elspeth Judith. b 53. Newc Univ CertEd 75 BPhil 88 MPhil 95. Lindisfarne Regional Tr Partnership 11. **d** 17 **p** 18. NSM Doddington, Ilderton, Kirknewton and Wooler *Newc* from 17. *The Crossings, Yeaverling, Kirknewton, Wooler NE71 6HG* T: (01668) 216098 M: 07778-465527

DOBSON, Geoffrey Norman. b 46. Leeds Univ CertEd 68 Open Univ BA 77 MA 05 ACP 70. Wells Th Coll 71. **d** 74 **p** 75. C Wanstead H Trin Hermon Hill *Chelmsf* 74–76; Colchester Adnry Youth Chapl 76–78; C Halstead St Andr w H Trin and Greenstead Green *Chelmsf* 76–78; Asst Dir Educn (Youth) *Carl* 78–82; P-in-c Kirkandrews-on-Eden w Beaumont and Grinsdale 78–82; V Illingworth *Wakef* 82–86; V Roxton w Gt Barford *St Alb* 86–93; Chapl N Man Health Care NHS Trust 93–98; P-in-c Newton Heath St Wilfrid and St Anne *Man* 93–97; C Newton Heath 97–98; P-in-c Alconbury cum Weston *Ely* 98–00; P-in-c Buckworth 98–00; P-in-c Gt w Lt Stukeley 98–00; PtO from 02. *30 Lees Lane, Southoe, St Neots PE19 5YG* T: (01480) 475474 E: geoffreyndobson@aol.com

DOBSON, Mrs Joanna Jane Louise. b 61. Coll of Ripon & York St Jo BEd 83. NEOC 98. **d** 01 **p** 02. NSM Scalby *York* 01–04; V Bridlington Em 04–08; P-in-c Skipsea w Ulrome and Barmston w Fraisthorpe 04–08; Pioneer Min Retford Deanery *S'well* 08–10; P-in-c Mitford and Hebron *Newc* 10–16; P-in-c Ulgham from 16; P-in-c Widdrington from 16. *The Vicarage, Grangemoor Road, Widdrington, Morpeth NE61 5PU* T: (01670) 458945 M: 07828-181506 E: revjoannadobson@yahoo.co.uk

DOBSON, The Very Revd John Richard. b 64. Van Mildert Coll Dur BA 87. Ripon Coll Cuddesdon 87. **d** 89 **p** 90. C Benfieldside *Dur* 89–92; C Darlington St Cuth 92–96; C-in-c Blackwell All SS and Salutation CD 96–98; V Blackwell All SS and Salutation 98–14; P-in-c Coniscliffe 04–14; AD Darlington 01–14; Hon Can Dur Cathl 08–14; Dean Ripon *Leeds* from 14. *Minster House, Bedern Bank, Ripon HG4 1PE* T: (01765) 602609 E: j.dobson991@btinternet.com

DOBSON, Judith. See DOBSON, Elspeth Judith

DOBSON, Michael William. b 66. Man Univ BA 89 Sussex Univ MSc 91 Open Univ PhD 99 FRSA 95. Regent Coll Vancouver MDiv 11. **d** 11 **p** 12. In Angl Network in Canada 11–14; R Maadi Egypt 14–19; C Pimlico St Gabr *Lon* from 19. *St Gabriel's Clergy House, Warwick Square, London SW1V 2AD* E: mike.w.dobson@gmail.com

DOBSON, Owen James. b 83. Ex Univ BA 04. Westcott Ho Cam 08. **d** 10 **p** 11. C St John's Wood *Lon* 10–14; C Paddington St Jas from 14. *61 Pembroke House, Hallfield Estate, London W2 6HQ* T: (020) 7706 1248 M: 07891-890837 E: owenjamesdobson@hotmail.com or owen@stjamespaddington.org.uk

DOBSON, Canon Peter David. b 88. St Andr Univ MTheol 10 Jes Coll Cam MPhil 11. Westcott Ho Cam 10. **d** 12 **p** 13. C Ch the King *Newc* 12–16; V Monkseaton St Pet 16–19; Can Res Newc Cathl from 19. *Cathedral House, 42 Mosley Street, Newcastle upon Tyne NE1 1DF* T: 0191-232 1939 M: 07940-706123 E: peterdobsonuk@yahoo.co.uk

DOBSON, Philip Albert. b 52. Lanc Univ BA 73 CertEd 74. Trin Coll Bris 89. **d** 89 **p** 90. C Grenoside *Sheff* 89–92; C Cove St Jo *Guildf* 92–93; TV 93–96; V Camberley St Martin Old Dean 96–07; TR Bushbury *Lich* 07–13; rtd 13; PtO *Man* from

14. *134 Old Moat Lane, Manchester M20 1DE* T: 0161-283 9697 E: philip297dobson.home@gmail.com

DOCKREE, Peter Martin. b 74. Keele Univ BA 96 Ox Univ MSc 00. Ox Min Course 07. **d** 10 **p** 11. C Wolverton *Ox* 10–14; V Swaythling *Win* from 14. *The Vicarage, 357 Burgess Road, Southampton SO16 3BD* T: (023) 8055 4231 M: 07972-439865 E: peter.dockree@outlook.com

DODD, Canon Andrew Patrick. b 68. Hatf Poly BEng 91 Selw Coll Cam BTh 00. Westcott Ho Cam 97. **d** 00 **p** 01. C New Addington *S'wark* 00–04; R Newington St Mary 04–11; AD S'wark and Newington 07–11; P-in-c Gt Grimsby St Mary and St Jas *Linc* 11–13; TR from 13; AD Grimsby and Cleethorpes from 11; Can and Preb Linc Cathl from 12. *The Rectory, 49 Park Drive, Grimsby DN32 0EG* T: (01472) 351815 E: andrew@vincerdodd.co.uk

DODD, Miss Denise Kate. b 72. Cranmer Hall Dur 07. **d** 09 **p** 10. C Porchester *S'well* 09–14; Bp's Dom Chapl *Dur* from 14; Hon Min Can Dur Cathl from 16. *Auckland Castle, Bishop Auckland DL14 7NR* T: (01388) 602576 F: 605264 E: denisekdodd@yahoo.co.uk or denise.dodd@durham.anglican.org

DODD, Graham Michael. b 38. St Jo Coll York CertEd 61 Hull Coll of Educn DipEd 67. NOC 93. **d** 96 **p** 97. NSM Golcar *Wakef* 96–99; NSM N Huddersfield 99–02; rtd 02; PtO *Wakef* 02–14; *Leeds* from 14. *9 Broombank, Huddersfield HD2 2DJ* T: (01484) 539832 or 687376 E: mikedodd184@btinternet.com

DODD, Michael Christopher. b 33. Ch Coll Cam BA 55 MA 59. Ridley Hall Cam 57. **d** 59 **p** 60. C Stechford *Birm* 59–62; V Quinton Road W St Boniface 62–72; TV Paston *Pet* 72–77; TR Hodge Hill *Birm* 77–89; rtd 90; PtO *Birm* from 90. *39 Regency Gardens, Birmingham B14 4JS* T: 0121-474 6945

DODD, Canon Peter Curwen. b 33. St Jo Coll Cam BA 57 FRSA 93. Linc Th Coll 58 Wm Temple Coll Rugby 59. **d** 60 **p** 61. C Eastwood *Sheff* 60–63; Ind Chapl 63–67; Ind Chapl *Newc* 67–98; RD Newc E 78–83 and 92–95; Hon Can Newc Cathl 82–98; rtd 98; PtO *Newc* from 98. *Glenesk, 26 The Oval, Benton, Newcastle upon Tyne NE12 9PP* T: 0191-266 1293

DODDS, Barry. See DODDS, Norman Barry

DODDS, Graham Michael. b 58. Liv Univ MA 01 Bris Univ PhD 08 LTCL 80 GTCL 80 York Univ PGCE 81. Trin Coll Bris 84. **d** 84 **p** 85. C Reigate St Mary *S'wark* 84–91; P-in-c Bath Walcot *B & W* 91–93; R 93–96; Dir Reader Studies 96–18; Lay Tr Adv 96–01; Asst Dir Min Development 01–04; Prin Sch of Formation *B&W* 04–10; Dir of Learning Communities 10–18; Preb Wells Cathl 03–10; Can Res and Treas Wells Cathl 10–18; Bps' Dom Chapl from 18. *2 The Canaries Path, Shepton Mallet BA4 4FP* T: (01749) 340925 M: 07702-658687 E: chaplain@bathwells.anglican.org

DODDS, Linda. b 54. **d** 08 **p** 09. OLM Bishop Auckland Woodhouse Close CD *Dur* 08–15; rtd 15; PtO *Dur* from 15. *30 Low Etherley, Bishop Auckland DL14 0EU* T: (01388) 832756 E: reverend.linda@yahoo.co.uk

DODDS, Canon Norman Barry. b 43. Open Univ BA. CITC 73. **d** 76 **p** 77. C Ballynafeigh St Jude *D & D* 76–80; I Belfast St Mich *Conn* 80–14; Chapl HM Pris Belfast 84–14; Can Belf Cathl 98–14; Adn Belfast *Conn* 07–13; rtd 14. *85 Bangor Road, Newtownards BT23 7BZ* T: (028) 9107 1347 M: 07763-935160 E: doddscavehill@yahoo.com

DODGSON, David. b 46. **d** 13 **p** 14. NSM Sandal St Cath *Leeds* 13–18; NSM Wakefield St Andr and St Mary and Belle Vue from 18. *St Catherine's Church, Doncaster Road, Belle Vue, Wakefield WF1 5HL* M: 07508-053587

DODHIA, Hitesh Kishorilal. b 57. Cranmer Hall Dur 85. **d** 88 **p** 89. C Leamington Priors All SS *Cov* 88–91; Chapl HM YOI Glen Parva 91–92; Asst Chapl 94–98; Chapl HM Pris Roch 92–94; The Mount 98–01; PtO *St Alb* from 02. HM Prison Wormwood Scrubs, Du Cane Road, London *W12 0AE* T: (020) 8588 3200 M: 07546-033740 E: hiteshdodhia@yahoo.co.uk

DODSON, Canon Gordon. b 31. Em Coll Cam BA 54 MA 58 LLB 55 LLM 01 Barrister 56. Ridley Hall Cam 57. **d** 59 **p** 60. C Belhus Park *Chelmsf* 59–60; C Barking St Marg 60–63; CMS 63–67; C New Malden and Coombe *S'wark* 67–69; V Snettisham *Nor* 69–81; RD Heacham and Rising 76–81; P-in-c Reepham and Hackford w Whitwell and Kerdiston 81–83; P-in-c Salle 81–83; P-in-c Thurning w Wood Dalling 81–83; R Reepham, Hackford w Whitwell, Kerdiston etc 83–94; Hon Can Nor Cathl 85–94; rtd 94; PtO *Nor* from 94. *Poppygate, 2 The Loke, Cromer NR27 9DH* T: (01263) 511811 E: dodlerpg@btinternet.com

DODWELL, Andrew. b 75. Man Univ BSc 96 MSc 98. SWMTC 06. **d** 08 **p** 09. C Barnstaple *Ex* 08–17; V Newport and Bishops Tawton from 17; RD Barnstaple from 17. *28 Old School Road, Barnstaple EX32 9DP* T: (01271) 371068

DOE, Laura Elizabeth. b 88. UEA BA 10. Trin Coll Bris BA 18. **d** 19. C Bedminster *Bris* from 19. *St Anne's Vicaraage, 75 Greenbank Road, Greenbank, Bristol BS5 6HD* M: 07717-790871 E: lauraedoe@gmail.com

✠**DOE, The Rt Revd Michael David.** b 47. St Jo Coll Dur BA 69 Bath Univ Hon LLD 02. Ripon Hall Ox 69. **d** 72 **p** 73 **c** 94. C St Helier *S'wark* 72–76; Hon C 76–81; Youth Sec BCC 76–81; C-in-c Blackbird Leys 81–88; V Blackbird Leys 88–89; RD Cowley 86–89; Soc Resp Adv *Portsm* 89–94; Can Res Portsm Cathl 89–94; Suff Bp Swindon *Bris* 94–04; Gen Sec USPG 04–11; rtd 11; Preacher Gray's Inn from 11; Asst Bp S'wark from 04. *405 West Carriage House, Royal Carriage Mews, London SE18 6GA* T: (020) 3259 3841 E: michaeldd@btinternet.com *or* michael.doe@graysinn.org.uk

DOE, Mrs Priscilla Sophia. b 41. LRAM 61. SEITE 97. **d** 00 **p** 01. NSM Maidstone All SS and St Phil w Tovil *Cant* 00–11; PtO from 11. *Mount St Laurence, High Street, Cranbrook TN17 3EW* T: (01580) 712330

DOERING, Monika Sigrid. b 72. Heidelberg Univ MA 00. St Steph Ho Ox BA 17. **d** 17 **p** 18. C W Barnsley *Leeds* from 17. *The Vicarage, 5 Church Lane, Cawthorne, Barnsley S75 4DW* M: 07719-934327 E: monikadoering72@gmail.com

DOERR, Mrs Anne. b 55. Man Univ BA 76. SEITE 06. **d** 09 **p** 10. NSM Belmont *S'wark* 09–13; NSM St Helier from 13; Chapl R Marsden NHS Foundn Trust from 14. *14 Central Way, Carshalton SM5 3NF* T: (020) 8669 2494 M: 07811-908731 E: aedoerr@btinternet.com *or* anne.doerr@rmh.nhs.uk

DOHERTY, Mrs Christine. b 46. SEN 72. STETS 97. **d** 00 **p** 01. NSM Framfield *Chich* 00–03; C Seaford w Sutton 03–11; rtd 11; PtO *Chich* 12–17. *27 Hawth Park Road, Seaford BN25 2RF* T: (01323) 351243 E: chris.doh@tiscali.co.uk

DOHERTY, Sean William. d 07 **p** 08. C Cricklewood St Gabr and St Mich *Lon* 07–10; Lect St Paul's Th Cen 08–10; Tutor St Mellitus Coll 10–19; Prin Trin Coll Bris from 19. *129 Reedley Road, Bristol BS9 1BE* T: 0117-968 2803 M: 07710-515800 E: principal@trinitycollegebristol.ac.uk

DOHERTY, Thomas Alexander. b 48. Chich Th Coll 73. **d** 76 **p** 77. V Choral Derry Cathl *D & R* 76–79; C Llandaff w Capel Llanilltern *Llan* 79–80; PV Llan Cathl 80–84; V Penmark w Porthkerry 84–90; R Merthyr Dyfan 90–02; V Margam 02–15; rtd 15; PtO *Llan* from 15. *Riverside Bungalow, 2 Library Lane, Port Talbot SA13 1LQ* E: tad.margham@ntlworld.com

DOICK, Paul Stephen James. b 70. Chich Univ BA 10. Ripon Coll Cuddesdon 03. **d** 05 **p** 06. C Hove Chich 09; TV 09–10; V Hove St Jo 10–14; R Henfield w Shermanbury and Woodmancote from 14; RD Hurst from 18. *Henfield Vicarage, Church Lane, Henfield BN5 9NY* T: (01273) 492017 M: 07742-868602 E: p.doick@btinternet.com

DOIDGE, Charles William. b 44. Univ Coll Lon BSc 65 MSc 67 PhD 72. EMMTC 93. **d** 93 **p** 94. NSM Blaby *Leic* 93–96; P-in-c Willoughby Waterleys, Peatling Magna etc 96–04; rtd 04. *21 Brunel Mews, Solsbro Road, Torquay TQ2 6QA* T: (01803) 690548 E: doidge@dmu.ac.uk *or* charlesdoidge@talktalk.net

DOIDGE, Valerie Gladys. b 49. STETS 98. **d** 01 **p** 02. C St Leonards St Ethelburga *Chich* 01–07; C Hollington St Leon 07–12; rtd 12; PtO *Chich* from 17. *6 Collinswood Drive, St Leonards-on-Sea TN38 0NU* T: (01424) 425651 E: val.doidge@outlook.com

DOIG, Allan George. b 51. Univ of BC BA 69 K Coll Cam BA 73 MA 80 PhD 82 FSA 98 FRHistS 15. Ripon Coll Cuddesdon 86. **d** 88 **p** 89. C Abingdon *Ox* 88–91; Chapl LMH Ox 91–19; Fell 96–19; Select Preacher Ox 95–96; rtd 19. *The Priory, Hudson Street, Deddington, Banbury OX15 0SW* M: 07595-003240

DOLBY, Mrs Christine Teresa. b 54. Nottm Univ MA 01 SRN 80. EMMTC 98. **d** 01 **p** 02. C Cropwell Bishop w Colston Bassett, Granby etc *S'well* 01–05; P-in-c Ancaster Wilsford Gp *Linc* 05–08; Chapl Qu Medical Cen Nottm Univ Hosp NHS Trust from 08. *16 Morley's Close, Lowdham, Nottingham NG14 7HN* T: 0115-966 5890 M: 07738-851181 E: c.dolby263@btinternet.com

DOLL, Canon Peter Michael. b 62. Yale Univ BA 84 Ch Ch Ox DPhil 89. Cuddesdon Coll BA 94. **d** 95 **p** 96. C Cowley St Jo *Ox* 95–99; Chapl Worc Coll Ox 98–02; TV Abingdon *Ox* 02–09; Can Res Nor Cathl from 09. *56 The Close, Norwich NR1 4EG* T: (01603) 218336 E: canonlibrarian@cathedral.org.uk

DOLLERY, Anne Mary Elizabeth. b 55. Hull Univ BA 78. Ridley Hall Cam 02. **d** 04. C Thundersley *Chelmsf* 04–09; V Walthamstow St Andr 09–15; V Feltham *Lon* from 15. *The Vicarage, St Elmo, Cardinal Road, Feltham TW13 5AL* T: (020) 8890 8347 E: annedollery@yahoo.co.uk

DOLMAN, Derek Alfred George Gerrit. b 40. ALCD 64. **d** 65 **p** 66. C St Alb St Paul 65–68; C Bishopwearmouth St Gabr *Dur* 68–72; R Jarrow Grange 72–80; V New Catton St Luke *Nor* 80–98; V New Catton St Luke w St Aug 98–00; R S Croxton

Gp *Leic* 00–06; rtd 06; PtO *Leic* 06–12; *Derby* 07–18; *Lich* 07–12. *17 Kestrel Way, Burton-on-Trent DE15 0DJ* T: (01283) 845330 E: derekdolman@uwclub.net

DOLMAN, William Frederick Gerrit. b 42. K Coll Lon MB, BS 65 Lon Univ LLB 87 MRCS 65 LRCP 65. SEITE 04. **d** 06 **p** 07. NSM Beckley and Peasmarsh *Chich* 06–14; rtd 15; PtO *Chich* 15–17. *Little Bellhurst Cottage, Hobbs Lane, Beckley, Rye TN31 6TT* T: (01797) 260203 E: hmcwd@aol.com

DOMINIAK, Paul Anthony. b 78. Univ of the S (USA) BA 05 SS Coll Cam BA 07 MPhil 08. Westcott Ho Cam 05. **d** 08 **p** 09. C Ingleby Barwick *York* 08–11; Chapl Trin Coll Cam 11–15; Dean Jes Coll Cam from 15; Asst Dir of Ords *Ely* from 16; Tutor Westcott Ho Cam from 17. *Jesus College, Cambridge CB5 8BL* T: (01223) 339339 E: pad39@cam.ac.uk *or* p.dominiak@jesus.cam.ac.uk

DOMINIC MARK, Brother. See IND, Dominic Mark

DOMINY, Canon Peter John. b 36. Qu Coll Ox BA 60 MA 64 Aber Univ MLitt 83 Ex Univ PhD 11. Oak Hill Th Coll 60. **d** 62 **p** 63. C Bedworth *Cov* 62–66; Nigeria 67–84; Sudan United Miss 67-72; V Jos St Piran 72–84; R Broadwater St Mary *Chich* 84–92; TR Broadwater 92–98; P-in-c Danehill 98–99; V 99–03; Can and Preb Chich Cathl 93–03; RD Uckfield 00–03; rtd 03; PtO *Sarum* from 03. *32 Bedwin Street, Salisbury SP1 3UT* T: (01722) 238635 E: peterd@uwclub.net

DOMMETT, Simon Paul. b 58. Warwick Univ BSc 79. St Jo Coll Nottm MA 99. **d** 99 **p** 00. C Weston Favell *Pet* 99–02; P-in-c Gt w Lt Harrowden and Orlingbury 02–06; P-in-c Isham w Pytchley 05–06; R Gt w Lt Harrowden and Orlingbury and Isham etc 06–12; RD Brackley 13–18; P-in-c Goldington *St Alb* from 18. *St Mary's Vicarage, Church Lane, Bedford MK41 0AP* E: the.revd.simon@gmail.com

DOMONEY, Canon Lynette May (Lyndy). b 44. Th Ext Educn Coll 90. **d** 92 **p** 93. S Africa 92–06; P-in-c Kessingland, Gisleham and Rushmere *Nor* 06–08; R 08–14; rtd 14; PtO *Nor* from 15. *25 Victory Court, Diss IP22 4GN* T: (01379) 650445 E: l.domoney@btinternet.com

DONAGHEY, Thomas Alfred. b 67. Trin Coll Bris 06. **d** 08 **p** 09. C Whittle-le-Woods *Blackb* 08–13; V Baxenden from 13. *The Vicarage, Langford Street, Accrington BB5 2RF* T: (01254) 384179 M: 07974-457544 E: tdonaghey@hotmail.com

DONALD, Brother. See GREEN, Donald Pentney

DONALD, Dennis Curzon. b 38. Oak Hill Th Coll 68. **d** 70 **p** 71. C Carl St Jo 70–73; LtO 73–77; Warden Blaithwaite Ho Chr Conf Cen Wigton 73–90; Chapl Cumberland Infirmary 85–92; Chapl Eden Valley Hospice Carl 92–98; rtd 98; PtO *Carl* 77–13. *5 The Old Bakery, Gretna DG16 5FZ* T: (01461) 338053

DONALD, Mrs Philippa Jane. b 58. Bath Univ BA 79 Moray Ho Edin DipEd 80. WEMTC 08. **d** 11 **p** 12. NSM Churchdown St Jo and Innsworth *Glouc* 11–15; NSM Twigworth, Down Hatherley, Norton, The Leigh etc from 15. *8 Seabroke Road, Gloucester GL1 3JH* T: (01452) 528569 E: talk2philippa@hotmail.com

DONALD, Robert Francis. b 49. St Jo Coll Nottm BTh 75 LTh. **d** 75 **p** 76. C New Barnet St Jas *St Alb* 75–79; C St Alb St Paul 79–86; C St Alb St Mary Marshalswick 86–87; LtO from 87; Dir Chr Alliance Housing Assn Ltd 87–98. *24 Meadowcroft, St Albans AL1 1UD* T: (01727) 841647 M: 07973-208289

DONALD, Rosemary Anne. b 52. STETS 99. **d** 02 **p** 03. NSM Blendworth w Chalton w Idsworth *Portsm* 02–07; P-in-c 07–18; rtd 18; PtO *Portsm* from 18. *1A Havant Road, Horndean, Waterlooville PO8 0DB* T: (023) 9259 2121 E: rosemary.donald3@gmail.com

DONALD, Steven. b 55. CertEd 76 Hull Univ MA 99. Oak Hill Th Coll BA 88. **d** 88 **p** 89. C Cheadle All Hallows *Ches* 88–91; C Ardsley *Sheff* 91; V Kendray 92–99; P-in-c Chadderton Ch Ch *Man* 99–03; V 03–05; V Carl St Jo from 05. *St John's Vicarage, London Road, Carlisle CA1 2QQ* T: (01228) 521601 E: stevedon1@aol.com

DONALDSON, Aron William Francis. b 92. Essex Univ BA 15. Wycliffe Hall Ox 16. **d** 19. C Corby Glen *Linc* from 19. *42 St John's Drive, Corby Glen, Grantham NG33 4NG*

DONALDSON, Miss Elizabeth Anne. b 55. Univ of Wales (Ban) BSc 76 Surrey Univ MSc 86 Nottm Univ BA 82. St Jo Coll Nottm 80. **dss** 83 **d** 87 **p** 94. Guildf Ch Ch 83–86; Cuddington 86–90; C 87–90; C Keresley and Coundon *Cov* 90–99; V Gt Amwell w St Margaret's and Stanstead Abbots *St Alb* from 00. *The Vicarage, 25 Hoddesdon Road, Stanstead Abbotts, Ware SG12 8EG* T: (01920) 870115 E: vicar@3churches.net *or* anne.donaldson@ntlworld.com

DONALDSON, Mrs Janet Elizabeth. b 53. GTCL 74 Whitelands Coll Lon CertEd 75. EAMTC 95. **d** 98 **p** 99. NSM Tolleshunt Knights w Tiptree and Gt Braxted *Chelmsf* 98–02; V Knights and Hospitallers Par 02–11; P-in-c Deeping St James *Linc* 11–13; P-in-c Welford w Sibbertoft and Marston

Trussell *Pet* 13–16; V 16–18; rtd 18. *11 Haddonian Road, Market Harborough LE16 9GD* E: rev.janet@donaldsonfamily.org.uk

DONALDSON, Malcolm Alexander. b 48. Cranmer Hall Dur 84. **d** 86 **p** 87. C Heworth H Trin *York* 86–89; Chapl York Distr Hosp 86–89; C Marfleet *York* 89–90; TV 90–96; R Collyhurst *Man* 96–05; rtd 05. *12 Clove Court, Tweedmouth, Berwick-upon-Tweed TD15 2FJ*

DONALDSON, Canon Roger Francis. b 50. Jes Coll Ox BA 71 MA 75. Westcott Ho Cam 72. **d** 74 **p** 75. C Mold *St As* 74–78; V Denio w Abererch *Ban* 78–95; TR Llanbeblig w Caernarfon and Betws Garmon etc from 95; AD Arfon 04–09; Hon Can Ban Cathl from 04. *The Rectory, 4 Ffordd Menai, Caernarfon LL55 1LF* T: (01286) 673750

DONALDSON, William Richard. b 56. St Cath Coll Cam BA 78 MA 81. Ridley Hall Cam 79. **d** 82 **p** 83. C Everton St Sav w St Cuth *Liv* 82–85; C Reigate St Mary *S'wark* 85–89; V Easton H Trin w St Gabr and St Lawr and St Jude *Bris* 89–99; V W Ealing St Jo w St Jas *Lon* 99–07; Dir of Ords Willesden Area 06–07; Dir Chr Leadership Wycliffe Hall Ox 07–12; Course Dir Part-Time Tr 12–13; Chapl St Edm Hall Ox from 13; C Ox St Aldate from 12; AD Ox from 15. *St Edmund Hall, Queens Lane, Oxford OX1 4AR* T: (01865) 279021 M: 07745-363540

DONCASTER, Archdeacon of. See HAWLEY, The Ven John Andrew

DONCASTER, Suffragan Bishop of. *Vacant*

DONE, Nigel Anthony. b 68. Wye Coll Lon BSc 89 St Jo Coll Dur 94. Cranmer Hall Dur. **d** 98 **p** 99. C Pilton w Croscombe, N Wootton and Dinder *B & W* 98–02; R Hardington Vale 02–12; V Ilminster and Whitelackington 12–18; RD Ilminster 17–18; Dioc Dir of Ords *Sarum* from 18; Co-ord of IME from 18. *Church House, Crane Street, Salisbury SP1 2QB* E: nigel.done@btinternet.com

DONEGAN-CROSS, Guy William. b 68. St Aid Coll Dur BA 90. Trin Coll Bris BA 98. **d** 99 **p** 00. C Swindon Ch Ch *Bris* 99–03; V Saltburn-by-the-Sea *York* 03–10; V Harrogate St Mark *Ripon* 10–14; *Leeds* 14–19; Hon Can Ripon Cathl 17–19; Dir Learning for Discipleship and Miss *Birm* from 19. *2 Geoffrey Close, Sutton Coldfield B76 1GB* T: 0121-426 0444 E: guydonegancross@yahoo.co.uk *or* guydc@cofebirmingham.com

DONEGAN-CROSS, Ruth Katherine. b 68. Dur Univ BA 90 Sheff Univ BA 16. Yorks Min Course 13. **d** 16 **p** 17. C Bilton *Leeds* from 16. *St Mark's Vicarage, 15 Wheatlands Road, Harrogate HG2 8BB* T: (01423) 504160 M: 07588-813343 E: ruthdonegancross@yahoo.co.uk

DONEY, Malcolm Charles. b 50. Lon Univ BA 71 Middx Univ BA 05. NTMTC 02. **d** 05 **p** 06. NSM Tufnell Park St Geo and All SS *Lon* 05–07; NSM W Holloway St Luke 07–12; NSM All Hallows Lon Wall 07–12; PtO *St E* from 10. *The Birdhouse, Old Angel Lane, Blythburgh, Halesworth IP19 9JW* T: (01502) 478229 E: malcolmdoney@me.com

DONKERSLEY, Mrs Christine Mary. b 44. K Alfred's Coll Win CertEd 65. STETS 98. **d** 01 **p** 02. NSM Baltonsborough w Butleigh, W Bradley etc *B & W* 01–06; P-in-c Fosse Trinity 06–13; rtd 13; PtO *B & W* 13–19. *7 Turnpike, Honiton EX14 2HX* M: 07866-531917 E: cm.donkersley@btinternet.com

DONKIN, Canon Robert. b 50. St Mich Coll Llan 71. **d** 74 **p** 75. C Mountain Ash *Llan* 74–77; C Coity w Nolton 77–79; V Oakwood 79–84; V Aberaman and Abercwmboi 84–91; V Aberaman and Abercwmboi w Cwmaman 91–99; R Penarth w Lavernock 99–04; R Penarth and Llandough 04–08; AD Penarth and Barry 04–08; R Caerphilly 08–14; AD 10–14; AD Merthyr Tydfil and Caerphilly 12–14; Hon Can Llan Cathl 06–14; rtd 14; PtO *Llan* from 14. *4 Heol-y-Gelli, Aberdare CF44 6LN* T: (01685) 884645 E: robert.donkin@hotmail.com

DONMALL, Michael Charles. b 53. Univ Coll Lon BSc 75 PhD 84 K Coll Lon PGCE 80 FFPH 06. Yorks Min Course 12. **d** 14 **p** 15. NSM Saddleworth *Man* from 14. *7 Higher Arthurs, Greenfield, Oldham OL3 7BE* T: (01457) 870427 E: michaeldonmall@cofeinsaddleworth.org.uk

DONNELLY, Juliet Ann. See EVANS, Juliet Ann

DONNELLY, Trevor Alfred. b 71. K Coll Lon BA 93 AKC 93. Cuddesdon Coll 94. **d** 97 **p** 98. C Southgate Ch Ch *Lon* 97–01; V Hinchley Wood *Guildf* 01–05; Sen Chapl Medway Secure Tr Cen 06–09; TV Deptford St Jo w H Trin and Ascension *S'wark* 09–17. *20 London Road, Stone, Dartford DA2 6DJ* E: trevordonnelly@mac.com

DONOGHUE, William Noel. b 80. Goldsmiths' Coll Lon BA 06. Trin Coll Bris MA 15. **d** 15 **p** 16. C Willowfield *D & D* 15–19; V Leyton St Cath and St Paul *Chelmsf* from 19. *The Vicarage, 2B Fairlop Road, London E11 1BL* T: (020) 8558 4607 M: 07719-754849 E: bill.donoghue@thecornerstone.org.uk

DONOVAN, Mrs Rosalind Margaret. b 48. Birm Univ LLB 69 Bedf Coll Lon DASS 73. SAOMC 95. **d** 98 **p** 99. NSM Seer Green and Jordans *Ox* 98–03; P-in-c Wexham 03–13; rtd 13; PtO *Ox* 14–15; *S'well* from 16. *2 The Dell, Chalfont St Peter, Gerrards Cross SL9 0JA* T: (01494) 871573 E: rev.ros.donovan@gmail.com

DONOVAN, Mrs Rosemary Ann. b 71. La Sainte Union Coll BTh 92 Birm Univ PGCE 93. Qu Coll Birm MA 01. **d** 01 **p** 02. C Kings Heath *Birm* 01–04; C Moseley St Mary and St Anne 04–11; V Epsom Common Ch Ch *Guildf* from 11; Bp's Adv for Women's Min from 16. *Christ Church Vicarage, 20 Christ Church Road, Epsom KT19 8NE* T: (01372) 720302 E: vicar@christchurchepsom.org.uk

DONSON, Miss Helen Cripps. b 32. Somerville Coll Ox DipEd 55 MA 58. Dalton Ho Bris 58 Gilmore Ho 69. dss 79 **d** 87. Staines St Pet *Lon* 80–83; Staines St Mary and St Pet 83–90; Par Dn 87–90; Par Dn Herne Bay Ch Ch *Cant* 90–92; rtd 93; Hon Par Dn Bexhill St Aug *Chich* 93–97; PtO 97–07. *Flat 27, Manormead, Tilford Road, Hindhead GU26 6RA* T: (01428) 601527

DONSON, Margaret Christine. See BARROW, Margaret Christine

DOODES, Peter John. b 45. STETS 98. **d** 01. NSM Ninfield and Hooe *Chich* 01–02; NSM Hastings H Trin 02–07; PtO *Roch* 09–14. *Catslide, The Common, Hooe, Battle TN33 9ET* T: (01424) 892329 M: 07718-302115 E: pjdoodes@hotmail.com

DOOGAN, Canon Simon Edward. b 70. Univ of Wales (Abth) LLB 92 Univ of Wales (Cardiff) LLM 01 TCD BTh 97. CITC 94. **d** 97 **p** 98. C Cregagh *D & D* 97–01; Dom Chapl to Bp Horsham *Chich* 01–04; I Aghalee *D & D* 04–08; I Ballyholme from 08; Dioc Registrar from 07; Can St Patr Cathl Dublin from 11. *Ballyholme Rectory, 3 Ward Avenue, Bangor BT20 5JW* T: (028) 9127 4901 *or* 9127 4912 F: 9146 6357 E: simon_doogan@hotmail.com

DOOLAN, Alison Ruth. b 59. Homerton Coll Cam BEd 93. Yorks Min Course 13. **d** 15 **p** 16. NSM Beverley St Mary *York* from 15. *25 Melrose Park, Beverley HU17 8JL* T: (01482) 864707 E: alidoolan@googlemail.com

DOOLAN, Benjamin. b 87. Sheff Univ BA 08 Anglia Ruskin Univ MA 13. Ridley Hall Cam 11. **d** 13 **p** 14. C York St Mich-le-Belfrey 13–18; C Newc Cathl from 19; Master Newc St Thos Prop Chpl from 19. *9 Chester Crescent, Newcastle upon Tyne NE2 1DH* M: 07849-024523 E: b.doolan@newcastle.anglican.org

DOOLAN, Canon Leonard Wallace. b 57. St Andr Univ MA 79 Ox Univ BA 82 MA 88. Ripon Coll Cuddesdon 80. **d** 83 **p** 84. C High Wycombe *Ox* 83–85; C Bladon w Woodstock 85–88; C Wootton by Woodstock 85–88; P-in-c 88–90; C Kiddington w Asterleigh 85–88; P-in-c 88–90; P-in-c Glympton 88–90; R Wootton w Glympton and Kiddington 90–91; TR Halesworth w Linstead, Chediston, Holton etc *St E* 91–98; RD Halesworth 95–98; TR Ifield *Chich* 98–08; V Cirencester *Glouc* 08–17; AD 11–15; Hon Can Glouc Cathl 12–17; Chapl Gtr Athens *Eur* from 17; Hon Can Douala Cameroon from 09. *St Paul, 27 Philellinon Street, Athens, Greece* E: anglican@otenet.gr

DOOLEY, Peter Martin. b 51. UEA BSc 72 Leic Univ PhD 77 Salford Univ DBA 96. St Mellitus Coll 18. **d** 19. NSM Cheadle *Ches* from 19. *48 Chorlton Drive, Cheadle SK8 2BG* T: 0161-491 1816 E: pm.dooley@ntlworld.com

DOORE, Sandra Patricia. b 61. **d** 16 **p** 17. C Gateacre *Liv* 16–18; TV from 18. *St Mark's Vicarage, Cranwell Road, Liverpool L25 1NZ* E: sandra.doore@gmail.com

DOORES, Jennifer Mary. See McKENZIE, Jennifer Mary

DOORES, Canon Peter George Herbert. b 46. Hull Univ BSc 67 Birm Univ PGCE 68. Linc Th Coll 92. **d** 92 **p** 93. C N Stoneham *Win* 92–96; V St Leonards and St Ives 96–03; P-in-c Alton St Lawr 03–09; V Alton 10–13; Hon Can Win Cathl 09–13; rtd 13; PtO *Win* from 13. *5 Cranford Gardens, Chandler's Ford, Eastleigh SO53 1PU* T: (023) 8025 3778 E: peterdoores@lineone.net *or* peter@doores.myzen.co.uk

DORAGH (née ELLIOTT), Mrs Sonya Jacqueline. b 72. Ox Brookes Univ BA 95. Trin Coll Bris MA 12. **d** 12 **p** 13. C Much Woolton *Liv* 12–16; TV Eccleston Team from 16. *Christchurch Vicarage, 34 Church Lane, Eccleston, St Helens WA10 5AD* T: (01744) 22698 M: 07852-244537 E: sonya@doragh.co.uk

DORAN, Clive. b 58. St Jo Coll Nottm 99. **d** 01 **p** 02. C Maghull *Liv* 01–05; V Huyton St Geo 05–13; TV Parr 13–16; TR from 16; Bp's Adv on Children and Communion from 06. *St Paul's Vicarage, 75 Chain Lane, St Helens WA11 9QF* T: (01744) 734335 E: revclivedoran@yahoo.co.uk

DORAN, Edward Roy. b 47. St Jo Coll Nottm. **d** 85 **p** 86. C Roby *Liv* 85–88; V Ravenhead 88–07; TV Eccleston Team

07–09; V Knotty Ash St Jo 09–16; rtd 16; PtO *Liv* from 17. *5 Moor Close, Southport PR8 3PA* T: (01704) 572387

DORBER, The Very Revd Adrian John. b 52. St Jo Coll Dur BA 74 K Coll Lon MTh 91. Westcott Ho Cam 76. **d** 79 **p** 80. C Easthampstead *Ox* 79–85; P-in-c Emmer Green 85–88; Chapl Portsm Poly 88–92; Chapl Portsm Univ 92–97; Lect 91–97; Public Orator 92–97; Hon Chapl Portsm Cathl 92–97; P-in-c Brancepeth *Dur* 97–01; Dir Min and Tr 97–05; Hon Can Dur Cathl 97–05; Dean Lich from 05. *The Deanery, 16 The Close, Lichfield WS13 7LD* T: (01543) 306250 F: 306109 E: adrian.dorber@lichfield-cathedral.org

DORCHESTER, Archdeacon of. *See* FRENCH, The Ven Judith Karen

DORCHESTER, Area Bishop of. *See* FLETCHER, The Rt Revd Colin William

DORÉ, Eric George. b 47. S Dios Minl Tr Scheme 87. **d** 90 **p** 91. NSM Hove Bp Hannington Memorial Ch *Chich* 90–92; C Burgess Hill St Andr 92–95; R Frant w Eridge 95–00; V Framfield 00–07; rtd 07; PtO *St E* from 08. *Oak House, 86A Southwold Road, Wrentham, Beccles NR34 7JF* T: (01502) 675777 E: ericdore@onetel.com *or* eric@ericdore.plus.com

DOREY, Miss Alison. b 77. Sheff Univ BA 98 Sheff Hallam Univ PGCE 01 St Jo Coll Dur MA 08. Cranmer Hall Dur 05. **d** 07 **p** 08. C Askern *Sheff* 07–11; Miss Development Co-ord N Sheff Estates 11–17; Dir Tr Fresh Expressions from 15. *85 Malton Street, Sheffield S4 7EA* T: 0114-272 6855 E: ali.dorey@sheffield.anglican.org *or* alidorey1@gmail.com

DOREY, Trevor Eric. b 30. ACIS 53. S Dios Minl Tr Scheme 87. **d** 90 **p** 91. NSM E Woodhay and Woolton Hill *Win* 90–96; P-in-c Manaccan w St Anthony-in-Meneage and St Martin *Truro* 96–99; rtd 99; PtO *Sarum* 01–05; *Ox* 07–17. *6 Marshall Court, Speen Lane, Newbury RG14 1RY* T: (01635) 551956 E: tandvdorey@btinternet.com

✠**DORGU, The Rt Revd Woyin Karowei.** b 58. MB, BS 85. Lon Bible Coll BA 93 Oak Hill Th Coll 93. **d** 95 **p** 96 **c** 17. C Tollington *Lon* 95–98; C Upper Holloway 98–00; TV 00–12; V 12–17; Preb St Paul's Cathl 16–17; Area Bp Woolwich *S'wark* from 17. *37 South Road, London SE23 2UJ* T: (020) 7939 9400 E: wdorgu@yahoo.com *or* bishop.karowei@southwark.anglican.org

DORKING, Archdeacon of. *See* BREADMORE, The Ven Martin Christopher

DORKING, Suffragan Bishop of. *See* WELLS, The Rt Revd Joanne Caladine Bailey

DORLING, Philip Julian. b 69. Edin Univ BSc 90. Ripon Coll Cuddesdon BTh 09. **d** 05 **p** 06. C Ulverston St Mary w H Trin *Carl* 05–09; R Vryheid St Pet S Africa 10–12; R Inglewood Gp *Carl* 13–19; Lead Chapl Scargill Ho from 19. *Scargill House, Kettlewell, Skipton BD23 5HU* T: (01756) 760500 E: philipdorling123@btinternet.com

DORMANDY, Richard Paul. b 59. Univ Coll Lon BA 81 St Edm Ho Cam BA 88. Ridley Hall Cam 86. **d** 89 **p** 90. C Sydenham H Trin *S'wark* 89–93; V 93–01; V Westminster St Jas the Less *Lon* 01–09; V Tulse Hill H Trin and St Matthias *S'wark* from 09. *Holy Trinity Vicarage, 49 Trinity Rise, London SW2 2QP* T: (020) 8674 6721 M: 07960-170851 E: richard@dormandy.co.uk *or* richard.dormandy@htth.org.uk

DORMOR, Duncan James. b 67. Magd Coll Ox BA 88 Lon Univ MSc 89. Ripon Coll Cuddesdon BA 94. **d** 95 **p** 96. C Wolverhampton *Lich* 95–98; Chapl St Jo Coll Cam 98–02; Fell and Dean 02–18; Chief Exec Officer USPG from 18; Public Preacher *S'wark* from 18. *USPG, Rise House, 5 Trinity Street, London SE1 1DB* T: (020) 7921 2200 E: duncand@uspg.org.uk

DORMOR, Preb Duncan Stephen. b 36. St Edm Hall Ox BA 60. Cuddesdon Coll 60. **d** 62 **p** 63. C Headington *Ox* 62–66; USA 66–72; R Hertford St Andr *St Alb* 72–88; RD Hertford 77–83; TR Tenbury Wells *Heref* 88–01; R Burford I, Nash and Boraston 88–01; R Whitton w Greete and Hope Bagot 88–01; R Burford III w Lt Heref 88–01; V Tenbury St Mich 94–01; RD Ludlow 96–01; Preb Heref Cathl 99–02; C Tenbury Wells 01–02; C Burford I, Nash and Boraston 01–02; C Whitton w Greete and Hope Bagot 01–02; C Burford III w Lt Heref 01–02; C Tenbury St Mich 01–02; rtd 02; PtO *Heref* 02–14; *Chelmsf* from 15. *30 Queen Anne Road, West Mersea, Colchester CO5 8BB*

DORNAN, Michael. CITC. **d** 09 **p** 10. C Hillsborough *D & D* 09–14; I Desertmartin w Termoneeny *D & R* from 14. *The Rectory, 25 Dromore Road, Desertmartin, Magherafelt BT45 5JZ* T: (028) 7963 2455 M: 07858-597416 E: mikedornan@gmail.com

DORRIAN, Adrian Terence Warren. b 82. QUB BA 03 TCD BTh 06. CITC 04. **d** 06 **p** 07. C Newtownards *D & D* 06–09; I Belfast St Pet and St Jas *Conn* 09–12; I Dundela St Mark *D & D* 12–15; Assoc Min Lecale Area Miss Partnership from

15. *40 English Street, Downpatrick BT30 6AB* T: (028) 4461 7469 M: 07760-664337 E: adriandorrian@gmail.com

DORRINGTON, Brian Goodwin. b 32. Leeds Univ CertEd 55. St Deiniol's Hawarden 65. **d** 66 **p** 67. C Poynton *Ches* 66–71; PtO *Truro* 71–78; Hd Master Veryan Sch Truro 71–84; Hon C Veryan *Truro* 78–83; Hon C Veryan w Ruan Lanihorne 83–84; C N Petherwin 84–87; C Boyton w N Tamerton 84–87; TV Bolventor 87–90; R Kilkhampton w Morwenstow 90–97; RD Stratton 92–97; rtd 97; PtO *Truro* 00–16. *Southcroft, 18 Elm Drive, Bude EX23 8EZ* T: (01288) 352467

DORRINGTON, Richard Bryan. b 48. Linc Th Coll 79. **d** 81 **p** 82. C Streetly *Lich* 81–84; C Badger, Ryton and Beckbury 84–85; R 85–88; V Geddington w Weekley *Pet* 88–98; P-in-c Bradworthy *Ex* 98–99; P-in-c Abbots Bickington and Bulkworthy 98–99; P-in-c Bradworthy, Sutcombe, Putford etc 99–00; R 00–13; RD Holsworthy 99–11; rtd 13; PtO *Truro* from 14. *3 Wassail Close, Bodmin PL31 2GG* T: (01208) 79156 E: r2b2d2@btinternet.com

DORSET, Archdeacon of. *See* MACROW WOOD, The Ven Antony Charles

DORSETT, Mark Richard. b 63. Univ of Wales (Lamp) BA 84 MTh 86 Birm Univ PhD 90. Ripon Coll Cuddesdon 91. **d** 93 **p** 94. C Yardley St Edburgha *Birm* 93–96; Chapl K Sch Worc from 96; Hon Can Worc Cathl from 96. *12A College Green, Worcester WR1 2LH* T: (01905) 25837

DOSSOR, Timothy Charles. b 70. Birm Univ BEng 94. Ridley Hall Cam BTh 99. **d** 99 **p** 00. C Ipswich St E *St E* 99–03; Asst Ldr Iwerne Holidays Titus Trust from 03; PtO *Ox* 08–19; C Ox St Ebbe w H Trin and St Pet from 19. *31 Southdale Road, Oxford OX2 7SE* T: (01865) 553226 *or* 310513 M: 07748-184503 E: tim@dossor.org

DOTCHIN, Andrew Steward. b 56. Federal Th Coll S Africa. **d** 84 **p** 85. C Standerton w Evender S Africa 84–87; Asst P St Martin's-in-the-Veld 87–89; R Belgravia St Jo the Divine 89–94; Chapl St Martin's Sch Rosettenville 94–01; TV Blyth Valley *St E* 01–04; P-in-c Whitton and Thurleston w Akenham 04–09; R 09–15; P-in-c Felixstowe St Jo from 15; RD Colneys from 15. *The New Vicarage, 54 Princes Road, Felixstowe IP11 7PL* M: 07814-949828 E: revdotchin@gmail.com

DOTCHIN, Canon Joan Marie. b 47. NEOC 84. **d** 87 **p** 94. C Newc St Gabr 87–92; Team Dn Willington 92–94; TV 94–95; TR 95–03; V Fenham St Jas and St Basil 03–08; Hon Can Newc Cathl 01–08; rtd 08; PtO *Newc* from 08. *12 St Aidan's Court, Mariners Lane, North Shields NE30 2SE*

DOUBLE, Richard Sydney (Brother Samuel). b 47. K Coll Lon BD 69 AKC 69. St Aug Coll Cant 69. **d** 70 **p** 71. C Walton St Mary *Liv* 70–74; SSF from 75; Guardian Hilfield Friary Dorchester 92–01; Can and Preb Sarum Cathl 95–01 and from 09; V Cambridge St Benedict *Ely* 01–05; PtO *Chelmsf* from 18; *Eur* from 19. *The Friary, Hilfield, Dorchester DT2 7BE* T: (01300) 341345 E: samuelssf@franciscans.org.uk

DOUBTFIRE, Canon Barbara. b 39. LMH Ox BA 61 MA 65. **d** 91 **p** 94. Par Development Adv *Ox* 88–04; NSM Kidlington w Hampton Poyle 91–04; Hon Can Ch Ch 98–04; rtd 04; PtO *Ox* from 05. *6 Meadow Walk, Woodstock OX20 1NR* T: (01993) 812095 E: spidir@oxford.anglican.org

DOUGAL, Stephen George. b 62. FICS. **d** 06 **p** 07. OLM Lyminge w Paddlesworth, Stanford w Postling etc *Cant* from 06. *Bereforstal Farm Bungalow, Canterbury Road, Elham, Canterbury CT4 6UE* T: (01303) 840750

DOUGHTY, The Ven Andrew William. b 56. K Coll Lon BD AKC. Westcott Ho Cam 80. **d** 82 **p** 83. C Alton St Lawr *Win* 82–85; TV Basingstoke 85–91; V Chilworth w N Baddesley 91–95; R Warwick St Mary V Bermuda from 95; Adn Bermuda from 04. *PO Box WK 530, Warwick WK BX, Bermuda* T: (001) (441) 236 5744 F: 236 3667 E: adoughty@ibl.bm

DOUGLAS, Ann Patricia. b 49. Lon Univ CertEd 71. Oak Hill NSM Course 85. **d** 88 **p** 94. Par Dn Chorleywood Ch Ch *St Alb* 88–94; V Oxhey All SS 94–02; TR Woodley *Ox* 02–06; rtd 06; Development Officer Li Tim-Oi Foundn 06–09; PtO *Sarum* from 07; Outreach Co-ord Refresh Weymouth and Portland 10–17. *20 Passage Close, Weymouth DT4 9GE* T: (01305) 788310 M: 07809-467717 E: annidouglas@gmail.com

DOUGLAS, Gavin Allan. b 52. Cardiff Univ BTh 08. St Mich Coll Llan 03. **d** 05 **p** 06. C Week St Mary Circle of Par *Truro* 05–08; R Castle Bromwich SS Mary and Marg *Birm* 08–16; rtd 16; PtO *Llan* from 17. *8 Cilgant y Meillion, Rhoose, Barry CF62 3LH* E: gavinadouglas@yahoo.co.uk

DOUGLAS, Jonathan William Dixon. b 75. QUB BSc 96 K Coll Lon MA 01 Spurgeon's Coll MTh 09. **d** 11 **p** 12. C Spitalfields Ch Ch w All SS *Lon* 11–14; C Northwood *Lon* 14–18; V Swanley St Paul *Roch* from 18. *The Vicarage, Rowhill Road, Swanley BR8 7RL* T: (01322) 662320 M: 07799-072845 E: revjohnnydouglas@gmail.com *or* office@stph.org.uk

DOUGLAS, Maureen Eleanor. b 43. Open Univ BA 87 Worc Coll of Educn CertEd 65. SWMTC 10. **d** 12. NSM Littleham w Exmouth *Ex* 12–13; NSM Littleham-cum-Exmouth w Lympstone 13–18; PtO from 18. *8A Elwyn Road, Exmouth EX8 2EL* T: (01395) 225963 E: medouglas@uwclub.net

DOUGLAS, Michael Williamson. b 51. Birm Univ BSc 72 Liv Univ PGCE 74. Trin Coll Bris 00. **d** 02 **p** 03. C Macclesfield Team *Ches* 02–06; TV Hawarden *St As* 06–10; PtO *Ches* from 17. *46 Far Meadow Lane, Wirral CH61 4XW* T: 0151-648 4071 E: mikedougie@yahoo.co.uk

DOUGLAS, Patrick John. b 62. Ox Brookes Univ BA 05. St Mellitus Coll BA 13. **d** 13 **p** 14. C Walbrook Epiphany *Derby* 13–17; P-in-c Newhall from 17. *8 Breadsall Close, Newhall, Swadlincote DE11 0QJ* M: 07968-503447 E: patrickdouglas62@gmail.com *or* revive67@virginmedia.com

DOUGLAS, Richard Norman Henry. b 37. SAOMC 94. **d** 97 **p** 98. NSM Watercombe *Sarum* 97–02; PtO 02–04; Ox 04–06; NSM Grove 06–07; rtd 07; PtO *Ox* 07–16. *36 Mallard Court, West Mills, Newbury RG14 5HL* T: (01635) 741613 E: dickandnan@talktalk.net

DOUGLAS LANE, Charles Simon Pellew. b 47. BNC Ox MA 71 MCIPD 79. Oak Hill Th Coll 91. **d** 94 **p** 95. C Whitton St Aug *Lon* 94–97; P-in-c Hounslow W Gd Shep 97–02; V 02–05; TV Riverside *Ox* 05–08; V Horton and Wraysbury 08–13; rtd 13; PtO *Ox* from 13; *Lon* from 13. *1 Magnolia Villas, 30A Belgrade Road, Hampton TW12 2AZ* T: (020) 8941 5027 E: simonsdl14@gmail.com

DOUGLASS, Kieran Christopher. b 89. **d** 16 **p** 17. C Histon *Ely* from 16; C Impington from 16. *The Vicarage, 60 Impington Lane, Impington, Cambridge CB24 9NJ* M: 07872-053231 E: kierandouglass@outlook.com

DOUGLASS, Michael Crone. b 49. Open Univ BA 96. NEOC 02. **d** 05 **p** 06. NSM Gosforth St Nic *Newc* 05–19; PtO from 19. *44 Regent Road, Newcastle upon Tyne NE3 1ED* T/F: 0191-285 0977 E: m.douglass@blueyonder.co.uk

DOUGLASS, Preb Philip. b 48. Open Univ BA 88. St Steph Ho Ox 87. **d** 89 **p** 90. C Peterlee *Dur* 89–92; V Crowan w Godolphin *Truro* 92–97; V Crowan and Treslothan 98–13; P-in-c Penponds 01–13; Preb St Endellion 02–13; rtd 13. *31 Bay View Terrace, Hayle TR27 4JY* T: (01736) 753382

DOULL, Canon Iain Sinclair. b 43. St Mich Coll Llan 86. **d** 88 **p** 89. C Malpas *Mon* 88–91; P-in-c Newport All SS 91–98; V 98–02; V Newport Ch Ch 02–12; Hon Can St Woolos Cathl 11–12; rtd 12. *Ty'r Ydlan, Fachelich, St Davids, Haverfordwest SA62 6QL*

DOULTON, Roderick John. b 55. Oak Hill Th Coll 91. **d** 93 **p** 94. C Hoddesdon *St Alb* 93–96; P-in-c Caldecote All SS 96–98; P-in-c Old Warden 97–98; V Caldecote, Northill and Old Warden 98–99; TV Macclesfield Team *Ches* 99–07; Chapl W Park Hosp Macclesfield 99–07; P-in-c Heydon, Gt and Lt Chishill, Chrishall etc *Chelmsf* 07–08; PtO *Ely* 14–19. *Darwin Oaks, Grange Road, Bronington, Whitchurch SY13 3HL* E: roddoulton@btinternet.com

DOVE, Giles Wilfred. b 62. St Andr Univ MA 85 MPhil 88 Glas Univ BD 08 FSAScot FRSA. TISEC 03. **d** 05 **p** 06. NSM Dunblane *St And* 05–07; Chapl Glenalmond Coll 07–19; Chapl Glamis Castle from 19; PtO *St And* from 19; *Edin* from 19. *South Eden, 8A High Road, Strathkinness, St Andrews KY16 9XY* E: gileswdove@gmail.com

DOVE, Ms Jacqueline McClintock. b 65. Natal Univ BSSc 86 DipEd 89 UEA MA 95. Ripon Coll Cuddesdon 15. **d** 17 **p** 18. C Schorne *Ox* from 17. *15 Offas Lane, Winslow, Buckingham MK18 3JS* T: (01296) 715242 M: 07775-387271 E: jacquelineleach.dove@gmail.com

DOVE, Lionel John. b 38. **d** 06 **p** 07. OLM N Bradley, Southwick, Heywood and Steeple Ashton *Sarum* 06–13; PtO from 13. *Chobham Cottage, Acreshot Lane, Steeple Ashton, Trowbridge BA14 6HD* T: (01380) 870013

DOVER, Suffragan Bishop of. *See* HUDSON WILKIN, The Rt Revd Rose Josephine

DOVEY, Andrew Michael Stanley. b 59. SEITE 00. **d** 06 **p** 07. NSM Selsdon St Jo w St Fran *S'wark* 06–10; PtO 10–14; NSM Shirley St Geo from 14; NSM Shirley St Jo from 14; Chapl Croydon Health Services NHS Trust 15–18; Lead Chapl from 18. *6 Stokes Road, Croydon CR0 7SD* T: (020) 8656 9911 *or* 8401 3105 M: 07527-818816 E: andy.dovey@me.com

DOW, Canon Andrew John Morrison. b 46. Univ Coll Ox BA 67 MA 71. Oak Hill Th Coll 69. **d** 71 **p** 72. C Watford St Luke *St Alb* 71–74; C Chadderton Ch Ch *Man* 75–78; V Leamington Priors St Paul *Cov* 78–88; V Knowle *Birm* 88–97; RD Solihull 95–97; V Clifton Ch Ch w Em *Bris* 97–04; P-in-c Cheltenham St Mary, St Matt, St Paul and H Trin *Glouc* 04–07; R Cheltenham St Mary w St Matt 07–10; AD Cheltenham 06–10; Hon Can Glouc Cathl 08–10; rtd 10; PtO *Cov* from 10. *17 Brownlow Drive, Stratford-upon-Avon CV37 9QS* T: (01789) 417852 E: andrewdow451@btinternet.com

✠DOW, The Rt Revd Geoffrey Graham. b 42. Qu Coll Ox BA 63 MA 68 BSc 65 MSc 81 Nottm Univ MPhil 82. Clifton Th Coll 66. **d** 67 **p** 68 **c** 92. C Tonbridge SS Pet and Paul *Roch* 67–72; Chapl St Jo Coll Ox 72–75; Lect St Jo Coll Nottm 75–81; V Cov H Trin 81–92; Can Th Cov Cathl 88–92; Area Bp Willesden *Lon* 92–00; Bp Carl 00–09; rtd 09; Hon Asst Bp Ches from 09; Hon Asst Bp Man from 11. *34 Kimberley Avenue, Romiley, Stockport SK6 4AB* T: 0161-494 9148 E: graham@gdow.co.uk

DOWD, Garfield George. b 60. QUB BSc. **d** 86 **p** 87. C Monkstown *D & G* 86–90; I Carlow w Urglin and Staplestown *C & O* 90–05; Can Ossory Cathl 96–05; I Glenageary *D & G* from 05. *St Paul's Vicarage, Silchester Road, Glenageary, Co Dublin, Republic of Ireland* T/F: (00353) (1) 280 1616 M: 87-926 6558 E: glenageary@dublin.anglican.org

DOWDING, Ms Clare Alice Elizabeth. b 74. Ch Ch Coll Cant BA 98 Greenwich Univ PGCE 99. Westcott Ho Cam BA 02. **d** 03 **p** 05. USA 03–04; C Longsight St Luke *Man* 04–07; Chapl Man HE Institutions 07–11; R Earlham *Nor* 11–14; R St Marylebone St Paul *Lon* from 14; Dean of Women's Min Two Cities Area from 16. *St Paul's House, 9 Rossmore Road, London NW1 6NJ* T: (020) 7262 9443 *or* 7724 8517 M: 07970-661534 E: caedowding@gmail.com

DOWDING, Canon Edward Brinley. b 47. St Mich Coll Llan 70 St D Coll Lamp BA 71. **d** 72 **p** 73. C Canton St Cath *Llan* 72–75; C Aberdare 75–78; V Aberavon H Trin 78–85; R Sully 85–13; R Wenvoe and St Lythans 10–13; RD Penarth and Barry 98–04; Hon Can Llan Cathl 11–13; rtd 13; PtO *Llan* from 13. *10 Clos Tawe, Barry CF62 7BN* T: (01446) 737180 E: edward.dowding@btinternet.com

DOWDING, Mrs Elizabeth Jean. b 43. Bath Coll of HE TCert 67. SAOMC 00. **d** 04 **p** 05. NSM Goring w S Stoke *Ox* 04–07; NSM Goring and Streatley w S Stoke from 07. *30 Milldown Avenue, Goring, Reading RG8 0AS* T: (01491) 873140 E: elizdowding@aol.com

DOWDING, Jeremy Charles. b 51. St Steph Ho Ox 89. **d** 91 **p** 92. C Newport St Steph and H Trin *Mon* 91–94; C Risca 94–96; P-in-c Whitleigh *Ex* 96–05; P-in-c Thorpe-le-Soken *Chelmsf* 05–17; V 17–19; P-in-c Weeley and Lt Clacton 17–19; rtd 19. *16 Cwmbeth Close, Crickhowell NP8 1DX* M: 07815-773262

DOWDLE, Canon Cynthia. b 48. Cranmer Hall Dur 88. **d** 90 **p** 94. C Allerton *Liv* 90–94; TR Halewood 94–00; V Knowsley 00–11; Dean of Women's Min 01–15; Hon Can Liv Cathl 01–10; Can Res Liv Cathl 10–15; rtd 16; PtO *Liv* from 16. *24 Borromeo Close, Liverpool L17 7DS* T: 0151-384 1887 E: cynthiadowdle@hotmail.com

DOWDY, Simon Mark Christopher. b 67. Trin Hall Cam BA 89 MA 93. Wycliffe Hall Ox 93. **d** 96 **p** 97. C Beckenham Ch Ch *Roch* 96–00; C St Helen Bishopsgate w St Andr Undershaft etc *Lon* 00–05; P-in-c St Botolph without Aldersgate from 02. *45 Woodwarde Road, London SE22 8UN* T: (020) 8299 1631 E: mail@stbotolphsaldersgate.org.uk

DOWER, Frances Helen. b 45. Lon Univ MB, BS 69. **d** 09 **p** 10. OLM Kirkwhelpington, Kirkharle, Kirkheaton and Cambo *Newc* 09–14; NSM 14–15; PtO from 15. *Cambo House, Front Row, Cambo, Morpeth NE61 4AY* T: (01670) 774297 E: frances.dower@dower.org.uk

DOWIE, Winifred Brenda McIntosh. b 57. Callendar Park Coll of Educn Falkirk DipEd 78. Trin Coll Bris BA 91. **d** 92 **p** 94. Par Dn Downend *Bris* 92–94; C 94–95; Chapl Asst Southmead Health Services NHS Trust 95–98; Chapl St Pet Hospice Bris 98–13; Hon Can Bris Cathl 02–13; Chapl Glos Hosps NHS Foundn Trust 13–16; Chapl N Bris NHS Trust from 16; Chapl Univ Hosps Bris NHS Foundn Trust 16–17; PtO Bris from 16. *Spiritual and Pastoral Care, The Chaplaincy, Gate 30, The Brunel Building, Southmead Hospital, Southmead Road, Westbury-on-Trym, Bristol BS10 5NB* T: 0117-414 3707 *or* 342 6795 E: brenda.dowie@nbt.nhs.uk *or* brenda.dowie@uhbristol.nhs.uk

DOWLAND, Martin John. b 48. Lon Univ BD 70 Southn Univ PGCE 71. Wycliffe Hall Ox 75. **d** 77 **p** 78. C Jesmond Clayton Memorial *Newc* 77–80; C Chadderton Ch Ch *Man* 80–85; R Haughton St Mary 85–14; rtd 14; PtO *Man* from 15; *Ches* from 19. *11 Overdale Drive, Glossop SK13 6GA* E: m.dowland@ntlworld.com

DOWLAND-OWEN, Edward Farrington. b 73. St D Coll Lamp BA 95 Trin Coll Carmarthen PGCE 96 FVCM 99. S Wales Ord Course 00 St Mich Coll Llan 03. **d** 04 **p** 05. C Llandaff *Llan* 04–08; P-in-c Llandyfodwg and Cwm Ogwr 08–10; C Penarth and Llandough 10–13; TV Cowbridge 13–17; P-in-c Margam from 17; Dioc Spirituality Adv from 12; P Assoc Shrine of Our Lady of Walsingham from 05. *Margam Vicarage, 3 Llys y Ddraenog, Margam, Port*

Talbot SA13 2TQ T: (01656) 749139 M: 07403-935555 E: vicar@parishofmargam.org.uk

DOWLAND-PILLINGER, Catherine Louise. b 60. New Hall Cam BA 82 MA 86 PhD 89. SEITE 05. **d** 08 **p** 09. C Addington *S'wark* 08–12; PtO 12–13; Chapl S'wark Cathl 13; TV Caterham from 13. *The Rectory, Station Road, Woldingham, Caterham CR3 7DD* T: (01883) 652192 M: 07768-065301 E: rev.catherine1@gmail.com

DOWLEN, Isabella McBeath. b 45. Man Univ CertEd 86 Edin Univ MTh 06 RGN 67 SCM 68 HVCert 69. STETS 96. **d** 99 **p** 01. NSM Branksome St Clem *Sarum* 99–04; NSM Clarkston *Glas* 04–06; P-in-c Glas St Oswald 06–08; R Pittenweem *St And* 10–14; R Elie and Earlsferry 10–14; rtd 14; LtO *Edin* from 15; PtO *Glas* from 16. *45 The Quarryknowes, Bo'ness EH51 0QJ* T: (01506) 826610 M: 07974-084657 E: isabel.dowlen@gmail.com

DOWLER, The Ven Robert Edward Mackenzie. b 67. Ch Ch Ox BA 89 Selw Coll Cam BA 09 Ox Univ PhD 07. Westcott Ho Cam 91. **d** 94 **p** 95. C Southgate Ch Ch *Lon* 94–97; C Somers Town 97–01; Tutor and Dir Past Th St Steph Ho Ox 01–09; Vice Prin 03–09; Asst Chapl Malvern Coll 09–10; V Clay Hill St Jo and St Luke *Lon* 10–16; CME Officer Edmonton Area 13–16; Adn Hastings *Chich* from 16. *Beechmount, Beacon Road, Crowborough TN6 1UQ* T: (01892) 611561 *or* (01273) 425040 M: 07990-675242 E: archhastings@chichester.anglican.org

DOWLEY, Mrs Ruth Ada. b 49. St Mellitus Coll 13. **d** 14 **p** 15. OLM Becontree St Cedd *Chelmsf* 14–17; NSM from 17. *68 Malvern Drive, Ilford IG3 9DW* T: (020) 8597 1988 M: 07817-163203 E: ruthdowley@hotmail.com

DOWLING, Donald Edward. b 43. St Andr Univ MA 66. Cranmer Hall Dur. **d** 74 **p** 75. C Thame w Towersey *Ox* 74–77; C Norton *St Alb* 77–80; V Wilbury 81–99; V Stevenage St Nic and Graveley 99–10; rtd 10; PtO *St Alb* from 10. *56 Caslon Way, Letchworth Garden City SG6 4QL* T: (01462) 678934 E: rev.don68@gmail.com

DOWLING, Graham Paul. b 62. NTMTC BA 09. **d** 09 **p** 10. C Rainham w Wennington *Chelmsf* 09–13; TV Barking 13–16; V Barking St Patr 17–18; Rural Adv Colchester Area from 18; NSM Witham and Villages from 18; Chapl Dioc Retreat Ho from 17. *The Rectory, New Road, Terling, Chelmsford CM3 2PN* M: 07889-286308 E: revgpd@btinternet.com

DOWLING, Canon Kingsley Avery Paul. b 60. Open Univ BA. Aston Tr Scheme 93 Ripon Coll Cuddesdon 95. **d** 97 **p** 98. C Headingley *Ripon* 97–99; C Far Headingley St Chad 99–01; V Wortley-de-Leeds 01–13; P-in-c Farnley 10–13; AD Armley 08–13; R Wortley and Farnley *Leeds* 13–15; V Meanwood 15–18; Hon Can Ripon Cathl 13–18; rtd 18. *70 Eaton Hill, Leeds LS16 6SE* M: 07810-212127 E: kingsley.dowling@hotmail.co.uk

DOWLING, Tracy Anne. b 59. SEITE 08. **d** 11 **p** 12. NSM Merton Priory *S'wark* 11–14; Chapl Dundee St Paul *Bre* 14–16; Hon Chapl Abertay Univ 14–16; P-in-c Auchterarder *St And* from 16; P-in-c Muthill from 16. *St Kessog's Rectory, High Street, Auchterarder PH3 1AD* T: (01764) 662525 M: 07788-239798 E: tadowling@btinternet.com

DOWMAN, Jonathan Robert. b 76. Westmr Coll Ox BEd 00. Trin Coll Bris 04. **d** 07 **p** 08. C Anglesey Gp *Ely* 07–10; Deanery Missr *Birm* 10–14; Bp's Adv on Fresh Expressions *Leic* from 14; PtO from 15. *Address temp unknown* E: jonathandowman@icloud.com *or* jonathan.dowman@leccofe.org

DOWMAN, Peter Robert. b 52. City Univ BSc 76. Wycliffe Hall Ox 82. **d** 84 **p** 85. C Cheltenham Ch Ch *Glouc* 84–87; C Danbury *Chelmsf* 87–90; R Woodham Ferrers and Bicknacre 90–95; Consultant E England CPAS 95–03; R Warboys w Broughton and Bury w Wistow *Ely* 03–14; rtd 14; PtO *Ely* from 16. *9 Peregrine Street, Hampton Vale, Peterborough PE7 8LH* T: (01733) 601935 E: peterdowman@me.com

DOWN, Andrew Stuart. b 77. Ex Univ BSc 99. Ripon Coll Cuddesdon BTh 14. **d** 14 **p** 15. C Ex St Jas 14–18; R Ipplepen w Torbryan, Denbury, Broadhempston and Woodland from 18. *The Rectory, Paternoster Lane, Ipplepen, Newton Abbot TQ12 5RY* M: 07443-458487 E: rev.andrew@gmail.com

DOWN, Edward William. b 91. Jes Coll Ox MChem 13. Trin Coll Bris MA 17. **d** 17 **p** 18. C St Jas in the City *Liv* from 17. *18 Lady Chapel Close, Liverpool L1 7BZ* E: rev.ed.down@gmail.com

DOWN, Martin John. b 40. Jes Coll Cam BA 62 MA 68. Westcott Ho Cam 63. **d** 65 **p** 66. C Bury St Mary *Man* 65–68; C Leigh St Mary 68–70; R Fiskerton *Linc* 70–75; V Irnham w Corby 75–79; RD Beltisloe 76–84; P-in-c Swayfield and Creeton w Swinstead 78–79; V Corby Glen 79–84; Good News Trust 84–88; PtO *Linc* 84–88; *Pet* 86–88; P-in-c Ashill w Saham Toney *Nor* 88–94; R 94–00; C Watton w Carbrooke

and Ovington 00–05; rtd 05; PtO *Nor* 05–12; *Ox* from 12. *36 Beechgate, Witney OX28 4JL* T: (01993) 709743

DOWN, The Ven Philip Roy. b 53. Hull Univ MA 93. Melbourne Coll of Div BTh 82 MTh 88. **d** 89 **p** 89. C Gt Grimsby St Mary and St Jas *Linc* 89–91; TV 91–95; R Hackington *Cant* 95–02; AD Cant 99–02; Adn Maidstone 02–11; Adn Ashford 11–17; rtd 17; PtO *Sarum* from 18. *4 Gooselands, Westbury BA13 3UQ* T: (01373) 822009

✠**DOWN, The Rt Revd William John Denbigh.** b 34. St Jo Coll Cam BA 57 MA 61 FNI 91. Ridley Hall Cam 57. **d** 59 **p** 60 **c** 90. C Fisherton Anger *Sarum* 59–63; Miss to Seamen 63–90; Australia 71–74; Dep Gen Sec Miss to Seamen 75; Gen Sec 76–90; Hon C Gt Stanmore *Lon* 75–90; Chapl St Mich Paternoster Royal 76–90; PtO *St Alb* 78–90; Hon Can Gib Cathl *Eur* 85–90; Hon Can Kobe Japan from 87; Bp Bermuda 90–95; Asst Bp Leic 95–01; P-in-c Humberstone 95–01; P-in-c Thurnby Lodge 01; rtd 01; Hon Asst Bp Ox from 01. *54 Dark Lane, Witney OX28 6LX* T: (01993) 706615 E: bishbill@aol.com

DOWN AND DROMORE, Bishop of. *Vacant*

DOWN, Archdeacon of. *See* MACCLAY, The Ven David Alexander

DOWN, Dean of. *See* HULL, The Very Revd Thomas Henry

DOWNER, Barry Michael. b 58. STETS 99. **d** 02 **p** 07. NSM Lake and Shanklin St Sav *Portsm* 02–05; NSM Bonchurch, Ventnor H Trin and Ventnor St Cath 05–08; NSM Oakfield St Jo 09–14; NSM Brading w Yaverland 14; PtO from 16. *44 Landguard Road, Shanklin PO37 7JX* T: (01983) 867150

DOWNES, Andrew Victor John. b 65. STETS 10. **d** 13 **p** 14. C Chiswick St Nic w St Mary *Lon* 13–16; V Sunbury from 16. *The Vicarage, Thames Street, Sunbury-on-Thames TW16 6AA* T: (01932) 779431 *or* 785448 M: 07939-290265 E: andrewvjd@gmail.com *or* vicar@stmarys-sunbury.org

DOWNEY, Jocelyn Stewart. b 69. Surrey Univ BSc 92 Lon Univ PhD 98 St Edm Coll Cam MPhil 14 Ch Coll Cam BTh 13. Ridley Hall Cam 11. **d** 14 **p** 15. C Bermondsey St Jas and St Anne *S'wark* 14–17; Miss Without Borders (UK) Ltd from 17. *Mission Without Borders, 175 Tower Bridge Road, London SE1 2AG* T: (020) 7940 1370

DOWNEY, Canon John Stewart. b 38. QUB CertEd 60 Open Univ BA 76. Oak Hill Th Coll 63. **d** 66 **p** 67. C Londonderry St Aug *D & R* 66–71; I Dungiven w Bovevagh 71–82; Bp's Dom Chapl 75–82; V Bishopwearmouth St Gabr *Dur* 82–91; V New Malden and Coombe *S'wark* 91–06; Hon Can S'wark Cathl 97–06; rtd 06; PtO *S'wark* from 08; *Newc* from 18. *171 Kenton Road, Newcastle upon Tyne NE3 4NR* T: 0191-597 2892 E: sdowney@mwbuk.org

DOWNEY, Olivia Margaret Grace. **d** 14 **p** 15. Aughaval w Achill, Knappagh, Dugort etc *T, K & A* 14–15; C Enniskillen *Clogh* 15–18; I Clogh w Errigal Portclare from 18. *The Rectory, 10 Augher Road, Clogher BT76 0AD* M: 07792-728495 E: odowney@clogher.anglican.org

DOWNHAM, Canon Peter Norwell. b 31. Man Univ BA 52. Ridley Hall Cam 54. **d** 56 **p** 57. C Cheadle *Ches* 56–62; V Rawtenstall St Mary *Man* 62–68; Chapl Rossendale Gen Hosp 62–68; V Denton Holme *Carl* 68–79; V Reading Greyfriars *Ox* 79–95; Hon Can Ch Ch 90–95; rtd 95; Hon C Cotehill and Cumwhinton *Carl* 95–00; PtO 98–07; *Ox* from 07. *17 Grange Close, Goring, Reading RG8 9DY* T: (01491) 875983 E: pndow@tiscali.co.uk

DOWNHAM, Simon Garrod. b 61. K Coll Lon LLB 84 Solicitor 87. Wycliffe Hall Ox BA 93. **d** 94 **p** 95. C Brompton H Trin w Onslow Square St Paul *Lon* 94–99; P-in-c Hammersmith St Paul 00–06; V from 06. *14 Lena Gardens, London W6 7PZ* T: (020) 7603 9662 *or* 8748 3855 E: simon.downham@sph.org

DOWNING, Francis Gerald. b 35. Qu Coll Ox BA 56 MA 60. Linc Th Coll. **d** 58 **p** 59. C Filwood Park CD *Bris* 58–60; Tutor Linc Th Coll 60–64; V Unsworth *Man* 64–80; Tutor NOC 80–82; Vice-Prin 82–90; V Bolton SS Simon and Jude *Man* 90–97; rtd 97; PtO *Blackb* from 97. *33 Westhoughton Road, Chorley PR7 4EU* T: (01257) 474240

DOWNS, Caroline Rebecca. b 58. UWIST BA 80 Univ of Wales (Cardiff) PGCE 81. St Mich Coll Llan 98. **d** 02 **p** 03. C Roath *Llan* 02–07; P-in-c Cathays from 07; Warden of Readers from 14; Asst Dir of Voc from 15. *6 Newminster Road, Roath, Cardiff CF23 5AP* T: (029) 2049 5699 E: carolinerebecca.downs@btinternet.com

DOWNS, John Alfred. b 58. Leic Univ BSc 79 PGCE 80 CBiol 80 MRSB 80. EMMTC 90. **d** 93 **p** 94. NSM Barlestone *Leic* 93–96; NSM Markfield, Thornton, Bagworth and Stanton etc 96–11; NSM Newbold de Verdun, Barlestone and Kirkby Mallory from 11; PtO *Cov* 13–15. *29 Meadow Road, Barlestone, Nuneaton CV13 0JG* T: (01455) 290195 E: revjohndowns@hotmail.co.uk

DOWSE, Ivor Roy. b 35. ARHistS MRSL. St Deiniol's Hawarden 66. **d** 68 **p** 70. C Harrow St Pet *Lon* 68–69; C Sudbury St Andr 69–71; C Weeke *Win* 71–73; Min Can Ban Cathl 73–78; V Hollym w Welwick and Holmpton *York* 78–81; R Bearwood *Ox* 81–82; P-in-c Rothesay *Arg* 83–86; C Boxmoor St Jo *St Alb* 86–92; Hon C Cowes H Trin and St Mary *Portsm* 92–94; PtO 94–98; P-in-c St Hilary w Perranuthnoe *Truro* 98–00; rtd 01; PtO *Win* from 06; Hon Chapl Win Cathl from 06; Hon Asst Chapl St Jo Win Charity from 09. *10 St Mary Magdalen Almshouses, Colebrook Street, Winchester SO23 9LR* T: (01962) 890877

DOWSETT, Andrew Christopher. b 72. Sheff Univ BA 95 PhD 99. St Jo Coll Nottm 07. **d** 09 **p** 10. C Clubmoor *Liv* 09–11; C Birkdale St Jas and Birkdale St Pet 11–13; Min Sunderland Minster *Dur* 13–17; Min P from 17. *St Nicholas' Vicarage, 200 Queen Alexandra Road, Sunderland SR3 1XQ* T: 0191-551 1209 M: 07783-760012 E: andrew@dowsetts.net *or* minsterpriest@sunderlandminster.org

DOWSETT, Ian Peter. b 71. Liv Univ BA 95 Lon Inst of Educn PGCE 96. Wycliffe Hall Ox BA 01. **d** 02. C Kensington St Helen w H Trin *Lon* 02–09; V S Harrow St Paul from 09; AD Harrow from 16. *St Paul's Vicarage, Eastcote Lane, Harrow HA2 8NJ* T: (020) 8864 0362 M: 07908-517934 E: irdowsett@talk21.com *or* iandowsett@stpaulsharrow.org.uk

DOWSON, Ruth Helen. b 59. Sheff Univ BA 81 MA 12 Bradf Univ MBA 85 Leeds Metrop Univ PGCE 09. Yorks Min Course 09. **d** 12 **p** 13. C Clayton *Leeds* 12–15; C Bingley All SS from 15. *2 Irving Terrace, Clayton, Bradford BD14 6LA* M: 07971-189599 E: r.dowson@leedsbeckett.ac.uk

DOWSON, Simon Paul. b 63. Bris Univ BSc 85 Cam Univ PGCE 89. Cranmer Hall Dur 95. **d** 97 **p** 98. C Bradf St Aug Undercliffe 97–99; C Werrington *Pet* 99–04; V Skirbeck H Trin *Linc* 04–14; RD Holland 13–14; TR Bilton *Leeds* from 14. *Bilton Vicarage, Bilton Lane, Harrogate HG1 3DT* T: (01423) 431513 E: simon.dowson@leeds.anglican.org

DOXSEY, Canon Roy Desmond. b 41. St D Coll Lamp 64. **d** 67 **p** 68. C Pembroke St Mary w St Mich *St D* 67–70; C Milford Haven 70–73; C Loughton *Ox* 73–75; Chapl Llandovery Coll 75–81 and 92–96; Zambia 81–86; Chapl Epsom Coll 86–92; V Roath St German *Llan* 96–11; Hon Can Llan Cathl 09–11; PtO from 12; *St D* from 12. *St Anne's Clergy House, 3 Snipe Street, Cardiff CF24 3RB* T: (029) 2048 9313

DOYE, Andrew Peter Charles. b 64. BNC Ox BA 85. Trin Coll Bris BA 93. **d** 93 **p** 94. C Surbiton St Matt *S'wark* 93–96; C Bourne *Guildf* 96–99; C The Bourne and Tilford 99–00; R Warhampstead *St Alb* 00–09; RD 06–08; PtO 15–17; R Westbourne *Chich* from 17. *The Rectory, Westbourne Road, Westbourne, Emsworth PO10 8UL* T: (01243) 372867 E: rector@westbourneparishchurch.org.uk

DOYLE, Andrew Michael. b 63. K Coll Lon BD 85 AKC 85. Ripon Coll Cuddesdon 86. **d** 88 **p** 89. C Lytchett Minster *Sarum* 88–92; TV Kirkby *Liv* 92–97; V Rotherhithe H Trin *S'wark* from 97; AD Bermondsey 00–08. *Holy Trinity Vicarage, Bryan Road, London SE16 5HF* T: (020) 7237 4098 E: andrewdoyle763@btinternet.com

DOYLE, Edward Michael. b 70. St Mich Coll Llan BTh 93. **d** 94 **p** 95. C Sketty *S & B* 94–96; C Llwynderw 96–00; R Rogate w Terwick and Trotton w Chithurst *Chich* from 00. *The Vicarage, Fyning Lane, Rogate, Petersfield GU31 5EE* T: (01730) 821576 E: edwarddoyle@uwclub.net

DOYLE, Eileen Ann. b 53. SEITE 08. **d** 11 **p** 12. NSM Coxheath, E Farleigh, Hunton, Linton etc *Roch* from 11. *63 Felderland Close, Maidstone ME15 9YD* T: (01622) 236170 E: eileen@leedoyle.co.uk

DOYLE, Michael Christopher. b 64. St Jo Coll Nottm 06. **d** 08 **p** 09. C Ashbourne St Oswald w Mapleton *Derby* 08–12; R N Bellisloe Gp *Linc* 12–16; P-in-c Devonport St Boniface *Ex* from 17; P-in-c Weston Mill from 17. *The Vicarage, 1 Normandy Way, Plymouth PL5 1SW* T: (01752) 368895 E: mike_c_doyle@hotmail.co.uk

DOYLE, Nigel Paul. b 55. MHort(RHS) 82. St Mich Coll Llan 00. **d** 03 **p** 04. NSM Landore w Treboeth *S & B* 03–09; NSM Swansea Deanery 09–15; NSM Gtr Gower *S & B* from 16. *3 Ael-y-Bryn, Penclawdd, Swansea SA4 3LF* T: (01792) 850659 E: tadnigel@yahoo.co.uk

DOYLE, Robin Alfred. b 43. Dur Univ BA 65. Westcott Ho Cam 66. **d** 68 **p** 69. C Edgbaston St Geo *Birm* 68–70; C Erdington St Barn 70–73; P-in-c Oldbury 73–81; R Maker w Rame *Truro* 81–11; rtd 11; PtO *Truro* from 14. *9 Camperknowle Close, Millbrook, Torpoint PL10 1QB* T: (01752) 822302

DOYLE, Mrs Tracey Elizabeth. b 58. Open Univ BA 00. SAOMC 94. **d** 97 **p** 98. OLM Winslow w Gt Horwood and Addington *Ox* 97–99; C 00–04; P-in-c Ivinghoe w Pitstone and Slapton 04–08; V Ivinghoe w Pitstone and Slapton and Marsworth 08–14; NSM Newton

Tracey, Horwood, Alverdiscott etc *Ex* 16–18; C from 18. *Stables Cottage, Nethergrove, High Bickington, Umberleigh EX37 9BQ* M: 07814-538208 E: revtracey@btinternet.com

DOYLE-BRETT, Mrs Jacqueline Margaret. b 62. Hull Univ BA 99 PGCE 00 Sheff Univ MA 13. Yorks Min Course 11. **d** 13 **p** 14. C Tadcaster *York* 13–16; V York St Luke from 16. *79 Burton Stone Lane, York YO30 6BZ* T: (01904) 628337 M: 07793-545755 E: jackiemdb@gmail.com

DRACKLEY, John Oldham. b 36. Em Coll Cam BA 57 MA 61. Wells Th Coll 57. **d** 59 **p** 60. C Eckington *Derby* 59–62; C Lee Gd Shep w St Pet *S'wark* 62–63; C Derby St Thos 63–67; C Matlock and Tansley 67–77; P-in-c Radbourne 77–82; P-in-c Dalbury, Long Lane and Trusley 77–82; P-in-c Longford 77–82; Sec Dioc Cttee for Care of Chs 82–98; rtd 95; PtO *Derby* 98–16. *26 Highfield Drive, Matlock DE4 3FZ* T: (01629) 55902

DRAIN, Walter. b 39. Open Univ BA 76 ACP 66. NW Ord Course 76. **d** 79 **p** 80. NSM Cheadle *Ches* 79–81; C 81–84; V Chatburn *Blackb* 84–02; Sub Chapl HM Pris Preston 94–02; rtd 02; PtO *Blackb* from 02. *Angels, 28 The Croft, Euxton, Chorley PR7 6LH* T: (01257) 249646 E: walterdrain@btinternet.com

DRAIN, William. b 84. Liv Hope Univ BDes 05 Edge Hill Univ PGCE 06. St Mellitus Coll BA 18. **d** 18 **p** 19. C Romiley *Ches* from 18. *21 Guywood Lane, Romiley, Stockport SK6 4AN* M: 07525-782787 E: will.drain1@gmail.com *or* will@stchadsromiley.co.uk

DRAISEY, Damon Allan. STETS 10. **d** 13 **p** 14. C Warblington w Emsworth *Portsm* 13–18; V S Downs Gateway Churches *Win* from 18. *Holy Trinity Church Centre, 154 Main Road, Colden Common, Winchester SO21 1TJ* T: (01962) 711216 M: 07906-346498

DRAKE, Graham. b 46. Linc Th Coll 81. **d** 83 **p** 85. C Alford w Rigsby *Linc* 83–84; PtO *Wakef* 84–85; Hon C Purston cum S Featherstone 85–89; NSM Castleford All SS 89–92; C Cudworth 92–95; rtd 11. *8A Broomhill, Castleford WF10 4QP* T: (01977) 518407

DRAKE, Canon Graham Rae. b 45. Fitzw Coll Cam BA 68 MA 72. Qu Coll Birm 70. **d** 73 **p** 74. C New Windsor *Ox* 73–77; TV 77–78; P-in-c Bath Ascension *B & W* 78–81; TV Bath Twerton-on-Avon 81–86; P-in-c Buxton w Oxnead *Nor* 86–90; P-in-c Lammas w Lt Hautbois 86–90; R Buxton w Oxnead, Lammas and Brampton 90–95; RD Ingworth 88–94; P-in-c Cockley Cley w Gooderstone 95–01; P-in-c Gt and Lt Cressingham w Threxton 95–01; P-in-c Didlington 95–01; P-in-c Hilborough w Bodney 95–01; P-in-c Oxborough w Foulden and Caldecote 95–01; P-in-c Mundford w Lynford 99–01; P-in-c Ickburgh w Langford 99–01; P-in-c Cranwich 99–01; V Thorpe St Matt 01–10; Chapl NW Anglia Healthcare NHS Trust 96–99; Hon Can Nor Cathl 99–10; Chapter Can Nor Cathl 02–05; rtd 10; PtO *Nor* from 10. *13 Needham Place, St Stephen's Square, Norwich NR1 3SD* T: (01603) 886084 E: grahamrdrake@btinternet.com

DRAKE, Jonathan Charles. b 81. Down Coll Cam MEng 03 MA 05. Wycliffe Hall Ox BA 11. **d** 12 **p** 13. C Wargrave w Knowl Hill *Ox* 12–16; C Maidenhead St Andr and St Mary from 16. *9 Castle Court, Maidenhead SL6 6DD* T: (01628) 638866 M: 07715-123856 E: jon.drake1981@gmail.com

DRAKE, Leslie Sargent. b 47. Boston Univ BA 69 MTh 72 Hull Univ BPhil 74 Anglia Poly Univ MSc 93. Coll of Resurr Mirfield 78. **d** 78 **p** 79. C Oldham *Man* 78–81; TV Rochdale 81–83; V Palmers Green St Jo *Lon* 83–89; St Mary's Sch Cheshunt 89–91; Hd RE St Mary's Sch Hendon 91–99; TV Wimbledon *S'wark* 99–03; V Clay Hill St Jo and St Luke *Lon* 03–09; V Aiken St Aug USA 09–12; V S Benfleet *Chelmsf* from 12. *St Mary's Vicarage, 105 Vicarage Hill, Benfleet SS7 1PD* T: (01268) 754268 E: frldrake@btinternet.com

DRAKE, Nicholas James. b 78. St Chad's Coll Dur BA 00 K Coll Lon MA 08. St Mellitus Coll 13. **d** 17 **p** 18. C Birm St Luke from 17. *12 Emerson Road, Birmingham B17 9LT* M: 07738-007005 *or* 07778-882802 E: nick.drake@gasstreet.org

DRAKE-SMITH, Jacqueline Ann. b 59. Ripon Coll Cuddesdon 12. **d** 14 **p** 15. C Merrow *Guildf* 14–18; V Wrecclesham from 18. *The Vicarage, 2 Kings Lane, Wrecclesham, Farnham GU10 4QB* M: 07806-775974 E: jackieds8@hotmail.com

DRAPER, Charles James. b 59. Dur Univ BSc 80 Cam Univ BA 86. Ridley Hall Cam 84. **d** 87 **p** 88. C Wareham *Sarum* 87–90; C Maltby *Sheff* 90–93; R The Claydons *Ox* 93–99; R Chinnor w Emmington and Sydenham etc 99–02; P-in-c Gt Faringdon w Lt Coxwell 02–07; V 07–15; AD Vale of White Horse 13–15; V Wolvercote and Wytham from 15. *The Vicarage, 1 Mere Road, Oxford OX2 8AN* T: (01865) 553992 E: charlesdraper@btinternet.com

DRAPER, Derek Vincent. b 38. Linc Th Coll 65. **d** 68 **p** 69. C Orpington All SS *Roch* 68–72; C Bramley *Guildf* 72–74; Min Kempston Transfiguration CD *St Alb* 74–79; V Kempston

Transfiguration 79–84; RD Bedford 79–84; V Bromham w Oakley 84–88; P-in-c Stagsden 84–88; V Bromham w Oakley and Stagsden 88–03; RD Elstow 00–02; Chapl Bromham Hosp 84–03; rtd 03; PtO *Ely* from 03; *St Alb* from 03. *24 Wilkinson Close, Eaton Socon, St Neots PE19 8HJ* T: (01480) 384031 E: drapers24@ntlworld.com

DRAPER, Elizabeth Ann. *See* BRADLEY, Elizabeth Ann

DRAPER, Ivan Thomas. b 32. Aber Univ MB, ChB 56 FRCP FRCPGlas. St Jo Coll Nottm 87. **d** 90 **p** 91. NSM Glas St Bride 90–06; P-in-c 96–99; LtO from 06. *13/1 Whistlefield Court, 2 Canniesburn Road, Bearsden, Glasgow G61 1PX* T: 0141-943 0954 E: muriel.draper@gmail.com

DRAPER, Canon John William. b 54. Win Univ MA 13. Qu Coll Birm 88. **d** 90 **p** 91. C Stepney St Dunstan and All SS *Lon* 90–94; C Leigh Park and Warren Park *Portsm* 94–96; R Rowner from 96; V Bridgemary 04–08; AD Gosport 09–14; Hon Can Portsm Cathl from 13; PtO *Eur* from 18. *The Rectory, 174 Rowner Lane, Gosport PO13 9SU* T: (023) 9258 1834 E: rownerrector@btinternet.com

DRAPER, Canon Martin Paul. b 50. Birm Univ BA 72 Southn Univ BTh 79. Chich Th Coll 72. **d** 75 **p** 76. C Primrose Hill St Mary w Avenue Road St Paul *Lon* 75–78; C Westmr St Matt 79–84; Chapl Paris St Geo *Eur* 84–02; adn France 91–02; Can Gib Cathl 94–02; PtO from 02; *Lon* from 10. *112 Bolanachi Building, Enid Street, London SE16 3EX* T: (020) 7740 1891

DRAPER, Patrick Hugh. b 43. S Dios Minl Tr Scheme 91. **d** 94 **p** 95. NSM Boscombe St Jo *Win* 94–99; P-in-c Southbourne St Chris 99–02; rtd 02; PtO *Win* 02–14. *82 Tuckton Road, Bournemouth BH6 3HT* T: (01202) 420190 E: rev.patdraper@hotmail.com

DRAPER (née TRIMMER), Mrs Penelope Marynice. b 65. STETS 01. **d** 04 **p** 05. C Talbot Village *Sarum* 04–08; TV Dunstable *St Alb* 08–16; TV N Poole Ecum Team *Sarum* 16; V Oakdale from 17. *St George's Rectory, 99 Darby's Lane, Poole BH15 3EU* T: (01202) 660612 M: 07842-317204 E: penny.draper1@outlook.com

DRAPER, Peter Raymond. b 57. Leeds Poly BSc 86 Leeds Univ CertEd 88 Hull Univ PhD 94 SRN 80. NEOC 01. **d** 04 **p** 05. NSM S Cave and Ellerker w Broomfleet *York* from 04. *122 The Stray, South Cave, Brough HU15 2AL* T: (01430) 425486 M: 07956-531002 E: p.r.draper@hull.ac.uk

DRAPER, Mrs Sylvia Edith. b 39. ARCM 60. NOC 86. **d** 89 **p** 94. C Aughton St Mich *Liv* 89–92; Par Dn Wigan St Jas w St Thos 92–94; Asst Chapl Wigan and Leigh Health Services NHS Trust 92–97; C Wigan St Jas w St Thos *Liv* 94–97; TV Walton-on-the-Hill 97–02; rtd 02; PtO *Liv* from 03. *6 Brookfield Lane, Aughton, Ormskirk L39 6SP* T: (01695) 422138

DRAX, Elizabeth Margaret. *See* ANSON, Elizabeth Margaret

DRAY, John. b 66. St Chad's Coll Dur BSc 87. St Steph Ho Ox BTh 95. **d** 95 **p** 96. C Byker St Ant *Newc* 95–98; C Cullercoats St Geo 98–01; P-in-c Platt *Roch* 01–05; Chapl to the Deaf 01–05. *14 Heol Fach, Caerbryn, Ammanford SA18 3DJ* E: john@flirdy.co.uk

DRAYCOTT, John Edward. b 54. EMMTC 99. **d** 01 **p** 02. C Calverton, Epperstone, Gonalston and Oxton *S'well* 01–05; TV Parr *Liv* 05–13; P-in-c E Scarsdale *Derby* 13–15; TR from 15. *The Rectory, Rectory Road, Upper Langwith, Mansfield NG20 9RE* T: (01623) 618972 E: john.draycott@sky.com

DRAYCOTT, Philip John. b 27. Sarum & Wells Th Coll. **d** 83 **p** 84. C Bishop's Cleeve *Glouc* 83–86; V Chedworth, Yanworth and Stowell, Coln Rogers etc 86–93; rtd 94; PtO *B & W* 94–12. *April Cottage, Newton Road, North Petherton, Bridgwater TA6 6NA* T: (01278) 662487

DRAYCOTT, Tina. *See* FOX, Tina

✠**DRAYSON, The Rt Revd Nicholas James Quested.** b 53. Keble Coll Ox BA 75 MA 83. Wycliffe Hall Ox 82. **d** 79 **p** 79 **c** 09. SAMS Argentina 79–82; 92–00; Pastor Tartagal and Chapl to Chorote Indians 79–82; P-in-c Seville Ascension Spain 83–91; Adn Andalucia 89–91; Translations Co-ord 92–98; Pastor Salta St Andr 98–00; C Beverley Minster *York* 00–09; Suff Bp N Argentina from 09. *Casilla 187, 4400 Salta, Argentina* T: (0054) (387) 431 1718 E: nicobispo@gmail.com

DRAYTON, James Edward. b 30. St Deiniol's Hawarden 81. **d** 84 **p** 86. Hon C Heald Green St Cath *Ches* 84–88; C Bollington St Jo 88–92; P-in-c Lt Leigh and Lower Whitley 92–96; P-in-c Aston by Sutton 92–96; P-in-c Antrobus 92–96; rtd 96; PtO *York* from 96. *64 Plaxton Court, Scarborough YO12 6QT* T: (01723) 372377

DREDGE, David John. b 32. Cranmer Hall Dur 69. **d** 71 **p** 72. C Goole *Sheff* 71–74; P-in-c Eastoft 74–77; V Whitgift w Adlingfleet 74–77; V Whitgift w Adlingfleet and Eastoft 77–78; V Walkley 78–81; TV Bicester w Bucknell, Caversfield and Launton *Ox* 81–86; V N Brickhill and Putnoe *St Alb* 86–90; P-in-c Sarratt 90–95; rtd 95; PtO *Lich* 95–14. *19 Waterdale, Wombourne, Wolverhampton WV5 0DH* T: (01902) 897467

DREDGE, David Julian. b 36. Sheff Univ BA 59 ALA 74. Cranmer Hall Dur 61 Ban Ord Course 85. **d** 87 **p** 88. NSM Dwygyfylchi *Ban* 87–92; R Llanllechid 92–97; rtd 97; PtO *Ban* from 97. *Westfield, Treforris Road, Penmaenmawr LL34 6RH* T: (01492) 623439 F: 0870-056 7258 M: 07721-941861 E: davidjuliandredge@gmail.com

DREW, Daniel Alexander Blair. b 86. Ox Brookes Univ BA 08. St Mellitus Coll BA 14 MA 16. **d** 16 **p** 17. C Hitchin and St Paul's Walden *St Alb* from 16. *113 Common Rise, Hitchin SG4 0HP* M: 07738-553264 E: blairdrew@me.com

DREW, Gerald Arthur. b 36. Bps' Coll Cheshunt 59. **d** 61 **p** 62. C Lyonsdown H Trin *St Alb* 61–67; C Tring 67–71; R Bramfield w Stapleford and Waterford 71–78; V Langleybury St Paul 78–90; P-in-c Hormead, Wyddial, Anstey, Brent Pelham etc 90–95; V 95–01; rtd 01; PtO *St E* from 01; *St Alb* 01–17. *33 The Glebe, Lavenham, Sudbury CO10 9SN* T: (01787) 248133

DREW (née ROY), Mrs Jennifer Pearl. b 53. SRN 75 CSS 91. Cranmer Hall Dur. **d** 01 **p** 02. C Hebburn St Jo and Jarrow Grange *Dur* 01–05; NSM Broom Leys *Leic* 05–08; PtO 08–11; NSM Loughborough Em and St Mary in Charnwood 11–14; PtO from 14. *5 Balmoral Road, Coalville LE67 4PE* T: (01530) 836329 E: revjen03@hotmail.co.uk

DREW, Jo Ann. b 57. Ripon Coll Cuddesdon 09. **d** 11 **p** 12. C Milton next Gravesend Ch Ch *Roch* 11–14; PtO *Blackb* from 15; *Roch* from 17; Chapl Burrswood Chr Hosp 16–17. *80 Main Street, Warton, Carnforth LA5 9PG* E: revjodrew@btinternet.com

DREW, Canon Rosemary. b 43. SRN 64. EAMTC 90. **d** 93 **p** 94. NSM Gt Dunmow *Chelmsf* 93–96; NSM Gt Dunmow and Barnston 96–11; Hon Can Chelmsf Cathl 01–11; rtd 11; Area Adv for Healing and Deliverance Min *Chelmsf* from 04; PtO from 13. *The Bowling Green, 8 The Downs, Dunmow CM6 1DT* T/F: (01371) 872662 E: rose.drew@btinternet.com

DREW, Simon Mark. b 68. Liv Univ BEng 89 CEng 94 MICE 94. St Jo Coll Nottm MA 98. **d** 99 **p** 00. C Torquay St Matthias, St Mark and H Trin *Ex* 99–03; St Marshfield w Cold Ashton and Tormarton etc *Bris* 03–11; V Middlewich w Byley *Ches* from 11; RD Middlewich from 12. *The Rectory, Poplar Fell, Nantwich Road, Middlewich CW10 9HG* T: (01606) 833440 E: revsdrew@btinternet.com *or* simon.drew@middlewichparishchurch.org.uk

DREWETT, Mrs Susan. b 56. **d** 06 **p** 07. NSM Bemerton *Sarum* 06–18; rtd 18; PtO *Sarum* from 19. *Melford House, 36 Bulford Road, Durrington, Salisbury SP4 8DJ* T: (01980) 652751 E: rev.susandrewett@btinternet.com

DREYER, Rodney Granville. b 55. Lon Univ MPhil 91 AKC 91. St Paul's Coll Grahamstown 79. **d** 81 **p** 82. S Africa 81–84; NSM Headstone St Geo *Lon* 84–86; NSM Northolt St Mary 86–87; C Portsea St Mary *Portsm* 87–90; V Sudbury St Andr *Lon* 90–94; Adn W and S Free State S Africa 94–95; V Hawkhurst *Cant* from 98. *The Vicarage, Moor Hill Road, Hawkhurst, Cranbrook TN18 4QB* T: (01580) 753397 E: rodneydreyer@sky.com

DRING (née PETTY), Alicia Christina Margaret. b 64. Wycliffe Hall Ox 01. **d** 03 **p** 04. C Ockbrook *Derby* 03–07; P-in-c Sawley 07–10; R 10–13; V Littleover from 13; P-in-c Blagreaves from 19; Dean of Women's Min from 11. *The Vicarage, 35 Church Street, Littleover, Derby DE23 6GF* T: (01332) 767802 E: alicia@stpeterlittleover.org.uk

DRINKWATER, Maximillian Luke Darryl. b 90. Jes Coll Cam BA 12 MA 16. Westcott Ho Cam 13. **d** 16 **p** 17. C Newmarket St Mary w Exning St Agnes *St E* from 16. *28 Exning Road, Newmarket CB8 0AB* M: 07989-779493 E: mlddrinkwater@cantab.net

DRISCOLL, Canon David. b 42. Lon Univ BSc 64. Linc Th Coll 68. **d** 71 **p** 72. C Walthamstow St Jo *Chelmsf* 71–76; Chapl NE Lon Poly 71–79; C-in-c Plaistow St Mary 76–79; P-in-c Stratford St Jo and Ch Ch w Forest Gate St Jas 79–89; V Theydon Bois 89–01; RD Epping Forest 92–00; Hon Can Chelmsf Cathl 01; C All Hallows by the Tower etc *Lon* 01–07; rtd 07; Educn Tutor R Foundn of St Kath in Ratcliffe 05–10; Exec Officer Miss in London's Economy 07–10; PtO *Chelmsf* 07–10; *Lon* 07–10; *Sarum* from 11; *B & W* from 11. *24 Baileys Barn, Bradford-on-Avon BA15 1BX* T: (01225) 865314 E: david_driscoll@btopenworld.com

DRISCOLL, Raymond Donald Charles. b 78. St Mellitus Coll 14. **d** 17 **p** 18. C Stoke Hill *Guildf* from 17. *87 Old Farm Road, Guildford GU1 1QR* M: 07597-692683 E: raydriscoll78@gmail.com

DRIVER, Arthur John Roberts. b 44. SS Coll Cam MA 70 FCIPA 73. Linc Th Coll 73. **d** 76 **p** 77. C S'wark H Trin w St Matt 76–80; TV N Lambeth 80–85; CMS Sri Lanka 86–92; V Putney St Marg *S'wark* 92–97; V Streatham St Paul 97–09; rtd 09; PtO *Chelmsf* from 09. *91 Ernest Road, Wivenhoe, Colchester CO7 9LJ* T: (01206) 822135 E: ajrdriver@gmail.com

DRIVER, Bruce Leslie. b 42. Lon Univ LLB 73. Linc Th Coll 76. d 78 p 79. C Dunstable St Alb 78–81; TV 81–86; V Rickmansworth 86–98; RD 91–98; V Northwood Hills St Edm Lon 98–08; rtd 08; PtO Roch from 09; S'wark from 12. 7 Bromley College, London Road, Bromley BR1 1PE T: (020) 8290 0366 E: brucedriver@gmx.com

DRIVER, Daniel John. b 93. Dur Univ BA 17. Ridley Hall Cam 14. d 17 p 19. C Gateshead St Geo Dur 17–18; C Cambridge St Barn Ely from 19. 122 Ditton Lane, Fen Ditton, Cambridge CB5 8SS M: 07929-972152 E: danny.driver@stbs.org.uk

DRIVER, Gordon Geoffrey. b 32. Garnett Coll Lon Dip Teaching 59. Trin Coll Bris. d 95 p 96. NSM Radipole and Melcombe Regis Sarum 95–03; rtd 03; PtO Sarum 03–17. 11 Greenway Close, Weymouth DT3 5BQ T: (01305) 814523 E: stephenedwardyoung52@gmail.com

DRIVER (née FRENCH), Janet Mary. Leeds Univ BA 65 PGCE 66 Surrey Univ BA 98. Linc Th Coll 74. dss 80 d 92 p 94. St Paul's Cathl Lon 80–82; N Lambeth S'wark 80–85; CMS Sri Lanka 86–92; NSM Putney St Marg S'wark 92–97; Hon C Streatham St Paul 97–09; rtd 09; PtO Chelmsf from 11. Address withheld by request E: janet@janetdriver.co.uk

DRIVER, Jennifer. b 63. Kent Univ BA. SEITE 05. d 08 p 09. NSM Farnborough Roch 08–13; NSM Orpington All SS 13–18. 3 Starts Hill Road, Orpington BR6 7AR T: (01689) 858766 M: 07599-957969 E: jen.driver63@gmail.com

DRIVER, John. See DRIVER, Arthur John Roberts

DRIVER, The Ven Penelope May. b 52. NOC. d 87 p 94. Dioc Youth Adv Newc 86–88; C Cullercoats St Geo 87–88; Youth Chapl Ripon 88–96; Dioc Adv on Women's Min 91–06; Assoc Dir of Ords 96–98; Dioc Dir of Ords 98–06; Min Can Ripon Cathl 96–06; Hon Can Ripon Cathl 98–06; Adn Ex 06–12; P-in-c Dawlish 09–10; Adn Westmorland and Furness Carl 12–17; rtd 17. 32 Priory Crescent, Grange-over-Sands LA11 7BL E: pennydriver52@gmail.com

DRIVER, Roger John. b 64. Liv Univ MA 08. Trin Coll Bris BA 88. d 90 p 91. C Much Woolton Liv 90–93; C Fazakerley Em 93–94; TV 94–00; P-in-c Bootle St Matt 00–03; P-in-c Bootle St Leon 00–03; P-in-c Litherland St Andr 00–03; TR Bootle 04–16; AD 07–16; Hon Can Liv Cathl 07–16; R Bath St Mich Without B & W from 16. The Rectory, 71 Priory Close, Bath BA2 5AP T: (01225) 833512 M: 07976-419981 E: rogerdriver@btinternet.com

DROBIG, Marion. See WOOD, Marion

DROMORE, Archdeacon of. See WEST, The Ven Thomas Roderic

DROMORE, Dean of. See WILSON, The Very Revd Samuel Geoffrey

DROWLEY, Arthur. b 28. Oak Hill Th Coll 54. d 56 p 57. C Longfleet Sarum 56–59; C Wallington S'wark 59–62; V Taunton St Jas B & W 62–73; RD Taunton N 72–73; V Rodbourne Cheney Bris 73–87; R Bigbury, Ringmore and Kingston Ex 87–94; rtd 94; PtO Ex 95–02; Man 03–08; Lich from 05. 4 Inglis Road, Park Hall, Oswestry SY11 4AN T: (01691) 671994

DRUCE, Brian Lemuel. b 31. MRICS 55. Bps' Coll Cheshunt 58. d 60 p 61. C Whitton St Aug Lon 60–63; C Minehead B & W 63–66; R Birch St Agnes Man 66–70; V Overbury w Alstone, Teddington and Lt Washbourne Worc 70–81; Ind Chapl 81–91; rtd 91; PtO Worc from 91. 2 Cherry Orchard, Pershore WR10 1EL T: (01386) 304504 E: bravo.delta@uwclub.net

DRUMMOND, John Malcolm. b 44. Nottm Univ CertEd 65. Edin Th Coll 68. d 71 p 72. C Kirkholt Man 71–74; C Westleigh St Pet 74–76; Hd of RE Leigh High Sch from 76; Lic Preacher Man 76–84; Hon C Leigh St Jo 84–90; Hon C Tonge Moor 90–10; PtO from 10. 14 Bull's Head Cottages, Tottington Road, Turton, Bolton BL7 0HS T: (01204) 852232 M: 07986-912442 E: revd.m.drummond@btinternet.com

DRUMMOND, Josceline Maurice Vaughan. b 29. Lon Univ BD 70. Wycliffe Hall Ox 55. d 58 p 59. C Tunbridge Wells St Jo Roch 58–60; C Walthamstow St Mary Chelmsf 60–62; V Oulton Lich 62–68; V Leyton St Cath Chelmsf 71–85; Gen Dir CMJ 85–94; Public Preacher St Alb from 94; PtO St Alb from 94. 73 King Harry Lane, St Albans AL3 4AS T: (01727) 857620

DRUMMOND, Matthew James. b 77. Roehampton Inst BSc 98 Birkbeck Coll Lon MSc. Westcott Ho Cam 12. d 14 p 15. C Limpsfield and Tatsfield S'wark 14–17; C Addington 17–19; TV Mardyke Chelmsf from 19. All Saints' Vicarage, 121 Foyle Drive, South Ockendon RM15 5HF E: revd.matt.drummond@gmail.com or purfleetvicar@gmail.com

DRUMMOND, Terence. b 50. d 16. NSM Norbury St Phil S'wark from 16. 29 Orchard Rise, Croydon CR0 7QZ T: (020) 8406 8371 E: terry.drummond@hotmail.com

DRURY, Anthony Desmond. b 42. NOC. d 99 p 00. NSM New Ferry Ches 99–15; rtd 15; PtO Ches from 15. 61 Church Road, Bebington, Wirral CH63 3DZ T: 0151-334 4797 E: des88@talktalk.net

DRURY, Benjamin Guy. b 84. Worc Coll Ox BA 05 MA 11 MPhil 07. St Steph Ho Ox BA 13. d 14 p 16. C Stony Stratford w Calverton Ox 14–16; C S Hinksey 16–19; P-in-c Prittlewell St Luke Chelmsf from 19. St Luke's Vicarage, St Luke's Road, Southend-on-Sea SS2 4AB E: benjamin.drury@gmail.com

DRURY, Caroline Norah. See BURNETT, Caroline Norah

DRURY, Desmond. See DRURY, Anthony Desmond

DRURY, The Very Revd John Henry. b 36. Trin Hall Cam MA 66. Westcott Ho Cam 61. d 63 p 64. C St John's Wood Lon 63–66; Chapl Down Coll Cam 66–69; Chapl Ex Coll Ox 69–73; Can Res Nor Cathl 73–79; Vice-Dean 78–79; Lect Sussex Univ 79–81; Dean K Coll Cam 81–91; Dean Ch Ch Ox 91–03; rtd 03; Chapl and Fell All So Coll Ox from 03. All Souls College, Oxford OX1 4AL T: (01865) 279379 F: 279299

DRURY, Michael Dru. b 31. Trin Coll Ox BA 55 MA 59. Wycliffe Hall Ox. d 58 p 59. C Fulham St Mary N End Lon 58–62; C Blackheath St Jo S'wark 62–64; Chapl and Asst Master Canford Sch 64–80; Chapl and Teacher Fernhill Manor Sch New Milton 80–81; P-in-c Stowe Ox 82–92; Asst Master Stowe Sch 82–92; R Rampton w Laneham, Treswell, Cottam and Stokeham S'well 92–96; rtd 96; PtO Sarum from 96. Tanfield, Giddylake, Wimborne BH21 2QT T: (01202) 881246 E: michaeldrury@talktalk.net

DRURY, Valerie Doreen. b 40. Univ of Wales (Cardiff) BA 62 K Coll Lon PGCE 63 MBATOD 80. Oak Hill Th Coll 85. d 87 p 94. NSM Becontree St Alb Chelmsf 87–89; NSM Becontree S 89–02; rtd 02; PtO Chelmsf from 02. 37 Blunts Hall Road, Witham CM8 1ES T: (01376) 517330

DRYDEN, Barry Frederick. b 44. Ches Coll of HE BTh 00. NOC 97. d 00 p 01. C Formby St Pet Liv 00–03; V Woolston 03–10; rtd 10; PtO Leic from 13; Eur from 17. 5 Briton Lodge Close, Moira, Swadlincote DE12 6DD T: (01283) 550920 E: revbarrydryden@btinternet.com

DRYDEN, Martin John. b 57. Loughb Univ BA 80 Univ of Wales (Lamp) MA 99. STETS 07. d 09 p 10. NSM Jersey St Clem Win from 09. Mont Ubé House, La rue de la Blinerie, St Clement, Jersey JE2 6QT T: (01534) 874668 M: 07797-729525 E: martin@mont-ube.net

DRYE, Douglas John. b 37. Man Univ BSc 61. Clifton Th Coll. d 63 p 64. C Whalley Range St Edm Man 63–66; C Drypool St Columba w St Andr and St Pet York 66–68; V Worsbrough Common Sheff 68–86; R Armthorpe 86–92; rtd 92; PtO Pet from 92. 25 Willow Crescent, Oakham LE15 6EQ T: (01572) 770429 E: djwillowoak@uwclub.net

D'SILVA, David Paul. b 90. St Steph Ho Ox. d 16 p 17. C Edlington and Hexthorpe Sheff 16–18; C Doncaster St Leon and St Jude from 18. The Vicarage, Barnsley Road, Doncaster DN5 8QE T: (01302) 971841 M: 07507-730569 E: fr.david.dsilva@gmail.com

D'SOUZA, Derek Emile. b 54. Trin Coll Bris. d 07 p 08. C Edgbaston St Germain Birm 07–11; P-in-c Prince's Park Roch 11–18; PtO Lich from 19. 23 Hilary Drive, Wolverhampton WV3 7NJ E: helennderek@yahoo.co.uk

du SAIRE, Canon Michele Marie. b 55. Leeds Poly BSc 78. ERMC 06. d 09 p 10. C Leavesden St Alb 09–13; R Sarratt and Chipperfield from 13; Hon Can St Alb from 18. The New Vicarage, The Street, Chipperfield, Kings Langley WD4 9BJ T: (01923) 265848 E: micheledusairehcstp@gmail.com

DUBLIN (Christ Church), Dean of. See DUNNE, The Very Revd Dermot Patrick Martin

DUBLIN, Archbishop of, and Bishop of Glendalough. See JACKSON, The Most Revd Michael Geoffrey St Aubyn

DUBLIN, Archdeacon of. See PIERPOINT, The Ven David Alfred

DUBREUIL, Yann. b 70. Birm Univ BA 04. Wycliffe Hall Ox 05. d 07 p 08. C Four Marks Win 07–11; R Bentley, Binsted and Froyle from 11. Holy Cross Vicarage, Church Street, Binsted, Alton GU34 4NX T: (01420) 23339 M: 07777-684533 E: yann@benbinfro.org

DUCE, Ms Catherine Veronica. b 81. Newc Univ BA 04 MA 05 Heythrop Coll Lon MA 11 Fitzw Coll Cam BTh 14. Westcott Ho Cam 12. d 15 p 16. C Westmr St Steph w St Jo Lon from 15. Flat C, 16 Hide Place, London SW1P 4NJ M: 07948-980024 E: curate@sswsj.org

DUCKERS, Miss Linda Jean. b 62. Univ of Wales (Abth) BSc 84 PGCE 85 Rob Coll Cam BTh 06. Ridley Hall Cam 04. d 06 p 07. C Leek and Meerbrook Lich 06–10; TV Warwick Cov from 10. St Nicholas' Vicarage, 184 Myton Road, Warwick CV34 6PS T: (01926) 496209 E: linda.duckers@gmail.com or linda.stnicswarwick@gmail.com

DUCKERS, Paul Gerrard. b 42. Qu Coll Birm 07. **d** 09 **p** 10. NSM Sutton Coldfield H Trin *Birm* 09–12; PtO from 12. *5 Moor Meadow Road, Sutton Coldfield B75 6BU* T: 0121-378 1835 E: paulduckers@talktalk.net

DUCKETT, Canon Brian John. b 45. ALCD 70. **d** 70 **p** 71. C S Lambeth St Steph *S'wark* 70–73; C Norwood St Luke 73–75; C Bushbury *Lich* 75–77; TV 77–79; V Dover St Martin *Cant* 79–92; TR Swindon Dorcan *Bris* 92–00; RD Highworth 95–99; V Clifton H Trin, St Andr and St Pet 00–09; Vulnerable Adults Policy Officer 07–09; Hon Can Bris Cathl 98–09; rtd 09; PtO *Chich* from 14. *52 The Fieldings, Southwater, Horsham RH13 9LZ* T: (01403) 733417

DUCKETT, Edward. b 36. Keble Coll Ox BA 59 MA 61 Portsm Poly CQSW 72. Cuddesdon Coll 59. **d** 61 **p** 62. C Portsea St Cuth *Portsm* 61–65; C Rotherham *Sheff* 65–68; LtO *Portsm* 68–69; Hon Chapl Portsm Cathl 69–75; PtO *Ely* 75–82; R Rampton 82–89; R Willingham 82–89; RD N Stowe 83–89; P-in-c Ramsey 89–90; P-in-c Upwood w Gt and Lt Raveley 89–90; TR The Ramseys and Upwood 90–92; RD St Ives 89–92; P-in-c Bassingbourn 93–95; V 95–96; P-in-c Whaddon 93–95; V 95–96; rtd 96. *3 Lancing Close, Battenhall, Worcester WR5 2HT* T: (01905) 357607

DUCKETT, Ms Helen Lorraine. b 71. Keble Coll Ox BA 92 Sheff Univ MA 94 Birm Univ MPhil 98. Qu Coll Birm 95. **d** 98 **p** 99. C Cannock *Lich* 98–01; TV Wednesfield 01–10; TV Cen Wolverhampton 10–14; Chapl K Sch Wolv 15–18; TV Bentley Em and Willenhall H Trin *Lich* from 16. *167 Colman Avenue, Wolverhampton WV11 3RU* T: (01902) 258862 E: revhelen.duckett@gmail.com

DUCKETT, John Dollings. b 41. Nottm Univ BA 62 BTh 81. Linc Th Coll 79. **d** 81 **p** 82. C Boston *Linc* 81–84; V Baston 84–86; V Langtoft Gp 86–88; V Sutterton and Wigtoft 88–89; R Sutterton w Fosdyke and Algarkirk 89–92; P-in-c Chapel St Leonards w Hogsthorpe 92–97; V 97–00; V Bracebridge 00–06; rtd 06; PtO *Linc* 15–18. *Old Post Office, Faldingworth Road, Spridlington, Market Rasen LN8 2DF* T: (01673) 860116

DUCKETT, Keith Alexander. b 69. Worc Coll of HE BA 93. Qu Coll Birm BD 97 MA 98. **d** 98 **p** 99. C Willenhall H Trin *Lich* 98–01; TV Blakenall Heath 01–03; Asst Chapl Sandwell and W Birm Hosps NHS Trust 03–06; Chapl 06–13; Chapl K Sch Wolv 12–15; Spiritual Care Lead John Taylor Hospice Birm 13; Chapl Karis Neighbour Scheme 15–16; C Oxley and Wednesfield St Greg *Lich* 15–16; Chapl Walsall Healthcare NHS Trust from 16; PtO *Birm* 16–17. *Walsall Palliative Care Centre, Goscote Lane, Walsall WS3 1SJ* M: 07972-525140 E: keith.duckett@sky.com

DUCKETT, Lee Christopher James. b 67. Wycliffe Hall Ox BTh 04. **d** 04 **p** 05. C Cranham Park *Chelmsf* 04–08; C Purley Ch Ch *S'wark* 08–12; V Ore Ch Ch *Chich* from 12. *103 Fairlight Road, Hastings TN35 5EJ* T: (01424) 429745 M: 07979-191747 E: lee@christchurchore.org

DUCKETT, Matthew Robert. b 64. UEA BSc 85 PGCE 88. NTMTC BA 09. **d** 09 **p** 10. NSM Old St Pancras *Lon* 09–13; P-in-c Friern Barnet St Pet le Poer 13–18; P-in-c Colindale St Matthias from 18. *St Matthias' Vicarage, 48 Rushgrove Avenue, London NW9 6QY* E: matthew_duckett@yahoo.co.uk

DUCKETT, Raphael Thomas Marie James. b 65. N Staffs Poly BA 87. Cranmer Hall Dur 01. **d** 03 **p** 04. C Madeley *Heref* 03–06; V Bradley St Martin *Lich* 06–19; Chapl RN from 19. *Royal Naval Chaplaincy Service, Mail Point 1-2, Leach Building, Whale Island, Portsmouth PO2 8BY* T: (023) 9262 5055 F: 9262 5134 E: revraphael@blueyonder.co.uk

DUCKWORTH, Angela Denise. See WATTS, Angela Denise

DUCKWORTH, Annette Jacqueline. b 54. Univ of Wales (Ban) BSc 75 PGCE 76. **d** 00 **p** 01. OLM Moxley *Lich* 00–14; OLM Darlaston and Moxley from 14; Chapl Blue Coat Comp Sch Walsall 07–10. *1 Sutton Road, Wednesbury WS10 8SG* E: annette.duckworth@hotmail.co.uk

DUCKWORTH, Brian George. b 47. Edin Th Coll 85. **d** 87 **p** 88. C Sutton in Ashfield St Mary *S'well* 87–95; C Sutton in Ashfield St Mich 89–95; P-in-c 95–98; TV Hucknall Torkard 98–03; R S Ockendon and Belhus Park *Chelmsf* 03–12; rtd 12; PtO *Cant* from 13. *24 Aspen Drive, Whitfield, Dover CT16 2EX* T: (01304) 827239 E: brian289@btinternet.com

DUDDLES (formerly MOORES), Samantha Jane. b 73. Man Metrop Univ BEd 96 Southn Univ MSc 01. Ripon Coll Cuddesdon. **d** 12 **p** 14. C Upper Dever *Win* 12–16; TV Portsea N End St Mark *Portsm* from 16. *St Peter's Vicarage, Playfair Road, Southsea PO5 1EQ* T: (023) 9307 0133 M: 07740-505271 E: samduddles@gmail.com

DUDGEON, Christopher Patrick. b 63. Portsm Poly BSc 86 Univ Coll Lon MSc 87. St Mellitus Coll 16. **d** 18 **p** 19. NSM N Hants Downs *Win* from 18. *43 High Street, Odiham, Hook RG29 1LF* T: (01256) 702918 M: 07810-544495 E: chrisdudgeon90@gmail.com

DUDLEY (formerly MORTIMER), Mrs Elizabeth Anne. b 69. RGN 92. Ripon Coll Cuddesdon 05. **d** 07 **p** 08. C Minehead *B & W* 07–10; P-in-c Castle Cary and Ansford from 10; RD Bruton and Cary from 16. *The Vicarage, Church Street, Castle Cary BA7 7EJ* T: (01963) 351615 E: fr.liz@talktalk.net *or* standrews.allsaints@gmail.com

DUDLEY, Mrs Janet Carr. b 36. EMMTC 86. **d** 89 **p** 94. NSM Countesthorpe w Foston *Leic* 89–94; NSM Arnesby w Shearsby and Bruntingthorpe 94–01; rtd 01; PtO *Leic* 01–02 and from 10; NSM Market Harborough and The Transfiguration etc 02–10. *13 The Broadway, Market Harborough LE16 7LZ* T: (01858) 467619

DUDLEY, John Donald Swanborough. b 34. Ox Univ BTh 95. SAOMC 96. **d** 97 **p** 98. NSM Emmer Green *Ox* 97–02; PtO from 02. *26 Russet Glade, Emmer Green, Reading RG4 8UJ* T/F: 0118-954 6664 E: johnd@stmparish.org.uk

DUDLEY, Ms Josephine. b 52. ERMC 04. **d** 06 **p** 07. NSM Tolleshunt Knights w Tiptree and Gt Braxted *Chelmsf* 06–11; P-in-c Lonan *S & M* 11–14; P-in-c Laxey 11–14; TV Onchan, Lonan and Laxey from 14. *The Vicarage, 56 Ard Reayrt, Ramsey Road, Laxey, Isle of Man IM4 7QQ* T: (01624) 861989 M: 07704-431790 E: jodudley56@gmail.com

DUDLEY, Martin Raymond. b 53. K Coll Lon BD 77 AKC 77 MTh 78 PhD 94 City Univ MSc 07 Hon DArts 14 FRHistS 95 FSA 97. St Mich Coll Llan 78. **d** 79 **p** 80. C Whitchurch *Llan* 79–83; V Weston *St Alb* 83–88; P-in-c Ardeley 87–88; V Owlsmoor *Ox* 88–95; Lect Simon of Cyrene Th Inst 92–95; R Smithfield St Bart Gt *Lon* 95–15; P-in-c St Bart Less 12–15; R Smithfield Gt St Bart 15–16; rtd 17; Hon Research Fell Qu Foundn Birm from 17. *13D Pitsford Street, Birmingham B18 6LJ* T: 0121-523 5708 M: 07957-246461 E: martin.dudley@btinternet.com

DUDLEY, Wendy Elizabeth. *See* KEAY, Wendy Elizabeth

DUDLEY-SMITH, James. b 66. Fitzw Coll Cam BA 89 MA 92. Wycliffe Hall Ox BTh 94. **d** 97 **p** 98. C New Borough and Leigh *Sarum* 97–01; C Hove Bp Hannington Memorial Ch *Chich* 01–06; R Yeovil w Kingston Pitney *B & W* from 06; RD Yeovil from 15. *The Rectory, 41 The Park, Yeovil BA20 1DG* T: (01935) 475352 E: jamesds100@outlook.com

✠**DUDLEY-SMITH, The Rt Revd Timothy.** b 26. Pemb Coll Cam BA 47 MA 51 Lambeth MLitt 91 Dur Univ Hon DD 09. Ridley Hall Cam 48. **d** 50 **p** 51 **c** 81. C Erith St Paul *Roch* 50–53; LtO *S'wark* 53–62; hd of Cam Univ Miss Bermondsey 53-55; Chapl 55–60; Ed Sec Evang Alliance and Ed Crusade 55–59; Asst Sec CPAS 59–65; Gen Sec 65–73; Adn Nor 73–81; Suff Bp Thetford 81–91; rtd 92; PtO *Sarum* from 12. *38 The Eights Marina, Mariner's Way, Cambridge CB4 1ZA*

DUDLEY, Archdeacon of. *See* GROARKE, The Ven Nicola Jane

DUDLEY, Suffragan Bishop of. *Vacant*

DUERDEN, Martin James. b 55. Liv Poly BA 77. Oak Hill Th Coll 86. **d** 88 **p** 89. C Tunbridge Wells St Jas *Roch* 88–92; V Southport SS Simon and Jude *Liv* 92–98; P-in-c Maghull 98–02; TR 02–07; P-in-c Marsh Green w Newtown 07; V 08–13; V Salesbury *Blackb* from 13; Hon C Langho Billington 13–16. *St Peter's Vicarage, 49A Ribchester Road, Blackburn BB1 9HU* T: (01254) 248072 E: martinduerden@hotmail.com

DUERR, Robert Kenneth. b 54. Univ of S California BMus 77 MMus 80. Ridley Hall Cam 99. **d** 04 **p** 06. NSM Cambridge Gt St Mary w St Mich *Ely* 04–05; C Marton-in-Cleveland *York* 06–07; C Scarborough St Martin and Scarborough St Sav w All SS 07–10. *258 Christiana Street, North Tonawanda NY 14120, USA* M: (001) (904) 671 2916 E: robert@robertduerr.com

DUFF, Alison. *See* FINCH, Alison

DUFF, Andrew John. b 57. Open Univ BSc 07. Sarum & Wells Th Coll 92. **d** 92 **p** 93. C Banbury *Ox* 92–95; C Bracknell 95–96; TV 96–98; CF 98–04; Chapl RN 04–12; rtd 12; PtO *Worc* from 12; *Glas* from 17. *50 Alyssum Crescent, Motherwell ML1 1DF*

DUFF, Miss Emma Cameron. b 73. St Andr Univ MA 95 Solicitor 99. Qu Coll Birm 12. **d** 14 **p** 15. C Willington *Newc* 14–18; C Wallsend St Jo from 18. *2 Burlington Court, Wallsend NE28 9YH* T: 0191-257 2405 E: eduff.willington@gmail.com

DUFF, Jeremy. b 71. MA DPhil. **d** 06 **p** 07. NSM Toxteth St Philemon w St Gabr and St Cleopas *Liv* 06–10; Dir Lifelong Learning and Can Liv Cathl 04–10; TV S Widnes *Liv* 10–16; Prin St Padarn's Inst from 16. *St Michael's Centre, 54 Cardiff Road, Llandaff, Cardiff CF5 2YJ* T: (029) 2056 3379 E: jeremy.duff@stpadarns.ac.uk

✠**DUFF, The Rt Revd Jillian Louise Calland.** b 72. Ch Coll Cam BA 93 MA 97 Worc Coll Ox DPhil 96. Wycliffe Hall Ox BA 02 MA 06. **d** 03 **p** 04 **c** 18. C Litherland St Phil *Liv* 03–05; Lic to Adn Liv 05–11; Chapl Liv Coll 09–16; Dir Tr for IME 2 and Dioc Voc Adv *Liv* 11–18; Dir St Mellitus NW 13–18; Suff Bp Lancaster *Blackb* from 18;

PtO *Liv* from 13; *Ches* from 17; *St As* from 18. *6 Marford Heights, Wrexham LL12 8TJ* E: jillduff@btinternet.com *or* bishop.lancaster@blackburn.anglican.org

DUFF, John Alexander. b 57. York Univ BA 78. EMMTC 91. **d** 94 **p** 95. NSM Linc St Geo Swallowbeck 94–00; PtO *Ripon* 02–14; *Leeds* from 14. *1 Butterbur Way, Harrogate HG3 2XH* T: (01423) 549987 M: 07788-432009 E: ffudnhoj@hotmail.com

DUFF, Michael Ian. b 63. Ox Univ BA 85. Trin Coll Bris BA 98 MA 99. **d** 99 **p** 00. C Southsea St Jude *Portsm* 99–03; CMS Bandung Indonesia 03–07; V Southsea St Jude *Portsm* 07–19; Hon Can Portsm Cathl 17–19. *Address temp unknown* E: all@theduffs.me.uk

DUFF, Timothy Cameron. b 40. G&C Coll Cam BA 62 LLM 63 MA 66 Solicitor 65. NEOC 90. **d** 93 **p** 94. NSM Tynemouth Priory *Newc* 93–96; NSM N Shields 96–05; TV 00–05; rtd 05; PtO *Newc* from 05. *24A Percy Gardens, Tynemouth, North Shields NE30 4HQ* T: 0191-257 1463 E: timothy@timothyduff.co.uk

DUFFELL, Lucy Margaret. See GARDNER, Lucy Margaret

DUFFETT-SMITH (née RUSHTON), Ms Patricia Mary. Lon Univ BPharm 76 Anglia Poly Univ MA 99 MRPharmS 77. EAMTC 94. **d** 97 **p** 98. NSM Haddenham and Wilburton *Ely* 97–00; Asst Chapl Hinchingbrooke Health Care NHS Trust 99–17; Asst Chapl NW Anglia NHS Foundn Trust from 17. *Address withheld by request* M: 07788-668900 E: trishads@gmail.com *or* trishads@googlemail.com

DUFFIELD, Ian Keith. b 47. K Coll Lon BD 71 AKC 71 MTh 73. NY Th Sem DMin 84. **d** 73 **p** 74. C Broxbourne *St Alb* 73–77; C Harpenden St Nic 77–81; TV Sheff Manor 81–87; V Walkley 87–02; V Sheff St Leon Norwood 02–13; rtd 13; PtO *Sheff* from 14. *17 Springwell Drive, Beighton, Sheffield S20 1XA*

DUFFIELD, Ronald Bertram Charles. b 26. Hull Univ Coll BA 49 TCert 50. Sarum & Wells Th Coll 91. **d** 92 **p** 93. NSM E Knoyle, Semley and Sedgehill *Sarum* 92–94; P-in-c 94–95; rtd 95; PtO *York* 95–99 and from 01; P-in-c Isfield *Chich* 99–01. *8 Beechdale, Cottingham HU16 4RH* T: (01482) 845086

DUFFUS, Barbara Rose. See HOBBS, Barbara Rose

DUFFY, Jennifer-Ann Lesley. b 71. Qu Foundn Birm 16. **d** 19. NSM Empingham, Edith Weston, Lyndon, Manton etc *Pet* from 19. *Lavender Cottage, 2 Water Lane, Ashwell, Oakham LE15 7LS* T: (01572) 720064 E: curate.rwb@gmail.com

DUGDALE, Angela Marion. b 33. ARCM 52 GRSM 54 UEA Hon MA 89. **d** 97 **p** 98. OLM Weybourne Gp *Nor* 97–03; rtd 03; PtO *Nor* from 03. *The Old Carpenter's Shop, Kelling, Holt NR25 7EL* T: (01263) 588389 F: 588594 E: dugdale@freeuk.com

DUGMORE, The Ven Barry John. b 61. STETS. **d** 01 **p** 02. C Cowplain *Portsm* 01–04; C-in-c Whiteley CD and Dioc Ecum Officer 04–07; P-in-c Tiverton St Geo and St Paul *Ex* 07–15; RD Tiverton and Cullompton 12–15; Dioc Miss Enabler 15–19; Adn Warwick *Cov* from 19. *Cathedral and Diocesan Office, 1 Hill Top, Coventry CV1 5AB* T: (024) 7652 1337 E: b.dugmore@ukgateway.net

DUGUID, Alison Audrey. b 52. STETS 99. **d** 02 **p** 03. C Appledore w Brookland, Fairfield, Brenzett etc *Cant* 02–06; P-in-c The Brents and Davington w Oare and Luddenham 06–12; P-in-c Eastling w Ospringe and Stalisfield w Otterden 06–12; V Marden from 12; Dir Dioc Poverty and Hope Appeal from 07; AD Weald 14–16. *The Vicarage, Haffenden Close, Marden, Tonbridge TN12 9DR* T: (01622) 831890 E: ali@dogooders.co.uk

DUKE, Canon Alan Arthur. b 38. Tyndale Hall Bris 59. **d** 64 **p** 65. C Whalley Range St Marg *Man* 64–67; C Folkestone H Trin w Ch Ch *Cant* 67–71; V Queenborough 71–76; V Bearsted w Thurnham 76–86; P-in-c Torquay St Luke *Ex* 86–91; R Barham w Bishopsbourne and Kingston *Cant* 91–00; Dioc Communications Officer 91–95; Hon Can Cant Cathl 99–03; Chapl to Bp Dover 00–03; Bp's Media Link Officer 00–03; rtd 03; PtO *Cant* from 03. *Roundways, Derringstone Hill, Barham, Canterbury CT4 6QD* T: (01227) 831817 F: 784985 M: 07751-833670 E: nail@alanaduke.com

DUKE, David Malcolm. b 40. Ch Ch Ox BA 61 MA 65 Newc Poly MPhil 80 CQSW 81. Cuddesdon Coll 63. **d** 65 **p** 66. C Sunderland Pennywell St Thos *Dur* 65–68; C Dur St Oswald 68–70; C Harton 70–74; PtO 85–96; Hon C Hedworth 96–13; Hon C The Boldons from 13. *43 Coquet Street, Jarrow NE32 5SW* T: 0191-430 1200 F: 537 4409 M: 07979-036977 E: david.duke@sky.com

DUKE, Miss Judith Mary. b 47. Leeds Univ LLB 68. Cranmer Hall Dur 03. **d** 04 **p** 05. NSM Buckrose Carrs *York* 04–07; R 07–12; rtd 12; PtO *York* from 13. *13 Sledgate Garth, Rillington, Malton YO17 8JS* T: (01944) 758408 E: judithduke347@btinternet.com

DULFER, John Guidi. b 37. Lich Th Coll 62. **d** 64 **p** 65. C Fenny Stratford and Water Eaton *Ox* 64–67; C Cheshunt *St Alb* 67–68; C Kennington Cross St Anselm *S'wark* 68–73; C N Lambeth 74–76; P-in-c Kensington St Phil Earl's Court *Lon* 76–79; V 79–84; V Jersey City St Jo & Jersey City St Matt USA 84–85; R New York Resurr 00–01; P-in-c Castleton 02–06. *110 West 15 Street, Apartment 1, New York NY 10011-6724, USA* E: johndulfer@hotmail.com

DULLEY, Priscilla Mary. b 72. St Aug Coll of Th 14. **d** 17 **p** 18. C Hythe *Cant* from 17. *23 Nursery Fields, Hythe CT21 4DL*

DUMAT, Mrs Jennifer. b 42. ARCM 62. Qu Coll Birm 80 EMMTC 82. **dss** 83 **d** 87 **p** 94. Chapl Asst Pilgrim Hosp Boston 83–94; P-in-c Friskney *Linc* 94–04; rtd 04; PtO *Linc* from 16. *11 Sea Lane, Butterwick, Boston PE22 0EY* T: (01205) 760883

DUMBRECK, Geoffrey James William. b 84. Peterho Cam BA 05 MA 09 MPhil 06 PhD 10. Ripon Coll Cuddesdon MTh 13. **d** 13 **p** 14. C Cambridge Ascension *Ely* 13–17; Asst Chapl Peterho Cam 15–19; Acting Dean 17–18; V S Croydon St Pet and St Aug *S'wark* from 19. *20 Haling Park Road, South Croydon CR2 6NE* T: (020) 8688 4715 M: 07727-968985 E: geoff.dumbreck@gmail.com

DUNCAN, Mrs Amanda Jayne. b 58. Balls Park Coll Hertford BEd 79. ERMC 08. **d** 11 **p** 12. C Harpenden St Jo *St Alb* 11–15; TV Bp's Hatfield, Lemsford and N Mymms 15–18; V High Cross from 18; V Thundridge from 18. *St Mary's House, Church Lane, Stapleford, Hertford SG14 3NB* T: (01992) 731904 M: 07506-715026 E: amanda.duncan2387@gmail.com

DUNCAN, Canon Bruce. b 38. Leeds Univ BA 60 FRSA. Cuddesdon Coll 65. **d** 67 **p** 68. C Armley St Bart *Ripon* 67–69; Dir Children's Relief Internat 69–71; Hon C Cambridge St Mary Less *Ely* 69–70; Chapl OHP and St Hilda's Sch Whitby 70–71; Chapl Vienna w Budapest and Prague *Eur* 71–75; V Crediton *Ex* 75–82; R Crediton and Shobrooke 82–86; RD Cadbury 76–81 and 84–86; Can Res Man Cathl 86–95; Prin Sarum Coll and Can and Preb Sarum Cathl 95–02; rtd 02; Chapl Ex Univ 03–04; PtO 02–08; *Sarum* from 08; *Eur* from 10; Hon C Salisbury St Martin and Laverstock *Sarum* 10–13; Hon C Salisbury St Martin 13–15. *92 Harnham Road, Salisbury SP2 8JW* T: (01722) 502227 M: 07851-737230 E: canon.duncan@gmail.com

DUNCAN, Christopher Robin. b 41. AKC 71. **d** 72 **p** 73. C Allington *Cant* 72–73; C Allington and Maidstone St Pet 73–77; P-in-c Wittersham 77–82; R Wittersham w Stone and Ebony 82–85; V Chilham 85–92; P-in-c Challock w Molash 87–92; V Chilham w Challock and Molash 92–11; RD W Bridge 92–95 and 02–03; rtd 12; PtO *Cant* from 12. *173 Shalmsford Street, Chartham, Canterbury CT4 7QP* T: (01227) 733813 E: rev.chris.duncan@gmail.com

DUNCAN, Colin Richard. b 34. SS Coll Cam BA 58 MA 60. Ripon Coll Cuddesdon 83. **d** 85 **p** 86. C Stafford *Lich* 85–89; C Wednesfield 89–90; TV 90–99; rtd 99; PtO *Glouc* 99–16; *B & W* 13–18. *92 Kingfisher Road, Portishead, Bristol BS20 7QD* T: (01275) 818607 M: 07891-528295 E: duncan.firtree@tiscali.co.uk

✠**DUNCAN, The Rt Revd Gregor Duthie.** b 50. Glas Univ MA 72 Clare Coll Cam PhD 77 Oriel Coll Ox BA 83. Ripon Coll Cuddesdon 81. **d** 83 **p** 84 **c** 10. C Oakham, Hambleton, Egleton, Braunston and Brooke *Pet* 83–86; Chapl Edin Th Coll 87–89; R Largs *Glas* 89–99; Dean Glas 96–10; R Glas St Ninian 99–10; Bp Glas 10–18; rtd 18; LtO *Glas* from 18. *3 Golf Road, Rutherglen, Glasgow G73 4JW*

DUNCAN, The Ven John Finch. b 33. Univ Coll Ox BA 57 MA 63. Cuddesdon Coll 57. **d** 59 **p** 60. C S Bank *York* 59–61; SSF 61–62; C Birm St Pet 62–65; Chapl Birm Univ 65–76; V Kings Heath 76–85; Hon Can Birm Cathl 83–85; Adn Birm 85–01; rtd 01; PtO *Birm* 01–18; *Pet* from 01. *66 Glebe Rise, King's Sutton, Banbury OX17 3PH* T: (01295) 812641 E: jfduncan66@gmail.com

DUNCAN, Richard William. b 87. Ch Coll Cam BA 09. Wycliffe Hall Ox BTh 15. **d** 16 **p** 17. C Moulton *Pet* 16–19; V Brackley St Pet w St Jas from 19. *The Vicarage, Old Town, Brackley NN13 7BZ* T: (01280) 702767 M: 07985-315034 E: richduncan100@gmail.com *or* brackleyvicar@gmail.com

DUNCAN, Thomas James. b 37. **d** 97 **p** 98. NSM Poplar *Lon* 97–17; PtO from 17. *1 Chardwell Close, London E6 5RR* T: (020) 7538 9198 *or* 7476 6465 M: 07732-666434 E: duncant1@sky.com

DUNCANSON, Derek James. b 47. AKC 69 Open Univ BA 80 Lon Univ MA(Ed) 93 FCollP 94. St Aug Coll Cant 69. **d** 70 **p** 71. C Norbury St Oswald *Cant* 70–72; CF (TAVR) 71–76 and 79–95; C Woodham *Guildf* 72–76; CF 76–79; V Burneside *Carl* 79–84; R Coppull St Jo *Blackb* 84–86; Chapl Bloxham Sch 86–99; V Pet St Mary Boongate 99–04; RD Pet 01–04; Chapl Pet Regional Coll 00–04; Chapl Heathfield Sch Ascot 04–08; rtd 08; PtO *Cant* from 08. *Old Forge Cottage, 235*

Canterbury Road, Birchington CT7 9TB T: (01843) 843289
E: dmduncanson@btinternet.com

DUNDAS, The Ven Edward Paul. b 67. NUU BSc 88. TCD Div Sch BTh 91. **d** 91 **p** 92. C Portadown St Mark *Arm* 91–95; I Ardtrea w Desertcreat 95–00; Dioc Youth Adv to Abp Armagh 99–00; I Belfast St Aid *Conn* 00–05; I Lisburn Ch Ch from 05; Adn Dalriada from 18. *Christ Church Rectory, 27 Hillsborough Road, Lisburn BT28 1JL* T: (028) 9266 2163 *or* 9267 3271 M: 07740-589465 E: paul_dundas@yahoo.com

DUNDAS, Gary Walter. b 56. EMMTC 04. **d** 07 **p** 08. NSM Stanton-by-Dale w Dale Abbey and Risley *Derby* 07–14; NSM Wilne and Draycott w Breaston from 14. *17-19 Victoria Road, Draycott, Derby DE72 3PS* T: (01332) 872893 F: 875371 M: 07971-783083 E: gdundas@aol.com

DUNDEE, Provost of. *See* AULD, The Very Revd Jeremy Rodger

DUNGAN, Hilary Anne. b 46. TCD BA 98 ARCM 68. CITC 98. **d** 00 **p** 01. C Arm St Mark 00–03; I Maryborough w Dysart Enos and Ballyfin *C & O* 03–11; Chapl Midlands and Portlaoise Pris 03–11; Chapl Midland Regional Hosp Portlaoise 03–11; rtd 11. *46 The Drive, Woodbrook Glen, Bray, Co Dublin, Republic of Ireland* T: (00353) (1) 200 5959 M: 087-6418125 E: hildungan@gmail.com

DUNGAN, Ivan Francis. b 49. CITC 06. **d** 09 **p** 10. NSM Bunclody w Kildavin, Clonegal and Kilrush *C & O* 09–14; NSM Ferns w Kilbride, Toombe, Kilcormack etc 14–16; P-in-c New w Old Ross, Whitechurch, Fethard etc 16–19; rtd 19. *Brookhaven, Lower Southknock, New Ross, Co Wexford, Republic of Ireland* T: (00353) (51) 422281 E: ivandungan@gmail.com

DUNHAM, Angela Mary. *See* CHEESEMAN, Angela Mary

DUNK, Mrs Carol Ann. b 65. EMMTC 08. **d** 11 **p** 13. NSM Retford Area *S'well* 11–12; NSM Tuxford w Weston, Markham Clinton etc 12–15; NSM Ollerton w Boughton 15–16; C Fleet *Guildf* from 16. *38 Oasthouse Drive, Fleet GU51 2UL* T: (01252) 444872 M: 07896-945636 E: dunkabiscuit@talktalk.net *or* carol@parishoffleet.org.uk

DUNK, Michael Robin. b 43. Oak Hill Th Coll BA 82. **d** 82 **p** 83. C Northampton All SS w St Kath *Pet* 82–86; Ind Chapl *Birm* 86–96; P-in-c Warley Woods 96; V 96–08; AD Warley 01–06; rtd 08; Hon C Shepshed and Oaks in Charnwood *Leic* 08–10; PtO *Birm* 11–14; *Guildf* from 15. *Glenesk, Church Street, Ewell, Epsom KT17 2AQ* T: (020) 3609 8013 E: michael.dunk@talk21.com

DUNKLEY, Canon Christopher. b 52. Edin Univ MA 74 Ox Univ BA 77 MA 81. St Steph Ho Ox 75. **d** 78 **p** 79. C Newbold w Dunston *Derby* 78–82; C Chesterfield St Mary and All SS 82; Chapl Leic Univ 82–85; TV Leic Ascension 85–92; Chapl Leics Hospice 85–87; V Leic St Aid 92–97; V Holbrooks *Cov* 97–16; Hon Can Cov Cathl 07–16; rtd 16. *79 Trueway Drive South, Shepshed, Loughborough LE12 9DY*

DUNLOP, Andrew James. b 76. Collingwood Coll Dur BSc 97 MA 16 PGCE 98. Wycliffe Hall Ox BTh 07. **d** 07 **p** 08. C Plymouth St Andr and Stonehouse *Ex* 07–10; Pioneer Min Gtr Northampton Deanery *Pet* 10–15; TV Duston 15; Tutor Cranmer Hall Dur 15–18; P Missr E Dur Miss Project 15–18; Tutor Ridley Hall Cam from 18. *Ridley Hall, Ridley Hall Road, Cambridge CB3 9HG* T: (01223) 741074 E: ajd232@cam.ac.uk

DUNLOP, Mrs Anne Cecilia. b 50. **d** 14 **p** 15. NSM Ex St Thos and Em 14–17; PV Ex Cathl 17. *14 Otterbourne Court, 6 Coastguard Road, Budleigh Salterton EX9 6HB* T: (01395) 446458 M: 07929-571522 E: revannedunlop@gmail.com

DUNLOP, Brian Kenneth Charles. b 49. Ex Univ BSc 73. WEMTC 07. **d** 10 **p** 11. NSM S Cheltenham *Glouc* 10–19; rtd 19. *31 Pickering Road, Cheltenham GL53 0LF* T: (01242) 515807 E: dogcollar@quinweb.net

DUNLOP, Mrs Frances Jane. b 57. New Hall Cam MA 82 ACA 84. STETS 06. **d** 09 **p** 10. NSM Clarendon *Sarum* from 09. *Little Paddock, Romsey Road, Whiteparish, Salisbury SP5 2SD* T: (01794) 884793 M: 07795-836653 E: fjdunlop@hotmail.com

DUNLOP, Jennifer Mary. b 51. Hull Univ LLB 72 Solicitor 73. Yorks Min Course 13. **d** 15 **p** 16. NSM Dukinfield St Mark *Ches* from 15. *180A Dowson Road, Hyde SK14 5BW* T: 0161-368 2149 E: revjenny15@gmail.com

DUNLOP, Neil Stuart. b 78. Qu Coll Birm. **d** 10 **p** 11. C Lighthorne *Cov* 10–12; C Newbold Pacey w Moreton Morrell 10–12; C Chesterton 10–12; Chapl N Warks and Hinckley Coll of FE 13–16; C Arden Marches *Cov* 13–16; R Alveley and Quatt *Heref* from 16. *The Rectory, Alveley, Bridgnorth WV15 6ND* T: (01746) 780882 E: nsdunlop@gmail.com

DUNLOP, Peter John. b 44. TCD BA 68 MA 72 Dur Univ CertEd 71. Cranmer Hall Dur. **d** 71 **p** 72. C Barking St Marg w St Patr *Chelmsf* 71–75; C Gt Malvern Ch Ch *Worc* 75–78; Chapl K Sch Tynemouth 78–89; V Monkseaton St Pet *Newc*

90–96; rtd 96; PtO *Newc* from 96. *19 Cliftonville Gardens, Whitley Bay NE26 1QJ* T: 0191-251 0983

DUNN, Canon Alastair Matthew Crusoe. b 40. Lon Univ LLB 64 AKC 64. Wycliffe Hall Ox 78. **d** 80 **p** 81. C Yardley St Edburgha *Birm* 80–83; R Bishop's Sutton and Ropley and W Tisted *Win* 83–90; V Milford 90–04; Hon Can Win Cathl 03–04; C Harrogate St Mark *Ripon* 04–05; Hon C 05–07; rtd 05; PtO *York* from 08. *13 Littlefield Close, Nether Poppleton, York YO26 6HX* T: (01904) 798487 E: asdunn@talk21.com

DUNN, David James. b 47. Leeds Univ CertEd 79 BA 82. Trin Coll Bris 88. **d** 90 **p** 91. C Magor w Redwick and Undy *Mon* 90–92; C St Mellons and Michaelston-y-Fedw 92–93; V Pontnewydd 93–11; P-in-c Llanfair Caereinion, Llanllugan and Manafon *St As* 11–16; rtd 16; Chapl Toc H from 90; PtO *St D* from 17; *Llan* from 17; *S & B* from 17. *100 Parc Gilbertson, Gelligron, Pontardawe, Swansea SA8 4PU* T: (01792) 862143 E: vicarddunn@btinternet.com

DUNN, Canon David Michael. b 47. AKC 70. St Aug Coll Cant 70. **d** 71 **p** 72. C Padgate *Liv* 71–74; C Halliwell St Marg *Man* 74–76; V Lever Bridge 76–84; V Bradshaw 84–01; TR Turton Moorland 01–12; Hon Can Man Cathl 12; rtd 12; PtO *Man* from 13. *1 Tottington Fold, Bolton BL2 4DX* T: (01204) 307199

DUNN, Derek William Robert. b 48. Open Univ BA 81 MA 01 Stranmillis Coll CertEd 70 AMusTCL 74 LTCL 75. **d** 85 **p** 87. Aux Min Carnalea *D & D* 85–97; Aux Min Bangor Abbey 97–05; C Ballymena w Ballyclug *Conn* 05–09; Bp's C Acton and Drumbanagher *Arm* from 09; V Choral Arm Cathl from 14. *Address temp unknown* M: 07745-584434 E: dwrdunn@gmail.com

DUNN, Florence Patricia. b 37. Ches Coll of HE BTh 02. NOC 99. **d** 02 **p** 03. NSM Basford *Lich* 02–17; PtO from 18. *213 Newcastle Road, Trent Vale, Stoke-on-Trent ST4 6PU* T: (01782) 846417 E: rev.patdunn@tesco.net

DUNN, John Frederick. b 44. Trin Coll Bris 71. **d** 74 **p** 75. C Carl St Jo 74–77; C Tooting Graveney St Nic *S'wark* 77–82; V Attleborough *Cov* 85; PtO *Cant* 86–02; V Tipton St Martin and St Paul *Lich* 02–14; rtd 14. *16 School Crescent, Godshill, Ventnor PO38 3JL*

DUNN, Julian. b 46. Open Univ BA 83. K Coll Lon 67 St Aug Coll Cant 70. **d** 71 **p** 72. C Hanworth All SS *Lon* 71–74; C Kidlington *Ox* 74–76; C-in-c Cleethorpes St Fran CD *Linc* 76–77; TV Cleethorpes 77–85; Chapl Friarage and Distr Hosp Northallerton 85–88; Chapl Broadmoor Hosp Crowthorne 88; Ind Chapl *York* 88–89; P-in-c Micklefield 88–89; PtO *Ox* from 95; rtd 11. *timbles brewery (sic), 1 Lewington Close, Great Haseley, Oxford OX44 7LS* T: (01844) 279687 E: eisendora@aol.com

DUNN (née LEE), Mrs Mary Elizabeth. b 49. Open Univ BA 81 Bp Grosseteste Coll CertEd 78. St Mich Coll Llan 08. **d** 09 **p** 10. NSM Malpas *Mon* 09–11; NSM Llanfair Caereinion, Llanllugan and Manafon *St As* 11–16; rtd 16; PtO *St D* from 17; *Llan* from 17; *S & B* from 17. *100 Parc Gilbertson, Gelligron, Pontardawe, Swansea SA8 4PU* T: (01792) 862143 E: ourmarylou@gmail.com

DUNN, Michael Henry James. b 34. Em Coll Cam BA 56 MA 62. Cuddesdon Coll 57 and 62. **d** 62 **p** 63. C Chatham St Steph *Roch* 62–66; C Bromley SS Pet and Paul 66–70; V Roch St Justus 70–83; P-in-c Malvern Wells and Wyche *Worc* 83–85; P-in-c Lt Malvern, Malvern Wells and Wyche 85–97; rtd 97. PtO *Worc* from 97. *253 Oldbury Road, Worcester WR2 6JT* T: (01905) 429938

DUNN, Pat. *See* DUNN, Florence Patricia

DUNN, Sharon Louise. *See* GOBLE, Sharon Louise

DUNN, Simon David. b 69. Trin Coll Bris BA 08. **d** 08 **p** 09. C Stoke Gifford *Bris* 08–11; TV Chippenham St Paul w Hardenhuish etc 11–14; P-in-c from 14; TV Kington St Michael 11–14. *Damsan House, Old Hardenhuish Lane, Chippenham SN14 6HH* T: (01249) 324944 M: 07904-733141 E: simon_dunn@hotmail.co.uk

DUNN, Canon Struan Huthwaite. b 43. Ch Coll Hobart 66 Moore Th Coll Sydney ThL 68 Clifton Th Coll 68. **d** 70 **p** 71. C Orpington Ch Ch *Roch* 70–74; C Cheltenham St Mary *Glouc* 74–76; C Welling *Roch* 76–79; Chapl Barcelona w Casteldefels *Eur* 79–83; R Addington w Trottiscliffe *Roch* 83–89; P-in-c Ryarsh w Birling 83–89; P-in-c S Gillingham 89–90; TR 90–96; RD Gillingham 91–96; R Meopham w Nurstead 96–08; Hon Can Roch Cathl 97–08; rtd 08; Chapl HM Pris Standford Hill 09–18; PtO *Cant* from 08; *Roch* from 08. *18 Blenheim Avenue, Faversham ME13 8NR* T: (01795) 531700 E: struanhdunn@talktalk.net

DUNNAN, Donald Stuart. b 59. Harvard Univ AB 80 AM 81 Ch Ch Ox BA 85 MA 90 DPhil 91. Gen Th Sem (NY) 86. **d** 86 **p** 87. USA 86–87; Lib Pusey Ho 87–89; LtO *Ox* 87–92; PtO *Cant* 87–92; Chapl Linc Coll Ox 90–92; USA from 92.

St James School, 17641 College Road, St James MD 21781-9900, USA E: dsdunnan@stjames.edu

DUNNE, The Very Revd Dermot Patrick Martin. b 59. Dub City Univ BA 04 MA 12. St Patr Coll Maynooth 78 CITC 98. **d** 83 **p** 84. In RC Ch 83–95; Dean's V Ch Ch Cathl Dublin *D & G* 99–01; I Crosspatrick Gp *C & O* 01–08; Prec Ferns Cathl 04–08; Adn Ferns 07–08; Dean Ch Ch Cathl Dublin *D & G* from 08. *Christ Church Deanery, Werburgh Street, Dublin 8, D08 WTC0, Republic of Ireland* T: (00353) (1) 677 8099 F: 679 8991 M: 87-986 5073 E: dean@christchurch.ie

DUNNE, Kevin Headley. b 43. Cranmer Hall Dur 85. **d** 87 **p** 88. C Chester le Street *Dur* 87–90; V S Hetton w Haswell 90–94; P-in-c Oxclose 94–02; R Chester le Street 02–08; AD Chester-le-Street 97–02 and 04–08; rtd 08; Chapl Sherburn Hosp Dur 09–13; PtO *Dur* from 13; Eur from 15. *7 Fir Tree Close, Durham DH1 1DT* T: 0191-375 0397 E: revdunne@btopenworld.com

DUNNE, The Very Revd Nigel Kenneth. b 66. TCD BA 88 BTh 90 MA 00 MPhil 00. **d** 90 **p** 91. C Dublin St Bart w Leeson Park *D & G* 90–93; C Taney 93–95; I Blessington w Kilbride, Ballymore Eustace etc 95–01; C Cork St Fin Barre's Cathl Dublin 01–03; I Bandon Union *C, C & R* 03–07; Dean Cork from 07; I Cork St Fin Barre's Union from 07. *The Deanery, Gilabbey Street, Cork, Republic of Ireland* T: (00353) (21) 431 8073 E: dean@cork.anglican.org

DUNNETT, John Frederick. b 58. SS Coll Cam MA 84 Worc Coll Ox MSc 83 CQSW 82. Trin Coll Bris BA 87. **d** 88 **p** 89. C Kirkheaton *Wakef* 88–93; V Cranham Park *Chelmsf* 93–06; Gen Dir CPAS from 06. *39 Crescent Road, Warley, Brentwood CM14 5JR* T: (01277) 221419 *or* (01926) 458427 E: jd@johndunnett.co.uk *or* jdunnett@cpas.org.uk

DUNNETT, Keith Owen. b 66. Cranfield Inst of Tech BSc 87. Trin Coll Bris BA 00. **d** 00 **p** 01. C Walton and Trimley *St E* 00–03; V Clayton *Bradf* 03–11; C Abingdon *Ox* 11–13; C N Abingdon 13–18; V from 18. *33 North Avenue, Abingdon OX14 1QW* M: 07974-081354 E: keith@cca.uk.net

DUNNETT, Nigella. *See* YOUNGS-DUNNETT, Elizabeth Nigella

DUNNETT, Robert Curtis. b 31. SS Coll Cam BA 54 MA 58. Oak Hill Th Coll 56. **d** 58 **p** 59. C Markfield *Leic* 58–60; C Bucknall and Bagnall *Lich* 60–73; Chapl and Tutor Birm Bible Inst 72–79; Vice-Prin 84–92; Hon Vice-Prin 92–05; PtO *Birm* 72–16; *Truro* from 16. *Potters Garden, Polcoverack Lane, Coverack, Helston TR12 6TD* T: (01362) 280964 E: dunnett670@btinternet.com

DUNNING, Adam Jonathan. b 73. Regent's Park Coll Ox BA 95 MA 99 Birm Univ PhD 00 Wolv Univ CertEd 05. Westcott Ho Cam 97. **d** 99 **p** 00. C Evesham w Norton and Lenchwick *Worc* 99–02; C Hamstead St Paul *Birm* 02–03; Hon C Moseley St Mary and Moseley St Anne 03–05; P-in-c The Ortons, Alwalton and Chesterton *Ely* 06–10; V Orton Longueville w Bottlebridge 10–11; Sen Chapl Cheltenham Coll from 11. *4 Waterfield Close, Cheltenham GL53 7NL* T: (01242) 228774 M: 07970-503909 E: a.dunning@cheltenhamcollege.org

DUNNINGS, Reuben Edward. b 36. Clifton Th Coll 62. **d** 66 **p** 67. C Longfleet *Sarum* 66–70; C Melksham 70–73; TV 73–78; R Broughton Gifford w Gt Chalfield 78–84; V Holt St Kath 78–84; R Broughton Gifford, Gt Chalfield and Holt 85–86; V Salisbury St Fran 86–99; P-in-c Stratford sub Castle 98–99; V Salisbury St Fran and Stratford sub Castle 99–01; rtd 01; PtO *Sarum* from 01. *11 Cornbrash Rise, Hilperton, Trowbridge BA14 7TS* T: (01225) 768834 E: reubendunnings@talktalk.net

DUNSETH, George William. b 52. Multnomah Sch of the Bible Oregon BRE 79. Oak Hill Th Coll BA 85. **d** 85 **p** 86. C Cheadle All Hallows *Ches* 85–88; C New Borough and Leigh *Sarum* 88–91; V Thurnby w Stoughton *Leic* 91–06; PtO 07–08; P-in-c Leic St Leon CD 08–14; rtd 14. *33 Nutfield Road, Leicester LE3 1AN* E: george.dunseth@sky.com

DUNSTAN, The Very Revd Gregory John Orchard. b 50. Cam Univ MA 75 TCD BTh 90. CITC 87. **d** 90 **p** 91. C Ballymena w Ballyclug *Conn* 90–93; I Belfast St Matt 93–11; Preb Swords St Patr Cathl Dublin 07–11; Dean Arm and Keeper of Public Lib from 11. *The Deanery, Library House, 43 Abbey Street, Armagh BT61 7DY* T: (028) 3751 8447 *or* 3752 3142 M: 07986-327333 E: dean@armagh.anglican.org

DUNSTAN, Kenneth Ian. b 40. Goldsmiths' Coll Lon BEd 71 ACP. Oak Hill Th Coll Course 86. **d** 88 **p** 89. NSM Creeksea w Althorne, Latchingdon and N Fambridge *Chelmsf* 88–94; P-in-c Woodham Mortimer w Hazeleigh 94–98; P-in-c Woodham Walter 94–98; NSM Bradwell on Sea 99–05; rtd 05; PtO *Chelmsf* 05–13; P-in-c Mayland 13–15. *35 Ely Close, Southminster CM0 7AQ* T: (01621) 772199 E: kandk@uwclub.net

DUNSTAN, Mark Philip. b 70. Middx Univ BSc 93. Oak Hill Th Coll BA 03. **d** 03 **p** 04. C Stranton *Dur* 03–06; P-in-c

Hunsdon w Widford and Wareside *St Alb* 06–15; R from 15. *The Rectory, Acorn Street, Hunsdon, Ware SG12 8PB* T: (01920) 877276 E: dunstan_mark@hotmail.com

DUNSTAN-MEADOWS, Victor Richard. b 63. Chich Th Coll BTh 90. **d** 90 **p** 91. C Clacton St Jas *Chelmsf* 90–93; C Stansted Mountfitchet 93–95; CF 95–00; Chapl RAF 00–10; P-in-c Up Hatherley *Glouc* 10–13; V 13–18; rtd 18. *Address withheld by request* M: 07712-050629 E: rev.rdm@gmail.com

DUNTHORNE, Paul. b 63. K Coll Lon LLB 85 St Jo Coll Dur BA 90 Dur Univ MA 98. Cranmer Hall Dur 88. **d** 91 **p** 92. C Heacham and Sedgeford *Nor* 91–95; C Eastbourne H Trin *Chich* 95–98; P-in-c Preston and Ridlington w Wing and Pilton *Pet* 98–00; Local Min Officer 98–00; CME Officer *Heref* 00–06; TR Ledbury 06–14; Preb Heref Cathl 12–14; Miss and Tr Adv Win Sch of Miss 14–18; Dean Lic Min Tr from 18. *School of Mission, Wolvesey, Winchester SO23 9ND* T: (01962) 710980 E: paul.dunthorne@winchester.anglican.org

DUNWICH, Suffragan Bishop of. *See* HARRISON, The Rt Revd Michael Robert

DUNWOODY, Stephen John Herbert. b 71. Glam Univ BA 92. St Steph Ho Ox BTh 96. **d** 96 **p** 97. C Skewen *Llan* 96–98; C Roath 98–99; C Stanley *Liv* 99–02; TV Colyton, Southleigh, Offwell, Widworthy etc *Ex* 02–03; V Offwell, Northleigh, Farway, Cotleigh etc 03–05; CF from 05; Chapl Guards Chpl Lon from 16. *c/o MOD Chaplains (Army)* T: (01264) 383430 F: 381824 E: stephendunwoody@hotmail.com *or* londist-snrchap@mod.uk

DUNWOODY, Thomas Herbert Williamson. b 35. TCD BA 58 MA 64. TCD Div Sch Div Test 59. **d** 59 **p** 60. C Newcastle *D & D* 59–61; Asst Missr Ballymacarrett St Martin 61–63; C Lurgan Ch the Redeemer 63–66; I Ardglass w Dunsford 66–74; OCM 66–74; V Urmston *Man* 74–85; I Wexford w Ardcolm and Killurin *C & O* 85–93; Can Ferns Cathl 88–93; I Newry *D & D* 93–02; rtd 02. *36 Godfrey Avenue, Bangor BT20 5LS* T: (028) 9145 3918 E: thw_d@tiscali.co.uk

DÜNZKOFER, Markus. b 69. Edin Univ MTh 94. Seabury-Western Th Sem MDiv 98. **d** 99 **p** 99. C Evanston St Matt USA 99–04; R Vancouver St Paul Canada 04–12; R Edin St Jo from 13. *1 Ainslie Place, Edinburgh EH3 6AR* T: 0131-225 5004 *or* 229 7565 M: 07962-536817 E: office@stjohns-edinburgh.org.uk *or* mduenz@gmail.com

DUPRÉ, Robin Charles. b 50. Nottm Univ BA 72 Worc Coll of Educn PGCE 76. SWMTC 08. **d** 11 **p** 12. NSM Jersey Grouville Win 11–18; PtO from 18. *Le Picachon, 4 Le Clos Royale, La Rue de la Ville es Renauds, Grouville, Jersey JE3 9DF* T: (01534) 856378 M: 07829-936250 E: dupre@freeuk.com

DUPREE, Hugh Douglas. b 50. Univ of the South (USA) BA 72 Virginia Th Sem MDiv 75 Ch Ch Ox MA 86 Ball Coll Ox DPhil 88. **d** 75 **p** 76. USA 75–80; Hon C Ox St Mich w St Martin and All SS 80–87; Asst Chapl Ball Coll Ox 84–87; Chapl 87–14; Dean 07–14; Chapl HM Pris Ox 88–97; rtd 14; R Bp's Inst for Min Florida USA from 15. *Diocesan House, 325 N Market Street, Jacksonville , Florida 32202 USA* T: (001) (904) 356 1328 M: 904-504-7042 E: ddupree@diocesefl.org

DUPUY, Alan Douglas William. b 48. SEITE 98. **d** 00 **p** 01. NSM Forest Hill St Aug *S'wark* 00–01; NSM S Dulwich St Steph 01–04; NSM Perry Hill St Geo w Ch Ch and St Paul 04–12; NSM Forest Hill w Lower Sydenham 12–18; PtO from 18. *323A Stansted Road, London SE6 4UE* T: (020) 3560 9100 M: 07837-011573 E: alandupuy1@aol.com

DURAND, Noel Douglas. b 33. Jes Coll Cam BA 57 MA 61 BD 76. Westcott Ho Cam 72. **d** 74 **p** 75. C Eaton *Nor* 74–78; V Cumnor *Ox* 78–01; rtd 01; PtO *Nor* from 01. *74 Amderley Drive, Norwich NR4 6JH* T: (01603) 501764 E: douglas.ismene@gmail.com

DURANT, Lucas Crain. b 85. Wheaton Coll Illinois BA 07 Leuven Univ Belgium MA 08. Wycliffe Hall Ox 15. **d** 15 **p** 16. C Wootton *St Alb* 15–19; PtO from 19. *9 Studley Road, Wootton, Bedford MK43 9DL* M: 07727-409641 E: lucas.durant@gmail.com

DURANT, Samuel John. b 85. Univ Coll Lon LLB 06. Wycliffe Hall Ox 12. **d** 15 **p** 16. C Linc St Pet in Eastgate 15–19; R Skellingthorpe w Doddington from 19. *The Rectory, Vicarage Drive, Skellingthorpe, Lincoln LN6 5UY* E: mrsamuel@gmail.com

DURANT, William John Nicholls. b 55. K Coll Lon BA 76 Southn Univ PGCE 11. St Jo Coll Nottm 77. **d** 80 **p** 81. C Norwood St Luke *S'wark* 80–83; C Morden 83–88; TV 88–92; V Frindsbury w Upnor *Roch* 92–00; CF 00–13; V Vale *Ox* from 13. *The Vicarage, Main Street, Grove, Wantage OX12 7LQ* T: (01235) 766484 E: vicar@valebenefice.org.uk

DURANT-STEVENSEN, Mrs Helen Mary. b 53. Saffron Walden Coll TCert 74. Trin Coll Bris BA 04. **d** 04 **p** 05. C S Croydon Em *S'wark* 04–08; C New Malden and Coombe 08–18; AD Kingston 16–18; rtd 18; PtO *Sarum* from 19. *7 Caspian Gardens, Westbury BA13 3GP*

DURBIN, James. b 70. Victoria Univ Wellington BA 93 MA 96 Ches Univ MA 18. Oak Hill Th Coll BA 13. **d** 13 **p** 14. C Barnston *Ches* 13–16; C Waverton w Aldford and Bruera 16–17; PtO 17; CF from 17. *c/o MOD Chaplains (Army)* T: (01362) 627972 M: 07411-226948 E: durbin1970@gmail.com

DURBIN, Roger. b 41. Bris Sch of Min 83. **d** 85 **p** 86. NSM Bedminster *Bris* 85–91; NSM Henbury 91–94; NSM Clifton All SS w St Jo 94–11; PtO from 11. *13 Charbury Walk, Bristol BS11 9UU* T: 0117-985 8404

DURHAM, Miss Bethany Helen. b 58. Cranmer Hall Dur 86. **d** 89 **p** 94. C Newark *S'well* 89–93; rtd 93; PtO *S'well* 93–14. *c/o Crockford, Church House, Great Smith Street, London SW1P 3AZ*

DURHAM, Mrs Eleanore Jane. b 62. St Andr Univ MTheol 84 Liv Hope Univ PhD 17. Trin Coll Bris MA 01. **d** 01 **p** 02. C Childwall All SS *Liv* 01–05; P-in-c Hunts Cross 05–12; TV Halewood and Hunts Cross 12–18; P-in-c Wheathill Priory Gp *B & W* from 18. *The Rectory, Church Street, Keinton Mandeville, Somerton TA11 6ER* T: (01458) 223417 M: 07421-700242 E: rev.jane.durham@gmail.com

DURHAM, Archdeacon of. *Vacant*

DURHAM, Bishop of. *See* BUTLER, The Rt Revd Paul Roger

DURHAM, Dean of. *See* TREMLETT, The Very Revd Andrew

DURIE, David James. b 63. Cen Lancs Univ BA 93 St Martin's Coll Lanc MA 99. CBDTI 97. **d** 99 **p** 00. C Briercliffe *Blackb* 99–01; P-in-c Edin St Dav 02–13. *20 Brucehaven Crescent, Limekilns, Dunfermline KY11 3JJ* T: (01890) 781542 E: patricia.durie@btinternet.com

DURING, Arthur Christopher. b 59. Sierra Leone Th Hall 80. **d** 83 **p** 85. C Freetown H Trin Sierra Leone 83–85; C St Geo Cathl 85–86; PtO *S'wark* 00–05. *22 Challice Way, London SW2 3RD* T: (020) 8671 7678 E: aduring@hotmail.co.uk

DURKIN, Anthony Michael. b 45. Sarum & Wells Th Coll 87. **d** 89 **p** 90. C Faversham *Cant* 89–92; V St Margarets-at-Cliffe w Westcliffe etc 92–09; rtd 09; PtO *Sarum* from 10. *Church Cottage, Leigh, Sherborne DT9 6HL* T: (01935) 872117 E: anthonyd916@btinternet.com

DURKIN, Mrs Derath May. b 52. N Staffs Poly LLB 87. SAOMC 01. **d** 02 **p** 03. C Harlington Ch Ch CD *Lon* 02–06; TV Brentford 06–14; rtd 14; PtO *Truro* from 14. *35 Fore Street, Newlyn, Penzance TR18 5JP* T: (01736) 369176 M: 07962-168440 E: derath@btinternet.com

DURLEY, Jonathan Richard Hall. b 66. Wolv Univ BA 97 Ch Ch Coll Cant MA 01. S Wales Ord Course 04. **d** 05 **p** 06. C Canton Cardiff *Llan* 05–07; C Newton Nottage 07–10; P-in-c Kenfig Hill from 10. *The Vicarage, 5 Redman Close, Kenfig Hill, Bridgend CF33 6BF* T: (01656) 670148 E: fatherjo@btinternet.com

DURNDELL, Miss Irene Frances. b 43. Trin Coll Bris 84. **dss** 86 **d** 87 **p** 94. Erith Ch Ch *Roch* 86–93; Par Dn 87–93; Par Dn Erith St Paul 93–94; C 94–98; Asst Dir of Tr 93–98; V Falconwood 98–07; rtd 07; PtO *Chich* 12–17. *17A Buxton Drive, Bexhill-on-Sea TN39 4BA* T: (01424) 810477

DURNFORD, Canon Catherine Margaret. b 36. St Mary's Coll Dur BA 57. Gilmore Course 78 NW Ord Course 77. **d** 87 **p** 94. Area Sec USPG York and Ripon 82–89; Par Dn Whitby *York* 89–92; Par Dn Redcar 92–94; C Selby Abbey 94–97; V New Marske and Wilton 97–03; Can and Preb York Minster 01–03; rtd 03. PtO *York* from 03. *18 Canongate, Cottingham HU16 4DG* T: (01482) 844868 E: cmdurnford@gmail.com

DUROSE, Harry William. b 54. **d** 14 **p** 15. OLM Stoke-upon-Trent and Fenton *Lich* from 14. *48 Lime Street, Stoke-on-Trent ST4 4EF* T: (01782) 863956 E: badger_bill1954@yahoo.co.uk

DURRAN, Ms Margaret. Surrey Univ MSc 96 Lady Spencer Chu Coll of Educn CertEd 70. S'wark Ord Course 88. **d** 91 **p** 94. Par Dn Brixton St Matt *S'wark* 91–94; C Streatham St Leon 94–95; V Walworth St Chris 95–99; Hon C S'wark St Geo w St Alphege and St Jude 99–09; Hist Churches Project Officer *Lon* 99–07; rtd 08; PtO *Ox* from 09. *8 Bath Terrace, Victoria Road, Bicester OX26 6PR* M: 07739-988742

DURRANS, Mrs Janet. b 58. Westcott Ho Cam 09. **d** 11 **p** 12. C Chislehurst St Nic *Roch* 11–16; P-in-c St Peter-in-Thanet *Cant* 16–18; V from 18. *St Peter's Vicarage, 14 Vicarage Street, Broadstairs CT10 2SG* T: (01843) 869169 M: 07585-660621 E: revjandurrans@gmail.com

DURRANT, James Mark. b 89. York Univ BSc 11. Cranmer Hall Dur BA 16. **d** 16 **p** 17. C Derby St Alkmund and St Werburgh 16–19; C Derby Cathl from 19. *25 Queen Mary Court, Derby DE22 1BB* E: jamesdurrant@sky.com *or* james@stalkmunds.org.uk

DURRANT, Melvyn Richard Bloomfield. b 59. Leeds Univ BA 82 St Luke's Coll Ex PGCE 86. Trin Coll Bris 01. **d** 03 **p** 04. C Watercombe *Sarum* 03–06; C Moreton and Woodsford w Tincleton 03–06; P-in-c Sixpenny Handley w Gussage

St Andrew etc 06–18; C Chase 06–18; rtd 18. *1 Knole Court, Knole Road, Bexhill-on-Sea TN40 1LN* E: durrant@talktalk.net

DURRANT, Simon James. b 82. R Academy of Music BMus 04 LRAM 03. Trin Coll Bris BA 11. **d** 12. C Tiverton St Geo and St Paul *Ex* 12–16; V Roxeth *Lon* from 16. *Christ Church Vicarage, Roxeth Hill, Harrow HA2 0JN* T: (020) 8423 3168 M: 07898-350791 E: simondurrant7@me.com

DURSTON, Canon David Michael Karl. b 36. Em Coll Cam BA 60 MA 64. Clifton Th Coll 61. **d** 63 **p** 64. C Wednesfield Heath *Lich* 63–66; Project Officer Grubb Inst 67–78; Ind Chapl *Lich* 78–84; P-in-c W Bromwich St Paul 78–82; V 82–84; Adult Educn Officer 84–92; Preb Lich Cathl 89–92; Can Res and Chan Sarum Cathl 92–03; Can and Preb Sarum Cathl 03–06; TR Wylye and Till Valley 03–06; rtd 06; PtO *Sarum* from 06. *26 Mill Road, Salisbury SP2 7RZ* T: (01722) 334017 E: david.durston36@btinternet.com

DURUEKE, Collins. b 71. St Mellitus Coll 12. **d** 12 **p** 17. PtO *S'wark* 15–17; NSM Camberwell St Luke from 17. *83 Dawes House, Orb Street, London SE17 1RD* T: (020) 3561 6910 M: 07862-285672 E: collinsdurueke@yahoo.com

DURWARD, Rosemary. b 58. **d** 10 **p** 11. NSM Notting Hill St Jo *Lon* 10–12; PtO *Win* from 14; Hon Chapl Win Cathl from 14; PtO *Guildf* 17–18; NSM E Horsley from 18. *Loral, Miles Lane, Cobham KT11 2EA* E: rdurward@msn.com

DUSSEK, Canon Jeremy Neil James Christopher. b 70. St Jo Coll Dur BA 92. Westcott Ho Cam 96. **d** 97 **p** 98. C Whickham *Dur* 97–00; C Fareham H Trin *Portsm* 00–01; TV 01–07; V Moseley St Mary and St Anne *Birm* 07–14; Can Res Ches Cathl from 14. *9 Abbey Street, Chester CH1 2JF* T: (01244) 500967 E: canon.precentor@chestercathedral.com

DUTHIE, Elliot Malcolm. b 31. Clifton Th Coll 63. **d** 66 **p** 67. C Eccleston St Luke *Liv* 66–69; Malaysia 70–75; P-in-c Bootle St Leon *Liv* 76–78; V 78–81; V Charlton Kings H Apostles *Glouc* 81–94; rtd 94; PtO *Glouc* 94–00; *Ex* 02–05; *Derby* 06–18. *25 De Ferrers Court, Tamworth Street, Duffield, Belper DE56 4HL* T: (01332) 843630 E: emduthie@btinternet.com

DUTTON, Antony John. b 82. Newc Univ BA 04 Liv Univ MTh 08 Ches Univ PGCE 08. Ripon Coll Cuddesdon BA 11 MSt 12. **d** 12 **p** 13. C Malpas and Threapwood and Bickerton *Ches* 12–14; V Gt Sutton from 14. *15 The Paddock, Great Sutton, Ellesmere Port CH66 2NN* T: 0151-339 9916 M: 07976-819114 E: ant_sjd@hotmail.com

DUTTON, Leonard Arthur. b 35. Bps' Coll Cheshunt 63. **d** 66 **p** 67. C Knighton St Jo *Leic* 66–70; C Chilvers Coton w Astley *Cov* 70–73; R Hathern *Leic* 73–79; V Ashby-de-la-Zouch H Trin 79–04; rtd 04; PtO *Leic* 04–16. *8 Merganser Way, Coalville LE67 4QA* T: (01530) 815420 E: lenmeg@uwclub.net

DUTTON, Sandra Rosemary. b 50. Ripon Coll Cuddesdon 03. **d** 04 **p** 05. NSM Chatham St Steph *Roch* 04–08; TV Hartshill, Penkhull and Trent Vale *Lich* 08–12; TR 12–13; R Loose *Roch* 13–14; P-in-c Rackheath and Salhouse *Nor* 14–17; rtd 17; PtO *Nor* from 17. *12 Blackthorn Close, Diss IP22 4ZA* T: (01379) 309012 E: sandydutton@hotmail.com

DUXBURY, Clive Robert. b 49. Open Univ BA(ThM) 06. St Jo Coll Nottm 90. **d** 92 **p** 93. C Horwich and Rivington *Man* 92–96; P-in-c Bury St Paul and Bury Ch King 98–00; P-in-c Freethorpe, Wickhampton, Halvergate w Tunstall *Nor* 00–02; P-in-c Reedham w Cantley w Limpenhoe and Southwood 00–02; R Freethorpe, Wickhampton, Halvergate etc 02–05; RD Blofield 04–05; R High Ongar w Norton Mandeville *Chelmsf* 05–08; Chapl HM Pris Everthorpe 08–14; Hon C Elloughton and Brough w Brantingham *York* 11–14; rtd 14; P-in-c S Rodings *Chelmsf* 14–17. *33 Mayfield Avenue, Holme, Carnforth LA6 1PT* T: (01524) 935261 M: 07777-602980 E: crduxbury1@sky.com

DWYER, James Richard. b 86. K Coll Lon BA 10 AKC 10. Wycliffe Hall Ox MTh 18. **d** 18 **p** 19. C Ox St Andr from 18. *5 Squitchey Lane, Oxford OX2 7LD* M: 07885-257932 E: jamesd522@gmail.com

DYAS, Stuart Edwin. b 46. Lon Univ BSc 67. Ridley Hall Cam 78. **d** 80 **p** 81. C w Kelston *B & W* 80–83; C Tunbridge Wells St Jas *Roch* 83–90; V Nottingham St Jude *S'well* 90–99; AD Nottingham Cen 93–98; V Long Eaton St Jo *Derby* 99–05; rtd 05; PtO *Derby* 05–15; *S'well* 14–15; *York* from 15. *50 Meadlands, York YO31 0NS* T: (01904) 427964

DYAS, Sylvia Denise (Dee). b 51. Bedf Coll Lon BA 72 Nottm Univ PhD 99. St Jo Coll Nottm MA 00. **d** 00 **p** 01. Dir Cen for Study of Christianity and Culture *York* from 99; Tutor St Jo Coll Nottm 00–12; PtO *Derby* 00–04; *S'well* 12–15; *York* from 15. *50 Meadlands, York YO31 0NS* T: (01904) 427964 E: dee.dyas@york.ac.uk

DYBALL, Rebecca Mary. b 82. Ridley Hall Cam 15. **d** 17 **p** 18. C The Ramseys and Upwood *Ely* from 17. *23 Signal Road, Ramsey, Huntingdon PE26 1NG* M: 07484-234961 E: beckycurate@gmail.com

DYBLE, Ian Hugh. b 64. Anglia Poly LLB 85 Leic Univ MSc 98. Ridley Hall Cam 08. **d** 10 **p** 11. C Onslow Square and S Kensington St Aug *Lon* 10–13; P-in-c Heigham St Thos *Nor* 13–17; C Nor Lakenham St Alb and St Mark 15–17; P-in-c Heigham St Barn w St Bart 17; V The Mitre Benefice from 17; RD Nor S 16–19; C Earlham from 18; C Costessey from 19; Dioc Dir Ch Revitalisation from 19. *St Thomas's Vicarage, 77 Edinburgh Road, Norwich NR2 3RL* T: (01603) 624390 M: 07770-592733 E: iandyble@live.co.uk *or* ian.dyble@stn.org.uk

DYE, Mrs Margaret Mary. b 48. NOC 95. **d** 98 **p** 99. C Morley St Pet w Churwell *Wakef* 98–02; TV Morley 02–08; TR 08–13; rtd 13; PtO *York* from 13. *5 Church Lane, Hutton, Driffield YO25 9PS* T: (01377) 271953 E: thedyes5@btinternet.com

DYE, Mervyn John. b 53. **d** 18 **p** 19. NSM Ipswich St Mary at Stoke w St Pet and St Fran *St E* from 18. *Address withheld by request* T: (01473) 601750 M: 07982-236074 E: revmerv@switmparish.org.uk

DYER, Adrian Louis. b 67. Cant Univ (NZ) BA 02 Auckland Univ BTheol 03. **d** 04 **p** 05. C Methven New Zealand 04–06; V Ellesmere 06–09; Chapl RAF from 09. *Chaplaincy Services (RAF), HQ Air Command, RAF High Wycombe HP14 4UE* T: (01494) 496800

✠**DYER, The Rt Revd Anne Catherine.** b 57. St Anne's Coll Ox MA 80 Lon Univ MTh 89. Wycliffe Hall Ox 84. **d** 87 **p** 94 **c** 18. NSM Beckenham St Jo *Roch* 87–88; NSM Beckenham St Geo 88–89; Hon Par Dn Luton Ch Ch 89–94; Chapl for Evang 93–98; NSM Istead Rise 94–98; Min Development Officer 98–04; Hon Can Roch Cathl 00–04; Warden Cranmer Hall Dur 05–11; Hon Can Dur Cathl 08–11; R Haddington *Edin* 11–18; Bp Ab from 18. *Ashley House, Ashley Gardens, Aberdeen AB10 6RQ* T: (01224) 208142 E: bishop@aberdeen.anglican.org

DYER, Ms Catherine Jane. b 46. Westf Coll Lon BA 68. Ox NSM Course 85. **d** 88 **p** 94. NSM Wokingham All SS *Ox* 88–90; C W Slough 95–01; TV W Slough 95–01; AD Mursley 03–06; rtd 07; PtO *Sarum* from 15. *45 Shady Bower, Salisbury SP1 2RG* T: (01722) 502781 E: catherine.dyer46@hotmail.co.uk

DYER, Canon Christine Anne. b 53. Nottm Univ BEd 75 MA 97. EMMTC 81. **dss** 84 **d** 87 **p** 94. Mickleover St Jo *Derby* 85–90; Par Dn 87–90; Dioc Voc Adv 86–90; Par Educn Adv 90–98; Dioc Youth Officer 91–98; P-in-c Morton and Stonebroom 98–99; P-in-c Shirland 98–99; R Morton and Stonebroom w Shirland 99–06; P-in-c Allestree 06–10; P-in-c Darley Abbey 06–10; V Allestree St Edm and Darley Abbey 10–15; Hon Can Derby Cathl 02–15; rtd 15; PtO *Derby* from 15. *7 Devonshire Drive, Mickleover, Derby DE3 9HA* T: (01332) 513397 E: c.a.dyer.t21@btinternet.com *or* c.a.dyer@talk21.com

DYER, Fraser Colin. b 65. SEITE. **d** 09 **p** 10. C De Beauvoir Town St Pet *Lon* 09–12; P-in-c S Lambeth St Anne and All SS *S'wark* 12–17; V from 17. *The Vicarage, 179 Fentiman Road, London SW8 1JY* T: (020) 7735 3191 E: revdfraserdyer@gmail.com

DYER, Mrs Gillian Marie. b 50. Sheff Univ BA 71 Leic Univ PGCE 72. S Dios Minl Tr Scheme 81. **dss** 84 **d** 87 **p** 94. Witney *Ox* 84–85; Carl St Cuth w St Mary 86–89; Par Dn 87–89; Dioc Communications Officer 86–89; Par Dn Kirkbride w Newton Arlosh 89–91; Par Dn Carl H Trin and St Barn 91–94; TV 94–97; P-in-c Arbroath *Bre* 01–03; P-in-c Lower Darwen St Jas *Blackb* 03–10; P-in-c Whalley 10–12; P-in-c Sabden and Pendleton 10–12; V W Pendleside 12–15; PtO from 15. *The Vicarage, 41 Rythergate, Cawood, Selby YO8 3TP* T: (01757) 268905 E: revvygilly141@btinternet.com

DYER, Janet. b 35. LNSM course 77. **dss** 85 **d** 86 **p** 94. Balerno *Edin* 85–86; NSM 86–93; Chapl Edin R Infirmary 88–93; Dn-in-c Roslin (Rosslyn Chpl) *Edin* 93–94; P-in-c 94–97; NSM Livingston LEP 97–00; Chapl Livingstone St Jo Hosp 97–00; NSM Dalmahoy *Edin* 02–11; LtO from 11. *499 Lanark Road West, Balerno EH14 7AL* T: 0131-449 3767 E: jdyer499@googlemail.com

DYER, Mrs Joanne. b 69. Cov Univ BA 99 FCIPD. Qu Foundn Birm 15. **d** 17 **p** 18. C Woodfield *Leic* from 17. *7 Packington Vicarage, Mill Street, Packington, Ashby-de-la-Zouch LE65 1WL* T: (01530) 415144 M: 07803-295282 E: jdyer269@btinternet.com

DYER, Mrs Kay. b 49. Open Univ BA 80. Qu Foundn Birm 14. **d** 15 **p** 16. NSM Shottery St Andr *Cov* 15–18; NSM Stratford-upon-Avon, Luddington etc from 18. *6 Sycamore Close, Stratford-upon-Avon CV37 0DZ* T: (01789) 298299 M: 07857-821168 E: revkaydyer@gmail.com

DYER, Ronald Whitfield. b 29. Solicitor 51. Guildf Dioc Min Course 91. **d** 95 **p** 96. NSM Fleet *Guildf* 95–99; rtd 99; PtO *Guildf* 99–17. *7 Dukes Mead, Fleet GU51 4HA* T: (01252) 621457

DYER, Stephen Roger. b 57. Brunel Univ BSc. Wycliffe Hall Ox 83. **d** 86 **p** 87. C Beckenham St Jo *Roch* 86–89; C Luton Ch Ch 89–94; V Istead Rise 94–01; V Frindsbury w Upnor 01–04; Hon C Easington, Easington Colliery and S Hetton *Dur* 05–09. *Ashley House, 16 Ashley Gardens, Aberdeen AB10 6RQ* T: (01224) 208142

DYER, Terence Neville. b 50. Sheff Univ BEng 71 Leic Univ PGCE 72 Open Univ MA 96. Carl Dioc Tr Course 86. **d** 89 **p** 90. NSM Kirkbride w Newton Arlosh *Carl* 89–91; NSM Carl H Trin and St Barn 91–97; NSM Arbroath *Bre* 01; P-in-c Monifieth 01–03; P-in-c Over Darwen St Jas *Blackb* 03–13; C Darwen St Pet w Hoddlesden 08–10; P-in-c Hoddlesden 10–13; V Over Darwen St Jas and Hoddlesden 13–16; rtd 16; PtO *Blackb* 16–17; P-in-c Cawood w Ryther and Wistow *York* from 17. *The Vicarage, 41 Rythergate, Cawood, Selby YO8 3TP* T: (01757) 268905 M: 07919-543475 E: terry255dyer@btinternet.com

DYKE, The Very Revd Elizabeth Muriel. b 55. St Mary's Coll Dur BSc 77 St Martin's Coll Lanc PGCE 78. Oak Hill Th Coll 92. **d** 94 **p** 95. C High Wycombe *Ox* 94–95; C W Wycombe w Bledlow Ridge, Bradenham and Radnage 95–97; TV Bedworth *Cov* 97–02; V Dunchurch 02–09; R Kidman Park and Mile End Australia 09–14; Adn Sturt 13–14; R Queanbeyan and Distr 14–18; Adn Queanbeyan, Monaro and Alpine Region 14–18; Dean Bendigo from 18. *38 Mafeking Street South, Kennington VA 3550, Australia* M: (0061) 40-950 4740 E: dean@bendigoanglican.org.au

DYKE, Kevin Robert. b 59. Sheff Univ BA 13. Coll of Resurr Mirfield 11. **d** 13 **p** 14. C Gainsborough and Morton *Linc* 13–16; TR Bottesford w Ashby from 16. *The Vicarage, St Paul's Road, Scunthorpe DN16 3DL* T: (01724) 852079 M: 07814-260467

DYKES, John Edward. b 33. Trin Coll Bris 82. **d** 84 **p** 85. C Rushden w Newton Bromswold *Pet* 84–87; R Heanton Punchardon w Marwood *Ex* 87–97; rtd 97; PtO *Guildf* 98–01; B & W from 02. *42 Ashley Road, Taunton TA1 5BP* T: (01823) 282507 E: johnvickydykes@gmail.com

DYKES, Mrs Katrina Mary. b 66. Trin Coll Bris BA 90. Guildf Dioc Min Course 03. **d** 04 **p** 05. NSM Windlesham *Guildf* 04–07; Chapl St Swithun's Sch Win 08–16; P-in-c Abbotts Ann and Upper Clatford and Goodworth Clatford *Win* from 16. *The Rectory, Upper Clatford, Andover SP11 7QP* T: (01264) 324428 M: 07922-153765 E: revdkatrina@gmail.com

DYKES, Philip John. b 61. Loughb Univ BSc 83. Trin Coll Bris 88. **d** 91 **p** 92. C Morden *S'wark* 91–95; C St Helier 95–98; TV Camberley St Paul *Guildf* 98–99; V Camberley Heatherside 99–08; Chapl Win Univ 08–11; Dioc Adult Discipleship Adv *Win* from 11. *The Diocesan Office, Old Alresford Place, Old Alresford, Alresford SO24 9DH* T: (01962) 737354 E: phil.dykes@winchester.anglican.org

DYSON, Mrs Clare Louise. b 63. WMMTC 02. **d** 05 **p** 06. C Tupsley w Hampton Bishop *Heref* 05–08; P-in-c Kingstone w Clehonger, Eaton Bishop etc 08–10; R Cagebrook 10–14; NSM Cheltenham St Mary w St Matt and St Luke *Glouc* from 14. *7 Apple Orchard, Prestbury, Cheltenham GL52 3EH* E: clared@stmstm.org.uk

DYSON, Mrs Debra Anne. b 62. **d** 08 **p** 09. C Lich St Mich w St Mary and Wall 08–11; V Wigginton from 11; RD Tamworth from 14. *The Vicarage, Comberford Lane, Wigginton, Tamworth B79 9DT* T: (01827) 690380 E: debdyson@btinternet.com

DYSON, Peter Whiteley. b 51. Man Univ BA 73 LLB 75. Qu Coll Birm 77. **d** 81 **p** 82. C Swindon Ch Ch *Bris* 81–84; P-in-c Brislington St Luke 84–91; V Bourne *Guildf* 91–92; PtO 02–04; P-in-c Herriard w Winslade and Long Sutton etc *Win* 04–08; P-in-c Newnham w Nately Scures w Mapledurwell etc 04–08; R N Hants Downs 08–16; RD Odiham 11–16; R Jersey St Sav from 16. *The Rectory, Rectory Lane, St Saviour's Hill, St Saviour, Jersey JE2 7NP* T: (01534) 736679 M: 07780-653588 E: pwdyson@btinternet.com

DYSON, Steven John. b 79. Univ of Wales (Ban) BSc 00. Trin Coll Bris BA 11. **d** 11 **p** 12. C Pinhoe and Broadclyst *Ex* 11–13; C Aylesbeare, Rockbeare, Farringdon etc 11–13; C Broadclyst, Clyst Honiton, Pinhoe, Rockbeare 13–16; V Biddulph *Lich* from 16. *7 Wrexham Close, Biddulph, Stoke-on-Trent ST8 6RZ* T: (01782) 513891 M: 07779-594037 E: revstevedyson@gmail.com

DYTHAM, Linda Alison. b 52. STETS 02. **d** 05 **p** 06. NSM Savernake *Sarum* 05–14; PtO from 14; Chapl Trizfarren Ho and Standon Lodge from 07. *10 Home Farm Close, Heddington, Calne SN11 0RH* T: (01380) 859571 M: 07921-123422 E: ladytham@btinternet.com

E

EADE, John Christopher. b 45. Ch Coll Cam BA 68 MA 72. Linc Th Coll 68. **d** 70 **p** 71. C Portsea N End St Mark *Portsm* 70–73; C Henleaze *Bris* 73–77; V Slad *Glouc* 77–82; V N Bradley, Southwick and Heywood *Sarum* 82–91; R Fovant, Sutton Mandeville and Teffont Evias etc 91–08; C Nadder Valley 06–08; TR 08–11; rtd 11; PtO *Sarum* from 15. *Odd Acre, Ryall Road, Ryall, Bridport DT6 6EG* T: (01297) 489633 E: john@thames.me.uk

EADES, David Julian John. b 74. Univ of Wales BA 95 St Jo Coll Dur BA 99. Cranmer Hall Dur. **d** 00 **p** 01. C Walbrook Epiphany *Derby* 00–04; Chapl Essex Univ *Chelmsf* 04–06; PtO *Ox* 16–17. *62 Headingley Avenue, Leeds LS6 3ER* M: 07926-649602 E: julian_eades@yahoo.co.uk

EADON, Benjamin Myles. b 85. Univ Coll Dur BA 07 Clare Coll Cam BA 10. Westcott Ho Cam 08. **d** 11 **p** 12. C Sunderland St Chad *Dur* 11–15; C Durrington *Chich* 15–16; P-in-c 16–19; V from 19. *The Vicarage, Bramble Lane, Worthing BN13 3JE* T: (01903) 694827 E: ben.eadon@btinternet.com

EADY, David Robert. b 43. Salford Univ BSc. Glouc Th Course 82. **d** 85 **p** 86. NSM Highnam, Lassington, Rudford, Tibberton etc *Glouc* 85–95; NSM Stratton, N Cerney, Baunton and Bagendon 95–99; P-in-c Swindon and Elmstone Hardwicke w Uckington 99–08; P-in-c N Cheltenham 08–10; rtd 10; PtO *Glouc* from 10. *117 Sussex Gardens, Hucclecote, Gloucester GL3 3SP*

EADY, Timothy William. b 57. Open Univ BA. Cranmer Hall Dur 82. **d** 85 **p** 86. C Boulton *Derby* 85–88; C Portchester *Portsm* 88–92; R Brighstone and Brooke w Mottistone 92–07; Relig Progr Adv Ocean Sound Radio 88–07; V Iver *Ox* 07–12; Miss Partner Bangkok Ch Ch Thailand 12–19; C Penn Fields *Lich* from 19. *100 Bellencroft Gardens, Wolverhampton WV3 8DU* E: timothy_eady@yahoo.co.uk

EAGER, Ms Rosemary Anne McDowall. b 65. St Andr Univ MA 87 Strathclyde Univ 88. Ridley Hall Cam 92. **d** 95 **p** 96. C Walthamstow St Mary w St Steph *Chelmsf* 95–97; C Walthamstow 97–01; TV Bushbury *Lich* 01–05; PtO 05–07. *37 Park Dale East, Wolverhampton WV1 4TD* T: (01902) 710340 or 553945 E: revdrosie@yahoo.co.uk

✠**EAGLES, The Rt Revd Peter Andrew.** b 59. K Coll Lon BA 82 AKC 82 Ox Univ BA 88. St Steph Ho Ox 86. **d** 89 **p** 90 **c** 17. C Ruislip St Martin *Lon* 89–92; CF 92–17; Chapl Guards Chpl Lon 07–08; Asst Chapl Gen 08–17; Adn for the Army 11–17; Can and Preb Sarum Cathl 15–17; Bp S & M from 17. *Thie yn Aspick, 4 The Falls, Tromode Road, Cronkbourne, Isle of Man IM4 4PZ* T: (01624) 622108 E: bishop@sodorandman.im

EAGLES, Thomas Ross. b 79. Southn Univ BSc 00 Dur Univ BA 17. St Mellitus Coll 14. **d** 17 **p** 18. C-in-c Cov St Mark Swanswell CD from 17. *29 Mary Herbert Street, Coventry CV3 5ER* M: 07968-985177 E: tom.eagles@stmarkscoventry.org

EALES, Canon Howard Bernard. b 46. Sarum & Wells Th Coll 73. **d** 76 **p** 77. C Timperley *Ches* 76–78; C Stockport St Thos 78–82; V Wythenshawe Wm Temple Ch *Man* 82–95; V Cheadle Hulme All SS *Ches* 95–11; RD Cheadle 02–09; Hon Can Ches Cathl 06–11; rtd 11; PtO *Ches* from 11. *8 Taxmere Close, Sandbach CW11 1WT* T: (01270) 763965 E: hbe.rev@gmail.com

EAMAN, Michael Leslie. b 47. Ridley Hall Cam 87. **d** 89 **p** 90. C Wharton *Ches* 89–93; V Buglawton 93–98; TV Congleton 98–10; rtd 10; Hon C Alcester and Arrow w Oversley and Weethley *Cov* 10–13; Hon C Kinwarton w Gt Alne and Haselor 10–13; P-in-c Potters Green 13–17; V from 17. *St Philip's Vicarage, Ringwood Highway, Coventry CV2 2GF* T: (024) 7661 2973 E: mikeeaman@virginmedia.com

EAMES, David John. b 80. Liv Hope Univ Coll BA 01 MA 04 St Jo Coll Dur MA 08. Cranmer Hall Dur 06. **d** 08 **p** 09. C Brigg, Wrawby and Cadney cum Howsham *Linc* 08–11; P-in-c Broughton from 11; P-in-c Scawby, Redbourne and Hibaldstow from 11. *St Hybald's Vicarage, Vicarage Lane, Scawby, Brigg DN20 9LX* T: (01652) 600860

EAMES (née WAKEHAM), Mrs Ellen Liesel. b 82. York Univ BA 04 CCC Cam BA 08. Westcott Ho Cam 06. **d** 09 **p** 10. C Frodingham *Linc* 09–12; Chapl St Gabr Coll Camberwell 12–18; Hon C Kennington St Jo w St Jas *S'wark* 12–19; PtO *Roch* 18–19; P-in-c Walworth St Chris *S'wark* from 19. *45 Aldbridge Street, London SE17 2RG* M: 07419-121950 E: mother.ellen@pembrokehouse.org.uk

EARDLEY, John. b 38. Ch Coll Cam BA 61. Ridley Hall Cam 60. **d** 62 **p** 63. C Barnston *Ches* 62–65; C Wilmslow 65–67; V Hollingworth 67–75; V Leasowe 75–91; Chapl Leasowe Hosp 75–82; RD Wallasey *Ches* 86–91; V Church Hulme and Chapl Cranage Hall Hosp 91–03; rtd 03; PtO *Ches* from 03. *7 Banks Road, Heswall, Wirral CH60 9JS* T: 0151-342 9537 E: johneardley@talktalk.net

EARDLEY, Canon John Barry. b 35. MEd 87. AKC 62. **d** 63 **p** 64. C Merton St Jas *S'wark* 63–66; C St Helier 66–69; C Bilton *Cov* 69–70; C Canley CD 70–74; P-in-c Church Lawford w Newnham Regis 74–80; P-in-c Leamington Hastings and Birdingbury 82–88; Dioc Educn Officer 82–00; Hon Can Cov Cathl 87–00; rtd 01; PtO *Cov* from 01. *8 Margetts Close, Kenilworth CV8 1EN* T: (01926) 748313 E: johnbarry.eardley@ntlworld.com

EARDLEY, Robert Bradford. b 44. St Alb Minl Tr Scheme 90. **d** 93 **p** 94. NSM Digswell and Panshanger *St Alb* 93–96; NSM Wheathampstead 97–98; NSM Tewin 98–05; P-in-c 98–04; rtd 05; PtO *St Alb* 05–07; *Sarum* from 06. *Bridge Cottage, Martin, Fordingbridge SP6 3LD* T: (01725) 519423 M: 07941-345895 E: rob.eardley@hotmail.co.uk

EARDLEY, William Robert. b 56. Oak Hill Th Coll 94. **d** 96 **p** 97. C Whitfield *Derby* 96–99; TV Dronfield w Holmesfield 99–19; rtd 19. *8 Brookfield Avenue, Nettleham, Lincoln LN2 2TB*

EAREY, Mark Robert. b 65. Loughb Univ BSc 87 St Jo Coll Dur BA 91. Cranmer Hall Dur 88. **d** 91 **p** 92. C Glen Parva and S Wigston *Leic* 91–94; C Luton Ch Ch *Roch* 94–97; Praxis Nat Educn Officer Sarum Coll 97–02; TR Morley *Wakef* 02–07; Tutor Qu Foundn Birm from 07; PtO *Birm* from 09. *The Queen's Foundation, Somerset Road, Edgbaston, Birmingham B15 2QH* T: 0121-452 2667 E: m.earey@queens.ac.uk

EARIS, Canon Stanley Derek. b 50. Univ Coll Dur BA 71 BCL 80. Ripon Hall Ox BA 73 MA 80. **d** 74 **p** 75. C Sutton St Jas and Wawne *York* 74–77; C Acomb St Steph and St Aid 77–81; V Skelmanthorpe *Wakef* 81–87; R Market Deeping *Linc* 87–02; V N Walsham and Edingthorpe *Nor* 02–13; C Bacton w Edingthorpe w Witton and Ridlington 04–07; Hon Can Nor Cathl 10–13; rtd 13; C York St Olave w St Giles from 13; C York St Denys from 13; C York St Helen w St Martin from 13; C York All SS Pavement w St Crux and St Mich from 13. *49 St John Street, York YO31 7QR* T: (01904) 654767 E: dereke569@gmail.com

EARL (formerly LAMB), Mrs Alison. b 60. Ches Coll of HE BTh 04. NOC 01. **d** 04 **p** 05. C Rossington *Sheff* 04–08; V Worsbrough w Elsecar 08–18; V Tickhill w Stainton from 18. *27 Herril Ings, Tickhill, Doncaster DN11 9UE* E: alison.lamb6@btinternet.com

EARL, Andrew John. b 61. Huddersfield Univ CertEd 01 Ches Coll of HE BTh 04. NOC. **d** 04 **p** 05. NSM Barnsley St Mary *Wakef* 04–08; NSM S Kirkby 08–09; Chapl W Yorks Police 04–09; CF from 09. *c/o MOD Chaplains (Army)* T: (01264) 383430 F: 381824 M: 07557-362130 E: padreearl@hotmail.co.uk

EARL, Simon Robert. b 50. Culham Coll of Educn CertEd 71 Open Univ BA 82. Linc Th Coll 94. **d** 96 **p** 97. C Bexhill St Aug *Chich* 96–99; R Ninfield 99–15; V Hooe 99–15; rtd 15; PtO *Chich* 15–19; TV Bexhill St Pet from 19. *6 Frant Avenue, Bexhill-on-Sea TN39 4NG* T: (01424) 842179 E: srearl@btinternet.com

EARL, Stephen Geoffrey Franklyn. b 53. Lon Univ BA 76 Goldsmiths' Coll Lon PGCE 77. Ridley Hall Cam 91. **d** 93 **p** 94. C Sawston *Ely* 93–96; V Burwell w Reach 96–10; RD Fordham and Quy 02–10; Hon Can Ely Cathl 07–10; P-in-c Lavenham w Preston *St E* 10–12; R from 12; RD Lavenham 12–17. *The Rectory, Church Street, Lavenham, Sudbury CO10 9SA* T/F: (01787) 247244 E: earls2222@btinternet.com

EARLE, Mrs Sylvia. b 51. St Aid Coll Dur BA 72. Cranmer Hall Dur 05. **d** 07 **p** 08. C Whitkirk *Ripon* 07–11; P-in-c Collingham w Harewood 12–14; *Leeds* from 14; P-in-c Spofforth w Kirk Deighton *Ripon* 12–14; *Leeds* from 14. *The Vicarage, Church Lane, Collingham, Wetherby LS22 5AU* T: (01937) 573975 E: sylvia.earle@tesco.net

EARLEY, Stephen John. b 48. Trin Coll Bris 91. **d** 93 **p** 94. C Stroud H Trin *Glouc* 93–98; C Leckhampton SS Phil and Jas w Cheltenham St Jas 98–02; V Nailsworth w Shortwood, Horsley etc 02–13; rtd 13; PtO *Glouc* from 13. *17 Whitecroft, Nailsworth, Stroud GL6 0NS* T: (01453) 836679 E: stevearl@earleys.f9.co.uk *or* stevejearley@gmail.com

EARNEY, Preb Graham Howard. b 45. AKC 67. **d** 68 **p** 69. C Auckland St Helen *Dur* 68–72; C Corsenside *Newc* 72–76; P-in-c 76–79; TV Willington 79–83; TR 83–87; Dioc

Soc Resp Officer *B & W* 87–95; Dir Bp Mascall Cen *Heref* 95–02; Hon TV Ludlow, Ludford, Ashford Carbonell etc 95–02; Dioc Development Rep 96–02; Local Min Officer 02–10; RD Condover 03–06; Preb Heref Cathl 02–10; rtd 10; PtO *Heref* from 10. *The Coppice, Castle Pulverbatch, Pulverbatch, Shrewsbury SY5 8DS* T: (01743) 718930 E: gandsearney@btinternet.com

EARNGEY, Mark Edward. b 80. Univ of NSW BSc 03. Moore Th Coll Sydney BD 11. **d** 12. C Toongabbie Australia 12–14; PtO *Ox* 15–18. *2 Court Place Gardens, Iffley, Oxford OX4 4EW* M: 07943-910520 E: mark.earngey@theology.ox.ac.uk

EARNSHAW, Alan Mark. b 36. CQSW 81. Lon Coll of Div LTh 60. **d** 60 **p** 61. C Fazakerley Em *Liv* 60–65; V Ovenden *Wakef* 65–79; NSM Halifax St Jude 79–90; V Coley 90–99; rtd 99; PtO *Wakef* 00–14; *Leeds* from 14. *4 Moor Royd, Halifax HX3 0HT* T: (01422) 381317

EARWICKER, Matthew Charles. b 77. St Jo Coll Ox BA 00 MA 03. Ridley Hall Cam 12. **d** 14 **p** 15. C Salisbury St Mark and Laverstock *Sarum* 14–18; R Oldbury from 18. *The Rectory, The Street, Cherhill, Calne SN11 8XR* T: (01249) 821329 E: mattearwicker@gmail.com

EASEMAN, Robert Leslie. b 44. **d** 00 **p** 01. OLM Hunstanton St Mary w Ringstead Parva etc *Nor* 00–09; rtd 09; PtO *Nor* from 09. *5 Lighthouse Close, Hunstanton PE36 6EL* T/F: (01485) 535258 M: 07941-323218 E: rleaseman@gmail.com

EAST, Bryan Victor. b 46. Oak Hill Th Coll 91. **d** 93 **p** 94. C Waltham Cross *St Alb* 93–96; C Wotton St Mary *Glouc* 96–99; V Humberston *Linc* 99–12; rtd 12; PtO *Glouc* from 15. *8 Ashway Court, Stroud GL5 4LL* T: (01453) 767261 E: bryan.east.be@gmail.com

EAST, Mark Richard. b 57. Trin Coll Bris BA 89. **d** 89 **p** 90. C Dalton-in-Furness *Carl* 89–93; TV Bucknall and Bagnall *Lich* 93–00; P-in-c Church Coniston *Carl* 00–12; P-in-c Torver 00–12; P-in-c Haughton le Skerne *Dur* 12–15; R from 15; P-in-c Sadberge 14–15; R from 15; AD Darlington from 19. *7 St Andrew's Close, Darlington DL1 2EB* T: (01325) 492993 E: east793@btinternet.com *or* revmark@standrewshaughton.org.uk

EAST, Martin James. b 47. STETS. **d** 10 **p** 11. NSM N Hants Downs *Win* 10–13; PtO from 13. *South Lodge, 112 London Road, Holybourne, Alton GU34 4EW* T: (01420) 549595 M: 07928-423762 E: martineast@btinternet.com

EAST, Peter Alan. *See* OSTLI-EAST, Peter Alan

EAST, Canon Richard Kenneth. b 47. Oak Hill Th Coll 86. **d** 88 **p** 89. C Necton w Holme Hale *Nor* 88–92; R Garsdon, Lea and Cleverton and Charlton *Bris* 92–12; P-in-c Gt Somerford, Lt Somerford, Seagry, Corston etc 10–12; C Brinkworth w Dauntsey 10–12; RD Malmesbury 93–99; Hon Can Bris Cathl 10–12; rtd 12; PtO *Sarum* from 13. *6 Ryeland Way, Trowbridge BA14 7SH* T: (01225) 282902 E: richardeast@homecall.co.uk

EAST, Stuart Michael. b 50. Chich Th Coll 86. **d** 88 **p** 89. C Middlesbrough St Martin *York* 88–92; R Upper Ryedale 92–97; V Macclesfield St Paul *Ches* 97–01; C Maidstone St Luke *Cant* 01–03; R Peopleton and White Ladies Aston w Churchill etc *Worc* 03–10; V Nunthorpe *York* 10–12; rtd 12. *12 Avon Drive, Guisborough TS14 8AX* M: 07754-244929

EAST RIDING, Archdeacon of. *See* BROOM, The Ven Andrew Clifford

EASTELL, Jane Rosamund. b 47. Sheff Univ BA 68 Univ of Wales (Lamp) MA 08 RIBA 73. Trin Coll Bris BA 99. **d** 99 **p** 00. C Backwell w Chelvey and Brockley *B & W* 99–03; C Chew Stoke w Nempnett Thrubwell 03–08; C Chew Magna w Dundry and Norton Malreward 03–08; Hon C Taunton St Jo 09–13; P-in-c 13–14; Hon C Taunton St Mary and St Jo from 14; Dioc Adv in Prayer and Spirituality 04–16. *Meadowside, Wild Oak Lane, Trull, Taunton TA3 7JT* T: (01823) 321069 E: jane.eastell458@btinternet.com

EASTER, Canon Ann Rosemarie. SRN 68 Univ of E Lon MBA 94. Gilmore Ho 78. **dss** 80 **d** 87 **p** 94. Stratford St Jo and Ch Ch w Forest Gate St Jas *Chelmsf* 80–89; Par Dn 87–89; Chapl Asst Newham Gen Hosp 80–89; PtO *Chelmsf* 89–08; Chief Exec Officer The Renewal Programme 95–15; AD Newham 97–07; NSM W Ham 08–15; NSM E Ham H Trin from 11; Hon Can Chelmsf Cathl from 00; Chapl to The Queen 07–17. *67 Disraeli Road, London E7 9JU* T: (020) 8555 6337 M: 07889-799290 E: anneaster5@gmail.com

EASTERN ARCHDEACONRY, Archdeacon of the. *See* KELHAM, Canon Adèle Mary

EASTOE, Canon Robin Howard Spenser. b 53. Lon Univ BD 75 AKC 75. Coll of Resurr Mirfield 77. **d** 78 **p** 79. C Gt Ilford St Mary *Chelmsf* 78–81; C Walthamstow St Sav 81–84; V Barkingside St Fran 84–92; V Leigh-on-Sea St Marg 92–08; RD Hadleigh 00–08; Chapl Southend Health Care NHS Trust 96–08; Hon Can Chelmsf Cathl 06–08; P-in-c Heavitree and

St Mary Steps *Ex* 08–14; TR from 14; RD Christianity 17–18; Preb Ex Cathl from 16. *The Rectory, 10 Victoria Park Road, Exeter EX2 4NT* T: (01392) 677150 E: theeastoes@btinternet.com *or* frrobin@heavitreeteam.org.uk

EASTON, Canon Christopher Richard Alexander. b 60. TCD BA 81. **d** 84 **p** 85. C Belfast St Donard *D & D* 84–89; I Inishmacsaint *Clogh* 89–95; I Magheralin w Dollingstown *D & D* 95–01; I Coleraine *Conn* 01–09; P-in-c Belfast Whiterock 09–14; I Armoy w Loughguile and Drumtullagh from 14; Can Conn Cathl from 16. *The Rectory, 181 Glenshesk Road, Armoy, Ballymoney BT53 8RJ* T: (028) 2075 1565 E: stpat@btinternet.com

EASTON, Donald Fyfe. b 48. St Edm Hall Ox BA 69 MA 85 Nottm Univ CertEd 70 Univ Coll Lon MA 76 PhD 90 Clare Hall Cam MA 85. Westcott Ho Cam 89. **d** 90 **p** 91. NSM Fulham St Andr *Lon* 90–97; Lic Preacher from 97. *12 Weltje Road, London W6 9TG* T: (020) 8741 0233 E: donaldfeaston@hotmail.com

EASTON, John. b 34. St Cath Soc Ox BA 59 MA 63. Chich Th Coll 59. **d** 61 **p** 62. C Rugeley *Lich* 61–64; TR 72–87; C Shrewsbury All SS 64–66; Ind Chapl *Sheff* 66–72; V Bolsover *Derby* 87–99; RD Bolsover and Staveley 93–98; rtd 99; PtO *Derby* 99–11; *York* from 11. *27 Dulverton Hall, Esplanade, Scarborough YO11 2AR*

EASTON, Robert Paul Stephen. b 62. Bris Univ BA 84. St Steph Ho Ox BTh 00. **d** 00 **p** 01. C Stoke Newington St Mary *Lon* 00–03; Chapl Brighton Coll 03–19; Chapl Highgate Sch Lon from 19. *Highgate School, North Road, London N6 4AY* T: (020) 8340 1524 M: 07793-417431 E: roberteaston1@onetel.com

EASTWOOD, David Dean. b 54. Newc Univ LLB 77. Ridley Hall Cam 06. **d** 08 **p** 09. C Westbrook St Phil *Liv* 08–10; P-in-c St Helens St Helen 10; TR St Helens Town Cen 10–18; AD St Helens 14–18; Hon Can Liv Cathl 14–18; rtd 18; PtO *Sheff* from 19. *Kairos, 199 Twentywell Lane, Sheffield S17 4QB* M: 07785-542594 E: davideastwood86@gmail.com

EASTWOOD, Canon Janet. b 54. Wycliffe Hall Ox 83. **dss** 86 **d** 87 **p** 94. Ainsdale *Liv* 86–90; Par Dn 87–90; Team Dn Kirkby Lonsdale *Carl* 90–94; TV 94–95; Dioc Youth Officer 90–94; R Wavertree H Trin *Liv* 95–18; P-in-c Wavertree St Thos 95–97; Hon Can Liv Cathl 06–18; Chapl Blue Coat Sch Liv 96–18; rtd 18. *Wavertree Rectory, Hunters Lane, Liverpool L15 8HL* T: 0151-733 2172

EASTWOOD, Mrs Nicola Jane. b 63. **d** 11 **p** 12. C Upton (Overchurch) *Ches* 11–18; V from 18. *20 Church Road, Upton, Wirral CH49 6JZ* E: nikkieastwood@gmail.com *or* nikki@stm-upton.org.uk

EATOCK, John. b 45. Lanc Univ MA 82. Lich Th Coll 67. **d** 70 **p** 71. C Crumpsall St Mary *Man* 70–73; C Atherton 73–74; C Ribbleton *Blackb* 74–77; V Ingol 77–83; V Laneside 83–92; RD Accrington 90–92; PtO 92–08; *Truro* from 08. *29 Wellington Road, Camborne TR14 7LH* T: (01209) 714899 E: john.eatock@tiscali.co.uk

EATON, Barry Anthony. b 50. St Martin's Coll Lanc MA 98. CBDTI 94. **d** 97 **p** 98. C W Burnley All SS *Blackb* 97–99; Dep Chapl HM Pris Leeds 99–00; Chapl HM Pris Buckley Hall 00–07; Chapl HM Pris Styal 07–10; Chapl HM Pris Preston from 10. *HM Prison Preston, 2 Ribbleton Lane, Preston PR1 5AB* T: (01772) 444550

EATON, Benjamin. *See* EATON, Oscar Benjamin

EATON, David Andrew. b 58. Man Univ BSc 79 ACA 83 FCA. Trin Coll Bris BA 89. **d** 89 **p** 90. C Barking St Marg w St Patr *Chelmsf* 89–92; C Billericay and Lt Burstead 92–95; P-in-c Vange 95–05; TV Sole Bay *St E* 05–10; CF (TA) from 94; rtd 10; PtO *St E* from 10. *The Cedars, School Lane, Great Barton, Bury St Edmunds IP31 2RQ* T: (01284) 787718 M: 07841-215182 E: davidaeaton@lineone.net

EATON, Canon David John. b 45. Nottm Univ LTh BTh 74. St Jo Coll Nottm 70. **d** 74 **p** 75. C Headley All SS *Guildf* 74–77; Ind Chapl *Worc* 77–82; TV Halesowen 80–82; V Rowledge *Guildf* 82–89; V Leatherhead 89–01; R Leatherhead and Mickleham 01–09; RD Leatherhead 93–98; Hon Can Guildf Cathl 02–09; rtd 09; PtO *Guildf* from 10; *S'wark* from 09. *Two Way House, Wheelers Lane, Brockham, Betchworth RH3 7LA* T: (01737) 843915 E: rev_davideaton@hotmail.com

✠**EATON, The Rt Revd Derek Lionel.** b 41. MA 78. Trin Coll Bris. **d** 71 **p** 71 **c** 90. C Barton Hill St Luke w Ch Ch *Bris* 71–72; Chapl Br Emb Tunisia 72–78; Provost All SS Cathl Cairo 78–83; Chapl Br Emb Egypt 78–83; Hon Can All SS Cathl Cairo 85; Assoc P Papanui St Paul New Zealand 84; V Sumner-Redcliffs 85–90; Bp Nelson 90–06; rtd 06. *67 Grove Street, The Wood, Nelson 7010, New Zealand* T: (0064) (3) 545 6998 E: eaton.d.a@gmail.com

EATON (née CRAIG), Mrs Julie Elizabeth. b 57. Open Univ BA 08 Essex Univ MA 13. Trin Coll Bris 87. **d** 89 **p** 94. Par Dn Gt Ilford St Andr *Chelmsf* 89–92; NSM Billericay and

Lt Burstead 92–95; C 95–96; TV 96–01; Chapl Thameside Community Healthcare NHS Trust 92–95; PtO *Chelmsf* 01–05; TV Sole Bay *St E* 05–10. *The Cedars, School Lane, Great Barton, Bury St Edmunds IP31 2RQ* T: (01284) 787718 E: julie@parkgates.plus.com

EATON, Mrs Margaret Anne. b 44. Ab Dioc Tr Course 82. **dss** 84 **d** 86 **p** 94. NSM Ellon and Cruden Bay *Ab* 84–95; C Bridge of Don 95–00; Co-ord Scottish Episc Renewal Fellowship 00–04; C Ellon *Ab* 01–03; C Elgin w Lossiemouth *Mor* 03–04 and 06–10; C Aberlour and Dufftown 06–10; LtO from 11. *Grianach, Tom-na-Muidh Road, Dufftown, Keith AB55 4AT* T: (01340) 821478 E: maggie-e@hotmail.co.uk

EATON, Canon Oscar Benjamin. b 37. Puerto Rico Th Coll STB 66. **d** 66 **p** 67. Ecuador 66–69; C Wandsworth St Anne *S'wark* 69–71; C Aldrington *Chich* 71–73; TV Littleham w Exmouth *Ex* 74–79; R Alphington 79–84; Chapl Barcelona w Casteldefels *Eur* 84–87; Chapl Barcelona 88; Chapl Maisons-Laffitte 88–02; P-in-c St Raphaël 02–10; Can Malta Cathl 96–10. *Flat 2, 104 Skipton Road, Ilkley LS29 9HE* T: (01943) 607205 E: beneatonsenior@gmail.com

✠**EATON, The Rt Revd Peter David.** b 58. K Coll Lon BA 82 AKC 82 Qu Coll Cam BA 85 MA 89 Magd Coll Ox MA 90. Westcott Ho Cam 83. **d** 86 **p** 87 **c** 15. C Maidstone All SS and St Phil w Tovil *Cant* 86–89; Fells' Chapl Magd Coll Ox 89–91; LtO *Ox* 89–06; PtO from 14; Assoc R Salt Lake City St Paul USA 91–95; R Lancaster St Jas Penn 95–01; Hon Can Th Utah 91–01; Dean St Jo Cathl Denver 02–15; Adjunct Angl Studies Iliff Sem Denver 05–15; Coadjutor Bp SE Florida 15–16; Bp SE Florida from 16. *The Diocese of Southeast Florida, 525 NE 15th Street, Miami FL 33132, USA* T: (001) (305) 373 0881 F: 375 8054 E: bishop@diosef.org

EATON, Miss Phyllis Mary. b 42. Qu Eliz Coll Lon BSc 63 UNISA BA 79 SRD. WMMTC 87. **d** 90 **p** 94. NSM Washwood Heath *Birm* 90–91; NSM Edgbaston SS Mary and Ambrose 91–95; PtO 95–05; NSM Oldbury, Langley and Londonderry 05–13; PtO from 13. *7 Milton Court, Sandon Road, Smethwick B66 4AD* T: 0121-420 3488 E: phyllis.eaton@btinternet.com

EAVES, Alan Charles. b 37. Tyndale Hall Bris 62. **d** 65 **p** 66. C Southport SS Simon and Jude *Liv* 65–66; C Eccleston Ch Ch 66–70; V Earlestown 70–79; V Orpington Ch Ch *Roch* 79–02; rtd 02; PtO *Ely* from 03. *4 Chervil Close, Folksworth, Peterborough PE7 3SZ* T: (01733) 241644 M: 07904-357476

EBBSFLEET, Suffragan Bishop of (Provincial Episcopal Visitor). See GOODALL, The Rt Revd Jonathan Michael

EBELING, Mrs Barbara. b 44. Hull Univ BA 67. St Alb Minl Tr Scheme 87. **d** 94 **p** 95. C Stevenage St Hugh and St Jo *St Alb* 94–99; R Riversmeet 99–08; rtd 08; PtO *St Alb* 08–09; *Chelmsf* 09–13; V High Cross *St Alb* 10–13; V Thundridge 10–13. *7 Wicklands Road, Hunsdon, Ware SG12 8PD* T: (01279) 842086 E: barbara.ebeling@sky.com

ECCLESTON, Mrs Frances Mary. b 61. Jes Coll Cam BA 83 York St Jo Coll MA 05 CQSW 88. NOC 00. **d** 03 **p** 04. C Ranmoor *Sheff* 03–06; C Sheff St Leon Norwood 06–09; P-in-c Crosspool 09–14; V 14–16; Dioc Ecum Officer 10–14; Bp's Adv in Past Care and Reconciliation 14–16; TR Aston cum Aughton w Swallownest and Ulley 16–19; Bp's Interim Min from 19; AD Laughton from 16. *The Rectory, 91 Worksop Road, Aston, Sheffield S26 2EB* T: 0114-287 3780 E: frances.eccleston@sheffield.anglican.org

ECCLESTONE, Canon Gary Edward. b 73. Ex Univ BA 95 PGCE 96. Cuddesdon Coll BTh 99. **d** 99 **p** 00. C Salisbury St Martin and Laverstock *Sarum* 99–03; P-in-c Hanslope w Castlethorpe *Ox* 03–09; V from 09; AD Newport from 17; Hon Can Ho Ghana from 14. *The Vicarage, Park Road, Hanslope, Milton Keynes MK19 7LT* T: (01908) 337936

ECKERSLEY, Mrs Nancy Elizabeth. b 50. York Univ BA 72 Leeds Univ CertEd 73. NEOC 86. **d** 89 **p** 94. C Clifton *York* 89–00; Chapl York Distr Hosp 90–93; Lay Tr Officer *York* 93–00; V Heslington 00–11; rtd 11; PtO *York* from 12. *14 Church Close, Flamborough, Bridlington YO15 1AF* T: (01626) 850515 E: revnance@yahoo.co.uk

ECKHARD, Robert Leo Michael. b 60. Middx Poly BA 87 Open Univ MA 96 La Sainte Union Coll PGCE 88. NTMTC BA 05. **d** 05 **p** 06. C Ealing St Paul *Lon* 05–08; C Hounslow H Trin w St Paul and St Mary 08–10; PtO from 14. *23 Ellerman Avenue, Twickenham TW2 6AA* M: 07985-003057 E: bob.eckhard50@gmail.com

EDDLESTON, Audrey Suzanne. b 65. Hull Univ BA 87 Ches Univ MA 19 Lon Inst of Educn PGCE 88. All SS Cen for Miss & Min 14. **d** 17 **p** 18. C Timperley *Ches* from 17. *17 Grange Avenue, Timperley, Altrincham WA15 6DS* T: 0161-973 3899 M: 07491-444014 E: revdsuzie@outlook.com

EDDY, Paul Anthony. b 67. St Jo Coll Nottm 07. **d** 09 **p** 10. C Grove *Ox* 09–12; V Stanford in the Vale w Goosey and Hatford from 13; Dioc Missr from 11. *The Vicarage, 24 Church* *Green, Stanford in the Vale, Faringdon SN7 8HU* T: (01367) 710267 M: 07958-905716 E: paul@pauleddy.uk

EDE, The Ven Dennis. b 31. Nottm Univ BA 55 Birm Univ MSocSc 73. Ripon Hall Ox 55. **d** 57 **p** 58. C Sheldon *Birm* 57–60; C Castle Bromwich SS Mary and Marg 60–64; Chapl E Birm Hosp 60–76; C-in-c Hodge Hill CD *Birm* 64–70; V Hodge Hill 70–72; TR 72–76; Chapl Sandwell Distr Gen Hosp 76–90; V W Bromwich All SS *Lich* 76–90; P-in-c W Bromwich Ch Ch 76–79; RD W Bromwich 76–90; Preb Lich Cathl 83–90; Adn Stoke-upon-Trent 90–97; rtd 97; Hon C Tilford *Guildf* 97–99; Hon C The Bourne and Tilford 99–02; PtO *S'wark* 03–16; *Guildf* 03–13. *Tilford, 13 Park Close, Carshalton SM5 3EU* T: (020) 8647 5891 M: 07946-324299

EDEN-JONES, Mrs Sarah Rachel. b 72. St Hilda's Coll Ox BA 93 MA 98. St Mellitus Coll 13. **d** 16 **p** 17. C Reading Greyfriars *Ox* from 16. *33 Highdown Hill Road, Emmer Green, Reading RG4 8QR* M: 07703-835704 E: sedenjones@gmail.com

EDGAR, David. b 59. Newc Univ BA 81. Linc Th Coll BTh 86. **d** 86 **p** 87. C Wednesbury St Paul Wood Green *Lich* 86–91; V Winterton *Gp Linc* 91–00; Chapl De Montford Univ *St Alb* 00–02; Chapl Linc Univ *York* 02–06; C Linc St Swithin 00–01; P-in-c 01–14; P-in-c Linc All SS 06–15; Chapl N Lincs Coll 00–15. *26 Holmfield, Fiskerton, Lincoln LN3 4GD* E: david.edgar1@tesco.net

EDGAR, Ian Henry. b 78. Huron Coll Ontario MDiv 18. **d** 18 **p** 19. C Durrington *Chich* from 18; C Maybridge and W Tarring from 18. *26 Vancouver Close, Worthing BN13 2SH* T: (01903) 694635 M: 07586-477191 E: st.kieran.st.luke@gmail.com *or* fr.ianedgar@gmail.com

EDGAR, Orion Burns. b 81. Nottm Univ BA 03 MA 07 PhD 12. Westcott Ho Cam 14. **d** 16 **p** 17. C Pershore w Pinvin, Wick and Birlingham *Worc* 16–17; C Malvern H Trin and St Jas 17–19; Chapl R Holloway and Bedf New Coll *Guildf* from 19. *Address temp unknown* M: 07779-357772 E: orionedgar@mac.com

EDGCUMBE, Irena Christine. See CZERNIAWSKA EDGCUMBE, Irena Christine

EDGE, Darren. b 69. Man Metrop Univ BEd 99 Staffs Univ PGCE 06. SNWTP 10. **d** 13 **p** 14. C Werrington and Wetley Rocks *Lich* 13–17; Dir Progress Blythe Bridge High Sch 14–15; PtO *Lich* 18–19; TV Bucknall from 19. *12 Tansey Close, Stoke-on-Trent ST2 9QX* M: 07940-555540 E: d.s.edge@hotmail.co.uk

EDGE, Michael MacLeod. b 45. St Andr Univ BSc 68 Qu Coll Cam BA 70 MA 74. Westcott Ho Cam 68. **d** 72 **p** 73. C Allerton *Liv* 72–76; R Bretherton *Blackb* 76–82; P-in-c Kilpeck *Heref* 82–84; P-in-c St Devereux w Wormbridge 82–84; TR Ewyas Harold w Dulas, Kenderchurch etc 82–93; RD Abbeydore 84–90; V Enfield St Andr *Lon* 93–13; rtd 13; PtO *St E* from 15. *19 Abbeyfields, Bury St Edmunds IP33 1AQ* T: (01284) 724178 E: michaeledge@cantab.net

EDGE, Philip John. b 54. Ripon Coll Cuddesdon 77. **d** 80 **p** 81. C N Harrow St Alb *Lon* 80–83; C St Giles Cripplegate w St Bart Moor Lane etc 83–86; P-in-c Belmont 86–88; V 88–92; V Ellesmere and Welsh Frankton *Lich* 92–97; V Ellesmere 97–19; RD 10–13; rtd 19. *127 Ellesmere Road, Shrewsbury SY1 2RA* T: (01743) 622842 E: philipedge@talktalk.net

EDGE, Timothy Peter. b 55. Brighton Poly BSc 80 K Coll Lon MA 10 CEng 85 MIET 85 FRAS 80. Westcott Ho Cam 85. **d** 88 **p** 89. C Norton *Ches* 88–91; C Bedworth *Cov* 91–96; TV Witney *Ox* 96–02; Asst Chapl HM Pris Bullingdon 02–04; Chapl 04–09; NSM Cogges and S Leigh *Ox* 03–11; PtO from 11. *27 Burford Road, Witney OX28 6DP* T: (01993) 773438 E: tim.edge@talk21.com

EDGERTON, Ms Hilary Ann. b 66. R Holloway & Bedf New Coll Lon BSc 88. Wycliffe Hall Ox BTh 93. **d** 93 **p** 94. Par Dn S Cave and Ellerker w Broomfleet *York* 93–94; C 94–97; TV Howden 97–00; V Hayfield and Chinley w Buxworth *Derby* 00–16; Chapl HM Pris Buckley Hall from 16; Hon C Saddleworth *Man* from 16. *HM Prison Buckley Hall, Buckley Farm Lane, Rochdale OL12 9DP* T: (01706) 514300 M: 07407-400261 E: hedgerton356@btinternet.com

EDIE, Jennifer Mary. b 40. Edin Univ MA 62 Hong Kong Univ PGCE 77. **d** 03 **p** 04. NSM Eyemouth *Edin* 03–09; P-in-c 06–09; rtd 09; LtO *Edin* from 09. *12 Barefoots Avenue, Eyemouth TD14 5JH* T: (018907) 50169 E: rev.jennifer@gmail.com

EDINBOROUGH, David. b 36. Nottm Univ BA 58 MEd 74. EMMTC 79. **d** 82 **p** 83. NSM Bramcote *S'well* 82–01; P-in-c 94–01; Dioc Officer for NSMs 89–94; rtd 01; PtO *S'well* 01–02; P-in-c Radford St Pet 02–04; PtO from 04; Bp's Chapl for Rtd Clergy 09–16. *105A Derby Road, Beeston, Nottingham NG9 3GZ* T: 0115-925 1066 E: david.edinborough@btopenworld.com *or* david.edinborough@googlemail.com

EDINBURGH, Bishop of. See ARMES, The Rt Revd John Andrew

EDINBURGH, Dean of. *See* BURBERRY, The Very Revd Frances Sheila

EDINBURGH, Provost of. *See* CONWAY, The Very Revd John Arthur

EDMANS, Mrs Jennifer. b 56. d 07 p 08. OLM Bernwode *Ox* 07–10; C from 10. *2 The Bungalow, Coldharbour Farm, Brill, Aylesbury HP18 9UA* T: (01844) 237855 M: 07808-347276 E: jennyedmans@aol.com

EDMONDS (née HARRIS), Mrs Catherine Elizabeth. b 52. Leic Coll of Educn CertEd 73 ACP 79. S Dios Minl Tr Scheme 91. d 95 p 96. NSM Basing *Win* 95–99; C Yeovil H Trin w Barwick *B & W* 99–01; Chapl Coll of SS Mark and Jo Plymouth *Ex* 01–06; TV Ottery St Mary, Alfington, W Hill, Tipton etc 06–17; C Broadhembury, Payhembury and Plymtree 09–16; Dioc Youth Adv 06–17; RD Ottery 14–17; rtd 17; RD Honiton *Ex* from 19. *Woodfield, Sidmouth Road, Lyme Regis DT7 3ES* T: (01297) 444465 E: cateedmonds@aol.com

EDMONDS, Clive Alway. b 42. ACII. S'wark Ord Course 78. d 81 p 82. C Horsell *Guildf* 81–85; R Bisley and W End 85–92; RD Surrey Heath 90–92; R Haslemere 92–00; Chapl Wispers Sch Haslemere 92–00; P-in-c Westbury-on-Severn w Flaxley and Blaisdon *Glouc* 00–02; V Westbury-on-Severn w Flaxley, Blaisdon etc 03–06; rtd 06; PtO *Heref* from 07; *Glouc* from 17. *3 Church Road, Longhope GL17 0LH* T: (01452) 831545 E: alwayedmonds@hotmail.com

EDMONDS, Michelle Kay. b 70. S Bank Univ BSc 98. Ripon Coll Cuddesdon BTh 08. d 06 p 07. C Croydon St Matt *S'wark* 06–09; TV Warlingham w Chelsham and Farleigh 09–16; TR from 16; Asst Dir of Ords Croydon Area from 13. *The Vicarage, 2 Chelsham Road, Warlingham CR6 9EQ* T: (01883) 623011 M: 07799-713957 E: revmichelle@btinternet.com

EDMONDS (née MAGUIRE), Ms Sarah Alison. b 65. Univ Coll Lon BSc 87 Southn Univ MSc 93. STETS 95. d 98 p 99. C Warwick St Paul *Cov* 98–02; P-in-c Hampton Lucy w Charlecote and Loxley 02–06; PtO 12–14; Hon C Ilmington w Stretton-on-Fosse etc 14–17; Hon C Tredington and Darlingscott 14–17; R Shipston-on-Stour w Honington and Idlicote from 17. *The Rectory, 8 Glen Close, Shipston-on-Stour CV36 4ED* T: (01608) 661210 E: sarah_edmonds@btconnect.com

EDMONDS, Stephen Harry James. b 77. SS Hild & Bede Coll Dur BA 99 Leeds Univ MA 08. Coll of Resurr Mirfield 06. d 08 p 09. C Hendon *Dur* 08–12; V Edlington and Hexthorpe *Sheff* from 12. *The Vicarage, 17 Heaton Gardens, Edlington, Doncaster DN12 1SY* T: (01709) 858358 M: 07882-443025 E: fr.s.edmonds@gmail.com

EDMONDS, Stephen Philip Augustine. Kent Univ BA 05 Heythrop Coll Lon MA 10 Selwyn Coll Cam PhD 16. Westcott Ho Cam 10. d 15 p 16. C Sydenham St Bart S'wark 15–19; TV Wimbledon from 19. *Address withheld by request* T: (020) 8544 0792 E: vicar@sedmonds.co.uk

EDMONDS, Tony Ernest. b 50. R Holloway Coll Lon BSc 71 Imp Coll Lon MSc 73 PhD 75 Nottm Univ MA 05. EMMTC 02. d 05 p 06. NSM Barrow upon Soar w Walton le Wolds *Leic* 05–10; TV Kegworth, Hathern, Long Whatton, Diseworth etc 10–16; Warden of Readers 10–13; AD Akeley E 11–16; rtd 16; PtO *Sarum* from 17. *Varhn, Agglestone Road, Studland, Swanage BH19 3BZ* T: (01929) 450097 M: 07837-009147 E: t.e.edmonds@btconnect.com

✠**EDMONDSON, The Rt Revd Christopher Paul.** b 50. St Jo Coll Dur BA 71 MA 81. Cranmer Hall Dur 71. d 73 p 74 c 08. C Kirkheaton *Wakef* 73–79; V Ovenden 79–86; Bp's Adv on Evang 81–86; Dioc Officer for Evang *Carl* 86–92; P-in-c Bampton w Mardale 86–92; V Shipley St Pet *Bradf* 92–02; Warden Lee Abbey 02–08; Suff Bp Bolton *Man* 08–16; rtd 16; Hon Asst Bp Leeds from 17. *16 Cavalier Drive, Apperley Bridge, Bradford BD10 0UF* T: (01274) 284031 E: chris.edmondson@me.com

EDMONDSON, Canon John James William. b 55. St Jo Coll Dur BA 83 MA 91 PhD 04. Cranmer Hall Dur 80. d 83 p 84. C Gee Cross *Ches* 83–86; C Camberley St Paul *Guildf* 86–88; TV 88–90; Chapl Elmhurst Ballet Sch 86–90; V Foxton w Gumley and Laughton and Lubenham *Leic* 90–94; R Bexhill St Mark *Chich* 94–05; V Battle 05–18; Dean Battle 05–18; P-in-c Sedlescombe w Whatlington 05–08; Dioc Voc Adv 98–02; Asst Dir of Ords 02–05; RD Battle and Bexhill 13–15; Can and Preb Chich Cathl 14–18; rtd 18; PtO *Nor* from 19. *Inglenooks, 49-53 Damgate Street, Wymondham NR18 0BJ*

EDMONTON, Area Bishop of. *See* WICKHAM, The Rt Revd Robert James

EDMUNDS, Andrew Charles. b 57. Whitelands Coll Lon BEd 80 CQSW 83. Oak Hill NSM Course 87. d 89 p 90. NSM Hawkwell *Chelmsf* 89–95; C Torquay St Matthias, St Mark and H Trin *Ex* 95–97; V Ripley *Derby* 97–09; RD Heanor 06–09; PtO 09–11; R Yateley *Win* 11–19; rtd 19. *Address temp unknown* M: 07715-377225 E: a.edmunds@me.com

EDMUNDS, Gary James William. b 56. K Coll Lon BD 78 RGN 89. STETS 12. d 15 p 16. NSM Norton sub Hamdon, W Chinnock, Chiselborough etc *B & W* 15–17; NSM Ham Hill Villages from 17; Chapl Taunton and Somerset NHS Foundn Trust from 17. *Hamdon Vale, West Street, Stoke-sub-Hamdon TA14 6QG* M: 07738-197880 E: gary.edmunds@hotmail.co.uk

EDMUNDSON, Susan Sharon. b 51. St Mellitus Coll 16. d 17 p 18. NSM Downham w S Hanningfield and Ramsden Bellhouse *Chelmsf* from 17. *19 Westerings, Danbury, Chelmsford CM3 4ND* T: (01245) 224181 E: suzy.edmundson@btinternet.com

EDSON, The Ven Michael. b 42. Birm Univ BSc 64 Leeds Univ BA 71. Coll of Resurr Mirfield 69. d 72 p 73. C Barnstaple St Pet w H Trin *Ex* 72–77; TV Barnstaple and Goodleigh 77–79; TV Barnstaple, Goodleigh and Landkey 79–82; V Roxbourne St Andr *Lon* 82–89; AD Harrow 85–89; P-in-c S Harrow St Paul 86–89; Warden Lee Abbey 89–94; LtO *Ex* 89–94; Adn Leic 94–02; Bp's Insp of Par Registers and Records 94–02; TR Bideford, Northam, Westward Ho!, Appledore etc *Ex* 02–09; rtd 09; PtO *Leeds* from 17. *11 Belmont Road, Ilkley LS29 8PE* T: (01943) 969874 E: ven.mike.edson@gmail.com

EDWARDS, Adam Peter Michael. b 78. Birm Univ BA 01. Qu Foundn (Course) 15. d 17 p 18. NSM Ettingshall *Lich* from 17. *35 Cherrington Gardens, Wolverhampton WV6 8AJ* M: 07523-907180 E: father.adam@hotmail.com

EDWARDS, Aiden James Alexander. b 82. Sheff Univ BA 17. Coll of Resurr Mirfield 14. d 17 p 18. C St Annes St Anne *Blackb* from 17. *66 Leach Lane, Lytham St Annes FY8 3AN* T: (01253) 728470 M: 07758-919144 E: curateofstannes@outlook.com

EDWARDS, Canon Aled. b 55. Univ of Wales (Lamp) BA 77. Trin Coll Bris 77. d 79 p 80. C Glanogwen *Ban* 79–82; V Llandinorwig w Penisa'r-waen 82–85; R Botwnnog 85–93; V Cardiff Dewi Sant *Llan* 93–99; Nat Assembly Liaison Officer from 99; Hon Chapl Llan Cathl from 99; Metrop Can Llan Cathl from 14. *20 Hilltop Avenue, Cilfynydd, Pontypridd CF37 4HZ* T: (01443) 407310

EDWARDS, Allen John. b 50. Univ of Wales (Cardiff) BSc 72 Imp Coll Lon PhD 81 York St Jo Univ MA 16 CEng 81 EurIng 88 FIMechE 93 FNucI 95 MCMI 95 MAPM 95. SAOMC 00. d 02 p 03. NSM Didcot All SS *Ox* 02–11; PtO *Eur* from 10; *Sarum* 12; NSM Warminster Ch Ch from 12. *10 Southdown Way, Warminster BA12 8FP* E: allen.edwards@btinternet.com

EDWARDS, Canon Andrew David. b 42. Tyndale Hall Bris 67. d 70 p 71. C Blackpool Ch Ch *Blackb* 70–73; C W Teignmouth *Ex* 73–76; P-in-c Ilfracombe SS Phil and Jas 76–85; C-in-c Lundy Is 79–89; V Ilfracombe SS Phil and Jas w W Down 85–89; TV Canford Magna *Sarum* 89–98; R Moresby *Carl* 98–07; RD Calder 02–07; Hon Can Carl Cathl 05–07; rtd 07; PtO *Carl* 07–14. *21 Grovelands Road, Headington, Oxford OX3 8HZ* T: (01865) 751591 E: a.edwards432@btinternet.com

EDWARDS, Andrew James. b 54. York Univ BA 76. Wycliffe Hall *Ox* 77. d 80 p 81. C Beckenham St Jo *Roch* 80–83; C Luton Ch Ch 83–87; V Skelmersdale Ch at Cen *Liv* 87–95; V Netherton 95–02; V Southport St Phil and St Paul 02–11; C Southport All SS 03–11; V W Derby Gd Shep 11–19; NSM Liv Cathl from 19. *4 Christchurch Close, Liverpool L11 3EN* T: 0151-474 1444 E: andrew@ajedwards.me.uk

EDWARDS, Andrew Jonathan Hugo (Joe). b 56. Ex Univ BA 78. Sarum & Wells Th Coll BTh 93. d 93 p 94. C Honiton, Gittisham, Combe Raleigh, Monkton etc *Ex* 93–97; P-in-c Queen Thorne *Sarum* 97–01; Chapl Clayesmore Sch Blandford 01–10; P-in-c Bridge Par *Sarum* 11–18; Chapl Qu Eliz Sch Wimborne 11–12; P-in-c Spetisbury w Charlton Marshall etc *Sarum* 13–18; rtd 18. *Church Farmhouse, Stourton Caundle, Sturminster Newton DT10 2JN*

EDWARDS, Anita Carolyn. *See* COLPUS, Anita Carolyn

EDWARDS, Canon Anne Joan. b 67. Lanc Univ BA 89 Liv Univ MTh 05 Salford Univ BSc 08. NOC 97. d 00 p 01. C Elton All SS *Man* 00–04; Chapl Bolton Hosps NHS Trust 02–04; Chapl and Spiritual Care Manager Wrightington, Wigan and Leigh NHS Foundn Trust from 04; Bp's Adv for Healthcare Chapl *Man* from 15; LtO *Blackb* from 10; Hon Can Man Cathl from 15. *9 Stocks Courts, 2 Harriet Street, Worsley, Manchester M28 3JW* T: (01942) 822324 E: anne.j.edwards@wwl.nhs.uk or anne@sajm.net

EDWARDS, Canon Arthur John. b 42. Qu Mary Coll Lon BA 64 MPhil 66 Cardiff Univ PhD 16. St Mich Coll Llan 66. d 68 p 69. C Newport St Woolos *Mon* 68–71; V Llantarnam 71–74; Chapl Bp of Llan High Sch 74–78; V Griffithstown *Mon* 78–86; Dioc Dir RE 86–91; TR Cwmbran 86–95; Hon Can St Woolos Cathl 88–91; Can St Woolos Cathl 91–12; V Caerleon 95–02; V Caerleon w Llanhennock 02–09; V Caerleon and Llanfrechfa 09–12; AD Newport 98–09; rtd

12; P-in-c Mynyddislwyn *Mon* 12–14; PtO from 14. *31 Candwr Park, Ponthir, Newport NP18 1HL* T: (01633) 430768 E: aandcedwards@talk21.com

EDWARDS, Carl Flynn. b 63. Cranmer Hall Dur 03. **d** 05 **p** 06. C Scartho *Linc* 05–09; P-in-c Fairfield *Derby* 09–18; C Buxton w Burbage and King Sterndale 09–12; P-in-c Peak Forest and Dove Holes 12–18; V Fairfield, Peak Forest and Dove Holes from 18. *Fairfield Vicarage, Cherry Tree Drive, Fairfield, Buxton SK17 7JN* T: (01298) 23629

EDWARDS, Miss Carol Rosemary. b 46. Trin Coll Bris 74. **dss** 81 **d** 87 **p** 94. Hengrove *Bris* 81–82; Filton 82–85; Brislington St Chris 85–99; Dn-in-c 87–94; P-in-c 94–99; P-in-c Brislington St Chris and St Cuth 99–00; Hon Can Bris Cathl 93–00; P-in-c California *Ox* 00–10; rtd 10; PtO *B & W* from 11. *44 Godwin Drive, Nailsea, Bristol BS48 2XF* T: (01275) 858168 M: 07879-536218 E: carol.edwards858@gmail.com

EDWARDS, Christopher Alban. b 27. Hertf Coll Ox. Th Ext Educn Coll. **d** 89 **p** 92. C Pietersburg Ch S Africa 89; C Montagu 90–96; C Harare Cathl Zimbabwe 96–01; PtO *Ripon* 01; *York* from 01. *1 Hastings House, Holyrood Lane, Ledsham, South Milford, Leeds LS25 5LL* T: (01977) 682117 M: 07780-543114 E: chrisalban@btopenworld.com

EDWARDS, David Arthur. b 26. Wadh Coll Ox BA 50 MA 51. Wycliffe Hall Ox. **d** 52 **p** 53. C Didsbury St Jas and Em *Man* 52–55; Liv Sec SCM 55–58; Chapl Liv Univ 55–58; R Burnage St Nic *Man* 58–65; V Yardley St Edburgha *Birm* 65–73; Org Sec CECS Blackb, Carl and Man 73–78; R Man Resurr 78–81; V Lorton and Loweswater w Buttermere *Carl* 81–87; USPG 87–92; Malaysia 87–92; rtd 92; PtO *Carl* 00–16. *46 Wainwright Court, Webb View, Kendal LA9 4TE* T: (01539) 739297

EDWARDS, The Rt Revd David John. b 60. Loughb Univ BA 81 Homerton Coll Cam PGCE 82 Kent Univ MA 95 Wycliffe Coll Toronto DD 15. CA Tr Coll 86 EAMTC 94. **d** 95 **p** 96. C High Ongar w Norton Mandeville *Chelmsf* 95–98; Prin Taylor Coll Saint John Canada 98–07; P-in-c Saint John St Jas 98–01; R Saint John St Mark 01–11; Adn Saint John 08–11; Adn St Andrews 11–14; Par Development Officer 11–14; Bp Fredericton from 14. *31 Carlile Crescent, Saint John NB E2J 5C3, Canada* T: (001) (506) 459 1801 E: dedwards@diofton.ca

EDWARDS, Diana Clare. b 56. Nottm Univ BTh 86 SRN 77 RSCN 81. Linc Th Coll 83. **dss** 86 **d** 87 **p** 94. S Wimbledon H Trin and St Pet *S'wark* 86–90; Par Dn 87–90; Par Dn Lingfield and Crowhurst 90–94; C 94–95; Chapl St Piers Hosp Sch Lingfield 90–95; R Bletchingley *S'wark* 95–04; RD Godstone 98–04; Hon Can S'wark Cathl 01–04; Dean of Women's Min 03–04; Can Res Cant Cathl 04–18; R Drybrook, Lydbrook and Ruardean *Glouc* from 18. *The Rectory, High Street, Ruardean GL17 9US*

EDWARDS, Gary Nord. St Mellitus Coll 17. **d** 19. NSM Ashingdon w S Fambridge, Canewdon and Paglesham *Chelmsf* from 19. *54 Durham Road, Southend-on-Sea SS2 4LU* T: (01702) 611777 E: gary-st.andrews@outlook.com

EDWARDS, Graham Charles. b 40. Qu Coll Birm BD 82 **p** 83. C Baswich *Lich* 82–86; C Tamworth 86–88; R Hertford St Andr *St Alb* 88–05; RD Hertford and Ware 96–99; rtd 05; PtO *Lich* 06–17. *The Old Forge, Main Road, Great Haywood, Stafford ST18 0RZ* T: (01889) 882868

EDWARDS, Guy. See EDWARDS, Jonathan Guy

EDWARDS, Helen. See HINGLEY, Helen

EDWARDS (née BENNETT), Canon Helen Anne. b 69. Coll of Ripon & York St Jo BEd 91 Bris Univ BA 01. Trin Coll Bris 99. **d** 01 **p** 02. C Beverley Minster *York* 01–05; P-in-c Liv Ch Ch Norris Green 05–09; V from 09; Hon Can Liv Cathl from 13. *4 Christchurch Close, Liverpool L11 3EN* T: 0151-474 1444 E: helenedwards@ymail.com

EDWARDS, Helen Glynne. See WEBB, Helen Glynne

EDWARDS, Canon Henry Victor. b 48. AKC 71 Open Univ BA 85 Middx Univ MSc 00. St Aug Coll Cant 72. **d** 73 **p** 74. C W Leigh CD *Portsm* 73–77; V Cosham 77–84; V Reydon *St E* 84–86; V Blythburgh w Reydon 86–96; Chapl St Felix Sch Southwold 86–96; Chapl Blythburgh Hosp 86–96; P-in-c Campsea Ashe w Marlesford, Parham and Hacheston *St E* 96–00; R 00–14; P-in-c Brandeston w Kettleburgh and Easton 07–14; Hon Can St E Cathl 00–14; rtd 14; PtO *St E* from 14; Dioc Adv for Counselling and Past Care 96–17. *Dunwich View, The Green, Walberswick, Southwold IP18 6TP* T: (01502) 722928 M: 07748-986022 E: harry@psalm23.demon.co.uk

EDWARDS, Canon James Frederick. b 36. ALCD 62. **d** 62 **p** 63. C Kenwyn *Truro* 62–68; V Tuckingmill 68–76; V St Columb Minor and St Colan 76–01; RD Pydar 84–93; Hon Can Truro Cathl 92–01; rtd 01; PtO *Truro* from 01. *45 Tretherras Road, Newquay TR7 2TF* T: (01637) 870967

EDWARDS, Jane. See EDWARDS, Wendy Jane

EDWARDS, Janet Margaret. b 41. TCert 62 Lon Bible Coll BD 73. WEMTC 98. **d** 01 **p** 02. NSM Coalbrookdale, Iron-Bridge and Lt Wenlock *Heref* from 01. *2 Madeley Wood View, Madeley, Telford TF7 5TF* T: (01952) 583254

EDWARDS, Mrs Jill Kathleen. b 48. Man Univ BA 69 CQSW 72. S'wark Ord Course 90. **d** 93 **p** 95. NSM Grays Thurrock and Ind Chapl *Chelmsf* 93–07; Asst Dioc Soc Resp Officer *Truro* 07–19; Public Preacher 07–08; P-in-c Gerrans w St Anthony-in-Roseland and Philleigh 08–19; rtd 19. *Trelowen, Rosevine, Portscatho, Truro TR2 5EW* T: (01872) 580117 E: jill@jilledwards.com

EDWARDS, Joe. See EDWARDS, Andrew Jonathan Hugo

EDWARDS, Joel Kim. b 69. Oak Hill Th Coll BA 02. **d** 09 **p** 10. NSM Leyton Ch Ch *Chelmsf* 09–14; PtO 14–15; P-in-c Dagenham 15–18; V from 18. *The Vicarage, Church Lane, Dagenham RM10 9UL* T: (020) 8215 2962 M: 07903-516456 E: joel.dagenham@gmail.com

EDWARDS, Canon John Ralph. b 50. Bris Univ BSc 71 FCA 74. SAOMC 98. **d** 01 **p** 02. NSM California *Ox* 01–06; NSM Finchampstead 06–11; NSM Finchampstead and California from 11; Hon Can Ch Ch from 13. *Green Hedges, 25 St John's Street, Crowthorne RG45 7NJ* T: (01344) 774586 F: 774056 M: 07850-602488

EDWARDS, Jonathan Guy. b 63. Bris Univ BA 85. Ridley Hall Cam BA 93 MA 96. **d** 94 **p** 95. C Preston Plucknett *B & W* 94–98; C Clevedon St Andr and Ch 98–02; V Farrington Gurney 02–06; V Paulton 02–06; P-in-c High Littleton 05–06; V Paulton w Farrington Gurney and High Littleton 07–18; R Bushey *St Alb* from 18. *The Rectory, High Street, Bushey WD23 1BD* T: (020) 8950 1546 M: 07837-672481 E: rector@busheyparish.org

EDWARDS, Judith Sarah. See McARTHUR-EDWARDS, Judith Sarah

EDWARDS (née EVANS), Mrs Linda Mary. b 49. Univ of Wales (Cardiff) BA 71 K Coll Lon BD 74 AKC 74. Yale Div Sch STM 76. **dss** 76 **d** 80 **p** 99. Llanishen and Lisvane *Llan* 76–78; Wrexham *St As* 78–80; C 80–82; Chapl Maudsley Hosp Lon 82–84; Chapl Bethlem R Hosp Beckenham 82–84; Chapl Lon Univ 84–87; NSM Llanfair-pwll and Llanddaniel-fab etc *Ban* 99–03; P-in-c Llangynog *St As* 03–06; C Llanrhaeadr ym Mochnant etc 07–10; rtd 10; PtO *St As* from 14. *15 The Meadows, Llandudno Junction LL31 9LP* T: (01492) 585063 M: 07791-467102 E: lindamaryedwards@yahoo.co.uk

EDWARDS, Malcolm Ralph. b 27. Man Univ 49. Cranmer Hall Dur 57. **d** 59 **p** 60. C Withington St Paul *Man* 59–62; C Chadderton 62–64; R Longsight St Jo 64–70; V Halliwell St Thos 70–81; V Milnrow 81–92; rtd 92; PtO *Man* from 92. *20 Upper Lees Drive, Westhoughton, Bolton BL5 3UE* T: (01942) 813279 M: 07791-294680 E: revmr.edwards@virgin.net

EDWARDS, Mark Anthony. b 61. Cranmer Hall Dur 91. **d** 95 **p** 97. C Ulverston St Mary w H Trin *Carl* 95–97; C Barrow St Jo 97–00; TV Barrow St Matt 00–08; TV Ch the King *Newc* from 08; Chapl Northumbria Police 08–12. *The Vicarage, 2 East Acres, Dinnington, Newcastle upon Tyne NE13 7NA* T: (01661) 872320 E: haydenfox9411@gmail.com

EDWARDS, Mrs Mary. b 47. St Jo Coll York CertEd 69 Birkbeck Coll Lon BSc 74 New Coll Edin BD 93. S Dios Minl Tr Scheme 96. **d** 96 **p** 97. NSM Avon Valley *Sarum* 96–00; TV Wexcombe 00–02; TV Savernake 02–12; RD Pewsey 10–12; rtd 12; LtO *Edin* from 16. *The Coach House, Glenmayne, Galashiels TD1 3NR* T: (01896) 668383 E: mary_avonvalley@hotmail.com

EDWARDS, Preb Nicholas John. b 53. UEA BA 75 Fitzw Coll Cam BA 77 MA 80. Westcott Ho Cam 75. **d** 78 **p** 79. C Kirkby *Liv* 78–81; V Cantril Farm 81–87; V Hale 87–94; R Chingford SS Pet and Paul *Chelmsf* 94–04; R Colyton, Musbury, Southleigh and Branscombe *Ex* 04–10; P-in-c Ex St Thos and Em 10–17; Preb Ex Cathl 13–17; rtd 17; PtO *Guildf* from 18. *2 Lawn Road, Guildford GU2 4DE* M: 07826-545315 E: fr.nicholasedwards@virginmedia.com

EDWARDS, Mrs Nita Mary. b 50. Univ of Wales (Ban) BD 72 Nottm Univ PGCE 73. Cranmer Hall Dur 93. **d** 93 **p** 94. C Ormesby *York* 93–95; C Billingham St Aid *Dur* 95–97; V 97–02; V Clayton *Lich* 02–17; rtd 17; PtO *St As* from 17. *13 Tŷ Gwylfa, Sandy Lane, Prestatyn LL19 7SB* T: (01745) 852106 E: nita.edwards@ntlworld.com

EDWARDS, Owen David. b 86. Ban Univ BA 07 Glyndŵr Univ PhD 15. St Seiriol Cen 12. **d** 16 **p** 18. C Carbonear Canada 16; C Prestwich St Mary *Man* 18–19; C Kersal Moor from 19. *25 Rectory Lane, Prestwich, Manchester M25 1RB* T: 0161-773 8801 M: 07512-760823 E: owen.edwards2@btinternet.com

EDWARDS, Peter Daniel. b 81. St Aid Coll Dur BA 02 Peterho Cam BA 09 MA 14. Ridley Hall Cam 07. **d** 10 **p** 11. C Gt Malvern St Mary *Worc* 10–14; P-in-c Walton le Soken *Chelmsf* from 15. *The Vicarage, Martello Road,*

Walton on the Naze CO14 8BP T: (01255) 675351
E: peter.edwards@allsaintswalton.co.uk

EDWARDS, Peter Richard Henderson. b 65. Nottm Univ BA 86. St Steph Ho Ox 03. **d** 05 **p** 06. C Uppingham w Ayston and Wardley w Belton *Pet* 05–08; TV Bridport *Sarum* 08–13; P-in-c Bath Bathwick *B & W* 13–17; R from 17. *The Rectory, Sham Castle Lane, Bath BA2 6JL* T: (01225) 447450 E: frpeteredwards@sky.com

EDWARDS, Canon Philip John. b 28. Lon Univ MRCS 51 LRCP 51. Chich Th Coll 58. **d** 60 **p** 61. C Orpington St Andr *Roch* 60–67; C Mayfield *Chich* 67–71; V Haywards Heath St Rich 71–91; Can and Preb Chich Cathl 84–91; rtd 91; PtO *Chich* from 91. *22 Hamsey Road, Sharpthorne, East Grinstead RH19 4PA* T: (01342) 810210

EDWARDS, Phillip Gregory. b 52. Lon Univ BSc 73 ARCS 73 MSOSc 90. Qu Coll Birm 78. **d** 81 **p** 82. C Lillington *Cov* 81–85; P-in-c Cov St Alb 85–86; TV Cov E 86–01; C Bury St Paul and Bury Ch King *Man* 01–03; Chapl Bolton Univ 03–15; C Westhoughton and Wingates 04–05; C Leverhulme 05–07; Lic Preacher from 11; PtO *Ches* from 19. *14 Howey Lane, Congleton CW12 4AE* E: philgedwards@outlook.com

EDWARDS, Robert James. b 52. Chich Univ BA 07. Cranmer Hall Dur 01. **d** 03 **p** 04. C Broadwater *Chich* 03–08; TV S Crawley from 08. *Holy Trinity House, Titmus Drive, Crawley RH10 5EU* T: (01293) 618214 E: rev.robedwards@outlook.com

EDWARDS, Roger Brian. b 41. Sarum & Wells Th Coll 87. **d** 89 **p** 90. C Wellington and Distr *B & W* 89–92; V Hursley and Ampfield *Win* 92–06; rtd 06; PtO *Win* from 06. *34 Heatherstone Avenue, Dibden Purlieu, Southampton SO45 4LH* T: (023) 8087 9689

EDWARDS, Canon Rowland Thomas. b 62. Univ of Wales BTh 91. St Mich Coll Llan 85. **d** 88 **p** 89. C Llangiwg *S & B* 88–90; C Morriston 90–91; V Llangorse, Cathedine, Llanfihangel Talyllyn etc 91–01; V Llyn Safaddan 01–06; V Talgarth w Bronllys w Llanfilo from 06; AD Hay 02–15; AD Gtr Brecon 16–17; Can Res Brecon Cathl from 08. *The Vicarage, Bronllys, Brecon LD3 0HS* T: (01874) 711200 E: rowlbar@talktalk.net

EDWARDS, Canon Ruth Blanche. b 39. Girton Coll Cam BA 61 MA 65 PhD 68 Aber Coll of Educn PGCE 75. Ab Dioc Tr Course 77. **d** 87 **p** 94. Lect Aber Univ *Ab* 77–90; Sen Lect 90–96; Lect Ripon Coll Cuddesdon 96–99; Hon Can St Andr Cathl *Ab* from 97; rtd 00; NSM Aberdeen St Jas *Ab* from 00; P-in-c 12–13. *99 Queen's Den, Aberdeen AB15 8BN* T: (01224) 312688

EDWARDS, Scott. b 71. Wolv Univ LLB 93 St Jo Coll Dur BA 00. Cranmer Hall Dur 97. **d** 00 **p** 01. C Halas *Worc* 00–03; V Frimley Green and Mytchett *Guildf* 03–12; V Chessington from 12. *The Vicarage, 1 Garrison Lane, Chessington KT9 2LB* T: (020) 8397 3016 E: scott_edwards@btinternet.com

EDWARDS, Stephen. b 44. S'wark Ord Course. **d** 82 **p** 83. C Benhilton *S'wark* 82–86; P-in-c Clapham Ch Ch and St Jo 86–87; TV Clapham Team 87–94; Chapl HM Pris Wormwood Scrubs 94–96; Chapl HM Pris Maidstone 96–01; Chapl HM Pris Wandsworth 01–04; rtd 04; PtO *S'wark* from 04. *12 Bucharest Road, London SW18 3AR* T: (020) 8870 1991

EDWARDS, Canon Stephen Michael. b 72. Lanc Univ BSc 93 Anglia Poly Univ MA 99 Man Univ DPT 16. Westcott Ho Cam 93. **d** 96 **p** 97. C Colwyn Bay *St As* 96–99; C Colwyn 99–02; P-in-c Brynymaen 99–02; P-in-c Birch-in-Rusholme St Agnes w Longsight St Jo etc *Man* 02–12; R 12; TR Wythenshawe 12–19; AD Withington 13–19; Can Res Worc Cathl from 19. *2 College Green, Worcester WR1 2LH* E: revdstephenedwards@yahoo.co.uk

EDWARDS, Mrs Susan. b 54. R Holloway Coll Lon BSc 75 SS Hild & Bede Coll Dur PGCE 76. Qu Coll Birm 78. **dss** 81 **d** 87 **p** 94. Lillington *Cov* 81–85; Cov E 85–01; Par Dn 87–94; C 94–01; P-in-c Woolfold *Man* 01–07; TV Leverhulme 07–12; TR 12–18; rtd 18; PtO *Ches* from 19. *14 Howey Lane, Congleton CW12 4AE* M: 07982-674902 E: sedwards327@outlook.com

EDWARDS, Mrs Susan Diane. b 48. St Alb Minl Tr Scheme 86 Cranmer Hall Dur 91. **d** 92 **p** 94. Par Dn Borehamwood *St Alb* 92–94; C 94–96; V Arlesey w Astwick 96–13; rtd 13; PtO *Ches* from 14. *31 School Road, Meadowbank, Winsford CW7 2PG* T: (01606) 559458 E: susan.d.edwards@ntlworld.com *or* granny.s@outlook.com

EDWARDS, Timothy Mark. b 79. St Aid Coll Dur BA 00. Oak Hill Th Coll MA 12. **d** 12 **p** 13. C Eden, Gelt and Irthing *Carl* 12–17; R Knockholt w Halstead *Roch* from 17. *The Rectory, Church Road, Halstead, Sevenoaks TN14 7HQ* T: (01959) 532133 M: 07980-826365 E: rev.tim.edwards@gmail.com

EDWARDS, Wendy Jane. b 49. Bingley Coll of Educn CertEd 71 Kent Univ BA 07. SEITE 03. **d** 06 **p** 07. C

Riverhead w Dunton Green *Roch* 06–11; P-in-c Belvedere All SS 11–12; V 12–18; rtd 18. *c/o Crockford, Church House, Great Smith Street, London SW1P 3AZ* M: 07858-483652 E: revjaneedwards@btinternet.com

EDY, Robert James. b 48. Southn Univ BA 70 CertEd 71. Ox Min Course 90. **d** 93 **p** 94. Dep Hd Master Henry Box Sch Witney 90–08; NSM Ducklington *Ox* 93–99; P-in-c 99–13; R 13–15; PtO from 15; Chapl Rendcomb Coll Cirencester from 15. *The Rectory Cottage, Rendcomb, Cirencester GL7 7EZ* T: (01285) 831391 E: bobedy21@gmail.com

EGAR, Miss Judith Anne. b 57. Somerville Coll Ox BA 79 MA 84 Solicitor 83. STETS 01. **d** 04 **p** 05. NSM Brighton St Nic *Chich* 04–07; LtO 09–15; NSM Lewes St Anne and St Mich and St Thos etc from 15; PtO *Lon* 08–10; RD Lewes and Seaford *Chich* from 17. *15 St Peter's Place, Lewes BN7 1YP*

EGERTON, George. b 28. S'wark Ord Course 70. **d** 73 **p** 74. NSM Shere *Guildf* 73–94; PtO 94–17. *Weyside, Lower Street, Shere, Guildford GU5 9HX* T: (01483) 202549

EGGERTSEN, Jacob Harold. b 85. Newc Univ BA 08. Oak Hill Th Coll 15. **d** 19. C Banbury St Paul *Ox* from 19. *10 Hardwick Park, Banbury OX16 1YD* M: 07890-620541 E: jakeeggertsen@hotmail.com

EGGLESTON, Hugh Patrick. b 60. LSE BSc(Econ) 82 Leeds Univ BA 10. Coll of Resurr Mirfield 08. **d** 10 **p** 11. C E Dulwich St Jo *S'wark* 10–14; TR Thamesmead from 14; Ecum Adv Woolwich Area from 17. *Thamesmead Rectory, 22 Manor Close, London SE28 8EY* T: (020) 8312 0731 M: 07788-563253 E: pegglseton@ymail.com

EGGLETON, Michael John. b 50. SAOMC 96 ERMC 06. **d** 07 **p** 08. NSM Northchurch and Wigginton *St Alb* from 07. *St Bartholomew's Vicarage, Vicarage Road, Wigginton, Tring HP23 6DZ* T: (01442) 823273 M: 07962-145398 E: mikeeggleton7@btopenworld.com

EGHTEDARIAN, Mohammad Reza. b 76. Wycliffe Hall Ox 12. **d** 15 **p** 16. C Liv Cathl 15–18; Chapl Ankara *Eur* 18–19. *C/o Church Mission Society, Watlington Road, Cowley, Oxford OX4 6BZ* M: 07709-903764

EGLIN, Ian Charles. b 55. St Jo Coll Dur BA 76. Coll of Resurr Mirfield 77. **d** 79 **p** 80. C Cov St Mary 79–83; TV Kingsthorpe w Northampton St Dav *Pet* 83–87; P-in-c Pitsford w Boughton 85–87; Chapl RN 87–03; V Ipplepen, Torbryan and Denbury *Ex* 03–12; RD Newton Abbot and Ipplepen 07–12; rtd 12; Dioc Chapl MU *Ex* 13–16; PtO *Eur* from 12; *Ex* from 13. *27 Riverside Walk, Yealmpton, Plymouth PL8 2LU* T: (01752) 881996 E: ian@eglins.co.uk

EKIN, Tom Croker. b 29. Linc Th Coll 59. **d** 60 **p** 61. C Leamington Priors All SS *Cov* 60–63; R Ilmington w Stretton-on-Fosse 63–72; S Africa 72–77; R Moreton-in-Marsh w Batsford *Glouc* 77–83; R Moreton-in-Marsh w Batsford, Todenham etc 83–94; rtd 95; Hon C Theale and Englefield *Ox* 96–04; PtO *B & W* from 04. *6 Old Bell Court, Wrington, Bristol BS40 5QH* T: (01934) 862398

ELBOURNE, Keith Marshall. b 46. Nottm Univ BTh 74 Lon Univ BD 76. St Jo Coll Nottm 70. **d** 74 **p** 75. C Romford Gd Shep *Chelmsf* 74–78; C Victoria Docks St Luke 78–81; P-in-c 81–92; V Walthamstow St Pet 92–02; TR Tettenhall Wood and Perton *Lich* 02–10; rtd 10; PtO *Lich* from 10. *11 Windsor Gardens, Codsall, Wolverhampton WV8 2EX*

ELBOURNE, Timothy. b 60. Selw Coll Cam BA 81 MA 85 PGCE 82. Westcott Ho Cam 84. **d** 86 **p** 87. C Tottenham H Trin *Lon* 86–88; Chapl York Univ 88–94; P-in-c Thorp Arch w Walton 94–98; Dir of Educn *Ely* 98–12; Hon Can Ely Cathl 99–12; Dir of Educn *Chelmsf* from 13; Public Preacher from 13. *10 Sherwood Way, Feering, Colchester CO5 9LJ* T: (01245) 294400 F: 294477 Pager: (04325) 320796 E: telbourne@chelmsford.anglican.org

ELCOCK, Jonathan. b 64. Westcott Ho Cam 07. **d** 09 **p** 11. C Aberavon *Llan* 09; C Salford All SS *Man* 10–13; R Failsworth St Jo 13–19. *Address withheld by request* E: oldsalopian@hotmail.com

ELDER, Andrew John. b 49. Sunderland Poly BSc 72 MSc 76. NEOC 91. **d** 94 **p** 95. NSM Wallsend St Luke *Newc* 94–02; NSM Wallsend St Pet and St Luke 02–03; C Monkseaton St Pet 03–06; V Blyth St Mary 06–19; Hon C Cowpen 18–19; rtd 19; PtO *Newc* from 19. *51 Rowantree Road, Newcastle upon Tyne NE6 4TE* E: andy.elder@btinternet.com

ELDER, Nicholas John. b 51. Hatf Poly BA 73. Cuddesdon Coll 73. **d** 76 **p** 77. C Mill End and Heronsgate w W Hyde *St Alb* 76–79; TV Borehamwood 79–85; V Bedford St Mich 85–90; V Bedford All SS 90–00; V Camberwell St Geo *S'wark* 00–17; Warden Trin Coll Cen Camberwell 00–17; rtd 17. *28 Cardigan Street, Ipswich IP1 3PF* E: 1nicholaselder@gmail.com

ELDERGILL, Sharon Alice. b 62. **d** 13 **p** 14. NSM Burnham *B & W* from 13. *Flat 4, 15 Esplanade, Burnham-on-Sea TA8 1BG* M: 07725-621437 E: sharon.eldergill@gmail.com

ELDRIDGE, John Frederick. b 48. Loughb Univ BSc 70 Golden Gate Sem (USA) MDiv 83 Fuller Th Sem California DMin 96. Oak Hill Th Coll 90. **d** 92 **p** 93. C Maidstone St Luke *Cant* 92–97; Min Prince's Park CD *Roch* 97–02; P-in-c Wickham Market w Pettistree *St E* 02–07; V 07–18; rtd 18. *23 Broad Road, Wickham Market, Woodbridge IP13 0RJ* M: 07835-733413 E: jeldridge@supanet.com

ELDRIDGE, John Kenneth Tristan. b 59. St Steph Ho Ox 90. **d** 92 **p** 93. C Brighton Resurr *Chich* 92–96; C Hangleton 96–98; TR Moulsecoomb 98–05; V W Worthing St Jo from 05; P-in-c Worthing St Andr from 18; Chapl Sussex Beacon Hospice from 00. *St John's Vicarage, 15 Reigate Road, Worthing BN11 5NF* T: (01903) 247340 *or* (01273) 694222 E: frjohn@live.co.uk

ELDRIDGE, Stephen William. b 50. Open Univ BA 98. Chich Th Coll 87. **d** 89 **p** 90. C Stroud and Uplands w Slad *Glouc* 89–92; C Glouc St Mary de Crypt w St Jo and Ch Ch 92–95; C Glouc St Mary de Lode and St Nic 92–95; Bp's Chapl 92–93; P-in-c Kingswood w Alderley and Hillesley 95–00; P-in-c Cheltenham St Pet 00–08; TV N Cheltenham 08–16; rtd 16; PtO *Glouc* from 17. *38 Stanwick Gardens, Cheltenham GL51 9LF* T: (01242) 321325 E: stephen.stanwick@outlook.com

ELEYAE, Mrs Adeola Winifred. b 63. Lagos Univ LLB 85 LLM 90 Bris Univ LLM 13. St Mellitus Coll 11. **d** 14 **p** 15. NSM E Ham St Paul *Chelmsf* 14–16; C Walthamstow 16–18; TV from 18. *St Gabriel's Vicarage, 17 Shernhall Street, London E17 3EU* T: (020) 8281 3366 M: 07821-710521 E: aweleyae333@gmail.com *or* ade@walthamstowchurch.org.uk

ELFICK, Brian Richard. b 76. Ex Coll Ox BA 98 Selw Coll Cam BA 04 MPhil 05. Ridley Hall Cam 02. **d** 06 **p** 07. C Cambridge H Sepulchre *Ely* 06–12; TR Toxteth St Philemon w St Gabr and St Cleopas *Liv* 12–18; R Toxteth St Philemon from 19. *The Vicarage, 40 Devonshire Road, Toxteth L8 3TZ* T: 0151-222 0814

ELFORD, Keith Anthony. b 59. Em Coll Cam BA 80 MA 84. Wycliffe Hall Ox 87. **d** 90 **p** 91. C Chertsey *Guildf* 90–94; P-in-c Ockham w Hatchford 94–98; Bp's Chapl 94–98; PtO 98–00; LtO from 01. *15 Canford Drive, Addlestone KT15 2HH* T: (01932) 885137 E: keith.elford@lineone.net

ELFORD, Canon Robert John. b 39. Man Univ MA 71 Ex Univ PhD 74. Brasted Th Coll 64 Ridley Hall Cam 66. **d** 68 **p** 69. C Denton St Lawr *Man* 68–71; P-in-c Gwinear *Truro* 71–74; R Phillack w Gwithian and Gwinear 74–78; Lect Man Univ 78–87; Hon C Withington St Paul *Man* 79–83; Warden St Anselm Hall 82–87; LtO *Man* 84–87; Pro-R Liv Inst of HE 88–99; Can Th Liv Cathl 92–04; rtd 04. *The Penthouse, 120 The Cliff, Wallasey CH45 2NW*

ELFRED, Michael William. b 48. BA 76 MPhil. Linc Th Coll 77. **d** 79 **p** 80. C Boultham *Linc* 79–82; C Croydon H Sav *Cant* 82–84; C Upper Norwood All SS *S'wark* 84–88; V Sanderstead St Mary 88–01; P-in-c Sanderstead 01–11; V 11–16; rtd 16; PtO *S'wark* from 17. *Gadbrook, Wonham Lane, Betchworth RH3 7AD* M: 07931-463661

ELGAR, Richard John. b 50. Charing Cross Hosp Medical Sch MB, BS 73 LRCP 73 MRCS 73 MRCGP 80. St Jo Coll Nottm 92. **d** 92 **p** 93. NSM Derby St Alkmund and St Werburgh 92–96; P-in-c Derby St Barn 96–01; V 01–08; RD Derby N 05–06; rtd 08; PtO *Derby* 08–18. *38 Holborn Drive, Derby DE22 4DX* T: (01332) 342553 *or* 344895 E: relgar1015@aol.com

ELIZABETH, Sister. *See* HEATON, Elizabeth Ann

ELKINGTON, The Ven Audrey Anne. b 57. St Cath Coll Ox BA 80 UEA PhD 83. St Jo Coll Nottm EAMTC 86. **dss** 88 **d** 92 **p** 94. Monkseaton St Mary *Newc* 88–91; Ponteland 91–93; Par Dn 92–93; C Prudhoe 93–02; RD Corbridge 99–02; Bp's Adv for Women in Min 01–11; Bp's Chapl 02–11; Dir of Ords 02–11; Hon Can Newc Cathl 06–11; Adn Bodmin *Truro* from 11; RD Trigg Major from 16. *4 Park Drive, Bodmin PL31 2QF* T: (01208) 892811 M: 07766-822872 E: audrey@truro.anglican.org

ELKINGTON, Canon David John. b 51. Nottm Univ BTh 76 Leic Univ MEd 81 Dur Univ MATM 05. St Jo Coll Nottm 73. **d** 76 **p** 77. C Leic Martyrs 76–78; C Kirby Muxloe 78–80; Asst Chapl Leic Univ 80–82; Hon C Leic H Spirit 82; Chapl UEA *Nor* 82–88; TV Newc Epiphany 88–91; TR 91–93; P-in-c Prudhoe 93–98; V 98–02; Can Res Newc Cathl 02–11; C St Tudy w St Mabyn and Michaelstow *Truro* 11–16; C Bodmin w Lanhydrock and Lanivet 11–16; RD Trigg Minor and Bodmin 13–16; rtd 16; PtO *Truro* from 16. *4 Park Drive, Bodmin PL31 2QF* T: (01208) 892811 E: djelk@btinternet.com

ELKINS, Alan Bernard. b 47. Sarum & Wells Th Coll 70. **d** 73 **p** 74. C Wareham *Sarum* 73–77; P-in-c Codford, Upton Lovell and Stockton 77–79; P-in-c Boyton w Sherrington

77–79; R Bishopstrow and Boreham 79–92; R Corfe Mullen 92–03; V W Byfleet *Guildf* 03–08; P-in-c 08–14; Bp's Adv for Spirituality 08–14; rtd 14; PtO *Nor* from 14; RD Burnham and Walsingham from 15. *4 The Lawn, Fakenham NR21 8DT* T: (01328) 855075 E: alanelkins@btinternet.com

ELKINS, Mrs Joy Kathleen. b 45. S Tr Scheme 93. **d** 96 **p** 97. NSM Corfe Mullen *Sarum* 96–03; NSM W Byfleet *Guildf* 03–08; C 08–14; rtd 14; PtO *Nor* from 14. *4 The Lawn, Fakenham NR21 8DT* T: (01328) 855075 E: joyelkins@btinternet.com

ELKINS, Canon Patrick Charles. b 34. St Chad's Coll Dur BA 57 DipEd 58. **d** 60 **p** 61. C Moordown *Win* 60–63; C Basingstoke 64–67; V Bransgore 67–04; Hon Can Win Cathl 89–04; rtd 04; PtO *Win* 04–19. *1 Tyrrells Court, Bransgore, Christchurch BH23 8BU* T: (01425) 673103

ELKS, Roger Mark. b 60. Imp Coll Lon BSc 83. Wycliffe Hall Ox 89. **d** 92 **p** 93. C St Austell *Truro* 92–95; V Carbis Bay w Lelant 95–01; I Holywood *D & D* 01–15; TV Appledore, Northam and Westward Ho! *Ex* from 19; C Abbotsham from 19. *7 Shepherds Meadow, Abbotsham, Bideford EX39 5BP* M: 07954-406680 E: vicarroger@gmail.com

ELLEM, Peter Keith. b 58. Nottm Univ BTh 90 Leeds Univ MA 99 CQSW. St Jo Coll Nottm 87. **d** 90 **p** 91. C Islington St Mary *Lon* 90–94; C Leeds St Geo *Ripon* 94–99; R Yagoona Australia 00–08; Chapl Westmead Hosp from 08. *46 Archibald Street, Padstow NSW 2211, Australia* T: (0061) (2) 9771 9369 *or* 9845 6038 E: prellem@yahoo.com.au

ELLERY, Ian Martyn William. b 56. K Coll Lon BD AKC. Chich Th Coll. **d** 82 **p** 83. C Hornsey St Mary w St Geo *Lon* 82–85; V Choral York Minster 85–89; Subchanter 86–89; R Patrington w Hollym, Welwick and Winestead 89–97; TR Howden 97–05; RD 97–02; P-in-c Cawood w Ryther and Wistow 05–11; R 11–16; rtd 16. *Address temp unknown* E: ianmwellery@hotmail.co.uk

ELLIN, Lindsey Jane. *See* GOODHEW, Lindsey Jane Ellin

ELLINGHAM, Fiona Madeleine. b 66. **d** 16 **p** 17. OLM Howell Hill *Guildf* 16–18; OLM Nork w Burgh Heath from 18. *3 Winkworth Road, Banstead SM7 2QJ* T: (01737) 212920 E: fiona.ellingham66@gmail.com

ELLIOT, William Brunton. b 41. Edin Dioc NSM Course 81. **d** 84 **p** 85. NSM Lasswade *Edin* 84–92; NSM Dalkeith 84–92; Assoc P Edin St Pet 92–94; R Selkirk 94–06; rtd 06; LtO *Edin* from 06. *157 Newbattle Abbey Crescent, Dalkeith EH22 3LR* T: 0131-663 1369 E: bille157@aol.com *or* billelsie@aol.com

ELLIOT-NEWMAN, Christopher Guy. b 43. Bede Coll Dur TCert 67 Hull Univ BTh 83 MEd 87. Westcott Ho Cam 67. **d** 70 **p** 71. C Ditton St Mich *Liv* 70–73; C Hazlemere *Ox* 73–77; R Stockton-on-the-Forest w Holtby and Warthill *York* 77–87; Dir of Educn *Cant* 87–94; P-in-c Warden w Newbrough *Newc* 99–01; PtO 95–99 and from 02. *15 Hextol Terrace, Hexham NE46 2DF* T: (01434) 600547 M: 07951-471189 E: christopher@firststandardltd.co.uk

ELLIOT, Anne. *See* ELLIOTT, Elizabeth Anne

ELLIOT, Mrs Antonia. b 66. St Mellitus Coll BA 14. **d** 14 **p** 15. C N Farnborough *Guildf* 14–17; C Finchampstead and California *Ox* from 18. *2 Oak Drive, Aborfield Green, Reading RG2 9GJ* M: 07871-047490 E: antonia_elliott@btinternet.com

ELLIOT, Ben. *See* ELLIOTT, William Henry Venn

ELLIOT, Canon Brian. b 49. Dur Univ BA 73. Coll of Resurr Mirfield 73. **d** 75 **p** 76. C Nunthorpe *York* 75–77; CF 77–09; Dep Asst Chapl Gen 96–09; rtd 09; PtO Cyprus and the Gulf from 09; OCM from 09; Hon Can St Paul's Cathl Nicosia from 18. *St Paul's Cathedral, PO Box 22014, 1516 Nicosia, Cyprus* E: brian@newport.org

ELLIOT, Christopher John. b 44. Sarum Th Coll 66. **d** 69 **p** 70. C Walthamstow St Pet *Chelmsf* 69–71; C Witham 71–74; P-in-c Gt and Lt Bentley 74–80; R Colchester Ch Ch w St Mary V 80–85; R Sible Hedingham 85–93; V Leigh-on-Sea St Aid 93–98; P-in-c Thornton Gp *Linc* 98–01; RD Horncastle 98–01; P-in-c Gt Leighs *Chelmsf* 01–05; P-in-c Lt Leighs 01–05; P-in-c Lt Waltham 01–05; R Gt and Lt Leighs and Lt Waltham 05–06; RD Chelmsf N 04–06; rtd 06; PtO *Chelmsf* 06–10; P-in-c Middleton-in-Teesdale w Forest and Frith *Dur* 10–13; P-in-c Eggleston 10–13; PtO *St E* from 14; *Chelmsf* from 18. *36 The Croft, Great Yeldham, Halstead CO9 4JD* T: 07899-905698 E: revchriselliott@gmail.com

ELLIOT, Elizabeth Anne. b 52. Lon Bible Coll BA 03 Win Univ MA 13. STETS 09. **d** 11 **p** 12. NSM Pennington *Win* from 11. *19 Heron Close, Sway, Lymington SO41 6ET* M: 07553-552540 E: anne19elliott@gmail.com

ELLIOT, Eveline Mary. *See* HALL, Eveline Mary

ELLIOT, Gordon. b 25. St Aid Birkenhead 63. **d** 65 **p** 66. C Latchford St Jas *Ches* 65–68; C Bollington St Jo 68–70; V Dukinfield St Mark 70–73; TV Tenbury Wells *Heref* 74–78; V Bromfield 78–82; R Culmington w Onibury 78–82; V

Stanton Lacy 78–82; P-in-c Withybrook w Copston Magna *Cov* 82–83; P-in-c Wolvey, Burton Hastings and Stretton Baskerville 82–83; V Wolvey w Burton Hastings, Copston Magna etc 83–90; rtd 90; PtO *Worc* 90–15; *Heref* 90–95. *17 Galanos House, Banbury Road, Southam CV47 2BL* T: (01926) 812185

ELLIOTT, Ian David. b 40. Qu Coll Cam BA 61 MA 65. Tyndale Hall Bris 64. d 66 p 67. C Halewood *Liv* 66–71; C Gt Crosby St Luke 71–74; C-in-c Dallam CD 74–80; V Dallam 80–83; TV Fazakerley Em 83–92; V Warrington H Trin 92–05; rtd 05; PtO *Carl* from 07. *High Bank, 1 West End Road, Orton, Penrith CA10 3RT* T: (015396) 24441 E: iandelliott@tiscali.co.uk

ELLIOTT, Ian Peter. b 58. d 16 p 17. OLM Barkingside St Laur *Chelmsf* from 16. *206 Ashurst Drive, Ilford IG6 1EW* E: ian7.elliott@gmail.com

ELLIOTT, Jane. b 49. d 08 p 09. NSM Hatcham St Cath *S'wark* from 08. *13 Seymour Gardens, London SE4 2DN* T: (020) 7277 7968 E: jane.elliott@kcl.ac.uk

ELLIOTT, Mrs Joanna Margaret. b 64. Bris Univ BA 85. STETS 03. d 06 p 07. NSM Haywards Heath St Wilfrid *Chich* from 06; Chapl Brighton and Sussex Univ Hosps NHS Trust from 19. *20 Courtlands, Haywards Heath RH16 4JD* T: (01444) 413799 M: 07710-273299 E: joanna@ctsn.co.uk

ELLIOTT, John Andrew. b 44. ACIB 68. SAOMC 95. d 98 p 99. NSM Bedgrove *Ox* 98–01; C Modbury, Bigbury, Ringmore w Kingston etc *Ex* 01–09; rtd 09; PtO *Ex* from 10. *Little Cumery, Aveton Gifford, Kingsbridge TQ7 4NN* T: (01548) 830688

ELLIOTT, Kathryn Georgina. b 50. d 08 p 17. NSM Manston *Ripon* 08–12; NSM Holbeck 12–14; *Leeds* from 14. *19 Roper Avenue, Leeds LS8 1LG* T: 0113-217 7805 M: 07979-954472 E: kelliott@ntlworld.com

ELLIOTT (née JUTSUM), Mrs Linda Mary. b 56. St Pet Coll Birm CertEd 77. WMMTC 92. d 95 p 96. NSM Longthorpe *Pet* 95–99; P-in-c Etton w Helpston and Maxey 99–04; Chapl Thorpe Hall Hospice 04–09; PtO *Pet* from 09; *Linc* from 17. *42 Frognall, Deeping St James, Peterborough PE6 8RR* T: (01778) 219167 E: revlinda.elliott@gmail.com

ELLIOTT, Marilyn Elizabeth. b 53. Ex Univ BTh 10. SWMTC 05. d 08 p 09. C Stoke Climsland *Truro* 08–13; C Linkinhorne 08–13; P-in-c Lanreath, Pelynt and Bradoc 13–16; R Lanreath and Pelynt 16–18; C Lanteglos by Fowey 13–15; P-in-c 15–18; C Talland 13–15; P-in-c 15–18; C Lansallos 13–15; P-in-c 15–18; R Trelawny from 18. *The Rectory, Lanreath, Looe PL13 2NU* T: (01503) 221159 E: marilynelliottm@btinternet.com

ELLIOTT, Mary. See HALL, Eveline Mary

ELLIOTT, Canon Maurice John. b 65. St Andr Univ MA 87 TCD BTh 92 MPhil 93 QUB PhD 01. CITC 89. d 93 p 94. C Coleraine *Conn* 93–98; I Greenisland 98–02; I Lurgan Ch the Redeemer *D & D* 02–08; Dir Ch of Ireland Th Inst from 08; Can Ch Cathl Dublin *D & G* from 15. *7 Coolgraney, Nutgrove Park, Clonskeagh, Dublin 14, Republic of Ireland* (1) 260 5737 *or* 492 3506 F: 492 3082 M: 87-968 5218 E: mauriceelliott@theologicalinstitute.ie

ELLIOTT, Michael James. b 54. Westmr Coll Ox MTh 96 Nottm Trent Univ PGCE 98. St Jo Coll Nottm LTh 83. d 83 p 84. C Pontypridd St Cath *Llan* 83–86; C Leamington Priors St Paul *Cov* 86–89; Chapl RAF 89–06 and 07–14; Chapl Kimbolton Sch 06–07; Chapl RAuxAF from 14; PtO *Ely* from 15; *Eur* from 17. *Chaplaincy Services (RAF), HQ Air Command, RAF High Wycombe HP14 4UE* T: (01494) 496800 F: 496343 E: elliott.michael50@yahoo.com

ELLIOTT, Neil Raymond. b 78. Trin Coll Bris 13. d 15 p 16. C Whalley Range St Edm and Moss Side etc *Man* 15–19; P-in-c Collyhurst from 19; P-in-c Harpurhey from 19. *Christ Church Rectory, 95 Church Lane, Manchester M9 5BG* E: revneilelliott@gmail.com

ELLIOTT, Nigel Harvey. b 55. St Jo Coll Nottm 90. d 92 p 93. C Radcliffe *Man* 92–95; V Kilnhurst *Sheff* 95–08; R Wombwell 08–14; AD Wath 06–11; P-in-c Sinfin *Derby* from 14. *St Stephen's Vicarage, 313 Sinfin Lane, Derby DE24 9GP* T: (01332) 760135 E: nigel520@btinternet.com

ELLIOTT, Rebecca Caroline. b 73. Qu Foundn Birm 15. d 17 p 18. C Worcs W Rural *Worc* from 17. *The Rectory, Church Road, Clifton-on-Teme, Worcester WR6 6DJ*

ELLIOTT, Richard David Clive. b 53. Portsm Poly BSc 74 MICE 79 MIStructE. STETS 03. d 06 p 07. NSM Sway *Win* 06–17; NSM Boldre w S Baddesley from 17. *19 Heron Close, Sway, Lymington SO41 6ET* T: (01590) 683778 M: 07836-760150 E: richard.elliott@uwclub.net

ELLIOTT, Simon Mark. b 76. Liv Hope Univ Coll BA 97. Ridley Hall Cam 05. d 08 p 09. C Gt Crosby St Luke *Liv* 08–12; C Netherton 12–14; TV 14–17; TV Netherton and Sefton from 17. *22 Moorbridge Close, Bootle L30 7RL* T: 0151-520 3141 E: revsielliott@gmail.com

ELLIOTT, Simon Richard James. b 66. Lon Univ BSc 88. Cranmer Hall Dur BA 95. d 95 p 96. C Hendon St Paul Mill Hill *Lon* 95–99; V Hull St Martin w Transfiguration *York* 99–17; V Hutton Cranswick w Skerne, Watton and Beswick from 17; V Nafferton w Wansford from 17. *5 Howl Lane, Hutton, Driffield YO25 9QA* T: (01377) 271592 M: 07776-143084 E: elliottrev66@gmail.com

ELLIOTT, Sonya Jacqueline. See DORAGH, Sonya Jacqueline

ELLIOTT, Stuart. b 75. Univ of Wales (Ban) BTh 98 MTh 00. St Mich Coll Llan 05. d 07 p 08. C Holywell *St As* 07–10; V Llanasa and Ffynnongroew 10–15; P-in-c Betws-y-Coed and Capel Curig w Penmachno etc *Ban* 15–16; P-in-c Bro Gwydyr from 16. *The Vicarage, Vicarage Road, Betws-y-Coed LL24 0AD* T: (01690) 710313 E: rev@stubiedoo.co.uk

ELLIOTT, William Henry Venn (Ben). b 34. K Coll Cam BA 55 MA 59. Wells Th Coll 59. d 61 p 62. C Almondbury *Wakef* 61–66; V Bramshaw *Sarum* 66–81; P-in-c Landford w Plaitford 77–81; V Mere w W Knoyle and Maiden Bradley 81–99; rtd 99. *3 St George's Close, Salisbury SP2 8HA* T: (01722) 338409

ELLIOTT, William James. b 38. Jes Coll Cam BA 62 MA 66 Birm Univ MA 69 PhD 74. Qu Coll Birm 62. d 64 p 65. C Hendon St Paul Mill Hill *Lon* 64–67; C St Pancras w St Jas and Ch Ch 67–69; P-in-c Preston St Paul *Blackb* 69–74; Chapl Preston R Infirmary 69–74; R Elstree *St Alb* 74–00; Research Fell Birm Univ 00–03; rtd 03; PtO *Nor* from 00. *23 Neil Avenue, Holt NR25 6TG* T/F: (01263) 713853 E: bill.elliott@akainternet.co.uk

ELLIOTT DE RIVEROL, Mrs Jennifer Kathleen. b 52. St Pet Coll Birm CertEd 75 UEA MA 88. ERMC 09. d 11 p 12. C Puerto de la Cruz Tenerife *Eur* 11–17; R Brinton, Briningham, Hunworth, Stody etc *Nor* from 17. *Rest Harrow, The Street, Swanton Novers, Melton Constable NR24 2QY* T: (01263) 502068 M: 07591-609397 E: revderiv@gmail.com

ELLIS, Anthony. See ELLIS, John Anthony

ELLIS, Brian Eric James. b 50. STETS 05. d 08 p 09. NSM Preston w Sutton Poyntz, Littlemoor etc *Sarum* 08–15; NSM Bincombe w Broadwey, Upwey and Buckland Ripers 12–15; NSM Weymouth Ridgeway from 15. *9 Windermere Crescent, Weymouth DT3 5HG* T: (01305) 549651 M: 07533-941686 E: brian-ellis@talktalk.net *or* brian9ellis@outlook.com

ELLIS, Canon Bryan Stuart. b 31. Qu Coll Cam BA 54 MA 58. Ridley Hall Cam 55. d 57 p 58. C Ramsgate St Luke *Cant* 57–59; C Herne Bay Ch Ch 59–62; V Burmantofts St Steph and St Agnes *Ripon* 62–81; RD Wakef 81–96; V Wakef St Andr and St Mary 81–00; Hon Can Wakef Cathl 89–00; rtd 00; PtO *Ripon* 01–14; *Leeds* from 14. *302 Oakwood Lane, Leeds LS8 3LE* T: 0113-240 3122

ELLIS, Charles Harold. b 50. NOC 78. d 81 p 82. C Davyhulme St Mary *Man* 81–85; V Tonge w Alkrington 85–91; P-in-c Radcliffe St Thos and St Jo 91; P-in-c Radcliffe St Mary 91; TR Radcliffe 91–99; AD Radcliffe and Prestwich 96–99; P-in-c Newchurch 99–00; TR Rossendale Middle Valley 00–04; AD Rossendale 00–04; V Ingleton w Chapel le Dale *Bradf* 04–14; TV Bentham, Burton-in-Lonsdale, Chapel-le-Dale etc *Leeds* 14–15; rtd 15. *2 Dallam Chase, Milnthorpe LA7 7DW* T: (015395) 62262 E: chasellis@btinternet.com

ELLIS, Christopher Duncan. b 67. Anglia Ruskin Univ BA 09. ERMC 05. d 08 p 09. C Thorpe St Andr *Nor* 08–11; V Thorpe St Matt 11–15; R Thurton w Ashby St Mary, Bergh Apton etc from 15; Hon PV Nor Cathl from 14. *The Rectory, 29 Ashby Road, Thurton, Norwich NR14 6AX* T: (01508) 484174 E: chris.ellis23@btinternet.com

ELLIS, Canon David Craven. b 34. Man Univ BA 56 MA 57. St Aid Birkenhead 59. d 61 p 62. C Gt Crosby St Luke *Liv* 61–65; Hong Kong 65–69; P-in-c Sawrey *Carl* 69–74; Dioc Youth Officer 69–74; V Halifax St Aug *Wakef* 74–84; R Greystoke, Matterdale and Mungrisdale *Carl* 84–87; R Watermillock 84–87; TR Greystoke, Matterdale, Mungrisdale etc 88–91; RD Penrith 87–91; TR Carl H Trin and St Barn 91–96; Hon Can Carl Cathl 91–96; rtd 96; PtO *Carl* 97–02 and 04–13; *Cov* 13–15; NSM Cartmel Peninsula *Carl* 02–04. *44 Cherry Orchard, Stratford-upon-Avon CV37 9AP* T: (01789) 269409 E: dandbellis4@btinternet.com

ELLIS, Dorothy Pearson. b 43. Sheff Univ BA 66 MA 67. Dioc OLM tr scheme 05. d 07 p 08. NSM Oakenshaw, Wyke and Low Moor *Bradf* 07–12; NSM Low Moor and Oakenshaw 12–14; *Leeds* from 14. *2 Woodrow Drive, Low Moor, Bradford BD12 0JN* T: (01274) 679048

ELLIS, Emma Louise. b 79. Coll of Ripon & York St Jo BA 00 Heythrop Coll Lon MTh 03. Ridley Hall Cam 05. d 07 p 08. C Addiscombe St Mary Magd w St Martin *S'wark* 07–10; TV Limpsfield and Tatsfield 10–15; Dioc Discipleship and Voc Missr 15–17; NSM S Croydon Em 15–16; NSM Sanderstead 16–17; Dioc Voc Adv 12–17; V Lilliput *Sarum* from 17.

The Vicarage, 55 Lilliput Road, Poole BH14 8JX T: (01202) 708567 M: 07470-226395

ELLIS, Hugh William. b 54. Sussex Univ BSc 76. Ridley Hall Cam 88. **d** 90 **p** 91. C Reading St Jo *Ox* 90–93; P-in-c Bradfield and Stanford Dingley 93–97; R 97–03; TR Langport Area *B & W* 03–12; TR High Wycombe *Ox* from 12. *The Vicarage, 6 Priory Avenue, High Wycombe HP13 6SH* T: (01494) 527526 E: hughelli@aol.com

ELLIS, Canon Ian Morton. b 52. QUB BD 75 MTh 82 TCD PhD 89. CITC. **d** 77 **p** 78. C Portadown St Columba *Arm* 77–79; C Arm St Mark w Aghavilly 79–85; Chapl Arm R Sch 79–85; Hon V Choral Arm Cathl 82–93; I Mullavilly 85–93; Dom Chapl to Abp Arm 86–93; Tutor for Aux Min (Arm) 90–93; Dioc Adv on Ecum 92–93; I Newcastle *D & D* from 93; Can Belf Cathl 00–03; Ed The Church of Ireland Gazette 01–17; Preb Newcastle St Patr Cathl Dublin from 01. *The Rectory, 1 King Street, Newcastle BT33 0HD* T: (028) 4372 2439 E: ian.m.ellis@btinternet.com

ELLIS, Jenny Susan. b 56. Bp Grosseteste Coll BEd 80. STETS 08. **d** 11 **p** 12. NSM Martock w Ash *B & W* 11–12; PtO *Ox* 13–17; NSM W Wycombe w Bledlow Ridge, Bradenham and Radnage from 17. *The Vicarage, 6 Priory Avenue, High Wycombe HP13 6SH* T: (01494) 444883 E: ellisjene@aol.com

ELLIS, John Anthony. b 47. Open Univ BA 80. Coll of Resurr Mirfield 70. **d** 72 **p** 73. C Sketty *S & B* 72–75; C Duston *Pet* 75–80; R Lichborough w Maidford and Farthingstone 80–85; V Stratfield Mortimer *Ox* 85–98; P-in-c Mortimer W End w Padworth 85–98; TR Kidlington w Hampton Poyle 98–12; AD Ox 04–12; Hon Can Ch Ch 07–12; rtd 13; PtO *Heref* from 13. *The Skirrid, Ullingswick, Hereford HR1 3JG* T: (01432) 820759 E: janthonychurch@gmail.com

ELLIS, John Franklin. b 34. Leeds Univ BA 58. Linc Th Coll 58. **d** 60 **p** 61. C Ladybarn *Man* 60–63; C Stockport St Geo *Ches* 63–66; V High Lane 66–81; V Chelford w Lower Withington 81–99; rtd 99; PtO *Ches* from 00. *3 Millers Croft, Adlington Street, Macclesfield SK10 1BD*

ELLIS, The Ven John Raymond. b 63. St Steph Ho Ox 95. **d** 97 **p** 98. C Clare w Poslingford, Cavendish etc *St E* 97–00; P-in-c Bury St Edmunds St Jo 00–02; P-in-c Bury St Edmunds St Geo 00–02; TV Bury St Edmunds All SS w St Jo and St Geo 02–04; Chapl RAF 04–18; Chapl-in-Chief RAF from 18; Can and Preb Linc Cathl from 18. *Chaplaincy Services (RAF), HQ Air Command, RAF High Wycombe HP14 4UE* T: (01494) 493802 F: 496343 E: john.ellis932@mod.gov.uk

ELLIS, John Roland. b 32. Wells Th Coll 67. **d** 69 **p** 70. C Kettering SS Pet and Paul 69–71; C Kingsthorpe 71–73; TV 73; TV Kingsthorpe w Northampton St Dav 73–74; TV Ebbw Vale *Mon* 74–76; V Llanddewi Rhydderch w Llanvapley etc 76–83; Miss to Seamen 79–86; V New Tredegar *Mon* 83–86; V Llanelli *S & B* 86–98; RD Crickhowell 91–98; rtd 99; P-in-c Rockfield and St Maughen's w Llangattock etc *Mon* 99–05; Hon C Rockfield and Dingestow Gp 05–07; PtO from 12. *Address temp unknown* E: revjohn32@gmail.com

ELLIS, Canon John Wadsworth. b 42. TCD BA 64. **d** 66 **p** 67. C Lisburn Ch Ch Cathl *Conn* 66–69; C Norbiton *S'wark* 69–72; C New Clee *Linc* 72–85; V 85–11; RD Grimsby and Cleethorpes 94–99; Can and Preb Linc Cathl 98–11; rtd 11; PtO *Linc* from 17. *9 Abbots Way, Grimsby DN32 0HB*

ELLIS, Kevin Stuart. b 67. Newc Univ BA 91 Lon Bible Coll PhD 97. Qu Coll Birm 99. **d** 01 **p** 02. C Matson *Glouc* 01–04; TV Maryport, Netherton and Flimby *Carl* 04–07; TR 07–09; V Bartley Green *Birm* 09–14; V Bro Cybi *Ban* 14–17; R Bro Eleth from 17. *The Rectory, Bull Bay Road, Amlwch LL68 9EA* T: (01407) 831525 M: 07535-557632 E: parchkevinellis@gmail.com

ELLIS, Sister Lilian. b 44. Keswick Hall Coll TCert 66. Oak Hill Th Coll 95. **d** 96 **p** 97. C Vange *Chelmsf* 96–00; C Pitsea w Nevendon 00–02; rtd 02; PtO *Chelmsf* 02–16; *Liv* from 16. *90 Moss Road, Southport PR8 4JQ* T: (01704) 565289 E: lilian.ellis@tesco.net *or* lilian.ellis@btinternet.com

ELLIS, Preb Mark Durant. b 39. Ex Univ BA 62. Cuddesdon Coll 62. **d** 64 **p** 65. C Lyngford *B & W* 64–67; V Weston-super-Mare St Andr Bournville 67–76; TV Yeovil 76–88; V Yeovil St Mich 88–09; Preb Wells Cathl 90–09; RD Yeovil 94–04; rtd 09; Hon C Bruton and Distr *B & W* 09–17; Hon C Bruton, Brewham, Pitcombe and Shepton Montague from 17; Hon C Alham Vale from 17. *The Parsonage, Gold Hill, Batcombe, Shepton Mallet BA4 6HF* T: (01749) 850074

ELLIS, Michael Edward. b 45. St Cath Coll Ox BA 67 MA 70 MSc 68 BM, BCh 72 Glos Univ BA 11 FRCP 92 FACP 05. St Steph Ho Ox 09. **d** 10 **p** 11. C Paphos Cyprus 10–12; PtO Cyprus and the Gulf from 12; PtO *Ex* from 13. *Lantern House, Maristow House, Roborough, Plymouth PL6 7BZ* T: (01752) 724178 E: mikeedwardellis@gmail.com

ELLIS, Paul. b 49. **d** 07 **p** 08. NSM Wakef St Jo 07–14; *Leeds* from 14. *98 Bradford Road, Wakefield WF1 2AH* T: (01924) 367976

ELLIS, Paul. b 56. Aston Tr Scheme 88 Trin Coll Bris 92. **d** 92 **p** 93. C Pennington *Man* 92–96; TV Deane 96–06; P-in-c Grassendale *Liv* 06–14; V from 14; P-in-c Liv All So Springwood 11–14; V from 14. *The Vicarage, 22 Eaton Road, Cressington, Liverpool L19 0PN* T: 0151-427 1474 E: rev.paul.ellis@gmail.com

ELLIS, Peter Andrew. b 46. St D Coll Lamp 65. **d** 69 **p** 70. C Milford Haven *St D* 69–71; R Walwyn's Castle w Robeston W 71–74; Miss to Seafarers 74–11; Hong Kong 74–75 and 92–11; Singapore 75–82; The Tees and Hartlepool 82–92; rtd 11; PtO *York* from 13. *The Forge, Home Farm, Hutton Village Road, Guisborough TS14 8EL* T: (01287) 348371 E: ellishongkong@gmail.com

ELLIS, Richard. b 47. **d** 02 **p** 03. OLM Leiston *St E* 02–13; NSM 13–17; PtO *St E* from 17. *9 Kings Road, Leiston IP16 4DA* T: (01728) 832168 M: 07759-349057 E: skinny.elephant@hotmail.co.uk

ELLIS, Robert Albert. b 48. K Coll Lon BD 70 AKC 70. St Aug Coll Cant 70. **d** 72 **p** 73. C Liv Our Lady and St Nic w St Anne 72–76; P-in-c Meerbrook *Lich* 76–80; Producer Relig Progr BBC Radio Stoke 76–80; V Highgate All SS *Lon* 80–81; P-in-c Longdon *Lich* 81–87; Dioc Communications Officer 81–01; Chapl Palma de Mallorca *Eur* 01–11; rtd 11; PtO *Lich* from 11; *Eur* from 16. *The Pump House, Jacks Lane, Marchington, Uttoxeter ST14 8LW* T: (01283) 820732 E: robertellis1948@gmail.com

ELLIS, Susannah Margaret. b 44. Open Univ BA 82 New Coll Dur CertEd 88. EAMTC 93. **d** 96 **p** 97. NSM S Elmham and Ilketshall *St E* 96–98; Warden Quiet Waters Chr Retreat Ho 96–98; C Worlingham w Barnby and N Cove *St E* 98–01; C Beccles St Mich 98–01; P-in-c Worlingham w Barnby and N Cove 01–03; R 03–14; rtd 14; P-in-c Worlingham w Barnby and N Cove *St E* 14–15; PtO *Nor* from 15; *St E* from 15. *97 High Road, Gorleston, Great Yarmouth NR31 0PE* T: (01493) 604512

✠**ELLIS, The Rt Revd Timothy William.** b 53. AKC 75 York Univ DPhil 98. St Aug Coll Cant 75. **d** 76 **p** 77 **c** 06. C Old Trafford St Jo *Man* 76–80; V Pendleton St Thos 80–87; Chapl Salford Coll of Tech 80–87; V Sheff St Leon Norwood 87–01; P-in-c Shiregreen St Hilda 94–01; RD Ecclesfield 94–99; Hon Can Sheff Cathl 00–01; Adn Stow *Linc* 01–06; Suff Bp Grantham 06–13; Dean Stamford 05–11; Can and Preb Linc Cathl 01–13; rtd 13; Hon Asst Bp Linc from 13; Hon Asst Bp Sheff from 14; Hon Asst Bp Derby from 15. *8 Mason Grove, Sheffield S13 8LL* E: fatherowl@gmail.com

ELLISDON, Canon Patrick Leon Shane. b 61. St Jo Coll Nottm 99. **d** 01 **p** 02. C Margate St Phil *Cant* 01–04; P-in-c Cliftonville 04–14; V from 14; Hon Can Cant Cathl from 14. *54 Bromstone Road, Broadstairs CT10 2HT* M: 07932-734932 E: stpaulscliftville@btinternet.com *or* pellisondon@diocant.org

ELLISON, John. b 37. FCA 64. Qu Coll Birm. **d** 04 **p** 05. NSM Northanger *Win* 04–07; PtO from 07. *High Candovers, Hartley Mauditt, Alton GU34 3BP* T: (01420) 511346 E: revjohnellison@hotmail.com

ELLISON, Mrs Margaret Helen. b 50. Edin Univ BSc 77 Leeds Univ BA 09 RN 72. Yorks Min Course 07. **d** 09 **p** 10. NSM York St Hilda and York St Lawr w St Nic 09–13; PtO 13–15; NSM Stamford Bridge Gp from 15. *17 Foresters Walk, Stamford Bridge, York YO41 1BB* T: (01759) 372696 E: maggs.ellison@gmail.com

ELLISON, Ms Sandra Anne. b 53. Anglia Poly Univ BA 96 RMN 74. EAMTC 99. **d** 02 **p** 03. C Hunstanton St Mary w Ringstead Parva etc *Nor* 02–05; R Ashmanhaugh, Barton Turf etc 05–15; rtd 15; PtO *Nor* from 15. *5 Howards Close, Old Hunstanton, Hunstanton PE36 6HR* T: (01485) 298852 E: sandraellison@homecall.co.uk

ELLISON, Simon John. b 51. SEITE 99. **d** 02 **p** 03. NSM Caterham *S'wark* 02–08; Asst Chapl Newcastle upon Tyne Hosps NHS Foundn Trust 08–09; Chapl Epsom and St Helier Univ Hosps NHS Trust from 09; PtO *S'wark* 09–14; NSM Caterham from 14. *Trust Headquarters, St Helier Hospital, Wrythe Lane, Carshalton SM5 1AA* T: (020) 8296 2000 E: simon.ellison@epsom-sthelier.nhs.uk *or* father.simon@tiscali.co.uk *or* simon.ellison@nhs.uk

ELLISON, John Ernest Nicholas. b 37. ALCD 61. **d** 61 **p** 62. C Gipsy Hill Ch Ch *S'wark* 61–64; C Whitton and Thurleston w Akenham *St E* 64–68; P-in-c New Clee *Linc* 68–71; V 75–76; V Grimsby St Steph 71–75; P-in-c Mildenhall *St E* 77–79; RD 81–84; R Barton Mills, Beck Row w Kenny Hill etc 80–84; V Ipswich St Aug 84–96; R Guernsey St Peter Port *Win* 96–02; Chapl Princess Eliz Hosp Guernsey 96–02; rtd 02; PtO *St E* from 03. *27 Wyvern Road, Ipswich IP3 9TJ* T: (01473) 726617 E: helenjohnelliston@talktalk.net

ELLOR, Preb Michael Keith. b 52. St Jo Coll Nottm 92. **d** 94 **p** 95. C Stafford St Jo and Tixall w Ingestre *Lich* 94–97; TV Bucknall and Bagnall 97–03; TR Bucknall 03–09; RD Stoke 02–06; V Branston 09–17; Local Min Adv (Stafford) 09–14; Local Par Development Adv Stafford Area 10–14; P-in-c Burton All SS w Ch Ch 14–17; Preb Lich Cathl 09–17; rtd 17; PtO *S & B* from 17. *28 Cae Folland, Penclawdd, Swansea SA4 3YJ* T: (01792) 852782 E: michael.ellor@btinternet.com

ELLSON, Montague Edward. b 33. Birm Univ BA 56 Cam Univ CertEd 67 Univ of Wales (Lamp) MA 08. EAMTC 84. **d** 87 **p** 88. Hon C Freethorpe w Wickhampton, Halvergate etc *Nor* 87–90; C Gaywood, Bawsey and Mintlyn 90–92; Miss to Seafarers from 90; R Pulham *Nor* 92–94; P-in-c Starston 93–94; R Pulham Market, Pulham St Mary and Starston 94–97; Dioc NSM Officer 94–97; RD Redenhall 95–97; rtd 97; PtO *Nor* from 97. *Barn Cottage, Neatishead Road, Horning, Norwich NR12 8LB* T: (01692) 630251 E: revmonty@btinternet.com

ELLSWORTH, Lida Elizabeth. b 48. Columbia Univ (NY) BA 70 Girton Coll Cam PhD 76. EMMTC 85. **d** 88 **p** 94. NSM Bakewell *Derby* 88–07; PtO 07–11; NSM Longstone, Curbar and Stony Middleton 11–18; rtd 18; PtO *Derby* from 18. *Apple Croft, Granby Gardens, Bakewell DE45 1ET* T/F: (01629) 814255 E: lidaellsworth@john-lewis.com

ELLWOOD, Keith Brian. b 36. Curwen Coll Lon BA 58 MMus 65 Bede Coll Dur CertEd 59 Hon DD 99 AIGCM 58 FRSA 64 ACP 66 FCollP 83. Bps' Coll Cheshunt 64. **d** 64 **p** 65. Asst Master R Wanstead Sch 60–66; Chapl 64–66; C Wanstead St Mary *Chelmsf* 64–66; CF 66–70; OCM 70–71 and 76–79; Chapl St Paul's Coll Hong Kong 70–71; P-in-c Bicknoller *B & W* 71–73; Chapl Roedean Sch Brighton 73–76; PtO *B & W* 74–79; Chapl Windsor Boys' Sch Hamm W Germany 76–79; Chapl Trin Coll Glenalmond 79–81; Hd Master St Chris Sch Burnham-on-Sea 82–86; Hon C Burnham *B & W* 82–86; R Staple Fitzpaine, Orchard Portman, Thurlbear etc 86–89; P-in-c Hugill and Dioc Educn Adv *Carl* 89–93; P-in-c Coldwaltham and Hardham *Chich* 93–95; rtd 96; PtO *Chich* 96–04; *Sheff* 04–17. *2 Lindrick Close, Doncaster DN4 7JL*

ELMAN, Simon Laurie. b 57. NTMTC. **d** 99 **p** 00. C Loughton St Jo *Chelmsf* 99–01; C Tye Green w Netteswell 01–07; PtO from 08. *26 Pakes Way, Theydon Bois, Epping CM16 7NA* T: (01992) 813057 E: simon.elman@btinternet.com

ELMES, Amanda Jane. b 53. Lon Univ BDS 76 RCS LDS 77 Herts Univ PhD 04. ERMC 06. **d** 08 **p** 09. NSM W w E Mersea *Chelmsf* 08–10; NSM W w E Mersea, Peldon, Gt and Lt Wigborough 10–14; P-in-c Langham w Boxted from 14; P-in-c W Bergholt and Gt Horkesley from 14; C Colchester St Mich Myland from 18; C Colchester St Luke from 18; C Wormingford, Mt Bures and Lt Horkesley from 18. *The Rectory, 1 Church Close, West Bergholt, Colchester CO6 3JZ* T: (01206) 240906 E: revmandyelmes@btinternet.com

ELMES, The Ven Ruth Katherine. b 65. TCD BTh 09 RGN 83. CITC 06. **d** 09 **p** 10. C Stillorgan w Blackrock *D & G* 09–12; I Crosspatrick Gp *C & O* from 12; Can Ferns Cathl 17–18; Adn Ossory and Leighlin from 18. *The Rectory, Churchlands, Tinahely, Co Wicklow, Republic of Ireland* T: (00353) (402) 28922 M: 86-062 1009 E: relmes@eircom.net

ELMS, Christian Grant. b 71. Salford Univ BSc 04. Trin Coll Bris 07. **d** 09 **p** 10. C Pennington *Man* 09–12; TV Worle *B & W* from 12. *Church Cottage, 2A St Marks Road, Weston-super-Mare BS22 7PW* T: (01934) 515438 M: 07796-988907 E: chriselms1@gmail.com

ELPHICK, Robin Howard. b 37. ALCD 63. **d** 64 **p** 65. C Clapham Common St Barn *S'wark* 64–67; C Woking St Pet *Guildf* 67–71; R Rollesby w Burgh w Billockby *Nor* 71–80; P-in-c Ashby w Oby, Thurne and Clippesby 79–80; R Rollesby w Burgh w Billockby w Ashby w Oby etc 80–84; R Frinton *Chelmsf* 84–94; P-in-c W w E Mersea and Peldon w Gt and Lt Wigborough 94–02; rtd 02; PtO *Nor* from 02. *5 Coralie Court, Westfield View, Norwich NR4 7FJ* T: (01603) 508061 E: robinelphick@btinternet.com

ELPHICK, Canon Vivien Margaret. b 53. Kent Univ BA 74 Solicitor 77. Trin Coll Bris BA 90. **d** 90 **p** 94. C Oulton Broad *Nor* 90–94; P-in-c Burlingham St Edmund w Lingwood, Strumpshaw etc 94–06; RD Blofield 98–04; Hon Can *Nor* Cathl 03–06; P-in-c Measham *Leic* 06–08; P-in-c Packington w Normanton-le-Heath 06–08; P-in-c Donisthorpe and Moira w Stretton-en-le-Field 06–08; TR Woodfield from 08; AD NW Leics from 11; Hon Can Leic Cathl from 16. *The Vicarage, High Street, Measham, Swadlincote DE12 7HZ* T: (01530) 270354

ELPHIN AND ARDAGH, Dean of. *See* WILLIAMS, The Very Revd Arfon

ELSDON, Mrs Janice Margaret. b 49. CITC 92. **d** 95 **p** 96. NSM Cloughfern *Conn* 95–99; NSM Ahoghill w Portglenone 99–02; NSM Belfast St Thos 02–05; LtO 05–08; NSM Belfast St Bart 08–13; NSM Belfast St Anne from 13. *128 Station Road, Greenisland, Carrickfergus BT38 8UW* T: (028) 9085 1963 E: janice@belfastcathedral.org

ELSDON, Ronald. b 44. St Jo Coll Cam BA 66 Trin Hall Cam PhD 69 K Coll Lon BD 86 Milltown Inst Dub PhD. CITC 97. **d** 99 **p** 00. C Ballymena w Ballyclug *Conn* 99–02; I Belfast St Bart 02–13; rtd 13. *128 Station Road, Greenisland, Carrickfergus BT38 8UW* T: (028) 9085 1963

ELSMORE, The Ven Guy Charles. b 66. Edin Univ BSc 88. Ridley Hall Cam 93. **d** 93 **p** 94. C Huyton St Mich *Liv* 93–98; V Hough Green St Basil and All SS 98–05; AD Widnes and Hon Can Liv Cathl 03–05; P-in-c St Luke in the City 05–10; TR 10–16; AD Toxteth and Wavertree 14–16; Hon Can Liv Cathl 14–16; Adn Buckingham *Ox* from 16. *Archdeacon's House, Stone, Aylesbury HP17 8RZ* T: (01865) 208266 E: archdeacon.buckingham@oxford.anglican.org

ELSOM, Neil. b 67. St Hild Coll 17. **d** 19. NSM Greasbrough *Sheff* from 19. *32 Whitehall Road, Rotherham S61 4JD* T: (01709) 324906 M: 07931-626988 E: elsom9@blueyonder.co.uk

ELSON, Alison Judith. b 66. Ch Ch Coll Cant BEd 89. SEITE 13. **d** 16 **p** 17. NSM Chipstead *S'wark* from 16. *4 Broadhurst Gardens, Reigate RH2 8AW* E: curate@smchipstead.org

ELSTOB, Stephen William. b 57. Sarum & Wells Th Coll. **d** 86 **p** 87. C Sunderland Springwell w Thorney Close *Dur* 86–88; C Upholland *Liv* 88–89; TV 89–96; V Cinnamon Brow 96–07; TV N Wearside *Dur* 07–11; TR from 11. *The Vicarage, Bootle Street, Sunderland SR5 4EY5* T: 0191-537 3744 E: steveelstob182@gmail.com

ELSTON, James Ian. b 70. City Univ BSc 95. SEITE 01. **d** 04 **p** 05. NSM Old St Pancras *Lon* 04–12; TV 12–15; TR from 15. *23 Albert Street, London NW1 7LU* T: (020) 7424 0724 E: fr.jameselston@gmail.com

ELSTON, Philip Herbert. b 35. Leeds Univ MA 76 K Coll Lon AKC 63 Leic Coll of Educn CertEd 67. St Boniface Warminster 63. **d** 64 **p** 65. C Thurnby Lodge *Leic* 64–66; Hon C 66–67; Chapl RNR 67–90; Chapl Malosa Sch Malawi 68–75; Hon C Far Headingley St Chad *Ripon* 75–79; V Knowl Hill w Littlewick *Ox* 79–84; Chapl RN Sch Haslemere 85–89; C Felpham w Middleton *Chich* 89–90; Asst S Regional Dir Miss to Seamen 91–93; Dep S Regional Dir 93–97; S Regional Dir 97–00; PtO *Win* 93–14; *Cant* 94–00; *Chich* from 97; Corps Chapl Sea Cadet Corps 83–95; rtd 00; Hon C Witchampton, Stanbridge and Long Crichel etc *Sarum* 00–04; Hon Chapl Miss to Seafarers from 00. *55A Queens Close, West Moors, Ferndown BH22 0HN* T: (01202) 854679 E: dee.elston1@btinternet.com

ELTRINGHAM, Anna. b 74. St Jo Coll Dur BA 96. SEITE 05. **d** 08 **p** 09. C S Norwood H Innocents *S'wark* 08–14; TV Oxted 14–19; TR from 19; Dean of Women's Min from 17. *The Vicarage, 14 Oast Road, Oxted RH8 9DU* T: (01883) 712674 M: 07826-524038 E: revd.anna@gmail.com

ELTRINGHAM, Mrs Fiona Ann. b 48. Bp Grosseteste Coll CertEd 69. NEOC 86. **d** 89 **p** 94. Par Dn Willington *Newc* 89–92; Chapl HM YOI Castington 92–95; Chapl HM Pris Dur 95–07; rtd 07; PtO *Dur* from 07. *Granary Cottage, Stockley House Farm, Oakenshaw, Crook DL15 0TJ* T: (01388) 746058 E: davefi122@btinternet.com

ELVERSON, Ronald Peter Charles. b 50. St Edm Hall Ox BA 73 MA 86. St Jo Coll Nottm 84. **d** 86 **p** 87. C Whitnash *Cov* 86–90; V Dunchurch 90–01; R Dersingham w Anmer and Shernborne *Nor* 01–05; P-in-c Ore Ch Ch *Chich* 05–08; V 08–11; rtd 11; PtO *Pet* from 12. *7 Cheltenham Close, Rushden NN10 0NY* T: (01933) 355716 E: ronelverson@hotmail.co.uk

ELVIDGE, Mrs Joanna. b 55. FCIPD 84. STETS BA 06. **d** 06 **p** 07. NSM Horsham *Chich* 06–14; P-in-c Hythe *Win* 14–18; V from 18. *The Vicarage, 14 Atheling Road, Hythe, Southampton SO45 6BR* T: (023) 8084 4336 E: joanna.elvidge@btinternet.com

ELVIN, Jonathan Paul Alistair. b 65. Bris Univ BSc 90 Fitzw Coll Cam BA 94. Ridley Hall Cam 92. **d** 95 **p** 96. C Gravesend St Geo *Roch* 95–98; C Ex St Leon w H Trin 98–07; Min Ex Trin CD 07–13; V Ex H Trin from 13. *23 Couper Meadows, Exeter EX2 7TF* T: (01392) 363627 E: jonny@trinityexeter.com

ELVY, Canon Peter David. b 38. Lon Univ BA 62 Fitzw Ho Cam BA 64 MA 68 Edin Univ PhD 95. Ridley Hall Cam. **d** 65 **p** 66. C Herne *Cant* 65–66; C New Addington 66–68; C Addiscombe St Mildred 69–71; Youth Chapl *Chelmsf* 71–80; V Gt Burstead 75–92; Can Chelmsf Cathl 80–92; V Chelsea All SS *Lon* 92–05; Can Ughelli from 98; Preb St Paul's Cathl *Lon* from 05; rtd 05; PtO *Lon* from 05; *Roch* 12–14; *S'wark* 12–14. *2 Honiton Mansions, Flood Street, London SW3 5TU* T: (020) 7795 0084 E: peterelvy@gmail.com

ELWIS, Malcolm John. b 42. Melbourne Univ DipEd 74 ACT ThL 74. St Jo Coll Morpeth 69. **d** 70 **p** 72. C Bentleigh St Jo Australia 70–72; C St Paul's Cathl Sale 72–73; PtO Melbourne 73–80; PtO *Chich* from 80; Chapl Eastbourne and Co Healthcare NHS Trust 88–93 and 93–02; Chapl E Sussex Co Healthcare NHS Trust 02–06; Chapl Sussex Partnership NHS Foundn Trust 06–13; Sub Chapl HM Pris Lewes 92–04; Chapl 04–06; rtd 13. *Adams Barn, 85 Church Street, Willingdon, Eastbourne BN22 0HS* T: (01323) 903102 E: malcolmelwis21@hotmail.co.uk

ELWOOD, Mrs Claire Siobhan. b 69. RGN 91. St Hild Coll BA 19. **d** 19. C Dur St Nic from 19. *20 Dickens Wynd, Durham DH1 3QY* M: 07751-358546 E: elwoodc42@gmail.com

ELY, Nigel Patrick. b 62. Thames Poly BA 83 Southn Univ BTh 92 Birm Univ MA 01. Chich Th Coll 89. **d** 92 **p** 93. C Rustington *Chich* 92–93; C Bexhill St Pet 93–96; Chapl St Geo Post 16 Cen *Birm* 96–99; PtO 02–06; *Lich* 11–13; Asst Chapl R Wolv NHS Trust 13–17; PtO *Birm* 14–17; C W Bromwich All SS *Lich* from 15; C W Bromwich St Andr w Ch Ch from 17. *St Andrew's Vicarage, Oakwood Street, West Bromwich B70 9SN* T: 0121-525 8086 E: nigel_stgeorge@excite.com

ELY, Bishop of. *See* CONWAY, The Rt Revd Stephen David

ELY, Dean of. *See* BONNEY, The Very Revd Mark Philip John

EMBLIN, Canon Richard John. b 48. BEd 71 MA 81. S Dios Minl Tr Scheme 83. **d** 86 **p** 87. C S w N Hayling *Portsm* 86–89; P-in-c Wootton 89–95; V Cowes H Trin and St Mary 95–13; RD W Wight 01–07; Hon Can Portsm Cathl 05–13; rtd 13; PtO *Win* from 14. *125 Sandy Lane, St Ives, Ringwood BH24 2LQ* T: (01425) 482742 E: remblin@yahoo.com

EMERSON, Arthur Edward Richard. b 24. Lich Th Coll 69. **d** 72 **p** 73. C Barton upon Humber *Linc* 72–74; V Chapel St Leonards 75–88; P-in-c Hogsthorpe 77–88; V Chapel St Leonards w Hogsthorpe 88–91; rtd 91; PtO *Linc* 91–09; *Liv* from 16. *119 Folkestone Road, Southport PR8 5PH* T: (01704) 514778

EMERSON, Mrs Jan Vivien. b 44. S Dios Minl Tr Scheme 89. **d** 92 **p** 95. NSM Chich St Paul and St Pet 92–94; NSM Bosham 94–02; asst Chapl R W Sussex NHS Trust 02–07; PtO *Chich* from 07. *Flete Cottage, Critchfield Road, Bosham, Chichester PO18 8HH* T: (01243) 574948 E: janvemerson@aol.com

EMERTON, Andrew Neil. b 72. York Univ BSc 93 Qu Coll Ox DPhil 96 Down Coll Cam BTh 05. Ridley Hall Cam 02. **d** 05 **p** 06. C Brompton H Trin w Onslow Square St Paul *Lon* 05–07; Asst Dean St Mellitus Coll 08–16; Dean from 16; Dir St Paul's Th Cen from 08; PtO *Chelmsf* from 08. *18 Collingham Road, London SW5 0LX* M: 07815-498162 E: andrew.emerton@stmellitus.ac.uk

EMERY, David John. b 37. Dur Univ BA 59. Chich Th Coll 63. **d** 65 **p** 66. C Upholland *Liv* 65–68; C Gt Crosby St Faith 68–70; V Warrington St Barn 70–73; rtd 02; PtO *Ches* 03–04. *86 Ullswater, Macclesfield SK11 7YP* T: (01625) 501179 E: d.emery433@btinternet.com

EMERY, Karen Maureen. *See* BECK, Karen Maureen

EMERY, Sandra Faith. b 50. **d** 10 **p** 11. NSM Minchinhampton w Box and Amberley *Glouc* from 10. *The Old Carriage House, Edge, Stroud GL6 6PQ* T: (01452) 814148 E: emery31@btinternet.com

EMINSON, Mark Franklin. b 79. Mert Coll Ox BA 01 MSt 03 MA 06 Trin Coll Cam BA 07. Westcott Ho Cam 05. **d** 08 **p** 09. C E Grinstead St Swithun *Chich* 08–12; V Pagham 12–19; TR Merton Priory *S'wark* from 19. *Holy Trinity Vicarage, 1 Trinity Road, London SW19 8QT* T: (020) 8542 2313 E: eminson.mark@gmail.com

EMMANUEL, Rufin. b 63. Punjab Univ BA 87. Nat Catholic Inst of Th Pakistan 89. **d** 96 **p** 96. In RC Ch 96–09; Chapl Mid-Essex Hosp Services NHS Trust 09–11; Chapl Lewisham Healthcare NHS Trust 12–14; Chapl Lewisham and Greenwich NHS Trust from 14. *8 Mendip Place, Chelmsford CM1 2WT* T: (01245) 357579 M: 07583-087984 E: rufi49@hotmail.com *or* rufin.emmanuel@nhs.net

EMMEL, Canon Malcolm David. b 32. Qu Coll Birm. **d** 58 **p** 59. C Hessle *York* 58–62; Canada 62–66; V Catterick *Ripon* 66–73; V Pateley Bridge and Greenhow Hill 73–77; P-in-c Middlesmoor w Ramsgill 76–77; V Upper Nidderdale 77–88; RD Ripon 79–86; Hon Can Ripon Cathl 84–97; R Bedale 88–97; P-in-c Leeming 88–97; rtd 97; PtO *Bradf* 97–14; *Leeds* from 14. *29 Greystone Close, Burley in Wharfedale, Ilkley LS29 7RS* T: (01943) 865047 E: malcolmemmel@hotmail.com

EMMETT, Kerry Charles. b 46. St Jo Coll Dur BA 68. St Jo Coll Nottm 71. **d** 73 **p** 74. C Attenborough w Chilwell *S'well* 73–75; C Chilwell 75–76; C Wembley St Jo *Lon* 76–79; V Hanworth St Rich 79–89; R Ravenstone and Swannington *Leic* 89–04; RD Akeley S 97–03; P-in-c Mountsorrel Ch Ch and St Pet 04–13; rtd 13; PtO *Leic* from 13. *1 Chamberlain's Field, Birstall, Leicester LE4 3LD* T: 0116-319 4736

EMMOTT, David Eugene. b 41. St Chad's Coll Dur BA 63. **d** 66 **p** 67. C Bingley H Trin *Bradf* 66–69; C Anfield St Marg *Liv* 69–70; C Kirkby 70–75; Chapl Newc Poly 75–78; Hon C Toxteth Park St Marg *Liv* 78–80; TV Upholland 80–88; V Southfields St Barn *S'wark* 88–99; TV Liv Our Lady and St Nic w St Anne 99–06; rtd 06; PtO *Liv* from 16; *Eur* from 16. *6A Eastern Drive, Liverpool L19 0NB* T: 0151-281 5493 E: davidemmott@mac.com

EMMOTT, Douglas Brenton. b 45. K Coll Lon BD 78 AKC 78 York Univ MA 97. Linc Th Coll 79. **d** 80 **p** 81. C Kingston upon Hull St Alb *York* 80–83; V Scarborough St Sav w All SS 83–91; V York St Chad 91–99; V Leeds All So *Ripon* 99–07; rtd 07. *Le Moulin de Vernay, 72500 Dissay-sous-Courcillon, France* T: (0033) 2 43 46 53 82 M: 6 37 79 26 45 E: douglas.emmott@mac.com

EMMOTT, John Charles Lionel. b 32. SEITE 96. **d** 96 **p** 97. NSM Tenterden St Mich *Cant* 96–02; rtd 02; PtO *Cant* from 02. *58 Grange Crescent, St Michaels, Tenterden TN30 6DZ* T: (01580) 762092 E: emmottjandc@gmail.com

EMPEY, Clement Adrian. b 42. TCD BA 64 MA 68 PhD 71. CITC. **d** 74 **p** 75. C Dublin St Ann *D & G* 74–76; I Kells-Inistioge Gp *C & O* 76–84; I Clane w Donadea and Coolcarrigan *M & K* 84–88; Hon Chapl Miss to Seafarers from 88; Sen Chapl Miss to Seamen (Irish Republic) 97–08; I Dublin St Ann and St Steph *D & G* 88–01; Preb Tassagard St Patr Cathl Dublin 82–89; Treas St Patr Cathl Dublin 89–91; Dean St Patr Cathl Dublin 91–96; Prec St Patr Cathl Dublin 96–01; Chapl Rotunda Hosp 98–08; Prin CITC 01–08; Prec Ch Ch Cathl Dublin *D & G* 01–08; rtd 08. *5 Callenders Mill, Simmonstown Manor, Celbridge, Co Kildare, W23 RP48, Republic of Ireland* T: (00353) (1) 503 7797 M: 87-902 2169 E: adrianempey@gmail.com

✠**EMPEY, The Rt Revd Walton Newcome Francis.** b 34. TCD BA 57 Hon FGCM 02. K Coll (NS) BD 68. **d** 58 **p** 59 **c** 81. C Glenageary *D & G* 58–60; Bp's C Grand Falls New Brunswick Canada 60–63; I Madawaska 63–66; I Stradbally *C & O* 66–71; Dean Limerick *L & K* 71–81; I Limerick St Mich 71–81; Preb Taney St Patr Cathl Dublin 73–81; Bp L & K 81–85; Bp M & K 85–96; Abp Dublin *D & G* 96–02; Preb Cualaun St Patr Cathl Dublin 96–02; rtd 02. *Rathmore Lodge, Rathmore, Tullow, Co Carlow, Republic of Ireland* T: (00353) (59) 916 1891 E: louempey@hotmail.com

EMTAGE, Miss Susan Raymond. b 34. St Mich Ho Ox 63. dss 79 **d** 87 **p** 94. SW Area Sec CPAS Women's Action 75–82; Leic St Chris 82–86; Bramerton w Surlingham *Nor* 86–88; C 87–88; C Rockland St Mary w Hellington, Bramerton etc 88–89; Par Dn W Bromwich St Jas and St Paul 89–94; C 94; rtd 94; Hon C Stapleton *Bris* 96–04; PtO *Glouc* 14–17. *23 Capel Court, The Burgage, Prestbury, Cheltenham GL52 3EL* T: (01242) 577535 E: sue.emtage@ukonline.co.uk

ENDALL, Peter John. b 38. Linc Th Coll 83. **d** 85 **p** 86. C Burley in Wharfedale *Bradf* 85–88; V Thwaites Brow 88–03; RD S Craven 96–02; rtd 03; Hon C Tamworth *Lich* 04–08; PtO 08–15; *Leic* 09–15; *Blackb* from 15. *21 Fosbrooke House, 8 Clifton Drive, Lytham St Annes FY8 5RQ* T: (01253) 667027 E: cpendall.red@outlook.com

ENDICOTT, Michael John. b 45. **d** 97. NSM Pontnewydd *Mon* 97; NSM Well Chr Healing Cen from 97. *The Order of Jacob's Well, Forge House, Clomendy Road, Cwmbran NP44 3LS* T: (01633) 483600

ENEVER, Canon Rosemary Alice Delande. b 45. Oak Hill Th Coll 86. **d** 88 **p** 94. NSM Gt Ilford St Jo *Chelmsf* 88–94; TV Waltham H Cross 94–02; Asst Area Dean Epping Forest 00–01; V St Ilford St Andr 02–10; RD Redbridge 06–08; Hon Can Chelmsf Cathl 06–10; rtd 10; PtO *Ex* from 12. *197 Pinhoe Road, Exeter EX4 8AB* T: (01392) 200510 E: rosemaryenever@gmail.com

ENEVER, Vivian John. b 61. Collingwood Coll Dur BA 82 Cam Univ PGCE 85 Man Univ BPhil 97. Westcott Ho Cam 88. **d** 91 **p** 92. C Gt Crosby St Faith *Liv* 91–95; C Cantril Farm 95–97; TV Halas *Worc* 97–03; TR Newark w Coddington *S'well* 03–13; R Queen Thorne *Sarum* 13–18; RD Sherborne 14–18; rtd 18. *Banksia, High Street, Queen Camel, Yeovil BA22 7NH* T: (01935) 851552 E: banksia2018@gmail.com

ENGA, Mrs Charis Amelia. b 84. Dur Univ BA 05. St Mellitus Coll 10. **d** 12 **p** 13. C Highbury Ch Ch w St Jo and St Sav *Lon* 12–16; P-in-c Stoke Newington St Andr from 16. *St Andrew's Vicarage, 106 Bethune Road, London N16 5DU* M: 07584-622091 E: revcharisenga@gmail.com

ENGEL, Jeffrey Davis. b 38. Man Univ BA 59 Liv Univ PGCE 60 Aston Univ MSc 82 FCP 83. St Deiniol's Hawarden 86. **d** 89 **p** 90. NSM Formby St Pet *Liv* 89–92; C Prescot 92–94; P-in-c Hale 94–03; Dioc Adv for Past Care and Counselling 94–03; rtd 04; Chapl MU from 05; PtO *Liv* from 16. *Church View, West Street, Prescot L34 1LQ*

ENGELSEN, Christopher James. b 57. Nottm Univ BTh 86. Linc Th Coll 83. **d** 86 **p** 87. C Sprowston *Nor* 86–89; C High Harrogate Ch Ch *Ripon* 89–92; TV Seacroft 92–95; P-in-c Foulsham w Hindolveston and Guestwick *Nor* 95–01; P-in-c Hevingham w Hainford and Stratton Strawless 01–05; R Coltishall w Gt Hautbois, Frettenham etc from 05. *The Rectory, Rectory Road, Coltishall, Norwich NR12 7HL* T: (01603) 737255

ENGH, Dwayne Darcy. b 72. Calgary Univ BMus 97 BEd 99 K Coll Lon MA 10 Wolfs Coll Cam BTh 15. Westcott Ho Cam 13. **d** 15 **p** 16. C Cov St Mary 15–18; V from 18. *63 Broad Lane, Coventry CV5 7AH* M: 07425-606421 E: dwayneengh@shaw.ca

ENGLAND, Mrs Elizabeth Anne. b 73. Qu Coll Birm BA 15. **d** 15 **p** 16. C Codsall *Lich* 15–19; TR Buxton w Burbage and King Sterndale *Derby* from 19. *7 Lismore Park, Buxton SK17 9AU* M: 07930-264857 E: reverendelizabethengland@gmail.com

ENGLAND, Richard Alan. b 74. Sheff Univ BA 97 Dur Univ MA 07. Wycliffe Hall Ox 06. **d** 08 **p** 09. C Whitfield *Derby* 08–13; C Gillingham St Mark *Roch* 13–16; V Crofton *Portsm* from 16. *The Vicarage, 40 Vicarage Lane, Fareham PO14 2JX* T: (01329) 661154 E: richardalanengland@gmail.com *or* richard@croftonparish.org.uk

ENGLAND-SIMON, Haydn Henry. b 57. Llan Dioc Tr Scheme 92. **d** 96 **p** 97. NSM Penydarren *Llan* 96–97; C Caerphilly 97–01; V Pentre 01–07; V Ystradyfodwg from 07; AD Rhondda 11–18. *The Vicarage, St David's Close, Pentre CF41 7AX* T: (01443) 433651

ENGLER, Mrs Margaret Dorothy. b 44. Lon Univ TCert 77. S'wark Ord Course 90. **d** 93 **p** 94. NSM Harlesden All So *Lon* 93–97; Dep Chapl HM Pris Wandsworth 97; Acting Chapl HM Pris Wormwood Scrubs 97–98; Chapl HM Pris High Down 98–04; rtd 04; PtO *Lon* 04–07 and from 13; NSM Harlesden All So 07–13; PtO *S'wark* from 18. *35 Sheppard's Colleges, London Road, Bromley BR1 1PE* T: (020) 8466 9384 M: 07929-300048 E: margaretengler@waitrose.com

ENGLISH, Dana Leigh. **d** 12 **p** 13. C Rome *Eur* 12–18. *via del Babuino 153, 00187 Rome, Italy* T: (0039) (06) 3600 1881 E: dlenglish@aya.yale.edu

ENGLISH, Helen Margaret (Sister Helen Julian). b 55. Newc Poly BA 76. Ripon Coll Cuddesdon 12. **d** 13. NSM Hanborough and Freeland *Ox* 13–14; NSM Edwinstowe S'well 14–17; NSM Clipstone 14–17; NSM Perlethorpe 14–17; Min Gen CSF from 17; PtO *Dur* from 17. *Address withheld by request* T: (01325) 462954 E: helenjuliancsf@franciscans.org.uk

ENGLISH, Philip Trevor. b 37. Dur Univ BSc 60 FLIA 81 MITPA 84. Cranmer Hall Dur 60. **d** 62 **p** 63. C Hall Green Ascension *Birm* 62–66; Chapl St Jo Cathl Hong Kong 66–67; V Dorridge *Birm* 67–72; PtO *Ox* from 04. *Churchlands, Appletree Road, Chipping Warden, Banbury OX17 1LN* T: (01295) 660222 F: 660725 M: 07831-446421 E: pteifs@aol.com

ENNION, Peter. b 56. Aston Tr Scheme 85 Coll of Resurr Mirfield 87. **d** 89 **p** 90. C Middlewich w Byley *Ches* 89–91; C Aylestone St Andr w St Jas *Leic* 91–92; C Coppenhall *Ches* 92–94; P-in-c Newton in Mottram 94–99; P-in-c Tranmere St Paul w St Luke 99–04; V Torrisholme *Blackb* 04–11; P-in-c Blackpool St Mary 11–13; V 13–19; V Blackpool H Cross 13–19; rtd 19; PtO *Blackb* from 19. *Address temp unknown* E: ennionpeter@gmail.com

ENNIS, Mrs Lesley. b 47. Bp Lonsdale Coll CertEd 68 Open Univ BA 84. OLM course 97. **d** 99 **p** 00. NSM Sowerby *Wakef* 99–13; NSM Norland 09–13; NSM Ryburn 13–14; Leeds from 14. *26 Springfield, Sowerby Bridge HX6 1AD* T: (01422) 832747 F: 842747 M: 07703-628897 E: lesleyennis@hotmail.co.uk

ENNIS, Martin Michael. b 58. Man Univ BSc 80 MCollP 98. Sarum & Wells Th Coll 87. **d** 89 **p** 90. C Newquay *Truro* 89–92; C Tewkesbury w Walton Cardiff *Glouc* 92–95; P-in-c Brockworth 95–96; V 96–03; Hon C Wotton St Mary 09–10; V Tividale *Lich* from 10; P-in-c Wednesbury St Jas and St Jo 14–17; RD Wednesbury from 16. *26 View Point, Tividale, Oldbury B69 1UU* T: (01384) 257888 E: frmennis@gmail.com

ENOCH, William Frederick Palmer. b 30. EMMTC 76. **d** 79 **p** 80. NSM Ilkeston St Mary *Derby* 79–85; P-in-c Ilkeston H Trin 85–95; rtd 95; PtO *Derby* 95–13. *82 Derby Road, Ilkeston DE7 5EZ* T: 0115-944 3003

ENTICOTT, Ian Peter. b 59. Sheff Univ BA 82 St Jo Coll Dur MA 00. Cranmer Hall Dur 97. **d** 99 **p** 00. C Higher Bebington *Ches* 99–02; P-in-c Kelsall 02–10; Dir African Pastors' Fellowship 10–14; PtO *Cov* 10–14; V Accrington St Jas and St Paul *Blackb* from 14; P-in-c Accrington Ch Ch from 19; AD Accrington from 16. *St Paul's Vicarage, Barnfield Street,*

Accrington BB5 2AQ T: (01254) 433590 M: 07941-389621 E: ian.enticott@dunelm.org.uk

ENTWISLE, George Barry. b 43. St Jo Coll Ox BA 66 MA 72 Massey Univ (NZ) MEd 99. Linc Th Coll 73. **d** 75 **p** 76. C Rawmarsh w Parkgate *Sheff* 75–78; C Ashburton New Zealand 78–80; V Upper Clutha 80–84; V Gore 84–94; Can St Paul's Cathl Dunedin 87–94; Hon C Upper Clutha 01–06; rtd 08. *5 Bruce Street, Cromwell 9310, New Zealand* T/F: (0064) (3) 445 1797 M: 27-426 5539 E: b.entwisle@xtra.co.nz

ENTWISTLE, Christopher John. b 47. NOC 79. **d** 82 **p** 83. NSM Colne H Trin *Blackb* 82–84; C Poulton-le-Fylde 84–87; V Blackpool St Paul 87–96; RD Blackpool 94–96; P-in-c Overton 96–01; V Ashton-on-Ribble St Andr 01–06; TV W Preston 06–10; AD Preston 04–09; rtd 10; PtO *Blackb* from 10. *9 Chatsworth Avenue, Warton, Preston PR4 1BQ* T: (01772) 462742

ENTWISTLE, Frank Roland. b 37. Dur Univ BA 59. Cranmer Hall Dur 59. **d** 61 **p** 62. C Harborne Heath *Birm* 61–65; S Area Sec BCMS 65–66; Educn Sec 66–73; Hon C Wallington *S'wark* 68–73; UCCF 73–02; Hon C Ware Ch Ch *St Alb* 73–76; Hon C Leic H Trin w St Jo 76–02; rtd 02. *50 Redlands Road, Fremington, Barnstaple EX31 2NY* T: (01271) 342449 E: entwistles@cwcom.net

ENWEREM, Christopher Onyemaechi. b 75. St Jo Coll Nottm BA 15. **d** 16 **p** 17. C Dudley Wood and Cradley Heath *Worc* from 16. *15 Morgan Close, Cradley Heath B64 6DH* T: (01384) 936309 M: 07773-719434 E: cfenwerem@talktalk.net *or* c.enwerem@outlook.com

ENWUCHOLA, The Ven Benjamin Ameh. b 56. Lon Bible Coll BA 94. **d** 95 **p** 98. NSM S Tottenham St Ann *Lon* 96–99; NSM W Kilburn St Luke w St Simon and St Jude 99–13; NSM W Kilburn St Luke and Harrow Road Em 13–16; Chapl Nigerian Congregation 99–16; Asst Gen Sec Ch of Nigeria from 16; Hon Can Ondo from 02. *24 Douala Street, Wuse Zone 5, Abuja, Nigeria* T: (00234) (9) 523 6950 E: benwuchola@yahoo.co.uk

EPPS, Christopher Derek. b 54. ACII 79. Linc Th Coll 95. **d** 95 **p** 96. C Clevedon St Jo *B & W* 95–98; R St John w Millbrook *Truro* 98–03; P-in-c Truro St Geo and St Jo 03–15; P-in-c Truro St Paul and St Clem 03–12; C 12–15; V Truro St Paul, St Geo and St Jo 15–18; rtd 19. *1 Penwethers Close, Truro TR1 3FS* E: frcdepps@gmail.com

EPPS, Gerald Ralph. b 31. Open Univ BA 79. Oak Hill Th Coll 52 K Coll Lon 54. **d** 57 **p** 58. C Slade Green *Roch* 57–60; V Freethorpe w Wickhampton *Nor* 60–70; P-in-c Halvergate w Tunstall 62–67; V 67–70; R Pulham St Mary Magd 70–80; P-in-c Alburgh 76–77; P-in-c Denton 76–77; P-in-c Pulham St Mary V 76–80; R Pulham 80–91; rtd 91; PtO *Nor* from 91. *10 Lime Close, Harleston IP20 9DG* T: (01379) 854532

EPPS (formerly REEVE), Mrs Sally Ann. b 55. SEITE 07. **d** 10 **p** 11. C Ringmer *Chich* 10–14; P-in-c Burwash 14–15; R Burwash, Burwash Weald and Etchingham from 15. *The Rectory, Rectory Close, Etchingham Road, Burwash, Etchingham TN19 7BH* T: (01435) 882301 E: sallyaepps@btinternet.com

EPTON, John Alan. b 47. EMMTC 08. **d** 10 **p** 11. NSM Morton and Stonebroom w Shirland *Derby* from 10. *Phare, 22 Fernwood Close, Shirland, Alfreton DE55 6BW* T: (01773) 834153

ERLANDSON, Gareth Leslie. b 84. St Cuth Soc Dur BA 05. St Padarn's Inst 16. **d** 19. C Borderlands Mission Area *St As* from 19. *11 Bron yr Eglwys, Mynydd Isa, Mold CH7 6YQ* T: (01352) 756392 M: 07731-827988 E: curate@hopeparishchurch.org

ERREY, Rosalind Elisabeth. *See* RUTHERFORD, Rosalind Elisabeth

ERRIDGE, David John. b 45. Tyndale Hall Bris 66. **d** 69 **p** 70. C Bootle St Matt *Liv* 69–72; C Horwich H Trin *Man* 72–77; R Blackley St Andr 77–00; AD N Man 85–94; V Acomb St Steph and St Aid *York* 00–10; rtd 10; PtO *York* from 11. *51 Barlow Street, Acomb, York YO26 5HS* T: (01904) 797614 M: 07751-879142 E: davidandsusan51@hotmail.co.uk

ERRIDGE, Timothy John. b 65. Wye Coll Lon BSc 86 Croydon Coll CertEd 90. St Jo Coll Nottm 08. **d** 10 **p** 11. C Congresbury w Puxton and Hewish St Ann *B & W* 10–14; P-in-c Bleadon 14–16; P-in-c Weston-super-Mare St Andr Bournville 14–16; R Bleadon and Bournville from 16. *The Rectory, 17 Coronation Road, Bleadon, Weston-super-Mare BS24 0PG* T: (01934) 815404 E: revtimerridge@gmail.com

ERRINGTON, Mrs Sarah. b 67. UEA BA 90. Wycliffe Hall Ox BTh 94. **d** 97 **p** 98. C Gateacre *Liv* 97–02; TV Halewood 02–10; TV Wrexham *St As* from 10. *The Vicarage, 160 Borras Road, Wrexham LL13 9ER* T: (01978) 266018 E: vicarstjohnswxm@gmail.com

ERVING, Christel Estelle Ann. *See* LANGDON-GRIFFITHS, Christel Estelle Ann

ESAU, John Owen. b 39. St Mich Coll Llan 93. **d** 95 **p** 96. Min Can St D Cathl 95–97; V Llanpumsaint w Llanllawddog

97–01; V Cydweli and Llandyfaelog 01–03; R Aberporth w Tremain w Blaenporth and Betws Ifan 03–04; rtd 04. *Nursery Cottage, 14 Grove Place, Cardiff CF14 4QS* T: (029) 2061 2190

ESDAILE, Canon Adrian George Kennedy. b 35. Mert Coll Ox BA 57 MA 61. Wells Th Coll 59. **d** 61 **p** 62. C St Helier *S'wark* 61–64; C Wimbledon 64–68; V Hackbridge and N Beddington 68–80; RD Sutton 76–80; TR Chipping Barnet w Arkley *St Alb* 80–01; RD Barnet 89–94; Hon Can St Alb 94–01; rtd 01; PtO *S'wark* 01–16; *Guildf* from 02. *29 Hereford Close, Epsom KT18 5DZ* T/F: (01372) 723770 E: esdaileadrian@yahoo.co.uk

ESPIN-BRADLEY, Richard John. b 61. Lanc Univ BSc 84. Oak Hill Th Coll 93. **d** 95 **p** 96. C Brundall w Braydeston and Postwick *Nor* 95–98; C St Helier *S'wark* 98–02; V Wolverhampton St Luke *Lich* from 02; PtO *Eur* from 19. *St Luke's Vicarage, 122 Goldthorn Hill, Wolverhampton WV2 3HU* T: (01902) 340261 E: vicar@stlukeswolverhampton.org *or* richard.eb@outlook.com

ESSEX, Mary Rose. b 50. **d** 02 **p** 03. NSM E and W Leake, Stanford-on-Soar, Rempstone etc *S'well* 02–08; P-in-c Kirkby Woodhouse 08–15; rtd 15; PtO *S'well* from 16. *1A Bley Avenue, East Leake, Loughborough LE12 6NX* T: (01509) 856521 E: rev.maryessex@btopenworld.com

ESTALL, John William. b 81. Moorlands Coll BA 04. Ripon Coll Cuddesdon 14. **d** 16 **p** 17. C Washington *Dur* from 16. *38 Brancepeth Road, Washington NE38 0LA* M: 07525-478336 E: revjestall@gmail.com

ETCHELL, Diane. b 54. St Hild Coll 16. **d** 18 **p** 19. NSM Greasbrough *Sheff* from 18. *35 Allendale Road, Rotherham S65 3BY* E: st.mary.curate@gmail.com

ETCHES, Haigh David. b 45. St Jo Coll Dur BA 71. Cranmer Hall Dur. **d** 73 **p** 74. C Whitnash *Cov* 73–77; C Wallingford w Crowmarsh Gifford etc *Ox* 77–83; P-in-c Bearwood 83–86; R 86–11; rtd 11; PtO *Heref* from 12. *Silver Birches, 6 Chelmick Drive, Church Stretton SY6 7BP* T: (01694) 723266 E: haigh.etches@gmail.com

ETHERIDGE, Alastair. b 60. **d** 10 **p** 11. NSM Woking Ch Ch *Guildf* 10–15; NSM Fisherton Anger *Sarum* from 15. *18 Angler Road, Salisbury SP2 9PB* E: ali@wearestpauls.church

ETHERIDGE, Canon Richard Thomas. b 32. Lon Univ BD 62. ALCD 61. **d** 62 **p** 63. C Wilmington *Roch* 62–65; C Rainham 65–69; V Langley St Jo *Birm* 69–01; P-in-c Oldbury 83–01; P-in-c Langley St Mich 95–01; Hon Can Birm Cathl 97–01; rtd 01; PtO *Birm* 01–12; *Worc* from 02. *23 Scobell Close, Pershore, Worcester WR10 1QJ* T: (01386) 554745

ETHERINGTON, Mrs Ferial Mary Gould. b 44. Open Univ BA. St Alb Minl Tr Scheme 86. **d** 93 **p** 94. NSM Luton St Chris Round Green *St Alb* 93–04; Selection Sec and Co-ord for OLM Min Division 97–04; rtd 04; PtO *Carl* 04–10; Dioc Min Review Officer 05–11; TV Cartmel Peninsula 10–14; PtO from 14. *North View, Durdar, Carlisle CA2 4TX* T: (01228) 599658 E: ferial.etherington@btinternet.com

ETHERINGTON, Robert Barry. b 37. Man Univ BA 62. Linc Th Coll 62. **d** 64 **p** 65. C Linc St Jo 64–67; C Frodingham 67–69; V Reepham 69–78; Ind Chapl 70–78; Ind Chapl *St Alb* 78–88; V Luton St Chris Round Green 88–04; RD Luton 98–02; rtd 04; PtO *Carl* 05–19. *North View, Durdar, Carlisle CA2 4TX* T: (01228) 599658 E: revdbarry@btinternet.com

ETHERTON, Christopher Charles. b 47. UMIST BSc 68. STETS 04. **d** 07 **p** 08. NSM Lower Sandown St Jo and Sandown Ch Ch *Portsm* 07–10; P-in-c Binstead 10–14; P-in-c Havenstreet St Pet 10–14; NSM Bourton-on-the-Water w Clapton etc *Glouc* 14–19; rtd 19. *9 Parkers Close, Faringdon SN7 7BD* T: (01367) 242884 M: 07906-238368 E: revc.etherton@uwclub.net

EUROPE, Bishop of Gibraltar in. See INNES, The Rt Revd Robert Neil

EUROPE, Suffragan Bishop in. See HAMID, The Rt Revd David

EVANS, Adrian John. b 81. St Jo Coll Nottm BA 13. **d** 13 **p** 14. C Walmley *Birm* 13–19; V from 19. *The Vicarage, 4 Walmley Road, Sutton Coldfield B76 1QN* T: 0121-313 0413 M: 07961-375769 E: adrianevans007@gmail.com *or* ade@stjw.org.uk

EVANS, Miss Alison Jane. b 66. Sheff Univ BSc 87 Bris Univ PGCE 93. Trin Coll Bris BA 04. **d** 04 **p** 05. C Finham *Cov* 04–08; V Cov St Geo 08–17; AD Cov N 15–17; V Attleborough from 17. *The Vicarage, 5 Fifield Close, Nuneaton CV11 4TS* T: (024) 7673 6002 E: htavicar1@gmail.com

EVANS, Alun John. b 86. Univ of Wales (Abth) BA 07 Univ of Wales (Lamp) MTh 09 Abth Univ PGCE 10. St Mich Coll Llan 13. **d** 16 **p** 17. C Haverfordwest *St D* 16–18; C Llanbadarn Fawr and Elerch and Penrhyncoch etc from 18. *The Vicarage, Maes-y-Garn, Bow Street SY24 5DS* M: 07949-826270 E: rev.alun@outlook.com

EVANS, Mrs Amanda Jane. b 66. Southn Univ BA 88 QTS 04. Ripon Coll Cuddesdon 13. **d** 16 **p** 17. C Mabe *Truro* from 16. *The Vicarage, Driftwood, Pellew Road, Falmouth TR11 2NS* M: 07544-527649 E: rev.amanda.evans@outlook.com

EVANS, Andrew. b 57. Southn Univ BEd 80. S Dios Minl Tr Scheme 88. **d** 91 **p** 92. NSM Cricklade w Latton *Bris* 91–97; C Yatton Keynell 97–99; TV By Brook 99–00; R Hullavington, Norton and Stanton St Quintin 00–09; P-in-c Sherston Magna, Easton Grey, Luckington etc 06–09; Bp's Adv for Rural Min 00–09; Hon Can Bris Cathl 05–09; AD N Wilts 06–09; TR Bridport *Sarum* 09–17; V Ashton-on-Ribble St Mich and All Angels w Preston St Mark *Blackb* from 17; OCM from 00. *St Michael's Vicarage, 2 Egerton Road, Ashton-on-Ribble, Preston PR2 1AJ* T: (01772) 726157 M: 07931-616329 E: canonandrewevans@gmail.com

EVANS, Andrew. See EVANS, John Andrew

EVANS, Andrew Eric. b 58. Sheff Univ LLB 80 Solicitor 83. Trin Coll Bris 01. **d** 03 **p** 04. C Gt Bookham *Guildf* 03–06; P-in-c Broughton Gifford, Gt Chalfield and Holt *Sarum* 06–14; R from 14; C Atworth w Shaw and Whitley from 07; C Melksham 07–10; TR 10–14; RD Bradford from 08. *The Rectory, Ham Green, Holt, Trowbridge BA14 7PZ* T: (01225) 782289 E: goodevansitsandrew@gmail.com

EVANS, Mrs Anna Rachel. b 77. Brunel Univ BA 00. St Mellitus Coll 16. **d** 19. C Hampton Wick *Lon* from 19. *16 Arlington Road, Ashford TW15 2LS*

EVANS, Anne. b 47. Ches Coll of HE MTh 99. **d** 05 **p** 06. OLM Broughton *Lich* 05–17; OLM Myddle 05–17; OLM Loppington w Newtown 05–17; rtd 17; PtO *Lich* from 17. *The Fields, Welshampton, Ellesmere SY12 0NP* T: (01948) 710206

EVANS, Canon Anthony Nigel. b 53. Nottm Univ BA 74 Fitzw Coll Cam BA 76. Westcott Ho Cam 74. **d** 77 **p** 78. C Sneinton St Cypr *S'well* 77–80; C Worksop Priory 80–83; V Nottingham St Geo w St Jo 83–88; R Ordsall 88–95; P-in-c Sutton in Ashfield St Mary 95–07; AD Newstead 01–05; Bp's Dom Chapl 07–11; Hon Can S'well Minster 04–11; P-in-c Edwinstowe 11–17; P-in-c Perlethorpe 11–17; P-in-c Clipstone 11–17; rtd 17; Warden Sacrista Prebend Retreat Ho *S'well* from 18; PtO from 18. *8 The Fields, Rainworth, Mansfield NG21 0GY* E: vicarfcep@btinternet.com

EVANS, Ashley Francis. b 58. Birm Univ BA 79. WEMTC 00. **d** 03 **p** 04. C Kington w Huntington, Old Radnor, Kinnerton etc *Heref* 03–07; P-in-c Ewyas Harold w Dulas, Kenderchurch etc 07–10; R 11–17; RD Abbeydore 09–14; V Ticehurst and Flimwell *Chich* from 17. *The Vicarage, Church Street, Ticehurst, Wadhurst TN5 7AB* T: (01580) 200316 M: 07763-070177 E: revdafe@gmail.com *or* revd@penandashley.co.uk

EVANS, Brian. b 34. Open Univ BA 86. St Deiniol's Hawarden 70. **d** 71 **p** 72. C Porthkerry *Llan* 71–72; C Barry All SS 72–75; V Abercynon 75–82; V Pendoylan w Welsh St Donats 82–87; R Maentwrog w Trawsfynydd *Ban* 87–99; rtd 99; PtO *Ban* 99–14 and from 16. *Madryn, 46 Glan Ysgethin, Talybont LL43 2BB* T: (01341) 247965

EVANS, Mrs Christine Elizabeth. b 54. RGN 75 RMHN 77. STETS. **d** 12 **p** 13. NSM Hanham *Bris* 12–17 and from 18; NSM Kingswood from 12; P-in-c 17–18. *3 Teewell Hill, Bristol BS16 5PA* T: 0117-957 0731 E: se007a4909_2@blueyonder.co.uk

EVANS, Christopher Idris. b 51. Chich Th Coll 74. **d** 77 **p** 78. C Gelligaer *Llan* 77–80; C St Andrews Major w Michaelston-le-Pit 80–81; V Llangeinor 81–87; V Wattlington w Pyrton and Shirburn *Ox* 87–97; R Icknield 97–16; rtd 16; PtO *Ox* from 17. *40 Croft Road, Wallingford OX10 0HH* E: c.idris.evans@gmail.com

EVANS, Christopher Jonathan. b 43. AKC 67 and 88. **d** 68 **p** 69. C Wednesfield St Thos *Lich* 68–71; C Dorridge *Birm* 71–74; V Marston Green 74–81; V Acocks Green 81–86; RD Yardley 84–86; V Hill 86–88; Area Officer COPEC Housing Trust 88–91; V Harborne St Pet *Birm* 91–08; rtd 08; PtO *Heref* 08–18. *3 Manor Road, Great Bedwyn, Marlborough SN8 3UF* E: s.evans761@btinternet.com

EVANS, Clive Roger. b 59. Worc Coll Ox BA 80 MA 84 Barrister (Middle Temple) 89. St Jo Coll Nottm 94. **d** 94 **p** 95. C Barton Seagrave w Warkton *Pet* 94–97; V Long Buckby w Watford 97–11; P-in-c W Haddon w Winwick and Ravensthorpe 03–11; V Long Buckby w Watford and W Haddon w Winwick 11–13; RD Brixworth 01–09; Can Pet Cathl 09–13; V Bromyard and Stoke Lacy *Heref* from 13; RD Bromyard from 17. *The Vicarage, 28 Church Lane, Bromyard HR7 4DZ* T: (01885) 788275 E: cliver.evans@tiscali.co.uk

EVANS, Canon Colin Rex. b 24. Reading Univ BA 49. Linc Th Coll. **d** 57 **p** 58. C Boultham *Linc* 57–59; C Linc St Nic w St Jo Newport 59–62; V Linc St Mary-le-Wigford w St Martin 62–66; P-in-c Linc St Faith 63–66; R Bassingham 66–74; V

Aubourn w Haddington 66–74; V Carlton-le-Moorland w Stapleford 66–74; R Skinnand 66–74; R Thurlby w Norton Disney 66–74; RD Graffoe 69–74; RD Elloe E 74–89; Can and Preb Linc Cathl 74–89; V Holbeach 74–89; rtd 90; Hon C Dawlish *Ex* 90–97; RD Kenn 95–97; PtO from 97. *87 West Cliff Park Drive, Dawlish EX7 9EL* T: (01626) 865191 E: canoncrevans@gmail.com

EVANS, Daniel Barri. b 70. St Steph Ho Ox 01. **d** 03 **p** 04. C Weymouth H Trin *Sarum* 03–07; V Llwynderw *S & B* 07–15; TV Hawarden *St As* from 15; TV Borderlands Miss Area from 17. *Address temp unknown* M: 07948-692927 E: revdannyevans@sky.com

EVANS, Miss Daphne Gillian. b 41. Bible Tr Inst Glas 67 Trin Coll Bris IDC 75. **dss** 83 **d** 87. Wenlock *Heref* 83–88; Team Dn 87–88; rtd 88. *3 Jean Lawrie Court, St Boswells, Melrose TD6 0BF* E: revevborders@gmail.com

EVANS, David. b 37. Open Univ BA 73 FRSA 95. St Mich Coll Llan 65. **d** 67 **p** 68. C Swansea St Pet *S & B* 67–70; C St Austell *Truro* 70–75; R Purley *Ox* 75–90; RD Bradfield 85–90; R Bryanston Square St Mary w St Marylebone St Mark *Lon* 90–99; P-in-c St Marylebone Ch Ch 90–91; R Nuthurst and Mannings Heath *Chich* 99–07; P-in-c 07–11; rtd 11; PtO *Chich* 12–17; S'wark from 15. *Flat 3, 4 Hardwicke Road, Reigate RH2 9AG* T: (01737) 479296 E: devans1662@gmail.com

EVANS, Canon David. b 37. Keble Coll Ox BA 60 MA 65 Lon Univ BD 64. Wells Th Coll 62. **d** 64 **p** 65. Min Can Brecon Cathl *S & B* 64–68; C Brecon w Battle 64–68; C Swansea St Mary and H Trin 68–71; Chapl Univ of Wales (Swansea) 68–71; Bp's Chapl for Samaritan and Soc Work *Birm* 71–75; Jt Gen Sec Samaritans 75–84; Gen Sec 84–89; R Heyford w Stowe Nine Churches *Pet* 89–96; R Heyford w Stowe Nine Churches and Flore etc 96–01; Chapl Northants Police 89–01; RD Daventry *Pet* 96–00; Can Pet Cathl 97–01; rtd 01; PtO *Ex* 01–17. *3 Elm Close, Tutshill, Chepstow NP16 7DA* T: (01291) 630398

EVANS, David Burton. b 35. Open Univ BA 87 Goldsmiths' Coll Lon BMus 93. K Coll Lon 58 Edin Th Coll 60. **d** 62 **p** 63. C Leeds St Hilda *Ripon* 62–63; C Cross Green St Sav and St Hilda 63–67; Min Can Dur Cathl 67–71; PV Chich Cathl 71–74; Chapl Prebendal Sch Chich 71–74; R Lynch w Iping Marsh *Chich* 74–79; V Easebourne 79–86; Chapl K Edw VII Hosp Midhurst 77–86; R St Mich Cornhill w St Pet le Poer etc *Lon* 86–96; rtd 96; Pau *Eur* 96–01; PtO from 05. *128 Little Breach, Chichester PO19 5UA* T: (01243) 773266 M: 07795-662991 E: evtherev@virginmedia.com

EVANS, David Elwyn. b 43. St Mich Coll Llan 71. **d** 73 **p** 74. C Llandybie *St D* 73–75; C Llanelli 75–78; V Tre-lech a'r Betws w Abernant and Llanwinio 78–02; rtd 02. *8 Ger y Llan, The Parade, Carmarthen SA31 1LY*

EVANS, David Julian James. b 65. Rob Coll Cam BA 87. Westcott Ho Cam 03. **d** 05 **p** 06. C W Hackney St Barn *Lon* 05–08; C St John-at-Hackney 08–10; V Walworth St Chris S'wark 10–18; Warden Pemb Coll Miss Walworth 10–18. *38 Marryat Road, London SW19 5BD* E: davidjjevans@me.com

EVANS, David Meurig Ashton. b 56. Univ of Wales (Cardiff) BSc 78 PhD 82 Lon Bible Coll BA 90. SEITE 12. **d** 13 **p** 14. C Lewisham St Mary S'wark 13–16; TR Brereton and Rugeley w Armitage *Lich* from 16. *20 Church Street, Rugeley WS15 2AB* M: 07919-416900 E: davidmaevans1@gmail.com

EVANS, Capt David Raymond. b 48. **d** 11 **p** 12. C Dale and St Brides w Marloes etc *St D* 11–14. *11 Lapwing Gardens, Weston-super-Mare BS22 8UP* M: 07814-699336 E: landevans79@aol.com

EVANS, David Richard. b 47. St Steph Ho Ox 68. **d** 72 **p** 73. C Cardiff St Jo *Llan* 72–76; PV Llan Cathl 76–80; V Cleeve Prior and The Littletons *Worc* 80–12; rtd 12. *Stone Barn, Main Street, Evesham WR11 8LG* T: (01789) 772299 E: father.richard@hotmail.co.uk

✠**EVANS, The Rt Revd David Richard John.** b 38. G&C Coll Cam BA 63 MA 66. Clifton Th Coll 63. **d** 65 **p** 66 **c** 78. C Enfield Ch Ch Trent Park *Lon* 65–68; SAMS Argentina 69–77; Peru 77–88; Bp Peru 78–88; Bp Bolivia 82–88; Asst Bp Bradf 88–93; Gen Sec SAMS 93–03; Hon Asst Bp Chich 94–97; Hon Asst Bp Roch 95–97; Hon Asst Bp Birm 97–03; rtd 03; Hon Asst Bp Cov from 03; Hon C Alderminster and Halford 03–07; Hon C Butlers Marston and the Pillertons w Ettington 03–07; Hon C Stourdene Gp 07–10. *30 Charles Street, Warwick CV34 5LQ* T: (01926) 258791 E: bishopdrjevans@talktalk.net

EVANS, David Russell. b 36. Liv Univ BA 57. Ripon Hall Ox 59. **d** 61 **p** 62. C Netherton CD *Liv* 61–65; Chapl Canon Slade Sch Bolton 65–93; Lic Preacher *Man* 65–09; PtO from 09. *2 Rushford Grove, Bolton BL1 8TD* T: (01204) 592981 E: revvyevvy@gmail.com

EVANS, Canon Derek. b 45. St D Coll Lamp. **d** 68 **p** 69. C Pembroke Dock *St D* 68–74; V Ambleston, St Dogwells, Walton E and Llysyfran 74–77; V Wiston w Ambleston, St Dogwells and Walton E 78–81; V Wiston w Ambleston, St Dogwells, Walton E etc 81–85; R Haverfordwest St Mary and St Thos w Haroldston 85–09; Dep Dioc Dir of Educn 92–97; Dir 97–09; Can St D Cathl 99–09; RD Roose 00–04; rtd 09; PtO *St D* from 09. *Thimble Cottage, 10 Milford Road, Haverfordwest SA61 1PJ* T: (01437) 765655

EVANS, Mrs Dorothi Madogwen Parry. **d** 16 **p** 17. NSM Corwen w Llangar w Glyndyfrdwy etc *St As* 16–17; NSM Valle Crucis Miss Area from 18. *Fron Heulog, 17 Ffrydan Road, Bala LL23 7RY* T: (01678) 520496 E: fronheulog@yahoo.co.uk

EVANS, Canon Edward John. b 47. St Mich Coll Llan 67. **d** 71 **p** 72. C Llantwit Fardre *Llan* 71–77; R Eglwysilan 77–88; V Laleston w Tythegston and Merthyr Mawr 88–09; V Laleston and Merthyr Mawr 09–13; V Laleston and Merthyr Mawr w Penyfai 13–15; RD Bridgend 94–04; AD 12–15; Hon Can Llan Cathl 07–15; rtd 15. *15 St Andrews Road, Bridgend CF31 1RX* T: (01656) 655511 M: 07968-044583 E: ejevans972@btinternet.com

EVANS, Elaine. *See* EVANS, Jennifer Elaine

EVANS, Elwyn David. b 36. Keble Coll Ox BA 58 MA 62. St Steph Ho Ox 58 St Mich Coll Llan 60. **d** 61 **p** 62. C Aberystwyth H Trin *St D* 61–63; C Llanelli St Paul 63–66; C Roath St German *Llan* 66–69; V Crynant 69–78; R Llanilid w Pencoed 79–95; rtd 95; PtO *Llan* from 95; *S & B* 95–14. *15 St Andrew's Road, Bridgend CF31 1RX* T: (01656) 655511 E: ejevans912@btinternet.com *or* ejevans972@btinternet.com

EVANS, Canon Freda Christine. b 48. NTMTC 96. **d** 99 **p** 00. C Hampton Hill *Lon* 99–02; V Kingshurst *Birm* 02–08; TR Erdington 08–16; V Erdington St Barn 16–19; Hon Can Birm Cathl 14–19; rtd 19. *Address withheld by request* M: 07957-666002 E: freda@fredaevans.co.uk

EVANS, Mrs Freda Mary Ann (Frieda). b 54. St D Coll Lamp 95. **d** 00 **p** 05. OLM Malpas *Mon* 00–09; NSM Caerleon and Llanfrechfa 09–13; NSM Cwmbran from 13. *3 The Firs, Malpas, Newport NP20 6YD* T: (01633) 850600 E: revfrieda@btinternet.com

EVANS, Canon Frederick John Margam. b 31. Magd Coll Ox BA 53 MA 57. St Mich Coll Llan 53. **d** 54 **p** 55. C New Tredegar *Mon* 54–58; C Chepstow 58–60; Asst Chapl United Sheff Hosps 60–62; Chapl Brookwood Hosp Woking 62–70; V Crookham *Guildf* 70–98; RD Aldershot 78–83; Hon Can Guildf Cathl 89–98; rtd 98; PtO *Guildf* from 98. *4 Radford Close, Farnham GU9 9AB* T/F: (01252) 710594 E: johnjunee@btinternet.com

EVANS, Genevieve Sarah. b 62. Univ of Wales (Cardiff) BA 04. St Mich Coll Llan 02. **d** 04 **p** 05. C Whalley Range St Edm and Moss Side etc *Man* 04–08; V Walsall Pleck and Bescot *Lich* 08–16; C Walsall St Matt 08–16; C Walsall St Paul 08–16; V Oxley and Wednesfield St Greg 16–19; R Comrie *St And* from 19; R Crieff from 19; R Killin from 19; R Lochearnhead from 19. *Strathearn Rectory, 3B Galvelmore Street, Crieff PH7 4DN* T: (01764) 656222 E: rev.gen@btinternet.com

EVANS, Geoffrey David. b 44. K Coll Lon BD 69 AKC 69 Ex Univ PGCE 74. St Aug Coll Cant 69. **d** 70 **p** 71. C Lawrence Weston *Bris* 70–73; Chapl Grenville Coll Bideford 74–79; Chapl Eastbourne Coll 79–82; Chapl Taunton and Somerset Hosp 83–91; Chapl Musgrove Park Hosp 83–91; Chapl Taunton Sch 92–04; rtd 09. *10 Chaucer Road, Bath BA2 4QU* E: suecebath@gmail.com

EVANS, Mrs Gillian. b 39. Imp Coll Lon BSc 61. Mon Dioc Tr Scheme 84. **d** 88 **p** 94. NSM Penallt and Trellech *Mon* 88–89; NSM Overmonnow w Wonastow and Michel Troy 89–92; Dioc Ecum Officer and C Ludlow, Ludford, Ashford Carbonell etc *Heref* 92–95; PtO *Heref* 96–06; Hon C Dawlish *Ex* 97–98; TV Golden Cap Team *Sarum* 98–01; rtd 01; PtO *Cov* 01–06; *Mon* 01–06; Hon C Wolford w Burmington *Cov* 06–08; Hon C Cherington w Stourton 06–08; Hon C Barcheston 06–08; Hon C Long Compton, Whichford and Barton-on-the-Heath 06–08; Hon C S Warks Seven Gp 08–16; PtO from 16. *8 Grange Park, Stratford-upon-Avon CV37 6XH* T: (01789) 269421

EVANS, Canon Glyn. b 59. Nene Coll Northn BA 80 Leic Univ BA 80 Ch Ch Coll Cant CertEd 82 Kent Univ PGCE 82. Qu Coll Birm 85. **d** 88 **p** 89. C Denton *Newc* 88–92; V Choppington 92–97; P-in-c Longhorsley and Hebron 97–01; Chapl HM Pris Acklington 97–01; P-in-c Newc St Andr and St Luke 01–17; City Cen Chapl 01–17; Chapl Northumbria Police from 11; Chapl to the Deaf from 16; TR N Shields from 17; Hon Can Newc Cathl from 11. *Christ Church Vicarage, 26 Cleveland Road, North Shields NE29 0NG* T: 0191-258 6653 E: office@northshieldsparish.org

EVANS, Canon Glyn Peter. b 54. Leeds Univ BA 75. Ripon Coll Cuddesdon 76. **d** 77 **p** 78. C Binley *Cov* 77–80; C Clifton upon Dunsmore w Brownsover 80–84; P-in-c Lacock w Bowden Hill *Bris* 84–89; P-in-c Lt Compton w Chastleton, Cornwell etc *Ox* 89–00; Agric Chapl 89–00; Dioc Rural Officer from 00; Hon Can Ch Ch from 05; PtO *Cov* from 16. *Chelmscote Cottage, Brailes, Banbury OX15 5JJ* T: (01608) 686749 M: 07581-491713 E: glynevans@gmail.com

EVANS, Canon Gwyneth Mary. b 43. Gilmore Ho 69 Linc Th Coll 70. **dss** 74 **d** 87 **p** 94. Stamford Hill St Thos *Lon* 74–79; Chapl Asst R Free Hosp Lon 79–89; Chapl Salisbury Health Care NHS Trust 89–01; Can and Preb Sarum Cathl 96–01; rtd 01; PtO *Sarum* from 01. *39 The Close, Salisbury SP1 2EL* T: (01722) 412546 E: gwyneth175@btinternet.com

EVANS, Ms Heather Rhiannon. b 14 **p** 15. NSM Llanbadarn Fawr and Elerch and Penrhyncoch etc *St D* from 14. *The Vicarage, Llanbadarn Fawr, Aberystwyth SY23 3TT* T: (01970) 624638 E: heather.melindwr@live.co.uk

EVANS, Hilary Margaret. b 49. Redland Coll of Educn TDip 71 Ches Coll of HE BTh 97. NOC 94. **d** 97 **p** 98. C Heald Green St Cath *Ches* 97–00; Dn-c Davyhulme Ch Ch *Man* 00–03; P-in-c Blackley St Pet 03–09; AD N Man 06–08; rtd 09; Hon C SW Gower *S & B* 09–14; PtO from 14. *10 Meadow Croft, Southgate, Swansea SA3 2DF* T: (01792) 234230 E: hilary@evanses.plus.com

EVANS, Ian David. b 61. Qu Coll Birm 13. **d** 15 **p** 16. NSM Ipsley *Worc* from 15. *27 Belmont Close, Redditch B97 5AW* T: (01905) 571243 *or* (01527) 404522 E: ianevans223@gmail.com

EVANS, Mrs Jane. b 59. W Midl Coll of Educn BEd 81. **d** 03 **p** 04. OLM Lilleshall and Muxton *Lich* from 03. *5 Collett Way, Priorslee, Telford TF2 9SL* T: (01952) 291340 E: revjane@talktalk.net

EVANS, Mrs Jennifer. b 41. Ilkley Coll DipEd 62. Sarum Th Coll 88. **d** 88 **p** 08. Par Dn Bramshott and Liphook *Portsm* 88–92; Par Dn Whippingham w E Cowes 92–95; Par Dn Sarisbury 95–05; Hon C Llawhaden w Bletherston and Llanycefn *St D* 08–10; Hon C Slebech and Uzmaston w Boulston 08; Hon C Uzmaston 08–10; Hon C Chaffcombe, Cricket Malherbie etc *B & W* 10–19. *Address temp unknown* M: 07932-746883 E: jennie.honeycombs@virgin.net

EVANS, Jennifer Elaine. b 59. Wolv Univ BA 92. Qu Coll Birm 00. **d** 02 **p** 03. C Stafford St Jo and Tixall w Ingestre *Lich* 02–06; TV Stafford 06–13; V Stafford St Bertelin and Whitgreave St Jo from 13; Dean's PV Lich Cathl from 17. *St Bertelin's Vicarage, 36 Holmcroft Road, Stafford ST16 1JF* T: (01785) 252874 E: elaine.dowevans@gmail.com

EVANS, Mrs Jennifer Mary. **d** 17. NSM Bro Cyfeiliog and Mawddwy *Ban* from 17. *Dolau, Llanbrynmair SY19 7DL* T: (01650) 521660 E: jenevans399@btinternet.com

EVANS, Jill. *See* EVANS, Gillian

EVANS, Mrs Joan. b 36. Nor Tr Coll TCert 57 UEA BEd 94. **d** 02 **p** 03. OLM Loddon, Sisland, Chedgrave, Hardley and Langley *Nor* 02–06; rtd 06; PtO *Nor* from 06. *13 Drury Lane, Loddon, Norwich NR14 6LB* T: (01508) 528656 E: joanevans936@btinternet.com

EVANS, John. *See* EVANS, Frederick John Margam

EVANS, John Andrew. b 53. Hull Univ BSc 74 Univ of Wales MSc 75 Bris Univ BA 96. Trin Coll Bris 94. **d** 96 **p** 97. C Walton H Trin *Ox* 96–98; C Caversham St Pet and Mapledurham etc *Sarum* 01–09; V N Hayes St Nic *Lon* from 09. *St Nicholas' Vicarage, Raynton Drive, Hayes UB4 8BG* T: (020) 8573 4122 M: 07725-805437 E: j_andrew_evans@btconnect.com

EVANS, John David Vincent. b 41. CGSW 78. Lich Th Coll 66. **d** 68 **p** 70. C Kingsthorpe *Pet* 68–69; C Corby Epiphany w St Jo 69–72; Bp's Adv in Children's Work 72–74; Probation Officer 74–90; PtO *Pet* 88–90; R Greens Norton w Bradden and Lichborough 90–96; V Northampton Ch Ch 96–06; rtd 06; PtO *Pet* 06–09. *Ivy Cottage, Creaton Road, Hollowell, Northampton NN6 8RP* T: (01604) 743878 E: johnevanssr203@gmail.com

EVANS, John Laurie. b 34. Pretoria Univ BSc 54 Imp Coll Lon BSc 55 Rhodes Univ BA 59. Ripon Coll Cuddesdon 84. **d** 86 **p** 87. C Bruton and Distr *B & W* 86–89; P-in-c Ambrosden w Merton and Piddington *Ox* 89–91; C Pet St Mary Boongate 91–93; V Michael *S & M* 93–96; R Ballaugh 93–96; rtd 96; Chapl Allnutt's Hosp Goring Heath 96–99; P-in-c Fochabers *Mor* 99–00; P-in-c Strathnairn St Paul 00–03; TV Langtree *Ox* 03–07; Hon C Kelso *Edin* 07–12; PtO from 12; Newc from 12. *2 Pressen Farm Cottage, Cornhill-on-Tweed TD12 4RS* T: (01890) 850309 M: 07909-986369 E: jonevansscotland@btinternet.com

EVANS, John Miles. b 39. Yale Univ BA 61 JD 67 St Cath Coll Cam BA 64 MA 68. NY Th Sem MDiv 93. **d** 95 **p** 95. Chapl St Jo Cathl Oban *Arg* 95–97; Interim R Lynbrook Ch Ch USA 98–99; R Davidsonville All Hallows 99–05. *PO Box 1272, Portsmouth NH 03802-1272, USA* E: johnmilesevans@comcast.net

EVANS, John Rhys. b 45. Hull Univ BSc 66. Sarum & Wells Th Coll 77. **d** 79 **p** 80. C Alton St Lawr *Win* 79–82; C Tadley St Pet 82–85; V Colden 85–91; V Bitterne Park 91–01; C Ringwood 01–11; Chapl R Bournemouth and Christchurch Hosps NHS Foundn Trust 01–11; rtd 11; PtO *Glouc* from 14. *The Cottage, Alderley, Wotton-under-Edge GL12 7QT* T: (01453) 845320 E: johnrhysevans@yahoo.co.uk

EVANS, John Stuart. b 57. Univ of Wales (Abth) BA 78 Bretton Hall Coll PGCE 81. Trin Coll Bris BA 98. **d** 98 **p** 99. C Connah's Quay *St As* 98–02; V Rhosllannerchrugog 02–10; AD Llangollen 05–10; R Ruthin w Llanrhydd and Llanfwrog 10–16; TV Dyffryn Clwyd Miss Area from 17. *The Cloisters, School Road, Ruthin LL15 1BL* T: (01824) 702068 E: cymrostu@gmail.com

EVANS, Canon John Thomas. b 43. St Mich Coll Llan 66. **d** 67 **p** 68. C Connah's Quay *St As* 67–71; C Llanrhos 71–74; Chapl Rainhill Hosp Liv 74–78; TV Wrexham *St As* 78–83; V Holywell 83–96; RD 95–96; V Colwyn Bay 96–99; V Colwyn Bay w Brynymaen 99–02; RD Rhos 00–02; R Caerwys and Bodfari 02–08; Can Cursal St As Cathl 96–08; rtd 08; PtO *St As* from 09. *4 Durham Drive, Prestatyn LL19 8DX* M: 07905-861174 E: johnbethevans@btinternet.com

✠**EVANS, The Rt Revd John Wyn.** b 46. FSA 88 FRHistS 94 Univ of Wales (Cardiff) BA 68 BD 71. St Mich Coll Llan 68. **d** 71 **p** 72 **c** 08. C St D Cathl 71–72; Min Can St D Cathl 72–75; PtO *Ox* 75–77; Dioc Archivist *St D* 76–82; R Llanfalteg w Clunderwen and Castell Dwyran etc 77–82; Warden of Ords 78–83; Dioc Dir of Educn 82–92; Chapl Trin Coll Carmarthen 82–90; Dean of Chpl 90–94; Hd Th and RS 91–94; Hon Can St D Cathl 88–90; Can St D Cathl 90–94; Dean St D 94–08; V St D Cathl 94–01; TR Dewisland 01–08; Bp St D 08–16; rtd 16; PtO *St D* from 16; *S & B* from 16. *12 Ffordd Caerfai, St Davids, Haverfordwest SA62 6QT* T: (01437) 729402

EVANS, Jonathan Alan. b 53. Fitzw Coll Cam BA 75 PGCE 77 MA 79. St Jo Coll Nottm MA 95. **d** 95 **p** 96. C Drypool York 95–98; V Beverley St Nic 98–12; V Rye Park St Cuth St Alb 12–18; rtd 18; PtO *Glouc* from 19. *38 Furlong Road, Gloucester GL1 4UT* E: jonathan@familyevans.org.uk

EVANS, Jonathan Edward. b 69. Oriel Coll Ox MA 91. Ripon Coll Cuddesdon 16. **d** 18 **p** 19. C Christchurch *Win* from 18. *6 Gleadowe Avenue, Christchurch BH23 1LR* E: revjonevans@gmail.com

EVANS, Mrs Judith Ann. b 55. SEITE 99. **d** 02 **p** 03. C Crayford *Roch* 02–06; P-in-c Kells *Carl* 06–13; Chapl N Cumbria Univ Hosps NHS Trust 06–13; V Northampton St Alb *Pet* from 13. *St Alban's Vicarage, Broadmead Avenue, Northampton NN3 2RA* T: (01604) 407074 M: 07929-978523 E: revdjudyevans@btinternet.com

EVANS, Ms Juliet Ann. b 70. K Coll Lon BD 92 AKC 92 PGCE 93. Ripon Coll Cuddesdon 01. **d** 05 **p** 06. C Bexley St Jo *Roch* 05–07; C Sidcup St Jo 07–08; Chapl Bp Justus C of E Sch Bromley 09–15; Chapl Trin Sch Lewisham from15; P-in-c Lewisham St Swithun *S'wark* from 17. *St Swithun's Vicarage, 191 Hither Green Lane, London SE13 6QE* M: 07955-229351 E: julietaevans@icloud.com

EVANS, Mrs Kathryn Louise. b 63. Birm Univ MHSc 96 RGN 86 RM 88. St Jo Coll Nottm 12. **d** 14 **p** 15. C Blackheath *Birm* 14–17; V Oldbury, Langley and Londonderry from 17. *The Vicarage, 2 St John's Road, Oldbury B68 9RP* T: 0121-557 4631 M: 07813-076628 E: kathrynevans3@sky.com

EVANS, Canon Keith. b 57. Trin Coll Carmarthen CertEd 81 BEd 82. St D Coll Lamp BA 84 Sarum & Wells Th Coll 84. **d** 85 **p** 86. C Swansea St Thos and Kilvey *S & B* 85–87; C Gorseinon 87–89; V Oxwich w Penmaen and Nicholaston 89–94; Dir Post-Ord Tr from 93; R Ystradgynlais 94–98; V Oystermouth from 98; Hon Can Brecon Cathl from 04. *The Vicarage, 9 Western Close, Mumbles, Swansea SA3 4HF* T: (01792) 369971 E: revkeithevans@talktalk.net

EVANS, Kevin Stuart. b 56. Bris Poly CQSW 80. Qu Coll Birm 93. **d** 95 **p** 96. C Madeley *Heref* 95–98; P-in-c Wombridge *Lich* from 98; TV Cen Telford 05–14; C St Georges' from 14. *Wombridge Vicarage, Wombridge Road, Telford TF2 6HT* T: (01952) 613334 E: wombridgechurch@hotmail.com

EVANS, Mrs Linda Joyce. b 54. Trin Coll Bris BA 06. **d** 06 **p** 07. NSM Weston super Mare Ch Ch and Em *B & W* 06–10; P-in-c Dale and St Brides w Marloes *St D* 10–11; P-in-c Herbrandston and Hasguard w St Ishmael's etc 10–11; P-in-c Dale and

St Brides w Marloes etc 11–14; rtd 14. *11 Lapwing Gardens, Weston-super-Mare BS22 8UP* E: landevans79@aol.com

EVANS, Linda Mary. *See* EDWARDS, Linda Mary

EVANS, Lloyd Russell. b 59. K Coll Lon BSc 81 York Univ MA 97. d 15 p 16. NSM Talgarth w Bronllys w Llanfilo *S & B* 15–18; PtO *Dur* from 17. *Denholme, Pinfold Lane, Butterknowle, Bishop Auckland DL13 5PS* T: (01388) 710394 E: l.evans758@btinternet.com

EVANS, Ms Margaret Elizabeth. b 48. Leeds Univ BA 69 Lon Inst of Educn CertEd 70. Oak Hill Th Coll 91. d 94 p 95. NSM Canonbury St Steph *Lon* 94–19; PtO from 19. *9 Compton Terrace, London N1 2UN* T: (020) 7359 4343

EVANS, Margaret Rose. b 48. d 12. NSM Ensbury Park *Sarum* 12–18; PtO from 18. *179 Redhill Drive, Bournemouth BH10 6AH* T: (01202) 513154

EVANS, Ms Marina Anne. b 58. d 14 p 15. NSM Pembroke Dock *St D* from 14. *43 Arthur Street, Pembroke Dock SA72 6EN* M: 07701-339490 E: rev.marina.evans@hotmail.com

EVANS, Martin Lonsdale. b 69. Man Univ BA 91. Ripon Coll Cuddesdon 93. d 95 p 96. C Morpeth *Newc* 95–98; Chapl RN from 98. *Royal Naval Chaplaincy Service, Mail Point 1-2, Leach Building, Whale Island, Portsmouth PO2 8BY* T: (023) 9262 5055 F: 9262 5134 E: padrecdo@aol.com

EVANS, Matthew Scott. b 72. Grey Coll Dur BA 93. Cranmer Hall Dur 96. d 98 p 99. C Fountains Gp *Ripon* 98–03; P-in-c Dacre w Hartwith and Darley w Thornthwaite 03–15; Jt AD Ripon 09–11; AD 11–14; P-in-c Dacre w Hartwith and Darley w Thornthwaite *Leeds* from 14; V High Harrogate Ch Ch from 15. *Christ Church Vicarage, 11 St Hilda's Road, Harrogate HG2 8JX* T: (01423) 530750 E: christchurch01@btconnect.com

EVANS, Michael. b 49. St Jo Coll Nottm 88. d 90 p 91. C Beeston *S'well* 90–93; P-in-c Kirkby in Ashfield St Thos 93–97; V 97–08; Chapl Notts Healthcare NHS Trust 93–08; rtd 08; PtO *S'well* from 10. *2 Westminster Avenue, Kirkby-in-Ashfield, Nottingham NG17 7HY* T: (01623) 759537 M: 07825-223189 E: munnamonk@aol.com

EVANS, Michael John. b 53. d 00 p 01. OLM Longnor, Quarnford and Sheen *Lich* 00–04; OLM Ipstones w Berkhamsytch and Onecote w Bradnop 04–11; P-in-c 11–15; V Butterton, Ipstones-w-Berkhamsytch etc from 15; RD Alstonfield from 16. *The Vicarage, Church Lane, Ipstones, Stoke-on-Trent ST10 2LF* T: (01538) 266313 E: revdmjevans@btinternet.com

EVANS, Preb Neil Robert. b 54. Lon Univ MA 93 K Coll Lon DMin 10. Coll of Resurr Mirfield. d 84 p 85. C Bethnal Green St Jo w St Bart *Lon* 84–86; C St Jo on Bethnal Green 87–88; P-in-c Stoke Newington Common St Mich 88–95; V 95–98; V Twickenham All Hallows 98–05; Kensington Area CME Officer 98–05; Par Min Development Adv Willesden Area 05–07; Area Dir Tr and Development 07–13; Dir Tr and Development Two Cities Area from 13; Dioc Dir of Min from 07; Preb St Paul's Cathl from 18. *23 St Albans Avenue, London W4 5LL* T: (020) 8987 7332 E: neil.evans@london.anglican.org

EVANS, Nicholas Anthony Paul. b 60. Sheff Univ BA 81 Liv Univ PGCE 86. Qu Coll Birm 81. d 84 p 87. C Ludlow *Heref* 84–85; C Sunbury *Lon* 86–92; hd RE Guildf Co Sch 93–99; NSM Crookham *Guildf* 94–99; CF 99–02; V Shenley Green *Birm* 02–15; R Newport Pagnell w Lathbury and Moulsoe *Ox* from 15. *The Rectory, 81 High Street, Newport Pagnell MK16 8AB* T: (01908) 611145 M: 07769-550204 E: nickevans49@btinternet.com

EVANS, Nigel William Reid. b 72. Sheff Hallam Univ BEd 96. Ridley Hall Cam BTh 01. d 01 p 02. C Ossett and Gawthorpe *Wakef* 01–05; V Loddon, Sisland, Chedgrave, Hardley and Langley *Nor* 05–10; RD Loddon 06–10; TR Bucknall *Lich* 10–18; RD Stoke 14–17; RD Stoke N 16–17; PtO *Lich* Stoke-on-Trent 17–18. *Address temp unknown*

EVANS, The Ven Patrick Alexander Sidney. b 43. Linc Th Coll 70. d 73 p 74. C Lyonsdown H Trin *St Alb* 73–76; C Royston 76–78; V Gt Gaddesden 78–82; V Tenterden St Mildred w Smallhythe *Cant* 82–89; Adn Maidstone 89–02; Hon Can Cant Cathl 89–02; Dir of Ords 89–93; Adn Cant and Can Res Cant Cathl 02–07; rtd 07; PtO *Truro* from 16. *Wills Tenement, Trehan, Saltash PL12 4QN* T: (01752) 847011 E: patrickevans120@hotmail.co.uk

EVANS, Paul David. b 54. Pemb Coll Cam BA 75 MA 79 Dur Univ BA 18 Lon Inst of Educn PGCE 76. SWMTC 11. d 14 p 15. NSM Cockington *Ex* from 14; NSM Torre All SS 14–16. *3 Hermosa, Higher Woodfield Road, Torquay TQ1 2LB* T: (01803) 215462 E: revpaulevans@gmail.com

EVANS, Peter Anthony. b 36. Imp Coll Lon BScEng 57. St Steph Ho Ox 58. d 60 p 61. C Surbiton St Mark *S'wark* 60–63; Asst Chapl Lon Univ 63–64; C S Kensington St Luke 64–68; C

Surbiton St Andr and St Mark *S'wark* 68–69; C Loughton St Jo *Chelmsf* 69–74; P-in-c Becontree St Geo 74–82; PtO 82–89; NSM Romford St Alb 89–93; NSM Coopersale 93–95; NSM Epping Distr 95–96; rtd 97; PtO *Chelmsf* from 97. *6 Woodhall Crescent, Hornchurch RM11 3NN* T: (01708) 702668

EVANS, Peter Gerald. b 41. Man Univ BA 71. AKC 65. d 65 p 66. C Kidbrooke St Jas *S'wark* 65–68; C Fallowfield *Man* 68–71; C Brockley Hill St Sav *S'wark* 71–73; P-in-c Colchester St Botolph w H Trin and St Giles *Chelmsf* 74–79; V 79–92; PtO from 93. *97 Northgate Street, Colchester CO1 1EY* T: (01206) 543297 E: p555evans@yahoo.com

EVANS, Richard. *See* EVANS, David Richard

EVANS, Richard Gregory. b 50. St Mich Coll Llan 69. d 73 p 74. C Oystermouth *S & B* 73–76; C Clydach 76–79; CF 78–81; V Llanddew and Talachddu *S & B* 79–83; Youth Chapl 79–83; Hon Min Can Brecon Cathl 79–83; Chapl Huntley Sch New Zealand 83–87; Chapl Nga Tawa Sch 83–90; Chapl Wanganui Sch from 90. *Wanganui Collegiate School, Private Bag 3002, Wanganui 4540, New Zealand* T: (0064) (6) 349 0281 ext 8750 F: 348 8302 E: rgevans@xtra.co.nz

EVANS, Richard Trevor. b 33. Jes Coll Ox MA 58 DipEd 58. St And Dioc Tr Course 73. d 76 p 76. NSM Leven *St And* 76–95; NSM St Andrews St Andr from 95. *33 Huntingtower Park, Whinnyknowe, Glenrothes KY6 3QF* T: (01592) 741670 E: revans9973@blueyonder.co.uk

EVANS, Robert. *See* EVANS, Simon Robert

EVANS, Robert Arnold Hughes. b 90. Ridley Hall Cam 12. d 15 p 16. C Cambridge St Andr Less *Ely* from 15. *Christ Church, Christchurch Street, Cambridge CB1 1HT* T: (01223) 750450 E: rob.evans@christchurchcambridge.org.uk

EVANS, Robert Charles. b 55. K Coll Lon BA 77 AKC 77 MA 78 MTh 89 Qu Coll Cam BA 80 MA 83 K Coll Lon CertEd 85 Qu Coll Ox DPhil 13. Westcott Ho Cam 79. d 81 p 87. C St Breoke *Truro* 81–83; C St Columb Minor and St Colan 83–84; Chapl Rob Coll Cam 87–92; Lect Ches Univ from 92. *University of Chester, Parkgate Road, Chester CH1 4BJ* T: (01244) 510000 E: r.evans@chester.ac.uk

EVANS, Robert George Roger. b 49. Cam Univ MA. Trin Coll Bris 74 St Jo Coll Nottm 94. d 77 p 78. C Bispham *Blackb* 77–80; C Chadwell *Chelmsf* 80–84; V Ardsley *Sheff* 84–09; P-in-c Kendray 04–09; Chapl Barnsley Community & Priority Services NHS Trust 98–00; rtd 09; PtO *Sheff* from 11. *73 High Street, Wombwell, Barnsley S73 8HS* T: (01226) 345635 E: rgrevans@gmail.com

EVANS, Robert Stanley. b 51. Univ of Wales (Lamp) BA 72 Univ of Wales (Cardiff) PGCE 73. St Mich Coll Llan 90. d 92 p 93. C Penarth All SS *Llan* 92–95; R Gelligaer 95–99; V Roath 99–04; R Coychurch, Llangan and St Mary Hill 04–06; rtd 06. *Ty Tudful, 5 Cook Road, Barry CF62 9HD* T: (01446) 420011 E: revrobertevans@hotmail.com

EVANS, Rupert Alexander. b 81. St Cath Coll Cam BA 02. Wycliffe Hall Ox MTh 10. d 10 p 11. C Crowborough *Chich* 10–14; Team Ldr Titus Trust from 14. *17 Clive Road, London SE21 8DA* T: (020) 8670 2736 E: rupertaevans@gmail.com

EVANS, Mrs Sarah Rosemary. b 64. Trevelyan Coll Dur BA 85. STETS 05. d 08 p 09. NSM Hullavington, Norton and Stanton St Quintin *Bris* 08–12; NSM Sherston Magna, Easton Grey, Luckington etc 08–12; NSM By Brook 12–17; Min Can Bris Cathl from 17. *Ashdown, Littleton Drew, Chippenham SN14 7NA* T: (01249) 782885 E: rev.sarahevans@gmail.com

EVANS, Selina Ann. b 62. ERMC 18. d 19. NSM Digswell *St Alb* from 19. *The Haven, Rabley Heath, Welwyn AL6 9UG* T: (01438) 813909 M: 07754-772445 E: saevans256@gmail.com

EVANS, Canon Simon. b 55. Newc Univ BA 77 Heythrop Coll Lon MA 06. St Steph Ho Ox 78. d 80 p 81. C Pet St Jude 80–84; Chapl Asst Pet Distr Hosp 80–84; C Wantage *Ox* 84–87; V W Leigh *Portsm* 87–96; Chapl E Hants Primary Care Trust 88–96; V Ruislip St Martin *Lon* from 96; AD Hillingdon 08–13; Can Wiawso Ghana from 08. *The Vicarage, 13 Eastcote Road, Ruislip HA4 8BE* T: (01895) 633040 or 625456 E: frsimonevans@outlook.com

EVANS, Simon Andrew. b 59. Sarum & Wells Th Coll 81. d 84 p 85. C Norbury St Steph and Thornton Heath *S'wark* 84–88; C Putney St Mary 88–92; P-in-c Telford Park St Thos 92–94; V 94–04; V Ensbury Park *Sarum* from 04. *St Thomas's Vicarage, 42 Coombe Avenue, Bournemouth BH10 5AE* T: (01202) 519735 E: simon@evansonline.info or vicar@ensburypark.org.uk

EVANS, Simon Robert. b 58. Reading Univ BSc 79. NOC 99. d 02 p 03. C Pudsey St Lawr and St Paul *Bradf* 02–04; P-in-c Low Moor 04–05; TV Oakenshaw, Wyke and Low Moor 06–07; TR 07–10; P-in-c Harden and Wilsden 10–13; P-in-c Denholme 10–13; P-in-c Cullingworth 10–13; TR Harden and Wilsden, Cullingworth and Denholme 13–14; *Leeds* 14–17; V Heeley *Sheff* from 17. *Heeley Vicarage,*

151 Gleadless Road, Sheffield S2 3AE T: 0114-255 7718 E: vicarbob999@gmail.com

EVANS, Stanley George. b 43. CITC 00. **d** 03 **p** 04. Aux Min Killaloe w Stradbally *L & K* 03–04; P-in-c Killarney w Aghadoe and Muckross 04–05; Aux Min Leighlin w Grange Sylvae, Shankill etc *C & O* 05–09; PtO *L & K* 09–13; P-in-c Omey w Ballynakill, Errislannan and Roundstone *T, K & A* 13–19; Can Tuam Cathl 16–19; Can Killala Cathl 16–19; Chapl Lanzarote *Eur* from 19. *Calle los Sabandeños 37, 35510 Puerto del Carmen, Lanzarote, Canary Islands, Spain* T: (0034) 928 514 241 E: revdstanevans@gmail.com

EVANS, Stephen Gary. b 66. ERMC 16. **d** 19. NSM Somersham w Pidley and Oldhurst and Woodhurst *Ely* from 19. *4 Clark Drive, St Ives PE27 6AD* E: gevans8@btinternet.com

EVANS, Stephen John. b 60. Dartmouth RN Coll 81 St Steph Ho Ox BA 85 MA 89 Aber Univ MPhil 94 DHC 17. **d** 86 **p** 87. Prec St Andr Cathl Inverness *Mor* 86–89; R Montrose *Bre* 89–91; P-in-c Inverbervie 89–91; Miss to Seamen 89–91; V Northampton St Paul *Pet* 91–98; CME Officer 94–00; Liturg Officer 96–03; P-in-c Ecton and Warden Ecton Ho 98–00; R Uppingham w Ayston and Wardley w Belton *Pet* 00–10; Can Pet Cathl 03–10; RD Rutland 03–10; R St Marylebone w H Trin *Lon* from 10. *21 Beaumont Street, London W1G 6DQ* T: (020) 7935 8965 E: rector@stmarylebone.org

EVANS, Steven Edward. b 52. CBDTI 97. **d** 00 **p** 01. NSM Caton w Littledale *Blackb* 00–05; NSM Hornby w Claughton and Whittington etc 05–06; NSM Slyne w Hest and Halton w Aughton 06–08; PtO from 08. *Old Bank House, Farleton, Lancaster LA2 9LF* T: (01524) 222034 M: 07808-795528

EVANS, Stuart. See EVANS, John Stuart

EVANS, Ms Susan Mary. b 55. St Jo Coll Dur BA 76 CertEd 77 Nottm Univ BCombStuds 84. Linc Th Coll 81. **dss** 84 **d** 87 **p** 94. Weaste *Man* 84–88; Par Dn 87–88; Par Dn Longsight St Luke 88–92; Par Dn Claydon and Barham *St E* 92–94; C 94–99; P-in-c Coddenham w Gosbeck and Hemingstone w Henley 95–99; Chapl HM YOI Hollesley Bay Colony 99–02; NSM Henley, Claydon and Barham *St E* 02–06; Chapl HM Pris Whatton 06–09; PtO *Linc* from 16. *8 Abbey Road, Bardney, Lincoln LN3 5XA* T: (01526) 397101 E: broadbentevans@btinternet.com

EVANS, Terence Robert. b 45. NOC 82. **d** 85 **p** 86. C Warrington St Elphin *Liv* 85–88; V Cantril Farm 88–94; V Rainhill 94–03; R Odd Rode *Ches* 03–10; rtd 10; PtO *Ches* from 10. *11 Harpur Crescent, Alsager, Stoke-on-Trent ST7 2SX* T: (01270) 878209 E: evans338@mac.com *or* evans238@btinternet.com

EVANS, Timothy Simon. b 57. York Univ BA 79 Sussex Univ MA 81 Fitzw Coll Cam BA 85 MA 88. Ridley Hall Cam 83. **d** 87 **p** 88. C Whitton St Aug *Lon* 87–90; C Ealing St Steph Castle Hill 90–93; P-in-c Shireshead *Blackb* 93–97; Asst Chapl Lanc Univ 93–97; Vice Prin LCTP 97–09; P-in-c Natland *Carl* 97–09; C Old Hutton and New Hutton 06–09; RD Kendal 00–03; Hon Can Carl Cathl 00–09; Dir Past Studies and Tutor Yorks Min Course 09–15; Dir Studies (Initial Tr) *Man* 15–18; Tr Officer CMD and IME 4-7 from 18; Lic Preacher from 15; PtO *Blackb* from 09. *Church House, 90 Deansgate, Manchester M3 2GH* T: 0161-828 1452 M: 07553-371165 E: timevans@manchester.anglican.org

EVANS, Trevor Owen. b 37. Univ of Wales BSc 59. Coll of Resurr Mirfield 59. **d** 61 **p** 62. C Llanaber w Caerdeon *Ban* 61–64; C Llandudno 64–70; TV 70–75; V Llanidloes w Llangurig 75–89; RD Arwystli 75–89; Can and Preb Ban Cathl 82–98; Spirituality Officer 84–03; R Trefdraeth 89–90; Dir of Min 89–98; R Llanfairpwll w Penmynydd *Ban* 90–97; R Llanfairpwll w Penmynydd and Llanddaniel-fab etc 98; Dean Ban 98–03; RD Ogwen 99–00; rtd 03. *Hafan, 3 Coed y Castell, Bangor LL57 1PH* T: (01248) 352855

EVANS, Mrs Wendy Nicola. b 59. St Jo Coll Dur BA 11. Cranmer Hall Dur 09. **d** 11 **p** 12. C Oulton Broad *Nor* 11–14; TV Diss 14–18; rtd 18; PtO *Nor* from 18. *5 Goshawk Way, Thetford IP24 3HX* M: 07971-082603 E: revwendi@icloud.com

EVANS, Wyn. See EVANS, John Wyn

EVANS-HILLS, Ms Bonnie Jean. b 57. Westcott Ho Cam. **d** 09 **p** 10. C Leic Resurr 09–10; C Oadby 10–14; Bp's Interfaith Adv 12–14; Dioc Interfaith Adv *St Alb* from 14; P-in-c Kimpton w Ayot St Lawrence 14–15; R 15–18. *The Vicarage, 11 High Street, Kimpton, Hitchin SG4 8RA* T: (01483) 833419

EVASON, Stuart Anthony. b 44. Salford Univ BSc. Chich Th Coll 79. **d** 81 **p** 82. C Heref St Martin 81–85; TV Cleethorpes *Linc* 85–87; TV Howden *York* 87–92; V Howsod St Jas *Man* 92–93; P-in-c Barrow St Jas *Carl* 03–10; TR Barrow St Matt 06–09; rtd 10; PtO *Man* from 10. *17 Drake Hall, Westhoughton, Bolton BL5 2RA* T: (01942) 810128 E: s.evason@gmail.com

EVE, David Charles Leonard. b 45. AKC 74. St Aug Coll Cant 74. **d** 75 **p** 76. C Hall Green Ascension *Birm* 75–79;

TV Kings Norton 79–84; V Rowley Regis 84–93; PtO *Heref* 94–98 and from 01; NSM Hallow and Grimley w Holt *Worc* 98–05; PtO from 05. *14 Orchard End, Cleobury Mortimer, Kidderminster DY14 8BA* T: (01299) 270510 E: gabrielle.davideve@btinternet.com

EVE, Gary Henry. b 68. SWMTC 12. **d** 15 **p** 16. NSM St Germans *Truro* 15–17; NSM Lanteglos by Fowey 17–18; NSM Lansallos 17–18; NSM Talland 17–18; NSM Lanreath and Pelynt 17–18; NSM Trelawny 18–19. *The Vicarage, 4 Ocean View, Polruan, Fowey PL23 1QJ* T: (01726) 870568 E: revgaryeve@gmail.com

EVE, Hilary Anne. See FIFE, Hilary Anne

EVELEIGH, Raymond. b 36. Univ of Wales (Cardiff) BSc 58. NW Ord Course 73. **d** 76 **p** 77. NSM S Cave and Ellerker w Broomfleet *York* 76–79; P-in-c Kingston upon Hull St Mary 79–82; Chapl Hull Coll of FE 79–01; V Anlaby Common St Mark *York* 82–94; V Langtoft w Foxholes, Butterwick, Cottam etc 94–01; rtd 01; PtO *York* from 04. *Pasture Lodge, West End, Kilham, Driffield YO25 4RR* T: (01262) 420060 E: rev@revray.co.uk

EVANS, Jonathan Adrian Harvey. b 63. Middx Poly BA 84 Middx Univ BA 03 ACIPD 90. NTMTC 00. **d** 03 **p** 04. C Barking St Marg w St Patr *Chelmsf* 03–06; V Gt Ilford St Jo 06–15; P-in-c St Steph Walbrook and St Swithun etc *Lon* 15–18; C St Martin-in-the-Fields from 15. *St Martin-in-the-Fields, 5 St Martin's Place, London WC2N 4JH* T: (020) 7766 1100 E: jonathan.evens@smitf.org

EVENS, Robert Alan. b 51. **d** 00 **p** 01. NSM Sharnbrook and Knotting w Souldrop *St Alb* 00–03; P-in-c Wymington w Podington 03–05; R Sharnbrook, Felmersham and Knotting w Souldrop 05–15; RD Sharnbrook 12–15; R Ashwell w Hinxworth and Newnham from 15. *109 High Street, Ashwell, Baldock SG7 5PQ* T: (01462) 742277 E: robert.evens@lineone.net

✠**EVENS, The Rt Revd Robert John Scott.** b 47. ACIB 74. Trin Coll Bris 74. **d** 77 **p** 78 **c** 04. C Southsea St Simon *Portsm* 77–79; C Portchester 79–83; V Locks Heath 83–96; RD Fareham 93–96; Adn Bath and Preb Wells Cathl *B & W* 96–04; Suff Bp Crediton *Ex* 04–12; Hon Asst Bp Glouc from 13; Hon Asst Bp Bris 13–18. *30 Highland Road, Charlton Kings, Cheltenham GL53 9LT* T: (01242) 251411 E: robertevens@hotmail.co.uk

EVERARD, Stephen Russell. b 54. Sarum Coll 13. **d** 16 **p** 17. NSM N Mundham w Hunston and Merston *Chich* from 16. *The Chestnuts, 30 The Drive, Emsworth PO10 8JP* T: (01243) 375858 E: jsne@talktalk.net

EVEREST, Canon John Cleland. b 45. Sarum Th Coll 66. **d** 68 **p** 69. C Moulsecoomb *Chich* 68–71; C Easthampstead *Ox* 71–74; C Southwick St Mich *Chich* 74–77; Dioc Soc Services Adv *Worc* 77–84; Ind Chapl 84–93; R Worc City St Paul and Old St Martin etc 84–93; RD Worc E 89–93; TR Halas 93–10; RD Dudley 95–98; Hon Can Worc Cathl 95–10; rtd 10; PtO *Worc* from 10. *18 Tunnel Hill, Worcester WR4 9RP* T: (01905) 723305 E: everestjc45@gmail.com

EVEREST, Alan Neil. b 57. St Cath Coll Ox BA 79 DPhil 96 SS Coll Cam BA 84. Westcott Ho Cam 82. **d** 85 **p** 86. C Hindley All SS *Liv* 85–88; Chapl Qu Mary Coll *Lon* 88–91; V S Hackney St Mich w Haggerston St Paul 94–10; V Notting Dale St Clem w St Mark and St Jas 10–19; Preb St Paul's Cathl 18–19; V W Dulwich All SS *S'wark* from 19. *Address temp unknown* E: alan@n16.org.uk

EVERETT, Anthony William. b 60. S Bank Poly BA 82. Oak Hill Th Coll BA 89. **d** 89 **p** 90. C Hailsham *Chich* 89–92; C New Malden and Coombe *S'wark* 92–97; V Streatham Park St Alb 97–02; V Herne Bay Ch Ch *Cant* from 02; Asst Dir of Ords 05–09; Jt AD Reculver 12–13; AD from 15. *Christ Church Vicarage, 38 Beltinge Road, Herne Bay CT6 6BU* T: (01227) 374906 *or* 366640

EVERETT, Mrs Christine Mary. b 46. St Osyth Coll of Educn CertEd 67. Westcott Ho Cam 90. **d** 92 **p** 94. Par Dn Ipswich St Fran *St E* 92–94; C 94–95; C Gt and Lt Bealings w Playford and Culpho 96; P-in-c 96–02; P-in-c The Creetings and Earl Stonham w Stonham Parva 02–11; PtO *St E* 11–17; *St D* from 17. *72 Charles Thomas Avenue, Pembroke Dock SA72 6UR* T: (01646) 684522 M: 07980-023236 E: c.everett65@btinternet.com

EVERETT, Colin Gerald Grant. b 44. Open Univ BA 77 Keswick Hall Coll CertEd. Ripon Coll Cuddesdon 79. **d** 81 **p** 82. C Aston cum Aughton *Sheff* 81–84; R Fornham All SS and Fornham St Martin w Timworth *St E* 84–92; P-in-c Old Newton w Stowupland 92–94; C Ipswich All Hallows 94–95; TV Ipswich St Fran 95–97; TV Ipswich St Mary at Stoke w St Pet and St Fran 97–09; rtd 09; PtO *St E* 09–17; *St D* from 17. *72 Charles Thomas Avenue, Pembroke Dock SA72 6UR* T: (01646) 684522 E: revcolin@btinternet.com

EVERETT, David John. b 51. Leeds Univ BA 07. NOC 04. **d** 07 **p** 08. NSM Moor Allerton and Shadwell *Ripon* 07–11; V Market Weighton *York* 11–17; R Goodmanham 11–17; V Sancton 11–17; rtd 17; PtO *St E* from 18. *24 Oxford Close, Mildenhall, Bury St Edmunds IP28 7RP* T: (01638) 718801 E: david.j.everett24@gmail.com

EVERETT, Nevsky James. b 89. G&C Coll Cam BA 10. Westcott Ho Cam 10. **d** 13 **p** 14. C Norton *St Alb* 13–16; Chapl Keble Coll Ox from 16. *Keble College, Parks Road, Oxford OX1 3PG* T: (01865) 272725 M: 07791-910050 E: nevsky.everett@hotmail.co.uk *or* chaplain@keble.ox.ac.uk

EVERETT, Robert Henry. b 60. Em Coll Cam BA 82 MA 86 Ox Univ BA 85 MA 90 Ex Univ MPhil 95. St Steph Ho Ox 83. **d** 86 **p** 87. C Ex St Thos and Em 86–88; C Plymstock 88–91; R St Dominic, Landulph and St Mellion w Pillaton *Truro* 91–96; P-in-c Reading All SS *Ox* 96–98; V 98–07; P-in-c Paddington St Mary Magd *Lon* 07–08; P-in-c Paddington St Pet 07–09; V Paddington St Mary Magd and St Pet from 09. *The Vicarage, 2 Rowington Close, London W2 5TF* T: (020) 7289 1818 *or* 7289 2011 E: frhenry@yahoo.co.uk

EVERETT, Robin Nigel. b 34. Dur Univ BA 55. Cranmer Hall Dur 57. **d** 59 **p** 60. C New Humberstone *Leic* 59–62; C Humberstone 62–66; V Quorndon 66–74; V Castle Donington 74–82; P-in-c Lockington w Hemington 81–82; V Castle Donington and Lockington cum Hemington 82–86; Antigua 86–87; R Ibstock w Heather *Leic* 87–98; rtd 98; PtO *Derby* 98–01; *Leic* 99–01. *30 Sevenlands Drive, Boulton Moor, Derby DE24 5AQ* T: (01332) 751879

EVERETT, Canon Simon Francis. b 58. Oak Hill Th Coll BA 89. **d** 89 **p** 90. C Wroughton *Bris* 89–93; TV Wexcombe *Sarum* 93–98; P-in-c The Iwernes, Sutton Waldron and Fontmell Magna 98–01; V Iwerne Valley 01–14; RD Milton and Blandford 01–13; TR Wareham from 14; RD Purbeck from 16; Can and Preb Sarum Cathl from 09. *The Rectory, 22 Worgret Road, Wareham BH20 4PN* T: (01929) 289236 M: 07879-658112 E: reveverett@btinternet.com

EVERETT-ALLEN, Canon Clive. b 47. AKC 70. St Aug Coll Cant 69. **d** 70 **p** 71. C Minera *St As* 70–72; C Hatcham St Cath *S'wark* 72–75; TV Beaconsfield *Ox* 75–83; R Southwick St Mich *Chich* 83–98; V E Grinstead St Swithun 98–15; RD E Grinstead 05–10; Can and Preb Chich Cathl 98–15; rtd 15; PtO *York* from 15. *2 Keble Park Crescent, Bishopthorpe, York YO23 2SY* T: (01904) 593969 E: cliveeval@gmail.com

EVERINGHAM, Miss Georgina Wendy. b 32. Tyndale Hall Bris BA 57. **d** 58 **p** 59. C Broadwater St Mary *Chich* 58–61; V Shipton Bellinger w S Tidworth *Win* 61–70; V Bournemouth St Paul 70–84; V Throop 84–95; rtd 95; PtO *Worc* from 96. *3 Harlech Close, Berkeley Alcester, Worcester WR4 0JU* T: (01905) 758631 M: 07940-851495 E: georgina@wordoflife.uk.com

EVERITT, Anthony David. b 64. Ex Univ BA 85 ACA 88. STETS 09. **d** 12 **p** 13. NSM Knowle St Martin *Bris* 12–17; NSM Knowle H Nativity 17–18; NSM Bris St Mary Redcliffe w Temple etc from 18. *23 Dunford Road, Bristol BS3 4PN* T: 0117-966 0563 M: 07792-330836

EVERITT, Mrs Jane. b 57. St Jo Coll Nottm 08. **d** 10 **p** 11. C Poulton Carleton and Singleton *Blackb* 10–14; TR Launceston *Truro* 14–18; P-in-c Long Itchington and Marton *Cov* from 18. *The Vicarage, Leamington Road, Long Itchington, Southam CV47 9PL* M: 07762-811170 E: revdjane@theeveritts.co.uk

EVERITT, Mark. b 34. Linc Coll Ox BA 58 MA 62. Wells Th Coll. **d** 60 **p** 61. C Hangleton *Chich* 60–63; Chapl Mert Coll Ox 63–02; rtd 02. *48 Annandale Avenue, Bognor Regis PO21 2EX* T: (01243) 823852 E: markeveritt934@btinternet.com

EVERITT, Canon Michael John. b 68. K Coll Lon BD 90 AKC 90. Qu Coll Birm 90 English Coll Rome 91. **d** 92 **p** 93. C Cleveleys *Blackb* 92–95; Succ Bloemfontein Cathl S Africa 95–98; Prec 96–98; Chapl and Asst Lect Univ of Orange Free State 96–98; Sen Chapl St Martin's Coll *Blackb* 98–02; Asst Dir of Ords 00–02; R Standish 02–11; P-in-c Appley Bridge 06–09; AD Chorley 04–11; Hon Can Blackb Cathl 10–11; Adn Lancaster 11–19; R Preston St Jo and St Geo 18–19; Can Res Dur Cathl from 19. *15 The College, Durham DH1 3EQ*

EVERITT, William Frank James. b 38. Dur Univ BA 68 FCA 63. Cranmer Hall Dur 65. **d** 69 **p** 70. C Leic St Phil 69–73; P-in-c Prestwold w Hoton 73–77; R Settrington w N Grimston and Wharram *York* 77–84; RD Buckrose 80–84; V Cheltenham St Pet *Glouc* 84–99; rtd 99; PtO *Ripon* 03–14; *Leeds* 14–16. *27 Lark Hill Crescent, Ripon HG4 2HN* T: (01765) 603683

EVETTS-SECKER, Ms Josephine. b 42. Univ Coll Lon BA 63 MPhil 65. Coll of Resurr Mirfield 06. **d** 07 **p** 08. NSM Hinderwell, Roxby and Staithes etc *York* 07–12; PtO from 12. *Lidgate, Victoria Square, Lythe, Whitby YO21 3RW* T/F: (01947) 893338 M: 07717-061343 E: revj@evetts-secker.co.uk

EWBANK, Canon Robin Alan. b 42. Ex Coll Ox BA 64 MA 88 Lon Univ BD 68. Clifton Th Coll 66. **d** 69 **p** 70. C Woodford Wells *Chelmsf* 69–72; Warden Cam Univ Miss Bermondsey 72–76; TV Sutton St Jas and Wawne *York* 76–82; R Bramshott *Portsm* 82–91; R Bramshott and Liphook 91–99; Hon Can Koforidua from 96; P-in-c Hartley Wintney, Elvetham, Winchfield etc *Win* 99–02; V 02–12; RD Odiham 04–11; rtd 12; Hon C Northanger *Win* 12–17; PtO *B & W* from 17. *Berry Farmhouse, Long Load, Langport TA10 9JX* E: robin.ewbank@gmail.com

EWEN, Keith John McGregor. b 43. Sarum & Wells Th Coll 77. **d** 79 **p** 80. C Kington w Huntington *Heref* 79–82; C Kington w Huntington, Old Radnor, Kinnerton etc 82–83; P-in-c Culmington w Onibury 83–89; P-in-c Bromfield 83–89; P-in-c Stanton Lacy 83–89; R Culmington w Onibury, Bromfield etc 90–01; R Llangenni and Llanbedr Ystrad Yw w Patricio *S & B* 01–08; rtd 08. *Ty Goleuddydd, 5 Goylands Close, Llandrindod Wells LD1 5RB* T: (01597) 825183

EWER, Edward Sydney John (Jonathan). b 36. Univ of New England BA 69 Lanc Univ MPhil 91 Ch Div Sch of the Pacific (USA) DMin 02. St Mich Th Coll Crafers ThL 63. **d** 62 **p** 63. Australia 62–83; SSM from 68; PtO *Blackb* 83–84; LtO *Dur* 84–98; Prior SSM Priory Dur 85–98; Dioc Dir of Ords *Dur* 94–98; PtO *S'wark* 00–05; Hon C Pimlico St Mary Bourne Street *Lon* 05–06; PtO 06–09; *Ox* from 09; *S'wark* 16–17. *3 Lawnsmead Gardens, Newport Pagnell MK16 8AY* M: 07915-377554 E: j_ewer@yahoo.com

EWINGTON, John. b 43. MRICS 65. Chich Th Coll 74. **d** 78 **p** 79. C Walthamstow St Jo *Chelmsf* 78–81; Papua New Guinea 81–87; V Southend St Sav Westcliff *Chelmsf* 87–96; TV Bideford, Northam, Westward Ho!, Appledore etc *Ex* 96–11; rtd 11. *The Ingle, Newland, Landkey, Barnstaple EX32 0LZ* T: (01271) 830949 E: jewington200@gmail.com

EWINS, Tiffany-Alice Letitia. b 74. Mansf Coll Ox BA 97. St Mellitus Coll MA 13. **d** 13 **p** 14. C Brixton St Paul w St Sav *S'wark* 13–16; PtO 16–17; P-in-c Battersea St Mich 17–18. *St Michael's Church, Cobham Close, London SW11 6SP* T: (020) 7924 3450 M: 07970-259580 E: tiffewins@gmail.com *or* vicar@stmichaelsbattersea.org

EXCELL, Bernadette Yasmin Carey. b 67. St Aug Coll of Th BA 19. **d** 19. C Balham St Mary and St Jo *S'wark* from 19. *42 Balham Park Road, London SW12 8DU* T: (020) 8675 3278 M: 07502-411918 E: curate@stmarybalham.org.uk

EXCELL, Robin Stanley. b 41. AKC 64. St Boniface Warminster 64. **d** 65 **p** 66. C Ipswich St Mary Stoke *St E* 65–68; C Melton Mowbray w Thorpe Arnold *Leic* 68–70; TV 70–71; R Gt and Lt Blakenham w Baylham *St E* 71–76; R Gt and Lt Blakenham w Baylham and Nettlestead 76–86; RD Bosmere 84–86; NSM Sproughton w Burstall 91–94; R Rattlesden w Thorpe Morieux, Brettenham etc 94–05; rtd 05; PtO *St E* from 05. *Hollywater, Upper Street, Baylham, Ipswich IP6 8JR* T: (01473) 830228 E: r.excell827@btinternet.com *or* robin.excell@btinternet.com

EXELL, Ernest William Carter. b 28. Qu Coll Cam BA 52 MA 53. Tyndale Hall Bris 49. **d** 52 **p** 53. C Sydenham H Trin *S'wark* 52–54; C E Ham St Paul *Chelmsf* 54–57; Uganda 57–65; Tanzania 66–70; R Abbess and Beauchamp Roding *Chelmsf* 70–71; P-in-c White Roding w Morrell Roding 70–71; R Abbess Roding, Beauchamp Roding and White Roding 71–94; RD Roding 75–79; rtd 94; PtO *St E* from 94. *8 Ickworth Drive, Bury St Edmunds IP33 3PX* T: (01284) 724726

EXELL, Michael Andrew John. b 45. FHCIMA MRIPHH 67 MICA 70. Sarum & Wells Th Coll 87. **d** 89 **p** 90. C Ryde H Trin *Portsm* 89–93; C Swanmore St Mich w Havenstreet 89–92; C Swanmore St Mich 92–93; P-in-c Carisbrooke St Mary 93–99; V 99–10; P-in-c Carisbrooke St Nic 93–99; V 99–10; rtd 10; PtO *Portsm* from 10. *3 Glossop Close, East Cowes PO32 6PD* T: (01983) 293686 E: mikeexell@aol.com

EXETER, Archdeacon of. *See* BEANE, The Ven Andrew Mark
EXETER, Bishop of. *See* ATWELL, The Rt Revd Robert Ronald
EXETER, Dean of. *See* GREENER, The Very Revd Jonathan Desmond Francis

EXLEY, Malcolm. b 33. Cranmer Hall Dur. **d** 67 **p** 68. C Sutton St Jas *York* 67–71; C Sutton St Jas and Wawne 71–73; V Mappleton w Goxhill 73–77; V Market Weighton 77–90; P-in-c Goodmanham 77–78; R 78–90; V Bridlington Em 90–98; rtd 98; PtO *York* from 00; *Eur* from 01. *11 The Chase, Driffield YO25 7FJ* T: (01377) 272312

EXON, Helier John Philip. b 44. BSc 70 CEng 87 MIET 87. STETS 96. **d** 99 **p** 00. NSM Milton Abbas, Hilton w Cheselbourne etc *Sarum* 99–05; NSM Piddletrenthide w Plush, Alton Pancras etc 02–05; NSM Piddle Valley, Hilton, Cheselbourne etc 05–14; rtd 14; PtO *Sarum* from 14. *The Monk's House, Hilton, Blandford Forum DT11 0DG* T: (01258) 881732 M: 07785-117773 E: helier@exon.me.uk *or* helier.exon@salisbury.anglican.org

EYEONS, Keith James. b 70. Clare Coll Cam BA 92 MA 96 Down Coll Cam PhD 10 Lon Inst of Educn PGCE 95. St Jo Coll Nottm MA(MM) 03. **d** 01 **p** 02. C Iffley *Ox* 01–03; Chapl Down Coll Cam from 03. *Downing College, Cambridge CB2 1DQ* T: (01223) 334810 E: kje11@cam.ac.uk

EYLES, Anthony John. b 34. Bris Univ BSc 57. Sarum Th Coll 61. **d** 63 **p** 64. C Wellington w W Buckland *B & W* 63–67; C Wilton 67–74; Ind Chapl *Dur* 74–85; Ind Chapl *Worc* 85–90; P-in-c Bickenhill w Elmdon *Birm* 90; P-in-c Bickenhill 90–00; Chapl Birm Airport 90–00; rtd 00; PtO *Ex* from 00. *5 Kersbrook Lane, Kersbrook, Budleigh Salterton EX9 7AD* T: (01395) 446084

EYNON, John Kenneth. b 56. Nottm Univ BA 77 BArch 80. **d** 96 **p** 97. OLM Croydon Ch Ch *S'wark* 96–05. *21 Rye Close, Saltdean, Brighton BN2 8PP* T: (01273) 308397 M: 07702-126362 E: johneynon@me.com

EYRE, Canon Richard Stuart. b 48. Bris Univ BEd 81 Nottm Univ MTh 86. Linc Th Coll 74. **d** 77 **p** 78. C Henbury *Bris* 77–81; C Bedminster 81–82; TV 82–84; Chapl Bp Grosseteste Coll Linc 84–95; Sen Tutor 89–95; P-in-c Long Bennington w Foston *Linc* 95; P-in-c Saxonwell 95–97; R 97–01; RD Grantham 96–01; TR Hykeham 01–13; R 13; RD Graffoe 02–09; Can and Preb Linc Cathl 03–13; rtd 13; PtO *Linc* from 17. *20 Quintin Close, Bracebridge Heath, Lincoln LN4 2LW* E: richard.eyre3@ntlworld.com

EZAT, Timothy. b 83. Wycliffe Hall Ox BTh 12. **d** 12 **p** 13. C Eastbourne All SS *Chich* 12–14; C Eastbourne St Mary 14–17; V Langney from 17. *St Richard's Rectory, 7 Priory Road, Eastbourne BN23 7AX* T: (01323) 760238 M: 07809-679421 E: timothy.ezat@gmail.com

EZE, Geoffrey Ejike. b 73. Trin Coll Bris 06. **d** 08 **p** 09. C Gt Ilford St Jo *Chelmsf* 08–12; TV Stoke-upon-Trent and Fenton *Lich* from 12. *23 Mere Side Close, Stoke-on-Trent ST1 5GH* T: (01782) 265129 E: geoffrey.e.eze@gmail.com

F

FACCINI (née LEGG), Sandra Christine. b 55. Surrey Univ BSc 78 PhD 82 Univ of Wales (Ban) BTh 07. **d** 04 **p** 05. OLM Howell Hill w Burgh Heath *Guildf* 04–09; P-in-c Ottershaw 09–14; V from 14; AD Runnymede from 16. *50 Slade Road, Ottershaw, Chertsey KT16 0HZ* T: (01932) 873160 M: 07743-675633 E: sandrafster@gmail.com

FACEY, Miss Jane. b 54. EMMTC 05. **d** 07 **p** 08. NSM W Hallam and Mapperley w Stanley *Derby* 07–11; V Chellaston from 11. *The Vicarage, Yews Drive, Chellaston, Derby DE73 6UT* T: (01332) 704835 E: bjfacey@btinternet.com

FAGAN, Jeremy David. b 75. Qu Coll Ox BA 98. Wycliffe Hall Ox 99. **d** 01 **p** 02. C Chell *Lich* 01–04; TV Kirkby Liv 04–12; TR from 12. *27 Shakespeare Avenue, Liverpool L32 9SH* T: 0151-547 2133 E: faganj@mac.com

FAGBEMI, Olubunmi Ayobami (Bunmi). b 57. Lagos Univ LLB 78 LSE LLM 81 Qu Mary Coll Lon PhD 91 Solicitor 79. Ripon Coll Cuddesdon 95. **d** 97 **p** 98. C Enfield St Andr *Lon* 97–01; V Tottenham H Trin from 01; AD E Haringey 11–16. *Holy Trinity Vicarage, Philip Lane, London N15 4GZ* T: (020) 8801 3021 E: bunmif@btinternet.com

✠**FAGBEMI, The Rt Revd Stephen Ayodeji Akinwale.** b 67. St Jo Coll Nottm BTh 96 Kent Univ PhD 04. Immanuel Coll Ibadan 87. **d** 90 **p** 91 **c** 17. C Iyere St Jo Nigeria 90–91; C Owo St Patr 91–92; P-in-c Wakajaye-Etile Ch Ch 92–93; V Emure-Ile St Sav 96–00; Can Owo from 99; PtO *Cant* 00–03; Hon C Murston w Bapchild and Tonge 03–05; Co-ord Chapl Sunderland Univ *Dur* 05–11; Hon C Sunderland Minster 05–11; Dean Abp Vining Coll of Th Nigeria 11–16; Gen Sec Ch of Nigeria 16–17; Bp Owo from 17. *Anglican Bishopscourt, PO Box 472, Owo, Ondo State, Nigeria* T: (00234) (80) 3695 6811 E: saaf95@hotmail.com or saaf90@yahoo.co.uk

FAGERSON, Joseph Leonard Ladd. b 35. Harvard Univ BA 57. Ridley Hall Cam 61. **d** 63 **p** 64. C Tonbridge SS Pet and Paul *Roch* 63–67; Afghanistan 67–74; P-in-c Marbury *Ches* 74–75; P-in-c Kinloch Rannoch *St And* 75–00; Chapl Rannoch Sch 75–00; rtd 00; Hon C Killin *St And* 00–12; PtO from 12. *Westgarth, Tomnacroich, Fortingall, Aberfeldy PH15 2LJ* T: (01887) 830569 E: laddandthea@gmail.com

FAHIE, Mrs Stephanie Bridget. b 48. St Jo Coll Nottm 85. **d** 87 **p** 94. Par Dn Leic St Chris 87–90; Chapl Scargill Ho 90–95; P-in-c Hickling w Kinoulton and Broughton Sulney *S'well* 95–00; R 00–10; rtd 11; PtO *Lich* from 12. *61 Monkmoor Avenue, Shrewsbury SY2 5ED* T: (01743) 588307 E: steph.fahie@gmail.com

FAINT, Paul Edward. b 38. Qu Coll Birm 85. **d** 87 **p** 88. C Cradley *Worc* 87–90; V Hanley Castle, Hanley Swan and Welland 90–94; V Northwood H Trin *Lon* 94–97; Miss to Seafarers from 97; Chapl Larnaca Cyprus 97–01; rtd 01; PtO *Ox* from 01; Hon Chapl Miss to Seafarers from 02. *17 Priory Orchard, Wantage OX12 9EL* T: (01235) 772297 E: thefaints@sky.com

FAIRALL, Hannah Marie. *See* MEARS, Hannah Marie

FAIRBAIRN, Andrew Graham. b 48. SEITE 06. **d** 09 **p** 10. NSM Surbiton Hill Ch Ch *S'wark* 09–12; NSM High Ongar w Norton Mandeville *Chelmsf* 13–17; rtd 17; PtO *Chelmsf* 17–19; *Win* from 19. *1 The Ferns, New Milton BH25 5WW* T: (01425) 619007 M: 07789-992843 E: gandlfairbairn@btinternet.com

FAIRBAIRN, Francis Stephen. b 41. **d** 98 **p** 99. OLM Orrell *Liv* 98–13; rtd 13; PtO *Liv* from 16. *27 Greenslate Road, Billinge, Wigan WN5 7BQ* T: (01695) 623127 or (01722) 812176 F: 815398

FAIRBAIRN, John Alan. b 46. Trin Coll Cam BA 67 MA 72. Wycliffe Hall Ox 84. **d** 86 **p** 87. C Boscombe St Jo *Win* 86–89; C Edgware *Lon* 89–95; R Gunton St Pet *Nor* 95–11; Chapl Jas Paget Healthcare NHS Trust 96–08; rtd 11; PtO *Win* from 11. *28 Clifton Road, Bournemouth BH6 3PA* T: (01202) 424466 E: jfairbairn2017@gmail.com

FAIRBAIRN, Mrs Stella Rosamund. b 30. Bris Univ CertEd 51 De Montfort Univ BA 13. **d** 87 **p** 94. NSM Banbury *Ox* 87–99; PtO *Pet* 88–94; *Ox* from 99. *Hillside, Overthorpe, Banbury OX17 2AF* T: (01295) 710648

FAIRBAIRN, Stephen. *See* FAIRBAIRN, Francis Stephen

FAIRBAIRN, William James. b 89. Cardiff Univ BSc 10. St Mellitus Coll BA 17. **d** 17 **p** 18. C Bitterne Park *Win* from 17. *24 Lacon Close, Southampton SO18 1JA* E: will@ascensionsouthampton.co.uk

FAIRBANK, Brian Douglas Seeley. b 53. AKC 75. St Steph Ho Ox 77. **d** 78 **p** 79. C Newton Aycliffe *Dur* 78–81; C Stocking Farm *Leic* 81–84; TV Ratby cum Groby 84–91; Chapl Min 91–04; R Bramfield, Stapleford, Waterford etc *St Alb* 04–12; R Culworth w Sulgrave and Thorpe Mandeville etc *Pet* from 12. *The Rectory, Queen's Street, Culworth, Banbury OX17 2AT* T: (01295) 768994 E: brianfairbank487@btinternet.com

FAIRCLOUGH, Miss Amanda Ann Catherine. b 68. Man Univ BSc 89. St Jo Coll Nottm 06 SNWTP 08. **d** 10 **p** 11. NSM Orford St Marg *Liv* 10–14; NSM Warrington E 14–17; P-in-c W Highland Region *Arg* from 17. *St Mary's Rectory, Glencoe, Ballachulish PH49 4HP* T: (01855) 811633 M: 07788-101178 E: a.fairclough@amandafairclough.co.uk

FAIRCLOUGH, Clive Anthony. b 54. TISEC 01. **d** 04 **p** 05. C Nadder Valley *Sarum* 04–08; R Abberton, The Flyfords, Naunton Beauchamp etc *Worc* 08–14; P-in-c Fladbury, Hill and Moor, Wyre Piddle etc 11–14; C Peopleton and White Ladies Aston w Churchill etc 11–14; Chapl Moscow *Eur* 14–17; P-in-c Mells w Buckland Dinham, Elm, Whatley etc *B & W* 17–18; R from 18. *The Rectory, Gay Street, Mells, Frome BA11 3PT* T: (01373) 673431 E: cliveatmellsgroup@gmail.com

FAIRCLOUGH, John Frederick. b 40. St Jo Coll Dur BA 63 MA 68 Keele Univ DASE 73 MBIM. Coll of Resurr Mirfield 81. **d** 83 **p** 84. C Horninglow *Lich* 83–87; V Skerton St Luke *Blackb* 87–94; V Thornton-le-Fylde 94–00; rtd 00; PtO *Blackb* 01–14. *18 Crosfield Avenue, Summerseat, Bury BL9 5NX* T: (01706) 825664

FAIRHURST, Rosemary Anne. b 63. Newnham Coll Cam BA 85 MA 85 Heythrop Coll Lon MTh 97 Lon Inst of Educn PGCE 86. Wycliffe Hall Ox MA 92. **d** 93 **p** 94. C Hackney Marsh *Lon* 93–97; C Islington St Mary 97–02; Dir Miss and Min Ripon Coll Cuddesdon 02–06; Organizational Analyst Grubb Inst 07–12; C St Martin-in-the-Fields *Lon* 12–14; PtO 12–14; Can Res and Chan Leic Cathl 14–18; V Bradf St Aug and St Clem *Leeds* from 18. *100 Harrogate Street, Bradford BD3 0LE* M: 07766-451316 E: rosy.fairhurst@leeds.anglican.org

FAIRHURST, Mrs Susan Mary. b 55. GBSM 80. Qu Coll Birm 12. d 14 p 15. NSM Lillington and Old Milverton *Cov* from 14. *23 Brese Avenue, Warwick CV34 4TS* T: (01926) 735254 M: 07906-610376 E: sue@fairhursts.me.uk

FAIRLAMB, Neil. b 49. Univ of Wales (Ban) BA 71 Jes Coll Ox BPhil 73 Univ of Wales (Abth) MTh 00 Pemb Coll Cam CertEd 74. S'wark Ord Course 90. d 93 p 94. NSM Dulwich St Barn *S'wark* 93–95; P-in-c Elerch w Penrhyncoch w Capel Bangor and Goginan *St D* 95–96; V 96–98; R Arthog w Fairbourne w Llangelynnin w Rhoslefain *Ban* 98–03; R Beaumaris 03–11; R Beaumaris w Llanddona and Llaniestyn 11–15; V Bro Seiriol 15–19; rtd 19; Hon C The Bourne and Tilford *Guildf* from 19. *All Saints' Vicarage, Tilford Road, Tilford, Farnham GU10 2DA* E: fairlamb49@gmail.com

FAIRLESS, Elizabeth Jane. See JONES, Elizabeth Jane

FAIRWEATHER, Colin Malcolm. b 72. Rob Coll Cam BA 94 Liv Univ MA 95 Rob Coll Cam PhD 00. Ridley Hall Cam 14. d 16 p 17. C Braintree St Paul *Chelmsf* from 16. *15 Trinovantian Way, Braintree CM7 3JN* T: (01376) 326140 M: 07791-188296 E: colinfairweather1972@gmail.com *or* curate@stpaulsbraintree.org.uk

FAIRWEATHER, John. b 39. K Coll Lon AKC 66 BD 72. d 67 p 68. C Plymouth St Jas Ham *Ex* 67–69; C Townstal w St Sav and St Petrox w St Barn 69–73; R Corringham w Springthorpe *Linc* 73–78; P-in-c Blyborough 76–78; P-in-c Heapham 76–78; P-in-c Willoughton 76–78; V Pinchbeck 78–82; V Exwick *Ex* 82–04; rtd 04. *52 Woodman's Crescent, Honiton EX14 2DY* T: (01404) 549711 E: john.fairweather6@btinternet.com

FAIRWEATHER, Sally Helen. See ROSS, Sally Helen

FALASCHI-RAY, Sonia Ofelia. Surrey Univ BSc 79 Wolfs Coll Cam BA 02 MA 06 CEng 86. Ridley Hall Cam 03. d 05 p 06. NSM Fowlmere, Foxton, Shepreth and Thriplow *Ely* 05–09; PtO from 09; *St Alb* from 09. *27 Church Lane, Barkway, Royston SG8 8EJ* T: (01763) 849057 M: 07747-844265 E: sonia@falaschi-ray.co.uk

FALCONER, Ian Geoffrey. b 40. BNC Ox BA 62 Newc Univ MA 93. Cuddesdon Coll 62. d 64 p 65. C Chiswick St Nic w St Mary *Lon* 64–68; C-in-c Hounslow Gd Shep Beavers Lane CD 68–76; P-in-c Hammersmith St Matt 76–84; P-in-c Byker St Silas *Newc* 84–93; V 93–95; P-in-c Newc St Phil and St Aug 95–98; P-in-c Newc St Matt w St Mary 95–98; P-in-c Newc St Phil and St Aug and St Matt w St Mary 98–00; V Seghill 00–06; rtd 06. *70 Lowgates, Staveley, Chesterfield S43 3TU* T: (01246) 471913 E: frianfalc@yahoo.co.uk

FALKINGHAM (née MOORE), Mrs Caroline Judith. b 57. Coll of Ripon & York St Jo BA 78 Leeds Univ MA 07. NOC 05. d 07 p 08. C Bilton *Ripon* 07–11; NSM Fountains Gp 11–12; R 12–14; *Leeds* 14–18; rtd 18. *111 Kirkby Road, Ripon HG4 2HH* E: carolinefalkingham@talktalk.net

FALKNER, Jonathan Michael Shepherd. b 47. Open Univ BA 74. Cranmer Hall Dur. d 79 p 80. C Penrith w Newton Reigny *Carl* 79–81; C Penrith w Newton Reigny and Plumpton Wall 81–82; C Dalton-in-Furness 82–84; V Clifton 84–90; P-in-c Dean 85–89; R 89–90; P-in-c Rumburgh w S Elmham w the Ilketshalls *St E* 90–92; R S Elmham and Ilketshall 92–99; RD Beccles and S Elmham 94–99; Hon Can St E Cathl 98–99; P-in-c W Newton and Bromfield w Waverton *Carl* 99–02; P-in-c Holme Cultram St Mary 00–02; P-in-c Holme Cultram St Cuth 00–02; TR Solway Plain 02–05; P-in-c Gosforth w Nether Wasdale and Wasdale Head 05–12; P-in-c Beckermet St Jo and St Bridget w Ponsonby 12; rtd 12; PtO *Carl* from 13. *22 Whole House Road, Seascale CA20 1QY* T: (019467) 21852 E: falcon626@btinternet.com

FALLA, Eric. b 60. d 18 p 19. NSM Whitton and Thurleston w Akenham *St E* from 18. *7 Stuart Close, Ipswich IP4 4BN* T: (01473) 290160 M: 07540-359993 E: eric.falla@cofesuffolk.org

FALLA, Miles. b 43. MCIM. EAMTC 93. d 96 p 97. NSM Buckden *Ely* 96–98; P-in-c Gretton w Rockingham *Pet* 98–99; V Gretton w Rockingham and Cottingham w E Carlton 99–01; RD Corby 01–02; rtd 04; PtO *Ely* from 05. *Bowlings, Silver Street, Buckden, St Neots PE19 5TS* T: (01480) 811335 E: miles@falla.ndo.co.uk

FALLOWS, Stuart Adrian. b 50. Moray Ho Edin 75. d 78 p 79. Hon C Forres w Nairn *Mor* 78–81; Hon C Elgin w Lossiemouth 81–86; Hon Dioc Chapl 86; C Brighton St Geo w St Anne and St Mark *Chich* 86–89; V Wivelsfield 89–98; P-in-c Kieth, Huntly and Aberchirder *Mor* 98–02; P-in-c Ringwould w Kingsdown *Cant* 02–04; R Ringwould w Kingsdown and Ripple etc 05–09; R W Highland Region *Arg* 09–15; rtd 15; PtO *Arg* from 16. *Duncroft, 25 Murray Crescent, Lamlash, Isle of Arran KA27 8NS* T: (01855) 811987 E: afallows222@aol.com

FALUDY, Alexander Raban Spencer. b 83. Peterho Cam BA 01 MA 05 Linc Coll Ox MSt 04. Coll of Resurr Mirfield 05.

d 08 p 09. C Tynemouth Cullercoats St Paul *Newc* 08–11; C Willington 11–14; P-in-c Wallsend St Jo 14–16; V 16–18; rtd 18. *33 Solent Road, Portsmouth PO6 1HH* T: (023) 9238 6325

FALVEY, Mrs Imogen Rosalind. b 62. Somerville Coll Ox BA 84 MA 89 Solicitor 88. ERMC 11. d 14 p 15. NSM Sawtry and Glatton *Ely* 14–17; NSM The Ortons 17–18; P-in-c from 18. *The New Rectory, 2A The Village, Orton Longueville, Peterborough PE2 7DN* T: (01733) 247329 E: revimogen@gmail.com

FANCOURT, Graeme. b 77. St Jo Coll Dur BA 00 DThM 11. Ripon Coll Cuddesdon 09. d 10 p 11. C Caversham Thameside and Mapledurham *Ox* 10–13; P-in-c Reading St Luke w St Bart 13–14; V 14–19; AD Reading from 17; C Reading St Mary the Virgin from 19. *The Vicarage, 50 London Road, Reading RG1 5AS* T: 0118-966 6389 E: fancourt@gmail.com

FANE DE SALIS, Mrs Mary. b 88. d 14 p 15. C Clothall, Rushden, Sandon, Wallington and Weston *St Alb* 14–17; R Holwell, Ickleford and Pirton from 17. *The Vicarage, 9 Crabtree Lane, Pirton, Hitchin SG5 3QE* T: (01462) 712230 M: 07866-890402 E: marydesalis@hotmail.com

FANTHORPE, Robert Lionel. b 35. Open Univ BA 80 CertEd 63 FCMI 81 FCP 90. Llan Dioc Tr Scheme. d 87 p 88. NSM Roath St German *Llan* 87–00; LtO from 00. *Rivendell, 48 Claude Road, Roath, Cardiff CF24 3QA* T: (029) 2049 8368 F: 2049 6832 M: 07767-207289 E: fanthorpe@aol.com

FARADAY, John. b 49. Leeds Univ BSc 71 MICE 78. Oak Hill Th Coll 81. d 83 p 84. C Sutton *Liv* 83–86; C Rainhill and Chapl Whiston Hosp 86–89; V Over Darwen St Jas *Blackb* 89–02; TR S Rochdale *Man* 02–08; TR Gorton and Abbey Hey 08–15; rtd 15; PtO *Man* from 15. *1 Magpie Lane, Oldham OL4 5PB* E: john.faraday@sky.com

FARAGHER, James Philip. b 77. St Jo Coll Nottm 12. d 14 p 15. C St Alb St Paul 14–17; V Coney Hill *Glouc* from 17. *St Oswald's Vicarage, Coney Hill Road, Gloucester GL4 4LX* T: (01452) 690750 M: 07800-908396 E: jamesfaragher@yahoo.co.uk *or* vicar@stoswaldconeyhill.com

FARAH, The Ven Mones Anton. b 64. Trin Coll Bris BA 88. d 88 p 89. C Aberystwyth *St D* 88–91; Chapl St D Coll Lamp 91–98; TV Gt Baddow *Chelmsf* 98–14; P-in-c Aberystwyth *St D* 14–19; Can St D Cathl from 18; Adn for New Ch Communities from 18. *The Rectory, 7 Laura Place, Aberystwyth SY23 2AU* T: (01970) 617184 E: archdeacon.farah@churchinwales.org.uk

FARBRIDGE, Nicholas Brisco. b 33. FCA. Sarum & Wells Th Coll 75. d 77 p 78. C Gt Bookham *Guildf* 77–80; C Ewell 80–83; V Addlestone 83–89; R Shere 89–95; rtd 96; PtO *Guildf* 96–17. *55 Curling Vale, Guildford GU2 7PH* T: (01483) 531140 E: nickfarbridge@msn.com

FARDELL, Rebecca Susan. b 70. Reading Univ BA 92 Leic Univ MA 94 Qu Coll Cam PGCE 93. Ridley Hall Cam 11. d 13 p 14. C Itchen Valley *Win* 13–17; V Sunnyside w Bourne End *St Alb* from 17. *The Vicarage, Ivy House Lane, Berkhamsted HP4 2PP* T: (01442) 865100 E: rebecca@sunnysidechurch.org.uk *or* vicar@sunnysidechurch.org.uk

FARISH, Alan John. b 58. Lanc Univ BA. St Jo Coll Nottm 83. d 86 p 87. C Bishopwearmouth St Gabr *Dur* 86–89; C Fatfield 89–98; P-in-c Preston on Tees 98–03; V Preston-on-Tees and Longnewton 03–10; P-in-c Stockton 08–16; C 16; Stockton Deanery Missr 16; rtd 17; PtO *Dur* from 17. *23 Deepdale Avenue, Stockton-on-Tees TS18 2QE* T: (01642) 611734

FARLEY, Claire Louise. See McCLELLAND, Claire Louise

FARLEY, David Stuart. b 53. Univ Coll Dur BA 75 Westmr Coll Ox MTh 00. St Jo Coll Nottm. d 84 p 85. C Bath Weston All SS w N Stoke *B & W* 84–87; Chapl Scargill Ho 87–90; Min Hedge End N CD *Win* 90–94; V Hedge End St Luke 94–00; Dep Chapl HM Pris Belmarsh 00; Chapl HM Pris Shrewsbury 00–13; Chapl HM Pris Featherstone 13–16; rtd 16; PtO *Lich* from 16. *c/o Athlone House, 68 London Road, Shrewsbury SY2 6PG* E: dfarley3@hotmail.co.uk

FARLEY, Ian David. b 56. Linc Coll Ox BA 78 MA 87 Dur Univ PhD 88. Cranmer Hall Dur 84. d 87 p 88. C Thorpe Acre w Dishley *Leic* 87–92; V S Lambeth St Steph *S'wark* 92–99; V Bacton w Edingthorpe w Witton and Ridlington *Nor* 99–03; Ind Chapl 99–03; TR Buckhurst Hill *Chelmsf* from 03. *St John's Rectory, High Road, Buckhurst Hill IG9 5RX* T: (020) 8504 1931 E: parish-office@buckhursthill.free-online.co.uk *or* ian.farley@sjbh.org.uk

FARLEY, James Trevor. b 37. IEng MIET FRSA. EMMTC 80. d 82 p 83. NSM Grantham St Wulfram *Linc* from 82; PtO *Leic* from 14. *Highfield Cottage, Station Road, Bottesford, Nottingham NG13 0EN* T/F: (01949) 843860 M: 07768-360592 E: jimfarley@talktalk.net

FARLEY-MOORE, Canon Peter James. b 72. Sheff Univ BA 94 UEA MA 00. Ridley Hall Cam. d 00 p 01. C Chapeltown

240

Sheff 00–03; Miss Cell Adv CMS 04–05; Asst Min Kowloon St Andr Hong Kong 05–07; V Blackheath St Jo *S'wark* 07–14; TR Deptford St Jo w H Trin and Ascension from 14; AD Deptford from 16; Hon Can Mara Tanzania from 16. *St John's Vicarage, St John's Vale, London SE8 4EA* E: peter.stjohnsdeptford@gmail.com

FARMAN, Joanne Margaret. b 46. Birkbeck Coll Lon BA 81 Leeds Univ MA 08 Southlands Coll Lon PGCE 82. SEITE 97. **d** 00 **p** 01. NSM Limpsfield and Titsey *S'wark* 00–04; Chapl St Geo Healthcare NHS Trust Lon 00–10; Lead Chapl R Hosp for Neuro-Disability 04–05; PtO *S'wark* 10–16; Nor from 16; *Roch* 12–16. *53B Colney Lane, Cringleford, Norwich NR4 7RG* T: (01603) 508380 E: joannefarman086@btinternet.com

FARMAN, Robert Joseph. b 54. Ridley Hall Cam 86. **d** 88 **p** 89. C Sutton St Nic *S'wark* 88–90; C Cheam Common St Phil 90–92; R Wootton w Glympton and Kiddington *Ox* 92–00; TV Kings Norton *Birm* 00–04; Chapl St Mary's Hospice 04–12; Chapl R Orthopaedic Hosp NHS Trust 05–06; Chapl Birm and Solihull Mental Health Trust 06–07; rtd 12; PtO *Birm* from 19. *121 The Hemisphere, 15 The Boulevard, Birmingham B5 7SU* M: 07766-054137 E: rjfarman@icloud.com

FARMER, Andrew. b 62. Birm Univ BSc 84 Bath Univ MBA 07 Ches Univ PGCE 12. SWMTC 14. **d** 17. C Buckland Monachorum *Ex* from 17. *Fernleigh, The Crescent, Crapstone, Yelverton PL20 7PS* T: (01822) 859328 M: 07500-948452 E: andrew.farmer99@btinternet.com

FARMER, Anne Louise. b 61. Warwick Univ BEd 84. Trin Coll Bris 04. **d** 06 **p** 07. C Stoke Bishop *Bris* 06–09; TV Worle *B & W* 09–17; P-in-c E Molesey *Guildf* 17–18; V E Molesey St Paul from 18. *101 Palace Road, East Molesey KT8 9DU* T: (020) 8941 2071 E: alf@rev21.co.uk *or* stpaulmolesey@gmail.com

FARMER, Diane Marcia (Diana). b 61. Warwick Univ BSc 82 PGCE 83. WMMTC 97 Cranmer Hall Dur 00. **d** 01 **p** 02. C Allesley Park and Whoberley *Cov* 01–05; Hd Tr and Development Rethink from 05; Hon C Pennsett *Worc* 05–07; PtO 07–09; Hon C Wollaston 09–17; Hon C Norton and Wollaston from 17. *13 Rectory Street, Stourbridge DY8 5QT* T: (01384) 295205

FARMER, Lorelie Joy. Southn Univ BA 65 MA 68 Univ of Mass EdD 88. Cranmer Hall Dur 97. **d** 99 **p** 00. C Newbury *Ox* 99–03; C Stratford-upon-Avon, Luddington etc *Cov* 03–05; C Warmington w Shotteswell and Radway w Ratley 05–06; rtd 08; Hon C Witchampton, Stanbridge and Long Crichel etc *Sarum* 08–10; Hon C Wimborne Minster 12–13; PtO 13–18. *1 Oakdene Close, Wimborne BH21 1TJ* T: (01202) 801470 E: loreliefarmer@dunelm.org.uk *or* lpor9146@aol.com

FARMER, Robert James. b 65. WMMTC 03. **d** 06 **p** 07. C Lich St Chad 06–10; C Longdon 08–10; P-in-c Longdon and C Heath Hayes 10–11; V Shelfield and High Heath 11–17; TR Worc SE 17–19; TV from 19. *33 Aconbury Close, Worcester WR5 1JD* E: teamoffice@tiscali.co.uk *or* revdrob@btinternet.com

FARMER, Robert John Thayer. b 62. Kent Univ BA 84. St Steph Ho Ox 91. **d** 93 **p** 94. C Leigh St Clem *Chelmsf* 93–96; P-in-c Wellingborough St Mary *Pet* 96–00; V from 00; Chapl Northants Healthcare NHS Foundn Trust from 99. *St Mary's Vicarage, 193 Midland Road, Wellingborough NN8 1NG* T: (01933) 225626 E: vicar@stmarywellingborough.org.uk

FARMILOE, Preb Trevor James. b 42. Sarum & Wells Th Coll. **d** 82 **p** 82. C S Petherton w The Seavingtons *B & W* 82–85; R Norton St Philip w Hemington, Hardington etc 85–93; Chapl Rural Affairs Wells Adnry 87–92; RD Frome 89–93; V Martock w Ash 93–07; RD Ivelchester 95–01 and 04–07; Preb Wells Cathl 96–07; rtd 07; PtO *B & W* from 07; C Yeovil St Mich 11–12. *38 Ashmead, Yeovil BA20 2SQ* T: (01935) 428952 E: revtrev.martock@btinternet.com

FARNHAM, Douglas John. b 30. SS Mark & Jo Univ Coll Plymouth TCert 52 Ex Univ MEd 75. S Dios Minl Tr Scheme 80. **d** 83 **p** 84. Lect Bp Otter Coll Chich 70–78; Sen Lect W Sussex Inst of HE 78–92; NSM Barnham and Eastergate *Chich* 83–85; NSM Aldingbourne, Barnham and Eastergate 85–92; R 92–96; rtd 96; PtO *Chich* from 96. *12 Summersdale Court, The Drive, Chichester PO19 5RF* T: (01243) 532251

FARNHAM, Mrs Rachael Theresa. b 87. Dur Univ BA 18. Ridley Hall Cam 15. **d** 18 **p** 19. C Bayston Hill *Lich* from 18. *15 Glebe Road, Bayston Hill, Shrewsbury SY3 0PJ* M: 07977-511119

FARNWORTH, Ms Joanna Helen. b 66. Jes Coll Cam BA 88 MA 92. St Jo Coll Nottm BTh 98 MA 99. **d** 99 **p** 00. C Middleton w Thornham *Man* 99–03; V Ashton 03–11; P-in-c Droylsden St Martin 11–16; R Droylsden St Andr and St Martin from 16; Dioc Ecum Officer from 16.

St James's Vicarage, Westbury Street, Ashton-under-Lyne OL6 9NL T: 0161-330 4925 E: revdjofarnworth@gmail.com

FARNWORTH, Roger. b 60. Man Univ BSc 81. St Jo Coll Nottm MA 99. **d** 99 **p** 00. C Tonge w Alkrington *Man* 99–03; TV Ashton 03–05; TR from 05; AD Ashton-under-Lyne 08–16; Borough Dean Tameside from 18. *St James's Vicarage, Westbury Street, Ashton-under-Lyne OL6 9NL* T: 0161-330 2771 E: rogerfarnworth@aol.com

FARNWORTH, Russell. b 60. Lon Bible Coll BA 82 Nottm Univ MTh 85. St Jo Coll Nottm 81. **d** 84 **p** 85. C Blackpool St Jo *Blackb* 84–87; TV Darwen St Pet w Hoddlesden 87–91; V Kidsgrove *Lich* 91–02; Chief Exec Officer Trans World Radio UK from 03. *28 Kingsway East, Newcastle ST5 3PZ* T: (01782) 637130 E: rfarnworth@twr.org.uk

FARQUHAR, Iain. b 45. **d** 05 **p** 06. OLM Catford St Laur *S'wark* 05–15; PtO from 15. *18 Birkhall Road, London SE6 1TE* T: (020) 8698 7438 E: iainfarquhar@googlemail.com

FARQUHAR, Preb Patricia Ann. b 42. **dss** 78 **d** 87 **p** 94. S Hackney St Jo w Ch Ch *Lon* 80–01; Par Dn 87–94; C 94–01; Preb St Paul's Cathl 97–01; rtd 01; PtO *Nor* from 15. *8 Holme Terrace, Bishopgate, Norwich NR1 4EJ* T: (01603) 610112

FARQUHARSON, The Very Revd Hunter Buchanan. b 58. ALAM LLAM. Edin Th Coll 85. **d** 88 **p** 89. C Dunfermline *St And* 88–91; R Glenrothes 91–97; R Leven 95–97; R Dunfermline 97–99; Provost St Ninian's Cathl Perth from 99; R Perth St Ninian from 99. *St Ninian's Cathedral, North Methven Street, Perth PH1 5PP* T: (01738) 632053 E: huntfar@gmail.com *or* provost@perthcathedral.co.uk

FARR, John. *See* FARR, William John

FARR, Richard William. b 55. Ridley Hall Cam. **d** 83 **p** 84. C Enfield Ch Ch Trent Park *Lon* 83–87; C Eastbourne H Trin *Chich* 87–90; P-in-c Henham and Elsenham w Ugley *Chelmsf* 90–91; V 91–09; C Tunbridge Wells St Jo *Roch* from 09. *112 Stephens Road, Tunbridge Wells TN4 9QA* T: (01892) 540897 E: dickthevic@btopenworld.com *or* rw.farr@stjohnstw.org

FARR, William John. b 66. QUB BTh 05 MTh 07. **d** 08 **p** 09. NSM Muckamore and Killead w Gartree *Conn* 08–11; P-in-c Stoneyford from 11. *1 Ballyvannon Road, Ballinderry Upper, Lisburn BT28 2LB* T: (028) 9442 2158 M: 07808-399579 E: j20far@hotmail.com

FARRAN, Canon George Orman. b 35. Worc Coll Ox BA 58 MA 62. Wycliffe Hall Ox 58. **d** 60 **p** 61. C Tyldesley w Shakerley *Man* 60–62; Tutor Wycliffe Hall Ox 62–64; V Netherton *Liv* 64–73; R Sefton 69–73; R Credenhill w Brinsop, Mansel Lacey, Yazor etc *Heref* 73–83; RD Heref Rural 81–83; R Ditcheat w E Pennard and Pylle *B & W* 83–94; Dir of Ords 86–89; Can and Chan Wells Cathl 85–97; rtd 97; PtO *B & W* 97–19. *6 The Empire, Grand Parade, Bath BA2 4DF* T: (01225) 339365 E: george.farran@btinternet.com

FARRANT, Canon Martyn John. b 38. AKC 61. **d** 62 **p** 63. C Hampton St Mary *Lon* 62–65; C Shere *Guildf* 65–67; V Stoneleigh 67–75; V Addlestone 75–83; V Dorking w Ranmore 83–98; RD Dorking 89–94; Hon Can Guildf Cathl 96–98; rtd 98; Chapl Phyllis Tuckwell Hospice Farnham 98–01; PtO *Guildf* 98–17. *42 Hampstead Road, Dorking RH4 3AE* T: (01306) 740916 E: mandrfarrant@talktalk.net *or* martyn.farrant@gmail.com

FARRAR, Ruth. b 43. Matlock Coll of Educn CertEd 64. **d** 04 **p** 05. OLM Leesfield *Man* 04–13; rtd 13; PtO *Man* from 13. *Belvoir, 43 Coverhill Road, Grotton, Oldham OL4 5RE* T: 0161-633 0374 M: 07894-466401 E: revruthfarrar@gmail.com

FARRELL, Mrs Joanna Susan Elizabeth. b 53. Southn Univ LLB 95. STETS 03. **d** 06 **p** 07. NSM Steep and Froxfield w Privett *Portsm* 06–16; Asst Chapl Portsm Hosps NHS Trust 11–14; PtO *Portsm* from 16. *Hurst Farm Cottage, Hurst Lane, Privett, Alton GU34 3PL* T: (01730) 828450 E: joanna@hfc.myzen.co.uk

FARRELL, Ms Katherine Lucy Anne. b 61. Westcott Ho Cam 00. **d** 02 **p** 03. C Forest Gate Em w Upton Cross *Chelmsf* 02–07; C Lt Ilford St Mich 03–07; V Bellingham St Dunstan *S'wark* 07–11; C Croydon St Jo 11–13; PtO 13–15; TV Gt Grimsby St Mary and St Jas *Linc* from 15. *62A Brighowgate, Grimsby DN32 0QW* M: 07904-653180 E: k.farrell916@btinternet.com

FARRELL, Lindsey Elaine. b 79. QUB BA 00. CITI 15. **d** 17 **p** 18. Rossorry *Clogh* 17–18; Bp's C Inver w Mountcharles, Killaghtee and Killybegs *D & R* from 18. *The Rectory, Inver, Co Donegal, Republic of Ireland* T: (00353) (74) 973 6013 M: 87-360 0896 E: lfarrell9@tcd.ie

FARRELL, Ms Margaret Ruth. b 57. Linc Inst Melbourne BAppSc(OT) 78. **d** 02 **p** 03. C Bury St Edmunds All SS w St Jo and St Geo *St E* 02–06; P-in-c Woolpit w Drinkstone 06–08; R from 08. *The Rectory, Rectory Lane, Woolpit, Bury St Edmunds IP30 9QP* T: (01359) 242244 E: ruthfarrell391@gmail.com

FARRELL, Peter Godfrey Paul. b 39. Sarum & Wells Th Coll 72. **d** 74 **p** 75. C St Just in Roseland *Truro* 74–77; C Kenwyn

77–80; V Knighton St Jo *Leic* 80–86; TR Clarendon Park St Jo w Knighton St Mich 86–89; V Woodham *Guildf* 89–99; V Wells St Cuth w Wookey Hole *B & W* 99–09; rtd 09; P-in-c E w W Harptree and Hinton Blewett *B & W* 09–12; PtO from 15. *Close Cottage, 1 Great Gardens, Gaol Lane, Shepton Mallet BA4 5LF* T: (01749) 345443 E: pgpfvic@gmail.com

FARRELL, Robert Edward. b 54. Univ of Wales (Abth) BA 74 Jes Coll Ox BA 77 MA 81. Qu Coll Birm 85. d 86 p 87. C Llanrhos *St As* 86–88; C Prestwich St Marg *Man* 89–91; V Moulsham St Luke *Chelmsf* 91–98; V Thorpe Bay 98–08; R Ardleigh and The Bromleys 08–13; rtd 13; PtO *Cant* 14–17. *Villa Derwen, 135 London Road, Temple Ewell, Dover CT16 3BY* E: robert_farrell21@hotmail.com

FARRELL, Ronald Anthony. b 57. Edin Univ BD 84 Birm Univ MA 86. Qu Coll Birm 84. d 86 p 87. C Shard End *Birm* 86–87; C Shirley 87–89; Bp's Officer for Schs and Young People 89–93; V Kingstanding St Mark 93–01; TR Swinton and Pendlebury *Man* 01–05; P-in-c Lower Broughton Ascension 02–05; V W Bromwich St Fran *Lich* from 05; V W Bromwich St Pet 17–18; RD W Bromwich from 17. *Friar Park Vicarage, Freeman Road, Wednesbury WS10 0HJ* T: 0121-556 5823 E: father.ron@btinternet.com

FARRELL, Stephen Andrew. b 84. Jes Coll Ox BA 05 MA 10 Cardiff Univ LLM 15. CITC BTh 08. d 08 p 09. C Taney *D & G* 08–11; I Dublin Zion Ch from 11; Prov and Dioc Registrar from 12. *Zion Rectory, 18 Bushy Park Road, Rathgar, Dublin 6, Republic of Ireland* T: (00353) (1) 492 2365 or 406 4730 E: zion@dublin.anglican.org

FARRELL, Thomas Stanley. b 32. Lon Univ BD 71. Ridley Hall Cam 69. d 71 p 72. C Much Woolton *Liv* 71–73; C Gt Sankey 73–74; Asst Chapl Dulwich Coll 74–76; Chapl 76–81; P-in-c Wonersh *Guildf* 81–86; V 86–90; RD Cranleigh 87–90; R St Marg Lothbury and St Steph Coleman Street etc *Lon* 90–00; P-in-c St Botolph without Aldersgate 90–97; rtd 00; Hon C Burford w Fulbrook, Taynton, Asthall etc *Ox* 00–04; PtO from 04. *17 Ridgeway Court, Crowmarsh, Wallingford OX10 9GU* T: (01491) 599433 E: tomfarrell@uwclub.net

FARRER, Canon Carol Elizabeth. b 47. Open Univ BA 88. Cranmer Hall Dur 81. dss 83 d 87 p 94. Newbarns w Hawcoat *Carl* 83–86; Egremont and Haile 86–91; Par Dn 87–91; Team Dn Penrith w Newton Reigny and Plumpton Wall 91–94; TV 94–01; Dioc Lay Min Adv 87–88; Assoc Dir of Ords 88–97; Dir of Ords 97–00; Dioc OLM Officer 00–05; TV S Barrow 01–07; Hon Can Carl Cathl 01–07; rtd 08; PtO *St As* from 09. *3 Marlow Terrace, Mold CH7 1HH* T: (01352) 756011 E: carolfarrer@hotmail.com

FARRIMOND, Sarah Lucy. b 67. Hertf Coll Ox BA 89 Leeds Univ BA 99 Dur Univ PhD 09. Qu Coll Birm 12. d 14 p 15. C Birkby and Birchencliffe *Leeds* 14–18; P-in-c High Hoyland, Scissett and Clayton W 18; R from 18 Clergy Development Officer Huddersfield Area from 18. *The Rectory, 19 Church Lane, Clayton West, Huddersfield HD8 9LY* T: (01484) 900025 M: 07943-738638 E: revsarahfarrimond@yahoo.co.uk

FARRINGTON, Canon Christine Marion. b 42. Birkbeck Coll Lon BA 65 Nottm Univ DASS 66 Middx Poly MA 75. St Alb Minl Tr Scheme 79. dss 82 d 87 p 94. Redbourn *St Alb* 82–87; Dir Past Studies Linc Th Coll 86–87; HM Pris Linc 86–87; Dir Sarum Chr Cen 87–93; Dn Sarum Cathl 87–93; Co-Dir of Ords and Dir of Women's Min *Ely* 93–02; Hon Can Ely Cathl 93–02; C Cambridge Gt St Mary w St Mich 93–96; V Cambridge St Mark 96–02; Chapl Wolfs Coll Cam 97–02; rtd 02; PtO *St Alb* 97–04; RD Wheathampstead 04–07; Chapl to The Queen 98–12. *4 Pondesmeade, Redbourn, St Albans AL3 7LD* E: canon.cmf@tiscali.co.uk

FARROW, Elizabeth Maud. b 43. Edin Th Coll. d 91 p 96. NSM Glas H Cross 91–96; TV Bearsden w Milngavie 96–00 and 03–05; Asst P Sanibel USA 06–11; LtO *Glas* from 08. *5 Campsie Road, Strathblane G63 9AB* T: (01360) 770936 E: liz.farrow@gmail.com

FARROW, Ian Edmund Dennett. b 38. S'wark Ord Course 70. d 72 p 73. C Tunbridge Wells St Jo *Roch* 72–78; Chapl N Cambs Gen Hosp Gp 78–92; P-in-c Walsoken *Ely* 78–80; R 80–92; V Bisley, Oakridge, Miserden and Edgeworth *Glouc* 92–04; rtd 04; PtO *Ox* from 18. *Wellspring, Brook Lane, Stonesfield, Witney OX29 8PR* T: (01993) 891293

FARROW, Canon Keith. b 59. Leeds Univ BA 05 RMN 91. NOC 02. d 05 p 06. C Sprotbrough *Sheff* 05–07; C Hillsborough and Wadsley Bridge 07–09; P-in-c 09–11; V 11–14; Can Missr Sheff Cathl from 14; Dir IME 4-7 from 12. *62 Kingfield Road, Sheffield S11 9AU* T: 0114-255 9093 E: keith.farrow@sheffield.anglican.org

FARROW, Peter Maurice. b 44. St Chad's Coll Dur BSc 65. d 68 p 69. C Gt Yarmouth *Nor* 68–71; C N Lynn w St Marg and St Nic 71–75; P-in-c Sculthorpe w Dunton and Doughton 75–77; PtO 78–89; TV Lowestoft and Kirkley 89–94; Ind Miss

89–94; Sen Ind Chapl 94–99; TV Gaywood 95–02; P-in-c Mundford w Lynford, Cranwich and Ickburgh w Langford 02–09; rtd 09; PtO *Nor* from 09. *21 Clifford Drive, Lowestoft NR33 9EX* T: (01502) 521817 E: farrpm@btinternet.com

FARTHING, Michael Thomas. b 28. St Cuth Soc Dur 48 Lambeth STh 81 Ox Univ CertHE 08. St Steph Ho Ox. d 58 p 59. C St Marylebone St Mark w St Luke *Lon* 58–63; C Newport Pagnell *Ox* 63–69; R Standlake 69–74; R Yelford 69–74; R Lower Windrush 74–82; V Wheatley w Forest Hill and Stanton St John 82–95; rtd 95; PtO *Ox* 95–15. *32 Falstaff Close, Eynsham, Oxford OX29 4QA* T: (01865) 883805

FARTHING, Paul Andrew. b 58. McGill Univ Montreal BA 80 STM 82. Montreal Dioc Th Coll. d 83 p 84. C Montreal W St Phil Canada 83–85; R Montreal St Jo Divine 85–96; R Montreal St Jo Ev 96–99; P-in-c Burton *Lich* 99–05; V Burton St Aid and St Paul 05–13; PV Lich Cathl 12–13; V Chislehurst Annunciation *Roch* from 13. *The Vicarage, 2 Foxhome Close, Chislehurst BR7 5XT* T: (020) 8467 3606 E: pafarthing@fmail.co.uk *or* annunciation.chislehurst@gmail.com

FASS, Michael John. b 44. Trin Coll Cam MA 75. Edin Dioc NSM Course 89. d 95 p 95. NSM Penicuik *Edin* 95–97; NSM W Linton 95–97; NSM Roslin (Rosslyn Chpl) 97–06; Bp's Officer for Min 03–09; LtO 06–17; PtO from 17; *Heref* from 08. *Old Gore Coach House, Old Gore, Ross-on-Wye HR9 7QT* T: (01989) 780339

FAULDS, Ian Craig. b 48. d 03 p 04. NSM Maughold *S & M* 03–12; NSM Maughold and S Ramsey 12–13; PtO 13–14; Min Can and Prec St German's Cathl from 14. *The Lynague, Ramsey Road, Lynague, Peel, Isle of Man IM5 2AQ* T: (01624) 842045

FAULKNER, Mrs Anne Elizabeth. b 38. Bp Otter Coll BA 58. d 00 p 01. NSM Aylesbury *Ox* 00–04; Chapl to Bp Buckingham 02–04; rtd 04; Hon C Wroxall *Portsm* 04–05; P-in-c 05–11; P-in-c St Lawrence 08–10; Hon C N Swindon St Andr *Bris* 11–17; PtO *Win* 17–19; Hon C Fawley from 19. *39 Clarendon Road, Southampton SO16 4GB* T: (023) 8051 2272 E: aefaulkner77@gmail.com

FAULKNER, Brian Thomas. b 48. S Dios Minl Tr Scheme. d 84 p 85. C W Leigh *Portsm* 84–88; R Foulsham w Hindolveston and Guestwick *Nor* 88–93; P-in-c Erpingham w Calthorpe, Ingworth, Aldborough etc 93–94; R 94–13; RD Ingworth 10–13; rtd 13; PtO *Nor* 14–15; Hon C Barningham w Matlaske w Baconsthorpe etc 15–16; Hon C Lt Barningham, Blickling, Edgefield etc 15–16; PtO from 16. *Oak Tree Cottage, Cherrytree Road, Plumstead, Norwich NR11 7LQ* T: (01263) 577868 E: briantfaulkner@gmail.com

FAULKNER, Bruce Stephen. b 63. Trin Coll Bris BA 97 St Jo Coll Dur MA 08. Cranmer Hall Dur 06. d 08 p 09. C Somerton w Compton Dundon, the Charltons etc *B & W* 08–12; P-in-c Ilchester w Northover, Limington, Yeovilton etc 12–17; R from 17; RD Ivelchester from 13. *3 The Paddocks, West Street, Ilchester, Yeovil BA22 8PS* T: (01935) 849441 M: 07796-283766 E: bsfaulkner1@aol.com *or* ilchestervicar@aol.com

FAULKNER, Mrs Catherine Evelyn. b 43. Man Poly RHV 82. d 01 p 02. OLM Urmston *Man* 01–11; P-in-c 11–14; NSM Davyhulme Ch Ch 13–14; rtd 14; PtO *Man* from 14. *5 Barnfield, Urmston, Manchester M41 9EW* T: 0161-748 3226 E: catherine.faulkner@ntlworld.com

FAULKNER, Henry Odin. b 35. G&C Coll Cam BA 56 MA 59. St Jo Coll Nottm 70. d 74 p 75. C Heigham H Trin *Nor* 74–76; C Heeley *Sheff* 76–80; TV Netherthorpe 80–84; PtO *St Alb* from 84; rtd 00. *69 Holywell Hill, St Albans AL1 1HF* T: (01727) 854177 M: 07719-642479 E: henry.faulkner@ntlworld.com

FAULKNER, Iain Stuart. d 12 p 14. NSM Balham St Mary and St Jo *S'wark* 12–17; P-in-c S Wimbledon St Andr 17; NSM Stockwell St Andr and St Mich from 18. *Address temp unknown* M: 07432-678139 E: iainsfaulkner@hotmail.com

FAULKNER (née RITCHIE), Ms June. b 41. UCD BA 64. d 05 p 06. OLM New Windsor *Ox* 05–11; PtO from 11. *69 Springfield Road, Windsor SL4 3PR* T: (01753) 622808 E: j.faulkner0406@gmail.com

FAULKNER, Margaret Evelyn. *See* WHITFORD, Margaret Evelyn

FAULKNER, Martin Trevor. b 62. Salford Univ BSc 83 Bretton Hall Coll PGCE 88 Leeds Univ BA 10 Sheff Univ MA 12. Coll of Resurr Mirfield 09. d 11 p 12. C Spilsby Gp *Linc* 11–14; C Bolingbroke Deanery 14–15; V S Holderness Coast *York* from 15. *28 Park Avenue, Withernsea HU19 2JU* T: (01964) 615060 M: 07908-703484 E: rev.martin@hotmail.co.uk

FAULKNER, Peter Graham. b 47. Lon Univ CertEd 69. Oak Hill Th Coll BA 87. d 82 p 83. C Crofton *Portsm* 87–89; R Mid Marsh Gp *Linc* 89–98; V S Cave and Ellerker w Broomfleet *York* 98–13; P-in-c N Cave w Cliffe 09–12; P-in-c Hotham 09–12; RD Howden 05–10; rtd 13; PtO *Linc* from 16; *Eur* from

18. *9 Hurn Close, Ruskington, Sleaford NG34 9FE* T: (01526) 832184 E: faulkner47peter@gmail.com

FAULKNER, Robert Sonny. b 59. ACMA 98 ACCA 13. Ripon Coll Cuddesdon 15. **d** 17 **p** 18. C Clapham Ch Ch and St Jo *S'wark* from 17. *49 Voltaire Road, London SW4 6DD* T: (020) 8771 5030 M: 07377-449607 E: robertsofaulkner@gmail.com

FAULKNER, Ms Susan Ann. b 70. Lanc Univ BA 96. Ripon Coll Cuddesdon 97. **d** 99 **p** 00. C Scotswood *Newc* 99–03; P-in-c Byker St Silas 03–10; P-in-c Badby w Newham and Charwelton w Fawsley etc *Pet* 10–12; R 12–19; V Dallington and St James from 19. *The Vicarage, 24A High Street, Silverstone, Towcester NN12 8US* T: (01327) 858018 M: 07786-265422 E: revsuefaulkner@aol.com

FAULKS, David William. b 45. EMMTC 82. **d** 86 **p** 87. C Market Harborough *Leic* 86–88; C Wootton Bassett *Sarum* 88–90; R Clipston w Naseby and Haselbech w Kelmarsh *Pet* 90–13; rtd 13; PtO *Leic* from 14. *7 Pochin Drive, Market Harborough LE16 7LP* E: david.faulks@btinternet.com

FAULKS, Simon George. b 73. Moorlands Th Coll BA 99. St Jo Coll Nottm 09. **d** 11 **p** 12. C Warminster Ch Ch *Sarum* 11–15; V Newton Longville, Mursley, Swanbourne etc *Ox* from 15. *The Rectory, 7 Main Street, Mursley, Milton Keynes MK17 0RT* T: (01296) 728531 M: 07795-154222 E: revsimon@notashamed.co.uk

FAULL, Janet Dorothy. b 60. SS Paul & Mary Coll Cheltenham PGCE 86 LGSM 82. WEMTC 05. **d** 08 **p** 09. C Cheltenham Ch Ch *Glouc* 08–12; V Tuffley 12–19; AD Glouc City 15–19; Hon Can Glouc Cathl 18–19; R Hook Norton w Gt Rollright, Swerford etc *Ox* from 19. *The Rectory, 2 Rectory Road, Hook Norton, Banbury OX15 5QQ* M: 07986-650459 E: janetfaull@btinternet.com

✠**FAULL, The Rt Revd Vivienne Frances.** b 55. St Hilda's Coll Ox BA 77 MA 82 Clare Coll Cam MA 90. St Jo Coll Nottm BA 81. **dss** 82 **d** 87 **p** 94 **c** 18. Mossley Hill St Matt and St Jas *Liv* 82–85; Chapl Clare Coll Cam 85–90; Chapl Glouc Cathl 90–94; Can Res Cov Cathl 94–00; Vice-Provost 95–00; Provost Leic 00–02; Dean Leic 02–12; Dean York 12–18; Bp Bris from 18. *Bishop's Office, Church Lane, Winterbourne, Bristol BS36 1SG* T: (01454) 777728

FAULTLESS, Mrs Patricia Doreen. b 53. **d** 05 **p** 06. OLM Glascote and Stonydelph *Lich* from 05. *40 Stephenson Close, Glascote, Tamworth B77 2DQ* T: (01827) 287171 M: 07980-434897 E: patriciafaultless@gmail.com

FAUX, Steven Paul. b 58. UEA BA 79. Trin Coll Bris BA 07. **d** 07 **p** 08. C Bath St Mich w St Paul *B & W* 07–14; PtO from 14; C Redland *Bris* from 16. *Fleetlands, Weston Park, Bath BA1 4AL* T: (01225) 313145 E: steven@stevenfaux.com

FAWCETT, Mrs Diane Elizabeth. b 49. Cant Univ (NZ) BA 72 Kent Univ MA 03. Westcott Ho Cam 03. **d** 04 **p** 05. C Egerton w Pluckley *Cant* 04–08; PtO 08–10; P-in-c St Margarets-at-Cliffe w Westcliffe etc from 10. *8 Luxmoore House, 75 New Dover Road, Canterbury CT1 3DZ* T: (01227) 760593 E: fawcett38@hotmail.com

FAWCETT, Mrs Joanna Mary. b 45. SRN 67 SCM 69. EAMTC 01. **d** 04 **p** 05. NSM Blakeney w Cley, Wiveton, Glandford etc *Nor* 04–12; PtO from 12. *14 The Cornfield, Langham, Holt NR25 7DQ* T: (01328) 830415 E: jofawcett@btinternet.com

FAWCETT, Mrs Laura Joy. b 82. Fitzw Coll Cam BA 03 Cen Sch Speech & Drama MA 07 Pemb Coll Cam MPhil 14. Westcott Ho Cam 13. **d** 15 **p** 16. C Putney St Mary *S'wark* 15–18; V Dalston H Trin w St Phil and Haggerston All SS *Lon* from 18. *All Saints' Vicarage, Livermere Road, London E8 4EZ* T: (020) 7254 5062 M: 07815-115826 E: vicar@trinitysaintsunited.co.uk

FAWCETT, Timothy John. b 44. K Coll Lon BD 66 AKC 67 PhD 71. St Boniface Warminster 66. **d** 67 **p** 68. C Blackpool St Steph *Blackb* 67–70; Hon C St Marylebone All SS *Lon* 68–70; C Southgate St Mich 70–72; Sacr Dur Cathl 72–75; V Wheatley Hill 75–79; V Torrisholme *Blackb* 79–84; V Thaxted *Chelmsf* 84–89; NSM Holt Deanery *Nor* 89–06; rtd 89; PtO *Nor* from 09. *Dowitchers, 14 The Cornfield, Langham, Holt NR25 7DQ* T: (01328) 830415 E: tjfawcett@btinternet.com

FAWNS, Canon Lynne. b 56. Thames Valley Univ BA 95. NTMTC 97. **d** 00 **p** 01. C Hillingdon All SS *Lon* 00–03; V London Colney *St Alb* 03–18; Hon Can St Alb 17–18; rtd 18. *Rowanlea, 55 Hull Road, Cottingham HU16 4PN*

FAYERS, Canon Robert Stanley. b 48. St Steph Ho Ox 82. **d** 84 **p** 85. C Deptford St Paul *S'wark* 84–88; V Beckenham St Mich w St Aug *Roch* 88–00; V Brighton St Mich *Chich* 00–11; P-in-c Brighton St Paul 06–11; V Brighton St Mich and St Paul 11–14; Can and Preb Chich Cathl 12–14; rtd 14; PtO *Nor* from 15; *Chich* from 15; *Ely* from 19. *Grampus House, 32 Pilot Street, King's Lynn PE30 1QL* M: 07706-067496 E: rsfayers@gmail.com

FAYLE, David Charles Wilfred. b 51. Sarum & Wells Th Coll. **d** 83 **p** 84. C Parkstone St Pet w Branksea and St Osmund *Sarum* 83–87; TV Dorchester 87–96; P-in-c Taunton All SS *B & W* 96–97; V 97–18; rtd 18. *Flat 2, 7 Fortfield Terrace, Sidmouth EX10 8NT* E: davidfayle@btinternet.com

FAZZANI, Keith. b 47. Portsm Poly BSc 70. Cant Sch of Min 93. **d** 96 **p** 97. NSM Appledore w Brookland, Fairfield, Brenzett etc *Cant* 96–01 and 05–13; Chapl Team Ldr E Kent Hosps Univ NHS Foundn Trust 01–12; rtd 13; PtO *Cant* 13–16. *Oakhouse Farm, Appledore, Ashford TN26 2BB* T: (01233) 758322 E: kfazzani@btinternet.com

FEAK, Christopher Martin. b 52. Keele Univ BA 75. Trin Coll Bris 92. **d** 94 **p** 95. C Handsworth St Mary *Birm* 94–97; P-in-c Perry Common 97–00; V 00–05; AD Aston 01–05; P-in-c Sandown Ch Ch *Portsm* 05–15; P-in-c Lower Sandown St Jo 05–15; AD E Wight 12–14; P-in-c Towyn *St As* 15–16; TV Aber-Morfa Miss Area from 17. *The Rectory, 7 Parc Gwellyn, Kinmel Bay, Rhyl LL18 5HN* T: (01745) 353955 E: cfeak173@gmail.com

FEARNLEY, Andrew Anthony. b 84. Nottm Univ BA 06. Oak Hill Th Coll MTh 13. **d** 13. C Sevenoaks St Nic *Roch* 13–17; C Fulwood *Sheff* from 17. *50 Brooklands Crescent, Sheffield S10 4GG* M: 07709-448080 E: andyfearnley1@gmail.com

FEARNLEY, Jeffrey Malcolm. b 46. Newc Univ BSc 69. St Jo Coll Nottm 90. **d** 92 **p** 93. C Bispham *Blackb* 92–95; C Bolton w Ireby and Uldale *Carl* 95–00; TV Binsey 00–02; C 02–07; rtd 07; PtO *Blackb* from 07. *32 Chestnut Court, Leyland PR25 3GN* T: (01772) 458696

FEARNSIDE, Mary Ingrid. b 44. **d** 98 **p** 99. OLM Shelton and Oxon *Lich* 98–08; Chapl Uplands Care Home 08–14; Chapl R Shrewsbury Hosps NHS Trust 98–04; Chapl Shrewsbury and Telford Hosp NHS Trust from 04; PtO *Lich* from 11. *23 Eastwood Road, Shrewsbury SY3 8YJ* T: (01743) 353290 E: revmfearnside1@btinternet.com

FEARON, Mrs Irene. b 51. CBDTI 00. **d** 03 **p** 04. NSM Maryport, Netherton and Flimby *Carl* 03–08; NSM Camerton, Seaton and W Seaton from 08. *Kirkborough Lodge, Ellenborough, Maryport CA15 7RD* T: (01900) 813108 E: irene@kirklodge.com

FEASTER, Mrs Sarah Catherine. b 67. St Hugh's Coll Ox BA 89 Sheff Univ BA 13. Yorks Min Course 10. **d** 13 **p** 14. C Manston *Ripon* 13–14; *Leeds* 14–17; V Gt and Lt Ouseburn w Marton cum Grafton etc from 17. *The Vicarage, Main Street, Great Ouseburn, York YO26 9RQ* T: (01423) 330928 E: sarahfeaster@btinternet.com   or gtouseburnvicarage@hotmail.com

FEATHER (formerly HESELTINE), Mrs Barbara Joan. b 42. Keele Univ BA 65. S'wark Ord Course 85. **d** 88 **p** 94. NSM Addington *S'wark* 88–98; PtO *Truro* 98–02; NSM Feock 02–13; rtd 13; PtO *Truro* from 16. *The Grange House, Feock, Truro TR3 6RG* T: (01872) 865497 M: 07767-264060 E: barbarafeather42@gmail.com

FEATHERSTON, Margery. *See* GRANGE, Alice Margery

FEATHERSTON, Nigel Havelock. b 56. SCRTP 15. **d** 17 **p** 18. OLM Wychert Vale *Ox* from 17. *Greenwood, New Road, Dinton, Aylesbury HP17 8UT* E: nfeatherston@btinternet.com

FEATHERSTONE (née HOWETT), Mrs Amanda Jane. b 68. Reading Univ BA 91 Birm Univ MPhil 08 Cam Univ BTh 11. Ridley Hall Cam 09. **d** 11 **p** 12. C Boldmere *Birm* 11–15; C Birm St Luke 15–19; V Wythall from 19. *15 Hawthorne Drive, Hollywood, Birmingham B47 5QT* T: (01564) 823248 E: churchoffice@wythallchurch.net

FEATHERSTONE, Gray. b 42. Stellenbosch Univ BA 62 LLB 64. Cuddesdon Coll 65. **d** 72 **p** 73. C Woodstock S Africa 67–70; Asst Master Waterford Sch Swaziland 70–72; P-in-c Maputo St Steph and St Lawr Mozambique 73–76; Miss to Seamen 73–80; V Upper Clapton St Matt *Lon* 80–83; V Stamford Hill St Thos 80–89; Chr Aid Area Sec (N & W Lon) 89–06; Chr Aid Area Sec (Lon) 06–07; rtd 07; PtO *Lon* 97–18. *20 Richmond Road, London N2 7JT* T: (020) 3602 2788 E: gray.featherstone@htef.org.uk

FEATHERSTONE, Jonathan Mark. b 88. Regent's Park Coll Ox BA 10. Ridley Hall Cam MA 17. **d** 17 **p** 18. C Enfield Ch Ch Trent Park *Lon* from 17. *13 Wilton Road, Cockfosters, Barnet EN4 9DX* T: (020) 8449 0556 M: 07903-309440 E: featherstone.jon@gmail.com

FEATHERSTONE, Robert Leslie. b 54. Leeds Univ MA 04 LLCM 74 Lon Univ CertEd 75. Chich Th Coll 84. **d** 86 **p** 87. C Crayford *Roch* 86–89; V Belvedere St Aug 89–94; V Crowborough St Jo *Chich* 94–01; P-in-c New Brompton St Luke *Roch* 01–06; Hon Succ Roch Cathl 03–06; PtO 07–08; P-in-c Hastings St Clem and All SS *Chich* 09–16; TV Bexhill St Pet 16–18; rtd 18. *St Michael's House, 20 Glassenbury Drive, Bexhill-on-Sea TN40 2NY* T: (01424) 576826 M: 07878-237312 E: frrobertf@live.co.uk

FEAVER, Nigel Conway McDonald. b 51. Leeds Univ BA 73 Brunel Univ MA 76 CQSW 76. Ripon Coll Cuddesdon 03. **d** 05 **p** 06. C Oxton *Ches* 05–08; R Wincanton *B & W* 08–18; R Pen Selwood 08–18; rtd 18. *Carisbrooke, Blandford Road, Sturminster Marshall, Wimborne BH21 4AG* E: revnigelfeaver@gmail.com

FEENEY, Damian Prescott Anthony. b 62. Grey Coll Dur BA 83 PGCE 84 ALCM 81. Chich Th Coll BTh 94. **d** 94 **p** 95. C Harrogate St Wilfrid *Ripon* 94–96; C Preston St Jo and St Geo *Blackb* 96–99; Bp's Miss P to Longsands 99–01; TR Ribbleton 01–04; V Woodplumpton 04–09; Vice-Prin St Steph Ho Ox 09–15; V Ettingshall *Lich* from 15; PtO *Ox* 12–15. *Holy Trinity Vicarage, Farrington Road, Wolverhampton WV4 6QH* T: (01902) 478679 M: 07949-570387 E: ettingshall.priest@gmail.com

FEIST, Canon Nicholas James. b 45. Solicitor 70. St Jo Coll Nottm. **d** 76 **p** 77. C Didsbury St Jas *Man* 76–80; TV Didsbury St Jas and Em 80; V Friarmere 80–88; R Middleton 88–94; TR Middleton w Thornham 94–10; R Middleton and Thornham 10–14; AD Heywood and Middleton 99–07; Hon Can Man Cathl 98–14; rtd 14; PtO *Man* from 14; *Ches* from 15. *86 Rossendale Road, Heald Green, Cheadle SK8 3HF* T: 0161-286 9440 M: 07808-159339 E: njfeist@gmail.com

FEITAL, Peterson. *See* DE ALMEIDA FEITAL, Peterson

FELIX, Canon David Rhys. b 55. Univ of Wales (Cardiff) LLB 76 Solicitor 81. Ripon Coll Cuddesdon 83. **d** 86 **p** 87. C Bromborough *Ches* 86–89; V Grange St Andr 89–99; Chapl Halton Gen Hosp NHS Trust 95–99; P-in-c Runcorn H Trin *Ches* 96–99; RD Frodsham 98–99; V Daresbury from 99; Sen Ind Chapl from 00; Hon Can Ches Cathl from 06. *All Saints' Vicarage, Daresbury Lane, Daresbury, Warrington WA4 4AE* T: (01925) 740348 F: 740799 E: david.felix@btinternet.com

FELL, Canon Alan William. b 46. Ball Coll Ox BA 69. Coll of Resurr Mirfield 68. **d** 71 **p** 72. C Woodchurch *Ches* 71–74; C Man Clayton St Cross w St Paul 74–75; C Prestwich St Marg 75–77; V Hyde St Thos *Ches* 77–80; R Tattenhall and Handley 80–86; V Sedbergh, Cautley and Garsdale *Bradf* 86–12; Hon C Firbank, Howgill and Killington 86–06; P-in-c 06–12; Hon Can Bradf Cathl 96–12; RD Ewecross 00–05; rtd 12; PtO *Lich* from 13. *The Wharfinger's House, Maesbury Marsh, Oswestry SY10 8JB* M: 07825-774588 E: fells.maesbury@gmail.com

FELL, David Edward. b 61. Bradf Univ BSc 84 Brunel Univ BA 05. ERMC 05. **d** 07 **p** 08. C Wootton *St Alb* 07–11; TV Barnsbury *Lon* from 11. *2 Brooksby Street, London N1 1HA* T: (020) 7697 4400 M: 07989-203429 E: ted_fell@hotmail.com

FELLOWS, Canon Grant. b 56. K Coll Lon BD 77 AKC 77. Coll of Resurr Mirfield 79. **d** 80 **p** 81. C Addington *Cant* 80–84; C S Gillingham *Roch* 84–86; V Heath and Reach *St Alb* 86–94; V Radlett 94–03; RD Aldenham 98–03; V Leighton Buzzard w Eggington, Hockliffe etc 03–05; TR Billington, Egginton, Hockliffe 06–08; TR Ouzel Valley 08–18; Hon Can St Alb 12–18; rtd 18; PtO *St Alb* from 18; *Ely* from 19; RD St Neots from 19. *8 Radland Close, St Neots PE19 6BQ* E: rev.grant.fellows@gmail.com

FELLOWS, Ian Christopher. b 73. Univ Coll Ox BA 94 MA 98 St Jo Coll Dur BA 99. Cranmer Hall Dur 96. **d** 99 **p** 00. C Bucknall and Bagnall *Lich* 99–03; TV Broughton *Man* 03–07; P-in-c Blackley St Andr 07–16; TV Wythenshawe from 16. *St Luke's Vicarage, Brownley Road, Manchester M22 4PT* T: 0161-998 2071 E: pointlessvicar@gmail.com

FELLOWS, John Lambert. b 35. LTCL 67 SS Mark & Jo Coll Chelsea CertEd 58. Portsm Dioc Tr Course 86. **d** 88. NSM Portsea St Cuth *Portsm* 88–94; NSM Farlington 94–05; PtO from 05. *7 Court Lane, Portsmouth PO6 2LG* T: (023) 9237 7270 E: 7courtlane@gmail.com

FELLOWS, Canon John Michael. b 46. Oriel Coll Ox MA 77. Coll of Resurr Mirfield 74. **d** 77 **p** 78. C Kings Heath *Birm* 77–80; TV E Ham w Upton Park and Forest Gate *Chelmsf* 80–85; P-in-c Wormingford 85–90; P-in-c Mt Bures 85–90; P-in-c Lt Horkesley 85–90; V Wormingford, Mt Bures and Lt Horkesley 90; R Wormingford w Shackleford and Peper Harow *Guildf* 90–12; RD Godalming 07–12; Chapl Prior's Field Sch 90–12; Hon Can Guildf Cathl 12; rtd 12; Hon C Balsham, Weston Colville, W Wickham etc *Ely* 12–16; Hon C Gt w Lt Abington 12–16; Hon C Hildersham 12–16; PtO *Nor* from 16; *St E* from 17. *29 Upper Olland Street, Bungay NR35 1BE* T: (01986) 894414 E: j.fellows321@btinternet.com

FELLOWS, Lesley June. *See* CRAWLEY, Lesley June

FELLOWS, Simon Peter. b 93. St Jo Coll Nottm BA 17. **d** 17 **p** 18. C Stapleford *S'well* from 17. *193 Toton Lane, Stapleford, Nottingham NG9 7JD* M: 07472-696609 E: simonfellows77@hotmail.com

FELLOWS, Mrs Susan Elizabeth. b 46. ATCL 65 LTCL 66 GTCL 67. SAOMC 99. **d** 02 **p** 03. NSM Weston Turville *Ox* from 02. *65 Craigwell Avenue, Aylesbury HP21 7AG* T: (01296) 424982 M: 07712-226999 E: susan.sefellows@btinternet.com

FELTHAM, Keith. b 40. **d** 75 **p** 76. In Bapt Ch 66–75; C Plympton St Mary *Ex* 75–79; TV Northam w Westward Ho! and Appledore 79–82; TR Lynton, Brendon, Countisbury, Lynmouth etc 82–85; P-in-c Bickleigh (Plymouth) 85–86; TR 86–91; Chapl R Bournemouth Gen Hosp 91–95; P-in-c Whimple, Talaton and Clyst St Lawr *Ex* 95–00; rtd 00; PtO *Ex* 00–14. *18 Oakland Walk, Dawlish EX7 9RS* T: (01626) 438663 E: keithfeltham@icloud.com

FENBY, Andrew Robert. b 66. Loughb Univ BSc 88. St Steph Ho Ox 03. **d** 05 **p** 06. C Leigh-on-Sea St Marg *Chelmsf* 05–09; V Barkingside St Fran 09–14; R Beddington *S'wark* from 14. *The Rectory, 18 Bloxworth Close, Wallington SM6 7NL* T: (020) 8647 1973 E: frandrew@me.com

FENBY, Mrs Sarah Louise. b 66. Kent Univ BA 88 Lon Bible Coll BA 96. Trin Coll Bris MA 00. **d** 00 **p** 01. C Stoke Gifford *Bris* 00–04; C S Croydon Em *S'wark* 04–10; Min Selsdon St Fran CD 07–10; P-in-c Woolaston w Alvington and Aylburton *Glouc* 10–18; P-in-c Lydney 10–18; Voc and Tr Officer *Worc* from 18. *7 Egremont Gardens, Worcester WR4 0QH* T: (01905) 20537 E: sfenby@cofe-worcester.org.uk

FENNELL (née PAVYER), Mrs Jennifer Elizabeth. b 75. Ex Univ BSc 96 Cam Univ BTh 02 Lon Univ MA 05. Westcott Ho Cam 99. **d** 02 **p** 03. C Stevenage St Andr and St Geo *St Alb* 02–05; C Harpenden St Nic 05–10; P-in-c Welwyn Garden City 10–14; V from 14; RD Welwyn Hatfield from 17. *The Vicarage, 48 Parkway, Welwyn Garden City AL8 6HH* T: (01707) 320960 E: jennyfennell@virginmedia.com

FENNELL, Julian. b 56. Dioc OLM tr scheme. **d** 08 **p** 09. OLM Ipswich St Mary at Stoke w St Pet and St Fran *St E* 08–13; NSM 13–14; C Bramford 14–18; C Gt and Lt Blakenham w Baylham and Nettlestead 14–18; TV Ipswich St Mary at Stoke w St Pet and St Fran from 18. *St Frances House, 190 Hawthorn Drive, Ipswich IP2 0QQ* M: 07449-972663 E: julianfennell@hotmail.co.uk

FENNEMORE, Catherine Edwina. b 63. Sarum Coll 13. **d** 16 **p** 17. NSM W Leigh *Portsm* 16–19. *Woodside, Christmas Hill, South Wonston, Winchester SO21 3ES* T: (01962) 883668 E: cefennemore@gmail.com

FENNEMORE, Canon Nicholas Paul. b 53. Wycliffe Hall Ox 76. **d** 79 **p** 80. C N Mymms *St Alb* 79–82; C Chipping Barnet w Arkley 82–83; TV 83–84; TV Preston w Sutton Poyntz, Littlemoor etc *Sarum* 84–86; Chapl St Helier Hosp Carshalton 86–90; Chapl Jo Radcliffe Hosp Ox 90–94; Chapl Ox Radcliffe Hosp NHS Trust 94–96; Sen Chapl Ox Radcliffe Hosps NHS Trust 96–06; Hon Can Ch Ch *Ox* 03–06; Hd Chapl Services Portsm Hosps NHS Trust 06–11; Dioc Adv for Healing *Portsm* 08–11; Chapl Martlets Hospice Hove 11–12; Lead Chapl St Wilfrid's Hospice Chich 12–14; Chapl Southern Health NHS Foundn Trust from 14; PtO *Chich* from 14; P-in-c Soberton w Newtown *Portsm* 17–18; Cathl Chapl and Min Can Win Cathl from 18; PtO *Portsm* from 11. *Woodside, Christmas Hill, South Wonston, Winchester SO21 3ES* T: (01962) 883668 M: 07919-547508 E: canonfennemore@btinternet.com *or* nick.fennemore@winchester-cathedral.org.uk

FENSOME, Canon Anthony David. b 49. Open Univ BA 89. Sarum & Wells Th Coll 82. **d** 84 **p** 85. C Gtr Corsham *Bris* 84–88; P-in-c Lyddington w Wanborough 88–91; P-in-c Bishopstone w Hinton Parva 88–91; P-in-c Lyddington and Wanborough and Bishopstone etc 91; V 91–93; V Chippenham St Pet 93–08; RD Chippenham 94–99; AD 06–08; Hon Can Bris Cathl 98–08; rtd 08. *42 Francis Crescent, Tiverton EX16 4EP* T: (01884) 256611 E: tonyfens@aol.com

FENSOME, Grant Lewis. b 91. Trin Coll Bris BA 17. **d** 17 **p** 18. C Broxbourne w Wormley *St Alb* from 17. *15 Trafalgar Avenue, Broxbourne EN10 7DJ* M: 07572-007918 E: revgrantfensome@gmail.com *or* grantfensome@broxbournewithwormley.org.uk

FENTIMAN, David Frank. b 43. RIBA 74 Roehampton Inst PGCE 94. S Dios Minl Tr Scheme 90. **d** 93 **p** 94. NSM Hastings St Clem and All SS *Chich* 93–98; P-in-c Blacklands Hastings Ch Ch and St Andr 98–01; V 01–05; rtd 05; PtO *Chich* from 15. *4 Barnfield Close, Hastings TN34 1TS* T: (01424) 421821 E: revdfentiman@tiscali.co.uk

FENTON, Ms Allison Jane. b 66. Grey Coll Dur BA 87 Dur Univ PGCE 90 St Jo Coll Dur MATM 08. Cranmer Hall Dur 06. **d** 08 **p** 09. C Newc St Geo and St Hilda 08–10; C Newc Ch Ch w St Ann 10–12; P-in-c Scotswood 12–14; NSM Dur St Giles 14–17; NSM Shadforth and Sherburn 14–17; Vice Prin IME *Carl* from 17. *Church House, 19-24 Friargate,*

Penrith CA11 7XR T: (01768) 807777 *or* 840225 F: 868918 E: allisonjfenton@gmail.com

FENTON, Barry Dominic. b 59. Leeds Univ BA 85. Coll of Resurr Mirfield 85. **d** 87 **p** 88. C Leigh Park *Portsm* 87–90; Chapl and Prec Portsm Cathl 90–95; Min Can and Prec Westmr Abbey 95–02; Chapl N Middx Hosp NHS Trust 02–04; Lead Chapl 04–16; P-in-c Broadstairs *Cant* 16–18; R from 18; Min Can Cant Cathl from 17; PV Westmr Abbey from 04. *The Rectory, Nelson Place, Broadstairs CT10 1HQ* T: (01843) 862921 M: 07846-629455 E: dominic.fenton11@btinternet.com

FENTON, David Frank. b 43. Open Univ BA 79 Matlock Coll of Educn CertEd 67. Wycliffe Hall Ox 07. **d** 08 **p** 09. NSM Win Ch Ch 08–12; PtO from 12. *5 Glenwood Avenue, Southampton SO16 3PY* T: (023) 8076 9574 M: 07967-419169 E: dave.fenton1@btinternet.com

FENTON, Geoffrey Eric Crosland. b 54. St Jo Coll Ox BA 75 MSc 76. WEMTC 98. **d** 01 **p** 02. NSM Wedmore w Theale and Blackford *B & W* 01–05; NSM Greinton and W Poldens 05–08; C Mark w Allerton 08–10; P-in-c 10–11; TV Ashburton, Bickington, Buckland in the Moor etc *Ex* from 11. *The Vicarage, Widecombe-in-the-Moor, Newton Abbot TQ13 7TF* T: (01364) 621334 E: geoffrey.fenton@wildyeast.co.uk

FENTON, Heather. b 48. Trin Coll Bris. **d** 87 **p** 97. C Corwen and Llangar *St As* 87–89; C Corwen and Llangar w Gwyddelwern and Llawrybetws 89–98; Dioc Rural Min Co-ord 87–98; LtO 98–01; C Deanery of Penllyn 01–03; P-in-c Bryneglwys 03–11; P-in-c Gwyddelwern 09–11; P-in-c Corwen w Llangar w Glyndyfrdwy etc 11; AD Penllyn and Edeirnion 10–12; PtO from 13. *7 Llys Trewithan, St Asaph LL17 0DJ* T: (01745) 583535 E: rev.heather@outlook.com

FENTON, Keith John. b 54. Coll of Resurr Mirfield 01. **d** 03 **p** 04. C St Annes St Anne *Blackb* 03–07; TV Ribbleton 07–12; C 12–14; R from 14. *140 Teil Green, Fulwood, Preston PR2 9PE* T: (01772) 791147 M: 07773-630784 E: keithjfenton@yahoo.co.uk *or* parishofribbleton@gmail.com

FENTON, Michael John. b 42. Linc Th Coll 67. **d** 69 **p** 70. C Guiseley *Bradf* 69–72; C Heswall *Ches* 72–75; TV Birkenhead Priory 75–81; V Alvanley 81–91; Chapl Crossley Hosp Cheshire 82–91; V Holbrook and Lt Eaton *Derby* 91–03; V Allenton and Shelton Lock 03–07; rtd 07; PtO *Derby* 07–18. *11 Nethercroft Lane, Danesmoor, Chesterfield S45 9DE* T: (01246) 250071 E: michaeljfenton@yahoo.co.uk

FENTON, Mrs Nicola Jane. b 70. York Univ BSc 91 Leeds Univ PGCE 94 St Jo Coll Dur BA 12. Cranmer Hall Dur 10. **d** 12 **p** 13. C Nottingham St Ann w Em *S'well* 12–16; P-in-c Hazelwood, Holbrook and Milford *Derby* from 16; Bp's Asst Chapl from 16; Spiritual Dir Advsr from 18. *The Vicarage, Hob Hill, Hazelwood, Belper DE56 4AL* T: (01332) 486100 M: 07811-957913 E: njfenton@aol.com *or* nicky.fenton@derby.anglican.org

FENTON, Miss Penelope Ann. b 41. Leic Univ BSc 64. Cant Sch of Min 92. **d** 95 **p** 96. NSM Eastling w Ospringe and Stalisfield w Otterden *Cant* 95–00; P-in-c 00–05; Asst to Bp's Officer for NSM 95–05; rtd 05; PtO *Cant* 05–08. *9 Brogdale Road, Faversham ME13 8SX* T: (01795) 536366 E: penny.fenton@lineone.net

FENTON, Canon Vincent Thompson. b 52. Cranmer Hall Dur 94. **d** 96 **p** 97. C Heworth St Mary *Dur* 96–99; C-in-c Bishop Auckland Woodhouse Close CD 99–06; Chapl S Durham Healthcare NHS Trust 01–02; Chapl Co Durham and Darlington Acute Hosps NHS Trust 02–05; P-in-c Crook *Dur* 06–16; V from 16; AD Stanhope 07–18; Hon Can Dur Cathl from 16. *The Rectory, 14 Hartside Close, Crook DL15 9NH* T: (01388) 760939 E: vincent.fenton@durham.anglican.org

FENWICK, Canon Malcolm Frank. b 38. Cranmer Hall Dur 62. **d** 65 **p** 66. C Tynemouth Cullercoats St Paul *Newc* 65–68; C Bywell 68–73; V Alnmouth 73–75; CF (TAVR) 75–83; V Lesbury w Alnmouth *Newc* 75–80; V Delaval 80–91; RD Bedlington 83–88; V Riding Mill 91–01; P-in-c Whittonstall 91–01; Chapl Shepherd's Dene Retreat Ho from 91; RD Corbridge *Newc* 93–99; P-in-c Slaley 97–99; P-in-c Healey 99–01; Hon Can Newc Cathl 97–01; rtd 01; PtO Newc from 01. *21 Welburn Close, Ovingham, Prudhoe NE42 6BD* T: (01661) 835565

✠**FENWICK, The Rt Revd Richard David.** b 43. Univ of Wales (Lamp) BA 66 MA 86 TCD MusB 79 MA 92 Univ of Wales (Lamp) PhD 95 FLCM 68 FTCL 76 Hon FGCM 04. Ridley Hall Cam 66. **d** 68 **p** 69 **c** 11. C Skewen *Llan* 68–72; C Penarth w Lavernock 72–74; PV, Succ and Sacr Roch Cathl 74–78; Min Can St Paul's Cathl *Lon* 78–83; Succ 79–83; Warden Coll Min Cans *Lon* 81–83; PV Westmr Abbey 83–90; V Ruislip St Martin *Lon* 83–90; Can Res and Prec Guildf

Cathl 90–97; Sub-Dean 96–97; Dean Mon 97–11; V Newport St Woolos 97–11; Warden Guild of Ch Musicians 98–11; Bp St Helena 11–18; rtd 18; PtO *Llan* from 18; *Eur* from 07. *St Anne's, 1 Insole Close, Cardiff CF5 2HQ* T: (029) 2021 9291 E: richard.d.fenwick@gmail.com

FERGUSON, Aean Michael O'Shaun. b 39. CITC 87. **d** 90 **p** 91. NSM Kilmallock w Kilflynn, Kilfinane, Knockaney etc *L & K* 90; NSM Killaloe w Stradbally 90–94; NSM Adare and Kilmallock w Kilpeacon, Croom etc 94–97; C Killala w Dunfeeny, Crossmolina, Kilmoremoy etc *T, K & A* 97–00; I Skreen w Kilmacshalgan and Dromard 00–08; Can Killala Cathl 05–08; rtd 08; Dioc Information Officer *T, K & A* 04–09. *Rathlee, Easkey, Co Sligo, Republic of Ireland* T: (00353) (96) 49865 M: 87-812 1020 E: amferguson@yahoo.com

FERGUSON, Caroline Maria. b 64. Sunderland Univ BA 08. Lindisfarne Regional Tr Partnership 10. **d** 13 **p** 14. NSM Darlington St Mark w St Paul *Dur* 13–17; PtO from 18. *Moss Glen, 248 North Road, Darlington DL1 2EN* T: (01325) 244907 M: 07816-154355 E: caroline.ferguson@ntlworld.com

FERGUSON, Mrs Kathleen. b 46. LMH Ox BA 68 MA 72 ALA 76. St As Minl Tr Course 86. **d** 88 **p** 97. NSM Llanidloes w Llangurig *Ban* 88–01; P-in-c Llandinam w Trefeglwys w Penstrowed 01–02; V 02–04; AD Arwystli 02–04; NSM Shelswell *Ox* 04–07; rtd 07; PtO *Ban* from 07. *Trawsnant, 18 Maes Trannon, Trefeglwys, Caersws SY17 5QX* T: (01686) 430666 E: kathy@oerle.co.uk

FERGUSON (*née* **PASTERFIELD), Laura Sophia.** b 85. Univ of the Arts Lon BA 07 Rob Coll Cam BTh 13. Ridley Hall Cam 11. **d** 13 **p** 14. C Liv All SS 13–16; PtO *Bris* 17–19. *14 Prince Albert Court, St Helens WA9 3GD* M: 07557-501582 E: laurasophiaferguson@gmail.com

FERGUSON, Michael Gary. b 89. Trin Coll Bris 16. **d** 19. C Sutton *Liv* from 19. *14 Prince Albert Court, St Helens WA9 3GD* M: 07535-497830 E: fergiebromik@gmail.com

✠**FERGUSON, The Rt Revd Paul John.** b 55. New Coll Ox BA 76 MA 80 K Coll Cam BA 84 MA 88 FRCO 75. Westcott Ho Cam 82. **d** 85 **p** 86 **c** 14. C Ches St Mary 85–88; Sacr and Chapl Westmr Abbey 88–92; Prec 92–95; Can Res and Prec York Minster 95–01; Adn Cleveland 01–14; Warden of Readers 04–14; Suff Bp Whitby from 14; Can and Preb York Minster from 01; Asst Bp S & M from 18. *21 Thornton Road, Stainton, Middlesbrough TS8 9DS* T: (01642) 593273 E: bishopofwhitby@yorkdiocese.org

FERGUSON, Paul Stephen. b 80. Trin Hall Cam BA 02 MA 05. St Mellitus Coll BA 16. **d** 16 **p** 17. C Onslow Square and S Kensington St Aug *Lon* 16–19; V Bath Odd Down w Combe Hay *B & W* from 19. *39 Frome Road, Bath BA2 2QF* M: 07557-597491

FERGUSON, Peter Armstrong. b 40. **d** 11. C Carrickfergus *Conn* 10–15; I Derg w Termonamongan *D & R* from 15. *The Rectory, 13 Strabane Road, Castlederg BT81 7HZ* T: (028) 8167 9433 E: peteferg50@hotmail.com *or* derg@derry.anglican.org

FERGUSON, Raymond. See FERGUSON, Wallace Raymond

FERGUSON, Richard Archie. b 39. Dur Univ BA 62. Linc Th Coll 62. **d** 64 **p** 65. C Stretford St Matt *Man* 64–68; Bp's Dom Chapl *Dur* 68–69; C Newc St Geo 69–71; V Glodwick *Man* 71–77; V Tynemouth Ch Ch *Newc* 77–82; V Tynemouth Ch Ch w H Trin 82–87; P-in-c Tynemouth St Aug 82–87; TR N Shields 87–90; TR Upton cum Chalvey *Ox* 90–95; V Kirkwhelpington, Kirkharle, Kirkheaton and Cambo *Newc* 95–04; AD Morpeth 95–04; rtd 04; PtO *Newc* from 04. *6 Green Close, Stannington, Morpeth NE61 6PE* T: (01670) 789795 E: r.ferguson1@btinternet.com

FERGUSON, Robert Garnett Allen. b 48. Leeds Univ LLB 70 Clare Coll Cam. Cuddesdon Coll 71. **d** 73 **p** 74. C Wakef Cathl 73–76; V Lupset 76–83; Chapl Cheltenham Coll 83–87; Sen Chapl Win Coll 87–05; PtO *S & M* from 09; *Eur* from 16. *Follaton, Highfield Drive, Baldrine, Isle of Man IM4 6EE*

FERGUSON, Robin Sinclair. b 31. Worc Coll Ox BA 53 MA 57 Lon Univ CertEd 63. ALCD 55 Wycliffe Coll Toronto 55. **d** 57 **p** 58. C Brompton H Trin *Lon* 57–60; C Brixton St Matt *S'wark* 60–63; Hon C Framlingham w Saxtead *St E* 63–65; Hon C Haverhill 65–67; Chapl St Mary's Sch Richmond 67–75; C Richmond St Mary w St Matthias *S'wark* 69–75; P-in-c Shilling Okeford *Sarum* 76–87; Chapl Croft Ho Sch Shillingstone 76–87; R Milton Abbas, Hilton w Cheselbourne etc *Sarum* 87–96; rtd 96; PtO *Sarum* from 98. *Durnovaria, East Walls, Wareham BH20 4NJ* T: (01929) 551340 E: revrob@btinternet.com

FERGUSON, Ronald Leslie. b 36. Open Univ BA 86 BA 89. Chich Th Coll 65. **d** 68 **p** 69. C Toxteth Park St Marg *Liv* 68–72; C Oakham w Hambleton and Egleton *Pet* 72–74; Asst Chapl The Dorothy Kerin Trust Burrswood 74–76; V Castleside *Dur* 76–96; C Washington 96–99; P-in-c

Eighton Banks 99–06; Chapl Gateshead Health NHS Trust 96–06; rtd 06; PtO *Dur* 07–18. *2 Lapwing Court, Burnopfield, Newcastle upon Tyne NE16 6LP* T: (01207) 271559 E: ronald.ferguson@mac.com

FERGUSON (*née* **PAMPLIN), Mrs Samantha Jane.** b 71. St Andr Univ MTheol 06. TISEC 06. **d** 08 **p** 09. C Aberdeen St Pet *Ab* 08–10; C Aberdeen St Jo 08–10; P-in-c Aberdeen St Ninian 10–14; Chapl Aber Univ 11–14; Chapl NHS Grampian 12–13; R Montrose *Bre* 14–17; R Inverbervie 14–17; R Pittenweem *St And* 17–18; R Elie and Earlsferry 17–18; Asst Chapl St Andr Univ from 19. *3 Silverdyke Gardens, Cellardyke, Anstruther KY10 3FH* T: (01333) 313798 M: 07971-231709 E: revsamferguson@gmail.com

FERGUSON, Wallace Raymond. b 47. Qu Coll Birm BTheol CITC 76. **d** 78 **p** 79. C Lurgan Ch the Redeemer *D & D* 78–80; I Newtownards w Movilla Abbey 80–84; I Mullabrack w Markethill and Kilcluney *Arm* 84–00; I Carnteel and Crilly 00–05; Hon V Choral Arm Cathl 86–05; Dioc Chapl to Rtd Clergy 92–05; Dean Kilmore *K, E & A* 05–14; I Kilmore w Ballintemple 05–14; All-Ireland Chapl MU 12–14; rtd 14. *81 Drumady Road, Stralustin, Newtownbutler, Enniskillen BT92 6NP* T: (028) 6775 1386 E: deanraymondferguson@gmail.com

FERGUSON, Mrs Zoë Marie. b 75. ERMC 09. **d** 12 **p** 13. C Trunch *Nor* 12–14; C Gaywood 14–16; P-in-c Mundford w Lynford from 16; C Hilborough w Bodney 16–17; P-in-c from 17; C Oxborough w Foulden and Caldecote 16–17; P-in-c from 17. *The Rectory, St Leonards Street, Mundford, Thetford IP26 5DW* M: 07767-878721 E: revzoe@hotmail.co.uk

FERGUSON-STUART, Hamish. b 51. Open Univ BA 92 Cardiff Univ MTh 10 RGN. **d** 99 **p** 00. OLM Burton St Chad *Lich* 99–05; Asst Chapl Rotherham NHS Foundn Trust 05–16; rtd 16; PtO *Lich* from 16. *210 Derby Road, Burton-on-Trent DE14 1RN* T: (01283) 510447 E: jacobus-senior@talk21.com

FERGUSSON, Norma. b 52. St Hilda's Coll Ox BA 73 MA 83. Sarum Coll 08. **d** 11 **p** 12. NSM Rowde and Bromham *Sarum* 11–14; NSM Shrivenham and Ashbury *Ox* 14–19; V from 19; PtO *Sarum* from 14. *St Andrew's Vicarage, High Street, Shrivenham, Swindon SN6 8AN* M: 07799-545035 E: rev.n.fergusson@btinternet.com

FERMER, Michael Thorpe. b 30. Lon Univ BSc 52 ARCS 52 St Cath Soc Ox BA 54. Wycliffe Hall Ox 52. **d** 54 **p** 55. C Upper Holloway All SS *Lon* 54–57; C Plymouth St Andr *Ex* 57–59; V Tamerton Foliot 59–63; Asst Chapl United Sheff Hosps 63–64; Chapl 64–66; LtO *Sheff* 66–73; V Holmesfield *Derby* 73–79; TR Old Brampton and Loundsley Green 79–83; V Brightside w Wincobank *Sheff* 83–89; V Loscoe *Derby* 89–94; rtd 94; PtO *Derby* 94–18; *Sheff* from 13. *39 Elm Lane, Sheffield S5 7TR* T: 0114-281 1267 E: fermermichael@gmail.com

FERMER, Richard Malcolm. b 71. St Pet Coll Ox BA 94 K Coll Lon MA 95 PhD 02 Surrey Univ PGCE 96. Coll of Resurr Mirfield 00. **d** 02 **p** 03. C Palmers Green St Jo *Lon* 02–05; USPG Brazil 05–09; Asst Chapl Paris St Geo Eur 09–12; P-in-c Grosvenor Chpl *Lon* from 12. *24 South Audley Street, London W1K 2PA* T: (020) 7499 1684 E: richard.fermer@grosvenorchapel.org.uk

FERN, John. b 36. Nottm Univ BA 57 MA 88. Coll of Resurr Mirfield 57. **d** 59 **p** 60. C Carlton *S'well* 59–61; C Hucknall Torkard 61–68; R Rainworth 68–97; rtd 97; PtO *S'well* 03–11. *4 Fosbrooke House, 8 Clifton Drive, Lytham St Annes FY8 5RQ*

FERNANDES, José Augusto dos Santos (Joseph). b 70. Lisbon Univ BA 95. Ripon Coll Cuddesdon BTh 15. **d** 15 **p** 16. C Horton and Wraysbury *Ox* 15–18; V Ashford St Hilda *Lon* from 18. *St Hilda's Vicarage, 8 Station Crescent, Ashford TW15 3HH* T: (01784) 245712 M: 07879-687301 E: joaufer@hotmail.com

FERNANDES, Sheila Maud. b 45. Punjab Univ MB, BS 69. NTMTC 05. **d** 08 **p** 09. NSM Leyton Em *Chelmsf* 08–12; NSM Tye Green w Netteswell 12–15; rtd 15; PtO *Chelmsf* from 15. *19 Wedgewood Drive, Harlow CM17 9PX* T: (01279) 629791

FERNÁNDEZ, Hugo. *See* ADÁN FERNÁNDEZ, Hugo Federico

FERNANDEZ, Mrs Valerie Anne. b 48. WMMTC 03. **d** 05 **p** 06. C Mile Cross *Nor* 05–08; P-in-c Doddington w Benwick and Wimblington *Ely* 08–11; rtd 11; PtO *Llan* from 11. *51 Glyn Bedw, Llanbradach, Caerphilly CF83 3PF* T: (029) 2088 2725 E: revval@btinternet.com

FERNANDO, Percy Sriyananda. b 49. St And Dioc Tr Course 85. **d** 88 **p** 89. NSM Blairgowrie *St And* 88–93; NSM Alyth and Coupar Angus 89–93. *Gowrie Cottage, Perth Road, Blairgowrie PH10 6QB* E: percyf@hotmail.com

FERNELEY, Alastair John. b 69. Roehampton Inst BA 93 K Coll Lon MA 94 Birm Univ MPhil 98 St Jo Coll Dur MA 02. Cranmer Hall Dur 00. **d** 02 **p** 03. C Skipton Ch Ch *Bradf* 02–05; P-in-c Scalby *York* 05–14; V 14–16; P-in-c Scarborough St Luke 05–14; V 14–16; V Ravenscar and Staintondale 14–16; V Hackness w Harwood Dale 14–16; V

Dacre w Hartwith and Darley w Thornthwaite *Leeds* from 16. *The Vicarage, Dacre Banks, Harrogate HG3 4ED* T: (01423) 780262 E: irreverend@btinternet.com

FERNS, Canon Stephen Antony Dunbar. b 61. St Chad's Coll Dur BA 84 MA 94. Ripon Coll Cuddesdon BA 87 MA 91. **d** 88 **p** 89. C Billingham St Cuth *Dur* 88–90; Chapl Dur Univ 91; Chapl Van Mildert and Trevelyan Colls Dur 91–95; V Norton St Mary 95–97; Bp's Dom Chapl *Blackb* 97–01; Voc Officer and Selection Sec Min Division 01–06; Sen Selection Sec 06–15; Sen Chapl to Bp Chich from 15; Can Res and Treas Chich Cathl from 16; PtO *Lon* 04–14. *The Palace, Chichester PO19 1PY* T: (01243) 782161 E: stephen.ferns@chichester.anglican.org

FERNS, Archdeacon of. *See* GRAY, The Ven Robert James

FERNS, Dean of. *See* MOONEY, The Very Revd Paul Gerard

FERNYHOUGH, Timothy John Edward. b 60. Leeds Univ BA 81. Linc Th Coll 81. **d** 83 **p** 84. C Daventry *Pet* 83–86; Chapl Tonbridge Sch 86–92; Chapl Dur Sch 92–02; Hd RS and Asst Chapl Radley Coll 02–17; R Lambfold *Pet* from 17. *The Lambfold Rectory, Collswell Lane, Blakesley, Towcester NN12 8RB* T: (01327) 860027 E: revtjef@gmail.com

FERRAR, Andrew Nicholas. b 46. Em Coll Cam MA 70 Liv Univ PhD 02. **d** 06 **p** 07. NSM St Alb St Sav from 06. *2 Tiberius Square, St Albans AL3 4GE* T: (01727) 685903 E: andrew.ferrar@gmail.com

FERRIER, Malcolm. b 38. Edmund Th Coll 65 St Mich Coll Llan 67. **d** 69 **p** 70. C Solihull *Birm* 69–73; C E Grinstead St Swithun *Chich* 73–75; V Saltley *Birm* 75–82; V Waterlooville *Portsm* 82–03; rtd 03. *44 Woodcock Gardens, Warminster BA12 9JG* T: (01985) 211344

FERRIS, Amanda Jane. b 61. RGN 83. SAOMC 02. **d** 03 **p** 04. NSM Letchworth St Paul w Willian *St Alb* from 03; Chapl E and N Herts NHS Trust 07–12; Chapl Milton Keynes Univ Hosp NHS Foundn Trust from 12; Spiritual Care Co-ord Garden Ho Hospice Letchworth from 18. *Rivendell, 33B Stotfold Road, Arlesey SG15 6XL* T: (01462) 834627 *or* (01908) 660033 M: 07780-670651 E: amanda.ferris@btinternet.com

FERRIS, Samuel Christopher. b 77. Univ of Wales (Lamp) BA 98. Trin Coll Bris 02. **d** 04 **p** 05. C Tunbridge Wells St Mark *Roch* 04–07; TV S Gillingham 07–11; C St John-at-Hackney *Lon* 11–14; Chapl Hackney Free and Paroch Sch 11–14; TR Chipping Barnet *St Alb* from 14. *The Rectory, 38 Manor Road, Barnet EN5 2JJ* T: (020) 8275 0648 M: 07910-077885 E: frchris@ymail.com

FERRITER, Felicity Eunice Myfanwy. b 54. Sheff Univ BA 76 Nottm Univ MA 98. EMMTC 95. **d** 98 **p** 99. NSM Retford *S'well* 98–03; Asst Chapl Rampton Hosp Retford 99–01; Asst Chapl Notts Healthcare NHS Trust 01–02; Chapl 02–03; Asst to AD Retford 03–04; C Rampton w Laneham, Treswell, Cottam and Stokeham *S'well* 04–11; C N and S Leverton 04–11; TV Retford Area 11–14; rtd 14; PtO *S'well* from 16. *The Gables, Treswell Road, Rampton, Retford DN22 0HU* T: (01777) 248580 E: felicityemferriter@btinternet.com *or* felicity.ferriter@btinternet.com

FERRY, Canon David Henry John. b 53. TCD BTh 88. **d** 88 **p** 89. C Enniskillen *Clogh* 88–90; I Leckpatrick w Dunnalong *D & R* 90–01; I Donagheady 01–12; I Balteagh w Carrick from 12; I Tamlaghtard w Aghanloo from 12; Bp's Dom Chapl from 96; Can Derry Cathl from 05. *Balteagh Rectory, 115 Drumsurn Road, Limavady BT49 0PD* T: (028) 7776 5806 M: 07813-983772 E: hdjferry@hotmail.com

FERRY, Malcolm Ronald Keith. b 66. QUB BEd 88. CITC BTh 94. **d** 96 **p** 97. C Agherton *Conn* 96–99; I Kilwaughter w Cairncastle and Craigy Hill 99–03; I Castlerock w Dunboe and Fermoyle *D & R* 03–08; I Clooney w Strathfoyle 08–14; I Londonderry St Aug 14–19; Can Derry Cathl 16–19; I Agherton *Conn* from 19. *Address temp unknown* E: weechurch@btinternet.com

FERWERDA, Ms Ilse. b 71. Westmr Univ BSc 00 RGN 93. Qu Foundn Birm 13 WEMTC 14. **d** 16 **p** 17. C Northleach w Hampnett and Farmington etc *Glouc* 16–19; P-in-c Deerhurst and Apperley w Forthampton etc from 19. *The Vicarage, 1 The Green, Apperley, Gloucester GL19 4DQ* T: (01452) 780546 *or* 780880 E: revferwerda@gmail.com

FESSEY, Mrs Annis Irene. b 40. St Mary's Coll Chelt CertEd 60. Ripon Coll Cuddesdon 88. **d** 90 **p** 94. Par Dn Bris St Andr Hartcliffe 90–94; C The Lydiards 94–95; C Penhill 95–00; rtd 00; PtO *Bris* 00–03; *Portsm* from 03. *Tintern, 17 Mayfield Road, Ryde PO33 3PR* T: (01983) 616466 E: annisfessey@gmail.com

FEWINGS, Peter Trenchard. b 53. WEMTC 12. **d** 14 **p** 15. NSM Sodbury Vale *Glouc* 14–15; Chapl Kingswood w Wickwar etc 15–17; NSM Sodbury Vale from 17. *8 Highlands Drive, North Nibley, Dursley GL11 6DX* T: (01453) 436703 E: ptfewings@gmail.com

FEWKES, Jeffrey Preston. b 47. Derby Univ MA 99 DMin 04. Wycliffe Hall Ox 72. **d** 75 **p** 76. C Chester le Street *Dur* 75–78; C Kennington St Mark *S'wark* 78–81; V Bulwell St Jo *S'well* 81–98; V Stapleford 98–02; Victim Support Nottinghamshire 02–12; rtd 12; PtO *Derby* from 06. *3 Monks Close, Ilkeston DE7 5EY* T: 0115-930 2482 E: j.fewkes@btopenworld.com

FFRENCH (née WILLIAMS), Mrs Janet Patricia (Trish). b 59. Bradf Univ BTech 81. Trin Coll Bris BA 02. **d** 02 **p** 03. C Quinton Road W St Boniface *Birm* 02–05; C Mamble w Bayton, Rock w Heightington etc *Worc* 05–07; C Elmsett w Aldham, Hintlesham, Chattisham etc *St E* 07–17; C Horsmonden *Roch* from 17. *The Rectory, Goudhurst Road, Horsmonden, Tonbridge TN12 8JU* T: (01892) 732055 E: revsffrench@gmail.com

FFRENCH, Timothy Edward. b 58. Ball Coll Ox MA 86. Trin Coll Bris BA 01 MA 03. **d** 03 **p** 04. C Pedmore *Worc* 03–07; R Elmsett w Aldham, Hintlesham, Chattisham etc *St E* 07–17; R Horsmonden *Roch* from 17. *The Rectory, Goudhurst Road, Horsmonden, Tonbridge TN12 8JU* T: (01892) 732055 E: revsffrench@gmail.com

FFRENCH-HODGES, Christina Caroline. b 64. RGN 86. Aston Tr Scheme 94. **d** 99 **p** 00. C Castle Church *Lich* 99–02; C Rugby *Cov* 02–03; TV 03–05; PtO *Sheff* 06–07; NSM Arbourthorne and Norfolk Park 07–14; P-in-c Sheff St Jo 14–16; PtO from 16. *All Hallows, Church Lane, High Hoyland, Barnsley S75 4BJ* M: 07850-660513 E: tina@transformationforall.com

FFRENCH-HODGES, Jasper Tor. See HODGES, Jasper Tor

FIDDIAN-GREEN, Anthony Brian. b 39. Sussex Univ MA 88 Birm Univ CertEd 60 ACP 66. Bps' Coll Cheshunt 62. **d** 64 **p** 65. C Batheaston w St Cath *B & W* 64–67; Chapl Aiglon Coll and Chapl Villars *Eur* 67–71; Hd Master Battisborough Sch Holbeton 71–81; Chapl R Gr Sch Worc 81–83; Hd Master Frewen Coll Rye 83–96; P-in-c New Groombridge *Chich* 97–11; rtd 11; PtO *Chich* from 16. *21 Chatham Green, Eastbourne BN23 5PQ* T: (01323) 478533 E: revtfg@googlemail.com

FIDDYMENT, Alan John. b 40. Cant Sch of Min 91. **d** 94 **p** 95. NSM Chatham St Wm *Roch* 94–96; NSM Spalding St Mary and St Nic *Linc* 96–99; R Barkston and Hough Gp 99–07; rtd 07; PtO *Linc* from 07; *Pet* from 14. *5 Ascot Close, Spalding PE11 3BZ* T: (01775) 712837 M: 07706-367387 E: alan.fiddyment@gmail.com

FIDLER, John Harvey. b 49. Hatf Poly BSc 72. St Alb Minl Tr Scheme 84. **d** 87 **p** 88. NSM Royston *St Alb* from 87; PtO *Ely* 00–14. *8 Stamford Avenue, Royston SG8 7DD* T: (01763) 241886

FIELD, David Hibberd. b 36. K Coll Cam BA 58. Oak Hill Th Coll 58. **d** 60 **p** 61. C Aldershot H Trin *Guildf* 60–63; C Margate H Trin *Cant* 63–66; Sec Th Students Fellowship 66–68; Tutor Oak Hill Th Coll 68–93; Vice Prin 79–93; Dean Minl Tr Course 88–93; Dir Professional Min Div CPAS 94–00; Patr Sec CPAS 94–00; PtO *Cov* 94–07; rtd 00. *25 Field Barn Road, Hampton Magna, Warwick CV35 8RX* T: (01926) 410291 E: d.field@sky.com

FIELD, The Very Revd Gerald Gordon. b 54. K Coll Lon BD 75 AKC 75. Coll of Resurr Mirfield 76. **d** 77 **p** 78. C Broughton *Blackb* 77–79; C Blackpool St Steph 79–82; V Skerton St Luke 82–86; NSM Westleigh St Pet *Man* 92–93; V Shap w Swindale and Bampton w Mardale *Carl* 93–97; P-in-c Netherton 97; V 98–01; I Tullamore w Durrow, Newtownfertullagh, Rahan etc *M & K* 01–14; Can Meath 10–14; Can Kildare Cathl 10–14; Dean Cashel *C & O* from 14; I Cashel w Magorban, Tipperary, Clonbeg etc from 14. *The Deanery, Boherclogh Street, Cashel, Co Tipperary, Republic of Ireland* T: (00353) (62) 61232 M: 87-908 3821 E: dean@cashel.anglican.org

FIELD, James Lewis. b 46. Open Univ BSc 96. SEITE 94. **d** 97 **p** 98. NSM Chatham St Mary w St Jo *Roch* 97–00; R Gravesend H Family w Ifield 00–08; P-in-c New Romney w Old Romney and Midley *Cant* 08–12; R Romney Marsh 12–14; rtd 14. *14 York Road, Littlehampton BN17 6EN* T: (01903) 713601 M: 07591-497378 E: revjamesfield@gmail.com

FIELD, Jeremy Mark. b 75. St Jo Coll Dur BA 96. Ridley Hall Cam 10. **d** 10 **p** 11. C Onslow Square and S Kensington St Aug *Lon* 10–13; C Teddington St Mark and Hampton Wick 13–17; V Hampton Wick from 17. *198 Broom Road, Teddington TW11 9PQ* T: (020) 8977 7733 M: 07767-784011 E: jerryfield@hotmail.com *or* jerry@stjohnshamptonwick.org

FIELD, Martin Richard. b 55. Keswick Hall Coll CertEd 76 Leic Univ MA 87. St Jo Coll Nottm BTh 82. **d** 82 **p** 83. C Gaywood, Bawsey and Mintlyn *Nor* 82–85; PtO *Leic* 85–87; Hon C S'well Minster 87–88; Hon C Stand *Man* 88–89; Dioc Press and Communications Officer 88–91; CUF 91–95; PtO *Cant* 96–99; Fundraising and Campaigns Dir Children's Soc 04–09; UK Dir of Fundraising Barnardo's from 09; PtO *Sarum* 13–18. *40 Elm Grove Road, Salisbury SP1 1JW* T: (01722) 502910 *or* (020) 8498 7647 M: 07827-859403 E: martin@fieldfamily.me.uk

FIELD, Preb Olwen Joyce. b 53. St Jo Coll Nottm 86. **d** 88 **p** 94. Par Dn Kensal Rise St Mark and St Martin *Lon* 88–91; Par Dn Northwood H Trin 91–94; C 94–95; Chapl Mt Vernon Hosp 91–99; P-in-c W Drayton 99–03; V 03–12; V Preston from 12; Dean of Women's Min Willesden Area 01–03; AD Hillingdon 03–08; Dir of Ords Willesden Area from 09; Preb St Paul's Cathl from 10. *The Rectory, 319 Preston Road, Harrow HA3 0QQ* T: (020) 8904 4062 M: 07901-563426 E: olwenfield123@btinternet.com

FIELD, Richard Colin. b 33. St Cath Soc Ox BA 54 MA 63. Clifton Th Coll 63. **d** 65 **p** 66. C Highbury Ch Ch *Lon* 65–70; V Hanger Lane St Ann 70–85; V Leytonstone St Jo *Chelmsf* 85–98; rtd 98; PtO *Chich* from 99. *3 St Thomas Court, Cliffe High Street, Lewes BN7 2AW* T: (01273) 472884 E: richard.field3@btinternet.com

FIELD, The Ven Susan Elizabeth. b 59. York Univ BA 80 Birm Univ CertEd 81 Ox Univ MTh 98. Qu Coll Birm 84. **d** 87 **p** 94. C Coleshill *Birm* 87–90; Chapl Loughb Univ *Leic* 91–98; TV Loughborough Em and St Mary in Charnwood 98–14; V Nanpantan St Mary in Charnwood 15–18; Dir Post-Ord Tr 95–04; Bp's Adv for Women's Min 97–04; Dioc Dir of Ords 04–18; Hon Can Leic Cathl 04–18; Adn Cov from 18; Chapl to The Queen from 17. *Cathedral and Diocesan Offices, 1 Hill Top, Coventry CV1 5AB* T: (024) 7669 7607 *or* 7652 1337 M: 07885-714829 E: sue.field@covcofe.org

FIELDEN, Elizabeth Ann. b 42. TCert 63. **d** 99 **p** 00. OLM Broughton Gifford, Gt Chalfield and Holt *Sarum* 99–12; OLM Atworth w Shaw and Whitley 07–12; OLM Melksham 07–12; rtd 12; PtO *Sarum* from 12. *19 The Street, Broughton Gifford, Melksham SN12 8PW* T: (01255) 782509 E: fieldenann@gmail.com

FIELDEN, Hugh. b 66. BNC Ox BA 88 Birm Univ PGCE 90. Qu Coll Birm 91. **d** 93 **p** 94. C Sholing *Win* 93–97; TV Bramley *Ripon* 97–02; TV Bingley All SS *Bradf* 02–07; P-in-c Earby 07; P-in-c Kelbrook 07; V Earby w Kelbrook 08–14; *Leeds* from 14. *The Vicarage, 40 Brookfield Way, Earby, Barnoldswick BB18 6YQ* T: (01282) 844877 E: hugh.fielden@leeds.anglican.org *or* hugh@fielden.me.uk

FIELDEN, Mrs Janice Winifred. b 46. Warwick Univ BEd 82 MEd 89. SAOMC 99. **d** 02 **p** 03. NSM Chipping Norton *Ox* 02–05; NSM Charlbury w Shorthampton from 05; AD Chipping Norton 12–15. *11 Broad Field Road, Yarnton, Kidlington OX5 1UL* T: (01608) 842072 E: jan@stmaryscharlbury.co.uk

FIELDER, Joseph Neil. b 67. Univ of Wales BSc 89. Wycliffe Hall Ox 93. **d** 96 **p** 97. C Cheadle All Hallows *Ches* 96–00; V Preston St Steph *Blackb* 00–09; P-in-c Baxenden 09–12; Supernumerary P Blackb and Darwen Deanery 12–13; Chapl Bradf Teaching Hosps NHS Foundn Trust from 13. *St Luke's Hospital, Little Horton Lane, Bradford BD5 0NA* T: (01274) 365819 M: 07944-182058 E: joe.fielder@bthft.nhs.uk

FIELDGATE, John William Sheridan. b 44. St Jo Coll Dur BA 68. Ox NSM Course 75. **d** 79 **p** 80. NSM Haddenham w Cuddington, Kingsey etc *Ox* 79–90; C Northleach w Hampnett and Farmington *Glouc* 90–92; C Cold Aston w Notgrove and Turkdean 90–92; P-in-c Upper and Lower Slaughter w Eyford and Naunton 92–01; P-in-c The Guitings, Cutsdean and Farmcote 92–01; V Acton w Gt Waldingfield *St E* 01–09; rtd 09; PtO *St E* 09–13; *Chelmsf* from 09. *Patmos, 23 Woodfield Drive, West Mersea, Colchester CO5 8PX* T: (01206) 386851 E: j.fieldgate123@btinternet.com

FIELDING, Robert David. b 67. Liv Univ BA 89 St Jo Coll Dur BA 08. Cranmer Hall Dur 07. **d** 08 **p** 09. C Formby St Pet *Liv* 08–10; Chapl Mersey Care NHS Trust 10–14; PtO *Blackb* 14–15; P-in-c Read and Simonstone from 15. *The Vicarage, George Lane, Read, Burnley BB12 7RQ* T: (01282) 548908 M: 07951-173434 E: robertdfielding@gmail.com

FIELDING, Stephen Aubrey. b 67. Ulster Univ BSc 89 TCD BTh 93. CITC 90. **d** 93 **p** 94. C Bangor Abbey *D & D* 93–97; I Templepatrick w Donegore *Conn* 97–07; I Agherton 07–18; I Belfast Malone St Jo from 18. *St John's Rectory, 86 Maryville Park, Belfast BT9 6LQ* T: (028) 9066 6644 *or* 9066 7861 E: malone@connor.anglican.org *or* secstjohns@btconnect.com

FIELDING, Canon Stephen Lister. b 52. Ch Ch Ox BA 73 MA 77 Barrister 74. SAOMC 04. **d** 07 **p** 08. NSM Welwyn *St Alb* 07–11; TV Albury, Braughing, Furneux Pelham, Lt Hadham etc 11–14; Can Res Cov Cathl 14–16; C Kensington St Mary Abbots *Lon* 16–19. *4 Kensington Church Court, London W8 4SP* T: (020) 7937 4106 M: 07760-287614 E: slfielding@hotmail.com

FIELDSEND, John Henry. b 31. Nottm Univ BSc 54 Lon Univ BD 61. Lon Coll of Div ALCD 59. **d** 61 **p** 62. C Pennington *Man* 61–64; C Didsbury Ch Ch 64–66; P-in-c Bayston Hill

Lich 66–67; V 67–88; UK Dir CMJ 89–91; Dir and Min at Large CMJ 91–96; rtd 96; PtO *St Alb* 96–00; *Ox* 01–18. *58 Cedar Crescent, Thame OX9 2AU* T: (01844) 212559 E: jandefieldsend@btinternet.com

FIELDSON, Canon Robert Steven. b 56. Qu Coll Cam BA 78 MA 81 Wye Coll Lon MSc 79. St Jo Coll Nottm BA 86. **d** 87 **p** 88. C Walmley *Birm* 87–90; Chapl Protestant Ch in Oman 90–95; P-in-c Cofton Hackett w Barnt Green *Birm* 95–98; V from 98; AD Kings Norton 00–06 and from 16; Hon Can Birm Cathl from 14. *The Vicarage, 8 Cofton Church Lane, Barnt Green, Birmingham B45 8PT* T: 0121-445 1269 *or* 447 7097 E: rob@fieldson.co.uk

FIFE (née EVE), Hilary Anne. b 57. Lon Univ BEd 80. Ripon Coll Cuddesdon 89. **d** 91 **p** 94. Par Dn Coulsdon St Andr *S'wark* 91–94; C 94–95; Chapl Croydon Coll 92–94; Chapl Harestone Marie Curie Cen Caterham 94–98; Asst Chapl Mayday Healthcare NHS Trust Thornton Heath 94–02; Sen Chapl 02–10; Sen Chapl Croydon Health Services NHS Trust 10–18; Hon C Shirley St Geo *S'wark* from 08. *19 Greenview Avenue, Croydon CR0 7QW* T: (020) 8654 8685 *or* 8401 3105 E: hilary.fife@croydonhealth.nhs.uk *or* h.fife@nhs.uk *or* thefifes19@gmail.com

FIFE, Janet Heather. b 53. Sussex Univ BA 77 Man Univ MPhil 98. Wycliffe Hall Ox 84. **d** 87 **p** 94. Chapl Bradf Cathl 87–89; Par Dn York St Mich-le-Belfrey 89–92; Chapl Salford Univ *Man* 92–00; Hon TV Pendleton St Thos w Charlestown 92–95; Hon TV Pendleton 95–96; V Upton Priory *Ches* 00–10; P-in-c Marske in Cleveland *York* 10–14; rtd 14; PtO *York* from 15. *12 Waterstead Crescent, Whitby YO21 1PY* T: (01947) 459604 E: jhfife@icloud.com

FIFE, Mrs Miriam Ann. b 64. ERMC 14. **d** 17 **p** 18. C Launditch and the Upper Nar *Nor* from 17. *The Rectory, Great Dunham, King's Lynn PE32 2LQ* E: miriam.fife@btinternet.com

FIGG, Robin Arthur Rex. b 62. RN Eng Coll Plymouth BScEng 84. Westcott Ho Cam 91. **d** 94 **p** 95. C Old Cleeve, Leighland and Treborough *B & W* 94–97; C Gt Berkhamsted *St Alb* 97–01; V Kildwick *Bradf* 01–14; Leeds 14–17; V Warton St Oswald w Yealand Conyers *Blackb* from 17. *The Vicarage, 92 Main Street, Warton, Carnforth LA5 9PG* T: (01524) 732946 E: robin.figg62@gmail.com

FIKSEAUNET, Mrs Torhild Holen. b 81. Norwegian Univ of Science and Tech MTech 07 Oslo Univ BA 14. ERMC 16. **d** 19. C Heathfield *Chich* from 19. *The Vicarage, Old Heathfield, Heathfield TN21 9AB* T: (01435) 862687 M: 07587-295676 E: torhild.fikseaunet@yahoo.no

FILES, Ian James. b 54. Loughb Univ BSc 76. Chich Th Coll 85. **d** 87 **p** 88. C Prestwich St Mary *Man* 87–89; C Man Clayton St Cross w St Paul 89–91; PtO *Blackb* from 12. *16 Stanah Gardens, Thornton-Cleveleys FY5 5JH* T: (01253) 854482 M: 07578-547081 E: ianfiles101@gmail.com

FILIPE LOPES, Marco Gonzaga. b 73. St Mellitus Coll MA 19. **d** 19. C E Ham H Trin *Chelmsf* from 19. *34 St Martin's Avenue, London E6 3DX* M: 07506-926443 E: rev.marco.lopes@gmail.com

FILLERY, Paul Leslie. b 61. Ex Univ BTh 14. SWMTC 08. **d** 11 **p** 12. C Crediton, Shobrooke and Sandford etc *Ex* from 11; NSM 11–16. *12 Linhay Park, Sandford, Crediton EX17 4LL* T: (01363) 777372 E: paul@fillery.plus.com

FILLERY, William Robert. b 42. Univ of Wales (Swansea) BA 65 St D Coll Lamp BD 69 PGCE 72 Surrey Univ MA 96. Bp Burgess Hall Lamp 65. **d** 68 **p** 69. C Llangyfelach *S & B* 68–71; C Morriston 71–72; LtO *Ox* 73–76; Chapl Windsor Girls's Sch Hamm W Germany 76–81; OCM 79–81; Chapl Reed's Sch Cobham 81–86; V Oxshott *Guildf* 86–89; P-in-c Seale 89–91; P-in-c Puttenham and Wanborough 89–91; Hd RE Streatham Hill & Clapham Sch for Girls 91–93; V Llanybydder and Llanwenog w Llanllwni *St D* 03–10; rtd 10; PtO *St D* from 10. *Afon Del, Falcondale Drive, Lampeter SA48 7SB* T: (01570) 421425 M: 07792-958431 E: fillerybill@gmail.com

FILMER, Paul James. b 58. Open Univ BA 88. Aston Tr Scheme 93 Oak Hill Th Coll 95. **d** 97 **p** 98. C Petham and Waltham w Lower Hardres etc *Cant* 97–00; P-in-c Patrixbourne w Bridge and Bekesbourne 00–06; P-in-c Lower Hardres w Nackington 00–06; Chapl Univ of Greenwich *Roch* 06–09; Chapl Univ for the Creative Arts 06–09; V Yalding w Collier Street 09–15; Chapl Kenward Trust 11–15; PtO *Roch* 16–19; V Prince's Park from 19. *6 Thrush Close, Chatham ME5 7TG* M: 07951-773426 E: vicarchristtheking@gmail.com

FILTNESS, Trevor Moshe. b 50. MNI MInstD. STETS 05. **d** 08 **p** 09. NSM Farlington *Portsm* 08–11; NSM Rowlands Castle 11–13; P-in-c 13–18. *24 Orchard Road, Brixton, Plymouth PL8 2FE* M: 07785-568056 E: trevor@filtness.org

FINCH, Alan James. b 51. **d** 06 **p** 07. OLM Orrell Hey St Jo and St Jas *Liv* 06–15; NSM Litherland St Phil 15–18; NSM Litherland and Orrell Hey from 19. *1 Kirkstone Road North, Liverpool L21 7NP* T: 0151-928 3919

FINCH, Mrs Alison. b 59. SEN 79. Sarum & Wells Th Coll 90. **d** 92 **p** 94. Par Dn Banbury *Ox* 92–94; C 94–95; C Wokingham All SS 95–98; C Binfield 98–99; C St Peter-in-Thanet *Cant* 99–02; R Kirkwall and P-in-c Stromness *Ab* 02–05; Ind Chapl and C Colchester St Pet and St Botolph *Chelmsf* 05–13; TV High Wycombe *Ox* 13–18; rtd 18. *Address temp unknown* M: 07762-744977

FINCH, Canon David Walter. b 40. Cam Univ MA 74 FIBMS 69. Ridley Hall Cam. **d** 91 **p** 92. C Ixworth and Bardwell *St E* 91–92; C Blackbourne 92–94; P-in-c Stoke by Nayland w Leavenheath 94–00; P-in-c Polstead 95–00; P-in-c Fressingfield, Mendham, Metfield, Weybread etc 00–08; C Hoxne w Denham, Syleham and Wingfield 06–08; RD Hoxne 00–07; Hon Can St E Cathl 05–08; rtd 08; PtO *St E* from 08; LtO *Ab* 08–12; Hon C Cen Buchan 10–12. *3 Fleetwood Avenue, Felixstowe IP11 9HR* T: (01394) 277061 E: canondavidfinch@btinternet.com

FINCH, Frank. b 33. Qu Coll Birm 72. **d** 74 **p** 75. C Bilston St Leon *Lich* 74–78; R Sudbury and Somersal Herbert *Derby* 78–87; Chapl HM Pris Sudbury 78–87; HM Det Cen Foston Hall 80–87; V Lilleshall and Sheriffhales *Lich* 87–90; R The Ridwares and Kings Bromley 90–98; rtd 98; PtO *Lich* 00–19. *11 Ferrers Road, Yoxall, Burton-on-Trent DE13 8PS* T: (01543) 472065

FINCH, Jeffrey Walter. b 45. Man Univ BA(Econ) 66 Liv Univ DASE 80. Linc Th Coll 82. **d** 84 **p** 85. C Briercliffe *Blackb* 84–87; P-in-c Brindle and Asst Dir of Educn 87–93; V Laneside 93–00; TV Fellside Team 00–08; TR 08–14; rtd 14; PtO *Blackb* from 14. *21 Cock Robin Lane, Catterall, Preston PR3 1YL* T: (01995) 601171 E: jeffinch187@yahoo.com

FINCH, Morag Anne Hamilton. b 64. EAMTC 97. **d** 00 **p** 01. C Cranham *Chelmsf* 00–05; V Gidea Park 05–13; V Shortlands *Roch* 13–18; NSM Leiston *St E* from 18; Chapl St Eliz Hospice Ipswich from 19. *The Vicarage, Church Road, Leiston IP16 4HG* E: revfinch@btinternet.com

FINCH, Paul William. b 50. Oak Hill Th Coll Lon Bible Coll. **d** 75 **p** 76. C Hoole *Ches* 75–78; C Charlesworth *Derby* 78–87; C Charlesworth and Dinting Vale 87–88; TV Radipole and Melcombe Regis *Sarum* 88–01; V Malvern St Andr and Malvern Wells and Wyche *Worc* 01–14; TR Malvern Chase 14–15; rtd 15. *Address withheld by request* E: paulwfinch@gmail.com

FINCH, Richard William. b 62. Glos Univ MA 16. Westcott Ho Cam 95. **d** 97 **p** 98. C Saffron Walden w Wendens Ambo and Littlebury *Chelmsf* 97–00; C Elm Park St Nic Hornchurch 00–01; V 01–10; Chapl and Faith Support Officer Forest YMCA 10–15; Hon C Gidea Park *Chelmsf* 11–13; Public Preacher from 13; NSM Shortlands *Roch* 13–18; P-in-c Leiston *St E* from 18. *The Vicarage, Church Road, Leiston IP16 4HG* E: rich.w.finch@gmail.com

FINCH, Miss Rosemary Ann. b 39. Leeds Univ CertEd 60. **d** 93 **p** 94. OLM S Elmham and Ilketshall *St E* 93–00; Asst Chapl Ipswich Hosp NHS Trust 00–11; rtd 11; PtO *St E* 11–15; *Glouc* from 14. *Grace House, 15 Weston Park, Weston under Penyard, Ross-on-Wye HR9 7FR* T: (01989) 565019 E: revrosie.finch@btinternet.com

FINCH, Canon Stanley James. b 31. Mert Coll Ox BA 55 MA 58. Wells Th Coll 55. **d** 57 **p** 58. C Lancaster St Mary *Blackb* 57–61; C Leeds St Pet *Ripon* 61–65; V Habergham All SS *Blackb* 65–73; V S Shore H Trin 73–84; V Broughton 84–98; RD Preston 86–92; Hon Can Blackb Cathl 91–98; rtd 98; P-in-c Alderton, Gt Washbourne, Dumbleton etc *Glouc* 98–02; PtO from 02. *14 Bellflower Road, Walton Cardiff, Tewkesbury GL20 7SB* T: (01684) 850544 E: goldfinches14@yahoo.com

FINCHAM, Nicholas Charles. b 56. St Jo Coll Dur BA 78 MA 80. Westcott Ho Cam 80 Bossey Ecum Inst Geneva 81. **d** 82 **p** 83. C Seaham w Seaham Harbour *Dur* 82–85; C Lydney w Aylburton *Glouc* 85–87; C Isleworth All SS *Lon* 87–95; P-in-c Chiswick St Mich 95–10; rtd 10; PtO *Chich* from 16. *7 Harding Avenue, Eastbourne BN22 8PH* T: (01323) 638273 E: nicholas.fincham@talk21.com

FINDLAY, Canon Brian James. b 42. Wellington Univ (NZ) BA 62 MA 63 BMus 66 Magd Coll Ox MA 75. Qu Coll Birm. **d** 72 **p** 73. C Deptford St Paul *S'wark* 72–75; Fell and Dean of Div Magd Coll Ox 75–84; V Tonge Moor *Man* 84–02; Hon Can Man Cathl 00–03; R Monks Eleigh w Chelsworth and Brent Eleigh etc *St E* 03–11; rtd 11; PtO *Carl* from 13. *The Bull Pen, Hallthwaites, Millom LA18 5HP* T: (01229) 770049 E: briankirsty@btinternet.com

FINDLAY, James. b 68. Bp Otter Coll BA 90 Westmr Coll Ox PGCE 92. Wycliffe Hall Ox 02. **d** 04 **p** 05. C Gillingham St Mark *Roch* 04–07; P-in-c Salisbury St Mark *Sarum* 07–13; V Salisbury St Mark and Laverstock 13–17; Asst

Dioc Dir of Ords 13–17; P-in-c Throop *Win* from 17. *1 Chesildene Avenue, Bournemouth BH8 0AZ* T: (01202) 525525 M: 07854-510569 E: office@stpaulsthroop.com *or* vicarjimfindlay@gmail.com

FINDLAYSON, Roy. b 44. Man Univ MA 89 CQSW 69. Sarum & Wells Th Coll 80. **d** 82 **p** 83. C Benwell St Jas *Newc* 82–83; Hon C 83–85; C Morpeth 85–88; C N Gosforth 88; TV Ch the King 88–94; V Newc St Fran 94–98; Asst Chapl Newcastle upon Tyne Hosps NHS Trust 98–06; rtd 06. *3 Balmoral Terrace, Stockton-on-Tees TS18 4DD* T: (01642) 601702 E: findlayson44@icloud.com

FINDLEY, Peter. b 55. Trin Coll Ox BA 77 MA 80 Barrister-at-Law (Gray's Inn) 78. Trin Coll Bris 90. **d** 92 **p** 93. C Yateley *Win* 92–97; V Westwood *Cov* 97–14; P-in-c Canley 09–14; Sen Miss P Philadelphia St Thos *Sheff* from 14. *30 Victoria Road, Sheffield S10 2DL* T: 0114-214 9560 E: peterfindley@ncsheffield.org

FINDON, John Charles. b 50. Keble Coll Ox BA 71 MA 75 DPhil 79. Ripon Coll Cuddesdon. **d** 77 **p** 78. C Middleton *Man* 77–80; Lect Bolton St Pet 80–83; V Astley 83–91; V Baguley 91–98; P-in-c Bury St Mary 98–05; R 05–17; rtd 17; PtO *Ox* from 17. *78 Oxford Road, Littlemore, Oxford OX4 4PE* T: (01865) 424356 E: john.findon@virginmedia.com

FINK-JENSEN, Thomas Karel. b 86. Ede Chr Coll BEd 11. Wycliffe Hall Ox BA 18. **d** 19. C Lancing St Mich *Chich* from 19. *1 Annington Gardens, Shoreham-by-Sea BN43 5GS* E: revthomasfj@gmail.com

FINLAY, Alison Mary. *See* CAW, Alison Mary

FINLAY, Canon Hueston Edward. b 64. TCD BA 85 BAI 85 BTh 89 MA 92 Cam Univ MA 98 Lon Univ PhD 98. CITC 86. **d** 89 **p** 90. C Kilkenny w Aghour and Kilmanagh *C & O* 89–92; Bp's Dom Chapl 89–92; Bp's V and Lib Kilkenny Cathl 90–92; Chapl Girton Coll Cam 92–95; C Cambridge Gt St Mary w St Mich *Ely* 92–95; Chapl and Fell Magd Coll Cam 95–99; Dean of Chpl 99–04; Can Windsor from 04; Treas St Patr Cathl Dublin 11–16. *8 The Cloisters, Windsor Castle, Windsor SL4 1NJ* T: (01753) 867094 F: 833806 E: hueston.finlay@stgeorges-windsor.org

FINLAY, Malcolm Armstrong. b 85. Univ Coll Lon BSc 10. Wycliffe Hall Ox BTh 13. **d** 13 **p** 14. C Southall Green St Jo *Lon* 13–16; C Broxbourne w Wormley *St Alb* 16–19; PtO *Lon* 16–19; LtO from 19. *69 Southdown Crescent, Harrow HA2 0QT* M: 07460-866562 E: rev.malcolm.finlay@gmail.com

FINLAY, Canon Michael Stanley. b 45. NOC 78. **d** 81 **p** 82. C Padgate *Liv* 81–85; V Newton-le-Willows 85–90; V Orford St Marg 90–98; P-in-c Warrington St Elphin 98–00; R 00–11; Hon Can Liv Cathl 07–11; rtd 11; PtO *Ches* from 12. *40 Chatteris Park, Runcorn WA7 1XE* T: (01928) 579354 E: finlay289@btinternet.com

FINLAY, Nicholas. b 47. Regent Coll Vancouver MCS 00. St Jo Coll Nottm 01. **d** 02 **p** 03. C Haydock St Mark *Liv* 02–03; C Bootle 03–04; Lic to Adn Warrington 04–05; V Sittingbourne St Mary and St Mich *Cant* 05–09; rtd 09; C Upper Ithon Valley and Lower Ithon Valley *S & B* 09–12; PtO *St D* from 11; *S & B* from 12; *Heref* 12–16; *Lich* 13–19. *31 Fosbrooke House, 8 Clifton Drive, Lytham St Annes FY8 5RQ* T: (01253) 667012 M: 07771-688812 E: nick.finlay047@gmail.com

FINLAYSON, Mrs Gladys Victoria. b 49. TCert 67. ERMC 05. **d** 09 **p** 10. NSM Luton St Anne w St Chris *St Alb* 09–11; PtO from 11. *St Andrew's Vicarage, 11 Blenheim Crescent, Luton LU3 1HA* T: (01582) 732380 E: gladysfinlayson@sky.com

FINLAYSON, Grantley Adrian. b 55. Wilson Carlile Coll 74 Chich Th Coll 87. **d** 89 **p** 90. C Watford St Mich *St Alb* 89–92; TV W Slough *Ox* 92–97; Dioc Officer for Race Relations *Glouc* 97–02; V Luton St Andr *St Alb* from 02. *St Andrew's Vicarage, 11 Blenheim Crescent, Luton LU3 1HA* T/F: (01582) 481711 E: grantleyfinlayson11@sky.com

FINLINSON, Paul. b 58. St Chad's Coll Dur BA 79 St Martin's Coll Lanc PGCE 81. Carl Dioc Tr Course 86. **d** 89 **p** 90. NSM Kirkby Lonsdale *Carl* 89–99; Chapl Worksop Coll Notts 99–19; Chapl Ranby Ho Sch Retford 11–19; PtO *Blackb* from 95; *Carl* 14–19; *Eur* from 19. *Address temp unknown*

FINN, Andrew David. b 79. Cant Ch Ch Univ Coll BA 00 PGCE 01 Glos Univ MA 14. Ridley Hall Cam 13. **d** 15 **p** 16. C Ingatestone w Fryerning *Chelmsf* 15–17; C Margaretting w Mountnessing and Buttsbury 15–17; C Gt Baddow 17–18; P-in-c Southsea St Simon *Portsm* from 18. *St Simon's Vicarage, 6 Festing Road, Southsea PO4 0NG* M: 07818-675100 E: revandyfinn@outlook.com

FINN, Gordon Frederick. b 33. Dur Univ BA 60. Ely Th Coll 60. **d** 62 **p** 63. C Kingswinford St Mary *Lich* 62–65; C Northampton St Mary *Pet* 65–67; Chapl Barnsley Hall Hosp Bromsgrove 67–71; Chapl Lea Hosp Bromsgrove 67–71; C Swanage *Sarum* 71–73; P-in-c Ford End *Chelmsf*

73–79; V S Shields St Oswin *Dur* 79–98; rtd 98. *58 Hutton Lane, Guisborough TS14 8AW* T: (01287) 619132 E: gffin@talktalk.net

FINN, Canon Ian Michael. b 58. AKC. Chich Th Coll 81. **d** 82 **p** 83. C Habergham All SS *Blackb* 82–83; C W Burnley All SS 83–85; C Torrisholme 85–87; V Lancaster Ch Ch w St Jo and St Anne 87–91; P-in-c Tillingham and Dengie w Asheldham *Chelmsf* 91–97; Chapl R Gr Sch Worc 97–99; P-in-c Denston w Stradishall and Stansfield *St E* 99–01; P-in-c Wickhambrook w Lydgate, Ousden and Cowlinge 00–01; R Bansfield 02–07; V Haverhill w Withersfield 07–19; RD Clare 06–17; Hon Can St E Cathl 11–19; rtd 19. *Huggens College, College Road, Northfleet, Gravesend DA11 9DL* E: ian.finn1@btinternet.com

FINN, Mrs Jane Lisa. b 65. Open Univ BSc 14. Coll of Resurr Mirfield BA 18. **d** 18 **p** 19. C Halifax w Siddal *Leeds* from 18. *41 Gibraltar Road, Halifax HX1 4HE* T: (01422) 355436 E: j.finn@halifaxminster.org.uk

FINN, Miss Sheila. b 30. LMH Ox BA 68 MA 69. Gilmore Ho 68. **dss** 78 **d** 87 **p** 94. Tettenhall Wood *Lich* 78–86; Dioc Ecum Officer 86–95; The Ridwares and Kings Bromley 86–87; Par Dn 87–94; C 94–95; rtd 95; PtO *Lich* from 97. *56 Pencric, Tildesley Close, Penkridge, Stafford ST19 5FG*

FINNEMORE, James Christopher. b 59. Pemb Coll Cam BA 81 MA 85. Coll of Resurr Mirfield. **d** 85 **p** 86. C Manston *Ripon* 85–88; C Hessle *York* 88–92; R Bishop Wilton w Full Sutton, Kirby Underdale etc 92–99; R Garrowby Hill 99–16; RD S Wold 07–12; PtO *Ox* from 17; *B & W* from 16; *York* from 16. *2 Carey Close, Oxford OX2 8HX* T: (01865) 558480 E: j.c.finnemore@btinternet.com

FINNERTY, Cynthia Ann. b 46. **d** 05 **p** 06. OLM E Greenwich *S'wark* 05–16; PtO from 16. *33 Ruthin Road, London SE3 7SJ* T: (020) 8858 2883 E: cynthiafin@hotmail.com

✠**FINNEY, The Rt Revd John Thornley.** b 32. Hertf Coll Ox BA 55. Wycliffe Hall Ox 56. **d** 58 **p** 59 **c** 93. C Highfield *Ox* 58–61; C Weston Turville 61–65; R Tollerton *S'well* 65–71; V Aspley 71–80; Bp's Adv on Evang 80–89; Bp's Research Officer 88–89; Hon Can S'well Minster 84–89; Officer for Decade of Evang in C of E 90–93; Suff Bp Pontefract *Wakef* 93–98; rtd 98; Hon Asst Bp S'well and Nottm from 98. *Greenacre, Crow Lane, South Muskham, Newark NG23 6DZ* T/F: (01636) 679791 E: john.finney2@talktalk.net

FINNIMORE, Keith Anthony. b 36. AKC 59. **d** 60 **p** 61. C Wanstead H Trin Hermon Hill *Chelmsf* 60–63; C Kingswood *S'wark* 63–65; V Bolney *Chich* 65–67; V Elmstead *Chelmsf* 67–73; R Pentlow, Foxearth, Liston and Borley 73–77; NSM Cockfield w Bradfield St Clare, Felsham etc *St E* 89–91; R Hawstead and Nowton w Stanningfield etc 91–96; P-in-c 96–01; rtd 96; PtO *St E* 01–09; *Chelmsf* from 09. *52B Summerhill Road, Saffron Walden CB11 4AJ* T: (01799) 521763

FIRBANK, Michael John. b 73. R Holloway Coll Lon BA 94 St Mary's Coll Twickenham PGCE 94. St Jo Coll Nottm MTh 05. **d** 05 **p** 06. C St Illogan *Truro* 05–07; P-in-c Camborne 07–13; P-in-c Tuckingmill 12–13; R Camborne and Tuckingmill 13–14; V Gresley *Derby* from 14. *The Vicarage, 120 Church Street, Church Gresley, Swadlincote DE11 9NR* T: (01283) 208947 M: 07814-033183 E: mjfirbank@hotmail.com

FIRMIN, Paul Gregory. b 57. Win Univ MA 11 ACIB 80. Trin Coll Bris BA 87. **d** 87 **p** 88. C Swindon Ch Ch *Bris* 87–91; V Shrewsbury H Trin w St Julian *Lich* 91–99; V Astley, Clive, Grinshill and Hadnall 99–01; V Southampton St Mary Extra *Win* 01–10; V Shrewsbury H Cross *Lich* 10–18; rtd 18. *Police House, Railway Road, Brymbo, Wrexham LL11 5EA* E: nimrifs@sky.com

FIRMSTONE, Ian Harry. b 44. Qu Coll Birm. **d** 82 **p** 83. C Warminster St Denys *Sarum* 82–84; C N Stoneham *Win* 84–88; R Freemantle 88–90; V Littleport *Ely* 90–91; TV Stanground and Farcet 91–97; P-in-c Holme w Conington 95–96; rtd 97; PtO *Worc* from 12; *Birm* 15–18. *Cotswold Cottage, School Lane, Alvechurch, Birmingham B48 7SA* T: 0121-445 1318 E: ianfirmstone@gmail.com

FIRTH, Mrs Ann Neswyn. b 40. St As Minl Tr Course 95. **d** 98 **p** 99. NSM Llanidloes w Llangurig *Ban* 98–05; LtO 05–11; PtO 11–18. *Springfield, Westgate Street, Llanidloes SY18 6HJ* T: (01686) 413098

FIRTH, Christopher John Kingsley. b 37. St Mich Coll Llan. **d** 66 **p** 67. C Sutton in Ashfield St Mary *S'well* 66–70; V Langold 70–74; C Falmouth K Chas *Truro* 74–77; P-in-c Mabe 77–81; V 81–95; RD Carnmarth S 90–94; rtd 99. *1 Boscawen, Cliff Road, Falmouth TR11 4AW* T: (01326) 316734

FIRTH, Geoffrey David. b 74. Lincs & Humberside Univ BA 96. Oak Hill Th Coll BA 08. **d** 06 **p** 07. C Poynton *Ches* 06–10; Chapl RAF from 10. *Chaplaincy Services (RAF), HQ Air Command, RAF High Wycombe HP14 4UE* T: (01494) 496800 E: geoffrey.firth485@mod.gov.uk *or* geoffreyfirth@gmail.com

FIRTH, Mrs Jennifer Anne. b 52. Goldsmiths' Coll Lon BMus 75 Kingston Poly PGCE 83. **d** 07 **p** 08. OLM Dorking St Paul *Guildf* from 07. *33 Downsview Gardens, Dorking RH4 2DX* T: (01306) 887051 M: 07970-102987 E: jennyafirth@aol.com *or* jenny@stpaulsdorking.org.uk

FIRTH, Matthew Paul. b 83. Magd Coll Cam BA 04 MA 08. Wycliffe Hall Ox BTh 09. **d** 09 **p** 10. C Triangle, St Matt and All SS *St E* 09–12; Chapl Cumbria Univ *Carl* 12–17; 18-30 Pioneer Min 12–17; P-in-c Darlington St Cuth *Dur* from 18; P-in-c Darlington H Trin from 18. *26 Upsall Drive, Darlington DL3 8RB* T: (01325) 353614 M: 07932-482929 E: mpf1983@hotmail.com

FIRTH, Neswyn. *See* FIRTH, Ann Neswyn

✠**FIRTH, The Rt Revd Peter James.** b 29. Em Coll Cam BA 52 MA 63. St Steph Ho Ox 53. **d** 55 **p** 56 **c** 83. C Barbourne *Worc* 55–58; C Malvern Link St Matthias 58–62; R Abbey Hey *Man* 62–66; Asst Network Relig Broadcasting BBC Man 66–67; Sen Producer/Org Relig Progr TV & Radio BBC Bris 67–83; Hon Can Bris Cathl 74–83; Suff Bp Malmesbury 83–94; Angl Adv HTV West 84–94; rtd 94; Hon Asst Bp Glouc from 03; Hon Asst Bp Bris from 09. *Mill House, Silk Mill Lane, Winchcombe, Cheltenham GL54 5HZ* T: (01242) 603669

FIRTH, Peter William Simpson. b 39. SEITE 99. **d** 11. NSM New Romney w Old Romney and Midley *Cant* 11–12; NSM Romney Marsh 12–14; rtd 14; PtO *Cant* 15–16. *114 Leonard Road, Greatstone, New Romney TN28 8RZ* T: (01797) 367296 E: firth166@btinternet.com

FIRTH, Canon Rachel Naomi. b 73. Huddersfield Univ BA 97 Leeds Univ BA 08 Sheff Univ MA 12. NOC 05. **d** 08 **p** 09. C Halifax *Wakef* 08–11; V Lindley 11–14; *Leeds* from 14; Adv for Women's Min Huddersfield Area from 15; Hon Can Wakef Cathl from 19. *The Vicarage, 2 The Clock Tower, Lidget Street, Huddersfield HD3 3JB* T: (01484) 645695 E: vicaroflindley@hotmail.co.uk

FIRTH, Richard Geoffrey. b 48. **d** 06 **p** 07. OLM Dur St Marg and Neville's Cross St Jo 06–08; PtO *York* from 08. *6 Vicarage Close, Seamer, Scarborough YO12 4QS* T: (01723) 867957 E: afirth9819@aol.com

FISH, Mrs Jacqueline Wendy. b 42. NTMTC 02. **d** 04 **p** 05. NSM Enfield Chase St Mary *Lon* 04–19; PtO from 19. *41 Churchbury Lane, Enfield EN1 3TX* T: (020) 8366 2235 E: jacquiefishie@aol.com

FISH, Michael. b 61. Lanc Univ BA 05. CBDTI 01. **d** 04 **p** 05. NSM Blackb St Mich w St Jo and H Trin 04–07; NSM Blackb St Thos w St Jude 04–07; P-in-c Cen Buchan *Ab* 07–08; P-in-c Shrewsbury All SS w St Mich *Lich* 08–16; TV Swinton and Pendlebury *Man* 16–18; V Blackfordby and Woodville *Leic* from 18. *The Vicarage, 11 Vicarage Close, Blackfordby, Swadlincote DE11 8AZ* M: 07867-760110 E: fr.michaelfish@btinternet.com

FISH, Thomas Ronald Huxley. b 59. Chu Coll Cam BA 81. Oak Hill Th Coll 11. **d** 13 **p** 14. C The Lye and Stambermill *Worc* 13–19; TV Wednesfield *Lich* from 19. *The Vicarage, St Albans House, Griffiths Drive, Wolverhampton WV11 2LJ* E: tomhelen@2fishes.org.uk

FISHER, Ms Alexandria Compton. b 53. Glas Univ MA 75. St Mellitus Coll 14. **d** 17 **p** 18. NSM Wilmslow *Ches* 17–18; C Brereton from 18. *The Rectory, Brereton Park, Brereton, Sandbach CW11 1RY* T: (01477) 533263 M: 07456-433103 E: fishersandi123@gmail.com

FISHER, Mrs Alison. b 48. Cranmer Hall Dur 04. **d** 05 **p** 06. NSM The Thorntons and The Otteringtons *York* 05–11; rtd 11; PtO *York* from 11. *31 Church Close, Marske-by-the-Sea, Redcar TS11 7AW* T: (01642) 488682 E: ali.fisher913@btinternet.com

FISHER, Andrew John. b 72. St Jo Coll Nottm BA 02 St Mich Coll Llan MTh 13. **d** 02 **p** 03. C Ilkeston St Jo *Derby* 02–05; P-in-c Hodge Hill *Birm* 05–08; Chapl Worcs Acute Hosps NHS Trust 08–13; V Wood End *Cov* 13–17; R Bulwell St Mary *S'well* from 17. *The Rectory, Station Road, Bulwell, Nottingham NG6 9AA* T: 0115-975 5358 E: a.j.fisher@outlook.com

FISHER, Brian Robert. b 36. **d** 02 **p** 03. OLM Sole Bay *St E* 02–07; rtd 07; PtO *St E* from 07. *Green Gates, The Street, Walberswick, Southwold IP18 6UH* T: (01502) 723023 M: 07766-216111 E: fishell@btopenworld.com

FISHER, David Benjamin. b 52. Bp Lonsdale Coll CertEd 74. Chich Th Coll 75. **d** 78 **p** 79. C Dovecot *Liv* 78–81; C Weymouth St Paul *Sarum* 81–82; R Lower Broughton Ascension *Man* 82–86; PtO *S'well* 10–14; *Derby* 14–15; P-in-c Salisbury St Martin *Sarum* 15–18; V from 18. *The Rectory, 42 Tollgate Road, Salisbury SP1 2JJ* T: (01722) 500896 M: 07734-200314 E: benevans002@mac.com

FISHER, David Stephen. b 66. Ripon Coll Cuddesdon BTh 99. **d** 98 **p** 99. C Stockport SW *Ches* 98–01; V Gatley 01–06; V Gt Sutton 06–13; RD Wirral S 11–13; Can and Prec Ban Cathl 13–18; Hon C Bro Deiniol 16–18; P-in-c Carshalton

FISHER, Eric Henry George. b 48. NTMTC 94. **d** 97 **p** 98. NSM Heydon, Gt and Lt Chishill, Chrishall etc *Chelmsf* 97–03; P-in-c Gt Oakley w Wix and Wrabness 03–08; rtd 08; PtO *Chelmsf* 09–15; *St E* from 09. *Sheldon, 12 Joseph Close, Hadleigh, Ipswich IP7 5FH* T: (01473) 832626 E: eric.fisher@ukgateway.net

FISHER, Eric William. b 30. Birm Univ BA 53. Coll of Resurr Mirfield 70. **d** 72 **p** 73. C Styvechale *Cov* 72–75; C Chesterfield St Mary and All SS *Derby* 75–78; Chapl Buxton Hosps 78–84; TV Buxton w Burbage and King Sterndale *Derby* 78–84; R Shirland 84–89; V Sheff St Matt 89–95; rtd 95; PtO *Lich* 95–15. *6 Wickstead Row, Main Road, Betley, Crewe CW3 9AB* T: (01270) 820653

FISHER, George Arnold. b 54. Lon Univ BD 75. NOC 81. **d** 84 **p** 85. C Conisbrough *Sheff* 84–92; V Blackpool St Thos *Blackb* 92–07; Dir Par Miss *Lich* 07–19; Hon C Walsall St Matt 07–19; rtd 19. *14 Lowther Close, Eastbourne BN23 8EZ* M: 07814-166951

FISHER, Gordon. b 44. NW Ord Course 74. **d** 77 **p** 78. NSM Airedale w Fryston *Wakef* 77–81; C Barkisland w W Scammonden 81–84; C Ripponden 81–84; V Sutton St Mich *York* 84–87; V Marton-in-Cleveland 87–96; R Kettering SS Pet and Paul 96–02; rtd 02. *8 Mount Pleasant Avenue, Marske-by-the-Sea, Redcar TS11 7BW* T: (01642) 489489

FISHER, Ian St John. b 59. Down Coll Cam BA 80 MA 84 Leic Univ PhD 84. St Steph Ho Ox BA 88. **d** 88 **p** 89. C Colwall w Upper Colwall and Coddington *Heref* 88–91; Chapl Surrey Univ *Guildf* 92–97; V Hurst *Man* 97–04; V N Shoebury *Chelmsf* 04–15; rtd 15; PtO *Chelmsf* 15–17; TV Linton *Ely* from 17. *The Camps Vicarage, Park Lane, Castle Camps, Cambridge CB21 4SR* T: (01799) 585977 E: ian.fisher@btconnect.com *or* ian59fisher@btinternet.com

FISHER, Mrs Joan. b 52. **d** 00 **p** 01. NSM Blackpool St Mark *Blackb* 00–04; NSM Blackpool St Thos 04–07; C Aldridge *Lich* 08–14; rtd 14; PtO *Lich* from 17. *14 Lowther Close, Eastbourne BN23 8EZ*

FISHER, John. b 62. **d** 16 **p** 17. C Darton w Staincross and Mapplewell *Leeds* 16–19. *Address temp unknown* E: john_fisher_801@outlook.com

FISHER, John Andrew. b 63. Bath Univ BSc 85 MA 97. Wycliffe Hall Ox BA 93. **d** 94 **p** 95. C Rayleigh *Chelmsf* 94–98; V Burton Joyce w Bulcote and Stoke Bardolph *S'well* 98–09; AD Gedling 00–05; Regional Leadership Adv (Midl) CPAS 09–11; Patr Sec 11–19; PtO *Sheff* 10–13; *York* 10–15; Dioc Dir of Ords *Ex* from 19. *The Bishop's Office, Palace Gate House, Palace Gate, Exeter EX1 1HX* T: (01392) 477702 E: john.fisher@exeter.anglican.org

FISHER, Mark Simon. b 52. K Coll Lon BD 76 AKC 76 Trin Coll Ox MA 82 DPhil 83. Kelham Th Coll 70 Perkins Sch of Th (USA) 76. **d** 78 **p** 78. SSF 78–80; Hon C Victoria Docks Ascension *Chelmsf* 78–79; LtO *Eur* 78–80; LtO *Lon* 78–80; LtO *Ox* 78–87; Chapl LMH Ox 80–86; R Glas St Matt 87–89; Hon Asst P W Derby St Jo *Liv* 97–05. *29A Rodney Street, Liverpool L1 9EH* T: 0151-707 9748

FISHER, Mary Christine. b 43. Bris Univ BA 64. LCTP 07. **d** 08 **p** 09. NSM Heaton St Barn *Bradf* 08–13; PtO 13–14; *Leeds* from 14. *423 Toller Lane, Bradford BD9 5NN* T: (01274) 541238

FISHER, Canon Michael Harry. b 39. Ex Univ BA 61. St Steph Ho Ox 61. **d** 63 **p** 64. C Wolverhampton St Pet *Lich* 63–67; C Newquay *Truro* 67–70; V Newlyn St Pet 70–75; P-in-c Launceston St Steph w St Thos 75–82; V Carbis Bay w Lelant 82–95; V Newquay 95–99; Hon Can Truro Cathl 85–99; RD Penwith 88–93; Chapl Costa del Sol W *Eur* 99–00; rtd 00; PtO *Truro* from 00; *Eur* 04–17. *Chymedda, Southway, Windmill, Padstow PL28 8RN* T: (01841) 521544 M: 07970-865049 E: mfisher39@aol.com

FISHER, Michael John. b 43. Leic Univ BA 64 Keele Univ MA 67. Qu Coll Birm 75. **d** 78 **p** 79. NSM Stafford St Mary and St Chad *Lich* 78–79; NSM Stafford 79–13; rtd 13; PtO *Lich* from 14. *35 Newland Avenue, Stafford ST16 1NL* T: (01785) 245069 E: mfisher25001@btinternet.com

FISHER, Nicholas. b 48. Newc Univ BA 71 MLitt 87 Man Univ MA 98 Leeds Univ PhD 04 Birm Univ BA 09. Qu Coll Birm 06. **d** 08 **p** 09. NSM Northleach w Hampnett and Farmington etc *Glouc* 08–13; P-in-c Sherborne, Windrush, the Barringtons etc 13–16; V 16–19; Dioc NSM Officer 13–19; rtd 19. *Providence House, High Street, Northleach, Cheltenham GL54 3EU* T: (01451) 861195 E: nick@5fishers.co.uk

FISHER, Paul Vincent. b 43. Worc Coll Ox BA 66 MA 70 ARCM 73. Qu Coll Birm. **d** 70 **p** 71. C Redditch St Steph *Worc* 70–73; C Chorlton upon Medlock *Man* 73–79; Chapl Man Univ 73–79; Exec Sec Community Affairs Division BCC 79–81; Asst Dir of Tr and Dir of Lay Tr *Carl*

81–86; P-in-c Raughton Head w Gatesgill 81–85; Lay Tr Team Ldr *S'wark* 86–90; Dir of Tr 90–94; V Kingswood 94–00; rtd 00; PtO *Bradf* 01–14; *Leeds* 14–16. *3 Buxton Park, Langcliffe, Settle BD24 9NQ* T: (01729) 824058 E: paul.v.fisher@btconnect.com

FISHER, Canon Peter Timothy. b 44. Dur Univ BA 68 MA 75. Cuddesdon Coll 68. **d** 70 **p** 71. C Bedford St Andr *St Alb* 70–74; Chapl Surrey Univ *Guildf* 74–78; Sub-Warden Linc Th Coll 78–83; R Houghton le Spring *Dur* 83–94; RD Houghton 87–92; Prin Qu Coll Birm 94–02; V Maney *Birm* 02–10; Hon Can Birm Cathl 00–10; rtd 10; PtO *Leeds* from 17. *Eden, Unicorn View, Bowes, Barnard Castle DL12 9HW* T: (01833) 628001

FISHER, Richard John. b 60. K Coll Lon BA 82 AKC 82 Selw Coll Cam BA 87 MA 95. Ridley Hall Cam 85. **d** 88 **p** 89. C Woodley St Jo the Ev *Ox* 88–91; C Acomb St Steph and St Aid *York* 91–95; Chapl Preston Acute Hosps NHS Trust 98–02; Chapl Lancs Teaching Hosps NHS Trust 02–06; PtO *Blackb* 08–09; NSM Rufford and Tarleton 09; C Loughton St Jo *Chelmsf* 09–18; TV Smestow Vale *Lich* from 18. *The Vicarage, School Road, Trysull, Wolverhampton WV5 7HR* T: (01902) 476843 E: vicarage@trysullchurch.org.uk

FISHER, Sandi. *See* FISHER, Alexandria Compton

FISHER, Mrs Sheila Janet. b 50. WEMTC 01. **d** 04 **p** 05. NSM Cam w Stinchcombe *Glouc* 04–11; NSM Thornbury and Oldbury-on-Severn w Shepperdine 11–15; rtd 15; PtO *Glouc* from 16. *Court Hayes, Rockhampton, Berkeley GL13 9DU* T: (01454) 269700 E: ashmead.fishers@btinternet.com

FISHER, Canon Simon John Plumley. b 80. St Jo Coll Dur BA 01. Ripon Coll Cuddesdon BA 04. **d** 05 **p** 06. C Bath Bathwick *B & W* 05–09; P-in-c Brigstock w Stanion and Lowick and Sudborough *Pet* 09–11; P-in-c Weldon w Deene 09–11; V W Derby St Jo *Liv* from 11; Hon Can Liv Cathl from 19. *The Vicarage, 685 West Derby Road, Liverpool L13 0BH* T: 0151-228 2023 M: 07525-617067 E: frsimonfisher@gmail.com

FISHER, Stephen Newson. b 46. Univ of Wales (Swansea) BSc 67 CEng 82 MIET 82. Linc Th Coll 84. **d** 86 **p** 87. C Nunthorpe *York* 86–89; P-in-c Middlesbrough St Oswald 89–90; V 90–94; V Redcar 94–02; P-in-c The Thorntons and The Otteringtons 02–11; Chapl N Yorks Police 01–11; PtO *Bradf* 02–11; rtd 11; PtO *York* from 11. *31 Church Close, Marske-by-the-Sea, Redcar TS11 7AW* T: (01642) 488682 E: stephen.fisher913@btinternet.com

FISHER, Stuart Frederick. b 48. **d** 11 **p** 12. OLM Swindon Dorcan *Bris* from 11; Chapl Swindon Coll from 16; PtO *Ox* 15–17 and from 18. *30 Blakeney Avenue, Swindon SN3 3NL* T: (01793) 497169 M: 07774-205640 E: sfisher111@btinternet.com

FISHER, Susan. b 49. Yorks Min Course 09. **d** 11. NSM Gomersal *Wakef* 11–12; NSM Griffin, Mango Hill and North Lakes Australia 12–13; C Culburra Beach, Callala and Currarong, NSW from 14. *21 Stott Crescent, Callala Bay, NSW 2540, Australia* T: (0061) (02) 8886 6684 M: 40-681 5449 E: sue@culburraanglican.asn.au

FISHER, Susan Alexandra. *See* NORTON, Susan Alexandra

FISHER, Thomas Ruggles. b 20. Cranmer Hall Dur 58. **d** 60 **p** 61. C Melton Mowbray w Thorpe Arnold *Leic* 60–63; R Husbands Bosworth 63–74; R Husbands Bosworth w Mowsley and Knaptoft etc 74–82; PtO 82–96; *Pet* 83–04; rtd 85. *12 The Dell, Oakham LE15 6JG* T: (01572) 757630 E: rigglesfisher@outlook.com

FISHER-BAILEY, Mrs Carol. b 56. **d** 96 **p** 97. C Eccleshill *Bradf* 96–99; TV Sutton St Jas and Wawne *York* 99–12; V Wawne 12; V Keyingham w Ottringham and Sunk Island 12–14; V Easington w Skeffling, Keyingham, Ottringham etc 14–19; R Lockington and Lund and Scorborough w Leconfield from 19. *Rectory House, 41 Church Lane, Lockington, Driffield YO25 9SU* E: ladyvicar@gmail.com

FISHLOCK, Christopher Douglas. b 70. Anglia Poly BA 91. Oak Hill Th Coll BA 06. **d** 07. C St Helen Bishopsgate w St Andr Undershaft etc *Lon* 07–12; C St Andr-by-the-Wardrobe w St Ann, Blackfriars and St Martin Ludgate from 12. *St Nicholas Cole Abbey, 114 Queen Victoria Street, London EC4V 4BJ* T: (020) 7248 5213 E: cfishlock@stnickstalks.org *or* chris@stnickschurch.org.uk

FISHWICK, Raymond Allen. b 42. St Fran Coll Brisbane 93 N Queensland Coll of Min ACP 96. **d** 91 **p** 92. P-in-c Charters Towers Australia 92–94; R 94–97; P-in-c Worthen *Heref* 98–02; P-in-c Hope w Shelve 98–02; P-in-c Middleton 98–02; P-in-c Weipa Australia 02–04; P-in-c Innisfail 04–08; CF 02–08; rtd 08. *217 Edward Road, Eagleton WA 6530, Australia* T: (0061) (8) 9921 5537 E: rfi64412@bigpond.net.au

FISKE, Paul Francis Brading. b 45. St Jo Coll Dur BA 68 PhD 72. Wycliffe Hall Ox 72. **d** 73 **p** 74. C Sutton *Liv*

73–76; TV Cheltenham St Mary, St Matt, St Paul and H Trin *Glouc* 76–80; C-in-c Hartplain CD *Portsm* 80–84; Hd of Miss UK CMJ 84–86; Hon C Edgware *Lon* 84–86; R Broughton Gifford, Gt Chalfield and Holt *Sarum* 86–95; TV Bourne Valley 95–97; Adv Chr Action 95–97; P-in-c Princes Risborough w Ilmer *Ox* 97–98; TR Risborough 98–08; rtd 08; PtO *Cov* 09–17; *Roch* from 17. *106 Ralph Perring Court, Stone Park Avenue, Beckenham BR3 3LX* M: 07969-112305 E: revpaulfiske@gmail.com

FISKEAUNET, Torhild. *See* FIKSEAUNET, Torhild Holen

FITCH, Capt Alan John. b 45. Open Univ BA 82 Warwick Univ MA 84. Wilson Carlile Coll 64 Qu Coll Birm 92. **d** 92 **p** 93. CA from 66; C Glouc St Jas and All SS 92–97; NSM Wotton St Mary 93–97; V Douglas All SS and St Thos *S & M* 97–02; Chapl HM Pris Is of Man 97–02; TR Walbrook Epiphany *Derby* 02–09; rtd 09; PtO *Derby* from 09; Dioc Adv on Racial Justice from 02. *16 Nether Slade Road, Ilkeston DE7 8ET* T: 0115-930 5768 E: iom123@btinternet.com *or* alaniomfitch@gmail.com

FITTER, Matthew Douglas. b 59. City of Lon Poly BSc 81. Trin Coll Bris MA 03. **d** 03 **p** 04. C Purley Ch Ch *S'wark* 03–07; C Beckenham Ch Ch *Roch* 07–10; TR Anerley from 10; P-in-c Penge St Jo 13–17. *The Vicarage, 234 Anerley Road, London SE20 8TJ* T: (020) 8778 4800 E: matthewfitter@hotmail.com

FITTER, Mrs Ruth Patricia. b 69. Chelt & Glouc Coll of HE BEd 99. WEMTC 08. **d** 11 **p** 12. C S Cheltenham *Glouc* 11–14; V Glouc St Paul and St Steph from 14. *84 Frampton Road, Gloucester GL1 5QB* T: (01452) 500537 M: 07553-758063 E: ruthfitter1@gmail.com *or* ruthfitter@paulstephenglos.org.uk

FITZGERALD, Elizabeth Anne. **d** 15 **p** 17. Donagheady *D & R* 15–17; C Gweedore, Carrickfin and Templecrone from 17. *The Rectory, Bunbeg, Co Donegal, Republic of Ireland* T: (00353) (74) 953 1043 M: 07771-728227 E: ea.fitzgerald1@btinternet.com

FITZGERALD, Miss Melanie Anne. b 52. Sheff Univ BMus 75. Westcott Ho Cam 96. **d** 98 **p** 99. C Rotherham *Sheff* 98–01; C Stannington 01–02; P-in-c Walkley 02–05; V from 05. *St Mary's Vicarage, 150 Walkley Road, Sheffield S6 2XQ* T: 0114-234 5029 E: melanie.fitzgerald@zen.co.uk

FITZGERALD CLARK, Mrs Diane Catherine. b 54. Rhode Is Univ BA 76. Gen Th Sem NY MDiv 86. **d** 86 **p** 87. USA 86–95; NSM Hampstead Em W End *Lon* 96–99; Chapl St Alb High Sch for Girls from 98; Assoc Min St Alb Abbey from 98. *13 Eleanor Avenue, St Albans AL3 5TA* T: (01727) 860099 E: dfc@stahs.org.uk

FITZGIBBON, Kevin Peter. b 49. St Jo Coll Nottm BTh 81. **d** 81 **p** 82. C Corby St Columba *Pet* 81–85; V Newborough 85–99; V Eaton Socon *St Alb* 99–07; Min Consultant CPAS from 07; P-in-c Christchurch and Manea and Welney *Ely* 07–15; P-in-c Doddington w Benwick and Wimblington 11–15; rtd 15; PtO *Ely* from 15; *Pet* from 15. *127 High Street, Eye, Peterborough PE6 7UX* T: (01733) 221530 E: k.fitzgibbon@care4free.net

FITZHARRIS, The Ven Robert Aidan. b 46. Sheff Univ BDS 71. Linc Th Coll 87. **d** 89 **p** 90. C Dinnington *Sheff* 89–92; V Bentley 92–01; RD Adwick 95–01; Hon Can Sheff Cathl 98–01; Adn Doncaster 01–11; rtd 12; PtO *Sheff* from 12. *Amberley, Old Bawtry Road, Finningley, Doncaster DN9 3BY* T: (01302) 773220 M: 07767-355357 E: lesleyfitzharris@waitrose.com

FITZMAURICE, Arthur William John. b 65. Leeds Univ BA 99 Heythrop Coll Lon MA 04 K Coll Lon PhD 14 Lon Inst of Educn PGCE 92 AGSM 89. Coll of Resurr Mirfield 97. **d** 99 **p** 00. C Spondon *Derby* 99–02; P-in-c Emscote *Cov* 02–03; TV Warwick 03–15; Dir of Ords *Worc* from 15. *The Old Palace, Deansway, Worcester WR1 2JE* T: (01905) 732814 E: jfitzmaurice@cofe-worcester.org.uk

FITZPATRICK, Paul Kevin. b 60. Open Univ BA 99 Univ of Wales (Lamp) MTh 05 Univ of Wales (Cardiff) PhD 11 Robert Gordon Univ Aber MSc 17 Plymouth Univ PGCE 07 FHEA 09 CPsychol 17. Cuddesdon Coll 96. **d** 98 **p** 99. C Okehampton w Inwardleigh, Bratton Clovelly etc *Ex* 98–02; P-in-c Whipton 02–04; V 04–07; RD Christianity 05–06; Co-ord Chapl Cardiff Metrop Univ *Llan* from 07. *Cardiff Metropolitan University, Chaplaincy, Cyncoed Campus, Cyncoed Road, Cardiff CF23 6XD* T: (029) 2041 7252 M: 07917-818524 E: pfitzpatrick@cardiffmet.ac.uk

FITZPATRICK, Paul Thomas. b 67. Coll of Resurr Mirfield 17. **d** 19. C S Beddington and Roundshaw *S'wark* from 19. *32 Waterer Rise, Wallington SM6 9DN* E: fr.paul.fitzpatrick@gmail.com

FITZSIMONS, Canon Kathryn Anne. b 57. Bedf Coll of Educn CertEd 78. NEOC 87. **d** 90 **p** 13. NSM Bilton *Ripon* 90–01; Soc Resp Development Officer Richmond Adnry

92–99; Urban Min Officer *Ripon* 99–14; P-in-c Leeds Gipton Epiphany 14 and 14–16; P-in-c Roundhay St Jo 15–16; V Gipton and Oakwood from 16; AD Allerton from 16; Hon Can Ripon Cathl from 04. *Epiphany Vicarage, 227 Beech Lane, Leeds LS9 6SW* T: 0113-225 6702 E: kathrynfitzsimons@hotmail.com

FLACH (*née* ROLLINS), **Canon Deborah Mary Rollins.** b 54. Sarum & Wells Th Coll 88. **d** 94 **p** 97. C Chantilly *Eur* 94–96; C Maisons-Laffitte 96–04; Asst Chapl 04–07; P-in-c Lille from 07; Can Gib Cathl from 07. *Christ Church, 14 rue Lyderic, 59000 Lille, France* T/F: (0033) 3 28 52 66 36 E: debbieflach@gmail.com

FLACK, Miss Heather Margaret. b 47. **d** 95 **p** 96. C Shenley Green *Birm* 95–00; TV Kings Norton 00–07; rtd 07; PtO *Birm* from 07; *Worc* from 08. *23 Stourport Road, Bewdley DY12 1BB* T: (01299) 400691 E: hm.flack@btinternet.com

✠**FLACK, The Rt Revd John Robert.** b 42. Leeds Univ BA 64. Coll of Resurr Mirfield 64. **d** 66 **p** 67 **c** 97. C Armley St Bart *Ripon* 66–69; C Northampton St Mary *Pet* 69–72; V Chapelthorpe *Wakef* 72–81; V Ripponden and Barkisland w W Scammonden 81–85; Chapl Rishworth Sch Ripponden 81–85; V Brighouse *Wakef* 85–88; TR Brighouse St Martin 88–92; RD Brighouse and Elland 86–92; Hon Can Wakef Cathl 89–92; Adn Pontefract 92–97; Suff Bp Huntingdon and Hon Can Ely Cathl 97–03; Abp's Rep H See and Dir Angl Cen Rome 03–08; P-in-c Nassington w Yarwell and Woodnewton w Apethorpe *Pet* 08–12; Can Pet Cathl 04–12; Hon Asst Bp Pet 03–17; Hon Asst Bp Eur from 03; PtO *Ely* 03–17; Hon Asst Bp Ely 13–17; Hon Asst Bp Leeds from 17; Bp's Adv for Healing Min *Pet* 14–17; PtO *Linc* from 16. *6 Oakhall Park, Crigglestone, Wakefield WF4 3HG* T: (01924) 259073 M: 07810-714056 E: johnflack67@yahoo.com

FLAGG, David Michael. b 50. CCC Cam BA 71 MA 75. St Jo Coll Nottm BA 76. **d** 77 **p** 78. C Hollington St Leon *Chich* 77–80; C Woodley St Jo the Ev *Ox* 80–86; Chapl The Dorothy Kerin Trust Burrswood 86–94; R Knockholt w Halstead *Roch* 94–99; Dir Chapl Services Mildmay UK 99–02; Hd Chapl Services Qu Eliz Hosp NHS Trust 02–11; Hd Chapl Services S Lon Healthcare NHS Trust 11–13; rtd 13; Chapl Burrswood Chr Hosp *Roch* 13–16; PtO *S'wark* from 13; *Roch* from 17. *61 Church Street, Edenbridge TN8 5BQ* T: (01732) 866058 M: 07910-141862 E: david.pastoral@mail.com

FLAHERTY, Jane Venitia. *See* ANDERSON, Jane Venitia

FLAHERTY, Miss Mandy Carol. b 63. Ches Coll of HE BA 86 Leic Univ PGCE 87. St Jo Coll Nottm MTh 04. **d** 04 **p** 05. C Oadby *Leic* 04–08; PtO *Ely* 09–10; NSM Alconbury cum Weston 10–14; NSM N Leightonstone 14–17; C 17–19; P-in-c 19; R from 19; Chapl K Sch Pet from 14. *5 Bramble End, Alconbury, Huntingdon PE28 4EZ* T: (01480) 896541 M: 07593-311568 E: heddamand@aol.com

FLANAGAN, James. b 17 **p** 18. C Pen-bre *St D* from 17. *10 Maes y Capel, Pembrey, Burry Port SA16 0EG* E: jimflanagan1662@gmail.com

FLANAGAN (*née* Malcolm), **Mrs Mercia Alana.** b 54. St Andr Univ MA 77. S'wark Ord Course 84. **d** 87 **p** 94. C Dartford Ch Ch *Roch* 87–91; Par Dn Stockport St Geo *Ches* 91–94; C Jordanstown *Conn* 95–99; Chapl Ulster Univ 95–03; I Carnmoney *Conn* 03–18; C Ballyholme *D & D* from 18. *95 Silverbirch Road, Bangor BT19 6FA* T: (028) 9147 9816 M: 07773-558326 E: merciaflanagan1@gmail.com

FLASHMAN (*née* WALLACE), **Sarah Louise.** b 63. Wycliffe Hall Ox MTh 18 RGN 85. STETS BA 13. **d** 13 **p** 14. NSM Southbourne w W Thorney *Chich* 13–16; PtO *Ox* 16–18; Chapl Wycliffe Hall Ox from 18; C Wolvercote and Wytham *Ox* from 19. *The Rectory, 27 Church Street, Quainton, Aylesbury HP22 4AW* T: (01296) 655237 M: 07443-637432 E: sarah@ontheboxmission.com

FLATT, Lynn Patricia. b 47. Univ of Wales (Ban) BA 73 Birm Univ MSocSc 75 Ex Univ DipSW 79 RGN 68. SWMTC 12. **d** 14 **p** 15. NSM S Molton w Nymet St George, High Bray etc *Ex* 14–16; NSM S Molton w Nymet St George, Chittlehamholt etc from 16. *1 Widgery Drive, South Molton EX36 4DP* T: (01769) 572076 E: lynnflatt@btinternet.com

FLATT, Stephen Joseph. b 57. SRN 79 RSCN 81. Sarum & Wells Th Coll 92. **d** 92 **p** 93. C Limpsfield and Titsey *S'wark* 92–96; TV Pewsey *Sarum* 96–97; Staff Nurse R Free Hampstead NHS Trust 97–99; Charge Nurse 99–00; Asst Chapl Univ Coll Lon Hosps NHS Trust 00–01; Chapl 01–03; PtO *S'wark* 98–99; NSM Clapham H Trin and St Pet 04–12; Lead Chapl St Mary's NHS Trust Paddington 03–10; Hd Spiritual and Past Care Imp Coll Healthcare NHS Trust 10–13; Clinical Service Manager W Middx Univ Hosp NHS Trust 13–14; Assoc Dir Nursing Barts Health NHS Trust 14–19; NSM St Marylebone Annunciation Bryanston Street *Lon* 14–19; Hd of Quality Governance Poole Hosp NHS Foundn Trust from 19; NSM Branksome St Aldhelm *Sarum* from 19. *Poole Hospital, Longfleet Road, Poole BH15 2JB* M: 07956-278566

FLATTERS, Clive Andrew. b 56. Sarum & Wells Th Coll 83. **d** 86 **p** 88. C Weston Favell *Pet* 86–87; C Old Brumby *Linc* 88–91; C Syston *Leic* 91–93; TV 93–99; V Knottingley *Wakef* 99–02; TR Knottingley and Kellington w Whitley 02–14; *Leeds* from 14. *The Vicarage, Chapel Street, Knottingley WF11 9AN* T: (01977) 672267

FLAVELL, Paul William Deran. b 44. St Mich Coll Llan 67. **d** 68 **p** 69. C W Cairns Australia 68–71; C Blaenavon w Capel Newydd *Mon* 71–74; V Ynysddu 74–84; R Llanaber w Caerdeon *Ban* 84–00; V Llanstadwel *St D* 00–10; rtd 10; PtO *St As* from 10; *Ban* from 10. *7 Park Grove, Abergele LL22 7NE* T: (01745) 823668 E: fish.foulkes1811@btinternet.com

FLEET, Daniel James Russell. b 60. Wye Coll Lon BSc 84 Keele Univ PGCE 02. St Jo Coll Nottm 86. **d** 89 **p** 90. C Boldmere *Birm* 89–92; C Caverswall and Weston Coyney w Dilhorne *Lich* 92–95; V Alton w Bradley-le-Moors and Oakamoor w Cotton 95–01; rtd 01; PtO *Lich* 01–10. *124 Byrds Lane, Uttoxeter ST14 7NB* T: (01889) 560214 E: danielfleet@btinternet.com

FLEMING (*formerly* LOOKER), **Miss Clare Margaret.** b 55. Liv Univ CertEd 78. Westcott Ho Cam 85. **d** 87 **p** 02. Par Dn Prestwood and Gt Hampden *Ox* 87–90; Hon C Olney w Emberton 90–92; Hon C Blunham, Gt Barford, Roxton and Tempsford etc *St Alb* 01–03; P-in-c Welford w Sibbertoft and Marston Trussell *Pet* 03–04; P-in-c Welford w Sibbertoft and Marston Trussell *Pet* 03–04; P-in-c Welford w Sibbertoft and Marston Trussell *Pet* 03–04; Hon C Wilden w Colmworth and Ravensden 05–08; PtO *Ely* 11–16; *St E* from 12. *Address temp unknown* M: 07519-590767 E: fleming.clare@yahoo.co.uk

FLEMING, The Ven David. b 37. Kelham Th Coll 58. **d** 63 **p** 64. C Walton St Marg Belmont Road *Liv* 63–67; Chapl HM Borstal Gaynes Hall 68–76; V Gt Staughton *Ely* 68–76; RD St Neots 72–76; V Whittlesey 76–85; RD March 77–82; Hon Can Ely Cathl 82–01; P-in-c Ponds Bridge 83–85; Adn Wisbech 84–93; V Wisbech St Mary 85–89; Chapl Gen of Pris 93–01; Chapl to The Queen 95–07; PtO *Ely* from 01. *Fair Haven, 123 Wisbech Road, Littleport, Ely CB6 1JJ* T: (01353) 862498 E: davidfleming@hotmail.com

FLEMING, Elizabeth Julie. b 57. Westhill Coll Birm CertEd 79 Ches Coll of HE BTh 00. NOC 97. **d** 00 **p** 01. C Widnes St Jo *Liv* 00–03; P-in-c Walton Breck Ch Ch 03–04; V Walton Breck 04–08; V Becontree St Mary *Chelmsf* 08–17; AD Barking and Dagenham 13–17; Hon Can Chelmsf Cathl 15–17; TR Worle *B & W* from 17. *93 Church Road, Worle, Weston-super-Mare BS22 9EA* E: lizjuliefleming@gmail.com

FLEMING, George. b 39. CITC. **d** 78 **p** 79. C Donaghcloney w Waringstown *D & D* 78–80; C Newtownards 80; I Movilla 80; C Heref St Pet w St Owen and St Jas 80–85; V Holmer w Huntington 85–96; P-in-c Worfield 96–98; V 98–04; rtd 04; PtO *Truro* 05–08; *Bris* from 08. *The Rectory, Kenwin Close, Swindon SN3 4NY* T: (01793) 831239

FLEMING, Canon Kathryn Claire. b 60. Trin Coll Cam BA 82 MA 91 Montessori TDip 92. WEMTC 01. **d** 04 **p** 05. C Charlton Kings St Mary *Glouc* 04–08; P-in-c Cainscross w Selsley 08–13; TV Stroud Team 13–14; Can Res Cov Cathl from 14. *Coventry Cathedral, 1 Hill Top, Coventry CV1 5AB* T: (024) 7652 1200 F: 7652 1220 E: kathryn.fleming@coventrycathedral.org.uk

FLEMING, Victoria Rosalie. b 58. WEMTC 01. **d** 04 **p** 05. NSM St Breoke and Egloshayle *Truro* 04–08; TV Stratton St Margaret w S Marston etc *Bris* 08–11; P-in-c 11–19. *The Rectory, Kenwin Close, Swindon SN3 4NY* T: (01793) 827021 E: vicky.fleming981@btinternet.com

FLEMING, William Edward Charlton. b 29. TCD BA 51 MA 65. CITC 52. **d** 52 **p** 53. C Dublin Santry *D & G* 52–56; C Arm St Mark w Aghavilly 56–61; I Tartaraghan 61–80; Prov Registrar 79–96; I Tartaraghan w Diamond 80–96; Can Arm Cathl 86–96; Treas Arm Cathl 88–92; Chan Arm Cathl 92–96; rtd 96. *65 Annareagh Road, Drumorgan, Richhill, Armagh BT61 9JT* T: (028) 3887 9612

FLENLEY, Benjamin Robert Glanville. b 50. Sarum & Wells Th Coll 86. **d** 88 **p** 89. C Eastleigh *Win* 88–92; V Micheldever and E Stratton, Woodmancote etc 92–03; R Bentworth, Lasham, Medstead and Shalden 03–15; rtd 15; Hon C Quantock Towers *B & W* from 15; RD Quantock from 17; Hon C Quantock Towers from 15. *Shardloes, Staple Lane, West Quantoxhead, Taunton TA4 4DE* T: (01984) 631190 E: flenbenley@btinternet.com

FLENLEY, Kathryn Alison. b 51. STETS. **d** 12 **p** 13. NSM Bentworth, Lasham, Medstead and Shalden *Win* 12–15; PtO *B & W* 15–17; C Watchet and Williton from 17. *Shardloes, Staple Lane, West Quantoxhead, Taunton TA4 4DE* T: (01984) 633568 E: kathryn.flenley@btinternet.com

FLETCHER, Anthony. *See* FLETCHER, James Anthony

FLETCHER, Anthony Peter Reeves. b 46. Bede Coll Dur CertEd Nottm Univ BTh 78. Ridley Hall Cam 71. **d** 74 **p** 75. C Luton St Mary *St Alb* 74–78; Chapl RAF 78–00; P-in-c Lyneham w Bradenstoke *Sarum* 98–99; P-in-c Kyrenia St Andr and Chapl N Cyprus 00–04; P-in-c Lyneham w Bradenstoke *Sarum* 04–07; rtd 07; PtO *Bris* from 08; *Glouc* from 14. *Glentworth House, Giles Avenue, Cricklade, Swindon SN6 6HS* T: (01793) 751333

FLETCHER, Barbara. b 41. ALAM 79. WMMTC 93. **d** 96 **p** 97. NSM Smethwick *Birm* 96–97; C 97–02; rtd 02; PtO *Birm* from 02; *Worc* from 12. *231 Abbey Road, Smethwick B67 5NN* T: 0121-429 9354 E: bfletcher@talktalk.net

FLETCHER, Bryce Clifford. b 45. ACIB. Cranmer Hall Dur. **d** 08 **p** 09. NSM Arle Valley *Win* 08–14; rtd 14; PtO *Win* from 14. *Camellia Cottage, Church Street, Ropley, Alresford SO24 0DS* E: bryce@newalresford.plus.com

FLETCHER, Christopher Ian. b 43. BSc PhD. Glouc Sch of Min. **d** 89 **p** 90. C Tenbury Wells *Heref* 89–93; R Bredenbury 93–09; RD Bromyard 99–05; rtd 09; PtO *Heref* from 10. *12 Geoffrey Avenue, Hereford HR1 1BZ* T: (01432) 273149 E: chris.fletcher@csfmail.co.uk

✠**FLETCHER, The Rt Revd Colin William.** b 50. Trin Coll Ox BA 72 MA 76. Wycliffe Hall Ox 72. **d** 75 **p** 76 **c** 00. C Shipley St Pet *Bradf* 75–79; Tutor Wycliffe Hall Ox 79–84; Hon C Ox St Andr 79–84; V Margate H Trin *Cant* 84–93; RD Thanet 88–93; Abp's Chapl 93–00; Area Bp Dorchester *Ox* from 00; Hon Can Dallas from 93. *Church House Oxford, Langford Locks, Kidlington OX5 1GF* T: (01865) 208218 F: 849003 E: bishopdorchester@oxford.anglican.org

FLETCHER, David Clare Molyneux. b 32. Worc Coll Ox BA 55 MA 59. Wycliffe Hall Ox 56. **d** 58 **p** 59. C Islington St Mary *Lon* 58–62; Hon C 62–83; Field Worker Scripture Union 62–86; R Ox St Ebbe w H Trin and St Pet 86–98; rtd 98; PtO *Ox* 06–18. *49 Erdington House, Cresswell Close, Yarnton, Kidlington OX5 1FZ* T: (01865) 579360 E: sanddfletcher@gmail.com

FLETCHER, David Mark. b 56. Chich Th Coll 84. **d** 87 **p** 88. C Taunton St Andr *B & W* 87–91; P-in-c Chard, Furnham w Chaffcombe, Knowle St Giles etc 91–95; P-in-c Tiverton St Andr *Ex* 95–11; RD Tiverton 02–08; Chapl Mid Devon Primary Care Trust 95–11; C Barnstaple *Ex* 11–17; V Barnstaple St Pet and St Mary from 17. *The Vicarage, Sowden Lane, Barnstaple EX32 8BU* T: (01271) 373837 E: davidfletcher56@btinternet.com

FLETCHER, Capt Frank. b 40. Wilson Carlile Coll 71 EAMTC 94. **d** 96 **p** 96. Asst Chapl HM Pris Highpoint 90–97; Chapl HM Pris Wealstun 97–05; rtd 05; PtO *York* from 05. *3 Pear Tree Close, Huntington, York YO32 9QZ* T: (01904) 765181 E: frank.fletcher2018@gmail.com

FLETCHER, Gordon Wolfe (Robin). b 31. Edin Th Coll. **d** 62 **p** 63. C Eston *York* 62–65; C Harton Colliery *Dur* 65–68; V Pelton 68–81; V Ryhope 81–96; rtd 96; PtO *Dur* from 04. *23 Swinburne Road, Darlington DL3 7TD* T: (01325) 265994 E: gordon.fletcher@btinternet.com

FLETCHER, Ian Paul. b 76. **d** 09 **p** 10. C Holdenhurst and Iford *Win* 09–13; P-in-c Eastleigh 14–19; V from 19. *Eastleigh Vicarage, 1 Cedar Road, Eastleigh SO50 9NR* T: (023) 8065 2295 E: ianpaulfletcher@gmail.com *or* ian@eastleighparish.com

FLETCHER, James Anthony. b 36. St Edm Hall Ox BA 60 MA 66. St Steph Ho Ox 60. **d** 62 **p** 63. C Streatham St Pet *S'wark* 62–65; C Hobs Moat CD *Birm* 65–66; C Hobs Moat 67–68; C Cowley St Jo *Ox* 68–77; V Hanworth All SS *Lon* 77–02; P-in-c Hanworth St Geo 89–91; rtd 02; PtO *Cant* from 02. *19 Strand Street, Sandwich CT13 9DX* T: (01304) 620506 E: franthonyfletcher@tiscali.co.uk

FLETCHER, James Arthur. b 71. Reading Univ BA 99. Trin Coll Bris 03. **d** 05 **p** 06. C Bexleyheath Ch Ch *Roch* 05–08; R Fawkham and Hartley 08–19; RD Cobham 13–18; R Gravesend St Geo from 19. *54 The Avenue, Gravesend DA11 0LX* T: (01474) 334965

FLETCHER, James John Gareth. b 79. Aber Univ MA 02 Selw Coll Cam BA 08 MA. Ridley Hall Cam 06. **d** 09 **p** 10. C Tooting Graveney St Nic *S'wark* 09–13; C Ox St Ebbe w H Trin and St Pet 13–18; V Summerstown *S'wark* from 18. *46 Wimbledon Road, London SW17 0UQ* T: (020) 8946 9853 E: jjgfletcher38@gmail.com

FLETCHER, Miss Janet. b 59. Lanc Univ MA 07. Cranmer Hall Dur 98. **d** 00 **p** 01. C Ainsdale *Liv* 00–04; TV Walton-on-the-Hill 04–09; Hon Chapl Liv Cathl 04–09; C Prescot 09–11; TV Bangor *Ban* 11–14; TV Bro Deiniol 14–15; Spirituality Officer from 15; C Bro Ystumaner 15–18; C Bro Enlli from 18. *Y Ficerdy, Aberdaron, Pwllheli LL53 8BP* T: (01758) 760587

FLETCHER, Jeremy James. b 60. Dur Univ BA 81. St Jo Coll Nottm 85. **d** 88 **p** 89. C Stranton *Dur* 88–91; C Nottingham St Nic *S'well* 91–94; P-in-c Skegby 94–00; P-in-c Teversal 96–00; Bp's Dom Chapl 00–02; Can Res

and Prec York Minster 02–09; V Beverley Minster 09–17; P-in-c Routh 09–17; RD Beverley 12–17; V Hampstead St Jo *Lon* from 17. *St John's Vicarage, 14 Church Row, London NW3 6UU* T: (020) 7794 5808 E: jeremy@jjfletcher.co.uk *or* vestry@hampsteadparishchurch.org.uk

FLETCHER, Canon John Alan Alfred. b 33. Oak Hill Th Coll 58. **d** 61 **p** 62. C Erith St Paul *Roch* 61–64; C Rushden *Pet* 64–67; R Hollington St Leon *Chich* 67–86; V Chadwell Heath *Chelmsf* 86–00; RD Barking and Dagenham 91–00; Chapl Chadwell Heath Hosp Romford 86–93; Chapl Redbridge Health Care NHS Trust 93–00; Hon Can Chelmsf Cathl 99–00; rtd 00; PtO *Chich* from 01. *41 Parkstone Road, Hastings TN34 2NR* T: (01424) 712345 M: 07860-128912 E: jaaf@btinternet.com

FLETCHER, Keith. b 47. Chich Th Coll 79. **d** 80 **p** 81. C Hartlepool St Paul *Dur* 80–82; V Eighton Banks 82–85; V Haydon Bridge *Newc* 85–96; RD Hexham 93–96; P-in-c Beltingham w Henshaw 93–96; R Ashmanhaugh, Barton Turf etc *Nor* 96–99; rtd 99. *2 Churchill Terrace, Sherburn Hill, Durham DH6 1PF* T: 0191-372 0362 E: keith16621980@gmail.com

FLETCHER, Linden Elisabeth. b 50. Lon Univ BEd 73 MA 80. St Jo Coll Nottm 87. **d** 89 **p** 94. C Fakenham w Alethorpe *Nor* 89–93; C Cumnor *Ox* 93–02; P-in-c Ringshall w Battisford, Barking w Darmsden etc *St E* 02–08; P-in-c Somersham w Flowton and Offton w Willisham 02–08; V Llanfair Caereinion, Llanllugan and Manafon *St As* 08–11; rtd 11. *Tanrallt, Cwrtnewydd, Llanybydder SA40 9YJ*

FLETCHER, Martin. b 60. Bradf Univ BEng 83 CEng MIMechE. Ripon Coll Cuddesdon. **d** 00 **p** 01. C Oatlands *Guildf* 00–04; R Tolleshunt Knights w Tiptree and Gt Braxted *Chelmsf* 04–10; V Hersham *Guildf* 10–18; R Richmond w Hudswell and Downholme and Marske *Leeds* from 18. *The Rectory, Church Wynd, Richmond DL10 7AQ* T: (01748) 323398 E: fletcher_martin@yahoo.co.uk

FLETCHER, Martin James. b 48. Ex Univ BA 03 MIFA 89. SWMTC 99. **d** 02 **p** 03. NSM Wolborough and Ogwell *Ex* 02–05; NSM Chudleigh w Chudleigh Knighton and Trusham from 05. *11 Troarn Way, Chudleigh, Newton Abbot TQ13 0PP* T: (01626) 853998 E: m.fletcher@uwclub.net

FLETCHER, Maurice. See FLETCHER, Ralph Henry Maurice

FLETCHER, Paul Gordon MacGregor. b 61. St Andr Univ MTheol 84. Edin Th Coll 84. **d** 86 **p** 87. C Cumbernauld *Glas* 86–89; C-in-c Glas H Cross 89–93; P-in-c Bearsden w Milngavie 93–99; R Clarkston 99–07; LtO *Arg* 08–10; R E Kilbride *Glas* from 10. *6 Kelvin Crescent, East Kilbride, Glasgow G75 0TY* T: (01355) 224895 E: paulmcgregorfletcher@hotmail.com

FLETCHER, Ralph Henry Maurice. b 43. St Luke's Coll Ex CertEd 65. St Steph Ho Ox 71. **d** 74 **p** 75. C Chislehurst Annunciation *Roch* 74–77; Chapl Quainton Hall Sch Harrow 77–87 and 94–00; Hon C Wallington All SS *Lon* 87–94; PtO 94–00; *Roch* 00–02; *Wakef* 05–14; *Leeds* from 14. *6 Joseph Court, Joseph Street, Barnsley S70 1LJ* T: (01226) 779928

FLETCHER, Robert Alexander. b 52. Ridley Hall Cam. **d** 84 **p** 85. C Chalfont St Peter *Ox* 84–88; C Bushey *St Alb* 88–93; TV Digswell and Panshanger 93–00; P-in-c Aldenham 00–05; TV Aldenham, Radlett and Shenley from 05. *The Vicarage, Church Lane, Aldenham, Watford WD25 8BE* T/F: (01923) 854209 E: r.afletcher@btconnect.com

FLETCHER, Robin. See FLETCHER, Gordon Wolfe

FLETCHER, Mrs Sheila Elizabeth. b 35. Nottm Univ BA 57 CertEd 58. NEOC 84. **d** 87 **p** 94. NSM Dringhouses *York* 87–90; Par Dn 90–94; C 94–97; P-in-c Sutton on the Forest 97–02; rtd 02; PtO *York* 02–15. *Mulberry Court Nursing Home, Clifton Park Avenue, York YO30 5PD* E: sheeliz@tiscali.co.uk

FLETCHER, Stephen. b 57. Man Univ BA 79 MA 84. St Jo Coll Nottm 82. **d** 84 **p** 85. C Didsbury St Jas and Em *Man* 84–88; R Kersal Moor 88–01; TR Horwich and Rivington from 01; C Blackrod 11–16. *The Rectory, Chorley Old Road, Horwich, Bolton BL6 6AX* T/F: (01204) 468263 E: horwichrectory@sandafletcher.myzen.co.uk

FLETCHER, Stephen William. b 62. Wolv Poly BA 84. Qu Coll Birm 85. **d** 88 **p** 89. C Rainham *Roch* 88–91; C Shottery St Andr *Cov* 91–97; Min Bishopton St Pet 91–97; V Llanrumney *Mon* 97–02; V Adderbury w Milton *Ox* 02–18; Hon C Ilmington w Stretton-on-Fosse etc *Cov* from 18; Hon C Tredington and Darlingscott from 18. *Tredington Rectory, Tredington, Shipston-on-Stour CV36 4NG* M: 07714-171143 E: revfletcher24@gmail.com

FLETCHER, Steven John Carylon. b 60. NCTJ 83. Aston Tr Scheme 89 Ripon Coll Cuddesdon 89. **d** 92 **p** 93. C Newquay *Truro* 92–93; NSM St Stythians w Perranarworthal and Gwennap from 15; NSM Chacewater w St Day and Carharrack from 15; NSM Feock from 15; NSM Devoran from

15. *5 Scorrier Street, St Day, Redruth TR16 5LH* T: (01209) 822584 E: steven.fletcher@btinternet.com

FLETCHER, Timothy John. b 63. Sheff Univ BA 88 St Jo Coll Dur MA 04. Cranmer Hall Dur 01. **d** 03 **p** 04. C Four Marks *Win* 03–06; V Walton le Soken *Chelmsf* 06–14; P-in-c Stannington *Sheff* from 14; Dir IME 4-7 from 14. *The Vicarage, 214 Oldfield Road, Stannington, Sheffield S6 6DY* T: 0114-234 9247 E: tim906fletcher@btinternet.com

FLEWKER, David William. b 53. Birm Univ BA 75. Wycliffe Hall Ox 76. **d** 78 **p** 79. C Netherton *Liv* 78–82; C Prescot 82–84; V Seaforth 84–88; TV Whitstable *Cant* 88–96; Miss to Seamen 88–96; V Bethersden w High Halden *Cant* 96–08; Asst Dir of Ords 02–06; P-in-c Deal St Leon w St Rich and Sholden etc 08–13; R 13–19; rtd 19. *24 Scholars Close, Deal CT14 9FA*

FLIGHT, Michael John. b 41. Sarum Th Coll 68. **d** 71 **p** 72. C Wimborne Minster *Sarum* 71–75; R Tarrant Gunville, Tarrant Hinton etc 75–78; P-in-c Tarrant Rushton, Tarrant Rawston etc 77–78; R Tarrant Valley 78–80; V Westbury 80–00; RD Heytesbury 83–87 and 96–00; R Broad Town, Clyffe Pypard, Hilmarton etc 00–07; RD Calne 03–06; rtd 07; PtO *Sarum* from 09. *11 Nursteed Close, Devizes SN10 3EU* T: (01380) 738493 E: michael@flightfamily.co.uk

FLINT, Howard Michael. b 59. Edge Hill Coll of HE BEd 81. Cranmer Hall Dur 95. **d** 97 **p** 98. C Chipping Campden w Ebrington *Glouc* 97–00; V Upper Wreake *Leic* 00–06; RD Framland 02–06; V Tunbridge Wells H Trin w Ch Ch *Roch* 06–16; V St Austell *Truro* from 16. *12 North Hill Park, St Austell PL25 4BJ* T: (01726) 64005 M: 07413-286491 E: rev4howard@hotmail.com or staustellparish@gmail.com

FLINT, Nicholas Angus. b 60. Chich Th Coll 84. **d** 87 **p** 88. C Aldwick *Chich* 87–91; Bp's Asst Chapl for the Homeless *Lon* 91–92; R Rusper *Chich* from 96. *The Rectory, High Street, Rusper, Horsham RH12 4PX* T: (01293) 871251

FLINT, Simon Paul. b 67. Trin Coll Bris 11. **d** 13 **p** 14. C Bath Weston All SS w N Stoke and Langridge *B & W* 13–16; C Streetsville Canada from 16. *69 Queen Street S, Mississauga ON L5M 1K5, Canada* M: 07864-910953 E: simonfredflint@gmail.com

FLINT, Tobias John Barnaby. b 76. Ex Univ BA 99. Wycliffe Hall Ox BA 08. **d** 08 **p** 09. C Brompton H Trin w Onslow Square St Paul *Lon* 08–11; C Onslow Square and S Kensington St Aug 11–18; C-in-c Bristol St Nic *Bris* from 18. *41 Lilymead Avenue, Bristol BS4 2BY* M: 07967-435080 E: toby@stnicholasbristol.org

FLINTHAM, Alan Jenkinson. b 45. Leeds Univ BSc 66 PGCE 67 MEd 74 Liv Univ PhD 09. EMMTC 98. **d** 00 **p** 01. NSM Melbourne *Derby* 00–10; NSM Melbourne, Ticknall, Smisby and Stanton 10–15; rtd 15; PtO *Derby* from 15; Chapl Derby Cathl from 18. *50 Burlington Way, Mickleover, Derby DE3 9BD* T: (01332) 512293 M: 07771-631370 E: alan@flintham.org.uk

FLINTOFT, Canon Ian Hugh. b 74. Pemb Coll Cam BA 97 MA 99 MPhil 98. Westcott Ho Cam 01. **d** 04 **p** 05. C Newc St Geo 04–06; C Newc St Geo and St Hilda 06–07; C Ch the King 07–08; TV 08–11; Bp's Chapl and Dioc Dir of Ords 11–17; Dir Discipleship and Min for Miss from 17; NSM Cowgate from 17; Hon Can Newc Cathl from 14. *Church House, St John's Terrace, North Shields NE29 6HS* T: 0191-270 4100 E: i.flintoft@newcastle.anglican.org or ianflintoft@hotmail.com

FLINTOFT-CHAPMAN, Mrs Margaret. b 47. Leeds Univ BA 68. NTMTC 03. **d** 05 **p** 06. NSM Barkingside St Cedd *Chelmsf* 05–12; NSM Barkingside H Trin 12–16; rtd 16. *84 Roding Lane North, Woodford Green IG8 8NG* T: (020) 8504 6750

FLIPSE, Miss Adriana Maria (Marja). b 82. Leiden Univ MA 05. St Mich Coll Llan 07. **d** 08 **p** 09. C Roath *Llan* 08–11; C Newton Nottage 11–14; TV Whitchurch from 14. *All Saints' Vicarage, 59 Station Road, Llandaff North, Cardiff CF14 2FB* T: (029) 2031 2510 E: marjaflipse@btinternet.com or marfli@zeelandnet.nl

FLITCROFT, Jonathan Frederick. b 62. Leeds Univ BA 85. Qu Coll Birm 13. **d** 15 **p** 16. C Four Oaks *Birm* 15–18; R Old Swinford Stourbridge *Worc* from 19. *The Rectory, Rectory Road, Stourbridge DY8 2HA* M: 07905-975601 E: johnflit@hotmail.co.uk

FLOATE, Miss Rhona Cameron. b 59. Univ of Wales (Cardiff) BA 80. Trin Coll Bris 01. **d** 03 **p** 04. C Lighthorne *Cov* 03–07; C Chesterton 03–07; C Newbold Pacey w Moreton Morrell 03–07; P-in-c Wool and E Stoke *Sarum* 07–15; R 15–16; RD Purbeck 15–16; P-in-c White Horse 16–19; TV Whitton from 19. *The Vicarage, Back Lane, Aldbourne, Marlborough SN8 2BP* E: rhonafloate@aol.com

FLOCKHART, Mrs Ruth. b 56. TISEC 96. **d** 99 **p** 00. NSM Strathpeffer *Mor* from 99; NSM Dingwall from 99. *Kilmuir*

Farm Cottage, North Kessock, Inverness IV1 3ZG T: (01463) 731580 E: kilmuirseabreeze@btinternet.com

FLOOD, Mrs Jean Anne. b 51. Liv Hope Univ MEd 00 Liv Univ CertEd 95. NOC 06. **d** 08 **p** 09. NSM Fazakerley Em *Liv* 08–11; Co-ord Miss in the Economy 11–16; NSM Walton-on-the-Hill 11–16; TV from 16. *19 Palm Close, Liverpool L9 1JD* T: 0151-525 0304 M: 07932-305963 E: revjflood@hotmail.com

FLOOD, Nicholas Roger. b 42. FCA. Ripon Hall Ox 71. **d** 92 **p** 93. NSM Romsey *Win* 92–94; Chapl Win and Eastleigh Healthcare NHS Trust 94–08; rtd 08; PtO *Win* from 09. *The Sanctuary, Salisbury Road, Plaitford, Romsey SO51 6EE* T: (01794) 323731

FLORANCE, James Andrew Vernon. b 44. MCIOB. Linc Th Coll 84. **d** 86 **p** 87. C Lt Ilford St Mich *Chelmsf* 86–90; TV Becontree S 90–93; R Orsett and Bulphan and Horndon on the Hill 93–97; P-in-c Liscard St Mary w St Columba *Ches* 97–02; RD Wallasey 99–02; Chapl St D Foundn Hospice Care Newport 02–03; P-in-c Abersychan and Garndiffaith *Mon* 03–08; rtd 08; PtO *Heref* 08–10; *Mon* 08–10; *St E* from 10. *1 Woodlands, Leiston IP16 4BT* T: (01728) 768124 E: jandp2florance@gmail.com

FLORANCE (*née* **WAINWRIGHT**), **Mrs Pauline Barbara.** b 40. Edge Hill Coll of HE CertEd 60. St Deiniol's Hawarden 83. **dss** 84 **d** 87 **p** 94. New Ferry *Ches* 84–90; Par Dn 87–90; Par Dn Hallwood 90–94; C 94–00; rtd 00; PtO *Ches* 00–03; *Mon* 04–08; *Heref* 08–10; Bp's Adv in Past Care and Counselling *Mon* 07–10; PtO *St E* from 10. *1 Woodlands, Leiston IP16 4BT* T: (01728) 768124 E: jandp2florance@gmail.com

FLORY, John Richard. b 35. Clare Coll Cam BA 59 MA 63. Westcott Ho Cam 69. **d** 71 **p** 72. C Shirehampton *Bris* 71–74; V Patchway 74–82; R Lydiard Millicent w Lydiard Tregoz 82–86; TR The Lydiards 86–93; R Box w Hazlebury and Ditteridge 93–01; rtd 01; PtO *Derby* from 02. *3 Fir Close, Poynton, Stockport SK12 1PD* E: jeanmaryflory@gmail.com

FLOWER, Roger Edward. b 45. AKC 68. **d** 69 **p** 70. C Gt Stanmore *Lon* 69–72; C Wells St Cuth w Coxley and Wookey Hole *B & W* 72–77; V Tatworth 77–82; P-in-c Taunton St Andr 82–84; V 84–96; RD Taunton 90–96; Preb Wells Cathl 92–96; V Dartmouth *Ex* 96–99; rtd 10. *6 Trinity Close, Burnham-on-Sea TA8 2HH* T: (01278) 788614 E: rogerflower@talktalk.net

FLOWERDAY, Andrew Leslie. b 53. Imp Coll Lon BSc 75. St Jo Coll Nottm. **d** 90 **p** 91. C Farnborough *Guildf* 90–95; TV Morden *S'wark* 95–12; V Patcham *Chich* from 12. *All Saints' Vicarage, 12 Church Hill, Brighton BN1 8YE* T: (01273) 552157 E: vicar.allsaintspatcham@gmail.com or fleurjour@tiscali.co.uk

FLOWERDEW, Martin James. b 56. Herts Coll CertEd 78 Pemb Coll Cam BEd 79. Sarum & Wells Th Coll 89. **d** 91 **p** 92. C Leagrave *St Alb* 91–95; C Radlett 95–99; TV Wilford Peninsula *St E* 99–01; V St Osyth *Chelmsf* 01–09; V Hoylake *Ches* 09–12; V Foremark and Repton w Newton Solney *Derby* from 12. *St Wystan's Vicarage, Willington Road, Repton, Derby DE65 6FH* T: (01283) 619686 E: thevicarforepton@gmail.com

FLYNN, Anna Therese. *See* LINDLEY, Anna Therese

FLYNN, Mrs Diane Mary. b 62. Yorks Min Course. **d** 09 **p** 10. C Roundhay St Edm *Ripon* 09–13; TV Kippax w Allerton Bywater 13–14; *Leeds* 14–16; TV Allerton Bywater, Kippax and Swillington from 16. *St Mary's Rectory, Wakefield Road, Swillington, Leeds LS26 8DS* T: 0113-286 4607 E: revdianeflynn@btinternet.com

FLYNN, Peter Murray. b 35. Oak Hill Th Coll 76. **d** 79 **p** 80. NSM Finchley St Mary *Lon* 79–83; NSM Mill Hill Jo Keble Ch 84–86; C Mill End and Heronsgate w W Hyde *St Alb* 86–92; V Chessington *Guildf* 92–05; rtd 05; PtO *Roch* from 05. *16 The Street, Plaxtol, Sevenoaks TN15 0QQ* T: (01732) 811304 E: revpeterflynn@yahoo.co.uk

FOBISTER, Mrs Wendy Irene. b 44. Lon Inst of Educn TCert 65. **d** 07 **p** 08. OLM Charminster and Stinsford *Sarum* 07–11; NSM 11–15; PtO from 15. *44 Meadow View, Charminster, Dorchester DT2 9RE* T: (01305) 251681 E: wenfob@gmail.com

FODEN, Mrs Janice Margaret. b 54. Sheff Univ BA 76 Sheff City Poly PGCE 77. NOC 98. **d** 01 **p** 02. NSM Kimberworth *Sheff* 01–05; P-in-c Barnby Dun 05–13; R Armthorpe from 13; AD Doncaster 10–18. *The Rectory, Church Street, Armthorpe, Doncaster DN3 3AD* T: (01302) 831231 E: janfoden@hotmail.com or jan.foden@sheffield.anglican.org

FODEN-CURRIE, Mary Agnes. b 43. Bp Grosseteste Coll BEd 64. St Jo Coll Nottm MA 97. **d** 98 **p** 99. NSM Skegby *S'well* 98–02; NSM Skegby w Teversal 02–03; rtd 03; PtO *S'well*

from 03. *40 Harvey Road, Mansfield NG18 4ES* T: (01623) 479838 E: revmaryfodencurrie@gmail.com

FOGDEN, Canon Elizabeth Sally. b 40. MCSP 61. Qu Coll Birm 76. **dss** 78 **d** 87 **p** 94. Chevington w Hargrave and Whepstead w Brockley *St E* 78–84; Honington w Sapiston and Troston 84–92; Par Dn 87–92; Par Dn Euston w Barnham, Elvedon and Fakenham Magna 90–92; Team Dn Blackbourne 92–94; TV 94–06; Chapl Center Parc Elvedon from 90; Dioc Adv for Women's Min *St E* 90–06; Hon Can St E Cathl 92–06; rtd 06; PtO *St E* from 06. *Meadow Farm, Coney Weston Road, Sapiston, Bury St Edmunds IP31 1RX* T: (01359) 268923 M: 07860-101980 E: sallyfogden@btinternet.com

FOGDEN, Mrs Patricia Lily Margaret. b 51. SRN 73. **d** 03 **p** 04. OLM Orlestone w Snave and Ruckinge w Warehorne etc *Cant* 03–10; NSM 10–11; NSM Appledore w Brookland, Fairfield, Brenzett etc 11–13; NSM Wittersham w Stone and Ebony 11–13; C Rother and Oxney 13–16; C Tenterden and Smallhythe 13–16; TV Tenterden, Rother and Oxney from 16; PtO *Eur* from 10. *The Vicarage, Appledore, Ashford TN26 2DB* T: (01233) 758250 M: 07885-285636 E: patricia.fogden@btinternet.com

FOGG, Mrs Margaret. b 37. CBDTI 04. **d** 05 **p** 06. NSM Allonby, Cross Canonby and Dearham *Carl* 05–08; PtO from 08. *Green Pastures, 59 Sycamore Road, Maryport CA15 7AE* T: (01900) 816203 E: margaretfogg@talktalk.net

FOLEY, Geoffrey Evan. b 30. Univ of New England BA 71 DipEd 73 MEd 79. St Jo Coll Morpeth 51. **d** 53 **p** 54. C Murwillumbah Australia 53–59; R Mallanganee 59–65; R Woodburn 65–72; P-in-c Lismore 84–85; P-in-c Bangalow 87–88; P-in-c Alstonville 88–89; PtO *S'wark* 90–91; Chapl Hamburg *Eur* 91; C Stoke-upon-Trent *Lich* 91; rtd 93; Perm to Offic Grafton Australia from 93; Dioc Archivist from 97. *25 Caroona Village, 65 Rous Road, Goonellabah NSW 2480, Australia* M: (0061) 41-452 8023 E: gefoley@bigpond.net.au

FOLKARD, Oliver Goring. b 41. Nottm Univ BA 63. Lich Th Coll 64. **d** 66 **p** 67. C Carlton *S'well* 66–67; C Worksop Priory 67–68; C Brewood *Lich* 68–71; C Folkingham w Laughton *Linc* 72–75; P-in-c Gedney Hill 76–77; V 77–84; V Whaplode Drove 76–84; V Sutton St Mary 84–94; RD Elloe E 89–94; P-in-c Sutton w E Ferry 94–99; R 99–06; R Scotton w Northorpe 99–06; rtd 06; PtO *Nor* from 06. *1 Barons Close, Fakenham NR21 8BE* T: (01328) 851468

FOLKES, Arwen Mary Caroline. b 76. Dur Univ BA 16 MA 19. Westcott Ho Cam 13. **d** 16 **p** 17. C St Just-in-Roseland and St Mawes *Truro* 16–19; R E Blatchington and Bishopstone *Chich* from 19. *The Rectory, 86 Belgrave Road, Seaford BN25 2HE* T: (01323) 892964 E: rectoryebb@gmail.com

FOLKS, Peter William John. b 30. FRCO 56 ARCM. Launde Abbey 72. **d** 72 **p** 73. C Leic St Aid 72–76; V Newfoundpool 76–84; V Whetstone 84–94; rtd 94; PtO *Leic* from 94. *4 Beaufort Close, Desford, Leicester LE9 9HS* T: (01455) 828090 E: peterfolks@hotmail.com

FOLLAND, Mrs Teresa Lorraine. b 61. SWMTC 13. **d** 16 **p** 17. C Launceston *Truro* from 16. *2 Church Lea, Launceston PL15 8QZ* T: (01566) 777651 M: 07932-385995 E: teresa.folland@gmail.com

FOLLETT, Jeremy Mark. b 60. Jes Coll Cam BA 82. St Jo Coll Nottm 90. **d** 91 **p** 92. C Newark *S'well* 91–95; C Hellesdon *Nor* 95–01; V St Alb Ch Ch from 01. *Christ Church Vicarage, 5 High Oaks, St Albans AL3 6DJ* T: (01727) 859806 E: vicar@ccstalbans.org.uk

FOLLETT, Samuel Joseph. b 90. Nottm Univ BSc 13. Ridley Hall Cam 13. **d** 16 **p** 17. C Onslow Square and S Kensington St Aug *Lon* from 16. *1 Osten Mews, London SW7 4HW* M: 07412-555039 E: sam.follett@gmail.com

FOLLIN, Michael Stuart. b 62. UMIST BSc 84. St Jo Coll Nottm MTh 02. **d** 02 **p** 03. C Aughton Ch Ch *Liv* 02–06; TV Maghull 06–09; TV Maghull and Melling 09–17; V Werrington and Wetley Rocks *Lich* from 17; RD Cheadle from 18. *360 Ash Bank Road, Werrington, Stoke-on-Trent ST9 0JS* T: (01782) 302954 M: 07813-794252 E: michael.follin@gmail.com or vicar.wwr@gmail.com

FONTAINE, Mrs Marion Elizabeth. b 39. RN 61 RM 62. SAOMC 96. **d** 99 **p** 00. OLM Thatcham *Ox* from 99. *24 Ferndale Court, Thatcham RG19 4PW* T: (01635) 827746

FOOT, Adam Julian David. b 58. Thames Poly BSc 80 Garnett Coll Lon CertEd 87. Trin Coll Bris 93. **d** 97 **p** 98. C Luton Ch Ch *Roch* 97–00; V Welling from 00; AD Erith from 17. *St John's Vicarage, Danson Lane, Welling DA16 2BQ* T: (020) 8303 1107 E: vicar@stjohnswelling.org.uk or adam_foot@lineone.net

FOOT, Daniel Henry Paris. b 46. Peterho Cam BA 67 MA 74. Ridley Hall Cam 77. **d** 79 **p** 80. C Werrington *Pet* 79–82; P-in-c Cranford w Grafton Underwood 82; R Cranford w Grafton Underwood and Twywell 83–16; P-in-c Slipton 94–16; rtd 16. *Address temp unknown* E: katinafoot@gmail.com

FOOT, Daniel James. b 87. Trin Coll Bris 12. **d** 15 **p** 16. C Sandy *St Alb* 15–18; R Guernsey St Martin *Win* from 18. *The Rectory, La Grande Rue, St Martin, Guernsey GY4 6RR* T: (01481) 238303 E: danieljamesfoot@yahoo.co.uk

FOOT, Elizabeth Victoria Anne. b 55. St Mich Coll Sarum BEd 77 Win Univ MA 19. Trin Coll Bris BA 04. **d** 04 **p** 05. C Linkinhorne and Stoke Climsland *Truro* 04–07; C Godrevy 07–08; TV 08–11; P-in-c Zennor from 11; P-in-c Towednack from 11; C Halsetown 11–15. *The Vicarage, Nancledra, Penzance TR20 8LQ* T: (01736) 741488 E: guenolesenara@hotmail.co.uk

FOOT, Jeremy Michael. b 67. Qu Mary Coll Lon BSc 88. St Mellitus Coll 07. **d** 10 **p** 11. NSM Enfield St Jas *Lon* 10–17; NSM Bush Hill Park St Mark from 17; NSM Bush Hill Park St Steph from 17. *24 St Andrews Road, Enfield EN1 3UB* T: (020) 8366 1456 M: 07725-474769 E: jeremy@thefeet.net *or* revjeremyfoot@gmail.com

FOOT, Joachim Paul Winwaloe. b 85. Collingwood Coll Dur BA 08 K Coll Lon MA 12. Westcott Ho Cam 13. **d** 15 **p** 16. C Duloe, Herodsfoot, Morval and St Pinnock *Truro* 15–17; C Looe and Morval 17–18; TR Probus, Ladock and Grampound w Creed and St Erme from 18. *The Sanctuary, Wagg Lane, Probus, Truro TR2 4JX* E: jpwfoot@outlook.com *or* rector@probusteam.com

FOOT, Keith George. b 45. Surrey Univ BSc 70 Lon Univ PhD 73 MRSC CChem. NTMTC 96. **d** 99 **p** 00. C New Thundersley *Chelmsf* 99–03; Min Prince's Park CD *Roch* 03–07; V Prince's Park 07–10; rtd 10; PtO *Roch* from 10. *51 Elmshurst Gardens, Tonbridge TN10 3QT* T: (01732) 365185 E: rev.keith.foot@btinternet.com

FOOT, Lynda. b 43. Reading Univ BEd 75 Loughb Univ MSc 82 Nottm Univ MA 00. EMMTC 97. **d** 00 **p** 01. NSM Coalville and Bardon Hill *Leic* 00–03; NSM Hickling w Kinoulton and Broughton Sulney *S'well* 04–05; NSM Bingham 05–08; rtd 08; PtO *S'well* from 08. *34 White Furrows, Cotgrave, Nottingham NG12 3LD* T: 0115-989 9724 M: 07799-662852 E: lyndafoot@btinternet.com

FOOT, Prof Sarah Rosamund Irvine. b 61. Newnham Coll Cam BA 84 MA 87 PhD 90. Ox Min Course 17. **d** 17 **p** 17. NSM Ch Ch Ox from 17; Can from 17. *Christ Church, Oxford OX1 1DP* T: (01865) 286078 E: sarah.foot@chch.ox.ac.uk

✠**FOOTTIT, The Rt Revd Anthony Charles.** b 35. K Coll Cam BA 57 MA 70. Cuddesdon Coll 59. **d** 61 **p** 62 **c** 99. C Wymondham *Nor* 61–64; C Blakeney w Lt Langham 64–67; P-in-c Hindringham w Binham and Cockthorpe 67–71; P-in-c Yarlington *B & W* 71–75; R N Cadbury 71–75; P-in-c S Cadbury w Sutton Montis 75; TR Camelot Par 76–81; RD Cary 79–81; Dioc Missr *Linc* 81–87; Can and Preb Linc Cathl 86–87; Dioc Rural Officer *Nor* 87; Adn Lynn 87–99; Suff Bp Lynn 99–03; rtd 03; Hon Asst Bp Nor from 04; Dioc Environmental Officer 04–09. *1 The Dial, Reepham, Norwich NR10 4LX* T: (01603) 870340 E: acfoottit@hotmail.com

FORAN, Andrew John. b 55. Aston Tr Scheme 84 Linc Th Coll 86. **d** 88 **p** 89. C Epping St Jo *Chelmsf* 88–92; TV Canvey Is 92–97; C Dorking w Ranmore *Guildf* 97–99; Chapl HM Pris Send 97–09; Chapl HM Pris Bullingdon 09–18; PtO *Ox* from 18. *Address withheld by request* M: 07753-677470 E: andrew.foran01@gmail.com

FORBES, Mrs Angela Laura. b 47. Ox Min Course 91. **d** 94 **p** 96. NSM Cowley St Jo *Ox* 94–04; PtO from 04. *6 Elm Crescent, Charlbury, Chipping Norton OX7 3PZ* T: (01608) 819121

FORBES, Elizabeth Karen. *See* FORBES STONE, Elizabeth Karen

FORBES, Graham John Thompson. b 51. Aber Univ MA 73 Edin Univ BD 76. Edin Th Coll 73. **d** 76 **p** 77. C Edin Old St Paul 76–82; Can St Ninian's Cathl Perth *St And* 82–90; R Stanley 82–88; Provost St Ninian's Cathl Perth 82–90; R St Ninian 82–90; Provost St Mary's Cathl Perth *Edin* 90–17; R Edin St Mary 90–17; rtd 17. *The Priory, 18 Priory Court, Pittenweem, Anstruther KY10 2LJ* T: (01333) 312061 M: 07711-199297 E: gjtforbes@outlook.com

FORBES, Iain William. b 56. Ex Univ BA 81. Chich Th Coll 83. **d** 85 **p** 86. C Upper Norwood St Jo *S'wark* 85–88; C Lewisham St Mary 88–90; Chapl St Martin's Coll of Educn *Blackb* 90–94; P-in-c Woodplumpton 94–99; Dioc Voc Adv 94–99; V Woodham *Guildf* from 99. *The Vicarage, 25 Woodham Waye, Woking GU21 5SW* T: (01483) 762857 E: fatheriainforbes@aol.com

FORBES, Canon Joyce Brinella. b 52. **d** 03 **p** 04. OLM Norbury St Steph and Thornton Heath *S'wark* from 03; Hon Can S'wark Cathl from 14. *36 Dalmeny Avenue, London SW16 4RT* T: (020) 8240 0283 *or* 7525 7982 E: petnard36@aol.com

FORBES, Moira Ruth. b 76. Birm Univ BA 99. Ridley Hall Cam 02. **d** 04 **p** 05. C Welling *Roch* 04–08; NSM Aldershot

H Trin *Guildf* 09–12; PtO 13–15; V Hazelwell *Birm* from
15. *St Mary Magdalen's Vicarage, 316 Vicarage Road,
Kings Heath, Birmingham B14 7NN* T: 0121-444 4469
E: hazelwellvicar@gmail.com

FORBES, Patrick. b 38. Open Univ BA 82. Linc Th Coll 64.
d 66 p 67. C Yeovil *B & W* 66–69; C Plumstead Wm
Temple Ch Abbey Wood CD *S'wark* 69–70; Thamesmead
Ecum Gp 70–73; TV Thamesmead *S'wark* 73–78; Dioc
Communications Officer *St Alb* 78–90; P-in-c Offley w Lilley
78–82; Info Officer Communications Dept Ch Ho Lon 91–95;
Press Officer Miss to Seamen 95–99; rtd 99; PtO *St Alb* from
04. *18 Francis Road, Hinxworth, Baldock SG7 5HL* T: (01462)
742015 E: patrickforbes06@gmail.com

FORBES, Raymond John. b 34. ALCD 58. d 58 p 59. C
Wandsworth St Steph *S'wark* 58–61; C Kewstoke *B & W*
61–63; V Fordcombe *Roch* 63–73; R Ashurst 64–73; P-in-c
Morden w Almer and Charborough *Sarum* 73–76; P-in-c
Bloxworth 73–76; V Red Post 76–84; P-in-c Hamworthy
84–92; P-in-c Symondsbury and Chideock 92–96; rtd 96;
PtO *Sarum* from 96. *3 Shelley Court, Library Road, Ferndown
BH22 9JZ* T: (01202) 897567

FORBES, Stuart. b 33. Lon Univ BD 59. Oak Hill Th Coll 56.
d 61 p 62. C Halliwell St Pet *Man* 61–64; P-in-c Wicker w
Neepsend *Sheff* 64–69; V Stainforth 69–77; V Salterhebble All
SS *Wakef* 77–89; V Toxteth Park St Mich w St Andr *Liv* 89–98;
rtd 98; PtO *Lich* 00–18. *29 Firbeck Gardens, Wildwood, Stafford
ST17 4QR* T: (01785) 663658

FORBES, Susan Margaret. *See* VAN BEVEREN, Susan Margaret

FORBES STONE, Elizabeth Karen (Buff). b 61. Birm Univ
MB, ChB 85. MRCGP 89. Ridley Hall Cam BA 99. d 00
p 01. C Brentford *Lon* 00–02; C Shaw cum Donnington
Ox 02–08; Chapl R Berks NHS Foundn Trust 09–10; PtO
Cov 10–12; C Cov St Fran N Radford 12–16; Min Stoke
Aldermoor CD 16–19; V Stoke Aldermoor and New Century
Park from 19; AD Cov E from 19. *55 Cotswold Drive,
Coventry CV3 6EZ* T: (024) 7641 9831 M: 07954-652824
E: buff@dandb.org.uk

FORD, Adam. b 40. Lanc Univ MA 72 K Coll Lon BD 63
AKC 63. d 65 p 65. C Cirencester *Glouc* 65–70; V Hebden
Bridge *Wakef* 70–76; Chapl St Paul's Girls' Sch Hammersmith
77–01; LtO *Lon* 77–98; P in O 84–91; rtd 05; PtO *Chich*
from 13. *Bramble, Weaver's Lane, Alfriston BN26 5TH*
E: adamfordspgs@hotmail.com

FORD, Alun James. b 73. Ex Univ BA 94 MA 96 Man Univ
PhD 09 St Jo Coll Cam BA 11. Westcott Ho Cam 08.
d 11 p 12. C Newc St Geo and St Hilda 11–14; V Sugley
14–17; P-in-c Fen Ditton *Ely* from 17; P-in-c Horningsea
from 17; P-in-c Teversham from 17. *The Rectory, 29 High
Street, Fen Ditton, Cambridge CB5 8ST* T: (01223) 295927
E: alun.ford@gmail.com

FORD, Canon Amanda Kirstine. b 61. Middx Univ
BA 83 Open Univ MA 97. St Steph Ho Ox 98. d 00 p 01.
C Leic Resurr 00–05; P-in-c Beaumont Leys 05–09; V
09–14; P-in-c Stocking Farm 11–14; AD City of Leic
11–14; Dioc CUF Officer 04–14; Hon Can Leic Cathl
13–14; Can Res and Chan S'wark Cathl from 14; Dir
Minl Educn from 14. *483C Southwark Park Road, London
SE16 2JP* T: (020) 7939 9449 E: mandyford@btinternet.com
or mandy.ford@southwark.anglican.org

FORD, Anthony. b 60. Oak Hill Th Coll 06. d 08 p 09. C
Chadderton Ch Ch *Man* 08–11; P-in-c Balderstone 11–13; V
13–18; P-in-c Barrow St Mark *Carl* from 18. *St Mark's Vicarage,
Rawlinson Street, Barrow-in-Furness LA14 1BX* T: (01229)
820405 M: 07816-596878 E: tonyford227@btinternet.com

FORD, Mrs Avril Celia. b 43. St Mary's Coll Dur BSc 64
Chelsea Coll Lon PGCE 65. d 92 p 94. OLM Horncastle w
Low Toynton *Linc* 92–98; NSM 98–06; OLM High Toynton
92–98; NSM 98–06; OLM Greetham w Ashby Puerorum
92–98; NSM 98–06; NSM Horncastle Gp 06–16; PtO from 16.
Frolic, Reindeer Close, Horncastle LN9 5AA T: (01507) 526234
or 525600 E: avrilford@btinternet.com

FORD, Brian. b 40. Imp Coll Lon BSc 62 Nottm Univ
MSc 66 PhD 74 Ox Univ MA 74 CMath FIMA ARCS.
SAOMC 96. d 99 p 00. NSM Witney *Ox* 99–02; NSM Forest
Edge 02–15; rtd 15; PtO *Ox* from 15. *Ramsden Farmhouse,
Ramsden, Oxford OX7 3AU* T: (01993) 868343 F: 868322
E: brianford2809@gmail.com

FORD, Carol Mary. *See* BARRETT FORD, Carol Mary

FORD (*née* HARRISON-WATSON), Mrs Carole. b 44. Reading
Univ BSc 66 St Martin's Coll Lanc PGCE 79. Carl Dioc Tr
Inst 92. d 95 p 96. NSM Windermere *Carl* 95–98; NSM
Borrowdale 98–01; NSM Thornthwaite cum Braithwaite,
Newlands etc 01–05; rtd 05; PtO *Carl* from 05. *4 Woodlands
Drive, Allithwaite, Grange-over-Sands LA11 7PZ*

FORD, David John. b 38. Lon Coll of Div BD 68. d 69 p 70.
C Blackheath St Jo *S'wark* 69–71; C Westlands St Andr

Lich 71–75; V Sheff St Steph w St Phil and St Ann 75–77;
R Netherthorpe 77–80; TR 80–84; R Thrybergh 82–84; R
Thrybergh w Hooton Roberts 84–94; Ind Chapl 86–87; TV
Parkham, Alwington, Buckland Brewer etc *Ex* 94–01; rtd
03; Hon C Knaresborough *Ripon* 01–05; PtO *York* 07–16. *19
Broom Drive, Rotherham S60 3NS* T: (01709) 641375

FORD, David Stuart. b 61. City of Lon Poly BA 82 Qu Coll
Birm MA 09. WMMTC 06. d 09 p 10. C Bramhope and
Ireland Wood *Ripon* 09–10; C Leeds City 10–11; Chapl Chapl
Abbey Grange High Sch 09–11; TV Hucknall Torkard *S'well*
11–14; Chapl Nat C of E Academy Hucknall 11–14; P-in-c
Northleach w Hampnett and Farmington etc *Glouc* 14–16; R
16–19; TR Bromsgrove *Worc* from 19; V Dodford from 19. *The
Vicarage, 15 Finstall Road, Bromsgrove B60 2EA* T: (01527)
873831 M: 07973-412625

FORD, Mrs Deborah Perrin. b 59. Leeds Univ BA 81 Birm Univ
MSocSc 85 Univ of Wales (Ban) BTh CQSW 85. EAMTC 00.
d 03 p 04. NSM Cambridge St Benedict *Ely* 03–12; NSM
Cambridge St Jas from 12; Chapl Cam Univ Hosps NHS
Foundn Trust from 03; Bp's Adv for Healthcare Chapl *Ely*
from 16. *102 Millington Lane, Cambridge CB3 9HA* T: (01223)
329321 *or* 363113 E: deborahford@gmail.com

FORD, Mrs Gaynor. b 47. Univ of Wales (Lamp) BA 99.
d 17 p 18. NSM Dale and St Brides w Marloes and
Hasguard w St Ishmael's *St D* from 17. *4 Pond Meadow,
Steynton, Milford Haven SA73 1HB* T: (01646) 693452
E: gaynorford2846@btinternet.com

FORD, Canon Henry Malcolm. b 33. Em Coll Cam BA 54
MA 58. Ely Th Coll 58. d 59 p 69. C Ipswich St Matt *St E*
59–61; Hon C Bury St Edmunds St Jo 66–76; Hon C Hawstead
and Nowton w Stanningfield etc 76–89; Hon Can St E Cathl
86–97; NSM Cockfield w Bradfield St Clare, Felsham etc
89–98; PtO 09–19. *Thatch on the Green, Cross Green, Cockfield,
Bury St Edmunds IP30 0LG* T: (01284) 828479

FORD, John. *See* FORD, William John

✠**FORD, The Rt Revd John Frank.** b 52. Chich Univ MA 04.
Chich Th Coll 76. d 79 p 80 c 05. C Forest Hill Ch Ch *S'wark*
79–82; V Lee St Aug 82–91; V Lower Beeding and Dom Chapl
to Bp Horsham *Chich* 91–94; Dioc Missr 94–00; Can and Preb
Chich Cathl 97–00; Can Res and Prec Chich Cathl 00–05;
Suff Bp Plymouth *Ex* 05–13; Asst Bp Truro 11–13; Bp The
Murray Australia from 13. *Diocese of The Murray, PO Box
394, Murray Bridge SA 5253, Australia* T: (0061) (8) 8532
2270 F: 8532 5760 E: registry@murray.anglican.org

FORD, Jonathan Laurence. *See* ALDERTON-FORD, Jonathan
Laurence

FORD, Mrs Kimberley Kaye. b 65. St Jo Coll Nottm 09. d 11
p 12. C Market Harborough and The Transfiguration etc
Leic 11–14; P-in-c Glen Magna cum Stretton Magna etc
14–19; TV Oadby Gt Glen from 19; Warden Past Assts from
18. *St Cuthbert's Vicarage, Church Road, Great Glen, Leicester
LE8 9FE* T: 0116-259 2238 E: kimberleykford@aim.com

FORD, Nancy Celia. b 48. Open Univ BA 02 FCIPD 00.
STETS 98. d 01 p 02. NSM Crookham *Guildf* 01–04; NSM
Aldershot St Mich 04–07; Asst Dioc Dir of Ords 04–05; Bp's
Chapl 05–10; Min Can Guildf Cathl 07–14; rtd 14; PtO *Chich*
from 14. *40 Orchard Avenue, Worthing BN14 7QB* T: (01903)
411523 E: nancyc.ford@sky.com

FORD, Peter. b 46. York Univ MA 96 Bede Coll Dur TCert 72
ACP 75. Linc Th Coll 76. d 78 p 79. OGS from 72; C
Hartlepool H Trin *Dur* 78–81; Dioc Youth Officer *Wakef*
81–84; C Mirfield Eastthorpe St Paul 82–84; C Upper Hopton
82–84; V Dodworth 84–88; Chapl and Hd RS Rishworth
Sch Ripponden 88–97; Ho Master 94–97; P-in-c Accrington
St Mary *Blackb* 97–99; C Torrisholme 99–01; V Warton
St Paul 01–08; Dioc Ecum Officer 02–08; Germany 08–09;
P-in-c Las Palmas *Eur* 09–13; P-in-c Oporto 13; rtd 13; Asst
Chapl Gib *Eur* 11–17; P-in-c Lanzarote 17–18; PtO from 18.
*Edificio Carlita 5F, Paseo de Maritimo 84, Los Boliches, 29640
Fuengirola (Malaga), Spain* T: (0034) 951 251 857 M: 692
301 288 E: pford@ogs.net

FORD, Canon Peter Hugh. b 43. St Cath Coll Cam BA 65
MA 69. Cuddesdon Coll 65. d 67 p 68. C Is of Dogs Ch Ch
and St Jo w St Luke *Lon* 67–70; C Tillsonburg St Jo Canada
70–71; St Catherine's St Thos 71–73; P-in-c Thorold South
Resurr 71–73; R Port Colborne St Brendan 73–78; R Milton
Grace Ch 78–80; Can Pastor Ch Ch Cathl Hamilton 80–86;
Adn Lincoln 86–91; R Niagara-on-the-Lake St Mark 86–91;
Hon Chapl Niagara from 91; Hon C Montserrat St Geo
Canada 91; R Saba 92–98; PtO *Chich* 98–99; V Newchurch
and Arreton *Portsm* 99–07; rtd 07; PtO *Portsm* from 15. *11
Vokins Rise, Esplanade, Ryde PO33 2AX* T: (01983) 568286
E: islandpeter@btinternet.com

FORD, Philippa. b 65. RVC(Lon) BVetMed 90. St Mellitus Coll
MA 18. d 16 p 17. C Burpham *Guildf* 16–17; C Guildf All

SS 17–19; C Woking Ch Ch from 19. *15A Woodruff Avenue, Guildford GU1 1XT* T: (01483) 457927 M: 07814-847436

FORD, Mrs Rachel Joy. b 83. York Univ BA 04 York St Jo Univ PGCE 05. St Hild Coll 16. **d** 19. C Abbeylands *Leeds* from 19. *The Vicarage, 1 Scotland Close, Horsforth, Leeds LS18 5SG* T: 0113-258 1719 E: rachel.ford@leeds.anglican.org

FORD, Richard. b 47. Grey Coll Dur BA 69 PGCE 70 FRSA 94. SEITE 06. **d** 09 **p** 10. NSM Sanderstead *S'wark* 09–15; NSM W Wickham St Fran and St Mary 15–17; NSM W Wickham St Jo 15–17; PtO from 17. *7 Sylvan Way, West Wickham BR4 9HA* T: (020) 8289 2432 M: 07706-998272 E: richard.ford73@ntlworld.com

FORD, Richard Graham. b 39. AKC 65 Open Univ BA 96. **d** 66 **p** 67. C Morpeth *Newc* 66–71; C Fordingbridge w Ibsley *Win* 71–73; TV Whorlton *Newc* 73–80; Chapl RNR 75–92; V Choppington *Newc* 80–92; V Tynemouth Priory 92–04; rtd 04; PtO *S'well* from 16. *13 St Mary's Drive, Edwinstowe, Mansfield NG21 9LY* T: (01623) 824985 E: richardford43@btinternet.com

FORD, Roger James. b 33. Sarum & Wells Th Coll 81. **d** 83 **p** 84. C Sidcup St Jo *Roch* 83–86; V Darenth 86–98; rtd 98; PtO *Cov* 02–04. *21 Hawthorn Way, Shipston-on-Stour CV36 4FD* T: (01608) 664875 E: roger585413@gmail.com

FORD, Roger Lindsay. b 47. Ex Univ LLB 68. Llan Dioc Tr Scheme 87. **d** 91 **p** 92. NSM Fairwater *Llan* 91–96; NSM Llandaff 96–01; NSM Arthog w Fairbourne w Llangelynnin w Rhoslefain *Ban* 12–14; NSM Bro Cymer from 14. *The Rectory, Llwyngwril LL37 2JB* T: (01341) 250888 E: lindsayrectory@hotmail.co.uk

FORD, Mrs Shirley Elsworth. b 40. AIMLS 67. Sarum & Wells Th Coll 89. **d** 91 **p** 94. C Farnham *Guildf* 91–96; V Wrecclesham 96–04; rtd 04; PtO *Chich* from 05. *19 St Luke's Terrace, Brighton BN2 9ZE* T: (01273) 674061

FORD, Canon William John. b 50. Linc Th Coll 89. **d** 91 **p** 92. C Marton-in-Cleveland *York* 91–94; V Whorlton w Carlton and Faceby 94–02; P-in-c Stainton w Hilton 02–12; P-in-c Brookfield 11–12; R Yarm from 12; P-in-c Crathorne from 17; P-in-c Kirklevington w Picton, and High and Low Worsall from 17; P-in-c Rudby in Cleveland w Middleton from 17; P-in-c Whorlton w Carlton and Faceby from 17; RD Stokesley from 03; Can and Preb York Minster from 13. *The Rectory, 6 Westgate, Yarm TS15 9QT* T: (01642) 964664 E: revjohnford@sky.com

FORDE, Barry George. **d** 07 **p** 08. C Coleraine *Conn* 07–10; Chapl and Dean of Residence QUB from 10. *20 Elmwood Avenue, Belfast BT9 6AY* T: (028) 9066 7754 or 9573 5980 E: barry@thehubbelfast.org

FORDE, The Very Revd Stephen Bernard. b 61. Edin Univ BSc. TCD Div Sch. **d** 86 **p** 87. C Belfast St Mary w H Redeemer *Conn* 86–89; Chapl QUB 89–95; Min Can Belf Cathl 89–91; Bp's Dom Chapl *Conn* 90–95; I Dublin Booterstown *D & G* 95–99; Dean of Res UCD 95–99; I Larne and Inver *Conn* 99–18; I Glynn w Raloo 99–18; Adn Dalriada 06–18; Dean Belf from 18. *The Deanery, 5 Deramore Drive, Belfast BT9 5JQ* T: (028) 9032 8332 or 9066 0980 E: stephenforde@btinternet.com or dean@belfastcathedral.org

FORDHAM, Richard George. b 34. AIMarE 60 TEng(CEI) 71 FBIM 74. **d** 91 **p** 92. NSM Cookham *Ox* 91–94; NSM Hedsor and Bourne End 94–01; PtO 01–03; *Ely* from 03. *6 Sorrel Way, Downham Market PE38 9UD* T: (01366) 384271 E: richardfordham939@btinternet.com

FORDYCE, Andrew Ian. b 70. K Alfred's Coll Win BA 94 Southn Univ PGCE 96. Trin Coll Bris BA 03. **d** 03 **p** 04. C Bramshott and Liphook *Portsm* 03–07; V Berechurch St Marg w St Mich *Chelmsf* 07–19; V Tenpenny Villages from 19. *The Rectory, St Andrew's Close, Alresford, Colchester CO7 8BL* M: 07790-543304 E: revdyce@gmail.com

FOREMAN, Mrs Jennifer Ruth. b 90. York Univ BA 11 St Jo Coll Dur BA 17. Cranmer Hall Dur 14. **d** 17 **p** 18. C Kingston upon Hull St Nic *York* from 17. *5 Gemsbok Way, Hull HU4 6UF* M: 07768-593395 E: jenni.r.foreman@gmail.com

FOREMAN, Canon Patrick Brian. b 41. CertEd. St Jo Coll Nottm 77. **d** 79 **p** 80. C Gainsborough All SS *Linc* 79–83; V Thornton St Jas *Bradf* 83–91; R Hevingham w Hainford and Stratton Strawless *Nor* 91–99; RD Ingworth 94–99; V Heacham 99–06; Hon Can Nor Cathl 03–06; rtd 06; PtO *Nor* from 06; RD Burnham and Walsingham 14–15; Bp's Officer for Rtd Clergy and Widows 08–15. *Seorah, 7 Mallard Close, Fakenham NR21 8PU* T: (01328) 853691 E: patrick@pandmforeman.eclipse.co.uk

FOREMAN, Mrs Penelope. b 47. Lon Inst of Educn TCert 68 Ch Ch Coll Cant BEd 90 MA 93. SEITE 04. **d** 06 **p** 07. NSM Roch St Justus 06–15; P-in-c Chatham St Mary w St Jo 15–17; AD Roch 14–17; rtd 17. *28 Kingsway, Chatham ME5 7HT* T: (01634) 571220 E: penny.foreman@btinternet.com

FOREMAN, Timothy. b 56. K Coll Lon BD 77. SEITE 97. **d** 99 **p** 00. C Camberwell St Giles w St Matt *S'wark* 99–02; R Buckland-in-Dover *Cant* 02–13; Hon Min Can Cant Cathl 04–13; V Walker *Newc* 13–18; P-in-c Eastchurch w Leysdown and Harty *Cant* from 18. *The Rectory, Warden Road, Eastchurch, Sheerness ME12 4EJ* T: (01795) 880825 E: fr.timforeman@gmail.com

FOREMAN, Vanessa Jane. *See* LAWRENCE, Vanessa Jane

FORESHEW-CAIN, Andrew David. b 63. Aber Univ BSc 86. Ripon Coll Cuddesdon BA 89. **d** 90 **p** 91. C Walworth St Jo *S'wark* 90–94; Bp's Dom Chapl *Ox* 94–98; P-in-c Kilburn St Mary w All So *Lon* 98–01; P-in-c W Hampstead St Jas 98–01; V Kilburn St Mary w All So and W Hampstead St Jas 01–17; AD N Camden 07–14. *The Old Vicarage, 23 High Street, Chapel-en-le-Frith, High Peak SK23 0HD* E: andynw6@icloud.com

FORMAN, Deborah Jayne. b 56. LMH Ox BA 78 MA 83 PGCE 79 Lambeth STh 07. STETS 05. **d** 08 **p** 09. C Churchdown St Jo and Innsworth *Glouc* 08–11; P-in-c Pebworth, Dorsington, Honeybourne etc 11–14; C Quinton and Welford w Weston 11–14; TV Vale and Cotswold Edge 14–16; V Addington *S'wark* from 16; Dir Ords Croydon Area from 17. *The Vicarage, Spout Hill, Croydon CR0 5AN* T: (01689) 847092 M: 07985-943371 E: deborah.forman2@btinternet.com

FORRER, Michael Dennett Cuthbert. b 34. St Pet Hall Ox BA 59 MA 63. Wycliffe Hall Ox 59. **d** 60 **p** 61. C Westwood *Cov* 60–63; C Cov Cathl 63–71; Ind Chapl 63–69; Sen Ind Chapl 69–71; Hon C All Hallows by the Tower etc *Lon* 76–99; Asst P Bangkok Ch Ch Thailand 81–89; PtO *Sarum* 99–01; *Ox* 01–02 and from 11; Hon C Sonning 02–11; rtd 04. *36 Ravensbourne Drive, Woodley, Reading RG5 4LJ* T: 0118-996 8050 M: 07899-926020 E: majing3008@gmail.com

FORREST, Antony William. b 60. Imp Coll Lon BSc 82 Sussex Univ PGCE 83 Leic Univ MBA 06 Win Univ MA 12 ARCS 82 FCollP 08. STETS 08. **d** 11 **p** 12. C Portsea N End St Mark *Portsm* 11–15; Chapl Portsm Coll 12–15; R Meon Bridge *Portsm* from 15; C Soberton, Newtown and Hambledon from 19. *The Rectory, Rectory Lane, Meonstoke, Southampton SO32 3NF* T: (01489) 877422

FORREST, Michael Barry Eric. b 38. Lon Univ BA 87 MA 89. NZ Bd of Th Studies LTh 62 Chich Th Coll 64. **d** 66 **p** 67. C Beckenham St Jas *Roch* 66–70; P-in-c Cape Vogel Papua New Guinea 70–73; P-in-c Alotau 74; R Lae 74–76; C Altarnon and Bolventor *Truro* 76–78; TV N Hill w Altarnon, Bolventor and Lewannick 78–79; R St Martin w E and W Looe 79–84; V Kensington St Phil Earl's Court *Lon* 84–04; rtd 04; PtO *Chich* from 04. *12 Riley Road, Brighton BN2 4AH* T: (01273) 690231 E: mbe.forrest@gmail.com

FORREST, Canon Robin Whyte. b 33. Edin Th Coll 58. **d** 61 **p** 62. C Glas St Mary 61–66; R Renfrew 66–70; R Motherwell 70–79; R Wishaw 75–79; R Forres *Mor* 79–98; R Nairn 79–92; Can St Andr Cathl Inverness 88–98; Hon Can St Andr Cathl Inverness from 98; Syn Clerk 91–92; Dean Mor 92–98; rtd 98. *Landeck, Cummingston, Elgin IV30 5XY* T/F: (01343) 835539 E: robin.forrest33@btinternet.com

FORREST (née Dinwiddy), Sarah Louise. b 72. Charing Cross Hosp Medical Sch MB, BS 97 MRCGP 07. ERMC 14. **d** 17 **p** 18. C Bishop's Stortford St Alb from 17. *Sarnia, 5 Church Manor, Bishop's Stortford CM23 5AF* T: (01279) 507825 M: 07488-914972 E: sarahforrest23@icloud.com

FORREST-REDFERN, Mrs Susan Michéle. b 57. S Bank Poly BEd 86. St Jo Coll Nottm 01. **d** 03 **p** 04. C Lostock St Thos and St Jo *Man* 03–06; C Bolton St Bede 05–06; Ch/Sch Missr E Bolton 06–15; C Tonge Fold 07–10; Chapl St Cath Academy Bolton 11–15; TV Morley *Leeds* from 15. *4 Lewisham Street, Morley, Leeds LS27 0LA* T: 0113-252 3783 M: 07738-407852 E: revsuefr@yahoo.co.uk

FORRESTER, Brenda Rose. b 72. Newc Univ BSc 93 Dur Univ MA 02. Lindisfarne Regional Tr Partnership 15. **d** 18 **p** 19. NSM Washington *Dur* from 18. *113 Rydal Road, Chester le Street DH2 3DS* T: 0191-387 3993 M: 07988-320368 E: forresterbrenda06@gmail.com

FORRESTER, Ian Michael. b 56. Chich Th Coll. **d** 82 **p** 83. C Leigh-on-Sea St Marg *Chelmsf* 82–84; Min Can, Succ and Dean's V Windsor 84–86; Prec and Chapl Chelmsf Cathl 86–91; Chapl Lancing Coll 91–99; P-in-c Boxgrove *Chich* from 99; Dioc Liturgy and Music Consultant from 95. *The Vicarage, Boxgrove, Chichester PO18 0ED* T: (01243) 774045 E: revdianforrester@hotmail.com

FORRESTER, James Oliphant. b 50. SS Coll Cam BA 72 MA 76. Wycliffe Hall Ox 73. **d** 76 **p** 77. C Hull St Jo Newland *York* 76–80; C Fulwood *Sheff* 80–87; V Lodge Moor St Luke 87–90; V Ecclesfield 90–01; AD 99–01; P-in-c Kingston upon Hull St Trin *York* 01–02; V and Lect 02–09; V Longnor, Quarnford and Sheen *Lich* 09–16; RD Alstonfield 12–16; rtd 16; PtO

Heref from 17. *4 Mortimer Drive, Orleton, Ludlow SY8 4JW*
E: james@forres50.plus.com

FORRESTER, Robin William. b 43. Kent Univ MA 84 Aston Univ MSc 90. All Nations Chr Coll 64. **d** 04 **p** 05. NSM Wharton *Ches* 04–06; P-in-c Moulton 06–11; rtd 11; PtO *Ches* from 11. *27 Leven Avenue, Winsford CW7 3TA* T: (01606) 215248 E: robinforrester@sky.com

FORSDIKE, Alan William. b 55. **d** 05 **p** 06. NSM Westerfield and Tuddenham w Witnesham *St E* from 05; P-in-c from 17. *Hill House, 2 Henley Road, Ipswich IP1 3SF* T: (01473) 252904 E: alan@wtandw.org.uk or alan.forsdike@btinternet.com

FORSE, Reginald Austin. b 43. Oak Hill Th Coll 77. **d** 79 **p** 80. C Crofton *Portsm* 79–84; NSM Gosport Ch Ch 91–96; NSM Alverstoke 96–13; PtO from 13. *40 Osprey Gardens, Lee-on-the-Solent PO13 8LJ* T: (023) 9255 3395 E: regforse@yahoo.co.uk

FORSHAW, David Oliver. b 27. Trin Coll Cam BA 50 MA 52. Qu Coll Birm. **d** 53 **p** 54. C Glen Parva and S Wigston *Leic* 53–55; Singapore 55–59; V Heptonstall *Wakef* 59–66; V Whitehaven St Nic *Carl* 66–76; P-in-c Whitehaven Ch Ch w H Trin 73–76; V Benchill *Man* 76–89; C Elton All SS 89–92; rtd 92; PtO *Carl* 92–18. *School House, Basingstoke Road, Old Alresford, Alresford SO24 9DR* T: (01962) 735343

FORSHAW, Mrs Frances Ann. b 52. Edin Univ BSc 74 Glas Univ MN 91 RGN 76 SCM 78. Moray Ord Course 91. **d** 98 **p** 02. NSM Elgin w Lossiemouth *Mor* 98–01; NSM Perth St Jo *St And* 01–05; P-in-c Pitlochry and Kilmaveonaig 05–09; NSM St Ninian's Cathl Perth 09–10; Miss P Fochabers *Mor* 10–15; rtd 15; PtO *St And* from 17. *Sunhaven, Caputh, Perth PH1 4JL* E: franceforshaw1@gmail.com

FORSHAW, Mrs Susan Margaret. b 47. Man Univ BSc 68 Makerere Univ Kampala DipEd 69. EMMTC 82. **dss** 82 **d** 87 **p** 95. Cinderhill *S'well* 82–85; Dioc Adv in Adult Educn 85–92; Par Dn Nottingham St Mary and St Cath 93–95; Lect 95–97; Asst Chapl Qu Medical Cen Nottm Univ Hosp NHS Trust 97–03; Sen Chapl 03–07; rtd 07; PtO *Leic* from 08. *33 Upton Close, Millers Reach, Castle Donington, Derby DE74 2GN* T: (01332) 858267 E: susanforshaw@talktalk.net

FORSTER, Alistair Marcus. b 68. Ch Ch Coll Cant BA 90. St Aug Coll of Th 15. **d** 18 **p** 19. C Norbury St Oswald *S'wark* from 18. *The Vicarage, 23 St Paul's Road, Thornton Heath CR7 8NB* M: 07710-405187 E: alistair.forster101@gmail.com

FORSTER, The Ven Andrew James. b 67. QUB BA 89. CITC BTh 92. **d** 92 **p** 93. C Willowfield *D & D* 92–95; Dean of Res QUB 95–02; C of I Adv Downtown Radio Newtownards 96–02; I Drumcliffe w Lissadell and Munninane *K, E & A* 02–07; Adn Elphin and Ardagh 02–07; I Drumglass w Moygashel *Arm* from 07; Adn Ardboe from 15. *The Rectory, 26 Circular Road, Dungannon BT71 6BE* T: (028) 8772 2614 E: drumglass@armagh.anglican.org

FORSTER, Gregory Stuart. b 47. Worc Coll Ox BA 69 MA 73. Wycliffe Hall Ox 69. **d** 72 **p** 73. C Bath Walcot *B & W* 72–74; C Bolton Em *Man* 74–76; C Bolton St Paul w Em 77–79; R Northenden 79–15; rtd 15; PtO *Heref* from 16. *43 Essex Road, Church Stretton SY6 6AY*

FORSTER, Jonathan William. b 82. St Mellitus Coll 15. **d** 18 **p** 19. C Huyton Quarry *Liv* from 18. *Address withheld by request* E: revjontyforster@gmail.com

✠**FORSTER, The Rt Revd Peter Robert.** b 50. Mert Coll Ox MA 73 Edin Univ BD 77 PhD 85. Edin Th Coll 78. **d** 80 **p** 81 **c** 96. C Mossley Hill St Matt and St Jas *Liv* 80–82; Sen Tutor St Jo Coll Dur 83–91; V Beverley Minster *York* 91–96; C Routh 91–96; Bp Ches from 96. *Bishop's House, 1 Abbey Street, Chester CH1 2JD* T: (01244) 350864 F: 314187 E: bpchester@chester.anglican.org

FORSTER, Canon Thomas Shane. b 72. QUB BA 93. CITC BTh 93. **d** 96 **p** 97. C Drumglass w Moygashel *Arm* 96–99; Hon V Choral Arm Cathl 97–99; I Donaghmore w Upper Donaghmore 99–06; I Ballymore from 06; Sen Dom Chapl to Abp Arm from 06; Dioc Communications Officer 02–09; Asst Dioc and Prov Registrar from 09; Can St Patr Cathl Dublin from 14. *Ballymore Rectory, 10 Glebe Hill Road, Tandragee, Craigavon BT62 2DP* T: (028) 3884 0234 E: ballymore@armagh.anglican.org

FORSTER, William. b 50. NOC 92. **d** 95 **p** 96. C Ashton-in-Makerfield St Thos *Liv* 95–00; TR Fazakerley Em 00–08; TV Eccleston Team 08–15; rtd 15; PtO *Liv* from 16. *7 Sunningdale Close, Liverpool L36 4QF* T: 0151-482 6623 E: william.forster1@btopenworld.com

FORSYTH, John Warren. b 38. Univ of W Aus BA 62 Princeton Th Sem DMin 98. St Mich Th Coll Crafers 65. **d** 65 **p** 66. C Busselton Australia 65–68; R Kondinin 68–72; C Warwick St Mary *Cov* 72–74; C Edin St Pet 74–76; R E Fremantle and Palmyra Australia 76–79; Chapl Abp Perth 79–82; Warden Wollaston 79–82; R Midland 82–89; Sen Angl Chapl R Perth Hosp 89–06; rtd 06; Perm to Offic Dio Perth Australia from

06. *40B Cookham Road, Lathlain WA 6100, Australia* T: (0061) (8) 9472 1893 M: 89-472 1893 E: forsyth@iinet.net.au

FORTNUM, Brian Charles Henry. b 48. Hertf Coll Ox MA Imp Coll Lon MSc. Wycliffe Hall Ox 82. **d** 84 **p** 85. C Tonbridge St Steph *Roch* 84–87; V Shorne 87–94; P-in-c Speldhurst w Groombridge and Ashurst 94–98; R 98–01; V Tunbridge Wells St Mark 01–12; rtd 12; PtO *Roch* from 13. *27 Ames Way, Kings Hill, West Malling ME19 4HT* E: brian.fortnum@btinternet.com

FORWARD, Canon Eric Toby. b 50. Nottm Univ BEd 72 Hull Univ MA 93. Cuddesdon Coll 74. **d** 77 **p** 78. C Forest Hill Ch Ch *S'wark* 77–80; Chapl Goldsmiths' Coll Lon 80–84; Chapl Westwood Ho Sch Pet 84–86; V Brighton St Aug and St Sav *Chich* 86–90; PtO *York* 90–95; V Kingston upon Hull St Alb 95–05; Can Res and Prec Liv Cathl 05–07; rtd 07. *2 Kingsway, Liverpool L22 4RQ* T: 0151-928 0681 E: roby.forward@blueyonder.co.uk

FORWARD, Miss Frances Mary. b 43. Bp Otter Coll Chich TCert 64. SEITE 96. **d** 99 **p** 00. NSM Ham St Andr *S'wark* 99–09; NSM Ham St Rich 09–13; NSM Petersham 09–13; PtO from 13. *66 Tudor Drive, Kingston upon Thames KT2 5QF* T: (020) 8546 1833

FORWARD, Toby. *See* FORWARD, Eric Toby

FOSS, David Blair. b 44. Bris Univ BA 65 Dur Univ MA 66 Fitzw Coll Cam BA 68 MA 72 K Coll Lon PhD 86. St Chad's Coll Dur 68. **d** 69 **p** 70. C Barnard Castle *Dur* 69–72; Sierra Leone 72–74; Chapl St Jo Coll York 74–75; Chapl Ch Ch Coll of HE Cant 75–80; Chapl Elmslie Girls' Sch Blackpool 80–83; Tutor Coll of Resurr Mirfield 83–88; V Battyeford *Wakef* 88–99; V Ryde All SS *Portsm* 99–01; TR Rochdale *Man* 01–09; R 09–10; rtd 10; PtO *Man* from 10. *11 Sims Close, Ramsbottom, Bury BL0 9NT* T: (01706) 828248

FOSS, Esther Rose. b 79. Regent's Park Coll Ox BA 00 MA 04 Clare Hall Cam MPhil 04 Univ of Wales (Trin St Dav) MA 12. Westcott Ho Cam 03. **d** 05 **p** 06. C Altrincham St Geo *Ches* 05–07; C Bramhall 07–09; TV Knaresborough *Ripon* 09–14; *Leeds* 14–15; P-in-c Coulsdon St Andr *S'wark* 15–18; V from 18; Dioc Chapl MU from 17. *St Andrew's Vicarage, Julien Road, Coulsdon CR5 2DN* T: (020) 3620 1885 E: esther.foss@live.co.uk or standrewsvicar@yahoo.co.uk

FOSSETT, Michael Charles Sinclair. b 30. Dur Univ BSc 54 CEng 59 MIMechE 59. NEOC 82. **d** 90 **p** 91. NSM Nether w Upper Poppleton *York* from 90. *20 Fairway Drive, Upper Poppleton, York YO26 6HE* T: (01904) 794712 E: michael_fossett@hotmail.com

FOSSEY (née HIRST), Margaret. b 52. Huddersfield Univ BA 96. NOC 06. **d** 09 **p** 10. NSM Birkby and Birchencliffe *Leeds* 09–16; NSM Almondbury w Farnley Tyas from 16. *103 Kirkstone Avenue, Dalton, Huddersfield HD5 9ES* T: (01484) 301242 E: m.fossey@ntlworld.com

FOSTEKEW, Canon Dean James Benedict. b 63. Bulmershe Coll of HE BEd 86. Chich Th Coll 89. **d** 92 **p** 93. C Boyne Hill *Ox* 92–95; P-in-c Lockerbie and Annan *Glas* 95–97; P-in-c Dalmahoy *Edin* 97–02; TV Edin St Mary 02–09; R Edin Gd Shep from 09; Dioc Miss 21 Co-ord 97–11; Prov Miss 21 Co-ord 01–11; Can St Mary's Cathl from 15. *The Rectory, 9 Upper Coltbridge Terrace, Edinburgh EH12 6AD* T: 0131-346 4127 M: 07968-099470 E: therector@uwclub.net or mission21@edinburgh.anglican.org

FOSTER, Antony John. b 39. Down Coll Cam BA 61 MA 65. Ridley Hall Cam 65. **d** 66 **p** 67. C Sandal St Helen *Wakef* 66–69; Uganda 69–74; V Mount Pellon *Wakef* 74–92; rtd 92; PtO *Wakef* 92–14; *Leeds* from 14. *32 Savile Drive, Halifax HX1 2EU* T: (01422) 344152

✠**FOSTER, The Rt Revd Christopher Richard James.** b 53. Univ Coll Dur BA 75 Man Univ MA 77 Trin Hall Cam BA 79 MA 83 Wadh Coll Ox MA 83. Westcott Ho Cam 78. **d** 80 **p** 81 **c** 01. C Tettenhall Regis *Lich* 80–82; Chapl Wadh Coll Ox 82–86; C Ox St Mary V w St Cross and St Pet 82–86; V Southgate Ch Ch *Lon* 86–94; CME Officer 88–94; Can Res and Sub-Dean St Alb 94–01; Suff Bp Hertford 01–10; Bp Portsm from 10. *Bishopsgrove, 26 Osborn Road, Fareham PO16 7DQ* T: (01329) 280247 E: bishop@portsmouth.anglican.org

FOSTER, Canon David Brereton. b 55. Selw Coll Cam BA 77 MA 81 Ox Univ BA 80. Wycliffe Hall Ox 78. **d** 81 **p** 82. C Luton St Mary *St Alb* 81–84; C Douglas St Geo and St Barn *S & M* 84–87; V S Ramsey St Paul 87–91; Dir Dioc Tr Inst 88–91; Asst Dir Buckingham Adnry Chr Tr Progr *Ox* 91–95; Dir 95–97; C W Wycombe w Bledlow Ridge, Bradenham and Radnage 91–97; TV High Wycombe 97–07; Tr Officer CME and Laity Development *Man* 07–12; Bp's Officer for Ord and Initial Tr *Nor* from 12; Hon Can Nor Cathl from 17. *Diocesan House, 109 Dereham Road, Easton, Norwich NR9 5ES* T: (01603) 882337 E: davidfoster@runbox.com or david.foster@dioceseofnorwich.org

FOSTER, Edward Philip John. b 49. Trin Hall Cam BA 70 MA 74. Ridley Hall Cam 76. **d** 79 **p** 80. C Finchley Ch Ch *Lon* 79–82; C Marple All SS *Ches* 82–86; P-in-c Cambridge St Matt *Ely* 86–90; V 90–07; rtd 07. *1 Barnfield, Common Lane, Hemingford Abbots, Huntingdon PE28 9AX* T: (01480) 399098 E: philip.foster12@ntlworld.com

FOSTER, Frances Elizabeth. *See* TYLER, Frances Elizabeth

FOSTER, Canon Gareth Glynne. b 44. Open Univ BA. Chich Th Coll 66. **d** 69 **p** 70. C Fairwater *Llan* 69–71; C Merthyr Tydfil and Cyfarthfa 71–76; TV 76–87; P-in-c Abercanaid and Dioc Soc Resp Officer 87–10; Exec Officer Dioc Bd Soc Resp 95–10; Can Llan Cathl 00–10; rtd 10; PtO *Llan* 12–18. *19 The Walk, Merthyr Tydfil CF47 8RW* T: (01685) 722375 M: 07850-823038

FOSTER, Gavin Richard. b 76. Regent's Park Coll Ox BA 97 MA 01 Cardiff Univ LLM 13 Barrister-at-Law (Gray's Inn) 98. Wycliffe Hall Ox BTh 09. **d** 09 **p** 10. C Radipole and Melcombe Regis *Sarum* 09–12; Bp's Dom Chapl *Win* 12–16; V Locks Heath *Portsm* from 16. *The Vicarage, 125 Locks Heath Park Road, Locks Heath, Southampton SO31 6LY* T: (01489) 578082 E: gavin@sjlh.org.uk

FOSTER, Mrs Gemma Michelle Hope. b 81. Lon Sch of Th BA 04 K Coll Lon MA 13. St Mellitus Coll 13. **d** 15 **p** 16. C Letchworth St Paul w Willian *St Alb* 15–19; P-in-c Cove St Jo *Guildf* from 19. *Fircroft, 21 St John's Road, Farnborough GU14 9RL* M: 07775-761518 E: revgemmafoster@gmail.com

FOSTER, Mrs Geraldine. b 55. RGN 77. SAOMC 00. **d** 03 **p** 04. C Flackwell Heath *Ox* 03–07; C Ashton-upon-Mersey St Mary Magd *Ches* 07–12; PtO *Nor* 12–13; C Wroxham w Hoveton and Belaugh 13–14; V Watton from 14; C Gt and Lt Cressingham w Threxton from 14. *St Mary's Vicarage, Norwich Road, Watton, Thetford IP25 6DB* T: (01953) 881252 M: 07730-586839 E: gerryfoster@runbox.com

FOSTER, Mrs Gillian Susan. b 62. Leeds Univ BA 09. NOC 06. **d** 09 **p** 10. C Frankby w Greasby *Ches* 09–13; C Ellesmere Port from 13. *4 Deeside Close, Whitby, Ellesmere Port CH65 6TH* T: 0151-356 2202 M: 07970-522365 E: revgill52@gmail.com

FOSTER, Graham Paul. b 66. Univ of W Aus BSc 86 DipEd 87 BEd 88 Murdoch Univ Aus BD 99 Qu Coll Ox MSt 00 DPhil 02. **d** 04 **p** 05. Lect NT Edin Univ from 03; NSM Edin St Mary from 04. *University of Edinburgh School of Divinity, New College, Mound Place, Edinburgh EH1 2LX* T: 0131-650 8917 E: paul.foster@ed.ac.uk

FOSTER, Mrs Jessica Beatrice. b 70. Birm Univ BA 91 Newman Univ MA 15. WEMTC 12. **d** 15. C Hall Green St Pet *Birm* 15–18; PtO from 19. *59 Addison Road, Kings Heath, Birmingham B14 7EN* T: 0121-443 2752 M: 07817-853452 E: jessbfoster3@gmail.com

FOSTER, Mrs Joan Alison. b 46. ARMCM 67. NOC 95. **d** 98 **p** 99. NSM Blundellsands St Nic *Liv* 98–02; Asst Chapl Southport and Ormskirk Hosp NHS Trust 98–02; V N Harrow St Alb *Lon* 02–16; rtd 16; PtO *Lon* from 17. *Arden Cottage, 12 Chapel Lane, Pinner HA5 1AB* T: (020) 8868 7589 M: 07713-819012 E: revjoanfoster@yahoo.co.uk

FOSTER, Leslie. b 49. Linc Th Coll 89. **d** 91 **p** 92. C Coseley Ch Ch *Lich* 91–93; C Coseley Ch Ch *Worc* 93–95; V Firbank, Howgill and Killington *Bradf* 95–00; C Sedbergh, Cautley and Garsdale 95–00; Dioc Rural Adv 96–00; P-in-c Ruyton XI Towns w Gt and Lt Ness *Lich* 00–10; V 10–14; RD Ellesmere 08–10; rtd 14. *1 Cambridge Court, Ellesmere SY12 0FN*

FOSTER, Luke Richard. b 78. St Anne's Coll Ox MA 00. Oak Hill Th Coll MTh 11. **d** 11 **p** 12. C Banbury St Paul *Ox* 11–15; Chile from 15. *2 Blenheim Court, High Street, Eynsham, Witney OX29 4NU*

FOSTER, Michael John. b 52. St Steph Ho Ox 76. **d** 79 **p** 80. C Wood Green St Mich *Lon* 79–82; TV Clifton *S'well* 82–85; P-in-c Aylesbury *Ox* 85–87; Dep Warden Durning Hall Chr Community Cen 87–89; V Lydbrook *Glouc* 89–97; R Hemsby, Winterton, E and W Somerton and Horsey *Nor* 97–99; P-in-c Tarrant Valley *Sarum* 99–01; P-in-c Tollard Royal w Farnham, Gussage St Michael etc 99–01; R Chase from 01; C Sixpenny Handley w Gussage St Andrew etc from 06. *The Rectory, Church Hill, Tarrant Hinton, Blandford Forum DT11 8JB* T: (01258) 830764 E: drmjf@church.prestel.co.uk

FOSTER, Paul. b 60. MAAT 80. Oak Hill Th Coll 91. **d** 93 **p** 94. C New Clee *Linc* 93–96; P-in-c Aldington w Bonnington and Bilsington *Cant* 96–02; P-in-c Sellindge w Monks Horton and Stowting etc 00–02; Chapl HM Pris Aldington 96–02; Chapl HM YOI Feltham from 02. *HM Young Offender Institution, Bedfont Road, Feltham TW13 4ND* T: (020) 8890 0061 *or* 8844 5325 E: pfozzy@hotmail.com *or* paul.foster01@justice.gov.uk

FOSTER, Paul. *See* FOSTER, Graham Paul

FOSTER, Philip. *See* FOSTER, Edward Philip John

FOSTER, Simon John Darby. b 57. Qu Mary Coll Lon BSc 78. Wycliffe Hall Ox 85. **d** 88 **p** 89. C Bedgrove *Ox* 88–92; C Glyncorrwg w Afan Vale and Cymmer Afan *Llan* 92–94; R Breedon cum Isley Walton and Worthington *Leic* 94–98; R Anstey 98–06; R Anstey and Thurcaston w Cropston 06–10; V Croydon St Matt *S'wark* from 10; P-in-c Croydon St Andr 17–18; AD Croydon Cen from 18. *The Vicarage, 7 Brownlow Road, Croydon CR0 5JT* T: (020) 8688 5055 *or* 8681 3147 E: revsimon@stmatthew.org.uk

FOSTER, Stephen. b 47. Leeds Univ CertEd 69. NEOC 83. **d** 86 **p** 87. NSM Kingston upon Hull St Nic *York* 86–87; NSM Aldbrough, Mappleton w Goxhill and Withernwick 87–98; TV Howden 98–05; RD 02–05; Chapl HM Pris Wolds 03–05; rtd 05; PtO *York* from 05; Chapl Costa Blanca *Eur* 13–16; PtO from 16; Chapl OHP from 17. *Wycliffe, Victoria Terrace, Robin Hoods Bay, Whitby YO22 4RJ* T: (01947) 880055 M: 07791-547727 E: tuftyclubbadge@gmail.com

FOSTER, Stephen. b 80. St Anne's Coll Ox BA 02 MA 11 Selw Coll Cam BTh 13 MPhil 14. Ridley Hall Cam 10. **d** 14 **p** 15. C Onslow Square and S Kensington St Aug *Lon* from 14. *Holy Trinity Brompton, 5-7 Cromwell Road, London SW7 2HR* E: stephen.foster@htb.org

FOSTER, Canon Stephen Arthur. b 54. Lon Univ BMus 75 BA 78 Potchefstroom Univ PhD 98. Coll of Resurr Mirfield 75. **d** 78 **p** 79. C Ches H Trin 78–82; C Tranmere St Paul w St Luke 82–83; V Grange St Andr 83–88; V Cheadle Hulme All SS 88–94; P-in-c Stockport St Matt 94–00; Asst Dir of Ords 96–04; V Sale St Anne 00–04; Can Res Leic Cathl 04–10; Prec Leic Cathl 04–10; Chapl Leic Univ 10–19; Hon Can Leic Cathl 11–19; rtd 19; PtO *Leic* from 19. *Flat 2, 5 Southampton Street, Leicester LE1 1SL* E: safpta6@gmail.com

FOSTER, Steven Francis. b 55. Lon Univ BD 74 AKC 76 Open Univ BA 91 FRSA 90. Coll of Resurr Mirfield 77. **d** 78 **p** 79. C Romford St Edw *Chelmsf* 78–80; C Leigh St Clem 80–83; Ed Mayhew McCrimmon Publishers 84–86; Hon C Southend *Chelmsf* 85–86; P-in-c Sandon 86–90; R 90–91; R Wanstead St Mary 91–93; R Wanstead St Mary w Ch Ch 93–00; PtO 00–05; Asst to Master R Foundn of St Kath in Ratcliffe 00–04; P-in-c Brighton Annunciation *Chich* 05–09; rtd 10; PtO *Chich* from 11. *55 Farm Road, Hove BN3 1FD* T: (01273) 206478 M: 07901-554866 E: stevenffoster@aol.com

FOSTER, Stuart Jack. b 47. Oak Hill Th Coll BA 80 Lambeth STh 86. **d** 80 **p** 81. C Worting *Win* 80–84; C-in-c Kempshott CD 84–88; R Hook 88–95; Chapl and Warden Bp Grosseteste Coll Linc 95–99; R Kirton in Lindsey w Manton *Linc* 99–05; R Grayingham 99–05; P-in-c Vale of Belvoir *Leic* 05–09; OCM 99–04; Chapl ATC 04–09; rtd 09; PtO *Leic* from 10; *Linc* from 16. *Sans Souci, 3 Marigold Close, Lincoln LN2 4SZ* T: (01522) 524918 M: 07887-701876 E: rafikimusoma@gmail.com

FOSTER, Susan. b 58. Nottm Univ BMedSci 80 BM, BS 82. WEMTC 00. **d** 03 **p** 05. NSM Tenbury *Heref* from 03; Chapl Kemp Hospice Kidderminster from 07. *Little Oaks Cottage, Hope Bagot, Ludlow SY8 3AE* T: (01584) 891092

FOSTER, Susan Anne. b 53. Trin Coll Bris BA 97. **d** 98 **p** 99. C Watton w Carbrooke and Ovington *Nor* 98–02; Min S Wonston CD *Win* 02–07; P-in-c Micheldever and E Stratton, Woodmancote etc 05–07; V Upper Dever 07–16; rtd 16; PtO *Chich* from 16. *10 Ham Way, Worthing BN11 2QH*

FOSTER, Mrs Susan Doreen. b 58. Win Sch of Art BA 02 Anglia Ruskin Univ MA 13. Coll of Resurr Mirfield 15. **d** 16 **p** 17. C Hadleigh, Layham and Shelley *St E* 16–19; V Rushmere from 19. *The Vicarage, 253 Colchester Road, Ipswich IP4 4SH* T: (01473) 270976 M: 07415-175745 E: revd.susanfoster@gmail.com

FOSTER, Thomas Andrew Hayden. b 43. CITC 70. **d** 73 **p** 74. C Dublin Clontarf *D & G* 73–78; I Drumcliffe w Clare Abbey and Kildysart *L & K* 78–80; P-in-c Polstead *St E* 78; I Kilscoran w Killinick and Mulrankin *C & O* 80–85; I Fanlobbus Union *C, C & R* 85–86; R Lasswade *Edin* 86–87; R Dalkeith 86–87; C Woodford St Mary w St Phil and St Jas *Chelmsf* 87–88; I New w Old Ross, Whitechurch, Fethard etc *C & O* 89–91; Dioc Info Officer (Ferns) 90–91; I Whitehouse *Conn* 03–10; rtd 10. *18 Marguerite Park, Belfast BT10 0HF* T: (028) 9061 6472 M: 07595-348856 E: tahf@me.com

FOTHERGILL, Richard Patrick. b 61. Newc Univ BA 83. Trin Coll Bris 91. **d** 95 **p** 96. C E Twickenham St Steph *Lon* 95–97; Assoc R Kirstenhof S Africa 97–04; Network Miss P *Bris* 04–06; Hon C Peasedown St John w Wellow and Foxcote etc *B & W* 08–15; PtO *Ox* 12–17; *B & W* 15–16. *Flossie's Cottage, Hodshill, South Stoke, Bath BA2 7ED* T: (01225) 832806 M: 07835-263706 E: richard@thefillingstation.org.uk

FOUHY, Giles. b 71. Oak Hill Th Coll. **d** 07 **p** 08. C Shoreditch St Leon w St Mich *Lon* 07–13; C W Hackney 13–19. *16 Albion Drive, London E8 4ET* T: (020) 7249 7119 E: gilesfouhy@hotmail.com

FOULDS, Samuel Richard. b 89. St Mellitus Coll BA 18. **d** 18 **p** 19. C Rusholme H Trin *Man* from 18. *2 Aldwych Avenue, Manchester M14 5NL* M: 07874-293776 E: sam-foulds@hotmail.co.uk

FOULGER, Jeffrey William. b 65. St Aug Coll of Th 15. **d** 17 **p** 18. NSM Beckenham St Barn *Roch* 17–18; NSM Beckenham St Geo and St Barn from 18. *1 Tudor Gardens, West Wickham BR4 9LX*

FOULGER, Wendy. b 43. St D Coll Lamp BA 90. St Jo Coll Nottm 04. **d** 11 **p** 12. NSM Cil-y-Cwm and Ystrad-ffin w Rhandir-mwyn etc *St D* 11–12; NSM Winchcombe *Glouc* 16–17; rtd 17; PtO *Glouc* from 17. *20 Gilders Paddock, Bishops Cleeve, Cheltenham GL52 8UJ* T: (01242) 679956 E: defld6@aol.com

FOULGER, William John. b 86. St Andr Univ MTheol 08 Princeton Th Sem MA 10. Cranmer Hall Dur 13. **d** 16 **p** 17. C Lenton Abbey *S'well* 16–19; Dir Miss and Evang Cranmer Hall Dur from 19. *Cranmer Hall, St John's College, 3 South Bailey, Durham DH1 3RJ* M: 07429-325560 E: foulger@me.com

FOULIS BROWN, Canon Graham Douglas. b 50. St Steph Ho Ox 80. **d** 82 **p** 83. C Hungerford and Denford *Ox* 82–84; Chapl Hungerford Hosp 83–84; C Bicester w Bucknell, Caversfield and Launton *Ox* 84–85; TV 85–90; V Kidmore End and Sonning Common 90–03; P-in-c Rotherfield Peppard 02–03; R Rotherfield Peppard and Kidmore End etc 03–15; AD Henley 06–11; Hon Can Ch Ch 11–15; rtd 15; PtO *Ox* from 15. *3 Hillview Place, West Street, Newbury RG14 1BF* T: (01635) 622634 M: 07703-267133 E: foulisbrown@gmail.com

FOULKES, Simon. b 58. Ox Poly BA 81. Oak Hill Th Coll BA 89. **d** 89 **p** 90. C St Austell *Truro* 89–92; C Boscombe St Jo *Win* 92–94; P-in-c Portswood St Denys 94–99; Par Evang Adv *Wakef* 99–04; TR Almondbury w Farnley Tyas 02–05; PtO *Cant* 07–09; P-in-c Bethersden w High Halden 09–11; Asst Dir of Educn 11–16; PtO 16–19. *53 Littlestone Road, Littlestone, New Romney TN28 8LN* T: (01797) 364517 E: vicar@idnet.co.uk

FOUNTAIN, John Stephen. b 43. RAF Coll Cranwell 65 Solicitor 80. LNSM course 91. **d** 93 **p** 94. NSM Nacton and Levington w Bucklesham and Foxhall *St E* 93–03; NSM Taddington, Chelmorton and Flagg, and Monyash *Derby* 03–11; NSM Taddington, Chelmorton and Monyash etc from 11. *The Old School, Chelmorton, Buxton SK17 9SL* T: (01298) 85009 E: johnfountain@fastmail.fm

FOUNTAIN, Miss Stephanie Ann Cecilia. b 58. Lon Univ BMus 81 Heythrop Coll Lon MA 06 Roehampton Inst PGCE 88. Westcott Ho Cam 00. **d** 02 **p** 03. C Tadworth *S'wark* 02–06; TV Boston *Linc* 07–10; P-in-c Bishop's Castle w Mainstone, Lydbury N etc *Heref* from 10; P-in-c Churchstoke w Hyssington and Sarn from 10; RD Clun Forest from 16. *The Vicarage, Church Lane, Bishops Castle SY9 5AF* T: (01588) 630324 E: stephaniefountain@yahoo.co.uk

FOUTS, Arthur Guy. b 44. Washington Univ BA 72 Seabury-Western Th Sem DMin 98. Ridley Hall Cam 78. **d** 81 **p** 82. C Alperton *Lon* 81–84; R Pinxton *Derby* 84–87; R Dublin St Patr USA 88–89; Pastor Warren St Mark 90–91; R Silver Spring St Mary Magd 91–99; Chapl St Andr Sch 99–00; P-in-c Point of Rocks St Paul 01–08. *603 Ramapo Avenue, Pompton Lakes NJ 07442, USA* T: (001) (973) 513 9810 E: rubberduck301@yahoo.com

FOWLER, Canon Colin. b 40. Linc Th Coll 80. **d** 82 **p** 83. C Barbourne *Worc* 82–85; TV Worc St Martin w St Pet, St Mark etc 85–86; TV Worc SE 86–92; P-in-c Moulton *Linc* 92–95; Chapl Puerto de la Cruz Tenerife *Eur* 95–01; Hon Can Madrid Cathl from 99; R Tangmere and Oving *Chich* 01–05; rtd 05; PtO *Nor* from 07. *10 Drakes Heath, Lowestoft NR32 2QQ* T: (01502) 564707

FOWLER, Canon David Mallory. b 51. Ian Ramsey Coll Brasted 74 Trin Coll Bris 75. **d** 78 **p** 79. C Rainhill *Liv* 78–81; C Houghton *Carl* 81–84; P-in-c Grayrigg 84–89; P-in-c Old Hutton w New Hutton 84–89; V Kirkoswald, Renwick and Ainstable 89–99; P-in-c Gt Salkeld w Lazonby 98–99; R Kirkoswald, Renwick w Croglin, Gt Salkeld etc 00–17; RD Penrith 99–06; Hon Can Carl Cathl 99–17; rtd 17; PtO *Carl* from 17; *Dur* from 18. *High Burnt Hills, Lanehead, Bishop Auckland DL13 1AJ* T: (01388) 537996 E: revdmf@btinternet.com

FOWLER, Mrs Janice Karen Brenda. b 56. Middx Univ BA 97. Oak Hill Th Coll 91. **d** 93 **p** 94. NSM Walton *St E* 93–96; Chapl Ipswich Hosp NHS Trust 94–00; NSM Combs *St E* 96–98; NSM Combs and Lt Finborough 98–00; C 00–04; P-in-c 04; C S Hartismere 04–07; PtO *Lich* 08–09; C *Lich* St Chad 09–10; P-in-c Worlingworth, Southolt, Tannington, Bedfield etc *St E* 10–11; NSM S Hartismere 11–13; PtO 13–17; Chapl Havebury Housing Partnership 13–18; Chapl HM Pris

Highpoint 14–18; V Alderney *Win* from 18. *Address withheld by request* E: jan.fowler@tesco.net

FOWLER, Mrs Jean Elsie. b 52. **d** 19. NSM Bridlington Priory *York* from 19. *3 Omega Road, Bridlington YO16 6RJ* T: (01262) 673019 M: 07971-914381 E: email@jeanfowler.plus.com

FOWLER, John Thomas. b 42. EAMTC. **d** 01 **p** 02. NSM Stoke by Nayland w Leavenheath and Polstead *St E* 01–11; rtd 11; PtO *St E* from 11. *Warners, Thorington Street, Stoke by Nayland, Colchester CO6 4SP* T/F: (01206) 337229 E: twam.johnf@gmail.com

FOWLER, Josephine Margaret. b 47. Worc Coll of Educn TCert 69 BEd 70. **d** 12 **p** 12. OLM Oulton Broad *Nor* 12–19; PtO from 19. *1 Swonnells Court, Lowestoft NR32 3PY* T: (01502) 572302 E: josephinefowler@talktalk.net

FOWLER, Margaret Joan. b 47. St Mellitus Coll 06. **d** 14 **p** 15. OLM Billericay and Lt Burstead *Chelmsf* 14–17; NSM from 17. *4 Chestwood Close, Billericay CM12 0PB* T: (01277) 630144 M: 07974-720510 E: margaret.fowler@billericaychurches.org

FOWLER, Rachel Mary. b 56. Linc Sch of Th and Min 15. **d** 17 **p** 18. NSM Waltham Gp *Linc* from 17. *80 Cheapside, Waltham, Grimsby DN37 0HW* E: rachel_m_fowler@hotmail.co.uk

FOWLER, Robert Charles Matthew. b 82. Wycliffe Hall Ox BTh 16. **d** 16. C Charles w Plymouth St Matthias *Ex* from 16. *32 Lancaster Gardens, Plymouth PL5 4AA* M: 07890-262863 E: robcharliefowler@hotmail.co.uk

FOX, Charles Ann. b 36. TISEC 98. **d** 99 **p** 00. NSM Ellon *Ab* from 99. *6 McDonald Drive, Ellon AB41 8BD* E: charlesandcarole@btinternet.com

FOX, Christopher. b 79. UWE BSc 01. Trin Coll Bris BA 10. **d** 11 **p** 12. C Ealing St Paul *Lon* from 11. *2 Nightingale Road, London W7 1DG* M: 07974-320324 E: chrispfox@gmail.com *or* chris@stpaulsealing.com

FOX, Colin George. b 46. Sarum & Wells Th Coll 73. **d** 75 **p** 76. C N Hammersmith St Kath *Lon* 75–79; CF (TA) 76–90; C Heston *Lon* 79–81; TV Marlborough *Sarum* 81–90; P-in-c Pewsey 90–91; TR 91–98; TR Pewsey and Swanborough 98–03; Chapl Pewsey Hosp 90–95; P-in-c Avon Valley *Sarum* 03–11; C Durrington 08–11; rtd 11; PtO *Sarum* from 12. *The Pightle, The Street, Teffont, Salisbury SP3 5QP* T: (01722) 716010 E: colingeorgefox@gmail.com

FOX, Canon Ian James. b 44. Selw Coll Cam BA 66 MA 70. Linc Th Coll 66. **d** 68 **p** 69. C Salford St Phil w St Steph *Man* 68–71; C Kirkleatham *York* 71–73; TV Redcar w Kirkleatham 73–77; V Bury St Pet *Man* 77–85; V Northallerton w Kirby Sigston *York* 85–03; RD Northallerton 85–91; Chapl Friarage and Distr Hosp Northallerton 88–91; Chapl Northallerton Health Services NHS Trust 92–03; Chapl Barlby and Riccall *York* 03–09; P-in-c Hemingbrough 06–09; rtd 09; Can and Preb York Minster 95–18; PtO from 10. *21 Springfield Close, Thirsk YO7 1FH* T: (01845) 526889 E: ianfox321@btinternet.com

FOX, Preb Jacqueline Frederica. b 43. Ripon Coll of Educn CertEd 66 Leeds Univ BEd 74 MEd 84 HonRCM 85. S Dios Minl Tr Scheme 83. **dss** 85 **d** 87 **p** 94. RCM *Lon* 85–86; Dioc FE Officer 87–96; Hon C Acton St Mary 87–96; R 96–08; Dean of Women's Min 96–08; Dir of Ords Willesden Area 01–08; Preb St Paul's Cathl 01–08; rtd 08; PtO *Leeds* from 17. *52 North Street, Ripon HG4 1EN* T: (01765) 603698 E: jackie@actonfox.co.uk

FOX, Mrs Jane. b 47. Open Univ BA 91 Bp Otter Coll Chich CertEd 75 ALA 70. S Dios Minl Tr Scheme 92. **d** 95 **p** 96. NSM W Blatchington *Chich* 95–98; C Peacehaven and Telscombe Cliffs 98–01; C Telscombe w Piddinghoe and Southease 98–01; TV Hitchin *St Alb* 01–08; P-in-c Harrold and Carlton w Chellington 08–15; rtd 15; PtO *St Alb* from 16. *14 Bedford Road, Barton-le-Clay, Bedford MK45 4JU* T: (01582) 882350 E: jandjsmfox@gmail.com

FOX (née COULDRIDGE), Mrs Janice Evelyn. b 49. Bognor Regis Coll of Educn CertEd 71. Glouc Sch of Min 89. **d** 92 **p** 94. C Tupsley w Hampton Bishop *Heref* 92–96; P-in-c Orleton w Brimfield 96–01; Dioc Ecum Officer 96–01; TV Worc SE 01–05; rtd 05; PtO *Worc* from 05. *6 Malvern View, Wichenford, Worcester WR6 6YY* T: (01886) 888637 E: janfox2@googlemail.com

FOX, June Kathryn. b 51. York St Jo Univ BA 11. St Hild Coll 18. **d** 19. NSM Woodhouse St Jas *Sheff* from 19. *12 Delves Avenue, Sheffield S12 4AB* T: 0114-248 8808 M: 07855-240978 E: junekfox@mail.com

FOX, Leonard. b 41. AKC 66. **d** 67 **p** 68. C Salford Stowell Memorial *Man* 67–68; C Hulme St Phil 68–72; C Portsea All SS w St Jo Rudmore *Portsm* 72–75; V Oakfield St Jo 75–92; P-in-c Portsea All SS 92–06; V 06; Dir All SS Urban Miss Cen 92–06; rtd 06; PtO *Portsm* from 07. *Middle Reach, Ashlake Farm Lane, Wootton Bridge, Ryde PO33 4LF* T: (01983) 880138 E: lenfox127@talktalk.net

FOX, Linda Margaret. b 58. **d** 08 **p** 09. NSM S Croydon St Pet and St Aug *S'wark* from 08. *67 Kingsdown Avenue, South Croydon CR2 6QJ* M: 07736-708828 E: linda.southcroydonbenefice@gmail.com

FOX, Michael Adrian Orme. b 47. Bris Univ BSc 68 PhD 72. WMMTC 01. **d** 04 **p** 05. NSM Codsall *Lich* 04–19; Ind Chapl Black Country Urban Ind Miss 04–12; PtO from 19. *1 Windsor Gardens, Codsall, Wolverhampton WV8 2EX* T: (01902) 843442 E: mike@maofox.me.uk

FOX, Michael Frederick. b 58. St Pet Coll Ox BA 80. All SS Cen for Miss & Min 12. **d** 14 **p** 15. NSM Bollington *Ches* 14–16; P-in-c Macclesfield St Paul from 16; Chapl to Bp Stockport 16–19. *Hordern Farm, Buxton New Road, Macclesfield SK11 0AN* M: 07714-216665 E: therevdfox@gmail.com

FOX, The Ven Michael John. b 42. Hull Univ BSc 63. Coll of Resurr Mirfield 64. **d** 66 **p** 67. C Becontree St Elisabeth *Chelmsf* 66–70; C Wanstead H Trin Hermon Hill 70–72; V Victoria Docks Ascension 72–76; V Chelmsf All SS 76–88; P-in-c Chelmsf Ascension 85–88; RD Chelmsf 86–88; R Colchester St Jas, All SS, St Nic and St Runwald 88–93; Hon Can Chelmsf Cathl 91–93; Adn Harlow 93–95; Adn W Ham 95–07; rtd 07; PtO *Chelmsf* from 08. *17A Northgate Street, Colchester CO1 1EZ* T: (01206) 710701 E: michael.fox510@ntlworld.com

FOX, Michael John Holland. b 41. Lon Univ BD 68. Oak Hill Th Coll 64. **d** 69 **p** 70. C Reigate St Mary *S'wark* 69–73; NSM 76–01; C Guildf St Sav 73–76; Asst Chapl Reigate Gr Sch 76–81; Chapl 81–01; NSM Reigate St Pet CD *S'wark* 96–01; P-in-c Reigate St Luke w Doversgreen 01–09; rtd 09; PtO *S'wark* from 09. *71 Blackborough Road, Reigate RH2 7BU* T: (01737) 226616 E: mikejh.fox@virgin.net

✠**FOX, The Rt Revd Peter John.** b 52. AKC 74. St Aug Coll Cant 74. **d** 75 **p** 76 **c** 02. C Wymondham *Nor* 75–79; Miss P Papua New Guinea 79–85; R Gerehu 80–85; Dioc Sec Port Moresby 84–85; P-in-c E w W Rudham *Nor* 85–88; P-in-c Syderstone w Barmer and Bagthorpe 85–88; P-in-c Tatterford 85–88; P-in-c Tattersett 85–88; P-in-c Houghton 85–88; R Coxford Gp 88–89; TR Lynton, Brendon, Countisbury, Lynmouth etc *Ex* 89–95; RD Shirwell 92–95; P-in-c Harpsden *Ox* 95–02; Gen Sec Melanesian Miss 95–02; Bp Port Moresby Papua New Guinea 02–06; Hon Asst Bp Nor from 06; P-in-c Nor Lakenham St Jo and All SS and Tuckswood 06–07; V 07–17; rtd 17; PtO *Leic* 18; Hon Asst Bp Leic from 18. *19 Cordwell Close, Castle Donington, Derby DE74 2JL* E: peterandangiefox@yahoo.co.uk

FOX, Raymond. b 46. QUB BSc 69. CITC 71. **d** 71 **p** 72. C Holywood *D & D* 71–75; C Min Can Down Cathl 75–78; I Killinchy w Kilmood and Tullynakill 78–81; I Belfast St Mary *Conn* 81–87; I Killaney w Carryduff *D & D* 88–02; Can Down Cathl 98–02; Chapter Clerk and V Choral Belf Cathl 00–02; I Donegal w Killymard, Lough Eske and Laghey *D & R* 02–10; Can Raphoe Cathl 09–10; rtd 10. *14 St Helens Court, High Street, Holywood BT18 9SS* T: (028) 9042 4560 M: 07511-752160 E: canonfox@btinternet.com

FOX, Robert. b 54. Man Univ BEd 76. NOC 89. **d** 91 **p** 92. NSM Stalybridge *Man* 91; NSM Ashton 91–16; PtO *Newc* from 18. *22 Queensbury Gate, Newcastle upon Tyne NE12 8JW* E: rob.fox36@gmail.com

FOX, Canon Sidney. b 47. Nottm Univ BTh 79 PhD 93. Linc Th Coll 75. **d** 79 **p** 80. C Middlesbrough St Oswald *York* 79–81; P-in-c 81–86; V 86–87; V Newby 87–92; R Brechin and Tarfside *Bre* 92–05; P-in-c Auchmithie 92–00; Can St Paul's Cathl Dundee 98–05; V Broughton *Blackb* 05–13; rtd 13; PtO *York* from 13. *15 Rawson Way, Hornsea HU18 1DH* E: revsfox@yahoo.co.uk

FOX, Timothy William Bertram. b 37. CCC Cam BA 61. Qu Coll Birm 66. **d** 68 **p** 69. C Cannock *Lich* 68–72; C Bilston St Leon 72–75; V Essington 75–81; R Buildwas and Leighton w Eaton Constantine etc 81–92; RD Wrockwardine 88–92; R Bradeley, Church Eaton and Moreton 92–04; rtd 04; Hon C Hanbury, Newborough, Rangemore and Tutbury *Lich* 04–08; PtO *Bradf* 09–14; *Leeds* from 14. *40 Lakeber Avenue, High Bentham, Lancaster LA2 7JN* T: (01524) 262575 E: wenningfoxes@btinternet.com

FOX (*née* DRAYCOTT), Tina. b 57. Win Univ BA 11. STETS 08. **d** 11 **p** 12. OLM Avon River *Sarum* 11–17; NSM Nadder Valley from 17. *The Pightle, The Street, Teffont, Salisbury SP3 5QP* T: (01722) 716010 M: 07747-033585 E: tina.fox@salisbury.anglican.org

FOXWOOD, Hugo Charles Amory. b 73. Bris Univ BA 95. St Mellitus Coll 15. **d** 18 **p** 19. C E Twickenham St Steph *Lon* from 18. *St Stephen's Church Office, 30 Crown Road, Twickenham TW1 3EE* T: (020) 8892 5258 M: 07931-578068 E: hugofoxwood@st-stephens.org.uk

FOY, Malcolm Stuart. b 48. Univ of Wales (Lamp) BA 71 Magd Coll Cam CertEd 72 K Coll Lon MA 89 ACP 80 FCollP

FRSA. Ox NSM Course 84. **d** 87 **p** 88. NSM Tilehurst St Mich *Ox* 87–90; C Ireland Wood *Ripon* 90–96; Adv RE Leeds Adnry 90–96; Dir Educn *Bradf* 96–99; C Otley 99; PtO 00–05; Hon C Keighley All SS 05–14; *Leeds* 14–16; Hon C Keighley from 16. *45 The Chase, Keighley BD20 6HU* T: (01535) 665112

FOY, Matthew John. b 81. Sheff Univ BA 04 Solicitor 07. Oak Hill Th Coll 13. **d** 16 **p** 17. C S Tottenham St Ann *Lon* 16–17; C Muswell Hill Grace Ch 17–19. *43 Mannock Road, London N22 6AB* M: 07752-787139 E: matthew.foy@btinternet.com

FOY, Peter James. b 59. **d** 08 **p** 09. NSM Warminster Ch Ch *Sarum* 08–15; Ind Chapl *St E* from 16. *2 Orford Road, Felixstowe IP11 2DY* M: 07557-922065 E: revpfoy@gmail.com

FRAIS, Jonathan Jeremy. b 65. Kingston Poly LLB 87. Oak Hill Th Coll BA 92. **d** 92 **p** 93. C Orpington Ch Ch *Roch* 92–96; Asst Chapl Moscow *Eur* 96–99; Chapl Kiev 99–05; R Bexhill St Mark *Chich* from 05; RD Battle and Bexhill from 15. *St Mark's Rectory, 11 Coverdale Avenue, Bexhill-on-Sea TN39 4TY* T/F: (01424) 843733 E: frais@tiscali.co.uk

FRAMPTON, Miss Marcia Ellen. b 36. SRN 65 SCM 66. Ripon Coll Cuddesdon 86. **d** 88 **p** 95. Par Dn Paston *Pet* 88–89; Par Dn Burford w Fulbrook and Taynton *Ox* 90–92; Par Dn Witney 92–93; NSM Heref S Wye 94–01; rtd 01; PtO *Heref* 02–17. *18 Brook Farm Court, Belmont, Hereford HR2 7TZ* T: (01432) 509007 E: revmframpton@talktalk.net

FRAMPTON, Samuel Francis. b 92. Dur Univ BA 18. Westcott Ho Cam 15. **d** 18 **p** 19. C Mill End and Heronsgate w W Hyde *St Alb* from 18. *St Thomas' House, 46 Chalfont Road, Maple Cross, Rickmansworth WD3 9TB* M: 07881-293543 E: s.frampton1992@hotmail.co.uk

FRANCE, Canon Charles Malcolm. b 48. Westmr Coll Ox BTh 01 ACA 71 FCA 76. EAMTC 94. **d** 97 **p** 98. C Gt Grimsby St Mary and St Jas *Linc* 97–02; P-in-c Skegness and Winthorpe 02–04; P-in-c Ingoldmells w Addlethorpe 02–04; R Skegness Gp 04–14; Can and Preb Linc Cathl 14–18; rtd 14; PtO *Nor* from 15; *Linc* from 17; *Eur* from 19. *7 High View Park, Cromer NR27 0HQ* T: (01263) 512861 E: malcolmfrance@aol.com

FRANCE (*née* PIERCY), Mrs Elizabeth Claire. b 66. Qu Mary Coll Lon BSc 87. Wycliffe Hall Ox 97. **d** 99 **p** 00. C Dronfield w Holmesfield *Derby* 99–03; V Allestree 03–05; P-in-c Etchingham *Chich* 11–12; PtO *Lon* 13–18; Chapl W Lon Univ from 18. *West London University, St Mary's Road, London W5 5RF* T: (020) 8231 2365 E: lizfrance@btinternet.com or liz.france@uwl.ac.uk

FRANCE, Evan Norman Lougher. b 52. Jes Coll Cam BA 74 MA 78. Wycliffe Hall Ox 76. **d** 79 **p** 80. C Hall Green Ascension *Birm* 79–82; CMS 82–84; C Bexhill St Pet *Chich* 84–87; V Westfield 87–11; R Buxted and Hadlow Down 11–15; rtd 15; PtO *Chich* from 17. *17 Lansdowne Way, Bexhill-on-Sea TN40 2UJ* E: enlfrance@gmail.com

FRANCE, Geoffrey. b 37. S Dios Minl Tr Scheme 87. **d** 90 **p** 91. NSM Uckfield *Chich* 90–92; C 92–94; R Warbleton and Bodle Street Green 94–02; rtd 02; PtO *Chich* from 15. *3 Osborne House, Rushlake Green, Heathfield TN21 9QL* T: (01435) 830309

FRANCE, Malcolm. See FRANCE, Charles Malcolm

FRANCE, Stephen Mark. b 66. Wycliffe Hall Ox BTh 00. **d** 00 **p** 01. C Newbold w Dunston *Derby* 00–03; P-in-c Darley Abbey 03–05; Dioc Duty Press Officer 03–04; P-in-c Burwash *Chich* 05–06; R 06–12; R Brondesbury Ch Ch and St Laur *Lon* from 12. *The Rectory, 46 The Avenue, London NW6 7NP* T: (020) 8451 1263 E: revfrance@btinternet.com

FRANCE, William Michael. b 43. Sydney Univ BA 68 Lon Univ BD 72 Chas Sturt Univ NSW MEd 96. Moore Th Coll Sydney LTh 70. **d** 73 **p** 73. C Turramurra Australia 73–75; C Barton Seagrave w Warkton *Pet* 76–78; R Dundas Australia 79–82; Chapl The K Sch 83–94; Chapl Sydney C of E Girls' Gr Sch 94–99; Assoc Chapl St Andr Cathl Sch 99–04; R Murchison 04–08; rtd 08. *6 Wesson Road, West Pennant Hills NSW 2125, Australia* T: (0061) (2) 9945 0939 E: billandjackie@optusnet.com.au or wfrance@sacs.nsw.edu.au

FRANCE, Archdeacon of. See WILLIAMS, The Ven Meurig Llwyd

FRANCES ANNE, Sister. See COCKER, Frances Rymer

FRANCIS, David Carpenter. b 45. Southn Univ BSc 66 Loughb Univ MSc 71 Sussex Univ MA 83. Westcott Ho Cam 85. **d** 87 **p** 88. C Ealing St Mary *Lon* 87–90; Chapl Ealing Coll of HE 87–90; Chapl Clayponds Hosp Ealing 88–90; P-in-c Wembley St Jo *Lon* 90–93; Chapl Wembley Hosp 90–93; V Platt *Roch* 93–01; Post Ord Tr Officer 93–98; RD Shoreham 99–01; R Stow on the Wold, Condicote and The Swells *Glouc* 01–11; AD Stow 04–09; rtd 11; PtO *Ex* from 12; RD Cadbury from 18. *East Forches, Alexandra Road, Crediton EX17 2DH* T: (01363) 776606 M: 07799-410370 E: stowrector@yahoo.co.uk

FRANCIS, Canon Graham John. b 45. St Mich Coll Llan 66. d 70 p 71. C Llanblethian w Cowbridge and Llandough etc *Llan* 70–76; V Penrhiwceiber w Matthewstown and Ynysboeth 76–02; V Cardiff St Mary w St Dyfrig and St Samson 02–16; V Grangetown 05–16; Can Llan Cathl 02–16; rtd 16; PtO *Llan* from 16. *84 Habershon Street, Cardiff CF24 2LB* T: (029) 2221 6123 M: 07907-985398 E: fathergraham@aol.com

FRANCIS, Canon James More MacLeod. b 44. Edin Univ MA 65 BD 68 PhD 74 Yale Univ STM 69. New Coll Edin 65. d 87 p 87. Sen Lect RS Sunderland Univ *Dur* from 82; NSM Sunderland St Chad 87–98; TV Sunderland 98–07; NSM Sunderland Minster 07–09; Tutor NEOC 89–98; Bp's Adv for NSM *Dur* 99–10; Prin Dioc OLM Course 02–09; Hon Can Dur Cathl 00–10; rtd 10; PtO *Dur* from 14. *11 Heatherdale Crescent, Durham DH1 2AP* T: 0191-386 6623 E: jamesfrancis@mac.com

FRANCIS, James Stephen. b 66. K Coll Lon MA 17 FInstD 97 FRSA 99. SEITE 95. d 99 p 07. NSM St Botolph Aldgate w H Trin Minories *Lon* 99–02; NSM Soho St Anne w St Thos and St Pet 02–05; Chapl RNR 05–07; NSM St Mary le Strand w St Clem Danes *Lon* 07; Chapl RN from 07. *Royal Naval Chaplaincy Service, Mail Point 1-2, Leach Building, Whale Island, Portsmouth PO2 8BY* T: (023) 9262 5055 F: 9262 5134 M: 07961-123811 E: james.francis118@hotmail.co.uk

FRANCIS, Jennifer Anne Harrison. b 45. Southn Univ BSc 67 Brunel Univ MA 74 CQSW 73. WEMTC 07. d 07 p 08. NSM Stow on the Wold, Condicote and The Swells *Glouc* 07–11; rtd 11; PtO *Ex* from 12. *East Forches, Alexandra Road, Crediton EX17 2DH* T: (01363) 776606 M: 07881-953769 E: jennyfrancis1@btinternet.com

FRANCIS, Jeremy Montgomery. b 31. BNC Ox BA 53 MA 56. Glouc Sch of Min 84. d 87 p 88. NSM Chedworth, Yanworth and Stowell, Coln Rogers etc *Glouc* 87–90; NSM Coates, Rodmarton and Sapperton etc 90–01; NSM Daglingworth w the Duntisbournes and Winstone 95–97; NSM Brimpsfield w Birdlip, Syde, Daglingworth etc 97–00; PtO from 01. *Old Barnfield, Duntisbourne Leer, Cirencester GL7 7AS* T: (01285) 821370

FRANCIS, John. b 56. Bris Poly BA 78 MCIH 81. d 98 p 99. OLM Hatcham Park All SS *S'wark* from 98. *4A Hatcham Park Mews, London SE14 5QA* T: (020) 7358 1769 M: 07703-567214 E: johnfrancis878@btinternet.com

FRANCIS, John Sims. b 25. Fitzw Ho Cam BA 54 MA 58. St D Coll Lamp BA 47 LTh 49. d 49 p 50. C Swansea St Barn *S & B* 49–52; C Chesterton St Andr *Ely* 52–54; C Swansea St Mary and H Trin *S & B* 54–58; V Newbridge-on-Wye and Llanfihangel Brynpabuan 58–65; R Willingham *Ely* 65–82; RD N Stowe 78–82; R Rampton 82; P-in-c Buckden 82–85; V 85–91; rtd 91; PtO *Linc* 92–01. *3 The Brambles, Bourne PE10 9TF* T: (01778) 426396

FRANCIS, Julian Montgomery. b 60. Selw Coll Cam BA 83 MA 83. S'wark Ord Course 88. d 91 p 92. C S Wimbledon H Trin and St Pet *S'wark* 91–95; V Cottingley *Bradf* 95–99; Minority Ethnic Angl Concerns Officer *Lich* 99–02; C W Bromwich St Andr w Ch Ch 99–02; TR Coventry Caludon *Cov* 02–08; Nat Tr Co-ord for Minority Ethnic Anglicans 08–11; V Edgbaston St Geo *Birm* from 11; Bp's Ecum Adv from 18. *The Vicarage, 3 Westbourne Road, Birmingham B15 3TH* T: 0121-454 4204 or 454 2303 M: 07837-910568 E: vicar@stgeorgesedgbaston.org.uk

FRANCIS, Miss Katherine Jane. b 67. St Jo Coll Dur BA 08 RGN 88 RM 92. Cranmer Hall Dur 06. d 08 p 09. C Sprotbrough *Sheff* 08–10; Chapl Newcastle upon Tyne Hosps NHS Foundn Trust 10–16; Chapl Marie Curie Cen Newc from 16. *Marie Curie Cancer Care, Marie Curie Drive, Newcastle upon Tyne NE4 6SS* T: 0191-219 1000

FRANCIS, Kenneth Charles. b 22. Oak Hill Th Coll 46. d 50 p 51. C Wandsworth All SS *S'wark* 50–53; V Deptford St Nic w Ch Ch 53–61; V Summerstown 61–77; R Cratfield w Heveningham and Ubbeston etc *St E* 77–87; rtd 87; PtO *Truro* 87–14. *Wheal Alfred, Chapel Hill, Bolingey, Perranporth TR6 0DQ* T: (01872) 571317

FRANCIS, Kevin. b 52. Glas Univ MA 83 PhD 88. TISEC 08. d 11 p 12. Hon C Glas St Bride 11–15; R from 15; Hon Chapl Glas Univ from 11. *33 Maxwell Avenue, Bearsden, Glasgow G61 1PA* T: 0141-570 0990 E: rev.kevinfrancis@gmail.com or anglicans@glasgow.ac.uk

FRANCIS, Prof Leslie John. b 47. Pemb Coll Ox BA 70 MA 74 BD 90 DD 01 Nottm Univ MTh 76 Qu Coll Cam PhD 76 ScD 97 Lon Univ MSc 77 Univ of Wales (Ban) DLitt 07 FBPsS 88 FCP 94 FAcSS 14. Westcott Ho Cam 70. d 73 p 74. C Haverhill *St E* 73–77; P-in-c Gt Bradley 78–82; Hon C Gt w Lt Wratting 79–82; Research Officer Culham Coll Inst 82–88; P-in-c N Cerney w Bagendon *Glouc* 82–85; PtO 85–95; Fell Trin Coll Carmarthen 89–99; Dean of Chpl 95–99; Prof

Th Univ of Wales (Lamp) 92–99; Prof Practical Th Univ of Wales (Ban) 99–07; Prof Religions and Educn Warw Univ *Cov* from 07; PtO *Ox* 95–01; *Ban* 99–06; Hon C Llanfairpwll and Llanddaniel-fab etc 06–12; Hon C Seintiau Braint a Chefni 12–14; Hon C Bro Dwynwen 15–17; Hon Can St D Cathl 98–99; Hon Can and Can Th Ban Cathl 06–16; Cursal Can 11–12; Treas 12–16; Hon Can Man Cathl from 16. *Llys Onnen, Abergwyngregyn, Llanfairfechan LL33 0LD* T: (01248) 681877 E: leslie.francis@warwick.ac.uk

FRANCIS, Mark Simon. b 77. Dur Univ BSc 98. Oak Hill Th Coll BA 10. d 10 p 11. C Egham *Guildf* 10–13; P-in-c Felbridge *S'wark* 13–16; V from 16. *The Vicarage, 8 The Glebe, Felbridge, East Grinstead RH19 2QT* T: (01342) 321524 M: 07774-324934 E: mark8sjf@gmail.com

FRANCIS, Martin Rufus. b 37. Pemb Coll Ox BA 60 MA 64. Linc Th Coll 60. d 63 p 64. C W Hartlepool St Paul *Dur* 63–67; C Yeovil St Jo w Preston Plucknett *B & W* 67–69; Chapl Tonbridge Sch 69–83; Chapl and Dep Hd St Jo Sch Leatherhead 83–94; R Herstmonceux and Wartling *Chich* 94–01; rtd 01; PtO *Sarum* 02–18. *4 Abbots Way, Sherborne DT9 6DT* E: venetiakfrancis@hotmail.co.uk or mrufus37@hotmail.com

FRANCIS, Canon Paul Edward. b 52. Southn Univ BTh 84. Sarum & Wells Th Coll 78. d 81 p 82. C Biggin Hill *Roch* 81–85; R Fawkham and Hartley 85–90; V Aylesford 90–99; V Riverhead w Dunton Green 99–11; Chapl Dioc Assn of Readers 01–11; RD Sevenoaks 05–11; R Beckenham St Geo 11–15; Hon Can Roch Cathl 10–15; Can Res Roch Cathl 15–17; rtd 17; PtO *Cant* from 18. *5 Russet Row, Grove Road, Preston, Canterbury CT3 1FS*

FRANCIS, Peter Alan. b 73. Wycliffe Hall Ox. d 09 p 10. C Horsham *Chich* 09–13; P-in-c Woodchester and Brimscombe *Glouc* 13–18; P-in-c Rodborough 16–18; R Rodborough, Woodchester and Brimscombe from 18. *The Rectory, Walkley Hill, Stroud GL5 3TX* T: (01453) 752659 E: peterfrancis777@gmail.com

FRANCIS, Peter Brereton. b 53. St Andr Univ MTheol 77. Qu Coll Birm 77. d 78 p 79. C Hagley *Worc* 78–81; Chapl Qu Mary Coll *Lon* 81–87; R Ayr *Glas* 87–92; Miss to Seamen 87–92; Provost St Mary's Cathl *Glas* 92–96; R Glas St Mary 92–96; Warden and Lib Gladstone's Lib Hawarden from 97; Visiting Prof Glyndŵr Univ from 09. *Gladstone's Library, Church Lane, Hawarden, Deeside CH5 3DF* T: (01244) 532350 E: peter.francis@gladlib.org

FRANCIS, Peter Philip. b 48. St Jo Coll Dur BA 73. Wycliffe Hall Ox 73. d 75 p 76. C Folkestone St Jo *Cant* 75–78; C Morden *S'wark* 78–83; P-in-c Barford St Martin, Dinton, Baverstock etc *Sarum* 83–88; P-in-c Fovant, Sutton Mandeville and Teffont Evias etc 83–86; R Newick *Chich* 88–14; rtd 14; PtO *Chich* from 15. *12 Downland Copse, Uckfield TN22 1SX* T: (01825) 763557 E: pandnfrancis@btinternet.com

FRANCIS, Mrs Sharon Edwina. b 57. Westmr Coll Ox BTh 99 Heythrop Coll Lon MA 14. STETS 98. d 08 p 09. NSM Langton Green *Roch* 08–12; P-in-c New Groombridge *Chich* 12–18; V from 18; RD Rotherfield from 18. *The Vicarage, Corseley Road, Groombridge, Tunbridge Wells TN3 9SE* T: (01892) 864265 M: 07527-396403 E: vicar@stthomasgroombridge.org.uk

FRANCIS, Canon Younis. b 66. d 95 p 95. C Addington *S'wark* 05–07; TV Cheam 07–11; P-in-c Norbury St Phil 11–16; V from 16; Hon Can S'wark Cathl from 17. *70 Pollards Hill North, London SW16 4NY* T: (020) 3172 1426 M: 07504-721294 E: revd.younis@gmail.com

✠**FRANCIS-DEHQANI, The Rt Revd Gulnar Eleanor (Guli).** b 66. Nottm Univ BA 89 Bris Univ MA 94 PhD 99. SEITE 95. d 98 p 99 c 17. C Mortlake w E Sheen *S'wark* 98–02; Chapl R Academy of Music *Lon* 02–04; Chapl St Marylebone C of E Sch 02–04; PtO *Pet* 04–11; C Tr Officer 11–17; Adv in Women's Min 12–17; Can Pet Cathl 16–17; Suff Bp Loughborough *Leic* from 17. *Bishop's House, 48 Mountsorrel Lane, Rothley, Leicester LE7 7PR* T: 0116-270 8985 E: bishop.loughborough@leccofe.org

FRANCIS-DEHQANI, Canon Lee Thomas. b 67. Nottm Univ BA 89. Sarum & Wells Th Coll 92 Trin Coll Bris BA 95. d 95 p 96. C Putney St Mary *S'wark* 95–98; TV Richmond St Mary w St Matthias and St Jo 98–04; P-in-c Oakham, Hambleton, Egleton, Braunston and Brooke *Pet* 04–10; P-in-c Langham 04–10; C Teigh w Whissendine and Market Overton 04–10; C Cottesmore and Barrow w Ashwell and Burley 04–10; TR Oakham, Ashwell, Braunston, Brooke, Egleton etc 11–18; RD Rutland 10–18; Can Pet Cathl 10–18; TR Fosse Team *Leic* from 18. *Bishop's House, 48 Mountsorrel Lane, Rothley, Leicester LE7 7PR* M: 07827-668169 E: leet.fd@gmail.com

FRANCK, Mrs Janet. b 53. MCSP 75. d 14 p 15. OLM Egham Hythe *Guildf* from 14. *56 Hazel Grove, Staines TW18 1JL* T: (01784) 465879 E: janetf56@aol.com

FRANK, Penelope Edith. b 45. WMMTC 96. **d** 99 **p** 00. NSM Edgbaston St Geo *Birm* 99–02; PtO *Cov* 03–04; NSM Stoneleigh w Ashow 04–10; CPAS 87–06; rtd 06; Asst Chapl Vevey w Château d'Oex *Eur* 10–12; PtO *Cov* from 15; *Glouc* from 16. *5 Townend Cottage, High Street, Moreton-in-Marsh GL56 0AD*

FRANK, Canon Richard Patrick Harry. b 40. St Chad's Coll Dur BA 66. **d** 68 **p** 69. C Darlington H Trin *Dur* 68–72; C Monkwearmouth St Andr 72–74; C-in-c Harlow Green CD 74–79; R Skelton and Hutton-in-the-Forest w Ivegill *Carl* 79–86; V Carl St Luke Morton 86–92; RD Carl 88–89; P-in-c Thursby 89–90; P-in-c Kirkbride w Newton Arlosh 89–92; TR Greystoke, Matterdale, Mungrisdale etc 92–98; P-in-c Patterdale 95–98; TR Gd Shep TM 98–99; RD Penrith 96–99; Hon Can Carl Cathl 97–99; rtd 99; PtO *Carl* 00–02; *York* from 02. *8 Taylors Rise, Walkington, Beverley HU17 8SF* T: (01482) 872262 E: taylors@taylors.karoo.co.uk

FRANK, Richard Stephen. b 70. Keble Coll Ox MEng 93 Fitzw Coll Cam MA 98. Ridley Hall Cam 96. **d** 99 **p** 00. C Cranham Park *Chelmsf* 99–04; P-in-c St Margaret's-on-Thames *Lon* 05–11; V from 11; AD Hounslow from 15. *295 St Margarets Road, Twickenham TW1 1PN* T: (020) 8891 3504 M: 07973-719730 E: richardfrank@allsoulschurch.org.uk

FRANKLAND, Angela Tara. b 65. Lon Bible Coll BA 96 MA 98. EAMTC 97. **d** 99 **p** 00. C Hornchurch St Andr *Chelmsf* 99–03; TV Wickford and Runwell 03–11; P-in-c Aveley and Purfleet 11–13; TR Mardyke from 13. *The Vicarage, Mill Road, Aveley, South Ockendon RM15 4SR* T: (01708) 891471 E: tfrankland@btinternet.com

FRANKLIN, Bryony Dean. b 69. Bath Univ BPharm 89 Sch of Pharmacy Lon MSc 93 PhD 99 FRPharmS 13. St Mellitus Coll BA 19. **d** 19. NSM W Acton St Martin *Lon* from 19. *4 King Edwards Gardens, London W3 9RG* E: bryonyfranklin@gmail.com

FRANKLIN, David John. b 67. Selw Coll Cam BA 88 MA 92. St Jo Coll Nottm MTh 06. **d** 06 **p** 07. C Windermere *Carl* 06–10; Hon C Bramley *Sheff* 10–12; V Askern from 12. *The Vicarage, Church Street, Askern, Doncaster DN6 0PH* T: (01302) 708081 E: david.franklin@sheffield.anglican.org

FRANKLIN, Dianne Mary. *See* COX, Dianne Mary

FRANKLIN (formerly WILKES), Mrs Elizabeth Ann. b 76. St Jo Coll Dur BA 97 UEA MA 01. **d** 13 **p** 14. C Blackheath Park St Mich *S'wark* 13–17; PtO *S'well* from 17. *Christ Church Vicarage, Boundary Road, Newark NG24 4AJ* T: (01636) 611345 E: liz.franklin@outlook.com

FRANKLIN, Jamie Andrew. b 87. Kent Univ BA 08 MA 09 K Coll Lon MA 15. Ripon Coll Cuddesdon 17. **d** 19. C Nottingham St Geo w St Jo *S'well* from 19. *7 Chancery Court, Wilford, Nottingham NG11 7EQ* M: 07783-184934 E: jamieandrewfranklin@gmail.com

FRANKLIN, Mrs Janet. b 67. Selw Coll Cam VetMB 91 MA 92 Cumbria Univ BA 10. LCTP 06. **d** 10 **p** 11. C Maltby and Thurcroft *Sheff* 10–13; P-in-c Stainforth 13–18; PtO from 18. *The Vicarage, Church Street, Askern, Doncaster DN6 0PH* T: (01302) 708081 E: janet.franklin@sheffield.anglican.org *or* janetfranklin3@hotmail.com

FRANKLIN, Miss Ola. b 55. Balls Park Coll Hertford CertEd 76 Open Univ BA 92 Birkbeck Coll Lon MA 95. NTMTC BA 09. **d** 09 **p** 10. C Harlow St Mary and St Hugh w St Jo the Bapt *Chelmsf* 09–13; PtO 13–14; V Woodford Bridge from 14. *St Paul's Vicarage, 4 Cross Road, Woodford Green IG8 8BS* T: (020) 8506 0662 E: ofrank@btinternet.com

FRANKLIN, Paul Steven. b 78. Portsm Univ BSc 01 Brighton Univ PGCE 02 Kent Univ MA 07. Wycliffe Hall Ox 11. **d** 13 **p** 14. NSM Kidbrooke St Nic *S'wark* 13–17; TV Newark w Coddington *S'well* 17; V Newark Ch Ch from 18. *Christ Church Vicarage, Boundary Road, Newark NG24 4AJ* T: (01636) 611345 E: rev.p.franklin@gmail.com

FRANKLIN, Canon Richard Charles Henry. b 48. Ch Ch Coll Cant CertEd 70 Heythrop Coll Lon MA 08. Sarum & Wells Th Coll 75. **d** 78 **p** 79. C Pershore w Pinvin, Wick and Birlingham *Worc* 78–80; Educn Chapl 80–85; V Wollescote 85–92; V Fareham SS Pet and Paul *Portsm* 92–98; V Luton All SS w St Pet *St Alb* 98–12; RD Luton 02–07; Hon Can St Alb 09–12; rtd 13. *Baldwin's Oak, Castle Tump, Newent GL18 1SL* T: (01531) 890289 E: richardfranklin@mail2world.com

FRANKLIN, Canon Richard Heighway. b 54. Southn Univ BA 75 MPhil 83. Sarum & Wells Th Coll 75. **d** 78 **p** 79. C Thame w Towersey *Ox* 78–81; Asst Chapl Southn Univ *Win* 81–83; Dir of Studies Chich Th Coll 83–89; P-in-c Stalbridge *Sarum* 89–94; V Weymouth H Trin 94–16; Can and Preb Sarum Cathl 02–16; RD Weymouth 02–08; rtd 16; PtO *Sarum* from 16. *3 d'Urberville Close, Dorchester DT1 2JT* E: richardfranklin@iname.com

FRANKLIN (née WESTMACOTT), Mrs Rosemary Margaret. b 41. WEMTC 03. **d** 05 **p** 06. NSM Cirencester *Glouc* 05–13; rtd 13; PtO *Glouc* from 17. *Waterton Farm House, Ampney Crucis, Cirencester GL7 5RR* T: (01285) 654282 E: revrmf@btinternet.com

FRANKLIN, Roxanne Fay. *See* HUNTE, Roxanne Fay

FRANKLIN, Preb Simon George. b 54. Bris Univ BA 75. Ridley Hall Cam 77. **d** 79 **p** 80. C Woodmansterne *S'wark* 79–83; C St Peter-in-Thanet *Cant* 83–86; R Woodchurch 86–96; P-in-c Ottery St Mary, Alfington, W Hill, Tipton etc *Ex* 96–99; TR 99–12; P-in-c Feniton and Escot 07–12; P-in-c Moretonhampstead, Manaton, N Bovey and Lustleigh 12–15; R 15–19; RD Moreton 15–19; Preb Ex Cathl 07–19; rtd 19. *2 Lanveoc Way, Modbury, Ivybridge PL21 0FW* E: safranklin@btinternet.com

FRANKUM, Matthew David Hyatt. b 65. Leic Poly BSc 87 Univ of Wales MA 13. Trin Coll Bris 97. **d** 99 **p** 00. C Bath St Luke *B & W* 99–03; TV Worle 03–08; P-in-c Bath St Luke 08–16; V from 16; RD Bath from 18. *St Luke's Vicarage, Hatfield Road, Bath BA2 2BD* T: (01225) 311904 E: matthew@stlukesbath.com

FRANSELLA, Cortland Lucas. b 48. Trin Hall Cam BA 70 MA 74 Heythrop Coll Lon MA 00 Open Univ BSc 05 MSc 11. NTMTC 95. **d** 98 **p** 99. NSM Palmers Green St Jo *Lon* 98–03 and 09–12; NSM Hornsey St Mary w St Geo 03–08; PtO from 08; Asst Chapl to Abp *Cant* 11–13; Lambeth Awards Officer from 14; Asst P Chpl R St Pet-ad-Vincula at HM Tower of Lon from 12; Dep P in O from 19. *17 Warner Road, London N8 7HB* T: (020) 8340 7706 E: fransella@btinternet.com *or* cortland.fransella@lambethpalace.org

FRANZ, Kevin Gerhard. b 53. Edin Univ MA 74 BD 79 PhD 92. Edin Th Coll 76. **d** 79 **p** 80. C Edin St Martin 79–83; R Selkirk 83–90; Provost St Ninian's Cathl and R Perth St Ninian *St And* 90–99; Gen Sec Action of Churches Together in Scotland 99–07; Hon Can St Ninian's Cathl Perth *St And* 00–05. *14 Comely Bank, Perth PH2 7HU* E: kgfranz53@gmail.com

FRASER, Alan Richard. b 69. Leeds Univ BA 91 MA 94. WMMTC 04. **d** 07 **p** 08. NSM Gravelly Hill *Birm* 07–16; PtO from 16. *41 Hobhouse Close, Birmingham B42 1HB* T: 0121-358 7576 E: alan-fraser@blueyonder.co.uk

FRASER, Andrew Thomas. b 52. Newc Univ Aus BA 81. St Jo Coll (NSW) ThL 79. **d** 81 **p** 82. Australia 81–87; C Prestbury *Glouc* 87–91; C Wotton St Mary 91–92. *79 Victoria Street, Gloucester GL1 4EP* T: (01452) 381082 E: andyinglos@live.co.uk

FRASER, Ann. *See* FRASER, Elizabeth Ann

FRASER, Charles Ian Alexander. b 45. Ex Univ BA Cam Univ PGCE Open Univ MA MCMI. ERMC. **d** 10 **p** 11. NSM Cherry Hinton St Jo *Ely* 10–13; NSM Lordsbridge from 13; Asst Master The Leys Sch from 10. *The Leys School, Fen Causeway, Cambridge CB2 7AD* T: (01223) 264974 *or* 508916 M: 07889-019157 E: ciaf@theleys.net *or* revd.charlesfraser@gmail.com *or* charlesfraser@lordsbridge.org

FRASER, Canon Christine Nancy. b 61. TISEC 98. **d** 02 **p** 03. NSM St Ninian's Cathl Perth *St And* 02–13; Chapl Perth High Sch 09–13; R Kirkcaldy *St And* from 13; R Kinghorn from 13; Can St Ninian's Cathl Perth from 19. *1 Longbraes Garden, Kirkcaldy KY2 5YJ* T: (01592) 204208 E: cnfraser@btinternet.com

FRASER, Darren Anthony. b 71. Wilson Carlile Coll 02. **d** 08 **p** 09. C Bucknall *Lich* 08–12; R Biddulph Moor and Knypersley from 12. *St John's Vicarage, 62 Park Lane, Knypersley, Stoke-on-Trent ST8 7AU* T: (01782) 512240 M: 07766-198455 E: rev.dfraser@gmail.com

FRASER, Duncan Piers. b 71. Bris Univ BA 93 Ch Ch Coll Cant PGCE 98. Wycliffe Hall Ox 11. **d** 13 **p** 14. C Eastbourne H Trin *Chich* 13–15; C Eastbourne All SS 15–17; V Eynsham and Cassington *Ox* from 17. *45 Acre End Street, Eynsham, Witney OX29 4PF* T: (01865) 682399 M: 07810-324088 E: duncanpfraser@gmail.com

FRASER, Mrs Elizabeth Ann. b 44. **d** 07 **p** 08. OLM Witley *Guildf* 07–14; PtO from 14. *Oakwood, Petworth Road, Milford, Godalming GU8 5BS* T: (01483) 417190 M: 07966-513450 E: ann.fraser@btinternet.com *or* revann@allsaintswitley.org.uk

FRASER, Canon Jane Alicia. b 44. Man Univ BA. Glouc Sch of Min 86. **d** 89 **p** 94. NSM Upton on Severn *Worc* 89–00; NSM Ripple, Earls Croome w Hill Croome and Strensham 97–00; Faith Adv Dept of Health's Adv Gp on Teenage Pregnancy from 00; NSM Upton-on-Severn, Ripple, Earls Croome etc *Worc* 00–14; Hon Can Worc Cathl 05–14; PtO from 14. *The Campanile, Church Lane, Stoulton, Worcester WR7 4RE* T: (01905) 840266

FRASER, Canon Jeremy Stuart. b 58. **d** 08 **p** 09. C E Greenwich *S'wark* 08–13; P-in-c Stratford St Paul and St Jas *Chelmsf* 13–15; V 15–18; P-in-c Forest Gate All SS from 16; AD Newham 15–19; Miss and Development Adv Bradwell Area from 18; V N Woolwich w Silvertown from 19; Hon Can Chelmsf Cathl from 15. *7 Duchess Drive, London E13 8FE* T: (020) 7473 5670 M: 07970-139881 E: jeremy@fraserwireless.co.uk *or* jfraser@chelmsford.anglican.org

FRASER, Juliet. d 16 **p** 17. C Rhyl w St Ann *St As* 16; C Aber-Morfa Miss Area 17–18; C Aberconwy Miss Area from 18. *The Rectory, 16 Y Bryn, Glan Conwy, Colwyn Bay LL28 5NJ* E: juliet@parishofrhyl.co.uk *or* squirt5@clive.co.uk

FRASER, Mark Adrian. b 69. Warwick Univ BSc 90 Birm Univ MSc 91. St Jo Coll Nottm MTh 04. **d** 05 **p** 06. C Astley Bridge *Man* 05–08; P-in-c Gamston and Bridgford *S'well* 08–11; V from 11; P-in-c Edwalton from 14; AD W Bingham 17–19. *10 Scafell Close, West Bridgford, Nottingham NG2 6RJ* T: 0115-982 2834 M: 07963-397688 E: mark@st-lukes-gamston.org *or* fraser5mark@gmail.com

FRASER, Simon Bernard Lovat. b 52. **d** 17 **p** 18. C Egham *Guildf* from 17. *5 Magnolia View, 77 Worple Road, Staines-upon-Thames TW18 1HJ*

FRASER-SMITH, Keith Montague. b 48. St Jo Coll Dur BA 70. Trin Coll Bris. **d** 73 **p** 74. C Bishopsworth *Bris* 73–75; CMS 76–84; Egypt 76–80; Jerusalem 80–84; Asst Chapl Marseille w St Raphaël, Aix-en-Provence etc *Eur* 84–90; Media Dir Arab World Min 84–92; E Area Dir 92–97; Dep Internat Dir 97–98; NSM Worthing Ch the King *Chich* 90–93; Cyprus 93–97; NSM Tranmere St Cath *Ches* 97–98; P-in-c Barnton 98–03; Dir Global Mobilisation Arab World Min 03–10; Min Ldr UK 10–13; rtd 13; PtO *Ches* 03–15; *Leeds* from 17. *8 Cockshott Close, Leeds LS12 2RJ* T: 0113-450 1844 E: kieth.fraser-smith@tiscali.co.uk

FRAY, Bernard Herbert. b 44. Open Univ BA 73 Worc Coll of Educn CertEd 65 LTCL 67. Cranmer Hall Dur 02. **d** 03 **p** 04. NSM Long Marston *York* 03–06; NSM Rufforth w Moor Monkton and Hessay 03–06; NSM Healaugh w Wighill, Bilbrough and Askham Richard 03–06; NSM Tockwith and Bilton w Bickerton 03–06; P-in-c Aberford w Micklefield 06–11; rtd 11; PtO *York* from 11; *Eur* from 11; *Lon* from 19. *31 Bromley College, London Road, Bromley BR1 1PE* T: (020) 3539 7650 M: 07967-232535 E: fraybernard985@gmail.com

FRAY, Vernon Francis. b 41. FCIOB 79. S'wark Ord Course 91. **d** 94 **p** 95. NSM Heston *Lon* 94–96; NSM Twickenham All Hallows 96–02; NSM Teddington St Mark and Hampton Wick 02–08; NSM Whitton SS Phil and Jas 08–11; PtO from 11; *S'wark* from 15. *1 Cavalier Court, 14 St Mark's Road, Teddington TW11 9DY* T: (020) 8614 1914 M: 07958-751915 E: v.fray@btinternet.com

FRAYLING, The Very Revd Nicholas Arthur. b 44. Ex Univ BA 69 Liv Univ Hon LLD 01. Cuddesdon Coll 69. **d** 71 **p** 72. C Peckham St Jo *S'wark* 71–74; V Tooting All SS 74–83; Can Res and Prec Liv Cathl 83–87; R Liv Our Lady and St Nic w St Anne 87–02; TR 90–02; Hon Can Liv Cathl 89–02; Dean Chich 02–14; rtd 14; PtO *Portsm* from 14. *Flat 5, 27 South Parade, Southsea PO5 2JF* T: (023) 9281 7041 E: nicholasfrayling@gmail.com

FRAYNE, The Very Revd David. b 34. St Edm Hall Ox BA 58 MA 62. Qu Coll Birm 58. **d** 60 **p** 61. C E Wickham *S'wark* 60–63; C Lewisham St Jo Southend 63–67; V N Sheen St Phil and All SS 67–73; R Caterham 73–83; RD 80–83; Hon Can S'wark Cathl 82–83; V Bris St Mary Redcliffe w Temple etc 83–92; RD Bedminster 86–92; Hon Can Bris Cathl 91–92; Provost Blackb 92–00; Dean Blackb 00–01; rtd 01; PtO *Sarum* from 02; *B & W* from 12. *30 Coleridge Vale Road South, Clevedon BS21 6PB* T: (01275) 873799 M: 07788-795698 E: davidfrayne666@btinternet.com

FRAZER, Canon James Stewart. b 27. TCD Div Sch. **d** 57 **p** 58. C Belfast Whiterock *Conn* 57–59; C Belfast St Matt 59–61; I Lack *Clogh* 61–64; I Camlough w Mullaglass *Arm* 64–65; I Milltown 65–70; I Heathcote w Axedale Australia 70–72; I Kangaroo Par w Marong, Lockwood etc 72–74; I Dromore *Clogh* 74–82; Bp's Dom Chapl 82; I Derryvullen S w Garvary 82–90; Can Clogh Cathl 83–85; Preb Clogh Cathl 85–94; I Clogh w Errigal Portclare 90–94; Glebes Sec 91–94; Chan Clogh Cathl 93–94; rtd 94. *8 Carsons Avenue, Ballygowan, Newtownards BT23 5GD* T: (028) 9752 1562

FREAR, Canon Philip Scott. b 45. Univ of Wales (Lamp) BA 66. Bris & Glouc Tr Course 77. **d** 80 **p** 81. Hon C Purton *Bris* 80–81; C Rodbourne Cheney 81–85; V Hengrove 85–95; V Braddan *S & M* 95–12; Chapl Isle of Man Dept of Health and Social Security 98–12; Can St German's Cathl *S & M* 04–12; rtd 12. *37 Hutchinson Square, Douglas, Isle of Man IM2 4HW* T: (01624) 615066 E: philipfrear@yahoo.com

FREARSON, Andrew Richard. b 57. Wolv Univ BA 80. Wycliffe Hall Ox. **d** 83 **p** 84. C Acocks Green *Birm* 83–86; C Moseley St Mary 86–89; P-in-c Holme *Blackb* 89–96; P-in-c Norcross Ch Ch USA 97–06; TV Bracknell *Ox* 06–10; R Dollar *St And* 10–18. *10 Lancaster Road, Brockworth, Gloucester GL3 4FN* E: andrewfrearsontron@hotmail.co.uk

FREATHY, Nigel Howard. b 46. Lon Univ BA 68 CertEd. Sarum & Wells Th Coll 79. **d** 81 **p** 82. C Crediton *Ex* 81–82;

C Crediton and Shobrooke 82–84; TV Ex St Thos and Em 84–86; V Beer and Branscombe 86–01; P-in-c Stockland, Dalwood, Kilmington and Shute 01–03; V Kilmington, Stockland, Dalwood, Yarcombe etc 03–08; RD Honiton 96–99; rtd 08; PtO *Ex* from 01. *7 Hawksdown View, Seaton EX12 2BJ* T: (01297) 22303 E: nigelfreathy@hotmail.co.uk

FREDERICK, John Bassett Moore. b 30. Princeton Univ BA 51 Birm Univ PhD 73. Gen Th Sem (NY) MDiv 54. **d** 54 **p** 55. C Cheshire St Pet USA 54–56; C All Hallows Barking *Lon* 56–58; C Ox SS Phil and Jas 58–60; R New Haven St Jo USA 61–71; R Bletchingley *S'wark* 74–95; Reigate Adnry Ecum Officer 90–95; RD Godstone 92–95; rtd 95. *22 Chestnut Street, Princeton NJ 08542-3806, USA* T: (001) (609) 924 7590 F: 924 1694 E: jf9642@netscape.net

FREDRIKSEN, Martin. b 47. St Chad's Coll Dur BA 69 Univ of Wales (Lamp) MA 03. **d** 70 **p** 71. C Bideford *Ex* 70–73; C Guildf St Nic 73–76; R Cossington *B & W* 76–82; V Woolavington 76–82; Asst Chapl K Coll Taunton 82–84; C Bp's Hatfield *St Alb* 84–94; P-in-c Broadstone *Sarum* 94; V 94–12; rtd 12; PtO *Sarum* from 12. *129 Stour View Gardens, Corfe Mullen, Wimborne BH21 3TN* T: (01202) 900198 E: fr.fred04@gmail.com

FREELAND, Nicolas John Michell. b 65. FNMSM 99 FCMI 10. STETS 07. **d** 10 **p** 11. NSM Jersey St Pet *Win* 10–13; C 13–15; C Jersey St Brelade 15–16; R Swanbourne w Mt Claremont Australia 16–18; R S Perth from 18. *3/9 Ridge Street, South Perth WA 6151, Australia* E: fr.nick@me.com

FREELAND, Paul William. b 77. Brunel Univ BSc 99. St Mellitus Coll 17. **d** 19. C Swindon St Aug *Bris* from 19. *80 Queen Elizabeth Drive, Swindon SN25 1UE* M: 07736-928126 E: paulwfreeland@gmail.com

FREEMAN, Anthony John Curtis. b 46. Ex Coll Ox BA 68 MA 72. Cuddesdon Coll 70. **d** 72 **p** 73. C Worc St Martin 72–74; C Worc St Martin w St Pet 74–75; Bp's Dom Chapl *Chich* 75–78; C-in-c Parklands St Wilfrid CD 78–82; V Durrington 82–89; P-in-c Staplefield Common 89–94; Bp's Adv on CME 89–93; Asst Dir of Ords 89–93; PtO from 13. *6 Winchester Drive, Chichester PO19 5DE* T: (01243) 783136 E: anthony.jcs@gmail.com

FREEMAN, Mrs Dorothy Lloyd (Dee). b 54. Lon Inst of Educn BEd 76 Nottm Univ MA 11. EMMTC 06. **d** 09 **p** 10. NSM Linc St Geo Swallowbeck 09–16; R Withamside from 16. *The Rectory, 11 Torgate Lane, Bassingham, Lincoln LN5 9HF* T: (01522) 788383 M: 07792-780683 E: revdee@withamsidechurches.org.uk

FREEMAN, Gordon Bertie. b 37. CITC BTh 95. **d** 95 **p** 96. C Lecale Gp *D & D* 95–98; I Ardara w Glencolumbkille, Inniskeel etc *D & R* 98–07; Bp's Dom Chapl 06–07; rtd 07. *3 Leyland Meadow, Ballycastle BT54 6JX* T: (028) 2076 8458 E: gordon.freeman2@btinternet.com

FREEMAN, Canon Jane. b 54. Dur Univ BA 75 PhD 80. Qu Coll Birm BD 00. **d** 00 **p** 01. C Waterloo St Jo w St Andr *S'wark* 00–03; TV E Ham w Upton Park and Forest Gate *Chelmsf* 03–11; TR Wickford and Runwell from 11; RD Basildon 16–19; Hon Can Chelmsf Cathl from 09. *8 Friern Walk, Wickford SS12 0HZ* T: (01268) 734077 M: 07702-922818 E: canjanefree@gmail.com

FREEMAN, Mrs Karen Lynn. b 62. San Diego State Univ USA BS 86 Leeds Univ BA 09. NOC 06. **d** 09 **p** 10. C New Brighton St Jas w Em *Ches* 09–12; P-in-c Birkenhead Ch Ch 13–18. *12510 Dennis Court, Auburn CA 95603, USA* E: k.freeman62@gmail.com

FREEMAN, Preb Karl Fredrick. b 57. St Luke's Coll Ex BEd 80. **d** 90 **p** 91. C Plymouth St Andr w St Paul and St Geo *Ex* 90–95; TV Plymouth St Andr and Stonehouse 95–96; Chapl Coll of SS Mark and Jo Plymouth 96–01; TR Plymouth Em, St Paul Efford and St Aug from 01; Preb Ex Cathl from 14; RD Plymouth City 15–17. *The Rectory, 9 Seymour Drive, Plymouth PL3 5BG* T: (01752) 248601 *or* 260317 E: karldesk@blueyonder.co.uk

FREEMAN, Keith Ian. b 66. St Jo Coll Nottm 10. **d** 12 **p** 13. C Shelley and Shepley *Leeds* 12–15; V Barnsley from 15. *The Vicarage, Green Road, Dodworth, Barnsley S75 3RT* T: (01226) 958737 M: 07958-328289 E: keithfreeman66@hotmail.com

FREEMAN, Malcolm Robin. b 48. Master Mariner 78. St And NSM Tr Scheme 85. **d** 88 **p** 89. NSM Kirkcaldy *St And* 88–94; NSM Westbury *Sarum* 99–02; R Tidworth, Ludgershall and Faberstown 02–13; rtd 13; PtO *Win* from 14. *26 Home Farm Gardens, Charlton, Andover SP10 4AX* M: 07810-862740 E: fgmastermariner@ntlworld.com *or* fgmastermariner@gmail.com

FREEMAN, Martin. *See* FREEMAN, Philip Martin

FREEMAN, Michael Charles. b 36. Magd Coll Cam BA 61 MA 68 Lon Univ BD 69 PhD 93. Clifton Th Coll 67. **d** 69 **p** 70. C Bedworth *Cov* 69–72; C Morden *S'wark* 72–77; P-in-c Westcombe Park St Geo 77–85; V Kingston Vale St Jo

85–94; rtd 99; PtO *B & W* from 11. *6 Wristland Road, Watchet TA23 0DH* T: (01984) 634378 E: freemmic@talktalk.net

FREEMAN, Michael Curtis. b 51. Lanc Univ BA 72 Liv Hope Univ Coll MA 96 PhD 05. Cuddesdon Coll 72. **d** 75 **p** 76. C Walton St Mary *Liv* 75–78; C Hednesford *Lich* 78–81; TV Solihull *Birm* 81–86; V Yardley Wood 86–90; V Farnworth *Liv* 90–03; AD Widnes 02–03; P-in-c Blundellsands St Mich 03–12; V 12; P-in-c Thornton and Crosby 05–12; rtd 12; PtO *Liv* from 16. *5 Lincoln Crescent, Bootle L20 7EB* E: michael.freeman6@mypostoffice.co.uk

FREEMAN, Preb Michael Raymond. b 58. Chu Coll Cam BA 80 MA 84 Ox Univ BA 87. St Steph Ho Ox 85. **d** 88 **p** 89. C Clifton All SS w St Jo *Bris* 88–92; TV Elland *Wakef* 92–01; V Horninglow *Lich* from 01; RD Tutbury from 10; Preb Lich Cathl from 16. *Horninglow Vicarage, 14 Rolleston Road, Burton-on-Trent DE13 0JZ* T: (01283) 568613 E: cft-rfreeman@supanet.com

FREEMAN, Preb Pamela Mary. b 45. Univ of Wales (Lamp) MA 08. WMMTC 83. **dss** 86 **d** 87 **p** 94. Cannock *Lich* 86–88; Par Dn 87–88; Min for Deaf (Salop Adnry) 88–95; Par Dn Shelton and Oxon *Lich* 88–94; C 94–95; TV Stafford 95–00; P-in-c High Offley and Norbury 00–02; R Adbaston, High Offley, Knightley, Norbury etc 02–10; Preb Lich Cathl 07–10; rtd 10; PtO *Lich* from 11; Chapl Severn Hospice from 11. *14 Meadow Close, Trentham Road, Wem, Shrewsbury SY4 5HP* T: (01939) 234672 E: revpmfreeman@gmail.com

FREEMAN, Peter Cameron Jessett. b 41. **d** 05 **p** 06. OLM Sturry w Fordwich and Westbere w Hersden *Cant* 05–11; rtd 11; PtO *Cant* from 11. *29 Cedar Road, Sturry, Canterbury CT2 0HZ*

FREEMAN, Philip Martin. b 54. Westcott Ho Cam 76. **d** 79 **p** 80. C Stanley *Liv* 79–82; C Bromborough *Ches* 82–84; V Runcorn H Trin 84–91; Chapl Halton Gen Hosp 84–91; R Ashton-upon-Mersey St Martin *Ches* 91–96; SSF 96–06; PtO *Sarum* 96–99; Asst Chapl HM Pris Birm 98–99; PtO *Lon* 99–02; *Ely* 02–05; Chapl Barts and The Lon NHS Trust 00–02 and 05–08; Chapl Guy's and St Thos' NHS Foundn Trust 05–08; PtO *S'wark* 05–08; Chapl Univ Coll Lon Hosps NHS Foundn Trust 08–16; Hon C Smithfield St Bart Gt *Lon* 06–08; rtd 16; PtO *Lon* from 16; *S'wark* from 16. *18 Foxley Gardens, Purley CR8 2DQ* T: (020) 3302 3099 M: 07985-512436 E: pmfreeman3@gmail.com

FREEMAN, Richard Alan. b 52. Ripon Coll Cuddesdon. **d** 83 **p** 84. C Crayford *Roch* 83–86; V Slade Green 86–94; R Eynsford w Farningham and Lullingstone 94–01; P-in-c Shoreham 01–12; V 12–15; Chapl St Mich Sch Otford 01–15; R Bradworthy, Sutcombe, Putford etc *Ex* 15; R Bradworthy, Sutcombe etc from 15; PtO Holsworthy from 19. *The New Rectory, St Peters Well Lane, Bradworthy, Holsworthy EX22 7TG* T: (01409) 241315 E: ricktherec@aol.com

✠**FREEMAN, The Rt Revd Robert John.** b 52. St Jo Coll Dur BSc 74 Fitzw Coll Cam BA 76 MA. Ridley Hall Cam 74. **d** 77 **p** 78 **c** 11. C Blackpool St Jo *Blackb* 77–81; TV Chigwell *Chelmsf* 81–85; V Leic Martyrs 85–99; Hon Can Leic Cathl 94–03; RD Christianity S 95–98; Nat Adv in Evang 99–03; LtO *Leic* 99–03; Adn Halifax *Wakef* 03–11; Suff Bp Penrith *Carl* 11–18; rtd 18; Hon Asst Bp Leic from 18. *40 Eastfield Road, Leicester LE3 6FE* E: frmnfrmn@gmail.com

FREEMAN, Rosemary. b 47. **d** 03 **p** 04. NSM Madeley *Heref* 03–17; PtO from 17. *5 Rowley Close, Madeley, Telford TF7 5RR* T: (01952) 583460 E: rosemary_freeman@sky.com

FREEMAN, Simon Thomas Allan. b 69. Univ of Wales (Trin St Dav) BTh 18. St Padarn's Inst 15. **d** 18 **p** 19. C Bro Gwydyr *Ban* from 18. *Hyfrydle, Dolwyddelan LL25 0EJ* T: (01690) 750458 E: revsimonfreeman18@gmail.com

FREESTONE, Anne Elizabeth. b 52. Bp Otter Coll Chich CertEd 73 Coll of Ripon & York St Jo MA 00. NEOC 04. **d** 07 **p** 08. NSM Middleton-in-Teesdale w Forest and Frith *Dur* 07–11; PtO from 11; *Leeds* from 14; Chapl Castle Howard 15–18; PtO *York* 18; *Ches* from 19. *5 Tedder Road, York YO24 3JD* M: 07939-964011 E: annefreestone22@btinternet.com

FREETH, Barry James. b 35. Birm Univ BA 60. Tyndale Hall Bris 60. **d** 62 **p** 64. C Selly Hill St Steph *Birm* 62–63; C Birm St Jo Ladywood 63–71; Chapl RAF 71–75; P-in-c Crudwell w Ashley *Bris* 75–81; P-in-c Lanreath *Truro* 81–84; R 84–87; P-in-c Pelynt 81–84; V 84–87; R Harvington and Norton and Lenchwick *Worc* 87–93; V Ramsden, Finstock and Fawler, Leafield etc *Ox* 93–99; rtd 99; PtO *Derby* 99–03; *Ox* 08–12. *16 Broad Meadow, Leonard Stanley, Stonehouse GL10 3PG* T: (01453) 823890

FREETH, Mrs Patricia. b 48. Wycliffe Hall Ox BTh 95. **d** 95 **p** 96. NSM Ramsden, Finstock and Fawler, Leafield etc *Ox* 95–99; TV Buxton w Burbage and King Sterndale *Derby* 99–03; V Shires' Edge *Ox* 03–12; AD Deddington 10–12; rtd 12; PtO *Glouc* from 13; AD Stroud from 18. *16 Broad Meadow,*

Leonard Stanley, Stonehouse GL10 3PG T: (01453) 823890 E: revpfreeth@gmail.com

FREMMER, Ludger. b 56. Ridley Hall Cam 02. **d** 04 **p** 05. C Mattishall w Mattishall Burgh, Welborne etc *Nor* 04–07; P-in-c Kibworth and Smeeton Westerby and Saddington *Leic* 07–17; R from 17. *The Rectory, 25 Church Road, Kibworth, Leicester LE8 0NB* T: 0116-279 2294 *or* 279 6577 M: 07753-213145 E: ludger.fremmer@gmail.com *or* wilfs.kibworth@gmail.com

FRENCH, Alexander James Watkins. b 70. Univ of Wales (Ban) BA 92 Univ Coll Worc PGCE 93. Qu Foundn Birm 13. **d** 16 **p** 17. C Old Swinford Stourbridge *Worc* from 16. *58 Arlington Court, Stourbridge DY8 1NN* T: (01384) 622400 M: 07745-780629 E: ajwfrench@yahoo.co.uk

FRENCH, Mrs Christine. b 68. Nottm Trent Univ PGCE 05. EMMTC MA 08. **d** 09 **p** 10. C Keyworth and Stanton-on-the-Wolds and Bunny etc *S'well* 09–13; P-in-c Norwell w Ossington, Cromwell and Caunton 13–14; P-in-c Kirk Hallam *Derby* from 14; C Ilkeston St Jo from 15. *The Vicarage, 71 Ladywood Road, Ilkeston DE7 4NF* T: 0115-783 1793 E: revchristine@outlook.com

FRENCH, Canon Clive Anthony. b 43. AKC 70. St Aug Coll Cant 70. **d** 71 **p** 72. C Monkseaton St Mary *Newc* 71–73; Dioc Youth Adv 73–76; Chapl RN 76–77; Dir of Ords RN 85–90; Chapl RN Coll Greenwich 95–97; R Cheam *S'wark* 97–06; TR Catford (Southend) and Downham 06–09; Hon Can S'wark Cathl 08–09; rtd 09; PtO *S'wark* 10 and 14–17; *Eur* from 18. *17 Kingslea, Leatherhead KT22 7SN* T: (01372) 375418

FRENCH, Daniel Alain. b 68. Kent Univ BSc 91. St Jo Sem Wonersh BTh 97. **d** 97 **p** 98. In RC Ch 97–01; C Aberdeen St Clem *Ab* 02–03; C Aberdeen St Mary 02–03; P-in-c Aberdeen St Clem 03–08; Chapl Robert Gordon Univ 04–08; V Salcombe and Malborough w S Huish *Ex* from 08; RD Woodleigh 12–16. *The Vicarage, Devon Road, Salcombe TQ8 8HJ* T: (01548) 842853 *or* 842626 E: cybervicar@gmail.com

FRENCH, Derek John. b 47. Man Univ BA 03. Ripon Coll Cuddesdon 93. **d** 95 **p** 96. C Stand *Man* 95–98; TV E Farnworth and Kearsley 98–00; P-in-c Halliwell St Marg 00–09; P-in-c Ringley w Prestolee 06–09; P-in-c Elton St Steph 09–11; V 11–15; rtd 15; PtO *Blackb* from 15. *22 Links Road, Knott End-on-Sea, Poulton-le-Fylde FY6 0DG* T: (01253) 812006 E: revdelboy@gmail.com

FRENCH, George Leslie. b 47. AIFST NE Lon Poly BSc 70. S'wark Ord Course 86. **d** 89 **p** 90. NSM Reading St Barn *Ox* 89–99. *Hawthorne House, 2 Cutbush Close, Lower Earley, Reading RG6 4XA* T: 0118-986 1886

FRENCH, Janet Mary. *See* DRIVER, Janet Mary

FRENCH, Jonathan David Seabrook. b 60. Westcott Ho Cam 84. **d** 87 **p** 88. C Loughton St Jo *Chelmsf* 87–90; Chapl St Bede's Ch for the Deaf Clapham 90–92; C Richmond St Mary w St Matthias and St Jo *S'wark* 92–95; TV 96–03; V Downham St Barn 03–10; Chapl RAD 92–03; Dioc Adv for Min of Deaf and Disabled People *S'wark* 03–10; R Southwick *Chich* from 10. *The Rectory, 22 Church Lane, Southwick, Brighton BN42 4GB* T: (01273) 592389 E: jo.nathan@btinternet.com

FRENCH, Mrs Joy Elizabeth. b 75. Sheff Univ BA 98 MA 17. St Hild Coll 14. **d** 17 **p** 18. C Owlerton *Sheff* from 17. *St Mark's Vicarage, 19 Graven Close, Grenoside, Sheffield S35 8QT* M: 07496-531257 E: joyfrench@hotmail.co.uk *or* joy@stjb.org.uk

FRENCH, The Ven Judith Karen. b 60. St D Coll Lamp BA 89. St Steph Ho Ox 89. **d** 91 **p** 94. Par Dn Botley *Portsm* 91–94; C Bilton *Cov* 94–97; V Charlbury w Shorthampton *Ox* 97–14; AD Chipping Norton 07–12; Hon Can Ch Ch 12–14; Adn Dorchester from 14. *11 Broad Field Road, Yarnton, Kidlington OX5 1UL* T: (01865) 208245 M: 07460-888482 E: archdeacon.dorchester@oxford.anglican.org

FRENCH, Michael John. b 37. WEMTC 92. **d** 95 **p** 96. OLM Cheltenham St Pet *Glouc* 95–01; NSM 01–08; NSM N Cheltenham from 08. *8 Alexandria Walk, Cheltenham GL52 5LG* T: (01242) 236661 E: mike.french@northchelt.org.uk

FRENCH, Peter Robert. b 65. Man Univ BTh 87. Qu Coll Birm 88. **d** 90 **p** 91. C Unsworth *Man* 90–93; C Bury Ch King w H Trin 93–95; V Bury Ch King 95–98; V Handsworth St Andr *Birm* 98–06; Sch Support Officer 06–18; PtO from 18. *Address temp unknown*

FRENCH, Richard John. b 34. Open Univ BA 82. Tyndale Hall Bris 62. **d** 64 **p** 65. C Rustington *Chich* 64–68; C Walton H Trin Ox 68–72; V Grove 72–99; rtd 99; PtO *Chich* from 01. *5 Green Meadows, The Welkin, Haywards Heath RH16 2PE* T: (01444) 487842

FRENCH, Stephen Robert James. b 52. St Jo Coll Nottm. **d** 87 **p** 88. C Chell *Lich* 87–91; TV 91–94; V Wednesfield Heath 94–01; TV Hemel Hempstead *St Alb* 01–06; P-in-c

Bugbrooke w Rothersthorpe *Pet* 06–10; P-in-c Kislingbury and Harpole 06–10; R Bugbrooke, Harpole, Kislingbury etc from 10. *The Rectory, Church Lane, Bugbrooke, Northampton NN7 3PB* T: (01604) 831621 E: srjfrench@hotmail.co.uk

FRENCH, William Stephen. b 49. STETS 07. **d** 10 **p** 11. NSM Verwood *Sarum* 10–16; NSM Wimborne Minster and the N Villages from 16. *Hollow Tree House, Chalbury, Wimborne BH21 7ER* T: (01258) 841061 M: 07771-560128 E: william.french4@btinternet.com

FRETT, Daniel Calvin. b 60. Univ of S Carolina 85. NTMTC 05 Oak Hill Th Coll BA 99. **d** 98 **p** 99. NSM Clerkenwell St Jas and St Jo w St Pet *Lon* 98–00; NSM Chelsea St Jo w St Andr 00–05; NSM Tulse Hill H Trin and St Matthias *S'wark* 05–08; NSM Cranleigh *Guildf* 09–16; PtO *Mon* from 16. *Headmaster's House, St John's on the Hill School, Castleford Hill, Tutshill, Chepstow NP16 7LE* M: 07966-196852 E: dfrett@mac.com

FREYHAN, Daniel Jonathan. b 83. Oriel Coll Ox MMath 06. Oak Hill Th Coll BA 14. **d** 14 **p** 15. C Stevenage St Nic and Graveley *St Alb* 14–17; V Prudhoe *Newc* from 17. *The Vicarage, 5 Kepwell Court, Prudhoe NE42 5PE* T: (01661) 836059

FRIARS, Ian Malcolm George. b 50. Sarum & Wells Th Coll 83. **d** 85 **p** 86. C Norton *St Alb* 85–88; C Ramsey *Ely* 88–90; TV The Ramseys and Upwood 90–93; P-in-c Cottenham 93–94; R 94–01; P-in-c Long Melford *St E* 01–02; R Chadbrook 02–13; rtd 13; PtO *Ely* from 12; *St Alb* from 13; *St E* from 13; *Eur* from 17. *Clanjenan, 3A Swan Street, Ashwell, Baldock SG7 5NY* T: (01462) 742441 E: ianmgfriars@gmail.com

FRIDD, Nicholas Timothy. b 53. Ch Ch Ox BA 74 MA 78. STETS 05. **d** 08 **p** 09. NSM Wells St Thos w Horrington *B & W* from 08. *The Old Bakery, 30 St Thomas Street, Wells BA5 2UX* T: (01749) 679832 M: 07831-209240 E: wellscottages@btconnect.com

FRIEDRICH, Robert Edmund. b 48. Houghton Coll (USA) BA 70 Gordon-Conwell Th Sem MDiv 74 DMin 96. Gen Th Sem NY 86. **d** 86 **p** 86. C Westfield Atonement USA 86–88; R Penfield 88–92; R Newport Epiphany 92–97; Meriden All SS 99–02; W Haven St Jo 04; Las Vegas Grace in the Desert 04–06; Olean 06–07; PtO *St As* from 15; *Ban* from 15. *Polyanna Cottage, Castle Street, Conwy LL32 8AY* E: bobfriedrich@gmail.com

FRIENDSHIP, Roger Geoffrey (John-Francis). b 46. ACII 72. WMMTC 90. **d** 93 **p** 94. SSF 76–02; NSM Harborne St Faith and St Laur *Birm* 93–94; Asst Novice Guardian Hilfield Friary 94–97; Novice Guardian 97–99; Gen Sec SSF 99–01; C Clerkenwell H Redeemer and St Mark *Lon* 00–01; R Romford St Andr *Chelmsf* 01–11; rtd 11; PtO *S'wark* from 12; *Chelmsf* from 15. *22 The Old Fire Station, Eaglesfield Road, London SE18 3BT* T: (020) 3583 9312 M: 07808-500717 E: jff2209@yahoo.com

FRIGGENS, Canon Maurice Anthony. b 40. Sheff Univ BA 65. Westcott Ho Cam 65. **d** 67 **p** 68. C Stocksbridge *Sheff* 67–70; C St Buryan, St Levan and Sennen *Truro* 70–72; R 72–84; RD Penwith 82–84; R St Columb Major w St Wenn 84–91; Dioc Dir of Ords 87–93; Hon Can Truro Cathl 87–00; V St Cleer 91–00; rtd 00; PtO *Ban* from 00; *Eur* from 01. *Tŷ Cernyw, Rhiw, Pwllheli LL53 8AF* T: (01758) 780365

FRISWELL, Caroline Anne. b 52. St Mary's Coll Chelt BEd 78 Sunderland Poly MA 90 Dur Univ PhD 99. Cranmer Hall Dur 06. **d** 09 **p** 10. NSM Greenside *Dur* 09–12; P-in-c Byers Green from 12. *St Peter's Rectory, Byers Green, Spennymoor DL16 7NL* T: (01388) 609436 E: caroline.friswell@btinternet.com

FRITH, Canon Christopher John Cokayne. b 44. Ex Coll Ox BA 65 MA 69. Ridley Hall Cam 66. **d** 68 **p** 69. C Crookes St Thos *Sheff* 68–71; C Rusholme H Trin *Man* 71–74; R Haughton St Mary 74–85; R Brampton St Thos *Derby* 85–02; V Alvaston 02–09; Hon Can Derby Cathl 99–09; rtd 09; PtO *Worc* from 10. *Cover Point, Back Lane, Bredon, Tewkesbury GL20 7LH* T: (01684) 773164

FRITH, Mrs Gillian. b 43. EAMTC 99. **d** 02 **p** 03. NSM Chipping Ongar w Shelley *Chelmsf* 02–06; P-in-c Doddinghurst 06–13; rtd 13; PtO *Chelmsf* 14–17. *29 Windmill Fields, Coggeshall, Colchester CO6 1PJ* T: (01376) 566815 M: 07890-376779 E: frithgill29@gmail.com

FRITH, Jonathan Paul (Jonty). b 72. Jes Coll Cam BA 94 MA 97. Wycliffe Hall Ox 95. **d** 97 **p** 98. C Houghton *Carl* 97–00; Chapl Cranleigh Sch Surrey 00–04; C Crowborough *Chich* 04–15; R Bathampton w Claverton *B & W* from 15. *The Vicarage, Bathampton Lane, Bathampton, Bath BA2 6SW* T: (01225) 338055 E: jontyfrith@gmail.com

FRITH, Canon Richard John. b 77. Warwick Univ BA 98 Sheff Univ MA 99 Trin Hall Cam PhD 04. Ripon Coll Cuddesdon BA 10. **d** 11 **p** 12. C Ox St Mary Magd 11–14; V Halifax H Trin and St Jude *Leeds* 14–19; Can Res S'well Minster from 19. *2 Vicars Close, Southwell NG25 0HP* T: (01636)

812649 M: 07754-524206 E: richard.frith@ymail.com or precentor@southwellminster.org.uk

✠**FRITH, The Rt Revd Richard Michael Cokayne.** b 49. Fitzw Coll Cam BA 72 MA 76. St Jo Coll Nottm 72. **d** 74 **p** 75 **c** 98. C Mortlake w E Sheen *S'wark* 74–78; TV Thamesmead 78–83; TR Keynsham *B & W* 83–92; Preb Wells Cathl 91–98; Adn Taunton 92–98; Suff Bp Hull *York* 98–14; Bp Heref from 14. *The Bishop's House, The Palace, Hereford HR4 9BN* T: (01432) 271355 F: 373346 E: bishop@hereford.anglican.org

FRITZE-SHANKS, Miss Annette. Sydney Univ BA 86 DipEd 87 LLB 89 Solicitor. SEITE 01. **d** 04 **p** 05. NSM Kilburn St Mary w All So and W Hampstead St Jas *Lon* 04–08; PtO 08–10; NSM Hampstead Em W End from 10. *13 Elm Grove, London NW2 3AE* M: 07771-544201 E: afritze-shanks@btconnect.com

FROGGATT, Peter Michael. b 65. St Hild Coll Dur BA 86 PGCE 88. Wycliffe Hall Ox BTh 95. **d** 95 **p** 96. C Bebington *Ches* 95–00; V Rock Ferry 00–11; RD Birkenhead 10–11; V Barnston from 11; RD Wirral N from 15. *The Vicarage, 87 Barnston Road, Heswall, Wirral CH61 1BW* T: 0151-648 1776 or 648 2404 E: peter@froggatt.org.uk

FROOM, Ian Leonard John. b 42. Sarum Th Coll 69. **d** 71 **p** 72. C Gillingham and Fifehead Magdalen *Sarum* 71–75; C Parkstone St Pet w Branksea and St Osmund 75–78; V Sedgley St Mary *Lich* 78–85; TV Weston-super-Mare Cen Par *B & W* 85–94; PtO 94–97; V Truro St Geo and St Jo 97–03; rtd 03; PtO *Truro* from 03. *11 Marlborough Crescent, Falmouth TR11 2RJ* T: (01326) 311760 E: sea2firechap@yahoo.co.uk

FROST, Christopher Dominic. b 83. Abth Univ BA 05 Cardiff Univ BTh 15. St Mich Coll Llan 12. **d** 15 **p** 16. C Cardigan w Mwnt and Y Ferwig w Llangoedmor *St D* 15–17; C Aberporth w Blaenporth w Betws Ifan 17–18; P-in-c Bro Teifi from 18. *Bronwydd, Parc y Plas, Aberporth, Cardigan SA43 2BJ* M: 07432-692179 E: christopher_dominic_frost@yahoo.co.uk

FROST, David John. b 48. **d** 86 **p** 87. Hon C Upper Norwood All SS *S'wark* 86–89; C Battersea St Luke 90–94; V Shirley St Geo 94–12; rtd 12; PtO *S'wark* from 12; *Cant* from 12. *19 Reculver Avenue, Birchington CT7 9NT* T: (01843) 844511 E: revdfrost1@gmail.com

FROST, Canon David Richard. b 54. Ridley Hall Cam 84. **d** 86 **p** 87. C Burgess Hill St Andr *Chich* 86–90; TV Rye 90–94; V Bexhill St Steph 94–10; RD Battle and Bexhill 06–10; TR Rye from 10; RD 11–18; Can and Preb Chich Cathl from 10. *The Rectory, Gungarden, Rye TN31 7HH* T: (01797) 222430 M: 07970-746545 E: david@drfrost.org.uk

FROST, Derek Charles. b 47. Lich Th Coll 69. **d** 71 **p** 72. C Woodley St Jo the Ev *Ox* 71–76; V Bampton w Clanfield 76–81; V Minster Lovell and Brize Norton 81–88; TV Upper Kennet *Sarum* 88–92; P-in-c Seend and Bulkington 92–97; P-in-c Seend, Bulkington and Poulshot 95–97; V 97–01; V Derry Hill w Bremhill and Foxham 01–10; rtd 10; PtO *Sarum* from 10. *Longhope Cottage, 93 North Street, Calne SN11 0HJ* T: (01249) 811565

FROST, The Ven George. b 35. Dur Univ BA 56 MA 61. Linc Th Coll 57. **d** 60 **p** 61. C Barking St Marg *Chelmsf* 60–64; C-in-c Marks Gate CD 64–70; V Tipton St Matt *Lich* 70–77; V Penn 77–87; RD Trysull 84–87; Preb Lich Cathl 85–87; Adn Salop 87–98; V Tong 87–98; P-in-c Donington 97–98; Adn Lich and Can Res and Treas Lich Cathl 98–00; rtd 00; PtO *Lich* from 00. *23 Darnford Lane, Lichfield WS14 9RW* T: (01543) 415109 E: frost151@btinternet.com

FROST, Mrs Jane Helena. b 59. St Aid Coll Dur BA 81 Newc Univ PGCE 82. SWMTC 12. **d** 15 **p** 16. C Totnes w Bridgetown, Berry Pomeroy etc *Ex* 15–19; TV Teignmouth, Ideford w Luton, Ashcombe etc from 19. *The Vicarage, 3 Moors Park, Bishopsteignton, Teignmouth TQ14 9RH* T: (01626) 870288 E: revjanefrost@gmail.com

✠**FROST, The Rt Revd Jonathan Hugh.** b 64. Aber Univ BD 88 Nottm Univ MTh 99 Surrey Univ DUniv 12 MSSTh 91. Ridley Hall Cam 91. **d** 93 **p** 94 **c** 10. C W Bridgford *S'well* 93–97; Police Chapl Trent Division 94–97; R Ash *Guildf* 97–02; Tutor Local Min Progr 99–10; Can Res Guildf Cathl 02–10; Chapl Surrey Univ 02–10; Co-ord Chapl 08–10; Bp's Adv Inter-Faith Relns *Guildf* 07–10; Suff Bp Southampton *Win* 10–19; Hon Asst Bp Portsm 16–19; Dean York from 19; Hon Asst Bp York from 19; PtO *Portsm* from 16. *The Deanery, Dean's Park, York YO1 7JQ* T: (01904) 557202 E: dean@yorkminster.org

FROST, Linda May. b 59. CITC MTh 14. **d** 13 **p** 14. Howth *D & G* 13–14; Bp's C Mohill w Farnaught, Aughavas, Oughteragh etc *K, E & A* 14–17; I from 17. *Corbo, Kilrooskey, Co Roscommon, F42 E671, Republic of Ireland* M: (00353) 86-601 0895 E: welcomefrost@iol.ie

FROST, Michael John. b 42. Westmr Coll Ox TCert 64. **d** 95 **p** 96. OLM Harwood *Man* 95–12; rtd 12; PtO *Man* from 12. *86 Harden Drive, Harwood, Bolton BL2 5BX* T: (01204) 418596 E: revmikefrost@live.co.uk

FROST, Paul William. b 75. Sheff Univ BA 97 Ox Univ PGCE 98. Wycliffe Hall Ox MTh 08. **d** 08 **p** 09. C Kettering Ch the King *Pet* 08–12; P-in-c Corby St Jo w Epiphany 12–17; R from 17. *16 Streather Drive, Corby NN17 1TN* M: 07979-547279 E: frost.pw@gmail.com

FROST, Richard John. b 49. Ch Ch Coll Cant CertEd 71 BA 00. SWMTC 95. **d** 97 **p** 98. NSM Bideford, Northam, Westward Ho!, Appledore etc *Ex* 97–00; C 00–03; TV 03–09; rtd 09; PtO *Ex* from 10; Chapl Kyrenia St Andr Cyprus 11–13; PtO *St E* from 15; *Eur* 10–19; Chapl Málaga 19–20. *Cana, 2 Tarka Falls, Old Barnstaple Road, Bideford EX39 4FL* E: richardjohnfrost@hotmail.co.uk

FROST, Stanley. b 37. Univ of Wales BSc 61 Liv Univ MSc 65 PhD 68 CBiol 66 MRSB 66 FAEB 82. NOC 79. **d** 82 **p** 83. NSM Lower Kersal *Man* 82–87; NSM Patricroft 87–89; NSM Convenor 87–95; Lic Preacher 89–03; P-in-c Pittenweem and Elie and Earlsferry *St And* 03–04; rtd 04; PtO *Derby* 04–18. *25 Somersall Park Road, Chesterfield S40 3LD* T: (01246) 567184 E: stan.frost@homecall.co.uk

FROSTICK, Paul Andrew. b 52. Stockwell Coll of Educn CertEd 73. Ripon Hall Ox 74. **d** 77 **p** 78. C Shepton Mallet *B & W* 77–80; TV Barton Mills, Beck Row w Kenny Hill etc *St E* 80–85; TV Mildenhall 85–86; TV Raveningham *Nor* 86–89; V Bottisham and P-in-c Lode and Longmeadow *Ely* 89–90; V Bottisham and Lode w Long Meadow 90–94; Hd RE Brittons Sch Romford 94–97; Hd RE The Grove Sch St Leonards 97–00; rtd 00; Assoc P Bexhill St Aug *Chich* 99–14; PtO 14–17; P-in-c Hooe from 17; P-in-c Ninfield from 17. *18 The Ridings, Bexhill-on-Sea TN39 5HU* T: (01424) 218126 M: 07713-243427 E: paul.frostick@sky.com

FROUD, Andrew William. b 65. Mansf Coll Ox BA 87 St Cath Coll Cam MPhil 92. Westcott Ho Cam 90. **d** 93 **p** 94. C Almondbury w Farnley Tyas *Wakef* 93–96; P-in-c Wootton *Portsm* 96–00; R 00–01; V Thornton-le-Fylde *Blackb* 01–05; Chapl St Geo C of E Sch Blackpool 05–09; P-in-c Clitheroe St Mary 09–13; V 13–17; P-in-c Chatburn and Downham 14–17; V Clitheroe St Mary and St Paul, Chatburn and Downham from 18. *The Vicarage, Church Street, Clitheroe BB7 2DD* T: (01253) 764467 E: andyfroud@gmail.com

FROUDE (née WOOLCOCK), The Ven Christine Ann. b 47. ACIB 73. S Dios Minl Tr Scheme 92. **d** 95 **p** 96. NSM Stoke Bishop *Bris* 95–99; Chapl United Bris Healthcare NHS Trust 99–01; P-in-c Shirehampton *Bris* 01–11; Dean of Women's Min 00–11; Hon Can Bris Cathl 01–11; Adn Malmesbury 11–18; Adn Bris 12–18; rtd 18. *24 Waterloo Street, Clifton, Bristol BS8 4BT* E: christine.froude@bristoldiocese.org

FRUEHWIRTH, Robert Alan. b 69. **d** 97 **p** 97. PtO *Nor* 11–13; Dir Julian Cen 13–15; C Nor St Pet Mancroft w St Jo Maddermarket 13–15; USA from 15. *302 Chesapeake Way, Chapel Hill NC 27516, USA* M: (001) (540) 406 3304 E: r.fruehwirth@icloud.com

FRY, Alison Jacquelyn (Sister Alison). b 65. Newnham Coll Cam BA 86 MA 90 Hertf Coll Ox DPhil 90 St Jo Coll Dur BA 95. Cranmer Hall Dur 93. **d** 96 **p** 97. C Milton *B & W* 96–00; V Batheaston w St Cath 00–12; OSB from 12; PtO *Worc* from 12. *Mucknell Abbey, Mucknell Farm Lane, Soulton, Worcester WR7 4RB* T: (01905) 345900 E: revajfry@gmail.com

FRY, Canon Barry James. b 49. K Alfred's Coll Win MA 03 Win Univ PhD 15 ACIB. Ripon Coll Cuddesdon 81. **d** 83 **p** 84. C Highcliffe w Hinton Admiral *Win* 83–87; V Southampton St Barn 87–19; rtd 19; Hon Can Ruvuma Cathl Tanzania from 02. *3 Sway Road, Brockenhurst SO42 7SH* T: (01590) 622486

FRY, David William. b 51. St Jo Coll Nottm. **d** 08 **p** 09. C Heeley and Gleadless Valley *Sheff* 08–10 and 12; V Ardsley 10–12; V Heeley 12–16; AD Attercliffe 13–16; rtd 16. *9 Ashfield Close, Sheffield S12 2QU*

FRY, John Edward. b 80. Univ of Wales (Swansea) BSc 01 PGCE 03. Wycliffe Hall Ox BTh 13. **d** 13 **p** 14. C Theydon Bois and Theydon Garnon *Chelmsf* 13–16; V 16–17; V Theydon Par from 17. *The Vicarage, 2 Piercing Hill, Theydon Bois, Epping CM16 7JN* T: (01992) 814725 M: 07719-469029 E: revjefry@gmail.com

FRY, Lynn Jane. b 60. **d** 03 **p** 04. OLM E w W Harling, Bridgham w Roudham, Larling etc *Nor* 03–19; Papua New Guinea 15 and 17–18. *Society of St Francis, The Friary, Hilfield, Dorchester DT2 7BE* M: 07554-930054 E: lynnandtony@outlook.com

FRY, Nigel Edward. b 57. St Jo Coll Nottm 91. **d** 93 **p** 94. C Wellingborough All Hallows *Pet* 93–96; R Peakirk w Glinton and Northborough 96–05; V Pet Ch Carpenter 05–16; TV Barby w Kilsby 16; TV Daventry from 16. *The Vicarage, 4 West End, West Haddon, Northampton NN6 7AY* M: 07854-810588 E: enfrys@gmail.com

FRY, Roger Joseph Hamilton. b 29. Em Coll Cam BA 52 MA 56. Clifton Th Coll 52. **d** 54 **p** 55. C Walcot *B & W*

54–57; C Gresley *Derby* 57–61; P-in-c Bowling St Bart and St Luke *Bradf* 61–65; V Bowling St Jo 61–87; V Ingleton w Chapel le Dale 87–95; rtd 95; PtO *Bradf* 95–14; *Leeds* from 14. *5 Margerison Crescent, Ilkley LS29 8QZ* T: (01943) 608738 E: rjhfry@gmail.com

FRYDAY, Canon Barbara Yvonne. b 47. Ch of Ireland Tr Coll TCert 67. CITC 90. **d** 92 **p** 93. NSM Cashel w Magorban, Tipperary, Clonbeg etc *C & O* 93–96; C Kilcooley w Littleon, Crohane and Fertagh 96–99; I 99–07; I Clonmel w Innislounagh, Tullaghmelan etc from 07; Can Ossory Cathl from 03; Warden of Readers from 08. *The Rectory, 7 Linden Lea, Silversprings, Clonmel, Co Tipperary, E91 CV63, Republic of Ireland* T/F: (00353) (52) 618 7464 M: 86-275 0735 E: frydayb@gmail.com

FRYER, Alison Jane. See BOWNASS, Alison Jane

FRYER, Cora Lynette. See YARRIEN, Cora Lynette

FRYER, Mrs Jenifer Anne. b 43. NOC 89. **d** 92 **p** 94. Par Dn Ecclesfield *Sheff* 92–94; C 94–95; Asst Chapl Cen Sheff Univ Hosps NHS Trust 93–96; Chapl Weston Park Hosp Sheff 94–96; Chapl Asst N Gen Hosp NHS Trust Sheff 96–04; Chapl Asst Sheff Teaching Hosps NHS Foundn Trust 04–07; rtd 07; PtO *Sheff* from 07. *5 Nursery Drive, Ecclesfield, Sheffield S35 9XU* T: 0114-246 1027 E: jeni_fryer@talktalk.net

FRYER, Mrs Suzanne Elizabeth. b 75. Sheff Univ BMus 96 Bretton Hall Coll PGCE 97. St Mellitus Coll BA 18. **d** 18 **p** 19. C Grays Thurrock *Chelmsf* from 18. *19 Martello Close, Grays RM17 6FL* T: (01375) 370884 E: revdsuziefryer@gmail.com

FRYER-SPEDDING, Mrs Clare Caroline. b 47. St Aid Coll Dur BA 69. LCTP 06. **d** 09 **p** 10. NSM Binsey *Carl* from 09. *West Mirehouse, Underskiddaw, Keswick CA12 4QE* E: cfs@mirehouse.com

FRYMANN, Mrs Janet Elizabeth. b 57. St Jo Coll Nottm BA 12. **d** 12 **p** 13. C N Wingfield, Clay Cross and Pilsley *Derby* 12–15; P-in-c Roughton and Felbrigg, Metton, Sustead etc *Nor* 15–17; R from 17. *The Rectory, Roughton, Norwich NR11 8SZ* T: (01263) 768075 M: 07766-712545 E: rev.roughton@gmail.com

FUDGE, Prof Erik Charles. b 33. Ch Coll Cam BA 55 MA 59 Southn Univ CertEd 58 Cam Univ PhD 68. Ox Min Course 91. **d** 93 **p** 94. NSM Wokingham St Sebastian *Ox* from 93. *4 South Close, Wokingham RG40 2DJ* T: 0118-978 6081

FUDGER, David John. b 53. Sheff Univ MMin 96. K Coll Lon 73 Coll of Resurr Mirfield 76. **d** 77 **p** 78. C Sutton in Ashfield St Mary *S'well* 77–80; P-in-c Duston *Pet* 80–82; V Radford All So w Ch Ch and St Mich *S'well* 82–91; Min Bermondsey St Hugh CD *S'wark* 91–97; P-in-c Blackheath Ascension 97–04; Hon Chapl S'wark Cathl 91–01; P-in-c Mansfield SS Pet and Paul *S'well* 04–11; V 11–17; P-in-c Mansfield St Mark 12–14; V 14–17; rtd 17; PtO *S'well* from 18. *Gardeners Cottage, Sherwood Grange, Mansfield NG18 2EJ* E: revfudger@mistral.co.uk

FUDGER, Michael Lloyd. b 55. K Coll Lon BD 77 AKC 77. Coll of Resurr Mirfield 77. **d** 78 **p** 79. C Weston Favell *Pet* 78–82; C Pet H Spirit Bretton 82–84; V Irchester 84–90; TV Darnall-cum-Attercliffe *Sheff* 90–96; TV Attercliffe, Darnall and Tinsley 96–97; TR 97–03; TR Attercliffe and Darnall 03–05; V 05–06; Chapl Nine o'Clock Community 04–06; RD Attercliffe 91–96; Hon Can Sheff Cathl 00–06; R Bedford St Pet w St Cuth *St Alb* 06–16; rtd 16. *64 The Promenade, Peacehaven BN10 8NH* E: fudgerm@yahoo.co.uk

FUERTE, Antonio. See GARCIA FUERTE, Antonio

FUHRI, Tessa Jane. See NISBET, Tessa Jane

FULFORD, Alison Jane. b 79. CCC Cam BA 00 MA 04. Ridley Hall Cam 01. **d** 04 **p** 05. C Old Catton *Nor* 04–07; Hon Chapl St Jo Coll Nottm 08–11; P-in-c Hickling w Kinoulton and Broughton Sulney *S'well* 11–13; R 13–14; P-in-c Baddiley and Wrenbury w Burleydam *Ches* from 14; Dean of Women in Min 15–18. *The Vicarage, The Green, Wrenbury, Nantwich CW5 8EY* T: (01270) 780742 E: revalisonfulford@hotmail.co.uk

FULFORD, Susan Yvonne. b 61. **d** 03. OLM Pemberton St Mark Newtown *Liv* 03–07; OLM Marsh Green w Newtown 08–14; OLM Newtown from 14. *13 Mitchell Street, Wigan WN5 9BY* T: (01942) 242369 E: sueandmike2003@yahoo.co.uk

FULHAM, Suffragan Bishop of. See BAKER, The Rt Revd Jonathan Mark Richard

FULKER, Lois Valerie. b 42. Keele Univ BA 64. Cranmer Hall Dur 04. **d** 04 **p** 05. NSM Egremont and Haile *Carl* 04–08; PtO 08–13. *3 Mill Farm, Calderbridge, Seascale CA20 1DN* T: (01946) 841475 E: lois-fulker@gmail.com

FULLAGAR, Michael Nelson. b 35. SS Coll Cam BA 57 MA 61. Chich Th Coll 57. **d** 59 **p** 60. C Camberwell St Giles *S'wark* 59–61; C Northolt Park St Barn *Lon* 61–64; C Hythe *Cant* 64–66; R Chipata Zambia 66–70; P-in-c Livingstone

70–75; P-in-c Chingola 75–78; R Freemantle *Win* 78–87; Buckingham Deanery Health Chapl and P-in-c Westbury w Turweston, Shalstone and Biddlesden *Ox* 87–94; Chapl S Bucks NHS Trust 94–96; rtd 96; P-in-c Burwash Weald *Chich* 97–04; PtO from 04. *1 Roffrey Avenue, Eastbourne BN22 0AE* T: (01323) 503212 E: michaelfullagar@aol.com

FULLALOVE, Brenda Hurst. *See* CRASTON, Brenda Hurst

FULLARTON, Mrs Heather Mary. b 42. Whitelands Coll Lon TCert 63. Qu Coll Birm 90. **d** 92 **p** 94. Par Dn Colwich w Gt Haywood *Lich* 92–94; C 94–97; P-in-c Swindon and Himley 97–01; V Prees and Fauls 01–02; rtd 02; PtO *Sarum* from 03. *26 Drovers, Sturminster Newton DT10 1QY* T: (01258) 269072 M: 07741-403539

FULLER, Alison Jane. *See* COZENS, Alison Jane

FULLER, Christopher John. b 53. Chich Th Coll 85. **d** 87 **p** 88. C Swinton and Pendlebury *Man* 87–90; C Chiswick St Nic w St Mary *Lon* 90–92; V Hounslow W Gd Shep 92–96; V Stoke Newington St Faith, St Matthias and All SS 96–05; V Enfield St Geo 05–13; P-in-c S Shields St Hilda w St Thos *Dur* 13–18; Chapl Miss to Seafarers 13–15; rtd 18. *Address withheld by request*

FULLER, Canon Graham Drowley. b 33. AKC 58. **d** 59 **p** 60. C E Grinstead St Swithun *Chich* 59–62; C Coulsdon St Andr *S'wark* 62–64; Chapl RN 64–68; V Battersea St Luke *S'wark* 68–75; V S Stoneham *Win* 75–90; R Eversley 90–96; Bp's Ecum Officer 84–95; Hon Can Win Cathl 93–96; rtd 96; PtO *Portsm* from 03. *Brookside Dairy, Nunnery Lane, Newport PO30 1YR* T: (01983) 525976 E: teasel@brooksidedairy.co.uk

FULLER, Ian David. b 60. St Mellitus Coll 16. **d** 17 **p** 18. OLM Springfield H Trin *Chelmsf* from 17. *8 Jasmine Close, Chelmsford CM1 6XL* T: (01245) 465777 E: iandavidfuller@gmail.com

FULLER, Canon John James. b 38. SS Coll Cam BA 63 MA 66. Chich Th Coll 63 Union Th Sem (NY) STM 64. **d** 65 **p** 66. C Westmr St Steph w St Jo *Lon* 65–71; Tutor Cuddesdon Coll 71–75; Tutor Ripon Coll Cuddesdon 75–77; Prin S Dios Minl Tr Scheme 77–96; Can and Preb Sarum Cathl 83–96; V Wheatley w Forest Hill and Stanton St John *Ox* 96–97; TR Wheatley 97–03; rtd 03; PtO *Sarum* from 13. *11 Ratcliffs Garden, Shaftesbury SP7 8HJ* T: (01747) 850079

FULLER, Matthew John. b 74. Birm Univ BA 95 PGCE 96. Oak Hill Th Coll BA 05. **d** 05 **p** 06. C St Helen Bishopsgate w St Andr Undershaft etc *Lon* from 05. *54 Monkton Street, London SE11 4TX* T: (020) 7735 2494 M: 07903-045667 E: matt@thebibletalks.org

FULLER, Michael George. b 46. Chich Th Coll 90. **d** 92 **p** 93. C Fulham All SS *Lon* 92–94; C Kensington St Mary Abbots w St Geo 94–06; V Holland Park 06–12; Dir Post-Ord Tr Kensington Area 94–99; Bp Kensington's Liaison Officer to Metrop Police *Lon* 99–12; rtd 12; R Vancouver St Jo Shaughnessy Canada 12–15; PtO *Lon* 15–16; Hon C St Marylebone St Cypr from 16. *21 Modern House, Harewood Avenue, London NW1 6NR* T: (020) 3536 6357 M: 07495-726006 E: michaelfuller1946@gmail.com

FULLER, Canon Michael Jeremy. b 63. Worc Coll Ox BA 85 MA 89 DPhil 89 Qu Coll Cam BA 91. Westcott Ho Cam 89. **d** 92 **p** 93. C High Wycombe *Ox* 92–95; C Edin St Jo 95–00; Prin TISEC 00–02; IME Officer 02–14; Pantonian Prof 00–14; Can St Mary's Cathl *Edin* 00–14; Hon Can St Mary's Cathl from 14; Hon Research Fell Glas Univ from 08. *28 Blackford Avenue, Edinburgh EH9 2PH* T: 0131-667 7273 E: michael.fuller@ed.ac.uk

FULLER (formerly MCCULLOCK), Mrs Patricia Ann. b 46. EMMTC 87. **d** 90 **p** 94. C Bottesford w Ashby *Linc* 90–95; P-in-c Wragby 95–98; Chapl N Lincs Coll of FE 95–98; Ind Chapl 98–01; rtd 01; PtO *Linc* 01–11; NSM Marden w Preston Grange and Billy Mill *Newc* 12–13; PtO from 14. *1 Orchard Close, Morpeth NE61 1XE* T: (01670) 519800 E: pat.fuller25@gmail.com

FULLER, Canon Terence James. b 30. Bris Univ BA 55. Clifton Th Coll 55. **d** 56 **p** 57. C Uphill *B & W* 56–60; V Islington St Jude Mildmay Park *Lon* 60–67; V Southgate *Chich* 67–80; R Stoke Climsland *Truro* 80–95; RD Trigg Major 85–91; P-in-c Lezant w Lawhitton and S Petherwin w Trewen 93–95; Hon Can Truro Cathl 94–96; rtd 96; PtO *Truro* 96–15. *9 Westover Road, Callington PL17 7EW* T: (01579) 384958

FULLERTON, Hamish John Neville. b 45. Ball Coll Ox BA 68 MA 73. S'wark Ord Course 76. **d** 79 **p** 80. Hd English Abp Tenison's Sch Kennington 79–88; Hon C Clapham Old Town *S'wark* 79–82; PtO 82–89; Hon C Brixton Road Ch Ch 89–91; C Streatham Ch Ch 91–96; C Purley St Mark 96–98; Asst P Tooting St Aug 98–01; PtO from 03. *Flat 4, 21 Offerton Road, London SW4 0DJ* T: (020) 7622 7890

FULLJAMES, Mrs Janet Kathleen Doris. b 43. Open Univ BA 79 Birm Univ MA 93. Qu Coll Birm 85. **d** 87 **p** 94. Par Dn Harborne St Pet *Birm* 87–93; Par Dn Smethwick SS Steph and Mich 93–94; C 94–95; C Smethwick Resurr 95–98; P-in-c

Dudley St Thos and St Luke *Worc* 98–04; P-in-c Dudley St Jo 98–04; rtd 04; PtO *B & W* from 04. *12 Obridge Road, Taunton TA2 7PX* T: (01823) 333585 E: fullj9@gmail.com

FULLJAMES, Michael William. b 36. K Coll Lon AKC 60. St Boniface Warminster 60. **d** 61 **p** 62. C Armley St Bart *Ripon* 61–64; C E Wells *B & W* 64–67; Chapl Mendip Hosp Wells 64–67; R Stanningley St Thos *Ripon* 67–73; Chapl St Aug Hosp Cant 73–88; Chapl St Martin's Hosp Cant 82–88; RD W Bridge Cant 87–88; Chapl Rotterdam *Eur* 88–94; Sen Chapl Rotterdam Miss to Seamen 88–94; Sen Chapl Burrswood Chr Cen *Roch* 94–01; rtd 01; PtO *Cant* from 01. *40 Somner Close, Canterbury CT2 8LJ* T: (01227) 766950 E: m.fulljames@gmail.com

FULLJAMES, Peter Godfrey. b 38. BNC Ox BA 60 MA 64 Birm Univ PhD 91. Qu Coll Birm. **d** 62 **p** 63. C Mexborough *Sheff* 62–65; Chapl Union Chr Coll India 65–69; Asst Master Wednesfield High Sch Wolverhampton 69–71; Asst Master Moorside High Sch Werrington 71–79; NSM Nairobi St Mark Kenya 80–85; Asst Master Nairobi High Sch 80–85; Research Fell Qu Coll Birm 85–87; Tutor WMMTC 87–90; Vice-Prin 90–93; Tutor Qu Coll Birm 93–94; Tutor Crowther Hall CMS Tr Coll Selly Oak 94–00; Hon Lect Th Birm Univ 97–03; rtd 00; PtO *B & W* from 04. *12 Obridge Road, Taunton TA2 7PX* T: (01823) 333585 E: fullj9@gmail.com

FULTON, Miss Ann Elizabeth. b 47. SWMTC 01. **d** 04 **p** 05. NSM Kingston St Mary w Broomfield etc *B & W* 04–11; NSM W Monkton 10–11; NSM W Monkton w Kingston St Mary, Broomfield etc 11–14; Chapl St Marg Hospice Taunton from 14; PtO *B & W* 14–16; LtO from 16. *St Margaret's Somerset Hospice, Heron Drive, Bishops Hull, Taunton TA1 5HA* T: (01823) 259394 M: 07765-925236 E: annfulton29@yahoo.co.uk *or* ann.fulton@st-margarets-hospice.org.uk

FULTON, John William. b 49. Ex Coll Ox BA 71 BPhil 72 MA 75 MPhil 79. Wycliffe Hall Ox 72. **d** 76 **p** 77. C Bexleyheath Ch Ch *Roch* 76–79; C Ealing Dean St Jo *Lon* 79–83; V Aldborough Hatch *Chelmsf* 83–87; Chapl Chantilly *Eur* 87–90; R Hepworth, Hinderclay, Wattisfield and Thelnetham *St E* 90–14; RD Ixworth 09–14; rtd 15; PtO *St E* from 15; *Eur* from 18. *11 Chancellery Mews, Bury St Edmunds IP33 3AB* T: (01284) 765744 E: jwfulton@btinternet.com

FUNNELL, Preb Norman Richard James. b 40. Univ of Wales (Lamp) BA 64. Ripon Hall Ox 64. **d** 66 **p** 67. C Hackney *Lon* 66–70; Hon C 71–85; TV 85–93; R S Hackney St Jo w Ch Ch 93–08; Chapl St Joseph's Hospice Hackney 93–08; Preb St Paul's Cathl *Lon* 05–08; rtd 08; PtO *Truro* from 14. *37 Brunel Quays, Great Western Village, Lostwithiel PL22 0JB* T: (01208) 873867 M: 07964-238934 E: jamesfunnell@btinternet.com

FURBER, Mrs Jennifer Margaret. b 50. WEMTC 98. **d** 01 **p** 02. NSM Malvern Link w Cowleigh *Worc* 01–08; rtd 09; PtO *Win* from 09. *3 Ravenswood, 23 Wimborne Road, Bournemouth BH2 6LZ* T: (01202) 296886 E: jenny@furber.me.uk

FURBER, Peter. b 43. Ex Univ BA. Sarum & Wells Th Coll 83. **d** 85 **p** 86. C Stanmore *Win* 85–88; TV Basingstoke 88–95; C Ringwood 95–98; P-in-c Gt Malvern Ch Ch *Worc* 98–99; V 99–08; rtd 09; PtO *Win* from 09. *3 Ravenswood, 23 Wimborne Road, Bournemouth BH2 6LZ* T: (01202) 296886 E: peter@furber.me.uk

FURBER, Sarah Anne. *See* COAKLEY, Sarah Anne

FUREY, Scott Robert. b 87. Ch Coll Cam MA 14. Oak Hill Th Coll BA 18. **d** 18 **p** 19. C Mayfair Ch Ch *Lon* from 18. *Flat 1, 86 Wilberforce Road, London N4 2SR* M: 07729-067651 E: scott@christchurchmayfair.org

FURLONG, Andrew William Ussher. b 47. TCD BA 69 Jes Coll Cam BA 71. Westcott Ho Cam 70 CITC 72. **d** 72 **p** 73. C Dundela St Mark *D & D* 72–76; C Dublin St Ann w St Mark and St Steph *D & G* 76–83; Zimbabwe 83–94; Adn W Harare 88–89; Can Harare 89–94; Asst Chapl Leeds Teaching Hosps NHS Trust 94–97; Dean Clonmacnoise *M & K* 97–02; I Trim and Athboy Gp 97–02; Prec Kildare Cathl 98–02. *12 Tubbermore Road, Dalkey, Co Dublin, Republic of Ireland* T: (00353) (1) 285 9817 E: awufurlong@gmail.com

FURLONG (née DAVIES), Mrs Catharine Mary. b 48. Philippa Fawcett Coll CertEd 73. EMMTC 85. **d** 88 **p** 95. C Spalding St Mary and St Nic *Linc* 88–92; Zimbabwe 92–94; C Gt w Lt Gidding and Steeple Gidding *Ely* 94–96; P-in-c 96–06; P-in-c Brington w Molesworth and Old Weston 96–06; P-in-c Leighton Bromswold 96–06; P-in-c Winwick 96–06; P-in-c Gt Gransden and Abbotsley and Lt Gransden etc 06–18; Asst Chapl Hinchingbrooke Health Care NHS Trust 06–17; rtd 18; PtO *Ely* from 18. *36 St Peters Road, Oundle, Peterborough PE8 4NT* T: (01832) 272650 E: catharinemfurlong@tiscali.co.uk

FURNESS, Barry Keith. b 47. Open Univ BSc 93. **d** 04 **p** 05. OLM High Oak, Hingham and Scoulton w Wood Rising *Nor* 04–09; P-in-c Smallburgh w Dilham w Honing and Crostwight 09–11; R 11–15; rtd 15; PtO *Nor* from 15. *Church*

View, 6 Alderfen Way, Hoveton NR12 8GA T: (01692) 536812
E: barry.furness6@btinternet.com

FURNESS, Christine Anne. b 51. Leic Coll of Educn CertEd 73
Open Univ BA 76 Man Univ MEd 84 PhD 91 Ches Coll of
HE MTh 02. NOC 99. **d** 02 **p** 03. C Offerton *Ches* 02–06; V
Brinnington w Portwood 06–12; rtd 13; PtO *Ches* 13–17; *Lich*
13–16 and from 18. *Address withheld by request* M: 07771-
601615 E: anne@afurness.co.uk

FURNESS, Dominic John. b 53. Bris Univ BA 76. Ridley Hall
Cam 82. **d** 84 **p** 85. C Downend *Bris* 84–88; V Stoke Hill
Guildf 88–05; V Milford *Win* 05–19; AD Lyndhurst 08–13;
rtd 19. *Red House Cottage, 88 Lower Road, Salisbury SP2 9NJ*
E: dominic.furness@talktalk.net

FURNESS, Edward Joseph. b 41. S'wark Ord Course 74.
d 77 **p** 78. NSM S Lambeth St Steph *S'wark* 77–81; Warden
Mayflower Family Cen Canning Town *Chelmsf* 82–96; P-in-c
Aston St Jas *Birm* 96–00; V 00–05; rtd 05; PtO *Birm* from
05. *304 New Oscott Village, 25 Fosseway Drive, Birmingham
B23 5GP* T: 0121-377 5304

FURSE, Adrian Thomas. b 76. Bris Univ BA 99 Univ of Wales
(Swansea) MA 01 Leeds Univ PhD 06. St Steph Ho Ox 08.
d 10 **p** 11. C Wistow *Leic* 10–14; TV Dewisland *St D* 14–18;
Min Can St D Cathl 14–18; P-in-c W Cemaes from 18. *The
Vicarage, Maenclochog, Clynderwen SA66 7LD* T: (01437)
532238 M: 07890-020849 E: adrian.t.furse@gmail.com

FUTCHER, Anne Elizabeth. b 57. Portsm Poly BA 78 Univ
of Wales (Swansea) MEd 83 PGCE 80 Ox Univ BTh 19.
Ripon Coll Cuddesdon 13. **d** 15 **p** 16. C Colyton,
Musbury, Southleigh and Branscombe *Ex* 15–19; NSM
Larnaca Cyprus from 19. *15 Odysseas Androutsou Street,
Aradippou, 7104 Larnaca, Cyprus* M: 07551-007123
E: anne.futcher@cypgulf.org

FUTCHER, The Ven Christopher David. b 58. Edin Univ
BD 80 Lon Univ MTh 04 K Coll Lon MA 11. Westcott
Ho Cam 80. **d** 82 **p** 83. C Borehamwood *St Alb* 82–85; C
Stevenage All SS Pin Green 85–88; V 88–96; V St Alb St Steph
96–00; R Harpenden St Nic 00–12; Adn Ex 12–19; Adn
Cyprus and Chapl Larnaca Cyprus and the Gulf from 19. *15
Odysseas Androutsou Street, Aradippou, 7104 Larnaca, Cyprus*
E: archdeacon.christopher@cypgulf.org

FUTERS, Michael Roger. b 58. Trin & All SS Coll Leeds BEd 80.
St Jo Coll Nottm 82. **d** 85 **p** 86. C Narborough and Huncote
Leic 85–87; C Spondon *Derby* 87–90; P-in-c Derby St Jas
90–95; TV Walbrook Epiphany 95–99; Hon C Derby St Mark
99–09; Community Development Officer Home Housing
from 99; Hon C Chaddesden St Phil w Derby St Mark from
09. *3 St Pancras Way, Derby DE1 3TH* T: (01332) 203075
E: futersm@hotmail.com

FYFE, Mrs Deirdre Bettina. b 44. STETS 05. **d** 07 **p** 08.
NSM S Petherton w The Seavingtons *B & W* 07–12; NSM
Winsmoor 12–19; PtO from 19. *1 Waldock Barton, South
Petherton TA13 5NZ* T: (01460) 241977 M: 07746-472445
E: dbfyfe@btinternet.com

FYFE, Stewart John. b 69. City Univ BSc 91. Ridley Hall
Cam 03. **d** 05 **p** 06. C Barony of Burgh *Carl* 05–07 and 08–10;
P-in-c Bolton 10–17; P-in-c Crosby Ravensworth 10–17;
P-in-c Morland, Thrimby, Gt Strickland and Cliburn 10–17;
R N Westmorland from 17; RD Appleby from 13; C Heart
of Eden from 18; Asst Dir of Ords from 18. *The Vicarage,
Morland, Penrith CA10 3AX* T: (01931) 714620 M: 07985-
900477 E: rectornwparishes@gmail.com

FYFFE, Timothy Bruce. b 25. New Coll Ox MA 54. Westcott
Ho Cam 54. **d** 56 **p** 57. C Lewisham St Mary *S'wark* 56–60; V
Enugu All SS Nigeria 60–68; TV Lowestoft St Marg *Nor* 69–80;
Chapl HM Pris Blundeston 70–78; TV Tettenhall Regis
Lich 80–85; Chapl Compton Hospice 85–87; rtd 90; NSM
Wolverhampton St Andr *Lich* 88–10; PtO 10–15; *Ely* from
16. *12 Chaston Road, Great Shelford, Cambridge CB22 5AP*
E: tim@timfyffe.plus.com

FYLES, Gordon. b 39. Trin Coll Bris 76. **d** 77 **p** 78. C
Islington St Mary *Lon* 77–81; Ext Sec BCMS 81–88;
C Wimbledon Em Ridgway Prop Chpl *S'wark* 88–97;
I Crinken *D & G* 97–04; rtd 04. *1 Marlowe House, 147
Durham Road, London SW20 0DQ* T: (020) 8715 1894
E: gordonandyvonne@yahoo.co.uk

FYSH, Leslie David. b 35. Glouc Sch of Min 88. **d** 91 **p** 92.
NSM Stonehouse *Glouc* 91–95; Asst Chapl Wycliffe Coll Glos
91–95; NSM W Walton *Ely* 95–00; PtO 00–11; Nor 08–12; PV
Ely Cathl 03–06; Sub-Warden Coll of St Barn Lingfield 14–16;
PtO *Ely* from 16. *3 King John House, Kings Walk, Wisbech
PE13 1HU* T: (01945) 589616 E: revfysh@gmail.com

G

GABBADON, Kenneth Fitz Arthur. b 53. NOC 97. **d** 99 **p** 00.
C Burnage St Marg *Man* 99–01; C Bury St Jo w St Mark 01–03;
P-in-c Newton Heath 03–08; R 08–09; Chapl HM Pris Leeds
09–14; Chapl HM Pris Wealstun 14–18; rtd 18; P-in-c Clifford
York from 09; P-in-c York All SS N Street 17–19. *The Vicarage,
19 Chapel Lane, Clifford, Wetherby LS23 6HU* T: (01937)
541165 E: kgabba7036@aol.com

GABEL, Lee. b 75. Ripon Coll Cuddesdon 11. **d** 14 **p** 15. C
Frodingham and New Brumby *Linc* 14–17; P-in-c Brocklesby
Park 17–18; P-in-c N Wolds Gp 17–18; P-in-c Brocklesby
Park, Croxton and North Wolds 18–19; R from 19. *The
Vicarage, Back Lane, Barnetby DN38 6JE* T: (01652)
680414 M: 07999-538824 E: leebbgabel@gmail.com

GABLE, Michael David. b 70. Poly of Wales BEng 92. St Mich
Coll Llan BTh 95. **d** 95 **p** 96. C Newton Nottage *Llan*
95–99; V Aberavon H Trin 99–01; TV Aberavon 01–05;
P-in-c Rhydyfelin w Graig 05–11; V Glyntaff, Rhydfelin
and the Graig 11–15; TV Pontypridd from 15; AD from
11. *St John's Vicarage, 28 Llantrisant Road, Graig, Pontypridd
CF37 1LW* T: (01443) 650336 E: michaeldgable@gmail.com

GADD, Alan John. b 44. Imp Coll Lon BSc 65 PhD 69 Heythrop
Coll Lon MA 07 FRMetS 67. S'wark Ord Course 68. **d** 71 **p** 72.
Asst Chapl Lon Univ 71–72; PtO *S'wark* 73–91; C Battersea
Park All SS 91–95; P-in-c 95–96; C Battersea Fields 96–05;
rtd 05; PtO *S'wark* from 05. *24 Holmewood Gardens, London
SW2 3RS* T: (020) 8678 8977 E: alangadd@yahoo.co.uk

GADD, Brian Hayward. b 33. Hatf Coll Dur BA 54 DipEd 55.
Glouc Sch of Min 82. **d** 85 **p** 87. NSM Cleobury Mortimer
w Hopton Wafers etc *Heref* 85–98; rtd 98; PtO *Heref*
99–12. *34 Lower Street, Cleobury Mortimer, Kidderminster
DY14 8AB* T: (01299) 270758

GADD, Bryan Stephen Andrew. b 56. Dur Univ BA Ox Univ
CertEd Univ of Qld MPhil Cen Qld Univ MLitt. Chich Th
Coll. **d** 81 **p** 82. C Newlyn St Pet *Truro* 81–86; R St Mawgan
w St Ervan and St Eval 86–90; Chapl Summer Fields Sch Ox
90–02; PtO *Truro* 90–00; Chapl Southport Sen Sch Australia
02–09; Sen Chapl Angl Ch Gr Sch from 09. *Anglican Church
Grammar School, Oaklands Parade, East Brisbane QLD
4169, Australia* T: (0061) (7) 3896 2281 F: 3891 5976
E: bryan.gadd@churchie.com.au

GADSBY, Alison. *See* HOGGER-GADSBY, Alison

GADSBY, Julian Timothy David Moritz. b 74. K Coll Lon
BA 96 AKC 96. Oak Hill Th Coll 02. **d** 04 **p** 05. C Chadwell
Chelmsf 04–09; P-in-c Bucklebury w Marlston *Ox* from
09. *The Vicarage, Burdens Heath, Upper Bucklebury, Reading
RG7 6SX* T: (01635) 866731 or 860220

GAFFIN, Jennifer Clare. b 78. Mansf Coll Ox BA 99 Man
Univ MA 00 Win Univ PhD 06. Ripon Coll Cuddesdon 07.
d 09 **p** 10. C Parkstone St Pet and St Osmund w Branksea
Sarum 09–12; Bp's Dom Chapl *Portsm* 12–16; P-in-c
N Hayling St Pet from 16; P-in-c S Hayling from 16;
P-in-c Hayling Is St Andr from 16. *St Mary's Vicarage, 34
Church Road, Hayling Island PO11 0NT* T: (023) 9307
0178 M: 07855-024789 E: jennyhaylingvicar@hotmail.com
or jennyhaylingisland@gmail.com

GAGE, Aëlla Rupert Fitzhardinge Berkeley. b 66. Bulmershe
Coll of HE BEd 92. Oak Hill Th Coll 98. **d** 00 **p** 02. C Muswell
Hill St Jas w St Matt *Lon* 00–05; C Hadley Wood St Paul
Prop Chpl 05–08; C Highgate Australia 08–10; C Fordham
Chelmsf 10–14; C Colchester St Pet and St Botolph from 14.
31 St Peter's Street, Colchester CO1 1ES M: 07796-475130
E: aella.gage@gmail.com

GAGE, Alan William. b 52. Univ of Wales (Cardiff) BMus 72
PGCE 73 Bris Univ MEd 90. WEMTC 98. **d** 00 **p** 01. NSM
Tuffley *Glouc* 00–08; NSM Hardwicke and Elmore w
Longney 08–09; PtO from 14. *Chadburn, 83 Dinglewell,
Hucclecote, Gloucester GL3 3HT* T: (01452) 614892
E: curatealan@blueyonder.co.uk

GAGE, Jennifer Anne. b 50. Girton Coll Cam MA 75 Open Univ BA 85 PhD 05 Keele Univ PGCE 86. ERMC 07. **d** 09 **p** 10. NSM Three Rivers Gp *Ely* 09–15; NSM Haddenham 15–19; NSM Wilburton 15–19; NSM Witchford w Wentworth 15–19; Bp's Adv for Self-Supporting Min from 14; NSM Ely Cathl from 19. *51 Henley Way, Ely CB7 4YH* T: (01353) 666426 E: revd.jennygage@gmail.com

GAGE, Canon Robert Edward. b 47. Whitman Coll Washington BA 69. Cuddesdon Coll BA 75 MA 81. **d** 76 **p** 77. C Cheshunt *St Alb* 76–79; C Harpenden St Nic 79–81; V S Mymms 81–82; P-in-c Ridge 81–82; V S Mymms and Ridge 82–97; Prec and Can Res Wakef Cathl 97–05; Can Res Newc Cathl 05–09; rtd 09; PtO *Newc* from 09. *44 Warkworth Avenue, Whitley Bay NE26 3PS* E: robertgage1@yahoo.co.uk

GAGE, Timothy Arthur John. b 85. Ridley Hall Cam 13. **d** 16 **p** 17. C Hove Bp Hannington Memorial Ch *Chich* from 16. *47 Nevill Avenue, Hove BN3 7NB* M: 07786-813724 E: revgage@outlook.com

GAGEN, Mrs Valerie Elizabeth. b 52. Ripon Coll of Educn BEd 75. NTMTC BA 10. **d** 10 **p** 11. NSM N Hinckford *Chelmsf* 10–14; NSM Pastrow *Win* 14–18; NSM Bury St Edmunds All SS w St Jo and St Geo *St E* from 18; NSM Lark Valley from 18. *The Vicarage, 16A Anselm Avenue, Bury St Edmunds IP32 6JY* M: 07874-067371 E: valgagen@hotmail.com

GAINER, Canon Jeffrey. b 51. Jes Coll Ox BA 73 MA 77 Univ of Wales LLM 94. Wycliffe Hall Ox 74. **d** 77 **p** 78. C Baglan *Llan* 77–81; V Cwmbach 81–85; V Tonyrefail w Gilfach Goch and Llandyfodwg 85–87; Dir NT Studies and Dir Past Studies St Mich Coll Llan 87–92; V Meidrim and Llanboidy and Merthyr *St D* from 92; P-in-c Abernant 07–18; AD St Clears 03–13; Cursal Can St D Cathl from 11; PtO *Eur* from 19. *The Vicarage, Meidrim, Carmarthen SA33 5QF* T: (01994) 231378 E: sieffremeidrim@googlemail.com

GAINES, Miss Atalie Clodia. b 78. Brighton Univ BA 00 Cam Univ BTh 14. Westcott Ho Cam 12. **d** 14 **p** 15. C Bedford St Andr *St Alb* 14–17; V Potters Bar K Chas from 17. *The Vicarage, 8 Dugdale Hill Lane, Potters Bar EN6 2DW* T: (01707) 661266

GAINSBOROUGH, Canon Jonathan Martin. b 66. SOAS Lon MA 91 MSc 95 PhD 01. STETS MA 10. **d** 10 **p** 11. NSM Barton Hill St Luke w Ch Ch and Moorfields *Bris* 10–13; P-in-c 13–16; Prof Development Politics Bris Univ 12–18; Can Th Bris Cathl 16–18; Dioc Soc Justice and Environmental Adv 17–18; Bp's Chapl *Bris* from 19; Can Res Bris Cathl from 19. *21 Cotham Lawn Road, Bristol BS6 6DS* T: (01454) 777728 E: bishop.chaplain@bristoldiocese.org

GAIR, Andrew Kennon. b 62. Westcott Ho Cam 88. **d** 91 **p** 92. C Clare w Poslingford, Cavendish etc *St E* 91–95; R Debden and Wimbish w Thunderley *Chelmsf* 95–06. *18-20 High Street, Wrentham, Beccles NR34 7HB*

✠**GAISFORD, The Rt Revd John Scott.** b 34. St Chad's Coll Dur BA 59 MA 76. **d** 60 **p** 61 **c** 94. C Audenshaw St Hilda *Man* 60–62; C Bramhall *Ches* 62–65; V Crewe St Andr 65–86; RD Nantwich 74–85; Hon Can Ches Cathl 80–86; Adn Macclesfield 86–94; Suff Bp Beverley (PEV) *York* 94–00; Asst Bp Ripon and Leeds 96–00; rtd 00; PtO *Ches* from 00; *Man* from 04. *5 Trevone Close, Knutsford WA16 9EJ* T: (01565) 633531 M: 07429-340155 E: jsandg.gaisford@gmail.com

GAIT, Canon David James. b 48. BNC Ox BA 71 BSc 72 MA 77 MSc 83. Ridley Hall Cam 71. **d** 74 **p** 75. C Litherland St Paul Hatton Hill *Liv* 74–77; C Farnworth 77–80; V Widnes St Jo 80–13; TV E Widnes 13; Chapl Widnes Maternity Hosp 86–90; AD Widnes *Liv* 07–13; Hon Can Liv Cathl 05–13; rtd 13. *Bryn Celyn, Betws Gwerfil Goch, Corwen LL21 9PP* T: (01490) 420759 E: dave.gait@btinternet.com

GAKURU, Griphus Stephen. b 59. Makerere Univ Kampala BSc 81 PGDE 83 Selw Coll Cam MPhil 92 PhD 95. Bp Tucker Coll Mukono BD 88. **d** 88 **p** 91. Uganda 89–91; Hon C Cambridge H Trin *Ely* 91–95; Chapl Selw Coll Cam 91–95; C Small Heath *Birm* 95–98; C Huyton St Mich *Liv* 98–01; P-in-c Brownswood Park *Lon* 01–03; PtO *St Alb* 03–05; P-in-c Stechford *Birm* 05–07; V from 07. *All Saints' Vicarage, Albert Road, Stechford, Birmingham B33 8UA* T/F: 0121-783 2463 M: 07795-206034

GALANZINO, Diego. b 80. St Steph Ho Ox BTh 11. **d** 11 **p** 12. C St Ives *Truro* 11–15; C Halsetown 11–15; P-in-c Houghton Regis *St Alb* from 15. *Clergy House, Lowry Drive, Houghton Regis, Dunstable LU5 5SJ* T: (01582) 867246 E: frdiego@mail.com

GALBRAITH, Alexander Peter James. b 65. Qu Coll Ox BA 86 MA 90. Wycliffe Hall Ox 87. **d** 90 **p** 91. C Southport Em *Liv* 90–94; C Mossley Hill St Matt and St Jas 94–97; V Kew from 97; Chapl Southport and Ormskirk Hosp NHS Trust 97–11. *20 Markham Drive, Kew, Southport PR8 6XR* T: (01704) 547758 E: alexgalbraith20@hotmail.com

GALBRAITH, Canon Jane Alexandra. **d** 95 **p** 96. NSM Kildare w Kilmeague and Curragh *M & K* 95–97; NSM Newbridge w Carnalway and Kilcullen 97–99; C Limerick *L & K* 03–14; C Tralee w Kilmoyley, Ballymacelligott etc 14–15; I Roscrea w Kyle, Bourney and Corbally from 15; Can Limerick, Killaloe and Clonfert Cathls from 16. *St Cronan's Rectory, Rosemount, Roscrea, Co Tipperary, Republic of Ireland* T: (00353) (505) 21725 M: 87-382 5336 E: galbraithjane@gmail.com

GALBRAITH, John Angus Frame. b 44. Sarum Th Coll 68. **d** 71 **p** 72. C Richmond St Mary w St Matthias *S'wark* 71–74; Chapl W Lon Colls 74–79; R S'wark H Trin w St Matt 79–95; V New Addington 95–02; Asst Chapl HM Pris Wandsworth 02–04; Chapl 04–09; rtd 09; PtO *S'wark* from 09. *35 Joseph Hardcastle Close, London SE14 5RN* T: (020) 7635 3607 E: angus.galbraith@talktalk.net

GALE, Ms Charlotte. b 70. Leeds Univ BEng 92 Nottm Univ MA 00. St Jo Coll Nottm 98. **d** 01 **p** 02. C Whitnash *Cov* 01–05; P-in-c Potters Green 05–08; P-in-c Lillington and Old Milverton 08–14; V 14–17; C Leamington Spa H Trin 08–17; AD Warwick and Leamington 14–17; C St Clare in Cov Cathl from 17. *6 Carthusian Road, Coventry CV3 6HA* T: (024) 7652 1200 E: charlotte.gale@sky.com

GALE, Canon Christopher. b 44. ALCD 67. **d** 68 **p** 69. C Balderton *S'well* 68–72; C Bilborough St Jo 72–75; P-in-c Colwick 75–78; V Radford St Pet 78–84; V Sherwood 84–98; AD Nottm N 90–98; P-in-c Bulwell St Mary 98–02; R 02–07; Hon Can S'well Minster 03–07; rtd 08. *11 Cliff Road, Carlton, Nottingham NG4 1BS* T: 0115-844 0209 E: rev.chrisgale@gmail.com

GALE, Colin Edward. b 49. Lon Univ PGCE 74. St Jo Coll Nottm BTh 73. **d** 79 **p** 80. C Hoole *Ches* 79–82; C Woodley St Jo the Ev *Ox* 82–87; V Clapham St Jas *S'wark* 87–96; V Sutton Ch Ch 96–05; R Burstow w Horne 05–14; rtd 14; PtO *Chich* from 16. *29 Kelmscott Way, Bognor Regis PO21 5DU* T: (01243) 870199 M: 07710-895463 E: revceg@aol.com

GALE, The Ven John. b 34. Univ of Wales (Lamp) 67. **d** 69 **p** 70. C Aberdare *Llan* 69–71; C Merthyr Dyfan 71–74; R Walmer St Sav S Africa 74–82; R Knysna St Geo 82–00; Adn Knysna 93–00; LtO *St D* from 00. *3 Connacht Way, Pembroke Dock SA72 6FB* T/F: (01646) 622219

GALE, Keith George. b 44. St Jo Coll Lusaka 68 Sarum Th Coll 69. **d** 70 **p** 71. C Sheff St Cuth 70–77; P-in-c Brightside All SS 72–77; C Birm St Martin 77–81; C Dwangwa Malawi 81–83; R Lilongwe St Pet 83–93; Adn Lilongwe 89–92; TV Sampford Peverell, Uplowman, Holcombe Rogus etc *Ex* 94–09; rtd 09. *101 Chapel Street, Tiverton EX16 6BU* T: (01884) 821879 E: keith@gale5.eclipse.co.uk

GALES, Bernard Henry. b 27. Lon Univ BSc(Econ) 51 Open Univ BA 02. Wells Th Coll 62. **d** 64 **p** 65. C Sholing *Win* 64–67; C Fordingbridge w Ibsley 67–71; C S Molton w Nymet St George *Ex* 71–73; C Thelbridge 73–77; P-in-c 77–78; P-in-c Creacombe 77–78; P-in-c W w E Worlington 77–78; P-in-c Meshaw 77–78; P-in-c Witheridge 77–78; C Witheridge, Thelbridge, Creacombe, Meshaw etc 79–80; R Bow w Broad Nymet 80–93; V Colebrooke 80–93; R Zeal Monachorum 80–93; RD Cadbury 90–93; rtd 93; PtO *Ex* from 93. *8 Old Rectory Gardens, Morchard Bishop, Crediton EX17 6PF* T: (01363) 877601 E: suebern.gales@btinternet.com

GALES, Simon Richard. b 59. Jes Coll Cam BA 81 MA 84 CEng 87 MICE 87. Wycliffe Hall Ox 91. **d** 93 **p** 94. C Houghton *Carl* 93–97; V Lindow *Ches* from 97. *St John's Vicarage, 137 Knutsford Road, Wilmslow SK9 6EL* T: (01625) 583251 or 586329 E: simongales22@gmail.com

GALLACHER, Owen Thomas. b 85. Nottm Univ BA 07. Wycliffe Hall Ox BA 13. **d** 14 **p** 15. C Worc St Nic and All SS w St Helen from 14. *160 Bath Road, Worcester WR5 3EP* E: owen@allsaintsworcester.org.uk

GALLAGHER, Mrs Barbara Jean. b 53. Ex Univ BA 73 Coll of Ripon & York St Jo PGCE 76 Open Univ MA 99. **d** 09 **p** 09. OLM The Creetings and Earl Stonham w Stonham Parva *St E* 08–13; NSM 13–18; P-in-c Weedon Bec w Everdon and Dodford *Pet* from 18. *The Vicarage, Church Street, Weedon, Northampton NN7 4PL* T: (01327) 340585 E: barbarajg@btopenworld.com

GALLAGHER, Canon Ian. BTh. **d** 90 **p** 91. C Annagh w Drumgoon, Ashfield etc *K, E & A* 90–93; I Drumcliffe w Lissadell and Munninane 93–01; Can Elphin Cathl 97–01; Dioc Sec (Elphin and Ardagh) 97–01; Preb Mulhuddart St Patr Cathl Dublin 98–01; I Stillorgan w Blackrock *D & G* from 01. *The Rectory, St Brigid's Church Road, Stillorgan, Blackrock, Co Dublin, Republic of Ireland* T: (00353) (1) 288 1091 F: 278 1833 M: 86-811 9544 E: stillorgan@dublin.anglican.org

GALLAGHER, Ian Míceál. b 71. Oberlin Coll (USA) BMus 93 Duke Univ (USA) MA 95. Westcott Ho Cam 06. **d** 08 **p** 09. C Walton-on-the-Hill *Liv* 08–12; R Frankfurt am Main Ch the K Germany 12–14; V Enfield St Jas *Lon* from 14. *St James's*

Vicarage, 144 Hertford Road, Enfield EN3 5AY T: (020) 8804 1966 E: ian.gallagher@stjameschurch.cc

GALLAGHER, Mrs Margaret. b 60. SRN 82 RM 84. Westcott Ho Cam 09. **d** 11 **p** 12. C Carrington *S'well* 11–14; V S Elmsall *Leeds* from 14; AD Pontefract from 18. *St Mary's Vicarage, Doncaster Road, South Elmsall, Pontefract WF9 2HS* T: (01977) 642861 E: revmgallagher@btinternet.com

GALLAGHER, Michael Collins Francis. b 48. St Jo Coll Dur BA 70. Sarum Th Coll 79. **d** 82 **p** 83. C Bridport *Sarum* 82–86; V Downton 86–01; RD Alderbury 93–99; R Crewkerne w Wayford *B & W* 01–07; R Wulfric Benefice 07–14; rtd 14; PtO *Heref* from 15. *Ridgeway, Woodleigh Road, Ledbury HR8 2BG* T: (01531) 635844 E: mcfgallagher@gmail.com

GALLAGHER, Neville Roy. b 45. Birm Univ CertEd 66 K Coll Lon AKC 70 BD 76 Open Univ BA 97. **d** 71 **p** 72. C Folkestone St Mary and St Eanswythe *Cant* 71–74; Hon C Sutton Valence w E Sutton and Chart Sutton 74–76; TV Cen Telford *Lich* 76–78; P-in-c Gt Mongeham *Cant* 78–80; P-in-c Ripple 78–80; R Gt Mongeham w Ripple and Sutton by Dover 80–83; V Kennington 83–88; Chapl and Dep Hd Bedgebury Sch Kent 88–05; P-in-c Appledore w Brookland, Fairfield, Brenzett etc *Cant* 05–11; P-in-c Woodchurch 06–11; P-in-c Wittersham w Stone and Ebony 08–11; AD Romney 08–10; rtd 11; PtO *Cant* from 11; *Chich* from 16. *1 Church Cottages, Church Road, Kilndown, Cranbrook TN17 2SF* T: (01892) 890426 E: nrwg45@aol.com

GALLAGHER, Robert. b 43. St Chad's Coll Dur BSc 65. **d** 67 **p** 68. C Crosland Moor *Wakef* 67–69; C Huddersfield SS Pet and Paul 69–71; Chapl Huddersfield Poly 72–79; Min Coulby Newham LEP *York* 79–90; V Toxteth St Marg *Liv* 90–13; rtd 13. *36 Bridge Road, Mossley Hill, Liverpool L18 5EG* T: 0151-903 1189

GALLAGHER, Canon Stephen. b 58. Southn Univ BTh 89. Chich Th Coll 86. **d** 89 **p** 90. C S Shields All SS *Dur* 89–92; C Hartlepool St Paul and Chapl Hartlepool Gen Hosp 92–94; R Loftus and Carlin How w Skinningrove *York* 94–97; P-in-c Lower Beeding and Dioc Youth Officer *Chich* 97–09; Shrine P and Youth Missr Shrine of Our Lady of Walsingham 09–16; P-in-c Enfield SS Pet and Paul *Lon* from 16. *177 Ordnance Road, Enfield EN3 6AB* M: 07969-367421

GALLANT, Mrs Joanna-Sue Sheena. b 62. Heythrop Coll Lon MA 18. SAOMC 99. **d** 02 **p** 03. C Amersham on the Hill *Ox* 02–05; NSM Gt Missenden w Ballinger and Lt Hampden 06–10; NSM Chenies and Lt Chalfont, Latimer and Flaunden 10–12; Dir Pelagos Spirituality and Retreat Cen from 09; PtO *Ox* 15–19; TV High Wycombe from 19. *51 Wellesbourne Crescent, High Wycombe HP13 5HF* M: 07791-839756 E: teamvicar@terrierschurch.org.uk

GALLEY, Giles Christopher. b 32. Qu Coll Cam BA 56 MA 60. Linc Th Coll 56. **d** 58 **p** 59. C Gt Yarmouth *Nor* 58–62; C N Lynn w St Marg and St Nic 62–66; C Leeds St Pet *Ripon* 66–69; V N Hull St Mich *York* 70–79; V Strensall 79–00; RD Easingwold 82–97; rtd 00; PtO *York* from 00. *19 St John's Road, Stamford Bridge, York YO41 1PH* T: (01759) 371592

✠**GALLIFORD, The Rt Revd David George.** b 25. Clare Coll Cam BA 49 MA 51. Westcott Ho Cam. **d** 51 **p** 52 **c** 75. C Newland St Jo *York* 51–54; C Eton w Boveney *Ox* 54–56; Min Can Windsor 54–56; V Middlesbrough St Oswald *York* 56–61; R Bolton Percy 61–71; Dioc Adult Tr Officer 61–71; Can and Preb York Minster 69–70; Can Res and Treas York Minster 70–75; Suff Bp Hulme *Man* 75–84; Suff Bp Bolton 84–91; rtd 91; Hon Asst Bp York 95–11; PtO from 11. *Connaught Court, St Oswalds Road, York YO10 4FA* T: (01904) 626208 E: galliford25e@btinternet.com

GALLON, Mrs Audrey Kay. b 41. SEITE 94. **d** 97 **p** 98. NSM Gt Mongeham w Ripple and Sutton by Dover *Cant* 97–98; NSM Eastry and Northbourne w Tilmanstone etc 97–98; NSM Walmer 98–04; PtO 04–05; *Roch* 07–17. *12 Arne Close, Tonbridge TN10 4DH* T: (01732) 355633 E: audreygallon@talktalk.net

GALLOWAY, Canon Peter John. b 54. Goldsmiths' Coll Lon BA 76 K Coll Lon PhD 87 Brunel Univ Hon DLitt 09 FRSA 88 FSA 00. St Steph Ho Ox 80. **d** 83 **p** 84. C St John's Wood *Lon* 83–86; C St Giles-in-the-Fields 86–90; Warden of Readers (Lon Episc Area) 87–92; P-in-c Hampstead Em W End *Lon* 90–95; V 95–08; AD N Camden 02–07; Chapl to RVO and Qu Chpl of the Savoy from 08; Hon Fell Goldsmiths' Coll Lon from 99; Visiting Prof Brunel Univ Lon from 08; Dep P in O from 16; Can Chpls R from 17. *The Queen's Chapel of the Savoy, Savoy Hill, London WC2R 0DA* T: (020) 7379 8088

GALVIN, Mrs Linda Susan. b 59. Ox Min Course 13. **d** 15 **p** 16. NSM W End *Win* from 15. *11A Westbury Court, Hedge End, Southampton SO30 0HN* T: (01489) 788880

GAMBLE, Bronwen. *See* GAMBLE, Edana Bronwen

GAMBLE, Miss Dianne Elizabeth. b 71. Hull Univ BSc 92 PGCE 94. Cranmer Hall Dur 13. **d** 15 **p** 16. C Sowerby

York 15–19; C Sessay 15–19; C Thirkleby w Kilburn and Bagby 15–19; P-in-c Osmotherley w Harlsey and Ingleby Arncliffe from 19; P-in-c Cowesby from 19; P-in-c Felixkirk w Boltby from 19; P-in-c Kirkby Knowle from 19; P-in-c Leake w Over and Nether Silton and Kepwick from 19. *Leake Vicarage, Knayton, Thirsk YO7 4AZ* M: 07761-125748 E: 229club.dg@gmail.com

GAMBLE, Canon Edana Bronwen. b 56. Hull Univ BSc(Econ) 78 Nottm Univ MA 02 FCA 82. EMMTC 99. **d** 02 **p** 03. NSM Nuthall *S'well* 02–06; R Wiverton in the Vale 06–18; AD E Bingham 16–18; C Retford Area from 18; Hon Can S'well Minster from 17. *The Rectory, Lincoln Road, East Markham, Newark NG22 0SH* T: (01777) 870848 E: brongamble@hotmail.com

GAMBLE, Kenneth Wesley. b 52. Ulster Univ BA 81. CITC 04. **d** 07 **p** 08. NSM Ballymacash *Conn* 07–17; NSM Derriaghy w Colin from 17. *21 Dalboyne Park, Lisburn BT28 3BU* T: (028) 9267 7498 E: kengamble@btinternet.com

GAMBLE, Norman Edward Charles. b 50. TCD BA 72 HDipEd 73 PhD 78. CITC 76. **d** 79 **p** 80. C Bangor St Comgall *D & D* 79–83; I Dunleckney w Nurney, Lorum and Kiltennel *C & O* 83–90; Warden of Readers 84–90; P-in-c Leighlin w Grange Sylvae, Shankill etc 89–90; Can Leighlin Cathl 89–90; Preb Ossory Cathl 89–90; I Malahide w Balgriffin *D & G* from 90; Abp's Dom Chapl 95–03. *The Rectory, Church Road, Malahide, Co Dublin, Republic of Ireland* T/F: (00353) (1) 845 4770 M: 86-815 3277 E: normanegamble@gmail.com

GAMBLE, Canon Robin Philip. b 53. Oak Hill Th Coll 74. **d** 77 **p** 78. C Kildwick *Bradf* 77–78; C Laisterdyke 78–80; C York St Paul 80–82; V Bradf St Aug Undercliffe 82–93; Dioc Adv in Evang 93–01; Can Ev Man Cathl 01–08; P-in-c Idle *Bradf* 08–14; *Leeds* 14–18; Dioc Ev *Bradf* 08–14; *Leeds* from 14; Hon Can Bradf Cathl from 13. *The Vicarage, 470 Leeds Road, Idle, Bradford BD10 9AA* T: (01274) 419754 *or* 615411 M: 07748-943541 E: robinp.gamble@blueyonder.co.uk

GAMBLE, Ronald George. b 41. Cant Sch of Min 92. **d** 95 **p** 96. NSM Loose *Cant* 95–00; P-in-c Boxley w Detling 00–07; Chapl NHS Ambulance Trust 99–07; rtd 07; PtO *Cant* from 07; *Roch* from 13. *18 Copper Tree Court, Maidstone ME15 9RW* T: (01622) 744455 E: r-gamble@sky.com

GAMBLE, Stanley Thomas Robert. b 82. QUB BA 03 MTh 05. CITC 05. **d** 07 **p** 08. C Knockbreda *D & D* 07–12; I Killinchy w Kilmood and Tullynakill from 12. *Killinchy Rectory, 11 Whiterock Road, Killinchy, Newtownards BT23 6PR* T: (028) 9754 1249 E: stanleygamble@gmail.com

GAMBLING, Paul Anthony. b 62. Middx Univ BA 06. NTMTC 03. **d** 06 **p** 07. C Warley Ch Ch and Gt Warley St Mary *Chelmsf* 06–10; TV Billericay and Lt Burstead 10–16; C Westcliff St Andr 16–19; P-in-c from 19; C Westcliff St Mich 16–19. *65 Electric Avenue, Westcliff-on-Sea SS0 9NN* M: 07821-201379 E: revpg@icloud.com

GAMLEN, Laurence William. b 59. STETS BA 07. **d** 07 **p** 08. NSM Chertsey, Lyne and Longcross *Guildf* 07–12; C from 12; Chapl Ashford and St Pet Hosps NHS Foundn Trust from 17. *The Vicarage, Lyne Lane, Lyne, Chertsey KT16 0AJ* T: (01932) 874405 *or* 872534 M: 07939-094851 E: laurence@intermissio.com *or* laurence@lyneparish.org.uk

GAMMON, Elizabeth Angela Myfanwy. b 47. SWMTC 06. **d** 09 **p** 10. NSM Sidmouth, Woolbrook, Salcombe Regis, Sidbury etc *Ex* 09–12; P-in-c Burley Ville *Win* from 12. *The Vicarage, Church Lane, Burley, Ringwood BH24 4AP* T: (01425) 402303 E: revd.angie@gmail.com

GANDIYA, Leonard Farirayi (Lee). b 64. Boston Coll (USA) MA 92. Gordon-Conwell Th Sem 90 Ridley Hall Cam 92. **d** 94 **p** 95. NSM Camberwell St Luke *S'wark* 94–95; C Lowestoft St Marg *Nor* 95–98; Dioc Rep for Black Anglican Concerns 96–98; CF from 98. *c/o MOD Chaplains (Army)* T: (01264) 383430 F: 381824

GANDON, Andrew James Robson. b 54. St Jo Coll Dur BA 76. Ridley Hall Cam 76. **d** 78 **p** 79. C Aston SS Pet and Paul *Birm* 78–82; CMS 82–95; Zaïre 82–88; Kenya 89–94; V Harefield *Lon* 95–10; Chapl R Brompton and Harefield NHS Trust 95–05; V Exhall *Cov* 10–18; rtd 18. *197 Bilford Road, Worcester WR3 8HL*

GANDON, James Noel. b 84. Leic Univ BSc 05. Trin Coll Bris BA 14. **d** 14 **p** 15. C Linc St Geo Swallowbeck 14–17; V Sneyd Green *Lich* from 17. *Sneyd Green Vicarage, 42 Granville Avenue, Stoke-on-Trent ST16BH* T: (01782) 363531 E: james@standrewssneydgreen.com

GANDY, Canon Nicholas John. b 53. Westf Coll Lon BSc 75 Reading Univ MSc 76 Ex Coll Ox PGCE 78 CBiol 79 MRSB. St Steph Ho Ox 86. **d** 88 **p** 89. C Crowthorne *Ox* 88–89; C Tilehurst St Mary 89–93; P-in-c Didcot St Pet 93–97; V 97–03; V Brackley St Pet w St Jas *Pet* 03–18; rtd 18; Past Care and Counselling Adv *Pet* from 18; Can Pet Cathl from

18; OGS from 96. *37 Debdale Road, Northampton NN3 2TR*
E: nicholas.gandy@btinternet.com

GANE, Canon Christopher Paul. b 33. Qu Coll Cam
BA 57 MA 61. Ridley Hall Cam 57. d 59 p 60. C Rainham
Chelmsf 59–62; C Farnborough *Guildf* 62–64; V Erith
St Paul *Roch* 64–71; V Ipswich St Marg *St E* 71–88; Hon
Can St E Cathl 82–98; R Hopton, Market Weston,
Barningham etc 88–98; rtd 98; PtO *St E* from 98. *5
Woodfields, Stradbroke, Eye IP21 5JQ* T: (01379) 388707
E: christopherpaulgane@gmail.com

GANN, Canon Anthony Michael. b 37. TCD BA 60 MA 64
BD 64. d 62 p 63. V Choral Derry Cathl *D & R* 62–66;
Lesotho 66–74; Dioc Officer for Miss and Unity *Carl*
75–80; P-in-c Bampton and Mardale 75–80; TV Cen
Telford *Lich* 80–89; TR Wolvercote w Summertown *Ox*
89–02; RD Ox 95–99; rtd 02; PtO *Worc* from 02. *Avalon, 84
Pickersleigh Road, Malvern WR14 2RS* T: (01684) 568114
E: connielightowler@agann.plus.com

GANN, John West. b 29. Ex Coll Ox BA 55 MA 59. Wells Th
Coll 55. d 57 p 58. C Wendover *Ox* 57–59; C Walton St Mary
Liv 59–62; R Didcot *Ox* 62–70; R Newbury St Nic 70–73; TR
Newbury 73–78; V Twickenham St Mary *Lon* 78–87; Dir of
Ords 81–87; TR Bridport *Sarum* 87–94; RD Lyme Bay 89–92;
rtd 94; PtO *Glouc* from 94; *Bris* 96–04. *3 Buttercross Lane,
Prestbury, Cheltenham GL52 5SF* T: (01242) 220787

GANNEY (née CHAMBERS), Mrs Rachel Jill. b 73. Hull Univ
BSc 94 MSc 96 Selw Coll Cam BTh 04. Ridley Hall Cam 01.
d 04 p 05. C Sutton St Jas and Wawne *York* 04–10; TV
Plaistow and N Canning Town *Chelmsf* 10–14. *26 Pentreath
Close, Fowey PL23 1ER* E: rachel@ganney.net

GANNON, James (Dub). b 75. W Sydney Univ BComm 98
BAppSc(Agric) 98. Moore Th Coll Sydney BTheol 08. d 10
p 11. NSM Henham and Elsenham w Ugley *Chelmsf* 10–13;
P-in-c High and Gd Easter w Margaret Roding 13–17; P-in-c
Gt Canfield w High Roding and Aythorpe Roding 13–17;
Rural Evang Adv Colchester Area 13–17; TV W Tamworth
Australia from 17. *16 Church Street, Tamworth NSW 2340,
Australia* E: dub1994@hotmail.com

GANT, Canon Brian Leonard. b 45. Ox Univ MTh 01. K Coll
Lon 72. d 73 p 74. C Hillmorton *Cov* 73–75; C Cov St Geo 76;
P-in-c Maldon St Mary *Chelmsf* 76–79; R Muthill, Crieff and
Comrie *St And* 79–81; V Walsall St Paul *Lich* 81–84; Chapl
K Sch Worc and Min Can Worc Cathl 84–89; V Tunbridge
Wells K Chas *Roch* 89–95; Hon Can Kumasi from 94; V
Wymondham *Nor* 95–01; P-in-c Haxby All SS N Street 01–03;
TV Haxby and Wigginton 03–09; CME Officer York Adnry
01–07; rtd 09; PtO *York* 09–14; *Worc* from 14. *122 Henwick
Road, Worcester WR2 5PB* T: (01905) 923933 M: 07944-
286915 E: brianlgant@aol.com

GANT, Joanna Elizabeth. See NORTHEY, Joanna Elizabeth

GANT, Peter Robert. b 38. BNC Ox BA 60 MA 64 G&C Coll
Cam BA 62 MA 67. Ridley Hall Cam 61. d 63 p 64. C Portsea
St Mary *Portsm* 63–67; V Blackheath *Birm* 67–73; Asst Master
Harold Malley Gr Sch Solihull 73–75; PtO *Birm* 73–75; *Guildf*
from 75; rtd 93. *8 Sandon Close, Esher KT10 8JE* T: (020)
8398 5107 E: gantpeter@btinternet.com

GANT, Russell William. b 77. Suffolk Coll BA 02 St Jo Coll
Dur BA 13. Cranmer Hall Dur 09. d 12 p 13. C Camberley
St Paul *Guildf* 12–16; V Rowledge from 16. *The Vicarage,
Church Lane, Rowledge, Farnham GU10 4EN* T: (01252)
792402 M: 07414-631359 E: vicar@stjamesrowledge.org.uk

GANT, Trevor Malcolm. b 56. Leeds Univ BSc 97. NEOC 05.
d 08 p 09. NSM York St Luke 08–16; NSM Skelton w Shipton
and Newton on Ouse from 16; NSM Alne from 17; NSM
Brafferton w Pilmoor, Myton-on-Swale etc from 17; NSM
Coxwold and Husthwaite from 17; NSM Crayke w Brandsby
and Yearsley from 17; NSM Easingwold w Raskelf from
17; NSM Strensall from 17; NSM Forest of Galtres from
17. *6 Lumley Road, York YO30 6DB* T: (01904) 654784
E: t.gant@st-peters.york.sch.uk

GARBUTT, Canon Mary Yvonne. b 45. Ridley Hall Cam 00.
d 02 p 03. C Desborough, Brampton Ash, Dingley and
Braybrooke *Pet* 02–05; P-in-c Arthingworth, Harrington
w Oxendon and E Farndon 05–07; R 07–15; P-in-c 15–17;
P-in-c Maidwell w Draughton, Lamport w Faxton 05–07; R
07–15; P-in-c 15–17; RD Brixworth 09–15; Can Pet Cathl
12–15; TV Daventry from 17; RD Daventry from 19. *The Vicarage,
19 Church Street, Staverton , Daventry NN11 6JJ* T: (01327)
700050 E: mygarbutt@gmail.com

GARCIA FUERTE, Antonio. b 77. St Damasus Univ Madrid
BST 02 Anglia Ruskin Univ MA 15. Westcott Ho Cam 13. d 15
p 16. C Paddington St Jo w St Mich *Lon* 15–18; Asst Chapl
St Chris Hospice Lon 18–19; C Dulwich St Barn *S'wark* 18–19;
C S'wark H Trin w St Matt from 19. *70 Frankfurt Road, London
SE24 9NY* M: 07939-997819 E: a.g.fuerte@gmail.com

GARDEN, Robert Andrew (Robin). b 26. Edin Univ BSc 49
Kent Univ MA 95 MInstP 58 FIMA 72. Cant Sch of Min 87.
d 90 p 91. NSM Sandwich *Cant* 90–97; Chapl St Bart Hosp
Sandwich 91–00; PtO *Cant* 97–15. *Naini, 164 St George's
Road, Sandwich CT13 9LD* T: (01304) 612116

GARDINER, Mrs Anika. b 84. Ox Brookes Univ BA 08. Trin
Coll Bris 13. d 16 p 17. C Warmley, Syston and Bitton *Bris*
16–19. *Address temp unknown*

GARDINER, Mrs Cathrine Leigh. b 64. STETS 05. d 08
p 09. C Bedminster *Bris* 08–11; TV Anerley *Roch* 11–15;
P-in-c Filwood Park *Bris* from 15. *Christ Church Vicarage,
7 Petherton Road, Bristol BS14 9BP* T: 0117-953 1060
E: cathrinegardiner@gmail.com

GARDINER, Gerald. See GARDINER, William Gerald Henry

GARDINER (née SAYERS), Ms Karen Jane. b 69. Sheff
Univ BMus 90 Heythrop Coll Lon MA 11. Ripon Coll
Cuddesdon 00. d 02 p 03. C Dunstable *St Alb* 02–05; TV
Elstree and Borehamwood 05–15; Hon C Escrick and
Stillingfleet w Naburn *York* 15–19; Hon C Bubwith w Skipwith
15–19; V Aldborough w Boroughbridge and Roecliffe *Leeds*
from 19. *The Vicarage, Church Lane, Boroughbridge, York
YO51 9BA* E: revkarenjg@gmail.com

GARDINER, Richard Allen. b 51. St Steph Ho Ox 12. d 13
p 14. C Bonn w Cologne *Eur* 13–17; Asst Chapl from
17. *Auf dem Kälberhof 12, D-53797 Lohmar-Krahwinkel,
Germany* T: (0049) (2247) 1472 M: 172-532 8025
E: richard.gardiner@web.de

GARDINER, Wendy Doreen. b 49. SRN 71. Trin Coll Bris 10.
d 12 p 13. OLM Barton Hill St Luke w Ch Ch and Moorfields
Bris from 12. *55 Whitehall Road, Bristol BS5 9BG* T: 0117-954
1645 M: 07902-318663 E: wdgardiner@btopenworld.com

GARDINER, Preb William Gerald Henry. b 46. Lon Univ
BD 72. Oak Hill Th Coll 68. d 72 p 73. C Beckenham St Jo
Roch 72–75; C Cheadle *Ches* 75–81; P-in-c Swynnerton
Lich 81–83; P-in-c Tittensor 81–83; R Swynnerton and
Tittensor 83–86; V Westlands St Andr 86–11; RD Newcastle
97–11; Preb Lich Cathl 05–11; rtd 11; PtO *Lich* from
12. *4 The Lindens, Stone ST15 0BD* T: (01785) 286460
E: geraldgardiner@btopenworld.com

GARDNER, Andrew Neil. b 64. d 16 p 17. C Luton St Mary *St Alb*
from 16. *30 Alexandra Avenue, Luton LU3 1HG* M: 07581-
292800 E: andygardner@stmarysluton.org

GARDNER, Benjamin James. b 84. St Jo Coll Dur BA 08.
St Barn Th Cen 13. d 16 p 17. C Loughborough Em *Leic* from
16. *47 Brookfield Avenue, Loughborough LE11 3LN* M: 07454-
836131 E: benjgardner@me.com

GARDNER, Brian Charles. b 46. FIBMS 71. d 04 p 05.
OLM Bodicote *Ox* 04–16; PtO from 16. *11 Farm Way,
Banbury OX16 9TB* T: (01295) 253309 M: 07967-859457
E: bri.jen@btopenworld.com

GARDNER, Clive Bruce. b 67. Selw Coll Cam BA 89 MA 93.
Wycliffe Hall Ox BA 95 MA 01. d 96 p 97. C Beverley Minster
York 96–98; Bp's Dom Chapl *Liv* 98–01; V Cumnor *Ox* 01–06;
TV Wimbledon *S'wark* from 11. *55 Alwyne Road, London
SW19 7AE* T: (020) 8944 0184 E: clivegardner@tesco.net *or*
clivegardner@outlook.com

GARDNER, Canon David. b 57. Oak Hill Th Coll BA 87. d 87
p 88. C Ogley Hay *Lich* 87–91; TV Mildenhall *St E* 91–98;
P-in-c Woodbridge St Jo 98–00; V 00–03; V Woodbridge St Jo
and Bredfield 03–12; P-in-c Ufford w Bredfield and Hasketon
01–03; Dir Miss from 12; Hon Can St E Cathl from 15.
St Nicholas Centre, 4 Cutler Street, Ipswich IP1 1UQ T: (01473)
298500 F: 298501 E: dave.gardner@cofesuffolk.org

GARDNER, Elizabeth Mary. b 47. Nottm Univ BA 01. Trin
Coll Bris 72 St Jo Coll Nottm 00. d 01 p 02. C Swindon
Dorcan *Bris* 01–04; P-in-c Runcorn St Jo Weston *Ches* 04–09;
V 09–13; rtd 13; PtO *Ches* from 13; Dioc Clergy Widows and
Retirement Officer 07–10; PtO from 13. *69 Ford Road, Wirral
CH49 0TD* T: 0151-792 5128 E: revbethgardner@gmail.com
or bethgardner@nhs.net

GARDNER, Geoffrey Maurice. b 28. K Coll Lon BA 51
Lon Inst of Educn PGCE 52 Bris Univ DipEd 74. Cranmer
Hall Dur. d 59 p 60. C Bowling St Jo *Bradf* 59–62; Nigeria
62–72; Hon C Bath St Luke *B & W* 72–73; PtO 73–90 and
94–99; NSM Bath Widcombe 90–94; rtd 94; PtO *Ex* from
99. *15 Bramley Gardens, Whimple, Exeter EX5 2SJ* T: (01404)
823235 E: 15geoffgardner@gmail.com

GARDNER, Mrs Helen Elizabeth. b 56. ERMC 05. d 08 p 09.
C Sunnyside w Bourne End *St Alb* 08–12; V Totternhoe,
Stanbridge and Tilsworth 12–16; rtd 16; PtO *St Alb* from 17.
7 Great Blakelands, Marston Moretaine, Bedford MK43 0WY
E: helerevg@gmail.com

GARDNER, Helen Lee. b 39. Man Univ BSc 61 PGCE 62.
WEMTC 93. d 96 p 97. NSM Stow on the Wold *Glouc* 96–00;
NSM Stow on the Wold, Condicote and The Swells 00–02;
NSM The Guitings, Cutsdean, Farmcote etc 03–04; PtO

04–07; NSM Stow on the Wold, Condicote and The Swells 07–12; rtd 12. *6 St Mary's Close, Lower Swell, Cheltenham GL54 1LJ* T: (01451) 832553 E: gardner269@btinternet.com

GARDNER, Ian Douglas. b 34. St Pet Hall Ox BA 58 MA 62. Oak Hill Th Coll 58. **d** 60 **p** 61. C Biddulph *Lich* 60–63; C Weston St Jo *B & W* 64; Nigeria 65–76; P-in-c Hurstbourne Tarrant and Faccombe *Win* 77–79; V Hurstbourne Tarrant, Faccombe, Vernham Dean etc 79–85; R Nursling and Rownhams 85–99; rtd 99; LtO *St D* from 99. *Wilderness Cottage, Haroldston Hill, Broad Haven, Haverfordwest SA62 3JP* T: (01437) 781592

GARDNER, Ian Norman. b 52. Open Univ BSc 96. WEMTC 03. **d** 05 **p** 06. NSM Dursley *Glouc* 05–18; NSM Dursley, Uley, Owlpen etc from 18. *9 Chestal Lodge, Chestal, Dursley GL11 5AA* T: (01453) 546895 M: 07960-287403 E: chestal@hotmail.com

GARDNER, Mrs Jacqueline Anne. b 49. WEMTC 95. **d** 98 **p** 99. NSM Fairford and Kempsford w Whelford *Glouc* 98–02; NSM Cirencester 02–05; PtO *Ox* 05–07; NSM Hanborough and Freeland 07–13; PtO 13–15. *11 Regency House, Humphris Place, Cheltenham GL53 7EW* T: (01242) 570264 E: jackiegardner@hotmail.com

GARDNER, Jane. *See* GARDNER, Helen Jane

GARDNER, Jason Matthew. b 71. Loughb Univ BA 94 Lon Sch of Th BA 98. St Mellitus Coll 14. **d** 16 **p** 17. C W Harrow *Lon* 16–19; C Preston St Jo and St Geo *Blackb* from 19. *248 Sharoe Green Lane, Fulwood, Preston PR2 9HD* M: 07816-775916 E: gardnerjason42@gmail.com

GARDNER, Mrs Lorna Olive. b 54. **d** 14 **p** 15. NSM Blaydon and Swalwell *Dur* from 14. *1 Kirkstone Close, Blaydon-on-Tyne NE21 6SY* T: 0191-414 5300 E: lornagardner6@gmail.com

GARDNER (*née* DUFFELL), Mrs Lucy Margaret. b 67. St Jo Coll Ox BA 90 MA 96. Ox Min Course 11. **d** 12 **p** 13. Tutor St Steph Ho Ox from 05; NSM Wheatley *Ox* 12–14; NSM Albury w Tiddington etc 14–16; PtO from 16. *St Stephen's House, 16 Marston Street, Oxford OX4 1JX* T: (01865) 613500 E: lucy.gardner@ssho.ox.ac.uk

GARDNER, Mrs Marian Elizabeth. b 50. Ripon Coll of Educn DipEd 71. WMMTC 00. **d** 03 **p** 04. NSM Kirkleatham *York* 03–07; P-in-c Easington w Liverton 07–15; rtd 15; PtO *York* from 17. *37 Bennison Street, Guisborough TS14 6HY* M: 07736-350643 E: marian@thegardners.com

GARDNER, Canon Mark Douglas. b 58. TCD BA 80 MA 83. **d** 83 **p** 84. C Ballymacarrett St Patr *D & D* 83–87; C Belfast St Steph w St Luke *Conn* 87–89; C Hendon and Sunderland *Dur* 89–90; TV Sunderland 90–95; I Dublin Santry w Glasnevin and Finglas *D & G* 95–01; PV and Chapter Clerk Ch Ch Cathl Dublin 96–10; Min Can St Patr Cathl Dublin 96; Treas V 96–01; Can Ch Ch Cathl Dublin *D & G* from 08; V Dublin St Patr Cathl Gp 10–12; I Dublin St Cath and St Jas w St Audoen from 12; Preb Tipperkevin St Patr Cathl Dublin 10–12; Preb Maynooth from 12. *248 South Circular Road, Dolphin's Barn, Dublin 8, Republic of Ireland* T: (00353) (1) 454 2274 M: 87-266 0228 E: markgardner@eircom.net

GARDNER, Paul Douglas. b 50. K Coll Lon BA 72 AKC 72 Reformed Th Sem Mississippi MDiv 79 SS Coll Cam PhD 89. Ridley Hall Cam 79. **d** 80 **p** 81. C Cambridge St Martin *Ely* 80–83; Lect Oak Hill Th Coll 83–90; V Hartford *Ches* 90–03; RD Middlewich 94–99; Adn Ex 03–05; USA 05–17; rtd 17. *30 Archibald Road, Exeter EX1 1SA* E: p.d.g@att.net

GARDNER (*née* JAMES), Mrs Sandra Kay. b 66. Westcott Ho Cam 97. **d** 99 **p** 00. C Whittlesey, Pondersbridge and Coates *Ely* 99–02; R Leverington 02–04; V Southea w Murrow and Parson Drove 02–04; R Leverington, Newton and Tydd St Giles from 05. *The Rectory, 35 Gorefield Road, Leverington, Wisbech PE13 5AS* T: (01945) 585850 E: sandra.gardner952@btinternet.com

GARDNER, Stephen John. b 70. Southn Univ MEng 92. St Jo Coll Nottm 00. **d** 02 **p** 03. C Brinsworth w Catcliffe and Treeton *Sheff* 02–03; C Rivers Team 03–05; V Woodlands from 05; AD Adwick 11–15. *All Saints' Vicarage, 9 Great North Road, Woodlands, Doncaster DN6 7RB* T: (01302) 339618 M: 07740-200942 E: stephen@all-saints-church.net

GARDNER, Susan Carol. *See* CLARKE, Susan Carol

GARDOM, James Theodore Douglas. b 61. St Anne's Coll Ox BA 83 K Coll Lon PhD 92. Ripon Coll Cuddesdon 88. **d** 90 **p** 91. C Witney *Ox* 90–92; Dean of Studies Bp Gaul Coll Harare Zimbabwe 93–97; V Chesterton St Andr *Ely* 97–06; Dean and Chapl Pemb Coll Cam from 06; PtO *S'wark* 18. *Pembroke College, Cambridge CB2 1RF* T: (01223) 338147 F: 338163 E: jtdg2@cam.ac.uk

GARFIELD, Diana Margaret. b 52. Leeds Poly BA 73 Anglia Poly Univ MA 02 Anglia Ruskin Univ PhD 12. St Mellitus Coll 16. **d** 17 **p** 18. NSM Broomfield *Chelmsf* from 17. *71 Pickwick Avenue, Chelmsford CM1 4UR* T: (01245) 443205 M: 07767-387959 E: dianagarfield@hotmail.com

GARLAND, Canon Michael. b 50. Sarum & Wells Th Coll 72. **d** 73 **p** 74. C Swansea St Thos and Kilvey *S & B* 73–76; C Boldmere *Birm* 76–79; V Kingshurst 79–88; P-in-c Curdworth w Castle Vale 88–90; R Curdworth 90–03; P-in-c Wishaw 99–00; V Charlton Kings St Mary *Glouc* 03–17; Hon Can Glouc Cathl 13–17; rtd 17; PtO *Glouc* from 18; AD Glouc City from 19. *6 Whimbrel Road, Quedgeley, Gloucester GL2 4LJ* T: (01452) 720872 M: 07974-066929 E: michaelgarland368@btinternet.com

GARLICK, Preb Kathleen Beatrice. b 49. Leeds Univ BA 71 Birm Univ PGCE 72. Glouc Sch of Min 87. **d** 90 **p** 94. NSM Much Birch w Lt Birch, Much Dewchurch etc *Heref* 90–03; P-in-c 03–07; R Wormelow Hundred 07–09; Chapl Heref Sixth Form Coll 96–03; Chapl Heref Cathl 09–14; Preb Heref Cathl 99–14; rtd 14; PtO *Heref* from 14; Chapl to The Queen from 11. *Birch Lodge, Much Birch, Hereford HR2 8HT* T: (01981) 540666 M: 07812-995442 E: kaygarlick@hotmail.com

GARLICK, Canon Peter. b 34. AKC 57. **d** 58 **p** 59. C Swindon New Town *Bris* 58–63; St Kitts-Nevis 63–66; V Heyside *Man* 66–73; R Stretford All SS 73–79; RD Wootton *Pet* 79–88; V Duston 79–91; TR 91–94; Can Pet Cathl 85–94; rtd 94; PtO *Pet* 94–18. *120 Worcester Close, Northampton NN3 9GD* T: (01604) 416511 E: garlick948@btinternet.com

GARLICK, William Frederick. b 51. **d** 98 **p** 99. OLM Bermondsey St Jas w Ch Ch and St Crispin *S'wark* 98–06; PtO *Chich* 12–17. *33 Penfolds Place, Arundel BN18 9SA*

GARMAN, Mrs Elaine Christine. b 60. Newc Poly BA 82 Glas Caledonian Univ MBA 95 Glas Univ MPH 01 FFPH 07. TISEC 14. **d** 15 **p** 16. C Dunoon *Arg* 15–18; C Rothesay 15–18; Dioc Miss Enabler 17–18; R Forfar *St And* from 18. *St John's Rectory, 24 St James Road, Forfar DD8 1LG* T: (01307) 463440 M: 07733-151458 E: revelainegarman@aol.com or rector@stjohnsforfar.co.uk

GARNELL, Paul Owen. b 81. ERMC 16. **d** 19. C Lordsbridge *Ely* from 19. *70 High Street, Coton, Cambridge CB23 7PL* M: 07761-454268 E: paulgarnell@hotmail.co.uk

GARNER, Alexander David. b 86. Dur Univ BA 07. St Steph Ho Ox BA 14. **d** 15 **p** 16. C Hendon St Alphage *Lon* 15–18; C Ashford St Matt from 18; C Stanwell from 18. *66 Oaks Road, Staines-upon-Thames TW19 7LG* M: 07528-513433 E: a.d.garner86@gmail.com

GARNER, Alistair Ross. b 58. Pemb Coll Ox BA 81 MA 86. St Jo Coll Nottm 90. **d** 92 **p** 93. C Ashton-upon-Mersey St Mary Magd *Ches* 92–96; P-in-c Bredbury St Mark 96–01; V 01–09; Miss Growth Team Ldr *Roch* 09–12; TR Walkden and Lt Hulton *Man* 12–17; TR Eccles from 17. *12B Westminster Road, Eccles, Manchester M30 9EB* T: 0161-661 6861 E: revrossgarner@gmail.com

GARNER, Canon Carl. b 42. Rhodes Univ BA 62 Keble Coll Ox BA 65 MA 70. St Paul's Coll Grahamstown 66. **d** 67 **p** 68. C Pietersburg S Africa 67–71; R Louis Trichardt 71–75; Chapl St Paul's Coll Grahamstown 75–84; Dioc Missr *St Alb* 84–98; Can Res St Alb 84–98; P-in-c Digswell and Panshanger 98–06; TR 06–12; Hon Can St Alb 99–12; Jt RD Welwyn Hatfield 01–12; rtd 12; PtO *St Alb* from 12. *2 Hill House, 38 Park Street, Hatfield AL9 5AZ*

GARNER, Mrs Carole. b 61. LCTP 05. **d** 08 **p** 09. NSM Oswaldtwistle St Paul *Blackb* 08–12; NSM Oswaldtwistle from 12. *17 Spinning Mill Close, Oswaldtwistle, Accrington BB5 4AB* E: carole.garner@blackburn.anglican.org

GARNER, Catherine Elizabeth. b 63. Univ of W of England BSc 02 PhD 07. Ripon Coll Cuddesdon 14. **d** 16 **p** 17. C E Meon *Portsm* 16–19; C W Meon and Warnford 16–19; C Langrish 16–19; R Backwell w Chelvey and Brockley *B & W* from 19. *The Rectory, 72 Church Lane, Backwell, Bristol BS48 3JJ* M: 07879-665767 E: revdrkatygarner@gmail.com

GARNER, David Henry. b 40. Trin Coll Bris 70. **d** 73 **p** 74. C Tunstead *Man* 73–75; C Fazeley *Lich* 76–78; V Sparkhill St Jo *Birm* 78–85; V Blackheath 85–01; Deanery P Warley Deanery 01–05; rtd 05; PtO *Birm* from 05; Chapl Sandwell and W Birm Hosps NHS Trust from 06; PtO *Worc* from 06. *94 Honeybourne Road, Halesowen B63 3HD* T: 0121-550 2498 M: 07779-948333 E: davidhenrygarner@yahoo.co.uk

GARNER, Geoffrey Walter. b 40. Ripon Hall Ox 69. **d** 71 **p** 72. C Stoke *Cov* 71–75; V Tile Hill 76–80; TV Hackney *Lon* 80–89; R Bow w Bromley St Leon 89–06; rtd 06. *98 Wordsworth Road, Plymouth PL2 2JQ*

GARNER, John David. b 47. **d** 03. OLM Kirkdale St Lawr *Liv* 03–15; rtd 15; PtO *Liv* from 15. *10 Doon Close, Liverpool L4 1XW* T: 0151-284 0388 E: johngarner65@aol.com

GARNER, John Howard. b 45. Univ of Wales (Swansea) BSc 67 Univ of Wales (Ban) PhD 75. SWMTC 95. **d** 98 **p** 99. NSM Upton *Ex* from 98; Sen Chapl S Devon Healthcare NHS Foundn Trust from 06. *Highgrove Lodge, Sunbury Hill, Upton, Torquay TQ1 3ED* T: (01803) 293640 or 654186

GARNER, Mark William John. b 50. Melbourne Univ BA 71 DipEd 73 Essex Univ MA 75 Aber Univ MTheol 08. TISEC 09. **d** 11. C Turriff *Ab* 11–12; Hd of Whitelands Coll Roehampton Univ *S'wark* from 12; PtO *Sarum* from 15. *Whitelands College, Holybourne Avenue, London SW15 4JD* T: (020) 8392 3501 E: mark.garner@roehampton.ac.uk

GARNER, Canon Rodney George. b 48. Lon Univ BA 87 Hull Univ MPhil 96 Man Univ PhD 01 MCIPD 75. Qu Coll Birm 75. **d** 78 **p** 79. C Tranmere St Paul w St Luke *Ches* 78–81; V Eccleston St Thos *Liv* 81–90; P-in-c Sculcoates St Paul w Ch Ch and St Silas *York* 90–95; Lay Tr Officer (E Riding Adnry) 90–95; P-in-c Southport H Trin *Liv* 95–96; V 96–18; Dioc Th Consultant 95–18; Hon Can Liv Cathl 07–18; rtd 18. *15 Carisbrooke Drive, Southport PR9 7JD* M: 07754-812915 E: rgcfgarner@gmail.com

GARNER, Ross. *See* GARNER, Alistair Ross

GARNER, Mrs Selina Clare. b 69. Newnham Coll Cam BA 90 K Coll Lon PGCE 93. EAMTC 00. **d** 06 **p** 07. C Fulbourn *Ely* 06–09; C Gt Wilbraham 06–09; C Lt Wilbraham 06–09; C Cullompton, Willand, Uffculme, Kentisbeare etc *Ex* 09–15; C Willand, Uffculme, Kentisbeare etc 15–16; Pioneer Youth Min Tiverton and Cullompton Deanery from 09 and 14–16; TV Wellington and Distr *B & W* from 16. *All Saints' Vicarage, 62 Rockwell Green, Wellington TA21 9BX* T: (01823) 662742 E: selina@thegarners.me.uk

GARNER, Thomas Richard. b 43. K Coll Lon. **d** 69 **p** 70. C Tynemouth Ch Ch *Newc* 69–73; C Fenham St Jas and St Basil 73–76; V Hamstead St Bernard *Birm* 76–80; V Greytown New Zealand 80–87; V Levin 87–96; Can Wellington 96–99; V Upper Riccarton w Yaldhurst 99–06; P-in-c Carterton 06–08; rtd 08; PtO Wellington New Zealand from 08. *267 Chester Road, RD 1, Carterton 5791, New Zealand* T: (0064) (6) 379 9375 M: 21-214 8897 E: rgarner@ihug.co.nz

GARNETT, Alyson Susan. *See* PEBERDY, Alyson Susan

GARNETT, The Ven David Christopher. b 45. Nottm Univ BA 67 Fitzw Coll Cam BA 69 MA 73. Westcott Ho Cam 67. **d** 69 **p** 70. C Cottingham *York* 69–72; Chapl Selw Coll Cam 72–77; P-in-c Patterdale *Carl* 77–80; Dir of Ords 78–80; V Heald Green St Cath *Ches* 80–87; R Christleton 87–92; TR Ellesmere Port 92–96; Adn Chesterfield *Derby* 96–09; P-in-c Beeley and Edensor 07–10; Hon Can Derby Cathl 96–10; rtd 10; PtO York from 13. *Wayside, Goslipgate, Pickering YO18 8EQ* E: davidcgarnett@aol.co.uk

GARNETT, Preb Ralph Henry. b 28. Cuddesdon Coll 58. **d** 60 **p** 61. C Broseley w Benthall *Heref* 60–64; V Leintwardine 64–69; P-in-c Downton w Burrington and Aston and Elton 66–69; RD Ludlow 72–75; R Whitton w Greete and Hope Bagot 69–87; R Burford III w Lt Heref 69–87; P-in-c Burford I, Nash and Boraston 72–74; R 74–87; V Tenbury Wells 69–74; TR 74–87; Preb Heref Cathl 82–93; P-in-c Fownhope 87–93; P-in-c Brockhampton w Fawley 87–93; RD Heref Rural 92–93; rtd 93; PtO *Heref* 93–12. *8 Butlers Place, Portsmouth Road, Milford, Godalming GU8 5EX*

GARNHAM, Laura Felicity. b 50. **d** 17 **p** 18. NSM Gt Oakley, Wix, Wrabness etc *Chelmsf* from 17. *1 Riverview, Church Road, Wrabness, Manningtree CO11 2TQ* E: landm.garnham@virgin.net

GARRARD, Mrs Christine Ann. b 51. Open Univ BA 86 LCST 75. EAMTC 87. **d** 90 **p** 94. Par Dn Kesgrave *St E* 90–94; C 94–96; V Ipswich All Hallows 96–02; R Higham, Holton St Mary, Raydon and Stratford 02–08; Asst Dioc Dir of Ords 03–08; Sen Chapl Burrswood Chr Hosp 08–14; rtd 14. *40 Oakbury Drive, Weymouth DT3 6JE* T: (01305) 833475 E: revdchris@aol.com

GARRARD, Mrs Elizabeth Helen. b 65. Dundee Univ BN 11 RGN 89. ERMC 09. **d** 11 **p** 12. OLM Broadside *Nor* from 11; Chapl Norfolk Community Health and Care NHS Trust 14–16; Lead Chapl James Paget Univ Hosps NHS Foundn Trust 16; Lead Chapl Norfolk Community Health and Care NHS Trust from 16. *Colman Hospital, Priscilla Bacon Lodge, Unthank Road, Norwich NR2 2PJ* T: (01603) 255728 M: 07920-528282 E: broadsidecurate@aol.com

GARRARD, Canon James Richard. b 65. Dur Univ BA 88 Keble Coll Ox DPhil 92 Leeds Univ MA 01 FRHistS 16. Westcott Ho Cam. **d** 94 **p** 95. C Elland *Wakef* 94–97; TV Brighouse and Clifton 98–01; P-in-c Balderstone *Blackb* 01–08; Warden of Readers 01–08; Can Res Ely Cathl from 08. *The Precentor's House, 32 High Street, Ely CB7 4JU* T: (01353) 660335 *or* 660300 F: 665658 E: j.garrard@elycathedral.org

GARRARD, Canon Nicholas James Havelock. b 62. Leeds Univ BA 83. Westcott Ho Cam 86. **d** 88 **p** 89. C Scotforth *Blackb* 88–91; C Eaton *Nor* 91–95; V Heigham St Thos 95–06; RD Nor S 03–06; R Broadside from 06; RD Blofield 14–17; Hon Can Nor Cathl from 14. *The Rectory, 23 The Street, South Walsham, Norwich NR13 6DQ* T: (01603) 270769 E: nickgarr39@aol.com

⌖GARRARD, The Rt Revd Richard. b 37. K Coll Lon BD 60 AKC 60. **d** 61 **p** 62 **c** 94. C Woolwich St Mary w H Trin *S'wark* 61–66; C Cambridge Gt St Mary w St Mich *Ely* 66–68; Chapl Keswick Hall Coll of Educn 68–74; Prin Wilson Carlile Coll of Evang 74–79; Can Res and Chan S'wark Cathl 79–87; Dir of Tr 79–87; Can Res St E Cathl 87–94; Dioc Adv for CME 87–91; Adn Sudbury 91–94; Suff Bp Penrith *Carl* 94–01; Hon Can Carl Cathl 94–01; Abp's Rep H See and Dir Angl Cen Rome 01–03; Hon Asst Bp Eur from 01; rtd 03; PtO *Nor* from 03; Hon Asst Bp Nor from 03. *26 Carol Close, Stoke Holy Cross, Norwich NR14 8NN* T: (01508) 494165 E: garrard.r.a@gmail.com

GARRARD, Miss Valerie Mary. b 48. K Alfred's Coll Win TCert 69 St Paul's Coll Chelt BEd 84. **d** 03 **p** 04. OLM Wylye and Till Valley *Sarum* 03–11; rtd 18; PtO *Sarum* from 18. *Cowslip Cottage, Wylye Road, Hanging Langford, Salisbury SP3 4NW* T: (01722) 790739 E: vmgarrard@btinternet.com

GARRATT, Alan William. b 54. **d** 04 **p** 05. NSM Hazlemere *Ox* 04–08; TR Thame from 08; AD Aston and Cuddesdon 13–17. *The Rectory, 3 Fish Ponds Lane, Thame OX9 2BA* T: (01844) 212225 E: alan.garratt@hotmail.co.uk

GARRATT, Peter James. b 37. ALCD 64. **d** 64 **p** 65. C Bingham *S'well* 64–67; C Mansfield SS Pet and Paul 67–69; V Purlwell *Wakef* 69–73; R Kirk Sandall and Edenthorpe *Sheff* 73–82; R Whippingham w E Cowes *Portsm* 82–87; V Soberton w Newtown 87–01; rtd 02; PtO *Portsm* from 02. *35 Fair Isle Close, Fareham PO14 3RT* T: (01329) 661162

GARRATT, Roger Charles. b 50. St Jo Coll Dur BA 72. Cranmer Hall Dur 72. **d** 74 **p** 75. C Leamington Priors St Paul *Cov* 74–77; Chapl Emscote Lawn Sch Warw 77–99; Chapl and Dep Hd Arden Lawn Sch 77–00; TV Warwick *Cov* 02–08; rtd 08; PtO *Cov* from 08. *8 Wasdale Close, Leamington Spa CV32 6NF* T: (01926) 335474 E: roger.garratt@btinternet.com

GARRETT, Clive Robert. b 54. Sheff Univ BA 75 PhD 80 Ex Univ PGCE 88. St Jo Coll Nottm MA 98. **d** 98 **p** 99. C Bath Weston St Jo w Kelston *B & W* 98–02; R 02–19; rtd 19. *3 Wheatfield Avenue, Worcester WR5 3HA* E: clivepics@uwclub.net

GARRETT, Miss Elizabeth Clare. b 46. Trin Coll Bris. **d** 94 **p** 95. C Ewyas Harold w Dulas, Kenderchurch etc *Heref* 94–96; C Tupsley w Hampton Bishop 96–00; TV Uttoxeter Area *Lich* 00–05; P-in-c Gt Canfield w High Roding and Aythorpe Roding *Chelmsf* 05–11; rtd 11. *10 Culverwell Gardens, Winchester SO23 9JG* M: 07790-878307 E: ecgarrett@btinternet.com

GARRETT, Geoffrey David. b 57. Oak Hill Th Coll 83. **d** 86 **p** 87. C Trentham *Lich* 86–90; V Rhodes *Man* 90–00; P-in-c Bardsley 00–05; V 05–08; V Watton *Nor* 08–13; C Cockley Cley w Gooderstone 10–13; R Condover w Frodesley, Acton Burnell etc *Heref* from 13; RD Condover from 18. *The Rectory, Condover, Shrewsbury SY5 7AA* T: (01743) 872251 E: revgeoff@live.co.uk

GARRETT, Ian Lee. b 60. MCSP 81. Sarum & Wells Th Coll 86. **d** 89 **p** 90. C Maidstone St Martin *Cant* 89–95; P-in-c S Ashford St Fran 95–07; TV Bishopsworth and Bedminster Down *Bris* 07–13; P-in-c Brislington St Anne from 13; C Brislington St Chris and St Cuth 07–08; P-in-c Brislington St Cuth from 08. *35 Wick Crescent, Bristol BS4 4HG* T: 0117-971 0523 E: ianlgarrett@gmail.com

GARRETT (née KIRK), Natalie Roberta. b 71. Leeds Univ BA 93. Wycliffe Hall Ox 03. **d** 05 **p** 06. C Gipsy Hill Ch Ch *S'wark* 05–06; Hon C Burford w Fulbrook, Taynton, Asthall etc *Ox* 06–10; Hon C Twickenham Common H Trin *Lon* from 10. *Holy Trinity Vicarage, 1 Vicarage Road, Twickenham TW2 5TS* T: (020) 8898 1168

GARRETT, Timothy Michael. b 70. Univ of Wales (Abth) BA 91. Wycliffe Hall Ox BA 01. **d** 02 **p** 03. C Ox St Andr 02–06; C Burford w Fulbrook, Taynton, Asthall etc 06–10; V Twickenham Common H Trin *Lon* from 10. *Holy Trinity Vicarage, 1 Vicarage Road, Twickenham TW2 5TS* T: (020) 8898 1168 E: revgaz@hotmail.com

GARROD, Mrs Christine Anne. b 49. EAMTC. **d** 00 **p** 01. C N w S Wootton *Nor* 00–04; P-in-c Brinklow *Cov* 04–09; P-in-c Harborough Magna 04–09; P-in-c Monks Kirby w Pailton and Stretton-under-Fosse 04–09; P-in-c Churchover w Willey 04–09; R Gt and Lt Plumstead w Thorpe End and Witton *Nor* 09–14; rtd 14; PtO *Nor* from 14. *17 Philip Nurse Road, Dersingham, King's Lynn PE31 6WJ* T: (01485) 543078 E: cagarrod@hotmail.com

GARROW, Alan John Philip. b 67. Lon Bible Coll BA 90 Wycliffe Hall Ox MPhil 94 Jes Coll Ox DPhil 00. **d** 93 **p** 94. C Waltham H Cross *Chelmsf* 93–97; C Akeman *Ox* 00–04; Tutor SAOMC 00–04; Dir Studies 04–05; Dir Studies Ox Min Course 05–06; V Th Bath Abbey w St Jas *B & W* 06–14; PtO *Sheff* 14–16; V High Harrogate St Pet *Leeds* from 16. *St Peter's*

274

Vicarage, 13 Beech Grove, Harrogate HG2 0ET T: (01423) 568218 M: 07761-017658 E: alan.garrow@gmail.com

GARSIDE, Geoffrey Malcolm. b 43. Huddersfield Poly CertEd Huddersfield Univ BEd. **d** 05 **p** 06. OLM Almondbury w Farnley Tyas *Wakef* 05–10; P-in-c Marsden 10–14; *Leeds* 14–15; rtd 15; PtO *Leeds* from 17. *16 Mountfield Avenue, Huddersfield HD5 8RD* E: ggarside@aol.com

GARSIDE, Melvin. b 42. NOC 85. **d** 88 **p** 89. C Lindley *Wakef* 88–91; C Shelf *Bradf* 91–93; V Lundwood *Wakef* 93–97; V Hanging Heaton 97–01; V Woodhouse and Bp's Adv in Racial Justice 01–05; rtd 05. *5 Hawthorne Close, Nether Poppleton, York YO26 6HP* M: 07803-250258 E: melgarside@melgarside.demon.co.uk

GARTHWAITE, Linda Petra. b 55. SWMTC 16. **d** 18 **p** 19. NSM Ludgvan, Marazion, St Hilary and Perranuthnoe *Truro* from 18. *Joyce's Farm, Higher Kenneggy, Rosudgeon, Penzance TR20 9AU* E: linda.garthwaite@kenneggycove.co.uk

GARTLAND, Christopher Michael. b 49. Man Univ BA 78 Leeds Univ MEd 99 Univ Coll Lon MSc 04. Coll of Resurr Mirfield 82. **d** 84 **p** 85. C Almondbury w Farnley Tyas *Wakef* 84–87; P-in-c Upperthong 87–89; TV Upper Holme Valley 89–91; Chapl Stanley Royd Hosp Wakef 91–94; Chapl Wakef HA (Mental Health Services) 91–95; Chapl Wakef and Pontefract Community NHS Trust 95–01; Hd Past/Spiritual Care SW Yorks Partnership NHS Foundn Trust from 02. *2 Weirside, Marsden, Huddersfield HD7 6BU* T: (01924) 327498 E: mike.gartland@swyt.nhs.uk *or* michaelgartland4@aol.com

GARTON, Mrs Anne-Marie. b 48. BA MSW CQSW. **d** 02 **p** 03. NSM Caterham *S'wark* 02–10 and from 14; PtO 10–14. *The Vicarage, 2 Churchview Close, Caterham CR3 6EZ* T: (01883) 343188 M: 07811-186526 E: anne-marie@garton.com

GARTON, Derek John. b 33. ALCD 59. **d** 59 **p** 60. C Bromley Common St Aug *Roch* 59–62; C Gravesend St Aid 62–64; Chapl Gordon High Sch Gravesend 64–73; LtO *Roch* 73–74; Chapl Plymouth Coll 74–82; Chapl Warrnambool High Sch Australia 83–87; C Traralgon 86–89; R Cann River 89–92; R Boolara w Yinnar 92–94; PtO Gippsland 96–98; rtd 98. *4 Rose Lodge, 225 Graham Street, Wonthaggi VIC 3995, Australia* T: (0061) (3) 5672 5554

GARTON, Capt Jeremy. b 56. Wilson Carlile Coll 78 SEITE 94. **d** 96 **p** 97. C Clapham Team *S'wark* 96–00; P-in-c Caterham Valley 00–03; TV Caterham from 03. *The Vicarage, 2 Churchview Close, Caterham CR3 6EZ* T: (01883) 343188 F: (020) 7863 4120 E: jerry@garton.com

GARVIE, Mrs Anna-Lisa Karen. b 48. Luton Univ BA 99 Leeds Univ MA 05. St Alb Minl Tr Scheme 89. **d** 96 **p** 97. NSM Caddington *St Alb* 96–99; NSM St Paul's Walden 99–01; Chapl Chelsea and Westmr Hosp NHS Foundn Trust 98–01; Co-ord Chapl Hinchingbrooke Health Care NHS Trust 01–09; Chapl Thorpe Hall Hospice 09–12; Chapl NHS Borders 12–16; rtd 16; PtO *Ely* from 09. *3 The Stiles, Godmanchester, Huntingdon PE29 2JF*

GARWOOD, Simon Frederick. b 62. Reading Univ BA 85 Lon Univ PGCE 93 Birm Univ BD 99. Qu Coll Birm MA 00. **d** 00 **p** 01. C Chelmsf All SS 00–03; TV Witham 03–14; P-in-c Kelvedon and Feering from 14. *The Vicarage, Church Street, Kelvedon, Colchester CO5 9AH* T: (01376) 573701 E: simongarwood@simonliz62.plus.com

GASCOIGNE, Philip. b 27. Oak Hill Th Coll. **d** 62 **p** 63. C Blackpool Ch Ch *Blackb* 62–65; V Bootle St Leon *Liv* 65–71; Staff Evang CPAS 71–74; V St Helens St Mark *Liv* 74–77; V Blackpool Ch Ch *Blackb* 77–81; V Blackpool Ch Ch w All SS 81–97; rtd 98; PtO *Blackb* from 98. *18 Grange Road, Blackpool FY3 8EJ* T: (01253) 315607

GASKELL, Barrie Stuart. b 56. SNWTP 07. **d** 10 **p** 11. NSM Bolton St Pet *Man* 10–11; NSM Bolton St Pet w St Phil from 11; Chapl Bolton NHS Foundn Trust from 10; Chapl Gtr Man W Mental Health NHS Foundn Trust from 13; PtO *Liv* from 16. *1 Old Vicarage Mews, Westhoughton, Bolton BL5 2EQ* T: (01942) 818797 E: barrie.gaskell@rbh.nhs.uk *or* barrie.gaskell@gmw.nhs.uk

GASKELL, David. b 48. Lon Univ BD 76. Trin Coll Bris 72. **d** 76 **p** 77. C Eccleston Ch Ch *Liv* 76–80; C Rainhill 80–83; V Over Darwen St Jas *Blackb* 83–88; V Livesey 88–95; V Preston St Cuth 95–01; V Copp w Inskip 01–13; rtd 13; PtO *Blackb* from 13. *4 St James Gardens, Leyland PR26 7XA* T: (01772) 452045 E: dabberoarer@btinternet.com

GASKELL, Canon Ian Michael. b 51. Nottm Univ BTh 81. Linc Th Coll 77. **d** 81 **p** 82. C Wakef St Jo 81–83; Ind Chapl *Sheff* 83–86; V Cleckheaton St Luke and Whitechapel *Wakef* 86–93; V Birkenshaw w Hunsworth 93–98; RD Birstall 96–98; Can Res Wakef Cathl 98–05; Dioc Soc Resp Adv 98–06; V Chapelthorpe 06–14; *Leeds* 14; Hon Can Wakef Cathl 05–14; rtd 15; PtO *Leeds* from 17. *21 Old Royston Avenue, Royston, Barnsley S71 4FZ*

GASKELL, Marion Ingrid. b 52. Wilson Carlile Coll 74 NOC 96. **d** 99 **p** 00. C Thorpe Edge *Bradf* 99–02; TV Shelf w Buttershaw St Aid 02–04; TR 04–18; rtd 18; PtO *Leeds* from 18. *12 Mayfield Gardens, Ossett WF5 9PW* T: (01924) 276451

GASKELL, Peter John. b 70. Bris Univ MS 93 ChB 93. Oak Hill Th Coll BA 03. **d** 03 **p** 04. NSM Poulton Lancelyn H Trin *Ches* 03–07; NSM Rusholme H Trin *Man* from 09. *47 Linden Park, Manchester M19 2PQ* T: 0161-224 7493 M: 07769-682142 E: peter@glod.co.uk

GASPER (*née* COHEN), Mrs Janet Elizabeth. b 47. Birm Univ CertEd 70. WMMTC 93. **d** 96 **p** 97. NSM Leominster *Heref* 96–99; C Letton w Staunton, Byford, Mansel Gamage etc 99–01; Hon Chapl RAF 97–01; R Baxterley w Hurley and Wood End and Merevale etc *Birm* 01–13; P-in-c Kingsbury 04–13; rtd 13; P-in-c The Langtons and Shangton *Leic* 14–17; P-in-c Welham, Glooston and Cranoe and Stonton Wyville 14–17; PtO from 18. *21 Northfold Road, Leicester LE2 3YG* E: janet.gasper@hotmail.co.uk

GASSON, Mrs Siân. b 68. **d** 12 **p** 13. C Collyhurst *Man* 12–15; V Bryn *Liv* 15–19; V Dingle from 19. *St Cleopas' Vicarage, Beresford Road, Liverpool L8 4SG* E: siangasson@gmail.com

GASTON, Mrs Lydia Madeleine. b 79. St Andr Univ MA 03 Rob Coll Cam BTh 09. Ridley Hall Cam 06. **d** 09 **p** 10. C Erdington Ch the K *Birm* 09–14; V Yardley Wood from 14. *The Vicarage, School Road, Yardley Wood, Birmingham B14 4EP* T: 0121-430 8367 M: 07779-006178 E: lydgaston@hotmail.co.uk *or* christchurchyardleywood@outlook.com

GASTON, Raymond Gordon. b 62. Leeds Univ BA 94 Nottm Univ MTh 97. Linc Th Coll 94. **d** 96 **p** 97. C Leeds Gipton Epiphany *Ripon* 96–99; V Leeds St Marg and All Hallows 99–07; Tutor Qu Coll Birm 08–16; PtO *Birm* 14–17; TV Cen Wolverhampton *Lich* from 15; Interfaith Officer Wolverhampton Area from 16. *St Chad's Vicarage, Manlove Street, Wolverhampton WV3 0HG* T: (01902) 652633 M: 07751-155124 E: revdray@hotmail.co.uk

GATENBY, Canon Simon John Taylor. b 62. Nottm Univ BA 83. St Jo Coll Nottm 84. **d** 87 **p** 88. C Haughton St Mary *Man* 87–90; C Newburn *Newc* 90–93; P-in-c Brunswick *Man* 93–96; R from 96; AD Hulme 99–05; Hon Can Man Cathl from 13; Tutor Westcott Ho Cam from 05. *The Rectory, Hartfield Close, Brunswick, Manchester M13 9YX* T: 0161-273 2470 E: simon@brunswickchurch.org.uk

GATES, Alan Raymond. b 46. EAMTC 98. **d** 01 **p** 02. C W w E Mersea and Peldon w Gt and Lt Wigborough *Chelmsf* 01–05; P-in-c Gt Barton *St E* 05–12; P-in-c Thurston 12; V Gt Barton and Thurston 12–14; RD Thingoe 08–14; rtd 14; Hon C Langtree *Ox* 16–19. *8 Waterside Drive, Purley on Thames, Reading RG8 8AQ* M: 07528-087733 E: pearleygates@outlook.com

GATES, Mrs Frances Margaret. b 44. STETS 01. **d** 04 **p** 05. NSM Portsea St Mary, Portsea St Geo and Portsea All SS *Portsm* 04–11; rtd 11; PtO *Portsm* from 11. *114 Kings Road, Southsea PO5 4DW* T: (023) 9282 0326 M: 07951-062226

GATES, John Richard. b 47. Oak Hill Th Coll 70. **d** 73 **p** 74. C Iver *Ox* 73–76; C Broadwater St Mary *Chich* 76–79; Dioc Youth Officer *Nor* 79–82; V Cosby *Leic* 82–86; Asst Chapl Bucharest w Sofia *Eur* 98–99; rtd 08; PtO *Leic* from 15. *103 Carrick Point, Falmouth Road, Leicester LE5 4WN* T: 0116-220 0990 M: 07851-628100 E: evingtonuk368@gmail.com

GATES, Richard James. b 46. Oak Hill Th Coll BA 85. **d** 85 **p** 86. C Heald Green St Cath *Ches* 85–89; V Norton 89–98; V Bunbury and Tilstone Fearnall 98–11; rtd 12; PtO *Ches* from 12; Chapl St Luke's Cheshire Hospice from 13. *Vicarage Cottage, Church Street, Tarvin, Chester CH3 8EB* T: (01829) 749134 M: 07715-178750 E: rickjgates@me.com

GATES, The Ven Simon Philip. b 60. St Andr Univ MA 82 St Jo Coll Dur BA 86. Cranmer Hall Dur 84. **d** 87 **p** 88. C Southall Green St Jo *Lon* 87–91; Assoc Min St Andr Ch Hong Kong 91–95; V Clapham Park St Steph *S'wark* 96–06; P-in-c Telford Park St Thos 05–06; V Telford Park 06–13; AD Lambeth S 06–13; Adn Lambeth from 13. *The Vicarage, 7 Hoadly Road, London SW16 1AE* T: (020) 8545 2440 E: simon.gates@southwark.anglican.org

GATFORD, The Ven Ian. b 40. AKC 65. **d** 67 **p** 68. C Clifton w Glapton *S'well* 67–71; TV Clifton 71–75; V Sherwood 75–84; Can Res Derby Cathl 84–99; Adn Derby and Hon Can Derby Cathl 93–05; rtd 05; PtO *Derby* from 05. *9 Poplar Nook, Allestree, Derby DE22 2DW* T: (01332) 557567

GATISS, Lee. b 72. New Coll Ox BA 96 MA 01 Westmr Th Sem Philadelphia ThM 09 Cam Univ PhD 14. Oak Hill Th Coll BA 00. **d** 01 **p** 02. C Barton Seagrave w Warkton *Pet* 01–04; C St Helen Bishopsgate w St Andr Undershaft etc *Lon* 04–09; PtO *Ely* from 10; Dir Ch Soc from 13. *Church Society, Ground Floor, Centre Block, Hille Business Estate, 132 St Albans Road, Watford WD24 4AE* T: (01923) 255410 F: 800362 E: director@churchsociety.org

GATLIFFE, David Spenser. b 45. Keble Coll Ox BA 67 Fitzw Coll Cam BA 69. Westcott Ho Cam 67. **d** 69 **p** 70. C Oxted S'wark 69–72; C Roehampton H Trin 72–75; C S Beddington St Mich 76–77; TV Clapham Old Town 78–87; P-in-c Clapham Ch Ch and St Jo 81–87; TV Clapham Team 87–89; V S Wimbledon H Trin and St Pet 89–01; R Lee St Marg 01–10; Ldr Post Ord Tr Woolwich Area 04–09; rtd 10; PtO *B & W* from 15. *47 Catherine Street, Frome BA11 1DA* T: (01373) 228757 M: 07527-424526 E: dgatliffe@yahoo.com

GATRILL, Canon Adrian Colin. b 60. Southn Univ BTh 82. Linc Th Coll 83. **d** 85 **p** 86. C W Bromwich St Andr *Lich* 85–88; C W Bromwich St Andr w Ch Ch 88–89; Chapl RAF 89–11; Dir of Ords 06–11; Sen Chapl Dur Constabulary from 11; PtO *St D* 90–95; *Ripon* 00–14; *Leeds* from 14; Hon Can Dur Cathl from 16. *Durham Constabulary Headquarters, Aykley Heads, Durham DH1 5TT* T: 0191-375 2361 E: adrian.gatrill@durham.pnn.police.uk

GAU, Justin Charles. b 65. Univ Coll Lon LLB 87 Down Coll Cam BTh 11. Westcott Ho Cam 09. **d** 11 **p** 12. Dep Chan *Linc* from 01; Dep Chan *B & W* from 11; Chan *Bris* from 11; NSM S Hackney St Jo w Ch Ch *Lon* 11–15; NSM Brownswood Park 15–17; NSM W Hackney from 17. *27 Arlington Square, London N1 7DP* T: (020) 7353 0711 M: 07771-711114 E: j.gau@pumpcourtchambers.com *or* justin@stpaulswesthackney.org

GAUDION, Craig Simon. b 84. Univ of Wales BA 08 Birm Univ MA 10. Trin Coll Bris 16. **d** 18 **p** 19. C S Widnes *Liv* from 18. *St Paul's Vicarage, Victoria Square, Widnes WA8 7QU* M: 07896-055484 E: craiggaudion@hotmail.co.uk

GAUGE, Canon Barrie Victor. b 41. St D Coll Lamp BA 62 Selw Coll Cam BA 64 MA 74 CQSW 81. Bp Burgess Hall Lamp. **d** 65 **p** 66. C Newtown w Llanllwchaiarn w Aberhafesp *St As* 65–68; C Prestatyn 68–73; R Bodfari and Dioc RE Adv 73–76; PtO *Ches* 76–84; V Birkenhead St Jas w St Bede 84–90; Dir of Resources 90–98; Hon Can Ches Cathl 94–98; C Lache cum Saltney 95–98; Par Development Adv *Derby* 98–06; Can Res Derby Cathl 99–06; Dioc Miss Adv 01–04; rtd 06; PtO *St As* from 09; *Ches* 10–14; *S & B* 11–14. *40 Swan Street, Wrexham LL13 7BD* T: (01978) 353715 E: bgauge254@btinternet.com

GAUNT, Adam. b 79. St Jo Coll Dur BA 00 MA 02. St Steph Ho Ox 03. **d** 05 **p** 06. C Middlesbrough Ascension *York* 05–09; R Loftus and Carlin How w Skinningrove from 09. *The Rectory, 11 Micklow Lane, Loftus, Saltburn-by-the-Sea TS13 4JE* T: (01287) 644047 E: adamgaunt@btinternet.com

GAUNT (née COTTELL), Mrs Avril Jane. b 50. SRN 72 SCM 74. S Dios Minl Tr Scheme 92. **d** 95 **p** 97. NSM Yatton Moor *B & W* 95–96 and 97–02; NSM Bourne *Guildf* 96–97; Chapl N Bris NHS Trust 02–14; rtd 14; PtO *B & W* from 05. *Myrtle Cottage, Ham Lane, Kingston Seymour, Clevedon BS21 6XE* T: (01934) 832995

GAUNT, Rachel. *See* SHUTTLEWORTH, Rachel

GAUNTLETT, Gilbert Bernard. b 36. Oriel Coll Ox BA 59 MA 62. Wycliffe Hall Ox 59. **d** 61 **p** 62. C Maidenhead St Andr and St Mary *Ox* 61–64; C Ox St Ebbe w St Pet 64–68; R Nottingham St Nic *S'well* 68–72; Asst Master Leys High Sch Redditch 73–79; Asst Master Stourport High Sch 79–85; rtd 97. *The Tower, Brynygwin Isaf, Dolgellau LL40 1YA* T: (01341) 423481 E: gauntlett278@btinternet.com

GAUSDEN, Canon Peter James. b 32. Qu Coll Birm 57. **d** 60 **p** 61. C Battersea St Pet and Chapl S Lon Ind Miss *S'wark* 60–63; C St Peter-in-Thanet *Cant* 63–68; V Sturry 68–74; R Sturry w Fordwich and Westbere w Hersden 74–97; Dioc Ecum Officer 91–96; Hon Can Cant Cathl 96–97; rtd 97; PtO *Cant* 97–99 and from 04; Hon C St Nicholas at Wade w Sarre and Chislet w Hoath 99–04. *2 The Paddocks, Collards Close, Monkton, Ramsgate CT12 4JZ* T: (01843) 825374 E: peter.gausden374@btinternet.com

GAWNE-CAIN, John. b 38. G&C Coll Cam BA 61 MA 66 CEng MICE. Cuddesdon Coll 74. **d** 76 **p** 77. C Cowley St Jas *Ox* 76–80; P-in-c Ox St Giles 80–85; V Ox St Giles and SS Phil and Jas w St Marg 85–92; P-in-c Uffington w Woolstone and Baulking 92–93; P-in-c Shellingford 92–93; R Uffington, Shellingford, Woolstone and Baulking 93–03; rtd 03; PtO *Ox* 04–08; *Win* 10–14. *51 Chesil Lodge, Chesil Street, Winchester SO23 0AH* E: j.gawne-cain@ruralnet.org.uk

GAWTHROP-DORAN, Mrs Sheila Mary. b 37. Birm Univ CertEd. Dalton Ho Bris 68. **dss** 79 **d** 87. Halliwell St Paul *Man* 79–82; New Bury 82–89; Par Dn 87–89; Par Dn Tonge w Alkrington 89–94; rtd 94; PtO *York* 95–15. *35 Swarthdale, Haxby, York YO32 3NZ* T: (01904) 761247

GAWTHROPE, Julie Anne. b 57. **d** 10 **p** 11. C Cherry Hinton St Jo *Ely* 10–15; TV Albury, Braughing, Furneux Pelham, Lt Hadham etc *St Alb* 15–16; R Braughing, Furneux Pelham and Stocking Pelham from 16. *The Vicarage, 1 Pentlows, Braughing, Ware SG11 2QD* M: 07789-838084 E: julie.gawthrope@ntlworld.com

GAY, Adam Garcia Hugh. b 57. STETS 02. **d** 05 **p** 06. C Bitterne *Win* 05–09; V Hedge End St Luke 09–13; PtO from 13; *Portsm* from 13. *14 Sissinghurst Road, Fareham PO16 9YA* T: (01329) 237126 E: adamgay@totalise.co.uk

GAY, John Charles Nankervis. b 58. ERMC 03. **d** 06 **p** 07. C Wilton *B & W* 06–10; R Itchingfield w Slinfold *Chich* 10–14; TV Brixham w Churston Ferrers and Kingswear *Ex* from 14; PtO *Eur* from 17. *13 Warborough Road, Churston Ferrers, Brixham TQ5 0JY* T: (01803) 845692 E: revjohngay@gmail.com

GAY, John Dennis. b 43. St Pet Coll Ox BA 64 MA 68 DPhil 69 MSc 78. Ripon Hall Ox 64. **d** 67 **p** 68. C Paddington St Jas *Lon* 67–71; P-in-c 71–72; Chapl Culham Coll Abingdon 72–79; Lect Ox Univ 78–80; Dir Culham Inst 80–11; Research Fell Dept of Educn Ox Univ from 11; LtO Ox 72–15; PtO 15–18; Visiting Prof Win Univ from 14. *Department of Educational Studies, 15 Norham Gardens, Oxford OX2 6PY* T: (01865) 611072 E: john.gay@education.ox.ac.uk

GAY, Canon Perran Russell. b 59. St Cath Coll Cam BA 81 MA 85 Ex Univ PGCE 82 FRGS 97 Hon FGCM 15. Ripon Coll Cuddesdon BA 86 MA 14. **d** 87 **p** 88. C Bodmin w Lanhydrock and Lanivet Truro 87–90; Bp's Dom Chapl 90–94; Dioc Officer for Unity 90–94; Can Res and Chan Truro Cathl 94–15; Prec 01–15; Dir of Tr *Truro* 94–99; Chapl Epiphany Ho 06–15; Chapl Is of Scilly from 15. *The Chaplaincy, Church Road, St Mary's, Isles of Scilly TR21 0NA* T: (01720) 423911 E: perran@perrangay.com *or* chaplain@scilly.church

GAYFORD, John. b 37. Lon Univ BDS 61 MB, BS 65 MD 78 Nottm Univ MA 13 FDSRCS 64 FRCPsych 86 Heythrop Coll Lon MA 05 Univ of Wales (Lamp) MTh 09. St Jo Sem Wonersh 02. **d** 03 **p** 04. NSM E Grinstead St Mary *Chich* from 03; PtO *S'wark* from 13. *Third Acre, 217 Smallfield Road, Horley RH6 9LR* T: (01342) 842752

GAYLE, Steve Anthony. b 74. Univ of W Indies BA 03 Heythrop Coll Lon MA 09. Ripon Coll Cuddesdon 13. **d** 15 **p** 16. C S Hackney St Jo w Ch Ch *Lon* 15–18; V Stoke Newington Common St Mich from 18. *St Michael's Vicarage, 55 Fountayne Road, London N16 7ED* M: 07903-175038 E: steveagayle@yahoo.com

GAYLER, Canon Roger Kenneth. b 44. Lich Th Coll 68. **d** 70 **p** 71. C Chingford St Anne *Chelmsf* 70–75; P-in-c Marks Gate 75–81; V 81–14; RD Barking and Dagenham 04–13; Hon Can Chelmsf Cathl 09–14; rtd 14; P-in-c Lambourne w Abridge and Stapleford Abbotts *Chelmsf* 14–19; TV Vale of Roding from 19. *The Vicarage, 1 The Poplars, Abridge, Romford RM4 1BB* T: (01992) 815838 E: rogergayler@btinternet.com

GAYNOR, Christopher Thomas. b 68. **d** 08 **p** 09. C Banbury St Fran *Ox* 08–13; V from 13. *26 Meadowsweet Way, Banbury OX16 1WE* T: (01295) 271403 E: allrevedup@hotmail.co.uk

GAYNOR, Mrs Mieke Aaltjen Cornelia. b 43. UEA BA 79. St Jo Coll Nottm 02. **d** 03 **p** 04. C Wollaton *S'well* 03–09; C Wollaton *S'well* 09–13; rtd 13; PtO *Ox* from 13. *5 Lodge Close, Marlow SL7 1RB* T: (01628) 487012 M: 07856-844554 E: mieke.gaynor@btopenworld.com

GAZE, The Ven Sally Ann. b 69. SS Coll Cam BA 91 MA 95 Birm Univ MPhil 98 PGCE 92. Qu Coll Birm 94. **d** 96 **p** 97. C Martley and Wichenford, Knightwick etc *Worc* 96–00; C Crickhowell w Cwmdu and Tretower *S & B* 00–02; TR Newton Flotman, Swainsthorpe, Tasburgh, etc *Nor* 02–17; Dioc Fresh Expressions Facilitator 09–17; Hon Can Nor Cathl 15–17; Dean for Rural Miss Consultancy *St E* 17–19; Adn for Rural Miss from 19; Can Res St E Cathl from 19. *5 Brook Lane, Playford, Ipswich IP6 9DY* T: (01473) 635113 *or* (01284) 748720 E: archdeacon.sally@cofesuffolk.org

GBEBIKAN, Canon Angela Maria Abike. b 56. Lon Univ MA 07. Westcott Ho Cam 02. **d** 04 **p** 05. C Norbury St Steph and Thornton Heath *S'wark* 04–07; P-in-c S Beddington and Roundshaw 07–08; V from 08; Asst Dir of Ords and Adv in Women's Min Croydon Area from 13; AD Sutton from 18; Hon Can S'wark Cathl from 16. *St Michael's Vicarage, Milton Road, Wallington SM6 9RP* T: (020) 8647 1201 E: gbebikan@cantab.net

GBONDA, Egerton Joe Fode. b 67. Univ of Sierra Leone BSc 94 MSc 03 E Lon Univ MA Heythrop Coll Lon MA. **d** 06 **p** 08. Sierra Leone 06–09; PtO *S'wark* 10–12; NSM Deptford St Jo w H Trin and Ascension 12–14; NSM Bermondsey St Kath w St Bart from 14; Chapl HM Pris High Down from 19. *HM Prison High Down, High Down Lane, Sutton SM2 5PJ* T: (020) 7147 6300 M: 07882-872830 E: father.egerton.gbonda@gmail.com *or* egerton.gbonda@justice.gov.uk

GEAR, John Arthur. b 37. St Aid Birkenhead 62. **d** 64 **p** 66. C Attleborough *Cov* 64–66; C Attercliffe *Sheff* 66–68; C Sheerness H Trin w St Paul *Cant* 68–73; Asst Youth Adv

S'wark 73–78; Youth Chapl *Lich* 78–88; V Stafford St Jo and Tixall w Ingestre 88–92; Gen Sec NCEC 92–97; rtd 97; PtO *Lich* 01–02 and 04–13; P-in-c Shrewsbury H Cross 02–03; PtO *Derby* 16–18. *50 Cadgwith Drive, Derby DE22 2AE*

GEARY, John Martin. b 52. LRSC 77. **d** 08 **p** 09. OLM Heywood *Man* 08–10; OLM Heywood St Marg and Heap Bridge 10–13; NSM Bagillt *St As* 13–16; NSM Flint 13–16; P-in-c Middlestown *Leeds* from 17. *The Vicarage, 6 Coxley Dell, Horbury, Wakefield WF4 5LF* T: (01924) 629269 M: 07753-462460 E: john@johngeary.co.uk

GEBAUER, George Gerhart. b 25. Sarum & Wells Th Coll 71. **d** 73 **p** 74. C Portsdown *Portsm* 73–78; V Purbrook 78–91; rtd 91; PtO *Portsm* from 91. *52 St John's Road, Locks Heath, Southampton SO31 6NF* T: (01489) 575172

GEDDES, Peter Henry. b 51. Trin Coll Bris 84. **d** 86 **p** 87. C Blackpool St Mark *Blackb* 86–88; C Barnston *Ches* 88–92; V Haslington w Crewe Green 92–04; V Partington and Carrington 04–16; rtd 16; PtO *Ches* from 17. *3 Elms Park, Thingwall, Wirral CH61 9PJ* T: 0151-648 9776 E: rev.peter.h.geddes@gmail.com

GEDGE, Richard John Anthony. b 70. Bath Univ BEng 92 CEng 96 MIMechE 96. St Jo Coll Nottm MTh 09. **d** 09 **p** 11. C Much Woolton *Liv* 09–16; C Halewood and Hunts Cross 17; C Liv Cathl 17–19. *4 Thackmore Way, Liverpool L19 4AE* T: 0151-427 9553 E: rjagedge@gmail.com

GEE, Anne Alison. b 43. Man Univ MB, ChB 66. STETS BA 01. **d** 01 **p** 02. NSM Canford Magna *Sarum* 01–06; NSM Horton, Chalbury, Hinton Martel and Holt St Jas 06–13; P-in-c 11–13; NSM Witchampton, Stanbridge and Long Crichel etc 06–13; P-in-c 11–13; rtd 13; PtO *Sarum* from 16; *Eur* from 16. *14 Merley Gardens, Wimborne BH21 1TB* T: (01202) 285819 E: a.gee@doctors.org.uk

GEE, Canon Edward. b 28. St Deiniol's Hawarden 59. **d** 61 **p** 62. C Hanging Heaton *Wakef* 61–65; V Brownhill 65–75; V Alverthorpe 75–84; R Castleford All SS 84–92; Hon Can Wakef Cathl 87–92; rtd 92; PtO *Bradf* 92–14; *Wakef* 92–14; *Leeds* 14–16. *1 Holme Ghyll, Colne Road, Glusburn, Keighley BD20 8RG* T: (01535) 630060 E: mandegee@btinternet.com

GEERING, Preb Anthony Ernest. b 43. Columbia Pacific Univ BSc. Kelham Th Coll 62. **d** 68 **p** 69. C Cov St Mary 68–71; New Zealand 71–75; P-in-c Brinklow *Cov* 75–77; R 77–81; V Monks Kirby w Pailton and Stretton-under-Fosse 77–81; R Harborough Magna 77–81; V Pilton w Ashford *Ex* 81–86; P-in-c Shirwell w Loxhore 83–86; R Crediton and Shobrooke 86–01; P-in-c Sandford w Upton Hellions 00–01; R Crediton, Shobrooke and Sandford etc 01; RD Cadbury 93–97; R Chagford, Drewsteignton, Hittisleigh etc 01–09; P-in-c 09–10; RD Okehampton 02–05; Preb Ex Cathl 02–09; rtd 09. *20 Iter Park, Bow, Crediton EX17 6BY* T: (01363) 881263 E: prebant43@gmail.com

GEILESKEY, Mrs Sarah Jane. b 73. ERMC 17. **d** 19. C St E Cathl Distr from 19. *Corner Mill, Hill Road, Westley, Bury St Edmunds IP33 3TR* T: (01284) 748720 E: curate@stedscathedral.org

GEILINGER, John Edward. b 27. Lon Univ BSc 53 BD 58 BA 76 MPhil 79. Tyndale Hall Bris. **d** 59 **p** 60. C Plymouth St Jude *Ex* 59–61; Lect Trin Th Coll Umuahia Nigeria 63–72; Lect Th Coll of N Nigeria 72–77; PtO *Portsm* from 79; rtd 92. *Emmaus House, Colwell Road, Freshwater PO40 9LY* T: (01983) 753030

GEISOW, Hilary Patricia. b 46. Salford Univ BSc 67 Warwick Univ PhD 71 Nottm Univ PGCE 94. St Jo Coll Nottm 01. **d** 03 **p** 04. C Linc St Faith and St Martin w St Pet 03–06; P-in-c Colsterworth Gp 06–08; P-in-c Peakirk w Glinton and Northborough *Pet* 08–16; P-in-c Etton w Helpston and Maxey 08–12; rtd 16; PtO *Linc* from 17. *73 Queens Road, Bourne PE10 9DR* T: (01778) 425842 E: hilary.geisow@btinternet.com

GELDARD, Preb Mark Dundas. b 50. Liv Univ BA 71 Bris Univ MA 75. Trin Coll Bris 73. **d** 75 **p** 76. C Aughton Ch Ch *Liv* 75–78; Tutor Trin Coll Bris 78–84; V Fairfield *Liv* 84–88; Dioc Dir of Ords *Lich* 88–07; C Lich St Mich w St Mary and Wall 95–07; P-in-c Wigginton 07–08; V 08–11; Preb Lich Cathl 00–11; rtd 11; PtO *Chich* from 12. *10 Fitzalan Court, Rackham Road, Rustington, Littlehampton BN16 2LE* T: (01903) 786665 E: mark.geldard2@btinternet.com

GELL, The Ven Anne Elizabeth. b 63. St Hugh's Coll Ox BA 85 MA 01 R Free Hosp Sch of Medicine MB, BS 90 Surrey Univ BA 01. STETS 98. **d** 01 **p** 02. C Headley All SS *Guildf* 01–05; V Wrecclesham 05–17; AD Farnham 10–17; Hon Can Guildf Cathl 13–17; Adn Wells and Can Res Wells Cathl *B & W* from 17. *6 The Liberty, Wells BA5 2SU* T: (01749) 685147 E: annegell@lineone.net *or* adwells@bathwells.anglican.org

GELL, Miss Margaret Florence. b 30. **d** 00 **p** 01. NSM Madeley *Lich* 00–04; rtd 04; PtO *Lich* 04–14. *19 Pear Tree Drive, Madeley, Crewe CW3 9EN* T: (01782) 750669 E: m.f.gell@btinternet.com

GELLI, Frank Julian. b 43. Birkbeck Coll Lon BA 78 K Coll Lon MTh 82. Ripon Coll Cuddesdon 84. **d** 86 **p** 87. C Chiswick St Nic w St Mary *Lon* 86–89; Chapl Ankara *Eur* 89–91; C Kensington St Mary Abbots w St Geo *Lon* 91–99; rtd 03. *58 Boston Gardens, Brentford TW8 9LP* T: (020) 8847 4533 E: numapomp@talk21.com

GELSTON, Anthony. b 35. Keble Coll Ox BA 57 MA 60 DD 85. Ridley Hall Cam 59. **d** 60 **p** 61. C Chipping Norton *Ox* 60–62; Lect Th Dur Univ 62–76; Sen Lect 76–88; Dean Div Faculty 77–79; Reader 89–95; LtO 62–95; rtd 95; PtO *Dur* from 95. *Lesbury, Hetton Road, Houghton le Spring DH5 8JW* T: 0191-584 2256 E: agelston35@btinternet.com

GEMMELL, Canon Ian William Young. b 52. ALAM. St Jo Coll Nottm. **d** 77 **p** 78. C Old Hill H Trin *Worc* 77–81; C Selly Park St Steph and St Wulstan *Birm* 81–83; V Leic St Chris 83–93; RD Christianity S 92–93; P-in-c Gt Bowden w Welham, Glooston and Cranoe 93–02; P-in-c Church Langton w Tur Langton, Thorpe Langton etc 93–99; P-in-c Church Langton cum Tur Langton etc 99–02; R Gt Bowden w Welham, Glooston and Cranoe etc 02–06; RD Gartree I 97–06; Hon Can Leic Cathl 03–06; P-in-c Welford w Sibbertoft and Marston Trussell *Pet* 06–12; P-in-c Foxton w Gumley and Laughton *Leic* 12–17; rtd 17; Hon C Foxton w Gumley and Laughton *Leic* 17; PtO from 18. *2 Marriott Drive, Kibworth Harcourt, Leicester LE8 0JX* E: budgemmell@mac.com

GENDALL, Stephen Mark. b 63. **d** 89 **p** 90. Lundi St Apollos Zimbabwe 89–01; Youth Chapl 93–01; Can Cen Zimbabwe 00–01; V Lingfield and Crowhurst *S'wark* 02–12; Chapl Crowhurst Chr Healing Cen from 12. *Crowhurst Christian Healing Centre, The Old Rectory, Crowhurst, Battle TN33 9AD* T: (01424) 830204 M: 07752-063150

GENDERS, Nigel Mark. b 65. Oak Hill Th Coll BA 92. **d** 92 **p** 93. C New Malden and Coombe *S'wark* 92–96; C Enfield Ch Ch Trent Park *Lon* 96–98; P-in-c Eastry and Northbourne w Tilmanstone etc *Cant* 98–03; P-in-c Woodnesborough w Worth and Staple 03–08; AD Sandwich 06–08; Min to Sandwich Secondary Schs 03–08; Dir of Educn *Cant* 08–12; C Margate H Trin 11–12; Hd of Sch Policy Bd of Educn and Dep Sec Nat Soc 12–14; Chief Educn Officer Abps' Coun from 14; PtO *Cant* from 12. *Church House, Great Smith Street, London SW1P 3AZ* T: (020) 7898 1500 E: nigel.genders@churchofengland.org

GENOE, Simon Alfred. b 82. Stranmillis Coll BEd 06 TCD BTh 09. CITC 06. **d** 09 **p** 10. C Lisburn Ch Ch Cathl *Conn* 09–13; V 13–16; I Magheralin w Dollingstown *D & D* from 16. *12 New Forge Road, Magheralin, Craigavon BT67 0QJ* T: (028) 9261 1273 M: 07501-288941 E: simon.genoe@gmail.com

GENT, David Robert. b 71. Surrey Univ BSc 94. Qu Coll Birm BD 97. **d** 98 **p** 99. C Wotton-under-Edge w Ozleworth and N Nibley *Glouc* 98–02; Chapl Yeovil Coll and C Yeovil H Trin w Barwick *B & W* 02–08; Churches' Development officer for FE 07–08; P-in-c Martock w Ash *B & W* 08–14; P-in-c Kingsbury Episcopi w E Lambrook, Hambridge etc 13–14; V Martock w Kingsbury Episcopi and Ash 14–18; R Wrington w Butcombe and Burrington from 18. *3 Alburys, Wrington, Bristol BS40 5NZ* T: (01934) 862348 E: david@rectory.org.uk

GENT, Emily Louise. *See* DAVIS, Emily Louise

GENT, Miss Susan Elizabeth. K Coll Lon LLB 78 Brunel Univ BA 95. Wycliffe Hall Ox MPhil 96. **d** 97 **p** 98. C Notting Hill St Jo and St Pet *Lon* 97–00; Chapl to City law firms 00–12; Hon Assoc P St Paul's Cathl 00–12; Dioc Visitor 01–02; P-in-c St Matthew Ludgate 05–12; Tutor Trin Coll Bris from 12. *4 Worrall Mews, Clifton, Bristol BS8 2HF* T: 0117-968 2803 E: sue.gent@trinity-bris.ac.uk

GENTILELLA, Barbara Catherine. b 55. SEITE 05. **d** 08 **p** 09. NSM Shirley St Jo *S'wark* 08–12; NSM Addington from 12. *42 Devonshire Way, Croydon CR0 8BR* T: (020) 8777 4462 M: 07977-190155 E: bb2ke@sky.com

GEOGHEGAN, Luke. b 62. SS Hild & Bede Coll Dur BA 83 Bedf Coll Lon MSc 87 CQSW 87 Bedfordshire Univ MA 13 FRSA 93. SAOMC 87. **d** 00 **p** 01. NSM Spitalfields Ch Ch w All SS *Lon* 00–03; NSM Gt Berkhamsted *St Alb* 03–05; NSM Gt Berkhamsted, Gt and Lt Gaddesden etc from 05; NSM Hemel Hempstead from 14; Warden Toynbee Hall 98–08; Visiting Prof Lon Metrop Univ 00–08; Chapl Ashridge Business Sch from 08. *1 Clapton Terrace, London E5 9BW*

GEORGE, Alexander Robert. b 46. K Coll Lon BD 69 AKC 69. St Aug Coll Cant. **d** 70 **p** 71. C Newmarket St Mary w Exning St Agnes *St E* 70–74; C Swindon Ch Ch *Bris* 74–76; C Henbury 76–79; LtO 79–80; TV Oldland 80–88; C Ipswich St Aug *St E* 89; C Hadleigh w Layham and Shelley 89–90; P-in-c Assington 90–91; R Assington w Newton Green and Lt Cornard 91–00; P-in-c Hundon 00–03; Hon C 03–04; C Stour Valley 04–11; Dioc Moderator for Reader Tr 95–03; Asst Liturg Officer (Formation and Educn) 00–03; Nat Moderator for Reader Tr 04–08; rtd 11; PtO *St E* from 11.

103 Bixley Road, Ipswich IP3 8NP T: (01473) 727351
E: alecrg@btinternet.com
GEORGE, Carole. b 64. St Mellitus Coll BA 19. **d** 18 **p** 19.
NSM Sunbury *Lon* from 18. *6 St Andrew's Close, Wraysbury, Staines-upon-Thames TW19 5DG* M: 07786-880392
E: carolegeorge1@sky.com
GEORGE, David. b 64. Wycliffe Hall Ox 01. **d** 03 **p** 04. C
Inkberrow w Cookhill and Kington w Dormston *Worc*
03–07; P-in-c Dudley St Jo 07–10; TV Kidderminster St Jo
and H Innocents 10–16; P-in-c Cockington *Ex* from 16. *The Vicarage, 22 Monterey Close, Torquay TQ2 6QW* T: (01803)
391425 M: 07824-885561 E: revdavegeorge@gmail.com
GEORGE, Henderson Rudolph. b 44. Open Univ BA 80
Chelsea Coll Lon MEd 85. NTMTC BA 07. **d** 07 **p** 08.
NSM Clapton St Jas *Lon* 07–11; NSM Enfield St Jas
from 11. *12 Cowland Avenue, Enfield EN3 7DX* T: (020)
8804 9224 E: henderson.george@stjameschurch.cc *or*
hendersonrgeorge@gmail.com
GEORGE, Nicholas Paul. b 58. St Steph Ho Ox 86. **d** 89 **p** 90.
C Leeds St Aid *Ripon* 89–92; C Leeds Richmond Hill 92–96;
Chapl Agnes Stewart C of E High Sch Leeds 93–96; V Leeds
Halton St Wilfrid *Ripon* 96–02; V Camberwell St Giles w
St Matt *S'wark* from 02. *St Giles's Vicarage, 200 Benhill Road,
London SE5 7LL* T: (020) 7703 4504 M: 07771-603217
E: mail@nickgeorge.org.uk
GEORGE-JONES, Canon Gwilym Ifor. b 26. K Coll (NS) 56.
d 57 **p** 57. R Seaforth St Jas Canada 57–61; V Kirton in
Lindsey *Linc* 61–71; R Grayingham 61–71; R Manton 61–71;
V Alford w Rigsby 71–92; R Maltby 71–92; R Well 71–92;
V Bilsby w Farlesthorpe 71–92; R Hannah cum Hagnaby w
Markby 71–92; R Saleby w Beesby 71–92; RD Calcewaithe
and Candleshoe 77–88; Can and Preb Linc Cathl
81–01; rtd 92. *42 Kelstern Road, Lincoln LN6 3NJ* T: (01522)
691896
GEORGE-ROGERS, Gillian Jean Richeldis. *See* WILLIAMS,
Gillian Jean Richeldis
GERAERTS, Virginia Gwynneth. b 50. **d** 15 **p** 16. NSM
Davenham *Ches* from 15. *The Old Coach House, 466
London Road, Davenham, Northwich CW9 8HW* T: (01606)
47111 M: 07709-049079 E: virginia_gray@hotmail.com
GERARD, Patrick Hoare. b 64. Man Univ BSc 86 MSc 88. Qu
Coll Birm 04. **d** 06 **p** 07. C Solihull *Birm* 06–10; R Baddesley
Clinton from 10; R Lapworth from 10; Bp's Adv for the
Environment from 12. *The Rectory, Church Lane, Lapworth,
Solihull B94 5NX* T: (01564) 782098 M: 07905-967930
E: patrick@gerard.net
GERD, Sister. *See* SWENSSON, Gerd Inger
GERRANS, Daniel. b 58. Em Coll Cam LLB 80 MA 83 Barrister-
at-Law (Middle Temple) 81. SEITE 02. **d** 05 **p** 06. NSM
De Beauvoir Town St Pet *Lon* 05–11; Chapl to Bp Stepney
07–11; V S Hackney St Mich w Haggerston St Paul from
11. *97 Lavender Grove, London E8 3LR* T: (020) 7249 2627
E: daniel.gerrans@xxiv.co.uk
GERRARD, The Ven David Keith Robin. b 39. St Edm Hall
Ox BA 61. Linc Th Coll 61. **d** 63 **p** 64. C Stoke Newington
St Olave *Lon* 63–66; C Primrose Hill St Mary w Avenue
Road St Paul 66–69; V Newington St Paul *S'wark* 69–79; V
Surbiton St Andr and St Mark 79–89; RD Kingston 84–88;
Hon Can S'wark Cathl 85–89; Adn Wandsworth 89–04;
rtd 05; PtO *Guildf* from 05; *S'wark* from 05. *15 Woodbourne
Drive, Claygate, Esher KT10 0DR* T: (01372) 467295
E: david.gerrard@btinternet.com
GERRY, Brian John Rowland. b 38. Oak Hill Th Coll 69.
d 71 **p** 72. C Hawkwell *Chelmsf* 71–74; C Battersea Park
St Sav *S'wark* 74–77; C Battersea St Geo w St Andr 74–77;
V Axmouth w Musbury *Ex* 77–86; R Upton 86–04; rtd 04.
49 Peasland Road, Torquay TQ2 8PA T: (01803) 322788
E: gerry113@btinternet.com
GERRY, Ulric James. b 67. Bris Univ BEng 89. Wycliffe Hall
Ox BA 96. **d** 97 **p** 98. C Hemel Hempstead *St Alb* 97–00; PtO
01–02; Crosslinks Tanzania 02–11; P-in-c Glas St Oswald
11–14; NSM Avondale Zimbabwe from 15. *20 Epping Road,
Mount Pleasant, Harare, Zimbabwe* T: (00263) (77) 722 3432
E: ulricgerry@gmail.com
GHEST, Richard William Iliffe. b 31. Em Coll Cam BA 53
MA 57 Lon Univ BA 66. Wells Th Coll 53. **d** 55 **p** 56. C
Weston-super-Mare St Jo *B & W* 55–57; India 58–63; C
Holborn St Geo w H Trin and St Bart *Lon* 63–67; Ceylon
67–68; C Combe Down *B & W* 68–73; C Combe Down w
Monkton Combe 73–74; R Tickenham 74–96; rtd 96. *120
Cottrell Road, Roath, Cardiff CF24 3EX* T: (029) 2048 1597
GIBAUT, Canon John St Helier. b 58. Toronto Univ BA 80.
Trin Coll Toronto MDiv 84 ThD 94. **d** 84 **p** 84. P-in-c Norton
Bay Canada 84–87; C St Jas Cathl Toronto 87–94; Prof Th
St Paul Univ Ottawa 94–07; Dir Faith and Order WCC
08–15; Dir Unity, Faith and Order Angl Communion Office

from 15; PtO *Lon* from 16; *Eur* from 16. *St Andrew's House,
16 Tavistock Crescent, London W11 1AP* M: 07479-167778
E: john.gibaut@anglicancommunion.org
GIBBENS, Gwyneth Andrea. b 52. Nottm Univ BA 73
PhD 78. WEMTC 07. **d** 10 **p** 11. NSM Kemble, Poole Keynes,
Somerford Keynes etc *Glouc* 10–13; V Wotton St Mary from
13. *Holy Trinity Vicarage, Church Road, Longlevens, Gloucester
GL2 0AJ* T: (01452) 524129
GIBBINS, Mrs Megan Ceinwen. b 59. Birm Univ MSc 03. St Jo
Coll Nottm 12. **d** 14 **p** 15. C Selly Park Ch Ch *Birm* 14–18;
R Ribbesford w Bewdley and Dowles and Wribbenhall *Worc*
from 18. *57 Park Lane, Bewdley DY12 2HA* T: 0121-345
2277 M: 07896-499640 E: megan.gibbins@talk21.com
GIBBON, Matthew. b 79. Trin Coll Carmarthen BA 00.
St Steph Ho Ox BTh 03. **d** 03 **p** 04. C Caerau w Ely *Llan* 03–05;
C Aberavon 05–08; P-in-c Treharris, Trelewis and Bedlinog
08–11; P-in-c Treharris, Trelewis, Bedlinog and Llanfabon
11–16; P-in-c Aberaman and Cwmaman from 16. *St Margaret's
Vicarage, Gladstone Street, Aberdare CF44 6SA* T: (01443)
410280 E: frmatthewgibbon@outlook.com
GIBBONS, David Austen. b 63. York Univ BSc 84. Ch Div Sch
of Pacific 93 Ripon Coll Cuddesdon BA 94. **d** 94 **p** 95. C Ryde
H Trin *Portsm* 94–97; C Swanmore St Mich 94–97; C Gosport
Ch Ch 97–01; R Havant 01–08; R Barrington Hills USA from
08. *337 Ridge Road, Barrington IL 60010-2331, USA* T: (001)
(847) 381 0596 E: dgibbons.stmarks@gmail.com
GIBBONS, Harvey Lloyd. b 62. Open Univ BA 12 York
St Jo Univ MA 16. Ripon Coll Cuddesdon 97. **d** 99 **p** 00.
C Verwood *Sarum* 99–00; C Gillingham 00–02; Dioc Voc
Adv and P-in-c Upavon w Rushall and Charlton 02–07; R
Warminster St Denys and Upton Scudamore 07–13; Asst
Dioc Dir of Ords 11–13; P-in-c Swindon All SS w St Barn
Bris 13–18; P-in-c Swindon St Aug 13–18; V Oswestry *Lich*
from 18; R Rhydycroesau from 18. *St Oswald's Vicarage,
Penylan Lane, Oswestry SY11 2AJ* T: (01691) 662253
E: revdharvey@gmail.com
GIBBONS, Jayne Lisa. *See* LEWIS, Jayne Lisa
GIBBONS, The Ven Kenneth Harry. b 31. Man Univ BSc 52.
Cuddesdon Coll 54. **d** 56 **p** 57. C Fleetwood St Pet *Blackb*
56–60; NE Sch Sec SCM 60–62; Hon C Leeds St Pet *Ripon*
60–62; C St Martin-in-the-Fields *Lon* 62–65; V New Addington
Cant 65–70; V Portsea St Mary *Portsm* 70–81; RD Portsm
73–79; Hon Can Portsm Cathl 76–81; Dir Post-Ord Tr *Blackb*
81–83; Dir of Ords and Dir IME 4-7 82–90; Adn Lancaster
81–97; P-in-c Weeton 81–85; V St Michaels-on-Wyre 85–97;
rtd 97; P-in-c St Magnus the Martyr w St Marg New Fish
Street *Lon* 97–03; P-in-c St Clem Eastcheap w St Martin Orgar
99–08. *15 The Oaks, Taunton TA1 2QX* T: (01823) 271140
E: margyandken@btinternet.com
GIBBONS, Lissa Melanie. *See* SCOTT, Lissa Melanie
GIBBONS, Paul James. b 37. Chich Th Coll 63. **d** 65 **p** 66. C
Croydon St Mich *Cant* 65–72; V Maidstone St Mich 72–12;
rtd 12. *19 Sterling Avenue, Maidstone ME16 0AY* T: (01622)
754812
GIBBONS, Ruth Banbury. b 91. York St Jo Univ BA 15.
Cranmer Hall Dur 14. **d** 16 **p** 17. C Fulford *York* 16–18; C
Dringhouses from 18. *2 Moor Lea Avenue, York YO24 2PA*
E: revdruthi@gmail.com
GIBBONS, Tobias Franklyn. b 89. Reading Univ BA 10 Ex
Univ MA 11 St Jo Coll Dur BA 17. Cranmer Hall Dur 14.
d 17 **p** 18. C York St Chad from 17. *2 Moor Lea Avenue, York
YO24 2PA* M: 07713-677269 E: revtobygibbons@gmail.com
GIBBONS, Mrs Valerie Mary Lydele. b 49. St Aid Coll Dur
BA 72 Solicitor 75. Wycliffe Hall Ox 98. **d** 03 **p** 04. OLM
Cholsey and Moulsford Ox from 03. *Kilifi, Caps Lane,
Cholsey, Wallingford OX10 9HF* T/F: (01491) 651377
E: val.gibbons@btinternet.com
GIBBONS, William Jacob. b 84. **d** 11 **p** 12. C E Carmarthen
St D 11–12; C Carmarthen St Pet 12–13; P-in-c Newtown *Liv*
from 13; TR Wigan All SS from 18. *22 Mabel Street, Wigan
WN5 9EJ* E: willgibbons@hotmail.co.uk
GIBBS, Ann Margaret. b 59. **d** 17 **p** 18. NSM Porlock and
Porlock Weir w Stoke Pero etc *B & W* from 17. *1 Rawles
Buildings, Porlock, Minehead TA24 8LB* T: (01643) 863593
GIBBS, Colin Wilfred. b 39. Man Univ BA 62 Birm Univ
CertEd 63. St Jo Coll Nottm 71. **d** 73 **p** 74. C Crowborough
Chich 73–76; C Rodbourne Cheney *Bris* 76–77; C Bickenhill
w Elmdon *Birm* 77–80; CF 80–96; Dir Ichthus Ho Homestay
96–06; Chapl Grenville Coll Bideford 99–02; P-in-c
Cowden w Hammerwood *Chich* 06–10; PtO 12–17. *11
The Gorses, Bexhill-on-Sea TN39 3BE* T: (01424) 845299
E: fayandcolin@me.com
GIBBS, Donna Louise. b 66. Sarum Coll 14. **d** 17 **p** 18. C Ipswich
St Mary at Stoke w St Pet and St Fran *St E* from 17. *46 Holcombe
Crescent, Ipswich IP2 9PW* T: (01473) 809843 M: 07765-
215661 E: donna.donnagibbs.gibbs@gmail.com

GIBBS (*née* **DE ROBECK**), **Canon Fiona Caroline.** b 74. St Martin's Coll Lanc BA 96. St Jo Coll Nottm MA(TS) 99. **d** 00 **p** 01. C Bitterne *Win* 00–05; C Chandler's Ford 05–13; P-in-c Hedge End St Luke 13–19; V from 19; AD Eastleigh 17–19; Hon Can Win Cathl from 17. *16 Elliot Rise, Hedge End, Southampton SO30 2RU* T: (01489) 795443

GIBBS, Mrs Fiorenza Silvia Elisabetta. b 49. SRN 71. St Alb Minl Tr Scheme 90. **d** 93 **p** 99. NSM Hitchin *St Alb* 93–96; NSM Pirton 97–99; Asst Chapl N Herts NHS Trust 99–00; Asst Chapl E and N Herts NHS Trust 00–02; Chapl 02–10; NSM Hitchin *St Alb* 10–16; NSM Hitchin and St Paul's Walden from 16. *12 Bunyon Close, Pirton, Hitchin SG5 3RE* T: (01462) 711846

GIBBS, Ian Edmund. b 47. Lon Univ BEd 69. St Steph Ho Ox 72. **d** 75 **p** 76. C Stony Stratford *Ox* 75–79; V Forest Town *S'well* 79–83; R Diddlebury w Munslow, Holdgate and Tugford *Heref* 83–12; R Abdon 83–12; rtd 12; PtO *Heref* from 12. *Dhustone Cottage, 10 High Street, Clee Hill, Ludlow SY8 3LZ* T: (01584) 890828

✠**GIBBS, The Rt Revd Jonathan Robert.** b 61. Jes Coll Ox MA 89 Jes Coll Cam PhD 90. Ridley Hall Cam 84. **d** 89 **p** 90 **c** 14. C Stalybridge H Trin and Ch Ch *Ches* 89–92; Chapl Basle w Freiburg-im-Breisgau *Eur* 92–98; R Heswall *Ches* 98–14; Suff Bp Huddersfield *Leeds* from 14. *Stone Royd, 9 Valley Head, Huddersfield HD2 2DH* T: (01484) 900656 *or* 471801 E: bishop.jonathan@leeds.anglican.org

GIBBS, Marcus Timothy. b 73. UMIST BSc 95. Trin Coll Bris BA 10. **d** 10 **p** 11. C Northampton St Giles *Pet* 10–13; V Balham Hill Ascension *S'wark* from 13; Dir IME Kingston Area from 17. *5 Rossiter Road, London SW12 9RY* T: (020) 8675 8626 F: 8673 3796 E: marcus.gibbs@ascensionbalhamhill.org

GIBBS, Peter Winston. b 50. Ex Univ BA 72 CQSW 75. St Jo Coll Nottm. **d** 90 **p** 91. C Hampreston *Sarum* 90–94; P-in-c Ipswich St Matt *St E* 94–99; Assoc P Attenborough *S'well* 99–01; V Toton 01–08; TV N Poole Ecum Team *Sarum* 08–15; rtd 15; PtO *Sarum* from 16. *98 Weymouth Bay Avenue, Weymouth DT3 5AA* T: (01305) 570241

GIBBS, Canon Philip Roscoe. b 33. Codrington Coll Barbados 57. **d** 60 **p** 61. C St Jo Cathl Belize Br Honduras 61–63; P-in-c S Distr Miss 63–70; V Pomona St Matt 70–71; R Corozal Belize 71–74; Hon Can Belize from 71; V Stoke Newington Common St Mich *Lon* 74–87; R Johnsonville New Zealand 87–96; rtd 96. *13 Sim Street, Johnsonville 6037, New Zealand* T: (0064) (4) 478 2886 E: philip.g@actrix.gen.nz

GIBBS, Raymond George. b 55. NTMTC 94. **d** 97 **p** 98. NSM Becontree S *Chelmsf* 97–99; C Dedham 99–04; C Colchester St Mich Myland 04–08; P-in-c from 08; Area Youth Officer 04–08; C Colchester St Luke from 18; C Langham w Boxted from 18; C W Bergholt and Gt Horkesley from 18; C Wormingford, Mt Bures and Lt Horkesley from 18. *352 Mill Road, Mile End, Colchester CO4 5JF* T: (01206) 843926 E: raymond359gibbs@btinternet.com

GIBBS, Richard James. b 68. St Paul's Coll Chelt BSc 90. St Jo Coll Nottm MTh 01. **d** 01 **p** 02. C Southport Ch Ch *Liv* 01–05; Min Banks St Steph CD 05–12; C Southport St Phil and St Paul 12–16; P-in-c Stilton w Denton and Caldecote etc *Ely* from 16. *The Rectory, Church Street, Stilton, Peterborough PE7 3RF* T: (01733) 248701 E: stiltonvicar@hotmail.com

GIBBS, Stewart Henry. b 77. CCC Cam BA 98 MA PGCE 99 Anglia Poly Univ BTh 05. Ridley Hall Cam 02. **d** 05 **p** 06. C Grays North *Chelmsf* 05–10; R Hatfield Heath and Sheering 10–15; PtO 15–17; NSM Blackmore and Stondon Massey 17–18; P-in-c High Ongar w Norton Mandeville from 18. *The Vicarage, Church Street, Blackmore, Ingatestone CM4 0RN* T: (01277) 821446 E: 07889-092559

GIBBS, William John Morris. b 71. Birm Univ BSc 94. Ripon Coll Cuddesdon BTh 00. **d** 00 **p** 01. C Staines St Mary and St Pet *Lon* 00–03; C Kensington St Mary Abbots w St Geo 03–06; V Redbourn *St Alb* from 06; RD Wheathampstead 10–15. *The Vicarage, 49 Church End, Redbourn, St Albans AL3 7DU* T: (01582) 791669

GIBLIN, Canon Brendan Anthony. b 64. K Coll Lon BD 86 AKC 93 Leeds Univ MA 95. Wycliffe Hall Ox 90. **d** 92 **p** 93. C Tadcaster w Newton Kyme *York* 92–96; R Stockton-on-the-Forest w Holtby and Warthill 96–02; P-in-c Middleham w Coverdale and E Witton etc *Ripon* 02–03; R 03–11; AD Wensley 10–11; P-in-c Wetherby 11–14; *Leeds* from 14; AD Harrogate 13–16; Hon Can Ripon Cathl from 19. *3 Lazenby Drive, Wetherby LS22 6WL* T: (01937) 520951 E: bgiblin@me.com

GIBRALTAR, Archdeacon of. *See* JOHNSTON, The Ven Geoffrey Stanley

GIBRALTAR, Dean of. *Vacant*

GIBSON, Catherine Snyder. b 39. Parson's Sch of Design (NY) 57. Ab Dioc Tr Course 81 Edin Th Coll 92. **d** 86 **p** 94. Colombia 86–87; NSM Aberdeen St Marg *Ab* 87–88; Dioc Hosp Chapl 88–92; C Aberdeen St Marv 93–94; Bp's Chapl for Tr and Educn 93–94; P-in-c Ballater 95–96; R 96–98; P-in-c Aboyne 95–96; R 96–98; P-in-c Braemar 95–97; Assoc P Fort Lauderdale USA 98–03; I Fermoy Union *C, C & R* 04–06; P-in-c Lugano *Eur* 06–07; P-in-C Dayton St Matt USA 09–10; Assoc P W Palm Beach 11–12; rtd 10; Dioc Supernumerary *Ab* 13–17; P-in-c Brechin *Bre* 17–18; Hon C Aberdeen St Jo *Ab* from 18. *65 Blenheim Place, Aberdeen AB25 2DZ* T: (01224) 611806 E: ecscanair@gmail.com

GIBSON, Charles Daniel. b 48. **d** 03 **p** 04. OLM Wisley w Pyrford *Guildf* 03–18; PtO from 18. *The Corner Cottage, Send Marsh Road, Ripley, Woking GU23 6JN* T: (01483) 225317 F: 223681

GIBSON, Colin Taylor. b 54. Trin Coll Cam BA 77. Oak Hill Th Coll 86. **d** 88 **p** 89. C Thrybergh w Hooton Roberts *Sheff* 88–91; P-in-c Tinsley 91–96; TV Attercliffe, Darnall and Tinsley 96–02; TR Walsall *Lich* 02–11; R Walsall St Matt 11–13; Hon C Walsall St Paul 05–13; Hon C Walsall Pleck and Bescot 05–13; V Horton and Wraysbury *Ox* from 13. *The Vicarage, 55 Welley Road, Wraysbury, Staines-upon-Thames TW19 5ER* T: (01784) 481258 E: vicar.hortonandwraysbury@gmail.com

GIBSON, Mrs Fiona Ruth. b 70. Homerton Coll Cam BEd 93. Oak Hill Th Coll MTh 11. **d** 11 **p** 12. C Bedford Ch Ch *St Alb* 11–14; V Cople, Moggerhanger and Willington from 14. *The Vicarage, 3 Grange Lane, Cople, Bedford MK44 3TT* T: (01234) 838145 E: cmwvicar@gmail.com

GIBSON, Canon Ian. b 48. Open Univ BA 85 Wolv Univ MSc 95 Liv Jo Moores Univ MA 09 FCIPD. S Dios Minl Tr Scheme 82. **d** 85 **p** 86. NSM Uckfield *Chich* 85–88; NSM Lt Horsted 85–88; NSM Isfield 85–88; V Fairwarp 88–93; P-in-c 94–00; NSM 00–04; V High Hurstwood 88–93; P-in-c 94–00; RD Uckfield 03–04; Bp's Dom Chapl and Research Asst 04–09; Acting Adn Lewes and Hastings 04–05; Episc V for Min and Bp's Sen Chapl 09–13; Can Res and Treas Chich Cathl 09–14; PtO *B & W* from 15; *Ex* from 15. *Windwhistle Down, Upton Lane, Seavington, Ilminster TA19 0PZ* T: (01460) 249566 M: 07843-672803 E: igchichester@gmail.com

GIBSON, James Campbell Ramsay. b 70. Southn Univ BEng 92 Cranfield Univ MSc 97 CEng 96 MIMechE 96. Trin Coll Bris 10. **d** 12 **p** 13. C Busbridge and Hambledon *Guildf* 12–16; V Hurdsfield *Ches* from 16. *197A Hurdsfield Road, Macclesfield SK10 2PX* T: (01625) 424587 E: jcrgibson@gmail.com *or* james@hthmacc.com

GIBSON, John Murray Hope. b 35. Dur Univ BA 58. Cranmer Hall Dur 58. **d** 60 **p** 61. C Chester le Street *Dur* 60–63; C Stockton 63–68; V Denton and Ingleton 68–75; V Swalwell 75–00; Chapl Dunston Hill Hosp Gateshead 80–93; Chapl Gateshead Health NHS Trust 94–99; rtd 00; PtO *Dur* 01–13; *Newc* from 01. *2 Cathedral Court, London Road, Gloucester GL1 3QE* T: (01452) 416397

GIBSON, Canon John Noël Keith. b 22. Ch Coll Cam MA 48 Lon Univ BD 59. Coll of Resurr Mirfield 45. **d** 47 **p** 48. C S Elmsall *Wakef* 47–51; Antigua 51–56; Virgin Is 56–13; Can All SS Cathl 89–92; rtd 92. *College of St Barnabas, Blackberry Lane, Lingfield RH7 6NJ* E: jnk.gibson24@gmail.com

GIBSON, Kenneth George Goudie. b 54. Glas Univ MA 83 Edin Univ BD 87 Strathclyde Univ PGCE 95. Edin Th Coll 83. **d** 88 **p** 89. C Glas St Marg 88–90; R E Kilbride 90–98; R Carnoustie *Bre* 98–07; PtO 08–14; P-in-c Monifieth from 14. *39 Durham Street, Monifieth, Dundee DD5 4PF* T: (01382) 533493 E: kenneth.gibson1@btinternet.com

GIBSON, Laura Mary. *See* WILFORD, Laura Mary

GIBSON, Lynne Margaret. b 65. St Andr Univ MA 88 TCD BTh 10. CITC 08. **d** 10 **p** 11. C Dundela St Mark *D & D* 10–16; I Ballymacash *Conn* from 16. *St Mark's Rectory, 97 Antrim Road, Lisburn BT28 3EA* T: (028) 9266 2393 M: 07828-516799 E: lynnetigger@gmail.com *or* lynneballym@gmail.com

GIBSON, Nigel Stephen David. b 53. St Barn Coll Adelaide 84. **d** 87 **p** 87. C N Adelaide Ch Ch Australia 87–89; Lect Boston *Linc* 90–91; P-in-c Stamford St Mary and St Mich 91–92; P-in-c Stamford Baron 91–92; R Stamford St Mary and St Martin 92–98; PtO 98–00; V Kempston Transfiguration *St Alb* 00–04; Chapl Milan w Cadenabbia and Varese *Eur* 04–10; Chapl St Jo Cathl and P-in-c Pokfulam Em Hong Kong 10–16; P-in-c Lugano *Eur* from 16. *St Edward the Confessor, via Maraini 6, 6900 Lugano, Switzerland* T: (0041) (92) 921 3938 E: frnigelgibson@gmail.com

GIBSON, Mrs Patricia Elizabeth. b 57. Nottm Univ MA 02. EMMTC 99. **d** 02 **p** 03. C Wigston Magna *Leic* 02–06; TV Gt Berkhamsted, Gt and Lt Gaddesden etc *St Alb* 06–10; Bp's Adv for Women in Min 07–10. *Venskab Barn, Morebath, Tiverton EX16 9AQ* E: revteg1@btinternet.com

GIBSON, Philip Nigel Scott. b 53. St Jo Coll Dur BA 78. Cranmer Hall Dur 79. **d** 79 **p** 80. C Yardley St Edburgha

Birm 79–82; C Stratford-on-Avon w Bishopton *Cov* 82–84; Chapl SW Hosp Lon 84–91; Chapl St Thos Hosp Lon 84–91; Assoc P Newington St Paul *S'wark* 91–92; Chapl Charing Cross Hosp Lon 92–93; Chapl R Lon Hosp (Whitechapel) 93–94; Chapl Bedford Hosp NHS Trust 95–08. *Sillwood, 1 Wood Lane, Aspley Guise, Milton Keynes MK17 8EJ* E: philip.gibson912@btinternet.com

GIBSON, Samuel James. b 89. Birm Univ BA 11 MA 12 PhD 16. St Steph Ho Ox MTh 17. **d** 17 **p** 18. C Solihull *Birm* from 17. *17 Church Hill Close, Solihull B91 3JB* T: 0121-709 0668 E: curate@solihullparish.org.uk

GIBSON, Timothy John. b 80. Ex Univ BA 01 MA 02 PhD 06. SWMTC 12. **d** 14 **p** 15. Dir Reader Tr and Lay Educn SWMTC from 11; NSM Isle Valley *B & W* 14–18; PtO from 18. *Wayside, Hare Lane, Broadway, Ilminster TA19 9LN* T: (01460) 54182 E: timjohngibson@hotmail.co.uk

GIDDINGS, Mrs Jaqueline Mary. b 44. St Aid Coll Dur BA 67. SWMTC 91. **d** 94 **p** 95. C Plympton St Mary *Ex* 94–02; rtd 02. *Grange End, Harrowbeer Lane, Yelverton PL20 6EA* T: (01822) 854825 E: anthonygiddings@btinternet.com

GIFFORD, David Christopher. b 53. Lon Univ BEd 75 Sussex Univ MA 85 Ox Brookes Univ BA 11. Ripon Coll Cuddesdon 08. **d** 11 **p** 12. Chief Exec Coun of Chrs and Jews 06–14; NSM Benson *Ox* 11–14; R Port Glas from 14; R Bridge of Weir from 14; R Kilmacolm from 14. *St Mary's Rectory, Bardrainney Avenue, Port Glasgow PA14 6HB* T: (01475) 705378 M: 07403-740185 E: dgdavid706@gmail.com

GIFFORD, Ms Elizabeth Ann. b 47. St Kath Coll Liv CertEd 72 Open Univ BSc 96. STETS 99. **d** 02 **p** 09. NSM Trowbridge H Trin *Sarum* 02–09; NSM Studley 09–16; PtO 17–18. *14 Innox Mill Close, Trowbridge BA14 9BA* T: (01225) 752756 M: 07903-269587

GIFFORD, Patricia Rose. b 47. **d** 10 **p** 11. NSM Glouc St Jas and All SS and Ch Ch 10–19; rtd 19. *49 Ducie Street, Gloucester GL1 4NZ* T: (01452) 306746 E: patgifford@btopenworld.com

GILBERT, Anne Elizabeth. b 66. Liv Univ BA 88 Bris Univ PGCE 89. All SS Cen for Miss & Min 15. **d** 18 **p** 19. C Dearnley, Wardle and Smallbridge *Man* from 18. *13 Wardle Gardens, Rochdale OL12 9EP* M: 07972-604381 E: annegilbert1966@gmail.com

GILBERT, Anthony John David. b 54. Open Univ BA 91 LRSC 83 MRSC 01. Ripon Coll Cuddesdon 83. **d** 86 **p** 87. C Exning St Martin w Landwade *St E* 86–89; Chapl RAF 89–14; QHC 10–14; TR Three Valleys *Sarum* from 14; RD Sherborne from 18. *The Rectory, Church Road, Thornford, Sherborne DT9 6QE* T: (01935) 873044 M: 07810-760680 E: rector3valleys@gmail.com

GILBERT, Canon Barry. b 46. Leeds Univ BA 67. Coll of Resurr Mirfield 67. **d** 69 **p** 70. C Malvern Link w Cowleigh *Worc* 69–73; P-in-c Bromsgrove All SS 73–81; V 81–83; P-in-c Lower Mitton 83–88; V 88–92; V Stourport and Wilden 92–06; RD Stourport 93–00 and 02–06; P-in-c Brierley Hill 06–07; TR 07–11; Hon Can Worc Cathl 09–11; rtd 11; LtO *Glas* from 11. *Allandale, High Street, New Galloway, Castle Douglas DG7 3RL* T: (01644) 420665 E: barry_gilbert@talk21.com

GILBERT, Clive Franklyn. b 55. City of Liv Coll of HE CertEd 76 BEd 77. SEITE 01. **d** 02 **p** 03. C Paddock Wood *Roch* 02–06; V Dartford St Alb 06–11; V Watchet and Williton *B & W* from 11. *The Vicarage, 24 Priest Street, Williton, Taunton TA4 4NJ* T: (01984) 631005 M: 07952-235762 E: clive.gilbert@btinternet.com

GILBERT, Frederick Joseph. b 29. Lich Th Coll 58. **d** 59 **p** 60. C Westhoughton *Man* 59–62; V Goodshaw 62–68; R Crumpsall St Matt 68–75; RD Cheetham 70–74; RD N Man 74–75; V Rochdale St Aid 75–78; TV Rochdale 78–80; V Westhoughton 80–84; TR 84–87; AD Deane 85–87; R W Bowbrook *Worc* 87–89; R Bowbrook N 89–93; rtd 93; PtO *Worc* from 93. *Freshways, Main Road, Peopleton, Pershore WR10 2EG* T: (01905) 841629 E: fsgilbert@btinternet.com

GILBERT, Hilda. b 57. Lon S Bank Univ BSc 01 Spurgeon's Coll BD 11 RGN 82. St Mellitus Coll 13. **d** 14 **p** 15. NSM Leyton St Mary w St Edw and St Luke *Chelmsf* 14–18; NSM Walthamstow St Andr from 18. *13 Priory Avenue, London E17 7QP* T: (020) 8521 8048 M: 07946-407294 E: gilberthil@aol.com

GILBERT, Canon Howard Neil. b 73. Southn Univ BA 96. Ripon Coll Cuddesdon BTh 05. **d** 05 **p** 06. C Dulwich St Barn *S'wark* 05–08; C Cirencester *Glouc* 09–19; AD 15–18; R Minchinhampton w Box and Amberley from 19; Hon Can Glouc Cathl from 18. *The Rectory, Butt Street, Minchinhampton, Stroud GL6 9JP* T: (01453) 889004 M: 07887-800478 E: father.howard@gmail.com

GILBERT, Mark. *See* GILBERT, Philip Mark

GILBERT, Michael Victor. b 61. Dur Univ BA 84. Trin Coll Bris 92. **d** 94 **p** 95. C Chapeltown *Sheff* 94–97; V Brightside w Wincobank 97–07; Adult Educator Wilson Carlile Coll of Evang 07–12; R Baslow and Eyam *Derby* from 12. *The Rectory, Church Street, Eyam, Hope Valley S32 5QH* T: (01433) 639637 E: thegilberts@thegilberts.f9.co.uk *or* rector@eyamchurch.org

GILBERT, Canon Philip Mark. b 62. Liv Univ BA 84. Coll of Resurr Mirfield 84. **d** 87 **p** 88. C Frodsham *Ches* 87–89; C Stockton Heath 89–92; R Tangmere and Oving *Chich* 92–01; Chapl Seaford Coll and P-in-c Graffham w Woolavington 01–09; P-in-c Chich St Wilfrid 09–10; V 10–15; Chapl Bp Luffa Sch Chich 09–15; RD Chich 11–15; P-in-c Petworth 15–16; R from 16; P-in-c Egdean 15–16; R from 16; RD Petworth from 16; Can and Preb Chich Cathl from 15. *The Rectory, Rectory Lane, Petworth GU28 0DB* T: (01798) 345278 M: 07810-004062 E: frmarkssc@msn.com

GILBERT, Raymond. b 34. AKC 61. **d** 62 **p** 63. C Newbold w Dunston *Derby* 62–66; PV and Succ S'wark Cathl 66–68; P-in-c Stuntney *Ely* 68–74; Prec and Sacr Ely Cathl 68–74; Min Can Cant Cathl 74–79; Hon Min Can from 79; P-in-c Patrixbourne w Bridge and Bekesbourne *Cant* 79–81; V 81–00; RD E Bridge 92–98; rtd 00; PtO *Cant* 09–16. *16 Green Acres, Eythorne, Dover CT15 4LX* T: (01304) 831485

GILBERT, Raymond Frederick. b 44. **d** 93 **p** 94. OLM Stowmarket *St E* 93–10; rtd 10; PtO *St E* from 10. *3 Violet Hill Road, Stowmarket IP14 1NE* T: (01449) 677700

GILBERT, Prof Robert John Crispin. b 74. Hatf Coll Dur BSc 95 Leic Univ PhD 99 Magd Coll Ox MA 05. Ripon Coll Cuddesdon 09. **d** 11 **p** 12. NSM Wolvercote and Wytham *Ox* 11–16; NSM Headington Quarry from 16; Fells' Chapl Magd Coll Ox from 14. *Magdalen College, High Street, Oxford OX1 4AU* T: (01865) 276070 E: gilbert@strubi.ox.ac.uk

GILBERT, Roger Charles. b 46. Ex Coll Ox BA 69 MA 74 Nottm Univ MEd 81. St Steph Ho Ox 69. **d** 71 **p** 72. NSM Bridgwater St Mary w Chilton Trinity *B & W* 71–74; NSM Rugeley *Lich* 74–81; NSM Cannock 81–83; NSM Wednesbury St Jas and St Jo 83–12; NSM Tividale 08–11; NSM W Bromwich St Pet 11–12; NSM Ettingshall 12–16; NSM Armitage 16; PtO 17–19; NSM Wolverhampton St Martin and St Steph from 19. *41 Stafford Road, Cannock WS11 4AF* T: (01543) 570531

GILBERT, Sean William. b 89. St Steph Ho Ox 12. **d** 15 **p** 16. C St Leonards Ch Ch and St Mary etc *Chich* 15–19; V S Norwood St Alb *S'wark* from 19. *6 Dagmar Road, London SE25 6HZ* M: 07535-445512 E: seanwgilbert@msn.com

GILBERTSON, The Ven Michael Robert. b 61. New Coll Ox BA 82 MA 92 St Jo Coll Dur BA 93 Dur Univ PhD 97. Cranmer Hall Dur. **d** 97 **p** 98. C Surbiton St Matt *S'wark* 97–00; V Stranton *Dur* 00–10; AD Hartlepool 02–10; Hon Can Dur Cathl 08–10; Adn Ches from 10; Chapter Can Ches Cathl from 17. *Church House, 5500 Daresbury Park, Daresbury, Warrington WA4 4GE* T: (01928) 718834 ext 253 M: 07921-040154 E: michael.gilbertson@chester.anglican.org

GILCHRIST, David John. b 51. Mert Coll Ox BA 75 MA 79 Maryvale Inst PGCE 08. St Jo Coll Nottm. **d** 79 **p** 80. C Gt Ilford St Andr *Chelmsf* 79–81; C Buckhurst Hill 81–84; Chapl Dover Coll 84–95; Chapl Brentwood Sch 95–12; rtd 12. *18B The Granville, Hotel Road, St Margarets Bay, Dover CT15 6DX* T: (01304) 851805 E: djgilx@btinternet.com

GILCHRIST, Gavin Frank. b 53. AKC 74. Coll of Resurr Mirfield 76. **d** 77 **p** 78. C Newbold w Dunston *Derby* 77–80; C Addlestone *Guildf* 80–84; V Blackpool St Mary *Blackb* 84–92; P-in-c Carl St Herbert w St Steph 92–97; V 97–01; V Tynemouth Cullercoats St Paul *Newc* 01–18; rtd 18. *1 Milton Close, Harrogate HG1 3NB* E: gg00217513@blueyonder.co.uk

GILDAY, Patrick Edward. b 84. Jes Coll Ox BA 05 MSt 07 DPhil 12 LRSM 02. Wycliffe Hall Ox BA 13. **d** 14 **p** 15. C Ascot Heath *Ox* 14–17; R Benson w Ewelme from 17. *Benson Vicarage, Church Road, Benson, Wallingford OX10 6SF* T: (01491) 201668

GILDER, James Bernard. b 85. Magd Coll Cam BA 07 MA Middx Univ PGCE 11. Westcott Ho Cam 16. **d** 19. C Chingford St Edm *Chelmsf* from 19. *44 Hurst Avenue, London E4 8DW* M: 07729-109638 E: jbgilder@hotmail.com

GILDERSLEVE, Paul. b 43. Lon Univ BD. Ridley Hall Cam. **d** 06 **p** 07. NSM Papworth *Ely* 06–17; PtO from 17. *Manor Farm, 14 Alms Hill, Bourn, Cambridge CB23 2SH* T: (01954) 713989 *or* 719318 E: paulg@miscom.co.uk

GILES, Anthony John. b 50. Aston Univ BSc 71 Surrey Univ MSc 78 Homerton Coll Cam PGCE 86 CEng 80 MIET 80. SAOMC 01. **d** 04 **p** 05. NSM Stevenage H Trin *St Alb* 04–09; NSM Norton 09–11; P-in-c High Wych and Gilston w Eastwick 11–15; R 15–17; RD Bishop's Stortford 14–17; rtd 17; PtO *St Alb* from 17. *8 Norton Road, Letchworth Garden City SG6 1AB* T: (01462) 620142 E: anthonyj.giles@ntlworld.com

GILES, Caroline Evelyn. *See* BECKETT, Caroline Evelyn

GILES, Christopher John. b 61. Westcott Ho Cam 14. **d** 16 **p** 17. C Pitsea w Nevendon *Chelmsf* 16–17; C Thorpe Bay from 17. *20 Wansfell Gardens, Southend-on-Sea SS1 3SW* M: 07970-370543 E: rev.christopherg34@gmail.com

GILES, Gordon John. b 66. Lanc Univ BA 88 Magd Coll Cam BA 95 MLitt 95 Middx Univ PhD 13. Ridley Hall Cam 92. **d** 95 **p** 96. C Chesterton Gd Shep *Ely* 95–98; Min Can and Succ St Paul's Cathl *Lon* 98–03; V Enfield Chase St Mary from 03; Dir Post-Ord Tr Edmonton Area from 08. *St Mary Magdalene Vicarage, 30 The Ridgeway, Enfield EN2 8QH* T: (020) 8363 1875 E: gordongiles@me.com

GILES, Graeme John. b 56. Linc Th Coll 82. **d** 85 **p** 86. C Prestbury *Glouc* 85–88; C Paulsgrove *Portsm* 88–96; V Friern Barnet St Pet le Poer *Lon* 96–04. *30A Vine Road, East Molesey KT8 9LF* M: 07981-708606 E: graeme@priest.com

GILES, Canon John Robert. b 36. Em Coll Cam BA 60 MA 65. Ripon Hall Ox 60. **d** 61 **p** 62. C Lowestoft St Marg *Nor* 61–65; Chapl UEA 65–72; R Kidbrooke St Jas *S'wark* 72–79; Sub-Dean Greenwich 74–79; V Sheff St Mark Broomhall 79–87; Ind Chapl 79–92; Can Res Sheff Cathl 87–92; V Lee Gd Shep w St Pet *S'wark* 92–98; rtd 98; PtO *St E* from 99. *25 The Terrace, Aldeburgh IP15 5HJ* T: (01728) 452319

GILES, Peter Michael Osmaston. b 40. Solicitor 65. S Dios Minl Tr Scheme 85. **d** 88 **p** 89. Hon C Wootton Bassett *Sarum* 88–90; Lic to RD Calne 91–13; RD Calne 98–03; Chapl St Mary's Sch Calne 00–13; PtO *Sarum* from 14. *The Old Vicarage, Honeyhill, Royal Wootton Bassett, Swindon SN4 7DY* T: (01793) 852643 E: gilesoldvic@talk21.com

GILES, The Very Revd Richard Stephen. b 40. Newc Univ BA 63 MLitt 88 MRTPI 71. Cuddesdon Coll 64. **d** 65 **p** 66. C Higham Ferrers w Chelveston *Pet* 65–68; PtO *Ox* 69; C Oakengates *Lich* 70; C Stevenage St Geo *St Alb* 71–75; P-in-c Howdon Panns *Newc* 75–76; TV Willington 76–79; Bp's Adv for Planning *Pet* 79–87; V Pet St Jude 79–87; Par Development Officer *Wakef* 87–99; P-in-c Huddersfield St Thos 87–93; V 93–99; Hon Can Wakef Cathl 94–99; Can Th Wakef Cathl 98–99; Dean Philadelphia USA 99–08; rtd 08; PtO *Newc* from 09. *5 Lovaine Row, North Shields NE30 4HF* T: 0191-258 7621 E: tynegiles@talktalk.net

GILES, Sarah Jayne. *See* MORRIS, Sarah Jayne

GILES, Susan Jane. b 58. BSc. **dss** 83 **d** 92 **p** 94. Balsall Heath St Paul *Birm* 83–85; Asst Chapl Southmead Hosp Bris 86–90; Asst Chapl HM Rem Cen Pucklechurch 90–96; Asst Chapl HM Pris Bris 92–98; Chapl HM Pris Shepton Mallet 98–01; P-in-c Stockton H Trin *Dur* 01–09; P-in-c Stockton H Trin w St Mark 09–12; Chapl Ian Ramsey Sch Stockton 01–09; V Anglesey Gp *Ely* from 12; RD Fordham and Quy from 17. *The Vicarage, 86 High Street, Bottisham, Cambridge CB5 9BA* T: (01223) 812726 E: suethevic@btinternet.com

GILES, Canon Timothy David. b 46. FCA 69. Oak Hill Th Coll 88. **d** 90 **p** 91. C Ipswich St Marg *St E* 90–94; C Reigate St Mary *S'wark* 94–99; P-in-c W Wickham St Jo 99–03; V 03–10; rtd 10; Hon Can Offa Nigeria from 06. *Lea Cottage, Hillhead Road, Kergilliack, Falmouth TR11 5PA* T: (01326) 377094

GILKES, Donald Martin. b 47. St Jo Coll Nottm 78. **d** 80 **p** 81. C Conisbrough *Sheff* 80–84; P-in-c Balne 84–86; P-in-c Hensall 84–86; TV Gt Snaith 86–88; V Whittle-le-Woods *Blackb* 88–02; V Normanton *Wakef* 02–12; rtd 12; PtO *Roch* from 12. *35 Tradescant Drive, Meopham, Gravesend DA13 0EL* E: don.gilkes1@gmail.com

GILKS, Canon Peter Martin. b 51. Nottm Univ BMus 72 SRN 77. Ripon Coll Cuddesdon 82. **d** 84 **p** 85. C Bitterne Park *Win* 84–87; TV Basingstoke 87–93; R Abbotts Ann and Upper Clatford and Goodworth Clatford 93–98; V Boyatt Wood 98–06; V Chilworth w N Baddesley 06–10; P-in-c Ampfield 08–10; V Ampfield, Chilworth and N Baddesley 10–15; TR Portway and Danebury 15–19; Hon Can Win Cathl 16–19; rtd 19. *1 Bramble Lane, Crediton EX17 1DA* E: peter.gilks@ntlworld.com

GILL, Canon Alan Gordon. b 42. Sarum & Wells Th Coll 73. **d** 75 **p** 76. C Wimborne Minster *Sarum* 75–78; R Winterbourne Stickland and Turnworth etc 78–86; V Verwood 86–00; TR Gillingham 00–04; V Gillingham and Milton-on-Stour 04–08; Can and Preb Sarum Cathl 99–08; rtd 09; PtO *Sarum* from 09. *1 Cheshire Close, Salisbury SP2 9JT* T: (01722) 325239 E: erznmine1@gmail.com

GILL, Alec John. b 79. Trin Coll Bris 11. **d** 13 **p** 14. C Thatcham *Ox* 13–16; C Vale from 16. *The Vicarage, Winter Lane, West Hanney, Wantage OX12 0LF* M: 07954-433513 E: revalec@hotmail.co.uk

GILL, Mrs Carol Ann. b 42. Lady Mabel Coll TCert 71. NOC 96. **d** 99 **p** 00. NSM Hanging Heaton *Wakef* 99–07; P-in-c 02–07; rtd 07; PtO *Wakef* 08–14; *Leeds* from 14. *6 Queen's Crescent, Ossett WF5 8AU* T: (01924) 276821 M: 07946-038562

GILL, David Alan. b 64. Coll of Resurr Mirfield 98. **d** 00 **p** 01. C Devizes St Jo w St Mary *Sarum* 00–04; P-in-c Brockworth *Glouc* 04–10; V 10–11; P-in-c Abenhall w Mitcheldean 11–17; R from 17; C Westbury-on-Severn w Flaxley, Blaisdon etc from 11; C Huntley and Longhope, Churcham and Bulley from 12. *The Rectory, The Stenders, Mitcheldean GL17 0HX* T: (01594) 542952 E: dgill@houseofgill.org *or* fr.d.gill@gmail.com

GILL, Preb David Brian Michael. b 55. Southn Univ BTh 88. Sarum & Wells Th Coll 83. **d** 86 **p** 87. C Honiton, Gittisham, Combe Raleigh, Monkton etc *Ex* 86–89; C Teignmouth, Ideford w Luton, Ashcombe etc 89–91; TV Ex St Thos and Em 91–05; RD Christianity 03–05; P-in-c Tamerton Foliot 05–17; C Southway 06–17; TR Tamerton Foliot and Southway from 17; RD Plymouth Moorside 09–15; RD Plymouth City from 17; Preb Ex Cathl from 17. *The Vicarage, 53 Whitson Cross Lane, Tamerton Foliot, Plymouth PL5 4NT* T: (01752) 771033 E: dbmgill@tiscali.co.uk

GILL, Miss Helen Barbara. b 61. K Alfred's Coll Win BEd 87. Cranmer Hall Dur. **d** 99 **p** 00. C Newc St Gabr 99–04; P-in-c Tynemouth St Jo 04–17; V Byker St Silas from 17. *40 Heaton Grove, Newcastle upon Tyne NE6 5NP* T: 0191-276 5005 E: helenbarbara1999@hotmail.co.uk

GILL, Michael John. b 59. K Coll Lon BA 81 AKC 81 Univ of Wales (Cardiff) BD 85. St Mich Coll Llan 82. **d** 85 **p** 86. Min Can St Woolos Cathl *Mon* 85–90; Chapl St Woolos Hosp Newport 87–90; Succ Heref Cathl and C Heref St Jo 90–93; TV Ebbw Vale *Mon* 93–96; V Tonypandy w Clydach Vale *Llan* 96–09; R Cranford *Lon* from 09. *The Rectory, 34 High Street, Cranford, Hounslow TW5 9RG* T: (020) 8897 8836 E: fathermichaelgill@gmail.com

GILL, Paul Joseph. b 45. Melbourne Coll of Div MMin 07. Ridley Coll Melbourne 73. **d** 74 **p** 74. C Applecross Australia 74–76; C Birm St Martin 77–79; V Pype Hayes 79–89; Perm to Offic Perth Australia 89–93; R Perth St Paul 93–00; Sen Chapl HM Min of Justice 00–10; rtd 10; Hon C Heref S Wye 11–13; PtO from 13. *7 Camelot Close, Hereford HR4 9XH* T: (01432) 507146 M: 07765-660418 E: pandagill@talktalk.net *or* pandagill1@gmail.com

GILL, Peter Stephen. b 48. FCA 79. **d** 09 **p** 10. OLM Exning St Martin w Landwade *St E* 09–13; NSM 13–18; rtd 18. *11 Isinglass Close, Newmarket CB8 8HX* T: (01638) 660335 M: 07762-608031 E: petergill861@btinternet.com

GILL, Canon Robin Morton. b 44. K Coll Lon BD 66 AKC 66 Lon Univ PhD 69 Birm Univ MSocSc 72. **d** 68 **p** 69. C Rugby St Andr *Cov* 68–71; Papua New Guinea 71–72; Lect Th Edin Univ 72–86; Sen Lect 86–88; Assoc Dean Faculty of Div 85–88; P-in-c Edin SS Phil and Jas 73–75; P-in-c Newc 75–87; P-in-c Coldstream *Edin* 87–92; Wm Leech Prof Applied Th Newc Univ 88–92; Mich Ramsey Prof Modern Th Kent Univ 92–11; Prof Th from 11; Hon Prov Can Cant Cathl from 92; AD N Downs 02–09; P-in-c Hollingbourne and Hucking w Leeds and Broomfield 03–11; Hon C 11–14; PtO from 14; Can Th *Eur* from 12. *2 Copse End, Hadley Gardens, Hollingbourne, Maidstone ME17 1UF* T: (01622) 884120 E: r.gill@kent.ac.uk

GILL, Canon Ruth Montcrieff. b 48. CITC 01. **d** 04 **p** 05. NSM Cloughjordan w Borrisokane etc *L & K* 04–06; NSM Birr w Lorrha, Dorrha and Lockeen from 06; Can Limerick, Killaloe and Clonfert Cathls from 16. *Kilgolan House, Kilcormac, Birr, Co Offaly, Republic of Ireland* T: (00353) (57) 913 5341 M: 87-948 4402 E: ruth_gill40@outlook.ie

GILL, Miss Sandra Julie. b 67. N Riding Coll of Educn BEd 90 Rolle Coll MEd 01 Ex Univ BTh 08. SWMTC 03. **d** 06 **p** 07. NSM Kingsteignton and Teigngrace *Ex* from 06. *58 Furze Cap, Kingsteignton, Newton Abbot TQ12 3TF* T: (01626) 355287

GILL, Miss Sarah Siddique. b 77. Punjab Univ BA 96 MA 01. Qu Coll Birm 08. **d** 11 **p** 12. C Shipley St Paul *Bradf* 11–14; *Leeds* 14–15; C-in-c Bishop Auckland Woodhouse Close CD *Dur* from 15. *18 Watling Road, Bishop Auckland DL14 6RP* T: (01388) 664268 M: 07584-498390 E: sarah_siddique_gill@yahoo.co.uk

GILL, Simon David. b 66. Southn Univ BSc 87 PhD 91. St Jo Coll Nottm BTh 00. **d** 01 **p** 02. C Frinton *Chelmsf* 01–05; P-in-c Sudbury w Ballingdon and Brundon *St E* 05–19; RD Sudbury 16–19; P-in-c Long Stanton w St Mich *Ely* from 19; P-in-c Over from 19; P-in-c Swavesey from 19; P-in-c Willingham from 19. *The Vicarage, Horseware, Over, Cambridge CB24 5NX* E: simon@5folds.org.uk

GILL, Miss Susan Mary. b 62. Girton Coll Cam BA 84 MA 87. CPFA 91. Ripon Coll Cuddesdon 13. **d** 16 **p** 17. NSM Amersham *Ox* from 16. *137 Carver Hill Road, High Wycombe HP11 2UQ* T: (01494) 451485 M: 07779-575702 E: susangill01@gmail.com

GILL, Timothy Charles. b 66. Newc Univ BA 88 Jes Coll Cam MPhil 93 Leeds Univ PhD 08. Westcott Ho Cam 89.

d 92 p 93. C N Hull St Mich *York* 92–96; P-in-c Sculcoates St Paul w Ch Ch and St Silas 96–98; P-in-c Hull St Mary Sculcoates 96–98; V York St Luke 98–02; R Adel *Ripon* 02–08; V Roby *Liv* 08–16; V Ecclesfield *Sheff* from 16. *The Vicarage, 230 The Wheel, Ecclesfield, Sheffield S35 9ZB* T: 0114-257 0002 M: 07853-293294 E: ttimgill@aol.com *or* tim.gill@sheffield.anglican.org

GILL, Wilson Ernest. b 55. SAOMC. d 05 p 06. C Walton H Trin *Ox* 05–09; V Southall Em *Lon* from 09. *37 Dormers Wells Lane, Southall UB1 3HX* T: (020) 8843 9556 E: wilsongill37@gmail.com *or* vicar.ecs@gmail.com

GILLANDERS, Jill Margaret. b 56. St Hild Coll 16. d 18 p 19. NSM Thirsk *York* from 18. *Finkle Cottage, Little Thirkleby, Thirkleby, Thirsk YO7 2AZ* T: (01845) 501174

GILLARD, David John. b 66. Ridley Hall Cam 96. d 98 p 99. C Seaford w Sutton *Chich* 98–02; P-in-c Eastbourne St Elisabeth 02–06; V from 06; RD Eastbourne from 15. *The Vicarage, 11 Baldwin Avenue, Eastbourne BN21 1UJ* T: (01323) 649728

GILLARD, Linda Ann. b 53. York St Jo Univ BA 09. Yorks Min Course 15. d 17 p 19. NSM Marfleet *York* 17–18; NSM Kingston upon Hull St Alb from 18. *15 Rillington Avenue, Cottingham HU16 5HP* M: 07955-891226 E: linda.gillard@hey.nhs.uk *or* revlinza2609@gmail.com

GILLARD-FAULKNER, Mrs Sarah Kate. b 80. Coll of Ripon & York St Jo BA 01 Glos Univ PGCE 02. St Mich Coll Llan BTh 06. d 09. C Abertillery w Cwmtillery *Mon* 09–10; C Abertillery w Cwmtillery w Llanhilleth etc 10–12; PtO *Llan* 13–14; Dn and Sub-Prior Abergavenny St Mary w Llanwenarth Citra *Mon* 14–17; Bp's Chapl 14–17; Chapl HM Pris Onley from 17. *HM Prison Onley, Willoughby, Rugby CV23 8AP* T: (01788) 523400

GILLESPIE, Bridget Jane. b 62. St Hild Coll 17. d 19. NSM Kirkbymoorside w Gillamoor, Farndale etc *York* from 19. *Fir Tree House, High Lane, Beadlam, Nawton, York YO62 7SX*

GILLESPIE, Canon David Ivan. b 68. TCD BTh 01. CITC 98. d 01 p 02. C Agherton *Conn* 01–04; I Moy w Charlemont *Arm* 04–09; I Dublin St Ann and St Steph *D & G* from 09; Can Ch Ch Cathl Dublin from 14. *88 Mount Anville Wood, Lower Kilmacud Road, Dublin 14, Republic of Ireland* T: (00353) (1) 288 0663 *or* 676 7727 M: 86-026 7528 E: digillespie@eircom.net

GILLESPIE, Jonathan Charles. b 64. NUU BSc 87 Cranfield Univ MSc 97 Oak Hill Th Coll BA 09. Cranmer Hall Dur 14. d 16 p 17. C Windermere St Mary and Troutbeck *Carl* from 16. *Burnthwaite, Kendal Road, Bowness-on-Windermere, Windermere LA23 3EW* M: 07951-922924 E: gillespie.jc@gmail.com

GILLETT, Brian Alan Michael. b 42. MRICS 73. Chich Th Coll. d 82 p 83. C Tupsley *Heref* 82–86; R Kingstone w Clehonger, Eaton Bishop etc 86–97; V Batonsborough w Butleigh, W Bradley etc *B & W* 97–09; Warden of Readers Wells Adnry 00–02; rtd 09; PtO *Bris* from 09; *B & W* from 15. *1 Barn Close, Somerton TA11 6PH* T: (01458) 272738 E: gillett546@btinternet.com *or* alary073@gmail.com

✠**GILLETT, The Rt Revd David Keith.** b 45. Leeds Univ BA 65 MPhil 68. Oak Hill Th Coll 66. d 68 p 69 c 99. C Watford St Luke *St Alb* 68–71; Sec Pathfinders and CYFA N Area 71–74; Lect St Jo Coll Nottm 74–79; Ch of Ireland Renewal Cen 79–82; V Luton Lewsey St Hugh *St Alb* 82–88; Prin Trin Coll Bris 88–99; Hon Can Bris Cathl 91–99; Suff Bp Bolton *Man* 99–08; rtd 08; Hon Asst Bp Nor from 08; Dioc Interfaith Adv from 10; PtO from 13. *10 Burton Close, Diss IP22 4YJ* T: (01379) 640309 E: dkgillett@btinternet.com

GILLEY, Margaret Mary. b 54. St Andr Univ MTheol 76 Dur Univ PhD 97. NEOC 97. d 00 p 01. C Birtley *Dur* 00–03; P-in-c Stockton St Mark 03; V 03–09; V Elton 03–09; Assoc P Lanchester Deanery 09–11; V Bensham and Teams from 11. *St Chad's Vicarage, Dunsmuir Grove, Gateshead NE8 4QL* T: 0191-478 6338 E: meg.gilley@durham.anglican.org

GILLHAM, Catherine Anne. b 73. Southn Univ BN 95. Trin Coll Bris BA 09. d 09 p 10. C Kempshott *Win* 09–13; CF from 13. *c/o MOD Chaplains (Army)* T: (01264) 383430 F: 381824 M: 07873-525602 E: catgillham@hotmail.com

GILLHAM, Martin John. b 45. Wilson Carlile Coll IDC 66 Qu Coll Birm 72. d 75 p 76. C Whitley Ch Ch *Ox* 75–78; TV Crowmarsh Gifford w Newnham Murren 78–79; TV Wallingford w Crowmarsh Gifford etc 79–83; V Kintbury w Avington 83–94; Dioc Lay Min Adv and Warden of Readers 89–97; P-in-c W Wycombe w Bledlow Ridge, Bradenham and Radnage 94–00; R 00; Prov Chapl Third Order SSF 95–99; P-in-c Norham and Duddo *Newc* 00–04; V 04–09; P-in-c Cornhill w Carham 00–09; P-in-c Branxton 00–09; AD Norham 05–09; rtd 09; PtO *Newc* 10–13; P-in-c Shilbottle 13–17; PtO from 17. *2 Duddo Farm Cottages,*

Duddo, Berwick-upon-Tweed TD15 2PS T: (01890) 820533 E: martingillham@btinternet.com

GILLHAM, Mrs Patricia Anne. b 40. Wilson Carlile Coll IDC 66 Ox Min Course 90. d 93 p 94. Par Dn Kintbury w Avington *Ox* 93–94; C 94–95; C W Wycombe w Bledlow Ridge, Bradenham and Radnage 95–00; rtd 00; PtO *Newc* from 00. *2 Duddo Farm Cottages, Duddo, Berwick-upon-Tweed TD15 2PS* T: (01890) 820533 E: gillysofduddo@gmail.com

GILLIAN, Patricia Julie. b 54. All SS Cen for Miss & Min 14. d 16 p 17. OLM Saddleworth *Man* from 16. *53 Burnedge Fold Road, Grasscroft, Oldham OL4 4EE* T: (01457) 870162 M: 07967-852149 E: patgillian54@gmail.com

GILLIBRAND, John Nigel. b 60. Ox Univ BA 82 MA 86 Lon Univ PGCE 83. St Steph Ho Ox BTh 87. d 88 p 89. C Dolgellau w Llanfachreth and Brithdir etc *Ban* 88–90; C Llanbeblig w Caernarfon and Betws Garmon etc 90–91; R Ffestiniog w Blaenau Ffestiniog 91–97; V Llandegfan w Llandysilio 97–02; Nat Co-ord (Wales) Nat Autistic Soc 02–04; P-in-c Llangeler w Pen-Boyr *St D* 04–10; V 10–16; V Llandeilo Tal-y-bont *S & B* from 16. *The Vicarage, 28 Bolgoed Road, Pontarddulais, Swansea SA4 8JE* T: (01792) 881965

GILLIBRAND, Margaret Ann Jane. b 43. d 01 p 02. OLM Deal St Leon and St Rich and Sholden *Cant* 01–04; PtO *Eur* 04–07; Asst Chapl Poitou-Charentes 07–09; NSM Whitstable *Cant* 11–13; rtd 13; PtO *Blackb* from 14. *128 Devonshire Road, Chorley PR7 2DJ* E: cornerstone161@yahoo.co.uk

GILLIES, Mrs Jennifer Susan. b 63. Westmr Coll Ox BEd 85. SNWTP 07. d 10 p 11. C Bidston *Ches* 10–13; R Bromborough from 13. *The Rectory, Mark Rake, Wirral CH62 2DH* T: 0151-201 9002 E: rector@stbarnabasbromborough.org.uk

✠**GILLIES, The Rt Revd Robert Arthur.** b 51. Edin Univ BD 77 St Andr Univ PhD 91. Edin Th Coll 73. d 77 p 78 c 07. C Falkirk *Edin* 77–80; C Edin Ch St 80–84; Chapl Napier Tech Coll 80–84; Chapl Dundee Univ *Bre* 84–90; R St Andrews St Andr *St And* 91–07; Dioc Dir of Ords 96–07; Can St Ninian's Cathl Perth 97–07; Dean St Andr 07; Bp Ab 07–16; rtd 16; PtO *Ab* from 19. *4 Kilrymont Place, St Andrews KY16 8DH* T: (01334) 476738 E: ragillies1@gmail.com

GILLIES, Miss Sheila Jennifer. b 50. St Martin's Coll Lanc TCert 71. d 06 p 07. OLM Childwall All SS *Liv* from 06. *190 Thomas Drive, Liverpool L14 3LE* T: 0151-228 4304

GILLINGHAM, Michael John. b 46. Hull Univ MA 90. Chich Th Coll 68. d 71 p 72. C Llanharan w Peterston-super-Montem *Llan* 71–73; C Skewen 73–76; PtO 79–80; TV Kirkby *Liv* 76–77; Youth Chapl Woodchurch *Ches* 77–79; Sen Youth Worker (Bedfordshire) *St Alb* 80–83; PtO 80–83; TV Sheff Manor 83–88; R Frecheville 88–16; Chapl RNR 90–92; Chapl S Yorks Police *Sheff* 93–16; rtd 16; PtO *Sheff* from 16. *14 Nethergreen Gardens, Killamarsh, Sheffield S21 1FX* T: 0114-327 7376 M: 07764-606456 E: mgillingham@talktalk.net

GILLINGHAM, Mrs Stephanie Ruth. b 60. W Lon Inst of HE CertEd 82 Open Univ BA 86 Man Univ MEd 06. NTMTC BA 09. d 09 p 10. C Galleywood Common *Chelmsf* from 09; P-in-c Widford 13–18; R from 18; C Moulsham St Jo from 13; C Moulsham St Luke from 13. *Widford Rectory, 3 Canuden Road, Chelmsford CM1 2SU* T: (01245) 477818 E: stephaniegillingham@hotmail.co.uk

GILLINGHAM, Prof Susan. b 51. St Jo Coll Nottm BTh 73 Keble Coll Ox PGCE 74 MA 80 DPhil 87 Ox Univ DD 15. d 18. C Ox St Barn and St Paul w St Thos from 18; Can Th Ex Cathl from 18. *43 Cranham Street, Oxford OX2 6DD* M: 07711-272076 E: susan.gillingham@worc.ox.ac.uk *or* susan.gillingham@theology.ox.ac.uk

GILLINGS, The Ven Richard John. b 45. St Chad's Coll Dur BA 67. Linc Th Coll 68. d 70 p 71. C Altrincham St Geo *Ches* 70–75; P-in-c Stockport St Thos 75–77; R 77–83; P-in-c Stockport St Pet 78–83; TR Birkenhead Priory 83–93; V Bramhall 93–05; RD Birkenhead 85–93; Hon Can Ches Cathl 92–94; Adn Macclesfield 94–10; rtd 11; PtO *Ches* from 11; Hon C Rothiemurchus *Mor* from 11; Hon C Grantown-on-Spey from 11. *Culvardie, Deshar Road, Boat of Garten PH24 3BN* T: (01479) 831365 E: richard.gillings698@btinternet.com

GILLINGS, Mrs Ruth Elizabeth. b 63. d 12 p 15. NSM Atworth w Shaw and Whitley *Sarum* from 12; Chapl St Monica Trust Bris from 18. *31 Westlands Lane, Beanacre, Melksham SN12 7QE* T: (01225) 700278 E: ruthgillings@sky.com

✠**GILLION, The Rt Revd Alan Robert.** b 51. LRAM 73. Sarum & Wells Th Coll 81. d 83 p 84 c 14. C E Dereham *Nor* 83–86; C Richmond St Mary w St Matthias and St Jo *S'wark* 86–90; P-in-c Discovery Bay CH Hong Kong 90–98; Chapl Shek Pik Pris 90–98; Bp Kensington's Officer for Evang *Lon* 98–01; P-in-c Upper Chelsea St Sav and St Simon 01–02; V 02–08; R Upper Chelsea H Trin 08–11; R Upper Chelsea H Trin and St Sav 11–14; AD Chelsea 04–11; Bp Riverina Australia 14–18; rtd 18; Hon Asst Bp Linc from 18.

7 Peachwood Close, Grantham NG31 8QP M: 07465-696419
E: robgillion@hotmail.com

GILLON, Patrick. b 51. WMMTC 05. **d** 08 **p** 09. NSM
Kingstanding St Mark *Birm* 08–11; PtO *Lich* 11–14;
NSM Small Heath *Birm* 12–13; Chapl HM Pris Birm
from 13. *HM Prison Birmingham, Winson Green Road,
Birmingham B18 4AS* T: 0121-598 8000 M: 07792-635831
E: patrick_gillon2000@yahoo.co.uk

GILLUM, Thomas Alan. b 55. Ex Univ BSc 76. Cranmer
Hall Dur 87. **d** 89 **p** 90. C Brompton H Trin w Onslow
Square St Paul *Lon* 89–94; P-in-c Paddington St Steph w
St Luke 94–04; P-in-c S Kensington St Jude 04–06; Warden
Community of St Jude 06–11; P-in-c Isleworth St Jo 11–12; V
12–14; V Isleworth St Jo w St Mary 15–17; Bp's Dom Chapl
S'well 17–18; V Nottingham St Mary Lace Market from 18. *20
Cavendish Road East, Nottingham NG7 1BB* T: 0115-958 2105
E: tom.gillum@stmarynotts.org

GILMARTIN, Frances. *See* CLARKE, Frances

GILMORE, David Samuel. b 70. Univ of Ulster BSc 92 QUB
MSSc 95 Anglia Poly Univ MA 05 CQSW 92. EAMTC 01.
d 03 **p** 04. C Basildon St Martin *Chelmsf* 03–04; C Danbury
04–08; R Soho St Anne w St Thos and St Pet *Lon* 08–10.
Address temp unknown E: davidgilmore@btinternet.com

GILMORE, Canon Henry. b 51. Man Univ BA 72 TCD
BD 82. CITC 75. **d** 75 **p** 76. C Arm St Mark w Aghavilly
75–78; C Dublin St Patr Cathl Gp *D & G* 78–81; I Stranorlar
w Meenglas and Kilteevogue *D & R* 81–84; I Achill w
Dugort, Castlebar and Turlough *T, K & A* 84–90; I Moville
w Greencastle, Donagh, Cloncha etc *D & R* 91–11;
I Tullyaughnish w Kilmacrennan and Killygarvan from
11; Can Raphoe Cathl from 01. *The Rectory, Ramelton,
Letterkenny, Co Donegal, Republic of Ireland* T: (00353) (74)
915 1013 E: tkkgparishes@hotmail.com

GILMOUR, Miss Erin Victoria. b 81. Trin Coll Bris 17. **d** 19.
C Reigate St Mary *S'wark* from 19. *3 St Clair Close, Reigate
RH2 0QB* M: 07719-830624 E: erin.gilmour@live.co.uk

GILMOUR, Ian Hedley. b 57. Ex Univ LLB Lon Univ BD.
Wycliffe Hall Ox 80. **d** 83 **p** 84. C Harold Wood *Chelmsf*
83–86; C Thame w Towersey *Ox* 86–91; V Streatham Vale
H Redeemer *S'wark* from 91. *The Vicarage, Churchmore Road,
London SW16 5UZ* T: (020) 8765 9923

GILPIN, Martin Leonard. b 49. Imp Coll Lon BSc 72
Magd Coll Ox DPhil 75. **d** 13 **p** 14. OLM Surrey
Weald *Guildf* from 13. *Yendaayar, Parkgate Road,
Newdigate, Dorking RH5 5DX* T: (01306) 631485
E: martin.gilpin@btinternet.com

GILPIN, Canon Richard John. b 45. Lon Univ BSc 66. Wells
Th Coll 67. **d** 70 **p** 71. C Davyhulme Ch Ch *Man* 70–74;
Pastor Gustav Adolf Berlin EKD 74–77; R Heaton Norris Ch
w All SS *Man* 77–83; R Chorlton-cum-Hardy St Clem 83–99;
AD Hulme 95–99; V Norley, Crowton and Kingsley *Ches*
99–07; RD Frodsham 03–06; Hon Can Ches Cathl 04–06;
rtd 07; PtO *Ches* from 08. *4 Smithy Close, Shocklach, Malpas
SY14 7BX* T: (01829) 250413 E: dick@shocklach.plus.com

GILROY, Peter William. b 62. Univ of Wales (Ban) MTh 09.
Ridley Hall Cam 09. **d** 11 **p** 12. C Kingsteignton *S'well* 11–14;
TV Eccleston Team *Liv* 14–18; TV Binsey *Carl* from 18.
The Vicarage, Ireby, Wigton CA7 1EX T: (016973) 71659
E: peterwgilroy@gmail.com

GIMSON, Francis Herbert. b 54. Reading Univ BSc 79. St Jo
Coll Nottm 83. **d** 86 **p** 87. C Menston w Woodhead *Bradf*
86–89; C Barnoldswick w Bracewell 89–91; V Langleybury
St Paul *St Alb* 91–02; P-in-c Downton *Sarum* 02–06; P-in-c
Redlynch and Morgan's Vale 04–06; TR Forest and Avon
from 06. *The Vicarage, Lode Lane, Downton, Salisbury
SP5 3QA* T: (01725) 510326 E: fhg@jf1990.co.uk

GINEVER, Paul Michael John. b 49. AKC 71. **d** 72 **p** 73. C
Davyhulme Ch Ch *Man* 72–75; Australia 76–77; C Tettenhall
Wood *Lich* 77–80; C Halesowen *Worc* 80; TV 80–86; P-in-c Gt
Malvern Ch Ch 86–98; V S Hayling *Portsm* 98–14; rtd 14; PtO
Portsm from 15. *33 Cotton Road, Portsmouth PO3 6FL* T: (023)
9217 4692

GINGRICH, Dale Robert. b 64. Midland Lutheran Coll (USA)
BSc 86 Lutheran Th Sem Gettysburg MDiv 93. EAMTC 03.
d 04 **p** 05. NSM Shingay Gp *Ely* 04–08; TV Gaywood *Nor*
08–16; Dioc Ecum Officer 09–16; V Bloxham w Milcombe
and S Newington *Ox* from 16. *St Mary's Vicarage, Church Street,
Bloxham, Banbury OX15 4ET* T: (01295) 720252 M: 07982-
627703 E: dalegingrich@hotmail.com

GINN, Canon Richard John. b 51. Lon Univ BD 77 Dur Univ
MLitt 05 ACIB 73 Lambeth STh 85. Oak Hill Th Coll 75
Cranmer Hall Dur 77. **d** 79 **p** 80. C Hornsey Ch Ch *Lon*
79–82; C Highgate St Mich 82–85; V Westleton w Dunwich
St E 85–08; V Darsham 85–08; P-in-c Yoxford, Peasenhall and
Sibton 01–08; P-in-c Middleton cum Fordley and Theberton
w Eastbridge 01–08; V Yoxmere 08–13; Hon Can St E Cathl

01–13; rtd 13; PtO *St E* from 13. *Wisteria Cottage, The Street,
Hacheston, Woodbridge IP13 0DS* E: r.ginn@btinternet.com

GINNELLY, Yvonne Anne. **d** 11 **p** 12. NSM Monkstown
D & G 11–14; NSM Dublin St Ann and St Steph
from 14. *Alexandra College, Milltown Road, Milltown,
Dublin 6, Republic of Ireland* M: (00353) 87-699 8238
E: yvonneginelly@gmail.com

GINNO, Albert Charles. b 31. CA Tr Coll 51 Lon Coll of
Div 66. **d** 68 **p** 69. C Kemp Town St Mark and St Matt
Chich 68–72; P-in-c E Hoathly 72–83; V Westham 83–96;
rtd 96; PtO *Chich* from 96. *106 Sorrel Drive, Eastbourne
BN23 8BJ* T: (01323) 761479

GIRLING, Andrew Martin. b 40. Em Coll Cam BA 63 MA 67.
Wycliffe Hall Ox 63. **d** 65 **p** 66. C Luton w E Hyde *St Alb*
65–69; Chapl Hull Univ *York* 69–75; V Dringhouses 75–00;
Can and Preb York Minster 97–00; P-in-c Thurlestone w S
Milton *Ex* 00–02; R Thurlestone, S Milton, W Alvington etc
02–08; rtd 08; PtO *Ex* from 08. *2 Mead Drive, Thurlestone,
Kingsbridge TQ7 3TA*

GIRLING, David Frederick Charles. b 33. Kelham Th Coll 49
Edin Th Coll 58. **d** 61 **p** 62. C Caister *Nor* 61–65; C Leigh
St Clem *Chelmsf* 65–66; CF 66–83; V Prittlewell St Luke
Chelmsf 83–98; rtd 98; PtO *Nor* 98–13. *37 Dell Road East,
Lowestoft NR33 9LA* T: (01502) 567426

GIRLING, Ian John. b 53. Oak Hill Th Coll 03. **d** 05 **p** 06. C
Hubberston St D 05–08; TV Aberystwyth 08–17; rtd 17; PtO
St D from 17; *B & W* from 17; *Eur* from 18. *22 Quantock
Road, Weston-super-Mare BS23 4DT* T: (01934) 420411
E: iangirling@yahoo.co.uk

GIRLING, Stephen Paul. b 61. Southn Univ BSc 83. Trin Coll
Bris BA 91. **d** 91 **p** 92. C Ogley Hay *Lich* 91–95; TV S Molton
w Nymet St George, High Bray etc *Ex* 95–01; RD S Molton
97–01; V Crofton *Portsm* 01–15; RD Fareham 08–13; Hon
Can Portsm Cathl 11–15; C Bath Abbey w St Jas *B & W* from
15. *26 Castle Gardens, Bath BA2 2AN* E: spgirling@gmail.com

GIRLING, Canon Timothy Havelock. b 43. St Aid
Birkenhead 63. **d** 67 **p** 68. C Wickford *Chelmsf* 67–70;
C Luton w E Hyde *St Alb* 70–74; C Luton All SS w St Pet
74–80; Chapl Luton and Dunstable Hosp 74–80; R Northill
w Moggerhanger *St Alb* 80–89; Chapl Glenfield Hosp NHS
Trust Leic 89–00; Chapl Glenfield Hosp 89–93; Chapl Univ
Hosps Leic NHS Trust 00–04; Hon Can Leic Cathl 97–04;
rtd 04; Chapl Leics Partnership NHS Trust from 04; PtO
Pet 04–08; *Leic* 04–10; *Blackb* from 17. *5 Jefferson Close,
Lancaster LA1 5EZ* T: (01524) 942113 M: 07947-026430
E: timothy.girling@gmail.com

GIRTCHEN, John Christopher. b 54. Linc Th Coll 94. **d** 96
p 97. C Bourne *Linc* 96–00; V Barrow and Goxhill from
00. *The Vicarage, Thornton Street, Barrow-upon-Humber
DN19 7AG* T: (01469) 530357

GISBOURNE, Canon Michael Andrew. b 65. Leeds Univ
BA 87 St Martin's Coll Lanc MA 09. St Jo Coll Nottm BTh 91.
d 92 **p** 93. C Gateacre *Liv* 92–95; C Marton *Blackb* 95–98;
V Freckleton 98–03; V Garstang St Thos 03–10; Chapl
Cumbria Univ 10–11; V Scotforth 11–18; AD Lancaster and
Morecambe 17–18; Can Res Ripon Cathl *Leeds* from 18.
St Wilfrid's House, Minster Close, Ripon HG4 1QP T: (01765)
600211 E: canonmichael@riponcathedral.org.uk

GISBY, Mrs Vivien Barbara. b 56. Wolv Poly BSc 78 Leeds
Univ BA 08. NOC 05. **d** 08 **p** 09. C Sutton St Jas *Ches* 08–14;
V Runcorn St Jo Weston from 14; Warden of Past Workers
from 11; Warden of Readers from 17. *St John's Vicarage, 225
Heath Road South, Weston, Runcorn WA7 4LY* T: (01928)
573798 E: vivien.gisby@btinternet.com

**GISLESKOG, Catharina Irene Gunilla Margaretha Elizabeth
Olsson.** b 65. St Mellitus Coll 16. **d** 18 **p** 19. NSM Isleworth
All SS *Lon* from 18. *28 Ashfield Road, London W3 7JJ* T: (020)
8740 8153 E: catharina.gisleskog@allsaints-isleworth.org

GISMONDI, Paul Arthur. b 55. Williams Coll Mass BA 77
Trin Hall Cam BTh 16. Westcott Ho Cam 14. **d** 16 **p** 17.
NSM Sandringham w W Newton and Appleton etc *Nor*
from 16; NSM Upper Chelsea H Trin and St Sav *Lon*
from 16. *Ken Hill House, Lynn Road, Snettisham, King's
Lynn PE31 7PG* T: (01485) 571111 M: 07770-500957
E: kenhillhouse@btinternet.com

GITTINGS, Graham. b 46. Qu Coll Birm 75. **d** 78 **p** 79. C
Caverswall *Lich* 78–81; C Wolverhampton St Matt 81–82;
C Walthamstow St Mary w St Steph *Chelmsf* 82–83; C
Dagenham 83–89; V Earl Shilton w Elmesthorpe *Leic* 89–11;
rtd 11; PtO *Leic* from 11; *Lich* 12–19. *21 Princetown Close,
Stoke-on-Trent ST3 7WN* T: (01782) 388866 M: 07711-
46063 E: graham.gittings77@btinternet.com

GITTOES, Julie Anne. b 76. Trevelyan Coll Dur BA 98 Graduate
Soc Dur MA 99 Selw Coll Cam PhD 04. Westcott Ho Cam 99.
d 03 **p** 04. C Hampton Hill *Lon* 03–06; V Hampton All SS
06–12; Can Res Guildf Cathl 12–19; V Hendon St Mary and

Ch Ch *Lon* from 19. *The Vicarage, 34 Parson Street, London NW4 1QR* M: 07702-151173 E: juliegittoes@gmail.com

GLADSTONE, Canon Robert Michael. b 60. Ch Ch Ox BA 82 MA 86. Wycliffe Hall Ox 92. **d** 94 **p** 95. C Trentham *Lich* 94–97; C Heigham H Trin *Nor* 97–01; V Rothley *Leic* from 01; AD Goscote from 06; Hon Can Leic Cathl from 10. *The Vicarage, 128 Hallfields Lane, Rothley, Leicester LE7 7NG* T: 0116-230 2241 E: rob.gladstone@btconnect.com

✠**GLADWIN, The Rt Revd John Warren.** b 42. Chu Coll Cam BA 65 MA 68. Cranmer Hall Dur. **d** 67 **p** 68 **c** 94. C Kirkheaton *Wakef* 67–71; Tutor St Jo Coll Dur 71–77; Dir Shaftesbury Project 77–82; Sec Gen Syn Bd for Soc Resp 82–88; Preb St Paul's Cathl *Lon* 84–88; Provost Sheff 88–94; Angl Adv Yorkshire TV 88–94; Bp Guildf 94–03; Bp Chelmsf 03–09; rtd 09; PtO *St Alb* from 10. *131A Marford Road, Wheathampstead, St Albans AL4 8NH* T: (01582) 834223 E: johnwgladwin@hotmail.com

GLADWIN, Thomas William. b 35. St Alb Minl Tr Scheme 78. **d** 81 **p** 82. NSM Hertford St Andr *St Alb* 81–82; NSM Digswell and Panshanger 82–86; C 86–96; rtd 96; PtO *St Alb* from 96. *99 Warren Way, Welwyn AL6 0DL* T: (01438) 714700

GLAISYER, Canon Hugh. b 30. Oriel Coll Ox BA 51 MA 55. St Steph Ho Ox 51. **d** 56 **p** 56. C Tonge Moor *Man* 56–62; C Sidcup St Jo *Roch* 62–64; V Milton next Gravesend Ch Ch 64–81; RD Gravesend 74–81; V Hove All SS *Chich* 81–91; Can and Preb Chich Cathl 82–91; RD Hove 82–91; P-in-c Hove St Jo 81–91; Adn Lewes and Hastings 91–97; rtd 97; PtO *Chich* 97–03; LtO from 03. *Florence Villa, Hangleton Lane, Ferring, Worthing BN12 6PP* T/F: (01903) 244688 M: 07712-317118 E: h.glaisyer@virgin.net *or* exarch2005@gmail.com

GLANVILLE-SMITH, Canon Michael Raymond. b 38. Leeds Univ MA 95 AKC 61. **d** 62 **p** 63. C St Marylebone St Mark w St Luke *Lon* 62–64; C Penzance St Mary *Truro* 64–68; R Worc St Andr and All SS w St Helen 68–74; Dioc Youth Chapl 68–74; V Catshill 74–80; P-in-c Worc St Martin w St Pet 80–81; TR Worc St Martin w St Pet, St Mark etc 81–86; TR Worc SE 86–90; Hon Can Worc Cathl 83–90; Can Res Ripon Cathl 90–07; RD Ripon 96–97; rtd 07; PtO *Ripon* 13–14; *Leeds* from 14. *13 Ure Bank Terrace, Ripon HG4 1JG* T: (01765) 609428 M: 07792-014055 E: mglansmith@hotmail.com

GLASBY, Alan Langland. b 46. St Jo Coll Nottm 74. **d** 77 **p** 78. C Erith St Paul *Roch* 77–80; C Moor Allerton *Ripon* 80–81; TV 81–87; V Middleton St Mary 87–92; V Bilton 92–00; V Barton and Manfield and Cleasby w Stapleton 00–04; TR E Richmond 04–11; rtd 11; PtO *Ripon* 13–14; *Leeds* from 14. *23 Westwinn View, Leeds LS14 2HY* T: 0113-265 5992 M: 07970-712484 E: alanglasby@btinternet.com

GLASGOW AND GALLOWAY, Bishop of. *Vacant*

GLASGOW AND GALLOWAY, Dean of. *See* BARCROFT, The Very Revd Ian David

GLASGOW, Provost of. *See* HOLDSWORTH, The Very Revd Kelvin

GLASS, Caroline Mary. b 57. Southn Univ BSc 79 Open Univ MA(Ed) 01. Trin Coll Bris BA 06. **d** 06 **p** 07. C Redhill H Trin *S'wark* 06–10; V Tunbridge Wells St Luke *Roch* from 10. *St Luke's Vicarage, 158 Upper Grosvenor Road, Tunbridge Wells TN1 2EQ* T: (01892) 521374 M: 07910-066837 E: caroline.glass957@btinternet.com

GLASS, Mrs Yvonne Elizabeth. b 58. EMMTC 94. **d** 97 **p** 98. NSM Bingham *S'well* 97–00; Chapl Nottm City Hosp NHS Trust 00–11; rtd 11; PtO *Glas* from 12. *Coigach, Laurieston Road, Gatehouse of Fleet, Castle Douglas DG7 2BE* T: (01557) 814045 E: yvonne.glass58@hotmail.co.uk

GLASSPOOL, John Martin. b 59. Kent Univ BA 83 Heythrop Coll *Lon* MTh 95 Leeds Univ MA 05 RGN 87. Westcott Ho Cam 88. **d** 90 **p** 91. C Forest Gate Em w Upton Cross *Chelmsf* 90–93; P-in-c Theydon Garnon 93–95; Chapl St Marg Hosp Epping 93–99; TV Epping Distr *Chelmsf* 95–99; Asst Chapl R Free Hampstead NHS Trust 99–02; Chapl Surrey and Sussex Healthcare NHS Trust 02–18; rtd 19. *50 Talfourd Way, Redhill RH1 6GF* M: 07375-045390 E: glasspool59@gmail.com

GLEAVES, John. b 39. Alsager Coll of Educn CertEd 60 Westmr Coll Ox BTh 03. NOC 99. **d** 00 **p** 01. NSM Alsager St Mary *Ches* 00–03; P-in-c Alvanley 03–08; rtd 08; PtO *Ches* from 10. *46 Linley Grove, Alsager, Stoke-on-Trent ST7 2PS* T: (01270) 878169 E: rev.johngleaves@gmail.com

GLEDHILL, Alan. b 43. Lon Univ BSc(Econ) 73. NOC 81. **d** 84 **p** 85. C Knaresborough *Ripon* 84–87; P-in-c Easby 87–88; P-in-c Bolton on Swale 87–88; V Easby w Brompton on Swale and Bolton on Swale 88–96; Teacher St Fran Xavier Sch Richmond 96–08; PtO *Ripon* 96–08; rtd 08; Hon C Gilling and Kirkby Ravensworth *Ripon* 08–14; *Leeds* 14–18. *75 High Street, Gilling West, Richmond DL10 5JW* T: (01748) 824466 M: 07906-195390 E: gledhill356@btinternet.com

✠**GLEDHILL, The Rt Revd Jonathan Michael.** b 49. Keele Univ BA 72 Hon DUniv 07 Bris Univ MA 75. Trin Coll Bris 72. **d** 75 **p** 76 **c** 96. C Marple All SS *Ches* 75–78; C Folkestone H Trin w Ch Ch *Cant* 78–83; V Cant St Mary Bredin 83–96; Tutor Cant Sch of Min 83–96; RD Cant 88–94; Hon Can Cant Cathl 92–96; Suff Bp Southampton *Win* 96–03; Bp Lich 03–15; rtd 15; PtO *Cant* from 16. *16 Cherry Garden Road, Canterbury CT2 8EL* T: (01227) 765062 E: jonathan.gledhill68@gmail.com

GLEESON, Robert Godfrey. b 49. Man Univ CQSW 74. Qu Coll Birm 83. **d** 85 **p** 86. C Hall Green St Pet *Birm* 85–88; Asst Chapl Mental Health & Elderly Care Services Birm HA 88–90; Chapl 90–94; Chapl Moseley Hall Hosp Birm 90–94; Chapl S Birm Mental Health NHS Trust 94–03; PtO *Birm* 03–12; rtd 14. *180 Pineapple Road, Birmingham B30 2TY* T: 0121-444 2793 *or* 678 2002 M: 07966-188006

GLEGHORN, Timothy. b 69. York Univ BA 92. St Jo Coll Nottm 10. **d** 12 **p** 13. C Win Ch Ch 12–16; R Bath Walcot *B & W* from 17. *Swallowgate, Lansdown Road, Bath BA1 5TD* T: (01225) 423013 M: 07754-801151 E: tim@stswithinswalcot.org.uk

GLEN, Mrs Dawn Andrea. b 64. Liv Univ BA 86. Westcott Ho Cam 07. **d** 09 **p** 10. C Derby Cathl 09–11; C Kirk Langley 11–15; C Mackworth All SS 11–15; C Mugginton and Kedleston 11–15; C Brailsford w Shirley, Osmaston w Edlaston etc 15–16; PtO from 17; *S'well* from 16. *41 Letchworth Crescent, Beeston, Nottingham NG9 5LL* T: 0115-783 8103 E: revdawnglen@gmail.com

✠**GLENFIELD, The Rt Revd Samuel Ferran.** b 54. QUB BA 76 TCD MLitt 90 MA 94 Ox Univ MTh 99. Wycliffe Hall Ox 88. **d** 91 **p** 92 **c** 13. C Douglas Union w Frankfield *C, C & R* 91–94; I Rathcooney Union 94–96; I Kill *D & G* 96–12; I Hillsborough *D & D* 12–13; Bp K, E & A from 13. *The See House, Kilmore, Cavan, Republic of Ireland* T: (00353) (49) 437 1551 E: bishop@kilmore.anglican.org

GLENNY, Robert Michael. b 90. **d** 14 **p** 15. C Marston w Elsfield *Ox* 14–17; R Radley, Sunningwell and Kennington from 17. *The Vicarage, Kennington Road, Radley, Abingdon OX14 2JN* T: (01235) 554739 M: 07871-644811 E: robertglenny@gmail.com

GLEW, Mark Roy. b 78. Bris Univ BSc 99 ACA 03. Oak Hill Th Coll BA 12. **d** 13 **p** 14. C Rusholme H Trin *Man* 13–17; P-in-c Haughton St Mary 17–19; R from 19. *St Mary's Rectory, Meadow Lane, Denton, Manchester M34 7GD* T: 0161-336 4529 E: markglew@hotmail.com *or* smhg.church@virginmedia.com

GLIDDON, Andrew James. b 86. LSE BSc 09 Nottm Trent Univ LLB 11. Trin Coll Bris 14. **d** 17 **p** 18. C Luton Lewsey St Hugh *St Alb* from 17. *247 Leagrave High Street, Luton LU4 0NA* M: 07746-212304 E: andrew@thegliddons.co.uk

GLITHERO, Mrs Helen Elizabeth. b 60. Nottm Univ BA 81 CQSW 83. Qu Coll Birm 11. **d** 14 **p** 15. NSM Highters Heath *Birm* 14–17; PtO from 17. *61 Stonerwood Avenue, Birmingham B28 0AX* T: 0121-778 3925 E: hglithero@btinternet.com *or* revdhelen@icloud.com

GLOSSOP, Jonathan Mark. b 55. Open Univ BA 91 Bradf Univ MA 93 Eaton Hall Coll of Educn CertEd 76. Linc Sch of Th and Min 11. **d** 14 **p** 15. OLM Wolds Gateway Group *Linc* from 14. *23 Pilgrims Way, Immingham DN40 2HD* T: (01469) 574522 E: jmseglossop@tiscali.co.uk

GLOUCESTER, Archdeacon of. *See* DAWSON, The Ven Hilary Joan

GLOUCESTER, Bishop of. *See* TREWEEK, The Rt Revd Rachel

GLOUCESTER, Dean of. *See* LAKE, The Very Revd Stephen David

GLOVER, Alan. b 47. SWMTC 96. **d** 99 **p** 00. NSM Bideford, Northam, Westward Ho!, Appledore etc *Ex* 99–17; NSM Bideford, Landcross, Littleham etc from 17. *West Fordlands, Heywood Road, Northam, Bideford EX39 3QA* T: (01237) 479542 E: alanglover2014@gmail.com

GLOVER, Canon David Charles. b 66. St Jo Coll Dur BA 87 St Jo Coll Cam MPhil 91. Ridley Hall Cam 87. **d** 90 **p** 91. C Wath-upon-Dearne w Adwick-upon-Dearne *Sheff* 90–92; Chapl Hatf Coll Dur 92–00; P-in-c Dur St Marg 95–00; R Dur St Marg and Neville's Cross St Jo 00–05; P-in-c Washington 05–07; R from 07; AD Chester-le-Street 08–18; AD Chester le Street and Houghton from 18; Hon Can Dur Cathl from 11; Chapl to The Queen from 17. *27 Wroxton, Washington NE38 7NU* T: 0191-418 7911 M: 07886-289311 E: htcwashington@tiscali.co.uk

GLOVER, Mrs Diana Mary. b 50. Kent Univ BA 73 MA 75. SAOMC. **d** 01 **p** 02. C Aylesbury *Ox* 01–05; P-in-c Amersham on the Hill 05–08; V 08–15; rtd 15; PtO *Ox* from 15. *11 Hamilton Close, Bicester OX26 2HX* E: diana.glover@btinternet.com

GLOVER, Elisabeth Ann. b 53. Univ Coll Ches BTh 99. **d** 98 **p** 99. NSM Thurstaston *Ches* 98–99; C Stockton Heath 00–04; V Eastham from 04; RD Wirral S from 13. *The Vicarage, 29 Ferry Road, Eastham, Wirral CH62 0AJ* T: 0151-327 2182 E: beth.glover@tesco.net

GLOVER, Janet Mary. b 58. Natal Univ BSc 79 UED 80 Anglia Ruskin Univ MA 05. EAMTC 98. **d** 01 **p** 02. NSM Cambridge St Phil *Ely* 01–04; NSM Histon 04–14; NSM Impington 04–14; Hon Asst Dir of Ords 07–18; NSM N Stowe from 15. *139 Waterbeach Road, Landbeach, Cambridge CB25 9FA* T: (01223) 864931 E: janet@theglovers.name

GLOVER, Canon John. b 48. Kelham Th Coll 67. **d** 71 **p** 72. C Foley Park *Worc* 71–75; TV Sutton *Liv* 75–79; P-in-c Churchill w Blakedown *Worc* 79–84; R 84–87; R Belbroughton w Fairfield and Clent 87–91; Chapl Children's Family Trust 91–13; NSM Flint *St As* 92–93; R Halkyn w Caerfallwch w Rhesycae 93–97; V Rhyl w St Ann 97–13; Can Cursal St As Cathl 02–08; Sacr 08–13; rtd 13; PtO *St As* from 15. *Bryn Oswald, James Park, Dyserth, Rhyl LL18 6AG* T: (01745) 571473 E: gloverjohn@btinternet.com

GLOVER, Canon Judith Rosalind. b 53. NEOC 93. **d** 95 **p** 96. C Glendale Gp *Newc* 95–99; P-in-c Alwinton w Holystone and Alnham 99–04; R Upper Coquetdale 04–09; R Alston Moor 09–13; V Beadnell 13–18; V N Sunderland 13–18; AD Bamburgh and Glendale 16–18; Hon Can Newc Cathl 10–18; rtd 18; PtO *Newc* from 18. *The Hemmel, Ellingham, Chathill NE67 5EU* T: (01665) 589628 E: judyglover432@btinternet.com

GLOVER, Richard John. b 47. Nottm Univ BTh 77. Linc Th Coll 73. **d** 77 **p** 78. C Barrow St Geo w St Luke *Carl* 77–79; C Netherton 79–80; P-in-c Addingham 80–83; P-in-c Edenhall w Langwathby and Culgaith 80–83; V Addingham, Edenhall, Langwathby and Culgaith 83–84; V Bishops Hull *B & W* 84–89; V Shilbottle *Newc* 89–96; V Whittingham and Edlingham w Bolton Chapel 96–00; P-in-c Barton, Pooley Bridge and Martindale *Carl* 00–04; Dioc Adv for Spiritual Direction and Healing 00–04; R Lower Swale *Ripon* 04–12; rtd 13; PtO *York* from 13. *45 Grovehill Road, Filey YO14 9NL*

GLOVER, Thomas Edward. b 85. Grey Coll Dur BA 06 Clare Coll Cam BA 09. Westcott Ho Cam 07. **d** 10 **p** 11. C Dur N 10–14; R Winlaton 14–18; AD Gateshead W 17–18; P-in-c Dur St Giles from 18; P-in-c Shadforth and Sherburn from 18. *St Giles's Vicarage, Gilesgate, Durham DH1 1QQ* T: 0191-384 2452 M: 07711-576522 E: vicarofsgss@gmail.com

GLYN, Aneirin. b 75. St Hugh's Coll Ox MMath 98 DPhil 02. Oak Hill Th Coll MTh 09. **d** 09 **p** 10. C St Helen Bishopsgate w St Andr Undershaft etc *Lon* from 09; P-in-c St Benet Paul's Wharf from 11. *28 Sharon Gardens, London E9 7RX* T: (020) 7283 2231 M: 07905-288078 E: aneirin@gmail.com *or* a.glyn@st-helens.org.uk

GLYN-JONES, Alun. b 38. CCC Cam BA 59 MA 63. Bps' Coll Cheshunt 60. **d** 61 **p** 62. C Portsea St Mary *Portsm* 61–65; Chapl Hampton Sch Middx 65–76; Hd Master Abp Tenison's Gr Sch Croydon 76–88; V Twickenham St Mary *Lon* 88–01; rtd 01; PtO *B & W* from 01; *Sarum* from 01; *Eur* from 01; *Bris* from 02. *2 Huntingdon Rise, Bradford-on-Avon BA15 1RJ* T: (01225) 866874 E: alunandchrisgj@gmail.com

GOALBY, George Christian. b 55. Leeds Univ BA 77. St Jo Coll Nottm 79. **d** 81 **p** 82. C Wakef St Andr and St Mary 81–84; Asst Chapl HM Pris Wakef 84–85; Chapl HM Youth Cust Cen Deerbolt 85–87; Chapl HM Pris Frankland 87–89; V Swinderby *Linc* 89–15; CF (ACF) from 04; R Washingborough w Heighington and Canwick *Linc* from 15. *The Rectory, Church Hill, Washingborough, Lincoln LN4 1EJ* T: (01522) 800240 F: 868430 M: 07923-546599 E: george.goalby@btconnect.com

GOATCHER, Mrs Sara Jacoba Helena. b 46. Oak Hill NSM Course 86. **d** 89 **p** 94. NSM S Croydon Em *S'wark* 89–95; C 95–96; R Sutton St Nic 96–06; Asst Chapl Old Palace Sch Croydon 06–11; C Croydon St Jo *S'wark* 07–12; rtd 13; PtO *S'wark* from 13. *8 Hornchurch Hill, Whyteleafe CR3 0DA* T: (020) 8660 6198 M: 07785-230983 E: sara.goatcher@btinternet.com

GOATER, Canon Michael Robert. b 46. York Univ BA MA. NOC 89. **d** 92 **p** 93. C Norton *Sheff* 92–94; V Endcliffe 94–99; Chapl Sheff Ind Miss 94–95; Assoc Chapl Sheff Hallam Univ 95–99; Asst Post-Ord Tr Officer 95–99; Dioc Voc Officer 96–99; C Stratford-upon-Avon, Luddington etc *Cov* 99–02; P-in-c Gt Shelford *Ely* 02–11; RD Shelford 04–09; RD Granta 09–11; Hon Can Ely Cathl 10–11; rtd 11; Master St Nic Hosp Salisbury 11–16; PtO *Sarum* from 17. *17 Chiselbury Grove, Salisbury SP2 8EP* T: (01722) 331899 E: michael@mickthevic.org.uk

GOATLY, Ms Ruth Christine. b 50. Leic Univ LLB 72 Herts Univ MA 98 CQSW 74. Westcott Ho Cam 08. **d** 09 **p** 10. NSM Boxmoor St Jo *St Alb* 09–13; NSM St Alb St Mary Marshalswick 13–15; NSM St Alb St Luke 15–16; PtO 16–18; NSM Boxmoor St Jo from 18. *30 Newgate Close, St Albans AL4 9JE* T: (01727) 751542 M: 07961-980158 E: ruthgoatly@hotmail.com

GOBBETT, Michael George Timothy. b 64. St Chad's Coll Dur BSc 86. St Steph Ho Ox BA 89 MA 98. **d** 90 **p** 91. C Hartlepool St Aid *Dur* 90–94; P-in-c Norton St Mich 94–95; V 95–05; TR Upper Skerne 05–16; TR Whitby w Ruswarp *York* from 16; AD Whitby from 17; CMP from 91. *The Rectory, Chubb Hill Road, Whitby YO21 1JP* T: (01947) 602590 E: michael.gobbett@btinternet.com

GOBEY, Ian Clifford. b 48. WEMTC 94. **d** 96 **p** 97. NSM Whiteshill and Randwick *Glouc* 96–00; NSM Painswick, Sheepscombe, Cranham, The Edge etc 00–07; P-in-c Westbury-on-Severn w Flaxley, Blaisdon etc 07–13; C Abenhall w Mitcheldean 11–13; C Huntley and Longhope, Churcham and Bulley 12–13; rtd 13; PtO *Glouc* from 13. *18 Blenheim Orchard, Shurdington, Cheltenham GL51 4TG* E: gobey910@btinternet.com *or* iangobey588@gmail.com

GOBLE, Christopher. b 75. Univ of Wales (Lamp) BA 96. Trin Coll Bris 96. **d** 98 **p** 99. C St Jo in Bedwardine *Worc* 98–01; P-in-c Worc St Clem 01–02; R Brington w Whilton and Norton etc *Pet* 02–08; P-in-c Ilmington w Stretton-on-Fosse etc *Cov* from 08; P-in-c Tredington and Darlingscott from 08. *The Rectory, Valenders Lane, Ilmington, Shipston-on-Stour CV36 4LB* T: (01608) 682282 E: ilmingtonrectory@btinternet.com

GOBLE, Clifford David. b 41. Oak Hill Th Coll 69. **d** 72 **p** 73. C Erith St Paul *Roch* 72–76; C Tunbridge Wells St Jas 76–79; R Southfleet 79–05; RD Gravesend 94–05; Hon Can Roch Cathl 99–05; rtd 05; PtO *Cant* from 06. *15 Martindown Road, Whitstable CT5 4PX* T: (01227) 263333 E: cliandjog@gmail.com

GOBLE (*née* **DUNN), Sharon Louise.** b 71. Univ of Wales (Swansea) BA 93 Fitzw Coll Cam BA 97 MA 01. Ridley Hall Cam 95. **d** 98 **p** 99. C Malpas *Mon* 98–01; C Cyncoed 01–02; R Heyford w Stowe Nine Churches and Flore etc *Pet* 02–04; PtO 04–08; Chapl Shakespeare Hospice 08–11; PtO *Cov* 08–13; P-in-c Stoneleigh w Ashow 13–17; R Stourdene Gp from 17. *The Rectory, Valenders Lane, Ilmington, Shipston-on-Stour CV36 4LB* T: (01608) 682282 M: 07799-220407 E: sharon.goble@btinternet.com

GODBOLD, Michelle Joanne. b 80. Bradf Univ BSc 01 BA 13. Linc Sch of Th and Min 09. **d** 13 **p** 14. C Boultham *Linc* 13–16; R Graffoe Gp from 16; Dioc Adv in Women's Min from 17. *The Rectory, 20 Temple Goring, Navenby, Lincoln LN5 0TX* T: (01522) 426723 E: michelle.godbold@hotmail.co.uk

GODDARD, Canon Charles <u>Douglas</u> James. b 47. CITC 67. **d** 70 **p** 71. C Orangefield *D & D* 70–73; C Stormont 73–75; Miss to Seafarers from 75; Sen Chapl and Sec N Ireland 77–09; rtd 10; Can Belf Cathl from 05. *9 Governors Gate Manor, Hillsborough BT26 6FZ* T: (028) 9268 3592 E: cdjgoddard@gmail.com

GODDARD, Christopher. b 45. Sarum & Wells Th Coll 79. **d** 81 **p** 82. C Whitehaven *Carl* 81–83; C Barrow St Geo w St Luke 83–85; P-in-c Hayton St Mary 85–90; V Brigham 90–98; V Mosser 90–98; PtO 00–03; Hon C Cockermouth w Embleton and Wythop 03–05; TV Cockermouth Area 05–10; rtd 10; PtO *Carl* from 11. *5 Craig Drive, Whitehaven CA28 6JX* T: (01946) 328099 E: chrisgoddardmail@gmail.com

GODDARD, Derek George. b 38. St Martin's Coll Lanc BA 97 CEng FIMechE FIMarEST FCMI. Cranmer Hall Dur 94 CBDTI 95. **d** 97 **p** 98. NSM Windermere St Mary and Troutbeck *Carl* 97–01; P-in-c Leven Valley 01–06; P-in-c Palermo w Taormina *Eur* 06–09; PtO *Blackb* 09–10; P-in-c Overton 10–12; rtd 13; PtO *Blackb* from 13; *Chich* from 16; *Eur* from 09. *15 The Towpath, Yapton, Arundel BN18 0FW* E: d.d.goddard@hotmail.co.uk

GODDARD, Mrs Doris. b 48. St Mary's Coll Twickenham CertEd 70 Open Univ BA 80. S'wark Ord Course 93. **d** 96 **p** 97. Chapl John Nightingale Sch W Molesley 96–00; NSM Addlestone *Guildf* 96–98; NSM Botleys and Lyne 98–04; NSM Long Cross 98–04; NSM Chertsey, Lyne and Longcross 04–05; NSM Blackdown *B & W* 05–09; P-in-c Puriton and Pawlett from 09; Chapl Bridgwater Hosp from 15. *The Vicarage, 1 The Rye, Puriton, Bridgwater TA7 8BZ* T: (01278) 683500 E: rev.doris.goddard@btinternet.com

GODDARD, Douglas. See GODDARD, Charles Douglas James

GODDARD, Mrs Elaine Clare. b 53. K Alfred's Coll Win CertEd 78. WEMTC 96. **d** 99 **p** 00. C Leominster *Heref* 99–04; P-in-c St Weonards 04–07; R 07–15; RD Ross and Archenfield 07–13; rtd 15. *Little Bylets House, Pembridge, Leominster HR6 9HY* E: email@ecgoddard.co.uk

GODDARD, Elisabeth Ann. b 64. St Hugh's Coll Ox BA 89 MA 99. Cranmer Hall Dur 94. **d** 96 **p** 97. C Cogges and S

Leigh *Ox* 96–99; Chapl Jes Coll Ox 99–04; Tutor Wycliffe Hall Ox 04–08; Hon C Ox St Andr 04–08; Hon C Stoke Bishop *Bris* 09–10; V Westminster St Jas the Less *Lon* from 10. *56 Tachbrook Street, London SW1V 2NA* T: (020) 7834 1343 E: goddardea@gmail.com

GODDARD, Canon Giles William. b 62. Clare Coll Cam MA 84. S'wark Ord Course 92. **d** 95 **p** 96. C N Dulwich St Faith *S'wark* 95–98; R Walworth St Pet 98–09; AD S'wark and Newington 02–07; P-in-c Waterloo St Jo w St Andr 09–14; V from 14; Hon Can S'wark Cathl from 07. *St John's Vicarage, 1 Secker Street, London SE1 8UF* T: (020) 7633 9819 E: giles@stjohnswaterloo.org

GODDARD, Canon Harold Frederick. b 42. Keble Coll Ox BA 63 MA 69. Cuddesdon Coll 64. **d** 66 **p** 67. C Birm St Pet 66–70; Chapl Dudley Road Hosp Birm 66–70; Chapl HM Pris Birm 68–70; C Alverstoke *Portsm* 70–72; Chapl Gosport Cottage Hosp Portsm 70–72; Chapl HM Det Cen Haslar 70–72; P-in-c Portsea St Geo CD *Portsm* 72–76; Chapl Portsm Cathl 73–76; Asst Chapl Portsm Gr Sch 73–75; P-in-c Stoke Prior *Worc* 76–78; P-in-c Wychbold and Upton Warren 77–78; R Stoke Prior, Wychbold and Upton Warren 78–80; Chapl Forelands Orthopaedic Hosp Worc 77–80; Chapl R Marsden Hosp 80–83; R Martley and Wichenford *Worc* 83–88; P-in-c Knightwick w Doddenham, Broadwas and Cotheridge 85–88; R Martley and Wichenford, Knightwick etc 89–90; Bp's Adv on Min of Healing 84–99; Chapl St Richard's Hospice Worc 87–94; RD Martley and Worc W 88–90; Chapl Kidderminster Gen Hosp 90–92; P-in-c Hallow *Worc* 91–92; P-in-c Sedgeberrow w Hinton-on-the-Green 92–00; Chapl Evesham Hosp 93–00; Chapl Worcs Community Healthcare NHS Trust 97–00; Co-ord W Midl Healing Advisers 94–99; RD Evesham *Worc* 97–00; TR Kidderminster St Jo and H Innocents 00–08; Hon Can Worc Cathl 03–08; rtd 08; PtO *Worc* 08–15; Hon C Gt Malvern Ch Ch from 15. *1 Springfield House, Como Road, Malvern WR14 2HS* T: (01684) 563350 M: 07768-106287 E: h.goddard@hotmail.com

✠**GODDARD, The Rt Revd John William.** b 47. St Chad's Coll Dur BA 69. **d** 70 **p** 71 **c** 00. C S Bank *York* 70–74; C Cayton w Eastfield 74–75; V Middlesbrough Ascension 75–82; RD Middlesbrough 81–87; V Middlesbrough All SS 82–88; Can and Preb York Minster 87–88; Vice-Prin Edin Th Coll 88–92; TR Ribbleton *Blackb* 92–00; Suff Bp Burnley 00–14; Bp's Adv on Hosp Chapls 01–14; Co-ord for Interfaith Work 07–14; rtd 14; PtO *Blackb* 14–17; Hon Asst Bp Blackb from 17; Hon Asst Bp Liv from 15; Hon Asst Bp Man from 15. *39 Kearsley Avenue, Tarleton, Preston PR4 6BP* T: (01772) 812532 M: 07779-786114 E: john.goddard39@gmail.com

GODDARD, Ms Marion. b 54. Sarum & Wells Th Coll 87. **d** 89 **p** 94. Par Dn Lewisham St Swithun *S'wark* 89–94; C 94–95; TV Thamesmead 96–04; rtd 04. *1 Hollows Close, Salisbury SP2 8JU* T: (01722) 338562

GODDARD, Matthew Francis. b 45. Kelham Th Coll 65. **d** 69 **p** 70. C Mansfield St Mark *S'well* 69–72; C Northolt Park St Barn *Lon* 72–78; P-in-c Acton Green St Pet 78–87; R Norwood St Mary 87–96. *27 Hounslow Avenue, Hounslow TW3 2DZ* T: (020) 8230 6591 E: mattandtrace@hotmail.com

GODDARD, Mrs Pamela Gay. b 53. LSE BSc(Econ) 74 CQSW 77. SAOMC 95 EAMTC 97. **d** 98 **p** 99. C New Catton St Luke w St Aug *Nor* 98–03; PtO 03–05; NSM Hamworthy *Sarum* 05–07; C Throop *Win* 07–08; C Hamworthy *Sarum* 08–17; rtd 17; PtO *Win* from 18. *180 Salisbury Road, Totton, Southampton SO40 3LQ* T: (023) 8206 0439 E: pam.goddard@gmail.com

GODDARD, Mrs Rosemary Joy. b 48. Philippa Fawcett Coll CertEd 69. EAMTC 00. **d** 03 **p** 04. C Linc St Nic w St Jo Newport 03–05; P-in-c Bicker 05–08; P-in-c Donington 08; P-in-c Fleet w Gedney 08–13; P-in-c Holbeach Marsh 08–13; rtd 13; PtO *Pet* 14–19; *Linc* 16–19. *9B Church Lane, Donington, Spalding PE11 4UD* T: (01775) 822398 M: 07740-203149 E: rogo9@btinternet.com

GODDARD, Stuart David. b 53. Cen Sch of Art Lon BA 76 Middx Poly PGCE 82. Trin Coll Bris 91. **d** 93 **p** 94. C Watling Valley *Ox* 93–97; P-in-c Bowthorpe *Nor* 97–00; TV 00–05; P-in-c Hamworthy *Sarum* 05–09; R 09–17; rtd 17; PtO *Win* from 18. *180 Salisbury Road, Totton, Southampton SO40 3LQ* T: (023) 8206 0439 E: goddard.stuart@gmail.com

GODDARD, Trevor Paul. b 63. NTMTC 03. **d** 06 **p** 07. NSM Kensal Rise St Mark and St Martin *Lon* 06–11; NSM Kensal Rise St Mark 11–13; NSM S Kenton from 13. *194 Windermere Avenue, Wembley HA9 8QT* T: (020) 8908 2252 E: trevorgoddard@mac.com

GODDEN, Canon Peter David. b 47. Leeds Univ BA 69 MA 04 ARCO 70. Linc Th Coll 85. **d** 87 **p** 88. C Bearsted w Thurnham *Cant* 87–90; C Hykeham *Linc* 90–91; TV 91–95; P-in-c Linc St Pet-at-Gowts and St Andr 95–99; Hon PV Linc Cathl 90–99; R Armthorpe *Sheff* 99–00; R

Owmby Gp *Linc* 00–12; RD Lawres 05–06 and 09–12; P-in-c Spring Line Gp 08–12; Can and Preb Linc Cathl 10–12; rtd 12; PtO *York* 13–16; *Nor* from 18. *7 Hampton Court, Nelson Street, King's Lynn PE30 5DX* T: (01553) 279954 E: petergodden65@gmail.com

GODDEN, Peter James Howard. b 86. St Jo Coll Dur BA 08 Clare Coll Cam BA 13. Westcott Ho Cam 11. **d** 14 **p** 15. C Northwood H Trin *Lon* 14–17; V Clay Hill St Jo and St Luke from 17. *St Luke's Vicarage, Browning Road, Enfield EN2 0HG* T: (020) 8363 6055 M: 07835-770610 E: revpetergodden@outlook.com

GODDEN, Timothy Richard James. b 62. Univ Coll Lon BA 84. St Jo Coll Nottm 89. **d** 89 **p** 90. C Tulse Hill H Trin and St Matthias *S'wark* 89–93; TV Horsham *Chich* 93–01; TR Bishopsworth and Bedminster Down *Bris* from 01. *St Peter's Vicarage, 61 Fernsteed Road, Bristol BS13 8HE* T/F: 0117-964 2734 E: goddenfamily@blueyonder.co.uk

GODFREY, Ann Veronica. *See* MacKEITH, Ann Veronica

GODFREY, David Samuel George. b 35. CITC 64. **d** 66 **p** 67. C Londonderry Ch Ch *D & R* 66–68; I Tomregan w Drumlane *K, E & A* 68–72; I Cloonclare 72–79; I Templebreedy *C, C & R* 79–85; I Bray *D & G* 85–97; Can Ch Ch Cathl Dublin 95–97; Dean Kilmore *K, E & A* 97–04; I Kilmore w Ballintemple 97–04; Preb Mulhuddart St Patr Cathl Dublin 01–04; rtd 04. *37 Earlsfort Meadows, Earlsfort, Lucan, Co Dublin, Republic of Ireland* T: (00353) (1) 624 1906 M: 86-238 9686 E: godfreyd@tcd.ie *or* dsggodfrey@gmail.com

✠**GODFREY, The Rt Revd Harold William.** b 48. AKC 71. St Aug Coll Cant 71. **d** 72 **p** 73 **c** 87. C Warsop *S'well* 72–75; TV Hucknall Torkard 75–86; Bp's Ecum Officer 81–82; United Soc 86–14; R and Adn Montevideo and Can Buenos Aires 86–88; Asst Bp Argentina and Uruguay 87–88; Bp Uruguay 88–98; Bp Peru 98–16; P-in-c Lastingham w Appleton-le-Moors, Rosedale etc *York* 16–17; V from 17. *The Vicarage, Anserdale Lane, Lastingham, York YO62 6TN* T: (01751) 417344 E: hwgodfrey@gmail.com

GODFREY, Jennifer Olwen. b 48. Hamilton Coll of Educn DipEd 70. TISEC 99. **d** 02 **p** 03. NSM Dalkeith *Edin* from 02; NSM Lasswade from 02. *131 Newbattle Abbey Crescent, Dalkeith EH22 3LP* T: 0131-660 6145 M: 07812-923159 E: jennie.o.godfrey@googlemail.com

GODFREY, Kesari Freeda. b 73. Nesamony Memorial Chr Coll Marthandam BSc 93 United Th Coll Bangalore BD 99. Princeton Th Sem ThM 01. **p** 05. PtO *Birm* 05–07; C Bridlington Priory *York* 07–10; V Southwater *Chich* from 10; Dioc Interfaith Adv from 18. *The Vicarage, Church Lane, Southwater, Horsham RH13 9BT* T: (01403) 730229 M: 07709-947056 E: revdgodfrey@yahoo.co.uk

GODFREY, Matthew Fenton. b 69. Univ Coll Dur BA 91 K Coll Lon MA 94. Ripon Coll Cuddesdon MTh 04. **d** 04 **p** 05. C Bodmin w Lanhydrock and Lanivet *Truro* 04–09; Chapl RN from 09. *Royal Naval Chaplaincy Service, Mail Point 1-2, Leach Building, Whale Island, Portsmouth PO2 8BY* T: (023) 9262 5055 F: 9262 5134 E: nitrogen_narcosis@hotmail.com

GODFREY, Michael. b 49. K Coll Lon BD 70 Wolv Univ PGCE 97. St Aug Coll Cant AKC 72. **d** 72 **p** 73. C Birtley *Dur* 72–75; Ind Chapl 76–79; TV Bilston *Lich* 79–86; TV Wolverhampton 86–93; Chapl Black Country Urban Ind Miss 79–86; Team Ldr 86–93; Preb Lich Cathl 87–93; PtO *Worc* 04–08; *Cov* 05–08; R Newport Pagnell w Lathbury and Moulsoe *Ox* 08–14; rtd 14; PtO *Cov* from 15; *Worc* from 15. *2 Dugdale Avenue, Bidford-on-Avon, Alcester B50 4QE* T: (01789) 773022 E: rev.michael.godfrey@gmail.com *or* rector_08@btinternet.com

GODFREY, Michael James. b 50. Sheff Univ BEd 77. St Jo Coll Nottm 79. **d** 82 **p** 83. C Walton H Trin *Ox* 82–86; C Chadderton Ch Ch *Man* 86–91; V Woodlands *Sheff* 91–03; V Wythall *Birm* 03–11; TV Morley *Wakef* 11–14; Leeds 14–18; rtd 18. *26 Wye Road, Brockworth, Gloucester GL3 4PP*

GODFREY, The Very Revd Nigel Philip. b 51. Ripon Coll Cuddesdon BA 78 MA 84 Lon Guildhall Univ MBA 00 K Coll Lon MSc 09 MRTPI 76. Ripon Coll Cuddesdon 77. **d** 79 **p** 80. C Kennington St Jo w St Jas *S'wark* 79–89; Community of Ch the Servant 84–93; V Brixton Road Ch Ch *S'wark* 89–01; Prin OLM Scheme 01–07; Chapl S'wark Cathl 02–07; V German *S & M* 07–12; P-in-c Patrick 11–12; V W Coast from 12; Vice-Dean St German's Cathl 07–11; Dean St German's Cathl from 11; Dir Voc and Tr from 10. *The Deanery, Albany Road, Peel, Isle of Man IM5 1JS* T: (01624) 844830 E: dean@sodoranddman.im

GODFREY, Mrs Patricia Ann. b 54. SEITE 01. **d** 04 **p** 05. NSM Dover St Mary *Cant* 04–14; NSM Dover Town 14–17; NSM Dover St Martin 14–17; rtd 17; PtO *Cant* from 17. *8 Longfield Road, Dover CT17 9QU* T: (01304) 206019 E: trishgodfrey8@yahoo.co.uk

GODFREY (née ROGERS), Canon Pauline Ann. b 58. LMH Ox BA 79 MA 83 Ox Univ Inst of Educn PGCE 80. S Dios Minl Tr Scheme 89. **d** 92 **p** 94. NSM Headley All SS *Guildf* 92–96; C 96–99; P-in-c Wyke 99–01; V 01–11; Past Tutor Local Min Progr 96–11; Dioc Voc Officer *Glouc* 11–18; Hd Discipleship and Voc and Dep Dir Dept Miss and Min from 18; Hon Can Glouc Cathl from 19. *3 Manston Way, Kingsway, Quedgeley, Gloucester GL2 2FB* T: (01452) 699803 *or* 835548 E: p.a.g@talktalk.net

GODFREY, Mrs Sarah Joy. b 64. Southn Univ BSc 85 Bath Univ PGCE 86. STETS 02. **d** 05 **p** 06. NSM Puddletown, Tolpuddle and Milborne w Dewlish *Sarum* 05–14; Asst Dioc Dir of Ords 11–14; V Milborne Port w Goathill etc *B & W* from 14. *The Vicarage, Bathwell Lane, Milborne Port, Sherborne DT9 5AN* T: (01963) 250248 E: sarah.godfrey@tiscali.co.uk

GODFREY, Simon. b 43. Kelham Th Coll 60. **d** 69 **p** 70. C Sutton Coldfield St Chad *Birm* 69–74; C Handsworth St Andr 74–76; TV Wyken *Cov* 75; TV Coventry Caludon 75–80; P-in-c Warwick St Paul 80–84; rtd 06. *123 High Street, Cottenham, Cambridge CB24 8SD* T: (01954) 251615 E: suffolkhouse@ntlworld.com

GODFREY, Canon Simon Henry Martin. b 55. K Coll Lon BD 80 AKC 80. St Steph Ho Ox 80. **d** 81 **p** 82. C Kettering SS Pet and Paul 81–84; R Crick and Yelvertoft w Clay Coton and Lilbourne 84–89; V Northampton All SS w St Kath 89–98; R Northampton All SS w St Kath and St Pet 98–09; Sen Chapl Malta and Gozo *Eur* from 09; Can and Chan St Paul's Pro-Cathl Valletta from 09; CF (TA) from 88. *St Paul's Anglican Pro-Cathedral, Independence Square, Valletta VLT 1535, Malta GC* T: (00356) 2122 5714 F: 2122 5867 E: simonhmgodfrey@gmail.com

GODFREY, William. *See* GODFREY, Harold William

GODIN, Mrs Mary Louise. b 42. SRN 64 QN 66. Oak Hill NSM Course 89. **d** 92 **p** 94. NSM Surbiton Hill Ch Ch *S'wark* 92–03; Chapl Kingston and Distr Community NHS Trust 97–01; Team Chapl SW Lon and St George's Mental Health NHS Trust 01–03; Chapl Taunton and Somerset NHS Foundn Trust 03–11; C Beercrocombe w Curry Mallet, Hatch Beauchamp etc *B & W* 11–17; rtd 17; PtO *B & W* from 18. *The Stables, Capland Court, Capland Lane, Hatch Beauchamp, Taunton TA3 6TP* T: (01823) 480606 E: revmarygodin@gmail.com

GODLINGTON, Ian Denis. b 58. All SS Cen for Miss & Min 13. **d** 14 **p** 15. OLM Mickleover *Derby* from 14; Chapl Rolls-Royce Derby from 14. *46 Bren Way, Hilton, Derby DE65 5HP* T: (01283) 730832 M: 07788-417819 E: godlingtons46@gmail.com

GODSALL, Canon Andrew Paul. b 59. Birm Univ BA 81. Ripon Coll Cuddesdon 86. **d** 88 **p** 89. C Gt Stanmore Lon 88–91; C Ealing All SS 91–94; V Hillingdon All SS 94–01; Dir of Ords Willesden Area 99–01; Bp's Chapl and Asst *Ex* 01–06; Dioc Dir of Min 06–14; PV Ex Cathl 04–06; Can Res and Chan Ex Cathl 06–14; Miss Community Min Development Adv from 14. *20 Newcourt Way, Exeter EX2 7SA* T: (01392) 294902 E: andrew.godsall@exeter.anglican.org

GODSALL, Peter. **d** 17 **p** 18. NSM Aberdare St Fagan *Llan* from 17. *Oaktree House, 60 Glan Road, Aberdare CF44 8BW* T: (01685) 883697 E: peteroaktree@aol.com

GODSALL, Canon Ralph Charles. b 48. Qu Coll Cam BA 71 MA 75. Cuddesdon Coll 73. **d** 75 **p** 76. C Sprowston *Nor* 75–78; Chapl Trin Coll Cam 78–84; V Hebden Bridge *Wakef* 84–93; V Westmr St Steph w St Jo *Lon* 93–01; Can Res Roch Cathl 01–08; rtd 08; PV Westmr Abbey from 08. *39 Vincent Square, London SW1P 2NP* T: (020) 7976 5899 M: 07786-959540 E: canonralph@hotmail.com

GODSELL, Philip Winston. b 66. Cardiff Univ BTh 15 MTh 16. St Mich Coll Llan 13. **d** 15 **p** 16. C Cyncoed *Mon* 15–17; C Upper Torfaen from 17. *The Vicarage, Freeholdland Road, Pontynewynydd, Pontypool NP4 8LW* T: (01495) 759980 M: 07411-667301 E: frgodsell@gmail.com

GODSELL, Stephen Philip. b 72. WEMTC 15. **d** 18 **p** 19. C Ashleworth, Corse, Hartpury, Hasfield etc *Glouc* from 18. *Whites Farm, Pillows Green Road, Corse, Gloucester GL19 3NX* M: 07752-463536 E: stevegodsell@gmail.com *or* curate.westof7@gmail.com

GODSMARK, Susan Mary. d 14 **p** 15. OLM Gt Totham and Lt Totham w Goldhanger *Chelmsf* 14–18; NSM from 18. *57 Mill Road, Great Totham, Maldon CM9 8DH* T: (01621) 891513 E: suegodsmark@aol.com

GODSON, Mark Rowland. b 61. K Coll Lon BD 83 AKC 83 CertEd 84. Linc Th Coll 84. **d** 86 **p** 87. C Hurst Green *S'wark* 86–88; C Fawley *Win* 88–90; TV Wimborne Minster and Holt *Sarum* 90–95; P-in-c Horton and Chalbury 90–93; P-in-c Vale of Allen 93–95; P-in-c Stalbridge 95–96; Chapl Forest Healthcare NHS Trust Lon 96–00; P-in-c Bicton, Montford w Shrawardine and Fitz *Lich* 00–06; Chapl Shropshire Co Primary Care Trust 01–06; TR Fordingbridge and Breamore

and Hale etc *Win* 06–10; R 10–12; AD Christchurch 10–12; Dir Lon Cen for Spirituality 12–16; Hon C Abinger and Coldharbour and Wotton and Holmbury St Mary *Guildf* 16–18; P-in-c Ewyas Harold w Dulas, Kenderchurch etc *Heref* from 18; PtO *Lon* from 17. *The Rectory, Ewyas Harold, Hereford HR2 0EZ* T: (01981) 240079 E: mrkgdsn@gmail.com

GODWIN, Canon David Harold. b 45. Glos Univ BA 09. Kelham Th Coll 67. **d** 71 **p** 72. C Camberwell St Phil and St Mark *S'wark* 71–75; Asst Chapl The Lon Hosp (Whitechapel) 75–79; Chapl R E Sussex Hosp Hastings 79–86; Chapl Over Hosp Glouc 86–92; Chapl Glos R Hosp 86–94; Chapl Glos R Hosp NHS Trust 94–02; Chapl Glos Hosps NHS Foundn Trust 02–05; Hon Can Glouc Cathl 03–05; rtd 05; PtO *Glouc* from 05. *61 The Barge Arm, The Docks, Gloucester GL1 2DN* T: (01452) 730435 M: 07989-046118 E: davidhgodwin@live.co.uk

GODWIN, Canon Michael Francis Harold. b 35. Nottm Univ BSc 57. Ely Th Coll 59. **d** 61 **p** 62. C Farnborough *Guildf* 61–65; V Epsom St Barn 66–85; V Bramley and Grafham 85–98; Hon Can Guildf Cathl 89–98; rtd 00; PtO *Chich* 13–17. *14 Lemmington Way, Horsham RH12 5JG* T: (01403) 273411

GOFF, Philip Francis Michael. b 52. K Coll Lon BD 73 AKC 73 FBS 00 FSA 08. St Aug Coll Cant 74. **d** 75 **p** 76. C Ruislip St Martin *Lon* 75–79; Chapl Aldenham Sch Herts 79–82; V Tokyngton St Mich *Lon* 82–89; In RC Ch 89–91; Primary Care Cllr NHS 91–98; PtO *Lon* 99–00; Chapl to Bp Edmonton 00–04; Asst Dir Post-Ord Tr Edmonton Area 03–06; P-in-c Highgate St Aug 04–14; V 14–15; AD W Haringey 11–14; rtd 15; PtO *Lon* 16–18. *51 Kingsmere, Benfleet SS7 3XN* M: 07768-920506 E: phildress@blueyonder.co.uk

GOFTON, Canon William Alder. b 31. Dur Univ BA 54. Coll of Resurr Mirfield 59. **d** 61 **p** 62. C Benwell St Aid *Newc* 61–64; C N Gosforth 64–69; V Seaton Hirst 69–77; V Newc H Cross 77–89; RD Newc W 85–89; Hon Can Newc Cathl 88–96; R Bolam w Whalton and Hartburn w Meldon 89–96; P-in-c Nether Witton 89–95; V 95–96; Chapl Kirkley Hall Coll 90–96; rtd 96; PtO *Newc* from 96. *4 Crossfell, Ponteland, Newcastle upon Tyne NE20 9EA* T: (01661) 820344 E: aggofton@yahoo.co.uk

GOGGIN, Philip Frederick de Jean. b 46. Rhodes Univ BA 66 Lon Univ MA 73 Keele Univ PhD 89 Leeds Univ MA 05. NOC 03. **d** 05 **p** 06. NSM Sandbach Heath w Wheelock *Ches* 05–07; P-in-c Leighton-cum-Minshull Vernon 07–11; V Leighton-cum-Minshull Vernon and Warmingham from 11. *The Vicarage, Middlewich Road, Minshull Vernon, Crewe CW1 4RD* T: (01270) 522213 E: gail.philip@virgin.net

GOLD, Stephen Eric. b 67. St Mellitus Coll 12. **d** 15 **p** 16. C Hillmorton *Cov* 15–18; P-in-c from 18. *2 Maxwell Road, Houlton, Rugby CV23 1AH* E: steve.gold2@me.com *or* steve@stjohnhillmorton.org.uk

GOLDBY, Miss Emma Lucy. b 73. Glos Univ BEd 97. Ripon Coll Cuddesdon 12. **d** 14 **p** 15. C Malvern H Trin and St Jas *Worc* 14–17; C Abberton, The Flyfords, Naunton Beauchamp etc from 17; C Fladbury, Hill and Moor, Wyre Piddle etc from 17; C Stoulton w Drake's Broughton and Pirton etc from 17. *The Rectory, 4 Manor Farm, Stoulton, Worcester WR7 4RS* T: (01905) 840752 E: revdemmagoldby@gmail.com

GOLDENBERG, Ralph Maurice. b 45. City Univ FBCO 67 FBOA 67. Trin Coll Bris 88. **d** 90 **p** 91. C Kinson *Sarum* 90–93; C Edgware *Lon* 93–97; TV Roxeth 97–01; V Bayston Hill *Lich* 01–10; rtd 10; PtO *Sarum* from 11. *2 Golf Links Road, Ferndown BH22 8BY* T: (01202) 893131 E: r.goldenberg@btopenworld.com

GOLDER, Rebecca Marie. *See* ROGERS, Rebecca Marie

GOLDIE, Prof James Stuart. b 46. Edin Univ BEd 73 Hon MEd 00 Cairo Univ Hon PhD 06. Lon Coll of Div BDQ 67 BTh 70 ALCD 69. **d** 69 **p** 70. C Blackpool St Paul *Blackb* 69–70; C St Sankey *Liv* 70–73; C-in-c Penketh CD 70–73; Asst Chapl Greystone Heath Sch 70–73; Chapl Kilmarnock Academy 73–75; V Flixton St Jo *Man* 75–78; Chapl Friars Sch Man 75–78; V Skelmersdale St Paul *Liv* 78–80; Chapl Trin Sch Liv 78–80; Lect Man Bible Coll and Dir Man City Miss 80–83; Hon Prof Cam Univ from 81; Chapl Westbrook Hay Sch Hemel Hempstead 83–89; V Pennington w Lindal and Marton *Carl* 89–90; Chapl Bp Wand Sch Sunbury-on-Thames 89–95; Chapl Queenswood Sch Herts 96–97; Hd Master Westcliff Prep Sch 97–03; V Red Sea Area (w ecum oversight) Egypt 04–12; Prin El Gouna Internat Sch 04–12; rtd 12. *23 Ffordd Naddyn, Glan Conway, Colwyn Bay LL28 4NH* T: (01492) 593996

GOLDIE, Katrina Ruth. *See* SCOTT, Katrina Ruth

GOLDING, Neil Christopher. b 47. Warwick Univ BA 69. S'wark Ord Course 92. **d** 95 **p** 96. C Mitcham Ascension *S'wark* 95–00; P-in-c Croydon Woodside 00–05; V 05–15;

rtd 15; PtO *Truro* from 15. *93 Retallick Meadows, St Austell PL25 3BZ* T: (01726) 69261 E: rev_neil@btopenworld.com

GOLDING, The Ven Simon Jefferies. b 46. Brasted Place Coll 70. Linc Th Coll 72. **d** 74 **p** 75. C Wilton *York* 74–77; Chapl RN 77–97; Chapl of the Fleet 97-98 and 00–02; Adn for the RN 97–02; Dir Gen Naval Chapl Service 00–02; QHC 97–02; Hon Can Gib Cathl *Eur* 98–02; rtd 02; PtO *Ripon* 02–11; Dioc Adv for NSM 08–11; Hon C E Richmond 11–14; *Leeds* 14–16; Hon C Wiske Benefice from 16. *Arlanza, Hornby Road, Appleton Wiske, Northallerton DL6 2AF* T: (01609) 881185 E: golding@clannet.co.uk

GOLDING, Stephen. b 57. Keele Univ BA 79 CertEd 79 Lon Bible Coll BA 86 Heythrop Coll Lon MA 09. Cant Sch of Min 93. **d** 95 **p** 96. NSM Ramsgate St Luke *Cant* 95–98; Chapl St Lawr Coll Ramsgate 95–98; Chapl Berkhamsted Sch Herts 98–10; Chapl Cn Hosp Horsham 10–19; rtd 19. *5 Loader Close, Kings Worthy, Winchester SO23 7TF* M: 07587-220706

GOLDING, Trevor. b 58. Ridley Hall Cam 07. **d** 09 **p** 10. C Highbury Ch Ch w St Jo and St Sav *Lon* 09–12; V Ipswich St Aug *St E* 13–19; TV Tollington *Lon* from 19. *Address temp unknown* M: 07511-870694 E: trevor.golding@gmail.com

GOLDINGAY, Prof John Edgar. b 42. Keble Coll Ox BA 64 Nottm Univ PhD 83 Lambeth DD 97. Clifton Th Coll 64. **d** 66 **p** 67. C Finchley Ch Ch *Lon* 66–69; Lect St Jo Coll Nottm 70–75; Dir Studies 76–79; Registrar 79–85; Vice-Prin 85–88; Prin 88–97; Prof OT Fuller Th Sem Pasadena 97–18. *4 Mill Stream House, Norfolk Street, Oxford OX1 1EB* T: (01865) 244090 E: johngold@fuller.edu

GOLDRING, Mrs Philippa Elizabeth Vincent. b 58. Southn Univ LLB 79 Spurgeon's Coll BD 05. SEITE BA 10. **d** 10 **p** 11. C Wednesfield Heath *Lich* 10–14; PtO 14–15; Hon C Heath Town from 15. *521 Cannock Road, Wolverhampton WV10 0RH* T: (01902) 731456

GOLDSMITH, Brian Derek. b 36. Leeds Univ BA 64. Coll of Resurr Mirfield 64. **d** 66 **p** 67. C Littlehampton St Mary *Chich* 66–69; C Guildf St Nic 69–73; V Aldershot St Aug 73–81; C-in-c Leigh Park St Clare CD *Portsm* 82–85; C Rowner 85–96; rtd 97; C Catherington and Clanfield *Portsm* 97–01; PtO *Win* 98–14. *27 White Dirt Lane, Catherington, Waterlooville PO8 0NB* T: (023) 9259 9462

GOLDSMITH, Christine Ann. b 63. Qu Coll Newfoundland BTh 18. **d** 15 **p** 16. Cyprus 15–19; R Brant Broughton and Beckingham *Linc* from 19; R Leadenham from 19; R Welbourn from 19. *The Rectory, Church End Fulbeck Road, Leadenham, Lincoln LN5 0PX* T: (01400) 679081 M: 07494-870701 E: rectorleadenham@gmail.com

✠**GOLDSMITH, The Rt Revd Christopher David.** b 54. York Univ BA 76 DPhil 79. NTMTC 97. **d** 00 **p** 01 **c** 13. NSM Pitsea w Nevendon *Chelmsf* 00–04; V Warley Ch Ch and Gt Warley St Mary 04–13; Suff Bp St Germans *Truro* 13–19; Dioc Warden of Readers 13–19; Dir Min Division Abps' Coun from 19. *Ministry Division, Church House, Great Smith Street, London SW1P 3AZ* T: (020) 7898 1390 E: chris.goldsmith@churchofengland.org

GOLDSMITH, Mrs Ellen Elizabeth. b 48. York Univ BA 77 Middx Univ BA 06. NTMTC 03. **d** 06 **p** 07. NSM Bentley Common, Kelvedon Hatch and Navestock *Chelmsf* 06–10; NSM Warley Ch Ch and Gt Warley St Mary 10–13; TV Probus, Ladock and Grampound w Creed and St Erme *Truro* 14–18; NSM 18–19; rtd 19. *Vounder, Tresillian, Truro TR2 4BW* T: (01872) 520192 M: 07906-979321 E: ellen.goldsmith@btinternet.com

GOLDSMITH, Kathryn Jane Alexandra. b 78. K Alfred's Coll Win BTh 01 Univ Coll Lon BSc 11 Qu Mary Coll Lon MSc 14 Leeds Univ PhD 19 FRAS 11. Coll of Resurr Mirfield MA 19. **d** 19. C Chapelthorpe *Leeds* from 19. *15 The Crimbles, Durkar, Wakefield WF4 3EX*

GOLDSMITH, Lesley Anne. NTMTC 02. **d** 05 **p** 06. C E Ham w Upton Park and Forest Gate *Chelmsf* 05–08; V Chingford St Edm from 08. *St Edmund's Vicarage, Larkswood Road, London E4 9DS* T: (020) 8529 5226 E: lesley.goldsmith@btinternet.com

GOLDSMITH, Canon Mary Louie. b 48. K Coll Lon BA 70 AKC 70. Qu Coll Birm 91. **d** 93 **p** 94. NSM Matlock Bank *Derby* 93–97; NSM Kirk Hallam 97–02; NSM Taddington, Chelmorton and Monyash etc 00–11; Hon Can Derby Cathl from 05. *9 Highfield Gardens, Highfield Road, Derby DE22 1HT* T: (01332) 209392 E: goldsmith681@btinternet.com *or* goldsmithjandm@aol.com

GOLDSMITH, Mrs Pauline Anne. b 40. Linc Th Coll 82. **dss** 84 **d** 87 **p** 94. Waddington *Linc* 86–88; Par Dn 87–88; Par Dn Gt and Lt Coates w Bradley 88–94; TV 94–96; TV Kidderminster St Mary and All SS w Trimpley etc *Worc* 96–01; rtd 01; PtO *Derby* from 01; *Sheff* 01–14. *143 Ravencar*

Road, Eckington, Sheffield *S21 4JR* T: (01246) 430083 E: paulnstevgoldsmith@gmail.com

GOLDSMITH, Stephen. b 32. Edin Th Coll. **d** 76 **p** 77. SPCK Staff 53–97; Bookshops Regional Manager SPCK 87–97; NSM Penicuik *Edin* 76–81; NSM Linc St Nic w St Jo Newport 81–90; NSM Gt and Lt Coates w Bradley 90–96; NSM Kidderminster St Mary and All SS w Trimpley etc *Worc* 96–01; PtO *Derby* from 01; *Sheff* 01–14. *143 Ravencar Road, Eckington, Sheffield S21 4JR* T: (01246) 430083

GOLDSPINK, David. b 35. Open Univ BA 81. Lon Coll of Div 62. **d** 65 **p** 66. C Mile Cross *Nor* 65–68; C St Austell *Truro* 68–70; TV Bramerton w Surlingham w Rockland St Mary 70–73; Min Gunton St Pet 73–75; R Mutford w Rushmere w Gisleham w N Cove w Barnby 75–81; Asst Chapl HM Pris Man 81–82; Chapl HM Youth Cust Cen Hollesley Bay Colony 82–84; Chapl HM Pris Blundeston 84–88; PtO *St E* 87–01; rtd 88; PtO *Nor* from 88. *14 Deepdale, Carlton Colville, Lowestoft NR33 8TU* T: (01502) 538138

GOLDSTONE-CREASEY, Graham. b 51. Trent Poly BA 73. Cranmer Hall Dur 80. **d** 83 **p** 84. C Birstall and Wanlip *Leic* 83–87; C-in-c Wheatley Park St Paul CD *Sheff* 87–92; V Wheatley Park 92–95; P-in-c Gleadless Valley 95–98. *281 Fleetwood Road North, Thornton-Cleveleys FY5 4LE* T: (01253) 862668 E: grahamgc10@gmail.com

GOLDTHORP, Ms Ann Lesley. b 59. Qu Coll Birm 08. **d** 11 **p** 12. C Harbury and Ladbroke *Cov* 11–15; V Deddington w Barford, Clifton and Hempton *Ox* from 15. *The Vicarage, 1 Earls Close, Deddington OX15 0TJ* T: (01869) 336880 E: reverendannie@hotmail.com

GOLDTHORPE, Duncan Robert. b 70. Herts Univ BA 99. ERMC 15. **d** 18 **p** 19. C Bedford St Andr *St Alb* from 18. *5 St Minver Road, Bedford MK40 3DQ* T: (01234) 268689 E: curate@standrewsbedford.org

GOLDTHORPE, Ms Shirley. b 42. Linc Th Coll 70. **dss** 76 **d** 87 **p** 94. Thornhill Lees *Wakef* 76–78; Birkenshaw w Hunsworth 78–80; Batley St Thos 80–85; Batley All SS 80–85; Purlwell 80–92; Par Dn 87–88; Dn-in-c 88–92; Dn-in-c Horbury Junction 92–94; P-in-c 94–01; rtd 02; PtO *Wakef* 02–14; *Leeds* from 14. *10 Orchid View, Alverthorpe, Wakefield WF2 0FG* T: (01924) 383181 M: 07885-462837

GOLLEDGE, Canon Patricia Anne. b 55. Trin Coll Bris BA 00. **d** 00 **p** 01. C Pontypool *Mon* 00–03; TV 03–09; V Griffithstown 09–13; R Panteg and Griffithstown from 13; AD Pontypool from 16; Can St Woolos Cathl from 17. *St Hilda's Vicarage, 2 Sunnybank Road, Griffithstown, Pontypool NP4 5LT* T: (01495) 763641 E: p.golledge@talktalk.net

GOLTON, Alan Victor. b 29. St Jo Coll Ox BA 51 MA 54 DPhil 54. **d** 85 **p** 86. NSM Barston *Birm* 85–95; P-in-c 87; rtd 95; PtO *Birm* 95–96; Hon C Grenoble *Eur* 97–00. *Chant du Matin, Les Michallons, 38250 St Nizier du Moucherotte, France* T: (0033) 4 76 53 43 77 E: avgolton@hotmail.com

GOMERSALL, Canon Ian Douglass. b 56. Birm Univ BSc 77 Fitzw Coll Cam BA 80 MA 85 Dur Univ MA 94. Westcott Ho Cam 78. **d** 81 **p** 82. C Darlington St Mark w St Paul *Dur* 81–84; C Barnard Castle w Whorlton 84–86; Chapl HM YOI Deerbolt 85–90; P-in-c Cockfield *Dur* 86–88; R 88–90; Dep Chapl HM Pris Wakef 90–91; Chapl HM Pris Full Sutton 91–97; P-in-c Kexby w Wilberfoss *York* 93–97; TV Man Whitworth 97–03; P-in-c Man Victoria Park 98–09; R from 09; Chapl Man Univ 97–03; Hon Chapl from 03; AD Ardwick Man 08–15; Hon Can Man Cathl from 11. *St Chrysostom's Rectory, 38 Park Range, Manchester M14 5HQ* T: 0161-224 6971 M: 07711-670225 E: ian.gomersall@btinternet.com

GOMERSALL, Richard. b 45. FCA 68. NOC 90. **d** 93 **p** 94. NSM Thurcroft *Sheff* 93–96; NSM Sheff St Matt 96–03; Ind Chapl 98–03; C-in-c Southey Green St Bernard CD 03–11. *Dale View House, 14 Wignall Avenue, Wickersley, Rotherham S66 2AX* T: (01709) 546441 F: 701900 E: fr.gomersall@btinternet.com

GOMM, Timothy Frank. b 64. St Jo Coll Nottm 00. **d** 02 **p** 03. C Kinson *Sarum* 02–04; C Heatherlands St Jo and Community Chapl Rossmore Community Coll 04–10; C Longfleet *Sarum* 10–11; TR Portland from 11. *St John's Vicarage, Ventnor Road, Portland DT5 1JE* T: (01305) 820103 E: rev.gomm@btinternet.com

GOMPERTZ, Mrs Charlotte. b 72. St Jo Coll Nottm 13. **d** 16 **p** 17. C Meole Brace *Lich* from 16. *7 Dargate Close, Shrewsbury SY3 9QE* M: 07769-349052 E: chargomp@gmail.com

GONIN, Christopher Willett. b 33. Man Univ DACE 87 MBA 92. AKC 59. **d** 60 **p** 61. C Camberwell St Geo *S'wark* 60–64; C Stevenage H Trin *St Alb* 64–69; C Bletchley *Ox* 70–73; R Newington St Mary *S'wark* 73–76; PtO *Bris* 76–77; Hon C Horfield H Trin 77–89; Hon C City of Bris 89–91; V Milton Ernest *St Alb* 92–97; V Thurleigh 92–97; rtd 97; PtO *St E* from 97. *24 Booth Court, Handford Road, Ipswich IP1 2GD* T: (01473) 232732 E: c.gonin@btinternet.com

GONZALEZ PENA, Heller. b 72. **d** 11 **p** 12. C La Coruña H Cross Spain 11–12; R 12–15; C Port Glas from 15; C Kilmacolm from 15; C Bridge of Weir from 15. *The Rectory, 4 Balmore Court, Kilmacolm PA13 4LX* T: (01505) 872961 M: 07496-841775 E: hellerg@hotmail.com

GOOCH, Michael Anthony. b 44. Nottm Coll of Educn TCert 66. Cant Sch of Min 90. **d** 93 **p** 94. NSM New Romney w Old Romney and Midley *Cant* 93–97; P-in-c Teynham w Lynsted and Kingsdown 97–08; Bp's Officer for NSM 98–03; rtd 08; PtO *Cant* from 08. *Little Owls, Tookey Road, New Romney TN28 8ET* T: (01797) 367858 E: manddgooch@hotmail.co.uk

GOOD, Andrew Ronald. b 60. Bris Univ BA 82. Linc Th Coll 83. **d** 85 **p** 86. C Epping St Jo *Chelmsf* 85–88; C Cheshunt *St Alb* 88–91; R Spixworth w Crostwick and Frettenham *Nor* 91–04; PtO 04–10; P-in-c Ashwellthorpe, Forncett, Fundenhall, Hapton etc 11–12; R Holkham w Egmere w Warham etc 12–14. *Ferrar House, Little Gidding, Huntingdon PE28 5RJ* E: andrewrgood@hotmail.com

GOOD, David Howard. b 42. Glouc Sch of Min 84. **d** 87 **p** 88. NSM Bromyard *Heref* 87–92; C Pontesbury I and II 92–95; P-in-c Ditton Priors w Neenton, Burwarton etc 95–98; R 98–02; rtd 02; PtO *Heref* from 02. *26 Farjeon Close, Ledbury HR8 2FU* T: (01531) 636474

GOOD, Preb John Hobart. b 43. Bps' Coll Cheshunt 66 Coll of Resurr Mirfield 68. **d** 69 **p** 70. C Ex St Jas 69–73; C Cockington 73–75; C Wolborough w Newton Abbot 75–78; P-in-c Exminster and Kenn 78–80; R 80–95; RD Kenn 89–95; TR Axminster, Chardstock, All Saints etc 95–09; Chapl All Hallows Sch Rousdon 98–09; Preb Ex Cathl 02–09; rtd 09; TV Dorchester *Sarum* 09–13; Hon C The Winterbournes and Compton Valence 09–13; PtO *Ex* from 13. *3 Home Farm Court, Deane Road, Stokeinteignhead, Newton Abbot TQ12 4QF* E: johngood1549@outlook.com

✠**GOOD, The Rt Revd Kenneth Raymond.** b 52. TCD BA 74 Nottm Univ BA 76 NUI HDipEd 81 MEd 84. St Jo Coll Nottm 75. **d** 77 **p** 78 **c** 02. C Willowfield *D & D* 77–79; Chapl Ashton Sch Cork 79–84; I Dungasntown w Redcross and Conary *D & G* 84–90; I Lurgan Ch the Redeemer *D & D* 90–02; Adn Dromore 97–02; Bp D & R 02–19; rtd 19. *Address temp unknown*

GOOD, The Ven Kenneth Roy. b 41. K Coll Lon BD 66 AKC 66. **d** 67 **p** 68. C Stockton St Pet *Dur* 67–70; Chapl Antwerp Miss to seamen *Eur* 70–74; Chapl Kobe Japan 74–79; Asst Gen Sec Miss to Seamen and Asst Chapl St Mich Paternoster Royal *Lon* 79–85; Hon Can Kobe from 85; V Nunthorpe *York* 85–93; RD Stokesley 90–93; Adn Richmond *Ripon* 93–06; rtd 06; PtO *York* 07–17; *Dur* from 10. *18 Fox Howe, Coulby Newham, Middlesbrough TS8 0RU* T: (01642) 594158 E: joken.good@ntlworld.com

GOOD, Stuart Eric Clifford. b 37. Wycliffe Hall Ox 63. **d** 64 **p** 65. C Walton H Trin *Ox* 64–66; C Nedlands Australia 66–67; R Mundaring 67–71; R Bassendean 71–78; R Como 78–85; Dir Chapl Services Angl Homes Inc 85–05; rtd 05. *135/27 Pearson Drive, Success WA 6164, Australia* M: (0061) 41-894 3337 E: sbargood@bigpond.net.au

GOODACRE, Canon David Leighton. b 36. AKC 59. **d** 60 **p** 61. C Stockton St Chad *Dur* 60–63; C Birtley 63–68; Chapl Sunderland Gen Hosp 69–74; P-in-c Ryhope *Dur* 75–81; V Ovingham *Newc* 81–01; Hon Can Newc Cathl 92–01; rtd 01; PtO *Newc* from 01. *9 Wilmington Close, Newcastle upon Tyne NE3 2SF* T: 0191-271 4382 E: david.goodacre29@sky.com

GOODACRE, Philip James. b 81. Ox Brookes Univ BA 04 Birm Univ MA 06 Anglia Ruskin Univ MA 13. Ridley Hall Cam 09. **d** 11 **p** 12. C Brightside w Wincobank *Sheff* 11–14; P-in-c Hillsborough and Wadsley Bridge from 14. *Christ Church Vicarage, 218 Fox Hill Road, Sheffield S6 1HJ* T: 0114-234 9376 E: philipgoodacre@gmail.com

GOODAIR, Jan. b 59. K Coll Lon BA 81 Leeds Univ PhD 02 Roehampton Inst PGCE 82. NEOC 97. **d** 00 **p** 01. NSM Tockwith and Bilton w Bickerton *York* 00–01; NSM York St Olave w St Giles 00–01; Chapl Harrogate Ladies' Coll 01–10; Chapl Haberdashers' Aske's Sch Elstree 10–15; Chapl Pocklington Sch 15–19; rtd 19. *47 North Moor, Huntington, York YO32 9RX* M: 07840-731137 E: jan.cheeseman@ntlworld.com

GOODALL, Alice Elizabeth. b 58. Keele Univ BA 80. STETS 09. **d** 12 **p** 13. C St Bartholomew *Sarum* 12–16; R Shelswell Ox from 16. *The Rectory, Water Stratford Road, Finmere, Buckingham MK18 4AT* T: (01280) 848192 M: 07447-933140 E: alicegoodall313@gmail.com

GOODALL, Canon John William. b 45. Hull Univ BA 69. Ripon Hall Ox 69. **d** 71 **p** 72. C Loughborough Em *Leic* 71–74; C Dorchester *Ox* 74–75; TV 75–80; Tutor Sarum & Wells Th Coll 80–88; Vice Prin S Dios Minl Tr Scheme

80–88; P-in-c Gt Wishford *Sarum* 80–83; P-in-c Colehill 88–96; V 96–13; Dioc Dir of Readers 88–95; Can and Preb Sarum Cathl 07–13; rtd 13; PtO *Sarum* 13–17. *27 Fishers Close, Blandford Forum DT11 7EL* E: canongoodall@gmail.com

✠**GOODALL, The Rt Revd Jonathan Michael.** b 61. R Holloway Coll Lon BMus 83. Wycliffe Hall Ox 86. **d** 89 **p** 90 **c** 13. C Bicester w Bucknell, Caversfield and Launton *Ox* 89–92; Asst Chapl HM Pris Bullingdon 90–92; Min Can, Chapl, and Sacr Westmr Abbey 92–98; Bp's Chapl and Research Asst *Eur* 98–05; Can Gib Cathl from 05; Abp's Personal Chapl and Ecum Sec *Cant* 05–13; Hon C Westmr St Matt *Lon* 99–03; PV Westmr Abbey 04–05; Suff Bp Ebbsfleet (PEV) *Cant* from 13; Hon Asst Bp Lich, Ox and Worc from 13; Cov and Ex from 14; Bris from 15; B & W from 16; Truro and Birm from 17; PV Westmr Abbey from 14. *Hill House, Treetops, The Mount, Caversham, Reading RG4 7RE* T: 0118-948 1038 E: office@ebbsfleet.org.uk

GOODBODY, Ruth Vivien. b 68. Surrey Univ BA 02. Wycliffe Hall Ox 96 STETS 00. **d** 02 **p** 03. C Bourne Valley *Sarum* 02–06; C Stebbing and Lindsell w Gt and Lt Saling *Chelmsf* 06–10; rtd 10; PtO *Chelmsf* from 12. *The Vicarage, 7 Ruffels Place, Stebbing, Dunmow CM6 3TJ* T: (01371) 856080 E: thegoodbodies@btinternet.com

GOODBODY, Steven John. b 70. Univ of Wales (Cardiff) BD 92. Wycliffe Hall Ox 00. **d** 02 **p** 03. C Tunbridge Wells St Jo *Roch* 02–05; C Ex St Leon w H Trin 05–10; TR Washfield, Stoodleigh, Withleigh etc 10–15; V Fremington from 15. *19 Lane End Close, Instow, Bideford EX39 4LG* T: (01271) 861082 M: 07768-645172 E: stevegoodbody@btinternet.com

GOODBURN, David Henry. b 41. S'wark Ord Course 73. **d** 76 **p** 77. NSM Enfield SS Pet and Paul *Lon* 76–82; PtO 83–85; NSM Potters Bar *St Alb* 85–88; Chapl RN 88–96; V Luton St Sav *St Alb* 96–09; rtd 09; PtO *St Alb* from 09; *Cant* from 12; *Lon* 17–18. *Major's, Barrack Hill, Hythe CT21 4BZ* T: (01303) 262736

GOODDEN, John Maurice Phelips. b 34. Sarum & Wells Th Coll 70. **d** 72 **p** 75. C Weymouth H Trin *Sarum* 72–74; C Harlow New Town w Lt Parndon *Chelmsf* 74–78; Ind Chapl and Chapl Princess Alexandra Hosp Harlow 78–82; V Moulsham St Jo *Chelmsf* 86–90; R Chipstead and Adv Rural Min *S'wark* 90–04; rtd 04; PtO *B & W* from 05; *Sarum* 05–16. *9 Royston House, 5 Duke Street, Bath BA2 4AH* T: (01225) 282246 E: goodden@msn.com

GOODDEN, Stephanie Anne. *See* NADARAJAH, Stephanie Anne

GOODE, Allan William. b 50. St Mellitus Coll 16. **d** 17 **p** 18. NSM Birkenhead Ch Ch *Ches* from 17. *49 Birch Road, Prenton CH43 5UF* T: 0151-652 1304 E: twogoodes@hotmail.com

GOODE, Claire Elizabeth. b 60. Nottm Univ BSc 82. EMMTC 04. **d** 08 **p** 09. C S Notts Cluster of Par *S'well* 08–11; P-in-c Thurgarton w Hoveringham and Bleasby etc 11–14; P-in-c Rolleston w Fiskerton, Morton and Upton 11–14; V Nottingham St Andr from 14. *St Andrew's Vicarage, 1 Chestnut Grove, Nottingham NG3 5AD* T: 0115-912 0098 E: revclairegoode@gmail.com

GOODE, John Laurence. b 48. W Cheshire Coll of Tech TEng 70 Federal Univ Minas Gerais Brazil Dip Teaching 78. Chich Th Coll 81. **d** 83 **p** 84. C Crewe St Andr *Ches* 83–86; USPG 87–94; Brazil 91–94; TV Ches 94–00; V Latchford Ch Ch from 00; P-in-c Latchford St Jas 15–18. *Christ Church Vicarage, Wash Lane, Warrington WA4 1HT* T: (01925) 630846 E: dida1@btopenworld.com

GOODE, Jonathan. b 67. St Martin's Coll Lanc BA 89. Qu Coll Birm. **d** 00 **p** 01. C Middleton St Mary *Ripon* 00–04; P-in-c Hartlepool St Hilda *Dur* 04–08; Chapl St Hilda's Sch 04–08; V Denton *Newc* 08–12; PtO 13–18; Chapl Northumberland, Tyne and Wear NHS Foundn Trust from 15. *St Mary's Vicarage, 77 Holywell Avenue, Whitley Bay NE26 3AG* T: 0191-280 3555 E: revjgoode@yahoo.com

GOODE, Michael Arthur John. b 40. K Coll Lon BD AKC 63. **d** 64 **p** 65. C Sunderland Springwell w Thorney Close *Dur* 64–68; C Solihull *Birm* 68–70; R Fladbury, Wyre Piddle and Moor *Worc* 70–75; P-in-c Foley Park 75–81; V 81–83; RD Kidderminster 81–83; TR Crawley *Chich* 83–93; TR Abingdon and V Shippon *Ox* 93–05; rtd 05; PtO *Worc* from 07. *13 Britannia Square, Worcester WR1 3DG* T: (01905) 616982 E: maj.goode@btinternet.com

GOODE, Canon Peter William Herbert. b 23. Oak Hill Th Coll 60. **d** 62 **p** 63. C Woodford Wells *Chelmsf* 62–65; V Harold Hill St Paul 65–76; V Gt Warley Ch Ch 76–93; RD Brentwood 89–93; Hon Can Chelmsf Cathl 90–93; rtd 93; PtO *St Alb* 93–18. *52 Slimmons Drive, St Albans AL4 9AP* T: (01727) 852150

GOODE, Timothy. b 69. Huddersfield Poly BA 90 Roehampton Inst PGCE 91. Ripon Coll Cuddesdon 07. **d** 09 **p** 10. C Croydon St Jo *S'wark* 09–12; TV Caterham 12–18; R Lee St Marg from 18; Dioc Disability Adv from 13. *St Margaret's Rectory, Brandram Road, London SE13 5EA* T: (020) 8318 5438 E: revtimgoode@gmail.com

GOODERHAM, Daniel Charles. b 24. St Fran Coll Brisbane 49. **d** 52 **p** 53. Australia 52–60; C Staveley *Derby* 60–61; C Ipswich St Thos *St E* 61–64; V Ipswich St Bart 64–71; R Drinkstone 71–78; R Rattlesden 71–78; RD Lavenham 75–78; V Beckenham St Mich w St Aug *Roch* 78–87; P-in-c Whiteparish *Sarum* 87–89; rtd 89; PtO *St E* from 89. *The Limes Retirement Home, Earlsford Road, Mellis, Eye IP23 8DY*

GOODEY, Philip Julian Frank. b 61. Aston Tr Scheme 87 Trin Coll Bris 89. **d** 92 **p** 93. C Iver *Ox* 92–94; C Hornchurch St Andr *Chelmsf* 94–99; V Wickham Market w Pettistree *St E* 99–01; TR Parkham, Alwington, Buckland Brewer etc *Ex* 01–06; P-in-c Lundy Is 01–06; R Botley *Portsm* 06–11; V Curdridge 06–11; R Durley 06–11; TR Drypool *York* 11–15; V Boughton Monchelsea *Cant* from 15. *The Vicarage, Church Hill, Boughton Monchelsea, Maidstone ME17 4BU* T: (01622) 743321 E: phil.goodey@gmail.com

GOODFELLOW, Ian. b 37. St Cath Coll Cam BA 61 MA 65 Lon Univ PGCE 76 Dur Univ PhD 83. Wells Th Coll 61. **d** 63 **p** 64. C Dunstable *St Alb* 63–67; Chapl Haileybury Coll 67–71; Asst Chapl St Bede Coll Dur 71–74; Lect and Tutor 71–75; Sen Lect and Tutor SS Hild and Bede Coll Dur 75–78; Sen Cllr Open Univ (SW Region) 78–97; PtO *Ex* from 89. *Crosslea, 206 Whitchurch Road, Tavistock PL19 9DQ* T: (01822) 612069 E: ian1@waitrose.com

GOODFELLOW, Richard Oliver. b 76. Goldsmiths' Coll Lon of Art & Design BA 00. St Jo Coll Nottm 14. **d** 16 **p** 17. C Aspatria w Hayton and Gilcrux *Carl* from 16. *Holme Cultram Vicarage, Abbeytown, Wigton CA7 4SP* M: 07720-784722 E: richard_goodfellow@yahoo.co.uk

GOODGER, The Very Revd Kenneth Andrew. b 67. Univ of Qld BA 96. St Fran Coll Brisbane BTh 97. **d** 93 **p** 96. C Milton Australia 93–96; C Caloundra 96–99; C Pimlico St Pet w Westmr Ch Ch *Lon* 99–02; R Moorooka and Salisbury Australia 02–04; R Caloundra 06–14; R Wangaratta and Dean H Trin Cathl from 14. *2 The Close, Wangaratta VIC 3677, Australia* T: (0061) (3) 5721 8292 E: kagoodger67@gmail.com

GOODHEW, David John. b 65. Collingwood Coll Dur BA 86 CCC Ox DPhil 92 St Jo Coll Dur BA 92. Cranmer Hall Dur 90. **d** 93 **p** 94. C Bedminster *Bris* 93–96; Chapl and Fell St Cath Coll Cam 96–01; V Fulford *York* 01–08; P-in-c York St Denys 01–04; Dir Minl Practice Cranmer Hall Dur 08–19; V Linthorpe *York* from 19. *St Barnabas' Vicarage, 8 The Crescent, Middlesbrough TS5 6SQ* E: d.j.goodhew@durham.ac.uk

GOODHEW, Lindsey Jane Ellin. b 66. UEA BA 87 St Jo Coll Dur BA 92. Cranmer Hall Dur 90. **d** 93 **p** 94. C Bishopsworth *Bris* 93–96; PtO *Ely* 96–97; Hon C Cambridge St Mark 97–01; PtO *York* 01–07; Hon C Fulford 07–08; PtO *Dur* 08–09; Hon C Dur St Nic 09–19; Hon C Linthorpe *York* from 19. *St Barnabas Church, 1A St Barnabas Road, Middlesbrough TS5 6JR* E: lindsey@st-barnabas.net

GOODING, Canon Ian Eric. b 42. Leeds Univ BSc 63 BCom 65 CEng 69 MIProdE 68. St Jo Coll Nottm 70. **d** 73 **p** 74. C Wandsworth All SS *S'wark* 73–77; P-in-c Stanton-by-Dale w Dale Abbey *Derby* 77–87; R 87–00; P-in-c Risley 94–00; R Stanton-by-Dale w Dale Abbey and Risley 00–12; RD Erewash 98–12; Bp's Ind Adv 77–12; Hon Can Derby Cathl 02–12; rtd 12; PtO *Derby* from 12; Older People's Adv from 13. *Holly Tree Cottage, 17 Bostocks Lane, Sandiacre, Nottingham NG10 5NL* T: 0115-849 8726 M: 07974-370330 E: ian.e.gooding@gmail.com

GOODING, Ms Karen Ann. b 55. LRAM 76 ARCM 77. **d** 11. OLM Alford w Rigsby *Linc* 11–12; NSM Enfield St Mich *Lon* 12–15; Chapl All SS Academy Dunstable 15–16; PtO *Lon* 15–18; C Wantsum Gp *Cant* from 16; P-in-c Westgate St Sav from 19. *The Vicarage, The Length, St Nicholas at Wade, Birchington CT7 0PW* T: (01843) 447791 E: karenanngooding@gmail.com

GOODING, Paul David Buchanan. b 76. Pemb Coll Ox MA 98 Green Coll Ox PGCE 01. Ox Min Course 06. **d** 08. NSM Grove Ox 08–12; NSM Vale from 12; Asst Chapl Abingdon Sch from 10. *c/o Crockford, Church House, Great Smith Street, London SW1P 3AZ* E: pdbgooding@hotmail.com

GOODING, Robert Henry. b 60. ACII 87. Trin Coll Bris 08. **d** 10 **p** 11. C Walton le Soken *Chelmsf* 10–13; V Iver *Ox* from 13. *St Peter's Church, 1 Thorney Lane North, Iver SL0 9JU* T: (01753) 652078 or 651001 E: rev.robert@goodingonline.co.uk

GOODISON, Miss Eleanor Mary. b 57. Leeds Univ BA 78. ERMC 11. **d** 14 **p** 15. NSM S Hartismere *St E* 14–17; NSM

Athelington, Denham, Horham, Hoxne etc from 17. *Catelyn's House, Wingfield, Diss IP21 5QZ* T: (01379) 384181 M: 07876-143579 E: eleanor.goodison@gmail.com

GOODLAD, Canon Martin Randall. b 39. Sheff City Coll of Educn TDip 60. Linc Th Coll 63. **d** 66 **p** 67. C Bramley *Ripon* 66–69; TV Daventry *Pet* 69–71; Asst Dioc Youth Officer 69–71; Asst Dir of Educn *Wakef* 71–74; Youth Work Officer Gen Syn Bd of Educn 74–83; P-in-c Cheam Common St Phil *S'wark* 83–85; V 85–97; RD Sutton 90–97; Hon Chapl St Raphael's Hospice *S'wark* 97–05; V Coulsdon St Andr *S'wark* 97–05; Hon Can S'wark Cathl 96–05; rtd 05; PtO *S'wark* from 06. *3 Cromer Mansions, Cheam Road, Sutton SM1 2SR* T: (020) 8915 0555 E: m.goodlad@sky.com

GOODLAND, Michael Eric. b 53. WEMTC 97. **d** 97 **p** 98. NSM Ilminster and Distr *B & W* 97–02; NSM Crewkerne w Wayford 02–07; PtO *Truro* 07–10; P-in-c Lanreath, Pelynt and Bradoc 10–12; P-in-c St Germans 12–14; V 14–17; C Saltash 12–17; RD E Wivelshire 12–17; rtd 17; PtO *B & W* from 18. *5 Lower Meadow, Ilminster TA19 9DR* M: 07947-719487 E: michaelgoodland08@gmail.com

GOODMAN, Ms Alice Abigail. b 58. Harvard Univ BA 80 Girton Coll Cam BA 82 MA 86 Boston Univ MDiv 97. Ripon Coll Cuddesdon 00. **d** 01 **p** 03. C Redditch, The Ridge *Worc* 01–02; C Kidderminster St Mary and All SS w Trimpley etc 02–06; Chapl Trin Coll Cam 06–11; R Fulbourn *Ely* from 11; V Gt Wilbraham from 11; R Lt Wilbraham from 11. *The Rectory, 2 Apthorpe Street, Fulbourn, Cambridge CB21 5EY* T: (01223) 880337 E: goodhill@appleinter.net

GOODMAN, Garry Gordon. b 52. **d** 09 **p** 10. OLM Bure Valley *Nor* 09–12; NSM Horsford, Felthorpe and Hevingham 12–19; rtd 19; PtO *Nor* from 19. *Heath Farm House, Coltishall Road, Buxton, Norwich NR10 5JD* T: (01603) 279393 E: garry.goodman@btinternet.com

GOODMAN, John Dennis Julian. b 35. Sarum & Wells Th Coll 74. **d** 76 **p** 77. C Cotmanhay *Derby* 76–79; TV Old Brampton and Loundsley Green 79–86; R Finningley w Auckley *S'well* 86–96; rtd 96; PtO *Pet* 96–19. *8 Springfield, Wootton, Northampton NN4 6HB* T: (01604) 706443 E: johndi.goodman@btinternet.com

GOODMAN, Brother Kevin Charles. b 54. Surrey Univ BA 06. STETS 03. **d** 06 **p** 07. NSM Buckland Newton, Cerne Abbas, Godmanstone etc *Sarum* 06–09; PtO *Cant* 09–10; C Cant St Dunstan w H Cross 10–17; C Cant St Dunstan, St Mildred and St Pet from 17. *Address temp unknown* E: kevinssf@franciscans.org.uk

GOODMAN, Mrs Mairion Kim (Mars). b 73. Leeds Univ BA 95. Trin Coll Bris BA 03. **d** 05 **p** 06. NSM Redland *Bris* 05–10 and 13–15. *6 Willoughby Road, Horfield, Bristol BS7 8QX* T: 0117-989 2597

GOODMAN, Mark Alexander Scott. b 61. Lanc Univ BA 84 Nottm Univ BTh 90 New Coll Edin MTh 97. Linc Th Coll 87. **d** 90 **p** 91. C Denton St Lawr *Man* 90–93; R Dalkeith and Lasswade *Edin* 93–96; Dioc Communications Officer 96–06; Can St Mary's Cathl and Syn Clerk 02–06; Chapl Stamford Sch from 06. *Stamford Endowed Schools, Brazenose House, St Paul's Street, Stamford PE9 2BE* T: (01780) 750363 M: 07947-032739 E: mgoodman@ses.lincs.sch.uk

GOODMAN, Mrs Penelope Jane. b 52. ERMC 06. **d** 09 **p** 10. OLM Bure Valley *Nor* 09–12; NSM Horsford, Felthorpe and Hevingham 12–17; C Easton, Colton, Marlingford and Bawburgh 17–19; NSM from 19; Chapl to Dioc Staff from 19. *Heath Farm House, Coltishall Road, Buxton, Norwich NR10 5JD* T: (01603) 279393 E: garry.goodman@btinternet.com

GOODMAN, Peter William. b 60. St Cath Coll Cam BA 82 Sheff Univ MPhil 98 PhD 11 Linc Univ PGCE 13. St Jo Coll Nottm 85. **d** 89 **p** 90. C Stapenhill w Cauldwell *Derby* 89–92; C Ovenden *Wakef* 92–94; P-in-c Halifax St Aug 94–98; Crosslinks Ethiopia 98–05; C Leic H Trin w St Jo 05–08; PtO 13–16; CMD Officer *Linc* 14–17; Asst Dir St Pet Coll and Dir CMD *Sheff* from 17. *Diocesan Church House, 95-99 Effingham Street, Rotherham S65 1BL* T: (01709) 309100 M: 07387-260826 E: bill.goodman@sheffield.anglican.org

GOODMAN, Victor Terence. b 46. Liv Univ BSc 67 CEng 92 MBCS 74. EMMTC 82. **d** 85 **p** 86. NSM Barwell w Potters Marston and Stapleton *Leic* 85–89; NSM Croft and Stoney Stanton 89–94; P-in-c Whetstone 94–03; TV Hugglescote w Donington, Ellistown and Snibston 03–07; C Coalville w Bardon Hill and Ravenstone 07–10; rtd 10; PtO *Leic* from 13. *21 New Inn Close, Broughton Astley, Leicester LE9 6SU* T: (01455) 285410 E: victor.goodman1@btinternet.com

GOODMAN, Mrs Victoria Elizabeth Stuart. b 51. RGN 74. Trin Coll Bris. **d** 98 **p** 99. C Ilminster and Distr *B & W* 98–02; R Blagdon w Compton Martin and Ubley 02–10; Dioc Chapl MU 01–10; rtd 10; PtO *Sarum* from 12; *B & W* 13–18. *Underhill,*

Castle Hill Lane, Mere, Warminster BA12 6JB T: (01747) 860070 E: vickieplum51@btinternet.com

GOODMAN, William. *See* GOODMAN, Peter William

GOODRICH, The Very Revd Derek Hugh. b 27. Selw Coll Cam BA 48 MA 54. St Steph Ho Ox 50. d 52 p 53. C Willesden St Andr *Lon* 52–57; W Lodge St Sidwell Guyana 57–67; V Port Mourant 67–71; R New Amsterdam All SS 71–84; Adn Berlice 81–84; V Gen Dio Guyana 82–94; Dean Georgetown 84–93; P-in-c St Aloysius 93–00; rtd 00; PtO *S'wark* 03–14. *The College of St Barnabas, Blackberry Lane, Lingfield RH7 6NJ* T: (01342) 872873

GOODRICH, Mrs Michelle Susan. b 69. All SS Cen for Miss & Min 13. d 16 p 17. C Prestbury *Ches* 16–18; P-in-c Alsager St Mary from 18. *The Vicarage, 37 Eaton Road, Alsager, Stoke-on-Trent ST7 2BQ* M: 07711-254708 E: rev.michelle.goodrich@gmail.com

GOODRICH, Mrs Nancy Elisabeth. b 66. St Hilda's Coll Ox BA 88 MA 09 ACA 93. WMMTC 06. d 09 p 10. C St Annes St Thos *Blackb* 09–12; V Bolton-le-Sands from 12; AD Tunstall from 16. *The Vicarage, 117 Main Road, Bolton le Sands, Carnforth LA5 8DX* T: (01524) 823106 M: 07974-250466 E: nancy@goodrich.myzen.co.uk

GOODRICH, Canon Peter. b 36. Dur Univ BA 58. Cuddesdon Coll 60. d 62 p 63. C Walton St Jo *Liv* 62–66; C Prescot 66–68; V Anfield St Marg 68–72; V Gt Crosby St Faith 72–83; P-in-c Seaforth 76–80; RD Bootle 78–83; TR Upholland 83–94; R Halsall 94–02; Dir Dioc OLM Scheme 94–02; Hon Can Liv Cathl 89–02; rtd 03; PtO *Liv* from 03. *Dunelm, 16 Hillside Avenue, Ormskirk L39 4TD* T: (01695) 573285

GOODRIDGE, Elizabeth Jane. b 57. SEITE 06. d 09 p 10. NSM S Beddington and Roundshaw *S'wark* 09–13; NSM Kenley from 13; NSM Purley St Barn from 13. *4 Gander Green Lane, Sutton SM1 2EJ* T: (020) 8661 5343 M: 07788-755752 E: elizabeth.goodridge1@btinternet.com

GOODRIDGE, John Francis James. b 49. Open Univ BA 86. WEMTC 04. d 07 p 08. Partnership P E Bris 07–13; NSM Two Mile Hill St Mich 07–13; NSM Hanham from 13; NSM Kingswood from 13. *153 Whittucks Road, Bristol BS15 3PY* T: 0117-940 1508

GOODRIDGE, Paul Charles. b 54. Leic Univ MSc 98 MCIPD 88. d 04 p 05. OLM Cheam *S'wark* 04–08; C Beddington 08–10; R Godstone and Blindley Heath 10–14; PtO *Eur* 15–16; Chapl Bucharest w Sofia 16–19. *Address temp unknown*

GOODRIDGE, Peter Warren. b 66. Liv Univ BA 87. Wycliffe Hall Ox 07. d 09 p 10. C Tonbridge SS Pet and Paul *Roch* 09–13; R Elmswell *St E* from 13. *The Rectory, Church Road, Elmswell, Bury St Edmunds IP30 9DY* T: (01359) 240512 E: elmswellrector@gmail.com

GOODSON, Sally Louise. b 64. BSc. STETS. d 13 p 14. C Win St Bart and St Lawr w St Swithun 13–17; C Harpenden St Nic *St Alb* from 17. *86 Tuffnells Way, Harpenden AL5 3HG* M: 07840-926507 E: sally.goodson21@gmail.com

GOODWIN, Canon Barry Frederick John. b 48. Birm Univ BSc 69 PhD 77. St Jo Coll Nottm 86. d 88 p 89. C Ware Ch Ch *St Alb* 88–91; P-in-c Stanstead Abbots 91–96; P-in-c Gt Amwell w St Marg 95–96; V Gt Amwell w St Margaret's and Stanstead Abbots 96–99; RD Hertford and Ware 96–99; V Clapham Park All SS *S'wark* 99–05; RD Clapham 02–05; Soc Resp (Par Development) Adv Croydon Adnry 05–11; Hon C Addiscombe St Mildred 09–11; Hon Can S'wark Cathl 11–13; rtd 13; PtO *S'wark* from 13. *57 South Way, Croydon CR0 8RH* M: 07967-917151 E: barry@bcgoodwin.me.uk

GOODWIN, Bruce William. b 56. W Aus BA 84 DipEd 85. Trin Coll Bris BA 09. d 09 p 10. C Thornbury and Oldbury-on-Severn w Shepperdine *Glouc* 09–12; Sen Chapl Glos Univ 12–17; V Oldland *Bris* from 17; P-in-c Longwell Green from 17. *St Anne's Vicarage, Grangevillle Close, Longwell Green, Bristol BS30 9YJ* T: (01454) 853213 M: 07720-772190 E: goodwins07@gmail.com

GOODWIN, Daphne Mary. b 35. Lon Univ MB, BS 60. STETS 94. d 97 p 98. NSM Ifield *Chich* 97–17; rtd 17; PtO *Chich* from 17. *1 Selbourne Close, Crawley RH10 3SA* T: (01293) 612906 E: dapheter@aol.com

GOODWIN, Mrs Gillian Sheila. b 54. NOC MTh 99. d 99 p 00. C Penkridge *Lich* 99–02; TV Wrockwardine Deanery 02–15; rtd 15; PtO *Ches* from 16. *4 Gloucester Road, Hyde SK14 5JG* T: 0161-368 6740 E: gillgoodwin61@gmail.com

GOODWIN, Mrs Josephine Anne. b 64. Ripon Coll Cuddesdon 09. d 12 p 13. C Stow on the Wold, Condicote and The Swells *Glouc* 12–16; C Cheltenham St Mark 16–17; Chapl Cheltenham Ladies' Coll from 17. *Rose Cottage, St Margaret's Road, Alderton, Tewkesbury GL20 8NN* T: (01242) 620391 M: 07718-089099 E: revdjosie.goodwin@btinternet.com

GOODWIN, Ronald Victor. b 33. S'wark Ord Course. d 86 p 87. NSM Wickford and Runwell *Chelmsf* 86–98; PtO 98–01; NSM W Hanningfield 01–03; P-in-c 03–06; rtd 06; PtO *Chelmsf* from 06. *164 Southend Road, Wickford SS11 8EH* T: (01268) 734447

GOODWIN, Stephen. b 58. Sheff Univ BA 80 Wolv Univ BSc 14. Cranmer Hall Dur 82. d 85 p 86. C Lytham St Cuth *Blackb* 85–87; C W Burnley All SS 88–90; TV Headley All SS *Guildf* 90–98; NSM Leek and Meerbrook *Lich* 98–03; Chapl Univ Hosp of N Staffs NHS Trust 03–08; Chapl Douglas Macmillan Hospice Blurton 08–17; PtO *Eur* from 17. *2 Lordshire Mews, Armshead Road, Werrington, Stoke-on-Trent ST9 0HJ* T: (01782) 302418 M: 07496-816239 E: stephen.goodwin@talktalk.net

GOODWIN, Mrs Susan Elizabeth. b 51. Leeds Poly BSc 74 Leeds Univ MSc 76. Cranmer Hall Dur 82. dss 84 d 87 p 94. Norton Woodseats St Chad *Sheff* 84–87; Par Dn 87; Chapl Scargill Ho 87–89; NSM W Burnley All SS *Blackb* 89–90; NSM Headley All SS *Guildf* 90–98; Past Asst Acorn Chr Healing Trust 91–93; P-in-c Wetley Rocks *Lich* 98–09; P-in-c Werrington 08–09; V Werrington and Wetley Rocks 09–16; RD Cheadle 14–16; rtd 16; PtO *Eur* from 18. *2 Lordshire Mews, Armshead Road, Werrington, Stoke-on-Trent ST9 0HJ* T: (01782) 302418 E: revsueg@gmail.com

GOODWIN-HUDSON, Anthony James Philip. b 76. d 14 p 15. C Appley Bridge and Parbold *Blackb* 14–16; C Leyland St Andr 16–18; PtO from 18; Chapl St Lawr Coll Ramsgate from 19. *St Lawrence College, College Road, Ramsgate CT11 7AE* T: (01843) 808080 E: jg-h@hotmail.com

GOODWIN HUDSON, Brainerd Peter de Wirtz. b 34. K Coll Lon BD 57 AKC 57. Westcott Ho Cam 57. d 59 p 60. C Morden *S'wark* 59–60; Australia 61–65; Asst Sec CCCS 65–68; Chapl St Lawr Coll Ramsgate 68–74; Chapl Repton Sch Derby 74–94; Chapl Santiago Chile 94–01; rtd 99; Hon C Broadwell, Evenlode, Oddington, Adlestrop etc *Glouc* 02–06; PtO from 19. *10 Old Forge Close, Bledington, Chipping Norton OX7 6XW* T: (01608) 658002 E: petergoodwinhudson@gmail.com

GOODWINS, Christopher William Hedley. b 36. St Jo Coll Cam BA 58 MA 62. Linc Th Coll 62. d 64 p 65. C Lowestoft St Marg *Nor* 64–69; V Tamerton Foliot *Ex* 69–78; P-in-c Southway 78–82; rtd 98; P-in-c Isleham *Ely* 99–04; PtO from 05; *St E* 10–15. *102 The Causeway, Isleham, Ely CB7 5ST* T: (01638) 780284 E: cwhgoodwins@gmail.com

GOODYEAR, Benjamin. b 76. LSE BSc 98. Ridley Hall Cam 03. d 06 p 07. C Balham Hill Ascension *S'wark* 06–09; P-in-c Brixton St Paul w St Sav 09–13; V 13–18; V Herne Hill from 18. *1 Finsen Road, London SE5 9AX* T: (020) 7737 4978 M: 07866-774354 E: vicar@hernehillparish.org.uk

GOODYEAR, Canon Edward Arthur. b 42. Witwatersrand Univ BA 63 SS Coll Cam BA 67 MA 70 Rhodes Univ MTh 91. St Paul's Coll Grahamstown 68. d 68 p 69. C Rosebank S Africa 69; R Vanderbijlpark 71–72; Chapl St Jo Coll Houghton Estate 73–75; R Stellenbosch 76–84; Can Cape Town 80–87; R Bramley S Africa 84–87; Chapl St Andr Coll Grahamstown 88–92; P-in-c Sidbury 90–92; R Alverstoke *Portsm* 92–12; P-in-c Gosport Ch Ch 97–01; rtd 12; Chapl Huggens Coll Northfleet 12–19; Hon Can Wusasa Nigeria from 99. *39 Burnt House Lane, Fareham PO14 2LP* M: 07952-194187 E: ego.lizg@gmail.com

GOOLJARY, Yousouf Azad. b 59. Ex Univ BSc 80 Man Poly PGCE 82. SEITE 07. d 10 p 11. C Greenwich St Alfege *S'wark* 10–13; C Becontree S *Chelmsf* 13–16; Chapl Dagenham Park C of E Sch 13–16; C Edin Ch Ch 16–18; R Edin St Martin from 18. *15 Ardmillan Terrace, Edinburgh EH11 2JW* M: 07563-366811 E: revgooljary@aol.com

GORDON, Alan Williamson. b 53. Strathclyde Univ BA 75 MCIBS 79. Wycliffe Hall Ox 98. d 98 p 99. C Win Ch Ch 98–02; R Headbourne Worthy 02–15; RD Win 07–13; V Tamworth *Lich* from 15. *The Vicarage, Hospital Street, Tamworth B79 7EE* T: (01827) 66776 or 68339 E: vicar.tamworth@gmail.com

GORDON, Canon Alexander Ronald. b 49. Nottm Univ BPharm 71. Coll of Resurr Mirfield 74. d 77 p 78. C Headingley *Ripon* 77–80; C Fareham SS Pet and Paul *Portsm* 80–83; V Cudworth *Wakef* 83–85; P-in-c Tain *Mor* 85–87; P-in-c Lairg Miss 87–01; P-in-c Brora *Mor* 88–01; P-in-c Dornoch 88–01; Dioc Dir of Ords 89–01; Can St Andr Cathl Inverness 95–01; Hon Can St Andr Cathl Inverness from 02; Chapl Strasbourg *Eur* 02–05; Provost St Andr Cathl Inverness *Mor* 05–14; Chapl Geneva *Eur* from 14. *rue de Montbrillant 84, CH-1202 Geneva, Switzerland* T: (0041) (22) 734 3817 M: 79-945 0605 E: canonalexgordon@outlook.com

GORDON, Anne. *See* LE BAS, Jennifer Anne

GORDON, Mrs Avis Patricia. b 52. Man Univ BA 73. d 08 p 09. OLM Clifton *Man* 08–12; NSM from 15; Assoc

Dir of Ords from 15. *47 Agecroft Road West, Prestwich, Manchester M25 9RF* T: 0161-798 8018 M: 07544-058011 E: avis.1968@hotmail.co.uk

GORDON, Bruce Harold Clark. b 40. Edin Univ MTh 96. Cranmer Hall Dur 65. **d** 68 **p** 69. C Edin St Jas 68–71; C Blackheath St Jo *S'wark* 71–74; R Duns *Edin* 74–90; R Lanark and Douglas *Glas* 90–05; rtd 05; LtO *Edin* from 05. *52 Foxknowe Place, Livingston EH54 6TX* T: (01506) 418466 M: 07769-927195 E: brucehc.gordon@btinternet.com

GORDON, David John. b 65. Edin Th Coll 90. **d** 93 **p** 94. Chapl St Andr Cathl *Ab* 93–95; P-in-c Alexandria *Glas* 95–00; Chapl Leven Distr Gen Hosp 95–00; Chapl Christie Park Primary Sch 95–00; Asst Chapl NE Lincs NHS Trust 00–01; Chapl Tayside Univ Hosps NHS Trust 01–06; Lead Chapl Acute Services NHS Tayside 06; Sen Staff Support Chapl from 13; PtO *Bre* from 13. *Wellbeing Centre, East Lodge, Royal Victoria Hospital, Jedburgh Road, Dundee DD2 1SP* T: (01382) 740830 E: davidjgordon@nhs.net

GORDON, Canon Jonathan Andrew. b 61. Keele Univ BA 83 MPhil 98 Southn Univ BTh 88 Southn Inst MPhil 04. Sarum & Wells Th Coll 84. **d** 87 **p** 88. C Wallingford w Crowmarsh Gifford etc *Ox* 87–91; C Tilehurst St Mich 91–93; TV Stoke-upon-Trent *Lich* 93–97; Chapl Southn Solent Univ *Win* 98–05; R Northchurch and Wigginton *St Alb* from 05; RD Berkhamsted from 14; Hon Can St Alb from 19. *St Mary's Rectory, 80 High Street, Northchurch, Berkhamsted HP4 3QW* T: (01442) 871547 E: revjogordonr@gmail.com

GORDON, Julia Kathryn. b 62. Dur Univ BA 17. SNWTP 15. **d** 17 **p** 18. OLM Harwood *Man* from 17. *163 Tottington Road, Bolton BL2 4DF* M: 07968-045893 E: dewhurst4@ntlworld.com

GORDON, Canon Kenneth Davidson. b 35. Edin Univ MA 57 Univ of Wales MTh 08. Tyndale Hall Bris 58. **d** 60 **p** 61. C St Helens St Helen *Liv* 60–66; V Daubhill *Man* 66–71; R Bieldside *Ab* 71–01; Can St Andr Cathl 81–01; Syn Clerk 96–01; rtd 01; Hon Can St Andr Cathl *Ab* from 01; PtO *Blackb* 01–07; *Liv* 01–07; Bp's Warrant Ab 06–12; Bp's Commn 12–16; P-in-c Aberdeen St Clem *Ab* 12–13 and 14–16; LtO from 16. *16 Reidford Gardens, Drumoak, Banchory AB31 5AW* T: (01330) 810260 M: 07715-169548 E: canonken@btopenworld.com

GORDON, Kristy. *See* PATTIMORE, Kristy

GORDON, Martin Lewis. b 73. Edin Univ MA 97. Wycliffe Hall Ox BA 09. **d** 10 **p** 11. C Stoke Gifford *Bris* 10–14; P-in-c Telford Park *S'wark* 14–15; V from 15. *The Vicarage, 2 Thornton Road, London SW12 0JU* T: (020) 8671 8276 E: martingordon2@gmail.com *or* martin.gordon@stwss.org.uk

GORDON, Mrs Pamela Anne. b 48. Brighton Coll of Educn CertEd 69 BEd 70. SAOMC 99. **d** 02 **p** 03. NSM Wargrave w Knowl Hill *Ox* 02–12; PtO from 12. *Rebeny, 2A Hawthorn Road, Caversham, Reading RG4 6LY* T: 0118-946 3727 M: 07714-256272 E: revpam.sdh@gmail.com

GORDON, Robert John. b 56. Edin Univ MA 81. Wycliffe Hall Ox 87. **d** 89 **p** 90. C Wilnecote *Lich* 89–91; C Bideford *Ex* 91–95; P-in-c Feniton, Buckerell and Escot 95–05; P-in-c Tiverton St Pet and Chevithorne w Cove 05–15; R from 15; P-in-c Tiverton St Andr from 11; RD Tiverton and Cullompton 05–17. *The Rectory, Withleigh, Tiverton EX16 8JQ* T: (01884) 242991 E: robert.j.gordon@btinternet.com

GORDON CLARK, John Vincent Michael. b 29. FCA. S'wark Ord Course 73. **d** 76 **p** 77. NSM Guildf H Trin w St Mary 76–81; NSM Albury w St Martha 81–91; Dioc Chapl to MU 92–95; LtO 95–99; Hon C Guildf Cathl 91–99; PtO 99–12; Newc from 12. *Bethany, 250 Western Way, Ponteland, Newcastle upon Tyne NE20 9ND* T: (01661) 598052

GORDON-CUMMING, Henry Ian. b 28. Barrister-at-Law (Gray's Inn) 56. Oak Hill Th Coll 54. **d** 57 **p** 58. C Southsea St Jude *Portsm* 57–60; Chapl to Bp Ankole-Kigezi Uganda 61–65; Chapl Ntari Sch 65–67; V Virginia Water *Guildf* 68–78; R Busbridge 78–87; R Lynch w Iping Marsh and Milland *Chich* 87–94; rtd 94; PtO *Chich* from 94. *Bay Cottage, Brookside, Runcton, Chichester PO20 1PX* T: (01243) 783395

GORDON-TAYLOR, Benjamin Nicholas. b 69. St Jo Coll Dur BA 90 MA 92 Leeds Univ BA 94 Dur Univ PhD 08 FRSA 99. Coll of Resurr Mirfield 92. **d** 95 **p** 96. C Launceston *Truro* 95–97; C Northampton St Matt *Pet* 97–99; Fell and Chapl Univ Coll Dur 99–04; Lect and Tutor Coll of Resurr Mirfield from 05; Visiting Lect Leeds Univ from 05; Dir Mirfield Liturg Inst from 08; Dioc Liturg Adv *Eur* from 13; PtO *Leeds* from 08. *College of the Resurrection, Stocks Bank Road, Mirfield WF14 0BW* T: (01924) 490441 E: bgordon-taylor@mirfield.org.uk

GORHAM, Canon Andrew Arthur. b 51. Bris Univ BA 73 Birm Univ MA 87. Qu Coll Birm 77. **d** 79 **p** 80. C Plaistow St Mary *Roch* 79–82; Chapl Lanchester Poly *Cov* 82–87;

TV Warwick 87–95; Chapl Birm Univ 95–00; Bp's Dom Chapl 00–11; Hon Can Birm Cathl 06–11; Master St Jo Hosp Lich 11–16; PtO *Cov* from 11; P-in-c Birm St Paul from 18. *St Paul's Church, St Paul's Square, Birmingham B3 1QZ* T: 0121-236 7858 E: andrewgorham@hotmail.co.uk *or* andrew.gorham@stpaulsjq.church

✠**GORHAM, The Rt Revd Karen Marisa.** b 64. Trin Coll Bris BA 95. **d** 95 **p** 96 **c** 16. C Northallerton w Kirby Sigston *York* 95–99; P-in-c Maidstone St Paul *Cant* 99–07; Asst Dir of Ords 02–07; AD Maidstone 03–07; Hon Can Cant Cathl 06–07; Adn Buckingham *Ox* 07–16; Area Bp Sherborne *Sarum* from 16; Hon Asst Bp Portsm from 19. *Sherborne House, Tower Hill, Iwerne Minster, Blandford Forum DT11 8NH* T: (01202) 659427 F: 691418 E: bishop.sherborne@salisbury.anglican.org

GORICK, The Ven Martin Charles William. b 62. Selw Coll Cam BA 84 MA 88. Ripon Coll Cuddesdon 85. **d** 87 **p** 88. C Birtley *Dur* 87–91; Bp's Dom Chapl *Ox* 91–94; V Smethwick *Birm* 94–01; AD Warley 97–01; R Stratford-upon-Avon, Luddington etc *Cov* 01–13; Adn Ox and Can Res Ch Ch from 13. *Christ Church, Oxford OX1 1DP* T: (01865) 208263 E: archdeacon.oxford@oxford.anglican.org

GORRINGE, Edward George Alexander. b 63. QUB BA 85 Strathclyde Univ MBA 00 FCMA 06. CITC 04. **d** 07 **p** 08. NSM Aghalee *D & D* 07–09; CF from 09; Dioc Sec *Dur* from 18. *Diocesan Office, Cuthbert House, Stonebridge, Durham DH1 3RY* T: (01388) 604515 E: diocesan.secretary@durham.anglican.org

GORRINGE, Prof Timothy Jervis. b 46. St Edm Hall Ox BA 69 MPhil 75. Sarum Th Coll 69. **d** 72 **p** 73. C Chapel Allerton *Ripon* 72–75; C Ox St Mary V w St Cross and St Pet 76–78; India 79–86; Chapl St Jo Coll Ox 86–96; Reader St Andr Univ from 96; Prof Th Ex Univ from 99. *Venbridge House, Cheriton Bishop, Exeter EX6 6HD* T: (01392) 264242 E: t.j.gorringe@exeter.ac.uk

GORTON, Angela Deborah. *See* WYNNE, Angela Deborah

GORTON (née CARTER), Sarah Helen Buchanan. b 44. St Andr Univ BSc 65 DipEd 66. TISEC 93. **d** 96 **p** 98. NSM Lenzie *Glas* 96–01; P-in-c Alexandria 01–12; Chapl Gtr Glas and Clyde NHS 01–12; rtd 12. *Northbank Gardens, 6B Northbank Road, Kirkintilloch, Glasgow G66 1EZ* T: 0141-775 1204 E: shbgorton@btinternet.com

GORWOOD, Duncan Brian. b 73. Huddersfield Univ BMus 95 Bretton Hall Coll PGCE 97. Ripon Coll Cuddesdon 17. **d** 19. C Horninglow *Lich* from 19. *62 Redhill Lane, Tutbury, Burton-on-Trent DE13 9JW* M: 07841-098465 E: revfrduncan@hotmail.com

GOSDEN, Angela. b 50. Ox Min Course 07. **d** 11 **p** 12. NSM Stanford in the Vale w Goosey and Hatford *Ox* 11–14; PtO 14–15; Chapl Gt Western Hosps NHS Foundn Trust from 15; PtO *Win* from 17; *Eur* from 17. *The Haven, 4 Garden Close, New Milton BH25 6NL* T: (01425) 629491 E: angela.gosden@btconnect.com

GOSDEN, Timothy John. b 50. Open Univ BA 86. Chich Th Coll 74. **d** 77 **p** 78. C Cant All SS 77–81; Asst Chapl Loughb Univ *Leic* 81–85; LtO *Cant* 85–87; Chapl Ch Ch Coll of HE Cant 85–87; Sen Chapl Hull Univ 87–94; V Taunton Lyngford *B & W* 94–98; V Harrow St Mary *Lon* 98–15; rtd 15; PtO *Lon* 15–16; *Nor* from 16. *24 Fletcher Close, Tunstead, Norwich NR12 8RA* T: (01603) 783973 E: fr.timgosden@gmail.com

GOSLER, Andrew Graham Gabriel. b 58. Aber Univ BSc 79 Reading Univ MSc 81 Wolfs Coll Ox DPhil 87 FLS 98 FRSB 16. Ox Min Course 15. **d** 18 **p** 19. NSM Marston w Elsfield *Ox* from 18. *Mansfield College, Mansfield Road, Oxford OX1 3TF* T: (01865) 761110 M: 07778-302488 E: andrew.gosler@zoo.ox.ac.uk

GOSLING, David. b 27. SAOMC 95. **d** 98 **p** 99. OLM High Wycombe *Ox* 98–03; PtO 02–09; *Nor* from 10. *18 Parsons Mead, Norwich NR4 6PG* T: (01603) 506025 E: greygoose@talktalk.net

GOSLING, David Lagourie. b 39. Man Univ MSc 63 Fitzw Coll Cam MA 69 Lanc Univ PhD 74 MInstP 69 CPhys 84. Ridley Hall Cam 63. **d** 73 **p** 74. Hon C Lancaster St Mary *Blackb* 73–74; Hon C Kingston upon Hull St Matt w St Barn *York* 74–77; Hon C Cottingham 78–83; Asst Chapl Geneva *Eur* 84–89; C Cambridge Gt St Mary w St Mich *Ely* 89–90; C Dry Drayton 90–94; USPG India 95–99; PtO *York* from 95; *Ely* 01–17; Fell Clare Hall Cam from 01; Prin Edwardes Coll Peshawar Pakistan from 06. *Clare Hall, Herschel Road, Cambridge CB3 9AL* T: (01223) 352450 F: 332333 E: dlg26@cam.ac.uk

GOSLING, Ms Dorothy Grace. b 57. St Martin's Coll Lanc BA 94 K Coll Lon MA 06. SNWTP 07. **d** 10 **p** 11. NSM Ches Cathl 10–14; Chapl Ches Univ 11–14; C Llanbedr DC, Llangynhafal, Llanychan etc. *St As* 14–16; V Llanasa and Ffynnongroew 16–17; I Bryn a Mor Miss

Area from 18. *The Vicarage, Llanasa Road, Gronant, Prestatyn LL19 9TL* T: (01745) 888797 M: 07976-274459 E: dotchka@icloud.com

GOSLING, John William Fraser. b 34. St Jo Coll Dur BA 58 MA 71 Ex Univ PhD 78 Win Univ MA 12. Cranmer Hall Dur 58. **d** 60 **p** 61. C Plympton St Mary *Ex* 60–68; V Newport 68–78; Org Sec CECS St Alb and Ox 78–82; C Stratford sub Castle *Sarum* 83–86; Adv on CME 83–86; PtO 86–91 and from 95; C Swindon Ch Ch *Bris* 91–95; rtd 95. *1 Wiley Terrace, Wilton, Salisbury SP2 0HN* T: (01722) 742788 E: jwfgosling@gmail.com

GOSNEY, Jeanette Margaret. b 58. Bath Univ BA 81 Univ Coll Ches MA 05 Nottm Univ PGCE 82. St Jo Coll Nottm BTh 93 MPhil 95. **d** 95 **p** 96. C Ipswich St Marg *St E* 95–98; Chapl Loughb Univ *Leic* 98; Sen Chapl 98–01; Tutor Trin Coll Bris 01–04; Chapl Repton Sch Derby 04–05; TV Albury, Braughing, Furneux Pelham, Lt Hadham etc *St Alb* 06–10; Par Development Officer 10–17; Bp's Min Officer *St E* from 17; NSM Ipswich St Mary-le-Tower from 18; Dioc Adv for Women's Min from 18. *8 Blandford Road, Ipswich IP3 8SL* T: (01473) 720270 M: 07710-479497 E: jeanette.gosney@cofesuffolk.org

GOSS, David James. b 52. Nottm Univ BCombStuds 83 York St Jo Univ MA 10. Linc Th Coll 80. **d** 83 **p** 84. C Wood Green St Mich w Bounds Green St Gabr etc *Lon* 83–86; TV Gleadless Valley *Sheff* 86–89; TR 89–95; V Wheatley Hills 95–15; V Wheatley Hills w Intake from 15. *The Vicarage, 18 Central Boulevard, Doncaster DN2 5PE* T: (01302) 342047 E: davidjamesgoss@gmail.com *or* david.goss@sheffield.anglican.org

GOSS, Canon Kevin Ian. b 56. LRAM 75 LTCL 76 GRSM 77 LGSM 80 Hughes Hall Cam PGCE 78 Heythrop Coll Lon MA 08. S Dios Minl Tr Scheme 89. **d** 92 **p** 93. NSM Ardingly *Chich* 92–98; Asst Chapl Ardingly Coll 92–98; Min Can, Prec and Sacr Cant Cathl 98–03; P-in-c Hockerill *St Alb* 04–13; V 13–14; Chapl Herts Community NHS Trust 04–14; RD Bishop's Stortford *St Alb* 12–14; V Bedford St Paul from 14; Hon Can St Alb from 18. *St Paul's Vicarage, 12 The Embankment, Bedford MK40 3PD* T: (01234) 364638 E: vicarstpaulsbedfd@btinternet.com

GOSS, Michael John. b 37. Chich Th Coll 62. **d** 65 **p** 66. C Angell Town St Jo *S'wark* 65–68; C Catford St Laur 68–71; P-in-c Lewisham St Swithun 71–81; V Redhill St Jo 81–88; V Dudley St Thos and St Luke *Worc* 88–98; C Small Heath *Birm* 98–02; rtd 02; PtO *Birm* from 02. *8 Mayland Road, Birmingham B16 0NG* T: 0121-429 6022 E: michael.goss@tinyworld.co.uk

GOSTELOW (née THOMPSON), Mrs Ruth Jean. b 47. St Alb Minl Tr Scheme 85. **d** 90 **p** 94. Par Dn Stonebridge St Mich *Lon* 90–94; C Ealing St Paul 94–96; TV W Slough *Ox* 96–03; V New Haw *Guildf* 03–13; rtd 13; TV Rye *Chich* from 16. *34 Oak Tree Court, Smallhythe Road, Tenterden TN30 7EQ* E: rev.ruth@btinternet.com

GOSWELL, Geoffrey. b 34. SS Paul & Mary Coll Cheltenham CertEd 68. Glouc Th Course 70. **d** 71 **p** 72. C Cheltenham Em *Glouc* 71–73; C Lydney w Aylburton 73–76; P-in-c Falfield w Rockhampton 76–79; Chapl HM Det Cen Eastwood Park 76–79; Area Sec CMS Ely 79–81; PtO *Linc* 79–86; Pet 79–86; Dep Regional Sec (UK) CMS 86–97; P-in-c Orton Waterville *Ely* 90–96; TV The Ortons, Alwalton and Chesterton 96–97; rtd 97; PtO *Pet* 01–07. *8 Lapwing Close, Northampton NN4 0RT* T: (01604) 701572 E: g.goswell@hotmail.co.uk

GOTHARD, Mrs Anne Marie. b 51. STETS. **d** 00 **p** 11. NSM E Meon and Langrish *Portsm* 00–04; NSM Catherington and Clanfield from 04. *27 Green Lane, Clanfield, Waterlooville PO8 0JU* T: (023) 9259 6315 M: 07939-472796 E: rev_gothard@hotmail.com

GOTT, Stephen. b 61. St Jo Coll Nottm 92. **d** 94 **p** 95. C Mount Pellon *Wakef* 94–97; V Greetland and W Vale 97–06; TR Em TM 06–16; V Queensbury *Leeds* from 16. *The Vicarage, 7 Russell Hall Lane, Queensbury, Bradford BD13 2AJ* E: revdsgott@gmail.com

GOUGH, Andrew Stephen. b 60. Sarum & Wells Th Coll 83. **d** 86 **p** 87. C St Leonards Ch Ch and St Mary *Chich* 86–88; C Broseley w Benthall *Heref* 88–90; V Ketley and Oakengates *Lich* 90–93; TV Bickleigh (Plymouth) *Ex* 93; TV Bickleigh and Shaugh Prior 94; P-in-c St Day *Truro* 94–96; V Chacewater w St Day and Carharrack 96–09; P-in-c St Ives 09–16; P-in-c Halsetown 09–16; V St Ives and Halsetown 16–17; Hon Can Truro Cathl 14–17; V Weymouth H Trin *Sarum* from 17. *Holy Trinity Vicarage, 7 Glebe Close, Weymouth DT4 9RL* T: (01305) 760354 M: 07590-695515 E: goughfr@hotmail.com

GOUGH, Andrew Walter. b 55. Bris Univ BA 78. Trin Coll Bris 90. **d** 92 **p** 93. C Mossley Hill St Matt and St Jas *Liv* 92–94; C Wavertree H Trin 94–96; Chapl Warw Sch 96–18; Chapl

Bp Wordsworth's Sch Salisbury from 18. *Bishop Wordsworth's School, Exeter Street, Salisbury SP1 2ED* T: (01722) 333851

GOUGH, Canon Colin Richard. b 47. St Chad's Coll Dur BA 69. Cuddesdon Coll 73. **d** 75 **p** 76. C Lich St Chad 75–78; C Codsall 78–84; V Wednesbury St Paul Wood Green 84–92; TR Tettenhall Wood 92–99; TR Tettenhall Wood and Perton 99–01; P-in-c Stannington *Newc* 01–10; Dioc Adv for CME 01–10; AD Morpeth 08–10; Hon Can Newc Cathl 06–10; rtd 10; PtO *Newc* from 10; Bp's Officer for Rtd Clergy 12–17. *44 Tyelaw Meadows, Shilbottle NE66 2JJ* T: (01665) 581100 E: canoncolin@gmail.com

GOUGH, David Norman. b 42. Oak Hill Th Coll 70. **d** 70 **p** 71. C Penn Fields *Lich* 70–73; C Stapenhill w Cauldwell *Derby* 73–77; V Heath 77–86; P-in-c Derby St Chad 86–95; TV Walbrook Epiphany 95–03; P-in-c Codnor and Loscoe 03–07; rtd 07. *7 Mulberry Close, Belper DE56 1RQ* T: (01773) 599013 E: thevic@dsl.pipex.com *or* heyhogough@yahoo.co.uk

GOUGH, Derek William. b 31. Pemb Coll Cam BA 55 MA 59. St Steph Ho Ox 55. **d** 57 **p** 58. C E Finchley All SS *Lon* 57–60; C Roxbourne St Andr 60–66; V Edmonton St Mary w St Jo 66–98; rtd 98; PtO *Chelmsf* 98–07; *St Alb* 00–07. *5 Old Priory Farm, Deeping St James, Peterborough PE6 8PW* T: (01778) 341421 E: derek.gough.1952@pem.cam.ac.uk

GOUGH, Elizabeth. b 54. CBDTI 97. **d** 00 **p** 01. OLM Eden, Gelt and Irthing *Carl* 00–06; TV 06–14; rtd 14; PtO *Carl* from 14. *Brackenside Barn, Brampton CA8 2QX* T: (016977) 746252 E: elizabeth.gough3@btinternet.com

GOUGH, Canon Ernest Hubert. b 31. TCD BA 53 MA 57. TCD Div Sch Div Test 54. **d** 54 **p** 55. C Glenavy *Conn* 54–57; C Lisburn Ch Ch 57–61; P-in-c Belfast St Ninian 61–62; I 62–71; I Belfast St Bart 71–85; I Templepatrick w Donegore 85–97; Can Conn Cathl from 91; rtd 97. *The Caim, 15 Swilly Road, Portstewart BT55 7DJ* T: (028) 7083 3253

GOUGH, Frank Peter. b 32. Lon Coll of Div 66. **d** 68 **p** 69. C Weymouth St Mary *Sarum* 68–70; C Attenborough w Chilwell *S'well* 70–73; R Barrow *Ches* 73–77; P-in-c Summerstown *S'wark* 77–88; RD Tooting 80–88; Dioc Past Sec 88–93; Tutor and Chapl Whittington Coll Felbridge 93–98; rtd 98; PtO *Roch* 03–07; *S'wark* 13–16. *The College of St Barnabas, Blackberry Lane, Lingfield RH7 6NJ* M: 07970-199135 E: frank_gough@msn.com

GOUGH, The Ven Jonathan Robin Blanning. b 62. Univ of Wales (Lamp) BA 83 Westmr Coll Ox MTh 96 FRSA 03. St Steph Ho Ox 83. **d** 85 **p** 86. C Braunton *Ex* 85–86; C Matson *Glouc* 86–89; CF 89–01; Abp's Officer for Ecum Cant 01–05; Can Gib Cathl *Eur* 02–05; Hon Can Nicosia from 06; CF 05–08; Sen CF 08–19; Chapl R Memorial Chpl Sandhurst 08–11; Adn Richmond and Craven *Leeds* from 19; PtO *Eur* from 05. *4 Appleby Way, Knaresborough HG5 9LX* T: (01423) 866717 E: jonathan.gough@leeds.anglican.org

GOUGH, Miss Lynda Elizabeth. b 54. SS Hild & Bede Coll Dur BA 94 RGN 83. Wycliffe Hall Ox 97. **d** 99 **p** 00. C Stranton *Dur* 99–03; V Spennymoor and Whitworth 03–11; C Darlington H Trin 11–16; AD Darlington 14–16; rtd 16. *19 Pentland Grove, Darlington DL3 8BA* T: (01325) 464799 E: lyndaegough@gmail.com

GOUGH, The Ven Martyn John. b 66. Univ of Wales (Cardiff) BTh 87 Univ of Wales (Lamp) MA 05 FRSA 04. St Steph Ho Ox 88. **d** 90 **p** 91. C Port Talbot St Theodore *Llan* 90–92; C Roath 92–94; Asst Chapl Milan w Genoa and Varese *Eur* 95–98; Chapl RN 98–14; Asst Dir of Ords 07–09; Dir of Ords 09–14; Voc Adv 07–14; Dir 09–14; Dep Chapl of the Fleet 14–17; Chapl of the Fleet and Adn for the RN from 18; QHC from 18. *Royal Naval Chaplaincy Service, Mail Point 1-2, Leach Building, Whale Island, Portsmouth PO2 8BY* T: (023) 9262 5055 M: 07867-720570 E: martyn.gough656@mod.gov.uk

GOUGH, Matthew James Charles. b 72. Hull Univ BA 94 MSW 98. Qu Coll Birm 17. **d** 19. C Knighton *Leic* from 19. *Knighton Parish Centre, Church Lane, Leicester LE2 3WG* T: 0116-270 2705 M: 07754-961997 E: revgough@gmail.com

GOUGH, Sally Elizabeth. b 56. St Hild Coll 16. **d** 18 **p** 19. NSM Thornton Dale w Allerston, Ebberston etc *York* from 18. *8 Westfield Terrace, Thornton-le-Dale, Pickering YO18 7SQ* E: theflyingphysio@hotmail.com

GOUGH, Stephen William Cyprian. b 50. Alberta Univ BSc 71. Cuddesdon Coll BA 80 MA. **d** 79 **p** 80. C Walton St Mary *Liv* 79–83; V New Springs 83–87; V Childwall St Dav 87–06; V Stoneycroft All SS 04–06; Co-ord Chapl HM Pris Risley 06–08; P-in-c Rainford *Liv* 08–11; V 11–13; TV Walton-on-the-Hill 13–16; rtd 16; PtO *Liv* from 17. *49 Grange Lane, Gateacre, Liverpool L25 4SA* T: 0151-421 1213 M: 07881-648037 E: gough_stephen@btopenworld.com

GOULD, Christine. b 52. **d** 10. NSM Darwen St Pet *Blackb* 10–14; rtd 14; PtO *Blackb* from 14. *15 Lamaleach*

Drive, Freckleton, Preston PR4 1AJ T: (01772) 755746 E: b.gould@yahoo.com

GOULD, David Robert. b 59. Cov Poly BA 81. Cranmer Hall Dur 87. **d** 90 **p** 91. C Rugby *Cov* 90–93; CF 93–94; PtO *Cov* 01–05; TV Kings Norton *Birm* 05–08; V Smethwick Resurr from 08. *The Vicarage, 69 South Road, Smethwick, Warley B67 7BP* T: 0121-558 0373 M: 07787-199998 E: davidgould1@btinternet.com

GOULD, Gary David. b 57. ERMC 17. **d** 19. OLM Hempton and Pudding Norton *Nor* from 19; OLM Walsingham, Houghton and Barsham from 19. *23 Priory Crescent, Binham, Fakenham NR21 0DB* T: (01328) 830715 M: 07469-921999 E: garygould57@gmail.com

GOULD, Gerald. b 37. Wilson Carlile Coll 60 S Dios Minl Tr Scheme 84. **d** 86 **p** 87. CA from 62; C Hedge End St Jo *Win* 86–89; V St Goran w Caerhays *Truro* 89–93; P-in-c Crook Peak *B & W* 93–94; R 94–99; rtd 99; PtO *Ex* 99–09. *2 Nightingale Lawns, Cullompton EX15 1UB* T: (01884) 38105 E: g.sj.gould@amserve.com

GOULD, Ms Janet. b 63. LTCL 85. Westcott Ho Cam 92. **d** 95 **p** 96. C Pet St Mary Boongate 95–98; C Fleet *Guildf* 98–04; C St Mellons *Mon* 04–05; P-in-c Glan Ely *Llan* from 06. *Church House, Grand Avenue, Cardiff CF5 2YJ* T: (029) 2067 9833 E: jan.gould2@btinternet.com

GOULD, Mrs Pamela Rosemarie. b 41. **d** 01 **p** 02. NSM New Bilton *Cov* 01–03; Asst Chapl HM YOI Onley 01–03; NSM Clifton upon Dunsmore and Newton *Cov* 03–05; P-in-c 05–06; PtO from 07. *19 Church Road, Church Lawford, Rugby CV23 9EG* T: (024) 7654 5745 E: revpamgould@aol.com

GOULD, Peter Richard. b 34. Univ of Wales BA 57. Qu Coll Birm. **d** 62 **p** 63. C Rothwell *Ripon* 62–68; Chapl Agnes Stewart C of E High Sch Leeds 65–68; V Allerton Bywater *Ripon* 68–73; Asst Master S'well Minster Gr Sch 73–76; Chapl Lic Victuallers' Sch Ascot 76–93; V Aberavon H Trin *Llan* 93–99; rtd 99. *Amber Cottage, 1 Load Lane, Weston Zoyland, Bridgwater TA7 0EQ* T: (01278) 691029

GOULD, Robert Ozburn. b 38. Williams Coll Mass BA 59 St Andr Univ PhD 63. **d** 78 **p** 83. NSM Edin St Columba 78–80; TV from 83; Hon Dioc Supernumerary 80–83; Hon Chapl Edin Univ 00–04. *80 Strathearn Road, Edinburgh EH9 2AF* T: 0131-447 8513 M: 07960-403872 E: bob@gould.ca

GOULD, Susan Judith. *See* MURRAY, Susan Judith

GOULDER, Canon Catherine Helen. b 44. Hull Univ BA 65 MA 67 Ox Univ DipEd 68. NEOC 96. **d** 98 **p** 99. NSM Sutton St Mich *York* 98–02; P-in-c N Cave w Cliffe 02–08; P-in-c Hotham 02–08; PtO from 08; Can and Preb York Minster from 05. *5 Bishops Croft, Beverley HU17 8JY* T: (01482) 880553 E: kategoulder@kategoulder.karoo.co.uk

GOULDING, Amanda. Win Univ BTh 01. STETS. **d** 07 **p** 08. NSM Upper Dever *Win* 07–08; NSM Win St Bart 08–10; NSM Win St Bart and St Lawr w St Swithun from 10. *St Lawrence Parish Office, Colebrook Street, Winchester SO23 9LH* T: (01962) 849434 E: threesaintswin@gmail.com

GOULDING, John Gilbert. b 29. Univ Coll Dur BA 54 MA 59. **d** 88 **p** 89. NSM Kemsing w Woodlands *Roch* 88–91; Hon Nat Moderator for Reader Tr ACCM 90-91; ABM 91–94; NSM Sevenoaks St Luke CD *Roch* 91–96; PtO 97–12. *Springwood, 50 Copperfields, Kemsing, Sevenoaks TN15 6QG* T: (01732) 762558 E: jonmar.611@btinternet.com

GOULDING, Nicolas John. b 56. Southn Univ BSc 78 PhD 82. NTMTC 94. **d** 97 **p** 98. NSM St Bart Less *Lon* 97–05; Chapl St Bart's and RLSMD Qu Mary and Westf Coll from 97; PtO *St Alb* 99–17; Dioc Adv on Faith and Science from 17; Public Preacher from 17. *5 Greatfield Close, Harpenden AL5 3HP* T: (01582) 461293 *or* (020) 7882 6128 F: 7982 6076 E: n.j.goulding@qmul.ac.uk

GOULDTHORPE, Rachel Carolyn. b 72. Bp Otter Coll 00. **d** 03 **p** 10. NSM Hove *Chich* 03–05; C Moulsecoomb 05–11; TV 11–12; V Bolsover *Derby* from 12. *The Vicarage, Church Street, Bolsover, Chesterfield S44 6HB* T: (01273) 824888 M: 07859-066557 E: rachelgouldthorpe@gmail.com

GOULSTON, Jeremy Hugh. b 68. St Aid Coll Dur BA 90. Ripon Coll Cuddesdon 01. **d** 03 **p** 04. C Henfield w Shermanbury and Woodmancote *Chich* 03–07; TV Wallingford *Ox* 07–15; R Uffington, Shellingford, Woolstone and Baulking from 15. *The Vicarage, Broad Street, Uffington, Faringdon SN7 7RA* T: (01367) 821143 E: jgoulston@btinternet.com

GOUNDREY-SMITH, Stephen John. b 67. Brighton Poly BSc 88 MRPharmS 89 City Univ MSc 94. Aston Tr Scheme 96 Wycliffe Hall Ox BTh 01. **d** 99 **p** 00. C Happisburgh, Walcott, Hempstead w Eccles etc *Nor* 99–01; PtO *Pet* 02–03; NSM Chenderit 03–08; PtO 09–11; P-in-c Chedworth, Yanworth and Stowell, Coln Rogers etc *Glouc* 10–16; V from 16; Hon C Northleach w Hampnett and Farmington etc 10–16; Hon C Sherborne, Windrush, the Barringtons etc

10–16. *The Vicarage, Cheap Street, Chedworth, Cheltenham GL54 4AA* T: (01285) 720392 M: 07771-741009 E: stephengoundreysmith@gmail.com

GOURDIE, Janice Elizabeth. *See* BROWN, Janice Elizabeth

GOURLAY, Wendy Elizabeth. b 50. DipOT 71. ERMC 08. **d** 11 **p** 12. NSM Boulge w Burgh, Grundisburgh and Hasketon *St E* 11–13; NSM Carlford 13–17; rtd 17; PtO *St E* from 17. *Tubric Cottage, The Street, Cretingham, Woodbridge IP13 7BL* T: (01728) 685335 E: rev.gourlay@gmail.com

GOURLEY, Malcolm Samuel. b 37. MRPharmS 58. NEOC 94. **d** 98 **p** 98. NSM Gt Smeaton w Appleton Wiske and Birkby etc *Ripon* 98–00; NSM Ainderby Steeple w Yafforth and Kirby Wiske etc 00–02; NSM Herrington, Penshaw and Shiney Row *Dur* 02–07; rtd 07; PtO *Dur* from 07. *Linden House, Lawn Drive, West Boldon, East Boldon NE36 0AZ* T: 0191-597 7548 E: malcolm.gourley@tombola.com

GOVAN, Kesh Rico. b 66. St Jo Coll Dur BA 96. Cranmer Hall Dur 93. **d** 96 **p** 97. C Astley Bridge *Man* 96–00; TV Walkden and Lt Hulton 00–04; I Blessington w Kilbride, Ballymore Eustace etc *D & G* 04–07; C Uttoxeter Area *Lich* 07–10; C Rocester and Croxden w Hollington 07–10; V 10–14; Chapl JCB Academy 10–14; R Nelson Bay Australia from 14. *29 Tomaree Street, Nelson Bay NSW 2315, Australia* T: (0061) (2) 4981 1839 E: revkesh@sky.com *or* allsaint@nelsonbay.com

GOVENDER, The Very Revd Rogers Morgan. b 60. Natal Univ BTh 97. St Paul's Coll Grahamstown 83. **d** 85 **p** 86. C Overport Ch Ch S Africa 85–87; R Greyville St Mary 88–92; R Hayfields St Matt 93–98; Adn Pietermaritzburg 97–98; R Berea St Thos S Africa 99–00; P-in-c Didsbury Ch Ch *Man* 01–06; P-in-c Withington St Chris 03–06; AD Withington 04–06; Dean Man from 06; Borough Dean Man from 18. *1 Booth Clibborn Court, Salford M7 4PJ* T: 0161-792 2801 *or* 833 2220 F: 839 6218 E: dean@manchestercathedral.org

GOWDEY, Michael Cragg. b 32. Oriel Coll Ox BA 56 MA 58 Keele Univ CertEd 73. Qu Coll Birm. **d** 58 **p** 59. C Ashbourne w Mapleton and Clifton *Derby* 58–63; V Chellaston 63–69; Asst Chapl Ellesmere Coll 69–74; Chapl Trent Coll Nottm 74–81; Educn Chapl *Worc* 81–97; Chapl K Edw Sixth Form Coll Worc 81–97; rtd 97; P-in-c Beeley and Edensor *Derby* 97–02; PtO 02–18. *18 Moorhall Estate, Bakewell DE45 1FP* T: (01629) 814121 E: jandmgowdey@uwclub.net

GOWER, Denys Victor. b 33. Cant Sch of Min 85. **d** 87 **p** 88. NSM Gillingham H Trin *Roch* 87–91; NSM Gillingham St Aug 89–91; C Perry Street 91–93; P-in-c Wateringbury w Teston and W Farleigh 93–96; R 96–00; rtd 00; PtO *Roch* from 00; Ind Chapl from 02; PtO *Cant* 03–09; Hon Chapl Medway NHS Foundn Trust from 05; PV Roch Cathl from 07. *4 Locarno Avenue, Gillingham ME8 6ET* T: (01634) 375765 M: 07985-781161

GOWER, Nikolas John . b 88. Wycliffe Hall Ox BA 17. **d** 17 **p** 18. C Romsey *Win* from 17. *15 Mount Temple, Romsey SO51 5UW* M: 07967-766070 E: nikolasgower@icloud.com

GOWER, Miss Patricia Ann. b 44. Wilson Carlile Coll IDC 79 Sarum & Wells Th Coll 88. **d** 88 **p** 94. Chapl Bris Univ 88–91; Hon Par Dn Clifton St Paul 88–91; Par Dn Spondon *Derby* 91–94; C 94–95; P-in-c Hatton 95–98; Asst Chapl HM Pris Sudbury 95–98; Chapl 98–04; rtd 04; PtO *Derby* from 04. *19 Heronswood Drive, Spondon, Derby DE21 7AX* T: (01332) 671031

GOWER, Miss Paulette Rose-Mary de Garis. b 70. Plymouth Univ BEd 93 St Jo Coll Dur MA 08. Cranmer Hall Dur 01. **d** 03 **p** 04. C Shrewsbury St Geo w Greenfields *Lich* 03–07; TV Hawarden *St As* 07–14; V Gwersyllt 14–16; I Alyn Miss Area from 17; AD Alyn from 16. *The Vicarage, Old Mold Road, Gwersyllt, Wrexham LL11 4SB* T: (01978) 756391 E: paulettegower@garyslth.plus.com

GOWER, Mrs Sarah Catherine. b 63. Ex Univ BA 84 Cam Univ BTh 09. Westcott Ho Cam 07. **d** 09 **p** 10. C St Neots *Ely* 09–13; C Eynesbury 12–13; Min Orton Goldhay CD from 13; Jt RD Yaxley 16–19; RD from 19. *Christ Church House, 1 Benstead, Orton Goldhay, Peterborough PE2 5JJ* T: (01733) 394411 E: sarahcgower@btinternet.com

GOWER, Archdeacon of. *See* DAVIES, The Ven Jonathan Byron

GOWING, Wilfred Herbert. b 50. QUB BSc 72. NEOC 03. **d** 06 **p** 07. NSM Ripon H Trin 06–14; *Leeds* from 14. *Littlemead, 20 Springfield Rise, Great Ouseburn, York YO26 9SE* T: (01423) 331177 F: 331178 E: wilfgowing@btinternet.com

GOWING-CUMBER, Alexander John. b 72. Fitzw Coll Cam MA 00 Moorlands Th Coll BA 94. Ridley Hall Cam 98. **d** 00 **p** 03. C Vange *Chelmsf* 00–02; C Rayleigh 02–05; TV Grays Thurrock 05–15; rtd 15; PtO *Chelmsf* from 15. *Trinity House, 5 Nevada Road, Canvey Island SS8 8EX* T: (01268) 698414 M: 07786-652286 E: fralexgc@aol.com

GOWLER, Simon Daniel Luke. b 60. Univ of Wales (Abth) LLB 83. All SS Cen for Miss & Min 16. **d** 18 **p** 19. NSM Knutsford St Cross *Ches* from 18. *Willow Tree Cottage, Knutsford Road, Mobberley, Knutsford WA16 7PU* T: (01565) 872358 M: 07881-912681 E: simon.gowler@jobling-gowler.co.uk

GRACE, Canon Andrew John. b 54. Univ of Wales (Abth) BMus 76 St Martin's Coll Lanc PGCE 78 FRCO 75 FTCL 76 LRAM 75. Sarum & Wells Th Coll 79. **d** 81 **p** 82. C Tenby w Gumfreston *St D* 81–84; C Llanelli 84–86; V Monkton 86–91; V Fairfield *Derby* 91–96; P-in-c Barlborough 96–01; R Barlborough and Renishaw 01–03; V Pembroke Dock *St D* 03–04; TR Carew 04–08; TR Tenby from 08; AD Pembroke 13–16; Can St D Cathl from 12. *The Rectory, Church Park, Tenby SA70 7EE* T: (01834) 842068

GRACE, David Leonard. b 55. Wilson Carlile Coll 89 Ripon Coll Cuddesdon 97. **d** 99 **p** 00. CA from 92; C St Leonards and St Ives *Win* 99–04; V 04–09; Chapl Basingstoke and N Hants NHS Foundn Trust 09–11; Chapl Hants Hosps NHS Foundn Trust 12–13; Chapl Weston Area Health NHS Trust from 13. *The Chaplaincy, Weston General Hospital, Grange Road, Uphill, Weston-super-Mare BS23 4TQ* T: (01934) 636363 ext 3611 M: 07825-896388 E: david.grace1@nhs.net

GRACE, Miss Michelle Elizabeth. b 59. St Jo Coll Nottm BA 12. **d** 12. C Chell *Lich* 12–13; C Oswestry 13–17; TV Tring *St Alb* from 17. *The Vicarage, Station Road, Aldbury, Tring HP23 5RS* T: (01442) 851200

GRACIE, Canon Bryan John. b 45. Open Univ BA 81. AKC 67. **d** 68 **p** 69. C Whipton *Ex* 68–72; Chapl St Jo Sch Tiffield 72–73; Chapl HM Borstal Stoke Heath 74–78; Asst Chapl HM Pris Liv 74; Chapl HM Youth Cust Cen Feltham 78–85; Chapl HM Pris Birm 85–10; Hon Can Birm Cathl 05–10; rtd 10; PtO *Birm* from 10. *346 Eachelhurst Road, Sutton Coldfield B76 1ER* T: 0121-351 6532 E: bryan_gracie@icloud.com

GRADY, Gary Brian. b 69. Bris Poly BA 92. WEMTC 10. **d** 13 **p** 14. C Cirencester *Glouc* 13–16; TV S Cheltenham from 16; AD Cheltenham from 18. *The Rectory, Kidnappers Lane, Cheltenham GL53 0NT* T: (01242) 242831 M: 07713-654074 E: garygrady@btinternet.com

GRAEME, Emma Jane. b 60. Southn Univ BA 00. Ripon Coll Cuddesdon 10. **d** 12 **p** 13. C E Grinstead St Swithun *Chich* 12–15; C New Fishbourne 15–17; R Beeding and Bramber w Botolphs from 17. *The Rectory, 73 Church Lane, Upper Beeding, Steyning BN44 3HP* T: (01903) 810265 M: 07403-114365 E: estonham@yahoo.co.uk *or* 3bsrector@gmail.com

GRAESSER, Adrian Stewart. b 42. Tyndale Hall Bris 63. **d** 67 **p** 68. C Nottingham St Jude *S'well* 67–69; C Slaithwaite w E Scammonden *Wakef* 69–72; CF 72–75; V Earl's Heaton *Wakef* 75–81; R Norton Fitzwarren *B & W* 81–86; R Bickenhill w Elmdon *Birm* 86–90; R Elmdon St Nic 90–00; P-in-c Dolton *Ex* 00–05; P-in-c Iddesleigh w Dowland 00–05; P-in-c Monkokehampton 00–05; RD Torrington 02–05; rtd 05; PtO *Worc* from 09. *7 Mortlake Drive, Martley, Worcester WR6 6QU* T: (01886) 888628 E: adrian.graesser@sky.com

GRAHAM, Alan Robert. b 44. St Edm Hall Ox BA 67 MA 71. St Steph Ho Ox BA 70. **d** 70 **p** 71. C Clifton All SS *Bris* 70–74; C Tadley St Pet *Win* 74–77; P-in-c Upper Clatford w Goodworth Clatford 77–79; R Abbotts Ann and Upper Clatford and Goodworth Clatford 79–84; V Lyndhurst and Emery Down 84–92; P-in-c Over Wallop w Nether Wallop 92–02; rtd 02; PtO *Win* from 08. *44 New Forest Drive, Brockenhurst SO42 7QW* T: (01590) 622324

GRAHAM, Alexander. *See* GRAHAM, Andrew Alexander Kenny

GRAHAM, Alfred. b 34. Bris Univ BA 57. Tyndale Hall Bris. **d** 58 **p** 59. C Chaddesden St Mary *Derby* 58–61; C Bickenhill w Elmdon *Birm* 61–64; V Kirkdale St Lawr *Liv* 64–70; V Stapleford *S'well* 70–83; V Burton Joyce w Bulcote 83–95; V Burton Joyce w Bulcote and Stoke Bardolph 95–97; rtd 97; PtO *S'well* 03–11; *Blackb* from 11. *16 Meadow View, Clitheroe BB7 2NT* T: (01200) 426805

✠**GRAHAM, The Rt Revd Andrew Alexander Kenny (Alec).** b 29. St Jo Coll Ox BA 52 MA 57 Lambeth DD 95. Ely Th Coll 53. **d** 55 **p** 56 **c** 77. C Hove All SS *Chich* 55–58; Chapl, Lect Th, and Tutor Worc Coll Ox 58–70; Warden Linc Th Coll 70–77; Can and Preb Linc Cathl 70–77; Suff Bp Bedford *St Alb* 77–81; Bp Newc 81–97; Chmn ACCM 84–87; Chmn Doctrine Commn 87–95; rtd 97; Hon Asst Bp Carl from 97. *Fell End, Butterwick, Penrith CA10 2QQ* T: (01931) 713147

GRAHAM, Canon Anthony Nigel. b 40. Univ of Wales (Abth) BA 62 CertEd 70. Ripon Hall Ox 62. **d** 64 **p** 65. C Heref H Trin 64–67; C Birm St Martin 67–69; C Selly Oak St Mary 71–75; V Edgbaston SS Mary and Ambrose 75–83; CMS Miss Partner Nigeria 84–88; Hon Can Jos from 88; V Highworth w Sevenhampton and Inglesham etc *Bris* 88–95; RD Highworth

93–95; P-in-c Coalpit Heath 95–99; V 99–00; rtd 00; PtO *Glouc* from 17. *19 Dormer Road, Cheltenham GL51 0AX*

GRAHAM, Benjamin Robert. b 85. **d** 16 **p** 17. C Wandsworth All SS *S'wark* from 16. *74 Haldon Road, London SW18 1QG* E: ben@wandsworthparish.co.uk

GRAHAM, Christopher John. b 55. EMMTC. **d** 03 **p** 04. NSM Ripley *Derby* 03–08; NSM Ilkeston St Jo 08–13; PtO from 13. *7 Derwent Drive, Merebrook Park, Whatstandwell, Matlock DE4 5PG* M: 07933-301562 E: revchrisg@hotmail.co.uk

GRAHAM, Clifton Gordon. b 53. ARCM 72 GRSM 74 FRCO 75 Coll of Ripon & York St Jo PGCE 76. St Steph Ho Ox 90. **d** 92 **p** 93. C Northfield *Birm* 92–93; C Perry Beeches 93–97; P-in-c S Yardley St Mich 97–00; V 00–06; Chapl Birm City Univ 06–10; Chapl Ex Univ 10–13; rtd 13. *Springwell, 31 Olympian Way, Cullompton EX15 1GB* T: (01884) 32545 E: jgccgg@gmail.com

GRAHAM, David. *See* GRAHAM, George David

GRAHAM, Fiona Karen. *See* WHEATLEY, Fiona Karen

GRAHAM, Frederick Lawrence. b 35. TCD BA 65. CITC 66. **d** 66 **p** 67. C Belfast St Matt *Conn* 66–69; TV Chelmsley Wood *Birm* 69–73; Ch of Ireland Youth Officer 73–78; Bp's C Stoneyford *Conn* 78–88; Bp's C Fahan Lower and Upper *D & R* 88–91; Can Raphoe Cathl 90–01; I Donagheady 91–01; Can Derry Cathl 95–01; rtd 01. *14 Greenmount Gardens, Lisburn BT27 5HD* T: (028) 9258 2639 M: 07719-529989 E: freka1@virginmedia.com

GRAHAM, George David. b 42. Jes Coll Cam BA 64 MA 68. St Jo Coll Nottm LTh Lon Coll of Div 66. **d** 71 **p** 72. C Corby St Columba *Pet* 71–74; C Deptford St Jo *S'wark* 74–77; P-in-c Deptford St Pet 77–82; C-in-c Wheatley Park St Paul CD *Sheff* 82–87; TV Dunstable *St Alb* 87–92; V Bromley Common St Luke *Roch* 92–02; R Hayes 02–12; rtd 12; PtO *Roch* from 13. *129 Warren Road, Orpington BR6 6JE* T: (01689) 850656 E: gd.graham77@gmail.com

GRAHAM, Canon George Edgar. b 55. QUB BA 91. Sarum & Wells Th Coll 74 CITC 77. **d** 78 **p** 79. C Lisburn Ch Ch *Conn* 78–81; C Mossley 81–83; I Broomhedge 83–91; I Derriaghy w Colin 91–96; I Ballywillan 96–05; I Dunluce from 05; Can Conn Cathl from 05; Preb from 06; Prec from 16; Chan from 16. *Dunluce Rectory, 17 Priestland Road, Bushmills BT57 8QP* T: (028) 2073 1221 *or* 2073 0537 E: g.k.graham@btinternet.com *or* admindunluce@btconnect.com

GRAHAM, Harry John. b 52. Magd Coll Cam BA 75 MA 86. Trin Coll Bris BA 94. **d** 96 **p** 97. C Walkden and Lt Hulton *Man* 96–99; Chapl Salford Coll of Tech 96–99; P-in-c Edgeside *Man* 99–00; TV Rossendale Middle Valley 00–02; Gen Sec Miss Without Borders (UK) Ltd from 02; PtO *S'wark* 07–13; *Lon* 09–19; NSM Edmonton St Aldhelm from 19. *69 Eyre Court, 3-21 Finchley Road, London NW8 9TX* T: (020) 7586 8336 *or* 7940 1370 F: 7403 7348 E: info_uk@mwbi.org *or* hgraham@mwbi.org

GRAHAM, Mrs Heather Karen. b 62. Keele Univ BA 83. Ripon Coll Cuddesdon 13. **d** 16 **p** 17. NSM High Wycombe Ox 16–19; TV from 19. *5 Manor Gardens, High Wycombe HP13 5HD* T: (01494) 526686 M: 07879-017667 E: heather.graham@standrewshw.co.uk

GRAHAM, Ian Maxwell. b 50. CertEd 76. Chich Th Coll 86. **d** 88 **p** 89. C Middlesbrough St Thos *York* 88–90; C Stainton-in-Cleveland 90–93; V Hemlington 93–00; V Grangetown 00–14; rtd 14; PtO *York* from 18. *19 Whitehouse Road, Thornaby, Stockton-on-Tees TS17 0AJ* T: (01642) 882323 E: ianmgraham50@gmail.com

GRAHAM, Kevin. *See* GRAHAM, Terence Kevin Declan

GRAHAM, Matthew John. b 78. Lon Guildhall Univ BSc 00. Oak Hill Th Coll BA 13. **d** 13 **p** 14. C Lt Heath *St Alb* 13–16; V Prenton *Ches* from 16. *The Vicarage, 1 Vicarage Close, Birkenhead CH42 8QX* T: 0151-608 1808

GRAHAM, Michael. b 51. CITC BTh 95. **d** 95 **p** 96. C Cork St Fin Barre's Union *C, C & R* 95–98; Min Can Cork Cathl 97–98; I Drogheda w Ardee, Collon and Termonfeckin *Arm* 98–16; Ch of Ireland Internet Co-ord 99–05; I Kilsaran w Drumcar, Dunleer and Dunany *Arm* 07–16; rtd 16; PtO Cyprus and the Gulf from 16. *PO Box 14, Esentepe Posta SB, Esentepe, 99400 Girne, Mersin 10, Turkey* T: (0090) (533) 8778307 E: mgraham597@gmail.com

GRAHAM, Michael John. b 50. Birm Univ BSc 72 Loughb Univ MSc 78 Bris Univ MEd 89. Trin Coll Bris 15. **d** 17 **p** 18. OLM Woodbridge *Bris* from 17. *Crosthwaite, Barnes Green, Brinkworth, Chippenham SN15 5AG* T: (01666) 510441 E: mike.graham@btinternet.com

GRAHAM, Nigel. *See* GRAHAM, Anthony Nigel

✠**GRAHAM, The Rt Revd Olivia Josephine.** b 56. UEA BA 84. SAOMC 94. **d** 97 **p** 98 **c** 19. NSM Wheatley *Ox* 97–98; C Risborough 98–01; TV Burnham w Dropmore, Hitcham and Taplow 01–07; Par Development Adv 07–13; Hon Can Ch Ch

12–13; Adn Berks 13–19; Area Bp Reading from 19. *Bishop's House, Tidmarsh Lane, Tidmarsh, Reading RG8 8HA* T: 0118-984 1216 E: bishopreading@oxford.anglican.org

GRAHAM, Richard William. b 63. Poly of Wales BA 86 ACA 91. Trin Coll Bris 03. **d** 05 **p** 06. C Savernake *Sarum* 05–09; TV Hemel Hempstead *St Alb* from 09. *St Barnabas' Vicarage, Everest Way, Hemel Hempstead HP2 4HY* T: (01442) 253681 E: randmgraham@hotmail.com

GRAHAM, Rory Malise. b 75. Southn Univ BSc 97. Oak Hill Th Coll BA 12. **d** 12 **p** 13. C Hove Bp Hannington Memorial Ch *Chich* 12–16; C Hailsham from 16. *1 Barn Close, Hailsham BN27 1TL* T: (01323) 844502 E: rorygraham@hailshamchurch.org

GRAHAM, Roy Richard Arthur. b 39. Lon Univ BD 63 Open Univ BA 78. ALCD 62. **d** 63 **p** 64. C Morden *S'wark* 66–70; V Tittensor *Lich* 70–79; R Hurworth and Dinsdale w Sockburn *Dur* 79–02; rtd 02. *Rose Cottage, Hackforth Road, Patrick Brompton, Bedale DL8 1JR* E: roygraham39@outlook.com

GRAHAM, Stephen Alan. b 78. QUB BA 99 MA 00 CCC Cam PGCE 01. St Steph Ho Ox. **d** 16 **p** 17. C Holt w High Kelling *Nor* from 16. *27 Neil Avenue, Holt NR25 6TG* T: (01263) 649985 M: 07856-071178 E: revdstephengraham@gmail.com

GRAHAM, Stig. *See* GRAHAM, William Stig

GRAHAM, Canon Terence Kevin Declan. b 67. NUI BSc 89 TCD BTh 02. CITC 99. **d** 02 **p** 03. C Knock *D & D* 02–05; J Carrowdore w Millisle 05–09; I Movilla 09–13; I Belfast St Bart *Conn* from 13; Can Belf Cathl from 19. *St Bartholomew's Rectory, 16 Mount Pleasant, Belfast BT9 5DS* T: (028) 9066 9995 M: 07964-663745 E: stbartholomew@connor.anglican.org

GRAHAM, William Stig. b 53. Newc Univ BSc 75. NEOC. **d** 99 **p** 00. C W Acklam *York* 99–02; Chapl Myton Hamlet Hospice from 02. *2 Winyates Road, Lighthorne Heath, Leamington Spa CV33 9TU* T: (01926) 640811 *or* 492518 E: stiggraham@netscape.net *or* stig.graham@mytonhospice.org

GRAHAM-BROWN, John George Francis. b 34. CA 60. Wycliffe Hall Ox 60. **d** 63 **p** 64. C Darlington St Cuth *Dur* 63–67; C Rufforth w Moor Monkton and Hessay *York* 67–73; Sec York Dioc Redundant Chs Uses Cttee 69–89; Asst Sec DBF 73–84; Dioc Past Cttee *York* 73–89; Hon C York St Barn 73–85; P-in-c 85–92; TV Marfleet 92–99; rtd 99; PtO *St Alb* from 00. *40 Hunters Oak, Hemel Hempstead HP2 7SW* T: (01482) 402226 E: f.graham-brown@tinyonline.co.uk

GRAINGER, Canon Bruce. b 37. Nottm Univ BA 62 Hull Univ MA 83. Cuddesdon Coll 62. **d** 64 **p** 65. C Bingley All SS *Bradf* 64–67; Chapl K Sch Cant 67–72; Hon Min Can Cant Cathl 69–72; V Baildon *Bradf* 72–88; V Oxenhope 88–04; Hon Can Bradf Cathl 84–04; Dir of Ords 88–96; Dioc Ecum Officer 96–04; Tutor Bradf Univ 99–03; RD S Craven 02–03; rtd 04; PtO *Bradf* 04–14; *Leeds* 14–15; Hon Chapl Bradf Cathl from 15. *Aspen Lodge, Low Shann Farm, High Spring Gardens Lane, Keighley BD20 6LN* T: (01535) 611989 E: bruce@graspen.gotadsl.co.uk

GRAINGER, Ian. b 66. Cranmer Hall Dur 89. **d** 92 **p** 93. C Whitehaven *Carl* 92–94; C Walney Is 94–97; P-in-c Barrow St Aid 97–02; V Camerton, Seaton and W Seaton from 02; Dioc World Development Officer from 11. *The Vicarage, Ling Beck Park, Seaton, Workington CA14 1JQ* T: (01900) 602162 E: ian.grainger66@btinternet.com

GRAINGER, Michael Noel Howard. b 40. Trin Coll Carmarthen. **d** 91 **p** 92. NSM Haverfordwest St Martin w Lambston *St D* 91–95; V Maenclochog and New Moat etc 95–05; rtd 05. *14 Swallowdale, Swindon SN3 5AZ*

GRAINGER-SMITH, James Edward. b 71. Nottm Univ BA 92. St Jo Coll Nottm MA 02. **d** 02 **p** 03. C Hordle *Win* 02–07; R Beeford w Frodingham and Foston *York* from 07; P-in-c Brandesburton and Leven w Catwick 11–13; V Brandesburton and Leven from 13; RD N Holderness 12–16. *The Rectory, 11 Glebe Gardens, Beeford, Driffield YO25 8BF* T: (01262) 488042 E: j.grainger-smith@sky.com

GRANGE (née FEATHERSTON), Mrs Alice Margery. b 55. Teesside Univ BA 97. NEOC. **d** 99 **p** 00. C Pickering w Lockton and Levisham *York* 99–02; TV Crosslacon *Carl* 02–07; P-in-c Middlesbrough St Agnes *York* 07–18; Chapl S Tees Hosps NHS Foundn Trust 07–18; rtd 18; PtO *York* from 18. *33 Marshall Drive, Pickering YO18 7JT* E: margery-grange@sky.com

GRANNER, Mrs Linda. b 52. Westmr Coll Ox BTh 00. WMMTC 01. **d** 03 **p** 04. NSM Bearwood *Birm* 03–06; C Edgbaston St Bart 06–08; C Edgbaston St Geo 06–08; P-in-c Hobs Moat from 08. *St Mary's House, 30 Hobs Meadow, Solihull B92 8PN* T: 0121-743 4955 E: l.granner@sky.com

GRANT, Andrew James. b 68. Cranmer Hall Dur 09. **d** 11 **p** 12. C Bramham *York* 11–15; V Marton-in-Cleveland

from 15; P-in-c Middlesbrough St Agnes from 18. *The Vicarage, Stokesley Road, Marton-in-Cleveland, Middlesbrough TS7 8JU* T: (01642) 316201 M: 07519-423552 E: vicar@stcuthbertmarton.org.uk

GRANT, Canon Andrew Richard. b 40. Univ of Wales BA 62. Chich Th Coll 63. **d** 65 **p** 66. C Kennington St Jo *S'wark* 65–68; Hon C 70–72; Hon C Stockwell Green St Andr 68–70; V Nunhead St Antony 72–79; TR N Lambeth 79–92; USPG Ghana 92–99; Hon Can Kumasi from 02; C Paddington St Jo w St Mich *Lon* 99–01; P-in-c Stockwell St Mich *S'wark* 01–03; P-in-c Stockwell St Andr and St Mich 03–04; V 04–09; rtd 09; PtO *S'wark* 09–13 and from 15. *48 Stannard Court, Culverley Road, London SE6 2LE* M: 07448-583179 E: argstockwell@hotmail.co.uk

GRANT, Antony Richard Charles. b 34. Ch Ch Ox BA 59 MA 64. Coll of Resurr Mirfield 72. **d** 74 **p** 75. C St John's Wood *Lon* 74–77; Novice CR 77–79; CR from 79; Lic to Offic *Wakef* 80–14; rtd 99; LtO *Leeds* from 14. *House of the Resurrection, Stocks Bank Road, Mirfield WF14 0BN* T: (01924) 483332 F: 490489 E: agrant@mirfield.org.uk

GRANT, Miss Frances Mary. b 52. Qu Coll Birm. **d** 12 **p** 13. NSM Etwall w Egginton *Derby* 12–18; NSM Brailsford w Shirley, Osmaston w Edlaston etc from 18; PtO *Lon* from 18. *177 Drewry Lane, Derby DE22 3QT* T: (01332) 364617 M: 07714-780668 E: franmgrant@gmail.com

GRANT, Canon Geoffrey Leslie. b 33. Trin Coll Cam BA 57 MA 61. Ridley Hall Cam 57. **d** 59 **p** 60. C Chelsea St Luke *Lon* 59–64; R Nacton w Levington *St E* 64–78; P-in-c Bucklesham w Brightwell and Foxhall 75–76; R Nacton and Levington w Bucklesham and Foxhall 78–06; P-in-c Kirton w Falkenham 96–06; R Nacton and Levington w Bucklesham etc 06–14; RD Colneys 86–11; Hon Can St E Cathl 94–14; Chapl Orwell Park Sch Nacton 64–14; rtd 14; PtO *St E* from 14. *Daisy Chain, The Common, Lavenham, Sudbury CO10 9RL* T: (01787) 247343 E: geoffrey@john-lewis.com

GRANT, James Nikolas. b 78. Glas Univ MA 07 Anglia Ruskin Univ MA 11. Westcott Ho Cam 09. **d** 11 **p** 12. C Chorlton-cum-Hardy St Clem *Man* 11–14; C Worth, Pound Hill and Maidenbower *Chich* 15; C Old Shoreham and Kingston Buci 15–19; R from 19. *Kingston Buci Rectory, Rectory Road, Shoreham-by-Sea BN43 6EB* T: (01273) 979811 M: 07753-456210 E: frjames.grant@gmail.com

GRANT, Julia Rosalind Russell. *See* RUSSELL GRANT, Julia Rosalind

GRANT, Ms Kes. b 65. SEITE 00. **d** 03 **p** 04. NSM Eltham St Sav *S'wark* 03–09; C Bermondsey St Hugh CD 09–11; Chapl Lewisham Hosp NHS Trust 05–09; Chapl St Sav and St Olave's Sch Newington *S'wark* 09–11; Chapl St Aug Academy Maidstone 11–16; rtd 16; PtO *Cant* from 16. *The Vicarage, Wallis Avenue, Maidstone ME15 9JJ* M: 07866-690527 E: revkes@ntlworld.com

GRANT, Canon Malcolm Etheridge. b 44. Edin Univ BSc 66 BD 69. Edin Th Coll 66. **d** 69 **p** 70. C St Mary's Cathl *Glas* 69–72; C Grantham w Manthorpe *Linc* 72; TV Grantham 72–78; P-in-c Invergordon St Ninian *Mor* 78–81; Provost St Mary's Cathl *Glas* 81–91; R Glas St Mary 81–91; Provost St Andr Cathl Inverness *Mor* 91–02; R Inverness St Andr 91–02; P-in-c Culloden St Mary-in-the-Fields 91–97; R Strathnairn St Paul 91–97; Hon Can St Andr Cathl Inverness from 02; V Eaton Bray w Edlesborough *St Alb* 02–09; RD Dunstable 04–09; rtd 09; PtO *St Alb* from 09; *Ox* from 09. *13 Rock Lane, Leighton Buzzard LU7 2QQ* T: (01525) 372771 E: mandkgrant@btinternet.com

GRANT, Murray William. b 36. Chich Th Coll 64. **d** 66 **p** 67. C Stanley *Liv* 66–70; C Munster Square St Mary Magd *Lon* 70–74; C Westmr St Sav and St Jas Less 74–82; P-in-c Albany Street Ch Ch 82; P-in-c Hammersmith H Innocents 83–94; V 94–99; Chapl Naples w Sorrento, Capri and Bari *Eur* 99–03; rtd 04; PtO *Lon* 12–18. *12 Ashdown Crescent, London NW5 4QB* T: (020) 7419 2519 E: mwgrant@gmail.com

GRANT, Patrick Iain Douglas. b 67. K Alfred's Coll Win BA 88. Cuddesdon Coll BTh 93. **d** 96 **p** 97. C Croydon Woodside *S'wark* 96–99; V S Beddington and Roundshaw 99–07; R Perth St Jo *St And* 07–14; rtd 14. *42 Bonhard Road, Scone, Perth PH2 6QB* T: (01738) 259663 M: 07948-270941 E: patrickidgrant@gmail.com

GRANT, Stuart Peter. b 64. Leeds Poly BSc 87 Leeds Univ BA 11. Yorks Min Course 08. **d** 12 **p** 13. NSM Gt and Lt Driffield *York* 12–17; V from 17; NSM Langtoft w Foxholes, Butterwick, Cottam etc 12–17; V from 17. *The Vicarage, Downe Street, Driffield YO25 6DX* T: (01377) 257712 M: 07795-560065 E: stuart@hastpace.co.uk

GRANTHAM, David George. b 70. **d** 07 **p** 08. C Bury St Edmunds Ch Ch *St E* 07–11; V Jersey All SS *Win* from 11; V Jersey St Simon from 11. *All Saints' Vicarage,*

Savile Street, St Helier, Jersey JE2 3XF T: (01534) 768323
E: godistheguy@hotmail.com

GRANTHAM, Michael Paul. b 47. Linc Th Coll. **d** 84 **p** 85.
C Gainsborough All SS *Linc* 84–87; R S Kelsey Gp 87–94;
R Dunster, Carhampton and Withycombe w Rodhuish
B & W 94–06; RD Exmoor 03–05; P-in-c Peakirk w Glinton
and Northborough *Pet* 06–07; P-in-c Etton w Helpston and
Maxey 06–07; rtd 07; PtO *Derby* 07–18; Hon C Albury w
Tiddington etc *Ox* 13–16. *22 The Covert, Tattersall, Lincoln
LN4 4GN* T: (01526) 344515 E: granthammichael@sky.com
or michaelgrantham@tiscali.co.uk

GRANTHAM, Suffragan Bishop of. *See* CHAMBERLAIN, The
Rt Revd Nicholas Alan

GRASBY, Derek. b 56. Bris Univ BA 80 MA 82. Wesley Coll
Bris 77 EAMTC 95. **d** 95 **p** 96. C Harlescott *Lich* 95–96; C
W Bromwich St Andr w Ch Ch 96–98; R Newton Heath
Man 98–02; Chapl UWE *Bris* 02–03; R Farnley *Ripon* 03–09;
rtd 09; PtO *Ripon* 10–13; *Nor* from 14. *9 Boundary Avenue,
Norwich NR6 5HY* T: (01603) 291211 M: 07834-276382
E: derek.grasby@gmail.com

GRASHAM, Mrs Frances Mary. b 68. Roehampton Inst BA 89
Kingston Poly PGCE 90. Yorks Min Course 11. **d** 13 **p** 14.
NSM Steeton *Bradf* 13–14; *Leeds* 14–16; NSM Newbridge w
Carnalway and Kilcullen *M & K* from 16; Chapl Defence
Forces from 16. *The Deanery, Post Office Hill, Curragh Camp,
Co Kildare, R56 XV50, Republic of Ireland* M: (00353) 83-826
3792 E: fran.grasham@gmail.com

GRASSKE, Christopher Karl. b 65. Ripon Coll Cuddesdon 12.
d 14 **p** 15. C Chagford, Gidleigh, Throwleigh etc *Ex*
14–17; R Eggardon and Colmers *Sarum* from 17. *The
Vicarage, Loders, Bridport DT6 3SA* T: (01308) 425161
E: cgrasske@outlook.com

GRATION, Phillip John. b 83. **d** 12 **p** 13. Chapl HM Pris
Linc 12–15; C Linc St Pet-at-Gowts and St Andr 12–15;
C Linc St Botolph 12–15; C Linc St Mary-le-Wigford w
St Benedict etc 12–15; Chapl Ellesmere Coll from 15.
Ellesmere College, Ellesmere SY12 9AB T: (01691) 622321
E: phillip.gration@ellesmere.com

GRATTON, Patricia Margaret. *See* MAGUIRE, Patricia
Margaret

GRATY, Canon John Thomas. b 33. Univ Coll Ox BA 58
MA 60. Coll of Resurr Mirfield 58. **d** 60 **p** 61. C Cov St Mark
60–63; C Hitchin St Mary *St Alb* 63–67; R Cov St Alb 67–75;
P-in-c Radway w Ratley 75–77; P-in-c Warmington w
Shotteswell 75–77; RD Dassett Magna 76–78; R Warmington
w Shotteswell and Radway w Ratley 77–84; Hon Can Cov
Cathl 80–96; P-in-c Nuneaton St Mary 84–89; V 89–96; rtd
96; PtO *Cov* from 96. *10 Kendall Avenue, Stratford-upon-Avon
CV37 6SG* T: (01789) 298856 E: gratyseniors@aol.com

GRAVELL, Canon John Hilary. b 45. Univ of Wales (Abth)
BA 65 DipEd 66. Bp Burgess Hall Lamp 66. **d** 68 **p** 69. C
Aberystwyth *St D* 68–72; R Llangeitho w Blaenpennal 72–73;
V Llangeitho, Blaenpennal and Betws Leucu 73–81; V Betws
Leuci 73–81; V Llan-non 81–95; Can St D Cathl 92–09; V
Llandybie 95–09; AD Dyffryn Aman 01–07; rtd 09; PtO *St D*
from 09. *16 Stewart Drive, Ammanford SA18 3BH* T: (01269)
594366

GRAVES, John Ivan. b 44. **d** 10 **p** 11. OLM Romney Deanery
Romney Marsh *Cant* 10–14; PtO 15; *Sarum* from 16. *22
Vicarage Road, Poole BH15 3AZ* E: gwthms44@gmail.com

GRAVES, Peter. b 33. EMMTC 78. **d** 81 **p** 82. NSM Roughey
Chich 81–89; NSM Itchingfield w Slinfold 89–98; PtO *S'wll*
98–18. *5 Fletcher Court, The Woodlands, Farnsfield, Newark
NG22 8LY* T: (01623) 882987 E: gravesp1@btinternet.com

GRAY, Alison Jane. b 63. New Hall Cam MB, BChir 87 MA 89
Birm Univ MMedSc 01 MRCPsych 95 FRCPsych 15. Qu Coll
Birm 07. **d** 10 **p** 11. NSM Malvern St Andr and Malvern Wells
and Wyche *Worc* 10–14; NSM Gt Malvern St Mary 14–18. *42
Wyche Road, Malvern WR14 4EG* T: (01684) 893637

GRAY, Andrew Stuart. b 70. LCTP. **d** 11 **p** 12. C Clitheroe
St Jas *Blackb* 11–18; Faith Sharing Enabler *B & W* from 18.
Diocesan Office, The Old Deanery, Wells BA5 2UG T: (01749)
670777

GRAY, Brett Christopher. b 71. Lon Bible Coll BA 95 Selw
Coll Cam MPhil 04 PhD 15. Ridley Hall Cam 02. **d** 04
p 05. C Sunnyside w Bourne End *St Alb* 04–07; V St Alb
St Mich 07–11; Asst Chapl Selw Coll Cam 11–15; Chapl
and Fell SS Coll Cam from 15. *Sidney Sussex College,
Cambridge CB2 3HU* T: (01223) 338837 M: 07795-580051
E: bcg24@cam.ac.uk *or* chaplain@sid.cam.ac.uk

GRAY, Ms Christine Angela (Kit). b 46. Nottm Univ
BA 67 CertEd 68. Cranmer Hall Dur 71. **dss** 80 **d** 87 **p** 94.
Rawthorpe *Wakef* 74–81; Chapl Nottm Univ *S'wll* 81–88; C
Rushmere St E 88–94; P-in-c Ringshall w Battisford, Barking
w Darmsden etc 94–00; P-in-c Nayland w Wiston 00–10; rtd

10; PtO *St E* 10–15; *Chelmsf* from 12. *Threeways, Bounstead
Hill, Layer-de-la-Haye, Colchester CO2 0LG* T: (01206) 734353

GRAY, Dale Armitage. b 42. Edin Th Coll 62. **d** 92 **p** 93.
Dioc Missr *Arg* 92–98; Chapl St Jo Cathl Oban 92–95; P-in-c
Cumbrae (or Millport) 95–98; rtd 98; PtO *Edin* from 98.
The Dovecote, Duke Street, Coldstream TD12 4BN T: (01890)
883247

GRAY, David. b 55. Oak Hill Th Coll. **d** 00 **p** 01. C Bestwood
Em w St Mark *S'wll* 00–04; P-in-c Bulwell St Jo 04–06; V from
06. *St John's Vicarage, Snape Wood Road, Bulwell, Nottingham
NG6 7GH* T: 0115-927 8025 E: davidgray72@hotmail.com

GRAY, David Cedric. b 53. RMN 77. **d** 97 **p** 98. OLM
Gorton Em w St Jas *Man* 97–06; OLM Gorton and
Abbey Hey 06–11. *Creoginity at St Francis Monastery, 89
Gorton Lane, Manchester M12 5WF* M: 07927-734419
E: rev.elation4.1@ntlworld.com

GRAY, David Michael. b 57. St Jo Coll Dur BA 99 ACIBS 80. CA
Tr Coll 90 Cranmer Hall Dur 97. **d** 99 **p** 00. C Newc H Cross
99–02; V Long Benton St Mary 02–11; V Killingworth 11–19;
TV Cramlington from 19. *119 Newlyn Drive, Cramlington
NE23 1RP* E: davidgray4316@aol.com

GRAY, Canon Donald Clifford. b 30. Liv Univ MPhil 81 Man
Univ PhD 85 FRHistS 88 FSA 07. AKC 55. **d** 56 **p** 57. C Leigh
St Mary *Man* 56–60; CF (TA) 58–67; V Westleigh St Pet *Man*
60–67; V Elton All SS 67–74; CF (TAVR) 67–77; QHC 74–77;
R Liv Our Lady and St Nic w St Anne 74–87; RD Liv 75–81;
Hon Can Liv Cathl 82–87; Chapl to The Queen 82–00; Can
Westmr Abbey 87–98; R Westmr St Marg 87–98; Chapl to
Speaker of Ho of Commons 87–98; rtd 98; PtO *Linc* from
98. *3 Barn Hill Mews, Stamford PE9 2GN* T: (01780) 765024

GRAY, Duncan Cowan. b 83. St Aug Coll of Th 5. **d** 18 **p** 19.
NSM Hackney Wick St Mary of Eton w St Aug *Lon* from 18.
27 Powell Road, London E5 8DJ

GRAY (née ROBERTS), Ms Jennifer. b 55. R Holloway Coll
Lon BA 76 Somerville Coll Ox PGCE 77. SAOMC 00. **d** 03
p 04. C Welwyn Garden City *St Alb* 03–13; P-in-c Bramfield,
Stapleford, Waterford etc 13–16; Min Aston St Mary CD
15–16; R Beane Valley from 16. *The Rectory, Church Lane,
Watton-at-Stone, Hertford SG14 3RD* T: (01920) 830035
E: jennygrayrectory@gmail.com

GRAY, Joan. *See* BURKITT-GRAY, Joan Katherine

GRAY, John David Norman. b 38. Oak Hill Th Coll 84.
d 86 **p** 87. C Portsdown *Portsm* 86–88; C Worthing St Geo
Chich 88–91; TV Swanborough *Sarum* 91–98; rtd 98;
PtO *Ex* 00–03; *Portsm* from 03. *15 Charminster Court, 46
Craneswater Park, Southsea PO4 0NU* T: (023) 9285 1299
E: johndngray@gmail.com

GRAY, Mrs Joy Dora. b 24. SRN 46 SCM 48. Gilmore Ho 79.
dss 81 **d** 87 **p** 95. Newick *Chich* 81–94; Hon Par D 87–94;
NSM Fletching 94–98; PtO from 98. *10 High Hurst Close,
Newick, Lewes BN8 4NJ* T: (01825) 722965

GRAY, Julian Francis. b 64. Univ of Wales (Lamp) BA 86
MA 09. Coll of Resurr Mirfield 86. **d** 88 **p** 89. Min
Can St Woolos Cathl *Mon* 88–91; C Bassaleg 91–93; V
Overmonnow w Wonastow and Michel Troy 93–98; V King's
Sutton and Newbottle and Charlton *Pet* 98–00; V Usk and
Monkswood w Glascoed Chpl and Gwehelog *Mon* 00–03; V
Usk and Gwehelog w Llantrisant w Llanllowell 03–14; P-in-c
Llantilio Pertholey w Bettws Chpl etc from 14. *The Vicarage,
10 The Pines, Mardy, Abergavenny NP7 6HQ* T: (01873)
859881 E: mardyvicarage@yahoo.co.uk

GRAY, Lindsay Doreen. b 50. Open Univ BA 83 Leic Univ
PhD 87. Coll of Resurr Mirfield 05. **d** 06 **p** 07. NSM Firbank,
Howgill and Killington *Bradf* 06–09; NSM Sedbergh, Cautley
and Garsdale 06–09; TV Egremont and Haile *Carl* 09–13;
P-in-c Seascale and Drigg 13–16; Ind Chapl 09–16; rtd 16;
Hon C Seascale and Drigg *Carl* 16; PtO *Bris* from 18. *The
Vicarage, The Banks, Seascale CA20 1QT* T: (019467) 28217
E: lgray782@btinternet.com

GRAY, The Ven Martin Clifford. b 44. Westcott Ho Cam 78.
d 80 **p** 81. C Gaywood, Bawsey and Mintlyn *Nor* 80–84;
V Sheringham 84–94; TR Lowestoft St Marg 94–99; Chapl
Lothingland Hosp 95–99; RD Lothingland *Nor* 97–99;
Adn Lynn 99–09; rtd 09; PtO *Nor* from 09. *11 Canns
Lane, Hethersett, Norwich NR9 3JE* T: (01603) 812610
E: mandpgray11@btinternet.com

GRAY, Melvyn Dixon. b 38. Lon Univ BD 86 Dur Univ
MA 89 PhD 07. NEOC 84. **d** 87 **p** 88. C Richmond w
Hudswell *Ripon* 87–90; P-in-c Downholme and Marske
88–90; P-in-c Forcett and Aldbrough and Melsonby
90–91; R 91–00; R Mobberley *Ches* 00–04; rtd 04; PtO
Dur from 04; *Ripon* 13–14; *Leeds* from 14. *51 The Orchard,
Sedgefield, Stockton-on-Tees TS21 3AQ* T: (01740) 629069
E: melandanne@gray19.plus.com

GRAY, Natty. *See* GRAY, Renate Kathrina

GRAY, Mrs Patricia Linda. b 51. Univ of Wales (Swansea) BA 73 Ches Coll of HE BTh 02. NOC 99. **d** 02 **p** 03. C Glazebury w Hollinfare *Liv* 02–12; rtd 12; PtO *Liv* from 16. *14 Bollin Close, Culcheth, Warrington WA3 5DU* T: (01925) 763750 M: 07747-772345 E: pat.gray@bollinclose.uk

GRAY, Paul Alfred. b 41. BA. Sarum & Wells Th Coll. **d** 82 **p** 83. C Harpenden St Jo *St Alb* 82–85; TV Lynton, Brendon, Countisbury, Lynmouth etc *Ex* 85–86; rtd 06. *28 Baymead Meadow, North Petherton, Bridgwater TA6 6QW* T: (01278) 661258

GRAY, Penelope Jane. *See* GRAYSMITH, Penelope Jane

GRAY, Canon Philip Charles. b 67. Nottm Univ BA 91. St Steph Ho Ox 91. **d** 93 **p** 94. C Scarborough St Martin *York* 93–97; TV Leek and Meerbrook *Lich* 97–01; Bp's Dom Chapl *Blackb* 02–07; P-in-c Ilkley St Marg *Bradf* 07–12; V 12–14; *Leeds* from 14; AD Ilkley 14–16; AD S Craven and Wharfedale from 17; Hon Can Ho Ghana from 04. *St Margaret's Vicarage, Wells Road, Ilkley LS29 9JH* T: (01943) 607015 *or* 607210

GRAY, Philip Thomas. Lon Univ BA 65. Chich Th Coll 66. **d** 68 **p** 69. C Leigh St Clem *Chelmsf* 68–74; V Mendlesham *St E* from 74; P-in-c Wickham Skeith 86–95; PtO *Nor* from 08. *The Vicarage, Mendlesham, Stowmarket IP14 5RS* T: (01449) 766359

GRAY, Renate Kathrina (Natty). b 52. SNWTP. **d** 13 **p** 14. OLM Deeplish and Newbold *Man* 13–18; NSM from 18. *669 Oldham Road, Rochdale OL16 4PE* T: (01706) 358550 M: 07577-825371 E: renate.gray@ntlworld.com *or* pabishopmark@manchester.anglican.org

GRAY, The Ven Robert James. b 70. TCD BA 92 HDipEd 93 MA 95 Irish Sch of Ecum MPhil 97. CITC 94. **d** 96 **p** 97. C Clooney w Strathfoyle *D & R* 96–99; I Ardamine w Kiltennel, Glascarrig etc *C & O* from 99; Treas Ferns Cathl from 04; Adn Ferns from 15; Adn Cashel, Waterford and Lismore from 15. *The Rectory, Knockroe, Courtown, Gorey, Co Wexford, Y25 NV02, Republic of Ireland* T: (00353) (53) 942 5423 M: 86-684 7621 E: ardamine@ferns.anglican.org

GRAY, Stephen James Norman. b 66. Lon Univ BA 89 Hughes Hall Cam PGCE 91. Ridley Hall Cam MA 00. **d** 00 **p** 01. C Cheltenham Ch Ch *Glouc* 00–03; Chapl RN 03–04; Chapl Sherborne Sch 04–10; Chapl Seaford Coll Petworth 10–13; P-in-c Graffham w Woolavington *Chich* 10–13; Chapl Bradfield Coll Berks 14–16; Conduct and Sen Chapl Eton Coll from 16. *3 Savile House, Eton College, Windsor SL4 6DW* T: (01753) 370864 E: s.gray@etoncollege.org.uk

GRAY, Mrs Susan Hazel. b 49. Kingston Univ BA 06. **d** 09 **p** 10. OLM Hersham *Guildf* 09–19; PtO from 19. *39 Misty's Field, Walton-on-Thames KT12 2BG* T: (01932) 242838 E: suehgray@btinternet.com *or* suegray@stpetershersham.com

GRAY, Mrs Trudy Ann Jennifer. b 48. Univ of Wales (Abth) BSc 69 Aston Univ MSc 72. **d** 05 **p** 06. NSM Gt Finborough w Onehouse, Harleston, Buxhall etc *St E* 05–10; NSM Upper Coquetdale *Newc* 10–13; rtd 13; PtO *Newc* from 13. *1 Greenside Avenue, Berwick-upon-Tweed TD15 1BZ* T: (01289) 331722 E: tajgrayfin@aol.com

GRAY, Mrs Ursula Mary. b 33. K Coll Lon BD 56 AKC 91 Univ of Wales (Lamp) MA 02. **d** 04 **p** 05. NSM Shaston *Sarum* 04–08; PtO 09; *Glouc* from 16. *27 Townsend Court, Priory Way, Malmesbury SN16 0FB* T: (01666) 824851 E: umg@shaston.plus.com

GRAY-HAMMOND, Betsy. b 58. Ripon Coll Cuddesdon BA 10. **d** 10 **p** 11. C Brighton St Nic *Chich* 10–14; TV Moulsecoomb from 14. *The Vicarage, Selham Drive, Brighton BN1 9EL* T: (01273) 601854 E: revbetsy@btinternet.com

GRAYSHON, Matthew Richard. b 47. St Jo Coll Nottm BTh 81. **d** 81 **p** 82. C Beverley Minster *York* 81–85; V Hallwood *Ches* 85–93; R Hanwell St Mary w St Chris *Lon* 93–16; rtd 16; Hon C Portway and Danebury *Win* from 16. *The Vicarage, Amport, Andover SP11 8BE* M: 07960-299434 E: revupmg@gmail.com

GRAYSHON, Paul Nicholas Walton. b 50. Cranmer Hall Dur 81. **d** 83 **p** 84. C Walkden Moor *Man* 83–87; V Radcliffe St Andr 87–07; P-in-c Matlock Bath and Cromford *Derby* from 07. *Holy Trinity Vicarage, 8 Derby Road, Matlock DE4 3PU* T: (01629) 583924 E: nickgrayshon@btopenworld.com

GRAYSMITH (née GRAY), Mrs Penelope Jane. b 63. SS Hild & Bede Coll Dur BA 85 Em Coll Cam MPhil 88. Westcott Ho Cam 86. **d** 89 **p** 94. Par Dn Evington *Leic* 89–92; Par Dn Cannock *Lich* 92–94; C 94–96; Chapl Asst Mid Staffs Gen Hosps NHS Trust 96–07; Hd Chapl Services Mid Staffs NHS Foundn Trust 07–12; Chapl Kath Ho Hospice Stafford 96–17; Chapl HM Pris Guernsey from 17. *HM Prison Guernsey, Les Nicolles, St Sampson, Guernsey GY2 4YF* T: (01481) 248376

GRAYSMITH, Peter Alexander. b 62. UEA BSc 83. Westcott Ho Cam 85. **d** 88 **p** 89. C Tettenhall Regis *Lich* 88–89; C Cannock 89–92; TV 92–99; V Rocester and Croxden w Hollington 99–01; V Baswich 01–16; Miss P Guernsey St Peter Port *Win* from 16; Miss P Guernsey St Jo from 16; Chapl Eliz Coll Guernsey from 16. *The Rectory, Cornet Street, St Peter Port, Guernsey GY1 1BZ* E: pgraysmith@elizabethcollege.gg

GRAYSON, Jane Elizabeth. b 71. **d** 07 **p** 08. OLM Moston St Mary *Man* 07–15; NSM Man Apostles w Miles Platting 15–18; PtO from 18. *296 St Mary's Road, Manchester M40 0BD* T: 0161-688 7073 E: janegrayson@aol.com

GRAYSON, Robin John. b 53. Mert Coll Ox BA 74 DPhil 78. Wycliffe Hall Ox 00. **d** 02 **p** 03. C Beaconsfield *Ox* 02–06; P-in-c Langley Marish 06–08; TR from 08. *The Vicarage, 3 St Mary's Road, Slough SL3 7EN* T: (01753) 542068 M: 07801-280475 E: r.j.grayson@btinternet.com

GREADY, Andrew John. b 63. Univ Coll Lon BSc 84 Newc Univ MA 93 Surrey Univ BSc 05. St Jo Coll Nottm 86. **d** 89 **p** 90. C Monkwearmouth St Andr *Dur* 89–92; C Bramley St Cath S Africa 92–96; R Sunninghill St Steph 96–99; Chapl St Pet Prep Sch 99; V Shottermill *Guildf* 00–06; Chapl Amesbury Sch 01–06; P-in-c Wynberg St Jo S Africa 06–08; R 08–12; Chapl W Prov Prep Sch 07–12; Chapl The Hague *Eur* 13–18; V Clifton York from 18. *Clifton Vicarage, Clifton, York YO30 6BH* T: (01904) 656788 E: andrew.gready12@gmail.com

GREANY, Canon Richard Andrew Hugh. b 44. Qu Coll Ox BA 67 MA 83. Coll of Resurr Mirfield 67. **d** 69 **p** 70. C Hartlepool St Oswald *Dur* 69–72; C Clifton All SS *Bris* 72–75; Tutor Coll of Resurr Mirfield 75–78; V Whitworth w Spennymoor *Dur* 78–83; P-in-c Byers Green 78–79; Asst Prin St Alb Minl Tr Scheme 83–88; V Flamstead *St Alb* 83–88; V Hessle *York* 88–94; V Cambridge St Mary Less *Ely* 94–11; Dioc Spirituality Officer 99–06; Hon Can Ely Cathl 05–11; RD Cambridge S 06–11; rtd 11; Chapl Laslett's *Worc* 11–14; Hon C Worc City 11–14; PtO *York* 14–19; *Ox* 15–18; *Nor* from 18; Chantry P Shrine of Our Lady of Walsingham from 18. *8 Guild Street, Walsingham NR22 6BU* M: 07791-632976 E: andrewgreany@btinternet.com

GREAR, Hugh Massey. b 60. Bris Univ LLB 82. SEITE. **d** 00 **p** 01. C Warlingham w Chelsham and Farleigh *S'wark* 00–04; V Upper Tooting H Trin w St Aug 04–10; R Worplesdon *Guildf* 10–15; P-in-c Ockham w Hatchford and Downside 15–17; R from 17. *The Rectory, Ockham Lane, Ockham, Woking GU23 6NP* E: hugh.grear@sky.com

GREASLEY, James Kenneth. b 39. K Coll Lon BD 66 AKC 66. **d** 67 **p** 68. C Stoke upon Trent *Lich* 67–70; P-in-c Lusaka St Pet Zambia 70–76; V Gt Staughton *Ely* 76–81; Chapl HM Borstal Gaynes Hall 76–81; V Melbourn and Meldreth *Ely* 81–96; RD Shingay 82–96; R Chalfont St Peter *Ox* 96–04; rtd 04; PtO *Heref* 05–19; *Sarum* from 19. *2 Bailey Mews, Old Sarum, Salisbury SP4 6FJ* T: (01722) 325017 E: jk.greasley@btinternet.com

GREATOREX, Mrs Susan Kathleen. b 58. St Hilda's Coll Ox BA 79 MA 04 Univ of Wales (Cardiff) PGCE 80. WEMTC 01. **d** 04 **p** 05. C Keynsham *B & W* 04–08; R Radstock w Writhlington 08–15; R Kilmersdon w Babington 08–15; V Lower Cam w Coaley *Glouc* from 15. *The Vicarage, 99 Fairmead, Cam, Dursley GL11 5JU* T: (01453) 542547 E: susangreatorex@btinternet.com

GREATREX, Richard Quintin. b 65. K Coll Lon BD 86 Surrey Univ BA 02. STETS 99. **d** 02 **p** 03. NSM Westbury-on-Trym St Alb *Bris* 02–06; NSM Flax Bourton and Barrow Gurney *B & W* 06–09; NSM Long Ashton w Barrow Gurney and Flax Bourton from 09. *The Rectory, Main Road, Flax Bourton, Bristol BS48 3QJ* T: (01275) 461179 E: rqg@hotmail.co.uk

GREAVES, Canon John Neville. b 29. Newc Univ MA 96 Dur Univ MLitt 03. St Aid Birkenhead 58. **d** 61 **p** 62. C Pendleton St Ambrose *Man* 61–62; P-in-c 62–63; C Benchill 63–65; C-in-c Peel Hall All SS CD 65–71; V Wythenshawe St Rich 71–73; R Sadberge *Dur* 73–78; V Dur St Cuth 78–94; Chapl New Coll Dur 78–92; Lect NEOC 79–84; Chapl Dur Co Fire Brigade 85–94; RD Dur 80–93; Dep Dir of Clergy Tr 91–94; Hon Can Dur Cathl 91–94; rtd 94; PtO *Ches* 94–97; P-in-c Salt and Sandon w Burston *Lich* 97–00; Past Aux Eccleshall Deanery 00–01; PtO 01–02; *Heref* from 03; *S & B* from 10. *3 Sitwell Close, Bucknell SY7 0DD* T: (01547) 530152 E: jngreaves5874@gmail.com

GREAVES, Kevin Adam Nathanael. b 65. Sheff Univ BA 13. Yorks Min Course 10. **d** 13 **p** 14. C Castleford *Wakef* 13–14; Leeds 14–16; V Chapelthorpe from 16; P-in-c Woolley from 19. *St James's Vicarage, 21 Stoney Lane, Chapelthorpe, Wakefield WF4 3JN* T: (01924) 256031 E: rev.kevingreaves@priest.com *or* kevin.greaves@leeds.anglican.org

GREAVES, Miss Rachel Miriam Jane. b 86. Univ of the Arts Lon BA 08. Trin Coll Bris BA 18. **d** 18 **p** 19. C Highgate St Mich *Lon* from 18. *Address withheld by request* E: rev.r.greaves@gmail.com

GREBE, Matthias. b 82. Tübingen Univ BA 07 Hughes Hall Cam MPhil 08 Ch Coll Cam PhD 12. Ridley Hall Cam 09. **d** 13 **p** 14. Asst Chapl Bonn w Cologne *Eur* 13–15; C Regent's Park St Mark *Lon* 15–17; C Cam St Edw *Ely* from 17; Adv Eur Ch Relns Coun for Chr Unity from 17. *15 Hillfield Road, Comberton, Cambridge CB23 7DB* M: 07919-445378 E: mgrebe471@gmail.com *or* grebe@uni-bonn.de

GREED, Frederick John. b 44. Trin Coll Bris 79. **d** 81 **p** 82. C Yateley *Win* 81–85; R Ore St Helen and St Barn *Chich* 85–95; R Street w Walton *B & W* 95–09; RD Glastonbury 08–09; rtd 09; PtO *B & W* from 09. *40 St Cleers Orchard, Somerton TA11 6QU* T: (01458) 272754 M: 07887-366698 E: john_greed@btinternet.com

GREEN, Adrian Paul. b 66. Trin Coll Bris 06. **d** 08 **p** 09. NSM Willowfield *D & D* 08–11; I Mt Merrion from 11; Dir of Ords from 15. *122 Mount Merrion Avenue, Belfast BT6 0FS* T: (028) 9029 4676 M: 07914-290193 E: adrian@mountmerrionchurch.org.uk

GREEN, Preb Alan John Enrique. b 56. Worc Coll Ox BA 78 MA 83. Linc Th Coll 83. **d** 85 **p** 86. C Kirkby *Liv* 85–88; TV 88–94; Chapl Knowsley Community Coll 87–90; Chapl Worc Coll and C Ox St Giles and SS Phil and Jas w St Marg 94–98; TR St Jo on Bethnal Green *Lon* from 98; AD Tower Hamlets 06–12; Preb St Paul's Cathl from 10. *St John's Rectory, 30 Victoria Park Square, London E2 9PB* T/F: (020) 8980 1742 E: alan.green@virgin.net

GREEN, Alison Iola. b 58. Glas Univ MB, ChB 81 Lon Univ MSc 97 Anglia Ruskin Univ BA 13 MRCPCH 96. Westcott Ho Cam 11. **d** 13 **p** 14. C Chich Cathl 13–17; NSM Westbourne 17–18; Chapl Chich Univ from 17. *61 Southleigh Road, Havant PO9 2QQ* M: 07581-070669 E: iolag1@yahoo.com *or* alison.green@chi.ac.uk

GREEN, Alison Mary. b 51. Boro Road Teacher Tr Coll BEd 74 Wesley Coll Bris MA 03 Roehampton Univ PhD 07. STETS 02. **d** 04 **p** 05. NSM Bath St Barn w Englishcombe *B & W* 04–06; NSM Monmouth w Overmonnow etc *Mon* 06–13; NSM Bradford on Avon H Trin, Westwood and Wingfield *Sarum* from 14. *36 Budbury Close, Bradford-on-Avon BA15 1QG* T: (01225) 868259 E: alig9@btinternet.com

GREEN, Arthur Edward. b 27. Chich Th Coll 58. **d** 59 **p** 60. C Malden St Jas *S'wark* 59–62; C Caterham 62–67; R Burgh Parva w Briston *Nor* 67–75; V Middleton 75–76; V Middleton w E Winch 76–84; R Neatishead w Irstead 84–90; V Barton Turf 84–90; R Neatishead, Barton Turf and Irstead 90–92; rtd 92; PtO *Portsm* 92–15. *10 James Butcher Court, 16 Eastern Villas Road, Southsea PO4 0TD* T: (023) 9275 0701

GREEN, Barrie. b 51. SS Coll Cam BA 72 MA 76. Wycliffe Hall Ox 75. **d** 78 **p** 79. C Castle Vale *Birm* 78–81; V W Heath 81–96; RD Kings Norton 87–95; TR Dronfield w Holmesfield *Derby* 96–09; P-in-c Bris St Paul's 09–15; rtd 15. *9 route de la Croix, 33220 Riocaud, France* E: barriegreen1951@gmail.com

GREEN, Benjamin Charles. b 83. Magd Coll Cam BA 04 MA 08. Wycliffe Hall Ox MTh 08. **d** 08 **p** 14. C Stockton *Dur* 08–09; C Arden Marches *Cov* 13–16; V Amington *Birm* from 16. *224 Tamworth Road, Amington, Tamworth B77 3DE* T: (01827) 62573 M: 07985-490173 E: ben@rev.me.uk

GREEN, Brian Robert. b 31. Bris Univ BA 55. Tyndale Hall Bris 52. **d** 56 **p** 57. C Toxteth Park St Philemon *Liv* 56–58; V Toxteth Park St Philemon w St Silas 58–69; P-in-c Toxteth Park St Gabr 64–69; P-in-c Toxteth Park St Jo and St Thos 64–69; P-in-c Toxteth Park St Jas and St Matt 68–69; V Elsenham *Chelmsf* 69–85; V Henham 69–85; P-in-c Ugley 84–85; V Henham and Elsenham w Ugley 85–89; RD Newport and Stansted 87–89; PtO *Ex* 90–91; V Tidenham w Beachley and Lancaut *Glouc* 91–97; RD Forest S 95–97; rtd 97; PtO *Ex* 97–11; *Sarum* 12–16. *3 Crosbys, Burbage, Marlborough SN8 3TL* T: (01672) 811655

GREEN, Brutus Zachary. b 78. Ex Univ BA 99 PhD 07 St Edm Coll Cam MPhil 04. Westcott Ho Cam 07. **d** 09 **p** 10. C Paddington St Jo w St Mich *Lon* 09–14; CF 14–18; P-in-c Putney St Marg *S'wark* from 18. *St Margaret's Vicarage, 46 Luttrell Avenue, London SW15 6PE* T: (020) 8355 2373 E: brutuszgreen@gmail.com

GREEN, Catherine Isabel. *See* HITCHENS, Catherine Isabel

GREEN, Christopher Frederick. b 46. Nottm Univ BTh 75 Birm Univ DipEd 85 Univ of Wales (Abth) MEd 94. Bp Otter Coll CertEd 69 Linc Th Coll 71. **d** 75 **p** 76. C Hodge Hill *Birm* 75–77; C S Lafford *Linc* 77–79; P-in-c Worc St Mich 79–82; Hd RS and Lib RNIB New Coll Worc 82–96; V Clipstone *S'well* 96–02; rtd 02; PtO *Linc* from 03. *Cobwebs, Middlefield Lane, Glentham, Market Rasen LN8 2ET* T: (01673) 878633

GREEN, Christopher Martyn. b 58. New Coll Edin BD 80. Cranmer Hall Dur 82. **d** 83 **p** 84. C Virginia Water *Guildf* 83–87; C Bromley Ch Ch *Roch* 87–91; Study Asst the Proclamation Trust 91–92; C Surbiton Hill Ch Ch *S'wark* 92–00; Vice Prin Oak Hill Th Coll 00–13; PtO *Lon* 02–13; V Muswell Hill St Jas w St Matt from 14. *St James's Vicarage, 2 St James's Lane, London N10 3DB* T: (020) 8442 2900

GREEN, Canon Daphne Mary. b 55. K Coll Cam BA 77 Bradf Univ MBA 91 Leeds Univ PhD 01 Lon Inst of Educn PGCE 79. NOC 95. **d** 98 **p** 99. C Headingley *Ripon* 98–02; Chapl Leeds Metrop Univ 00–02; R Stanningley St Thos 02–08; Abp's Chapl and Researcher *York* from 08; Can and Preb York Minster from 16. *Bishopthorpe, York YO23 2GE* T: (01904) 772372 F: 709204 M: 07796-084264

GREEN, David Allen. b 61. Sheff City Poly BA 90. Cranmer Hall Dur 00. **d** 02 **p** 03. C Huyton St Geo *Liv* 02–06; TV Walkden and Lt Hulton *Man* 06–10; P-in-c Thorne *Sheff* 10–14; V from 14. *The Vicarage, 2 Brooke Street, Thorne, Doncaster DN8 4AZ* T: (01405) 814055 E: redrev@talktalk.net

GREEN, David Michael. b 62. Lanc Univ BSc 83. St Mellitus Coll BA 12. **d** 12 **p** 13. NSM Ruislip St Martin *Lon* 12–17; V Hatch End St Anselm from 17. *The Vicarage, 50 Cedar Drive, Pinner HA5 4DE* M: 07962-057767 E: fr.david@live.co.uk

GREEN, David Norman. b 37. Magd Coll Cam BA 60. Clifton Th Coll 60. **d** 62 **p** 63. C Islington St Mary *Lon* 62–65; C Burley *Ripon* 65–68; Kenya 69–80; P-in-c Brimscombe *Glouc* 81–90; R Woodchester and Brimscombe 90–96; P-in-c Coberley w Cowley 96–97; P-in-c Colesborne 96–97; P-in-c Coberley, Cowley, Colesbourne and Elkstone 97–04; Dioc Rural Adv 96–04; rtd 04; Tanzania 04–13; PtO *S'well* from 13. *8 Cherrywood Gardens, Nottingham NG3 6LQ* T: 0115-950 2958 E: revdavidngreen@hotmail.com

GREEN, David Robert John. b 73. Sheff Univ BA 96 Anglia Ruskin Univ MA 12. Ridley Hall Cam 06. **d** 08 **p** 09. C Chatham St Phil and St Jas *Roch* 08–11; P-in-c W Malling w Offham 11–18; V from 18. *The Vicarage, 138 High Street, West Malling ME19 6NE* T: (01732) 842245 E: mail@revdgreen.org.uk *or* vicar@stmaryswestmalling.org.uk

GREEN, David William. b 53. CertEd 75 Nottm Univ BCombStuds 84. Linc Th Coll 81. **d** 84 **p** 85. C S Merstham *S'wark* 84–88; C Walton-on-Thames *Guildf* 88–91; V Gillingham H Trin and Chapl Lennox Wood Elderly People's Home *Roch* 91–99; V Strood St Nic w St Mary from 99; RD Strood 12–17. *18 Honeypot Close, Rochester ME2 3DU* T: (01634) 719052 E: revdavidgreen@blueyonder.co.uk

GREEN, Canon Denise Penelope. b 57. Bedf Coll of Educn BEd 80 MPhil 89 Nottm Univ MA 05. EMMTC 03. **d** 06 **p** 07. C Skirbeck H Trin *Linc* 06–10; P-in-c S Lawres Gp 10–14; R from 14; V Barlings from 14; Can and Preb Linc Cathl from 18. *The Vicarage, 14 Church Lane, Cherry Willingham, Lincoln LN3 4AB* T: (01522) 595596 M: 07812-006295 E: revdpg@virginmedia.com

GREEN, Donald Pentney (Brother Donald). b 25. Leeds Univ MA 50. Coll of Resurr Mirfield 50. **d** 52 **p** 53. C Ardwick St Benedict *Man* 52–55; SSF from 55; Sec for Miss SSF 78–96; LtO *Chelmsf* 58–60 and 69–72; Papua New Guinea 60–63; Chapl HM Pris Kingston (Portsm) 72–76; LtO *Edin* 76–77; Org Sec Catholic Renewal 77; LtO *Lich* from 78; rtd 95. *85 Crofton Road, London E13 8QT* T: (020) 7474 5863 E: donaldssf@freeuk.com

GREEN, Mrs Dorothy Mary. b 36. Westf Coll Lon BA 58. Selly Oak Coll 75. **dss** 83 **d** 87 **p** 94. Ryde All SS *Portsm* 83–91; C 87–91; Hon C Hempnall *Nor* 91–96; rtd 96; PtO *B & W* 97–07. *12 Monica Wills House, Cromwell Street, Bristol BS3 3NH* T: 0117-239 4257

GREEN, The Ven Duncan Jamie. b 52. Sarum & Wells Th Coll 82. **d** 84 **p** 85. C Uckfield *Chich* 84–87; Dioc Youth Officer *Chelmsf* 87–96; Warden and Chapl St Mark's Coll Res Cen 93–96; TR Saffron Walden w Wendens Ambo, Littlebury etc *Chelmsf* 96–07; RD Saffron Walden 05–07; C of E Olympic and Paralympic Co-ord 07–13; Hon Can Chelmsf Cathl 03–13; Adn Northolt *Lon* from 13; P-in-c Ealing Common St Matt 16–17. *9 Sheridan Gardens, Harrow HA3 0JT* T: (020) 7932 1274 M: 07741-246521 E: archdeacon.northolt@london.anglican.org

GREEN, Edward Marcus. b 66. Mert Coll Ox BA 88 MA 92. Wycliffe Hall Ox 90. **d** 94 **p** 95. C Glyncorrwg w Afan Vale and Cymmer Afan *Llan* 94–96; C Aberystwyth St D 96–99; P-in-c Pontypridd St Cath *Llan* 00–01; V 01–11; PtO *Bradf* 11–13; R Steeple Aston w N Aston and Tackley *Ox* from 13; PtO *Eur* from 17. *The Rectory, Fir Lane, Steeple Aston, Bicester OX25 4SF* T: (01869) 340903 E: steeplerector@hotmail.co.uk

GREEN, Mrs Elizabeth Pauline Anne. b 29. Gilmore Ho 69. **dss** 76 **d** 87 **p** 94. Chorleywood Ch Ch *St Alb* 76–87; Par Dn 87–90; C Chipping Sodbury and Old Sodbury *Glouc* 90–95;

Asst Dioc Missr 90–95; rtd 95; NSM Chipping Sodbury and Old Sodbury *Glouc* 95–99; PtO from 99; *Bris* from 99. *The Old House, The Common, Chipping Sodbury, Bristol BS37 6PX* T: (01454) 311936

GREEN, Ernest James. b 31. Pemb Coll Cam BA 55 MA 62. Linc Th Coll 55. **d** 57 **p** 58. C Rawmarsh w Parkgate *Sheff* 57–60; Sec Th Colls Dept SCM 60–62; Prec and Sacr Bris Cathl 62–65; Min Can 62–65; V Churchill *B & W* 65–78; RD Locking 72–78; V Burrington and Churchill 78–82; Preb Wells Cathl 81–82; V Ryde All SS *Portsm* 82–91; P-in-c Ryde H Trin 82–86; RD E Wight 83–88; TR Hempnall *Nor* 91–96; rtd 96; PtO *B & W* 97–07. *12 Monica Wills House, Cromwell Street, Bristol BS3 3NH* T: 0117-239 4257 E: revdern17@yahoo.co.uk

GREEN, Ms Fiona Jenifer. b 67. Rob Coll Cam BA 89 MA 93. Ridley Hall Cam 02. **d** 05 **p** 06. C Highbury Ch Ch w St Jo and St Sav *Lon* 05–08; C St Jo on Bethnal Green 08–12; Co-ord Reader Tr Stepney Area 08–12; Intern Programme Dir from 12. *The Rectory Flat, Hereford Street, London E2 6EX* T: (020) 7033 3446 or 3837 5237 M: 07786-541559 E: fionajgreen@yahoo.co.uk or fiona.green@london.anglican.org

GREEN, Canon Fleur Estelle. b 72. Univ of Wales (Ban) BD 94. Ripon Coll Cuddesdon 95. **d** 97 **p** 98. C Blackpool St Jo *Blackb* 97–00; C Lancaster St Mary w St John and St Anne 00–03; P-in-c Blackb St Luke w St Paul 03–04; P-in-c Witton 03–04; V Blackb Christ the King 04–12; V Darwen St Pet from 12; AD Blackb and Darwen from 18; Asst Dir of Ords 06–12; Women's Min Adv from 11; Hon Can Blackb Cathl from 11. *The Rectory, St Peter's Close, Darwen BB3 2EA* T: (01254) 702411 E: chauntry1@live.co.uk

GREEN, Frank Gilbert. b 23. Kelham Th Coll 46. **d** 50 **p** 51. C Sheff St Cecilia Parson Cross 50–56; SSM from 52; C Nottingham St Geo w St Jo *S'well* 56–58; Basutoland 59–62; S Africa 62–69 and 84–88; Lesotho 69–84; PtO *Ox* 88–16; rtd 93. *Society of the Sacred Mission, Provincial Office, St Michael's Priory, The Well, Newport Road, Willen, Milton Keynes MK15 9AA*

GREEN, Gary Henry. b 64. Univ of Wales (Cardiff) BD 87. St Mich Coll Llan 93. **d** 95 **p** 96. C Baglan *Llan* 95–97; C Neath w Llantwit 97–01; TV Neath 01–02; V Llangiwg *S & B* from 02. *1 Clos yr Hen Ysgol, Pontardawe, Swansea SA8 4AZ* T: (01792) 862003 E: gary.green890@btinternet.com

GREEN, Gillian. b 41. Balls Park Coll Hertford TCert 61 Open Univ BA 83. EAMTC 03. **d** 05 **p** 06. NSM Stour Valley St E 05–11; PtO from 11; *Nor* from 16. *7 Haling Way, Thetford IP24 1EY* T: (01842) 338355 M: 07979-502840 E: revgillgreen@gmail.com

GREEN, Gloria. *See* SHERBOURNE, Gloria

GREEN, Graham Herbert. b 53. City Univ BSc 74. Westcott Ho Cam 75. **d** 78 **p** 79. C Hatcham St Cath *S'wark* 78–82; C S Ashford Ch Ch *Cant* 82–88; V Cheriton All So w Newington 88–97; P-in-c Milton next Sittingbourne 97–02; V 02–06; PtO *Roch* 12–13; V Helsby and Dunham-on-the-Hill *Ches* from 13; Dioc Adv in Spirituality from 13. *St Paul's Vicarage, Vicarage Lane, Helsby, Frodsham WA6 9AB* T: (01928) 722151 M: 07988-850261 E: millett1006@btinternet.com

GREEN, Imogen Elizabeth. *See* VIBERT, Imogen Elizabeth

GREEN, Mrs Janice Anne. b 48. NTMTC BA 07. **d** 07 **p** 08. NSM Gt Hallingbury and Lt Hallingbury *Chelmsf* 07–18; P-in-c 09–18; rtd 18. *Langham, Latchmore Bank, Little Hallingbury, Bishop's Stortford CM22 7PH* E: rev.janicegreen@btinternet.com

GREEN, Miss Jennifer Mary. b 55. SEN 78 SRN 81 RM 84. Trin Coll Bris 87. **d** 90 **p** 95. C Tong *Bradf* 90–93; Chapl Bradf Cathl 93; CMS Uganda 94–15; C Lt Horton *Leeds* from 15. *St Matthew's Vicarage, Carr Bottom Road, Bradford BD5 9AA* T: (01274) 928033 E: jennykisoro@hotmail.com

GREEN, Jeremy Nigel. b 52. St Andr Univ MA. St Jo Coll Nottm 80. **d** 83 **p** 84. C Dorridge *Birm* 83–86; V Scrooby *S'well* 86–94; V Bawtry w Austerfield and Misson 94–06; AD Bawtry 01–06; P-in-c Haxey *Linc* 06–12; V 12–18; P-in-c Owston 06–12; V 12–18; rtd 18. *6 Harvester Close, Epworth, Doncaster DN9 1QZ* E: jngreen@live.co.uk

GREEN, The Ven John. b 53. Nottm Univ BCombStuds 83. Linc Th Coll 80. **d** 83 **p** 84. C Watford St Mich *St Alb* 83–86; C St Alb St Steph 86–91; Chapl RN 91–06; Chapl of the Fleet and Adn for the RN 06–10; QHC 2006–10; Hon Can Portsm Cathl 06–10; PtO *Cov* 11–12; Adn Cov 12–17; C Cov St Mary 14–17; PtO *Birm* 12–16; rtd 17. *Tigh Callum, Culkein, Drumbeg, Lairg IV27 4NL* M: 07929-003361 E: venjgreen@gmail.com

GREEN, Canon John Francis Humphrey. b 44. Ex Univ BA 65 Heythrop Coll Lon MA 96. Westcott Ho Cam 91. **d** 93 **p** 94. C Tadworth *S'wark* 93–96; Chapl St Geo Sch Harpenden 96–01; P-in-c Flamstead *St Alb* 01–12; P-in-c Markyate Street 01–12; V Flamstead and Markyate Street 12–14; RD

Wheathampstead 09–10; Hon Can St Alb 13–14; rtd 14; P-in-c Barlavington, Burton w Coates, Sutton and Bignor *Chich* from 14. *The Rectory, The Street, Sutton, Pulborough RH20 1PS* T: (01798) 869023 E: johnfhgreen@gmail.com

GREEN, Canon John Henry. b 44. K Coll Lon BD 72 AKC. **d** 73 **p** 74. C Tupsley *Heref* 73–77; Asst Chapl Newc Univ 77–79; V Stevenage St Hugh Chells *St Alb* 79–85; V St Jo in Bedwardine *Worc* 85–92; Dir of Ords 92–08; P-in-c Guarlford and Madresfield w Newland 92–99; C Fladbury w Wyre Piddle and Moor etc 99–08; P-in-c Bowbrook N 08–12; P-in-c Bowbrook S 08–12; Hon Can Worc Cathl 94–12; rtd 12; PtO *Worc* from 12. *25 Station Road, Alcester B49 5ET* T: (01789) 400213 M: 07778-585746 E: ddocropthorne@waitrose.com

GREEN, Jonathon Samuel McKibbin. b 58. LCTP 10. **d** 13 **p** 14. Gen Manager Rydal Hall *Carl* 07–16; NSM Windermere St Mary and Troutbeck 13–14; NSM Grasmere 14–16; NSM Rydal 14–16; Dir Foxhill Retreat and Conf Cen *Ches* from 16. *The Bungalow, Foxhill Conference Centre, Tarvin Road, Frodsham WA6 6XB* T: (01928) 733777 E: jsmamgreen@gmail.com or jonathon.green@chester.anglican.org

GREEN, Mrs Joy Elizabeth. b 53. Open Univ BA 00. SEITE 04. **d** 07 **p** 08. NSM Maidstone St Martin *Cant* 07–14; rtd 14; PtO *Cant* from 14. *50 Anglesey Avenue, Maidstone ME15 9SU* T: (01622) 741616 E: joy.green50@tiscali.co.uk

GREEN, Julia Ann. *See* CARTWRIGHT, Julia Ann

GREEN, Canon Karina Beverley. b 61. Ripon Coll Cuddesdon 87. **d** 90 **p** 94. C Lee-on-the-Solent *Portsm* 90–93; Dioc Youth Officer *Guildf* 94–99; Youth and Children's Work Adv *Portsm* 99–03; P-in-c Portsea St Geo 03–05; V 05–12; P-in-c W Leigh from 12; CME Officer 03–13; Jt Dir Havant from 14; Hon Can Portsm Cathl from 06. *St Alban's Vicarage, Martin Road, Havant PO9 5TE* T: (023) 9307 6871 E: canonkarina@talktalk.net

⬧**GREEN, The Rt Revd Laurence Alexander.** b 45. K Coll Lon BD 68 AKC 68 NY Th Sem STM 69 DMin 82. St Aug Coll Cant 70. **d** 70 **p** 71 **c** 93. C Kingstanding St Mark *Birm* 70–73; V Erdington St Chad 73–83; Prin Aston Tr Scheme 83–89; Hon C Birchfield *Birm* 84–89; TR Poplar *Lon* 89–93; Area Bp Bradwell *Chelmsf* 93–11; rtd 11; Hon Asst Bp Chich from 11; Hon Asst Bp Roch from 18. *Belclare, 86 Belle Hill, Bexhill-on-Sea TN40 2AP* T: (01424) 217872 M: 07891-938647 E: mail@lauriegreen.org

GREEN, Mrs Linda Anne. b 60. Westcott Ho Cam 84. **dss** 86 **d** 87 **p** 94. Borehamwood *St Alb* 86–89; Par Dn 87–89; Par Dn Sheff St Cuth 89–90; Chapl Asst N Gen Hosp Sheff 89–91; Chapl 91–95; Chapl Qu Mary's Sidcup NHS Trust 96–05; P-in-c Crockenhill All So *Roch* 06–10; P-in-c Brasted 10–12; R from 12. *The Rectory, Coles Lane, Brasted, Westerham TN16 1NR* T: (01959) 565829 E: revlindagreen@aol.com

GREEN, Canon Linda Jeanne. b 50. R Holloway Coll Lon BSc 72 RGN 74 RCNT 79. SAOMC 01. **d** 04 **p** 05. C Headington Quarry *Ox* 04–09; P-in-c Banbury 09–13; R 13–15; Hon Can Ch Ch 14–15; rtd 15; PtO *Chich* from 16. *118 Marine Parade, Seaford BN25 2QR* M: 07973-802863 E: revlindagreen@gmail.com

GREEN, Malcolm Colin Robert. b 59. St Mellitus Coll 14. **d** 17 **p** 18. NSM St Mary-at-Latton *Chelmsf* from 17. *5 The Gowers, Harlow CM20 2JP* E: malcolm.green23@ntlworld.com

GREEN, Marcus. *See* GREEN, Edward Marcus

GREEN, Mark Richard. b 66. York Univ BA 87. All SS Cen for Miss & Min 14. **d** 17 **p** 18. NSM Witton *Ches* 17–19; P-in-c Moulton from 19. *15 Park Lane, Moulton, Northwich CW9 8QG* T: (01606) 557712 M: 07940-950311 E: mark@markrgreen.co.uk

GREEN, Martin Charles. b 59. Bris Univ BA 81 MPhil 86. Wycliffe Hall Ox 82. **d** 84 **p** 85. C Margate H Trin *Cant* 84–88; V Kingston upon Hull St Aid Southcoates *York* 88–94; P-in-c Bishop's Itchington *Cov* from 94; Dioc Children's Officer 94–05; P-in-c Radford Semele from 05; AD Southam from 16. *The Vicarage, 1 Manor Road, Bishop's Itchington, Southam CV47 2QJ* T: (01926) 613466 E: revmcg@kerrins.net

GREEN, Mrs Maureen. b 49. Avery Hill Coll CertEd 70 Lon Univ BEd 71. EAMTC 95. **d** 98 **p** 02. NSM Ipswich St Jo *St E* 98–10; Asst Chapl Ipswich Hosp NHS Trust 98–05; Asst Chapl Local Health Partnerships NHS Trust 98–02; Asst Chapl Cen Suffolk Primary Care Trust 02–05; PtO *Ox* 11–15; *St E* from 15. *Church House, Lower Farm Road, Ringshall, Stowmarket IP14 2JE* T: (01473) 657472 E: maureengreen@talk21.com

GREEN, Michael Alan. b 87. St Mellitus Coll BA 19. **d** 19. C Brownhill *Leeds* from 19. *26 Burnley's Mill Road, Gomersal, Cleckheaton BD19 4PQ* T: (01274) 871570 M: 07403-069879

GREEN, Paul John. b 48. Sarum & Wells Th Coll 72. **d** 73 **p** 74. C Tuffley *Glouc* 73–76; C Prestbury 76–82; P-in-c Highnam w Lassington and Rudford 82–83; P-in-c Tibberton w Taynton 82–83; R Highnam, Lassington, Rudford, Tibberton etc 84–92; Hon Min Can Glouc Cathl 85–96; V Fairford 92–96; RD 93–96; rtd 96; PtO *Glouc* 98–17. *15 Roselle Drive, Brockworth, Gloucester GL3 4GG*

GREEN, Pauline. *See* GREEN, Elizabeth Pauline Anne

GREEN, Penny. *See* GREEN, Denise Penelope

GREEN, Peter. b 38. Ex Univ BSc 59. Sarum Th Coll 59. **d** 61 **p** 62. C Romford St Edw *Chelmsf* 61–66; Chapl Trin Coll Kandy Ceylon 66–70; V Darnall *Sheff* 71–80; TV Stantonbury *Ox* 80–87; TV Stantonbury and Willen 87–91; Dep Chapl HM Pris Belmarsh 91–92; Chapl HM Pris Woodhill 92–03; rtd 03; PtO *Ox* from 04; *St D* from 06. *34 North Twelfth Street, Milton Keynes MK9 3BT* T: (01908) 240634 F: 240635 M: 07808-556213 E: peter@pg34.eclipse.co.uk

GREEN, Peter Geoffrey. b 59. St Andr Univ MA 83 Open Univ MA 01 PhD 10 BA 15. Coll of Resurr Mirfield 85. **d** 88 **p** 89. C Pershore w Pinvin, Wick and Birlingham *Worc* 88–91; V Dudley St Barn 91–99; V W Bromwich St Fran *Lich* 99–04; RD W Bromwich 02–04; Chapl Abbots Bromley Sch 04–12; P-in-c Hoar Cross w Newchurch *Lich* 07–12; Dean of Chpl and Chapl Bp Grosseteste Univ from 13; PV Linc Cathl from 15; PtO *Leeds* from 17. *Bishop Grosseteste University, Longdales Road, Lincoln LN1 3DY* T: (01522) 583607 E: peter.green@bishopg.ac.uk

GREEN, Peter Jamie. b 63. Aston Tr Scheme 87 Oak Hill Th Coll BA 93. **d** 93 **p** 94. C Brigg *Linc* 93–97; C Brigg, Wrawby and Cadney cum Howsham 97; P-in-c Billinghay 97–01; V Carr Dyke Gp 01–02; R Kelsey Gp 02–09; P-in-c St Mark's Bermuda 09–12; R Old Brampton and Great Barlow *Derby* from 12; P-in-c Loundsley Green from 12. *The Rectory, 25 Oldridge Close, Chesterfield S40 4UF* T: (01246) 558112 E: peter.green_99@tiscali.co.uk

GREEN, Philip Charles. b 53. NOC 91. **d** 94 **p** 95. C Southport Em *Liv* 94–98; P-in-c Crossens 98–03; TV N Meols 03–05; TR 05–18; AD 09–18; Hon Can Liv Cathl 09–18; rtd 18; PtO *Blackb* from 19. *45 Seacroft Crescent, Southport PR9 9FR* E: revphilgreen@talktalk.net

GREEN, Philip Stuart. b 69. Man Poly BA 90 Man Univ PGCE 91. ERMC 11. **d** 14 **p** 15. NSM London Colney *St Alb* from 14; Asst Chapl Aldenham Sch Herts from 17. *Aldenham School, Aldenham Road, Elstree, Borehamwood WD6 3AJ* T: (01923) 851636 M: 07934-335793 E: revphilipgreen@btinternet.com *or* psg@aldenham.com

GREEN, Richard Alistair. b 76. Ex Univ BA 97. St Steph Ho Ox BA 01. **d** 01 **p** 02. C Cockerton *Dur* 01–05; TV Ludlow *Heref* 05–13; Chapl Shropshire Co Primary Care Trust 05–13; V Aberdare St Fagan *Llan* from 13. *The Vicarage, 5 Redwood Court, Aberdare CF44 8RX* T: (01685) 881435 E: vicar.stfagans@btconnect.com

GREEN, Robert Henry. b 57. K Coll Lon BD 79. Wycliffe Hall Ox 81. **d** 83 **p** 84. C Norbury *Ches* 83–86 and 91–19; C Knutsford St Jo and Toft 86–88. *122 Cavendish Road, Hazel Grove, Stockport SK7 6JH* T: (01625) 858680 E: rob.green122@btinternet.com

GREEN, Robert Leonard. b 44. Open Univ BA 98. Sarum & Wells Th Coll 82. **d** 84 **p** 85. C Battersea St Luke *S'wark* 84–89; CF 89–04; P-in-c Southwick w Boarhunt *Portsm* 05–16; PtO *Sarum* from 16; *Win* from 16. *5 Grouse Road, Old Sarum, Salisbury SP4 6GE* T: (01722) 321870 M: 07876-426384 E: robertgreen7@btinternet.com

GREEN, Robert Stanley. b 42. Dur Univ BA 65. Wells Th Coll 65. **d** 67 **p** 68. C Ashford *Cant* 67–73; R Otham 73–80; V Bethersden w High Halden 80–87; R Winterbourne Stickland and Turnworth etc *Sarum* 87–99; R Monkton Farleigh, S Wraxall and Winsley 99–05; rtd 05; PtO *Sarum* from 06. *The Bungalow, Wootton Grove, Sherborne DT9 4DL* T: (01935) 817066 E: robertgreen@hotmail.com

GREEN, Robin. b 47. St as Minl Tr Course. **d** 06 **p** 07. NSM Llangystennin *St As* 06–09; NSM Rhos-Cystennin 09–11; rtd 11; PtO *St As* from 12; *Ban* from 15. *140 Queens Road, Llandudno LL30 1UE* T: (01492) 876451 E: robandjoy_@hotmail.com

GREEN, Roderick Ernest Alexander. b 74. Reading Univ BA 95 Brunel Univ MA 99. Wycliffe Hall Ox MTh 07. **d** 07 **p** 08. C Spitalfields Ch Ch w All SS *Lon* 07–11; C Shadwell St Paul w Ratcliffe St Jas 11–14; V W Harrow from 14. *22 Butler Avenue, Harrow HA1 4EH* M: 07957-247239 E: rodeagreen@gmail.com *or* rod@stpetersharrow.org

GREEN, Rodney William. b 52. **d** 93 **p** 94. OLM Flixton St Jo *Man* from 93; PtO *Eur* from 16. *85 Arundel Avenue, Flixton, Manchester M41 6MG* T: 0161-748 7238

GREEN, Roger Thomas. b 43. Oak Hill Th Coll. **d** 79 **p** 80. C Paddock Wood *Roch* 79–83; R High Halstow w All Hallows and Hoo St Mary 83–89; Chapl HM Pris Brixton 89–90; Chapl HM Pris Standford Hill 90–94; Chapl HM Pris Swaleside 94–99; Chapl HM Pris Roch 99–03; Chapl HM Pris Blantyre Ho 03; Chapl HM Pris Brixton 03–06; rtd

06; PtO *Sarum* from 11. *86 Tatnam Road, Poole BH15 2DS* E: rogert.green@gmail.com

GREEN, Ruth. b 54. Pittsburgh Th Sem DMin 18 RGN 76. New Coll Edin BD 11. **d** 11 **p** 12. C Edin St Pet 11–14; R Edin St Dav 14–19; Prin-c Aberdeen St Jas *Ab* from 19. *95 Gray Street, Aberdeen AB10 6JH* M: 07941-552768 E: revruthstjames@hotmail.com

GREEN, Ruth Valerie. *See* JAGGER, Ruth Valerie

GREEN, Ryan Albert. b 77. Nottm Univ BA 99. St Steph Ho Ox MTh 05. **d** 05 **p** 06. C The Cookhams *Ox* 05–09; R Swanbourne w Mt Claremont Australia 09–17; V Hove All SS *Chich* from 17. *24 Denmark Villas, Hove BN3 3TE* T: (01273) 733331 E: rev_green@hotmail.co.uk *or* frryan@allsaintshove.org

GREEN, Samuel John Mckibben. b 90. **d** 16 **p** 17. C Ashton-in-Makerfield St Thos *Liv* from 16. *79 Greenfields Crescent, Ashton-in-Makerfield, Wigan WN4 8QY* T: (01942) 272277 M: 07553-936123 E: samhcsp@gmail.com

GREEN, Sidney Leonard. b 44. K Coll Lon MTh 86 Montessori DipEd 84 Tabor Coll (Australia) ThD 13. Oak Hill Th Coll BD 72. **d** 72 **p** 73. C Skelmersdale St Paul *Liv* 72–74; C Denton Holme *Carl* 74–76; In Bapt Min 76–85; Chapl Qu Eliz Gr Sch Blackb 85–91; Chapl Epsom Coll 91–01; P-in-c Sway *Win* 01–03; V 03–04; rtd 04; Australia from 04; Asst Min Adelaide H Trin 05; R Adelaide St Luke 06; Chapl Kensington St Matt 07–12; Asst Min Adelaide St Jude from 12. *Bethany, 44/7 Sommer Place, Pasadena, Adelaide SA 5042, Australia* T: (0061) (8) 8277 7944 M: 43-989 5117 E: sidneygreen@adam.com.au

GREEN, Ms Stella Louise. b 61. Kent Univ BA 84 Cardiff Univ MTh 05 Anglia Ruskin Univ MA 16. St Mich Coll Llan 01. **d** 03 **p** 04. C Stamford Hill St Thos *Lon* 03–06; R Horsford, Felthorpe and Hevingham *Nor* 06–10; Chapl Norfolk and Nor Univ Hosps NHS Foundn Trust 10–18; Lead Chapl Qu Eliz Hosp King's Lynn NHS Foundn Trust from 18. *Chaplaincy Department, Queen Elizabeth Hospital, Gayton Road, King's Lynn PE30 4ET* T: (01553) 613441 E: stella.green@qehkl.nhs.uk

GREEN, Canon Steven Douglas. b 57. Univ of Wales BA 97. Sarum & Wells Th Coll 81. **d** 82 **p** 83. C Hawarden *St As* 82–86; V Mostyn 86–93; V Ffynnongroew 86–93; V Mostyn w Ffynnongroyw 93–99; R Trefnant w Tremeirchion 99–01; R Cefn w Trefnant w Tremeirchion 01–07; V Shotton 07–16; TV Borderlands Miss Area from 17; Warden of Readers from 10; Hon Can St As Cathl from 19. *The Vicarage, Chester Road East, Shotton, Deeside CH5 1QD* T: (01244) 836991 E: sdgreen1957@gmail.com

GREEN, The Very Revd Susan Denise. b 66. TCD BA 89 HDipEd 90. **d** 92 **p** 93. C Antrim All SS *Conn* 92–95; Dioc Youth Officer (Cashel) *C & O* 95–00; Chapl Adelaide and Meath Hosp Dublin 00–09; Chapl Kilkenny Coll *C & O* 10–18; Can Ossory Cathl 13–18; Dean Cloyne *C, C & R* from 18; I Cloyne Union from 18. *13 The Pinnacles, Midleton, Co Cork, Republic of Ireland* T: (00353) (21) 463 7913 E: s2011green@gmail.com

GREEN, Mrs Susan Margaret. b 54. Univ of Wales (Abth) BSc 75. SWMTC 92. **d** 95 **p** 96. NSM Wiveliscombe w Chipstable, Huish Champflower etc *B & W* 95–05; R Blackdown 05–14; C Trull w Angersleigh 05–14; rtd 14; PtO *B & W* 15–18. *Stonehouse, Allenslade Close, Wiveliscombe, Taunton TA4 2BS* T: (01942) 623012 E: suegreen@summit.me.uk

GREEN, Susannah Ruth. *See* CURTIS, Susannah Ruth

GREEN, Canon Trevor Geoffrey Nash. b 45. BA. Oak Hill Th Coll 81. **d** 84 **p** 85. C Stalybridge H Trin and Ch Ch *Ches* 84–89; V 89–96; V Lache cum Saltney 96–10; Hon Can *Ches* Cathl 08–10; rtd 10; PtO *Ches* from 10; *Man* 13–18; *Derby* 15–18. *27 Winchester Road, Dukinfield SK16 5DH* T: 0161-304 7796 M: 07837-424038 E: trevlaine10@aol.co.uk

GREEN, Trevor Howard. b 37. Sarum & Wells Th Coll 72. **d** 74 **p** 75. C Bloxwich *Lich* 74–77; C Willenhall St Steph 77–79; P-in-c 79–80; V 80–82; V Essington 82–90; V Bishopswood and Brewood 90–02; P-in-c Coven 00–02; RD Penkridge 94–01; rtd 02; PtO *Lich* from 02. *113 Stafford Street, Cannock WS12 2EN* T: (01543) 271159

GREEN, Mrs Veronica Gale. b 62. All SS Cen for Miss & Min 12. **d** 14 **p** 15. C Bunbury and Tilstone Fearnall *Ches* 14–15; C Marbury w Tushingham and Whitewell 15–17; P-in-c from 17. *The Vicarage, Marbury, Whitchurch SY13 4LN* T: (01948) 663758 M: 07928-792337 E: veronicarom838@aol.com

GREENALL, Canon Ronald Gilbert. b 41. St Aid Birkenhead 61. **d** 64 **p** 65. C Adlington *Blackb* 64–67; C Ribbleton 67–69; R Coppull St Jo 69–84; V Garstang St Thos 84–99; RD Garstang 89–96; Hon Can Blackb Cathl 95–99; rtd 99; PtO *Blackb* from 99. *40 Duckworth Drive, Catterall, Preston PR3 1YS* T: (01995) 606135 E: canon.ron@tiscali.co.uk

GREENAWAY-ROBBINS, Mark. b 72. Ox Univ BA 95. Qu Coll Birm 96. **d** 99 **p** 00. C Redruth w Lanner and Treleigh *Truro* 99–01; Consultant on Other Faiths 00–01; TV Whitchurch *Llan* 02–06; Canada 06–15; TR Eglwysilan and Caerphilly *Llan* from 15. *The Rectory, Rectory Close, Caerphilly CF81 1EQ* T: (029) 2085 1991 E: rector.rbec@gmail.com

GREENE, Colin John David. b 50. QUB BA 73 Fitzw Coll Cam MA 75 Nottm Univ PhD. St Jo Coll Nottm 78. **d** 80 **p** 81. NSM Sandiacre *Derby* 80–81; C Loughborough Em *Leic* 81–84; V Thorpe Acre w Dishley 84–89; Evang Tr Consultant Bible Soc 89–91; Tutor Trin Coll Bris 91–95; Th Consultant Bible Soc and Springdale Coll 95–96; Hd Th and Public Policy Bible Soc 96–03; Dean Th and Prof Seattle Pacific Univ USA 03–05; Prof Seattle Sch of Th and Psychology 05–08; Research Prof New York Th Sem from 11; Progr Ldr Sarum Coll 11–19; P-in-c Marnhull *Sarum* 11–13; R 13–15. *4 Old Manor Farm, Hinton Martell, Wimborne BH21 7HR* E: colin.greeneuk@gmail.com

GREENE, Ms Rachel Elizabeth. b 78. Virginia Univ BA 01 Peterho Cam MPhil 04. Westcott Ho Cam 05 Yale Div Sch 06. **d** 08 **p** 09. C Sturminster Newton, Hinton St Mary and Lydlinch *Sarum* 08–11; C Ox St Mary V w St Cross and St Pet 11–13; Chapl Trin Coll Cam 14–15; R Chiddingfold *Guildf* from 19. *The Rectory, Coxcombe Lane, Chiddingfold, Godalming GU8 4QA* T: (01428) 682008 E: rector.chiddingfold@gmail.com

GREENE, Richard Francis. b 47. TCD BAI 70 BA 70 MA 86 AMIMechE. CITC 03. **d** 06 **p** 07. NSM Waterford w Killea, Drumcannon and Dunhill *C & O* 06–10; NSM New w Old Ross, Whitechurch, Fethard etc 10–11; P-in-c 11–15. *Shallon, 2 Pleasant Avenue, Mount Pleasant, Waterford, Republic of Ireland* T: (00353) (51) 878477 M: 87-825 0418 E: rev.greene@gmail.com

GREENE, Valerie. b 45. Sheff Univ MA 04. Linc Th Coll 09. **d** 11 **p** 12. OLM Kirkby Laythorpe *Linc* from 11. *68 Church Lane, Kirkby-la-Thorpe, Sleaford NG34 9NU* T: (01529) 413148

GREENER, The Very Revd Jonathan Desmond Francis. b 61. Trin Coll Cam BA 83 MA 87. Coll of Resurr Mirfield 89. **d** 91 **p** 92. C S'wark H Trin w St Matt 91–94; Bp's Dom Chapl *Truro* 94–96; V Brighton Gd Shep Preston *Chich* 96–03; Adn Pontefract *Wakef* 03–07; Dean Wakef 07–17; Dean Ex from 17. *The Deanery, 10 Cathedral Close, Exeter EX1 1EZ* T: (01392) 255573 *or* 256730 E: jonathan.greener@exeter-cathedral.org.uk

GREENFIELD, Brian James. b 62. Liv Poly BSc 86 Leeds Univ PGCE 02. St Hild Coll 15. **d** 18 **p** 19. C Sutton w Cowling and Lothersdale *Leeds* from 18. *21 Walker Close, Glusburn, Keighley BD20 8PW* T: (01535) 637123 E: revd.brian.greenfield@gmail.com

GREENFIELD, Daniel James. b 82. Sheff Univ BA 03. St Mellitus Coll BA 18. **d** 18 **p** 19. C Crofton *Portsm* from 18. *7 Darren Close, Fareham PO14 2LU* T: (01329) 661154 E: dan@croftonparish.org.uk

GREENFIELD, Diana Marion. b 71. NTMTC. **d** 10 **p** 11. C Glastonbury w Meare *B & W* from 10; C Street w Walton and Compton Dundon from 13; Adv on New Relig Movements etc from 15. *25 Brookfield Way, Street BA16 0UE* T: (01458) 446838 E: dmgreenfield@me.com

GREENFIELD, Mrs Judith Clare. b 81. Sheff Univ BA 02. St Mellitus Coll BA 17. **d** 18 **p** 19. C Crofton *Portsm* from 18. *7 Darren Close, Fareham PO14 2LU* T: (01329) 661154 E: jude@croftonparish.org.uk

GREENFIELD, Canon Martin Richard. b 54. Em Coll Cam MA 75. Wycliffe Hall Ox MA 78. **d** 79 **p** 80. C Enfield Ch Ch Trent Park *Lon* 79–83; CMS 84–94; Nigeria 85–94; Hon Can Aba from 89; C Langdon Hills *Chelmsf* 94–95; R Brampton *Ely* 95–13; RD Huntingdon 99–04; P-in-c Sanderstead *S'wark* from 13; PtO *Eur* from 17. *53 Glebe Hyrst, South Croydon CR2 9JJ* T: (020) 8657 1366 E: rector@sanderstead-parish.org.uk

GREENHALGH, Harry. b 54. **d** 11 **p** 13. NSM Winwick *Liv* 11–15; NSM Leigh St Mary *Man* 16–17. *Address withheld by request*

GREENHALGH, Canon Ian Frank. b 49. Wycliffe Hall Ox 74. **d** 77 **p** 78. C Parr *Liv* 77–80; V Wigan St Barn Marsh Green 80–84; Chapl RAF 84–04; V Clapham-with-Keasden and Austwick *Bradf* 04–14; *Leeds* 14–17; RD Ewecross *Bradf* 05–14; RD Bowland 14; AD *Leeds* 14–16; AD Ewecross 14–16; AD Bowland and Ewecross 17; Hon Can Bradf Cathl 11–17; rtd 17; PtO *Eur* from 16. *1 Riversdale, Giggleswick, Settle BD24 0AW* E: iangreenhalgh49@gmail.com

GREENHALGH, Jane. b 64. **d** 11 **p** 12. OLM New Bury w Gt Lever *Man* 11–14; TV 14–18; V Freckleton and Warton St Paul *Blackb* from 18. *The Vicarage, Church Road, Warton, Preston PR4 1BD* T: (01772) 631885 M: 07843-

266881 E: jane.greenhalgh@hotmail.com *or* jane.greenhalgh@freckletonparishchurch.org.uk

GREENHALGH, Philip Adrian. b 52. Dur Univ MA 05. Ian Ramsey Coll Brasted 75 Wycliffe Hall Ox 76. **d** 79 **p** 80. C Gt Clacton *Chelmsf* 79–82; P-in-c Stalmine *Blackb* 82–86; Rep Leprosy Miss E Anglia 86–87; Area Org CECS 88–90; NSM Alston Team *Newc* 90–92; NSM Chulmleigh *Ex* 92–93; NSM Chawleigh w Cheldon 92–93; NSM Wembworthy w Eggesford 92–93; P-in-c Gilsland w Nether Denton *Carl* 93–95; V Millom 95–00; P-in-c Heatherycleugh *Dur* 00–04; P-in-c Westgate 00–04; P-in-c St John in Weardale 00–04; P-in-c Stanhope w Frosterley 02–04; P-in-c Eastgate w Rookhope 02–04; R Upper Weardale 04–07; AD Stanhope 00–07; R Bewcastle, Stapleton and Kirklinton etc *Carl* 07–12; RD Brampton 12–15; P-in-c Veryan w Ruan Lanihorne *Truro* from 17. *The Haven, Veryan Green, Truro TR2 5QE* T: (01872) 501950

GREENHALGH, Mrs Rosalyn. b 61. S Bank Poly BSc 83. WEMTC 09. **d** 12 **p** 13. C Cheltenham St Mark *Glouc* 12–16; V Quinton, Welford, Weston and Marston Sicca from 16. *The Rectory, Church Lane, Welford on Avon, Stratford-upon-Avon CV37 8EL* M: 07581-235524 E: revdrosgreenhalgh@gmail.com

GREENHILL, Anthony David. b 39. Bris Univ BSc 59. Tyndale Hall Bris 61. **d** 63 **p** 64. C Southsea St Jude *Portsm* 63–65; India 65–78; C Kinson *Sarum* 78–81; V Girlington *Bradf* 81–97; C Platt Bridge *Liv* 97–00; rtd 00; PtO *Bradf* 01–05; *Man* 05–17. *65 Lymbridge Drive, Blackrod, Bolton BL6 5TH* T: (01204) 696509 E: green-hill@ntlworld.com

GREENHOUGH, Alan Kenneth. b 40. St D Coll Lamp. **d** 66 **p** 67. C Allestree *Derby* 66–70; C Ilkeston St Mary 70–73; V Bradwell 73–85; R Twyford w Guist w Bintry w Themelthorpe etc *Nor* 85–95; P-in-c Stibbard 94–95; R Twyford, Guist, Bintree, Themelthorpe etc 95–05; rtd 05; PtO *Linc* from 17. *10 Newton Close, Metheringham, Lincoln LN4 3EQ* T: (01526) 328642

GREENHOUGH, Andrew Quentin. b 68. E Lon Poly BSc 89. Wycliffe Hall Ox BTh 94. **d** 94 **p** 95. C Partington and Carrington *Ches* 94–98; C Davenham 98–05; P-in-c Moulton 01–05; V New Ferry from 05. *St Mark's Vicarage, New Chester Road, Wirral CH62 1DG* T: 0151-645 2638 E: andy@macvicar.org.uk

GREENHOUGH, Arthur George. b 30. Fitzw Ho Cam BA 52 MA 56. Tyndale Hall Bris 55. **d** 57 **p** 58. C Wakef St Andr 57–63; R Birkin w Haddlesey *York* 63–85; RD Selby 77–84; P-in-c Hambleton 84–85; R Haddlesey w Hambleton and Birkin 85–00; rtd 00; PtO *York* from 01. *4 Sandway Drive, Camblesforth, Selby YO8 8JX* T: (01757) 617347 E: rev.greenhough@btinternet.com

GREENHOUGH, Geoffrey Herman. b 36. Sheff Univ BA 57 Lon Univ BD 71. St Jo Coll Nottm 74. **d** 75 **p** 76. C Cheadle Hulme St Andr *Ches* 75–78; R Tilston and Shocklach 78–82; V Hyde St Geo 82–87; V Pott Shrigley 87–00; rtd 00; PtO *Ches* from 01. *9 Spey Close, Winsford CW7 3BP* T: (01606) 556275 E: ghgreenhough@uwclub.net

GREENIDGE (*formerly* LARKIN)**, Mrs Karen Maria.** b 74. Qu Coll Birm BA 08. **d** 08 **p** 09. C Coleshill and Maxstoke *Birm* 08–12; Chapl Lon City YMCA 12–16; NSM Southall Em 16–18; P-in-c N Greenford All Hallows from 18. *72 Horsenden Lane North, Greenford UB6 0PD* M: 07956-923653 E: karengreenidge@hotmail.co.uk

GREENLAND, Hazel. b 64. ERMC 14. **d** 17 **p** 18. C Colchester St Mich Myland *Chelmsf* from 17. *Myland Parish Hall, Mile End Road, Colchester CO4 5DY* T: (01206) 855040 E: hazel@mylandchurch.org.uk

GREENLAND, Martin. b 65. Warwick Univ BSc 87. Westcott Ho Cam 94. **d** 97 **p** 98. C Scarborough St Martin *York* 97–00; TV Bramley and Ravenfield w Hooton Roberts etc *Sheff* 00–04; V Ravenfield, Hooton Roberts and Braithwell 04–08; R Acle w Fishley, N Burlingham, Beighton w Moulton *Nor* 08–15; R Acle and Bure to Yare from 15; Jt RD Blofield from 17. *The Rectory, Norwich Road, Acle, Norwich NR13 3BU* T: (01493) 750393 E: rector@aclechurch.plus.com

GREENLAND, Paul Howard. b 59. Bath Univ BA 80 ACA 85. Trin Coll Bris 98. **d** 00 **p** 01. C Caverswall and Weston Coyney w Dilhorne *Lich* 00–03; P-in-c Chelmsf St Andr 03–05; V from 05. *The Vicarage, 88 Chignal Road, Chelmsford CM1 2JB* T/F: (01245) 496722 M: 07811-539328 E: paulhgreenland@care4free.net

GREENLAND, Roy Wilfrid. b 37. St Steph Ho Ox 71. **d** 73 **p** 74. C Wanstead St Mary *Chelmsf* 73–76; V Harlow St Mary Magd 76–83; P-in-c Huntingdon All SS w St Jo *Ely* 83–84; P-in-c Huntingdon St Barn 83–84; P-in-c Huntingdon St Mary w St Benedict 83–84; Bermuda 84–89; V Northampton St Alb *Pet* 89–92; R Waldron *Chich* 92–02; rtd 02; PtO *Pet* 05–07; *Cov* from 08. *7 Margetts Close, Kenilworth CV8 1EN* T: (01926) 852560

GREENMAN, David John. b 35. Lon Univ BA 59. Oak Hill Th Coll 57. **d** 61 **p** 62. C Wandsworth St Steph *S'wark* 61–63; C Bishopwearmouth St Gabr *Dur* 63–66; C-in-c Bedgrove CD *Ox* 66–74; P-in-c Macclesfield Ch Ch *Ches* 74–77; V 77–81; P-in-c Glouc All SS 81–85; V Glouc St Jas 81–85; V Bare *Blackb* 85–91; V Market Lavington and Easterton *Sarum* 91–99; rtd 99; PtO *Sarum* from 00; *Win* from 00. *3 Bure Lane, Christchurch BH23 4DJ* T: (01425) 241034 E: davidjeangreenman@hotmail.co.uk

GREENMAN (née CHESTER), Mrs Irene Mary. b 51. Dioc OLM tr scheme 97. **d** 99 **p** 00. OLM Cornholme *Wakef* 99–00; OLM Cornholme and Walsden 00–11. *8 Glen View Street, Cornholme, Todmorden OL14 8LT* T/F: (01706) 817296 E: revgreenman@aol.com

GREENSLADE, Canon Gillian Carol. b 43. Leic Univ BA 64 Essex Univ MA 78 Nottm Univ PGCE 65. EAMTC 93. **d** 96 **p** 97. NSM Dovercourt and Parkeston w Harwich *Chelmsf* 96–00; NSM Colchester, New Town and The Hythe 00–02; R Broxted w Chickney and Tilty etc 02–08; Hon Can Chelmsf Cathl 07–08; rtd 08; Adv for Women's Min (Colchester Area) *Chelmsf* 05–08; PtO from 08. *15 The Grand, 6 The Esplanade, Frinton-on-Sea CO13 9DS* T: (01255) 676755 E: gcgreenslade@googlemail.com

GREENSLADE, Timothy Julian. b 63. St Jo Coll Ox BA 86. Oak Hill Th Coll BA 95. **d** 95 **p** 96. C Broadwater *Chich* 95–99; TV Radipole and Melcombe Regis *Sarum* 99–16; TR Melbury from 16. *The Vicarage, Tollerford Lane, Higher Frome Vauchurch, Dorchester DT2 0AT* T: (01300) 748675 E: the.greenslades@tiscali.co.uk

GREENSMITH, Mrs Sharon Suzanne. b 68. RGN 89. Qu Foundn Birm 12. **d** 14 **p** 15. NSM Clayton *Lich* 14–18; C from 18. *26 Crown Bank, Talke, Stoke-on-Trent ST7 1PU* M: 07962-139947 E: sharon116@btinternet.com

GREENWAY, Gayle Kimberley. b 86. St Jo Coll Nottm 14. **d** 17 **p** 18. C Wolverhampton St Matt *Lich* from 17. *47 Lincoln Green, Wolverhampton WV10 8HW*

GREENWAY, John Michael. b 34. **d** 96 **p** 97. OLM Gt Yarmouth *Nor* 96–04; PtO from 04. *17 Hamilton Road, Great Yarmouth NR30 4ND* T: (01493) 853558 E: john.greenway3@ntlworld.com

GREENWELL, Christopher. b 49. Linc Th Coll 79. **d** 81 **p** 82. C Scarborough St Martin *York* 81–84; V S Bank 84–89; R Bolton by Bowland w Grindleton *Bradf* 89–92; V Nether Hoyland St Andr *Sheff* 92–96; V Kirkleatham *York* 96–07; rtd 07. *79 Hillshaw Park Way, Ripon HG4 1JU* T: (01765) 600467

GREENWELL, Canon Paul. b 60. Magd Coll Ox BA 81 MA 85. St Steph Ho Ox 82. **d** 85 **p** 86. C Hendon and Sunderland *Dur* 85–88; Min Can and Prec Ripon Cathl 88–93; Chapl Univ Coll of Ripon and York St Jo 88–93; V Hunslet St Mary *Ripon* 93–02; Chapl Harrogate and Distr NHS Foundn Trust 02–08; Chapl St Mich Hospice Harrogate 02–08; Convenor Dioc Adv Gp for Chr Healing *Ripon* 03–08; Can Res Ripon Cathl 08–17; Master Charterhouse Hull from 17; Chapl MU 09–14. *The Master's House, Charterhouse Lane, Hull HU2 8AF* T: (01482) 329307 E: master@thecharterhouse.karoo.co.uk

GREENWOOD, Caroline Elizabeth. b 63. Lanc Univ BSc 85 Open Univ BSc 96 Trent Poly PGCE 88. St Jo Coll Nottm MTh 14. **d** 14 **p** 15. C Hillock and Unsworth *Man* 14–18; PtO from 18; V Warley and Halifax St Hilda *Leeds* from 18. *The Vicarage, 466 Burnley Road, Halifax HX2 7LW* T: (01422) 363623 M: 07771-858404 E: karis1763@gmail.com *or* caroline.greenwood@leeds.anglican.org

GREENWOOD, Claire. *See* GREENWOOD, Helen Claire

GREENWOOD, David. *See* GREENWOOD, Norman David

GREENWOOD, Canon David Michael. b 57. Univ of New Brunswick BBA 79 St Thos Aquinas Pontifical Univ Rome MA(Theol) 10 STL 14. Vancouver Sch of Th MDiv 95. **d** 95 **p** 96. C Nanaimo Canada 95–97; CF 97–08; PtO *Eur* 08–10; Course Resource Research Development Officer Forces Chapl Sch Canada 10–13; PtO *Eur* 13–15; P-in-c Marseille w Aix-en-Provence 15–17; PtO from 17. *Suite 1201, 31 King's Wharf Place, Dartmouth NS B2Y 0C1, Canada* E: dmgcag1@msn.com

GREENWOOD, David Neal. b 70. New Coll Edin PhD 13. **d** 14 **p** 15. C Banchory *Ab* 14–17; C Kincardine O'Neil 14–17; P-in-c 17–18. *Address temp unknown* E: dngreenwood@abdn.ac.uk

GREENWOOD, Elizabeth. *See* GREENWOOD, Margaret Elizabeth

GREENWOOD, Canon Gerald. b 33. Leeds Univ BA 57 Sheff Poly MSc 81 Surrey Univ Hon MA 93. Linc Th Coll 57. **d** 59 **p** 60. C Rotherham *Sheff* 59–62; V Elsecar 62–70; V Wales 70–77; P-in-c Thorpe Salvin 74–77; Dioc Sch Officer 77–84; P-in-c Bramley and Ravenfield 77–78; P-in-c Hooton Roberts 77–78; R 78–84; Hon Can Sheff Cathl 80–84; Dioc

Dir of Educn 81–84; Hon Can S'wark Cathl 84–97; Dir of Educn 84–97; rtd 97; PtO *Cant* from 97. *Home Farm Cottage, Westmarsh, Canterbury CT3 2LW* T: (01304) 812160 E: gegreenwood@btinternet.com

GREENWOOD, Helen Claire. b 54. Cranmer Hall Dur 05. **d** 06 **p** 07. C Willington *Newc* 06–10; V Marden w Preston Grange 10–13; V Billy Mill 10–13; rtd 13; Hon C Barnoldswick w Bracewell *Bradf* 14; *Leeds* 14–18. *158 Keighley Road, Skipton BD23 2QT* T: (01756) 799253 E: hcgreenwood@yahoo.com

GREENWOOD, Ian Richard. b 74. Liv Hope BEd 96. St Jo Coll Nottm MTh 09. **d** 09. C Burscough Bridge *Liv* 09–13; P-in-c Aigburth 13–14; V from 14. *St Anne's Vicarage, 389 Aigburth Road, Liverpool L17 6BH* T: 0151-727 1101 M: 07840-829956 E: reviangreenwood@gmail.com

GREENWOOD, James Peter. b 61. Univ Coll Lon BSc 83 St Jo Coll Dur BA 90 RIBA 87. Cranmer Hall Dur 88. **d** 91 **p** 92. C Belper *Derby* 91–94; CMS Pakistan 95–01; V Islamabad St Thos 95–00; V Silsden *Bradf* 01–09; Dioc Spirituality Adv 05–09; RD S Craven 07–09; P-in-c Gillingham and Milton-on-Stour *Sarum* 09–16; V 16–19; R Gillingham, Milton-on-Stour and Silton from 19. *The Rectory, High Street, Gillingham SP8 4AJ* T: (01747) 822435 *or* 821598

GREENWOOD, John Newton. b 44. St Chad's Coll Dur BA 69. **d** 70 **p** 71. C Hartlepool H Trin *Dur* 70–72; LtO from 72; Hd Master Archibald Primary Sch Cleveland 84–97; Asst Chapl HM Pris Holme Ho 99–11. *1 Brae Head, Eaglescliffe, Stockton-on-Tees TS16 9HP* T: (01642) 783200

GREENWOOD, Leslie. b 37. Dur Univ BA 59. Cranmer Hall Dur. **d** 61 **p** 62. C Birstall *Wakef* 61–63; C Illingworth 64–70; Chapl H Trin Sch Halifax 64–89; V Charlestown *Wakef* 70–91; TV Upper Holme Valley 91–97; PtO 97–14; *Leeds* from 14; rtd 00. *2 Trenance Gardens, Greetland, Halifax HX4 8NN* T/F: (01422) 373926 E: kyandles@aol.com

GREENWOOD, Mrs Margaret Elizabeth. b 34. St Mary's Coll Chelt TCert 65 Surrey Univ MA 93. St Mich Ho Ox 60. **d** 00. NSM Shepperton *Lon* 00–01; NSM Whitton SS Phil and Jas 01–04; PtO from 04. *Bundoran Cottage, Vicarage Lane, Staines TW18 1UE* T: (01784) 458115 E: elizabethgreenwood@btinternet.com

GREENWOOD, Canon Michael Eric. b 44. Oak Hill Th Coll 78. **d** 80 **p** 81. C Clubmoor *Liv* 80–83; V Pemberton St Mark Newtown 83–94; V Grassendale 94–00; V Ashton-in-Makerfield St Thos 00–09; Hon Can Liv Cathl 08–09; rtd 09. *1 Fardon Close, Wigan WN3 6SN* T: (01942) 825670 E: mikeg09@btinternet.com

GREENWOOD, Norman David. b 52. Edin Univ BMus 74 Lon Univ BD 78 Nottm Univ MPhil 90. Oak Hill Th Coll 76. **d** 78 **p** 79. C Gorleston St Andr *Nor* 78–81; SAMS 81–83; C Cromer *Nor* 83–84; R Appleby Magna and Swepstone w Snarestone *Leic* 84–94; P-in-c Chesterfield H Trin *Derby* 94–95; P-in-c Chesterfield Ch Ch 94–95; R Chesterfield H Trin and Ch Ch 95–99; V S Ramsey St Paul *S & M* 99–12; Dir Voc and Tr 01–12; RD Ramsey 08–11; Chapl HM Pris Is of Man 05–12; Hon Can St German's Cathl *S & M* 09–12; Chapl St Pet Viña del Mar Chile 12–15; Chapl Rio de Janeiro Ch Ch Brazil 15–16; PtO *S & M* from 16; *Eur* from 17. *24 St Paul's Mews, Ramsey, Isle of Man IM8 1EE* M: 07624-234414 E: davidgreenwood@manx.net

GREENWOOD, Peter. *See* GREENWOOD, James Peter

GREENWOOD, Canon Robin Patrick. b 47. St Chad's Coll Dur BA 68 MA 71 Birm Univ PhD 92. **d** 70 **p** 71. C Adel *Ripon* 70–73; Min Can and Succ Ripon Cathl 73–78; V Leeds Halton St Wilfrid 78–86; Dioc Can Res Glouc Cathl 86–95; Dioc Missr and Dir Lay and Post-Ord Tr 86–95; Dir of Min and Hon Can Chelmsf Cathl 95–00; Prov Officer for Min Ch in Wales 01–05; Hon C Canton St Jo *Llan* 02–05; V Monkseaton St Mary *Newc* 05–13; rtd 13; C Kincardine O'Neil *Ab* 14–17; C Banchory 14–17; PtO *Leeds* from 17. *158 Keighley Road, Skipton BD23 2QT* T: (01756) 799253 E: robingreenwood1@gmail.com

GREENWOOD, Sharon. b 44. **d** 07 **p** 08. NSM Welling *S'wark* 07–18. *Address temp unknown* E: sharon.greenwood44@tiscali.co.uk

GREENWOOD, Stella Jane. b 68. Teesside Poly BSc 90. All SS Cen for Miss & Min 15. **d** 17 **p** 18. NSM Swadlincote *Derby* 17–18; C from 18; NSM Hartshorne and Bretby 17–18; C from 18. *64 Castle Road, Castle Gresley, Swadlincote DE11 9LH* T: (01283) 558330 M: 07802-963817 E: greenwoodstella@yahoo.com

GREEVES, Roger Derrick. b 43. TCD BA 66 MA 70 Fitzw Coll Cam BA 68 MA 73. Westcott Ho Cam 98. **d** 98 **p** 99. In Methodist Ch 68–98; NSM Cam St Edw *Ely* 98–00; Chapl Oakington Immigration Reception Cen 00–01; Chapl Peterho Cam 00–01; Dean Clare Coll Cam 01–08; rtd 08; PtO *Ely* from 08; *Eur* from 15. *The Cart Lodge, 5 Home Farm,*

89 High Street, Harston, Cambridge CB22 7PZ T: (01223) 977988 M: 07817-032301 E: rdg20@cam.ac.uk

GREGG, David William Austin. b 37. Lon Univ BD 66 Bris Univ MA 69. Tyndale Hall Bris 63. **d** 68 **p** 69. C Barrow St Mark *Carl* 68–71; P-in-c Lindal w Marton 71–75; Communications Sec Gen Syn Bd for Miss and Unity 76–81; Prin Romsey Ho Coll Cam 81–88; V Haddenham w Cuddington, Kingsey etc *Ox* 88–96; P-in-c Newton Longville w Stoke Hammond and Whaddon 96–02; rtd 03; PtO *Carl* from 03. *Lowick Farm House, Lowick Green, Ulverston LA12 8DX* T: (01229) 885258

GREGORY, Alan Paul Roy. b 55. K Coll Lon BD 77 MTh 78 Emory Univ Atlanta PhD 94 AKC 77. Ripon Coll Cuddesdon 78. **d** 79 **p** 80. C Walton-on-Thames *Guildf* 79–82; Lect Sarum & Wells Th Coll 82–88; Dir Studies 85–88; Assoc R Atlanta St Patr USA 88-94; R Athens Em 94–95; Assoc Prof Ch Hist Episc Th Sem of the SW 95–04; Academic Dean and Prof Ch Hist 04–12; P-in-c Stannington *Newc* 12–14; Dioc CMD Officer 12–14; Prin St Aug Coll of Th from 14; PtO *S'wark* 14–15; Public Preacher from 15. *St Augustine's College of Theology, 52 Swan Street, West Malling ME19 6JX* T: (01732) 252656 M: 07969-335562 E: principal@seite.co.uk *or* alan@scrivenersgloom.com

GREGORY, Andrew Forsythe. b 71. St Jo Coll Dur BA 92 Linc Coll Ox DPhil 01. Wycliffe Hall Ox BA 96 MA 00. **d** 97 **p** 98. C E Acton St Dunstan w St Thos *Lon* 97–99; Asst Chapl Keble Coll Ox 97–99; Chapl and Jun Research Fell Linc Coll Ox 99–03; Research Fell Keble Coll Ox 03–05; Chapl and Fell Univ Coll Ox from 05; LtO *Ox* from 08. *University College, High Street, Oxford OX1 4BH* T: (01865) 276663 E: andrew@theology.ox.ac.uk

GREGORY, Anthony Lawrence. b 43. Lon Univ BD 71. Tyndale Hall Bris 67. **d** 71 **p** 72. C Branksome St Clem *Sarum* 71–74; SAMS from 74; rtd 08. *Molina Campos 507, V Vega San Martin, San Martin de los Andes, Q8370 Neuquen, Argentina* T: (0054) (2972) 425191 E: anthmollie@gmail.com

GREGORY, Brian. b 43. Trin Coll Bris. **d** 82 **p** 83. C Burscough Bridge *Liv* 82–85; V Platt Bridge 85–92; V Ben Rhydding *Bradf* 92–06; rtd 06; PtO *Bradf* 07–14; *Leeds* 14–16; *Blackb* from 15. *6 Hawthorn Close, Hesketh Bank, Preston PR4 6EP* T: (01772) 812234 E: gregory.brian@btinternet.com

✠**GREGORY, The Rt Revd Clive Malcolm.** b 61. Lanc Univ MA 84 Qu Coll Cam BA 87 MA 89 Warwick Univ Hon MA 99. Westcott Ho Cam 85. **d** 88 **p** 89 **c** 07. C Margate St Jo *Cant* 88–92; Chapl Warw Univ *Cov* 92–98; TR Cov E 98–07; Area Bp Wolverhampton *Lich* from 07. *61 Richmond Road, Wolverhampton WV3 9JH* T: (01902) 824503 F: 824504 E: bishop.wolverhampton@lichfield.anglican.org

GREGORY, Mrs Elizabeth Louise Annunciata. b 83. UWE LLB 05 Univ of Wales (Swansea) MA 07 Lucy Cavendish Coll Cam BA 11. Westcott Ho Cam 09. **d** 12 **p** 13. C Sole Bay *St E* 12–15; R Filton *Bris* from 15. *The Rectory, Rectory Lane, Filton, Bristol BS34 7BE* T: 0117-979 1128 M: 07528-518968 E: elizabeth.gregory@talk21.com

GREGORY, Miss Mary Emma. b 70. Birm Univ BA 92 St Jo Coll Dur BA 04 MA 06. Cranmer Hall Dur 02. **d** 05 **p** 06. C Hatfield *Sheff* 05–08; R Kirk Sandall and Edenthorpe 08–15; Dean of Women's Min 13–15; Hon Can Sheff Cathl 14–15; TR Ashby-de-la-Zouch and Breedon on the Hill *Leic* from 15. *The Rectory, 4 Upper Packington Road, Ashby-de-la-Zouch LE65 1EF* T: (01530) 534672 M: 07734-052524 E: revmarygregory@aol.co.uk

GREGORY, Peter. b 35. Cranmer Hall Dur 59. **d** 62 **p** 63. C Pennington *Man* 62–65; C N Ferriby *York* 65–68; V Tonge Fold *Man* 68–72; V Hollym w Welwick and Holmpton *York* 72–77; P-in-c Foston w Flaxton 77–80; P-in-c Crambe w Whitwell and Huttons Ambo 77–80; R Whitwell w Crambe, Flaxton, Foston etc 81–94; rtd 94; PtO *York* from 13. *6 High Terrace, Northallerton DL6 1BG* T: (01609) 776956

GREGORY, Richard Branson. b 33. Fitzw Ho Cam BA 58 MA 62. Sarum Th Coll 58 Ridley Hall Cam 59. **d** 60 **p** 61. C Sheff St Cuth 60–62; Asst Chapl Leeds Univ *Ripon* 62–64; V Yeadon St Jo *Bradf* 64–71; R Keighley 71–74; TR Keighley St Andr 74–82; Hon Can Bradf Cathl 71–82; RD S Craven 71–73 and 78–82; P-in-c Broadmayne, W Knighton, Owermoigne etc *Sarum* 82–85; R 85–98; rtd 98; PtO *Sarum* 98–08. *2 Huish Cottages, Sydling, Dorchester DT2 9NS* T: (01300) 341835

GREGORY, Canon Stephen Simpson. b 40. Nottm Univ BA 62 CertEd 63. St Steph Ho Ox. **d** 68 **p** 69. C Aldershot St Mich *Guildf* 68–71; Chapl St Mary's Sch Wantage 71–74; R Edgefield *Nor* 74–88; R Holt 74–94; R Holt w High Kelling 94–95; RD Holt 79–84 and 95–96; Hon Can Nor Cathl 94–95; V Prestbury *Glouc* 95–03; P-in-c Pittville All SS 99–03; TR Prestbury and All SS 03–06; RD Cheltenham 00–05; Hon Can Glouc Cathl 04–06; rtd 06; PtO *Nor* from 08; *Glouc*

from 14. *Mulberry Cottage, Balfour Road, West Runton, Cromer NR27 9QJ* T: (01263) 838049

GREGORY-WITHAM, Ms Katherine Fiona Marie. b 90. Ches Univ BA 12. Cranmer Hall Dur BA 18. **d** 19. C Burnley St Matt w H Trin *Blackb* from 19. *229 Coal Clough Lane, Burnley BB11 4DL* E: kfmwitham@gmail.com

GREGSON (née ROBERTSON), Fiona Jane Robertson. b 76. Birm Univ BA 98 Lon Sch of Th PhD 14. Wycliffe Hall Ox BA 05 MA 10. **d** 06 **p** 07. C Aston SS Pet and Paul *Birm* 06–08; C Aston St Jas 06–08; C Nechells 06–08; C Aston and Nechells 08–10; P-in-c Girlington *Bradf* 10–13; V 13; C Manningham 10–12; PtO *Birm* 14–18; C Harborne Heath from 18. *18 Willow Avenue, Birmingham B17 8HD* M: 07958-494560 E: fionajanerobertson@yahoo.co.uk *or* fionagregson@stjohnsharborne.org

GREGSON, Gillian Amy. b 33. Westmr Coll Ox BTh 02 CQSW 78. **d** 98 **p** 99. OLM Coulsdon St Jo *S'wark* 98–05; PtO 05–18. *21 Canons Hill, Coulsdon CR5 1HB* T: (01737) 479689 E: gillgregson21@gmail.com

GREGSON, Peter John. b 36. Univ Coll Dur BSc 61. Ripon Hall Ox 61. **d** 63 **p** 64. C Radcliffe St Thos *Man* 63–65; C Baguley 65–67; Chapl RN 68–91; V Ashburton w Buckland in the Moor and Bickington *Ex* 91–01; RD Moreton 95–98; rtd 01; PtO *Sarum* 01–11; *Blackb* from 11. *26 Astley Road, Chorley PR7 1RR* T: (01257) 247999

GREIFF, Andrew John. b 64. Huddersfield Univ BA 98 Leeds Univ PGCE 99 St Jo Coll Dur BA 05. Cranmer Hall Dur 03. **d** 05 **p** 06. C Pudsey St Lawr and St Paul *Bradf* 05–08; P-in-c Thornton St Jas 08–12; P-in-c Fairweather Green 08–12; TV Shelf w Buttershaw St Aid 12–14; *Leeds* from 14. *80 Carr House Road, Halifax HX3 7RJ* T: (01274) 671576 *or* 676335 E: andrew.greiff667@gmail.com

GREIG, George Malcolm. b 28. CA 53 St Andr Univ BD 95. LNSM course 75. **d** 81 **p** 82. NSM Dundee St Mary Magd *Bre* 81–84; NSM Dundee St Jo 82–84; P-in-c Dundee St Ninian 84–85; Chapl St Paul's Cathl Dundee 85–98; rtd 98; Hon C Dundee St Salvador *Bre* 98–16; PtO from 16. *61 Charleston Drive, Dundee DD2 2HE* T: (01382) 566709 E: gmg28@btinternet.com

GREIG, Martin David Sandford. b 45. Bris Univ BSc 67. St Jo Coll Nottm 72. **d** 75 **p** 76. C Keresley and Coundon *Cov* 75–79; C Rugby 79–83; TV 83–86; V Cov St Geo 86–93; TV Southgate *Chich* 93–01; R Maresfield 01–06; P-in-c Nutley 01–06; rtd 06. *Bodawen, Llangrannog, Llandysul SA44 6SH* T: (01239) 654257 E: mg@bodawen.org.uk

GREIG, Philip. b 76. Ox Brookes Univ BA 02. Ridley Hall Cam 09. **d** 11 **p** 12. C Chartham *Cant* 11–14; C Cant All SS from 14. *Glebe House, Military Road, Canterbury CT1 1PA* T: (01227) 450669 M: 07411-936354 E: revphilgreig@me.com

GRENFELL, Canon James Christopher. b 69. Qu Coll Ox BA 93 MA 96 MPhil 95 Ox Univ DPhil 00. Westcott Ho Cam 98. **d** 00 **p** 01. C Kirkby *Liv* 00–03; P-in-c Sheff Manor 03–06; TR 06–09; P-in-c Ranmoor 09–13; AD Hallam 12–13; PtO *Portsm* 13–16; Dir Portsm Pathway Ripon Coll Cuddesdon from 16; Hon Can Portsm Cathl from 19. *63 Coborn Road, London E3 2DB* M: 07759-974332 E: jamescgrenfell@gmail.com *or* portsmouthpathway@rcc.ac.uk

✠**GRENFELL, The Rt Revd Joanne Woolway.** b 72. Oriel Coll Ox BA 93 DPhil 97 Univ of BC MA 94. Westcott Ho Cam 98. **d** 00 **p** 01 **c** 19. C Kirkby *Liv* 00–03; Jt P-in-c Sheff Manor 03–06; Can Res Sheff Cathl 06–13; Dioc Dir of Ords 06–13; Dean of Women's Min 08–13; Adn Portsdown *Portsm* 13–19; Area Bp Stepney *Lon* from 19. *63 Coborn Road, London E3 2DB* M: 07936-043945

GRENHAM-THOMPSON, Mrs Sharon Carmel. b 66. Reading Univ LLB 87 Solicitor 92. Trin Coll Bris 94 SAOMC 96. **d** 98 **p** 00. C Buckingham *Ox* 98–02; C Milton Keynes 00–02; Miss Adv USPG Lon, Ox and St Alb 02–03; NSM Wilshamstead and Houghton Conquest *St Alb* 03–04; Chapl Oakhill Secure Tr Cen 04–05; PtO *St Alb* from 04; Asst Chapl HM Pris Woodhill 08–11; Chapl HM Pris Bedf 11–16; TV Watling Valley *Ox* from 16. *Address withheld by request* M: 07891-892550

GRESHAM, Karen Louise. *See* SMEETON, Karen Louise

GRETTON-DANN, Judith Adrienne. b 75. St Andr Univ MSci 97 PhD 01. St Mich Coll Llan 12. **d** 14 **p** 15. NSM Chesterton Gd Shep *Ely* from 14. *45 Darwin Drive, Cambridge CB4 3HQ* T: (01223) 750013 M: 07900-523959 E: goodshepherdcurate@gmail.com

GREW, Nicholas David. b 52. Surrey Univ BSc 74 MSc 75. Wycliffe Hall Ox 93. **d** 95 **p** 96. C Biddulph *Lich* 95–99; P-in-c Knaphill *Guildf* 99–00; V Knaphill w Brookwood 00–15; V Luton St Fran *St Alb* from 15. *The Vicarage, 145 Hollybush Road, Luton LU2 9HQ* T: (01582) 451132 M: 07527-269373 E: nickthevic@talktalk.net

GREW, Timothy Richard. b 65. SS Coll Cam MA 88. WEMTC 03. **d** 06 **p** 07. NSM Cheltenham H Trin and St Paul *Glouc* 06–10; TV from 10. *208 Prestbury Road, Cheltenham GL52 3ER* T: (01242) 321473 E: tim.grew@trinitycheltenham.com

GREY, Mrs Nicola Jane Francis. b 61. **d** 13 **p** 14. C Burton St Chad *Lich* 13–16; Chapl HM YOI Werrington Ho 16–18; Chapl HM Pris Drake Hall 16–18; R Cheadle w Freehay *Lich* from 18. *The Rectory, Church Street, Cheadle, Stoke-on-Trent ST10 1HU* T: (01538) 753337 E: rector@cheadlefreehay.org.uk

GREY, Richard Thomas. b 50. St D Coll Lamp BA 73 Ripon Hall Ox 73. **d** 75 **p** 76. C Blaenavon w Capel Newydd *Mon* 75–77; Ind Chapl 77–02; C Newport St Paul 77–80; CF (TA) from 78; Chapl Aberbargoed Hosp 80–88; V Bedwellty *Mon* 80–88; R Llanwenarth Ultra 88–92; R Govilon w Llanfoist w Llanelen 92–02; RD Abergavenny 98–02; V Brynmawr *S & B* 02–09. *Rivendell, Cefn Rhoss, Tredegar NP22 3PA* E: rev.richard.grey@outlook.com

GREY, Canon Roger Derrick Masson. b 38. AKC 61. **d** 62 **p** 63. C Darlington H Trin *Dur* 62–63; C Bishopwearmouth St Mich 63–67; V Mabe *Truro* 67–70; Dioc Youth Chapl 67–70; Youth Chapl *Glouc* 70–77; V Stroud H Trin 77–82; Dioc Can Res Glouc Cathl 82–03; Dir of Educn 82–94; Bp's Chapl 94–03; rtd 03; Clergy Widows' Officer (Glouc Adnry) *Glouc* from 03; PtO from 04. *12 Buckingham Close, Walton Cardiff, Tewkesbury GL20 7QB* T: (01684) 275742

GREY, Stephen Bernard. b 56. Linc Th Coll 86. **d** 88 **p** 89. C Worsley *Man* 88–93; V Bamford 93–04; P-in-c Rochdale St Geo w St Alb 99–04; P-in-c Preesall *Blackb* 04–05; P-in-c Hambleton w Out Rawcliffe 04–05; V Waterside Par 05–10; P-in-c Garstang St Thos 10–13; V 13–17; TV Newton *Liv* from 17; AD Winwick from 17. *8 The Parchments, Newton-le-Willows WA12 0DY* M: 07910-854911 E: revstephengrey@gmail.com

GRIBBEN, John Gibson. b 44. K Coll Lon BD 75 QUB MTh 81. CITC 73. **d** 75 **p** 76. C Dunmurry *Conn* 75–78; CR from 79; Lic to Offic *Wakef* 83–14; rtd 09; LtO *Leeds* from 14. *House of the Resurrection, Stocks Bank Road, Mirfield WF14 0BN* T: (01924) 483339 E: jgribben@mirfield.org.uk

GRIBBIN, Canon Bernard Byron. b 35. Bradf Univ MPhil 84. St Aid Birkenhead 58. **d** 60 **p** 61. C Maghull *Liv* 60–63; C Prescot 63–65; V Denholme Gate *Bradf* 65–71; V Bankfoot 71–79; Dioc Stewardship Adv 79–86; Prec and Chapl Choral Ches Cathl 86–91; V Ringway 91–96; Dioc Tourism Officer 91–96; Hon Can Ches Cathl 91–96; rtd 96; PtO *Bradf* 96–14; *Leeds* from 14. *5 Heather Court, Ilkley LS29 9TZ* T: (01943) 816253 E: b.b.gribbin@btinternet.com

GRIBBLE, Malcolm George. b 44. Chu Coll Cam BA 67 MA 71. Linc Th Coll 79. **d** 81 **p** 82. C Farnborough *Roch* 81–84; V Bostall Heath 84–90; V Bexleyheath Ch Ch 90–02; P-in-c Hever, Four Elms and Mark Beech 02–06; R 06–09; rtd 10. *26 Neville Road, Tewkesbury GL20 5ED* T: (01684) 290641 E: m@griblog.net *or* mgg@myphone.coop

GRICE, Charles. b 24. **d** 58 **p** 59. C Stocksbridge *Sheff* 58–61; R Armthorpe 61–66; Ind Missr 66–69; Ind Chapl 69–76; V Tinsley 69–73; V Oughtibridge 73–76; Gen Sec Ch Lads' and Ch Girls' Brigade 77–91; R Braithwell w Bramley *Sheff* 88–91; rtd 89; PtO *Sheff* from 89. *57 Deepdale Road, Rotherham S61 2NR* T: (01709) 557551

GRICE, Canon David Richard. b 32. Keble Coll Ox BA 55 MA 59. St Steph Ho Ox 55. **d** 57 **p** 58. C Leeds St Aid *Ripon* 57–61; C Middleton St Mary 61–62; V Woodlesford 62–69; V Leeds St Wilfrid 69–78; TR Seacroft 78–93; Hon Can Ripon Cathl 92–99; P-in-c Thorner 93–95; V 95–99; rtd 99; PtO *Ripon* 00–14; *Leeds* from 14. *15 Mead Road, Leeds LS15 9JR* T: 0113-260 4371

GRIER, James Emerson. b 74. St Pet Coll Ox BA 95 MA 01. Wycliffe Hall Ox 96. **d** 98 **p** 99. C Ox St Andr 98–02; C Harborne Heath *Birm* 02–07; TV Pinhoe and Broadclyst *Ex* 07–12; Dioc Youth Adv 07–12; Ldr Unlimited Ch from 12. *St Thomas's Rectory, 57 Cowick Street, Exeter EX4 1HR* M: 07825-610288 E: james.grier@exeter.anglican.org

GRIERSON, Peter Stanley. b 42. Lon Univ BD 68 Leeds Univ MPhil 74. Linc Th Coll 68. **d** 69 **p** 70. C Clitheroe St Mary *Blackb* 69–71; C Aston cum Aughton *Sheff* 71–74; V Preston St Jude w St Paul *Blackb* 74–81; V Blackb St Luke w St Phil 89–97; RD Blackb 91–97; V Burnley St Matt w H Trin 97–02; PtO *Bradf* 03–13; *Blackb* from 13. *21 Fosbrooke House, 8 Clifton Drive, Lytham St Annes FY8 5RQ* T: (01253) 667014 E: olwen62@sky.com

GRIEVE, David Campbell. b 51. St Jo Coll Dur BA 74. Wycliffe Hall Ox 74. **d** 76 **p** 77. C Upton (Overchurch) *Ches* 76–80; C Selston *S'well* 80–82; V Pelton *Dur* 82–89; rtd 89; PtO *Dur* from 04. *The Old Rectory, The Village, Castle Eden, Hartlepool TS27 4SL* T: (01388) 718447 E: david@grieve.org.uk *or* davidgrieve0@icloud.com

GRIEVE (*née* PIERSSENÉ), Canon Frances Jane. b 55. St Jo Coll Dur BA 76. Cranmer Hall Dur 99. **d** 01 **p** 02. C Barnard Castle w Whorlton *Dur* 01–05; P-in-c Cockfield 05–14; R 14–15; P-in-c Lynesack 05–14; V 14–15; P-in-c Evenwood 09–14; V 14–15; P-in-c Wheatley Hill, Thornley and Wingate w Hutton Henry from 15; AD Easington from 15; Adv for Women's Min from 10; Hon Can Dur Cathl from 10. *The Old Vicarage, The Village, Castle Eden, Hartlepool TS27 4SL* T: (01429) 835479 E: jane.grieve@durham.anglican.org

GRIFFIN, Alan Howard Foster. b 44. TCD BA 66 MA 69 Peterho Cam PhD 71. Sarum & Wells Th Coll 75. **d** 78 **p** 79. Lect Ex Univ 78–01; Asst to Lazenby Chapl 78–92; Sub-Warden Duryard Halls 78–81; Warden 81–84; Sen Warden 84–98; PtO *Ex* 92–98; C Heavitree w Ex St Paul 98–01; Ex Campus Chapl Plymouth Univ 98–01; R St Andr-by-the-Wardrobe w St Ann, Blackfriars *Lon* 01–11; R St Jas Garlickhythe w St Mich Queenhithe etc 01–11; CME Officer Two Cities Area 01–08; rtd 11. *24 Cinnamon Street, London E1W 3NJ* T: (020) 7265 1851 M: 07583-251931 E: a.h.f.griffin@gmail.com

GRIFFIN, Christopher Donald. b 59. Reading Univ BA 80 CertEd 81. Wycliffe Hall Ox 82. **d** 85 **p** 86. C Gerrards Cross *Ox* 85–88; Chapl Felsted Sch 88–98; Chapl Sedbergh Sch 98–06; Ho Master 00–17. *39 Dial Hill Road, Clevedon BS21 7EL* E: chrisdgriffin1@outlook.com

GRIFFIN, Eugene Thomas. MTh FCCA. **d** 13 **p** 14. C Castleknock and Mulhuddart w Clonsilla *D & G* 14–18; Abp's Dom Chapl 15–18; I Dunboyne and Rathmolyon *M & K* from 18. *The Rectory, 1 The Close, Plunkett Hall, Dunboyne, Co Meath, A86 E167, Republic of Ireland* T: (00353) (1) 825 3288 M: 86-382 6646 E: eugenethomasgriffin@gmail.com

GRIFFIN, Canon Joseph William. b 48. St Mich Coll Llan 70. **d** 74 **p** 75. C Killay *S & B* 74–78; C Swansea St Thos and Kilvey 78–81; V Troedrhiwgarth *Llan* 81–91; V Llanrhidian w Llanmadoc and Cheriton *S & B* 91–99; RD Gower 94–99; V Swansea St Nic 99–04; RD Swansea 02–04; P-in-c SW Gower 04–05; R 05–15; AD Gower 11–14; Hon Can Brecon Cathl 98–01; Can Res 01-11; Can Treas 11–15; rtd 15; PtO *S & B* from 15. *25 Maes-y-Coed, Gorseinon, Swansea SA4 6RN* T: (01792) 410321 E: joe.griffin3@hotmail.com

GRIFFIN, Judith. Wycliffe Hall Ox. **d** 12 **p** 12. C Onslow Square and S Kensington St Aug *Lon* 12–15; Chapl R Brompton and Harefield NHS Foundn Trust 15–16. *Address withheld by request*

GRIFFIN, Keith. b 66. Nottm Trent Univ BA 88. Cranmer Hall Dur BA 94. **d** 95 **p** 96. C Gedling *S'well* 95–98; V Barkingside St Geo *Chelmsf* 99–02; TV Upper Holme Valley *Wakef* 02–14; *Leeds* from 14. *The Vicarage, 3 Vicarage Meadows, Holmfirth HD9 1DZ* T: (01484) 682644 E: revdkg@tiscali.co.uk

GRIFFIN, Malcolm Roger. b 46. Goldsmiths' Coll Lon TCert 67 Open Univ BA 73. S'wark Ord Course. **d** 83 **p** 84. NSM Romford St Andr *Chelmsf* 83–87; NSM Romford St Jo 87–91; NSM Gt Ilford St Alb 91–97; PtO 97–98; P-in-c Romford St Jo 98–00; P-in-c Cratfield w Heveningham and Ubbeston etc *St E* 00–02; Dioc Dir of Educn 05–06; PtO *Nor* 02–08; *St E* 02–05 and 06–08; *Nor* from 15; *St E* from 15. *4 Old Forge Court, Brockdish, Diss IP21 4JE* T: (01379) 669252 E: father.malcolm@outlook.com

GRIFFIN, Mark Richard. b 68. Trin Coll Bris BA 93. Westcott Ho Cam 94. **d** 96 **p** 97. C Walmer *Cant* 96–00; V Wingham w Elmstone and Preston w Stourmouth 00–07; V Sevenoaks St Luke *Roch* 07–17; RD Sevenoaks 11–16; Hon Can Roch Cathl 15–17; R Cant St Martin and St Paul from 17. *The Rectory, 13 Ersham Road, Canterbury CT1 3AR* T: (01227) 768072 E: revd.mark.griffin@talk21.com

GRIFFIN, Niall Paul. b 37. TCD BA 61 Div Test 61. **d** 61 **p** 62. C Newtownards *D & D* 61–63; C Arm St Mark w Aghavilly 63–64; C Cross Roads Jamaica 64–66; C Lurgan Ch the Redeemer *D & D* 66–69; Chapl RAF 69–84; Missr Chr Renewal Cen *D & D* 84–89; Nat Dir (Ireland) SOMA UK 89–07; rtd 07. *7 Cloughmore Park, Rostrevor, Newry BT34 3AX* T/F: (028) 4173 8959 E: nandg@griffin.go-plus.net *or* niallpgriffin@gmail.com

GRIFFIN, Nicholas Philip. b 84. Moorlands Coll BA 06. Wycliffe Hall Ox 09. **d** 11 **p** 12. C Frome H Trin *B & W* 11–15; Chapl Univ of St Mark and St Jo *Ex* 15–18; Tutor St Mellitus Coll from 18; Hon C Blackdown *B & W* from 18. *5 Barton Green, Trull, Taunton TA3 7NA* M: 07947-672547 E: ngriffin84@gmail.com *or* nick.griffin@stmellitus.ac.uk

GRIFFISS, Canon Helen Mary. b 48. Univ of Wales (Ban) CertEd 69 K Alfred's Coll Win MA 98. STETS 97. **d** 00 **p** 01. Miss Adv USPG Bris, Sarum and Win 00–03; NSM Bransgore Win 00–03; C Milton 04–06; P-in-c Mudeford 06–09; V

09–17; rtd 17; Hon Can Win Cathl from 16; PtO from 17. *35A River Way, Christchurch BH23 2QQ* T: (01202) 474067 E: revhelengriffiss@gmail.com

GRIFFITH, Benedict Lloyd Thomas. b 64. Trin Coll Carmarthen BA 86. Ripon Coll Cuddesdon 04. **d** 06 **p** 07. C Kempston Transfiguration *St Alb* 06–09; V Upper Wye *S & B* 09–14; P-in-c Erwood Gp w Painscastle Gp 14–16; R Kington w Huntington, Old Radnor, Kinnerton etc *Heref* from 16. *The Vicarage, Church Road, Kington HR5 3AG* T: (01544) 230525 M: 07960-947137 E: vicar@kingtonparishes.org.uk

GRIFFITH, The Ven David Vaughan. b 36. St D Coll Lamp BA 60. Lich Th Coll 60. **d** 62 **p** 63. C Llanfairfechan *Ban* 62–66; C Dolgellau 66–70; R Llanfair Talhaiarn *St As* 70–82; R Llanfairtalhaiarn and Llansannan 82–85; P-in-c Llangernyw and Gwytherin 77–85; V Colwyn 85–98; Warden of Readers 91–99; Can Cursal St As Cathl 95–98; P-in-c Berriew and Manafon 98–99; V 99–02; Preb St As Cathl and Adn Montgomery 98–02; rtd 02; PtO *St As* from 09. *1 Bishop's Walk, St Asaph LL17 0SU* T: (01745) 582903

GRIFFITH, Glyn Keble Gethin. b 37. St D Coll Lamp BA 59. Ridley Hall Cam 67. **d** 69 **p** 70. C Derby St Aug 69–72; C Coity w Nolton *Llan* 72–75; P-in-c Heage *Derby* 75–81; V Allestree St Nic 81–92; R Wilne and Draycott w Breaston 92–01; rtd 01; PtO *Mon* from 02; *Heref* 02–08. *3 Cornford Close, Osbaston, Monmouth NP25 3NT* T: (01600) 719740

GRIFFITH, Canon John Vaughan. b 33. St D Coll Lamp 53. **d** 58 **p** 59. C Holyhead w Rhoscolyn *Ban* 58–63; R Maentwrog w Trawsfynydd 63–68; Chapl RAF 68–72; V Winnington *Ches* 72–76; V Northwich St Luke and H Trin 76–81; V Sandiway 81–98; Dioc Communications Officer 84–86; Ed Chester Diocesan News 84–92; Hon Can Ches Cathl 89–98; rtd 98; PtO *Ches* 99–14. *41 Moss Lane, Cuddington, Northwich CW8 2PT*

GRIFFITH, Sandra. b 44. Open Univ BA 94. EAMTC 01. **d** 04 **p** 05. NSM The Ortons, Alwalton and Chesterton *Ely* 04–06; NSM Sawtry and Glatton 06–11; Asst Chapl Hinchingbrooke Health Care NHS Trust from 05. *14 Nene Way, Oundle, Peterborough PE8 4LR* M: 07450-470685 E: sandra@revgriffith.com

GRIFFITH, Stephen. *See* GRIFFITH, William Stephen

GRIFFITH, Steven Ellsworth. b 63. Univ of Wales BTh 91. St Steph Ho Ox. **d** 87 **p** 88. C Holyhead w Rhoscolyn w Llanfair-yn-Neubwll *Ban* 87–90; CF 90–08; Sen CF 08–13; PtO *S & B* 12–13; Min Can Brecon Cathl 13–15; PV Brecon Cathl from 15; P-in-c Brecon St Mary from 14; AD Gtr Brecon from 17. *The Clergy House, Cathedral Close, Brecon LD3 9DP* T: (01874) 622044 M: 07540-609029 E: frstevengriffith@outlook.com

GRIFFITH, Mrs Wendy Margaret. b 41. **d** 01 **p** 02. NSM Sixpenny Handley w Gussage St Andrew etc *Sarum* 01–06; NSM Wimborne Minster 06–08; NSM Somerton w Compton Dundon, the Charltons etc *B & W* 08–14; NSM Ivelchester Deanery 14–16; PtO *B & W* from 17; *Sarum* from 18. *Homelea, 5 Church Walk, Cross Lane, Long Sutton, Langport TA10 9LR* T: (01458) 241771 M: 07720-942996 E: wendymgriffith@gmail.com

GRIFFITH, William Stephen. b 50. Univ of Wales (Ban) BA 71 FRAS 92. Westcott Ho Cam 71. **d** 73 **p** 74. C Llandudno *Ban* 73–76; C Calne and Blackland *Sarum* 76–78; P-in-c Broadwindsor w Burstock and Seaborough 78–79; TV Beaminster Area 79–81; PtO 81–83; Chapl St Pet Sch York 83–87; C Leeds St Pet *Ripon* 87; Chapl Bearwood Coll Wokingham 87–92; CMS Jordan 92–95; Sen Chapl Univ of Wales (Cardiff) *Llan* 95–96; Chapl Damascus 96–02; P-in-c Yerevan, Baku and Tbilisi *Eur* 03; V Denton *Newc* 04–08; TV Mortlake w E Sheen *S'wark* 09–15; rtd 15; PtO *York* from 15. *14 North Parade, York YO30 7AB* T: (01904) 626819 M: 07729-278294 E: haywales@hotmail.com

GRIFFITH-JONES, David Laugharne. b 79. Pemb Coll Cam MA 06. Wycliffe Hall Ox BTh 12. **d** 12 **p** 13. C Toxteth St Philemon w St Gabr and St Cleopas *Liv* 12–16; TR Drypool *York* from 16. *139 Laburnum Avenue, Garden Village, Hull HU8 8PA* T: (01482) 786553 M: 07775-563126 E: dave_gj@hotmail.com

GRIFFITH-JONES, Robin Guthrie. b 56. New Coll Ox BA 78 Ch Coll Cam BA 88. Westcott Ho Cam 86. **d** 89 **p** 90. C Cantril Farm *Liv* 89–92; Chapl Linc Coll Ox 92–99; Master of The Temple from 99. *The Master's House, Temple, London EC4Y 7BB* T: (020) 7353 8559 E: master@templechurch.com

GRIFFITHS, Ainsley. *See* GRIFFITHS, John Mark Ainsley

GRIFFITHS, Alan Charles. b 46. Dur Univ BA 67. Cranmer Hall Dur 66. **d** 69 **p** 70. C Leic H Apostles 69–72; Leic York 73–77; V Lea Hall *Birm* 77–87; Asst Dir of Educn *Sheff* 87–92; V W Bessacarr 92–02; V Conisbrough 02–13; rtd 13; PtO *Sheff* 13–14; P-in-c Barnburgh w Melton on the Hill etc 14–16; PtO

from 16. *356C Thorne Road, Doncaster DN2 5AN* T: (01302) 365164 E: alan.c.griffiths@btinternet.com

GRIFFITHS, Canon Andrew Taylor. b 68. Jes Coll Ox BA 92 MA 96. Cranmer Hall Dur 98. **d** 00 **p** 01. C Paris St Mich *Eur* 00–04; C Galleywood Common *Chelmsf* 04–05; V 05–17; C Moulsham St Luke 13–17; C Moulsham St Jo 13–17; C Widford 13–17; RD Chelmsf S 07–17; Chelmsf IME Co-ord and Bradwell Area CMD Adv from 17; Public Preacher *Chelmsf* from 17; Hon Can Chelmsf Cathl from 15. *Chelmsford Diocesan Board of Finance, 53 New Street, Chelmsford CM1 1AT* T: (01245) 294400 M: 07969-605059 E: agriffiths@chelmsford.anglican.org

GRIFFITHS, Beatrice Mary. b 29. Chelsea Coll Lon CertEd 60. Westcott Ho Cam 85. **dss** 86 **d** 87 **p** 94. W Bridgford *S'well* 86–87; NSM Wilford Hill 87–99; rtd 99; PtO *S'well* from 99. *7 Stella Avenue, Tollerton, Nottingham NG12 4EX* T: 0115-937 4155

GRIFFITHS, Benjamin David. b 78. Ches Univ MA 14. St Jo Coll Nottm BA 12. **d** 13 **p** 14. C Brampton St Thos *Derby* 13–16; V Newbold w Dunston from 16; Asst Dir of Ords from 18. *Newbold Rectory, Littlemoor, Chesterfield S41 8QN* T: (01246) 450374 M: 07813-285445 E: revbengriffiths@gmail.com

GRIFFITHS, Brian John. b 45. Brunel Univ PhD 82. **d** 05 **p** 06. OLM Iver *Ox* 05–14; PtO from 14; *Win* 11–15. *7 Benton Drive, Chinnor OX39 4DP* T: (01844) 355953

GRIFFITHS, Christopher Rhys. b 82. Leeds Univ BA 06 Anglia Ruskin Univ MA 14. Westcott Ho Cam 10. **d** 13 **p** 14. C Wimbledon *S'wark* 13–16; R Horringer *St E* from 16. *The Rectory, Manor Lane, Horringer, Bury St Edmunds IP29 5PY* T: (01284) 736839 E: revdchrisgriffiths@gmail.com

GRIFFITHS, Canon David. b 38. St Mich Coll Llan. **d** 67 **p** 68. C Llangollen *St As* 67–71; C Rhyl w St Ann 71–74; V Kerry 74–77; V Kerry and Llanmerewig 77–82; R Caerwys and Bodfari 82–87; V Gresford 87–97; V Gresford w Holt 97–03; RD Wrexham 97–01; RD Gresford 01–03; Can St As Cathl 98–03; rtd 03; PtO *St As* 09–17. *16 Heol-y-Wal, Bradley, Wrexham LL11 4BY* T: (01978) 751416 E: revdavidgriffiths@btinternet.com

GRIFFITHS, David Bruce. b 44. Sussex Univ BA 69 Hull Univ MA 83. Linc Th Coll. **d** 82 **p** 83. C Springfield All SS *Chelmsf* 82–84; TV Horwich *Man* 84–92; V Heaton Ch Ch 92–03; P-in-c Ainsworth 03–09; rtd 09; PtO *Man* from 09. *Woodford, Mill Lane, Horwich, Bolton BL6 6AQ* T: (01204) 469621 M: 07854-769119 E: dandbgriffiths@googlemail.com

GRIFFITHS, David John. b 53. St Jo Coll Nottm BTh 93. **d** 94 **p** 95. C Retford St Sav *S'well* 94–96; NSM Thwaites Brow *Bradf* 96–98; P-in-c Oakenshaw cum Woodlands 98–03; V Buttershaw St Paul 03–10; V Silsden 10–14; *Leeds* from 14; Asst Chapl Airedale NHS Foundn Trust from 96. *The Vicarage, Briggate, Silsden, Keighley BD20 9JS* T: (01535) 652204 E: david.griffiths@bradford.anglican.org

GRIFFITHS, David Mark. b 59. Kent Univ BA 80. Chich Th Coll 81. **d** 83 **p** 84. C Clydach *S & B* 83–84; C Llwynderw 84–88; V Swansea St Nic 88–98; Chapl Swansea Inst of HE 88–98; V Swansea St Gabr from 98; P-in-c Swansea St Barn from 17; Chapl Swansea NHS Trust from 98. *3 Trafalgar Place, Brynmill, Swansea SA2 0BU* T: (01792) 464011 E: mark.griffiths35@btinternet.com

GRIFFITHS, David Mark. b 41. Univ of Wales (Cardiff) BA 67 CertEd 71. St Mich Coll Llan 92. **d** 94 **p** 95. C Llwynderw *S & B* 94–96; R Llanbadarn Fawr, Llandegley and Llanfihangel etc 96–02; P-in-c Slebech and Uzmaston w Boulston *St D* 02–06; rtd 06; PtO *St D* from 06. *17 Catherine's Gate, Merlins Bridge, Haverfordwest SA61 1NB* T: (01437) 783950 M: 07811-647910 E: davidgriffiths41@mypostoffice.co.uk

GRIFFITHS, David Rowson Hopkin. b 38. Oak Hill Th Coll 59. **d** 62 **p** 63. C Barrow St Mark *Carl* 62–65; OMF Internat 66–09; Japan 66–88; Philippines 88–09; rtd 03. *4 Warwick Place, West Cross, Swansea SA3 5JG* T: (01792) 402885 E: david.griffiths@omfmail.com

GRIFFITHS, Dorothy Anastasia de Jaegher. b 55. **d** 14 **p** 15. NSM Cheltenham St Mary w St Matt and St Luke *Glouc* 14–16; NSM Charlton Kings St Mary 16–17; PtO from 17. *35 St Mary's Square, Gloucester GL1 2QT* T: (01452) 453429 E: anna.dejaegher.griffiths@gmail.com

GRIFFITHS, Ms Elizabeth Leigh. b 61. St Hugh's Coll Ox BA 83 MA 87 Warwick Univ PGCE 84. Ripon Coll Cuddesdon 96. **d** 98 **p** 99. C Bettws *Mon* 98–99; C Maindee Newport 99–01; TV Cen Swansea and Dioc Chapl Tertiary Educn *S & B* 01–03; C St Martin-in-the-Fields *Lon* 03–09; Dir Past Studies ERMC and Nor Dioc Min Course 09–10; Dir Past Studies and Vice Prin ERMC 10–11; V Cardiff City Par *Llan* 11–12; Dioc Dir of Ords 12; TV Basingstoke *Win* 14–17; Dir Tr Bridge Builders Min from 17; PtO *Bris* from 17. *20*

Grantham Close, Freshbrook, Swindon SN5 8NZ T: (01793) 432738 E: lizgriff999@btinternet.com

GRIFFITHS, Mrs Frances Karen Bernadette. b 62. St Mellitus Coll 17. **d** 19. C Kirkholt *Man* from 19. *St Thomas's Vicarage, Gainsborough Drive, Rochdale OL11 2QU* M: 07592-191504 E: griffclan2@gmail.com

GRIFFITHS, Garrie Charles. b 53. St Jo Coll Nottm. **d** 77 **p** 78. Canada 77–78; C Stalybridge H Trin and Ch Ch *Ches* 78–81; C Moreton 81–84; V Godley cum Newton Green 84–89; V Bayston Hill *Lich* 89–01; TR Mildenhall *St E* 01–04; V Hadfield *Derby* 04–10; RD Glossop 06–10; V Youlgreave, Middleton, Stanton-in-Peak etc 10–16; Spiritual Dir Adv 13–16; rtd 16. *8 Main Road, Martlesham, Woodbridge IP12 4SF*

GRIFFITHS, Gerald Brian. b 41. Open Univ BA 88. SEITE 97. **d** 00 **p** 01. NSM Cliftonville *Cant* 00–03; TV St Laur in Thanet 04–09; rtd 09; Chapl Costa Blanca *Eur* 10–12; PtO *Cant* from 13; *Eur* from 14. *11 Wellesley Court, Ramsgate CT11 8NU* T: (01843) 850229 E: gbgriffiths41@gmail.com

GRIFFITHS, Gordon John. b 31. Univ of Wales (Cardiff) BA 53. S'wark Ord Course 72. **d** 75 **p** 76. NSM Sutton St Nic S'wark 75–78; Asst Chapl Eastbourne Coll 78–81; PtO *Chich* from 81. *15 Buckhurst Close, Willingdon, Eastbourne BN20 9EF* T: (01323) 505547

GRIFFITHS, Griff. *See* GRIFFITHS, Stephen David

GRIFFITHS, Harvey Stephen. b 35. Linc Coll Ox BA 58 MA 62. Linc Th Coll 62. **d** 62 **p** 63. C Frodingham *Linc* 62–65; C Darlington St Cuth *Dur* 65–70; Chapl RN 70–92; P-in-c Southwick w Boarhunt *Portsm* 92–05; rtd 05; PtO *Portsm* from 05. *27 Burnham Wood, Fareham PO16 7UD* T: (01329) 232915 M: 07747-093365 E: harveysgriffiths@virginmedia.com

GRIFFITHS, Hugh. b 44. Nottm Univ BEd 78. Clifton Th Coll 69. **d** 71 **p** 72. C Mansfield SS Pet and Paul *S'well* 71–77; NSM Stockport St Geo *Ches* 08–09; rtd 09; PtO *Ches* from 09. *1 Heath Crescent, Stockport SK2 6JN* T: 0161-285 9772 E: hugh.griffiths@norburychurch.org.uk

GRIFFITHS, James Brian. b 69. Man Univ BSocSci 92. Oak Hill Th Coll BA 13. MA 15. **d** 15 **p** 16. C Gabalfa *Llan* from 15. *27 Pen-y-Bryn Road, Gabalfa, Cardiff CF14 3LG* E: j.b.griffiths69@gmail.com

GRIFFITHS, Jason Anthony. b 70. St Jo Coll Nottm 14. **d** 17 **p** 18. C Britwell *Ox* from 17. *99 Haymill Road, Slough SL2 2NP* T: (01908) 566728 M: 07717-496770 E: griff205@gmail.com

GRIFFITHS, Mrs Jean Rose. b 36. Avery Hill Coll TCert 56. S'wark Ord Course 93. **d** 95 **p** 96. NSM Charlton *S'wark* 95–03; Asst Chapl HM Pris Brixton 95–03; Chapl 03–04; rtd 04; PtO *S'wark* 04–18. *32 Weyman Road, London SE3 8RY* T: (020) 8319 8676 E: jean.peterg@hotmail.com

GRIFFITHS, John. b 57. Coll of Ripon & York St Jo BEd 83. LCTP 12. **d** 14 **p** 15. C Heart of Eden *Carl* 14–15; C Cockermouth Area 15–18; V Garstang St Thos *Blackb* from 18. *The Vicarage, Church Street, Garstang, Preston PR3 1PA* M: 07984-895722 E: johntherev@btinternet.com

GRIFFITHS, John Gareth. b 44. Lich Th Coll 68. **d** 71 **p** 72. C Shotton *St As* 71–73; C Rhyl w St Ann 73–76; V Llanasa 76–95; RD Holywell 89–95; V Rhuddlan 95–10; rtd 10; PtO *St As* from 10. *13 Llwyn Harlech, Bodelwyddan, Rhyl LL18 5WG* T: (01745) 539955 E: jg.griffiths@btinternet.com

GRIFFITHS, John Mark Ainsley. b 68. Man Univ BSc 90 MSc 91 PGCE 92 Nottm Univ PhD 15. Ripon Coll Cuddesdon BA 97. **d** 98 **p** 99. Min Can Bangor 98–01; P-in-c Denio w Abererch 01–02; V 02–05; Chapl Univ of Wales (Trin St Dav) 05–18; CMD Officer *St D* 05–18; Dir Faith, Order and Unity Ch in Wales from 18. *The Church in Wales, 2 Callaghan Square, Cardiff CF10 5BT* E: ainsleygriffiths@churchinwales.org.uk

GRIFFITHS, Mrs Linda Betty. b 48. Trin Coll Carmarthen CertEd 69 Gwent Coll of HE BEd 96 Open Univ MA 97. Mon Dioc Tr Scheme 05. **d** 06 **p** 11. NSM Newbridge *Mon* 06–10; NSM Risca 10–13; NSM Lower Islwyn 13–16; rtd 16; PtO *Mon* from 16. *19 Cromwell Road, Risca, Newport NP11 7AF* T: (01495) 270455 E: griff.l@btinternet.com

GRIFFITHS, Malcolm. b 47. St Alb Minl Tr Scheme. **d** 82 **p** 83. NSM Hemel Hempstead *St Alb* 82–86; C Bedc 87–96; TV Liskeard, St Keyne, St Pinnock, Morval etc *Truro* 87–96; V Landrake w St Erney and Botus Fleming 96–12; rtd 12. *12 Lowertown Close, Landrake, Saltash PL12 5DG*

GRIFFITHS, Margaret. *See* MacLACHLAN, Margaret

GRIFFITHS, Mrs Margarett. b 29. ATCL 47 LRAM 48. CA Tr Coll 50. **dss** 81 **d** 87. Hackington *Cant* 81–83; Ashford 84–89; Par Dn 87–89; rtd 89. *39 Newington Way, Craven Arms SY7 9PS* T: (01588) 673848

GRIFFITHS, Mark. b 68. Nottm Univ PhD 09. St Jo Coll Nottm 04. **d** 07 **p** 08. C Stoke Poges *Ox* 07–10; P-in-c Warfield 10–16; Tutor St Padarn's Inst from 17; Hd Children, Young People and Family Min Development Ch in Wales from 17;

Hd C and Lic Min Tr and Development from 18; PtO *Llan* from 17; *St As* from 19; *Ban* from 19; *St D* from 19; *Mon* from 19; *S & B* from 19. *83 Picca Close, Cardiff CF5 6XR* T: (029) 2056 3379 M: 07592-242303 E: mark.griffiths@stpadarns.ac.uk *or* revmarkgriff@hotmail.com

GRIFFITHS, Mark. *See* GRIFFITHS, David Mark

GRIFFITHS, Canon Martyn Robert. b 51. Nottm Univ BTh 74 St Martin's Coll Lanc PGCE 75. Kelham Th Coll 70. **d** 74 **p** 75. C Kings Heath *Birm* 74–77; C-in-c Elmdon Heath CD 77–79; TV Solihull 79–81; Asst Admin Shrine of Our Lady of Walsingham 81–85; V Oldham St Steph and All Martyrs *Man* 85–89; TR Swinton and Pendlebury 89–98; Hon Can Man Cathl 96–98; R Preston St Jo and St Geo *Blackb* 98–05; Hon Can Blackb Cathl 00–05; R Henley w Remenham *Ox* 05–18; rtd 18; PtO *Ox* from 18. *1 Southby Close, Cholsey, Wallingford OX10 9FQ* T: (01491) 659040 E: rector.hwr@btinternet.com

GRIFFITHS, Michael James. b 76. St Mellitus Coll BA 15. **d** 15 **p** 16. C Yateley *Win* 15–18; P-in-c E Win from 18. *All Saints' Rectory, 19 Petersfield Road, Winchester SO23 0JD* M: 07866-727146 E: officeeastwinchester@gmail.com

GRIFFITHS, Neil Timothy. b 62. Portsm Poly BSc 84 De Montfort Univ MSc 01. Qu Coll Birm 12. **d** 14 **p** 15. C Broom Leys *Leic* 14–18; P-in-c Colsterworth Gp *Linc* from 18. *The Rectory, 13A Back Lane, Colsterworth, Grantham NG33 5NJ* M: 07879-620041 E: neilgriffiths01@btinternet.com

GRIFFITHS, Neville. b 39. Univ of Wales BA 63. St D Coll Lamp LTh 66. **d** 66 **p** 67. C Newport St Mark *Mon* 66–68; C Cardiff St Jo *Llan* 68–70; Chapl Greystoke Coll Carl 70–76; C Greystoke w Matterdale *Carl* 70–75; TV Greystoke, Matterdale and Mungrisdale 75–76; Chapl Grey Coll Dur 76–81; C Croxdale *Dur* 76–81; R Didsbury Ch Ch *Man* 81–83; P-in-c Lowther and Askham *Carl* 83–84; R 84–88; V Guernsey St Matt *Win* 88–93; R Guernsey St Pierre du Bois 93–02; R Guernsey St Philippe de Torteval 93–02; Vice-Dean Guernsey 99–02; rtd 03; PtO *Dur* from 02; *Eur* from 17. *6 Howlcroft Villas, Neville's Cross, Durham DH1 4DU* T: 0191-386 4778 E: gtiff.nevboy@yahoo.co.uk

GRIFFITHS, Nigel Timothy. b 64. Sheff Univ BSc 86 Imp Coll Lon PhD 90. Wycliffe Hall Ox 13. **d** 15 **p** 16. C Southborough St Pet w Ch Ch and St Matt etc *Roch* 15–19; C Bidborough St Lawr and Southborough St Pet 19; C Southborough Ch Ch 19; C Reigate St Mary *S'wark* from 19. *Address temp unknown* M: 07879-427944 E: nigegriffiths@hotmail.com

GRIFFITHS, Mrs Pamela Verley. **d** 07 **p** 10. NSM Ebbw Vale *Mon* 07–13; NSM Upper Ebbw Valleys from 13. *221 Marine Street, Cwm, Ebbw Vale NP23 7TA* T: (01495) 371819

GRIFFITHS, Paul Edward. b 48. St Jo Coll Nottm 86. **d** 88 **p** 89. C Ipswich St Andr *St E* 88–92; P-in-c Tollerton *S'well* 92–00; P-in-c Plumtree 95–97; Ind Chapl and Dioc Adv on Ind Soc 97–00; V Hellesdon *Nor* 00–13; rtd 13; PtO *Leic* 13–15; *St E* from 15. *111 Colneis Road, Felixstowe IP11 9LH* E: revgriffiths@btinternet.com

GRIFFITHS, Ms Paula Whitmore Llewellyn. b 49. LMH Ox BA 71 MA 75 Anglia Ruskin Univ BA 09. Westcott Ho Cam 08. **d** 09 **p** 10. NSM Saffron Walden and Villages *Chelmsf* from 09. *Greatford Cottage, Stocking Green, Radwinter, Saffron Walden CB10 2SS* E: paula.greatford@btinternet.com

GRIFFITHS, Richard Barré Maw. b 43. CCC Ox BA 65 MA 69 St Jo Coll Dur BA 71. Cranmer Hall Dur. **d** 71 **p** 72. C Fulwood *Sheff* 71–74; Hon C Sheff St Jo 74–76; Fell Dept of Bibl Studies Sheff Univ 74–76; C Fulham St Matt *Lon* 76–78; P-in-c 78–83; R Chich St Pancras and St Jo 83–09; rtd 09. *24 Beechcroft, Humshaugh, Hexham NE46 4ON* E: richardgriff@clara.co.uk

GRIFFITHS, Prof Richard Mathias. b 35. K Coll Cam BA 57 MA 61 PhD 62 BNC Ox MA 66 FIL 91 FKC 95. Ox Min Course 89 SAOMC 96. **d** 97 **p** 98. Prof French K Coll Lon 90–00; NSM W Woodhay w Enborne, Hampstead Marshall etc *Ox* 97–00; NSM Llantrisant *Llan* 01–02; NSM Penarth and Llandough from 03. *Waltham House, Bradford Place, Penarth CF64 1AG* T: (029) 2070 7828 F: 2070 9699 E: richardgriffiths477@gmail.com

GRIFFITHS, The Ven Robert Herbert. b 53. Chich Th Coll 75. **d** 76 **p** 77. C Holywell *St As* 76–80; CF (TA) 79–87; P-in-c Gyffylliog *St As* 80–84; V Llanfair Dyffryn Clwyd 80–84; V Llanfair DC, Derwen, Llanelidan and Efenechtyd 84–88; Asst Dioc Youth Chapl 81–86; Dioc Youth Chapl 86–91; PV St As and Tremeirchion w Cefn 88–97; Chapl H M Stanley Hosp 88–97; Bp's Visitor and Dioc RE Adv *St As* 88–93; Chapl Glan Clwyd Distr Gen Hosp 93–97; V Llanrhos *St As* 97–09; TR Rhos-Cystennin 09–14; R Llandegla and Bryneglwys 14–18; Can St As Cathl 98–18; AD Llanrwst 01–09; Chapl NW Wales NHS Trust 97–18; Adn Wrexham *St As* 14–18; rtd 18; PtO *Ban* from 18. *26 St Anne's Gardens, Llandudno LL30 1SD* T: (01492) 584890

GRIFFITHS, Robert James. b 52. Nottm Univ BTh 82. St Jo Coll Nottm 79. **d** 82 **p** 83. C Kettering St Andr *Pet* 82–85; C Collier Row St Jas and Havering-atte-Bower *Chelmsf* 86–89; R High Ongar w Norton Mandeville 89–97; R Ilmington w Stretton-on-Fosse etc *Cov* 97–99; V Newport *Chelmsf* 99–03; V Newport and Widdington 03–06; PtO *Ely* 09–10; R Horringer *St E* 10–15; rtd 15. *31 Castle View Gardens, Westham, Pevensey BN24 5HP* T: (01323) 461511 E: r.griffiths45@btinternet.com

GRIFFITHS, Roger Michael. b 47. Wycliffe Hall Ox 83. **d** 86 **p** 87. Min Can St D Cathl 86–88; V Pen-boyr 88–94; V Fishguard w Llanychar and Pontfaen w Morfil etc 94–03. *Nevern Cottage, 10 Feidr Gongol, Fishguard SA65 9BA* T: (01348) 218073

GRIFFITHS, Sarah. *See* BICK, Sarah

GRIFFITHS, Canon Shane Owen. b 63. Ripon Coll Cuddesdon 01. **d** 04 **p** 04. C Icknield *Ox* 04–07; P-in-c Mullion *Truro* 07–16; P-in-c Cury and Gunwalloe 07–16; V Mullion and Cury w Gunwalloe from 16; Hon Can Truro Cathl from 18. *The Vicarage, Nansmellyon Road, Mullion, Helston TR12 7DH* T: (01326) 240325 E: shaneowengriffiths@yahoo.co.uk

GRIFFITHS, The Ven Shirley Thelma. b 48. Univ of Wales (Ban) CertEd 69 Open Univ BA 83 Coll of Ripon & York St Jo MA 01. St Deiniol's Hawarden 79. **d** 82 **p** 95. NSM Dyserth and Trelawnyd and Cwm *St As* 82–91; RE Officer 89–95; Min Can St As Cathl 91–95; P-in-c The Cowtons *Ripon* 95–02; RE Adv 95–02; V Abergele *St As* 02–08; V Abergele and St George 08–10; Adn Wrexham 10–13; R Llandegla 10–11; V Bryneglwys 11; R Llandegla and Bryneglwys 11–13; rtd 13; PtO *Dur* from 14. *The Gables, 22 Greenways, Sunnybrow, Crook DL15 0LX* T: (01388) 747035 E: shirleytgriffiths@gmail.com

GRIFFITHS, Canon Simon Mark. b 62. Ch Ch Coll Cant BA 84 Kent Univ MA 95. Chich Th Coll. **d** 87 **p** 88. C Cardiff St Jo *Llan* 87–91; Sub Chapl HM Pris Cardiff 87–91; Chapl and Succ Roch Cath 91–96; Chapl Univ Coll Chich 96–01; V Sheff St Matt 01–11; TR Cen Swansea *S & B* 11–16; Can Prec Truro Cathl from 16. *52 Daniell Road, Truro TR1 2DA* T: (01872) 450779 E: simongriffiths@trurocathedral.org.uk

GRIFFITHS, Stephen David (Griff). b 70. Oak Hill Th Coll BA 96 Trin Coll Bris. **d** 00 **p** 01. C Cranleigh *Guildf* 00–04; TV Thetford *Nor* 04–10; Chapl Cam Univ Hosps NHS Foundn Trust 10–17; Chapl W Suffolk NHS Foundn Trust from 17. *89 Sycamore Drive, Bury St Edmunds IP32 7PW* T: (01284) 712704 M: 07802-224140 E: revgriff70@gmail.com *or* stephen.griffiths@wsh.nhs.uk

GRIFFITHS, Stephen Robert. b 78. Oak Hill Th Coll BA 00 Anglia Poly Univ MA 05. Ridley Hall Cam 02. **d** 04 **p** 05. C Normanton *Derby* 04–08; P-in-c Moresby *Carl* 08–13; RD Calder 12–13; TR Cherwell Valley *Ox* 13–18; AD Bicester and Islip 14–18; TR Oakham, Ashwell, Braunston, Brooke, Egleton etc *Pet* from 18. *All Saints' Vicarage, 2 Vicarage Road, Oakham LE15 6EG* T: (01572) 724007 M: 07504-320597 E: steph78griff@hotmail.com

GRIFFITHS, Mrs Susan Angela. b 61. St Jo Coll Nottm BTh 94. **d** 94 **p** 95. C Ingrow w Hainworth *Bradf* 94–98; V Wyke 98–03; C Buttershaw St Paul 03–10; C Silsden 10–14; *Leeds* from 14; RD S Craven *Bradf* 10–14; AD Keighley *Leeds* 14–16. *The Vicarage, Briggate, Silsden, Keighley BD20 9JS* T: (01535) 652204 E: susan.griffiths@leeds.anglican.org

GRIFFITHS, Canon Sylvia Joy. b 50. Gipsy Hill Coll of Educn CertEd 71. St Jo Coll Nottm 85. **dss** 86 **d** 87 **p** 94. Woodthorpe *S'well* 86–90; Par Dn 87–90; Min Bestwood/Rise Park LEP 90–94; Team Dn Bestwood 90–94; TR 94–99; P-in-c Sherwood 99–01; V 01–16; Hon Can S'well Minster 04–11; rtd 16; PtO *S'well* from 17. *2 Islay Close, Arnold, Nottingham NG5 8FL* T: 0115-920 8090 E: sylvia.griffiths1@outlook.com

GRIFFITHS, Timothy James. b 60. Edge Hill Coll of HE BEd 92. All SS Cen for Miss & Min 17. **d** 19. C Clubmoor *Liv* from 19. *1 Westonby Court, Ashton-in-Makerfield, Wigan WN4 8WB* M: 07894-051153 E: tgriffiths30@sky.com

GRIFFITHS, Canon Tudor Francis Lloyd. b 54. Jes Coll Ox BA 76 MA 81 Wycliffe Hall Ox BA 78 MA 81 Leeds Univ PhD 99. Wycliffe Hall Ox 76. **d** 79 **p** 80. C Brecon w Battle *S & B* 79–81; Min Can Brecon Cathl 79–81; C Swansea St Mary w H Trin 81–83; R Llangattock and Llangynidr 83–88; CMS Uganda 89–95; C Newton St Pet *S & B* 96; Dioc Missr *Mon* 96–03; V Goldcliffe and Whitson and Nash 96–98; TV Magor 98–03; TR Hawarden *St As* 03–11; Can Cursal St As Cathl 05–08; Chan St As Cathl 08–11; R Cheltenham St Mary w St Matt *Glouc* 11–12; R Cheltenham St Mary w St Matt and St Luke 12–17; AD Cheltenham 11–17; Sen Interim Min from 17; Hon Can Glouc Cathl from 13. *35 St Mary's Square, Gloucester GL1 2QT* M: 07718-906066 E: tgriffiths@glosdioc.org.uk

GRIFFITHS, William Thomas Gordon. b 48. York Univ BA 70 Fitzw Coll Cam BA 79. Ridley Hall Cam 78. **d** 80 **p** 81. C Dulwich St Barn *S'wark* 80–83; C Egglescliffe *Dur* 83–85; Ind Chapl 85–90; V Stockton St Jas 90–98; NSM Leamington Hastings and Birdingbury *Cov* 98–03; NSM Grandborough w Willoughby and Flecknoe 98–03; NSM Leam Valley 03–06; PtO from 06. *24 Park Road, Rugby CV21 2QH* T: (01788) 547815 E: wtg.griffiths@btopenworld.com

GRIGG, Deborah Ann. b 56. R Holloway Coll Lon BA 79 Kingston Poly PGCE 80. SWMTC 09. **d** 12 **p** 14. C Liskeard and St Keyne *Truro* 12–13; C Bodmin w Lanhydrock and Lanivet 13–16; Public Preacher from 16; TV Redruth w Lanner and Treleigh from 19. *2 The Old Orchard, Trewirgie Road, Redruth TR15 2SX* M: 07742-865618 E: deb@redruthchurch.org.uk

GRIGG, Robin Harold. b 44. **d** 07 **p** 08. NSM St Mewan w Mevagissey and St Ewe *Truro* 07–15; Chapl R Cornwall Hosps Trust 07–11; PtO *Truro* from 15. *33 Tregolls Lodge, St Clements Hill, Truro TR1 1GW* E: robingrigg124@btinternet.com

GRIGG, Simon James. b 61. Warwick Univ BA 82 MA 83 Southn Univ BTh 90. Chich Th Coll 87. **d** 90 **p** 91. C Cowley St Jas *Ox* 90–94; C W Hampstead St Jas *Lon* 94–95; V Munster Square Ch Ch and St Mary Magd 95–06; R Covent Garden St Paul from 06. *Flat 4, 19 Bedford Street, London WC2E 9HP* T: (020) 3509 9374 M: 07958-472568 E: simon.grigg@btopenworld.com

GRIGGS, Alan Peter. b 71. St Jo Coll Nottm. **d** 15 **p** 16. NSM Derby St Barn 15–18; NSM Fenny Bentley, Thorpe, Tissington, Parwich etc from 18. *4 Ravenscourt Road, Derby DE22 4DL* T: (01332) 361534 M: 07804-735556 E: alandeut6@gmail.com

GRIGGS, Canon Alan Sheward. b 33. Trin Hall Cam BA 56 MA 60. Westcott Ho Cam 58. **d** 60 **p** 61. C Arnold *S'well* 60–63; Succ S'wark Cathl 63–66; Ind Chapl 66–71; C Leeds H Trin *Ripon* 71–81; V 81–90; Soc and Ind Adv 71–81; Hon Can Ripon Cathl 84–98; Soc Resp Officer 91–98; rtd 98; PtO *Ripon* 98–14; *Leeds* from 14. *32 St Chad's Avenue, Leeds LS6 3QF* T: 0113-275 8100 E: alangriggs32@gmail.com

GRIGGS, Mrs Anthea Mary. b 37. Homerton Coll Cam TCert 57 New Coll Edin BA 86. SAOMC. **d** 00 **p** 01. NSM Sunningdale *Ox* 00–05; LtO *Edin* from 06. *8/1 Rattray Drive, Edinburgh EH10 5TH* T: 0131-447 2448 E: antheagriggs@me.com

⚑**GRIGGS, The Rt Revd Ian Macdonald.** b 28. Trin Hall Cam BA 52 MA 56. Westcott Ho Cam. **d** 54 **p** 55 **c** 87. C Portsea St Cuth *Portsm* 54–59; Dioc Youth Chapl *Sheff* 59–64; Bp's Dom Chapl 59–64; V Sheff St Cuth 64–71; V Kidderminster St Mary *Worc* 71–82; Hon Can Worc Cathl 77–84; TR Kidderminster St Mary and All SS, Trimpley etc 82–84; Preb Heref Cathl 84–94; Adn Ludlow 84–87; P-in-c Tenbury St Mich 84–87; Suff Bp Ludlow 87–94; rtd 94; Hon Asst Bp Carl from 94. *Rookings, Patterdale, Penrith CA11 0NP* T: (01768) 482064 E: ian.griggs@virgin.net

GRIGSON, Preb Richard John Stephen. b 60. Man Univ BA 83. Qu Coll Birm 86. **d** 88 **p** 89. C W Bromwich St Fran *Lich* 88–92; V Smallthorne 92–14; P-in-c Brown Edge 05–14; V Stafford St Mary and Marston from 14; V Stafford St Chad from 14; Preb Lich Cathl from 11. *The Vicarage, Victoria Terrace, Stafford ST16 3HA* T: (01785) 223600 E: richard.grigson@staffordchurches.uk

GRIMLEY, The Very Revd Robert William. b 43. Ch Coll Cam BA 66 MA 70 Wadh Coll Ox BA 68 MA 76 UWE Hon DLitt 04 Bris Univ Hon LLD 09. Ripon Hall Ox 66. **d** 68 **p** 69. C Radlett *St Alb* 68–72; Chapl K Edw Sch Birm 72–84; Hon C Moseley St Mary *Birm* 72–84; V Edgbaston St Geo 84–97; Dean Bris 97–09; rtd 09; PtO *Ox* from 10. *88 Old High Street, Headington, Oxford OX3 9HW* T: (01865) 308219 E: robertgrimley88@gmail.com

GRIMSBY, Suffragan Bishop of. *See* COURT, The Rt Revd David Eric

GRIMSTER, Barry John. b 49. Ex Univ BA 70. Trin Coll Bris 72. **d** 74 **p** 75. C S Lambeth St Steph *S'wark* 74–77; C New Malden and Coombe 77–82; P-in-c Deptford St Jo 82–84; V Deptford St Jo w H Trin 84–89; V Woking St Pet *Guildf* 89–01; TR 02–13; rtd 13; PtO *Ex* from 15. *16 Littlefield, Bishopsteignton, Teignmouth TQ14 9SG* T: (01626) 870921 E: bjgrimster@live.co.uk

GRIMWOOD, Canon David Walter. b 48. Lon Univ BA 70 K Coll Lon BD 73 AKC 73. **d** 74 **p** 75. C Newc St Geo 74–78; C Whorlton 78–80; TV Totton *Win* 80–93; Adv to Coun for Soc Resp Roch and Cant 93–02; Chief Exec Ch in Soc Roch and Cant 02–09; Hon Can Roch Cathl 97–09; PtO *Cant* from 09; *Roch* from 12. *56 Postley Road, Maidstone ME15 6TR* T: (01622) 764625 M: 07960-369681 E: d.grimwood@zedakah.co.uk *or* dwgrimwood@gmail.com

GRINDROD (née UTTIN), Suzanne. b 72. Trin Coll Bris 09. **d** 11 **p** 12. C Lydney *Glouc* 11–15; P-in-c Ashchurch and Kemerton from 15. *The Rectory, Northleach, Cheltenham GL54 3HL* E: revsuttin@hotmail.co.uk

GRINDVOLL, Morten. b 92. Norwegian Sch of Th BA 14. Westcott Ho Cam 15. **d** 17 **p** 18. C Ch the King *Newc* 17–18. *c/o Bjerregaards Gate 56G, 0174 Oslo, Norway* T: (0047) 9570 9902 M: 07936-555910 E: morten.grindvoll@hotmail.com

GRINHAM, Julian Clive. b 39. Birkbeck Coll Lon BA 65. Oak Hill Th Coll 79. **d** 81 **p** 82. C Blackb Ch Ch w St Matt 81–83; Nat Sec Pathfinders CPAS 83–89; Dir CYPECS 89–94; V Normanton *Derby* 94–00; rtd 00; PtO *Nor* 01–17; *Roch* from 17. *104 Ralph Perring Court, Stone Park Avenue, Beckenham BR3 3LX* T: (020) 3105 2668 E: grinham@pobroadband.co.uk

GRINSTED, Richard Anthony. b 43. Leic Univ BSc 65. Oak Hill Th Coll 67. **d** 70 **p** 71. C Egham *Guildf* 70–73; C Woodford Wells *Chelmsf* 73–76; P-in-c Havering-atte-Bower 76–84; R Ditton *Roch* 84–94; R Chulmleigh *Ex* 94–96; R Chawleigh w Cheldon 94–96; R Wembworthy w Eggesford 94–96; R Chulmleigh, Chawleigh w Cheldon, Wembworthy etc 96–00; rtd 00. *Stone House, Village Road, Christow, Exeter EX6 7NF* T: (01647) 252653

GRISCOME, David. b 47. Oak Hill Th Coll BA 88 TCD Div Sch 89. **d** 89 **p** 90. C Glendermott *D & R* 89–91; I Clondehorkey w Cashel 91–95; I Mevagh w Glenalla 91–95; Bp's C Calry *K, E & A* 95–97; I 97–00; Dean Elphin and Ardagh 99–04; I Sligo w Knocknarea and Rosses Pt 99–04; PtO *Cant* 04–06; I Convoy w Monellan and Donaghmore *D & R* 06–13; Bp's Dom Chapl 07–13; rtd 13; Hon C Clondevaddock w Portsalon and Leatbeg *D & R* from 16. *Keida, 15 Birchill Upper, Creeslough, Letterkenny, Co Donegal, Republic of Ireland* T: (00353) (74) 913 8395 E: keida@eircom.net

GROARKE, The Ven Nicola Jane. b 62. Lanc Univ BA 84. Ridley Hall Cam. **d** 00 **p** 01. C Balham Hill Ascension *S'wark* 00–08; V Canonbury St Steph *Lon* 08–14; Adn Dudley *Worc* from 14. *15 Worcester Road, Droitwich WR9 8AA* T/F: (01905) 773301 E: ngroarke@cofe-worcester.org.uk

GROOCOCK, Christopher John. b 59. Cardiff Univ MTh 12. St Jo Coll Nottm LTh 92. **d** 92 **p** 93. C Shawbury *Lich* 92–95; V Hengoed w Gobowen 95–00; CF 00–16; P-in-c Ashington *Newc* from 16. *Holy Sepulchre Vicarage, Wansbeck Road, Ashington NE63 8HZ* T: (01661) 886638 E: chrisgroocock@hotmail.com

GROOCOCK, Craig Ronald. Open Univ BA 11. WMMTC 03. **d** 05 **p** 06. C Kenilworth St Nic *Cov* 05–08; P-in-c Harbury and Ladbroke 08–19; AD Southam 11–15; V Shottery St Andr from 19. *St Andrew's Vicarage, Church Lane, Shottery, Stratford-upon-Avon CV37 9HQ* M: 07811-395169 E: kankudai43@aol.co.uk

GROOM, The Ven Susan Anne. b 63. Univ of Wales BA 85 Hughes Hall Cam MPhil 86 Lon Bible Coll MA 94 Open Univ MPhil 00 Dur Univ DThM 16. St Jo Coll Nottm 94. **d** 96 **p** 97. C Harefield *Lon* 96–99; C Eastcote St Lawr 99–01; P-in-c Yiewsley 01–03; V 03–07; Dir Lic Min Kensington Area 07–09; P-in-c Henlow and Langford *St Alb* 09–16; Asst Dir of Ords 09–11; Dir of Ords 11–16; Adn Wilts *Sarum* from 16; Can and Preb Sarum Cathl from 16. *Southbroom House, London Road, Devizes SN10 1LT* T: (01722) 438662 *or* (01380) 738097 E: adwilts@salisbury.anglican.org

GROOMBRIDGE, Jeremy Carl. b 55. SEITE 13. **d** 15 **p** 16. NSM Sanderstead *S'wark* from 15. *Lothlorien, 7 Callow Field, Purley CR8 4DU* T: (020) 8668 7795 M: 07590-262866 E: jeremy@sanderstead-parish.org.uk

GROOMBRIDGE, Mrs Sonia Elizabeth. b 58. NTMTC. **d** 12 **p** 13. OLM Hornchurch St Andr *Chelmsf* from 12. *300 Goodwood Avenue, Hornchurch RM12 6DH* T: (01708) 440585 E: segroombridge@gmail.com

GROSSCURTH, Stephen. b 55. Sarum & Wells Th Coll 81. **d** 84 **p** 85. C Southport H Trin *Liv* 84–87; C Amblecote *Worc* 87–89; V Walton St Jo *Liv* 89–95; Chapl Univ Hosp of S Man NHS Foundn Trust 95–12; rtd 12. *68 Lincoln Close, Woolston, Warrington WA1 4LU* T: (01925) 821124

GROSSE, Anthony Charles Bain. b 30. Oak Hill Th Coll 58. **d** 61 **p** 62. C Chislehurst Ch Ch *Roch* 61–65; C Washfield *Ex* 65–71; TV Washfield, Stoodleigh, Withleigh etc 71–73; R Hemyock 73–86; P-in-c Clayhidon 76–86; R Hemyock w Culm Davy and Clayhidon 87–93; R Hemyock w Culm Davy, Clayhidon and Culmstock 93–96; rtd 96; PtO *Ex* from 98. *8 Fore Street, Bampton, Tiverton EX16 9ND* T: (01398) 331981 E: tony.grosse@btinternet.com

GROSSE, Peter George. b 43. St Steph Ho Ox 02. **d** 03 **p** 04. NSM Reading St Matt *Ox* 03–06; NSM Tilehurst St Geo and St Mary 06–12; PtO from 12. *18 Rangewood Avenue, Reading RG30 3NN* T: 0118-959 4573 E: revdpetergrosse@talktalk.net

GROSSE, Canon Richard William. b 52. Mid Essex Tech Coll LLB 73 Solicitor 77. Ridley Hall Cam 86. **d** 88 **p** 89. C Soham *Ely* 88–91; C Bedale *Ripon* 91–93; C-in-c Thornton Watlass w Thornton Steward 91–93; V Barton and Manfield w Cleasby 93–95; V Barton and Manfield and Cleasby w Stapleton 95–99; R Keelby Gp *Linc* 99–04; R Callander *St And* from 04; R Aberfoyle from 04; Syn Clerk from 15; Can St Ninian's Cathl Perth from 15. *St Mary's Rectory, Main Street, Aberfoyle, Stirling FK8 3UJ* T/F: (01877) 382887 E: richard_grosse@hotmail.com

GROSU, Iosif. b 60. Iasi Univ BTh 92. RC Inst Iasi. **d** 89 **p** 89. In RC Ch 89–93; C Darlington St Cuth *Dur* 96–99; C Stockton St Jo and Stockton St Jas 99–02; TV Ch the K 02–08; P-in-c Purston cum S Featherstone *Wakef* 08–09; P-in-c Featherstone 08–09; V 09–14; *Leeds* from 14. *St Thomas's House, 32 Victoria Street, Featherstone, Pontefract WF7 5EZ* T: (01977) 792280 E: iosifgrosu@btinternet.com

GROSVENOR, Royston Johannes Martin. b 47. K Coll Lon BD 70 AKC. **d** 71 **p** 72. C Pontesbury I and II *Heref* 71–75; C Bishopston *Bris* 75–79; P-in-c Croydon St Pet S End *Cant* 79–81; V Croydon St Pet 81–84; V Croydon St Pet *S'wark* 85–87; R Merstham and Gatton 87–97; V Tidenham w Beachley and Lancaut *Glouc* 97–11; P-in-c St Briavels w Hewelsfield 05–11; AD Forest S 04–09; rtd 11; PtO *Bris* from 12; *B & W* from 14. *75 King's Drive, Bishopston, Bristol BS7 8JQ* T: 0117-924 7919 E: royston.grosvenor@hotmail.co.uk

GROVE, Lynn. b 43. Lon Univ MB, BS 67. Cranmer Hall Dur 03. **d** 04 **p** 05. NSM Pickering w Lockton and Levisham *York* 04–11; NSM Helmsley 12–17; NSM Upper Ryedale 12–17; rtd 17; PtO *York* from 18. *Hillcrest, Newton-on-Rawcliffe, Pickering YO18 8QA* T: (01751) 475928 E: revlynn625@gmail.com

GROVER, Paul Anthony. b 53. St Mellitus Coll 15. **d** 17 **p** 18. C N Hinckford *Chelmsf* from 17. *Spring House, Cross End, Pebmarsh, Halstead CO9 2NU* T: (01787) 269223 E: paulgrover.pebmarsh@gmail.com

GROVES, Caroline Anne. b 41. **d** 05 **p** 06. OLM Norbiton *S'wark* 05–11; PtO from 11; *Lon* from 15. *16 Beaufort Road, Kingston upon Thames KT1 2TQ* T: (020) 8549 1585 E: sicaro@blueyonder.co.uk

GROVES, Elizabeth Ann. b 36. Bp Otter Coll 94. **d** 97 **p** 09. NSM Soberton w Newtown *Portsm* 97–01; NSM Botley, Durley and Curdridge 01–06; NSM Wickham 06; NSM Shedfield and Wickham 07–12; rtd 12; PtO *Portsm* from 12. *54 Privett Road, Gosport PO12 3SU* T: (023) 9258 6168 E: rev.elizabeth@btinternet.com

GROVES, James Alan. b 32. CCC Cam BA 58 MA 62. Wells Th Coll 58. **d** 60 **p** 61. C Milton next Gravesend Ch Ch *Roch* 60–64; C Beckenham St Jas 64–66; V Orpington St Andr 66–98; rtd 98; PtO *Chich* from 98. *9 Wykeham Road, Hastings TN34 1UA* T: (01424) 200839

GROVES, Preb Jill. b 61. Univ Coll Lon BSc 82. St Jo Coll Nottm MA 93. **d** 93 **p** 94. C Tenbury Wells *Heref* 93–98; P-in-c Hope Bowdler w Eaton-under-Heywood 98–11; P-in-c Cardington 98–11; P-in-c Rushbury 98–11; Asst Chapl St Mich Hospice Hereford from 11; Preb Heref Cathl from 09. *St Michael's Hospice, Bartestree, Hereford HR1 4HA* T: (01432) 851000 E: jill@grovesfamily.co.uk

GROVES, Justin Simon John. b 69. Lon Bible Coll BA 93. Ridley Hall Cam 00. **d** 02 **p** 03. C Glouc St Cath 02–05; C Newport St Paul *Mon* 05–07; P-in-c 07–17; P-in-c Newport Maesglas St Paul w St Steph and H Trin from 17; AD Newport from 16. *52 Oakfield Road, Newport NP20 4LX* T: (01633) 842317 E: justtherev@gmail.com

GROVES, Canon Peter John. b 70. New Coll Ox BA 92 MA 96 DPhil 96. Westcott Ho Cam 95. **d** 97 **p** 98. C Leigh-on-Sea St Marg *Chelmsf* 97–99; Lib Pusey Ho 99–01; Asst Chapl and Tutor Keble Coll Ox 01–02; Chapl and Fell BNC Ox 02–06; Hon C Ox St Mary Magd 01–04; P-in-c 05–13; V from 13; Hon Can Ch Ch from 16. *15 Beaumont Street, Oxford OX1 2NA* T: (01865) 247836 E: peter.groves@theology.ox.ac.uk

GROVES, Canon Philip Neil. b 62. Man Univ BA 84 Birm Univ PhD 10. St Jo Coll Nottm 86. **d** 88 **p** 89. C Holbeck *Ripon* 88–91; CMS 91–99; Lect St Phil Th Coll Kongwa Tanzania 93–98; Hon Can Mpwapwa from 98; TV Melton Mowbray *Leic* 99–05; Listening Process Facilitator on Human Sexuality Angl Communion 06–09; Project Dir for Continuing Indaba 09–16; PtO *Ox* 15–16; C Wychert Vale from 16. *7 Badgers Rise, Stone, Aylesbury HP17 8RR* T: (01296) 748390 M: 07875-438244 E: drphilgroves@gmail.com

GROVES, Robert John. b 42. Trin Coll Bris 74. **d** 76 **p** 77. C Norwood St Luke *S'wark* 76–79; P-in-c Clapham Park All SS 79–86; V Anerley *Roch* 86–95; TV Canford Magna *Sarum* 95–98; TR Tollington *Lon* 98–02; rtd 02; PtO *Cant* 02–09; *Roch* 02–15; *Chich* from 15. *23 Ramsay Hall, 9-13 Byron Road, Worthing BN11 3HN*

GRUBB, Greville Alexander (Alex). b 36. Saltley Tr Coll Birm CertEd 60. St Jo Coll Nottm 72. **d** 74 **p** 75. C Rushden w Newton Bromswold *Pet* 74–77; Chapl St D Coll Llandudno 77–89; Chapl Casterton Sch Lancs 90–96; rtd 96; PtO *Blackb* 96–11; *Bradf* 02–14; *Leeds* 14–16; *Chich* from 15. *5 Cambridge Lodge, 10 Southey Road, Worthing BN11 3HT* T: (01903) 368580

GRUMBALL, Kevin. b 67. St Steph Ho Ox. **d** 11 **p** 12. NSM Temple Grafton w Binton *Cov* 11–15; NSM Exhall w Wixford 11–15; NSM Salford Priors 11–15; NSM Heart of England 15–19; NSM Vale and Cotswold Edge *Glouc* from 19. *Stone Croft, Ardens Grafton, Alcester B49 6DR*

GRUNDY, Anthony Brian. b 36. Pemb Coll Cam BA 62 MA 87. Ridley Hall Cam 61. **d** 63 **p** 64. C Hatcham St Jas *S'wark* 63–66; C Margate H Trin *Cant* 66–68; C Brixton Hill St Sav *S'wark* 68–70; V Assington *St E* 70–76; TV Much Wenlock w Bourton *Heref* 76–81; TV Wenlock 81–82; TR 82–88; RD Condover 86–88; R Burghfield *Ox* 88–02; rtd 02; PtO *Chich* from 03. *18 Victoria Court, Henley-on-Thames RG9 1XG*

GRUNDY, Canon Christopher John. b 49. ACA 72 FCA 79. Trin Coll Bris 74. **d** 77 **p** 78. C Maidstone St Luke *Cant* 77–81; Argentina 81–82; Chile 82–84; PtO *Guildf* 84–95; C Seale 95; NSM Guildf Ch Ch w St Martha-on-the-Hill 96–99; C Shere, Albury and Chilworth 99–06; TV Drypool *York* 06–12; rtd 12; PtO *Guildf* from 16; Hon Can Wusasa Nigeria from 03. *The Lyttons, Elstead Road, Seale, Farnham GU10 1HZ* E: chris@grundy.org.uk

GRUNDY, Judith Michal Towers Mynors. b 54. Lady Spencer Chu Coll of Educn CertEd 76 Ox Univ BEd 77. Trin Coll Bris 85. **d** 93 **p** 94. NSM Kensal Rise St Mark and St Martin *Lon* 93–95; NSM Snettisham w Ingoldisthorpe and Fring *Nor* 95–04; R Denver and Ryston w Roxham etc *Ely* from 04. *The Rectory, Ryston Road, Denver, Downham Market PE38 0DP* T: (01366) 383226

GRUNDY, Canon Malcolm Leslie. b 44. Open Univ BA 76 Leeds Univ PhD 14. St Boniface Warminster AKC 68. **d** 69 **p** 70. C Doncaster St Geo *Sheff* 69–72; Ind Chapl 72–80; Dir of Educn *Lon* 80–86; TR Huntingdon *Ely* 86–91; Hon Can Ely Cathl 88–94; Dir Avec 91–94; Adn Craven *Bradf* 94–05; Dir Foundn for Ch Leadership 05–09; rtd 09; PtO *York* from 09. *11 Givendale Grove, York YO10 3QF* T: (01904) 422999 M: 07950-816641 E: mlgweg@gmail.com

GRUNDY, Paul. b 55. BD 77 AKC. Linc Th Coll 79. **d** 80 **p** 81. C Ryhope *Dur* 80–82; C Ferryhill 82–85; TV Cramlington *Newc* 85–87; TV Swinton and Pendlebury *Man* 87–90; V Wingate Grange *Dur* 90–95; R Willington and Sunnybrow 95–07; P-in-c Usworth 07–09; R 09–13; rtd 13; PtO *Dur* from 13. *14 Kellsway, Gateshead NE10 8NB* E: p-grundy@ntlworld.com

GRUNDY, Simon. b 80. St Jo Coll Dur BA 02. Cranmer Hall Dur 15. **d** 17 **p** 18. C Herrington, Penshaw and Shiney Row *Dur* from 17. *The Rectory, Bournmoor, Houghton le Spring DH4 6EX* E: simon_grundy@hotmail.com

GRÜNEBERG, Keith Nigel. *See* BEECH-GRÜNEBERG, Keith Nigel

GRÜNEWALD, Gottfried Johannes. b 38. Loyola Univ Chicago MPS 92. Th Faculty Frankfurt 66. **d** 69 **p** 69. Denmark 70–95; C Dunbar *Edin* 95–97; R Dollar *St And* 98–05; rtd 05. *Teglparken 8, 8860 Ulstrup, Denmark* T: (0045) 864 6341 E: grunewald@email.dk

GRYLLS, Canon Catherine Anne. b 70. **d** 00 **p** 01. C Hall Green St Pet *Birm* 00–04; P-in-c Balsall Heath St Paul 04–07; P-in-c Edgbaston SS Mary and Ambrose 04–07; P-in-c Balsall Heath and Edgbaston SS Mary and Ambrose 07–08; V 08–16; PtO 16–17; V Stirchley from 17; Warden of Readers from 17; AD Moseley 13–17; Hon Can Birm Cathl from 15. *18 Pineapple Grove, Birmingham B30 2TJ* T: 0121-443 1371 E: gryllsc@btinternet.com

GRYLLS, Canon Michael John. b 38. Qu Coll Cam BA 62 MA 66. Linc Th Coll 62. **d** 64 **p** 65. C Sheff Gillcar St Silas 64–67; C-in-c Dunscroft CD 67–70; V Herringthorpe 70–78; V Amport, Grateley, Monxton and Quarley *Win* 78–89; RD Andover 85–89; V Whitchurch w Tufton and Litchfield 89–03; Hon Can Win Cathl 01–03; rtd 03; PtO *Worc* from 04. *41 Church Street, Evesham WR11 1DY* T: (01386) 442086

GUBBINS, Andrew Martin. b 65. York Univ BA 86 Keele Univ 93. St Jo Coll Nottm LTh 93. **d** 96 **p** 97. C Harrogate St Mark *Ripon* 96–00; P-in-c Osmondthorpe St Phil 00–03; V Leeds All SS w Osmondthorpe 03–09; P-in-c Chippenham St Pet *Bris* from 09. *St Peter's Vicarage, 32 Lords Mead, Chippenham SN14 0LL* T: (01249) 448530 E: gubbinsrevs@sky.com

GUBBINS (née O'BRIEN), Mrs Mary Veronica. b 68. Leeds Univ BSc 90. St Jo Coll Nottm BTh 93. **d** 94 **p** 95. C Middleton St Mary *Ripon* 94–96; C Bilton 96–99; PtO 09–09; *Bris* 10–19; NSM By Brook from 19. *St Peter's Vicarage, 32 Lords Mead, Chippenham SN14 0LL* T: (01249) 448530

GUDGEON, Canon Michael John. b 40. Qu Coll Cam BA 63 MA 67. Chich Th Coll 65. **d** 66 **p** 67. C Kings Heath *Birm* 66–72; Asst Chapl K Edw Sch Birm 69–72; Chapl and Tutor Cuddesdon Coll 72–75; V Hawley H Trin *Guildf* 75–80; V Minley 75–80; Adult Educn Adv *Chich* 80–87; Can Res Portsm Cathl 87–90; Dioc Dir of Educn 87–90; V Hove St Thos *Chich* 90–93; TV Hove 93–94; Bp's Chapl *Eur* 94–98; Dir of Ords 94–97; Can Gib Cathl 96–06; P-in-c Worthing St Andr *Chich* 98–05; rtd 05; PtO *Chich* from 15; S'wark from 16; *Roch* from 16; *Eur* from 18. *36 Ariel Court, Essenden Road, Belvedere DA17 5EG* E: michaelgudgeon@aol.com

GUERNSEY, Dean of. *See* BARKER, The Very Revd Timothy Reed

GUEST, Miss Alexandra Jodie. b 92. Heythrop Coll Lon BA 14 Dur Univ MA 17. Ridley Hall Cam 15. **d** 17 **p** 18. C Waltham H Cross *Chelmsf* from 17. *15 Deer Park Way, Waltham Abbey EN9 3YN* T: (01992) 679332 M: 07393-203544 E: alexandrajguest@gmail.com

GUEST, David Andrew. b 61. Chich Th Coll BTh 92. **d** 92 **p** 93. C Prenton *Ches* 92–94; C Ches H Trin 94–97; Assoc P Douglas All SS and St Thos *S & M* 97–00; Dioc Communications Officer 97–00; Relig Adv Manx Radio 97–00; Bp's Dom Chapl *S & M* 98–00; Dioc Communications Officer *Chich* 00–09; C Hove 00–03; C Southwick 03–09; P-in-c Heathfield 09–13; V 13–16; TV Mortlake w E Sheen *S'wark* from 16. *Christ Church Vicarage, 17 Sheen Gate Gardens, London SW14 7PD* T: (020) 8876 5914 E: davidguest.christchurch@gmail.com

GUEST, Derek William. b 55. NOC 90. **d** 93 **p** 94. C Cheadle Hulme St Andr *Ches* 93–99; V 99–16; V Runcorn All SS w H Trin from 16; RD Frodsham from 18. *The Vicarage, 1 Highlands Road, Runcorn WA7 4PS* T: (01928) 572417 M: 07941-874259 E: revdguest@yahoo.co.uk

GUEST, Miss Elizabeth Judy. b 76. Qu Foundn Birm 16. **d** 18 **p** 19. C Oxhey All SS *St Alb* from 18. *14 The Hoe, Watford WD19 5AY* M: 07545-328187 E: lizzie_1976@hotmail.co.uk

GUEST, Ernest Anthony. b 64. NTMTC 99. **d** 02 **p** 03. C Gt Ilford St Jo *Chelmsf* 02–05; V Barkingside St Laur 05–13; P-in-c Tye Green w Netteswell 13–19; P-in-c Ashingdon w S Fambridge, Canewdon and Paglesham from 19. *35 Henry Crescent, Rochford SS4 1GU* T: (01702) 904558 M: 07810-516356 E: ernieguest@btinternet.com

GUEST, Canon Helen. b 54. Totley Thornbridge Coll CertEd 75 Nottm Univ MA 02. EMMTC 99. **d** 02 **p** 03. NSM Brimington *Derby* 02–05; C Hatton 05–07; P-in-c Killamarsh 07–13; C Barlborough and Renishaw 07–13; R Killamarsh and Renishaw from 13; RD Bolsover and Staveley 11–16; Hon Can Derby Cathl from 12. *The Rectory, Sheepcote Road, Killamarsh, Sheffield S21 1DU* T: 0114-248 2769 E: revsguest@btinternet.com *or* revshmguest@gmail.com

GUEST, John Andrew Kenneth. b 55. Univ of Wales (Lamp) BA 78. Wycliffe Hall Ox 78. **d** 80 **p** 81. C Eastwood *S'well* 80–84; TV Toxteth St Philemon w St Gabr and St Cleopas *Liv* 84–89; C Cranham Park *Chelmsf* 89–93; P-in-c Stanford-le-Hope w Mucking 93–03; R from 03. *The Rectory, The Green, Stanford-le-Hope SS17 0EP* T: (01375) 672271 E: gof4god@aol.com

GUEST, Michael. b 52. EMMTC. **d** 99 **p** 00. NSM Heath *Derby* 99–07; NSM Killamarsh and Barlborough and Renishaw 07–13. *The Rectory, Sheepcote Road, Killamarsh, Sheffield S21 1DU* T: 0114-248 2769 E: revsguest@btinternet.com *or* revshmguest@gmail.com

GUILDFORD, Bishop of. *See* WATSON, The Rt Revd Andrew John

GUILDFORD, Dean of. *See* GWILLIAMS, The Very Revd Dianna Lynn

GUILFORD, John Edward. b 50. S & M Dioc Tr Inst 94. **d** 99 **p** 00. OLM Lonan *S & M* 99–12; OLM Laxey 99–12; OLM Onchan, Lonan and Laxey 12–15; NSM Douglas St Geo and All SS 15–17; NSM Douglas St Ninian from 17. *Tremissory House, Strathallan Road, Douglas, Isle of Man IM2 4PN* T: (01624) 672001 M: 07624-353475 E: revjohnnyg@manx.net

GUILIANO, Zachary Morgan. b 86. Evangel Univ (USA) BA 09 Harvard Univ MDiv 12 St Jo Coll Cam PhD 16. Westcott Ho Cam 15. **d** 17 **p** 18. NSM Cambridge St Benedict *Ely* 17–19; C from 19. *130 Hulatt Road, Cambridge CB1 8TH* M: 07986-816854 E: zack@stbenetschurch.org

GUILLE, The Very Revd John Arthur. b 49. Southn Univ BTh 79. Sarum & Wells Th Coll 73. **d** 76 **p** 77. C Chandler's Ford *Win* 76–80; P-in-c Bournemouth St Jo 80–84; P-in-c Bournemouth St Mich 83–84; V Bournemouth St Jo w St Mich 84–89; R Guernsey St Andr 89–99; Adn Win 99–07; Can Res Win Cathl 99–07; Dean S'well 07–14; rtd 14; PtO *Win* from 14. *Pelerins, La Planque Road, St Martin, Guernsey GY4 6TH* T: (01481) 237168

GUILLEBAUD, Mrs Jette Margaret (Maggie). b 48. Ex Univ BA 70 UWE Hon MA 98 FRSA 95. Ripon Coll Cuddesdon 03. **d** 05 **p** 06. NSM Sarum Cathl 05–12; Asst Chapl Sarum Coll 10–12; Chapl Ch Ho *Sarum* from 12. *178 The Close, Salisbury SP1 2EZ* T: (01722) 411922 M: 07985-576739 E: maggieguillebaud@gmail.com

GUILLEBAUD, Canon Margaret Jean. b 43. Edin Univ BSc 66. Cranmer Hall Dur 79. **dss** 80 **d** 87 **p** 94. New Malden and Coombe *S'wark* 80–84; Carlton Colville w Mutford and Rushmere *Nor* 84–91; Par Dn 87–91; Par Dn Rodbourne Cheney *Bris* 91–94; C 94–95; CMS Rwanda 95–08; rtd 08; PtO *Birm* from 08; Can Res Byumba from 10. *7 Poplar Road, Dorridge, Solihull B93 8DD* T: (01564) 770113 E: mguillebaud@gmail.com

GUILLEMIN, Thierry Jean-Louis. b 62. Coll of Resurr Mirfield 08. **d** 01 **p** 01. In RC Ch 01–07; PtO *Wakef* 08–09; C Heckmondwike 09–11; C Liversedge w Hightown 09–11; P-in-c Wibsey St Paul *Bradf* 11–14; *Leeds* 14–17; V from 17. *St Paul's Vicarage, 42A Wibsey Park Avenue, Bradford BD6 3QA* T: (01274) 676359 M: 07778-577008 E: t.guillemin@btinternet.com

GUINNESS, Alexander. *See* GUINNESS, Graham Alexander

GUINNESS, Canon Garry Grattan. b 40. Em Coll Cam BA 64 MA 68. Ridley Hall Cam 64. **d** 66 **p** 67. C Wallington *S'wark* 66–69; C St Marylebone All So w SS Pet and Jo *Lon* 69–72; P-in-c Clifton H Trin, St Andr and St Pet *Bris* 72–79; V Watford St Luke *St Alb* 79–90; TR Worthing Ch the King *Chich* 90–05; Hon Can Kigeme from 02; rtd 05; PtO *Sarum* from 05. *37 Stowell Crescent, Wareham BH20 4PT* T: (01929) 550215 E: gguinness@talktalk.net

GUINNESS, Graham Alexander. b 60. Edin Th Coll 82. **d** 85 **p** 86. Dioc Youth Chapl *Mor* 85–88; C Elgin w Lossiemouth 85–88; Asst P Glas St Ninian 88–90; R Tighnabruaich *Arg* 90–91 and 94–99; R Dunoon 90–99; Miss to Seamen 90–99; R Fort William *Arg* from 99. *St Andrew's Rectory, Parade Road, Fort William PH33 6BA* T/F: (01397) 702979 E: ftwilliam@argyll.anglican.org *or* alexinness@ymail.com

GUINNESS, Canon Peter Grattan. b 49. Man Univ BSc 71 CertEd 73. St Jo Coll Nottm 80. **d** 82 **p** 83. C Normanton *Wakef* 82–87; V Fletchamstead *Cov* 87–91; V Lancaster St Thos *Blackb* 91–10; Hon Can Blackb Cathl 04–10; P-in-c Gillingham St Mark *Roch* 10–14; rtd 14; PtO *Roch* from 15. *56 Malvern Road, Gillingham ME7 4BB* E: peter.guinness@yahoo.co.uk

GUINNESS, Sarah Helen. b 76. Cant Ch Ch Univ Coll BSc 98. STETS 11. **d** 14 **p** 15. C Buckhurst Hill *Chelmsf* 14–18; P-in-c Brentford *Lon* from 18. *The Rectory, 3 The Butts, Brentford TW8 8BJ* T: (020) 8568 7442 E: sarah.guinness@gmx.com

GUISE, John Christopher. b 29. Cheltenham & Glouc Coll of HE MA 94 MRPharmS 51. WMMTC 80. **d** 83 **p** 84. NSM Alfrick, Lulsley, Suckley, Leigh and Bransford *Worc* 83–94; NSM Martley and Wichenford, Knightwick etc 94–00; PtO from 00. *Marsh Cottage, Leigh, Worcester WR6 5LE* T: (01886) 832336

GUISE, Stephen. b 48. Win Sch of Art BA 75. Chich Th Coll 85. **d** 87 **p** 88. C Bexhill St Pet *Chich* 87–90; TV Haywards Heath St Wilfrid 90–94; V Kirdford 94–97; Chapl Community of Servants of the Cross 97–01; P-in-c Amberley w N Stoke and Parham, Wiggonholt etc *Chich* 99–03; TV Bridport *Sarum* 03–07; rtd 07; PtO *Chich* 07–09; P-in-c Sidlesham from 09. *The Vicarage, Church Farm Lane, Sidlesham, Chichester PO20 7RE* T: (01243) 641237

GUITE, Ayodeji Malcolm. b 57. Pemb Coll Cam BA 80 MA 84 Newc Poly PGCE 82 Dur Univ PhD 93. Ridley Hall Cam 88. **d** 90 **p** 91. C Ely 90–93; TV Huntingdon 93–98; Chapl Anglia Poly Univ 98–03; Chapl Girton Coll Cam from 03. *Girton College, Cambridge CB3 0JG* T: (01223) 338999 E: mg320@cam.ac.uk

GUITE, Mrs Frances Clare. b 56. Leeds Univ BA 08. Coll of Resurr Mirfield 06. **d** 08 **p** 09. C Westleigh St Pet *Man* 08–11; C Westleigh St Paul 09–11; P-in-c Castleton Moor 11–16; V from 16; AD Heywood and Middleton from 16. *St Martin's Vicarage, Vicarage Road North, Rochdale OL11 2TE* T: (01706) 632353 M: 07791-328624 E: francesguite@yahoo.co.uk

GUITE, Canon Margaret Ann. b 53. Girton Coll Cam BA 74 MA 78 St Jo Coll Dur PhD 81. Cranmer Hall Dur 75. **dss** 79 **d** 87 **p** 94. Warlingham w Chelsham and Farleigh *S'wark* 79–82; Cherry Hinton St Jo *Ely* 82–86; Tutor Westcott Ho Cam 82–90; Tutor Wesley Ho Cam 87–90; NSM Ely 90–93; NSM Chettisham 90–93; NSM Prickwillow 90–93; NSM Huntingdon 93–99; V Fenstanton 99–06; V Hilton 99–06; RD Huntingdon 05–06; P-in-c Cambridge St Mark 06–15; TR Linton from 15; Hon Can Ely Cathl from 04. *The Rectory, 11A Joiners Road, Linton CB21 4NP* T: (01223) 327621 E: margaret.guite@icloud.com

GUIVER, George Paul Alfred. b 45. St Chad's Coll Dur BA 68. Cuddesdon Coll 71. **d** 73 **p** 74. C Mill End and Heronsgate w W Hyde *St Alb* 73–76; P-in-c Bishop's Frome *Heref* 76–82; P-in-c Castle Frome 76–82; P-in-c Acton Beauchamp and Evesbatch w Stanford Bishop 76–82; CR from 83; Superior CR 02–18; Lic to Offic *Wakef* 85–14; LtO *Leeds* from 14. *House of the Resurrection, Stocks Bank Road, Mirfield WF14 0BN* T: (01924) 483317 E: gguiver@mirfield.org.uk

GULL, William John. b 42. Ripon Hall Ox 63. **d** 65 **p** 66. C Worksop Priory *S'well* 65–69; C Newark St Mary 69–71; P-in-c Mansfield St Lawr 71–77; V 77–78; Chapl HM YOI Lowdham Grange 78–90; R Lambley *S'well* 78–91; V Sneinton St Cypr 91–99; rtd 99; PtO *S'well* 03–11. *37 Hazel Grove, Mapperley, Nottingham NG3 6DQ* T: 0115-920 8071 E: wjgull@btopenworld.com

GULLAND, John Robertson. b 46. Open Univ BA 76 Chelsea Coll Lon MA 82 Avery Hill Coll CertEd 70 ACIB. Oak Hill Th Coll 88. **d** 90 **p** 91. NSM Woodside Park St Barn *Lon* 90–92; LtO *S & M* 91–09; NSM Castletown 92–09; Chapl K Wm's Coll Is of Man 92–09; P-in-c Corfu *Eur* 09–12; PtO *S & M* from 13; Dir Studies from 14; PtO *Eur* from 18. *3 Snaefell House, Promenade, Port Erin, Isle of Man IM9 6LE* T: (01624) 834548 E: gulland@talk21.com

GULLIDGE, Philip Michael Nowell. b 60. Univ of Wales (Swansea) BSc 82 Univ of Wales (Cardiff) BD 93. St Mich Coll Llan 90. **d** 93 **p** 94. C Neath w Llantwit *Llan* 93–97; V Treharris w Bedlinog 97–03; V Treharris, Trelewis and Bedlinog 04–08; V Llantwit Fardre from 08. *The Vicarage, Church Village, Pontypridd CF38 1EP* T: (01443) 202538 E: philipgullidge@aol.com

GULLIFORD, Canon William Douglas FitzGerald. b 69. Selw Coll Cam BA 91 MA 95. Westcott Ho Cam. **d** 94 **p** 95. C Banstead *Guildf* 94–97; C Wilton Place St Paul *Lon* 97–00; Chapl Guildhall Sch of Music and Drama 97–01; P-in-c St Dunstan in the West 00–08; V 08–12; Gen Sec Angl and E Churches Assn 00–05; Bp's Chapl *Lon* 00–02; R St Mary le Strand w St Clem Danes 02–08; Bp's Chapl for E Orthodox Affairs 02–12; V Regent's Park St Mark from 12; Dioc Dir of Ords *Eur* from 03; Hon Can from 12; PtO from 03. *St Mark's Vicarage, 4 Regent's Park Road, London NW1 7TX* T: (020) 7485 6340 E: william.gulliford@london.anglican.org

GULLY, Mrs Carol Glenys. b 57. Coll of Ripon & York St Jo BEd 79. NOC 02. **d** 05 **p** 06. NSM Castleton Moor *Man* 05–09; NSM Kirkholt 09–10; Asst Chapl Pennine Acute Hosps NHS Trust 08–10; PtO *Portsm* 10–11; NSM Portsea St Cuth from 11; Asst Chapl Portsm Hosps NHS Trust 12–13; Chapl The Rowans Hospice from 13. *The Rectory, 27 Farlington Avenue, Cosham, Portsmouth PO6 1DF* T: (023) 9237 5145 *or* 9225 0001 E: revdcarolgully@gmail.com *or* carol.gully@rowanshospice.co.uk

GULLY, Canon Paul David. b 59. Shoreditch Coll Lon BEd 81. Trin Coll Bris BA 95. **d** 95 **p** 96. C Radcliffe *Man* 95–99; TV New Bury 99–05; V Oakenrod and Bamford 05–10; R Farlington *Portsm* from 10; Hon Can Ho Ghana from 17. *The Rectory, 27 Farlington Avenue, Cosham, Portsmouth PO6 1DF* T: (023) 9237 5145 E: paul@farlingtonparish.co.uk

GUMBEL, Jonathan Philip. b 82. Oriel Coll Ox BA 05. NTMTC 07. **d** 09 **p** 10. C Brighton St Pet *Chich* from 09. *9 St Peter's Place, Brighton BN1 4SA* T: (01273) 698182

GUMBEL, Nicholas Glyn Paul. b 55. Trin Coll Cam MA 76. Wycliffe Hall Ox MA 86. **d** 86 **p** 87. C Brompton H Trin w Onslow Square St Paul *Lon* 86–05; V 05–11; V Onslow Square and S Kensington St Aug from 11. *Holy Trinity Vicarage, 73 Princes Gate Mews, London SW7 2PP* T: (020) 7052 0263 *or* 7052 0264 F: 7589 3390 E: nicky.gumbel@htb.org.uk

GUNASEKERA, Nilanka Keith (Kit). b 72. Ridley Hall Cam 04. **d** 06 **p** 07. C Brentford *Lon* 06–09; P-in-c Clapham St Jas *S'wark* 09–15; V from 15. *The Vicarage, 8A West Road, London SW4 7DN* M: 07968-591695 E: kit.gunasekera2014@gmail.com

GUNDERSON, Ross. b 79. Westcott Ho Cam 13. **d** 15 **p** 16. C Dulwich St Barn *S'wark* 15–18; V Fulham St Etheldreda w St Clem *Lon* from 18; C Fulham All SS from 18. *St Etheldreda's Vicarage, Doneraile Road, London SW6 6EL* M: 07962-274381 E: gunderson_ross@hotmail.com

GUNN, Jeffrey Thomas. b 47. St Chad's Coll Dur BA 77 Kent Univ MA 95. Coll of Resurr Mirfield 77. **d** 79 **p** 80. C Prestbury *Glouc* 79–82; P-in-c Coldham, Elm and Friday Bridge *Ely* 82–87; V Larkfield *Roch* 87–94; P-in-c Leybourne 87–94; V Petts Wood 94–99; Dean Ballarat Australia 99–04; V Eastbourne St Sav and St Pet *Chich* 05–15; RD Eastbourne 10–15; rtd 15; PtO *Glouc* from 16. *4 Victoria Circus, Tewkesbury GL20 5GF* T: (01684) 290972

GUNN-JOHNSON, The Ven David Allan. b 49. Lambeth STh 85 MA 95. St Steph Ho Ox 79. **d** 81 **p** 82. C Oxhey St Matt *St Alb* 81–84; C Cheshunt 84–88; TR Colyton,

Southleigh, Offwell, Widworthy etc *Ex* 88–03; RD Honiton 90–96; Preb Ex Cathl 99–03; Adn Barnstaple 03–14; Warden of Readers 04–14; rtd 14; Hon PV Ex Cathl from 18. *12 Hylton Gardens, Exeter EX4 2QE* T: (01392) 496877 M: 07921-150428 E: dgunnjohnson549@btinternet.com

GUNNER, Canon Laurence François Pascal. b 36. Keble Coll Ox BA 59 MA 63. Wells Th Coll 59. **d** 61 **p** 62. C Charlton Kings St Mary *Glouc* 61–65; C Hemel Hempstead *St Alb* 65–69; Hd RE Adeyfield Secondary Modern Sch 67–69; Chapl Bloxham Sch 69–86; Chapl Tudor Hall Sch 70–84; Sen Chapl Marlborough Coll 86–96; Can Windsor 96–06; Can Steward 97–06; rtd 06; LtO *Mor* from 07; PtO *Eur* from 05. *Contin Mains, Contin, Strathpeffer IV14 9ES* T/F: (01997) 421996 M: 07836-369729 E: laurence@gunner.co.uk

GUNNER, Mrs Susanna Mary. b 58. St Jo Coll Dur BA 08 Anglia Ruskin Univ MA 10 SS Coll Cam PGCE 81. ERMC 05. **d** 08 **p** 09. Dioc Lay Development and Tr Co-ord *Nor* 07–16; C N Walsham and Edingthorpe 08–11; NSM 13–16; Bp's Chapl from 16; Dioc Spirituality and Discipleship Adv from 19; Hon Chapl from 16. *Bishop's House, Norwich NR3 1SB* T: (01603) 629001 *or* 614172 E: susanna.gunner@gmail.com *or* bishops.chaplain@dioceseofnorwich.org *or* susanna.gunner@dioceseofnorwich.org

GUNSTONE, Peter Wilfrid. b 77. Leeds Univ BA 99 St Jo Coll Dur BA 18. Wycliffe Hall Ox 15 Cranmer Hall Dur 16. **d** 19. C Inner Bradford and Outer Bradford Deaneries from 19. *35 Scarborough Road, Shipley BD18 3DW* M: 07932-792373 E: petegunstone@gmail.com

GUNTER, Benjamin Luke William. b 65. Coll of Ripon & York St Jo BEd 89. Cranmer Hall Dur 15. **d** 17 **p** 18. C Norton juxta Malton *York* from 17. *St Michael's House, Crambe, York YO60 7JR* M: 07902-670311 E: revbengunter@gmail.com

GUNTER, Timothy Wilson. b 37. Leeds Univ BA 59 St Jo Coll Cam BA 62 MA 66. Ridley Hall Cam 59. **d** 62 **p** 63. C Beverley Minster *York* 62–65; C Hornsea and Goxhill 65–70; V Silsden *Bradf* 70–80; V Sunninghill *Ox* 80–03; rtd 03; PtO *Worc* from 04. *2 Hillstone Court, Victoria Road, Malvern WR14 2TE* T: (01684) 899377 E: gunters@gmail.com

GUNTON, Helen Louise. b 71. Lanc Univ BA 93. Sarum Coll MA 17. **d** 17 **p** 18. NSM Jersey St Ouen w St Geo *Win* from 17. *Rosevale House, La Rue du Craslin, St Peter, Jersey JE3 7BU* T: (01534) 499950 M: 07700-339356 E: hlgunton@gmail.com

GURD, Brian Charles (Simon). b 44. Sarum & Wells Th Coll 72. **d** 74 **p** 75. OSP from 67; LtO *Win* 74–82; Prior Alton Abbey 79–82; C Shepherd's Bush St Steph w St Thos *Lon* 82–84; NSM Willesborough *Cant* 85–87; V Bethersden w High Halden 87–95; R Etchingham and V Hurst Green *Chich* 95–97; V Langney 97–01; R Yarm from 01–10; rtd 10; PtO *Chich* 11–15; *Leeds* from 15. *27 Jubilee Road, Askew, Bedale DL8 1FD* T: (01677) 427440 E: simongurd@btinternet.com

GURNER (formerly RAVEN), Mrs Margaret Ann. b 54. Westmr Univ BSc 76 City Univ MSc 87 Anglia Ruskin Univ BA 08. Ridley Hall Cam 03. **d** 05 **p** 06. C Woodhall Spa Gp *Linc* 05–08; P-in-c Cheveley Ely 08–12; P-in-c Wood Ditton w Saxon Street 08–12; P-in-c Kirtling 08–12; P-in-c Ashley w Silverley 08–12; rtd 12; PtO *B & W* 12–16; C Norton sub Hamdon, W Chinnock, Chiselborough etc 16–17; C Stoke sub Hamdon 16–17; C Odcombe, Brympton, Lufton and Montacute 16–17; C Ham Hill Villages from 17. *Oswalds, Church Street, Lopen, South Petherton TA13 5JX* M: 07765-216818 E: revgurner@btinternet.com

GURNEY, Miss Ann. b 27. Lambeth STh 92. Gilmore Ho 45. dss 54 **d** 87 **p** 94. Lewisham St Jo Southend *S'wark* 54–56; Warden Berridge Ho Coll of Educn 56–59; Prin Gilmore Ho 59–70; Bp's Adv for Lay Min *Lon* 70–87; rtd 87; Hon C Eltham H Trin *S'wark* 94–98; PtO 98–17. *3 Brecon Court, Greenacres, London SE9 5BG* T: (020) 8850 4083

GURNEY, Canon Dennis Albert John. b 31. Lon Coll of Div. **d** 67 **p** 68. C Boscombe St Jo *Win* 67–70; V Hurstbourne Tarrant and Faccombe 70–77; R Jersey St Ouen w St Geo 77–84; Hon Chapl Miss to Seafarers from 84; Chapl ICS UAE 84–01; Can Bahrain from 98; rtd 01; PtO *Ex* from 02; *B & W* from 02. *3 Stevens Cross Close, Sidford, Sidmouth EX10 9QJ* T: (01395) 515362 M: 07789-111226 E: d.gurney123@btinternet.com

GURNEY, Jean Elizabeth. *See* MAYHEW, Jean Elizabeth

GURR, Mrs Mary Sandra. b 42. SAOMC 95. **d** 98 **p** 99. C Easthampstead *Ox* 98–02; TV High Wycombe 02–09; rtd 09; Chapl Pipers Corner Sch 04–17; Chapl to the Homeless *Ox* from 11. *12 Navigation Way, Oxford OX2 6XW* T: (01865) 552010 M: 07745-601046 E: mary.gurr1@btinternet.com

GURR, Stephen John. b 72. Kent Univ BA 94. Trin Coll Bris MLitt 97. **d** 97 **p** 98. C Ore St Helen and St Barn *Chich* 97–00; C Goring-by-Sea 00–03; V Findon w Clapham and Patching 03–06; Chapl St Barn Ho Worthing from 07; Chapl Chestnut Tree Ho Arundel from 07; PtO *Chich* from 07. *c/o St Barnabas House, Titnore Lane, Worthing BN12 6NZ* T: (01903) 706374 E: stephen.gurr@stbh.org.uk

GUSSMAN, Canon Robert William Spencer Lockhart. b 50. Ch Ch Ox BA 72 MA 76. Coll of Resurr Mirfield BA 74. **d** 75 **p** 76. C Pinner *Lon* 75–79; C Northolt St Jos 79–81; P-in-c Sutton *Ely* 81–82; V 82–89; P-in-c Witcham w Mepal 81–82; R 82–89; RD Ely 86–89; V Alton St Lawr *Win* 89–02; Hon Can Win Cathl 99–02; rtd 02; PtO *Win* 02–10. *6A Patrick's Close, Liss GU33 7ER* T: (01730) 893545

GUTHRIE, Adrian Malcolm. b 57. Goldsmiths' Coll Lon BEd 80. Wycliffe Hall Ox 01. **d** 03 **p** 04. C Ickenham *Lon* 03–05; R 05–13; R Alcester Minster *Cov* from 13. *St Nicholas' Rectory, Old Rectory Garden, Alcester B49 5DB* E: rector@alcesterminster.org

GUTHRIE, Preb Nigel. b 60. Bris Univ BA 82 LRAM 78 ARCO 80 ARCM 81. Ripon Coll Cuddesdon BA 87 MA 91. **d** 88 **p** 89. C Cov St Jo 88–91; Chapl Cov Cathl 91–94; V Chellaston *Derby* 94–02; RD Melbourne 99–02; R Crediton, Shobrooke and Sandford etc *Ex* 02–18; RD Cadbury 13–18; V Ex St Dav from 18; Preb Ex Cathl from 10. *St David's Vicarage, 95 Howell Road, Exeter EX4 4LH* E: rev.guthrie@btinternet.com

GUTSELL, Canon David Leonard Nicholas. b 35. Sheff Univ BA 59. ALCD 61. **d** 61 **p** 62. C Clapham Common St Barn *S'wark* 61–65; V Upper Tulse Hill St Matthias 65–76; RD Clapham and Brixton 74–75; V Patcham *Chich* 76–93; Can and Preb Chich Cathl 89–00; V Polegate 93–00; rtd 00; C Peacehaven and Telscombe Cliffs *Chich* 01–05; C Southease 01–05; C Piddinghoe 01–05; PtO from 05. *6 Solway Avenue, Brighton BN1 8UJ* T: (01273) 554434 E: davidgutsell@googlemail.com

GUTSELL, Eric Leslie. b 44. Goldsmiths' Coll Lon TCert 65. Ox NSM Course 79. **d** 82 **p** 83. NSM Gt Faringdon w Lt Coxwell *Ox* 82–88; NSM Shrivenham w Watchfield and Bourton 82–99; Asst Chapl HM Pris Wormwood Scrubs 99–00; Chapl HM Pris Coldingley 00–03; Chapl HM Pris Erlestoke 03–04; rtd 04; PtO *Ox* 05–18. *54 Folly View Road, Faringdon SN7 7DH* T: (01367) 240886 E: eric.gutsell@gmail.com

GUTTERIDGE, David Frank. b 39. Man Univ BSc 61 Lon Inst of Educn PGCE 62 DipEd 67 Birkbeck Coll Lon MSc 73. WMMTC 82. **d** 85 **p** 87. NSM Droitwich *Worc* 85–87; NSM Droitwich Spa 87–93; C Shrawley, Witley, Astley and Abberley 93–98; Chapl Abberley Hall Sch *Worc* 93–97; Dioc Tertiary Educn Officer *Worc* 97–99; NSM Ombersley w Doverdale 98–99; TV Malvern Link w Cowleigh 99–02; rtd 02; PtO *Worc* from 12. *79 Tan House Lane, Malvern WR14 1LQ* T: (01886) 832627 M: 07962-129241 E: david@mlwc.co.uk

GUTTERIDGE, John. b 34. Oak Hill Th Coll 60. **d** 63 **p** 64. C Deptford St Luke *S'wark* 63–66; C Southgate *Chich* 66–70; P-in-c Brixton Road Ch Ch *S'wark* 70–73; P-in-c Manuden w Berden *Chelmsf* 73–76; Distr Sec (N Lon, Herts and Essex) BFBS 76–82; Hon C Walthamstow St Gabr *Chelmsf* 79–82; V 82–95; Chapl Thorpe Coombe Psycho-Geriatric Hosp 83–95; rtd 95; PtO *Chelmsf* 95–12. *52 Hatch Road, Pilgrims Hatch, Brentwood CM15 9PX* T: (01277) 375401

GUTTRIDGE, John William. b 54. Surrey Univ BSc 75 Cardiff Coll of Educn PGCE 76 MRSC 95. STETS 08. **d** 11 **p** 12. NSM Aisholt, Enmore, Goathurst, Nether Stowey etc *B & W* 11–15; PtO from 15. *The Vicarage, 47A Brendon Road, Watchet TA23 0HU* T: (01984) 631228 M: 07813-350710 E: jwguttridge@hotmail.com

GUTWEIN, Martin. b 45. Hobart Coll (NY) BA 67. Episc Th Sch Cam Mass MA 69 MDiv 72. **d** 72 **p** 72. USA 72–78 and from 80; C Toxteth St Marg Liv 78–80; rtd 10; PtO *S'wark* from 16. *527 N 2nd Street, Camden NJ 08102-2101, USA* E: revgutwein@yahoo.com

GUY, Mrs Alison. b 43. CQSW 69. WMMTC 95. **d** 98 **p** 99. NSM Minchinhampton *Glouc* 98–04; C Bisley, Chalford, France Lynch, and Oakridge 04–08; PtO from 14. *7 Tooke Road, Minchinhampton, Stroud GL6 9DA* T: (01453) 883906 E: alisonguy@metronet.co.uk

GUY, Ian Towers. b 47. Newc Univ MB, BS 70 MSc 89 MRCGP. NEOC. **d** 83 **p** 84. NSM Saltburn-by-the-Sea *York* 83–88; NSM Skelton w Upleatham 88–92; PtO from 92. *14 North Terrace, Skelton-in-Cleveland, Saltburn-by-the-Sea TS12 2ES* T: (01287) 650309 M: 07092-298033 E: iantguy@mac.com

GUY, John Richard. *See* MORGAN-GUY, John Richard

GUY, Peter-John. b 71. Bournemouth Univ BA 93. Oak Hill Th Coll BA 03. **d** 03 **p** 04. C Eastbourne All So *Chich* 03–07; C Lindfield 07–11; V Horam from 11. *The Vicarage, Horebeech Lane, Horam, Heathfield TN21 0DT* T: (01435) 813372 E: pjgerdaguy@hotmail.com

GUY, Simon Edward Walrond. b 39. St Andr Univ MA 61. St D Coll Lamp LTh 67. **d** 67 **p** 68. C Bris St Mary Redcliffe w Temple etc 67–68; C Knowle St Martin 68–71; C Bishopston

71–75; V Westwood *Sarum* 75–81; TV Melksham 81–82; TV Wednesfield *Lich* 82–90; R Heaton Moor *Man* 90–02; P-in-c Heaton Norris Ch w All SS 99–01; TV Heatons 02–04; rtd 04. *1 Holley Close, Exminster, Exeter EX6 8SS* T: (01392) 823084 E: sewguy@supanet.com *or* sewguy@uwclub.net

GUYMER, Canon Raymond John. b 41. AKC 64. St Boniface Warminster. **d** 65 **p** 66. C W Bromwich All SS *Lich* 65–70; Chapl HM Pris Wormwood Scrubs 70–71 and 84–93; Chapl HM Borstal Portland 71–78; Chapl HM Youth Cust Cen Hollesley Bay Colony 78–84; Chapl HM Pris Win 93–01; Hon C Upper Itchen *Win* 02–06; Hon Can Win Cathl 99–06; rtd 06; PtO *Sarum* from 14. *39A Horse Road, Hilperton Marsh, Trowbridge BA14 7PF*

GUZEK, Mrs Bridget Louise. b 47. York Univ BA 70 Keswick Hall Coll PGCE 79. STETS 05. **d** 08 **p** 09. NSM E Clevedon w Clapton in Gordano etc *B & W* 08–12; P-in-c St Buryan, St Levan and Sennen *Truro* 12–13; C St Stythians w Perranarworthal and Gwennap 14–15; C Chacewater w St Day and Carharrack 14–15; C Feock 14–15; C Devoran 14–15; PtO *B & W* 15–16; *Truro* from 17. *4 Hendra Terrace, Stithians, Truro TR3 7AJ* M: 07985-977666 E: blguzek@gmail.com

GWALCHMAI, Mrs Alison Clare. b 63. N Lon Poly BA 84. **d** 16 **p** 17. NSM Bro Arwystli *Ban* from 16. *1 Wesley Place, Llandinam SY17 5DW* T: (01686) 689142 M: 07789-860066 E: alisong@care4free.net

GWILLIAMS, The Very Revd Dianna Lynn. b 57. California Univ BA 78 K Coll Lon MA 01. S'wark Ord Course 89. **d** 92 **p** 94. NSM Peckham St Sav *S'wark* 92–97; C Dulwich St Barn 97–99; V 99–13; P-in-c Peckham St Sav 07–11; AD Dulwich 05–12; Dean of Women's Min 09–12; Chapl Alleyn's Foundn Dulwich 99–13; Hon Can S'wark Cathl 06–13; Dean Guildf from 13. *The Deanery, Cathedral Close, Guildford GU2 7TL* T: (01483) 547860 F: 303350 E: dean@guildford-cathedral.org

GWILLIM, Allan John. b 51. Coll of Resurr Mirfield 87. **d** 89 **p** 90. C Skerton St Luke *Blackb* 89–94; P-in-c Ellel 94–98; V Fleetwood St Pet 98–06; V Leyland St Jas 06–08; V Ocker Hill *Lich* 08–16; RD Wednesbury 13–16; rtd 16; PtO *Worc* from 17; *Lich* from 17. *2 Little Holt Cottages, Quatt, Bridgnorth WV15 6QW* T: (01746) 780798 E: allan.gwillim@btinternet.com

GWINN, Brian Harvey. b 35. MIQA 75. St Alb Minl Tr Scheme 83. **d** 86 **p** 87. NSM Wheathampstead *St Alb* 86–88; Ind Chapl 88–95; RD Hatfield 93–95; P-in-c Watton at Stone 95–99; R Bramfield, Stapleford, Waterford etc 99–01; rtd 01; PtO *St Alb* from 01. *18 Kingfisher Close, Wheathampstead, St Albans AL4 8JJ* T: (01582) 629903 M: 07966-469754 E: gwinns@ntlworld.com

GWINNETT, Clifton Harry. b 57. Cranmer Hall Dur 08. **d** 10 **p** 11. C Golcar and Longwood *Wakef* 10–13; V Thornton St Jas *Bradf* 13–14; *Leeds* from 14. *The Vicarage, Thornton Road, Thornton, Bradford BD13 3AB* M: 07817-526342 E: harry@james4u.org

GWYN-THOMAS, James John. b 82. Ex Univ BA 03. Wycliffe Hall Ox BTh 13. **d** 13 **p** 14. C Leyland St Andr *Blackb* 13–17; Min Buckshaw Village Ch CD from 17. *1 Bridgewater Drive, Buckshaw Village, Chorley PR7 7EU* T: (01772) 453205 M: 07988-66360 E: jamesgwynthomas@gmail.com *or* james.gt@buckshawvillagechurch.org.uk

GWYNN, Mrs Fiona Jane. b 67. **d** 15 **p** 16. OLM Haslemere and Grayswood *Guildf* from 15. *The Gables, Park Close, Grayswood, Haslemere GU27 2DT* T: (01428) 654728 M: 07929-935179 E: revfigwynn@gmail.com

GWYNN, Canon Phillip John. b 57. Univ of Wales (Lamp) BA 87 MA 04. St Mich Coll Llan 87. **d** 89 **p** 90. C Clydach *S & B* 89–93; V Swansea St Thos and Kilvey 93–00; Hon Chapl Miss to Seafarers 93–00; V Tycoch *S & B* from 00; V Killay from 16; AD Clyne 12–15; Chapl Swansea NHS Trust from 00; Hon Can Brecon Cathl *S & B* from 17. *68 Ffordd yr Olchfa, Sketty, Swansea SA2 7RF* T: (01792) 204758 M: 07946-351787 E: phillip@gwynn.org.uk

GWYNNE, Robert Durham. b 44. Qu Coll Birm 67. **d** 70 **p** 72. C N Hammersmith St Kath *Lon* 70–75; C Ramsey *Ely* 76–78; TV Old Brumby *Linc* 78–81; P-in-c Goxhill and Thornton Curtis 81–83; C Edmonton All SS w St Mich *Lon* 83–84; rtd 86. *127 Eastfield Road, Louth LN11 7AS* T: (01507) 600966

GWYTHER, Canon Geoffrey David. b 51. St D Coll Lamp. **d** 74 **p** 75. C Pembroke Dock *St D* 74–77; C Milford Haven 77–81; V Llawhaden w Bletherston and Llanycefn 81–88; R Prendergast w Rudbaxton 88–16; AD Daugleddau 01–12; Can St D Cathl 01–16; Treas 14–16; rtd 16; PtO *St D* from 18. *30 Gibbas Way, Pembroke SA71 5JA* T: (01646) 685591

GYLE, Alan Gordon. b 65. Aber Univ MA 87 Ox Univ BA 91 Univ of E Lon MA 09 FRSA 99. St Steph Ho Ox. **d** 92 **p** 93. C Acton Green *Lon* 92–94; Min Can, Succ and Dean's V Windsor 94–99; Chapl Imp Coll and R Coll of Art 99–04; P-in-c Wilton Place St Paul *Lon* 01–03; V from 03; PV Westmr Abbey from 07; Dir Development Two Cities Area *Lon* 08–12. *St Paul's Vicarage, 32 Wilton Place, London SW1X 8SH* T: (020) 7201 9990 *or* 7201 9999 F: 7201 9990 E: alan@stpaulsknightsbridge.org

GYLES, Canon Sonia. b 76. TCD BTh 01. CITC 98. **d** 01 **p** 02. C Taney *D & G* 01–04; I Dublin Sandford w Milltown from 04; Chan V St Patr Cathl Dublin 01–07; Can Ch Ch Cathl Dublin *D & G* from 17. *The Rectory, Sandford Close, Ranelagh, Dublin 6, Republic of Ireland* T: (00353) (1) 497 2983 E: sandford@dublin.anglican.org

H

HAARHOFF, Preb Robert Russell. b 46. St Paul's Coll Grahamstown 89 Th Ext Educn Coll 91. **d** 90 **p** 91. Harare Cathl Zimbabwe 91–94; I Makonde 94–02; P-in-c Astley, Clive, Grinshill and Hadnall *Lich* 02–17; RD Wem and Whitchurch 08–13; Preb Lich Cathl 11–17; rtd 17; PtO *Lich* from 17. *25 Fismes Way, Wem, Shrewsbury SY4 5YD* E: rob.haarhoff@gmail.com

HABERSHON, Kenneth Willoughby. b 35. New Coll Ox BA 57 MA 60. Wycliffe Hall Ox 57. **d** 59 **p** 60. C Finchley Ch Ch *Lon* 59–66; Sec CYFA 66–74; CPAS Staff 74–90; Hon C Slaugham *Chich* 84–10; Hon C Slaugham and Staplefield Common from 10; Ldr Mayfield CYFA 90–00; rtd 00; Sec Ch Patr Trust 90–07; Sec Peache Trustees 90–11. *Truckers Ghyll, Horsham Road, Handcross, Haywards Heath RH17 6DT* T: (01444) 400274 E: kandmhab@btopenworld.com

HABGOOD, Simon. *See* LAWRENCE, Simon Peter

HABGOOD, Stephen Roy. b 52. Open Univ MBA 95 Fitzw Coll Cam MSt 01. St Mich Coll Llan 75. **d** 77 **p** 78. C Whitchurch *Llan* 77–80; PtO *Worc* 85–91; *Lich* from 18. *Yew Tree Cottage, Wharf Road, Gnosall, Stafford ST20 0DA* T: (01785) 824244

HACKER, The Rt Revd George Lanyon. b 28. Ex Coll Ox BA 52 MA 56. Cuddesdon Coll 52. **d** 54 **p** 55 **c** 79. C Bris St Mary Redcliffe w Temple 54–59; Chapl St Boniface Coll Warminster 59–64; V Bishopwearmouth Gd Shep *Dur* 64–71; R Tilehurst St Mich *Ox* 71–79; Suff Bp Penrith *Carl* 79–94;

Hon Can Carl Cathl 79–94; Episc Adv for the Angl Young People's Assn 87–94; rtd 94; Hon Asst Bp Carl from 94. *Keld House, Milburn, Penrith CA10 1TW* T: (01768) 361506 E: bishhack@outlook.com

HACKER HUGHES, Katherine Lucy. b 60. York Univ BA 81. Westcott Ho Cam 90. **d** 92 **p** 94. Par Dn S Woodham Ferrers *Chelmsf* 92–94; C 94–95; NSM Maldon All SS w St Pet 95–98; Chapl Chelmsf Cathl 98–01; P-in-c Gt Waltham w Ford End 01–05; Adv relationship and family issues (Bradwell Area) 01–03; PtO 05–09; Chapl Mid-Essex Hosp Services NHS Trust 06–07; Chapl Farleigh Hospice 07–14; P-in-c Newington St Paul *S'wark* 14–19; V 19; C St Marylebone w H Trin *Lon* from 19. *St Marylebone Parish Church, 17 Marylebone Road, London NW1 5LT* T: (020) 7935 7315 E: katyhh@hotmail.co.uk

HACKETT, Bryan Malcolm. b 66. Magd Coll Ox BA 88 MA 93 SS Coll Cam BA 92 MA 03. Westcott Ho Cam 90. **d** 93 **p** 94. C Willington *Newc* 93–97; TV Radcliffe *Man* 97–03; P-in-c Prestwich St Mary 03–13; C Prestwich St Marg 10–13; C Prestwich St Gabr 10–13; V Baguley 13–15; PtO *Carl* 15–16; P-in-c Portsea N End St Mark *Portsm* from 16; P-in-c Portsea St Sav 17–18; P-in-c Portsea Ascension 17–18. *St Mark's Rectory, 3A Wadham Road, Portsmouth PO2 9ED* T: (023) 9265 5654 E: bryan.hackett@btinternet.com

HACKETT, The Ven Ronald Glyndwr. b 47. Hatf Coll Dur BA 70. Cuddesdon Coll 70. **d** 72 **p** 73. C Pembroke St Mary w St Mich *St D* 72–75; C Bassaleg *Mon* 75–78; V Blaenavon w Capel Newydd 78–84; Chapl R Gwent Hosp 84–90; V Newport St Paul 84–90; V Newport Ch Ch 90–01; Adn Mon 01–08; R Mamhilad and Llanfihangel Pontymoile 01–03; R Mamhilad w Monkswood and Glascoed Chapel 03–08; Adn Newport 08–12; rtd 12. *71 Castle Lea, Caldicot NP26 4PJ* E: glyndwr.hackett@btinternet.com

HACKING, Philip Henry. b 31. St Pet Hall Ox BA 53 MA 57. Oak Hill Th Coll 53. **d** 55 **p** 56. C St Helens St Helen *Liv* 55–58; C-in-c Edin St Thos 59–68; V Fulwood *Sheff* 68–97; rtd 97. PtO *Sheff* from 98. *61 Sefton Court, Sefton Road, Sheffield S10 3TP* T: 0114-230 4324 E: philiphacking@fulwood-s10.me.uk

HACKING, Rodney Douglas. b 53. K Coll Lon BD 74 AKC 74 Man Univ MA 83. St Aug Coll Cant 75. **d** 76 **p** 78. C Byker St Mich *Newc* 76–77; C Eltham St Jo *S'wark* 77–79; Ind Chapl *Ripon* 80–85; R Upwell St Pet and Outwell *Ely* 85–88; Vice Prin S Dios Minl Tr Scheme 89–93; V Bolton-le-Sands *Blackb* 93–97; In Orthodox Ch 01–03; R The Wainfleet Gp *Linc* 03–06; rtd 06. *135 The Close, Salisbury SP1 2EY* T: (01722) 417289 E: rodhacking@btinternet.com

HACKING, Stuart Peter. b 60. St Pet Coll Ox BA 82 MA. Oak Hill Th Coll 83. **d** 85 **p** 86. C Shipley St Pet *Bradf* 85–88; C Darfield *Sheff* 88–91; V Thornton St Jas *Bradf* 91–00; P-in-c Frizinghall St Marg 00–12; Chapl Immanuel Coll from 00. *33 Cyprus Gardens, Idle, Bradford BD10 8JF* T: (01274) 616473 or 425900 E: stuart.hacking@btinternet.com

HACKL, Aileen Patricia. b 41. Wycliffe Hall Ox 00. **d** 01 **p** 02. C Vienna *Eur* 01–09; NSM 09–11; rtd 11. *Hardtmuthgasse 28/3/20, A-1100 Vienna, Austria* T/F: (0043) (1) 600 3083 E: aileen_hackl@hotmail.com

HACKSHALL, Brian Leonard. b 33. K Coll Lon BD 53 AKC 53. **d** 57 **p** 58. C Portsea St Mary *Portsm* 57–62; C Westbury-on-Trym St Alb *Bris* 62–64; V Avonmouth St Andr 64–71; Miss to Seamen 71–79; C Crawley *Chich* 79; TV 79–98; Ind Chapl 89–98; rtd 98. *5 St Michael Street, Brecon LD3 9AB* T: (01874) 611319 E: b.hackshakk319@btinternet.com

HACKWOOD, Canon Paul Colin. b 61. Huddersfield Poly BSc 84 Bradf Univ MBA 05. Qu Coll Birm 86. **d** 89 **p** 90. C Horton *Bradf* 89–93; Soc Resp Adv *St Alb* 93–97; V Thornbury *Bradf* 97–05; Adn Loughborough *Leic* 05–09; Can Res Leic Cathl 07–15; Exec Chair CUF from 15; PtO *Leic* from 15; Hon Can Leic Cathl from 15. *Church View Farmhouse, 4 St Mary's Close, Osgathorpe, Loughborough LE12 9SY* T: (01530) 223265 M: 07738-286428 E: paulhackwood@me.com

HADDEN, Timothy. b 48. Brighton Poly BSc 72 Surrey Univ MSc 75. **d** 05 **p** 06. OLM Watling Valley *Ox* 05–16; PtO from 16. *13 Weavers Lane, Oakridge Park, Milton Keynes MK14 6FQ* M: 07889-614386 E: tim.hadden@btinternet.com

HADDOCK, Malcolm George. b 27. Univ of Wales (Cardiff) BA 56 CertEd 73. St Deiniol's Hawarden 87. **d** 80 **p** 81. NSM Newport Ch Ch *Mon* 80–85; NSM Risca 85–87; C 87–89; C Caerleon 89–96; rtd 96; LtO *Mon* from 96. *48 Cambria Close, Caerleon, Newport NP18 1LF* T: (01633) 422960

HADDON-REECE (née STREETER), Mrs Christine Mary. b 50. St Jo Coll Nottm BTh 81 LTh 81. dss 83 **d** 87 **p** 94. Monkwearmouth St Andr *Dur* 83–85; Stranton 85–87; Par Dn 87–90; Par Dn Lastingham w Appleton-le-Moors, Rosedale etc *York* 90–94; C 94–97; V Topcliffe, Baldersby w Dishforth, Dalton etc 97–08; V Middle Esk Moor 08–15; rtd 16; PtO *York* from 16. *Thorgill House, Rosedale Abbey, Pickering YO18 8SE* T: (01751) 417401 E: c.haddonreece@btinternet.com

HADDON-REECE, David. b 45. Liv Univ BEng 69 Bradf Univ MPhil 81 FRSA 72 CEng 77 MIEE 76. **d** 19. NSM Lastingham w Appleton-le-Moors, Rosedale etc *York* from 19. *Thorgill House, Rosedale Abbey, Pickering YO18 8SE* T: (01751) 417401 E: d.haddonreece@btinternet.com

HADFIELD, Prof Brigid. b 50. Edin Univ LLB 72 QUB LLM 77 Essex Univ PhD 03. EAMTC 02. **d** 03 **p** 04. NSM Wivenhoe *Chelmsf* 03–06; NSM Shrub End 06–11; P-in-c Harston w Hauxton and Newton *Ely* 11–18; rtd 18; PtO *Ely* from 18; *Chich* from 18. *6 Cornfield Road, Seaford BN25 1SW* E: bhadfield216@gmail.com

HADFIELD, Christopher John Andrew Chad. b 39. Jes Coll Cam BA 61. Wells Th Coll 63. **d** 65 **p** 66. C Wigton w Waverton *Carl* 65–68; Teacher Newlands Sch Seaford 70–06; LtO *Mor* from 92; PtO *Chich* from 96. *15 The Fridays, East Dean, Eastbourne BN20 0DH* T: (01323) 422050

HADFIELD, David William. b 53. Newc Univ BA 74 MA 76 PhD 83 Barrister 82 Solicitor 88. SEITE 10. **d** 13 **p** 14. NSM E Grinstead St Mary *Chich* from 13. *Highgate House, Tomtits Lane, Forest Row RH18 5AT* T: (01342) 823105 M: 07526-792889 E: revdhad@gmail.com

HADFIELD, Derek. b 34. **d** 01 **p** 02. OLM Folkestone H Trin w Ch Ch *Cant* 01–04; OLM Sandgate St Paul w Folkestone St Geo 01–04; rtd 04; PtO *Cant* 04–11; *York* from 11. *Mon Abri, South Duffield Road, Osgodby, Selby YO8 5HW* T: (01757) 705940 E: dhaddy1146@gmail.com

HADFIELD, Graham Francis. b 48. Bris Univ BSc 69. Cranmer Hall Dur 70. **d** 73 **p** 74. C Blackpool St Thos *Blackb* 73–76; CF 76–99; Asst Chapl Gen 99–04; QHC 02–04; P-in-c Nottingham St Jude *S'well* 04–11; V 11–12; rtd 12; PtO *Chelmsf* from 13; *Eur* from 17. *22 Coast Road, West Mersea, Colchester CO5 8LH* T: (01206) 382458

HADFIELD, Jonathan Benedict Philip John. b 43. Lon Univ BA 64 Jes Coll Cam BA 67 MA 72. Edin Th Coll 66. **d** 68 **p** 69. C Fort William *Arg* 68–70; Chapl K Sch Glouc and Hon Min Can Glouc Cathl 70–03; rtd 03. *36 Corsend Road, Hartpury, Gloucester GL19 3BP*

HADFIELD, Norman. b 39. Doncaster Coll of Educn TEng 78. St Mich Coll Llan 89 Llan Dioc Tr Scheme 83. **d** 86 **p** 87. NSM Ferndale w Maerdy *Llan* 86–90; C Llanblethian w Cowbridge and Llandough etc 90–92; V Resolven w Tonna 92–04; RD Neath 01–03; rtd 04; PtO *Llan* from 04. *42 Lakeside, Cwmdare, Aberdare CF44 8AX* T: (01685) 872764

HADJIOANNOU, John. b 56. Ch Coll Cam BA 78 MA 81. SAOMC 95. **d** 97 **p** 98. C Linslade *Ox* 97–00; V Kinsley w Wragby *Wakef* 00–14; *Leeds* from 14; P-in-c Felkirk *Wakef* 05–12. *Kinsley Vicarage, Wakefield Road, Fitzwilliam, Pontefract WF9 5BX* T: (01977) 610497 E: john@minster.co.uk

HADLEY, Adam Richard. b 82. York Univ BA 03 Essex Univ MA 05. Qu Foundn Birm 16. **d** 18 **p** 19. C Stourbridge St Thos *Worc* from 18. *10 Bernwall Close, Stourbridge DY8 1SD* M: 07759-900947 E: adam@stthomasstourbridge.org

HADLEY, Ann. *See* HADLEY, Elizabeth Ann

HADLEY, Charles Adrian. b 50. Trin Coll Cam BA 71 MA 75. Cuddesdon Coll 73. **d** 75 **p** 76. C Hadleigh w Layham and Shelley *St E* 75–78; C Bracknell *Ox* 78–82; R Blagdon w Compton Martin and Ubley *B & W* 82–92; RD Chew Magna 88–92; R Somerton w Compton Dundon, the Charltons etc 92–04; Chapl Ex Univ 04–10; Chemin Neuf Community Israel 10–15; Hon C Storrington *Chich* from 15. *28 Meadowside, Storrington, Pulborough RH20 4EG* T: (01903) 740787 E: charles.felicity@gmail.com

HADLEY, David Charles. b 42. **d** 02 **p** 03. NSM Kenley *S'wark* 02–13; NSM Purley St Barn 08–13; PtO from 13. *21 Park Road, Kenley CR8 5AQ* T: (020) 8763 6206

HADLEY, Preb Elizabeth Ann. b 33. St Jo Coll Nottm 80. dss 81 **d** 87 **p** 94. Aspley *S'well* 81–85; Stone St Mich w Aston St Sav *Lich* 85–92; Par Dn 87–92; P-in-c Myddle 92–97; R 97–99; P-in-c Broughton 92–97; V 97–99; Dioc Voc Officer 92–99; Preb Lich Cathl 97–99; rtd 99; P-in-c Harvington *Worc* 99–00; PtO from 00. *6 Peninsula Road, Brockhill Village, Norton, Worcester WR5 2SE* T: (01905) 353710 E: revannhadley@gmail.com

HADLEY, Georgina Ann Lacy. b 53. De Montfort Univ BA 95 PGCE 96. Linc Sch of Th and Min 12. **d** 13 **p** 14. NSM Retford Area *S'well* 13–16; C Averham w Kelham from 16; C N and S Muskham from 16. *43 Great North Road, Sutton on Trent, Newark NG23 6PL* T: (01636) 821343 M: 07811-393920 E: georgie.hadley@gmail.com

HADLEY, Canon John Spencer Fairfax. b 47. Ch Ch Ox BA 70 MA 73. Coll of Resurr Mirfield BA 72. **d** 73 **p** 74. C Stoke Newington St Mary *Lon* 73–77; C High Wycombe *Ox* 77–81; TV 82–87; P-in-c Clifton St Paul *Bris* 87–91; Sen Chapl Bris Univ 87–91; Chapl Hengrave Hall Ecum Cen 91–94; Ecum Assoc Min Chelsea Methodist Ch 94–97; Hon C Chelsea St Luke and Ch Ch *Lon* 94–97; Chapl Westcott Ho Cam 97–02; P-in-c Horfield H Trin *Bris* 02–15; R 15–17; Hon Can Bris Cathl 12–17; rtd 17. *14 Picton Street, Bristol BS6 5QA* T: 0117-944 6153 E: john-hadley@tiscali.co.uk

HADLEY, Stuart James. b 55. K Coll Lon BD 76 AKC 76. St Steph Ho Ox 77. **d** 78 **p** 79. C Mansfield St Mark *S'well* 78–82; V Cowbit *Linc* 82–86; PtO 86–88; NSM W w E Allington and Sedgebrook 88–95; NSM Saxonwell 95–96; NSM Woolsthorpe 88–95; NSM Harlaxton Gp 95–96; PtO 97–99; NSM Barkston and Hough Gp 99–17; P-in-c 17–18; P-in-c Copythorne 17–18; R S Cliff Villages Gp from 18. *35 Wensleydale Close, Grantham NG31 8FH* T: (01476) 575854 M: 07398-390549 E: rectorsouthcliff@outlook.com

HADLOW, Mrs Jennifer Lesley. b 48. **d** 01 **p** 02. OLM Reculver and Herne Bay St Bart and Hoath *Cant* 01–18; rtd 18. *2 Hicks Forstal Cottages, Hicks Forstal Road, Hoath, Canterbury CT3 4NA* T: (01227) 711516

HAGAN, Matthew Henry. b 59. TCD MPhil 09. CITC. **d** 06 **p** 07. NSM Derryloran *Arm* 06–10; P-in-c Tynan w Middletown and Aghavilly 10–12; Bp's C 12–13; I from 13. *The Rectory, 16 Derryhaw Road, Tynan, Armagh BT60 4SS* T: (028) 3756 8619 M: 07778-038454 E: mhhagan@hotmail.com

HAGAN, Yvonne Joan Katherine. b 59. Yorks Min Course 14. **d** 17 **p** 18. NSM Mixenden and Illingworth *Leeds* from 17. *6 Roseberry Terrace, Halifax HX1 4AW*

HAGAN-PALMER, David Edward. b 66. UEA BSc 88 PGCE 96. ERMC 10. **d** 13 **p** 14. C Lowestoft St Marg *Nor* 13–14; C Drayton 14–16; C Taverham 14–16; C Cawston w Booton and Brandiston etc 16–17; TV Aylsham and Distr from 17. *The Rectory, 24 Brook Street, Buxton, Norwich NR10 5HF* M: 07880-660900 E: revdavepalmer@gmail.com

HAGENBUCH, Mrs Andrea. b 63. STETS 05. **d** 08 **p** 09. C Corfe Castle, Church Knowle, Kimmeridge etc *Sarum* 08–12; V Stour Vale 12–16; R Milngavie *Glas* from 16. *1 Westbourne Drive, Bearsden, Glasgow G61 4BD* T: 0141-942 0029 E: stephenhagenbuch@hotmail.com

HAGGIS, Richard. b 66. Ch Ch Ox BA 88 MA 95 Nottm Univ MA 95. Linc Th Coll. **d** 95 **p** 96. C Romford St Edw *Chelmsf* 95–98; Chapl Trin Coll Cam 98–00; C St Giles-in-the-Fields *Lon* 00–03; C Upper Chelsea H Trin 04–06. *Flat 5, 14-16 Mather Road, Barton-Upon-Bayswater, Oxford OX3 9PG* T: (01865) 750068 M: 07788-704044 E: rh.giles@btopenworld.com

HAGGIS, Timothy Robin. b 52. New Coll Ox BA 75 MA 79. St Jo Coll Nottm. **d** 82 **p** 83. C Chilwell *S'well* 82–86; TV Hucknall Torkard 86–94; Chapl Trent Coll Nottm 94–11; rtd 11. *86 Trowell Grove, Long Eaton, Nottingham NG10 4BB* T: 0115-972 9589 E: timhaggis@hotmail.com

HAGON, Roger Charles. b 58. Nottm Univ BA 80. St Steph Ho Ox 82. **d** 85 **p** 86. C Charlton St Luke w H Trin *S'wark* 85–88; C St Helier 88–95; V Kenley 95–10; P-in-c Purley St Barn 01–10; V Addiscombe St Mildred from 10. *St Mildred's Vicarage, Sefton Road, Croydon CR0 7HR* T: (020) 8676 1569 E: vicar@stmildredchurch.org.uk

HAGUE, Canon David Hallett. b 59. Univ Coll Lon BScEng 81 MSc 82. Ridley Hall Cam 91. **d** 93 **p** 94. C Luton St Mary *St Alb* 93–96; V Stevenage St Pet Broadwater 96–09; P-in-c Romford Gd Shep *Chelmsf* 09–14; V from 14; AD Havering 14–18; Hon Can Chelmsf Cathl from 15. *Good Shepherd Vicarage, 97 Collier Row Lane, Romford RM5 3BA* T: (01708) 753395 E: vicargs@thegoodshepherd.co.uk

HAIG, Alistair Alexander Matthew. b 39. K Coll Lon BD 63 AKC 63. **d** 64 **p** 65. C Forest Gate St Edm *Chelmsf* 64–67; C Laindon w Basildon 67–71; V S Woodham Ferrers 71–78; P-in-c Bath H Trin *B & W* 78–83; R 83–89; R Bocking St Mary *Chelmsf* 89–95; Dean Bocking 89–95; rtd 00. *17 Maidenburgh Street, Colchester CO1 1UB* T: (01206) 530530 E: aam.haig@ntlworld.com

HAIG, Canon Andrew Livingstone. b 45. Keble Coll Ox BA 67. Coll of Resurr Mirfield 67. **d** 69 **p** 70. C Elton All SS *Man* 69–75; R Brantham *St E* 75–76; R Brantham w Stutton 76–82; RD Samford 81–82; P-in-c Haverhill 82; TR Haverhill w Withersfield, the Wrattings etc 82–90; RD Clare 84–87; Chapl Qu Eliz Hosp King's Lynn 90–10; Hon Can Nor Cathl 07–10; rtd 10; PtO *Nor* from 10; C P-in-c *Ely* from 13; *Eur* from 17. *46 Elvington, King's Lynn PE30 4TA* T: (01553) 761389 E: bandahaig@yahoo.co.uk

HAIGH, Nicholas James. b 71. Sheff Univ BA 00 St Jo Coll Dur MA 04. Cranmer Hall Dur 02. **d** 04 **p** 05. C Bredbury St Mark *Ches* 04–06; P Missr Huddersfield *Wakef* 06–09; C Crookes St Thos *Sheff* 09–15; V Haydock St Mark *Liv* 15–17; Miss Chapl Lee Abbey from 17. *Lee Abbey, Lynton EX35 6JJ* T: (01598) 752621 E: nickhaigh@leeabbey.org.uk *or* missionpriest@gmail.com

HAIGH, Nicolas Peter. b 57. Teesside Poly BEd 84. Ripon Coll Cuddesdon 07. **d** 09 **p** 10. C Eastbourne St Mary *Chich* 09–12; P-in-c Fernhurst 12–14; V 14–16; V Fernhurst, Lynchmere and Camelsdale from 16. *The Vicarage, Church Road, Fernhurst, Haslemere GU27 3HZ* T: (01428) 652229 M: 07966-187349 E: nickhaigh95@hotmail.com

HAIGH, Richard Michael Fisher. b 30. Dur Univ BA 57. Cranmer Hall Dur 57. **d** 59 **p** 60. C Stanwix *Carl* 59–62; CMS India 63–67; 68–70; R Salford St Clem w St Cypr Ordsall *Man* 71–75; R Holcombe 75–85; V Unsworth 85–93; R Brough w Stainmore, Musgrave and Warcop *Carl* 93–97; rtd 97; PtO *Carl* 98–19. *21 Templand Park, Allithwaite, Grange-over-Sands LA11 7QS* T: (015395) 32312

HAIGH, Samuel Edward. b 85. Anglia Ruskin Univ BA 11. Ridley Hall Cam 08. **d** 11 **p** 12. C Wootton *St Alb* 11–14; TV Tollington *Lon* 14–18; C Onslow Square and S Kensington St Aug 18–19; R Preston St Jo and St Geo *Blackb* from 19. *The Rectory, 13 Ribblesdale Place, Preston PR1 3NA* M: 07429-022977 E: revhaigh@me.com

HAILES, Derek Arthur. b 38. Coll of Resurr Mirfield. **d** 82 **p** 83. C Sneinton St Cypr *S'well* 83–84; V Kneesall w Laxton 84–85; P-in-c Wellow 84–85; V Kneesall w Laxton and Wellow 85–88; V Sneinton St Steph w St Alb 88–95; P-in-c Bury H Trin *Man* 95–03; rtd 03; PtO *S'well* from 05. *14 Manor Road, Carlton, Nottingham NG4 3AY* T: 0115-987 3314 E: derek.hailes@hotmail.com

HAILS, Canon Brian. b 33. ACMA 62 FCMA 76. NEOC 77. **d** 81 **p** 82. NSM Harton *Dur* 81–87; Ind Chapl 87–99; Hon Can Dur Cathl 93–99; TR Sunderland 96–99; rtd 99; PtO *Dur* from 99. *The Coach House, Church Lane, Whitburn, Sunderland SR6 7JL* T: 0191-529 5297 E: bhails@btinternet.com

HAINE, Mrs Joanne Elizabeth. b 78. RMN 00. St Jo Coll Nottm 13. **d** 15 **p** 16. C Dorchester and the Winterbournes *Sarum* 15–18; TV Radipole and Melcombe Regis from 18. *The Vicarage, 74 Field Barn Drive, Weymouth DT4 0EF* M: 07530-255684 E: revjohaine@gmail.com

HAINES, Andrew Philip. b 47. LSE BSc 68. Oak Hill Th Coll 84. **d** 87 **p** 88. C Enfield Ch Ch Trent Park *Lon* 87–91; V Hillmorton *Cov* 91–12; PtO *Cov* from 12. *69 Waverley Road, Kenilworth CV8 1JL* T: (01926) 855518 E: revaph@btinternet.com *or* andrew@haines.uk.com

HAINES, Fiona Elizabeth. b 56. Open Univ BA 95 York Univ MA 00. LCTP 14. **d** 16 **p** 17. NSM Freckleton and Warton St Paul *Blackb* from 16. *19 Derbe Road, Lytham St Annes FY8 1NJ* M: 07850-422566 E: fiona_haines@outlook.com

HAINSWORTH, Richard John. b 79. Jes Coll Cam BA 01 MA 03. St Mich Coll Llan 04. **d** 06 **p** 07. C Newtown w Llanllwchaiarn w Aberhafesp *St As* 06–07; C Llanllwchaiarn and Newtown w Aberhafesp 07–08; C Wrexham 08–09; TV 09–14; V Northop 14–16; TV Mold Miss Area 17–19; Dioc Dir for Exploring Faith from 18. *The Vicarage, Sychdyn Road, Northop, Mold CH7 6AW* T: (01352) 840842 M: 07886-117922 E: rich_hainsworth@yahoo.co.uk

HAIR, James Eric. b 48. Lon Univ BA 69 MPhil 92. St Steph Ho Ox 69. **d** 72 **p** 73. C Fishponds St Jo *Bris* 72–75; C Bushey *St Alb* 75–79; P-in-c Lake *Portsm* 79–81; V 81–88; P-in-c Shanklin St Sav 79–81; V 81–88; TV Totton *Win* 88–95; C Portchester *Portsm* 96–97; Community Mental Health Chapl Portsm Health Care NHS Trust 97–00; Community Portsm Hosps NHS Trust 01–02; Community Mental Health Chapl Hants Partnership NHS Trust 02–13; Chapl Team Ldr E Hants Primary Care Trust 99–13; Asst to RD Fareham *Portsm* 97–98 and 99; Dioc Adv for Mental Health from 12; PtO *Win* 09–14; *Portsm* from 16. *26 Bayly Avenue, Fareham PO16 9LD*

HAITH, James Rodney. b 69. Ex Univ BA. Ridley Hall Cam 02. **d** 04 **p** 05. C Brompton H Trin w Onslow Square St Paul *Lon* 04–11; C Onslow Square and S Kensington St Aug 11–12; USA 12–19; C Holborn St Geo w H Trin and St Bart *Lon* from 19. *13 Doughty Street, London WC1N 2PL* T: (020) 7430 2272 M: 07833-705271

HAKE, Darren Mark. b 73. Plymouth Univ BSc 00 Lanc Univ MRes 01 FGS 01. Wycliffe Hall Ox 09. **d** 11 **p** 12. C Wembdon *B & W* 11–14; PtO 14–18; C Peacehaven and Telscombe Cliffs w Piddinghoe etc *Chich* from 18. *79 Ambleside Avenue, Telscombe Cliffs, Peacehaven BN10 7LN* M: 07545-379112 E: revd.mark.hake@gmail.com

HAKE (*née* JACKSON), Mrs Ruth Victoria. b 75. Univ Coll Dur BA 99 Fitzw Coll Cam BA 01 MA 05. Ridley Hall Cam 99. **d** 02 **p** 03. C York St Mich-le-Belfrey 02–05; CF(V) 04–05; Chapl RAF from 05. *Chaplaincy Services (RAF), HQ Air Command, RAF High Wycombe HP14 4UE* T: (01494) 496800

HALDON-JONES, The Hon Mark Vincent. b 60. St Mich Coll Llan 81. **d** 84 **p** 85. C Whitchurch *Llan* 84–89; V Pwllgwaun w Llanddewi Rhondda 89–00; PtO 19; Hon Can Cant Cathl 00–02; P-in-c Folkestone St Pet from 19; PtO *Lon* from 19. *Address temp unknown*

HALE, Antony Jolyon (Jon). b 56. Newc Univ BA 79 MRTPI 89. Sarum & Wells Th Coll 86. **d** 88 **p** 89. C Monkseaton St Mary *Newc* 88–92; P-in-c Tandridge *S'wark* 92–97; C Oxted 92–97; C Oxted and Tandridge 97–98; V Crawley Down All SS *Chich* 98–16; R Alderley w Birtles *Ches* from 16. *St Mary's Rectory, Congleton Road, Nether Alderley, Macclesfield SK10 4TW* T: (01625) 586467 E: rector@alderleychurch.co.uk *or* aj@jkcahale.co.uk

HALE, David Nigel James. b 43. SEITE 00. **d** 03 **p** 04. NSM Aylesham w Adisham *Cant* 03–12; NSM Nonington w Wymynswold and Goodnestone etc 03–12; NSM Canonry 12–13; rtd 14; PtO *Cant* from 14; Chapl Northbourne Park Sch from 14. *Chilton House, 43 The Street, Ash, Canterbury CT3 2EN* T: (01304) 813161 *or* (01843) 862991 E: halenigelval@hotmail.com

HALE, Jon. See HALE, Antony Jolyon

HALE, Canon Keith John Edward. b 53. Sheff Poly BSc 75. St Jo Coll Nottm MA 94. **d** 91 **p** 92. C Greasbrough *Sheff* 91–94; P-in-c Tankersley 94–95; R Tankersley, Thurgoland

and Wortley from 95; Ind Chapl 96–01; Bp's Rural Adv from 01; AD Tankersley 07–19; Hon Can Sheff Cathl from 10. *The Rectory, 9 Chapel Road, Tankersley, Barnsley S75 3AR* T: (01226) 744140 E: revkeith.hale@virgin.net

HALE (*née* McKAY)**, Mrs Margaret McLeish (Greta).** b 37. RN 76. WEMTC 92. **d** 95 **p** 96. OLM Bream *Glouc* 95–01; NSM 01–04; NSM Newland and Redbrook w Clearwell 04–06; NSM Coleford, Staunton, Newland, Redbrook etc 06–13. *14 Meadow Walk, Sling, Coleford GL16 8LR* T: (01594) 832400 E: gretahale@hotmail.com

HALE, Nigel. *See* HALE, David Nigel James

HALE, Roger Anthony. b 41. MCIH 85. Brasted Th Coll 68 Oak Hill Th Coll 70. **d** 72 **p** 73. C Blackb Sav 72–75; C Burnley St Pet 75–77; Chapl Burnley Gen Hosp 75–77; V Fence in Pendle *Blackb* 77–82; Chapl Lancs Ind Miss 77–82; NSM Tottenham St Mary *Lon* 88–91; R Cheddington w Mentmore and Marsworth *Ox* 91–06; rtd 06; PtO *Ox* from 06. *9 Ridgeway Place, 8 Hale Road, Wendover, Aylesbury HP22 6BJ* E: rogertherector@yahoo.co.uk

HALE, Susan Mary. b 55. Dur Univ BA 77 Newman Coll Birm PGCE 96. Qu Foundn Birm 13. **d** 16 **p** 17. NSM Pensnett *Worc* from 16; PtO *Birm* from 16. *20 Links View, Halesowen B62 8SS* M: 07946-700236 E: revsuehale@gmail.com

HALE-HEIGHWAY, Catherine Anne. b 58. Lanc Univ BEd 79 Cumbria Univ BA 16. LCTP 10. **d** 12 **p** 13. NSM Colne and Villages *Blackb* 12–14; NSM Colne 14–18; NSM Clitheroe St Mary and St Paul, Chatburn and Downham from 18. *The Vicarage, St Paul's Street, Clitheroe BB7 2LS* E: revdcahale@gmail.com

HALES, Peter John. b 45. Open Univ BSc 02. ERMC 08. **d** 08 **p** 09. C Coutances *Eur* 08–09; P-in-c 09–14; PtO from 18. *4 rue le Mascaret, 50220 Précey, France* T: (0033) 2 33 58 86 76 F: 6 87 53 20 13 E: halesphx2@aol.com

HALFORD, David John. b 47. Didsbury Coll Man CertEd 69 Open Univ BA 75 DipEd 86 Man Univ MEd 79 ACP 72. **d** 96 **p** 97. OLM Royton St Anne *Man* 96–12; NSM Royton from 12. *33 Broadway, Royton, Oldham OL2 5DD* T: 0161-633 4650 M: 07966-178836 E: djhalford81@hotmail.com

HALFPENNY, Brian Norman. b 36. St Jo Coll Ox BA 60 MA 64. Wells Th Coll 60. **d** 62 **p** 63. C Melksham *Sarum* 62–65; Chapl RAF 65–83; Sen Chapl RAF Coll Cranwell 82–83; Asst Chapl-in-Chief RAF 83–88; Chapl-in-Chief RAF 88–91; QHC 85–91; Can and Preb Linc Cathl 89–91; TR Redditch, The Ridge *Worc* 91–01; rtd 01; PtO *Glouc* from 02. *80 Roman Way, Bourton-on-the-Water, Cheltenham GL54 2EW* T: (01451) 821589 E: bnhalfpenny@gmail.com

HALIFAX, Archdeacon of. *See* DAWTRY, The Ven Anne Frances

HALKES, Canon John Stanley. b 39. SWMTC 87. **d** 90 **p** 91. NSM St Buryan, St Levan and Sennen *Truro* 90–92; P-in-c Lanteglos by Fowey 92–04; P-in-c Lansallos 03–04; Hon Can Truro Cathl 03–08; rtd 04; PtO *Truro* from 16. *Creek Cottage, Lerryn, Lostwithiel PL22 0QB*

HALL, Canon Alfred Christopher. b 35. Trin Coll Ox BA 58 MA 61. Westcott Ho Cam 58. **d** 61 **p** 62. C Frecheville *Derby* 61–64; C Dronfield 64–67; V Smethwick St Matt *Birm* 67–70; V Smethwick St Matt w St Chad 70–75; Can Res Man Cathl 75–83; Hon Can Man Cathl 83–90; Dioc Adult Educn Officer 75–83; Dioc World Development Officer 76–88; V Bolton St Pet 83–90; Co-ord Chr Concern for One World 90–00; Hon Sec Li Tim-Oi Foundn 93–17; Hon Can Ch Ch *Ox* 00–01; PtO from 03. *The Knowle, Philcote Street, Deddington, Banbury OX15 0TB* T: (01869) 338225 E: gaedoh@icloud.com

HALL, Andrew David. b 62. Mattersey Hall MA 09 St Jo Coll Dur MATM 12. Cranmer Hall Dur 10. **d** 12 **p** 13. C Brighouse and Clifton *Leeds* 12–15; R Burbage w Aston Flamville *Leic* from 15. *The Rectory, New Road, Burbage, Hinckley LE10 2AW* M: 07507-561216 E: 1andrewdavidhall@gmail.com

HALL, Barry George. b 38. Solicitor 62. Oak Hill Th Coll 78. **d** 81 **p** 82. NSM Stock Harvard *Chelmsf* 81–90; NSM W Hanningfield 90–02; P-in-c 93–02; PtO from 02. *Harvard Cottage, Swan Lane, Stock, Ingatestone CM4 9BQ* T: (01277) 840387

HALL, Brian. b 59. Aston Tr Scheme 90 Oak Hill Th Coll 92. **d** 94 **p** 95. C Mansfield St Jo *S'well* 94–96; C Skegby 96–99; P-in-c Sutton in Ashfield St Mich 99–04; R Carlton-in-the-Willows 04–16; V Gorleston St Andr *Nor* from 16. *St Andrew's Vicarage, 16 Duke Road, Gorleston, Great Yarmouth NR31 6LL* T: (01493) 296950 E: revbhall@sky.com

HALL, Canon Brian Arthur. b 48. Ex Univ BEd 70. Cuddesdon Coll 73. **d** 75 **p** 76. C Hobs Moat *Birm* 75–79; V Smethwick 79–93; R Handsworth St Mary 93–13; AD Handsworth 99–05 and 06–08; Hon Can Birm Cathl 05–13; rtd 13; PtO *Birm* from 13. *97 Perry Hill Road, Oldbury B68 0AH* E: brian.a.hall@btinternet.com

HALL, Mrs Carolyn Ruth. **d** 08 **p** 09. NSM Builth and Llanddewi'r Cwm w Llangynog etc *S & B* 08–11; NSM Builth Deanery 11–15; NSM Radnor and Builth *S & B* from 16. *Coedmor, Broadway, Llandrindod Wells LD1 5HT* T: (01597) 829637

HALL, Ms Christine Beryl. b 52. Southn Univ BSc 73 Leeds Univ MA 06. NTMTC BA 08. **d** 08 **p** 09. NSM Stepney St Dunstan and All SS *Lon* 08–13; NSM St Jo on Bethnal Green from 13; Chapl Guy's and St Thos' NHS Foundn Trust from 08; Chapl Lon Fire Brigade from 08. *15 Lidfield Road, London N16 9NA* T: (020) 7254 9185 E: christine.b.hall@btinternet.com

HALL, Canon Christine Mary. K Coll Lon BD 67 MPhil 86. **d** 87. NSM Bickley *Roch* 87–92; Vice-Prin Chich Th Coll 92–94; LtO *Chich* 95–03; Can and Preb Chich Cathl from 15; PtO *Portsm* from 15. *The Old School, East Marden, Chichester PO18 9JE* T: (01243) 535244 E: dcnchall@eastmarden.net

HALL, Christopher. *See* HALL, Alfred Christopher

HALL, Clive Richard. b 61. Lindisfarne Regional Tr Partnership 15. **d** 18 **p** 19. NSM Stranton *Dur* from 18. *10 Clarkson Court, Hartlepool TS25 5HP* T: (01429) 278504 M: 07804-530120 E: clive.hall7@ntlworld.com

HALL, David Anthony. b 43. Reading Univ BA 66. Qu Coll Birm 79. **d** 81 **p** 82. C Norton *St Alb* 81–85; TV Hitchin 85–93; P-in-c Bidford-on-Avon *Cov* 93; V 93–08; RD Alcester 05–08; rtd 08; PtO *Cov* from 09; *Worc* from 14. *1 Abbey Close, Alcester B49 5QW* T: (01789) 763252 E: davidahall@onetel.com

HALL, David Martin. b 66. Greenwich Univ BA 89. Oak Hill Th Coll BA 00. **d** 00 **p** 01. C Bebington *Ches* 00–03; P-in-c Danehill *Chich* 03–05; V 05–12; RD Uckfield 11–12; V Chorleywood Ch Ch *St Alb* from 12; RD Rickmansworth from 16. *Christ Church Vicarage, Rickmansworth Road, Chorleywood, Rickmansworth WD3 5SG* T: (01923) 282149 or 284325 E: david.andmaryhall@tiscali.co.uk

HALL, Denis. b 43. Lon Coll of Div 65. **d** 69 **p** 70. C Netherton *Liv* 69–71; C Roby 72–75; V Wigan St Steph 75–90; V Newton-le-Willows 90–13; rtd 13; PtO *Liv* from 16. *39 Tracy Drive, Newton-le-Willows WA12 8PX* E: allsaints@3tc4u.net *or* lastresort1943@gmail.com

HALL, Derek. *See* HALL, John Derek

HALL, Derek Guy. b 26. Tyndale Hall Bris 50. **d** 51 **p** 52. C Preston All SS *Blackb* 51–54; C Halliwell St Pet *Man* 54–56; C-in-c Buxton Trin Prop Chpl *Derby* 56–58; V Blackb St Jude 58–67; R Fazakerley Em *Liv* 67–74; TR 74–81; V Langdale *Carl* 81–86; rtd 86; PtO *Carl* 86–10. *14 Gale Park, Ambleside LA22 0BN* T: (01539) 433144

HALL, Diana Mary. b 76. Edin Univ MA 98 LLB 00. **d** 14. C St Andrews St Andr *St And* 14–17; R Dunbar *Edin* from 17. *St Anne's House, 1 Westgate, Dunbar EH42 1JL* E: rector@stannesdunbar.org.uk

HALL, Canon Elaine Chegwin. b 59. Liv Univ MTh 01 RGN 82. NOC 94. **d** 97 **p** 98. C Frankby w Greasby *Ches* 97–01; V Stretton and Appleton Thorn 01–13; RD Gt Budworth 08–10; V Stockport St Geo from 13; Hon Can Ches Cathl from 12. *17 Frewland Avenue, Stockport SK3 8TZ* E: petera.hall@care4free.net

HALL, Elizabeth. *See* SNOWDEN, Elizabeth

HALL (*née* Elliott)**, Mrs Eveline Mary.** b 39. Bedf Coll Lon BA 60 Cam Univ 92 ALA 63. EAMTC 92. **d** 95 **p** 96. NSM Bury St Edmunds St Mary *St E* 95–97; NSM Lark Valley 97–07; rtd 07; PtO *St E* 07–17; *St And* from 17. *15 High Street, Elie, Leven KY9 1BY* T: (01333) 330216

HALL, Frances. *See* SHOESMITH, Judith Frances

HALL, Geoffrey Hedley. b 33. Bris Univ BA 55. St Steph Ho Ox 63. **d** 65 **p** 66. C Taunton H Trin *B & W* 65–67; CF 67–80; Sen CF 80–86; P-in-c Ambrosden w Arncot and Blackthorn *Ox* 72–75; V Barnsley St Edw *Wakef* 86–98; rtd 98; PtO *St And* from 98; *Bre* from 99. *Montana Villa, 39 Haston Crescent, Perth PH2 7XD* T: (01738) 636802 M: 07803-578499 E: geoffreyhall@blueyonder.co.uk

HALL, George Richard Wyndham. b 49. Ex Univ LLB 71. Wycliffe Hall Ox BA 74 MA 78. **d** 75 **p** 76. C Walton H Trin *Ox* 75–79; C Farnborough *Guildf* 79–84; Bp's Chapl *Nor* 84–87; R Saltford w Corston and Newton St Loe *B & W* 87–14; Chapl Bath Coll of HE 88–90; RD Chew Magna *B & W* 97–03; rtd 14; PtO *Carl* from 15. *45 Howard Park, Greystoke, Penrith CA11 0TU* T: (01768) 483394 E: revrichardhall45@gmail.com

HALL, Canon George Rumney. b 37. Westcott Ho Cam 60. **d** 62 **p** 63. C Camberwell St Phil *S'wark* 62–65; C Waltham Cross *St Alb* 65–67; R Buckenham w Hassingham and Strumpshaw *Nor* 67–74; Chapl St Andr Hosp Thorpe 67–72; Chapl HM Pris Nor 72–74; V Wymondham *Nor* 74–87; RD Humbleyard 86–87; R Sandringham w W Newton 87–94; P-in-c Flitcham 87–94; P-in-c Wolferton w Babingley 87–94; R Sandringham w W Newton and Appleton etc 95–03; P-in-c

Castle Rising 87–03; P-in-c Hillington 87–03; Hon Can Nor Cathl 87–03; RD Heacham and Rising 89–01; Dom Chapl to The Queen 87–03; Chapl to The Queen 89–07; rtd 03; PtO Nor from 03. *Town Farm Cottage, 95 Lynn Road, Great Bircham, King's Lynn PE31 6RJ* T: (01485) 576134 M: 07889-627940

HALL, Mrs Gillian Louise. b 45. Univ of Wales (Ban) MPhil 06. NOC 87. **d** 90 **p** 94. NSM Earby *Bradf* 90–96; NSM Gisburn 96–01; NSM Hellifield 96–01; PtO 01–02; Chapl Airedale NHS Trust 02–04; PtO *Bradf* 05–14; *Leeds* from 14. *Mitton House, Lothersdale, Keighley BD20 8HR* T: (01535) 636144 E: miltonhouse@dsl.pipex.com

HALL, Gillian Mary. b 58. Linc Sch of Th and Min. **d** 12 **p** 13. NSM Bilborough w Strelley *S'well* 12–15; NSM Bilborough and Strelley 15–19; NSM Kimberley and Nuthall from 19. *30 Parkside, Nottingham NG8 2NN* E: gillhall30@gmail.com

HALL (*née* JACKSON), Hannah Louise. b 81. St Cuth Soc Dur BA 04 St Jo Coll Dur MA 06. St Mellitus Coll 10. **d** 12 **p** 13. C Pitsmoor Ch Ch *Sheff* 12–15; V Nottingham St Sav *S'well* from 15. *St Saviour's Vicarage, Arkwright Walk, Nottingham NG2 2JU* M: 07702-163138 E: hannah3hall@gmail.com

HALL, Harry. b 41. Open Univ BA 93. Chich Th Coll 91. **d** 91 **p** 92. C Boston *Linc* 91–92; C Bourne 92–94; P-in-c Sutterton w Fosdyke and Algarkirk 94–97; R Sutterton, Fosdyke, Algarkirk and Wigtoft 97–99; V Barnsley St Edw *Wakef* 99–05; Chapl ATC 99–05; R Ardstraw w Baronscourt, Badoney Lower etc *D & R* 05–10; rtd 10; PtO *Linc* from 11. *18 Kings Road, Metheringham, Lincoln LN4 3HT* T: (01526) 320308 E: slk248@hotmail.com

HALL, Canon Hubert William Peter. b 35. Ely Th Coll 58. **d** 60 **p** 61. C Louth w Welton-le-Wold *Linc* 60–62; C Gt Grimsby St Jas 62–69; C Gt Grimsby St Mary and St Jas 69–71; Hon Chapl Miss to Seafarers 71–01; V Immingham *Linc* 71–01; RD Haverstoe 86–01; Can and Preb Linc Cathl 89–01; rtd 01; PtO *Linc* from 01. *6 Abbey Rise, Barrow-upon-Humber DN19 7TF* T: (01469) 531504 E: hwphall@gmail.co.uk

HALL, Mrs Jane Daphne. b 60. Trent Poly BA 92 Solicitor 93. **d** 09 **p** 10. NSM Clopton w Otley, Swilland and Ashbocking *St E* 09–13; NSM Carlford 13–17; rtd 17. *Lark Rise, 230 Ferry Road, Felixstowe IP11 9RU* E: jane.d.pearse@gmail.com

HALL, Jeffrey Ernest. b 42. Linc Th Coll 73. **d** 75 **p** 76. C Brampton St Thos *Derby* 75–78; C Whittington and New Whittington 78–81; TV Riverside *Ox* 81–90; Ind Chapl Slough Deanery 81–89; R Anstey *Leic* 90–97; TR Hugglescote w Donington, Ellistown and Snibston 97–08; rtd 08; PtO *Sarum* from 10; *B & W* from 17. *21 Woodsage Drive, Gillingham SP8 4UE* T: (01747) 823480 M: 07876-540343 E: jeffreyhall123@btinternet.com

HALL, Jennifer. *See* HALL, Margaret Jennifer

HALL, The Ven John Barrie. b 41. Sarum & Wells Th Coll 82. **d** 84 **p** 85. Chapl St Edward's Hosp Cheddleton 84–88; C Cheddleton *Lich* 84–88; V Rocester 88–94; V Rocester and Croxden w Hollington 94–98; RD Uttoxeter 91–98; Adn Salop 98–11; V Tong 98–11; P-in-c Donington 98–00; rtd 11; PtO *Lich* 11–13; Hon C Hanbury, Newborough, Rangemore and Tutbury 13; PtO from 13. *16 Mill House Drive, Cheadle, Stoke-on-Trent ST10 1XL* T: (01538) 750628 E: j.hall182@btinternet.com

HALL, John Bruce. b 33. Covenant Th Sem St Louis MTh 80 DMin 85. ALCD 60. **d** 60 **p** 61. C Kingston upon Hull H Trin *York* 60–67; C Beverley Minster 67–68; V Clapham Park St Steph *S'wark* 68–76; R Tooting Graveney St Nic 76–03; rtd 03; PtO *S'wark* from 03; *Eur* from 04. *44 Mayford Road, London SW12 8SD* T: (020) 8673 6869 E: jbewhall@gmail.com

HALL, John Charles. b 46. Hull Univ BA 71 Spurgeon's Coll MTh 05. Ridley Hall Cam 71. **d** 73 **p** 74. C Bromley Common St Aug *Roch* 73–77; C Westbury-on-Trym St Alb *Bris* 78–80; Oman 80–82; C-in-c Bishop Auckland Woodhouse Close CD *Dur* 82–90; P-in-c Gt and Lt Glemham, Blaxhall etc *St E* 90–91; P-in-c Rodney Stoke w Draycott *B & W* 91–01; Dioc Ecum Officer 91–01; V Southmead *Bris* 01–11; rtd 11; PtO *B & W* from 15. *8 Ridgeway Close, West Harptree, Bristol BS40 6EF* T: (01761) 221881 M: 07771-848412 E: sarasgarden@hotmail.co.uk

HALL, John Curtis. b 39. CEng 73 MIMechE 73. Coll of Resurr Mirfield 80. **d** 82 **p** 83. C Pet Ch Carpenter 82–86; TV Heavitree w Ex St Paul 86–93; R Bow w Broad Nymet 93–04; V Colebrooke 93–04; R Zeal Monachorum 93–04; RD Cadbury 97–02; rtd 04. *37 Lawn Drive, Chudleigh, Newton Abbot TQ13 0LS* T: (01626) 853245

HALL, Canon John Derek. b 25. St Cuth Soc Dur BA 50. Linc Th Coll 50. **d** 52 **p** 53. C Redcar *York* 52–54; C Newland St Jo 54–57; V Boosbeck w Moorsholm 57–61; V Middlesbrough St Oswald 61–68; Chapl St Luke's Hosp Middlesbrough 61–67; V York St Chad 68–90; Chapl Bootham Park Hosp 68–85; Can and Preb York Minster 85–90; rtd 90; Chapl

Castle Howard 90–02; PtO *York* 98–15. *25 Fairfields Drive, Skelton, York YO30 1YP* T: (01904) 470978

HALL, Canon John Edmund. b 49. Open Univ BA 84 Birm Univ MPhil 05 Warwick Univ PhD 06 CQSW 76. Trin Coll Bris BA 89. **d** 89 **p** 90. C Winchmore Hill East Barnet 89–92; V Edmonton St Aldhelm 92–01; Dir Soc Resp *Cov* 01–10; Dir Interfaith Relns and Dir St Phil Cen *Leic* 10–14; Hon Can Leic Cathl 10–14; rtd 14. *7 Riverside View, Ottery St Mary EX11 1YA*

HALL, Canon John Michael. b 62. Leeds Univ BA. Coll of Resurr Mirfield 83. **d** 86 **p** 87. C Ribbleton *Blackb* 86–89; C Carnforth 89–92; V Lt Marsden 92–98; V Lt Marsden w Nelson St Mary 98; V Warton St Oswald w Yealand Conyers 98–08; AD Tunstall 05–08; P-in-c Fleetwood St Pet 08–11; V 11–14; P-in-c Fleetwood St Dav 08–14; V Fleetwood St Pet and St Dav from 14; Hon Can Bloemfontein Cathl from 01; Hon Can Blackb Cathl from 09. *The Vicarage, 49 Mount Road, Fleetwood FY7 6QZ* T: (01253) 876176 E: johnbloem@aol.com

HALL, John Michael. b 47. BD. Oak Hill Th Coll 68. **d** 73 **p** 74. C Walthamstow St Mary w St Steph *Chelmsf* 73–76; C Rainham 76–79; P-in-c Woodham Mortimer w Hazeleigh 79–93; P-in-c Woodham Walter 79–93; Ind Chapl 79–93; R Fairstead w Terling and White Notley etc 93–13; RD Witham 01–07; rtd 13; PtO *Ely* from 14. *43 Northwold, Ely CB6 1BG* T: (01353) 969089 E: rev.johnhall@tiscali.co.uk

HALL, The Very Revd John Robert. b 49. St Chad's Coll Dur BA 71 FRSA 02 FSA 14 Hon FCollT 09 Roehampton Univ Hon DD 07 Ches Univ Hon DTheol 08 Westmr Univ Hon DLitt 14 Hull Univ Hon DLitt 16. Cuddesdon Coll 73. **d** 75 **p** 76. C Kennington St Jo *S'wark* 75–78; P-in-c S Wimbledon All SS 78–84; V Streatham St Pet 84–92; Dioc Dir of Educn *Blackb* 92–98; Hon Can Blackb Cathl 92–94 and 98–00; Can Res Blackb Cathl 94–98; Gen Sec Nat Soc 98–06; Gen Sec C of E Bd of Educn 98–02; Chief Educn Officer and Hd Educn Division Abps' Coun 03–06; Hon C S Norwood St Alb *S'wark* 03–06; Dean Westmr 06–19; rtd 19; Wiccamical Preb Chich Cathl from 18. *15 Little London, Chichester PO19 1NZ* M: 07973-418859

HALL, Canon John Terence Peter. b 67. St Jo Coll Dur BA 98. Cranmer Hall Dur. **d** 98 **p** 99. C Towcester w Easton Neston *Pet* 98–01; P-in-c Blakesley w Adstone and Maidford etc 01–07; C Greens Norton w Bradden and Lichborough 06–07; R Lambfold 07–11; RD Towcester 09–11; P-in-c Irthlingborough 11–12; P-in-c Gt w Lt Addington and Woodford 11–12; R Irthlingborough, Gt Addington, Lt Addington etc from 13; Warden of Readers 14–19; Warden Lay Min Oakham Adnry from 19; Can Pet Cathl from 10. *The Rectory, 79 Finedon Road, Irthlingborough, Wellingborough NN9 5TY* T: (01933) 650278 E: canon.johnhall@gmail.com *or* fr.john@nenecrossings.org.uk

HALL, Jonathan. b 62. Ch Ch Coll Cant BA 83 MCIPD 94. STETS BTh 99. **d** 99 **p** 00. C Weymouth H Trin *Sarum* 99–03; R Whippingham w E Cowes *Portsm* 03–10; RD W Wight 07–10; Chapl Burrswood Chr Hosp *Roch* 10–16; V Aylesford 16–18; PtO *Portsm* 14–18; P-in-c Lower Sandown St Jo from 18; P-in-c Shanklin St Blasius from 18. *10 Elmbank Gardens, Sandown PO36 9SA*

HALL, Judith Frances. *See* SHOESMITH, Judith Frances

HALL, The Very Revd Kenneth Robert James. b 59. St Jo Coll Nottm 95. **d** 98 **p** 99. NSM Derryloran *Arm* 98–02; C Drumglass w Moygashel 02–03; C Brackaville w Donaghendry and Ballyclog 03–04; I 04–10; Dean Clogh from 10; I Enniskillen from 10. *St Macartin's Deanery, 13 Church Street, Enniskillen BT74 7DW* T: (028) 6632 2465 *or* 6632 2917 E: krjhall@btinternet.com

HALL, Mrs Linda Charlotte. b 50. Cam Inst of Educn CertEd 72. St Alb Minl Tr Scheme 85 Oak Hill Th Coll 91. **d** 92 **p** 94. NSM St Alb St Steph 92–98; NSM Sandridge 98–99; C Ipswich All Hallows *St E* 99–00; PtO 01; TV Cwmbran *Mon* 01–08; P-in-c Maesglas and Duffryn 08–15; rtd 16; PtO *Mon* from 16. *32 Woodlands Park, Pontypool NP4 6UP* T: (01495) 760472 E: rev.linda.chall@gmail.com

HALL, Malcolm. b 67. Lindisfarne Regional Tr Partnership 15. **d** 18 **p** 19. NSM N Shields *Newc* from 18. *4 Allendale Crescent, Shiremoor, Newcastle upon Tyne NE27 0UE* T: 0191-295 4760 M: 07833-497208

HALL, Margaret Jennifer. b 44. Univ Coll Lon BSc 67 Brunel Univ MA 83. Trin Coll Bris 10. **d** 12 **p** 13. OLM Stoke Bishop *Bris* from 12. *Dial Cottage, 34 Julian Road, Bristol BS9 1JY* T: 0117-968 5959 E: mjenniferhall@btinternet.com

HALL, Mary. *See* HALL, Eveline Mary

HALL, Ms Melanie Jane. b 55. Ex Univ BA 78. Ripon Coll Cuddesdon 01. **d** 03 **p** 04. C Stepney St Dunstan and All SS *Lon* 03–06; rtd 06; PtO *Lon* 14–19. *Gramarye House, Bush Road,*

Spaxton, Bridgwater TA5 1BX T: (01278) 671034 M: 07788-440078 E: melanie.jh@btopenworld.com

HALL, Michael Alan. b 76. Univ of Wales (Lamp) BA 98. Ripon Coll Cuddesdon 99. **d** 01 **p** 02. C Wellington Ch Ch *Lich* 01–05; V Chelmsf All SS 05–14; P-in-c Gt Burstead w Ramsden Crays from 14. *The Vicarage, 111 Church Street, Billericay CM11 2TR* T: (01277) 632060 E: revd.michael@btinternet.com

HALL, Canon Michael Anthony. b 41. St Paul's Coll Grahamstown LTh 64. **d** 64 **p** 65. C E London St Alb S Africa 65–67; C Queenstown St Mich 67–69; R Port Elizabeth All SS 70–78; R E London All SS 78–81; R Queenstown St Mich w Tarkastad St Mary 81–91; Adn Aliwal N 81–01; R Barkly E St Steph 91–01; P-in-c Dordrecht St Aug 91–02; Hon Can Grahamstown from 01; P-in-c Lapford, Nymet Rowland and Coldridge *Ex* 01–03; TV N Creedy 03–11; rtd 11; PtO *Ex* from 02. *10 Blagdon Rise, Crediton EX17 1EN* T: (01363) 776574 M: 07751-798670 E: micksandhall@btopenworld.com

HALL, Michael Edward. b 32. Fitzw Ho Cam BA 57 MA 61. Ridley Hall Cam 68. **d** 69 **p** 70. C Aspley *S'well* 69–73; P-in-c Bulwell St Jo 73–75; V 75–81; P-in-c Tyler's Green *Ox* 81–90; V 90–00; rtd 00. *5 Hawkings Meadow, Marlborough SN8 1UR* T: (01672) 511713

HALL, Nicholas Charles. b 56. **d** 86 **p** 87. C Hyde St Geo *Ches* 86–89; C Cheadle 89–91; NSM 91–11; PtO from 11. *58 Warren Avenue, Cheadle SK8 1ND* T: 0161-491 6758 F: 491 0285 E: kairosmedia@swissmail.org

HALL (née WANSTALL), Canon Noelle Margaret. b 53. Wolfs Coll Cam BEd 76. Sarum & Wells Th Coll 84. **dss** 86 **d** 87 **p** 94. Hythe *Cant* 86–89; Par Dn 87–89; Par Dn Reculver w Herne Bay St Bart 89–94; C 94–95; Dioc Adv in Women's Min 92–99; Asst Dir Post-Ord Tr 94–97; P-in-c Sittingbourne St Mary 95–00; P-in-c Cant St Martin and St Paul 00–02; R 02–16; P-in-c Blean 07–09; P-in-c Cant All SS 14–16; AD Cant 05–11; Hon Can Cant Cathl 96–16; rtd 16; PtO *Cant* from 17. *127 Rylands Road, Kennington, Ashford TN24 9LR* M: 07743-629975 E: nmhall1556@gmail.com

HALL, Peter. *See* HALL, Hubert William Peter

HALL, Canon Peter Douglas. b 60. Oak Hill Th Coll BA 92. **d** 92 **p** 93. C Bromyard *Heref* 92–96; C Dorridge *Birm* 96–01; V Fareham St Jo *Portsm* 01–13; P-in-c Crookhorn 13–18; C Purbrook 13–18; C Portsdown 13–18; Dioc Dir Voc and Ord from 18; Hon Can Portsm Cathl from 15. *269 Hawthorn Crescent, Cosham, Portsmouth PO6 2TL* T: (023) 9221 0283 E: revpdhall@gmail.com or peter.hall@portsmouth.anglican.org

HALL, Philip Edward Robin. b 36. Oak Hill Th Coll 64. **d** 67 **p** 68. C Ware Ch Ch *St Alb* 67–70; C Rayleigh *Chelmsf* 70–73; R Leven w Catwick *York* 73–85; P-in-c Mayfield *Lich* 85–95; P-in-c Ilam w Blore Ray and Okeover 89–95; Res Min Canwell 95–01; Res Min Hints 95–01; Res Min Drayton Bassett 95–01; rtd 01; PtO *Sheff* from 01; *Derby* 02–13. *22 Kings Court, 358 Manchester Road, Sheffield S10 5DQ* T: 0114-438 2564 E: per.hall13@uwclub.net

HALL, Richard. *See* HALL, George Richard Wyndham

HALL, Richard Alexander Bullock. b 71. Ex Univ BA 93 Edin Univ MTh 95 BD 98. TISEC 95. **d** 98 **p** 99. C Boxmoor St Jo *St Alb* 98–01; CF 01–09; Hon Min Can Ripon Cathl 06–09; P-in-c Kirkby Stephen w Mallerstang etc *Carl* 09–11; CF from 11. *c/o MOD Chaplains (Army)* T: (01264) 383430 F: 381824 E: richard.moonhall@btinternet.com

HALL, Robert Arthur. b 35. Lon Univ BSc 66. NW Ord Course 74. **d** 77 **p** 78. C York St Paul 77–79; R Elvington w Sutton on Derwent and E Cottingwith 79–82; Chapl Tiffield Sch Northants 82–84; V Bessingby and Carnaby *York* 84–88; V Fulford 88–00; P-in-c York St Denys 97–00; rtd 00; PtO *York* from 00. *11 Almond Grove, Filey YO14 9EH* T: (01723) 518355 E: robertandjune@cwctv.net

HALL, Canon Robert Stainburn. b 72. Qu Coll Cam BA 93. St Steph Ho Ox 96. **d** 98 **p** 99. C Worc SE 98–01; TV Halas 01–10; P-in-c 10–15; TR from 15; Hon Can Worc Cathl from 17. *St Margaret's Vicarage, 55 Quarry Lane, Halesowen B63 4PD* T: 0121-550 8744

HALL, Canon Roger John. b 53. Linc Th Coll. **d** 84 **p** 85. C Shrewsbury St Giles w Sutton and Atcham *Lich* 84–87; CF 87–07; Warden Amport Ho 98–01; Chapl Guards Chpl Lon 01–03; Asst Chapl Gen 03–07; Dir Ords 98–02 and Warden of Readers 98–07; QHC 06–07; Dep P in O from 07; Chapl St Pet-ad-Vincula at HM Tower of Lon from 07; Can Chpls R from 12; Chapl Bacon's Coll from 07. *The Chaplain's Residence, HM Tower of London, London EC3N 4AB* T: (020) 3166 6796 E: roger.hall@hrp.org.uk

HALL, Mrs Rosalyn. b 58. NEOC 04. **d** 07 **p** 08. C Washington *Dur* 07–11; V Hartlepool H Trin from 11. *Holy Trinity*

Vicarage, Davison Drive, Hartlepool TS24 9BX T: (01429) 869618 M: 07985-134577 E: rosalyn44@hotmail.com

HALL, Sandra June. b 58. Westcott Ho Cam. **d** 10 **p** 11. C Cuckfield *Chich* 10–15; P-in-c Itchingfield w Slinfold 15–16; R from 16. *The Rectory, The Street, Slinfold, Horsham RH13 0RR* T: (01403) 790197 M: 07817-056986

HALL, Sonia Winifred. *See* RUDD, Sonia Winifred

HALL, Stephen Philip. b 56. Ripon Coll Cuddesdon. **d** 84 **p** 85. C Camberwell St Giles *S'wark* 84–88; Chapl Brighton Poly *Chich* 88–92; TV Bicester w Bucknell, Caversfield and Launton *Ox* 92–02; Sub Chapl HM Pris Bullingdon 92–02; TV Southampton (City Cen) *Win* 02–12; V Lewisham St Mary *S'wark* from 12; AD E Lewisham from 17; Chapl Colfe's Sch Lon from 15. *48 Lewisham Park, London SE13 6QZ* T: (020) 8690 2682

HALL, Prof Stuart George. b 28. New Coll Ox BA 52 MA 55 BD 72. Ripon Hall Ox 53. **d** 54 **p** 55. C Newark w Coddington *S'well* 54–58; Tutor Qu Coll Birm 58–62; Lect Th Nottm Univ 62–73; Sen Lect 73–78; Prof Ecclesiastical Hist K Coll Lon 78–90; PtO *St Alb* 80–86; *S'wark* 86–90; R Pittenweem *St And* 90–98; R Elie and Earlsferry 90–98; rtd 93. *Hopedene, 15 High Street, Elie, Leven KY9 1BY* T: (01333) 330216 E: s.hall579@btinternet.com

HALL, Timothy Patrick. b 63. Bucks Coll of Educn BSc 87 Oak Hill Th Coll BA 93. Trin Coll Bris 99. **d** 01 **p** 02. C Kingsnorth and Shadoxhurst *Cant* 01–04; P-in-c Crowfield w Stonham Aspal and Mickfield *St E* 04–12; P-in-c Coddenham w Gosbeck and Hemingstone w Henley 04–12; RD Bosmere 07–08; V W Sheppey *Cant* 12–18; Chief Exec Officer Through Faith Miss from 18; PtO *Ely* from 19. *14 Bowthorpe Road, Wisbech PE13 2DX* E: tim@throughfaithmissions.org

HALL, Timothy Robert. b 52. Dur Univ BA 74. St Jo Coll Nottm LTh 87. **d** 87 **p** 88. C Hawarden *St As* 87–89; Chapl St D Coll Llandudno from 90. *Woodpecker Cottage, St David's College, Llandudno LL30 1RD* T: (01492) 581224 M: 07887-874487 E: revtimhall@stdavidscollege.co.uk

HALL, William. b 34. Hull Univ BSc(Econ) 56. NEOC 89. **d** 92 **p** 93. NSM Bishopwearmouth St Nic *Dur* 92–01; rtd 01. *31 Nursery Road, Silksworth Lane, Sunderland SR3 1NT* T: 0191-528 4843

HALL-MATTHEWS, Preb John Cuthbert Berners. b 33. Univ of Qld BA 55 K Coll Lon PGCE 65. Coll of Resurr Mirfield 58. **d** 60 **p** 61. C Woodley St Jo the Ev *Ox* 60–63; C Is of Dogs Ch Ch and St Jo w St Luke *Lon* 63–65; Asst Chapl Ch Hosp Horsham 65–72; Chapl R Hosp Sch Holbrook 72–75; V Tupsley *Heref* 75–90; P-in-c Hampton Bishop and Mordiford w Dormington 77–90; RD Heref City 84–90; Preb Heref Cathl 85–90; TR Wolverhampton *Lich* 90–98; TR Cen Wolverhampton 98–02; Preb Lich Cathl 01–02; rtd 02; PtO *Heref* 11–15. *26 Plover Close, Stratford-upon-Avon CV37 9EN* T: (01789) 414182 E: jotricia@btinternet.com

HALLAM, Mrs Janet Kay. b 59. EN(G) 79 RGN 01. STETS 05. **d** 08 **p** 13. NSM Newport St Jo *Portsm* 08–18; NSM Newport St Thos 08–18; Chapl Isle of Wight NHS Trust from 13. *Maranatha, 10 Broadwood Lane, Newport PO30 5NE* T: (01983) 529973 M: 07955-381319 E: jezjanet@btinternet.com

HALLAM, Leslie. b 50. All SS Cen for Miss & Min 13. **d** 17 **p** 17. OLM Ramsbottom and Edenfield *Man* 17.. 25 *Rochdale Road, Ramsbottom, Bury BL0 0JT* T: (01706) 823240 E: leshallam50@gmail.com

HALLAM, Mrs Marilyn. b 61. **d** 03 **p** 04. NSM Hayes *Roch* 03–19; PtO from 19. *83 Pickhurst Rise, West Wickham, Bromley BR4 0AE* T: (020) 8777 2246

HALLAM, Canon Nicholas Francis. b 48. Univ Coll Ox BA 71 MA 81 Glas Univ PhD 76 MB, ChB 81 FRCPath 00. Ox NSM Course 84. **d** 87 **p** 88. NSM Ox St Clem 87–93; NSM Balerno *Edin* 93–05; NSM Hawkshead and Low Wray w Sawrey and Rusland etc *Carl* from 06; NSM Ambleside w Brathay 06–10; NSM Loughrigg from 10; Hon Can Carl Cathl from 18. *Wetherlam, Hawkshead, Ambleside LA22 0NR* T: (01539) 436069 E: nick.hallam@uwclub.net

HALLAM, Stuart Peter. b 66. St Martin's Coll Lanc BA 92 Wolfs Coll Cam BTh 99. Westcott Ho Cam 96. **d** 99 **p** 00. C Battersea St Mary *S'wark* 99–02; Chapl RN 02–18; R Vancouver St Phil Canada from 18. *3691 West 27th Avenue, Vancouver BC V6S 1RS, Canada* E: revhallam@aol.com

✠**HALLATT, The Rt Revd David Marrison.** b 37. Southn Univ BA 59 St Cath Coll Ox BA 62 MA 66. Wycliffe Hall Ox 59. **d** 63 **p** 64 **c** 94. C Maghull *Liv* 63–67; PC Totley *Derby* 67–75; R Didsbury St Jas *Man* 75–80; R Barlow Moor 76–80; TR Didsbury St Jas and Em 80–89; Adn Halifax *Wakef* 89–94; Area Bp Shrewsbury *Lich* 94–01; Asst Bp Sheff 01–10; rtd 02; Hon Asst Bp Sarum from 11; PtO *Win* 11–15. *10 St Nicholas Hospital, St Nicholas Road, Salisbury SP1 2SW* T: (01722) 413360 E: david.hallatt@btopenworld.com

HALLETT, Miss Caroline Morwenna. b 51. Nottm Univ BSc 72 PGCE 74 Univ of Wales (Ban) BTh 05. EAMTC 03. **d** 05 **p** 06. C Sole Bay *St E* 05–09; P-in-c Acton w Gt Waldingfield from 09. *The Vicarage, Melford Road, Acton, Sudbury CO10 0BA* T: (01787) 377287 E: revhallett@yahoo.co.uk

HALLETT, Howard Adrian. b 43. Man Univ MPhil 90. Oak Hill Th Coll BA 81. **d** 81 **p** 82. C Walshaw Ch Ch *Man* 81–84; V Stoke sub Hamdon *B & W* 84–99; RD Ivelchester 91–95; V Kea *Truro* 99–05; rtd 05; PtO *Truro* 05–14. *Address temp unknown*

HALLETT, Keith Philip. b 37. Tyndale Hall Bris 61. **d** 64 **p** 65. C Higher Openshaw *Man* 64–68; C Bushbury *Lich* 68–71; P-in-c Drayton Bassett 71–72; R 72–90; V Fazeley 71–90; P-in-c Hints 78–83; V 83–90; C-in-c Canwell CD 78–83; V Canwell 83–90; RD Tamworth 81–90; P-in-c Buckhurst Hill *Chelmsf* 90–93; TR 93–02; rtd 02; PtO *B & W* from 03. *46 Balmoral Way, Weston-super-Mare BS22 9AL* T: (01934) 413711 E: keithkph@talktalk.net

HALLETT, Peter. b 49. Bath Univ BSc 72. Oak Hill Th Coll. **d** 76 **p** 77. C Brinsworth w Catcliffe *Sheff* 76–79; P-in-c Doncaster St Jas 80–81; V 81–86; R Henstridge and Charlton Horethorne w Stowell *B & W* 86–07; P-in-c Abbas and Templecombe w Horsington 06–07; R Abbas and Templecombe, Henstridge and Horsington 07–17; rtd 17; PtO *Bris* from 18. *27 Atherston, Bristol BS30 8YB* T: 0117-961 6262 E: halatvic@gmail.com

HALLETT, Peter Duncan. b 43. CCC Cam BA 66 MA 68. Westcott Ho Cam 69. **d** 71 **p** 72. C Sawston *Ely* 71–73; C Lyndhurst and Emery Down *Win* 73–78; C Skegness and Winthorpe *Linc* 78–80; P-in-c Samlesbury *Blackb* 80–91; Asst Dir RE 80–00; C Leyland St Ambrose 91–94; V Lostock Hall 00–09; P-in-c Farington Moss 03–09; V Lostock Hall and Farington Moss 09; rtd 09; PtO *Blackb* from 09. *121 Pleasington Close, Blackburn BB2 1TU*

HALLETT, Stephen Jonathan. b 70. Trin Coll Bris BA 96. Ripon Coll Cuddesdon 17. **d** 19. C Water Eaton *Ox* from 19. *Water Eaton Church Centre, Drayton Road, Bletchley, Milton Keynes MK2 3RR* M: 07702-098719 E: mkstevehallett@gmail.com

HALLIDAY, Christopher Norton Robert. b 48. Bradf Univ PhD 99. NOC 82. **d** 85 **p** 86. C Davyhulme St Mary *Man* 85–87; Lect Bolton St Pet 87–90; I Rathdrum w Glenealy, Derralossary and Laragh *D & G* 90–00; R Valley Lee St Geo USA 00–05; PtO *Man* 07–08; TR Saddleworth 08–16; rtd 16; PtO *Man* from 16. *2A Gatehead Mews, Delph, Oldham OL3 5QA* E: frchristopher@waitrose.com

HALLIDAY, Mrs Diana Patricia. b 40. ALA 66. NOC 89. **d** 92 **p** 94. NSM Burley in Wharfedale *Bradf* 92–95; NSM Harden and Wilsden 95–97; P-in-c Cullingworth 97–05; Chapl Airedale NHS Foundn Trust 04–11; PtO *Bradf* 11–14; *Leeds* from 14. *8 Malham Court, Silsden, Keighley BD20 0QB* T: (01535) 656777 E: revdi.halliday@btinternet.com

HALLIDAY, Jean Douglas. b 47. NTMTC 99. **d** 01 **p** 02. NSM Forest Gate Em w Upton Cross *Chelmsf* 01–02; NSM E Ham w Upton Park and Forest Gate 02–05; NSM Becontree S 05–09; P-in-c Margaretting w Mountnessing and Buttsbury 09–13; Dioc Child Protection Adv 05–13; rtd 13. *27 Lynns Hall Close, Great Waldingfield, Sudbury CO10 0FW* T: (01787) 466921 E: jeanhalliday456@gmail.com

HALLIDAY, Louisa. b 42. Open Univ BA 77 BA 94. STETS. **d** 00 **p** 01. NSM Wylye and Till Valley *Sarum* 00–09; rtd 09; PtO *Sarum* from 10. *Station House, Great Wishford, Salisbury SP2 0PA* T: (01722) 790618 E: louisahalliday@rocketmail.com

HALLIDAY, Paula Patricia. *See* ROBINSON, Paula Patricia

✠**HALLIDAY, The Rt Revd Robert Taylor.** b 32. Glas Univ MA 54 BD 57. Edin Th Coll 55. **d** 57 **p** 58 **c** 90. C St Andrews St Andr *St And* 57–60; C Glas St Marg 60–63; Lect NT Edin Th Coll 63–74; R Edin H Cross 63–83; Tutor Edin Univ 69–71; Can St Mary's Cathl *Edin* 73–83; R St Andrews St Andr *St And* 83–90; Tutor St Andr Univ 84–90; Bp Bre 90–96; rtd 96; LtO *Edin* from 97; NSM Edin Ch Ch 97–09; NSM Edin St Pet 09–18. *28 Forbes Road, Edinburgh EH10 4ED* T: 0131-221 1490

HALLIDIE SMITH, William. b 35. Pemb Coll Cam BA 58 MA 62. Coll of Resurr Mirfield 59. **d** 60 **p** 62. C Poplar *Lon* 60–67; rtd 00. *69 Park Road, Chilwell, Beeston, Nottingham NG9 4DD* T: 0115-943 1896

HALLIGAN, Adrian Ronald. b 69. Ulster Univ MSc 96 PGCE 05. CITC 06. **d** 11. NSM Antrim All SS *Conn* 11–14; NSM Skerry w Rathcavan and Newtowncrommelin 14–18; NSM Craigs w Dunaghy and Killagan from 18. *35 Castle Manor, Ballynure, Ballyclare BT39 9GW* T: (028) 9334 2572 M: 07846-451932 E: adrian.halligan@sky.com

HALLISSEY, Catherine Jane. **d** 14 **p** 15. Kilternan *D & G* 14–15; C Taney 15–19; I Powerscourt w Kilbride from 19. *Address temp unknown* M: (00353) 86-358 3104 E: cathyhallissey@hotmail.com

HALLIWELL, Christopher Eigil. b 57. Newc Univ BA 78. Trin Coll Bris 89. **d** 91 **p** 92. C Mildenhall *St E* 91–94; R Wrentham w Benacre, Covehithe, Frostenden etc 94–97; TV Sileby, Cossington and Seagrave *Leic* 97–01; V Preston St Cuth *Blackb* 01–12; V Grimsargh 12–17; Rural and Environmental Officer 11–17; rtd 17; PtO *Blackb* from 17. *14 Durham Avenue, Lancaster LA1 4ED* E: chris.halliwell@btinternet.com

HALLIWELL, Ivor George. b 33. St Cath Coll Cam BA 57 MA 60. Wells Th Coll 58. **d** 60 **p** 60. C Hanworth St Geo *Lon* 60–62; C Willenhall *Cov* 62–65; C-in-c Whitley St Jas CD 65–68; V Whitley 68–72; V Corton *Nor* 72–77; P-in-c Hopton 72–74; V 74–77; Asst Chapl HM Pris Pentonville 77; Chapl HM Pris Ex 77–83; Chapl HM Pris Wakef 83–85; P-in-c Bickington *Ex* 85–87; P-in-c Ashburton w Buckland-in-the-Moor 85–87; V Ashburton w Buckland in the Moor and Bickington 87–90; Chapl HM Pris Channings Wood 90–97; LtO *Ex* 90–97; rtd 97; PtO *Ex* from 97. *Anastasis, Avenue Road, Bovey Tracey, Newton Abbot TQ13 9BQ* T: (01626) 834899 E: ivor@ivorhalliwell.com

HALLIWELL, Canon Michael Arthur. b 28. St Edm Hall Ox BA 50 MA 53. Ely Th Coll 52. **d** 54 **p** 55. C Welling *S'wark* 54–57; C Bournemouth St Alb *Win* 57–59; Asst Gen Sec C of E Coun on Foreign Relns 59–62; C St Dunstan in the West *Lon* 60–62; Chapl Bonn w Cologne *Eur* 62–67; Chapl RAF 66–67; V Croydon St Andr *Cant* 67–71; R Jersey St Brelade *Win* 71–96; Chapl HM Pris Jersey 75–80; Vice-Dean Jersey *Win* 85–99; Tutor S Dios Minl Tr Scheme 92–96; rtd 96; Hon C Jersey Grouville *Win* 96–99; Hon Can Win Cathl 98–99; PtO from 99. *1 Alliance Cottages, Awbridge Hill, Awbridge, Romsey SO51 0HF* T: (01794) 830395 E: michaelandsusan@halliwell.info

HALLS, Canon Peter Ernest. b 38. Bris Univ BA 62. Tyndale Hall Bris 59. **d** 64 **p** 65. C Blackb St Barn 64–67; C Bromley Ch Ch *Roch* 67–70; V Halvergate w Tunstall *Nor* 70–79; V Freethorpe w Wickhampton 71–79; P-in-c Beighton and Moulton 77–79; V Tuckswood 79–90; RD Nor S 86–90; R Brooke, Kirstead, Mundham w Seething and Thwaite 90–03; RD Depwade 91–97 and 01–03; Hon Can Nor Cathl 99–03; rtd 03; PtO *Nor* from 03. *1 Church Farm Close, Weston Longville, Norwich NR9 5JY* T: (01603) 880835 E: pandm.halls@gmail.com

HALLS, Susan Mary. *See* HEMSLEY HALLS, Susan Mary

HALLSWORTH, Peter Michael. b 59. Nottm Univ BSc 81 PGCE 82 York St Jo Univ MA 05. Wilson Carlile Coll 00. **d** 12 **p** 13. C Bridlington Quay Ch Ch *York* 12–15; C Clifton 15–19; C Langley Mill and Aldercar *Derby* from 19. *The Vicarage, Church Street, Horsley, Derby DE21 5BR* M: 07772-549088 E: petermhallsworth@gmail.com

HALMSHAW, Mrs Stella Mary. b 36. Brighton Coll of Educn TCert 57. St Alb Minl Tr Scheme 81. **dss** 84 **d** 87 **p** 96. Radlett *St Alb* 84–01; Par Dn 87–93; Hon C 93–01; Chapl Herts Univ 93–96; rtd 96; NSM Wittersham w Stone and Ebony *Cant* 01–12; PtO from 13. *Orchard Field House, Grove Lane, Iden, Rye TN31 7PX* T: (01797) 280435 E: stellashaw@gmail.com

HALSALL, Graham. b 61. Sheff Univ BA 82 Westmr Coll Ox PGCE 84. St Steph Ho Ox MTh 00. **d** 00 **p** 01. C Preston St Jo and St Geo *Blackb* 00–02; C Torrisholme 02–04; P-in-c Bamber Bridge St Sav 04–12; V from 12. *St Saviour's Vicarage, Church Road, Bamber Bridge, Preston PR5 6AJ* T: (01772) 335374 E: graham@stsavioursbb.org.uk

HALSALL, Mrs Isobel Joan. b 47. Liv Univ CertEd 71. **d** 94 **p** 95. OLM Walshaw Ch Ch *Man* 94–05; NSM Cockermouth Area *Carl* 05–13; rtd 13; PtO *Carl* from 13. *1 London Head, Santon Bridge, Holmrook CA19 1UY*

HALSEY, David Mark. b 61. Qu Coll Cam BA 83 MA 87 Cranfield Inst of Tech PhD 87. ERMC 16. **d** 18 **p** 19. NSM St Alb St Luke from 18. *32 Wordsworth Road, Harpenden AL5 4AF* T: (01582) 462322 E: david.halsey@clara.co.uk

HALSEY, Brother John Walter Brooke. b 61. Cam Univ BA 57. Westcott Ho Cam 61. **d** 61 **p** 62. C Stocksbridge *Sheff* 61–65; Community of the Transfiguration Midlothian from 65; Ind Chapl Edin 65–69. *The Hermitage, 70E Clerk Street, Loanhead EH20 9RG* T: 0131-440 3028

HALSON, Bryan Richard. b 32. Jes Coll Cam BA 56 MA 60 Liv Univ MA 72 Geneva Univ 59. Ridley Hall Cam 57. **d** 59 **p** 60. C Coulsdon St Andr *S'wark* 59–62; LtO *Ches* 63–68; Tutor St Aid Birkenhead 63–65; Sen Tutor 65–68; Vice-Prin 68–69; Lect Alsager Coll of Educn 69–72; Prin Lect Crewe and Alsager Coll of HE 72–90; PtO *Ches* from 97. *1 Victoria Mill Drive, Willaston, Nantwich CW5 6RR* T: (01270) 652393 E: bbhalson@gmail.com

HALSTEAD, James. b 74. Nottm Univ BA 97. Oak Hill Th Coll MTh 09. **d** 09 **p** 10. C Gee Cross *Ches* 09–12; V Mottram in

Longdendale 12–19; Prin Sch of Discipleship *S'well* from 19. *8 Ridgeway, Southwell NG25 0DU*

HALSTEAD, Stuart. NTMTC 02. **d** 05 **p** 06. C Houghton Regis *St Alb* 05–08; C Kilburn St Aug w St Jo *Lon* 08–10; P-in-c Gt Ilford St Alb *Chelmsf* 10–14; V from 14. *The Vicarage, 99 Albert Road, Ilford IG1 1HS* T: (020) 8478 2031 E: sh927b@hotmail.com

HAM, Mark Peter. b 65. Sheff Univ BA 86 Birkbeck Coll Lon MSc 96. Ripon Coll Cuddesdon BA 15. **d** 14 **p** 15. C Staplehurst *Cant* 14–15; C The Six 15–18; P-in-c Dartford St Alb *Roch* from 18; P-in-c Dartford St Edm from 18. *St Edmund's Vicarage, St Edmund's Road, Dartford DA1 5ND* T: (01322) 229261 M: 07790-430805 E: m.ham904@gmail.com

HAM, Robin Peter. b 84. St Aid Coll Dur BA 07. Oak Hill Th Coll MA 15. **d** 15 **p** 16. C S Barrow *Carl* from 15. *33 Holebeck Road, Barrow-in-Furness LA13 0HR* M: 07828-333106 E: robinpeterham@gmail.com

HAM-RICHE, Mrs Emma Louise. b 73. Univ of Wales (Abth) BA 95 Surrey Univ PGCE 96. St Aug Coll of Th 17. **d** 19. C E Preston w Kingston *Chich* from 19. *20 The Ridings, East Preston, Littlehampton BN16 2TN* M: 07720-709119 E: ehamriche@gmail.com

HAMBIDGE, John Robert. b 29. Birm Univ MA 02. Sarum Th Coll. **d** 55 **p** 56. C Tynemouth H Trin W Town *Newc* 55–57; C Middlesbrough St Jo the Ev *York* 58–63; C Clerkenwell H Redeemer w St Phil *Lon* 63–64; C Richmond St Mary w St Matthias *S'wark* 64–66; V Richmond St Jo 66–76; R Swanscombe *Roch* 76–84; V Aberedw w Llandeilo Graban and Llanbadarn etc *S & B* 84–91; P-in-c Sibson w Sheepy and Ratcliffe Culey *Leic* 91–94; P-in-c Orton-on-the-Hill w Twycross etc 92–94; R The Sheepy Gp 95–97; rtd 97; PtO *Lich* 99–18. *99 Elizabeth Drive, Tamworth B79 8DE* T: (01827) 61526 E: john@hambidge.com

HAMBLIN, Derek Gordon Hawthorn. b 35. SWMTC 94. **d** 96 **p** 97. NSM S Brent and Rattery *Ex* 96–01; Chapl Larnaca Cyprus 01–02; Asst Chapl Dubai UAE 03–04; PtO *Ex* from 04. *2 Brookwood Close, South Brent TQ10 9DH* T: (01364) 72388 *or* (00357) (24) 620455 E: derekthecleric1@aol.com

HAMBLIN, Canon Karen Elizabeth. b 59. St Mary's Coll Dur BA 80 Homerton Coll Cam PGCE 82. St Jo Coll Nottm 05. **d** 07 **p** 08. C Long Eaton St Jo *Derby* 07–11; TV N Wingfield, Clay Cross and Pilsley 11–16; P-in-c Brampton St Mark from 16; C Chesterfield St Mary and All SS from 16; C Chesterfield H Trin and Ch Ch from 16; C Chesterfield SS Aug from 16; RD Chesterfield 15–18; AD NE Derbyshire from 18; Hon Can Derby Cathl from 17. *1 Whitecotes Lane, Chesterfield S40 3HJ* T: (01246) 913688 M: 07432-705255 E: khndeanery@gmail.com

HAMBLIN, Canon Roger Noel. b 42. Ripon Hall Ox 67. **d** 70 **p** 71. C Scotforth *Blackb* 70–73; C Altham w Clayton le Moors 73–76; V Cockerham w Winmarleigh 76–87; V Cockerham w Winmarleigh and Glasson 87–00; P-in-c Wray w Tatham and Tatham Fells 00–03; V E Lonsdale 03–09; Agric Chapl 01–09; Hon Can Blackb Cathl 04–09; rtd 09; PtO *Blackb* from 09. *Wycoller, School Lane, Pilling, Preston PR3 6AA* T: (01253) 790555 E: rogerhamblin@yahoo.co.uk

HAMBORG, Canon Graham Richard. b 52. Bris Univ BSc 73 Nottm Univ BA 76 MTh 77. St Jo Coll Nottm 74. **d** 77 **p** 78. C Tile Cross *Birm* 77–80; C Upton cum Chalvey *Ox* 80–82; TV 82–86; V Ruscombe and Twyford 86–04; AD Sonning 03–04; CME Adv *Chelmsf* 04–12; Ord Min Development Adv 12–17; C Gt Baddow 04–17; C Lt Baddow 05–17; Hon Can Chelmsf Cathl 12–17; rtd 17; PtO *Portsm* from 18. *3 Hatchlands, Huntsbottom Lane, Liss GU33 7EU* E: revghamborg@hotmail.com

HAMBORG, Peter Graham. b 79. BMus 00. Trin Coll Bris BA 09. **d** 10 **p** 11. C Fulwood Ch Ch *Blackb* 10–14; V Lea from 14; V Preston Em from 14. *45 Abingdon Drive, Ashton-on-Ribble, Preston PR2 1EY* T: (01772) 726987 M: 07771-993004 E: revpete@emmanelpreston.org

HAMEEM, Samuel. b 77. **p** 17. NSM Kingsbury H Innocents *Lon* from 15. *458B Church Lane, London NW9 8UA* M: 07481-753258 E: hameem_77@gmail.com

HAMER, Irving David. b 59. **d** 84 **p** 85. C Newton Nottage *Llan* 84–88; C Roath 88–90; V Llansawel, Briton Ferry 90–00; V Roath St Martin from 00; Miss to Seafarers from 90. *St Martin's Vicarage, Strathnairn Street, Roath, Cardiff CF24 3JL* T: (029) 2048 2295 E: fr.irving.hamer@ntlworld.com

HAMER, Mrs Jeanette Estelle. b 55. Wall Hall Coll Aldenham CertEd 76. SNWTP 10. **d** 12 **p** 13. NSM Douglas St Geo *S & M* 12–14; NSM W Coast from 14. *15 Faaie Ny Cabbal, Kirk Michael, Isle of Man IM6 2HS* T/F: (01624) 877814 M: 07624-462251 E: manxmiffy55@gmail.com

HAMER, Penelope Ann. *See* WEST, Penelope Ann

HAMER, Canon Val. b 52. Leeds Univ BA 74. S'wark Ord Course 83. **dss** 86 **d** 87 **p** 94. Warlingham w Chelsham and Farleigh *S'wark* 86–88; Par Dn 87–88; Par Dn Caterham 88–94; C 94–96; RD 95–96; Sub Chapl HM Pris Wandsworth 88–95; V Addiscombe St Mildred *S'wark* 96–02; Ldr Post Ord Tr Croydon Area 94–99; Can Res and Chan Heref Cathl 02–08; Dioc Missr and P-in-c Coychurch, Llangan and St Mary Hill *Llan* 08–12; rtd 12; PtO *Chich* from 13. *Noddfa Fach, 126 West Hill Road, St Leonard's-on-Sea TN38 0AY* T: (01424) 254564 E: val_hamer@hotmail.com

HAMES, Daniel Lewis. b 84. Leic Univ BSc 06. Wycliffe Hall Ox BA 11 MSt 12. **d** 15 **p** 16. NSM Ox St Aldate w H Trin from 15. *Flat 8, 25-27 Fairacres Road, Oxford OX4 1TH* E: danielhames@gmail.com *or* daniel.hames@staldates.org.uk

✠**HAMID, The Rt Revd David.** b 55. McMaster Univ Ontario BSc 78. Trin Coll Toronto MDiv 81 Hon DD 05. **d** 81 **p** 82 **c** 02. C Burlington St Chris Canada 81–83; R Burlington St Jo 83–87; Miss Co-ord Gen Syn of Angl Ch of Canada 87–96; Hon Can Santo Domingo 93–02; Dir Ecum Affairs ACC 96–02; Suff Bp Eur from 02; Hon Asst Bp Roch 03–11; hon C Orpington St Andr 03–09. *14 Tufton Street, London SW1P 3QZ* T: (020) 7898 1160 F: 7898 1166 E: david.hamid@churchofengland.org

HAMIL, Sheila. b 49. Northd Coll of Educn TCert 71. NEOC 92. **d** 95 **p** 98. NSM Wallsend St Luke *Newc* 95–97; NSM Long Benton St Mary 97–02; NSM Willington 02–06; rtd 06; PtO *Newc* from 06. *5 Kings Road, Wallsend NE28 7QT* T: 0191-287 3449 E: sheila@sheilahamil.co.uk

HAMILL-STEWART, Simon Francis. b 32. Pemb Coll Cam BA 56. NOC 77. **d** 80 **p** 81. NSM Neston *Ches* 80–83; C 83–86; V Over St Jo 86–00; Dioc Ecum Officer 92–00; rtd 00; PtO *Ches* 00–01 and from 04; C Middlewich w Byley 01–03. *87 Warmingham Lane, Middlewich CW10 0DJ* T: (01606) 737329

HAMILTON, Graham. *See* HAMILTON, William Graham

HAMILTON, Janice Patricia. b 64. Ch Ch Coll Cant BEd 86. Ox Min Course 14. **d** 17 **p** 18. C Tidenham w Beachley and Lancaut *Glouc* from 17. *Caradoc, Sedbury Lane, Tutshill, Chepstow NP16 7DU* T: (01291) 626158 M: 07749-130323 E: janice-hamilton@outlook.com

HAMILTON, John Hans Patrick. b 44. K Coll Lon BD 66 AKC 67 Lon Univ DipAdEd 76 FCMI 96. St Boniface Warminster 66. **d** 67 **p** 68. C Cleobury Mortimer w Hopton Wafers *Heref* 67–69; C Sanderstead All SS *S'wark* 69–73; V Battersea St Mary-le-Park 73–75; PtO *Ely* 75–90; Dir of Educn *Derby* 90–95; P-in-c Cliddesden and Ellisfield w Farleigh Wallop etc *Win* 95–00; PtO 00–03; P-in-c Dungeon Hill and The Caundles w Folke and Holwell *Sarum* 03–07; TR Wylye and Till Valley 07–11; rtd 11; PtO *Sarum* from 11. *Hillview, Duck Street, Tisbury, Salisbury SP3 6LJ* T: (01722) 790117

HAMILTON, John Nicholas. b 49. Trin Coll Cam BA 71 MA 75. Ridley Hall Cam 72. **d** 75 **p** 76. C Ealing Dean St Jo *Lon* 75–79; C Stoughton *Guildf* 79–83; R Denton St Lawr *Man* 83–88; R The Sherbornes w Pamber *Win* 88–19; rtd 19. *54 Little Hivings, Chesham HP5 2LU* E: jt77hamilton@waitrose.com

HAMILTON, Nigel John. *See* TABER-HAMILTON, Nigel John

HAMILTON, Canon Paul Stuart. b 69. Univ of Wales (Ban) BTh 02. EAMTC. **d** 02 **p** 03. C Hawkwell *Chelmsf* 02–06; V Ingrave St Nic and St Steph from 06; AD Brentwood from 15; Hon Can Chelmsf Cathl from 15. *The Rectory, Thorndon Gate, Ingrave, Brentwood CM13 3RG* T: (01277) 812452 E: psh@btinternet.com

HAMILTON, Reid Henry. b 56. **d** 98 **p** 98. C Kansas City St Paul USA 98–01; R Kent Ch Ch 01–04; Chapl Canterbury Ho Ann Arbor 04–17; Chapl Algarve *Eur* from 18. *Casa São Vicente, Apartado 2135, 8100-070 Boliqueime, Portugal* E: stvincentsalgarve.east@gmail.com

HAMILTON, Sarah Louise. *See* BRUSH, Sarah Louise

HAMILTON, Sebastian John Marie. b 91. Coll of Resurr Mirfield BA 18. **d** 18 **p** 19. C Tewkesbury w Walton Cardiff and Twyning *Glouc* from 18. *40 Church Street, Tewkesbury GL20 5SN* E: curate@tewkesburyabbey.org.uk

HAMILTON, William Graham. b 63. New Coll Ox BA 86. Wycliffe Hall Ox BA 95. **d** 95 **p** 96. C Ivybridge w Harford *Ex* 95–99; V Bovey Tracey SS Pet, Paul and Thos w Hennock from 99. *The Vicarage, Coombe Cross, Bovey Tracey, Newton Abbot TQ13 9EP* T: (01626) 833813 E: pptbovey@mac.com

HAMILTON, William Joseph Taylor. b 40. Univ Coll Ches MTh 00. **d** 97 **p** 98. NSM Ches 97–02; C Thurstaston, S Milton, W Alvington etc *Ex* 02–07; rtd 07; PtO *Ches* from 07. *51 Vincent Drive, Chester CH4 7RQ* T: (01244) 428457 E: william-hamilton3@sky.com

HAMILTON-BOX, William Michael. b 90. Cant Ch Ch Univ BMus 13 MMus 15. St Steph Ho Ox BA 19. **d** 19. NSM

Hammersmith St Luke *Lon* from 19. *28 Cowper Road, London W3 6PZ*

HAMILTON-BROWN, James John. b 35. Lon Univ BSc 59. Ridley Hall Cam 59. **d** 61 **p** 62. C Attenborough w Bramcote *S'well* 61–67; V Bramcote 67–76; R and D Officer Abps' Coun on Evang 76–79; LtO *Sarum* 76–81 and 91–95; TR Dorchester 81–91; Sec Par and People 91–95; P-in-c Tarrant Valley *Sarum* 95–99; C Tollard Royal w Farnham, Gussage St Michael etc 99–00; rtd 00; PtO *Sarum* from 00. *April Cottage, West Street, Winterborne Stickland, Blandford Forum DT11 0NT* T: (01258) 880627 E: jumperhb@btinternet.com

HAMILTON-GREY, Mrs Deborah. b 66. Birm Univ BA 99 MA 03 Sheff Univ BA 14. Coll of Resurr Mirfield 12. **d** 14 **p** 15. C Diss *Nor* 14–15; C Watton 15–17; V Ludham, Potter Heigham, Hickling and Catfield 17–19; PtO from 19. *51A Station Road, Sheringham NR26 8RG* M: 07896-658373 E: deborah.hamiltongrey@gmail.com

HAMILTON-MANON, Phillipp Robert Christian. b 49. BA 88. St Steph Ho Ox 89. **d** 90 **p** 91. C Norton St Mary *Dur* 90–94; P-in-c Cleadon Park 94–95; V 95–97; TV Lewes All SS, St Anne, St Mich and St Thos *Chich* 97–00; R Lewes St Anne 00–10; R Lewes St Anne and St Mich and St Thos etc 10–12; rtd 12; PtO *Chich* from 13. *9 Belgrave Crescent, Seaford BN25 3AX* E: phm1949@aol.com

HAMLET, Paul Manning. b 42. Open Univ BA 81 Ex Univ MEd 96 Univ of Wales (Lamp) MTh 04 PhD 12 Lambeth STh 84 FCollP 96. Kelham Th Coll 61. **d** 66 **p** 67. C Rumboldswyke *Chich* 66–69; C Ely 69–73; Hon C Ipswich St Bart *St E* 73–84; Chapl Wellington Sch Somerset 84–94; Chapl Ipswich Sch 94–02; CF (TAVR) 88–99; CF (ACF) 99–09; rtd 02; PtO *St E* from 02; *Chelmsf* from 18. *5 Wincanton Close, Ipswich IP4 3EE* T: (01473) 724413 E: paul.hamlet@btopenworld.com

HAMLETT, David. b 50. All SS Cen for Miss & Min 13. **d** 15 **p** 16. OLM Wigan All SS *Liv* 15–19; TV Maghull and Melling from 19. *17 Woodedge, Ashton-in-Makerfield, Wigan WN4 9JY* T: (01942) 740812 M: 07972-577801 E: dhamlett@blueyonder.co.uk

HAMLEY, Isabelle Maryvonne. b 75. Orléans Univ BA 95 MA 96 Birm Univ BA 03 Ches Univ PhD 17. St Jo Coll Nottm 09. **d** 11 **p** 12. C W Bridgford *S'well* 11–12; C Wilford Hill 12–14; C Edwalton 14–17; Abp's Chapl *Cant* from 17; PtO *S'wark* from 17; *Lon* from 17. *Lambeth Palace, London SE1 7JU* T: (020) 7898 1200 M: 07850-402321 E: isabellehamley@yahoo.co.uk *or* isabelle.hamley@lambethpalace.org.uk

HAMMERSLEY, Peter Angus Ragsdale. b 35. Linc Th Coll 74. **d** 76 **p** 77. C Stafford *Lich* 76–79; P-in-c W Bromwich St Andr 79–83; V 83–88; P-in-c W Bromwich Ch Ch 85–88; V Streetly 88–98; RD Walsall 90–98; C Ledbury *Heref* 98–00; Team Chapl W Heref 98–00; rtd 01; Assoc TV Ledbury *Heref* 01–04; PtO from 04. *15 Pound Close, Tarrington, Hereford HR1 4AZ* T: (01432) 890609

HAMMERSLEY, Susan. b 67. Nottm Univ BA 90. Ripon Coll Cuddesdon BA 07. **d** 07 **p** 08. C Ecclesfield *Sheff* 07–10; C Sheff St Mark Broomhill 10–15; V from 15. *The Vicarage, 4 St Mark's Crescent, Sheffield S10 2SG* T: 0114-327 6908 *or* 266 0260 E: suehammersley@tiscali.co.uk *or* sue.hammersley@sheffield.anglican.org

HAMMETT, The Ven Barry Keith. b 47. Magd Coll Ox BA 71 MA 74. St Steph Ho Ox 71. **d** 74 **p** 75. C Plymouth St Pet *Ex* 74–77; Chapl RN 77–02; Chapl of the Fleet and Adn for the RN 02–06; Dir Gen Naval Chapl Service 02–06; Hon Can Portsm Cathl 02–06; Can Gib Cathl *Eur* 03–06; rtd 06; QHC 99–06; PtO *Portsm* 07–15; *Ox* from 15. *26 Penhurst Gardens, Chipping Norton OX7 5ED*

HAMMILL, Anthony Lawrence. b 71. Linc Coll Ox BA 92 MA 97 Univ Coll Lon MSc 95 Anglia Ruskin Univ MA 08 Fitzw Coll Cam MPhil 08. Ridley Hall Cam 05. **d** 08 **p** 09. C Chalk *Roch* 08–11; C Tonbridge SS Pet and Paul 11–18; CMD Officer from 18. *3 Annexe Close, Tunbridge Wells TN2 3PA* E: anthony.hammill@rochester.anglican.org

HAMMOND, Mrs Barbara Watson. b 33. Lanc Univ MA 79 Bp Otter Coll TCert 53 ACP 70. S'wark Ord Course 89. **d** 92 **p** 94. NSM Upper Norwood St Jo *S'wark* 92–94; Hon C Spring Park All SS 94–97; PtO 97–02; *Portsm* from 98; *Chich* 12–17. *28 Church Path, Emsworth PO10 7DP* T: (01243) 370531 E: barbarawh@virginmedia.com

HAMMOND, Carolyn John-Baptist. b 64. St Jo Coll Ox MA 90 Univ Coll Ox DPhil 93 CCC Cam BA 97 MA 02. Westcott Ho Cam 95. **d** 98 **p** 99. C Gamlingay w Hatley St George and E Hatley *Ely* 98–99; C Gamlingay and Everton 99–01; R 01–05; Dean G&C Coll Cam from 05. *Gonville and Caius College, Trinity Street, Cambridge CB2 1TA* T: (01223) 332400 F: 332336 E: cjbh2@cam.ac.uk *or* dean@cai.cam.ac.uk

HAMMOND, Kathryn Mary. b 49. LCTP 07. **d** 08 **p** 09. NSM Linton in Craven and Burnsall w Rylstone *Bradf* 08–11; NSM Adbaston, High Offley, Knightley, Norbury etc *Lich* 11–16; R from 16. *The Vicarage, Glebe Lane, Gnosall, Stafford ST20 0ER* E: rev.kathrynh@gmail.com

HAMMOND, Canon Lindsay John. b 57. Southn Univ BA 83. Sarum & Wells Th Coll 84. **d** 86 **p** 87. C Ashford *Cant* 86–90; V Appledore w Brookland, Fairfield, Brenzett etc 90–95; P-in-c Wittersham w Stone and Ebony 95–03; RD S Lympne 95–01; P-in-c Westwell and Hothfield 03–11; P-in-c Charing w Charing Heath and Lt Chart 06–11; AD Ashford 09–11; V Tenterden and Smallhythe 11–16; TR Tenterden, Rother and Oxney from 16; Hon Min Can Cant Cathl 93–08; Hon Can Cant Cathl from 08; AD Romney and Tenterden 13–19. *The Vicarage, Church Road, Tenterden TN30 6AT* T: (01580) 761591 *or* 765414 E: tentvic@gmail.com

HAMMOND, Martin James. b 62. St Jo Coll Nottm 03. **d** 05 **p** 06. C Walmley *Birm* 05–08; C Erdington 08–09; TV Bedworth *Cov* 09–18; Chapl Geo Eliot Hosp NHS Trust Nuneaton from 14. *The George Eliot Hospital NHS Trust, Lewes House, College Street, Nuneaton CV10 7DJ* T: (024) 7635 1351 E: revmartinh@btinternet.com

HAMMOND, Peter Clark. b 27. Linc Coll Ox BA 49 MA 53. Wells Th Coll 51. **d** 52 **p** 53. C Willesborough *Cant* 52–55; C Croydon St Jo 55–59; R Barham 60–66; V Walmer 66–85; V Rolvenden 85–89; rtd 89; PtO *Ely* 89–15. *19 Hardwick Street, Cambridge CB3 9JA* T: (01223) 467425

HAMNETT, Mrs Karen. b 63. All SS Cen for Miss & Min. **d** 16 **p** 17. OLM Middleton and Thornham *Man* from 16. *15 Cragg Road, Oldham OL1 2RX* M: 07759-286653 E: thehamnetts@btinternet.com

HAMPEL, Canon Michael Hans Joachim. b 67. Univ Coll Dur BA 89 St Chad's Coll Dur MA 02 FRSA 02. Westcott Ho Cam 90. **d** 93 **p** 94. C Whitworth w Spennymoor *Dur* 93–97; Min Can, Prec and Sacr Dur Cathl 97–02; Sen Tutor St Chad's Coll Dur 02–04; Can Res St E Cathl 04–11; Sub Dean 08–11; Can Res and Prec St Paul's Cathl *Lon* 11–18; Can Res Dur Cathl from 18. *7 The College, Durham DH1 3EQ* E: michael.hampel@dunelm.org.uk

HAMPSON, David. b 46. Chich Th Coll 69. **d** 72 **p** 73. C Penrith *Carl* 72–78; V Crosscrake 78–95; V Crosscrake and Preston Patrick 95; P-in-c Arnside 95–97; rtd 97. *81 Rectory Road, Ashton-in-Makerfield, Wigan WN4 0QD* T: (01942) 728760

HAMPSON, Miss Judith Elizabeth. b 50. I M Marsh Coll of Physical Educn Liv BEd 72 Open Univ BA 89. Ripon Coll Cuddesdon 90. **d** 92 **p** 94. C Alnwick *Newc* 92–96; R Allendale w Whitfield 96–05; V Haydon Bridge and Beltingham w Henshaw 05–13; rtd 13. *5 St Aidan's Terrace, Trimdon Station TS29 6BT* T: (01429) 551022 E: judithhmpsn19@gmail.com

HAMPSON, Michael John. b 67. Jes Coll Ox BA 88. Ripon Coll Cuddesdon 88. **d** 91 **p** 92. C W Burnley All SS *Blackb* 91–93; C Harlow St Mary Magd *Chelmsf* 93–00; V Church Langley 00–04; PtO *Blackb* 10–12; V Hornby w Claughton and Whittington etc from 12. *Station House, Arkholme, Carnforth LA6 1AZ* T: (015242) 21712 M: 07712-477003 E: michael.hampson.mobile@googlemail.com

HAMPSON, Michele Elizabeth. b 55. Univ Coll Lon MB, BS 79 Edin Univ MPhil 85. Ridley Hall Cam 15. **d** 17 **p** 18. NSM Lenton *S'well* from 17. *Address withheld by request* T: 0115-845 7985

HAMPSTEAD, Archdeacon of. See HAWKINS, The Ven John Edward Inskipp

HAMPTON, Alison Jean. b 61. St Mary's Coll Twickenham BA 98. SEITE 98. **d** 01 **p** 02. C Notting Dale St Clem w St Mark and St Jas *Lon* 01–04; P-in-c Burrough Hill Pars *Leic* 04–06; Chapl Brooksby Melton Coll 04–06; P-in-c Husbands Bosworth w Mowsley and Knaptoft etc *Leic* 06–09; P-in-c Arnesby w Shearsby and Bruntingthorpe 06–09; R Hexagon 09–10; PtO *Cov* 10–11; Chapl Shakespeare Hospice 11–13; Dominican Republic 13–15; V Millfield St Mark and Pallion St Luke *Dur* 15–19. *2 Garth Terrace, Porthmadog LL49 9BE* E: alijhampton@gmail.com

HAMPTON, Canon Carla Irene. b 47. ARCM 67 GRSM 68. NTMTC 96. **d** 99 **p** 00. Asst Chapl Mid-Essex Hosp Services NHS Trust 98–02; Chapl Team Ldr 02–04; NSM Chelmsf St Andr 99–04; NSM Gt and Lt Leighs and Lt Waltham 04–06; P-in-c Gt Waltham w Ford End 06–10; V 10–12; rtd 12; RD Chelmsf N 07–14; Hon C Springfield All SS 12–17; Hon Can Chelmsf Cathl 08–12; PtO from 17; *Nor* from 17. *14 Fairfield Close, Mundesley, Norwich NR11 8BZ* M: 07850-913452 E: revcarlahampton@gmail.com

HAMPTON, Canon John Waller. b 28. Linc Coll Ox BA 51 MA 58. Westcott Ho Cam 51. **d** 53 **p** 54. C Rugby St Andr *Cov* 53–56; Chapl St Paul's Sch Hammersmith 56–65; Chapl St Paul's Girls' Sch Hammersmith 60–65; V Gaydon w

Chadshunt *Cov* 65–69; Asst Dir RE 65–70; C-in-c Warwick St Nic 69–75; Fell Qu Coll Birm 75–76; P-in-c Wetton *Lich* 76–82; P-in-c Alstonfield 76–82; P-in-c Sheen 76–80; RD Alstonfield 80–82; P-in-c Butterton 80–82; P-in-c Warslow and Elkstones 80–82; P-in-c Broadway *Worc* 82–91; V 91–93; RD Evesham 87–93; Hon Can Worc Cathl 88–93; rtd 93; PtO *Ab* from 93. *29 Midmar Gardens, Edinburgh EH10 6DY* T: 0131-447 3520

HAMPTON, Stephen William Peter. b 72. Magd Coll Cam BA 93 MA 97 Ex Coll Ox MSt 99 DPhil 02. Wycliffe Hall Ox BA 95 MA 98. **d** 96 **p** 97. C St Neots *Ely* 96–98; Chapl and Fell Ex Coll Ox 98–03; Sen Tutor St Jo Coll Dur 04–07; Hon Min Can Dur Cathl 05–07; Fell and Dean Peterho Cam from 07. *Peterhouse, Cambridge CB2 1RD* T: (01223) 338217 F: 337578 E: swph2@cam.ac.uk

HANCE, Mrs Joy. b 47. Cam Inst of Educn. SAOMC 99. **d** 02 **p** 03. NSM Cherbury w Gainfield *Ox* 02–14; C Witney from 14. *1 Grangers Place, Witney OX28 4BS* T: (01993) 707935 M: 07752-187014 E: joysmail@talk21.com

HANCE, Mrs Marion. b 49. **d** 01 **p** 02. OLM Cheddington w Mentmore and Marsworth *Ox* 01–08; NSM Quantock Coast *B & W* 08–13; PtO from 13; rtd 13. *14 Parnell Way, Burnham-on-Sea TA8 2EG* T: (01278) 792082 E: marionhance@yahoo.co.uk

HANCE, The Very Revd Stephen John. b 66. Portsm Poly BSc 89 Nottm Univ BTh 92 MA 93. St Jo Coll Nottm 90. **d** 93 **p** 94. C Southsea St Jude *Portsm* 93–96; TV Tollington *Lon* 96–99; V Balham Hill Ascension *S'wark* 99–13; Can Res S'wark Cathl 13–17; Dean Derby from 17. *The Deanery, 27A Penny Long Lane, Derby DE22 1AX* E: stephen.hance@btinternet.com

HANCOCK, Christopher David. b 54. Qu Coll Ox BA 75 MA 80 St Jo Coll Dur BA 78 PhD 84. Cranmer Hall Dur. **d** 82 **p** 83. C Leic H Trin w St Jo 82–85; Chapl Magd Coll Cam 85–88; USA 88–94; V Cambridge H Trin *Ely* 94–02; Dean Bradf 02–04. *3 College Farm Cottages, Garford, Abingdon OX13 5PF* T: (01865) 392804 E: chancock@btinternet.com

HANCOCK, Christopher Michael Jefferies. b 67. Ex Coll Ox MA 90 ACA 93. **d** 16 **p** 17. OLM Epsom St Martin *Guildf* 16–17; NSM Headley and Box Hill w Walton on the Hill from 17. *Cleaver House, Headley Common Road, Headley, Epsom KT18 6NR* T: (01372) 362386 M: 07901-715882 E: cmjhancock@gmail.com

HANCOCK, Dorothy Myfanwy. *See* WOFFENDEN, Dorothy Myfanwy

HANCOCK, Mrs Eleanor Mary Catherine. b 55. Huddersfield Univ CertEd 91. CBDTI. **d** 05 **p** 06. C Carl H Trin and St Barn 05–08; P-in-c 08–17; rtd 17. *111 Holmrook Road, Carlisle CA2 7TQ* T: (01228) 527106 M: 07763-482542 E: eleanor.hancock55@gmail.com

HANCOCK, Preb Frances Margaret. b 34. LMH Ox BA 56 MA 94. Gilmore Course IDC 81. **dss** 81 **d** 87 **p** 94. Isleworth All SS *Lon* 81–87; Team Deacon Ross w Brampton Abbotts, Bridstow and Peterstow *Heref* 87–93; rtd 94; Dioc Adv on Women in Min *Heref* 93–99; NSM Peterchurch w Vowchurch, Turnastone and Dorstone 93–00; NSM Madley w Tyberton, Peterchurch, Vowchurch 00–04; Preb Heref Cathl 96–99; PtO from 06. *Flat 4, 102 East Street, Hereford HR1 2LW* T: (01981) 550457

HANCOCK, Miss Gillian. b 59. St Jo Coll Nottm 05. **d** 07 **p** 08. C Iffley *Ox* 07–11; Chapl Mary Ann Evans Hospice from 11. *Mary Ann Evans Hospice, Eliot Way, Nuneaton CV10 7QL* T: (024) 7686 5440 M: 07919-064612 E: gillhancock@btinternet.com *or* gill.hancock@geh.nhs.uk

HANCOCK, Mrs Helen Margaret. b 62. Rob Coll Cam MA 85. SEITE 06. **d** 09 **p** 10. NSM New Malden and Coombe *S'wark* 09–11; C Surbiton St Andr and St Mark 11–12; P-in-c Surbiton St Matt 12–14; TR 14–15; TR Tolworth, Hook and Surbiton from 15. *The Vicarage, 20A Kingsdowne Road, Surbiton KT6 6JZ* T: (020) 8942 6987 E: helenccnm@gmail.com *or* teamrector@tolworthtm.org

HANCOCK, Jill Catherine. b 72. Coll of Resurr Mirfield BA 18. **d** 18 **p** 19. C E Scarsdale *Derby* from 18. *114 Horsehead Lane, Bolsover, Chesterfield S44 6XH* M: 07746-668257 E: jillhancock@outlook.com

HANCOCK, Canon John Clayton. b 36. Dur Univ BA 58. Cranmer Hall Dur. **d** 60 **p** 61. C Newbarns w Hawcoat *Carl* 60–65; V Church Coniston 65–76; R Torver 66–76; P-in-c Heversham 76–77; V 77–93; V Heversham and Milnthorpe 93–05; Hon Can Carl Cathl 98–05; rtd 05; P-in-c Levens *Carl* 04–06; PtO from 06. *Fairfield, Sandside, Milnthorpe LA7 7HW* T: (015395) 63659

HANCOCK, John Llewellyn. b 14. **d** 14 **p** 15. NSM Llanstadwell St D 14–16; NSM Llanstadwell and Burton and Rosemarket from 16. *Mill House, Llanstadwell, Milford Haven SA73 1EG* T: (01646) 600610 E: john.hancock3@me.com

HANCOCK, John Martin. b 55. Ealing Coll of Educn BA 78. Wycliffe Hall Ox 97. **d** 99 **p** 00. C Bedford St Jo and St Leon *St Alb* 99–04; V Old Hill H Trin *Worc* 04–12; P-in-c Hengrove *Bris* 12–19; P-in-c Whitchurch 12–15; V Whitchurch St Nic 15–19; rtd 19. *40A Queen Alexandra Road, Salisbury SP2 9LN* E: martin@hancocks.plus.com

HANCOCK, Canon John Mervyn. b 38. St Jo Coll Dur BA 61 MA 70 Hertf Coll Ox BA 63 MA 66. Cranmer Hall Dur 63. **d** 64 **p** 65. C Bishopwearmouth St Gabr *Dur* 64–67; V Hebburn St Jo 67–87; RD Jarrow 83–92; V S Westoe 87–03; C-in-c S Shields St Aid w St Steph 92–95; Hon Can Dur Cathl 88–03; rtd 03; PtO *Dur* from 04. *9 Railway Cottages, Dubmire, Houghton le Spring DH4 6LE* T: 0191-385 7491 E: canonhancock21@talktalk.net

HANCOCK, Malcolm James. b 50. Leeds Univ MA 02 AGSM 73. Sarum & Wells Th Coll 85. **d** 87 **p** 88. C Sandhurst *Ox* 87–90; P-in-c Bradbourne and Brassington *Derby* 90–92; TV Wirksworth 92–95; V Tunbridge Wells K Chas *Roch* 95–02; R Beckenham St Geo 02–10; Asst Chapl Lewisham Healthcare NHS Trust 10–11; Chapl Lewisham and Greenwich NHS Trust 11–15; rtd 15. *3 Seymour Place, Totnes TQ9 5AY* T: (01803) 866147 E: malcolm.j.hancock@btinternet.com

HANCOCK, Martin. *See* HANCOCK, John Martin

HANCOCK, Mrs Mary. b 52. Imp Coll Lon BSc 73 ARCS 73. Ridley Hall Cam 04. **d** 07 **p** 08. C Fen Orchards *Ely* 07–11; P-in-c Witcham w Mepal 11–17; R from 17; P-in-c Sutton 11–17; V from 17. *The Vicarage, 7 Church Lane, Sutton, Ely CB6 2RQ* T: (01353) 778722 E: mhancock@waitrose.com

HANCOCK, Ms Mary Joy. b 40. Auckland Univ BA 61 Auckland Teachers' Coll PGCE 62 Man Univ CQSW 69. S'wark Ord Course 91. **d** 94 **p** 95. NSM Merton St Mary *S'wark* 94–01; NSM Colliers Wood Ch Ch 01–06; NSM Upper Tooting H Trin w St Aug 06–12; PtO 12–18. *55 Huntspill Street, London SW17 0AA* T: (020) 8946 8984

HANCOCK, Nigel John. b 35. K Coll Cam BA 63 MA 67. EAMTC 86. **d** 89 **p** 91. NSM Cambridge St Mary Less *Ely* 89–00; PV St Jo Coll Cam 95–99; PtO *Ely* 00–12. *5 Atherton Close, Cambridge CB4 2BE* T: (01223) 355828

HANCOCK, Preb Paul. b 43. AKC 66. **d** 67 **p** 68. C Wednesbury St Paul Wood Green *Lich* 67–70; C Rugeley 70–73; V Rickerscote 73–75; R Blisland w St Breward *Truro* 75–78; V Mansfield St Lawr *S'well* 78–82; P-in-c Charleton *Ex* 82–83; P-in-c E Portlemouth, S Pool and Chivelstone 82–83; R Charleton w Buckland Tout Saints etc 83–95; RD Woodleigh 88–95; P-in-c Plymouth Crownhill Ascension 95–99; V 99–09; Preb Ex Cathl 03–09; rtd 09; PtO *Ex* from 11. *27 Paddock Drive, Ivybridge PL21 0UB* T: (01752) 690655 E: hazelnut330@gmail.com

HANCOCK, Paul David. Oak Hill Th Coll. **d** 10 **p** 11. C Buxton Trin Prop Chpl *Derby* 10–14. *24 Bath Road, Buxton SK17 6HH* T: (01298) 23104 M: 07816-409476 E: paulhancock2001@hotmail.com

✠**HANCOCK, The Rt Revd Peter.** b 55. Selw Coll Cam BA 76 MA 79. Oak Hill Th Coll BA 80. **d** 80 **p** 81 **c** 10. C Portsdown *Portsm* 80–83; C Radipole and Melcombe Regis *Sarum* 83–87; V Cowplain *Portsm* 87–99; Adn The Meon 99–10; RD Havant 93–98; Hon Can Portsm Cathl 97–10; Dioc Dir Miss 03–06; Suff Bp Basingstoke *Win* 10–14; Bp B & W from 14. *The Palace, Wells BA5 2PD* T: (01749) 672341 F: 679355 E: bishop@bathwells.anglican.org

HANCOCK, Peter Thompson. b 31. G&C Coll Cam BA 54 MA 58. Ridley Hall Cam 54. **d** 56 **p** 57. C Beckenham Ch Ch *Roch* 56–59; Chapl St Lawr Coll Ramsgate 59–62; Chapl Stowe Sch 62–67; Asst Chapl and Lect Br Embassy Ch Paris *Eur* 67–70; V Walton H Trin *Ox* 70–80; Canada 80–84; V Northwood H Trin *Lon* 84–94; rtd 94; PtO *Ox* 99–07; *Guildf* 07–10. *High Lawns, Woodhouse Lane, Holmbury St Mary, Dorking RH5 6NN* T: (01483) 205430 E: suemhancock@gmail.com

HANCOCK, Mrs Rebecca Jane. b 72. St Jo Coll Nottm 14. **d** 17 **p** 18. C Bawtry w Austerfield, Misson, Everton and Mattersey *S'well* from 17. *12 Dalton Grove, Bawtry, Doncaster DN10 6XS* E: revbeckyhancock@gmail.com

HANCOCK, Canon Richard Manuel Ashley. b 69. LRPS 02. Linc Th Coll 94 Westcott Ho Cam 95. **d** 97 **p** 98. C Didcot St Pet *Ox* 97–00; P-in-c Shrivenham w Watchfield and Bourton 00–03; V Shrivenham and Ashbury 03–18; AD Vale of White Horse 05–12; Hon Can Ch Ch 12–18; P-in-c Sixpenny Handley w Gussage St Andrew etc *Sarum* from 18. *The Vicarage, 60 High Street, Sixpenny Handley, Salisbury SP5 5ND* T: (01725) 552608 E: canonrick@icloud.com

HANCOCK, Mrs Sarah. b 80. Ches Univ BSc 01. Ridley Hall Cam 15. **d** 17 **p** 18. C Luton St Fran *St Alb* from 17. *15 Lancing Road, Luton LU2 8JN* M: 07738-441486 E: sarah.hancock293@gmail.com

HANCOCK, Ms Vittoria Ruth. b 74. Univ of Wales (Ban) BSc 95 BD 99. Cranmer Hall Dur 91. **d** 01 **p** 02. C Llanberis w Llanrug Ban 01–03; C Llanberis, Llanrug and Llandinorwig 03–04; C Dolgellau w Llanfachreth and Brithdir etc 04–05; Chapl St As Cathl and Dioc Evang Officer 06–12; P-in-c Ballater Ab from 14; P-in-c Aboyne from 14. 7 Invercauld Road, Ballater AB35 5RP　T: (013397) 55919 E: vittoriahancock@gmail.com

HANCOCK, Graeme. b 58. Univ of Wales (Ban) BD 79 Oslo Univ 87. Linc Th Coll 79. **d** 81 **p** 82. C Denbigh and Nantglyn St As 81–84; Asst Chapl Oslo St Edm Eur 84–88; Chapl Stockholm 88–89; Chapl Marseille w St Raphaël, Aix-en-Provence etc 89; Chapl Gothenburg w Halmstad, Jönköping etc 90–93; Chapl Southn Univ Hosps NHS Trust 93–98; Chapl Trafford Healthcare NHS Trust 98–02; Chapl Leeds Teaching Hosps NHS Trust 02–09; rtd 09; PtO Bradf 09–14; Leeds 14–16. 7 Woodfield Road, Cullingworth, Bradford BD13 5JL　T: (01535) 271551

HANCOX, Ms Sarah Anne. b 85. Edin Univ BD 07. Cranmer Hall Dur 09. **d** 11 **p** 12. C Kirk Sandall and Edenthorpe Sheff 11–14; P-in-c Methley w Mickletown Leeds 14–15; P-in-c Oulton w Woodlesford 14–15; TV Rothwell, Lofthouse, Methley etc from 15. The Rectory, Church Side, Methley, Leeds LS26 9BJ E: hancoxsa@gmail.com

HAND, Michael. See HAND, Peter Michael

HAND, Michael Anthony (Tony). b 63. York Univ BA 84 DipCOT 88 SROT. St Jo Coll Nottm MA 95. **d** 95 **p** 96. C Lutterworth w Cotesbach Leic 95–98; C Lutterworth w Cotesbach and Bitteswell 99–01; V Acomb H Redeemer York from 01; Chapl Manor Sch from 01. The Vicarage, 108 Boroughbridge Road, York YO26 6AB　T: (01904) 798593 E: tony@holyredeemeryork.com

HAND, Canon Nigel Arthur. b 54. St Jo Coll Nottm. **d** 84 **p** 85. C Birm St Luke 84–88; C Walton H Trin Ox 88–89; TV 89–97; C Selly Park St Steph and St Wulstan Birm 97–04; P-in-c Selly Park Ch Ch 04–08; AD Moseley 04–07; Can Res Birm Cathl 08–19; rtd 19; PtO Birm from 19. 12 Nursery Drive, Handsworth, Birmingham B20 2SW E: nigelhand@me.com

HAND, Peter Michael. b 42. Univ Coll Ox BA 63 Lon Univ BSc 75. Sarum & Wells Th Coll 77. **d** 80 **p** 81. NSM Shaston Sarum 80–81; C Tisbury 81–83; C Glastonbury St Jo w Godney B & W 83–84; C Glastonbury w Meare, W Pennard and Godney 84–87; V High Littleton 87–99; RD Midsomer Norton 92–98; R Winford w Felton Common Hill 99–07; Warden of Readers Bath Adnry 98–06; rtd 07; TV Winchcombe Glouc 10–13; PtO from 17. 27 Stancombe View, Winchcombe, Cheltenham GL54 5LE　T: (01242) 609575 E: anne_michael_hand@yahoo.co.uk

HAND, Philip Ronald. b 53. Spurgeon's Coll BA 78. **d** 03 **p** 04. NSM Southampton (City Cen) Win 03–18; NSM Southampton St Mich from 18. 21 The Greenwich, Gloucester Square, Southampton SO14 2GJ E: philand@newporteducational.co.uk

HANDCOCK, Mrs Alison Dawn. **d** 15. C Preston Plucknett B & W 15–19; PtO 19–20. Address withheld by request M: 07791-546435 E: rev.alisonh@yahoo.co.uk

✠**HANDFORD, The Rt Revd George Clive.** b 37. Hatf Coll Dur BA 61. Qu Coll Birm 61. **d** 63 **p** 64 **c** 90. C Mansfield SS Pet and Paul S'well 63–67; Lebanon 67–74; Dean Jerusalem 74–78; UAE 78–83; Adn Gulf 78–83; V Kneesall w Laxton S'well 83–84; P-in-c Wellow 83–84; RD Tuxford and Norwell 83–84; Adn Nottingham 84–90; Suff Bp Warw Cov 90–96; Bp Cyprus and the Gulf 96–07; Pres Bp Episc Ch Jerusalem and Middle E 02–07; rtd 07; Hon Asst Bp Ripon and Leeds 07–14; Asst Bp Leeds from 14. Wayside, 1 The Terrace, Kirby Hill, Boroughbridge, York YO51 9DQ　T: (01423) 325406 E: cpdhandford@gmail.com

HANDFORTH, Canon Richard Brereton. b 31. St Pet Coll Ox BA 55 MA 60. Westcott Ho Cam 63. **d** 64 **p** 65. C Hornchurch St Andr Chelmsf 64–65; Warden St Steph Coll Hong Kong 65–73; Chapl CMS Fellowship Ho Chislehurst 73–75; Hon C Chislehurst St Nic Roch 73–75; Home Educn Sec CMS 75–83; V Biggin Hill Roch 83–88; Inter-change Adv CMS 88–96; Hon C Plaistow St Mary Roch 95–04; Hon Can Lagos from 95; rtd 96; PtO Roch from 01. 1 Bromley College, London Road, Bromley BR1 1PE　T: (020) 8460 0238 E: r.handforth1@btinternet.com

HANDLEY, The Ven Anthony Michael. b 36. Selw Coll Cam BA 60 MA 64. Chich Th Coll 60. **d** 62 **p** 63. C Thorpe St Andr Nor 62–66; C Gaywood, Bawsey and Mintlyn 66–72; V Hellesdon 72–81; RD Nor N 80–81; Adn Nor 81–93; Adn Norfolk 93–02; rtd 02; PtO Nor from 02. 25 New Street, Sheringham NR26 8EE　T: (01263) 820928 E: amhandley@yahoo.co.uk

HANDLEY, Canon Dennis Francis. b 57. MIE 79 TEng(CEI) 80. Coll of Resurr Mirfield 82. **d** 85 **p** 86. C Headingley Ripon

85–88; C Rothwell 88–92; V Liversedge Wakef 92–97; V Ripponden and Barkisland w W Scammonden 97–06; TR Almondbury w Farnley Tyas 06–14; Dioc Rural Officer 04–14; V Berwick H Trin and St Mary Newc from 14; Hon Can Newc Cathl from 19. The Vicarage, Parade, Berwick-upon-Tweed TD15 1DF　T: (01289) 306136

HANDLEY, James William. b 74. Imp Coll Lon MEng 96 Leeds Univ PhD 04 Dur Univ BA 17. St Hild Coll 14. **d** 17 **p** 18. NSM Harrogate St Mark Leeds from 17. 32 St Helens Road, Harrogate HG2 8LD　M: 07392-599699 E: revjameshandley@gmail.com

HANDLEY, John. b 38. Oak Hill Th Coll. **d** 83 **p** 84. C Witton w Brundall and Braydeston Nor 83–86; R Reedham w Cantley w Limpenhoe and Southwood 86–93; P-in-c E w W Harling and Bridgham w Roudham 93–95; R E w W Harling, Bridgham w Roudham, Larling etc 95–05; P-in-c Garboldisham w Blo' Norton, Riddlesworth etc 94–96; RD Thetford and Rockland 95–98; rtd 05; PtO Nor from 05. 6 Barton Close, Swaffham PE37 7SB　T: (01760) 336328 E: john.handley@hotmail.co.uk

HANDLEY, Mrs Kathryn Emma. b 70. **d** 14 **p** 15. C Bredbury St Mark Ches 14–16; P-in-c Stalybridge St Paul from 16. St Paul's Vicarage, Huddersfield Road, Stalybridge SK15 2PT　T: 0161-338 2966 E: kehandley@btinternet.com

HANDLEY, Michael. See HANDLEY, Anthony Michael

HANDLEY, Timothy John. b 63. Glos Univ BTh 01. St Steph Ho Ox 94. **d** 96 **p** 97. C St Marychurch Ex 96–98; PtO Cant 06–10; Lon 15–17; P-in-c St Jas Garlickhythe w St Mich Queenhithe etc from 17. 35 Buckhurst Street, London E1 5QT　T: (01227) 720765　M: 07912-583201 E: frtimhandley@gmail.com

HANDLEY MACMATH, Terence. b 59. Goldsmiths' Coll Lon BA 80 K Coll Cam MA 98. Westcott Ho Cam 91. **d** 94 **p** 95. NSM Southwold St E 94–95; PtO St Alb 96–99; C St Alb St Pet 99–05; PtO 09–19; V Harrow Weald All SS Lon 05–07; Chapl R Free Hampstead NHS Trust 07–09; Chapl R Brompton and Harefield NHS Foundn Trust 09–16; rtd 16; PtO Sarum from 17. 32 Priests Road, Swanage BH19 2RW E: terencehandleymacmath@gmail.com

HANDY, Miss Laura Jane. b 82. Regents Th Coll BA 13. St Mellitus Coll 13. **d** 15 **p** 16. C Droitwich Spa Worc 15–18; TV from 18; C Salwarpe and Hindlip w Martin Hussingtree from 18. 7 College Green, Droitwich WR9 8QY　M: 07921-524394 E: revlaurahandy@gmail.com

HANDY, Thomas. b 79. Ex Univ BA 02 Bris Univ PGCE 05. Trin Coll Bris MA 09. **d** 09 **p** 10. C Shepton Mallet w Doulting B & W 09–12; R S Petherton w The Seavingtons 12–14; C Kingsbury Episcopi w E Lambrook, Hambridge etc 13–14; R S Petherton w The Seavingtons and The Lambrooks from 14. The Rectory, Hele Lane, South Petherton TA13 5DY　T: (01460) 249443 E: revdtomhandy@hotmail.com

HANFORD, Karen Anne. b 60. **d** 17 **p** 18. NSM Wollaton S'well from 17. 6 Beeston Fields Drive, Beeston, Nottingham NG9 3DB

HANFORD, Richard James. b 90. St Andr Univ MTheol 12. Trin Coll Bris 16. **d** 18 **p** 19. C Worksop St Anne S'well from 18; C Norton Cuckney from 18. 129 Stubbing Lane, Worksop S80 1NF E: richard.hanford@btinternet.com

HANFORD, Canon William Richard. b 38. Keble Coll Ox BA 60 MA 64 Lon Univ BD 66 Univ of Wales LLM 95. St Steph Ho 60. **d** 63 **p** 64. C Roath St Martin Llan 63–66; C Llantwit Major 67–68; PV Llan Cathl 68–72; Chapl RN 72–76; Hon Chapl Gibraltar Cathl Eur 74–76; Hon C Eastbourne St Sav and St Pet Chich 76–77; C Brighton St Pet 77–78; Can Res and Prec Guildf Cathl 78–83; Hon Can Guildf Cathl 03–09; V Ewell 83–09; Tutor and Lect Chich Th Coll 79–86; rtd 09; PtO Guildf 09–10; Llan from 09. 15 Austin Avenue, Laleston, Bridgend CF32 0LG　T: (01656) 656892 E: wrhanford@btinternet.com

HANILY, Séan Jerome Keanspark. b 90. TCD BA 12 MA 15 MTh 18 FRAS 16 LLCM 17. CITI. **d** 17 **p** 18. Dublin Rathfarnham D & G 17–18; C Drumragh w Mountfield D & R from 18. 12 Crevenagh Way, Omagh BT79 0JE　T: (028) 8216 0883　M: (00353) 87-778 2387 E: hanilys@tcd.ie

HANKEY, Miss Dorothy Mary. b 38. CertEd 65. Trin Coll Bris 75. **dss** 78 **d** 87 **p** 94. Wigan St Jas w St Thos Liv 78–84; Middleton Man 84–85; Litherland Ch Ch Liv 85–89; Par Dn 87–89; Par Dn Blackpool St Mark Blackb 89–94; C 94–95; C Blackpool St Paul 95–98; rtd 98; PtO Blackb from 98. 89 Rutland Avenue, Poulton-le-Flyde FY6 7RX　T: (01253) 890635

HANKEY, Rupert Christopher Alers. b 60. Sheff Univ LLB 82. Wilson Carlile Coll 86 St Jo Coll Nottm MTh 06. **d** 07 **p** 08. C Bedford St Jo and St Leon St Alb 07–11; V Sidcup St Andr Roch from 11. The Vicarage, St Andrew's Road, Sidcup DA14 4SA　T: (020) 8300 4712　M: 07539-319545 E: ruperth5@btinternet.com

HANKINS, Clifford James. b 24. Chich Th Coll 70. **d** 72 **p** 73. C Henfield Chich 72–76; V Fernhurst 76–84; V Mithian w

Mount Hawke *Truro* 84–89; rtd 89; Hon C W Wittering and Birdham w Itchenor *Chich* from 90. *Flat 1, 10 Sarum Terrace, Bow Common Lane, London E3 4HJ*

HANKS, John Martin. b 57. St Chad's Coll Dur BA 80 Univ of Wales (Cardiff) LLM 94 Selw Coll Cam PGCE 82. St Steph Ho Ox 10. **d** 12. NSM Ox St Barn and St Paul 12–15; NSM Ox St Thos 12–15; Chapl to Suff Bp Ebbsfleet (PEV) *Cant* 12–13; PtO *York* 16–18; NSM York All SS N Street from 18. *20 Ogleforth, York YO1 7JG* T: (01904) 731636 E: hanksj@gmail.com

HANLEY, Máirt Joseph. b 74. Univ Coll Ches BA 95. CITC BTh 03. **d** 03 **p** 04. NSM Tralee w Kilmoyley, Ballymacelligott etc *L & K* 03–11; Bp's C Kilcolman w Kiltallagh, Killorglin, Knockane etc 11–15; I Baltinglass w Ballynure etc *C & O* from 15. *The Rectory, Church Lane, Baltinglass, Co Wicklow, W91 T8X6, Republic of Ireland* T: (00353) (59) 648 1321 M: 87-619 4733 E: baltinglassgroup@gmail.com

HANLON, Canon Thomas Kyle. b 72. QUB BA 94 TCD BTh 97. **d** 97 **p** 98. C Bangor St Comgall *D & D* 97–00; I Dromore *Clogh* 00–06; I Fivemiletown from 06; Chapl to Bp Clogh from 03; Can Clogh Cathl from 16; Prec from 19. *St John's Rectory, 160 Ballagh Road, Fivemiletown BT75 0QP* T: (028) 8952 1030 *or* 8952 2422 E: fivemiletown@clogher.anglican.org

HANMER, Sister Phoebe Margaret. b 31. Edin Univ MA 54. **d** 96 **p** 97. NSM Brakpan S Africa 96–00; NSM Actonville 00–03; PtO *Ox* 99–00; *Birm* 04–15; *Ox* from 16. *St Mary's Convent, Denchworth Road, Wantage OX12 9AU* T: (01235) 763141 E: srphoebe@csmr.org.uk

HANMER, Canon Richard John. b 38. Peterho Cam BA 61 MA 65. Linc Th Coll 62. **d** 64 **p** 65. C Sheff St Swithun 64–69; Bp's Chapl *Nor* 69–73; V Cinderhill *S'well* 73–81; V Eaton *Nor* 81–94; Dioc Chapl MU 91–04; Hon Can Nor Cathl 93–94; Can Res Nor Cathl 94–04; P-in-c Nor St Mary in the Marsh 94–04; rtd 04; PtO *Nor* from 04. *18 Quebec Road, Dereham NR19 2DR* T: (01362) 655092 E: richard.hanmer@tiscali.co.uk

HANNA, Miss Elizabeth. b 50. QUB BA 73 Lon Bible Coll BA 79 Milltown Inst Dub MA 01. CITC 99. **d** 01 **p** 02. C Bangor Abbey *D & D* 01–04; I Magherally w Annaclone 04–08; I Belfast St Nic *Conn* 08–18; rtd 18. *9 Bignian Avenue, Kilkeel, Newry BT34 4NF* T: (028) 4176 5851 M: 07801-946909 E: hannamanor15@btinternet.com

HANNA, John. b 44. Lon Bible Coll BA 83. Westcott Ho Cam 86. **d** 87 **p** 88. C Denton Ch Ch *Man* 87–91; V Higher Walton *Blackb* 91–98; C Marple All SS *Ches* 98–02; TV Burrington, Chawleigh, Cheldon, Chulmleigh etc *Ex* 02–09; RD S Molton 03–09; rtd 09; PtO *S & B* 10–12 and from 16; P-in-c Beguildy and Heyope and Llangynllo and Bleddfa 12–16. *Victoria House, Victoria Road, Knighton LD7 1BD* T: (01547) 529296

HANNA, Patricia Elizabeth. *See* McKEE HANNA, Patricia Elizabeth

HANNA, Peter Thomas. b 45. ACII 66 GIFireE 75. CITC 85. **d** 88 **p** 89. NSM Cork St Fin Barre's Union *C, C & R* 88–95; Min Can Cork Cathl from 92; Dioc Info Officer 94–95; Aux Min Cork St Luke Union 95–00; Aux Min Kinsale Union 00–04; Aux Min Douglas Union w Frankfield from 04. *Mount Windsor, Farnahoe, Inishannon, Co Cork, Republic of Ireland* T/F: (00353) (21) 477 5470 E: peterthanna@gmail.com

HANNA, Canon Robert Charles. b 49. Oak Hill Th Coll 75. **d** 77 **p** 78. C Coleraine *Conn* 77–82; I Convoy w Monellan and Donaghmore *D & R* 82–94; Can Raphoe Cathl 88–94; I Drumcliffe w Kilnasoolagh *L & K* 94–18; Can Limerick, Killaloe and Clonfert Cathls 00–18; Chan 04–18; rtd 18. *Seafield Cottage, Baile an tSagart, Tromara West, Quilty, Co Clare, V95 YOP4, Republic of Ireland* T: (00353) (65) 708 7965 M: 86-6216 7040 E: bobhanna@eircom.net

HANNAFIN (née Lewis), Angela Jane. b 69. Portsm Univ BA 92. St Jo Coll Nottm 13. **d** 15 **p** 16. C Uxbridge *Lon* 15–18; P-in-c Bardsey *Leeds* 18–19; V from 19; Lay Tr Officer from 18. *The Vicarage, Woodacre Lane, Bardsey, Leeds LS17 9DG* M: 07860-824314 E: angelalewisjane@gmail.com

HANNAFORD, Prof Robert. b 53. Ex Univ BEd 76 MA 78 PhD 87. St Steph Ho Ox 78. **d** 80 **p** 81. C Ex St Jas 80–83; Chapl Ex Univ 83–88; Tutor St Steph Ho Ox 89–92; Sen Lect Cant Ch Ch Univ Coll 92–99; Prof Chr Th Univ Coll Chich 99–01; Hon C Bury w Houghton and Coldwaltham and Hardham 99–01; Th Consultant Bp Horsham 99–01; Can and Preb Chich Cathl from 00; Prof Th St Martin's Coll Lanc 02–05; Dean of Faculty 05–07; Dean of Faculty Cumbria Univ Carl from 07; Hon C Tunstall w Melling and Leck *Blackb* 02–03; Hon C E Lonsdale 03–15; P-in-c Workington St Jo *Carl* 15–19; Dir Cumbria Chr Learning from 18. *Cumbria Christian Learning, Church*

House, 19-24 Friargate, Penrith CA14 4DP T: (01768) 807765 E: rhannaford@ucsm.ac.uk

HANNAH, Darrell Dale. b 62. Grand Canyon Univ BA 85 S Bapt Th Sem MDiv 89 Regent Coll Vancouver ThM 92 Magd Coll Cam PhD 96. WMMTC 00. **d** 03 **p** 03. NSM Edgbaston St Geo *Birm* 03–04; NSM Iffley *Ox* 04–07; NSM Earley St Pet 07–08; R Ascot Heath from 08; AD Bracknell 16–19. *All Saints' Rectory, London Road, Ascot SL5 8DQ* T: (01344) 621200 E: drddhannah@yahoo.co.uk

HANNAM, Robert Stephen. b 46. CertEd 69. **d** 05 **p** 06. NSM Rastrick St Matt *Wakef* 05–08; NSM Rastrick 08–14; *Leeds* from 14. *33 Lyndhurst Road, Brighouse HD6 3RX* T: (01484) 716053 E: stephenr.hannam@btinternet.com

HANNEN, Robert John. *See* DAVIES-HANNEN, Robert John

HANNING, Christopher William Arthur. b 80. Edin Univ MA 04 MSc 05. Oak Hill Th Coll BA 16. **d** 18 **p** 19. C Blackheath St Jo *S'wark* from 18. *Flat A, 15 St John's Park, London SE3 7TD* M: 07743-828309 E: cwahanning@gmail.com

✠**HANNON, The Rt Revd Brian Desmond Anthony.** b 36. TCD BA 59 MA 62. TCD Div Sch Div Test 61. **d** 61 **p** 62 **c** 86. C Clooney *D & R* 61–64; I Desertmartin 64–69; I Londonderry Ch Ch 69–82; I Enniskillen *Clogh* 82–86; Preb Clogh Cathl 82–84; Dean Clogh 85–86; Bp Clogh 86–01; rtd 01. *Drumconnis Top, 202 Mullaghmeen Road, Ballinamallard, Enniskillen BT94 2DZ* T: (028) 6638 8557 F: 6638 8086

HANSCOMBE, Stephen John. b 63. Bp Grosseteste Coll BEd 84 Hughes Hall Cam MEd 05. Yorks Min Course BA 16. **d** 16 **p** 17. NSM Bedale and Leeming and Thornton Watlass *Leeds* 16–19; V Leyburn w Bellerby from 19. *The Vicarage, I'Anson Close, Leyburn DL8 5LF* M: 07734-138431 E: hanscombe63@gmail.com *or* stephen.hanscombe@leeds.anglican.org

HANSELL, Anupama. b 76. Pune Univ India BSc 97 Serampore Univ BD 03 Birm Univ MA 06. **d** 02 **p** 04. C Birm St Martin w Bordesley St Andr 04–08; Chapl Aston Univ 05–08; TV Coventry Caludon *Cov* 08–10; PtO *Nor* 10–11; C Bure Valley 11–13; PtO *Derby* 13–14; *Bris* 14–18; Chapl Univ Hosps Bris NHS Foundn Trust 16–18; PtO *Ox* from 19. *Mill Cottage, Church Road, Bradfield, Reading RG7 6BX* E: revd.akh@btinternet.com

HANSELL, Peter Michael. b 76. Selw Coll Cam BA 97 MA 01 MPhil 99 PhD 02. Qu Coll Birm 03. **d** 05 **p** 06. C Moseley St Mary *Birm* 05–07; C Moseley St Mary and St Anne 07–09; Reader Initial Tr Adv *Cov* 09–10; R Bure Valley *Nor* 10–13; Chapl Trent Coll Nottm 13–14; Chapl Clifton Coll Bris 14–16; Chapl Bradfield Coll Berks from 16; PtO *Ox* from 16. *Bradfield College, Bradfield, Reading RG7 6AU* T: 0118-964 4776 M: 07825-714728 E: chaplain@bradfieldcollege.org.uk

HANSEN, Ernest Paul. b 46. Linc Th Coll 78. **d** 80 **p** 81. C Greenside *Dur* 80–83; rtd 11. *34 Riversley Road, Gloucester GL2 0QT* T: (01452) 415923 E: ernie.hansen46@gmail.com

HANSEN, James Edwin. b 41. Concordia Coll (USA) BSc 64 San Jose State Univ MA 71. Ch Div Sch of the Pacific (USA) MDiv 86. **d** 86 **p** 87. C Swansea St Pet *S & B* 86–87; C Sketty 87–89; C Hornchurch St Andr *Chelmsf* 89–91; P-in-c Chelmsf St Andr 91–94; USA from 94; rtd 06. *PO Box 7830, Brookings OR 97415-0370, USA* T: (001) (541) 412 9993 E: jimehansen@charter.net

HANSFORD, Gordon John. b 40. Southn Univ BSc 61. Trin Coll Bris 77. **d** 79 **p** 80. C Ex St Leon w H Trin 79–82; C Shirley *Win* 82–87; R Landcross, Littleham, Monkleigh etc *Ex* 87–96; TV Bideford, Northam, Westward Ho!, Appledore etc 96–99; P-in-c Monkleigh 96–99; RD Hartland 96–99; V Paul *Truro* 99–07; rtd 07. Address withheld by request

HANSFORD, Ruth Patricia. b 68. K Coll Lon BSc 90 Surrey Univ MSc 96 Sch of Pharmacy Lon PhD 00. Trin Coll Bris BA 02. **d** 03 **p** 04. C Parkham, Alwington, Buckland Brewer etc *Ex* 03–07; P-in-c Hatherleigh, Meeth, Exbourne and Jacobstowe 07–11; TV Okehampton, Inwardleigh, Belstone, Sourton etc 12–18; RD Okehampton 12–16; V Bro Ystumaner *Ban* from 18. *Y Ficerdy, Ffynnon Arian, Tywyn LL36 9BF* T: (01654) 710255 E: maggiethecat@waitrose.com

HANSHAW, Eugene Edward. b 73. ERMC 13. **d** 16 **p** 17. C Chipping Barnet *St Alb* 16–19; TV Cheshunt from 19. *The Vicarage, Churchgate, Cheshunt, Waltham Cross EN8 9DY* M: 07795-195728 E: rev.eugene@outlook.com

HANSON, Barry James. b 70. Qld Univ of Tech DipEd 91 BEd 94 Lon Inst of Educn MA 03. Ripon Coll Cuddesdon 15. **d** 19. C Merrow *Guildf* from 19. *42 Finches Rise, Guildford GU1 2UW* M: 07949-654988 E: revbarryhanson@outlook.com

HANSON, David John. b 59. All SS Cen for Miss & Min. **d** 14 **p** 15. C Chadderton Ch Ch *Man* 14–17; V Preston St Steph *Blackb* from 17. *6 Woodfield Close, Penwortham, Preston PR1 0SJ*

HANSON, Edward William. b 51. Salem State Coll (USA) BA 73 Tufts Univ MA 78 Boston Coll PhD 92 Episc Div Sch MDiv 00. Ripon Coll Cuddesdon 00. **d** 01 **p** 02. C Linc St Botolph and Linc St Pet-at-Gowts and St Andr 01–04; P-in-c Orsett and Bulphan and Horndon on the Hill *Chelmsf* 04–06; R 06–14; RD Thurrock 08–11; rtd 14; PtO *Lon* from 15; *Eur* from 16. *14 Erncroft Way, Twickenham TW1 1DA* E: ed.hanson@alumni.tufts.edu

HANSON, Michael Beaumont. b 49. Univ Coll Ox MA 70 PGCE 71. NOC 81. **d** 84 **p** 85. Chapl Leeds Gr Sch 84–99; Hon C Leeds St Geo *Ripon* 84–99; rtd 99; PtO *Carl* from 99. *5 The Crofts, Crosby, Maryport CA15 6SP* T: (01900) 816630 E: mikeandchristinehanson@sky.com

HANSON, Philip Arthur. b 46. Loughb Univ BTech 69 City Univ MSc 73 St Jo Coll Nottm MA 04 CEng 72 FRSA 96. Qu Coll Birm MA 12. **d** 12 **p** 13. NSM Claverdon w Preston Bagot *Cov* from 12. *Lion Hill Cottage, Station Road, Claverdon, Warwick CV35 8PE* T: (01926) 843421 M: 07879-400947 E: phil@philiphanson.net

HANSON, Robert Arthur. b 35. Keele Univ BA 57. St Steph Ho Ox 57 St Mich Coll Llan 59. **d** 60 **p** 61. C Longton St Mary and St Chad *Lich* 60–65; Chapl St Mary's Cathl Edin 65–69; R Glas St Matt 69–79; R Paisley H Trin 79–87; V Walsall St Andr *Lich* 87–93; PtO *Worc* 94–97; C Kentish Town *Lon* 97–01; Hon C 02–06; rtd 02; PtO *Lon* from 06. *7B Fraser Regnart Court, Southampton Road, London NW5 4HU* T: (020) 7284 3634 M: 07951-154384 E: bob.hanson@btinternet.com

HANWELL, David John. b 46. Leic Univ CertEd 74 UEA BEd 94. **d** 98 **p** 99. OLM Mundford w Lynford, Cranwich and Ickburgh w Langford *Nor* 98–04; OLM Cockley Cley w Gooderstone 99–04; P-in-c 04–13; OLM Gt and Lt Cressingham w Threxton 99–04; C 04–13; OLM Hilborough w Bodney 99–04; C 04–13; OLM Oxborough w Foulden and Caldecote 99–04; C 04–13; rtd 13; PtO *Nor* from 15. *Cherry Tree Cottage, Back Lane, Castle Acre, King's Lynn PE32 2AR* T: (01760) 755812 E: david.hanwell@btopenworld.com

HARALD, Claire Louise. b 76. St Mellitus Coll 16. **d** 19. C Norton *St Alb* from 19. *2 Common View, Letchworth Garden City SG6 1DA* M: 07739-515172 E: claire_harald@hotmail.com

HARBAGE, Matthew Michael. b 86. York Univ MMath 10 Cam Univ BTh 15. Westcott Ho Cam 12. **d** 15 **p** 16. C Louth *Linc* 15-18; C Regent's Park St Mark *Lon* from 18. *Flat C, 16 Hide Place, London SW1P 4NJ* E: mharbage@hotmail.com

HARBIDGE, The Ven Adrian Guy. b 48. St Jo Coll Dur BA 70. Cuddesdon Coll 73. **d** 75 **p** 76. C Romsey *Win* 75–80; V Bournemouth St Andr 80–86; V Chandler's Ford 86–99; RD Eastleigh 93–99; Adn Bournemouth 99–02; P-in-c Seale, Puttenham and Wanborough *Guildf* 10–15; R 15–16; rtd 17. *2 Tudor Cottages, 309 Catherington Lane, Waterlooville PO8 0TE* E: adrianharbidge@gmail.com

HARBORD, Canon Paul Geoffrey. b 56. Keble Coll Ox BA 78 MA 86. Chich Th Coll 81. **d** 83 **p** 84. C Rawmarsh w Parkgate *Sheff* 83–86; C Doncaster St Geo 86–90; C-in-c St Edm Anchorage Lane CD 90–95; V Masbrough 95–03; Bp's Chapl from 03; Hon Can Sheff Cathl from 07. *4 Clarke Drive, Sheffield S10 2NS* T: 0114-266 1932 *or* 230 2170 M: 07898-485428 E: geoffrey.harbord@sheffield.anglican.org

HARBORD, Philip James. b 56. St Cath Coll Ox BA 77. Cranmer Hall Dur 78. **d** 80 **p** 81. C Enfield St Andr *Lon* 80–83; CMS Pakistan 84–88; C Clay Hill St Jo and St Luke *Lon* 88–91; Chapl Wexham Park Hosp Slough 91–92; Chapl Upton Hosp Slough 91–92; Chapl Heatherwood and Wexham Park Hosps NHS Trust 92–95; Chapl Leic Gen Hosp NHS Trust 95–98; Chapl Fosse Health NHS Trust 98–99; Chapl Leics and Rutland Healthcare NHS Trust 99–01; P-in-c Cosby *Leic* 01–07; P-in-c Whetstone 03–07; rtd 07; PtO *Leic* 15–18. *122 Durban Road, Grimsby DN32 8AY*

HARBRIDGE, Philip Charles Anthony. b 65. K Coll Lon LLB 88 AKC 88 Ch Coll Cam BA 98 MA 02. Westcott Ho Cam. **d** 99 **p** 00. C Hampton All SS *Lon* 99–02; Chapl Ch Coll Cam 02–07; Chapl Millfield Sch Somerset from 07. *Millfield School, Street BA16 0YD* T: (01458) 442291 E: pch@millfieldschool.com

HARCOURT, Canon Giles. b 36. Westcott Ho Cam 68. **d** 71 **p** 72. C Bishopwearmouth St Mich w St Hilda *Dur* 71–73; C Fishponds St Mary *Bris* 73–75; Bp's Dom Chapl *S'wark* 75–78; LtO 78–79; V S Wimbledon H Trin and St Pet 79–88; V Greenwich St Alfege 88–04; Hon Chapl RN Coll Greenwich 89–99; RD Greenwich Thameside *S'wark* 94–98; Boro Dean Greenwich 94–98; Hon Can S'wark Cathl 96–04; rtd 05; PtO *Chich* from 05. *1A Trinity Trees, Eastbourne BN21 3LA* T: (01323) 638790

HARCOURT, Paul George. b 67. Em Coll Cam BA 88 MA 92. Wycliffe Hall Ox BA 91 MA 17. **d** 92 **p** 93. C Moreton *Ches* 92–95; C Woodford Wells *Chelmsf* 95–00; V from 00; P-in-c Barkingside St Cedd from 16; AD Redbridge 10–14; Nat Ldr New Wine from 16. *All Saints' Vicarage, 4 Inmans Row, Woodford Green IG8 0NH* T: (020) 8504 0266 F: 8504 9640 E: paul@asww.org.uk *or* paul.harcourt@new-wine.org

HARCOURT-NORTON, Michael Clive. See NORTON, Michael Clive Harcourt

HARDACRE (née BROOKFIELD), Mrs Patricia Anne. b 50. St Mary's Coll Dur BA 72 St Jo Coll Dur MA 74. Cranmer Hall Dur. **dss** 84 **d** 87 **p** 94. Kingston upon Hull St Nic *York* 84–86; Acomb St Steph and St Aid 86–96; Par Dn 87–94; C 94–96; rtd 07; PtO *Blackb* from 07. *17 Fairfield Drive, Clitheroe BB7 2PE* T: (01200) 429341 E: annderekh@talktalk.net

HARDCASTLE, Ian Kenneth Dalton. b 56. Auckland Univ BE 78 ME 80. St Jo Coll Nottm MTh 04. **d** 04 **p** 05. C Denton Holme *Carl* 04–09; V Whangaparaoa Peninsular New Zealand from 09. *20 Rakino Avenue, Manly, Whangaparaoa 0930, New Zealand* T: (0064) (9) 424 0939 E: vicar@ststephenswgp.org.nz

HARDCASTLE, Nigel John. b 47. Reading Univ BSc 68. Qu Coll Birm. **d** 72 **p** 73. C Weoley Castle *Birm* 72–75; C Handsworth St Andr 75–78; V Garretts Green 78–86; Exec Sec Ch Computer Project BCC 86–89; R Emmer Green *Ox* 89–99; V Reading St Luke w St Bart 99–12; rtd 12; PtO *Ox* from 13. *67 Dunstall Close, Tilehurst, Reading RG31 5AY* T: 0118-943 1258 E: nigel.hardcastle@btinternet.com

HARDCASTLE, Roger Clive. b 52. Southn Univ BSc 73. Qu Coll Birm. **d** 78 **p** 79. C Walton St Mary *Liv* 78–82; V Pemberton St Fran Kitt Green 82–94; TV Padgate 94–96; V Birchwood 96–06; rtd 06. *15 Ullswater Avenue, Orrell, Wigan WN5 8PF* T: (01942) 513568

HARDING, Alan. b 45. St Jo Coll Ox BA 67 MA 73 Pemb Coll Ox DPhil 92. Oak Hill NSM Course 89. **d** 93 **p** 94. NSM Lt Heath *St Alb* 93–99; P-in-c S Mymms and Ridge 99–05; PtO *St E* 05–08; NSM S Hartismere 08–13; PtO *St Alb* 05–17; *St E* from 13. *The Old Guildhall, Mill Street, Gislingham, Eye IP23 8JT* T: (01379) 783361 E: alansharon.harding@googlemail.com

HARDING, Canon Alec James. b 61. St Andr Univ MA 83 DTh. Cranmer Hall Dur 86. **d** 89 **p** 90. C Thirsk *York* 89–93; TV Heref St Martin w St Fran 93–95; TV Heref S Wye 95–00; V Barnard Castle w Whorlton *Dur* from 00; AD Barnard Castle from 03; Hon Can Dur Cathl from 11. *The Vicarage, Parson's Lonnen, Barnard Castle DL12 8ST* T: (01833) 637018 E: alec.harding@durham.anglican.org

HARDING, Mrs Allison Joan. b 65. Sheff Univ BA 96 Northumbria Univ BSc 04. Cranmer Hall Dur 11. **d** 13 **p** 14. C Benwell *Newc* 13–15; C Benwell and Scotswood 15–17; V Newburn from 17. *The Vicarage, High Street, Newburn, Newcastle upon Tyne NE15 8LQ* T: 0191-229 0522 E: revallisonharding@gmail.com

HARDING, Canon Brenda Kathleen. b 39. Bedf Coll Lon BA 60 K Coll Lon BD 62 Lon Inst of Educn PGCE 65. St Deiniol's Hawarden 91. **d** 92 **p** 94. NSM Lancaster Ch Ch *Blackb* 92–13; Acting Vice-Prin CBDTI 04–05; Hon Can Blackb Cathl 05–13; rtd 13; PtO *Blackb* from 13. *14 Ascot Close, Lancaster LA1 4LT* T: (01524) 66071 E: brendakharding@hotmail.com

HARDING, Canon Brian Edward. b 38. ALCD 65. **d** 65 **p** 66. C Chislehurst Ch Ch *Roch* 65–68; P-in-c Baxenden *Blackb* 68–70; V 70–88; V Douglas 88–07; Hon Can Blackb Cathl 96–07; rtd 07; PtO *St As* from 08. *8 Lon Eirlys, Prestatyn LL19 9JZ* T: (01745) 851615 E: bnbharding@tiscali.co.uk

HARDING, Carl Julius. b 64. St Jo Coll Dur BA 15. Cranmer Hall Dur 12. **d** 15 **p** 16. C Stanwix *Carl* from 15. *54 Eden Street, Carlisle CA3 9LH* T: (01228) 524436 M: 07961-862956 E: carljharding@gmail.com

HARDING, Mrs Christine Joan. b 54. St Mellitus Coll. **d** 11 **p** 12. NSM Chadwell Heath *Chelmsf* from 11. *69 Eric Road, Romford RM6 6JH* T: (020) 8599 6174 E: christine@romfordhardings.me.uk

HARDING, Derek Gordon Edward. b 50. Open Univ BA 89 MIAP 95. **d** 01 **p** 02. OLM Godstone and Blindley Heath *S'wark* 01–09; C Blenheim New Zealand 09; PtO Dio Nelson 10–15; 16–18; rtd 15; PtO *S'wark* 15–16. *27 Moran Street, Redwoodtown, Blenheim 7201, New Zealand* E: peripatetic.padre@gmail.com

HARDING, Mrs Elise. b 44. RGN 65. STETS 07. **d** 10 **p** 11. NSM Wimborne Minster *Sarum* 10–15; NSM Witchampton, Stanbridge and Long Crichel etc 15; NSM Horton, Chalbury, Hinton Martel and Holt St Jas 15; NSM Wimborne Minster and the N Villages 15–17; rtd 17; PtO *Sarum* from 17. *The Beaches, 210 Middlehall Road, Wimborne BH21 2SD* T: (01202) 884775 E: fur_elise_h@yahoo.co.uk

HARDING, Elizabeth. See BUNKER, Elizabeth

HARDING, James Alexander. b 78. Trin Coll Bris BA 11. **d** 11 **p** 12. C Fulham Ch Ch *Lon* 11–16; CF from 16. *c/o MOD Chaplains (Army)* T: (01264) 383430 F: 381824 M: 07956-222940 E: hardingjamesa@gmail.com

HARDING, James Owen Glyn. b 42. Sussex Univ BA 65. NEOC 04. **d** 06 **p** 07. NSM Acomb H Redeemer *York* 06–12; PtO from 12. *63 Station Road, Upper Poppleton, York YO26 6PZ* T: (01904) 784495 E: jim2sal65@yahoo.co.uk

HARDING, John Stuart Michael. b 45. St Jo Coll Nottm 79. **d** 81 **p** 82. C Clifton *S'well* 81–87; V Broxtowe 87–98; PtO *Chelmsf* 98–01; Perm to Offic *M & K* 01–02; rtd 07. *Greystone Farm, 9 Liscable Road, Newtownstewart BT78 4EF* E: john@greystomefarming.org

HARDING, Lesley Anne. *See* ATKINS, Lesley Anne

HARDING, Mrs Mary Elizabeth. b 46. SRN 67. STETS 97. **d** 00 **p** 01. NSM Shaftesbury *Sarum* 00–13; Chapl Westmr Memorial Hosp Shaftesbury 02–13; rtd 13. *Greenacres, Boxfield Road, Axminster EX13 5LD* T: (01297) 32155

HARDING, Michael Anthony John. b 37. Brasted Th Coll 67 Sarum Th Coll 68. **d** 71 **p** 72. C Forest Hill Ch Ch *S'wark* 71–72; C Catford St Laur 72–74; C Leominster *Heref* 74–77; R Neenton and V Ditton Priors 77–86; P-in-c Aston Botterell w Wheathill and Loughton 77–86; P-in-c Burwarton w Cleobury 77–86; R Ditton Priors w Neenton, Burwarton etc 86–94; V E Budleigh w Bicton and Otterton *Ex* 94–03; rtd 03; PtO *Sarum* from 03. *The Beaches, 22 Middlehill Road, Wimborne BH21 2SD* T: (01202) 884775 E: michaelharding@talktalk.net

HARDING, Preb Michael David. b 38. Man Univ BA 61. Lich Th Coll 61. **d** 63 **p** 64. C Hednesford *Lich* 63–67; C Blurton 67–70; V Newcastle St Paul 70–99; RD Newcastle 87–97; Preb Lich Cathl 89–99; rtd 99; PtO *Lich* from 00. *7 Staines Court, Stone ST15 8XF* T: (01785) 811737 E: church@mdharding.org.uk

HARDING, Peter Gordon. b 45. Lon Univ BA 70 Open Univ BA 88 MA 90. Cranmer Hall Dur 77. **d** 79 **p** 80. C Kirkheaton *Wakef* 79–82; NSM New Sleaford *Linc* 90–00. *77 The Drove, Sleaford NG34 7AS* T: (01529) 306055 E: peter@harding67.plus.com

HARDING, Mrs Ren Elaine Lois. b 56. Glos Univ BA 05. Trin Coll Bris MA 07. **d** 07 **p** 08. C Rainham *Roch* 07–11; V Joydens Wood St Barn 11–18; TR Bexley from 18. *The Vicarage, 6 Tile Kiln Lane, Bexley DA5 2BB* T: (01322) 528923 M: 07836-644782 E: renharding@hotmail.com

HARDING, Richard Warrington. b 60. Trin Coll Bris 05. **d** 07 **p** 08. C Broadway w Wickhamford *Worc* 07–09; C Old Hill H Trin 09–11; TV Ipsley from 11. *Matchborough Vicarage, Winward Road, Redditch B98 0SX* T: (01527) 523768

HARDINGHAM, Paul David. b 52. Lon Univ BSc 74 Fitzw Coll Cam BA 77. Ridley Hall Cam 75. **d** 78 **p** 79. C Cambridge St Martin *Ely* 78–81; C Jesmond Clayton Memorial *Newc* 81–88; C Harborne Heath *Birm* 88–91; R Ipswich St Matt *St E* 91–04; V Halliwell St Pet *Man* from 04. *St Peter's Vicarage, 1 Sefton Road, Bolton BL1 6HT* T: (01204) 848567 E: paulharding@googlemail.com

HARDINGHAM, Timothy Kenneth. b 49. G&C Coll Cam BA 70. ERMC 08. **d** 11 **p** 12. NSM Saffron Walden and Villages *Chelmsf* from 11. *Steading, West End, Wendens Ambo, Saffron Walden CB11 4UJ* T: (01799) 542874 M: 07894-537990 E: tim@hardingham.net

HARDISTY, Gloria. b 62. **d** 10 **p** 11. NSM Thornton St Jas *Bradf* 10–14; Leeds from 14. *1 Wembley Avenue, Thornton, Bradford BD13 3BY* T: (01274) 833280 E: john-hardisty@sky.com

✠**HARDMAN, The Rt Revd Christine Elizabeth.** b 51. Lon Univ BSc(Econ) 73. St Alb Minl Tr Scheme 81. **dss** 84 **d** 87 **p** 94. Markyate Street *St Alb* 84–88; Par Dn 87–88; Tutor St Alb Minl Tr Scheme 88–91; Course Dir 91–96; C Markyate Street *St Alb* 94–96; V Stevenage H Trin 96–01; RD Stevenage 99–01; Adn Lewisham *S'wark* 01–08; Adn Lewisham and Greenwich 08–12; NSM Lewisham St Mary 12–15; PtO *St Alb* 13–15; Bp Newc from 15. *The Bishop's House, 29 Moor Road South, Newcastle upon Tyne NE3 1PA* T: 0191-285 2220 E: bishop@newcastle.anglican.org

HARDMAN, Geoffrey James. b 41. Birm Univ BA 63. NOC 77. **d** 80 **p** 81. NSM Latchford St Jas *Ches* 80–93; NSM Haydock St Jas *Liv* 94–06; rtd 06; PtO *Ches* from 16; *Liv* from 16. *48 Denbury Avenue, Stockton Heath, Warrington WA4 2BW* T: (01925) 264064 E: geoffrey.hardman1@ntlworld.com

HARDMAN, Canon Peter George. b 35. Man Univ BSc 56. Ridley Hall Cam 58. **d** 60 **p** 61. C Oldham St Paul *Man* 60–63; NW England Area Sec SCM 63–64; NW England Area Sec CEM 64–67; Asst Chapl Marlborough Coll 67–72; Chapl 72–79; P-in-c Wareham *Sarum* 79–80; TR 80–00; Chapl Wareham Hosp 80–92; Chapl Dorset HealthCare University NHS Foundn Trust 92–00; Can and Preb Sarum Cathl 87–00; RD Purbeck 89–99; rtd 00; PtO *Sarum* from 00; *B & W* 02–14. *55 Palairet Close, Bradford-on-Avon BA15 1US* T: (01225) 867198 E: peterhardman@onetel.com

HARDWICK, Christopher George. b 57. Open Univ BA 94 Birm Univ MA 96 PhD 00 ACIB 79. Ripon Coll Cuddesdon 90. **d** 92 **p** 93. C Worc SE 92–95; R Ripple, Earls Croome w Hill Croome and Strensham 95–00; R Upton-on-Severn, Ripple, Earls Croome etc 00–05; RD Upton 97–05; Hon Can Worc Cathl 03–05; Dean Truro 05–11; R Truro St Mary 05–11; P-in-c Pyworthy, Pancrasweek and Bridgerule *Ex* 11–15; P-in-c Tavistock and Gulworthy 15; V Tavistock, Gulworthy and Brent Tor from 15. *The Rectory, 5A Plymouth Road, Tavistock PL19 8AU* T: (01822) 617432 E: veryrevdchristopher.hardwick@btinternet.com

HARDWICK, Mrs Daphne Anne. b 45. Reading Univ BA 97 SRN 67 SCM 69 HVCert 79. Trin Coll Bris 10. **d** 12 **p** 13. OLM Swindon Ch Ch *Bris* from 12. *6 St Margaret's Road, Swindon SN3 1RU* T: (01793) 693721 M: 07881-281843 E: daphne@christchurchswindon.co.uk

HARDWICK, Canon Graham John. b 42. Qu Coll Birm 68. **d** 70 **p** 71. C Watford St Mich *St Alb* 70–73; C N Mymms 73–75; Youth Officer Cov Cathl 75–81; Chapl Lanchester Poly 76–81; V Nuneaton St Nic 81–95; Ind Chapl and P-in-c New Bilton 95–07; Hon Can Cov Cathl 04–07; rtd 08; PtO *Cov* from 08. *150 Pytchley Road, Rugby CV22 5NG* T: (01788) 544011 F: 333256 E: revgjh@btinternet.com

HARDWICK, Canon Susan Frances. b 44. Warwick Univ BA 81. Qu Coll Birm 82. **dss** 85 **d** 87 **p** 94. Chilvers Coton w Astley *Cov* 85–91; C 87–91; Dioc Disabilities Officer 91–96; Chapl Hereward Coll 91–96; Chapl FE Colls *Cov* 94–09; Hon C New Bilton 96–98; FE Field Officer Team Co-ord (W Midl) 97–09; Chapl Rainsbrook Secure Tr Cen 99–09; Hon Can Cov Cathl 04–09; rtd 09; PtO *Cov* from 09. *150 Pytchley Road, Rugby CV22 5NG* T: (01788) 544011 F: 333256

HARDY, Ms Alison Jane. b 61. St Anne's Coll Ox BA 82 MA 96. NOC 92. **d** 95 **p** 96. C Flixton St Mich *Man* 95–98; Lect Bolton St Pet 98–00; P-in-c Irlam 00–05; R Stand 05–18; AD Radcliffe and Prestwich 13–18; P-in-c Embleton w Rennington and Rock *Newc* from 18; AD Alnwick from 18. *The Vicarage, Embleton, Alnwick NE66 3UW* E: embleton.vicar@btinternet.com

HARDY, Alison Jane. b 60. **d** 14 **p** 15. C Stratton and Launcells *Truro* 14–16; C Bude Haven and Marhamchurch 14–16; C N Kernow 16–18; C Kilkhampton w Morwenstow 16–18; C Launceston from 18. *St Mary's Church Hall, Tower Street, Launceston PL15 8BQ* T: (01566) 772771 E: reverendalisonhardy@gmail.com

HARDY, Anthony. b 36. **d** 86 **p** 87. NSM Malden St Jas *S'wark* 86–06; PtO 06–10. *48 Blake's Lane, New Malden KT3 6NR* T: (020) 8949 0703 E: aehardy@waitrose.com

HARDY, Anthony William. b 56. Man Univ BEd 79 MEd 86 Open Univ BSc 00. St Jo Coll Nottm LTh 88. **d** 88 **p** 89. C Pennington *Man* 88–91; V Eccleston St Luke *Liv* 91–00; Min Consultant CPAS 00–09; Dioc Evang *Liv* 00–02; Can Ev Man Cathl 09–14; R Whalley Range St Edm and Moss Side etc from 14; AD Hulme from 16. *St Edmund's Rectory, 1 Range Road, Manchester M16 8FS* T: 0161-226 4554 E: tonybillhardy@gmail.com *or* stedsandstjames@gmail.com

HARDY, Canon Brian Albert. b 31. St Jo Coll Ox BA 54 MA 58. Westcott Ho Cam 55. **d** 57 **p** 58. C Rugeley *Lich* 57–62; Chapl Down Coll Cam 62–66; C-in-c Livingston Miss *Edin* 66–74; Preb Heref Cathl 74–78; Ch Planning Officer Telford 74–78; RD Telford Severn Gorge 75–78; Chapl Edin Th Coll 78–82; Chapl Edin R Infirmary 82–86; R Edin St Columba 82–91; Dean Edin 86–91; Hon Can St Mary's Cathl from 91; R St Andrews All SS *St And* 91–96; rtd 96; LtO *Edin* from 10. *3/3 Starbank Road, Edinburgh EH5 3BN* T: 0131-551 6783

HARDY, Christopher Richard. b 52. R Holloway Coll Lon BMus 77 Southn Univ BTh 90. Chich Th Coll 87. **d** 90 **p** 91. C Kenton *Lon* 90–95; V E Finchley All SS 95–19; rtd 19. *Address temp unknown* M: 07785-728272 E: christopherhardy@btinternet.com

HARDY, Miss Janet Frances. b 59. Newc Univ BA 81 CertEd 82. Trin Coll Bris 87. **d** 89 **p** 94. Par Dn Sheff St Paul 89–92; Team Dn Gt Snaith 92–94; TV 94–96; V Pitsmoor Ch Ch 96–01; V Thorpe Hesley 01–14; Dioc Ecum Officer 11–14; V Barmby Moor Gp *York* from 14. *The Vicarage, St Helen's Square, Barmby Moor, York YO42 4HF* T: (01759) 307042 E: rev.j.hardy@btinternet.com

HARDY, John Christopher. b 61. St Jo Coll Dur BA 83 Dur Univ MA 95 New Coll Edin BD 92 Ox Univ MLitt 00. Aston Tr Scheme 87 Coates Hall Edin 89. **d** 92 **p** 93. C Walker *Newc* 92–95; Fell Chapl Magd Coll Ox 95–98; TV Benwell *Newc* 98–03; R Alston Moor 03–08; R Newmarket St Mary w Exning St Agnes *St E* from 08; P-in-c Exning St Martin w Landwade from 18; RD Mildenhall 16–18. *The Rectory, 21 Hamilton Road, Newmarket CB8 0NY* T: (01638) 660729 E: jhardy153@btinternet.com

HARDY, Mrs Julie Anne. b 68. St Mellitus Coll BA 16. **d** 16 **p** 17. C Broomfield *Chelmsf* from 16. *65 School Lane, Broomfield, Chelmsford CM1 7DR* E: revjuliehardy@btinternet.com

HARDY, Lesley Anne. b 53. Nottm Univ BA 75 St Luke's Coll Ex PGCE 76. **d** 05 **p** 06. OLM Lydd *Cant* 05–09; NSM Barham Downs 09–16; rtd 16; PtO *Cant* from 17. *Russets, Maidstone Road, Marden, Tonbridge TN12 9AE* M: 07752-517903

HARDY, Michael Henry. b 33. Qu Coll Birm 85. **d** 86 **p** 87. C Leic St Jas 86–88; R Arnesby w Shearsby and Bruntingthorpe 88–94; RD Guthlaxton I 91–94; TV Bradgate Team 94–99; rtd 99; PtO *Leic* 99–12; *Pet* from 99. *14 Dean's Street, Oakham LE15 6AF* T: (01572) 722591

HARDY, Miss Pauline. b 41. CertEd. Linc Th Coll 85. **d** 87 **p** 94. Par Dn Walsall Wood *Lich* 87–89; Par Dn Buckingham *Ox* 89–93; C Buckingham w Radclive cum Chackmore 93–97; C Nash w Thornton, Beachampton and Thornborough 96–97; C Buckingham 97–03; C Watling Valley 03–06; rtd 06. *32 Campbell Road, Plymouth PL9 8UE* E: pauline@revhardy.plus.com

✠**HARDY, The Rt Revd Robert Maynard.** b 36. Clare Coll Cam BA 60 MA 64 Hull Univ Hon DD 92. Cuddesdon Coll 60. **d** 62 **p** 63 **c** 80. C Langley St Aid CD *Man* 62–64; C Langley All SS and Martyrs 64–65; Chapl and Lect Th Selw Coll Cam 65–72; V Boreham Wood All SS *St Alb* 72–75; Dir St Alb Minl Tr Scheme 75–80; P-in-c Aspley Guise *St Alb* 75–79; P-in-c Husborne Crawley w Ridgmont 76–79; R Aspley Guise w Husborne Crawley and Ridgmont 80; Suff Bp Maidstone *Cant* 80–87; Bp Linc 87–01; Bp HM Pris 85–01; rtd 01; Hon Asst Bp Carl from 01. *Carleton House, Back Lane, Langwathby, Penrith CA10 1NB* T: (01768) 881210

HARDY, Sam Richard Ian. b 71. Wall Hall Coll Aldenham BEd 95 Open Univ MA 00. Wycliffe Hall Ox BTh 04. **d** 04. C Parr *Liv* 04–05. *Knarrside, Woodhead Road, Tintwistle, Glossop SK13 1JX* E: sam.hardy@tiscali.co.uk

HARDY, Stephen John Arundell. b 49. SEITE 95. **d** 97 **p** 98. NSM Marden *Cant* 97–00; P-in-c Lydd 00–09; AD Romney 03–08; P-in-c Barham w Bishopsbourne and Kingston 09–12; C Nonington w Wymynswold and Goodnestone etc 11–12; P-in-c Barham Downs 12–16; AD E Bridge 11–16; AD W Bridge 11–14; rtd 16; PtO *Cant* from 17. *Russets, Maidstone Road, Marden, Tonbridge TN12 9AE* M: 07752-517903 E: stephenhardy1@mac.com

HARE, Christopher Sumner. b 49. Solicitor 73. WEMTC 92. **d** 95 **p** 96. NSM Saltford w Corston and Newton St Loe *B & W* 95–01; P-in-c Timsbury and Priston 01–10; R Timsbury w Priston, Camerton and Dunkerton 10–12; Bp's Officer for Ord NSM (Bath Adnry) 07–08; RD Midsomer Norton 07–12; rtd 12; PtO *B & W* 15–17; Acting Adn Bath from 17; PtO *B & W* from 12. *Cuckoo Hill, 61 Packsaddle Way, Frome BA11 2RW* T: (01373) 469788 M: 07779-825348

HARE, David. b 46. Qu Coll Birm 81. **d** 83 **p** 83. SSF 67–94; Bp's Dom Chapl *Birm* 83–87; V Handsworth St Mich 87–97; R Newton Regis w Seckington and Shuttington 97–03; rtd 03; PtO *Birm* 03–12. *34 The Charters, Lichfield WS13 7LX* E: dandjhare7@gmail.com

HARE, Richard William. b 66. Bris Univ BSc 88 PhD 94. Cranmer Hall Dur BA 95. **d** 95 **p** 96. C Coulsdon St Jo *S'wark* 95–98; C Coventry Caludon *Cov* 98–99; TV 99–07; AD Cov E 01–07; TR Bedworth 07–16; AD Nuneaton 12–16; V Bridlington Em and Barmston w Fraisthorpe *York* from 16. *72 Cardigan Road, Bridlington YO15 3JT* M: 07871-194435 E: thehares@live.net

HARE (née CALDWELL), Mrs Sarah Louise. b 75. St Jo Coll Nottm 11. **d** 13 **p** 14. C Bishop's Castle w Mainstone, Lydbury N etc *Heref* 13–16; TV Wenlock 16–19; V Yaxley and Holme w Conington *Ely* from 19. *The Vicarage, 43 Church Street, Yaxley, Peterborough PE7 3LH* M: 07709-056177 E: sarah.hare@aol.co.uk

HARES, David Ronald Walter. b 40. Qu Coll Cam BA 63 MA 67 CertEd. Westcott Ho Cam 64. **d** 66 **p** 67. C Cannock *Lich* 66–69; Chapl Peterho Cam 69–72; Asst Master Chesterton Sch Cam 72–74; V Kesgrave *St E* 74–98; R Lt Barningham, Blickling, Edgefield etc *Nor* 98–05; rtd 05; PtO *Nor* from 05. *17 Trory Street, Norwich NR2 2RH* T: (01603) 626392 E: david.hares@gmail.com

HARFORD, Paul Roger. b 83. York Univ BA 04 Selw Coll Cam BA 09. Ridley Hall Cam 07. **d** 10 **p** 11. C Stokesley w Seamer *York* 10–13; R Bishop Thornton, Burnt Yates, Markington etc *Ripon* 13–14; *Leeds* from 14. *The Vicarage, Westerns Lane, Markington, Harrogate HG3 3PB* T: (01765) 677123 *or* (01423) 771820 E: revpaulharford@gmail.com

HARGER, Robin Charles Nicholas. b 49. BTh. Sarum & Wells Th Coll 78. **d** 81 **p** 82. C Charlton Kings St Mary *Glouc* 81–85; C Folkestone St Mary and St Eanswythe *Cant* 85–89; TV Langley and Parkfield *Man* 89–95; TV Bournemouth

Town Cen *Win* 95–12; rtd 12; PtO *Win* from 17. *1 Northover Gardens, 5 Dunbar Road, Bournemouth BH3 7AZ* T: (01202) 318126 E: robin.cn.harger@gmail.com

HARGRAVE, Canon Alan Lewis. b 50. Birm Univ BSc 73 PhD 77. Ridley Hall Cam 87. **d** 89 **p** 90. C Cambridge H Trin w St Andr Gt *Ely* 89–92; C Cambridge H Trin 92–93; C-in-c Fen Ditton 93–94; V Cambridge H Cross 94–04; Can Res Ely Cathl 04–16; rtd 16; PtO *S'well* from 16. *16 Foxhollies Grove, Nottingham NG5 2NP*

HARGRAVES, Mrs Christobel Mary Kathleen. b 58. Man Poly BSc 79 Open Univ MBA RGN 83. SAOMC 03. **d** 06 **p** 07. C Goring and Streatley w S Stoke *Ox* 06–09; R Shelswell 09–14; AD Bicester and Islip 13–14; PtO *S & B* from 15; *Heref* from 15. *Pye Corner, Llangunilo, Knighton LD7 1ST* T: (01547) 550311 E: hargraves391@btinternet.com

HARGREAVE, James David. b 44. K Coll Lon BA 66 PGCE 68 ALCM 89 LTCL 90. Coll of Resurr Mirfield 70. **d** 73 **p** 74. C Houghton le Spring *Dur* 73–77; C Gateshead St Cuth w St Paul 77–79; V Trimdon 79–87; C-in-c Stockton Green Vale H Trin CD 87–94; V Hedon w Paull *York* 94–02; rtd 02; PtO *York* from 03. *1 The Avenue, Crescent Street, Cottingham HU16 5QT* T: (01482) 844297 E: j.hargr25@gmail.com

HARGREAVES, Andrew David. b 74. Homerton Coll Cam BEd 97. Trin Coll Bris BA 08. **d** 08 **p** 09. C Shirley *Win* 08–12; V Whitfield *Derby* 12–17; Miss Development Officer *Portsm* from 17. *Diocese of Portsmouth, First Floor, Peninsular House, Wharf Road, Portsmouth PO2 8HB* T: (023) 9289 9676 E: andrew.hargreaves@portsmouth.anglican.org

HARGREAVES, John. b 43. St Jo Coll Nottm 86. **d** 88 **p** 89. C Werneth *Man* 88–91; TV Rochdale 91–96; C Man Gd Shep 96–97; PtO *Liv* 96–97; C Manchester Gd Shep and St Barn *Man* 97–98; rtd 98; PtO *Man* 06–08. *Water House, Wyebank, Bakewell DE45 1BH* M: 07922-004930 E: johnatbakewell@gmail.com

HARGREAVES, John Wilson. b 46. Aber Univ BScFor 67. Westcott Ho Cam 84. **d** 86 **p** 87. C Rugby *Cov* 86–90; TV Daventry, Ashby St Ledgers, Braunston etc *Pet* 90–97; Chapl Daventry Tertiary Coll 94–97; P-in-c Pinxton *Derby* 97–01; R 01–02; TR E Scarsdale 02–11; rtd 11; PtO *Leeds* from 17. *66 Bishopton Lane, Ripon HG4 2QN* T: (01765) 609413

HARGREAVES, Julia Gay. b 61. EMMTC 04. **d** 07 **p** 08. NSM Glenfield *Leic* 07–08; NSM Upper Soar 08–11; TV Bosworth and Sheepy Gp from 11; C Nailstone and Carlton w Shackerstone from 11. *The Rectory, Church Lane, Sheepy Magna, Atherstone CV9 3QS* T: (01827) 881389 E: julia.hargreaves17@gmail.com

HARGREAVES, Ms Marise. b 60. Leeds Univ BA 81. Cranmer Hall Dur 82. **dss** 83 **d** 94 **p** 95. Yeadon St Jo *Bradf* 85–87; NSM Bradf St Clem 94–96; NSM Buttershaw St Paul 96–00; C Eccleshill 00–03; PtO 03–09; Chapl Derby Teaching Hosps NHS Foundn Trust from 09. *Chaplaincy, Royal Derby Hospital, Uttoxeter Road, Derby DE22 3NE* T: (01332) 340131 E: ma6591@hotmail.com

HARGREAVES, Mark Kingston. b 63. Oriel Coll Ox BA 85 MA 89 Rob Coll Cam PhD 91 W Lon Inst of HE PGCE 86. Ridley Hall Cam 87. **d** 91 **p** 92. C Highbury Ch Ch w St Jo and St Sav *Lon* 91–94; C Ealing St Steph Castle Hill 94–97; C Notting Hill St Jo and St Pet 97–02; V Notting Hill St Pet 03–16; AD Kensington 06–11; R La Jolla USA from 16. *743 Prospect Street, La Jolla, CA 92037-4229, USA* T: (001) (858) 459 3421 E: mark@sjbts.org

HARKER, Harold Aidan. b 35. **d** 82 **p** 83. OSB from 53; C Reading St Giles *Ox* 82–83; LtO 83–87; C Halstead St Andr w H Trin and Greenstead Green *Chelmsf* 87–89; P-in-c Belchamp St Paul 89–97; R Belchamp Otten w Belchamp Walter and Bulmer etc 97–00; rtd 00; LtO *Chelmsf* from 00; PtO *Lon* from 15. *38 Sheppard's College, London Road, Bromley BR1 1PE* T: (020) 8464 1206

HARKER, Ian. b 39. Dur Univ BA 61. Lich Th Coll Moray Ho Edin 66. **d** 63 **p** 64. C Knottingley *Wakef* 63–66; PtO 66–70; C Notting Hill *Lon* 70–75; Chapl Newc Univ 75–83; Master Newc St Thos Prop Chpl 75–83; PtO *Chelmsf* 99–01; C Plaistow and N Canning Town 01; C Loughton St Jo 01–02; V Leytonstone H Trin and St Aug Harrow Green 02–11; rtd 11; PtO *Chelmsf* 11–13; *Cant* 14–19. *70 Sturry Hill, Canterbury CT2 0NH* T: (01227) 711247 E: harkatvic@aol.com *or* i.harker@aol.com

HARKER, Stephan John. b 47. Em Coll Cam BA 68 MA 72. Westcott Ho Cam 70. **d** 72 **p** 73. C Marton *Blackb* 72–76; C Preston St Matt 76–79; C Fleetwood St Pet 79–80; Sen Chapl Charterhouse Sch Godalming 81–07; Chapl 07–16; rtd 16; PtO *Blackb* from 16. *17 The Millrace, Damside Street, Lancaster LA1 1BL* T: (01524) 555740 M: 07850-915725 E: stephanjh@btinternet.com

HARKIN, Canon John Patrick. b 53. Oak Hill Th Coll 87. **d** 89 **p** 90. C Wisley w Pyrford *Guildf* 89–93; P-in-c Mickleham

93–98; Chapl Box Hill Sch Surrey 93–98; R Jersey St Ouen w St Geo *Win* 98–10; Vice-Dean Jersey 01–10; P-in-c Andover 10–11; V 11–18; RD 10–18; Hon Can Win Cathl 09–18; Hon C Leatherhead and Mickleham *Guildf* from 18. *The Rectory, London Road, Mickleham, Dorking RH5 6EB* T: (01372) 378335 E: harkin12@btinternet.com

HARKIN, Terence James. b 46. Lon Bible Coll BA 82 New Coll Edin MTh 94. **d** 95 **p** 96. In Bapt Min 86–95; C Edin H Cross 95–96; C S Queensferry 95–96; P-in-c from 96; R Edin Clermiston Em 09–18; rtd 18. *6 Wellhead Close, South Queensferry EH30 9WA* T: 0131-331 1958 *or* 319 1099 E: tjharkin@priorychurch.com

HARKNETT, David Philip. b 74. St Pet Coll Ox BA 97. Oak Hill Th Coll BA 03. **d** 03 **p** 04. C Radipole and Melcombe Regis *Sarum* 03–07; TV Melbury 07–17; P-in-c Upper Wreake *Leic* from 17. *2 Carrfields Lane, Frisby on the Wreake, Melton Mowbray LE14 2NT*

HARKNETT, Mrs Helen. b 78. Loughb Univ BA 00. Westcott Ho Cam 14. **d** 16 **p** 17. C Clapham H Spirit *S'wark* 16–18; C Kennington St Jo w St Jas from 18. *60 Wix's Lane, London SW4 0AQ* M: 07557-093585 E: hhharknett@gmail.com

HARKNETT, Linda. b 48. Open Univ BA 81 Croydon Coll CertEd 92. SEITE 97. **d** 00 **p** 01. NSM Sutton St Nic *S'wark* 00–03; Chapl Epsom and St Helier NHS Trust 00–03; Chapl Whitelands Coll Roehampton Univ *S'wark* 03–07; Dioc FE and HE Chapl Officer 03–07; P-in-c Headley w Box Hill *Guildf* 07–16; rtd 16. *7 Bridge Place, Edinburgh EH3 5JJ* M: 07796-903167 E: lindaharknett@gmail.com

HARLAND, Brenda. b 53. **d** 08. NSM Thatcham *Ox* from 08. *St Mary's Church Office, Church Gate, Thatcham RG19 3PN* T: (01635) 862277 E: brenda.harland@ntlworld.com

HARLAND, Canon Harold William James. b 35. Hertf Coll Ox BA 59 MA 63. Clifton Th Coll 59. **d** 61 **p** 62. C Reigate St Mary *S'wark* 61–64; C Farnborough *Guildf* 64–68; V Walmley *Birm* 68–74; V Bromley Ch Ch *Roch* 74–86; V Folkestone St Jo *Cant* 86–00; Dir Post-Ord Tr 93–97; Hon Can Cant Cathl 94–00; rtd 00; PtO *Cant* from 00. *121 Station Road West, Canterbury CT2 8DE* T: (01227) 764699 E: harland672@btinternet.com

HARLE, Michael Richardson. b 58. BA 80 Man Univ MBM 91. **d** 11 **p** 12. NSM Claygate *Guildf* from 11. *1 The Green, Claygate, Esher KT10 0JL* T: (01372) 463898 M: 07788-160040 E: mikeharle@btinternet.com *or* mikeharle@holytrinityclaygate.org.uk

HARLEY, Canon Brian Nigel. b 30. Clare Coll Cam BA 53 MA 57. Cuddesdon Coll 53. **d** 55 **p** 56. C Basingstoke *Win* 55–60; TV 71–73; TR 73–80; C W End 60–61; C-in-c Southn St Chris Thornhill CD 61–71; V Eastleigh 80–93; RD 85–93; rtd 93; PtO *Win* 93–13; Bp's Dom Chapl 94–96. *18 Phillimore Road, Southampton SO16 2NR* T: (023) 8055 1049

HARLEY, Mrs Carol Anne. b 46. **d** 00 **p** 01. OLM Tettenhall Wood and Perton *Lich* 00–19; PtO from 19. *27 Tyrley Close, Compton, Wolverhampton WV6 8AP* T: (01902) 755316

HARLEY, Christopher David. b 41. Selw Coll Cam BA 63 MA 69 Bris Univ PGCE 64 Columbia Bible Sem DMin 92 Utrecht Univ PhD 02. Clifton Th Coll 64. **d** 66 **p** 67. C Finchley Ch Ch *Lon* 66–69; Hon C 75–78; Ethiopia 70–75; Hd of UK Miss CMJ 75–78; Lect All Nations Chr Coll Ware 78–85; Prin 85–93; Chmn Lon Inst of Contemporary Christianity 88–89; Chmn CMJ 89–90; Crosslinks 93–06; Gen Dir OMF Internat 93–05; NSM Bromley Ch Ch *Roch* 93–96; NSM Singapore 96–06; rtd 06; PtO *Ex* from 06. *12 Harrington Drive, Exeter EX4 8PD* T: (01392) 460457 E: cdrkharley@gmail.com

HARLEY, The Ven Michael. b 50. AKC 73 Ch Ch Coll Cant CertEd 74 Lambeth STh 92 Kent Univ MPhil 95. St Aug Coll Cant 74. **d** 75 **p** 76. C Chatham St Wm *Roch* 75–78; C-in-c Weeke *Win* 78–81; V Southampton St Mary Extra 81–86; V Hurstbourne Tarrant, Faccombe, Vernham Dean etc 86–99; ACORA Link Officer 91–94; Dioc Rural Officer 94–97; RD Andover 95–99; V Chandler's Ford 99–09; Tutor STETS 03–06; Hon Can Win Cathl 06–15; Adn Win 09–15; P-in-c Win St Cross w St Faith and Master St Cross Hosp 09–11; rtd 15; PtO *Win* from 16; *Sarum* from 16; *Ox* from 17. *28 Simmons Field, Thatcham RG18 4ET* E: mharley50@gmail.com

HARLEY, Nigel. *See* HARLEY, Brian Nigel

HARLEY, Peter David. b 59. Sheff Univ BSc 82 Warwick Univ MBA 86. **d** 09 **p** 10. OLM Horwich and Rivington *Man* from 09; OLM Blackrod 11–15. *6 Barford Grove, Lostock, Bolton BL6 4NQ* T: (01204) 694611

HARLEY, Canon Robert Patterson. b 53. St Andr Univ MA 75 Cam Univ CertEd 76 Glas Univ PhD 89 Edin Univ BD 97. **d** 97 **p** 98. C Edin St Thos 97–00; Chapl Lothian Univ Hosps NHS Trust 98–00; P-in-c Kirriemuir *St And* from 00; Can

St Ninian's Cathl Perth from 08. *128 Glengate, Kirriemuir DD8 4JG* T: (01575) 575515 E: robert.harley@gmx.co.uk

HARLEY, Roger Newcomb. b 38. Ely Th Coll 61. **d** 64 **p** 65. C Plymouth St Pet *Ex* 64–66; C Heston *Lon* 66–69; C Maidstone All SS w St Phil and H Trin *Cant* 69–73; R Temple Ewell w Lydden 73–79; P-in-c Shirley St Geo 79–81; V 81–84; V Croydon H Sav *S'wark* 85–95; V Forest Row *Chich* 95–03; rtd 03; PtO *Cant* 03–16; *Lich* from 17. *34 Milltown Way, Leek ST13 5SZ* T: (01538) 387369 E: rogerharley@btinternet.com

HARLING, Timothy Charles. b 80. Southn Univ BSc 01 Fitzw Coll Cam BA 04 Qu Coll Cam MA 13. Westcott Ho Cam 02. **d** 05 **p** 06. C Romsey *Win* 05–09; Chapl HM Pris Peterborough 09–13; Chapl Qu Coll Cam 13–17; Dean of Chpl from 17. *Queens' College, Silver Street, Cambridge CB3 9ET* T: (01223) 335511 E: tch42@cam.ac.uk

HARLOW, Mark Jonathan. b 80. Man Univ BSc 01 K Coll Lon MA 10. Ridley Hall Cam 11. **d** 14 **p** 15. C Leeds St Geo 14–17; P-in-c Ireland Wood 17–19; V from 19. *St Paul's Vicarage, Raynel Drive, Leeds LS16 6BS* M: 07725-625900 E: mark.harlow@stpaulsirelandwood.org

HARLOW, Canon Richard John St Clair. b 63. Cam Univ BA 85 MA 88. Cranmer Hall Dur 87. **d** 89 **p** 90. C Basford w Hyson Green *S'well* 89–94; C Mansfield SS Pet and Paul 94–97; TV Newark 97–01; Chapl Brighton and Sussex Univ Hosps NHS Trust 01–10; Lead Chapl Sussex Partnership NHS Foundn Trust 10–13; Chapl St Pet and St Jas Hospice N Chailey 02–05; R Tadley w Pamber Heath and Silchester *Win* from 13; AD Basingstoke from 15; Hon Can Win Cathl from 17. *The Rectory, The Green, Tadley RG26 3PB* T: 0118-981 4860 M: 07875-969128 E: richard73harlow@aol.com *or* minister@st-marys-church-tadley.org.uk

HARLOW, Archdeacon of. *See* HERRICK, The Ven Vanessa Anne

HARMAN, Karin. *See* VOTH HARMAN, Karin

HARMAN, Kathleen Joyce. b 49. **d** 03 **p** 04. C Llangynwyd w Maesteg *Llan* 03–08; R Dowlais and Penydarren 08–16; rtd 16. *33 Orchard Way, Stretton on Dunsmore, Rugby CV23 9HP*

HARMAN, Canon Leslie Davies. b 46. Nottm Univ BTh 76. St Jo Coll Nottm LTh 75. **d** 76 **p** 77. C Wandsworth All SS *S'wark* 76–78; C Godstone 78–82; V Thorncombe w Winsham and Cricket St Thomas *B & W* 82–87; TV Hitchin *St Alb* 87–95; V Royston 95–11; RD Buntingford 96–01; Hon Can St Alb 09–11; rtd 11. *1 Berry Meadow, Kingsteignton, Newton Abbot TQ12 3BL* T: (01626) 351757 E: leslie.harman@btopenworld.com

HARMAN, Michael John. b 48. Chich Th Coll 71. **d** 74 **p** 75. C Blackpool St Steph *Blackb* 74–79; Chapl RN 79–06; rtd 06; PtO *Ex* 06–08; *Truro* 06–13; P-in-c Wembury *Ex* 08–14; PtO from 14. *18 Furzeacre Close, Plymouth PL7 5DZ* T: (01752) 338910 M: 07836-377820 E: revmikeharman@blueyonder.co.uk

HARMAN, Theodore Allan. b 27. Linc Coll Ox BA 52 MA 56 Hatf Coll Dur MA 90. Wells Th Coll 52. **d** 54 **p** 55. C Hawkshead and Low Wray *Carl* 54–55; C Kirkby Stephen w Mallerstang 55–57; Asst Chapl Sedbergh Sch 57–84; Sen Chapl 84–87; Tutor Hatf Coll Dur from 88; Admissions Tutor 89–90; Lib and Coll Officer 91–02; Acting Chapl 99–00; Fell from 00; PtO *Dur* from 88. *2 Palmers Close, Church Street Head, Durham DH1 3DN* T: 0191-386 7213 F: 334 3101 E: theoharman@gmail.com

HARMER, Timothy James. b 47. Birm Univ CertEd 68. St Jo Coll Nottm BA 95. **d** 95 **p** 96. C Studley *Cov* 95–98; V Tanworth *Birm* 98–05; P-in-c Helsington *Carl* 05–12; P-in-c Underbarrow 05–12; RD Kendal 08–12; rtd 12; PtO *Carl* 12–13; P-in-c Church Coniston 13–15; P-in-c Torver 13–15; R Coniston and Torver 13–16; PtO from 16. *Address temp unknown* E: tharmer246@btinternet.com

HARMON, Michael Edgar. b 54. Birm Univ BEd 76. Wycliffe Hall Ox 10. **d** 12 **p** 13. NSM Aston and Nechells *Birm* 12–15; R Chelmsley Wood from 15. *28 Stokesay Close, Chelmsley Wood, Birmingham B37 7QW* T: 0121-788 2464 M: 07900-405455 E: vicar.standrewschelmsleywood@gmail.com

HARMSWORTH, Canon Roger James. b 46. Univ of W Ontario BA 87. Huron Coll Ontario MDiv 90. **d** 90 **p** 90. Canada 90–96; I Maryborough w Dysart Enos and Ballyfin *C & O* 96–01; I Killanne w Killegney, Rossdroit and Templeshanbo 01–17; Treas Ferns Cathl 03–04; Chan 04–17; rtd 17. *Ballinastoll, Killanne, Enniscorthy, Co Wexford, Republic of Ireland* T: (00353) (53) 925 6517 E: precentor.1@hotmail.com

HARNDEN, Peter John. b 63. Coll of Resurr Mirfield 96. **d** 98 **p** 99. C Staplehurst *Cant* 98–02; V Tokyngton St Mich *Lon* 02–11; P-in-c Benhilton *S'wark* 11–15; V 15–17; R Harbledown *Cant* from 17. *The Rectory, Summer Hill, Harbledown, Canterbury CT2 8NW* T: (01227) 479377 E: rector.harbledown@btconnect.com

HARNEY, Janice. b 56. **d** 02 **p** 03. OLM Pennington *Man* 02–06; PtO 06–11 and from 18; NSM Astley, Tyldesley and Mosley Common 11–18; NSM Glazebury w Hollinfare *Liv* from 18. *10 Hesnall Close, Glazebury, Warrington WA3 5PB* T: (01942) 671481 M: 07811-764355 E: jan.harney29@gmail.com

HARONSKI, Boleslaw. b 46. Pemb Coll Ox BA 68 MA 72 DPhil 73. St Mich Coll Llan 80 Westcott Ho Cam 82. **d** 82 **p** 83. C Maindee Newport *Mon* 82–85; V Llanishen w Trellech Grange and Llanfihangel etc *Mon* 85–89; V Blackwood 89–92; rtd 11. *Tir Llandre, Llanarthney, Carmarthen SA32 8JE*

⊕ **HARPER, The Rt Revd Alan Edwin Thomas.** b 44. Leeds Univ BA 65. CITC 75. **d** 78 **p** 79 **c** 02. C Ballywillan *Conn* 78–80; I Moville w Greencastle, Upper Moville etc *D & R* 80–82; I Londonderry Ch Ch 82–86; I Belfast Malone St Jo *Conn* 86–02; Preb St Audoen St Patr Cathl Dublin 90–01; Adn Conn 96–02; Prec Belf Cathl 96–02; Bp Conn 02–07; Abp Arm 07–12; rtd 12. *Forth Cottage, 67 Lisnacroppan Road, Rathfriland, Newry BT61 9AU* T: (028) 4065 1649 M: 07713-954758 E: a.e.t.harper@gmx.com

HARPER, Canon Alan Peter. b 50. Man Univ BA 73 FCA 83. Ripon Coll Cuddesdon 86. **d** 88 **p** 89. C Newport w Longford and Chetwynd *Lich* 88–91; P-in-c Wilnecote 91–94; V 94–98; V Codsall 98–07; Preb Lich Cathl 02–07; RD Penkridge 06–07; Bp's Dom Chapl *Derby* 07–11; P-in-c Mackworth All SS 11–17; P-in-c Kirk Langley 11–17; P-in-c Mugginton and Kedleston 11–17; Hon Can Derby Cathl 12–17; rtd 17. *78 Moatbrook Avenue, Codsall, Wolverhampton WV8 1DH* E: revd.alan8@btinternet.com

HARPER, Andrew. b 61. Leic Poly BA 83. St Mellitus Coll BA 16. **d** 16 **p** 17. C Ramsbottom and Edenfield *Man* from 16. *16 Maple Grove, Ramsbottom, Bury BL0 0AN* T: (01706) 823525 M: 07825-081861 E: revandyharper@gmail.com

HARPER, Barry. *See* HARPER, Malcolm Barry

HARPER, The Ven Brian John. b 61. Liv Univ BA 82. CITC. **d** 85 **p** 86. C Portadown St Columba *Arm* 85–88; C Drumglass w Moygashel 88–89; I Errigle Keerogue w Ballygawley and Killeshil 89–93; I Mullavilly 93–12; Adn Clogh from 12; Can Clogh Cathl from 14. *27 Craghan Road, Ballinamallard, Enniskillen BT94 2BT* T: (028) 6638 8238 M: 07898-743545 E: magheracross@btinternet.com

HARPER, Clive Stewart. b 35. FCIS 71. Ridley Hall Cam 80. **d** 82 **p** 83. C Bromyard *Heref* 82–85; P-in-c Bredenbury and Wacton w Grendon Bishop 85–89; P-in-c Edwyn Ralph and Collington w Thornbury 85–89; P-in-c Pencombe w Marston Stannett and Lt Cowarne 85–89; R Bredenbury w Grendon Bishop and Wacton etc 89–92; R Bilton *Cov* 92–02; rtd 02; Hon C Churchover w Willey *Cov* 02–05; PtO 05–19. *6 Arcade Park, North Shields NE30 4HP* T: 0191-296 6800 E: harperclival@btinternet.com

HARPER, David Laurence. b 51. Qu Coll Cam BA 73 MA 77 PhD 78. Wycliffe Hall Ox BA 80. **d** 80 **p** 81. C Mansfield SS Pet and Paul *S'well* 80–84; C Wollaton 84–87; V Brinsley w Underwood 87–94; R Bingham 94–16; AD 00–03; AD E Bingham 03–07; rtd 16; PtO *S'well* from 16. *13 Holmsfield, Keyworth, Nottingham NG12 5RD* T: 0115-937 5776 M: 07814-548150 E: dl.harper@btinternet.com

HARPER, Canon Geoffrey Roger. b 57. Jes Coll Cam BA 79 MA 83. St Jo Coll Nottm 81. **d** 84 **p** 85. C Belper *Derby* 84–87; C Birstall and Wanlip *Leic* 87–90; TV Tettenhall Regis *Lich* 90–97; C Aldridge 97–02; PtO 02–07; Chapl Douglas MacMillan Hospice Stoke-on-Trent 04–07; C W Bromwich Gd Shep w St Jo *Lich* 07–09; PtO *Derby* 07–10; P-in-c Burton Joyce w Bulcote and Stoke Bardolph *S'well* 10–11; V 11–15; Chapl HM Pris Whatton 15–17; Chapl HM Pris Thameside from 17; Hon Can W Ankole *Uganda* from 05. *HM Prison Thameside, Griffin Manor Way, London SE28 0FJ* T: (020) 8317 9777 M: 07954-409635 E: harperrog@gmail.com

HARPER, Gordon William Robert. b 48. Wellington Univ (NZ) BA 70 St Chad's Coll Dur BA 74 Nottm Univ PhD 89. Coll of Resurr Mirfield 74. **d** 75 **p** 76. C Battyeford *Wakef* 75–76; New Zealand 76–80; P-in-c Byers Green *Dur* 80–83; V Evenwood 83–89; R Wolviston 89–00; V Billingham St Mary 97–01; P-in-c Winlaton 01–06; R 06–13; rtd 13; PtO *Dur* from 13. *66 Rochester Road, Durham DH1 5QD* T: 0191-383 1348 E: gordonharper89@gmail.com

HARPER, Canon Ian. b 51. AKC 78. Oak Hill Th Coll 79. **d** 80 **p** 81. C Sidcup St Jo *Roch* 80–83; C Bushey *St Alb* 83–87; TV Thamesmead *S'wark* 87–92; TR N Lambeth 92–00; V Homerton St Luke *Lon* 00–10; AD Hackney 04–09; V Ladywood St Jo and St Pet *Birm* from 10; AD Cen Birm 12–16; Hon Can Birm Cathl from 16. *St John's Vicarage, Darnley Road, Birmingham B16 8TF* T: 0121-454 0973 *or* 218 5530 M: 07961-537487 E: harper-i1@sky.com

HARPER, James. b 35. St Luke's Coll Ex TDip 57. SWMTC. **d** 90 **p** 91. NSM Pendeen w Morvah *Truro* 90–97; PtO *Win* from

09. *1 Millstream Mews, 50 Beaconsfield Road, Christchurch BH23 1QT* T: (01202) 477138

HARPER, John Anthony. b 46. AKC 69. **d** 70 **p** 71. C Pet St Mary Boongate 70–73; C Abington 73–75; V Grendon w Castle Ashby 75–82; Asst Dioc Youth Chapl 75–82; R Castor w Sutton and Upton *Pet* 82–94; TV Riverside *Ox* 94–04; V Meppershall and Shefford *St Alb* 04–11; RD Shefford 08–10; RD Ampthill and Shefford 11; rtd 11; PtO *St Alb* 11–18; *Ely* from 12; *Pet* from 12. *54 Chapel Street, Yaxley, Peterborough PE7 3LN* T: (01733) 688923 E: revjohnharper@talktalk.net

HARPER, Joseph Frank. b 38. Hull Univ BA 60 MA 86 MPhil 98 Dur Univ PhD 10. Linc Th Coll 80. **d** 81 **p** 82. C Preston St Cuth *Blackb* 81–83; C Lancaster St Mary 83–87; V Bamber Bridge St Aid 87–92; V Kinsley w Wragby *Wakef* 92–99; R Newhaven *Chich* 99–04; rtd 04; PtO *Dur* from 04. *30 Greenways, Consett DH8 7DE* T: (01207) 507466 E: j925harper@btinternet.com

HARPER, Ms Lisa Rae. b 67. Cranmer Hall Dur 13. **d** 15 **p** 16. C Cen Telford *Lich* 15–18; C Oakengates, Priors Lee and Wrockwardine Wood from 18. *16 Highgrove Meadows, Priorslee, Telford TF2 9RJ* M: 07808-924223 E: lisataraharper@yahoo.co.uk

HARPER, Canon Malcolm Barry. b 37. Dur Univ BSc 59. Wycliffe Hall Ox 59. **d** 61 **p** 62. C Harold Wood *Chelmsf* 61–65; C Madeley *Heref* 65–68; V Slaithwaite w E Scammonden *Wakef* 68–75; V Walmley *Birm* 75–03; Hon Can Birm Cathl 96–03; rtd 03; PtO *Birm* from 03. *1 Welcombe Drive, Sutton Coldfield B76 1ND* T: 0121-351 3990 M: 07866-216154 E: canonbarryharper@gmail.com

HARPER, Mrs Margaret. b 51. Nottm Coll of Educn TCert 73 Nottm Univ BEd 74. SAOMC 98. **d** 01 **p** 02. C Slough *Ox* 01–05; P-in-c Leeds St Cypr Harehills *Ripon* 05–09; P-in-c Burmantofts St Steph and St Agnes 05–09; TV Ely 09–14; rtd 14; Hon C Bishop's Cleeve and Woolstone w Gotherington etc *Glouc* 16–17; PtO *Leic* from 19. *14 Peter Laslett Close, Loughborough LE11 2PT* E: margaretharper@waitrose.com

HARPER, Martin Nigel. b 48. Cant Ch Ch Univ Coll PGCE 95 FRICS 88. S Dios Minl Tr Scheme 82. **d** 85 **p** 86. NSM St Leonards Ch Ch and St Mary *Chich* 85–93; NSM Rye 94–95; R Brede w Udimore 08–14; R Brede w Udimore and Beckley and Peasmarsh 14–19; rtd 19. *31 Manor Road, Bexhill-on-Sea TN40 1SP* M: 07760-197954 E: martin.harper48@icloud.com

HARPER, Michael Sydney. b 36. Portsm Dioc Tr Course 86. **d** 87. NSM Leigh Park St Clare CD *Portsm* 87–88; NSM Warren Park 88–05; NSM Leigh Park 96–05; rtd 05; PtO *Portsm* from 07. *17 Hampage Green, Warren Park, Havant PO9 4HJ* T: (023) 9245 4275 E: michael_harper06@tiscali.co.uk *or* michael.harper1936@gmail.com

HARPER, Roger. b 43. Man Univ BSc 64 FCA 80. Local Minl Tr Course 84. **d** 87 **p** 88. NSM Onchan *S & M* 87–97; NSM Douglas St Geo 97–06. *The Barns, Strawberry Fields, Croit-e-Caley, Colby, Isle of Man IM9 4BZ* T: (01624) 842466 E: roger.harper@mcb.net

HARPER, Roger. *See* HARPER, Geoffrey Roger

HARPER, Canon Rosemary Elizabeth. b 55. Birm Univ BA 76 ARCM 75 LRAM 78. NTMTC 96. **d** 99 **p** 00. C Amersham *Ox* 99–03; P-in-c Gt Missenden w Ballinger and Lt Hampden 03–07; V from 07; Chapl to Bp Buckingham from 06; Hon Can Ch Ch from 11. *The Rectory, Church Street, Amersham HP7 0BD* T: (01494) 728988 E: rosie51619@aol.com

HARPER, Canon Timothy James Lincoln. b 54. Lon Univ BMus 76 MA 96 CertEd LRAM. Wycliffe Hall Ox 84. **d** 86 **p** 87. C Morden *S'wark* 86–90; V Deptford St Pet 90–97; R Amersham *Ox* from 97; Jt AD from 17; Hon Can Ch Ch from 18. *The Rectory, Church Street, Amersham HP7 0DB* T: (01494) 724426 *or* 729380 F: 08701-639596 E: harpervic@yahoo.co.uk

HARPHAM, Mrs Diana Joan. b 44. MCSP 66. St Alb Minl Tr Scheme 94. **d** 98 **p** 99. NSM Harrold and Carlton w Chellington *St Alb* 98–01; NSM Bromham w Oakley and Stagsden 01–15; PtO from 15. *129 Stagsden Road, Bromham, Bedford MK43 8QJ* T: (01234) 918691 E: diharpham@gmail.com

HARRATT, James Michael. b 87. Univ of Wales (Ban) BSc 08. Ripon Coll Cuddesdon BA 14. **d** 15 **p** 16. C Rainham *Roch* 15–18; V Bromley SS Pet and Paul from 18. M: 07969-293648 E: jharratt@outlook.com

HARRATT, Philip David. b 56. Magd Coll Ox BA 79 MA 83. Ripon Coll Cuddesdon 82. **d** 85 **p** 86. C Ewyas Harold w Dulas, Kenderchurch etc *Heref* 85–88; V Chirbury 88–09; V Marton 88–09; V Trelystan w Leighton 88–09; P-in-c Middleton 02–09; RD Pontesbury 01–08; Preb Heref Cathl 03–09; V Embleton w Rennington and Rock *Newc* 09–16; rtd 16; PtO *St As* from 17; *Heref* from 18. *The Rectory,*

Lions Bank, Montgomery SY15 6PT T: (01686) 668418 E: philipharratt@mypostoffice.co.uk

HARREX, David Brian. b 54. Trin Coll Bris 87. **d** 89 **p** 90. C Bedminster St Mich *Bris* 89–93; V Pilning w Compton Greenfield 93–00; RD Westbury and Severnside 97–99; AD Bris W 99–00; TR Yate New Town 00–12; C Frampton Cotterell and Iron Acton 07–12; Hon Can Bris Cathl 10–12; TV Yatton Moor *B & W* 12–17; rtd 17; PtO *Bris* from 19. *Address temp unknown* M: 07798-830172 E: davidharrex@gmail.com

HARRE-YOUNG, Steven Nicholas. b 86. Trin Coll Bris 14. **d** 17 **p** 18. NSM Patchway *Bris* from 17. *48 Rock Lane, Stoke Gifford, Bristol BS34 8PF*

HARRIES, John Edward. b 60. Bris Univ BSc 81 PhD 84. Wycliffe Hall Ox 94. **d** 96 **p** 97. C Hyde St Geo *Ches* 96–00; P-in-c Walton 00–15; C Latchford St Jas 00–15; Chapl Sir Thos Boteler High Sch 03–15; V Sutton, Wincle, Wildboarclough and Bosley *Ches* from 15; RD Macclesfield from 19. *St James' Vicarage, Church Lane, Sutton, Macclesfield SK11 0DS* T: (01260) 253945 E: vicar@peakparishes.org.uk

HARRIES, Malcolm David. b 44. BA 99. Oak Hill Th Coll 94. **d** 96 **p** 97. C Rock Ferry *Ches* 96–00; P-in-c Godley cum Newton Green 00–14; rtd 14. *17 Barnes Court, Durham Avenue, Woodford Green IG8 7NJ* E: malcolmharries2@btinternet.com

HARRIES, Sebastian David Tudor. b 86. Man Univ MusB 11 Jes Coll Cam BTh 15. Westcott Ho Cam 13. **d** 16 **p** 17. C Lingfield and Dormansland *S'wark* 16–19; Chapl St Gabr Coll Camberwell from 19; NSM Kennington St Jo w St Jas *S'wark* from 19. *St Gabriel's College, Langton Road, London SW9 6UL* T: (020) 7793 3901 M: 07732-773303 E: sebastian.harries@cantab.net

✠**HARRIES OF PENTREGARTH, The Rt Revd Lord (Richard Douglas).** b 36. Selw Coll Cam BA 61 MA 65 Lon Univ Hon DD 94 FKC 83 FRSL 96. Cuddesdon Coll 61. **d** 63 **p** 64 c 87. C Hampstead St Jo *Lon* 63–69; Chapl Westf Coll Lon 67–69; Tutor Wells Th Coll 69–71; Warden Sarum & Wells Th Coll 71–72; V Fulham All SS *Lon* 72–81; Dean K Coll Lon 81–87; Consultant to Abps Cant and York on Inter-Faith Relns 86–06; Bp Ox 87–06; rtd 06; Asst Bp S'wark from 06; Hon Prof Th K Coll Lon from 06; Hon Asst Bp Lon from 14. *House of Lords, London SW1A 0PW* E: harriesr@parliament.uk

HARRIGAN, David Michael. b 84. Ox Min Course 15. **d** 18 **p** 19. C Romford Gd Shep *Chelmsf* from 18. *103 Highfield Road, Romford RM5 3AE* T: (01708) 941789 M: 07598-291807 E: dmharrigan@gmail.com *or* dmharrigan@thegoodshepherd.co.uk

HARRINGTON, Christopher Robert. b 57. Wilson Carlile Coll 99 ERMC 06. **d** 08 **p** 09. C Middle Rasen Gp *Linc* 08–12; P-in-c Heckington Gp 12–13; P-in-c Helpringham w Hale 12–13; R Heckington and Helpringham Gp from 13. *The Rectory, 10 Cameron Street, Heckington, Sleaford NG34 9RW* T: (01529) 460904 E: c.r.harrington@btinternet.com

HARRINGTON, John Christopher Thomas. b 43. Qu Coll Birm 71. **d** 74 **p** 75. C Northampton St Mich *Pet* 74–76; C Paston 76–79; R Doddington *Ely* 79–82; R Benwick St Mary 79–82; R Doddington w Benwick 82–83; CF (TA) 75–85; Chapl Doddington Co Hosp 79–83; V Eastbourne St Mich *Chich* 83–02; R Selsey 02–11; Chapl RNLI 03–11; rtd 11; Custos St Mary's Hosp Chich 11–18. *43 Kingston Way, Seaford BN25 4NG* T: (01323) 351816 E: jctharrington@tiscali.co.uk

HARRIS, Mrs Alanna Jane. b 87. Regent's Park Coll Ox BA 08 Anglia Ruskin Univ MA 19. Ridley Hall Cam 16. **d** 19. C St Geo-in-the-East w St Paul *Lon* from 19. *Address temp unknown*

HARRIS, Mrs Alison Ann. b 54. Univ of Wales (Abth) BA 75 Westmr Coll Ox PGCE 76 Ches Univ MTh 07. Qu Coll Birm 07. **d** 08 **p** 09. C Neston *Ches* 08–12; V Witton 12–18; rtd 18; PtO *Ches* from 18. *12 Moorlands Avenue, Cuddington, Northwich CW8 2LU* M: 07969-005978 E: alisonannharris@hotmail.co.uk

HARRIS, Arthur Emlyn Dawson. b 27. Ex Univ BSc 47. S'wark Ord Course 83. **d** 86 **p** 87. NSM Frant w Eridge *Chich* 86–87; P-in-c Withyham St Mich 87–95; rtd 95; PtO *Sarum* 96–07; *Chich* from 13. *Pine Lodge, Beacon Gardens, Crowborough TN6 1BD* E: closecelts@btinternet.com

HARRIS, Bernard Malcolm. b 29. Leeds Univ BA 54. Coll of Resurr Mirfield 54. **d** 56 **p** 57. C Shrewsbury St Chad *Lich* 56–60; C Porthill 60–61; V Birches Head 61–66; V W Bromwich St Jas 66–78; V Sedgley All SS 78–93; rtd 93; PtO *Worc* 93–12; *Lich* from 09. *6 Beacon Lane, Sedgley, Dudley DY3 1NB* T: (01902) 663134 E: bernardharris30@hotmail.com

HARRIS, Brian. b 33. Man Univ BSc. Qu Coll Birm 79. **d** 80 **p** 81. C Lich St Chad 80–81; PtO *Ches* 82–87; NSM Warburton 87–88; P-in-c 88–92; R Gt and Lt Casterton w Pickworth and Tickencote *Pet* 92–98; RD Barnack 94–98; rtd 98; PtO *Pet*

99–07; *St Alb* 06–07; *Ches* 10–14. *16 Westminster Green, Chester CH4 7LE* T: (01244) 675824 E: meadowbrook@waitrose.com *or* brookmeadow@btinternet.com

HARRIS, Brian. See HARRIS, Reginald Brian

HARRIS, Brian William. b 38. K Coll Lon BD 61 AKC 61. St Boniface Warminster 61. **d** 62 **p** 63. C Liversedge *Wakef* 62–65; C Kirkby *Liv* 65–70; V Dalton 70–79; V Aberford w Saxton *York* 79–91; V Hemingbrough 91–95; rtd 95; PtO *York* from 95; Dom Chapl to Bp Selby 95–03; Rtd Clergy and Widows Officer (York Adnry) 99–19. *2 Furness Drive, Rawcliffe, York YO30 5TD* T: (01904) 638214 E: harrischap@talktalk.net

HARRIS, Mrs Carol. b 66. Dur Univ BSc 87. Lindisfarne Regional Tr Partnership BA 17. **d** 17 **p** 18. C Wheatley Hill, Thornley and Wingate w Hutton Henry *Dur* from 17. *72 North Road East, Wingate TS28 5AY* T: (01429) 835272 E: carol.harris@durham.anglican.org

HARRIS, Catherine Elizabeth. See EDMONDS, Catherine Elizabeth

HARRIS, David Anthony. b 68. **d** 96. Canada 96–11; R Reading St Giles Ox from 11. *St Giles's Rectory, Church Street, Reading RG1 2SB* T: 0118-957 2831 E: sgiles.vicar@gmail.com

HARRIS, David Rowland. b 46. Ch Ch Ox BA 69 MA 72. Wycliffe Hall Ox 70. **d** 73 **p** 74. C Virginia Water *Guildf* 73–76; C Clifton Ch Ch w Em *Bris* 76–79; Scripture Union 79–85; V Bedford Ch Ch *St Alb* 85–99; R Ex St Leon w H Trin 99–12; rtd 12; P-in-c Ilsington *Ex* 12–15; V from 15. *The Vicarage, Ilsington, Newton Abbot TQ13 9RW* T: (01364) 661781 E: dandsharris@hotmail.com

HARRIS, Mrs Elaine Sarah. b 43. SWMTC 02. **d** 03 **p** 04. NSM Dyffryn *Llan* 03–06; P-in-c Penyfai 06–12; rtd 12; PtO *Llan* 17–18. *15 Neath Road, Fforest Goch, Pontardawe, Swansea SA8 3JB* T: (01656) 651719 E: revel07@hotmail.com

HARRIS, Elizabeth Anne. b 55. Qu Foundn (Course) 15. **d** 17 **p** 18. OLM Coventry Caludon *Cov* 17–19; OLM Caludon H Cross Cov from 19. *48 Coombe Park Road, Coventry CV3 2NX* T: (024) 7672 3364 E: curate@holy-cross.org.uk

HARRIS, Ernest John. b 46. QUB BD 75. **d** 75 **p** 76. C Lisburn Ch Ch *Conn* 75–78; C Coleraine 78–83; I Belfast St Kath 83–90; I Ballinderry 90–11; Preb Conn Cathl 06–11; rtd 11. *10 Little Wenham, Moira, Craigavon BT67 0NN* T: (028) 9210 7385 M: 07842-114854

HARRIS, Geoffrey Daryl. b 39. Open Univ BA 83. St Aid Birkenhead 63. **d** 66 **p** 67. C Eston *York* 66–70; C Iffley *Ox* 70–75; V Bubwith *York* 75–78; V Bubwith w Ellerton and Aughton 78–79; P-in-c Stillingfleet w Naburn 79–80; R Escrick and Stillingfleet w Naburn 80–95; Chapl Qu Marg Sch York 83–94; Hon C Okehampton w Inwardleigh, Bratton Clovelly etc Ex 96–99; P-in-c Ashwater, Halwill, Beaworthy, Clawton etc 99–01; R 01–03; rtd 03; C Okehampton w Inwardleigh, Bratton Clovelly etc *Ex* 07–11. *The Old Barnside, 7 Crossley Moor Road, Kingsteignton, Newton Abbot TQ12 3LE* E: revgdh@btinternet.com

HARRIS, Harriet Anne. b 68. Oriel Coll Ox BA 90 New Coll Ox DPhil 94. St Steph Ho Ox. **d** 00 **p** 01. C Ox St Mary V w St Cross and St Pet 00–06; Chapl Wadham Coll 00–10; Chapl Edin Univ from 10; NSM St Mary's Cathl 10–12. *Chaplaincy Centre, The University of Edinburgh, 1 Bristo Square, Edinburgh EH8 9AL* T: 0131-650 2595 M: 07896-244792 E: h.harris@ed.ac.uk

HARRIS, James Philip. b 59. Westf Coll Lon BA 82 Cardiff Univ MPhil 12 Univ of Wales PGCE 97. St Mich Coll Llan BD 86. **d** 86 **p** 87. C Newport St Paul *Mon* 86–89; C Bedwellty 89–91; V Newport St Matt 91–96; Chapl Univ of Wales Inst Cardiff *Llan* 97–99; Chapl Glam Univ 99–03; V Gwernaffield and Llanferres *St As* 03–09; Dioc Dir of Ords 03–09; V Bwlchgwyn and Minera *St As* 09–10; V Minera w Coedpoeth and Bwlchgwyn 10–14; V Minera w Coedpoeth 14–16; TV Alyn Miss Area from 17; AD Alyn 12–16. *The Vicarage, Church Road, Minera, Wrexham LL11 3DA* T: (01978) 753133 M: 07757-595154 E: jamespharris03@aol.com

HARRIS, Canon Jeremy David. b 63. Leeds Metrop Univ MA 00 Univ of Wales (Lamp) BA 04 Cardiff Univ MPhil 07 FCCA 92. St Mich Coll Llan 05. **d** 07 **p** 08. C Monmouth w Overmonnow etc *Mon* 07–09; C Magor 09–10; TV 10–12; TR from 12; AD Netherwent from 14; Can St Woolos Cathl from 17. *The Rectory, Redwick Road, Magor, Caldicot NP26 3GU* M: 07710-410950

HARRIS, Jeremy Michael. b 64. St Steph Ho Ox BTh 93. **d** 93 **p** 94. C Newport St Julian *Mon* 93–95; C Ebbw Vale 95–97; TV 97–98; Dioc Youth Chapl 96–98; TV Bracknell *Ox* 98–05; V Boyne Hill from 05. *The Vicarage, Westmorland Road, Maidenhead SL6 4HB* T: (01628) 626921

HARRIS, The Very Revd John. b 32. Univ of Wales (Lamp) BA 55. Sarum Th Coll 55. **d** 57 **p** 58. V Pontnewynydd *Mon* 57–60; C Bassaleg 60–63; V Penmaen 63–69; V Newport

St Paul 69–84; RD Newport 77–93; V Maindee Newport 84–93; Can St Woolos Cathl 84–93; Dean Brecon *S & B* 93–98; V Brecon St Mary and Battle w Llanddew 93–98; rtd 98; LtO *Mon* from 98. *40 Mounton Drive, Chepstow NP16 5EH* T: (01291) 621233

HARRIS, John. b 54. Leeds Univ BSc 75. St Jo Coll Nottm LTh 86. **d** 86 **p** 87. C S Ossett *Wakef* 86–90; V Moldgreen 90–97; P-in-c S Ossett 97–04; V 04–10; P-in-c Luddenden w Luddenden Foot 10–13; rtd 18; PtO *Leeds* 17–18; P-in-c Woolley 18–19. *Address temp unknown* E: nettletonscottage@gmail.com

HARRIS, Canon John. b 45. St Steph Ho Ox 72. **d** 75 **p** 76. C Wanstead St Mary *Chelmsf* 75–84; V Penponds *Truro* 84–91; V St Gluvias 91–12; RD Carnmarth S 00–12; Hon Can Truro Cathl 01–12; rtd 12; PtO *Truro* from 15. *The Anchorage, 2 Penlee View Terrace, Penzance TR18 4HY* T: (01736) 351026 E: john.harris25116@btinternet.com

HARRIS, John Brian. b 53. Hertf Coll Ox BA 76. Ripon Coll Cuddesdon 87. **d** 89 **p** 90. C Witton *Ches* 89–93; R Thurstaston 93–99; V Stockton Heath 99–04; P-in-c Gt Saughall 04–12; P-in-c Lostock Gralam 12–15; V 15–18; rtd 18; PtO *Ches* from 18. *12 Moorlands Avenue, Cuddington, Northwich CW8 2LU* E: revjohnbrianharris@gmail.com

HARRIS, Joshua Lloyd. b 89. Keble Coll Ox BA 10 Trin Coll Cam BA 18. Ridley Hall Cam 16. **d** 19. NSM St Geo-in-the-East w St Paul *Lon* from 19. *Address temp unknown*

HARRIS, Mrs Judith Helen. b 42. Chelsea Coll Lon TCert 64 Westmr Coll Ox MTh 03. St Alb Minl Tr Scheme 83. **dss** 86 **d** 87 **p** 94. Leagrave *St Alb* 86–87; Hon Par Dn 87–91; Team Dn Dunstable 91–94; TV 94–03; rtd 03; PtO *Truro* from 03. *Belmont, Fore Street, Porthleven, Helston TR13 9HN* T: (01326) 563090 E: revdjhharris@btopenworld.com

HARRIS, Julie Christine. b 61. Sarum Coll 15. **d** 17 **p** 18. NSM Wraxall *B & W* from 17. *2 Moorlands Close, Nailsea, Bristol BS48 2DR* E: jules.curate@gmail.com

HARRIS, Linda Margaret. b 55. Man Univ BSc 76 UMIST MSc 78 Birkbeck Coll Lon MSc 98. Wycliffe Hall Ox 03. **d** 05 **p** 06. C Cannock *Lich* 05–08; P-in-c Hatch Warren and Beggarwood *Win* 08–13; V Birchwood *Linc* from 13. *St Luke's Vicarage, 78 Jasmin Road, Lincoln LN6 0YR* E: revlinda@btinternet.com

HARRIS, Mrs Mandy June. b 63. Qu Foundn Birm 16. **d** 18 **p** 19. C Sheldon *Birm* 18; C Sheldon and Tile Cross from 18. *St Peter's Church Vicarage, Haywood Road, Birmingham B33 0LH* T: 0121-770 1377 M: 07598-122307 E: mandyjharris@virginmedia.com

HARRIS, Margaret Claire (Sister Margaret Joy). b 53. RGN 85 Homerton Coll Cam BEd 78. Ridley Hall Cam 90. **d** 92. Par Dn Stevenage All SS Pin Green *St Alb* 92–93; C 93–95; CSMV 95–99; OSB from 99. *St Mary's Abbey, 52 Swan Street, West Malling ME19 6JX* T: (01732) 843309

HARRIS, Mark. b 72. Ox Univ MA 94 K Coll Lon MA 12. Oak Hill Th Coll 16. **d** 18 **p** 19. C Kensington Ch Ch *Lon* from 18. *St Mary Abbots Vicarage, Vicarage Gate, London W8 4HN* E: mark.harris@parliament.uk

HARRIS, Mark Andrew. b 69. Heythrop Coll Lon BD 92 K Coll Lon MA 05 Jes Coll Cam PhD 12. Ridley Hall Cam 06. **d** 10 **p** 11. C Meopham w Nurstead *Roch* 10–13; C Blockhouse Bay New Zealand 13–14; P-in-c Henderson 14–16; Lect St Jo Coll Auckland from 16. *194 St John's Road, Meadowbank, Auckland 1072, New Zealand* T: (0064) (9) 869 4253 E: m.harris@stjohnscollege.ac.nz

HARRIS, Mark Jonathan. b 66. St Cath Coll Cam BA 88 MA 92 PhD 92. Ripon Coll Cuddesdon BA 01 MA 05. **d** 02 **p** 03. C Cowley St Jas *Ox* 02–04; Chapl Oriel Coll Ox 04–10; Can and Vice Provost St Mary's Cathl Edin 10–12; Prec 12–13; LtO *Edin* from 14; Lect Edin Univ from 12. *Edinburgh University Faculty of Divinity, New College, Mound Place, Edinburgh EH1 2LX* M: 07813-676892 E: mark.harris@ed.ac.uk

HARRIS, Canon Martin John. b 54. Trin Coll Cam BA 76 MA. Wycliffe Hall Ox 82. **d** 85 **p** 86. C Lindfield *Chich* 85–88; C Galleywood Common *Chelmsf* 88–91; V Southchurch Ch Ch 91–08; RD Southend 00–05; TR Harlow Town Cen w Lt Parndon from 08; RD Harlow from 09; Hon Can Chelmsf Cathl from 15. *The Rectory, 43 Upper Park, Harlow CM20 1TW* T: (01279) 411100 *or* 434243 E: martin.harris@messages.co.uk

HARRIS, Mary Noreen Cecily. See SOKANOVIC, Mary Noreen Cecily

HARRIS, Michael. b 34. St Mark & St Jo Coll Lon CertEd 56 ACP 65 MIL 76. Qu Coll Birm. **d** 83 **p** 84. NSM Bournville *Birm* 83–90; NSM Stirchley 90–96; Chapl Univ of Cen England in Birm 92–99; Dean NSMs 96–99; rtd 00; PtO *Birm* 00–12; *Cov* from 00. *33 Bosley Close, Shipston-on-Stour CV36 4QA* T/F: (01608) 661672 M: 07811-489713 E: mike.harris@pikkle.net

HARRIS, Michael Andrew. b 53. Ian Ramsey Coll Brasted 74 Trin Coll Bris 75. **d** 78 **p** 79. C St Paul's Cray St Barn *Roch* 78–82; C Church Stretton *Heref* 82–87; Res Min Penkridge w Stretton *Lich* 87–90; Res Min Penkridge Team 90–92; V Amington *Birm* 92–15; AD Polesworth 07–14; V Highley w Billingsley, Glazeley etc *Heref* from 15. *The Rectory, Church Street, Highley, Bridgnorth WV16 6NA* E: mikeharassed@gmail.com

HARRIS, Nicholas Bryan. b 60. Down Coll Cam BA 81 MA 85. Ridley Hall Cam 82. **d** 85 **p** 86. C Walney Is *Carl* 85–88; C S'wark Ch Ch 88–92; PtO *Chich* 92–08. *Wheelwrights, High Street, Fairwarp, Uckfield TN22 3BP* E: box534@yahoo.co.uk

✠**HARRIS, The Rt Revd Patrick Burnet.** b 34. Keble Coll Ox BA 58 MA 63. Clifton Th Coll 58. **d** 60 **p** 61 **c** 73. C Ox St Ebbe w St Pet 60–63; SAMS 63–81; Adn N Argentina 70–73; Bp N Argentina 73–80; R Kirkheaton *Wakef* 81–85; Asst Bp Wakef 81–85; Sec C of E Partnership for World Miss 86–88; Asst Bp Ox 86–88; Bp S'well 88–99; rtd 99; Asst Bp Linc 99–05; Asst Bp Eur from 99; Hon Asst Bp Glouc from 05. *Apartment B, Ireton House, Pavilion Gardens, Cheltenham GL50 2SR* T: (01242) 231376 E: pandvharris@blueyonder.co.uk

HARRIS, Paul Ian. b 45. MSc. Qu Coll Birm. **d** 82 **p** 83. C The Quinton *Birm* 82–86; V Atherstone *Cov* 86–13; rtd 13; PtO *Cov* from 13; *Leic* from 13. *31 Woodside, Ashby-de-la-Zouch LE65 2NJ* T: (01530) 589873 E: pigmharris@talktalk.net *or* starpentree@gmail.com

HARRIS, Paul Michael. b 58. Chelsea Coll Lon BSc 79 Oak Hill Th Coll BA 89 Bath Coll of HE CertEd 82 Open Univ BA 04 MA 14. **d** 89. C Finchley Ch Ch *Lon* 89–90; Asst Master St Luke's Sch W Norwood 90–91; Master and Asst Chapl Brent Internat Sch Philippines 91–92; Volunteer Miss Movement Sunningdale 93–94; Past Asst St Joseph's RC Ch Dorking 94–95; Form Master Merton Court Prep Sch Sidcup 95–97; Asst Master Clewborough Ho Prep Sch Camberley 98–01; Teacher St Nic Sch for Girls Church Crookham 01–02; Culford Sch Bury St Edmunds 02–04; Teacher St Marg Prep Sch Calne 05–07. *Maes-yr-Haf, 4 Penllain, Penparc, Cardigan SA43 1RJ* T: (01239) 571082 E: paul.harris.007@hotmail.co.uk

HARRIS, Peter Malcolm. b 52. Em Coll Cam BA 74 MA 79. Trin Coll Cam **d** 80 **p** 81. C Upton (Overchurch) *Ches* 80–83; Crosslinks from 83; Portugal 93–97; France from 97. *rue de Meunier 4, Ribet, 13990 Fontvieille, France* M: (0033) 8 77 35 61 53 E: harris@crosslinks.org

HARRIS, Peter Samuel. b 68. Dundee Univ BA 98 St Jo Coll Dur BA 04. Cranmer Hall Dur 02. **d** 04 **p** 05. C Walton and Trimley *St E* 04–07; R Dalkeith *Edin* from 07; R Lasswade from 07. *11 Peacock Parkway, Bonnyrigg EH19 3RQ* T: 0131-663 7000 E: revpharris@gmail.com

HARRIS, Raymond. b 36. Nottm Univ BA 58. Lich Th Coll 58. **d** 60 **p** 61. C Clifton St Fran *S'well* 60–63; C Davyhulme St Mary *Man* 63–66; V Bacup Ch Ch 66–82; R Dunsby w Dowsby *Linc* 82–87; R Rippingale 82–87; R Rippingale Gp 87–94; rtd 94. *2 The Bungalow, Swaton Lane, Swaton, Sleaford NG34 0JU* T: (01529) 421343

HARRIS, Rebecca Jane. See SWYER, Rebecca Jane

HARRIS (née LEE), Mrs Rebecca Susan. b 62. Man Univ BA 85. Trin Coll Bris 93. **d** 95 **p** 96. C Cirencester *Glouc* 95–99; TV Gt Chesham *Ox* 99–11; V Creech St Michael and Ruishton w Thornfalcon *B & W* from 11; RD Taunton from 18. *The Rectory, Creech St Michael, Taunton TA3 5PP* E: harrisrs211@gmail.com

HARRIS, The Ven Reginald Brian. b 34. Ch Coll Cam BA 58 MA 61. Ridley Hall Cam. **d** 59 **p** 60. C Wednesbury St Bart *Lich* 59–61; C Uttoxeter w Bramshall 61–64; V Bury St Pet *Man* 64–70; V Walmsley 70–80; RD 70–80; Adn Man 80–98; Can Res Man Cathl 80–98; rtd 98; PtO *Derby* 98–18. *9 Cote Lane, Hayfield, High Peak SK22 2HL* T: (01663) 746321 E: aandbharris@btinternet.com

HARRIS, Robert. See WYNFORD-HARRIS, Robert William

HARRIS, Preb Robert Douglas. b 57. Ex Univ BEd 80 Bris Univ MEd 96. Chich Th Coll 80. **d** 82 **p** 83. C Portsea St Mary *Portsm* 82–87; V Clevedon St Jo *B & W* 87–92; R Felpham w Middleton *Chich* 92–99; R Felpham 99–04; RD Arundel and Bognor 98–04; P-in-c Southwick 04–06; R 06–10; RD Hove 09–10; P-in-c Ilfracombe, Lee, Woolacombe, Bittadon etc *Ex* 10–16; TR Plympton from 16; Preb Ex Cathl from 17. *St Mary's Vicarage, 209 Ridgeway, Plymouth PL7 2HP* T: (01752) 658762 E: robdharris@btinternet.com

HARRIS, Robert James. b 45. Nottm Univ MA 02 ALCD 73. St Jo Coll Nottm 69. **d** 72 **p** 73. C Sheff St Jo 72–76; C Goole 76–78; V Bramley and Ravenfield 78–91; P-in-c Boulton *Derby* 91–99; RD Melbourne 96–99; P-in-c Hazlewood 99–02; P-in-c Hazlewood and Milford 02–05; V Hazelwood, Holbrook and Milford 05–10; rtd 10. *13 Mill Close, Findern, Derby DE65 6AP* T: (01283) 703024 E: jrjubilate@btinternet.com

HARRIS, Mrs Ruth. b 60. Hull Univ BA 82 Liv Univ MArAd 84 MTh 06. NOC 01. **d** 04 **p** 05. C Kinsley w Wragby *Wakef* 04–07; C Felkirk 05–07; P-in-c Wrenthorpe 07–14; *Leeds* 14–15; V Skipton Ch Ch w Carleton from 15; AD Skipton from 17. *Christ Church Vicarage, Carleton Road, Skipton BD23 2BE* T: (01756) 793612 M: 07779-648336 E: ruth.harris@leeds.anglican.org

HARRIS, Sian Elizabeth. b 54. Kingston Poly BSocSc 75. WEMTC 03. **d** 06 **p** 07. NSM Leominster *Heref* 06–09; Chapl St Mich Hospice Hereford 09–11; TV Tenbury *Heref* 11–16; TR from 16. *The Rectory, Burford, Tenbury Wells WR15 8HG* T: (01584) 819792 M: 07866-492863 E: sianharris@f2s.com

HARRIS, Thomas William. b 54. Univ of Wales (Lamp) MA 04 AKC 76. Linc Th Coll 77. **d** 78 **p** 79. C Norton Woodseats St Chad *Sheff* 78–81; V Barnby Dun 81–91; P-in-c Kirk Bramwith and Fenwick 81–85; Chapl RN 91–94; R Draycot Bris 94–02; P-in-c Cawston w Booton and Brandiston etc *Nor* 02–12; Chapl Norfolk and Nor Univ Hosp NHS Trust 02–07; Chapl Cawston Park Hosp 07–12; P-in-c Gt w Lt Massingham, Harpley, Rougham etc *Nor* 12–13; rtd 13; PtO *Nor* from 14. *Blake House, The Common, Hanworth, Norwich NR11 7HP* T: (01263) 761570 E: revtomharris@gmail.com

HARRIS, William Edric Mackenzie. b 46. Sarum & Wells Th Coll 72. **d** 75 **p** 76. C Langney *Chich* 75–79; C Moulsecoomb 80–81; TV 81–85; R W Grinstead 85–16; rtd 16. *Address temp unknown* E: williamemharris@gmail.com

HARRIS, William Fergus. b 36. CCC Cam BA 59 MA 63 Edin Univ DipEd 70. Yale Div Sch 59 Westcott Ho Cam 60. **d** 62 **p** 63. C St Andrews St Andr *St And* 62–64; Chapl Edin Univ 64–71; R Edin St Pet 71–83; R Perth St Jo *St And* 83–90; Hon C 90–08; rtd 90; Prov Archivist 91–02; LtO *St And* from 08. *35 St Mary's Drive, Perth PH2 7BY* T: (01738) 621379 E: ruth.harris1@tesco.net

HARRIS-EVANS, William Giles. b 46. AKC 68. Bangalore Th Coll. **d** 70 **p** 71. C Clapham H Trin *S'wark* 70–74; Sri Lanka 75–78; V Benhilton *S'wark* 78–86; TR Cov E 86–93; TR Brighouse and Clifton *Wakef* 93–99; V Petersfield and R Buriton *Portsm* 99–10; rtd 10; PtO *Portsm* from 11. *11 Great Southsea Street, Southsea PO5 3BY* E: wghevans@talktalk.net

HARRIS-WHITE, John Emlyn. b 34. St Aid Birkenhead 59. **d** 62 **p** 63. C Cricklade w Latton *Bris* 62–63; C Kingswood 63–66; C Ashton-on-Ribble St Andr *Blackb* 66–69; V Heyhouses 69–71; Chapl Roundway Hosp Devizes 71–77; Chapl R Variety Children's Hosp and K Coll Hosp Lon 77–89; Chapl Belgrave Hosp Lon 77–89; Regional Community Relns Co-ord 89–93; rtd 94; Hon C Folkestone St Pet *Cant* 97–01. *40 Tippet Knowes Road, Winchburgh, Broxburn EH52 6UL* E: johnharriswhite@aol.com

HARRISON, Alison Edwina. *See* HART, Alison Edwina

HARRISON, Mrs Barbara Ann. b 41. Man Univ BA 63 Leic Univ CertEd 64. EMMTC 85. **d** 88 **p** 94. C Immingham *Linc* 88–94; P-in-c Habrough Gp 94–99; V 99–01; rtd 02; PtO *Linc* from 02. *3 Windsor Mews, Louth LN11 9AY* T: (01507) 610015

HARRISON, Canon Barbara Anne. b 34. Westf Coll Lon BA 56 CertEd 57 Hull Univ MA 85. Linc Th Coll 76. **dss** 79 **d** 87 **p** 94. Lakenham St Jo *Nor* 79–80; Chapl York Univ 80–88; Team Dn Sheff Manor 88–93; Par Dn Holts CD *Man* 93–94; C-in-c 94–98; Dioc UPA Officer 93–98; Chapl Rochdale Healthcare NHS Trust 98–02; Chapl Pennine Acute Hosps NHS Trust 02–04; C Bury Ch King *Man* 98–01; C Bury St Paul 98–04; P-in-c Kirkholt 01–04; Hon Can Man Cathl 02–04; rtd 04; PtO *Man* from 04; *Ches* from 17. *36 Homebeck House, Gatley Green, Gatley, Cheadle SK8 4NF* M: 07513-160794 E: barbara.harrison34@hotmail.com

HARRISON, Bruce. b 49. Linc Th Coll 86. **d** 88 **p** 89. C Syston *Leic* 88–90; C Whitby *York* 90–93; V Glaisdale 93–99; R Brotton Parva 99–04; V Coatham and Dormanstown 04–08; Chapl Tees and NE Yorks NHS Trust 04–07; rtd 08; PtO *York* from 08. *St Peter's Vicarage, 66 Aske Road, Redcar TS10 2BP* T: (01642) 489842 *or* 484833 E: bruce.harrison@live.co.uk

HARRISON, Bruce Mountford. b 49. AKC 71. **d** 72 **p** 73. C Hebburn St Cuth *Dur* 72–75; C Bethnal Green St Jo w St Simon *Lon* 75–77; P-in-c Bethnal Green St Bart 77–78; TV Bethnal Green St Jo w St Bart 78–80; C-in-c Pennywell St Thos and Grindon St Oswald CD *Dur* 80–85; V Sunderland Pennywell St Thos 85–90; V Gateshead St Helen 90–14; rtd 14. *18 Salkeld Road, Gateshead NE9 5UD*

HARRISON, Sister Cécile. b 29. Bp Lonsdale Coll TCert 51. St Steph Ho Ox 97. **d** 97 **p** 97. CGA from 66; LtO *Eur* 97–12; PtO *Ex* from 13. *19 Gracey Court, Woodland Road, Broadclyst, Exeter EX5 3GA* E: cga.prasada@gmail.com

HARRISON, Christine Amelia. b 47. STETS 94. **d** 98 **p** 99. NSM Goldsworth Park *Guildf* 98–12; rtd 12; PtO *Guildf* from

---

12. *2 Abercorn Way, Woking GU21 3NY* T: (01483) 750645 E: revchrissie@btinternet.com

HARRISON, Christopher Dennis. b 57. Clare Coll Cam BA 79 BA 86. Westcott Ho Cam 84. **d** 87 **p** 88. C Camberwell St Geo *S'wark* 87–92; V Forest Hill 92–96; P-in-c Fenny Bentley, Kniveton, Thorpe and Tissington *Derby* 96–98; P-in-c Parwich w Alsop-en-le-Dale 96–98; R Fenny Bentley, Thorpe, Tissington, Parwich etc 98–09; RD Ashbourne 98–09; P-in-c Nottingham All SS, St Mary and St Pet *S'well* 09–11; R 11–17; R Nottingham St Pet and All SS from 18. *24 Pelham Crescent, Nottingham NG7 1AW* T: 0115-941 8927 E: christopher.d.harrison@btinternet.com

HARRISON, Christopher Joseph. b 38. AKC 61 Hull Univ CertEd 68 Bris Univ BEd 75. **d** 62 **p** 63. C Bottesford *Linc* 62–67; C Elloughton *York* 67–68; Asst Master Bishop's Cleeve Primary Sch 68–74; Sen Master 74–78; Dep Hd 78–96; P-in-c Farmington *Glouc* 69–73; C Tredington w Stoke Orchard and Hardwicke 74–86; rtd 96; PtO *Glouc* from 87. *Appledore, 93 Stoke Road, Bishops Cleeve, Cheltenham GL52 8RP* T: (01242) 673452 E: c.harrison@btinternet.com

HARRISON, Crispin. *See* HARRISON, Michael Burt

HARRISON, David Daniel. b 62. St Paul's Coll Chelt BA 84 Leeds Univ MA 85 Westmr Coll Ox PGCE 88. Westcott Ho Cam 03. **d** 05 **p** 06. C Beckenham St Geo *Roch* 05–09; P-in-c Woodnesborough w Worth and Staple *Cant* 09–12; Chapl Univ Campus Suffolk *St E* 13; PtO 13–16; P-in-c Ringshall w Battisford, Barking w Darmsden etc 16–19; R S Bosmere from 19. *The Rectory, Willisham, Ipswich IP8 4SP* E: ddh25@btinternet.com

HARRISON, David Henry. b 40. Tyndale Hall Bris 65. **d** 68 **p** 69. C Bolton St Paul *Man* 68–72; V Bircle 72–83; V Southport SS Simon and Jude *Liv* 83–91; TR Fazakerley Em 91–99; V Toxteth Park Ch Ch and St Mich w St Andr 99–05; rtd 05; PtO *Blackb* from 06. *55 The Oval, Shevington, Wigan WN6 8EN* T: (01257) 400084 E: revdave@live.co.uk

HARRISON, Miss Doreen. b 32. Leeds Univ BA 53 PGCE 54 Lanc Univ MLitt 78 MA(Ed) 79. **d** 92 **p** 94. C Ambleside w Brathay *Carl* 92–96; Asst P Colton 96–01; P-in-c 01–02; Asst P Rusland 96–01; P-in-c 01–02; Asst P Satterthwaite 96–01; P-in-c 01–02; rtd 02; PtO *Carl* from 02. *Fox How, Ambleside LA22 9LL* T: (015394) 33021

HARRISON, Fred Graham. b 41. Lon Univ BSc 62. Ridley Hall Cam 80. **d** 82 **p** 83. C Lenton *S'well* 82–85; V Ruddington 85–04; rtd 04; PtO *Ches* from 05. *18 Holly Bank, Hollingworth, Hyde SK14 8QL* T: (01457) 765955 E: fg.harrison@talktalk.net

HARRISON, Gloria. b 55. Qu Foundn (Course) 14. **d** 17 **p** 18. OLM Hanley H Ev *Lich* 17–19; NSM Stoke-upon-Trent and Fenton from 19. *18 Ashbourne Grove, Stoke-on-Trent ST1 5QW* T: (01782) 252820

HARRISON, Guy Patrick. b 58. Ox Univ MTh 99 Middx Univ DPsych 16 MBACP 04. Sarum & Wells Th Coll 92. **d** 94 **p** 95. C Wimborne Minster and Holt *Sarum* 94–96; C Wimborne Minster 96–97; Chapl Dorothy House Hospice Winsley 97–01; Chapl Stoke Mandeville Hosp NHS Trust 01–02; Chapl Team Ldr 02–05; Team Ldr and Bereavement Service Manager Bucks Hosps NHS Trust 05–07; Hd Spiritual and Past Care W Lon Mental Health NHS Trust 07–12; Hd Spiritual and Past Care Ox Health NHS Foundn Trust from 12. *Littlemore Mental Health Centre, Sandford Road, Littlemore, Oxford OX4 4XN* T: 08452-191145 M: 07786-843878 E: guy.harrison@oxfordhealth.nhs.uk

HARRISON, Ian David. b 45. Imp Coll Lon BSc 66. Oak Hill Th Coll 93. **d** 96 **p** 97. NSM Tunbridge Wells St Jo *Roch* 96–99; P-in-c Chiddingstone w Chiddingstone Causeway 99–10; rtd 10; PtO *Roch* from 10. *3 Brunswick Terrace, Tunbridge Wells TN1 1TR* T: (01892) 871639 E: ian.harrison.tw@gmail.com

HARRISON, Canon John. b 49. Fitzw Coll Cam BA 71 MA 74. Westcott Ho Cam 74. **d** 77 **p** 78. C Nunthorpe *York* 77–81; C Acomb St Steph and St Aid 81–83; V Heptonstall *Wakef* 83–91; R Stamford Bridge Gp *York* 91–02; V Easingwold w Raskelf 02–14; RD Easingwold 05–14; Can and Preb York Minster 10–14; rtd 14; PtO *York* from 14. *24 The Manor Beeches, Dunnington, York YO19 5PX* E: john.harrison8@hotmail.co.uk

HARRISON, John. *See* HARRISON, Steven John

HARRISON, John Christopher. b 69. Liv Univ BA 90 MSc 98 Liv Jo Moores Univ PhD 06. SNWTP 07. **d** 10 **p** 11. NSM Hoylake *Ches* from 10. *St Hildeburgh's Vicarage, 1 Stanley Road, Hoylake, Wirral CH47 1HL* T: 0151-632 3897 M: 07834-262166 E: j.c.harrison@ljmu.ac.uk

HARRISON, John Northcott. b 31. St Jo Coll Cam BA 54. Westcott Ho Cam 54. **d** 56 **p** 57. C Moor Allerton *Ripon* 56–59; C Bedale 59–61; V Hudswell w Downholme 61–64; Youth Chapl *Dur* 64–68; V Auckland St Andr and St Anne 68–76; Community Chapl Stockton-on-Tees 76–83;

TR Southampton (City Cen) *Win* 83–88; V Bris Ch the Servant Stockwood 88–96; RD Brislington 89–95; Chapl St Brendan's Sixth Form Coll 90–96; rtd 96; PtO *B & W* 96–12; *Bris* 96–12. *3 Dulverton Hall, Esplanade, Scarborough YO11 2AR* T: (01723) 449828

HARRISON, Mrs Kathryn Maxine. b 70. Ox Min Course 13. **d** 15 **p** 16. C New Windsor *Ox* 15–18; V St Marylebone St Mark Hamilton Terrace *Lon* from 18. *St Mark's Vicarage, 114 Hamilton Terrace, London NW8 9UT* M: 07794-113782 E: mail.kmh22@gmail.com

HARRISON, Keith. *See* HARRISON, Peter Keith

HARRISON, Canon Lyndon. b 47. St Mich Coll Llan 91. **d** 93 **p** 94. C Ebbw Vale *Mon* 93–96; TV 96–01; TV Caldicot 01–05; TR 05–14; Can St Woolos Cathl 12–14; rtd 14; PtO *Mon* from 14. *14 Swallow Drive, Caldicot NP26 5RD* T: (01291) 430041

HARRISON, Mrs Marion Jeanne. b 56. SAOMC 04. **d** 07 **p** 08. C Watercombe *Sarum* 07–11; P-in-c Lt Barningham, Blickling, Edgefield etc *Nor* 11–15; C 15–17; P-in-c Barningham w Matlaske w Baconsthorpe etc 15–17; P-in-c The Lavingtons, Cheverells, and Easterton *Sarum* 17–18; R from 18. *The Vicarage, 25 White Street, West Lavington, Devizes SN10 4LW* T: (01380) 816963 M: 07932-521776 E: marion681@btinternet.com *or* lavingtonrector@gmail.com

HARRISON, Mark. b 60. Global Univ Missouri BA 95 Open Univ BSc 14 St Jo Coll Dur BA 18. Cranmer Hall Dur 16. **d** 18 **p** 19. C Chester le Street *Dur* from 18. *16 Park Road North, Chester le Street DH3 3SD* M: 07975-782891 E: mark.ofelton@gmail.com

HARRISON, Martin. b 58. DCR(R) 78. Trin Coll Bris BA 89. **d** 89 **p** 90. C Heworth H Trin *York* 89–94; Chapl York Distr Hosp 89–94; P-in-c Skelton w Shipton and Newton on Ouse *York* 94–95; R 95–01; V Strensall from 01; RD Easingwold 00–05; C Alne from 17; C Brafferton w Pilmoor, Myton-on-Swale etc from 17; C Coxwold and Husthwaite from 17; C Crayke w Brandsby and Yearsley from 17; C Easingwold w Raskelf from 17; C Skelton w Shipton and Newton on Ouse from 17; C Forest of Galtres from 17. *The Vicarage, 10 York Road, Strensall, York YO32 5UN* T: (01904) 490683 E: revmartinharrison@gmail.com

HARRISON, Maureen Ann. b 39. **d** 08 **p** 09. OLM Sutton *Liv* 08–13; rtd 13. *89 Farndon Avenue, Sutton Manor, St Helens WA9 4DN*

HARRISON, Michael Anthony. b 48. Westhill Coll Birm CertCYW 72 Huddersfield Poly CertEd 88 Leeds Poly BA 91 Leeds Univ MA 98. NOC 94. **d** 97 **p** 98. NSM Thornhill and Whitley Lower *Wakef* 97–99; TV Wrexham *St As* 99–03; V Ruabon 03–11; rtd 11; PtO *St As* from 11; *Ban* from 12. *15 Vicarage Gardens, Llandudno LL30 1RG* T: (01492) 870701 M: 07910-141410 E: mikeonorme@gmail.com

HARRISON, Michael Burt (Crispin). b 36. Leeds Univ BA 59 Trin Coll Ox BA 62 MA 66. Coll of Resurr Mirfield 59. **d** 63 **p** 64. C W Hartlepool St Aid *Dur* 63–64; C Middlesbrough All SS *York* 64–66; Lic to Offic *Wakef* 67–69 and 78–87 and 97–02 and 06–14; CR from 68; S Africa 69–78 and 87–97 and 03–06; Registrar Coll of the Resurr Mirfield 78–84; Vice-Prin 84–87; Superior CR 97–02; LtO *Leeds* from 14. *Community of the Resurrection, Stocks Bank Road, Mirfield WF14 0BN* T: (01924) 483337 E: charrison@mirfield.org.uk

✠**HARRISON, The Rt Revd Michael Robert.** b 63. Selw Coll Cam BA 84 K Coll Lon PhD 97 Bradf Univ MA 99. Ripon Coll Cuddesdon 88 Union Th Sem (NY) STM 90. **d** 90 **p** 91 **c** 16. C S Lambeth St Anne and All SS *S'wark* 91–94; Bp's Chapl to Students *Bradf* 94–98; Chapl Bradf Univ 94–98; Chapl Bradf and Ilkley Community Coll 94–98; V Eltham H Trin *S'wark* 98–06; RD Eltham and Mottingham 05–06; Dir Min and Miss *Leic* 06–16; Hon Can Leic Cathl 06–16; Suff Bp Dunwich *St E* from 16; Dioc Warden of Readers and Lic Lay Min from 16. *Robin Hall, Chapel Road, Mendlesham, Stowmarket IP14 5SQ* T: (01473) 252829

HARRISON, Mrs Nona Margaret. b 50. Open Univ BA 80. S Dios Minl Tr Scheme 92. **d** 95 **p** 96. NSM E w W Wellow and Sherfield English *Win* 95–99; NSM Barton Stacey and Bullington etc 99; NSM Hurstbourne Priors, Longparish etc 00–08; PtO 08–15; *Sarum* from 18. *35 Blackthorn Way, Verwood BH31 6TA* T: (01202) 020374 E: nonaharrison@mypostoffice.co.uk

HARRISON, Miss Patricia Mary. b 35. St Kath Coll Lon CertEd 65 Open Univ BA 74. St Mich Ho Ox IDC 59. **dss** 85 **d** 87 **p** 94. NSM Nunthorpe *York* 85–98; rtd 98; PtO *York* from 98. *22 Lamonby Close, Nunthorpe, Middlesbrough TS7 0QG* T: (01642) 313524 E: marie.pat@btinternet.com

HARRISON, Paul Graham. b 53. Univ of Wales (Lamp) MA 10. Sarum & Wells Th Coll 76. **d** 79 **p** 80. C Brixham w Churston Ferrers *Ex* 79–82; C Portsea N End St Mark *Portsm* 82–87; V Tiverton St Andr *Ex* 87–94; Chapl Tiverton and Distr Hosp

90–94; P-in-c Astwood Bank *Worc* 94–05; TV Redditch Ch the K 05–08; P-in-c Churchill-in-Halfshire w Blakedown and Broome 08–17; Chapl to Deaf People 94–08; Dioc Adv for Disability Issues 03–08; Hon C Belbroughton w Fairfield and Clent 15–17; RD Stourbridge 15–17; rtd 17; PtO *Lich* from 17. *8 Truro Close, Lichfield WS13 7SR* T: (01543) 326458 E: connectpharrison@hotmail.com

HARRISON, Mrs Penelope Ann. b 58. St Andr Univ MA 79. Qu Coll Birm MA 09. **d** 09 **p** 10. C Hamstead St Paul *Birm* 09–13; V Marston Green from 13. *The Vicarage, 32 Elmdon Road, Marston Green, Birmingham B37 7BT* T: 0121-788 2654 M: 07722-446222 E: revdpenny13@gmail.com

HARRISON, Peter. *See* HARRISON, Robert Peter

HARRISON, Peter Keith. b 44. Open Univ BA 85. St Aid Birkenhead. **d** 68 **p** 69. C Higher Bebington *Ches* 68–71; C Walmsley *Man* 71–74; V Lumb in Rossendale 74–79; V Heywood St Marg 79–87; V Hey 87–95; AD Saddleworth 93–95; Chapl Athens w Kifissia *Eur* 95–98; V Aston Cantlow and Wilmcote w Billesley *Cov* 98–02; V W Burnley All SS *Blackb* 02–09; rtd 09; PtO *Blackb* from 09. *57 West Cliffe, Lytham St Annes FY8 5DR* T: (01253) 735128 E: keithharrison207@gmail.com

HARRISON, The Ven Peter Reginald Wallace. b 39. Selw Coll Cam BA 62. Ridley Hall Cam 62. **d** 64 **p** 65. C Barton Hill St Luke w Ch Ch *Bris* 64–69; Chapl Greenhouse Trust 69–77; Dir Northprep Hall Trust 77–84; TR Drypool *York* 84–98; AD E Hull 88–98; Adn E Riding 98–06; Can and Preb York Minster 94–06; rtd 06; PtO *York* from 06. *10 Priestgate, Sutton-on-Hull, Hull HU7 4QR* T: (01482) 797110 E: peter@harrisons.karoo.co.uk

HARRISON, Phillip Roger Neil. b 74. Trin Coll Bris 12. **d** 15 **p** 16. C Gtr Corsham and Lacock *Bris* 15–18; V Wroughton and Wichelstowe from 18. *The Vicarage, Church Hill, Wroughton, Swindon SN4 9JS* T: (01793) 812050 M: 07749-355334 E: philliprnharrison@yahoo.com

HARRISON, Canon Rachel Elizabeth. b 53. NEOC 98. **d** 01 **p** 02. C Skelton w Upleatham *York* 01–04; P-in-c New Marske 04–06; V 06–12; P-in-c Wilton 04–06; V 06–12; V Redcar from 12; Ind Chapl from 04; RD Guisborough 13–19; Can and Preb York Minster from 16. *St Peter's Vicarage, 66 Aske Road, Redcar TS10 2BP* T: (01642) 489842 *or* 490700 E: rachelhere@hotmail.com

HARRISON, Richard Kingswood. b 61. Linc Coll Ox BA 83 MA 88 Leeds Univ BA 90. Coll of Resurr Mirfield 88. **d** 91 **p** 92. C Reading St Giles *Ox* 91–93; Asst Chapl Merchant Taylors' Sch Northwood 93–96; Chapl Ardingly Coll 96–02; R Shill Valley and Broadshire *Ox* 02–04; Chapl Uppingham Sch 04–09; Chapl Lancing Coll from 09; PtO *Ox* 11–19. *Ladywell House, Lancing College, Lancing BN15 0RW* T: (01273) 465961 E: rkh@lancing.org.uk

HARRISON, Robert Peter. b 28. Chich Th Coll. **d** 60 **p** 61. C Ealing Ch the Sav *Lon* 60–64; C Hammersmith SS Mich and Geo White City Estate CD 64–66; P-in-c Fulham St Pet 66–73; V 73–94; rtd 94; PtO *Chich* from 94. *8 Broadwater Way, Worthing BN14 9LP* T: (01903) 217073

HARRISON, Robert William. b 62. Mansf Coll Ox BA 84. Qu Coll Birm 87. **d** 89 **p** 90. C Sholing *Win* 89–93; Communications Adv to Bp Willesden *Lon* 93–97; C Cricklewood St Gabr and St Mich 93–97; V Hillingdon St Jo 97–15; V Neasden St Cath w St Paul from 15. *9 Midstrath Road, London NW10 1TD* T: (020) 8452 7322 M: 07961-011040 E: rob.harrison@london.anglican.org *or* st.catherines@gmx.com

HARRISON, Miss Rosemary Elizabeth. b 57. Lindisfarne Regional Tr Partnership 16. **d** 19. NSM Humshaugh w Simonburn and Wark *Newc* from 19. *20A North Side, Stamfordham, Newcastle upon Tyne NE18 0LA* T: (01661) 855128 M: 07888-834961 E: rosemaryharrison@ymail.com

HARRISON, Miss Ruth Margaret. b 33. FRSA 94. Ripon Coll Cuddesdon 02. **d** 02 **p** 03. NSM Baddiley and Wrenbury w Burleydam *Ches* 02–08; PtO from 08. *2 Heywood Cottages, Heywood Lane, Audlem, Crewe CW3 0EX* T: (01270) 812010

HARRISON, Stephen George. b 66. Rhodes Univ BA 96. **d** 95 **p** 96. C Newlands S Africa 95–97; R Northlands 97–11; R Westville 11–17; Adn Pinetown 15–16; TR Stroudwater Team *Glouc* from 17. *The Rectory, Church Road, Leonard Stanley, Stonehouse GL10 3NP* M: 07466-858975 E: speedyharrison@gmail.com

HARRISON, Steven John. b 47. Univ of Wales (Abth) BSc 68 PhD 74 FRMetS 74. St And Dioc Tr Course 87. **d** 90 **p** 91. NSM Alloa *St And* 90–94; NSM Bridge of Allan 94–02; NSM Spittal *Newc* 02–10; NSM Scremerston 02–10; P-in-c 06–10; rtd 10; PtO *Newc* from 10. *East Cottage, Plunderheath, Haydon Bridge, Hexham NE47 6JU* T: (01434) 684994 E: johnandaveril@aol.com

HARRISON-SMITH, Ms Fiona Jane. b 74. Huddersfield Univ BMus 96 Ox Brookes Univ BA 03 Leeds Univ MA 07. Coll of Resurr Mirfield 05. **d** 07 **p** 08. C Redcar *York* 07–11; TV Seacroft *Leeds* 11–16; V Weoley Castle *Birm* from 16. *83 Marston Road, Birmingham B29 5LS* M: 07709-914786 E: revdfiona@gmail.com

HARRISON-WATSON, Carole. *See* FORD, Carole

HARRISON, John Anthony Lomax. b 47. Ex Univ BA 72. Qu Coll Birm 72. **d** 74 **p** 75. C Loughton St Jo *Chelmsf* 74–81; V Chingford St Anne 81–98; TV Aldrington *Chich* 98–04; TV Golden Cap Team *Sarum* 04–09; rtd 09. *82 Chestnut Way, Honiton EX14 2XF* E: john.harrison@yahoo.co.uk

HARROLD, Canon Jeremy Robin. b 31. Hertf Coll Ox BA 54 BSc 56 MA 58. Wycliffe Hall Ox. **d** 59 **p** 60. C Rushden *Pet* 59–61; Bp's Chapl *Lon* 61–64; Australia 64–67; V Harlesden St Mark *Lon* 67–72; V Hendon St Paul Mill Hill 72–84; V Stowmarket *St E* 84–96; RD 90–96; Hon Can St E Cathl 94–96; rtd 96; PtO *St E* 96–19. *18 Wilkinson Way, Woodbridge IP12 1SS* T: (01394) 380127 E: jeremy@harrold1931.plus.com

HARRON, Canon Gareth Andrew. b 71. QUB BA 92. CITC BTh 95. **d** 95 **p** 96. C Willowfield *D & D* 95–98; C Dromore Cathl 98–02; I Magheralin w Dollingstown 02–15; I Holywood from 15; Can Dromore Cathl from 12; Can Belf Cathl from 16. *The Vicarage, 156 High Street, Holywood BT18 9HT* T: (028) 9042 2069 E: garethharron@btinternet.com

HARRON, James Alexander. b 37. GIMechE 61. St Aid Birkenhead 63. **d** 65 **p** 66. C Willowfield *D & D* 65–69; I Desertmartin *D & R* 69–80; Dep Sec BCMS (Ireland) 80–84; I Aghalee *D & D* 84–03; Preb Dromore Cathl 02–03; Chapl HM Pris Maghaberry 86–03; rtd 03. *8 Churchill Avenue, Lurgan, Craigavon BT66 7BW* T/F: (028) 3834 6543 E: jmeli3harron@gmail.com

HARROP, Mrs Eileen Khean Geok. b 59. Keele Univ BA 83 MA 89 PGCE 83 Wolfs Coll Cam BTh 11. Ridley Hall Cam 08. **d** 12 **p** 13. C Tenterden and Smallhythe *Cant* 12–16; C Rother and Oxney 13–16; C Bishop Auckland *Dur* from 16; P-in-c Gainford from 16; P-in-c Winston from 16. *The Vicarage, Low Green, Gainford, Darlington DL2 3DS* T: (01325) 733154 M: 07976-676098 E: ekgharrop@gmail.com

HARROP, Stephen Douglas. b 48. St Jo Coll York CertEd 74 Man Univ DipAdEd 90. Edin Th Coll 77. **d** 79 **p** 82. C Middlesbrough St Martin *York* 79–80; C Cayton w Eastfield 80–81; C Oldham *Man* 82–84; V Oldham St Barn 84–89; P-in-c Em Ch Hong Kong 89–93; Ind Chapl and TV Kidderminster St Mary and All SS w Trimpley etc *Worc* 93–95; Chapl Kidderminster Coll 93–95; Sandwell Chs Link Officer *Birm* 95–96; Dep Chapl HM Pris Brixton 96–97; Chapl Taichung St Jas Taiwan 97–98; R Lower Merion St Jo USA 98–99; R Essington *Lich* 99–03; PtO *Man* 03–04 and 09–13; C Elton St Steph 04–05; P-in-c 05–08; Chapl HM Pris Forest Bank 08–13; P-in-c Petton w Cockshutt, Welshampton and Lyneal etc *Lich* 13–17; Hon C Adbaston, High Offley, Knightley, Norbury etc 17–18; R Harlaxton Gp *Linc* from 18. *The Rectory, 6 Rectory Lane, Harlaxton, Grantham NG32 1HD* T: (01476) 594608 M: 07871-987455 E: steph60en@aol.com

HARRY, Bruce David. b 40. Culham Coll Ox CertEd 60. NOC 83. **d** 86 **p** 87. NSM Liscard St Thos *Ches* 86–91; NSM Eastham 91–94; C New Brighton St Jas 94–96; C New Brighton Em 94–96; C New Brighton St Jas w Em 96–98; NSM 98–02; NSM New Brighton All SS 98–02; P-in-c 02–03; PtO from 03. *21 Sandymount Drive, Wallasey CH45 0LJ* T: 0151-639 7232 E: rev_bdh@tiscali.co.uk

HARRY, Usha Praful. b 26. **d** 98 **p** 02. PtO *Lon* 98–14; NSM Wembley St Jo 14–18; PtO from 18. *157 Ealing Road, Wembley HA0 4BY* T: (020) 8903 8873 E: ushaharry157@yahoo.com

HART (formerly HARRISON), Mrs Alison Edwina. b 53. Newc Univ BEd 75. Linc Th Coll 84. **dss** 86 **d** 87 **p** 94. Loughborough Em *Leic* 86–89; Par Dn 87–89; C Stockton *Dur* 89–92; P-in-c Lynesack and Cockfield 92–95; P-in-c Ebchester 95–96; R 96–97; V Medomsley 96–97; V Newc H Cross 97–01; P-in-c Ulgham and Widdrington 01–06; P-in-c Beckermet St Jo and St Bridget w Ponsonby *Carl* 06–10; rtd 10; PtO *Newc* from 10; *Mor* from 10. *1 Braeval, Carrbridge PH23 3AA* E: coolingstreams@yahoo.co.uk

HART, Allen Sydney George. b 38. Chich Th Coll 64. **d** 67 **p** 68. C N Bradley St Cuth *Lon* 67–71; C W Bromwich All SS *Lich* 71–74; TV Hucknall Torkard *S'well* 74–80; V Annesley Our Lady and All SS 80–86; V Bilborough St Jo 86–99; RD Nottingham W 94–99; P-in-c Clarborough w Hayton 99–03; Asst Chapl HM Pris Ranby 99–03; rtd 03; PtO *S'well* 03–15. *3 Castleton Close, Hucknall, Nottingham NG15 6TD* T: 0115-955 2067 E: a.hart557@ntlworld.com

HART, André Hendrik. b 62. Cape Town Univ BA 86. St Steph Ho Ox 89. **d** 91 **p** 92. C Newbold w Dunston *Derby* 91–95; P-in-c Clifton and Norbury w Snelston 95–02; Chapl S

Derbyshire Community Health Services NHS Trust 95–01; Chapl Derbyshire Mental Health Services NHS Trust 01–02; V Westbury-on-Trym H Trin *Bris* from 02. *Holy Trinity Vicarage, 44 Eastfield Road, Westbury-on-Trym, Bristol BS9 4AG* T: 0117-962 1536 *or* 950 8644

HART, Anthony. b 35. St Mich Coll Llan 77. **d** 79 **p** 80. NSM Jersey St Helier *Win* 79–81; C Heref All SS 81–82; C Kingstone 82–84; C Eaton Bishop 82–84; C Clehonger 82–84; R Sutton St Nicholas w Sutton St Michael 84–88; R Withington w Westhide 84–88; R Jersey St Mary *Win* 88–01; rtd 01; PtO *Win* from 02. *Villa Rapallo, Mont de la Trinite, St Helier, Jersey JE2 4NJ* T: (01534) 739146 M: 07797-750435 E: hartjsy@gmail.com

HART, Colin Edwin. b 45. Leeds Univ BA 66 PGCE 67 MPhil 89 Fitzw Coll Cam BA 73 MA 77 K Coll Lon MTh 76 Man Univ PhD 98. Trin Coll Bris 74. **d** 74 **p** 75. C Ware Ch Ch *St Alb* 74–78; TV Sheff Manor 78–80; V Wombridge *Lich* 80–87; Lect St Jo Coll Nottm 87–01; Public Preacher *S'well* 87–01; Hon C Chilwell 87–91; Hon C Trowell 91–01; PtO *Ches* from 09. *47 Deveraux Drive, Wallasey CH44 4DG* T: 0151-630 0749 E: ceh2397@gmail.com

HART, Dagogo. b 50. Birm Bible Inst 77. **d** 82 **p** 83. Nigeria 82–00; C St Cypr Niger Delta 82–88; V 93–96; Chapl to Bp 83–88; Res Min Niger Delta Ch Ch 89–92; Can Res St Steph Cathl Niger Delta 97–00; C W Bromwich St Jas w St Paul *Lich* 01–06; V 06–15; rtd 15. *43 Ravenscar Road, Surbiton KT6 7PJ* M: 07469-761906

HART, David John. b 58. K Coll Lon BD 80. St Mich Coll Llan 83. **d** 85 **p** 86. C Denbigh and Nantglyn *St As* 85–88; Chapl RAF 88–89; C Llanrhos *St As* 89–91; V Rhosllannerchrugog 91–01; PtO *Lich* 11–14 and from 17. *Address temp unknown* E: davidjhart@lineone.net

HART, David Maurice. b 35. Univ Coll Dur BSc 57. Clifton Th Coll 59. **d** 61 **p** 62. C Bolton St Paul *Man* 61–64; C Hamworthy *Sarum* 64–70; R W Dean w E Grimstead 70–81; R Farley w Pitton and W Dean w E Grimstead 81–90; V Steeple Ashton w Semington and Keevil 90–03; rtd 03; PtO *Sarum* from 04. *9 Field Close, Westbury BA13 3AG* T: (01373) 827912 E: rotherham1935@gmail.com

HART, Debbie. *See* HORE, Debbie

HART, Dennis William. b 30. Open Univ BA. Oak Hill Th Coll 75. **d** 78 **p** 79. NSM Clacton St Paul *Chelmsf* 78–04; PtO 04–07. *Maranatha, 15 Albert Gardens, Clacton-on-Sea CO15 6QN* T: (01255) 431794

HART, Geoffrey Robert. b 49. TISEC 93. **d** 95 **p** 96. P-in-c Edin St Salvador 95–98; C Edin St Cuth 96–98; LtO 98–00; TV Edin St Marg 00–04; NSM Edin St Dav 04–09; P-in-c Edin St Marg 09–12; rtd 12; LtO *Edin* from 16. *27 Links View, Port Seton, Prestonpans EH32 0EZ* T: (01875) 814520 M: 07963-463551

HART, Canon Gillian Mary. b 57. Sheff City Poly BA 79. Carl Dioc Tr Inst 92. **d** 95 **p** 96. C Burgh-by-Sands and Kirkbampton w Kirkandrews etc *Carl* 95–99; C Aikton 95–99; C Orton St Giles 95–99; Dioc Youth Officer 99–03; Chapl St Martin's Coll Carl 99–03; R Barony of Burgh *Carl* 03–10; TR Maryport, Netherton and Flimby 10–15; P-in-c Brigham, Gt Broughton and Broughton Moor 14–15; P-in-c Eskdale, Irton, Muncaster and Waberthwaite 15–17; R Black Combe, Drigg, Eskdale etc from 17; Adv for Women in Min from 08; Hon Can Carl Cathl from 10. *2 Smithy Banks, Holmrook CA19 1TP* T: (019467) 24724 E: hart.gill@btopenworld.com

HART, Jane Elizabeth. *See* WARHURST, Jane Elizabeth

HART, Mark. b 61. Chu Coll Cam BA 82 Cam Univ MA 86 PhD 86. Trin Coll Bris BA 98. **d** 98 **p** 99. C Bromborough *Ches* 98–02; V Plemstall w Guilden Sutton 02–18; RD Ches 09–13; R Nantwich from 18. *The Rectory, Church Lane, Nantwich CW5 5RQ* T: (01270) 620668 E: markhart61@gmail.com

HART, Canon Michael Anthony. b 50. AKC 71. St Aug Coll Cant 72. **d** 73 **p** 74. C Southwick St Columba *Dur* 73–76; C Hendon St Alphage *Lon* 76–78; P-in-c Eltham Park St Luke *S'wark* 78–83; V 83–85; R Newington St Mary 85–96; P-in-c Camberwell St Mich w All So w Em 85–96; RD S'wark and Newington 93–96; P-in-c Chaldon 96–97; P-in-c Caterham 96–97; TR 98–05; RD 98–05; Hon Can S'wark Cathl 01–05 and 10–15; Can Missr 05–10; TR Catford (Southend) and Downham 10–15; rtd 15; PtO *S'wark* from 15; *Chich* from 15. *1 High Beeches, Worthing BN11 4TJ* E: michael.hart@southwark.anglican.org

HART, Preb Michael Stuart. b 39. Univ of Wales (Lamp) BA 61 Lanc Univ MA 72. Wycliffe Hall Ox 61. **d** 63 **p** 64. C W Bromwich St Jas *Lich* 63–66; C Tarrington w Stoke Edith *Heref* 66–67; C Putney St Mary *S'wark* 67–70; V Accrington St Mary *Blackb* 70–82; RD Accrington 76–82; Hon Can Blackb Cathl 81–91; V Walton-le-Dale 82–91; TR Heavitree w Ex St Paul 91–02; P-in-c Ex St Mary Steps 01–02; TR Heavitree and St Mary Steps 02–07; P-in-c Exwick 05–07; Preb Ex Cathl

02–07; rtd 07; P-in-c Bath H Trin *B & W* 09–11; PtO 11–13. *14 Maes yr Ysgol, Templeton, Narberth SA67 8TZ* M: 07786-516076 E: m.hart254@btinternet.com

HART, Mrs Mildred Elizabeth. b 49. **d** 10 **p** 11. OLM Len Valley *Cant* 10–14; NSM from 14. *15 Mercer Drive, Harrietsham ME17 1AY* T: (01622) 859753 E: millie.hart@uwclub.net

HART, Mrs Pauline Jayne. b 58. St Mellitus Coll 13. **d** 15 **p** 16. NSM Alresford and Frating w Thorrington *Chelmsf* 15–17; NSM Elmstead 16–17; NSM Tenpenny Villages from 17. *8A Manor Road, Wivenhoe, Colchester CO7 9LN* T: (01206) 826318 E: curate@alresfordchurch.net

HART, Preb Peter Osborne. b 57. St Jo Coll Nottm. **d** 92 **p** 93. C Shipley St Pet *Bradf* 92–97; TV Walsall *Lich* 97–03; TV Cannock 03–09; TV Cannock and Huntington 09–10; V 10–17; V Hatherton 10–17; TV Brereton and Rugeley w Armitage from 17; Preb Lich Cathl from 13. *3 Church Lane, Armitage, Rugeley WS15 4BA*

HART, Peter William. b 60. Liv Univ BA 82 Université de Haute Normandie MèsL 84 Univ of Wales (Swansea) MPhil 92. Sarum & Wells Th Coll 86. **d** 88 **p** 89. C Llansamlet *S & B* 88–89; C Sketty 89–92; P-in-c Warndon St Nic *Worc* 92–97; R Berkhamsted St Mary *St Alb* 97–04; V Kew St Phil and All SS w St Luke *S'wark* from 04; Ecum Adv Kingston Area from 05; AD Richmond and Barnes from 18. *St Philip's Vicarage, 70 Marksbury Avenue, Richmond TW9 4JF* T: (020) 8392 1425 *or* 8332 1324 E: pwhart1@aol.com

HART, Robert William. b 76. R Holloway & Bedf New Coll Lon BSc 97 Leeds Univ BA 01 MA 04. Coll of Resurr Mirfield 99. **d** 02 **p** 03. C Haydock St Jas *Liv* 02–06; R Hemsworth *Wakef* 06–14; *Leeds* from 14. *The Rectory, 3 Church Close, Hemsworth, Pontefract WF9 4SJ* T: (01977) 610507 E: frrobert@parishofhemsworth.org.uk

HART, Ronald George. b 46. BSc CQSW 77. Sarum & Wells Th Coll. **d** 85 **p** 86. C Sittingbourne St Mich *Cant* 85–88; C Walton H Trin *Ox* 88–89; TV 89–96; R Broughton Gifford, Gt Chalfield and Holt *Sarum* 96–05; Chapl UWE *Bris* 05–07; C Mangotsfield 06–07; R Vale of White Hart *Sarum* 07–11; rtd 11; PtO *Sarum* from 11. *Lavenders, 6 Squarey Close, Downton, Salisbury SP5 3LQ* T: (01725) 514772 E: ronhart1@yahoo.co.uk

HART, Mrs Sheila Elizabeth. b 49. ERMC. **d** 08 **p** 09. NSM Whinlands *St E* 08–17; NSM Alde Sandlings from 17; RD Saxmundham from 18. *3 Keats Close, Saxmundham IP17 1WJ* T: (01728) 602456 E: sheila.hart49@gmail.com

HART, Mrs Susan Clare. b 67. Ripon Coll Cuddesdon 15. **d** 17 **p** 18. C River Were *Sarum* from 17. *10 Manor Gardens, Warminster BA12 8PW*

HARTE, Matthew Scott. b 46. TCD BA 70 MA 74. CITC 71. **d** 71 **p** 72. C Bangor Abbey *D & D* 71–74; C Ballynafeigh St Jude 74–76; I Ardara w Glencolumbkille, Inniskeel etc *D & R* 76–98; I Dunfanaghy, Raymunterdoney and Tullaghbegley 98–13; Adn Raphoe 83–13; Preb Howth St Patr Cathl Dublin 07–13; rtd 13. *Largymore, Kilcar, Co Donegal, Republic of Ireland* T: (00353) (74) 973 8434 M: 87-756 5081 E: msharte1@eircom.net

HARTER, Andrew Michael Hatfeild. b 44. K Coll Cam BA 66 MA 69. Ripon Coll Cuddesdon 12. **d** 13 **p** 14. NSM Grosmont and Skenfrith and Llangattock etc *Mon* 13–16; PtO from 16; *Heref* from 17. *Ferry Bank, Breinton, Hereford HR4 7PR* T: (01432) 356320 E: andrew@harter.co.uk

HARTERINK, Mrs Joy Frances. b 49. Essex Univ BA 71 Hughes Hall Cam CertEd 72 Lon Univ MSc 87. Oak Hill NSM Course 89. **d** 92 **p** 94. NSM Richmond H Trin and Ch Ch *S'wark* 92–05; Chapl Richmond Coll 97–01; PtO *Guildf* 05–15; *Chich* from 16. *8 Portland Close, Littlehampton BN17 6SJ* E: joyharterink@yahoo.com

HARTLAND, Ian Charles. b 49. K Coll Lon BD 72 MTh 76 AKC 72 Lon Inst of Educn PGCE 73. Sarum & Wells Th Coll 83. **d** 84 **p** 85. C Orpington All SS *Roch* 84–87; Sen Lect Ch Ch Coll Cant 87–95; Adv RE Kent Coun 96–03; HMI of Schs 03–07; PtO *Heref* from 17. *Dormington House, Dormington, Hereford HR1 4ES* T: (01432) 851465 E: ian.c.hartland@hotmail.co.uk

HARTLAND (née CLARKE), Mrs Rachel Frances. b 69. Univ of Wales (Abth) BSc 90. Ox Min Course 12. **d** 14 **p** 15. NSM Old Basing and Lychpit *Win* 14–18; NSM Darby Green and Eversley from 18. *Ramtops, 26 Cornfields, Yateley GU46 6YT* E: ramtopsrac@yahoo.co.uk

HARTLESS, Berengaria Isabella de la Tour. b 52. Univ of Wales (Cardiff) BSc 74 Goldsmiths' Coll Lon PGCE 76 Liv Univ MA 03 K Coll Lon DThMin 15. Ox Min Course 90. **d** 93 **p** 94. Par Dn High Wycombe *Ox* 93–94; C 94–97; P-in-c Seer Green and Jordans 97–00; OLM Tr Officer (Bucks) 97–00; Dioc Prin of OLM 00–18; Dir of IME (2) from 11; PtO *Cov* 10–18; Hon C Edgehill Churches from 18. *Lloyd's*

House, Banbury Street, Kineton, Warwick CV35 0JS T: (01926) 642975 E: beren.hartless@btinternet.com

HARTLEY, Mrs Anne Theresa. b 52. St Cuth Soc Dur BSc 74 Worc Coll of Educn PGCE 75. **d** 03 **p** 04. OLM Wychwood *Ox* 03–17; PtO from 17. *The Old House, Upper Milton, Milton-under-Wychwood, Chipping Norton OX7 6EX* T: (01993) 830160 M: 07976-025101 E: anne@thartley.net *or* anne@wychwoodbenefice.org.uk

HARTLEY, Brian. b 41. NOC 82. **d** 85 **p** 86. NSM Royton St Paul *Man* 85–91; NSM Oldham St Steph and All Martyrs 91–94; TV E Farnworth and Kearsley 94–97; TR New Bury 97–06; P-in-c Gt Lever 03–06; AD Farnworth 98–05; rtd 06; PtO *Man* from 06. *21 Penryn Avenue, Royton, Oldham OL2 6JR* T: (01706) 849132 E: brian_hartley@tiscali.co.uk

HARTLEY, Christopher Neville. b 56. Hull Univ BA 82 SS Paul & Mary Coll Cheltenham PGCE 84. SNWTP 08. **d** 10 **p** 11. OLM Man Victoria Park from 10. *8 Bronte Street, Manchester M15 6QL* T: 0161-232 0644 M: 07783-932386 E: christopherhartley@ymail.com

HARTLEY, Daniel George. b 73. Leeds Univ BA 95. Coll of Resurr Mirfield 96. **d** 99 **p** 00. C Richmond w Hudswell *Ripon* 99–03; Chapl HM YOI Deerbolt 03–10; V Ecclesfield *Sheff* 11–15; P-in-c Thurlestone, S Milton, W Alvington etc *Ex* 15; R Thurlestone, S Milton, Churchstow etc from 15. *The Rectory, Thurlestone, Kingsbridge TQ7 3LF*

HARTLEY, Denis. b 54. NTMTC BA 07. **d** 07 **p** 15. NSM Wood Green St Mich w Bounds Green St Gabr etc *Lon* 07–12; Chapl HM Pris Thameside 12–16; NSM Thamesmead *S'wark* 15–16; PtO *Cant* 16–17; C Margate All SS from 17. *23A Palm Bay Avenue, Margate CT9 3DQ* M: 07957-227764 E: fr-denis@outlook.com

HARTLEY, Dianna Lynn. *See* GWILLIAMS, Dianna Lynn

✠**HARTLEY, The Rt Revd Helen-Ann Macleod.** b 73. St Andr Univ MTheol 95 Princeton Th Sem ThM 96 Worc Coll Ox MPhil 00 DPhil 05. SAOMC 03. **d** 05 **p** 06 **c** 14. C Wheatley *Ox* 05–07; C Littlemore 07–12; Lect Ripon Coll Cuddesdon 05–12; Tutor 09–12; Tutor St Jo Coll Auckland New Zealand 12–14; Bp Waikato 14–17; Suff Bp Ripon *Leeds* from 18. *Redwood, New Road, Sharow, Ripon HG4 5BS* M: 07568-536408 E: bishop.helenann@leeds.anglican.org

HARTLEY, John Peter. b 56. Cam Univ BA 78 Leeds Univ PhD 82 Dur Univ BA 84. Cranmer Hall Dur 82. **d** 85 **p** 86. C Spring Grove St Mary *Lon* 85–88; C Bexleyheath St Pet *Roch* 88–91; P-in-c Hanford *Lich* 91–00; Faith in the City Officer (Potteries) 91–00; V Eccleshill *Bradf* 00–14; *Leeds* from 14. *The Vicarage, 2 Fagley Lane, Bradford BD2 3NS* T: (01274) 636403 M: 07811-915320 E: john.hartley@leeds.anglican.org

HARTLEY, Julian John. b 57. Oak Hill Th Coll BA 85. **d** 85 **p** 86. C Eccleston Ch Ch *Liv* 85–89; V Goose Green 89–00; P-in-c Mosley Common *Man* 00–06; TV Astley, Tyldesley and Mosley Common 06–19; AD Leigh 15–19; V Astley Bridge from 19; AD Walmsley from 19. *St John's Vicarage, Mosley Common Road, Worsley, Manchester M28 1AN* T: 0161-790 2957 F: 799 0314 E: rev.hartley@hartley.me.uk

HARTLEY, Martin John Edward. b 67. Ridley Hall Cam 11. **d** 13 **p** 14. C Newton Flotman, Swainsthorpe, Tasburgh, etc *Nor* 13–17; V Mile Cross from 17. *St Catherine's Vicarage, Aylsham Road, Norwich NR3 2RJ* M: 07876-643560 E: mjehartley@gmail.com

HARTLEY, Canon Michael Leslie. b 56. Leeds Univ BSc 77. Ripon Coll Cuddesdon 87. **d** 89 **p** 90. C Standish *Blackb* 89–93; V Bamber Bridge St Aid 93–98; TR Colne and Villages 98–08; P-in-c Warton St Paul 08–16; P-in-c Freckleton 16; V Freckleton and Warton St Paul 17–17; Dioc Ecum Officer 08–17; Hon Can Blackb Cathl 15–17; rtd 17; PtO *Blackb* from 17. *31 Southdown Drive, Thornton-Cleveleys FY5 5BL* T: (01253) 975435 E: canonmichaelhartley@gmail.com

HARTLEY, Canon Nigel John. b 48. Portsm Poly BA. St Jo Coll Nottm. **d** 83 **p** 84. C Ipswich St Marg *St E* 83–86; P-in-c Hintlesham w Chattisham 86–95; Dioc Radio Officer 86–95; P-in-c Gt Finborough w Onehouse, Harleston, Buxhall etc 95–04; RD Stowmarket 96–99; V Aldeburgh w Hazlewood 04–14; RD Saxmundham 05–12; Hon Can St E Cathl 10–14; rtd 14; PtO *St E* 14–18; *Chich* from 14. *Sheppens, Newham Lane, Steyning BN44 3LR* E: nigel.hartley2@btinternet.com

HARTLEY, Paul. b 51. Nottm Univ BTh 88. Linc Th Coll 85. **d** 88 **p** 89. C Clitheroe St Mary *Blackb* 88–91; TV Guiseley w Esholt *Bradf* 91–97; R Ackworth *Wakef* 97–14; *Leeds* 14–17; rtd 17. *27 Upper Carr Lane, Calverley, Pudsey LS28 5PL* E: rev.paulhartley@yahoo.co.uk

HARTLEY, Canon Peter. b 44. St Cath Coll Cam BA 66 MA 69 Avery Hill Coll PGCE 67. Sarum & Wells Th Coll 77. **d** 78 **p** 79. Hon C Freemantle *Win* 78–79; Chr Educn Officer Pet 79–81; Dir of Educn 81–90; Dir Coun of Educn and Tr *Chelmsf* 90–09; Hon Can Chelmsf Cathl 92–09; rtd 09; PtO *Nor* from

04. *3 St Mary's Lane, Langham, Holt NR25 7AF* T: (01328) 830624 E: peter.hartley49@btinternet.com

HARTLEY, Peter Mellodew. b 41. Qu Coll Cam BA 63 MA 66 Lon Univ MSc 71 FICE. S'wark Ord Course 80. **d** 83 **p** 84. NSM Salfords *S'wark* 83–97; Chapl Surrey and Sussex Healthcare NHS Trust 97–02; rtd 02; PtO *Chich* from 00; *S'wark* from 02; *Eur* from 05; *Lon* from 14. *Old Timbers, North Lane, West Hoathly, East Grinstead RH19 4QF* T: (01342) 811238 E: petermhartley@btinternet.com

HARTLEY, Sarah Elizabeth. *See* ARCHER, Sarah Elizabeth

HARTLEY, Stewart John Ridley. b 47. St Jo Coll Nottm 78. **d** 80 **p** 81. C Altham w Clayton le Moors *Blackb* 80–84; P-in-c Nelson St Phil 84–91; V 91–98; V Gt Marsden w Nelson St Phil 99–03; Hon Can Blackb Cathl 99–03; V Bermondsey St Anne and St Aug *S'wark* 03–12; V Bermondsey St Jas w Ch Ch and St Crispin 03–12; rtd 12; PtO *Leeds* from 17. *8 Weston Park View, Otley LS21 2DU* T: (01943) 464106 E: sr.hartley47@gmail.com

HARTLEY, Susan Mary. b 49. Newc Univ MB, BS 73 MRCGP 77. SEITE 99. **d** 02 **p** 03. NSM Spitalfields Ch Ch w All SS *Lon* 02–07; NSM Hainault *Chelmsf* 07–16; Asst Chapl St Joseph's Hospice Hackney 06; PtO *Chelmsf* from 16; Chapl Barking Havering and Redbridge Hosps NHS Trust from 17. *272 New North Road, Ilford IG6 3BT* T: (020) 8500 4592 M: 07741-468576 E: suemhartley@btinternet.com

HARTMAN, Mrs Jill Norma. b 57. Cen Sch of Art Lon BA 80. SEITE 08. **d** 11 **p** 16. NSM Upper St Leonards St Jo *Chich* from 11. *21 Nelson Road, Hastings TN34 3RX* T: (01424) 716126 M: 07952-950316 E: jillhartman39@gmail.com

HARTNELL, Canon Bruce John. b 42. Ex Univ BA 64 Linacre Coll Ox BA 66 MA. Ripon Hall Ox 64. **d** 66 **p** 67. C S Stoneham *Win* 66–69; Chapl and Tutor Ripon Hall Ox 69–74; V Knowl Hill w Littlewick *Ox* 74–78; Chapl Southn Univ *Win* 78–83; V Sholing 83–07; AD Southampton 93–01; Hon Can Win Cathl 92–07; rtd 07; PtO *Win* from 07. *9 Ash Close, Southampton SO19 5SD* T: (023) 8090 5420 E: bruce.hartnell@ukgateway.net

HARTNELL, Graham Philip. b 50. **d** 08 **p** 08. NSM Flackwell Heath *Ox* 08–15; PtO *Lich* from 15. *93 Planks Lane, Wombourne, Wolverhampton WV5 8DX* T: (01902) 593086 E: g.hartnell@icloud.com

HARTOPP, Mrs Penelope Faye. b 55. Ripon Coll Cuddesdon. **d** 03 **p** 04. C Studley *Cov* 03–04; C Cov E 04–07; TV Godalming *Guildf* 07–11; V Over St Chad *Ches* 11–15; C Budleigh Salterton, E Budleigh w Bicton etc *Ex* 15–19; Chapl HM Pris Channings Wood from 19. *HM Prison Channings Wood, Denbury, Newton Abbot TQ12 6DW* T: (01803) 814647 M: 07884-314752 E: penniehartopp@googlemail.com

HARTREE, Steven John. b 65. FFA 78. WEMTC 96. **d** 99 **p** 00. NSM Highbridge *B & W* 99–03; P-in-c Tintinhull w Chilthorne Domer, Yeovil Marsh etc 03–09; rtd 09; PtO *B & W* from 10. *Chestnuts, Chestnut Lane, Bleadon, Weston-super-Mare BS24 0QD* T: (01934) 811849 M: 07899-660422 E: stevenhartree194@btinternet.com

HARTROPP, Andrew James. b 59. Southn Univ BSc 80 PhD 85 K Coll Lon PhD 03. Oak Hill Th Coll BA 95. **d** 98 **p** 99. C Watford *St Alb* 98–01; C Watford Ch Ch 01–08; Teacher Henrietta Barnett Sch 01–06; NSM White Waltham w Shottesbrooke and Waltham St Lawrence *Ox* 08–12; Research Tutor Ox Cen for Miss Studies 12–16; PtO *Ox* from 12. *4 Pembroke Way, Bicester OX26 4TX* T: (01869) 242223 E: a.hartropp@btinternet.com

HARTSHORNE, Kim. *See* BROWN, Kim

HARTWELL, Mrs Jeanette May. b 65. Aston Univ BSc 88. Qu Coll Birm BA 07. **d** 07 **p** 08. C Brereton and Rugeley *Lich* 07–10; TV Smestow Vale 10–16; Dir Reader Tr from 16; Tutor Qu Coll Birm from 16. *The Vicarage, School Road, Trysull, Wolverhampton WV5 7HR* T: (01902) 896650

HARVEY, Anne. *See* HARVEY, Ruth Anne

HARVEY, Brian. b 51. Hatf Poly BA 74. St As Minl Tr Course 02. **d** 05 **p** 06. NSM Cilcain and Nannerch and Rhydymwyn *St As* 05–09; P-in-c 06–09; R Flint 09–16; P-in-c Bagillt 13–16; TV Estuary and Mountain Miss Area from 17. *The Rectory, Allt Goch, Flint CH6 5NF* T: (01352) 733274 E: brianharvey@mac.com

HARVEY, The Ven Cyril John. b 30. Univ of Wales (Lamp) BA 51. Coll of Resurr Mirfield 51. **d** 53 **p** 54. C Caerau w Ely *Llan* 53–57; C Milford Haven *St D* 57–61; V Castlemartin and Warren 61–65; R Begelly w Ludchurch and Crunwere 65–73; V Haverfordwest St Martin w Lambston 73–88; Can St D Cathl from 85; R Tenby 88–96; Adn St D 91–96; rtd 96; PtO *St D* from 05. *5 Paxton Court, White Lion Street, Tenby SA70 7ET* T: (01834) 845747 E: johnofwales@hotmail.co.uk

HARVEY, Desmond Victor Ross. b 37. QUB BA 59. Princeton Th Sem ThM 63 Fuller Th Sem California DMin 93 St Mich Coll Llan 95. **d** 95 **p** 96. Presbyterian Min 65–95; C Cwmbran *Mon* 95–97; TV 97; PtO from 97; OCM from 98. *Mallory, Llanmaes, Llantwit Major CF61 2XR* T/F: (01446) 792753 E: mallory06@talktalk.net

HARVEY, James. *See* HARVEY, Thomas James

HARVEY, John Christopher. b 65. Univ of Wales (Lamp) BA 86 Nottm Univ BTh 89. Linc Th Coll 86. **d** 89 **p** 90. C Dwygyfylchi *Ban* 89–93; V Llangrannog w Llandysiliogogo w Penbryn *St D* 93–02; RD Glyn Aeron 99–02; P-in-c Llangystennin *St As* 02–04; R 04–09; V Meliden and Gwaenysgor 09–17; P-in-c Bryn a Mor Miss Area from 18; Dioc Voc Adv from 08. *The Vicarage, Ffordd Penrhwylfa, Prestatyn LL19 8HN* T: (01745) 856220

HARVEY, Lt Col John William Arthur. b 43. Guildf Dioc Min Course 98. **d** 01 **p** 02. OLM Aldershot St Aug *Guildf* 01–13; PtO from 13. *59 Knoll Road, Fleet GU51 4PT* T: (01252) 622793 E: father.john@talktalk.net

HARVEY, Jonathan Bromley. b 72. BSc BA PGCE. St Mellitus Coll. **d** 14 **p** 15. C Eastleigh *Win* 14–18; C N Stoneham and Bassett from 18. *St Francis House, Nightingale Avenue, Eastleigh SO50 9JH* M: 07515-287108

HARVEY, Margaret Claire. b 41. Univ of Wales (Abth) BA 62 DipEd 63 Lon Univ BD 68. Dalton Ho Bris 66. **dss** 68 **d** 80 **p** 97. Flint *St As* 68–74; Lect Trin Coll Bris 74–80; Connah's Quay *St As* 79–80; C 80–86; Bp's Adv for Continuing Clerical Educn 86–98; Hon C Corwen and Llangar 86–87; Dn-in-c Bryneglwys 87–97; P-in-c 97–02; rtd 02; PtO *St As* from 09. *7 Llys Trewithan, St Asaph LL17 0DJ* T: (01745) 583535 E: rev.maggie@outlook.com

✠**HARVEY, The Rt Revd Murray Alexander.** b 63. Univ of Qld BA 85 Deakin Univ Australia DHSc 03 MAPsS 87. St Fran Coll Brisbane BTh 91. **d** 91 **p** 92 **c** 18. C Milton Australia 92–93; C Stafford 94–95; P-in-c Tamborine Mt St Geo 95–02; V Glen Gp *Linc* 02–11; R Clayfield Australia 11–18; Can Res Brisbane 14–18; Bp Grafton from 18. *Bishopsholme, 35 Victoria Street, Grafton NSW 2460, Australia* T: (0061) (2) 6642 4122 E: bishop@graftondiocese.org.au

HARVEY, Nicola Joan. b 70. Liv Ho Moores Univ BEd 93. St Aug Coll of Th 14. **d** 17 **p** 18. C Hadlow *Roch* from 17. *45 The Cherry Orchard, Hadlow, Tonbridge TN11 0HU* M: 07919-075470 E: harveynj@hotmail.com

HARVEY, Canon Norman Roy. b 43. Nottm Univ DipAE 86. Wycliffe Hall Ox 66. **d** 69 **p** 70. C Clay Cross *Derby* 69–72; C Dronfield 72–76; TV 76–79; P-in-c Rowsley 79–89; Dioc Youth Officer 79–83; Dioc Adv in Adult and Youth Educn 83–89; TR Eckington w Handley and Ridgeway 89–01; R Eckington and Ridgeway 01–08; RD Bolsover and Staveley 00–05; Hon Can Derby Cathl 00–08; rtd 08; PtO *Derby* 08–13; *Sheff* 09–11. *62 Parklands View, Aston, Sheffield S26 2GW* T: 0114-287 2243 E: norman.harvey3@gmail.com

HARVEY, Oliver Paul. b 33. Magd Coll Ox BA 55 MA 59. Cuddesdon Coll 57. **d** 59 **p** 60. C S Norwood St Mark *Cant* 59–61; C Hythe 61–64; Zambia 64–71; Chapl Cant Coll of Tech 71–77; Hon C Cant St Martin and St Paul 73–77; Chapl K Sch Roch 77–88; C Roch 88–90; V Gillingham St Mary 90–00; RD Gillingham 98–00; rtd 00; PtO *Roch* 00–03; *B & W* from 05. *11 Henley Road, Taunton TA1 5BN* T: (01823) 272825

HARVEY, Miss Pamela Betty. b 33. Dalton Ho Bris IDC 59. **dss** 68 **d** 87 **p** 95. Nottingham St Ann *S'well* 68–72; Bestwood St Matt 72–76; CPAS Staff 76–93; Dir Consultants Division CPAS 93–99; rtd 99; Hon C Glenfield *Leic* 95–04; PtO from 04. *72 Chestnut Road, Glenfield, Leicester LE3 8DB* T: 0116-232 2959 E: pamela.harvey@mypostoffice.co.uk

HARVEY, Canon Patrick Arnold. b 58. TCD MA. CITC 82. **d** 85 **p** 86. C Bandon Union *C, C & R* 85–88; Dean's V Limerick St Mich *L & K* 88–91; Dioc Info Officer 88–91; I Abbeyleix w Ballyroan etc *C & O* from 91; Can Ossory Cathl from 97; Chan from 11; Chan Leighlin Cathl *C & O* from 10; Can St Patr Cathl Dublin from 13; Can Ferns Cathl *C & O* from 14. *The Rectory, Abbeyleix, Portlaoise, Co Laois, R32 C6N1, Republic of Ireland* T/F: (00353) (57) 873 1243 E: patrickharveyone@gmail.com

HARVEY, Paul. *See* HARVEY, Oliver Paul

HARVEY, Philip Ian. b 61. Macquarie Univ (NSW) DipEd 85 BA 85 New England Univ NSW MA 94. Cam Th Federation 14. **d** 17 **p** 18. C Sprowston w Beeston *Nor* from 17. *62 Avocet Rise, Sprowston, Norwich NR7 8ES* T: (01603) 948222 E: philip@sprowston.org.uk

HARVEY, Robert Martin. b 30. S'wark Ord Course 69. **d** 70 **p** 71. C Sutton New Town St Barn *S'wark* 70–75; C Leatherhead *Guildf* 76–78; V Wadworth w Loversall *Sheff* 78–96; RD W Doncaster 94–97; rtd 96; PtO *Sheff* 96–13. *58 Thomson Avenue, Doncaster DN4 0NU* T: (01302) 857599

HARVEY, Robin Grant. b 43. Clare Coll Cam BA 64 MA 68 Univ of NSW PhD 74. Linc Th Coll 85. **d** 87 **p** 88. C Keynsham

B & W 87–91; R E w W Harptree and Hinton Blewett 91–97; Chapl Surrey Univ *Guildf* 98–02; P-in-c Cuddington 02–07; V 07–08; rtd 08; PtO *B & W* 09–19. *21 St Cadoc House, Temple Street, Keynsham, Bristol BS31 1HD* T: 0117-986 2295 E: rgharvey.194@btinternet.com

HARVEY, Canon Roland. b 68. St Jo Coll Nottm 99. **d** 01 **p** 02. C Skelmersdale St Paul *Liv* 01–05; P-in-c Pemberton St Fran Kitt Green 05–12; P-in-c Garston 12–14; V from 14; AD Liv S 14–19; Hon Can Liv Cathl from 14. *St Michael's Vicarage, 49 Harbour Drive, Liverpool L19 8AB* T: 0151-345 7475 M: 07817-901455 E: rolandharvey68@gmail.com

HARVEY, Ruth Anne. b 59. Leic Univ MB, ChB 83 Open Univ BA 02. St Mellitus Coll BA 12. **d** 13 **p** 14. NSM Broomfield *Chelmsf* from 13. *Ladyhope House, Mill Lane, Broomfield, Chelmsford CM1 7BQ* T: (01245) 443871 E: rev.anneharvey@gmail.com

HARVEY, Simon John. b 63. Trin Coll Bris BA 00. **d** 00 **p** 01. C Walsall St Paul *Lich* 00–03; TV Oadby *Leic* 03–10; Warden of Readers 05–10; V Islington St Mary *Lon* 10–19; V Bury St Edmunds St Mary *St E* from 19. *11 Sicklesmere Road, Bury St Edmunds IP33 2BN* M: 07376-060101 E: simon.harvey@sjharvey.org.uk

HARVEY, Canon Steven Charles. b 58. Reading Univ BA 79 Cam Univ PGCE 80 Ox Univ BA 83 MA 88. Ripon Coll Cuddesdon 81. **d** 84 **p** 85. C Oldham *Man* 84–87; Chapl and Hd RS St Pet Sch York 87–96; Sen Dep Hd Kingswood Sch Bath 96–03; Educn Officer and Sen Provost Woodard Corp 03–06; PtO *B & W* 96–03; *Lich* 03–06; Hd Master Bury Gr Sch 06–13; PtO *Blackb* 06–13; *Man* 06–13; Can Res Newc Cathl 13–19; rtd 19. *32 Ascot Close, Northallerton DL7 8BF* E: harveysteven@btinternet.com

HARVEY, Mrs Susan Esther. b 44. **d** 11 **p** 12. OLM Sherston Magna, Easton Grey, Luckington etc *Bris* 11–16; OLM Hullavington, Norton and Stanton St Quintin 15–16; OLM Gauzebrook from 16. *55 The Tarters, Sherston, Malmesbury SN16 0NT* T: (01666) 840696

HARVEY, Thomas James. b 71. Nottm Univ BA 92 Leic Univ MA 96 DipSW 96. Cranmer Hall Dur 09. **d** 11 **p** 12. C Cramlington *Newc* 11–14; P-in-c Felton from 14; P-in-c Longframlington w Brinkburn from 14. *The Vicarage, 1 Benlaw Grove, Felton, Morpeth NE65 9NG* T: (01670) 787263 M: 07722-405253 E: james.harvey@live.com

HARVEY, Mrs Tracey Louise. b 74. St Mellitus Coll 13. **d** 16 **p** 17. C Coggeshall w Markshall *Chelmsf* from 16; C Cressing w Stisted and Bradwell etc from 16. *109C Tilkey Road, Coggeshall, Colchester CO6 1QN* M: 07546-464175 E: tlharvey74@gmail.com

HARVEY, Mrs Verity Margaret. b 48. Bris Univ BA 69 Saltley Tr Coll Birm DipEd 70. SAOMC 99. **d** 02 **p** 03. NSM Radlett *St Alb* 02–05; NSM Bushey 05–11; Chapl Herts Partnership Univ NHS Foundn Trust from 10; PtO *St Alb* from 12. *28 Field Road, Watford WD19 4DR* T: (01923) 492863 E: verity.harvey@yahoo.co.uk

HARVEY, Wendy Marion. b 46. SEITE 06. **d** 09 **p** 10. NSM Hurst Green *S'wark* 09–14; NSM Limpsfield and Tatsfield 14–16 and from 18; Chapl HM Pris Downview 11–18; PtO *Lon* from 14; *Guildf* from 16; *S'wark* from 18. *St Andrew's House, Kent Hatch Road, Oxted RH8 0TB* T: (01883) 723153 M: 07973-428683 E: wendyharvey@talktalk.net

HARVIE, Robert. b 53. **d** 04 **p** 05. OLM Godalming *Guildf* from 04. *4 Bargate Court, Godalming GU7 2NA* T: (01483) 414378 E: robert.harvie@btinternet.com

HARWOOD (formerly SOUTH), Mrs Gillian. b 51. NEOC 87. **d** 90 **p** 94. C Rothbury *Newc* 90–93; C Morpeth 93–97; V Amble 97–06; Chapl Northumbria Healthcare NHS Foundn Trust 06–15; rtd 15; PtO *Newc* from 15. *7 Hedgerow Mews, Fallowfield, Ashington NE63 8LH* T: (01670) 810478 E: gillian.harwood@sky.com

HARWOOD, Canon Robin Rossiter. b 26. Selw Coll Cam BA 51 MA 55. Wycliffe Hall Ox 51. **d** 53 **p** 54. C Handsworth St Mary *Birm* 53–55; Tutor Trin Coll Umuahia Nigeria 57–64; Warden Minl Tr Cen Freetown Sierra Leone and Bp's Dom Chapl 64–67; Home Educn Sec CMS 67–75; V Cheltenham Ch Ch *Glouc* 75–91; RD Cheltenham 84–89; Hon Can Glouc Cathl 85–91; rtd 91; PtO *Ex* 91–99; *Chich* 00–18; *Portsm* from 00. *14 Nile Street, Emsworth PO10 7EE* T: (01243) 372215

HARWOOD, Mary Ann. b 46. Cam Inst of Educn CertEd 68. Ox Min Course 04. **d** 07 **p** 08. NSM Burghfield *Ox* 07–10; NSM W Downland 10–18; rtd 18; PtO *Ox* from 18. *10 Brook View, South Street, Letcombe Regis, Wantage OX12 9RG* M: 07721-437316 E: maryharwood695@btinternet.com

HARWOOD, Peter James. b 64. Birm Univ MB 88 ChB 88 K Coll Lon MA 02. Wycliffe Hall Ox BA 93 MA 98. **d** 94 **p** 95. C Cov H Trin 94–97; C Kensington St Barn *Lon* 97–02; V Woking Ch Ch *Guildf* from 02; Chapl Woking Hospice from 02; AD Woking *Guildf* from 16. *Christ Church Vicarage,*

10 Russetts Close, Woking GU21 4BH T: (01483) 762100 E: peter.harwood@christchurchwoking.org

HARWOOD, William Francis. b 78. Pemb Coll Ox MA 00 Keble Coll Ox MSt 19 New Coll Ox PGCE 05. Wycliffe Hall Ox BA 18. **d** 19. C Kea *Truro* from 19. *169 Treffry Road, Truro TR1 1UF* M: 07823-886788 E: will_harwood@me.com

HASELHURST (née STERLING), Mrs Anne. b 51. Macalester Coll (USA) BA 73. EAMTC 89. **d** 92 **p** 94. Par Dn Bury St Edmunds St Jo *St E* 92–94; C 94–95; V Fordham St Pet *Ely* 95–06; P-in-c Kennett 95–06; P-in-c Isleham 05–06; R Cupar *St And* 06–15; R Ladybank 06–15; rtd 15; PtO *St And* from 17. *7 Newmill Gardens, St Andrews KY16 8RY* T: (01334) 209068 E: annehaselhurst@talktalk.net

HASELOCK, Canon Jeremy Matthew. b 51. York Univ BA 73 BPhil 74. St Steph Ho Ox BA 82 MA 86. **d** 83 **p** 84. C Pimlico St Gabr *Lon* 83–86; C Paddington St Jas 86–88; Bp's Dom Chapl *Chich* 88–91; P-in-c Boxgrove 91–94; V 94–98; Dioc Adv on Liturgy 91–98; Can and Preb Chich Cathl 94–98; Can Res and Prec Nor Cathl 98–17; rtd 17; Chapl to The Queen from 13; PtO *Lon* from 17. *3 The Terrace, Old Ford Road, London E2 9PH* T: (020) 8980 6087

HASKETT, Mrs Fiona Ann. b 55. SEITE 01. **d** 04 **p** 05. NSM Leigh *Roch* 04–09; V Whittington w Weeford and Hints *Lich* 09–15; V Headcorn and The Suttons *Cant* from 15. *The Vicarage, 64 Oak Lane, Headcorn, Ashford TN27 9TB* E: fiona.haskett@btopenworld.com

HASKETT, Stephen Ian. b 78. Cranmer Hall Dur. **d** 13 **p** 14. C Anchorsholme *Blackb* 13–17; V Blackpool St Jo from 17. *St John's Vicarage, 32 Forest Gate, Blackpool FY3 9AW* T: (01253) 623190 M: 07890-248917 E: stevehaskett78@gmail.com

HASKINS, Thomas. b 41. TCD BA 72. CITC 71. **d** 73 **p** 74. C Larne and Inver *Conn* 73–78; C Antrim All SS 78–83; I Belfast St Mark 83–90; I Dublin Clontarf *D & G* 90–02; I Dublin St Ann and St Steph 02–08; Can Ch Ch Cathl Dublin 99–08; rtd 08. *7 Gorse Haven, Coolboy, Tinahely, Co Wicklow, Republic of Ireland* T: (00353) (402) 34997 E: tomhaskins2@gmail.com

HASLAM, Andrew James. b 57. Univ Coll Dur BSc 78 Coll of Ripon & York St Jo PGCE 79 Lambeth STh 84. Trin Coll Bris 80. **d** 83 **p** 84. C Leyland St Andr *Blackb* 83–86; C Hartford *Ches* 86–88; V Grimsargh *Blackb* 88–98; V St Helens St Mark *Liv* 98–05; V Birkenhead Ch Ch *Ches* 05–13; PtO from 13. *2 Millview Drive, Wirral CH63 8PL* T: 0151-792 6201 E: andrew.haslam@live.co.uk

HASLAM, John Gordon. b 32. Birm Univ LLB 53. Qu Coll Birm 75. **d** 77 **p** 77. Hon C Bartley Green *Birm* 77–79; Hon C Moseley St Mary 79–96; Chapl to The Queen 89–02; PtO *Heref* 97–18. *16 Mill Street, Ludlow SY8 1BE* T/F: (01584) 876663

HASLAM, Michael Henry. b 72. Buckingham Univ BA 93. Trin Coll Bris BA 94 MA 94. **d** 97 **p** 98. C Minehead *B & W* 97–00; Chapl Newc Univ 00–04; C Purton and Dioc Ecum Officer *Bris* 04–06; P-in-c N Swindon St Andr 06–09; NSM Alfred Jewel *B & W* from 10; Chapl Taunton Academy 11–17; Chapl Richard Huish Coll Taunton 16–17; Chapl Development Adv *B & W* from 17. *The New Rectory, Cliff Road, North Petherton, Bridgwater TA6 6NY* T: (01278) 662429 M: 07530-677493 E: mike.haslam@hotmail.co.uk

HASLER, Catherine Lesley. b 54. St Mellitus Coll 16. **d** 18 **p** 19. OLM Grays Thurrock *Chelmsf* from 18. *28 Orchard Drive, Grays RM17 5AF*

HASLER, Canon John Joseph. b 45. Univ of Wales (Cardiff) MPhil 99. Qu Coll Birm 89. **d** 90 **p** 91. C Horfield H Trin *Bris* 90–93; V Bris St Andr Hartcliffe 93–01; V Bris Lockleaze St Mary Magd w St Fran 01–15; AD City 03–06; Hon Can Bris Cathl 08–15; rtd 15. *Address withheld by request* E: joehasler@btinternet.com

HASLER, Kevin John. b 56. RGN 80 RMN 80. St Mich Coll Llan 03. **d** 06 **p** 07. NSM Raglan w Llandenny and Bryngwyn *Mon* 06–08; P-in-c Llangwm Uchaf and Llangwm Isaf w Gwernesney etc 08–12; PtO 13–15; V Usk Min Area from 15. *The Vicarage, 10 Cassia Drive, Usk NP15 1TZ* M: 07836-795753 E: kevin@hasler.org.uk *or* kevin@deanery.info

HASSALL, Mrs Elizabeth Claire. b 80. R Holloway Coll Lon BSc 01 Trin Coll Bris MA 11. BA 08. **d** 09 **p** 10. C Bempton w Flamborough, Reighton w Speeton *York* 09–13; V Coxwold and Husthwaite from 13; R Crayke w Brandsby and Yearsley from 13; RD Easingwold from 14; C Alne from 17; C Brafferton w Pilmoor, Myton-on-Swale etc from 17; C Easingwold w Raskelf from 17; C Skelton w Shipton and Newton on Ouse from 17; C Strensall from 17; C Forest of Galtres from 17. *The Rectory, Church Hill, Crayke, York YO61 4TA* T: (01347) 822809 E: revliz@trundlebug.co.uk

HASSALL, William Edwin. b 41. St Jo Coll Nottm 75. **d** 77 **p** 78. C Wellington w Eyton *Lich* 77–80; C Farewell 80–82; V 82–93; C Gentleshaw 80–82; V 82–93; P-in-c Cheddleton

93–94; PtO 97–09; Asst Chapl Birm Heartlands and Solihull NHS Trust 98–01; Chapl Team Ldr 01–06; rtd 06; PtO *Birm* 06–13; C Hatherton *Lich* 09–16; PtO from 16. *The Vicarage, Buds Road, Rugeley WS15 4NB* T: (01543) 670739 E: revbillhassall@outlook.com

HASSAN, Brian Joseph. b 67. CITC 05. d 08 p 09. NSM Clooney w Strathfoyle *D & R* 08–09; NSM Faughanvale from 09. *59 Newton Road, Limavady BT49 0UD* T: (028) 7776 6281 M: 07828-668342 E: brian.hassan2@btinternet.com

HASSELL, David Edwin. b 38. WMMTC 87. d 90 p 91. NSM Worc SE 90–93; C Abberton, Naunton Beauchamp and Bishampton etc 93–94; P-in-c 94; R Abberton, The Flyfords, Naunton Beauchamp etc 94–04; rtd 04; PtO *Worc* from 04. *14 Napleton Lane, Kempsey, Worcester WR5 3PT* T: (01905) 828096 E: davidhassellrev@aol.com

HASTED, Marcus Arthur David. b 35. Qu Coll Birm 63. d 66 p 67. C Woodchurch *Ches* 66–69; C W Kirby St Bridget 69–72; V Farndon 72–76; V Farndon and Coddington 76–79; PtO 98–00 and 02–14; NSM Liscard St Mary w St Columba 00–02. *62 South Road, West Kirby, Wirral CH48 3HQ* T: 0151-625 0428

HASTIE-SMITH, Timothy Maybury. b 62. Magd Coll Cam MA 84. Wycliffe Hall Ox 85. d 88 p 89. C Ox St Ebbe w H Trin and St Pet 88–91; Chapl Stowe Sch 91–98; Hd Master Dean Close Sch 98–08; TV S Cotswolds *Glouc* from 08. *The Parsonage, High Street, Kempsford, Fairford GL7 4ET* T: (01285) 810773 E: tim.hastie-smith@hotmail.com

HASTINGS, David Kerr. b 40. St Luke's Coll Ex CertEd 63. Ox NSM Course 84. d 87 p 88. Hd Master St Edburg's Sch Bicester 82–89; Asst Chapl HM Pris Grendon and HM Pris Spring Hill 87–89; NSM Bicester w Bucknell, Caversfield and Launton *Ox* 87–89; Chapl HM Pris Reading 90–92; P-in-c Gt Wishford *Sarum* 92; P-in-c S Newton 92; P-in-c Stapleford w Berwick St James 92; P-in-c Winterbourne Stoke 92; R Lower Wylye and Till Valley 92–95; Chapl HM Pris Ex 96–01; PtO *Ex* from 01; rtd 01. *26 Hoopern Street, Exeter EX4 4LY* T: (01392) 498233 E: david.godsquad@sky.com

HASTINGS, Canon Gary Lea. b 56. NUU BA 82 MA 87 TCD BTh 93. CITC 90. d 93 p 94. C Galway w Kilcummin *T, K & A* 93–95; I Aughaval w Achill, Knappagh, Dugort etc 95–09; I Galway w Kilcummin 09–18; Dom Chapl to Bp Tuam 94–12; Can Tuam Cathl 00–18; Adn Tuam 06–18; Can St Patr Cathl Dublin from 10; Can Killala Cathl *T, K & A* 13–18; I Killiney H Trin *D & G* from 18; Treas Ch Ch Cathl Dublin from 18. *Holy Trinity Rectory, Killiney Road, Killiney, Co Dublin, A96 HD62, Republic of Ireland* T: (00353) (01) 285 2695 E: gryh@me.com *or* rector.htkilliney@dublin.anglican.org

HASTWELL, James Sydney. b 37. Roch Th Coll 67. d 69 p 70. C Croydon St Aug *Cant* 69–73; C Hurstpierpoint *Chich* 73–75; P-in-c Twineham 76; P-in-c Sayers Common 76; P-in-c Albourne 76; R Albourne w Sayers Common and Twineham 76–88; V Forest Row 88–94; rtd 94; PtO *Chich* 97–09; *Nor* from 11. *4 East End Close, Caister-on-Sea, Great Yarmouth NR30 5PG* T: (01692) 678574 E: jen-jim@hotmail.co.uk

HASWELL, Jeremy William Drake. b 60. Qu Mary Coll Lon BSc 84. Ridley Hall Cam 06. d 08 p 09. C St Alb St Paul 08–13; PtO 13–15; C Grayshott *Guildf* 15–18; V from 18. *The Vicarage, 10 Vicarage Gardens, Grayshott, Hindhead GU26 6NH* T: (01428) 605254 E: revjeremy.grayshott@gmail.com

HATCHER, Mark. b 54. Ox Univ BA 77 MA 82 Barrister (Middle Temple) 78 FRSA 94 MCIPR 10. SEITE 09. d 12 p 13. NSM Brockley Hill St Sav *S'wark* 12–15; Reader of The Temple from 15; PtO *S'wark* from 17. *Temple Church Offices, 1 Inner Temple Lane, London EC4Y 1AF* T: (020) 8293 4969 *or* 7353 8559 M: 07801-038389 E: reader@templechurch.com

HATCHETT, Mrs Ruth Merrick. b 54. K Coll Lon BD 77 AKC 77 Open Univ BA 92. EAMTC 03. d 05 p 06. NSM Tolleshunt Knights w Tiptree and Gt Braxted *Chelmsf* 05–06; NSM Melton and Ufford *St E* 06–10; TV Wilford Peninsula from 10. *The Vicarage, 6 Rectory Road, Hollesley, Woodbridge IP12 3JS* T: (01394) 412052 E: ruth.hatchett@yahoo.com

HATHAWAY, John Albert. b 24. Sarum Th Coll 59. d 60 p 61. C Fleet *Guildf* 60–64; C Cowley St Jas *Ox* 64–66; V Holmwood *Guildf* 66–71; V Westborough 71–74; V Newmarket All SS *St E* 74–82; V Acton w Gt Waldingfield 82–85; R W Downland *Sarum* 85–90; rtd 90; PtO *Sarum* 94–10. *15 Stuart Court, High Street, Kibworth Beauchamp, Leicester LE8 0LR* T: 0116-279 2447

HATHAWAY, Martin Charles. b 48. St Jo Coll Nottm 93. d 95 p 96. C Weddington and Caldecote *Cov* 95–99; V Potters Green 99–04; C The Heyfords w Rousham and Somerton *Ox* 04–05; C Fritwell w Souldern and Ardley w Fewcott 04–05; TV Dunstable *St Alb* 05–13; rtd 13; PtO *Pet* from 15. *61 Symington Way, Market Harborough LE16 7XA* T: (01858) 288701 E: revd.martinhathaway@tiscali.co.uk

HATHORNE (née MARSH), Mrs Carol Ann. b 44. W Midl Coll of Educn BA 83. WMMTC 88. d 91 p 94. Par Dn Wednesbury St Paul Wood Green *Lich* 91–93; NSM Pensnett *Worc* 93–97; TV Cannock *Lich* 97–01; NSM Willenhall H Trin 05–11; NSM Bentley Em and Willenhall H Trin 11–12; PtO 12–17. *3 Kirton Grove, Wolverhampton WV6 8RX* E: hathorne@btinternet.com

HATHORNE, Mark Stephen. b 51. Boston Univ MDiv 76. d 00 p 00. C Willenhall H Trin *Lich* 00–01; TV 01–06; TR 06–11; P-in-c Bentley 06–09; TR Bentley Em and Willenhall H Trin 11–13; TV Bilston 13–17; rtd 17; PtO *Lich* from 18. *3 Kirton Grove, Wolverhampton WV6 8RX* E: mchathorne@virginmedia.com

HATTAWAY, Judith Helen Alison. b 53. Kent Univ BA 79 PGCE 80 Liv Univ MA 02 MBACP 00. STETS 07. d 10 p 11. NSM Hurst *Ox* 10–11; Asst Chapl Broadmoor Hosp Crowthorne 10–11; NSM Frimley *Guildf* 11–14; Asst Chapl Frimley Park Hosp NHS Foundn Trust 11–12; Lead Chapl 12–14; NSM Wokingham St Paul *Ox* from 15. *15 Rayner Drive, Arborfield, Reading RG2 9FB* T: 0118-976 1197 M: 07798-723232 E: judihattaway@mac.com

HATTON, Canon Jane Elizabeth. b 53. SAOMC 95. d 98 p 99. NSM Stevenage St Pet Broadwater *St Alb* 98–04; Chapl E and N Herts NHS Trust 03–17; Hon Can St Alb 16–17; rtd 18; PtO *St Alb* from 18. *2 Dancote, Park Lane, Knebworth SG3 6PB* T: (01438) 811039 E: janehatton@virginmedia.com

HATTON, Janet Ann. b 56. d 18 p 19. NSM Bromsgrove *Worc* from 18. *255 Pennine Road, Bromsgrove B61 0TN* E: janet.hatton1@btinternet.com

HATTON, Jeffrey Charles. b 49. K Coll Lon BD 70 Bris Univ MA 72. Westcott Ho Cam 72 Episc Th Sch Cam Mass 73. d 74 p 75. C Nor St Pet Mancroft 74–78; C Earlham St Anne 78–79; Relig Broadcasting Asst IBA 79–82; Hon C Kensington St Barn *Lon* 79–84; Hon C Fulham All SS 85–89; R Win All SS w Chilcomb and Chesil 89–94; Dioc Communications Officer 89–94; P-in-c Salisbury St Thos and St Edm *Sarum* 94–99; R 99–05; rtd 05; Hon C Chalke Valley *Sarum* 06–11; Hon C E Coker w Sutton Bingham and Closworth *B & W* 11–13; Hon C W Coker w Hardington Mandeville, E Chinnock etc 11–13; Hon C Coker Ridge 13–15. *35 Harnwood Road, Salisbury SP2 8DD* T: (01722) 505504

HATTON, Michael Samuel. b 44. St Jo Coll Dur BA 72. Cranmer Hall Dur. d 74 p 75. C Dudley St Jas *Worc* 74–75; C N Lynn w St Marg and St Nic *Nor* 75–77; C Walsall Wood *Lich* 78–79; Min Shelfield St Mark CD 79–89; V Middleton St Cross *Ripon* 89–97; V Ingol *Blackb* 97–11; rtd 11; PtO *Blackb* from 11. *7 Laurel Avenue, Euxton, Chorley PR7 6AY* T: (01257) 274584

HATWELL, Timothy Rex. b 53. Oak Hill Th Coll BA 85. d 85 p 86. C Tonbridge St Steph *Roch* 85–90; V Cudham and Downe 90–07; V Falconwood 07–15; R Ightham from 15; RD Shoreham from 16. *The Rectory, Bates Hill, Ightham, Sevenoaks TN15 9BG* T: (01732) 886827 M: 07799-601546 E: revtim.hatwell@gmail.com

HAUGH, Geoffrey Norman. d 13 p 14. Ballymore *Arm* 13–14; C Holywood *D & D* 14–17; I Knocknamuckley from 17. *The Rectory, 30 Moss Bank Road, Craigavon BT63 5SL* T: (028) 3883 2121 M: 07568-364573 E: geoff_karen@hotmail.co.uk *or* revghaugh@hotmail.com

HAUGHTON, Peter Steele. b 57. K Coll Lon BD 84 MA 90. Westcott Ho Cam 84. d 86 p 87. C Cheam Common St Phil *S'wark* 86–90; Chapl Lon Univ Medical Schs 90–94; Educn Adv 94–95; P-in-c Kingston Vale St Jo 95–03; Adv in Ethics and Law K Coll Lon 03–13; PtO *Win* 03–13; C Southampton (City Cen) 13–18; PtO from 18. *95 Bullar Road, Southampton SO18 1NT* T: (023) 8033 5187 M: 07815-803920 E: pshaughton@virginmedia.com

HAUGHTY, Miss Rebecca Mary. b 69. Coll of Resurr Mirfield 09. d 11 p 12. C Pocklington Wold and Londesborough Wold *York* 11–15; V Coatham and Dormanstown from 15. *9 Blenheim Terrace, Redcar TS10 1QP* M: 07518-412149 E: r.haughty@btinternet.com

HAVELL, Edward Michael. b 38. Dur Univ BA 65. Ridley Hall Cam 66. d 68 p 69. C Ecclesall *Sheff* 68–71; C Roch St Justus 71–74; P-in-c Holbeach Hurn *Linc* 74–75; C Hollington St Jo *Chich* 75–85; TV Rye 85–92; C E Dereham and Scarning *Nor* 92; rtd 93; PtO *Chich* from 99. *4 Gammons Way, Sedlescombe, Battle TN33 0RQ* T: (01424) 870864 E: lavell01@btinternet.com

HAVEY, Kenneth Richard. b 61. St Steph Ho Ox 95. d 97 p 98. C Corringham *Chelmsf* 97–98; C Leigh St Clem 98–02; R 02–13; P-in-c Hockley from 13. *The Vicarage, 6A Silvertree Close, Hockley SS5 4SP* T: (01702) 203668 E: kenneth.havey@btinternet.com

HAVILAND, Canon Andrew Mark James. b 65. Leeds Univ BEd 87. STETS 02. d 05 p 06. NSM N Holmwood *Guildf*

05–08; Chapl Bryanston Sch 08–19; Can and Preb Sarum Cathl 15–19; Sen Chapl Epsom Coll from 19; CF(V) from 15. *Epsom College, College Road, Epsom KT14 4JQ* T: (01372) 821000 M: 07756-698565

HAVILAND, Edmund Selwyn. b 24. K Coll Cam BA 49 MA 51. Wells Th Coll 49. d 51 p 52. C St Helier *S'wark* 51–55; C-in-c Bermondsey St Hugh CD 55–58; V Ockbrook *Derby* 58–68; V E Peckham *Roch* 68–78; R E Peckham and Nettlestead 78–84; S Africa 84–85; Dep Chapl HM Pris Brixton 85–89; rtd 89; PtO *Guildf* 89–19. *143 The Close, Salisbury SP1 2EY* T: (01722) 333140 M: 07880-682194 E: edmundshaviland@gmail.com

HAWES, Canon Andrew Thomas. b 54. Sheff Univ BA 77 Em Coll Cam MA 79. Westcott Ho Cam 77. d 80 p 81. C Gt Grimsby St Mary and St Jas *Linc* 80–84; P-in-c Gedney Drove End 84–86; P-in-c Sutton St Nicholas 84–86; V Lutton w Gedney Drove End, Dawsmere 86–89; V Edenham w Witham on the Hill 89–00; V Edenham w Witham on the Hill and Swinstead 00–18; RD Beltisloe 97–13; Can and Preb Linc Cathl 09–18; rtd 18. *Pilkingtons Lodge, Little Bytham, Grantham NG33 4RD* T: (01778) 590035

HAWES, The Ven Arthur John. b 43. UEA BA 86. Chich Th Coll 65. d 68 p 69. C Kidderminster St Jo *Worc* 68–72; P-in-c Droitwich 72–76; R Alderford w Attlebridge and Swannington *Nor* 76–92; Chapl Hellesdon and David Rice Hosps and Yare Clinic 76–92; RD Sparham *Nor* 81–91; Mental Health Act Commr 86–94; Hon Can Nor Cathl 88–95; TR Gaywood 92–95; Adn Linc and Can and Preb Linc Cathl 95–08; rtd 08; PtO *S'wark* 10–13; *Nor* 12–17; Hon C Barnham Broom and Upper Yare from 17. *29 Market Street, Shipdham, Thetford IP25 7LY* T: (01362) 822441 M: 07803-249834 E: arthur.hawes@yahoo.co.uk

HAWES, Mrs Joy Elizabeth. b 58. STETS 12. d 15 p 16. NSM Isle of Wedmore *B & W* 15–19; NSM Yeovil St Mich from 19. *Glencoe, Fishers Hill, Glastonbury BA6 8AH* T: (01458) 830659 M: 07968-156910 E: therevjoy@gmail.com

HAWES, Mary Elizabeth. b 56. SEITE 94. d 00 p 01. Dioc Children's Adv *Lon* 98–06; Nat Children's Adv Abps' Coun 06–12; Nat Going for Growth (Children and Youth) Adv from 12; NSM Streatham St Leon *S'wark* 00–11; NSM Teddington St Mary w St Alb *Lon* from 11. *47 Traherne Lodge, 64 Walpole Road, Teddington TW11 8PW* T: (020) 7898 1504 E: mary.hawes@churchofengland.org

HAWES, Ms Rachel. b 54. St Hugh's Coll Ox BA 76 MA 80. STETS 05. d 07 p 08. NSM Kensington St Mary Abbots w Ch Ch and St Phil *Lon* 07–10; NSM Notting Hill St Jo 10–16; P-in-c St Martin Ludgate 14–16; PtO *Chich* 17; NSM Chich St Paul and Westhampnett from 17. *Downcote Cottage, Summersdale Road, Chichester PO19 6PN* T: (01243) 539150 M: 07768-875590 E: rachel.hawes@outlook.com

HAWKEN, Andrew Robert. b 58. K Coll Lon BD 81 AKC 81. St Steph Ho Ox 83. d 85 p 86. C Ex St Dav 85–88; TV Witney *Ox* 88–93; V Benson 93–10; AD Aston and Cuddesdon 02–07; Hon Can Ch Ch 09–10; Chapl Midi-Pyrénées and Aude *Eur* 10–16; V E Grinstead St Swithun *Chich* from 16. *The Vicarage, Church Lane, East Grinstead RH19 3AZ* T: (01342) 323307 M: 07503-573486 E: vicareg16@gmail.com

HAWKEN, Rosalind Mary. b 56. York Univ BA 77 Univ of Wales (Cardiff) BTh 02. St Mich Coll Llan 99. d 02 p 03. C Swansea St Thos and Kilvey *S & B* 02–03; C Gorseinon 03–07. *Society of the Sacred Cross, Tymawr Convent, Lydart, Monmouth NP25 4RN* T: (01600) 860244

HAWKER, The Ven Alan Fort. b 44. Hull Univ BA 65. Clifton Th Coll 65. d 68 p 69. C Bootle St Leon *Liv* 68–71; C Fazakerley Em 71–73; V Goose Green 73–81; TR Southgate *Chich* 81–98; Can and Preb Chich Cathl 91–98; RD E Grinstead 94–98; Hon Can Bris Cathl 98–10; Adn Swindon 98–99; Adn Malmesbury 99–10; rtd 10; PtO *Cov* from 11. *21 Paddocks Close, Wolston, Coventry CV8 3GW* T: (024) 7654 4021 E: alanandjen68@gmail.com *or* p.winchester123@btinternet.com

HAWKER, Alan John. b 53. K Coll Lon BD 76 AKC 76. Sarum & Wells Th Coll 77. d 78 p 79. C Coleford w Staunton *Glouc* 78–81; C Up Hatherley 81–84; V Plymouth St Jas Ham *Ex* 84–92; TV Worc SE 92–99; TR Leic Presentation 99–03; P-in-c Leic St Chad 02–03; PtO 09–10; NSM Eyres Monsell 10–11; R Narborough and Huncote 11–19; rtd 19. *318 Victoria Park Road, Leicester LE2 1XE* T: a.hawker87@btinternet.com

HAWKER, Brian Henry. b 34. AKC 61 St Boniface Warminster 61. d 62 p 63. C Hemel Hempstead *St Alb* 62–66; R Stone w Hartwell w Bishopstone *Ox* 66–69; Chapl St Jo Hosp 66–69; V W Wycombe *Ox* 69–72; Past Consultant Clinical Th Assn 72–83; Past Consultant 83–94; Public Preacher *S'well* 76–95; PtO *B & W* 76–83; *Truro* 83–90; rtd 94; PtO *Leic* 99–09. *12 Burfield Avenue, Loughborough LE11 3AZ* T: (01509) 261439

HAWKER, Canon Peter John. b 37. Ex Univ BA 59. Wycliffe Hall Ox 69. d 70 p 71. Asst Chapl Berne *Eur* 70–76; Chapl Berne w Neuchâtel 76–89; Switzerland 86–04; Chapl Zürich w St Gallen, Baden and Zug 90–00; Can Brussels Cathl 86–04; rtd 04. *Schulgasse 10, 3280 Murten, Switzerland* T: (0041) (26) 670 6221 F: 670 6219 E: phawker@anglican.ch

HAWKES, Canon Cecilia Mary (Cilla). b 48. Reading Univ BSc 69 Canley Coll of Educn DipEd 71. EAMTC 99. d 02 p 03. NSM Takeley w Lt Canfield *Chelmsf* 02–10; NSM Stebbing and Lindsell w Gt and Lt Saling from 10; NSM Broxted w Chickney and Tilty etc from 18; Voc Officer Colchester Area from 08; RD Dunmow and Stansted from 10; Hon Can Chelmsf Cathl from 15. *Greenfields, Felsted, Dunmow CM6 3LF* T/F: (01371) 856480 E: cilla@hawkesfarming.co.uk

HAWKES, Mrs Elisabeth Anne. b 56. GRNCM 78 PGCE 80 Kent Univ MA 97. Linc Th Coll 86. d 88 p 97. Hon Par Dn Finham *Cov* 88–90; Hon Par Dn Bexhill St Pet *Chich* 90–97; Asst to RD Oundle *Pet* 97–98; NSM 98–00; NSM Benefield and Southwick w Glapthorn 99–00; PtO *Cant* 00–04; Hon Min Can Cant Cathl 03–12; NSM Reculver and Herne Bay St Bart 04–12; NSM St Nicholas at Wade w Sarre and Chislet w Hoath 04–12; Dioc Adv in Liturgy 04–12; NSM Wykeham *Ox* 12–20; rtd 20. *The New Rectory, Sibford Gower, Banbury OX15 5RW* T: (01295) 780555 E: revlizhawkes@gmail.com

HAWKES, Mrs Helen Vanda. b 50. Surrey Univ BA 01. STETS 98. d 01 p 02. NSM N Hayling St Pet and Hayling Is St Andr *Portsm* 01–05; NSM Bedhampton 05–11; rtd 11; PtO *Portsm* from 11. *67 East Lodge Park, Farlington, Portsmouth PO16 1BZ* T: (023) 9221 9005 M: 07719-828113 E: vanda.hawkes@btinternet.com

HAWKES, Keith Andrew. b 28. Oak Hill Th Coll 72. d 74 p 75. C Gt Yarmouth *Nor* 74–77; C-in-c Bowthorpe CD 77; Chapl Düsseldorf *Eur* 77–83; TV Quidenham *Nor* 83–88; TR 88–90; RD Thetford and Rockland 86–90; R Wickmere w Lt Barningham, Itteringham etc 90–96; Dioc Rural Officer 90–94; P-in-c Saxthorpe w Corpusty, Blickling, Oulton etc 94–96; R Lt Barningham, Blickling, Edgefield etc 96–98; Bp's Chapl 98; rtd 98; PtO *Nor* 98–00 and from 04; P-in-c Guiltcross 00–03; Chapl Norwich Primary Care Trust 00–02; Chapl Riddlesworth Hall Sch Nor from 04. *Peel Cottage, West Church Street, Kenninghall, Norwich NR16 2EN* T/F: (01953) 888533 E: revkahawkes@aol.com

HAWKES, Nigel Anthony Robert. b 59. UEA BSc 80 Edin Univ MSc 82. Ripon Coll Cuddesdon 00. d 02 p 03. C Chase *Ox* 02–04; C Chipping Norton 04–05; TV Dorchester 05–11; P-in-c Wheatley 11–14; V Albury w Tiddington etc from 14. *The Vicarage, 18 London Road, Wheatley, Oxford OX33 1YA* T: (01865) 872224 E: vicar.wheatley@gmail.com

HAWKES, Vanda. *See* HAWKES, Helen Vanda

HAWKETT, Graham Kenneth. b 20. Bps' Coll Cheshunt 61. d 63 p 64. C Farncombe *Guildf* 63–67; V Wyke 67–85; rtd 85; PtO *Guildf* 85–14. *Bede House, Beech Road, Haslemere GU27 2BX* T: (01428) 656430 E: grahamhawkett@yahoo.com

HAWKEY, Canon James Douglas Thomas. b 79. Girton Coll Cam BA 01 MA 05 Selw Coll Cam MPhil 02 PhD 08. Westcott Ho Cam 03 St Thos Aquinas Pontifical Univ Rome 06. d 07 p 08. C Portsea St Mary *Portsm* 07–10; Min Can and Sacr Westmr Abbey 10–13; Prec Westmr Abbey 13–15; Dean Clare Coll Cam 15–19; Asst Dir of Ords *Ely* 16–19; PV Westmr Abbey 15–19; Can Th Westmr Abbey from 19; Visiting Lect K Coll Lon from 19; Chapl to The Queen from 17. *The Chapter Office, 20 Dean's Yard, London SW1P 3PA* T: (020) 7222 5152 M: 07792-908026 E: jdth2@cam.ac.uk

HAWKINGS, Timothy Denison. b 55. Ex Univ BA 78. St Jo Coll Nottm BA 80. d 81 p 82. C Penn *Lich* 81–85; TV Stafford 85–94; TR Stratton St Margaret w S Marston etc *Bris* 94–05; P-in-c Axbridge w Shipham and Rowberrow *B & W* 05–11; R from 11; P-in-c Mark w Allerton 08–10; RD Axbridge 08–14. *The Rectory, Cheddar Road, Axbridge BS26 2DL* T: (01934) 732261 E: revhawkings@googlemail.com

HAWKINS, The Very Revd Alun John. b 44. K Coll Lon BA 66 AKC 66 Univ of Wales (Ban) BD 81. St Deiniol's Hawarden 78. d 81 p 82. C Dwygyfylchi *Ban* 81–84; R Llanberis 84–89; Tutor Ban Dioc NSM Course 85–90; Dir of Ords Ban 86–90; V Knighton and Norton *S & B* 89–93; Chapl Knighton Hosp 89–93; TR Bangor *Ban* 93–06; Adult Educn Officer 93–11; Sec Dioc Bd of Miss 93–11; Can Res and Can Missr Ban Cathl 93–00; Adn Ban 00–04; Dean Ban 04–11; rtd 11; PtO *Ban* from 11. *9 Cil y Craig, Llanfairpwllgwyngyll LL61 5NZ* T: (01248) 717403

HAWKINS (née BRAZIER), Mrs Annette Michaela. b 56. Brighton Univ BEd 95 Homerton Coll Cam BTh. Ridley Hall Cam 07. d 09 p 10. C Ore St Helen and St Barn *Chich* 09–16; V Salehurst, Hurst Green and Robertsbridge from

16. *4 Glenleigh Walk, Robertsbridge TN32 5DQ* T: (01424) 423859 M: 07900-332791 E: annette@jhbd.co.uk

HAWKINS, Canon Bruce Alexander. b 44. Qu Coll Ox BA 66 MA 71. Sarum Th Coll 66. d 68 p 69. C Epsom St Martin *Guildf* 68–71; Dioc Youth Chapl *Cant* 72–81; Hon Min Can Cant Cathl 75–99; Dep Dir of Educn 81–86; V Walmer 86–05; RD Sandwich 94–00; Hon Can Cant Cathl 99–05; rtd 05; PtO *Cant* from 05. *88 The Gateway, Dover CT16 1LQ* T: (01304) 240820 E: brucehawkins0701@gmail.com

HAWKINS, Mrs Christine Ann. b 56. SEITE 98. d 01 p 02. NSM Epping Distr *Chelmsf* 01–02; C Woodford St Mary w St Phil and St Jas 02–05; P-in-c Hatfield Broad Oak and Bush End 05–07; Ind Chapl Harlow 05–07; Chapl Princess Alexandra Hosp NHS Trust 07–14; TV Louth *Linc* 15–17; P-in-c Fyfield, Moreton w Bobbingworth etc *Chelmsf* from 17; P-in-c High Laver w Magdalen Laver and Lt Laver etc from 18. *The Rectory, 6 Forest Drive, Fyfield, Ongar CM5 0TP* T: (01277) 899866 E: revcah56@gmail.com

HAWKINS, Canon Clive Ladbrook. b 53. St Pet Coll Ox BA 76 MA 79. Trin Coll Bris 80. d 82 p 83. C Win Ch Ch 82–86; R Eastrop from 86; AD Basingstoke 00–08; Hon Can Win Cathl from 05. *Eastrop Rectory, 2A Wallis Road, Basingstoke RG21 3DW* T: (01256) 355507 *or* 464249 E: clive.hawkins@stmarys-basingstoke.org.uk

HAWKINS, David Kenneth Beaumont. b 36. Em Coll Saskatoon LTh 63. d 63 p 64. C Northminster Canada 63–69; C Belleville Ch Ch 69–71; I Wellington 71–79; I Barriefield w Pittsburgh 80–85; C St Alb St Paul 85–87; C Hednesford *Lich* 87–92; R Buildwas and Leighton w Eaton Constantine etc 92–95; TV Wrockwardine Deanery 95–01; rtd 01. *PO Box 454, 131 Westwind Crescent, Wellington ON K0K 3L0, Canada* T: (001) (613) 399 5666 E: rowenadavid@sympatico.ca

HAWKINS, Mrs Dorothy. b 56. RGN 77 RM 79. All SS Cen for Miss w Min 07. d 14 p 15. OLM Worsley *Man* from 14. *4 Ryecroft Lane, Worsley, Manchester M28 2PN* T: 0161-794 5072 E: dh89@btinternet.com

HAWKINS, Ivor Geoffrey. b 15 p 16. NSM Garthbeibio, Llanerfel and Llangadfan *St As* 15–16; NSM Caereinion Miss Area from 17. *Ceunant, Pont Robert, Meifod SY22 6JN* T: (01938) 500483 E: hawkinsceunant@aol.com

HAWKINS, James Reginald. b 39. Ex Univ BA 61 Hull Univ MA 00. Westcott Ho Cam 61. d 63 p 64. C Cannock *Lich* 63–66; C Wem 66–67; C Cheddleton 67–69; R Yoxall 69–77; R The Quinton *Birm* 77–84; V Bosbury w Wellington Heath etc *Heref* 84–96; P-in-c Ancaster Wilsford Gp *Linc* 96–99; R 99–04; RD Loveden 97–03; rtd 04; PtO *Bris* from 05. *14 Pound Pill, Corsham SN13 9JA* T: (01249) 715353 E: jrhawkins74@outlook.com

HAWKINS, John Colin. b 50. SEITE 97. d 00 p 01. NSM W Wickham St Jo *S'wark* 00–04; P-in-c Burwash Weald *Chich* 04–11; PtO from 11. *Bell Cottage, Vinehall Road, Mountfield, Robertsbridge TN32 5JN* E: john.c.hawkins@btinternet.com

HAWKINS, The Ven John Edward Inskipp. b 63. K Coll Lon BD 85. Qu Coll Birm 86. d 88 p 89. C Birchfield *Birm* 88–92; C Poplar *Lon* 92–93; TV 93–99; V W Hendon St Jo 99–15; P-in-c Colindale St Matthias 07–15; AD W Barnet 04–09; Adn Hampstead from 15; Preb St Paul's Cathl from 13. *13 Kingscroft Road, London NW2 3QE* E: jeih.stj@tiscali.co.uk *or* archdeacon.hampstead@london.anglican.org

HAWKINS, Jonathan Desmond. b 53. FRICS 93. Ox Min Course 04. d 07 p 08. NSM Walton H Trin *Ox* 07–09; NSM Southcourt 09–10; NSM Haddenham w Cuddington, Kingsey etc 10–16; NSM Wychert Vale from 16. *Croft End, 1A White Hart Lane, Haddenham, Aylesbury HP17 8BB* T: (01844) 299429 M: 07976-281699 E: jon@jdhawkins.co.uk

HAWKINS, Nicholas Milner. b 45. Univ of Wales (Swansea) BA 69 MSc 71. d 01 p 05. Par Dn Dingestow and Llangovan w Penyclawdd etc *Mon* 01–02; PtO *Ban* 02–03; NSM Nefyn w Tudweiliog w Llandudwen w Edern 03–08; P-in-c Botwnnog w Bryncroes w Llangwnnadl w Penllech 08–12; rtd 12; C Dawlish *Ex* 12–15; C Kenton, Mamhead, Powderham, Cofton and Starcross 12–15; C Dawlish, Cofton and Starcross 15–18. *Harlea, The Strand, Starcross, Exeter EX6 8PA* T: (01626) 899166 M: 07870-264385 E: rev.starcross@gmail.com

HAWKINS, Noel. b 46. St Jo Coll Nottm 82. d 84 p 85. C Worksop St Jo *S'well* 84–86; C Wollaton Park 86–89; TV Billericay and Lt Burstead *Chelmsf* 89–95; TV Keynsham *B & W* 95–00; V Brislington St Chris and St Cuth *Bris* 00–08; V Brislington St Chris 08–12; P-in-c Hengrove 06–12; rtd 12; PtO *B & W* from 13. *17 White Horse Drive, Frome BA11 2DA* T: (01373) 451305 E: henbriznl@gmail.com

HAWKINS, Canon Patricia Sally. b 59. LMH Ox BA 80 MA 84 Ex Univ BPhil 85 Ox Univ BTh 04 CQSW 83. St Steph Ho Ox 99. d 01 p 02. C Stafford *Lich* 01–04; V Oxley 04–14; AD Wolverhampton 08–11; RD Wulfrun

11–14; Can Res Lich Cathl from 14; Preb Lich Cathl from 09. *23 The Close, Lichfield WS13 7LD* T: (01543) 306142 E: pat.hawkins@lichfield-cathedral.org

HAWKINS, Paul Henry Whishaw. b 46. Ex Coll Ox BA 68 MA 74 SS Coll Cam MA 84. St Steph Ho Ox 70. d 72 p 73. C Fawley *Win* 72–75; C Ealing St Steph Castle Hill *Lon* 75–77; P-in-c Dorney *Ox* 77–78; TV Riverside 78–81; Chapl SS Coll Cam 82–87; V Plymstock *Ex* 87–97; RD Plymouth Sutton 91–96; TR Plymstock and Hooe 97–00; Preb Ex Cathl 98–00; P-in-c St Pancras w St Jas and Ch Ch *Lon* 00–02; V 02–11; rtd 11; PtO *Bris* from 11. *Ground Floor Flat, 9 Buckingham Place, Clifton, Bristol BS8 1LJ* T: 0117-946 7506 E: jackie.schubert@hotmail.com

HAWKINS, Peter Edward. b 35. Leeds Univ BA 60. Coll of Resurr Mirfield 60. d 62 p 63. C Forest Gate St Edm *Chelmsf* 62–65; C Sevenoaks St Jo *Roch* 65–68; Chapl Metrop Police Cadet Corps Tr Sch 68–73; P-in-c Knowle H Nativity *Bris* 73; TV Knowle 73–79; V Westbury-on-Trym H Trin 79–87; TR Solihull *Birm* 87–96; Hon Can Birm Cathl 92–96; rtd 00. *Back Street Cottage, 15 St Andrew's Road, Stogursey, Bridgwater TA5 1TE* T/F: (01278) 733635 E: peterhawkins15@googlemail.com *or* peh.stogursey@tiscali.co.uk

HAWKINS, Peter Michael. b 38. Kelham Th Coll 58. d 63 p 64. Ox Miss to Calcutta India 63–64; C Calcutta Cathl 64–66; C-in-c Kidderpore 66–68; V Asansol w Burnpur 68–69; C Manningham St Paul and St Jude *Bradf* 70–72; C Bradf Cathl 72–75; V Allerton 75–90; V Pet H Spirit Bretton 90–07; P-in-c Marholm 90–95; rtd 07. *Le Pavillon, Mané Gouélo, RD 765, 56690 Landaul, France* T: (0033) 2 97 59 90 83 M: 6 48 42 78 70 E: peterhawkins@sfr.fr

HAWKINS, Mrs Rachel Ann. b 76. Trin Coll Bris 09. d 11 p 12. C Long Eaton St Jo *Derby* 11–15; V Rushden St Pet Pet from 15. *St Peter's Vicarage, 12 Kensington Close, Rushden NN10 6RR* T: (01933) 356398 E: revrach@hotmail.co.uk

✠**HAWKINS, The Rt Revd Richard Stephen.** b 39. Ex Coll Ox BA 61 MA 65 Ex Univ BPhil 76. St Steph Ho Ox 61. d 63 p 64 c 88. C Ex St Thos 63–66; C Clyst St Mary 66–75; TV Clyst St George, Aylesbeare, Clyst Honiton etc 75–78; TV Cen Ex 78–81; Bp's Officer for Min and Jt Dir Ex and Truro NSM Scheme 78–81; Dioc Dir of Ords 79–81; Adn Totnes 81–88; P-in-c Oldridge and Whitestone 81–87; Suff Bp Plymouth 88–96; Suff Bp Crediton 96–04; rtd 04; Hon Asst Bp Ex from 05. *3 Westbrook Close, Exeter EX4 8BS* T: (01392) 462622 E: valrid@aol.com

HAWKINS, Canon Richard Whishaw. b 51. Coll of Resurr Mirfield 93. d 95 p 96. C Weymouth H Trin *Sarum* 95–99; P-in-c Hey *Man* 99–06; TR Medlock Head 06–16; AD Saddleworth 03–09; Hon Can Man Cathl 12–16; rtd 16; PtO *Man* from 16. *45 Otmoor Way, Royton, Oldham OL2 6SD* T: (01706) 844391 M: 07801-241428 E: richardhawkins190@gmail.com

HAWKINS, Roger David William. b 33. K Coll Lon BD 58 AKC 58. d 59 p 60. C Twickenham St Mary *Lon* 59–61; C Heston 61–64; C Dorking w Ranmore *Guildf* 64–65; V Mitcham St Mark *S'wark* 65–74; V Redhill St Matt 74–91; P-in-c Warlingham w Chelsham and Farleigh 91–97; TR 97–98; rtd 98; PtO *Guildf* 11–13. *26 Ramsay Hall, 9-13 Byron Road, Worthing BN11 3HN* T: (01903) 411060 E: rdwhawki@hotmail.com

HAWKINS, Roger Julian. b 32. Ripon Hall Ox 59. d 61 p 62. C-in-c Newall Green CD *Man* 61–63; Chapl RAF 63–67; R Mawgan in Pyder *Truro* 67–75; R Lanteglos by Camelford w Advent 75–78; R Newmarket St Mary w Exning St Agnes *St E* 78–85; P-in-c Coltishall w Gt Hautbois *Nor* 85–87; R Coltishall w Gt Hautbois and Horstead 87–90; Chapl Whiteley Village *Guildf* 90–94; rtd 97; PtO *Win* 01–02; *Sarum* 02–08; *Nor* from 10. *3 Norman Cockaday Court, Holt NR25 6JA* T: (01263) 710004

HAWKINS, Susan. b 47. Doncaster Coll of Educn CertEd 69 Ches Coll of HE BTh 99. NOC 95. d 99 p 00. NSM Prestbury *Ches* 99–02; P-in-c Marthall and Chapl David Lewis Cen for Epilepsy 02–09; rtd 09; PtO *Ches* from 09; *Eur* from 18. *3 Thorne Close, Prestbury, Macclesfield SK10 4DE* T: (01625) 829833 E: suehawkins03@virginmedia.com

HAWKINS, Timothy St John. b 59. CCC Ox BA 82. Trin Coll Bris BA 87. d 87 p 88. C Cheltenham St Mary, St Matt, St Paul and H Trin *Glouc* 87–90; C Cowplain *Portsm* 90–94; V Pennycross *Ex* 94–96; P-in-c St Keverne *Truro* 96–05; P-in-c Gulval and Madron 05–16; V from 16. *The Vicarage, Church Road, Madron, Penzance TR20 8SW* T: (01736) 360992 E: revtimhawkins@gmail.com

HAWKSLEY, Katharine Mary. b 82. d 16 p 17. C Chard St Mary w Combe St Nicholas, Wambrook etc *B & W* from 16. *83 Brutton Way, Chard TA20 2HB* M: 07812-488991

HAWKSWORTH, Maldwyn Harry. b 45. Aston Univ CertEd 74. St Jo Coll Nottm 87. **d** 89 **p** 90. C Penn *Lich* 89–94; TV Bloxwich 94–09; Local Min Adv (Wolverhampton) 09–15; Local Par Development Adv Wolverhampton Area 10–15; P-in-c Yoxall 09–17; rtd 17; PtO *Lich* from 17. *118 Haymoor, Lichfield WS14 9SX*

HAWKSWORTH, Peter John Dallas. b 54. St Jo Coll Ox BA 75 MA 79 Solicitor 79. Sarum & Wells Th Coll 89. **d** 91 **p** 92. C Warminster St Denys, Upton Scudamore etc *Sarum* 91–95; P-in-c Salisbury St Mark 95–99; V 99–05; RD Salisbury 03–05; PtO from 07. *6 Newton Rise, Swanage BH19 2QP* E: onehundredkilos@btinternet.com or confluence@btinternet.com

HAWLEY, Canon Anthony Broughton. b 41. St Pet Coll Ox BA 67 MA 71. Westcott Ho Cam 67. **d** 69 **p** 70. C Wolverhampton St Pet *Lich* 69–72; C-in-c Bermondsey St Hugh CD *S'wark* 73–84; Hon PV S'wark Cathl 83–84; TR Kirkby *Liv* 84–02; AD Walton 93–02; Hon Can Liv Cathl 96–02; Can Res Liv Cathl 02–11; rtd 11; PtO *Sarum* from 12. *Pimlico Cottage, Black Lane, Lover, Salisbury SP5 2PQ* T: (01794) 390607 E: anthonybhawley@gmail.com

HAWLEY, The Ven John Andrew. b 50. K Coll Lon BD 71 AKC 71. Wycliffe Hall Ox 72. **d** 74 **p** 75. C Kingston upon Hull H Trin *York* 74–77; C Bradf Cathl Par 77–80; V Woodlands *Sheff* 80–91; TR Dewsbury *Wakef* 91–02; Hon Can Wakef Cathl 98–02; Adn Blackb 02–15; Bp's Adv on UPA 02–15; Bp's Adv on Hospice and Hosp Chapl 13–15; Bp's Adv on Pris Chapl 14–15; rtd 15; PtO *Sheff* from 15; *York* from 15; *Leeds* from 17; Acting Adn Doncaster *Sheff* from 19. *35 Woodland Avenue, Goole DN14 6QT* T: (01405) 762678 M: 07980-945035 E: john.hawley627@gmail.com

HAWLEY, Nigel David. b 51. Coll of Resurr Mirfield 77. **d** 80 **p** 81. C Birch w Fallowfield *Man* 80–84; P-in-c Moston St Jo 84–85; R 85–93; R Reddish 93–06; Co-ord Chapl HM Pris Forest Bank 06–07; Co-ord Chapl HM Pris Risley 08–16; Lic Preacher *Man* 07–16; rtd 16; PtO *Leeds* from 16. *Rosa Mystica, 31 Barnsley Road, Cawthorne, Barnsley S75 4HW* M: 07812-489776 E: nigelhawley@gmail.com

HAWORTH, Canon Mark Newby. b 50. Aber Univ BSc 73 MICFor 81. Westcott Ho Cam 88. **d** 90 **p** 91. C Cherry Hinton St Andr *Ely* 90–93; C Teversham 90–93; P-in-c Swaffham Bulbeck and Swaffham Prior w Reach 93–94; V 94–02; Sub Warden of Readers 95–02; RD Fordham 96–02; Chapl Framlingham Coll and Brandeston Hall Sch 03; Chapl to Bp Pet 03–05; TR Pendleton *Man* 05–09; P-in-c Lower Kersal 06–09; TR Salford All SS 09–12; Borough Dean Salford 10–12; R Rochdale 12–13; Hon Can Man Cathl 12–13; TR Bury St Edmunds All SS w St Jo and St Geo *St E* from 13; P-in-c Lark Valley from 14; RD Thingoe from 14; Hon Can St E Cathl from 16. *The Rectory, 59 Bennett Avenue, Bury St Edmunds IP33 3JJ* T/F: (01284) 755374 M: 07932-160009 E: rectornorthburyteam@btinternet.com

HAWORTH, Paul. b 47. G&C Coll Cam BA 68 MA 72. Westcott Ho Cam 75. **d** 78 **p** 79. C Hornchurch St Andr *Chelmsf* 78–81; C Loughton St Mary and St Mich 81–88; TV Waltham H Cross 88–92; TR Becontree S 92–00; P-in-c S Woodham Ferrers 00–11; rtd 11; PtO *Chelmsf* from 11. *25 Cambridge Street, Normanton WF6 1ET* T: (01924) 219360 M: 07986-535425 E: onthemat@btconnect.com

HAWORTH, Stanley Robert. b 48. St Jo Coll Dur BA 69. Sarum & Wells Th Coll 71. **d** 73 **p** 74. C Skipton H Trin *Bradf* 73–76; C Bradf Cathl 76–78; C Grantham *Linc* 78–82; V Deeping St James 82–96; V Middlewich w Byley *Ches* 96–01; P-in-c Forcett and Aldbrough and Melsonby *Ripon* 01–12; AD Richmond 08–12; rtd 12; PtO *Pet* from 12. *45 Finedon Road, Irthlingborough, Wellingborough NN9 5TY* T: (01933) 653798 E: stantherevman@hotmail.com

HAWORTH, Stuart. b 43. **d** 94 **p** 95. OLM Bradshaw *Man* 94–01; OLM Turton Moorland 01–08; rtd 08; PtO *Man* from 08. *39 Patterdale Road, Bolton BL2 3LX* T: (01204) 384006

HAWRISH, Mary-Beth Louise Ladine. b 51. **d** 09 **p** 10. OLM Oxshott *Guildf* 09–17; NSM N Hants Downs *Win* from 17. *The Parsonage, Gaston Lane, South Warnborough, Hook RG29 1RH* E: mhawrish@yahoo.co.uk

HAWTHORN, The Ven Christopher John. b 36. Qu Coll Cam BA 60 MA 64. Ripon Hall Ox 60. **d** 62 **p** 63. C Sutton St Jas *York* 62–66; V Kingston upon Hull St Nic 66–72; V E Coatham 72–79; V Scarborough St Martin 79–91; RD Scarborough 82–91; Can and Preb York Minster 87–01; Adn Cleveland 91–01; rtd 01; PtO *York* from 01. *Wetherlam, 11 Holly Tree Lane, Haxby, York YO32 3YJ* T: (01904) 591008

HAWTHORN, David. b 63. Chich Th Coll 87. **d** 90 **p** 91. C Hartlepool H Trin *Dur* 90–94; C Middlesbrough All SS *York* 94–95; P-in-c Thornaby on Tees 95–96; V S Thornaby 96–02; P-in-c Brighton Annunciation *Chich* 02–04; V Hollinwood and Limeside *Man* 04–18; rtd 18. *Hawthorn Cottage, Sloothby,*

Alford LN13 9NS, or *Casa São Oscar Romero, Rua da Fonta Velha 1, Salgueiro, 2540-435 Bombarral, Portugal* T: 0161-241 9424 or (00351) 262 608 230

HAWTHORN, Philip Alan. b 58. Essex Univ BSc 79. Ripon Coll Cuddesdon 05. **d** 07 **p** 08. C Hardington Vale *B & W* 07–10; P-in-c Charlcombe w Bath St Steph 10–16; R from 16. *The Rectory, Richmond Place, Bath BA1 5PZ* T: (01225) 466114 M: 07973-350560 E: philiphawthorn@btinternet.com or philip@ststephensbath.org.uk

HAWTHORNE, John William. b 32. St Aug Coll Cant 74. **d** 77 **p** 78. C Boxley *Cant* 77–80; P-in-c Otham 80–82; P-in-c Langley 80–82; R Otham w Langley 82–83; TR Preston w Sutton Poyntz, Littlemoor etc *Sarum* 83–87; R Tetbury w Beverston *Glouc* 87–01; rtd 01; PtO *Ex* 02–16; *Sarum* from 06; *Bris* from 12. *19 Long Street, Devizes SN10 1NN* T: (01380) 728056 E: j.hawthorne146@btinternet.com

✠**HAWTIN, The Rt Revd David Christopher.** b 43. Keble Coll Ox BA 65 MA 70. Wm Temple Coll Rugby 65 Cuddesdon Coll 66. **d** 67 **p** 68 **c** 99. C Pennywell St Thos and Grindon St Oswald CD *Dur* 67–71; C Stockton St Pet 71–74; C-in-c Leam Lane CD 74–79; R Washington 79–88; Dioc Ecum Officer 88–91; Adn Newark *S'well* 92–99; Suff Bp Repton *Derby* 99–06; rtd 06; Hon Asst Bp Sheff from 07. *29 Arran Way, Rothwell, Leeds LS26 0WB*

HAY, David Frederick. b 38. Pemb Coll Ox BA 62 MA 67. Qu Coll Birm 82. **d** 84 **p** 85. C Prenton *Ches* 84–88; V Stockport St Sav 88–96; P-in-c Gt Saughall 96–03; rtd 03; PtO *Ches* from 04; Hon Min Can Ches Cathl from 04; PtO *St As* from 09. *2 Moel View Road, Buckley CH7 2BT* T: (01244) 541342 E: dfhay@talktalk.net

HAY, Jack Barr. b 31. Bps' Coll Cheshunt 57. **d** 60 **p** 61. C Byker St Ant *Newc* 60–63; C Killingworth 63–68; V Cowgate 68–77; V Woodhorn w Newbiggin 77–96; rtd 96; PtO *Newc* from 96. *7 Glebelands, Corbridge NE45 5DS* T: (01434) 632979

HAY, Joanna Jane Louise. See DOBSON, Joanna Jane Louise

HAY, John. b 43. St D Coll Lamp 63. **d** 67 **p** 68. C Ynyshir *Llan* 67–70; C Cardiff St Mary and St Steph w St Dyfrig etc 70–74; V Llanwynno 74–78; P-in-c Weston-super-Mare All SS *B & W* 78–80; TV Weston-super-Mare Cen Par 80–85; P-in-c Handsworth St Mich *Birm* 85–86; NSM Eastbourne St Sav and St Pet *Chich* 88–91; V Buckley *St As* 91–96; P-in-c Ardwick St Benedict *Man* 96–99; C Hollinwood and Oldham St Chad Limeside 99–01; rtd 01; Hon C Hampden Park and The Hydnye *Chich* 09–12; PtO from 14. *Flat 2, 16A Beach Road, Littlehampton BN17 5HT*

HAY, Miss Lesley Jean Hamilton. b 48. St Andr Univ MA 71. Westcott Ho Cam 04 Yale Div Sch 05. **d** 06 **p** 07. C Shrivenham and Ashbury *Ox* 06–08; C Bethany USA 08; Asst R Hamden 08–10; R Mentone St Jos from 10. *PO Box 161, Mentone AL 35984-0161, USA* T: (001) (256) 634 4476 E: lesleyhay@yahoo.co.uk

HAY, Margaret Ann. b 47. Brunel Univ BTech 71 W Sussex Inst of HE PGCE 95. STETS 02. **d** 05 **p** 06. NSM Elson *Portsm* from 05. *Bodinnick, 12 Longwater Drive, Gosport PO12 2UP* T: (023) 9234 3303

HAY, Mark Alastair. b 71. St Martin's Coll Lanc BA 94. Trin Coll Bris 11. **d** 14 **p** 15. C Longfleet *Sarum* from 14. *32 Linthorpe Road, Poole BH15 2JS* T: (01202) 677573 M: 07792-405805 E: mark.hay@smlpoole.org.uk

HAY, Canon Nicholas John. b 56. Sheff Poly BSc 85. St Jo Coll Nottm 85. **d** 88 **p** 89. C Blackb Redeemer 88–91; C Hellesdon *Nor* 91–95; R Widford *Chelmsf* 95–01; Sen Chapl HM Pris Ashfield 01–09; C Bedminster *Bris* 09–15; P-in-c from 15; C Whitchurch 09–15; V Whitchurch St Aug 15–18; AD Bris S from 16; Hon Can Bris Cathl from 09. *St Paul's Vicarage, 2 Southville Road, Bristol BS3 1DG* T: 0117-971 1465 M: 07534-249338 E: nickthevichay@googlemail.com

HAY, Richard. b 42. Ball Coll Ox BA 63. Cranmer Hall Dur 94. **d** 96 **p** 97. C Hastings St Clem and All SS *Chich* 96–99; V Addlestone *Guildf* 99–07; RD Runnymede 02–07; rtd 07; PtO *Guildf* from 07. *15 Fox Close, Woking GU22 8LP* T: (01932) 343585 E: richard.hay3@btinternet.com

HAY, Robin Andrew. b 72. WEMTC 16. **d** 17 **p** 18. NSM Evington *Leic* 17–19; NSM Avon-Swift from 19; Hd Learning and Min Development from 17. *St Martin's House, 7 Peacock Lane, Leicester LE1 5PZ* T: 0116-261 5317 E: rob.hay@leccofe.org

HAYCRAFT, Brian Roger Norman. b 43. Oak Hill Th Coll 69. **d** 73 **p** 74. C Belsize Park *Lon* 73–76; C Yardley St Edburgha *Birm* 76–79; V Hornchurch H Cross *Chelmsf* 79–03; rtd 03; PtO *Chelmsf* from 04. *12 Hannards Way, Hainault IG6 3TB* T: (020) 8501 1718

HAYDAY, Canon Alan Geoffrey David. b 46. Kelham Th Coll 65. **d** 69 **p** 70. C Evington *Leic* 69–72; C Spalding St Mary and St Nic *Linc* 72–78; V Cherry Willingham w Greetwell

78–86; RD Lawres 84–86; TR Brumby 86–02; RD Manlake 93–99; Can and Preb Linc Cathl 00–02; Dean St Chris Cathl Bahrain 02–09; Adn Gulf 06–09; Hon Can Bahrain from 09; rtd 09. *22 Kestral Drive, Louth LN11 0GE* T: (01507) 600877 M: 07709-873224 E: windhover22@live.co.uk

HAYDEN, Carol Toni. b 64. Leeds Univ BA 05. NOC 02. **d** 05 **p** 06. NSM Ainsworth *Man* 05–09; NSM Bury SE 09–11; TV Radcliffe 11–17; TR 17; TV Turton Moorland from 17; Assoc Dir of Ords from 16. *2 Higher Dunscar, Egerton, Bolton BL7 9TE* T: (01204) 587150 M: 07434-365971 E: c_hayden1@sky.com

HAYDEN, The Ven David Frank. b 47. Lon Univ BD 71. Tyndale Hall Bris 67. **d** 71 **p** 72. C Silverhill St Matt *Chich* 71–75; C Galleywood Common *Chelmsf* 75–79; R Redgrave cum Botesdale w Rickinghall *St E* 79–84; RD Hartismere 81–84; V Cromer *Nor* 84–02; P-in-c Gresham 84–98; Chapl Cromer and Distr Hosp Norfolk 84–94; Chapl Norfolk and Nor Health Care NHS Trust 94–00; Chapl Fletcher Hosp Norfolk 85–00; RD Repps *Nor* 95–02; Hon Can Nor Cathl 96–12; Adn Norfolk 02–12; rtd 12; PtO *Nor* 12–17 and from 19; P-in-c Oulton Broad 17–19; P-in-c Oulton St Mich 18–19. *Church Farm House, Church Lane, Lowestoft NR32 3JN* T: (01502) 456001 E: davidf.hayden@gmail.com

✠**HAYDEN, The Rt Revd John Donald.** b 40. Lon Univ BD 62. Tyndale Hall Bris 63. **d** 65 **p** 66 **c** 03. C Macclesfield Ch Ch *Ches* 65–68; C H Spirit Cathl Dodoma Tanzania 68–69; V Moshi 70–77; Home Sec USCL 77–83; TV Ipswich St Mary at Stoke w St Pet *St E* 83–94; P-in-c Bury St Edmunds St Mary 94–99; V 99–04; Asst Bp Mt Kilimanjaro from 04; Hon Asst Bp *Ches* from 08; PtO *Liv* from 16. *45 Birkenhead Road, Hoylake, Wirral CH47 5AF* T: 0151-632 0448 E: johndhayden@gmail.com

HAYDEN, Canon Mark Joseph James. b 68. St Thos Aquinas Pontifical Univ Rome BD 93. H Cross Coll Clonliffe 86. **d** 92 **p** 93. In RC Ch 92–99; C Monkstown *D & G* 99–01; I Gorey w Kilnahue, Leskinfere and Ballycanew *C & O* from 01; Can Treas Ferns Cathl from 07. *The Rectory, The Avenue, Gorey, Co Wexford, Republic of Ireland* T/F: (00353) (53) 942 1383 E: gorey@ferns.anglican.org

HAYDOCK, Canon Alan. b 41. Kelham Th Coll 60. **d** 65 **p** 66. C Rainworth *S'well* 65–68; C Hucknall Torkard 68–71; TV 71–74; V Bilborough St Jo 74–80; R E Bridgford 80–82; R E Bridgford and Kneeton 82–06; RD Bingham 84–94; Hon Can S'well Minster 86–06; rtd 06; PtO *Leic* from 15; *S'well* from 06. *29 The Teasels, Bingham, Nottingham NG13 8TY* T: (01949) 875805 M: 07944-569661

HAYDON, Keith Frank Michael. b 46. Cuddesdon Coll 73. **d** 75 **p** 76. C De Beauvoir Town St Pet *Lon* 75–77; C Wells St Thos w Horrington *B & W* 77–80; TV Weston-super-Mare Cen Par 80–84; TV Cowley St Jas *Ox* 84–87; TR 87–95; V Walsingham, Houghton and Barsham *Nor* 95–96; P-in-c 96–99; rtd 01; C Sutton on Plym *Ex* 09–11; C Plymouth St Simon and St Mary 09–11; P-in-c Sutton-on-Plym, Plymouth St Simon and St Mary 11–16; P-in-c Plymouth St Gabr 11–16; PtO from 17. *Address withheld by request*

HAYES, Bruce John. b 75. UCD BA 97 TCD BTh 01. CITC 98. **d** 01 **p** 02. C Cregagh *D & D* 01–04; I Abbeystrewry Union *C, C & R* 04–13; Warden of Readers 08–13; I Dalkey St Patr *D & G* from 13. *The Rectory, Barnacoille Park, Church Road, Dalkey, Co Dublin, Republic of Ireland* T: (00353) (1) 280 3369 M: 86-232 7349 E: brucejohnhayes@gmail.com

HAYES, Carmen Miranda. b 61. TCD BTh 08. **d** 08 **p** 09. C Portadown St Mark *Arm* 08–11; I Kilcronaghan w Draperstown and Sixtowns *D & R* 11–19; I Errigal w Garvagh from 19; Bp's Dom Chapl from 12. *Address temp unknown* M: 07907-579913 E: carmenmirandahayes@hotmail.com

HAYES, David Malcolm Hollingworth. b 42. K Coll Lon BD 68 AKC 68 MPhil 97. **d** 69 **p** 70. C Upper Teddington SS Pet and Paul *Lon* 69–70; C Ruislip St Martin 70–75; P-in-c Ludford *Heref* 75–80; P-in-c Ashford Carbonell w Ashford Bowdler 75–80; V Eastcote St Lawr *Lon* 80–90; R Cant St Pet w St Alphege and St Marg etc 90–07; P-in-c Blean 03–07; Master Eastbridge Hosp 90–07; Guardian of the Greyfriars 97–07; rtd 07; PtO *Sarum* from 07. *Forge Cottage, 3 North Row, Warminster BA12 9AD* T: (01985) 212929 E: dmhforge@btinternet.com

HAYES, David Thomas. b 70. Leeds Univ BA 09. NOC. **d** 09 **p** 10. NSM Leeds Belle Is St Jo and St Barn *Ripon* 09–12; NSM Aberford w Micklefield *York* 12–18; NSM Sherburn in Elmet w Saxton 12–18; Chapl Mid Yorks Hosps NHS Trust from 17. *15 Windsor Mount, Leeds LS15 7DD* M: 07739-364755

HAYES, Denise Angela. b 62. NOC 02. **d** 05 **p** 06. C Ashton-in-Makerfield St Thos *Liv* 05–10; P-in-c Litherland St Phil 10–14; P-in-c Pemberton St Fran Kitt Green 14–15; V 15–16; P-in-c Marsh Green 14–15; V 15–16; V Kitt Green and Marsh Green 16–19; P-in-c Hattersley *Ches* from 19. *St Barnabas'*

Vicarage, Hattersley Road East, Hyde SK14 3EQ M: 07736-523168 E: denisehayes4@aol.com

HAYES, Helen. b 45. **d** 10 **p** 11. NSM Bradgate Team *Leic* 10–13; Pioneer P among homeless in W *Leic* 13–19; PtO from 19. *32 Hawthorne Drive, Thornton, Leicester LE67 1AW* T: (01530) 231401

HAYES, Jane. **d** 16. NSM Parkham, Alwington, Buckland Brewer etc *Ex* from 16. *16 Pengilly Way, Hartland, Bideford EX39 6HR*

HAYES, Canon John Henry Andrew. b 52. BSc. Wycliffe Hall Ox 82. **d** 84 **p** 85. C Moreton *Ches* 84–87; R Barrow 87–94; Bp's Chapl 87–94; P-in-c Runcorn St Mich 94–04; P-in-c Runcorn All SS 94–05; P-in-c Runcorn H Trin 04–05; V Runcorn All SS w H Trin 05–15; Hon Can Ches Cathl 08–15; rtd 15; PtO *Ches* from 15. *Crosbies Cottage, Buxworth, High Peak SK23 7NE* E: johnh552@outlook.com

HAYES, Mrs Marion Anne. b 51. Leeds Univ BA 05 Liv Inst of Educn CertEd 72. NOC 02. **d** 05 **p** 06. NSM Runcorn All SS w H Trin *Ches* 05–15; rtd 15; PtO *Ches* from 15. *Crosbies Cottage, Buxworth, High Peak SK23 7NE* E: mrsmahayes@gmail.com

HAYES, Michael Gordon William. b 48. St Cath Coll Cam BA 69 MA 73 PhD 73. Ridley Hall Cam 73. **d** 75 **p** 76. C Combe Down w Monkton Combe *B & W* 75–78; C Cambridge H Trin *Ely* 78–81; V Bathampton *B & W* 81–88; V Clevedon St Andr and Ch Ch 88–95; C Belper *Derby* 95–00; P-in-c Drayton in Hales *Lich* 00–07; RD Hodnet 01–06; P-in-c Chilton Cantelo, Ashington, Mudford, Rimpton etc *B & W* 07–13; rtd 13; PtO *B & W* from 13. *10 Paddock Close, Creech St Michael, Taunton TA3 5DZ* T: (01823) 444766 E: mhhayes@outlook.com

HAYES, Michael John. b 52. Lanc Univ BA 73. Coll of Resurr Mirfield 75. **d** 78 **p** 79. C Notting Hill *Lon* 78–81; C-in-c Hammersmith SS Mich and Geo White City Estate CD 81–88; PtO 98–00; NSM Norwood St Mary 00–03; Chapl Heart of Kent Hospice 05–12; P-in-c Burham and Wouldham *Roch* 12–16; R from 16. *22 Ridley Road, Rochester ME1 1UL* M: 07964-697556 E: mikejhayes@hotmail.co.uk

HAYES, Canon Miranda Jane. b 57. STETS BA 06. **d** 06 **p** 07. C Dorking w Ranmore *Guildf* 06–10; P-in-c Earls Barton *Pet* 10–16; RD Wellingborough 15–18; P-in-c Welford w Sibbertoft and Marston Trussell 19; P-in-c Clipston w Naseby and Haselbech w Kelmarsh 19; R Clipston, Haselbech, Kelmarsh, Marston Trussell etc from 19; Can Pet Cathl from 17. *The Rectory, 18 Church Lane, Clipston, Market Harborough LE16 9RW* T: (01858) 525342 E: mirandahayes@outlook.com *or* vicar.welfordclipston@outlook.com

HAYES, Peter Rowland. b 53. Melbourne Coll of Div BD 82 MMin 05. **d** 82 **p** 83. C Hamilton Australia 82–83; R Wongan Hills w Dalwallinu 84–87; R Kwinana 87–91; CF 91–09; P-in-c Lurgashall *Chich* 14–19; P-in-c N Chapel w Ebernoe 14–19; rtd 19. *c/o Ms C Hayes, Unit 17, 36 Jerdanefield Road, St Lucia QLD 4067, Australia* E: rowls3613@gmail.com

HAYES, Richard. b 39. K Coll Lon BD 68 AKC 68. **d** 69 **p** 70. C Dartford H Trin *Roch* 69–72; C S Kensington St Steph *Lon* 72–76; V Ruislip Manor St Paul 76–82; V Ealing St Pet Mt Park 82–91; R St Edm the King and St Mary Woolnoth etc 91–99; rtd 99; PtO *Lich* 99–04; *Heref* from 00; Hon C Shrewsbury St Alkmund *Lich* 04–07; Hon C Shrewsbury St Chad, St Mary and St Alkmund 07–15; PtO from 15; OCM from 09. *53 Stiperstones Court, Abbey Foregate, Shrewsbury SY2 6AL* T: (01743) 244668 E: l.r.hayes@btinternet.com

HAYES, Richard Henry. b 65. St Jo Coll Nottm 89. **d** 92 **p** 93. C Southborough St Pet w Ch Ch and St Matt *Roch* 92–95; C Downend *Bris* 95–97; V Gravesend St Mary *Roch* 97–02; R Clymping and Yapton w Ford *Chich* from 02. *The Rectory, St Mary's Meadow, Yapton, Arundel BN18 0EE* T: (01243) 552962 M: 07944-804933 E: revrichhayes@me.com

HAYES, Canon Rosemarie Eveline. b 51. Brighton Coll of Educn CertEd 72. NOC 88. **d** 91 **p** 94. Par Dn Manston *Ripon* 91–94; C 94–95; C Beeston 95–00; V Horsforth 00–11; P-in-c Kirkstall 06–11; TR Abbeylands 11–12; P-in-c Kippax w Allerton Bywater 12–14; *Leeds* 14–16; P-in-c Swillington *Ripon* 12–14; *Leeds* 14–16; TR Allerton Bywater, Kippax and Swillington from 16; AD Whitkirk 17; Hon Can Ripon Cathl from 10. *The Rectory, Church Lane, Kippax, Leeds LS25 7HF* T: 0113-286 2710 E: rosemariehayes@live.co.uk

HAYES, Sarah Caroline. b 61. Man Univ BA 84 Solicitor 90. St Jo Coll Nottm 05 Qu Coll Birm 07. **d** 09 **p** 10. NSM Hall Green St Pet *Birm* 09–13; NSM Edgbaston St Germain 13–19; V from 19. *180 Portland Road, Birmingham B16 9TD* T: 0121-429 3431 M: 07891-136654 E: sarahhayes2@me.com *or* sarah@stgermains.org

HAYES, Sarah Elizabeth. b 63. Ch Coll Cam BA 85 MA 89. Wycliffe Hall Ox 08. **d** 10 **p** 11. C Chipping Campden w Ebrington *Glouc* 10–13; V Horsell *Guildf* from 13. *The*

Vicarage, Wilson Way, Woking GU21 4QJ T: (01483) 721901 *or* 772134 M: 07878-455644

HAYES, Stephen Anthony. b 57. St Jo Coll Dur BA 80 S Bank Univ PGCE 96. SAOMC 97. **d** 99 **p** 00. NSM Kingham w Churchill, Daylesford and Sarsden *Ox* 99–01; NSM Chipping Norton 01–06; Chapl Kingham Hill Sch Oxon 99–06; Teacher Arnold Lodge Sch Leamington Spa 06–12; Teacher St Mary's Sch Ascot 15–16; PtO *Ox* 06–16; R Ray Valley from 16. *The Vicarage, Church Walk, Ambrosden, Bicester OX25 2UJ* T: (01869) 247813 E: hayesfamily@freeuk.com

HAYES, Timothy James. b 62. **d** 89 **p** 90. C Lache cum Saltney *Ches* 89–94; P-in-c Dukinfield St Jo 94–99; V from 99; P-in-c Millbrook from 17. *37 Harold Avenue, Dukinfield SK16 5NH* T: 0161-308 4708 E: revtimhayes@hotmail.com

HAYHOE, Geoffrey John Stephen. b 57. Portsm Univ BSc 00. Qu Coll Birm 01. **d** 03 **p** 04. C Felixstowe St Jo *St E* 03–06; V Geraldine New Zealand 06–17; R Broadhembury, Dunkeswell, Luppitt, Plymtree, Sheldon, and Upottery *Ex* from 17. *The Rectory, Dunkeswell, Honiton EX14 4RE* M: 07864-048575 E: john@hayhoe.net *or* rector.dunkeswell@gmail.com

HAYLER, Peter John. b 65. R Holloway Coll Lon BSc 87 Univ of Wales (Cardiff) MPhil 01 Anglia Ruskin Univ DProf 16. Wilson Carlile Coll 89 St Mich Coll Llan 99. **d** 00 **p** 04. Ind Chapl *Mon* 95–03; C Pontnewydd 00–03; C Magor 03–06; TV 06–09; C Cambridge Gt St Mary w St Mich *Ely* 09–17; Chapl Univ Staff Cam 09–17; R Shipbourne w Plaxtol *Roch* from 17. *The Rectory, The Street, Plaxtol, Sevenoaks TN15 0QG* T: (01732) 811081 E: rectorswp@gmail.com

HAYLETT, David William. b 44. **d** 05 **p** 06. OLM Dorchester *Ox* 05–16; PtO from 16. *8 Westfield Road, Long Wittenham, Abingdon OX14 4RF* T: (01865) 407382 E: familyhaylett@yahoo.com

HAYLOCK, Mrs Jill Caroline. b 54. ERMC 12. **d** 15 **p** 16. OLM Loddon, Sisland, Chedgrave, Hardley and Langley *Nor* from 15. *Lodge Farm, Sisland, Norwich NR14 6EE* T: (01508) 520248 E: jillhaylock@aol.com

HAYMAN, Mrs Audrey Doris. b 41. St Mary's Coll Chelt 61 Bris Univ CertEd 61 Cov Coll of Educn 65. Glouc Sch of Min 88. **d** 91 **p** 94. NSM Matson *Glouc* 91–98; P-in-c Falfield w Rockhampton 98–02; P-in-c Oldbury-on-Severn 98–02; PtO 02–04; NSM Barnwood from 04. *32 Corncroft Lane, Matson, Gloucester GL4 6XU* T: (01452) 411786 E: audrey.hayman@gmail.com

HAYNES, Miss Catherine Mary. b 68. Man Univ BA 90 Win Univ MA 11. St Mich Coll Llan BD 95. **d** 96 **p** 97. C Llantwit Major *Llan* 96–99; C Coity w Nolton 99–01; Dioc Children's Officer 99–01; P-in-c Llangammarch w Llanganten and Llanlleonfel etc *S & B* 01–03; P-in-c Irfon Valley 03–06; R 06–10; V Blaenau Irfon 06–10; Dioc Dir of Educn 02–08; Chapl Haberdashers' Monmouth Sch for Girls from 12; C Monmouth w Overmonnow etc *Mon* from 14; Dioc Children's Adv from 14. *St Thomas's Vicarage, St Thomas Square, Monmouth NP25 5ES* T: (01600) 715159 E: revcmhaynes@btinternet.com

HAYNES, Jonathan Kenneth. b 84. R Cen Sch Speech & Drama BA 07. Ripon Coll Cuddesdon BA 19. **d** 19. C Putney St Mary *S'wark* from 19. *8 Deodar Road, London SW15 2NN* M: 07507-606958　　　E: jonathanhaynes838@gmail.com *or* jonathan.haynes@parishofputney.co.uk

HAYNES, Canon Michael Thomas Avery. b 32. AKC 61. St Boniface Warminster 61. **d** 62 **p** 63. C Hebden Bridge *Wakef* 62–64; C Elland 64–68; V Thornhill Lees 68–82; V Lindley 82–97; Hon Can Wakef Cathl 82–97; rtd 97; PtO *Wakef* 97–14; *Leeds* 14–16. *Longwood Edge Cottage, 86 Lamb Hall Road, Huddersfield HD3 3TJ*

HAYNES, Canon Stuart Edward. b 69. Edge Hill Coll of HE BA 91. SNWTP 07. **d** 10 **p** 11. NSM Ormskirk *Liv* from 10; Hon Can Liv Cathl from 19. *11 Fairfield Close, Ormskirk L39 1RN* M: 07534-218122 E: stuart.haynes@liverpool.anglican.org

HAYNES, Valerie Elizabeth Mary-Benedict. b 53. Cant Ch Ch Univ BA 09. St Steph Ho Ox 03. **d** 05 **p** 06. C Sheerness H Trin w St Paul *Cant* 05–09; PtO 09–10; P-in-c Skelton w Upleatham *York* 10–14; R from 14; P-in-c Boosbeck and Lingdale 10–14; V from 14. *2 Nidderdale, Skelton-in-Cleveland, Saltburn-by-the-Sea TS12 2FY* T: (01287) 654040 M: 07803-798475 E: revhaynes@btinternet.com

HAYNS, Mrs Clare Julia Yates. b 69. Warwick Univ BA 91 R Holloway Coll Lon MSc 95 DipSW 95. Ripon Coll Cuddesdon 08. **d** 11 **p** 12. C Blenheim *Ox* 11–15; Chapl Ch Ch Ox from 15; LtO *Ox* from 17. *Christ Church, St Aldates, Oxford OX1 1DP* T: (01865) 276236 M: 07801-930702 E: clare.hayns@chch.ox.ac.uk

HAYSMORE, Geoffrey Frederick. b 39. Bps' Coll Cheshunt 63. **d** 66 **p** 67. C St Marylebone St Mark w St Luke *Lon* 66–69; C Stockton St Chad *Dur* 69–72; C-in-c

Town End Farm CD 72–77; PtO *York* from 95; rtd 01. *139 Lambton Road, Middlesbrough TS4 2ST* T: (01642) 275259 E: g.haymore@ntlworld.com

HAYTER, Mark Harrison George. b 49. Newc Univ BA 72. WEMTC 10. **d** 12 **p** 13. NSM St Weonards *Heref* 12–14; C Nadder Valley *Sarum* from 14. *High Spinney, Sutton Road, Fovant, Salisbury SP3 5LF* E: revmarkh@icloud.com

HAYTER, Mary Elizabeth. *See* BARR, Mary Elizabeth

HAYTER, Canon Raymond William. b 48. Oak Hill Th Coll 74. **d** 77 **p** 78. C Bermondsey St Jas w Ch Ch *S'wark* 77–80; C Sydenham H Trin 81–83; Asst Chapl HM Pris Brixton 83–84; Chapl HM Youth Cust Cen Stoke Heath 84–88; Chapl HM Pris Maidstone 88–91; CF 91–08; Chapl HM Pris Standford Hill 08–11; Min Can St Woolos Cathl *Mon* 11–14; Can Pastor 14–16; rtd 16. *Address withheld by request* E: raymondhayter@hotmail.com

HAYTER, Sandra. *See* RAILTON, Sandra

HAYTON, John Anthony. b 45. Heythrop Coll Lon MA 00 ACII 70. Oak Hill Th Coll 93. **d** 96 **p** 97. NSM St Alb St Mich 96–15; PtO from 15; OCM 02–08. *89 Harpenden Road, St Albans AL3 6BY* T: (01727) 761719 *or* 835037 F: 811744 E: john.hayton@ntlworld.com

HAYTON, Mark William. b 59. St Steph Ho Ox 85. **d** 88 **p** 89. C Sittingbourne St Mich *Cant* 88–91; C Kennington 91–94; R Broadstairs 94–07; RD Thanet 96–01; P-in-c Folkestone Trin 07–11; V 11–14; AD Elham 11–14; V Fleet *Guildf* from 14; AD Aldershot from 19. *The Vicarage, Branksomewood Road, Fleet GU51 4JU* T: (01252) 219281 E: vicar@parishoffleet.org.uk

HAYWARD, Canon Christopher Joseph. b 38. TCD BA 63 MA 67. Ridley Hall Cam 63. **d** 65 **p** 66. C Hatcham St Jas *S'wark* 65–69; Warden Lee Abbey Internat Students' Club Kensington 69–74; Chapl Chelmsf Cathl 74–77; P-in-c Darlaston All SS *Lich* 77–83; Ind Chapl 77–83; Can Res Bradf Cathl 83–92; Sec Bd Miss 83–92; R Linton in Craven *Bradf* 92–03; P-in-c Burnsall w Rylstone 97–03; RD Skipton 93–98; Hon Can Bradf Cathl 92–03; rtd 03; PtO *Bradf* 04–14; *Leeds* from 14. *12 Ron Lawton Crescent, Burley in Wharfedale, Ilkley LS29 7ST* T: (01943) 865261 E: chrisannh@talktalk.net

HAYWARD, Jane. *See* HAYWARD, Pamela Jane

HAYWARD, Jeffrey Kenneth. b 47. St Jo Coll Nottm BTh 74. **d** 74 **p** 75. C Stambermill *Worc* 74–77; C Woking St Jo *Guildf* 77–83; V Springfield H Trin *Chelmsf* 83–98; Chapl HM Pris Chelmsf 86–00; Area RD Chelmsf 86–88; RD Chelmsf 88–93; RD Chelmsf N 93–95; Hon Can Chelmsf Cathl 93–98; Chapl HM Pris Wakef 00–05; Chapl HM Pris Long Lartin 05–12; rtd 12; PtO *Chelmsf* from 14. *4 Durham Close, Great Bardfield, Braintree CM7 4UA* T: (01371) 810837

HAYWARD, Mrs Jennifer Dawn. b 38. WMMTC 85. **d** 88 **p** 94. NSM Gt Malvern St Mary *Worc* 88–90; NSM Gt Malvern Ch Ch 88–90; Par Dn 90–94; C 94–96; TV Wirksworth *Derby* 96–04; rtd 04; PtO *Worc* from 04. *26 Barley Crescent, Long Meadow, Worcester WR4 0HW* T: (01905) 29545 M: 07963-089437 E: revjenniehayward@gmail.com

HAYWARD, John Andrew. b 63. Nottm Univ BTh 89 MHCIMA 83. Linc Th Coll 86. **d** 89 **p** 90. C Seaford w Sutton *Chich* 89–92; C St Pancras H Cross w St Jude and St Pet *Lon* 92–95; V Kentish Town St Martin w St Andr 95–08; AD S Camden 05–08; V Merton St Mary *S'wark* from 08. *The Vicarage, 3 Church Path, London SW19 3HJ* T: (020) 8543 6192 E: vicar@stmarysmerton.org.uk

HAYWARD, Preb John Talbot. b 28. Selw Coll Cam BA 52 MA 56. Wells Th Coll 52. **d** 54 **p** 55. C S Lyncombe *B & W* 54–58; R Lamyatt 58–71; V Bruton w Wyke Champflower and Redlynch 58–71; RD Bruton 62–71; R Weston-super-Mare St Jo 71–75; Preb Wells Cathl 73–03; TR Weston-super-Mare Cen Par 75–92; rtd 92; PtO *B & W* from 92. *5 Chelswood Avenue, Weston-super-Mare BS22 8QP* T: (01934) 628431

HAYWARD, Martin. b 45. WMMTC 04. **d** 07 **p** 08. Dir Internat Min *Cov* 07–08; NSM Cov St Fran N Radford 07–12; Dean's V Cov Cathl 10–12; rtd 12; PtO *S'wark* from 12; *Cov* 12–15. *31 Waterside Court, Millpond Place, Carshalton SM5 2JT* T: (020) 3652 0551 M: 07917-182579 E: martin.hayward12@sky.com

HAYWARD, Ms Pamela Jane. b 52. RGN 82. Westcott Ho Cam 84. **d** 87 **p** 94. Par Dn Northampton St Mary *Pet* 87–90; Par Dn Bris St Mary Redcliffe w Temple etc 90–94; C 94–96; V Eastville St Anne w St Mark and St Thos 96–13; rtd 13. *18 Tilley Hill Close, Oundle, Peterborough PE8 4PU* E: janehayward266@btinternet.com

HAYWARD, Timothy David Mark. b 78. St Andr Univ MTheol 00. Westcott Ho Cam 07. **d** 09 **p** 10. C Buckden w the Offords *Ely* 09–12; V Bunbury and Tilstone Fearnall *Ches* from 12. *The New Vicarage, Vicarage Lane, Bunbury, Tarporley CW6 9PE* T: (01829) 261511 M: 07988-994481 E: revtimhayward@gmail.com

HAYWOOD, Christopher John. b 69. Poly Cen Lon BSc 92 Brighton Univ BSc 95 St Jo Coll Lon BA 17. Cranmer Hall Dur 15. **d** 17 **p** 18. C Hugglescote w Donington, Ellistown and Snibston *Leic* from 17. *7 Parkers Close, Ellistown, Coalville LE67 1DW* T: (01530) 261930 M: 07810-224133 E: rev.chrishaywood@btinternet.com

HAYWOOD, Preb Keith Roderick. b 48. Oak Hill Th Coll 84. **d** 86 **p** 87. C Fazeley *Lich* 86–90; TV Leek and Meerbrook 90–01; Acting TR Hanley H Ev 01–03; TR 03–13; Preb Lich Cathl 07–13; rtd 13; PtO *Lich* from 14. *135 Chase Road, Burntwood WS7 0EB* E: keithrhaywood@gmail.com

HAZEL, Sister. *See* SMITH, Hazel Ferguson Waide

HAZELTON, Michael John. b 53. UEA BA 76 Bedf Coll Lon PhD 81. Heythrop Coll Lon BD 89. **d** 90 **p** 91. Asst Chapl Helsinki *Eur* 94–95; Asst Chapl Zürich w Winterthur 95–98; R Mablethorpe w Trusthorpe *Linc* 98–02; R Saxonwell 02–05; V Danby w Castleton and Commondale *York* 05–17; V Westerdale 05–17; V Moorsholm 09–17; RD Whitby 16–17; rtd 17; PtO *S'wark* from 17. *19 St Elmos Road, London SE16 6SA* E: mjh_uk@hotmail.com

HAZELWOOD, Ms Jillian. b 32. Bp Otter Coll CertEd 52 St Alb Minl Tr Scheme 82. **d** 87 **p** 94. NSM Wheathampstead *St Alb* 87–02; rtd 02; PtO *St Alb* 02–19. *14 Butterfield Road, Wheathampstead, St Albans AL4 8PU* T/F: (01582) 833146 E: woodhazel@waitrose.com

HAZLEHURST, Anthony Robin. b 43. Man Univ BSc 64. Tyndale Hall Bris 65. **d** 68 **p** 69. C Macclesfield Ch Ch *Ches* 68–71; C Bushbury *Lich* 71–75; P-in-c New Clee *Linc* 75–85; TV Deane *Man* 85–96; V Harwood 96–07; rtd 07; PtO *Man* from 07. *6 Vale End, Nailsea, Bristol BS48 2JS* T: (01275) 819024 E: robinhaz@btinternet.com

HAZLETT, Stephen David. b 56. TCD BTh 88. CITC. **d** 88 **p** 89. C Ballywillan *Conn* 88–90; I Rathcoole 90–95; I Dunluce 95–00; Ind Chapl *Dur* 00–12; TV Sunderland 00–07; Chapl Sunderland Minster 07–12; Chapl Rotterdam w Schiedam Miss to Seafarers *Eur* 12–16; Hon C Rotterdam 12–16; R Kirkcudbright *Glas* from 16; R Gatehouse of Fleet from 16. *The Rectory, 18 Castledykes Road, Kirkcudbright DG6 4AN* M: 07900-231360

HAZLEWOOD, Canon Andrew Lord. b 54. Essex Univ BSc 76. Wycliffe Hall Ox. **d** 82 **p** 83. C Leckhampton SS Phil and Jas w Cheltenham St Jas *Glouc* 82–85; C Waltham H Cross *Chelmsf* 85–89; R Pedmore *Worc* 89–15; P-in-c Wollaston 09–13; RD Stourbridge 07–13; Hon Can Worc Cathl 10–15; rtd 15; PtO *B & W* from 15. *Wychbury, 3 Cuzco Gardens, Periton Road, Minehead TA24 8DU* T: (01643) 818916 E: andrewhazlewood@gmail.com

HAZLEWOOD, David Paul. b 47. Sheff Univ MB, ChB 70 Campion Hall Ox BA 72 MA 77. Wycliffe Hall Ox 70. **d** 73 **p** 74. C Chapeltown *Sheff* 73–75; Singapore 76; Indonesia 76–88; V Blackpool St Helen *St E* 88–97; V Shirley *Win* 97–11; rtd 11; PtO *Llan* 11–14; *Truro* from 14. *2 Hazelmead, Liskeard PL14 4PY* T: (01579) 324848 E: dphazlewood@gmail.com

HAZLEWOOD, Preb William Peter Guy. b 71. De Montfort Univ BA 97. St Steph Ho Ox BTh 01. **d** 01 **p** 02. C Knowle H Nativity and Easton All Hallows *Bris* 01–04; P-in-c Iver Heath *Ox* 08–11; P-in-c Dartmouth and Dittisham *Ex* 11–15; V from 15; Preb Ex Cathl from 17. *The Vicarage, 79 Seymour Drive, Dartmouth TQ6 9GE* T: (01803) 414767 E: frwill@hazlewoodhq.co.uk

HEAD, David Nicholas. b 55. Pemb Coll Cam BA 77 MA 81 Westmr Coll of Educn MTh 01. Westcott Ho Cam 78. **d** 81 **p** 82. C Surbiton St Andr and St Mark *S'wark* 81–84; C St Marylebone w H Trin *Lon* 84–89; TV Clapham Team *S'wark* 89–96; Chapl Trin Hospice Lon 89–96; Chapl Princess Alice Hospice Esher 96–03; R Lyng, Sparham, Elsing, Bylaugh, Bawdeswell etc *Nor* 03–14; RD Sparham 13–14; R Aylmerton, Runton, Beeston Regis and Gresham 14–19; rtd 19. *Dane House, The Street, Kettlestone, Fakenham NR21 0AU* T: (01328) 878455 E: david@davidhead.plus.com

HEAD, Peter Ernest. b 38. Lon Univ BSc 59. Ridley Hall Cam 61. **d** 63 **p** 64. C Fulwood *Sheff* 63–66; C Belper *Derby* 66–68; Hd RE Shoeburyness Sch Southend-on-Sea 69–74; Hd RE Bilborough Coll 74–79; Public Preacher *S'well* 74–79; NSM Bramcote 74–79; Vice-Prin Totton Coll Southn 79–93; Hon C Hordle *Win* 94–02; rtd 03; PtO *Win* from 02. *44 Lentune Way, Lymington SO41 3PF* T/F: (01590) 678097 E: peter_head@bigfoot.com

HEADING, Margaret Anne. b 66. Leeds Univ BSc 88 Man Univ PhD 91 Aston Univ PGCE 99. Wycliffe Hall Ox BA 01. **d** 02 **p** 03. C Fletchamstead *Cov* 02–05; V Ingleby Greenhow, Bilsdale Priory etc *York* from 05. *3 Holmemead, Great Broughton, Middlesbrough TS9 7HQ* T: (01642) 710045 E: anne.heading@tesco.net

HEADING, Canon Richard Vaughan. b 43. Lon Univ BSc 65 ARCS 65. Coll of Resurr Mirfield 66. **d** 68 **p** 69. C Heref St Martin 68–75; P-in-c Birches Head and Northwood *Lich* 75–77; TV Hanley H Ev 77–82; V Heref H Trin 82–92; TR Bedminster *Bris* 92–08; AD Bris S 01–06; Hon Can Bris Cathl 01–08; rtd 08; PtO *Worc* from 09. *18 Timberdine Avenue, Worcester WR5 2BD* T: (01905) 360998 E: ric.heading@gmail.com

HEADLEY, Miss Carolyn Jane. b 50. K Coll Lon MA 94 MCSP 71. Oak Hill Th Coll BA 83. dss 83 **d** 87 **p** 94. Kensal Rise St Mark and St Martin *Lon* 83–87; Par Dn Uxbridge 87–90; Team Dn 90–92; Warden of Readers (Willesden Area) 88–92; Tutor Wycliffe Hall Ox 94–05; P-in-c W Meon and Warnford *Portsm* 05–07; Chapl Portsm Hosps NHS Trust 07–11; Chapl Team Ldr 11–13; PtO *Portsm* 13–14; Chapl Epsom and St Helier Univ Hosps NHS Trust 14–18; rtd 18; PtO *S'wark* from 18. *17 Hawkwood Rise, Bookham, Leatherhead KT23 4JS* T: (01372) 456330 M: 07777-617516 E: carolynheadley@btinternet.com

HEAGERTY, Alistair John. b 42. Oriel Coll Ox BA 63 MA 67. Lon Coll of Div BD 68. **d** 68 **p** 69. C Margate H Trin *Cant* 68–72; CF 72–97; Chapl R Memorial Chpl Sandhurst 92–97; TV Kingswood *Bris* 97–08; rtd 08; PtO *St Alb* from 08. *44 Ferney Road, East Barnet, Barnet EN4 8LF* T: (020) 3234 1003 E: ajheagerty@gmail.com

HEAK, Philip George. b 70. QUB BA 92. CITC BTh 95. **d** 95 **p** 96. C Ballymacash *Conn* 95–98; C Galway w Kilcummin *T, K & A* 98–00; Dioc Youth Officer (Cashel) *C & O* 00–06; I Naas w Kill and Rathmore *M & K* from 06. *15 Spring Gardens, Naas, Co Kildare, Republic of Ireland* T: (00353) (45) 897206 M: 86-817 2356 E: pheak@eircom.net

HEAL, Miss Felicity Joan. b 42. Portsm Dioc Tr Course 89. **d** 92. NSM Bramshott and Liphook *Portsm* 92–95; NSM Blendworth w Chalton w Idsworth 95–97; PtO from 97. *25 College Street, Petersfield GU31 4AG* T: (01730) 260410 M: 07712-249608 E: felicity.heal@gmail.com

HEALE, Nicholas James. b 67. St Cath Coll Ox BA 89 DPhil 95 Leeds Univ BA 94. Coll of Resurr Mirfield 95. **d** 95 **p** 96. C Syston *Leic* 95–99; V Blackpool St Mich *Blackb* 99–10; P-in-c Skerton St Chad 10–15; V 15–19; P-in-c N and E Blackb from 19. *St Jude's Vicarage, Didsbury Street, Blackburn BB1 3JL*

HEALE, Walter James Grenville. b 40. Wycliffe Hall Ox 77. **d** 79 **p** 80. C Walsall *Lich* 79–82; TV Marfleet *York* 82–89; TR 89–94; R Easington w Skeffling, Kilnsea and Holmpton 94–05; P-in-c Owthorne and Rimswell w Withernsea 00–05; rtd 05; P-in-c Easington w Skeffling, Kilnsea and Holmpton *York* 05–06; PtO from 06. *18 Sloe Lane, Beverley HU17 8ND* T: (01482) 865915

HEALEY, Mrs Hilary Louise. b 51. RSCN 73 SRN 73. STETS 10. **d** 13 **p** 14. NSM Ampfield, Chilworth and N Baddesley *Win* 13–16; NSM Win St Cross w St Faith from 16. *178 Oliver's Battery Road South, Winchester SO22 4LF* T: (01962) 865923 M: 07443-437472 E: hilaryhealey24@gmail.com

HEALEY, Michael Harry Edmund. b 74. Mansf Coll Ox MA 01 Leeds Univ BA 03. Coll of Resurr Mirfield 01. **d** 04 **p** 05. C Norton *Sheff* 04–07; P-in-c Beighton from 07. *The Vicarage, 27 Tynker Avenue, Beighton, Sheffield S20 1DX* T: 0114-248 7635 E: mhehealey@hotmail.com

HEALY (née THOROLD), Mrs Alison Susan Joy. b 59. St Jo Coll Dur BA 80. Ripon Coll Cuddesdon 97 SEITE 03. **d** 06 **p** 07. NSM Shooters Hill Ch Ch *S'wark* 06–11; PtO 12–13; R Brant Broughton and Beckingham *Linc* 13–17; R Leadenham 13–17; R Welbourn 13–17; P-in-c Caythorpe 13–17; Chapl Trin Sch Belvedere from 17; NSM Footscray w N Cray *Roch* 17–18; NSM Sidcup St Jo 17–18; NSM Sidcup St Jo w Footscray from 18. *3 Holt Close, Sidcup DA14 5EQ* M: 07962-318728 E: vicardancer@supanet.com *or* ahealy@trinity.bexley.sch.uk

HEANEY, Eileen. b 59. SNWTP 08. **d** 11 **p** 12. NSM Burscough Bridge *Liv* 11–13; NSM Scarisbrick 13–15; P-in-c 15–18; V from 19. *473 Southport Road, Scarisbrick, Ormskirk L40 9RF* T: (01704) 880463 E: reveileenheaney@hotmail.co.uk

HEANEY, Canon James Roland. b 59. **d** 85 **p** 86. C Ballynafeigh St Jude *D & D* 85–88; C Lisburn Ch Ch Cathl *Conn* 88–90; I Dunganstown w Redcross and Conary *D & G* from 90; Can Ch Ch Cathl Dublin from 05. *The Rectory, Redcross, Co Wicklow, Republic of Ireland* T/F: (00353) (404) 41637 E: rolyheaney@gmail.com

HEANEY, Michael Roger. b 43. TCD BA 66 HDipEd 67 MA 69. CITC 74. **d** 76 **p** 77. Chapl St Columba's Coll Dub 76–09; rtd 09. *Montana, Scholarstown Road, Dublin 16, Republic of Ireland* T: (00353) (1) 493 1167 M: 86-265 1791 E: revmheaney@gmail.com

HEANEY, Robert Stewart. b 40. **d** 01 **p** 02. C Dunboyne Union *M & K* 01–04; PtO *Ox* 05–08; Sen Lect St Jo Univ Tanzania 10–12; Asst Prof Virginia Th Sem USA from 13; Dir Cen for Angl Communion Studies from 13. *Virginia Theological Seminary, 3737 Seminary Road, Alexandria, VA 22304, USA* T: (001) (703) 370 6600 E: robert.s.heaney@gmail.com

HEANEY, Samuel Stewart. b 44. Open Univ BA 79 Ulster Univ BEd 83 Lon Univ BD 93 QUB MPhil 99. St Deiniol's Hawarden 92. **d** 92 **p** 93. In Presbyterian Ch 85–92; C Knockbreda *D & D* 92–96; I Belfast H Trin and St Silas *Conn* 96–02; I Ballyrashane w Kildollagh 02–09; rtd 09. *3 Edgewood Court, Antrim BT41 4PG* T: (028) 9446 1076 E: stewartheaney@yahoo.co.uk

HEANEY, Wendy Anne. b 42. St Alb Minl Tr Scheme 90. **d** 95 **p** 96. NSM Clifton and Southill *St Alb* 95–99; Asst Chapl HM Pris Bedf 95–99; Chapl 99–02; LtO *St Alb* 99–02; rtd 02; PtO *St Alb* from 03. *34 Meadow Way, Letchworth Garden City SG6 3JB* T: (01462) 641303

HEAP, David Leonard. b 58. Man Univ BA 79. Cranmer Hall Dur 82. **d** 85 **p** 86. C Clitheroe St Jas *Blackb* 85–88; C Blackb St Gabr 88–92; V Bare from 92. *St Christopher's Vicarage, 12 Elm Grove, Morecambe LA4 6AT* T: (01524) 411363 E: davidleonardheap@gmail.com

HEAPS, Richard Peter. b 35. Bernard Gilpin Soc Dur 58 Qu Coll Birm 58. **d** 61 **p** 62. C Castle Bromwich SS Mary and Marg *Birm* 61–65; C-in-c Erdington St Chad CD 65–70; V Nechells 70–81; RD Aston 75–81; V Marston Green 81–86; P-in-c Shrawley and Witley w Astley *Worc* 86–92; R Shrawley, Witley, Astley and Abberley 92–01; rtd 01; PtO *Worc* from 01. *9 Timberdyne Close, Rock, Kidderminster DY14 9RT* T: (01299) 832376

HEARD, James Barrie. b 66. Brunel Univ BA 98 K Coll Lon MA 01. Ridley Hall Cam 03. **d** 06 **p** 07. C Fulham All SS *Lon* 06–09; C Chelsea St Luke and Ch 09–13; P-in-c Holland Park 13–18; V from 18. *2 Aubrey Walk, London W8 7JG* M: 07867-508919

HEARD, Richard Adrian. b 72. Univ of Wales (Swansea) BSc 94 Hull Univ PGCE 96. St Jo Coll Nottm 06. **d** 08 **p** 09. C Hackenthorpe *Sheff* 08–11; V W Bessacarr from 11; Jt AD Doncaster from 18. *The Vicarage, 39 Sturton Close, Doncaster DN4 7JG* T: (01302) 953342 M: 07818-850347 E: rev.richardheard@yahoo.co.uk *or* richard.heard@sheffield.anglican.org

HEARD, Stephen Edward. b 53. NTMTC 02. **d** 04 **p** 08. NSM Bush Hill Park St Mark *Lon* 04–19; NSM Bush Hill Park St Steph 13–19; Parliamentary Chapl to Bp Lon 07–13; rtd 19. *43 Speed House, Barbican, London EC2Y 8AT* M: 07939-253657 E: seh3@me.com

HEARL, Maria Christina. b 47. New Hall Cam BA 69 Ex Univ MA 98 PhD 07 PGCE 70. SWMTC 03. **d** 07 **p** 08. NSM Ex St Dav 07–13; PtO *B & W* 13–15; NSM Wellington and Distr from 15. *16 Twyford Place, Tiverton EX16 6AP* T: (01884) 256380

HEARN, John Henry. b 49. Trin Coll Bris. **d** 82 **p** 83. C Epsom Common Ch *Guildf* 82–85; C Ringwood *Win* 85–88; Chapl Basingstoke Distr Hosp 88–91; Chapl Luton and Dunstable Hosp 91–96; C Ampthill w Millbrook and Steppingley *St Alb* 96–99; P-in-c Wymington w Podington 99–03; V W Acklam *York* 03–14; rtd 14; PtO *Dur* from 14. *18 Thurso Close, Stockton-on-Tees TS19 7JD* E: jhhearn4@gmail.com

HEARN, Jonathan. b 58. Leeds Univ BA 81 GradIPM 85. Westcott Ho Cam 89. **d** 91 **p** 92. C Tuffley *Glouc* 91–94; C Milton *Win* 94–02; P-in-c Warwick St Paul *Cov* 02–03; TV Warwick from 03. *St Paul's Vicarage, 33 Stratford Road, Warwick CV34 6AS* T: (01926) 419814

HEARN, Canon Peter Brian. b 31. St Jo Coll Dur 52. **d** 55 **p** 56. C Frodingham *Linc* 55–59; R Belton SS Pet and Paul 59–64; PC Manthorpe w Londonthorpe 59–64; V Billingborough 64–73; V Sempringham w Pointon and Birthorpe 64–73; V Flixborough w Burton upon Stather 73–96; RD Manlake 87–93; Can and Preb Linc Cathl 92–01; rtd 96; PtO *Linc* from 01. *7 St Andrews Drive, Burton-upon-Stather, Scunthorpe DN15 9BY* T: (01724) 720510 E: peter_hearnl@sky.com

HEARN, Trevor. b 36. Sarum Th Coll 61. **d** 64 **p** 65. C Hounslow St Steph *Lon* 64–67; Miss to Seafarers 67–01; UAE 92–01; rtd 01; PtO *Bris* from 01. *37 Elberton Road, Bristol BS9 2PZ* T: 0117-983 6526 E: tvhearn37@btinternet.com

HEATH, Mrs Cynthia Grace. b 46. St Mark & St Jo Coll Lon TCert 68 Open Univ BA 85 ARCM 66 GRSM 68. WMMTC 94. **d** 97 **p** 98. NSM Penkridge *Lich* 97–00; TV 00–07. *2 Hall Farm Road, Brewood, Stafford ST19 9EZ* T: (01902) 850175 E: cynthgren@btinternet.com

HEATH, Henry. b 40. FCII 77. Oak Hill Th Coll 77. **d** 80 **p** 81. NSM Lexden *Chelmsf* 80–86; C Colne Engaine 86; NSM Halstead St Andr w H Trin and Greenstead Green 86–90; NSM W w E Mersea 90–95; R Stanway 95–02; rtd 02; PtO *Chelmsf* 02–05; P-in-c Wormingford, Mt Bures and Lt Horkesley 05–12; PtO *St E* from 13. *The Mews, Hill House, High*

Street, Long Melford, Sudbury CO10 9BD M: 07885-306699 E: hillhousemews@aol.com *or* revhenryheath@gmail.com

HEATH, John Henry. b 41. Chich Th Coll 69. **d** 71 **p** 72. C Crediton *Ex* 71–74; C Tavistock and Gulworthy 74–76; C Brixham 76–77; C Brixham w Churston Ferrers 77–79; R Bere Ferrers 79–85; P-in-c Moretonhampstead, N Bovey and Manaton 85–88; R 88–93; P-in-c Lifton 93–99; P-in-c Kelly w Bradstone 93–99; P-in-c Broadwoodwidger 93–99; R Lifton, Broadwoodwidger, Coryton, Stowford etc 99–01; V Lifton, Broadwoodwidger, Stowford etc 01–03; rtd 03; PtO *Heref* 04–10. *30 Wye Way, Hereford HR1 2NP*

HEATH, Julie Ann. b 62. Nottm Univ BA 09. EMMTC. **d** 06 **p** 07. NSM Kegworth, Hathern, Long Whatton, Diseworth etc *Leic* 06–08; Workplace Chapl 08–14; Chapl Leic Univ 09–13; Chapl Leic Cathl 12–14; PtO from 14. *Fairmount House, 87 Leicester Road, Ashby-de-la-Zouch LE65 1DD* T: (01530) 414549 M: 07801-467348 E: julieannheath@pottersmaze.co.uk

HEATH, Martin Jonathan. b 68. St Jo Coll Nottm 07. **d** 09 **p** 10. C Gt Wyrley *Lich* 09–12; C Harlescott from 12. *Emmanuel Vicarage, Mount Pleasant Road, Shrewsbury SY1 3HY* T: (01743) 350907 M: 07847-370572 E: martinjheath@talktalk.net

HEATH-WHYTE, David Robert. b 68. Fitzw Coll Cam BA 89. Wycliffe Hall Ox BTh 98. **d** 98 **p** 99. C Gt Chesham *Ox* 98–02; V Frogmore St Alb 02–14; TR Morden *S'wark* from 14. *The Rectory, London Road, Morden SM4 5QT* T: (020) 8648 3920 *or* 8685 0012 E: david.hw@hotfrog.info

HEATHER, Mark Duncan Grainger. b 62. Leic Poly LLB 83 Leeds Univ BA 99. Coll of Resurr Mirfield 97. **d** 99 **p** 00. C Leeds St Aid *Ripon* 99–03; V Leeds Halton St Wilfrid 03–10; Bp's Chapl *Guildf* 10–17; R Ashurst *Chich* from 17; V Steyning from 17. *The Vicarage, Station Road, Steyning BN44 3YL* T: (01903) 879877 E: vicarofsteyning@gmail.com *or* rectorofashurst@gmail.com

HEATHER, Mrs Sally Patricia. b 51. Avery Hill Coll BEd 73. STETS 99. **d** 02 **p** 03. NSM Michelmersh and Awbridge and Braishfield etc *Win* 02–06; TV Basingstoke 06–11; rtd 11; PtO *Win* from 11. *8 Sparkford Road, Winchester SO22 4NL* T: (01962) 622550 E: spheather@gmail.com

HEATHFIELD, Rachel Jane. b 70. Surrey Univ BA 91 MA 93. St Mellitus Coll BA 16. **d** 16 **p** 17. C The Quinton *Birm* from 16. *175 Harborne Lane, Selly Oak, Birmingham B29 6SS* T: 0121-258 3771 M: 07968-077453 E: rachel.heathfield@gmail.com

HEATHFIELD, The Ven Simon David. b 67. Birm Univ BMus 88 Fitzw Coll Cam BTh 99. Ridley Hall Cam 96. **d** 99 **p** 00. C Heswall *Ches* 99–02; Voc and Min Adv CPAS 02–05; TR Walthamstow *Chelmsf* 06–14; AD Waltham Forest 12–14; Adn Aston *Birm* from 14. *175 Harborne Lane, Selly Oak, Birmingham B29 6SS* T: 0121-258 3771 M: 07968-077453 E: simonh@cofebirmingham.com

HEATLEY, Cecil. *See* HEATLEY, William Cecil

HEATLEY, David Henry. b 50. Kent Univ BA 72. Qu Coll Birm 86. **d** 88 **p** 89. C Liss *Portsm* 88–91; V Newchurch and Arreton 91–99; R Greatham w Empshott and Hawkley w Prior's Dean 99–13; Dioc Rural Officer 98–13; rtd 13; PtO *Portsm* from 14. *1 Osborne Chase, Cowes PO31 7FA* T: (01983) 290567 E: dhheatley@aol.com

HEATLEY, Canon William Cecil. b 39. QUB BA 61. Ridley Hall Cam 62. **d** 64 **p** 65. C Ballymacarrett St Patr *D & D* 64–69; C Herne Hill St Paul *S'wark* 69–74; TV Sanderstead All SS 75–82; P-in-c Peckham St Sav 82–87; V 87–07; RD Dulwich 97–02; Hon Can S'wark Cathl 01–07; rtd 07; PtO *S'wark* from 07; *Roch* from 07. *37 Bromley College, London Road, Bromley BR1 1PE* T: (020) 8460 9505 E: cecilheatley@yahoo.com

HEATON, Alan. b 36. K Coll Lon BD 64 AKC 64 Nottm Univ MTh 76. **d** 65 **p** 66. C Stockton St Chad *Dur* 65–68; C Englefield Green *Guildf* 68–70; C Winlaton *Dur* 70–74; Chapl Derby Lonsdale Coll 74–79; V Alfreton 79–87; RD 81–86; TR Clifton *S'well* 87–93; P-in-c Rolleston w Fiskerton, Morton and Upton 93–96; rtd 97; PtO *Liv* from 97. *29 The Parchments, Newton-le-Willows WA12 0DX* T: (01925) 292209 E: a.ms-heaton@tiscali.co.uk

HEATON, Sister Elizabeth Ann. b 65. Bath Coll of HE BSc 87. Ripon Coll Cuddesdon 98. **d** 00 **p** 01. C Lostwithiel, St Winnow w St Nectan's Chpl etc *Truro* 00–03; CSF from 03; PtO *B & W* 03–10; *Linc* 10–12; C Branston w Nocton and Potterhanworth 12–15; C Metheringham w Blankney and Dunston 12–15; PtO *Leic* from 17. *Address withheld by request* T: (01455) 289831 E: lizcsf@franciscans.org.uk

HEATON, Canon Joseph Anthony Turnley. b 70. Univ of Wales (Abth) BSc 91 PhD 95 St Jo Coll Dur BA 08. Cranmer Hall Dur 06. **d** 08 **p** 09. C Ribbesford w Bewdley *Worc* 08–11; P-in-c Rushen *S & M* 11–13; V from 13; Can St German's Cathl from 16. *Rushen Vicarage, Barracks*

Road, Port St Mary, Isle of Man IM9 5LP T: (01624) 832275 E: rev.joeheaton@gmail.com

HEATON, Julian Roger. b 62. LSE BSc(Econ) 83. St Steph Ho Ox BA 86 MA 92. **d** 87 **p** 88. C Stockport St Thos w St Pet Ches 87–90; Chapl Asst Qu Medical Cen and Univ Hosp Nottm 90–92; V Knutsford St Cross Ches 92–01; P-in-c Altrincham St Jo 01–05; Voc Officer (Macclesfield Adnry) 01–05; V Sale St Anne 05–17; RD Bowdon 12–17; R Bury St Mary Man from 17; V Bury St Paul from 17. Bury Rectory, Tithebarn Street, Bury BL9 0JR T: 0161-764 2452 M: 07564-721331 E: julian.heaton_1@outlook.com

HEATON, Robert Anthony. b 56. **d** 16 **p** 17. C Sprotbrough Sheff from 16. 24 Field House Road, Sprotbrough, Doncaster DN5 7RP T: (01302) 570209 M: 07762-929763 E: r.heaton1956@virgin.net or robert.heaton@sheffield.anglican.org

HEATON, Timothy. b 59. STETS 08. **d** 08 **p** 10. NSM Upper Stour Sarum 08–11; NSM Gillingham and Milton-on-Stour 11–19; NSM Gillingham, Milton-on-Stour and Silton from 19. Grange Cottage, Chaffeymoor, Bourton, Gillingham SP8 5BY T: (01747) 840936 E: tim4heaton@yahoo.co.uk

HEAVISIDES, Canon Neil Cameron. b 50. Selw Coll Cam BA 72 MA 76 Ox Univ BA 74 MA 85. Ripon Hall Ox 72. **d** 75 **p** 76. C Stockton St Pet Dur 75–78; Succ S'wark Cathl 78–81; V Seaham w Seaham Harbour Dur 81–88; P-in-c Edington and Imber, Erlestoke and E Coulston Sarum 88–89; R 89–93; Can Res Glouc Cathl 93–15; rtd 15; Asst Chapl St Jo Coll Cam 15–16. 218 Myreside Street, Glasgow G32 6DX E: neil.heavisides@gmail.com

HEAZELL, Pamela Fletcher. b 50. NTMTC 96. **d** 99 **p** 00. NSM Hayes St Nic CD Lon 99–01; NSM N Greenford All Hallows 01–04; P-in-c 04–08; V 08–17; rtd 17; PtO B & W from 18. 3 Wells Road, Glastonbury BA6 9DN T: (01458) 833752 E: pfheazell@aol.com

HEBBERN, Geoffrey Alan. b 43. **d** 05 **p** 06. NSM Radipole and Melcombe Regis Sarum from 05; Asst Chapl HM Pris The Verne from 05. 11 Hawthorn Close, Weymouth DT4 9UG T/F: (01305) 772205 E: ghebbern@hotmail.com

HEBBLETHWAITE, Brian Leslie. b 39. Magd Coll Ox BA 61 MA 67 Magd Coll Cam BA 63 MA 68 BD 84 DD 06. Westcott Ho Cam 62. **d** 65 **p** 66. C Elton All SS Man 65–68; Chapl Qu Coll Cam 68; Dean of Chpl and Fell 69–94; Asst Lect Div Cam Univ 73–77; Lect 77–99; Can Th Leic Cathl 82–00; rtd 99; PtO Ely 02–17. The Old Barn, 32 High Street, Stretham, Ely CB6 3JQ T: (01353) 648279 M: 07740-307568 E: blh1000@cam.ac.uk

HEBBLEWHITE, David Ernest. b 52. Hull Univ BA 81 Nottm Univ MA 82 CQSW 82. St Jo Coll Nottm MA 95. **d** 97 **p** 98. C Melton Mowbray Leic 97–00; TV Cannock Lich 00–07; P-in-c Countesthorpe w Foston Leic 07–16; R Four Saints 16–19; Warden of Ev 10–14; RD Guthlaxton 10–18; rtd 19. 24 Waverley Road, Blaby, Leicester LE8 4HH

HEBDEN, Canon Cynthia Margaret. b 47. Univ of Wales (Ban) BTh 94. **d** 94 **p** 97. NSM Llanfairpwll w Penmynydd Ban 94–95; C Twrcelyn Deanery 95–96; C Knighton St Mary Magd Leic 96–99; P-in-c Higham-on-the-Hill w Fenny Drayton and Witherley 99–02; P-in-c Stoke Golding w Dadlington 01–02; R Fenn Lanes Gp 02–03; V Shepshed and Oaks in Charnwood 03–16; RD Akeley E 06–11; Hon Can Leic Cathl 13–16; rtd 16; PtO Leic 16–18; R Hallaton and Allexton, w Horninghold, Tugby etc from 18. 3 Stonton Road, Church Langton, Market Harborough LE16 7SZ M: 07740-433871 E: cynthia.hebden47@gmail.com

HEBDEN, Keith Oliver. b 76. Univ of Wales (Ban) BD 98 MTh 00 Warwick Univ PGCE 01 Birm Univ PhD 08. Qu Coll Birm 07. **d** 09 **p** 10. C Matson Glouc 09–12; C Mansfield SS Pet and Paul S'well 12–16; C Mansfield St Mark 12–16; Dir Urban Th Unit Sheff from 16; PtO Leic from 16. 151 Letchworth Road, Leicester LE3 6FP E: keithhebden@gmail.com

HEBER, Andrew John. b 63. Nottm Univ BA 86 MA 89 CQSW 89. Trin Coll Bris BA 99. **d** 99 **p** 00. C Parr Liv 99–03; TV Kirkby 03–12; R Clogherny w Seskinore and Drumnakilly Arm 12–18; I Carnmoney Conn from 18. 20 Glebe Road, Newtownabbey BT36 6UW T: (028) 9083 6637 M: 07804-340912 E: andy.heber@googlemail.com

HEBER PERCY, Canon Christopher John. b 41. St Jo Coll Cam BA 64 MA 68. Wells Th Coll 66. **d** 68 **p** 69. C Leigh St Mary Man 68–71; Asst Ind Chapl 71–80; P-in-c Oldham St Andr 75–78; TV Oldham 78–80; Ind Chapl Win 80–90; N Humberside Ind Chapl York 90–06; AD E Hull 98–06; Can and Preb York Minster 05–06; rtd 06. 59 Swarcliffe Road, Harrogate HG1 4QZ T: (01423) 884076

HEBER-PERCY, Colin Michael. b 68. Birkbeck Coll Lon BA 99 K Coll Lon MA 00 PhD 06. Ripon Coll Cuddesdon MTh 16. **d** 16 **p** 17. C Vale of Pewsey Sarum from 16. Tidcombe

Manor Cottage, Tidcombe, Marlborough SN8 3SL T: (01264) 731386 M: 07823-772043 E: colinheberpercy@gmail.com

HECTOR, Preb Noel Antony. b 61. Sheff Univ LLB 83 Barrister-at-Law 84. Oak Hill Th Coll BA 91. **d** 91 **p** 92. C Rodbourne Cheney Bris 91–92; C Bris St Mary Redcliffe w Temple etc 92–95; R Wrington w Butcombe B & W 95–03; R E Clevedon w Clapton in Gordano etc from 03; Chapl N Bris NHS Trust from 03; RD Portishead B & W 10–17; Preb Wells Cathl from 17. The Rectory, All Saints' Lane, Clevedon BS21 6AU T/F: (01275) 873257 E: eastcleveub@blueyonder.co.uk

HEDDERLY, Katherine. b 63. St Hugh's Coll Ox BA 85 MA 94. NTMTC BA 06. **d** 06 **p** 07. C Bedford Park Lon 06–09; C St Martin-in-the-Fields 09–19; V All Hallows by the Tower etc from 19; AD The City from 19. All Hallows, 43 Trinity Square, London EC3N 4DJ M: 07855-161415 E: vicar@ahbtt.org.uk

HEDDLE, Duncan. b 34. Wadh Coll Ox BA 57 MA 61 DPhil 64. **d** 86 **p** 86. Chapl Aber Univ Ab from 86; P-in-c Bucksburn from 90. 2 Douglas Place, High Street, Aberdeen AB24 3EA T: (01224) 485975 or 272137

HEDGECOCK, Jonathan James. b 64. Imp Coll Lon BScEng 86 Ban Univ BTh 09 CEng MIET 89. **d** 07 **p** 08. OLM Guildf H Trin w St Mary from 07. 8 Foxglove Gardens, Guildford GU4 7ES T: (01483) 502199 M: 07785-766631 E: jonathanjhedgecock@hotmail.com

HEDGER, Canon Graham. b 57. Lon Bible Coll BA 79. Ridley Hall Cam 81. **d** 83 **p** 84. C Walton St E 83–86; TV Mildenhall 86–91; R Swainsthorpe w Newton Flotman Nor 91–94; Dioc Evang Officer 91–94; PtO St E 95–99; Bp's Chapl and Liaison Officer 99–07; Bp's Policy and Liaison Officer 07–11; P-in-c Clopton w Otley, Swilland and Ashbocking 09–12; Asst Dioc Sec 10–18; Hd of Stewardship 17–18; P-in-c Orebeck St E from 18; Hon Can St E Cathl 04–15. 14 St Peter's Close, Charsfield, Woodbridge IP13 7RG T: (01473) 737280 M: 07388-117656 E: revgrahamhedger@outlook.com

HEDGES, Mrs Anne Violet. b 53. Ripon Coll Cuddesdon 87. **d** 89 **p** 94. C Thetford Nor 89–94; P-in-c Garboldisham w Blo' Norton, Riddlesworth etc 94–97; R Guiltcross 97–00; Chapl Riddlesworth Hall Sch Nor 93–00; Dep Chapl HM Pris Leeds 00–01; Chapl HM Pris Leic 01–05; Chapl HM Pris Highpoint 05–09; Chapl HM Pris Bure 09–16; rtd 16; PtO Nor from 16. Address withheld by request

HEDGES, Ian Charles. b 55. Sarum & Wells Th Coll 79. **d** 82 **p** 83. C Chessington Guildf 82–85; C Fleet 85–90; Dioc Adv on Homelessness from 87; V S Farnborough from 90; Tr Officer for Past Assts 91–00. The Vicarage, 1 St Mark's Close, Farnborough GU14 6PP T: (01252) 544711 E: smarksfbro@btinternet.com

HEDGES, The Very Revd Jane Barbara. b 55. St Jo Coll Dur BA 78. Cranmer Hall Dur 78. dss 80 **d** 87 **p** 94. Fareham H Trin Portsm 80–83; Southampton (City Cen) Win 83–87; Par Dn 87–88; Dioc Stewardship Adv Portsm 88–93; Can Res Portsm Cathl 93–01; P-in-c Honiton, Gittisham, Combe Raleigh, Monkton etc Ex 01–03; TR 03–06; RD Honiton 03–06; Can Steward Westmr Abbey 06–14; Dean Nor from 14. The Deanery, The Close, Norwich NR1 4EG T: (01603) 218300 E: dean@cathedral.org.uk

HEDGES, Mrs Jane Rosemary. b 44. RGN 65. S Dios Minl Tr Scheme 86. **d** 89 **p** 94. NSM Gillingham Sarum 89–04; NSM Gillingham and Milton-on-Stour 04–08; Lic to RD Blackmore Vale 08–12; PtO Ox from 16. 89 Derwent Avenue, Headington, Oxford OX3 0AS T: (01865) 429494 M: 07966-548127 E: denehollow@msn.com

HEDGES, John Michael Peter. b 34. Leeds Univ BA 60. Ripon Hall Ox 60. **d** 61 **p** 62. C Weaste Man 61–65; V Ashton St Pet 65–74; C Easthampstead Ox 74–85; V Tilehurst St Geo 85–91; C Thatcham 91–94; TV 94–99; rtd 99; PtO Ox 99–19. 39 Mallard Way, Grove, Wantage OX12 0QG

HEDLEY, Charles John Wykeham. b 47. R Holloway Coll Lon BSc 69 PhD 73 Fitzw Coll Cam BA 75 MA 79. Westcott Ho Cam 73. **d** 76 **p** 77. C Chingford St Anne Chelmsf 76–79; C St Martin-in-the-Fields Lon 79–84 and 85–86; P-in-c 84–85; Chapl Ch Coll Cam 86–90; TR Gleadless Sheff 90–99; R Westmr St Jas Lon 99–09; rtd 09. 95 Brighton Belle, 2 Stroudley Road, Brighton BN1 4ZD E: chequal@googlemail.com

HEDWORTH, Paul Simon James. b 56. Worc Coll of Educn BEd 78. Qu Coll Birm BA(Theol) 84. **d** 04 **p** 05. NSM Bacup and Stacksteads Man 04–06; Chapl Qu Eliz Gr Sch Blackb 98–06; Chapl Bromsgrove Sch from 06. Bromsgrove School, Worcester Road, Bromsgrove B61 7DU T: (01527) 579679 M: 07966-503194 E: hedworthfamily@yahoo.co.uk or phedworth@bromsgrove-school.co.uk

HEELEY, Mrs Janet. b 45. **d** 00 **p** 01. OLM Lich St Chad 00–10; rtd 10; PtO Lich from 10. 43 High Grange, Lichfield WS13 7DU T: (01543) 251600

HEELEY, Robert Francis. b 54. NOC 06. **d** 08 **p** 09. NSM Hadfield *Derby* 08–12; NSM Charlesworth and Dinting Vale 12–14; NSM Dinting Vale 14–19; rtd 19. *3 Chesham Close, Hadfield, Glossop SK13 1QX* T: (01457) 855541 E: rob.heeley@uwclub.net

HEELEY, Mrs Ruth Mary. b 41. Qu Coll Birm 04. **d** 06 **p** 07. NSM Halas *Worc* 06–11; rtd 11; PtO *Worc* 11–17. *24 Willow View Park, Whimple, Exeter EX5 2QT* T: (01404) 758708 E: ruthmh@hotmail.co.uk

HEENAN, Vivienne Mary. b 48. Univ of Wales (Abth) BA 70 SS Paul & Mary Coll Cheltenham PGCE 90. STETS 03. **d** 06 **p** 07. NSM Whitwell and Niton *Portsm* 06–11; NSM Ventnor St Cath 11–13; NSM Ventnor H Trin 11–13; NSM Bonchurch 11–13; PtO 13–18; *Worc* from 18. *The Risings, Kington, Worcester WR7 4DH* M: 07740-780767 E: vivienneheenan@outlook.com

HEGARTY, Ms Bernadette Grace. b 58. Man Poly BA 81 Leeds Univ BA 11 CQSW 90. Coll of Resurr Mirfield 09. **d** 11 **p** 12. C High Harrogate St Pet *Ripon* 11–14; *Leeds* 14; V Bow Common *Lon* from 14. *St Paul's Vicarage, Leopold Street, London E3 4LA* E: bhgrace@hotmail.co.uk

HEGEDUS, Frank Michael. b 48. St Louis Univ BA 71 Michigan State Univ MA 76 Univ of St Thos St Paul MBA 84. Colgate-Rochester Div Sch DMin 80. **d** 74 **p** 74. P-in-c St Paul St Paul's-on-the-Hill USA 87–89; P-in-c Northfields All SS & Dundas H Cross 88–90; R Farmington Advent 89–96; Asst P Orange Trin Ch 97–98; P-in-c Norwalk St Fran 98–99; NSM Budapest *Eur* 99–01; Asst P Huntington Beach St Wilfrid USA 01–02; P-in-c Redlands Trin Ch 02–03; P-in-c Plymouth St Jo 04–05; P-in-c El Cajon St Alb 05–08; P-in-c Del Mar St Pet 08–09; P-in-c El Centro St Pet and St Paul 09; P-in-c Episc Ch in Almaden San Jose 09–10; P-in-c Budapest *Eur* from 11. *1117 Budapest, Szerémi út 7/A - 603, Hungary* T: (0036) (20) 269 5161 E: anglicanbudapest@gmail.com

HEIGHT (formerly WATKINS), Susan Jane. b 58. Qu Coll Birm. **d** 01 **p** 02. C Edgbaston St Germain *Birm* 01–05; TV Salter Street and Shirley 05–11; P-in-c N Dulwich St Faith *S'wark* 11–18; V from 18; AD Dulwich from 16. *St Faith's Vicarage, 62 Red Post Hill, London SE24 9JQ* T: (020) 7274 3924 E: office@stfaithschurch.org

HEIGHTON, George. b 55. Qu Coll Birm 08. **d** 11 **p** 12. NSM Bilton *Cov* 11–14; C Willenhall 14–17; C Whitley 14–17; V Brailes from 17; R Sutton under Brailes from 17; P-in-c Tysoe w Oxhill and Whatcote from 17. *The Vicarage, Peacock Lane, Tysoe, Warwick CV35 0SG* M: 07730-009098 E: revgeorgeh@outlook.com

HEIGHTON, Miss Janet Elizabeth. b 67. Leeds Poly BSc 92. Ripon Coll Cuddesdon. **d** 00 **p** 01. C Leeds Gipton Epiphany *Ripon* 00–04; P-in-c 04–07; TV Upholland *Liv* 07–14; V Rainford from 14. *1 Tudor Close, Rainford, St Helens WA11 8SD* T: (01744) 882200

HEIL, Janet. b 53. Liv Univ BEd 75 St Jo Coll Dur BA 84. Cranmer Hall Dur. **dss** 85 **d** 87 **p** 94. Ashton Ch Ch *Man* 85–91; Par Dn 87–91; Par Dn Scotforth *Blackb* 91–94; C 94–95; V Gt Harwood St Bart 95–06; P-in-c Gt Harwood St Jo 02–06; Hon Can Blackb Cathl 04–06; Chapl Oslo w Bergen, Trondheim and Stavanger *Eur* 06–13; rtd 13; PtO *Blackb* 14–17. *4 Hornby Court, Beaumont Park, Lancaster LA1 2LB* E: janetheil@btinternet.com

HEINE, John Karl. b 62. Simpson Univ (USA) BA 84 California State Univ BA 87 Univ of the Pacific MA 89. Wycliffe Hall Ox 16. **d** 18. C Ashtead *Guildf* 18–19; C Gt Bookham from 19. *17 Loraine Gardens, Ashtead KT21 1PD* M: 07930-126622 E: skyehiker@gmail.com

HEININK, Mrs Jennifer Ann. b 54. K Coll Lon BD 75 Sarum Coll MA 10. St Mellitus Coll 13. **d** 14 **p** 15. OLM Cranham Park *Chelmsf* 14–17; NSM from 17. *14 Grosvenor Gardens, Upminster RM14 1DJ* T: (01708) 227374 E: jennyheinink@hotmail.com

HEITZMANN, Pamela. *See* BARRIE, Pamela

HELD, Ms Catherine Jane. b 54. Edin Univ BA 77. **d** 18 **p** 19. NSM Blyth Valley *St E* from 18. *Oak Cottage, The Street, Rumburgh, Halesworth IP19 0JX* T: (01986) 781760 M: 07771-556391

HELEN, Sister. *See* LODER, Helen

HELEN JULIAN, Sister. *See* ENGLISH, Helen Margaret

HELEY, John. b 28. Lon Univ BA 72. Bps' Coll Cheshunt 54. **d** 56 **p** 57. C Claremont St Sav S Africa 57–61; C Wimborne Minster *Sarum* 61–62; V Narborough w Narford *Nor* 62–67; R Pentney St Mary Magd w W Bilney 62–67; V Catton 67–69; LtO *Ox* 69–72; R E w W Rudham *Nor* 72–75; P-in-c Houghton 72–74; V 74–75; V Hunstanton St Edm 75–82; V Hunstanton St Edm w Ringstead 82–83; rtd 88. *24 Kestrel Close, Burnham Market, King's Lynn PE31 8EF* T: (01328) 730036

HELKVIST, Samuel James. **d** 16 **p** 17. NSM Newport St Julian and St Teilo *Mon* from 16. *104 Worcester*

Court, Tonyrefail, Porth CF39 8JT M: 07827-932821 E: frsamuel@stteilonewport.org.uk

HELLARD, Dawn Yvonne Lorraine. b 47. St Mich Coll Llan 89. **d** 91 **p** 97. C Llantwit Major *Llan* 91–95; TV Cowbridge 95–05; rtd 05; PtO *Llan* from 05. *10 Maes Lloi, Aberthin, Cowbridge CF71 7HA* T: (01446) 772460 E: dawnhellard05@gmail.com

HELLEWELL, John. b 63. Bris Univ BSc 86 BTh 93 Nottm Univ MA 94. St Jo Coll Nottm 93. **d** 94 **p** 95. C Greasbrough *Sheff* 94–98; P-in-c High Hoyland, Scissett and Clayton W *Wakef* 98–04; V Mount Pellon 04–09; V Halifax St Aug and Mount Pellon 09–14; *Leeds* from 14; Warden of Readers *Wakef* 04–12. *The Vicarage, Church Lane, Halifax HX2 0EF* T: (01422) 365027 E: revjhell@blueyonder.co.uk

HELLICAR, Hugh Christopher. b 37. Qu Coll Birm 69. **d** 70 **p** 71. C Bromyard *Heref* 70–73; C Bishop's Castle w Mainstone 73–75; PtO *S'wark* 77–85; *Chich* 83–93; NSM Hove 93–98; rtd 02. *74 Marina, St Leonards-on-Sea TN38 0BJ* T: (01424) 444072 E: rainbow.poctry@hotmail.com

HELLIER, Jeremy Peter. b 53. K Coll Lon BD 75 AKC 75. St Aug Coll Cant 75. **d** 76 **p** 77. C Walton *St E* 76–79; C Ipswich St Fran 79–80; C Wolborough w Newton Abbot *Ex* 80–82; CF 82–84; R Pendine w Llanmiloe and Eglwys Gymyn w Marros *St D* 84–89; TR Widecombe-in-the-Moor, Leusdon, Princetown etc *Ex* 89–94; CF (TAVR) 90–03; RD Moreton *Ex* 91–94; Chapl and Hd RE Wellington Sch Somerset 94–15; rtd 16; Hon Chapl Miss to Seafarers from 02; PtO *B & W* from 15; Dioc Secondary Relig Educn Adv from 18; PtO *Eur* from 17. *Overside, Hillcommon, Taunton TA4 1DU* T: (01823) 400655 E: jeremyhellier@hotmail.com

HELLINGS, Mrs Tara Charmian Lashmar. b 68. Ch Ch Ox MA 90. STETS 06. **d** 09 **p** 10. NSM Alton *Win* 09–12; Chapl Alton Coll 11–12; V Crondall and Ewshot *Guildf* from 12. *The Vicarage, Farm Lane, Crondall, Farnham GU10 5QE* M: 07932-184873 E: tartzhellings@yahoo.co.uk

HELLMUTH, Miss Lynn Margaret. b 61. Lon Bible Coll BA 82 Birm Univ PGCE 83. Wycliffe Hall Ox 00. **d** 02 **p** 03. C Twickenham Common H Trin *Lon* 02–05; TV Crawley *Chich* 05–08; V Stoneleigh *Guildf* 08–18; V Hackness w Harwood Dale *York* from 18; V Ravenscar and Staintondale from 18; V Scalby from 18; V Scarborough St Laur from 18. *1 Queen Elizabeth Drive, Scalby, Scarborough YO13 0SR* E: lynnhellmuth@yahoo.co.uk

HELLYER, Stephen John. b 56. St Cath Coll Cam BA 77 MA 81. Wycliffe Hall Ox 82. **d** 84 **p** 85. C Plymouth St Andr w St Paul and St Geo *Ex* 84–88; Chapl Lee Abbey 88–89; Lon and SE Consultant CPAS 90–94; C Nottingham St Nic *S'well* 94–98; P-in-c Ox St Matt 98–10; R 10–18; rtd 18. *6 Millers Cottages, 17A Mill Street, Eynsham, Witney OX29 4JX* T: (01865) 881246 M: 07811-001712 E: stevejohnhellyer@yahoo.co.uk

HELM, Canon Alistair Thomas. b 53. Aston Univ BSc 75. EAMTC 88. **d** 91 **p** 92. NSM Leic St Jas 91–95; NSM Humberstone 95–04; NSM Emmaus Par Team 04–12; NSM Giggleswick and Rathmell w Wigglesworth *Bradf* 09–12; NSM Settle 09–12; P-in-c Manningham 12–13; V *Leeds* 13–18; Acting Adn Bradf 15–16; AD Inner Bradford 17–18; rtd 18; Hon C Market Harborough and The Transfiguration etc *Leic* from 19. *61 Tungstone Way, Market Harborough LE16 9GA* M: 07557-375844 E: alistair.helm@btinternet.com

HELM, Catherine Mary. b 64. St Martin's Coll Lanc BEd 86. St Jo Coll Nottm 03. **d** 05 **p** 06. C Heswall *Ches* 05–09; V Burton and Shotwick from 09. *The Vicarage, Vicarage Lane, Burton, Neston CH64 5TJ* T: 0151-353 0453 E: chelm@shotwick.org.uk

HELM, Preb Nicholas. b 57. Surrey Univ BSc 81. St Jo Coll Nottm 85. **d** 88 **p** 89. C Old Ford St Paul w St Steph and St Mark *Lon* 88–92; TV Netherthorpe *Sheff* 92–93; V Sheff St Bart 93–98; Bp's Chapl 99–03; Bp's Adv in Spirituality 99–09; Chapl Whirlow Grange Conf Cen Sheff 99–09; CMD Officer *Heref* from 10; Preb Heref Cathl from 16. *Diocese of Hereford, 8-9 The Business Quarter, Eco Park Road, Ludlow SY8 1FD* T: (01584) 871082 E: n.helm@hereford.anglican.org

HELMS, David Clarke. b 50. Boston Univ BA 72. Yale Div Sch MDiv 77. **d** 77 **p** 77. USA 77–88; Ind Chapl *Worc* 88–97; Ind Chapl Teesside York 97–02; Dir Workplace Min for Ch in Soc Roch 05–12; P-in-c Dartford St Alb 12–16; rtd 16. *3 Royal Oak Terrace, Gravesend DA12 1JU* T: (01474) 321593 M: 07957-193816

HEMINGRAY, Raymond. b 47. Leeds Univ LLB 68 Solicitor 71. ERMC 04. **d** 07 **p** 08. Dioc Registrar *Pet* 74–14; NSM Castor w Sutton and Upton w Marholm 07–14; PtO from 14; *Ely* from

11. *4 Holywell Way, Peterborough PE3 6SS* T: (01733) 262523
E: rh@raymondhemingray.co.uk

HEMMING, Andrew Martyn. b 56. Bath Univ BSc 78.
STETS 08. **d** 11 **p** 12. NSM Axbridge w Shipham and
Rowberrow *B & W* 11–14; NSM Wrington w Butcombe
and Burrington from 14. *Eleuthera, Garston Lane, Blagdon,
Bristol BS40 7TF* T: (01761) 462582 M: 07584-124198
E: andrewmhemming@btinternet.com

HEMMING, Terry Edward. b 47. Calvin Coll Michigan MA 84.
S Dios Minl Tr Scheme 88. **d** 90 **p** 91. NSM E Win 90–09;
Chapl St Swithun's Sch Win 95–07; NSM Hurstbourne
Priors, Longparish etc *Win* 09–18; rtd 18; PtO *Win* from
18; *Eur* from 19. *10 Portland Grove, Andover SP10 1DB*
E: revhemm@yahoo.co.uk

HEMMING-CLARK, Stanley Charles. b 29. Peterho Cam BA 52
MA 56. Ridley Hall Cam 52. **d** 54 **p** 55. C Redhill St Matt
S'wark 54–56; C Woking St Jo *Guildf* 56–59; V Crockenhill
All So *Roch* 59–97; rtd 97; PtO *Guildf* from 97. *St Anthony's,
22 Ashcroft, Shalford, Guildford GU4 8JT* T: (01483) 568197

HEMMINGS, Ms Jane Marie. b 68. Lon Univ BD 91 AKC 91
Heythrop Coll Lon MTh 95 Southn Univ PGCE 08.
NTMTC 01. **d** 03 **p** 04. C Bishop's Waltham *Portsm* 03–08;
NSM 07–08; C Upham 03–08; NSM 07–08; NSM Akeman
Ox 08–12; R 12–16; Dir of Ords (Dorchester Area) from
16. *1 The Rookery, Kidlington OX5 1AW* T: (01869) 350224
E: Jane.Hemmings@oxford.anglican.org

HEMMINGS, Roy Anthony. b 48. Univ of Wales (Cardiff)
BD 85 MTh 00. St Mich Coll Llan 82. **d** 86 **p** 87. C Rhyl w
St Ann *St As* 86–90; CF 90–08; V Maybush and Southampton
St Jude *Win* 08–18; rtd 18. *81 Hebron Road, Clydach, Swansea
SA6 5EH* M: 07710-774431 E: padreroy48@aol.com

HEMP, Mrs Julia. b 61. Reading Univ BA 82. ERMC 10. **d** 13
p 14. C Earlham *Nor* 13–16; C Gressenhall w Longham w
Wendling etc 16–18; C Wellingham 17–18; TV Launditch
and the Upper Nar *Nor* from 18. *4 Lodge Farm Meadows,
Gressenhall, Dereham NR20 4TN* M: 07702-665000
E: reverendjulia@gmail.com

HEMPHILL, John James. b 44. TCD BA 68 MA 72. Oak Hill Th
Coll 71. **d** 73 **p** 74. C Dundonald *D & D* 73–78; I Balteagh w
Carrick *D & R* 78–02; I Ballyhalbert w Ardkeen *D & D* from 02.
*Ballyeasboro Rectory, 187 Main Road, Portavogie, Newtownards
BT22 1DA* T: (028) 4277 1234 M: 07890-012843

HEMSLEY HALLS, Susan Mary. b 59. Cranmer Hall Dur 93.
d 95 **p** 96. C Wilnecote *Lich* 95–00; P-in-c Attenborough
S'well 00–11; V 11–13; Dioc Chapl amongst Deaf People
00–12; Dioc Dir of Ords 12–18; P-in-c S Trin Broads *Nor*
from 18. *The Rectory, Main Road, Fleggburgh, Great Yarmouth
NR29 3AG*

HEMSTOCK, Canon Julian. b 51. Trent Poly BSc 74 CEng
MIProdE. Sarum & Wells Th Coll 89. **d** 91 **p** 92. C Carrington
S'well 91–94; C Basford St Aid 94–97; Asst Chapl Qu Medical
Cen Nottm Univ Hosp NHS Trust 97–03; Chapl from 03; Hon
Can S'well Minster from 13. *Queen's Medical Centre University
Hospital, Derby Road, Nottingham NG7 2UH* T: 0115-924
9924 ext 43799 E: julian.hemstock@qmc.nhs.uk

HEMSTOCK, Mrs Pat. b 51. Sarum & Wells Th Coll 89. **d** 91
p 95. Par Dn Carrington *S'well* 91–94; Par Dn Basford St Aid
94–95; C 95–97; P-in-c 97–05; V Calverton 05–16; rtd 16;
PtO *S'well* from 17. *8 Peacock Drive, Eastwood, Nottingham
NG16 3HW*

HEMSWORTH, John Alan. b 45. FGA 67. **d** 02 **p** 03. OLM
Droylsden St Andr *Man* 02–10; P-in-c 10–16; C Droylsden
St Martin 13–16; rtd 16; PtO *Man* from 16. *13 Keston
Avenue, Droylsden, Manchester M43 6BL* M: 07544-306713
E: john.hemsworth@ntlworld.com

HENDERSON, Andrew Douglas. b 36. Trin Coll Cam BA 60
MA 64 Liv Univ DASS 65 MBASW. Cuddesdon Coll 60. **d** 62
p 63. C Newington St Paul *S'wark* 62–64; Hon C Camberwell
St Luke 65–80; PtO *Lon* 85–06; *Chich* from 06. *4 Western
Terrace, Brighton BN1 2LD* T: (01273) 327829

HENDERSON, Ashley. *See* HENDERSON, Peter Ashley

HENDERSON, Daniel Thomas. b 81. Nottm Univ BSc 03. Oak
Hill Th Coll BTh 10. **d** 10 **p** 11. C Hailsham *Chich* 10–14; C Hove
St Andr 14–18; P-in-c from 18; RD Hove from 18. *St Andrew's
Vicarage, 17 Vallance Gardens, Hove BN3 2DB* M: 07734-
928877 E: dan-henderson@hotmail.com

HENDERSON, David. *See* HENDERSON, Robert David Druitt

HENDERSON, Mrs Elizabeth. b 42. CITC 96. **d** 99 **p** 00. C
Ballymacash *Conn* 99–00; C Finaghy 00–15; Asst Chapl
Belfast City Hosp Health and Soc Services Trust 99–05; Asst
Chapl Down Lisburn Health and Soc Services Trust 05–15;
rtd 15. *39 Garvey Court, Lisburn BT27 4DG* T: (028) 9260
7146 E: lilabethhenderson@yahoo.com

HENDERSON, Mrs Janet Elizabeth. b 53. N Lon Poly BSc 75.
Ripon Coll Cuddesdon 05. **d** 06 **p** 07. NSM Ellesborough,
The Kimbles and Stoke Mandeville *Ox* 06–09; R 09–18; rtd

18; PtO *Ox* from 18. *Brook Farm, Marsh Road, Little Kimble,
Aylesbury HP22 5XS* E: jeh@brook-farm.supanet.com

HENDERSON, Mrs Joanne Sarah. b 63. Ripon Coll
Cuddesdon 10. **d** 12 **p** 13. C Abu Dhabi St Andr UAE
12–16; TV Knaresborough *Leeds* 16–19. *3/17 Western
Harbour Breakwater, Edinburgh EH6 6PA* M: 07577-150543
E: revjohenderson@gmail.com

⌖**HENDERSON, The Rt Revd Julian Tudor.** b 54. Keble Coll
Ox BA 76 MA 81. Ridley Hall Cam 77. **d** 79 **p** 80 **c** 13. C
Islington St Mary *Lon* 79–83; V Hastings Em and St Mary
in the Castle *Chich* 83–92; V Claygate *Guildf* 92–05; RD
Emly 96–01; Adn Dorking 05–13; Hon Can Guildf Cathl
02–13; Bp Blackb from 13. *Bishop's House, Ribchester Road,
Clayton le Dale, Blackburn BB1 9EF* T: (01254) 248234
E: bishop@bishopofblackburn.org.uk

HENDERSON, Nicholas Paul. b 48. Selw Coll Cam BA 73
MA 77 Univ of Wales (Lamp) PhD 09. Ripon Hall Ox 73.
d 75 **p** 76. C St Alb St Steph 75–78; Warden J F Kennedy
Ho Cov Cathl 78–79; C Bow w Bromley St Leon *Lon* 79–85;
P-in-c W Acton St Martin 85–96; V 96–18; P-in-c Ealing All
SS 89–95; V 96–14; rtd 18. *38 Caledonian Wharf, London
E14 3EW* E: nicholashenderson@btinternet.com

HENDERSON, Olive Elizabeth. b 48. St Jo Coll Nottm. **d** 97
p 98. Aux Min Tallaght *D & G* 97–99; P-in-c Moviddy Union
C, C & R 99–01; P-in-c Rathdrum w Glenealy, Derralossary
and Laragh *D & G* 01–04; C 04–07; I 07–08; I Killeshin w
Cloydagh and Killabban *C & O* 08–10; Chapl Kingston
Coll Mitchelstown 10–12; I Donoughmore and Donard w
Dunlavin *D & G* 12–14; rtd 14. *Strathmore, Grangemellon,
Athy, Co Kildare, Republic of Ireland* M: (00353) 87-218 1891
E: oliveernest@hotmail.com

HENDERSON, Patrick James. b 57. R Holloway Coll Lon
BA 78 St Mary's Univ Coll Twickenham MA 12 Surrey
Univ PGCE 01. St Steph Ho Ox 83. **d** 86 **p** 87. C Hornsey
St Mary w St Geo *Lon* 86–90; V Whetstone St Jo 90–95;
In RC Ch 95–01; PtO *Lon* 01–02; C Hornsey H Innocents
02–07; C Stroud Green H Trin 02–04; P-in-c 04–07; V from
07; C Hornsey H Innocents from 07; C Harringay St Paul
from 10; Chapl Greig City Academy from 02. *Holy Trinity
Vicarage, Granville Road, London N4 4EL* T: (020) 8340 2051
E: pjhenderson2001@yahoo.co.uk

HENDERSON, Peter Ashley. b 59. St Martin's Coll Lanc
PGCE 00. CBDTI 02. **d** 05 **p** 06. NSM Arnside *Carl* 05–08;
NSM Kendal H Trin from 08. *2 Lowther Park, Kendal
LA9 6RS* T: (01539) 736079 E: janash@btinternet.com

HENDERSON, Richard. b 69. St Jo Coll Nottm 04. **d** 06 **p** 07.
C Beccles St Mich and St Luke *St E* 06–09; TV Sole Bay 09–16;
P-in-c Beccles St Mich and St Luke 16–18; R from 18. *The
Rectory, 44 Ringsfield Road, Beccles NR34 9PF* T: (01502)
349143 E: richhenderson@btinternet.com

⌖**HENDERSON, The Rt Revd Richard Crosbie Aitken.** b 57.
Magd Coll Ox MA 84 DPhil 84. St Jo Coll Nottm 83. **d** 86
p 87 **c** 98. C Chinnor w Emmington and Sydenham etc *Ox*
86–89; I Abbeystrewry Union *C, C & R* 89–95; I Ross Union
95–98; Dean Ross 95–98; Chan Cork Cathl 95–98; Bp T, K
& A 98–11; TV Heart of Eden *Carl* 11–12; Hon Asst Bp Carl
from 11. *Tralispean, Skibbereen, Co Cork, Republic of Ireland*
E: rcah57@gmail.com

HENDERSON, Robert. b 43. TCD 66 Lambeth STh 94. **d** 69
p 70. C Drumglass *Arm* 69–72; Chapl Miss to Seamen 72–77;
Sen Chapl Mombasa Kenya 77–78; I Mostrim w Granard,
Clonbroney, Killoe etc *K, E & A* 78–82; I Belfast St Matt *Conn*
82–92; I Kilroot and Templecorran 92–98; rtd 98. *39 Garvey
Court, Lisburn BT27 4DG* T: (028) 9260 7146

HENDERSON, Robert David Druitt. b 41. St Edm Hall Ox
MA 64 Brunel Univ MA 77 K Alfred's Coll Win PGCE 88.
d 03 **p** 04. OLM Wylye and Till Valley *Sarum* 03–10; rtd
10; PtO *Sarum* from 11. *Orchard House, Salisbury Road,
Steeple Langford, Salisbury SP3 4NQ* T: (01722) 790388
E: henderson.family@virgin.net

HENDERSON, Terry James. b 45. St Deiniol's Hawarden 76.
d 77 **p** 77. C Wrexham *St As* 77–79; Wilson Carlile Coll of
Evang 79–81; TV Langtree *Ox* 81–87; P-in-c Aston Cantlow
and Wilmcote w Billesley *Cov* 87–90; V 90–97; V St Peter-in-
Thanet *Cant* 97–02; R Elmley Castle w Bricklehampton and
Combertons *Worc* 02–12; C Overbury w Teddington, Alstone
etc 09–12; rtd 12; PtO *Cov* from 13. *8 Birdhaven Close,
Banbury Road, Lighthorne, Warwick CV35 0BE* T: (01926)
640350 E: terryhenderson15@gmail.com

HENDERSON, William Ernest. b 53. CEng 81 MICE 81 Southn
Univ BSc 75. St Jo Coll Nottm 87. **d** 89 **p** 90. C Win Ch Ch
89–93; V Stanley *Wakef* 93–14; *Leeds* 14–17; V Outwood,
Stanley and Wrenthorpe 17–18; rtd 18. *1 Drake Hill Cottage,
Cumberworth, Huddersfield HD8 8YD*

HENDERSON SMITH, Mrs Judith Hazel. b 55. De Montfort
Univ BSc 00 Nottm Univ MA 11. EMMTC 08. **d** 11 **p** 12.

NSM Alvaston *Derby* 11–15; NSM Sawley 15–16; V Ault Hucknall and Scarcliffe from 16; Jt Dioc Ecum Officer 12–16. *11 Devonshire Cottages, Churchside, Scarcliffe, Chesterfield S44 6TE* T: (01246) 241835 M: 07810-580340 E: judyh.hs@gmail.com

HENDRICKSE, Canon Clarence David. b 41. Nottm Univ PGCE 73 MPhil 95 CEng MIMechE 71. St Jo Coll Nottm 71. d 74 p 75. C St Helens St Helen *Liv* 74–76; C Netherley Ch Ch CD 76–77; TV 78–87; V Liv Ch Ch Norris Green 87–93; V Eccleston Ch Ch 93–06; Hon Can Liv Cathl 96–06; rtd 06; PtO *Carl* from 07; PtO Saldanha Bay from 11. T: (015394) 43058 E: canon.clarence.hendrickse@talktalk.net

HENDRY, Mrs Helen Clare. b 58. Lanc Univ BA 79 Cam Univ PGCE 80. Reformed Th Sem Mississippi MA 85 Oak Hill Th Coll 94. d 95. Lect Oak Hill Th Coll 86–08; NSM Muswell Hill St Jas w St Matt *Lon* from 95. *44 The Grove, London N13 5JR* T: (020) 8882 2186 *or* 8442 0276 E: clare.hendry@gracech.org.uk

HENDRY, Malcolm Graham. b 54. d 13 p 14. NSM Wrose *Bradf* 13–14; *Leeds* 14; C Shipley St Paul 15–17; V Cottingley from 17. *81 Littlelands, Bingley BD16 1AL* T: (01274) 560761 M: 07545-073075 E: malg6031@gmail.com

HENDY, Canon Graham Alfred. b 45. St Jo Coll Dur BA 67 MA 75 Fitzw Coll Cam CertEd Univ of Wales (Lamp) MTh 03 MPhil 07. Sarum Th Coll 67. d 70 p 71. C High Wycombe *Ox* 70–75; TV 75–78; R Upton cum Chalvey 78–83; TR 83–90; R S Walsham and Upton *Nor* 90–97; Dioc Lay Tr Officer 90–97; Can Res S'well Minster 97–02; R Upper Itchen *Win* 02–08; rtd 08; PtO *B & W* from 09. *74 Bath Road, Wells BA5 3LJ* T: (01749) 677003 E: grahamhendy@dunelm.org.uk

HENGIST, Barry. b 59. N Lon Poly BA 88. Ripon Coll Cuddesdon 07. d 09 p 10. C Weybridge *Guildf* 09–13; P-in-c Shirley St Geo *S'wark* 13–17; V from 17. *The Vicarage, 2 The Grove, West Wickham BR4 9JS* T: (020) 8654 8747 M: 07947-068209 E: barryhengist@gmail.com

HENIG, Martin Edward. b 42. St Cath Coll Cam BA 63 MA 66 Worc Coll Ox DPhil 72 DLitt 98 FSA 75. St Steph Ho Ox 08. d 10 p 11. NSM Osney *Ox* 10–18; PtO from 18. *16 Alexandra Road, Oxford OX2 0DB* T: (01865) 241118 *or* 278265 E: martin.henig@arch.ox.ac.uk

HENLEY, Christopher Charles. b 57. St Mellitus Coll BA 16. d 16 p 17. NSM Staines *Lon* 16–18; NSM Staines St Mary and St Pet from 18. *11 Hartington Court, Hartington Road, London W4 3TT* T: (020) 8582 5898 M: 07920-104009 E: christopherhenley57@gmail.com *or* christopher@stainesparish.org.uk

HENLEY, Dean. b 64. St Chad's Coll Dur BA 93. Westcott Ho Cam 93. d 95 p 96. C Farncombe *Guildf* 95–99; TV Hale w Badshot Lea 99–06; R Campton, Clophill and Haynes *St Alb* 06–19. *Address temp unknown*

HENLEY, James Andrew. d 15 p 16. C Newport St Paul *Mon* 15–17; TR Cyncoed from 17. *The Rectory, 256 Cyncoed Road, Cardiff CF23 6RU* T: (029) 2075 2138 E: james.henley@gmail.com

HENLEY, John Francis Hugh. b 48. SS Mark & Jo Coll Chelsea CertEd 69. St Mich Coll Llan. d 82 p 83. C Griffithstown *Mon* 82–85; V St Hilary Greenway 85–90; P-in-c Fulham St Etheldreda w St Clem *Lon* 90–11; V 11–18; C 18; rtd 18; PtO *Lon* from 18; *Nor* from 19. *11 Beatty Road, Great Yarmouth NR30 4BT* T: (01493) 298867

HENNING, Mrs Judy. b 49. Portsm Univ MSc 99. S Dios Minl Tr Scheme 85. d 88 p 97. C Catherington and Clanfield *Portsm* 88–91; C Leigh Park 91–92; PtO 94–96; Min in Whiteley and Asst to RD Fareham 96–99; C-in-c Whiteley CD 99–04; P-in-c Old Cleeve, Leighland and Treborough *B & W* 04–06; R 06–11; P-in-c Rainham *Roch* 11–13; V 13–17; rtd 17; PtO *Portsm* from 18. *17 Orpine Close, Fareham PO15 5TE* T: (01329) 845946 E: judy.henning@btinternet.com

HENNINGS, John Richard. b 58. Sheff Univ BA 80. Spurgeon's Coll BA 87. d 07 p 08. SSF from 05; PtO *Ripon* 09–10; *Sheff* 10–11; *Newc* 11–17; *Birm* from 17. *113 Gillott Road, Birmingham B16 0ET* T: 0121-454 8302 E: johnssf@franciscans.org.uk

HENRY, Cornelius Augustus. b 70. K Coll NY BA 92 Heythrop Coll Lon MA 06. NTMTC 07. d 09 p 10. C Hornchurch St Andr *Chelmsf* 09–13; V Forest Gate St Sav and St Jas from 13. *St Saviour's Rectory, Sidney Road, London E7 0EF* T: (020) 8534 6109 E: revcahenry@gmail.com

HENRY, Miss Jacqueline Margaret. b 40. Open Univ BA 82. Trin Coll Bris 77. dss 83 d 87 p 94. Deptford St Jo *S'wark* 79–82; Catshill and Dodford *Worc* 83–86; The Lye and Stambermill 86–87; Par Dn 87–89; Educn Chapl 89–93; C Tolleshunt Knights w Tiptree and Gt Braxted *Chelmsf* 94–97; Chapl amongst Deaf People 94–97; TV Stantonbury and

Willen *Ox* 97–02; rtd 02; PtO *Cant* 02–09; *Roch* from 09. *110 Ballens Road, Chatham ME5 8PG* T: (01634) 829183

HENRY, Peter. b 49. BTh. St Jo Coll Nottm. d 84 p 85. C Sinfin Moor and Blagreaves St Andr CD *Derby* 84–89; V Guernsey St Jo *Win* 89–97; P-in-c Sawley *Derby* 97–01; R 01–06; rtd 06. *23 Mulberry Close, Stotfold, Hitchin SG5 4NL* T: (01462) 834902 E: henmusic@cwgsy.net

HENRY, Canon Stephen Kenelm Malim. b 37. Brasted Th Coll 58 Bps' Coll Cheshunt 60. d 62 p 63. C Leic St Phil 62–67; CF 67–70; V Woodhouse *Wakef* 70–01; Hon Can Wakef Cathl 00–01; rtd 01; PtO *Wakef* 01–14; *Leeds* from 14. *1 Yorkstone, Crosland Moor, Huddersfield HD4 5NQ* T: (01484) 644807 E: mandsmalim64@btinternet.com

HENRYHOLLAND, Miss Anne. b 56. d 12 p 13. NSM Ludgvan, Marazion, St Hilary and Perranuthnoe *Truro* 12–17; Public Preacher from 17. *Tremorran, Truthwall, St Just, Penzance TR19 7QJ* M: 07768-166309 E: missanniehenry@hotmail.com

HENSHALL, Keith. *See* HENSHALL, Ronald Keith

HENSHALL, The Very Revd Nicholas James. b 62. Wadh Coll Ox BA 84 MA 88. Ripon Coll Cuddesdon 85. d 88 p 89. C Blyth St Mary *Newc* 88–92; V Scotswood 92–02; Can Res Derby Cathl 02–08; V High Harrogate Ch Ch *Ripon* 08–14; Dean Chelmsf from 14. *3 Harlings Grove, Chelmsford CM1 1YQ* T: (01245) 294492 E: nicholas.henshall@chelmsfordcathedral.org.uk

HENSHALL, Ronald Keith. b 54. Loughb Coll of Educn CertEd 76. Chich Th Coll 87. d 89 p 90. C Ribbleton *Blackb* 89–92; TV 95–98; P-in-c Charlestown and Lowland St Kitts-Nevis 92–95; V Ellel w Shireshead *Blackb* 98–02; Cyprus 02–05; Chapl R Alexandra and Albert Sch Reigate 05–06; P-in-c Lerwick and Burravoe *Ab* 06–10; V Hunwick-in-Cliviger w Worsthorne *Blackb* 10–16; rtd 16; PtO *Man* from 17. *Flat 203, 5 Munday Street, Manchester M4 7AY* M: 07540-133357 E: r.k.henshall@gmail.com

HENSON, Carolyn. b 44. Bedf Coll Lon BA 65 Nottm Univ MTh 88 PhD 97 Solicitor 75. EMMTC 82. dss 85 d 87 p 94. Braunstone *Leic* 85–89; Par Dn 87–89; Adult Educn and Tr Officer *Ely* 89–91; NSM Sutton and Witcham w Mepal 89–95; Chapl Gt Ormond Street Hosp for Children NHS Trust 95–96; NSM Cainscross w Selsley *Glouc* 96–97; Vice Prin EMMTC *S'well* 97–01; R Morley w Smalley and Horsley Woodhouse *Derby* 02–05; rtd 05; Chapl St Mich Hospice Harrogate 09–10; PtO *York* from 09. *45 Harvest Drive, Malton YO17 7BF* E: carolyn.henson2@gmail.com

HENSON, Joanna. b 62. d 06 p 07. NSM Egton-cum-Newland and Lowick and Colton *Carl* 06–12; rtd 12; PtO *Carl* from 13. *Woodside Cottage, Colton, Ulverston LA12 8HE* T: (01229) 861800 E: joannahenson@aol.com

HENSON, John David. b 48. EMMTC. d 00 p 01. NSM Beckingham w Walkeringham *S'well* 00–02; NSM Gringley-on-the-Hill 00–02; NSM Misterton and W Stockwith 02–05; C 06–07; C Beckingham w Walkeringham and Gringley 06–07; P-in-c Beckingham and Walkeringham and Misterton etc 07–11; V 11–15; Asst Chapl HM Pris Whatton 00–05; V Beckingham, Walkeringham, Misterton, etc *S'well* from 15; Sen Police Chapl from 03. *The Vicarage, 4 Church Lane, Misterton, Doncaster DN10 4AL* T: (01427) 890270 E: jd.henson@btinternet.com

HENSON, Canon John Richard. b 40. Selw Coll Cam BA 62 MA 66. Ridley Hall Cam 62. d 65 p 66. C Ollerton *S'well* 65–68; Univs sec CMS 68–73; Chapl Scargill Ho 73–78; V Shipley St Paul *Bradf* 78–83; TR Shipley St Paul and Frizinghall 83–91; V Ilkeston St Mary *Derby* 91–99; V Mickleover St Jo 99–05; Dioc Ecum Officer 96–05; Hon Can Derby Cathl 00–05; rtd 05; PtO *Derby* 05–16; *S'well* from 06; Asst P St Geo Cathl Jerusalem 13–15. *6 Ganton Close, Nottingham NG3 3ET* E: john.henson3@ntlworld.com

HENSTRIDGE, Edward John. b 31. Ex Coll Ox BA 55 MA 59 FCIPD 77. Wells Th Coll 55. d 57 p 58. C Milton *Portsm* 57–62; V Soberton w Newtown 62–69; LtO *Derby* 69–71; PtO *Guildf* 72–84 and from 02; LtO 84–02; Bp's Officer for NSMs 97–01. *Hunters Moon, Lower Ham Lane, Elstead, Godalming GU8 6HQ* T: (01252) 702272 E: johnhn@globalnet.co.uk

HENTHORNE, Thomas Roger. b 30. EAMTC. d 79 p 80. Hd Master St Mary's Sch St Neots 67–93; NSM St Neots *Ely* 79–04; PtO from 04. *Stapeley, 45 Berkley Street, Eynesbury, St Neots PE19 2ND* T: (01480) 472548 E: roger.henthorne@uwclub.net

HENWOOD (née RENNIE), Mrs Gillian Kathleen. b 56. Lanc Univ MA 97 ABIPP 81. CBDTI 94. d 97 p 98. NSM Whitechapel w Admarsh-in-Bleasdale *Blackb* 97–00; NSM Fellside Team 00–01; Rural Chapl 00–03; Chapl Myerscough Coll 00–03; Bp's Adv for Leisure and Tourism 01–03; C Westmr St Jas *Lon* 03–04; V Nunthorpe *York* 04–09; P-in-c Riding Mill *Newc* 09–10; Chapl Shepherd's

Dene Retreat Ho 09–10; Adv for Spirituality and Spiritual Direction 09–10; P-in-c Ribchester w Stydd *Blackb* 10–11; R 11–16; PtO 16–17; P-in-c Grasmere *Carl* 17–19; P-in-c Rydal 17–19; rtd 19; PtO *Carl* from 19. *Keen Ground, Hawkshead, Ambleside LA22 0NW* M: 07712-526719 E: gillkhenwood@hotmail.com

HENWOOD, Canon Peter Richard. b 32. St Edm Hall Ox BA 55 MA 69. Cuddesdon Coll 56. **d** 57 **p** 58. C Rugby St Andr *Cov* 57–62; C-in-c Gleadless Valley CD *Sheff* 62–71; V Plaistow St Mary *Roch* 71–97; RD Bromley 79–96; Hon Can Roch Cathl 88–97; rtd 97; PtO *Cant* 99–14. *Wayside, 1 Highfield Close, Sandling Road, Saltwood, Hythe CT21 4QP* T: (01303) 230039

HENWOOD (née OAKLEY), Mrs Susan Mary. b 55. Salford Univ BSc 76. St Jo Coll Nottm 84. **d** 87 **p** 94. Par Dn Armthorpe *Sheff* 87–91; C Howell Hill *Guildf* 91–96; PtO *Cov* 02–04; NSM Bidford-on-Avon 04–15; NSM Heart of England 15–16; NSM Alcester Minster from 16. *Kinwarton Rectory, Spernall Lane, Great Alne, Alcester B49 6HY*

HEPBURN, Ian Malcolm George. b 76. Napier Univ Edin BSc 00. St Mellitus Coll 16. **d** 19. C Bolton St Pet w St Phil *Man* from 19. *24 Ingleby Close, Westhoughton, Bolton BL5 3QZ* T: (01942) 814045 E: curate@boltonparishchurch.co.uk

HEPBURN, Julia Mary. b 61. St Andr Univ BSc 82 Man Univ MB, ChB 85. Linc Sch of Th and Min 04. **d** 12 **p** 13. OLM Spring Line Gp *Linc* 12–16; OLM Owmby Gp 12–16; NSM Linc St Mary Magd w St Paul and St Mich from 16. *27 Lee Road, Lincoln LN2 4BQ* M: 07707-027804 E: julia.hepburn@lincoln.anglican.org

HEPPER, Canon Christopher Michael Alan. b 55. Wolv Univ BSc 78. St Jo Coll Nottm 90. **d** 92 **p** 93. C High Harrogate Ch Ch *Ripon* 92–95; Bp's Dom Chapl 95–99; Dioc Communications Officer 95–97; NSM Ripon H Trin 98–99; P-in-c Poitou-Charentes *Eur* 99–11; P-in-c Leyburn w Bellerby *Leeds* 11–15; V 15–18; AD Wensley 13–18; Hon Can Ripon Cathl 17–18; NSM Felton *Newc* from 18; NSM Longframlington w Brinkburn from 18. *West Moor Farm, Longhorsley, Morpeth NE65 8QX* E: revmichael@btinternet.com

HEPPER, William Raymond. b 62. Kingston Poly BA 83. Trin Coll Bris BA 98. **d** 98 **p** 99. C Spring Grove St Mary *Lon* 98–01; CMS Egypt 01–04; NSM Greenford H Cross *Lon* 05–08; PtO from 08. *92 Beechmount Avenue, London W7 3AQ* T: (020) 8578 3437 M: 07917-336657 E: williamhepper@hotmail.com

HEPTINSTALL, Canon Lillian. b 49. EMMTC 99. **d** 02 **p** 03. NSM Chilwell *S'well* 02–15; Hon Can S'well Minster 12–15; rtd 15; PtO *S'well* from 16. *8 Cranston Road, Bramcote, Nottingham NG9 3GU* T: 0115-916 4588 E: heptinstall@ntlworld.com

HEPTINSTALL, Mrs Susan Margaret. b 56. Yorks Min Course 08. **d** 10 **p** 11. NSM Halifax St Aug and Mount Pellon *Wakef* 10–14; *Leeds* 14–17; NSM Bradshaw and Holmfield from 17. *26 Sandbeds Road, Pellon, Halifax HX2 0JF* T: (01422) 341436 M: 07510-510359 E: vicarsue@gmail.com

HEPWORTH, Canon Ernest John Peter. b 42. K Coll Lon BD 65 AKC 65 Hull Univ MA 87. **d** 66 **p** 67. C Headingley *Ripon* 66–69; Asst Chapl St Geo Hosp Lon 69–71; C Gt Grimsby St Mary and St Jas *Linc* 71–72; TV 72–74; V Crosby 74–80; V Barton upon Humber 80–04; RD Yarborough 86–92; Can and Preb Linc Cathl 94–04; rtd 04. *63 Ferriby Road, Barton-upon-Humber DN18 5LQ* T: (01652) 661363 E: ehep01@aol.com

HEPWORTH, Michael David Albert. b 37. Em Coll Cam BA 59 MA 63 Lon Inst of Educn PGCE 60. Ridley Hall Cam 65. **d** 67 **p** 68. C Eastbourne All SS *Chich* 67–69; Teacher Eastbourne Coll 67–69; Asst Chapl Bedford Sch 69–72; Chapl 72–83; Hd Master Birkdale Sch 83–98; PtO *Sheff* 83–09; *Derby* 83–09; *Guildf* from 10. *6 Elm Gardens, Claygate, Esher KT10 0JS* T: (01372) 466651 E: michaelhepworth@talktalk.net

HERAPATH, Jonathan James. b 67. Westmr Coll Ox BTh 96 Ox Brookes Univ PGCE 02. St Steph Ho Ox MTh 06. **d** 05 **p** 06. C Cowley St Jo Ox 05–07; Chapl SS Helen and Kath Sch Abingdon 07–10; Chapl Wadh Coll Ox 10–12; PtO *Portsm* from 12; *Lon* 16–17; NSM St Vedast w St Mich-le-Querne etc 17–19. *11 Dial Place, Warkworth, Morpeth NE65 0UR* M: 07745-405150 E: jonathanherapath@gmail.com

HERBERT, Christopher. b 63. Yorks Min Course 14. **d** 17 **p** 18. NSM Burghwallis and Campsall *Sheff* from 17. *4 Highfield Villas, High Street, Norton, Doncaster DN6 9EJ* T: (01302) 702615 E: bluefin040@gmail.com or chris.herbert@sheffield.anglican.org

HERBERT, Christopher John. b 37. Dur Univ BA 60. Cranmer Hall Dur 60. **d** 62 **p** 63. C Huyton Quarry *Liv* 62–65; C Rainford 65–68; V Impington *Ely* 68–78; RD N Stowe 76–78; V Gt Shelford 78–97; RD Shelford 80–85; rtd 97. *North Place, Crown Street, Great Bardfield, Braintree CM7 4ST* T: (01371) 810516

✠**HERBERT, The Rt Revd Christopher William.** b 44. Univ of Wales (Lamp) BA 65 Bris Univ PGCE 65 Leic Univ MPhil 02 PhD 08 Herts Univ Hon DLitt 03. Wells Th Coll 65. **d** 67 **p** 68 **c** 95. C Tupsley *Heref* 67–71; Dioc RE Adv 71–76; Dioc Dir RE 76–81; Preb Heref Cathl 76–81; V Bourne *Guildf* 81–90; Hon Can Guildf Cathl 85–95; Adn Dorking 90–95; Bp St Alb 95–09; rtd 09; Hon Asst Bp Guildf from 09; Hon Asst Bp Win from 09; Hon Asst Bp Chich 10–14. *1 Beacon Close, Wrecclesham, Farnham GU10 4PA* T: (01252) 795600 E: cherbert@threeabbeys.org.uk

HERBERT, Clare Marguerite. b 54. St Hild Coll Dur BA 76 New Coll Edin MTh 78 Anglia Ruskin Univ DProf 17. Linc Th Coll 79. **dss** 83 **d** 87 **p** 94. Clifton St Paul and Asst Chapl Bris Univ 81–84; Hon Par Dn Bris St Mary Redcliffe w Temple etc 87–90; Dioc Past Care Adv *Lon* 92–95; Hon C Clapham Team *S'wark* 94–96; C St Martin-in-the-Fields *Lon* 96–98; R Soho St Anne w St Thos and St Pet 98–07; Dean of Women's Min Two Cities Area 01–07; Nat Co-ord Inclusive Ch 07–10; Lect St Martin-in-the-Fields *Lon* 10–14; Tutor St Aug Coll of Th 14–18; rtd 18; Assoc Tutor (Lead) St Aug Coll of Th from 18; PtO *S'wark* from 14. *Fiere, 15 Queen Street, Emsworth PO10 7BJ* T: (01243) 430765 M: 07841-032751 E: herbert.clare@googlemail.com

HERBERT, Canon David Alexander Sellars. b 39. Bris Univ BA 60. St Steph Ho Ox 65. **d** 67 **p** 68. C St Leonards Ch Ch *Chich* 67–81; V Bickley *Roch* 81–09; Hon Can Roch Cathl 92–09; rtd 09; PtO *Roch* from 09. *54 High Street, Chislehurst BR7 5AQ* T: (020) 8467 5230 M: 07545-645316 E: fatherdavidherbert@btinternet.com

HERBERT, Canon David Roy. b 51. K Coll Lon BD 73 AKC 73 Ches Univ MTh 12. **d** 74 **p** 75. C Sheff St Aid w St Luke 74–75; C Sheff Manor 75–78; TV Gleadless Valley 78–83; TV Ellesmere Port *Ches* 83–93; V Tarvin 93–09; Continuing Minl Tr Officer 03–09; CMD Officer and IME (4-7) Officer from 09; Hon Can Ches Cathl from 08. *25 Blackstairs Road, Ellesmere Port CH66 1TX* T: 0151-356 4554 E: david.herbert@chester.anglican.org

HERBERT, Mrs Denise Bridget Helen. b 42. Win Univ MA 11 SRN 72 SCM 74. Ripon Coll Cuddesdon. **d** 95 **p** 96. C Ocean View S Africa 95–97; C Grahamstown Cathl 97–99; Sub-Dean 99–00; R Jedburgh *Edin* 00–08; rtd 08; R Newport-on-Tay *St And* 09–15; PtO *Bre* 15–18; LtO from 18; Protection of Vulnerable Gps Officer from 17; PtO *St And* from 15; *Edin* from 16. *43 Bridieswell Gardens, Gauldry, Newport-on-Tay DD6 8RY* T: (01382) 330411 E: dbh.herbert@btinternet.com

HERBERT, Geoffrey William. b 38. Ox Univ MA 62 Birm Univ PhD 72. Qu Coll Birm 80. **d** 82 **p** 83. C Hall Green Ascension *Birm* 82–85; R Sheldon 85–95; rtd 95; PtO *Birm* from 95; Co-ord for Spiritual Direction 00–05. *28 Lulworth Road, Birmingham B28 8NS* T: 0121-777 2684

HERBERT, Graham Victor. b 61. St Jo Coll Nottm BA 02. **d** 02 **p** 03. C Strood St Nic w St Mary *Roch* 02–06; P-in-c Grain w Stoke 06–09; R Milton next Gravesend w Denton from 09. *The Rectory, Church Walk, Gravesend DA12 2QU* T: (01474) 533434 E: rector@miltonchurch.org.uk or grahamherbert@hotmail.co.uk

HERBERT, Ian Charles. b 65. Trin Coll Bris 10. **d** 12 **p** 13. C Haddenham w Cuddington, Kingsey etc *Ox* 12–16; TV Grays Thurrock *Chelmsf* 16–17; R Woughton *Ox* from 17. *7 Stonebridge Grove, Monkston Park, Milton Keynes MK10 9PB* M: 07740-081457 E: ian.herbert@yahoo.co.uk

HERBERT, Jonathan Patrick. b 62. Bris Univ BA 86. Linc Th Coll 86. **d** 88 **p** 89. C Kirkby *Liv* 88–91; TV Blakenall Heath *Lich* 91–96; Pilsdon Community 96–10; Chapl to Travelling People *Sarum* from 15. *The Friary, Hilfield, Dorchester DT2 7BE* T: (01300) 341345 E: jonathanherbert1@hotmail.co.uk

HERBERT, Peter David. b 83. Pemb Coll Cam BA 05 MSci 05 MA 08 Herts Univ PhD 12. Oak Hill Th Coll BA 13. **d** 13 **p** 14. C Cromer *Nor* 13–18; TR Thetford from 18. *The Rectory, 6 Redcastle Road, Thetford IP24 3NF* T: (01842) 763579 E: revpeterherbert@gmail.com

HERBERT, Canon Ronald. b 53. Worc Coll Ox BA 75 MA 80 Lon Univ BD 78 W Kentucky Univ MA 79. Oak Hill Th Coll 75. **d** 79 **p** 80. C Welling *Roch* 79–89; V Falconwood 89–90; V Becontree St Mary *Chelmsf* 90–07; Hon Can Chelmsf Cathl 02–07; V Stonebridge St Mich *Lon* 07–18; rtd 18; PtO *Cant* from 18. *111 Somerset Road, Folkestone CT19 4NW* T: (01303) 279859 E: ronald.herbert53@gmail.com

HERBERT, Canon Stephen Edward. b 54. Hastings Coll Nebraska BA 76 Bemidji State Univ MA 81. Seabury-Western Th Sem MDiv 87. **d** 87 **p** 87. V Lake City Grace Ch USA 87–90; Asst P Vancouver St Jas Canada 90–00; TV Wythenshawe *Man* 00–06; TR 06–09; P-in-c Byker St Martin *Newc* 09–16; V from 16; P-in-c Byker St Mich w St Lawr 09–12; P-in-c Byker St Ant 12–16; V from 16; Hon Can Newc Cathl from 17. *St Martin's Vicarage, 152 Roman Avenue, Newcastle upon Tyne NE6 2RJ* T: 0191-265 5931

HERBERT, Canon Timothy David. b 57. Man Univ BA 78 MPhil 88 PhD 04. Ridley Hall Cam 79. **d** 81 **p** 82. C Macclesfield St Mich *Ches* 81–85; V Wharton 85–93; Asst CME Officer 90–93; P-in-c Thanington *Cant* 93–98; Dir of Ords 93–98; Dir Dioc Tr Inst *Carl* 99–14; C Cotehill and Cumwhinton 99–00; C Scotby and Cotehill w Cumwhinton 00–14; P-in-c Aspatria w Hayton and Gilcrux from 14; RD Solway from 16; Hon Can Carl Cathl from 99. *The Vicarage, King Street, Aspatria, Wigton CA7 3AL* T: (016973) 22712 E: therbert@globalnet.co.uk

HEREFORD, Archdeacon of. *See* CHEDZEY, The Ven Derek Christopher

HEREFORD, Bishop of. *See* FRITH, The Rt Revd Richard Michael Cokayne

HEREFORD, Dean of. *See* TAVINOR, The Very Revd Michael Edward

HERKES, Richard Andrew. b 54. Kent Univ BA 75. STETS 99. **d** 02 **p** 03. NSM Polegate *Chich* from 02. *31 Wannock Lane, Eastbourne BN20 9SB* T: (01323) 488328

HERKLOTS, Canon John Radu. b 31. Trin Hall Cam BA 53 MA 61. Westcott Ho Cam 54. **d** 55 **p** 56. C Attercliffe w Carbrook *Sheff* 55–60; C Stoke Damerel *Ex* 60–65; V Devonport St Bart 65–72; V Denmead *Portsm* 72–97; RD Havant 82–87; Hon Can Portsm Cathl 86–97; rtd 97; PtO *Heref* 97–02; *Portsm* from 03. *14 Derwent Road, Lee-on-the-Solent PO13 8JG* T: (023) 9255 2652 E: dencliff1@hotmail.com

HERMO, Ole Bertin. b 66. Spurgeon's Coll BA 14. St Mellitus Coll 14. **d** 16 **p** 17. C Hounslow H Trin *Lon* 16–19; V Leic Martyrs from 19. *The Vicarage, 17 Westcotes Drive, Leicester LE3 0QT* M: 07950-644390 E: bertin.hermo@yahoo.com

HERON, David George. b 49. AKC 72. **d** 73 **p** 74. C Stockton St Chad *Dur* 73–77; C Beamish 77–81; R Willington and Sunnybrow 81–95; V Dipton and Leadgate 95–11; rtd 11; PtO *Dur* from 15. *31 Hill Top, Stanley DH9 0UZ* E: fatherheron@talktalk.net

HERON, George Dobson. b 34. Cranmer Hall Dur 58. **d** 61 **p** 62. C Benfieldside *Dur* 61–65; C Winlaton 65–68; V Dunston St Nic 68–77; P-in-c Dunston Ch Ch 74–77; V Dunston 77–82; V Gateshead St Helen 82–89; rtd 94; PtO *Dur* 94–17; *Newc* from 94. *9 Beech House, Snows Green Road, Consett DH8 0HS*

HERON, Nicholas Peter. b 60. Man Univ BA 81 Southn Univ BTh 86. Sarum & Wells Th Coll. **d** 84 **p** 85. C Brinnington w Portwood *Ches* 84–87; Chapl RAF 87–14; P-in-c Wem *Lich* 14–15; P-in-c Lee Brockhurst 14–15; R Wem, Lee Brockhurst etc from 16. *The Rectory, Ellesmere Road, Wem, Shrewsbury SY4 5TU*

HERON, Canon Simon Alexander. b 68. Ridley Hall Cam 05. **d** 07 **p** 08. C Frindsbury w Upnor and Chattenden *Roch* 07–11; P-in-c Lawford *Chelmsf* 11–17; C Ardleigh and The Bromleys 16–17; C Tendring and Lt Bentley w Beaumont cum Moze 16–17; V Lawford, Lt Bentley and The Bromleys from 17; AD Harwich from 16; Hon Can Chelmsf Cathl from 16. *The Rectory, Church Hill, Lawford, Manningtree CO11 2JX* T: (01206) 392659 E: simon.heron@mac.com *or* vicar@lawfordchurch.co.uk *or* simon.heron@lawfordchurch.co.uk

HERRICK, The Ven Andrew Frederick. b 58. Univ of Wales (Lamp) BA 80. Wycliffe Hall Ox 80. **d** 82 **p** 83. C Aberystwyth *St D* 82–85; P-in-c Llangeitho and Blaenpennal w Betws Leucu etc 85–86; R 86–88; Youth Chapl 86–88; R Aberporth w Tremain and Blaenporth 88–91; Succ St D Cathl 91–94; V Betws w Ammanford 94–00; TV Aberystwyth 00–15; P-in-c Lampeter w Maestir and Silian and Llangybi and Betws Bledrws 15–18; Hon Can St D Cathl 14–18; V Bro Cybi *Ban* from 18; Adn Anglesey from 18. *Bryn Llewellyn, Penrallt Road, Trearddur Bay, Holyhead LL65 2UG* T: (01407) 861084 E: andyherrick101@gmail.com *or* archdeacon.anglesey@churchinwales.org.uk

HERRICK, Canon David William. b 52. Middx Poly BSc 73. St Jo Coll Nottm 79. **d** 82 **p** 83. C Ipswich St Matt *St E* 82–85; C Nor St Pet Mancroft w St Jo Maddermarket 85–88; V Bury St Edmunds St Geo *St E* 88–96; P-in-c Gt Barton 96–99; Dir Studies Dioc Min Course 99–12; Vice Prin 04–12; Lay Min Tr Officer 12–16; Dioc Warden of Readers and Lic Lay Min 14–16; Hon Can St E Cathl 13–16; rtd 16; PtO *Sarum* 13–17; *Chelmsf* 17–18; P-in-c Gt Hallingbury

and Lt Hallingbury from 18. *Glebe House, Church Lane, Sheering, Bishop's Stortford CM22 7NR* T: (01279) 734524 E: davidherrick103@gmail.com

HERRICK (formerly COWLEY), Mrs Jean Louie Cameron. b 39. Sarum Dioc Tr Coll CertEd 59. SAOMC 94. **d** 96 **p** 97. NSM Chorleywood Ch Ch *St Alb* 96–02; NSM Hermitage *Ox* 02–05; PtO *Glouc* from 05. *1 The Maltings, Station Street, Tewkesbury GL20 5NN* T: (01684) 295598 E: jean.herrick@talktalk.net

HERRICK (née RENAUT), The Ven Vanessa Anne. b 58. York Univ BA 80 Anglia Poly Univ MA 96 LTCL 75. St Jo Coll Nottm 80 Ridley Hall Cam 94. **d** 96 **p** 97. C St E Cathl Distr 96–99; Chapl Fitzw Coll Cam 99–02; Fell 01–02; Tutor Ridley Hall Cam 99–02; Dir Min and Vocation *Ely* 03–12; Hon Can Ely Cathl 03–12; R Wimborne Minster *Sarum* 12–15; P-in-c Witchampton, Stanbridge and Long Crichel etc 15; P-in-c Horton, Chalbury, Hinton Martel and Holt St Jas 15; R Wimborne Minster and the N Villages 15–17; Can and Preb Sarum Cathl 14–17; Adn Harlow *Chelmsf* from 17. *Glebe House, Church Lane, Sheering, Bishops Stortford CM22 7NR* T: (01279) 734524 F: 734426 E: a.harlow@chelmsford.anglican.org

HERROD, Kathryn. b 59. Warwick Univ BSc 80 Matlock Coll of Educn PGCE 81. St Jo Coll Nottm MA 97. **d** 98 **p** 99. C Wollaton *S'well* 97–01; R Warsop 01–10; TR Hucknall Torkard 10–17; Dean of Women's Min 15–17; Hon Can S'well Minster 11–17; P-in-c Barnburgh w Melton on the Hill etc *Sheff* from 17; P-in-c Bilham from 17; Asst Dioc Dir of Ords from 17. *1 Fitzwilliam Drive, Harlington, Doncaster DN5 7HY* T: (01709) 898538 E: kathryn.herrod@sheffield.anglican.org *or* revkathryn@btinternet.com

HERRON, Robert Gordon John. b 36. MCIPD 75. Wycliffe Hall Ox 65. **d** 77 **p** 78. C Ditton St Mich *Liv* 77–80; C W Kirby St Bridget *Ches* 80–82; R Gorton Our Lady and St Thos *Man* 82–00; rtd 00; PtO *Ches* from 10. *The Gables, 13 West Road, Bowdon, Altrincham WA14 2LD* E: revgordon@bowdonchurch.org *or* rgjherron@gmail.com

HERTFORD, Archdeacon of. *See* MACKENZIE, The Ven Janet

HERTFORD, Suffragan Bishop of. *See* BEASLEY, The Rt Revd Noel Michael Roy

HERTH, Daniel Edwin. b 36. Xavier Univ Cincinnati BS 58. Ch Div Sch of Pacific MDiv 83. **d** 83 **p** 84. C Oakland St Paul USA 83–86; R Alameda Ch Ch 86–97; NSM Gt and Lt Ouseburn w Marton cum Grafton etc *Ripon* 98–01; Chapl HM YOI Wetherby from 99. *The Garden House, 32 Mallorie Park Drive, Ripon HG4 2QF* T/F: (01765) 602558 M: 07779-379420 E: danielhevthsr@btinternet.com

HERVÉ, Canon John Anthony. b 49. Open Univ BA 81 Wolv Univ PGCE 95. Lich Th Coll 70. **d** 73 **p** 74. C Middlesbrough All SS *York* 73–76; CF 76–81; CF (TAVR) 81–08; P-in-c Handsworth St Andr *Birm* 81–86; Hon C Cowley St Jo *Ox* 86–90; Tutor St Steph Ho Ox 86–90; V Sparkbrook St Agatha w Balsall Heath St Barn *Birm* 90–14; P-in-c Highgate 05–10; Hon Can Birm Cathl 05–14; rtd 14. *29 Lytton House, St Luke's Road South, Torquay TQ2 5PA* T: (01803) 295887

HERVEY, Mrs Mary Diana. b 41. St Hugh's Coll Ox BA 63. St And Dioc Tr Course 83 TISEC 96. **d** 92 **p** 94. Par Dn Cupar *St And* 92–94; Asst Chapl St Andr Univ 94–97; Asst P Cen Fife Team 94–97; C Ulverston St Mary w H Trin *Carl* 97–00; P-in-c Barrow St Jo 00–06; rtd 06; PtO *Carl* 08–14; *Bradf* 11–14; *Leeds* 14–16; *Ab* from 18. *Nor Hamar, Baltasound, Unst, Shetland ZE2 9DS* T: (01957) 711331

HESELTINE, Barbara Joan. *See* FEATHER, Barbara Joan

HESELWOOD, Eric Harold. b 43. Oak Hill Th Coll 84. **d** 86 **p** 87. C Farnborough *Roch* 86–88; V Biggin Hill 88–96; V Orpington All SS 96–98; V Bromley Common St Aug 98–05; rtd 05; PtO *Roch* 06–08; P-in-c Cudham and Downe 08–10; PtO from 10. *34 Victoria Gardens, Biggin Hill, Westerham TN16 3DJ* T/F: (01959) 509131 E: eric.heselwood@ntlworld.com

HESFORD-LOCKE, Richard Nigel. b 61. Coll of Resurr Mirfield 92. **d** 94 **p** 95. C Middlesbrough Ascension *York* 94–97; C Paignton St Jo *Ex* 97–98; rtd 98. *2 Windyhill Drive, Bolton BL3 4TH*

HESKETH, Derrick. b 61. **d** 12 **p** 13. OLM Blackwell w Tibshelf *Derby* from 12. *61 Peveril Road, Tibshelf, Alfreton DE55 5LR* T: (01773) 872146 E: derrickhesketh61@btinternet.com

HESKETH, The Very Revd Philip John. b 64. K Coll Lon BD 86. AKC 86 PhD 94. Ripon Coll Cuddesdon 92. **d** 94 **p** 95. C Bearsted w Thurnham *Cant* 94–98; V Chatham St Steph *Roch* 98–05; Can Res Roch Cathl 05–16; Dean Roch from 16. *Chapter Office, Garth House, The Precinct, Rochester ME1 1SX* T: (01634) 843366 F: 401410 E: dean@rochestercathedral.org

HESKETH, The Ven Ronald David. b 47. Bede Coll Dur BA 68 FRGS 02. Ridley Hall Cam 69 St Mich Coll Llan 71.

d 71 **p** 72. C Southport H Trin *Liv* 71–74; Asst Chapl Miss to Seamen 74–75; Chapl RAF 75–98; Command Chapl RAF 98–01; Chaplain-in-Chief RAF 01–06; Can and Preb Linc Cathl 01–06; Voc Officer *Worc* 06–11; Co-ord Chapl W Mercia Police from 09; QHC from 01; PtO *Glouc* from 15; *Worc* from 16. *Whistledown, Twyning Green, Twyning, Tewkesbury GL20 6DQ* T: (01684) 299773 E: ron@hesketh.org.uk

HESKINS, Georgiana Mary. *See* BELL, Georgiana Mary

HESKINS, Canon Jeffrey George. b 55. Heythrop Coll Lon MA 94 Princeton Th Sem DMin 00 AKC 78. Chich Th Coll 80. **d** 81 **p** 82. C Primrose Hill St Mary w Avenue Road St Paul *Lon* 81–85; Enfield Deanery Youth Officer 85–88; C Enfield Chase St Mary *Lon* 85–88; TV Kidbrooke St Jas *S'wark* 88–95; R Charlton St Luke w H Trin 95–02; P-in-c Old Charlton St Thos 02; R Charlton 02–07; Dioc Dir of Ords *Linc* 07–18; Min Can and PV Linc Cathl 08–10; Dir IME 4-7 10–18; Can and Preb Linc Cathl from 10. *Address temp unknown*

HESKINS, Rachel. b 70. Trevelyan Coll Dur BA 92 Ox Univ PGCE 97. Westcott Ho Cam 15. **d** 16 **p** 17. C Welton and Dunholme w Scothern *Linc* from 16. *The Rectory, Main Street, Hackthorn, Lincoln LN2 3PF* E: rachel@heskins.plus.com

HESLAM, Peter Somers. b 63. Hull Univ BA 89 Keble Coll Ox DPhil 94 Trin Coll Cam BA 96 MA 01. Ridley Hall Cam 93. **d** 96 **p** 97. C Huntingdon *Ely* 96–99; Min Stukeley Meadows LEP 99; Dir Studies EAMTC 99–00; Tutor Ridley Hall Cam 99–05; Dir Capitalism Project Lon Inst of Contemporary Chr 00–04; Fell Faculty of Div Cam Univ from 05; Hon C Cherry Hinton St Jo *Ely* from 00. *Glebe House, 64A Glebe Road, Cambridge CB1 7SZ* T: (01223) 722822 E: psh20@cam.ac.uk

HESLOP, Alan. *See* WILSON, James Alan

HESLOP, Andrew James. b 66. Man Univ BA 87 PGCE 88. **d** 03 **p** 04. OLM Turton Moorland *Man* 03–18; Chapl Wrightington, Wigan and Leigh NHS Foundn Trust 07–10; Chapl Springhill Hospice 10–14; Chapl Salford R NHS Foundn Trust from 14; PtO *Blackb* 07–10; *Man* from 18. *The Chaplaincy, Salford Royal NHS Foundation Trust, Stott Lane, Salford M6 8HD* T: 0161-789 7373 E: andrew.heslop@srft.nhs.uk

HESLOP, Caroline Susan. *See* WILSON, Caroline Susan

HESLOP, David Anthony. b 45. BSc DipEd MTh Birm Univ MLitt 97. St Jo Coll Nottm 81. **d** 83 **p** 84. C Willenhall H Trin *Lich* 83–86; V Gresley *Derby* 86–92; V Marston on Dove w Scropton 92–95; Chapl Derby Univ 95–99; V Castle Donington and Lockington cum Hemington *Leic* 99–03; Chapl E Midl Airport 99–03; Prin OLM and Integrated Tr *Sarum* 03–07; Co-ord for Learning and Discipleship 07–10; rtd 11; Dir of Ords (Berks) *Ox* 11–13; PtO *B & W* from 15. *4 Bakers Buildings, Wrington, Bristol BS40 5LQ* T: (01934) 862473 E: revdave@heslops.co.uk

HESLOP, James Alan. b 37. Codrington Coll Barbados 61. **d** 64 **p** 65. C Bartica Guyana 64–68; P-in-c Long Is Nassau Bahamas 68–71; C Ch Ch Cathl 71–72; C Haxby w Wigginton *York* 72–74; TV 74–76; V York St Olave w St Giles 76–87; V Northampton All SS w St Kath *Pet* 87–88; R Felpham w Middleton *Chich* 88–92; TR Howden *York* 92–94; Warden Coll of St Barn Lingfield 94–95; Warden Morley Retreat and Conf Ho Derby 95–98; R Kirkbride and V Lezayre St Olave Ramsey *S & M* 98–99; P-in-c Woburn w Eversholt, Milton Bryan, Battlesden etc *St Alb* 99–03; rtd 03; Chapl Soc of St Marg 04–05; P-in-c Pau *Eur* 05–06. *1 Coniston Close, Bognor Regis PO22 8ND* T: (01243) 869499

HESLOP, Neil. b 73. Sunderland Univ BSc 95 MSc 03 Sheff Univ BA 15. Coll of Resurr Mirfield 13. **d** 15 **p** 16. C Fenham St Jas and St Basil *Newc* 15–18; C Sugley 18; P-in-c from 18. *Sugley Vicarage, Sugley Drive, Lemington, Newcastle upon Tyne NE15 8RD* T: 0191-267 4633 E: frneil.heslop@gmail.com

HETHERINGTON, Andrew. b 50. Sheff Univ BSc 71. Wycliffe Hall Ox 71. **d** 74 **p** 75. C Leic H Trin w St Jo 74–78; C Leic H Apostles 78–82; V Bootle St Mary w St Paul *Liv* 82–93; TR W Swindon and the Lydiards 93–01; P-in-c Chebsey, Ellenhall and Seighford-with-Creswell *Lich* 01–06; V Chebsey, Creswell, Ellenhall, Ranton etc 06–15; rtd 15; PtO *Liv* from 15. *67 Maliston Road, Great Sankey, Warrington WA5 1JS* E: andrewhetherington@btinternet.com

HETHERINGTON, Mrs Charlotte Elizabeth. b 52. Girton Coll Cam BA 74 Maria Grey Coll Lon PGCE 75 Heythrop Coll Lon MA 02. SAOMC 95. **d** 98 **p** 99. NSM Stratfield Mortimer and Mortimer W End etc *Ox* 98–04; C Portsea St Mary *Portsm* 04–17; rtd 17; PtO *Portsm* from 17. *Pitts Farm House, Langrish, Petersfield GU32 1RQ* E: charlottehetherington@hotmail.com

HETHERINGTON, John Carl. b 52. Hull Univ BTh 93. Linc Th Coll 82. **d** 84 **p** 85. C Crosby *Linc* 84–88; TV Cleethorpes 88–93; Chapl RAF 93–07; R Monk Fryston and S Milford *York* 07–17; rtd 17; PtO *York* from 17. *12 Longbridge Drive,*

Easingwold, York YO61 3FH T: (01347) 469087 M: 07709-827122 E: easingwoldrev@gmail.com

HETHERINGTON, Mrs Rachel Marie. b 65. ERMC 05. **d** 08 **p** 12. NSM Northampton Ch Ch *Pet* 08–11; NSM Northampton H Sepulchre w St Andr and St Lawr 08–11; NSM Northampton St Mich w St Edm 08–11; NSM Northampton H Trin and St Paul 08–11; Asst Chapl St Andr Healthcare from 11; C Kingsthorpe *Pet* 12–16; TV from 16. *St David's Vicarage, 88 Eastern Avenue South, Northampton NN2 7QB* T: (01604) 717005 E: rhetherington10@gmail.com

HEWERDINE, Mark Richard. b 77. Man Univ BA 99. Qu Coll Birm MA 13. **d** 13 **p** 14. C W Didsbury and Withington St Chris *Man* 13–16; P-in-c Ladybarn 16–19; R from 19; C Burnage St Nic from 17. *1 St Chad's Road, Manchester M20 4WH* T: 0161-445 1185 M: 07772-538491 E: markhewerdine@gmail.com

HEWES, John. b 29. Nottm Univ BA 50. Chich Th Coll 79. **d** 81 **p** 82. C Buckland in Dover w Buckland Valley *Cant* 81–84; P-in-c Elmsted w Hastingleigh 84–89; P-in-c Crundale w Godmersham 84–89; RD W Bridge 88–89; R Lydd 89–95; RD S Lympne 89–95; rtd 95; PtO *Cant* from 95. *Brambledown, Tamley Lane, Hastingleigh, Ashford TN25 5HW* T: (01233) 750214 E: john.hewes@btinternet.com

HEWES, Timothy William. b 50. Sheff Univ BDS 74. SAOMC 98. **d** 01. NSM Abingdon *Ox* 01–14; NSM Sutton Courtenay w Appleford 14–17; PtO from 17. *25 New Road, Charney Bassett, Wantage OX12 0ER* M: 07771-880117 E: timothy.hewes@btinternet.com

HEWETSON, The Ven Christopher. b 37. Trin Coll Ox BA 60 MA 64. Chich Th Coll 67. **d** 69 **p** 70. C Leckhampton St Pet *Glouc* 69–71; C Wokingham All SS *Ox* 71–73; V Didcot St Pet 73–82; R Ascot Heath 82–90; RD Bracknell 86–90; P-in-c Headington Quarry 90–94; Hon Can Ch Ch 92–94; RD Cowley 94; Adn Ches 94–02; rtd 02; Bp's Adv for Spirituality *Ex* 03–07; PtO *Ches* 05–10; *B & W* 09–13. *70 East Street, South Molton EX36 3DQ* E: christopher.hewetson@sky.com

HEWETSON, Canon Robin Jervis. b 39. AKC 63 K Coll Lon MA 93. **d** 64 **p** 65. C Thorpe St Andr *Nor* 64–67; C E Dereham w Hoe 67–69; TV Mattishall w Mattishall Burgh 69–72; R Ingham w Sutton 72–78; R Catfield 75–78; R Taverham w Ringland 78–89; P-in-c Marsham 89–92; P-in-c Burgh 89–92; Dioc Ecum Officer 89–04; Exec Officer Norfolk Ecum Coun 89–04; R Marsham w Burgh-next-Aylsham *Nor* 92–04; Hon Can Nor Cathl 01–04; rtd 04; PtO *Nor* from 04. *83 Soame Close, Aylsham, Norwich NR11 6JF* T: (01263) 734325 E: robin.hewetson@gmail.com

HEWETSON, Canon Valerie Patricia. b 44. St Mary's Coll Dur BSc 66 MSc 70 Leeds Univ MA 75. Linc Th Coll 89. **d** 91 **p** 94. C Kingston upon Hull St Nic *York* 91–94; V Barmby Moor w Allerthorpe, Fangfoss and Yapham 94–98; V Barmby Moor Gp 98–10; RD S Wold 01–06; Can and Preb York Minster 01–10; rtd 10; PtO *York* from 11. *27 Briarsfield, Barmby Moor, York YO24 4HN* T: (01759) 303816 E: valerie.hewetson@btinternet.com

HEWISH, Mrs Lesley Gillian. b 60. Trin Coll Bris 08. **d** 10 **p** 11. C Tetbury, Beverston, Long Newnton etc *Glouc* 10–13; Chapl HM Pris Eastwood Park 13–18; Chapl HM Pris Leyhill from 18. *HM Prison Leyhill, Wootton-under-Edge GL12 8BT* T: (01454) 264041 M: 07876-775290 E: lesley.hewish@justice.gov.uk

HEWISON, Miss Catherine Ann. b 75. Univ of Wales (Ban) BSc 98. Trin Coll Bris 17. **d** 19. C Gorton and Abbey Hey *Man* from 19. *St Philip's Rectory, Lavington Grove, Manchester M18 7EQ* M: 07732-082537 E: cathhewison@hotmail.com

HEWITT, Caroline Doris. b 62. Man Univ BSc 83 PhD 87. All SS Cen for Miss & Min 12. **d** 15 **p** 16. C Salford All SS *Man* 15–19; TV Wythenshawe from 19; P-in-c Lawton Moor from 19. *St Michael and All Angels Vicarage, Orton Road, Manchester M23 0LH* T: 0161-998 2715 E: revd.caroline.hewitt@gmail.com

HEWITT, Christopher James Chichele (Chich). b 45. Witwatersrand Univ BSc 68 UNISA BA 78 MTh 92 LTCL 69. St Paul's Coll Grahamstown. **d** 78 **p** 79. S Africa 78–99; Chapl St Paul's Coll Grahamstown 84–86; Warden 86–92; Can Grahamstown Cathl 88–93; Chan 92; Sub-Dean 93; Dean and Adn Grahamstown 93–98; USA 99; TR Radcliffe *Man* 00–09; AD Radcliffe and Prestwich 02–09; P-in-c Swinton H Rood 09–13; V 13–14; C Worsley 13–14; rtd 14; PtO *Man* from 14. *79 Long Lane, Bolton BL2 6EU* T: (01204) 436374 E: chich@rink-hewitt.co.uk

HEWITT, Christopher William. b 63. Nottm Trent Univ BEng 98 PGCE 05 Linc Univ BA 14 CEng 01 MIET 01. Linc Sch of Th and Min 10. **d** 15 **p** 16. C Barlings *Linc* 15–18; C S Lawres Gp 15–18; V Walesby Gp from 18. *The Rectory, Otby Lane, Walesby, Market Rasen LN8 3UT* M: 07853-277065 E: cwhewitt@btinternet.com or chris.hewitt@lincoln.anglican.org

HEWITT, Colin Edward. b 52. Man Poly BA 80 Em Coll Cam BA 82 MA 86 Maryvale Inst PGCE 08. Westcott Ho Cam 81. **d** 83 **p** 84. C Radcliffe St Thos and St Jo *Man* 83–84; C Langley and Parkfield 84–86; R Byfield w Boddington *Pet* 86–89; R Byfield w Boddington and Aston le Walls 89–91; Chapl RAF 91–09; V Brentwood St Thos *Chelmsf* 09–17; rtd 17; PtO *St E* from 19. *Address withheld by request* M: 07704-495001 E: colinhewitt@hotmail.com

HEWITT, David Warner. b 33. Selw Coll Cam BA 56 MA 60. Wells Th Coll 57. **d** 59 **p** 60. C Longbridge *Birm* 59–61; C Sheldon 61–64; V Smethwick Old Ch 64–70; V Smethwick 70–78; P-in-c Littlehampton St Jas *Chich* 78–85; P-in-c Wick 78–85; V Littlehampton St Mary 78–85; TR Littlehampton and Wick 86–89; PtO *Eur* from 95; rtd 98; Hon Asst Chapl Gtr Athens *Eur* 00–03; PtO *Chelmsf* from 07. *18 Orchard Close, Weaverhead Lane, Thaxted, Dunmow CM6 2JX* T: (01371) 830591 E: tangulls1@mac.com

HEWITT, Canon Francis John Adam. b 42. St Chad's Coll Dur BA 64. **d** 66 **p** 67. C Dewsbury Moor *Wakef* 66–69; C Huddersfield St Jo 69–73; V King Cross 73–81; V Lastingham w Appleton-le-Moors, Rosedale etc *York* 81–94; RD Helmsley 85–94; V Pickering 94–95; V Pickering w Lockton and Levisham 95–07; RD Pickering 94–06; rtd 07; PtO *York* from 07; Can and Preb York Minster from 97. *Michaelmas Cottage, 3 Lime Chase, Kirkbymoorside, York YO62 6BX* T: (01751) 430322 E: fandb.michaelmas1@btinternet.com

HEWITT, Canon Garth Bruce. b 46. St Jo Coll Dur BA 68. Lon Coll of Div LTh 70. **d** 70 **p** 71. C Maidstone St Luke *Cant* 70–73; Staff Evang CPAS 73–79; Hon C W Ealing St Jo w St Jas *Lon* 73–81; Amos Trust from 85; Dir 88–11; World Affairs Adv *Guildf* 94–96; Regional Co-ord (Lon and SE) Chr Aid 96–12; PtO *S'wark* 96–04; P-in-c All Hallows Lon Wall 97–99; V 99–13; Hon C St Clem Eastcheap w St Martin Orgar 13–18; Hon Can Jerusalem from 06. *Amos Trust, St Clement's Church, 1 St Clement's Court, London EC4N 7HB* T: (020) 7588 2638 E: garth@amostrust.org.uk

HEWITT, Guy Arlington Kenneth. b 67. Univ of W Indies BSc 92 MSc 94. SEITE 00. **d** 04 **p** 05. C Ch Ch Barbados 04–06; P-in-c Ruby H Trin 06–07; C Ch Ch 07–08; PtO *S'wark* 15–19. *9 Roehampton Gate, London SW15 5JR* T: (020) 8878 0260 *or* 7299 1160 E: guyhewitt@gmail.com

HEWITT, Jason Lawrence. b 87. St Steph Ho Ox 16. **d** 19. C Cen Barnsley *Leeds* from 19. *St George's Vicarage, 100 Dodworth Road, Barnsley S70 6HL* M: 07395-522289 E: jaylhewitt@hotmail.co.uk

HEWITT, Kenneth Victor. b 30. Lon Univ BSc 49 CertEd 51 MSc 53. Cuddesdon Coll 60. **d** 62 **p** 63. C Maidstone St Martin *Cant* 62–64; C Croydon St Mich 64–67; P-in-c S Kensington St Aug *Lon* 67–73; V 73–95; Asst Chapl Lon Univ 67–73; rtd 95; PtO *Roch* 95–16. *41 Bromley College, London Road, Bromley BR1 1PE* T: (020) 8464 0014

HEWITT, Laura Jane. b 67. Cranmer Hall Dur 01. **d** 03 **p** 04. C Kingston upon Hull St Aid Southcoates *York* 03–07; V Seamer w East Ayton 07–14; TR Billingham *Dur* 14–17; V New Barnet St Jas *St Alb* from 17. *St James' Vicarage, 11 Park Road, New Barnet, Barnet EN4 9QA* M: 07500-345058 E: revlaurajane@yahoo.co.uk

HEWITT, Michael David. b 49. K Coll Lon BD 79 AKC 79 CertEd. Qu Coll Birm 79. **d** 80 **p** 81. C Bexleyheath Ch Ch *Roch* 80–84; C Buckland in Dover w Buckland Valley *Cant* 84–89; R Ridgewell w Ashen, Birdbrook and Sturmer *Chelmsf* 89–13; rtd 13. *22 Bromley College, London Road, Bromley BR1 1PE*

HEWITT, Paul Stephen Patrick. b 59. TCD BA 82 MA 87. CITC 83. **d** 86 **p** 87. C Ballymacash *Conn* 86–89; C Ballymena w Ballyclug 89–91; I Glencraig *D & D* 91–12; rtd 12. *18A Old Cultra Road, Holywood BT18 0AE* T: (028) 9042 1847 E: paulsphewitt@btconnect.com *or* wphewitt@gmail.com

HEWITT, Stephen Wilkes. b 49. Fitzw Coll Cam MA 71. St Jo Coll Nottm 88. **d** 90 **p** 91. C Eaton *Nor* 90–93; V Warwick St Paul *Cov* 93–01; PtO *Newc* 01–02; P-in-c High Spen and Rowlands Gill *Dur* 02–05; V 05–09; TR Cramlington *Newc* 09–14; rtd 15; PtO *Newc* from 15. *54 Prior Road, Tweedmouth, Berwick-upon-Tweed TD15 2EH*

HEWITT, Canon Timothy James. b 67. St D Coll Lamp BD 88. Ripon Coll Cuddesdon 89. **d** 91 **p** 92. C Milford Haven *St D* 91–94; C Llanelli 94–96; P-in-c Llan-non 96–97; V Clydach *S & B* 98–07; V Ystalyfera from 07; Dioc Voc Adv 07–17; Bp's Officer for Tr and Minl Development from 18; Can Res Brecon Cathl from 18. *The Vicarage, Glan yr Afon Road, Ystalyfera, Swansea SA9 2EP* T: (01639) 842257 E: timothyhewitt@outlook.com

HEWLETT, Mrs Caroline Joan. b 68. Coll of Ripon & York St Jo BEd 92 St Jo Coll Dur BA 01. Cranmer Hall Dur 99. **d** 01 **p** 02. C Leeds St Geo *Ripon* 01–04; C Aldborough w Boroughbridge and Roecliffe 04–06; Chapl Leeds Combined Court Cen

03–06; V Swaledale 06–14; *Leeds* from 14. *The Vicarage, Reeth, Richmond DL11 6TR* T: (01748) 884706 M: 07866-750211 E: carolinejhewlett@btinternet.com

HEWLETT, David Bryan. b 49. Bris Univ BEd 72. Qu Coll Birm 77. **d** 79 **p** 80. C Ludlow *Heref* 79–81; TV 81–84; V Marden w Amberley and Wisteston 84–92; Lect Glouc Sch for Min 84–92; Field Officer for Lay Min *Heref* 84–91; CME Officer 86–92; Dir Post-Ord Tr 91–92; Hd Master St Fran Sch Pewsey 92–94; Co-ord Chapl Frenchay Healthcare NHS Trust Bris 94–99; Chapl N Bris NHS Trust 99–00; Dir Past Studies OLM Scheme and CME Adv *Linc* 00–04; Par Development Adv (South) 00–04; R Pontesbury I and II *Heref* 04–08; V Corbridge w Halton and Newton Hall *Newc* 08–17; AD Corbridge 09–17; rtd 17; PtO *Heref* from 17. *Broxmere, Bodenham, Hereford HR1 3JB* T: (01568) 797568 E: david.hewlett3@btopenworld.com

HEWLETT, Canon David Jonathon Peter. b 57. Dur Univ BA 79 PhD 83. Ridley Hall Cam 82. **d** 83 **p** 84. C New Barnet St Jas *St Alb* 83–86; Lect CITC 86–90; P-in-c Feock *Truro* 91–95; Jt Dir SWMTC 91–95; Prin 95–03; Adv Local Ord Min 91–95; Hon Can Truro Cathl 01–03; Prin Qu Coll Birm from 03; Hon Can Birm Cathl from 14. *The Queen's Foundation, Somerset Road, Edgbaston, Birmingham B15 2QH* T: 0121-452 2612 *or* 452 2603 F: 454 8171 E: d.hewlett@queens.ac.uk

HEWLETT, Guy Edward. b 59. Thames Poly CertEd 89 Open Univ BA 90. Oak Hill Th Coll 96. **d** 96 **p** 97. NSM Sudbury St Andr *Lon* 96–99; C Harrow Trin St Mich 99–05; V Harrow Weald St Mich 05–13; Chapl Worcs Acute Hosps NHS Trust 13–17; TR Gornal and Sedgley *Worc* from 17. *The Vicarage, Vicar Street, Sedgley, Dudley DY3 3SD* E: guyhewlett18@gmail.com

HEWLINS, Pauline Elizabeth. *See* SEAMAN, Pauline Elizabeth

HEWSON, Douglas Peter. b 43. **d** 12 **p** 13. OLM Milford *Guildf* 12–16; PtO from 16. *Meijendel, Sandy Lane, Milford, Godalming GU8 5BL* T: (01483) 425131 E: peter_hewson@sky.com

HEWSON, Mrs Mandy Carol. b 61. Anglia Ruskin Univ BSc 05. St Mellitus Coll BA 11. **d** 11 **p** 13. NSM E Springfield *Chelmsf* 11–16; PtO from 16. *33 Meon Close, Chelmsford CM1 7QG* T: (01245) 287710 E: mandyhewson@gmail.com

HEYCOCKS, Christian John. b 71. Univ of Wales (Ban) BA 93 MA 96. Westcott Ho Cam 94 CITC 97. **d** 97 **p** 98. C Rhyl w St Ann *St As* 97–00; Chapl RN 00–06; Chapl Univ Staff Cam and C Cambridge Gt St Mary w St Mich *Ely* 06–09; V Sheringham *Nor* from 09; RD Repps from 14. *The Vicarage, 10 North Street, Sheringham NR26 8LW* T: (01263) 822089 E: rev.heycocks15@btinternet.com

HEYES, Robert John. b 46. STETS 00. **d** 03 **p** 04. NSM Bramley and Grafham *Guildf* 03–08; NSM Shamley Green 08–11; rtd 11. *Juniper Cottage, 22 Eastwood Road, Bramley, Guildford GU5 0DS* T: (01483) 893706 F: 894001 E: bobheyes@onetel.com

HEYGATE, Stephen Beaumont. b 48. Loughb Univ BSc 71 CQSW 73 PhD 89. St Jo Coll Nottm 86. **d** 88 **p** 89. C Aylestone St Andr w St Jas *Leic* 88–90; V Cosby 90–00; V Evington 00–11; P-in-c Leic St Phil 00–04; rtd 12; PtO *Leic* from 12; *Pet* from 12; Bp's Adv for Healing and Deliverance *Leic* from 04. *4 Gapstile Close, Desborough, Kettering NN14 2TZ* T: (01536) 764106 E: stephenheygate@btinternet.com

HEYHOE, Jonathan Peter. b 53. Man Univ BA 75. Trin Coll Bris 77. **d** 80 **p** 81. C Woking St Pet *Guildf* 80–83; C Heatherlands St Jo *Sarum* 83–91; Chr Renewal Cen Rostrevor 91–95; PtO *D & D* 91–97; I Ballybay w Mucknoe and Clontibret *Clogh* 98–11; Preb Clogh Cathl 06–11; rtd 11. *11 Rowallon, Warrenpoint, Newry BT34 3TR* T: (028) 4175 4659 M: 07503-920902 E: jheyhoe@iol.ie

HEYN, Lucinda Jane. *See* MORRISS, Lucinda Jane

HEYWARD, Daniel James. b 74. Ex Univ BA 97 MCIPD. Wycliffe Hall Ox 09. **d** 11 **p** 12. C Reading Greyfriars *Ox* 11–15; C Bris St Phil and St Jacob w Em 15–16; V Ox St Andr from 16. *46 Charlbury Road, Oxford OX2 6UX* M: 07508-346550 E: daniel_heyward@hotmail.com *or* dan.heyward@standrewsoxford.org

HEYWOOD, Mrs Anne Christine. b 44. Sarum Th Coll. **d** 97 **p** 98. C Talbot Village *Sarum* 97–01; TV Shaston 01–09; rtd 10; PtO *Sarum* from 10; *Ox* from 18. *26 Casterbridge Way, Gillingham SP8 4FG* T: (01747) 825259

HEYWOOD, Anthony. *See* HEYWOOD, Richard Anthony

HEYWOOD, David Stephen. b 55. Selw Coll Cam BA 76 MA 80 SS Hild & Bede Coll Dur PhD 89. Cranmer Hall Dur 80. **d** 86 **p** 87. C Cheltenham St Luke and St Jo *Glouc* 86–90; TV Sanderstead All SS *S'wark* 90–98; V Edensor *Lich* 98–03; Deanery and Min Development Officer 03–06; Lect Past Th Ripon Coll Cuddesdon 06–15; Dep Dioc Dir of Miss *Ox* from 17. *Church House Oxford, Langford Locks,*

Kidlington OX5 1GF T: (01865) 595244 M: 07823-788173 E: david.heywood@oxford.anglican.org

HEYWOOD, Deiniol John Owen. *See* KEARLEY-HEYWOOD, Deiniol John Owen

HEYWOOD, Mrs Margaret Anne (Meg). b 52. Luton Coll of HE BSc 81. EMMTC 04. **d** 07 **p** 07. Chapl Ox Min Course from 06; NSM Ox St Clem 07–08; NSM Thame 09–10; PtO 10–17; NSM DAMASCUS from 17. *The Vicarage, 8 Gravel Lane, Drayton, Abingdon OX14 4HY* E: meg_heywood@hotmail.com

HEYWOOD, Peter. b 46. Cranmer Hall Dur 72. **d** 75 **p** 76. C Blackley St Andr *Man* 75–78; C Denton Ch Ch 78–80; V Constable Lee 80–01; rtd 01; PtO *Man* from 01. *1 Millgate Road, Rossendale BB4 7AS* T: (01706) 212297 M: 07881-543973 E: peterheywood1@sky.com

HEYWOOD, Richard Anthony. b 77. St Jo Coll Dur BA 99. Oak Hill Th Coll 04. **d** 07 **p** 08. C Lt Shelford *Ely* 07–11; TV Thetford *Nor* from 11. *44 Nunsgate, Thetford IP24 3EL* M: 07804-671405 E: tony.heywood@talk21.com

HEZEL, Adrian. b 43. Chelsea Coll Lon BSc 64 PhD 67. NOC 78. **d** 81 **p** 82. NSM Mirfield *Wakef* 81–89; C 89–90; V Shelley and Shepley 90–99; V Hoylake *Ches* 99–08; rtd 08; PtO *Ches* from 09. *32 Ffordd Byrnwr Gwair, Mold CH7 1FQ* T: (01352) 756922 E: ahezel@btinternet.com

HIBBERD, Brian Jeffery. b 35. Fitzw Coll Cam MA 62 Southn Univ MA 84. Ridley Hall Cam 58. **d** 60 **p** 61. C Cambridge H Trin *Ely* 60–63; C Doncaster St Mary *Sheff* 63–66; Asst Master Price's Sch Fareham 66–69; Warblington Sch Havant 69–71; Hd Soc and RS Carisbrooke High Sch 71–84; Distr Health Promotion Officer Is of Wight 84–88; SW Herts 88–90; Hd RS Goffs Sch Cheshunt 90–95; rtd 95; Teacher Qu Sch Bushey 95–97; Teacher R Masonic Sch for Girls Rickmansworth 97–00; Hon C Abbots Langley *St Alb* 00–01; PtO from 01. *50 Rosehill Gardens, Abbots Langley WD5 0HF* T: (01923) 267391

HIBBERD, John. b 60. Wadh Coll Ox MA 82. Trin Coll Bris BA 89. **d** 89 **p** 90. C Northolt St Mary *Lon* 89–92; C-in-c Southall Em CD 92–94; Min of Miss Through Faith Miss *Ely* 95–14; Miss Development Adv Sheff and Rotherham Adnry from 14. *14 Hollingswood Way, Sunnyside, Rotherham S66 3ZN* T: (01709) 700351 E: jhibberd14@btinternet.com

HIBBERD, John Charles. b 38. Bernard Gilpin Soc Dur 62 Chich Th Coll 63. **d** 66 **p** 67. C W Drayton *Lon* 66–70; C Noel Park St Mark 70–72; C Ealing St Steph Castle Hill 72–75; V Gunnersbury St Jas 75–84; V Whitton SS Phil and Jas 84–86; Finance and Trust Sec Lon Dioc Fund 87–98; PtO *Lon* 87–98; rtd 98. *18 Pursley Close, Sandown PO36 9QP* T: (01983) 401036 E: johnhibberd0138@talktalk.net

HIBBERT, Gillian Mary. **d** 09 **p** 10. Chapl Countess of Chester Hosp NHS Foundn Trust from 09. *Whitehaven, Church Walks, Christleton, Chester CH3 7AF* T: (01244) 336544

HIBBERT, Canon Peter John. b 43. Hull Univ BA 71 Lon Univ CertEd 72 MA 79. Sarum & Wells Th Coll 85. **d** 88 **p** 89. C Newsome and Armitage Bridge *Wakef* 88–92; P-in-c Newton Flowery Field *Ches* 92–00; P-in-c Hyde St Thos 97–00; V Handsworth St Jas *Birm* 00–08; P-in-c Altarnon w Bolventor, Laneast and St Clether *Truro* 08–09; P-in-c Micklehurst *Ches* 09–13; P-in-c Hyde St Thos w Godley cum Newton Green 10–17; PtO *Man* 16–18; NSM Hulme Ascension from 18; NSM Chorlton-cum-Hardy St Werburgh from 18; PtO *Ches* from 17; Hon Can Ches Cathl 11–18. *203 Petersburg Road, Stockport SK3 9RA* T: 0161-474 1601 E: hibbert631@btinternet.com

HIBBERT, Prof Peter Rodney. b 53. Man Univ LLB 74 Nottm Univ MA 99 Solicitor 77. EMMTC 96. **d** 99 **p** 00. C Knighton St Mary Magd *Leic* 99–01; PtO 01–12; *Birm* from 03; *Leic* from 15. *Grange Cottage, 37 Rushes Lane, Lubenham, Market Harborough LE16 9TN* T: (01858) 433174 E: for.peter@hotmail.com

HIBBERT, Canon Richard Charles. b 62. Trin Coll Bris BA 93. **d** 96 **p** 97. C Luton St Mary *St Alb* 96–00; V Bedford Ch Ch from 00; RD Bedford from 10; Hon Can St Alb from 13. *Christ Church Vicarage, 115 Denmark Street, Bedford MK40 3TJ* T/F: (01234) 359342 E: vicar@ccbedford.org

HIBBINS, Neil Lance. b 58. St Anne's Coll Ox BA 82 MA 87. St Mich Coll Llan 83. **d** 85 **p** 86. C Griffithstown *Mon* 85–87; C Pontypool 87–88; TV 88–92; Walsall Hosps NHS Trust 92–96; Asst Chapl Manor Hosp Walsall 92–96; R Norton Canes *Lich* from 96. *The Rectory, 81 Church Road, Norton Canes, Cannock WS11 9PQ* T: (01543) 278969 E: neil_hibbins@lycos.com

HIBBS, Peter Wilfred. b 56. NOC 05. **d** 08 **p** 09. NSM Gt Snaith *Sheff* from 08. *Peveril, High Street, Snaith, Goole DN14 9HJ* T: (01405) 862517 M: 07885-348498 E: peter.hibbs@sheffield.anglican.org

HICKEN, Kathryn Elizabeth. b 69. Moorlands Coll BA 10. St Mellitus Coll 11. **d** 13 **p** 14. C Holdenhurst and Iford *Win*

13–16; P-in-c Southampton St Mark from 16. *The Vicarage, 54 Archers Road, Southampton SO15 2LU* M: 07590-211015 E: kathy.iford@icloud.com

HICKLING, John. b 34. Handsworth Coll Birm 56. Launde Abbey 69. **d** 69 **p** 70. In Methodist Ch 59–69; C Melton Mowbray w Thorpe Arnold *Leic* 69–71; TV 71–75; R Waltham on the Wolds w Stonesby and Saltby 75–84; R Aylestone St Andr w St Jas 84–93; R Husbands Bosworth w Mowsley and Knaptoft etc 93–96; rtd 96; PtO *Leic* 99–19. *28 Oxford Drive, Melton Mowbray LE13 0AL* T: (01664) 560770 E: revd.johnhickling@btinternet.com

HICKMAN, John William. b 38. Barrister-at-Law (Middle Temple) 69 Qu Coll Cam LLM 81. Oak Hill Th Coll 92. **d** 95 **p** 96. NSM Sevenoaks St Nic *Roch* 95–98; P-in-c Stedham w Iping *Chich* 98–04; rtd 04; PtO *Chich* from 05. *Bywood, Selham Road, West Lavington, Midhurst GU29 0EG* T: (01730) 810821

HICKS, Miss Barbara. b 42. Cranmer Hall Dur BA 71. dss 85 **d** 87 **p** 94. Norton Woodseats St Paul *Sheff* 85–87; Par Dn Sheff St Jo 87–94; C 94–02; Chapl Shrewsbury Hosp 96–02; rtd 02; PtO *Sheff* from 06. *87 Underwood Road, Sheffield S8 8TG* T: 0114-255 8087

HICKS, Clive Anthony. b 58. Man Univ BA 79 Bris Univ PhD 88. Coll of Resurr Mirfield 09. **d** 11 **p** 12. C Budbrooke *Cov* 11–14; V Ossett and Gawthorpe *Leeds* from 14. *The Vicarage, 12 Fearnley Avenue, Ossett WF5 9ET* M: 07397-984358 E: cliveahicks@gmail.com

HICKS, Ms Eunice. b 41. Trin Coll Bris BA 00. WEMTC 01. **d** 01 **p** 02. NSM Chew Magna w Dundry and Norton Malreward *B & W* 01–06; NSM Rowledge and Frensham *Guildf* 06–10; rtd 10; PtO *B & W* 11–14; *Eur* from 16. *Apartado 319, 8601-929 LUZ-LGS, Algarve, Portugal* T: (00351) (282) 799064 E: revehicks@gmail.com

HICKS, Hazel Rebecca. b 54. Open Univ BA 92. CITC 05. **d** 08 **p** 09. NSM Annagh w Drumaloor, Cloverhill and Drumlane *K, E & A* 08–11; P-in-c Arvagh w Carrigallen, Gowna and Columbkille from 11; Dioc Sec (Elphin and Ardagh) from 16. *Garvary Lodge, 49 Teemore Road, Garvary, Derrylin, Enniskillen BT92 9QB* T: (028) 6774 8422 *or* (00353) (89) 459 3219 M: 07770-852362 E: diocsechazel@gmail.com *or* revhazel08@yahoo.com

HICKS, Miss Joan Rosemary. b 60. Homerton Coll Cam BEd 83. Westcott Ho Cam 87. **d** 90 **p** 94. C Wendover *Ox* 90–95; C Earley St Pet 95–98; P-in-c Beech Hill, Grazeley and Spencers Wood 98–05; P-in-c Cox Green 05–17; V from 17. *The Vicarage, 9 Warwick Close, Maidenhead SL6 3AL* T: (01628) 622139

HICKS, John Michael. *See* PEARSON-HICKS, John Michael

HICKS (née HODGSON), Julia Ruth. b 66. Somerville Coll Ox BA 88 UEA PGCE 89. Westcott Ho Cam 06. **d** 08 **p** 09. C Bridgwater St Mary and Chilton Trinity *B & W* 08–11; R Merriott w Hinton, Dinnington and Lopen from 11; Adv in Women's Min Taunton Adnry from 18. *The Rectory, Church Street, Merriott TA16 5PS* T: (01460) 76406 E: juliahicks1@gmail.com

HICKS, Richard Barry. b 32. Dur Univ BA 55. Sarum Th Coll 59. **d** 61 **p** 62. C Wallsend St Luke *Newc* 61–64; C Tynemouth Ch Ch 64–69; V Tynemouth St Jo 69–75; V Prudhoe 75–82; TV Swanborough *Sarum* 82–86; R Hilperton w Whaddon and Staverton etc 86–97; rtd 97; PtO *Newc* 97–18; *Carl* 98–19. *Lane House, Sawmill Lane, Brampton CA8 1DA* T: (016977) 2156 E: hicks323@btinternet.com

HICKS, Robert Buxton. b 66. Ex Univ BSc 90. Westcott Ho Cam 06. **d** 08 **p** 09. C Bridgwater St Fran *B & W* 08–11; C Merriott w Hinton, Dinnington and Lopen from 11. *The Rectory, Church Street, Merriott TA16 5PS* T: (01460) 76406 E: bobhicks66@googlemail.com

HICKS, Mrs Valerie Joy. b 47. SRN 69. Cant Sch of Min 82. dss 85 **d** 87 **p** 94. Roch 85–89; Hon Par Dn 87–89; Par Dn Thatcham *Ox* 89–93; Team Dn Aylesbury 93–94; TV 94–00; P-in-c Dordon *Birm* 00–09; V 09–10; Dioc Chapl MU 01–06; rtd 10; PtO *Birm* from 10; *Lich* from 11. *12 Rocklands Crescent, Lichfield WS13 6DH* E: val.hicks@virginmedia.com

HICKS, Canon William Trevor. b 47. Hull Univ BA 68 Fitzw Coll Cam BA 70 MA 74. Westcott Ho Cam 68. **d** 70 **p** 71. C Cottingham *York* 70–73; C Elland *Wakef* 73–76; V Walsden 76–81; V Knottingley 81–92; R Castleford All SS 92–96; P-in-c Womersley and Kirk Smeaton 96–00; RD Pontefract 94–99; V Bolsover *Derby* 00–11; RD Bolsover and Staveley 05–11; Hon Can Derby Cathl 07–11; rtd 11. *18 Spittal Green, Bolsover, Chesterfield S44 6TP* T: (01246) 827856 E: wtrevorhicks@gmail.com *or* trevorhicks1@aol.com

HICKSON, Gordon Crawford Fitzgerald. b 51. CCC Cam MA 76. **d** 06 **p** 07. NSM Ox St Aldate 06–10; PtO 10–11; NSM Cowley St Jas 11–15; PtO from 13. *31 Orchard Road,*

Oxford OX2 9BL T: (01865) 862981 M: 07713-688079
E: gordon.hickson@gmail.com

HIDDEN, Jonathan Martin. b 79. Portsm Univ BSc 00. Wycliffe Hall Ox BTh 13. **d** 13 **p** 14. C Guildf Ch Ch 13–17; V Anston *Sheff* from 17. *The Vicarage, 17 Rackford Road, North Anston, Sheffield S25 4DE* M: 07790-018645 E: jonhidden@yahoo.co.uk

HIDER, David Arthur. b 46. Lon Univ BSc 67. Sarum & Wells Th Coll 86. **d** 89 **p** 90. NSM Southbourne w W Thorney *Chich* 89–91; C Goring-by-Sea 91–94; P-in-c Peacehaven and Telscombe Cliffs 94–99; V 99–09; P-in-c Telscombe w Piddinghoe and Southease 94–99; V Telscombe Village 99–09; V Piddinghoe 99–09; V Southease 99–09; rtd 09; PtO *Chich* from 09. *74 Park Road, Emsworth PO10 8NY* T: (01243) 377636 E: revd_d_hider@msn.com

HIDER, Mrs Melanie Anne. b 53. UEA BA 91 Homerton Coll Cam PGCE 92. **d** 06 **p** 07. OLM Nor Lakenham St Alb and St Mark 06–15; NSM Sprowston w Beeston from 15. *10 Brian Avenue, Norwich NR1 2PH* T: (01603) 622373 E: melanie@sprowston.org.uk

HIGGINBOTTOM, Richard. b 48. Lon Univ BD 74. Oak Hill Th Coll. **d** 74 **p** 75. C Kenilworth St Jo *Cov* 74–77; C Finham 77–79; P-in-c attleborough 79–81; V 81–84; Asst Chapl HM Pris Brixton 84–85; Chapl HM Pris Roch 85–92; Camp Hill 92–00; HM YOI Dover 00–03; rtd 03; PtO *Cant* 03–07; *Cov* 09–19. *c/o Crockford, Church House, Great Smith Street, London SW1P 3AZ* M: 07779-775081

HIGGINBOTTOM, Richard William. b 51. Man Univ BA 73 MA 75. Edin Th Coll 83. **d** 85 **p** 86. C Knighton St Mary Magd *Leic* 85–87; C Northleach w Hampnett and Farmington *Glouc* 87–89; V Hayfield *Derby* 89–93; CPAS Min Adv for Scotland 93–08; Community Development Officer Tulloch NET 08–14; rtd 14; PtO *Newc* from 16; *Eur* from 16. *2 Horsley Place, Christon Bank, Alnwick NE66 3FB* M: 07548-209922 E: richwhigg@gmail.com

HIGGINS, Anthony Charles. b 46. **d** 97 **p** 98. OLM Swanage and Studland *Sarum* 97–09; PtO from 09. *The Old School House, School Lane, Studland, Swanage BH19 3AJ* T: (01929) 450691 E: revtonyhiggins@btinternet.com

HIGGINS, Bernard. b 42. Leic Poly BPharm 63 PhD 66 MRPharmS 68. St Jo Coll Nottm 89. **d** 91 **p** 92. C Stockport St Geo *Ches* 91–94; C Stockport SW 94–95; P-in-c Dunham Massey St Marg and St Mark 95–98; V 98–00; rtd 00; PtO *Blackb* 01–11; *Carl* 01–13; *Leic* from 13. *20 Kingfisher Close, Great Glen, Leicester LE8 9DG* T: 0116-259 2624

HIGGINS (née JAMIESON), Mrs Emma Victoria. b 89. Edin Univ MA 12 Fitzw Coll Cam MPhil 15. Ridley Hall Cam 13. **d** 15 **p** 16. C Rugby W *Cov* 15–18; Chapl HM Pris Gartree from 19; PtO *Cov* from 19. *HM Prison Gartree, Market Harborough LE16 7RP* T: (01858) 426600 M: 07843-878636 E: revemmahiggins@gmail.com *or* emma.higgins@justice.gov.uk

HIGGINS, Canon Godfrey. b 39. St Chad's Coll Dur BA 61 DipEd 63. **d** 63 **p** 64. C Brighouse *Wakef* 63–66; C Huddersfield St Jo 66–68; R High Hoyland w Clayton W 68–75; V Marsden 75–83; V Pontefract St Giles 83–04; Hon Can Wakef Cathl 93–04; rtd 04; PtO *Bradf* 05–14; *Leeds* from 14. *2 Holme View, Ilkley LS29 9EL* T: (01943) 603861 E: godfrey.higgins@talktalk.net

HIGGINS, Canon John Leslie. b 43. Open Univ BA 79 Birm Univ MEd 89 PhD 07 CQSW 75. Lich Th Coll 64. **d** 66 **p** 67. C Sale St Anne *Ches* 66–69; C Bredbury St Mark 69–72; V Wharton 72–74; Hon C Annan and Lockerbie *Glas* 75–79; V Coseley Ch Ch *Lich* 79–89; R Arthuret *Carl* 89–96; Soc Resp Officer and Child Protection Co-ord 96–00; C Brampton and Farlam and Castle Carrock w Cumrew 96–00; Hon Can Carl Cathl 96–00; Hon C Annan *Glas* 00–12; Child Protection Adv and Researcher Abps' Coun 00–03; PtO *Carl* from 01; *Eur* 09–12; P-in-c Ankara 12–15. *Green Croft Cottage, The Haggs, Ecclefechan, Lockerbie DG11 3ED* T: (01576) 300796 F: 300790 M: 07867-505644 E: john-higgins@vodafoneemail.co.uk *or* canon-higgins@hotmail.co.uk

HIGGINS, Canon Kenneth. b 56. TCD BTh 93. CITC 90. **d** 93 **p** 94. C Cregagh *D & D* 93–96; Bp's C Movilla 96–00; I 01–09; I Belfast St Donard from 09; Can Down Cathl from 06; Treas Down Cathl from 12. *St Donard's Rectory, 421 Beersbridge Road, Belfast BT5 5DU* T: (028) 9065 2321 M: 07986-866690 E: revkenhiggins@hotmail.com

HIGGINS, The Very Revd Michael John. b 35. Birm Univ LLB 57 G&C Coll Cam LLB 59 PhD 62. Ridley Hall Cam 63. **d** 65 **p** 65. C Ormskirk *Liv* 65–67; Selection Sec ACCM 67–74; Hon C St Marylebone St Mary w St Luke *Lon* 69–74; P-in-c Woodlands *B & W* 74–80; V Frome St Jo 74–80; TR Preston St Jo *Blackb* 80–91; Dean Ely 91–03; rtd 03; PtO *Ely* from 05; *Nor* from 13; *Eur* from 16. *Twin Cottage, North Street,*

Great Dunham, King's Lynn PE32 2LR T: (01328) 701058 E: michaelj.higgins@btinternet.com

HIGGINS, Natasha Caroline. *See* WOODWARD, Natasha Caroline

HIGGINS, Rupert Anthony. b 59. Man Univ BA 80. Wycliffe Hall Ox 82. **d** 85 **p** 86. C Plymouth St Andr w St Paul and St Geo *Ex* 85–90; C-in-c St Paul 88–90; Assoc V Clifton Ch Ch w Em *Bris* 90–95; V S Croydon Em *S'wark* 95–02; C Langham Place All So *Lon* 02–05; P-in-c Clifton Ch Ch w Em *Bris* 05–09; Asst Vacancy Development Adv Strategy Support 09–10; V Talbot Village *Sarum* from 10. *The Vicarage, 20 Alton Road, Bournemouth BH10 4AE* T: (01202) 939799 E: rupert.higgins@gmail.com

HIGGINS, Mrs Sheila Margaret. b 46. STETS 09. **d** 10 **p** 11. NSM Aldingbourne, Barnham and Eastergate *Chich* from 10. *2 Orchard Terrace, The Street, Walberton, Arundel BN18 0PH* T: (01243) 553901 M: 07884-495916 E: smhandaway@tiscali.co.uk *or* smhandaway@hotmail.co.uk

HIGGINS, Canon Timothy John. b 45. Bris Univ BEd 70 Lanc Univ MA 74. Cranmer Hall Dur. **d** 79 **p** 80. C Northampton All SS w St Kath *Pet* 79–82; V Whitton St Aug *Lon* 82–90; AD Hampton 86–90; TR Aylesbury *Ox* 90–06; RD 94–04; Hon Can Ch Ch 00–06; Can Res Bris Cathl 06–14; P-in-c City of Bris 06–08; P-in-c Bris St Steph w St Jas and St Jo w St Mich etc 08–14; rtd 14; PtO *Ban* from 15. *Cae Helyg, Tudweiliog, Pwllheli LL53 8PB* T: (01758) 770303 E: tim.tssf@gmail.com

HIGGINSON, Andrew John. b 62. Bradf Univ BTech 85. Trin Coll Bris 02. **d** 04 **p** 05. C Quarrington w Old Sleaford *Linc* 04–08; C Silk Willoughby 04–08; P-in-c Freiston, Butterwick w Bennington, and Leverton from 08; RD Holland from 19. *The Rectory, Butterwick Road, Freiston, Boston PE22 0LF* T: (01205) 760480 E: revonline@btopenworld.com

HIGGINSON (née BROOKS), Hannah Victoria. b 90. **d** 14 **p** 15. C Finchampstead and California *Ox* 14–18; C Wokingham All SS from 18. *69 Bishops Drive, Wokingham RG40 1WA* M: 07976-309668

HIGGINSON, Richard Andrew. b 53. St Jo Coll Cam BA 74 Man Univ PhD 82. EAMTC 02. **d** 04 **p** 05. Lect Ridley Hall Cam 89–18; rtd 18; NSM Cambridge St Phil *Ely* 04–11; PtO from 12. *66 Winstanley Court, Cromwell Road, Cambridge CB1 3UR* T: (01223) 246616 M: 07551-249351 E: rah41@cam.ac.uk *or* richard.higginspn@cantab.net

HIGGINSON, Stanley. b 53. **d** 08 **p** 09. NSM Wigan St Mich *Liv* 08–15; TV Wigan All SS from 15. *12 Clifton Crescent, Wigan WN1 2LB* T: (01942) 235900 E: stanley.higginson33@yahoo.co.uk

HIGGON, David. b 49. Univ of Wales (Swansea) BA 75 Birm Univ MBA 96 Nottm Univ MA 99. EMMTC 96. **d** 00 **p** 01. NSM Crich and S Wingfield *Derby* 00–04; Chapl HM Pris Dovegate 04–05; PtO *Derby* 05–07; Chapl HM Pris Ranby 07–11; NSM Crich and S Wingfield *Derby* 11–17; Lic Mor from 17. *Brackloch Cottage, Dundonnell, Garve IV23 2QW* T: (01854) 633226 E: dhiggon@btopenworld.com

HIGGOTT, Bryn Graham. b 54. Birm Poly BA 76 Solicitor 79. NEOC 03. **d** 06 **p** 07. NSM Thirsk *York* 06–08. *15 Spencelayh Close, Wellingborough NN8 4UU* E: bghiggott@gmail.com

HIGGS, Andrew Richard Bowen. b 53. Man Univ BSc 75. St Jo Coll Nottm 81. **d** 85 **p** 86. C Droylsden St Mary *Man* 85–88; C Harlow Town Cen w Lt Parndon *Chelmsf* 88–95; TV 95–02; Chapl Princess Alexandra Hosp NHS Trust 96–02; R Stifford *Chelmsf* from 02. *The Rectory, High Road, North Stifford, Grays RM16 5UE* T: (01375) 372733 E: rector@parishofstifford.co.uk

HIGGS, Mrs Karen Elizabeth. b 66. SEITE 12. **d** 16 **p** 17. NSM Hartfield w Coleman's Hatch *Chich* 16–18; NSM E Grinstead St Swithun from 18. *34 Mallard Place, East Grinstead RH19 4TF*

HIGGS, Owen Christopher Goodwin. b 63. St Anne's Coll Ox BA 84 MA 88. St Steph Ho Ox 90. **d** 93 **p** 94. C Teddington St Mark and Hampton Wick *Lon* 93–96; C Lon Docks St Pet w Wapping St Jo 96–00; V Petts Wood *Roch* 00–09; V Bickley 09–14; V Pimlico St Gabr *Lon* from 14. *St Gabriel's Vicarage, 30 Warwick Square, London SW1V 2AD* T: (020) 7834 7520 E: frowen@stgabrielspimlico.com

HIGHAM, Gerald Norman. b 40. St Aid Birkenhead 64. **d** 68 **p** 69. C Garston *Liv* 68–71; C Blundellsands St Nic 71–73; V Bolton All So w St Jas *Man* 73–78; V Tonge w Alkrington 78–84; P-in-c Edenfield 84–86; P-in-c Stubbins 84–86; V Edenfield and Stubbins 86–03; rtd 03; PtO *Blackb* from 03; *Man* from 08. *71 Cherry Tree Way, Rossendale BB4 4JZ* T: (01282) 210143 E: g_higham@sky.com

HIGHAM, John Leonard. b 39. Wycliffe Hall Ox 62. **d** 65 **p** 66. C Prescot *Liv* 65–71; V Hollinfare 71–74; Adult and Youth Service Adv Knowsley 74–76; TV Padgate *Liv* 76–84; V

Farnworth 84–89; TR Sutton 89–02; rtd 02; PtO *Liv* from 03. *86 Ormskirk Road, Rainford, St Helens WA11 8DB*

HIGHAM (née ANNS), Canon Pauline Mary. b 49. Bris Univ BEd 71. EMMTC 87. **d** 90 **p** 94. Par Dn Wirksworth w Alderwasley, Carsington etc *Derby* 90–92; Par Dn Lt Berkhamsted and Bayford, Essendon etc *St Alb* 92–94; C 94–96; P-in-c 96–05; R 05–18; Jt RD Hertford and Ware 05–15; Hon Can St Alb 06–18; Hon C Combs and Finborough *St E* from 18. *The Rectory, Woodland Close, Onehouse, Stowmarket IP14 3HL*

HIGHTON, Philip William. b 70. Liv Univ BSc 91 Nottm Univ MSc 92. Oak Hill Th Coll BA 05. **d** 05 **p** 06. C Knutsford St Jo and Toft *Ches* 05–09; V Cheadle All Hallows 09–14; NSM Hartford from 14; Chapl Hartford C of E High Sch from 14. *2 Trafalgar Close, Northwich CW9 8WQ* T: (01606) 810685 E: phil@stjohnshartford.org

HIGHTON, William James. b 31. St Deiniol's Hawarden. **d** 82 **p** 83. NSM Thornton Hough *Ches* 82–84; C Cheadle 84–88; V Walton 88–99; rtd 99; PtO *Carl* from 01. *15 Mowbray Drive, Burton-in-Kendal, Carnforth LA6 1NF* T: (01524) 782073 E: mo.l@wjhighton.plus.com

HIGHWAY, Andrew David Carnell. b 67. St Mich Coll Llan 09. **d** 12 **p** 13. NSM Llanishen *Llan* 12–15; C Eglwysilan and Caerphilly from 16. *18 Y Groes, Cardiff CF14 6DX* M: 07969-757742 E: a.highway30@btinternet.com

HIGSON, Peter James. b 55. Glas Univ BD 13. TISEC 06. **d** 19. NSM Middle Esk Moor *York* from 19. *Ashling, Goathland, Whitby YO22 5LA* T: (01947) 896155 M: 07724-434444 E: peterjhigson@hotmail.com

HIGTON, Anthony Raymond. b 42. Lon Sch of Th BD 65. Oak Hill Th Coll 65. **d** 67 **p** 68. C Newark Ch Ch *S'well* 67–69; C Cheltenham St Mark *Glouc* 70–75; R Hawkwell *Chelmsf* 75–99; Gen Dir CMJ 99–05; R Jerusalem Ch Ch Israel 03–06; R N w S Wootton *Nor* 06–09; rtd 09; PtO *Ely* 09–15; *Nor* 09–15; Hon C Brough w Stainmore *Carl* 15–17. *2 Heggerscales Cottages, Kaber, Kirkby Stephen CA17 4HZ* T: (017683) 72159 M: 07815-891582 E: tony@higton.info

HILARY, Sister. *See* JORDINSON, Vera

HILBORN, David Henry Kyte. b 64. Nottm Univ BA 85 PhD 94 Mansf Coll Ox MA 88 SFHEA 18. **d** 02 **p** 02. C Acton St Mary *Lon* 02–06; Dir Studies NTMTC 06–07; Prin 07–12; Asst Dean St Mellitus Coll *Lon* 07–12; Lic Preacher from 06; Prin St Jo Coll Nottm 12–19; Prin Moorlands Coll Christchurch from 19; PtO *Win* from 19. *Moorlands College, Sopley, Christchurch BH23 7AT* T: (01425) 674500 M: 07792-350701 E: david.hilborn@moorlands.ac.uk

HILBORN, Mrs Mia Alison Kyte. b 63. City Univ BSc 84 Mansf Coll Ox MA 87. **d** 02 **p** 02. Chapl Team Ldr Guy's and St Thos' NHS Foundn Trust from 01; NSM N Lambeth *S'wark* from 02; NSM S Lambeth St Anne and All SS from 13. *Guy's & St Thomas' NHS Foundation Trust, St Thomas Street, London SE1 9RT* T: (020) 7188 5588 M: 07740-779585 E: mia.hilborn@gstt.nhs.uk

HILDING OHLSSON, Nicolas. b 82. Buenos Aires Bible Inst BA 08. **d** 09 **p** 13. Argentina 09–15; PtO *Guildf* 16–17; C Ashtead from 17. *1 Oakfield Road, Ashtead KT21 2RE* M: 07928-987835 E: ho.nico@gmail.com

HILDITCH, Janet. b 59. St Andr Univ MTheol 81 PhD 87. NOC 92. **d** 94 **p** 95. C Kirkholt *Man* 94–98; Chapl Rochdale Healthcare NHS Trust 97–98; Chapl N Man Health Care NHS Trust 98–00; Chapl Tameside Hosp NHS Foundn Trust 00–15; Hon Can Man Cathl 04–15; LtO *Ab* from 15. *6 Sunnyside, Mid Yell, Shetland ZE2 9BS* T: (01957) 702258 E: janetofhoulland@hotmail.co.uk

HILDITCH, Mrs Rachel Helen. b 87. SS Coll Cam BA 07 MA 11 Clare Coll Cam BTh 15. Ridley Hall Cam 13. **d** 16 **p** 17. C Hampton *Ely* from 16. *8 Tabor Court, Hampton Centre, Peterborough PE7 8GF* M: 07817-737401 E: rhh31@cantab.net

HILDRED, David. b 61. Bath Univ BSc 83 CertEd 83. Wycliffe Hall Ox 86. **d** 89 **p** 90. C Westcliff St Mich *Chelmsf* 89–92; C Rayleigh 92–96; V Sidcup St Andr *Roch* 96–10; AD Sidcup 03–08; R Darfield *Sheff* from 10. *The Rectory, Church Street, Darfield, Barnsley S73 9JX* T: (01226) 752236 E: david.hildred@talktalk.net

HILDRETH, Steven Marcus. b 47. Leeds Univ LLB 69 Solicitor 78. SNWTP 08. **d** 11 **p** 12. NSM Ches St Paul 11–14; rtd 15; PtO *Ches* from 15. *3 Field Close, Tarvin, Chester CH3 8DL* T: (01829) 749303 E: shildr1027@aol.com

HILES, John Michael. b 32. Qu Coll Cam BA 57 MA 61. Sarum Th Coll 57. **d** 59 **p** 60. C Clifton St Jas *Sheff* 59–62; V Bramley St Fran 62–69; Hon C Holmfirth *Wakef* 69–89; Hon C Upper Holme Valley 89–91; Lic to Offic 91–97; PtO 97–03; *Sarum* from 03. *22 Oldfield Road, Bishopdown, Salisbury SP1 3GQ* T: (01722) 349951 E: mike.hiles@btinternet.com

HILL, Mrs Alison Elizabeth. b 67. Glos Univ BEd 89. St Mellitus Coll BA 18. **d** 18 **p** 19. C Southampton (St Mary) *Win* from 18. *The Rectory, 32B Morris Road, Southampton SO15 2BR* M: 07810-544710 E: fivehills@hotmail.co.uk

HILL, Andrew Nicholas Luke. b 70. Glam Univ BA 95. Ripon Coll Cuddesdon 15. **d** 19. NSM Cam w Stinchcombe *Glouc* from 19. *15 Marment Road, Dursley GL11 6LA* T: (01453) 519754 M: 07413-278171 E: andrewnlhill@hotmail.com

HILL, Mrs Anne Doreen. b 40. **d** 88 **p** 94. Par Dn Bexleyheath St Pet *Roch* 88–90; Sub Chapl HM Pris Belmarsh 91–96; Dep Chapl 96–99; Hon C Lee St Mildred *S'wark* 93–04; rtd 04; PtO *Sarum* 05–08 and from 14. *64 St Mary's Road, Poole BH15 2LL* T: (01202) 666076 E: adhill40@hotmail.com

HILL, Barry Leon. b 79. Wycliffe Hall Ox BTh 05. **d** 05 **p** 06. C Loughborough Em and St Mary in Charnwood *Leic* 05–09; Dioc Miss Enabler 09–17; TR Market Harborough and The Transfiguration etc from 17; Dioc Resource Ch Enabler from 17. *The Rectory, Rectory Lane, Market Harborough LE16 8AS* E: barry@hill-home.co.uk *or* barry@harborough-anglican.org.uk

HILL, Mrs Carol. b 52. SCRTP 13. **d** 15 **p** 16. OLM Bicester w Bucknell, Caversfield and Launton *Ox* 15–19; NSM from 19. *25 Shaw Close, Bicester OX26 2FN* T: (01869) 600680 E: carolghill@hotmail.co.uk

HILL, Charles Bernard. b 50. Sheff Univ BA 71 Qu Coll Ox DPhil 76. Cant Sch of Min 91. **d** 94 **p** 95. NSM Sandgate St Paul w Folkestone St Geo *Cant* 94–98; NSM Folkestone H Trin w Ch Ch 98–04; Eur Sec Coun for Chr Unity 99–08; PtO *Eur* from 03; Can Gib Cathl 03–08; P-in-c Benenden *Cant* 08–10; P-in-c Sandhurst w Newenden 08–10; P-in-c Benenden and Sandhurst 10–13; rtd 13; PtO *Cant* from 14. *39 Cinque Ports Avenue, Hythe CT21 6HP* T: (01303) 269886 M: 07746-621448 E: cbhill18@hotmail.com

HILL, Christopher David. b 84. Moorlands Coll BA 07. St Mellitus Coll BA 12. **d** 12 **p** 13. C Cricklewood St Gabr and St Mich *Lon* 12–15; R Northolt St Mary from 15. *The Rectory, Ealing Road, Northolt UB5 6AA* T: (020) 8841 5691 E: chris.hill@northolt.org

HILL, Christopher Glynn. b 43. Tyndale Hall Bris 66. **d** 70 **p** 71. C Longfleet *Sarum* 70–74; LtO *Chelmsf* 74–82; rtd 05. *7 Paddock Close, Benson, Wallingford OX10 6RS* E: clministries@btinternet.com

✠**HILL, The Rt Revd Christopher John.** b 45. K Coll Lon BD 67 AKC 67 MTh 68. **d** 69 **p** 70 **c** 96. C Tividale *Lich* 69–73; C Codsall 73–74; Abp's Asst Chapl on Foreign Relns *Cant* 74–81; ARCIC from 74; Sec 74–90; Abp's Sec for Ecum Affairs *Cant* 82–89; Hon Can Cant Cathl 82–89; Chapl to The Queen 87–96; Can Res and Prec St Paul's Cathl *Lon* 89–96; Select Preacher Ox Univ 90; Area Bp Stafford *Lich* 96–04; Bp Guildf 04–13; rtd 13; Hon Asst Bp Glouc from 14; Clerk of the Closet 05–14. *Hillview, West End, Ruardean GL17 9TP* T: (01594) 541831 E: christopher.j.hill@outlook.com

HILL, Christopher Murray. b 57. Lanchester Poly Cov BA 78. Ox Min Course 05. **d** 07 **p** 08. NSM Warfield *Ox* 07–11; C 11–13; P-in-c Ely 13–17; TR from 17. *The Vicarage, St Mary's Street, Ely CB7 4HF* T: (01353) 662308 M: 07788-206361 E: chris.hill@stmarysely.org

HILL, The Ven Colin. b 42. Leic Univ BSc 64 Open Univ PhD 88. Ripon Hall Ox 64. **d** 66 **p** 67. C Leic Martyrs 66–69; C Braunstone 69–71; Lect Ecum Inst Thornaby Teesside 71–72; V Worsbrough St Thos and St Jas *Sheff* 72–78; Telford Planning Officer *Lich* 78–96; RD Telford and Telford Severn Gorge *Heref* 80–96; Preb Heref Cathl 83–96; Can Res Carl Cathl 96–04; Dioc Sec 96–04; Adn W Cumberland 04–08; rtd 08; PtO *Carl* from 09. *1A Briery Bank, Arnside, Carnforth LA5 0HW* T: (01524) 762629 E: hill69@tiscali.co.uk

HILL, Canon Colin Arnold Clifford. b 29. Bris Univ 52 Univ of Wales (Ban) MPhil 03. Ripon Hall Ox 55. **d** 57 **p** 58. C Rotherham *Sheff* 57–61; V Brightside St Thos 61–64; R Easthampstead *Ox* 64–73; Chapl RAF Coll Bracknell 68–73; V Croydon St Jo *Cant* 73–84; V Croydon St Jo *S'wark* 85–94; Chapl Abp Whitgift Foundn 73–94; Hon Can Cant Cathl 75–84; Hon Can S'wark Cathl 85–94; Chapl to The Queen 90–99; rtd 94; PtO *Ox* from 11. *Silver Birches, 70 Preston Crowmarsh, Wallingford OX10 6SL* M: 07837-249949 E: colinstb@clara.co.uk

HILL, David Rowland. b 34. Lon Univ BSc 55. Qu Coll Birm. **d** 59 **p** 60. C Upper Tooting H Trin *S'wark* 59–61; C Cheam 61–63; C Richmond St Mary w St Matthias 63–68; V Sutton St Nicholas *Linc* 68–82; V Pinchbeck 82–99; rtd 99; PtO *Linc* 99–02 and from 05; *Pet* 04–11. *24 London Road, Spalding PE11 2TA* T: (01775) 768912 E: revdavidhill1934@gmail.com

HILL, David Royston. b 68. Westmr Coll Ox BTh 96. ERMC 04. **d** 06 **p** 07. C Dereham and Distr *Nor* 06–09; R Quidenham Gp 09–14; R Upper St Leonards St Jo

Chich from 14; CF(V) 09–17. *St John's Rectory, 53 Brittany Road, St Leonards-on-Sea TN38 0RD* T: (01424) 423367 M: 07827-815247 E: fatherdavid68@icloud.com *or* david.hill007@btinternet.com

HILL, Derek Stanley. b 28. AKC 53. **d** 53 **p** 54. C Rushmere *St E* 53–55; S Africa 55–57; C Boreham Wood All SS *St Alb* 57–59; V Crowfield *St E* 59–67; P-in-c Stonham Aspal 59–61; R 61–67; V Bury St Edmunds St Geo 67–73; P-in-c Ampton w Lt Livermere and Ingham 68–73; V Gazeley w Dalham 73–75; P-in-c Lidgate w Ousden 73–74; P-in-c Gt Bradley 74–78; V Gazeley w Dalham and Moulton 75–78; V Gt Barton 78–86; V Bury St Edmunds All SS 86–93; rtd 93; PtO *St E* from 93. *Whinwillow, 38 Maltings Garth, Thurston, Bury St Edmunds IP31 3PP* T: (01359) 230770

HILL, Eugene Mark. b 48. Univ of Wales (Lamp) BA 71. Sarum Th Coll 71. **d** 73 **p** 74. C Sutton St Nic *S'wark* 73–77; Hon C 77–80; Asst Chapl Fern Sch Wandsworth 77–87; Chapl 87–04; Hon C St Helier *S'wark* 83–84; Hon C Caterham 84–98; Dir Chr Studies Course 85–04; PtO 98–07 and from 10; Hon C Croydon St Jo 07–10. *129A Honor Oak Park, London SE23 3LD* M: 07771-708893 E: eugenemarkhill@btinternet.com

HILL, Giles. *See* HILL, Michael John Giles

HILL, Canon Gillian Beryl. b 53. Open Univ BA 86 Portsm Univ PhD 06. S Dios Minl Tr Scheme 87. **d** 90 **p** 94. NSM Southsea St Jude *Portsm* 90–95; C Southsea St Pet 95–01; V Catherington and Clanfield 01–18; Hon Can Portsm Cathl 03–18; rtd 18. *53 Highfield, Lapford, Crediton EX17 6PY* E: gill.vicar@gmail.com

HILL, Ian Maxwell. b 60. Loughb Univ BSc 81 MCIT 85. EMMTC 92. **d** 95 **p** 96. NSM Thurnby Lodge *Leic* 95–00; NSM Thurmaston 00–08; NSM Fosse Team from 08. *Shady Ash, 4 Sturrock Close, Thurnby, Leicester LE7 9QP* T: 0116-243 1609

HILL, Ian Richard. b 69. Wycliffe Hall Ox 04. **d** 06 **p** 07. C Fareham St Jo *Portsm* 06–09; P-in-c Aspenden, Buntingford and Westmill *St Alb* 09–13; R from 13. *The Vicarage, Vicarage Road, Buntingford SG9 9BH* T: (01763) 271552

HILL, James. *See* HILL, Kenneth James

HILL, James Aidan Stuart. b 75. Ridley Hall Cam 06. **d** 09 **p** 10. C Cov H Trin 09–13; Asst Chapl Amsterdam w Den Helder and Heiloo *Eur* 13–19; P-in-c Mildmay Grove St Jude and St Paul *Lon* from 19. *71 Marquess Road, London N1 2PT* E: jamesincitycentre@gmail.com

HILL, James Alexander Hart. b 82. K Coll Lon BA 05. St Steph Ho Ox 05. **d** 07 **p** 08. C Tottenham St Paul *Lon* 07–11; C Tottenham St Benet Fink 10–11; P-in-c 11–16; V from 16; P-in-c Tottenham St Phil 14–18. *St Benet Fink Vicarage, Walpole Road, London N17 6BH* T: (020) 8888 4541 E: frjameshill@hotmail.co.uk

HILL, Mrs Janice. Sheff Univ BEd 79 Nottm Univ MA 10. St Jo Coll Nottm 05. **d** 07 **p** 08. C Formby H Trin *Liv* 07–10; TV N Meols 10–14; PtO 14–16; Dioc Missr 15–16; P-in-c Blundellsands St Mich 16–17; TR Maghull and Melling from 17. *28B Willow Hey, Liverpool L31 3DL* E: janicehill.htc@gmail.com

HILL, Mrs Jennifer Clare. b 50. City Univ BSc 71 FBCO 72. EMMTC 94. **d** 97 **p** 98. NSM Bottesford and Muston *Leic* 97–98; C Glen Parva and S Wigston 98–01; C Walsall Wood *Lich* 01–08; V Shelfield and High Heath 08–10; RD Walsall 05–10; TV Hemel Hempstead *St Alb* 10–13; TR 13–16; Dioc Adv for Women's Min 11–16; rtd 16; PtO *St Alb* from 16; Ely 16–18; P-in-c Long Stanton w St Mich 18–19; P-in-c Over 18–19; P-in-c Swavesey 18–19; P-in-c Willingham 18–19; PtO from 19. *57 Water Lane, Oakington, Cambridge CB24 3AL* T: (01223) 635076 M: 07970-949331 E: jennyhill@pawstime.co.uk

HILL, Jonathan Carey. b 68. St Jo Coll Nottm 12. **d** 14 **p** 15. C Cheylesmore *Cov* 14–16; C Fletchamstead 16–18; V Hull St Martin w Transfiguration *York* from 18. *942 Anlaby Road, Hull HU4 6AH* M: 07810-652011 E: jonathan.carey.hill@gmail.com

HILL, Kenneth James. b 43. Leic Univ BA 64 Lon Univ BD 68. Oak Hill Th Coll 65. **d** 69 **p** 70. C Southall Green St Jo *Lon* 69–72; C Blackheath Park St Mich *S'wark* 72–75; C Bath Abbey w St Jas *B & W* 75–83; P-in-c Bath St Mich w St Paul 75–82; R 82–83; V Huntspill 83–91; Omega Order 91–98; PtO *B & W* 91–98; *Bris* 91–98; C Somerton w Compton Dundon, the Charltons etc *B & W* 98–07; rtd 07; PtO *B & W* 08–18; *Sarum* from 14. *14 White Horse Road, Winsey, Bradford-on-Avon BA15 2JZ* T: (01225) 864119 E: kjhill23@btinternet.com

HILL, Laurence Bruce. b 60. Open Univ BA 97. AKC 67. **d** 69 **p** 70. C Feltham *Lon* 69–72; C-in-c Hampstead St Steph 72–77; V Finchley H Trin 77–10; rtd 10. *49 Abbots Gardens, London N2 0JG* T: (020) 8444 0510 E: lorenzohill@yahoo.co.uk

HILL, Mrs Leonora Anne. b 59. Bath Univ BSc 81 Westmr Coll Ox PGCE 93. Ox Min Course 05. **d** 08 **p** 09. C Charlton Kings St Mary *Glouc* 08–12; R Ridgeway *Ox* from 12. *Ridgeway Rectory, Warborough Road, Letcombe Regis, Wantage OX12 9LD* T: (01235) 760112 M: 07867-420234 E: revd.lahill@btinternet.com

HILL, Malcolm Crawford. b 43. Oak Hill Th Coll 68. **d** 71 **p** 72. C Maidstone St Luke *Cant* 71–74; C Longfleet *Sarum* 74–79; V Bexleyheath St Pet *Roch* 79–90; V Lee St Mildred *S'wark* 90–04; rtd 04; PtO *Sarum* from 05. *64 St Mary's Road, Poole BH15 2LL* T: (01202) 666076 E: adhill40@hotmail.com

HILL, Mrs Marjorie Ann. b 38. MCSP 60. St Jo Coll Nottm 92. **d** 94 **p** 95. C Hull St Martin w Transfiguration *York* 94–99; P-in-c Willerby w Ganton and Folkton 99–03; rtd 03; PtO *York* 03–06 and from 10; P-in-c Sigglesthorne w Nunkeeling and Bewholme 06–09; RD N Holderness 07–08. *31 White Gap Road, Little Weighton, Cottingham HU20 3XE* T: (01482) 840544 E: marjoriehill28@googlemail.com

HILL, Mark. *See* HILL, Eugene Mark

HILL, Martyn William. b 43. Man Univ BSc 64 Univ of Wales (Ban) PhD 70 MInstP 68 CPhys 85. Westcott Ho Cam 90. **d** 92 **p** 93. C Horninglow *Lich* 92–95; TV Hawarden *St As* 95–00; V Bistre 00–05; rtd 05; PtO *St As* 05–16. *Llys Penmaen, Penmaenpool, Dolgellau LL40 1YD* T: (01341) 423305 M: 07835-238522 E: machilpenmden@aol.com

HILL, Matthew Anthony Robert. b 71. Leeds Univ BA 93 Univ of Wales (Cardiff) BD 96 MPhil 00 Univ of Wales (Trin St Dav) PhD 16. St Mich Coll Llan 94. **d** 97 **p** 98. C Cardiff St Jo *Llan* 97–00; PV Llan Cathl 00–04; P-in-c Dowlais and Penydarren 04–05; R 05–07; Tutor Cardiff Univ and St Mich Coll Llan 04–07; Chapl Univ of Wales (Trin St Dav) *St D* 07–13; Voc Adv Cardigan Adnry 09–13; Co-ord Voc Adv *St D* 10–13; P-in-c Llanfihangel Ystrad and Cilcennin w Trefilan etc 13–19; P-in-c Carmarthen St Pet and Abergwili etc from 19. *6 Ael y Bryn, Tanerdy, Carmarthen SA31 2HB* T: (01267) 468432 M: 07964-631997 E: ystrad.matthew@outlook.com

✠**HILL, The Rt Revd Michael Arthur.** b 49. Ridley Hall Cam 74. **d** 77 **p** 78 **c** 98. C Addiscombe St Mary *Cant* 77–81; C Slough *Ox* 81–83; P-in-c Chesham Bois 83–90; R 90–92; RD Amersham 89–92; Adn Berks 92–98; Area Bp Buckingham 98–03; Bp Bris 03–17; rtd 17; Hon Asst Bp B & W from 18. *13 Lime Kiln Lane, Clevedon BS21 6BX* M: 07808-290908 E: mhill1949@gmail.com

HILL, The Rt Revd Michael John Giles. b 43. S Dios Minl Tr Scheme 82. **d** 84 **p** 86. Community of Our Lady and St John from 67; Abbot from 90; PtO *Win* 84–92 and from 13; Public Preacher 92–13; PtO *Portsm* from 04; Hon Can Win Cathl from 15. *Abbey of Our Lady and St John, Abbey Road, Beech, Alton GU34 4AP* T: (01420) 562145 *or* 563575 F: 561691 E: giles@altonabbey.com

HILL, Miss Naomi Jean. b 75. Coll of Ripon & York St Jo BA 96. Wycliffe Hall Ox BTh 06. **d** 06 **p** 07. C Northampton St Giles *Pet* 06–10; C Nottingham St Nic *S'well* 10–14; C Sneinton St Chris w St Phil 10–14; P-in-c from 14; C Nottingham St Ann w Em from 14. *St Christopher's Vicarage, 180 Sneinton Boulevard, Nottingham NG2 4GL* T: 0115-924 0046 M: 07855-060410 E: naomihillster@gmail.com

HILL, Nicholas John. b 66. St Mellitus Coll BA 15. **d** 17 **p** 18. C Stoke-next-Guildf *Guildf* from 17. *35 Woking Road, Guildford GU1 1QD* T: (01483) 874827 M: 07974-228961 E: nick66hill@gmail.com *or* nickhill@stjohnstoke.com

HILL, Peppie. *See* HILL, Stephanie Jane

HILL, Canon Peter. b 36. AKC 60. St Boniface Warminster 60. **d** 61 **p** 62. C Gt Berkhamsted *St Alb* 61–67; R Bedford St Mary 67–69; P-in-c 69–70; V Goldington 69–79; V Biggleswade 79–90; RD 80–85; Hon Can St Alb 85–90; V Holbeach *Linc* 90–01; RD Elloe E 94–99; P-in-c The Suttons w Tydd 99–01; rtd 01; PtO *Nor* 01–12; *Ely* 06–19. *40 Walnut Tree Crescent, Fenstanton, Huntingdon PE28 9LE* T: (01480) 461005

✠**HILL, The Rt Revd Peter.** b 50. Man Univ BSc 71 Nottm Univ MTh 90. Wycliffe Hall Ox 81. **d** 83 **p** 84 **c** 14. C Porchester *S'well* 83–86; V Huthwaite 86–95; P-in-c Calverton 95–04; RD S'well 97–01; Dioc Chief Exec 04–07; Adn Nottingham 07–14; Hon Can S'well Minster 01–07; Area Bp Barking *Chelmsf* from 14. *Barking Lodge, 35A Verulam Avenue, London E17 8ES* T: (020) 8509 7377 E: b.barking@chelmsford.anglican.org

HILL, Canon Richard Brian. b 47. Dur Univ BA 68. Cranmer Hall Dur 68 Westcott Ho Cam 70. **d** 71 **p** 72. C Cockermouth All SS w Ch Ch *Carl* 71–74; C Barrow St Geo w St Luke 74–76; V Walney Is 76–83; Dir of Clergy Tr 83–90; P-in-c Westward, Rosley-w-Woodside and Welton 83–90; V Gosforth All SS *Newc* 90–05; rtd 05; Hon Can Newc Cathl from 05; Chapl St Mary Magd and H Jes Trust 06–19; Asst Dioc Ecum Officer *Newc* 08–19; PtO from 19. *56 St Mary Magdalene Hospital,*

Claremont Road, Newcastle upon Tyne NE2 4NN T: 0191-261 2648 E: r.b.hill@lineone.net

HILL, Richard Hugh Oldham. b 52. CCC Ox BA 74 BA 77 MA 78. Wycliffe Hall Ox 75. **d** 78 **p** 79. C Harold Wood *Chelmsf* 78–81; C Hampreston *Sarum* 81–86; TV N Ferriby *York* 86–97; V Swanland 97–08; R Church Stretton *Heref* 08–18; RD Condover 11–18; rtd 18; PtO *Heref* from 19. *5 Whitbatch Close, Ludlow SY8 2PA* T: (01584) 318093

HILL, Robert Joseph. b 45. Oak Hill Th Coll BA 81. **d** 81 **p** 82. C W Derby St Luke *Liv* 81–84; P-in-c Devonport St Mich *Ex* 84–97; Chapl Morden Coll Blackheath 97–99; TV Manningham *Bradf* 99–04; P-in-c Davyhulme Ch Ch *Man* 04–13; rtd 13; PtO *Ches* from 17; *Man* from 19. *52 Wellfield Road, Stockport SK2 6AT* T: 0161-456 2450 E: rjandh@gmail.com *or* bobhillmsc@mailas.com

HILL, Rodney Maurice. b 44. Leeds Univ BA 67 FCIPD. Ripon Coll Cuddesdon 04. **d** 05 **p** 06. NSM N Hinksey and Wytham *Ox* 05–10; NSM Osney 10–12; PtO from 12. *13 Hobson Road, Oxford OX2 7JX* T: (01865) 426804 E: rodneymauricehill@hotmail.com

HILL, Canon Roger Anthony John. b 45. Liv Univ BA 67 Linacre Coll Ox BA 69 MA. Ripon Hall Ox 67. **d** 70 **p** 71. C St Helier *S'wark* 71–74; C Dawley Parva *Lich* 74–75; C Cen Telford 76–77; TV 77–81; TR 81–88; TR Newark *S'well* 88–02; RD 90–95; Hon Can S'well Minster 98–02; R Man St Ann 02–07; AD Hulme 05–07; Bp's Missr 07–11; Hon Can Man Cathl 02–11; rtd 11; PtO *Man* from 11; Chapl to The Queen 01–15. *4 Four Stalls End, Littleborough OL15 8SB* T: (01706) 374719 E: hillraj@gmail.com

HILL, Simon George. b 53. Reading Univ BSc 75 MSc 78 K Coll Lon MA 02 Lon Univ DMin 10. S'wark Ord Course 80. **d** 83 **p** 84. NSM Croydon St Aug *Cant* 83–84; Swaziland 84–86; Fiji 86–88; NSM Croydon St Aug *S'wark* 88–90; Tanzania 90–94; Uganda 94–96; Swaziland 96–98; PtO *S'wark* 99–02; *Chich* 99–02; P-in-c Cockfield w Bradfield St Clare, Felsham etc *St E* 02–04; R Bradfield St Clare, Bradfield St George etc 04–11; RD Lavenham 09–11; V Copthorne *Chich* 11–17; R Chevington w Hargrave, Chedburgh w Depden etc *St E* from 17. *The Rectory, New Road, Chevington, Bury St Edmunds IP29 5QL* T: (01284) 850857 M: 07840-038384 E: mlima001@btinternet.com

HILL, The Ven Simon James. b 64. Sheff Univ BA 85 Ex Univ PGCE 88 Bris Univ MA 09. Ripon Coll Cuddesdon BA 94. **d** 95 **p** 96. C Manston *Ripon* 95–98; TV Dorchester *Ox* 98–03; Dir Berinsfield Progr Ripon Coll Cuddesdon 98–03; R Backwell w Chelvey and Brockley *B & W* 03–10; Dioc Dir of Clergy Development 10–16; Preb Wells Cathl 14–16; Adn Taunton from 16. *2 Monkton Heights, West Monkton, Taunton TA2 8LU* T: (01823) 413315 E: adtaunton@bathwells.anglican.org

HILL, Stephanie Jane (Peppie). b 67. K Coll Lon LLB 88. Wycliffe Hall Ox BTh 05. **d** 05 **p** 15. C Loughborough Em and St Mary in Charnwood *Leic* 05–06; NSM Leic H Trin w St Jo 14–17; Assoc P Evang Development Market Harborough and The Transfiguration etc from 17. *The Rectory, Rectory Lane, Market Harborough LE16 8AS* E: pep@hill-home.co.uk *or* pep@harborough-anglican.org.uk

HILL, Stuart Graeme. b 64. Ripon Coll Cuddesdon BTh 97. **d** 97 **p** 98. C Usworth *Dur* 97–99; C Monkwearmouth 99–01; TV 01–06; V Upper Derwent *York* 06–19; C Jarrow and Simonside *Dur* from 19. *St Simon's Vicarage, 134 Wenlock Road, South Shields NE34 9AL* T: 0191-660 7927 E: revd.stuarthill@icloud.com

HILL (formerly SAYERS), Susan. b 46. Bp Otter Coll Chich BEd 69 Middx Univ BA 02. NTMTC 99. **d** 02 **p** 03. NSM Southend *Chelmsf* 02–12; TV 05–12; Asst Chapl HM Pris Bullwood Hall 02–06; rtd 12; PtO *Chelmsf* 13–16; Hon C Chingford SS Pet and Paul 16–18. *17 Claremont Close, Westcliff-on-Sea SS0 7UA* T: (01702) 431843 M: 07557-101314 E: susansayers@yahoo.com

HILL, Walter Henry. **d** 06 **p** 07. Aux Min Cloyne Union *C, C & R* 06–14; NSM Fermoy Union from 14. *Quetta, Glenatore, Conna, Co Cork, Republic of Ireland* M: (00353) 87-629 6545 E: whill911@gmail.com

HILL, William. b 44. Man Univ BSc 66 CEng 73 MICE 73. SEITE 95. **d** 98 **p** 99. NSM Farnham *Guildf* 98–01; P-in-c Smallburgh w Dilham w Honing and Crostwight *Nor* 01–05; rtd 05; PtO *Nor* from 05; RD St Benet 07–12. *65 New Road, Hethersett, Norwich NR9 3HJ* T: (01603) 812220 E: revd.william.hill@btinternet.com

HILL-BROWN, Rachel Judith. b 65. Westmr Coll Ox BEd 88. St Jo Coll Nottm MTh 07. **d** 07 **p** 09. C Knowle *Birm* 07–10; C Tanworth 10–11; Hon C Dorridge from 11; Hon Chapl Birm Children's Hosp NHS Foundn Trust from 11. *54 Glendon Way, Dorridge, Solihull B93 8SY* T: (01564) 772472 E: rhillbrown@googlemail.com

HILL-TOUT, Mark Laurence. b 50. AKC 73. **d** 74 **p** 75. C Brighton Resurr *Chich* 74–77; C Old Shoreham and New Shoreham 77–79; Dioc Stewardship Adv Lewes and Hastings 79–84; P-in-c Stonegate 79–83; R Horsted Keynes 84–89; V St Helens and Sea View *Portsm* 89–95; P-in-c Wymering 95–99; V 99–06; rtd 06. *c/o Crockford, Church House, Great Smith Street, London SW1P 3AZ* M: 07758-260936 E: m-m.h-t@hotmail.co.uk

HILLEL, Laurence Christopher Francis. b 54. Bris Univ BA 76 Sheff Univ PGCE 78 SOAS Lon MA 84. Cuddesdon Coll 98. **d** 98 **p** 99. C Pinner *Lon* 98–00; Chapl Bp Ramsey Sch 01–14; Inter Faith Adv Willesden Area *Lon* 14–19; NSM Eastcote St Lawr 01–04; NSM Brondesbury St Anne w Kilburn H Trin 04–19; rtd 19. *10 Cross Street, Lynton EX35 6HG* M: 07801-286819 E: revhillel@aol.com

HILLER, Ms Frances. b 53. Greenwich Univ BA 93. NTMTC 07. **d** 09. Chapl to Suff Bp Eur from 09; PtO *S'wark* from 09. *14 Tufton Street, London SW1P 3QZ* T: (020) 7898 1161 E: frances.hiller@churchofengland.org

HILLER, Ms Jane Alison Summer. b 69. Univ of W of England BA 96. Trin Coll Bris 17. **d** 19. C Penhill *Bris* from 19; C Upper Stratton from 19. *St Peter's Vicarage, Bremhill Close, Swindon SN2 5DS* T: (01793) 703322 E: thegreenvicar@gmail.com

HILLIAM, Mrs Cheryl. b 49. EMMTC. **d** 94 **p** 95. C Linc St Faith and St Martin w St Pet 94–98; P-in-c S Ormsby Gp 98–16; rtd 16; PtO *Linc* from 17. *17 Queen Street, Horncastle LN9 6BD* T: (01507) 523936

HILLIARD, Canon David. b 57. TCD BTh 91. CITC 88. **d** 91 **p** 92. C Holywood *D & D* 91–94; C Seagoe 94–96; I Tartaraghan w Diamond *Arm* from 96; Can Arm Cathl from 06. *The Rectory, 5 Tarthlogue Road, Portadown BT62 1RB* T/F: (028) 3885 1289 E: tartaraghan@armagh.anglican.org

HILLIARD, Ms Lorelli Alison. b 60. St Mary's Coll Dur BSc 82 Dur Univ MA 07. Cranmer Hall Dur 04. **d** 06 **p** 07. C Drypool *York* 06–10; P-in-c Gt Marsden w Nelson St Phil *Blackb* 10–13; V from 13. *St Philip's Vicarage, 1 Victory Close, Nelson BB9 9ED* T: (01282) 697011 E: lorelli.hilliard@googlemail.com

HILLIARD, Martin. b 45. TCD BA 69 BTh 08. CITC 05. **d** 08 **p** 09. C Larne and Inver and Glynn w Raloo *Conn* 08–11; I Kells Gp *C & O* 11–17; rtd 17. *21 Crannagh Road, Dublin 14, D14 AY10, Republic of Ireland* T: (00353) (1) 490 8676 M: 86-108 7432 E: revmartinhilliard@gmail.com *or* hilliarm@gmail.com

HILLIARD, Robert Godfrey. b 52. Portsm Univ BA(Ed) 97 MA 03. St Mich Coll Llan 72. **d** 75 **p** 76. C Whitchurch *Llan* 75–80; Chapl RNR 77–80; Chapl RN 80–06; Hon Chapl Portsm Cathl 03–06; Chapl Bradfield Coll Berks 06–12; C Cobham and Stoke D'Abernon *Guildf* 13–19; R Stoke D'Abernon from 19. *The Rectory, Blundel Lane, Stoke D'Abernon, Cobham KT11 2SE* T: (01932) 868428 M: 07786-257395 E: godfreyhilliard@hotmail.co.uk

HILLIER, Andrew. b 68. Cardiff Univ MTh RGN 92. SWMTC 99. **d** 02 **p** 03. C Castle Cary w Ansford *B & W* 02–05; Chapl RN from 05. *Royal Naval Chaplaincy Service, Mail Point 1-2, Leach Building, Whale Island, Portsmouth PO2 8BY* T: (023) 9262 5055 F: 9262 5134 E: revandrewhillier@gmail.com

HILLIER, Derek John. b 30. Sarum Th Coll 61. **d** 63 **p** 64. C Salisbury St Mark *Sarum* 63–65; C Weymouth H Trin 65–66; R Caundle Bishop w Caundle Marsh and Holwell 66–75; R The Caundles and Holwell 75–81; R The Caundles w Folke and Holwell 81–02; P-in-c Pulham 70–78; rtd 02; PtO *Sarum* 02–18; *B & W* 02–18. *Sarum House, Bishop's Caundle, Sherborne DT9 5ND* T/F: (01963) 23243 E: hillier899@btinternet.com *or* hilliers899@brimvernd.com

HILLIER, John Frederick. b 43. ARIBA 67. **d** 01 **p** 02. OLM Merton St Mary *S'wark* 01–06; PtO *St Alb* 07; NSM Sandridge 07–13; rtd 13; PtO *St Alb* 13; *Ely* from 14. *70 Royal Way, Trumpington, Cambridge CB2 9AX* T: (01223) 844282 M: 07802-646374 E: johnfhillier@gmail.com

HILLIER (née CHAPMAN), Mrs Linda Rosa. b 54. Middx Univ BA 04. NTMTC 01. **d** 04 **p** 05. C W Drayton *Lon* 04–07; Faith and Work Development Officer Slough *Ox* 07–13; NSM Upton cum Chalvey from 12. *79 Torbay Road, Harrow HA2 9QG* T: (020) 8864 5728 E: lindarosahillier@msn.com

HILLIER, Ms Marilyn Jean. b 51. Ches Coll of HE CertEd 73. NTMTC BA 08. **d** 08 **p** 09. NSM Gt Parndon *Chelmsf* 08–12; PtO from 13. *23 Chapel Hill, Stansted CM24 8AD* T: (01279) 819176 E: lynhillier@btinternet.com

HILLIER, Canon Timothy John. b 55. Westmr Coll Ox CertEd 77. Oak Hill Th Coll 94. **d** 96 **p** 97. C Chertsey *Guildf* 96–00; V 00–04; V Chertsey, Lyne and Longcross from 04; RD Runnymede 07–13; Hon Can Guildf Cathl from 18. *The Vicarage, London Street, Chertsey KT16 8AA* T/F: (01932) 563141 E: timjhillier@gmail.com

HILLMAN, Clive Ralph. b 71. York Univ BSc 92. St Steph Ho Ox BA 93. **d** 96 **p** 97. C Kingston upon Hull St Alb *York* 96–00; Chapl St Jo Coll Cam 02–06; V Betws-y-Coed and Capel Curig w Penmachno etc *Ban* 06–13; P-in-c Leigh St Clem *Chelmsf* from 14. *The Rectory, 80 Leigh Hill, Leigh-on-Sea SS9 1AR* T: (01702) 475967 E: clivehillman@btinternet.com

HILLMAN, John Anthony. b 32. St Chad's Coll Dur BA 53. St Mich Coll Llan 54. **d** 55 **p** 56. C Llangollen *St As* 56–60; C Silvertown S Africa 60–64; P-in-c Matroosfontein 64–72; R Noorder Paarl 72–75; R Durbanville 75–80; R Somerset W 80–86; TV Wolstanton *Lich* 86–91; P-in-c E Goscote w Ratcliffe and Rearsby *Leic* 91–93; TV Syston 93–98; rtd 98; PtO *St As* 09–13. *20 Plas Mariandir, Deganwy Road, Llanrhos, Llandudno LL30 1NB*

HILLMAN, Jonathan. b 68. Man Univ BEng 90. Ridley Hall Cam. **d** 00 **p** 01. C N Wingfield, Clay Cross and Pilsley *Derby* 00–03; TV Cove St Jo *Guildf* 03–10; R Windlesham from 10; AD Surrey Heath from 17. *The Rectory, Kennel Lane, Windlesham GU20 6AA* T: (01276) 472363 E: rector@windleshamchurch.org.uk

HILLMAN, Peter. b 69. Spurgeon's Coll Lon BD. NTMTC. **d** 07 **p** 08. C Rayleigh *Chelmsf* 07–11; Public Preacher 12–19; C New Thundersley from 19. *20 Lambeth Road, Benfleet SS7 4BN* T: (01268) 461753 E: pete@legacyweb.org or pete.hillman@stmarkscollege.co.uk

HILLMAN, Sarah Catherine. b 68. Selw Coll Cam BA 90 MA 94. St Jo Coll Nottm MA 05. **d** 03 **p** 04. C Sandy *St Alb* 03–06; P-in-c Barkway, Reed and Buckland w Barley 06–11; P-in-c Puddletown, Tolpuddle and Milborne w Dewlish *Sarum* 11–15; R from 15. *The Vicarage, The Square, Puddletown, Dorchester DT2 8SL* T: (01305) 848784 E: sarah.c.hillman@tesco.net

HILLS, Alan Arthur. b 49. Sussex Univ BA 73 Ches Coll of HE MEd 94. **d** 09 **p** 10. OLM Ashton Ch Ch *Man* from 09. *41 Bollington Road, Stockport SK4 5ER* T: 0161-432 2964 F: 477 7459 M: 07752-162333 E: alan@cahills.co.uk or alan.hills@chills.me

HILLS, Elaine. b 45. RN 67. Mon Dioc Tr Scheme 02. **d** 04 **p** 08. NSM Caerleon w Llanhennock *Mon* 04–09; NSM Caerleon and Llanfrechfa 09–18. *15 Church Street, Caerleon, Newport NP18 1AW* M: 07967-349096 E: rev.elaine@btinternet.com

HILLS, Kenneth Hugh. b 30. Univ of NZ BCom 54. Ripon Hall Ox 55. **d** 57 **p** 58. C Handsworth St Mary *Birm* 57–59; V Wanganui Paroch Distr New Zealand 59–61; V Porirua 67–74; Ind Chapl *Birm* 67–74; Chapl Aston Univ 74–82; rtd 91; Community Member Cluny Hill Coll 93–00. *2 O'Neills Place, Church Road, Holywood BT18 9BU* T: (028) 9042 1545 E: ken.hills1@btinternet.com

HILLS, Michael John. b 58. Open Univ BA 10. Westcott Ho Cam 87. **d** 88 **p** 89. C Workington St Jo *Carl* 88–91; C Gosforth All SS *Newc* 91–93; TV Seaton Hirst 93–98; Chapl RN 98–19; PtO *Glas* 00–03; *Bre* 03–06; *Newc* 06–19; *Sarum* 10–15; *Portsm* from 16; V Newc St Andr from 19; City Cen Chapl from 19; Chapl RNR from 19. *21 Treherne Road, Newcastle upon Tyne NE2 3NP* T: 0191-285 4464 M: 07900-583922 E: revmikehills@hotmail.com

HILLS, Michael William John. b 54. Univ of Wales (Lamp) BA 84. Westcott Ho Cam 85. **d** 87 **p** 88. C Reddish *Man* 87–91; V Bolton St Phil 91–00; V Northampton St Mich w St Edm *Pet* from 00; P-in-c Northampton H Sepulchre w St Andr and St Lawr 04–07; V from 07. *The Vicarage, 94 St Georges Avenue, Northampton NN2 6JF* T: (01604) 230316 or 717855 F: 635673 M: 07932-141428 E: mickhills54@gmail.com

HILLS, Roger Malcolm. b 42. Oak Hill Th Coll 83. **d** 86 **p** 87. NSM Mill Hill Jo Keble Ch *Lon* 86–98; NSM Mill Hill St Mich 86–98; PtO 98–00; V Queensbury All SS 00–07; rtd 07; PtO *Lon* from 08. *22 Sefton Avenue, London NW7 3QD* T: (020) 8959 1931 E: roger.hills2@btinternet.com

HILLS, Canon Sarah Ann St Leger. b 65. Sheff Univ MB, Chb 89 Leeds Univ MA 07. NOC 04. **d** 07 **p** 08. C Millhouses H Trin *Sheff* 07–10; PtO 10–11; Hon C Sheff St Pet and St Oswald 11–14; Bp's Adv in Past Care and Reconciliation 13–14; Can for Reconciliation Min Cov Cathl 14–19; V Holy Is *Newc* from 19. *The Vicarage, Holy Island, Berwick-upon-Tweed TD15 2RX* M: 07557-054641 E: incumbentholyisland@gmail.com

HILLS, Stephen Alan. b 59. Sheff Univ BA 81. Ridley Hall Cam 97. **d** 99 **p** 00. C Southborough St Pet w Ch Ch and St Matt etc *Roch* 99–02; TV 02–19; R Bidborough St Lawr and Southborough St Pet from 19. *The Rectory, Rectory Drive, Bidborough, Tunbridge Wells TN3 0UL* T: (01892) 528081 E: stephen.bidborough@yahoo.co.uk

HILTON, Mrs Barbara Anne. b 59. Lindisfarne Regional Tr Partnership BA 14. **d** 14 **p** 15. C Heighington and Darlington St Matt and St Luke *Dur* 14–17; P-in-c Croxdale and Tudhoe from 17; P-in-c Merrington from 17. *St David's Vicarage, 21 York Villas, Spennymoor DL16 6LP* M: 07456-082231 E: barbara17hilton@yahoo.co.uk

HILTON, Clive. b 30. K Coll Lon 54. **d** 58 **p** 59. C Wythenshawe Wm Temple Ch CD *Man* 58–61; C Newton Heath All SS 61–62; C-in-c Oldham St Chad Limeside CD 62–65; V Oldham St Chad Limeside 65–70; P-in-c Gravesend H Family *Roch* 70–71; R Killamarsh *Derby* 71–88; R Broughton w Loddington and Cransley etc *Pet* 88–91; rtd 92; PtO *Man* 92–95; *Pet* from 98; *Ches* 95–99; *Linc* from 98; *Ely* 05–08. *73A Tattershall Drive, Market Deeping, Peterborough PE6 8BZ* T: (01778) 346217

HILTON, Canon Ian Anthony. b 57. St Jo Coll Nottm 83. **d** 86 **p** 87. C Nottingham St Sav *S'well* 86–90; C Aspley 90–97; P-in-c Colchester, New Town and The Hythe *Chelmsf* 97–02; R 02–18; RD Colchester 06–14; CME Adv from 18; Public Preacher from 18; Hon Can Chelmsf Cathl from 12. *Chelmsford Diocesan Board of Finance, 53 New Street, Chelmsford CM1 1AT* M: 07813-538926 E: ihilton@chelmsford.anglican.org

HILTON, John. b 49. Ex Univ BA 70. Cuddesdon Coll 71. **d** 73 **p** 74. C W Derby St Jo *Liv* 73–79; V Orford St Andr 79–96; V Leeds St Wilfrid *Ripon* 96–14 and 14; rtd 14; PtO *Man* from 15. *42 College Avenue, Oldham OL8 4DS* T: 0161-624 9172 M: 07970-476406 E: fr.john@btinternet.com

HILTON, Steven Craig. b 79. Southn Univ BA 01 FRSA 16. Westcott Ho Cam 02 Ripon Coll Cuddesdon 17. **d** 19. C Man Cathl from 19. *237 Great Clowes Street, Salford M7 2DZ* M: 07779-604781 E: curate@manchestercathedral.org

HILTON-TURVEY, Geoffrey Michael. b 34. Oak Hill Th Coll 80. **d** 81 **p** 82. C Bispham *Blackb* 81–85; V Inskip 85–99; rtd 99; PtO *Heref* from 00. *20 Cralves Mead, Tenbury Wells WR15 8EX* T: (01584) 811153

HILTON-TURVEY, Keith Geoffrey Michael. b 59. Oak Hill Th Coll BA 03. **d** 03 **p** 04. C S Mimms Ch Ch Lon 05–09; P-in-c Cricklewood St Pet 09–15; P-in-c Ledbury w Eastnor *Heref* 15–17; V from 17. *The Rectory, Worcester Road, Ledbury HR8 1PL* E: kwrbht@zoho.com or rector@ledburyparishchurch.org.uk

HINCHCLIFFE, Garry Anthony Frank. b 68. New Coll Edin BD 94. Edin Th Coll 90. **d** 94 **p** 95. C Dumfries *Glas* 94–97; P-in-c Motherwell and Wishaw 97–00; V Hampsthwaite and Killinghall *Ripon* 00–04; V Hampsthwaite and Killinghall and Birstwith 04–13; TR Knaresborough 13–14; *Leeds* 14–18; P-in-c Nidd 14–18; TR Knaresborough, Goldsborough, Nidd and Brearton from 19. *The Rectory, High Bond End, Knaresborough HG5 9BT* T: (01423) 202092 E: garry.hinchcliffe@btinternet.com

HINCHCLIFFE, Lesley. b 56. Huddersfield Univ CertEd 02. LCTP 13. **d** 16 **p** 17. NSM Salesbury *Blackb* 16–19; V Fence-in-Pendle and Higham from 19. *10 Lynwood Avenue, Clayton le Moors, Accrington BB5 5RR* T: (01254) 396485 M: 07711-585645 E: lesleyhinchcliffe@hotmail.com

HINCKLEY, Paul Frederick. b 61. Cranfield Inst of Tech MSc 85. Ridley Hall Cam 92. **d** 94 **p** 95. C Ovenden *Wakef* 94–99; TV Billericay and Lt Burstead *Chelmsf* 99–06; R Yateley *Win* 06–10; TV Gt Marlow w Marlow Bottom, Lt Marlow and Bisham *Ox* 10–13; TV Stoke Gifford *Bris* 13–15; V Bradley Stoke from 15. *106 Cooks Close, Bradley Stoke, Bristol BS32 0BB* T: (01454) 880065 E: paul@bradleystokeparish.org.uk

✠**HIND, The Rt Revd John William.** b 45. Leeds Univ BA 66 Lambeth DD 09. Cuddesdon Coll 70. **d** 72 **p** 73 **c** 91. C Catford (Southend) and Downham *S'wark* 72–76; V Forest Hill Ch Ch 76–82; P-in-c Forest Hill St Paul 81–82; Prin Chich Th Coll 82–91; Wiccamical Preb Chich Cathl 82–91; Area Bp Horsham 91–93; Bp Eur 93–01; Asst Bp Chich 93–01; Bp Chich 01–12; rtd 12; Hon Asst Bp Portsm from 12; PtO from 16. *1 Stanley Road, Emsworth PO10 7BD* M: 07768-081106 E: johnwhind@gmail.com

HIND, Ruth Elizabeth. See NEWTON, Ruth Elizabeth

HINDER, Richard Alan. b 46. Birm Univ BSc 67 CCC Cam PhD 71 FRAS 70 CEng 82 FIEE 80. S'wark Ord Course 04. **d** 07 **p** 08. NSM Croydon St Matt *S'wark* 07–16; PtO from 16. *18 Mapledale Avenue, Croydon CR0 5TB* T: (020) 8123 5256 E: richard@richardhinder.com or rahinder@gmail.com

HINDLE (formerly PARKER), Anne Margaret. b 57. Leeds Univ BSc 78. EAMTC 96. **d** 99 **p** 00. C Greenstead w Colchester St Anne *Chelmsf* 99–04; TV 04–08; P-in-c Kingsley and Foxt-w-Whiston *Lich* 08–10; R Kingsley and Foxt-w-Whiston and Oakamoor etc 10–11; P-in-c Clifton and Southill *St Alb* 11–15; R 15–16; V Warmington, Tansor and Cotterstock etc *Pet* 16–19; rtd 19. *Address temp unknown* M: 07738-230985 E: annehindle12@gmail.com

HINDLE, Miss Penelope Jane Bowyn. b 45. Trin Coll Bris 76. dss 84 **d** 87 **p** 94. Stoneycroft All SS *Liv* 84–89; Par Dn 87–89; Asst Chapl Broadgreen Hosp Liv 87–89; Asst Chapl R Free Hosp Lon 89–93; Chapl N Herts NHS Trust 93–00; Chapl E and N Herts NHS Trust 00–02; rtd 02; PtO *B & W* from 07. *Cleeve House, Level Lane, Charlton Horethorne, Sherborne DT9 4NN* T: (01963) 220055 E: jane.hindle@btinternet.com

HINDLEY, Canon Anthony Talbot. b 41. Bernard Gilpin Soc Dur 61 Oak Hill Th Coll 62. **d** 66 **p** 67. C Stoke next Guildf St Jo 66–69; C Eldoret Kenya 70–72; V Menengai 72–78; C Redhill H Trin *S'wark* 78–79; P-in-c Eastbourne All So *Chich* 79–83; V 83–86; V S Malling 86–89; R Wainford *St E* 98–06; RD Beccles and S Elmham 00–03; Hon Can St E Cathl 05–06; rtd 06; PtO *St E* 07–13; *Nor* 07–13; *Ex* from 15. *19 Thorne Park Road, Torquay TQ2 6RU* T: (01803) 445885 M: 07766-546601 E: anthonyhindley1@gmail.com

HINDLEY, Michael Alexander. b 72. Man Metrop Univ BA 94. Wycliffe Hall Ox BTh 05. **d** 05 **p** 06. C Clubmoor *Liv* 05–09; TV Fazakerley Em from 09. *Emmanuel Rectory, Higher Lane, Liverpool L9 9DJ* T: 0151-525 5229 M: 07980-912768 E: revd.mike@btinternet.com

HINDLEY, Roger Dennis. b 48. Birm Univ BA 70 Ox Univ BA 77 MA 83. Ripon Coll Cuddesdon 75 Qu Coll Birm 77. **d** 78 **p** 79. C Rubery *Birm* 78–81; C Henbury *Bris* 81–83; V Erdington St Chad *Birm* 83–89; V Hill 89–05; AD Sutton Coldfield 96–02; Hon Can Birm Cathl 00–05; TR Willington *Newc* 05–11; rtd 11; PtO *Lich* from 11. *29 Thacker Drive, Lichfield WS13 6NS* T: (01543) 253686

HINDMARSH, Valerie Gail. b 54. Edin Univ BA 75 Jordanhill Coll Glas CertEd 76 Man Metrop Univ CertEd 98 Lon Inst of Educn MA 06 EdD 12. All SS Cen for Miss & Min 15. **d** 17 **p** 18. NSM Norbury *Ches* from 17. *1 Clumber Close, Poynton, Stockport SK12 1PG* T: (01625) 873820 E: val_hindmarsh@hotmail.com

HINDS, Kenneth Arthur Lancelot. b 30. K Coll Lon BA 00 Birkbeck Coll Lon MA 04. Bps' Coll Cheshunt. **d** 64 **p** 65. C Sawbridgeworth *St Alb* 64–67; C Gt Berkhamsted 67–71; V Boreham Wood St Mich 71–75; Trinidad and Tobago 75–79; P-in-c St Ilford St Luke *Chelmsf* 79–81; V 81–95; rtd 95; PtO *Chelmsf* from 95. *214 Aldborough Road South, Ilford IG3 8HF* T: (020) 8598 2963 M: 07824-808664 E: frkalhinds@ntlworld.com

HINE, John Victor. b 36. Open Univ BA 82. Carl Dioc Tr Course 85. **d** 88 **p** 89. NSM Dean *Carl* 88–92; NSM Clifton 88–92; C Millom 92–94; P-in-c Gt Broughton and Broughton Moor 94–02; P-in-c Brigham 99–02; rtd 02; PtO *Carl* from 02. *4 The Paddocks, Thursby, Carlisle CA5 6PB* T: (01228) 712704 E: john.v.hine@btinternet.com

HINE, Keith Ernest. b 50. Bradf Univ BA Leeds Univ CertEd. NOC 89. **d** 89 **p** 90. C Wilmslow *Ches* 89–94; V Bowdon 94–08; R Tarporley 08–14; C Acton and Worleston, Church Minshull etc 10–14; RD Malpas 10–14; rtd 14; PtO *Ches* from 14. *18 Statham Drive, Lymm WA13 9NW* T: (01925) 752213 E: keithehine@gmail.com

HINE, Patrick Lewis. b 45. **d** 06 **p** 07. OLM Horfield H Trin *Bris* 06–15; PtO 15–19. *16 Red House Lane, Bristol BS9 3RZ* T: 0117-962 3861 E: revpatrickhine@gmail.com

HINES, Mrs Ashley Jane. b 64. Qu Coll Birm 11. **d** 14 **p** 15. OLM Horninglow *Lich* 14–17; Chapl Burton Hosps NHS Foundn Trust from 17; PtO *Lich* from 18. *24 Church View, Burton-on-Trent DE13 0NQ* T: (01283) 563115 E: ashleyhines1964@hotmail.com

HINES, Richard Arthur. b 49. Imp Coll Lon MSc 73 PhD 76 K Coll Lon MTh 89. Oak Hill Th Coll 82. **d** 84 **p** 85. C Mile Cross *Nor* 84–87; Lect Oak Hill Th Coll 87–97; Vice-Prin NTMTC 94–97; R Happisburgh, Walcott, Hempstead w Eccles etc *Nor* 97–07; C Bacton w Edingthorpe w Witton and Ridlington 04–07; R Falkland Is 07–14; rtd 14; P-in-c Aberdeen St Jas *Ab* 15–18; PtO *Ely* from 19; RD Wisbech Lynn Marshland from 19. *47B Ramnoth Road, Wisbech PE13 2JA* T: (01945) 587742 M: 07933-198943 E: richard.hines@outlook.com

HINEY, Thomas Bernard Felix. b 35. Open Univ BA 07. Ridley Hall Cam 67. **d** 69 **p** 70. C Edgbaston St Aug *Birm* 69–71; CF 71–91; Chapl R Hosp Chelsea 91–01; Chapl Mercers' Coll Holborn 99–01; rtd 01. *7B Dagmar Road, Exmouth EX8 2AN* T: (01395) 270688 E: sevenbdagmar@gmail.com

HINGE, Derek Colin. b 36. Imp Coll Lon BSc 58 CChem 60 MRSC 60. St Alb Minl Tr Scheme 84. **d** 88 **p** 89. NSM Bishop's Stortford St Mich *St Alb* 88–08; PtO from 08. *12 Avenue Road, Bishop's Stortford CM23 5NU* T: (01279) 652173 E: derekhinge@gmail.com

HINGLEY, Christopher James Howard. b 48. Trin Coll Ox BA 69 MA 71. Wycliffe Hall Ox 81. **d** 80 **p** 81. C St Jo Cathl Bulawayo Zimbabwe 80–81; C Hillside Ascension 82–84; Tutor Wycliffe Hall Ox 84–88; Chapl Whitestone Sch

Bulawayo Zimbabwe 89–04; Headmaster Petra High Sch 04–06; R Petra Schs Bulawayo from 06. *Whitestone School, Private Bag 4, Bulawayo, Zimbabwe* E: hingley@yoafrica.com

HINGLEY (née EDWARDS), Canon Helen. b 55. Natal Univ BSW 75. St Steph Ho Ox 94. **d** 96 **p** 97. C Gravelly Hill *Birm* 96–01; TV Cen Wolverhampton *Lich* 01–05; P-in-c Hamstead St Bernard *Birm* 05–08; V 08–14; AD Handsworth 08–11; Hon Can Birm Cathl 11–14; rtd 14; PtO *Birm* from 14. *4 Adrian Croft, Birmingham B13 9YF* T: 0121-777 2171 E: h.hingley@btinternet.com

HINGLEY, Robert Charles. b 46. Ball Coll Ox BA 69 MA 74 Birm Univ CertEd 73. Qu Coll Birm 70. **d** 73 **p** 74. C Charlton St Luke w H Trin *S'wark* 73–76; Asst Warden Iona Abbey 76–77; TV Langley Marish *Ox* 77–83; V Balsall Heath St Paul *Birm* 83–90; PtO 90–91; V Birm St Luke 91–96; LtO 96–05; Hon C Hamstead St Bernard 05–14; rtd 14; PtO *Birm* from 14; *Lich* 01–16. *4 Adrian Croft, Birmingham B13 9YF* T: 0121-777 2171 E: rob.hingley@btinternet.com

HINGLEY, Roderick Stanley Plant. b 51. St Chad's Coll Dur BA 72. St Steph Ho Ox 74. **d** 75 **p** 76. C Lower Gornal *Lich* 75–79; C Tividale 79–82; C Broseley w Benthall *Heref* 82–84; C Wanstead St Mary *Chelmsf* 84–92; V Romford St Alb from 92. *St Alban's Vicarage, 3 Francombe Gardens, Romford RM1 2TH* T: (01708) 473580

HINGSTON, Barry David. b 63. LSE BSc(Econ) 84. NTMTC BA 08. **d** 08 **p** 09. C Ealing St Paul *Lon* 08–12; P-in-c Greenhill St Jo 12–14; V from 14. *11 Flambard Road, Harrow HA1 2NB* T: (020) 8907 7956 M: 07710-359483 E: barryhingston@btinternet.com or barry@stjohnsharrow.org

HINKLEY, Mrs Maureen. b 41. **d** 04. NSM Hollington St Jo *Chich* from 04. *8 Wadhurst Close, St Leonards-on-Sea TN37 7AZ* T: (01424) 754872 E: hinkley872@btinternet.com

HINKS, Margaret Anne. b 47. Birm Univ MB, ChB 65. Qu Coll Birm 08. **d** 10 **p** 11. NSM Birm St Geo 10–14; NSM Hampton-in-Arden w Bickenhill 14–17; PtO 17–18; P-in-c Leam Valley Cov from 18. *The Vicarage, Lower Street, Willoughby, Rugby CV23 8BX* M: 07854-329892 E: anne.hinks@outlook.com

HINKS (née CHAMBERS), Mrs Marion Patricia. b 48. Univ of Wales BDS 72. SWMTC 97. **d** 97 **p** 98. NSM Plymstock and Hooe *Ex* 97–02; NSM Ivybridge w Harford 02–15; rtd 15; PtO *Ex* from 16. *52 Southland Park Road, Wembury, Plymouth PL9 0HQ* T: (01752) 862439

HINKSMAN, Barrie Lawrence James. b 41. K Coll Lon BD 64 AKC 64 Birm Univ PhD 02. St Boniface Warminster 64. **d** 65 **p** 66. C Crosby *Linc* 65–67; Ecum Development Officer Scunthorpe Coun of Chs 67–69; C Chelmsley Wood *Birm* 69–72; TV 72–75; P-in-c Hurchurch *Cov* 75–79; Dioc Lay Tr Adv 75–79; PtO 89–90; Hon Chapl Cov Cathl 90–01; PtO *Birm* 01–12; Hon Sen Fell Warw Univ *Cov* 02–09; PtO *Heref* 12–18; *Worc* 16–17. *c/o Crockford, Church House, Great Smith Street, London SW1P 3AZ*

HINSLEY, Robert Charles. b 77. Univ of Wales (Abth) BTh 98 St Jo Coll Dur MATM 06. Cranmer Hall Dur 03. **d** 05 **p** 06. C Carlton-in-Lindrick and Langold w Oldcotes *S'well* 05–08; P-in-c Felixstowe St Jo *St E* 08–14; RD Colneys 11–14; TR Ipswich St Mary at Stoke w St Pet and St Fran from 14. *The Rectory, 1 Salmet Close, Ipswich IP2 9BA* T: (01473) 807119 E: rev.roberthinsley@gmail.com

HINTON, Mrs Frances Mary. b 43. EN(G) 85. EMMTC 89. **d** 92 **p** 94. Par Dn Hornsey Rise Whitehall Park Team *Lon* 92–94; C 94–97; C Upper Holloway 97; TV Barking St Marg w St Patr *Chelmsf* 97–04; rtd 04; PtO *Linc* from 17. *5 Little Thorpe Lane, Thorpe-on-the-Hill, Lincoln LN6 9BL* T: (01522) 688886

HINTON, Canon James William. b 63. Cov Poly BSc 84 Leeds Univ PGCE 86. St Jo Coll Nottm 00. **d** 02 **p** 03. C Thornbury *Bradf* 02–05; P-in-c Bowling St Steph 05–15; P-in-c Bankfoot 09–15; V Bankfoot and Bowling St Steph *Leeds* from 15; C Lt Horton from 05; Hon Can Bradf Cathl from 17. *St Stephen's Vicarage, 48 Newton Street, Bradford BD5 7BH* T: (01274) 720784 or 391537 E: jimmy4hinton@gmail.com or jimmy.hinton@leeds.anglican.org

HINTON, Michael Ernest. b 33. K Coll Lon 53 St Boniface Warminster 56. **d** 57 **p** 58. C Babbacombe *Ex* 57–60; S Africa 60–66; P-in-c Limehouse St Pet *Lon* 66–68; R Felmingham *Nor* 68–72; R Suffield 68–72; P-in-c Colby w Banningham and Tuttington 68–72; Bahamas 72–76; P-in-c Mylor w Flushing *Truro* 77–80; R The Deverills *Sarum* 82–87; Bermuda 87–89; Virgin Is 89–91; Chapl Sequoian Retreat and Conf Progr from 91; rtd 98; PtO *St E* 00–01; *Ex* from 02. *Le Petit Plan, St Ann's Chapel, Kingsbridge TQ7 4HQ* T: (01548) 810124 E: lactonint@btinternet.com

HINTON, Michael George. b 27. Mert Coll Ox BA 48 MA 51 Reading Univ PhD 59. S Dios Minl Tr Scheme 81. **d** 83 **p** 84. NSM Weston-super-Mare St Paul *B & W* 83–85; NSM Sibertswold w Coldred *Cant* 85–87; NSM Eythorne and Elvington w Waldershare etc 87–95; PtO 95–19. *212 The Gateway, Dover CT16 1LL* T/F: (01304) 204198 E: michael@hintonm.demon.co.uk

HINTON, Nigel Keith. b 49. Univ Coll Lon BSc 70 Lon Inst of Educn MA 87 Worc Coll of Educn PGCE 73. Oak Hill NSM Course 89. **d** 92 **p** 93. NSM Cudham and Downe *Roch* 92–07; Asst Chapl St Paul's Sch Barnes 92–07; PtO *Lon* 03–13; NSM Ootacamund St Steph India 08–12; PtO *Roch* 13–15; NSM Dormansland *S'wark* from 15. *St John's Vicarage, The Platt, Dormansland, Lingfield RH7 6QU* T: (01342) 832391 E: nigelk.hinton@gmail.com

HINTON, Paul Robin George. b 64. St Jo Coll Dur BA 86. Qu Coll Birm BA 05. **d** 05 **p** 06. C Rowley Regis *Birm* 05–09; V Warley Woods 09–19; Asst Dioc Dir of Ords 18–19; Hd of Min Formation from 19; PtO from 19. *St Hilda's Vicarage, Abbey Road, Smethwick, Warley B67 5NQ* T: 0121-429 1384 F: 420 2386 M: 07777-603188 E: revpaulhinton@btinternet.com *or* paulh@cofebirmingham.com

HINTON, Robert Matthew. b 69. Lanc Univ BA 91. Cranmer Hall Dur BA 97. **d** 97 **p** 98. C Lache cum Saltney *Ches* 97–99; C Cheadle Hulme St Andr 99–02; V Hale Barns w Ringway 02–09; Ind Chapl *Ripon* 09–13; V Beckenham Ch Ch *Roch* from 13; AD Beckenham from 15. *Christ Church Vicarage, 18 Court Downs Road, Beckenham BR3 6LR* T: (020) 8650 3487 E: revrobhinton@hotmail.com

HIPPISLEY-COX, Stephen David. b 63. Sheff Univ BSc 85 PhD 92 Peterho Cam BA 98 MA 02. Westcott Ho Cam 96. **d** 99 **p** 00. C Ollerton w Boughton *S'well* 99–02; NSM Wilford Hill 02–07; P-in-c Willoughby-on-the-Wolds w Wysall and Widmerpool 07–11; R from 11; AD E Bingham from 18. *The Rectory, Keyworth Road, Wysall, Nottingham NG12 5QQ* T: (01509) 889706 E: s.d.hippisley.cox@gmail.com

HIRONS, Malcolm Percy. b 36. Oriel Coll Ox BA 59 MA 62. Wycliffe Hall Ox 59. **d** 61 **p** 62. C Edgbaston St Aug *Birm* 61–64; Chapl Warw Sch 64–65; C Beverley Minster *York* 65–69; V Barnby upon Don *Sheff* 69–80; P-in-c Kirk Bramwith 75–80; P-in-c Fenwick 75–80; V Norton Woodseats St Paul 80–98; rtd 98; PtO *Nor* 98–16. *Broome Lodge, 8 Lincoln Square, Hunstanton PE36 6DL* T: (01485) 532385

HIRST, David William. b 37. Man Univ MA 78. Brasted Th Coll 59 St Aid Birkenhead 61. **d** 63 **p** 64. C Clayton *Man* 63–64; C Bury St Jo 64–66; C Wythenshawe Wm Temple Ch 67–70; V Oldham St Chad Limeside 70–79; V Friezland 79–91; R Ashton St Mich 91–95; Chapl HM Pris Buckley Hall 95–00; Chapl HM Pris Wolds 00–02; rtd 02; PtO *Blackb* from 09. *8 Priory Mews, Lytham St Annes FY8 4FT* T: (01253) 730945 M: 07833-353837 E: davidwilliamhirst@btinternet.com

HIRST, Canon Godfrey Ian. b 41. Univ of Wales (Lamp) BA 63 MBIM. Chich Th Coll 63. **d** 65 **p** 66. C Brierfield *Blackb* 65–68; Ind Chapl *Liv* 68–71; TV Kirkby 71–75; Ind Chapl *Blackb* 75–94; P-in-c Treales 75–87; Hon Can Blackb Cathl 83–87 and 94–06; Can Res Blackb Cathl 87–94; V Lytham St Cuth 94–06; AD Kirkham 98–06; rtd 06; PtO *Blackb* from 06. *11 Arundel Road, Lytham St Annes FY8 1AF* T: (01253) 732474 M: 07885-118331 E: godfrehirst@btinternet.com

HIRST, John Adrian. b 49. St Jo Coll Nottm BTh 78. **d** 78 **p** 79. C Cheltenham St Mark *Glouc* 78–84; TV 84–85; TV Swan *Ox* 85–89; R Denham 89–15; rtd 15; PtO *Ox* from 15. *15 Riverview, Flackwell Heath, High Wycombe HP10 9AT*

HIRST, Canon Judith. b 54. St Mary's Coll Dur BA 76 LMH Ox PGCE 77 Hull Univ MA 86 St Jo Coll Dur BA 94. Cranmer Hall Dur 91. **d** 94 **p** 95. Bp's Adv in Past Care and Counselling *Dur* 94–00; C Dur St Oswald 94–00; Dir Min Formation Cranmer Hall Dur 00–07; Local Min Development Officer Dur and Newc 07–11; Local Ch Growth and Development Adv (Missr) *Dur* from 11; NSM Dur St Marg and Neville's Cross St Jo from 12; Hon Can Dur Cathl from 11. *5 Beechways, Durham DH1 4LG* T: 0191-370 9505 E: judy.hirst@durham.anglican.org

HIRST, Margaret. *See* FOSSEY, Margaret

HIRST, Mrs Rachel Ann. b 58. Portsm Poly BA 79 Hull Univ PGCE 81 ACII 85. NEOC 99. **d** 02 **p** 03. NSM Clifton *York* 02–04; C 04–06; Par Development and Tr Officer (York Adnry) 06–11; V Norton juxta Malton from 11; RD S Ryedale 13–18. *The Vicarage, 80 Langton Road, Norton, Malton YO17 9AE* T: (01653) 699222 M: 07896-204121 E: rachel.hirst40@googlemail.com

HISCOCK, Gary Edward. b 43. Oak Hill Th Coll BA 90. **d** 90 **p** 91. C Cheltenham St Luke and St Jo *Glouc* 90–94; C Hardwicke, Quedgeley and Elmore w Longney 95–96; rtd 96. *25 Bournside Road, Cheltenham GL51 3AL* T: (01242) 513002

HISCOCK, Phillip George. b 47. Southn Univ CertEd 68 MPhil 90 MCIPD 83. STETS 95. **d** 98 **p** 99. NSM Portchester and Chapl Portsm Docks 98–02; Chapl Dunkirk Miss

to Seafarers *Eur* 02–08; C Alverstoke *Portsm* 08–15; rtd 15; PtO *Portsm* from 15. *15 Winnham Drive, Fareham PO16 8QE* T: (01329) 314345 M: 07830-362149 E: phillip.hiscock@ntlworld.com *or* philhiscock@gmail.com

HISCOCKS, Nicholas Robin Thomas. b 75. Keble Coll Ox BA 96 MA 01 Anglia Poly Univ MA 01. Ridley Hall Cam 99. **d** 01 **p** 02. C Bromley Ch Ch *Roch* 01–11; V Westbourne Ch Ch Chpl *Win* from 11. *134 Alumhurst Road, Bournemouth BH4 8HU* T: (01202) 767881 E: nick@christchurchwestbourne.com

HISCOX, Miss Denise. b 47. Lon Univ TCert 68 Lanchester Poly Cov BSc 78. WMMTC 98. **d** 01 **p** 02. NSM Cov St Mary 01–05; NSM Leamington Priors All SS 05–07; NSM Leamington Spa H Trin and Old Milverton 05–07; PtO 07–08; NSM Willenhall 08–10; PtO *Newc* from 11. *1 Rogerson Road, Belford NE70 7DB* E: denise@dhiscox.co.uk

HISLOP, Martin Gregory. b 55. Jas Cook Univ Townsville BA 78 Univ of S Aus MEd 88. **d** 92 **p** 93. C N Mackay St Ambrose Australia 92–93; Dir Studies St Barn Coll of Min 93–94; Chapl Ballarat Univ 95–98; Asst Chapl St Mich Gr Sch 98; Assoc P E St Kilda 98; C Kingston St Luke *S'wark* 00–01; P-in-c 01–05; V from 05. *St Luke's Vicarage, 4 Burton Road, Kingston upon Thames KT2 5TE* T: (020) 8546 4064 E: mhislop@btinternet.com

HISLOP, Mrs Patricia Elizabeth. b 42. Heythrop Coll Lon MA 03. **d** 08 **p** 09. OLM Ewhurst *Guildf* 08–12; PtO from 12; Birtley Ho Bramley 12–16. *2 Napper Place, Cranleigh GU6 8DG* T: (01483) 274359 E: patricia.hislop@phrh.co.uk

HITCH, Canon Kim William. b 54. Leic Univ BSc 75 K Coll Lon MA 84 Birm Univ MPhil 08. Trin Coll Bris 76. **d** 78 **p** 79. C Becontree St Mary *Chelmsf* 78–80; C Huyton Quarry *Liv* 80–83; V Hatcham St Jas *S'wark* 83–91; TR Kidbrooke 91–02; R Kidbrooke St Jas from 02; Lewisham Adnry Ecum Officer 03–06; Dir Ords (Woolwich Area) 05–12; AD Charlton 06–19; Hon Can S'wark Cathl from 08; Dioc Voc Adv 12–17; Dir Ords Woolwich Area from 13. *St James's Rectory, 62 Kidbrooke Park Road, London SE3 0DU* T: (020) 8856 3438 E: k.w.hitch@btinternet.com

HITCHEN, Carol Ann. *See* CLOSE, Carol Ann

HITCHEN, Gillian Françoise Helene. b 71. Wycliffe Hall Ox 16. **d** 18 **p** 19. C Parr *Liv* from 18. *St Philip's Vicarage, 459 Fleet Lane, St Helens WA9 2NQ*

HITCHEN, Lisa Jan. *See* MacINNES, Lisa Jan

HITCHENS (née GREEN), Mrs Catherine Isabel. b 48. Cant Sch of Min 89. **d** 92 **p** 94. C Willesborough *Cant* 92–96; Sen Asst P E Dereham and Scarning *Nor* 96–97; Asst Chapl HM Pris Wayland 96–97; Chapl HM Pris Leic 97–00; Chapl HM YOI Castington 00–02; Chapl HM Pris Cant 02–12; rtd 12. *Dan y Coed, 6 Gybbons Road, Rolvenden, Cranbrook TN17 4LL* E: cathandfred@hotmail.com

HITCHINER, Mrs Elizabeth Ann. b 59. Birm Univ BSc 80. WEMTC 03. **d** 06 **p** 07. NSM Cagebrook *Heref* from 06. *Dunan House, Clehonger, Hereford HR2 9SF* T: (01432) 355980

HITCHING, His Honour Judge Alan Norman. b 41. Ch Ch Ox BA 62 MA 66 BCL 63 Barrister-at-Law (Middle Temple) 64. **d** 01 **p** 02. NSM High Ongar w Norton Mandeville *Chelmsf* 01–06; PtO from 06. *9 Monkhams Drive, Woodford Green IG8 0LG* T: (020) 8504 4260 E: anhitching@btinternet.com

HITCHINS, Graham Edward David. b 54. S Dios Minl Tr Scheme 91. **d** 94 **p** 95. C Bishop's Waltham *Portsm* 94–97; C Upham 94–97; C Honiton, Gittisham, Combe Raleigh, Monkton etc *Ex* 97–98; TV 98–03; Chapl RN 03–10; R Burnham Gp of Par *Nor* 09–18; Corps Chapl Sea Cadet Corps from 10; Chapl RNR from 16; PtO *Ex* from 18. *Stapleford House, Gold Street, Stalbridge, Sturminster Newton DT10 2LX* E: revdgrahamhitchins@hotmail.com

HITCHMAN, Keith John. b 62. Middx Univ BSc 90. Trin Coll Bris BA 95. **d** 95 **p** 96. C Bestwood *S'well* 95–99; Chapl Glos Univ 99–04; C Cheltenham St Mary, St Matt, St Paul and H Trin *Glouc* 04–07; TV Cheltenham H Trin and St Paul 07–10; Pioneer Min River in the City *Liv* 10–16; V Toxteth Park Ch Ch and St Mich w St Andr from 16. *St Michael's Vicarage, 1B St Michael's Church Road, Liverpool L17 7BD*

HIZA, Douglas William. b 38. Richmond Univ Virginia BA 60 MDiv 63 Mankato State Univ MS 70. Virginia Th Sem 60. **d** 63 **p** 64. C Calvary Cathl Sioux Falls USA 63–65; V Sioux Falls Gd Shep 65–66; V Vermillion St Paul 66–69; V New Ulm St Pet 71–80; Chapl Mankato State Univ 74–80; Chapl Hackney Hosp Gp Lon 80–95; Chapl Homerton Hosp Lon 80–95; PtO *Lon* 96–04; Hon C Smithfield St Bart Gt 04–06; PtO from 06; *S'wark* 06–15. *10 Meynell Crescent, London E9 7AS* T: (020) 8985 7832 *or* 7253 3107 E: hiza@btinternet.com

HOAD, Anne Elizabeth. b 42. Bris Univ BA 63. **dss** 69 **d** 94 **p** 95. Asst Chapl Imp Coll *Lon* 69–74; S'wark Lay Tr Scheme 74–77; Brixton St Matt *S'wark* 77–80; Charlton St Luke w H

Trin 80–94; Project Worker Community of Women and Men 88–91; Voc Adv Lewisham from 91; Asst Chapl Lewisham Hosp *S'wark* 92–03; Hon C Lee Gd Shep w St Pet 94–03; C 03–10; rtd 10; PtO *S'wark* from 11. *14 Silk Close, London SE12 8DL* T: (020) 8297 8761 E: hoadanne@yahoo.co.uk

HOAD, Miss Rosemary Claire. b 60. Cranmer Hall Dur 92. **d** 94 **p** 95. C Epsom St Martin *Guildf* 94–97; TV Brentford *Lon* 97–05; V Spring Grove St Mary 05–18; V Egham Hythe *Guildf* from 18. *17 Old School Mews, Staines-upon-Thames TW18 3HX* E: vicar@speh.org.uk

HOAD, Mrs Shona Mary. b 66. Newc Univ BA 88. STETS 07. **d** 10 **p** 11. C Dorking St Paul *Guildf* 10–14; V Atworth w Shaw and Whitley *Sarum* 14–18; NSM Whitewater *Win* from 18. *Mattingley Rectory, Vicarage Lane, Hound Green, Hook RG27 8LF* T: 0118-932 6075 M: 07871-740158 E: shonahoad@whitewaterchurches.co.uk

HOARE, Carol. b 46. Lon Univ BA 68 Birm Univ CertEd 69. Qu Coll Birm 86 WMMTC 86. **d** 91 **p** 94. NSM Curdworth *Birm* 91–00; PtO from 00. *14 Elms Road, Sutton Coldfield B72 1JF* T: 0121-354 1117 E: c.hoare@btinternet.com

HOARE, Canon David Marlyn. b 33. Bps' Coll Cheshunt 60. **d** 63 **p** 64. C Ampthill w Millbrook and Steppingley *St Alb* 63–67; C Bushey 67–70; V Harlington 70–76; V Oxhey All SS 76–81; V Hellesdon *Nor* 81–98; Hon Can Nor Cathl 95–98; rtd 98; PtO *Nor* from 98. *14 Cottinghams Drive, Norwich NR6 6PS* T: (01603) 423418 E: dmhoare@icloud.com

HOARE, Diana Charlotte. Kent Univ BA 78. WEMTC 02. **d** 05 **p** 06. C Bishop's Castle w Mainstone, Lydbury N etc *Heref* 05–09; P-in-c Bucknell w Chapel Lawn, Llanfair Waterdine etc 09–14; V Middle Marches 14–15; P-in-c Walton W w Talbenny and Haroldston W *St D* 15–18; P-in-c Gtr Dewisland from 18. *The Rectory, Calbern, Simpson Cross, Haverfordwest SA62 6EP* T: (01437) 721205 E: diana.hoare540@btinternet.com *or* starstonewell@gmail.com

HOARE (née CULLING), Elizabeth Ann. b 58. St Mary's Coll Dur BA 76 St Jo Coll Dur PhD 87 Rob Coll Cam BA 88 PGCE 80. Ridley Hall Cam 86. **d** 89 **p** 94. Par Dn S Cave and Ellerker w Broomfleet *York* 89–92; Tutor Cranmer Hall Dur 93–95; P-in-c Cherry Burton *York* 95–00; Abp's Sen Adv on Rural Affairs 95–98; Spiritual Dir York Angl Cursillo 98–00; Chapl Bp Burton Coll *York* from 07; PtO *York* 01–02; NSM Cowesby 02–07; NSM Felixkirk w Boltby 02–07; NSM Kirkby Knowle 02–07; NSM Leake w Over and Nether Silton and Kepwick 02–07; Tutor and Lect Cranmer Hall Dur 02–07; Tutor Wycliffe Hall Ox from 07. *Wycliffe Hall, 54 Banbury Road, Oxford OX2 6PW* T: (01865) 274200 *or* 873412 E: eahoare@googlemail.com

HOARE, Janet Francis Mary. *See* MILES, Janet Francis Mary
HOARE, Patrick Gerard. *See* GERARD, Patrick Hoare
HOARE, Patrick Reginald Andrew Reid (Toddy). b 47. Hull Univ MA 90. Wycliffe Hall Ox 77. **d** 80 **p** 81. Rotterdam w Schiedam *Eur* 76–77; C Guisborough *York* 80–83; P-in-c Felixkirk w Boltby 83–07; P-in-c Kirkby Knowle 83–07; P-in-c Leake w Over and Nether Silton and Kepwick 83–07; P-in-c Cowesby 83–07; Chapl Yorks Agric Soc 92–09; CF (TA) 82–99; rtd 07; PtO *Ox* from 07. *Pond Farm House, Holton, Oxford OX33 1PY* T: (01865) 873412 E: toddy100@btinternet.com

HOARE, Roger John. b 38. Tyndale Hall Bris 63. **d** 66 **p** 67. C Stoughton *Guildf* 66–70; C Chesham St Mary *Ox* 70–73; V Bath St Bart *B & W* 73–83; V Gt Faringdon w Lt Coxwell *Ox* 83–89; Deputation Appeals Org (NE Lon) Children's Soc 89–93; P-in-c Lambourne w Abridge and Stapleford Abbotts *Chelmsf* 93–03; Ind Chapl 93–03; rtd 03; PtO *Chelmsf* from 04. *44 Anchor Road, Tiptree, Colchester CO5 0AP* T: (01621) 817236 E: randd@hoare44.plus.com

✠**HOARE, The Rt Revd Rupert William Noel.** b 40. Trin Coll Ox BA 61 MA 66 Fitzw Ho Cam BA 64 MA 84 Birm Univ PhD 73. Kirchliche Hochschule Berlin 61 Westcott Ho Cam 62. **d** 64 **p** 65 **c** 93. C Oldham St Mary w St Pet *Man* 64–67; Lect Qu Coll Birm 68–72; Can Th Cov Cathl 70–76; R Man Resurr 72–78; Can Res Birm Cathl 78–81; Prin Westcott Ho Cam 81–93; Area Bp Dudley and Hon Can Worc Cathl 93–00; Dean Liv 00–07; rtd 07; Hon Asst Bp Man from 08; PtO *Eur* from 16. *14 Shaw Hall Bank Road, Greenfield, Oldham OL3 7LD* T: (01457) 820375 E: rupert.gesinehoare@gmail.com

HOARE, Canon Simon Gerard. b 37. AKC 61. **d** 62 **p** 63. C Headingley *Ripon* 62–65; C Adel 65–68; R Spofforth 68–71; R Spofforth w Kirk Deighton 71–77; V Rawdon *Bradf* 77–85; Hon Can Bradf Cathl 85–02; R Carleton and Lothersdale 85–02; Dioc Ecum Officer 85–94; rtd 02; PtO *Ripon* 02–14; *Leeds* from 14. *Skell Villa, 20 Wellington Street, Ripon HG4 1PH* T: (01765) 692187 E: sghoare@talktalk.net

HOARE, Toddy. *See* HOARE, Patrick Reginald Andrew Reid

HOARE, Mrs Valerie Mary. b 54. Ex Univ BTh 07. SWMTC 04. **d** 07 **p** 08. NSM Chard St Mary *B & W* 07–10; C Chard St Mary w Combe St Nicholas, Wambrook etc 10–14; NSM Ilminster and Whitelackington 15–18; rtd 18; PtO *B & W* from 18. *Nyleve, Church Lane, Horton, Ilminster TA19 9RN* T: (01460) 54542 E: cherrybrook@hotmail.co.uk

HOBBINS, Mrs Susan. b 47. Birm Univ CertEd 68. STETS 04. **d** 07 **p** 08. NSM Hatherden w Tangley, Weyhill and Penton Mewsey *Win* 07–09; C Pastrow 09–13; rtd 13; PtO *Win* from 13. *Rose Cottage, Upton, Andover SP11 0JP* T: (01264) 736166 E: susanhobbins@icloud.com

HOBBS, Alexander. b 85. Ex Univ BA 07 Leeds Univ MMus 08 Sheff Univ BA 16 AKC 15. Coll of Resurr Mirfield 14. **d** 17 **p** 18. C Heavitree and St Mary Steps *Ex* from 17. *10 Sherwood Close, Exeter EX2 5DX* T: (01392) 677153 E: fralexanderhobbs@gmail.com

HOBBS, Mrs Alison Clare. b 58. Imp Coll Lon BSc 80. Lindisfarne Regional Tr Partnership 09. **d** 12 **p** 13. NSM Brancepeth *Dur* from 12. *Brancepeth Castle, Brancepeth, Durham DH7 8DF* T: 0191-378 9670 M: 07504-489089 E: alison@brancepethcastle.org.uk *or* alisonhobbs@stbrandon.org.uk

HOBBS (formerly DUFFUS), Mrs Barbara Rose. b 51. EMMTC 95. **d** 98 **p** 99. C Linc St Faith and St Martin w St Pet 98–00; C Grantham St Wulfram 00–02; P-in-c Brothertoft Gp 02–04; Mental Health Chapl SE Lincs 02–04; P-in-c Hastings St Clem and All SS *Chich* 04–08; rtd 08; PtO *Chich* from 08. *Courtyard Cottage, Main Road, Westfield, Hastings TN35 4QE* T: (01424) 756479 M: 07724-410292 E: barbara.r.hobbs@googlemail.com

HOBBS, Christopher Bedo. b 61. Jes Coll Cam BA 83 BTh 90. Ridley Hall Cam 88. **d** 91 **p** 92. C Langham Place All So *Lon* 91–95; C Hull St Jo Newland *York* 95–00; V Selly Park St Steph and St Wulstan *Birm* from 00. *18 Selly Wick Road, Selly Park, Birmingham B29 7JA* T: 0121-472 0050 *or* 472 8253 E: chris.hobbs@sssw.org.uk

HOBBS, Christopher John Pearson. b 60. Sydney Univ BA 82 K Coll Lon BD 89 AKC 89. Wycliffe Hall Ox 89. **d** 91 **p** 92. C S Mimms Ch Ch *Lon* 91–94; C Jesmond Clayton Memorial *Newc* 94–97; V Oakwood St Thos *Lon* 97–17; V Cheadle Hulme St Andr *Ches* from 17. *2 Orrishmere Road, Cheadle Hulme, Cheadle SK8 5HP* E: christopher.hobbs@blueyonder.co.uk

HOBBS, Edward Quincey. b 74. Bris Univ BSc 95. Wycliffe Hall Ox BA 99. **d** 00 **p** 01. C Stapenhill w Cauldwell *Derby* 00–03; C Newbury *Ox* 03–08; C Brompton H Trin w Onslow Square St Paul *Lon* 08–09; P-in-c Cullompton, Willand, Uffculme, Kentisbeare etc *Ex* 09–15; R Cullompton from 15. *Windyridge, 10 Willand Road, Cullompton EX15 1AP* E: eqhobbs@gmail.com

HOBBS, Ian. *See* HOBBS, Kenneth Ian

HOBBS, James. b 42. K Alfred's Coll Win CertEd 64 Open Univ BA 89 Hull Univ MA 94 Win Univ BUniv 15. Linc Th Coll 66. **d** 68 **p** 69. C Moseley St Mary *Birm* 68–73; V Kingstanding St Mark 73–77; R Rushbrooke *St E* 77–78; R Bradfield St Geo w Rushbrooke 77–78; R Bradfield St Geo 78–80; P-in-c Bradfield St Clare 77–80; P-in-c Felsham w Gedding 77–80; R Bradfield St George w Bradfield St Clare etc 80–84; P-in-c Gt and Lt Whelnetham 84–85; R Gt and Lt Whelnetham w Bradfield St George 85–90; Ecum Chapl for F&HE Grimsby *Linc* 90–97; Chapl Lincs and Humberside Univ (Grimsby Campus) 90–97; Gen Preacher 92–97; V Ingham w Cammeringham w Fillingham 97–01; R Aisthorpe w Scampton w Thorpe le Fallows etc 97–01; P-in-c N w S Carlton 97–01; P-in-c Burton by Linc 97–01; rtd 01; PtO *Linc* 01–04; *Chich* from 04. *Courtyard Cottage, Main Road, Westfield, Hastings TN35 4QE* T: (01424) 756479 M: 07726-302341 E: hobbs.jim1@gmail.com

HOBBS, Jason Michael. b 74. Northumbria Univ BSc 97 Sunderland Univ BA 00. TISEC 07. **d** 10 **p** 11. C Aberdeen St Mary *Ab* from 10. *98 Burnieboozle Crescent, Aberdeen AB15 8NQ* M: 07446-113014 E: jhobbs10@gmail.com

HOBBS, Kenneth Brian. b 47. Sussex Univ BA 68 Lon Inst of Educn PGCE 70. NTMTC 98. **d** 98 **p** 99. NSM Howell Hill *Guildf* 98–01; NSM Shere, Albury and Chilworth 01–11; rtd 11; PtO *Guildf* from 11; Rtd Clergy Officer from 18. *5 Burdon Park, Cheam SM2 7PS* T: (020) 8643 7878 E: revken.hobbs@gmail.com

HOBBS, Kenneth Ian. b 50. Oak Hill Th Coll 74. **d** 77 **p** 78. C Southborough St Pet w Ch Ch and St Matt *Roch* 77–80; C Hoole *Ches* 80–84; V Barnston 84–95; P-in-c Bedworth *Cov* 95; TR 95–01; RD Nuneaton 00–01; TR Radipole and Melcombe Regis *Sarum* 01–15; RD Weymouth and Portland 08–12; rtd 15; PtO *Ches* from 16. *4 Daryl Road, Wirral CH60 5RD* T: 0151-342 8353 E: kijahobbs@gmail.com

HOBBS, Leslie Robert. b 42. Sussex Univ BA 64 Lon Bible Coll BD 67. EAMTC 02. **d** 02 **p** 03. NSM Somerleyton, Ashby,

Fritton, Herringfleet etc *Nor* 02–09; R 09–12; rtd 12; PtO *Nor* from 13. *Nether End Cottage, Blacksmiths Loke, Lound, Lowestoft NR32 5LS* T: (01502) 732536 E: hobbsnec@btinternet.com

HOBBS, Preb Maureen Patricia. b 54. Surrey Univ BSc 76. Westcott Ho Cam 95. **d** 97 **p** 98. C Shrewsbury St Chad w St Mary *Lich* 97–01; R Baschurch and Weston Lullingfield w Hordley 01–09; P-in-c Pattingham w Patshull 09–14; V from 14; RD Trysull 09–19; Dioc Adv for Women in Min 04–11; Preb Lich Cathl from 12. *The Vicarage, 20 Dartmouth Avenue, Pattingham, Wolverhampton WV6 7DP* T: (01902) 700257 E: vicar@pattinghamchurch.org.uk

HOBBS, Michael Bedo. b 30. Fitzw Ho Cam BA 58 MA 62. Clifton Th Coll 58. **d** 60 **p** 61. C Southsea St Jude *Portsm* 60–63; Paraguay 63–65; Argentina 65–67; V Potters Green *Cov* 68–75; Distr Sec BFBS 75–82; R Plaxtol *Roch* 82–96; Dioc Miss Audits Consultant 90–96; rtd 96; PtO *Sarum* from 96. *Falcons, Barkers Hill, Semley, Shaftesbury SP7 9BH* T: (01747) 828920 E: mandehobbs@btinternet.com

HOBBS, Mrs Nicola. b 77. **d** 14 **p** 15. C Broughton w Loddington and Cransley etc *Pet* 14–18; R Broughton w Cransley and Mawsley from 18. *15 Loddington Way, Mawsley, Kettering NN14 1GE* E: revnicki@familyhobbs.org.uk

HOBBS, Ms Sarah Kathleen. b 72. Liv Univ BA 94 UMIST BSc 98 PGCE 95. Wycliffe Hall Ox BA 05. **d** 05 **p** 06. C W Ealing St Jo w St Jas *Lon* 05–08; V Blockhouse Bay New Zealand from 08. *429A Blockhouse Bay Road, Blockhouse Bay, Auckland 0600, New Zealand* T: (0064) (9) 627 8779 E: sarah@churchofthesaviour.org.nz

HOBBS, Sarah Louise. b 47. WEMTC 01. **d** 04 **p** 05. NSM Westbury-on-Severn w Flaxley, Blaisdon etc *Glouc* 05–14; NSM Abenhall w Mitcheldean 11–14; NSM Huntley and Longhope, Churcham and Bulley 12–14; rtd 14; PtO *Glouc* from 15. *Wedgewood House, High Street, Newnham GL14 1AD* T: (01594) 517157 E: shobbs001@btinternet.com

HOBBS, Simon John. b 59. St Steph Ho Ox BA 82 MA. **d** 83 **p** 84. C Middlesbrough Ascension *York* 83–85; C Stainton-in-Cleveland 85–88; C St Marylebone All SS *Lon* 88–90; P-in-c Paddington St Pet 90–94; C-in-c Grosvenor Chpl 94–08; C Hanover Square St Geo 94–08; Chapl Bonn w Cologne *Eur* 08–11; Chapl Sussex Partnership NHS Foundn Trust from 13. *Address temp unknown*

HOBDAY, Hannah Elizabeth. b 80. Jes Coll Ox BA 04 MA 15 Selw Coll Cam BA 06 MA 15. Ridley Hall Cam 04. **d** 07 **p** 08. C Margate H Trin *Cant* 07–09; C Cliftonville 07–09; Hon C Chesterton St Geo *Ely* 09–15; C Earley St Pet *Ox* from 15. *69 Eastcourt Avenue, Earley, Reading RG6 1HN* T: 0118-966 6701 E: hannah@earleystpeters.org.uk

HOBDAY, Philip Peter. b 81. Ex Coll Ox BA 02 MA 09 Fitzw Coll Cam BA 05 MA 09 Nottm Univ MA 14. Ridley Hall Cam 03. **d** 06 **p** 07. C St Peter-in-Thanet *Cant* 06–09; Chapl Cant Ch Ch Univ 06–09; Chapl and Fell Magd Coll Cam 09–14; Dean of Chpl 15; V Earley St Pet *Ox* from 15. *69 Eastcourt Avenue, Earley, Reading RG6 1HH* T: 0118-966 6701 M: 07894-219629 E: philip@earleystpeters.org.uk

HOBDEN, Christopher Martin. b 49. Lon Univ BSc 71. Oak Hill Th Coll 80. **d** 87 **p** 88. NSM St Marylebone All So w SS Pet and Jo *Lon* 87–88; NSM Langham Place All So 88–95. *10 Kent Terrace, London NW1 4RP*

HOBDEN, David Nicholas. b 54. K Coll Lon BD 76 AKC 76 Cam Univ PGCE. Ripon Coll Cuddesdon 77. **d** 78 **p** 79. C Marlborough *Sarum* 78–80; C Salisbury St Thos and St Edm 81–85; V Shalford *Guildf* 85–99; Asst Chapl R Surrey Co Hosp NHS Trust 99–00; Sen Chapl R Surrey Co Hosp NHS Foundn Trust 00–15; rtd 15; PtO *Guildf* from 15. *Greenwood, Oakdene Road, Godalming GU7 1QF* T: (01483) 410177 E: dnhobden@gmail.com

HOBDEN, Geoffrey William. b 46. Trin Coll Bris 80. **d** 82 **p** 83. C Ex St Leon w H Trin 82–86; V Weston-super-Mare Ch Ch *B & W* 86–06; V Weston super Mare Ch Ch and Em 06–11; RD Locking 93–99; rtd 11; PtO *B & W* from 11. *21 Burrington Avenue, Weston-super-Mare BS24 9LP* T: (01934) 707981 M: 07531-648609 E: hobdenshouse@gmail.com

HOBLEY, Ms Susan Elizabeth. b 51. Newc Univ BA 74 Dur Univ PGCE 75. NEOC 98. **d** 01 **p** 02. NSM Millfield St Mark and Pallion St Luke *Dur* 01–05; C Sheff St Mark Broomhill 05–09; V Wath-upon-Dearne 09–16; rtd 16; PtO *Leeds* from 17; *Sheff* from 18. *6 Greenway, Honley, Holmfirth HD9 6NQ*

HOBMAN, David John. b 52. **d** 17. NSM York All SS Pavement w St Crux and St Mich from 17; NSM York H Trin Micklegate from 17; NSM York St Denys from 17; NSM York St Helen w St Martin from 17; NSM York St Lawr w St Nic from 17; NSM York St Olave w St Giles from 17. *41 Manor Park Road, York YO30 5UB*

HOBSON, Alexander. *See* HOBSON, John Alexander

HOBSON, Anthony Peter. b 53. St Jo Coll Cam BA 74. St Jo Coll Nottm 75. **d** 77 **p** 78. C Brunswick *Man* 77–82; R Stretford St Bride 82–92; TR Hackney Marsh *Lon* 92–00; V Leic Martyrs 00–08; Dir St Martin's Ho 09–16; Project Dir Leic Cathl Common Ground Project from 16; PtO *Leic* 15–16. *4 Church Road, Aylestone, Leicester LE2 8LB* T: 0116-283 3251 *or* 261 5363 E: petehobson@me.com *or* pete.hobson@leccofe.org

HOBSON, Barry Rodney. b 57. Open Univ BA 98. Wilson Carlile Coll 82 EAMTC 97. **d** 98 **p** 99. CA from 85; C Warboys w Broughton and Bury w Wistow *Ely* 98–01; P-in-c Roxwell *Chelmsf* 01–07; RD Chelmsf N 06–07; V Hornchurch St Andr from 07. *The Vicarage, 222 High Street, Hornchurch RM12 6QP* T: (01708) 454594 *or* 441571 E: b.hobson@btinternet.com

HOBSON, John Alexander (Alex). b 70. LMH Ox BA 91 MA 02 York Univ MA 94. Wycliffe Hall Ox BA 01. **d** 02 **p** 03. C Aynho and Croughton w Evenley etc *Pet* 02–05; Chapl RAF from 05. *Chaplaincy Services (RAF), HQ Air Command, RAF High Wycombe HP14 4UE* T: (01494) 496800 E: alexhobson17@gmail.com

HOBSON, Canon Patrick John Bogan. b 33. Magd Coll Cam BA 56 MA 60 Ox Brookes Univ BA 08. S'wark Ord Course 75 Qu Coll Birm 77. **d** 79 **p** 80. C St Jo in Bedwardine *Worc* 79–81; R Clifton-on-Teme, Lower Sapey and the Shelsleys 81–88; TR Waltham H Cross *Chelmsf* 88–98; Hon Can Chelmsf Cathl 95–98; rtd 98; PtO *Ox* from 09. *24 Cunliffe Close, Oxford OX2 7BL* T/F: (01865) 556206 E: patrick.hobson@btinternet.com

HOBSON, Peter. *See* HOBSON, Anthony Peter

HOBSON, Miss Trudy. b 82. Open Univ BA 09. Coll of Resurr Mirfield BA 15. **d** 16 **p** 17. C Brigg, Wrawby and Cadney cum Howsham *Linc* 16–19; P-in-c Upper Wylye Valley *Sarum* from 19. *1 Bests Lane, Sutton Veny, Warminster BA12 7AU* M: 07508-066222 E: cowpy27@hotmail.co.uk

HOBSON, Mrs Yvonne Mary. b 45. Ex Univ BTh 03. SWMTC 00. **d** 03 **p** 04. C St Illogan *Truro* 03–06; C Paul 06–10; rtd 10; PtO *Truro* from 16. *8 Donnithorne Road, Penzance TR18 4PQ* T: (01736) 364354 E: yvonnehobson@btinternet.com

HOCKEN, Glen Rundle. b 59. Kent Univ BA 80 Southlands Coll Lon PGCE 90 ACA 84. Wycliffe Hall Ox 90. **d** 92 **p** 93. C Cogges *Ox* 92–94; C Cogges and S Leigh 94–96; C Boldmere *Birm* 96–99; TV Southgate *Chich* 99–06; Chapl HM Pris Lewes 06–13; Chapl St Pet and St Jas Hospice N Chailey 05–13; Chapl HM Pris Onley 13–16; Chapl HM Pris Moorland 16–19; Chapl HM Pris Wealstun from 19. *HM Prison Wealstun, Walton Road, Wetherby LS23 7AZ* T: (01937) 444725 E: glen.hocken@justice.gov.uk

HOCKEY (née LOOMES), Gaenor Mary. b 65. Hull Univ BA 92 RGN 86. St Jo Coll Nottm MPhil 93. **d** 96 **p** 97. C Charles w Plymouth St Matthias *Ex* 96–00; C Devonport St Aubyn 00–05; PtO 05–06; P-in-c Seer Green and Jordans *Ox* 06–13; R Yeovil H Trin w Barwick *B & W* 13–19; C Marnhull *Sarum* from 19. *The Rectory, New Street, Marnhull, Sturminster Newton DT10 1PY* E: rev@gaenorhockey.plus.com

HOCKLEY, Paul William. b 47. Chu Coll Cam BA 68 MA 72 Nottm Univ BA 73. St Jo Coll Nottm 71. **d** 74 **p** 75. C Chatham St Phil and St Jas *Roch* 74–78; C Tunbridge Wells St Jo 78–81; V Penketh *Liv* 81–14; TV Warrington W 14–15; rtd 15; PtO *Sarum* from 16. *76 Vale Road, Poole BH14 9AY* T: (01202) 730626

HOCKLEY-STILL, Tanya. b 89. Cardiff Univ BA 10 Anglia Ruskin Univ MA 14. Westcott Ho Cam 12. **d** 14 **p** 15. C Stone Cross St Luke w N Langney *Chich* 14–17; P-in-c Ex St Mark, St Sidwell and St Matt 17–18; R Ex St Mark from 18. *St Mark's Rectory, 8 Lamacraft Drive, Exeter EX4 8QS* T: (01392) 423311 M: 07971-442264 E: tanya@stmarksexeter.uk

HOCKNULL, Canon Mark Dennis. b 63. Surrey Univ BSc 85 Univ Coll Lon PhD 89 St Jo Coll Dur BA 93. Cranmer Hall Dur 91. **d** 94 **p** 95. C Prenton *Ches* 94–96; C Runcorn All SS and Runcorn St Mich 96–99; V Gt Meols 99–05; CME Officer *Linc* 05–09; Lic Preacher 05–09; Can Res and Chan *Linc* Cathl 09–17; Hd of Min Tr (Dioc Min Course) 09–17; Tutor Linc Univ from 17. *University of Lincoln, Campus Way, Lincoln LN6 7TS* T: (01522) 886076 E: mhocknull@lincoln.ac.uk

HODDER, Anthony Mark. b 56. Univ of Wales (Newport) CertEd 00 FCCA 90. Ridley Hall Cam 08. **d** 11 **p** 13. C Heref S Wye 11–12; C Ledbury 12–17; PtO from 17. *21 Biddulph Way, Ledbury HR8 2HP* M: 07977-063294 E: tony.hodder@gmail.com

HODDER, Christopher John. b 75. Huddersfield Univ BA 96. St Jo Coll Nottm BTh 00. **d** 01 **p** 02. C Loughborough Em and St Mary in Charnwood *Leic* 01–05; Chapl Derby Univ and Derby Cathl 05–10; P-in-c Wilford Hill *S'well* 10–11; V 11–18; Chapl Heref from 18; PtO *Nor* from 18. *Chaplaincy Service (RAF), HQ Air Command, RAF High Wycombe HP14 4UE* T: (01494) 496800 M: 07833-592800

HODDER, John Kenneth. b 45. Edin Univ MA 68. Cuddesdon Coll 71. **d** 73 **p** 74. C Kibworth Beauchamp *Leic* 73–76; C Whittlesey *Ely* 76–80; R Downham 80–87; P-in-c Coveney 80–81; R 81–87; R Nunney and Witham Friary, Marston Bigot etc *B & W* 87–10; rtd 10; PtO *B & W* from 10. *95 Nunney Road, Frome BA11 4LF* T: (01373) 466063 E: hodderhodder@btinternet.com

HODGE, Anthony Charles. b 43. AKC 66. **d** 67 **p** 68. C Carrington *S'well* 67–69; C Bawtry w Austerfield 69–72; C Misson 69–72; Grenada 72–74; Trinidad and Tobago 74–76; V Tuckingmill *Truro* 76–78; V Worksop St Paul *S'well* 78–81; P-in-c Patrington w Hollym, Welwick and Winestead *York* 81–86; R 86–88; V York St Olave w St Giles 88–08; V York St Helen w St Martin 97–08; Chapl York Coll for Girls 88–96; rtd 08; P-in-c Duloe, Herodsfoot, Morval and St Pinnock *Truro* 08–14; PtO from 14. *3 Tower Hill Gardens, Rhind Street, Bodmin PL31 2FD* T: (01208) 892929 M: 07717-877430 E: achodge@live.co.uk

HODGE, Mrs Joanne Lesley. b 64. Bris Univ BA 87 Open Univ BSc 06 Univ of Wales (Cardiff) PGCE 88. Trin Coll Bris 17. **d** 19. OLM Fromeside *Bris* from 19; OLM Yate from 19. *3 Chatterton Road, Yate, Bristol BS37 4BJ* T: (01454) 880152 M: 07758-648264 E: nijo.hodge@blueyonder.co.uk

HODGE, Canon Michael Robert. b 34. Pemb Coll Cam BA 57 MA 61. Ridley Hall Cam 57. **d** 59 **p** 60. C Harpurhey *Ch Ch Man* 59; C Blackpool St Mark *Blackb* 59–62; V Stalybridge Old St Geo *Man* 62–67; R Cobham w Luddesdowne and Dode *Roch* 67–81; Hon Can Roch Cathl 81–99; R Bidborough 81–99; rtd 99; Hon C Chale *Portsm* 99–06; Hon C Gatcombe 99–06; Hon C Shorwell w Kingston 99–06; Asst to RD W Wight 99–06; PtO from 06. *Braxton Cottage, Halletts Shute, Norton, Yarmouth PO41 0RH* T/F: (01983) 761121 M: 07941-232983 E: michael.hodge.1954@pem.cam.ac.uk

HODGES, Christina Caroline. See FFRENCH-HODGES, Christina Caroline

HODGES, Ian Morgan. b 72. Glam Univ BSc 95 Cam Univ BTh(Min) 05. Ridley Hall Cam. **d** 05 **p** 06. C Llantrisant *Llan* 05–11; R Llanilid w Pencoed from 11; AD Bridgend from 18. *The Rectory, 60 Coychurch Road, Pencoed, Bridgend CF35 5NA* T: (01656) 860337 E: revian@lphparish.org.uk

HODGES, Mrs Jane Anne Christine. b 62. Leeds Univ BA 84. SEITE 06. **d** 09 **p** 10. C Poplar *Lon* 09–11; TV 11–15; TR from 15. *164 St Leonard's Road, London E14 6PW* E: revjanehodges@hotmail.com

HODGES, Jasper Tor. b 62. Leeds Univ BSc 84 Sheff Univ MEng 85 Lon Univ PGCE 87. Trin Coll Bris BA 94. **d** 94 **p** 95. C Holbeck *Ripon* 94–97; C Ealing St Steph Castle Hill *Lon* 97–04; V Arbourthorne and Norfolk Park *Sheff* 04–18. *All Hallows, Church Lane, High Hoyland, Barnsley S75 4BJ* M: 07850-660513 E: jasplive@gmail.com

HODGES, Keith Michael. b 53. Southn Univ BTh 82 Heythrop Coll Lon MA 04. Chich Th Coll 77. **d** 80 **p** 81. C Sydenham St Phil *S'wark* 80–84; PtO 85; C Leatherhead *Guildf* 86–89; V Aldershot St Aug from 89. *St Augustine's Vicarage, Holly Road, Aldershot GU12 4SE* T: (01252) 320840 E: father.keith@ntlworld.com

HODGES, Wayne Anthony. **d** 90 **p** 91. PtO *Ban* from 17. *The Rectory, Newtown Road, Machynlleth SY20 8HE* T: (01654) 703467 E: awdhodges63@gmail.com

HODGETT, Ms Tina Elizabeth. b 64. Leic Univ MBA 05 Sheff Univ PGCE 90. St Mary's Coll Dur BA 88. Ridley Hall Cam 06. **d** 08 **p** 09. C Bestwood Em w St Mark *S'well* 08–11; TV Portishead *B & W* 11–17; Evang Team Ldr Min for Miss from 17. *110 Brampton Way, Portishead, Bristol BS20 6YT* M: 07759-909106

HODGETTS, Canon Alan Paul. b 54. Birm Poly BSc 78 Heythrop Coll Lon MA 96. St Steph Ho Ox 79. **d** 82 **p** 83. C Perry Barr *Birm* 82–85; C Broseley w Benthall *Heref* 85–87; V Effingham w Lt Bookham *Guildf* 87–96; R Merrow 96–06; Chapl HM Pris Woodhill from 06; Hon Can Ch Ch Ox from 16. *The Chaplaincy Department, HM Prison Woodhill, Tattenhoe Street, Milton Keynes MK4 4DA* T: (01908) 722000 ext 2097 E: alan.hodgetts@justice.gov.uk

HODGETTS, Colin William John. b 40. St D Coll Lamp BA 61. Ripon Hall Ox 61. **d** 63 **p** 64. C Hackney St Jo *Lon* 63–68; Hon C St Martin-in-the-Fields 70–76; C Creeksea w Althorne *Chelmsf* 76–79; PtO *Ex* 84–03; C Parkham, Alwington, Buckland Brewer etc 03–07; AD Gambella Ethiopia 11–12; rtd 12; PtO *Ex* 12–17; P-in-c Abbotsham 17–18; PtO *Edin* from 18. *5 Brunton Terrace, Edinburgh EH7 5EH* E: colin@colinhodgetts.co.uk

HODGETTS, Harry Samuel. b 30. Chich Th Coll 63. **d** 65 **p** 66. C Harton Colliery *Dur* 65–68; C Penzance St Mary *Truro* 68–70; V Penwerris 70–79; V Kettering St Mary Pet 79–94; rtd 95; PtO *Win* 03–09. *The Flat, Etal Manor,*

Etal, Cornhill-on-Tweed TD12 4TL T: (01890) 820378 E: airchandmin@btinternet.com

HODGINS, Miss Kylie Anne. b 68. SEITE 98 Ridley Hall Cam 00. **d** 02 **p** 03. C Histon and Impington *Ely* 02–07; Chapl Sherborne Sch for Girls 07–08; P-in-c Cottenham *Ely* 08–16; P-in-c Rampton 09–16; V Bricket Wood *St Alb* from 16. *20 West Riding, Bricket Wood, St Albans AL2 3QP* E: kh2@gumnut.me.uk

HODGINS, Philip Arthur. b 57. Lanc Univ BA 78 Bradf Univ MBA 90 MCIPD 94. Linc Th Coll 82. **d** 85 **p** 86. C Norton *Ches* 85–88; C Whitkirk *Ripon* 88–89; PtO *Bradf* 89–90; Chich 91–02; Hon C Chiddingly w E Hoathly 02–04; P-in-c 04–09; R from 09; RD Uckfield 06–11. *The Rectory, Rectory Close, East Hoathly, Lewes BN8 6EG* T: (01825) 840270 E: philhodgins@btinternet.com

HODGKINS, Christopher Thomas Alan. b 73. Westcott Ho Cam. **d** 13 **p** 14. C G7 Benefice *Cant* 13–16; C Tenterden, Rother and Oxney from 16. *The Vicarage, Rolvenden, Cranbrook TN17 4ND*

HODGKINSON, Mrs Jennifer Mary. b 57. **d** 12 **p** 13. OLM Cromer *Nor* from 12. *29 Fulcher Avenue, Cromer NR27 9SG* T: (01263) 510153 E: jenniehodgkinson1997@gmail.com

HODGKINSON, John David. b 57. Birm Univ BA 78 Edin Univ BD 89. Edin Th Coll 86. **d** 89 **p** 90. C Briercliffe *Blackb* 89–92; C Darwen St Cuth w Tockholes St Steph 92–94; R Harrington *Carl* 94–00; V Walney Is 00–12; TV N Barrow 12–17; P-in-c Barrow St Jo 15–17; rtd 17; PtO *Carl* from 17. *St Francis House, 158 Schneider Road, Barrow-in-Furness LA14 5ER*

HODGSON, Ms Amanda Jane. b 66. Westmr Coll Ox BA 88 Heythrop Coll Lon MA 99. Westcott Ho Cam 94. **d** 96 **p** 97. C Epping Distr *Chelmsf* 96–01; TV Wythenshawe *Man* 01–07; R Streatham St Leon *S'wark* 07–16; TR Wimbledon from 16; Adv for Women's Min Kingston Area from 12. *14 Arthur Road, London SW19 7DZ* T: (020) 8946 2830 *or* 8946 2605 E: mandy@stmaryswimbledon.org

HODGSON, Antony Robert. b 66. Dundee Univ MA 88 Jes Coll Cam BA 92 MA 96 Lanc Univ MA 04 K Coll Lon MPhil 10 AKC 10 Lambeth PhD 15 FSAScot 15. Westcott Ho Cam 90 Ven English Coll Rome 92. **d** 93 **p** 94. C Chorley St Geo *Blackb* 93–96; C Lytham St Cuth 96–99; V St Annes St Marg from 99. *St Margaret's Vicarage, 24 Chatsworth Road, Lytham St Annes FY8 2JN* T: (01253) 722329

HODGSON, Barbara Elizabeth. b 46. N Riding Coll of Educn BEd 85. NEOC 06. **d** 08 **p** 09. NSM Bridlington Em *York* 08–11; NSM Burton Fleming w Fordon, Grindale etc 11–15; NSM Rudston, Boynton, Carnaby etc from 15. *The Vicarage, Back Street, Burton Fleming, Driffield YO25 3PD* T: (01262) 470873 M: 07907-593234 E: vidara1972@talktalk.net

HODGSON, Canon David Peter. b 56. Fitzw Coll Cam BA 77 MA 81 Nottm Univ BA 82 MTh 85. St Jo Coll Nottm 80. **d** 83 **p** 84. C Guiseley w Esholt *Bradf* 83–86; Asst Chapl Loughb Univ *Leic* 86–89; P-in-c Hatfield Broad Oak *Chelmsf* 89–90; P-in-c Bush End 89–90; P-in-c Hatfield Broad Oak and Bush End 90–97; Ind Chapl Harlow 89–97; R Wokingham All SS *Ox* from 97; AD Sonning 04–13; Hon Can Ch Ch from 09. *The Rectory, 2A Norreys Avenue, Wokingham RG40 1TU* T: 0118-979 2999 E: david@allsaintswokingham.org.uk

HODGSON, Canon Gary Stuart. b 65. Ridley Hall Cam 95. **d** 98 **p** 99. C S Ossett *Wakef* 98–01; V Kirkburton 01–07; Chapl Huddersfield Univ and Hon C Fixby and Cowcliffe 07–09; P-in-c Cottingley *Bradf* 09–14; V 14; *Leeds* 14–16; RD Airedale *Bradf* 10–14; AD *Leeds* 14–16; R Tong and Laisterdyke from 16; Hon Can Bradf Cathl from 13. *The Vicarage, 74 Holme Wood Road, Bradford BD4 9EJ* E: gshodgson@sky.com

HODGSON, John. b 35. St Jo Coll Cam MA 62 Lon Univ BD 61. St Deiniol's Hawarden 80. **d** 81 **p** 82. Hon C Padiham *Blackb* 81–84; C W Burnley All SS 85–87; V 87–95; rtd 95; PtO *Worc* 95–02; *Glouc* 98–02; Win from 12. *33 Ticonderoga Gardens, Southampton SO19 9HB* T: (023) 8043 2895

HODGSON, Julia Ruth. See HICKS, Julia Ruth

HODKINSON, George Leslie. b 48. Qu Coll Birm 86. **d** 88 **p** 89. C Hall Green St Pet *Birm* 88–91; TV Solihull 91–96; P-in-c Billesley Common 96–00; V 00–05; AD Moseley 01–02; rtd 05; Chapl Countess of Chester Hosp NHS Foundn Trust 05–11; Chapl Cheshire and Wirral Partnership NHS Foundn Trust 05–11; PtO *Lich* from 09. *2 Birch Close, Four Crosses, Llanymynech SY22 6NH* T: (01691) 839946

HODSON, Gordon George. b 35. St Chad's Coll Dur BA 59. **d** 60 **p** 61. C Tettenhall Regis *Lich* 60–64; C Rugeley 64–68; V Shrewsbury St Mich 68–74; V Kinnerley w Melverley 74–87; P-in-c Knockin w Maesbrook 75–87; P-in-c Chebsey 87–91; P-in-c Seighford, Derrington and Cresswell 87–91; V Chebsey, Ellenhall and Seighford-with-Creswell

91–00; rtd 00; PtO *Lich* from 01. *27 Oak Drive, Oswestry SY11 2RU* T: (01691) 662849

HODSON, Keith. b 53. Hatf Coll Dur BA 74. Wycliffe Hall Ox 77. **d** 80 **p** 81. C Ashton-upon-Mersey St Mary Magd *Ches* 80–84; C Polegate *Chich* 84–92; V Baddesley Ensor w Grendon *Birm* 92–08; R Beckbury, Badger, Kemberton, Ryton, Stockton etc *Lich* from 08; RD Edgmond and Shifnal from 10. *The Rectory, Beckbury, Shifnal TF11 9DG* T: (01952) 750474 E: keithhodson@talk21.com

HODSON, Mrs Margot Rosemary. b 60. Bris Univ BSc 82 PGCE 83 Ox Brookes Univ BA 06. All Nations Chr Coll 87 SAOMC 99. **d** 01 **p** 02. C Grove *Ox* 01–04; Chapl Jes Coll Ox 04–09; P-in-c Haddenham w Cuddington, Kingsey etc *Ox* 09–16; R Wychert Vale 16–19; C Shill Valley and Broadshire from 19; Dir Th and Educn The John Ray Initiative from 19. *The Vicarage, Filkins, Lechlade GL7 3JQ* E: margot.hodson@jri.org.uk

HODSON, Canon Raymond Leslie. b 42. St Chad's Coll Dur BSc 64. **d** 66 **p** 67. C Adlington *Blackb* 66–68; C Cleveleys 68–72; V Ewood 72–77; V Nazeing *Chelmsf* 77–84; R Ampthill w Millbrook and Steppingley *St Alb* 84–95; Chapl Madrid *Eur* 95–04; Can Gib Cathl 02–04; rtd 04. *Los Alcazares 3, 03726 Benitachell (Alicante), Spain* M: (0034) 607 706 904 E: m2813341g@yahoo.co.uk

HODSON, Trevor. b 57. Sheff Univ BA 78 Padgate Coll of Educn PGCE 79 Leeds Univ MA 06. NOC 04. **d** 06 **p** 07. NSM Broadheath *Ches* 06–13; NSM Latchford Ch Ch 13–18; PtO *Liv* 18; TV Lowton and Golborne from 18. *40 Riversdale, Woolston, Warrington WA1 4PZ* T: (01925) 811952 M: 07935-198009 E: th57dearden@outlook.com

HOEY, David Paul. b 57. QUB BD 79. CITC 79. **d** 81 **p** 82. C Belfast Whiterock *Conn* 81–83; C Portadown St Mark *Arm* 83–84; I Cleenish w Mullaghdun *Clogh* 84–90; I Magheracross 90–03; Dir of Ords 91–03; Can Clogh Cathl 95–03; Min Consultant for Ireland CPAS 03–11; Dioc Par Development Officer and P-in-c Clondevaddock w Portsalon and Leatbeg *D & R* 11–15. *St Canice's Rectory, 21 Main Street, Eglinton, Londonderry BT47 3AB* T: (028) 7181 2462 E: dphoey@btinternet.com

HOEY, Raymond George. b 46. TCD BA 70 MA. **d** 72 **p** 73. C Portadown St Mark *Arm* 72–78; I Camlough w Mullaglass 78–14; Dom Chapl to Abp Arm 86–14; Adn Arm 92–14; rtd 14. *252A Armagh Road, Newry BT35 6NL* T: (028) 3082 1222 M: 07767-270982 E: rghoey@btinternet.com

HOEY, William Thomas. b 32. CITC 64. **d** 66 **p** 67. C Belfast St Mary *Conn* 66–68; C Lisburn Ch Ch 69–72; I Ballinderry 72–78; I Belfast St Simon w St Phil 78–02; rtd 02. *11 Cairnshill Court, Belfast BT8 6TX* T: (028) 9079 0595

HOFBAUER, Canon Andrea Martina. b 71. Johannes Gutenberg Univ Mainz Ox Univ MTh 04. St Steph Ho Ox 00. **d** 02 **p** 03. C Teignmouth, Ideford w Luton, Ashcombe etc *Ex* 02–05; Chapl Ex Univ 05–09; Tutor SWMTC 05–09; PV Ex Cathl 06–09; Prec Wakef Cathl 09–15; P-in-c Leeds All So and St Aid 15–16; V Leeds St Aid from 16; Hon Can Bradf Cathl from 17. *St Aidan's Vicarage, Elford Place West, Leeds LS8 5QD* E: andihofb@gmail.com

HOFFMANN, Miss Rosalind Mary. b 49. **d** 10 **p** 11. OLM Loddon, Sisland, Chedgrave, Hardley and Langley *Nor* from 10. *Oakhurst, Briar Lane, Hales, Norwich NR14 6SY* T: (01508) 548200 E: ros@hoffman2011.plus.com

HOFREITER, Christian. b 75. Wycliffe Hall Ox BA 08 MA 12 Keble Coll Ox MSt 09 Innsbruck Univ MPhil 01. Ox Min Course 09. **d** 10 **p** 10. NSM Ox St Aldate 10–17; PtO *Eur* from 17. *Ebendorferstrasse 8/1, A-1220 Vienna, Austria* M: 07771-781130 E: chofreiter@gmail.com

HOGAN, Edward James Martin. b 46. Trin Coll Bris. **d** 85 **p** 86. C St Austell *Truro* 85–88; V Gt Broughton and Broughton Moor *Carl* 88–94; V St Stythians w Perranarworthal and Gwennap *Truro* 94–10; RD Carnmarth N 03–08; rtd 10; PtO *Heref* 15–18. *444 Buckfield Road, Leominster HR6 8SD* T: (01568) 620064 E: martin@houseofhogan.org *or* martinhogan@me.com

HOGARTH, Alan Francis. b 58. Oak Hill Th Coll BA 89. **d** 89 **p** 90. C Felixstowe SS Pet and Paul *St E* 89–93; R Beckington w Standerwick, Berkley, Rodden etc *B & W* 93–04; P-in-c Basildon w Aldworth and Ashampstead *Ox* 04–08; P-in-c Heapey and Withnell *Blackb* 08–12; V from 12. *34 Kittiwake Road, Heapey, Chorley PR6 9BA* T: (01257) 231868 E: alan.hogarth@gmail.com

HOGG, Matthew. b 79. **d** 08 **p** 09. C Brompton H Trin w Onslow Square St Paul *Lon* 08–10; C Hammersmith St Paul 10–11; P-in-c Fulham St Alb w St Aug 11–13; V from 13. *St Alban's Vicarage, 4 Margravine Road, London W6 8HJ* T: (020) 7610 2151 E: matt@stalbansfulham.org

HOGG, Neil Richard. b 46. BSc 69. Ridley Hall Cam 82. **d** 84 **p** 85. C Bingham *S'well* 84–87; TV Bushbury *Lich*

87–00; V Worksop St Jo *S'well* 00–11; rtd 11; PtO *York* from 18. *4 Lowick, York YO24 2RF* M: 07585-816697 E: hogg350@btinternet.com

HOGG, William John. b 49. New Coll Ox MA 71 Lon Univ CertEd 72 Crewe & Alsager Coll MSc 88. Edin Th Coll 86. **d** 88 **p** 89. C Oxton *Ches* 88–93; R Bromborough 93–04; P-in-c Radlett *St Alb* 04–05; TR Aldenham, Radlett and Shenley 05–12; rtd 12; PtO *St And* from 12. *Craigwood, Brae Street, Dunkeld PH8 0BA* T: (01350) 727053 E: wijoho@btinternet.com

HOGG, William Ritson. b 47. Leeds Univ BSc 69. Qu Coll Birm. **d** 72 **p** 73. C Bordesley St Oswald *Birm* 72–76; TV Seacroft *Ripon* 76–82; V Hunslet St Mary 82–88; V Catterick 88–97; rtd 97. *c/o Crockford, Church House, Great Smith Street, London SW1P 3AZ* E: bill.denise@yahoo.co.uk

HOGGARD, Mrs Jean Margaret. b 36. NW Ord Course 76. **dss** 79 **d** 87 **p** 94. Northowram *Wakef* 79–94; Par Dn 87–94; C Ovenden 94–00; rtd 00; PtO *Wakef* 01–14; *Leeds* from 14. *13 Joseph Avenue, Northowram, Halifax HX3 7HJ* T: (01422) 201475

HOGGER, Clive Duncan. b 70. Sheff Univ BA 92. Ridley Hall Cam 06. **d** 08 **p** 09. C Fletchamstead *Cov* 08–11; TV Cov E 11–16; R Cov All SS from 16; AD Cov E 14–18; Acting Adn Cov 17–18. *St Margaret's Vicarage, 18 South Avenue, Coventry CV2 4DR* T: (024) 7665 1642 E: clive.hogger@gmail.com

HOGGER-GADSBY, Alison. b 71. **d** 14 **p** 15. C Coventry Caludon *Cov* 14–18; V Foleshill St Paul from 18; Chapl K Henry VIII Sch Cov from 15. *St Margaret's Vicarage, 18 South Avenue, Coventry CV2 4DR* M: 07788-593805 E: alison.hogger@gmail.com

HOLBEN, Bruce Frederick. b 45. STETS 99. **d** 02 **p** 03. NSM W Wittering and Birdham w Itchenor *Chich* from 02. *3 Elmstead Gardens, West Wittering, Chichester PO20 8NG* T: (01243) 514129 M: 07940-759060

HOLBIRD, Derek John. b 50. **d** 17 **p** 18. C Churt and Hindhead *Guildf* from 17. *The Old School House, Fieldway, Haslemere GU27 2AX* T: (01428) 642988

HOLBIRD, Thomas James. b 79. Leeds Univ BSc 00 Cam Univ BTh 11. Ridley Hall Cam 08. **d** 11 **p** 12. C Gerrards Cross and Fulmer *Ox* 11–15; C Brighton St Pet *Chich* from 15; P-in-c Brighton St Matthias from 17. *45 Hollingbury Park Avenue, Brighton BN1 7JQ* T: (01273) 553246 M: 07870-682853 E: tomh@stpetersbrighton.org

HOLBROOK, Canon Barbara Mary. b 58. Nottm Trent Univ BA 94 Nottm Univ MA 04. EMMTC 02. **d** 04 **p** 05. C Chesterfield H Trin and Ch Ch *Derby* 04–08; P-in-c Kimberley *S'well* 08–15; P-in-c Nuthall 08–15; R Kimberley and Nuthall from 15; Hon Can S'well Minster from 13. *The Rectory, 1 Eastwood Road, Kimberley, Nottingham NG16 2HX* T: 0115-938 3565 M: 07766-732514

✠**HOLBROOK, The Rt Revd John Edward.** b 62. St Pet Coll Ox BA 83 MA 87. Ridley Hall Cam 82. **d** 86 **p** 87 **c** 11. C Barnes St Mary *S'wark* 86–89; C Bletchley *Ox* 89–93; C N Bletchley CD 89–93; V Adderbury w Milton 93–02; RD Deddington 00–02; R Wimborne Minster *Sarum* 02–11; P-in-c Witchampton, Stanbridge and Long Crichel etc 02–11; P-in-c Horton, Chalbury, Hinton Martel and Holt St Jas 06–11; RD Wimborne 04–11; Chapl S and E Dorset Primary Care Trust 02–11; Can and Preb Sarum Cathl 06–11; Suff Bp Brixworth *Pet* from 11; Can Pet Cathl from 11. *Orchard Acre, 11 North Street, Mears Ashby, Northampton NN6 0DW* T: (01733) 562492 E: bishop.brixworth@peterborough-diocese.org.uk

HOLCOMBE, Canon Graham William Arthur. b 50. Open Univ BA 99. St Mich Coll Llan. **d** 80 **p** 81. C Neath w Llantwit *Llan* 80–84; Asst Youth Chapl 81–84; PV Llan Cathl 84–86; V Pentyrch 86–00; V Pentyrch w Capel Llanillterne 00–02; Can Llan Cathl 02–14; Can Res from 14. *1 White House, Cathedral Green, Llandaff, Cardiff CF5 2EB* T: (029) 2056 9521 E: grahamw.holcombe@gmail.com

HOLDAWAY, Graham Michael. b 51. Southn Univ BSc 73. Sarum & Wells Th Coll 74. **d** 77 **p** 78. C Walton-on-Thames *Guildf* 77–81; TV Westborough 81–86; PtO 86–01; NSM Walton-on-Thames 01–02; rtd 06. *7 Mampitts Lane, Shaftesbury SP7 8FN* E: grahamholdaway@mac.com

HOLDAWAY, Mark Daniel James. b 78. Selw Coll Cam BA 99 MA 02. Oak Hill Th Coll BA 07. **d** 07 **p** 08. C Bury St Edmunds St Mary *St E* 07–11; R Kirby-le-Soken w Gt Holland *Chelmsf* from 11. *The Rectory, 10 Thorpe Road, Kirby Cross, Frinton-on-Sea CO13 0LT* T: (01255) 675997 E: mdjholdaway@gmail.com

HOLDAWAY, Canon Stephen Douglas. b 45. Hull Univ BA 67. Ridley Hall Cam 67. **d** 70 **p** 71. C Southampton Thornhill St Chris *Win* 70–73; C Tardebigge *Worc* 73–78; Ind Chapl 73–78; Ind Chapl *Linc* 78–93; Co-ord City Cen Group Min 81–93; TR Louth *Linc* 93–11; RD Louthesk 95–11; rtd 11;

Can and Preb Linc Cathl from 00. *36 Wesley Way, Horncastle LN9 6RY* E: stephen.holdaway@btinternet.com

HOLDEN, Christopher Charles. b 54. d 11 p 12. OLM Codnor *Derby* 11–19; OLM Horsley and Denby 11–19; OLM Denby Gp from 19. *62 Waingroves Road, Waingroves, Ripley DE5 9TD* T: (01773) 746411 E: cholden123@aol.com

HOLDEN, Geoffrey. b 26. FCII 54. Oak Hill Th Coll 57. d 59 p 60. C Crookes St Thos *Sheff* 59–61; C Belper *Derby* 61–63; C Woking St Jo *Guildf* 63–66; R Bath St Mich w St Paul *B & W* 66–73; Chapl Bath Gp Hosps 73–91; rtd 91; PtO *B & W* from 91. *32 Crescent Gardens, Bath BA1 2NB* T: (01225) 427933

HOLDEN, James. b 87. Keble Coll Ox BA 09. Ripon Coll Cuddesdon 15. d 17 p 18. C Ludgershall and Faberstown *Sarum* 17–18; C Ludgershall and Tidworth from 18. *6 Laurence Court, Ludgershall, Andover SP11 9QN* T: (01264) 791770 E: ludgershall.curate@gmail.com

HOLDEN, James Bryan. b 60. Sheff Univ BA 81. St Steph Ho Ox 14. d 16. NSM Claverdon w Preston Bagot *Cov* 16–18; NSM Wootton Wawen 16–18; C Aston Cantlow and Wilmcote w Billesley from 18. *49 Cocksparrow Street, Warwick CV34 4ED* M: 07767-321086 E: james.holden@leader.co.uk

HOLDEN, Canon John. b 33. Sheff Univ MA 02 ACMA 62. Ridley Hall Cam 65 Selly Oak Coll 71. d 67 p 68. C Flixton St Jo CD *Man* 67–71; Uganda 71–75; V Aston SS Pet and Paul *Birm* 75–87; RD Aston 86–87; Hon Can Birm Cathl 86–87; R Ulverston St Mary w H Trin *Carl* 87–98; RD Furness 90–94; Hon Can Carl Cathl 91–94; rtd 98; PtO *Carl* 98–16; *Heref* from 99. *3 Alison Road, Church Stretton SY6 7AT* T: (01694) 724167

HOLDEN, Mark Noel. b 61. Collingwood Coll Dur BA 82 Birm Univ MA 95 Edin Univ CQSW 85 Warwick Univ TCert 93. Qu Coll Birm 93. d 95 p 96. C Brumby *Linc* 95–99; P-in-c Wragby 99–00; R Wragby Gp from 00; RD Horncastle from 12. *The Vicarage, Church Street, Wragby, Lincoln LN8 5RA* T: (01673) 857825

HOLDEN, Paul Edward. b 53. BSc 75 CEng 79 MIM MIBF. Trin Coll Bris 82. d 86 p 87. C Harpurhey Ch Ch *Man* 86–88; C Harpurhey St Steph 88–93; Sen Min Harpurhey LEP 88–93. *2 Baywood Street, Harpurhey, Manchester M9 5XJ* T: 0161-205 2938

HOLDEN, Richard Gary. d 04 p 05. C Louth *Linc* 04–07; P-in-c Clee 07–16; P-in-c Cleethorpes St Aid 07–16; R Skegness Gp from 16. *The Parsonage, 18 Danial Close, Skegness PE25 1RQ* E: richard.holden70@ntlworld.com

HOLDEN, Mrs Rita. b 45. SAOMC 98. d 01 p 03. OLM Burghfield *Ox* 01–02; NSM Droitwich Spa *Worc* 02–15; PtO from 15. *40 Nightingale Close, Droitwich WR9 7HB* T: (01905) 772787 M: 07814-621389 E: rita.openv@btinternet.com

HOLDEN, Tony. b 55. Lindisfarne Regional Tr Partnership 07. d 16 p 17. NSM Esh and Hamsteels *Dur* from 16; NSM Langley Park from 16; NSM Waterhouses from 16. *27 Middridge Road, Langley Park, Durham DH7 9FH* T: 0191-373 2715 M: 07425-150040 E: tony-holden@outlook.com

HOLDER, John William. b 41. Chester Coll CertEd 61 Open Univ BA 73 Bath Univ MEd 85. Trin Coll Bris MA 94. d 87 p 88. C Brockworth *Glouc* 87–91; P-in-c Avening w Cherington 91–95; V Cinderford St Jo 95–05; P-in-c Lydbrook 99–03; P-in-c Coberley, Cowley, Colesbourne and Elkstone 05–13; Hon Can Glouc Cathl 03–13; rtd 13. *8 Elmfield Road, Seaton EX12 2EG* T: (01297) 24351 E: canon.john@holder-net.co.uk

HOLDER, Jonathan Mark. b 83. Ox Brookes Univ BA 08. Trin Coll Bris 16. d 19. C Turnham Green Ch Ch *Lon* from 19. *64A Grove Park Road, London W4 3SB* M: 07590-013277 E: jon@christchurchw4.com

HOLDER, Mrs Lydia Jayne. b 89. Univ Coll Falmouth BA 11. Trin Coll Bris BA 19. d 19. C Turnham Green Ch Ch *Lon* from 19. *64A Grove Park Road, London W4 3SB* M: 07443-564286 E: lydia@christchurchw4.com

HOLDER, Rodney Dennis. b 50. Trin Coll Cam BA 71 MA 75 Ch Ch Ox MA 75 DPhil 78 FRAS 75 CPhys 91 MInstP 91 CMath 95 FIMA 95. Wycliffe Hall Ox BA 96. d 97 p 98. C Long Compton, Whichford and Barton-on-the-Heath *Cov* 97–01; C Wolford w Burmington 97–01; C Cherington w Stourton 97–01; C Barcheston 97–01; PtO 01–02; P-in-c The Claydons *Ox* 02–05; Course Dir Faraday Inst for Science and Relig 06–13; rtd 13; PtO *Eur* from 02; *Ely* from 06. *44 St Margaret's Road, Girton, Cambridge CB3 0LT* T: (01223) 364577 E: drandmrsr.holder@virginmedia.com

HOLDING (formerly SMITH), Mrs Georgina Leah. b 83. Nottm Univ MA 05. Ripon Coll Cuddesdon 07. d 10 p 11. C Gt and Lt Coates w Bradley *Linc* 10–14; TV Brereton and Rugeley w Armitage *Lich* from 14. *The Vicarage, 72 Main Road, Rugeley WS15 1DU* E: rev.georgesmith@hotmail.com

HOLDING, Kenneth George Frank. b 27. Sarum & Wells Th Coll 75. d 77 p 78. C Bexley St Mary *Roch* 77–80; Min

Joydens Wood St Barn CD 80–85; R Mereworth w W Peckham 85–92; rtd 92; PtO *Roch* 92–04; P-in-c Willerby w Ganton and Folkton 04–18. *Address temp unknown*

HOLDRIDGE, The Ven Bernard Lee. b 35. Lich Th Coll 64. d 67 p 68. C Swinton *Sheff* 67–71; V Doncaster St Jude 71–81; R Rawmarsh w Parkgate 81–88; RD Rotherham 86–88; V Worksop Priory *S'well* 88–94; Adn Doncaster *Sheff* 94–01; rtd 01; PtO *Sheff* 01–06; *Guildf* 06–15. *33 Denehyrst Court, York Road, Guildford GU1 4EA* T: (01483) 570791

HOLDSTOCK, Adrian Charles. b 51. Peterho Cam BA MA 75 Nottm Univ MA 03 CMgr FCMI. EMMTC 00. d 03 p 04. NSM Bosworth and Sheepy Gp *Leic* 03–12; NSM Nailstone and Carlton w Shackerstone 07–12; P-in-c Pet St Mark 12–16; V from 16; Asst Dir Ords from 14. *The Vicarage, 82 Lincoln Road, Peterborough PE1 2SN* M: 07792-452669 E: adrian.holdstock@peterborough-diocese.org.uk

HOLDSWORTH, Canon Ian Scott. b 52. Sheff Poly BA 75. Oak Hill Th Coll BA 81. d 81 p 82. C Denham *Ox* 81–84; P-in-c S Leigh 84–89; P-in-c Cogges 84–88; V 88–89; PtO *Pet* 95; NSM Brackley St Pet w St Jas 96–99; P-in-c Northampton St Mary 99–04; V 04–19; Can Pet Cathl 17–19; rtd 19. *62 Cardigan Road, Bridlington YO15 3JT* T: (01262) 308078 M: 07912-639980 E: canonianh@gmail.com

HOLDSWORTH, Canon John Ivor. b 49. Univ of Wales (Abth) BA 70 Univ of Wales (Cardiff) BD 73 MTh 75 Univ of Wales (Lamp) PhD 96. St Mich Coll Llan 70. d 73 p 74. C Newport St Paul *Mon* 73–77; CF (TAVR) 75–90; V Abercraf and Callwen *S & B* 77–86; Bp's Chapl for Th Educn 80–97; V Gorseinon 86–97; Hon Lect Th Univ of Wales (Swansea) 88–96; Prin and Warden St Mich Coll Llan 97–03; Lect Th Cardiff Univ *Llan* 97–10; Adn St D and V Steynton *St D* 03–10; Adn Cyprus, Chapl Larnaca and Exec Adn Cyprus and the Gulf 10–19; rtd 19; Dir Min Cyprus and the Gulf from 19; Can Th Nicosia from 19. *Ty Newydd, Llansaint, Kidwelly SA17 5HZ* T: (01267) 267350 or (01970) (22) 671220 M: (00357) 99-658147 E: archdeaconjohn32@gmail.com

HOLDSWORTH, The Very Revd Kelvin. b 66. Man Poly BSc 89 St Andr Univ BD 92 Edin Univ MTh 96. TISEC 95. d 97 p 98. Prec St Ninian's Cathl Perth *St And* 97–00; R Bridge of Allan 00–06; Chapl Stirling Univ 00–06; Provost St Mary's Cathl *Glas* from 06; R Glas St Mary from 06. *300 Great Western Road, Glasgow G4 9JB* T: 0141-530 8643 E: provost@thecathedral.org.uk

HOLE, The Very Revd Derek Norman. b 33. De Montfort Univ Hon DLitt 99 Leic Univ Hon LLD 05. Linc Th Coll 57. d 60 p 61. C Knighton St Mary Magd *Leic* 60–62; Dom Chapl to Abp Cape Town 62–64; C Kenilworth St Nic *Cov* 64–67; R Burton Latimer *Pet* 67–73; V Leic St Jas 73–92; Hon Can Leic Cathl 83–92; RD Christianity S 83–92; Provost Leic 92–99; Chapl to The Queen 85–93; rtd 99; PtO *Leic* from 00. *25 Southernhay Close, Leicester LE2 3TW* T: 0116-270 9988 M: 07799-892615 E: dnhole@btinternet.com

HOLE, Samuel Richard. b 84. Trin Hall Cam BA 06 MA 10 PGCE 07 K Coll Lon MA 11 Selw Coll Cam PhD 16. Westcott Ho Cam 12. d 16 p 17. C S'wark St Geo w St Alphege and St Jude from 16. *St Alphege House, Pocock Street, London SE1 0BJ* T: (020) 7357 7331 M: 07792-786442 E: samhole@gmail.com

HOLE, Toby Kenton. b 72. Dur Univ BA 94 MA 95 Cam Univ BTh 06. Ridley Hall Cam 03. d 06 p 07. C Islington St Mary *Lon* 06–10; V Woodseats St Chad *Sheff* from 10; C Norton from 17; C Greenhill from 17; C Norton Lees St Paul from 17; AD Ecclesall from 14. *St Chad's Vicarage, 9 Linden Avenue, Sheffield S8 0GA* T: 0114-274 9302 or 274 5086 M: 07906-312998 E: toby.hole@gmail.com or toby.hole@sheffield.anglican.org

HOLFORD, Canon Andrew Peter. b 62. Nottm Univ BSc 84. Cranmer Hall Dur 87. d 90 p 91. C Waltham Cross *St Alb* 90–93; C Northampton St Benedict *Pet* 93–95; V Pet Ch Carpenter 95–04; TR Baldock w Bygrave and Weston *St Alb* 04–13; R Baldock w Bygrave from 13; Hon Can St Alb from 18. *The Rectory, 9 Pond Lane, Baldock SG7 5AS* T: (01462) 896273 E: 2008luddite@googlemail.com

HOLFORD, Canon John Alexander. b 40. Chich Th Coll 65. d 67 p 68. C Cottingley *Bradf* 67–71; C Baildon 71–73; P-in-c Bingley H Trin 73–74; V 74–86; V Woodhall 86–93; C Shelf 93–94; TV Shelf w Buttershaw St Aid 94–99; rtd 99; P-in-c Embsay w Eastby *Bradf* 99–04; Hon Can Bradf Cathl 03–04; PtO 04–14; *Leeds* from 14. *3 Wheelwrights Court, Hellifield, Skipton BD23 4LX* T: (01729) 851740 E: john.holford720@gmail.com

HOLFORD, Margaret Sophia. b 39. SAOMC 95. d 98 p 99. NSM Stevenage St Andr and St Geo *St Alb* 98–03; NSM Ickleford w Holwell 03–05; NSM Holwell, Ickleford and Pirton from 05. *Icknield House, Westmill Lane, Ickleford, Hitchin SG5 3RN* T: (01462) 432794 F: 436618

HOLGATE, Audrey Elizabeth. *See* KAY, Audrey Elizabeth

HOLGATE, Canon David Andrew. b 54. Cape Town Univ BA 77 Port Eliz Univ BA 89 Rhodes Univ MTh 90 PhD 94. All Nations Chr Coll 80. **d** 82 **p** 84. C Uitenhage St Kath S Africa 82–84; Asst P Port Elizabeth St Hugh 84–87; P-in-c Somerset E All SS 88–89; St Paul's Coll Grahamstown 90–93; CME Officer *Chelmsf* 93–96; P-in-c Felsted 93–96; V Felsted and Lt Dunmow 96–97; Dean of Studies STETS 97–14; Vice-Prin 01–11; Prin 11–14; Can Res Man Cathl from 14. *3 Booth Clibborn Court, Salford M7 4PJ* E: daholgate@googlemail.com

✠**HOLLAND, The Rt Revd Alfred Charles.** b 27. St Chad's Coll Dur BA 50. **d** 52 **p** 53 **c** 70. C W Hackney St Barn *Lon* 52–54; R Scarborough Australia 55–70; Asst Bp Perth 70–77; Bp Newcastle 78–92; rtd 92; Bp Jerusalem 93–94; Australia from 94. *21 Sullivan Crescent, Wanniassa ACT 2903, Australia* T: (0061) (2) 6231 8368 E: acjmholland@bigpond.com

✠**HOLLAND, The Rt Revd Edward.** b 36. AKC 64. **d** 65 **p** 66 **c** 86. C Dartford H Trin *Roch* 65–69; C Mill Hill Jo Keble Ch *Lon* 69–72; Prec Gib Cathl *Eur* 72–74; Chapl Naples Ch Ch 74–79; Chapl Bromley Hosp 79–86; V Bromley St Mark *Roch* 79–86; Suff Bp Eur 86–95; Dean Brussels 86–95; Area Bp Colchester *Chelmsf* 95–01; rtd 01; Hon Asst Bp Lon from 02; Hon Asst Bp Eur from 02. *37 Parfrey Street, London W6 9EW* T: (020) 8746 3636 E: ed.holland@uwclub.net

HOLLAND, Mrs Elizabeth Ann. b 91. Dur Univ BA 12. St Mellitus Coll 15. **d** 17 **p** 18. C Berkswell *Cov* from 17. *45 Steinway, Coventry CV4 9ZG* T: (024) 7798 1526 M: 07377-449873 E: lizzyholland@berkswellchurch.org.uk

HOLLAND, Mrs Gillaine. b 67. Kent Inst of Art & Design BA 89. STETS 05. **d** 08 **p** 09. C Epsom St Martin *Guildf* 08–09; C Woking St Mary 09–12; Asst Chapl HM Pris Send 11–12; Chapl St Columba's Retreat and Conf Cen 12–16; C Woodham *Guildf* from 16. *St Michael's Shared Church, Dartmouth Avenue, Woking GU21 5PJ* T: (01932) 341694 M: 07969-067116 E: stmichaels.bmo@virginmedia.com *or* rev.gillaine.holland@stmichaelssheerwater.org.uk

HOLLAND, Glyn. b 59. Hull Univ BA Bris Univ CertEd. Coll of Resurr Mirfield 83. **d** 85 **p** 86. C Brighouse St Martin *Wakef* 85–89; V Ferrybridge 89–96; Chapl Pontefract Gen Infirmary 89–96; V Middlesbrough All SS *York* from 96. *All Saints' Vicarage, 14 The Crescent, Middlesbrough TS5 6SQ* T: (01642) 820304

HOLLAND, Jesse Marvin Sean. b 66. Westmr Coll Ox MTh 03. Oak Hill Th Coll BA 97. **d** 98 **p** 99. C Thundersley *Chelmsf* 98–02; P-in-c Tedburn St Mary, Whitestone, Oldridge etc *Ex* 02–06; V Buller New Zealand 06–08; P-in-c Lyneham w Bradenstoke *Sarum* 08–10; Chapl RAF from 10. *Chaplaincy Services (RAF), HQ Air Command, RAF High Wycombe HP14 4UE* T: (01494) 496800 E: revdjmsholland@aol.com

HOLLAND, John Stuart. b 52. Sarum & Wells Th Coll 77. **d** 80 **p** 81. C Wylde Green *Birm* 80–83; C Swanage and Studland *Sarum* 83–85; P-in-c Handley w Pentridge 85–88; TV Preston w Sutton Poyntz, Littlemoor etc 88–95; P-in-c Failsworth St Jo *Man* 95–01; V Ashton Ch Ch 01–07; P-in-c Carbis Bay w Lelant *Truro* 07–10; P-in-c Towednack and Zennor 08–10; P-in-c Oswaldtwistle Immanuel and All SS *Blackb* 10–12; P-in-c Oswaldtwistle St Paul 10–12; V Oswaldtwistle 12–16; AD Accrington 14–16; rtd 16; PtO *Newc* from 16. *33 Tyelaw Meadows, Shilbottle, Alnwick NE66 2JJ* M: 07718-483817 E: johnholland703@yahoo.co.uk

HOLLAND, Lesley Anne. *See* LEON, Lesley Anne

HOLLAND, Mrs Lisa Jayne. b 67. RGN 94. Ridley Hall Cam 16. **d** 18 **p** 19. C Duston and Upton *Pet* from 18. *St Francis House, Eastfield Road, Duston, Northampton NN5 6TQ* T: (01604) 590052 E: lisaholland@dustonanduptonparish.org.uk

HOLLAND, Matthew Francis. b 52. Lon Univ BA 73. Qu Coll Birm. **d** 79 **p** 80. C Ecclesall *Sheff* 79–83; TV Gleadless Valley 83–86; TR 86–88; V Sheff Gillcar St Silas 88–92; V Sheff St Silas Broomhall 92–98; V Southsea St Simon *Portsm* 98–15; rtd 15; PtO *York* from 15. *6 Rifts Avenue, Saltburn-by-Sea TS12 1QE* T: (01287) 624915 E: matthew758@btinternet.com

HOLLAND, Canon Simon Paul. b 56. Westcott Ho Cam 79. **d** 81 **p** 82. C Uckfield *Chich* 81–84; TV Lewes All SS, St Anne, St Mich and St Thos 84–88; TR 88–91; R Glas St Matt 91–95; P-in-c Glas St Kentigern 95–96; R Aldingbourne, Barnham and Eastergate *Chich* 96–12; R Chich St Paul and Westhampnett from 12; P-in-c Chich St Wilfrid from 17; PtO *Portsm* from 15; Can and Preb Chich Cathl from 10. *The Rectory, Tower Close, Chichester PO19 1QN* T: (01243) 779089 E: simonholland578@btinternet.com

HOLLAND, Mrs Tessa Christine. b 59. Hull Univ BA 81 Heythrop Coll Lon MA 12. STETS 00. **d** 03 **p** 04. NSM Storrington *Chich* 03–05; NSM Pulborough 05–07; LtO from 07. *Wild Fortune, Sandgate Lane, Storrington, Pulborough RH20 3HJ* T: (01903) 740487 E: wildfortune@btinternet.com

HOLLETT, Catherine Elaine. *See* DAKIN, Catherine Elaine

HOLLEY, Paul Robert. b 65. Cranmer Hall Dur 91. **d** 94 **p** 95. C Tonge w Alkrington *Man* 94–98; P-in-c Salford St Phil w St Steph 98–00; P-in-c Salford Sacred Trin 99–00; R Salford Sacred Trin and St Phil 00–03; P-in-c La Côte *Eur* 03–10; PtO 10–15; Hon C S Dulwich St Steph *S'wark* 12–14; P-in-c Colbury *Win* 14–16; P-in-c Bodmin w Lanhydrock and Lanivet *Truro* 16–17; TR Bodmin from 17; RD Trigg Minor and Bodmin from 18. *The Rectory, Barons Meadow, Bodmin PL31 2DD* M: 07470-192378 E: paul.holley@mac.com

HOLLIDAY, Canon Andrew. b 62. St Steph Ho Ox 89. **d** 92 **p** 93. C Marton *Blackb* 92–95; C Poulton-le-Fylde 95–97; V Leyland St Jas 97–04; AD Leyland 02–04; P-in-c Darwen St Pet w Hoddlesden 04–10; V Darwen St Pet 10–11; R Standish from 11; Chapl MU from 12; Warden of Readers *Blackb* from 16; Hon Can Blackb Cathl from 12. *The Rectory, 13 Rectory Lane, Standish, Wigan WN6 0XA* T: (01257) 421396 E: andrew.holliday@tesco.net *or* holliday321@btinternet.com

HOLLIDAY, Canon Peter Leslie. b 48. Birm Univ BCom 70 MA 92 FCA 79. Qu Coll Birm 81. **d** 83 **p** 84. C Burton *Lich* 83–87; P-in-c Longdon 87–93; PV and Subchanter Lich Cath 87–93; TV Stratford-on-Avon w Bishopton *Cov* 93–00; Chief Exec St Giles Hospice Lich 00–17; Chan's V Lich Cathl 02–13; Can Custos Lich Cathl 13–18; Chapl to The Queen 15–18; rtd 18; PtO *Lich* from 18. *60 Needlers End Lane, Balsall Common, Coventry CV7 7AB* T: (01676) 533305 E: plh@europe.com

HOLLIDAY, William John. b 49. Middleton St Geo Coll of Educn TCert 72. CBDTI 05. **d** 07 **p** 08. NSM Kendal St Thos *Carl* 07–12; TV Loughrigg 12–13; rtd 13; PtO *Carl* from 13. *2 Michaelson Road, Kendal LA9 5JQ* T: (01539) 730701 E: billholliday@googlemail.com

✠**HOLLINGHURST, The Rt Revd Anne Elizabeth.** b 64. Trin Coll Bris BA 96 Hughes Hall Cam MSt 10. **d** 96 **p** 97 **c** 15. C Nottingham St Sav *S'well* 96–99; Chapl Derby Univ and Derby Cathl 99–05; Bp's Dom Chapl and Can Res Man Cathl 05–10; V St Alb St Pet 10–15; Suff Bp Aston *Birm* from 15. *16 Coleshill Street, Sutton Coldfield B72 1SH* T: 0121-426 0400 E: bishopofaston@cofebirmingham.com

HOLLINGHURST, Preb Stephen. b 59. St Jo Coll Nottm 81. **d** 83 **p** 84. C Hyde St Geo *Ches* 83–86; C Cropwell Bishop w Colston Bassett, Granby etc *S'well* 86–90; R Pembridge w Moor Court, Shobdon, Staunton etc *Heref* 90–02; R Presteigne w Discoed, Kinsham, Lingen and Knill from 02; RD Kington and Weobley 95–02 and 07–12 and from 14; Preb Heref Cathl from 08. *The Rectory, St David's Street, Presteigne LD8 2BP* T: (01544) 267777 E: revsteve.hollinghurst@gmail.com

HOLLINGHURST, Stephen Patrick. b 63. Hull Univ BA 84. Trin Coll Bris BA 93 MA 93. **d** 96 **p** 97. C Nottingham St Sav *S'well* 96–99; Chapl Nottm Trent Univ 99–03; Researcher CA from 03; PtO *Derby* 00–04; Chapl Derby Cathl 04–05; PtO *Birm* from 16. *16 Coleshill Street, Sutton Coldfield B72 1SH* M: 07834-070246 E: stevehollinghurst@hotmail.com

HOLLINGS, Ms Daphne. b 46. WMMTC 02. **d** 05 **p** 06. NSM Adbaston, High Offley, Knightley, Norbury etc *Lich* 05–09; C Edstaston, Fauls, Prees, Tilstock and Whixall 09–15; C Whitchurch 13–15; rtd 15; PtO *Ban* 15–16; Hon C Uwch Gwyrfai Beuno Sant from 16. *Nythfa, County Road, Penygroes, Caernarfon LL54 6EY* T: (01286) 880853 E: daphne.hollings785@btinternet.com

HOLLINGS, Robert George. b 48. St Jo Coll Nottm. **d** 94 **p** 95. C Cotmanhay *Derby* 94–97; TV Godrevy *Truro* 97–02; V Newhall *Derby* 02–12; rtd 12; P-in-c Six Pilgrims *B & W* 12–13; PtO *Lich* from 15. *2 Meadow View, Rolleston-on-Dove, Burton-on-Trent DE13 9AN* E: bobandjacqui@btinternet.com

HOLLINGSBEE, Thomas Richard. b 86. Sheff Univ BSc 07. Oak Hill Th Coll 13. **d** 16 **p** 17. C Higher Openshaw *Man* from 16. *1455 Ashton Old Road, Manchester M11 1HH* T: 0161-371 1697 M: 07841-538516 E: tomhollingsbee@gmail.com

HOLLINGSHURST, Christopher Paul. b 63. St Chad's Coll Dur BA 85 Westmr Coll Ox PGCE 86 Anglia Poly Univ MA 04. Ridley Hall Cam 96. **d** 99 **p** 00. C Bourn and Kingston w Caxton and Longstowe *Ely* 99–00; C Papworth 00–03; V Hook *S'wark* 03–14; Voc Adv Wandsworth Adnry 09–12; Dioc Voc Adv 12–13; Dir Ords Kingston Area 13–14; P-in-c W Byfleet *Guildf* 14–16; V from 16. *3 Clare Close, West Byfleet KT14 6RD* T: (01932) 400198 E: chris@stjohnswestbyfleet.org.uk

HOLLINGSWORTH, Geoffrey. b 53. MCIPD 85. NOC 86. **d** 86 **p** 87. C Thorne *Sheff* 86–89; V Rawcliffe 89–96; V Airmyn, Hook and Rawcliffe 96–09; P-in-c Pocklington and Owsthorpe and Kilnwick Percy etc *York* 09–10; P-in-c Burnby 09–10; P-in-c Londesborough 09–10; P-in-c Nunburnholme and Warter and Huggate 09–10; P-in-c Shiptonthorpe and Hayton 09–10; R Pocklington Wold 10–18; R Londesborough Wold 10–18; rtd 18; PtO *York* from 18; *Sheff* from 18; *Eur* from 18. *8 Barn Hill Farm, Selby Road, Howden, Goole DN14 7JP* E: geoff.holly145@btinternet.com

HOLLINGSWORTH, James William. b 69. Southn Univ BA 91 SS Coll Cam BA 96. Aston Tr Scheme 92 Ridley Hall Cam 94. **d** 97 **p** 98. C Mildenhall *St E* 97–01; R Barcombe *Chich* from 01; P-in-c Newick from 16. *The Rectory, 1 The Grange, Barcombe, Lewes BN8 5AT* T: (01273) 400260 E: james@barcombe.net

HOLLINGSWORTH, Mrs Lucy Jane. b 70. SEITE. **d** 16 **p** 17. NSM Ringmer *Chich* 16–17; NSM Scaynes Hill from 17. *The Rectory, 1 The Grange, Barcombe, Lewes BN8 5AT* T: (01273) 400260 E: lucyjhollingsworth@gmail.com

HOLLINGSWORTH, Preb Paula Marion. b 62. Van Mildert Coll Dur BSc 83 Univ of Wales (Lamp) MA 08. Trin Coll Bris BA 91. **d** 91 **p** 94. C Keynsham *B & W* 91–95; C Balsall Heath St Paul *Birm* 95–98; Tutor Crowther Hall CMS Tr Coll Selly Oak 95–01; P-in-c Houghton-on-the-Hill, Keyham and Hungarton *Leic* 01–10; Bp's Adv for CME 01–04; P-in-c Westbury sub Mendip w Easton *B & W* 10–12; V from 12; V Priddy from 12; Sub-Dean and Preb Wells Cathl from 14; Dean of Women's Min from 15. *The Vicarage, Crow Lane, Westbury sub Mendip, Wells BA5 1HB* T: (01749) 870293 M: 07909-631977 E: pmhollingsworth@btinternet.com

HOLLINS, Canon Beverley Jayne. b 68. Univ of Wales (Abth) BLib 90. SAOMC 00. **d** 03 **p** 04. C Milton Keynes *Ox* 03–06; LtO 06–07; Newport Deanery Development Facilitator 07–12; P-in-c Hardingstone and Piddington w Horton *Pet* 12–15; V Hardingstone, Piddington w Horton and Quinton and Preston Deanery from 15; RD Gtr Northn from 16; Can Pet Cathl from 18. *The Vicarage, 29 Back Lane, Hardingstone, Northampton NN4 6BY* T: (01604) 945818 E: beverley.hollins@gmail.com

HOLLINS, John Edgar. b 35. St Jo Coll Cam BA 58 MA 62. Oak Hill Th Coll 58. **d** 60 **p** 61. C Whalley Range St Edm *Man* 60–63; C Highbury Ch Ch *Lon* 63–66; C St Alb St Paul 66–71; Hon C Halliwell St Paul *Man* 71–72; C Ravenhill St Jo 72–73; PtO *Birm* 79–81; V Millbrook *Ches* 81–89; rtd 89; PtO *Truro* from 89. *3 Victoria Close, Liskeard PL14 3HU* T: (01579) 349963 E: johnhollins@live.co.uk

HOLLINS (formerly SHIPP), Patricia Susan. b 54. Univ of Wales BA 76. St Paul's Coll Grahamstown 77 Linc Th Coll 81. **d** 83 **p** 94. C Cyncoed *Mon* 83–87; Par Dn Lawrence Weston *Bris* 89–91; Par Dn Henbury 91–94; V Longwell Green 94–99; Hon Can Bris Cathl 97–99; Chapl Mt Vernon and Watford Hosps NHS Trust 99–00; Sen Co-ord Chapl W Herts Hosps NHS Trust 00–04; Lead Chapl (E) Caring for the Spirit NHS Project 04–09; P-in-c Boxley w Detling *Cant* 09–14; AD N Downs 09–14; Chapl Cam St Edw *Ely* 14–15; Lead Chapl Qu Eliz Hosp King's Lynn NHS Foundn Trust 15–17; PtO *Nor* 17–18. *63 Dorset Avenue, Exeter EX4 1ND* M: 07918-671476 E: susan@susanhollins.com

HOLLIS, The Ven Arnold Thaddeus. b 33. Stockton State Coll New Jersey BA 74 NY Th Sem MDiv 74 STM 76 DMin 78. Codrington Coll Barbados 56. **d** 59 **p** 60. C Wakef St Jo 60–62; Br Guiana 62–64; P-in-c Horbury Bridge *Wakef* 64–66; C Loughton St Jo *Chelmsf* 66–69; USA 69–77; Hon Chapl RN Bermuda from 77; Chapl HM Pris from 77; Chapl Miss to Seafarers from 90; Hon Can Bermuda Cathl from 87; Adn Bermuda 96–03; rtd 03. *3 Middle Road, Sandys SB 02, Bermuda* T: (001441) 234 0834 or 234 2025 F: 234 2723 E: athol@logic.bm

HOLLIS, Derek. b 60. Loughb Univ BA 82. Cranmer Hall Dur 83. **d** 86 **p** 87. C Evington *Leic* 86–89; C Arnold *S'well* 89–93; V Beckingham w Walkeringham 93–03; P-in-c Gringley-on-the-Hill 95–03; V Beckingham w Walkeringham and Gringley 03–05; P-in-c Elston w Elston Chapelry 05–11; P-in-c E Stoke w Syerston 05–11; P-in-c Shelton 05–11; P-in-c Sibthorpe 05–11; P-in-c Staunton w Flawborough 05–11; P-in-c Kilvington 05–11; Hon Chapl Miss to Seafarers 03–04; Bp's Adv on Rural Affairs *S'well* 04–11; V Stourhead *St E* 11–18; rtd 18. *13 Queens Gardens, Hunstanton PE36 6HD*

HOLLIS, Miss Elizabeth Jane. b 92. Ex Univ BA 14 St Jo Coll Dur MA 15. Cranmer Hall Dur 16. **d** 19. C Belmont and Pittington Dur from 19. *83 Birkdale Gardens, Durham DH1 2UJ* M: 07985-984827 E: liz_hollis@live.co.uk

HOLLIS, Mrs Lorna Mary. b 40. Cranmer Hall Dur 05. **d** 06 **p** 07. NSM Scarborough St Jas w H Trin *York* 06–19; Asst Chapl Scarborough and NE Yorks Healthcare NHS Trust 06–12; Asst Chapl York Teaching Hosp NHS Foundn Trust from 12; PtO *York* from 19. *30 Hartford Court, Filey Road, Scarborough YO11 2TP* T: (01723) 351935 E: mary.hollis3@btinternet.com

HOLLIS, Rebecca Catherine. See MATHEW, Rebecca Catherine

HOLLIS, Timothy Knowles. b 28. RN Coll Dartmouth 45. St Steph Ho Ox 54. **d** 58 **p** 59. C Oatlands *Guildf* 58–60; C Crawley *Chich* 60–63; C Sotterley w Willingham *St E* 63–69; C Sotterley, Willingham, Shadingfield, Ellough etc 69; R 69–76; Gen Sec L'Arche UK 77–93; rtd 93; PtO *Chich* 93–02; *Glouc* from 03. *9 Abbots Court Drive, Twyning, Tewkesbury GL20 6JJ* T: (01684) 274903

HOLLIS, Mrs Valerie Elizabeth. b 40. Maria Grey Coll Lon CertEd 61. St Alb Minl Tr Scheme 89. **d** 92 **p** 94. NSM Kempston Transfiguration *St Alb* 92–06; NSM Officer Bedford Adnry 06–10; PtO 06–18. *33 Silverdale Street, Kempston, Bedford MK42 8BE* T: (01234) 853397 E: nsmobeds@stalbans.anglican.org

HOLLOWAY, Canon David Dennis. b 43. Lich Th Coll 65. **d** 68 **p** 69. C Cricklade w Latton *Bris* 68–71; C Bris St Agnes and St Simon w St Werburgh 71–74; V Bitton 74–78; TV E Bris 78–80; P-in-c Tormarton w W Littleton 80–83; Dioc Ecum and Global Partnership Officer 83–93; Hon C Bris St Mich 89–93; V Horfield St Greg 93–00; RD Horfield 97–99; Chapl St Monica Home Westbury-on-Trym 00–07; Hon Can Bris Cathl 92–07; rtd 07; PtO *Ox* from 09; *St Alb* from 16. *76 Marsworth Road, Pitstone, Leighton Buzzard LU7 9AS* T: (01296) 662765 M: 07974-648556

HOLLOWAY, David Ronald James. b 39. Univ Coll Ox BA 62 MA 66. Ridley Hall Cam 65. **d** 67 **p** 68. C Leeds St Geo *Ripon* 67–71; Tutor Wycliffe Hall Ox 71–72; V Jesmond Clayton Memorial *Newc* from 73. *7 Otterburn Terrace, Newcastle upon Tyne NE2 3AP* T: 0191-281 2001 or 212 7400 M: 07702-175399 E: david.holloway@church.org.uk

HOLLOWAY, Graham Edward. b 45. Chich Th Coll 69. **d** 72 **p** 73. C W Drayton *Lon* 72–75; P-in-c Hawton *S'well* 75–80; V Ladybrook 80–85; P-in-c Babworth 85–87; R Babworth w Sutton-cum-Lound 87–97; RD Retford 88–93; C Mansfield Woodhouse 97–04; P-in-c Mansfield St Aug 04–12; P-in-c Pleasley Hill 04–12; rtd 12; PtO *S'well* from 13. *6 Aylesbury Way, Forest Town, Mansfield NG19 0GJ* T: (01623) 414616 E: padreg@btinternet.com

HOLLOWAY, Keith Graham. b 45. Linc Coll Ox BA 67. Cranmer Hall Dur. **d** 73 **p** 74. C Gt Ilford St Andr *Chelmsf* 73–78; Hon C Squirrels Heath 78–80; Min Chelmer Village CD 80–87; V E Springfield 87–89; P-in-c Gt Dunmow 89–96; R Gt Dunmow and Barnston 96–02; R Upper Colne 02–10; rtd 10; PtO *Chelmsf* from 10. *5 Martens Meadow, Braintree CM7 3LB* T: (01376) 334976 E: kanddway@aol.com

HOLLOWAY, Michael Sinclair. b 50. UEA BSc 74 Southn Univ PGCE 75. STETS 99. **d** 02 **p** 03. NSM Catherington and Clanfield *Portsm* 02–07; C Bishop's Cleeve *Glouc* 07–08; TV Bishop's Cleeve and Woolstone w Gotherington etc 08–13; V Painswick, Sheepscombe, Cranham, The Edge etc 13–18; rtd 18. *10 Orchard Road, Winchcombe, Cheltenham GL54 5QB* T: (01242) 603421 E: revmike.holloway@gmail.com

✠**HOLLOWAY, The Rt Revd Prof Richard Frederick.** b 33. Lon Univ BD 63 NY Th Sem STM 68 Strathclyde Univ DUniv 94 Aber Univ Hon DD 95 Napier Univ Edin DLitt 00 Glas Univ DD 01 FRSE 95. Edin Th Coll 58. **d** 59 **p** 60 **c** 86. C Glas St Ninian 59–63; P-in-c Glas St Marg 63–68; R Edin Old St Paul 68–80; R Boston The Advent MA USA 80–84; V Ox St Mary Magd 84–86; Bp Edin 86–00; Primus 92–00; rtd 00; Gresham Prof of Div 97–01. *6 Blantyre Terrace, Edinburgh EH10 5AE* T: 0131-446 0696 M: 07710-254500 E: richard@docholloway.org.uk

HOLLOWAY, Simon Anthony. b 50. Sussex Univ BSc 72 Univ of Wales MA 03. Trin Coll Bris 76. **d** 79 **p** 81. C Bushbury *Lich* 79–81; C Castle Church 81–84; P-in-c Sparkbrook Ch Ch *Birm* 84–91; V 91–02; AD Bordesley 92–99; TV Horley *S'wark* 02–11; Chapl SE Cyprus 11–14; P-in-c Kilmington, Stockland, Dalwood, Yarcombe etc *Ex* from 14. *The Vicarage, Whitford Road, Kilmington, Axminster EX13 7RF* M: 07986-274393 E: simonholloway55@yahoo.co.uk

HOLLOWOOD, Graham. b 56. Anglia Ruskin Univ MA 07. St Steph Ho Ox 97. **d** 99 **p** 00. C Newport St Julian *Mon* 99–02; V Newport All SS 02–08; V Glodwick *Man* 08–18; AD Oldham E 14–18; V Royton from 18. *St Mark's Vicarage, 1 Skipton Street, Oldham OL8 2JF* T: 0161-624 4964 M: 07748-106718 E: 1frgraham@gmail.com

HOLLYWELL, Mrs Catherine Ann Mary. b 62. Qu Coll Birm 12. **d** 15 **p** 16. C Derby St Jo 15–16; C Pride Park, Wilmorton, Allenton and Shelton Lock from 16. *St Werburgh's Vicarage, Gascoigne Drive, Spondon, Derby DE21 7GL* M: 07745-735060 E: chollywell@btinternet.com

HOLMAN, Francis Noel. b 37. Sarum Th Coll 62. **d** 65 **p** 66. C Weston Favell *Pet* 65–68; C Eckington *Derby* 68–71; Asst Chapl St Thos Hosp Lon 72–77; Chapl Hope Hosp Salford 77–02; Chapl Salford R Hosp 77–93; Chapl Ladywell Hosp 77–99; Chapl Man and Salford Skin Hosp 88–94;

rtd 02; PtO *Man* 03–18. *90 Rocky Lane, Eccles, Manchester M30 9LY* T: 0161-707 1180 E: fnholman@talktalk.net

HOLMAN, Mrs Lesley Anita. b 50. SWMTC 11. **d** 14 **p** 15. NSM Littleham-cum-Exmouth w Lympstone *Ex* from 14. *6 Dukes Close, Otterton, Budleigh Salterton EX9 7EY* T: (01395) 567255 E: lesley.holman@btinternet.com

HOLMDEN, Miss Maria Irene. b 50. Trent Poly TCert 72 BEd 73. Oak Hill Th Coll 90. **d** 92 **p** 94. Par Dn Stratford St Jo and Ch Ch w Forest Gate St Jas *Chelmsf* 92–94; C 94–96; P-in-c Leyton All SS 96–01; V from 01. *All Saints' Vicarage, 47 Melbourne Road, London E10 7HF* T: (020) 8558 8139 E: mholmden@tiscali.co.uk

HOLME, Thomas Edmund. b 49. Selw Coll Cam BA 71 MA 75. Coll of Resurr Mirfield 71. **d** 73 **p** 74. C Wyther *Ripon* 73–76; C Wimbledon *S'wark* 76–78; TV 78–79; V Bermondsey St Anne 79–81; V Stamford Baron *Pet* 83–89; P-in-c Tinwell 83–89; Hon Min Can Pet Cathl 84–89; Prec Worc Cathl 89–95; P-in-c Penshurst and Fordcombe *Roch* 95–05; R from 05; P-in-c Chiddingstone w Chiddingstone Causeway from 19. *The Rectory, High Street, Penshurst, Tonbridge TN11 8BN* T: (01892) 870316

HOLMES, Miss Alexandra Jane. b 74. Ox Brookes Univ BA 96 Portsm Univ MSc 11. Ripon Coll Cuddesdon 13. **d** 16 **p** 17. C Blagdon w Compton Martin and Ubley *B & W* from 16. *Sirinor, Liberty Lane, Blagdon, Bristol BS40 7TJ* M: 07979-667324 E: holmesaj@yahoo.com

HOLMES, Andrew Keith. b 69. Univ of Wales BEng 93. St Mich Coll Llan BTh 96. **d** 96 **p** 97. C Clydach *S & B* 96–98; C Swansea St Thos and Kilvey 98–00; P-in-c New Radnor and Llanfihangel Nantmelan etc 00–03; V Penrhiwceiber, Matthewstown and Ynysboeth *Llan* 03–16; Voc Adv 13–16; V Manselton and Cwmbwrla *S & B* 16–18; R Fish Hoek S Africa from 18. *4 Fourth Avenue, Fish Hoek 7975, South Africa* E: andrewkeithholmes@gmail.com

HOLMES (née PLATT), Mrs Anne Cecilia. b 46. Birm Univ BA 67 Anglia Ruskin Univ MA 09 Ox Univ DipEd 68 MInstGA 96. SAOMC 99. **d** 02 **p** 03. Chapl Headington Sch 02–04; Asst Chapl Oxon & Bucks Mental Health Partnership NHS Trust 04–09; NSM Marston w Elsfield *Ox* 02–12; PtO from 12. *Trinity Cottage, 27 Mill Street, Eynsham, Witney OX29 4JX* T: (01865) 881397 M: 07831-254727 E: administrator@acholmes.demon.co.uk or anne@acholmes.demon.co.uk

HOLMES, Brian. b 41. NEOC 92. **d** 95 **p** 96. NSM Darlington St Matt and St Luke *Dur* 95–98; V 98–08; rtd 08; PtO *Dur* from 08. *2 Christchurch Close, Darlington DL1 2YL* T: (01325) 482255 E: revbholmes@hotmail.co.uk

HOLMES (née KENYON), Caroline Elizabeth. b 40. SRN 62. NOC 04. **d** 05 **p** 06. NSM Hale and Ashley *Ches* 05–10; PtO from 10. *1 Broomfield House, 134 Hale Road, Hale, Altrincham WA15 9HJ* T: 0161-233 0761 E: caroline.holmes@rgsit.com

HOLMES, Craig Walter. b 72. Southn Univ BSc 95 R Holloway & Bedf New Coll Lon PhD 01 Fitzw Coll Cam BA 03 MA 07 CCC Cam MPhil 06. Ridley Hall Cam 01. **d** 07 **p** 08. C Egham *Guildf* 07–10; V Hanworth St Rich *Lon* from 10. *St Richard's Vicarage, 35 Forge Lane, Feltham TW13 6UN* T: (020) 8893 4935 E: craigholmes@strichardshanworth.org

HOLMES (formerly WARD), Mrs Elizabeth Joyce. b 42. Open Univ BA. WEMTC 04. **d** 06 **p** 07. OLM Painswick, Sheepscombe, Cranham, The Edge etc *Glouc* 06–11; rtd 11; PtO *Truro* from 16. *Arbour Cottage, Mount Hawke, Truro TR4 8EE* T: (01209) 890388 E: e.holmes154@btinternet.com

HOLMES, Geoffrey Robert. b 70. Nottm Univ BSc 89 Sheff Univ PhD 13. Ridley Hall Cam BA 92. **d** 93 **p** 94. C Clifton St Jas *Sheff* 93–98; V Worsbrough St Thos and St Jas 98–05. *Address withheld by request* E: geoff.r.holmes@sheffield.ac.uk

HOLMES, Grant Wenlock. b 54. St Steph Ho Ox BA 78 MA 83. **d** 79 **p** 80. C Benhilton *S'wark* 79–82; C-in-c S Kenton Annunciation CD *Lon* 82–86; Tutor Chich Th Coll 86–87; Bp's Dom Chapl *Chich* 86–88; V Mayfield 88–99; P-in-c Mark Cross 97–99; Asst Chapl Lewisham Hosp NHS Trust 99–01; Lead Chapl Kingston Hosp NHS Foundn Trust Surrey 01–14; Hon C Barnes *S'wark* 01–06; V St Alb St Mary Marshalswick from 14. *The Old Rectory, Sumpter Yard, Holywell Hill, St Albans AL1 1BY* T: (01727) 890260 E: wenlockholmes@gmail.com

HOLMES, Jane Margaret. b 57. Ridley Hall Cam 05. **d** 07 **p** 08. C Stamford Ch Ch *Linc* 07–11; P-in-c Gayton, Gayton Thorpe, E Walton, E Winch etc *Nor* 11–15; P-in-c Grimston, Congham and Roydon 14–15; P-in-c Gt w Lt Massingham, Harpley, Rougham etc 14–15; TR Ashwicken w Leziate, Bawsey etc from 15. *The Rectory, Grimston Road, Gayton, King's Lynn PE32 1QA* T: (01553) 636227 E: jmh200@btinternet.com

HOLMES, Mrs Janet Ellen. b 61. Wolv Univ BSc 95 RCN MSc 99 RGN 82. Qu Coll Birm MA 09. **d** 09 **p** 10. C Hadley and Wellington Ch Ch *Lich* 09–12; C Cen Telford

11–12; TV from 12; Chapl Severn Hospice from 15. *Sutton Bank Farm, Sutton, Newport TF10 8DD* T: (01952) 813658 M: 07980-521064 E: janeteholmes@btinternet.com or janet@telfordchurch.co.uk

HOLMES, Canon John Robin. b 42. Leeds Univ BA 64. Linc Th Coll 64. **d** 66 **p** 67. C Wyther *Ripon* 66–69; C Adel 69–73; V Beeston Hill St Luke 73–76; V Holbeck 76–86; RD Armley 82–86; V Manston 86–93; Hon Can Ripon Cathl 89–98; Dioc Missr 93–98; Can Missr *Wakef* 98–07; rtd 07; PtO *Leeds* from 17; *York* from 17. *54 West Crayke, Bridlington YO16 6XW* T: (01262) 424101 M: 07712-044364 E: canon.john@sky.com

HOLMES, Jonathan Michael. b 49. Qu Coll Cam BA 70 MA 74 VetMB 73 PhD 78 MRCVS 73. Ridley Hall Cam 87. **d** 88 **p** 89. Chapl Qu Coll Cam 88–13; Dean of Chpl 94–14; rtd 14; PtO *Ely* from 15. *Queens' College, Cambridge CB3 9ET* T: (01223) 335545 F: 335522 E: jmh38@cam.ac.uk

HOLMES, Nigel Peter. b 48. Nottm Univ BTh 72 Lanc Univ CertEd 72 Lon Univ BD 76 Sheff Univ MEd 84. Kelham Th Coll. **d** 72 **p** 73. C Barrow St Matt *Carl* 72–75; C Derby St Bart 75–78; P-in-c Gt Barlow 78–84; V Carl St Herbert w St Steph 84–91; V Keswick St Jo 91–94; V Mexborough *Sheff* 94–97; P-in-c Nether Hoyland St Pet 97–98; P-in-c Nether Hoyland St Andr 97–98; V Hoyland 98–07; AD Tankersley 04–07; V Monk Bretton *Wakef* 07–09; rtd 09. *6 The Signals, Widdrington, Morpeth NE61 5QU* E: paxlives@btinternet.com

HOLMES, Peter Anthony. b 55. Univ of Wales (Ban) BA 77 Brighton Poly CertEd 78. Trin Coll Bris. **d** 88 **p** 89. C Croydon Ch Ch *S'wark* 88–93; V Norbiton from 93; RD Kingston 97–00. *The Vicarage, 21 Wolsey Close, Kingston upon Thames KT2 7ER* T: (020) 8942 8330 or 8546 3212 E: revdrock@yahoo.co.uk

HOLMES, Prof Peter Geoffrey. b 32. Bris Univ BSc 59 MSc 69 Leic Univ PhD 74 CEng FIEE. St Deiniol's Hawarden 74. **d** 76 **p** 77. NSM Glen Parva and S Wigston *Leic* 76–02; Prof Nottm Poly 85–92; Prof Nottm Trent Univ 92–96; rtd 02; PtO *Leic* 02–16. *19 Windsor Avenue, Glen Parva, Leicester LE2 9TQ* T: 0116-277 4534 E: peterholmes@iee.org

HOLMES, Peter John. b 41. Reading Univ TCert 63 Open Univ BA 76 K Coll Lon BA 96 AKC 96 MA 97 Glas Univ PhD 02. St Steph Ho Ox 03. **d** 04 **p** 05. NSM Beaconsfield *Ox* 04–08; PtO 08–10; *Pet* 11–13 and from 16. *14 Bayley Close, Uppingham, Oakham LE15 9TG* T: (01572) 821834 E: peterholmes734@gmail.com or p.holmes4@icloud.com

HOLMES, Roger Cockburn. b 46. Jes Coll Ox BA 70 MA 84 Edin Univ BD 76. Edin Th Coll 73. **d** 84 **p** 85. Canada 84–88; R Ditchingham w Pirnough *Nor* 88–90; R Hedenham 88–90; R Broome 88–90; R Ditchingham, Hedenham and Broome 90–93; V Helmsley *York* 93–97; PtO *Wakef* 07. *7 Bishopgate, Howden, Goole DN14 7AD* T: (01430) 430880 E: fatherholmes@hotmail.com

HOLMES, Roy Grant. b 37. Ox NSM Course 83. **d** 86 **p** 87. NSM Wokingham St Paul *Ox* from 86. *58 Copse Drive, Wokingham RG41 1LX* T: 0118-978 4141

HOLMES, Stephen. b 54. St Andr Univ MTheol 84. Chich Th Coll 84. **d** 86 **p** 87. C Croydon St Jo *S'wark* 86–89; C Tewkesbury w Walton Cardiff *Glouc* 89–92; P-in-c Bournemouth St Luke *Win* 92–94; V 94–10; P-in-c N Stoneham and Bassett 10–15; rtd 15; PtO *Win* from 16; *Sarum* from 16. *Palmyra House, 7 St Luke's Road, Bournemouth BH3 7LR* T: (01202) 252201 E: liberanos7@gmail.com

HOLMES, Canon Stephen John. b 50. CertEd 72. Trin Coll Bris 81 Sarum & Wells Th Coll 88. **d** 89 **p** 90. C Skegness and Winthorpe *Linc* 89–93; P-in-c Mablethorpe w Trusthorpe 93–97; V Hadleigh St Barn *Chelmsf* 97–07; R Gt and Lt Leighs and Lt Waltham 07–14; rtd 14; PtO *Chelmsf* from 16; Can Roray Tanzania from 18. *105 Grand Parade, Leigh-on-Sea SS9 1DW* T: (01702) 875381 E: familyholmes@hotmail.co.uk

HOLMES, Stephen Mark. b 65. St Andr Univ MA 87 Pontifical Univ Maynooth BD 04 Edin Univ PhD 13 CCC Cam PGCE 88 FSAScot 98 FRHistS 15. TISEC 11. **d** 04 **p** 04. In RC Ch 04–08; NSM Edin Old St Paul 12–14; P-in-c Edin St Marg 13–14; C Edin St Jo 14–18; R Padstow, St Merryn and St Issey w St Petroc Minor *Truro* from 18; Tutor Scottish Episc Inst from 16. *The Rectory, 46 Treverbyn Road, Padstow PL28 8DN* M: 07584-091870 E: rectorpmil@gmail.com

HOLMES, Susan. b 46. Leeds Univ LLB 68 Univ of Wales LLM 00. **d** 06 **p** 07. NSM Scotby and Cotehill w Cumwhinton *Carl* 06–11; rtd 11; PtO *Carl* from 11. *Woodside, Great Corby, Carlisle CA4 8LL* T: (01228) 560617 E: susan@gtcorby.plus.com

HOLMES, Trevor Norman. b 61. TCD BSc 82 NUI MBA 94. CITC MTh 15. **d** 13 **p** 15. NSM Julianstown and Colpe w Drogheda and Duleek *M & K* 13–15; NSM Mullingar, Portnashangan, Moyliscar, Kilbixy etc from 15; Vice Pres

External and Strategic Affairs Dublin City Univ *D & G* from 14; PtO from 15. *45 Parsons Hall, Rathcoffey Road, Maynooth, Co Kildare, Republic of Ireland* T: (00353) (1) 629 0182 M: 87-242 5560 E: trevor.n.holmes@gmail.com

HOLMES, William John. b 49. d 97 p 98. Aux Min Billy w Derrykeighan *Conn* 97–02; Aux Min Ballymoney w Finvoy and Rasharkin 02–14; NSM Killowen *D & R* from 14. *14 Glenlough Park, Coleraine BT52 1TY* T: (028) 7035 5993 M: 07780-916795 E: william149@btinternet.com *or* billyh851@gmail.com

HOLROYD, John Richard. b 54. Liv Univ BA 75 PGCE 77. Wycliffe Hall Ox 78. d 81 p 82. C Gt Stanmore *Lon* 81–84; Min Can, V Choral and Prec St E Cathl 84–89; TV Wolverton *Ox* 89–96; P-in-c Maidenhead St Luke 96–10; P-in-c Cotham St Sav w St Mary and Clifton St Paul *Bris* 10–14; V 14–17; rtd 17. *Bredon, Church Lane, Whittington, Worcester WR5 2RQ* E: richardholroyd@mac.com

HOLROYD, Stephen Charles. b 56. UEA BA 79. St Jo Coll Nottm 84. d 87 p 88. C Barton Seagrave w Warkton *Pet* 87–91; V Eye 91–97; V Silsoe, Pulloxhill and Flitton *St Alb* 97–14; P-in-c The Stodden Churches from 14. *Stodden Rectory, High Street, Upper Dean, Huntingdon PE28 0ND* E: stephenholroyd@btinternet.com

HOLROYD-THOMAS, Dominic John. b 94. Dur Univ BA 18. Westcott Ho Cam 14. d 17 p 18. C Welwyn *St Alb* from 17. *St Michael's House, 3 London Road, Woolmer Green, Knebworth SG3 6JU* T: (01438) 813043 E: curate@welwyn.org.uk

HOLT, Andrew Michael. b 82. K Coll Lon LLB 05. Oak Hill Th Coll BA 18. d 18 p 19. C Kensington St Helen w H Trin *Lon* from 18. *First Floor Flat, 79 St Quintin Avenue, London W10 6PB* M: 07747-843018 E: andrewmholt@outlook.com

HOLT, Mrs Claire Frances. b 66. Bris Univ BSc 88 Kingston Poly PGCE 89. STETS 02. d 05 p 06. C N Farnborough *Guildf* 05–12; P-in-c Tongham 12–14; V from 14. *The Vicarage, Poyle Road, Tongham, Farnham GU10 1DU* T: (01252) 782790 E: clairefholt@hotmail.com *or* claire@stpaulstongham.org.uk

HOLT, Canon David. b 44. St Jo Coll Dur BSc 67. d 70 p 71. C Blackley St Pet *Man* 70–73; C Radcliffe St Thos 73–74; C Radcliffe St Thos and St Jo 74–75; V Ashton St Pet 75–79; Dioc Youth Officer *Guildf* 80–85; V Bagshot 85–97; RD Surrey Heath 92–97; V Fleet 97–03; RD Aldershot 98–03; Hon Can Guildf Cathl 99–03; rtd 03; PtO *Guildf* from 03; *Ox* from 06. *62 Lynwood Drive, Mytchett, Camberley GU16 6BY* T: (01276) 507538 M: 07974-354411 E: david.holt10@ntlworld.com

HOLT, Canon Douglas Robert. b 49. MA. Ridley Hall Cam. d 82 p 83. C Cambridge St Barn *Ely* 82–84; P-in-c 84–86; V 86–91; V Ealing St Mary *Lon* 91–98; Dioc Dir Strategy Support *Bris* 98–09; Can Res Bris Cathl 98–10; Hon Can and Dioc Dir Strategy Support 10–14; rtd 14; PtO *Bris* 14–16; P-in-c Hove St Jo *Chich* 14–18; PtO *Bris* from 19. *71 High Street, Malmesbury SN16 9AG* E: douglas.holt49@gmail.com

HOLT, Francis Thomas. b 38. Edin Th Coll 79. d 81 p 82. C Cullercoats St Geo *Newc* 81–83; C Ponteland 83–86; Chapl Worc Coll of HE 86–89; R Worc St Clem 86–93; V Finstall 93–96; Chapl Menorca *Eur* 96–97; rtd 98; PtO *Worc* 97–13; *Newc* from 13. *34 Meadow Grange, Berwick-upon-Tweed TD15 1NW*

HOLT, Jack Derek. b 38. Trin Coll Bris 71. d 73 p 74. C Daubhill *Man* 73–76; P-in-c Thornham w Gravel Hole 76–79; V 79–83; R Talke *Lich* 83–93; V Cotmanhay *Derby* 93–03; Chapl Derbyshire Mental Health Services NHS Trust 93–03; rtd 03; PtO *Lich* 03–19. *31 Hatherton Close, Newcastle ST5 7SN* T: (01782) 560845

HOLT, James Edward. b 49. St Martin's Coll Lanc BA 94 PGCE 95. NOC 99. d 02 p 04. NSM Holme-in-Cliviger w Worsthorne *Blackb* 02–03; NSM Whalley 03–12; NSM W Pendleside 12–19; PtO from 19. *15 Wheatley Close, Fence, Burnley BB12 9QH* T: (01282) 778319 E: jimeholt@btinternet.com

HOLT, Mrs Lucinda Jane. b 65. Open Univ BSc 00. Wycliffe Hall Ox 01. d 03 p 04. C Newton Longville and Mursley w Swanbourne etc *Ox* 03–06; TV Riverside 06–08; V Eton w Eton Wick, Boveney and Dorney 08–13; R Poole *Sarum* from 13; RD Poole and N Bournemouth from 16. *The Rectory, 10 Poplar Close, Poole BH15 1LP* T: (01202) 672694 E: revlucy@tiscali.co.uk *or* lucy.stjamespoole@hotmail.co.uk

HOLT, Michael. b 38. Univ of Wales (Lamp) BA 61. St D Coll Lamp. d 63 p 64. C Stand *Man* 63–69; V Bacup St Jo 69–03; AD Rossendale 98–00; rtd 03; PtO *Man* from 03. *22 Windermere Road, Bacup OL13 9DN* T: (01706) 877976 M: 07884-241575 E: hoplite@talktalk.net

HOLT, Shirley Ann. b 48. d 98 p 99. OLM High Oak, Hingham and Scoulton w Wood Rising *Nor* 98–14; PtO from 14. *Westfield, 59 Church Lane, Wicklewood, Wymondham NR18 9QH* T: (01953) 603668 E: saholt@talk21.com

HOLT, Stephen Richard. b 64. Leeds Univ BA 11. Coll of Resurr Mirfield 09. d 11 p 12. C Gt Grimsby St Mary and St Jas *Linc* 11–14; C Boston 14–18; V Carr Dyke Gp from 18. *The Vicarage, 6 Walcott Road, Billinghay, Lincoln LN4 4EH* T: (01526) 580654 M: 07722-117519 E: steve.carrdyke@gmail.com

⊕**HOLTAM, The Rt Revd Nicholas Roderick.** b 54. Collingwood Coll Dur BA 75 K Coll Lon BD 78 AKC 78 FKC 05 Dur Univ MA 89 Hon DCL 05. Westcott Ho Cam 78. d 79 p 80 c 11. C Stepney St Dunstan and All SS *Lon* 79–83; Tutor Linc Th Coll 83–88; V Is of Dogs Ch Ch and St Jo w St Luke *Lon* 88–95; V St Martin-in-the-Fields 95–11; Bp Sarum from 11. *South Canonry, 71 The Close, Salisbury SP1 2ER* T: (01722) 334031 F: 413112 E: bishop.salisbury@salisbury.anglican.org

HOLTH, Øystein Johan (Stein). b 31. Open Univ BA 75. AKC 54. d 54 p 55. C Greenford H Cross *Lon* 54–56; Br N Borneo and Sarawak 56–63; E Malaysia 63–67; Chapl OHP and St Hilda's Sch Whitby 67–75; P-in-c Pimlico St Barn *Lon* 75–97; Ind Chapl 75–97; rtd 97; PtO *Lon* from 97. *13 Dollis Park, London N3 1HJ* T: (020) 8346 8131 E: steinandclare@holth.de

HOLZAPFEL, Mrs Christine Anne. b 53. Ex Univ BA 74 PGCE 75. WMMTC 04. d 07 p 08. C Worc SE 07–10; P-in-c Finstall 10–12; C Catshill and Dodford 10–12; TV Bromsgrove 12–14; TR 14–17; V Dodford 14–17; Harnhill Cen of Chr Healing from 17; PtO *Glouc* from 19. *The Harnhill Centre of Christian Healing, Harnhill Manor, Harnhill, Cirencester GL7 5PX* T: (01285) 850283 M: 07749-898698 E: c.holzapfel15@gmail.com *or* christineh@harnhillcentre.org.uk

HOMDEN, Peter David. b 56. Roehampton Coll BA 06. STETS 07. d 09 p 10. C Heatherlands St Jo *Sarum* from 09. *72 Alexandra Road, Poole BH14 9EW* T: (01202) 241437 M: 07841-699094 E: homdenhome@virginmedia.com

HOMER, Rosemary Louise. b 86. Ripon Coll Cuddesdon 15. d 18 p 19. C Coplow *Leic* from 18. *20A Weare Close, Billesdon, Leicesster LE7 9DY* E: rosiehomer1@gmail.com

HOMFRAY, Kenyon Lee James. b 55. TCD BTh 99 MA 03 Univ of Wales (Cardiff) LLM 02. CITC 96. d 99 p 00. C Convoy w Monellan and Donaghmore *D & R* 99–02; I 02–05; I Bunclody w Kildavin, Clonegal and Kilrush *C & O* 05–11; rtd 12. *Garrankyle, Cloneen, Fethard, Co Tipperary, Republic of Ireland* E: homfrayk@eircom.net

HONES, Simon Anthony. b 54. Sussex Univ BSc 75. Qu Coll Birm. d 79 p 80. C Win Ch Ch 79–82; C Basing 82–88; Min Chineham CD 88–90; V Surbiton St Matt *S'wark* 90–08; TR 08–11; P-in-c Marchwood *Win* from 11. *St John's Vicarage, Vicarage Road, Marchwood, Southampton SO40 4SX* T: (023) 8086 1496 E: simon.hones@btinternet.com

HONEY, Mrs Elizabeth Katherine. b 81. Keble Coll Ox MA 07. Wycliffe Hall Ox 06. d 09 p 10. C Furze Platt *Ox* 09–13; Pioneer Min *Derby* from 13. *119 Francis Street, Derby DE21 6DE* T: (01332) 299110 M: 07883-470158 E: revhoney@live.co.uk *or* benandbethderby@gmail.com

HONEY, Canon Frederick Bernard. b 22. Selw Coll Cam BA 48 MA 72. Wells Th Coll 48. d 50 p 51. C S'wark St Geo 50–52; C Claines St Jo *Worc* 52–55; V Wollaston 55–87; RD Stourbridge 72–83; Hon Can Worc Cathl 75–87; rtd 87. *38 Park Farm, Bourton-on-the-Water, Cheltenham GL54 2HF* T: (01451) 822218

HONEY, Canon Thomas David. b 56. Lon Univ BA 78. Ripon Coll Cuddesdon 80. d 83 p 84. C Mill End and Heronsgate w W Hyde *St Alb* 83–86; C Stepney St Dunstan and All SS *Lon* 86–89; TV High Wycombe *Ox* 89–95; P-in-c Headington Quarry 95–07; Can Res and Treas Ex Cathl 07–10; V Ex St Dav 10–17; Chapl St Mich Hosp Basingstoke from 17. *St Michael's Hospice, Park Prewett, Aldermaston Road, Basingstoke RG24 9NB* T: (01256) 844744 E: tom.honey@stmichaelshospice.org.uk

HONEYMAN, Jennifer Mary. *See* LANE, Jennifer Mary

HONOR MARGARET, Sister. *See* McILROY, Honor Margaret

HONOUR, Colin Reginald. b 44. Lanc Univ CertEd 69 Man Univ AdDipEd 75 Newc Univ MEd 80. NOC 88. d 91 p 92. NSM Walmsley *Man* 91; C Middleton 92–94; R Holcombe 94–01; P-in-c Hawkshaw Lane 99–01; P-in-c Aldingham, Dendron, Rampside and Urswick *Carl* 01–03; R 03–09; rtd 09; PtO *Carl* from 10. *1 Crow Wood, Heversham, Milnthorpe LA7 7ER* T: (015395) 64357 E: cnchonour@btinternet.com

HONOUR, Derek Gordon. b 59. Bath Univ BSc 84. St Jo Coll Nottm. d 89 p 90. C High Wycombe *Ox* 89–91; C Brightside w Wincobank *Sheff* 91–94; P-in-c Dawley St Jerome *Lon* 94–01; C Derby St Alkmund and St Werburgh 01–05; V Stoke Hill *Guildf* 05–09; P-in-c Derby St Barn 09–13; V from 13. *St Barnabas' Vicarage, 122 Radbourne Street, Derby DE22 3BU* T: (01332) 342553 E: dghonour@ad.co.uk

HONOUR, Mrs Joanna Clare. b 61. Westmr Coll Ox BEd 83. St Jo Coll Nottm 86. **d** 89 **p** 94. Par Dn High Wycombe *Ox* 89–91; Par Dn Brightside w Wincobank *Sheff* 91–94; C 94; Dep Chapl HM Pris Wandsworth 95–97; Chapl HM Pris The Mount 97; NSM Dawley St Jerome *Lon* 96–01; Chapl HM Pris Foston Hall 01–05; Chapl HM Pris Coldingley 06–09; Chapl HM Pris Whatton 09–16; Hon Can S'well Minster 15–16; Chapl HM Pris Stafford from 16. *HM Prison, 54 Gaol Street, Stafford ST16 3AW* T: (01785) 773000 E: jo.honour@justice.gov.uk

HONOUR, Jonathan Paul. b 68. Ox Brookes Univ BSc 90 Greenwich Univ PGCE 91. St Jo Coll Nottm MA 98. **d** 99 **p** 00. C Tonbridge St Steph *Roch* 99–03; TV Woodley *Ox* 03–08; V Guernsey H Trin *Win* from 08. *Holy Trinity Vicarage, Brock Road, St Peter Port, Guernsey GY1 1RS* T: (01481) 724382 M: 07752-241255 E: jonhonour@googlemail.com

HOOD, Mrs Doreen. b 38. Open Univ BA 90 SRN 59 RFN 61. NEOC 90. **d** 93 **p** 94. NSM Cullercoats St Geo *Newc* 93–99; NSM Monkseaton St Pet 99–00; P-in-c Newc St Hilda 00–03; rtd 03; PtO *Newc* from 03. *24 Keswick Drive, North Shields NE30 3EW* T: 0191-253 1762

HOOD, Mrs Elizabeth Mary. b 57. Ex Univ BA 79. ERMC 05. **d** 08 **p** 09. C Boxmoor St Jo *St Alb* 08–12; TV Langelei 12–18; TR from 18; AD Hemel Hempstead from 15. *The Vicarage, 14 Pancake Lane, Hemel Hempstead HP2 4NB* T: (01442) 264860 E: lizziehood@aol.com

HOOD, Miss Jennifer Louise. St Mich Coll Llan. **d** 10 **p** 11. C Glanogwen and Llanllechid w St Ann's and Pentir *Ban* 10–13; Chapl Salford R NHS Foundn Trust from 14. *Salford Royal NHS Foundation Trust, Hope Hospital, Stott Lane, Salford M6 8HD* T: 0161-789 7373 E: jenniferhood.7@hotmail.co.uk *or* jennifer.hood@srft.nhs.uk

HOOD, Mrs Linda. b 47. Leeds Univ BA 68. St Jo Coll Nottm 07. **d** 09 **p** 10. NSM Chase Terrace *Lich* 09–15; NSM Burntwood, Chase Terrace etc 15–17; rtd 17; PtO *Lich* from 18. *13 Mossbank Avenue, Burntwood WS7 4UN* T: (01543) 301728 M: 07786-987114 E: linda_hoodburntwood@hotmail.co.uk

HOOD, Peter Michael. b 47. Sheff Univ BSc 68. Wycliffe Hall Ox 70. **d** 73 **p** 74. C Soundwell *Bris* 73–76; P-in-c Walcot St Andr CD 76–77; TV Swindon St Jo and St Andr 77–80; V Esh and Hamsteels *Dur* 80–88; V Stockton St Paul 88–00; P-in-c Herrington 00–05; P-in-c Penshaw 00–05; P-in-c Shiney Row 00–05; R Herrington, Penshaw and Shiney Row 05–07; Lic to Adn Sunderland and Houghton Deanery 07–12; rtd 12; PtO *Dur* from 12. *1 Victory Street East, Hetton le Hole, Houghton le Spring DH5 9DN* T: 0191-526 9187 E: revphood@talktalk.net

HOOD, Stephen William. b 61. **d** 13 **p** 14. NSM New Milverton *Cov* 13–16; NSM Wellesbourne from 16; NSM Walton d'Eiville from 16. *Millbrook House, Wasperton, Warwick CV35 8EB* T: (01926) 624579 E: steve.hood@accel.org.uk

HOOK, Canon Ian Kevin. b 57. Trin Coll Bris 93. **d** 95 **p** 96. C Dalton-in-Furness *Carl* 95–98; C Newbarns w Hawcoat 98–01; V Barrow St Mark 01–17; P-in-c Barrow 06–11; Hon Can Carl Cathl 10–17; rtd 17. *Craiglea, Brodick, Isle of Arran KA27 8AJ* E: ianhook@dsl.pipex.com

HOOK (*née* KAMINSKI), Mrs Julia Ann. b 55. WEMTC 07. **d** 10 **p** 11. NSM Winchcombe *Glouc* from 10; TV from 14. *18 Ratcliff Lawns, Southam, Cheltenham GL52 3PA* T: (01242) 519346 M: 07715-953076 E: julia.hook@btinternet.com

HOOK, Neil. b 73. Univ of Wales (Swansea) BA 94 Univ of Wales (Cardiff) BD 96. St Mich Coll Llan 94. **d** 97 **p** 98. C Brecon St Mary and Battle w Llanddew *S & B* 97–99; Min Can Brecon Cathl 97–99; P-in-c Llanllyr-yn-Rhos w Llanfihangel Helygen 99–00; V Upper Wye 00–05; P-in-c Trallwng w Bettws Penpont w Aberyskir etc 05–09; P-in-c Cynog Honddu 08–09; V Dan yr Eppynt 10–12; V Builth and Llanddewi'r Cwm w Llangynog etc 12–15; V Buallt from 15. *The Vicarage, 1 North Road, Builth Wells LD2 3BT* T: (01982) 552355 E: frhooky@gmail.com

HOOPER, Preb Derek Royston. b 33. St Edm Hall Ox BA 57 MA 65. Cuddesdon Coll 57. **d** 59 **p** 60. C Gt Walsingham *Nor* 59–62; C Townstall w Dartmouth *Ex* 62–65; V Lynton and Brendon 65–69; C Littleham w Exmouth 70–72; TV 72–79; R Wrington w Butcombe *B & W* 79–94; Preb Wells Cathl 93–94; rtd 94; PtO *Ex* from 95; *B & W* 95–00 and 16–19. *23 Dagmar Road, Exmouth EX8 2AN* T: (01395) 272831

HOOPER, Geoffrey Michael. b 39. Univ of Wales (Ban) MA 07. K Coll Lon 61. **d** 66 **p** 67. C Chesterfield St Mary and All SS *Derby* 66–69; Chapl RAF 69–74; P-in-c Hook Norton w Swerford and Wigginton *Ox* 74–80; P-in-c Gt Rollright 75–80; R Hook Norton w Gt Rollright, Swerford etc 80–82; Warden Mansf Ho Univ Settlement Plaistow 82–00; Dir 86–00; rtd 03; PtO *Ban* from 09. *2 Mount Pleasant, Corris, Machynlleth SY20 9RL* T: (01654) 761392 M: 07740-467426 E: geoffrey.hooper678@btinternet.com

HOOPER, Ian. b 44. St Jo Coll York CertEd 67. Trin Coll Bris. **d** 88 **p** 89. C Martlesham w Brightwell *St E* 88–92; R Pakenham w Norton and Tostock 92–09; RD Ixworth 03–09; rtd 09; PtO *St E* from 09; Dioc Retirement Officer from 10. *26 Drake Close, Stowmarket IP14 1UP* T: (01449) 770179 E: ianavrilhooper126@btinternet.com

✠**HOOPER, The Rt Revd Michael Wrenford.** b 41. Univ of Wales (Lamp) BA 63. St Steph Ho Ox 63. **d** 65 **p** 66 **c** 02. C Bridgnorth St Mary *Heref* 65–70; P-in-c Habberley 70–78; R 78–81; V Minsterley 70–81; RD Pontesbury 75–80; Preb Heref Cathl 81–02; V Leominster 81–85; TR 85–97; P-in-c Eyton 81–85; RD Leominster 81–97; P-in-c Eye, Croft w Yarpole and Lucton 91–97; Adn Heref 97–02; Suff Bp Ludlow 02–09; Adn Ludlow 02–09; rtd 09; Hon Asst Bp Worc from 10. *6 Avon Drive, Eckington, Pershore WR10 3BU* T: (01386) 751589 E: bishopmichael@btinternet.com

HOOPER, The Ven Paul Denis Gregory. b 52. Man Univ BA 75 Ox Univ BA 80 MA 87. Wycliffe Hall Ox 78. **d** 81 **p** 82. C Leeds St Geo *Ripon* 81–84; Dioc Youth Officer 84–87; Bp's Dom Chapl 87–95; Dioc Communications Officer 87–97; V Harrogate St Mark 95–09; AD Harrogate 05–09; Dir Clergy Development 09–12; Adn Leeds 12–16; Hon Can Ripon Cathl 08–16; rtd 16. *9 Fulwith Gate, Harrogate HG2 8HS* E: ven.paul.hooper@outlook.com

HOOPER, Canon Peter George. b 62. BSc PhD. Catholic Inst of Toulouse 04. **d** 06 **p** 07. C Melton Mowbray *Leic* 06–10; TR Bradgate Team 10–15; R Groby and Ratby 15–16; R Peckleton 15–16; AD Sparkenhoe E 11–16; P-in-c Ab Kettleby and Holwell w Asfordby from 16; C Old Dalby, Nether Broughton, Saxelbye etc from 18; AD Framland from 16; Dioc Rural Officer from 11; Hon Can Leic Cathl from 16. *2 Church Lane, Asfordby, Melton Mowbray LE14 3RU* T: (01664) 812191 E: peter.hooper@live.com

HOPE, Charles Henry. b 64. Regent's Park Coll Ox BA 87 MA 90 St Jo Coll Dur BA 90 FRGS 82. Cranmer Hall Dur. **d** 90 **p** 91. C Tynemouth St Jo *Newc* 90–94; V 94–03; P-in-c Prudhoe 03–07; V 07–16; P-in-c Keswick St Jo *Carl* 16–18; C Upper Derwent 16–18; V Keswick St Jo w Borrowdale from 18; P-in-c St John's-in-the-Vale, Threlkeld and Wythburn from 18; RD Derwent from 17; CF(V) from 94. *St John's Vicarage, Ambleside Road, Keswick CA12 4DD* T: (01768) 775855 E: charleshope@btopenworld.com

HOPE, Colin Frederick. b 49. St Mich Coll Llan 73. **d** 76 **p** 77. C Warrington St Elphin *Liv* 76–80; V Newton-le-Willows 80–84; CSWG from 84; LtO *Chich* from 88. *The Monastery, Crawley Down, Crawley RH10 4LH* T: (01342) 712074 E: father.colin@cswg.org.uk

HOPE, Robert. b 36. Dur Univ BSc 61. Clifton Th Coll 61. **d** 63 **p** 64. C Woking St Mary *Guildf* 63–66; C Surbiton Hill Ch Ch *S'wark* 66–68; Th Students' Sec IVF 68–71; Hon C Wallington *S'wark* 69–71; C Ox St Ebbe w St Pet 71–74; V Walshaw Ch Ch *Man* 74–87; TR Radipole and Melcombe Regis *Sarum* 87–93; rtd 93; PtO *St D* from 93. *1A Swiss Valley, Felinfael, Llanelli SA14 8BS* T: (01554) 759199

HOPE, Canon Susan. b 49. St Jo Coll Dur BA 83 Sheff Univ MA 04. Cranmer Hall Dur 80. **dss** 83 **d** 87 **p** 94. Boston Spa *York* 83–86; Brightside w Wincobank *Sheff* 86–97; Par Dn 87–89; Dn-in-c 89–94; V 94–97; V Chapeltown 97–02; Dioc Missr 02–07; RD Tankersley 00–02; Dir Tr Wilson Carlile Coll of Evang 07–08; Six Preacher Cant Cathl 99–09; Hon Can Sheff Cathl 00–09; P-in-c Shipley St Paul *Bradf* 09–14; V 14; *Leeds* 14–16; Dioc Adv in Evang *Bradf* 09–14; *Leeds* 14–16; Hon Can Bradf Cathl 12–16; rtd 16; Chapl Wycliffe Hall Ox 16–18; PtO *Dur* from 18. *14 Sunderland Bridge, Durham DH6 5HD* T: 0191-908 5400 M: 07736-774937 E: shope12443@aol.com

✠**HOPE OF THORNES, The Rt Revd and Rt Hon Lord (David Michael).** b 40. Nottm Univ BA 62 Linacre Ho Ox DPhil 65 Hon FGCM 94. St Steph Ho Ox 62. **d** 65 **p** 66 **c** 85. C W Derby St Jo *Liv* 65–67 and 68–70; Chapl Bucharest *Eur* 67–68; V Orford St Andr *Liv* 70–74; Prin St Steph Ho Ox 74–82; V St Marylebone All SS *Lon* 82–85; Master of Guardians Shrine of Our Lady of Walsingham 82–93; Bp Wakef 85–91; Bp Lon 91–95; Dean of HM Chpls Royal 91–95; Abp York 95–05; rtd 05; PtO *Ilkley St Marg Bradf* 05–06; Hon Asst Bp Bradf 05–14; Hon Asst Bp Eur 07–12; Hon Asst Bp Blackb from 08; PtO *Leeds* from 17; Hon Asst Bp Leeds from 19. *35 Hammerton Drive, Hellifield, Skipton BD23 4LZ* E: dmhhellifield@gmail.com

HOPE-BELL, Mrs Vanessa Anne. b 45. TCD BA 67 Univ of Wales (Swansea) MEd 98. **d** 14 **p** 15. NSM Catheiniog *St D* from 14. *The Mill House, Llansadwrn, Llanwrda SA19 8LW* T: (01550) 777239 E: v.hopebell@btinternet.com

HOPEGOOD JONES, Mrs Emma Kate. b 88. K Coll Lon BMus 09. Ripon Coll Cuddesdon 14. **d** 17 **p** 18. C Hanborough and Freeland *Ox* from 17. *4 The Cairns, Swan*

Lane, Long Hanborough, Witney OX29 8LT M: 07896-558932
E: emma.hopegood.jones@gmail.com

HOPEWELL, Canon Jeffery Stewart. b 52. Leic Univ BA 75 ACA 79. EMMTC 82. **d** 85 **p** 86. NSM Houghton on the Hill w Keyham *Leic* 85–88; NSM Houghton-on-the-Hill, Keyham and Hungarton 88–91; C Syston 91–93; TV 93–97; Bp's Ecum Adv 91–97; P-in-c Wymeswold and Prestwold w Hoton 97–04; V Old Dalby, Nether Broughton, Saxelbye etc 04–15; Dioc Ecum Officer 03–06; Hon Can Leic Cathl 14–15; rtd 15; PtO *Leic* from 15. *23 Weare Close, Billesdon, Leicester LE7 9DY* T: 0116-259 9760 E: jshopewell@btinternet.com

HOPKIN, David James. b 67. Birm Univ BTh 94 Univ of Wales MA 14. Ripon Coll Cuddesdon 98. **d** 99 **p** 00. C Wickford and Runwell *Chelmsf* 99–02; TV Penistone and Thurlstone *Wakef* 02–06; TR 06–14; TR Penistone and Thurlstone *Sheff* from 14; AD Tankersley from 19. *The Vicarage, Shrewsbury Road, Penistone, Sheffield S36 6DY* T: (01226) 370954 or 370006 E: david.hopkin@sheffield.org or fatherdavid.pen@outlook.com

HOPKIN WILLIAMS, Jeffrey. *See* WILLIAMS, Robert Jeffrey Hopkin

HOPKINS, Mrs Angela Joan. b 42. Bp Otter Coll Chich CertEd 64. S Dios Minl Tr Scheme 92. **d** 95 **p** 96. NSM Kingsbury H Innocents *Lon* 95–13; PtO from 13. *3 Regal Way, Harrow HA3 0RZ* T: (020) 8907 1045 E: ahopkins762@btinternet.com

HOPKINS, Brenda Alison. b 63. St Martin's Coll Lanc BA 95 Anglia Poly Univ MA 97. Westcott Ho Cam 95. **d** 97 **p** 98. C Camberwell St Geo *S'wark* 97–00; Chapl Nor City Coll of F&HE 00–03. *Rose Tree Cottage, The Green, Stokesby, Great Yarmouth NR29 3EX*

HOPKINS, Christopher John. b 61. Trin Coll Bris 11. **d** 13 **p** 14. C Somerton w Compton Dundon, the Charltons etc *B & W* 13–16; P-in-c Baltonsborough w Butleigh, W Bradley etc from 16. *The Vicarage, Ham Street, Baltonsborough, Glastonbury BA6 8PX* T: (01458) 851681 E: bruebeneficevicar@btinternet.com

HOPKINS, Gillian Frances. b 55. Bedf Coll Lon BA 76 SS Mark & Jo Univ Coll Plymouth PGCE 77 Cam Inst of Educn MA 91. NTMTC BA 07. **d** 07 **p** 08. C Wickford and Runwell *Chelmsf* 07–10; TV Waltham H Cross 10–16; PtO from 16. *15 Ferndown, Woodford Road, London E18 2ED* M: 07973-289801 E: gill_hopkins@yahoo.co.uk

HOPKINS, Henry Charles. b 46. Edin Th Coll 65. **d** 71 **p** 72. C Dundee St Salvador *Bre* 71–74; C Dundee St Martin 71–74; Chapl RNVR 72–81; R Monifieth *Bre* 74–78; Chapl Miss to Seamen Kenya 78–85; Singapore 85–92; Offg Chapl NZ Defence Force 89–92; Chapl Miss to Seamen Teesside 92–94; V Middlesbrough St Thos *York* 94–97; V N Thornaby 97–18; rtd 18; PtO *York* from 18. *28 Windsor Oval, Thornaby, Stockton-on-Tees TS17 8PP* E: hopkins.347@btinternet.com

HOPKINS, Hugh. b 33. TCD BA. **d** 62 **p** 63. C Ballymena w Ballyclug *Conn* 62–64; C Belfast Ch Ch 64–67; I Ballintoy 67–72; I Belfast St Ninian 72–81; I Mossley 81–86; I Ballywillan 86–96; Can Belf Cathl 94–96; rtd 96. *2 Bush Gardens, Ballyness, Bushmills BT57 8AE* T: (028) 2073 2981 E: hopkins.347@btinternet.com

HOPKINS, Ian Richard. b 70. Collingwood Coll Dur BA 92. Wycliffe Hall Ox BTh 00. **d** 00 **p** 01. C Edin St Thos 00–04; I 04–13; C Haydock St Mark *Liv* 13–17; C Liv Cathl from 17. *11 Wagon Lane, Haydock, St Helens WA11 0HZ* T: (01744) 302265

HOPKINS, John Dawson. b 39. Chich Th Coll 85. **d** 87 **p** 88. C Walker *Newc* 87–89; C Newc St Fran 89–92; V Horton 92–00; rtd 00; PtO *Newc* from 01. *Amen Cottage, 31 High Fair, Wooler NE71 6PA* T: (07790) 915763

HOPKINS, Kenneth Victor John. b 45. Univ Coll Lon BA 66 Lon Univ BD 69 Hull Univ PhD 84. Tyndale Hall Bris 66. **d** 69 **p** 70. C S Mimms Ch Ch *Lon* 69–72; C Branksome St Clem *Sarum* 72–75; P-in-c Trowbridge St Thos 75–76; V 76–81; R Wingfield w Rowley 76–81; Chapl and Lect NE Surrey Coll of Tech 81–84; Hd Student Services Essex Inst of HE 84–88; Kingston Poly 88–92; Kingston Univ 92–98; Dean of Students 98–03; Pro Vice-Chan 04–06; rtd 06. *Quarry Cottage, Duke Street, Withington, Hereford HR1 3QD* T: (01432) 850933

HOPKINS, Lionel. b 48. Open Univ BA 82. St D Coll Lamp. **d** 71 **p** 72. C Llandeilo Tal-y-bont *S & B* 71–74; C Morriston 74–78; P-in-c Waunarllwydd 78–80; V 80–86; Youth Chapl 84–86; V Llangyfelach 86–96; P-in-c Swansea Ch Ch 96–00; Chapl HM Pris Swansea 96–13; rtd 13. *1051 Llangyfelach Road, Tirdeunaw, Swansea SA5 7HY* E: lionelhopkins22@gmail.com

HOPKINS, Neil James. b 72. Brunel Univ BTh 97 MTh 01. Trin Coll Bris 10. **d** 12 **p** 13. C Portswood Ch Ch *Win* 12–16; V Knaphill w Brookwood *Guildf* from 16. *Trinity House, 2 Trinity Road, Knaphill, Woking GU21 2SY* M: 07557-908383 E: neiljuleshopkins@me.com

HOPKINS, Miss Patricia Mary. b 46. Kingston Poly BEd 78. Trin Coll Bris 83. **dss** 85 **d** 87 **p** 94. Gorleston St Andr *Nor* 85–88; C 87–88; C Woking St Jo *Guildf* 88–90; Team Dn Barnham Broom *Nor* 90–94; TV 94–97; V Otford *Roch* 97–07; rtd 07; PtO *Nor* from 08. *Hill Cottage, Broomhill, East Runton, Cromer NR27 9PF* T: (01263) 512338 E: popkins@greenbee.net

HOPKINS, Peter. b 54. Nottm Univ BSc 75 Imp Coll Lon MSc 79. Oak Hill Th Coll BA 86. **d** 86 **p** 87. C Gee Cross *Ches* 86–90; R Gt Gonerby *Linc* 90–95; R Barrowby and Gt Gonerby 95–19; RD Grantham 01–09; rtd 19. *1 Gregory Close, Harlaxton, Grantham NG32 1JG* E: peterhoppy@gmail.com

HOPKINS, Robert James Gardner. b 42. Bris Univ BSc 64 ACA 76 FCA 81. St Alb Minl Tr Scheme. **d** 79 **p** 80. NSM Chorleywood Ch Ch *St Alb* 79–83; NSM Parr Mt *Liv* 83–97; NSM Crookes St Thos *Sheff* 97–09; NSM Philadelphia St Thos 09–15; PtO from 15; Dir Angl Ch Planting Initiatives from 92; Missr Fresh Expressions from 05. *70 St Thomas Road, Sheffield S10 1UX* T: 0114-267 8266 or 278 9378 E: hopkins.the@gmail.com

HOPKINS, Victor John. b 44. UEA LLB 82. CBDTI 06. **d** 07 **p** 08. NSM Sedbergh, Cautley and Garsdale *Bradf* 07–12; NSM Sedbergh, Cautley and Garsdale *Carl* 12–14; PtO *St E* from 15; *Pet* from 15. *94 Chediston Street, Halesworth IP19 8BJ* T: (01986) 875934 E: csninefour@btinternet.com

HOPKINSON, The Ven Barnabas John. b 39. Trin Coll Cam BA 63 MA 67. Linc Th Coll 63. **d** 65 **p** 66. C Langley All SS and Martyrs *Man* 65–67; C Cambridge Gt St Mary w St Mich *Ely* 67–71; Asst Chapl Charterhouse Sch Godalming 71–75; P-in-c Preshute *Sarum* 75–76; TV Marlborough 76–81; RD 77–81; TR Wimborne Minster and Holt 81–86; Can and Preb Sarum Cathl 83–04; RD Wimborne 85–86; Adn Sarum 86–98; P-in-c Stratford sub Castle 87–98; Adn Wilts 98–04; rtd 04; PtO *B & W* 09–15. *Tanners Cottage, 22 Frog Street, Bampton, Tiverton EX16 9NT* T: (01398) 331611 E: barneyesme@onetel.net

HOPKINSON, Benjamin Alaric. b 36. Trin Coll Ox BA 59. Chich Th Coll 59. **d** 61 **p** 62. C Pallion *Dur* 61–66; Rhodesia 66–67; Botswana 67–74; Hon C Sherwood *S'well* 74–77; Hon C Carrington 74–77; V Lowdham 77–85; R Whitby *York* 85–95; Miss to Seafarers from 85; V Stainton w Hilton *York* 95–01; Chapl Cleveland Constabulary 95–01; rtd 01; PtO *Newc* from 01. *11 Watershaugh Road, Warkworth, Morpeth NE65 0TT* T/F: (01665) 714213 E: benjamin.hopkinson@gmail.com

HOPKINSON, Colin Edward. b 57. BA LLB. Ridley Hall Cam. **d** 84 **p** 85. C Chadwell *Chelmsf* 84–87; C Canvey Is 87–90; P-in-c E Springfield 90–98; RD Chelmsf N 95–99; R Langdon Hills from 98. *The Rectory, 105A Berry Lane, Langdon Hills, Basildon SS16 6AN* T: (01268) 542156 E: cchopkinson@aol.com

HOPKINSON, David John. b 47. Ox NSM Course. **d** 79 **p** 80. NSM Wardington *Ox* 79; Hon C Didcot St Pet 80–83; C Headingley *Ripon* 83–87; P-in-c Leeds All So 87–91; R Middleton Tyas w Croft and Eryholme 91–95; V Leeds Belle Is St Jo and St Barn 95–98; rtd 98; PtO *Ripon* 98–06; *Wakef* 07–12. *11 Old Well Head, Halifax HX1 2BN* T: (01422) 361226

HOPKINSON, William Humphrey. b 48. Lon Univ BSc 69 Dur Univ MA 78 Nottm Univ MPhil 84 Man Poly MSc 90 California State Univ MEd 00 ARIC 73. Cranmer Hall Dur. **d** 77 **p** 78. C Normanton *Derby* 77–80; C Sawley 80–82; V Birtles *Ches* 82–87; Dir Past Studies NOC 82–94; Dir Course Development 90–94; CME Officer *Ches* 87–94; P-in-c Tenterden St Mich *Cant* 94–96; Dir Min and Tr 94–02; Hon Can Cant Cathl 01–02; PtO 03–06; World Faith Manager Harmondsworth Immigration Removal Cen 03–05; Registrar Lon Academy of HE 05–06; Manager Independent Newham Users Forum 07; Asst Prof California State Univ USA from 07; rtd 13. *91 Chobham Road, London E15 1LX* M: 07057-111933 E: bill@bhopkinson.co.uk

HOPLEY, David. b 37. Wells Th Coll 62. **d** 65 **p** 66. C Frome St Jo *B & W* 65–68; R Staunton-on-Arrow w Byton and Kinsham *Heref* 68–81; P-in-c Lingen 68–81; P-in-c Aymestrey and Leinthall Earles w Wigmore etc 72–81; R Buckland Newton, Long Burton etc Sarum 81–02; rtd 02; PtO *B & W* 07–19. *Sunnyside, Clatworthy, Taunton TA4 2EH* T: (01984) 623842

HOPPER, Canon Robert Keith. b 45. Cranmer Hall Dur 74. **d** 77 **p** 78. C Oxclose *Dur* 77–80; C Hebburn St Jo 80–82; V Lobley Hill 82–04; P-in-c Marley Hill 02–04; V Hillside 04–16; Hon Can Dur Cathl 09–16; rtd 16; PtO *Dur* from 16. *3 Hallgarth View, High Pittington, Durham DH6 1AS* M: 07960-754744 E: canonbob@durham.uk.net

HOPPERTON, Thomas. b 38. Chich Th Coll 71. **d** 73 **p** 74. C Cheam *S'wark* 73–89; P-in-c St Alb 76–89; P-in-c Rotherhithe St Kath w St Barn 89–92; P-in-c S Bermondsey

St Bart 91–92; P-in-c Bermondsey St Kath w St Bart 92; V 92–01; rtd 01; PtO *York* 03–11. *8 Croft Heads, Sowerby, Thirsk YO7 1ND* T: (01845) 524210 E: fathertom21@aol.com

HOPTHROW, Mrs Elizabeth Rosemary Gladys. b 45. **d** 01 **p** 02. NSM Aylesham w Adisham *Cant* 01–04; NSM Nonington w Wymynswold and Goodnestone etc 01–04; NSM Barham w Bishopsbourne and Kingston 04–11; Chapl Pilgrims Hospice Cant 01–11; Warden The Quiet View from 11; PtO *Cant* from 11. *146 The Street, Kingston, Canterbury CT4 6JQ* T: (01227) 830070 *or* 812610 M: 07977-754920 E: lizziehopthrow@gmail.com

HOPWOOD OWEN, Mrs Karen. b 58. Padgate Coll of Educn CertEd 79 St Martin's Coll Lanc DASE 90. **d** 95 **p** 96. OLM Peel *Man* 95–99; OLM Walkden and Lt Hulton 99–13; TV Worsley from 13; AD Eccles from 16. *8 Landrace Drive, Worsley, Manchester M28 1UY* M: 07964-663225 E: karen.h.owen@ntlworld.com

HORAN, Helene. b 57. Qu Foundn (Course) 14. **d** 17 **p** 18. NSM Chelmsley Wood *Birm* from 17. *7 Rotherby Grove, Marston Green, Birmingham B37 7XL*

HORAN, Joan Anne. b 53. BA 74 DipEd 75. **d** 05 **p** 06. Australia 05–09; R Grimshoe *Ely* from 09. *The Rectory, 7 Oak Street, Feltwell, Thetford IP26 4DD* T: (01842) 828034

HORBURY, Prof William. b 42. Oriel Coll Ox BA 64 MA 67 Clare Coll Cam BA 66 PhD 71 DD 00 FBA 97. Westcott Ho Cam 64. **d** 69 **p** 70. Fell Clare Coll Cam 68–72; CCC Cam from 78; R Gt w Lt Gransden *Ely* 72–78; Lect Div Cam Univ 84–98; Prof Jewish and Early Chr Studies from 98; P-in-c Cambridge St Botolph *Ely* 90–14; PtO from 15. *5 Grange Road, Cambridge CB3 9AS* T: (01223) 363529 F: 462751 E: wh10000@cam.ac.uk

HORDER, Mrs Catharine Joy. b 51. Battersea Coll of Educn CertEd 72 UWE BA 98. S Dios Minl Tr Scheme 92. **d** 95 **p** 96. C Burrington and Churchill *B & W* 95–00; TV Yatton Moor 00–11; rtd 11. *The Sanctuary, Bridford, Exeter EX6 7HS* T: (01647) 252750

HORE (*formerly* **HART), Debbie.** b 56. **d** 11 **p** 16. NSM St Marylebone St Paul *Lon* 11–17; NSM Sawbridgeworth *St Alb* from 17. *St Mary's Lodge, Knight Street, Sawbridgeworth CM21 9AX* M: 07985-649120 E: deacondebs@gmail.com

HORE, Leslie Nicholas Peter. b 40. SWMTC 99. **d** 02 **p** 03. OLM Treverbyn *Truro* 02–10; rtd 10; PtO *Truro* from 16. *Tremore Noweth, Hallaze Road, Penwithick, St Austell PL26 8YW* T: (01726) 851750 E: peterhore@hotmail.co.uk

HORLESTON, Kenneth William. b 50. Oak Hill Th Coll BA 86. **d** 86 **p** 87. C Wednesfield Heath *Lich* 86–89; V Blagreaves *Derby* 89–00; P-in-c Horsley 00–02; P-in-c Denby 00–02; V Horsley and Denby 02–10; C Morley w Smalley and Horsley Woodhouse 06–07; rtd 10. *11 Pegasus Way, Hilton, Derby DE65 5HW* T: (01283) 735600 E: kwh@gmx.co.uk *or* kwhorleston@gmail.com

HORLOCK, Andrew John. b 51. Bath Univ BSc 74 Open Univ MPhil 89 Nottm Univ PhD 99. Ridley Hall Cam 03. **d** 05 **p** 06. C Crich and S Wingfield *Derby* 05–08; P-in-c Lugano *Eur* 08–15; rtd 15; PtO *Eur* from 15. *20 Duffield Court, Chapel Street, Duffield, Belper DE56 4EQ* T: (01332) 842408 E: andyhorlock@hotmail.com

HORLOCK, The Very Revd Brian William. b 31. Univ of Wales (Lamp) BA 55. Chich Th Coll 55. **d** 57 **p** 58. C Chiswick St Nic w St Mary *Lon* 57–61; C Witney *Ox* 61–62; V N Acton St Gabr *Lon* 62–68; Chapl Oslo w Bergen, Trondheim and Stavanger *Eur* 68–79; RD Scandinavia 75–79; Adn 80–89; Hon Can Brussels Cathl 80–89; Dean Gib 89–98; Chapl Gib 89–98; rtd 98; PtO *Eur* from 98; *Sarum* 98–16. *1 Richard's Close, Royal Wootton Bassett, Swindon SN4 7LE* T: (01793) 848344 F: 848378 E: brian@horlocks.com

HORLOCK, Peter Richard. b 76. UWE BA 97. Oak Hill Th Coll BA 04. **d** 04 **p** 05. C Rusholme H Trin *Man* 04–12; Missr to Business Community from 12; C Man St Ann from 12. *63 Burnside Drive, Burnage, Manchester M19 2NA* M: 07890-860022 E: petehorlock@googlemail.com *or* pete@ministry2business.com

HORLOCK, Timothy Edward. b 72. Anglia Poly Univ BSc 94 Bath Univ PGCE 96. Ridley Hall Cam 05. **d** 07 **p** 08. C Bedford Ch Ch *St Alb* 07–10; P-in-c Stevenage St Pet Broadwater 10–14; V 14–16; RD Stevenage 13–16; V Chorleywood St Andr from 16. *The Vicarage, 37 Quickley Lane, Chorleywood, Rickmansworth WD3 5AE* M: 07787-968843 E: tim.horlock@st-andrews.org.uk

HORN, Colin Clive. b 39. CEng MIMechE FEI. Cant Sch of Min. **d** 83 **p** 84. NSM Yalding w Collier Street *Roch* 83–91; V Kemsing w Woodlands 91–98; RD Shoreham 94–98; rtd 99; PtO *B & W* from 00. *Saw Mill Cottage, Leigh Street, Leigh upon Mendip, Radstock BA3 5QQ* T/F: (01373) 812736 M: 07885-523190 E: colinhorn@hotmail.com

HORN, David Henry. *See* RANDOLPH-HORN, David Henry

HORNBUCKLE, Eric Wayne. b 67. **d** 07. USA 07–08; C Tonbridge St Steph *Roch* 16–17. *2277 Longview Drive, Woodbridge VA 22191, USA* T: (001) (703) 492 9279 E: eric.hornbuckle@gmail.com

HORNBY (*née* **CHRISTIAN), Mrs Helen.** b 47. K Coll Lon BA 68 AKC 68 Lon Inst of Educn PGCE 69. Cranmer Hall Dur 00. **d** 02 **p** 03. C Briercliffe *Blackb* 02–07; C Blackpool St Jo 07–11; C Layton and Staining 11–12; rtd 12; PtO *Blackb* from 12. *2 Arnside Avenue, Lytham St Annes FY8 3SA* T: (01253) 711215 E: revhelenhornby@yahoo.co.uk

HORNBY, Matthew. b 75. **d** 13 **p** 14. C S Barrow *Carl* 13–17; R Coppull *Blackb* from 17. *The Vicarage, 209 Chapel Lane, Coppull, Chorley PR7 4NA* T: (01257) 791218 M: 07903-136128 E: hornbymatt@gmail.com

HORNE, Brian Edward. b 37. Lon Univ BSc 62 PhD 78 CEng 82 MRAeS 68 MIET 68 EurIng 92. WEMTC 92. **d** 95 **p** 96. OLM Cheltenham St Mark *Glouc* 95–12; rtd 12; PtO *Glouc* from 16. *87A Rowanfield Road, Cheltenham GL51 8AF* T: (01242) 236786 E: lynbrihorne@btinternet.com

HORNER, Graham. b 57. Grey Coll Dur BSc 78 ACA 81. St Jo Coll Nottm 93. **d** 93 **p** 94. C Longdon-upon-Tern, Rodington, Uppington etc *Lich* 93–95; C Wrockwardine Deanery 95–96; TV 96–02; TR 02–07; RD Wrockwardine 02–07; V Gt Wyrley 07–18; V Riccall, Barlby and Hemingbrough *York* from 18. *The Vicarage, 10 Grove Park, Barlby, Selby YO8 5LP* E: gandjhorner123@btinternet.com

HORNER, Ian. b 13 **p** 14. C Bailieborough w Knockbride, Shercock and Mullagh *K, E & A* 14–16; I from 16. *The Rectory, Bailieborough, Co Cavan, Republic of Ireland* T: (00353) (42) 967 5822 M: 87-622 3609 E: ianewhorner@gmail.com

HORNER, Richard Murray. b 61. Dur Univ BSc 83. NTMTC 93. **d** 96 **p** 97. C Sherborne w Castleton and Lillington *Sarum* 96–99; Chapl Rugby Sch from 99. *Tudor House, 4 Horton Crescent, Rugby CV22 5DL* T: (01788) 544939 E: rmh@rugbyschool.net

HORNER, Sally Jane. b 68. City Univ BSc 94 Cam Univ BTh 08 Cant Ch Ch Univ MA 13. Westcott Ho Cam 06. **d** 08 **p** 09. C Peckham St Jo w St Andr *S'wark* 08–12; Chapl Notts Healthcare NHS Foundn Trust 12–15; Chapl W Lon Mental Health NHS Trust 15–18; PtO *S'wark* 14–18; Chapl Ox Health NHS Foundn Trust from 18. *Oxford Health NHS Foundation Trust, Corporate Services Building, Littlemore Mental Health Centre, Sandford Road, Littlemore, Oxford OX4 4XN* T: (01865) 902760 E: sally.horner@oxfordhealth.nhs.uk

HOROBIN, Canon Timothy John. b 60. St Jo Coll Nottm 92. **d** 94 **p** 95. C Nelson St Phil *Blackb* 94–98; P-in-c Blackpool St Paul 98–00; PtO 05–06; LtO 06–10; P-in-c Lower Darwen St Jas 10–11; V from 11; P-in-c Over Darwen St Jas and Hoddlesden from 17; Hon Can Blackb Cathl from 18. *The Vicarage, Johnson New Road, Hoddlesden, Darwen BB3 3NN* T: (01254) 53898 M: 07811-074063 E: stjameschurch.lowerdarwen@aol.co.uk

HORREX, Mrs Gay Lesley. b 42. **d** 96 **p** 97. OLM Walton-on-Thames *Guildf* 96–07; rtd 07; PtO *Guildf* 07–17; *Portsm* from 08. *25 Pine Walk, Liss GU33 7AT* T: (01730) 893827 E: glhorrex@gmail.com

HORROCKS, Judith Anne. b 53. Univ of Calgary BSc 76 Keele Univ MA 99. St Jo Coll Nottm. **dss** 82 **d** 87 **p** 94. Denton Ch Ch *Man* 82–85; Whalley Range St Edm 85–97; Par Dn 87–97; C 94–97; Chapl Man R Infirmary 88–90; Chapl Christie Hosp NHS Trust Man 95–03; Chapl S Man Univ Hosps NHS Trust 98–03; Lic Preacher *Man* 97–03; Hon Can Man Cathl 02–03; Multifaith Chapl Co-ord Sheff Hallam Univ 03–05; Chapl St Ann's Hospice Manchester 05–09; Lect Bolton St Pet *Man* 09–11; Lect Bolton St Pet w St Phil 11–14; Ch in Sch Development Worker 14–17; Lic Preacher 14–17; rtd 17; PtO *Eur* from 17. *Calle Cardon 76, Tamaragua, 35660 Corralejo, Fuerteventura, Spain* T: (0035) 928 345 360 M: 660 068 782 E: judie.horrocks@ymail.com

HORROCKS, Oliver John. b 30. Clare Coll Cam BA 53 MA 57. Westcott Ho Cam 53. **d** 55 **p** 56. C Moss Side Ch Ch *Man* 55–58; C Arnold *S'well* 58–60; R Ancoats *Man* 60–67; R Barthomley *Ches* 67–96; rtd 96; PtO *Ches* 98–14. *36 Station Road, Alsager, Stoke-on-Trent ST7 2PD* T: (01270) 877284

HORROCKS, Robert James. b 56. Grey Coll Dur BSc 78. St Jo Coll Nottm. **d** 82 **p** 83. C Denton Ch Ch *Man* 82–85; R Whalley Range St Edm 85–97; P-in-c Bolton St Paul w Em 97–06; P-in-c Daubhill 05–06; TR New Bury w Gt Lever 06–16; P-in-c Fuerteventura *Eur* from 17. *Calle Cardon 76, Tamaragua, 35660 Corralejo, Fuerteventura, Spain* T: (0034) 928 345 360 E: revbobhorrocks@yahoo.co.uk

HORSFALL, Canon Andrew Stuart. b 64. Qu Coll Birm 93. **d** 06 **p** 06. Methodist Min 95–06; Chapl E Lancs Hosps NHS Trust 05–09; Chapl Co-ord from 09; NSM Feniscowles *Blackb* 06–07; Hon C Accrington Ch the King 11–12; Can Res Blackb Cathl from 16. *Royal Blackburn Hospital, Haslingden*

Road, Blackburn BB2 3HH T: (01254) 263555 *or* 736849 E: andrew.horsfall@blackburncathedral.co.uk

HORSFALL, David John. b 55. Bris Poly BA 77. St Jo Coll Nottm 87. **d** 89 **p** 90. C Chaddesden St Mary *Derby* 89–92; V Swadlincote 92–11; RD Repton 99–09; R Chesterfield H Trin and Ch Ch from 11. *Holy Trinity Rectory, 31 Newbold Road, Chesterfield S41 7PG* T: (01246) 220860 E: djhorsfall@hotmail.com

HORSFALL, Deborah. *See* NASH, Deborah

HORSFALL, Keith. b 39. Tyndale Hall Bris 62. **d** 65 **p** 66. C Walton Breck *Liv* 65–68; C Fazakerley Em 68–70; C Mile Cross *Nor* 70–73; V Gayton 73–80; TR Parr *Liv* 80–90; V Leyland St Andr *Blackb* 90–00; P-in-c Willand *Ex* 00–01; TV Cullompton, Willand, Uffculme, Kentisbeare etc 01–05; rtd 05; PtO *Nor* from 13. *Honeycroft, 9 Sporle Road, Swaffham PE37 7HL* T: (01760) 723112 E: ritaandkeith@hotmail.com

HORSHAM, Archdeacon of. *See* WINDSOR, The Ven Julie Fiona

HORSHAM, Area Bishop of. *Vacant*

HORSINGTON, Timothy Frederick. b 44. Dur Univ BA 66. Wycliffe Hall Ox 67. **d** 69 **p** 70. C Halewood *Liv* 69–72; C Farnworth 72–75; C-in-c Widnes St Jo 72–75; P-in-c Llangarron w Llangrove *Heref* 75–82; P-in-c Whitchurch w Ganarew 77–82; R Llangarron w Llangrove, Whitchurch and Ganarew 83–84; R Highclere and Ashmansworth w Crux Easton *Win* 84–09; rtd 09; PtO *B & W* from 12; *Win* 12–17. *27 Arlington Close, Yeovil BA21 3TB* T: (01935) 410731 E: timhordington@ticomail.com

HORSLEY, Canon Alan Avery. b 36. St Chad's Coll Dur BA 58 Pacific States Univ MA 84 PhD 85. Qu Coll Birm 58. **d** 60 **p** 61. C Daventry *Pet* 60–63; C Reading St Giles *Ox* 63–64; C Wokingham St Paul 64–66; V Yeadon St Andr *Bradf* 66–71; R Heyford w Stowe Nine Churches *Pet* 71–78; RD Daventry 76–78; V Oakham w Hambleton and Egleton 78–81; V Oakham, Hambleton, Egleton, Braunston and Brooke 81–86; Can Pet Cathl 79–86; V Lanteglos by Fowey *Truro* 86–88; Provost St Andr Cathl Inverness *Mor* 88–91; R Inverness St Andr 88–91; P-in-c Culloden St Mary-in-the-Fields 88–91; P-in-c Strathnairn St Paul 88–91; V Mill End and Heronsgate w W Hyde *St Alb* 91–01; RD Rickmansworth 00–01; rtd 01; PtO *Pet* 03–14. *22 Vyner Close, Thorpe Astley, Braunstone, Leicester LE3 3EJ* T: 0116-289 2695 M: 07503-321553 E: canonalanahorsley@gmail.com

HORSLEY, Peter Alec. b 56. Leeds Metrop Univ CertEd 98. Cranmer Hall Dur 99. **d** 01 **p** 02. C Acomb St Steph and St Aid *York* 01–05; P-in-c Wheldrake w Thorganby 05–08; R Derwent Ings 08–11; V Acomb St Steph and St Aid 11–15; rtd 15; PtO *York* from 15. *38 Campbell Avenue, Holgate, York YO24 4LA* T: (01904) 799095 E: peterhorsley1@icloud.com

HORSMAN, Andrew Alan. b 49. Otago Univ BA 70 Man Univ MA 72 PhD 75. St Steph Ho Ox BA 80 MA 87. **d** 81 **p** 82. C Hillingdon All SS *Lon* 81–84; C Lt Stanmore St Lawr 84–87; TV Haxby w Wigginton *York* 87–98; V Acomb Moor 98–15; P-in-c York All SS N Street 03–15; rtd 15; PtO *York* from 49. *24 Mayfair House, Piccadilly, York YO1 9QJ* E: andrew@horsmanz.plus.com

HORSWELL, Kevin George. b 55. Jes Coll Cam BA 77 MA 81 Nottm Univ BA 81. St Jo Coll Nottm 79. **d** 82 **p** 83. C Bootle Ch Ch *Liv* 82–86; Chapl LMH Ox 86–91; C Ox St Giles and SS Phil and Jas w St Marg 86–91; R Dodleston *Ches* 91–00; R Llanaber w Caerdeon *Ban* 00–15; AD Ardudwy 12–15; V Mold St *Ban* from 15–16; TV Mold Miss Area from 17. *The Vicarage, 8 Church Lane, Mold CH7 1BW* T: (01352) 752960

HORTON, Anne. *See* HORTON, Roberta Anne

HORTON, David Harold. b 49. St Jo Coll Dur BA 72. NEOC 82. **d** 86 **p** 87. C Enfield St Jas *Lon* 86–90; Min Joydens Wood St Barn CD *Roch* 90–93; V Joydens Wood St Barn 93–99; P-in-c Rusherville 99–04; rtd 04; PtO *Roch* 09–18. *6 Blaisdon Way, Cheltenham GL51 0WR* T: (01242) 241350 E: davidhhorton@gmail.com

HORTON, Jane. *See* HORTON, Margaret Jane

HORTON, John. b 49. STETS 05. **d** 07 **p** 08. NSM Exhall *Cov* 07–11; NSM Stourdene Gp 11–19; rtd 19. *Address temp unknown* E: john.horton123@btinternet.com

HORTON, Mrs Joy. b 52. CertEd 73 Kent Univ MA 98. SEITE 94. **d** 97 **p** 98. C Dartford St Edm *Roch* 97–01; Chapl Bromley Hosps NHS Trust 01–02; C Erith St Jo *Roch* 02–03; PtO 03–04; Chapl Burrswood Chr Cen 04–08; PtO *St E* from 09. *3 Furze Close, Thurston, Bury St Edmunds IP31 3PR* T: (01359) 230649

HORTON, Mrs Margaret Jane. b 60. ARCM 83. Ripon Coll Cuddesdon 13. **d** 15 **p** 16. C Truro St Mary 15–18; Prayer and Discipleship Co-ordinator from 18; Public Preacher from 18. *22 Stret Myghtern Arthur, Nansledan, Newquay TR8 4GJ* T: (01872) 360028 E: jane.horton@truro.anglican.org

HORTON, Ralph Edward. b 41. S'wark Ord Course 75. **d** 78 **p** 79. C Streatham St Leon *S'wark* 78–81; TV Catford (Southend) and Downham 81–88; V Ashford St Matt *Lon* 88–12; rtd 12. *12 Convent Fields, Sidmouth EX10 8QR*

HORTON, Canon Roberta Anne. b 44. Leic Univ BSc 66 CertEd 67 Nottm Univ BCombStuds 82. Linc Th Coll 79. **dss** 82 **d** 87 **p** 94. Cambridge St Jas *Ely* 82–86; Beaumont Leys *Leic* 86–91; Par Dn 87–91; Dioc Dir of Tr 91–00; P-in-c Swithland 94–99; R Woodhouse, Woodhouse Eaves and Swithland 00–14; Hon Can Leic Cathl 94–14; rtd 14; PtO *Leic* 14–17. *8B Copeland Road, Birstall, Leicester LE4 3AA* E: rahorton@outlook.com

HORTON, Simon James. b 65. **d** 12 **p** 13. C Goring-by-Sea *Chich* 12–16; P-in-c Saltdean from 16. *The Vicarage, 51 Saltdean Vale, Saltdean, Brighton BN2 8HE* T: (01273) 271683

HORWELL, Elizabeth. b 54. Southn Univ BSc 76 Essex Univ MA 77 Birm Univ PhD 84 Wolv Univ PGCE 94. ERMC 04. **d** 07 **p** 08. C Wanstead St Mary w Ch Ch *Chelmsf* 07–11; R 11–16; rtd 16; PtO *Chelmsf* from 16. *32 Tumulus Way, Colchester CO2 9SD* T: (01206) 521995 M: 07835-450837 E: ehorwell@hotmail.com

HORWOOD, Mrs Juliet Joy. b 51. Ex Univ BSc 73. SWMTC 09. **d** 11. NSM Topsham and Wear *Ex* from 11; Chapl R Devon and Ex NHS Foundn Trust from 11. *20 Higher Shapter Street, Topsham, Exeter EX3 0AW* T: (01392) 875558 E: juliet_horwood@yahoo.co.uk

HOSKIN, Canon David William. b 49. Hatf Coll Dur BSc 71. Wycliffe Hall Ox 72. **d** 75 **p** 76. C Bridlington Priory *York* 75–78; C Rodbourne Cheney *Bris* 78–79; C Bebington *Ches* 79–82; R Lockington and Lund and Scarborough w Leconfield *York* 82–88; V Beverley St Mary 88–10; RD Beverley 97–07; Can and Preb York Minster 05–10; rtd 10. *24 Chestnut Avenue, Driffield YO25 6SH* T: (01377) 538172 E: david@hoskin.eu

HOSKINS, Hugh George. b 46. S Dios Minl Tr Scheme. **d** 84 **p** 85. NSM Hilperton w Whaddon and Staverton etc *Sarum* 84–87; C Calne and Blackland 87–90; R W Lavington and the Cheverells 90–97; TR Upper Wylye Valley 97–04; RD Heytesbury 00–03; TR Pewsey and Swanborough 04–10; P-in-c Upavon w Rushall and Charlton 07–10; TR Vale of Pewsey 10–11; rtd 11; PtO *Sarum* from 11. *42 St Mary's Close, Hilperton Marsh, Trowbridge BA14 7PW* T: (01225) 781579 E: hughhoskins9@gmail.com

HOSKINS, John Paul. b 74. Univ Coll Dur BA 95 MA 96 MLitt 07 Trin Coll Cam BA 99 MA 04 Ox Univ MTh 10. Westcott Ho Cam 97 Ripon Coll Cuddesdon 05. **d** 07 **p** 08. C Bakewell *Derby* 07–11; Bp's Chapl *Glouc* 11–16; Min Can Glouc Cathl 13–16; P-in-c Winchcombe from 16. *The Rectory, Langley Road, Winchcombe, Cheltenham GL54 5QP* T: (01242) 603640 E: johnpaul@winchcombeparish.org.uk

HOSKINS, Preb Rosemary Anne. b 56. Surrey Univ BA 03. Wesley Coll Bris 99 STETS 01. **d** 02 **p** 03. NSM Camelot Par *B & W* 02–06; NSM Cam Vale from 06; Warden of Readers Wells Adnry 05–09; RD Bruton and Cary 10–16; Preb Wells Cathl from 09. *Springfields, Weston Bampfylde, Yeovil BA22 7HZ* T: (01963) 440026 E: revroseanne@gmail.com

HOST, Mrs Charmaine Anne. b 54. Birm Univ BA 00. WMMTC 87. **d** 90 **p** 94. C Westwood *Cov* 90–94; C Whitnash 94–96; V Kineton 96–08; V Combroke w Compton Verney 96–08; P-in-c Warmington w Shotteswell and Radway w Ratley 07–08; Asst Chapl Paris St Mich *Eur* 08–09; P-in-c Bishopswood *Lich* 09–11; V 11–15; P-in-c Brewood 09–11; V 11–15; TV Smestow Vale from 15. *Swindon Vicarage, 12 St John's Close, Swindon, Dudley DY3 4PQ* E: charmainehost@yahoo.co.uk *or* charmainehost@btinternet.com

HOTCHEN, Stephen Jeffrie. b 50. Bradf Coll of Educn. Linc Th Coll 85. **d** 87 **p** 88. C Morpeth *Newc* 87–90; TV High Wycombe *Ox* 90–91; R Dingwall and Strathpeffer *Mor* 91–94; V Rickerscote *Lich* 94–04; R Aylmerton, Runton, Beeston Regis and Gresham *Nor* 04–07; P-in-c Altofts *Wakef* 07–13; P-in-c Badsworth 13–14; *Leeds* 14–19; Dioc Adv on Disability Issues *Wakef* 13–14; *Leeds* 14–19; Chapl Princess of Wales Hospice 13–19; rtd 19. *36 Devereux Gardens, Great Haywood, Stafford ST18 0WY* M: 07976-387199 E: stephenhorton@btinternet.com

HOTCHIN, Mrs Hilary Moya. b 52. Birm Univ CertEd 73. WMMTC 85. **d** 88 **p** 94. NSM Redditch St Steph *Worc* 88–91; Par Dn Handsworth *Sheff* 91–94; C 94–96; TV Maltby 96–98; NSM Marfleet *York* 06–08; NSM Sutton St Mich 08–15; PtO 16–17 and 18–19. *8 Whisperwood Way, Bransholme, Hull HU7 4JT* T: (01482) 828015

HOTCHKISS, Mrs Mary. b 79. Cape Town Univ BSocSc 01. Trin Coll Bris 17. **d** 19. C Bristol St Aid w St Geo *Bris* from 19; C Fishponds St Jo from 19; C Two Mile Hill St Mich from 19. *2 Jockey Lane, Bristol BS5 8NZ* M: 07570-100775 E: revmhotchkiss@gmail.com

HOUGH, Adrian Michael. b 59. Hertf Coll Ox BA 80 MA 84 DPhil 84 MRSC LRPS. Ripon Coll Cuddesdon BA 91. **d** 92 **p** 93. C Martley and Wichenford, Knightwick etc *Worc* 92–96; Asst P Evesham Deanery 96–97; V Badsey w Aldington and Offenham and Bretforton 97–04; C Lerwick and Burravoe *Ab* 04–05; PtO *Worc* 05–06; Bp's Chapl and Asst *Ex* 06–11; Episc V and Chapl 11–16; Dioc Miss and Past Sec from 16; Dir IME 4-7 08–15; NSM Broadclyst, Clyst Honiton, Pinhoe, Rockbeare etc from 19. *The Old Deanery, The Cloisters, Cathedral Close, Exeter EX1 1HS* T: (01392) 294910 E: ah@exeter.anglican.org

HOUGH, Miss Carole Elizabeth. b 59. Lon Hosp SRN 81. St Jo Coll Nottm 87. **d** 91 **p** 94. C Beoley *Worc* 91–95; Asst Chapl Addenbrooke's NHS Trust 95–98; Chapl Milton Keynes Hosp NHS Foundn Trust 98–09; Chapl Milton Keynes Primary Care Trust 98–09; Chapl St Jo Hospice Moggerhanger 10–12; Chapl Bucks Healthcare NHS Trust from 13; Chapl Florence Nightingale Hospice 13–19; Chapl MHA Westbury Grange Care Home and Dementia Care from 19. *2 Pettigrew Close, Walnut Tree, Milton Keynes MK7 7LL* M: 07947-257425 E: carolehough59@gmail.com

HOUGH, Peter George. b 40. Dur Univ BA 62. Wells Th Coll 62. **d** 64 **p** 65. C Stocking Farm CD *Leic* 64–68; V Leic St Aid 68–76; V Knutton *Lich* 76–05; P-in-c Silverdale and Alsagers Bank 93–94; V Alsagers Bank 01–05; rtd 05. *2 Station Road, Keele, Newcastle ST5 5AH* T: (01782) 624282 E: phough@pobroadband.co.uk

HOUGH, Sharron Lesley. b 54. **d** 01 **p** 02. OLM Willenhall H Trin *Lich* 01–05; C Bentley 05–09; P-in-c 09–11; TV Bentley Em and Willenhall H Trin from 11. *10 Pineneedle Croft, Willenhall WV12 4BY* T: (01902) 410458

HOUGHTON, Christopher Guy. b 64. W Surrey Coll of Art & Design BA 86. Oak Hill Th Coll BA 89. **d** 89 **p** 90. C Mossley Hill St Matt and St Jas *Liv* 89–92; C Ashton-in-Makerfield St Thos 92–95; C Southport St Phil and St Paul 95–96; Chapl Chorley and S Ribble NHS Trust 96–01; rtd 01; PtO *Blackb* from 03. *35 Deerfold, Chorley PR7 1UD* E: rev.chris.htn@hotmail.co.uk

HOUGHTON, David John. b 47. Edin Univ BSc(Econ) 68. Cuddesdon Coll 69. **d** 71 **p** 72. C Prestbury *Glouc* 71–74; Prec Gib Cathl *Eur* 74–76; Chapl Madrid 76–78; C Croydon St Jo *Cant* 78–80; Chapl Warw Sch 80–85; P-in-c Isleworth St Fran *Lon* 85–90; USA 90–91; TV Clapham Team *S'wark* 91–01; RD Clapham 93–01; V Clapham H Spirit 02; Chapl Paris St Geo *Eur* 02–07; P-in-c Surbiton St Andr and St Mark *S'wark* 07–10; V 10–12; AD Kingston 09–12; rtd 12; PtO *Chich* from 13; *Roch* from 13; *S'wark* from 14; *Eur* from 18. *2 Milton Drive, Tunbridge Wells TN2 3DE* T: (01892) 541988 E: houghton308@btinternet.com

HOUGHTON, Canon Geoffrey John. b 59. Ridley Hall Cam 87. **d** 90 **p** 91. C Sholing *Win* 90–94; P-in-c Jersey All SS 94–99; V 99–09; P-in-c Jersey St Simon 94–99; V 99–19; P-in-c Jersey H Trin 05–06; R from 06; Vice-Dean Jersey from 99; Hon Chapl Jersey Hospice from 96; Hon Can Win Cathl from 11. *Holy Trinity Rectory, La Rue du Presbytère, Trinity, Jersey JE3 5JB* T/F: (01534) 861110 E: geoffhoughton51@gmail.com

HOUGHTON, Graham. *See* HOUGHTON, Peter Graham

HOUGHTON, Hugh Alexander Gervase. b 76. St Jo Coll Cam BA 97 MPhil 98 MA 01 Leeds Univ BA 02 Birm Univ PhD 06. Coll of Resurr Mirfield 00. **d** 03 **p** 04. NSM Weoley Castle *Birm* 03–06; NSM Headington Quarry *Ox* 06–09; PtO *Birm* from 09; Research Fell Birm Univ 06–15; Reader NT Textual Scholarship from 15. *ITSEE, Department of Theology and Religion, University of Birmingham, Edgbaston, Birmingham B15 2TT* T: 0121-415 8440 E: h.a.g.houghton@bham.ac.uk

HOUGHTON, Ian David. b 50. Lanc Univ BA 71 Newc Univ CertEd 74. Sarum & Wells Th Coll 80. **d** 82 **p** 83. C Newc St Geo 82–85; Chapl Newc Poly 85–92; Chapl Northumbria Univ 92–95; Master Newc St Thos Prop Chpl 90–95; Ind Chapl Black Country Urban Ind Miss *Lich* 95–04; Res Min Bilston 95–04; Chapl Pet City Cen 04–08; C Pet St Jo 04–08; P-in-c Osmotherley w Harlsey and Ingleby Arncliffe *York* 08–09; V 09–18; P-in-c Leake w Over and Nether Silton and Kepwick 08–09; V 09–18; P-in-c Felixkirk w Boltby 08–09; V 09–18; P-in-c Kirkby Knowle 08–09; V 09–18; P-in-c Cowesby 08–09; R 09–18; RD Mowbray 14–17; rtd 18. *19 Weavers Green, Northallerton DL7 8FJ* M: 07742-563519

HOUGHTON, Canon Josephine Elizabeth Mayer. b 80. Birm Univ BA 01 PhD 07. St Steph Ho Ox BA 09 MA 14. **d** 09 **p** 10. C Handsworth St Andr *Birm* 09–13; P-in-c Stirchley 13–15; V 15–16; Bp's Dom Chapl 16–19; Asst Dioc Learning Adv *Cov* 16–17; Can Res Birm Cathl from 19. *Birmingham*

Cathedral, Colmore Row, Birmingham B3 2QB T: 0121-262 1840 E: canonprecentor@birminghamcathedral.com

HOUGHTON, Matthew Walker. b 71. Ridley Hall Cam 14. **d** 16 **p** 17. C Gt Baddow *Chelmsf* 16–19; C Margaretting w Mountnessing and Buttsbury from 19; C Ingatestone w Fryerning from 19. *45 Riffhams Drive, Great Baddow, Chelmsford CM2 7DE* M: 07758-228443 E: matthoughton1@hotmail.co.uk

HOUGHTON, Peter Graham. b 51. St Jo Coll Nottm 85. **d** 87 **p** 88. C Toxteth Park St Clem *Liv* 87–91; Chapl Winwick Hosp Warrington 91–92; Chapl Warrington Community Health Care NHS Trust 93–98; Chapl HM Pris Styal 98–01; Asst Chapl St Helens and Knowsley Hosps NHS Trust 03–04; rtd 04; PtO *Liv* from 04. *10 Burlington Drive, Great Sankey, Warrington WA5 8AB* T: (01925) 711451

HOUGHTON, Prof Peter John. b 47. Chelsea Coll Lon BPharm 68 PhD 73 Cant Ch Ch Univ MA 13 FRPharmS 94 FRSC 95 CChem 95. Dioc OLM tr scheme 05. **d** 08 **p** 09. NSM Balham Hill Ascension *S'wark* 08–12; PtO 12–13; NSM Heref S Wye 13–18; V S Wye Rural Par 18; rtd 18; PtO *Heref* from 19. *The Lodge, Ballingham, Hereford HR2 6NN* T: (01432) 840443 F: 352412 M: 07734-747688 E: peter.houghton@kcl.ac.uk

HOUGHTON, Mrs Rosemary Margaret Anne. b 46. **d** 00 **p** 01. OLM Earlham *Nor* 00–16; PtO from 16. *74 St Mildred's Road, West Earlham, Norwich NR5 8RS* T: (01603) 502752 M: 07808-774811

HOULDERSHAW, Michelle Louse. b 67. **d** 12 **p** 13. OLM Brothertoft Gp *Linc* 12–17; OLM Sibsey w Frithville 12–17; C Skegness Gp from 17. *6 Bayes Road, Skegness PE25 3AN* M: 07986-433358 E: michelle@sheafhf.com

HOULDING, Preb David Nigel Christopher. b 53. AKC 76. **d** 77 **p** 78. C Hillingdon All SS *Lon* 77–81; C Holborn St Alb w Saffron Hill St Pet 81–85; V Hampstead St Steph w All Hallows from 85; AD N Camden 01–04; Preb St Paul's Cathl from 04. *All Hallows' House, 52 Courthope Road, London NW3 2LD* T: (020) 7267 7833 *or* 7267 6317 F: 7267 6317 M: 07710-403294 E: fr.davidhoulding@gmail.com

HOULTON, David Andrew. b 58. Bradf Univ BEng 80 MPhil 86 Wycliffe Hall Ox BTh 11 CEng 90 EurIng 90 FIChemE 98 SOSc 13. Wycliffe Hall Ox 07. **d** 09 **p** 10. C Old Trafford St Bride *Man* 09–12; NSM Stoke Bishop *Bris* 12–13; V Gargrave w Coniston Cold *Leeds* 13–18; Rural Adv 13–17; I Conwal Union w Gartan *D & R* from 18. *Conwal Rectory, New Line Road, Letterkenny, Co Donegal, F92 PCC2, Republic of Ireland* T: (00353) (74) 912 2573 E: david.houlton@wycliffe.oxon.org

HOULTON, Heather Joy. Bradf Univ BA 83 Open Univ MA 03. Trin Coll Bris MA 14. **d** 13 **p** 14. C Linton in Craven *Leeds* 13–15; C Burnsall w Rylstone 13–15; C Skipton H Trin 15–17; C Keighley 16–17; PtO 17–18; D & R from 18. *Address withheld by request*

HOULTON, Neil James. b 54. STETS 04. **d** 07 **p** 08. NSM Pokesdown St Jas *Win* 07–10; NSM Boscombe St Andr from 10; P-in-c from 12. *3 Wilfred Road, Bournemouth BH5 1NB* T: (01202) 462476 E: neil.houlton@ntlworld.com

HOUNSELL, Mrs Susan Mary. b 49. STETS BA 10. **d** 07 **p** 08. NSM W Monkton *B & W* 07–11; NSM W Monkton w Kingston St Mary, Broomfield etc 11–13; rtd 13; PtO *B & W* from 14. *33 Home Orchard, Hatch Beauchamp, Taunton TA3 6TG* T: (01823) 480545 E: susan@sackbuts.co.uk

HOUSE, Graham Ivor. b 44. Oak Hill Th Coll BA 80. **d** 80 **p** 81. C Ipswich St Jo *St E* 80–84; V Ipswich St Andr 84–00; R Monks Eleigh w Chelsworth and Brent Eleigh etc 00–03; PtO *St E* from 03. *6 Through Duncans, Woodbridge IP12 4EA* T: (01394) 386066 M: 07966-169372 E: graham.house44@gmail.com

HOUSE, Jack Francis. b 35. Bris Univ BEd 70 Lon Univ MA 80 Univ of Wales MTh 94. Bris & Glouc Tr Course 79. **d** 80 **p** 81. NSM Bedminster *Bris* 80–92; PtO 92–94; NSM Knowle H Nativity 94–03; NSM Easton All Hallows 98–03; NSM Brislington St Anne 03–05; rtd 05; PtO *Bris* from 05. *48 Hendre Road, Bristol BS3 2LR* T: 0117-966 1144 E: rhouse3766@virginmedia.com

HOUSE, Mrs Janet. b 45. UEA BA 67 Keswick Hall Coll PGCE 68 Sussex Univ MA 80. Ripon Coll Cuddesdon 93. **d** 95 **p** 96. C Swindon Ch Ch *Bris* 95–99; TV Worc SE 99–06; rtd 06; PtO *Nor* from 06. *11 Caernarvon Road, Norwich NR2 3HZ* T: (01603) 762259 E: jhouse@waitrose.com

HOUSE, Simon Hutchinson. b 30. Peterho Cam BA 65 MA 67. Cuddesdon Coll 61. **d** 64 **p** 65. C Sutton St Jas *York* 64–67; C Acomb St Steph and St Aid 67–69; V Allestree St Nic *Derby* 69–81; RD Duffield 74–81; V Bitterne Park *Win* 81–91; rtd 91; PtO *Win* 91–12. *22 Stanley Street, Southsea PO5 2DS* T: (023) 9283 8592

HOUSEMAN, Patricia Adele. *See* CAMPION, Patricia Adele

HOUSMAN, Arthur Martin Rowand. b 53. MA CertEd. Trin Coll Bris 81. **d** 83 **p** 84. C Croydon Ch Ch Broad Green *Cant* 83–84; C Croydon Ch Ch *S'wark* 85–87; TV Stratton St Margaret w S Marston etc *Bris* 87–93; Chapl Peterhouse Sch Zimbabwe 93–98; Chapl Nor Sch 98–07; Hon PV Nor Cathl 98–07; Hon C Raveningham Gp from 08. *Orchards, Beccles Road, Raveningham, Norwich NR14 6NW* T: (01508) 548322 M: 07790-944860 E: housemartin54@yahoo.com

HOUSSEMAYNE du BOULAY, Miss Sarah Elizabeth. b 82. Kent Univ BA 03 Staffs Univ BA 12. Ripon Coll Cuddesdon 17. **d** 19. C Needham Market w Badley *St E* from 19. *20 Flint Drive, Needham Market, Ipswich IP6 8FL*

HOUSTON, Canon Arthur James. b 54. Trin Coll Bris BA 87. **d** 87 **p** 88. C Chatham St Phil and St Jas *Roch* 87–91; I Carrigaline Union *C, C & R* 91–99; Can Cork Cathl 95–99; Can Ross Cathl 95–99; Dir of Ords 96–99; V Margate H Trin *Cant* 99–08; P-in-c Maidstone St Paul 08–10; AD Thanet 02–08; AD Maidstone 08–10; P-in-c Minster-in-Sheppey 10–12; C Eastchurch w Leysdown and Harty 10–12; C Sheerness H Trin w St Paul 10–12; Min Parkwood CD from 12; C Maidstone St Luke 12–15; P-in-c Maidstone St Faith from 15; Hon Can Cant Cathl from 03. *11 Maidstone Road, Lenham, Maidstone ME17 2QH* T: (01622) 858020 E: arthurjhouston@googlemail.com

HOUSTON, David William James. b 52. Th Ext Educn Coll. **d** 93 **p** 95. C Lyttelton S Africa 93–96; R Sabie w Lydenburg 96–00; P-in-c Elmsted w Hastingleigh *Cant* 00–06; P-in-c Petham and Waltham w Lower Hardres etc 00–06; V Stone Street Gp 06; R Southfleet *Roch* 06–17; rtd 17. *The Lime Pick Cottage, 105 Bridge Street, Wye, Ashford TN25 5ED* E: david@houstonclan.net

HOUSTON, Helen Sarah. b 70. Bris Univ BA 91. St Jo Coll Nottm MA 95. **d** 95 **p** 96. C Bourne *Guildf* 95–98; PtO *Bris* 98–99; Hon C Chippenham St Pet 99–00; C Ballyholme *D & D* 02–04; C Stretton and Appleton Thorn *Ches* 04–05; Asst to RD Gt Budworth 05; Chapl St Rocco's Hospice 05–11; Hon C Stockton Heath *Ches* 08–11; Chapl Rossall Sch Fleetwood 11–12; Chapl St Geo Sch Blackpool 12–19; Chapl Blackpool Teaching Hosps NHS Foundn Trust from 19. *Blackpool Wyre & Fylde Health Authority, Victoria Hospital, Whinney Heys Road, Blackpool FY3 8NR* E: helen.davehouston@btinternet.com

HOUSTON, Kenneth. *See* HOUSTON, Samuel Kenneth

HOUSTON, Mark Russell. b 68. Bretton Hall Coll BEd 92. St Mellitus Coll 15. **d** 18 **p** 19. C Cross Fell Gp *Carl* from 18. *The New Vicarage, Plumpton, Penrith CA11 9PA* E: houstonmark@ymail.com

HOUSTON, Prof Samuel Kenneth. b 43. QUB BSc 64 PhD 67 FIMA 73 MILT. CITC 81. **d** 85 **p** 86. NSM Belfast St Jas w St Silas *Conn* 85–91; NSM Belfast St Andr 91–18; Prof Mathematical Studies Ulster Univ 96–06; PtO *Conn* from 18. *29 North Circular Road, Belfast BT15 5HB* T: (028) 9077 1830 M: 07929-725319 E: skhouston43@gmail.com

HOUSTON, Thomas Michael. b 89. Trin Coll Bris 14. **d** 17 **p** 18. C Burton Latimer *Pet* from 17. *3 Virginia Crescent, Burton Latimer, Kettering NN15 5GB*

HOVER, David James. b 83. Birm Univ LLB 04 Called to the Bar (Lincoln's Inn) 05. Qu Foundn Birm 13. **d** 16 **p** 17. C Four Saints *Leic* 16–19; C Avon-Swift 19; P-in-c Braunstone Town w Thorpe Astley from 19. P-in-c Leicester Forest East from 19. *The Rectory, 36 Woodcote Road, Leicester LE3 2WD* E: revddavehover@gmail.com

HOVEY, Richard Michael. b 58. Imp Coll Lon BScEng 79 Cranfield Inst of Tech MBA 84 CEng 83 MIET 83 EurIng 92. Cranmer Hall Dur 93. **d** 95 **p** 96. C Cheddar *B & W* 95–99; TV Gtr Corsham *Bris* 04–06; PtO *Bris* from 05. *80 High Street, Corsham SN13 0HF* T: (01249) 715407 E: richard@richardhovey.co.uk

HOVIL, Jeremy Richard Guy. b 65. K Coll Lon BSc 86 Spurgeon's Coll Lon MTh 99 Stellenbosch Univ ThD 05. Wycliffe Hall Ox BTh 95. **d** 95 **p** 96. C Kensington St Barn *Lon* 95–99; Crosslinks Uganda and S Africa 00–13; Crosslinks UK from 13; PtO *B & W* 14–16; NSM Bath St Bart from 16. *10 The Firs, Bath BA2 5ED* T: (01225) 833850 M: 07860-337113 E: hovil@crosslinks.org

HOWARD, Andrew. b 63. Man Univ BA 95 Leeds Univ MA 97. Coll of Resurr Mirfield 95. **d** 97 **p** 98. C Worksop Priory *S'well* 97–01; V Hemlington *York* 01–05; Chapl Teesside Univ 05–13; C Middlesbrough St Jo the Ev and Middlesbrough St Columba w St Paul 05–13; V Cantley *Sheff* from 13; Jt AD Doncaster from 18. *St Wilfrid's Vicarage, 200 Cantley Lane, Doncaster DN4 6PA* T: (01302) 285316 E: fatherahoward@gmail.com *or* andrew.howard@sheffield.anglican.org

HOWARD, Arthur Calvin. b 60. Leeds Univ LLB 82 Barrister 83. Wycliffe Hall Ox 00. **d** 03 **p** 04. C Heswall *Ches* 03–04; C Weston 04–07; Chapl E Lancs Hospice 09–11; C

Bispham *Blackb* 11–13; V Copp w Inskip 13–17; rtd 17; PtO *Blackb* from 18. *189 Common Edge Road, Blackpool FY4 5DL* E: calvina.howard@gmail.com

HOWARD, Charles William Wykeham. b 52. Southn Univ BTh 81. Sarum & Wells Th Coll 76. **d** 79 **p** 80. C St Mary-at-Latton *Chelmsf* 79–82; Chapl RN 82–06; Chapl Midi-Pyrénées and Aude *Eur* 06–09; V Funtington and Sennicotts *Chich* 10–15; R W Stoke 10–15; R Funtington and W Stoke w Sennicotts 15–17; rtd 17; PtO *Portsm* from 19. *10 Heather Close, Waterlooville PO7 8EE* T: (023) 9225 4123 E: ch@scwwh.com

HOWARD, Clive Eric. b 65. Oak Hill Th Coll BA 99. **d** 99 **p** 00. C Chipping Sodbury and Old Sodbury *Glouc* 99–03; V Tipton St Matt *Lich* 03–13; RD Wednesbury 12–13; V Woodbridge St Jo and Bredfield *St E* from 13. *The Vicarage, St John's Hill, Woodbridge IP12 1HS* T: (01394) 382083 E: clive.howard65@gmail.com

HOWARD, Daniel James. b 71. Nottm Univ BA 94. Oak Hill Th Coll 04. **d** 06 **p** 07. C Deane *Man* 06–09; V Thornton Hough *Ches* 09–18. *54 Neston Road, Thornton Hough, Wirral CH63 1JF* T: 0151-336 3429 *or* 336 1654 E: vicar@allsaintsth.org.uk

HOWARD, Daniel Thomas. b 90. Liv Hope Univ BA 11. St Steph Ho Ox MSt 13. **d** 14 **p** 15. C Anfield St Columba *Liv* 14–17; V Orford St Marg from 17. *The Vicarage, St Margaret's Avenue, Warrington WA2 8DT* E: fr.danielhoward@gmail.com

HOWARD, David John. b 51. Lon Univ BSc 73. Oak Hill Th Coll 74. **d** 77 **p** 78. C Radipole and Melcombe Regis *Sarum* 77–83; R Tredington and Darlingscott w Newbold on Stour *Cov* 83–90; P-in-c Binley 90–94; V 94–04; RD Cov E 95–99; V Potterne w Worton and Marston *Sarum* 04–16; rtd 16; PtO *Cov* from 17. *53 Ivybridge Road, Coventry CV3 5PF* E: dahoward@waitrose.com

HOWARD, David John. b 47. Brasted Th Coll 68 Ripon Hall Ox 70. **d** 72 **p** 73. C Benchill *Man* 72–75; C Sedgley All SS *Lich* 75–77; C-in-c Lostock CD *Man* 77–85; V Lt Hulton 85–88; PtO 90–91; C E and W Leake, Stanford-on-Soar, Rempstone etc *S'well* 91–94; P-in-c Bilborough w Strelley 94–98; Chapl HM YOI Werrington Ho 98–03; Chapl HM Pris Drake Hall 03–14; rtd 14; PtO *Lich* from 14. *c/o Crockford, Church House, Great Smith Street, London SW1P 3AZ* E: davidjohnhoward@virginmedia.com

HOWARD, Mrs Erika Kathryn. b 49. SRN 70 SCM 72 FRSA. S Dios Minl Tr Scheme 88. **d** 91 **p** 94. NSM New Shoreham and Old Shoreham *Chich* 91–94; C Kingston Buci 94–03; V Sompting 03–17; rtd 17. *207 Upper Shoreham Road, Shoreham-by-Sea BN43 6BE* E: rev.erikahoward@ntlworld.com

HOWARD, Frank Thomas. b 36. Lon Univ BSc 57. Bps' Coll Cheshunt 59. **d** 61 **p** 62. C Macclesfield St Mich *Ches* 61–64; C Claughton cum Grange 64–66; V Lache cum Saltney 66–76; R Stanton *St E* 76–97; RD Ixworth 79–85; P-in-c Hempnall *Nor* 97–01; rtd 01; PtO *Nor* from 01; *St E* from 19. *55 Heywood Avenue, Diss IP22 4DN* T: (01379) 640819 E: fandrhoward@hotmail.com

HOWARD, Geoffrey. b 30. Barrister-at-Law 83 Lon Univ LLB 77. EMMTC. **d** 85 **p** 86. NSM Barton *Ely* 85–87; NSM Coton 85–87; C W Walton 87–92; TV Daventry, Ashby St Ledgers, Braunston etc *Pet* 92–97; rtd 97; PtO *Ely* 97–00 and 07–17. *11 Porson Court, Pembroke Road, Cambridge CB2 8ER* T: (01223) 300738 E: geoffreyhoward@mail.com

HOWARD, Geoffrey. b 45. St Jo Coll Dur BA 68. Cranmer Hall Dur 67. **d** 71 **p** 72. C Cheetham Hill *Man* 71–74; C Denton Ch Ch 74–77; V Pendleton St Ambrose 77–91; TR Pendleton St Thos w Charlestown 91–94; AD Salford 86–94; PtO from 04. *20 May Road, Swinton, Manchester M27 5FR* T: 0161-950 7778 E: geoffrey.howard@ntlworld.com

HOWARD, Ian Barry. b 57. Trin Coll Cam BA 81 MA 87 Homerton Coll Cam PGCE 82. SEITE 13. **d** 16 **p** 17. NSM Brize Norton and Carterton *Ox* from 16; Chapl Cokethorpe Sch Witney from 16. *39 Bluebell Way, Carterton OX18 1JY* T: (01993)   837677   M: 07867-784693 E: ibhoward@btinternet.com *or* ian.barry.howard@gmail.com

HOWARD, John. *See* HOWARD, Nicolas John

HOWARD, Canon John Robert. b 60. NUI BA HDipEd. **d** 84 **p** 85. C Donaghcloney w Waringstown *D & D* 84–88; I Belfast St Ninian *Conn* 88–94; Bp's Dom Chapl 88–94; Chapl Ulster Univ 88–94; I Annahilt w Magherahamlet *D & D* from 94; Chapl HM Pris Maghaberry from 96; Can Dromore Cathl *D & D* from 06; Chan Dromore Cathl from 12. *Annahilt Rectory, 15 Ballykeel Road, Hillsborough BT26 6NW* T: (028) 9263 8218 E: jrobert.howard@btinternet.com

HOWARD, Keith. b 55. St Jo Coll Nottm 81. **d** 84 **p** 85. C Llanidloes w Llangurig *Ban* 84–87; R Llansantffraid Glan Conwy and Eglwysbach *St As* 87–00; V Heapey and Withnell *Blackb* 00–07; V Hooton *Ches* from 07. *Hooton*

Vicarage, Chester Road, Childer Thornton, Ellesmere Port CH66 1QF T: 0151-339 2020

HOWARD, Canon Michael Charles. b 35. Selw Coll Cam BA 58 MA 63 CQSW 72. Wycliffe Hall Ox 58. **d** 60 **p** 61. C Stowmarket *St E* 60–64; CMS Nigeria 64–71; Hon Can Ondo 70–71; Hon C Southborough St Pet w Ch Ch and St Matt *Roch* 72–73; PtO *Ox* 73–18; rtd 00. *17 Milton Road, Bloxham, Banbury OX15 4HD* T: (01295) 720470

HOWARD, Michael John. b 51. Redland Coll of Educn CertEd 74 Open Univ BA 78. **d** 09 **p** 10. OLM Ness Gp *Linc* from 09; RD Elloe W from 19. *East Dean House, East End, Langtoft, Peterborough PE6 9LP* T: (01778) 349576 E: michaelj.howard@virgin.net

HOWARD, Nicolas John. b 61. Nottm Univ BTh 90. Aston Tr Scheme 85 Linc Th Coll 87. **d** 90 **p** 91. C Bracknell *Ox* 90–94; P-in-c Oldham St Chad Limeside *Man* 94–96; PtO *Birm* 96–99. *11 Chesterfield Court, Middleton Hall Road, Birmingham B30 1AF* T: 0121-459 4975

HOWARD, Paul David. b 47. Lanchester Poly Cov BA 69. St Jo Coll Nottm 74. **d** 77 **p** 78. C Bedworth *Cov* 77–83; V Newchapel *Lich* 83–93; V Stretton w Claymills 93–04; P-in-c Talke 04–10; R 10–13; Chapl Newcastle-under-Lyme Primary Care Trust 07–13; rtd 13; PtO *Lich* from 13. *30 Fairfax Close, Biddulph, Stoke-on-Trent ST8 6ER* M: 07824-099577 E: paulhoward510@gmail.com

HOWARD, Canon Peter Leslie. b 48. Nottm Univ BTh 77 Birm Univ MA 80 Leeds Univ MEd 91. St Jo Coll Nottm LTh 77. **d** 77 **p** 78. C Gospel Lane St Mich *Birm* 77–81; P-in-c Nechells 81–85; V Stanley *Wakef* 85–92; P-in-c Nor Heartsease St Fran 92–16; Hon Can Nor Cathl 10–16; RD Nor E 06–14; rtd 16; PtO *Nor* from 16; Dioc UPA/CUF Link Officer from 02; PtO *Eur* from 16. *Chapel Cottage, 17 Chapel Lane, Coltishall, Norwich NR12 7DR* T: (01603) 738835 E: plhoward@btinternet.com

HOWARD, Robert. *See* HOWARD, John Robert

HOWARD, Canon Robert Weston (Robin). b 28. Pemb Coll Cam BA 49 MA 53. Westcott Ho Cam 51. **d** 53 **p** 54. C Bishopwearmouth St Mich *Dur* 53–56; C Cambridge Gt St Mary w St Mich *Ely* 56–60; Hong Kong 60–66; V Prenton *Ches* 66–75; RD Frodsham 74–82; P-in-c Dunham-on-the-Hill 75–77; V Helsby and Ince 75–77; V Helsby and Dunham-on-the-Hill 77–82; Hon Can Ches Cathl 78–82; V Moseley St Mary *Birm* 82–88; V Chalke Valley W *Sarum* 88–93; rtd 93; PtO *St D* 93–08; *Heref* 93–08; *Ox* 08–18. *4 Hitchmans Drive, Chipping Norton OX7 5BG* T: (01608) 641248 E: roberthoward5@sky.com

HOWARD, Ronald. b 40. AMIBF 65 AMICME 01. Cranmer Hall Dur 86. **d** 88 **p** 89. C Baildon *Bradf* 88–92; P-in-c Sutton 92–96; P-in-c St Tudy w St Mabyn and Michaelstow *Truro* 96–00; P-in-c Keyingham w Ottringham, Halsham and Sunk Is *York* 00–03; R 03–08; RD S Holderness 04–06; rtd 08; PtO *York* from 08. *Silver Gates, Withernsea Road, Hollym, Withernsea HU19 2QH* T: (01964) 611270 E: ronaldhoward146@btinternet.com

HOWARD, Simon Charles. b 60. Birm Univ BA 81. Ridley Hall Cam 90. **d** 92 **p** 93. C Cambridge St Martin *Ely* 92–96; Chapl St Bede's Sch Cam 92–96; P-in-c Earley Trin *Ox* 96–05; P-in-c Ruscombe and Twyford 05–12; V Ruscombe and Twyford w Hurst 12–16; Chapl Lee Abbey from 16. *Lee Abbey, Lynton EX35 6JJ* T: (01598) 752621 E: simonhoward@leeabbey.org.uk

HOWARD, Thomas Norman. b 40. St Aid Birkenhead 64. **d** 67 **p** 68. C Farnworth and Kearsley *Man* 67–70; C Prestwich St Marg 70–73; V Heyside 73–85; Warden Lamplugh Ho Angl Conf Cen 85–90; Hon C Langtoft w Foxholes, Butterwick, Cottam etc *York* 85–87; C 87–90; V Fence and Newchurch-in-Pendle *Blackb* 90–00; Dioc Ecum Officer 90–95; rtd 00; Hon C Stalybridge H Trin and Ch Ch *Ches* 01–03; PtO 03–04; *Blackb* from 00. *5 Mount Gardens, Morecambe LA4 6AS* E: revd.t.n.h@gmail.com

HOWARD, William Alfred. b 47. St Jo Coll Dur BA 69. Wycliffe Hall Ox 74. **d** 77 **p** 79. C Norbiton *S'wark* 77–80; C Mile Cross *Nor* 80–84; R Grimston, Congham and Roydon 84–13; Chapl Norfolk Constabulary 00–13; rtd 13; PtO *Cov* from 14; *Eur* from 16. *21 Daniell Road, Wellesbourne, Warwick CV35 9UD* T: (01789) 508831 E: william.howard@dunelm.org.uk

HOWARTH, Christopher Robin. b 41. **d** 10 **p** 12. NSM Canley *Cov* 10–18; NSM Westwood 14–18; PtO 18–19. *The Vicarage, 47 Glebe Close, Coventry CV4 8DJ* T: (024) 7642 1721 M: 07730-409778 E: christopherrobin41@gmail.com

HOWARTH, David Alexander. b 81. Wycliffe Hall Ox BTh 14. **d** 14 **p** 15. C Bromley Ch Ch *Roch* 14–18; C Hove Bp Hannington Memorial Ch *Chich* from 18. *43 Hogarth Road, Hove BN3 5RH* M: 07740-361097 E: dahowarth1@gmail.com *or* daveholycross@gmail.com

HOWARTH, Delphine. *See* HOWARTH, Victoria Elizabeth Delphine

HOWARTH, Mrs Henriette. b 66. Utrecht Univ MTh 94. Wycliffe Hall Ox 91. **d** 04 **p** 05. C Sparkbrook Ch Ch *Birm* 04–05; C Springfield 05–09; PtO 09–11; Chapl St Mich C of E Academy 11–14; NSM Peckham All SS *S'wark* 12–14; V Shipley St Paul *Leeds* from 17. *47 Kirkgate, Shipley BD18 3EH* T: (01274) 407471 E: henhowarth@gmail.com

HOWARTH, Maxine. b 71. Westcott Ho Cam 17. **d** 19. C Langelei *St Alb* from 19. *1 Linden Glade, Hemel Hempstead HP1 1XB* E: curateht@gmail.com

HOWARTH, Michael Scott. b 42. SNWTP. **d** 13 **p** 14. NSM Dearnley *Man* 13–14; NSM Dearnley, Wardle and Smallbridge 14–18; PtO from 18. *5 Starfield Avenue, Littleborough OL15 0NG* T: (01706) 371544 M: 07977-164848 E: michael.howarth@zen.co.uk

HOWARTH, Miles. b 58. **d** 08 **p** 09. OLM Failsworth St Jo *Man* 08–12; Spiritual Care Co-ord Dr Kershaw's Hospice Oldham 11–16; NSM Kirkholt *Man* 12–14; P-in-c Denton Ch Ch from 14; C Audenshaw St Steph from 14; C Denton St Lawr from 14; C Haughton St Anne from 14. *15 Grimshaw Street, Failsworth, Manchester M35 0DF* T: 0161-688 7710 M: 07718-326321 E: mhowarth175@gmail.com

HOWARTH, Robert Francis Harvey. b 31. S'wark Ord Course 71. **d** 72 **p** 73. C St Marylebone All So w SS Pet and Jo *Lon* 72–73; C St Helen Bishopsgate w St Martin Outwich 73–78; V Harlow St Mary and St Hugh w St Jo the Bapt *Chelmsf* 78–88; P-in-c Victoria Docks Ascension 88–96; rtd 96; PtO *Chelmsf* 12–16. *14 Quinlan Court, 78 Mill Lane, Danbury, Chelmsford CM3 4HX* T: (01245) 698142

HOWARTH, Canon Ronald. b 26. TCD BA 51 MA 54. Linc Th Coll 50. **d** 52 **p** 53. C Gannow *Blackb* 52–55; Chapl Victory Coll Ikare Nigeria 55–60; Chapl St Paul's Abeokuta 60–66; Chapl Egbado Coll Ilaro 66–84; Vice Prin 75–84; P-in-c Ilaro All So 84–86; Bp's Sec and P-in-c Abeokuta St Paul 86–89; Hon Can Abeokuta 83–86; Can from 86; rtd 91. *c/o Mrs H Howarth Downey, 35 Alford Road, West Bridgford, Nottingham NG2 6GJ*

✠**HOWARTH, The Rt Revd Toby Matthew.** b 62. Yale Univ BA 86 Birm Univ MA 91 Free Univ of Amsterdam PhD 01. Wycliffe Hall Ox 89. **d** 92 **p** 93 **c** 14. C Derby St Aug 92–95; Crosslinks India 95–00; The Netherlands 00–02; Vice Prin and Tutor Crowther Hall CMS Tr Coll Selly Oak 02–04; P-in-c Springfield *Birm* 04–11; Bp's Adv on Inter-Faith Relns 05–11; Abp's Sec for Inter-Relig Affairs *Cant* 11–14; Suff Bp Bradf *Leeds* from 14. *47 Kirkgate, Shipley BD18 3EH* T: (01274) 407471 *or* 0113-353 0290 M: 07811-467999 E: bishop.toby@leeds.anglican.org

HOWARTH, Victoria Elizabeth Delphine. b 50. Keele Univ MSc 06. **d** 11 **p** 12. OLM Penkridge *Lich* 11–15; C from 15. *Lower Farm House, Bednall, Stafford ST17 0SA* T: (01785) 714527 M: 07412-617211 E: delphine.howarth@ifdev.net

HOWAT, Jeremy Noel Thomas. b 35. Em Coll Cam BA 59 MA 62. Ridley Hall Cam 59. **d** 63 **p** 64. C Sutton *Liv* 63–65; C Kirk Ella *York* 65–66; C Bridlington Quay Ch Ch 66–69; R Wheldrake 69–78; Dioc Youth Officer 69–74; SAMS Argentina 78–81; 90–97; P-in-c Newton upon Ouse *York* 81–82; V Shipton w Overton 81–82; P-in-c Skelton by York 81–82; R Skelton w Shipton and Newton on Ouse 82–89; C Elloughton and Brough w Brantingham 97–99; rtd 99; PtO *York* from 00. *18 Petersway, York YO30 6AR* T: (01904) 628946 E: nowell@ntlworld.com

HOWDEN, Canon John Travis. b 40. RIBA 62. Sarum Th Coll 66. **d** 69 **p** 70. C S Gillingham *Roch* 69–72; C Banbury *Ox* 72–73; LtO *York* 73–74; Hon C Hull St Jo Newland 74–81; Hon C Stock Harvard *Chelmsf* 82–86; R Doddinghurst and Mountnessing 86–91; P-in-c Pleshey 91–00; Warden Pleshey Retreat Ho 91–00; R Wickham Bishops w Lt Braxted *Chelmsf* 00–05; Hon Can Chelmsf Cathl 97–05; rtd 05; PtO *Chelmsf* from 05. *12A Back Road, Writtle, Chelmsford CM1 3PD* T: (01245) 422023 E: johnhowden7@gmail.com

HOWE, Canon Alan Raymond. b 52. Nottm Univ BTh 79. St Jo Coll Nottm 76. **d** 80 **p** 81. C Southsea St Simon *Portsm* 80–83; C Bexleyheath St Pet *Roch* 83–86; TV Camberley St Paul *Guildf* 86–93; P-in-c Mansfield St Jo *S'well* 93–96; P-in-c Wollaton Park 96–02; V 02–05; AD Nottingham W 99–05; V Chilwell 05–16; P-in-c Lenton Abbey 09–16; rtd 16; P-in-c Tollerton *S'well* from 16; Hon Can S'well Minster from 11; PtO *Eur* from 18. *The Rectory, Tollerton Lane, Tollerton, Nottingham NG12 4FW*

HOWE, Canon Anthony Graham. b 72. Qu Coll Ox BA 93 MA 99. St Steph Ho Ox BA 00. **d** 01 **p** 02. C Newbury *Ox* 01–04; Dioc Communications Officer *Wakef* 04–05; C Athersley and Monk Bretton 05–06; V Staincliffe and Carlinghow 06–14; *Leeds* 14–15; Chapl Chpl Royal Hampton Court Palace from 15; Dep P in O from 15;

Can Chpls R from 17. *Chapel Royal, Hampton Court Palace, East Molesey KT8 9AU* T: (020) 3166 6515 M: 07795-095157 E: chapelroyal@hrp.org.uk or anthony.howe@hrp.org.uk

HOWE, The Ven George Alexander. b 52. St Jo Coll Dur BA 73. Westcott Ho Cam 73. **d** 75 **p** 76. C Peterlee *Dur* 75–79; C Norton St Mary 79–81; V Hart w Elwick Hall 81–85; R Sedgefield 85–91; RD 89–91; V Kendal H Trin *Carl* 91–00; RD Kendal 94–00; Hon Can Carl Cathl 94–15; Adn Westmorland and Furness 00–11; Bp's Adv for Ecum Affairs 01–11; Bp's Chapl and Chief of Staff and Dioc Dir of Ords 11–15; rtd 15; PtO *Heref* from 16. *29 Forge Bank, Bosbury, Ledbury HR8 1QU* T: (01531) 641998 M: 07879-452763 E: gahowe@hotmail.co.uk

HOWE, Canon Rex Alan. b 29. Ch Coll Cam BA 53 MA 57. Coll of Resurr Mirfield 53. **d** 55 **p** 56. C Barnsley St Pet *Wakef* 55–57; C Helmsley *York* 57–60; V Middlesbrough St Martin 60–67; V Redcar 67–73; V Kirkleatham 67–73; RD Guisborough 67–73; Dean Hong Kong 73–76; Adn Hong Kong 75–76; TR Grantham *Linc* 77–85; RD 78–85; Can and Preb Linc Cathl 81–85; V Canford Cliffs and Sandbanks *Sarum* 85–94; RD Poole 92–94; rtd 94; PtO *Sarum* 94–17. *2 St Nicholas Hospital, 5 St Nicholas Road, Salisbury SP1 2SW* T: (01722) 326677

HOWE, Roy William. b 38. ALCD 67. **d** 66 **p** 67. C Bradf Cathl 66–70; C Barnoldswick w Bracewell 70–72; V Yeadon St Jo 72–79; P-in-c Bainton *York* 79–86; P-in-c Middleton-on-the-Wolds 79–86; P-in-c N Dalton 79–86; RD Harthill 81–87; C Watton w Beswick and Kilnwick 82–86; R Bainton w N Dalton, Middleton-on-the-Wolds etc 86–87; TV Penrith w Newton Reigny and Plumpton Wall *Carl* 87–92; Dioc Chapl to Agric and Rural Life 87–92; V Cornhill w Carham *Newc* 92–98; V Branxton 92–98; P-in-c Lowick w Gosbeck and Hemingstone w Henley *St E* 98–03; rtd 03; PtO *Truro* from 04. *Ballaclague, 2 Halvasso Vean, Longdowns, Penryn TR10 9DN* T: (01209) 860552

HOWELL, Andrew John. b 44. Clifton Th Coll 68. **d** 71 **p** 72. C Halliwell St Pet *Man* 71–77; V Facit 77–95; P-in-c Wardle and Smallbridge 95–13; rtd 13; PtO *Man* from 13. *21 Bateman Avenue, Rochdale OL12 9ST* T: (01706) 375082 E: a.howell554@btinternet.com

HOWELL (formerly WILLIAMS), David Paul. b 61. Coll of Resurr Mirfield 91. **d** 93 **p** 94. C Leic St Aid 93–97; P-in-c Edvin Loach w Tedstone Delamere etc *Heref* 97–16; R Ariconium from 16. *The Rectory, Weston under Penyard, Ross-on-Wye HR9 7QA* T: (01886) 821285

HOWELL, Geoffrey Peter. b 52. Selw Coll Cam BA 75 MA 78 Leeds Univ MA 01 K Alfred's Coll Win PGCE 77 LTCL 82. Cranmer Hall Dur 85. **d** 87 **p** 88. C Hartlepool St Luke *Dur* 87–90; C Whitton w Greete and Hope Bagot 90–94; TV Burford III w Lt Heref 90–94; TV Tenbury Wells 90–94; P-in-c Cradley w Mathon and Storridge 94–97; Succ Heref Cathl 97–99; Chapl Heref Cathl Jun Sch 97–99; PtO *Heref* 99–16; Min Can St Woolos Cathl *Mon* 02–10; TV Monkton *St D* 10–16; rtd 16; PtO *Ox* from 17. *33 Brook End, Weston Turville, Aylesbury HP22 5RQ* T: (01296) 614826 E: gphowell@btinternet.com

HOWELL, Mrs Heather Ellen. b 40. Bp Otter Coll Chich TCert 60 Sussex Univ BA 83. Ripon Coll Cuddesdon 00. **d** 01 **p** 02. NSM Newhaven *Chich* 01–06; P-in-c Fletching 06–11; rtd 11; PtO *Chich* from 17. *1 Rookery Way, Seaford BN25 2SA* T: (01323) 873643 E: heather.howell@tiscali.co.uk

HOWELL, Miss Julie. b 65. Ox Univ BA 98 Ox Brookes Univ MA 04. Ripon Coll Cuddesdon 17. **d** 19. C W Downland *Ox* from 19. *The Rectory, Main Street, Chaddleworth, Newbury RG20 7EW* T: (01488) 638566 M: 07919-207137 E: j.howell826@btinternet.com

HOWELL, Mrs Pamela Isobel Anne. b 62. Sheff Univ LLB 84 Solicitor 87. Qu Coll Birm 09. **d** 12 **p** 13. C Whitnash *Cov* 12–15; V Willenhall from 15; AD Cov E 18–19. *St John's Vicarage, Robin Hood Road, Coventry CV3 3AY* T: (024) 7630 3266 E: revpamhowell@gmail.com

HOWELL, Roger Brian. b 43. ALCD 67. **d** 67 **p** 68. C Battersea Park St Sav *S'wark* 67–71; C Southgate *Chich* 71–76; V Pendeen and P-in-c Sancreed *Truro* 76–81; V Bedgrove *Ox* 81–91; R Purley 91–08; RD Bradfield 94–04; rtd 08; PtO *Ox* from 08. *246 Burwell Meadow, Witney OX28 5JJ* T: (01993) 706893 E: roger@lvcerne1.plus.com

HOWELL, Simon Gordon. b 63. Sheff Univ BMus 84 Bath Coll of HE PGCE 85 Anglia Ruskin Univ MA 07 ACII 90. Ridley Hall Cam 00. **d** 03 **p** 04. C Northwood Em *Lon* 03–06; TV Keynsham *B & W* 06–14; Bp's Inter Faith Officer 10–14; TV Stroud Team *Glouc* from 14; Interfaith Adv from 15. *Holy Trinity Vicarage, 10 Bowbridge Lane, Stroud GL5 2JW* T: (01453) 350387 M: 07971-582332 E: revsimonhowell@blueyonder.co.uk

HOWELL, Thomas William. b 75. New Coll Ox MBiochem 99 Ox Univ Inst of Educn PGCE 00. St Mellitus Coll 16. **d** 19. NSM Ox St Andr from 19. *33 Wentworth Road, Oxford OX2 7TH* T: (01865) 552496 M: 07986-044254 E: tcabmhowell@gmail.com

HOWELL-JONES, The Very Revd Peter. b 62. Huddersfield Poly BMus 84 Bretton Hall Coll PGCE 85. St Jo Coll Nottm 90 MA 96. **d** 93 **p** 94. C Walsall *Lich* 93–98; V Boldmere *Birm* 98–05; Can Res Birm Cathl 05–11; Bp's Adv for Miss 05–11; Asst Dean 07–11; Acting Dean 08–10; Vice-Dean and Can Res Ches Cathl 11–17; Dean Blackb from 17. *The Deanery, Cathedral Close, Blackburn BB1 5AA* M: 07435-969256 E: dean@blackburncathedral.co.uk

HOWELLS, Chan Arthur Glyn. b 32. Univ of Wales (Lamp) BA 54. St Mich Coll Llan 54. **d** 56 **p** 57. C Oystermouth *S & B* 56–58; C Llangyfelach 58–64; R Llandefalle and Llyswen w Boughrood etc 64–69; Youth Chapl 67–71; V Landore 70–80; Dioc Missr 80–89; Can Brecon Cathl 80–89; Can Tres Brecon Cathl 89–94; Dir St Mary's Coll Swansea 82–89; V Swansea St Jas *S & B* 89–98; Chan Brecon Cathl 94–98; RD Swansea 96–98; rtd 98. *2 Lilliput Lane, West Cross, Swansea SA3 5AQ* T: (01792) 402123 E: aghow@hotmail.com

HOWELLS (formerly SMITHAM), Canon Elizabeth Ann. b 62. St D Coll Lamp BA 90 Univ of Wales (Lamp) MA 04. St Mich Coll Llan. **d** 92 **p** 97. C Llangiwg *S & B* 92–94; C Morriston 94–98; P-in-c Llanfair-is-gaer and Llanddeiniolen *Ban* 98–00; V 00–03; V Llanddeiniolen w Llanfair-is-gaer etc 03–04; V Clydau w Egremont and Llanglydwen etc *St D* 04–06; P-in-c Llanpumsaint w Llanllawddog 06–08; V Llanilar w Rhostie and Llangwyryfon etc 09–10; V Llandybie 10–17; P-in-c Llan-llwch w Llangain and Llangynog and Llansteffan etc 17–18; P-in-c Bro Sancler from 18; Hon Can St D Cathl from 18. *The New Vicarage, Millbank Lane, Johnstown, Carmarthen SA31 3HW* T: (01267) 468136

HOWELLS, Euryl. b 60. Univ of Wales (Cardiff) BD 93. St Mich Coll Llan 90. **d** 93 **p** 94. C Deanery of Emlyn *St D* 93–97; V Llangeler w Pen-Boyr 97–03; P-in-c Tre-lech a'r Betws w Abernant and Llanwinio 03–06; Chapl Carmarthenshire NHS Trust 06–08; Chapl R Devon and Ex NHS Foundn Trust 08–09; V Grwp Bro Ystwyth a Mynach *St D* 09–10; PtO from 10; Sen Chapl Hywel Dda Health Bd from 11. *Chaplaincy Office, Glangwili Hospital, Dolgwili Road, Carmarthen SA31 2AF* T: (01267) 227563 E: euryl.howells@virgin.net

HOWELLS, Gordon. b 39. Univ of Wales (Cardiff) BSc 61 DipEd 62. Ripon Coll Cuddesdon 86. **d** 88 **p** 89. C Atherstone *Cov* 88–89; C Lillington 89–92; R Clymping and Yapton w Ford *Chich* 92–97; P-in-c Rackheath and Salhouse *Nor* 97–04; Chapl among Deaf People 97–04; rtd 04; PtO *St As* from 09; *Ban* 14–17. *53 Abbey Road, Rhos on Sea, Colwyn Bay LL28 4NR* T: (01492) 525899 E: ghowells@idnet.com

HOWELLS, Richard Grant. b 62. Univ of Wales (Lamp) BA 83 Anglia Ruskin Univ MA 05. Westcott Ho Cam 83 and 92. **d** 93 **p** 94. NSM Harston w Hauxton and Newton *Ely* 93–15; NSM Nar Valley *Nor* from 15. *Church Farm House, South Acre, King's Lynn PE32 2AD* T: (01223) 871902 E: rhowells@harvardup.co.uk

HOWES, Alan. b 49. Chich Th Coll 76. **d** 79 **p** 80. C Bilborough St Jo *S'well* 79–82; TV Newark w Hawton, Cotham and Shelton 82–89; TV Newark 89–94; V Coseley St Chad *Worc* 94–19; rtd 19. *46 Himley Close, Bilston WV14 0LL* M: 07941-284048 E: alan.howes.49@gmail.com

HOWES, David. b 30. Open Univ BA 75. Roch Th Coll 62. **d** 64 **p** 65. C Highweek *Ex* 64–67; C Clyst St George 67–71; P-in-c Woolfardisworthy w Kennerleigh 71–72; P-in-c Washford Pyne w Puddington 71–72; TR N Creedy 72–73; PtO 74–77; C Walworth *S'wark* 77–78; P-in-c Roundshaw LEP 78–83; R S'wark St Geo 83–90; P-in-c S'wark St Jude 84–90; P-in-c Risley *Derby* 90–93; Bp's Ind Adv 90–93; rtd 93; PtO *Derby* 93–00; *S'well* 95–00; *Win* 01–13; *Lich* 13–14; *Birm* 16–17. *8C Cliff Road, Bridgnorth WV16 4EY* M: 07415-506476

HOWES, Miss Judith Elizabeth. b 44. SRN RSCN. Ripon Coll Cuddesdon 83. **d** 89 **p** 94. Par Dn Ex St Sidwell and St Matt 89–92; Par Dn Brixham w Churston Ferrers and Kingswear 92–94; C 94–95; TV E Darlington *Dur* 95–97; TR 97–02; P-in-c Washington 02–04; P-in-c S Shields St Simon 04–08; C Hedworth 04–08; rtd 08; PtO *Dur* from 08. *25 Firtree Avenue, Harraton, Washington NE38 9BA* E: judithehowes@gmail.com

HOWES, Canon Norman Vincent. b 36. AKC 61. **d** 62 **p** 63. C Radford *Cov* 62–66; V Napton on the Hill 66–72; V Exhall 72–83; R Walton d'Eiville and V Wellesbourne 83–03; RD Fosse 87–93; Hon Can Cov Cathl 89–03; rtd 03; PtO *Cov* from 03. *6 Brookside Avenue, Wellesbourne, Warwick CV35 9RZ* T: (01789) 470902 E: howes.howes@btinternet.com

HOWES, Stuart James. b 78. Wolv Univ BA 03 Worc Univ PGCE 04. Qu Foundn Birm 15. **d** 17 **p** 18. C

Shrewsbury St Giles w Sutton and Atcham *Lich* from 17. *14 Langholm Drive, Shrewsbury SY2 5UN* M: 07800-894416 E: rev_stu@outlook.com

HOWETT, Amanda Jane. *See* FEATHERSTONE, Amanda Jane

HOWITT, Ivan Edward. b 56. Kent Univ BA 81. Sarum & Wells Th Coll 83. **d** 85 **p** 86. C Herne Bay Ch Ch *Cant* 85–87; C St Laur in Thanet 87–90; R Owmby and Normanby w Glentham *Linc* 90–91; P-in-c Spridlington w Saxby and Firsby 90–91; R Owmby Gp 91–99; RD Lawres 96–99; Chapl Hull Miss to Seafarers 99–03; V Hedon w Paull *York* 03–09; P-in-c Sand Hutton 09–12; P-in-c Whitwell w Crambe and Foston 09–12; R Harton 12–13; rtd 13; PtO *York* from 14; *Linc* 16–19. *40 Clipson Crest, Barton-upon-Humber DN18 5GW* T: (01652) 781491 M: 07739-316019 E: ivan.howitt@btinternet.com

HOWITZ (*formerly* TEDD), Christopher Jonathan Richard. b 74. Ch Ch Ox MEng 96. Oak Hill Th Coll BA 00. **d** 00 **p** 01. C Harpurhey Ch Ch *Man* 00–04; P-in-c Higher Openshaw 05–12; Co-Chapl Oman from 12; PtO *Eur* from 16. *PO Box 1982, Ruwi 112, Sultanate of Oman* E: cjhowitz@hotmail.com

HOWLAND, David John. b 55. SEITE 12. **d** 15. NSM Horsted Keynes *Chich* 15–18; NSM W Green 18–19; NSM Colgate and Roffey from 19; PtO *S'wark* from 15. *13 Holtye Avenue, East Grinstead RH19 3EG* T: (01342) 313094 E: david@davidhowland.co.uk

HOWLES, Gareth Harry. b 80. Ridley Hall Cam 15. **d** 17 **p** 19. C Burley in Wharfedale *Leeds* 17–19; C Morton and Riddlesden from 19. *1 Grange Road, Burley in Wharfedale, Ilkley LS29 7NF* M: 07795-268997 E: gnhowles@hotmail.co.uk

HOWLES, Kenneth. b 56. Oak Hill Th Coll 91. **d** 93 **p** 94. C Leyland St Andr *Blackb* 93–96; C Livesey 96–97; C Ewood 96–97; P-in-c 97–99; V 99–03; P-in-c Blackb Sav 01–03; V Chorley St Jas 03–10; rtd 10. *20 Waverley Drive, Tarleton, Preston PR4 6XX* T: (01772) 815752

HOWLES, Timothy David. b 80. Qu Coll Cam BA 02 LSE MSc 04 Keble Coll Ox MSt 13. Wycliffe Hall Ox BA 12. **d** 17 **p** 18. C Headington *Ox* from 17. *84 Oxford Road, Old Marston, Oxford OX3 0RD* M: 07775-733846 E: timhowles@outlook.com

HOWLETT, Mrs Elizabeth Mary. b 58. Southn Univ BA 80. WMMTC 99. **d** 01 **p** 02. C Salter Street and Shirley *Birm* 01–04; Bp's Adv for Lay Adult Educn and Tr 04–18; PtO from 19. *6 Greenside, Shirley, Solihull B90 4HH* T: (01564) 702233 E: lizhowlett@outlook.com

HOWLETT, Philip John. b 60. St Mellitus Coll 14. **d** 17 **p** 18. NSM Black Notley, Gt Notley and Rayne *Chelmsf* from 17. *1 Blackwater Avenue, Colchester CO4 3UY* E: howlettphilip@hotmail.com

HOWLETT, Richard Laurence. b 56. Kent Univ BA 79. Trin Coll Bris. **d** 94 **p** 95. C Louth *Linc* 94–98; R Marston Morteyne w Lidlington *St Alb* 98–05; V Goldington 05–17; TV Langelei from 17. *St Benedict's Vicarage, Peascroft Road, Hemel Hempstead HP3 8EP* T: (01442) 243934 E: revrhowlett@gmail.com

HOWLETT, Mrs Susannah Elizabeth. b 62. RGN 84. St Mellitus Coll BA 14. **d** 14 **p** 15. C Boreham *Chelmsf* 14–18; TV Greenstead w Colchester St Anne from 18. *1 Blackwater Avenue, Colchester CO4 3UY* E: sue_howlett@hotmail.co.uk *or* sue@greensteadwithstanne.org.uk

HOWLETT, Victor John. b 43. S Dios Minl Tr Scheme 90. **d** 93 **p** 94. NSM Bris St Andr w St Bart 93–95; NSM Bishopston and Bris St Matt and St Nath 95–96; C Gtr Corsham 96–99; V Wick w Doynton and Dyrham 99–05; AD Kingswood and S Glos 02–05; P-in-c Stratton St Margaret w S Marston etc 05–10; rtd 10; PtO *Bris* from 10; *B & W* from 15. *11 Moor Park, Neston, Corsham SN13 9YJ* T: (01225) 819954 E: victorhowlett@hotmail.co.uk

HOWLETT-SHIPLEY, Ruth Mary. b 65. Univ Coll Lon BSc 86 MB, BS 89 Birm Univ MPH 03. Portsm Dioc Tr Course 17. **d** 19. C Shedfield and Wickham *Portsm* from 19. *12 Greenwood Close, Fareham PO16 7UF* M: 07970-407176 E: ruthshipley@hotmail.co.uk

HOWMAN, Anne Louise. b 43. Ex Univ BA 97. SWMTC 97. **d** 99 **p** 00. NSM Ex St Dav 99–02; C Salcombe and Malborough w S Huish 02–07; rtd 08. *28 Sentrys Orchard, Exminster, Exeter EX6 8UD*

HOWORTH, Andrew John. b 59. **d** 15 **p** 16. NSM Addingham *Leeds* 15–18; NSM Menston w Woodhead from 18; Chapl Bradf Univ from 17. *75 Silverdale Drive, Guiseley, Leeds LS20 8BE* T: (01943) 879267 E: revahoworth@icloud.com

HOWSE, Martin David. b 58. St Steph Ho Ox 97. **d** 99 **p** 00. C Colchester St Jas and St Paul w All SS etc *Chelmsf* 99–03; V Rush Green from 03. *St Augustine's Vicarage, 78 Birkbeck Road, Romford RM7 0QP* T: (01708) 741460 F: 732093 M: 07770-928167 E: martin.howse@virgin.net

HOWSON, Mrs Anne Margaret. b 56. Qu Mary Coll Lon BA 95 Anglia Ruskin Univ BA 09 Lon Inst of Educn PGCE 96. Westcott Ho Cam 07. **d** 09 **p** 10. C Saffron Walden w Wendens Ambo, Littlebury etc *Chelmsf* 09–11; C Saffron Walden and Villages 12; P-in-c Brightlingsea 12–17; rtd 17. *Marshwood House, Whitchurch Canonicorum, Bridport DT6 6RQ* E: revhowson@gmail.com

HOWSON, Edwin John. b 51. ERMC. **d** 13 **p** 14. NSM St Osyth *Chelmsf* 13–15; NSM St Osyth and Great Bentley 15–16. *Marshwood House, Whitchurch Canonicorum, Bridport DT6 6RQ* T: (01297) 489238 E: eddiehowson@gmail.com

HOWSON, James Edward. b 62. Ridley Hall Cam 97 EAMTC 98. **d** 00 **p** 01. C Cogges and S Leigh *Ox* 00–05; PtO 05–06; *Eur* 05–06; P-in-c Kiev 06–08; R Alfriston w Lullington, Litlington and W Dean *Chich* 09–14; PtO *Pet* from 14; *Ox* from 17. *1 The Mansions, Pevers Lane, Western Underwood, Olney MK46 5JU* E: jameshowson@rocketmail.com

HOWSON, Philip Michael. b 68. St Jo Coll Nottm 14. **d** 16 **p** 17. C Ollerton w Boughton *S'well* 16–19; C Bilsthorpe 18–19; C Eakring 18–19; C Egmanton 18–19; C Kirton 18–19; C Kneesall w Laxton and Wellow 18–19; C Walesby 18–19; V S Leightonstone *Ely* from 19. *The Rectory, Church Lane, Tilbrook, Huntingdon PE28 0JS* M: 07545-325789

HOY, Michael John. b 30. Reading Univ BSc 52. Oak Hill Th Coll 57. **d** 59 **p** 60. C Worthing St Geo *Chich* 59–62; C Tulse Hill H Trin *S'wark* 62–66; R Danby Wiske w Yafforth and Hutton Bonville *Ripon* 66–76; V Camelsdale *Chich* 76–87; V Gt Marsden *Blackb* 87–96; rtd 96. *35 Hardwick Park, Banbury OX16 1YF* T: (01295) 268744

HOY, Stephen Anthony. b 55. Leeds Poly BA 76. Linc Th Coll 92. **d** 94 **p** 95. C Glen Parva and S Wigston *Leic* 94–98; V Linc St Jo 98–18; Can and Preb Linc Cathl 15–18; rtd 18; PtO *Chich* from 19. *4 Gordon Avenue, Chichester PO19 8QY* T: (01243) 786374

HOYAL, Richard Dunstan. b 47. Ch Ch Ox BA 67 MA 71 BA 78. Ripon Coll Cuddesdon 76. **d** 79 **p** 80. C Stevenage St Geo *St Alb* 79–83; V Monk Bretton *Wakef* 83–89; V Ilkley St Marg *Bradf* 89–04; Dir of Ords 96–04; Hon Can Bradf Cathl 03–04; P-in-c Clifton All SS w St Jo *Bris* 04–12; P-in-c Easton All Hallows 04–12; P-in-c Bris Ch Ch w St Ewen, All SS and St Geo 09–12; rtd 12; PtO *Chich* from 13. *15 Garland Close, Petworth GU22 0QZ* E: richardhoyal@btinternet.com

HOYLAND, John Gregory. b 50. Sussex Univ BEd 73. Wycliffe Hall Ox 75. **d** 78 **p** 79. C Pudsey St Lawr *Bradf* 78–81; P-in-c Long Preston 81–84; V Long Preston w Tosside 84; CPAS Staff 85–87; Chapl York St Jo Coll 87–01; Lect York St Jo Univ from 01; PtO *York* from 01. *18 Caxton Avenue, York YO26 5SN* T: (01904) 784140 *or* 876533 E: greg@hoyland.me.uk

HOYLE, David Fredric. b 46. Lon Bible Coll. **d** 02 **p** 03. NSM Northwood Em *Lon* 02–05; PtO *Win* from 11. *23 Cranleigh Gardens, Bournemouth BH6 5LE* T: (01202) 386305

HOYLE, The Very Revd David Michael. b 57. CCC Cam BA 80 MA 83 Magd Coll Cam PhD 91. Ripon Coll Cuddesdon 84. **d** 86 **p** 87. C Chesterton Gd Shep *Ely* 86–88; Chapl Magd Coll Cam 88–91; Dean and Fell 91–95; V Southgate Ch Ch *Lon* 95–02; Dir Post-Ord Tr Edmonton Area 00–02; Dioc Officer for Min *Glouc* 02–10; Dioc Can Res Glouc Cathl 02–10; Dean Bris 10–19; Dean Westmr from 19. *The Chapter Office, 20 Dean's Yard, London SW1P 3PA* T: (020) 7654 4801 E: david.hoyle@westminster-abbey.org

HOYLE, Pamela Margaret. *See* CLOCKSIN, Pamela Margaret

HOYTE, David Anthony. St Mellitus Coll BA 15. **d** 15 **p** 16. OLM Forest Gate All SS *Chelmsf* 15–16; C 16–19; V Plaistow SS Phil and Jas and St Mary from 19. *The Rectory, 19 Abbey Street, London E13 8DT* T: (020) 7473 5734

HRYZIUK, Petro. b 57. Lanc Univ BEd 80 Open Univ MA 95. St Jo Coll Nottm 89. **d** 90 **p** 91. C Huyton St Geo *Liv* 90–93; C Goose Green 93–96; C Wavertree H Trin 96–98; TV Maghull 98–05; Chapl Shrewsbury and Telford NHS Trust 05–13; Lead Chapl Shrewsbury and Telford Hosp NHS Trust from 13. *Chaplaincy Department, Royal Shrewsbury Hospital, Mytton Oak Road, Shrewsbury SY3 8XQ* T: (01743) 261000 E: petroh@hotmail.com *or* petro.hryziuk@sath.nhs.uk

HUBAND, Richard William. b 39. Trin Coll Cam BA 62 MA 66. Qu Coll Birm 76. **d** 78 **p** 79. C Norton *St Alb* 78–81; R Aspley Guise w Husborne Crawley and Ridgmont 81–91; V Elstow 91–03; rtd 03; PtO *Sarum* from 04. *5 Shooters Paddock, Layton Lane, Shaftesbury SP7 8AB* T: (01747) 854741

HUBBARD, Mrs Gillian Carol. b 63. RGN 84. WEMTC 05. **d** 08 **p** 09. NSM Glouc St Paul and St Steph 08–12; P-in-c Mow Cop *Lich* 12–16; V from 16. *The Vicarage, 5 Congleton Road, Mow Cop, Stoke-on-Trent ST7 3PJ* T: (01782) 515077 M: 07525-039323 E: gillyhubbard@hotmail.co.uk

HUBBARD, Ian Maxwell. b 43. Surrey Univ BEd 84 Goldsmiths' Coll Lon MA 86 FCollP 83 ACP 83. Sarum &

Wells Th Coll 69. **d** 73 **p** 74. Hon C S'wark H Trin w St Matt 73–78; Hon C Camberwell St Mich w All So w Em 78–87; Hon C Dulwich St Barn 87–90; C Battersea St Mary 90–92; V Winscombe *B & W* 92–98; TR Yatton Moor 98–13; RD Portishead 02–10; rtd 13; PtO *B & W* 13–18. *38 Wemberham Lane, Yatton, Bristol BS49 4BP* T: (01934) 835859 E: ian.hubbardi@gmail.com

HUBBARD, Ms Judith Frances. b 49. St Alb Minl Tr Scheme 79. **dss** 82 **d** 87 **p** 94. Hemel Hempstead *St Alb* 82–86; Longden and Annscroft w Pulverbatch *Heref* 86–87; Hon C 87–91; Vice Prin WEMTC 91–97; Acting Prin 94–95; Hon C Leominster *Heref* 94–97; Cathl Chapl and Visitors' Officer *Glouc* 97–02; I Kinneigh Union *C, C & R* 02–09; Warden of Readers 05–08; P-in-c Frampton on Severn, Arlingham, Saul etc *Glouc* 09–10; rtd 10. *63 The Meadows, Leominster HR6 8QY* T: (01568) 612779 M: 07958-505881 E: judithfrances@gmail.com

HUBBARD, Julian Richard Hawes. b 55. Em Coll Cam BA 76 MA 81. Wycliffe Hall Ox 80 MA 85. **d** 81 **p** 82. C Fulham St Dionis *Lon* 81–84; Chapl Jes Coll and Tutor Wycliffe Hall Ox 84–89; Selection Sec ACCM 89–91; Sen Selection Sec ABM 91–93; V Bourne *Guildf* 93–99; P-in-c Tilford 97–99; RD Farnham 96–99; Can Res Guildf Cathl and Dir Minl Tr 99–05; Adn Ox and Can Res Ch Ch 05–11; Dir Min Division Abps' Coun 11–18. *48 Manor Way, Guildford GU2 7RP* E: julianrhhubbard@gmail.com

HUBBARD, Laurence Arthur. b 36. Qu Coll Cam BA 60 MA 64. Wycliffe Hall Ox 60 CMS Tr Coll Chislehurst 65 CMS Tr Coll Selly Oak 93. **d** 62 **p** 63. C Widcombe *B & W* 62–65; CMS Kenya 66–73; V Pype Hayes *Birm* 73–79; P-in-c Norwich-over-the-Water Colegate St Geo *Nor* 79–85; P-in-c Nor St Aug w St Mary 79–85; CMS 85–97; Area Sec Cant and Roch 85–93; Chapl Damascus, Syria 93–97; Miss to Seamen Aqaba, Jordan 97–00; rtd 00; PtO *Glouc* from 01. *31 Saddlers Road, Quedgeley, Gloucester GL2 4SY* T: (01452) 728061 E: laurencehubbard@supanet.com

HUBBARD, Peter James. b 72. York Univ BA 93 Nottm Univ PGCE 97. Trin Coll Bris BA 03. **d** 04 **p** 05. C Hinckley H Trin *Leic* 04–08; R Karrinyup Australia 08–12; C Meole Brace *Lich* 12–16; V Bayston Hill from 16; Chapl Prestfelde Sch Shrewsbury 12–16. *42 Eric Lock Road West, Bayston Hill, Shrewsbury SY3 0QA* M: 07951-444269 E: peterhubbard1972@hotmail.com

HUBBARD, Roy Oswald. b 32. Lich Th Coll 62. **d** 64 **p** 65. C Baswich *Lich* 64–68; P-in-c Ash 68–70; V Stevenage St Pet Broadwater *St Alb* 71–78; V Flitwick 78–90; RD Ampthill 87–90; R Sharnbrook and Knotting w Souldrop 90–96; rtd 96; PtO *St Alb* 96–16; *Pet* from 96. *27 Cottington Court, Sidmouth EX10 8HD* T: (01395) 708599 E: roynpam11@gmail.com

HUBBLE, Canon Raymond Carr. b 30. Wm Temple Coll Rugby 60. **d** 61 **p** 62. C Newbold w Dunston *Derby* 61–64; Chapl RAF 64–80; Asst Chapl-in-Chief RAF 80–85; QHC 84–85; P-in-c Odiham w S Warnborough and Long Sutton *Win* 85; P-in-c Odiham 85–86; V 86–95; RD 88–95; Hon Can Win Cathl 94–95; rtd 95; PtO *Win* from 95. *Dormers, Centre Lane, Everton, Lymington SO41 0JP*

HUBBUCK, Dominic George. b 75. Univ of Wales (Newport) BA 07. Trin Coll Bris 14. **d** 16 **p** 17. C Yare Valley *Nor* 16–18; C Thorpe St Andr 18–19; Chapl Koinonia Federation from 19. *Address temp unknown* M: 07984-022700 E: dghubbuck@gmail.com

HUCKETT, Andrew William. b 50. AKC 72. St Aug Coll Cant 72. **d** 73 **p** 74. C Chipping Sodbury and Old Sodbury *Glouc* 73–76; Miss to Seafarers 76–14; Chapl Flushing 76–79; Chapl Teesside 79–82; Chapl Lagos Nigeria 82–85; Chapl Mombasa Kenya 85–86; Chapl Milford Haven 86–92; Chapl Medway Ports 92–03; Staff Chapl and Chapl Thames/Medway 03–05; Chapl Southampton 05–14; rtd 14; PtO *Cant* from 14. *24 Chegworth Gardens, Tunstall, Sittingbourne ME10 1RH* M: 07836-261324 E: andrewhuckett@outlook.com

HUCKLE, Peter. b 46. Ox Univ Inst of Educn CertEd 69 Auckland Univ DipEd 71. Educn for Min (NZ). **d** 90 **p** 91. New Zealand 90–91; Hon C N Walsham w Antingham *Nor* 91–92; C Gt Yarmouth 92–94; TV 94–96; Min Can and Chapl St Paul's Cathl *Lon* 96–97; Asst Chapl Athens and PtO *Eur* 97; SSJE from 97; Superior from 02. *Address withheld by request* T: (01760) 788014 E: superior@ssje.org.uk

HUCKLE, Stephen Leslie. b 48. Ch Ch Ox BA 70 BA 72 MA 74. Coll of Resurr Mirfield 73. **d** 75 **p** 76. C Wednesbury St Paul Wood Green *Lich* 75–78; C Aylesbury *Ox* 78–85; C Farnham Royal w Hedgerley 85–88; V Fenny Stratford 88–98; V Stirchley *Birm* 98–05; P-in-c Kempston All SS *St Alb* 05–15; V 15–16; P-in-c Biddenham 05–15; V 15–16; rtd 16; PtO *Linc* from 16. *15 Hall Road, Great Hale, Sleaford NG34 9LJ* T: (01529) 461704 E: stephenhuckle48@gmail.com

HUDD, Philip Simon Gorman. b 68. Westmr Coll Ox BA 90 Lanc Univ MA 06. Westcott Ho Cam 91. **d** 93 **p** 94. C Kirkby *Liv* 93–97; TV 97–99; V Lancaster Ch Ch *Blackb* 99–19; AD Lancaster 04–10. *7 Dumbarton Road, Lancaster LA1 3BX*

HUDDERSFIELD, Suffragan Bishop of. See GIBBS, The Rt Revd Jonathan Robert

HUDDLESON, Robert Roulston. b 32. QUB BA 55 TCD Div Test 57. **d** 57 **p** 58. C Ballymena w Ballyclug *Conn* 57–59; C Belfast St Pet and St Jas 59–63; Ethiopia 65–69; Exec Asst WCC Geneva 69–75; Dep Sec Gen Syn Bd for Miss and Unity 75–81; Admin Sec *Dur* 81–86; Dioc Sec *Ex* 86–97; rtd 97; PtO *Ex* from 97. *6 Newton Court, Bampton, Tiverton EX16 9LG* T: (01398) 331412

HUDDLESTON, Geoffrey Roger. b 36. TCD BA 63 MA 67. Ridley Hall Cam 63. **d** 65 **p** 66. C Tonbridge SS Pet and Paul *Roch* 65–69; Chapl RAF 69–85; V Lyonsdown H Trin *St Alb* 85–00; RD Barnet 94–99; rtd 00; PtO *Lich* 01–17. *12 Island Green, Stafford ST17 0QB* T: (01785) 501728 E: grhuddleston@gmail.com

HUDGHTON, Deborah Elizabeth. See MOYO, Deborah Elizabeth

HUDGHTON, Emily Victoria. b 89. York Univ BA 11 Sheff Univ PGCE 14. Cranmer Hall Dur 14. **d** 17 **p** 18. C Stockton Par Ch *Dur* from 17. *The Vicarage, 61 Bishopton Road, Stockton-on-Tees TS18 4PD* T: (01642) 611734 E: emily@stocktonparishchurch.org.uk

HUDGHTON, John Francis. b 56. BA. Cranmer Hall Dur 81. **d** 83 **p** 84. C Stockport St Geo *Ches* 83–85; C Witton 85–87; C Stockport St Alb Hall Street 87–90; V Thornton-le-Moors w Ince and Elton 90–95; Chapl RAF 95–01; P-in-c Burnby *York* 01–03; P-in-c Londesborough 01–03; P-in-c Nunburnholme and Warter and Huggate 01–03; P-in-c Shiptonthorpe and Hayton 01–03; TR Buxton w Burbage and King Sterndale *Derby* 03–17; RD Buxton 11–14; V Hayfield and Chinley w Buxworth from 17. *The Vicarage, 8 Bluebell Close, Hayfield, High Peak SK22 2PG* E: vicarhcb@outlook.com

HUDSON, Alison Margaret. b 64. St Jo Coll Nottm 14. **d** 17 **p** 18. NSM Bradwell and Porthill *Lich* 17–18; NSM Stone St Mich and St Wulfad w Aston St Sav from 18. *Meadow View, Shallowford House, Shallowford, Stone ST15 0NZ* M: 07725-467246 E: alison.hudson4@gmail.com

HUDSON, Andrew Julian. b 57. Cranmer Hall Dur 93. **d** 93 **p** 94. C Moldgreen *Wakef* 93–97; P-in-c Lundwood 97–01; V Dodworth 01–04; Ind Chapl *Chelmsf* from 04; C Aveley and Purfleet 04–13; TV Maryke 13–17; P-in-c Thundersley from 17. *St Peter's Rectory, Church Road, Benfleet SS7 3HG* M: 07946-115396 E: andyhudson483@btinternet.com

HUDSON, Anthony George. b 39. NOC. **d** 84 **p** 85. C Harrogate St Mark *Ripon* 84–87; P-in-c Hampsthwaite 87–94; P-in-c Killinghall 87–94; P-in-c Hampsthwaite and Killinghall 94–96; V 96–99; rtd 99; PtO *Ripon* 00–14; *Leeds* from 14. *26 Beckwith Crescent, Harrogate HG2 0BQ* T: (01423) 858740

HUDSON, Brainerd Peter de Wirtz Goodwin. See GOODWIN HUDSON, Brainerd Peter de Wirtz

HUDSON, Charles Edward Cameron. b 73. Univ Coll Ox BA 94 MA 08. Wycliffe Hall Ox BA 07. **d** 08 **p** 09. C St Margaret's-on-Thames *Lon* 08–11; R Broxbourne w Wormley *St Alb* from 11; RD Cheshunt from 17. *The Vicarage, Churchfields, Broxbourne EN10 7AU* T: (01992) 444117 E: bwparishoffice@btinternet.com

HUDSON, Christopher John. b 45. Bedf Coll Lon BSc 68 MCIH 73. Cranmer Hall Dur. **d** 77 **p** 78. C Bath Weston St Jo *B & W* 77–80; Youth Chapl 77–80; P-in-c Baltonsborough w Butleigh and W Bradley 80–84; V 84–87; P-in-c Shirwell w Loxhore *Ex* 87–89; P-in-c Kentisbury, Trentishoe, E Down and Arlington 88–89; TR Shirwell, Loxhore, Kentisbury, Arlington, etc 90–91; P-in-c Trentishoe 90–91; RD Shirwell 88–91; R Huntspill *B & W* 91–94; rtd 01; PtO *B & W* 98–09; *Ex* from 06; *B & W* from 17. *Achray, 5 Conigar Close, Hemyock, Cullompton EX15 3RE* T: (01823) 680170 E: revchris@mhbruton.eclipse.co.uk

HUDSON, Daniel James. b 76. Sussex Univ BSc 97. Wycliffe Hall Ox 17. **d** 19. C Gt Aycliffe *Dur* from 19. *St Francis's Vicarage, Burnhope, Newton Aycliffe DL5 7ER* E: revdanielhudson@gmail.com

HUDSON, Mrs Elizabeth Rachel Ann. b 60. Newc Univ BA 81 Avery Hill Coll PGCE 83 Derby Univ MSc 03. Cranmer Hall Dur 15. **d** 17 **p** 18. C Morpeth *Newc* 17–18; C Cramlington from 18; Adv for Counselling and Wellbeing from 19. *24 Lindsey Close, Cramlington NE23 8EJ* T: (01670) 731418 M: 07974-410409 E: revrachelhudson@gmail.com

HUDSON, John. b 51. Oak Hill Th Coll 84. **d** 86 **p** 87. C Leyland St Andr *Blackb* 86–89; V Coppull 89–16; P-in-c Coppull St Jo 10–11; R 11–16; rtd 16. *12 Mallom Way, Euxton, Chorley PR7 6PU*

HUDSON, John Peter. b 42. AKC 64. St Boniface Warminster 64. **d** 65 **p** 66. C S Shields St Hilda w St Thos *Dur* 65–68; Chapl RN 68–84; V Mellor *Blackb* 84–07; rtd 07; PtO *Blackb* from 07. *Hazel Mount, Bailrigg Lane, Bailrigg, Lancaster LA1 4XP* T: (01524) 848693 E: jpeterhudson@btinternet.com

HUDSON, John Stephen Anthony. b 49. S Dios Minl Tr Scheme 85 Chich Th Coll 86. **d** 88 **p** 89. C Horsham *Chich* 88–91; TV Littlehampton and Wick 91–15; rtd 15. *166 Little Breach, Chichester PO19 5UA* T: (01243) 931557 E: stephen.hudson@outlook.com

HUDSON, Peter. *See* HUDSON, John Peter

HUDSON, Peter John. b 66. **d** 03 **p** 04. OLM Deptford St Paul *S'wark* 03–07; NSM Lewisham St Steph and St Mark from 07. *7A Blackheath Rise, London SE13 7PN* T: (020) 8318 0483 M: 07908-640369 E: frpeter@sky.com

HUDSON, Rachel. *See* HUDSON, Elizabeth Rachel Ann

HUDSON, Robert Antony. b 82. York Univ BA 04. Wycliffe Hall Ox BA 09. **d** 10 **p** 11. C Elburton *Ex* 10–14; C Harold Wood *Chelmsf* 14–18; V from 18. *The Vicarage, 15 Athelstan Road, Romford RM3 0QB* T: (01708) 376400 M: 07799-600147 E: roberthudson79@btinternet.com *or* robhudson@stpetersharoldwood.org

HUDSON, Stephen. *See* HUDSON, John Stephen Anthony

HUDSON, Walter Gerald. b 29. **d** 95 **p** 96. Hon C Eccleston Park *Liv* 95–99; PtO from 99. *31 Springfield Lane, Eccleston, St Helens WA10 5EW* T: (01744) 24919

✠**HUDSON-WILKIN, The Rt Revd Rose Josephine.** b 61. Birm Univ BPhil 00. WMMTC 89. **d** 91 **p** 94 **c** 19. Par Dn Wolverhampton St Matt *Lich* 91–94; C 94–95; C W Bromwich Gd Shep w St Jo 95–98; Black Anglican Concern 95–98; V Dalston H Trin w St Phil and Haggerston All SS *Lon* 98–14; P-in-c St Mary at Hill w St Andr Hubbard etc 14–19; Chapl to The Queen 07–19; Chapl to Speaker of Ho of Commons 10–19; PV Westmr Abbey 10–19; Preb St Paul's Cathl *Lon* 13–19; Suff Bp Dover *Cant* from 19. *The Bishop's Office, Old Palace, Canterbury CT1 2EE* T: (01227) 459382 E: revdrose@aol.com *or* rhudson-wilkin@diocant.org

HUDSPETH, Ralph. b 46. **d** 06 **p** 07. NSM Ripley w Burnt Yates *Ripon* 06–12; NSM Lower Wharfedale 12–14; *Leeds* from 14. *10 Winksley Grove, Harrogate HG3 2SZ* T: (01423) 561918 M: 07810-631826 E: ralphhudspeth@hotmail.com

HUDSPITH, Colin John. b 46. Nottm Univ BA 67. SWMTC 93. **d** 96 **p** 97. C Pilton w Ashford *Ex* 96–97; C Barnstaple 97–99; C Shirwell, Loxhore, Kentisbury, Arlington, etc 99–00; TV 00–11; rtd 11. *Brackendale, Heanton, Barnstaple EX31 4DG* T: (01271) 813547

HUDSPITH, Mrs Susan Mary. b 49. St Alb Minl Tr Scheme 79. **dss** 82 **d** 87 **p** 94. Luton St Chris Round Green *St Alb* 82–92; Par Dn 87–88; NSM 88–92; PtO 92–94 and 00–05; NSM Luton St Mary 94–00; NSM Stevenage St Pet Broadwater 05–08; PtO 08–18. *15 Waverley Close, Stevenage SG2 8RU* T: (01438) 725030

HUFFMAN, John Phillip. b 81. Pittsburgh Univ BA 04 MS 07. St Aug Coll of Th 16. **d** 19. C Margate H Trin *Cant* from 19. *61 Addiscombe Road, Margate CT9 2SY* M: 07999-479202 E: johnhuffman7@gmail.com

HUGGETT, John Victor James. b 39. Dur Univ BA 64. Tyndale Hall Bris 64. **d** 66 **p** 67. C Hailsham *Chich* 66–69; C Worthing St Geo 69–71; C Woking St Pet *Guildf* 71–73; C Buckhurst Hill *Chelmsf* 73–76; V Meltham Mills *Wakef* 76–78; V Wilshaw 76–78; rtd 79; Jt Ldr Breath Fellowship from 79; PtO *Wakef* 79–84; *Roch* from 84; *Chich* from 15. *Breath Ministries, 3 Cannon House, St John's Close, Tunbridge Wells TN4 9GE* T: (01892) 512520 E: cjphuggett@yahoo.co.uk

HUGGETT, Kevin John. b 62. St Jo Coll Dur BA 83. Trin Coll Bris 88. **d** 91 **p** 92. C Gt Ilford St Andr *Chelmsf* 91–94; Regional Manager for Uganda and Sudan CMS 94–01; Hon C Tonbridge SS Pet and Paul *Roch* 98–01; Chapl Lanc Univ *Blackb* from 01. *11 Alderman Road, Lancaster LA1 5FW* T: (01524) 843091 *or* 594082 *or* 594071 E: k.huggett@lancaster.ac.uk

HUGGETT, Michael George. b 38. Bris Univ BA 60 Birm Univ CertEd 61. EMMTC 85. **d** 88 **p** 89. C Sawley *Derby* 88–92; C Chaddesden St Phil 92–95; P-in-c Alkmonton, Cubley, Marston Montgomery etc 93–99; R 99–04; rtd 04. *12 Murray Road, Mickleover, Derby DE3 9LE* T: (01332) 511259 E: m.huggett152@btinternet.com

HUGGINS, Jonathan Paul (John). b 59. Leeds Univ BSc 80 Bris Univ PhD 83. SEITE 12. **d** 14 **p** 15. C Kingsdown and Creekside *Cant* 14–17; P-in-c Len Valley from 17. *Lenham Vicarage, Old Ashford Road, Lenham, Maidstone ME17 2PX* T: (01622) 851407 E: john.p.huggins1@gmail.com

HUGGINS, Stephen David. b 53. Sussex Univ BEd 75 K Coll Lon MA 80 Leic Univ DipEd 79. STETS 98. **d** 01 **p** 02. NSM Bexhill St Aug *Chich* 01–02; NSM Sedlescombe w

Whatlington 02–07; P-in-c Turners Hill 07–09; Angl Chapl Worth Sch 07–09; TV Bexhill St Pet *Chich* 09–15; rtd 15; PtO *Chich* 16–17; Hon C Bexhill St Barn from 17. *10 Constable Way, Bexhill-on-Sea TN40 2UH* M: 07926-569152 E: frshuggins@googlemail.com

HUGHES, Canon Adrian John. b 57. Newc Univ BA 78 St Jo Coll Dur BA 82. Cranmer Hall Dur 80. **d** 83 **p** 84. C Shard End *Birm* 83–86; TV Solihull 86–90; TV Glendale Gp *Newc* 90–94; P-in-c Belford 94–95; V Belford and Lucker 95–06; V Ellingham 95–02; AD Bamburgh and Glendale 97–06; Asst Dioc Dir of Ords 98–06; V Cullercoats St Geo from 06; AD Tynemouth 09–14; Hon Can Newc Cathl from 05. *St George's Vicarage, 1 Beverley Gardens, North Shields NE30 4NS* T: 0191-252 1817 E: revajh@btinternet.com *or* revajh@virginmedia.com

HUGHES, Canon Alan. b 46. Edin Th Coll 71. **d** 74 **p** 75. C Edin St Cuth 74–76; P-in-c Wester Hailes St Luke 76–78; C Marske in Cleveland *York* 78–81; V New Marske 81–84; V Kirkbymoorside w Gillamoor, Farndale etc 84–94; CF 84–94; V Berwick H Trin and St Mary *Newc* 94–13; Hon Can Newc Cathl 08–13; rtd 13; PtO *Newc* from 13. *12 Governors Gardens, Berwick-upon-Tweed TD15 1JF* T: (01289) 307640 E: skypilot60@btinternet.com

HUGHES, The Ven Alexander James. b 75. Greyfriars Ox BA 97 MA 04 St Edm Coll Cam MPhil 99 PhD 11. Westcott Ho Cam 98. **d** 00 **p** 01. C Headington Quarry *Ox* 00–03; Bp's Dom Chapl *Portsm* 03–08; P-in-c Portsea St Luke 08–13; P-in-c Southsea St Pet 08–13; V Southsea St Luke and St Pet 13–14; Adn Cam *Ely* from 14; Hon Can Ely Cathl from 14. *1A Summerfield, Cambridge CB3 9HE* T: (01223) 350424 E: archdeacon.cambridge@elydiocese.org

HUGHES, Allan Paul. b 45. Open Univ BA 91 Glam Coll of Educn CertEd 69. Abp's Sch of Min 01. **d** 02 **p** 03. Chapl St Olave's Sch York 02–05; NSM Skelton w Shipton and Newton on Ouse York 02–03; Asst to RD Easingwold 03–04; NSM York All SS Pavement w St Crux and St Mich 04–12; NSM York St Denys 04–12; rtd 12; PtO *York* from 12; Asst Dioc Dir of Ords from 10; Voc Advr *Eur* from 14; PtO *Win* from 17; *Eur* from 18. *11 Farmers Way, Copmanthorpe, York YO23 3XU* T: (01904) 269557 M: 07443-518645 E: revd_al@hotmail.co.uk

HUGHES, Miss Angela Mary. b 52. Avery Hill Coll CertEd 75. St Steph Ho Ox 90. **d** 92 **p** 94. Par Dn Kidderminster St Mary and All SS w Trimpley etc *Worc* 92–94; C 94–96; P-in-c Gilmorton w Peatling Parva and Kimcote etc *Leic* 96–01; RD Guthlaxton II 99–01; R Wyberton *Linc* 01–09; V Frampton 01–09; RD Holland W 04–09; R Carnoustie *Bre* 09–13; R Monifieth 09–13; P-in-c Clipston w Naseby and Haselbech w Kelmarsh *Pet* 13–18; rtd 18; P-in-c Lancercost, Walton, Gilsland and Nether Denton *Carl* from 18. *The Vicarage, Lanercost, Brampton CA8 2HQ* T: (016977) 2478 E: ahughes@webleicester.co.uk

HUGHES, Arthur John. b 41. MCIOB 71 MRICS 78. WEMTC 03. **d** 05 **p** 06. NSM Church Stretton *Heref* 05–11; rtd 11. *Jacey, 4 Lawley Close, Church Stretton SY6 6EL* T: (01694) 722582 E: jonhughes@uwclub.net

HUGHES, Arthur Lewis. b 36. St Deiniol's Hawarden 65. **d** 68 **p** 69. C Holywell *St As* 68–71; Lect Watford St Mary *St Alb* 71–73; C Watford 73–75; V Thornton in Lonsdale w Burton in Lonsdale *Bradf* 75–84; V Daubhill *Man* 84–89; V Castle Town *Lich* 89–00; Chapl Staffs Univ 91–00; rtd 00; PtO *Ches* 00–04; *Pet* from 05. *31 Hunt Close, Towcester NN12 7AD* T: (01327) 358257

HUGHES, Bernard Patrick. b 35. Oak Hill Th Coll. **d** 65 **p** 66. C Fulham St Matt *Lon* 65–69; Chapl St Steph Hosp Lon 69–89; Chapl St Mary Abbots Hosp Lon 69–97; Chapl Chelsea and Westmr Hosp Lon 89–94; Chapl Westmr Children's Hosp Lon 89–94; Sen Chapl Chelsea and Westmr Hosp NHS Foundn Trust 94–97; rtd 97; PtO *Sarum* from 97. *Charis, 6 Priory Park, Bradford-on-Avon BA15 1QU* T: (01225) 868679

HUGHES, Miss Carol Lindsay. b 51. Cam Inst of Educn CertEd 72 Nottm Univ BEd 86. Trin Coll Bris 91. **d** 93 **p** 94. C Ilkeston St Mary *Derby* 93–97; P-in-c Langley Mill 97–02; V 02–06; P-in-c Oakwood 06–11; RD Heanor 99–06; rtd 11; PtO *Cov* from 12. *13 Harris Drive, Rugby CV22 6DX*

HUGHES, Clive. b 54. Univ of Wales BA 77 MA 82. St Mich Coll Llan BD 95. **d** 95 **p** 96. C Carmarthen St Dav *St D* 95–97; TV Aberystwyth 97–04; P-in-c Hanmer, Bronington, Bettisfield, Tallarn Green *St As* 04–09; P-in-c Hanmer and Bronington and Bettisfield 09–12; V Hanmer, Bronington, Bettisfield and Penley 12–16; TV Maelor Miss Area from 17. *The Vicarage, Hanmer, Whitchurch SY13 3DE* T: (01948) 830468 E: clivehughes54@gmail.com

HUGHES, Cynthia May. b 45. **d** 10 **p** 11. NSM Middlewich w Byley *Ches* from 10. *The Vicarage, 50 Norley Road,*

Sandiway, Northwich CW8 2JU T: (01606) 883286
E: thiahughes@hotmail.com

HUGHES, David Anthony. b 25. Trin Coll Cam BA 48 MA 55.
Linc Th Coll 74. **d** 76 **p** 77. C Boston *Linc* 76–78; R Graffoe
78–90; rtd 90; PtO *Linc* from 91. *27 St Clement's Road,
Ruskington, Sleaford NG34 9AF* T: (01526) 832618

HUGHES, David Howard. b 55. Univ of Wales (Ban). St Mich
Coll Llan. **d** 79 **p** 80. C Llanrhos *St As* 79–82; C Eckington w
Handley and Ridgeway *Derby* 82–83; C Staveley and Barrow
Hill 83–85; TV 85–89; V Whitworth St Bart *Man* 89–00. *2
Cromwell Road, Chesterfield S40 4TH* T: (01246) 277361

HUGHES, Canon David Michael. b 41. Oak Hill Th Coll
BD 67. **d** 68 **p** 69. C Tunbridge Wells St Jo *Roch* 68–73;
C Crookes St Thos *Sheff* 73–81; V Normanton *Wakef*
81–90; TR Didsbury St Jas and Em *Man* 90–09; AD
Withington 00–04; Hon Can Man Cathl 06–09; rtd 09;
PtO *Ches* from 09; *Man* from 09. *41 Cross Lane, Marple,
Stockport SK6 6DG* T: 0161-434 3829 M: 07929-114143
E: davidmhughes11@googlemail.com

HUGHES, Canon Elizabeth Jane. b 58. K Coll Lon BD 81
AKC 81. Ripon Coll Cuddesdon 84. **dss** 83 **d** 87 **p** 94.
Chipping Barnet w Arkley *St Alb* 83–86; Dunstable 86–93;
Hon Par Dn 87–93; NSM Boxmoor St Jo 93–03; Chapl
Hospice of St Fran Berkhamsted 99–13; Sen Chapl Luton
Airport *St Alb* from 13; Hon Can St Alb from 13. *London
Luton Airport Operations Ltd, Navigation House, Airport Way,
London Luton Airport, Luton LU2 9LY* T: (01582) 405100
E: liz.hughes@stfrancis.org.uk

HUGHES, Canon Evelyn. b 31. Gilmore Ho 73. **dss** 79 **d** 87
p 94. Fetcham *Guildf* 79–82; Dioc Adv Lay Min 82–86;
Farnborough 83–87; C 87–92; Bp's Adv for Women's Min
87–94; Dn-in-c Badshot Lea CD 92–94; C-in-c 94–96; Hon
Can Guildf Cathl 94–96; rtd 96; PtO *Guildf* from 96. *4
Oaklands, Haslemere GU27 3RD* T: (01428) 651576

HUGHES, Gareth Francis. b 73. St Jo Coll Dur MSc 94 Wolfs
Coll Ox MSt 07 GInstP 94. St Mich Coll Llan BD 98. **d** 98
p 99. C Haughton le Skerne *Dur* 98–02; TV White Horse
Sarum 02–06; PtO *Lon* 09–11; Chapl Hertf Coll Ox 11–16;
Prec Perth Cathl Australia from 16. *St George's Cathedral, 38
St George's Terrace, Perth WA 6000, Australia* T: (0061) (8)
9325 5766 E: gareth.hughes@perthcathedral.org

HUGHES, The Very Revd Geraint Morgan Hugh. b 34. Keble
Coll Ox BA 58 MA 63. St Mich Coll Llan 58. **d** 59 **p** 60. C
Gorseinon *S & B* 59–63; C Oystermouth 63–68; R Llanbadarn
Fawr, Llandegley and Llanfihangel etc 68–76; R Llandrindod
w Cefnllys 76–86; R Llandrindod w Cefnllys and Disserth
87–98; Can Brecon Cathl 89–98; Prec Brecon Cathl 95–98;
RD Maelienydd 95–98; Dean Brecon 98–00; V Brecon
St Mary and Battle w Llanddew 98–00; rtd 00. *Hafod, Cefnllys
Lane, Penybont, Llandrindod Wells LD1 5SW* T: (01597)
851830

HUGHES, Canon Gerald Thomas. b 30. Lon Univ BD 63
MTh. Qu Coll Birm 72. **d** 72 **p** 73. LtO *Cov* 72–80; P-in-c
Birdingbury 80–81; P-in-c Leamington Hastings 80–81; V
Leamington Hastings and Birdingbury 81–82; V Dunchurch
82–89; RD Rugby 85–89; Can Res Cov Cathl 89–94; rtd
94; PtO *Cov* from 94; *Worc* from 94. *Loafers' Cottage, Lazy
Lane, Fladbury, Pershore WR10 2QL* T: (01386) 860650
E: gerald@loafers.plus.net

HUGHES, Canon Gwilym Berw. b 42. St Mich Coll Llan.
d 68 **p** 69. C Conwy w Gyffin *Ban* 68–71; V Llandinorwig
71–75; TV Llandudno 75–80; V Dwygyfylchi 80–96; RD
Archllechwedd 88–96; V Bodelwyddan *St As* 96–09; Can
Cursal St As Cathl 08–09; rtd 09; PtO *Ban* from 09; *St As*
from 10. *Glanfa, Glanyrafon Road, Dwygyfylchi, Penmaenmawr
LL34 6UD* T: (01492) 623365

HUGHES, Gwilym Lloyd. b 48. Univ of Wales (Cardiff) BD 76
MA 79 Univ of Wales (Ban) CertEd 84. St Mich Coll Llan 71.
d 99 **p** 00. NSM Caerwys and Bodfari *St As* 99–14; Warden
of Readers 99–02; PtO from 14. *Grove Hall, Bodfari, Denbigh
LL16 4DE* E: lloyd.hughes@btconnect.com

HUGHES, Ian Peter. b 55. Fitzw Coll Cam BA 76 MA 93. Ridley
Hall Cam 05. **d** 07 **p** 08. C Wadhurst *Chich* 07–11; C Howell
Hill w Burgh Heath *Guildf* 11–17; PtO from 18. *2 Meadow
Close, Westcott, Dorking RH4 3GG* E: ian@hughes.name

HUGHES, Preb Ivor Gordon. b 45. Westmr Coll Ox MTh 94
Culham Coll of Educn CertEd 68. Ripon Coll Cuddesdon 75.
d 77 **p** 78. C Newport w Longford *Lich* 77–79; Children's
Work Officer CMS 79–82; V Gt and Lt Bedwyn and Savernake
Forest *Sarum* 82–86; P-in-c Urchfont w Stert 86–90; TR
Redhorn 90–92; Nat Children's Officer Gen Syn Bd of Educn
92–95; R Yeovil w Kingston Pitney *B & W* 95–06; Preb Wells
Cathl 02–06; RD Yeovil 04–06; Chapl St Marg Hospice
Yeovil 04–06; P-in-c Klamath Falls and Bonanza USA 06–08;
rtd 08; PtO *B & W* from 08; *Sarum* from 13. *15 Leventon*

Place, Hilperton, Trowbridge BA14 7US T: (01225) 760275
E: hughes6cm@btinternet.com

HUGHES, Canon Jacqueline Louise. b 50. Birm Poly BEd 86
ACP 81. WMMTC 89. **d** 92. NSM Edgbaston St Geo *Birm*
92–95; Tutor Qu Coll Birm 96–00; Educn Chapl Birm
City Coun 00–10; Dir of Educn *Birm* 10–15; Hon Can
Birm Cathl 14–15; rtd 15; PtO *Birm* 05–16. *267 Stoney
Lane, Yardley, Birmingham B25 8YG* T: 0121-628 4184
E: jackielhughes1950@gmail.com

HUGHES, James Thomas. b 74. St Anne's Coll Ox BA 95 Liv
Hope PGCE 97. Oak Hill Th Coll BA 02. **d** 03 **p** 04. C Virginia
Water *Guildf* 03–07; C Hartford *Ches* 07–16; V Duffield and Lt
Eaton *Derby* from 16. *The Vicarage, 2 Vicarage Lane, Duffield,
Belper DE56 4EB* E: james.t.hughes@btopenworld.com

HUGHES, John. *See* HUGHES, Arthur John

HUGHES, John David. b 58. Leeds Univ BA 79 Man
Univ PGCE 82. Ripon Coll Cuddesdon 97. **d** 99 **p** 00.
C Wythenshawe *Man* 99–06; P-in-c Old Trafford St Jo
06–18; R from 18; AD Stretford 10–15. *St John's Rectory, 1
Lindum Avenue, Manchester M16 9NQ* T: 0161-872 0500
E: john_dhughes@yahoo.co.uk

HUGHES, John Malcolm. b 47. Man Univ BSc 68. Coll of
Resurr Mirfield 68. **d** 71 **p** 72. C Newton Nottage *Llan* 71–78;
V Llanwynno 78–92; R Cadoxton-juxta-Barry 92–11; AD
Penarth and Barry 08–11; rtd 11; PtO *Llan* from 14; *Mon* from
14. *3 The Terrace, Rhymney, Tredegar NP22 5LY* T: (01685)
555374 E: fr.johnhughessc@hotmail.com

HUGHES, Canon John Patrick. b 41. Oak Hill Th Coll.
d 67 **p** 68. C Chorleywood St Andr *St Alb* 67–71; C E
Twickenham St Steph *Lon* 71–76; TV High Wycombe *Ox*
77–92; Chapl Wycombe Gen Hosp 77–83; V Harborne
Heath *Birm* 92–09; Hon Can Birm Cathl 99–09; rtd 09;
PtO *Ox* from 10. *59 Witney Road, Ducklington, Witney
OX29 7TS* T: (01993) 358781 M: 07817-465996
E: johnandanniehughes@googlemail.com

HUGHES, Canon John Tudor. b 59. Nottm Univ BSc 81 Univ
of Wales (Cardiff) BD 84. St Mich Coll Llan 81. **d** 84 **p** 85.
C Mold *St As* 84–88; Asst Dioc Youth Chapl 86–90; Dioc
Youth Chapl 90–97; Min Can St As Cathl 88–90; Min St As
and Tremeirchion 88–90; V Holt 90–96; V Buckley 96–04;
RD Mold 00–03; V Gresford 04–09; V Holt and Gresford
09–16; TV Alyn Miss Area from 17; Can Cursal St As Cathl
05–13; Can Res, Preb and Sacr from 13. *The Vicarage, Church
Green, Gresford, Wrexham LL12 8RG* T: (01978) 852236
E: tudorhughes53@gmail.com

HUGHES, Jonathan William Llewelyn. b 83. Fitzw Coll Cam
BA 05 MA 09. St Mellitus Coll 14. **d** 16 **p** 17. C Lenton Abbey
S'well from 16. *7 Kingston Road, West Bridgford, Nottingham
NG2 7AQ* M: 07720-540302

HUGHES, Katherine. *See* HACKER HUGHES, Katherine Lucy

HUGHES, Lindsay. *See* HUGHES, Carol Lindsay

HUGHES, Lloyd. *See* HUGHES, Gwilym Lloyd

HUGHES, Martin Conway. b 40. Ex Coll Ox BA 61 MA 67.
Chich Th Coll. **d** 63 **p** 64. C Roehampton H Trin *S'wark*
63–67; C Addlestone *Guildf* 67–71; V Burpham 71–88;
V Shamley Green 88–05; RD Cranleigh 90–95; rtd 05;
PtO *Portsm* from 05; *Win* from 08. *22 Siskin Close, Bishops
Waltham, Southampton SO32 1RQ* T: (01489) 890365
E: martin@mchughes.org.uk

HUGHES, Matthew James. b 66. K Coll Lon BD 88. Westcott
Ho Cam 89. **d** 91 **p** 92. C Heston *Lon* 91–94; C Fulham All
SS 94–96; TV St Laur in Thanet *Cant* 96–01; R Farnborough
Roch from 01. *The Rectory, Farnborough Hill, Orpington
BR6 7EQ* T: (01689) 856931 E: jmath@btinternet.com

HUGHES, Michael John Minto. b 50. Liv Univ MB, ChB 74
Westmr Coll Ox MTh 94. Wycliffe Hall Ox 76. **d** 79
p 80. C Stranton *Dur* 79–82; Chapl Intercon Ch Soc
Peru 82–86; PtO *Dur* 86–87; *Carl* 87–89; TV Thetford
Nor 89–97; P-in-c Downham *Ely* 97–05; Hon C Ely
05–13; CMS Uganda 13–18; rtd 18. *44 Merchant Gate,
Riverside Square, Bedford MK40 1AS* M: 07542-840685
E: mikeandsue.hughes@gmail.com

HUGHES, Neville Joseph. b 52. NUU BA 79 MBIM 93.
CITC 97. **d** 91 **p** 92. NSM Mullabrack w Markethill and
Kilcluney *Arm* 91–98; I 00–18; C Portadown St Mark 98–00;
Can Arm Cathl 14–18; rtd 18. *24 Derryhale Road, Portadown,
Craigavon BT62 4HE* T: (028) 3833 3647

HUGHES, The Ven Paul Vernon. b 53. Ripon Coll
Cuddesdon 79. **d** 82 **p** 83. C Chipping Barnet w Arkley *St Alb*
82–86; TV Dunstable 86–93; P-in-c Boxmoor St Jo 93–98; V
98–03; RD Hemel Hempstead 96–03; Adn Bedford 03–19; rtd
19. *156 Buckingham Drive, Luton LU2 9RE*

HUGHES, Mrs Penelope Patricia. b 47. Sheff Univ LLB.
WMMTC 95. **d** 98 **p** 99. NSM Whitley *Cov* 98–01; NSM
Leamington Spa H Trin and Old Milverton 01–03; P-in-c
Berkswell 03–08; rtd 08; PtO *Cov* from 08. *8 Albany*

Terrace, Leamington Spa CV32 5LP T: (01926) 330204 E: penhughes@aol.com

HUGHES, Peter John. b 59. Wolv Poly BA 83 Lon Univ PGCE 85. Wycliffe Hall Ox 90. **d** 92 **p** 93. C Ecclesall *Sheff* 92–96; V Kimberworth 96–05; R Wickersley from 05; P-in-c Ravenfield, Hooton Roberts and Braithwell from 17; AD Rotherham from 17. *The Rectory, 5 Church Lane, Wickersley, Rotherham S66 1ES* T: (01709) 543111 E: peter.j.hughes59@btinternet.com

HUGHES, Canon Philip. b 47. St Jo Coll Nottm 79. **d** 81 **p** 82. C Dolgellau w Llanfachreth and Brithdir etc *Ban* 81–83; Asst Youth Chapl 82–83; R Llaneugrad w Llanallgo and Penrhosllugwy etc 83–95; R Llanberis w Llanrug 95–03; R Llanberis, Llanrug and Llandinorwig 03; Dioc Youth Chapl 93–98; RD Arfon 00–02; R Llanfair-pwll and Llanddaniel-fab etc 03–12; AD Tindaethwy and Menai 07–10; Can Ban Cathl 10–12; rtd 12; PtO *Ban* from 12. *Afallon, 27 Pengarth, Conwy LL32 8RW* T: (01492) 562866 E: revphiliphughes@yahoo.co.uk

HUGHES, Philip Geoffrey John. b 60. Nottm Univ BCombStuds 82. Qu Coll Birm 86. **d** 89 **p** 90. C Sedgley All SS *Worc* 89–94; V Boscoppa *Truro* 94–96; Chapl Gatwick Airport and Chapl Sussex Police 96–02; P-in-c Harmondsworth *Lon* 02–07; Chapl Heathrow Airport 02–07; Chapl Metrop Police 02–07; V Seghill *Newc* from 07; AD Bedlington from 13; Chapl Northumbria Police 07–13. *Seghill Vicarage, Mares Close, Seghill NE23 7EA* T: 0191-298 0925 E: phil.hughes@pobroadband.co.uk

HUGHES, Philip Stephen. b 34. Dur Univ BA 59. Coll of Resurr Mirfield 59. **d** 62 **p** 63. C Horfield St Greg *Bris* 62–66; C Bedminster St Mich 66–69; P-in-c Chippenham St Pet 69–71; V 71–83; TR Bedminster 83–91; V Ashton Keynes, Leigh and Minety 91–00; rtd 00; PtO *Worc* from 00. *19 Fairways, Pershore WR10 1HA* T: (01386) 552375 E: p-jhughes@outlook.com

HUGHES, Poppy. *See* HUGHES, Veronica Jane

HUGHES, Richard Millree. b 33. Univ of Wales BA 56 MA 79. St Mich Coll Llan 56. **d** 58 **p** 59. C Mold *St As* 58–61; V Choral St As Cathl 61–64; V Towyn 64–67; Asst Master Marlborough Sch Woodstock 77–79; R Whitchurch St Mary *Ox* 79–00; rtd 00; PtO *St As* 13–14; P-in-c Llansilin w Llangadwaladr and Llangedwyn 14–16; TV Tanat Valley Miss Area 17–18; PtO from 18. *The Vicarage, Llansilin, Oswestry SY10 7PX* T: (01691) 791876 M: 07798-790369 E: rmillree@aol.com

HUGHES, Robert Elistan-Glodrydd. b 32. Trin Coll Ox BA 54 MA 58 Birm Univ MLitt 85. Westcott Ho Cam 55. **d** 57 **p** 58. C Stoke *Cov* 57–61; Ind Chapl *S'wark* 61–64; Chapl Birm Univ 64–69; Lodgings Warden and Student Welfare Adv 69–87; Dir Housing Study Overseas Students Trust 88–91; PtO *Ban* 88–94; V Harlech and Llanfair-juxta-Harlech etc 94–99; rtd 97. *Clogwyn Melyn, Ynys, Talsarnau LL47 6TP* T: (01766) 780257 E: shebob.clog1@virgin.net

HUGHES, Rodney Thomas. b 39. Dur Univ BA 60. Wycliffe Hall Ox 60. **d** 62 **p** 63. C Edin St Thos 62–65; C Harlow New Town w Lt Parndon *Chelmsf* 65–67; R Haworth *Bradf* 67–74; R W Knighton w Broadmayne *Sarum* 74–77; R Broadmayne, W Knighton, Owermoigne etc 77–82; V Crosthwaite Keswick *Carl* 82–02; PtO *Carl* from 02. *2 Bewcastle Close, Carlisle CA3 0PU* T: (01228) 401680

HUGHES, Canon Sally Lorraine. b 59. Open Univ BA 98. EAMTC 99. **d** 02 **p** 03. NSM Gretton w Rockingham and Cottingham w E Carlton *Pet* 02–05; Asst Chapl Kettering Gen Hosp NHS Trust 02–04; P-in-c Stoke Albany w Wilbarston and Ashley etc *Pet* 05–06; R 16–18; Rural Adv Oakham Adnry 05–06; Can Pet Cathl 17–18; rtd 19. *28 Rushton Road, Wilbarston, Market Harborough LE16 8QL* T/F: (01536) 770998 E: sally@hughes.uk.com

HUGHES, Mrs Sheila. b 52. NOC 92. **d** 95 **p** 96. NSM Birkenhead Priory *Ches* 95–97; C 97–99; P-in-c Northwich St Luke and H Trin 99–01; V 01–07; Bp's Adv for Women in Min 00–07; Chapl Mid Cheshire Hosps Trust 99–07; P-in-c Barrow St Jo *Carl* 07–14; rtd 14; P-in-c Lorton and Loweswater w Buttermere *Carl* 14–17. *7 Pine Tree Avenue, Prenton CH43 9RX* T: 0151-678 4233 E: vicarlolobu@hotmail.com

HUGHES, Sheila Norah. b 40. **d** 06 **p** 07. NSM Ellesmere Port *Ches* 06–10; rtd 10; PtO from 10. *13 Bridle Way, Great Sutton, Ellesmere Port CH66 2NJ* T: 0151-339 9777 E: sheila.hughes67@ntlworld.com

HUGHES, Timothy David Llewelyn. b 77. St Mellitus Coll. **d** 13 **p** 14. C Onslow Square and S Kensington St Aug *Lon* 13–15; P-in-c Birm St Luke from 15. *38 Carpenter Road, Birmingham B15 2JJ* M: 07590-692535 E: tim@worshipcentral.org

HUGHES, Trystan Owain. b 72. Univ of Wales (Ban) BD 94 PhD 98. Wycliffe Hall Ox MTh. **d** 05 **p** 07. C Llantwit Major *Llan* 05–09; C Whitchurch 09; Chapl Cardiff Univ 09–13;

P-in-c Cardiff Ch Ch Roath Park from 13; Dioc Dir of Ords 13–15; Dir of Voc from 15. *Christ Church Vicarage, 154 Lake Road East, Cardiff CF23 5NQ* T: (029) 2075 8588 *or* 2075 7190 E: trystanhughes@churchinwales.org.uk

HUGHES, Tudor. *See* HUGHES, John Tudor

HUGHES, Ms Valerie Elizabeth. b 53. Birm Univ BA 75 CertEd 76. Wycliffe Hall Ox 85. **d** 87 **p** 94. C Hallwood *Ches* 87–90; Par Dn Garston *Liv* 90–93; Asst Chapl Liv Univ 93; Team Dn Gateacre 93–94; TV 94–00; C St Helens St Helen 00–09; TV Newton 09–19; rtd 19. *21 Coronation Drive, Chirk, Wrexham LL14 5LF* E: val.hughes@live.co.uk

HUGHES, Veronica Jane (Poppy). b 60. Ex Univ BA 82 Birkbeck Coll Lon MSc 04. SEITE 07. **d** 10 **p** 11. C Dulwich St Clem w St Pet *S'wark* 10–13; P-in-c Tetbury, Beverston, Long Newnton etc *Glouc* 13–14; R from 14; R Avening w Cherington 14–16; AD Cirencester from 18. *The Vicarage, 6 The Green, Tetbury GL8 8DN* T: (01666) 502333 E: poppy_hughes@hotmail.co.uk

HUGHES, Canon William Piers Maximillian. b 76. Ex Univ BA 99. Ripon Coll Cuddesdon 99. **d** 01 **p** 02. C Cley Hill Warminster *Sarum* 01–05; V Blackmoor and Whitehill *Portsm* 05–11; V Petersfield from 11; R Buriton from 11; AD Petersfield 11–16; Hon Can Portsm Cathl from 15. *12 Dragon Street, Petersfield GU31 4AB* T: (01730) 260464 E: revwilliamhughes@btinternet.com

HUGHESDON, James Carlyle. b 82. Ex Univ BA 05 Anglia Ruskin Univ MA 12. Westcott Ho Cam 10. **d** 12 **p** 13. C Old Ford St Paul and St Mark *Lon* 12–15; V from 15. *The Vicarage, St Stephen's Road, London E3 5JL* M: 07841-123869 E: james@stpauloldford.com

HUGHMAN, June Alison. b 58. Kingston Poly BSc 81 Southn Univ PhD 84. Trin Coll Bris 86. **d** 89 **p** 94. Par Dn Penge St Jo *Roch* 89–93; C Woking Ch Ch *Guildf* 93–98; V Croydon Ch Ch *S'wark* 98–00; C Uxbridge *Lon* from 00; Town Cen Min from 00. *84 Harefield Road, Uxbridge UB8 1PN* T: (01895) 254121 *or* 258766 F: 254121 E: junehughman@tiscali.co.uk *or* june.hughman@uxbridgeparish.org

HUGO, Canon Keith Alan. b 41. Nottm Univ BA 62. Chich Th Coll 62. **d** 64 **p** 65. C Pontefract St Giles *Wakef* 64–68; C Chesterfield St Mary and All SS *Derby* 68–71; V Allenton and Shelton Lock 71–77; Dioc Communications Officer *Sarum* 77–89; V Potterne 77–84; V Worton 77–84; V Potterne w Worton and Marston 84–89; R Wyke Regis 89–06; Can and Preb Sarum Cathl 84–06; RD Weymouth 94–04; rtd 06; PtO *Sarum* from 06; *Eur* from 18. *15 Steepdene, Poole BH14 8TE* T: (01202) 734971 E: keith.hugo@ntlworld.com

HUISH, Barnaby Thomas. b 71. St Chad's Coll Dur BA 94 MA 95. Ripon Coll Cuddesdon BA 98. **d** 99 **p** 00. C Darlington H Trin *Dur* 99–02; Prec and Min Can St Alb Abbey 02–06; R Dur St Marg and Neville's Cross St Jo from 06. *St Margaret's Rectory, 10 Westhouse Avenue, Durham DH1 4FH*

HUITSON, Christopher Philip. b 45. Keble Coll Ox BA 66 MA 70. Cuddesdon Coll 67. **d** 69 **p** 70. C Croydon St Sav *Cant* 69–71; Soc Service Unit St Martin-in-the-Fields Lon 71–73; C St Alb St Pet 73–77; V Cople 77–78; P-in-c Willington 77–78; V Cople w Willington 78–89; V Leavesden 89–96; V Totteridge 96–11; RD Barnet 99–05; rtd 11; PtO *Sarum* from 12; *St Alb* 11–16. *Abbotsleigh, 1A Gainsborough Drive, Sherborne DT9 6DS* T: (01935) 815187 E: c.huitson33@btinternet.com

HULBERT, John Anthony Lovett. b 40. Trin Coll Cam BA 63 MA 67. Wells Th Coll 64. **d** 66 **p** 67. C Fareham H Trin *Portsm* 66–70; R Wickham 70–79; RD Bishop's Waltham 74–79; V Bedford St Andr *St Alb* 79–92; RD Bedford 87–92; V Leighton Buzzard w Eggington, Hockliffe etc 92–03; Hon Can St Alb 91–03; C Stansted *Chich* 03–04; P-in-c Lynch w Iping Marsh and Milland 04–10; rtd 10; PtO *Chich* from 10; *Portsm* from 11. *Cherry Trees, Buckshead Hill, Meonstoke, Southampton SO32 3NA* T: (01489) 878289 E: anthonic@btinternet.com

HULBERT, Canon Martin Francis Harrington. b 37. Dur Univ BSc 58 MA 62. Ripon Hall Ox 58. **d** 60 **p** 61. C Buxton *Derby* 60–63; C Eglingham *Newc* 63–67; C-in-c Loundsley Green Ascension CD *Derby* 67–71; P-in-c Frecheville 71–72; R Frecheville and Hackenthorpe *Sheff* 73–77; P-in-c Hathersage *Derby* 77–83; V 83–90; RD Bakewell and Eyam 81–90; R Brailsford w Shirley and Osmaston w Edlaston 90–93; V Tideswell 93–02; RD Buxton 96–99; Hon Can Derby Cathl 89–02; rtd 02; PtO *Derby* from 02. *18 Yokecliffe Crescent, Wirksworth, Matlock DE4 4ER* T: (01629) 825148 E: martin.hulbert1@btinternet.com

HULKS, Mrs Nicola Ann. b 84. Ripon Coll Cuddesdon 12. **d** 15 **p** 16. C Maidenhead St Luke *Ox* 15–19; TV Thatcham from 19. *1 Cowslip Crescent, Thatcham RG18 4DE* M: 07884-264131 E: nicola.hulks@hotmail.co.uk

HULL, Mrs Bernadette Mary. b 46. E Lon Univ BA 92 PGCE 93. NTMTC 99. **d** 02 **p** 03. NSM Becontree S *Chelmsf* 02–04; NSM Marks Gate 04–09; P-in-c Romford Ascension Collier Row 09–17; rtd 17; PtO *Chelmsf* 18–19. *1 Colin Pond Court, 21 Longhayes Avenue, Romford RM6 5HB* T: (020) 8598 8027 M: 07506-377414 E: revbernadettehull@gmail.com

HULL, David John. b 44. Linc Th Coll 88. **d** 90 **p** 91. C Mansfield Woodhouse *S'well* 90–93; P-in-c Mansfield St Lawr 93–00; V Mosborough *Sheff* 00–03; V Elmton *Derby* 03–09; P-in-c Whitwell 05–09; rtd 10; PtO *Derby* from 10; *S'well* 10–16. *5 Beeley Close, Creswell, Worksop S80 4GA* T: (01909) 724104 E: rev.dhull@tiscali.co.uk

HULL, The Very Revd Thomas Henry. b 55. QUB BD 79. NTMTC 94. **d** 97 **p** 98. C Kidbrooke *S'wark* 97–99; TV 99–01; I Lecale Gp *D & D* from 01; Min Can Down Cathl 03–06; Dean Down from 06. *Lecale Rectory, 9 Quoile Road, Downpatrick BT30 6SE* T: (028) 4461 3101 *or* 4461 4922 F: 4461 4456 E: henryhull@downcathedral.org

HULL, Timothy David. b 60. Lon Bible Coll 87 K Coll Lon PhD 97. St Jo Coll Nottm BTh 90. **d** 90 **p** 91. C Leyton St Mary w St Edw *Chelmsf* 90–95; Chapl Havering Coll of F&HE 94–98; C Harold Hill St Geo *Chelmsf* 95–98; TV Becontree W 98–05; Co-ord NTMTC 98–01; Registrar 01–05; Tutor St Jo Coll Nottm from 05. *St John's College, Chilwell Lane, Bramcote, Nottingham NG9 3DS* T: 0115-925 1114 E: t.hull@stjohns-nottm.ac.uk

HULL, Suffragan Bishop of. *See* WHITE, The Rt Revd Alison Mary

HULLYER, Paul Charles. b 68. Anglia Poly Univ MA 98 Lambeth MA 04 FRSA 04. Aston Tr Scheme 92 Westcott Ho Cam 94. **d** 97 **p** 98. C Stoke Newington St Mary *Lon* 97–00; C Addlestone *Guildf* 00–03; V Hillingdon All SS *Lon* 03–08; V Pinner from 08; Dir Post-Ord Tr 10–15; CF from 12. *The Vicarage, 2 Church Lane, Pinner HA5 3AA* T: (020) 8866 3869

HULME, Alan John. b 60. Birm Univ BSc 81. Wycliffe Hall Ox BA 90. **d** 91 **p** 92. C Chilwell *S'well* 91–96; TV Roxeth *Lon* 96–02; V S Harrow St Paul 02–08; TR Ely 08–13; Dioc Dir Par Development and Evang *Guildf* 13–18. *16 Lyons Drive, Guildford GU2 9YP*

HULME (née ASHLEY), Mrs Jane Isobel. b 59. Birm Univ BSc 81. **d** 05 **p** 06. NSM S Harrow St Paul *Lon* 05–08; NSM Ely 08–13; PtO *Guildf* 13–18. *16 Lyons Drive, Guildford GU2 9YP* T: (01483) 234046 E: janehulme59@gmail.com

HULME, Ms Juliette Mary. b 57. Whitelands Coll Lon BEd 81. Cranmer Hall Dur 94. **d** 94 **p** 95. C Crayford *Roch* 94–98; C Leatherhead *Guildf* 98–01; CF 02–05; PtO *Sarum* 05–08; Chapl Wells Cathl Sch 06–18; TV Nadder Valley *Sarum* from 18. *The Rectory, Park Road, Tisbury, Salisbury SP3 6LF* T: (01747) 871957 E: revjmhulme@gmail.com

HULME, Susan. b 52. **d** 08 **p** 09. NSM Kinsley w Wragby *Wakef* 08–12; NSM Brotherton 12–14; *Leeds* from 14; NSM Ferrybridge *Wakef* 12–14; *Leeds* from 14; Chapl Mid Yorks Hosps NHS Trust from 13. *4 Balmoral Drive, Knottingley WF11 8RQ* T: (01977) 676808 E: bedeuk@talk21.com

HULME, Suffragan Bishop of. Vacant

HULSE (formerly WHITTINGHAM), Mrs Janet Irene. b 49. **d** 03 **p** 04. OLM Pendleton *Man* 03–09; OLM Salford All SS 09–16; Chapl Salford R NHS Foundn Trust from 14; PtO *Man* from 16. *24 Aylesbury Close, Salford M5 4FQ* T: 0161-736 5878 M: 07905-667308 E: revjhulse@gmail.com

HULSE, Mrs Ruth Carole. b 80. Ripon Coll Cuddesdon 11. **d** 13 **p** 14. C W Heref 13–16; TV from 16. *The Vicarage, Vowles Close, Hereford HR4 0DF* T: (01432) 273086 M: 07733-323290 E: ruthhulse@hotmail.co.uk

HULSE, William John. b 42. Dur Univ BA 65. Linc Th Coll 65. **d** 67 **p** 68. C S Westoe *Dur* 67–70; LtO *Newc* 70–72; C Far Headingley St Chad *Ripon* 72–76; R Swillington 76–88; V Shadwell 88–95; V Oulton w Woodlesford 95–02; P-in-c Spennithorne w Finghall and Hauxwell 02–12; Chapl MU 03–09; rtd 12; PtO *Ripon* 13–14; *Leeds* from 14. *5 Hargill Close, Harmby, Leyburn DL8 5QE* T: (01969) 623396 E: wjhulse@btinternet.com

HUMBLE, Reid Thomas. b 87. Oklahoma Chr Univ BA 09 Sheff Univ MA 11. Westcott Ho Cam 12. **d** 16 **p** 17. C Rotherham *Sheff* 16–18; C Walkley 18–19; Asst Chapl Sheff Univ 18–19; P-in-c Southchurch H Trin *Chelmsf* from 19. *The Rectory, 8 Pilgrims Close, Southend-on-Sea SS2 4XF* M: 07577-769450 E: reverend.reidhumble@gmail.com

HUME, Mrs Barbara Christine. b 56. NTMTC 94. **d** 97 **p** 98. NSM Romford St Edw *Chelmsf* 97–01; C 01–11; P-in-c Upper Colne 11–17; P-in-c Sible Hedingham w Castle Hedingham 16–17; R The Hedinghams and Upper Colne 17; rtd 18; PtO *Chelmsf* from 18. *Robins Rest, Moat Street, Gestingthorpe, Halstead CO9 3AT* M: 07707-680562 E: revbarbara8@gmail.com

HUME, Miss Clephane Arrol. b 46. Open Univ BA 87 Edin Univ MTh 98 DipOT 68. Edin Dioc NSM Course 88. **d** 92 **p** 94. NSM Edin St Jo from 92. *26 Findhorn Place, Edinburgh EH9 2JP* T: 0131-667 2996 F: 668 3568 E: cah@clephane.plus.com

HUME, Ernest. b 45. Linc Th Coll 77. **d** 79 **p** 80. C Ilkeston St Mary *Derby* 79–81; C Sheff Manor 81–82; TV 82–88; V Norton Woodseats St Chad 88–99; V Woodhouse St Jas 99–02; rtd 02. *Shadwell, 6 Canal Bridge, Killamarsh, Sheffield S21 1DJ* T: 0114-248 1769

HUME, Martin. b 54. Coll of Resurr Mirfield 89. **d** 91 **p** 92. C Brentwood St Thos *Chelmsf* 91–94; P-in-c Corringham 94–04; V E Wickham *S'wark* 04–10; rtd 10; PtO *Chich* from 11. *55 Farm Road, Hove BN3 1FD* T: (01273) 206478 M: 07901-553522 E: martinhume@aol.com

HUME, Richard Fletcher. b 68. Qu Foundn (Course) 14. **d** 17 **p** 18. OLM Longton St Mary and St Chad *Lich* 17–18; C Walsall St Gabr Fulbrook from 19. *1A Orchard Road, Walsall WS5 4UT* M: 07887-761147

HUMM, Andrew James. b 72. St Jo Coll Nottm 10. **d** 12 **p** 13. C Loughborough Em and St Mary in Charnwood *Leic* 12–14; C Loughborough Em 15–16; P-in-c Tiverton St Geo and St Paul *Ex* from 16. *St Paul's Vicarage, Bakers Hill, Tiverton EX16 5NE* E: as_humm@yahoo.com

HUMPHREY, Alan. b 48. Open Univ BA 74. Qu Coll Birm 07. **d** 10 **p** 11. C Kirby Muxloe *Leic* 10–15; R Leicester Forest East 15–18; Warden Community of the Tree of Life from 18; PtO *Leic* from 18. *The Community of the Tree of Life, St Martin's House, 7 Peacock Lane, Leicester LE1 5PZ* T: 0116-261 5200 M: 07768-374200 E: alan.humphrey@icloud.com

HUMPHREY, David Lane. b 57. Maine Univ BA 79. St Jo Coll Nottm 84. **d** 88 **p** 89. C Springfield All SS *Chelmsf* 89–91; C Thundersley 91–96; V Standon *St Alb* 96–04; RD Bishop's Stortford 01–04; R Portland St Matt USA from 04. *11229 NE Prescott Street, Portland OR 97220-2457, USA* T: (001) (503) 252 5720 E: humphrey@iinet.com

HUMPHREY, Timothy Martin. b 62. Ex Univ BA 83. St Jo Coll Nottm 86. **d** 89 **p** 90. C Wallington *S'wark* 89–92; P-in-c 92–97; C Oakley w Wootton St Lawrence *Win* 97–02; Faith Development Field Officer 97–02; V Kensington St Barn *Lon* 02–15; V Tunbridge Wells Ch Ch *Roch* from 17. *The Vicarage, 63 Claremont Road, Tunbridge Wells TN1 1TE* T: (01892) 526644

HUMPHREYS, Mrs Anne-Marie (Anna). b 44. SRN 67 K Coll Lon BD 92 AKC 92 Man Univ MA 96. NOC 92. **d** 95 **p** 96. NSM Manchester Gd Shep and St Barn *Man* 95–98; NSM Burnage St Nic 98–03; Chapl Cen Man Healthcare NHS Trust 96–01; Chapl Cen Man/Man Children's Univ Hosp NHS Trust 01–06; rtd 06; PtO *Ban* 10–17; *St As* from 17. *Eryl Mor, 60 Deganwy Road, Deganwy, Conwy LL31 9DN* T: (01492) 573396

HUMPHREYS, Brian Leonard. b 29. MChS 51 SRCh. Bp Attwell Tr Inst. **d** 87 **p** 88. NSM Maughold *S & M* 87–91; NSM S Ramsey St Paul 91–92; NSM Andreas 92–94; PtO 94–10. *1 Seafield, Ballure Road, Ramsey, Isle of Man IM8 1NL* T: (01624) 813694

HUMPHREYS, John Louis. b 51. Jes Coll Cam BA 72 MA 76 Nottm Univ BA 75. St Jo Coll Nottm 73. **d** 76 **p** 77. C W Bromwich Gd Shep w St Jo *Lich* 76–79; C Woodford Wells *Chelmsf* 79–83; V Werrington *Lich* 83–08; Chapl HM YOI Werrington Ho 83–98; PtO *Lich* 09–18. *61 Josephine Avenue, Lower Kingswood, Tadworth KT20 7AB* T: (01737) 832922

HUMPHREYS, Canon Kenneth Glyn. b 28. Bps' Coll Cheshunt 64. **d** 66 **p** 67. C New Windsor St Jo *Ox* 66–67; C Whitley Ch Ch 67–70; V Compton 70–74; R Compton w E Ilsley 74–75; C Wokingham All SS 75–77; Chapl Lucas Hosp Wokingham (Almshouses) 77–81; V California *Ox* 81–94; RD Sonning 86–88; Hon Can Ch Ch 91–94; rtd 95; PtO *Ox* 96–18. *36 Kennet Court, Wokingham RG41 3DB* E: canonkenh@gmail.com

HUMPHREYS, Canon Roger John. b 45. CertEd 66 Open Univ BA 76. Wycliffe Hall Ox 81. **d** 83 **p** 84. Chapl Dragon Sch Ox 83–87; C Ox St Andr 83–87; V Carterton 87–94; R Bladon w Woodstock 94–05; TR Blenheim 05–09; AD Woodstock 01–06; Chapl Cokethorpe Sch Witney 09–13; Hon Can Ch Ch *Ox* 05–14; PtO from 09; *Eur* from 15. *12 The Pieces, Bampton, Oxford OX18 2JZ* T: (01993) 850199 M: 07788-717214 E: rev.rog@zen.co.uk

HUMPHREYS, Stephen Robert Beresford. b 52. K Coll Lon BA 98. 74. **d** 76 **p** 77. C Northwood Hills St John *Lon* 76–79; C Manningham St Mary and Bradf St Mich 79–81; Chapl Bradf R Infirmary 82–86; C Leeds St Pet *Ripon* 87–90; PtO *B & W* 94–99; C Selworthy, Timberscombe, Wootton Courtenay etc 02–07; C Porlock and Porlock Weir w Stoke Pero etc from 07. *Stowey Farm, Timberscombe, Minehead TA24 7BW* T: (01643) 841265 M: 07973-409536 E: srbh@mac.com

HUMPHRIES, Anthony Roy. b 49. Lon Univ BSc 73. Wycliffe Hall Ox. **d** 94 **p** 95. C Worksop St Jo *S'well* 94–96; C Retford St Sav 96–98; TV Grantham *Linc* 98–00; TV Bestwood *S'well* 00–03; V Branston w Tatenhill *Lich* 03–07; P-in-c Gisburn *Bradf* 12–14; P-in-c Gisburn *Blackb* 14–16. *Fell Cottage, 9 High Town, Westgate, Bishop Auckland DL13 1JR* T: (01388) 517283 M: 07809-177343 E: revtonyhumphries@hotmail.com

HUMPHRIES, Benjamin Paul. b 56. Man Univ BA 77 FRGS 85. Qu Coll Birm 82. **d** 85 **p** 86. C Hall Green Ascension *Birm* 85–88; P-in-c Belmont *Man* 88–96; Fieldworker USPG Blackb, Bradf, Carl and Wakef 96–98; Area Co-ord Chr Aid (Cumbria, Lancs and Isle of Man) 98–07; C Shepherd's Bush St Steph w St Thos *Lon* 07–12; Chapl Mombasa Miss to Seafarers Kenya 12–15; Chapl Dunkirk Miss to Seafarers *Eur* 15–17; C Shepherd's Bush St Steph w St Thos *Lon* 17–19; V White City from 19. *Church of St Michael and St George, 1 Commonwealth Avenue, London W12 7QR* M: 07712-460860 E: ben.humphries@london.anglican.org

HUMPHRIES, Catherine Elizabeth. See NICHOLLS, Catherine Elizabeth

HUMPHRIES, Canon Christopher William. b 52. St Jo Coll Cam BA 73 MA 77 Lon Inst of Educn CertEd 74. St Jo Coll Nottm 77. **d** 79 **p** 80. C Eccleshill *Bradf* 79–82; Chapl Scargill Ho 82–86; TV Guiseley w Esholt *Bradf* 86–91; V Filey *York* 91–05; RD Scarborough 98–04; Can Res Ches Cathl 05–14; V Whitegate w Lt Budworth 14–18; Hon Can Ches Cathl 14–18; rtd 18; PtO *York* from 19. *The Meadows, Bempton Lane, Flamborough, Bridlington YO15 1PS*

HUMPHRIES, David. See HUMPHRIES, William David

HUMPHRIES, David Graham. b 48. St Mich Coll Llan 67. **d** 71 **p** 72. C Neath w Llantwit *Llan* 71–72; C Bishop's Cleeve *Glouc* 81–83; C Cirencester 83–87; V Glouc St Steph 87–96; P-in-c Mickleton 96–03; Assoc P Up Hatherley 03–06; rtd 06; Chapl Glouc Charities Trust from 06. *19 Gurney Avenue, Tuffley, Gloucester GL4 0YJ* T: (01452) 529582 E: fr.didds@virginmedia.com

HUMPHRIES, David John. b 51. BSc CertEd BD. Edin Th Coll. **d** 84 **p** 85. C Styvechale *Cov* 84–88; V Greetland and W Vale *Wakef* 88–96; V Shawbury *Lich* 96–15; R Moreton Corbet 96–15; V Stanton on Hine Heath 96–15; rtd 15; PtO *Lich* from 16. *New Vicarage, Church Street, Shawbury, Shrewsbury SY4 4NH*

HUMPHRIES, Mrs Janet Susan. b 46. SAOMC 02. **d** 04 **p** 05. NSM Potton w Sutton and Cockayne Hatley *St Alb* 04–07; NSM Caldecote, Northill and Old Warden 07–16; PtO from 16. *7 Shakespeare Drive, Upper Caldecote, Biggleswade SG18 9DD* T: (01767) 220365 E: janet.humphries1@ntlworld.com

HUMPHRIES, Mrs Julie Ann. b 64. Birm Univ BA 02 MA 08. Qu Coll Birm 06. **d** 08 **p** 09. C Redditch H Trin *Worc* 08–12; TV Salter Street and Shirley *Birm* 12–17; V Salter Street 17–19. *Minfford, Waresley Road, Hartlebury, Kidderminster DY11 7XT* E: juliehumphries27@yahoo.co.uk

HUMPHRIES, Richard James Robert. b 44. Anglia Ruskin Univ MA 12 FRAM 95. EAMTC 99. **d** 01 **p** 02. NSM Heybridge w Langford *Chelmsf* 01–02; NSM Maldon All SS w St Pet 02–09; Asst Chapl Mid-Essex Hosp Services NHS Trust 01–04; Chapl Colchester Hosp Univ NHS Foundn Trust 04–09; rtd 09; PtO *Chelmsf* from 09. *20 Rosewood Park, Mistley, Manningtree CO11 1UH* T: (01206) 393240 M: 07803-281036 E: richard.humphries1@btopenworld.com

HUMPHRIES, Robert William. b 36. Open Univ BA 87. SWMTC 96. **d** 99 **p** 00. OLM Kenwyn w St Allen *Truro* from 99. *27 Penhalls Way, Playing Place, Truro TR3 6EX* T: (01872) 862827 E: rev.bobh@btinternet.com

HUMPHRIES, Sara Ann. b 59. Qu Foundn (Course) 15. **d** 18 **p** 19. OLM Ashley and Mucklestone and Broughton and Croxton *Lich* from 18. *12 Martin Dale, Loggerheads, Market Drayton TF9 4DH* T: (01630) 673740 M: 07989-731978 E: sarahumphries2@gmail.com

HUMPHRIES, Sidney Mark. b 53. **d** 13 **p** 14. NSM Littleham-cum-Exmouth w Lympstone *Ex* 13–17; C 17–18; V Aylesbeare, Clyst St George, Clyst St Mary etc 18–19. *36 Trafalgar Road, Lympstone, Exeter EX8 5HX* M: 07922-117556 E: revsidh@gmail.com

HUMPHRIES, Mrs Susan Joy. b 45. Open Univ BSc 98. Cranmer Hall Dur 05. **d** 06 **p** 07. NSM Beverley Minster *York* 06–09; NSM N Cave w Cliffe and Hotham 09–12; P-in-c 12; PtO *Worc* from 12. *119 Old Station Road, Bromsgrove B60 2AS* T: (01527) 577808 M: 07930-803601 E: rev.s.humphries@btinternet.com

HUMPHRIES, Canon William David. b 57. QUB BEd LTCL. CITC. **d** 86 **p** 87. C Ballyholme *D & D* 86–90; Min Can Belf Cathl 89–12; V Choral Belf Cathl 90–93; Can Belf Cathl from 12; C Belfast St Anne *Conn* 90–93; I Stormont *D & D* 93–16;

I Kilbride *Conn* from 16. *Kilbride Rectory, 7 Rectory Road, Doagh, Ballyclare BT39 0PT* E: wdhumphries@hotmail.com

HUMPHRIS, Richard. b 44. Sarum & Wells Th Coll 69. **d** 72 **p** 73. C Cheltenham St Luke and St Jo *Glouc* 72–77; C Lydney w Aylburton 77–82; Chapl RAF 82–85; TV Kippax w Allerton Bywater *Ripon* 85–92; RSPCA 92–95; rtd 95; PtO *York* 98–14. *4 Belle Vue Terrace, Bellerby, Leyburn DL8 5QL* T: (01969) 622004

HUMPHRISS, Canon Reginald George. b 36. Kelham Th Coll 56. **d** 61 **p** 62. C Londonderry *Birm* 61–63; Asst Dir RE *Cant* 63–66; Dioc Youth Chapl 63–66; V Preston next Faversham 66–72; P-in-c Goodnestone St Bart and Graveney 71–72; V Spring Park 72–76; R Cant St Martin and St Paul 76–90; R Saltwood 90–01; RD Cant 82–88; Hon Can Cant Cathl 85–01; RD Elham 93–00; rtd 01; PtO *Cant* from 01. *Winsole, Faussett, Lower Hardres, Canterbury CT4 7AH* T: (01227) 765264 E: reg@humphriss1.plus.com

HUMPHRYS, Kevin Luke. b 73. Surrey Univ BA 97. St Steph Ho Ox. **d** 99 **p** 00. C Moulsecoomb *Chich* 99–03; NSM Colgate and Roffey 16–19; NSM Brighton St Mich and St Paul from 19. *2 Adur Court, 463 Brighton Road, Lancing BN15 8LF* T: (01903) 609260 E: kevin_humphrys@hotmail.com

HUNDLEBY, Alan. b 41. **d** 86 **p** 87. OLM Fotherby *Linc* 86–02; NSM Barnoldby le Beck 02–14; NSM Waltham Gp from 14. *35 Cheapside, Waltham, Grimsby DN37 0HE* T: (01472) 827159

HUNG, Frank Yu-Chi. b 45. Birm Univ BSc 68 BA 75 Liv Univ MSc 71. Wycliffe Hall Ox 76. **d** 78 **p** 79. C Walton H Trin *Ox* 78–82; C Spring Grove St Mary *Lon* 82–85; TV Wexcombe *Sarum* 85–92; V Hatcham St Jas *S'wark* 92–98; Chapl Goldsmiths' Coll Lon 95–98; Chapl Lon S Bank Univ 98–10; rtd 10; Hon C S'wark St Geo w St Alphege and St Jude from 10. *151 Graham Road, London SW19 3SL* T: (020) 8542 1612

HUNGERFORD, Robin Nicholas. b 47. Redland Coll of Educn CertEd 74. Trin Coll Bris 86. **d** 88 **p** 89. C Swindon Dorcan *Bris* 88–92; TV Melbury *Sarum* 92–01; P-in-c Winterbourne Stickland and Turnworth etc 01–05; V Winterborne Valley and Milton Abbas 05–12; rtd 12; PtO *Sarum* from 12; B & W from 19. *Church House, 53A High Street, Heytesbury, Warminster BA12 0EA* T: (01985) 840522

HUNNISETT, John Bernard. b 47. AKC 73. **d** 73 **p** 74. C Charlton Kings St Mary *Glouc* 73–77; C Portsea St Mary *Portsm* 77–80; V Badgeworth w Shurdington *Glouc* 80–87; R Dursley 87–99; TR Ross *Heref* 99–07; RD Ross and Archenfield 02–07; Chapl Huggens Coll Northfleet 07–12; rtd 12; PtO *Glouc* from 12. *1 Fernleigh Villas, Old Bristol Road, Nailsworth, Stroud GL6 0LQ* T: (01453) 833491 M: 07970-280274 E: john.hunnisett@me.com

HUNNYBUN, Martin Wilfrid. b 44. Oak Hill Th Coll 67. **d** 70 **p** 71. C Ware Ch St Alb 70–74; C Washfield, Stoodleigh, Withleigh etc *Ex* 74–75; TV 75–80; R Braunston *Pet* 80–85; Asst Chapl HM Pris Onley 80–85; R Berry and Kangaroo Valley Sydney Australia 85–94; Sen Chapl Angl Retirement Village 94–98; TV Parkham, Alwington, Buckland Brewer etc *Ex* 98–00; Dioc Ecum Adv 98–00; R Glebe Australia 00–03; rtd 03. *204 Beacon Road, North Tambrine QLD 4272, Australia* T: (0061) (7) 5545 4310 E: m.hunnybun@bigpond.com

HUNT, Andrew Collins. b 54. Reading Univ BA 77 Hull Univ PGCE 79. St Alb Minl Tr Scheme 82 Sarum & Wells Th Coll 89 WEMTC 99. **d** 00 **p** 01. NSM Cainscross w Selsley *Glouc* 00–02; NSM Wells St Thos w Horrington *B & W* 07–10; PtO 10–12; NSM Polden Wheel 12–16; PtO from 16. *58A Cowl Street, Shepton Mallet BA4 5EP* E: r54hunt@btinternet.com *or* dandj@wisteria33.plus.com

HUNT, Ashley Stephen. b 50. St Jo Coll Nottm 81. **d** 83 **p** 84. C Southchurch H Trin *Chelmsf* 83–86; TV Droitwich *Worc* 86–87; USA 88–91; TV Melton Gt Framland *Leic* 92–93; TV Melton Mowbray 93–98; TV Grantham *Linc* 98–00; Chapl Mental Health 98–01; C Stamford All SS w St Jo *Linc* 00–01; TV Mynyddislwyn *Mon* 02–18. *5 Laurel Drive, The Bryn, Pontllanfraith, Blackwood NP12 2PR*

HUNT, Mrs Beverley Cecilia. b 49. **d** 08 **p** 09. NSM E Molesey *Guildf* 08–11; TV Godalming 11–15; PtO 15; P-in-c E Molesey 15–17; C Woking St Pet 17–18; rtd 19; PtO *Guildf* from 19. *1 St John's Rise, Woking GU21 7PN* E: revbevppm@btinternet.com

HUNT, Mrs Christina. b 24. Qu Mary Coll Lon BSc 45. S Dios Minl Tr Scheme 78. **dss** 81 **d** 87 **p** 94. Alderbury and W Grimstead *Sarum* 81–87; Hon Par Dn 87–91; Hon Par Dn Alderbury Team 91–94; rtd 94; PtO *Sarum* 94–08 and from 11. *37 Elizabeth Court, Crane Bridge Road, Salisbury SP2 7UX* T: (01722) 336002 E: chrishunt37@btinternet.com

HUNT, Christopher Paul Colin. b 38. Ch Coll Cam BA 62 MA 62. Clifton Th Coll 63. **d** 65 **p** 66. C Widnes St Paul *Liv* 65–68; Singapore 68–70; Malaysia 70–71; Hon C

Folkestone St Jo *Cant* 72–73; Iran 74–80; Overseas Service Adv CMS 81–91; P-in-c Claverdon w Preston Bagot *Cov* 91–02; rtd 02; PtO *Worc* from 04. *Birchfield House, 18 Oaklands, Malvern WR14 4JE* T: (01684) 578803 E: pauldianamalvern@gmail.com

HUNT, Craig Adam. b 86. St Jo Coll Dur BSc 07. St Mellitus Coll BA 12. **d** 12 **p** 13. C Cant St Mary Bredin 12–19; Dioc Dir of Ords *S'well* from 19. *Diocese of Southwell and Nottingham, Jubilee House, 8 Westgate, Southwell NG25 0JH* T: (01636) 814331 M: 07837-830231 E: craig.hunt@dunelm.org.uk

HUNT, David John. b 35. Kelham Th Coll 60. **d** 65 **p** 66. C Bethnal Green St Jo w St Simon *Lon* 65–69; C Mill Hill St Mich 69–73; R Staple Fitzpaine, Orchard Portman, Thurlbear etc *B & W* 73–79; P-in-c E Coker w Sutton Bingham 79–88; V E Coker w Sutton Bingham and Closworth 88–00; RD Merston 85–94; rtd 00; PtO *B & W* 01–11. *Meadowside, Head Street, Tintinhull, Yeovil BA22 8QH* T: (01935) 824554

HUNT, Ernest Gary. b 36. Univ Coll Dur BA 57. Carl Dioc Tr Inst 90. **d** 93 **p** 94. NSM Salesbury *Blackb* 93–95; NSM Blackb St Mich w St Jo and H Trin 95–98; NSM Balderstone 98–01; rtd 01; PtO *Blackb* from 01. *Dunelm, 10 Pleckgate Road, Blackburn BB1 8NN* T: (01254) 52531 E: eg.andk.hunt@talktalk.net

HUNT, Miss Gabrielle Ann. b 59. STETS BA 10. **d** 08 **p** 09. C Salisbury St Fran and Stratford sub Castle *Sarum* 08–12; C Bourne Valley 09–12; TV Avon River from 12. *The Vicarage, High Street, Netheravon, Salisbury SP4 9QP* T: (01980) 670326 E: galehunt@btinternet.com

HUNT, Giles Butler. b 28. Trin Hall Cam BA 51 MA 55. Cuddesdon Coll 51. **d** 53 **p** 54. C N Evington *Leic* 53–56; C Northolt St Mary *Lon* 56–58; Bp's Dom Chapl *Portsm* 58–59; Bp's Chapl *Nor* 59–62; R Holt 62–67; R Kelling w Salthouse 63–67; C Pimlico St Pet w Westmr Ch Ch *Lon* 67–72; V Barkway w Reed and Buckland *St Alb* 72–79; V Preston next Faversham, Goodnestone and Graveney *Cant* 79–92; rtd 92; PtO *Nor* from 92. *The Cottage, The Fairstead, Cley-next-the-Sea, Holt NR25 7RJ* T: (01263) 740471 E: gileshunt@btinternet.com

HUNT, James Castle. b 66. Univ of Ulster BSc 90 MRICS 92. Wycliffe Hall Ox 02. **d** 04 **p** 05. C N Farnborough *Guildf* 04–08; R Bishop's Waltham *Portsm* from 08; R Upham from 08. *The Rectory, Maypole Green, Bishops Waltham, Southampton SO32 1PW* T: (01489) 892618 E: jameshunt1966@gmail.com

HUNT, John Barry. b 46. Lich Th Coll 70 Qu Coll Birm 72. **d** 73 **p** 74. C Auckland St Andr and St Anne *Dur* 73–77; C Consett 77–79; R Lyons 79–89; P-in-c Hebburn St Cuth 89–05; P-in-c Hebburn St Oswald 01–05; V Hebburn St Cuth and St Oswald 05–11; rtd 11; PtO *Dur* from 11. *11 Parklands, Gateshead NE10 8YP* T: 0191-438 3022 E: tyneheaven2@outlook.com

HUNT, John Edwin. b 38. ARCO Dur Univ BA 60 DipEd. EMMTC 78. **d** 81 **p** 82. NSM Newbold w Dunston *Derby* 81–92; NSM Chesterfield St Mary and All SS 92–02. *4 Ardsley Road, Ashgate, Chesterfield S40 4DG* T: (01246) 275141 E: fredwin@cwcom.net

HUNT, John Stewart. b 37. Nor Ord Course 75. **d** 78 **p** 79. NSM Hunstanton St Edm *Nor* 78–81; NSM Hunstanton St Mary w Ringstead Parva, Holme etc 81–86; NSM Sedgeford w Southmere 84–86; C Lowestoft and Kirkley 86–89; R Blundeston w Flixton and Lound 89–93; P-in-c Kessingland w Gisleham 93–99; R Kessingland, Gisleham and Rushmere 99–00; rtd 00; PtO *Nor* from 00. *31 Eckling Grange, Dereham NR20 3BB* E: chippyhunt@binternet.com

HUNT, Canon Judith Mary. b 57. Bris Univ BVSc 80 Lon Univ PhD 85 Fitzw Coll Cam BA 90 MRCVS 80. Ridley Hall Cam 88. **d** 91 **p** 94. Par Dn Heswall *Ches* 91–94; C 94–95; P-in-c Tilston and Shocklach 95–03; Bp's Adv for Women in Min 95–00; Can Res Ches Cathl and Dioc Dir of Min 03–09; Adn Suffolk *St E* 09–12; R Whitchurch *Lich* from 12; P-in-c Edstaston, Fauls, Prees, Tilstock and Whixall 13–18; C from 18. *The Rectory, Church Street, Whitchurch SY13 1LB* T: (01948) 667253 E: revjudyhunt@gmail.com

HUNT, Canon Kevin. b 59. St Jo Coll Dur BA 80 Ox Univ BA 84 MA 88. St Steph Ho Ox 81. **d** 84 **p** 85. C Mansfield St Mark *S'well* 84–85; C Hendon and Sunderland *Dur* 85–88; V Sunderland St Mary and St Pet 88–95; TR Jarrow 95–02; V Walker *Newc* 02–12; AD Newc E 04–12; Hon Can Newc Cathl 10–12; Can Res Newc Cathl 12–15; Asst Dioc Dir of Ords 03–15; PtO 15–19; P-in-c Vancouver St Jas Canada 15–17; R from 17. *2305-1501 Haro Street, Vancouver BC V6G 1G4, Canada* E: kevin@hunt10.plus.com

HUNT, Michael David. b 64. Southn Univ BSc 86. Ox Min Course 09. **d** 12 **p** 13. NSM Wendover and Halton *Ox* 12–16; NSM Risborough from 16. *Autumn Winds, Aylesbury Road, Princes Risborough HP27 0JP* T: (01844) 344150 M: 07712-851381 E: midahunt@yahoo.co.uk

HUNT, Paul. *See* HUNT, Christopher Paul Colin

HUNT, Paul Edwin. b 47. Ripon Coll Cuddesdon 93. **d** 95 **p** 96. C Cleobury Mortimer w Hopton Wafers etc *Heref* 95–98; P-in-c Fritwell w Souldern and Ardley w Fewcott *Ox* 98–05; TR Cherwell Valley 05–12; AD Bicester and Islip 05–08; rtd 12; PtO *Pet* from 13. *32 Dalestones, Northampton NN4 9UU* T: (01604) 460539 E: paul.jehu@mac.com *or* paul.e.hunt@me.com

HUNT, Canon Peter John. b 35. AKC 58. St Boniface Warminster. **d** 59 **p** 60. C Chesterfield St Mary and All SS *Derby* 59–61; C Matlock and Tansley 61–63; Chapl Matlock Hosp 61–63; Lect Matlock Teacher Tr Coll 61–63; V Tottington *Man* 63–69; CF (TA) 65–67 and from 75; V Bollington St Jo *Ches* 69–76; R Wilmslow 76–98; Hon Can Ches Cathl 94–02; P-in-c Brereton w Swettenham 98–02; rtd 02; PtO *Ches* from 02. *1 Varden Town Cottages, Birtles Lane, Over Alderley, Macclesfield SK10 4RZ* T: (01625) 829593 E: canonhari@gmail.com

HUNT, Canon Richard William. b 46. G&C Coll Cam BA 67 MA 71. Westcott Ho Cam 68. **d** 72 **p** 73. C Bris St Agnes and St Simon w St Werburgh 72–77; Chapl Selw Coll Cam 77–84; V Birchfield *Birm* 84–01; R Chich St Paul and Westhampnett 01–11; RD Chich 06–11; Can and Preb Chich Cathl 10–11; rtd 11; PtO *Sarum* from 12; *B & W* from 15. *76 Warminster Road, Bath BA2 6RU* T: (01225) 938529 M: 07504-089009 E: richardhunt040246@gmail.com

HUNT, Canon Rosalind Edna Mary. b 55. Man Univ BA 76. St Steph Ho Ox 86. **d** 88 **p** 94. Chapl Jes Coll Cam 88–92; Hon Chapl to the Deaf *Ely* 92–04; C Cambridge St Jas 00; PtO *Man* from 05; *Ely* from 15. *4 Silverwood Close, Cambridge CB1 3HA* M: 07775-508900 E: ros.hunt@virgin.net

HUNT, Canon Russell Barrett. b 35. NY Univ Virginia Univ Fitzw Ho Cam. Westcott Ho Cam 73. **d** 75 **p** 76. C Leic St Mary 75–78; V Leic St Gabr 78–82; Chapl Leic Gen Hosp 82–95; Hon Can Leic Cathl 88–95; rtd 95; PtO *Leic* from 15. *33 Braunstone Avenue, Leicester LE3 0JH* T: 0116-254 9101 E: c.p.k@btinternet.com

HUNT, Simon John. b 60. Pemb Coll Ox BA 81 MA 85. St Jo Coll Nottm 87. **d** 90 **p** 91. C Stalybridge St Paul *Ches* 90–93; C Heysham *Blackb* 93–99; V Higher Walton 99–18; rtd 18. *The Ancient Shepherd, Wrights Lane, Cridling Stubbs, Knottingley WF11 0AS* T: (01977) 679854 E: simon.hunt15@btinternet.com

HUNT, Stephen. b 38. Man Univ BSc 61 MSc 62 PhD 64 DSc 80. Carl Dioc Tr Inst 88. **d** 91 **p** 92. C Broughton *Blackb* 91–95; Chapl Preston Acute Hosps NHS Trust 94–95; V Preston Em *Blackb* 95–03; rtd 03; PtO *Blackb* from 05. *8 Wallace Lane, Forton, Preston PR3 0BA* T: (01524) 792563

HUNT, Timothy Collinson. b 65. Univ of Wales (Cardiff) BD 95 Ox Univ MTh 98. Ripon Coll Cuddesdon 95. **d** 97 **p** 98. C Ex St Dav 97–01; Chapl Blundell's Sch Tiverton from 01. *1B Hillands, 39 Tidcombe Lane, Tiverton EX16 4EA* T: (01884) 242343 E: tch@blundells.org *or* timothy.collinson.hunt@gmail.com

HUNT, Vera Susan Henrietta. b 33. S Dios Minl Tr Scheme 88. **d** 91 **p** 94. Hon Chapl RAD from 91; PtO *Lon* from 03; *Ox* from 08. *54 Highway Avenue, Maidenhead SL6 5AQ* T: (01628) 623909

HUNTE (née FRANKLIN), Canon Roxanne Fay. b 60. Gama Filho Univ Brazil BSc 93 Huron Univ MBA 94 Leeds Univ BA 08. Coll of Resurr Mirfield 07. **d** 09 **p** 10. C Newington St Mary *S'wark* 09–13; P-in-c S Norwood H Innocents 13–18; P-in-c S Norwood St Mark 15–18; V S Norwood H Innocents and St Mark from 18; Dioc Minority Ethnic Voc Champion from 16; Hon Can S'wark Cathl from 17. *The Vicarage, 192A Selhurst Road, London SE25 6XX* T: (020) 8916 1830 M: 07472-662323 E: mtrroxanne@gmail.com

HUNTER, Edwin Wallace. b 43. NUI BA 83 FCIM. CITC 91. **d** 94 **p** 95. NSM Cork St Fin Barre's Union C, C & R 94–18; Min Can Cork Cathl 95–18; Bp's Dom Chapl 03–18; rtd 18. *Cedar Lodge, Church Road, Carrigaline, Co Cork, Republic of Ireland* T: (00353) (21) 437 2338 E: enjhunter@eircom.net

HUNTER, Graham. b 78. K Coll Lon BA 02. Ridley Hall Cam 05. **d** 07 **p** 08. C Holloway St Mary Magd *Lon* 07–10; C Hoxton St Jo w Ch Ch 10–11; V from 11. *St John's Vicarage, Crondall Street, London N1 6PT* T: (020) 7739 9823 E: graham@stjohnshoxton.org.uk

HUNTER, Ian Roy. *See* WILLIAMS-HUNTER, Ian Roy

HUNTER, James. b 38. Union Th Coll Belf BD 90. **d** 92 **p** 92. In Presbyterian Ch of Ireland 82–92; V Werneth *Man* 92–98; V Woking St Paul *Guildf* 98–05; Asst Chapl HM Pris Coldingley 01–05; rtd 06; PtO *Pet* from 06. *31 The Ridings, Desborough, Kettering NN14 2LP* T: (01536) 660328 E: jimo.hunter2@gmail.com

HUNTER, John Crichton. b 38. Univ of Wales (Cardiff) BA 59 DipEd 60 LTCL. St Steph Ho Ox 98. **d** 99 **p** 00. NSM Walham Green St Jo w St Jas *Lon* 99–05; NSM S Kensington St Steph

05–08; PtO from 08. *57 Manor Court, 23 Bagleys Lane, London SW6 2BN* T: (020) 7736 7544 E: frjohnhunter@hotmail.com *or* reverendwilliams@btinternet.com

HUNTER, Canon John Gaunt. b 21. St Jo Coll Dur BA 49 Leeds Univ MA 94 Lanc Univ MA 01 MPhil 09. Ridley Hall Cam 49. **d** 51 **p** 52. C Bradf Cathl 51–54; C Compton Gifford *Ex* 54–56; V Bootle St Matt *Liv* 56–62; Prin Bp Tucker Coll Uganda 62–65; V Altcar *Liv* 65–78; Dioc Missr 65–71; Abp's Miss Adv *York* 71–78; Hon Can Liv Cathl 71–78; TR Buckhurst Hill *Chelmsf* 78–89; Dioc Adv in Evang *Bradf* 89–92; rtd 92; PtO *Bradf* 92–14; *Leeds* from 14. *Westhouse Lodge, Lower Westhouse, Ingleton, Carnforth LA6 3NZ* T: (015242) 41305 E: canonjgh@gmail.com

HUNTER, Matthew Gawain. b 83. LMH Ox BA 04 Man Univ MA 08 Northumbria Univ MA 11. Ripon Coll Cuddesdon 10. **d** 12 **p** 13. C Halifax *Wakef* 12–15; C Hexham *Newc* 15–18; P-in-c Whorlton from 18. *St John's Vicarage, Whorlton, Newcastle upon Tyne NE5 1NN* E: mwg_hunter@yahoo.co.uk

HUNTER, Michael John. b 45. CCC Cam BA 67 MA 71 PhD 71 Ox Univ BA 75. Wycliffe Hall Ox 73. **d** 76 **p** 77. C Partington and Carrington *Ches* 76–79; CMS 80–90; Uganda 80–89; C Penn Fields *Lich* 90–02; RD Trysull 97–02; V Dore *Sheff* 02–12; rtd 12; PtO *Sheff* 12–14; *Carl* from 13. *18 Linnet Grove, Kendal LA9 7RP* T: (01539) 725093 E: mutagwok@aol.com

HUNTER, Canon Michael Oram. b 40. K Coll Lon BD 64 AKC 64. **d** 65 **p** 66. C Tividale *Lich* 65–68; C Harrogate St Wilfrid *Ripon* 68–70; V Hawksworth Wood 70–78; V Whitkirk 78–86; TR Gt Grimsby St Mary and St Jas *Linc* 86–10; Can and Preb Linc Cathl 89–10; rtd 10; PtO *Leeds* from 17. *12 Osborne Road, Harrogate HG1 2EA* T: (01423) 313825 E: mo.hunter@talktalk.net

HUNTER, Paul Andrew. b 55. Trin Coll Bris 09. **d** 11 **p** 12. OLM Brislington St Chris *Bris* 11–18; NSM Whitchurch St Aug from 18. *17 Friendship Road, Bristol BS4 2RW* T: 0117-971 9390 E: paulzhunter@blueyonder.co.uk

HUNTER, Paul Graham. b 64. Sheff Univ LLB 85 Solicitor 86. St Jo Coll Nottm MA 96. **d** 04 **p** 05. Prin Morogoro Bible Coll Tanzania 04–06; PtO *Blackb* 08–19; C Copp w Inskip from 19. *St Peter's Vicarage, Preston Road, Inskip, Preston PR4 0TT* M: 07731-924289 E: pp.hunter@sky.com

HUNTER, Peter Wells. b 52. Bris Univ BSc 73. Trin Coll Bris BA 91. **d** 91 **p** 92. C New Borough and Leigh *Sarum* 91–97; P-in-c Warminster Ch Ch 97–18; rtd 18; PtO *Sarum* from 19. *15 Tilting Road, Thornbury, Bristol BS35 1EP* E: peter.wh@btopenworld.com

HUNTER, Stephanie Louise. b 89. Aber Univ MA 13. Ripon Coll Cuddesdon 15. **d** 17 **p** 18. C Cumberworth, Denby, Denby Dale etc *Leeds* from 17. *The Rectory, 43 Hollybank Avenue, Upper Cumberworth, Huddersfield HD8 8NY*

HUNTER, Stephen Albert Paul. b 52. NOC 01. **d** 04 **p** 05. NSM Ecclesall *Sheff* 04–13; Bp's Adv for SSM 10–14; Dioc Dir of Ords from 13. *Overhill, Townhead Road, Dore, Sheffield S17 3GE* T: 0114-236 9978 F: 275 9769 M: 07739-949473 E: stephenaphunter@btinternet.com

HUNTER DUNN, Jonathan. b 69. Sussex Univ BSc 91 Uppsala Univ PhD 98. Oak Hill Th Coll BA 09. **d** 10 **p** 11. C Burford w Fulbrook, Taynton, Asthall etc *Ox* 10–15; R Shepton Mallet w Doulting *B & W* from 15. *11 Naisholt Road, Shepton Mallet BA4 5GD* T: (01749) 342420 E: jonathanhunterdunn@btinternet.com

HUNTER JONES, Karen Elizabeth. See JONES, Karen Elizabeth

HUNTER SMART, Ian Douglas. b 60. St Jo Coll Dur BA 83 MA 99. Edin Th Coll 83. **d** 85 **p** 86. C Cockerton *Dur* 85–89; TV Jarrow 89–92; TV Sunderland 92–98; Chapl Sunderland Univ 92–98; Ecum Chapl Newcastle Coll 98–00; PtO *Dur* from 98; *Ripon* 12–14; *Leeds* from 14. *Gardeners Cottage, Carlton, Richmond DL11 7AG* T: (01325) 710481 E: ihs@dunelm.org.uk

HUNTER SMART, William David. b 75. Bris Univ BSc 97. Wycliffe Hall Ox BA 01. **d** 02 **p** 03. C Watford *St Alb* 02–05; C Muswell Hill St Jas w St Matt *Lon* 05–11; TR Newbury *Ox* 11–15; R Newbury St Nic and Speen from 15. *The Rectory, 64 Northcroft Lane, Newbury RG14 1BN* T: (01635) 47018 E: rector@st-nicolas-newbury.org

HUNTINGDON AND WISBECH, Archdeacon of. See MACCURDY, The Ven Hugh Kyle

HUNTINGDON, Suffragan Bishop of. See WINTER, The Rt Revd Dagmar

HUNTLEY, David Anthony. b 32. AMInstT 56 MRTvS 78 MILT 98. Lon Bible Coll BA 60 Fuller Sch of World Miss MTh 81 Trin Coll Singapore 65. **d** 64 **p** 65. OMF Internat from 61; Singapore 61–71; Indonesia 72–73; Philippines 74–75; Hong Kong 77–81; Seychelles 82–87; Thailand 88–97; NSM S Croydon Em *Cant* 76–77 and 81–82; NSM S Croydon Em *S'wark* 87–88 and 91–92 and 98–04; PtO from 05. *42*

Farnborough Avenue, South Croydon CR2 8HD T: (020) 8657 5673

HUNTLEY, Denis Anthony. b 56. Saltley Tr Coll Birm CertEd 77. Qu Coll Birm 77. **d** 80 **p** 81. C Llanblethian w Cowbridge and Llandough etc *Llan* 80–83; TV Glyncorrwg w Afan Vale and Cymmer Afan 83–86; R 86–89; Chapl Asst Walsgrave Hosp Cov 89–92; Chapl Halifax Gen Hosp 92–94; Chapl Calderdale Healthcare NHS Trust 94–97; C Leeds City *Ripon* 97–02; Chapl to the Deaf 97–02; Chapl amongst Deaf People and Adv for Deaf Min 02–06; Chapl amongst Deaf and Deaf-blind People *Chelmsf* 06–14; Lead Min Deaf Community 15–19; Adv on Disability Issues *Chelmsf* 06–19. *17 Oakham Close, Langdon Hills, Basildon SS16 6NX* T: (01268) 546026 E: denishuntley@gmail.com

HUNTLEY, Heidi Anne. b 71. Ripon Coll Cuddesdon 07. **d** 09 **p** 10. C Sydenham St Bart *S'wark* 09–12; V Royston *St Alb* from 12. *The Vicarage, 20 Palace Gardens, Royston SG8 5AD* T: (01763) 243145 E: hahlive@gmail.com

HUNTLEY, Stuart Michael. b 73. BEng BA. Trin Coll Bris. **d** 08 **p** 09. C Jersey St Lawr *Win* 08–09; C Jersey St Helier 09–11; R Port Washington St Steph USA 11–15; R Wulfric Benefice *B & W* from 15. *The Rectory, 67A North Street, Crewkerne TA18 7AX* M: 07479-532355 E: revshuntley@gmail.com

HUNTON, Thomas Mark. b 80. Trin Coll Bris 16. **d** 18 **p** 19. C Chippenham St Paul w Hardenhuish etc *Bris* from 18. *33 Fallow Field Close, Chippenham SN14 6YA* M: 07570-477540 *or* 07464-505800 E: tomhunton@hotmail.co.uk

HUPFIELD, Mrs Hannah Elizabeth. b 84. New Hall Cam BA 06 MA 10 Anglia Ruskin Univ BA 14 Selw Coll Cam MPhil 17. Westcott Ho Cam 08. **d** 11 **p** 12. C Woodbridge St Mary *St E* 11; C Saxilby Gp *Linc* 12–15; C Stow Gp 12–15; PtO *Ely* 15–20; Asst Chapl Selw Coll Cam 16–18; PtO *Worc* from 19. *3 Orchard Grove, Ferry Lane, Offenham, Evesham WR11 8GZ* T: (01386) 769432 E: hannahhupfield@cantab.net

HUPFIELD, Timothy. b 83. K Coll Cam MSci 06 BA 06 MA 09 PGCE 09 Jes Coll Cam BTh 17. Westcott Ho Cam 15. **d** 18 **p** 19. C E Vale and Avon Villages *Worc* from 18. *3 Orchard Grove, Ferry Lane, Offenham, Evesham WR11 8GZ* T: (01386) 769432 M: 07812-982196 E: timothyhupfield@cantab.net

HURCOMBE, Thomas William. b 45. BD 74 AKC 76. **d** 76 **p** 77. C Hampstead All So *Lon* 76–79; C Is of Dogs Ch Ch and St Jo w St Luke 79–83; C Bromley All Hallows 83–89; C E Greenwich Ch Ch w St Andr and St Mich *S'wark* 89–96; Ind Chapl 89–97; Dioc Urban Missr 90–96; Greenwich Waterfront Chapl 96–98; C Charlton St Luke w H Trin 97–98; P-in-c S Norwood St Mark 98–14; rtd 14; PtO *S'wark* from 16. *39A Warminster Road, London SE25 4DL* M: 07939-289196 E: hurcomt@aol.com

HURD, Alun John. b 52. Trin Coll Bris BA 86 New Coll Edin MTh 97. **d** 86 **p** 87. C Chertsey *Guildf* 86–90; Chapl St Pet Hosp Chertsey 86–90; V W Ewell *Guildf* 90–04; Chapl NE Surrey Coll Ewell 01–05; CF (TA) 99–05; Distr P Lower Yorke Peninsula 05–07; P-in-c Gt Wakering w Foulness *Chelmsf* 08–17; P-in-c Barling w Lt Wakering 08–17; P-in-c Rochford and Sutton w Shopland 14–17; P-in-c High Westmorland *Carl* from 17. *The Vicarage, Shap, Penrith CA10 3LB* M: 07941-417135 E: alunjhurd@gmail.com

HURD, Brenda Edith. b 44. Sittingbourne Coll DipEd 75. Cant Sch of Min 87. **d** 92 **p** 94. NSM Birling, Addington, Ryarsh and Trottiscliffe *Roch* 92–02; P-in-c Wrotham 02–12; R 12–14; RD Shoreham 06–11; Hon Can Roch Cathl 09–14; rtd 14; PtO *Roch* from 15. *South View, London Road, Ryarsh, West Malling ME19 5AW* T: (01732) 842255 E: b.hurd@virgin.net

HURFORD, Colin Osborne. b 33. Qu Coll Ox BA 55 MA 59. Wells Th Coll 55. **d** 57 **p** 58. C Barnoldswick w Bracewell *Bradf* 57–61; C Warrington St Elphin *Liv* 61–63; Malaysia 63–70; P-in-c Annscroft *Heref* 71–79; P-in-c Longden 71–79; P-in-c Pontesbury III 71–79; R Longden and Annscroft 79–85; P-in-c Church Pulverbatch 81–85; R Longden and Annscroft w Pulverbatch 85–86; Tanzania 86–87; TR Billingham St Aid *Dur* 87–96; rtd 96; PtO *Heref* from 96; *Lich* 01–19. *14 Station Road, Pontesbury, Shrewsbury SY5 0QY* T: (01743) 792605

HURLE, Canon Anthony Rowland. b 54. Lon Univ BSc Em Coll Cam PGCE. Wycliffe Hall Ox 80. **d** 83 **p** 84. C Ipswich St Mary at Stoke w St Pet *St E* 83–87; TV Barking St Marg w St Patr *Chelmsf* 87–92; V St Alb St Paul from 92; RD St Alb 95–05; Hon Can St Alb from 05. *St Paul's Vicarage, 7 Brampton Road, St Albans AL1 4PN* T: (01727) 836810 *or* 846281 F: 836810 E: tony@stpauls-stalbans.org *or* vicar@stpauls-stalbans.org

HURLE (*née* POWNALL), Mrs Lydia Margaret. b 53. SRN SCM. Wycliffe Hall Ox 78. **dss** 81 **d** 94 **p** 95. Ipswich St Mary at Stoke w St Pet etc *St E* 81–83; NSM St Alb St Paul from 93; PtO *Chelmsf* from 19. *St Paul's Vicarage, 7 Brampton Road, St Albans AL1 4PN* T/F: (01727) 836810 E: lydiahurle@gmail.com

HURLEY, Robert. b 64. Univ of Wales (Cardiff) BD 86. Ridley Hall Cam 88. **d** 90 **p** 91. C Dagenham *Chelmsf* 90–93; C Egg Buckland *Ex* 93–96; C Devonport St Budeaux 96; P-in-c Camberwell All SS *S'wark* 96–99; V 99–02; R Oldbury *Sarum* 02–04; Chapl Grenoble *Eur* 13–18; C W Cheltenham *Glouc* from 18. *St Barnabas' Vicarage, 152 Alstone Lane, Cheltenham GL51 8HL* E: janeandbobhurley@aol.com

HURLEY, Susan Elizabeth. b 65. Leeds Univ BA 87 Leic Univ PGCE 88. St Mellitus Coll 14. **d** 16 **p** 17. C Stebbing and Lindsell w Gt and Lt Saling *Chelmsf* from 16; C Broxted w Chickney and Tilty etc from 17. *The Rectory, Park Road, Little Easton, Dunmow CM6 2JJ* T: (01371) 859158 E: sue@hurleyathome.com

HURLSTON, Canon Jean Margaret. b 54. Crewe Coll of Educn CertEd 75 Keele Univ BEd 76. **d** 06 **p** 07. OLM High Crompton *Man* 06–10; OLM Oldham 10–11; NSM Oldham St Mary w St Pet from 11; Borough Dean Oldham from 18; Chapl Man Airport from 18; Chapl Tameside and Glossop Integrated Care NHS Foundn Trust from 18; Hon Can Man Cathl from 18. *24 Taunton Lawns, Ashton-under-Lyne OL7 9EL* T/F: 0161-344 2854 M: 07885-406808 E: jeanhurlston@btinternet.com

HURN, Mrs June Barbara. b 32. Birm Univ CertEd 53. Cant Sch of Min 87. **d** 90 **p** 94. NSM Chislehurst St Nic *Roch* from 90. *Hawkswing, Hawkwood Lane, Chislehurst BR7 5PW* T: (020) 8467 2320 E: junehurn@yahoo.co.uk

HURREN, Timothy John. b 46. York Univ BA 74 ACIB 70. NEOC 99. **d** 02 **p** 03. C High Harrogate St Pet *Ripon* 02–14; *Leeds* from 14. *1 South Park Road, Harrogate HG1 5QU* T: (01423) 541696 E: tim.hurren@ntlworld.com

HURRY, Lynn Susan. b 59. Middx Univ BA 05. NTMTC 02. **d** 05 **p** 06. C Southchurch H Trin *Chelmsf* 05–08; V St Mary-at-Latton from 08. *St Mary-at-Latton Vicarage, The Gowers, Harlow CM20 2JP* T: (01279) 424005 E: revlynn@btinternet.com

HURST, Canon Brian Charles. b 58. Nottm Univ BA Sheff Univ MA 07. Ripon Coll Cuddesdon 82. **d** 84 **p** 85. C Cullercoats St Geo *Newc* 84–87; C Prudhoe 87–88; TV Willington 88–95; V Denton 95–03; RD Newc W 97–98; TV Glendale Gp 03–09; V Bamburgh 09–17; V Ellingham 09–17; AD Bamburgh and Glendale 06–16; V Newc St Geo and St Hilda from 17; Hon Can Newc Cathl from 10. *St George's Vicarage, St George's Close, Newcastle upon Tyne NE2 2TF* T: 0191-281 1628 E: brian.hurst1@btopenworld.com

HURST, Colin. b 49. Linc Th Coll 88. **d** 90 **p** 91. C Wavertree H Trin *Liv* 90–93; C Croft and Stoney Stanton *Leic* 93–95; V Wigan St Andr *Liv* 97–14; AD Wigan W 03–05; AD Wigan 05–08; Hon Can Liv Cathl 03–08; rtd 14; PtO *Liv* from 15; *Blackb* 16–17. *19 Foxfield Grove, Shevington, Wigan WN6 8AJ* T: (01257) 402261 E: churst6000@gmail.com

HURST, Colin. b 58. Westmr Coll Ox BA 90. St Jo Coll Nottm MA 95. **d** 95 **p** 96. C Warboys w Broughton and Bury w Wistow *Ely* 95–98; P-in-c Wisbech St Mary 98–04; P-in-c Guyhirn w Ring's End 98–04; V Wisbech St Mary and Guyhirn w Ring's End etc 05–07; P-in-c Eye *Pet* 07–14; P-in-c Newborough 07–14; P-in-c Thorney Abbey *Ely* 07–14; V Eye, Newborough and Thorney *Pet* from 14. *The Vicarage, Thorney Road, Eye, Peterborough PE6 7UN* T: (01733) 222334 E: cehurst@globalnet.co.uk

HURST, Edward. b 57. SEITE 09. **d** 11 **p** 12. NSM S Gillingham *Roch* 11–17; V Shorne from 17; PtO *Cant* from 14; Chapl Kent & Medway NHS and Soc Care Partnership Trust from 13. *The Vicarage, Butchers Hill, Shorne, Gravesend DA12 3EB* T: (01474) 822239 M: 07791-994933 E: notfatherted@gmail.com

HURST, Canon Jeremy Richard. b 40. Trin Coll Cam BA 61 MA MPhil FCP. Linc Th Coll 62. **d** 64 **p** 65. C Woolwich St Mary w H Trin *S'wark* 64–69; PtO *Ex* 69–76; Ox 76–84; TV Langley Marish 84–85; TR 85–05; Hon Can Ch Ch 05; Chapl Thames Valley Univ *Lon* 92–98; rtd 05; PtO *Ox* from 18. *Hortus Lodge, 22A Bolton Avenue, Windsor SL4 3JF* T: (01753) 863693

HURST, Mrs Joanna. b 74. Cranmer Hall Dur 13. **d** 15 **p** 16. C Kendal H Trin *Carl* 15–18; Chapl Eden Valley Hospice *Carl* from 18; PtO *Carl* from 18. *Eden Valley Hospice, Durdar Road, Carlisle CA2 4SD* T: (01228) 810801

HUSBAND, Mrs Caroline Elizabeth. b 72. STETS BA 14. **d** 14 **p** 15. NSM Paulton w Farrington Gurney and High Littleton *B & W* 14–17; Lic to RD Midsomer Norton 17–18; TV White Horse *Sarum* from 18. *The Vicarage, The Hollow, Dilton Marsh, Westbury BA13 4BU* T: (01373) 596104 M: 07887-621580 E: husbandcc@gmail.com

HUSS, The Ven David Ian. b 75. Jes Coll Ox MPhys 97. Wycliffe Hall Ox BA 07. **d** 07 **p** 08. C Banbury St Paul *Ox* 07–11; I Donegal w Killymard, Lough Eske and Laghey *D & R* from 11; Adn Raphoe from 13. *The Rectory, The*

Glebe, Donegal, Republic of Ireland T: (00353) (74) 972 1075 E: donegal@raphoe.anglican.org

HUSTWAYTE, Samantha Jane. b 73. Lon Univ BD 96 Ches Univ MTh 13. St Jo Coll Nottm LTh 13. **d** 13 **p** 14. C Arnold *S'well* 13–17; V Calverton from 17. *The Vicarage, 18 Crookdole Lane, Calverton, Nottingham NG14 6GF* M: 07801-364984 E: revsam@hustwayte.co.uk

HUSTWICK, Mrs Joanne Patricia. b 59. Trin Coll Bris 11. **d** 13 **p** 14. C Tong *Bradf* 13–14; *Leeds* 14–15; C Tong and Laisterdyke 15–17; V Birkby and Birchencliffe from 17. *The Vicarage, 4 Brendon Drive, Huddersfield HD2 2DF* E: jhustwick13@gmail.com

HUTCHEON, Mrs Elsie. b 39. RGN 63 CertEd UEA MEd 98. EAMTC 89. **d** 92 **p** 94. NSM Heigham St Thos *Nor* 92–02; P-in-c Heigham St Barn w St Bart 02–15; RD Nor S 06–09; rtd 15; PtO *Nor* from 16. *6 St Julian's Alley, Norwich NR1 1QD* T: (01603) 629912 E: elsie.hutcheon@tiscali.co.uk *or* elsie.hutcheon@me.com

HUTCHERSON, Justin Francis. b 87. Jes Coll Cam BA 08 MA 11 Univ of E Lon PGCE 11 Open Univ MEd 12 Heythrop Coll Lon MA 12. St Steph Ho Ox BA 12 MA 12. **d** 14 **p** 15. C Corringham and Fobbing *Chelmsf* 14–18; V Clacton St Jas from 18. *St James's Vicarage, 44 Wash Lane, Clacton-on-Sea CO15 1DA* T: (01255) 426602 M: 07515-946575 E: frjustin@cantab.net

HUTCHIN, David William. b 37. Man Univ MusB 58 CertEd 59 DipEd 59 LRAM ARCM LTCL. Glouc Sch of Min 85. **d** 88 **p** 89. NSM Northleach w Hampnett and Farmington *Glouc* 88–94; NSM Cold Aston w Notgrove and Turkdean 88–94; NSM Chedworth, Yanworth and Stowell, Coln Rogers etc 94–01; RD Northleach 96–99; PtO *Leic* 01–06; *Derby* 02–06; *Ripon* 06–14; *Leeds* from 14. *Bank Side Garden, Glasshouses, Harrogate HG3 5QY* T: (01423) 712733

HUTCHINGS, Colin Michael. b 36. Clifton Th Coll 66. **d** 68 **p** 69. C Worksop St Jo *S'well* 68–71; C Hampreston *Sarum* 71–76; TV Tisbury 76–82; R Waddesdon w Over Winchendon and Fleet Marston *Ox* 82–00; rtd 00; PtO *Pet* from 01. *Nimrod, 4 The Beeches, Pattishall, Towcester NN12 8LT* T: (01327) 830563

HUTCHINGS, Ian James. b 49. Ches Coll of HE MA 03. Clifton Th Coll 69 Trin Coll Bris 72. **d** 73 **p** 74. C Parr *Liv* 73–77; C Timperley *Ches* 77–81; V Partington and Carrington 81–96; V Huntington 96–12; Chapl Bp's Blue Coat C of E High Sch 96–08; rtd 12; PtO *Ches* from 12; *Lich* from 12; *Liv* from 16. *52 Hillcrest, Ellesmere SY12 0LJ* T: (01691) 622304 E: ihutchings@aol.com

HUTCHINGS, James Benjamin Balfour. b 62. Ex Univ BA 84. STETS 03. **d** 06 **p** 07. C Ex St Jas 06–09; C Cen Ex 09–11; P-in-c Littleham w Exmouth 11–13; TR Littleham-cum-Exmouth w Lympstone 13–19; RD Aylesbeare 15–19; TR Barnes *S'wark* from 19. *25 Glebe Road, London SW13 0DZ* E: hutchingsjames@sky.com

HUTCHINGS, Thomas George. b 84. Qu Coll Cam BA MPhil 07 BA 13. Ridley Hall Cam 11. **d** 14 **p** 15. C Sileby, Cossington and Seagrave *Leic* 14–17; C Cambridge H Sepulchre *Ely* from 17. *1 Pretoria Road, Cambridge CB4 1HD* M: 07484-663325 E: tghutchings@gmail.com

HUTCHINS, Miss Katrina Mary. b 62. Ripon Coll Cuddesdon 13. **d** 15 **p** 16. C Kingsthorpe *Pet* 15–18; R Mears Ashby and Hardwick and Sywell etc from 18. *The Vicarage, 46 Wellingborough Road, Mears Ashby, Northampton NN6 0DZ* T: (01604) 812907 M: 07710-464675 E: katrinahutchins94@yahoo.co.uk

HUTCHINS, Canon Paul. b 79. Coll of Resurr Mirfield 99 NOC 04. **d** 05 **p** 06. C Royton St Paul *Man* 05–10; TV Swinton and Pendlebury 10–13; P-in-c Southport St Luke *Liv* 13–18; R Failsworth H Family *Man* from 18; Can Wiawso Ghana from 15. *Holy Family Rectory, 190 Lord Lane, Failsworth, Manchester M35 0QS* T: 0161-681 3644 M: 07572-075990 E: fr.hutchins@btinternet.com

HUTCHINS, Richard Frank. b 70. Ox Min Course 14. **d** 17 **p** 18. C Liss *Portsm* from 17. *13 Kelsey Close, Liss GU33 7HR*

HUTCHINSON, Alison Joyce. b 62. Leeds Univ BA 84 RMN 90. Aston Tr Scheme 92 Ripon Coll Cuddesdon 94. **d** 97 **p** 98. C Benfieldside *Dur* 97–00; C Bishopwearmouth St Nic 00–02; PtO *Carl* 02–07; C Penrith w Newton Reigny and Plumpton Wall 07–08; PtO 09; Hon C Crathorne *York* 09–16 and from 18; Hon C Kirklevington w Picton, and High and Low Worsall 09–16 and from 18; Hon C Rudby in Cleveland w Middleton 09–16 and from 18; Hon C Whorlton w Carlton and Faceby from 16; Asst Chapl HM Pris Kirklevington Grange from 16. *HM Prison, Kirklevington Grange, Yarm TS15 9PA* T: (01642) 792600 E: alison.hutchinson@btinternet.com

HUTCHINSON, Canon Andrew Charles. b 63. Univ of Wales (Ban) BA 84 MEd 96. Aston Tr Scheme 85 Chich Th Coll 87. **d** 89 **p** 90. C Burnley St Cath w St Alb and St Paul *Blackb*

89–92; C Shrewsbury St Chad w St Mary *Lich* 92–94; Chapl Heref Cathl Sch 94–97; Succ Heref Cathl 94–97; Chapl Solihull Sch from 97; Can St Jo Pro-Cathl Katakwa from 00. *36 Avenbury Drive, Solihull B91 2QZ* T: 0121-704 0171 E: andrewcapecoast@gmail.com *or* hutcha@solsch.org.uk

HUTCHINSON, Andrew George Pearce. b 78. Glos Univ BA 01 PGCE 02. Oak Hill Th Coll BA 08. **d** 08 **p** 09. C Normanton *Derby* 08–15; Chapl Monkton Combe Sch Bath from 15. *Monkton Combe School, Church Lane, Monkton Combe, Bath BA2 7HG* T: (01225) 721208 M: 07877-831506 E: andy_hutchinson@hotmail.com

HUTCHINSON, Andrew Paul. b 65. Trin Hall Cam BA 87 MA 91 Solicitor 90. Aston Tr Scheme 92 Ripon Coll Cuddesdon BTh 97. **d** 97 **p** 98. C Stanley *Dur* 97–99; C Sunderland 99–01; TV 01–02; Chapl Sunderland Univ 99–02; TV Penrith w Newton Reigny and Plumpton Wall *Carl* 02–09; Chapl Cumbria Campus Cen Lancs Univ 02–07; Chapl Cumbria Univ *Carl* 07–09; R Stokesley w Seamer *York* from 09. *The Rectory, Leven Close, Stokesley, Middlesbrough TS9 5AP* T: (01642) 710405 E: paul.hutchinson5@btinternet.com

HUTCHINSON, Anthony Hugh. b 47. Open Univ BSc 00 Liv Univ MA 09. **d** 10 **p** 11. OLM Stafford St Chad *Lich* 10–15; NSM Rough Hills 15; NSM Wolverhampton St Martin and St Steph from 15. *Kilsall Hall, Kilsall, Shifnal TF11 8PL* T: (01902) 373145 E: fr.tony@softersolutions.co.uk

HUTCHINSON, Canon Cyril Peter. b 37. Dur Univ BA 61. Wm Temple Coll Rugby 61. **d** 63 **p** 64. C Birm St Paul 63–67; Prin Community Relns Officer 66–69; Dir Bradf SHARE 69–76; Hon C Manningham *Bradf* 75–76; V Clayton 76–83; RD Bowling and Horton 80–83; TR Keighley St Andr 83–94; Hon Can Bradf Cathl 84–03; rtd 94; Hon C Keighley All SS *Bradf* 94–03; PtO 04–14; *Leeds* from 14. *Wellcroft, Laycock Lane, Laycock, Keighley BD22 0PN* T: (01535) 606145 E: peter_hutchinson@hotmail.co.uk

HUTCHINSON, David. *See* HUTCHINSON, William David

HUTCHINSON, Mrs Janice Vivien. b 50. All SS Cen for Miss & Min 17. **d** 18 **p** 19. OLM W Hallam and Mapperley w Stanley *Derby* from 18. *1 Spencer Street, Stanley Common, Ilkeston DE7 6GA* T: 0115-752 6116

HUTCHINSON, Jeremy Olpherts. b 32. Oriel Coll Ox BA 55 MA 60. Cranmer Hall Dur. **d** 57 **p** 58. C Shoreditch St Leon *Lon* 57–60; V Hoxton St Jo w Ch 60–78; Hon C Hackney 78–85; C Highbury Ch Ch w St Jo and St Sav 85–91; P-in-c Hanley Road St Sav w St Paul 91–92; TV Tollington 92–96; rtd 96; PtO *Lon* 96–19. *8 Casimir Road, London E5 9NU* T: (020) 8806 6492 E: jeremy.hutch@virgin.net *or* janddhutchinson@gmail.com

HUTCHINSON, John Charles. b 44. K Coll Lon 64. **d** 69 **p** 70. C Portsea All SS *Portsm* 69–71; C Portsea All SS w St Jo Rudmore 71–73; TV Fareham H Trin 73–78; P-in-c Pangbourne *Ox* 78–86; P-in-c Tidmarsh w Sulham 84–86; R Pangbourne w Tidmarsh and Sulham 86–96; PtO from 07. *90 Fir Tree Avenue, Wallingford OX10 0PL* T: (01491) 832445 E: cavea@tiscali.co.uk

HUTCHINSON, Prof John Maxwell. b 48. PPRIBA Robert Gordon Univ Aber Hon DDes 07 Linc Univ DA 15. **d** 14. NSM St Jo on Bethnal Green *Lon* 14–16; C Chingford SS Pet and Paul *Chelmsf* from 16. *95 Falmouth Avenue, London E4 9QR* E: m.hutchinson@blueyonder.co.uk

HUTCHINSON, Jonathan Graham. b 62. Bris Univ BA 01. Trin Coll Bris 98. **d** 01 **p** 02. C Church Stretton *Heref* 01–04; P-in-c Aspley *S'well* 04–11; V 11–17; V Sunningdale *Ox* from 17. *The Vicarage, Sidbury Close, Ascot SL5 0PD* T: (01344) 620061 E: jghutchinson@btinternet.com

HUTCHINSON, Jonathan Mark. b 45. Open Univ BA 73 E Lon Univ MSc 94. Cant Sch of Min 85. **d** 89 **p** 90. NSM Wickham Market w Pettistree and Easton *St E* 89–93; V Thorington w Wenhaston, Bramfield etc 94–97; TV Ipswich St Mary at Stoke w St Pet and St Fran 97–02; PtO *B & W* from 02. *35A Milton Lane, Wells BA5 2QS* T: (01749) 938779 E: drmark.hutchinson@hotmail.com

HUTCHINSON, Canon Julie Lorraine. b 55. WMMTC 90. **d** 93 **p** 94. C Northampton St Mary *Pet* 93–95; P-in-c Morcott w Glaston and Bisbrooke 95–97; P-in-c Lyddington w Stoke Dry and Seaton etc 97–02; V 03; Dir of Ords and Voc 03–10; Bp's Chapl 11–15; TV Oakham, Ashwell, Braunston, Brooke, Egleton etc 15–18; Can Pet Cathl 04–18; Hon C High Framland Par *Leic* from 18; Hon C S Framland from 18. *5 Croxton Lane, Harston, Grantham NG32 1PP* M: 07949-199135 E: revdjulie@icloud.com

HUTCHINSON, The Ven Karen Elizabeth. b 64. LMH Ox BA 85 MA 89 Kent Univ MA 06 Solicitor 89. Wycliffe Hall Ox. **d** 01 **p** 02. C Alton St Lawr *Win* 01–06; V Crondall and Ewshot *Guildf* 06–12; V The Bourne and Tilford 12–16; Hon Can Guildf Cathl 13–16; Adn Nor from

16. *31 Bracondale, Norwich NR1 2AT* T: (01603) 620007 E: archdeacon.norwich@dioceseofnorwich.org

HUTCHINSON, Mark. *See* HUTCHINSON, Jonathan Mark

HUTCHINSON, Maxwell. *See* HUTCHINSON, John Maxwell

HUTCHINSON, Michael Thomas. b 87. St Cath Coll Cam BA 08 MA 12. St Mellitus Coll BA 19. **d** 19. C Preston St Cuth *Blackb* from 19. *58 Garstone Croft, Fulwood, Preston PR2 3WY* M: 07933-533205 E: hutchi44@hotmail.com

HUTCHINSON, Paul. *See* HUTCHINSON, Andrew Paul

HUTCHINSON, Peter. *See* HUTCHINSON, Cyril Peter

HUTCHINSON, Peter Francis. b 52. Sarum & Wells Th Coll 87. **d** 89 **p** 90. C Honiton, Gittisham, Combe Raleigh, Monkton etc *Ex* 89–93; V Valley Park *Win* 93–17; rtd 17; PtO *Portsm* from 18. *9 Albert Way, East Cowes PO32 6GA* T: (01983) 294615

HUTCHINSON, Canon Raymond John. b 51. Liv Univ BSc 73. Westcott Ho Cam 73. **d** 76 **p** 77. C Peckham St Jo *S'wark* 76–78; C Peckham St Jo w St Andr 78–79; C Prescot *Liv* 79–81; V Edgehill St Dunstan 81–87; P-in-c Litherland Ch Ch 87–89; P-in-c Waterloo Park 87–89; V Waterloo Ch Ch and St Mary 90–97; Chapl Wigan and Leigh Health Services NHS Trust 97–01; Chapl Wrightington, Wigan and Leigh NHS Foundn Trust 01–15; P-in-c Wigan All SS *Liv* 04–08; P-in-c Wigan St Geo 05–08; R Wigan All SS and St Geo 08–15; TR Wigan All SS 15; Hon Can Liv Cathl 13–15; rtd 15; PtO *Liv* from 16. *9 Chequers Gardens, Liverpool L19 3PD* T: 0151-291 5803 E: rayh365@gmail.com

HUTCHINSON, Roy William. b 69. Oak Hill Th Coll BA 94. **d** 17 **p** 18. C W Hendon St Jo and Cricklewood St Pet *Lon* from 17. *102 Claremont Road, London NW2 1AP* T: (020) 8455 9820 M: 07790-317721 E: roy.hutchinson@gmail.com

HUTCHINSON, Canon Stephen. b 38. St Chad's Coll Dur BA 60. **d** 62 **p** 63. C Tividale *Lich* 62–68; V Walsall St Andr 68–73; R Headless Cross *Worc* 73–81; TR Redditch, The Ridge 81–91; RD Bromsgrove 85–91; V Stourbridge St Thos 91–03; Hon Can Worc Cathl 88–03; rtd 03; PtO *Worc* from 03. *251 Stourbridge Road, Kidderminster DY10 2XJ* T: (01562) 631658 E: stephen.hutchinson71@virginmedia.com

HUTCHINSON, Canon William Davld. b 27. Wycliffe Hall Ox 55. **d** 57 **p** 58. C Ipswich St Jo *St E* 57–60; R Combs 60–65; V Ipswich St Aug 65–76; R Ewhurst *Guildf* 76–81; V Aldeburgh w Hazlewood *St E* 81–92; RD Saxmundham 83–88; Hon Can St E Cathl 87–92; rtd 92. *Hazelwood, 1 Birch Close, Woodbridge IP12 4UA* T: (01394) 383760 E: wdhutchinson@tiscali.co.uk

HUTCHINSON CERVANTES, Canon Ian Charles. b 62. Cant Univ (NZ) BSc 84 Reading Univ MSc 86 Jes Coll Cam BA 89 MA 92. Westcott Ho Cam 86. **d** 89 **p** 90. C Iffley *Ox* 89–92; USPG 92–04; Locum P Caracas Cathl Venezuela 93; P-in-c El Cayo St Andr Belize 93–97; USPG Staff 97–04; Chapl Madrid *Eur* 04–12; World Miss Officer and P-in-c Nuthurst and Mannings Heath *Chich* 12–15; R 15–18; Regional Dir Miss to Seafarers from 18; Hon Can Madrid Cathl from 01; Hon Can Buenos Aires from 02; Hon Can Pelotas from 06; Can Gib Cathl *Eur* from 10. *Mission to Seafarers, St Michael Paternoster Royal, College Hill, London EC4R 2RL* M: 07733-023880

HUTCHISON, Geoffrey John. b 52. Trin Hall Cam MA 76 Lon Univ CertEd 76. Ridley Hall Cam 77. **d** 79 **p** 80. C Harold Wood *Chelmsf* 79–83; CF 83–89; Warden Viney Hill Chr Adventure Cen 89–96; P-in-c Viney Hill *Glouc* 89–96; V Wadsley *Sheff* 96–11; Chapl Sheff Children's NHS Foundn Trust 11–14; PtO *Sheff* from 16. *14 Canterbury Crescent, Sheffield S10 3RX* T: 0114-230 9286 E: rev.hutch@gmail.com

HUTCHISON, Ross. b 61. Wadh Coll Ox BA 83 MA 86 DPhil 88. SEITE 03. **d** 06 **p** 07. NSM Newington St Mary *S'wark* 06–10; NSM Kilburn St Mary w All So and W Hampstead St Jas *Lon* from 10. *12A Cumberland Mansions, West End Lane, London NW6 1LL* T: (020) 7794 6087 E: rossnw6@gmail.com

HUTSON, Mark Arthur. b 69. Linc Sch of Th and Min 10. **d** 13 **p** 16. OLM Barrow and Goxhill *Linc* 13–15; NSM Gt Grimsby St Mary and St Jas 15–18; C Wolds Gateway Group from 18. *Lindum Lodge, Spruce Lane, Ulceby DN39 6UL* M: 07745-369630 E: prayerhut1@gmail.com

HUTT, Canon David Handley. b 38. Lambeth MA 05 AKC 68. **d** 69 **p** 70. C Bedford Park *Lon* 69–70; C Westmr St Matt 70–73; PV and Succ S'wark Cathl 73–78; Chapl K Coll Taunton 78–82; V Bordesley SS Alb and Patr *Birm* 82–86; V St Marylebone All SS *Lon* 86–95; Can Steward Westmr Abbey 95–05; Sub-Dean and Adn Westmr 99–05; rtd 05; PtO *Lon* 06–13; *Eur* from 06. *14A The Quadrangle, Morden College, 19 St Germans Place, London SE3 0PW*

HUTTON, Christopher. b 81. Sussex Univ BSc 04. Wycliffe Hall Ox BTh 10. **d** 10 **p** 11. C Southgate *Chich* 10–14; R Ditchingham, Hedenham, Broome, Earsham etc *Nor* from 14. *The Rectory, School Road, Earsham, Bungay NR35 2TF* T: (01986) 895423 E: chrishutton@hotmail.com

HUTTON, Elizabeth. *See* HUTTON, Susan Elizabeth

HUTTON, Griffith Arthur Jeremy. b 31. Trin Hall Cam BA 56 MA 59. Linc Th Coll 56. **d** 58 **p** 59. C Hexham *Newc* 58–60; C Gosforth All SS 60–65; V Whitegate *Ches* 65–71; V Whitegate w Lt Budworth 71–78; R Dowdeswell and Andoversford w the Shiptons etc *Glouc* 78–91; V Newnham w Awre and Blakeney 91–96; rtd 96; PtO Heref from 99; *Glouc* from 15. *12 Kent Close, Churchdown, Gloucester GL3 2HQ* T: (01452) 712626 E: behindthemower@gmail.com

HUTTON, Matthew Charles Arthur. b 53. Ch Ch Ox BA 75 MA 79. St Mellitus Coll BA 14. **d** 14 **p** 15. OLM Nor St Steph 14–18; PtO 18–19; NSM The Mitre Benefice from 19. *Broom Farm, Chedgrave, Norwich NR14 6BQ* T: (01508) 520775 *or* 528388 F: 528099 E: mhutton@paston.co.uk

HUTTON, Sarah Fielding. b 63. **d** 11 **p** 12. NSM Shere, Albury and Chilworth *Guildf* from 11; Spiritual Growth Facilitator from 14. *Netley House, Shere Road, Gomshall, Guildford GU5 9QA* T: (01483) 203800 E: sarah@handr.co.uk *or* sarah.hutton@cofeguildford.org.uk

HUTTON, Mrs Serena Quartermaine. b 35. Nottm Univ BA 57 Lon Univ BA 73 Stranmillis Coll PGCE 68 FRSA 87. SAOMC 95. **d** 98 **p** 99. OLM Chinnor, Sydenham, Aston Rowant and Crowell *Ox* 98–06; PtO from 06. *Robin Cottage, The Green, Kingston Blount, Chinnor OX9 4SE* T: (01844) 354173

HUTTON, Susan Elizabeth. b 70. Univ of Wales (Cardiff) BD 91. Ripon Coll Cuddesdon 93. **d** 95 **p** 96. C W Parley *Sarum* 95–99; C Trowbridge H Trin 99–05; P-in-c 05–09; PtO 09–14; Lic to RD Devizes 14–16; TV Clarendon from 16. *The Rectory, 5 The Copse, Alderbury, Salisbury SP5 3BL* T: (01722) 238504 E: beth.hutton@clarendonteam.org

HUXHAM, Canon Peter Richard. b 38. Worc Coll Ox BA 61 MA 74. St Steph Ho Ox 61. **d** 63 **p** 64. C Gillingham *Sarum* 63–67; C Osmondthorpe St Phil *Ripon* 67–70; V Parkstone St Osmund *Sarum* 70–75; TR Parkstone St Pet w Branksea and St Osmund 75–92; RD Poole 85–92; Can and Preb Sarum Cathl 85–92; Chapl Taunton and Somerset NHS Trust 92–03; rtd 03; PtO *Sarum* from 04. *Salterns House, 34 Brownsea View Avenue, Poole BH14 8LQ* T: (01202) 707431

HUXLEY, Canon Stephen Scott. b 30. Linc Th Coll 53. **d** 56 **p** 57. C Cullercoats St Geo *Newc* 56–59; C Eglingham 59–60; C N Gosforth 63–65; V Nether Witton and Hartburn and Meldon 63–65; V Tynemouth Priory 65–74; V Warkworth and Acklington 74–78; P-in-c Tynemouth St Jo 78–81; V 81–87; Hon Can Newc Cathl 82–92; V Wylam 87–92; rtd 92; PtO *Newc* 92–10. *7 Langside Drive, Comrie, Crieff PH6 2HR* T: (01764) 679877

HUXLEY-JONES, Craig John. b 85. Cant Ch Ch Univ BA 06 MCollT 09. SEITE 11. **d** 14 **p** 15. NSM Hackington *Cant* 14–15; NSM Goudhurst w Kilndown 15–19; Chapl Benenden Sch 14–19; Sen Chapl Ch Hosp Horsham from 19. *2 West Gun Copse, The Avenue, Christ's Hospital, Horsham RH13 0JE* M: 07872-554044

HUXTABLE, Christopher Michael Barclay. b 61. Ex Univ BA 83 Qu Coll Cam PGCE 84. St Steph Ho Ox 93. **d** 95 **p** 96. C Chich 95–98; C Haywards Heath St Wilfrid 98–99; TV 99–01; Chapl Geelong Gr Sch (Timbertop) Australia 01–04; Chapl St Mary's Sch Wantage 04–05; C Blewbury, Hagbourne and Upton *Ox* 05–06; C S w N Moreton, Aston Tirrold and Aston Upthorpe 05–06; R Mansfield Australia 06–11; Chapl Westbourne Gr Sch 11; Chapl Stowe Sch 12–16; NSM Newport Pagnell w Lathbury and Moulsoe *Ox* 16–17; R Funtington and W Stoke w Sennicotts *Chich* from 17. *The Vicarage, Church Lane, Funtington, Chichester PO18 9LH* T: (01243) 575127 M: 07469-177919 E: cmbhux@gmail.com

HUXTABLE, Canon Peter Alexander. b 68. Southn Univ BEng 90. St Jo Coll Nottm MTh 01. **d** 01 **p** 02. C Kidderminster St Geo *Worc* 01–05; V Bestwood Em w St Mark S'well 05–10; P-in-c Stapleford 10–11; V from 11; AD Nottm N 16–19; Hon Can S'well Minster from 17. *The Vicarage, 61 Church Street, Stapleford, Nottingham NG9 8GA* T: 0115-854 0196

HUYTON, Canon Susan Mary. b 57. Birm Univ BA 79. Qu Coll Birm 83. **d** 86 **p** 97. C Connah's Quay *St As* 86–89; C Wrexham 89–90; Dn-in-c 90–91; TV 91–99; V Gwersyllt 99–14; AD Gresford 05–12; R Bangor Monachorum, Worthenbury and Marchwiel 14–16; I Maelor Miss Area from 17; AD Dee Valley from 14; Can Cursal St As Cathl from 08. *The Rectory, 8 Ludlow Road, Bangor-on-Dee, Wrexham LL13 0JG* T: (01978) 780608 E: suehuyton@aol.com

HUZZEY, Canon Peter George. b 48. Trin Coll Bris 74. **d** 76 **p** 77. C Bishopsworth *Bris* 76–79; V 86–96; C Downend 79–80; TV Kings Norton *Birm* 80–86; TR Bishopsworth and Bedminster Down *Bris* 97–00; RD Bedminster 98–99; TR Kingswood 00–15; P-in-c Hanham 12–15; Hon Can Bris Cathl 12–15; rtd 15; PtO *Bris* from 16. *134 Guest Avenue, Emersons Green, Bristol BS16 7DA* T: 0117-983 0725 M: 07397-208088 E: peterhuzzey67@gmail.com

HYATT, Robert Keith. b 34. Em Coll Cam BA 59 MA 63. Ridley Hall Cam 58. **d** 60 **p** 61. C Cheltenham St Mary *Glouc* 60–63; Asst Chapl K Edw Sch Witley 63–65; C Godalming *Guildf* 65–69; Hong Kong 69–78; V Claygate *Guildf* 78–91; TV Whitton *Sarum* 91–96 and 99–00; TR 96–99; rtd 00; PtO *B & W* 00–04; *Bris* from 02; May Moore Chapl Malmesbury w Westport and Brokenborough 02–05; Chapl Kennet and N Wilts Primary Care Trust 02–05. *19 Dark Lane, Malmesbury SN16 0BB* T: (01666) 829026 E: bobnhelen@dsl.pipex.com

HYDE, Canon Denise. b 54. WEMTC 05. **d** 08 **p** 09. OLM Fairford Deanery *Glouc* 08–12; NSM S Cotswolds from 12; Hon Can Glouc Cathl from 18. *14 Park Street, Fairford GL7 4JJ* T: (01285) 713285 *or* 850283 M: 07816-500269 E: denisehyde15@gmail.com

HYDE, Canon Jacqueline Diane. b 66. Glos Univ BA 12. WEMTC 06. **d** 09 **p** 10. NSM S Cheltenham *Glouc* 09–15; V Churchdown St Jo and Innsworth from 15; Dioc Ecum Officer from 13; Hon Can Glouc Cathl from 19. *The Vicarage, 2 St John's Avenue, Churchdown, Gloucester GL3 2DB* T: (01452) 713421 E: revdjacqui@talktalk.net

HYDE, Jane. b 56. All SS Cen for Miss & Min 17. **d** 18 **p** 19. NSM Clarksfield and Waterhead *Man* from 18. *2 Old Rectory Gardens, Mellalieu Street, Middleton, Manchester M24 5DN* E: janehyde10@hotmail.com

HYDE, Jeremy Richard Granville. b 52. Sch of Pharmacy Lon BPharm 75 PhD 80. SAOMC 01. **d** 04 **p** 05. NSM Furze Platt *Ox* 04–11; AD Maidenhead and Windsor 08–11; V Hanham *Cov* 11–17; rtd 17; PtO *Lon* 17–18; NSM Hanwell St Mellitus w St Mark from 18. *4A Castlebar Park, London W5 1BX* T: (020) 8997 9380 E: jeremy.hyde@btinternet.com

HYDE, Karen. b 68. Univ of Wales (Cardiff) BSc 89 St Hugh's Coll Ox DPhil 94. Ox Min Course 14. **d** 17 **p** 18. NSM DAMASCUS *Ox* from 17. *Address withheld by request* M: 07526-985395 E: revdkaren.hyde@gmail.com

HYDER-SMITH, Brian John. b 45. FInstAM MCMI MBIM. EAMTC 84. **d** 87 **p** 88. NSM Huntingdon *Ely* 87–90; P-in-c Abbots Ripton w Wood Walton 90–98; P-in-c Kings Ripton 90–98; C Whittlesey, Pondersbridge and Coates 98–99; TV 99–04; rtd 04; Hon C Ironstone *Ox* 10–12; PtO *Ely* from 13. *The Cherry Trees, New Road, Woodwalton, Huntingdon PE28 5YT* T: (01487) 773960 E: revbh-s@hotmail.com *or* hydersmith@icloud.com

HYDON, Canon Veronica Weldon. b 52. N Lon Poly BA 73 Maria Grey Coll Lon CertEd 74. Aston Tr Scheme 87 Westcott Ho Cam 89. **d** 91 **p** 94. Par Dn Poplar *Lon* 91–94; C 94–95; P-in-c Roxwell *Chelmsf* 95–00; Lay Development Officer 95–00; V Forest Gate Em w Upton Cross 00–03; Assoc V Timperley *Ches* 03–07; V Bollington from 07; RD Macclesfield 14–19; Hon Can Ches Cathl from 14. *6 Merlin Close, Macclesfield SK10 2AS* T: (01625) 422849 E: vhydon@hotmail.com

HYGATE, Paul. b 72. Bolton Inst of HE BA 95. EMMTC 07. **d** 10 **p** 11. NSM Aston on Trent, Elvaston, Weston on Trent etc *Derby* from 10. *38 Oaklands Avenue, Littleover, Derby DE23 2QH* T: (01332) 772779 E: frpaulhygate@gmail.com

HYLAND, Cecil George. b 38. TCD BA 62 MA 78. CITC Div Test. **d** 63 **p** 64. C Belfast St Nic *Conn* 63–66; C Monkstown *D & G* 66–68; Ch of Ireland Youth Officer 68–73; Chapl TCD 73–79; I Tullow *D & G* 79–90; I Howth 90–05; Dir of Ords (Dub) 91–98; Can Ch Ch Cathl Dublin 91–05; Cen Dir of Ords 98–05; rtd 05. *34 The Vale, Skerries Rock, Skerries, Co Dublin, Republic of Ireland* T: (00353) (1) 810 6884 M: 86-838 5317 E: cecilhyland@hotmail.com

HYLTON, Jane Lois. *See* NURSEY, Jane Lois

HYSLOP, Mrs Catherine Graham Young. b 53. Carl Dioc Tr Inst 90. **d** 92 **p** 94. NSM St Bees *Carl* 92–95; NSM Upperby St Jo 95–98; C Upperby 98–19; Adv for Post-Ord Tr 00–03; Chapl Cumbria Partnership NHS Foundn Trust 05–19; rtd 19. *Address temp unknown* E: katie.hyslop2010@gmail.com

HYSLOP, Canon Thomas James. b 54. St Andr Univ BD 76. Edin Th Coll 76. **d** 78 **p** 79. C Whitehaven *Carl* 78–81; C Walney Is 81–83; P-in-c Gt Broughton and Broughton Moor 83–85; V 85–88; V Kells 88–95; P-in-c Upperby St Jo 95–97; V 97–03; TR S Carl 03–12; R Upperby 12–19; Dioc Chapl MU 02–19; Hon Can Carl Cathl 06–19; rtd 19. *Address temp unknown* E: jim.hyslop@talk21.com

HYSON, Peter Raymond. b 51. Open Univ BA 80 Bris Univ MSc 05. Oak Hill Th Coll BA 86. **d** 87 **p** 88. C Billericay and Lt Burstead *Chelmsf* 87–92; TV Whitton *Sarum* 92–99; PtO *Lon* 07–14. *53 Plough Way, London SE16 2LS* T: (020) 3509 2796 M: 07951-767113 E: peter@change-perspectives.com

I

I'ANSON, Frederick Mark. b 43. MRAC 68. Carl Dioc Tr Inst 89. d 92 p 93. NSM Sedbergh, Cautley and Garsdale *Bradf* 92–98; P-in-c Kirkby-in-Malhamdale w Coniston Cold 98–08; rtd 08; PtO *Bradf* 09–12; *Carl* from 12. *The Bowers, Firbank, Sedbergh LA10 5EG* T: (015396) 21757 M: 07815-552778 E: mark.mmia43@gmail.com

IBBOTSON, David Paul. b 64. Man Univ BSc 85 PGCE 86. STETS 09. d 12 p 13. C Tewkesbury w Walton Cardiff and Twyning *Glouc* 12–14; Chapl Monmouth Schs 14–16; Chapl Eastbourne Coll 16–18; PtO *Glouc* 16–17; *Chich* from 17; Chapl Malvern Coll from 19. *24 College Road, Malvern WR14 3DD* M: 07876-333390 E: dpibbotson@tesco.net

IBBOTSON, Miss Tracy Alexandra. b 63. Cranmer Hall Dur 01. d 03 p 04. C Todmorden *Wakef* 03–08; V Airedale w Fryston 08–14; *Leeds* from 14; Adv on Urban Issues *Wakef* 12–14; *Leeds* from 14. *Holy Cross Vicarage, The Mount, Castleford WF10 3JN* T: (01977) 553157 E: ibbotson457@btinternet.com

IBIAYO, David Akindayo Oluwarotimi. b 71. Lagos Univ BSc. Ridley Hall Cam. d 06 p 07. C Barking St Marg w St Patr *Chelmsf* 06–10; R Vange from 11; P-in-c Bowers Gifford w N Benfleet from 11. *Vange Rectory, 782 Clay Hill Road, Basildon SS16 4NG* T: (01268) 581404 M: 07904-846028 E: david_ibiayo@hotmail.com

ICKE, Robert John. b 69. Regents Th Coll BA 98. All SS Cen for Miss & Min 17. d 19. C Stockton Heath *Ches* from 19; C Latchford St Jas from 19. *St James's Vicarage, 14 Manx Road, Warrington WA4 6AJ* M: 07791-611128 E: r.icke@btinternet.com

IDDON, Fiona Margaret Hastings. b 74. Regent's Park Coll Ox BA 95 MA 99 Westmr Coll Ox PGCE 97. St Mellitus Coll 14. d 17 p 18. C Shrewsbury St Geo w Greenfields *Lich* from 17. *18A Meole Walk, Shrewsbury SY3 9EU* T: (01743) 357262 E: fionamhiddon@gmail.com

IDDON, Roy Edward. b 40. TCert 61 Lanc Univ MA 88. NOC 83. d 83 p 84. Hd Teacher St Andr Primary Sch Blackb from 83; NSM Bolton St Matt w St Barn *Man* 83–88; Lic to AD Walmsley 88–93; NSM 93–01; NSM Turton Moorland 01–04; NSM Bolton St Phil 04–10; PtO from 11. *28 New Briggs Fold, Egerton, Bolton BL7 9UL* T: (01204) 306589 M: 07792-654445 E: raiddon@aol.com

IDLE, Christopher Martin. b 38. St Pet Coll Ox BA 62. Clifton Th Coll 62. d 65 p 66. C Barrow St Mark *Carl* 65–68; C Camberwell Ch Ch *S'wark* 68–71; P-in-c Poplar St Matthias *Lon* 71–76; R Limehouse 76–89; R N Hartismere *St E* 89–95; PtO *S'wark* 95–03; *St E* 01–03; rtd 03; PtO *Roch* 04–16; *S'wark* from 13. *50 Park View House, Hurst Street, London SE24 0EH* T: (020) 3490 7828 E: christophermidle@gmail.com

✠IDOWU-FEARON, The Rt Revd Josiah Atkins. b 49. Birm Univ MA. Immanuel Coll Ibadan 67. d 71 p 71 c 90. Gen Sec Evang Fellowship Angl Communion Nigeria 71–90; Warden St Fran Th Coll Wusasa 81–84; Provost St Mich Cathl 84–90; Bp Sokoto 90–98; Bp Kaduna 98–15; Abp 02–09; Sec Gen Angl Communion Office from 15; Hon Asst Bp Lon from 15; Hon Asst Bp S'wark from 18; PV Westmr Abbey from 16; Six Preacher Cant Cathl from 07. *Anglican Consultative Council, St Andrew's House, Tavistock Crescent, London W11 1AP* T: (020) 7313 3900

IEVINS, Mrs Catherine Ruth. b 54. LMH Ox BA 77 MA 80 Solicitor 81. EAMTC 98. d 01 p 02. C Pet Ch Carpenter 01–05; PtO 05–06; P-in-c Polebrook and Lutton w Hemington and Luddington 06–07; C Barnwell w Tichmarsh, Thurning and Clapton 06–07; R Barnwell, Hemington, Luddington in the Brook etc 07–16; Warden of Readers 12–14; rtd 16; PtO *Ely* 17–18; Hon C Cambridge St Phil from 18. *18 Hemingford Road, Cambridge CB1 3BZ* T: (01223) 242945 E: ci.life9@gmail.com

IEVINS, Paul Janis. b 58. Linc Sch of Th and Min 12. d 15 p 16. NSM Welton and Dunholme w Scothern *Linc* from 15. *5 Oak Avenue, Dunholme, Lincoln LN2 3QX*

IEVINS, Peter Valdis. b 54. St Jo Coll Ox BA 75 MA 81 Solicitor 79. Westcott Ho Cam 86. d 88 p 89. C Sawston and Babraham *Ely* 88–91; NSM Pet Ch Carpenter 01–06; LtO 06–16; PtO *Ely* 16–17; NSM Cherry Hinton St Andr from 17. *18 Hemingford Road, Cambridge CB1 3BZ* T: (01223) 242945 M: 07708-216974 E: peterievins54@gmail.com

IJAZ, Luke Anthony. b 76. Univ Coll Lon MSci 99 Lon Inst of Educn PGCE 01. Wycliffe Hall Ox BA 06. d 07 p 08. C Wallington *S'wark* 07–11; C Redhill H Trin 11–13; C

Langham Place All So *Lon* from 14. *25 Fitzroy Street, London W1T 6DR* M: 07803-244543 E: luke_ijaz@hotmail.com *or* luke.ijaz@allsouls.org

IKECHUKWU, Eliakim Chinonyerem. b 62. Calabar Univ Nigeria BA 01 Wolv Univ MA 16 MRes 17. Trin Coll Umuahia 08. d 07 p 08. Chapl Calabar Univ Nigeria 07–10; Chapl Calabar Pris 10–15; C Calabar Cathl 11–13; Chapl 13–15; PtO *Birm* 15–18; NSM Kings Norton from 18. *53 Wychall Park Grove, Birmingham B38 8AG* T: 0121-458 3289 M: 07958-600772 E: eliakimike@yahoo.com

IKIN, Gordon Mitchell. b 30. AKC 57. d 58 p 59. C Leigh St Mary *Man* 58–61; V Westleigh St Paul 61–72; V Thornham St Jas 72–95; rtd 95; PtO *Man* 95–08; *Worc* from 14. *3 Lygon Lodge, Newland, Malvern WR13 5AX* T: (01684) 564948

ILIFFE, Mrs Alison Jane. b 63. Birm Poly BA 86. Qu Coll Birm 13. d 15 p 16. NSM Avon-Swift *Leic* 15–18; TV Market Harborough and The Transfiguration etc from 18. *44 Northampton Road, Market Harborough LE16 9HE* E: ajiliffe@gmail.com

ILIFFE, Mrs Felicity Mary. b 57. Glam Univ BA 79 Normal Coll Ban PGCE 82. SEITE 06 WEMTC 07. d 09 p 10. C Ledbury *Heref* 09–13; V Highley w Billingsley, Glazeley etc 13–14; PtO *Pet* from 16. *70 Chapel Road, Weldon, Corby NN17 3HP* T: (01536) 266842 E: revfliss@gmail.com

ILLING, Eric James. b 33. Kelham Th Coll 54 Chich Th Coll 55. d 57 p 58. C Leeds St Aid *Ripon* 57–60; C Leeds All SS 60–62; C E Grinstead St Swithun *Chich* 62–65; V Middleton St Mary *Ripon* 65–74; R Felpham w Middleton *Chich* 74–81; Chapl R Devon and Ex Hosp (Wonford) 81–91; TR Heavitree w Ex St Paul 81–91; R Bradninch and Clyst Hydon 91–94; rtd 94; PtO *B & W* from 94; *Eur* from 98. *12 Barlinch Close, Taunton TA2 7HL* T: (01823) 275278 E: ericilling@btinternet.com

ILSLEY (*née* ROGERS), Mrs Anne Frances. b 50. Heythrop Coll Lon BA 00 RGN 72. Wycliffe Hall Ox 00. d 02 p 03. NSM Harefield *Lon* 02–06; NSM Dorchester *Ox* 06–15; rtd 15; PtO *Sarum* from 16. *1-2 Charlton Hill, Edington, Westbury BA13 4PL* M: 07956-374624 E: annefi36@aol.com

ILSLEY (*formerly* PHILLIPS), Mary Alice. b 53. Ripon Coll Cuddesdon 97. d 99 p 00. C Addiscombe St Mildred *S'wark* 99–02; TV Basingstoke *Win* 02–12; rtd 13; PtO *Win* from 15. *42 Topaz Drive, Andover SP10 3EE*

ILTON, Mrs Jennifer Jane. b 38. S Dios Minl Tr Scheme 92. d 95 p 96. NSM Jersey St Sav *Win* 95–08; PtO from 08. *38 Maison St Louis, St Saviour, Jersey JE2 7LX* T: (01534) 722327

ILYAS, Marilyn. b 51. Oak Hill Th Coll 92. d 95 p 96. C Roch 95–98; TV S Chatham H Trin 98–01; TR 01–12; rtd 12; PtO *Roch* from 12. *5 Pepperidge Way, Hoo, Rochester ME3 9FY* T: (01634) 255897

IMPEY, Miss Joan Mary. b 35. Dalton Ho Bris 65. dss 74 d 87 p 94. Kennington St Mark *S'wark* 67–75; Barking St Marg w St Patr *Chelmsf* 75–81; Harwell w Chilton *Ox* 81–87; Par Dn 87–92; Par Dn Didcot All SS 92–94; C 94–97; rtd 98; PtO *Ox* from 99. *15 Loder Road, Harwell, Didcot OX11 0HR* T: (01235) 820346

IMPEY, Canon Patricia Irene. b 45. Birm Univ BA 67 Lanc Univ MPhil 01. Carl Dioc Tr Course 88. d 90 p 94. Par Dn Blackpool St Paul *Blackb* 90–94; C 94–95; Chapl Asst Victoria Hosp Blackpool 94–95; Asst Chapl Norfolk and Nor Health Care NHS Trust 95–96; Hon C Sprowston w Beeston Nor 96; R King's Beck 96–02; V Ecclesfield *Sheff* 02–10; Dean of Women's Min 03–06 and 06–08; Hon Can Sheff Cathl 04–10; rtd 10; PtO *Blackb* from 11. *22 Hala Grove, Lancaster LA1 4PS* T: (01524) 36617 E: patriciaimpey@btinternet.com

IMPEY, Richard. b 41. Em Coll Cam BA 63 MA 67 Harvard Univ ThM 67 Ches Univ DProf 13. Ridley Hall Cam 67. d 68 p 69. C Birm St Martin 68–72; Dir of Tr *B & W* 72–79; Dir of Ords 76–79; V Blackpool St Jo *Blackb* 79–95; RD Blackpool 84–90; Hon Can Blackb Cathl 89–95; Dioc Dir of Tr *Nor* 95–00; P-in-c Heigham St Barn w St Bart 00–02; V Wentworth *Sheff* 02–06; Bp's Adv in Par Development 04–10; rtd 06; PtO *Blackb* from 10. *22 Hala Grove, Lancaster LA1 4PS* T: (01524) 36617 E: richardimpey@btinternet.com

INALL, Mrs Elizabeth Freda. b 47. Univ of Wales (Lamp) MA 06. St Alb Minl Tr Scheme 88. d 92 p 94. NSM Tring St Alb 92–01; C Harpenden St Nic 01–09; P-in-c Milton Ernest, Pavenham and Thurleigh 09–13; rtd 13; PtO *Ches* from 14. *Grange House, Village Road, Christleton, Chester CH3 7AS* T: (01244) 336500 E: elizabeth@inall.co.uk

INBADAS, Hamilton. b 77. Nesamony Memorial Chr Coll Marthandam BA 97 Leuven Univ Belgium MSc 10

Nottm Univ PhD 15. United Th Coll Bangalore BD 02. **p** 09. Chapl Chr Medical Coll Vellore India 09–10; PtO *S'well* 11–14; LtO *Glas* 15–17; P-in-c Forres *Mor* from 18. *St John's Rectory, Victoria Road, Forres IV36 3BN* T: (01309) 672856   E: clergystjohnsforres@gmail.com   *or* clergy@stjohnsforres.org.uk

INCH, Vivian Ann. b 57. **d** 13 **p** 14. OLM High Wycombe *Ox* 13–16. *Address temp unknown* E: vainch73@gmail.com

IND, Dominic Mark. b 63. Lanc Univ BA 87. Ridley Hall Cam 87. **d** 90 **p** 91. C Birch w Fallowfield *Man* 90–93; SSF 93–95; PtO *Glas* 95–96; C Byker St Martin *Newc* 96–98; C Walker 96–98; P-in-c Cambuslang and Uddingston *Glas* 98–07; R Bridge of Allan *St And* 07–18; Chapl Stirling Univ 07–18; Bp's Chapl 07–18; Can St Ninian's Cathl Perth 10–18; Dioc Dir of Ords 11–18; R Helensburgh *Glas* from 18. *The Rectory, 16 William Street, Helensburgh G84 8BD* T: (01436) 670297 E: ind.dominic@gmail.com

IND, Philip William David. b 35. K Coll Lon BD 82. Wycliffe Hall Ox 74 Cranmer Hall Dur 59. **d** 65 **p** 66. C Ipswich St Jo *St E* 65–67; C Charlton Kings St Mary *Glouc* 67–71; R Woolstone w Gotherington and Oxenton 71–74; Chapl Alleyn's Sch Dulwich 76–81; C Beckenham St Geo *Roch* 83–85; V Bromley St Jo 85–87; PtO *Ox* 88–91 and 95–12; P-in-c Hurley 91–92; P-in-c Stubbings 91–92; rtd 92; PtO *St E* from 12. *Ostlers' End, Station Road, Melton, Woodbridge IP12 1PX* T: (01394) 384392

✠**IND, The Rt Revd William.** b 42. Leeds Univ BA 64. Coll of Resurr Mirfield 64. **d** 66 **p** 67 **c** 87. C Feltham *Lon* 66–71; C Northolt St Mary 71–73; TV Basingstoke *Win* 73–87; Vice-Prin Aston Tr Scheme 79–82; Dioc Dir of Ords *Win* 82–87; Hon Can Win Cathl 84–87; Suff Bp Grantham *Linc* 87–97; Dean Stamford 87–97; Can and Preb Linc Cathl 87–97; Bp Truro 97–08; PtO *Sarum* from 16. *15 Dean Close, Melksham SN12 7EZ* T: (01225) 340979 E: frances.bill@blueyonder.co.uk

INESON, David Antony. b 36. ALCD 62. **d** 62 **p** 63. C Sandal St Helen *Wakef* 62–65; C Birm St Geo 66–71; V Horton *Bradf* 71–80; RD Bowling and Horton 78–80; V Sedbergh, Cautley and Garsdale 80–86; C Firbank, Howgill and Killington 81–86; TV Langley and Parkfield *Man* 86–88; TR Banbury *Ox* 92–98; R 98–01; rtd 01; PtO *Ripon* 01–14; *Leeds* from 14. *11 Church Close, Redmire, Leyburn DL8 4HF* T: (01969) 624631 E: d.ine70@btinternet.com

✠**INESON, The Rt Revd Emma Gwynneth.** b 69. Birm Univ BA 92 MPhil 93 PhD 98. Trin Coll Bris BA 99. **d** 00 **p** 01 **c** 19. C Dore *Sheff* 00–03; Chapl Lee Abbey 03–06; Partnership P Inner Ring Partnership *Bris* 06–13; Tutor Trin Coll Bris 07–13; Bp's Chapl *Bris* 13–14; Prin Trin Coll Bris 14–19; NSM Bris St Matt and S Nath 06–14; NSM Stoke Bishop 15–19; Chapl to The Queen 16–19; Suff Bp Penrith *Carl* from 19; Cen Chapl MU from 19. *Holm Croft, 13 Castle Road, Kendal LA9 7AU* T: (01539) 727836 E: bishop.penrith@carlislediocese.org.uk

INESON, John Michael. b 57. Leeds Univ BA 12 MA 14 MIGEM 12 FRSA 16. Yorks Min Course 09. **d** 12 **p** 13. NSM Utley *Bradf* 12–14; *Leeds* 14–16; NSM Keighley from 16; NSM Ingrow w Hainworth from 19. *7 Badger Gate, Wilsden, Bradford BD15 0NP* T: (01535) 273670 M: 07850-204114 E: ineson50@btinternet.com

INESON, Mathew David. b 69. Birm Univ BEng 91. Trin Coll Bris BA 99 MA 00. **d** 00 **p** 01. NSM Dore *Sheff* 00–03; Chapl Lee Abbey 03–06; P-in-c Bris St Matt and S Nath 06–14; V 14; Min Inner Ring Partnership 06–14; AD City 10–14; P-in-c Stoke Bishop 14–15; V 15–19; AD Bris W 16–19; P-in-c Crosscrake *Carl* from 19. *Holmcroft, 13 Castle Road, Kendal LA9 7AU* M: 07896-997604 E: matineson@blueyonder.co.uk

INGALL, David Lenox. b 81. Jes Coll Cam MA 08. Wycliffe Hall Ox BA 08. **d** 09 **p** 10. C Holborn St Geo w H Trin and St Bart Lon 09–12; C Onslow Square and S Kensington St Aug 12–13; P-in-c St Sepulchre w Ch Ch Greyfriars etc from 13. *The Watch House, 10 Giltspur Street, London EC1A 9DE* T: (020) 7236 1145 M: 07968-119017 E: davidingall@gmail.com *or* david@stsepulchres.org

INGAMELLS, Ronald Sidney. b 32. FCIPD 92. AKC 56. **d** 57 **p** 58. C Leeds Gipton Epiphany *Ripon* 57–59; C Gt Yarmouth *Nor* 59–64; Dioc Youth Officer 64–79; Hon C Nor St Pet Mancroft 64–79; P-in-c Lemsford *St Alb* 79–02; Sec Tr Development and Chr Educn Nat Coun YMCAs 79–92; Consultant to Romania Euro Alliance YMCAs 93–97; rtd 02; PtO *Ely* 03–16; *Nor* from 16. *5 Riverview Drive, Upton, Norwich NR13 6BH* E: rjingamells@btinternet.com

✠**INGE, The Rt Revd John Geoffrey.** b 55. St Chad's Coll Dur BSc 77 MA 94 PhD 02 Keble Coll Ox PGCE 79. Coll of Resurr Mirfield. **d** 84 **p** 85 **c** 03. Asst Chapl Lancing Coll 84–86; Jun Chapl Harrow Sch 86–89; Sen Chapl 89–90; V Wallsend

St Luke *Newc* 90–96; Can Res Ely Cathl 96–03; Vice-Dean 99–03; Suff Bp Huntingdon *Ely* 03–07; Bp Worc from 07; Ld High Almoner from 13. *The Bishop's Office, The Old Palace, Deansway, Worcester WR1 2JE* T: (01905) 731599 F: 739382 E: bishop@cofe-worcester.org.uk

INGHAM, Anthony William. b 55. Ven English Coll Rome PhB 75 STB 78 NOC 98. **d** 78 **p** 79. In RC Ch 78–98; NSM Tottington *Man* 99–01; CF 01–15; P-in-c Beaulieu-sur-Mer *Eur* from 15. *Presbytère Anglican, 9 rue Paul-Doumer, 06310 Beaulieu-sur-Mer, France* T: (0033) 4 93 01 45 61 E: chaplain@stmichaelsbeaulieusurmer.org

INGHAM, Carol Helen. *See* PHARAOH, Carol Helen

INGHAM, John Edmund. b 34. Reading Univ BA 56. Clifton Th Coll 58. **d** 60 **p** 61. C Rodbourne Cheney *Bris* 60–63; C Tunbridge Wells St Jo *Roch* 63–67; V Sevenoaks Weald 67–82; V Farrington Gurney *B & W* 82–92; V Paulton 82–92; RD Midsomer Norton 88–91; R Aspley Guise w Husborne Crawley and Ridgmont *St Alb* 92–99; rtd 99; PtO *B & W* 00–18. *42 Hyatt Place, Shepton Mallet BA4 5XY* T: (01749) 345403 E: jsingham@talktalk.net

INGHAM, Malcolm John. b 68. Wycliffe Hall Ox BTh 99. **d** 99 **p** 00. C Moreton-in-Marsh w Batsford, Todenham etc *Glouc* 99–03; C Leckhampton SS Phil and Jas w Cheltenham St Jas 03–04; TV The Ortons, Alwalton and Chesterton *Ely* 04–10; P-in-c Elton w Stibbington and Water Newton 06–10; V Alwalton and Chesterton from 10. *St Andrew's Rectory, 4 Alwalton Hall, Alwalton, Peterborough PE7 3UN* T: (01733) 239289 E: malcolm.ingham@yahoo.com

INGHAM, Mrs Pamela. b 47. NEOC 93. **d** 96 **p** 97. C Newc Epiphany 96–99; C Fawdon 99–00; P-in-c 00–06; Dioc Development Officer for Partners in Community Action 06–10; rtd 10; Hon C Tynemouth St Jo *Newc* from 12; PtO from 15. *15 St George's Road, Cullercoats NE30 3JZ* E: pimbe@o2.co.uk

INGLE-GILLIS, William Clarke. b 68. Baylor Univ (USA) BA 90 MA 95 K Coll Lon PhD 04. Westcott Ho Cam 02. **d** 04 **p** 05. C Caldicot *Mon* 04–08; Dioc Soc Resp Officer 06–08; P-in-c Caerwent w Dinham and Llanvair Discoed etc 08–14; P-in-c Wentwood 14–17; Tutor St Mich Coll Llan 07–16; V Newport Maindee and Lliswerry *Mon* from 17. *St John's Vicarage, St John's Road, Newport NP19 8GR* T: (01633) 674155 M: 07722-500805 E: w.c.ingle-gillis@cantab.net

INGLEBY, Canon Anthony Richard. b 48. Keele Univ BA 72. Trin Coll Bris. **d** 83 **p** 84. C Plymouth St Jude *Ex* 83–88; R Lanreath *Truro* 88–97; V Pelynt 88–97; RD W Wivelshire 96–97; P-in-c Stoke Climsland 97–05; P-in-c Linkinhorne 03–05; P-in-c Liskeard and St Keyne 05–16; Chapl Cornwall and Is of Scilly Primary Care Trust 05–09; Hon Can Truro Cathl 04–16; RD W Wivelshire 08–13; C Duloe, Herodsfoot, Morval and St Pinnock 10–16; rtd 16. *91 Compton Avenue, Plymouth PL3 5DD* E: revtonyingleby@gmail.com

INGLEDEW, Peter David Gordon. b 48. AKC 77 Jo Dalton Coll Man CertEd 73 Croydon Coll DASS 92 CQSW 92 Univ Coll Chich BA 03. St Steph Ho Ox 77. **d** 78 **p** 79. C Whorlton *Newc* 78–81; C Poplar *Lon* 81–83; TV 83–85; V Tottenham H Trin 85–90; PtO *Chich* from 90. *11 St Luke's Terrace, Brighton BN2 2ZE* T: (01273) 689765 F: 389115 E: david.ingledew2@ntlworld.com

INGLE-GILLIS, Mrs Sally. b 66. **d** 18 **p** 19. C Wentwood *Mon* from 18. *The Vicarage, 25 St John's Road, Newport NP19 8GR* M: 07813-264429 E: sallyinglegillis@wentwood.church

INGLES, Daniel Edward. b 78. Plymouth Univ BA 00. Ridley Hall Cam 12. **d** 14 **p** 15. C Beaminster Area *Sarum* 14–17; TV Melbury from 17. *The Vicarage, Corscombe, Dorchester DT2 0NU* T: (01935) 891858 E: revdanielingles@hotmail.com

INGLESBY, Richard Eric. b 47. Birm Univ BSc 69 Bris Univ CertEd 74. Wycliffe Hall Ox 85. **d** 87 **p** 88. C Cheltenham Ch Ch *Glouc* 87–92; P-in-c Paulton *B & W* 92–94; V 94–01; P-in-c Farrington Gurney 92–94; V 94–01; P-in-c Moxley Lich 01–09; V 09–13; C Darlaston All SS 01–13; C Darlaston St Lawr 01–13; Ecum Adv (Wolverhampton Area) 04–08; RD Wednesbury *Lich* 05–12; Preb Lich Cathl 09–13; rtd 13; PtO *Glouc* from 14. *32 Sandycroft Road, Churchdown, Gloucester GL3 1JH* T: (01452) 541509 E: r_inglesby@hotmail.com

INGLIS, Kelvin John. b 62. Ripon Coll Cuddesdon MTh 00. **d** 00 **p** 01. C Southampton Maybush St Pet *Win* 00–04; V Whitchurch w Tufton and Litchfield 04–17; AD Whitchurch 14–17; R Salisbury St Thos and St Edm *Sarum* from 17; RD Salisbury from 18. *Little Bower, Campbell Road, Salisbury SP1 3BG* T: (01722) 239463

INGRAM, Canon Bernard Richard. b 40. Lon Coll of Div 66. **d** 66 **p** 67. C Bromley Common St Aug *Roch* 66–70; C Gravesend St Geo 70–74; Chapl Joyce Green Hosp Dartford 75–83; V Dartford St Edm *Roch* 75–83; V Strood St Fran

83–04; RD Strood 91–97; Hon Can Roch Cathl 00–04; rtd 04; PtO *Heref* from 05. *1 Hillview Cottage, Upper Colwall, Malvern WR13 6DH* T/F: (01684) 540475

INGRAM, Mrs Clodagh Mary. b 65. Man Poly BA 87. WEMTC 07. **d** 10 **p** 11. C Tuffley *Glouc* 10–13; NSM Churchdown 13–17; P-in-c Upton St Leonards from 17. *2 Coxmore Close, Hucclecote, Gloucester GL3 3SA* M: 07583-754960 E: rev.clodaghingram@gmail.com

INGRAM, Gary Simon. b 58. K Coll Lon BD AKC. Ripon Coll Cuddesdon. **d** 83 **p** 84. Chapl Nelson and Colne Coll 92–98; C Spalding St Mary and St Nic *Linc* 83–87; C Heaton Ch Ch *Man* 87–89; V Colne H Trin *Blackb* 89–98; RD Pendle 96–98; R Poulton-le-Sands w Morecambe St Laur 98–09; AD Lancaster 98–04; P-in-c Ferring *Chich* 09–11; V from 11. *The Vicarage, 19 Grange Park, Ferring, Worthing BN12 5LS* T: (01903) 241645 E: revgaryingram@googlemail.com

INGRAM, Miss Jennifer Rebecca. b 90. Nottm Univ BA 12 St Jo Coll Nottm MA 13. Cranmer Hall Dur 14. **d** 16 **p** 17. C Wootton *Pet* 16–19; V Earls Barton from 19. *The Vicarage, 7 High Street, Earls Barton, Northampton NN6 0JG* M: 07743-593700 E: revjennyingram@outlook.com

INGRAM, Canon Peter Anthony. b 53. NOC 83. **d** 86 **p** 87. C Maltby *Sheff* 86–89; TV Gt Snaith 89–92; R Adwickle-Street w Skelbrooke 92–05; AD Adwick 01–05; V Millhouses H Trin 05–15; P-in-c Abbeydale St Jo 11–15; V Abbeydale and Millhouses from 15; AD Ecclesall 07–11; Hon Can Sheff Cathl from 05. *The Vicarage, 80 Millhouses Lane, Sheffield S7 2HB* T: 0114-236 2838 E: peter.ingram@sheffield.anglican.org

INGRAMS, Canon Peter Douglas. b 56. Wheaton Coll Illinois BA 77 Ox Univ BA 80. Wycliffe Hall Ox 78. **d** 83 **p** 84. C Rowner *Portsm* 83–86; C Petersfield w Sheet 86–90; V Sheet 90–96; V Locks Heath 96–07; Local Min Officer *Cant* 07–15; Local Min and Growth Adv from 15; Hon Can Cant Cathl from 19. *12 Guildford Road, Canterbury CT1 3QD* E: pdingrams@lineane.net

INKPIN, David Leonard. b 32. Liv Univ BSc 54 CChem MRSC 55. EMMTC 83. **d** 86 **p** 87. NSM Legsby, Linwood and Market Rasen *Linc* 86–04; PtO from 04. *Weelsby House, Legsby Road, Market Rasen LN8 3DY* T: (01673) 843360 E: inkypens@yahoo.co.uk

INMAN, Canon Daniel David. b 84. Wycliffe Hall Ox BA 05 Qu Coll Ox MSt 06 DPhil 09. Ripon Coll Cuddesdon 07. **d** 10 **p** 11. C Deddington w Barford, Clifton and Hempton *Ox* 10–13; Chapl Win Coll 13; Chapl Qu Coll Ox 13–16; Dioc Dir of Ords *Chich* 16–19; C Hove All SS 19; Can Res and Chan Chich Cathl from 19. *2 Vicars Close, Chichester PO19 1PT* M: 07747-016370 E: daniel.inman@queens.ox.ac.uk *or* daniel.inman@chichester.anglican.org *or* chancellor@chichestercathedral.org.uk

INMAN, Malcolm Gordon. b 33. Edin Th Coll 58. **d** 60 **p** 61. C Lundwood *Wakef* 60–63; C Heckmondwike 63–70; V Wrenthorpe 70–75; Chapl Cardigan Hosp 70–73; Asst Chapl Pinderfields Gen Hosp Wakef 72–73; V Cleckheaton St Jo *Wakef* 75–98; rtd 98; PtO *Wakef* 00–07; Hon C Staincliffe and Carlinghow 07–14; *Leeds* from 14. *14 Briestfield Road, Thornhill Edge, Dewsbury WF12 0PW* T: (01924) 437171

INMAN, Canon Thomas Jeremy. b 45. Rhodes Univ BA 67. St Steph Ho Ox 67. **d** 69 **p** 70. C Deptford St Paul *S'wark* 69–72; C Bellville S Africa 72–73; R Malmesbury 73–76; P-in-c Donnington *Chich* 76–80; V Hangleton 80–86; V Bosham 86–10; RD Westbourne 91–99; Can and Preb Chich Cathl 00–10; rtd 10; PtO *Bris* from 10; *Chich* from 13. *35 Hunters Road, Bristol BS15 3EZ* T: 0117-960 5045 M: 07941-834914 E: tjinman45@gmail.com

INNES, Donald John. b 32. St Jo Coll Ox BA 54 MA. Westcott Ho Cam 56. **d** 56 **p** 57. C St Marylebone St Mark Hamilton Terrace *Lon* 56–58; C Walton-on-Thames *Guildf* 58–67; Chapl Moor Park Coll Farnham 67–76; P-in-c Tilford *Guildf* 76–97; rtd 97; PtO *Guildf* from 97. *Watchetts, 67A Upper Hale Road, Farnham GU9 0PA* T: (01252) 734597

INNES, Donald Keith. b 33. St Jo Coll Ox BA 56 MA 60 Lon Univ BD 58 Bris Univ MPhil 01. Clifton Th Coll 56. **d** 58 **p** 59. C Harold Hill St Paul *Chelmsf* 58–61; C Ealing Dean St Jo *Lon* 61–65; V Westacre and R Gayton Thorpe w E Walton *Nor* 65–70; V Woking St Paul *Guildf* 70–78; R Alfold and Loxwood 78–88; V Doddington w Wychling *Cant* 88–90; V Newnham 88–90; V Doddington, Newnham and Wychling 90–97; rtd 97; PtO *Chich* from 98. *Terrys Cross House, Brighton Road, Woodmancote, Henfield BN5 9SX* T: (01273) 492821

✠**INNES, The Rt Revd Robert Neil.** b 59. K Coll Cam BA 82 MA 85 St Jo Coll Dur BA 91 Dur Univ PhD 95. Cranmer Hall Dur 89. **d** 95 **p** 96 **c** 14. C Dur St Cuth 95–97; C Shadforth and Sherburn w Pittington 97–99; Lect St Jo Coll Dur 95–99; P-in-c Belmont *Dur* 99–00; V 00–05;

Sen Chapl and Chan Brussels Cathl *Eur* 05–14; Chapl to The Queen 12–14; Bp Eur from 14. *avenue Princesse Paola 15, 1410 Waterloo, Belgium* T: (0032) (2) 213 7480 E: bishop.europe@churchofengland.org

INNES, Canon Ruth. b 56. New Coll Edin BD 00. TISEC 97. **d** 00 **p** 01. Prec St Ninian's Cathl Perth *St And* 00–02; P-in-c Linlithgow and Bathgate *Edin* 02–06; P-in-c Edin St Mark 06–10; R Falkirk 10–16; R Edin St Fillan from 16; Synod Clerk from 17. *St Fillan's Rectory, 8 Buckstone Drive, Edinburgh EH10 6PD* M: 07765-908829 E: ruth@ruthinnes.me.uk

INSLEY, Canon Michael George Pitron. b 47. Trin Coll Ox BA 69 MA 70 Nottm Univ MPhil 85. Wycliffe Hall Ox 69. **d** 72 **p** 73. C Beckenham Ch Ch *Roch* 72–76; P-in-c Cowden 76–79; Lect St Jo Coll Nottm 79–85; V Tidebrook and Wadhurst *Chich* 85–98; P-in-c Stonegate 95–98; Can and Preb Chich Cathl 94–98; P-in-c Horsmonden and Dioc Rural Officer *Roch* 98–03; V Bromley Common St Luke 03–12; Hon Can Th Roch Cathl 06–12; rtd 12; PtO *Sarum* from 12; *Roch* 13–15. *22 Bridport Road, Dorchester DT1 1RS* T: (01305) 262412 E: michaelinsley@uwclub.net

INSTON, Brian John. b 47. SAOMC 95. **d** 98 **p** 99. C Bentley *Sheff* 98–01; V Balby 01–12; AD W Doncaster 07–11; rtd 12; PtO *Sheff* from 12. *62 Hindburn Close, Doncaster DN4 7RP* T: (01302) 534976 M: 07990-513120 E: bjinston@yahoo.co.uk

INVERNESS, Provost of. See STRANGE, The Most Revd Mark Jeremy

✠**IPGRAVE, The Rt Revd Michael Geoffrey.** b 58. Oriel Coll Ox BA 78 MA 94 St Chad's Coll Dur PhD 00 SOAS Lon MA 04. Ripon Coll Cuddesdon BA 81. **d** 82 **p** 83 **c** 12. C Oakham, Hambleton, Egleton, Braunston and Brooke *Pet* 82–85; Asst P Chiba Resurr Japan 85–87; TV Leic Ascension 87–90; TV Leic H Spirit 91–95; TR 95–99; P-in-c Leic St Mary 93–94; Bp's Adv on Relns w People of Other Faiths 91–99; Bp's Dom Chapl 92–99; Hon Can Leic Cathl 94–04; Adv Inter-Faith Relns Abp's Coun 99–04; Sec Ch's Commission Inter Faith Relns 99–04; Hon C Leic Presentation 02–04; Adn S'wark 04–12; P-in-c S'wark St Geo w St Alphege and St Jude 06–07; P-in-c Peckham St Jo w St Andr 09–10; Can Missr 10–12; Area Bp Woolwich 12–16; Dioc Warden of Readers 14–16; Bp Lich from 16. *Bishop's House, 22 The Close, Lichfield WS13 7LG* T: (01543) 306001 F: 306009 E: bishop.michael@lichfield.anglican.org

IPSWICH, Archdeacon of. See KING, The Ven Rhiannon Elizabeth

IQBAL, Javaid. b 71. Birm Univ MA 09. St Jo Coll Nottm BA 97. **d** 97 **p** 99. C Lahore St Thos Pakistan 97–99; P-in-c Lashore Ch Ch 99–00; Dir Miss and Evang Raiwind 98–99; PtO *Leic* 00–05; C Evington 05–07; P-in-c Thurmaston 07–08; TV Fosse Team 08–13; Hon Can Leic Cathl 11–13; TR Aldenham, Radlett and Shenley *St Alb* from 13. *The Vicarage, Church Field, Watling Street, Radlett WD7 8EE* T: (01923) 856606 M: 07782-169987 E: canoniqbal@gmail.com

IREDALE, Hilary Grace. b 59. Guy's Hosp Medical Sch MB, BS 82 FRCA 90. Qu Coll Birm 06. **d** 09 **p** 10. NSM Rugby *Cov* 09–13; V Rugby St Geo 13–19; rtd 19. *241 Hillmorton Road, Rugby CV22 5BD* T: (01788) 540355 E: mike.iredale@btinternet.com

IREDALE, Simon Peter. b 56. Cam Coll of Arts & Tech BA 78 Cam Univ MPhil 80 Univ of Wales PhD 04 FRSA 06. Wycliffe Hall Ox 83. **d** 86 **p** 87. C Thirsk *York* 86–89; Asst Chapl Norfolk and Nor Hosp 89–90; P-in-c Kexby w Wilberfoss *York* 90–93; Sub-Chapl HM Pris Full Sutton 90–93; Chapl RAF 93–06; PtO *Lich* 14–19; V Coven from 19. *5 Grange Road, Albrighton, Wolverhampton WV7 3LD* T: (01902) 791923 M: 07847-280162 E: spiredale@gmail.com

IRELAND, David Arthur. b 45. Mert Coll Ox BA 67 MA 71 MICFM 87. Cuddesdon Coll 67. **d** 69 **p** 70. C Chapel Allerton *Ripon* 69–72; C Harpenden St Nic *St Alb* 72–76; R Clifton 76–84; PtO *Guildf* 91–00; NSM Tattenham Corner and Burgh Heath 01–02; NSM Leatherhead and Mickleham 02–12; Chapl Box Hill Sch 05–12; rtd 12; PtO *Guildf* from 12. *St Michael's Lodge, Old London Road, Mickleham, Dorking RG5 6DU* E: rev.ireland43@btinternet.com

IRELAND, Leslie Sydney. b 55. York Univ BA 76. St Jo Coll Nottm 83. **d** 86 **p** 87. C Harwood *Man* 86–89; C Davyhulme St Mary 89–90; V Bardsley 90–99; R Levenshulme St Andr and St Pet 99–06; P-in-c Levenshulme St Mark 05–06; R Levenshulme 06–12; AD Heaton 04–12; R Lenzie *Glas* from 12. *58 Waverley Park, Kirkintilloch, Glasgow G66 2BP* T: 0141-776 3866 M: 07757-946184 E: rector@stcyprianslenzie.com *or* les949@btinternet.com

IRELAND, Mrs Lucy Annabel. b 53. Univ of Zimbabwe BSc 74. St Jo Coll Nottm. **dss** 85 **d** 87 **p** 95. Mansfield St Jo *S'well* 85–87; Hon Par Dn Harwood *Man* 87–89; NSM Bardsley 90–99; C Levenshulme St Andr and St Pet 99–06;

C Levenshulme 06–12; NSM Glas E End from 13. *58 Waverley Park, Kirkintilloch, Glasgow G66 2BP* T: 0141-776 3866 M: 07583-884358 E: irelandla@hotmail.com

IRELAND, The Ven Mark Campbell. b 60. St Andr Univ MTheol 81 Sheff Univ MA 01. Wycliffe Hall Ox 82. **d** 84 **p** 85. C Blackb St Gabr 84–87; C Lancaster St Mary 87–89; Sub-Chapl HM Pris Lanc 87–89; V Baxenden *Blackb* 89–97; Dioc Missr *Lich* 98–07; TV Walsall 98–07; V Wellington All SS w Eyton 07–16; Adn Blackb from 16. *19 Clarence Park, Blackburn BB2 7FA* T: (01254) 958836 M: 07866-778791 E: mark.ireland@blackburn.anglican.org

IRELAND, Mrs Mary Janet. b 52. EMMTC 96. **d** 99 **p** 00. NSM Kibworth and Smeeton Westerby and Saddington *Leic* 99–02; C Lutterworth w Cotesbach and Bitteswell 02–05; P-in-c Glen Magna cum Stretton Magna etc 05–13; R Gt w Lt Harrowden and Orlingbury and Isham etc *Pet* 13–17; rtd 17; PtO *Leic* from 18. *19 Links Road, Kibworth Beauchamp, Leicester LE8 0LD* T: 0116-279 6892 E: mary_ireland@btinternet.com

IRELAND, Mrs Sharran. b 49. SEITE 95. **d** 98 **p** 99. C Appledore w Brookland, Fairfield, Brenzett etc *Cant* 98–01; TV St Laur in Thanet 01–03; TR 03–13; rtd 13; PtO *Cant* from 13. *Jamark, 13 Norman Road, Faversham ME13 8PX*

IRESON, David Christopher. b 45. Man Univ TCert 67 Birm Univ BEd 80. St Steph Ho Ox. **d** 93 **p** 94. C Minehead *B & W* 93–97; V St Decumans 97–08; rtd 08; PtO *B & W* 11–14. *50 Camperdown Terrace, Exmouth EX8 1EQ* T: (01395) 263307 M: 07786-943967 E: decuman@hotmail.co.uk

IRESON, Philip. b 52. Newc Univ BSc 73. St Jo Coll Nottm. **d** 84 **p** 85. C Owlerton *Sheff* 84–87; V The Marshland 87–94; PtO *Linc* 90–93; Chapl HM YOI Hatfield 91–92; Bp's Rural Adv *Sheff* 91–00; R Firbeck w Letwell 94–01; V Woodsetts 94–01; Chapl HM Pris and YOI Doncaster 01–11; V Piston R Ch Ch *Sheff* 11–16; P-in-c Ellesmere St Pet 13–16; rtd 16; PtO *Portsm* from 17; *Sheff* from 17. *19 Stradbroke Road, Sheffield S13 8LR* M: 07882-027473 E: ireson61@gmail.com

IRETON, Elliott John. b 83. Cranmer Hall Dur 15. **d** 17 **p** 18. C Burscough Bridge *Liv* from 17. *20 Warpers Moss Lane, Burscough, Ormskirk L40 4AQ* M: 07872-952961 E: elliottireton@gmail.com

IRETON, Robert John. b 56. Bris Univ BEd. Oak Hill Th Coll BA. **d** 84 **p** 85. C Bromley Ch Ch *Roch* 84–87; TV Greystoke, Matterdale, Mungrisdale etc *Carl* 87–90; V Falconwood *Roch* 90–97; V Stanwix *Carl* 97–04; P-in-c Erith St Jo *Roch* 04–10; Chapl Trin Sch Belvedere 04–10; P-in-c Brinklow *Cov* 10–11; P-in-c Harborough Magna 10–11; P-in-c Monks Kirby w Pailton and Stretton-under-Fosse 10–11; P-in-c Churchover w Willey 10–11; R Revel Gp 11–13; rtd 13. *7 The Meadows, Bempton, Bridlington YO15 1LU*

IRONS, Nigel Richard. b 55. Aston Univ BSc 77. St Jo Coll Nottm MA 96. **d** 97 **p** 98. C Newchapel *Lich* 94–00; V Burton All SS w Ch Ch 00–14; TR Leek and Meerbrook from 14. *St Edward's Vicarage, 24 Ashenhurst Way, Leek ST13 5SB* E: mail@nigelirons.co.uk

IRONSIDE, John Edmund. b 31. Peterho Cam BA 55 MA 59. Qu Coll Birm 55. **d** 57 **p** 58. C Spring Park *Cant* 57–60; C Guernsey St Sampson *Win* 60–63; Thailand 63–66; V Guernsey St Jo *Win* 66–72; V Sholing 72–82; R Guernsey St Sampson 82–98; Miss to Seamen 82–98; rtd 98; PtO *Win* 98–07; P-in-c Guernsey St Andr 07–11; PtO *Chich* from 11. *1 Johnson Way, Ford, Arundel BN18 0TD* T: (01903) 722884 E: sarniaford@hotmail.co.uk

IRVINE, Mrs Andrea Mary. b 49. Sussex Univ BA 70 Ox Univ PGCE 71. NTMTC 99. **d** 02. NSM Cov H Trin 02–05; PtO 05–06; NSM Cov Cathl 06–12; PtO *Ely* 13–16. *42 Pretoria Road, Cambridge CB4 1HE* T: (01223) 364128 E: andreairvine12@gmail.com

IRVINE (formerly SADLER), Ann Penrith. b 50. STETS 98. **d** 01 **p** 02. C Len Valley *Cant* 01–04; P-in-c Aylesham w Adisham 04–08; C Nonington w Wymynswold and Goodnestone etc 04–08; PtO 08–10. *Pilgrim Cottage, 16 Kilmahamogue Road, Moyarget, Ballycastle BT54 6JH* T: (028) 2076 3748 E: revann@uwclub.net

IRVINE, Mrs Catherine Frances. b 70. K Coll Lon BA 97. Ripon Coll Cuddesdon 99. **d** 01 **p** 02. C Romsey *Win* 01–05; TV Richmond St Mary w St Matthias and St Jo *S'wark* 05–11; Chapl R Holloway and Bedf New Coll *Guildf* 11–19; TR Ouzel Valley *St Alb* from 19. *The Vicarage, Pulford Road, Leighton Buzzard LU7 1AB* T: (01525) 373217 E: rectorcate@gmail.com

IRVINE, Canon Christopher Paul. b 51. Nottm Univ BTh 75 Lanc Univ MA 76 St Martin's Coll Lanc PGCE 77. Kelham Th Coll 73. **d** 76 **p** 76. Chapl Lanc Univ *Blackb* 76–77; C Stoke Newington St Mary *Lon* 77–80; Chapl Sheff Univ 80–85; Chapl St Edm Hall Ox 85–90; Tutor St Steph Ho Ox 85–90; Vice-Prin 91–94; V Cowley St Jo *Ox* 94–98; Prin Coll of Resurr Mirfield 98–07; Can Res and Lib Cant

Cathl 07–17; rtd 17; P-in-c Ewhurst *Chich* from 17; P-in-c Bodiam from 17; RD Rye from 18. *The Rectory, Ewhurst Green, Robertsbridge TN32 5TB* T: (01580) 830268 *or* 830925 E: canonchristopher@outlook.com

IRVINE, Clyde. *See* IRVINE, James Clyde

IRVINE, David John. b 50. Trin Coll Cam BA 72 MA 75. NOC 91. **d** 94 **p** 95. C Hexham *Newc* 94–99; P-in-c Blanchland w Hunstanworth and Edmundbyers etc 99–13; P-in-c Slaley 99–13; P-in-c Healey 03–13; P-in-c Whittonstall 03–13; rtd 13; PtO *St And* 14–20. *25 Charles Street, Pittenweem, Anstruther KY10 2QH* T: (01333) 311868 E: davidirvine190@btinternet.com

IRVINE, Donald Andrew. b 45. Trin Coll Bris 94. **d** 96 **p** 97. C Allington and Maidstone St Pet *Cant* 96–99; P-in-c Harrietsham w Ulcombe 99–02; P-in-c Lenham w Boughton Malherbe 00–02; R Len Valley 02–07; TV Whitstable 07–10. *Pilgrim Cottage, 16 Kilmahamogue Road, Moyarget, Ballycastle BT54 6JH* T: (028) 2076 3748 M: 07932-149495 E: don.irvine35@gmail.com

IRVINE, James Clyde. b 35. QUB BA 57 NUU BPhil(Ed) 83. CITC 59. **d** 59 **p** 60. C Belfast St Luke *Conn* 59–62; C Lisburn Ch Ch Cathl 62–65; R Duneane w Ballyscullion 65–69; I Kilbride 69–74; Hd of RE Ballyclare High Sch 73–98; Bp's C Killead w Gartree 98–05; rtd 05. *1A Rathmena Avenue, Ballyclare BT39 9HX* T: (028) 9332 2933 E: irvineclyde@live.co.uk

IRVINE, Mrs Jennifer Anne. b 81. Warwick Univ BSc 03. St Mellitus Coll BA 12. **d** 12 **p** 13. C Westwood *Cov* 12–16; PtO 17–18; NSM Foleshill St Laur from 18. *The Vicarage, 142 Old Church Road, Coventry CV6 7ED* T: (024) 7668 8271

IRVINE, The Very Revd John Dudley. b 49. Sussex Univ BA 70. Wycliffe Hall Ox 80. **d** 81 **p** 82. C Brompton H Trin w Onslow Square St Paul *Lon* 81–85; P-in-c Kensington St Barn 85–94; V 94–01; Dean Cov 01–12; P-in-c Cov St Fran N Radford 06–12; C Cambridge H Trin *Ely* 12–16; rtd 16. *42 Pretoria Road, Cambridge CB4 1HE* T: (01223) 364128 E: jdirvine@lineone.net

IRVINE-CAPEL, The Ven Luke Thomas. b 75. Greyfriars Ox BA 97 MA 01 Leeds Univ MA 99. Coll of Resurr Mirfield 97. **d** 99 **p** 00. C Abertillery w Cwmtillery w Six Bells *Mon* 99–01; Chapl Coleg Gwent 99–01; Min Can St Woolos Cathl 01–03; Sub-Chapl HM Pris Cardiff 02–03; R Cranford *Lon* 03–08; V Pimlico St Gabr 08–13; P-in-c St Leonards Ch Ch and St Mary etc *Chich* 13–14; R 14–19; P-in-c Hastings St Clem and All SS 17–19; Adn Chich from 19. *The Palace, Canon Lane, Chichester PO19 1PY* T: (01273) 425799 M: 07775-526858 E: ltic75@hotmail.com *or* archchichester@chichester.anglican.org

IRVING, Alexander John Dolman. b 87. UEA BA 08 Lon Sch of Th BTh 13 MTh 14. Wycliffe Hall Ox 14. **d** 17 **p** 18. C Nor St Steph from 17. *1 Aurania Avenue, Norwich NR1 2RD* M: 07788-413238 E: alex.irving3@gmail.com *or* curate@ststephensnorwich.org

IRVING, Canon Michael John Derek. b 43. BEd 80. Qu Coll Birm 80. **d** 81 **p** 82. C Coleford w Staunton *Glouc* 81–84; V Dean Forest H Trin 84–91; RD Forest S 88–91; P-in-c Hempsted and Dir of Ords 91–96; R Minchinhampton 96–08; Hon Can Glouc Cathl 94–08; rtd 08; PtO *Glouc* from 17. *9 Canton Acre, Painswick, Stroud GL6 6QX* T: (01452) 814242 E: mi@vale-view.co.uk

IRVING, Paul John. b 74. Univ of Wales (Ban) BA 96 Bris Univ PGCE 97. Trin Coll Bris BA 08. **d** 10 **p** 11. C Galmington *B & W* 10–14; TV Redditch H Trin *Worc* from 14. *St Leonard's Vicarage, Church Hill, Beoley, Redditch B98 9AR* E: revpaulirving@outlook.com

IRWIN, Canon Alan David. b 65. TCD BTh 09. CITC 07. **d** 09 **p** 10. C Ballymena w Ballyclug *Conn* 09–12; I Lack *Clogh* from 12; Can Clogh Cathl from 19. *The Rectory, Main Street, Lack, Enniskillen BT93 0DN* T: (028) 6863 1689 E: alan.irwin7@gmail.com

IRWIN, Andrew Trevor Ronald. QUB BEng. CITI. **d** 17 **p** 18. Donaghcloney w Waringstown *D & D* 17–18; C Seapatrick from 18. *61 Burn Brae Court, Banbridge BT32 4GD* T: (028) 3884 1323 M: 07543-702570 E: irwinan@tcd.ie *or* andrewirwin80@gmail.com *or* andrew@bchurch.com

IRWIN, John Henry. b 60. ACA 92 FCA 02. St Aug Coll of Th 17. **d** 19. NSM S Hackney St Mich w Haggerston St Paul *Lon* from 19. *Flat 28, 73A Drayton Park, London N5 1DW* M: 07957-579680 E: curate@stmichaelslondonfields.org.uk

IRWIN, Mrs Patricia Jane. b 49. CBDTI 02. **d** 05 **p** 06. NSM S *Carl* 05–10; rtd 10; PtO *Carl* from 11. *31 Blackwell Road, Carlisle CA2 4AB* T: (01228) 526885

IRWIN, Patrick Alexander. b 55. BNC Ox BA 77 MA 81 Edin Univ BD 81. Edin Th Coll 77 Liturgisches Inst Trier 79. **d** 81 **p** 82. Hon C Cambridge St Botolph *Ely* 81–84; Chapl BNC Ox 84–92; Lect Th 86–92; CF 92–99; Sen CF 99–10;

Chapl Guards Chpl Lon 05–07; Dir of Ords 05–07; Chapl Udruga Hvrata Sv Dominik Gorazde 94–95; PtO *D & G* from 87; *Arm* from 96; *Guildf* 99–02; *Ripon* 00–14; *Leeds* 14–16; Hon V Choral Arm Cathl 02–07; PtO *Eur* 08–10 and from 13; Chapl Bucharest w Sofia 10–13; Lect St Trivelius Inst Sofia Bulgaria 13–14. *Hedgebank, 8 Paganel Road, Minehead TA24 5ET* T: (01643) 703509 E: patalexirwin@yahoo.co.uk

IRWIN, Stewart. b 53. Sarum & Wells Th Coll 80. **d** 83 **p** 84. C Brighouse *Wakef* 83–87; V Stockton St Jo *Dur* 87–95; V Howden-le-Wear and Hunwick 95–13; rtd 13; PtO *Dur* from 13. *22 South View, Hunwick, Crook DL15 0JW* E: stewart_irwin@talktalk.net

IRWIN, Miss Susan Elizabeth. b 47. Cranmer Hall Dur 77. dss 79 **d** 87 **p** 94. Harborne St Faith and St Laur *Birm* 79–82; Caterham *S'wark* 82–88; Par Dn 87–88; Par Dn Kidlington w Hampton Poyle *Ox* 88–94; C 94–95; TV Gt Marlow w Marlow Bottom, Lt Marlow and Bisham 95–06; R Powick and Guarlford and Madresfield w Newland *Worc* 06–17; Chapl St Oswald's Almshouses from 17; PtO *Eur* from 13. *The Chaplain's House, St Oswald's Hospital, Upper Tything, Worcester WR1 1HR* T: (01905) 29438 M: 07703-350301 E: revsueirwin@gmail.com

IRWIN, Canon William George. b 53. QUB BSc 77. CITC 80. **d** 80 **p** 81. C Lisburn St Paul *Conn* 80–83; C Seagoe *D & D* 83–85; C Newtownards w Movilla Abbey 85–88; I Ballymacash *Conn* 88–16; Preb Conn Cathl 04–16; Treas 12-16; Chan 16; rtd 16. *11 The Willows, Sion Mills, Strabane BT82 9FQ* E: wgirwin@btopenworld.com

IRWIN-CLARK, Peter Elliot. b 49. Univ Coll Lon LLB 71 Barrister 72. Cranmer Hall Dur BA 80. **d** 81 **p** 82. C Kirkheaton *Wakef* 81–86; V Shirley Win 86–96; PtO *Chich* 96–97; *S'wark* 97; V Prestonville St Luke *Chich* 97–03; Missr Warham Trust and Faith Development Officer (Basingstoke Adnry) *Win* 03–08; TR Broadwater *Chich* 08–15; rtd 15. *Desmond Castle, London Road, Handcross, Haywards Heath RH17 6HA* T: (01444) 400307 E: picvic@btinternet.com

ISAAC, Canon David Thomas. b 43. Univ of Wales BA 65. Cuddesdon Coll 65. **d** 67 **p** 68. C Llandaff w Capel Llanilltern *Llan* 67–71; P-in-c Swansea St Jas *S & B* 71–73; Chapl Ch in Wales Youth Coun 73–77; V Llangiwg *S & B* 77–79; Dioc Youth Officer *Ripon* 79–83; Nat Officer for Youth Work Gen Syn Bd of Educn 83–90; Can Res Portsm Cathl 90–14; Dioc Dir of Educn 90–06; Hd Miss and Discipleship 06–14; Warden of Readers 11–14; rtd 14; PtO *Portsm* from 15; AD Is of Wight 16–17; AD Bishop's Waltham from 19. *The Rectory, Southwick Road, Wickham, Fareham PO17 6HR* M: 07768-997220 E: dtisaac@btinternet.com

ISAAC, Mrs Patricia Jane. b 59. Leeds Univ BA 80 Univ Coll Lon MA 82. STETS 11. **d** 14 **p** 15. C Ryde All SS *Portsm* 14–17; C Swanmore St Mich 14–17; R Shedfield and Wickham from 17. *The Rectory, Southwick Road, Wickham, Fareham PO17 6HR* E: pjisaac@btinternet.com

ISAACS, James Alexander. b 84. Ex Univ BA 06. Oak Hill Th Coll BA 15. **d** 15 **p** 16. C Hailsham *Chich* 15–18; V Riseley w Bletsoe *St Alb* from 18. *The Vicarage, 16 Church Lane, Riseley, Bedford MK44 1ER* M: 07872-111354 E: jisaacs11@gmail.com

ISAACSON, Alan Timothy. b 55. York Univ BA 77 Sheff Univ PGCE 84 Leeds Univ MA 97. NOC 94. **d** 96 **p** 97. C Kimberworth *Sheff* 96–99; TV Brinsworth w Catcliffe and Treeton 99–03; TV Rivers Team 03–07; R Bradfield from 07; Dioc Discipleship Development Officer from 07; AD Ecclesfield from 14. *The Rectory, High Bradfield, Bradfield, Sheffield S6 6LG* T: 0114-285 1225 E: alan.isaacson@sheffield.anglican.org

ISAACSON, Hilda Ruth. b 57. Leeds Univ BA 10. NOC 07. **d** 09 **p** 10. C Deepcar *Sheff* 09–13; P-in-c 13–18; P-in-c Bolsterstone 14–18; V Cornerstone from 18. *The Rectory, High Bradfield, Bradfield, Sheffield S6 6LG* T: 0114-285 1225 M: 07762-075687 E: hilda.isaacson@sheffield.anglican.org

ISABEL, Sister. *See* KEEGAN, Frances Ann

ISHERWOOD, Mrs Claire Virginia. b 54. Liv Univ BDS 76 K Alfred's Coll Win PGCE 92. OLM from 10. *37 Watchetts Drive, Camberley GU15 2PQ* T: (01276) 505015 M: 07854-549154 E: claire.isherwood@ntlworld.com *or* claire.isherwood@stpaulscamb.co.uk

ISHERWOOD, Canon David Owen. b 46. BA 68 Lon Univ MA 95 MPhil 87. Ridley Hall Cam 76. **d** 78 **p** 79. C Sanderstead All SS *S'wark* 78–82; C Horley 82–84; TV 84–88; P-in-c Streatham Immanuel and St Andr 88–89; V 89–95; TR Clapham Team 95–01; V Clapham H Trin and St Pet 02–15; Hon Can S'wark Cathl 06–15; rtd 15; PtO *Portsm* from 16. *15 Streamleaze, Fareham PO14 4NP* E: davidowenisherwood@gmail.com

ISHERWOOD, Robin James. b 56. Hull Univ BA 78 Uppsala Univ MDiv 92. Ripon Coll Cuddesdon 92. **d** 94 **p** 95. C Bramhall *Ches* 94–98; V Alsager St Mary 98–14; Chapl Charterhouse from 14; Hon Chapl ATC from 99. *Charterhouse Sutton's Hospital, The Charterhouse, Charterhouse Square, London EC1M 6AN* T: (020) 7253 9503 E: robinjisherwood@googlemail.com *or* robin.isherwood@thecharterhouse.org

ISHERWOOD, Samuel Peter. b 34. Lon Coll of Div ALCD 62 LTh 74. **d** 62 **p** 63. C Bacup St Sav *Man* 62–65; C Man Albert Memorial Ch 65–67; V Livesey *Blackb* 67–79; V Handforth *Ches* 79–99; RD Cheadle 92–99; rtd 99; PtO *York* from 00. *1 Andrew Drive, Huntington, York YO32 9YF* T: (01904) 438116

ISIORHO, David John Phillip. b 58. Liv Poly BA 80 Warwick Univ MA 93 Bradf Univ PhD 98. Westcott Ho Cam 87. **d** 90 **p** 91. C Nuneaton St Mary *Cov* 90–93; P-in-c Bradf St Oswald Chapel Green 93–96; P-in-c Brereton *Lich* 96–00; P-in-c Arthingworth, Harrington w Oxendon and E Farndon *Pet* 00–05; P-in-c Maidwell w Draughton, Lamport w Faxton 01–05; V Kempston Transfiguration *St Alb* 05–09; V Handsworth St Jas *Birm* 09–17; P-in-c Charlestown *Truro* from 17; P-in-c Par from 17; P-in-c Tywardreath w Tregaminion from 17. *The Parsonage, 2 Nursery Close, Tywardreath, Par PL24 2QW* T: (01726) 815588 E: david.isiorho@outlook.com

ISIORHO (née NORTHALL), Mrs Linda Barbara. b 50. Birm Univ BA 72 Birm City Univ MA 15 Worc Coll of Educn PGCE 75. Qu Coll Birm 88. **d** 90 **p** 94. C Wood End *Cov* 90–91; PtO 91–93; *Bradf* 93–94; NSM Low Moor St Mark 94–96; PtO *Lich* 96–97; NSM Arewas 97–00; PtO *Pet* 01–05; *Birm* 10–17. *The Parsonage, 2 Nursery Close, Tywardreath, Par PL24 2QW* T: (01726) 815588

ISKANDER, Mrs Susan Mary Mackay. b 64. Ox Univ BA 85 MBA 93. NTMTC 05. **d** 08 **p** 09. NSM Writtle w Highwood *Chelmsf* 08–12; PtO 12–13; P-in-c E Hanningfield 13–15; P-in-c Springfield All SS from 15. *The Rectory, 4 Old School Field, Springfield, Chelmsford CM1 7HU* M: 07710-646297 E: revsusaniskander@gmail.com

ISLE OF WIGHT, Archdeacon of. *See* LEONARD, The Ven Peter Philip

ISON, Canon Andrew Phillip. b 60. Imp Coll Lon BEng 82 Penn Univ MSE 83 Univ Coll Lon PhD 87 CEng 92 MIChemE 92. Trin Coll Bris BA 01. **d** 01 **p** 02. C Cleethorpes *Linc* 01–05; V Bestwood Park w Rise Park *S'well* 05–07; Chapl Voorschoten *Eur* 07–12; V Gt and Lt Driffield *York* 12–16; V Langtoft w Foxholes, Butterwick, Cottam etc 12–16; I Ballisodare w Collooney and Emlaghfad *T, K & A* from 16; Can Tuam Cathl from 18; Can Killala Cathl from 18. *The Rectory, Ballisodare, Co Sligo, Republic of Ireland* M: (00353) 71-913 3217 E: rev.andrew.ison@gmail.com

ISON, The Very Revd David John. b 54. Leic Univ BA 76 Nottm Univ BA 78 K Coll Lon PhD 85. St Jo Coll Nottm 76. **d** 79 **p** 80. C Deptford St Nic and St Luke *S'wark* 79–85; Lect CA Tr Coll Blackheath 85–88; V Potters Green *Cov* 88–93; Jt Dir SWMTC *Ex* 93–95; Dioc Officer for CME 93–05; Bp's Officer for NSMs 97–05; Can Res Ex Cathl 95–05; Chan 97–05; Dean Bradf 05–12; Dean St Paul's *Lon* from 12. *The Chapter House, St Paul's Churchyard, London EC4M 8AD* T: (020) 7246 8360 E: dean@stpaulscathedral.org.uk

ISON, Mrs Hilary Margaret. b 55. Leic Univ BA 76 E Lon Univ MA 02 Man Univ MA 09. Gilmore Course 77. **d** 87 **p** 94. NSM Deptford St Nic and St Luke *S'wark* 87–88; NSM Potters Green *Cov* 88–90; C Rugby 90–93; Chapl Ex Hospiscare 93–00; C Ex St Mark, St Sidwell and St Matt 99–02; Bp's Adv for Women in Min 02–05; Area Tutor SWMTC 03–05; PV Ex Cathl 04–05; Tutor Coll of Resurr Mirfield 05–08; Selection Sec Min Division 08–17; Hon C Calverley Deanery Bradf 06–12; PtO *Lon* from 14. *The Deanery, 9 Amen Court, London EC4M 7BU* E: hilary@isons.org.uk

ISON-STIERER, Susan Jane. b 79. Ripon Coll Cuddesdon 16. **d** 18 **p** 19. C Bridgwater St Mary and Chilton Trinity *B & W* from 18. *9 Park Avenue, Bridgwater TA6 7EF* M: 07934-804889 E: revsuse@gmail.com

ISSBERNER, Norman Gunther Erich. b 34. Fitzw Ho Cam BA 58 MA 61. Clifton Th Coll 57. **d** 59 **p** 60. C Croydon Ch Ch Broad Green *Cant* 59–61; C Surbiton Hill Ch Ch *S'wark* 61–66; V Egham *Guildf* 66–75; V Wallington *S'wark* 75–86; UK Chmn Africa Inland Miss from 77; Adv on Miss and Evang *Chelmsf* 86–91; P-in-c Castle Hedingham 91–93; V Clacton St Paul 93–99; RD St Osyth 94–99; rtd 99; PtO *Chelmsf* from 99. *14 Darcy Close, Frinton-on-Sea CO13 0RR* T: (01255) 673548 E: nissb@talktalk.net

ISTED, Elisabeth. b 66. Bris Univ BA 87 PhD 94. Ripon Coll Cuddesdon 16. **d** 18 **p** 19. C Yeovil St Mich *B & W* from 18. *26 Redwood Road, Yeovil BA21 5XE* M: 07890-464201 E: revd.elisabeth.isted@gmail.com

ITALY AND MALTA, Archdeacon of. *Vacant*
ITUMU, John Murithi. b 65. Lon Sch of Th BA 04 Heythrop Coll Lon MA 10. Lon Bible Coll 01. **d** 02 **p** 03. C Cricklewood St Gabr and St Mich *Lon* 02–07; C Herne Hill *S'wark* 07–10; P-in-c Glouc St Cath 10–12; V 12–18; V St Helier *S'wark* from 18. *193 Bishopsford Road, Morden SM4 6BH* M: 07946-000364 E: vicarsthelier@gmail.com
IVE, Jeremy George Augustus. b 57. Rhodes Univ BA 81 Ch Coll Cam PhD 86 K Coll Lon MPhil 95 PhD 12. Wycliffe Hall Ox 89. **d** 91 **p** 92. NSM Ivybridge w Harford *Ex* 91–95; P-in-c Abbotskerswell 95–99; P-in-c Tudeley cum Capel w Five Oak Green *Roch* 99–12; V 12–19; V Capel United Ben from 19; Dioc Lay Min Adv 99–01. *The Vicarage, Sychem Lane, Five Oak Green, Tonbridge TN12 6TL* T/F: (01892) 836653 E: jeremy@tudeley.org
IVESON, Robert George. b 70. Oak Hill Th Coll BA 01. **d** 01 **p** 02. C Cheadle All Hallows *Ches* 01–04; C-in-c Cheadle Hulme Em CD 04–14; R Davenham from 14. *4 Waystead Close, Northwich CW9 8NN* T: (01606) 42450 E: rob.iveson@btinternet.com
IVESON, Canon Ronald Edward. b 68. Ches Coll of HE RMN 92. Aston Tr Scheme 95 Oak Hill Th Coll BA 00. **d** 00 **p** 01. C Lache cum Saltney *Ches* 00–03; V Bidston from 03; RD Birkenhead from 16; Hon Can Ches Cathl from 18. *The Vicarage, 6 Statham Road, Prenton CH43 7XS* T: 0151-652 4852 *or* 653 4584 E: roniveson@hotmail.com
IVES-SMITH, Mrs Susan Margaret. **d** 15 **p** 16. C Tideswell *Derby* 15–18; P-in-c Newbold de Verdun, Barlestone and Kirkby Mallory *Leic* from 18; P-in-c Peckleton from 18. *The Rectory, 6 The Paddock, Newbold Verdon, Leicester LE9 9NW* T: (01455) 821122 E: sueivessmith@live.co.uk
IVISON, Norman William. b 54. Hull Univ BA 75 DipEd 76 Dur Univ MA(Theol) 12. Trin Coll Bris. **d** 82 **p** 83. C Barrow St Mark *Carl* 82–85; Ecum Liaison Officer BBC Radio Furness 82–85; Chapl Barrow Sixth Form Coll 83–85; Dioc Broadcasting Officer *Lich* 85–91; Relig Progr Producer BBC Radio Stoke 85–91; Hon C Bucknall and Bagnall *Lich* 85–91; Asst Producer Relig Progr BBC TV Man 91–93; Producer Relig and Ethics BBC TV Man 93–05; Dir Tr and

Events Fresh Expressions 05–08; Dir Communications and Resources 08–15; Dir BowlandMedia 15–18; PtO *Blackb* from 98. *3 Claremont Drive, Clitheroe BB7 1JW* M: 07885-866317 E: norman.ivison@btinternet.com
IVORSON, David. b 51. Mansf Coll Ox MA 73 York Univ BPhil 75 ACA 80. SEITE 05. **d** 08 **p** 09. NSM E Grinstead St Swithun *Chich* 08–11; Chapl Whittington Coll Felbridge from 11; PtO *Chich* from 15. *Woodhurst, Portland Road, East Grinstead RH19 4DZ* T: (01342) 316451 M: 07787-155154 E: david@ivorson.com *or* davidivorson@gmail.com
IVORY, Canon Christopher James. b 54. Reading Univ BSc 76. Qu Coll Birm. **d** 81 **p** 82. C Waltham Cross *St Alb* 81–84; C Is of Dogs Ch Ch and St Jo w St Luke *Lon* 84–88; V Streatham Ch Ch *S'wark* 88–03; Lambeth Adnry Ecum Officer 90–95; RD Streatham 00–03; R King's Lynn St Marg w St Nic *Nor* 03–17; TR from 17; RD Lynn 08–13; Hon Can Nor Cathl from 08. *St Margaret's Vicarage, St Margaret's Place, King's Lynn PE30 5DL* T: (01553) 767090 E: vicar@stmargaretskingslynn.org.uk
IZOD, Mrs Wendy Janet. b 47. Sheff Univ BA(Econ) 68. SEITE 98. **d** 01 **p** 02. NSM Hever, Four Elms and Mark Beech *Roch* 01–16; P-in-c 16–19; Chapl ATC 01–19; rtd 19. *West Lodge, Stick Hill, Edenbridge TN8 5NJ* T: (01342) 850738 M: 07703-107496 E: izodiham@gmail.com
IZZARD, David Antony. b 55. Trin Coll Bris 92. **d** 94 **p** 95. C E Bris 94–98; V Sea Mills 98–16; R Radstock w Writhlington *B & W* from 16; R Kilmersdon w Babington from 16. *Westfield Vicarage, 5 Wellsway, Wells Road, Radstock BA3 3UW* E: david.izzard@btinternet.com
IZZARD, Canon Susannah Amanda. b 59. Hatf Poly BA 82 Birm Univ MEd 93 Wolv Univ PGCE 92. Trin Coll Bris BA 86. **dss** 86 **d** 87 **p** 01. Birm St Martin w Bordesley St Andr 86–89; Par Dn 87–89; C Handsworth St Jas 89–91; Asst Chapl Qu Eliz Hosp Birm 90–91; Lect Birm Univ 93–02; NSM Selly Oak St Mary 01–12; PtO 12–17; Bp's Adv for Pastoral Care 07–16; Hon Can Birm Cathl 16; PtO *St E* from 17; Bp's Adv for Past Care of Clergy 17–19. *Corner House, Mill Lane, Barnby, Beccles NR34 7PX* M: 07702-571760 E: susannah.izzard@cofesuffolk.org

J

JABLONSKI, Andrew Philip. b 54. St Jo Coll Cam MA 76 Nottm Univ MBA 90 Anglia Ruskin Univ MA 10 CEng 90 FIMechE 02. Ridley Hall Cam 07. **d** 09 **p** 10. NSM Grantham, Harrowby w Londonthorpe *Linc* 09–12; C Bromley SS Pet and Paul *Roch* 12–18; P-in-c Mudeford *Win* from 18. *22 Kestrel Drive, Christchurch BH23 4DE* T: (01425) 240018 M: 07736-649401 E: andrewjab@gmail.com
JABLONSKI, Mrs Anne Judith. b 54. Girton Coll Cam BA 76 MA 79. Ridley Hall Cam 07. **d** 09 **p** 10. C Grantham St Wulfram *Linc* 09–12; V Bromley SS Pet and Paul *Roch* 12–18; NSM Mudeford *Win* from 18. *22 Kestrel Drive, Christchurch BH23 4DE* T: (01425) 240018 M: 07759-661836 E: annejab1@virginmedia.com
JACK, Judith Ann. *See* JEFFERY, Judith Ann
JACK, Philip Andrew. b 76. Nottm Univ BA 98. Oak Hill Th Coll BA 08. **d** 08 **p** 09. C Ox St Ebbe w H Trin and St Pet 08–12; NSM 12–13; Chapl Canford Sch from 13. *Canford School, Canford Magna, Wimborne BH21 3AD* T: (01202) 841254 M: 07972-078148 E: phil.a.jack@gmail.com *or* paj@canford.com
JACKLIN, John Frederick. b 30. Oak Hill Th Coll 72. **d** 72 **p** 72. Chile 72–75; C Roxeth Ch Ch *Lon* 75–78; V Selston *S'well* 78–95; rtd 95; PtO *Derby* 97–18. *5 Rose Avenue, Borrowash, Derby DE72 3GA* T: (01332) 669670
JACKMAN, Aaron Anthony. b 83. Leeds Univ BA 04 MMus 06. Westcott Ho Cam 14. **d** 17 **p** 18. C Saddleworth *Man* from 17. *The Vicarage, Woods Lane, Dobcross, Oldham OL3 5AN* M: 07717-893466 E: aaronajackman@gmail.com
JACKS, David. Nottm Univ BTh 87 Birm Univ MA 95 PhD 08. Linc Th Coll 84. **d** 87 **p** 88. C Oakham, Hambleton, Egleton, Braunston and Brooke *Pet* 87–90; V Weedon Bec w Everdon 90–96; V Weedon Bec w Everdon and Dodford 96–01; V Llandrillo-yn-Rhos *St As* 01–16; AD Llanrwst and Rhos 14–15; V Ashton Ch Ch *Man* from 16. *Christ Church Vicarage, Vicarage Road, Ashton-under-Lyne OL7 9QY* T: 0161-330 1601 M: 07974-937517 E: david.jacks@live.co.uk

JACKSON, Alan. b 44. Newc Univ BA 67 DipEd 68 MEd 79. NEOC 79. **d** 81 **p** 82. NSM Jesmond H Trin *Newc* 81–82; Chapl Bp Wand Sch Sunbury-on-Thames 82–89; V Hanworth St Rich *Lon* 89–10; rtd 10; PtO *Lon* from 11. *7 Uxbridge Road, Feltham TW13 5EG* T: (020) 8898 3093 E: alan11144@gmail.com
JACKSON, Alison. b 58. St Mellitus Coll. **d** 14 **p** 15. NSM Rye Park St Cuth *St Alb* 14–17; Fresh Expressions Development Officer from 18. *95 New Road, Ware SG12 7BY* T: (01727) 818113 E: ajackson@stalbans.anglican.org
JACKSON, Barry. b 30. St Jo Coll Cam BA 53 DipEd 54 MA 57. Westcott Ho Cam 63. **d** 65 **p** 66. C Stockport St Geo *Ches* 65–68; C Bridgwater St Mary, Chilton Trinity and Durleigh *B & W* 68–70; P-in-c Thurloxton 70–75; Chapl Wycliffe Coll Glos 75–88; V Heathfield *Chich* 88–97; rtd 97; PtO *Chich* from 98. *11 Glenleigh Walk, Robertsbridge TN32 5DQ* T: (01580) 880067
JACKSON, Barry James. b 65. Sheff Univ BEng 87. St Jo Coll Nottm 05. **d** 07 **p** 08. C Leamington Priors St Mary *Cov* 07–10; P-in-c Kineton 10–14; P-in-c Combroke w Compton Verney 10–14; P-in-c Warmington w Shotteswell and Radway w Ratley 10–14; R Edgehill Churches from 14. *The Vicarage, Warwick Road, Kineton, Warwick CV35 0HW* T: (01926) 640248 E: revbarryjackson@btinternet.com
JACKSON, The Very Revd Brandon Donald. b 34. Liv Univ LLB 56 Bradf Univ Hon DLitt 90. Wycliffe Hall Ox. **d** 58 **p** 59. C New Malden and Coombe *S'wark* 58–61; C Leeds St Geo *Ripon* 61–65; V Shipley St Pet *Bradf* 65–77; Relig Adv Yorkshire TV 69–79; Provost Bradf 77–89; Dean Linc 89–97; rtd 97; PtO *Ripon* 98–14; *Leeds* 14–16. *1 Kingston Way, Market Harborough LE16 7XB* T: (01858) 462425 E: brandon.j1@btinternet.com
JACKSON, Mrs Brenda Joan. b 51. All SS Cen for Miss & Min 18. **d** 19. NSM Bakewell, Ashford w Sheldon and Rowsley *Derby* from 19. *27 Castle Mount Crescent, Bakewell DE45 1AT* T: (01332) 554820 *or* (01629) 813143 M: 07805-949918 E: rev.brendajackson@gmail.com

JACKSON, Charlotte Lucy. b 88. St Andr Univ MA 10 Middx Univ MA 14 Cam Univ BTh 18. Ridley Hall Cam 16. **d** 19. C Willenhall *Cov* from 19. *St James's Church Vicarage, Abbey Road, Coventry CV3 4BG* T: (024) 7630 3266 M: 07591-474231 E: revcharlottejackson@gmail.com

JACKSON, Christopher John Wilson. b 45. St Pet Coll Ox BA 67 MA 87. Ridley Hall Cam 69. **d** 72 **p** 73. C Putney St May *S'wark* 72–76; C Battersea St Pet and St Paul 76–79; TV Preston St Jo *Blackb* 79–87; P-in-c Sandal St Cath *Wakef* 87–90; V Shenley Green *Birm* 90–01; AD Kings Norton 95–99; P-in-c Chesterfield H Trin and Ch Ch *Derby* 01–10; R 10; rtd 10; PtO *Blackb* from 10. *5 Beech Grove, Ashton-on-Ribble, Preston PR2 1DX* T: (01772) 721772 E: chrisaliz76@virginmedia.com

JACKSON, Miss Cynthia. b 42. Open Univ BA 07. S'wark Ord Course 93. **d** 96 **p** 97. NSM Wimbledon *S'wark* 96–12; PtO from 12. *39 Panmuir Road, London SW20 0PZ* T: (020) 8947 5940 E: revcynthia@timetalk.co.uk *or* cynthia@stmaryswimbledon.org

JACKSON, David. b 48. Open Univ BA 85. St Deiniol's Hawarden 91. **d** 91 **p** 92. C Scotforth *Blackb* 91–95; Chapl Ox Radcliffe Hosps NHS Trust 95–00; C Banbury *Ox* 95–96; TV 96–98; V Banbury St Hugh 98–07; V Banbury St Fran 07–12; rtd 12; PtO *Eur* from 12. *16 rue Soeur Marie Antoinette, 50720 Barenton, France* E: davyjax.dj@gmail.com

JACKSON, David Reginald Estcourt. b 25. Qu Coll Cam BA 45 MA 49. Cranmer Hall Dur 80. **d** 81 **p** 82. Hon C Douglas *Blackb* 81–82; C 82–87; rtd 90. *64 The Common, Parbold, Wigan WN8 7EA* T: (01257) 462671

JACKSON, David Robert. b 51. Lon Univ BDS. Linc Th Coll 81. **d** 83 **p** 84. C Hatcham St Cath *S'wark* 83–87; V Sydenham St Bart 87–93; PtO *Lon* 03–05 and 11–16; C St Martin-in-the-Fields 05–11; PtO *Ox* from 16. *Hunter's Rest, 1 Field Court, Duns Tew, Bicester OX25 6LD* M: 07973-657260 E: djsaab@aol.com

JACKSON, Canon Derek Reginald. b 49. K Coll Lon BD 72 AKC 72. **d** 73 **p** 74. C Westhoughton *Man* 73–75; C Kendal H Trin *Carl* 75–78; V Pennington w Lindal and Marton 78–83; Warden of Readers 82–92; V Kendal St Geo 83–94; Hon Can Carl Cathl 89–00; V Applethwaite 94–96; P-in-c Troutbeck 94–96; V Windermere St Mary and Troutbeck 96–00; RD Windermere 98–00; Can Res Bradf Cathl 00–03; P-in-c Bingley All SS 03–10; RD Airedale 05–10; rtd 10; PtO *Carl* from 11. *3 Ellas Orchard, Green Lane, Flookburgh, Grange-over-Sands LA11 7JT* T: (015395) 59086 E: derekjackson2901@hotmail.com

JACKSON, Mrs Elizabeth Mary. b 41. Man Univ BA 67 Leeds Univ MA 01. Ox Min Course 90. **d** 92 **p** 94. Chapl Reading Hosps 86–95; NSM Reading St Mary the Virgin *Ox* 92–94; Chapl R Berks and Battle Hosps NHS Trust 95–02; NSM Reading Deanery *Ox* 02–07; PtO *Carl* from 08. *The Hayloft, 2 Hall Court, Tallentire, Cockermouth CA13 0PU* T: (01900) 825799 E: mjack2bl@aol.com

JACKSON, The Ven Frances Anne (Peggy). b 51. Somerville Coll Ox BA 72 MA 76 ACA 76 FCA 81. Ripon Coll Cuddesdon 85. **d** 87 **p** 94. C Ilkeston St Mary *Derby* 87–90; TM Hemel Hempstead *St Alb* 90–94; TV 94–98; TR Mortlake w E Sheen *S'wark* 98–09; RD Richmond and Barnes 00–05; Hon Can S'wark Cathl 03–09; Dean of Women's Min 04–09; Adn Llan from 09; P-in-c Penmark w Llancarfan w Llantrithyd 09–14; P-in-c St Fagans and Michaelston-super-Ely from 14. *The Rectory, Greenwood Lane, St Fagans, Cardiff CF5 6EL* T: (029) 2056 7393 E: archdeacon.llandaff@churchinwales.org.uk

JACKSON, Miss Freda. b 41. Bp Otter Coll TCert 61. **d** 92 **p** 94. OLM Middleton *Man* 92–94; OLM Middleton and Thornham 94–12; rtd 12; PtO *Man* from 12. *17 Craiglands, Rochdale OL16 4RA* T: (01706) 523520 M: 07974-971683

JACKSON, Ms Gillian Rosemary. b 52. Newc Univ BA 75 PGCE 76 Aber Univ MLitt 80 Nottm Univ MA 04 AFBPsS. EMMTC 01. **d** 04 **p** 05. NSM Bosworth and Sheepy Gp *Leic* 04–08; Dioc Dir Soc Resp 04–08; Bp's Exec Asst 08–10; PtO *S & B* from 17. *3 Oxford Villas, Oxford Road, Hay-on-Wye, Hereford HR3 5BW*

JACKSON, Hannah Louise. *See* HALL, Hannah Louise

JACKSON, Mrs Isobel Margaret. b 69. Uganda Chr Univ BD 04. **d** 04. CMS Uganda 04–05; C Lismore w Cappoquin, Kilwatermoy, Dungarvan etc *C & O* 05–10; I Templebreedy w Tracton and Nohoval *C, C & R* from 10. *Templebreedy Rectory, Church Road, Crosshaven, Co Cork, Republic of Ireland* T: (00353) (21) 483 1236 M: 86-743 5424 E: isobel@nijackson.com *or* templebreedyrector@ccrd.ie

JACKSON, Mrs Janet Lesley. b 45. CQSW 78. NEOC 93. **d** 96 **p** 97. NSM Whorlton *Newc* 96–98; Chapl St Oswald's Hospice Newc 98–07; Bereavement Services Co-ord Tynedale Hospice 10–12; Chapl from 12; PtO *Newc* from 10.

1 St Andrews Road, Hexham NE46 2EY T: (01434) 602929 E: revjan307@btinternet.com

JACKSON, Mrs Joan. b 44. Bolton Coll of Educn CertEd 71 Lanc Univ MA 98. CBDTI 95. **d** 98 **p** 99. NSM Staveley, Ings and Kentmere *Carl* 98–00; Chapl Furness Hosps NHS Trust 98–00; Asst Chapl Bradf Hosps NHS Trust 00–04; NSM Bingley H Trin *Bradf* 03–07; PtO 07–10; *Carl* from 11. *3 Ellas Orchard, Green Lane, Flookburgh, Grange-over-Sands LA11 7JT* T: (015395) 59086 E: jjacksonddp@yahoo.co.uk

JACKSON, Miss Kathryn Dianne. b 64. Leeds Univ BA 87 MA 01. St Steph Ho Ox 87. **d** 90 **p** 94. Par Dn Headingley *Ripon* 90–94; C Hawksworth Wood 94–00; P-in-c Scarborough St Columba *York* 00–14; Chapl St Cath Hospice Scarborough 00–14; R Haxby and Wigginton *York* from 14. *The Rectory, 5 Back Lane, Wigginton, York YO32 2ZH* T: (01904) 765155 E: rectorkathryn@btinternet.com

JACKSON, Lisa Helen. *See* BARNETT, Lisa Helen

JACKSON, Miss Lynne Margaret. b 74. St Mellitus Coll 16. **d** 19. C Rainhill *Liv* from 19. *26 Calder Drive, Rainhill, Prescot L35 0NW* M: 07444-793958 E: lynn-ej@hotmail.com

JACKSON, Malcolm. b 58. NEOC 01. **d** 04 **p** 05. C Guisborough *York* 04–08; V Kirkleatham 08–14; C Whitby w Ruswarp 14–18; P-in-c Hinderwell, Roxby and Staithes etc 18; R from 18. *27 Runswick Lane, Hinderwell, Saltburn-by-the-Sea TS13 5HP* E: maljackoagain@gmail.com

JACKSON, Mrs Margaret Elizabeth. b 47. Lon Univ BSc 68 MSc 95 Univ of Wales (Lamp) MTh 05 FCIPD 91. S'wark Ord Course 80. **dss** 83 **d** 92 **p** 94. Surbiton Hill Ch Ch *S'wark* 83–84; Saffron Walden w Wendens Ambo and Littlebury *Chelmsf* 84–85; Dulwich St Barn *S'wark* 86–97; Hon C 92–97; Personal Asst to Bp S'wark 92–94; Selection Sec Min Division 96–00 and from 03; NSM Churt *Guildf* 98–00; NSM The Bourne and Tilford 00–10; NSM Churt and Hindhead 10–12; Convenor STETS 00–02; Dioc Dir of Ords *S'wark* 05–06; Dir of Ords Kingston Area 11–17; PtO *Guildf* from 14. *62 Wheelwrights Lane, Grayshott, Hindhead GU26 6EB* T: (01428) 714411 E: revjackson@btinternet.com

JACKSON, Margaret Jane. b 50. RGN 72 RHV 74. S'wark Ord Course 89. **d** 92 **p** 94. Par Dn Hatcham St Cath *S'wark* 92–94; C 94–98; V Mottingham St Edw 98–17; rtd 17; Hon C Dunster, Carhampton, Withycombe w Rodhuish etc *B & W* from 17. *5 Winsors Lane, Carhampton, Minehead TA24 6NJ* T: (01643) 822501 E: rev.mjackson@gmail.com

JACKSON, Mark Benjamin. b 77. Dur Univ BSc 00. Wycliffe Hall Ox BTh 13. **d** 13 **p** 14. C Langham Place All So *Lon* from 13; C Clerkenwell St Jas and St Jo w St Pet from 18. *4 Owen's Row, London EC1V 4NP* T: (020) 7251 1190 E: mark@inspirelondon.org

JACKSON, Mark Harding. b 51. Open Univ BA 87. Sarum & Wells Th Coll 78. **d** 79 **p** 80. C Hobs Moat *Birm* 79–83; Chapl RN from 83; PtO *Eur* from 17. *Bush House, 12 Palmer Street, South Petherton TA13 5DB* T: (01460) 242171 M: 07960-733472 E: maundycottage@talktalk.net

JACKSON, Martin. b 56. Clare Coll Cam BA 77 MA 81 St Jo Coll Dur BA 80 MA 97. Cranmer Hall Dur. **d** 81 **p** 82. C Houghton le Spring *Dur* 81–84; C Bishopwearmouth St Mich w St Hilda 84–86; TV Winlaton 86; V High Spen and Rowlands Gill 86–97; P-in-c Benfieldside 94–97; V from 97; P-in-c Castleside from 11; AD Lanchester 00–06. *St Cuthbert's Vicarage, Church Bank, Consett DH8 0NW* T: (01207) 503019 E: martin.jackson@durham.anglican.org

JACKSON, Matthew Christopher. b 75. Univ of Wales (Abth) BD 96 MTh 98. Ripon Coll Cuddesdon. **d** 01 **p** 02. C King's Lynn St Marg w St Nic *Nor* 01–05; V Pembury *Roch* 05–10; R Attleborough w Besthorpe *Nor* from 10; RD Thetford and Rockland from 11. *The Rectory, Surrogate Street, Attleborough NR17 2AW* T: (01953) 453185 E: therectory@me.com

JACKSON, Mrs Melanie Jane Susann. b 60. UWE BA 83 Leic Univ MA 94. SWMTC 97. **d** 00 **p** 01. C Ottery St Mary, Alfington, W Hill, Tipton etc *Ex* 00–04; PtO 04–08; NSM Linc St Jo 08–14; Chapl Bp Grosseteste Univ from 15; PtO *Linc* 15–18. *Chaplaincy Office, Bishop Grosseteste University, Longdales Road, Lincoln LN1 3DY* E: melanie.jackson@bishopg.ac.uk

✠**JACKSON, The Most Revd Michael Geoffrey St Aubyn.** b 56. TCD BA 79 MA 82 St Jo Coll Cam BA 81 MA 85 PhD 86 Ch Ch Ox MA 89 DPhil 89. CITC 86. **d** 86 **p** 87 **c** 02. C Dublin Zion Ch *D & G* 86–89; Chapl Ch Ch Ox 89–97; Student 93–97; Dean Cork *C, C & R* 97–02; I Cork St Fin Barre's Union 97–02; Chapl and Asst Lect Univ Coll Cork 98–02; Chapl Cork Inst of Tech 98–02; Bp Clogh 02–11; Abp Dublin *D & G* from 11. *The See House, 17 Temple Road, Dartry, Dublin 6, Republic of Ireland* T: (00353) (1) 497 7849 F: 497 6355 E: archbishop@dublin.anglican.org

JACKSON, Michael Ian. b 51. Southn Univ BA 73. STETS 00. **d** 03 **p** 04. Dir St Jo Win Charity 87–13; NSM Twyford and

Owslebury and Morestead etc *Win* 03–13; V Kirkby-in-Malhamdale *Leeds* 13–16; rtd 16; PtO *Win* from 17. *Hill Farm Lodge, Morestead, Winchester SO21 1LZ* T: (01962) 777277 E: michael.jackson@morestead.net

JACKSON, Canon Michael James. b 44. Liv Univ BEng 65 Newc Univ PhD 84 CEng 69 MICE 69. NEOC 82. **d** 84 **p** 85. C Houghton le Spring *Dur* 84–87; V Millfield St Mark 87–95; V Ponteland *Newc* 95–07; AD Newc W 03–07; Hon Can Newc Cathl 06–07; rtd 07; PtO *Newc* from 07. *1 St Andrews Road, Hexham NE46 2EY* T: (01434) 602929

JACKSON, Michael Richard. b 31. Selw Coll Cam BA 54 MA 58. Westcott Ho Cam 54. **d** 56 **p** 57. C Gosforth All SS *Newc* 56–62; R Dinnington *Sheff* 62–76; V Swinton 76–97; rtd 97; PtO *Sheff* from 97. *10 Elmhirst Drive, Rotherham S65 3ED* T: (01709) 531065

JACKSON, Nicholas David. b 54. Wadh Coll Ox MA 75 Bris Univ PGCE 76. Wycliffe Hall Ox 06. **d** 08 **p** 09. C Branksome Park All SS *Sarum* 08–12; V Southlake *Ox* 12–17; rtd 17; PtO *Win* from 17. *77 Carbery Avenue, Bournemouth BH6 3LW* T: (01202) 388140 E: rev.nickj@gmail.com

JACKSON, Patricia Ann. b 56. **d** 16 **p** 17. NSM Mow Cop *Lich* from 16. *65 Hollington Drive, Stoke-on-Trent ST6 6TZ* T: (01782) 790376 E: patjackson@mypostoffice.co.uk

JACKSON, Paul Andrew. b 65. NEOC 05. **d** 08 **p** 09. NSM Haxby and Wigginton *York* 08–16; V Middle Esk Moor from 16. *The Vicarage, Egton, Whitby YO21 1UT* T: (01947) 895833 E: pjacko99@aol.com

JACKSON, Peggy. *See* JACKSON, Frances Anne

JACKSON, Peter Jonathan Edward. b 53. St Pet Coll Ox BA 74 MA 78 PGCE 78. St Steph Ho Ox 79. **d** 79 **p** 80. Lect Westmr Coll Ox 79–80; Hon C Ox St Mich w St Martin and All SS 79–80; C Malvern Link w Cowleigh *Worc* 79–82; Chapl Aldenham Sch Herts 82–89; Chapl and Hd RE Harrow Sch 89–01; Lect K Coll Lon 92–99; Dir Chr Educn and Assoc R Washington St Patr USA 01–03; V Southgate Ch Ch *Lon* 03–14; Chapl Nice w Vence *Eur* from 14. *Holy Trinity, 11 rue de la Buffa, 06000 Nice, France* T: (0033) 4 93 87 19 83 M: 7 83 28 39 53 E: peterjejackson@aol.com

JACKSON, Philip Michael. b 74. Chelt & Glouc Coll of HE BA 95 Brunel Univ PGCE 97. Trin Coll Bris BA 05. **d** 06 **p** 07. C W Kilburn St Luke w St Simon and St Jude *Lon* 06–09; C Reigate St Mary *S'wark* 09–13; P-in-c Chipstead 13–14; R 14–17; Chapl Reigate Gr Sch from 17; PtO *S'wark* from 17. *Reigate Grammar School, Reigate Road, Reigate RH2 0QS* T: (01737) 222231 M: 07545-054022 E: phil.jackson74@gmail.com

JACKSON (*née* PRICE), Mrs Rachel Anne. b 57. **d** 03 **p** 04. OLM Barnham Broom and Upper Yare *Nor* 03–18; PtO from 18. *Red Hall, Red Hall Lane, Southburgh, Thetford IP25 7TG* T: (01362) 821032 E: revrachel@edwardjacksonltd.com

✠JACKSON, The Rt Revd Richard Charles. b 61. Ch Ch Ox BA 83 Cranfield Inst of Tech MSc 85. Trin Coll Bris 92. **d** 94 **p** 95 **c** 14. C Lindfield *Chich* 94–98; V Rudgwick 98–09; RD Horsham 05–09; Dioc Adv for Miss and Renewal 09–14; Area Bp Lewes from 14. *Ebenezer House, Kingston Ridge, Kingston, Lewes BN7 3JU* T: (01273) 425009 E: bishop.lewes@chichester.anglican.org

JACKSON, Richard Hugh. b 44. St Jo Coll York CertEd 66 UEA MA 84. **d** 98 **p** 99. OLM Stalham and E Ruston w Brunstead *Nor* 98–00; OLM Stalham, E Ruston, Brunstead, Sutton and Ingham 00–14; PtO from 14. *The Croft, Camping Field Lane, Stalham, Norwich NR12 9DT* T: (01692) 581389 E: richard.jackson@intamail.com

JACKSON, Robert. b 69. Nottm Univ BA 01. St Jo Coll Nottm 01 **d** 01 **p** 02. C Altham w Clayton le Moors *Blackb* 01–03; C Blackb St Gabr 03–05; TV Westhoughton and Wingates *Man* 05–10; TV Cartmel Peninsula *Carl* 10–15; P-in-c Whitehaven from 15; Lay Development Co-ord from 10. *Autumn Garth, Harras Road, Harras Moor, Whitehaven CA28 6SG* M: 07863-377777 E: revrobjackson@live.co.uk

JACKSON, Robert Brandon. b 61. Lanchester Poly Cov BA 86 Ox Univ BA 88 MA 95. Wycliffe Hall Ox 86. **d** 89 **p** 90. C Bromley Common St Aug *Roch* 89–92; P-in-c Stowe *Ox* 92–97; Asst Chapl Stowe Sch 92–97; Chapl 02–11; Chapl Lord Wandsworth Coll Hook 97–02; PtO *Ox* 11–18; Chapl RNR from 18. *Royal Naval Chaplaincy Service, Mail Point 1-2, Leach Building, Whale Island, Portsmouth PO2 8BY* T: (023) 9262 5055 F: 9262 5134 E: hittiterev@msn.com

JACKSON, Robert Fielden. b 35. St D Coll Lamp BA 57. Sarum Th Coll 57. **d** 59 **p** 60. C Altham w Clayton le Moors *Blackb* 59–62; C Lytham St Cuth 62–64; V Skerton St Chad 64–69; V Preesall 69–90; RD Garstang 85–89; V Wray w Tatham and Tatham Fells 90–00; rtd 00; PtO *Blackb* 00–14. *8 Squirrel's Chase, Lostock Hall, Preston PR5 5NE* T: (01772) 338756

JACKSON, The Ven Robert William. b 49. K Coll Cam MA 73 Man Univ MA. St Jo Coll Nottm 78. **d** 81 **p** 82. C Fulwood

---

Sheff 81–84; V Grenoside and Chapl Grenoside Hosp 84–92; V Scarborough St Mary w Ch Ch and H Apostles *York* 92–01; Springboard Missr 01–04; Adn Walsall and Hon Can Lich Cathl 05–09; rtd 09. *4 Glebe Park, Eyam, Hope Valley S32 5RH* T: (01433) 631212 E: archbob@gmail.com *or* venerablebob@gmail.com

JACKSON, Roger. b 57. Chich Th Coll 85. **d** 88 **p** 89. C Hale *Guildf* 88–92; V Barton w Peel Green *Man* 92–95; P-in-c Long Crendon w Chearsley and Nether Winchendon *Ox* 95–00; V 00–08; V Clevedon St Jo *B & W* 08–14; P-in-c Fareham SS Pet and Paul *Portsm* from 14. *The Vicarage, 22 Harrison Road, Fareham PO16 7EJ* T: (01329) 281521 E: frrjackson@gmail.com

JACKSON, Canon Ronald William. b 37. Lon Univ MA 71 ALCD. **d** 69 **p** 70. C Crofton *Portsm* 69–74; V Wolverhampton St Matt *Lich* 74–85; V Bloxwich 85–89; C Tamworth 89–92; Bp's Officer for Par Miss and Development *Bradf* 92–98; Hon Can Bradf Cathl 94–98; rtd 98; PtO *Bradf* 99–14; *Leeds* 14–16; *Blackb* from 14. *24 Fosbrooke House, Clifton Drive, Lytham St Annes FY8 5RQ* T: (01253) 667024 E: rw.jackson@icloud.com

JACKSON, Ruth Ellen. b 69. Dub City Univ BBS 91. CITC BTh 02. **d** 02 **p** 03. C Portadown St Mark *Arm* 02–05; C Carrigrohane Union *C, C & R* 05–10; I Mountmellick w Coolbanagher, Rosenallis etc *M & K* 10–15; I Dublin Crumlin w Chapelizod *D & G* from 15. *St Mary's Rectory, 118 Kimmage Road West, Dublin 12, Republic of Ireland* M: (00353) 87-052 3450 E: ruthjnoble@gmail.com

JACKSON, Ruth Victoria. *See* HAKE, Ruth Victoria

JACKSON, Sarah Diana. b 53. Birkbeck Coll Lon MSc 01 Dorset Ho Sch of Occupational Therapy DipCOT 74. SEITE 09. **d** 12 **p** 13. NSM Wandsworth Common St Mary *S'wark* 12–15; NSM Upper Tooting H Trin w St Aug from 15. *25 Mantilla Road, London SW17 8DY* T: (020) 8767 4667 M: 07719-876610 E: mail@sarahjackson.me

JACKSON (STAFF), Mrs Susan. b 59. Leeds Univ BA 82. Ridley Hall Cam 88. **d** 90 **p** 94. Par Dn Mickleover All SS *Derby* 90–93; Par Dn Chatham St Wm *Roch* 93–94; C 94–97; TV Walton Milton Keynes *Ox* 97–13; PtO from 13. *11 Herdwyck Close, Oakridge Park, Milton Keynes MK14 6GR* T: (01908) 317515 E: s.jackson201@btinternet.com

JACKSON, Wendy Pamela. *See* JACKSON-HILL, Wendy Pamela

JACKSON, William Stafford. b 48. Sunderland Poly DCYW 83 Sunderland Univ CertEd 96. Linc Th Coll 86. **d** 89 **p** 90. C Heworth St Mary *Dur* 89–91; C Tudhoe Grange 91–92; Churches' Regional Commn in the NE 97–01; NSM Dipton and Leadgate 03–08; V Burnham *Ox* 08–19; rtd 19. *10 Woodland Terrace, Nettlesworth, Chester le Street DH2 3PW* M: 07793-750652

JACKSON, Canon William Stanley Peter. b 39. St Mich Coll Llan 63. **d** 66 **p** 67. C Llandrindod w Cefnllys *S & B* 66–69; C Gowerton w Waunarlwydd 69–73; V Crickadarn w Gwenddwr and Alltmawr 73–79; R Llanfeugan w Llanthetty etc 79–04; Dioc GFS Chapl 84–92; Can Res Brecon Cathl *S & B* 90–04; Prec Brecon Cathl 98–99; Treas Brecon Cathl 99–00; Chan Brecon Cathl 00–04; Dioc Communications Officer 92–94; RD Crickhowell 98–02; rtd 04. *9 St Peter's Avenue, Fforestfach, Swansea SA5 5BX* T: (01792) 541229

JACKSON-HILL, Mrs Wendy Pamela. b 45. Th Ext Educn Coll 99. **d** 00 **p** 02. Community P Woodlands S Africa 02–03; C Crediton, Shobrooke and Sandford etc *Ex* 03–05; P-in-c Southway 05–15; C Tamerton Foliot 06–15; rtd 15; PtO *Cant* from 16. *33 Colmanton Grove, Sholden, Deal CT14 0FF* E: wendyjacksonhill@gmx.com

JACKSON NOBLE, Ruth Ellen. *See* JACKSON, Ruth Ellen

JACKSON-STEVENS, Preb Nigel. b 42. St Steph Ho Ox. **d** 68 **p** 69. C Babbacombe *Ex* 68–73; V Swimbridge 73–75; P-in-c W Buckland 73–75; V Swimbridge and W Buckland 75–84; P-in-c Mortehoe 84–85; P-in-c Ilfracombe, Lee, W Down, Woolacombe and Bittadon 84–85; TR Ilfracombe, Lee, Woolacombe, Bittadon etc 85–08; RD Barnstaple 93–97; Preb Ex Cathl 95–08; rtd 08. *Rose Cottage, Eastacombe, Barnstaple EX31 3NT* T: (01271) 325283 E: jacksonstorens@btinternet.com

JACOB, Mrs Amelia Stanley. b 52. Punjab Univ BA 73. Oak Hill Th Coll. **d** 90 **p** 94. NSM Asian Chr Congregation All SS Tufnell Park *Lon* 90–92; NSM Alperton 92–12; C from 13. *39 Chester Drive, Harrow HA2 7PX* T: (020) 8902 4592 E: ameliastanley39@yahoo.com

JACOB, John Lionel Andrew. b 26. Selw Coll Cam BA 50 MA 54. Westcott Ho Cam 50. **d** 52 **p** 53. C Brightside St Thos *Sheff* 52–55; C Maltby 55–58; V Doncaster Intake 58–67; V Sheff St Aid w St Luke 67–75; TR Sheff Manor 75–82; R Waddington *Linc* 82–91; rtd 91; PtO *Linc* 91–00. *Flat 21,*

Manormead, Tilford Road, Hindhead GU26 6RA　T: (01428) 602559

JACOB, Neville Peter. b 60. Kent Univ BA 82 Leeds Metrop Univ PGCE 86. Ripon Coll Cuddesdon 94. **d** 96 **p** 97. C Market Harborough *Leic* 96–97; C Market Harborough Transfiguration 96–97; C Market Harborough and The Transfiguration etc 97–99; Chapl Miss to Seafarers 99–03; P-in-c Copythorne *Win* 03–11; Chapl Ibex 03–09; PtO *Win* 11–16. *3 Elmsleigh Court, Glen Eyre Road, Southampton SO16 3NT* E: raveknave@tinyworld.co.uk

JACOB, The Ven William Mungo. b 44. Hull Univ LLB 66 Linacre Coll Ox BA 69 MA 73 Ex Univ PhD. St Steph Ho Ox 70. **d** 70 **p** 71. C Wymondham *Nor* 70–73; Asst Chapl Ex Univ 73–75; Dir Past Studies Sarum & Wells Th Coll 75–80; Vice-Prin 77–80; Selection Sec and Sec Cttee for Th Educn ACCM 80–86; Warden Linc Th Coll 85–96; Can and Preb Linc Cathl 86–96; Hon C Linc Minster Gp 88–96; Adn Charing Cross *Lon* 96–14; Bp's Sen Chapl 96–00; R St Giles-in-the-Fields 00–15; P-in-c Soho St Anne w St Thos and St Pet 11–13; rtd 15; P-in-c E Dulwich St Jo *S'wark* 15–16; PtO *Lon* from 17; *Nor* from 18. *4 St Mary's Walk, London SE11 4UA*　T: (020) 7735 8201 E: wmjacob15@gmail.com

JACOBS, Mrs Brenda Mary. b 61. Birm Univ BA 85 Glos Univ PGCE 04. WEMTC 06. **d** 09 **p** 10. C Holmer w Huntington *Heref* 09–10; C W Heref 10–12; R Pembridge w Moor Court, Shobdon, Staunton etc 12–16; TR Parkham, Alwington, Buckland Brewer etc *Ex* 16–18; PtO from 18. *18 Higher Road, Fremington, Barnstaple EX31 3BG*　T: (01271) 345743 E: jacobs200@btinternet.com

JACOBS, Kevin David. b 55. Dur Univ BA 18. SEITE 11. **d** 14 **p** 15. NSM Tunstall and Bredgar *Cant* from 14. *2 Acacia Terrace, Cryalls Lane, Sittingbourne ME10 1NU*　M: 07572-690460 E: frkevin.0614@gmail.com

JACOBS, Prof Michael David. b 41. Ex Coll Ox BA 63 MA 67. Chich Th Coll 63. **d** 65 **p** 66. C Walthamstow St Pet *Chelmsf* 65–68; Chapl Sussex Univ *Chich* 68–72; Student Cllr Leic Univ 72–84; Lect 84–97; Sen Lect 97–00; Dir Past Care Derby, Linc and S'well 84–94; Visiting Prof Bournemouth Univ *Sarum* from 03. *12 Atlantic Road, Swanage BH19 2EG*　T/F: (01929) 423068

JACOBS, Peter John. b 33. MICFM. SEITE 96. **d** 96 **p** 97. NSM Boughton under Blean w Dunkirk and Hernhill *Cant* 96–99; NSM Murston w Bapchild and Tonge 99–02; rtd 02; PtO *Cant* from 02. *16 Temple Road, Canterbury CT2 8JD*　M: 07780-353108 E: pjacobs631@gmail.com

JACOBSON, Ian Andrew. b 61. FRGS 94. STETS 02. **d** 05 **p** 06. NSM Ewell St Fran *Guildf* 05–08; NSM Headley w Box Hill 08–11; Asst Chapl Gibraltar Cathl *Eur* 11–14; P-in-c St Laur in Thanet *Cant* from 14; P-in-c Ramsgate St Mark 16–17; AD Thanet 15–17; C TA) 07–10; OCM 11–14; PtO *Eur* from 15. *The Rectory, 2 Newington Road, Ramsgate CT11 0QT*　T: (01843) 582672　M: 07711-716254 E: andrew.jacobson@waitrose.com

JACQUES, Barry John. b 52. Open Univ BSc 95. Wycliffe Hall Ox 00. **d** 02 **p** 03. NSM Attleborough *Cov* 02–03; C Weddington and Caldecote 03–07; PtO from 07. *23 Ferndale Close, Nuneaton CV11 6AQ*　T: (024) 7767 7044 E: bazjac1702@gmail.com

JACQUES, Mrs Margaret Irene. b 53. St Jo Coll Nottm BA 03 Birm Univ MPhil 10. **d** 03 **p** 04. C W Hallam and Mapperley w Stanley *Derby* 03–07; P-in-c Morton and Stonebroom w Shirland 07–12; R 12–16; rtd 16; PtO *Derby* from 16. *63 Jubilee Close, Melbourne, Derby DE73 8GR*　T: (01332) 865842 E: margaret@ajacques.plus.com

JACQUES, Martin. b 62. Ch Ch Coll Cant BA 05. Coll of Resurr Mirfield 00. **d** 02 **p** 03. C Margate St Jo *Cant* 02–06; P-in-c Bucharest w Sofia *Eur* 06–09; P-in-c Gainford *Dur* 09–15; P-in-c Winston 09–15; V Tynemouth Priory *Newc* 15–18; V Budleigh Salterton, E Budleigh w Bicton etc *Ex* from 18. *The New Vicarage, Vicarage Road, East Budleigh, Budleigh Salterton EX9 7EF*　M: 07706-875741 E: revmartinjacques@gmail.com

JACQUET, Linda. b 44. Hatf Poly BA 84. ERMC 06. **d** 08 **p** 09. NSM Bungay *St E* 08–14; rtd 15. *Roseheath, 10 Sun Road, Broome, Bungay NR35 2RW*　T: (01986) 896780　M: 07890-216889 E: l.jacquet@talktalk.net

JACQUET, Trevor Graham. b 56. Man Univ BSc 77. Oak Hill Th Coll BA 88. **d** 88 **p** 89. C Deptford St Nic and St Luke *S'wark* 88–92; Chapl HM Pris Brixton 92–95; Chapl HM Pris Elmley 95–08; Chapl HM Pris Belmarsh from 08. *HM Prison Belmarsh, Western Way, London SE28 0EB*　T: (020) 8331 4400　F: 8331 4401 E: trevor.jacquet@justice.gov.uk

JACSON, Edward Shallcross Owen. b 38. St Steph Ho Ox 61. **d** 64 **p** 65. C Yate *Glouc* 64–67; C Churchdown 67–70; P-in-c Sandhurst 70–75; V Sherborne w Windrush and the Barringtons 75–76; V Sherborne, Windrush, the Barringtons etc 76–80; TV Shaston *Sarum* 80–87; LtO 87–03;

PtO 03–14. Grove Farm House, Melbury Abbas, Shaftesbury SP7 0DE　T: (01747) 853688

JAGANNATH, Julia Rosemary. b 67. St Mellitus Coll 16. **d** 19. C Oak Tree Angl Fellowship *Lon* from 19. *3 Roman Close, London W3 8HE*　M: 07954-572682 E: juliajag@hotmail.co.uk

JAGE-BOWLER, Canon Christopher William. b 61. Nottm Univ BA 83 Ch Ch Ox PGCE 84 Down Coll Cam BA 89 MA 95. Ridley Hall Cam 87. **d** 90 **p** 91. C Downend *Bris* 90–94; Chapl Bris Univ 94–96; C Bris St Mich and St Paul 94–96; Asst Chapl Berlin *Eur* 96–97; Chapl from 97; Can Malta Cathl from 10. *Goethestrasse 31, 13158 Berlin, Germany*　T/F: (0049) (30) 917 2248 E: office@stgeorges.de

JAGGER, The Ven Ian. b 55. K Coll Cam BA 77 MA 81 St Jo Coll Dur BA 80 MA 87. Cranmer Hall Dur 78. **d** 82 **p** 83. C Twickenham St Mary *Lon* 82–85; P-in-c Willen *Ox* 85–87; TV Stantonbury and Willen 87–94; TR Fareham H Trin *Portsm* 94–98; Dioc Ecum Officer 94–96; RD Fareham 96–98; Can Missr 98–01; Adn Auckland *Dur* 01–06; Dioc Rural Development Officer 01–06; Adn Dur and Can Res Dur Cathl 06–19; rtd 19. *20 The Timbers, Fareham PO15 5NB* E: ruth.ian@jagfam.co.uk

JAGGER (née GREEN), Mrs Ruth Valerie. b 56. Ex Univ CertEd 77. Ox NSM Course 87. **d** 90 **p** 94. NSM Stantonbury and Willen *Ox* 90–94; NSM Fareham H Trin *Portsm* 94–98; NSM Portsm Deanery 98–01; PtO *Dur* 01–19; *Portsm* from 19. *20 The Timbers, Fareham PO15 5NB*　E: ruth.jagger@durham.anglican.org　or ruth.ian@jagfam.co.uk

JAGGS-FOWLER, Robert Mark. b 60. Charing Cross Hosp Medical Sch MB, BS 85 De Montfort Univ LLM 11 St Jo Coll Dur MA 16 FRCGP 09 FRSA 13. Linc Sch of Th and Min 15. **d** 19. NSM Barton upon Humber *Linc* from 19; NSM S Ferriby from 19; NSM Horkstow from 19; NSM Saxby All Saints from 19. *The Retreat, 6 Park View, Barton-upon-Humber DN18 6AX*　T: (01652) 633727　M: 07538-988944 E: bartoncurate@theretreat-barton.com

JAGO, Christine May. b 52. Ex Univ BA 01 SRN 73. SWMTC 92. **d** 94 **p** 95. OLM St Buryan, St Levan and Sennen *Truro* 94–11; rtd 11; PtO *Truro* from 14. *Boscarne House, St Buryan, Penzance TR19 6HR*　T: (01736) 810374 E: christinejago331@btinternet.com

JAGO, David. b 48. Shoreditch Coll Lon CertEd 69 Birm Univ BPhil 77. St Steph Ho Ox 95. **d** 97 **p** 98. C S Bank *York* 97–00; V Middlesbrough St Martin w St Cuth 00–05; V Kingston upon Hull St Alb 05–17; rtd 17; PtO *Carl* from 18. *10 Albert Court, Brook Street, Penrith CA11 7XH*　T: (01768) 862674

JAKEMAN, Francis David. b 47. Leeds Univ BSc 69. Cuddesdon Coll 71. **d** 74 **p** 75. C Gt Grimsby St Mary and St Jas *Linc* 74–77; Ind Chapl *Lon* 77–88; V Harrow Weald All SS 88–03; V Bexleyheath Ch Ch *Roch* 03–13; AD Erith 04–09; rtd 13; PtO *Ox* from 14. *50 Eastern Avenue, Reading RG1 5SE*　T: 0118-327 3326　M: 07899-922883 E: francis.jakeman@gmail.com

JALLAND, Hilary Gervase Alexander. b 50. Ex Univ BA 72. Coll of Resurr Mirfield 74. **d** 76 **p** 77. C Ex St Thos 76–80; C Portsea St Mary *Portsm* 80–86; V Hampton and Pudding Norton *Nor* 86–90; TV Hawarden *St As* 90–93; R Llandysilio and Penrhos and Llandrinio etc 93–03; V Towyn and St George 03–06; rtd 06; PtO *B & W* from 15; *Sarum* from 15. *Flat 7, Sexeys Hospital, Bruton BA10 0AS*　T: (01749) 813700　M: 07814-132259 E: hgaj@jalland1504.plus.com

JAMES, Andrew Nicholas. b 54. BSc 76. Trin Coll Bris 77. **d** 80 **p** 81. C Prescot *Liv* 80–83; C Upholland 83–85; V Hindley Green 85–91; V Dean Forest H Trin *Glouc* 91–06; RD Forest S 97–03; P-in-c Hardwicke and Elmore w Longney 06–09; V 09–19; rtd 19. *Address temp unknown*

JAMES, Andrew Peter. b 69. Glam Univ BSc 96 Univ of Wales (Cardiff) BTh 99. St Mich Coll Llan 96. **d** 99 **p** 00. C Roath *Llan* 99–01; C Radyr 01–06; TV Whitchurch 06–14; P-in-c St Andrews Major w Michaelston-le-Pit from 14; AD Penarth and Barry from 16. *The Rectory, Lettons Way, Dinas Powys CF64 4BY*　T: (029) 2051 2555 E: andrewjames@churchinwales.org.uk

JAMES, Anne Loraine. b 45. St Jo Coll Nottm. **d** 90 **p** 94. NSM Ellon and Cruden Bay *Ab* 90–99; NSM Alford 99–02; P-in-c 02–17; rtd 17. *9 Stewart Place, Alford AB33 8UH*　T: (01975) 564151 E: revanne.alford@outlook.com

JAMES, Barry Paul. b 49. BSc. Sarum & Wells Th Coll. **d** 82 **p** 83. C Bitterne Park *Win* 82–86; V Southampton St Mary Extra 86–00; R Fawley 00–14; rtd 14; PtO *Win* from 14. *7 Cleveland Drive, Dibden Purlieu, Southampton SO45 5QR*　T: (023) 8087 9872

JAMES, Brunel Hugh Grayburn. b 70. Selw Coll Cam BA 93 MA 97 Leeds Univ MA 02. Wycliffe Hall Ox BA 97. **d** 98 **p** 99. C Thornbury *Bradf* 98–02; R Barwick in Elmet *Ripon* 02–08; Abp's Dom Chapl *York* 08–10; P-in-c Cleckheaton

St Luke and Whitechapel *Wakef* 10–13; P-in-c Cleckheaton St Jo 10–13; V Cleckheaton *Leeds* from 13; PtO *York* from 15. *Wayside, Eldon Place, Cleckheaton BD19 5DH* T: (01274) 873471 M: 07811-195280

JAMES, Miss Carolyn Anne. b 65. Coll of Ripon & York St Jo BA 87 Nottm Univ BTh 91 Leeds Univ MA 03. Linc Th Coll 88. **d** 91 **p** 94. Par Dn Middleton St Mary *Ripon* 91–94; C Wetherby 94–97; V Kirkstall 97–05; Chapl and Sen Warden Bp Grosseteste Coll Linc 05–12; P-in-c Manston *Leeds* 12–16; V from 16. *Manston Vicarage, Church Lane, Leeds LS15 8JB* T: 0113-264 2685 E: carolyn.james117@btinternet.com

JAMES, Christyan Elliot. b 68. Westcott Ho Cam. **d** 09 **p** 10. C Maidstone St Martin *Cant* 09–11; rtd 11; Hon C Brighton Gd Shep Preston *Chich* 11–14; PtO from 16. *Wickham Cottage, 20 Deneside, East Dean, Eastbourne BN20 0JG* T: (01323) 423070 E: christyanj@yahoo.co.uk

JAMES, Colin Robert. b 39. Magd Coll Ox BA 61 MA 65 DipEd 62. SAOMC 93. **d** 96 **p** 97. NSM Wokingham All SS *Ox* 96–13; PtO from 13. *7 Sewell Avenue, Wokingham RG41 1NT* T: 0118-978 1515 E: colinjames@waitrose.com

JAMES, David. *See* JAMES, Richard David

✠**JAMES, The Rt Revd David Charles.** b 45. Ex Univ BSc 66 PhD 71. St Jo Coll Nottm BA 73. **d** 73 **p** 74 **c** 98. C Portswood Ch Ch *Win* 73–76; C Goring-by-Sea *Chich* 76–78; Chapl UEA *Nor* 78–82; V Ecclesfield *Sheff* 82–90; RD 87–90; V Portswood Ch Ch *Win* 90–98; Hon Can Win Cathl 98; Suff Bp Pontefract *Wakef* 98–02; Bp Bradf 02–10; rtd 10; Hon Asst Bp York from 10. *7 Long Lane, Beverley HU17 0NH* T: (01482) 871240 E: david@davidjames43.karoo.co.uk

JAMES, David Clive. b 40. Bris Univ BA 61 K Coll Lon DipEd 87. Lich Th Coll 62 St Steph Ho Ox 64. **d** 65 **p** 66. C Portslade St Nic *Chich* 65–68; C Haywards Heath St Wilfrid 68–71; Chapl Brighton Poly 71–75; PtO from 75. *The Old Stables, 5 De Warrenne Road, Lewes BN7 1BP* T: (01273) 471851 E: davidcjames@talktalk.net

JAMES, David Henry. b 45. Univ of Wales MB, BCh 68 Univ of Wales (Swansea) MA 92 MRCPsych 75. SWMTC 95. **d** 98. NSM Truro Cathl 98–00; rtd 00; PtO *Truro* 00–03; *Sarum* 03–05; LtO *Arg* from 06. *Glencruitten House, Glencruitten, Oban PA34 4QB* T: (01631) 562431 E: david.james.855@btinternet.com

JAMES, Preb David Howard. b 47. Ex Univ BA 70 MA 73 Pemb Coll Cam CertEd 72. Linc Th Coll 81. **d** 83 **p** 84. C Tavistock and Gulworthy *Ex* 83–86; C E Teignmouth 86–88; C W Teignmouth 86–88; P-in-c Bishopsteignton 88–89; P-in-c Ideford, Luton and Ashcombe 88–89; TV Teignmouth, Ideford w Luton, Ashcombe etc 90–95; P-in-c Sidmouth, Woolbrook, Salcombe Regis, Sidbury etc 95–97; TR 97–13; Preb Ex Cathl 99–13; RD Ottery 03–13; rtd 13; PtO *Ex* from 13. *1 Farm Close, Exeter EX2 5PJ* T: (01392) 424690 E: rev.davidjames@btinternet.com

JAMES, Glyn. *See* JAMES, Henry Glyn

JAMES, Canon Godfrey Walter. b 36. Univ of Wales (Lamp) BA 58 Univ of Wales (Cardiff) MA 60 St Pet Coll Ox DipEd 61 BA 63 MA 67. St Mich Coll Llan 63. **d** 64 **p** 65. C Canton St Jo *Llan* 64–71; V Dinas and Penygraig w Williamstown 71–85; V Kenfig Hill 85–01; Hon Can Llan Cathl 96–01; rtd 01; PtO *Llan* from 04. *Albert Edward Prince of Wales Court, Penylan Avenue, Porthcawl CF36 3LY*

✠**JAMES, The Rt Revd Graham Richard.** b 51. Lanc Univ BA 72 Hon FGCM 92. Cuddesdon Coll 72. **d** 75 **p** 76 **c** 93. C Pet Ch Carpenter 75–79; C Digswell St Alb 79–82; TV Digswell and Panshanger 82–83; Sen Selection Sec and Sec Cand Cttee ACCM 83–87; Abp's Chapl *Cant* 87–93; Hon Can Dallas from 89; Suff Bp St Germans *Truro* 93–99; Bp Nor 99–19; rtd 19. *Address temp unknown*

JAMES, Helen Alice. *See* JONES, Helen Alison

JAMES, Henley George. b 31. Sarum & Wells Th Coll 79. **d** 81 **p** 82. C Tottenham H Trin *Lon* 81–85; C Cricklewood St Pet 85–88; P-in-c 88–89; V Bearwood *Birm* 89–97; rtd 97; PtO *Birm* from 97. *32 Antrobus Road, Birmingham B21 9NZ* E: henleyjames12000@yahoo.com

JAMES, Henry Glyn. b 26. Keble Coll Ox BA 50 MA 58 Toronto Univ MEd 74. Wycliffe Hall Ox 50. **d** 52 **p** 53. C Edgbaston St Aug *Birm* 52–54; C Surbiton St Matt *S'wark* 54–57; Housemaster Kingham Hill Sch Oxon 57–62; Chapl St Lawr Coll Ramsgate 62–68; Canada 68–73; Hon C Kidmore End *Ox* 74–77; K Jas Coll of Henley 74–87; Hon C Remenham *Ox* 77–88; Chapl The Henley Coll 87–88; Chapl Toulouse *Eur* 88–91; rtd 91; PtO *Win* from 93. *13 Harbour Road, Bournemouth BH6 4DD* T: (01202) 427697 E: glyn.james55@gmail.com

JAMES, Prof Ian Nigel. b 48. Leeds Univ BSc 69 Man Univ PhD 74. SAOMC 99. **d** 02 **p** 03. NSM Bracknell *Ox* 02–04; NSM Winkfield and Cranbourne 04–10; P-in-c

Bootle, Corney, Whicham and Whitbeck *Carl* 10–15; rtd 15; PtO *Carl* from 15. *High Pasture, Crook Road, Kendal LA8 8LY* M: 07808-207422 E: dr.i.n.james@btinternet.com

JAMES, Jane Eva. b 55. Birm Univ BSc 76 W Midl Coll of Educn PGCE 77. St Mich Coll Llan 08. **d** 11 **p** 12. NSM Llansantffraid-ym-Mechain and Llanfechain *St As* 11–13; P-in-c Meifod w Llangynyw w Pont Robert w Pont Dolanog 13–16; I Caereinion Miss Area from 17. *The Vicarage, Meifod SY22 6DH* T: (01938) 500231 M: 07748-697112 E: janevicaragemeifod@btinternet.com

JAMES, Jeffrey Aneurin. b 53. Univ of Wales (Cardiff) BScEcon 80 Bris Univ MSc 85 MHSM 83. WEMTC 98. **d** 01 **p** 02. NSM Minchinhampton *Glouc* 01–07; NSM Painswick, Sheepscombe, Cranham, The Edge etc 07–13; NSM Mylor w Flushing *Truro* from 13. *17 Olivey Place, Bells Hill, Mylor Bridge, Falmouth TR11 5RX* T: (01326) 374408 E: jayscott@dsl.pipex.com

JAMES, Canon Jeremy Richard. b 52. Jes Coll Cam BA 73 MA 77 York Univ CertEd 77. Cranmer Hall Dur 86. **d** 88 **p** 89. C Broxbourne w Wormley *St Alb* 88–91; C Hailsham *Chich* 91–99; V Wadhurst 99–18; V Tidebrook 99–18; P-in-c Stonegate 99–18; RD Rotherfield 03–14; Can and Preb Chich Cathl 12–18; rtd 18; PtO *Ely* from 18. *6 Downham Road, Ely CB6 1AH* E: jeremy@jrjames.me

JAMES, Mrs Joanna Elizabeth. b 72. SAOMC. **d** 06 **p** 07. C Northwood Em *Lon* 06–10; C S Mimms Ch 10–18; V Hendon St Paul Mill Hill from 18. *St Paul's Vicarage, Hammers Lane, London NW7 4EA* T: (020) 8906 3793 E: revjoannajames@btinternet.com

JAMES, John Charles. b 35. Keble Coll Ox BA 59. Linc Th Coll 68. **d** 70 **p** 71. C S Shields St Hilda w St Thos *Dur* 70–77; P-in-c Jarrow Docks 77–78; Adn Seychelles 78–92; V Mylor w Flushing *Truro* 92–05; rtd 06; PtO *Dur* from 11. *172 Westoe Road, South Shields NE33 3PH*

JAMES, Mrs Julie Margaret. b 55. Shenstone Coll of Educn TCert 76 BEd 77. Qu Coll Birm 01. **d** 04 **p** 05. NSM Salwarpe and Hindlip w Martin Hussingtree *Worc* 04–06; NSM St Jo in Bedwardine 06–09; NSM Abberton, The Flyfords, Naunton Beauchamp etc 09–14; R Berrow w Pendock, Eldersfield, Hollybush etc from 14. *Thistledown, Pendock, Gloucester GL19 3PW* T: (01531) 650563 M: 07751-465241 E: julie.m.james@btinternet.com

JAMES, Keith Edwin Arthur. b 38. Sarum & Wells Th Coll 85. **d** 87 **p** 88. C Hempnall *Nor* 87–91; R Roughton and Felbrigg, Metton, Sustead etc 91–98; V Ascension Is 98–01; rtd 02; Chapl Laslett's *Worc* 02–04; PtO *Nor* from 05. *30 Woodland Rise, Tasburgh, Norwich NR15 1NF* T: (01508) 470032 E: keith.james2011@btinternet.com

JAMES, Canon Keith Nicholas. b 69. Leeds Univ BA 91 Univ of Wales (Lamp) MA 06. St Jo Coll Nottm MA 93. **d** 93 **p** 94. C Crosby *Linc* 93–96; P-in-c Cherry Willingham w Greetwell 96–00; R S Lawres Gp 00–03; RD Lawres 01–03; R Ribbesford w Bewdley *Worc* 03–11; R Ribbesford w Bewdley and Dowles and Wribbenhall 11–15; RD Kidderminster 07–13; Can Res Nor Cathl from 15; CMD Officer from 15. *25 The Close, Norwich NR1 4DZ* T: (01603) 882339 E: keith.james@dioceseofnorwich.org

JAMES, Malcolm. b 37. CEng MICE MIStructE. NOC 80. **d** 83 **p** 84. NSM Ripponden *Wakef* 83–10; PtO 10–14; *Leeds* from 14. *Lower Stones, Bar Lane, Rishworth, Sowerby Bridge HX6 4EY* T: (01274) 677439 E: malcolm@mjconsultancy.demon.co.uk

JAMES, Manon Ceridwen. b 69. Poly of Wales BA 90 Selw Coll Cam BA 93 MA 97 Birm Univ PhD 15. Ridley Hall Cam. **d** 94 **p** 97. C Llandudno *Ban* 94–98; P-in-c Glanogwen w St Ann's w Llanllechid 98–99; V 99–05; V Pentir 04–05; Dir of Ords 02–05; C Llanrhos *St As* 05–07; Dioc Dir Lifelong Learning 05–08; R Llanddulas and Llysfaen 08–16; Bp's Adv for Min 12–13; Dir Min 14–18; LtO 15–18; Hon Can St As Cathl 17–18; Dir Formation for Lic Min St Padarn's Inst from 18. *St Padarn's Institute, 54 Cardiff Road, Llandaff, Cardiff CF5 2YJ* T: (029) 2056 3379 M: 07776-591799 E: manoncjames@churchinwales.org.uk

JAMES, Mark Nicholas. b 55. Jes Coll Ox BA 77 MA 80 PGCE 79. Ridley Hall Cam 03. **d** 05 **p** 06. C Gt Dunmow and Barnston *Chelmsf* 05–09; R Bentley Common, Kelvedon Hatch and Navestock 09–19; P-in-c Doddinghurst 14–19; rtd 19. *11 Keith Way, Southend-on-Sea SS2 6SG* E: revmarkjames@btinternet.com

JAMES, Martin. b 40. ACII. **d** 94 **p** 95. OLM N Farnborough *Guildf* 94–08; OLM Camberley St Martin Old Dean 08–09; NSM 09–10; rtd 10; PtO *Guildf* from 10. *43 Ashley Road, Farnborough GU14 7HB* T: (01252) 544698 E: martinjean.james@ntlworld.com

JAMES, Michael Howard. b 55. Bris Univ LLB 73 Solicitor 92. WEMTC 04. **d** 06 **p** 07. NSM Clifton H Trin, St Andr and

St Pet *Bris* 06–08; NSM Westbury Park LEP 08–15; Chapl Partis Coll Bath 15–19; PtO *Bris* from 15; rtd 19. *10 Hill Drive, Failand, Bristol BS8 3UX* T: (01275) 393729

JAMES, Canon Peter David. b 42. Keble Coll Ox BA 63 Lon Univ BD 67. Tyndale Hall Bris 64. **d** 67 **p** 68. C Haydock St Mark *Liv* 67–69; C Ashton-in-Makerfield St Thos 69–74; V Whiston 74–80; V Harlech and Llanfair-juxta-Harlech etc *Ban* 80–94; R Botwnnog w Bryncroes 94–99; V Botwnnog w Bryncroes w Llangwnnadl w Penllech 99–07; Hon Can Ban Cathl 02–07; rtd 07. *Tabor, Llithfaen, Pwllheli LL53 6NL* T: (01758) 750202 E: peter@llithfaen.org.uk

JAMES, Richard Andrew. b 44. Mert Coll Ox BA 67 MA 70. Tyndale Hall Bris. **d** 70 **p** 71. C Bebington *Ches* 70–73; C Histon *Ely* 73–77; Chapl Guildf Coll of Tech 77–80; C Guildf St Sav w Stoke-next-Guildford 77–80; Ecum Chapl Bedf Coll of HE *St Alb* 81–83; TV Ipsley *Worc* 84–89; R Mulbarton w Kenningham *Nor* 89–92; rtd 93. *5 Links Way, Harrogate HG2 7EW* T: (01423) 889410 E: e4jameses@icloud.com

JAMES, Richard David. b 45. Cheltenham & Glouc Coll of HE MA 97. Lon Coll of Div 66. **d** 70 **p** 71. C Boultham *Linc* 70–74; C New Waltham 74–77; TV Cleethorpes 77–87; TR E Bris 87–99; Partnership P E Bris 99–15; V E Bris St Ambrose and St Leon 99–15; rtd 15; PtO *Bris* from 16. *87 Victoria Park, Kingswood, Bristol BS15 1RZ* T: 0117-329 3528 M: 07824-888427 E: rd.james@live.co.uk

JAMES, Richard David. b 65. Clare Coll Cam MA 88 Lon Hosp MB, BChir 90. Ridley Hall Cam 92. **d** 95 **p** 96. C Clifton Ch Ch w Em *Bris* 95–98; C Enfield Ch Ch Trent Park *Lon* 98–00; V 00–17; AD Enfield 09–16; R Heigham H Trin *Nor* from 17. *The Rectory, 17 Essex Street, Norwich NR2 2BL* T: (01603) 622225

JAMES, Richard Lindsay. b 39. Kelham Th Coll 61. **d** 66 **p** 67. C Seacroft *Ripon* 66–74; rtd 04. *3 Cavendish Mews, Hove BN3 1AZ* T: (01273) 324672 E: rljames@supanet.com

JAMES, Robert William. b 79. Kent Univ BA 01 SOAS Lon MA 02 PhD 10 CCC Cam MPhil 03 St Andr Univ MLitt 13 Nottm Univ MA 17. Westcott Ho Cam 02. **d** 05 **p** 06. C St Edm Way and Bradfield St Clare, Bradfield St George etc *St E* 05–07; PtO *Glouc* 12–13; NSM Coleford, Staunton, Newland, Redbrook etc 13–14; V Newnham w Awre and Blakeney from 14. *The Vicarage, 1 Whetstones, Unlawater Lane, Newnham GL14 1BT* T: (01594) 516671 E: robdogcollar@yahoo.co.uk

JAMES, Roger Michael. b 44. K Coll Lon BD 66 AKC 66. **d** 69 **p** 70. C Frindsbury w Upnor *Roch* 69–72; LtO *St Alb* 73–78; C Digswell 78–81; R Knebworth 81–92; P-in-c Upper Tean and Local Min Adv (Stafford) *Lich* 92–99; Dir Cottesloe Chr Tr Progr *Ox* 99–03; R Cusop w Blakemere, Bredwardine w Brobury etc *Heref* 03–09; RD Abbeydore 06–09; rtd 09. *Ty Siloh, Llandeilo'r Fan, Brecon LD3 8UD* T: (01874) 636126 E: tysiloh@googlemail.com

JAMES, Sandra Kay. See GARDNER, Sandra Kay

JAMES, Ms Sheridan Angharad. b 71. Univ of Wales (Abth) BA 93 PGCE 94 MPhil 00. SEITE 04. **d** 07 **p** 08. C Catford (Southend) and Downham *S'wark* 07–11; V Hatcham St Cath from 11; Dean of Women's Min Woolwich Area from 12. *St Catherine's Vicarage, 102A Pepys Road, London SE14 5SG* T: (020) 7639 1050 M: 07703-291594 E: revsheridanjames@gmail.com

JAMES, Canon Stephen Lynn. b 53. Oak Hill Th Coll BA 86. **d** 86 **p** 87. C Heigham H Trin *Nor* 86–89; C Vancouver St Jo Canada 89–93; R Bebington *Ches* 93–06; R Rusholme H Trin *Man* 06–19; Hon Can Man Cathl 18–19; rtd 19; PtO *Man* from 19. *81 Piper's Lane, Heswall, Wirral CH60 9HR*

JAMES, Canon Stephen Nicholas. b 51. Reading Univ MA 87 Bris Univ EdD 95 ARCM 72 LTCL 72 FTCL 73. SAOMC 01. **d** 04 **p** 05. NSM Hanney, Denchworth and E Challow Ox 04–07; P-in-c Goetre w Llanover Mon 07–13; Dioc Dir Educn 11–15; Bp's Chapl from 15; Hon Can St Woolos Cathl from 14. *Pear Tree Cottage, Llanfair Kilgeddin, Abergavenny NP7 9DY* T: (01873) 840229 E: sueandstephen1973@gmail.com

JAMES, Thomas Martin St John. b 85. St Jo Coll Cam MA 12. Westcott Ho Cam 09. **d** 12 **p** 13. C Petersfield *Portsm* 12–15; Chapl RN from 15. *72 Redmill Drive, Lee-on-the-Solent PO13 9JE* T: (023) 9262 5055 F: 9262 5134

JAMES, Canon Veronica Norma. b 59. STETS 99. **d** 02 **p** 03. NSM Ashton Keynes, Leigh and Minety *Bris* 02–05; R Merriott w Hinton, Dinnington and Lopen *B & W* 05–10; R The Guitings, Cutsdean, Farmcote etc *Glouc* 10–14; AD N Cotswold 10–14; Hon Can Glouc Cathl 12–14; R Skipton H Trin *Leeds* 14–19; Hon Can Ripon Cathl 19; rtd 19. *42 Back Lane, Settrington, Malton YO17 8NP* E: veronica.james690@gmail.com

JAMESON, Miss Beverley Joyce. b 60. St Jo Coll Nottm 09. **d** 11 **p** 12. C Cen Telford *Lich* 11–15; TV Droitwich Spa

Worc 15–17; C Salwarpe and Hindlip w Martin Hussingtree 15–17; Dean of Women's Min 16–17; R Lymm *Ches* from 17. *46 Rectory Lane, Lymm WA13 0AL* T: (01925) 757081 M: 07817-379583 E: bevjameson@live.co.uk

JAMESON, Canon Dermot Christopher Ledgard. b 27. TCD BA 49 MA 54. CITC 49. **d** 50 **p** 51. C Seagoe *D & D* 50–53; C Holywood 53–57; I Kilkeel 57–62; I Donaghcloney w Waringstown 62–79; Can Dromore Cathl 77–93; I Kilbroney 79–93; Treas Dromore Cathl 81–83; Prec Dromore Cathl 83–90; Chan Dromore Cathl 90–93; rtd 93. *Concord, 10B Kilbroney Road, Rostrevor, Newry BT34 3BH* T: (028) 4173 9728 E: jameson.dermot@gmail.com

JAMESON, Howard Kingsley. b 63. Warwick Univ BSc 84. Trin Coll Bris 99. **d** 02 **p** 03. C Wareham *Sarum* 02–05; P-in-c Monkton Farleigh, S Wraxall and Winsley 05–11; P-in-c Bradford-on-Avon Ch Ch 10–11; R N Bradford on Avon and Villages 11–12; P-in-c Patchway *Bris* from 12. *86 Oakleaze, Patchway, Bristol BS34 5AW* T: 0117-370 8279 E: revh.jameson@gmail.com

JAMIE, Mrs Katherine Elizabeth. b 81. Cranmer Hall Dur 12. **d** 15 **p** 16. C Easington and Easington Colliery *Dur* 15–18; V Heworth St Mary from 18. *Heworth Vicarage, High Heworth Lane, Gateshead NE10 0PB* M: 07792-159154 E: rev.katejamie@gmail.com

JAMIESON, Christopher Donald. b 50. Man Univ MEd 89 Westmr Coll Ox BEd 72. SNWTP. **d** 13 **p** 14. OLM Turton Moorland *Man* from 13. *25 Timberbottom, Bolton LB2 3DG* T: (01204) 302346 M: 07726-349195 E: roscanvel2@gmail.com

JAMIESON, Douglas. See JAMIESON, William Douglas

JAMIESON, Emma Victoria. See HIGGINS, Emma Victoria

JAMIESON, Guy Stuart. b 66. Leeds Univ BA 98. Ripon Coll Cuddesdon. **d** 00 **p** 01. C Woodhall *Bradf* 00–03; V Southowram and Claremount *Wakef* 03–14; Leeds 14–16; V Lt Marsden w Nelson St Mary and Nelson St Bede *Blackb* from 16; AD Pendle from 18. *St Paul's Vicarage, Bentley Street, Nelson BB9 0BS* T: (01282) 615888 M: 07983-678356 E: guyjamieson@btinternet.com

JAMIESON, Ian David. b 73. Leeds Univ BA 99 PGCE 00. St Jo Coll Nottm 11. **d** 13 **p** 14. C Em TM *Leeds* 13–17; P-in-c Bradley from 17; P-in-c Fixby and Cowcliffe from 17. *The Vicarage, 3 St Thomas Gardens, Bradley, Huddersfield HD2 1SL* T: (01484) 427838 M: 07594-552519 E: revianjamieson@gmail.com

JAMIESON, Kenneth Euan Oram. b 24. Roch Th Coll 60. **d** 62 **p** 63. C Bromley SS Pet and Paul *Roch* 62–66; R Colchester St Mary Magd *Chelmsf* 66–71; V Bexleyheath St Pet *Roch* 71–78; P-in-c Maidstone St Faith *Cant* 78–83; P-in-c Maidstone St Paul 78–83; Ind Chapl *St Alb* 83–89; rtd 89; PtO *B & W* 89–19. *4 Ashley Road, Taunton TA1 5BP* T: (01823) 289367 E: ken@keoj4.plus.com or kenjy@uwclub.net

JAMIESON, Canon Marilyn. b 52. Cranmer Hall Dur IDC 80. **d** 91 **p** 94. Par Dn Bensham *Dur* 91–93; Par Dn Ryton w Hedgefield 93–94; Chapl Metro Cen Gateshead 94–02 and from 06; Bp's Sen Chapl 02–05; Hon C Ryton 05–06; Hon Can Dur Cathl from 97; PtO *Newc* from 06. *2 Westburn Cottages, Ryton NE40 4EY* T: 0191-493 0259

JAMIESON, Mrs Moira Elizabeth. b 50. **d** 08 **p** 09. C Lenzie *Glas* 08–13; P-in-c Cumbernauld 13–19; rtd 19. *3 Cawder Place, Cumbernauld, Glasgow G68 0BG* T: (01236) 597633 M: 07977-096446 E: jamiemoi60@sky.com

JAMIESON, Peter Grant. b 64. Liv Univ BA 87. Coll of Resurr Mirfield 90. **d** 93 **p** 94. C Charlton Kings St Mary *Glouc* 93–96. *56 East Street, Thame OX9 3JS* M: 07779-148898 E: peterjamieson2@gmail.com

JAMIESON, Miss Rosalind Heather. b 49. CertEd 71. Cranmer Hall Dur 79. **dss** 81 **d** 87 **p** 94. Queensbury All SS *Lon* 81–85; Richmond H Trin and Ch Ch *S'wark* 85–87; Par Dn 87–91; Par Dn Burmantofts St Steph and St Agnes *Ripon* 91–94; C 94–99; TV Seacroft 99–14; *Leeds* 14; rtd 14; PtO *Leeds* from 17; Man from 18. *7 Alford Close, Bolton BL2 6NR* E: heather.jameson2@gmail.com

JAMIESON, Thomas Lindsay. b 53. N Lon Poly BSc 74. Cranmer Hall Dur. **d** 77 **p** 78. C Gateshead Fell *Dur* 77–80; C Gateshead 80–84; TV 84–90; P-in-c Gateshead St Cuth w St Paul 90–91; TV Bensham 91–93; P-in-c Ryton w Hedgefield 93–95; R 95–05; R Ryton 05–17; AD Gateshead W 94–98; rtd 17; P-in-c Ryton *Dur* 17–19. *2 Westburn Cottages, Ryton NE40 4EY* E: tomjbees@outlook.com

JAMIESON, William Douglas. b 38. Oak Hill Th Coll 63. **d** 66 **p** 67. C Shrewsbury St Julian *Lich* 66–68; C Bucknall and Bagnall 68–70; C Otley *Bradf* 70–74; TV Keighley 74–81; V Utley 81–00; rtd 00; PtO *Ches* from 00. *11 The Quay, Frodsham, Warrington WA6 7JG* T: (01928) 731085 M: 07974-947838 E: douglasjamieson@tiscali.co.uk or wdouglasjamieson@gmail.com

JAMISON, William Mervyn Noel. b 66. CITC 03. **d** 07 **p** 08. NSM Ballybeen *D & D* 07–10; NSM Comber 10–15; P-in-c Belvoir 15–17; P-in-c Drumbo from 17. *1 Old Ballygowan Road, Comber, Newtownards BT23 5NP* T: (028) 9187 1881 M: 07808-481669 E: rev.merv@me.com

JANES, Austin Steven. b 75. York Univ BA 97. Ripon Coll Cuddesdon 06. **d** 08 **p** 09. C Crewe St Andr w St Jo *Ches* 08–11; Min Can St Alb Abbey 11–14; TV Hemel Hempstead from 14. *33 Craigavon Road, Hemel Hempstead HP2 6BA* E: revaustin@sky.com

JANES, David Edward. b 40. Lon Univ BSc 67. Glouc Sch of Min 86. **d** 89 **p** 90. NSM Church Stretton *Heref* 89–00; rtd 00; PtO *Heref* from 00. *Bourton Westwood Farm, 3 Bourton Westwood, Much Wenlock TF13 6QB* T: (01952) 727393

JANICKER, Laurence Norman. b 47. SS Mark & Jo Coll Chelsea DipEd 69. St Jo Coll Nottm 83. **d** 85 **p** 86. C Beverley Minster *York* 85–89; R Lockington and Lund and Scorborough w Leconfield 89–94; V Cov St Geo 94–08; rtd 08; PtO *Nor* from 09. *136 Manor Road, Newton St Faith, Norwich NR10 3LG* T: (01603) 898614 E: winnieaurens@gmail.com

JANSSON, The Very Revd Maria Patricia. b 55. Milltown Inst Dub MRelSc 92. CITC 00. **d** 01 **p** 02. C Galway w Kilcummin *T, K & A* 01–02; C Wexford w Ardcolm and Killurin *C & O* 02–04; I 04–09; C Kilscoran w Killinick and Mulrankin 02–04; P-in-c 04–09; I Wexford and Kilscoran Union 10–11; Dean Waterford from 11; I Waterford w Killea, Drumcannon and Dunhill from 11; Preb Ossory Cathl from 12. *The Deanery, 41 Grange Park Road, Waterford, Republic of Ireland* T: (00353) (51) 874119 or (51) 858958 M: 87-225 5793 E: miajansson@eircom.net or dean@waterford.anglican.org

JANVIER, Philip Harold. b 57. Trin Coll Bris BA 87. **d** 87 **p** 88. C Much Woolton *Liv* 87–90; TV Toxteth St Philemon w St Gabr and St Cleopas 90–99; TR Gateacre from 97. *St Stephen's Rectory, Belle Vale Road, Liverpool L25 2PQ* T/F: 0151-487 9338 E: philjanvier@btinternet.com

JAQUET, Didier Francis. b 76. K Coll Lon LLB 97. ERMC 06. **d** 11 **p** 12. NSM Tring *St Alb* from 11. *Address withheld by request* T: (01525) 240465 M: 07420-656955 E: didier@tringteamparish.org.uk

JAQUISS, Mrs Gabrielle Clair. b 56. Clare Coll Cam BA 79 MA 85 LRAM 76. NOC 06. **d** 08 **p** 09. NSM Bowdon *Ches* 08–11; NSM Hale Barns w Ringway 11–16; V from 16; RD Bowdon from 17. *Ingersley, Belgrave Road, Bowdon, Altrincham WA14 2NZ* T: 0161-928 0717 M: 07843-375494 E: clairjq@aol.com

JARAM, Peter Ellis. b 45. Lon Univ BSc 70 CEng 77 MIET 77 MBIM 88. Linc Th Coll 94. **d** 94 **p** 95. C Bridlington Priory *York* 94–96; C Rufforth w Moor Monkton and Hessay 96–97; C Healaugh w Wighill, Bilbrough and Askham Richard 96–97; P-in-c 97–01; Chapl Askham Bryan Coll 97–01; V Brompton by Sawdon w Hutton Buscel, Snainton etc *York* 01–05; rtd 05; PtO *York* from 05. *74 Eastgate, Pickering YO18 7DY* T: (01751) 477831 E: pwj74@btinternet.com

JARDINE, Canon Anthony. b 38. Qu Coll Birm 64. **d** 67 **p** 68. C Baldock w Bygrave and Clothall *St Alb* 67–71; C N Stoneham *Win* 71–73; P-in-c Ecchinswell cum Sydmonton 73–79; P-in-c Burghclere w Newtown 78–79; R Burghclere w Newtown and Ecchinswell w Sydmonton 79–87; R Wonston and Stoke Charity w Hunton 87–97; P-in-c Chawton and Farringdon 97–04; Dioc Rural Officer 97–04; Hon Can Win Cathl 99–04; rtd 04; Hon C Knight's Enham and Smannell w Enham Alamein *Win* 04–08; PtO *Heref* from 09. *9 Park Green, Kington HR5 3AP*

JARDINE, Canon David John (Brother David). b 42. QUB BA 65. CITC 67. **d** 67 **p** 68. C Ballymacarrett St Patr *D & D* 67–70; Asst Chapl QUB 70–73; SSF from 73; Asst Chapl HM Pris Belfast 75–79; Chapl 79–85; USA 85–88; Sen Asst Warden Ch of Ireland Min of Healing 88–92; Dir Divine Healing Min 92–08; Can Belf Cathl from 07. *3 Richmond Park, Stranmillis, Belfast BT9 5EF* T: (028) 9066 6200 or 9031 1532 E: divinehealing@live.co.uk or davidjjardine@gmail.com

JARDINE, Canon Norman. b 47. QUB BSc 72. Trin Coll Bris 74. **d** 76 **p** 77. C Magheralin *D & D* 76–78; C Dundonald 78–80; Bp's C Ballybeen 80–88; I Willowfield 88–00; Dir Think Again 00–04; I Ballynafeigh St Jude 04–16; Can Belf Cathl 03–16; rtd 16. *273 Orby Drive, Belfast BT5 6BG* T: (028) 9050 0012 E: norman.jardine2@ntlworld.com

JARDINE, Thomas Andrew. b 44. Oak Hill Th Coll BA 87. **d** 87 **p** 88. C Crowborough *Chich* 87–91; R Dersingham w Anmer and Shernborne *Nor* 91–00; P-in-c Southport SS Simon and Jude *Liv* 00–03; V Southport SS Simon and Jude w All So 03–09; C Southport All SS 03–09; rtd 09; PtO *Win* 10–19. *16 Donnelly Road, Bournemouth BH6 5NW* E: tomandannjardine@googlemail.com

JARMAN, Christopher (Kit). b 38. QUB BA 63. Wells Th Coll 69. **d** 71 **p** 72. C Leckhampton SS Phil and Jas *Glouc* 71–73; Chapl RN 73–93; Chapl Rossall Sch Fleetwood 94; R Stirling *St And* 94–03; Chapl ATC 97–03; rtd 03; LtO *Arg* 04–17. *Ground Floor Flat 2, 4 Branksome Park, Longsdale Road, Oban PA34 5JZ* T/F: (01631) 563535

JARMAN, Michael Robert. b 48. Trin Coll Bris 07. **d** 09 **p** 10. NSM Caerleon and Llanfrechfa *Mon* 09–12; P-in-c Newport Ch Ch 12–18; rtd 18; Chapl Madeira *Eur* from 19. *rua do Quebra Costas 18, 9000-034 Funchal, Portugal* T: (00351) (291) 220674 E: jarmanmichael48@gmail.com or htcchaplain@gmail.com

JARRATT, David. b 70. Herts Univ BSc 92 Univ of N Lon PhD 97 UEA PGCE 97. Ox Min Course 10. **d** 12 **p** 13. C Felpham *Chich* 12–16; R Lavant from 16; RD Chich from 19. *The Rectory, Pook Lane, East Lavant, Chichester PO18 0AH* T: (01243) 527313 M: 07911-132417 E: david.jarratt@btinternet.com or rector@lavantchurches.net

JARRATT, Canon Robert Michael. b 39. K Coll Lon BD 62 AKC 62 NY Th Sem DMin 85. **d** 63 **p** 64. C Corby St Columba *Pet* 63–67; Lay Tr Officer *Sheff* 67–71; Ind Chapl S'wark 72–80; P-in-c Betchworth 76–80; V Ranmoor *Sheff* 80–01; P-in-c Worsbrough and Dir Post-Ord Tr 01–05; RD Hallam 87–94; Hon Can Sheff Cathl 95–05; rtd 05; PtO *Sheff* from 05. *69 Barley House, 211 Ecclesall Road, Sheffield S11 8HR* T: 0114-273 7545 M: 07805-017426

JARRATT, Stephen. b 51. Edin Univ BD 76 St Kath Coll Liv CertEd 77. **d** 78 **p** 79. C Horsforth *Ripon* 78–81; C Stanningley St Thos 81–84; P-in-c Fishponds St Jo *Bris* 84–85; V 85–92; V Chapel Allerton *Ripon* 92–04; AD Allerton 97–04; TR Clifton *S'well* 04–08; AD W Bingham 07–08; P-in-c Haxby and Wigginton *York* 08–09; R 09–13; rtd 13; PtO *York* from 14. *The Lighthouse, 18 Longbridge Drive, Easingwold, York YO61 3FH* T: (01347) 823047 E: jarratt312@btinternet.com

✠**JARRETT, The Rt Revd Martyn William.** b 44. K Coll Lon BD 67 AKC 67 Hull Univ MPhil 91. **d** 68 **p** 69 **c** 94. C Bris St Geo 68–70; C Swindon New Town 70–74; C Northolt St Mary *Lon* 74–76; V Northolt St Jos 76–81; V Hillingdon St Andr 81–83; P-in-c Uxbridge Moor 82–83; V Uxbridge St Andr w St Jo 83–85; Selection Sec ACCM 85–88; Sen Selection Sec 89–91; V Chesterfield St Mary and All SS *Derby* 91–94; Suff Bp Burnley *Blackb* 94–00; Hon Can Blackb Cathl 94–00; Suff Bp Beverley (PEV) *York* 00–12; Hon Asst Bp S'well and Nottm from 01; Hon Asst Bp Dur, Ripon and Sheff 00–12; Man and Wakef 01–12; Bradf 02–12; Liv 03-12; Newc 10–12; Hon Can Wakef Cathl 01–10; rtd 12. *91 Beaumont Rise, Worksop S80 1YG* T: (01909) 477847 E: martyn.jarrett@yahoo.co.uk

JARRETT, René Isaac Taiwo. b 49. Milton Margai Teachers' Coll Sierra Leone TCert 79 Lon Inst of Educn BEd 94. Sierra Leone Th Hall 80. **d** 83 **p** 85. Dn Freetown St Luke Sierra Leone 83–85; C Freetown Bp Elwin Memorial Ch 85–89; Hon C St Pancras w St Jas and Ch Ch *Lon* 89–95; C Bloomsbury St Geo w Woburn Square Ch 95–11; rtd 11; PtO *Lon* from 11; *S'wark* from 13. *2 Woburn Mansions, Torrington Place, London WC1E 7HL* T: (020) 7580 5165 M: 07853-348143 E: jarrorene@yahoo.co.uk

JARROW, Suffragan Bishop of. *See* CLARK, The Rt Revd Sarah Elizabeth

JARVIS, Benjamin Joseph Francis. b 86. Coll of Resurr Mirfield BA 19. **d** 19. C Monkseaton St Mary *Newc* from 19. *2 Seacombe Avenue, North Shields NE30 3DR* M: 07972-717783 E: revd.bjarvis@gmail.com

JARVIS, Ian Frederick Rodger. b 38. Bris Univ BA 60. Tyndale Hall Bris 61. **d** 63 **p** 64. C Chepp Ch Ch w H Trin *Roch* 63–67; C Bilston St Leon *Lich* 67–71; V Lozells St Silas *Birm* 71–76; V Chaddesden St Mary *Derby* 76–95; V Newhall 95–02; rtd 02; PtO *Derby* from 02. *29 Springfield Road, Midway, Swadlincote DE11 0BZ* T: (01283) 551589 E: ianandirenejarvis@btinternet.com

JARVIS, Canon Nathan John. b 73. Ox Brookes Univ BA 97 Leeds Univ MA 04. St Steph Ho Ox BTh 06. **d** 06 **p** 07. C Hartlepool H Trin *Dur* 06–09; V Kingstanding St Luke *Birm* 09–12; TV Blenheim *Ox* 12–17; Chapl Lic Victuallers' Sch Ascot from 16; Chapl Ban Univ from 18; Hon Can Ban Cathl from 18. *Bangor University, College Road, Bangor LL57 2DG* T: (01248) 351151 E: fr.nathan@yahoo.com

JARVIS, Mrs Pamela Ann. b 51. Sussex Univ BEd 74. SWMTC 97. **d** 00 **p** 01. C Braunton *Ex* 00–03; C Combe Martin, Berrynarbor, Lynton, Brendon etc 03–04; TV 04–10; rtd 10. *Crocnamac, Tomouth Road, Appledore, Bideford EX39 1QD* T: (01237) 420454 M: 07773-900523 E: revpajarvis@btinternet.com

JARVIS, Stephen John. b 55. WEMTC 04. **d** 07 **p** 08. NSM Bisley, Chalford, France Lynch, and Oakridge etc *Glouc* 07–18; NSM Nailsworth w Shortwood, Horsley etc from 18.

8 Ollney Road, Minchinhampton, Stroud GL6 9BX T: (01453) 884545 M: 07975-565156 E: stephenjarvis88@talktalk.net

JARVIS, Steven Roy. b 73. NE Wales Inst of HE BA 05. WEMTC 04. **d** 07 **p** 08. NSM Ludlow *Heref* 07–10; Dioc Youth Officer *Glouc* 10–13; TV White Horse *Sarum* 13–17; C Stratford-upon-Avon, Luddington etc *Cov* from 17. *3 Coopers Close, Stratford-upon-Avon CV37 0RS* M: 07879-442751 E: steve.the.vicar@btinternet.com

JARY, Ms Helen Lesley. b 69. Lanc Univ BA 91. St Jo Coll Nottm 05. **d** 07 **p** 08. C Oulton Broad *Nor* 07–11; TV Thetford from 11. *Cloverfield Vicarage, 24 Foxglove Road, Thetford IP24 2XF* T: (01842) 755769 M: 07990-501683 E: helenjary@btinternet.com

JASPER, Canon David. b 51. Jes Coll Cam BA 72 MA 76 Keble Coll Ox BD 80 Dur Univ PhD 83 Ox Univ DD 02 Uppsala Univ Hon ThD 07 FRSE 06. St Steph Ho Ox BA 75 MA 79. **d** 76 **p** 77. C Buckingham *Ox* 76–79; C Dur St Oswald 80; Chapl Hatf Coll Dur 81–88; Dir Cen Study of Lit and Th Dur 88–91; Prin St Chad's Coll Dur 88–91; Reader and Dir Cen Study of Lit and Th Glas Univ from 91; Vice-Dean of Div 95–98; Dean of Div 98–02; LtO *Glas* 91–08; NSM Hamilton from 08; P-in-c Cambuslang 14–16; P-in-c Uddingston 14–16; Can Th St Mary's Cathl from 17. *Netherwood, 124 Old Manse Road, Wishaw ML2 0EP* T/F: (01698) 373286 E: david.jasper@glasgow.ac.uk

JASPER, David Julian McLean. b 44. Dur Univ BA 66. Linc Th Coll 66. **d** 68 **p** 69. C Redruth *Truro* 68–72; TV 72–75; V St Just in Penwith 75–86; P-in-c Sancreed 82–86; C Reading St Matt *Ox* 96–00; P-in-c 00–02; R S Petherton w The Seavingtons *B & W* 02–11; rtd 11; RD Trigg Major *Truro* 12–16; PtO from 14. *39 Fore Street, Plympton, Plymouth PL7 1LZ* T: (01752) 331536 M: 07767-814533 E: davidjasper5dy@btinternet.com

JAVELLE, Stéphane Jean Michel. b 71. Provence Univ BA 98. Ripon Coll Cuddesdon 15. **d** 17 **p** 18. C Salisbury Plain *Sarum* from 17. *11 The Limes, High Street, Shrewton, Salisbury SP3 4BW* T: (01980) 621318 M: 07740-775070 E: rev.stephane.javelle@eclipso.eu

JAY, Canon Colin. b 62. Keble Coll Ox BA 85 St Jo Coll Dur BA 89. Cranmer Hall Dur 87. **d** 90 **p** 91. C Bishopwearmouth St Gabr *Dur* 90–94; C Newton Aycliffe 94; TV 94–96; TV Gt Aycliffe 96–03; AD Sedgefield 99–03; Chapl Co Dur & Darlington Priority Services NHS Trust 03–06; Chapl Tees, Esk and Wear Valleys NHS Foundn Trust from 06; Hon Can Dur Cathl from 18. *The Chaplaincy, West Park Hospital, Edward Pease Way, Darlington DL2 2TS* T: (01325) 552045 E: colin.jay@tewv.nhs.uk *or* colin.jay@nhs.net

JAY, Mrs Sarah Clare. b 65. **d** 12 **p** 13. NSM Stranton *Dur* 12–15; NSM Blackwell All SS and Salutation from 15. *All Saints Church, Ravensdale Road, Darlington DL3 8DT* E: colsarjay@yahoo.co.uk

JAYNE, Martin Philip. b 49. Man Univ BA 71 MRTPI 73. Carl Dioc Tr Course 87. **d** 90 **p** 91. NSM Natland *Carl* from 90; Dioc Officer for NSM 04–08. *12 Longmeadow Lane, Natland, Kendal LA9 7QZ* T: (01539) 560942 E: martjay@btinternet.com

JEAL, David James. b 66. **d** 15 **p** 16. NSM Bris Lockleaze St Mary Magd w St Fran 15–16; C 16–19; Chapl RN from 19. *Royal Naval Chaplaincy Service, Mail Point 1-2, Leach Building, Whale Island, Portsmouth PO2 8BY* M: 07814-024321 E: davejeal@blueyonder.co.uk

JEANES, Gordon Paul. b 55. Ox Univ BA 79 MA 82 BD 90 Univ of Wales (Lamp) PhD 99. St Steph Ho Ox 80. **d** 82 **p** 83. C S Wimbledon H Trin and St Pet *S'wark* 82–85; C Surbiton St Andr and St Mark 85–90; Chapl St Chad's Coll Dur 90–93; Sub-Warden St Mich Coll Llan 94–98; Lect Th Univ of Wales (Cardiff) 94–98; V Wandsworth St Anne *S'wark* 98–08; P-in-c Wandsworth St Faith 05–08; V Wandsworth St Anne w St Faith from 08; Dioc Voc Adv from 99. *St Anne's Vicarage, 182 St Ann's Hill, London SW18 2RS* T: (020) 8874 2809 E: gordon.jeanes@virgin.net

JEANS, The Ven Alan Paul. b 58. MIAAS 84 MIBCO 84 Southn Univ BTh 89 Univ of Wales (Lamp) MA 03. Sarum & Wells Th Coll 86. **d** 89 **p** 90. C Parkstone St Pet w Branksea and St Osmund *Sarum* 89–93; P-in-c Bishop's Cannings, All Cannings etc 93–98; Par Development Adv from 98; Can and Preb Sarum Cathl from 02; Adn Sarum from 03; RD Alderbury 05–07; Dioc Dir of Ords 07–13. *Herbert House, 118 Lower Road, Salisbury SP2 9NW* T: (01722) 336290 F: 411990 E: adsarum@salisbury.anglican.org

JEANS, David Bockley. b 48. Mert Coll Ox BA 71 MA 80 PGCE 73 Man Univ MPhil 98. Trin Coll Bris 83. **d** 85 **p** 86. C Clevedon St Andr and Ch Ch *B & W* 85–88; V Wadsley *Sheff* 88–96; Dir Studies Wilson Carlile Coll of Evang 96–06; Prin 97–06; Dean Coll of S Cross New Zealand 06–08; P-in-c Deepcar *Sheff* 08–13; rtd 13; PtO *Sheff* from

13. *112 Airedale Road, Sheffield S6 4AW* T: 0114-221 7829 E: d.jeans1948@gmail.com

JEANS, Miss Eleanor Ruth. b 75. Man Univ BMus 97 GRNCM 97. Ridley Hall Cam 09. **d** 11 **p** 12. C Thurnby w Stoughton *Leic* 11–14; C Kettering Ch the King *Pet* from 14. *11 Churchill Way, Kettering NN15 5DP* M: 07795-660144 E: eleanor@thisman.co.uk

JEAPES (née PORTER), Mrs Barbara Judith. b 47. Cam Inst of Educn TCert 68. Carl Dioc Tr Inst 91. **d** 94 **p** 95. NSM Egremont and Haile *Carl* 94–14; TV 09–14; rtd 14; PtO *Carl* 14–19. *15 Millfields, Beckermet CA21 2YY* T: (01946) 841489 E: barbara.jeapes@btinternet.com

JEAVONS, Mrs Margaret Anne. b 51. Liv Poly BA 72 Bris Univ BA 01 St Kath Coll Liv PGCE 74. Trin Coll Bris 99. **d** 01 **p** 02. C Totnes w Bridgetown, Berry Pomeroy etc *Ex* 01–05; V Sutton St Mich *York* 05–19; P-in-c Bilton St Pet 15–19; AD E Hull 13–19; rtd 19. *4 Collison House, Trinity Lane, Beverley HU17 0AR* E: maggieannejeavons@gmail.com

JEE, Jonathan Noel. b 63. BNC Ox BA 84 MA 88. Wycliffe Hall Ox 85. **d** 88 **p** 89. C Brampton St Thos *Derby* 88–92; TV Hinckley H Trin *Leic* 92–00; V Leamington Priors St Paul *Cov* from 00. *The Vicarage, 15 Lillington Road, Leamington Spa CV32 5YS* T: (01926) 772132 *or* 427149 E: jonathan@stpl.org.uk

JEE, Thomas Peter. b 91. St Jo Coll Ox BA 13 Trin Coll Cam BA 17 MPhil 18 Birm City Univ PGCE 14. Ridley Hall Cam 15. **d** 18 **p** 19. C Woodford Wells *Chelmsf* from 18. *55B Montalt Road, Woodford Green IB8 9RS* M: 07403-463755 E: thomas_jee@hotmail.co.uk

JEEWAN, Alexander. b 71. Univ of E Lon BA 95 PGCE 97. Westcott Ho Cam 13. **d** 15 **p** 16. C Witham and Villages *Chelmsf* 15–18; TV Saffron Walden and Villages from 18. *The Vicarage, Church Street, Great Chesterford, Saffron Walden CB10 1NP* M: 07801-946217 E: alex_jeewan@hotmail.com *or* vicar.camvillages@gmail.com

JEFF, Canon Gordon Henry. b 32. St Edm Hall Ox BA 56 MA 60. Wells Th Coll 59. **d** 61 **p** 62. C Sydenham St Bart *S'wark* 61–64; C Kidbrooke St Jas 64–66; V Clapham St Paul 66–72; V Raynes Park St Sav 73–79; RD Merton 77–79; V Carshalton Beeches 79–86; P-in-c Petersham 86–90; Chapl St Mich Convent 90–96; Hon Can S'wark Cathl 93–96; rtd 96; PtO *B & W* 07–12. *9 Barnetts Well, Draycott, Cheddar BS27 3TF* T: (01934) 744943 E: rumpus9bw@hotmail.com

JEFFCOAT, Rupert Edward Elessing. b 70. St Cath Coll Cam BA 92 MA 96 Salford Univ PhD 16 FRCO 91. WMMTC 02. **d** 05 **p** 06. NSM Brisbane Cathl Australia 05–10. *Arden House, 25 Saunders Avenue, Bedworth CV12 8RJ* T: (024) 7673 4799 E: ruperteejeffcoat@gmail.com

JEFFERIES, Preb Phillip John. b 42. St Chad's Coll Dur BA 65 MA 91. **d** 67 **p** 68. C Tunstall Ch Ch *Lich* 67–71; C Wolverhampton St Pet 71–74; P-in-c Oakengates 74–80; V 80–82; P-in-c Ketley 78–82; V Horninglow 82–00; RD Tutbury 97–00; TR Stafford 00–07; Bp's Adv on Hosp Chapl 82–06; Preb Lich Cathl 99–07; rtd 07; PtO *Lich* from 07; *Truro* from 16. *16 Morley's Hill, Burton-on-Trent DE13 0TA* T: (01283) 544013 E: pjjefferies@talktalk.net

JEFFERS, Cliff Peter. b 69. CITC BTh 98. **d** 98 **p** 99. C Limerick City *L & K* 98–01; I Clonenagh w Offerlane, Borris-in-Ossory etc *C & O* 01–04; I Athy w Kilberry, Fontstown and Kilkea *D & G* 04–13; Chapl Dub Inst of Tech 13–14; I Fanlobbus Union *C, C & R* from 14. *The Rectory, Sackville Street, Dunmanway, Co Cork, Republic of Ireland* T: (00353) (23) 884 5151 E: cliff4b@gmail.com

JEFFERS, Neil Gareth Thompson. b 78. St Jo Coll Ox BA 99 MA 05. Oak Hill Th Coll MTh 07. **d** 07 **p** 08. C Lowestoft Ch Ch *Nor* 07–11; Chapl Pangbourne Coll from 11. *Sunbeam, Bere Court Road, Pangbourne, Reading RG8 8JY* T: 0118-976 7449 M: 07769-586260 E: neiljeffers2003@yahoo.co.uk

JEFFERSON, Charles Dudley. b 55. St Pet Coll Ox BA 78 MA 81. Ridley Hall Cam 79. **d** 81 **p** 82. C Chadkirk *Ches* 81–84; C Macclesfield St Pet 84–85; C Macclesfield Team 85–89; R Elworth and Warmingham 89–99; Chapl Framlingham Coll 99–01; Chapl Rendcomb Coll Cirencester and P-in-c Rendcomb *Glouc* 01–09; R Thrapston, Denford and Islip *Pet* 09–15; R Chenderit 15–17; V Balderstone, Mellor and Samlesbury *Blackb* 17–19; P-in-c Walton-on-Trent w Croxall, Rosliston etc *Derby* from 19; P-in-c Seale and Lullington w Coton in the Elms from 19; P-in-c Stapenhill Immanuel from 19. *The Rectory, 2 Station Lane, Walton-on-Trent, Swadlincote DE12 8NA* E: revcjefferson@uwclub.net

JEFFERSON, David Charles. b 33. Leeds Univ BA 57. Coll of Resurr Mirfield 57. **d** 59 **p** 60. C Kennington Cross St Anselm *S'wark* 59–62; C Richmond St Mary w St Matthias 62–64; Chapl Wilson's Gr Sch Camberwell 64–93; Chapl Wilson's Sch Wallington 75–99; Public Preacher *S'wark* 64–74; Hon C Carshalton Beeches 74–04; rtd 93; PtO *S'wark* 04–13.

15 Sandown Drive, Carshalton SM5 4LN T: (020) 8669 0640 *or* 8773 2931

JEFFERY, Graham. b 35. Qu Coll Cam BA 58. Wells Th Coll 58. **d** 60 **p** 61. C Southampton Maybush St Pet *Win* 60–63; Australia 63–66; C E Grinstead St Swithun *Chich* 66–68; C-in-c The Hydneye CD 68–74; V Wick 74–76; C Hove 76–78; P-in-c Newtimber w Pyecombe 78–82; R Poynings w Edburton, Newtimber and Pyecombe 82–92; P-in-c Sullington and Thakeham w Warminghurst 92–95; rtd 96; NSM Edburton *Chich* 97–99; PtO 00–17; NSM Poynings w Edburton, Newtimber and Pyecombe 17–18. *6 Orchard Close, Small Dole, Henfield BN5 9YA*

JEFFERY (née CAW), Canon Hannah Mary. b 69. Birm Univ BMus 90. St Jo Coll Nottm MA 95. **d** 95 **p** 96. C Northampton St Giles *Pet* 95–99; Hon C Hanger Hill Ascension and W Twyford St Mary *Lon* 99–04; TV Northampton Em *Pet* 04–11; CMD Officer 11–16; Chapl Bp Stopford Sch 11–16; R Desborough, Brampton Ash, Dingley and Braybrooke *Pet* from 16; RD Kettering from 17; Can Pet Cathl from 19. *19 Rosemount Road, Kettering NN15 6EU* T: (01536) 660415 M: 07761-288326 E: revhj@outlook.com

JEFFERY, Harry Ernest. b 59. **d** 11. NSM Bardney *Linc* from 11. *28 Station Road, Bardney, Lincoln LN3 5UD*

JEFFERY, Mrs Jennifer Ann. b 45. Philippa Fawcett Coll CertEd 66. STETS. **d** 02 **p** 03. NSM Wilton *B & W* 02–15; Chapl Bp Henderson Sch from 07; rtd 15; PtO *B & W* from 15. *4 Southwell, Trull, Taunton TA3 7HU* T: (01823) 286589 M: 07979-285607 E: revjen@sky.com

JEFFERY, Jonathan George Piers. b 63. Man Univ LLB 84. Ripon Coll Cuddesdon 95. **d** 97 **p** 98. C Lee-on-the-Solent *Portsm* 97–01; V Leigh Park from 01; V Warren Park from 01; AD Havant 09–14. *The Vicarage, Riders Lane, Havant PO9 4QT* T: (023) 9247 5276 E: jonathanjeffery7@btinternet.com

JEFFERY (née JACK), Mrs Judith Ann. b 54. Wycliffe Hall Ox 03. **d** 05 **p** 06. C Tetbury, Beverston and Long Newnton and Shipton Moyne *Glouc* 05–10; P-in-c Baltonsborough w Butleigh, W Bradley etc *B & W* 10–15; R Crook Peak from 15. *The Rectory, Sparrow Hill Way, Weare, Axbridge BS26 2LE* E: judithjack@talktalk.net

JEFFERY, Kenneth Charles. b 40. Univ of Wales BA 64 Linacre Coll Ox BA 67 MA 70. St Steph Ho Ox 64. **d** 67 **p** 68. C Swindon New Town *Bris* 67–68; C Summertown *Ox* 68–71; C Brighton St Pet *Chich* 71–77; V Ditchling 77–00; rtd 01; PtO Ox from 19. *Carrick House, 2 South Street, Caulcott, Bicester OX25 4NE* T: (01869) 343114 E: fruitlands@live.co.uk

JEFFERY, Michael Frank. b 48. Linc Th Coll 74. **d** 76 **p** 77. C Caterham Valley *S'wark* 76–79; C Tupsley *Heref* 79–82; P-in-c Stretton Sugwas 82–84; P-in-c Bishopstone 83–84; P-in-c Kenchester and Bridge Sollers 83–84; V Whiteshill *Glouc* 84–92; P-in-c Randwick 92; V Whiteshill and Randwick 93–02; TV Bedminster *Bris* 02–09; P-in-c 09–13; rtd 13. *Old Hall House, Ham Street, Baltonsborough, Glastonbury BA6 8PX* E: michael@not2arty.com

JEFFERY, Peter James. b 41. Leeds Univ BSc 63. Oak Hill Th Coll 64. **d** 66 **p** 67. C Streatham Park St Alb *S'wark* 66–70; C Northampton St Giles *Pet* 70–73; C Rushden St Pet 73–76; C Rushden w Newton Bromswold 77–78; V Siddal *Wakef* 78–85; V Sowerby Bridge w Norland 85–98; P-in-c Cornholme 98–00; P-in-c Walsden 98–00; V Cornholme and Walsden 00–05; rtd 06; PtO *Wakef* 07–14; *Leeds* from 14. *12 Highcroft Road, Todmorden OL14 5LZ* T: (01706) 839781 E: pandm.jeffery@tiscali.co.uk

JEFFERY, Richard William Christopher. b 43. Ex Univ BA 65. Coll of Resurr Mirfield 66. **d** 68 **p** 69. C Widley w Wymering *Portsm* 68–71; C Salisbury St Mich *Sarum* 71–74; TV Ridgeway 74–80; V Stanford in the Vale w Goosey and Hatford *Ox* 80–89; V Topsham *Ex* 89–09; RD Aylesbeare 01–07; rtd 09; P-in-c Topsham and Wear *Ex* 09–13; PtO from 13. *5 Brownlees, Exminster, Exeter EX6 8SW* T: (01392) 823526 E: richardwcj@gmail.com

JEFFORD, Peter Ernest. b 29. AKC 53. **d** 54 **p** 55. C Berkeley *Glouc* 54–57; C Petersfield w Sheet *Portsm* 57–61; Chapl Churcher's Coll 57–61; R Rollesby w Burgh w Billockby *Nor* 62–71; V Watton 71–81; V Watton w Carbrooke and Ovington 81–82; OCM 71–82; P-in-c Brampford Speke *Ex* 82–83; P-in-c Cadbury 82–83; P-in-c Thorverton 82–83; P-in-c Upton Pyne 82–83; TR Thorverton, Cadbury, Upton Pyne etc 83–92; rtd 92; PtO *Ox* 92–96 and 03–18; Hon C Ox St Mary V w St Cross and St Pet 96–99; P-in-c Whitchurch St Mary 00–03; Chapl Plater Coll 94–05. *27 Ashlong Road, Headington, Oxford OX3 0NH* T: (01865) 760593

JEFFREY, Katrina. See METZNER, Katrina

JEFFREY, William Kenneth. CITI. **d** 17 **p** 18. Killaney w Carryduff *D & D* 17–18; C Ballymacash *Conn* from 18. *79 Kings*

Road, Belfast BT6 7BU T: (028) 9070 3949 M: 07443-462265 E: jeffreyw@tcd.ie *or* williamjeffrey01@btinternet.com

JEFFREYS, David John. b 45. S Dios Minl Tr Scheme 89. **d** 92 **p** 93. NSM Bexhill St Barn *Chich* 92–95; Chapl Hastings and Rother NHS Trust 95–02; Chapl E Sussex Hosps NHS Trust 02–05; Chapl Team Ldr 05–09; rtd 09; PtO *Chich* from 10. *4 Osbern Close, Bexhill-on-Sea TN39 4TJ* T: (01424) 843672 E: frdavid@onetel.com

JEFFREYS (née DESHPANDE), Lakshmi Anant. b 64. Liv Univ BSc 86 St Luke's Coll Ex PGCE 87. Wycliffe Hall Ox BTh 94. **d** 94 **p** 95. C Long Eaton St Jo *Derby* 94–97; Chapl Nottm Trent Univ *S'well* 98–03; PtO *Derby* 03–04; Dioc Miss Adv 04–13; P-in-c Wootton w Quinton and Preston Deanery *Pet* 13–15; V Wootton from 15; Asst Dir Ords from 14. *The Rectory, Water Lane, Wootton, Northampton NN4 6HH* T: (01604) 962061 E: woottonvicar@talktalk.net

JEFFREYS, Timothy John. b 58. Man Univ BSc 79. Cranmer Hall Dur 83. **d** 86 **p** 87. C Goodmayes All SS *Chelmsf* 86–88; PtO *S'wark* 92–93; Hon C S Lambeth St Anne and All SS 93–96; C Croydon St Jo 96–96; P-in-c Brixton Road Ch Ch 06–12; V from 12. *The Vicarage, 96 Brixton Road, London SW9 6BE* T: (020) 7793 0621 E: vicar@christchurchbr.org.uk

JELLEY, Ian. b 54. Newc Univ MA 94 Dur Univ MA 03. NEOC 89. **d** 91 **p** 92. C Jarrow *Dur* 91–95; P-in-c Leam Lane 95–96; Chapl HM Pris Holme Ho 96–01; R Grindon, Stillington and Wolviston *Dur* 01–03; rtd 03; PtO *Dur* from 03. *1 Rievaulx Avenue, Billingham TS23 2BP* E: lun1204@hotmail.co.uk

JELLEY, James Dudley. b 46. Linc Th Coll 78. **d** 80 **p** 81. C Stockwell Green St Andr *S'wark* 80–85; V Camberwell St Phil and St Mark 85–93; PtO 93–96; V Camberwell St Luke 96–13; RD Camberwell 00–06; rtd 13; PtO *S'wark* 13–18; Hon C Brede w Udimore and Beckley and Peasmarsh *Chich* from 18. *Vine Cottage, Main Street, Peasmarsh, Rye TN31 6UL*

JELLEY (née CAPITANCHIK), Canon Sophie Rebecca. b 72. Leeds Univ BA 93. Wycliffe Hall Ox MPhil 97. **d** 97 **p** 98. C Shipley St Pet *Bradf* 97–00; CMS Uganda 00–03; C Churt and Hindhead *Guildf* 03–10; V Burgess Hill St Andr *Chich* 10–15; Dir Miss, Min and Discipleship *Dur* from 15; Can Res Dur Cathl from 15. *3 The College, Durham DH1 3EQ* T: (01388) 604515 E: sophiejelley@gmail.com *or* sophie.jelley@durham.anglican.org

JELLEYMAN, Susan. b 53. WEMTC 14. **d** 18 **p** 19. NSM Apedale Gp *Heref* from 18. *35 Stretton Farm Road, Church Stretton SY6 6DX* T: (01694) 724031 E: suejellsincs@btinternet.com *or* apedalecurate@gmail.com

JEMMETT, Melanie Jane. b 72. Surrey Univ BA 93 Cam Univ BTh 14 Middx Univ PGCE 96. Westcott Ho Cam 12. **d** 14 **p** 15. C Fawkham and Hartley *Roch* 14–17; V Lamorbey H Redeemer from 17; AD Sidcup from 19. *Holy Redeemer Vicarage, 64 Day's Lane, Sidcup DA15 8JR* T: (020) 8300 1508 E: melaniejemmett@btinternet.com

JENKIN, Canon Charles Alexander Graham. b 50. BScEng. Westcott Ho Cam 81. **d** 84 **p** 85. C Binley *Cov* 84–88; TV Canvey Is *Chelmsf* 88–94; TR Melton Mowbray *Leic* 94–08; RD Framland 98–02; Hon Can Leic Cathl 06–08; V Ipswich St Mary-le-Tower *St E* from 08; Bp's Interfaith Adv from 09; RD Ipswich 12–17; Hon Can St E Cathl from 17. *The Vicarage, 18 Kingsfield Avenue, Ipswich IP1 3TA* T/F: (01473) 289001 E: charles@jenkin.uk.net

JENKIN, Christopher Cameron. b 36. BNC Ox BA 61 MA 64. Clifton Th Coll 61. **d** 63 **p** 64. C Walthamstow St Mary *Chelmsf* 63–68; C Surbiton Hill Ch Ch *S'wark* 68–78; V Newport St Jo *Portsm* 78–88; TR Newbarns w Hawcoat *Carl* 88–01; rtd 01; PtO *Carl* from 01. *Beckside, Orton, Penrith CA10 3RX* T: (01539) 624410 E: chriscjenkin@aol.com

JENKINS, Alan David. b 60. Bris Poly BA 83 Spurgeon's Coll MTh 02. Wycliffe Hall Ox 93. **d** 95 **p** 96. C Tunbridge Wells St Jas w St Phil *Roch* 95–01; TV S Gillingham 01–07; R Gt Bookham *Guildf* from 07; AD Leatherhead from 15. *The Rectory, 2A Fife Way, Bookham, Leatherhead KT23 3PH* T: (01372) 452405 E: alan.jenkins@stnicolasbookham.org.uk

JENKINS, Audrey Joan. b 36. TCert 61. St D Coll Lamp. **d** 01 **p** 06. Par Dn Marshfield and Peterstone Wentloog etc *Mon* 01–06; NSM Llanrumney from 06. *10 Cwrt Pencraig, 8 Caerau Crescent, Newport NP20 4HG* T: (01633) 263470

JENKINS, Clifford Thomas. b 38. Westmr Coll Ox MTh 02 IEng MIEIecIE. Sarum & Wells Th Coll 74. **d** 77 **p** 78. Chapl Yeovil Coll 77–86; Hon C Yeovil w Kingston Pitney *B & W* 77–80; P-in-c 80–86; Chs FE Liaison Officer B & W, Bris and Glouc 87–90; PtO *B & W* 87–19; FE Adv Gen Syn Bd of Educn and Meth Ch 90–98; rtd 98. *Bethany, 10 Grove Avenue, Yeovil BA20 2BB* T: (01935) 475043

JENKINS, Clive Ronald. b 57. Chich Univ BA 08. Ripon Coll Cuddesdon 81. **d** 84 **p** 85. C E Grinstead St Swithun *Chich* 84–87; C Horsham 87–88; TV 88–90; Dioc Youth

Chapl 90–96; P-in-c Amberley w N Stoke and Parham, Wiggonholt etc 93–96; V Southbourne w W Thorney 96–15; RD Westbourne 11–15; P-in-c Wisborough Green from 15. *The Vicarage, Billingshurst Road, Wisborough Green, Billingshurst RH14 0DZ* T: (01403) 700339 M: 07812-740720 E: candmjenkins@hotmail.com

JENKINS, David. *See* JENKINS, Richard David

JENKINS, David. *See* JENKINS, William Gordon Frederick

JENKINS, David Alan. b 62. Linc Sch of Th and Min 15. **d** 18 **p** 19. C Quarrington w Old Sleaford *Linc* from 18. *16 Dove Close, Sleaford NG34 9UT* T: (01529) 306557 M: 07908-738039 E: ajenkins016@gmail.com

JENKINS, The Ven David Harold. b 61. SS Coll Cam BA 84 MA 87 Ox Univ BA 88 MA 94 Univ of Wales (Lamp) PhD 08. Ripon Coll Cuddesdon 86. **d** 89 **p** 90. C Chesterton Gd Shep *Ely* 89–91; C Earley St Pet *Ox* 91–94; V Blackpool St Mich *Blackb* 94–99; V Broughton 99–04; AD Preston 04; Can Res Carl Cathl 04–10; Dir of Educn 04–10; Adn Sudbury *St E* from 10; NSM St Edm Way 16–18. *Sudbury Lodge, Stanningfield Road, Great Whelnetham, Bury St Edmunds IP30 0TL* T: (01284) 386942 M: 07900-990073 E: archdeacon.david@cofesuffolk.org

JENKINS, Prof David Harrison. b 52. **d** 15 **p** 16. NSM St Ishmael's w Llan-saint and Ferryside *St D* 15–18. *17 Parc Y Ffynnon, Ferryside SA17 5TQ* T: (01267) 268230

JENKINS, David Thomas. b 43. Ox Univ MA 94 RIBA 70. S'wark Ord Course 76. **d** 79 **p** 80. NSM Merthyr Tydfil and Cyfarthfa *Llan* 79–86; NSM Brecon St David w Llanspyddid and Llanllltyd *S & B* 86–91; P-in-c Llangiwg 91–92; V 92–01; Chapl Puerto de la Cruz Tenerife *Eur* 02–09; rtd 09. *15 Highmoor, Maritime Quarter, Swansea SA1 1YE* M: 07974-748476 E: djenkins@tinyonline.co.uk

JENKINS, David William. b 43. **d** 12 **p** 13. OLM Busbridge and Hambledon *Guildf* from 12. *Medlar House, 6 Quartermile Road, Godalming GU7 1TG* T: (01483) 416084 E: david.jenkins@djturfcare.co.uk

JENKINS, Canon Eric Robert. b 52. Poly Cen Lon BSc 74. STETS 97. **d** 00 **p** 01. C Weybridge *Guildf* 00–04; R Cobham and Stoke D'Abernon 04–17; RD Leatherhead 08–15; Hon Can Guildf Cathl 15–17; rtd 17. *69 The Glade, Fetcham, Leatherhead KT22 9TF* M: 07747-844689 E: er.jenkins@btinternet.com

JENKINS, Mrs Fiona. b 59. Dur Univ BSc 80 York St Jo Coll MA 04. St Jo Coll Nottm 04. **d** 06 **p** 07. C Settle *Bradf* 06–08; C Linton in Craven 08–14; *Leeds* 14–15; C Kettlewell w Conistone, Hubberholme etc *Bradf* 08–14; *Leeds* 14–15; C Burnsall w Rylstone *Bradf* 08–14; *Leeds* 14–15; V Chipping and Whitewell *Blackb* 15–18; V Chipping from 18. *The Vicarage, Garstang Road, Chipping, Preston PR3 2QH* E: revdfiona.chipping@icloud.com

JENKINS, Garry Frederick. b 48. Southn Univ BTh 79. Chich Th Coll 75. **d** 79 **p** 80. C Kingsbury St Andr *Lon* 79–84; C Leigh St Clem *Chelmsf* 84–88; P-in-c Brentwood St Geo 88–94; V 94–18; Chapl NE Lon Foundn Trust 02–18; rtd 18; P-in-c New Brompton St Luke *Roch* from 19. *51 Trinity Road, Gillingham ME7 1JA* E: g.jenkins197@btinternet.com

JENKINS, Canon Gary John. b 59. York Univ BA 80 CertEd 81. Oak Hill Th Coll BA 89. **d** 89 **p** 90. C Norwood St Luke *S'wark* 89–94; P-in-c St Helier 94–95; V 95–01; V Redhill H Trin 01–12; AD Reigate 12; V Bermondsey St Jas and St Anne from 13; AD Bermondsey from 18; Hon Can S'wark Cathl from 06. *St James's Vicarage, 4 Thurland Road, London SE16 4AA* T: (020) 7394 1482 E: garyjjenkins@outlook.com

JENKINS, Glyn Frank. b 34. Keble Coll Ox BA 55 MA 59 DipEd 58. **d** 14 **p** 14. NSM Bassaleg *Mon* from 14. *10 Cwrt Pencraig, 9 Caerau Crescent, Newport NP20 4HG*

JENKINS, Canon Jeanette. b 42. St Jo Coll Nottm 83. **dss** 84 **d** 86 **p** 94. NSM Kilmarnock *Glas* 84–94; NSM Irvine St Andr LEP 84–94; NSM Ardrossan 84–94; Asst Chapl Crosshouse Hosp 86–94; Chapl Ayrshire Hospice 90–02; Can St Mary's Cathl *Glas* from 99; LtO from 12. *4 Gleneagles Avenue, Kilwinning KA13 6RD* T: (01294) 553383 M: 07775-595109 E: revj.jenkins@btinternet.com

JENKINS, John. b 49. **d** 14 **p** 15. NSM Uxbridge *Lon* from 14. *39 Church Road, Uxbridge UB8 3ND* T: (01895) 812670 E: john.jenkins@uxbridgeparish.org

JENKINS, John Francis. b 46. Ripon Hall Ox 77 Ripon Coll Cuddesdon 75. **d** 77 **p** 78. C Filton *Bris* 77–79; C Bris St Andr Hartcliffe 79–84; P-in-c Bris H Cross Inns Court 84–85; V 85–95; R Odcombe, Brympton, Lufton and Montacute *B & W* 95–14; rtd 14. *10 Cursley Path, Wells BA5 1FF* E: johnjenkins382@btinternet.com

JENKINS, John Rhys. b 64. Southn Univ BM 89 MRCGP 94 DRCOG 93. St Mich Coll Llan 09. **d** 13 **p** 14. NSM Roath *Llan* 13–19; NSM Canton Cardiff from 19. *1 Thompson Avenue, Cardiff CF5 1EX* E: jrhysj@ntlworld.com

JENKINS, Julian James. b 56. St Mich Coll Llan 97. **d** 99 **p** 00. C Whitchurch *Llan* 99–01; TV Aberavon 01–05; TV Cowbridge 05–11; P-in-c Llandyfodwg and Cwm Ogwr from 11. *The Vicarage, Coronation Street, Ogmore Vale, Bridgend CF32 7HE* T: (01656) 840248

JENKINS, Canon Lawrence Clifford. b 45. Open Univ BA 77 AKC 70. St Aug Coll Cant. **d** 71 **p** 72. C Osmondthorpe St Phil *Ripon* 71–74; C Monkseaton St Mary *Newc* 74–78; V Shiremoor 78–84; V Wheatley Hills *Sheff* 84–95; RD Doncaster 92–95; V Greenhill 95–10; Hon Can Sheff Cathl 08–10; rtd 10; PtO *Sheff* from 11. *10 Chiltern Crescent, Sprotbrough, Doncaster DN5 7PE* T: (01302) 856587 E: lawriejenkins@virginmedia.com

JENKINS, Canon Paul Morgan. b 44. Sussex Univ BEd 68 Fitzw Coll Cam BA 73 MA 76. Westcott Ho Cam 71. **d** 74 **p** 75. C Forest Gate St Edm *Chelmsf* 74–77; Chapl Bryanston Sch 77–85; P-in-c Stourpaine, Durweston and Bryanston *Sarum* 77–83; Asst Chapl and Housemaster Repton Sch Derby 84–89; Dean of Chpl 89–91; R Singleton *Chich* 91–97; V E Dean 91–97; V W Dean 91–97; Dir St Columba's Retreat and Conf Cen 97–07; Chapl Community of St Pet Woking 03–07; P-in-c Dunsfold and Hascombe *Guildf* 07–12; Hon Can Guildf Cathl 05–12; Master Hugh Sexey's Hosp Bruton from 12; PtO *B & W* 17–19. *The Master's House, Sexey's Hospital, Bruton BA10 0AS* T: (01749) 813369 M: 07973-848941 E: jenkins44@aol.com

JENKINS (née RICHARDSON), Pauline Kate. b 41. RGN 62 Nottm Univ CertEd 80 RNT 83. St Jo Coll Nottm 91. **d** 94 **p** 98. Uganda 94–96; PtO *S'well* 96–98; NSM Selston 98–01; NSM Annesley w Newstead 01–03; rtd 03; PtO *S'well* 03–15; *Leic* 07–17; *S'wark* from 17. *45 March Court, Warwick Drive, London SW15 6LE* T: (020) 8789 3396 E: revd.p.k.jenkins@gmail.com

JENKINS, Rhys. *See* JENKINS, John Rhys

JENKINS, Preb Richard David. b 33. Magd Coll Cam BA 58 MA. Westcott Ho Cam 59. **d** 61 **p** 62. C Staveley *Derby* 61–64; C Billingham St Aid *Dur* 64–68; V Walsall Pleck and Bescot *Lich* 68–73; R Whitchurch 73–97; RD Wem and Whitchurch 85–95; P-in-c Tilstock and Whixall 92–95; Preb Lich Cathl 93–97; rtd 97; PtO *Lich* 99–17. *The Council House, Council House Court, Castle Street, Shrewsbury SY1 2AU* T: (01743) 270051

JENKINS, Richard Morvan. b 44. St Mich Coll Llan 65. **d** 69 **p** 70. C Tenby *St D* 69–73; V Llanrhian w Llanhywel and Carnhedryn etc 73–80; R Johnston w Steynton 80–93; V St Ishmael's w Llan-saint and Ferryside 93–09; rtd 09; PtO *St D* from 11. *Geirionydd, 7 Dwynant, Furnace Road, Burry Port SA16 0YQ* T: (01554) 834761

JENKINS, Robert. *See* JENKINS, Eric Robert

JENKINS, Rosemary Edith. b 47. Nottm Univ MA 04 RGN 68 RHV 71. EMMTC 01. **d** 04 **p** 05. NSM Bassingham Gp *Linc* 04–08; P-in-c Sibsey w Frithville 08–13; V 13–17; P-in-c Brothertoft Gp 10–13; V 13–17; rtd 17; PtO *Linc* from 18. *11 Deepdale Drive, Leasingham, Sleaford NG34 8LR* T: (01529) 306816 E: rev.rosemaryt@btinternet.com

JENKINS, Mrs Sarah Jean. b 65. Westcott Ho Cam 16. **d** 18 **p** 19. C Nacton and Levington w Bucklesham etc *St E* from 18; C Waldringfield w Hemley and Newbourne from 18. *25 Weir Place, Kirton, Ipswich IP10 0QA* T: (01394) 448936 M: 07900-667089 E: revdsarahjenkins@gmail.com

JENKINS, Timothy David. b 52. Pemb Coll Ox BA 73 MLitt 77 MA 82 St Edm Ho Cam BA 84 PhD 01. Ridley Hall Cam 82. **d** 85 **p** 86. C Kingswood *Bris* 85–87; Sen Chapl Nottm Univ *S'well* 88–92; Dean of Chpl Jes Coll Cam 92–10; Fell from 92; Can Th Leic Cathl 04–09. *50 Stanley Road, Cambridge CB5 8BL* T: (01223) 363185 *or* 339302 E: tdj22@jesus.cam.ac.uk

JENKINS, Canon William David. b 42. Birm Univ BA 63. St D Coll Lamp LTh 65. **d** 65 **p** 66. C Gorseinon *S & B* 65–67; C Llanelli *St D* 67–72; V Clydach *S & B* 72–82; Chapl Gwynedd Hosp NHS Trust 82–97; V Llanrhos *St As* 82–97; RD Llanrwst 84–96; Can Cursal St As Cathl 93–97; TR Tenby *St D* 97–07; rtd 07; PtO *St As* from 09; *St D* from 11. *Kildare, 96 Conway Road, Llandudno LL30 1PP* T: (01492) 860176 M: 07791-738018

JENKINSON, Margaret. b 40. MCSP 62. Carl Dioc Tr Inst 89. **d** 92 **p** 94. NSM Preesall *Blackb* 92–96; NSM Lanercost, Walton, Gilsland and Nether Denton *Carl* 96–04; P-in-c Lorton and Loweswater w Buttermere 04–13; rtd 13; PtO *Blackb* from 14. *10 The Conifers, Hambleton, Poulton-le-Fylde FY6 9EP* T: (01253) 702237 E: margaretjenkinson@btinternet.com

JENKYNS, John Thomas William Basil. b 30. Univ of Wales (Lamp) BA 54 St Cath Coll Ox BA 57 MA 62. Wycliffe Hall Ox 54. **d** 57 **p** 58. C Neasden cum Kingsbury St Cath *Lon* 57–60; C S Lyncombe *B & W* 60–64; V Gt Harwood St Bart

Blackb 64–66; R Colne St Bart 66–69; V Chard St Mary B & W 69–87; Preb Wells Cathl 87; V Swaffham *Nor* 87–89; V Overbury w Teddington, Alstone etc *Worc* 89–95; rtd 95; PtO *St E* 10–14. *9 Aldeburgh Road, Leiston IP16 4JY*

JENNER, Peter David. b 67. **d** 95 **p** 96. C Staines *Lon* 15–18; V Hinchley Wood *Guildf* from 18. *The Vicarage, 98 Manor Road North, Esher KT10 0AD* T: (020) 8398 9095 M: 07824-323815 E: vicar@stchristopherschurch.org.uk

JENNER, Canon Peter John. b 56. Chu Coll Cam BA 77 PhD 80 MA 81. St Jo Coll Nottm 82. **d** 85 **p** 86. C Upperby St Jo *Carl* 85–88; Chapl Reading Univ *Ox* 88–96; P-in-c Mellor *Derby* 96–99; V 99–06; V Mellor *Ches* 06–12; RD Chadkirk 08–11; Can Res Ches Cathl 12–15; Chapl Ches Univ from 12. *22 Balmoral Park, Chester CH1 4BQ* E: jennerfamily@btinternet.com *or* p.jenner@chester.ac.uk

JENNER, William George. b 37. Nottm Univ BSc 59 K Coll Lon PGCE 60. **d** 97 **p** 98. OLM Gillingham w Geldeston, Stockton, Ellingham etc *Nor* 97–05; PtO from 05. *3 Woodland Drive, Kirby Cane, Bungay NR35 2PT* T: (01508) 518229 E: williamgjenner@gmail.com

JENNETT, The Ven Maurice Arthur. b 34. St Jo Coll Dur BA 60. Cranmer Hall Dur 60. **d** 62 **p** 63. C Marple All SS *Ches* 62–67; V Withnell *Blackb* 67–75; V Stranton *Dur* 75–91; Crosslinks Zimbabwe 92–99; Asst P Nyanga Mary Magd 92–93; R 93–99; Can and Adn Manicaland N 97; rtd 99; PtO *Ripon* 01–14; *Leeds* 14–16; *York* from 17. *1 Dulverton Hall, Esplanade, Scarborough YO11 2AR* T: (01723) 372954

JENNINGS, Clive John. b 57. Trin Coll Bris. **d** 00 **p** 01. C Milton *B & W* 00–02; C Clevedon St Andr and Ch Ch 02–18; V Clevedon Ch Ch from 18. *12 Princes Road, Clevedon BS21 7SZ* T: (01275) 872134 E: vicar@christchurch-clevedon.org.uk

⊞**JENNINGS, The Rt Revd David Willfred Michael.** b 44. AKC 66. **d** 67 **p** 68 **c** 00. C Walton St Mary *Liv* 67–69; C Christchurch *Win* 69–73; V Hythe 73–80; V Romford St Edw *Chelmsf* 80–92; RD Havering 85–92; Hon Can Chelmsf Cathl 87–92; Adn Southend 92–00; Suff Bp Warrington *Liv* 00–09; rtd 09; PtO *Ox* 10–13; Hon Asst Bp Ox from 13; Hon Asst Bp Glouc from 10. *The Laurels, High Street, Northleach, Cheltenham GL54 3ET* T: (01451) 860743 E: bishopdavidjennings@gmail.com

JENNINGS, Duncan William. b 54. UWE MA. STETS 05. **d** 08 **p** 09. C Southampton Thornhill St Chris *Win* 08–11; P-in-c from 11. *St Christopher's Vicarage, 402 Hinkler Road, Southampton SO19 6DF* T: (023) 8122 5911

JENNINGS, Canon Frederick David. b 48. K Coll Lon BD 73 AKC 73 Loughb Univ MPhil 98. St Aug Coll Cant 73. **d** 74 **p** 75. C Halesowen *Worc* 74–77; PtO *Birm* 78–80; *Leic* 78–80 and 85–87; P-in-c Snibston 80–85; Community Relns Officer 81–84; P-in-c Burbage w Aston Flamville 87–91; R 91–14; Hon Can Leic Cathl 03–10; Project officer for Ch and Soc 11–14; rtd 14; Can Th Leic Cathl from 10; PtO from 14. *59 Pipistrelle Drive, Market Bosworth, Nuneaton CV13 0NW* T: (01455) 698805 M: 07710-205582 E: revdavidjennings@talktalk.net

JENNINGS, Ian Matheson. b 47. Leeds Univ MA 98. NOC 95. **d** 97 **p** 97. NSM Hackenthorpe *Sheff* 97–01; Asst Chapl HM Pris and YOI Doncaster 97–98; Chapl 98–01; V Sheff St Cuth 01–06; TR Aston cum Aughton w Swallownest and Ulley 06–15; rtd 15; PtO *Sheff* from 16; Hon C Denham *Ox* from 19. *The Annexe, Kayalami, The Pyghtle, Denham, Uxbridge UB9 5BD* E: ianjennings@denhamparish.church

JENNINGS, Ian Richard. b 65. Liv Univ BA 88 Wolv Poly PGCE 91. Trin Coll Bris 07. **d** 09 **p** 10. C Pedmore *Worc* 09–13; C The Lye and Stambermill 13–14; V Low Moor and Oakenshaw *Leeds* from 14. *The Vicarage, Oak Lane Road, Low Moor, Bradford BD12 0HR* M: 07722-019096 E: ianrichardjennings@gmail.com

JENNINGS, Janet. b 38. SCM 71 SRN 74. Oak Hill Th Coll BA 87. **d** 88 **p** 97. Par Dn Stevenage St Pet Broadwater *St Alb* 88–90; PtO *St As* 92–14. *5 Elsted Road, Bexhill-on-Sea TN39 3BG* T: (01424) 843669 E: wandjjennings@hotmail.com

JENNINGS, Jonathan Peter. b 61. K Coll Lon BD 83. Westcott Ho Cam 84. **d** 86 **p** 87. C Peterlee *Dur* 86–89; C Darlington St Cuth 89–92; Dioc Communications Officer *Man* 92–95; Broadcasting Officer Gen Syn 95–01; PtO *S'wark* 95–98; Hon C Banstead *Guildf* 98–04; Abp Cant's Press Sec 01–08; PtO *Cant* 05–08; *Roch* 05–08; P-in-c Gillingham St Aug 08–16; RD Gillingham 10–11; C Rainham from 16. *7 Elmstone Road, Gillingham ME8 9BD* E: revjpj@aol.com

JENNINGS, Robert Henry. b 46. St Jo Coll Dur BA 69 MA 79. Qu Coll Birm. **d** 72 **p** 73. C Dursley *Glouc* 72–74; C Coleford w Staunton 75–78; TV Bottesford w Ashby *Linc* 78–83; TV Witney *Ox* 83–89; V Lane End w Cadmore End 89–16; rtd 16; PtO *Ox* from 16. *3 Fall Close, Aylesbury HP19 9XR* M: 07866-027542 E: revrobjennings@gmail.com

JENNINGS, Mrs Susan Mary. b 61. MCSP 82. St Jo Coll Nottm BA 15. **d** 15 **p** 16. C Manningham *Leeds* 15–18; C Girlington, Heaton and Manningham from 18. *The Vicarage, Park House Road, Low Moor, Bradford BD12 0HR* T: (01274) 421077 M: 07963-279153 E: suemaryjennings@gmail.com

JENNINGS, Walter James. b 37. Birm Univ BMus 60 MA 90. Qu Coll Birm 77. **d** 80 **p** 81. Hon C Hampton in Arden *Birm* 80–84; Chapl St Alb Aided Sch Highgate Birm 84–86; C Wotton-under-Edge w Ozleworth and N Nibley *Glouc* 86–89; V Pittville All SS 89–98; rtd 98; Chapl Beauchamp Community 98–00; PtO *Worc* 98–18. *1 Elgar Court, 27 Hampton Park Road, Hereford HR1 1TH* T: (01432) 271841 E: walterlinda.jennings@gmail.com

JENSEN, Alexander Sönderup. b 68. Tübingen Univ 94 St Jo Coll Dur PhD 97 Ox Univ MTh 01. St Steph Ho Ox 97. **d** 99 **p** 00. C Norton St Mich *Dur* 99–02; Lect CITC 02–05; Hon C Ch Ch Cathl Dublin *D & G* 02–05; Lect Murdoch Univ w Perth Th Hall Australia 05–07; Sen Lect 08–15; Prin Perth Th Hall 06–12; Hon C Perth Cathl 05–15; Prin ERMC from 16. *Eastern Region Ministry Course, 1A The Broad, Lady Margaret Road, Cambridge CB3 0BJ* T: (01223) 760444 E: asj43@cam.ac.uk

JENSEN, Juliet Helen. b 68. Man Univ MB, ChB 92 Univ Coll Lon MSc 97. STETS 11. **d** 13 **p** 14. C Forest Gate Em w Upton Cross *Chelmsf* 13–16; V Glouc St Jas and All SS and Ch Ch from 16. *The Vicarage, 1 The Conifers, Gloucester GL1 4LP* M: 07946-869324 E: juliet.jensen@btinternet.com

JENSON, Philip Peter. b 56. Ex Coll Ox BA 78 MA 82 Down Coll Cam BA 80 MA 86 PhD 88. Ridley Hall Cam 80. **d** 87 **p** 88. C Gt Warley Ch Ch *Chelmsf* 87–89; Lect Trin Coll Bris 89–05; Lect Ridley Hall Cam from 05. *Ridley Hall, Cambridge CB3 9HG* T: (01223) 746580 F: 746581 E: ppj22@cam.ac.uk

JEPP, Malcolm Leonard. b 44. SWMTC 06. **d** 09 **p** 10. NSM Meneage *Truro* 09–14; rtd 14; PtO *Truro* from 14. *Polpidnick Cottage, Porthallow, St Keverne, Helston TR12 6PL* T/F: (01326) 281031 M: 07797-505539 E: lenjepp@jeppassociates.co.uk

JEPP (*née* NUGENT), Mrs Mary Patricia. b 55. Mt St Vincent Univ Canada BA 79 Univ of New Brunswick BEd 80 Open Univ MA 03. ERMC 05. **d** 08 **p** 09. C Godmanchester *Ely* 08–11; P-in-c Alconbury cum Weston 11–14; P-in-c Winwick 11–14; P-in-c Hamerton 11–14; P-in-c Gt w Lt Gidding and Steeple Gidding 11–14; P-in-c Upton and Copmanford 11–14; P-in-c Buckworth 11–14; R N Leightonstone 14–17; R Kilmarnock *Glas* from 17. *The Rectory, 1 Dundonald Road, Kilmarnock KA1 1EQ* T: (01563) 535997 E: m.jepp@btinternet.com

JEPSON, Mrs Ann Brenda. b 46. Open Univ BA 81 Hockerill Coll Cam CertEd 68. LCTP 10. **d** 11 **p** 12. NSM Hurst Green and Mitton *Bradf* 11–13; NSM Ribchester w Stydd *Blackb* 13–15; rtd 15; PtO *Blackb* from 15; *Man* from 18. *Ribblesdale View, Greenside, Ribchester, Preston PR3 3ZJ* T: (01254) 878177 E: annjepson@btinternet.com

JEPSON, Joanna Elizabeth. b 76. Trin Coll Bris BA 99 Cam Univ MA 03. Ridley Hall Cam 01. **d** 03 **p** 04. C Plas Newton *Ches* 03–06; Chapl Lon Coll of Fashion 06–11; P-in-c Fulham St Pet 06–09; PtO *Portsm* 12–13; CF (TA) 13–19; Chapl Wells Cathl Sch from 19. *4 The Liberty, Wells BA5 2SU* T: (01749) 673489 E: joeyjep@yahoo.com

JEPSON-BIDDLE, Canon Nicholas Lawrence. b 71. K Coll Lon BA 94 Leeds Univ MA 98. Coll of Resurr Mirfield 96. **d** 98 **p** 99. C Bedford St Andr *St Alb* 98–01; Bp's Dom Chapl and Research Asst *Chich* 01–04; P-in-c Brighton Gd Shep Preston 04–05; TV Putney St Mary *S'wark* 07–10; PV Westmr Abbey 08–10; Can Res Portsm Cathl 10–13; Can Res and Prec Wells Cathl *B & W* from 13. *4 The Liberty, Wells BA5 2SU* T: (01749) 673489 M: 07825-322326 E: nicklb@hotmail.co.uk

JEREMIAH, Anderson Harris Mithra. b 75. Madras Univ BA 95 MA 97 MPhil 98 Edin Univ PhD 09. United Th Coll Bangalore BD 02. **d** 03 **p** 04. C Ranipet St Mary India 03; Chapl Chr Medical Coll and Hosp Vellore 03–05; LtO *Edin* 06–08; C Edin Ch Ch 08–11; PtO *Blackb* 12–14; P-in-c Gisburn 14–16; NSM Lancaster St Mary w St John and St Anne 16–17; PtO 17; Bp's Adv for Black, Asian and Minority Ethnic Affairs from 18. *6 Beechwood Gardens, Lancaster LA1 4PH* T: (01524) 298442 E: a.jeremiah@lancaster.ac.uk

JERMAIN, Jessica-Jil Stapleton. *See* AIDLEY, Jessica-Jil Stapleton

JERSEY, Dean of. *See* KEIRLE, The Very Revd Michael Robert

JERUSALEM AND THE MIDDLE EAST, President Bishop of the Episcopal Church in. *See* LEWIS, Michael Augustine Owen

JERVIS, Christopher. b 53. Loughb Univ BEd 75. Wycliffe Hall Ox 80. **d** 82 **p** 83. C Woodford Wells *Chelmsf* 82–85; Chapl Felsted Sch 85–87; Chapl Canford Sch 87–13; C Jersey

St Helier *Win* 13–17; Provost Milton Abbey Community from 17; PtO *Sarum* from 17. *7 Woodlands, Hazelbury Bryan, Sturminster Newton DT10 2DD*   T: (01258) 817969 E: cjervis7@gmail.com

JERVIS, William Edward. b 47. MRICS 74. Linc Th Coll 74. **d** 77 **p** 78. C W Bromwich All SS *Lich* 77–80; C Horsham *Chich* 80–86; R W Tarring 86–14; rtd 14; PtO Cyprus and the Gulf from 15. *5 Broadmark Beach, Broadmark Lane, Rustington, Littlehampton BN16 2JF*   T: (01903) 367214 E: eandj.jervis@gmail.com

JERWOOD, Eleanor Alice Jerwood. *See* CLACK, Eleanor Alice Jerwood

JESSETT, David Charles. b 55. K Coll Lon BD 77 AKC 77 MTh. Westcott Ho Cam 78. **d** 79 **p** 80. C Walthamstow St Pet 82–85; P-in-c Hunningham *Cov* 85–91; P-in-c Wappenbury w Weston under Wetherley 85–91; Progr Dir Exploring Chr Min Scheme 85–91; Dir CME 87–90; PtO *Cov* 90–97; P-in-c Barford w Wasperton and Sherbourne 97–19; P-in-c Hampton Lucy w Charlecote and Loxley 07–19; rtd 19. *Address temp unknown*

JESSIMAN, Timothy Edward. b 58. Portsm Univ MA 06. Oak Hill Th Coll 88. **d** 91 **p** 92. C Baldock w Bygrave *St Alb* 91–95; C Bideford *Ex* 95–96; TV Bideford, Northam, Westward Ho!, Appledore etc 96–00; Chapl Grenville Coll Bideford 95–00; Chapl N Devon Healthcare NHS Trust 98–00; P-in-c Hartplain *Portsm* 00–06; V 06–13; P-in-c Stokesay *Heref* 13–17; P-in-c Halford w Sibdon Carwood 13–17; P-in-c Wistanstow 13–17; P-in-c Acton Scott 13–17; P-in-c Churchill and Langford *B & W* from 17. *Park View, Maysmead Lane, Langford, Bristol BS40 5HX*

JESSON, Alan Francis. b 47. Ealing Coll of Educn 70 Loughb Univ MLS 77 Selw Coll Cam MA 87 ALA 70 FLA 91 MBIM 82. EAMTC 88. **d** 91 **p** 92. NSM Swavesey *Ely* 91–95; NSM Fen Drayton w Conington and Lolworth etc 95–00; CF (ACF) 92–96; Sen Chapl ACF from 96; R Outwell *Ely* 00–12; R Upwell St Pet 00–12; rtd 12; PtO *Ely* from 12; *Nor* from 01. *9 Lawn Lane, Sutton, Ely CB6 2RE*   T: (01353) 776172

JESSON, Julia Margaret. b 54. St Matthias Coll Bris CertEd 75 Nottm Univ MA 04. EMMTC 01. **d** 04 **p** 05. NSM Stapleford *S'well* 04–07; C Kimberley 07–08; P-in-c E Markham w Askham, Headon w Upton and Grove 08–11; P-in-c Dunham w Darlton, Ragnall, Fledborough etc 08–11; TV Retford Area 11–17; AD Bassetlaw and Bawtry 16–17; V Knotty Ash St Jo *Liv* from 17. *The Vicarage, Thomas Lane, Liverpool L14 5NR* E: julia.jesson@btinternet.com

JESSOP, Canon Gillian Mary. b 48. Hatf Poly BSc 71 Nottm Univ MEd 85 Homerton Coll Cam PGCE 80. EAMTC 91. **d** 94 **p** 95. C Gt Yarmouth *Nor* 94–97; R Gt w Lt Addington and Woodford *Pet* 97–02; R Paston 02–15; Asst Dir Tr for Readers 00–02; Dir 02–10; RD Pet 10–15; Can Pet Cathl 11–15; rtd 15; PtO *Pet* from 15; *Ely* from 15. *35 Gidding Road, Sawtry, Huntingdon PE28 5TS*   T: (01487) 832237 E: rev.gill69@gmail.com

JESSOP, Ms Tracy Jane. b 65. ERMC 16. **d** 19. C Wroxham w Hoveton, Belaugh and Tunstead etc *Nor* from 19. *2 Burnt Fen Way, Hoveton, Norwich NR12 8GJ*   T: (01603) 784651   M: 07402-165485 E: tracy_jessop@btinternet.com

JESTY, Mrs Helen Margaret. b 51. York Univ BA 72. Cranmer Hall Dur BA 81. **dss** 82 **d** 87. S Lambeth St Steph *S'wark* 82–86; Norbiton 86–93; Par Dn 87–90; Hon Par Dn 91–93; Chapl Naomi Ho Hospice 05–13; rtd 13. *Fairfield, 1 Downside Road, Winchester SO22 5LT*   T: (01962) 849190 E: helen.jesty@btinternet.com

JESUDASON, Leslie Peter Prakash. b 58. Wycliffe Hall Ox 05. **d** 07 **p** 08. C Throop *Win* 07–11; TV Bracknell *Ox* 11–19; V Croydon Ch Ch *S'wark* from 19. *The Vicarage, 34 Longley Road, Croydon CR0 3LH*   T: (020) 8649 7620 E: ljesudason@outlook.com

JEVONS, The Ven Alan Neil. b 56. Ex Univ BA 77 Selw Coll Cam BA 80 MA 84. Ridley Hall Cam. **d** 81 **p** 82. C Halesowen *Worc* 81–84; C Heywood St Luke w All So *Man* 84–87; TV Heref St Martin w St Fran 87–93; P-in-c Much Birch w Lt Birch, Much Dewchurch etc 93–02; RD Ross and Archenfield 98–02; TR Tenbury Wells 02–07; Preb Heref Cathl 02–07; RD Ludlow 05–07; V Llyn Safaddan *S & B* 07–15; C from 15; C The Beacons from 15; Dioc Tourism Officer 07–13; Asst Dioc Soc Resp Officer 09–13; Adn Brecon from 13. *The Vicarage, Llangorse, Brecon LD3 7UG*   T: (01874) 658298 E: archdeacon.brecon@churchinwales.org.uk

JEVONS, Harry Clifford. b 56. Otter Coll 01. **d** 04 **p** 05. C Ifield *Chich* 04–07; C Milton *Win* 07–11; rtd 11; C Ermington and Ugborough *Ex* 11–14; C Diptford, N Huish, Harberton, Harbertonford etc 11–14; P-in-c Torquay St Luke 14–16; C Paignton St Jo 16–19. *St Luke's Vicarage, 1 Mead Road, Torquay TQ2 6TE*   T: (01803) 368047   M: 07881-527050 E: fr.harry@hotmail.co.uk

JEWELL, Alan David John. b 59. St Cath Coll Ox MA 86. Wycliffe Hall Ox 83. **d** 86 **p** 87. C Walton H Trin *Ox* 86–91; TV Sutton *Liv* 91–97; TV Halewood 97–01; TR 01–12; TR Halewood and Hunts Cross 12–14; V Stretton and Appleton Thorn *Ches* from 14. *The Vicarage, Stretton Road, Stretton, Warrington WA4 4NT*   T: (01925) 730276 E: alandjjewell@btopenworld.com

JEWISS, Anthony Harrison. b 39. Virginia Th Sem MDiv 92. **d** 92 **p** 93. Chapl to Bp Los Angeles USA 92–99; Can Prec Los Angeles 99; Dep Exec Officer Episc Ch Cen New York 99–07; rtd 07; Asst Chapl Midi-Pyrénées and Aude *Eur* from 09. *3 rue Mandrière, 11580 Alet-les-Bains, France*   T: (0033) 4 68 69 01 22 E: tonyjewiss@gmail.com

JEWITT, Martin Paul Noel. b 44. AKC 69. St Aug Coll Cant. **d** 70 **p** 71. C Usworth *Dur* 70–74; TV 77–78; Tutor Newton Coll Papua New Guinea 74–77; V Balham Hill Ascension *S'wark* 78–93; R N Reddish *Man* 93–95; V Thornton Heath St Paul *S'wark* 99–10; rtd 10; PtO *Cant* from 10. *12 Abbott Road, Folkestone CT20 1NG*   T: (01303) 211491   M: 07981-754738 E: martin.jewitt@virginmedia.com

JEWSON, Dawn. b 56. St Mellitus Coll BA 13. **d** 13 **p** 14. C Southall St Geo *Lon* 13–16; P-in-c Hatfield Heath and Sheering *Chelmsf* from 16. *The Vicarage, Broomfields, Hatfield Heath, Bishop's Stortford CM22 7EH*   T: (01279) 730288   M: 07930-902507 E: rev.dawn.jewson@gmail.com

JEYES, Caroline Helen. *See* WALKER, Caroline Helen

JEYNES, Anthony James. b 44. AKC 68. St Boniface Warminster 68. **d** 69 **p** 70. C Ellesmere Port *Ches* 69–73; C Birkenhead St Pet w St Matt 73–74; R Oughtrington 75–80; C Timperley 80–85; C Eastham 85–89; V New Brighton St Jas 89–96; P-in-c New Brighton Em 94–96; R Tarleton *Blackb* 96–04; P-in-c Kyrenia St Andr and Chapl N Cyprus 04–07; Chapl Paphos 07–09; rtd 09; PtO Cyprus and the Gulf from 09; PtO *Ches* from 19. *6 Maidwell Close, Winsford CW7 3UG*   T: (01606) 860120   M: 07485-000839 E: tonyirenejeynes@gmail.com

JINKS, Mrs Elizabeth. b 60. St Aug Coll of Th 16. **d** 19. NSM Holbrook *Chich* from 19. *St Mark's Church, St Mark's Lane, Horsham RH12 5PU*   T: (01403) 275403 E: curate@stmarksholbrook.org.uk

JOACHIM, Margaret Jane. b 49. St Hugh's Coll Ox BA 70 MA 74 Birm Univ PhD 77 W Midl Coll of Educn PGCE 71 FGS 91. S Dios Minl Tr Scheme 91. **d** 94 **p** 95. NSM Ealing St Barn *Lon* 94–97; NSM Ealing St Pet Mt Park 97–19; PtO from 19. *8 Newburgh Road, London W3 6DQ*   T: (020) 8723 4514 E: margaret.joachim@london.anglican.org

JOBBER, Barry William. b 38. N Staffs Poly BA 84. Cuddesdon Coll 73. **d** 75 **p** 76. C Fenton *Lich* 76–79; V Goldenhill 79–80; PtO *Ches* 90–02 and from 12; NSM Middlewich w Byley 02–08; NSM Witton 08–12; rtd 12. *16 Angus Grove, Middlewich CW10 9GR*   T: (01606) 737386   M: 07974-380234 E: barry.jobber@uwclub.net

JOBBINS, John Clive. b 46. Bournemouth Univ BSc 06 Win Univ MA 11. Sarum Coll 08. **d** 15 **p** 16. NSM Winkleigh *Ex* 15–17; NSM Ashreigney 15–17; NSM Broadwoodkelly 15–17; NSM Brushford 15–17; NSM Burrington, Chawleigh, Cheldon, Chulmleigh etc from 17. *Vine Croft, Vine Street, Winkleigh EX19 8HN*   M: 07745-684505 E: jclivejobbins@gmail.com

JOBLING, Mary. *See* ROLLS, Mary

✠**JOHN, The Rt Revd Andrew Thomas Griffith.** b 64. Univ of Wales LLB. St Jo Coll Nottm BA. **d** 89 **p** 90 **c** 08. C Cardigan w Mwnt and Y Ferwig *St D* 89–91; C Aberystwyth 91–92; TV 92–99; V Henfynyw w Aberaeron and Llanddewi Aberarth etc 99–06; V Pencarreg and Llanycrwys 06–08; Adn Cardigan 06–08; Bp Ban from 08. *Ty'r Esgob, Upper Garth Road, Bangor LL57 2SS*   T: (01248) 362895 E: bishop.bangor@churchinwales.org.uk

JOHN, Canon Arun Andrew. b 54. **d** 77 **p** 78. India 77–96; S Africa 97–04; TV Manningham *Bradf* 04–11; P-in-c Blackb St Steph 11–12; P-in-c Blackb St Jas 11–12; V Blackb St Steph and St Jas 12–18; AD Blackb and Darwen 16–18; TR Rothwell, Lofthouse, Methley etc *Leeds* from 18. *Holy Trinity Vicarage, 1 Beech Grove, Rothwell, Leeds LS26 0EF*

JOHN, Barbara. b 34. Gilmore Ho. **dss** 67 **d** 80 **p** 97. Merthyr Tydfil *Llan* 67–71; Loughton St Jo *Chelmsf* 71–73; Newport St Woolos *Mon* 73–78; Asst Chapl Univ Hosp of Wales Cardiff 78–85; C Radyr *Llan* 85–00; rtd 00; PtO *Llan* from 04. *14 Pace Close, Cardiff CF5 2QZ*   T: (029) 2055 2989

JOHN, Canon Beverley Hayes. b 46. Qu Coll Birm 83. **d** 85 **p** 86. C Oystermouth *S & B* 85–87; C Morriston 87–88; V Cefn Coed w Vaynor 88–14; P-in-c Penderyn Mellte 12–14; AD Brecon 99–14; Can Res Brecon Cathl 04–14; rtd 14; PtO *S & B* from 14. *63 Kingrosia Park, Clydach, Swansea SA6 5PL*   T: (01792) 842911

JOHN, Brother. *See* HENNINGS, John Richard

JOHN, Canon David Michael. b 36. Univ of Wales (Lamp) BA 57. St Mich Coll Llan 57. **d** 59 **p** 60. C Pontypool *Mon* 59–61; C Roath *Llan* 61–66; Asst Chapl HM Pris Liv 66–67; Chapl HM Pris Ex 67–68; V Ystrad Rhondda *Llan* 68–76; V Pontyclun w Talygarn 76–84; R Newton Nottage 84–91; Can Llan Cathl 85–91; rtd 91; PtO *Llan* from 91; *Mon* from 91. *Hastings House, OPH, 130 Barnards Green Road, Malvern WR14 3NA* T: (01684) 585015

JOHN, David Wyndham. b 61. Lon Bible Coll. NTMTC. **d** 01 **p** 02. NSM Hampstead Em W End *Lon* 01–04; NSM W Hampstead St Cuth 04–15; P-in-c 06–15; V Iwerne Valley *Sarum* from 15. *The Vicarage, Iwerne Minster, Blandford Forum DT11 8NF* M: 07719-333389 E: david.john6@btopenworld.com

JOHN, The Very Revd Jeffrey Philip Hywel. b 53. Hertf Coll Ox BA 75 Magd Coll Ox DPhil 84. St Steph Ho Ox BA 77 MA 78. **d** 78 **p** 79. C Penarth w Lavernock *Llan* 78–80; Asst Chapl Magd Coll Ox 80–82; Fell and Dean of Div 84–91; Chapl and Lect BNC Ox 82–84; V Eltham H Trin *S'wark* 91–97; Chan and Can Th S'wark Cathl 97–04; Bp's Adv for Min 97–04; Dean St Alb from 04. *The Deanery, Sumpter Yard, St Albans AL1 1BY* T: (01727) 890203 F: 890227 E: dean@stalbanscathedral.org

JOHN, Michael Ioannou. b 86. City Univ BA 09. Wycliffe Hall Ox BTh 15. **d** 15 **p** 16. C Muswell Hill St Jas w St Matt *Lon* 15–18; C Clapham H Trin *S'wark* from 18. *7 Buckmaster Road, London SW11 1EN* M: 07540-469052 E: michael.john@holytrinityclapham.org

JOHN, Napoleon. b 55. Punjab Univ BA 76. Lahetysteologisen Inst Ryttyla Finland 84 Oak Hill Th Coll BA 93. **d** 93 **p** 94. C Leyton St Mary w St Edw *Chelmsf* 93–96; C Leyton St Mary w St Edw and Luke 96–97; P-in-c Beccontree St Elisabeth 97–04; V 04–07; TR Walton and Trimley *St E* 07–13; R Hayes *Roch* from 13. *The Rectory, Hayes Street, Hayes, Bromley BR2 7LH* T: (020) 8462 1373 E: napojohn@gmail.com

JOHN, Robert Michael. b 46. Edin Univ BSc 67 Man Univ MSc 68 PhD 70 Otago Univ BD 78. St Jo Coll Auckland 76. **d** 78 **p** 79. C Tauranga New Zealand 78–80; C Hastings 80–83; V Waipaoa 83–87; C Swansea St Jas *S & B* 87–88; V Otumoetai New Zealand 88–94; Chapl Auckland Hosps 94–09; Chapl Univ Hosps of Morecambe Bay NHS Trust 09–11; C N Barrow *Carl* 11–13; rtd 13; PtO *Carl* 13–15; New Zealand 15–16; P-in-c Onehunga 16. *11 Palmerston Road, Birkenhead, Auckland 0626, New Zealand* E: robertmichaeljohn@btinternet.com

JOHNES, Philip Sydney. b 45. St Mich Coll Llan 90. **d** 92 **p** 93. C Cardigan w Mwnt and Y Ferwig *St D* 92–95; V Llanegwad w Llanfynydd 95–10; rtd 10; PtO *St D* from 10. *Keeper's Cottage, Ferryside SA17 5TY* T: (01267) 267081 E: pjohnes@phonescoop.coop

JOHN-FRANCIS, Brother. *See* FRIENDSHIP, Roger Geoffrey

JOHNS, Adam Aubrey. b 34. TCD BA 57 MA 76 NUU BA 75. CITC Div Test 58. **d** 58 **p** 59. C Aghalee *D & D* 58–61; C Derriaghy *Conn* 61–63; I Billy 63–77; I Billy w Derrykeighan 77–03; Can Conn Cathl 98–03; rtd 03. *26 Chatham Road, Armoy, Ballymoney BT53 8TT* T: (028) 2075 1978 E: chathambrae@btinternet.com

JOHNS, Canon Bernard Thomas. b 36. Birm Univ BSc 58. St Mich Coll Llan 61. **d** 63 **p** 64. C Aberavon *Llan* 63–65; C St Andrews Major w Michaelston-le-Pit 65–70; V Cardiff St Andr and St Teilo 70–76; Asst Dioc Dir of Educn 72–91; V Roath 76–88; R Wenvoe and St Lythans 88–02; Dioc Dir Community Educn 91–02; Can Llan Cathl 96–02; rtd 02. *Bay Tree Cottage, 13 Badgers Meadow, Pwllmeyric, Chepstow NP16 6UE* T: (01291) 623254

JOHNS, Mrs Patricia Holly. b 33. Girton Coll Cam BA 56 MA 60 Hughes Hall Cam PGCE 57. Ox NSM Course 87. **d** 90 **p** 94. NSM Wantage Ox 90–94; NSM Marlborough *Sarum* 94–95; rtd 95; PtO *Sarum* from 95. *1 Priory Lodge, 93 Brown Street, Salisbury SP1 2BX* T: (01722) 328007 E: payjohns70@hotmail.com

JOHNS, Thomas Morton. b 43. Oak Hill Th Coll 67. **d** 70 **p** 71. C N Meols *Liv* 70–73; C Farnborough *Guildf* 73–76; P-in-c Badshot Lea *Guildf* 76–83; Dep Chapl HM Pris Man 83; Chapl HM Youth Cust Cen Wellingborough 83–88; Chapl HM YOI Swinfen Hall 88–90; Chapl Tr Officer 88–95; Chapl HM Pris Service Coll 90–95; Asst Chapl Gen of Pris (HQ) 95–01; Acting Chapl Gen 00–01; P-in-c Colbury *Win* 02–08; Chapl Hants Constabulary 02–08; rtd 08; PtO *Portsm* from 02. *18 Southbrook Mews, Bishops Waltham, Southampton SO32 1RZ* T: (01489) 891585 M: 07988-314928 E: tomjohns585@btinternet.com

JOHNS-PERRING, Michael James. b 85. York Univ BA 07 Edin Univ MSc 09 Selw Coll Cam BTh 18. Westcott Ho Cam 16. **d** 19. C Surbiton St Andr and St Mark *S'wark* from 19. *1 The Mall, Surbiton KT6 4EH*

JOHNSEN, Edward Andrew. b 67. Birm Univ BTheol 89. Qu Coll Birm 95. **d** 97 **p** 98. C Birm St Luke 97–01; C Handsworth St Mary 01–04; PtO 05–06; TV Eden, Gelt and Irthing *Carl* from 06; RD Brampton from 18. *The Vicarage, Hayton, Brampton CA8 9HR* T: (01228) 670248 E: edwardajohnsen@gmail.com

JOHNSON, Dom Andrew Edmond. b 59. **d** 08 **p** 09. OSB from 85; PtO *Win* from 09. *Abbey of Our Lady and St John, Abbey Road, Beech, Alton GU34 4AP* T: (01420) 562145 F: 561691

JOHNSON, Andrew Paul. b 56. W Surrey Coll of Art & Design BA 79 Kent Coll for Careers CertEd 82 TCD BTh 96. CITC 93. **d** 96 **p** 97. C Penarth w Lavernock *Llan* 96–99; R Walton W w Talbenny and Haroldston W *St D* 99–15; P-in-c Dale and St Brides w Marloes etc from 14. *The Vicarage, Castle Way, Dale, Haverfordwest SA62 3RN* T: (01646) 636966 E: frandrewj@btinternet.com

JOHNSON, Andrew Paul. b 69. **d** 14 **p** 15. C W Ealing St Jo w St Jas *Lon* 14–17; P-in-c Perivale from 17. *5 Bethlehem Close, Perivale, Greenford UB6 7FQ* M: 07958-604708 E: revandyjohnson@me.com

JOHNSON, Andrew Peter. **d** 12 **p** 15. NSM Ex Cathl 12–17; NSM Heavitree and St Mary Steps from 17. *Elm Brook House, 348 Topsham Road, Exeter EX2 6HF* T: (01392) 271059 E: andrewjohnson1@btinternet.com

JOHNSON, Andrew Peter. b 67. Westf Coll Lon BA 89 St Jo Coll Nottm MA 98 LTh 99. Aston Tr Scheme 94. **d** 99 **p** 00. C Hitchin *St Alb* 99–03; V Batley All SS and Purlwell *Wakef* 03–13; R Barton-le-Cley w Higham Gobion and Hexton *St Alb* from 13. *The Rectory, 2 Manor Farm Close, Barton-le-Clay, Bedford MK45 4TB* T: (01582) 881873 E: johnsons@care4free.net

JOHNSON, Mrs Angela Carolyn Louise. b 52. RGN 76. STETS 00. **d** 03 **p** 04. NSM Catherington and Clanfield *Portsm* 03–07; NSM Denmead from 07. *90 Downhouse Road, Waterlooville PO8 0TY* T: (023) 9264 4595

JOHNSON, Anthony Peter. b 45. K Coll Lon BD 76 AKC 76 MTh 79. Wells Th Coll 67. **d** 70 **p** 71. C Goldington *St Alb* 70–73; C Hainault *Chelmsf* 73–76; TV Loughton St Mary 76–81; V Scunthorpe All SS *Linc* 81–85; V Alkborough 85–87; Chapl Man Univ and TV Man Whitworth 87–96; P-in-c Chorlton-cum-Hardy St Werburgh 96–00; R 00–05; P-in-c Yardley St Cypr Hay Mill *Birm* 05–08; V 08–10; rtd 10; PtO *Birm* 10–16. *St Barnabas' Vicarage, 51 Over Green Drive, Kingshurst, Birmingham B37 6EY* M: 07842-151492 E: ajohnson940@btinternet.com

JOHNSON, Anthony Warrington. b 40. Goldsmiths' Coll Lon CertEd 60. St Jo Coll Nottm 86. **d** 88 **p** 89. C Lutterworth w Cotesbach *Leic* 88–92; V Countesthorpe w Foston 92–06; P-in-c Arnesby w Shearsby and Bruntingthorpe 94–01; rtd 06; Hon C Lutterworth w Cotesbach and Bitteswell *Leic* 06–09; PtO 13–17. *15 Constable Drive, Barton Seagrave, Kettering NN15 5UA* T: (01536) 515033 E: tonywjohnson@btinternet.com

JOHNSON, Miss Barbara. b 45. St Jo Coll Nottm 04. **d** 07 **p** 08. NSM Royston *St Alb* 07–08; NSM Goldington 08–10; Chapl Beds and Luton Fire and Rescue Service from 07; PtO *Ely* 10–15 and from 16; Ox from 11. *4 Hicks Lane, Girton, Cambridge CB3 0JS* T: (01223) 276282 M: 07768-560646

JOHNSON, Barry Charles Richard. b 48. EAMTC 96. **d** 99 **p** 00. C Gt Burstead *Chelmsf* 99–02; C Bowers Gifford w N Benfleet 02–04; P-in-c Woodham Mortimer w Hazeleigh 04–06; R Vange 06–10; P-in-c Bowers Gifford w N Benfleet 07–10; V Folkestone St Mary, St Eanswythe and St Sav *Cant* 10–12; rtd 12; P-in-c Gt Parndon *Chelmsf* 13–14; V Staple Tye 14–15; P-in-c Mayland 15–16; C Althorne and Latchingdon w N Fambridge 15–16; V Mayland and Latchingdon 16; PtO 16–18. *Lyndon, London Road, Bowers Gifford, Basildon SS13 2HE* T: (01268) 726318 E: revbj@btinternet.com

JOHNSON, Mrs Brenda Margaret. b 47. TISEC 93. **d** 00. NSM Edin St Salvador 00–03; NSM Wester Hailes St Luke 00–03; NSM Edin Gd Shep 03–17. *58 Ratho Park Road, Ratho, Newbridge EH28 8PQ* T: 0131-333 1742 M: 07713-154744 E: brenmj@btinternet.com

JOHNSON, Brian. b 42. S'wark Ord Course 84. **d** 87 **p** 88. NSM Dulwich St Barn *S'wark* 87–92; NSM Herne Hill 92–94; PtO 94–96; Chapl HM Pris Man 96–01; P-in-c Rotterdam *Eur* 01–02; Operations Manager ICS 03; PtO *Cov* 03; *Ches* from 04; *Man* 11–17; *Newc* from 18. *42 Sunningdale, Whitley Bay NE25 9YF* T: 0191-340 0659 E: revbfg13@gmail.com

JOHNSON, Bruce Graham. b 67. All SS Cen for Miss & Min 15. **d** 18 **p** 19. NSM Heanor *Derby* 18–19; NSM Langley Mill and Aldercar 18–19; NSM Marlpool 18–19; NSM Belper Ch Ch w Turnditch from 19. *31 Porterhouse Road, Ripley DE5 3FL* T: (01773) 449001 E: revbruce18@gmail.com

JOHNSON, Christopher Frederick. b 43. MRICS 67. Ripon Hall Ox 71. **d** 74 **p** 75. C Chatham St Steph *Roch*

74–78; V Slade Green 78–85; V Wilmington 85–95; R Chevening 95–09; rtd 09; PtO *Roch* from 09. *7 Kennedy Gardens, Sevenoaks TN13 3UG* T: (01732) 456626 E: c.f.johnson@btinternet.com

JOHNSON, Christopher James. b 88. Cant Ch Ch Univ BA 11. Ripon Coll Cuddesdon MTh 13. **d** 13 **p** 14. C Weobley w Sarnesfield and Norton Canon *Heref* 13–16; C Wigston *Leic* from 16. *St Thomas's Vicarage, 9 Hindoostan Avenue, Wigston LE18 4UD* M: 07969-432481 E: christopher.johnson121@gmail.com

JOHNSON, Christopher Neil. b 87. St Benet's Hall Ox BA 10 MA 14. St Steph Ho Ox MSt 10 MLitt 14. **d** 13 **p** 14. C Pickering w Lockton and Levisham *York* 13–17; V Horbury w Horbury Bridge *Leeds* from 17. *St Peter's Vicarage, Northgate, Horbury, Wakefield WF4 6AS* E: fr.christopher.johnson@gmail.com

JOHNSON, Christopher Paul. b 47. Leeds Univ MA 01. St Jo Coll Nottm BTh 74. **d** 74 **p** 75. C Normanton *Wakef* 74–78; P-in-c Dewsbury St Mark 78–82; V Harden and Wilsden *Bradf* 82–88; P-in-c Holbeck *Ripon* 88–94; V 94–97; Asst Chapl Leeds Teaching Hosps NHS Trust 97–00; Chapl Bradf Hosps NHS Trust 00–13; rtd 13; PtO *Leeds* from 13. *6 Suffield Road, Gildersome, Morley, Leeds LS27 7WA* T: 0113-285 4953 E: christopherjohnson1947@live.co.uk

JOHNSON, Christopher Robert. b 43. Lon Coll of Div 66. **d** 70 **p** 71. C Everton St Geo *Liv* 70–71; C Childwall All SS 71–75; TV Gateacre 75–76; TV Bushbury *Lich* 76–87; R Burslem 87–10; rtd 10; PtO *Lich* from 11. *102 Chell Green Avenue, Stoke-on-Trent ST6 7LA* T: (01782) 850169 E: rob.johnson60@talk21.com

JOHNSON, Colin Leslie. b 41. Trin Coll Cam MA 65. Cheshunt Coll Cam 62. **d** 93 **p** 94. Publications Dir *Chr Educn* Movement from 89; NSM Brailsford w Shirley and Osmaston w Edlaston *Derby* 93–04; PtO from 04. *33 The Plain, Brailsford, Ashbourne DE6 3BZ* T: (01335) 360591 E: cj@acjohnson.plus.com

JOHNSON, Colin Stewart. b 46. SEITE 99. **d** 02 **p** 03. NSM Borden *Cant* 02–05; C Charlton-in-Dover 05–06; P-in-c 06–13; rtd 13; PtO *Cant* from 14. *423 Minster Road, Minster on Sea, Sheerness ME12 3NS* T: (01795) 857175 M: 07740-775277 E: frcj@dsl.pipex.com

JOHNSON, David. b 68. Cranmer Hall Dur 13. **d** 15 **p** 16. C Monk Fryston and S Milford *York* 15–19; C Northallerton w Kirby Sigston from 19. *6 Mayfair Court, Northallerton DL7 8WG* M: 07515-288105 E: davidjohnsonihs@gmail.com

JOHNSON, David. *See* JOHNSON, John David

JOHNSON, David Alan. b 43. Lon Univ BSc 63 PhD 67. Trin Coll Bris 78. **d** 80 **p** 81. C Watford St Alb 80–85; V Idle *Bradf* 85–08; P-in-c Greengates 08; rtd 08; PtO *Dur* from 09. *15 Blackburn Close, Bearpark, Durham DH7 7TQ* T: 0191-373 7953 E: david@festsoft.co.uk

JOHNSON, David Bryan Alfred. b 36. Kelham Th Coll 56. **d** 61 **p** 62. C Streatham St Paul *S'wark* 61–63; C St Thos Cathl Kuching Malaysia 63–66; V Sibu 66–71; V Worc St Mich 71–74; Warden Lee Abbey Internat Students' Club Kensington 74–77; V Plumstead St Mark and St Marg *S'wark* 77–86; Chapl W Park Hosp Epsom 86–96; Chapl Laslett's *Worc* 96–01; rtd 96; PtO *Ox* from 18. *3 St Birinus Cottages, Wessex Way, Bicester OX26 6DX* T: (01869) 320839 E: dbajohnson1@gmail.com

JOHNSON, David Francis. b 32. Univ Coll Ox BA 55 MA 59. Westcott Ho Cam 55. **d** 57 **p** 58. C Earlsdon *Cov* 57–59; C Willenhall 59–61; C Attenborough w Bramcote *S'well* 61–62; V Ravenstone w Weston Underwood *Ox* 62–66; V Crewe Ch Ch *Ches* 66–70; P-in-c Crewe St Pet 67–70; V Thornton w Allerthorpe *York* 70–79; V N Hull St Mich 79–81; V Leyburn w Bellerby *Ripon* 81–88; V Coxwold and Husthwaite *York* 88–97; rtd 97; PtO *York* 98–03; *Heref* 05–13; *Glouc* from 17. *Fleur de Lys, Coleford Road, Tutshill, Chepstow NP16 7BU* T: (01291) 621636 E: dfjjaj@btinternet.com

JOHNSON, David John. b 49. Lanc Univ BA 72. Linc Th Coll 78. **d** 81 **p** 82. C Stockport St Thos *Ches* 81–84; OGS from 83; C Stockton Heath *Ches* 84–88; V Tranmere St Paul w St Luke 88–99; P-in-c Antrobus 99–02; P-in-c Aston by Sutton 99–02; V Antrobus, Aston by Sutton, Lt Leigh etc 02–07; C Coppenhall 07–10; rtd 11; PtO *Ches* from 11. *14 Manor Way, Crewe CW2 6JX* T: (01270) 250256

JOHNSON, David William. b 40. Oak Hill Th Coll BD 64. **d** 65 **p** 66. C Tunbridge Wells St Jas *Roch* 65–68; C Kirby Muxloe *Leic* 68–72; V Burton Joyce w Bulcote *S'well* 72–83; V Mitford and Chapl Northgate Mental Handicap Unit Morpeth 83–87; Asst Chapl R Victoria Infirmary Newc 87–89; Chapl R Shrewsbury Hosps NHS Trust 89–04; rtd 04. *42 Hartlands, Bedlington NE22 6JG* T: (01670) 828693

JOHNSON, Preb Derek John. b 36. St Aid Birkenhead 65. **d** 68 **p** 69. C Eccleshall *Lich* 68–73; C Stafford St Mary 73–74; C Stafford St Mary and St Chad 74–75; Chapl New Cross Hosp Wolv 75–96; Preb Lich Cathl 83–96; rtd 96; PtO *St E* from 96. *6 St Paul's Close, Aldeburgh IP15 5BQ* T: (01728) 452474

JOHNSON, Diana. b 54. RMCS BSc 79 Qu Coll Cam MPhil 92 Anglia Ruskin Univ MA 06. ERMC 16. **d** 17 **p** 18. C Girton *Ely* from 17. *13 Gretton Court, Girton, Cambridge CB3 0QN* T: (01223) 276291 E: diana.johnson@cantab.net

JOHNSON, Canon Diana Margaret. b 46. MCSP 68 SRP 68. Cranmer Hall Dur 92. **d** 94 **p** 95. C Birtley *Dur* 94–99; TV Gateshead 99–06; AD 03–06; P-in-c Belmont 06–07; V Belmont and Pittington 07–12; Hon Can Dur Cathl 06–12; rtd 12; PtO *Dur* from 12. *3 Avenue Street, High Shincliffe, Durham DH1 2PT* T: 0191-386 1660 E: dmjohnson462@gmail.com

JOHNSON, Mrs Diane Pearl. b 47. Leeds Univ BA 68 Cam Univ PGCE 69. EAMTC 95. **d** 98 **p** 99. NSM Gt Bowden w Welham, Glooston and Cranoe *Leic* 98–01; C Evington and Leic St Phil 01–04; P-in-c 04–07; rtd 07; PtO *Pet* from 10; *Leic* from 15. *16 Oaklands Park, Market Harborough LE16 8EU* T: (01858) 434118 E: gandi2007@btinternet.com

JOHNSON, Mrs Dorothy. Leic Univ BSc 89 Ox Univ MTh 95 Ox Brookes Univ MA 14 RGN FRSH 91. Qu Coll Birm 77. **dss** 80 **d** 87 **p** 94. Coventry Caludon *Cov* 80–81; Wolston and Church Lawford 81–86; NSM Stoneleigh w Ashow 87–08; Bp's Asst Officer for Soc Resp 87–96; PtO 11–15; *Win* from 16. *119 Hillside Drive, Christchurch BH23 2SZ* M: 07975-893114 E: e.djohnson@btinternet.com

JOHNSON, Douglas Leonard. b 45. St Paul's Coll Chelt CertEd 67 Lon Bible Coll MA 95 Roehampton Univ PhD 13. Tyndale Hall Bris 70. **d** 73 **p** 74. C New Malden and Coombe *S'wark* 73–76; P-in-c Upper Tulse Hill St Matthias 76–82; CPAS Staff 82–88; Lect and Tutor CA Coll 88–91; Dir Crossways Chr Educn Trust 92–08; Hon C Wimbledon Em Ridgway Prop Chpl *S'wark* 91–94; Lect Cornhill Tr Course 94–06; Crosslinks Kenya 08–10; rtd 11; PtO *B & W* from 12. *The Stables, Mudford, Yeovil BA21 5TD* T: (01935) 432304 E: douglasjohnson@btinternet.com

JOHNSON, Emma Louise. *See* PARKER, Emma Louise

JOHNSON, Emma Louise. *See* COLEY, Emma Louise

JOHNSON, Eric. b 38. Nottm Univ BSc 60 Man Univ CertEd 65 Open Univ BA 92 SS Paul & Mary Coll Cheltenham MA 94 Birm Univ BA 06. Qu Coll Birm 74. **d** 77 **p** 78. Sen Lect Cov Tech Coll 66–91; NSM Earlsdon *Cov* 77–81; NSM Wolston and Church Lawford 81–86; NSM Stoneleigh w Ashow and Baginton 90–98; FE Liaison Officer B & W, Bris and Glouc 91–93; Dioc Dir of Educn *Worc* 93–98; rtd 98; PtO *Cov* 11–15; *Win* from 16. *119 Hillside Drive, Christchurch BH23 2SZ* M: 07773-748967 E: e.djohnson@btinternet.com

JOHNSON, Frances Josephine. b 53. Leeds Univ CertEd 74 Open Univ BA 90. NOC 02. **d** 05 **p** 06. C Hall Green St Pet *Birm* 05–08; V Kingshurst from 08. *St Barnabas' Vicarage, 51 Over Green Drive, Birmingham B37 6EY* T: 0121-770 3972 E: revjohnson@btinternet.com

JOHNSON, Geoffrey Stuart. b 39. ALCD 65 Wolv Poly DipEd Sussex Univ DPhil 01. **d** 65 **p** 66. C Worksop St Jo *S'well* 65–68; Taiwan 68–71; C St Andr Cathl Singapore 71–76; Aber Univ *Ab* 76–78; PtO *Heref* 78–82; P-in-c Hoarwithy, Sellack and Hentland 82–84; Chapl Horton Hosp Epsom 84–90; Distr Chapl Brighton HA 90–94; Managing Chapl Brighton Healthcare NHS Trust 94–99; rtd 99; Chapl S Downs Health NHS Trust 99–00; Chapl S Downs Health NHS Trust 00–06; Chapl Sussex Partnership NHS Foundn Trust 06–13; PtO *Chich* 01–14. *Kingfisher, Rope Walk, Ross-on-Wye HR9 7BU* T: (01989) 562002 E: g.johnson479@btinternet.com

JOHNSON, Gillian Margaret. b 55. Bretton Hall Coll CertEd 76 Coll of Ripon & York St Jo MA 03. NOC 00. **d** 03 **p** 04. C Thornhill and Whitley Lower *Wakef* 03–07; C Mirfield 07–10; Curriculum Development Officer Dioc Bd Educn 07–10; Dioc Educn Development Officer 10–14; Dioc Schs' Adv *Leeds* 14–18; Sec Coll of Resurr Mirfield from 18. *College of the Resurrection, The Mirfield Centre, Stocks Bank Road, Mirfield WF14 0BW* T: (01924) 481900 M: 07804-477867 E: gjohnson@mirfield.org.uk

JOHNSON, Harriet. b 69. St Aug Coll of Th 15. **d** 17 **p** 18. NSM Kingsdown *Roch* from 17. *150 Brownspring Drive, London SE9 3LD* E: revharrietjohnson@gmail.com

JOHNSON, Helen Louise. b 74. **d** 13 **p** 14. C Bedminster *Bris* 13–16; C Whitchurch 13–15; C Whitchurch St Aug 15–16; P-in-c Shirehampton from 16. *8 Priory Gardens, Shirehampton, Bristol BS11 0BZ* E: revhelenjohnson@btinternet.com

JOHNSON, Canon Hilary Ann. b 51. RGN 72 RHV 74. S'wark Ord Course 82. **dss** 85 **d** 87 **p** 94. Hon Par Dn Salfords *S'wark* 85–90; Chapl St Geo Hosp Lon 90–94; Chapl St Geo Healthcare NHS Trust Lon 94–15; NSM Wimbledon *S'wark*

95–10; Bp's Adv for Healthcare Chapl 11–15; Hon Can S'wark Cathl 07–15; NSM Chessington *Guildf* from 10; rtd 15. *203 Moor Lane, Chessington KT9 2AB* T: (020) 8397 0952 M: 07764-221116 E: hilary1j@gmail.com

JOHNSON, Ian Lawrence. b 44. Wells Th Coll 68. **d** 71 **p** 72. C Benhilton *S'wark* 71–73; C Weymouth H Trin *Sarum* 73–76; R Pewsey 76–81; R Maiden Newton and Valleys 81–83; Youth Officer (Sherborne Area) 81–83; Dioc Youth Officer *Sarum* 83–88; TR Langley and Parkfield *Man* 88–95; P-in-c Haughton St Anne 95–99; Dioc Adv on Evang 95–99; TR Southampton (City Cen) *Win* 99–08; rtd 08. *Farthing Cottage, 71 St Andrew Street, Tiverton EX16 6PL* T: (01884) 251974

JOHNSON, Ian Leslie. b 51. Bede Coll Dur TCert 73. Wycliffe Hall Ox 91. **d** 93 **p** 94. C Evington *Leic* 93–96; C Foxton w Gumley 96–00; P-in-c Foxton w Gumley and Laughton 00–12; Sub Chapl HM Pris Gartree 96–04; Chapl 04–15; Co-ord Chapl 12; rtd 15; PtO *Nor* from 15. *59 Lower Street, Horning, Norwich NR12 8AA* T: (01692) 631287 E: ijoh270951@aol.com

JOHNSON (née SILINS), Ms Jacqueline. b 62. Coll of Ripon & York St Jo BA 85 York St Jo Univ MA 15. Ripon Coll Cuddesdon 01. **d** 03 **p** 04. C Torpoint *Truro* 03–08; P-in-c Harworth *S'well* 08–12; Dioc Min Development Adv from 12; PtO from 19. *Jubilee House, 8 Westgate, Southwell NG25 0JH* M: 07827-291724 E: jackie.johnson@southwell.anglican.org or jackie@benedict.f9.co.uk

JOHNSON, John David. b 38. Claremont Sch of Th 65 St Deiniol's Hawarden 71. **d** 71 **p** 72. C Heref St Martin 71–73; P-in-c Ewyas Harold w Dulas 73–79; P-in-c Kilpeck 73–79; P-in-c St Devereux w Wormbridge 73–79; P-in-c Kenderchurch 73–79; P-in-c Bacton 78–79; TR Ewyas Harold w Dulas, Kenderchurch etc 79–81; R Kentchurch w Llangua, Rowlestone, Llancillo etc 79–81; Chapl Napsbury Hosp St Alb 81–96; Chapl Horizon NHS Trust Herts 96–00; Chapl Barnet Healthcare NHS Trust 96–00; Chapl Barnet and Chase Farm Hosps NHS Trust 00–05; Chapl Herts Partnerships NHS Trust 02–03; rtd 03. *10 Highcroft Road, Sharpthorne, East Grinstead RH19 4NX* T: (01342) 810314

JOHNSON, Josephine. *See* JOHNSON, Frances Josephine

JOHNSON, Mrs Julie Margaret. b 47. **d** 98 **p** 99. OLM Welton and Dunholme w Scothern *Linc* 98–07; NSM Edgeley and Cheadle Heath *Ches* from 07. *10 Delaford Close, Stockport SK3 8XA* T: 0161-456 6463 E: johnson-julie2@sky.com

JOHNSON, Kathryn Ann. **d** 03 **p** 04. C Wrexham *St As* 03–04; C Prestatyn 04–11; V Abergele and St George 11–16; TV Aled Miss Area from 17. *The Vicarage, 28 Lon Dinon, Abergele LL22 8PX* T: (01745) 822493 M: 07801-541380 E: pastorkate@btinternet.com

JOHNSON, Keith Henry. b 64. Keele Univ BA 91 Leeds Univ BA 97 MA 09 CQSW 91. Coll of Resurr Mirfield 95. **d** 97 **p** 98. C W Bromwich St Fran *Lich* 97–00; P-in-c Willenhall St Giles 00–05; V 05–06; PtO *Lon* 06–08; *Sheff* 08; P-in-c Handsworth 08–10; R from 10. *St Mary's Rectory, Handsworth Road, Handsworth, Sheffield S13 9BZ* T: 0114-269 3983 E: keithhjohnson@hotmail.com

JOHNSON, Keith Martyn. b 68. St Jo Coll Nottm 04. **d** 06 **p** 07. C Ipsley *Worc* 06–10; V Chatham St Paul w All SS *Roch* 10–16; V Hughenden *Ox* from 16. *The Vicarage, Valley Road, Hughenden Valley, High Wycombe HP14 4PF* T: (01634) 811536 M: 07772-642393 E: keiththevicar@gmail.com

JOHNSON, The Very Revd Keith Winton Thomas William. b 37. K Coll Lon BD 63 Open Univ MA 06 AKC 63. **d** 64 **p** 65. C Dartford H Trin *Roch* 64–69; Chapl Kuwait 69–73; V Erith St Jo *Roch* 73–80; V Bexley St Jo 80–91; V Royston *St Alb* 91–94; R Sandon, Wallington and Rushden w Clothall 94–97; Dean St Chris Cathl Bahrain 97–02; rtd 02; Hon C Balsham, Weston Colville, W Wickham etc *Ely* 04–10; RD Linton 07–09; PtO from 10. *17 The Rookery, Balsham, Cambridge CB21 4EU* T: (01223) 890835 E: jkeith1412@gmail.com

JOHNSON, Kenneth William George. b 53. Hull Univ BA 76 PGCE 77. EMMTC 92. **d** 95 **p** 96. NSM Ilkeston H Trin *Derby* 95–99; NSM Sandiacre from 99; Chapl Bluecoat Sch Nottm 02–11; PtO *S'well* from 96. *18 Park Avenue, Awsworth, Nottingham NG16 2RA* T: 0115-930 7830 E: kwjohnson@ntlworld.com

JOHNSON, Miss Lesley Denise. b 47. WMMTC 95. **d** 98 **p** 99. NSM Stockingford *Cov* 98–01; TV Cov E 01–10; rtd 10; PtO *Cov* from 12. *212 Sedgemoor Road, Coventry CV3 4DZ* T: (024) 7630 1241

JOHNSON, Malcolm Arthur. b 36. Univ Coll Dur BA 60 MA 64 Lon Metrop Univ Hon MA 02 Lambeth MA 06 K Coll Lon PhD 10 FSA 04. Cuddesdon Coll 60. **d** 62 **p** 63. C Portsea N End St Mark *Portsm* 62–67; Chapl Qu Mary Coll *Lon* 67–74; V St Botolph Aldgate w H Trin Minories 74–92; P-in-c St Ethelburga Bishopsgate 85–89; AD The City 85–90; Master

R Foundn of St Kath in Ratcliffe 93–97; Bp's Adv for Past Care and Counselling *Lon* 97–01; rtd 02; PtO *Lon* from 07; *Guildf* 09–17. *1 Foxgrove Drive, Woking GU21 4DZ* T: (01483) 720684 E: malcolm.johnson4@btinternet.com

JOHNSON, Canon Malcolm Stuart. b 35. AKC 60. **d** 61 **p** 62. C Catford St Laur *S'wark* 61–64; Hon C Hatcham St Cath 66–76; P-in-c Kingstanding St Luke *Birm* 76–77; V 77–82; P-in-c Peckham St Jo w St Andr *S'wark* 82–92; V 92–03; Hon Can Sabongidda-Ora from 98; rtd 04. *34 Sheppard's College, London Road, Bromley BR1 1PF* T: (020) 8466 5276

JOHNSON, Canon Margaret Anne Hope. b 52. Fitzw Coll Cam BA 95 MA 99. Ridley Hall Cam 93. **d** 95 **p** 96. C Northampton Em *Pet* 95–97; P-in-c 97–98; TR 98–16; Adv in Women's Min 03–06; Can Pet Cathl 04–16; rtd 16; PtO *Pet* from 17. *3 The Drive, Wellingborough NN8 2DB* T: (01933) 384628 M: 07752-183574 E: revmahj@gmail.com

JOHNSON, Margaret Joan (Meg). b 41. S'wark Ord Course 92. **d** 95 **p** 96. NSM Sanderstead St Mary *S'wark* 95–04; PtO 13–17. *Rose Cottage, 89 Durrington Lane, Worthing BN13 2TQ* E: megjohnson@uwclub.net

JOHNSON, Preb Mark. b 62. Leic Poly BSc 84 Loughb Univ PhD 88. Ripon Coll Cuddesdon 88. **d** 94 **p** 95. C Bishop's Cleeve *Glouc* 94–98; TV Heref S Wye 98–09; R Wormelow Hundred from 09; RD Ross and Archenfield from 13; Preb Heref Cathl from 16. *Becket House, Much Birch, Hereford HR2 8HT* T: (01981) 540390

JOHNSON, Michael. b 42. Birm Univ BSc 63. S'wark Ord Course 68. **d** 71 **p** 72. C Kidbrooke St Jas *S'wark* 71–74; NSM Eynsford w Farningham and Lullingstone *Roch* 74–89; NSM Selling w Throwley, Sheldwich w Badlesmere etc *Cant* 89–12; rtd 12; PtO *Cant* from 12. *1 Halke Cottages, North Street, Sheldwich, Faversham ME13 0LR* T: (01795) 536583 M: 07860-635728 E: onehalke@aol.com

JOHNSON, Canon Michael Anthony. b 51. Ex Univ BA 76. Ripon Coll Cuddesdon 76 Ch Div Sch of the Pacific (USA) 77. **d** 78 **p** 79. C Primrose Hill St Mary w Avenue Road St Paul *Lon* 78–81; C Hampstead St Jo 81–85; TV Mortlake w E Sheen *S'wark* 85–93; V Wroughton *Bris* 93–17; RD 97–99; AD Swindon 99–06; Hon Can Bris Cathl 99–17; PtO from 17; Acting Adn Bris 18–19. *20 Brettingham Gate, Swindon SN3 1NH* T: (01793) 434696 M: 07985-963031 E: michaeljohnson@bristoldiocese.org

JOHNSON, Michael Colin. b 37. S'wark Ord Course 77. **d** 80 **p** 81. NSM New Eltham All SS *S'wark* 80–84; NSM Woldingham 84–98; rtd 98; PtO *Chich* 99–07. *The College of St Barnabas, Blackberry Lane, Lingfield RH7 6NJ* T: (01342) 872832 E: tandem@collegeofstbarnabas.com

JOHNSON, Michael Douglas. b 64. St Jo Coll Nottm 11. **d** 13 **p** 14. C Woodthorpe *S'well* 13–17; R Gedling from 17; P-in-c Lambley from 17. *The Rectory, Rectory Drive, Gedling, Nottingham NG4 4BG* E: michael.johnsons@hotmail.com

JOHNSON, Michael Gordon. b 45. Kelham Th Coll 64. **d** 68 **p** 69. C Holbrooks *Cov* 68–72; C Cannock Lich 72–75; V Coseley Ch Ch 75–79; P-in-c Sneyd 79–82; R Longton 82–88; Chapl Pilgrim Hosp Boston 88–96; TV Jarrow *Dur* 96–98; Chapl Monkton and Primrose Hill Hosp 96–98; R Burghwallis and Campsall *Sheff* 98–10; rtd 10; PtO *Sheff* 10–18; *Leeds* from 17. *8 Harmby Close, Skellow, Doncaster DN6 8PA* T: (01302) 330700 E: junejohnson@btinternet.com

JOHNSON, Mrs Nancy May. b 46. TCert 67 Sheff Poly MA 86. NOC 00. **d** 02 **p** 03. NSM Sheff Cathl 02–04; Asst Chapl Sheff Teaching Hosps NHS Foundn Trust 04–10; rtd 10; PtO *Sheff* from 10. *121 Rustlings Road, Sheffield S11 7AB* T: 0114-266 6456 E: nancyjohnson@hotmail.co.uk

JOHNSON, Nicholas Ronald. b 84. Man Univ LLB 05 Cardiff Univ LLM 11 Called to the Bar (Lincoln's Inn) 06. St Steph Ho Ox BA 16. **d** 17 **p** 18. C Glodwick *Man* 17–18; C Royton from 18. *The Vicarage, Yates Street, Oldham OL1 4AR* M: 07817-912245 E: father.nicholas@icloud.com

JOHNSON, Canon Nigel Victor. b 48. ARCM 68 LTCL 75 Cam Univ DipEd 69. Linc Th Coll 80. **d** 82 **p** 83. C Lindley *Wakef* 82–85; P-in-c Upperthong 85–87; PtO *Derby* 88–89; NSM Calow and Sutton cum Duckmanton 89–90; R 90–00; RD Bolsover and Staveley 98–00; V Newbold w Dunston 00–15; RD Chesterfield 02–11; Hon Can Derby Cathl 05–15; rtd 15; PtO *Derby* from 15; Spiritual Dir Adv 16–18. *Yew Tree Cottage, Wheatley Road, Two Dales, Matlock DE4 2FF* E: nvjohnson@tiscali.co.uk

JOHNSON, Paul James. b 56. Teesside Coll of Educn BEd 80 Dur Sch of Educn MA 95. NEOC 06. **d** 09 **p** 10. NSM Whorlton w Carlton and Faceby *York* 09–12; PtO from 12; Chapl Ian Ramsey Sch Stockton 12–14; NSM Norton St Mary *Dur* 13–19; NSM Norton St Mich 13–19; NSM Billingham from 19. *18 Priorwood Gardens, Ingleby Barwick, Stockton-on-Tees TS17 0XH* T: (01642) 761941 E: pauljohnson452@btinternet.com

JOHNSON, Canon Peter Frederick. b 41. Melbourne Univ BA 63 Ch Ch Ox BA 68 MA 72. St Steph Ho Ox 68. d 69 p 70. C Banbury *Ox* 69–71; Tutor St Steph Ho Ox 71–74; Chapl St Chad's Coll Dur 74–80; Vice-Prin 78–80; Chapl K Sch Cant 80–90; PtO *Cant* 80–81; Hon Min Can Cant Cathl 81–90; Can Res Bris Cathl 90–08; rtd 08; PtO *Ox* from 08. *4 St John's Road, Windsor SL4 3QN* T: (01753) 865914 E: pf.johnson@btinternet.com

JOHNSON, Prof Peter Stewart. b 44. Nottm Univ BA 65 PhD 70. Cranmer Hall Dur 01. d 03 p 04. NSM Dur St Nic 03–14; PtO from 14. *126 Devonshire Road, Durham DH1 2BH* T: 0191-386 6334 M: 07949-680467 E: psjohnson969@gmail.com

JOHNSON, Philip Anthony. b 69. All Nations Chr Coll BA 97 MA 98 FIBMS 94. Ridley Hall Cam 00. d 02 p 03. C Witham *Chelmsf* 02–06; P-in-c Holland-on-Sea 06–13; V Sleaford *Linc* from 13. *1A Northfield Road, Quarrington, Sleaford NG34 8RT* E: revdphilip@aol.com

JOHNSON, Phillip Thomas. b 75. City Univ BA 03 Ox Univ BTh 12 Open Univ MA 14 Roehampton Univ MA 14 FRSA. Ripon Coll Cuddesdon 06. d 08 p 09. C Cheam *S'wark* 08–11; V Weston *Guildf* 11–18; AD Emly 17–18; V Malvern Link w Cowleigh *Worc* from 18. *12 Lambourne Avenue, Malvern WR14 1NL* M: 07815-018846 E: vicar@mlwc.church

JOHNSON (*née* DAVIES), Canon Rhiannon Mary Morgan. b 69. St Anne's Coll Ox BA 90 MA 96 Univ of Wales (Cardiff) PhD 94 BD 96. St Mich Coll Llan 94. d 97 p 98. C Whitchurch *Llan* 97–99; NSM Walton W w Talbenny and Haroldston W *St D* 99–00; Chapl Trin Coll Carmarthen 00; NSM Walton W w Talbenny and Haroldston W *St D* 00–08; P-in-c Walwyn's Castle 08–14; P-in-c Walwyn's Castle and Robeston W from 15; Dioc Course Dir for Exploring Faith from 11; Can St D Cathl from 15. *The Vicarage, Castle Way, Dale, Haverfordwest SA62 3RN* T: (01646) 636966 E: rhiannonjohnson@churchinwales.org.uk

JOHNSON, Richard Miles. b 59. Bris Univ BSc 82. St Jo Coll Nottm 87. d 90 p 91. C Bromley SS Pet and Paul *Roch* 90–94; USPG/CMS Philippines 94–97; Ind Chapl *Roch* 97–06; C Bexleyheath Ch Ch 97–06; Ind Chapl *Worc* from 06; TV Redditch H Trin 06–17. *124 Lyttleton Avenue, Bromsgrove B60 3LB* E: dickim@globalnet.co.uk

JOHNSON, Richard William. b 76. St Cath Coll Cam BA 98 MA Glos Univ PhD 05. Westmr Th Cen. d 05 p 06. C Symonds Street St Paul New Zealand 05–09; C Worc City 09–14; V Worc St Nic and All SS w St Helen from 14. *All Saints' Church Centre, Unicorn Chambers, Chapel Walk, Worcester WR1 3LD* T: (01905) 734625 E: rich@allsaintsworcester.org.uk

JOHNSON, Robert. *See* JOHNSON, Christopher Robert

JOHNSON, Robert Anthony. b 59. Trans Min Course 14. d 16 p 17. NSM Thornbury *Leeds* 16–17; NSM Woodhall 16–17; NSM Thornbury, Woodhall and Waterloo from 17. *13 Plumpton Drive, Bradford BD2 1PJ* T: (01274) 618330 E: revdjohnson13@gmail.com

JOHNSON, Ronald George. b 33. Chich Th Coll 75. d 76 p 77. NSM Shipley *Chich* 76–79; C Brighton St Matthias 79–82; R Barlavington, Burton w Coates, Sutton and Bignor 82–93; rtd 93; PtO *Chich* from 93. *1 Highdown Drive, Littlehampton BN17 6HJ* T: (01903) 732210

JOHNSON, Ruth Alice Edna. *See* LAMBERT, Ruth Alice Edna

JOHNSON (*née* ROWE), Mrs Shiela. b 43. CITC 93. d 96 p 97. Aux Min Urney w Denn and Derryheen *K, E & A* 96–97; Aux Min Boyle and Elphin w Aghanagh, Kilbryan etc 97–01; Aux Min Roscommon w Donamon, Rathcline, Kilkeevin etc 97–01; P-in-c Clondevaddock w Portsalon and Leatbeg *D & R* 02–08; rtd 08. *Rainbow's End, Carrickmacafferty, Derrybeg, Co Donegal, Republic of Ireland* T: (00353) (74) 953 2843 M: 087-635 0776 E: revshjohnson@gmail.com

JOHNSON, Simon Benjamin. b 73. Univ Coll Lon BEng 94. Trin Coll Bris 16. d 18 p 19. C S Harrow St Paul *Lon* from 18. *39 Eastcote Lane, Harrow HA2 8DF* M: 07810-180102 E: simonbjohnson1973@gmail.com

JOHNSON, Stanley. b 42. QUB BSc 63 TCD BTh 89. CITC 86. d 89 p 90. C Kilmore w Ballintemple, Kildallan etc *K, E & A* 89–96; Adn Elphin and Ardagh 97–01; Can Elphin Cathl 97–01; I Templemichael w Clongish, Clooncumber etc 97–01; I Clondehorkey w Cashel *D & R* 01–09; Can Raphoe Cathl 08–09; rtd 09. *Rainbow's End, Carrickmacafferty, Derrybeg, Co Donegal, Republic of Ireland* T: (00353) (74) 953 2843 M: 87-973 5775 E: revshjohnson@gmail.com *or* sjohnsons@eircom.net

JOHNSON, Stephen Ashley. b 79. York Univ BA 01 MA 02. Wycliffe Hall Ox BTh 06. d 06 p 07. C Sunningdale *Ox* 06–09; V Sunninghill and S Ascot from 09. *Sunninghill Vicarage, Church Lane, Ascot SL5 7DD* T: (01344) 873202 M: 07799-834250 E: vicar@ssaparish.org

JOHNSON, Stephen George. b 75. Ch Ch Coll Cant BA 97. Ridley Hall Cam 14. d 16 p 17. C Goring and Streatley w S Stoke *Ox* 16–19; R Church Stretton *Heref* from 19. *The Rectory, 4 Ashbrook Meadow, Carding Mill Valley, Church Stretton SY6 6JF* T: 07855-850667 E: stevejohn18@hotmail.com

JOHNSON, Stephen William. b 63. Trent Poly BEd 86 Keele Univ MA 94 Univ Coll Ches BA 05 ALCM 85. NOC 02. d 05 p 06. NSM Silverdale *Lich* 05–08; PtO *Linc* 09–10; Lich 10–12; Community Chapl *Linc* 13–14; P-in-c Market Rasen from 14; P-in-c Legsby from 14; P-in-c Linwood from 14; P-in-c Lissington from 14; RD W Wold from 17. *The Rectory, 3B Caistor Road, Market Rasen LN8 3HY* T: (01673) 844770 M: 07766-411090 E: stephenjohnson1963@icloud.com

JOHNSON, Stuart. *See* JOHNSON, Geoffrey Stuart

JOHNSON, Mrs Susan Constance. b 46. EAMTC 01. d 03 p 04. NSM Heald Green St Cath *Ches* 03–07; PtO from 10; *Newc* from 18. *42 Sunningdale, Whitley Bay NE25 9YF* T: 0191-340 0659 E: revsusan@talktalk.net

JOHNSON, Miss Susan Elaine. b 44. R Holloway Coll Lon BA 66. EAMTC 99. d 03 p 03. C Münich Ascension and V Ingolstadt H Trin Germany 03–06; NSM Cwmbran *Mon* 06–09; TV Papworth *Ely* 09–11; rtd 11. *96 The Green, Weasenham, King's Lynn PE32 2TD* T: (01328) 838124 M: 07919-232211 E: revsusan44@btinternet.com

JOHNSON, Mrs Suzanne Joan. b 61. Ripon Coll Cuddesdon 16. d 19. NSM Taplow and Dropmore *Ox* from 19. *32 Ferrers Avenue, West Drayton UB7 7AA* M: 07971-240645 E: rev.suzanne@btinternet.com

JOHNSON, Terence John. b 44. Cov Poly BA 89. ALCD 70. d 69 p 70. C Woodside *Ripon* 69–72; C Leeds St Geo 72–76; C Heworth H Trin *York* 76–81; V Budbrooke *Cov* 81–97; Chapl Wroxall Abbey Sch 83–93; V Stone Ch Ch and Oulton *Lich* 97–02; P-in-c Collingtree w Courteenhall and Milton Malsor *Pet* 02–08; rtd 08; PtO *Pet* from 09. *18 Northgate, Towcester NN12 6HT* T: (01327) 351408 E: terencejohnson194@btinternet.com

JOHNSON, Thomas Bernard. b 44. BA CertEd. Oak Hill Th Coll. d 84 p 85. C Birkenhead St Jas w St Bede *Ches* 84–88; R Ashover and Brackenfield *Derby* 88–01; P-in-c Wessington 99–01; R Ashover and Brackenfield w Wessington *Derby* 01–03; RD Chesterfield 97–02; V Swanwick and Pentrich 03–10; Hon Chapl Derbyshire St Jo Ambulance 91–09; rtd 10; PtO *Derby* from 10. *11 The Spinney, Ripley DE5 3HW* T: (01773) 570375 E: t.b.johnson2000@gmail.com

JOHNSON, Canon Victoria Louise. b 75. Leic Univ BSc 96 PhD 00 SS Coll Cam BA 06. Westcott Ho Cam 04 Yale Div Sch 06. d 07 p 08. C Baguley *Man* 07–10; P-in-c Flixton St Mich 10–15; Can Res Ely Cathl from 15. *The Black Hostelry, The College, Ely CB7 4DL* T: (01353) 660302 M: 07713-478609 E: v.johnson@elycathedral.org *or* vickyjohnson@cantab.net

JOHNSTON, Alexander Irvine. b 47. Keele Univ BA 70 LRAM. St Alb Minl Tr Scheme 77. d 80 p 81. NSM Hockerill *St Alb* 80–95; NSM High Wych and Gilston w Eastwick 95–96; TV Bottesford w Ashby *Linc* 96–01; P-in-c St Germans *Truro* 01–12; rtd 12; PtO *Truro* 12–16. *31 Longmeadow Road, Saltash PL12 6DP* T: (01752) 842328 E: alecjohnston@btinternet.com

JOHNSTON, Allen Niall. b 61. Southn Univ BTh 92 Kent Univ MA 97 AMBIM 87 MISM 87 MInstD 00. Sarum & Wells Th Coll 89. d 92 p 93. C Roehampton H Trin *S'wark* 92–95; Dir Past Services Richmond, Twickenham and Roehampton NHS Trust 95–98; Tutor SEITE 95–97; PtO *Eur* 01–02; Sierra Leone 02–03; Asst P St Jo Cathl Freetown 03; PtO *Ely* 03–08; *D & R* 04–12; rtd 12. *4 Patrick's Hill, Dunfanaghy , Co Donegal, F92 FP78, Republic of Ireland* E: niall@nialljohnston.org

JOHNSTON, Austin. b 50. Huddersfield Poly CertEd 76 BEd 90. Chich Th Coll 92. d 94 p 95. C Peterlee *Dur* 94–97; C Stockton St Pet 97–00; TR Stanley and Tanfield 00–01; TR Ch the K 01–15; V Stanley and S Moor 15–16; rtd 16. *12 Selwyn House, 29 Selwyn Road, Eastbourne BN21 2LF*

JOHNSTON, Brian. *See* JOHNSTON, Wilfred Brian

JOHNSTON, Mrs Carole Ann. b 58. Worc Coll of Educn BA 84. St Jo Coll Nottm 04. d 06 p 07. C Ilkley All SS *Bradf* 06–09; TV Turton Moorland *Man* 09–11; PtO *St Alb* from 15. *21A Orchard Road, Beeston, Sandy SG19 1PJ* T: (01767) 699934 E: carole.johnston@virgin.net

JOHNSTON, Charles James Andrew. b 60. d 16 p 17. NSM St Mary le Strand w St Clem Danes *Lon* 16–19; PtO *Eur* 19; Chapl Marseille w Aix-en-Provence from 19. *All Saints, 4 rue de Belloi, 13006 Marseille, France* M: 07808-054572

JOHNSTON, David George Scott. b 66. Avery Hill Coll BA 88. SEITE 00. d 03 p 04. C Frindsbury w Upnor and Chattenden *Roch* 03–06; R Longfield 06–11; C Chislehurst Ch Ch 11–15; V from 15. *The Vicarage, 62 Lubbock Road, Chislehurst BR7 5JK* T: (020) 8467 3185 E: rev.dj@btinternet.com

JOHNSTON, Edith Violet Nicholl. b 28. d 87. Par Dn Bentley *Sheff* 87–88; rtd 88; PtO *Sheff* 88–08. *30 Sharman Road, Belfast BT9 5FW* T: (028) 9066 6776

JOHNSTON, Frank. *See* JOHNSTON, William Francis

JOHNSTON, The Ven Geoffrey Stanley. b 44. Aston Univ MBA 81 Birm Univ CertEd 78. Kelham Th Coll 64. d 68 p 69. C Blakenall Heath *Lich* 68–72 and 73–75; C St Buryan, St Levan and Sennen *Truro* 72–73; P-in-c Willenhall St Steph *Lich* 75–76; C W Bromwich All SS 76–77; Lect W Bromwich Coll of Commerce and Tech 78–82; Ind Chapl *Worc* 82–94; TV Halesowen 82–94; NSM Dudley St Fran 94–99; P-in-c 99–08; P-in-c Dudley St Edm 04–08; rtd 08; P-in-c Nerja and Almuñécar *Eur* 08–14; Adn Gib from 14; Adn Italy and Malta 19. *29 Little Fallows, Milford, Belper DE56 0RY* T: (01773) 270972   M: 07507-391297   E: vengeoffrey@gmail.com *or* geoff.johnston@europe.anglican.org

JOHNSTON, Mrs Helen Kay. b 48. SRN 70. SAOMC 95. d 98 p 99. OLM Banbury St Paul *Ox* 98–01; P-in-c Flimby *Carl* 01–03; C Netherton 01–03; PtO *Derby* 04–11; *Lich* from 11. *Merryfields, Whitehorn Avenue, Barleston, Stoke-on-Trent ST12 9EF* T: (01782) 372618

JOHNSTON, Miss Henrietta Elizabeth Ann. b 59. St Jo Coll Dur BA 03. Cranmer Hall Dur 01. d 03 p 04. C Cov H Trin 03–07; C Dorridge *Birm* 07–11; V Lache cum Saltney *Ches* from 11; P-in-c Chester St Pet 16–17; RD Ches from 19. *St Mark's Vicarage, 5 Cliveden Road, Chester CH4 8DR* T: (01244) 671702 *or* 675372   M: 07796-948904 E: hennie.johnston@gmail.com

JOHNSTON, Ian. b 61. Hull Univ CertEd 82 BEd 84. LCTP 08. d 13 p 14. NSM Carl H Trin and St Barn from 13; Asst Dir of Ords from 16. *Watch Hill, Burgh-by-Sands, Carlisle CA5 6AQ* T: (01228) 576097

JOHNSTON, Ian Harold. b 50. Ex Univ BA 72 McMaster Univ Ontario MA 74 Sheff Univ BA 13. Yorks Min Course 10. d 13 p 14. NSM Adel *Leeds* 13–16; NSM Ireland Wood 13–16; NSM Hampsthwaite and Killinghall and Birstwith 16–18; Min to Business Leeds from 14; rtd 18. *4 Buttercup Close, Killinghall, Harrogate HG3 2WU* M: 07914-750969 E: revianjohnston@gmail.com

JOHNSTON, James. *See* JOHNSTON, Charles James Andrew

JOHNSTON, Kay. *See* JOHNSTON, Helen Kay

JOHNSTON, Lee. b 91. Glas Univ BD 15 MTh 16. d 18. C Lanark *Glas* from 18. *21B High Street, Lanark ML11 7LU* T: (01555) 450095 E: l.johnston.gla@gmail.com

JOHNSTON, Michael David Haigh. b 44. S Dios Minl Tr Scheme 88. d 91 p 92. NSM Wootton *Portsm* 91–95; NSM Ryde H Trin 95–99; NSM Swanmore St Mich 95–99; P-in-c Cowes St Faith 99–03; Asst Chapl Isle of Wight NHS Primary Care Trust 03–11; Chapl HM Pris Kingston (Portsm) 03–05; P-in-c St Lawrence *Portsm* 11–14; rtd 14; PtO *Portsm* from 14. *8 Coniston Drive, Ryde PO33 3AE* T: (01983) 611291 E: rvdmikej@fastmail.fm

JOHNSTON, Niall. *See* JOHNSTON, Allen Niall

JOHNSTON, Canon Robert John. b 31. Oak Hill Th Coll 64. d 64 p 65. C Bebington *Ches* 64–68; I Lack *Clogh* 68–99; Can Clogh Cathl 89–99; rtd 99. *Flat 16, 8 Eastermede Park, Ballymoney BT53 6HP* T: (028) 2766 9317

JOHNSTON, Trevor Samuel. b 72. Ulster Univ BMus 96 TCD BTh 01. CITC 98. d 01 p 02. C Carrickfergus *Conn* 01–04; C Jordanstown and Chapl Jordanstown and Belf Campuses Ulster Univ 04–09; Crosslinks Ireland Team Ldr 09–14; I Belfast All SS *Conn* from 14. *All Saints' Rectory, 171 Malone Road, Belfast BT9 6TA* M: 07776-178248 E: trev@tjohnston.net

JOHNSTON, Volet. *See* JOHNSTON, Edith Violet Nicholl

JOHNSTON, Wilfred Brian. b 44. TCD BA 67 MA 70. Div Test 68. d 68 p 70. C Seagoe *D & D* 68–73; I Inniskeel *D & R* 73–82; I Castlerock w Dunboe and Fermoyle 82–02; Bp's C Gweedore, Carrickfin and Templecrone 02–08; Dioc Registrar 89–06; Can Derry Cathl 92–02; Preb 99–02; Can Raphoe Cathl *D & R* 05–08; rtd 08. *2 The Apple Yard, Coleraine BT51 3PP* T: (028) 7032 6406 E: b.johnston@talk21.com *or* johnston.brian1944@gmail.com

JOHNSTON, William Francis (Frank). b 30. TCD BA 55 MA 69. d 55 p 56. C Orangefield *D & D* 55–59; CF 59–77; Asst Chapl Gen 77–80; Chapl Gen 80–87; P-in-c Winslow *Ox* 87–91; RD Claydon 89–94; R Winslow w Gt Horwood and Addington 91–95; rtd 95; PtO *Ex* from 95. *Lower Axehill, Chard Road, Axminster EX13 5ED* T: (01297) 33259 E: revjeu@talktalk.net

JOHNSTON, Canon William John. b 35. Lon Univ BA 85 MA 90 PhD. CITC 67. d 70 p 71. C Belfast St Donard *D & D* 70–72; C Derg *D & R* 72–78; I Drumclamph w Lower and Upper Langfield 78–91; I Kilskeery w Trillick *Clogh* 91–10; Preb Clogh Cathl 04–10; Prec 09–10; rtd 10. *Ernedene, 61 Dublin Road, Enniskillen BT74 6HN* T: (028) 6632 2268

JOHNSTON, William McConnell. b 33. TCD BA 57. d 58 p 59. C Ballymena w Ballyclug *Conn* 58–61; C Belfast St Thos 61–63; C Finaghy 63–66; R Kambula S Africa 66–74; Dean Eshowe 74–86; R Mtubatuba 86–99; rtd 00; PtO *Chich* from 04. *Honeysuckle Cottage, Redford, Midhurst GU29 0QG* T: (01428) 741131

JOHNSTONE, Debra Jayne. b 62. All SS Cen for Miss & Min 15. d 17 p 18. OLM Ainsworth *Man* from 17. *51 Green Bank, Bolton BL2 3NQ*

JOINT, Canon Michael John. b 39. Sarum & Wells Th Coll 79. d 79 p 79. CA from 61; Hon C Chandler's Ford *Win* 79–83; Youth Chapl 79–83; V Lymington 83–95; Co-ord Chapl R Bournemouth and Christchurch Hosps NHS Trust 96–03; Hon Can Win Cathl 00–03; rtd 03; PtO *Win* 03–04 and from 12. *20 Wavendon Avenue, Barton on Sea, New Milton BH25 7LS* T: (01425) 628952 E: michjoin@aol.com

JOLLEY, Mrs Alice Elizabeth. b 95. Grey Coll Dur BA 17 Dur Univ MA 19. Westcott Ho Cam 17. d 19. C Linc St Nic w St Jo Newport from 19. *14 Nettleham Close, Lincoln LN2 1SJ* T: (01522) 402315   M: 07891-695963 E: mthr.alicejolley@outlook.com

JOLLEY, The Ven Andrew John. b 61. Nottm Univ BSc 83 PhD 06 Warwick Univ MBA 88 CEng 88 MIMechE 88. St Jo Coll Nottm BTh 97. d 98 p 99. C Sparkhill w Greet and Sparkbrook *Birm* 98–02; V Aston SS Pet and Paul 02–08; P-in-c Aston St Jas 05–08; P-in-c Nechells 05–08; V Aston and Nechells 08–16; AD Aston 05–12; Hon Can Birm Cathl 15–16; Adn Bradf *Leeds* from 16. *1 Selborne Grove, Bradford BD9 4NL* T: (01274) 405720 E: andy.jolley@leeds.anglican.org

JONAS, Alan Charles. b 56. Leeds Univ BA 79 Univ of Wales (Abth) PGCE 80. Wycliffe Hall Ox 92. d 94 p 95. C Hersham *Guildf* 94–98; P-in-c Westcott 98–08; V from 08; Chapl Priory Sch 01–07; AD Dorking *Guildf* 14–19. *The Vicarage, Guildford Road, Westcott, Dorking RH4 3QB* T: (01306) 885309 E: alchasjonas@aol.com

JONAS, Canon Ian Robert. b 54. St Jo Coll Nottm BTh 80. d 80 p 81. C Portadown St Mark *Arm* 80–82; C Cregagh *D & D* 82–85; BCMS Sec *D & G* 85–90; V Langley Mill *Derby* 90–97; I Kilgariffe Union *C, C & R* 97–09; I Carrigrohane Union from 09; Can Cork Cathl from 11; Can Cloyne Cathl from 11. *The Rectory, Church Hill, Carrigrohane, Co Cork, Republic of Ireland* T: (00353) (21) 487 1106 E: revianjonas@yahoo.co.uk

JONES, Adrian. *See* JONES, Michael Adrian

JONES, Alan Pierce. *See* PIERCE-JONES, Alan

JONES, Canon Alison. b 61. NE Surrey Coll of Tech BSc 86 Cardiff Univ BTh 12. d 10 p 11. NSM Swansea St Pet *S & B* 10–11; NSM Cen Swansea 11; C Sketty 11–15; V Swansea St Nic and St Jude from 15; Can Res Brecon Cathl from 18; Bp's Officer for Lay Min from 18; Warden of Readers from 18. *St Nicholas' Vicarage, 58A Dyfed Avenue, Townhill, Swansea SA1 6NG* T: (01792) 418478   M: 07890-707117 E: alison.rhossili@hotmail.co.uk

JONES, Alison. *See* JONES, Helen Alison

JONES, Alison. *See* WAGSTAFF, Alison

JONES, Alison Fiona Kay. b 67. St Mellitus Coll 11. d 13 p 14. C Burghfield *Ox* 13–17; LtO *S'well* from 17. *Willow Cottage, Norwell Woodhouse, Newark NG23 6NG* M: 07818-806403 E: alison.jones@thepottingshedchurch.com

JONES, Alun. b 52. Leeds Univ BA 96. Cuddesdon Coll 94. d 96 p 97. C Newc St Geo 96–98; C Cowgate 98–99; C Fenham St Jas and St Basil 99–04; P-in-c Carl St Herbert w St Steph 04–07; V from 07. *St Herbert's Vicarage, Blackwell Road, Carlisle CA2 4RA* T: (01228) 523375 E: alun52@sky.com

JONES, Alyson Elizabeth. *See* DAVIE, Alyson Elizabeth

JONES, Ms Amanda Louise. b 69. Cranmer Hall Dur 14. d 16 p 17. C Penrith w Newton Reigny and Plumpton Wall *Carl* from 16. *18 Skirsgill Close, Penrith CA11 8QF* T: (01768) 744687 E: mandyjoness@aol.co.uk

JONES, Mrs Andrea Margaret. b 46. Qu Coll Birm 88. d 90 p 94. Par Dn Kidderminster St Geo *Worc* 90–94; TV 94–95; C Penn Fields *Lich* 95–00; C Gt Wyrley 00–06; rtd 06; PtO *Worc* from 07. *50 Woodward Road, Kidderminster DY11 6NY* T: (01562) 823555 E: aam57@blueyonder.co.uk

JONES, Ms Andrea Susan. b 55. SNWTP 08. d 10 p 11. OLM Davyhulme St Mary *Man* 10–11; C Newton Heath 11–13; C Moston St Jo 11–13; C Moston St Chad 11–13; R Manchester Gd Shep and St Barn 13–17; Borough Dean Man 12–17; Hon Can Man Cathl 16–17; TV Borderlands Miss Area *St As* from 17. *The Rectory, 2 Birch Rise, Hawarden, Deeside CH5 3DD* T: (01244) 520992 E: andysjones@hotmail.co.uk

JONES, The Ven Andrew. b 61. Univ of Wales (Ban) BD 82 PGCE 82 TCD BTh 85 MA 91 Univ of Wales MPhil 93. CITC 82 St Geo Coll Jerusalem 84. d 85 p 86. Min Can Ban Cathl 85–88; R Dolgellau w Llanfachreth and Brithdir etc

88–92; Warden of Readers 91–92; Dir Past Studies St Mich Coll Llan 92–96; Lect Th Univ of Wales (Cardiff) 92–96; Visiting Prof St Geo Coll Jerusalem from 94; Research Fell from 96; R Llanbedrog w Llannor w Llanfihangel etc *Ban* 96–01; R Llanbedrog w Llannor and Llangian 01–12; Dioc CME and NSM Officer 96–00; AD Llyn and Eifionydd 99–10; Hon Can Ban Cathl 04–05; Can Ban Cathl from 05; Dioc Dir of Ords from 06; Adn Meirionnydd from 10; C Bro Enlli 12–16; V from 16. *Ty'n Llan Rectory, Llanbedrog, Pwllheli LL53 7TU* T/F: (01758) 740919 E: archdeacon.meirionnydd@churchinwales.org.uk

JONES, Andrew. b 64. York Univ BA 85. Westmr Th Sem (USA) MDiv 91 St Jo Coll Nottm 92. **d** 94 **p** 95. C Win Ch Ch 94–98; C St Helen Bishopsgate w St Andr Undershaft etc *Lon* 98–04; C Hoxton St Anne w St Columba from 04. *89 Forest Road, London E8 3BL* T: (020) 7254 5942 M: 07534-669528 E: rev.aj64@btinternet.com *or* info@gracechurchhackney.org.uk

JONES, Andrew. *See* JONES, Ian Andrew

JONES, Andrew Edward. b 71. Ridley Hall Cam 10. **d** 12 **p** 13. C Sprowston w Beeston *Nor* 12–15; R Trunch Group from 15. *The Rectory, Knapton Road, Trunch, North Walsham NR28 0QE* T: (01603) 418296 E: revandrewjones@gmail.com

JONES, Mrs Anna Holt. b 75. Mert Coll Ox BA 96 Univ Coll Lon MA 98 Peterho Cam MPhil 99. Westcott Ho Cam 17. **d** 19. C Three Rivers Gp *Ely* from 19. *13 Mayfield Close, Ely CB6 3AB* T: (01353) 645944 M: 07425-168933 E: ahjones@cantab.net

JONES, Anne. *See* FURNESS, Christine Anne

JONES, Anthony. b 43. WEMTC 99. **d** 01 **p** 02. OLM Lydney *Glouc* 01–07; NSM Woolaston w Alvington and Aylburton 07–17; rtd 17; PtO *Glouc* from 19. *2 The Lodge, High Street, St Briavels, Lydney GL15 6TB* T: (01594) 531134 M: 07860-331755 E: jones_rev@yahoo.co.uk

JONES, April Elizabeth. b 46. WEMTC. **d** 12 **p** 13. NSM Badgeworth, Shurdington and Witcombe w Bentham *Glouc* 12–17; rtd 17. *Charnwood, Bryerland Road, Witcombe, Gloucester GL3 4TA* T: (01452) 864469 E: alanjones1944@hotmail.com

JONES, Barbara Christine. b 48. St Hugh's Coll Ox BA 71 MA 74 Lady Spencer Chu Coll of Educn PGCE 74. CBDTI 97. **d** 00 **p** 01. NSM Bolton-le-Sands *Blackb* 00–13; Bp's Adv on Healing 09–16; PtO from 13. *11 Sandown Road, Lancaster LA1 4LN* T: (01524) 65598

JONES, Barry Mervyn. b 46. St Chad's Coll Dur BA 68. **d** 70 **p** 71. C Bloxwich *Lich* 70–72; C Norwood All SS *Cant* 72–76; C New Addington 76–78; Chapl Mayday Univ Hosp Thornton Heath 78–86; Chapl Qu Hosp Croydon 78–86; Chapl St Mary's Hosp Croydon 78–86; Chapl Bromsgrove and Redditch DHA 86–94; Chapl Alexandra Healthcare NHS Trust Redditch 94–00; Chapl Worcs Acute Hosps NHS Trust 00–03; Chapl Team Ldr 03–05; PtO *Worc* from 05. *46 Barlich Way, Redditch B98 7JP* T: (01527) 520659

JONES, Benjamin Jenkin Hywel. b 39. Univ of Wales BA 61. St Mich Coll Llan 61. **d** 64 **p** 65. C Carmarthen St Pet *St D* 64–70; V Cynwyl Gaeo w Llansawel and Talley 70–79; R Llanbadarn Fawr 79–82; V Llanbadarn Fawr w Capel Bangor and Goginan 82–92; V Llanychaearn w Llanddeiniol 92–05; Warden of Readers from 82; Can St D Cathl 86–90; RD Llanbadarn Fawr 89–90; Adn Cardigan 90–06; rtd 06. *Dowerdd, Waun Fawr, Aberystwyth SY23 3QF* T: (01970) 617100 E: lywelandanne@btinternet.com

JONES, Benjamin Mark Oscar. b 79. Kent Univ BA 00 Cant Ch Ch Univ PGCE 01. Trin Coll Bris BA 11 MPhil 12. **d** 12 **p** 13. C Folkestone St Jo *Cant* 12–15; C S Croydon Em *S'wark* from 15. *12 Hurst View Road, South Croydon CR2 7AG* M: 07779-494372 E: benmarkjones@hotmail.com

JONES, Bernard Lewis. b 48. Llan Dioc Tr Scheme 89. **d** 93 **p** 94. NSM Aberaman and Abercwmboi w Cwmaman *Llan* 93–99; V Hirwaun 99–13; AD Cynon Valley 08–12; rtd 13; PtO *Llan* from 13. *21 Parc Aberaman, Aberaman, Aberdare CF44 6EY* T: (01685) 870607

JONES, Brenda. b 50. Cranmer Hall Dur 02. **d** 04 **p** 05. C Jarrow *Dur* 04–07; C-in-c Bishop Auckland Woodhouse Close CD 07–14; rtd 14; PtO *Dur* from 17. *33 Walden Close, Ouston, Chester le Street DH2 1TF*

JONES, Brenda. *See* CAMPBELL, Brenda

JONES, Canon Brian Howell. b 35. Univ of Wales MPhil 96. St Mich Coll Llan. **d** 61 **p** 62. C Llangiwg *S & B* 61–63; C Swansea St Mary and H Trin 63–70; R New Radnor w Llanfihangel Nantmelan etc 70–75; V Llansamlet 75–89; Dioc Dir of Stewardship 82–89; P-in-c Capel Coelbren 89–94; Dioc Missr 89–95; Can Res Brecon Cathl 89–00; Can Tres Brecon Cathl 98–00; Chan Brecon Cathl 99–00; RD

Cwmtawe 89–93; V Killay 95–00; rtd 00. *125 Homegower House, St Helen's Road, Swansea SA1 4DW* T: (01792) 652466 E: b.h.jones@outlook.com

JONES, Canon Brian Michael. b 34. Trin Coll Bris 79 Oak Hill Th Coll BA 82. **d** 84 **p** 84. CMS 82–93; Sierra Leone 84–93; Can Bo from 91; C Frimley *Guildf* 93–99; rtd 99; PtO *Newc* 00–01; Hon C N Tyne and Redesdale 01–08; PtO *Carl* from 09. *20 Campfield Road, Ulverston LA12 9PB* T: (01229) 480380 E: bmj.retired@btopenworld.com

JONES, Brian Robert. b 53. Surrey Univ BSc 76. SAOMC 02. **d** 05 **p** 06. NSM Greenham *Ox* from 05. *27 Three Acre Road, Newbury RG14 7AW* T: (01635) 34875

JONES, Canon Bryan Maldwyn. b 32. St Mich Coll Llan. **d** 62 **p** 63. C Swansea St Barn *S & B* 62–69; V Trallwng and Betws Penpont 69–75; V Trallwng, Bettws Penpont w Aberyskir etc 75–00; RD Brecon 80–91 and 91–99; Hon Can Brecon Cathl 92–00; rtd 00. *Plas Newydd, 8 Camden Crescent, Brecon LD3 7BY* T: (01874) 625063 E: bryanandmary8@gmail.com

JONES, Bryn Parry. b 49. Univ of Wales BSc 98 MCIH 98 FCIH 03. St As Minl Tr Course 04. **d** 06 **p** 10. NSM Connah's Quay *St As* 06–15; C Pontrobin 15–16; TV Borderlands Miss Area 17–19; rtd 19. *Address temp unknown*

JONES, Bryon. b 34. Open Univ BA 84. St D Coll Lamp 61. **d** 64 **p** 65. C Port Talbot St Theodore *Llan* 64–67; C Aberdare 68–69; C Up Hatherley *Glouc* 69–71; C Oystermouth *S & B* 71–74; V Camrose *St D* 74–77; V Camrose and St Lawrence w Ford and Haycastle 77–04; rtd 04. *31 New Road, Haverfordwest SA61 1TU* T: (01437) 760596

JONES, Cameron Charles Wallace. **d** 14 **p** 15. Carrickfergus *Conn* 14–15; C from 15. *1 Coates Park, Carrickfergus BT38 7XA* M: 07742-617224 E: cameron.cw.jones@gmail.com

JONES, Miss Celia Lynn. b 54. Univ of Wales (Lamp) MTh 09. Trin Coll Bris. **d** 01 **p** 08. C Bris St Paul's 01–08; C Barton Hill St Luke w Ch Ch and Moorfields 08–09; TV Magor *Mon* from 09. *The Vicarage, Station Road, Llanwern, Newport NP18 2DW* T: (01633) 413647 E: clynnjones@talktalk.net

JONES, Charles Derek. b 37. K Coll Lon BD 60 AKC 60. **d** 61 **p** 62. C Stockton St Chad *Dur* 61–64; C Becontree St Elisabeth *Chelmsf* 64–66; C S Beddington St Mich *S'wark* 66–73; LtO *Ex* 73–77; PtO *Liv* 77–99; rtd 02. *4 Bryn Glas, Graigfechan, Ruthin LL15 2EX* T: (01824) 705015 E: derek620jones@btinternet.com

JONES, Christopher Howell. b 50. BA FCCA. Oak Hill Th Coll 80. **d** 83 **p** 84. C Leyton St Mary w St Edw *Chelmsf* 83–86; C Becontree St Mary 86–90; P-in-c Bootle St Matt *Liv* 90–93; V 93–99; AD Bootle 97–99; V Ormskirk 99–15; Chapl W Lancashire NHS Trust 99–11; C Liv Cathl 15–18; rtd 18. *9 Mersey Court, Liverpool L23 3AQ* T: 0151-932 1674

JONES, Christopher Mark. b 56. St Jo Coll Cam BA 78 MA 82 Wycliffe Hall Ox BA 81 MA 85. **d** 82 **p** 83. C Walsall *Lich* 82–84; Chapl St Jo Coll Cam 84–89; Chapl Eton Coll from 89; Ho Master 97–10. *2 Hodgson House, Eton College, Windsor SL4 6DE* T: (01753) 671330 M: 07794-136258 E: c.m.jones@etoncollege.org.uk

JONES, Christopher Yeates. b 51. STETS 97. **d** 00 **p** 01. NSM Yeovil St Mich *B & W* 00–12; rtd 12; PtO *B & W* from 15. *26 Glenthorne Avenue, Yeovil BA21 4PG* T: (01935) 420886 M: 07944-461154

JONES, Mrs Claire Rachel. b 90. Worc Coll Ox BA 13. Cranmer Hall Dur 17. **d** 19. C Bodmin *Truro* from 19. *Address withheld by request* E: revclairejones@gmail.com

JONES, Clive. b 51. BA 82. Oak Hill Th Coll 79. **d** 82 **p** 83. C Brunswick *Man* 82–85; V Pendlebury St Jo 85–96; V Attleborough *Cov* 96–16; rtd 16; PtO *Derby* 17–19. *25 Bedford Road, Burton-on-Trent DE15 9JG*

JONES, Clive Morlais Peter. b 40. Univ of Wales (Cardiff) BA 63 CertEd 64 LTCL 71. Chich Th Coll 64. **d** 66 **p** 67. C Llanfabon *Llan* 66–70; PV Llan Cathl 70–75; R Gelligaer 75–85; Prec and Can Llan Cathl 84–85; R Tilehurst St Mich *Ox* 85–96; Chapl Costa Blanca *Eur* 94–97; V Newton St Pet *S & B* 97–06; P-in-c Haarlem *Eur* 07–10; PtO *Ox* from 10; *Eur* from 16. *31 Lowbury Gardens, Compton, Newbury RG20 6NN* T: (01635) 579409 E: clive.jones857@btinternet.com

JONES, Clive Wesley. b 68. St Steph Ho Ox 95. **d** 98 **p** 99. C Swanley St Mary *Roch* 98–02; P-in-c Belvedere St Aug 02–07; V from 07; Chapl Trin Sch Belvedere 02–04; PtO *Chelmsf* from 14. *The Vicarage, St Augustine's Road, Belvedere DA17 5HH* T: (020) 8311 6307 E: frclive@tiscali.co.uk

JONES, Colin Stuart. b 56. Southn Univ LLB 77. Coll of Resurr Mirfield 81. **d** 84 **p** 85. C Mountain Ash *Llan* 84–86; C Castle Bromwich SS Mary and Marg *Birm* 86–89; V Kingstanding 89–94; V Perry Barr 94–05; P-in-c Wordsley *Worc* 05–07; TR from 07; RD Kingswinford 10–16. *The Rectory, 13 Dunsley Drive, Stourbridge DY8 5RA* T: (01384) 400709

JONES, Collette Moyra Yvonne. b 50. Liv Univ BSc 71 PhD 75 ALCM 91. SNWTP 08. **d** 11 **p** 12. NSM Gt Sutton *Ches* 11–14; V Aston by Sutton, Lt Leigh and Lower Whitley from 14. *The Vicarage, Street Lane, Lower Whitley, Warrington WA4 4EN* T: (01925) 730158 E: collettejones868@gmail.com

JONES, Daniel. b 78. St Andr Univ MTheol 01 PGCE 02. Qu Coll Birm 06. **d** 08 **p** 09. NSM Barbourne *Worc* 08–11; Chapl St Pet Sch York from 11. *St Peter's School, Clifton, York YO30 6AB* T: (01904) 527412 E: daniel_a_jones@btopenworld.com

JONES, David. b 55. CA Tr Coll 74 St Steph Ho Ox 83. **d** 85 **p** 86. C Fleur-de-Lis *Mon* 85–87; V Ynysddu 87–93; V Blackwood 93–08; AD Bedwellty 06–08; V Landore and Treboeth *S & B* from 08. *St Alban's Vicarage, Heol Fach, Treboeth, Swansea SA5 9DE* T: (01792) 310586

JONES, David. *See* JONES, Wilfred David

JONES, David. *See* JONES, William David

JONES, David Arthur. b 44. Liv Univ BA 66 Sussex Univ MA 68. St D Coll Lamp LTh 74. **d** 74 **p** 75. C Tenby *St D* 74–76; C Chepstow *Mon* 76–78; P-in-c Teversal *S'well* 78–81; R 81–91; Chapl Sutton Cen 78–89; V Radford All So w Ch Ch and St Mich 91–04; Adv to Urban Priority Par 96–01; Officer for Urban Life and Miss 04–09; rtd 09; PtO *S'well* from 19. *37 Devonshire Road, Nottingham NG5 2EW* T: 0115-962 2115 E: urbanrover@gmail.com

JONES, David Eric. b 72. St Mellitus Coll BA 16. **d** 16 **p** 17. C Croxley Green All SS *St Alb* 16–19; V Beckenham St Jo *Roch* from 19. *The Vicarage, 249 Eden Park Avenue, Beckenham BR3 3JN* M: 07540-120077 E: djones007@me.com

JONES, David Gordon. b 78. Trin Coll Bris 17. **d** 19. C Fromeside *Bris* from 19. *The Vicarage, Mautravers Close, Bradley Stoke, Bristol BS32 8ED* M: 07737-529687 E: davidjones75@msn.com

JONES, David Ian Stewart. b 34. Selw Coll Cam BA 57 MA 61. Westcott Ho Cam 57. **d** 59 **p** 60. C Oldham *Man* 59–63; V Elton All SS 63–66; Chapl Eton Coll 66–70; Sen Chapl 70–74; Hd Master Bryanston Sch 74–82; P-in-c Bris Ch Ch w St Ewen and All SS 82–84; P-in-c Bris St Steph w St Nic and St Leon 82–84; Soc Resp Adv 84–85; Dir Lambeth Endowed Charities 85–94; Hon PV S'wark Cathl 85–94; rtd 94; PtO *Ox* 08–12. *33 St Lucian's Lane, Wallingford OX10 9ER* T: (01491) 836052 E: davidandsuejones@aol.com

JONES, David Mark. b 73. St Mich Coll Llan 03. **d** 06 **p** 07. C Llansamlet *S & B* 06–08; Min Can Brecon Cathl 08–13; P-in-c Rhondda Fach Uchaf *Llan* from 13. *Ty Nant, Margaret Street, Pontygwaith, Ferndale CF43 3EH* T: (01443) 732321 E: revdmj@yahoo.co.uk

JONES, David Michael. b 48. Oral Roberts Univ BA 09. Chich Th Coll 75. **d** 78 **p** 79. C Yeovil *B & W* 78–84; C Barwick 81–84; V Cleeve w Chelvey and Brockley 84–92; V Heigham St Barn w St Bart *Nor* 92–00; V Writtle w Highwood *Chelmsf* 00–14; rtd 14; PtO *Sarum* from 15. *5 Rope Yard Court, Rope Yard, Royal Wootton Bassett, Swindon SN4 7FD* E: revjmjoneswrittle@aol.com

JONES, David Raymond. b 34. Univ of Wales (Lamp) BA 54 St Cath Coll Ox BA 57 MA 61. Wycliffe Hall Ox 58. **d** 58 **p** 59. C Ex St Dav 58–60; C Bideford 60–63; Chapl Grenville Coll Bideford 63–66; Chapl RN 66–89; QHC 84–89; Dir and Warden Divine Healing Miss Crowhurst 89–97; rtd 97; PtO *Chich* from 97. *9 Perrots Lane, Steyning BN44 3NB* T: (01903) 815236 E: maureenroy9@gmail.com

JONES, David Sebastian. b 43. St Cath Coll Cam BA 67 MA 73. Linc Th Coll 66. **d** 68 **p** 69. C Baguley *Man* 68–71; C Bray and Braywood *Ox* 71–73; V S Ascot 73–07; AD Bracknell 96–04; Chapl Heatherwood Hosp E Berks 81–94; Chapl Heatherwood and Wexham Park Hosps NHS Trust 94–07; rtd 07. *Fairhaven, 1 St Clement's Terrace, Mousehole, Penzance TR19 6SJ* T: (01736) 732938

JONES, David Victor. b 37. St Jo Coll Dur BA 59. Cranmer Hall Dur Bossey Ecum Inst Geneva 61. **d** 62 **p** 63. C Farnworth *Liv* 62–65; CF 65–68; Asst Master Hutton Gr Sch Preston 68–97; rtd 02. *10 Houghton Close, Penwortham, Preston PR1 9HT* T: (01772) 745306

JONES, Denise Gloria. b 56. Cov Univ BA 93 Leeds Univ MA 06. WMMTC 95. **d** 98 **p** 99. C Hobs Moat *Birm* 98–02; C Olton and Chapl Birm and Solihull Mental Health Trust 02–06; Chapl Manager Birm Women's NHS Foundn Trust 06–08; TV Bridgnorth, Tasley, Astley Abbotts, etc *Heref* 08–10; PtO *Birm* 10–11; Chapl Co-ord Birm Women's NHS Foundn Trust from 11; Hon C Yardley Wood *Birm* 14–15; P-in-c Hamstead St Bernard from 15. *Birmingham Women's NHS Foundation Trust, Mindelsohn Way, Birmingham B15 2TG* T: 0121-472 1377 *or* 472 4208 M: 07747-385006 E: revddee@aol.com

JONES, Derek Alan. b 81. Reading Univ BA 03. Cranmer Hall Dur 15. **d** 17 **p** 18. C Lt Horton *Leeds* from 17. *10 Anstone Drive, Bradford BD5 9AF* M: 07880-508174 E: derekalanjones@me.com

JONES, Miss Diana. b 46. Qu Coll Birm 89. **d** 91 **p** 94. Par Dn Harnham *Sarum* 91–94; C 94–95; C Tidworth, Ludgershall and Faberstown 95–00; P-in-c Hazelbury Bryan and the Hillside Par 00–06; rtd 06. *47 Gloucester Road, Trowbridge BA14 0AB* T: (01225) 755826

JONES, Canon Dick Heath Remi. b 32. Jes Coll Cam BA 56. Linc Th Coll 56. **d** 58 **p** 59. C Ipswich St Thos *St E* 58–61; C Putney St Mary *S'wark* 61–65; P-in-c Dawley Parva *Lich* 65–75; P-in-c Lawley 65–75; RD Wrockwardine 70–72; P-in-c Malins Lee 72–75; RD Telford 72–80; P-in-c Stirchley 74–75; TR Cen Telford 75–80; Preb Lich Cathl 76–80; TR Bournemouth St Pet w St Swithun, H Trin etc *Win* 80–96; RD Bournemouth 90–95; Hon Can Win Cathl 91–96; rtd 96; PtO *Sarum* 96–17. *Maltings, Church Street, Fontmell Magna, Shaftesbury SP7 0NY* T: (01747) 812071 E: dick.jones@uwclub.net

JONES, Dominic Jago Francis. St Jo Coll Nottm 09. **d** 11 **p** 12. C Ludgvan, Marazion, St Hilary and Perranuthnoe *Truro* 11–15; C Feock 15–17; C Devoran 15–17; C St Stythians w Perranarworthal and Gwennap 15–17; C Chacewater w St Day and Carharrack 15–17; Chapl Hants Constabulary from 17. *19 Gatcombe, Netley Abbey, Southampton SO31 5PX* M: 07904-500882

JONES, Donald. b 50. BA BSc. St Jo Coll Nottm 79. **d** 82 **p** 83. C Hutton *Chelmsf* 82–86; C E Ham w Upton Park and Forest Gate 86–88; TV 88–96; V Nuneaton St Nic *Cov* 96–14; P-in-c Weddington and Caldecote 09–14; RD Nuneaton 01–06; rtd 14; C Atherstone *Cov* 14–15; PtO *S'well* from 19. *28 Holkham Avenue, Beeston, Nottingham NG9 5EQ* T: 0115-837 8852 E: don.jones4718@gmail.com

JONES, Edward. b 36. Dur Univ BA 60. Ely Th Coll 60. **d** 62 **p** 63. C S Shields St Hilda w St Thos *Dur* 62–65; C Cleadon Park 65–68; V Hebburn St Cuth 68–79; R Winlaton 79–00; rtd 00; PtO *Newc* from 01. *10 Melkridge Gardens, Benton, Newcastle upon Tyne NE7 7GQ* T: 0191-266 4388

JONES, Elaine. b 52. SNWTP. **d** 10 **p** 11. C Wavertree St Mary *Liv* 10–14; V Toxteth St Bede w St Clem from 14; C Wavertree St Bridget and St Thos from 19; AD Toxteth and Wavertree from 17. *29 Moel Famau View, Liverpool L17 7ET* M: 07787-550622

JONES, Miss Elaine Edith. b 58. St Jo Coll Nottm BA 99. **d** 99 **p** 00. C Gainsborough and Morton *Linc* 99–02; C Netherton *Carl* 02–04; TV Maryport, Netherton and Flimby 04–05; Lay Tr Officer 02–05; V Binley *Cov* 05–14; V Peterlee *Dur* from 14. *St Cuthbert's Vicarage, Manor Way, Peterlee SR8 5QW* T: 0191-586 2630 E: reveej@hotmail.co.uk

JONES, Canon Elaine Joan. b 50. Oak Hill Th Coll. **d** 87 **p** 94. Par Dn Tottenham H Trin *Lon* 87–92; Par Dn Clay Hill St Jo and St Luke 92–94; C St Botolph Aldgate w H Trin Minories 94–96; V Hackney Wick St Mary of Eton w St Aug 96–04; AD Hackney 99–04; Can Res Derby Cathl 04–13; rtd 13; Hon Can Derby Cathl from 13; C Derby St Jo from 13. *The Vicarage, 2 Glebe Crescent, Stanley, Ilkeston DE7 6FL* T: 0115-930 2080 M: 07749-867347 E: canonelaine.stjohns@gmail.com

JONES, Mrs Elizabeth. b 52. St Mich Coll Llan 09. **d** 12 **p** 13. NSM Tredegar *Mon* from 12. *Allesley, Ashville, Tredegar NP22 4LN* T: (01495) 726251 E: ejones8@talktalk.net

JONES, Elizabeth Anne. b 66. **d** 14 **p** 16. Chapl Univ Hosps Cov and Warks NHS Trust 14–17; C Bulkington *Cov* 14–18; C Burton Hastings 17–18; Chapl Univ Hosps Cov and Warks NHS Trust from 18. *Morahill, Tamworth Road, Corley, Coventry CV7 8BX*

JONES, Mrs Elizabeth Jane. b 57. Derby Univ BSc 00. St Jo Coll Nottm MTh 02. **d** 02 **p** 03. C Leek and Meerbrook *Lich* 02–05; C Harlescott and Chapl Shropshire Co Primary Care Trust 05–11; R Darlaston St Lawr *Lich* 11–14; TR Darlaston and Moxley 14–18; P-in-c Rocester and Croxden w Hollington from 18; C Alton w Bradley-le-Moors and Denstone etc from 18; Chapl JCB Academy from 18. *The Vicarage, Church Lane, Rocester, Uttoxeter ST14 5JZ* T: (01889) 591748 M: 07923-403395 E: revdlizjones@gmail.com

JONES, Mrs Elizabeth Somerset. b 49. St Jo Coll Nottm. **d** 88 **p** 94. NSM Duns *Edin* 88–99; NSM Selkirk 89–90; Dioc Dir of Ords 95–05; NSM Dalkeith from 02; NSM Lasswade from 02. *255 Carnethie Street, Rosewell EH24 9DR* T: 0131-440 2602 E: esomersetjones@btinternet.com

JONES, Lt Col Ellis Glyn. b 42. Victoria Univ Man BDS 67. St Mich Coll Llan. **d** 15 **p** 16. NSM Garthbeibio, Llanerfel and Llangadfan *St As* 15–16; NSM Caereinion Miss Area from 17. *1 High Street, Llanfair Caereinion, Welshpool SY21 0QS* T: (01938) 811031 E: eglyn@eglynjones.plus.com

JONES, Ernest Edward Stephen. b 39. Lon Univ BD 76. St D Coll Lamp. **d** 66 **p** 67. C N Meols *Liv* 66–69; C Kirkby

69–71; V Farnworth All SS *Man* 71–75; P-in-c Bempton *York* 75–78; R Rufford *Blackb* 78–84; V Cropredy w Gt Bourton and Wardington *Ox* 84–90; R York St Clem w St Mary Bishophill Senior 90–98; P-in-c York All SS N Street 90–98; V Northampton St Benedict *Pet* 98–05; rtd 05; P-in-c Wootton w Glympton and Kiddington *Ox* 05–15; R from 15; AD Woodstock 09–12. *The Rectory, 22 Castle Road, Wootton, Woodstock OX20 1EG* T: (01993) 812543

JONES, Mrs Eva Frances. d 16 p 17. NSM Newport All SS *Mon* from 16. *16 The Maltings, Llantarnam, Cwmbran NP44 7BB* E: garethandfrancesjones@btinternet.com

JONES, Evan Hopkins. b 38. St Mich Coll Llan 65. d 67 p 68. C Churston Ferrers w Goodrington *Ex* 67–70; C Tavistock and Gulworthy 70–73; R Ashprington and V Cornworthy 73–78; R S Hackney St Jo w Ch Ch *Lon* 78–92; AD Hackney 84–89; V Islington St Jas w St Pet 92–08; rtd 08; PtO *Lon* from 08. *5 St James's Close, Bishop Street, London N1 8PH* T: (020) 7226 0104 E: fatherevanjones@btinternet.com

JONES, Evan Trefor. b 32. Univ of Wales (Ban) BA 54. Coll of Resurr Mirfield 54. d 56 p 57. C Ban St Mary 56–62; V Llandinorwig 62–71; TV Llanbeblig w Caernarfon and Betws Garmon etc 71–84; Ed dioc magazine The Link 79–89; R Llanfairfechan w Aber *Ban* 84–97; Can Ban Cathl 95–97; rtd 97. *19 Marlborough Place, Vaughan Street, Llandudno LL30 1AE* T: (01492) 878411 E: jonesevan223@email.com

JONES, Frances. *See* JONES, Eva Frances

JONES, Gareth Edward John Paul. b 79. Leeds Univ BA 06 FRSA 15. Coll of Resurr Mirfield 03. d 06 p 07. C Brighton St Mich *Chich* 06–10; P-in-c Gt Ilford St Mary *Chelmsf* 10–14; V from 14; Dioc Refugee Co-ord from 18; Chapl Snaresbrook Crown Court from 18. *St Mary's Vicarage, 26 South Park Road, Ilford IG1 1SS* T: (020) 8478 0546 E: vicar@stmarysilford.org.uk

JONES, Gareth Lewis. b 42. K Coll Lon BD 64 AKC 64. d 65 p 66. C Risca *Mon* 65–70; PtO *Win* 70–74; Keswick *Man* 74–75; Sarum 75; C Pontesbury I and II *Heref* 75–77; P-in-c Presteigne w Discoed 77–79; TV Hemel Hempstead *St Alb* 79–86; R Longden and Annscroft w Pulverbatch *Heref* 86–93; TV Leominster 93–07; rtd 07; PtO *Heref* from 08. *33 Danesfield Drive, Leominster HR6 8HP* T: (01568) 620453

JONES, Prof Gareth Lloyd. b 38. Univ of Wales BA 61 Selw Coll Cam BA 63 MA 67 Yale Univ STM 69 TCD BD 70 Lon Univ PhD 75. Episc Sem Austin Texas Hon DD 90 Westcott Ho Cam 62. d 65 p 66. C Holyhead w Rhoscolyn *Ban* 65–68; USA 68–70; P-in-c Merton *Ox* 70–72; Tutor Ripon Hall Ox 72; Sen Tutor 73–77; Lect Ex Coll Ox 73–77; Tutor and Lib Ripon Coll Cuddesdon 75–77; Lect Th Univ of Wales (Ban) 77–89; Sen Lect 89–95; Reader and Hd of Sch from 95; Prof from 98; Sub-Dean Faculty of Th 80–89; Dean 89–92; Chan Ban Cathl 90–09; Select Preacher Ox Univ 89. *22 Bron-y-Felin, Llandegfan, Menai Bridge LL59 5UY* T: (01248) 712786

JONES, Gary. b 60. d 18 p 19. NSM Kesgrave *St E* from 18. *30 Maycroft Close, Ipswich IP1 6RG* T: (01473) 412329 M: 07714-614095 E: gary.jones590@ntlworld.com

JONES, Canon Glyndwr. b 35. St Mich Coll Llan. d 62 p 63. C Clydach *S & B* 62–64; C Llangyfelach 64–67; C Sketty 67–70; V Bryngwyn and Newchurch and Llanbedr etc 70–72; Miss to Seafarers 72–00; Swansea 72-76; Port of Lon 76-81; Aux Min Sec 81–85; Asst Gen Sec 85-90; Sec Gen 90–00; V St Mich Paternoster Royal *Lon* 91–00; rtd 01; Hon Can Kobe Japan from 88; Chapl to The Queen 90–05; PtO *Chelmsf* from 91. *5 The Close, Grays RM16 2XU* T: (01375) 375053 E: glynita.tomdavey@blueyonder.co.uk

JONES, Glynn. b 56. Ches Univ MA 14. NEOC 91. d 94 p 95. NSM Glendale Gp *Newc* 94–97; Chapl HM Pris Leeds 97–99; Chapl HM Pris Dur 99–00; Co-ord Chapl HM YOI Wetherby 00–05; Co-ord Chapl HM Pris Wymott 06–07; Co-ord Chapl HM Pris Haverigg 07–16; Chapl from 16; Carl Dioc Chapl to Chapl from 16; Regional Dir (N) Daylight Chr Pris Trust from 16. *10 Blencathra View, Threlkeld Quarry, Keswick CA12 4TY* T: (017687) 79082 E: glynnandlizjones@aol.com *or* glynn@daylightcpt.org

JONES, Godfrey Caine. b 36. Dur Univ BA 59 Lon Univ CertEd 60 Birm Univ MEd 71. St Deiniol's Hawarden 76. d 78 p 79. Hd Humanities Denbigh High Sch 75–81; NSM Ruthin w Llanrhydd *St As* 78–81; C 83–84; Sen Lect Matlock Coll 81–83; P-in-c Llanfwrog and Clocaenog and Gyffylliog *St As* 84–85; R 85–93; V Ruabon 93–02; RD Llangollen 93–02; rtd 02; Min Pradoe *Lich* 02–08; PtO 08–16; *St As* from 09. *14 Adlington House, Abbey Road, Rhos on Sea, Colwyn Bay LL28 4PU* T: (01492) 471312 E: dodie2822@gmail.com

JONES, Griffith Trevor. b 56. BSc MPS Univ of Wales BD. d 87 p 88. C Llandrygarn w Bodwrog and Heneglwys etc *Ban* 87–89; R Llangefni w Tregaean and Llangristiolus etc 89–91; TV Bangor 91–94; Chapl Ysbyty Gwynedd 91–94; LtO *Ban* 94–00; Hon C Bro Tysilio from 14. *8 Carreg-y-Gad Estate,*

Ffordd Penmynydd, Llanfairpwllgwyngyll LL61 5QF T: (01248) 713094 E: gjones2747@aol.com

JONES, Gwynn Rees. b 32. St D Coll Lamp BA 55. d 57 p 58. C Llangystennin *St As* 57–59; C Llanrhos 59–64; R Cefn 64–68; R Llanfyllin 68–80; V Bistre 80–89; R Flint 89–97; rtd 97; PtO *St As* 09–13. *3 Lon Derw, Abergele LL22 7EA* T: (01745) 825188

JONES, Harold Philip. b 49. Leeds Univ BA 72 St Jo Coll Dur BA 84. Cranmer Hall Dur 82. d 85 p 86. C Scartho *Linc* 85–88; V Dodworth *Wakef* 88–91; C Penistone and Thurlstone 91–95; C Scunthorpe All SS *Linc* 95–96; TV Brumby 96–02; Chapl Derby Hosps NHS Foundn Trust 02–14; rtd 14. *53 Beech Avenue, Alvaston, Derby DE24 0EA* E: haroldofderby@yahoo.co.uk

JONES, Haydn Llewellyn. b 42. Edin Th Coll 63. d 65 p 66. C Towcester w Easton Neston *Pet* 65–68; C Northampton St Matt 68–72; C Northampton St Paul *Roch* 97–98; Ex from 98; rtd 99. *11 Lady Park Road, Livermead, Torquay TQ2 6UA* T: (01803) 690483

JONES (née JAMES), Ms Helen Alison. b 59. St Andr Univ BSc 81. EMMTC 93. d 96 p 97. C Brocklesby Park *Linc* 96–98; PtO 06–08; C Bassingham Gp 08–10; R Dundee St Jo *Bre* 10–14; R Dundee St Marg 10–14; R Dundee St Martin 10–14; NSM Alexandria and Dumbarton *Glas* 14–15. *Shillinghill, 16 School Road, Rhonehouse, Castle Douglas DG7 1UA* M: 07814-789817 E: halisonjones@gmail.com

JONES, Hester. *See* JONES, Susannah Hester Everett

JONES, Hugh Vaughan. b 44. d 07 p 08. C Holyhead *Ban* 07–09; P-in-c Bodedern w Llanfaethlu 09–11; P-in-c Amlwch 11–15; rtd 15; PtO *Ban* from 15. *116 Foryd Road, Kinmel Bay, Rhyl LL18 5LR* M: 07795-578932 E: hughvaughan.santelbod@btinternet.com

JONES, Hugh William Fawcett. b 68. Ripon Coll Cuddesdon. d 10 p 11. C Boston *Linc* 10–14; V Linc St Nic w St Jo Newport from 14; RD Christianity from 17. *The Vicarage, 95 Yarborough Crescent, Lincoln LN1 3NE* E: hugh.wf.jones@talk21.com

JONES, Ian Andrew. b 65. Lanc Univ BA 87. St Mich Coll Llan. d 90 p 91. C Caerphilly *Llan* 90–96; Chapl RAF from 96. *Chaplaincy Services (RAF), HQ Air Command, RAF High Wycombe HP14 4UE* T: (01494) 496800

JONES, Ian Robert. b 69. Sheff Univ BA 92. Trin Coll Bris 11. d 13 p 14. C Burscough Bridge *Liv* 13–17; P-in-c Kirkheaton *Leeds* 17–18; R from 18. *The New Rectory, Church Lane, Kirkheaton, Huddersfield HD5 0BH* T: (01484) 532410 M: 07957-502260 E: rector@kirkheatonchurch.org.uk

✠**JONES, The Rt Revd Idris.** b 43. St D Coll Lamp BA 64 NY Th Sem DMin 86. Edin Th Coll 64. d 68 p 98. C Stafford St Mary *Lich* 67–70; Prec St Paul's Cathl Dundee *Bre* 70–73; P-in-c Gosforth All SS *Newc* 73–80; R Montrose and Inverbervie *Bre* 80–89; Can St Paul's Cathl Dundee 84–92; Chapl Angl Students Dundee Univ 89–92; P-in-c Invergowrie 89–92; TR S Ayrshire TM 92–98; Bp Glas 98–09; Primus 06–09; rtd 09; Hon Fell Univ of Wales (Trin St Dav) from 07; LtO *Glas* from 10. *27 Donald Wynd, Largs KA30 8TH* T: (01475) 674919 E: idrisjones43@hotmail.co.uk

JONES, Jacqueline Dorian. b 58. K Coll Lon BD 80 AKC 80 MTh 81. Westcott Ho Cam 84. dss 86 d 87 p 94. Epsom St Martin *Guildf* 86–91; C 87–91; Chapl Chelmsf Cathl 91–97; V Bridgemary *Portsm* 97–03; Can Res S'well Minster 03–18; P-in-c Danbury *Chelmsf* from 18; P-in-c Lt Baddow from 18. *The Rectory, 55 Main Road, Danbury, Chelmsford CM3 4NG*

JONES, Mrs Jacqueline Mary Shore. b 65. York St Jo Univ BA 14. Yorks Min Course 15. d 17 p 18. NSM Warmsworth *Sheff* from 17. *31 Chamberlain Avenue, Doncaster DN5 9BH* T: (01302) 783239 M: 07921-387793 E: threadsjj@gmail.com

JONES, Jacqueline Primrose. b 47. d 09 p 10. NSM Chipping Norton *Ox* 09–12; Chapl Ox Univ Hosps NHS Trust 12–13; C Chipping Norton *Ox* from 13; Chapl Kath Ho Hospice from 13. *Old Appleyard, 18 Kingham Road, Churchill, Chipping Norton OX7 6NE* T: (01608) 658616 E: jackiejones.churchill@gmail.com

JONES, James Richard. b 65. SS Hild & Bede Coll Dur BA 87 Open Univ MBA 95. Wycliffe Hall Ox 02. d 04 p 05. C Ashtead *Guildf* 04–08; P-in-c Burscough Bridge *Liv* 08–15; V 15; R Ashtead *Guildf* from 15. *Ashdene, Dene Road, Ashtead KT21 1EE* T: (01372) 805182 E: jrj37@aol.com *or* richard.jones@ashteadparish.org

✠**JONES, The Rt Revd James Stuart.** b 48. Ex Univ BA 70 PGCE 71 Hull Univ Hon DD 99 Lincs & Humberside Univ Hon DLitt 01. Wycliffe Hall Ox 81. d 82 p 83 c 94. C Clifton Ch Ch w Em *Bris* 82–90; V S Croydon Em *S'wark* 90–94; Suff Bp Hull *York* 94–98; Bp Liv 98–13; Bp HM Pris 07–13; rtd 13; Asst Bp York from 14. *The Diocese of York, Amy Johnson House, Amy Johnson Way, York YO30 4XT* T: (01904) 699500

JONES, Jeffrey Lloyd. b 66. Univ of Wales (Abth) BD 87 PGCE 90. Wycliffe Hall Ox 95. **d** 97 **p** 98. C Lampeter Pont Steffan w Silian *St D* 97; C Carmarthen St Dav 97–00; TV Llantwit Major *Llan* 00–08; V Llanddeiniolen w Llanfair-is-gaer etc *Ban* 08–13; AD Arfon 09–12; V Uwch Gwyrfai Beuno Sant from 13; AD Synod Bangor from 18. *Y Ficerdy, Clynnogfawr, Caernarfon LL54 5PE* T: (01286) 660656

JONES, Jennifer Margaret. b 49. Lon Univ CertEd. Cranmer Hall Dur 87. **d** 89 **p** 94. C Musselburgh *Edin* 89–93; Dn-in-c 93–94; P-in-c 94–95; R 95–02; C Prestonpans 89–93; Dn-in-c 93–94; P-in-c 94–95; R 95–02; NSM Rothiemurchus *Mor* from 07. *Meadowbank, Main Street, Newtonmore PH20 1DD* T: (01540) 673532 E: jennifer.jones32@btinternet.com

JONES, Mrs Joanne. b 64. Warwick Univ BA 88. St Mellitus Coll BA 10. **d** 10 **p** 11. C Maldon All SS w St Pet *Chelmsf* 10–14; P-in-c Writtle w Highwood 14–17; P-in-c Roxwell 15–17; PtO from 18. *Address withheld by request* T: (01245) 842598 E: jojonesb@outlook.com

JONES, John Bernard. b 49. Qu Coll Birm 86. **d** 88 **p** 89. C Mold *St As* 88–91; P-in-c Treuddyn and Nercwys and Eryrys 91–92; V Treuddyn w Nercwys 92–14; RD Mold 95–00; rtd 14; PtO *St As* from 15. *18 Willow Walk, Leeswood, Mold CH7 4UJ* T: (01352) 770919 M: 07952-071657 E: revjbj@hotmail.com

JONES, John David Emrys. b 36. Trin Coll Carmarthen. **d** 96 **p** 97. NSM Llanfihangel Ystrad and Cilcennin w Trefilan etc *St D* 96–97; P-in-c Llangeitho and Blaenpennal w Betws Leucu etc 97–06; PtO from 06. *Dolfor, Ciliau Aeron, Lampeter SA48 8DE* T: (01570) 470569

JONES, Canon Joyce Rosemary. b 54. Newnham Coll Cam BA 76 MA 82 Coll of Ripon & York St Jo MA 97 Solicitor 79. NOC 94. **d** 97 **p** 98. C Pontefract All SS *Wakef* 97–00; NSM Cumberworth, Denby and Denby Dale 00–01; Dioc Voc Adv 00–01; Asst Chapl Kirkwood Hospice Huddersfield 00–01; P-in-c Shelley and Shepley *Wakef* 01–14; Leeds 14–16; R Cumberworth, Denby, Denby Dale etc from 16; AD Kirkburton 11–18; Hon Can Wakef Cathl from 10. *15 Busker Lane, Scissett, Huddersfield HD8 9JU* T/F: (01484) 862350 E: joycerjones@aol.com

JONES, Julie Ann. b 59. STETS. **d** 10 **p** 11. NSM W Meon and Warnford *Portsm* 10–11; NSM Portchester 11–14; NSM Purbrook 14–19; Chapl Qu Alexandra Hosp Portsm from 19. *Orchard View, Hill Pound, Swanmore, Southampton SO32 2UN* T: (01489) 891402 M: 07800-553920 E: jones59ja@btinternet.com

JONES, Mrs Julie Denise. b 63. CBDTI 03. **d** 06 **p** 07. C Darwen St Pet w Hoddlesden *Blackb* 06–09; P-in-c Wesham and Treales 09–11; V 11–16; rtd 16. *191 Reads Avenue, Blackpool FY1 4HZ* M: 07814-500855 E: juliejones449@btinternet.com

JONES, Karen Elizabeth. b 64. Univ of Ulster BA 87. Wycliffe Hall Ox 04. **d** 06 **p** 07. C Northolt Park St Barn *Lon* 06–07; NSM Longwell Green *Bris* 08–10; Chapl UWE 10–11; C Stoke Gifford 10–16; NSM Woodchester and Brimscombe *Glouc* 16–18; C Chacewater w St Day and Carharrack *Truro* from 18; C Devoran from 18; C Feock from 18; C St Stythians w Perranarworthal and Gwennap from 18. *The Vicarage, 2 Old Vicarage Close, Stithians, Truro TR3 7DZ* T: (01209) 860803 M: 07799-028802 E: karenhunterjones@outlook.com *or* kehunterjones@outlook.com

JONES, Karen Sheila Frances. *See* ROOMS, Karen Sheila Frances

JONES, Karl Rupert Barker. b 63. Salford Univ BSc 87 Lon Univ BD 93 York St Jo Coll MA 01. NOC 05. **d** 07 **p** 08. NSM Utley *Bradf* 07–08; NSM Thwaites Brow 08–10; Lect Dur Univ 10–18; PtO *Dur* 11–18; NSM Waverton w Aldford and Bruera *Ches* from 18. *The Rectory, Green Lake Lane, Aldford, Chester CH3 6HW*

JONES, Kathryn Mary. *See* BUCK, Kathryn Mary

JONES (née SANDELLS-REES), The Very Revd Kathy Louise. b 68. Univ of Wales (Ban) BTh 96 Leeds Univ MA 13 Northumbria Univ PGCE 11. Qu Coll Birm 90. **d** 92 **p** 97. C Holyhead w Rhoscolyn w Llanfair-yn-Neubwll *Ban* 92–94; C Bangor 94–95; Chapl Gwynedd Hosp Ban 94–99; P-in-c Bangor *Ban* 95–99; C Betws-y-Coed and Capel Curig w Penmachno etc 99–06; Chapl Newcastle upon Tyne Hosps NHS Foundn Trust 06–12; Chapl Team Ldr Northumbria Healthcare NHS Foundn Trust 12–16; Dean Ban from 16; TR Bro Deiniol from 16. *Erw Fach, Hwfa Road, Bangor LL57 2BN* T: (01248) 352515 E: kathyjones@esgobaethbangor.org

JONES, Mrs Kay Sandra. b 61. Linc Univ BA 01. **d** 12 **p** 13. OLM New Clee *Linc* 12–17; P-in-c from 17. *The Rectory, 41 Dunbar Avenue, New Waltham, Grimsby DN36 4PY* T: (01472) 884434 M: 07811-747569 E: revsok@virginmedia.com

JONES, The Very Revd Keith Brynmor. b 44. Selw Coll Cam BA 65 MA 69. Cuddesdon Coll 67. **d** 69 **p** 70. C Limpsfield and Titsey *S'wark* 69–72; Dean's V St Alb Abbey 72–76; P-in-c Boreham Wood St Mich 76–79; TV Borehamwood 79–82; V Ipswich St Mary-le-Tower *St E* 82–96; RD Ipswich 92–96; Hon Can St E Cathl 93–96; Dean Ex 96–04; Dean York 04–12; rtd 12; PtO *St E* from 13. *7 Broughton Road, Ipswich IP1 3QR* T: (01473) 413436 E: keithbjones@gmail.com *or* keithbjones2012@gmail.com

JONES, Keith Ellison. b 47. Wycliffe Hall Ox 72. **d** 75 **p** 76. C Everton St Chrys *Liv* 75–79; C Buckhurst Hill *Chelmsf* 79–81; TV 81–88; TR Leek and Meerbrook *Lich* 88–99; V Formby H Trin *Liv* 99–11; AD Sefton 05–08; Hon Can Liv Cathl 05–08; rtd 11; PtO *Lich* 13–15 and from 17. *77 Woodhouse Lane, Biddulph, Stoke-on-Trent ST8 7EN*

JONES, Kingsley Charles. b 45. Birm Univ BSc 66 Open Univ BA 75. Sarum Th Coll 66. **d** 69 **p** 70. C Penwortham St Mary *Blackb* 69–72; C Broughton 72–74; P-in-c Gt Wollaston *Heref* 74–77; Chapl RAF 77–83; V Colwich w Gt Haywood *Lich* 83–94; V Winshill *Derby* 94–01; P-in-c Glouc St Aldate 01–11; rtd 11. *Orchard House, Sandhurst Road, Gloucester GL1 2SE* T: (01452) 690406

JONES, Lesley Anne. b 46. Luton Coll of HE CertEd 77. SAOMC 01. **d** 04 **p** 06. NSM Gravenhurst, Shillington and Stondon *St Alb* 04–06; NSM Leagrave 06–16; NSM Officer Bedford Adnry 14–16; rtd 16; PtO *St Alb* from 16. *91 Manton Drive, Luton LU2 7DL* T: (01582) 616888 E: lesleyjones31647@aol.com

JONES, Mrs Lesley Marie. b 66. **d** 12 **p** 13. NSM N Wearside *Dur* 12–13; C Milton Regis w Murston, Bapchild and Tonge *Cant* 13–17; TV Sittingbourne w Bobbing from 17. *32 Valenciennes Road, Sittingbourne ME10 1EN* M: 07881-555580 E: revlesleyjones@gmail.com

JONES, Lloyd. *See* JONES, Gareth Lloyd

JONES, Lloyd. *See* JONES, Jeffrey Lloyd

JONES, Miss Mair. b 41. Cartrefle Coll of Educn TCert 61. St Mich Coll Llan 91. **d** 93 **p** 97. C Llangollen w Trevor and Llantysilio *St As* 93–97; V Llandrillo and Llandderfel 97–00; R Llanelian w Betws-yn-Rhos w Trofarth 00–03; R Llanelian 03–08; P-in-c Brynymaen 04–08; rtd 08; PtO *St As* from 09. *5 Ffordd Bugail, Colwyn Bay LL29 8TN* T: (01492) 517866 E: jonesmair41@gmail.com

JONES, Malcolm. *See* JONES, Philip Malcolm

JONES, Canon Malcolm Francis. b 44. Open Univ BA 88 Hull Univ MA 96 Univ of Wales (Cardiff) LLM 05 FInstLM 10. Chich Th Coll 67. **d** 70 **p** 71. C Prestbury *Ches* 70–73; Chapl RAF 73–81; R Heaton Reddish *Man* 81–84; CF (ACF) 82–84 and 98–14; CF (TA) 83–84; CF 84–93; CF (R of O) 93–99; TV Cleethorpes *Linc* 93–97; V Ryde H Trin *Portsm* 97–10; V Swanmore St Mich 97–10; rtd 10; P-in-c Win H Trin 10–11; R 11–16; P-in-c 16–17; Hon Can Win Cathl 14–17; PtO *Eur* from 15; *Win* from 17. *Rue des Aubépines, 56580 Bréhan, France* T: (0033) (0) 2 56 22 00 45 M: 07710-543155 E: frmalcolmjones@hotmail.com

JONES, Malcolm Stuart. b 41. Sheff Univ BA 62. Linc Th Coll 64. **d** 66 **p** 67. C Monkseaton St Mary *Newc* 66–69; C Ponteland 69–72; Chapl Lake Maracaibo Venezuela 73–75; C Hexham *Newc* 75–77; P-in-c Killingworth 77–92; V Delaval 92–01; TV Ch the King 01–07; rtd 07; PtO *Newc* from 07. *13 Valeside, Newcastle upon Tyne NE15 9LA* T: 0191-267 7829 E: malcolmjonespcdc@hotmail.com

JONES, Mrs Margaret Angela. b 53. Wolv Univ CertEd 91 Univ of Wales (Lamp) MA 04. Qu Coll Birm BA 99. **d** 99 **p** 00. C Pershore w Pinvin, Wick and Birlingham *Worc* 99–03; TV Solihull *Birm* 03–11; P-in-c Pontesbury I and II *Heref* 11–18; RD Pontesbury 13–17; rtd 18; PtO *Blackb* from 19. *9 Fairview Close, Walmer Bridge, Preston PR4 5RF* E: magz.stgeorges@talktalk.net

JONES, Mrs Margaret Anne. b 47. Luton Univ TCert 68 Ches Coll of HE BTh 04. NOC 01. **d** 04 **p** 05. NSM Altrincham St Geo *Ches* 04–07; C 07–12; C Altrincham St Jo 07–12; P-in-c Whaley Bridge from 12; Chapl Trin C of E High Sch Man 05–07. *46 Buxton Road, Whaley Bridge, High Peak SK23 7JE* M: 07748-645596 E: margaret_jones@talk21.com

JONES, Margaret Mary. b 47. Oak Hill Th Coll 92. **d** 95 **p** 96. C Sydenham H Trin *S'wark* 95–98; V Anerley St Paul *Roch* 98–09; TV Anerley 09–11; rtd 11; PtO *S'wark* from 12. *10 Lower Road, Redhill RH1 6NN* T: (01737) 247998 E: maggi.jones99@gmail.com

JONES, Mark. *See* JONES, Christopher Mark

JONES, Mark Andrew. b 60. Southn Univ BSc 82 Sussex Univ PGCE 83. Oak Hill Th Coll BA 91. **d** 91 **p** 92. C Wolverhampton St Luke *Lich* 91–96; I Inishmacsaint *Clogh* 96–01; V Padiham w Hapton and Padiham Green

Blackb from 01; AD Burnley 10–19. *The Vicarage, 1 Arbory Drive, Padiham, Burnley BB12 8JS* T: (01282) 772442 E: jones.padiham@btinternet.com

JONES, Mark Vincent. *See* HALDON-JONES, Mark Vincent

JONES, Martin. b 58. Leeds Univ BA 07. NOC 04. **d** 07 **p** 08. NSM Winwick *Liv* 07–13; Chapl St Helens and Knowsley Hosps NHS Trust 09–13; NSM Aisholt, Enmore, Goathurst, Nether Stowey etc *B & W* 13–17; Chapl Somerset Partnership NHS Foundn Trust 13–17; PtO *Truro* 17–18; P-in-c Duloe and Herodsfoot from 18. *April Cottage, Tredinnick, Liskeard PL14 4PJ* T: (01503) 265862 M: 07943-706693 E: revmartinjones@icloud.com

JONES, Martin David. b 50. Liv Univ MB, ChB 73. **d** 13 **p** 14. OLM Codnor *Derby* 13–19; OLM Horsley and Denby 13–19; OLM Horsley Woodhouse 13–19; OLM Loscoe 13–19; OLM Denby Gp from 19. *Meadow Rise, Smalley Mill Road, Horsley, Derby DE21 5BL* T: (01332) 882929 M: 07788-641946 E: martinjones2812@gmail.com

JONES, Martin Patrick. b 62. K Coll Lon BDS 85. Dioc OLM tr scheme 02. **d** 05 **p** 06. NSM Kingsnorth and Shadoxhurst *Cant* 05–09; PtO 09–11; NSM Aldington w Bonnington and Bilsington etc 11–13; C Saxon Shoreline 13–18; P-in-c Haywards Heath Ascension *Chich* from 18. *Ascension Vicarage, 1 Redwood Drive, Haywards Heath RH16 4ER* E: martin.jones62@icloud.com

JONES, Mary Catherine Theresa Bridget. b 41. Westhill Coll Birm CertEd 77 Birm Univ BA 80 MA 09 Leic Univ PhD 17. Qu Coll Birm 04. **d** 05 **p** 06. NSM Bromsgrove St Jo *Worc* 05–08; PtO from 08; *Birm* from 11. *262 Dickens Heath Road, Shirley, Solihull B90 1QJ* T: (01564) 822687 E: theresaj1@btinternet.com

JONES, Canon Mary Nerissa Anna. b 41. Qu Mary Coll Lon BA 86 FRSA 91. Ripon Coll Cuddesdon 86. **d** 88 **p** 94. Par Dn St Botolph Aldgate w H Trin Minories *Lon* 88–93; P-in-c Wood End *Cov* 93–95; V 95–01; Hon Can Cov Cathl 01; rtd 01; P-in-c Askerswell, Loders and Powerstock *Sarum* 01–10; P-in-c Symondsbury 07–10; PtO from 11. *Church Farm Cottage, West Milton, Bridport DT6 3SL* T: (01308) 485304 E: revnerissa@gmail.com

JONES, Canon Mary Valerie. b 37. Univ of Wales (Ban) BD 84. St Deiniol's Hawarden 84. **d** 85 **p** 97. C Holyhead w Rhoscolyn w Llanfair-yn-Neubwll *Ban* 85–87; C Ynyscynhaearn w Penmorfa and Porthmadog 87–90; Dn-in-c Llansantffraid Glyn Ceirog and Llanarmon etc *St As* 90–97; V 97–98; R Overton and Erbistock and Penley 98–04; RD Bangor Isycoed 98–04; Can Cursal St As Cathl 01–04; rtd 04; PtO *St As* 09–18. *Cysgod y Coed, 12 Church View, Ruabon, Wrexham LL14 6TD* T: (01978) 822206

JONES, Maurice Maxwell Hughes. b 32. Clifton Th Coll 56. **d** 60 **p** 61. C Islington St Andr w St Thos and St Matthias *Lon* 60–63; Argentina 63–71; C Whitchurch *Llan* 72–73; Area Sec (NW England) SAMS 73–77; V Haydock St Mark *Liv* 78–87; V Paddington Em Harrow Road *Lon* 87–97; rtd 98. *Glyn Orig, Cemmaes, Machynlleth SY20 9PR* T/F: (01650) 511632

JONES, Canon Melville Kenneth. b 40. Open Univ BA 82. St D Coll Lamp. **d** 66 **p** 67. C Aberdare *Llan* 66–71; C Caerau w Ely 71–72; Chapl Pontypridd Hosps 72–89; V Graig *Llan* 72–89; P-in-c Cilfynydd 86–89; V Llantwit Fardre 89–07; Chapl E Glam NHS Trust 89–97; RD Pontypridd *Llan* 99–05; Hon Can Llan Cathl 04–07; Chapl Pontypridd and Rhondda NHS Trust 99–01; rtd 07; PtO *Llan* from 07. *Nanteos, 7 Meadow Hill, Church Village, Pontypridd CF38 1RX* T: (01443) 217213 E: melville_k.jones@virgin.net

JONES, Michael. b 49. Leeds Univ BA 71 Man Univ MA 73 Padgate Coll of Educn PGCE 73. Qu Coll Birm 83. **d** 85 **p** 86. C Leigh St Mary *Man* 85–88; C-in-c Holts CD 88–93; V Hamer 93–05; rtd 09; PtO *Man* 06–12; *St As* 09–16. *Ty Coch Cottage, Llangynhafal, Ruthin LL15 1RT* T: (01824) 703037 E: mike@ashborn.force9.co.uk

JONES, Michael. *See* JONES, David Michael

JONES, Michael Adrian. b 62. Reading Univ BSc 83 PGCE 84. Trin Coll Bris 07. **d** 09 **p** 10. C Bath Weston All SS w N Stoke and Langridge *B & W* 09–13; Bp's Chapl and Policy Adv *Leic* 13–17; V Knighton from 17. *Knighton Vicarage, 5 Church Lane, Leicester LE2 3WG* T: 0116-270 4268 E: adrian.jones@zoho.com

JONES, Michael Barry. b 48. MCIEH 88 MIOSH 88. ERMC 04. **d** 07 **p** 08. NSM Whittlesey, Pondersbridge and Coates *Ely* 07–12; PtO from 12; Chapl Peterborough and Stamford Hosps NHS Foundn Trust from 13. *Chaplaincy Department, Peterborough City Hospital, Bretton Gate, Peterborough PE3 9GZ* T: (01733) 673115 E: michael.jones@pbh-tr.nhs.uk

JONES, Michael Christopher. b 67. Southn Univ BSc 88. St Jo Coll Nottm MTh 03 MA 04. **d** 04 **p** 05. C Aldridge *Lich* 04–07; V Lilleshall and Muxton 07–13; V Luton St Mary *St Alb* from 13; P-in-c Luton St Matt High Town from 17; P-in-c Luton St Paul 18–19. *32 Whitehill Avenue, Luton LU1 3SP*

JONES, Michael Denis Dyson. b 39. CCC Cam BA 62 MA 66 Lon Univ MSc 73. Wycliffe Hall Ox. **d** 76 **p** 77. C Plymouth St Andr w St Paul and St Geo *Ex* 76–81; V Devonport St Budeaux 81–00; RD Plymouth Devonport 93–95; TV Barnstaple 00–07; RD 03–07; rtd 07. *The Spinney, 40 West Drive, Harrow HA3 6TS* T: (020) 8954 1530

JONES, Michael Kevin. b 57. Llan Ord Course 94. **d** 98 **p** 99. NSM Caerau w Ely *Llan* 98–00; NSM Cen Cardiff 01; P-in-c Tremorfa St Phil CD 02–05; Area Fundraising Manager Children's Soc Llan and Mon 98–00; Ch Strategy Manager Wales 01–02; LtO *Llan* 05–09; V Mountain Ash and Miskin from 09; AD Cynon Valley from 13. *5 Lon-y-Felin, Cefn Pennar, Mountain Ash CF45 4ES* T: (01443) 473700 E: jonesm78@sky.com

JONES, Nerissa. *See* JONES, Mary Nerissa Anna

JONES, Canon Neville George. b 36. Univ of Wales (Ban) BA 59. St Mich Coll Llan 59. **d** 61 **p** 62. C Broughton *St As* 61–65; C Newcastle Llan 65–68; V Laleston w Tythegston 68–83; V Llanishen and Lisvane 84–93; V Llanishen 93–02; Hon Can Llan Cathl 96–02; rtd 02; PtO *Llan* from 10. *21 Cwm Gwynlais, Tongwynlais, Cardiff CF15 7HU* T: (029) 2081 1150 E: nevilliegjones@btinternet.com

JONES, Nicholas Godwin. b 58. St Jo Coll Cam BA 81 MA 84 Hughes Hall Cam PGCE 90. Ridley Hall Cam 91. **d** 93 **p** 94. C Cambridge H Trin *Ely* 93–97; Chapl St Bede's Sch Cam 97–00; C Fulbourn w Gt and Lt Wilbraham 97–00; V Harston w Hauxton and Newton 00–03; V Gt Horton *Bradf* 03–10; Chapl HM Pris Man 10–11; Chapl HM Pris Hindley 10–15; Hon C Halifax *Leeds* 13–15; Hon C Siddal 13–15; P-in-c Acton St Mary *Lon* 15–16; R from 16. *The Rectory, 14 Cumberland Park, London W3 6SX* T: (020) 8992 8876 *or* 8993 0422 E: nickjones114@gmail.com

JONES, Nicholas Peter. b 55. St Mich Coll Llan. **d** 82 **p** 83. C St Andrews Major w Michaelston-le-Pit *Llan* 82–84; C Aberdare 84–88; Youth Chapl 85–89; V Abercynon 88–96; R Llanilid w Pencoed 96–10; AD Bridgend 10; Chapl Miss to Seafarers 12–17; P-in-c Burry Port and Pwll *St D* from 17. *The Vicarage, Cae Ffwrnes, Burry Port SA16 0FW* T: (01554) 832936 E: revnickjones@gmail.com

JONES, Nigel David. b 69. Qu Coll Cam MA 95. Westcott Ho Cam 97. **d** 00 **p** 01. C Abbots Langley *St Alb* 00–03; TV Dunstable 03–08; V Caversham St Andr *Ox* from 08. *St Andrew's Vicarage, Harrogate Road, Reading RG4 7PW* T: 0118-947 2788

JONES, Nigel Ivor. b 54. Sheff Univ MMin 04. WMMTC 91. **d** 94 **p** 95. C Shirley *Birm* 94–99; TV Salter Street and Shirley 99–01; V Olton 01–08; Chapl HM Pris Rye Hill 10–17; PtO *Birm* from 13. *62 Balmoral Way, Birmingham B14 4NT* E: revnigel@aol.com

JONES, Norman. b 50. Oak Hill Th Coll BA 83. **d** 83 **p** 84. C Ulverston St Mary w H Trin *Carl* 83–87; Hong Kong 88–92; TR Eccles *Man* 92–01; AD 95–00; R Haslemere and Grayswood *Guildf* 01–10; RD Godalming 02–07; Chapl Wispers Sch Haslemere 01–10; rtd 11; PtO *Ches* from 11; Chapl E Cheshire Hospice 12–13. *51 Freshwater Drive, Weston, Crewe CW2 5GR* T: (01270) 829141 E: normanjones1950@gmail.com

JONES, Norman Burnet. b 52. St Andr Univ BSc 74 Man Univ PhD 78 CChem 81 CBiol 78. SEITE 08. **d** 11 **p** 12. NSM Southgate *Chich* 11–15; PtO *St Alb* from 15. *6 Aldridge Way, Buntingford SG9 9FX* M: 07766-367983 E: normanbjones1@virginmedia.com *or* normanbjones1@gmail.com

JONES, Mrs Patricia Ann. b 43. **d** 97 **p** 98. OLM Bincombe w Broadwey, Upwey and Buckland Ripers *Sarum* 97–05; NSM 06–10; rtd 11; PtO *Sarum* from 11. *23 Camedown Close, Weymouth DT3 5RB* T: (01305) 813056

JONES, Mrs Patricia Anne. b 55. CSS 81. Oak Hill Th Coll 92. **d** 95 **p** 00. NSM Mill Hill Jo Keble Ch *Lon* 95–01; NSM Queensbury All SS 01–08; PtO 08–12; TV Thatcham *Ox* 12–19; V London Colney *St Alb* from 19. *St Peter's Vicarage, Riverside, London Colney, St Albans AL2 1QA* E: revpatsy55@gmail.com

JONES, Canon Patrick Geoffrey Dickson. b 28. Ch Ch Ox BA 51 MA 55 Aber Univ MLitt 98. St Deiniol's Hawarden 79. **d** 82 **p** 83. NSM Sandbach *Ches* 82–84; R Aboyne *Ab* 84–96; R Ballater 84–96; P-in-c Braemar 84–96; rtd 96; P-in-c Cen Buchan *Ab* 96–98; LtO 06–16; P-in-c Cuminestown 09–15; PtO from 16; Hon Can St Andr Cathl from 01. *2 Kingston Cross, Kingston, Sturminster Newton DT10 2AR* T: (01258) 817967 E: patrickj786@btinternet.com

JONES, Patrick George. b 42. Cant Ch Ch Univ Coll MA 99. Lich Th Coll 69. **d** 72 **p** 73. C Chesterton St Geo *Ely* 72–75; P-in-c Waterbeach 75–78; P-in-c Landbeach 76–78; R Charlton-in-Dover *Cant* 78–90; Chapl Cautley

Ho Chr Cen 90–06; rtd 06. *36 Windmill Grange, Windmill Lane, Histon, Cambridge CB24 9JF* T: (01223) 232505 E: patrickjones303@btinternet.com

JONES, Paul Evan. b 62. York Univ BA 84 Sarum Coll MA 13 CPFA 89. SEITE 02. **d** 05 **p** 06. C Kingstanding St Luke *Birm* 05–09; P-in-c Babbacombe *Ex* 09–17; V from 17; RD Torbay 13–16. *Babbacombe Vicarage, 4 Cary Park, Torquay TQ1 3NH* T: (01803) 323002 E: liberty.hall@me.com

JONES, Pauline Edna. b 55. Liv Univ BA 77. **d** 10 **p** 11. OLM Langley *Man* 10–17; Chapl Pennine Acute Hosps NHS Trust 13–17; NSM Bro Eleth *Ban* from 17. *The Rectory, 3 Swn-y-Don, Benllech, Tyn-y-Gongl LL74 8PR* E: broeleth@pjones.wales

JONES, Canon Peter Anthony Watson. b 53. AKC 75. Sarum & Wells Th Coll 76. **d** 77 **p** 78. C Hessle *York* 77–81; C Stainton-in-Cleveland 81–82; P-in-c Weston Mill *Ex* 82–84; Chapl Plymouth Poly 82–90; V Gt Ayton w Easby and Newton-in-Cleveland *York* 90–92; C Devonport St Aubyn *Ex* 92–98; P-in-c Yealmpton and Brixton 98–01; Team Chapl Portsm Hosps NHS Trust 01–05; Chapl Portsm Univ 05–09; Can Res Portsm Cathl 05–09; R Havant 09–14; Dioc Interfaith Adv 06–11; rtd 14; Hon C York All SS Pavement w St Crux and St Mich 14–16; Hon C York St Olave w St Giles 14–16; Hon C York St Helen w St Martin 14–16; Hon C York St Denys 14–16; P-in-c Farnsfield *S'well* 16–18; P-in-c Kirklington w Hockerton 16–18; P-in-c Winkburn 16–18; P-in-c Maplebeck 16–18. *28 Blakeney Road, Radcliffe-on-Trent, Nottingham NG12 2GX*

JONES, Peter Brian. b 81. Ulster Univ BA 02 PGCE 03. MTh 14. **d** 13 **p** 14. Maghera w Killelagh *D & R* 13–14; C Drumglass w Moygashel *Arm* 14–17; I Mossley *Conn* from 17; Dioc Warden of Readers from 19. *1 Woodford Manor, Newtownabbey BT36 6FF* E: peterjones917@hotmail.com

JONES, Peter Charles. b 60. Univ of Wales BA 81 MA 82 PGCE 97. St Mich Coll Llan 80. **d** 83 **p** 84. C Pontnewynydd *Mon* 83–85; C Bassaleg 85–87; TV Cwmbran 87–94; V Blaenavon w Capel Newydd 94–01; Chapl CME 00–01; Chapl and Fell Trin Coll Carmarthen 01–05; V Llangennech and Hendy *St D* 05–11; AD Cydweli 08–11; V Keele *Lich* from 11; V Silverdale from 11. *The Vicarage, 21 Pepper Street, Silverdale, Newcastle ST5 6QJ* T: (01782) 624455 E: tadjones@btinternet.com

JONES, Peter David. b 48. S'wark Ord Course 89. **d** 92 **p** 93. NSM Coulsdon St Andr *S'wark* 92–04; PtO from 04. *79 Beverley Road, Whyteleafe CR3 0DU* T: (020) 8668 6398 E: revpeter79@gmail.com

JONES, Peter Owen. b 64. Hull Univ BSc 86. Oak Hill Th Coll BA 08. **d** 08 **p** 09. C Hubberston *St D* 08–11; P-in-c Llanfihangel Genau'r Glyn and Llangorwen 11–17; AD Llanbadarn Fawr 14–17; P-in-c Monkton from 17. *The Vicarage, Church Terrace, Monkton, Pembroke SA71 4LW* E: rev.peterjones@outlook.com

JONES, Peter Robin. b 42. Open Univ BA 75 Bp Otter Coll Chich CertEd 68. EMMTC 79. **d** 82 **p** 83. NSM Doveridge *Derby* 82–97; NSM Doveridge, Scropton, Sudbury etc 98–10; NSM S Dales from 11; Bp's Inspector of Th Colls and Courses from 98; PtO *Lich* 93–10. *4 Cross Road, Uttoxeter ST14 7BN* T: (01889) 565123 E: rev.john@talktalk.net

JONES, Canon Peter Russell. b 48. St Jo Coll Cam BA 71 MA 75 Univ of Wales MTh 86. Wycliffe Hall Ox. **d** 75 **p** 76. C Northampton All SS w St Kath *Pet* 75–79; C Ban Cathl 79–81; Min Can Ban Cathl 79–81; R Pentraeth and Llanddyfnan 81–85; P-in-c Heathfield St Rich *Chich* 08–13; V Conwy w Gyffin 85–14; Lect Univ of Wales (Ban) 89–95; AD Archllechwedd Ban 96–09; Can and Treas Ban Cathl 99–09; Chan Ban Cathl 09–14; rtd 14; PtO *St As* from 14; *Ban* from 14. *Encilfa, 14 Victoria Park, Colwyn Bay LL29 7AX* T: (01492) 531711

JONES, The Ven Philip Hugh. b 51. Solicitor. Chich Th Coll 92. **d** 94 **p** 95. C Horsham *Chich* 94–97; V Southwater 97–05; RD Horsham 02–04; Adn Hastings 05–16; rtd 16; P-in-c Slindon, Eartham and Madehurst *Chich* from 16. *The Rectory, Dyers Lane, Slindon, Arundel BN18 0RE* T: (01825) 763326 E: archlandh@chichester.anglican.org

JONES, Philip Malcolm. b 43. Qu Coll Birm. **d** 04 **p** 05. NSM Birm St Paul 04–08; P-in-c Heathfield St Rich *Chich* 08–13; V 13–15; rtd 15; PtO *Cant* from 16. *2 The Oast, Gate Court Farm, Station Road, Northiam, Rye TN31 6QT* T: (01797) 252563 E: malcolm@peri.co.uk

JONES, Philip Thomas Henry. b 34. Qu Coll Birm 58. **d** 60 **p** 61. C Castle Bromwich SS Mary and Marg *Birm* 60–67; C Reading St Mary V *Ox* 67–72; C-in-c Reading All SS CD 72–75; V Reading All SS 75–95; PtO *Portsm* from 97; Hon Chapl Portsm Cathl from 97. *13 Oyster Street, Portsmouth PO1 2HZ* T: (023) 9275 6676 E: johnmortiboys@gmail.com

JONES, Canon Phillip Bryan. b 34. St Mich Coll Llan. **d** 61 **p** 62. C Hope *St As* 61–64; C Llanrhos 64–67; V Kerry 67–74; R Newtown w Llanllwchaiarn w Aberhafesp 74–97; RD

Cedewain 76–97; Sec Ch in Wales Prov Evang Cttee 80–83; Hon Can St As Cathl 86–93; Can St As Cathl 93–97; rtd 97. *7 Dalton Drive, Shrewsbury SY3 8DA* T: (01743) 351426

JONES, Phillip Edmund. b 56. Man Poly BA 78 Fitzw Coll Cam BA 84 MA 88 GradCIPD 79. Westcott Ho Cam 82. **d** 85 **p** 86. C Stafford St Jo and Tixall w Ingestre *Lich* 85–89; TV Redditch, The Ridge *Worc* 89–95; TV Worc SE 95–08; Ind Chapl 89–08; Team Ldr Worcs Ind Miss 01–08; Team Ldr and Chapl Faith at Work in Worcs 08–11; Miss Development Officer 11–17; C Worc St Barn w Ch Ch 08–17; TR Hanley H Ev *Lich* from 17. *19 Widecombe Road, Stoke-on-Trent ST1 6SL* T: (01782) 922540 M: 07586-303831 E: phillip.e.jones@talktalk.net

JONES, Phyllis Gwendoline Charlotte. b 44. **d** 05 **p** 06. OLM Talbot Village *Sarum* 05–12; rtd 13; PtO *Sarum* 13–15; Hon C Tralee w Kilmoyley, Ballymacelligott etc *L & K* from 15. *The New Rectory, Kilgobbin, Camp, Co Kerry, Republic of Ireland* T: (00353) (66) 713 0767 M: (00353) 85-855 8594 E: phyllisjones@eircom.net

JONES, Ray. See JONES, David Raymond

JONES, Raymond. b 43. NOC 99. **d** 02 **p** 03. NSM Ashton-in-Makerfield St Thos *Liv* 02–03; C Widnes St Mary w St Paul 03–05; V 05–08; rtd 08; Hon C Farnworth *Liv* 10–13; Hon C E Widnes 13; PtO from 16. *4 Norlands Park, Widnes WA8 5BH*

JONES, Raymond Alban. b 34. RGN 55 RMN 63. Chich Th Coll 64. **d** 67 **p** 68. C Ocker Hill *Lich* 67–70; C Truro St Paul 70–71; Chapl Selly Oak Hosp Birm 71–76; USPG Bahamas 76–79; Chapl Willen Hospice Milton Keynes 80–83; Chapl St Jas Hosp Balham 83–87; NSM Leamington Spa H Trin and Old Milverton *Cov* 87–92; TV Probus, Ladock and Grampound w Creed and St Erme *Truro* 92–94; In Orthodox Ch 95–09; rtd 94; PtO *Sarum* 09–19. *2 St Catherine's Terrace, Rodden Row, Abbotsbury, Weymouth DT3 4JL* T: (01305) 871836 E: ajmck66@gmail.com

JONES, Canon Raymond Trevor. b 35. Linc Th Coll. **d** 82 **p** 83. C Rushmere *St E* 82–85; Bp's Dom Chapl 85–86; CF 86–91; TV Ridgeway *Sarum* 91–97; Relig Programmes Producer BBC Wiltshire Sound 91–97; Chapl Fuengirola *St Andr Eur* 97–00; P-in-c Ypres 00–10; P-in-c Ostend 06–08; Can Gib Cathl 04–10; PtO *Portsm* 10–16. *Easter Moy, Afton Road, Freshwater PO40 9TP*

JONES (née WELCH), Mrs Rebecca Anne. b 79. Leic Univ BSc 00. Wycliffe Hall Ox BTh 10. **d** 09 **p** 10. C Cov Cathl 09–12; C Aston and Nechells *Birm* 12–18; V Leamington Priors St Mary *Cov* from 18. *28 St Mary's Road, Leamington Spa CV31 1JP* M: 07712-632504

JONES, Rhiannon Elizabeth. See KING, Rhiannon Elizabeth

JONES, Rhys. b 69. TCD Div Sch MTh 17. **d** 15 **p** 17. Castledawson *D & R* from 15; C Clooney w Strathfoyle from 17. *72 Craigadick Road, Maghera BT46 5DH* T: (028) 7964 3861 M: 07907-386327 E: rhjones@tcd.ie *or* analogkid04@hotmail.com

JONES, Richard. See JONES, James Richard

JONES, Richard Christopher Bentley. b 53. Pemb Coll Ox BA 77 MA 79. SEITE 03. **d** 06 **p** 07. NSM Clapham H Trin and St Pet *S'wark* 06–13; PtO *Heref* 13–17; NSM Wye Brooks Benefice from 17. *Langstone Court, Llangarron, Ross-on-Wye HR9 6NR* T: (01989) 770254 E: richard.jones@langstone-court.org.uk

JONES, Robert. b 45. Culham Coll Ox CertEd 67. St Steph Ho Ox. **d** 85 **p** 86. C High Wycombe *Ox* 85–89; V Beckenham St Barn *Roch* 89–90; C Swanley St Mary 90–91; C Edenbridge and Crockham Hill H Trin 91–13; rtd 13. *23 Bromley College, London Road, Bromley BR1 1PE* E: r.jones52@btinternet.com

JONES, Robert Cecil. b 32. Univ of Wales (Abth) BA 54 DipEd 55. Qu Coll Birm 84. **d** 86 **p** 87. C Llanbadarn Fawr w Capel Bangor and Goginan *St D* 86–88; R Llanllwchaearn and Llanina 88–91; R Newport w Cilgwyn and Dinas w Llanllawer 91–98; rtd 98; PtO *Derby* 05–18. *Old Craigstead Works, High Street, Stoney Middleton, Hope Valley S32 4TL* T: (01433) 631857 E: revrobbiejones02@gmail.com

JONES, Robert David. b 73. UCD BSc 97 TCD BTh 07. CITC 04. **d** 07 **p** 08. C Dublin St Patr Cathl Gp *D & G* 07–10; V Dublin Rathmines w Harold's Cross 10–17; R from 17. *25 Airfield Road, Rathgar, Dublin 6, Republic of Ireland* M: (00353) 86-285 4098

JONES, The Ven Robert George. b 55. Hatf Coll Dur BA 77. Ripon Coll Cuddesdon BA 79 MA 87. **d** 80 **p** 81. C Foley Park *Worc* 80–84; V Dudley St Fran 84–92; TR Worc St Barn w Ch Ch 92–06; Dir Development 06–14; RD Worc E 99–05; Hon Can Worc Cathl 03–14; Adn Worc from 14; V Gt Malvern Ch Ch from 15. *The Archdeacon's House, Walkers Lane, Whittington, Worcester WR5 2RE* T: (01905) 773301 E: rjones@cofe-worcester.org.uk *or* archdeacon.worcester@cofe-worcester.org.uk

JONES, Canon Robert George. b 42. St Mich Coll Llan 93. d 95 p 96. NSM Treboeth *S & B* 95–02; P-in-c 02–07; P-in-c Landore 03–07; Can Res Brecon Cathl 06–07; rtd 07. *106 Plunch Lane, Mumbles, Swansea SA3 4JE* E: robertgeorgejones@yahoo.co.uk

JONES, Robert William. b 55. Open Univ BA 85 MA 88. Ian Ramsey Coll Brasted 75 Chich Th Coll 76 TCD Div Sch 77. d 79 p 80. C Seapatrick *D & D* 79; C Bangor Abbey 81–83; I Drumgath w Drumgooland and Clonduff 83–89; I Finaghy *Conn* 89–93; I Kilwaughter w Cairncastle and Craigy Hill 94–98; I Athlone w Benown, Kiltoom and Forgney *M & K* 98–02; Dean Clonmacnoise 02–12; I Trim and Athboy Gp 02–12; I Belfast Malone St Jo *Conn* 12–18; Can Belf Cathl 13–18; I Kiltegan w Hacketstown, Clonmore and Moyne *C & O* from 18. *The Rectory, Kiltegan, Co Wicklow, W91 D2E6, Republic of Ireland* T: (00353) (59) 647 3368 M: 85-257 3139 E: kilteganrectory@gmail.com

JONES, Robin Dominic Edwin. b 78. St Chad's Coll Dur BA 00 K Coll Lon MA 01. St Steph Ho Ox MTh 07. d 04 p 05. C Ealing Ch the Sav *Lon* 04–08; V Hammersmith St Luke 08–12; V Sevenoaks St Jo *Roch* from 12. *St John's Clergy House, 62 Quakers Hall Lane, Sevenoaks TN13 3TX* T: (01732) 451710 M: 07779-299924

JONES, Roderick. b 48. Leeds Univ BA 70 PGCE 72. Westmr Th Sem (USA) 73 Oak Hill Th Coll 74. d 76 p 77. C Beckenham Ch Ch *Roch* 76–80; C Uphill *B & W* 80–84; R Springfield All SS *Chelmsf* 84–90; Selection Sec ABM 91–96; V Horsell *Guildf* 96–13; rtd 13; PtO *Guildf* from 13. *3 Pine Close, New Haw, Addlestone KT15 3BW* E: revrodjones@btinternet.com

JONES, Canon Roger. b 49. St Mich Coll Llan 84. d 86 p 87. C Llangynwyd w Maesteg *Llan* 86–90; V Wiston w Walton E and Clarbeston *St D* 90–01; V Pembroke Gp 01–04; V Monkton 04–16; Can St D Cathl 09–16; rtd 16; PtO *St D* from 17. *32 Oakfield Drive, Kilgetty SA68 0UD* T: (01834) 811797 M: 07971-528933 E: canonrog@gmail.com

JONES, Mrs Rose-Mary Harriett. b 90. Westmr Univ BA 11 St Jo Coll Dur BA 18. Cranmer Hall Dur 16. d 19. C N Cornwall Cluster *Truro* from 19. *Address withheld by request* E: revrosejones@gmail.com

JONES, Russell Frederick. b 55. Man Univ BA 77 Edin Univ BD 84. Edin Th Coll 81. d 84 p 85. C Croxteth *Liv* 84–87; V Edgehill St Dunstan 87–98; R Glas St Bride 98–08; Hon Chapl Glas Univ 00–06; Chapl Marie Curie Hospice Glasgow 08–14; Chapl Gtr Glas and Clyde NHS from 15. *The Chaplaincy, Gartnavel General Hospital, 1053 Great Western Road, Glasgow G12 0YN* T: 0141-211 3026 E: russell.jones@ggc.scot.nhs.uk

JONES, Mrs Sally Ann. b 41. d 09 p 10. NSM Teme Valley N *Worc* 09–13. *2 Old School House, Eastham, Tenbury Wells WR15 8PB* T: (01584) 781526 E: revsally@live.com

JONES, Samuel. b 44. CITC. d 86 p 87. C Agherton *Conn* 86–88; I Connor w Antrim St Patr 88–97; I Whitehead and Islandmagee 97–01; Bp's C Kilbroney *D & D* 01–10; rtd 10. *2 The Brambles, Coleraine BT52 1PN* T: (028) 7031 0076

JONES, Sarah. *See* EDEN-JONES, Sarah Rachel

JONES, Sarah Charlotte. b 57. SRN 79. SAOMC 01. d 04 p 05. NSM Forest Edge *Ox* 04–18; rtd 18; PtO *Ox* from 18. *4 Tower Hill, Witney OX28 5ER* T: (01993) 200483 E: sarahtandem@hotmail.com

JONES, Ms Sarah Jane. b 61. St Hugh's Coll Ox BA 95 MA 03 Northumbria Univ MSc 02. Westcott Ho Cam 02. d 04 p 05. C Ross *Heref* 04–07; P-in-c 07–08; R Ross w Walford and Brampton Abbotts 08–18; P-in-c Cardiff City Par *Llan* from 18. *The Vicarage, 16 Queen Anne Square, Cardiff CF10 3ED* T: (029) 2022 4956

JONES, Sebastian. *See* JONES, David Sebastian

JONES, Canon Sharon Ann. b 60. St Kath Coll Liv BA 82. Cranmer Hall Dur 83. dss 85 d 87 p 94. Rubery *Birm* 85–89; Par Dn 87–89; C-in-c Chelmsley Wood St Aug CD 89–92; PtO *Newc* 92–93; Chapl HM Pris Acklington 93–97; Chapl HM YOI Castington 97–00; Chapl HM Pris Forest Bank 00–06; P-in-c Dearnley *Man* 06–14; P-in-c Wardle and Smallbridge 13–14; V Dearnley, Wardle and Smallbridge 14–16; AD Salford 03–06; AD Rochdale 06–15; TR Saddleworth from 16; Hon Can Man Cathl from 13. *Saddleworth Vicarage, Station Road, Uppermill, Oldham OL3 6HQ* T: (01457) 879977 M: 07738-966271 E: sharonjones@cofesaddleworth.org *or* sharonjones@cofeinsaddleworth.org.uk

JONES, Mrs Shelagh Deirdre. b 46. St Mary's Coll Dur BA 68. NEOC 01. d 04 p 05. NSM Burnby *York* 04–07; NSM Londesborough 04–07; NSM Nunburnholme and Warter and Huggate 04–07; NSM Shiptonthorpe and Hayton 04–07; PtO from 07; Chapl HM YOI Wetherby 04–10; PtO *Eur* from 13. *Red Gables, Fair View, Town Street, Shiptonthorpe, York YO43 3PE* T/F: (01430) 871612 E: revd-shelagh@red-gables.org.uk

JONES, Canon Simon. b 63. Trin Coll Bris BA 89. d 89 p 90. C Hildenborough *Roch* 89–93; C Crofton *Portsm* 93–96; C Northwood Em *Lon* 96–01; Min in charge Ignite 01–07; R Stoke Gifford *Bris* from 07; AD Kingswood and S Glos 11–19; Hon Can Bris Cathl from 17. *119 North Road, Stoke Gifford, Bristol BS34 8PE* T: 0117-979 1656 *or* 969 2486 F: 959 9264 E: simon@stmichaelsbristol.org

JONES, Canon Simon Matthew. b 72. SS Hild & Bede Coll Dur BA 93 MA 94 Selw Coll Cam PhD 00 Ox Univ MA 02 DPhil 03. Westcott Ho Cam 95. d 99 p 00. C Tewkesbury w Walton Cardiff and Twyning *Glouc* 99–02; Chapl and Fell Mert Coll Ox from 02; Hon Can Ch Ch *Ox* from 15; Can and Preb Chich Cathl from 16. *Merton College, Oxford OX1 4JD* T: (01865) 276365 *or* 281793 F: 276361 E: simon.jones@merton.ox.ac.uk

JONES, Stephen. *See* JONES, Ernest Edward Stephen

JONES, Stephen Frederick. b 53. Magd Coll Ox BA 75 MA 79 Lon Univ BD 89 Leeds Univ MA 96. Linc Th Coll BCombStuds 84. d 84 p 85. C Kingswinford St Mary *Lich* 84–87; Min Can, Succ and Dean's V Windsor 87–94; C Howden *York* 94–96; Chapl St Elphin's Sch Matlock 96–01; C Worksop Priory *S'well* 01–03; R Longton *Lich* 03–13; TR Staveley and Barrow Hill *Derby* from 13. *The Rectory, Church Street, Staveley, Chesterfield S43 3TN* T: (01246) 498603 E: sfjones53@googlemail.com

JONES, Stephen John. b 56. d 14 p 15. NSM Rednal *Birm* from 14; Bp's Adv on Disability from 16. *19 Meadowfield Road, Rubery, Rednal, Birmingham B45 9BY* T: 0121-460 1173 M: 07866-748932 E: stephen.jones@forumpm.com *or* revdstevejones@gmail.com

JONES, Canon Stephen Leslie. b 59. Hull Univ BA 80 Lanc Univ MA 06. Sarum & Wells Th Coll 82. d 85 p 86. C Perry Barr *Birm* 85–88; C Blackpool St Steph *Blackb* 88–90; V Greenlands 90–95; V Carnforth from 95; Hon Can Blackb Cathl from 11. *The Vicarage, North Road, Carnforth LA5 9LJ* T: (01524) 732948 E: stephenjones17@hotmail.com

JONES, Stephen Richard. b 49. Heythrop Coll Lon MA 01. Oak Hill Th Coll 72. d 75 p 76. C Welling *Roch* 75–79; C Cheltenham St Mark *Glouc* 79–82; V Shiregreen St Jas and St Chris *Sheff* 82–86; P-in-c Harold Hill St Geo *Chelmsf* 86–88; V 88–97; P-in-c Harold Hill St Paul 94–95; V Kippington *Roch* 97–08; RD Sevenoaks 00–05; R Ightham 08–14; RD Shoreham 11–14; rtd 14; PtO *B & W* 15–18; Hon C Beercrocombe w Curry Mallet, Hatch Beauchamp etc from 18. *The Rectory, Hatch Beauchamp, Taunton TA3 6AB* E: srjones49@greenbee.net

JONES, Steven Charles. b 64. Ex Univ LLB 93 Barrister-at-Law. Trin Coll Bris 16. d 16. C Totnes w Bridgetown, Berry Pomeroy etc *Ex* from 16. *The Vicarage, 1 Love Lane Close, Marldon, Paignton TQ3 1TH* M: 07711-833178 E: stevencharlesjones@icloud.com

JONES, Stewart William. b 57. Heriot-Watt Univ BA 79 Bris Univ BA 88. Trin Coll Bris 86. d 88 p 89. C Stoke Bishop *Bris* 88–92; P-in-c Brislington St Luke 92–97; Abp's Chapl and Dioc Missr *Cant* 97–03; P-in-c Cant All SS 01–05; AD Cant and Hon Prov Can Cant Cathl 02–05; R Birm St Martin w Bordesley St Andr 05–17; Hon Can Birm Cathl 11–17; V Barlaston *Lich* from 17. *The Vicarage, 2 Longton Road, Stoke-on-Trent ST12 9AA* M: 07793-724949 E: canonstewart@icloud.com

JONES, Susan Catherine. *See* ASHTON, Susan Catherine

JONES, The Very Revd Susan Helen. b 60. Trin Coll Carmarthen BEd 92 MPhil 94 Univ of Wales (Ban) PhD. Ripon Coll Cuddesdon 93. d 95 p 97. Chapl Univ of Wales (Swansea) *S & B* 95–98; Hon C Sketty 95–98; Dir Past Studies St Mich Coll Llan 98–00; Lect Univ of Wales (Cardiff) *Llan* 98–00; TV Bangor *Ban* 00–09; AD Ogwen 07–09; Can Missr Ban Cathl 10–11; Dean Ban 11–15; TR Bro Deiniol 14–15; Dir of Miss and Min *Derby* 15–18; Can Res Derby Cathl 15–18; Acting Dean Derby 16–17; Dean Liv from 18; Research Fell Glyndŵr Univ from 09. *1 Cathedral Close, Liverpool L1 7BR* T: 0151-702 7202 E: sue.jones@liverpoolcathedral.org.uk

JONES, Susan Jean. b 47. Bp Grosseteste Coll CertEd 68 Heythrop Coll Lon MA 01. SAOMC 93. d 96 p 97. C S Ascot *Ox* 96–07; NSM 01–07; rtd 07. *Fairhaven, 1 St Clement's Terrace, Mousehole, Penzance TR19 6SJ* T: (01736) 732938

JONES, Susannah Hester Everett. b 67. d 07 p 08. NSM Bris St Mary Redcliffe w Temple etc 07–13; P-in-c Abbots Leigh w Leigh Woods 13–14; V from 14. *The Vicarage, 51 Church Road, Abbots Leigh, Bristol BS8 3QU* E: hester.jones2@googlemail.com

JONES, Theresa. *See* JONES, Mary Catherine Theresa Bridget

JONES, Canon Timothy Llewellyn. b 67. York Univ BA 90. Ripon Coll Cuddesdon BA 94. d 94 p 95. C Middlesbrough St Martin *York* 94–96; P-in-c Rounton w Welbury 96–02;

Chapl HM YOI Northallerton 96–99; Adv for Young Adults and Voc (Cleveland) 99–02; R Corinth St Paul USA 02–07; P-in-c York St Hilda 07–14; P-in-c York St Lawr w St Nic 07–14; Dioc Dir of Ords *St E* from 14; Hon C Lark Valley from 14; Hon C Bury St Edmunds All SS w St Jo and St Geo from 14; Hon Can St E Cathl from 17. *The Rectory, West Stow, Bury St Edmunds IP28 6ET* T: (01284) 729148 M: 07468-474065 E: tim.jones@cofesuffolk.org

JONES, Timothy Richard Nigel. b 54. Collingwood Coll Dur BSc 75 Birm Univ MSc 76 FGS. Trin Coll Bris 84. **d** 86 **p** 87. C Hailsham *Chich* 86–91; V Madley w Tyberton, Preston-on-Wye and Blakemere *Heref* 91–00; R Madley w Tyberton, Peterchurch, Vowchurch etc 00–06; V Taunton St Jas *B & W* 06–17; rtd 17. *Clover Cottage, Little Silver, Tiverton EX16 4LW* T: (01884) 595001 E: tim@bankend.net

JONES, Tracey Anne. b 62. Ripon Coll Cuddesdon 18. **d** 19. NSM Hughenden *Ox* from 19. *101 Cedar Avenue, Hazlemere, High Wycombe HP15 7EF* E: rev.funkyfish@gmail.com

JONES, Trevor Blandon. b 43. Oak Hill Th Coll 77. **d** 80 **p** 81. NSM Homerton St Barn w St Paul *Lon* 80–83; NSM Harlow New Town w Lt Parndon *Chelmsf* 83–90; C 90–92; V Leyton Em 92–01; rtd 02; PtO *Chelmsf* from 03. *5 Wheatley Close, Sawbridgeworth CM21 0HS* T: (01279) 600248

JONES, Trevor Edwin. b 49. Heythrop Coll Lon MA 05 K Coll Lon DThMin 12. Ripon Coll Cuddesdon 74. **d** 76 **p** 77. C Cannock *Lich* 76–79; C Middlesbrough Ascension *York* 79–81; V Oldham St Steph and All Martyrs *Man* 81–84; V Perry Beeches *Birm* 84–90; P-in-c Saltley 90–93; P-in-c Shaw Hill 90–93; V Saltley and Shaw Hill 93–97; R Lon Docks St Pet w Wapping St Jo 97–17; rtd 17; PtO *Nor* from 17. *30 Cleaves Drive, Walsingham NR22 6EQ* T: (01328) 821415 M: 07977-260559 E: father.jones@btinternet.com *or* frtejones@aol.com

JONES, The Ven Trevor Pryce. b 48. Southn Univ SEd 76 BTh 79 Univ of Wales (Cardiff) LLM 04 St Jo Coll Dur DThM 13 Herts Univ Hon LLM 18. Sarum & Wells Th Coll 73. **d** 76 **p** 77. C Glouc St Geo 76–79; Warden Bp Mascall Cen *Heref* 79–84; Dioc Communications Officer 81–86; TR Heref S Wye 84–97; Preb Heref Cathl 93–97; OCM 85–97; Adn Hertford and Hon Can St Alb 97–16; Hon Can St Alb 97–16; PtO *Ex* 16–17; Chapter Can Ex Cathl from 17. *3 South Terrace, Longmeadow Road, Lympstone, Exmouth EX8 5LN* T: (01395) 268745 E: tprycejones@gmail.com

JONES, Miss Victoria Kay. b 83. St Mich Coll Llan 09. **d** 12 **p** 13. C Llangwm w Freystrop and Johnston *St D* 12–15; P-in-c Llanedi w Tycroes and Saron from 15; P-in-c Gorslas from 15. *The Vicarage, 56 Black Lion Road, Gorslas, Llanelli SA14 6RU* T: (01269) 845505 M: 07976-836209 E: rev.vjones@gmail.com

JONES, Preb Wilfred David. b 22. Keble Coll Ox BA 47 MA 48. St Mich Coll Llan 47. **d** 48 **p** 49. C Aberaman *Llan* 48–50; C Cardiff St Jo 50–55; Chapl Kelly Coll Tavistock 55–62; V St Decumans *B & W* 62–76; V Ilminster w Whitelackington 76–92; RD Ilminster 78–87; Preb Wells Cathl 81–05; rtd 92; PtO *B & W* 92–06. *Dragons, Lambrook Road, Shepton Beauchamp, Ilminster TA19 0NA* T: (01460) 240967 E: dado@gmail.com

JONES, Wilfred Lovell. b 39. Lon Univ BD 71 Cam Univ CertEd. St D Coll Lamp. **d** 63 **p** 64. C Llanllyfni *Ban* 63–65; C Llanbeblig w Caernarfon 65–68; V Llanwnog w Penstrowed 68–72; V Llanwnnog and Caersws w Carno 72–75; Asst Chapl Dover Coll 77–90; Chapl Wrekin Coll Telford 91–94; V Llangollen w Trevor and Llantysilio *St As* 94–04; AD Llangollen 03–04; rtd 04; PtO *St As* 09–16; *Guildf* from 16. *21 Ashley Drive, Blackwater, Camberley GU17 0PR* T: (01276) 600643 E: wlwaj@btinternet.com

JONES, Canon William David. b 28. St D Coll Lamp BA 48 Lon Univ BD 57 Leeds Univ MA 73. St Mich Coll Llan 48. **d** 51 **p** 52. C Risca *Mon* 51–54; C Chepstow St Arvan's w Penterry 54–55; C St Geo-in-the-East w Ch Ch w St Jo *Lon* 55–59; C Farnham Royal *Ox* 59–64; Lect Div Culham Coll 65–67; Hd RS Doncaster Coll of Educn 67–74; Vice-Prin St Bede Coll Dur 74; Vice-Prin SS Hild and Bede Coll Dur 75–89; Lect Th Dur Univ 75–89; Dir of Miss Ch in Wales 89–93; Metropolitical and Hon Can St D Cathl 90–93; rtd 93; PtO *Glouc* 93–08; *Llan* 12–18. *Triscombe Lodge, 55 Llantrisant Road, Cardiff CF5 2PU* T: (029) 2019 3914 E: wdavidjones@ntlworld.com

JONES, Mrs Wyn. b 49. **d** 01 **p** 02. OLM Linslade *Ox* 01–08; OLM Ouzel Valley *St Alb* from 08. *2 Woodside Way, Linslade, Leighton Buzzard LU7 7PN* T: (01525) 373638 E: wjones255@aol.com

JONES-BLACKETT, Enid Olive. b 40. Reading Univ BA 61. **d** 97 **p** 98. OLM Hellesdon *Nor* 97–10; rtd 10; PtO *Nor* from 10. *8 Fastolf Close, Hellesdon, Norwich NR6 5RE* T: (01603) 424769 E: enidjonesblackett@btinternet.com

JONGMAN, Canon Kären Anngel Irene. b 43. EMMTC 97. **d** 01 **p** 02. NSM Northampton St Mary *Pet* 01–03; NSM Guilsborough w Hollowell and Cold Ashby 03–04; P-in-c Walgrave w Hannington and Wold and Scaldwell 04–18; R Pattishall w Cold Higham and Gayton w Tiffield from 18; Chapl Northants Fire and Rescue Service from 03; Can Pet Cathl 12–13. *The Vicarage, 17 Church Street, Pattishall, Towcester NN12 8NB* M: 07980-881252 E: karenajongman@gmail.com

JORDAN, Anne. b 42. RGN 66. **d** 02 **p** 03. OLM Crofton *Wakef* 02–14; *Leeds* from 14. *95 Ashdene Avenue, Crofton, Wakefield WF4 1LY* T: (01924) 865527 M: 07450-475184

JORDAN, Anthony John. b 50. Birm Univ BEd 73. LNSM course. **d** 83 **p** 84. Asst Chapl Uppingham Sch 83–86; NSM Uppingham w Ayston and Wardley w Belton *Pet* 83–86; Asst Chapl Sherborne Sch 86–87; NSM Bournemouth St Fran *Win* 88–03; PtO *Leic* 04–06; NSM Leic St Aid 06–08; V Eyres Monsell 08–13; rtd 13. *67 Lethbridge Close, Leicester LE1 2EB* T: 0116-278 0940 M: 07798-860106

JORDAN, Elizabeth Ann. b 58. New Hall Cam MA 82 Anglia Ruskin Univ DProf 16. St Jo Coll Nottm 82. **d** 87 **p** 94. Par Dn Blackpool St Jo *Blackb* 87–90; Par Dn Ewood 90–94; C 94–95; Asst Dir of Ords 90–95; Min Shelfield St Mark CD *Lich* 95–00; Local Min Adv (Wolverhampton) 95–05; OLM Course Ldr and Team Ldr Min Division 03–05; Dir Local Min Development 06–10; C Blakenall Heath 10–11; Lay Educn and Tr Adv *Chelmsf* from 11; Hon C Rawreth from 12. *Diocesan Office, 53 New Street, Chelmsford CM1 1AT* T: (01245) 294454 F: 294477 E: ejordan@chelmsford.anglican.org

JORDAN, John Charles. b 37. CQSW 81. NOC 84. **d** 87 **p** 88. C Southport Em *Liv* 87–90; V Abram and Bickershaw 90–95; V Bempton w Flamborough, Reighton w Speeton *York* 95–00; rtd 01; PtO *York* from 05. *35 Hollycroft, Barmston, Driffield YO25 8PP* T: (01262) 468925   E: barmstonbonnie@yahoo.co.uk *or* bonnie.35@btinternet.com

JORDAN, Lucy Charlotte Tansley. b 87. St Cuth Soc Dur BA 08 St Mary's Coll Dur PGCE 09. Ripon Coll Cuddesdon 17. **d** 19. C Wells St Cuth w Wookey Hole *B & W* from 19. *7 Deckle Edge Close, Wells BA5 2GP* M: 07983-307197 E: rev.lucy.jordan@outlook.com

JORDAN, Miss Pamela Mary. b 43. Univ of Wales (Cardiff) BSc 64 Ox Univ DipEd 65. WEMTC 02. **d** 05 **p** 06. NSM Coalbrookdale, Iron-Bridge and Lt Wenlock *Heref* from 05. *2 Madeley Wood View, Madeley, Telford TF7 5TF* T: (01952) 583254

JORDAN, Patrick Glen. b 69. SEITE 01. **d** 04 **p** 05. C Charlton *S'wark* 04–07; C Catford (Southend) and Downham 07–08; TV 08–16; V Thorpe St Matt *Nor* from 16; C Nor Heartsease St Fran from 19. *St Matthew's Vicarage, Albert Place, Norwich NR1 4JL* T: (01603) 494015 *or* 763695 E: revpatrickjordan@gmail.com

JORDAN, Peter Harry. b 42. Leeds Univ BA 64 Leeds Coll of Educn PGCE 65. Cranmer Hall Dur 70. **d** 73 **p** 74. C Nottingham St Ann w Em *S'well* 73–77; C Edgware *Lon* 77–82; V Everton St Chrys *Liv* 82–94; Dioc Ev and V Bootle St Mary w St Paul 94–02; Chapl Barcelona *Eur* 02–08; rtd 08; PtO *Eur* from 08; *Ches* from 10. *11 Stanford Avenue, Wallasey CH45 5AP* T: 0151-639 7860 E: peterybarbara@gmail.com

JORDAN, Canon Richard William. b 56. Lanchester Poly Cov BSc 78 Sheff Univ MA 07. St Jo Coll Nottm 84. **d** 87 **p** 88. C Blackpool St Jo *Blackb* 87–90; V Ewood 90–95; PtO *Lich* 95–97; Co-ord Walsall Town Cen Min 97–00; Ch Links Projects Officer 00–06; Dioc Ch and Soc Officer *Derby* 06–11; P-in-c Rawreth *Chelmsf* from 11; P-in-c Rettendon and Hullbridge from 17; AD Rochford 15–18; Hon Can Chelmsf Cathl from 15. *The Rectory, Church Road, Rawreth, Wickford SS11 8SH* T: (01268) 766565 E: rev.richard.jordan@gmail.com

JORDAN, Steven Paul. b 52. **d** 11 **p** 12. NSM Church Lench w Rous Lench and Abbots Morton etc *Worc* 11–15; PtO New Zealand 15–16; NSM Nelson Cathl 16–17; Sub Dean from 17. *48 Weka Street, The Wood, Nelson 7010, New Zealand* M: (0064) 21-294 6105 E: bspj@live.co.uk

JORDAN, Tansley. *See* JORDAN, Lucy Charlotte Tansley

JORDAN, Thomas. b 36. NW Ord Course 76. **d** 79 **p** 80. NSM Prenton *Ches* 79–84; NSM Egremont St Jo 84–91; C 91–96; Ind Chapl 91–96; TV Birkenhead Priory 96–01; rtd 01; PtO *Ches* from 02. *13 Corniche Road, Wirral CH62 5HA* E: thomas.t.jordan@btinternet.com

JORDAN, Trevor. b 44. Lon Hosp MB, BS 67 LRCP 68 MRCS 68 Nottm Univ MA 99. EMMTC 96. **d** 03 **p** 04. NSM Seamer *York* 03–07; PtO 07–11; NSM Long Buckby w Watford and W Haddon w Winwick *Pet* 11–16; rtd 16; PtO *Leic* from 16. *5 Pretoria Road, Ibstock LE67 6LP* T: (01530) 459619 M: 07887-537244 E: trevor@trevorsweb.net

JORDINSON, Vera (Sister Hilary). b 37. Liv Univ BA 60 CertEd 61. Westcott Ho Cam 88. **d** 89 **p** 94. CSF from 74; Prov Sec 90–01; Gen Sec 96–02; Sec for Miss SSF 96–99; Gift Aid Sec 01–11; LtO *Heref* 89–92; PtO *Lich* 90–92; *Birm* 92–94, 97–06 and from 12; *B & W* 06–10; NSM Birchfield *Birm* 94–96. *37 Firs Close, Watery Lane, Smethwick B67 6DQ* E: hilarycsf@franciscans.org.uk

JØRGENSEN (née BURGESS), Mrs Laura Jane. b 74. Imp Coll Lon BSc 95 ARSM 95. Ripon Coll Cuddesdon BTh 00. **d** 00 **p** 01. C St Alb Abbey 00–01; C Boxmoor St Jo 01–04; Min Can and Sacr St Paul's Cathl *Lon* 04–09; V St Botolph Aldgate w H Trin Minories from 09; PV Westmr Abbey from 10. *St Botolph's Church, Aldgate High Street, London EC3N 1AB* T: (020) 7283 2154 E: rector@stbotolphs.org.uk

JORYSZ, Canon Ian Herbert. b 62. Van Mildert Coll Dur BSc 84 MA 95 Liv Univ PhD 87. Ripon Coll Cuddesdon BA 89 MA 95. **d** 90 **p** 91. C Houghton le Spring *Dur* 90–93; C Ferryhill 93–95; Research Officer to Bp of Bradwell 95–15; P-in-c S Weald *Chelmsf* 95–00; V 00–15; RD Brentwood 08–15; Bp's Sen Chapl *Man* from 15; Hon Can Man Cathl from 15. *Bishopscourt, Bury New Road, Salford M7 4LE* T: 0161-792 2096 E: chaplain@bishopscourt.manchester.anglican.org

JOSEPH EMMANUEL, Brother. See DICKSON, Colin James

JOSS, Capt Martin James Torquil. b 60. Univ of Wales (Lamp) BA 79. EAMTC 03. **d** 03 **p** 04. C Harlow Town Cen w Lt Parndon *Chelmsf* 03–07; P-in-c Coalville and Bardon Hill *Leic* 07–09; C Ravenstone and Swannington 07–09; V Coalville w Bardon Hill and Ravenstone 09–17; V Oswaldtwistle *Blackb* from 17. *The Vicarage, 29 Mayfield Avenue, Oswaldtwistle, Accrington BB5 3AA* T: (01254) 231038 M: 07875-494588 E: vicarofossy@gmail.com

JOSS-POTHEN, Bethany Deborah Keziah. b 92. Westcott Ho Cam 16. **d** 19. C St Mary-at-Latton *Chelmsf* from 19. *21 Huntley Road, Harlow CM20 2PR* E: reverendbethany@gmail.com

JOSS-POTHEN, Nathan James. b 93. Westcott Ho Cam 16. **d** 19. C Harlow Town Cen w Lt Parndon *Chelmsf* from 19. *21 Huntley Road, Harlow CM20 2PR*

JOWETT, Ms Hilary Anne. b 54. Hull Univ BA 75. Cranmer Hall Dur IDC 80. **dss** 82 **d** 87 **p** 94. Sheff St Jo 80–83; Brampton Bierlow 83–87; Par Dn 87–89; Hon Par Dn Sharrow St Andr 89–95; Chapl Nether Edge Hosp Sheff 89–95; C Sheff St Mark Broomhill 95–97; C Mosborough 97–00; TR Gleadless 00–12; R Dinnington w Laughton and Throapham 12–17; R Dinnington from 17. *The Rectory, 217 Nursery Road, Dinnington, Sheffield S25 2QU* T: (01909) 562335 E: hilary.jowett@sheffield.anglican.org

JOWETT, Canon Nicholas Peter Alfred. b 44. St Cath Coll Cam BA 66 MA Bris Univ CertEd 67. Qu Coll Birm 72. **d** 75 **p** 76. C Wales *Sheff* 75–78; TV Sheff Manor 78–83; V Brampton Bierlow 83–89; V Psalter Lane St Andr 89–95; V Bramley Adv 01–09; Hon Can Sheff Cathl 06–12; rtd 12; PtO *Sheff* from 12. *The Rectory, 217 Nursery Road, Dinnington, Sheffield S25 2QU* T: (01909) 562335 E: mail@njowett.plus.com

JOWITT, Andrew Robert Benson. b 56. Down Coll Cam BA 78 PGCE 79 MA 81. Wycliffe Hall Ox 88. **d** 90 **p** 91. C Northampton Em *Pet* 90–94; C Barking St Marg w St Patr *Chelmsf* 94–98; TV 98–00; TV Stantonbury and Willen *Ox* 00–17; Bp's Officer for Evang 00–17; rtd 17. *12 Fields View, Sudbury CO10 1BJ* E: jowitts@btinternet.com

JOY, Bernard David. b 50. Sarum & Wells Th Coll 90. **d** 92 **p** 93. C Shortlands *Roch* 92–94; C Henbury *Bris* 94–96; V Bristol St Aid w St Geo 96–03; P-in-c Bridgwater St Fran *B & W* 03–07; V 07–16; rtd 16; PtO *Sarum* from 17; *B & W* from 18. *40 Wessex Way, Gillingham SP8 4LX* T: (01747) 834427 M: 07745-291113 E: rev.obejoyful@gmail.com

JOY, Canon Matthew Osmund Clifton. b 40. St Edm Hall Ox BA 62 MA 66. St Steph Ho Ox 62. **d** 64 **p** 65. C Brinksway *Ches* 64–66; C Southwick St Columba *Dur* 66–69; V Hartlepool H Trin 69–85; V Rotherham St Paul, St Mich and St Jo Ferham Park *Sheff* 85–88; V Masbrough 88–95; RD Rotherham 88–93; P-in-c Bordesley St Benedict *Birm* 95–01; V 01–05; Bp's Adv on Chr/Muslim Relns 95–05; rtd 05; PtO *Wakef* 05–14; *Leeds* from 14; *Sheff* 06–18; *Leic* from 19. *22 Stuart Court, High Street, Kibworth Beauchamp, Leicester LE8 0LR* T: 0116-367 0332 E: joy313.matthew@gmail.com

JOYCE, Canon Alison Jane. b 59. Univ of Wales (Swansea) BA 81 Bris Univ MLitt 87 Birm Univ PhD 00 SS Coll Cam PGCE 84. Ripon Coll Cuddesdon BA 87 MA 94. **d** 88 **p** 94. Par Dn Chalgrove w Berrick Salome *Ox* 88–90; Tutor WMMTC 90–95; Tutor Qu Coll Birm 95–96; NSM Moseley St Anne *Birm* 96–04; Dean NSMs 00–03; NSM Birm Cathl 04–05; P-in-c Edgbaston St Bart 05–11; V 11–14; Chapl Birm Univ 05–14; Chapl Elmhurst Sch for Dance 11–14; Hon Can Birm Cathl 06–14; R St Bride Fleet Street w Bridewell etc *Lon* from 14. *St Bride's Rectory, St Bride's Avenue, London EC4Y 8AU* T: (020) 7427 0133 E: alison.joyce@stbrides.com

JOYCE, Anthony Owen. b 35. Selw Coll Cam BA 60 MA 64. Wycliffe Hall Ox 60. **d** 62 **p** 63. C Birm St Martin 62–67; Rhodesia 67–70; V Birm St Luke 70–79; V Downend *Bris* 79–01; RD Stapleton 83–89; rtd 01; PtO *Bris* from 01. *116 Jellicoe Avenue, Stapleton, Bristol BS16 1WJ* T: 0117-956 2510 E: anthonyjoyce@gmail.com

JOYCE, Graham Leslie. b 49. Lon Univ CertEd 71. Trin Coll Bris 87. **d** 89 **p** 90. C Heald Green St Cath *Ches* 89–93; R Church Lawton 93–14; rtd 14; PtO *Ches* from 14. *11 Fields Close, Alsager, Stoke-on-Trent ST7 2ND* T: (01270) 883621 E: revglj@gmail.com

JOYCE, Jennifer Claire. See BRIDGMAN, Jennifer Claire

JOYCE, Miss Joanna Lucy. b 76. Ridley Hall Cam 16. **d** 18 **p** 19. C Stockingford *Cov* from 18. *10 Rossendale Way, Nuneaton CV10 7NS* M: 07730-474129 E: revjoannajoyce@outlook.com

JOYCE, John Barnabas Altham. b 47. St Chad's Coll Dur BA 69 Lon Univ DipEd 86. St Steph Ho Ox 72. **d** 74 **p** 75. C Reading St Giles *Ox* 74–77; C Cowley St Jo 77–80; Dioc Youth and Community Officer 80–87; V Hangleton *Chich* 87–94; Dioc Adv for Schs and Dir Educn 94–99; R Hurstpierpoint 99–13; rtd 13; PtO *Chich* 13–17. *3 Wolstonbury Road, Hove BN3 6EJ* T: (01273) 773150

JOYCE, Margaret. b 47. Oak Hill NSM Course 86. **d** 89 **p** 94. NSM Chadwell Heath *Chelmsf* 89–92; NSM Bath Odd Down w Combe Hay *B & W* from 92; Chapl Bath and West Community NHS Trust from 95. *69 Bloomfield Rise, Bath BA2 2BN* T: (01225) 840864 M: 07841-053454 E: margaretjoyce@stphilipstjames.org

JOYCE, Paul David. b 70. Qu Coll Birm 00. **d** 02 **p** 03. C Perry Beeches *Birm* 02–05; V Eastwood St Dav *Chelmsf* from 05. *St David's Vicarage, 400 Rayleigh Road, Leigh-on-Sea SS9 5PT* T: (01702) 523126 E: joycefamily400@btinternet.com

JOYCE, Miss Penelope Anne. b 53. St Mary's Coll Chelt CertEd 74. Wycliffe Hall Ox. **d** 00 **p** 01. C Ox St Clem 00–03; C Cogges and S Leigh 03–09; Hon C Bourne Valley *Sarum* 11–16; Hon C Salisbury St Fran and Stratford sub Castle 11–16; PtO from 17; rtd 18. *60 Endless Street, Salisbury SP1 3UH* T: (01722) 416054 M: 07808-181885 E: pennyre.joyce@gmail.com

JOYCE, Philip Rupert. b 38. Selw Coll Cam BA 68 MA 72. Cranmer Hall Dur 68. **d** 70 **p** 71. C Newland St Jo *York* 70–73; C Woolwich St Mary w H Trin *S'wark* 73–77; Chapl Thames Poly 73–77; Chapl S Bank Poly 77–79; rtd 03. *37 Fulcher Avenue, Cromer NR27 9SG* T: (01263) 519405

JOYCE, Canon Terence Alan. b 57. St Jo Coll Nottm BTh 84. **d** 84 **p** 85. C Mansfield SS Pet and Paul *S'well* 84–88; V Greasley 88–00; Dioc Dir of Ords 99–11; Dir Post-Ord Support and Tr 01–11; Hon Can S'well Minster 02–11; York Adnry Tr Adv and Dioc Adv for Clergy CMD from 12; NSM Rural E York from 12. *The Rectory, Sandy Lane, Stockton-on-the-Forest, York YO32 9UR* T: (01904) 400811 E: terry.joyce@yorkdiocese.org

JOYNER, Mrs Susan Diane. b 58. Nene Coll Northn BA 79 Open Univ MA 99 Leic Univ PGCE 84. NEOC 05. **d** 08 **p** 09. NSM Upper Coquetdale *Newc* from 08. *The Old Church, Harbottle, Morpeth NE65 7DQ* T: (01669) 650385 E: suejoyner2@aol.com

JOYNES, David. b 51. Leeds Univ BSc 74. Ripon Coll Cuddesdon 12. **d** 13 **p** 14. OLM The Cookhams *Ox* 13–16; NSM from 16. *1 Keeleys Cottages, High Street, Cookham, Maidenhead SL6 9SF* T: (01628) 528622 M: 07753-749228 E: revdavidjoynes@gmail.com

JOYNSON, Gillian Marion. b 57. **d** 16 **p** 17. OLM Cannock and Huntington *Lich* from 16; OLM Hatherton from 16. *2 Deer Close, Huntington, Cannock WS12 4UL* M: 07803-931828 E: gill.joynson@deerbahn.co.uk

JUCKES, Jonathan Sydney. b 61. St Andr Univ MA 83. Ridley Hall Cam BA 87. **d** 88 **p** 89. C Sevenoaks St Nic *Roch* 88–92; Proclamation Trust 92–95; C St Helen Bishopsgate w St Andr Undershaft etc *Lon* 95–98; TR Kirk Ella and Willerby *York* 98–14; R 14–17; Pres Oak Hill Coll from 18; Public Preacher *Lon* from 18. *Oak Hill College, Chase Side, London N14 4PS* T: (020) 8449 0467 E: johnnyj@oakhill.ac.uk

JUCKES, Canon Nigel Patrick. b 49. St Jo Coll Nottm 74. **d** 77 **p** 78. C Westville S Africa 78–80; R Addington 80–86; R Stanger All So 86–92; R Kloof 93–15; Adn Pinetown 01–06; Hon Can Pietermaritzburg from 06; P-in-c Llandogo w Whitebrook Chpl and Tintern Parva *Mon* from 15. *The Rectory, Llandogo, Monmouth NP25 4TW* T: (01594) 530041 E: nigelpj49@icloud.com

JUDD, Adrian Timothy. b 67. Lanc Univ BA 88 St Jo Coll Dur BA 92 St Thos Aquinas Pontifical Univ Rome MA 18 Huddersfield Univ MSc 18 PGCE 13. Cranmer Hall Dur 90

Trin Coll Singapore 92. **d** 93 **p** 94. C Dudley St Aug Holly Hall *Worc* 93–97; V Stockbridge Village *Liv* 97–99; V Went Valley *Wakef* 00–14; Leeds from 14. *The Vicarage, Marlpit Lane, Darrington, Pontefract WF8 3AB* T: (01977) 704744 E: revjudd@gmail.com

JUDD, Colin Ivor. b 35. Dur Univ BA 61. Ridley Hall Cam 61. **d** 63 **p** 64. C Stratford St Jo w Ch Ch *Chelmsf* 63–66; C Kimberworth *Sheff* 66–68; Area Sec CMS Bradf and Wakef 68–80; V Bradf St Columba w St Andr 80–00; rtd 00; PtO *Bradf* 00–14; Leeds from 14. *57 Grosvenor Road, Shipley BD18 4RB* T: (01274) 584775 E: thejudds@saltsvillage.co.uk

JUDD, Mrs Nicola Jane. b 51. K Alfred's Coll Win CertEd 72. S Dios Minl Tr Scheme 87. **d** 90 **p** 94. NSM Abbotts Ann and Upper Clatford and Goodworth Clatford *Win* 90–11; Chapl 00–92; Adv for NSM *Win* 01–05; rtd 11; PtO *Win* 11–17; NSM Abbotts Ann and Upper Clatford and Goodworth Clatford from 17. *13 Belmont Close, Andover SP10 2DE* T: (01264) 729075 E: revdnickyannabenefice@gmail.com

JUDD, The Very Revd Peter Somerset Margesson. b 49. Trin Hall Cam BA 71. Cuddesdon Coll 71. **d** 74 **p** 75. C Salford St Phil w St Steph *Man* 74–76; Chapl Clare Coll Cam 76–81; C Burnham *Ox* 81–82; TV Burnham w Dropmore, Hitcham and Taplow 82–88; V Iffley 88–97; RD Cowley 94–97; Provost Chelmsf 97–00; Dean Chelmsf 00–13; rtd 13; PtO *Ely* 13–17; Acting Dean Clare Coll Cam 14–15; P-in-c Cambridge Gt St Mary w St Mich *Ely* 17–18; PtO from 18. *18 Baycliffe Close, Cambridge CB1 8EE* T: (01223) 214205 M: 07740-456844 E: peterjudd19@yahoo.co.uk

JUDD, Susan Elizabeth. b 48. Bris Univ BSc 74 Univ of Wales MA 04 ACA 80. STETS 05. **d** 08 **p** 09. NSM Portsm Cathl 08–12; PtO from 12. *16 Bepton Down, Petersfield GU31 4PR* T: (01730) 266819 E: susan.judd@ntlworld.com

JUDGE, Mrs Alison Gwendolyn. b 60. Ch Ch Coll Cant BA 13. SEITE BA 10. **d** 10 **p** 11. C W Wickham St Fran and St Mary *S'wark* 10–14; PtO 14–16; TV Merton Priory from 16. *Christ Church Vicarage, Christchurch Road, London SW19 2NY* T: (020) 8616 5794 E: revalisonjudge@gmail.com

JUDGE, Andrew Duncan. b 50. Cape Town Univ BCom 72 Keble Coll Ox MA 81. Pietermaritzburg Th Sem 82. **d** 83 **p** 84. C Westville S Africa 84–87; R Prestbury 88–94; R Westville 94–01; TV Keynsham *B & W* 01–18; rtd 18. *4 Alum Close, Trowbridge BA14 7HD* T: (01225) 777491 E: adjudge27@outlook.com

JUDSON, Miss Christine Alison. b 64. Surrey Univ BSc 86 Birm Univ PGCE 88. Ripon Coll Cuddesdon 05. **d** 07 **p** 08. C Highbridge *B & W* 07–10; TV Portishead from 10. *77 Nightingale Rise, Portishead, Bristol BS20 8LX* T: (01275) 397232 E: c.judson@btinternet.com *or* pastor@portisheadparish.co.uk

JUDSON, Mrs Mary Ruth. b 47. Bretton Hall Coll DipEd 68. NEOC 89. **d** 92 **p** 94. Par Dn Chester le Street *Dur* 92–94; C 94–96; V Millfield St Mark and Pallion St Luke 96–04; V Hartlepool St Luke 04–11; rtd 11; PtO *Dur* from 12. *5 Caxton Way, Chester le Street DH3 4BW* T: 0191-388 0512 E: maryjudson7@gmail.com

JUDSON, Paul Wesley. b 46. Leic Poly ATD 71. Cranmer Hall Dur 87. **d** 89 **p** 90. C Lobley Hill *Dur* 89–92; C Chester le Street 92–96; Ed Dioc Publications and Sec Dioc Bd of Soc Resp 96–98; C Millfield St Mark and Pallion St Luke 96–04; C Hartlepool St Luke 04–11; Dioc Publications Officer 98–11; Dioc Dir of Communications 02–11; rtd 11; PtO *Dur* from 12. *5 Caxton Way, Chester le Street DH3 4BW* T: 0191-388 0512 E: pwjudson@gmail.com

JUDSON, Peter. b 39. Lon Univ BSc 61 Plymouth Univ PGCE 87. SWMTC 99. **d** 02 **p** 03. OLM Bude Haven and Marhamchurch *Truro* 02–09; rtd 09; PtO *Truro* from 15; Portsm from 19. *25 Limewood, St Mary's Road, Hayling Island PO11 9FE* M: 07970-115538 E: mepmeadowcroft@gmail.com

JUKES, John Christopher. b 61. Ex Univ BTh 13 MA 17. SWMTC 10. **d** 13 **p** 14. C Saltash *Truro* 13–16; TV Cen Telford *Lich* 16–17; TV Uttoxeter Area 17–19; P-in-c Todmorden w Cornholme and Walsden *Leeds* from 19. *The Vicarage, 7 Fern Valley Chase, Todmorden OL14 7HB* M: 07443-414436 E: johnjukes101@yahoo.co.uk *or* john.jukes@leeds.anglican.org

JUKES (née WEATHERHOGG), Mrs Susanne. b 56. Leeds Univ BA 77 Coll of Ripon & York St Jo PGCE 78. NEOC 98. **d** 01 **p** 02. C Monk Fryston and S Milford *York* 01–05; P-in-c 05–07; Assoc Min Aldborough w Boroughbridge and Roecliffe *Ripon* 07–09; Asst Dir of Ords 07–09; Chapl HM Pris Full Sutton 09–14; V Topcliffe, Baldersby w Dishforth, Dalton etc *York* from 14. *The Vicarage, Front Street, Topcliffe, Thirsk YO7 3RU*

JUNIPER, Sandra Elizabeth. b 42. SWMTC. **d** 11 **p** 12. NSM Bideford, Northam, Westward Ho!, Appledore etc *Ex* 11–17; NSM Appledore, Northam and Westward Ho! from 17. *6 Acacia Close, Bideford EX39 3BA* T: (01237) 425982 E: sandra.juniper@talktalk.net

✠**JUPP, The Rt Revd Roger Alan.** b 56. St Edm Hall Ox BA 78 MA 82 Surrey Univ PGCE 96. Chich Th Coll 79. **d** 80 **p** 81 **c** 03. C Newbold w Dunston *Derby* 80–83; C Cowley St Jo *Ox* 83–85; C Islington St Jas w St Phil *Lon* 85–86; V Lower Beeding *Chich* 86–90; Dom Chapl to Bp Horsham 86–91; V Burgess Hill St Jo 90–93; TR Burgess Hill St Jo w St Edw 93–94; PtO 97–98; C Aldwick 98–00; Prin Newton Th Coll Papua New Guinea 00–03; Bp Popondota 03–05; P-in-c St Leonards Ch Ch and St Mary *Chich* 05–06; R St Leonards Ch Ch and St Mary etc 06–12; Hon Asst Bp Chich 05–12; V Long Eaton St Laur *Derby* 12–18; P-in-c Ilkeston H Trin 12–18; rtd 18; PtO *Chich* from 19. *2 Redgeland Rise, St Leonards-on-Sea TN38 9JT* T: (01424) 432364 E: rajupp1@hotmail.com

JUPP, Vincent John. b 64. St Jo Coll Nottm BA(ThM) 06. **d** 00 **p** 01. C Evington *Leic* 00–03; TV Ascension TM 03–07; TR 07–11; AD City of Leic 09–11; V Birstall and Wanlip from 11. *The Rectory, 251 Birstall Road, Birstall, Leicester LE4 4DJ* T: 0116-267 4517 *or* 267 1797 E: stjames.birstall@btconnect.com *or* vincejupp@btinternet.com

JUSTICE, Keith Leonard. b 42. Wolv Univ BSc 68 CEng 83 MIMechE 83. Wycliffe Hall Ox 91. **d** 93 **p** 94. C Penwortham St Mary *Blackb* 93–96; C Dovercourt and Parkeston w Harwich *Chelmsf* 96–98; V Wentworth *Sheff* 98–01; Chapl Rotherham Gen Hosps NHS Trust 98–01; Chapl Rotherham Priority Health Services NHS Trust 98–01; R Melrose *Edin* 01–04; P-in-c Royton St Anne *Man* 04–08; P-in-c Lawton Moor 08–13; rtd 13; PtO *Man* from 13; Ches from 16. *228A Wythenshawe Road, Manchester M23 0PH* T: 0161-215 1113 E: keithjustice123@gmail.com

JUSTICE, Simon Charles. b 66. Univ of Wales (Lamp) BD 88 Edin Univ MTh 90. Cranmer Hall Dur 90. **d** 92 **p** 93. C Tilehurst St Mich *Ox* 92–95; R Troy St Paul USA 95–01; R Tigard St Jas 02–04; Can All SS Cathl Albany 98–04; R Edin Ch Ch 04–06; R Corvallis Gd Samaritan USA from 06. *445 NW Elizabeth Drive, Corvallis OR 97330, USA* E: simon.justice@googlemail.com

JUTSUM, Linda Mary. *See* ELLIOTT, Linda Mary

K

KABOLEH, David Reardon. b 64. Westmr Coll Ox MTh 00. Trin Coll Nairobi 88. **d** 90 **p** 91. C-in-c Nairobi St Phil Kenya 90–92; TV Nairobi St Luke and Immanuel 93–95; NSM Hoddesdon *St Alb* 95–97; NSM Ox St Matt 97–99; NSM Blackbird Leys 99–02; NSM Ox St Aldate 03–04; NSM Akeman 04–07; P-in-c Worminghall w Ickford, Oakley and Shabbington 07–10; R from 10. *The Rectory, 32A The Avenue, Worminghall, Aylesbury HP18 9LE* T: (01844) 338839 E: kaboleh@btinternet.com

KACHIWANDA, Evans Esau. b 62. Univ of Malawi BA 97. Bp Patteson Th Coll (Solomon Is) 87 Virginia Th Sem MTh 04. **d** 89 **p** 91. Chapl to Bp S Malawi 91–92; Sch and Coll Chapl 92–93; Angl Progr Dir 97–98; Chapl and Teacher Malosa Sch 99–04; Headmaster 01–02; Prov Sec Cen Africa 04–05; Lect+Dean Studies Leonard Kamungu Th Coll 05–06; PtO

Blackb 07–09; Malawi from 09. *All Saints' Church, PO 309, Ntcheu, Malawi* E: ekachiwanda@hotmail.com

KAGGWA, Nelson Sonny. b 58. E Lon Univ BA 91. Bp Tucker Coll Mukono 77. **d** 80 **p** 80. Kenya 80–83; USA 83; Hon C Ox SS Phil and Jas w St Marg 84–85; C W Ham *Chelmsf* 86–87; TV Walthamstow St Mary w St Steph 87–92; PtO *Sheff* 92–95; V Sheff St Paul 96–97; rtd 98. *Al-Salam, 36 Standish Gardens, Sheffield S5 8YD* T: 0114-273 1428 F: 273 1348 M: 07989-261278 E: kaggwanelsonibrahim@msn.com

KAKURU (née ASHBRIDGE), Mrs Clare Patricia Esther. b 80. QUB BTh 03 MTh 07. **d** 07 **p** 08. C Donaghcloney w Waringstown *D & D* 07–12; V Lurgan Ch the Redeemer 12–17; P-in-c Maghaberry from 17. *48 Birchdale, Lurgan, Craigavon BT66 7TR* T: (028) 3832 9420 *or* 3832 5673 E: weedoll@gmail.com

KALENIUK, Nicholas George. b 69. WEMTC. **d** 09 **p** 10. C Claines St Jo *Worc* 09–13; P-in-c Wollaston 13–17; P-in-c Stourbridge St Mich Norton 13–17; V Norton and Wollaston from 17. *The Wollaston Vicarage, 46 Vicarage Road, Wollaston, Stourbridge DY8 4NP*

KALSI, Mrs Gina Louise. b 68. Leeds Univ BA 09. NOC 06. **d** 09 **p** 10. C Netherthorpe St Steph *Sheff* 09–13; V Malin Bridge from 13; P-in-c Wadsley 15–16. *St Polycarp's Vicarage, 33 Wisewood Lane, Sheffield S6 4WA* T: 0114-234 3450 M: 07787-578721 E: ginalkalsi@hotmail.co.uk *or* gina.kalsi@sheffield.anglican.org

KAMBLE HANSELL, Anupama. *See* HANSELL, Anupama

KANE, Peter David Colin. b 72. K Coll Lon BMus 92 Fitzw Coll Cam BA 05 MA 09 Chich Univ MA 13 ARCO 91 ARCM 94. Wycliffe Hall Ox BA 08. **d** 09 **p** 10. C Chich St Paul and Westhampnett 09–13; V Clacton St Jas *Chelmsf* 13–17; P-in-c Heene *Chich* from 18. *Heene Rectory, 4 Lansdowne Road, Worthing BN11 4LY* T: (01903) 339656 E: p.kane.03@cantabgold.net

KANERIA, Rajni. b 57. Bath Univ BPharm 82. Wycliffe Hall Ox 83. **d** 86 **p** 87. C Hyson Green *S'well* 86–87; C Hyson Green St Paul w St Steph 87–89; C Harold Hill St Geo *Chelmsf* 89–91; TV Oadby *Leic* 91–97; PtO from 15. *32 Rendall Road, Leicester LE4 6LE* T: 0116-266 6613 E: kanerias@ntlworld.com

KAOMA, Canon John Kafwanka. b 66. Trin Coll Melbourne BTh 97 Ridley Coll Melbourne MA 00. St Jo Sem Lusaka 90. **d** 93 **p** 94. C Chingola St Barn Zambia 93–94; PtO Melbourne Australia 94–00; Lect St Jo Coll Kitwe Zambia 00–03; Prin 01–03; Regional Manager (S Africa) CMS 03–06; PtO Lusaka Zambia 04–06; Research Officer Miss Dept Angl Communion Office 06–09; Dir for Miss from 09; PtO *Lon* 06–12; Hon C Isleworth St Jo 12–14; PtO 15–17; Hon C Heston from 17; Hon Can Lusaka from 15. *19 Passingham House, Ferraro Close, Hounslow TW5 0BF* T: (020) 7313 3940 F: 7313 3999 M: 07901-987239 E: john.kafwanka@anglicancommunion.org

KARAMURA, Grace Patrick. b 62. Nat Teachers' Coll Uganda DipEd 89 Rob Coll Cam MPhil 95 Leeds Univ PhD 98. Bp Tucker Coll Mukono BD 92. **d** 92 **p** 93. C All SS Cathl Kampala Uganda 92–93; C Ebbw Vale Mon 98–01; TV 01–03; V Pontyclun w Talygarn *Llan* 03–14. *17 Muchelney Way, Yeovil BA21 3RB* T: (01935) 700371

KAROON, David. b 69. FRAS. Westcott Ho Cam 16. **d** 17. C Trumpington *Ely* 17–19; P-in-c W Norfolk Priory Gp from 19. *The Rectory, Church Road, Wimbotsham, King's Lynn PE34 3QQ* M: 07596-707469 E: davidshirley@hotmail.com

KASHOURIS, Peter Zacharias. b 66. Peterho Cam BA 89 MA 93. St Steph Ho Ox 92. **d** 94 **p** 95. C Hampstead St Jo *Lon* 94–97; R Hartlepool St Hilda *Dur* 97–03; P-in-c Dur St Oswald 03–06; P-in-c Dur St Oswald and Shincliffe from 06; Dioc Ecum Officer 03–09. *St Oswald's Vicarage, Church Street, Durham DH1 3DG* T: 0191-374 1681 E: p.j.kashouris@durham.anglican.org

KASIBANTE, Amos Sebadduka. b 54. Trin Coll Cam BA 83 MA 87 Yale Univ STM 89. Bp Tucker Coll Mukono 76. **d** 79 **p** 80. C Lyantonde Uganda 79–80; Tutor Bp Tucker Coll Mukono 83–92; Tutor Coll of Ascension Selly Oak 92–95; Prin Simon of Cyrene Th Inst 95–97; Vice Prin St Mich Coll Llan 97–02; Chapl Leic Univ and Co-ord Reader Tr *Leic* 02–09; P-in-c Burmantofts St Steph and St Agnes *Ripon* 10–14; *Leeds* 14–16; P-in-c Leeds St Cypr Harehills 10–16; V Burmantofts and Harehills from 16; Racial Justice Officer *Ripon* 12–14; *Leeds* from 14. *St Agnes' Vicarage, 21 Shakespeare Close, Leeds LS9 7UQ* T: 0113-248 2648 M: 07990-938122 E: amos.kasibante@virgin.net

KASIBANTE, Sonia Ann. b 69. Open Univ BSc 08. Yorks Min Course BA 16. **d** 16 **p** 17. C Gipton and Oakwood *Leeds* from 16. *St Agnes' Vicarage, 21 Shakespeare Close, Leeds LS9 7UQ* T: 0113-248 2648 M: 07789-308067 E: sonia.kasibante@yahoo.co.uk

KASSELL, Colin George Henry. b 42. Ripon Coll Cuddesdon 76. **d** 68 **p** 69. In RC Ch 69–75; PtO *Ox* 76–77; C Denham 77–80; V Brotherton *Wakef* 80–84; Chapl and Past Ldr St Cath Hospice Crawley 84–91; R Rogate w Terwick and Trotton w Chithurst *Chich* 91–94; C Heene 94–06; Chapl Worthing Hosp 94–07; rtd 07; P-in-c Worthing St Andr *Chich* 06–15; RD Worthing 10–16; PtO 16–17. *6 Benedict Close, Worthing BN11 2NZ* M: 07802-259310 E: c.kassell@virginmedia.com

KATE, Sister. *See* BURGESS, Kate Lamorna

KAUNHOVEN, Canon Anthony Peter. b 55. Leeds Univ BA 78 Coll of Ripon & York St Jo PGCE 79. Edin Th Coll 79. **d** 81 **p** 82. C Leeds St Aid *Ripon* 81–84; C Hawksworth Wood 84–89; V Upper Nidderdale 89–91; Hon C Rawdon *Bradf* 96–99; P-in-c Old Brampton *Derby* 99–07; P-in-c Gt

Barlow 04–07; P-in-c Bakewell 07–11; C Ashford w Sheldon and Longstone 07–11; P-in-c Rowsley 07–11; V Bakewell, Ashford w Sheldon and Rowsley from 11; RD Bakewell and Eyam 12–15; Dioc Ecum Officer from 01; Hon Can Derby Cathl from 11. *The Vicarage, South Church Street, Bakewell DE45 1FD* T: (01629) 814462 E: jazzyrector@aol.com

KAUTZER, Benjamin Allen. b 85. Pt Loma Nazarene Univ (USA) BA 07 Nottm Univ MA 08 St Jo Coll Dur PhD 15. Ripon Coll Cuddesdon 13. **d** 15 **p** 16. C Earley St Nic *Ox* 15–19; R Oakley w Wootton St Lawrence *Win* from 19. *9 The Drive, Oakley, Basingstoke RG23 7DA* T: (01256) 420903 M: 07787-838384 E: ben@oww.church

KAVANAGH, The Ven Michael Lowther. b 58. York Univ BA 80 Newc Univ MSc 82 Leeds Univ BA 86 MBPsS 90. Coll of Resurr Mirfield 84. **d** 87 **p** 88. C Boston Spa *York* 87–91; C Clifford 89–91; Chapl Martin House Hospice for Children Boston Spa 87–91; V Beverley St Nic *York* 91–97; RD Beverley 95–97; Abp's Dom Chapl and Dioc Dir of Ords 97–05; Chapl HM Pris Full Sutton 05–08; Angl Adv HM Pris Service 08–12; Hd Chapl and Faith Services 12–18; Chapl Gen of Pris and Adn to HM Pris 13–18; rtd 18; NSM Garrowby Hill *York* from 19; Can Th Liv Cathl from 09. *The Rectory, Worsendale Road, Bishop Wilton, York YO42 1ST* T: (01759) 369974 M: 07828-849823 E: mikekavanagh@hotmail.co.uk

KAY, Alasdair Stewart. b 61. St Jo Coll Nottm MA 15. **d** 14 **p** 15. NSM Walbrook Epiphany *Derby* 14–15; C Mackworth St Fran 15–18; P-in-c 18–19; R Wyke Regis *Sarum* from 19. *Address temp unknown* M: 07885-858709 E: revaskay@gmail.com

KAY, Mrs Audrey Elizabeth. b 60. NOC 04. **d** 07 **p** 08. NSM Ramsbottom and Edenfield *Man* 07–10; V Cadishead from 10; Chapl Salford City Academy from 10. *St Mary's Vicarage, Penry Avenue, Cadishead, Manchester M44 5ZE* T: 0161-775 2171 M: 07752-526140 E: kaynacg@aol.com

KAY, Clifford. b 60. Leeds Metrop Univ BA 94 Ban Univ MA 09. Ridley Hall Cam 10. **d** 12 **p** 13. C Warley *Wakef* 12–14; *Leeds* 14–15; C Halifax St Hilda *Wakef* 12–14; *Leeds* 14–15; V Belton Gp *Linc* from 15; RD Is of Axholme from 17. *All Saints Rectory, 118 High Street, Belton DN19 1NS* E: cliffkay1@gmail.com *or* cliff.kay@cantab.net

KAY, Dennis. b 57. St as Minl Tr Course 96. **d** 99 **p** 00. NSM Llangystennin *St As* 99–01; NSM Colwyn Bay w Brynymaen 01–03; NSM Petryal 03–07. *41 Ffordd Ffynnon, Rhuddlan, Rhyl LL18 2SP* M: 07748-312067

KAY, Peter Richard. b 72. St Cath Coll Cam BA 93 MA 00 PGCE 95. Trin Coll Bris 09. **d** 11 **p** 12. C Letchworth St Paul w Willian *St Alb* 11–14; P-in-c Milton Ernest, Pavenham and Thurleigh from 14. *The Vicarage, Thurleigh Road, Milton Earnest, Bedford MK44 1RF* M: 07718-201449 E: rev.peterkay@outlook.com

KAYE, Canon Alistair Geoffrey. b 62. Reading Univ BSc 85. St Jo Coll Nottm 87. **d** 90 **p** 91. C Gt Horton *Bradf* 90–94; C Rushden w Newton Bromswold *Pet* 94–98; V Upper Armley *Ripon* 98–08; Armley Deanery Missr 08–13; AD Armley 05–08; P-in-c Beeston Hill and Hunslet Moor 13–14; Hon Can Ripon Cathl *Leeds* from 13. *St Luke's Vicarage, Malvern View, Leeds LS11 8SG* M: 07881-804104

KAYE, Canon Gerald Trevor. b 32. Man Univ BSc 54. Oak Hill Th Coll. **d** 56 **p** 57. C Widnes St Ambrose *Liv* 56–58; C St Helens St Mark 58–62; V Brixton Hill St Sav *S'wark* 62–65; Canada 65–85; Hon Can Keewatin 70–75; Adn Patricia 75–78; V Slough *Ox* 85–97; rtd 97; LtO *Arg* from 08. *Craiguanach, Torlundy, Fort William PH33 6SW* T: (01397) 705395 E: eleanorado@aol.com

KAYE, Peter Alan. b 47. K Coll Lon BD 71 AKC 71 Leic Univ MA 82 CQSW 82. St Aug Coll Cant 71. **d** 72 **p** 73. C Fulham All SS *Lon* 72–74; Chapl Rubery Hill, Jo Conolly and Jos Sheldon Hosps Birm 74–80; Hon C Northfield *Birm* 80–83; PtO 99–06; P-in-c Stirchley 06–12; rtd 12; PtO *Birm* from 12; Ban from 12. *Ty Gwyn, Factory Place, Tremadog, Porthmadog LL49 9RE* T: (01766) 513732 M: 07769-944070 E: peterakaye@gmail.com

KAYE, Simon Keith. b 66. Ridley Hall Cam 11. **d** 13 **p** 14. C Eye and Newborough *Pet* 13–14; C Eye, Newborough and Thorney 14–17; V Pet Ch Carpenter from 17. *The Vicarage, 93A Chestnut Avenue, Peterborough PE1 4PE* E: simonkaye748@gmail.com

KAYE, Stephen Michael. b 72. Trin Coll Bris 06. **d** 08 **p** 09. C Calverley *Bradf* 08–12; C Washburn and Mid-Wharfe 12–13; C Abbeylands *Ripon* 13–14; *Leeds* 14–18; TV from 18. *St Mary's Vicarage, 50 Cragside Walk, Leeds LS5 3QE* T: 0113-228 6359 M: 07756-274011 E: revstephenkaye@gmail.com

KAYE, Timothy Henry. b 52. Linc Th Coll 77. **d** 80 **p** 81. C Warsop *S'well* 80–83; C Far Headingley St Chad *Ripon* 83–86; P-in-c Birkby *Wakef* 86; TV N Huddersfield 86–91; R Stone St Mich w Aston St Sav *Lich* 91–95; V S Kirkby *Wakef* 95–14;

Leeds 14–18; rtd 18; PtO *Blackb* from 18. *87 Marsden Hall Road North, Nelson BB9 8JH* E: kayetimothy62@gmail.com

KAYLA, Ms Giyanow Sophia. b 62. St Jo Coll Nottm 13. **d** 15 **p** 16. NSM Aston and Nechells *Birm* from 15. *11 Tansley Road, Birmingham B44 0DN* T: 0121-384 1795 M: 07944-365778 E: giyanow@yahoo.co.uk

KAZICH, Ms Anne. b 69. Cranmer Hall Dur 12. **d** 14 **p** 15. C Tanhouse The Oaks CD *Liv* 14–18; NSM Skelmersdale St Paul from 18. *63 Enstone, Skelmersdale WN8 6AW* M: 07935-320832 E: revannekazich@gmail.com

KAZIRO, Godfrey Sam. b 48. BDSc Lon Univ MSc FDSRCPSGlas FFDRCSI. **d** 02 **p** 03. OLM Waterloo St Jo w St Andr *S'wark* 02–12; NSM from 12; PtO *Lon* from 09. *19 Hampshire Road, Hornchurch RM11 3EU* T: (01708) 441609 M: 07845-281593 E: godfrey_kaziro@yahoo.co.uk

KEAL, Barry Clifford. b 57. Leeds Univ BA 06. NOC 03. **d** 06 **p** 07. NSM Halsall, Lydiate and Downholland *Liv* 06–11. *46 Eastway, Liverpool L31 6BS* T: 0151-526 4508 E: barry@keal.me.uk

KEAN, Robert John. b 64. St Mellitus Coll BA 11. **d** 11 **p** 12. C Black Notley *Chelmsf* 11–14; P-in-c Fairstead w Terling and White Notley etc 14; TV Witham and Villages 14–17; Chapl Algarve *Eur* from 17. *Casa do Jardim, rua José de Conceição Conde, 8600-169 Luz (Lagos), Portugal* T: (00351) (282) 789660 E: revrobkean@gmail.com

KEANE, Christian John. b 74. Rob Coll Cam BA 95 MA 99. Wycliffe Hall Ox BA 06 MA 06. **d** 06 **p** 07. C Eastrop *Win* 06–11; C Ex St Leon w H Trin from 11. *St Leonard's Church, Topsham Road, Exeter EX2 4NG* T: (01392) 286995 E: chris.keane@stleonards.church

KEAR, Mrs Cara Lindsay. b 70. St Mellitus Coll BA 19. **d** 19. C Twickenham Common H Trin *Lon* from 19. *404 Chertsey Road, Twickenham TW2 6LP* M: 07704-889852 E: carakear@gmail.com

KEARLEY-HEYWOOD, Deiniol John Owen. b 73. K Coll Lon BA 95 Peterho Cam MPhil 03. Westcott Ho Cam 02. **d** 04 **p** 05. C Paddington St Jo w St Mich *Lon* 04–08; R Prestwood and Gt Hampden *Ox* from 08; AD Wendover from 16. *The Rectory, 140 Wycombe Road, Prestwood, Great Missenden HP16 0HJ* T: (01494) 866530 E: rector@htprestwood.org.uk

KEARNEY, Mrs Sandra. b 55. Bolton Inst of HE BSc 89 Univ Coll Ches BTh 04. NOC 01. **d** 04 **p** 05. C Blackpool Ch Ch w All SS *Blackb* 04–08; P-in-c Ordsall and Salford Quays *Man* 08–18; R from 18. *The Rectory, Parsonage Close, Salford M5 3GS* T: 0161-872 0800 E: rev.sandra@sky.com

KEARNS, Andrew Philip. b 76. Wycliffe Hall Ox. **d** 09 **p** 10. C Maidenhead St Andr and St Mary *Ox* 09–15; PtO from 18. *5 Walden Avenue, Arborfield, Reading RG2 9HR* E: andrewpkearns@gmail.com

✠**KEARON, The Rt Revd Kenneth Arthur.** b 53. TCD BA 76 MA 79 MPhil 91. CITC 78. **d** 81 **p** 82 **c** 15. C Raheny w Coolock *D & G* 81–84; Lect TCD 82–90; Dean of Res TCD 84–90; I Tullow *D & G* 91–99; Can Ch Ch Cathl Dublin 95–15; Dir Irish Sch Ecum 99–05; Sec Gen Angl Communion Office 05–15; Hon Prov Can Cant Cathl 06–15; Bp L & K from 15. *Kilbrane House, Golf Links Road, Castletroy, Limerick, V94 X0EF, Republic of Ireland* T: (00353) (61) 333635 E: bishop@limerick.anglican.org

KEARTON, Canon Janet Elizabeth. b 54. Univ Coll Lon BSc 78 Birkbeck Coll Lon MSc 81. NEOC 01. **d** 04 **p** 05. C Richmond w Hudswell and Downholme and Marske *Ripon* 04–08; V Hipswell 08–13; Can Res Carl Cathl from 13. *3 The Abbey, Carlisle CA3 8TZ* T: (01228) 521857 M: 07816-278267 E: canonwarden@carlislecathedral.org.uk

KEAST, William. b 43. Univ Coll Ox BA 65 DipEd 66. **d** 88 **p** 89. OLM Scotton w Northorpe *Linc* 88–16; OLM Messingham w E Butterwick, Scotter w E Ferry and Scotton w Northorpe from 16. *4 Crapple Lane, Scotton, Gainsborough DN21 3QT* T: (01724) 763190 E: wkeast@hotmail.com

KEATES, Stephanie Louise. b 87. Univ of Wales (Newport) BA 08. Coll of Resurr Mirfield BA 17. **d** 18 **p** 19. C Newc St Geo and St Hilda from 18. *Close House, St George's Close, Newcastle upon Tyne NE2 2TF* M: 07968-951665 E: revdskeates@gmail.com

KEATES, Thomas Frederick. b 45. Southn Univ BSc 96. WEMTC 09. **d** 12 **p** 13. NSM Thornbury and Oldbury-on-Severn w Shepperdine *Glouc* 12–17. *80 Knapp Road, Thornbury, Bristol BS35 2HJ* T: (01454) 885058 F: 856981 M: 07905-834870 E: tomkeates@blueyonder.co.uk

KEATING, Mrs Ann Barbara. b 53. Open Univ BA 85. STETS 06. **d** 09 **p** 10. NSM Fisherton Anger *Sarum* 09–11; NSM Avon River 11–13; Asst Chapl Win Univ 12–13; R N Bradford on Avon and Villages *Sarum* from 13. *The Rectory, 6 Milbourn Close, Winsley, Bradford-on-Avon BA15 2NN* T: (01225) 722230 M: 07510-588007 E: rev.ann.keating@btinternet.com

KEATING, Christopher Robin. b 39. K Coll Lon BD AKC 84. Sarum Th Coll 62. **d** 65 **p** 66. C Baildon *Bradf* 65–67; CF 67–72; V Thornton Heath St Paul *Cant* 72–79; C Harold Hill St Geo *Chelmsf* 85–89; V Goodmayes All SS 89–07; rtd 07; PtO *York* from 09; *Newc* from 19. *Brigwood, Highford Lane, Hexham NE46 2DD* T: (01434) 605793

KEATING, Geoffrey John. b 52. Open Univ BA 94. St Steph Ho Ox 81. **d** 84 **p** 85. C Lancaster Ch Ch w St Jo and St Anne *Blackb* 84–85; C Rotherham *Sheff* 85–87; V Bentley 87–91; V Penponds *Truro* 91–96; V Pet St Jude 96–19; rtd 19. *47 Borthwick Park, Orton Wistow, Peterborough PE2 6YY* E: geoffrey.keating@btinternet.com

KEATING, Mrs Valerie. b 54. Leeds Metrop Univ BSc 87 Huddersfield Univ MEd 92 CertEd 89 FHEA 06. Yorks Min Course 12. **d** 14 **p** 15. NSM Batley All SS and Purlwell *Leeds* 14–16 and from 14; P-in-c Lepton 17–18; P-in-c Emley 17–18; P-in-c Flockton cum Denby Grange 17–18; R Lepton, Emley and Flockton w Denby Grange from 18. *138 Wakefield Road, Lepton, Huddersfield HD8 0LU* T: (01484) 606126 M: 07505-134105 E: valkeating@sky.com

KEAY, Charles Edward. b 70. Glos Univ BA 94. St Steph Ho Ox 01. **d** 03 **p** 04. C Havant *Portsm* 03–07; P-in-c Alford w Rigsby *Linc* 07–11; TV Portsea N End St Mark *Portsm* 11–15; TV Ex St Thos and Em from 15. *The Vicarage, 78 Queens Road, Exeter EX2 9EW* T: (01392) 672996 M: 07948-600619 E: fathercharles04@gmail.com

KEAY (*née* Dudley), **Mrs Wendy Elizabeth.** b 46. City of Sheff Coll CertEd 68. Cranmer Hall Dur 79. **dss** 81 **d** 87 **p** 94. Cumnor *Ox* 81–89; Par Dn 87–89; Par Dn Hodge Hill *Birm* 89–94; C 94–95; TV 95–98; TV Bucknall *Lich* 98–06; rtd 06; PtO *Lich* from 08. *26 Swallow Croft, Lichfield WS13 7HF* T: (01543) 306509

KEDDIE, Canon Tony. b 37. Qu Coll Birm 63. **d** 66 **p** 67. C Barnoldswick w Bracewell *Bradf* 66–69; C New Bentley *Sheff* 69–71; TV Seacroft *Ripon* 71–79; V Kippax 79–84; TR Kippax w Allerton Bywater 84–92; R Fountains Gp 92–02; Hon Can Ripon Cathl 94–02; rtd 02; PtO *Ripon* 02–14; *Bradf* 03–14; *Leeds* from 14. *4A Stone Acre Heights, Meltham, Holmfirth HD9 4EF* E: tbmk@metronet.co.uk

KEDDILTY, Matthew Paul. b 79. St Jo Coll Nottm 12. **d** 14 **p** 15. C Ulverston St Mary w H Trin *Carl* 14–17; V Bishop Auckland *Dur* from 17. *The Vicarage, 4 Conway Grove, Bishop Auckland DL14 6AF* M: 07872-620605 E: matthew.keddilty@hotmail.com

KEEBLE, Philip Wade. b 47. St Seiriol Cen 09. **d** 13. Min Can Ban Cathl 13–14. *12 Glasffordd, Marianglas, Anglesey LL73 8PH* T/F: (01248) 853802 M: 07944-671444 E: keeblephil@gmail.com

KEECH, April Irene. b 52. Penn State Univ BA 76. Trin Coll Bris BA 89. **d** 89 **p** 92. C Walthamstow St Luke *Chelmsf* 89–92; USA 92–95; V Deptford St Jo w H Trin *S'wark* 95–02; Asst Dioc Dir of Ords 96–00; Hon Can S'wark Cathl 99–02; V Hoxton St Jo w Ch Ch *Lon* 02–10; Chapl St Mary Magd Academy Lon from 10; PtO *Lon* 10–15; NSM Old Ford St Paul and St Mark from 15. *13 Regents Wharf, Wharf Place, London E2 9BD* T: (020) 7739 7621 or 7697 0123 E: april.keech@smmacademy.org.uk or april.keech@btinternet.com

KEECH, Dominic. b 83. Keble Coll Ox BA 05 MA 14 MSt 06 DPhil 10. St Steph Ho Ox 10. **d** 12 **p** 13. C Wantage Ox 12–14; Chapl BNC Ox 14–17; C Ox St Mary Magd 14–16; LtO 16–17; V Brighton St Nic *Chich* from 17. *2 Windlesham Road, Brighton BN1 3AG* M: 07920-761546

KEEGAN, Frances Ann (Sister Isabel). b 44. Open Univ BA 11 Sarum Coll MA 16 SEN 74. Franciscan Study Cen 87. **d** 99 **p** 00. NSM Sherborne w Castleton and Lillington *Sarum* 99–01; NSM Golden Cap Team 01–08; NSM Crosslacon *Carl* 08–11; P-in-c Brigham, Gt Broughton and Broughton Moor 11–12; rtd 12; PtO *Truro* 13–14; *Sarum* 14–18; P-in-c Kilcolman w Kiltallagh, Killorglin, Knockane etc *L & K* from 18. *Seaview House, Gurrane West, Sunhill, Killorglin, Co Kerry, V93 T2C1, Republic of Ireland* T: (00353) (66) 979 0359 E: revik@hotmail.co.uk

KEEGAN, Graham Brownell. b 40. Nottm Univ CertEd 68. NOC 81. **d** 84 **p** 85. C Highfield *Liv* 84–87; V Ince St Mary 87–95; V Newton in Makerfield St Pet 95–05; rtd 05; PtO *Liv* from 16. *5 Scott Road, Lowton, Warrington WA3 2HD* T: (01942) 713809

KEELER, Alan. b 58. City Univ BSc 81. St Jo Coll Nottm MA 01. **d** 90 **p** 91. C Paddock Wood *Roch* 90–94; V Blendon 94–06; V Plaistow St Mary from 06; AD Bromley from 15. *St Mary's Vicarage, 74 London Lane, Bromley BR1 4HE* T: (020) 8460 1827 E: agkeeler@tiscali.co.uk

KEELING, Peter Frank. b 34. Kelham Th Coll. **d** 58 **p** 59. C S Elmsall *Wakef* 58–63; C Barnsley St Mary 63–67; V Ravensthorpe 67–73; V Cudworth 73–83; R Downham Market w Bexwell *Ely* 83–00; RD Fincham 83–94; V

Crimplesham w Stradsett 85–00; rtd 00; P-in-c Hempton and Pudding Norton *Nor* 00–04; PtO from 04. *23 Cleaves Drive, Walsingham NR22 6EQ* T: (01328) 820310

KEEN, David Mark. b 69. Oriel Coll Ox BA 91. St Jo Coll Nottm BTh 96 MPhil 98. **d** 98 **p** 99. C Yeovil w Kingston Pitney *B & W* 98–02; C Haughton le Skerne *Dur* 02–06; C Preston Plucknett *B & W* 06–17; V from 17. *3 Poplar Drive, Yeovil BA21 3UL* T: (01935) 422286 E: revdmkeen@btinternet.com

KEEN, Michael Spencer. b 41. St Pet Coll Ox BA 68 MA 72 GRSM 62 ARCM Reading Univ CertEd. Westcott Ho Cam 68. **d** 73 **p** 74. NSM W Derby St Jo *Liv* 73–74; NSM Stanley 74–76; Chs Youth and Community Officer Telford *Lich* 77–82; Dioc Unemployment Officer *Sheff* 82–89; NSM Brixton Road Ch Ch *S'wark* 89–92; Employment Development Officer 89–92; PtO 92–99; NSM Camberwell St Giles w St Matt 99–01. *40 Sheppard's College, London Road, Bromley BR1 1PF* T: (020) 8313 0490 E: keen3045@gmail.com

KEEN, Ms Miriam Frances. b 65. Ex Univ BSc 87 Glos Univ MA 10 Westmr Coll of Educn PGCE 88. Wycliffe Hall Ox 04. **d** 05 **p** 06. C Cogges and S Leigh *Ox* 05–14; C N Leigh 13–14; TV Marlborough *Sarum* 14–18; R W Downland *Ox* from 18. *The Rectory, Church Street, Great Shefford, Hungerford RG17 7DU* T: (01488) 649927 M: 07954-117093 E: miriwestdownland@gmail.com

KEEP, Andrew James. b 55. Collingwood Coll Dur BA 77 Yale Univ STM 84 K Coll Lon MA 14. Sarum & Wells Th Coll 78. **d** 80 **p** 81. C Banstead *Guildf* 80–83; Chapl Qu Eliz Hosp Banstead 80–83; USA 83–84; Chapl Cranleigh Sch Surrey 84–98; Chapl Wells Cathl Sch 98–06; PV Wells Cathl *B & W* 01–06; Chapl Mill Hill Sch Lon 07–10; PtO *Lon* 10–14; NSM St Marg Pattens from 14. *193 Foundling Court, Brunswick Centre, London WC1N 1QF* T: (020) 7837 5327 M: 07740-647813 E: andrew.keep@me.com *or* vicar@stmargaretpattens.org

KEEP, Hugh Charles John Martin. b 45. Qu Coll Birm 90. **d** 92 **p** 93. C Aston Cantlow and Wilmcote w Billesley *Cov* 92–95; P-in-c Hampton Lucy w Charlecote and Loxley 95–02; Chapl Rainsbrook Secure Tr Cen 02–05; rtd 05; PtO *Cov* from 05. *4 Old Town, Stratford-upon-Avon CV37 6BG* T: (01789) 414142 E: hrkeepnet@aol.com

KEFFORD, Canon Peter Charles. b 44. Nottm Univ BTh 74. Linc Th Coll 70. **d** 74 **p** 75. C W Wimbledon Ch Ch *S'wark* 74–77; C All Hallows by the Tower etc *Lon* 77–81; C-in-c Pound Hill CD *Chich* 81; TV Worth 82–83; TR 83–92; R Henfield w Shermanbury and Woodmancote 92–01; Can Res and Treas Chich Cathl 01–09; Adv for Ord Min and Dioc Dir of Ords 01–06; Dioc Adv for Min 07–09; rtd 09. *17 North Close, Mickleover, Derby DE3 9JA* T: (01332) 549534 E: peter_kefford@hotmail.com

KEIGHLEY, Mrs Amanda Jane. b 56. Garnett Coll Lon CertEd 85 Leeds Univ MA 98. Cranmer Hall Dur 04. **d** 07 **p** 08. NSM Is of Dogs Ch Ch and St Jo w St Luke *Lon* 07–12; P-in-c Elm Park St Nic Hornchurch *Chelmsf* 12–13; V from 13. *The Vicarage, 17 St Nicholas Avenue, Hornchurch RM12 4PT* T: (01708) 474639 M: 07889-486354 E: akeighley@clara.co.uk

KEIGHLEY, Andrew Kenneth. b 62. Nottm Univ LLB 84 Solicitor 85. Wycliffe Hall Ox 94. **d** 97 **p** 98. C Westminster St Jas the Less *Lon* 97–00; NSM 00–04; C Brompton H Trin w Onslow Square St Paul 04–06; P-in-c W Hampstead Trin 06–09; V from 09. *10 Lisburne Road, London NW3 2NR* M: 07747-611577

KEIGHLEY, David John. b 48. Open Univ BA 88 CertEd. Sarum & Wells Th Coll 82. **d** 83 **p** 84. C Sawbridgeworth *St Alb* 83–86; TV Saltash *Truro* 86–89; V Lanlivery w Luxulyan 89–00; P-in-c The Candover Valley *Win* 00–08; P-in-c Wield 03–08; P-in-c Hurstbourne Tarrant, Faccombe, Vernham Dean etc 08–16; rtd 16. *Drokensford, Chapel Road, Meonstoke, Southampton SO32 3NJ* T: (01489) 877983 M: 07736-799262 E: davidkeighley@hotmail.com

KEIGHLEY, Martin Philip. b 61. Edin Univ MA 83. Westcott Ho Cam 86. **d** 88 **p** 89. C Lytham St Cuth *Blackb* 88–91; C Lancaster St Mary 91–93; R Halton w Aughton 93–00; V Poulton-le-Fylde 00–04; V Poulton Carleton and Singleton from 04; AD Poulton from 08. *The Vicarage, 7 Vicarage Road, Poulton-le-Fylde FY6 7BE* T: (01253) 883086 E: martinkeighley@btconnect.com

KEIGHLEY, Thomas Christopher. b 51. Open Univ BA 85 K Coll Lon PhD 15. NEOC 00. **d** 03 **p** 04. NSM Upper Nidderdale *Ripon* 03–06; NSM Dacre w Hartwith and Darley w Thornthwaite 06–07; NSM Is of Dogs Ch Ch and St Jo w St Luke *Lon* 07–12; Chapl St Joseph's Hospice Hackney 09–10; NSM Elm Park St Nic Hornchurch *Chelmsf* from 12; Dean SSM Stepney Area *Lon* 09–12; Dean SSM Barking Area from 15. *The Vicarage, 17 St Nicholas Avenue, Hornchurch*

KEILLER, Canon Jane Elizabeth. b 52. Westmr Coll Ox BEd 74. Cranmer Hall Dur 76. **dss** 80 **d** 87 **p** 94. Cambridge H Trin w St Andr Gt *Ely* 80–86; NSM Cambridge St Barn 86–88 and 90–94; NSM Cambridge H Cross 95–02; Chapl and Tutor Ridley Hall Cam 96–14; Hon Can Ely Cathl from 05; Bp's Adv for Spirituality from 14; PtO from 16. *68 Pierce Lane, Cambridge CB21 5DL* T: (01223) 575776 *or* 741076 F: 741076 E: jk271@cam.ac.uk *or* jane.keiller@gmail.com

KEIR, Mrs Gillian Irene. b 44. Westf Coll Lon BA 66 Somerville Coll Ox BLitt 70 Lon Univ MA 95. SAOMC 95. **d** 98 **p** 99. NSM St Alb St Steph 98–08; PtO from 08; NSM Officer St Alb Adnry 06–14. *17 Battlefield Road, St Albans AL1 4DA* T: (01727) 854885 E: gillikeir@gmail.com

KEIRLE, The Very Revd Michael Robert. b 62. Trin Coll Bris BA 89. **d** 89 **p** 90. C Orpington Ch Ch *Roch* 89–92; Zimbabwe 92–95; R Keston *Roch* 95–03; R Guernsey St Martin *Win* 03–17; Vice-Dean Guernsey 13–17; R Jersey St Helier from 17; Dean Jersey from 17. *The Deanery, David Place, Jersey JE2 4TE* T: (01534) 720001 E: dean@jerseydeanery.je

KEITH, Elisabeth Grace. b 77. Sheff Univ BA 02 York St Jo Univ MA 09. Cranmer Hall Dur 13. **d** 16 **p** 17. C Sheff Cathl 16–19; C Ecclesall from 19. *9 Greystones Grange Road, Sheffield S11 7JH* M: 07904-979713 E: beth.keith@sheffield.anglican.org

KEITH, John. b 25. LRAM 50 LGSM 50 AGSM 51. Cuddesdon Coll 60. **d** 62 **p** 63. C Lee-on-the-Solent *Portsm* 62–65; C Raynes Park St Sav *S'wark* 65–68; rtd 90. *7 Torr An Eas, Glenfinnan PH37 4LS* T: (01397) 722314

KELHAM, Canon Adèle Mary. b 46. St Andr Univ BSc 69. Cranmer Hall Dur. **d** 98 **p** 99. Asst Chapl Zürich *Eur* 98–01; P-in-c Bishop Middleham *Dur* 01–05; AD Sedgefield 03–05; P-in-c Lausanne *Eur* 05–13; P-in-c Lausanne w Neuchâtel 13–16; Dioc Adv for Women's Min 05–08; Hon Can from 16; Acting Adn Switzerland from 16; Acting Adn E Adnry from 19. *Lindenstrasse 4, 5303 Würenlingen, Switzerland* T: (0041) (56) 281 1025 E: kelham@bluewin.ch *or* adele.kelham@europe.anglican.org

KELK, Michael Anthony. b 48. Sarum & Wells Th Coll. **d** 83 **p** 84. C Ross w Brampton Abbotts, Bridstow and Peterstow *Heref* 83–86; P-in-c Burghill 86–97; P-in-c Stretton Sugwas 86–97; P-in-c Walford and St John w Bishopswood, Goodrich etc 97–02; P-in-c Llangarron w Llangrove, Whitchurch and Ganarew 02–08; PtO from 11. *Highland Cottage, Fownhope, Hereford HR1 4NX* T: (01432) 860565

KELLEN, David. b 52. St Mich Coll Llan 70. **d** 75 **p** 76. C Mynyddislwyn *Mon* 75–77; C Risca 77–78; C Malpas 78–81; V Newport All SS 81–88; V St Mellons from 88; R Michaelston-y-Fedw 89–96. *The Vicarage, Ty'r Winch Road, St Mellons, Cardiff CF3 5UP* T: (029) 2079 6560 E: hyweldda1067@gmail.com

KELLETT, Canon Richard. b 64. Leeds Univ BSc 85 PhD 89. St Jo Coll Nottm BTh 95 MA 96. **d** 96 **p** 97. C Nottingham St Jude *S'well* 96–00; P-in-c Skegby 00–02; P-in-c Teversal 00–02; R Skegby w Teversal 02–17; AD Newstead 06–17; P-in-c Lenton Abbey from 16; Hon Can S'well Minster from 10. *Jubilee House, Westgate, Southwell NG25 0JH* T: (01636) 814331 E: richard.kellett@southwell.anglican.org

KELLEY, Neil George. b 64. ARCM 85. Westcott Ho Cam 88. **d** 91 **p** 92. C E Bedfont *Lon* 91–93; C Chiswick St Nic w St Mary 93–97; C Kirkby *Liv* 97–99; V Gt Crosby St Faith and Waterloo Park St Mary 99–12; Dioc Adv on Worship and Liturgy 06–12; R Bushey *St Alb* 12–17; R Chorley St Laur *Blackb* from 17; PtO *Lon* 13–18. *The Rectory, Rectory Close, Chorley PR7 1QW* M: 07980-872203 E: frneilkelley@gmail.com

KELLEY, Peter John. b 55. Poly of the S Bank BSc 85 Kingston Univ MBA 97 Cant Ch Ch Univ BA 12. SEITE 06. **d** 09 **p** 10. NSM Hook *S'wark* 09–15; NSM Tolworth, Hook and Surbiton 15–17; P-in-c Raynes Park St Sav from 17. *95 Lime Grove, New Malden KT3 3TR* T: (020) 8336 1639 M: 07542-961809

KELLOW, Richard James. b 78. Kent Univ BA 00 Cam Univ PGCE 01. Trin Coll Bris MA 12. **d** 12 **p** 13. C Histon *Ely* 12–16; C Impington 12–16; TV Duston and Upton *Pet* from 16. *22 Berrywood Drive, Northampton NN5 6GB* E: revrkellow@gmail.com

KELLS, Ms Jill Elizabeth. b 70. Univ of Wales (Cardiff) BSc 91. Trin Coll Bris 16. **d** 19. C Bursledon *Win* from 19. *St Paul's Church, 2 Oak Road, Bursledon, Southampton SO31 8DU* M: 07731-838797 E: revjillkells@gmail.com

KELLS, Mary Eileen. b 65. St Andr Univ MA 87 LSE PhD 00. Ripon Coll Cuddesdon 15. **d** 17 **p** 18. C Bridgemary *Portsm* 17–18; C Elson 17–18; C Lee-on-the-Solent from 18. *5 Caspar John Close, Fareham PO14 2DQ* M: 07846-951285 E: maryeileenkells@gmail.com

KELLY, Canon Brian Horace. b 34. St Jo Coll Dur BA 57 MA 69. **d** 58 **p** 59. C Douglas St Geo and St Barn *S & M* 58–61; V Foxdale 61–64; V Bolton All So w St Jas *Man* 64–73; V Maughold *S & M* 73–77; Dir of Ords 76–93; V German 77–06; Can and Prec St German's Cathl 80–06; RD Castletown and Peel 97–04; rtd 06; PtO *S & M* from 09. *16 Slieau Whallian Park, St Johns, Isle of Man IM4 3JH* T: (01624) 801479 E: revkelly@manx.net

KELLY, Desmond Norman. b 42. Oak Hill Th Coll BA 95. **d** 90 **p** 91. C Braintree *Chelmsf* 90–94; P-in-c Sible Hedingham 94–95; P-in-c Castle Hedingham 94–95; R Sible Hedingham w Castle Hedingham 95–08; rtd 08; PtO *St E* from 11; *Chelmsf* from 11. *Wykhams, Mill Common, Westhall, Halesworth IP19 8RQ* T: (01502) 575493 E: rev.des@btinternet.com

KELLY, John Adrian. b 49. Qu Coll Birm 70. **d** 73 **p** 74. C Formby St Pet *Liv* 73–77; Org Sec CECS Liv, Blackb and S & M 77–92; Deputation Appeals Org (Lancs and Is of Man) 88–92; PtO *Liv* 77–05; *Blackb* 77–00; *Man* 88–97. *4 Blandford Close, Southport PR8 2DB* E: karin.kelly@btopenworld.com

KELLY, Canon John Dickinson. b 42. Nottm Univ BA 63. Ripon Hall Ox 63. **d** 65 **p** 66. C Egremont *Carl* 65–67; C Upperby St Jo 67–70; V Arlecdon 70–73; V Barrow St Aid 73–79; V Milnthorpe 79–83; V Beetham and Milnthorpe 83–85; V Camerton St Pet 85–88; P-in-c Camerton H Trin W Seaton 86–88; V Camerton, Seaton and W Seaton 88–01; P-in-c Kells 01–05; Hon Can Carl Cathl from 00; Chapl N Cumbria Acute Hosps NHS Trust 03–05; rtd 05; P-in-c Kirkland, Lamplugh w Ennerdale *Carl* 05–07; Hon C Whitehaven 07–12; PtO from 12. *10 Stonyhurst Drive, Whitehaven CA28 7RZ* T: (01946) 692630

KELLY, Malcolm Bernard. b 46. St Mich Coll Llan 72. **d** 74 **p** 75. C Tranmere St Paul w St Luke *Ches* 74–77; C Barnston 77–80; R Thurstaston 80–92; R Grappenhall 92–11; rtd 11; PtO *Ches* from 11. *22 Boswell Avenue, Warrington WA4 6DQ* T: (01925) 423871 E: malcolmkelly25@yahoo.co.uk

KELLY, Martin Herbert. b 55. Selw Coll Cam MA 90. Aston Tr Scheme 78 Ripon Coll Cuddesdon 80. **d** 83 **p** 84. C Clapham Old Town *S'wark* 83–87; Chapl and Fell Selw Coll Cam 87–92; Chapl Newnham Coll Cam 87–92; Chapl St Piers Hosp Sch Lingfield *S'wark* 95–01; C Limpsfield and Titsey 95–01; Chapl Basildon and Thurrock Gen Hosps NHS Trust 03–04; Chapl Dartford and Gravesham NHS Trust 04–18; PtO *S'wark* 14–15. *Cygnets, Hosey Hill, Westerham TN16 1TB* E: martinkelly300@gmail.com

KELLY, Paul. b 60. Qu Coll Birm 02. **d** 04 **p** 05. C Ogley Hay *Lich* 04–07; V Stafford St Paul Forebridge 07–11; V Hednesford from 11. *The Vicarage, Church Hill, Hednesford, Cannock WS12 1BD* T: (01543) 426954 M: 07815-452616

KELLY, Canon Peter Hugh. b 46. Sarum & Wells Th Coll 81. **d** 84 **p** 85. C Fareham H Trin *Portsm* 84–87; Chapl and Prec Portsm Cathl 87–90; V Eastney 90–97; P-in-c Swanmore St Barn 97–06; V 07–11; RD Bishop's Waltham 03–09; Hon Can Portsm Cathl 07–11; rtd 11; PtO *Portsm* from 11. *16 Rosedale Close, Fareham PO14 4EL* T: (01329) 849567 E: peterkelly@swanmore.net

KELLY, Canon Stephen Alexander. b 61. Man Univ BSc 84. Ridley Hall Cam 03. **d** 05 **p** 06. C Meole Brace *Lich* 05–08; C Cen Telford 08–13; Fresh Expressions Adv 12–13; V Northampton St Giles *Pet* from 13; Can Pet Cathl from 18. *St Giles's Vicarage, 2 Spring Gardens, Northampton NN1 1LX* T: (01604) 627680 E: revstevekelly@gmail.com

KELLY, Canon Stephen Paul. b 55. Keble Coll Ox BA 77 MA 07 Leeds Univ MA 06. Linc Th Coll 77. **d** 79 **p** 80. C Illingworth *Wakef* 79–82; C Knottingley 82–84; V Alverthorpe 84–93; Dioc Ecum Officer 88–93; TR Bingley All SS *Bradf* 93–03; P-in-c Woolley *Wakef* 03–14; *Leeds* 14–17; Dioc CME Officer *Wakef* 03–14; *Leeds* 14–17; RD Wakef 11–14; AD *Leeds* 14–17; Hon Can Wakef Cathl 08–17; rtd 17. *416 Leeds Road, Dewsbury WF12 7QE* E: s.p.kelly1995@gmail.com

KELLY, Timothy Patrick. b 73. Trin Hall Cam MA 94 York Univ DPhil 99. St Hild Coll 16. **d** 19. C Beverley Minster *York* from 19. *23 Outer Trinities, Beverley HU17 0HN* M: 07818-456834 E: tim.kelly@duvelle.co.uk

KELLY-MOORE, The Ven Joanne. b 68. Victoria Univ Wellington BA LLB. Bible Coll of NZ BD 99. **d** 00 **p** 01. C Remuera St Aidan New Zealand 00–04; V Remuera St Aidan 04–10; Dean Auckland 10–17; Adn Cant from 17. *29 The Precincts, Canterbury CT1 2EP* T: (01227) 865238 E: archdeacon@canterbury-cathedral.org

KELSEY, Canon George Robert Joseph. b 61. Imp Coll Lon BSc 83 Newc Univ MSc 84 PhD 92. Cranmer Hall Dur 95. **d** 97 **p** 98. C Denton *Newc* 97–01; TV Glendale Gp 01–10; V Norham and Duddo from 10; P-in-c Cornhill w Carham from 10; P-in-c Branxton from 10; AD Norham from 10; Hon Can Newc Cathl from 16. *The Vicarage, Church Lane,*

Norham, Berwick-upon-Tweed TD15 2LF T: (01289) 382325 E: robert.josephkelsey@live.com

KELSEY, Michael Ray. b 22. FEPA 57. Wycliffe Hall Ox 60. **d** 62 **p** 63. C Lower Broughton St Clem *Man* 62–64; V Ingleby Greenhow *York* 64–68; V Scarborough St Jas 68–71; Asst to the Gen Sec USCL 71–74; V Blackheath St Jo *S'wark* 74–87; rtd 87; PtO *St E* 88–05. *20 Sweet Briar, Marcham, Abingdon OX13 6PD* T: (01865) 391835 E: mjkelsey08@btinternet.com

KELSEY, Mrs Tina Jane. b 69. Chich Univ BA 10. Ripon Coll Cuddesdon 11. **d** 13 **p** 14. C Beckenham St Geo *Roch* 13–17; V Edmonton St Pet w St Martin *Lon* from 17. *The Vicarage, St Peter's Road, London N9 8JP* T: (020) 8807 7431 M: 07512-710085 E: tina.jk42@yahoo.co.uk

KELSO, Andrew John. b 47. Lon Univ BA 70 LRAM 73. St Jo Coll Nottm 83. **d** 85 **p** 86. C Gorleston St Mary *Nor* 85–87; C Hellesdon 87–90; TV Ipsley *Worc* 90–09; rtd 09; PtO *Worc* from 11. *2 The Close, Throckmorton, Pershore WR10 2JU* T: (01386) 462087 M: 07795-431382 E: andy.kelso@sky.com

KEMBALL, Sister Heather Susan. b 61. St Mellitus Coll 18. **d** 19. NSM Alsager Ch Ch *Ches* from 19. *54 Obelisk Way, Congleton CW12 4FY* T: (01260) 278362 M: 07762-914673 E: heather@kemball.com

KEMBER, Ms Ann Elizabeth. b 58. ERMC 12. **d** 15 **p** 16. C Wolverton *Ox* 15–18; R Chard St Mary w Combe St Nicholas, Wambrook etc *B & W* from 18. *The Vicarage, Forton Road, Chard TA20 2HJ* M: 07855-470522 E: annkember@hotmail.com

KEMP, Canon Alice Mary Elizabeth. b 59. Kent Univ BA 82 Thames Poly PGCE 91. STETS 07. **d** 10 **p** 11. NSM Box w Hazlebury and Ditteridge *Bris* 10–18; NSM Colerne w N Wraxall 11–18; NSM Marshfield w Cold Ashton and Tormarton etc from 18; Hon Can Bris Cathl from 17. *Barn House, Barn Piece, Box, Corsham SN13 8LF* T: (01225) 742128 E: revalicekemp@btinternet.com

KEMP, Canon Allan. b 43. Bps' Coll Cheshunt 65 Oak Hill Th Coll 67. **d** 68 **p** 69. C Tunbridge Wells St Jas *Roch* 68–76; V Becontree St Mary *Chelmsf* 76–90; RD Barking and Dagenham 81–86; V Gt w Lt Chesterford 90–07; Hon Can Chelmsf Cathl 99–07; rtd 07; PtO *Glouc* from 16. *6 Freemans Orchard, Newent GL18 1TX* T: (01531) 822041 E: canonkemp@waitrose.com

KEMP, Prof Anthony Eric. b 34. St Mark & St Jo Coll Lon CertEd 57 LTCL 63 FTCL 63 Lon Inst of Educn DipEd 70 Sussex Univ MA 71 DPhil 79 Hon FLCM 83 CPsychol 89 FBPsS 97 Helsinki Univ Hon MusDoc 03. SAOMC 96. **d** 98 **p** 99. NSM Wokingham All SS *Ox* 98–05; NSM Wokingham St Paul 05–09; PtO 09–13; *Portsm* from 14. *40 Sea Grove Avenue, Hayling Island PO11 9EU* T: (023) 9378 6659 E: ae.kemp@yahoo.co.uk

KEMP, Christopher Michael. b 48. K Coll Lon BD 71 AKC 71. St Aug Coll Cant 75. **d** 76 **p** 77. C Weaverham *Ches* 76–79; C Latchford St Jas 79–82; P-in-c Sandbach Heath 82–88; V Macclesfield St Paul 88–89; C Cheadle Hulme All SS 89–93; C Oxton 93–98; P-in-c Seacombe 98–02; P-in-c Brereton w Swettenham 02–05; P-in-c Brereton w Eaton and Hulme Walfield 05–10; rtd 10. *1 Orchard Rise, Droitwich WR9 8NU* T: (01905) 774372

KEMP, Hilary Anne. b 65. ERMC 15. **d** 18 **p** 19. NSM Hemel Hempstead *St Alb* from 18. *6 Granville Dene, Bovingdon, Hemel Hempstead HP3 0JE* E: hilarykemp65@gmail.com

KEMP, John Graham Edwin. b 29. Bris Univ BA 51 PGCE 52 Lon Univ BD 65. Wells Th Coll 63. **d** 65 **p** 66. C Maidenhead St Luke *Ox* 65–70; R Rotherfield Greys 70–78; V Highmore 70–78; Dep Dir Tr Scheme for NSM 78–84; P-in-c Taplow 78–82; TV Burnham w Dropmore, Hitcham and Taplow 82–84; Prin EAMTC 84–92; rtd 92; Chapl Kyrenia Cyprus 92–95; PtO *St E* from 95. *Lea Cottage, The Street, Middleton, Saxmundham IP17 3NJ* T: (01728) 648324 E: revdjgk@waitrose.com

KEMP, John Robert Deverall. b 42. City Univ BSc 65 BD 69. Oak Hill Th Coll 66. **d** 70 **p** 71. C Fulham Ch Ch *Lon* 70–73; C Widford *Chelmsf* 73–79; P-in-c New Thundersley 79–84; V 84–98; Chapl HM Pris Bullwood Hall 79–98; R S Shoebury *Chelmsf* 98–09; rtd 09; PtO *Chelmsf* from 09. *36 Macmurdo Road, Leigh-on-Sea SS9 5AQ* T: (01702) 525978

KEMP, Mrs Pamela Ann. b 52. Coll of St Matthias Bris CertEd 73 RMN 98. Ripon Coll Cuddesdon BTh 07. **d** 02 **p** 03. C Portland All SS w St Pet *Sarum* 02–04; C Verwood 04–06; R Highnam, Lassington, Rudford, Tibberton etc *Glouc* 06–11; P-in-c Stokenham, Slapton, Charleton w Buckland etc *Ex* 11–14; P-in-c Slapton, Charleton w Buckland etc 14–19; rtd 19. *Plot 177, 5 Sanderling Close, Bude EX23 8GJ* M: 07989-604543 E: pamelakemp@btinternet.com

KEMP, Ralph John. b 71. Wye Coll Lon BSc 93 Trin Hall Cam BTh 04. Ridley Hall Cam 01. **d** 04 **p** 05. C Astbury and

Smallwood *Ches* 04–07; V Burton and Shotwick 07–08; NSM Plas Newton w Ches Ch Ch 09–11; NSM Ches Ch Ch from 11. *38 Ethos Court, City Road, Chester CH1 3AT* M: 07762-847211 E: ralphjkemp@googlemail.com *or* ralph.kemp@christchurchchester.com

KEMP, William. b 67. St Anne's Coll Ox BA 91 Brunel Univ PGCE 92 Wolfs Coll Cam BTh 99. Ridley Hall Cam 96. **d** 99 **p** 00. C Kensington St Barn *Lon* 99–04; C Hurstpierpoint *Chich* 04–16; P-in-c Mid-Sussex Network Ch from 04. *12 Western Road, Hurstpierpoint BN6 9TA* T: (01273) 835829

KEMPSTER, Miss Helen Edith. b 49. **d** 00 **p** 01. OLM Weybridge *Guildf* 00–06; OLM Esher 06–14; PtO 14–15; NSM Headley All SS from 15. *Perrymead, May Close, Headley, Bordon GU35 8LR* T: (01428) 713973 E: helen.kempster@btinternet.com

KEMPTHORNE, Renatus. b 39. Wadh Coll Ox BA 60 MA 64. Wycliffe Hall Ox 60. **d** 62 **p** 63. C Stoke *Cov* 62–65; Lect St Jo Coll Auckland New Zealand 65–68; R Wytham *Ox* 68–75; Chapl Bp Grosseteste Coll Linc 75–83; V Waimea New Zealand 83–90; Th Consultant 90–96; Researcher and Educator from 97; rtd 04. *140 Nile Street, Nelson 7010, New Zealand* T: (0064) (3) 546 7447 E: kempthorne@xtra.co.nz

KENCHINGTON, Mrs Jane Elizabeth Ballantyne. b 58. Hull Univ BSc 79 Trin Coll Bris MA 05 Hughes Hall Cam PGCE 83. Westcott Ho Cam 88. **d** 90 **p** 94. C Winchcombe, Gretton, Sudeley Manor etc *Glouc* 90–96; PtO 96–99; NSM Dursley 99–02; Dir Reader Tr and Tutor WEMTC 01–06; Dean of Women Clergy 06–09; R Sodbury Vale 09–15; AD Wotton 13–15; Hon Can Glouc Cathl 06–15; TR Solihull *Birm* from 15. *The Rectory, 45 Park Avenue, Solihull B91 3EJ* T: 0121-705 0069 M: 07743-402229 E: rector@solihullparish.org.uk

KENCHINGTON, Paul Henry. b 54. Worc Coll Ox MA 76. St Jo Coll Nottm BA 81. **d** 82 **p** 83. C Scarborough St Mary w Ch Ch and H Apostles York 82–85; C Caversham St Pet and Mapledurham etc *Ox* 85–89; V Hucclecote *Glouc* 89–00; V Kowloon St Andr Hong Kong 00–05; Chapl Versailles w Chevry *Eur* 05–11; P-in-c Combe Down w Monkton Combe and S Stoke *B & W* 11–16; V 16–17; rtd 17; PtO *Glouc* from 19. *4 Painswick Heights, Yokehouse Lane, Stroud GL6 7QS* M: 07825-482225

KENDAL, Gordon McGregor. b 46. Dundee Univ MA 70 Mansf Coll Ox BA 72 MA 76 Lon Univ BA 73 PhD 79 MA 98 St Andr Univ PhD 08 Jordanhill Coll Glas PGCE 88. Edin Th Coll 72. **d** 74 **p** 75. C Bracknell *Ox* 74–77; C Wokingham All SS 77–79; Chapl and Fell Linc Coll Ox 79–83; R Edin St Pet 83–87; Man Gr Sch 88–92; Gen Sec Fellowship of St Alb and St Sergius 92–96; V S Lambeth St Anne and All SS *S'wark* 96–00; rtd 11. *10 Bamff Road, Alyth, Blairgowrie PH11 8DT* T: (01828) 633400 E: gkendal@tesco.net

KENDAL, Henry David. b 59. ASVA 83. Lon Bible Coll 90 Oak Hill NSM Course 92. **d** 94 **p** 95. C Roxeth *Lon* 94–99; C Woodside Park St Barn 99–06; V from 06. *78 Woodside Avenue, London N12 8TB* T: (020) 8343 7776 *or* 8343 5775 F: 8446 7492 *or* 8343 5771 M: 07977-521656 E: henrykendal@stbarnabas.co.uk

KENDALL, Edward Jonathan. b 76. Nottm Univ BA 98 Ox Univ PGCE 99. Oak Hill Th Coll BA 10. **d** 10 **p** 11. C Fulham St Pet *Lon* 10–14; C Teddington SS Pet and Paul and Fulwell 14–19; V Fulwell from 19. *45 St James's Avenue, Hampton Hill, Hampton TW12 1HL* M: 07813-610977 E: ed@stmichaelsfulwell.co.uk

KENDALL, Frank. b 40. CCC Cam BA 62 MA 68 FRSA 90. S'wark Ord Course 74. **d** 74 **p** 75. NSM Lingfield *S'wark* 74–75 and 78–82; NSM Sketty *S & B* 75–78; NSM Limpsfield and Titsey *S'wark* 82–84; LtO *Man* 84–89; LtO *Liv* 89–96; NSM Adnry St Helens 96–00; PtO from 01; NSM Farington Moss and Lostock Hall *Blackb* 03–06; PtO from 06. *52 Kingsway, Penwortham, Preston PR1 0ED* T: (01772) 748021 E: fandbkendall@hotmail.com

KENDALL, Giles. b 57. Lon Univ BA 80 Univ Coll Lon BSc 86 Lon Univ PhD 90. STETS BTh 98. **d** 98 **p** 99. C Wareham *Sarum* 98–01; V Sawston *Ely* 01–08; P-in-c Babraham 01–08; P-in-c Kingswinford St Mary *Worc* 08–17; R from 17. *15 Penzer Street, Kingswinford DY6 7AA* E: revg.kingswinford@virginmedia.com

KENDALL, Gordon Sydney. b 41. **d** 72 **p** 74. NSM Old Ford St Paul w St Steph and St Mark *Lon* 72–82; NSM Homerton St Luke 86–92; Asst Chapl Hackney and Homerton Hosp Lon 87–92; Chapl S Devon Healthcare NHS Trust 92–06; rtd 06. *Shiloh, Beech Trees Lane, Ipplepen, Newton Abbot TQ12 5TW* T: (01803) 814054 E: kendallg@uwclub.net

KENDALL, Miss Jacqueline Ann. b 63. Univ of Wales (Abth) BA 85. Cranmer Hall Dur 88. **d** 91 **p** 94. Par Dn Stockport St Sav *Ches* 91–94; C 94–95; C Acton and Worleston, Church Minshull etc 95–96; C Alvanley and Helsby and Dunham-

on-the-Hill 96–97; C Timperley 97–01 and 07–10; P-in-c Dodleston 01–07; rtd 10. *Address withheld by request*

KENDRA, Neil Stuart. b 46. Leeds Univ BA 67 Bradf Univ MSc 80 PhD 84. Linc Th Coll 67. **d** 69 **p** 70. C Allerton *Liv* 69–72; Ldr Leeds City Cen Detached Youth Work Project 73–75; Dioc Youth Officer *Ripon* 75–77; Lect Ilkley Coll 77–78; Sen Lect Bradf and Ilkley Community Coll 78–88; Hd Community and Youth Studies St Martin's Coll 88–94; Hd Applied Soc Sciences 94–06; Hd Sch Soc Sciences and Business Studies 01–06; P-in-c Settle *Bradf* 06–11; P-in-c Giggleswick and Rathmell w Wigglesworth 08–11; rtd 11; PtO *Bradf* 11–14; Leeds from 14. *Cravendale, Belle Hill, Giggleswick, Settle BD24 0BA* T: (01729) 825307 E: neil.kendra@totalise.co.uk

KENDREW, Geoffrey David. b 42. K Coll Lon BD 66 AKC 66. **d** 67 **p** 68. C Bourne *Guildf* 67–70; C Haslemere 70–76; V Derby St Barn 76–95; R Deal St Leon w St Rich and Sholden etc *Cant* 95–07; Chapl E Kent NHS and Soc Care Partnership Trust 00–06; Chapl Kent & Medway NHS and Soc Care Partnership Trust 06–07; rtd 07; PtO *Linc* 15–18. *2 Mill Lane, Butterwick, Boston PE22 0JE* T: (01205) 760977 E: david-kendrew@supanet.com

KENDRICK, Dale Evans. b 62. Ch Ch Coll Cant BA 86 Nottm Univ MA 87 Leeds Univ MA 95 Birm Univ PhD 13. Coll of Resurr Mirfield 94. **d** 95 **p** 96. C Tividale *Lich* 95–96; C Blakenall Heath 96–97; C Stafford 97–98; Dep Chapl HM Pris Birm 98–01; Chapl HM Pris Drake Hall 01–03; Chapl RAF 03–04; Chapl HM YOI Werrington Ho 04–08; Chapl HM Pris Lewes 08–17. *Roskhill House, Roskhill, Dunvegan, Isle of Skye IV55 8ZD*

KENDRICK, Mrs Helen Grace. b 66. Bris Univ BA 88. SAOMC 96. **d** 99 **p** 00. C Icknield *Ox* 99–03; P-in-c Sutton Courtenay w Appleford 03–17; R DAMASCUS from 17; AD Abingdon from 17. *The Vicarage, 3 Tullis Close, Sutton Courtenay, Abingdon OX14 4BD* T: (01235) 848297 E: rector@damascusparish.org.uk

KENNAR, Canon Thomas Philip. b 66. Surrey Univ BA 08. STETS 02. **d** 05 **p** 06. C Warblington w Emsworth *Portsm* 05–08; Chapl Portsm Coll 06–08; TR Portsea N End St Mark *Portsm* 08–15; P-in-c Havant from 15; Hon Can Cape Coast Ghana from 11; Hon Can Ho from 13; Hon Can Portsm Cathl from 18. *St Faith's Rectory, 5 Meadowlands, Havant PO9 2RP* T: (023) 9307 1946 M: 07881-025592 E: tomkennar@gmail.com

KENNARD, Mark Philip Donald. b 60. Man Univ BSc 82 Cardiff Univ MTh 08. Cranmer Hall Dur 85. **d** 88 **p** 89. C Newark w Hawton, Cotham and Shelton *S'well* 88–89; C Newark 89–91; C Cropwell Bishop w Colston Bassett, Granby etc 91–93; P-in-c Shireoaks 93–99; Chapl Bassetlaw Hosp and Community Services NHS Trust 93–96; Chapl RAF 99–16; PtO *Linc* 17–18; P-in-c Digby Gp from 18. *2 Thomas à Becket Close, Digby, Lincoln LN4 3GA* E: digbyrectory@outlook.com

KENNEDY, Alan. b 52. Liv Univ BSc 95. NOC 01. **d** 03 **p** 04. C Westbrook St Phil *Liv* 03–07; TV Mossley Hill 07–16; TR from 16. *The Vicarage, Rose Lane, Liverpool L18 8DB* T: 0151-724 1915

KENNEDY, Canon Alison Mary. b 66. K Coll Lon BMus 87 Heythrop Coll Lon MA 95 LTCL 90. NTMTC 96. **d** 99 **p** 00. C De Beauvoir Town St Pet *Lon* 99–02; TV Walthamstow *Chelmsf* 02–07; TV N Lambeth *S'wark* 07–18; Can Res Chelmsf Cathl from 18; Tutor St Mellitus Coll from 18. *1A Harlings Grove, Chelmsford CM1 1YQ* T: (01245) 491599 E: alison_m_kennedy@hotmail.com

KENNEDY, Ms Caroline Jane. b 62. St Andr Univ MA 85 York Univ PGCE 86. LCTP 11. **d** 14 **p** 15. NSM Harraby *Carl* 14–15; NSM Aspatria w Hayton and Gilcrux from 15; Chapl Trin Sch Carl from 15; Chapl Cumbria Univ *Carl* from 19. *4 The Courtyard, Broadwath, Heads Nook, Brampton CA8 9BL* T: (01228) 561885 M: 07506-563393

KENNEDY, Carolyn Ruth. b 59. Univ of Wales (Ban) BA 81 GradCertEd(FE) 85. Ripon Coll Cuddesdon BA 90. **d** 91 **p** 94. C Frodingham *Linc* 91–95; Chapl Cov Univ 95–00; R Uffington Gp *Linc* 00–18; rtd 18. *21 Plantagenet Way, Gillingham SP8 4TD* T: (01747) 835981 E: ccd@crk.me.uk

KENNEDY, Christopher John. b 82. Brunel Univ BSc 10. St Mellitus Coll BA 17. **d** 17 **p** 18. C Hanworth St Rich *Lon* from 17. *35 Oxford Way, Feltham TW13 6RY* M: 07941-435622 E: kennes777@yahoo.co.uk

KENNEDY, David George. b 46. Hull Univ BEd 71 MA 76. Linc Th Coll 77. **d** 79 **p** 80. C Linc St Faith and St Martin w St Pet 79–82; V Bilton St Pet *York* 82–90; V New Seaham *Dur* 90–92; Chapl Lincs and Humberside Univ 92–97; P-in-c Barrow St Matt *Carl* 97–99; TR 99–03; Chapl Furness Coll 97–03; P-in-c Blackb St Aid 03–04; V Blackb St Fran and St Aid 04–06; Chapl Nord Pas de Calais *Eur* 06–08; P-in-c Bierley *Bradf* 08–12; V 12–14; Leeds 14–15; PtO *Blackb* from 15. *53 Parklands Way, Blackburn BB2 4QS* T: (01254) 600515

KENNEDY, Canon David John. b 57. St Jo Coll Dur BA 78 Nottm Univ MTh 81 Birm Univ PhD 96. St Jo Coll Nottm 79. d 81 p 82. C Tudhoe Grange *Dur* 81–87; C Merrington 84–87; Tutor Qu Coll Birm 88–96; R Haughton le Skerne *Dur* 96–01; Can Res Dur Cathl 01–18; Chapl Grey Coll Dur 01–09; V Corbridge w Halton and Newton Hall *Newc* from 18. *The Vicarage, Greencroft Avenue, Corbridge NE45 5DW*

KENNEDY, Gary. b 63. Qu Coll Birm BA 02. d 03 p 04. C New Bury *Man* 03–06; C New Bury w Gt Lever 06; P-in-c Bolton SS Simon and Jude 06–11; TR Broughton 11–16; Chapl Pennine Acute Hosps NHS Trust from 16; PtO *Blackb* from 18. *Pennine Acute Hospitals NHS Trust, Fairfield General Hospital, Rochdale Old Road, Bury BL9 7TD* T: 0161-624 0420 E: therev.wolf@gmail.com

KENNEDY, Ian Duncan. b 53. d 04 p 05. OLM Whitnash *Cov* 04–07; NSM Leek Wootton 07–08; P-in-c Fillongley and Corley 08–15; V 15–18; rtd 18; PtO *Cov* from 18. *27 Primrose Drive, Bedworth CV12 0GL* E: reviankennedy@aol.com

KENNEDY, Mrs Jane Rowston. b 47. Dudley Coll of Educn CertEd 70 Leic Univ DipEd 93. EMMTC 04. d 07 p 08. NSM Avon-Swift *Leic* 04–17; rtd 17; PtO *Leic* from 17. *11 Cromwell Close, Walcote, Lutterworth LE17 4JJ* T: (01455) 554065

KENNEDY, Jason Grant. b 68. Oak Hill Th Coll BA 95. d 98 p 99. C Beccles St Mich *St E* 98–01; R Hollington St Leon *Chich* 01–05; C Tonbridge St Steph *Roch* 05–10; V Ripley *Derby* 10–14; Ch Growth Officer Derby Adnry from 14. *Church House, Full Street, Derby DE1 3DR* T: (01332) 388691 E: jason.kennedy@derby.anglican.org

KENNEDY, John Frederick. b 42. Birm Univ BSc 64 PhD 67 DSc 73 BA 12. Qu Coll Birm 05. d 06 p 07. NSM Edgbaston St Geo *Birm* 06–10; PtO from 11; *Heref* from 11; *Worc* from 15. *Kyrewood House, Kyrewood, Tenbury Wells WR15 8FF* M: 07801-624749

KENNEDY, Joseph. b 69. Edin Univ BSc 91 BD 94 Moray Ho Coll of Educn PGCE 97 St Hugh's Coll Ox MSt 00 Keble Coll Ox DPhil 06. St Steph Ho Ox 98. d 02 p 03. C Stratfield Mortimer and Mortimer W End etc *Ox* 02–03; C Abingdon 03–05; Dean of Chpl, Chapl and Fell Selw Coll Cam 05–08; Chapl Newnham Coll Cam 05–08; Prin Coll of Resurr Mirfield 08–11; Hon Can Wakef Cathl 10–11; V Oxton *Ches* from 11. *The Vicarage, 7 Willow Lea, Prenton CH43 2GQ* T: 0151-652 2402 E: revd.j.kennedy@gmail.com

KENNEDY, Michael Charles. b 39. TCD BA 79 BD 79 Open Univ PhD 87. TCD Div Sch 61. d 63 p 64. C Drumglass *Arm* 63–66; I Lisnadill w Kildarton 66–14; Warden Dioc Guild of Lay Readers from 74; Hon V Choral Arm Cathl 75–14; Tutor for Aux Min (Arm) 82–14; Preb Yagoe St Patr Cathl Dublin 92–14; rtd 14. *8 Vicar's Hill, Armagh BT61 7ED* T: (028) 3752 3630 E: michaelkennedy2@btinternet.com

KENNEDY, Paul Alan. b 67. ACA 92. St Steph Ho Ox BA 95. d 95 p 96. C Romford St Andr *Chelmsf* 95–98; C Cheam *S'wark* 98–01; V Steep and Froxfield w Privett *Portsm* 01–08; Bp's Adv on Healing 04–08; R E Win 08–17; AD Win 13–17; P-in-c Win St Cross w St Faith 15–17; P-in-c St Vedast w St Mich-le-Querne etc *Lon* from 17; P-in-c St Mary Aldermary from 17. *St Vedast's Rectory, 4 Foster Lane, London EC2V 6HH* T: (020) 7606 3998 M: 07877-211307 E: priest@vedast.org.uk *or* paul@moot.uk.net

KENNEDY, Paul Joseph Alan. b 57. Newc Univ MA 93. Sarum & Wells Th Coll 81. d 84 p 85. C Shildon w Eldon *Dur* 84–86; C Shotton w E Waterhouses *Dur* 88–93; V Denton *Newc* 93–95; CF 95–98; P-in-c Leam Lane *Dur* 98–99; V 99–05; P-in-c S Westoe 05–15; V 15–16; V Seaham and Dawdon from 16. *Seaham Harbour Vicarage, Maureen Terrace, Seaham SR7 7SN*

KENNEDY, Miss Penelope Ann Cheney. b 49. STETS 08. d 11 p 12. NSM Buckland Newton, Cerne Abbas, Godmanstone etc *Sarum* 11–13; NSM Charminster and Stinsford 13–17; NSM Charminster, Stinsford and the Chalk Stream villages from 17. *Church House, 4 Meadow Bottom, Stratton, Dorchester DT2 9WH* T: (01305) 251422 E: penekennedy@yahoo.co.uk

KENNEDY, Brother Philip Bartholomew. b 47. STETS 95. d 98 p 99. SSF from 77; C Plaistow and N Canning Town *Chelmsf* 08–16; PtO from 17. *Address temp unknown* E: philipbartholomewssf@gmail.com

KENNEDY, Philip Richard John. b 90. G&C Coll Cam BA 13 MA 17. St Steph Ho Ox BA 16. d 17 p 18. C Croydon St Mich w St Jas *S'wark* from 17; CMP from 19. *3 St Michael's Court, 5 Poplar Walk, Croydon CR0 1UA* T: (020) 3609 4184 E: fr.kennedy20@gmail.com

KENNEDY, Ross Kenneth. b 40. Edin Th Coll 83. d 85 p 86. C Hexham *Newc* 85–89; TV Glendale Gp 89–93; TR Ch the King 93–05; rtd 05. *12 Calaisburn Place, Dunfermline KY11 4RD* T: (01383) 625887 E: rk.kennedy@talktalk.net

KENNEDY, Samuel (Uell). b 51. Heriot-Watt Univ BSc 72. CBDTI 06. d 07 p 08. NSM Baildon *Bradf* 07–14; *Leeds* 14; Development Officer Min and Miss 02–18; PtO *Leeds* from 15. *The Moorings, Hunsingore, Wetherby LS22 5HY* T: (01423) 358993 E: uell_kennedy@yahoo.co.uk

KENNEDY, Canon Wendy Patricia. b 58. STETS 00. d 03 p 04. NSM Warren Park and Leigh Park *Portsm* 03–07; Dioc Sec 07–18; rtd 18; PtO *Portsm* 07–11 and from 18; Public Preacher 11–18; Interim Dir Discipleship, Voc and Min and Par Development and Evang *Guildf* from 18; Hon Can Portsm Cathl from 18. *13 Ashcroft Lane, Waterlooville PO8 0AX* T: (023) 9241 3190 E: wendy.kennedy234@gmail.com

KENNERLEY, Katherine Virginia (Ginnie). Somerville Coll Ox BA 58 MA 65 TCD BA 86 Princeton Th Sem DMin 98. CITC 86. d 88 p 90. Lect Applied Th CITC 88–93; NSM Bray *D & G* 88–93; I Narraghmore and Timolin w Castledermot etc 93–05; Can Ch Ch Cathl Dublin 96–05; rtd 05. *4 Seafield Terrace, Dalkey, Co Dublin, Republic of Ireland* T: (00353) (1) 275 0737 M: 87-647 5092 E: vkennerley@gmail.com

KENNETT, Mrs Jeanette Tracy. b 71. Kent Univ BA 94. St Aug Coll of Th 15. d 18 p 19. C Tenterden, Rother and Oxney *Cant* from 18. *14 Abbott Way, Tenterden TN30 7BZ* M: 07888-998874 E: caulkhead7@talktalk.net

KENNEY, Canon Peter. b 50. Edin Univ BD 75 Dur Univ MA 97 Essex Univ MA 05. Edin Th Coll 73. d 76 p 77. C Cullercoats St Geo *Newc* 76–81; TV Whorlton 81–88; TR Ch the King 88–93; P-in-c Newc St Jo 93–02; P-in-c Gosforth St Hugh 02–09; P-in-c Chapel House 09–12; Dioc Adv in Past Care and Counselling 02–12; Min Development Officer 12–18; Hon Can Newc Cathl 04–18; rtd 18; PtO *Newc* from 18. *17 North Farm Court, Throckley, Newcastle upon Tyne NE15 9DW* T: 0191-267 5989 M: 07890-628251 E: peter.kenney5@btinternet.com

KENNING, Canon Michael Stephen. b 47. St Chad's Coll Dur BA 68. Westcott Ho Cam 69. d 71 p 72. C Hythe *Cant* 71–75; TV Bow w Bromley St Leon *Lon* 75–77; C-in-c W Leigh CD *Portsm* 77–81; V Lee-on-the-Solent 81–92; R N Waltham and Steventon, Ashe and Deane *Win* 92–10; RD Whitchurch 03–08; Hon Can Win Cathl 09–10; rtd 10; PtO *Win* from 10. *20 Teal Crescent, Basingstoke RG22 5QX* T: (01256) 817989 E: michael.kenning@telorycoed.co.uk

KENNINGTON, The Very Revd John Paul. b 61. Collingwood Coll Dur BA 85. St Steph Ho Ox BA 87 MA 92. d 88 p 89. C Headington *Ox* 88–91; C Dulwich St Clem w St Pet *S'wark* 91–94; TV Mortlake w E Sheen 94–01; V Battersea St Mary 01–10; Dean Montreal Canada 11–16; NSM Leytonstone St Andr *Chelmsf* 16–18; P-in-c 18; V from 18. *St Andrew's Vicarage, 7 Forest Glade, London E11 1LU* T: (020) 8989 0942 E: jpaulkennington@gmail.com *or* priest.standrews.leytonstone@gmail.com

KENNY, Charles John. b 39. QUB BA 61 MEd 78 LGSM 74. CITC 69. d 69 p 70. C Belfast St Paul *Conn* 69–71; Hd of RE Grosvenor High Sch 71–94; V Choral Belf Cathl 94–00; Can Ellerker w Broomfleet 15–18; Chapl HM Pris Humber 18–19; TV Howden *York* from 19. *The Vicarage, 3 Thimblehall Lane, Newport, Brough HU15 2PX* T: (01430) 266394 M: 07545-471474 E: revd_lyn@yahoo.co.uk

KENNY, Mrs Lynda Ann. b 57. Sheff Univ BA 14 MA 17. Yorks Min Course 11. d 14 p 16. C N Ormesby *York* 14–15; C S Cave and Ellerker w Broomfleet 15–18; Chapl HM Pris Humber 18–19; TV Howden *York* from 19. *The Vicarage, 3 Thimblehall Lane, Newport, Brough HU15 2PX* T: (01430) 266394 M: 07545-471474 E: revd_lyn@yahoo.co.uk

KENRICK, Kenneth David Norman. b 44. RMN. Ripon Hall Ox 70 NW Ord Course 77. d 77 p 78. C Stockport St Geo *Ches* 77–83; R Stockport St Thos 83–85; R Stockport St Thos w St Pet 86–12; Chapl St Thos Hosp 88–12; Chapl Cheadle R Hosp 88–12; rtd 12; PtO *Ches* from 12. *88 Woodlands Drive, Stockport SK2 5AP* E: truefaith_@hotmail.com

KENSINGTON, Area Bishop of. *See* TOMLIN, The Rt Revd Graham Stuart

KENT, Alan Gilbert. b 56. Univ of Wales (Ban) BTh 09 Univ of Wales (Trin St Dav) MTh 15. d 14 p 15. NSM Cardigan w Mwnt and Y Ferwig w Llangoedmor *St D* 14–18; NSM Bro Teifi from 18. *44 Bro Teifi, Cardigan SA43 1DQ* T: (01239) 613907 E: albewaiting@googlemail.com

KENT, Barry James. b 41. d 02 p 03. OLM Kinson *Sarum* 02–07; NSM Hordle *Win* 07–12; rtd 12; PtO *Win* from 12. *6 Orchard Leigh, 2 Herbert Road, New Milton BH25 6BX* T: (01202) 611348 M: 07733-048534 E: barrykent@minister.com

KENT, Christopher Alfred. b 48. Birm Univ BSc 69 PhD 72 CEng 77 MIChemE 77. St Jo Coll Nottm 82. d 84 p 85. C Bucknall and Bagnall *Lich* 84–86; Hon C Halesowen *Worc* 86–96; NSM Reddal Hill St Luke 96–01; NSM The Lye and Stambermill from 01. *40 County Park Avenue, Halesowen B62 8SP* T: 0121-550 3132 E: c.a.kent@bham.ac.uk

KENT, Miss Cindy. b 45. SEITE 05. **d** 07 **p** 08. NSM Whetstone St Jo *Lon* 07–16; P-in-c 10–16; rtd 16; PtO *Cant* from 16. *170 Southsea Avenue, Minster on Sea, Sheerness ME12 2LU* T: (01795) 876469 M: 07879-642100 E: cindykent58@hotmail.com

KENT, David. b 44. CEng MIMechE. NOC. **d** 83 **p** 84. NSM Huddersfield St Pet and All SS *Wakef* 83–98; NSM Newsome and Armitage Bridge 98–03; NSM Em TM 03–14; Newsome and Armitage Bridge and S Crosland *Leeds* from 14. *2 Hillside Crescent, Huddersfield HD4 6LY* T: (01484) 324049 M: 07949-762186 E: david.kent3@ntlworld.com

KENT, Frank. b 44. Open Univ BA 82 ARCM 76. Ridley Hall Cam. **d** 86 **p** 87. C Faversham *Cant* 86–89; R Lyminge w Paddlesworth, Stanford w Postling etc 89–99; P-in-c Sittingbourne St Mich 99–00; V Sittingbourne St Mary and St Mich 01–04; R Eastry and Northbourne w Tilmanstone etc 04–07; rtd 07; PtO *Cant* from 14. *3 Balfour Road, Walmer, Deal CT14 7HU* T: (01304) 375080 *or* 619366 E: francikeut@tiscali.co.uk

KENT, Hugh. *See* KENT, Richard Hugh

KENT, Mrs Mary. b 51. Birm Univ BA 72. St Steph Ho Ox 06. **d** 08 **p** 09. NSM Alveston *Cov* 08–13; PtO 13–14; P-in-c Wexham *Ox* 14–18; rtd 18; PtO *Ox* from 18. *16 Ash Road, Princes Risborough HP27 0BQ* M: 07597-382594

KENT, Richard Hugh. b 38. Worc Coll Ox BA 61 MA 63. Chich Th Coll 61. **d** 63 **p** 64. C Emscote *Cov* 63–66; C Finham 66–70; V Parkend *Glouc* 70–75; V Glouc St Aldate 75–86; Chapl and Warden Harnhill Healing Cen 86–96; R N Buckingham *Ox* 96–04; AD Buckingham 00–04; rtd 04; PtO *Pet* from 05; *Ox* 06–12 and from 17. *10 Booth Close, Pattishall, Towcester NN12 8JP* T: (01327) 830231 E: hugh.hilary38@btinternet.com

KENTIGERN-FOX, Canon William Poyntere Kentigern. b 38. AKC 63. **d** 64 **p** 65. C S Mimms St Mary and Potters Bar *Lon* 64–67; C S Tottenham 67–70; R Barrowden and Wakerley *Pet* 70–76; P-in-c Duddington w Tixover 70–76; P-in-c Morcott w S Luffenham 75–76; R Barrowden and Wakerley w S Luffenham 77–79; R Byfield w Boddington 79–86; V Northampton St Mich w St Edm 86–95; V Raunds 95–03; Can Pet Cathl 94–03; RD Higham 97–02; rtd 03; PtO *Linc* from 17. *41 Parkfield Road, Ruskington, Sleaford NG34 9HT* T: (01526) 830944

KENT-WINSLEY, Cindy. *See* KENT, Cindy

KENWARD, Roger Nelson. b 34. Selw Coll Cam BA 58 MA 62. Ripon Hall Ox 58. **d** 60 **p** 61. C Paddington St Jas *Lon* 60–63; Chapl RAF 64–82; Asst Chapl-in-Chief RAF 82–89; P-in-c Lyneham w Bradenstoke *Sarum* 72–76; QHC 85–89; R Laughton w Ripe and Chalvington *Chich* 90–95; Chapl Laughton Lodge Hosp 90–95; rtd 95; NSM Chiddingly w E Hoathly *Chich* 96; PtO from 96. *The Coach House, School Hill, Old Heathfield, Heathfield TN21 9AE* T: (01435) 862618 E: kenwardroger@gmail.com

KENWAY, Ian Michael. b 52. Leeds Univ BA 74 Bris Univ PhD 86. Coll of Resurr Mirfield 74. **d** 76 **p** 77. C Cov E 76–79; C Southmead *Bris* 79–81; P-in-c Shaw Hill *Birm* 82–88; Asst Sec Gen Syn Bd for Soc Resp 88–93; Chapl Essex Univ *Chelmsf* 93–99; Dir Studies Cen for Study of Th 93–99; PtO *S & B* 01–19. *Katerina's House, Symi, 85600 Dodecanese, Greece* M: 07927-429237 E: iankenway@phidoc.net

KENWAY, Robert Andrew. b 56. Bris Univ BA 78. Westcott Ho Cam 80. **d** 82 **p** 83. C Birchfield *Birm* 82–85; C Queensbury All SS *Lon* 87–89; R Birm St Geo 89–97; V Calne and Blackland *Sarum* 97–10; TR Marden Vale from 10. *The Vicarage, 4 Vicarage Close, Calne SN11 8DD* T: (01249) 812340 E: rakenway@gmail.com

KENYON, Caroline Elizabeth. *See* HOLMES, Caroline Elizabeth

KENYON, Robert Fletcher. b 52. K Coll Lon BSc 73 PhD 80. SEITE 02. **d** 05 **p** 17. C Ashford *Cant* 05–06; PtO *S'wark* 15–16; NSM Brockham Green 16; NSM Leigh 16; NSM Brockham Green and Leigh 17–19; Faith in the Countryside Officer from 19. *156 Croydon Road, Reigate RH2 0NG* M: 07979-707529 E: robfleckenyon@gmail.com

KEOGH, Robert Gordon. b 56. CITC. **d** 84 **p** 85. C Mossley *Conn* 84–87; I Taunagh w Kilmactranny, Ballysumaghan etc *K, E & A* 87–90; I Swanlinbar w Tomregan, Kinawley, Drumlane etc 90–02; Preb Kilmore Cathl 95–02; I Drumclamph w Lower and Upper Langfield *D & R* from 02. *Drumclamph Rectory, 70 Greenville Road, Castlederg BT81 7NU* T: (028) 8167 1433 E: rkeogh10@hotmail.co.uk

KEOWN, Paul Gabriel. b 53. Univ of Wales (Swansea) BA 95 PGCE 97 LGSM 76. Ripon Coll Cuddesdon 00 St Steph Ho Ox BTh 06. **d** 02 **p** 03. C Llansamlet *S & B* 02–04; P-in-c Swansea St Nic 04–07; R Haddington *Edin* 07–08; V Salfords *S'wark* 08–12; P-in-c Beckenham St Mich w St Aug *Roch* 12–15; P-in-c Footscray w N Cray 15–16; Dioc Dir of Ords

15–16; P-in-c Erwood Gp w Painscastle Gp *S & B* from 16. *Trefechan, Aberedw, Builth Wells LD2 3UH* T: (01982) 560653 E: frpaulkeown@mac.com

KER, Robert Andrew. **d** 05 **p** 06. Aux Min Larne and Inver *Conn* 05–13; Dioc C 13–16; I Templepatrick w Donegore 16–18. *24 Ravensdale, Newtownabbey BT36 6FA* T: (028) 9083 6901 E: a.ker@btinternet.com

KERL, Ms Elizabeth. b 72. **d** 13 **p** 14. NSM Bassaleg *Mon* 13–18; TV Cwmbran from 18. *St Peter's Vicarage, 30 Longhouse Grove, Henllys, Cwmbran NP44 6HQ* T: (01633) 974973

KERLEY, Patrick Thomas Stewart. b 42. Linc Th Coll. **d** 85 **p** 86. Hon C Thorpe St Andr *Nor* 85–90; C Wymondham 90–94; C Gt Yarmouth 94–95; TV 95–00; TV Wilford Peninsula *St E* 00–07; rtd 07; PtO *Nor* from 08. *3 St Leonard's Close, Wymondham NR18 0JF* T: (01953) 606618 M: 07940-739769 E: patrick_kerley@sky.com

KERNEY, Barbara. *See* SHERLOCK, Barbara Lee Kerney

KERNOHAN, Jason William. b 79. TCD BTh 10. CITC 07. **d** 10 **p** 11. C Drumachose *D & R* 10–15; I Eglantine *Conn* from 15. *All Saints' Rectory, 16 Eglantine Road, Lisburn BT27 5RQ* T: (028) 9266 1406 E: jasonkernohan79@gmail.com

KERR, Mrs Alison. b 76. Ripon Coll Cuddesdon 06. **d** 09 **p** 10. C Lytchett Minster *Sarum* 09–10; C The Lytchetts and Upton 10–12; P-in-c Whippingham w E Cowes *Portsm* 12–17; P-in-c Newport St Jo 17–19; AD Is of Wight 17–19; V Portsea St Cuth from 19. *St Cuthbert's Vicarage, 2 Lichfield Road, Portsmouth PO3 6DE* T: (023) 9307 1792

KERR, Andrew Harry Mayne. b 41. TCD BA 63. Melbourne Coll of Div MMin 98. **d** 65 **p** 66. C Belfast St Luke *Conn* 65–68; SCM Sec (Ireland) 68–72; C Clooney *D & R* 72–74; C Swinburne Australia 74–80; I Dallas 80–88; I Mont Albert 88–94; P-in-c W Geelong from 96. *101 Katrina Street, Blackburn North Vic 3130, Australia* T: (0061) (3) 5221 6694 *or* (3) 9893 4946 F: 9893 4946 E: ahmker@hotmail.com

KERR, Mrs Anita Dawn Christina. b 63. SRN 81 SCM 86 PGCE 04. CITC 04. **d** 07 **p** 08. Aux Min Sligo w Knocknarea and Rosses Pt *K, E & A* 07–09; LtO *Clogh* 09–10; Chapl to Bp Clogh from 10; NSM Devenish w Boho 10–12; NSM Garrison w Slavin and Belleek 12–13; Dioc C Galloon w Drummully and Sallaghy 13–15; I from 15. *The Rectory, 23 Drumcru Road, Aghagay, Newtownbutler, Enniskillen BT92 8GP* T: (028) 6773 8245 E: st_kerr@btopenworld.com

KERR, Bryan Thomas. b 70. QUB BD 91 TCD MPhil 96. CITC 94. **d** 96 **p** 97. C Enniskillen *Clogh* 96–99; I Garrison w Slavin and Belleek 99–05; I Lisbellaw 05–14; Dioc Communications Officer 00–13; Can Clogh Cathl 12–14; Dean Dromore *D & D* 14–15; I Dromore Cathl 14–15; P-in-c Heversham and Milnthorpe *Carl* from 19; P-in-c Levens from 19. *The Vicarage, Vicarage Road, Levens, Kendal LA8 8PY* E: brykerr@sky.com

KERR, Charles. *See* KERR, Ewan Charles

KERR, David James. b 36. TCD BA 58 MA 61 BD 61 HDipEd 66. TCD Div Sch Div Test 59. **d** 60 **p** 61. C Belfast Trin Coll Miss *Conn* 60–63; Dean's V St Patr Cathl Dublin 63–66; Chapl Beechwood Park Sch St Alb 66–01; Hon C Flamstead *St Alb* 74–00; PtO 00–13; rtd 01. *Trumpton Cottage, 12A Packhorse Road, Markyate, St Albans AL3 8RU* T: (01582) 841191 E: kerr_david@hotmail.com *or* kerr-david66@hotmail.com

KERR, Canon Derek Preston. b 64. TCD BTh 90. Oak Hill Th Coll 85. **d** 90 **p** 91. C Belfast St Donard *D & D* 90–93; C Carrickfergus *Conn* 93–96; I Devenish w Boho *Clogh* 96–07; I Drummaul w Duneane and Ballyscullion *Conn* from 07; Preb Conn Cathl from 16. *The Vicarage, 1A Glenkeen, Randalstown, Antrim BT41 3JX* T: (028) 9447 2561 E: derekpkerr@gmail.com

KERR, Miss Dora Elizabeth. b 41. QUB BA 65 Southn Univ DipEd 66. St Jo Coll Nottm 82. **dss** 84 **d** 87 **p** 94. Becontree St Mary *Chelmsf* 84–88; Par Dn 87–88; Par Dn Rushden w Newton Bromswold *Pet* 88–93; C Finham and Chapl Walsgrave Hosps NHS Trust 94–00; C Belper *Derby* 00–07; rtd 07; PtO *Cov* from 08. *23 Worcester Close, Allesley, Coventry CV5 9FZ* T: (024) 7640 2413 E: elizabeth@ekerr1.plus.com

KERR, Ewan Charles. b 74. Fitzw Coll Cam BA 96 MA 00. Ripon Coll Cuddesdon MTh 01. **d** 02 **p** 02. C Nor St Pet Mancroft w St Jo Maddermarket 01–04; Chapl Glenalmond Coll *St And* 04–07; Chapl St Edw Sch Ox 07–18; LtO *Ox* from 18. *31 Stone Meadow, Oxford OX2 6TD* E: charlie.kerr@oxford.anglican.org

KERR, Canon Jean. b 46. Man Univ MA 93 SS Hild & Bede Coll Dur CertEd 69. NOC 84. **d** 87 **p** 94. NSM Peel *Man* 87–93; Par Dn Dixon Green 88–89; Par Dn New Bury 89–93; Par Dn Gillingham St Mark *Roch* 93–94; C 94–98; Chapl Medway Secure Tr Cen 98–01; Warden of Ev *Roch* 98–05; NSM Roch St Justus 01–05; Hon Can Roch Cathl 03–05; Can Missr 05–16; Tr Officer for Lay Minl Educn *Roch* 03–05; Bp's Officer for Miss and Unity 05–16; rtd 16; PtO *Cant* from 17;

Roch from 17. *30 Scholars Close, Deal CT14 9FA* T: (01304) 360546 M: 07791-503123 E: jeankerr146@yahoo.co.uk

KERR, Karlene Theresa Kamella. b 58. **d** 13 **p** 14. C Harefield *Lon* 13–14; C Wealdstone H Trin 14–16; PtO 16–18; C Gaywood *Nor* 17–18; TV from 18; Dioc Ecum Officer from 18. *28 Jermyn Road, King's Lynn PE30 4AE* T: (01553) 768264 M: 07989-467276 E: karlenekerr@aol.com *or* vicar@stfaithsgaywoodlep.org.uk

KERR, Canon Nicholas Ian. b 46. Em Coll Cam BA 68 MA 72. Westcott Ho Cam 74. **d** 77 **p** 78. C Merton St Mary *S'wark* 77–80; C Rainham *Roch* 80–84; Chapl Joyce Green Hosp Dartford 84–90; V Dartford St Edm *Roch* 84–90; V Lamorbey H Redeemer 90–11; RD Sidcup 98–03; Hon Can Roch Cathl 02–11; rtd 11; PtO *Roch* from 11. *11 Cobdown Grove, Rainham, Gillingham ME8 7PN* T: (01634) 389960 M: 07885-619595 E: mizeki@mac.com

KERR, Canon Paul Turner. b 47. Man Univ MA 92. Cranmer Hall Dur 68. **d** 71 **p** 72. C Kingston upon Hull St Martin *York* 71–72; C Linthorpe 72–76; C Cherry Hinton St Jo *Ely* 76–78; Chapl Addenbrooke's Hosp Cam 76–78; TV Rochdale *Man* 78–84; Chapl Birch Hill Hosp 78–84; V New Bury *Man* 84–87; TR 87–93; C Gillingham St Mark *Roch* 93–98; RD Gillingham 96–98; V Roch St Justus 98–11; RD Roch 02–11; CF (ACF) 99–03; Chapl Roch Cathl 11–16; Hon Can Roch Cathl 11–16; rtd 12; PtO *Cant* from 17; *Roch* from 17. *30 Scholars Close, Deal CT14 9FA* T: (01304) 360546 E: ptkerr@hotmail.co.uk

KERR, Canon Stephen Peter. b 46. TCD BA 68 Edin Univ BD 71 MPhil 80. **d** 71 **p** 72. C Belfast H Trin *Conn* 72–76; C Ballywillan 76–78; Lect Linc Th Coll 78–87; Dioc Officer for Adult Educn and Minl Tr *Worc* 87–99; P-in-c Ombersley w Doverdale 87–13; P-in-c Hartlebury 08–13; P-in-c Elmley Lovett w Hampton Lovett and Elmbridge etc 10–13; Bp's Th Adv 99–07; RD Droitwich 07–13; Hon Can Worc Cathl 93–13; rtd 13; PtO *Worc* from 13. *27 Witton Avenue, Droitwich WR9 8NX* T: (01905) 776423 E: stephen.kerr46@yahoo.co.uk

KERR, Terence Philip. b 54. QUB BD 97. CITC 97. **d** 99 **p** 00. C Antrim All SS *Conn* 99–01; I Drummaul w Duneane and Ballyscullion 01–07; I Belfast St Aid 07–12; rtd 13; P-in-c Maghera w Killelagh *D & R* 16–17; I from 17. *The Rectory, 20 Church Street, Maghera BT46 5EA* T: (028) 7964 2252 M: 07727-877830 E: terryrevkerr@talktalk.net

KERRIDGE, Benjamin. b 82. Clare Coll Cam BA 04. Coll of Resurr Mirfield 11. **d** 14 **p** 15. C Hornsey St Mary w St Geo *Lon* 14–17; V Hornsey H Innocents from 17. *99 Hillfield Avenue, London N8 7DG*

KERRY, Martin John. b 55. Ox Univ MA 78. St Jo Coll Nottm BA 81 MTh 83. **d** 82 **p** 83. C Everton St Geo *Liv* 82–85; LtO *S'well* 85–04; Chapl Asst Nottm City Hosp 85–89; Chapl 89–94; Hd Chapl Nottm City Hosp NHS Trust 94–04; Lead Chapl (NE) Caring for the Spirit NHS Project 04–07; Chapl Manager Sheff Teaching Hosps NHS Foundn Trust 07–18; rtd 18. *14 Avondale Road, Chesterfield S40 4TF* T: (01246) 202144 E: martinkerry101@gmail.com

KERSHAW, Johanna. b 81. Clare Coll Cam BA 12 St Andr Univ MA 04 Oriel Coll Ox MSt 05 DPhil 10. Westcott Ho Cam 10. **d** 13 **p** 14. C Todmorden w Cornholme and Walsden *Leeds* 13–17; C Wrenthorpe 17; C Outwood, Stanley and Wrenthorpe from 17. *St Anne's Vicarage, 121 Wrenthorpe Road, Wrenthorpe, Wakefield WF2 0JS* T: (01924) 373758 M: 07979-042694 E: johanna.kershaw@gmail.com

KERSHAW, Savile. b 37. Bernard Gilpin Soc Dur 60 Chich Th Coll 61. **d** 64 **p** 65. C Staincliffe *Wakef* 64–66; C Saltley *Birm* 66–68; C Birm St Aid Small Heath 68–72; PtO 88–02; rtd 02. *74 Longmore Road, Shirley, Solihull B90 3EE* T: 0121-744 3470

KERSLAKE, Marc Richard. b 67. SWMTC 14. **d** 17 **p** 18. C Whimple, Talaton, Clyst St Lawr and Clyst Hydon *Ex* from 17. *The Old Goods Yard, Station Road, Whimple, Exeter EX5 2QH* T: (01392) 462731 M: 07958-557068 E: marckerslake@hotmail.co.uk

KERSLEY, Stuart Casburn. b 40. CEng MIET. Trin Coll Bris. **d** 82 **p** 83. C Lancing w Coombes *Chich* 82–87; TV Littlehampton and Wick 87–90; R Kingston Buci 90–98; V Kirdford 98–06; rtd 06; Hon C Appleshaw, Kimpton, Thruxton, Fyfield etc *Win* 06–12; PtO *Chich* 12–17. *7 Hormare Crescent, Storrington, Pulborough RH20 4PW*

KERSWILL, Canon Anthony John. b 39. Lambeth STh 85. Linc Th Coll 72. **d** 73 **p** 73. C Boultham *Linc* 73–76; P-in-c N Kelsey and Cadney 76–83; V Gainsborough St Geo 83–91; V Bracebridge 91–00; P-in-c Linc St Swithin 00–01; V Linc All SS 01–05; RD Christianity 96–02; Can and Preb Linc Cathl 02–05; rtd 05; Chapl Trin Hosp Retford 05–12; PtO *S'well* from 12. *Tenterflat Cottage, Tenterflat Walk, Retford DN22 7PZ* T: (01777) 862533 E: kerswill@btinternet.com

KERSYS-HULL, Mrs Polly Ruth. b 91. Cant Ch Ch Univ BA 13. St Mellitus Coll MA 17. **d** 17 **p** 18. C Leytonstone St Jo *Chelmsf* from 17. *34 Leyspring Road, London E11 3BX* M: 07510-053841 E: polly@kersys-hull.co.uk

KERTON-JOHNSON, Peter. b 41. St Paul's Coll Grahamstown. **d** 81 **p** 82. S Africa 81–99; PtO *Sarum* 99–00; P-in-c Stoke sub Hamdon *B & W* 00–11; Chapl St Marg Hospice Yeovil 07–08; rtd 11. *50 Brutton Way, Chard TA20 2HB* T: (01460) 419761 M: 07932-753872 E: kertonjohnson@sky.com

KESLAKE, Peter Ralegh. b 33. Sarum & Wells Th Coll. **d** 83 **p** 84. C Glouc St Geo w Whaddon 83–86; P-in-c France Lynch 86–91; V Chalford and France Lynch 91–03; rtd 03; PtO *Glouc* from 04. *4 Farmcote Close, Eastcombe, Stroud GL6 7EG* E: qml@live.co.uk

KESTER, Jonathan George Frederick. b 66. Ex Univ BA 90 FRSA 14. Coll of Resurr Mirfield 91. **d** 93 **p** 94. C Cheshunt *St Alb* 93–96; Chapl to Bp Edmonton *Lon* 96–00; Hon C Munster Square Ch Ch and St Mary Magd 96–00; V Gt Ilford St Mary *Chelmsf* 00–08; P-in-c Hampstead Em W End *Lon* 08–13; V from 13; P-in-c W Hampstead St Cuth from 16; Asst Dir of Ords 09–17; CMP 00–14; AD N Camden *Lon* from 16; AD S Camden from 18. *Emmanuel Vicarage, Lyncroft Gardens, London NW6 1JU* T: (020) 7435 1911 E: frjonathan@mac.com

KESTERTON, David William. b 59. Man Univ BSc 80. Cranmer Hall Dur 85. **d** 88 **p** 89. C Cheddleton *Lich* 88–92; TV Dunstable *St Alb* 92–97; Chapl Dunstable Coll 92–97; PtO *St Alb* 12–13; C Luton All SS w St Pet 13–14; V from 14; AD Luton from 19. *All Saints' Vicarage, Shaftesbury Road, Luton LU4 8AH* T: (01582) 526662 M: 07957-228102 E: dkesterton01@gmail.com

KESTEVEN, Elizabeth Anne. b 79. Newc Univ LLB 01. St Steph Ho Ox 05. **d** 08 **p** 09. C Bris St Steph w St Jas and St Jo w St Mich etc 08–12; C Bedminster 12–13; C Whitchurch 12–13; P-in-c Fishponds All SS 13–19; P-in-c Fishponds St Mary 13–19; V Fishponds All SS and St Mary from 19. *11 Vicar's Close, Bristol BS16 3TH* T: 0117-965 7740 M: 07973-917720 E: lizzie.kesteven@live.co.uk

KESTON, Marion. b 44. Glas Univ MB, ChB 68 Edin Univ MTh 95. St And Dioc Tr Course 87 Edin Th Coll 92. **d** 90 **p** 94. NSM W Fife Team Min *St And* 90–93; C Dunfermline 93–96; Priest Livingston LEP *Edin* 96–04; P-in-c Kinross *St And* 04–11; rtd 11; LtO *St And* 11–18; LtO *Mor* from 18. *60 Manse Road, Nairn IV12 4RS* T: (01667) 456587 E: marionkeston2@gmail.com

KETLEY, Christopher Glen. b 62. Aston Tr Scheme 91 Coll of Resurr Mirfield 93. **d** 95 **p** 96. C Gt Crosby St Faith *Liv* 95–98; C Swinton and Pendlebury *Man* 98–00; V Belfield 00–08; R Elgin w Lossiemouth *Mor* 08–18; R Dufftown 08–12; R Aberlour 08–12; Syn Clerk 14–18; R Castle Douglas *Glas* from 18; R Dalbeattie from 18. *Address temp unknown* M: 07932-183069

KETLEY, Michael James. b 39. Oak Hill Th Coll 79. **d** 81 **p** 82. C Bedhampton *Portsm* 81–85; R St Ive w Quethiock *Truro* 85–86; NSM Basildon St Andr w H Cross *Chelmsf* 89–90; C Barkingside St Cedd 90–92; P-in-c 92–95; R Hadleigh St Jas 95–08; rtd 08; PtO *Chelmsf* from 08. *40 Commonhall Lane, Hadleigh, Benfleet SS7 2RN* T: (01702) 428971 E: mikeketley@aol.com

KETTLE, Alan Marshall. b 51. Leeds Univ BA 72. Wycliffe Hall Ox MA 78. **d** 78 **p** 79. C Llantwit Fardre *Llan* 78–81; Prov RE Adv Ch in Wales 81–84; Chapl Llandovery Coll 84–92; P-in-c Cil-y-Cwm and Ystrad-ffin w Rhandir-mwyn etc *St D* 85–92; Chapl W Buckland Sch Barnstaple 92–11; rtd 11; PtO *Llan* 11–12; P-in-c Castleton, Llandow and Llysworney from 12; PtO *St D* from 15. *Moat Farm, Llysworney, Cowbridge CF71 7NQ* T: (01446) 679186 E: kettlesatmoat@hotmail.co.uk

KETTLE, Martin Drew. b 52. New Coll Ox BA 74 Selw Coll Cam BA 76 Cam Univ MA 85. Ridley Hall Cam 74. **d** 77 **p** 78. C Enfield St Andr *Lon* 77–80; Chapl Ridley Hall Cam 80–84; V Hendon St Paul Mill Hill *Lon* 85–98; AD W Barnet 90–95; PtO *Ely* 03–04; Hon C Huntingdon 04–06; Hon C E Leightonstone 06–10; Hon C Hamerton, Winwick and Gt w Lt Gidding and Steeple Gidding 09–10; PtO *Ox* 11–19. *Apple Tree House, 97 New Road, Bampton OX18 2NP* T: (01993) 852454 E: mdkettle@msn.com

KETTLE, Mrs Patricia Mary Carole. b 41. Worc Coll of Educn CertEd 61. Dalton Ho Bris 66. **d** 87 **p** 94. C Wonersh *Guildf* 87–98; C Wonersh w Blackheath 98–01; rtd 01; PtO *Guildf* from 02; Dioc Widow/Widowers' Officer from 13. *Wakehurst Cottage, Links Road, Bramley GU5 0AL* T: (01483) 898856 E: patsykettle@talktalk.net

KETTLE, Peter. b 51. K Coll Lon BD 74 AKC 74. St Aug Coll Cant 74. **d** 75 **p** 76. C Angell Town St Jo *S'wark* 75–78; C Putney St Mary 78–80; V Raynes Park St Sav 80–85; PtO from

85; *Lon* 03–13; NSM S Kensington H Trin w All SS from 13. *46 Allenswood, Albert Drive, London SW19 6JX* T: (020) 8785 3797 E: peter@levelsix.plus.com

KEULEMANS, Andrew Francis Charles. b 68. Univ of Wales (Abth) BSc 90. St Jo Coll Nottm BTh 93. d 94 p 95. C Mold *St As* 94–97; TV Wrexham 97–02; Chapl Loretto Sch Musselburgh 02–10; R Musselburgh and Prestonpans *Edin* 10–15; PtO 15–17; Chapl Shrewsbury Sch from 17. *Shrewsbury School, Kingsland, Shrewsbury SY3 7BA* T: (01743) 280500 E: andrewkeulemans@btinternet.com *or* ak@shrewsbury.org.uk

KEULEMANS, Michael Desmond. b 42. SS Mark & Jo Univ Coll Plymouth TCert 65 Univ of Wales (Ban) MTh 06 DMin 10. St As Minl Tr Course 02. d 92 p 93. PtO *St As* 03–11; Hon C Llanfyllin, Bwlchycibau and Llanwddyn 11–13; PtO *Lich* 13–15; *Blackb* 16–18. *4 Wakefield Crescent, Standish, Wigan WN6 0AU* T: (01257) 425320 E: mdkeulemans43@gmail.com

KEVILL-DAVIES, Christopher Charles. b 44. AKC 69. St Aug Coll Cant 70. d 70 p 71. C Folkestone St Sav *Cant* 70–75; V Yaxley *Ely* 75–78; R Chevington w Hargrave and Whepstead w Brockley *St E* 78–86; PtO *St Alb* 86–89; NSM Stansted Mountfitchet *Chelmsf* 87–89; R Barkway, Reed and Buckland w Barley *St Alb* 89–97; R Chelsea St Luke and Ch Ch *Lon* 97–05; rtd 06; PtO *S'wark* from 06; Hon Min Can S'wark Cathl from 06; PtO *Lon* from 19. *York House, 35 Clapham Common South Side, London SW4 9BS* T: (020) 7622 9647 E: christopherkd@hotmail.com

KEVIN, Brother. *See* GOODMAN, Kevin Charles

KEVIS, Lionel William Graham. b 55. York Univ BA. Wycliffe Hall Ox 83. d 86 p 87. C Plaistow St Mary *Roch* 86–90; R Ash 90–00; R Ridley 90–00; P-in-c Bidborough 00–02; P-in-c Leigh 00–09; V from 09; RD Tonbridge 03–10. *The Vicarage, The Green, Leigh, Tonbridge TN11 8QJ* T: (01732) 833022

KEW, Canon William Richard. b 45. Lon Univ BD 69. ALCD 68. d 69 p 70. C Finchley St Paul Long Lane *Lon* 69–72; C Stoke Bishop *Bris* 72–76; C Hamilton and Wenham USA 76–79; R Rochester All SS 79–85; Exec Dir SPCK 85–95; Co-ord Russian Min Network 95–00; Convenor US Angl Congregation 00–02; V Franklin Apostles 02–06; R Franklin Resurr 06–07; Development Dir Ridley Hall Cam 07–15; rtd 15; PtO *Ely* 12–16; Hon Can Missr Owerri from 12. *2272 Lewisburg Pike, Franklin TN 37064, USA* E: richardkew@aol.com

KEY, Christopher Halstead. b 56. St Jo Coll Dur BA 77 K Coll Lon MTh 78. Ridley Hall Cam 79. d 81 p 82. C Balderstone *Man* 81–84; C Wandsworth All SS *S'wark* 84–88; C-in-c W Dulwich Em CD 88–93; V W Dulwich Em 93–95; R Ore St Helen and St Barn *Chich* 95–13; RD Hastings 03–13; V Maidstone St Luke *Cant* from 13. *St Luke's Vicarage, 24 Park Avenue, Maidstone ME14 5HN* T: (01622) 762995 E: revchriskey@gmail.com

KEY, Roderick Charles Halstead. b 57. MTh. d 84 p 85. C Up Hatherley *Glouc* 84–87; V Glouc St Paul 87–04; TR Trunch *Nor* 04–14; V Chippenham St Andr w Tytherton Lucas *Bris* from 14. *St Andrew's Vicarage, 54A St Mary Street, Chippenham SN15 3JW* T: (01249) 652788

KEY, Roger Astley. b 49. Coll of Resurr Mirfield 72. d 74 p 75. PtO *Wakef* 74–75; P-in-c Khomasdal Grace Ch Namibia 75–77; R Luderitz 77–81; Adn The South 80–86; R Walvis Bay 81–85; Personal Asst to Bp Windhoek 85–86; Dean Windhoek 86–00; V Hopton w Corton *Nor* 00–19; rtd 19; PtO *Nor* from 19. *The Fairstead, 1 Back Street, Horsham St Faith, Norwich NR10 3JP* M: 07733-028048 E: thekeybunch@aol.com

KEYES, Graham George. b 44. St Cath Coll Cam BA 65 MA 68 Lanc Univ MA 74 Nottm Univ MTh 85 MPhil 92. EMMTC 82. d 84 p 85. C Evington *Leic* 84–86; Vice-Prin NEOC 86–89; C Monkseaton St Mary *Newc* 86–89; P-in-c Newc St Hilda 89–94; TV Ch the King 94–99; rtd 99; PtO *Newc* from 09. *1 East Avenue, Newcastle upon Tyne NE12 9PH* T: 0191-259 9024 E: graham.keyes@btinternet.com

KEYT, Fitzroy John. b 34. Linc Th Coll. d 67 p 68. C Highters Heath *Birm* 67–70; Hon C Sheldon 70–73; V Miles Australia 73–76; R Rayton 76–84; R Coolangatta 86–98; P-in-c Clayfield 98–01. *58 Thompson Street, Zillmere QLD 4034, Australia* T: (0061) (7) 3314 3011 E: dskeyt@optusnet.com.au

KEYTE, Mrs Christine Evi. b 73. UNISA BA 98. Westcott Ho Cam 13. d 14 p 15. C Rustington *Chich* 14–17; V Crawley Down All SS from 17. *The Vicarage, Vicarage Road, Crawley Down, Crawley RH10 4JJ* T: (01342) 718741 E: vicar@allsaintscrawleydown.org

KHAKHRIA, Rohitkumar Prabhulal (Roy). b 60. Sheff Univ BSc 82 PGCE 83. Oak Hill Th Coll 94. d 96 p 97. C Muswell Hill St Jas w St Matt *Lon* 96–01; C Stoughton *Guildf* 01–04; V Boscombe St Jo *Win* from 04. *St John's Vicarage, 17 Browning*

Avenue, Bournemouth BH5 1NR T: (01202) 396667 *or* 301916 F: 301916 E: roykhakhria@me.com

KHAMBATTA, Neville Holbery. b 48. St Chad's Coll Dur BA 74. S'wark Ord Course 81. d 84 p 85. Asst Chapl Em Sch Wandsworth 84–87; Hon C Thornton Heath St Jude w St Aid *S'wark* 84–87; Asst Warden Horstead Cen 87–01; Hon C Coltishall w Gt Hautbois and Horstead *Nor* 87–01; V Ludham, Potter Heigham, Hickling and Catfield 01–11; rtd 11; PtO *Nor* from 11. *The Spinney, Butchers Common, Neatishead, Norwich NR12 8XH* T: (01692) 630231 E: nevilleandval@gmail.com

KHAN, Rana Youab. b 71. St Thos Th Coll Karachi MDiv 99. d 99 p 01. C Lahore St Andr Pakistan 99–01; V Lahore St Paul 01–03; V Lahore St Jo 03–09; Pris Chapl and Bp's Interfaith Adv 04–09; Internat Inter-Faith Dialogues Asst ACC 09–13; NSM Belmont *Lon* 13–15; C Mill Hill Jo Keble Ch 16–17; V Crickhowell w Cwmdu and Tretower *S & B* from 17. *The Rectory, Rectory Road, Crickhowell NP8 1DW* T: (01873) 810944 M: 07729-805100 E: revrana@hotmail.com *or* rector@crickhowellparish.org.uk

KHARITONOVA, Natalia. *See* CRITCHLOW, Natalia

KHOVACS, Ivan Patricio. b 68. d 14 p 15. NSM Willesborough w Sevington *Cant* 14–15; NSM Westmr St Jas *Lon* from 15. *3 St Peter's House, 119 Eaton Square, London SW1W 9AL* M: 07540-418621 E: ivankhovacs@gmail.com

KHOVACS, Mrs Julie Marie. b 67. Regent Coll Vancouver MA 00 Leeds Univ MA 05. Westcott Ho Cam 09. d 11 p 12. C Ashford *Cant* 11–15; C Pimlico St Pet w Westmr Ch Ch *Lon* from 15. *3 St Peter's House, 119 Eaton Square, London SW1W 9AL* M: 07540-418623 E: revjuliekho@gmail.com *or* julie.khovacs@stpeteraetonsquare.co.uk

KICHENSIDE, David Alexander. b 78. St Jo Coll Nottm BA 10. d 10 p 11. C Lilleshall and Muxton *Lich* 10–14; TV S Chatham H Trin *Roch* from 14. *26 Mayford Road, Chatham ME5 8SZ* E: david.kichenside@gmail.com

KICHENSIDE, Mark Gregory. b 53. Nottm Univ BTh 83. St Jo Coll Nottm 80. d 83 p 84. C Orpington Ch Ch *Roch* 83–86; C Bexley St Jo 86–90; V Blendon 90–93; V Welling 93–00; R Flegg Coastal Benefice *Nor* 00–05; RD Gt Yarmouth 02–05; TV Walton and Trimley *St E* 10–17; V Felixstowe Ch Ch 17–18; rtd 18. *36 Coombe Meadows, Chillington, Kingsbridge TQ7 2JL* M: 07933-997480 E: mgkichenside@gmail.com

KIDD, Anthony John Eric. b 38. Solicitor. Oak Hill NSM Course. d 89 p 90. NSM Rawdon *Bradf* 89–91; C Ilkley All SS 91–93; PtO 93–95; *York* 95–96; Hon C Gt and Lt Driffield 96–98; PtO 98–04; P-in-c The Beacon 04–08; PtO from 08; *Chich* from 08; *Bradf* 12–14; *Leeds* from 14. *23 Sitwell Grove, York YO26 5JG* T: (01904) 849488 M: 07795-109090 E: tony.kidd546@gmail.com

KIDD, Maurice Edward. b 26. d 55 p 56. C Wembley St Jo 54–58; C Middleton *Man* 58–61; Chapl Pastures Hosp Derby 61–69; Chapl Guild of Health Lon 69–72; R Hanworth St Geo *Lon* 72–82; R Chartham *Cant* 82–91; rtd 91; PtO *Cant* 91–13; *Lon* 96–97. *2 Sextries Farmhouse, Church Lane, Nackington, Canterbury CT4 7AF* T: 07730-360252 E: ck10072@gmail.com

KIDD, Mrs Ruth. b 62. Southn Univ BSc 83 Westmr Coll of Educn PGCE 84. d 12 p 13. OLM Lightwater *Guildf* from 12. *11 Aplin Way, Lightwater GU18 5TY* T: (01276) 471193 M: 07738-263057 E: ruth.kidd@btinternet.com

KIDDLE, The Ven John. b 58. Qu Coll Cam BA 80 MA 83 Heythrop Coll Lon MTh 02. Ridley Hall Cam 79. d 82 p 83. C Ormskirk *Liv* 82–86; V Huyton Quarry 86–91; V Watford St Luke *St Alb* 91–08; RD Watford 99–04; Officer for Miss and Development 08–15; Hon Can St Alb 05–10; Can Res St Alb 10–15; Dir Miss 11–15; Adn Wandsworth *S'wark* from 15. *Kingston Episcopal Area Office, 620 Kingston Road, London SW20 8DN* T: (020) 8545 2440 E: john.kiddle@southwark.anglican.org

KIDDLE, Mark Brydges. b 34. ACP 61. Wycliffe Hall Ox. d 63 p 64. C Scarborough St Luke *York* 63–66; C Walthamstow St Sav *Chelmsf* 66–71; V Nelson St Bede *Blackb* 71–76; V Perry Common *Birm* 76–79; R Grayingham *Linc* 79–84; V Kirton in Lindsey 79–84; R Manton 79–84; Hon C St Botolph Aldgate w H Trin Minories *Lon* 85–91; Hon C St Clem Eastcheap w St Martin Orgar 91–08. *12 Tudor Rose Court, 35 Fann Street, London EC2Y 8DY* E: mk@fpsi.org

KIDDLE, Martin John. b 42. Open Univ BA 80. St Jo Coll Nottm 74. d 76 p 77. C Gt Parndon *Chelmsf* 76–80; Asst Chapl HM Pris Wakef 80–81; Asst Chapl HM Youth Cust Cen Portland 81–88; Chapl HM Pris Cardiff 88–97; Chapl HM Pris Channings Wood 97–02; rtd 02; PtO *Ex* 02–09. *2 Cricketfield Close, Chudleigh, Newton Abbot TQ13 0GA* T: (01626) 853980 E: mkiddle@talktalk.net

KIDDLE, Miss Susan Elizabeth. b 44. Birm Univ BSc 66 Nottm Univ CertEd 67. d 89 p 95. OLM Waddington *Linc* 89–97;

OLM Bracebridge 98–06; PtO from 06. *Rose Cottage, 30 Finningley Road, Lincoln LN6 0UP*

KIDDY, Claire Elizabeth. b 60. ERMC 15. **d** 18 **p** 19. NSM Beccles St Mich and St Luke *St E* from 18. *Wissett Lodge, Lodge Lane, Wissett, Halesworth IP19 0JQ* T: (01986) 873173 E: revclairekiddy@gmail.com

KIGGELL, Mrs Anne Kirk. b 36. Liv Univ BA 57. SAOMC 99. **d** 02 **p** 03. OLM Basildon w Aldworth and Ashampstead *Ox* 02–09; PtO from 09. *6 Quarry Hollow, Headington, Oxford OX3 8JR* T: (01865) 766235 E: anne.kiggell@btinternet.com

KILCOOLEY, Christine Margaret Anne. *See* ROBINSON, Christine Margaret Anne

KILDARE, Dean of. *See* WRIGHT, The Very Revd Timothy

KILFORD, William Roy. b 38. Bris Univ BA 60. Sarum & Wells Th Coll 82. **d** 84 **p** 85. C Herne *Cant* 84–87; Chapl Wm Harvey Hosp Ashford 87–93; R Mersham w Hinxhill *Cant* 87–93; P-in-c Sevington 87–93; V Reculver and Herne Bay St Bart 93–95; Chapl Paphos Cyprus 95–98; P-in-c Doddington, Newnham and Wychling *Cant* 98–02; P-in-c Teynham w Lynsted and Kingsdown 98–02; P-in-c Norton 98–02; AD Ospringe 01–02; rtd 02; Chapl Nord Pas de Calais *Eur* 02–04; Hon C Burton Fleming w Fordon, Grindale etc *York* 04–08; Chapl St Jo Hosp *Cant* 08–09; P-in-c Burpham *Chich* 09–13; P-in-c Poling 09–13; PtO *Leic* 14–17; Hon C Daventry *Pet* 14–17; PtO *Cant* from 18. *12A St Nicholas' Hospital, Church Hill, Harbledown, Canterbury CT2 9AD* E: revkilford@aol.com

KILGOUR, Christine Mary. *See* CROMPTON, Christine Mary

KILGOUR, Christopher Richard Hargrave. b 74. York Univ BSc 97 MSc 00. Oak Hill Th Coll BA 13. **d** 13 **p** 14. C Chalk *Roch* 13–17; V Northaw and Cuffley *St Alb* from 17. *The Vicarage, 58 Hill Rise, Cuffley, Potters Bar EN6 4RG* M: 07446-516945 E: chris@kilgour.org.uk

KILGOUR, Richard Eifl. b 57. Edin Univ BD 85. Edin Th Coll 81. **d** 85 **p** 86. C Wrexham *St As* 85–88; V Whitford 88–97; Ind Chapl 89–97; R Newtown w Llanllwchaiarn w Aberhafesp 97–03; RD Cedewain 01–03; Provost St Andr Cathl *Ab* 03–15; R Aberdeen St Andr 03–15; P-in-c Aberdeen St Ninian 03–15; Gen Sec Internat Chr Maritime Assn 15–16; R Motherwell *Glas* from 18; R Wishaw from 18. *Flat 0/1, 4 Caledon Street, Glasgow G12 9DX* T: 0141-328 9861 E: newrect@hotmail.com

KILLALA AND ACHONRY, Archdeacon of. *See* MACWHIRTER, The Ven Stephen Joseph

KILLALOE, KILFENORA AND CLONFERT, Dean of. Hull Univ BA 81 QUB PhD 94. Ripon Coll Cuddesdon BA 84. C Redcar *York* 85–88; P-in-c Gweedore, Carrickfinn and Templecrone *D & R* 88–92; Bp's Dom Chapl 91–92; Dean Raphoe 92–02; I Raphoe w Raymochy and Clonleigh 93–01; Dean Killaloe and Clonfert *L & K* 02–12; Chan St Patr Cathl Dublin 11–12; P-in-c Dunsfold and Hascombe *Guildf* 12–19. *The Rectory, Church Green, Dunsfold, Godalming GU8 4LT* T: (01483) 200048 E: stephenwhite14@btinternet.com

KILLALOE, KILFENORA, CLONFERT AND KILMACDUAGH, Archdeacon of. *See* CARNEY, The Ven Richard Wayne

KILLWICK, Canon Simon David Andrew. b 56. K Coll Lon BD 80 AKC 80. St Steph Ho Ox 80. **d** 81 **p** 82. C Worsley *Man* 81–84; TV 84–97; P-in-c Moss Side Ch 97–06; R from 06; Hon Can Man Cathl from 04; AD Hulme 07–12. *Christ Church Rectory, Monton Street, Manchester M14 4LT* T/F: 0161-226 2476 E: frskillwick@btinternet.com

KILMISTER, David John. b 46. Open Univ BA 88. **d** 06 **p** 07. OLM Chippenham St Paul w Hardenhuish etc *Bris* from 06; OLM Kington St Michael from 06. *22 The Common, Langley Burrell, Chippenham SN15 4LQ* T/F: (01249) 650926 M: 07747-331971 E: djkilmster@sky.com

KILMORE, Archdeacon of. *See* MACCAULEY, The Ven Craig William Leslie

KILMORE, ELPHIN AND ARDAGH, Bishop of. *See* GLENFIELD, The Rt Revd Samuel Ferran

KILNER, Canon Frederick James. b 43. Qu Coll Cam BA 65 MA 69. Ridley Hall Cam 67. **d** 70 **p** 71. C Harlow New Town w Lt Parndon *Chelmsf* 70–74; C Cambridge St Andr Less *Ely* 74–79; P-in-c Milton 79–88; R 88–94; P-in-c Ely 94–96; P-in-c Chettisham 94–96; P-in-c Prickwillow 94–96; P-in-c Stretham w Thetford 94–96; P-in-c Stuntney 95–96; TR Ely 96–08; Hon Can Ely Cathl 88–08; Hon C Somersham w Pidley and Oldhurst and Woodhurst from 08; RD St Ives from 10. *125 High Street, Somersham, Huntingdon PE28 3EN* T: (01487) 842864 E: kilner@btinternet.com

KILNER, Mrs Valerie June. b 42. Univ of Wales (Abth) BSc 64 Hughes Hall Cam PGCE 65 MICFM 91. EAMTC 98. **d** 98 **p** 99. NSM Ely 98–08; PtO from 08. *125 High Street, Somersham, Huntingdon PE28 3EN* T: (01487) 842864 E: vjkilner@btinternet.com

KILPATRICK, Alan William. b 64. Oak Hill Th Coll BA 96. **d** 96 **p** 97. C Ealing St Paul *Lon* 96–01; Assoc R Mt Pleasant USA 01–04; P-in-c Prestonville St Luke *Chich* 04–09; R Diep River S Africa 09–13; I Knocknamuckley *D & D* 13–15; Min Hope Community Ch Craigavon 15–17; PtO *B & W* from 18. *139A Bleary Road, Portadown, Craigavon BT63 5NG* E: alanwkilpatrick@gmail.com

KILPATRICK, Edmund Stuart. b 52. **d** 12 **p** 13. NSM Southowram and Claremount *Leeds* from 12. *17 Athol Green, Halifax HX3 5RN* T: (01422) 259196

KIM, Byung Jun. b 82. Yonsei Univ S Korea BTh 10. Angl Th Sem Seoul MDiv 13. **d** 13 **p** 16. C Yaksu-dong and Dioc Officer Dept of Tr and Educn Seoul Korea 13–14; C Pet All SS 15–19; R Abington from 19. *15 Honeysuckle Way, Northampton NN3 3QE* M: 07961-469048 E: prayandwork@gmail.com

KIMARU, Benson Mbure. b 54. St Andr Coll Kabare 81. **d** 83 **p** 84. V Mitinguu Kenya 85; Dioc Radio Producer 86–88; Asst to Provost Nairobi 88; V Kangaru 89–90; V Kayole 91–94; V Nyari 95–98; V Maringo 99–02; V Githurai 03–05; PtO *Sheff* 06–07; NSM Brightside w Wincobank 07; NSM Penistone and Thurlstone *Wakef* 07–09; Chapl SW Yorks Partnership NHS Foundn Trust from 09; Chapl Leeds and York Partnership NHS Foundn Trust from 13; PtO *Leeds* from 17. *41 Holgate Mount, Worsbrough, Barnsley S70 6SR* T: (01226) 891185 M: 07919-988131 E: benititu@gmail.com

KIMBER, Geoffrey Francis. b 46. Univ Coll Lon BA 67 Birm Univ MPhil 01. St Jo Coll Nottm 86. **d** 88 **p** 89. C Buckhurst Hill *Chelmsf* 88–92; R Arley *Cov* 92–02; P-in-c Ansley 97–02; CMS Romania 02–07; R Birm Bp Latimer w All SS 07–12; rtd 12; PtO *Eur* from 18. *10A Belle Vue Road, Paignton TQ4 6ER* T: (01803) 556773 E: geoff.kimber@gmail.com

KIMBER, Mrs Gillian Margaret. b 48. Bedf Coll Lon BA 70. Oak Hill Th Coll 89. **d** 91. NSM Buckhurst Hill *Chelmsf* 91–92; C Arley *Cov* 92–97; C Ansley 97–02; CMS Romania 02–07; PtO *Birm* 08–11; rtd 11; PtO *Eur* from 18. *10A Belle Vue Road, Paignton TQ4 6ER* T: (01803) 556773 E: deacon_gill@yahoo.co.uk

KIMBER, Mrs Jennifer Carole Mary. Keele Univ BA 70. **d** 15 **p** 16. NSM Lampeter w Maestir and Silian and Llangybi and Betws Bledrws *St D* from 15. *Creuddyn, Bryn Steffan, Lampeter SA48 8BS* T: (01570) 422770 M: 07740-463486 E: jcm.kimber@gmail.com

KIMBER, John Keith. b 45. Bris Univ BSc 66. St Mich Coll Llan. **d** 69 **p** 70. C Caerphilly *Llan* 69–72; Chapl Birm Univ 72–75; TR Bris St Agnes and St Simon w St Werburgh 75–82; P-in-c Bris St Paul w St Barn 80–82; Hon C Westbury-on-Trym H Trin 82–83; Area Sec (Wales) USPG 83–89; TR Halesowen *Worc* 89–92; Chapl Geneva *Eur* 92–01; Chapl Monte Carlo 01–02; TR Cen Cardiff *Llan* 02–06; V Cardiff City Par 07–10; rtd 10; PtO *Llan* from 10; *Eur* from 15. *13 Meadow Street, Cardiff CF11 9PY* T: (029) 2023 5809 E: johnkeith.k@gmail.com

KIMBER, Canon Jonathan Richard. b 69. K Coll Cam BA 91 MA 95 St Jo Coll Dur MA 02 K Coll Lon PhD 15. Cranmer Hall Dur 99. **d** 02 **p** 03. C Weston Favell *Pet* 02–05; P-in-c Northampton St Benedict 05–10; V 10–15; Can Pet Cathl 14–15; Dioc Dir Min and Discipleship *Worc* from 15. *The Old Palace, Deansway, Worcester WR1 2JE* E: jkimber@cofe-worcester.org.uk

KIMBER, Stuart Francis. b 53. Qu Eliz Coll Lon BSc 74 Fitzw Coll Cam BA 79 MA 83. Ridley Hall Cam 77. **d** 80 **p** 81. C Edgware *Lon* 80–83; C Cheltenham St Mark *Glouc* 83–84; TV 84–92; C Hawkwell *Chelmsf* 92–01; V Westcliff St Andr 01–15; rtd 15; PtO *Birm* from 18. *210 Staple Lodge Road, Birmingham B31 3DL* M: 07758-468052 E: revskimber@blueyonder.co.uk

KIMBERLEY, Canon Carol Lylie Wodehouse, Countess of. b 51. St Hugh's Coll Ox BA 73 MA 77 CertEd 74. Ripon Coll Cuddesdon 87. **d** 89 **p** 94. NSM Hambleden Valley *Ox* 89–02; P-in-c Hormead, Wyddial, Anstey, Brent Pelham etc *St Alb* 02–12; P-in-c Sandon, Wallington and Rushden w Clothall 10–11; RD Buntingford 06–11; Hon Can St Alb 10–12; rtd 12; PtO *Ox* from 12; *St Alb* from 12. *Fieldfares, Ferry Lane, Medmenham, Marlow SL7 2EZ* T: (01491) 413155 E: ck@womvic.demon.co.uk

KIMMIS, Ms Sally Elizabeth. b 59. Westcott Ho Cam 08. **d** 10 **p** 11. C King's Lynn St Marg w St Nic *Nor* 10–14; P-in-c Foulsham, Guestwick, Stibbard, Themelthorpe etc 14–17; P-in-c N Elmham, Billingford, Bintree, Guist etc 16–17; P-in-c Bawdeswell w Foxley 16–17; TR Heart of Norfolk from 17. *The Vicarage, 48 Holt Road, North Elmham, Dereham NR20 5JQ* T: (01362) 668850 M: 07548-741159 E: sally.kimmis@live.co.uk *or* heartofnorfolkrector@gmail.com

KINAHAN, Canon Timothy Charles. b 53. Jes Coll Cam BA 75. CITC 77. **d** 78 **p** 79. C Carrickfergus *Conn* 78–81; Papua New Guinea 81–84; I Belfast Whiterock *Conn* 84–90; I Gilnahirk

D & D 90–06; I Helen's Bay from 06; Can Belf Cathl from 04; Preb Monmohenock St Patr Cathl Dublin from 12. *The Rectory, 2 Woodland Avenue, Helen's Bay, Bangor BT19 1TX* T: (028) 9185 3601 E: timothykinahan@btinternet.com

KINCH, Christopher David. b 81. K Alfred's Coll Win BTh 02. St Steph Ho Ox 03. **d** 05 **p** 06. C Long Eaton St Laur *Derby* 05–09; TV Swindon New Town *Bris* 09–11; Partnership P Bris S 11–15; P-in-c Knowle H Nativity 12–16; CF(V) 10–16; CF from 16. *c/o MOD Chaplains (Army)* T: (01264) 383430 F: 381824 E: frchristopherkinch@gmail.com *or* artycen-14ra-rhq-padre@mod.uk

KINCHIN-SMITH, John Michael. b 52. Fitzw Coll Cam MA. Ridley Hall Cam 79. **d** 82 **p** 83. C Sanderstead All SS *S'wark* 82–87; TV Halesworth w Linstead, Chediston, Holton etc *St E* 87–92; R Mursley w Swanbourne and Lt Horwood *Ox* 92–02; R Newton Longville and Mursley w Swanbourne etc 03–06; R Chinnor, Sydenham, Aston Rowant and Crowell 06–13; rtd 13; PtO *Nor* from 13; RD Gt Yarmouth from 16; PtO *Eur* from 16. *The Old Vicarage, Duke Road, Gorleston, Great Yarmouth NR31 6LL* T: (01493) 717739 E: johnks1881@aol.com

KINDER, David James. b 55. EAMTC 01. **d** 04 **p** 05. NSM Warboys w Broughton and Bury w Wistow *Ely* 04–08; Chapl HM Pris Littlehey from 08. *Chaplain, HM Prison Littlehey, Perry, Huntingdon PE28 0SR* T: (01480) 335252 E: david.kinder@justice.gov.uk

KINDER, Mrs Sylvia Patricia. b 61. Ridley Hall Cam 03. **d** 05 **p** 06. C Warboys w Broughton and Bury w Wistow *Ely* 05–09; C Werrington *Pet* 09–12; P-in-c Hampton *Ely* 13–18; V from 18. *105 Eagle Way, Hampton Vale, Peterborough PE7 8EL* T: (01733) 240196 M: 07876-204624 E: vicar@hamptonchurch.co.uk *or* sylvia@5kinders.com

KING, Mrs Angela Margaret. b 45. Bedf Coll Lon BA 67 Lon Inst of Educn PGCE 68. SEITE 00. **d** 03 **p** 04. NSM Bromley St Andr *Roch* 03–15; P-in-c 11–15; rtd 15; PtO *Roch* from 16. *4 Avondale Road, Bromley BR1 4EP* T/F: (020) 8402 0847 E: angelaking45@hotmail.com

KING, Annabel Ingrid. b 57. SWMTC 14. **d** 16 **p** 17. NSM Callington Cluster *Truro* from 16. *12 Trefloyd Close, Kelly Bray, Callington PL17 8DP* T: (01579) 382765 E: annabelking@gmail.com

KING, Mrs Barbara Anne. b 55. St Mich Coll Sarum BEd 78. SNWTP 07. **d** 13 **p** 14. NSM Christleton *Ches* 13–16; NSM Tarvin from 16. *17 Cathcart Green, Guilden Sutton, Chester CH3 7SR* T: (01244) 300756 E: barbara.king65@yahoo.com

KING, Benjamin John. b 74. Down Coll Cam BA 96 MA 00 Harvard Univ MTh 03 Dur Univ PhD 07. Westcott Ho Cam 97. **d** 00 **p** 00. C Boston the Advent USA 00–06; Chapl Harvard Univ 06–09; Asst Prof Ch Hist Univ of the South 09–14; Assoc Prof from 14. *University of the South, 335 Tennessee Avenue, Sewanee TN 37383, USA* T: (001) (931) 598 1619 E: bjking@sewanee.edu

KING, Benjamin William. b 76. Dijon Univ BA 97 Man Univ BA 98 Univ Coll Lon MA Cam Univ 03. Ridley Hall Cam 03. **d** 06 **p** 07. C Stanwix *Carl* 06–10; TV Chigwell and Chigwell Row *Chelmsf* 10–15; TR 15–19; V Forest Gate St Mark from 19. *The Vicarage, 4A Tylney Road, London E7 0LS* T: (020) 8555 2988 M: 07752-708207 E: kingbw2001@yahoo.com

KING, Caroline Naomi. b 62. New Coll Edin BD 94. Ripon Coll Cuddesdon 95. **d** 97 **p** 98. C Wheatley *Ox* 97–12; TV Dorchester from 12. *The Vicarage, 49 The Green North, Warborough, Wallingford OX10 7DW* T: (01865) 858525 M: 07540-051798 E: reverend.caroline@gmail.com

KING, Charles Edward Bruce. b 81. St Cath Coll Cam BA 04. St Mellitus Coll MA 18. **d** 18 **p** 19. C St Alb St Mich from 18. *1 Blue House Hill, St Albans AL3 6AD*

KING, Clare Maria. b 68. St Andr Univ BD 91 K Coll Lon MPhil 98. Westcott Ho Cam 91. **d** 94. C Nor Norbury St Phil *S'wark* 94–96; Chapl Croydon Coll 95–96; Asst Chapl Cen Sheff Univ Hosps NHS Trust 96–01; C Leic Presentation 02–08; C Leic St Chad from 08. *The Vicarage, 12 Saddington Road, Fleckney, Leicester LE8 8AW* T: 0116-240 2215 E: cmking@leicester.anglican.org

KING, David Charles. b 52. K Coll Lon 73 Coll of Resurr Mirfield 77. **d** 78 **p** 79. C Saltburn-by-the-Sea *York* 78–81; Youth Officer 81–85; P-in-c Crathorne 81–85; Par Educn Adv *Wakef* 85–91; Min Coulby Newham LEP *York* 91–94; P-in-c Egton w Grosmont 94–00; P-in-c Goathland and Glaisdale 99–00; V Middle Esk Moor 00–07; PtO 12–13; V Middlesbrough St Martin w St Cuth 13–19; Chapl Cleveland Police 13–19; rtd 19. *16 Ellerby Lane, Runswick, Saltburn-by-the-Sea TS13 5HS* M: 07977-729612 E: meaux1@hotmail.co.uk

KING, David John. b 67. W Sussex Inst of HE BEd 91. St Steph Ho Ox 98. **d** 00 **p** 01. C Bexhill St Pet *Chich* 00–03; TV 03–08; V Eastbourne St Andr from 08. *St Andrew's Vicarage,*

425 Seaside, Eastbourne BN22 7RT T: (01323) 723739 E: frdavidking@talktalk.net *or* frdavid@tiscali.co.uk

KING, David Michael. b 73. St Jo Coll Dur BA 95 PGCE 96 Cam Univ BA 02. Ridley Hall Cam 00. **d** 03 **p** 04. C Claygate *Guildf* 03–07; C Redhill H Trin *S'wark* 07–10; C Wallington 10–11; V Wallington St Patr from 12. *12 Mallard Way, Wallington SM6 9LZ* M: 07901-700958 E: david.king@stpats.org.uk

KING, Canon David Russell. b 42. Univ of Wales (Lamp) BA 67. St D Coll Lamp. **d** 68 **p** 69. C Barrow St Geo w St Luke *Carl* 68–72; P-in-c Kirkland 72–74; V Edenhall w Langwathby 72–73; P-in-c Culgaith 72–73; V Edenhall w Langwathby and Culgaith 73–74; V Flookburgh 75–79; V Barrow St Jas 79–82; P-in-c Bolton w Ireby and Uldale 82–83; R 83–90; R Burgh-by-Sands and Kirkbampton w Kirkandrews etc 90–00; P-in-c Aikton and Orton St Giles 95–00; R Barony of Burgh 00–02; P-in-c Gt Broughton and Broughton Moor 02–05; V Brigham, Gt Broughton and Broughton Moor 05–07; Hon Can Carl Cathl 01–07; rtd 07; PtO *Carl* 08–10; Hon C Aspatria w Hayton and Gilcrux from 10. *27 King Street, Aspatria, Wigton CA7 3AF* T: (016973) 23580 E: candrking@gmail.com

KING, David William Anthony. b 42. Ch Ch Ox BA 63 MA 68. Westcott Ho Cam 63. **d** 65 **p** 66. C Cayton w Eastfield *York* 65–68; C Southbroom *Sarum* 68–71; V Holt St Jas 71–72; R Hinton Parva 71–72; V Holt St Jas and Hinton Parva 72–75; P-in-c Horton and Chalbury 73–75; R Holt St Jas, Hinton Parva, Horton and Chalbury 75–79; TV Melton Mowbray w Thorpe Arnold *Leic* 79–83; V Foxton w Gumley and Laughton and Lubenham 83–90; P-in-c Boreham *Chelmsf* 90–00; R Tendring and Lt Bentley w Beaumont cum Moze 00–06; rtd 06; PtO *Ely* from 06. *14 The Hythe, Reach, Cambridge CB5 0JQ* T: (01638) 742924 E: dking66@btinternet.com

KING, Mrs Elaine Rosemary. b 55. Qu Coll Birm. **d** 13 **p** 14. NSM Ward End w Bordesley Green *Birm* 13–17; NSM Birm Cathl from 17. *283 George Road, Erdington, Birmingham B23 7SD* M: 07582-407188 E: rev.eking@hotmail.co.uk

KING, Eleanor Olwen. b 61. Leeds Univ BSc 82 Strathclyde Univ MSc 84. STETS 11. **d** 14 **p** 15. C Alfred Jewel *B & W* 14–18; R Aisholt, Enmore, Goathurst, Nether Stowey etc from 18. *The Rectory, 25 St Mary Street, Nether Stowey, Bridgwater TA5 1LJ* M: 07803-243823 E: eleanor.king@hotmail.com

KING, Ellen Francis. *See* LOUDON, Ellen Francis

KING, Canon Fergus John. b 62. St Andr Univ MA Edin Univ BD 89 UNISA DTh 06. Edin Th Coll 86. **d** 89 **p** 90. Chapl St Jo Cathl Oban *Arg* 89–92; C Oban St Jo 89–92; Tanzania 92–98; Hon Can and Can Th Tanga from 01; PtO *S'wark* 99–03; Hon C Thamesmead 03–05; R Kotara South Gd Shep Australia from 05. *The Rectory, 10 Melissa Avenue, Adamstown Heights NSW 2289, Australia* T: (0061) (2) 4943 0103 M: 40-377 2431 E: revfking@bigpond.net.au

KING, Helen Sarah Elizabeth. *See* BLAINE, Helen Sarah Elizabeth

KING, James Anthony. b 46. K Coll Lon BA 69 AKC 69 Lon Inst of Educn DipEd 77. SAOMC 99. **d** 01 **p** 02. NSM Gerrards Cross and Fulmer *Ox* 01–03; NSM S Tottenham St Ann *Lon* 03–08; NSM Chalfont St Peter *Ox* 08–15; PtO from 15. *7 Meadowcroft, Chalfont St Peter, Gerrards Cross SL9 9DH* T: (01753) 887386

KING, Canon Jeffrey Douglas Wallace. b 43. AKC 67. **d** 68 **p** 69. C S Harrow St Paul *Lon* 68–71; C Garforth *Ripon* 71–74; V Potternewton 74–83; TR Moor Allerton 83–99; RD Allerton 85–89; P-in-c Thorner and Dioc Ecum Officer 99–08; Hon Can Ripon Cathl 90–08; rtd 08; PtO *Ripon* 09–14; *Leeds* from 14. *17 Barleyfields Terrace, Wetherby LS22 6PW* T: (01937) 520646

KING, Jennifer. b 48. **d** 08 **p** 09. OLM Chorlton-cum-Hardy St Clem *Man* from 08. *8 St Clements Road, Manchester M21 9HU* T: 0161-861 0898 M: 07918-702572 E: jen.king@stclement-chorlton.org.uk

KING, Mrs Joanna Claire. b 72. Chelt & Glouc Coll of HE BEd 96. Ripon Coll Cuddesdon 12. **d** 14 **p** 15. C Pagham *Chich* 14–18; P-in-c N Bersted 18–19; V from 19. *71 St James's Road, Chichester PO19 7HR* M: 07960-286601 E: joannaclaireking@gmail.com

KING, John. b 47. **d** 05 **p** 06. NSM Buckingham *Ox* from 05. *Wood End Farm, 2 Wood End, Nash, Milton Keynes MK17 0EL* T: (01908) 501860 E: john@kingsfold100.co.uk

KING, John Andrew. b 50. Qu Coll Birm 72. **d** 75 **p** 76. C Halesowen *Worc* 75–77; C Belper Ch Ch and Milford *Derby* 78–81; PtO from 87. *3 Holly House Lane, Blackbrook, Belper DE56 2DE* T: (01773) 823467 E: jaking49@hotmail.com

KING, Joseph Stephen. b 39. St Chad's Coll Dur BA 62 MPhil 83. **d** 64 **p** 65. C Lewisham St Mary *S'wark* 64–69; Hon C Milton next Gravesend Ch Ch *Roch* 70–85; V 85–07; rtd 07; PtO *Roch* from 07. *13 Bannister Drive, Hutton, Brentwood CM13 1YX* T: (01277) 201900 E: patandjoe48@hotmail.com

KING, Mrs Katharine Mary. b 63. St Hugh's Coll Ox BA 85 MA 89 SS Coll Cam BA 88. Ridley Hall Cam 86. **d** 89 **p** 94. C Ipswich St Aug *St E* 89–91; NSM Bures 92–02; NSM Bures w Assington and Lt Cornard 02–13; PtO *Chelmsf* 14–15; NSM Coggeshall w Markshall from 15; NSM Cressing w Stisted and Bradwell etc from 15. *The House, The Street, Bradwell, Braintree CM77 8EL* T: (01376) 563357 E: kkingchurch@gmail.com

KING, Malcolm Charles. b 37. Chich Th Coll 67. **d** 70 **p** 71. C Mill End *St Alb* 70–72; Chapl RAF 72–76; R W Lynn *Nor* 76–81; V Croxley Green All SS *St Alb* 81–90; V Grimsby St Aug *Linc* 90–99; Asst Local Min Officer 90–95; V Bury w Houghton and Coldwaltham and Hardham *Chich* 99–02; rtd 02; OGS from 90; PtO *Chich* 02–11; Warden Community of St Pet Woking 02–03. *20 The Quadrangle, Morden College, 19 St Germans Place, London SE3 0PW* T: (020) 8858 5313

KING, Malcolm Stewart. b 56. Univ of Wales (Lamp) MA 09. Sarum & Wells Th Coll 77. **d** 80 **p** 81. C Farnham *Guildf* 80–83; C Chertsey and Chapl St Pet Hosp Chertsey 83–86; V Egham Hythe *Guildf* 86–91; TR Cove St Jo 91–98; RD Aldershot 93–98; V Dorking w Ranmore 98–04; Hon Can Guildf Cathl 99–04; RD Dorking 01–04; P-in-c Portsea N End St Mark *Portsm* 04–06; TR 06–07; Warden Iona Community *Arg* 07–10; R Robina w Mermaid Beach Australia 10–12; PtO *Carl* 12–13; TR Stroud Team *Glouc* 13–16; AD Stroud 13–16; rtd 16. *The Rectory, School Hill, Bourton-on-the-Water, Cheltenham GL54 2AW* T: (01451) 821282 E: malcolmsking@btinternet.com

KING (née COWIE), Mrs Margaret Harriet. b 53. Glas Univ BSc 76 AMA 85 FMA 97. TISEC 95. **d** 98 **p** 99. NSM Montrose and Inverbervie *Bre* 98–05; Dioc Dir of Ord 00–05; TV N Hinckford *Chelmsf* 05–13; TR from 13. *The Vicarage, Great Henny, Sudbury CO10 7NW* T: (01787) 269385 M: 07855-558056 E: mandgking39@hotmail.com

KING, Marie. b 40. CertEd 78. **d** 03 **p** 04. OLM Addiscombe St Mildred *S'wark* 03–10; PtO from 10. *8 Annandale Road, Croydon CR0 7HP* T: (020) 8654 2651 E: marie.king@virgin.net

KING, Martin Harry. b 42. St Jo Coll Cam MA 68 MBCS 85. SAOMC 03. **d** 05 **p** 06. NSM Wheathampstead *St Alb* 05–12; Dioc Environment Officer 08–09; rtd 12; PtO *St Alb* from 13. *29 Parkfields, Welwyn Garden City AL8 6EE* T: (01707) 328905 E: revdmartin.king@cantab.net

KING, Martin Peter James. b 73. Bris Univ BEng 95. Oak Hill Th Coll BA 05. **d** 05 **p** 06. C Leamington Priors St Paul *Cov* 05–09; V Rudgwick *Chich* from 10. *The Vicarage, Cox Green, Rudgwick, Horsham RH12 3DD* T: (01403) 822127 E: martinthevicar@googlemail.com or vicar@rudgwickchurch.org.uk

KING, Martin Quartermain. b 39. Reading Univ BA 61. Cuddesdon Coll 62. **d** 64 **p** 65. C S Shields St Hilda w St Thos *Dur* 64–66; C Newton Aycliffe 66–71; V Chilton Moor 71–78; R Middleton St George 78–91; R Sedgefield 91–04; RD 91–96; Chapl Co Dur & Darlington Priority Services NHS Trust 91–04; rtd 04; PtO *Dur* from 04; Chapl Dur from 09. *3 White House Drive, Sedgefield, Stockton on Tees TS21 3BX* T: (01740) 620424 E: martin.king@durham.anglican.org or mqking@btinternet.com

KING, Mrs Melanie Jane. b 58. Lindisfarne Regional Tr Partnership 13. **d** 15 **p** 16. Northumbria Univ *Newc* 92 and 92–93; NSM Brompton w Deighton *York* 15–18; PtO from 19. *19 Weavers Green, Northallerton DL7 8FJ* M: 07938-054338 E: revmelking@gmail.com

KING, Nicholas Bernard Paul. b 46. Wycliffe Hall Ox 72. **d** 75 **p** 76. C Pitsmoor w Wicker *Sheff* 75–78; C Erdington St Barn *Birm* 78–80; C Sutton Coldfield H Trin 80–84; V Lynesack *Dur* 84–92; rtd 93. *16 Chatsworth Avenue, Bishop Auckland DL14 6AX* T: (01388) 605614

KING, Nigel Edward. b 44. St Cath Coll Ox BA 66 MA 69. **d** 16 **p** 17. NSM Three Cliffs *S & B* from 16. *36 East Cliff, Pennard, Swansea SA3 2AS* T: (01792) 233124 M: 07850-583153 E: nigeledward.king@btopenworld.com

KING, Patrick Stewart. b 84. St Chad's Coll Dur BA 06 Jes Coll Cam MPhil 10. Westcott Ho Cam 08. **d** 10 **p** 11. C Dorchester *Sarum* 10–13; C Wokingham St Paul *Ox* 13–16; Voc Advocate Wollaston Th Coll Australia 16–17; R Fremantle and Palmyra from 17. *St John's Anglican Church, 24 Adelaide Street, Fremantle WA 6160, Australia* T: (0061) (8) 9335 2213 F: 9335 2005 E: patrick.s.king@gmail.com

KING, Paul Derwent. b 39. Ball Coll Ox BA 62 MA 65. Cuddesdon Coll 63. **d** 65 **p** 66. C Portsea N End St Mark *Portsm* 65–67; C Iffley *Ox* 67–70; Asst Chapl Nottm Univ *S'well* 70–72; Chapl Southn Univ *Win* 72–78; V Headington *Ox* 78–86; RD Cowley 81–86; V Ox St Mary Magd 86–89; rtd 04. *60 Abingdon Road, Oxford OX1 4PE* T: (01865) 437066

KING, Penelope Ann. b 86. Cant Ch Ch Univ BA 07 Sheff Univ MA 13. Coll of Resurr Mirfield 11. **d** 13 **p** 14. C

Reddish *Man* 13–16; TV Rossendale Middle Valley 16–17; V Newchurch from 17. *The Rectory, 539 Newchurch Road, Rossendale BB4 9HH* T: (01706) 211122 M: 07747-836411 E: revdpennyking@outlook.com

KING, Peter Duncan. b 48. K Coll Lon LLB 70 AKC 70 Fitzw Coll Cam BA 72 MA 77. Westcott Ho Cam 70. **d** 80 **p** 81. NSM Notting Hill *Lon* 80–84; NSM Mortlake w E Sheen *S'wark* 84–18; Dean MSE 99–16; PtO 18–19. *49 Leinster Avenue, London SW14 7JW* T: (020) 8876 8997 F: 8287 9329 E: kingpd@hotmail.com

KING, Canon Philipa Ann. b 65. Westcott Ho Cam 91. **d** 95 **p** 96. C Cambridge Ascension *Ely* 95–00; TV 00–02; TR from 02; Hon Can Ely Cathl from 11. *2 Stretten Avenue, Cambridge CB4 3EP* T: (01223) 366665 or 315000 M: 07816-833363 E: pipking@btinternet.com or rectoratcastle@btinternet.com

KING (née JONES), The Ven Rhiannon Elizabeth. b 72. Ex Univ BA 93 Brunel Univ MA 95 Anglia Poly Univ MA 05. Ridley Hall Cam 98. **d** 00 **p** 01. C Huntingdon *Ely* 00–04; R Fulbourn 04–10; V Gt Wilbraham 04–10; R Lt Wilbraham 04–10; Transforming Ch Co-ord *Birm* 10–14; Dir of Miss 14–19; Adn Ipswich *St E* from 19. *Address temp unknown* M: 07595-880584 E: archdeacon.rhiannon@cofesuffolk.org

KING, Richard Andrew. b 51. Linc Th Coll. **d** 84 **p** 85. C Bramhall *Ches* 84–87; V Heald Green St Cath 87–92; P-in-c Ashprington, Cornworthy and Dittisham *Ex* 92–99; RD Totnes 97–99; P-in-c Torquay St Jo and Ellacombe 99–02; P-in-c Stoneleigh and Dioc Spirituality Adv *Guildf* 02–07; P-in-c S Framland *Leic* 08–11; rtd 12; PtO *Linc* 15–18. *18 Whitehall Grove, Lincoln LN1 1PG* T: (01522) 524003 E: rking11@hotmail.com

KING, Robert Dan. b 57. Sarum & Wells Th Coll 92. **d** 94 **p** 95. C Heref H Trin 94–97; TV W Heref 97–00; V Weobley w Sarnesfield and Norton Canon 00–14; P-in-c Letton w Staunton, Byford, Mansel Gamage etc 00–04; R 04–14; Preb Heref Cathl 10–14; R Kelso *Edin* from 14. *St Andrew's Rectory, 6 Forestfield, Kelso TD5 7BX* T: (01573) 224163 E: rectorofkelso@gmail.com

KING, The Ven Robin Lucas Colin. b 59. Dundee Univ MA 81. Ridley Hall Cam 87. **d** 89 **p** 90. C Ipswich St Aug *St E* 89–92; V Bures 92–02; C Assington w Newton Green and Lt Cornard 00–02; V Bures w Assington and Lt Cornard 02–13; RD Sudbury 06–13; Dean St E Cathl 08–13; Adn Stansted *Chelmsf* from 13. *The House, The Street, Bradwell, Braintree CM77 8EL* T: (01376) 563357 M: 07813-633096 E: a.stansted@chelmsford.anglican.org

KING, Mrs Rowena Niesje. b 77. Univ of Qld BAppSc 97 Chas Sturt Univ NSW BTh 13 Ox Univ MTh 15. WEMTC 13. **d** 15 **p** 16. C Dursley *Glouc* 15–18; R Bourton-on-the-Water w Clapton etc from 18. *The Rectory, School Hill, Bourton-on-the-Water, Cheltenham GL54 2AW* T: (01451) 821282 E: revrowena@gmail.com

KING, Canon Walter Raleigh. b 45. New Coll Ox BA 67 MA 74. Cuddesdon Coll 71. **d** 74 **p** 75. C Wisbech SS Pet and Paul *Ely* 74–77; C Barrow St Geo w St Luke *Carl* 77–79; P-in-c Clifford *Heref* 79–83; P-in-c Cusop 79–83; P-in-c Hardwick 79–83; P-in-c Whitney w Winforton 81–84; R Cusop w Clifford, Hardwicke, Bredwardine etc 83–86; R Heref St Nic 86–92; Dir of Ords 86–92; Preb Heref Cathl 86–92; TR Huntingdon *Ely* 92–01; RD 94–99; Hon Can Ely Cathl 99–01; Vice Dean and Can Res Chelmsf Cathl 01–10; rtd 10; PtO *S'wark* from 13; *Lon* from 11. *8 Woodlands, Clapham Common North Side, London SW4 0RJ* E: walterking@btinternet.com

KING, William. b 46. **d** 14 **p** 15. OLM N Beltisloe Gp *Linc* from 14. *Tanglewood, Grantham Road, Old Somerby, Grantham NG33 4AB* M: 07568-075680 E: bill.king@hotmail.co.uk

KING-BROWN, Ian Barry. b 53. St Cuth Soc Dur BA 80 PGCE 81. Sarum & Wells Th Coll 84. **d** 86 **p** 87. C Winchmore Hill St Paul *Lon* 86–89; Hon Chapl Chase Farm Hosp Enfield 86–88; Hon Chapl Harley Street Area Hosps 88–90; Hon Chapl RAM 89; C St Marylebone w H Trin *Lon* 89–94; rtd 94; Hon Chapl Regent's Coll Lon 96–05; PtO *Lon* from 11. *Flat 4, 9 Welbeck Street, London W1G 9YB* T: (020) 3624 4433 E: ibkb13@gmail.com

KING-SMITH, Preb Giles Anthony Beaumont. b 53. Univ Coll Ox BA 75. Trin Coll Bris 86. **d** 88 **p** 89. C Gtr Corsham *Bris* 88–92; V Two Mile Hill St Mich 92–96; TV Ilfracombe, Lee, Woolacombe, Bittadon etc *Ex* from 96; RD Barnstaple 14–17; Preb Ex Cathl from 14. *The Vicarage, Springfield Road, Woolacombe EX34 7BX* T: (01271) 870467

KINGDOM, Paul Anthony. b 62. Ex Univ BA 83 Win Univ MA 18 FCA 86 ATII 87. STETS 07. **d** 10 **p** 11. NSM Burnham *B & W* 10–14; NSM Wedmore w Theale and Blackford 15–16; NSM Chapel Allerton 15–16; NSM Dulverton w Brushford, Brompton Regis etc from 16. *The Vicarage, Brompton Regis, Dulverton TA22 9NL* T: (01398) 371572 M: 07803-922605 E: revpaulkingdom@gmail.com

KINGMAN, Paul Henry Charles. b 64. Reading Univ BSc 86. Wycliffe Hall Ox BTh 95. **d** 95 **p** 96. C Whitton *Sarum* 95–99; C Harold Wood *Chelmsf* 99–03; V Stone Ch Ch and Oulton *Lich* from 03. *Christ Church Vicarage, Bromfield Court, Stone ST15 8ED* T: (01785) 812669

✠**KINGS, The Rt Revd Graham Ralph.** b 53. Hertf Coll Ox BA 77 MA 80 Utrecht Univ PhD 02. Ridley Hall Cam 78. **d** 80 **p** 81 **c** 09. C Harlesden St Mark *Lon* 80–84; CMS Kenya 85–91; Dir Studies St Andr Inst Kabare 85-88; Vice Prin 89–91; Lect Miss Studies Cam Th Federation 92–00; Overseas Adv Henry Martyn Trust 92–95; Dir Henry Martyn Cen Westmr Coll Cam 95–00; Hon C Cambridge H Trin *Ely* 92–96; Hon C Chesterton St Andr 96–00; V Islington St Mary *Lon* 00–09; Area Bp Sherborne *Sarum* 09–15; Can and Preb Sarum Cathl 09–15; Miss Th Angl Communion 15–17; Hon Asst Bp S'wark from 15; Hon Asst Bp Dur 16–17; P-in-c S'wark H Trin w St Matt 17–18; Hon C from 18. *483B Southwark Park Road, London SE16 2JP* T: (020) 3539 5722 *or* 7357 8532 M: 07786-071677 E: grahamrkings@gmail.com

KINGS, Jean Alison. *See* THORN, Jean Alison

KINGSLEY, Miss Mary Phyllis Lillian. b 48. K Coll Lon BSc 76 Lon Inst of Educn MA 87. ERMC 96. **d** 09 **p** 10. NSM Croxley Green All SS *St Alb* 09–13; NSM Bushey 13–18; C 18–19; rtd 19. *19 The Cloisters, Rickmansworth WD3 1HL* T: (01923) 771172 E: mplk@waitrose.com

KINGSMILL-LUNN, Brooke. *See* LUNN, Brooke Kingsmill

KINGSTON, Desmond. *See* KINGSTON, John Desmond George

KINGSTON, Eric. b 24. **d** 69 **p** 70. C Ballymacarrett St Patr *D & D* 69–72; C Knock 72–76; I Annahilt w Magherahamlet 76–93; Can and Prec Dromore Cathl 93; rtd 93. *38 Kinedale Park, Ballynahinch BT24 8YS* T: (028) 9756 5715

KINGSTON, John Desmond George. b 40. TCD BA 63 MA 66. CITC 64. **d** 64 **p** 65. C Arm St Mark w Aghavilly 64–70; Hon V Choral Arm Cathl 69–70; Chapl Portora R Sch Enniskillen 70–01; LtO *Clogh* 70–01; Can Clogh Cathl 96–01; rtd 01. *Ambleside, 45 Old Rossory Road, Enniskillen BT74 7LF* T: (028) 6632 4493

KINGSTON, Kenneth Robert. b 42. TCD BA 65 MA 69. **d** 66 **p** 67. C Enniscorthy *C & O* 66–69; C Ballymena w Ballyclug *Conn* 70–72; C Drumragh w Mountfield *D & R* 72–78; I Badoney Lower w Greenan and Badoney Upper 78–84; I Desertmartin w Termoneeny 84–13; Can Derry Cathl 97–13; rtd 13. *1 Fairlea Heights, Moneymore, Magherafelt BT45 7UQ* T: (028) 8674 7905 E: kennethkingstonfairlea@gmail.com

KINGSTON, Malcolm Trevor. b 75. QUB BSc 97 MSc 98 TCD BTh 04. CITC 01. **d** 04 **p** 05. C Portadown St Mark *Arm* 04–07; I Kilmore St Aid w St Sav 07–14; I Arm St Mark from 14. *St Mark's Rectory, 14 Portadown Road, Armagh BT61 9EE* T: (028) 3752 2970 E: malcolm.kingston@btinternet.com

KINGSTON, Canon Michael Joseph. b 51. K Coll Lon BD 73 AKC 73. St Aug Coll Cant 73. **d** 74 **p** 75. C Reading H Trin Ox 74–77; C New Eltham All SS *S'wark* 77–83; V Plumstead Ascension 83–94; Sub-Dean Greenwich N 92–94; V Sydenham St Bart 94–18; RD W Lewisham 04–16; Hon Can S'wark Cathl 15–18; rtd 18; PtO Ox from 19. *23 Windmill Avenue, Bicester OX26 3DX* T: (01869) 354990 E: michaelkingston@btinternet.com

KINGSTON, Robert George. b 46. TCD BA 68 Div Test 69. **d** 69 **p** 72. C Belfast St Thos *Conn* 69–72; C Kilkenny St Canice Cathl *C & O* 72–75; I Ballinasloe w Taughmaconnell *L & K* 77–79; I Maryborough w Dysart Enos and Ballyfin *C & O* 79–85; I Lurgan w Billis, Killinkere and Munterconnaught *K, E & A* 85–88; Registrar Kilmore 87–92; I Lurgan etc w Ballymachugh, Kildrumferton etc *K, E & A* 88–92; I Tallaght *D & G* 92–98; Warden of Readers 93–98; I Mallow Union *C, C & R* 98–07; I Carrickmacross w Magheracloone *Clogh* 07–13; Chapl Mageough Home *D & G* from 13. *Chaplain's Apartment, The Mageough, Cowper Road, Dublin 6, Republic of Ireland* T: (00353) (1) 555 2179 M: 89-400 1720 E: rgk@eircom.net

KINGSTON-UPON-THAMES, Area Bishop of. *See* CHEETHAM, The Rt Revd Richard Ian

KINGTON, Canon David Bruce. b 45. Trin Coll Bris 72. **d** 72 **p** 73. C Wellington w Eyton *Lich* 72–77; C Boscombe St Jo *Win* 77–81; R Michelmersh, Timsbury, Farley Chamberlayne etc 81–98; R Michelmersh and Awbridge and Braishfield etc 98–01; RD Romsey 95–05; Hon Can Win Cathl 02–10; rtd 11; PtO *Win* from 11. *St Swithun's Cottage, Main Road, Littleton, Winchester SO22 6QS* T: (01962) 882698 E: dbruce.kington245@btinternet.com

KINKEAD, John Alfred Harold. b 84. TCD BA 06. CITC BTh 10. **d** 10 **p** 11. C Cregagh *D & D* 10–13; C Taney *D & G* 13–15; Chan V St Patr Cathl Dublin 13–15; P-in-c Wicklow w Killiskey *D & G* 15–18; I from 18. *6 Glendasan Drive, Wicklow,*

Co Wicklow, A67 C822, Republic of Ireland M: (00353) 86-172 7654 E: kinkeadj@gmail.com

KINNA, Preb Michael Andrew. b 46. Chich Th Coll 84. **d** 86 **p** 87. C Leominster *Heref* 86–90; TV Wenlock 90–93; R Broseley w Benthall, Jackfield, Linley etc 94–11; P-in-c Coalbrookdale, Iron-Bridge and Lt Wenlock 07–11; RD Telford Severn Gorge 03–10; Preb Heref Cathl 07–11; rtd 11; PtO *Heref* from 11; *Lich* from 18. *15 Underwood, Broseley TF12 5NZ* T: (01952) 881169

KINNAIRD, Jennifer. b 41. Hull Univ BA 62 Ex Univ PGCE 63. NEOC 94. **d** 97 **p** 98. NSM Corbridge w Halton and Newton Hall *Newc* 97–11; rtd 11; PtO *Newc* from 11. *17 Glebelands, Corbridge NE45 5DS* T: (01434) 632695 E: j.kinnaird@btopenworld.com *or* j.kinnaird1356@btinternet.com

KINNAIRD, Keith. b 42. Chich Th Coll 72. **d** 75 **p** 76. C Didcot St Pet *Ox* 75–78; C Abingdon w Shippon 78–82; P-in-c Sunningwell 82–90; P-in-c Radley 88–90; R Radley and Sunningwell 90–95; Chapl Abingdon Hosp 79–92; V Old Shoreham *Chich* 95–00; V New Shoreham 95–00; V Caversham St Andr Ox 00–07; Voc Adv and Adv for Min of Healing 00–07; rtd 07; PtO *Ox* 07–18. *2 Weaver Row, Garston Lane, Wantage OX12 7DZ* T/F: (01235) 760867 E: keithkinnaird@btinternet.com

KINNEY, Robert Scott. b 81. Univ of Chicago BA 04 Univ of Illinois MS 08 Bris Univ PhD 15. **d** 14 **p** 16. PtO *Eur* 16–19; Hon C Vienna from 19. *Schottengasse 7/2/4/11A, Wien 1010, Austria* T/F: (001) (773) 771 0771 E: rkinney@simeontrust.org

KINRADE, Nicol Wendy. b 73. St Chad's Coll Dur BA 97 Newc Univ MA 98. Westcott Ho Cam 13. **d** 15 **p** 16. C Ditchling, Streat and Westmeston *Chich* 15–18; P-in-c Highbrook and W Hoathly from 18. *The Vicarage, North Lane, West Hoathly, East Grinstead RH19 4QF* T: (01342) 810183 E: mother.nicol@gmail.com

KINSELLA, Nigel Paul. b 66. Wolv Univ LLB 95. Westcott Ho Cam 00. **d** 02 **p** 03. C Attleborough w Besthorpe *Nor* 02–03; C Quidenham Gp 03–05; R E w W Harling, Bridgham w Roudham, Larling etc 05–10; CF from 10. *c/o MOD Chaplains (Army)* T: (01264) 383430 F: 381824 E: nigelkinsella@btinternet.com

KINSEY, Canon Bruce Richard Lawrence. b 59. K Coll Lon BD 81 AKC 81 MTh 86 MA 94 Down Coll Cam MA 95 Balliol Coll Ox MA 15. Wycliffe Hall Ox. **d** 84 **p** 85. C Gt Stanmore *Lon* 84–88; C Shepherd's Bush St Steph w St Thos 88–91; Chapl and Fell Down Coll Cam 91–01; Hd Philosophy and RS Perse Sch Cam 01–10; Sen Tutor 10–14; Fell and Chapl Ball Coll Ox from 14; PtO *Ely* 07–18; *Ox* from 17; Hon Can Ely Cathl from 17. *Balliol College, Broad Street, Oxford OX1 3BJ* T: (01865) 277777 E: bruce@balliol.ox.ac.uk

KINSEY, Russell Frederick David. b 34. Sarum Th Coll 59. **d** 62 **p** 63. C Twerton *B & W* 62–66; C N Cadbury 66–75; P Yarlington 66–75; P-in-c Compton Pauncefoot w Blackford 66–75; P-in-c Maperton 66–75; P-in-c N Cheriton 66–75; TV Camelot Par 76–79; V Pill 79–82; P-in-c Easton-in-Gordano w Portbury and Clapton 80–82; V Pill w Easton in Gordano and Portbury 82–92; rtd 94. *25 Newbourne Road, Weston-super-Mare BS22 8NF*

KINYANJUI, Peter Thiongo. b 65. St Paul's Coll Limuru 91. **d** 94 **p** 94. C Jericho St Phil Kenya 94; V Kajiado St Jo 94–95; Adn Loitokitok 95–96; V Thogoto 97–00; USA 01–06; PtO *Chelmsf* from 11. *91 Blake Avenue, Barking IG11 9SB* M: 07557-243106 E: mabipeter@yahoo.co.uk

KIPLING, Miss Susan Jane. b 49. Girton Coll Cam BA 70 MA 73. Westcott Ho Cam 04. **d** 06 **p** 08. C Old Basing and Lychpit *Win* 06–07; C N Hants Downs 07–10; R Brington w Whilton and Norton etc *Pet* 10–17; rtd 17; PtO *Win* from 18. *Westbourne, Goodworth Clatford, Andover SP11 7QX* T: (01264) 352579 E: suekipling@btinternet.com

KIPPAX, Canon Michael John. b 48. Open Univ BA 82. SWMTC 89. **d** 92 **p** 93. C Camborne *Truro* 92–95; C Woughton Ox 95–96; TV 96–98; R St Illogan *Truro* 98–12; Hon Can Truro Cathl 08–12; rtd 12; PtO *Glouc* from 16. *33 Berkeley Crescent, Lydney GL15 5SH* T: (01594) 840497 E: mikekippax@gmail.com

KIRBY, Antony Philip. b 60. Leeds Univ BA 11. Yorks Min Course 08. **d** 11 **p** 12. C Richmond w Hudswell and Downholme and Marske *Leeds* 11–15; P-in-c Barningham w Hutton Magna and Wycliffe 15–18; P-in-c Gilling and Kirkby Ravensworth 15–18; R Holmedale from 19. *The Vicarage, Gilling West, Richmond DL10 5JG* T: (01748) 850349 M: 07594-615190 E: antonykirby01@btinternet.com

KIRBY, David Graham. b 58. Univ of Wales (Cardiff) BA 80. Wycliffe Hall Ox BA 85 MA 92. **d** 86 **p** 87. C Northallerton w Kirby Sigston *York* 86–89; C Southport Ch Ch *Liv* 89–92; R Bishop Burton w Walkington *York* 92–07; R Weston Favell

Pet from 07; Warden Lay Past Min from 10. *The Rectory, Church Way, Northampton NN3 3BX* T: (01604) 413218 E: kirbydg@gmail.com

KIRBY, Mrs Elizabeth. b 56. City Univ BSc 79. ERMC 06. **d** 10 **p** 11. NSM Bury St Edmunds All SS w St Jo and St Geo *St E* 10–12; C Ipswich St Mary at Stoke w St Pet and St Fran 12–14; P-in-c Elmton *Derby* 14–18; P-in-c Whitwell 14–18; R Elmton w Creswell and Whitwell w Steetley 18–19; rtd 19. *Address temp unknown* E: liz.kirby@btinternet.com

KIRBY, Miss Kathryn Margaret. b 52. Girton Coll Cam BA 74 MA 78 Hughes Hall Cam PGCE 75 Leeds Univ MA 08 MCLIP 82. Coll of Resurr Mirfield 06. **d** 07 **p** 08. NSM Sale St Paul *Ches* 07–09; NSM Gatley 09–10; V Macclesfield St Paul 10–15; rtd 15; PtO *Truro* from 15; *Ches* from 15. *Chy Lowen, 1 Rowan Road, Wadebridge PL27 7SN* T: (01208) 369963 M: 07745-434266 E: k.m.kirby@btinternet.com

KIRBY, Michael Christopher. b 63. BSc BTh MSc MA PhD CSci FHEA. **d** 13 **p** 14. NSM Blackb Cathl 13–16; PV Ches Cathl 16–18; Chapl Countess of Chester Hosp NHS Foundn Trust 17; PtO *Ches* from 17; *Liv* from 18; Chapl Liv Cathl from 18. *22 Elstree Road, Liverpool L6 8NU* T: 0151-228 6178 E: mkirby1821@aol.com

KIRBY, Paul Michael. b 51. Wycliffe Hall Ox 74 Seabury-Western Th Sem Illinois 99. **d** 76 **p** 77. C Gateacre *Liv* 76–79; C Barton Seagrave w Warkton *Pet* 79–83; V Bidston *Ches* 83–93; V Ormskirk *Liv* 93–99; Team Ldr Chapl E Kent Hosps NHS Trust 99–00; Sen Team Ldr Chapl E Kent Hosps Univ NHS Foundn Trust 00–14; Chapl Manager E and Coastal Kent Primary Care Trust 08–14; Bp's Adv for Hosp Chapl *Cant* 02–14; rtd 14. *74 Churchfield Way, Wye, Ashford TN25 5ET* T: (01233) 812347 M: 07811-134383 E: kirby74@btinternet.com

KIRBY, Richard Arthur. b 48. Lon Univ BSc 69. **d** 05 **p** 06. OLM Wellington All SS w Eyton *Lich* 05–07; NSM 11–16; PtO 07–11; rtd 16; PtO *S'well* from 17. *16 Dover Back Close, Ravenshead, Nottingham NG15 9ER*

KIRBY, Simon Thomas. b 67. Lon Bible Coll BA 92. NTMTC 00. **d** 03 **p** 04. C Woodside Park St Barn *Lon* 03–06; Lic Preacher 06–11; Chapl Wren Academy 08–12; C Friern Barnet St Jas *Lon* 11–12; V Cogges and S Leigh *Ox* from 13; V N Leigh 13–16. *Cogges Priory, Church Lane, Witney OX28 3LA* T: (01993) 702155 M: 07862-254540 E: simonkirby@gmail.com

KIRBY, Stennett Roger. b 54. St Pet Coll Ox BA 75 MA 79. Sarum & Wells Th Coll 75. **d** 77 **p** 78. C Belsize Park *Lon* 77–79; NSM Plumstead St Nic *S'wark* 88; C Leic Ch Sav 90–91; TV Hanley H Ev *Lich* 91–95; P-in-c Walsall St Pet 95–01; V 01–07; V W Ham *Chelmsf* 07–18; rtd 18. *11 Aulton Crescent, Hinckley LE10 0XA* T: (01455) 371542 E: srkirby2016@outlook.com

KIRK, Alastair James. b 71. St Jo Coll Dur BSc 93 PhD 98 Fitzw Coll Cam BA 06. Ridley Hall Cam 04. **d** 07 **p** 08. C Tong *Bradf* 07–10; C Laisterdyke 08–10; Chapl Warw Univ *Cov* 10–14; V Burley in Wharfedale *Leeds* from 14. *The Vicarage, 21 Southfield Road, Burley in Wharfedale, Ilkley LS29 7PB* T: (01943) 863216 M: 07725-991073 E: alastair_kirk@yahoo.co.uk

KIRK, Andrew. See KIRK, John Andrew

KIRK, Clive John Charles. b 37. FIBMS 66. Guildf Dioc Min Course 95. **d** 98 **p** 99. OLM E Molesey St Paul *Guildf* 98–04; NSM E Horsley and Ockham w Hatchford and Downside 04–10; rtd 10; PtO *Guildf* from 10. *63 Send Barns Lane, Send, Woking GU23 7BS* T: (01483) 211799 E: candakirk@btinternet.com

KIRK, Miss Erika Cottam. b 55. Nottm Univ LLB 76. St Jo Coll Nottm MA 98. **d** 98 **p** 99. NSM Epperstone *S'well* 98–03; NSM Gonalston 98–03; NSM Oxton 98–03; NSM Calverton 98–03; NSM Woodborough 98–03; NSM Burton Joyce w Bulcote and Stoke Bardolph 03–08; NSM Edingley w Halam 08–10; NSM Gedling 11–16; Warden Sacrista Prebend Retreat Ho 16–18; PV S'well Minster from 18. *24 St Helen's Crescent, Burton Joyce, Nottingham NG14 5DW* T: 0115-931 4125 E: erika.kirk@btinternet.com

KIRK, The Ven Gavin John. b 61. Southn Univ BTh Heythrop Coll Lon MA. Chich Th Coll 83. **d** 86 **p** 87. C Seaford w Sutton *Chich* 86–89; Chapl and Succ Roch Cathl 89–91; Min Can 89–91; Hon PV 91–98; Asst Chapl K Sch Roch 91–98; Can Res Portsm Cathl 98–03; Can Res and Prec Linc Cathl 03–16; Adn Linc from 16; PtO *S'well* from 06. *Edward King House, The Old Palace, Lincoln LN2 1PU* T: (01522) 504039 E: archdeacon.lincoln@lincoln.anglican.org

KIRK, Geoffrey. b 45. Keble Coll Ox BA 67. Coll of Resurr Mirfield 71. **d** 72 **p** 73. C Leeds St Aid *Ripon* 72–74; C St Marylebone St Mark w St Luke *Lon* 74–76; C Kennington St Jo *S'wark* 77–79; C Kennington St Jo w St Jas 79–81; P-in-c

Lewisham St Steph and St Mark 81–87; V 87–12; rtd 12. *60 Burnt Ash Road, London SE12 8PY* E: gkirkuk@aol.com

KIRK, Miss Geraldine Mercedes. b 49. Hull Univ MA 89. **d** 87 **p** 94. Ind Chapl *Linc* 87–99; P-in-c Bridgwater St Jo *B & W* 99–14; Chapl Somerset Primary Care Trust 99–14; rtd 14; PtO *B & W* from 15. *121 Newton Road, Bath BA2 1RU* T: (01225) 400688 E: revkirk52@gmail.com

KIRK, Henry Logan. b 52. Adelaide Univ BA 74 New Coll Edin BD 77 K Coll Lon MA 96. **d** 80 **p** 81. Chapl Dioc Coll Cape Prov S Africa 80–85; Asst Master Haileybury Coll 86; Asst Chapl Rugby Sch 86–93; Dep Hd Dulwich Coll Prep Sch 93–94; NSM S Dulwich St Steph *S'wark* 93–94; C Linslade *Ox* 94–96; Chapl Birkenhead Sch 96–03; Chapl Abingdon Sch 04–11; Chapl R Russell Sch Croydon from 12. *Royal Russell School, Coombe Lane, Croydon CR0 5RN* T: (020) 8657 4433 E: hkirk@royalrussell.co.uk

KIRK, John Andrew. b 37. Lon Univ BD 61 AKC 61 MPhil 75 Fitzw Ho Cam BA 63. Ridley Hall Cam 61. **d** 63 **p** 64. C Finchley Ch Ch *Lon* 63–66; Argentina 66–79; SAMS 79–81; CMS 82–90; Dean of Miss Selly Oak Coll Birm 90–99; Dept of Th Birm Univ 99–02; PtO *Glouc* from 99; rtd 02. *The Old Stable, Market Square, Lechlade GL7 3AB* T: (01367) 253254

KIRK, Natalie Roberta. See GARRETT, Natalie Roberta

KIRK, Canon Steven Paul. b 59. Ex Univ LLB 80 Univ of Wales (Cardiff) BD 87 LLM 94. St Mich Coll Llan 84. **d** 87 **p** 88. C Ebbw Vale *Mon* 87–89; PV Llan Cathl 89–91; PV and Succ 91–94; V Port Talbot St Agnes w Oakwood *Llan* 94–01; TR Aberavon 01–07; AD Margam 06–07; V Ystrad Mynach w Llanbradach from 07; Can Llan Cathl from 07; AD Merthyr Tydfil and Caerphilly from 14. *The Vicarage, Cedar Way, Ystrad Mynach, Hengoed CF82 7DR* T: (01443) 813246

KIRKBRIDE, Martin Lea. b 51. Oak Hill Th Coll BA 94. **d** 97 **p** 98. C Lancaster St Thos *Blackb* 97–00; TV Hampreston *Sarum* 00–05; V Lenton *S'well* 05–11; Dioc Learning Adv *Cov* 11–14; Assoc Min Cov Cathl 12–14; P-in-c Wembury *Ex* from 14 and 14–18; C 19; PtO *B & W* from 19. *17 The Fairways, Sherford, Taunton TA1 3PA* M: 07983-852456 E: martinkirkbride@aol.com

KIRKBY, Canon John Victor Michael. b 39. Lon Univ BScEng 62 BD 73. Ridley Hall Cam 65. **d** 67 **p** 68. C Muswell Hill St Jas *Lon* 67–70; Chapl Hatf Poly *St Alb* 71–75; V Wootton 75–86; RD Elstow 82–86; R Byfleet *Guildf* 86–92; P-in-c Potten End w Nettleden *St Alb* 92–97; V 97–05; TV Gt Berkhamsted, Gt and Lt Gaddesden etc 05–08; Chapl Ashridge Business Sch 92–08; rtd 08; PtO *St Alb* from 08; Can Masindi Uganda from 09. *3 Hillside Gardens, Berkhamsted HP4 2LE* T: (01442) 872725 E: jvmkirkby@aol.com

KIRKER, Richard Ennis. b 51. Sarum & Wells Th Coll 72. **d** 77. C Hitchin *St Alb* 77–78; Chief Exec LGCM 79–08. *10 Coopers Close, London E1 4BB* T: (020) 7791 1802 M: 07798-805428 E: richard@richardkirker.com

✠**KIRKHAM, The Rt Revd John Dudley Galtrey.** b 35. Trin Coll Cam BA 59 MA 63. Westcott Ho Cam 60. **d** 62 **p** 63 **c** 76. C Ipswich St Mary le Tower *St E* 62–65; Bp's Chapl *Nor* 65–69; P-in-c Rockland St Mary w Hellington 67–69; Papua New Guinea 69–70; C St Martin-in-the-Fields *Lon* 70–72; C Westmr St Marg 70–72; Abp's Dom Chapl *Cant* 72–76; Area Bp Sherborne *Sarum* 76–81 and 81–01; Can and Preb Sarum Cathl 77–01; Abp's Adv to the Headmasters' Conf from 90; Bp HM Forces 92–01; rtd 01; Hon Asst Bp Sarum from 01; Can and Preb Sarum Cathl from 02. *Flamstone House, Flamstone Street, Bishopstone, Salisbury SP5 4BZ* T: (01722) 780221

KIRKHAM, Mrs Judith Mary. b 52. **d** 13 **p** 14. OLM Stalmine w Pilling *Blackb* from 13; OLM Waterside Par from 13. *4 Stalmine Country Park, Neds Lane, Stalmine, Poulton-le-Fylde FY6 0LW* T: (01253) 702711 M: 07508-884528 E: judithkirkham@hotmail.com

KIRKHAM, June Margaret. b 54. EMMTC 99. **d** 02 **p** 03. C Nottingham St Jude *S'well* 02–06; P-in-c Broxtowe 06–11; V 11–19; rtd 19. *12 Lyndhurst Avenue, Grimsby DN33 2AW*

KIRKLAND, Richard John. b 53. Leic Univ BA 75. Cranmer Hall Dur 76. **d** 79 **p** 80. C Knutsford St Jo and Toft *Ches* 79–82; C Bebington 82–89; V Poulton Lancelyn H Trin 89–95; V Hoole from 95. *All Saints' Vicarage, 2 Vicarage Road, Chester CH2 3HZ* T: (01244) 322056 E: j.kirkland@hender.org.uk

KIRKMAN, Richard Marsden. b 55. Cranmer Hall Dur. **d** 87 **p** 88. C Bridlington Priory *York* 87–90; TV Thirsk 90–96; R Escrick and Stillingfleet w Naburn from 96; RD Derwent 01–11; P-in-c Bubwith w Skipwith from 11. *The Rectory, York Road, Escrick, York YO19 6EY* T: (01904) 728406 E: richarmk.777@gmail.com or rectorofescrick@outlook.com

KIRKPATRICK, Nigel David Joseph. b 68. CITC BTh 96. **d** 96 **p** 97. C Portadown St Columba *Arm* 96–99; C Lecale Gp *D & D* 99–01; I Killinchy w Kilmood and Tullynakill 01–07;

I Gilnahirk 07–19; I Kilroot and Templecorran *Conn* from 19. *Address temp unknown*

KIRKPATRICK, Reginald. b 48. **d** 07 **p** 08. OLM Ditchingham, Hedenham, Broome, Earsham etc *Nor* from 07. *18 Clark Road, Ditchingham, Bungay NR35 2QQ* T: (01986) 893645 E: revregkirk@uwclub.net

KIRK-SPRIGGS, Graham Voysey. b 91. Sheff Hallam Univ BA 12. Ripon Coll Cuddesdon BA 17. **d** 17 **p** 18. C Nor St Pet Mancroft w St Jo Maddermarket from 17. *63 Recreation Road, Norwich NR2 3PA* T: (01603) 456112 M: 07787-041810 E: graham.kirk-spriggs@outlook.com

KIRKUP, Nigel Norman. b 54. K Coll Lon BD 79 AKC 79. **d** 80 **p** 80. Hon C Catford (Southend) and Downham *S'wark* 80–83; Hon C Surbiton St Andr and St Mark 83–85; Hon C Shirley St Geo 85–93; PtO *Lon* 96–09. *10 Norfolk Buildings, Brighton BN1 2DZ* M: 07817-458076 E: nigelkirkup@hotmail.com

KIRKWOOD, Canon David Christopher. b 40. Pemb Coll Ox BA 63. Clifton Th Coll 63. **d** 65 **p** 66. C Wilmington *Roch* 65–68; C Green Street Green 68–72; Youth and Area Sec BCMS 72–73; Educn and Youth Sec 73–80; Hon C Sidcup Ch Ch *Roch* 74–80; V Rothley *Leic* 80–92; RD Goscote II 84–88; RD Goscote 88–90; P-in-c Toxteth St Philemon w St Gabr and St Cleopas *Liv* 92–95; TR 95–01; TR Harlow Town Cen w Lt Parndon *Chelmsf* 01–07; AD Toxteth and Wavertree *Liv* 96–01; AD Harlow *Chelmsf* 04–07; Hon Can Chelmsf Cathl 07; rtd 07. *7 Dunoon Close, Sinfin, Derby DE24 9NF* E: davidk@minternet.org

KIRLEW, John Richard Francis. b 52. STETS 92. **d** 05 **p** 06. NSM Castle Cary w Ansford *B & W* 05–08; P-in-c Colwyn *S & B* 08–13; V 13–15; Dioc Rural Life Adv 09–15; TV Three Valleys *Sarum* from 15. *The Rectory, Holwell, Sherborne DT9 5LF* T: (01963) 23570 E: richard.kirlew@btinternet.com

KIRTON, Canon Richard Arthur. b 43. Dur Univ BA 67 MA 73. Wycliffe Hall Ox 68. **d** 69 **p** 70. C Warsop *S'well* 69–72; C Newark St Mary 72–75; Lect Kolej Theolojo Malaysia 76–79; Dean of Studies Th Sem Kuala Lumpur 79–82; P-in-c Kuala Lumpur St Gabr 79–81; Hon Can Kuala Lumpur from 88; P-in-c Bleasby w Halloughton *S'well* 83–89; V Thurgarton w Hoveringham 83–89; V Thurgarton w Hoveringham and Bleasby etc 89–91; Bp's Adv on Overseas Relns 85–91; Tutor Wilson Carlile Coll of Evang 91–98; P-in-c Ollerton w Boughton *S'well* 98–08; rtd 08; PtO *S'well* from 08. *Hill Top, Mosscar Close, Warsop, Mansfield NG20 0BW* T: (01623) 842915 M: 07803-627574 E: richardkirton1@btinternet.com

KISA, Robert. b 82. St Jo Coll Nottm BA 16. **d** 16 **p** 17. C Liv All SS from 17. *1 Callander Road, Liverpool L6 8NT* M: 07815-690760 E: kisarobert2@gmail.com

KISH, Paul Alexander. b 68. K Coll Lon BD 92 AKC 92 Leeds Univ MA 96. St Steph Ho Ox 96. **d** 98 **p** 99. C Prestbury *Glouc* 98–01; Chapl Sutton Valence Sch Kent 01–13; PtO *Cant* 14–16; V Yalding w Collier Street *Roch* from 16. *The Vicarage, Vicarage Road, Yalding, Maidstone ME18 6DR* T: (01622) 814182 M: 07760-355434 E: pkish@btinternet.com *or* vicar@yaldingchurches.co.uk

KISSEL, Mathias. b 65. **d** 19. NSM Basle *Eur* from 19. *Uhlandstrasse 4, 4053 Basle, Switzerland* E: mathias.kissel@anglicanbasel.ch

KISSELL, Barrington John. b 38. Lon Coll of Div 64. **d** 67 **p** 68. C Camborne *Truro* 67–71; C Chorleywood St Andr *St Alb* 71–00; C Bryanston Square St Mary w St Marylebone St Mark *Lon* from 00; Dir Faith Sharing Min from 74. *Garden Flat, 19 Lena Gardens, London W6 7PY* T: (020) 7258 5040 E: bkissell1@aol.com

KISSELL, Jonathan Mark Barrington. b 66. Glos Univ BA 93. Trin Coll Bris 99. **d** 01 **p** 02. C Stevenage St Pet Broadwater *St Alb* 01–05; C Dublin St Patr Cathl Gp *D & G* 05–11; Chapl Arbour Hill Pris 05–11; PtO *S'wark* 12–13; Asst Chapl YMCA from 14; C Surbiton St Matt *S'wark* 13–15; C Tolworth, Hook and Surbiton 15–15; PtO *Lon* 16; C Teddington St Mark from 16. *83 Beresford Avenue, Surbiton KT5 9LW* T: (020) 8977 7733 M: 07708-934268 E: jonkissell@mac.com *or* jon@stjohnshamptonwick.org

KITCHEN, Ian Brian. b 60. Worc Coll Ox BA 81 Southn Univ PGCE 82. Wycliffe Hall Ox 98. **d** 00 **p** 01. C Brandesburton and Leven w Catwick *York* 00–03; P-in-c Coxwold and Husthwaite 03–11; V 11–12; P-in-c Crayke w Brandsby and Yearsley 03–11; R 11–12; R Derwent Ings from 12. *The Rectory, Church Lane, Wheldrake, York YO19 6AW* T: (01904) 448230 E: dulloldman@gmail.com

KITCHEN, Martin. b 47. N Lon Poly BA 71 K Coll Lon BD 76 AKC 77 Man Univ PhD 88. S'wark Ord Course 77. **d** 79 **p** 80. Lect CA Tr Coll Blackheath 79–83; Hon C Kidbrooke St Jas *S'wark* 79–83; Chapl Man Poly 83–88; TV Man Whitworth 83–86; TR 86–88; Adv In-Service Tr *S'wark* 88–95; Dioc Co-ord of Tr 95–97; Can Res S'wark Cathl 88–97; Can Res Dur

Cathl 97–05; Sub-Dean 99–05; Dean Derby 05–07; P-in-c S Rodings *Chelmsf* 08–11; rtd 11; PtO *Newc* from 12. *4 Town Farm Close, Wall, Hexham NE46 4DH* T: (01434) 689696

KITCHENER, Christopher William. b 46. Open Univ BA. Sarum & Wells Th Coll 82. **d** 84 **p** 85. C Bexleyheath Ch Ch *Roch* 84–88; V Gravesend St Mary 88–97; V Biggin Hill 97–07; V St Mary Cray and St Paul's Cray 07–11; rtd 11; Bp's Officer for Retired Clergy Widows and Widowers *Roch* from 11; PtO from 11. *22 Renton Drive, Orpington BR5 4HH* T: (01732) 761766 E: chriskitchener4@gmail.com

KITCHENER, Mrs Evarina Carol. b 51. Stockwell Coll of Educn CertEd 70 Heythrop Coll Lon MA 00. Cant Sch of Min 89. **d** 92 **p** 94. NSM Gravesend St Mary *Roch* 92–97; NSM Biggin Hill 97–07; Asst Chapl Bromley Hosps NHS Trust 98–99; Distr Evang Miss Enabler S Prov URC 99–01; Par Development Officer *Roch* 01–07; C Chislehurst St Nic 07–11; P-in-c Seal St Lawr 11–12; V 12–16; P-in-c Underriver 11–12; V 12–16; V Seal Chart w Underriver 16; rtd 16. *22 Renton Drive, Orpington BR5 4HH* E: carolkitchener2@gmail.com

KITCHENER, Canon Michael Anthony. b 45. Trin Coll Cam BA 67 MA 70 PhD 71. Cuddesdon Coll 70. **d** 71 **p** 72. C Aldwick *Chich* 71–74; C Caversham *Ox* 74–77; Tutor Coll of Resurr Mirfield 77–83; Prin NEOC *Dur* 83–90; Hon Can Newc Cathl 84–90; Can Res and Chan Blackb Cathl 90–95; P-in-c Rydal *Carl* 95–99; Warden Rydal Hall 95–99; Warden Rydal Hall and Ldr Rydal Hall Community 95–99; Can Res Nor Cathl 99–05; Dioc Dir of Ords 99–04; Bp's Officer for Ord and Initial Tr 04–05; rtd 05; LtO *Edin* 06–10; LtO *Arg* from 10. *Croft Cottage, Creag an Tairbh Beag, Ford, Lochgilphead PA31 8RH* T: (01546) 810062 E: kitcheners@yahoo.co.uk

KITCHIN, Kenneth. b 46. Trin Coll Bris. **d** 89 **p** 90. C Barrow St Mark *Carl* 89–93; C Dalton-in-Furness 93–95; P-in-c Dearham 95–01; P-in-c Clifton 01–07; P-in-c Dean 01–07; P-in-c Mosser 01–07; R Clifton, Dean and Mosser 07–10; rtd 10; PtO *Carl* from 10. *7 Allerdale, Cockermouth CA13 0BN* E: kenkitchin@yahoo.co.uk

KITCHING, Daphne. b 48. Yorks Min Course. **d** 09 **p** 10. NSM Swanland *York* 09–17; PtO from 17. *23 Old Pond Place, North Ferriby HU14 3JE* T: (01482) 635159 E: daphnekitching@hotmail.com

KITCHING, Miss Elizabeth. b 49. Trent Park Coll of Educn CertEd 74. St Jo Coll Nottm. **d** 01 **p** 02. C Northallerton w Kirby Sigston *York* 01–05; V Cloughton and Burniston w Ravenscar etc 05–13; V Hackness w Harwood Dale 05–13; rtd 13; PtO *York* from 13. *31 Osgodby Crescent, Scarborough YO11 3JP* M: 07889-425025 E: elizabethkitching@btinternet.com

KITE, Paul Anthony. b 64. SEITE BA 14. **d** 14 **p** 15. C W Sheppey *Cant* 14–17; TV N Downs from 17. *The Vicarage, Upper Street, Hollingbourne, Maidstone ME17 1UJ* T: (01622) 880243 E: revkite@btinternet.com

KITELEY, Robert John. b 51. Hull Univ BSc 73 Univ of Wales (Abth) MSc 75 Lon Univ PhD 82. Trin Coll Bris. **d** 83 **p** 84. C Bebington *Ches* 83–88; C Hoole 88–91; V Plas Newton 91–99; R Ashtead *Guildf* 99–14; rtd 14. *2 Doreen Close, Farnborough GU14 9HB* T: (01276) 428834 E: johntew51@gmail.com

KITLEY, Canon David Buchan. b 53. St Jo Coll Dur BA. Trin Coll Bris 78. **d** 81 **p** 82. C Tonbridge St Steph *Roch* 81–84; C-in-c Southall Em CD *Lon* 84–91; V Dartford Ch Ch *Roch* 91–09; RD Dartford 98–07; V Kippington 09–20; rtd 20; Bp's Adv for Overseas Links *Roch* from 09; Hon Can Roch Cathl from 05; Hon Can Mpwapwa from 05. *The Vicarage, 59 Kippington Road, Sevenoaks TN13 2LL* T: (01732) 452112 E: kitley@clara.net

KITSON, Kevin. b 64. **d** 14 **p** 15. NSM Dur N 14–16; PtO from 17. *24 Village Gate, Howden le Wear, Crook DL15 8EF* T: (01388) 763775 M: 07950-341110 E: kevinkitson64@gmail.com

KIVETT, Michael Stephen. b 50. Bethany Coll W Virginia BA 72. Chr Th Sem Indiana MDiv 76 Sarum & Wells Th Coll 76. **d** 77 **p** 78. C Harnham *Sarum* 77–80; C E Dereham *Nor* 80–83; R S Walsham and V Upton 83–88; Chapl Lt Plumstead Hosp 84–88; V Chard St Mary *B & W* 88–99; TR Chard and Distr 99–04; RD Crewkerne and Ilminster 93–98; R Staplegrove w Norton Fitzwarren from 04. *The Rectory, Rectory Drive, Staplegrove, Taunton TA2 6AP* T: (01823) 270211 E: kivett@btinternet.com

KIYAGA, Innocent Nathan. b 87. Redcliffe Coll Glouc BA 12. Lon Sch of Th MA 13. **d** 15 **p** 16. Min for Internat Miss Dio Mbeere Kenya 15–16; NSM Upton *Ex* from 16; Asst Chapl Univ of St Mark and St Jo from 16. *Brunel Manor, Teignmouth Road, Torquay TQ1 4SF* M: 07964-532187 E: nathan@kiyaga.com

KLAIR, Sarbjit Singh. b 65. Bath Univ BSc 88 FCA 92. Ridley Hall Cam 15. **d** 17 **p** 18. C Thames Ditton *Guildf* from 17. *4 Quinton Road, Thames Ditton KT7 0AX* M: 07711-752778 E: sarb.klair@gmail.com

KLIMAS, Canon Lynda. b 58. Jes Coll Cam BA 89 MA 93. Cranmer Hall Dur 89. **d** 90 **p** 94. Par Dn Sandy *St Alb* 90–93; Par Dn Bishop's Stortford St Mich 93–94; C 94–98; P-in-c Weston and C Baldock w Bygrave 98–03; TV Baldock w Bygrave and Weston 03–04; V Cople, Moggerhanger and Willington 04–13; R Maulden from 13; RD Ampthill and Shefford from 13; Hon Can St Alb from 13. *The Rectory, Clophill Road, Maulden, Bedford MK45 2AA* E: rev.l.klimas@btinternet.com

KNAPP, Antony Blair. b 48. Imp Coll Lon BSc 68. NOC 86. **d** 89 **p** 90. C Bolton St Jas w St Chrys *Bradf* 89–92; V Kettlewell w Conistone, Hubberholme etc 92–00; TR Swindon Dorcan *Bris* 00–13; rtd 13; PtO *Llan* from 14. *5 Mountjoy Place, Penarth CF64 2TB* T: (01793) 525130

KNAPP, Canon Bryan Thomas. b 61. Trin Coll Bris BA 91. **d** 91 **p** 92. C S Gillingham *Roch* 91–95; V Chatham St Paul w All SS 95–09; V Paddock Wood from 09; RD 13–19; Hon Can Roch Cathl from 15. *The Vicarage, 169 Maidstone Road, Paddock Wood, Tonbridge TN12 6DZ* T: (01892) 833917 E: bryan@standrewspw.org.uk

KNAPP (née STOCKER), Canon Rachael Ann. b 64. Bris Univ BA 86. Trin Coll Bris BA 91. **d** 91 **p** 94. C Ditton *Roch* 91–95; C Chatham St Paul w All SS 95–08; Chapl Bennett Memorial Dioc Sch Tunbridge Wells from 08; Hon Can Roch Cathl from 18. *The Vicarage, 169 Maidstone Road, Paddock Wood, Tonbridge TN12 6DZ* T: (01892) 833917 *or* 521595 E: knapp@bennett.kent.sch.uk

KNEEBONE, Canon Patricia Jane. b 53. Man Univ BA 74 Lon Univ BD 94. SWMTC 08. **d** 10 **p** 11. NSM Newquay *Truro* from 10; Hon Can Truro Cathl from 15. *34 Henver Road, Newquay TR7 3BN* M: 07966-703924 E: janekneebone@gmail.com

KNEEN, Preb Michael John. b 55. Univ Coll Lon BSc 76 MSc 77 St Jo Coll Dur BA 85. Cranmer Hall Dur 83. **d** 86 **p** 87. C Bishop's Castle w Mainstone *Heref* 86–90; TV Bridgnorth, Tasley, Astley Abbotts, etc 90–08; TV Leominster 08–10; TR from 10; RD from 14; Preb Heref Cathl from 18. *The Rectory, Church Street, Leominster HR6 8NH* T: (01568) 615709 E: mjkneen@btinternet.com

KNIBBS, Peter John. b 55. Birm Univ BDS 78 DDS 93. SWMTC 04. **d** 07 **p** 08. NSM St Illogan *Truro* 07–11; P-in-c Chacewater w St Day and Carharrack 11–14; C 14; P-in-c St Stythians w Perranarworthal and Gwennap 11–14; P-in-c Devoran 11–14; P-in-c Feock 11–14; V Monkseaton St Mary *Newc* 14–16; rtd 16; Hon C N Shields *Newc* from 17; PtO from 16. *85 Holywell Drive, Blyth NE24 3UZ* T: (01670) 302546 E: peter.knibbs@lineone.net

KNIGHT, The Very Revd Alexander Francis (Alec). b 39. St Cath Coll Cam BA 61 MA 65. Wells Th Coll. **d** 63 **p** 64. C Hemel Hempstead *St Alb* 63–68; Chapl Taunton Sch 68–75; Dir Bloxham Project 75–81; Dir of Studies Aston Tr Scheme 81–83; P-in-c Easton and Martyr Worthy *Win* 83–91; Adn Basingstoke 90–98; Can Res Win Cathl 91–98; Dean Linc 98–06; rtd 06; PtO *Sarum* from 15. *Shalom, Clay Street, Whiteparish, Salisbury SP5 2ST* T: (01794) 884402 E: sheelagh_knight@hotmail.com

KNIGHT, Canon Andrew James. b 50. Grey Coll Dur BA 72 Ox Univ BA 74 MA 81. Wycliffe Hall Ox 72. **d** 75 **p** 76. Min Can Brecon Cathl *S & B* 75–78; C Brecon w Battle 75–78; C Morriston 78–82; V 89–00; V Llanwrtyd w Llanddulas in Tir Abad etc 82–89; RD Cwmtawe 97–00; V Sketty 00–15; Can Res Brecon Cathl 98–04; Treas Brecon Cathl 04–15; rtd 15; PtO *S & B* from 15. *105 Frampton Road, Gorseinon, Swansea SA4 4YE* T: (01792) 736159 E: andrewknight@phonecoop.coop

KNIGHT, Andrew Ronald. b 67. **d** 06 **p** 07. C Wolstanton *Lich* 06–09; V 09–14; Chapl Staffs and Stoke on Trent Partnership NHS Trust 14; R Shrewsbury St Giles w Sutton and Atcham *Lich* from 14. *The Rectory, 127 Abbey Foregate, Shrewsbury SY2 6LY* T: (01743) 600691 E: andykn@talktalk.net

KNIGHT, Andrew William. b 71. Hull Univ BSc 92 PhD 96. St Jo Coll Nottm 12. **d** 14 **p** 15. C Mottram in Longdendale *Ches* 14–17; P-in-c Partington and Carrington from 17. *St Mary's Vicarage, Manchester Road, Partington, Manchester M31 4FB* M: 07899-724760 E: andrewknight247@gmail.com

KNIGHT, Mrs Barbara. b 46. St Alb Minl Tr Scheme 86. **d** 90 **p** 94. NSM Weston and Ardeley *St Alb* 90–95; C Norton 95–97; R Barkway, Reed and Buckland w Barley 97–05; rtd 05; PtO *Glouc* from 14. *332 London Road, Charlton Kings, Cheltenham GL52 6YJ*

KNIGHT, Mrs Barbara Mary. b 43. SRN 64 SCM 70. EMMTC 94. **d** 97 **p** 98. NSM Market Harborough and The Transfiguration etc *Leic* 97–99; C Church Langton cum Tur Langton etc 99–02; P-in-c Billesdon and Skeffington 02; R Church Langton cum Tur Langton etc 02–07; rtd 07; PtO *Blackb*

from 07. *1 Whittlewood Drive, Accrington BB5 5DJ* T: (01254) 395549 E: revbarbarak@btopenworld.com

KNIGHT, David Alan. b 59. Lanc Univ BA 81. Ripon Coll Cuddesdon 82. **d** 85 **p** 86. C Stretford All SS *Man* 85–88; C Charlestown 88–89; TV Pendleton St Thos w Charlestown 89–94; V Tysoe w Oxhill and Whatcote *Cov* 94–05; RD Shipston 04–05; Chapl Marie Curie Cen Solihull 06–08; Chapl St Richard's Hospice Worc 06–15; Chapl Mary Stevens Hospice Stourbridge 15–17; Bp's Health Service Adv *Worc* 12–17; Chapl St Wilfrid's Hospice Eastbourne 17–19; Lead Chapl Sussex Community NHS Foundn Trust from 19. *Sussex Community NHS Fouindation Trust, Brighton General Hospital, Elm Grove, Brighton BN2 3EW* T: (01273) 696011 E: davidalanknight@outlook.com

KNIGHT, Canon David Charles. b 45. Lon Univ BA 66 St Edm Hall Ox BA 68 MA 73 ATCL 63. St Steph Ho Ox 68. **d** 70 **p** 71. C Northwood H Trin *Lon* 70–73; C Stevenage All SS Pin Green *St Alb* 73–77; C Cippenham CD *Ox* 77–78; TV W Slough 78–83; Dep Min Can Windsor 81–08; R Lt Stanmore St Lawr *Lon* 83–91; Ecum Officer to Bp Willesden 83–91; Prec and Can Res Chelmsf Cathl 91–01; V Ranmoor *Sheff* 01–08; rtd 08; PtO *Ox* from 09. *12 Bankside, Headington, Oxford OX3 8LT* T: (01865) 761476 E: davidcknight45@gmail.com

KNIGHT, Canon David Lansley. b 33. Em Coll Cam BA 58 MA 61 PGCE 76. Ridley Hall Cam 57. **d** 59 **p** 60. C Chatham St Steph *Roch* 59–63; C Plymouth St Andr *Ex* 63–65; V Gravesend St Aid *Roch* 65–71; V Bexley St Mary 71–98; RD Sidcup 93–97; Hon Can Roch Cathl 97; rtd 98; PtO *Chich* from 98. *1 Newlands Avenue, Bexhill-on-Sea TN39 4HA* T: (01424) 212120

KNIGHT, Mrs Dawn Marie. b 68. RGN 90. Qu Foundn (Course) 16. **d** 19. C Allestree St Nic *Derby* from 19; C Quarndon from 19. *28 Earlswood Drive, Mickleover, Derby DE3 9LN* M: 07789-070260 E: dawnmarieknight@hotmail.co.uk

KNIGHT (née SMITH), Frances Mary. b 48. St Jo Coll York CertEd 69. EMMTC 98. **d** 03 **p** 04. NSM Braunstone *Leic* 03–07; NSM The Abbey Leic 07–12; rtd 12; PtO *Leic* from 15. *32 Aster Way, Burbage, Hinckley LE10 2UQ* T: (01455) 618218 E: frances.knight@mypostonline.co.uk

KNIGHT, Gavin Rees. b 65. St Andr Univ MTheol 94. Ripon Coll Cuddesdon MTh 96. **d** 98 **p** 99. C Solihull *Birm* 98–02; P-in-c Fulham St Andr *Lon* 02–05; P-in-c Fulham St Alb w St Aug 04–05; Chapl Mon Sch 05–11; V Summertown *Ox* from 11. *The Vicarage, 33 Lonsdale Road, Oxford OX2 7ES* T: (01865) 557079 E: vicar@stmichaels-summertown.org.uk

KNIGHT, Isaac John. b 91. St Jo Coll Dur BA 13. Wycliffe Hall Ox 16. **d** 19. C Flackwell Heath *Ox* from 19. *12 Green Crescent, Flackwell Heath, High Wycombe HP10 9JQ* M: 07494-409303 E: revisaacknight@gmail.com

KNIGHT, Joel Matthew. b 88. Nottm Univ BA 11. Wycliffe Hall Ox 14. **d** 17 **p** 18. C Ox St Ebbe w H Trin and St Pet from 17. *81 Marlborough Road, Oxford OX1 4LX* M: 07773-780998 E: jknightgy@gmail.com

KNIGHT, Canon John Bernard. b 34. Fuller Th Sem California DMin 91 ACIS 60. Oak Hill Th Coll 61. **d** 65 **p** 66. C Morden *S'wark* 65–69; USA 69–71; V Summerfield *Birm* 71–80; Hon Can Birm Cathl 01–07; rtd 07; PtO *Birm* from 07; *Worc* from 08. *102 High Haden Road, Cradley Heath B64 7PN* T: 0121-559 0108 E: home@jandmknight.go-plus.net

KNIGHT, Canon John Francis Alan Macdonald. b 36. Coll of Resurr Mirfield 59. **d** 61 **p** 62. C Gwelo Rhodesia 61–66; R Melfort 66–68; C Highlands and P-in-c Chikwaka, Mrewa, Hoyuyu, and Mtoko 68–70; LtO Mashonaland 70–75; R Umtali Zimbabwe 76–81; Dean Mutare 81–87; TR Northampton Em *Pet* 87–97; RD Northn 88–92; P-in-c Greens Norton w Bradden and Lichborough 97–05; Bp's Adv for Min of Healing 99–05; Can Pet Cathl 01–05; rtd 05; PtO *Pet* 06–11; P-in-c Weedon Bec w Everdon and Dodford 11–17; PtO from 17. *The Rectory, High Street, Marston St Lawrence, Banbury OX17 2DB* T: (01295) 368682 E: theknights16@tiscali.co.uk

KNIGHT, Jonathan Morshead. b 59. Fitzw Coll Cam BA 81 MA 85 Jes Coll Cam PhD 91 Jes Coll Ox MA 87 Worc Coll Ox DPhil 02 W Lon Inst of HE PGCE 82 Sheff Univ PGCE 00. Wycliffe Hall Ox 86. **d** 88 **p** 89. C Hillingdon St Jo *Lon* 88–91; NSM Baslow *Derby* 91–92; NSM Curbar and Stoney Middleton 91–92; Lect Bibl Studies Sheff Univ 91–92; Research Fell 92–94; NSM Sheff St Paul 92–94; Bp's Research Asst *Ely* 94–98; Min Whittlesford LEP 95–96; Bp's Dom Chapl 96; Sec Doctrine Commn 96–98; P-in-c Holywell w Needingworth *Ely* 98–01; Tutor Westcott Ho Cam 98–99; OCM from 99; CF (TAVR) 00–03; Hon Lect Th Kent Univ 00–03; Chapl Worc Coll Ox 02–03; Visiting Fell York St Jo Univ from 07; Tutor Grey Coll Dur from 10. *36 Ninth Street, Peterlee SR8 4LZ* M: 07549-170031 E: jonathanknight5@hotmail.com

KNIGHT, Joseph Daniel. b 83. Trin Coll Bris MA 18. **d** 18 **p** 19. C Newnham w Awre and Blakeney *Glouc* from 18. *The Old Library, High Street, Newnham GL14 1AD* M: 07950-712282 E: joeknight@outlook.com

KNIGHT, Keith Kenneth. b 36. Southn Univ BSc 58. Wycliffe Hall Ox 59. **d** 62 **p** 63. C Lower Darwen St Jas *Blackb* 62–64; C Leyland St Andr 64–68; P-in-c Blackb All SS 68–71; Dioc Youth Chapl 71–88; Hon C Burnley St Pet 71–88; Warden Scargill Ho 88–01; rtd 01; PtO *Bradf* 01–14; *Leeds* from 14. *4 The Hawthorns, Sutton-in-Craven, Keighley BD20 8BP* T: (01535) 632920

KNIGHT, Mrs Margaret Owen. b 34. Oak Hill Th Coll 78. **dss** 80 **d** 87 **p** 94. Chorleywood St Andr *St Alb* 80–04; Par Dn 87–94; C 94–04; rtd 94; PtO *St Alb* 04–19. *15A Blacketts Wood Drive, Chorleywood, Rickmansworth WD3 5PY* T: (01923) 283832 E: moknight@waitrose.com

KNIGHT, Canon Michael Richard. b 47. St Jo Coll Dur BA 69 MA 79 Fitzw Coll Cam BA 73 MA 78 St Cross Coll Ox MA 92. Westcott Ho Cam 71. **d** 74 **p** 75. C Bishop's Stortford St Mich *St Alb* 74–75; C Bedford St Andr 75–79; Chapl Angl Students Glas 79–86; V Riddings and Ironville *Derby* 86–91; Lib Pusey Ho 91–94; Fell St Cross Coll Ox 92–94; V Chesterfield St Mary and All SS *Derby* 94–13; P-in-c Chesterfield SS Aug 05–09; Hon Can Derby Cathl 06–13; rtd 13; PtO *S'well* from 14. *1 Leabrook Close, Nottingham NG11 8NW*

KNIGHT, Paul Jeremy. b 53. **d** 94 **p** 95. CA 77–04; C Moreton Say *Lich* 94–96; C Adderley, Ash, Calverhall, Ightfield etc 96–97; V Birstall *Wakef* 97–14; *Leeds* from 14; AD 14–18. *St Peter's Vicarage, King's Drive, Birstall, Batley WF17 9JJ* T/F: (01924) 473715 E: vicar@stpetersbirstall.co.uk

KNIGHT, Peter John. b 51. AKC 73 Ch Ch Coll Cant CertEd 77. Sarum & Wells Th Coll 79. **d** 80 **p** 81. C Greenford H Cross *Lon* 80–83; C Langley Marish *Ox* 83; NSM W Acton St Martin *Lon* 88–90; C E Acton St Dunstan w St Thos 90–92; V Malden St Jo *S'wark* 92–02; Co-ord Chapl HM Pris Long Lartin 02–05; TR Malvern Link w Cowleigh *Worc* 05–10; V 10–17; RD Malvern 13–17; rtd 17. *29 Albert Road, Evesham WR11 4JZ* E: pjknight1951@gmail.com

KNIGHT, Peter Malcolm. b 55. Cam Univ BA 76 Lon Hosp MB, BS 76 MRCGP 85. Trin Coll Bris BA 94. **d** 94 **p** 95. C Quidenham *Nor* 94–97; R Thurton w Ashby St Mary, Bergh Apton etc 97–14; RD Loddon 99–05; NSM Tunis St Geo Tunisia 14–19; PtO *Nor* 14–19; P-in-c Trigg Major CD *Truro* from 19. *The Rectory, Dunheved Road, Launceston PL15 9JE* T: (01566) 777607 E: pandcknight@gmail.com or tl.triggmaj@gmail.com

KNIGHT, Philip Stephen. b 46. Ian Ramsey Coll Brasted 74 Oak Hill Th Coll 75. **d** 77 **p** 78. C Pennycross *Ex* 77–80; C Epsom St Martin *Guildf* 80–83; V Clay Hill St Jo *Lon* 83–86; TV Washfield, Stoodleigh, Withleigh etc *Ex* 86–90; Chapl ATC from 86; Chapl S Warks Hosps 90–94; Chapl S Warks Health Care NHS Trust 94–05; PtO *Cov* from 05; *Ex* from 10; rtd 11. *Coombeside, 122 Alexandria Road, Sidmouth EX10 9HG* T: (01395) 514166 E: psk54@hotmail.co.uk

KNIGHT, Rhona Anton. b 60. Lon Univ MB, BS 85 Surrey Univ MA 04 FRCGP 06. Ridley Hall Cam 14. **d** 16 **p** 17. C Sleaford *Linc* from 16. *56 Clay Hill Road, Sleaford NG34 7TF* T: (01529) 300237 M: 07599-447431 E: revrhona@btinternet.com

KNIGHT, Canon Roger George. b 41. Culham Coll Ox CertEd 63. Linc Th Coll 65. **d** 67 **p** 68. C Bris St Andr Hartcliffe 67–69; Hd Master Twywell Sch Kettering 69–74; V Naseby *Pet* 74–79; P-in-c Haselbech 74–79; R Clipston w Naseby and Haselbech 79–82; C Arthingworth w Kelmarsh and Harrington 79–82; TR Corby SS Pet and Andr w Gt and Lt Oakley 82–88; R Irthlingborough 88–99; RD Higham 89–94; R Burton Latimer 99–03; Can Pet Cathl 92–03; rtd 03; PtO *Pet* from 03. *9 Hollow Wood Road, Burton Latimer, Kettering NN15 5RB* T: (01536) 669618 E: rogerknight41@outlook.com

KNIGHT, Roger Ivan. b 54. K Coll Lon BD 79 AKC 79. Ripon Coll Cuddesdon 79. **d** 80 **p** 81. C Orpington All SS *Roch* 80–84; C St Laur in Thanet *Cant* 84–87; R Cuxton and Halling *Roch* from 87. *The Rectory, 6 Rochester Road, Cuxton, Rochester ME2 1AF* T: (01634) 717134 E: roger@cuxtonandhalling.org.uk

KNIGHT, Stephen. See KNIGHT, Philip Stephen

KNIGHT, Ms Sue Elizabeth. b 47. Southlands Coll Lon CertEd 68. SEITE 01. **d** 03 **p** 04. NSM Lee St Mildred *S'wark* 03–09; NSM Cheltenham St Mary w St Matt and St Luke *Glouc* from 12. *11 Giffard Way, Leckhampton, Cheltenham GL53 0PW* T: (01242) 234363

KNIGHT, Mrs Susan Jane. b 57. Open Univ BSc 99. NTMTC BA 09. **d** 09 **p** 10. C Harlow Town Cen w Lt Parndon *Chelmsf*

09–12; TV 12–16; P-in-c Roydon 15–16; rtd 16. *11 Sweetbriar Lane, Holcombe, Dawlish EX7 0JZ* E: sue@kerryknight.co.uk

KNIGHT, Mrs Susan Margaret. **d** 02 **p** 03. C Clydach *S & B* 02–03; C Cen Swansea 04–05; TV 05–16; rtd 16; PtO *S & B* from 16. *21 Parklands Court, Sketty, Swansea SA2 8LZ* T: (01792) 683049

KNIGHT, William Lawrence. b 39. Univ Coll Lon BSc 61 PhD 65. Coll of Resurr Mirfield 75. **d** 77 **p** 78. C Bp's Hatfield *St Alb* 77–81; Asst Chapl Brussels Cathl *Eur* 81–84; V Pet H Spirit Bretton 84–89; P-in-c Marholm 84–89; TR Riverside *Ox* 89–04; rtd 04; PtO *Chich* from 15. *90 Norfolk Gardens, Littlehampton BN17 5PF* T: (01903) 716750 E: wlnight@tiscali.co.uk

KNIGHT-SCOTT, Catherine Mary. Selw Coll Cam BA 83 MA 00 Goldsmiths' Coll Lon PGCE 11. Ripon Coll Cuddesdon 12. **d** 14 **p** 15. C Orpington All SS *Roch* 14–18; P-in-c Footscray w N Cray 18; P-in-c Sidcup St Jo 18; V Sidcup St Jo w Footscray from 18. *St John's Vicarage, Church Avenue, Sidcup DA14 6BU* E: revcathyks@gmail.com

KNIGHTS, Christopher Hammond. b 61. St Jo Coll Dur BA 83 PhD 88. Linc Th Coll 87. **d** 89 **p** 90. C Stockton St Pet *Dur* 89–92; C Chich St Paul and St Pet 92–94; Tutor Chich Th Coll 92–94; V Ashington *Newc* 94–00; V Monkseaton St Mary 00–04; Dioc Moderator Reader Tr 03–10; P-in-c Scotswood 04–11; R Kelso *Edin* 11–13; P-in-c Coldstream 11–13; Development Worker Hawick Acorn Project 13–14; Ch and Community Development Worker Musselburgh 14–16; PtO *Edin* 13–16; *Newc* 14–16; P-in-c Southampton Lord's Hill and Lord's Wood *Win* from 16. *The Vicarage, 1 Tangmere Drive, Southampton SO16 8GY* T: (023) 8073 1091 M: 07486-425069 E: revchrisknights@gmail.com

KNIGHTS, James William. b 34. AKC 66. **d** 67 **p** 68. C Kettering St Andr *Pet* 67–71; V Braunston w Brooke 71–81; V Dudley St Jo *Worc* 81–97; rtd 97; PtO *Worc* from 98. *192 Brook Farm Drive, Malvern WR14 3SL* T: (01684) 561358

KNIGHTS JOHNSON, Nigel Anthony. b 52. Ealing Tech Coll BA 74 Westmr Coll Ox MTh 99. Wycliffe Hall Ox 78. **d** 80 **p** 81. C Beckenham Ch Ch *Roch* 80–84; CF 84–07; R Ockley, Okewood and Forest Green *Guildf* 07–17; rtd 17; PtO *Ox* from 17; *Eur* from 16. *134 Main Road, Long Hanborough, Witney OX29 8JY* E: nigelknightsjohnson@gmail.com

KNOTT, Barry James Frederick. b 64. Cant Ch Ch Univ BSc 00. St Aug Coll of Th 15. **d** 17 **p** 18. C Allington and Maidstone St Pet *Cant* from 17; C Barming Heath from 17. *17 Paynes Lane, Maidstone ME15 9QU* T: (01622) 749605 M: 07891-199459 E: barryjfknott@msn.com

KNOTT, The Ven Graham Keith. b 53. Oak Hill Th Coll BA 80. **d** 80 **p** 81. C Normanton *Derby* 80–83; C Ripley 83–87; TV Newark w Hawton, Cotham and Shelton *S'well* 87–89; TV Newark 89–97; P-in-c Mansfield St Jo 97–06; AD Mansfield 03–06; P-in-c Croajingolong Australia 06–09; P-in-c Watford *St Alb* 09–11; R Maffra Australia 11–15; R Leongatha from 15; Adn Gippsland from 15. *PO Box 271, Leongatha VIC 3953, Australia* T: (0061) (3) 5662 5043 E: grahamjune74@gmail.com

KNOTT, Preb Janet Patricia. b 50. Avery Hill Coll CertEd 71. S Dios Minl Tr Scheme MTS 91. **d** 92 **p** 94. NSM Clutton w Cameley *B & W* 92–99; Chapl R Sch Bath 94–98; Chapl R High Sch Bath 98–99; R Farmborough, Marksbury and Stanton Prior *B & W* from 99; Chapl Bath Spa Univ from 99; RD Chew Magna *B & W* 04–14; Preb Wells Cathl from 07. *The Rectory, Church Lane, Farmborough, Bath BA3 1AN* T: (01761) 479311 E: jpknott@btinternet.com

KNOTT, Wendy Gillian. b 47. Adelaide Univ BA 78. Melbourne Coll of Div BD 95. **d** 94 **p** 96. NSM Sandy Bay Australia 94–98; NSM New Town St Jas 98–01; NSM Franklin w Esperance 01–05; Hon Chapl Ch Coll Tasmania 97–06; R Wick *Mor* 06–17; P-in-c Thurso 06–17; rtd 17. *39 Ormlie Road, Thurso KW14 7EB* E: rev.wendy@btinternet.com

KNOWERS, Stephen John. b 49. K Coll Lon BD 72 AKC 72. **d** 73 **p** 74. C Bp's Hatfield *St Alb* 73–77; C Cheshunt 77–81; P-in-c Barnet Vale St Mark 81–83; V 83–85; Chapl S Bank Poly *S'wark* 85–92; Chapl S Bank Univ 92–94; V Croydon St Pet 94–06; P-in-c Croydon St Aug 04–06; V S Croydon St Pet and St Aug 06–07; V Shirley St Jo 07–15; AD Croydon Addington 11–15; rtd 15; PtO *Eur* from 15. *Narva Mnt 6-19, Tallinn 10117, Estonia* T: (00372) 5802 4920 E: frstiiv@hotmail.com

KNOWLES, Andrew John. b 66. Wimbledon Sch of Art BA 88. St Jo Coll Nottm 05. **d** 07 **p** 08. C Long Buckby w Watford and W Haddon w Winwick and Ravensthorpe *Pet* 07–11; V Camberley St Mary *Guildf* from 11; Asst Dioc Dir of Ords from 15. *St Mary's Vicarage, 37 Park Road, Camberley GU15 2SP* T: (01276) 22085 or 685167 E: vicar@stmaryscamberley.org.uk

KNOWLES, Canon Andrew William Allen. b 46. St Cath Coll Cam BA 68 MA 72. St Jo Coll Nottm 69. **d** 71 **p** 72. C Leic H Trin 71–74; C Cambridge H Trin *Ely* 74–77; C Woking St Jo *Guildf* 77–81; V Goldsworth Park 81–93; V Wyke 93–98; Dioc Officer Educn and Development of Lay People 93–98; Can Res Chelmsf Cathl 98–11; rtd 11; PtO *Carl* from 12. *68 Appleby Road, Kendal LA9 6HE* T: (01539) 723478 E: andrew.knowles@btinternet.com

KNOWLES, Charles Howard. b 43. Sheff Univ BSc 65 Fitzw Coll Cam BA 69 MA 73. Westcott Ho Cam 67. **d** 69 **p** 70. C Bilborough St Jo *S'well* 69–72; V Choral S'well Minster 72–82; V Cinderhill 82–94; AD Nottingham W 91–94; V Cov St Mary 94–06; AD Cov S 96–02; C Burnsall w Rylstone *Bradf* 06–08; C Linton in Craven 06–08; C Kettlewell w Conistone, Hubberholme etc 06–08; rtd 08; PtO *Bradf* 08–14; *Leeds* 14–16. *Ivy Cottage, Linton, Skipton BD23 5HH*

KNOWLES, Clay. *See* KNOWLES, Melvin Clay

KNOWLES, Clifford. b 35. Open Univ BA 82. NW Ord Course 74. **d** 77 **p** 78. C Urmston *Man* 77–80; V Chadderton St Luke 80–87; V Heywood St Luke w All So 87–95; AD Heywood and Middleton 92–95; PtO *Linc* 95–98; rtd 00; PtO *Linc* from 02. *12B Far Lane, Coleby, Lincoln LN5 0AH* T: (01522) 810720

KNOWLES, Canon Eric Gordon. b 44. WMMTC 79. **d** 82 **p** 83. NSM Gt Malvern St Mary *Worc* 82–83; NSM Malvern H Trin and St Jas 83–90; NSM Lt Malvern, Malvern Wells and Wyche 90–99; NSM Lt Malvern 99–00; P-in-c 00–13; V from 13; Hon Can Worc Cathl from 05. *45 Wykewane, Malvern WR14 2XD* T: (01684) 567439 E: skypilot@homecall.co.uk

✠**KNOWLES, The Rt Revd Graeme Paul.** b 51. AKC 73 FKC 11. St Aug Coll Cant 73. **d** 74 **p** 75 **c** 03. C St Peter-in-Thanet *Cant* 74–79; C Leeds St Pet *Ripon* 79–81; Chapl and Prec Portsm Cathl 81–87; Chapter Clerk 85–87; V Leigh Park *Portsm* 87–93; RD Havant 90–93; Adn Portsm 93–99; Dean Carl 99–03; Bp S & M 03–07; Dean St Paul's *Lon* 07–12; Hon Asst Bp St E from 12; Hon Asst Bp Ely from 12; PtO *Lon* from 12; PV Westmr Abbey from 14; PtO *Linc* 16–19; Can Res St E Cathl 17–18. *102A Barons Road, Bury St Edmunds IP33 2LY* T: (01284) 723823 E: graemeknowles@hotmail.co.uk

KNOWLES, James Russell. b 80. Sydney Univ BA 01. Oak Hill Th Coll BTh 13. **d** 13 **p** 14. C High Ongar w Norton Mandeville *Chelmsf* 13–16; C Enfield Ch Ch Trent Park *Lon* from 16. *2 Chalk Lane, Cockfosters, Barnet EN4 9JQ* M: 07791-371808 E: jamesknowles@gmail.com *or* james.knowles@cockfosters.org.uk

KNOWLES, Mrs Jane Frances. b 44. GGSM 66 Lon Inst of Educn TCert 67. Ox Min Course 90. **d** 93 **p** 94. NSM Sandhurst *Ox* 93–97; C Wargrave 97–99; P-in-c Ramsden, Finstock and Fawler, Leafield etc 99–01; V Forest Edge 01–09; rtd 09; PtO *Sarum* from 10. *41 Martin's Road, Keevil, Trowbridge BA14 6NA* T: (01380) 870325 E: jane.knowles2@btinternet.com

KNOWLES, John Geoffrey. b 48. Man Univ BSc 69 Lon Univ MSc 75 Ox Univ PGCE 70 FRSA. WMMTC 95. **d** 98 **p** 99. NSM The Lickey *Birm* 98–99; R Hutcheson's Gr Sch 99–04; P-in-c Woodford *Ches* 05–12; V 12; Dioc Warden of Readers 05–16; NSM Norbury 13–14; NSM Handforth 13–18; rtd 18; PtO *Ches* from 18. *15 Clare Avenue, Handforth, Wilmslow SK9 3EQ* T: (01625) 526531 E: john.knowles92@btinternet.com

KNOWLES, Melvin Clay. b 63. Stetson Univ (USA) BA 66 Ex Univ MA 73. Ripon Coll Cuddesdon 75. **d** 77 **p** 78. C Minchinhampton *Glouc* 77–80; St Helena 80–82; TV Haywards Heath St Wilfrid *Chich* 82–88; Adult Educn Adv 88–94; TR Burgess Hill St Jo w St Edw 94–00; V Burgess Hill St Jo 00–09; rtd 09; PtO *Chich* from 14. *20 Fairfield Road, Burgess Hill RH15 8QA* T: (01444) 254429 E: cknowles@waitrose.com *or* mclayknowles@gmail.com *or* mclayknowles@gmail.com

KNOWLES, Philip Andrew. b 63. Leeds Univ BA 07. NOC 04. **d** 07 **p** 08. C Blackb St Mich w St Jo and H Trin 07–10; C Blackb St Thos w St Jude 07–10; P-in-c Lt Marsden w Nelson St Mary and Nelson St Bede 10–11; V 11–15; V Sheff St Cath Richmond Road from 15; Jt AD Attercliffe from 18. *St Catherine's Vicarage, 300 Hastilar Road South, Sheffield S13 8EJ* T: 0114-239 9598 M: 07813-966257 E: philip.knowles1@btinternet.com *or* philip.knowles@sheffield.anglican.org

KNOWLES, Philip John. b 48. MA PhD BTh LTCL ALCM LLAM. CITC 76. **d** 76 **p** 77. C Lisburn St Paul *Conn* 76–79; I Cloonclare w Killasnett and Lurganboy *K, E & A* 79–87; I Gorey w Kilnahue *C & O* 87–89; I Gorey w Kilnahue, Leskinfere and Ballycanew 89–95; Preb Ferns Cathl 91–95; Dean Cashel 95–13; I Cashel w Magorban, Tipperary, Clonbeg etc 95–13; Chan Waterford Cathl 95–13; Chan

Lismore Cathl 95–13; Can Ossory and Leighlin Cathls 96–13; Preb Stagonil St Patr Cathl Dublin 09–13; rtd 13. *99 Kingsgrove, Athy, Co Kildare, Republic of Ireland* T: (00353) (59) 863 8936 M: 87-264 3111 E: philipknowles65@gmail.com

KNOX, Canon Geoffrey Martin. b 44. Dur Univ BA 66 Sheff City Coll of Educn DipEd 73. St Chad's Coll Dur 63. **d** 67 **p** 68. C Newark St Mary *S'well* 67–72; PtO *Derby* 72–74; V Woodville 74–81; RD Repton 79–81; V Long Eaton St Laur 81–00; V Somercotes 00–09; RD Alfreton 04–09; Hon Can Derby Cathl 08–09; rtd 09; PtO *Truro* from 16. *9 Treveryn Parc, Budock Water, Falmouth TR11 5EH* T: (01326) 373142

KNOX, Canon Ian Stephen. b 44. Leeds Univ LLB 64 Solicitor 66 Brunel Univ MPhil 03. **d** 05 **p** 05. PtO *Cov* 05–06; *Newc* from 06; Exec Dir 40:3 Trust from 05. *16 East Moor, Loughoughton, Alnwick NE66 3JB* T: (01665) 572939 E: office@fortythreetrust.com *or* ian@knox.org.uk

KNOX, Canon Janet. b 57. **d** 11 **p** 12. NSM Quinton Road W St Boniface *Birm* from 11; Hon Can Birm Cathl from 18. *405 Simmons Drive, Quinton, Birmingham B32 2UH* T: 0121-426 3575 *or* 426 3166 E: janet_405@hotmail.com

KOBUS van WENGEN (née SHUTE), Rosemary Margaret. b 38. Westf Coll Lon BA 60 Leiden Univ MA 77 PhD 81. SEITE 98. **d** 01 **p** 02. NSM Benenden *Cant* 01–10; NSM Sandhurst w Newenden 04–10; NSM Benenden and Sandhurst 10–11; PtO from 11. *Beach House, Grange Road, St Michaels, Tenterden TN30 6EF* T: (01580) 764857 E: rosemaryvanwengen@gmail.com

KOCH, John Dunbar. b 77. Washington & Lee Univ BA 00 Humboldt Univ Berlin PhD 14. Trin Episc Sch for Min Penn MDiv 07. **d** 07 **p** 08. C Wiesbaden Austria 07–09; C Vienna *Eur* 09–12; R Harrods Creek St Fran USA from 12. *436 Club Lane, Louisville KY 40207, USA* T: (001) (502) 544 5711 E: jadykoch@gmail.com

KOEPPING, Elizabeth Rosalind. b 47. Edin Univ MA 71 Man Univ MA 73 Univ of Qld PhD 81 Westmr Coll Ox MTh 98. **d** 09 **p** 10. NSM Edin Ch Ch 09–14; PtO *Eur* 11–14; P-in-c Heidelberg 14–16; PtO *Ox* from 16. *Blenheim Cottage, The Slade, Charlbury, Chipping Norton OX7 3SJ* T: (01608) 811400 E: e.koepping@ed.ac.uk

KOH, Mrs Yunghee. b 68. Roehampton Inst MA 00 PGDE 08 Dur Univ BA 17. St Aug Coll of Th 15. **d** 17 **p** 18. C Wimbledon *S'wark* from 17. *9 Thornton Road, London SW19 4NE* T: (020) 8543 8526 M: 07533-386918 E: yungheekoh05@yahoo.co.uk *or* yunghee@stmaryswimbledon.org

KOMOR, The Ven Michael. b 60. Univ of Wales BSc 83. Chich Th Coll 83. **d** 86 **p** 87. C Mountain Ash *Llan* 86–89; C Llantwit Major 89–91; TV 91–00; V Ewenny w St Brides Major 00–05; R Coity, Nolton and Brackla 05–14; R Coity, Nolton and Brackla w Coychurch from 14; AD Bridgend 04–10 and 15–18; Can Llan Cathl from 14; Adn Margam from 18; C Llansantffraid, Bettws and Aberkenfig from 18. *Nolton Rectory, Merthyr Mawr Road North, Bridgend CF31 3NH* T: (01656) 652247 E: archdeacon.margam@churchinwales.org.uk

KONIG, Peter Montgomery. b 44. Univ of Wales (Lamp) MA 10. Westcott Ho Cam 80. **d** 82 **p** 83. C Oundle *Pet* 82–86; Chapl Westwood Ho Sch Pet 86–92; Chapl Pet High Sch 92–95; Chapl Worksop Coll Notts 95–99; Chapl Glenalmond Coll *St And* 99–04; rtd 04; PtO *Pet* from 04. *Crossways, Main Street, Yarwell, Peterborough PE8 6PR* T: (01780) 782873 M: 07764-586619 E: pandakonig@talktalk.net

KOPSCH, Hartmut. b 41. Sheff Univ BA 63 Univ of BC MA 66 Lon Univ PhD 70. Trin Coll Bris 78. **d** 80 **p** 81. C Cranham Park *Chelmsf* 80–85; V Springfield *Birm* 85–92; V Dover St Martin *Cant* 92–96; R Bath Walcot *B & W* 96–06; rtd 06; PtO *Glouc* 07–09; *Bris* from 09. *10 St Edyths Road, Bristol BS9 2ES* T: 0117-968 8683 E: hartmuvandjane@gmail.com

KORMI, Emmanuel Barine. b 58. **d** 16. NSM Hatcham St Cath *S'wark* from 16; Chapl Lewisham and Greenwich NHS Trust from 18. *50 Wild Goose Drive, London SE14 5LL*

KORMOS, Endre. b 86. Coll of Resurr Mirfield BA 16. **d** 16 **p** 17. C Wallsend St Pet and St Luke *Newc* from 16. *148 Park Road, Wallsend NE28 7QS* T: 0191-209 2274 E: frkormos@protonmail.com

KORN, Sam Christopher. b 89. Trin Hall Cam MA 14. Westcott Ho Cam 12 Bossey Ecum Inst Geneva 13. **d** 14 **p** 15. C E Barnet St Alb 14–17; V Aintree St Giles w St Pet *Liv* 17–19; Chapl St Mary Magd Academy Lon from 19. *St Mary Magdalene Academy, 475 Liverpool Road, London N7 8PG* T: (020) 7697 0123 M: 07900-827371 E: sam.korn@cantab.net

KORNAHRENS, Canon Wallace Douglas. b 43. St Andr Univ PhD 08. The Citadel Charleston BA 66 Gen Th Sem (NY) STB 69. **d** 69 **p** 70. USA 69–72; C Potters Green *Cov* 72–75; Chapl Community of Celebration Wargrave Oxon 75–76;

P-in-c Cumbrae (or Millport) *Arg* 76–78; R Grantown-on-Spey *Mor* 78–83; R Rothiemurchus 78–83; R Edin H Cross 83–18; Hon Can St Mary's Cathl from 14; rtd 18. *114 Broomfield Crescent, Edinburgh EH12 7NF*

KOSLA, Mrs Ann Louise. b 56. Middx Univ BA 04. NTMTC 01. **d** 04 **p** 05. NSM Thorley *St Alb* 04–07; NSM Chelmsf S Deanery 08–10; NSM Boreham *Chelmsf* 10–12; V Church Langley from 12. *The Vicarage, Clockhouse Lane, Grays RM16 6YW* M: 07563-548337 E: annkosla@gmail.com

KOSLA, Charles Antoni. b 58. Cam Th Federation MA 12. Ridley Hall Cam 97. **d** 99 **p** 00. C Widford *Chelmsf* 99–03; C Thorley *St Alb* 03–07; Dioc Adv for Miss and Evang *Chelmsf* 07–17; Hon C E Springfield 08–12; Hon C Church Langley 12–18; TV Grays Thurrock from 18. *The Vicarage, Clockhouse Lane, Grays RM16 6YW* M: 07753-634021 E: charliekosla@gmail.com

KOUBLE (née MACKIE), Fiona Mary. b 66. Anglia Ruskin Univ BA 94 MSc 95 St Jo Coll Dur BA 09 RGN 88. Cranmer Hall Dur 07. **d** 11 **p** 12. C Hillsborough and Wadsley Bridge *Sheff* 11–13; V Ardsley from 13. *Christ Church Vicarage, Doncaster Road, Barnsley S71 5EF* M: 07817-167386 E: fionakouble@yahoo.co.uk

KOUSSEFF, Mrs Karen Patricia. b 60. Ex Univ BA 83. STETS 06. **d** 09 **p** 10. NSM Lower Dever *Win* 09–17; NSM Win St Bart and St Lawr w St Swithun 18–19; P-in-c from 19; AD Win from 17. *St Bartholomew's House, 1 Abbey Hill Close, Winchester SO23 7AZ* E: karen.kousseff@outlook.com

KOZAK, Robert Jozef. b 84. SS Coll Cam BTh 15 K Coll Lon MA 18. Westcott Ho Cam 12. **d** 15 **p** 16. C Leavesden *St Alb* 15–18; P-in-c Letchworth from 18. *The Rectory, 39 South View, Letchworth Garden City SG6 3JJ* T: (01462) 684822 E: father.kozak@gmail.com

KRAFT (née STEVENS), Mrs Jane. b 45. SRN 66 SCM 68. NTMTC 01. **d** 03 **p** 04. NSM Finchley St Mary *Lon* 03–07; TV Chipping Barnet *St Alb* 07–14; rtd 15; PtO *St Alb* 15–17; *Ox* from 15. *66 Yeovil Road, Owlsmoor, Sandhurst GU47 0TE* T: (01276) 36402 M: 07803-868482 E: revd.janekraft@btinternet.com

KRAMER, Mrs Caroline Anne. b 70. Wycliffe Hall Ox BTh 98. **d** 98. C Oatlands *Guildf* 98–99; USA 00–10; C Wokingham All SS *Ox* 10–13; C Ponte Vedra Beach USA from 13. *304 S Mill View Way, Ponte Vedra Beach FL 32082, USA* E: revcarolinekramer@googlemail.com

KRAMER, Maxwell James. b 85. Ball Coll Ox BA 07 MA 11 St Jo Coll Cam BA 10 MPhil 11 MA 15. Westcott Ho Cam 08. **d** 13 **p** 14. NSM Cambridge St Mary Less *Ely* 13–17; Min Can and Prec Cant Cathl from 17. *5 The Precincts, Canterbury CT1 2EE* M: 07796-673081 E: max_kramer@hotmail.com

KRAWIEC, Christopher James Michael. b 86. St Jo Coll Dur BA 16. Cranmer Hall Dur 12. **d** 15 **p** 16. C Gt Harwood *Blackb* 15–19; R Poulton-le-Sands w Morecambe St Laur from 19. *The Rectory, Church Walk, Morecambe LA4 5PR* M: 07596-669987 E: c.krawiec@icloud.com

KREJCI, Kvetoslav Tomas. b 68. Chas Univ Prague PhD 01 PhD 17 Blackfriars Ox MPhil 16 Solicitor 07. St Steph Ho Ox 16. **d** 18 **p** 19. C Reading St Giles *Ox* from 18. *10 Jesse Terrace, Reading RG1 7RT* M: 07984-838866 E: pater_tomas@outlook.com

KRINKS, Philip Lewis. b 72. Magd Coll Ox BA 95 MA 99 INSEAD MBA 00 K Coll Lon PhD 11 MA 12. Westcott Ho Cam 12. **d** 14 **p** 15. C Battersea St Mary *S'wark* 14–16; C E Win 16–17; C Win St Cross w St Faith 16–17; P-in-c from 17. *St Anne's, Petersfield Road, Winchester SO23 0JD* M: 07899-813650 E: philip@krinks.com

KRONBERGS, Paul Mark. b 55. NEOC 02. **d** 05 **p** 06. NSM Middlesbrough St Columba w St Paul *York* from 05. *39 Northumberland Grove, Stockton-on-Tees TS20 1PB* T: (01642) 365160 E: fr-paul.kronbergs@hotmail.co.uk

KRONENBERG, John Simon. b 59. Greenwich Univ BSc 85 Open Univ BA 00 MRICS 87 MBEng 94. Ripon Coll Cuddesdon BTh 06. **d** 02 **p** 03. C Chandler's Ford *Win* 02–06; V Hinchley Wood *Guildf* 06–15; V Redhill St Jo *S'wark* from 15. *St John's Vicarage, Church Road, Redhill RH1 6QA* M: 07500-954963 E:: js.kronenberg@btinternet.com

KROUKAMP, Nigel John Charles. b 53. Cen Lancs Univ BSc 93 Bolton Inst of HE CertEd 86 RNMH 75 RGN 78. LCTP 05. **d** 08 **p** 09. NSM Colne and Villages *Blackb* 08–14; rtd 14; PtO *Blackb* from 14. *56 Kelswick Drive, Nelson BB9 0SZ* T: (01282) 698261 M: 07725-858433 E: nigelkroukamp@googlemail.com

KTORIDES, Nicholas. b 59. Sheff Univ MA 97. Ridley Hall Cam. **d** 14 **p** 15. C Gorleston St Andr *Nor* 14–16; C Lowestoft St Andr 16–18; C Oulton St Mich 18–19; PtO *Ox* from 19. *9 Williams Road, Upper Heyford, Bicester OX25 5AX* M: 07812-170911

KUHRT, The Ven Gordon Wilfred. b 41. Lon Univ BD 63 Middx Univ DProf 01. Oak Hill Th Coll 65. **d** 67 **p** 68. C Illogan *Truro* 67–70; C Wallington *S'wark* 70–73; V Shenstone *Lich* 73–79; P-in-c S Croydon Em *Cant* 79–81; V S Croydon Em *S'wark* 81–89; RD Croydon Cen *Cant* 81–84; RD Croydon Cen *S'wark* 85–86; Hon Can S'wark Cathl 87–89; Adn Lewisham 89–96; Dir Chief Sec ABM 96–98; Min Division Abps' Coun 99–06; rtd 06; Hon C Ilmington w Stretton-on-Fosse etc *Cov* 06–12; PtO *Ox* from 12. *87 Churchway, Haddenham, Aylesbury HP17 8DT* T: (01844) 292870 E: omkuhrt@tiscali.co.uk

KUHRT, Martin Gordon. b 66. Nottm Univ LLB 88. Trin Coll Bris 93. **d** 96 **p** 97. C Morden *S'wark* 96–00; Chapl Lee Abbey 00–02; TV Melksham *Sarum* 02–08; C Atworth w Shaw and Whitley 07–08; C Broughton Gifford, Gt Chalfield and Holt 07–08; P-in-c Bedgrove *Ox* 08–09; V from 09. *2 Earlswood Close, Aylesbury HP21 7PG* T: (01296) 435546 E: makuhrt555@btinternet.com or martin@holyspiritbedgrove.org

KUHRT, Stephen John. b 69. Man Univ BA 91 Lon Inst of Educn PGCE 93. Wycliffe Hall Ox BA 03. **d** 03 **p** 04. C New Malden and Coombe *S'wark* 03–07; P-in-c 07–17; V from 17. *The Vicarage, 6 Filbert Terrace, Cambridge Avenue, New Malden KT3 4JZ* T: (020) 8942 0915 E: stephenkuhrt@ccnm.org

KUIN LAWTON, Theresa (Tess). b 69. St Aid Coll Dur BA 91 TCD MPhil 96 Bris Univ PhD 11 Dur Univ PGCE 92. Ox Min Course 05. **d** 07 **p** 08. NSM Bampton w Clanfield *Ox* 07–10 and from 17; Chapl Magd Coll Sch Ox 09–17; Chapl Worc Coll Ox from 17; Voc Adv Ox Univ from 17. *Manor Croft, Church Close, Bampton OX18 2LW* T: (01993) 278371 E: chaplain@worc.ox.ac.uk

KURK, Pamela Ann. b 56. Univ of Wales (Ban) BTh 06. **d** 04 **p** 05. NSM Wandsworth St Mich w St Steph *S'wark* 04–11; Chapl St Cecilia's Wandsworth C of E Sch from 07; P-in-c Battersea St Mich *S'wark* 13–17; NSM Clapham Common St Barn 17–19; TV Caterham from 19. *St Cecilia's C of E School, Sutherland Grove, London SW18 5JR* T: (020) 8780 1244 M: 07774-437471 E: thekurks@aol.com or akurk@saintcecilias.london.uk

KURZ, Nathaniel William. b 84. Trin Coll Bris BA 15. **d** 15 **p** 16. C Esher *Guildf* 15–18; C E Molesey St Mary from 18. *The Vicarage, St Mary's Road, East Molesey KT8 0ST* M: 07912-037246

KUSTNER, Ms Jane Lesley. b 54. Lanchester Poly Cov BA 76 FCA 79. St Steph Ho Ox 03. **d** 05 **p** 06. C Waterloo St Jo w St Andr *S'wark* 05–08; P-in-c Lewisham St Swithun 08–17; AD E Lewisham 13–17; P-in-c Mariannridge S Africa 17–19; Chapl Bromley Coll from 19. *Chaplain's House, Bromley College, London Road, Bromley BR1 1PE* T: (020) 8460 4712 E: bromleysheppardscolleges@btinternet.com or janetkustner@gmail.com

KUTIWULU, Calixte. b 63. Qu Coll Birm 12. **d** 92 **p** 93. In RC Ch Democratic Republic of Congo 92–03; C Pet St Mary Boongate 14–16; C Paston 16–18. *1A Mead Close, Peterborough PE4 6BS* M: 07417-433229 E: ckutiwulu@yahoo.co.uk

KYRIACOU, Brian George. b 42. Lon Univ LLB 64. Oak Hill Th Coll 79. **d** 81 **p** 82. C Becontree St Mary *Chelmsf* 81–83; C Becontree St Cedd 83–85; C Becontree W 85; TV 85–87; V Shiregreen St Jas and St Chris *Sheff* 87–92; TV Schorne *Ox* 92–98; V Edmonton All SS w St Mich *Lon* 98–07; rtd 07; PtO *Chelmsf* from 07. *3 Cranford Close, Frinton-on-Sea CO13 9LF* T: (01255) 763782 M: 07970-719094 E: briankyriacou71@gmail.com

KYRIAKIDES-YELDHAM, Preb Anthony Paul Richard. b 48. Birkbeck Coll Lon BSc 82 Warwick Univ MSc 90 Univ of Wales (Lamp) MMin 10 Ex Univ PhD 17 CQSW 83 CPsychol 91. K Coll Lon BD 73 AKC 73. **d** 74 **p** 75. C Dalston H Trin w St Phil *Lon* 74–78; NSM Lon Docks St Pet w Wapping St Jo 79–81; NSM Hackney Wick St Mary of Eton w St Aug 81–85; NSM Wandsworth Common St Mary *S'wark* 85–87; Chapl Wandsworth HA Mental Health Unit 87–93; Chapl Springfield Univ Hosp Lon 87–93; PtO *Ex* 94–98; LtO 98–08; Sen Chapl Plymouth Hosps NHS Trust 98–08; P-in-c Kingsbridge and Dodbrooke *Ex* 08–11; Preb Ex Cathl 07–11; Chapl Imp Coll Healthcare NHS Trust 11–12; rtd 13; PV Westmr Abbey from 13; Chapl 13–15; Chapl Marie Curie Hospice from 15; Bp's Adv for Healthcare Chapl *Lon* from 18. *Marie Curie Hospice Hampstead, 11 Lyndhurst Gardens, London NW3 5NS* M: 07929-775228 E: aprkyriakides@mac.com

KYTE, Eric Anthony. b 62. Leeds Univ BSc 84 PGCE 85. Trin Coll Bris BA 98. **d** 98 **p** 99. C Pudsey St Lawr and St Paul *Bradf* 98–01; P-in-c Gisburn and Hellifield 01–11; New Zealand from 11. *353 Highgate, Roslyn, Dunedin, New Zealand* E: thereverick@aol.com

KYUMU MOTUKO, Norbert. *See* CHUMU MUTUKU, Norbert

L

LA TOUCHE, Francis William Reginald. b 51. Linc Th Coll 73. d 76 p 77. C Yate *Bris* 76–77; C Yate New Town 77–79; Chapl Vlissingen (Flushing) Miss to Seamen *Eur* 79–83; Port Chapl Hull Miss to Seamen 83–91; V Burstwick w Thorngumbald *York* 91–02; PtO *Ches* 11–14; *York* from 16. *45 Lee Street, Hull HU8 8NN* E: frank.latouche@gmail.com

LABRAN, Stuart. b 79. Leeds Univ BA 00 PGCE 02 Clare Coll Cam MPhil 09. Westcott Ho Cam 07. d 09 p 10. C Stratford-upon-Avon, Luddington etc *Cov* 09–12; Asst Chapl Em Sch Wandsworth from 17; NSM Kennington St Jo w St Jas *S'wark* from 19. *Flat 3, 24 Peckham Rye, London SE15 4JR* E: stuartlabran@hotmail.com

LACEY, Canon Allan John. b 48. Sheff Univ MA 02. Wycliffe Hall Ox. d 82 p 83. C Greasbrough *Sheff* 82–85; R Treeton 85–92; V Thorpe Hesley 92–00; R Rossington 00–07; CMS Uganda 07–13; Can Em Cathl Arua from 12; rtd 13; PtO *Leic* 14–16; *Derby* from 17. *45 High Street, Staveley, Chesterfield S43 3UU* T: (01246) 470422 M: 07887-473540 E: allanandanne@btinternet.com

LACEY, Carol Ann. b 62. Qu Coll Birm 07. d 09 p 10. NSM Leic St Anne, St Paul w St Aug 09–14; V Brampton Bierlow *Sheff* 14–18; Chapl LOROS Hospice from 19. *22A Chapel Street, Blaby, Leicester LE8 4GB* T: 0116-231 3771 M: 07971-519705 E: carolannlacey@gmail.com

LACEY, Colin Brian. d 10 p 11. C Ballymena w Ballyclug *Conn* 10–13; I Belfast St Pet and St Jas from 13. *St Peter's Rectory, 17 Waterloo Park South, Belfast BT15 5HX* T: (028) 9077 7053 M: 07563-531082 E: brianlacey@hotmail.co.uk

LACEY, Eric. b 33. Cranmer Hall Dur 69. d 71 p 72. C Blackpool St Jo *Blackb* 71–75; V Whittle-le-Woods 75–88; R Heysham 88–98; rtd 98; PtO *Blackb* from 98. *143 Bredon Avenue, Chorley PR7 6NS* T: (01257) 273040

LACEY, Nigel Jeremy. b 59. St Jo Coll Nottm BTh 94. d 94 p 95. C Mildenhall *St E* 94–97; C Selly Park St Steph and St Wulstan *Birm* 97–01; Chapl St Mary's Hospice 97–01; P-in-c W Wycombe w Bledlow Ridge, Bradenham and Radnage *Ox* 01–09; R 09–16. *The Vicarage, Preston Lane, Burton, Christchurch BH23 7JU* T: (01202) 473834 M: 07761-852619 E: nigellacey405@btinternet.com

LACK, Miss Catherine Mary. b 59. Clare Coll Cam BA 81 Ox Univ MTh 00 ARCM 78. Qu Coll Birm 90. d 92 p 94. C Leiston *St E* 92–95; TV Ipswich St Mary at Stoke w St Pet and St Fran 95–98; Chapl Keele Univ *Lich* 98–07; Cultural and Relig Affairs Manager Yarl's Wood Immigration Removal Cen 07–08; Warden Ferrar House Lt Gidding 08–09; Chapl Newc Univ 09–18; Master Newc St Thos Prop Chpl 09–18. *67 Main Street, Felton, Morpeth NE65 9PT* M: 07852-033125 E: catherine.lack50@gmail.com

LACK, Martin Paul. b 57. St Jo Coll Ox MA 79 MSc 80. Linc Th Coll 83. d 86 p 87. C E Bowbrook and W Bowbrook *Worc* 86–89; C Bowbrook S and Bowbrook N 89–90; R Teme Valley S 90–01; rtd 01. *Colbridge Cottage, Bottom Lane, Whitbourne, Worcester WR6 5RT* T: (01886) 821978

LACKENBY, George Joseph. b 48. d 13 p 14. NSM Harlow Green and Lamesley *Dur* from 13. *68 Ashford, Gateshead NE9 6YG* T: 0191-421 9173 E: george.lackenby@hotmail.co.uk

LACKEY, Michael Geoffrey Herbert. b 42. Oak Hill Th Coll 73. d 75 p 76. C Hatcham St Jas *S'wark* 75–81; V New Barnet St Jas *St Alb* 81–91; V Hollington St Jo *Chich* 91–02; Dir Crowhurst Chr Healing Cen 02–05; rtd 05; Hon C Gt Amwell w St Margaret's and Stanstead Abbots *St Alb* 05–09; PtO from 10. *5 Vicarage Close, St Albans AL1 2PU* E: glackey@virginmedia.com

LACY, Melanie June. b 75. TCD BA 98 All Hallows Coll Dublin MA 00. CITC 98. d 00. C Bangor St Comgall *D & D* 00–02; N Ireland Regional Co-ord Crosslinks 02–06; C Knutsford St Jo and Toft *Ches* 06–09; Dir Youth and Children's Min Oak Hill Coll from 10. *Oak Hill College, Chase Side, London N14 4PS* T: (020) 8449 0467 F: 8441 5996 E: mell@oakhill.ac.uk

LADD, Mrs Anne de Chair. b 56. Nottm Univ BA 78 Birm Univ CQSW 80. St Jo Coll Nottm 83. dss 86 d 87 p 94. Bucknall and Bagnall *Lich* 86–91; Par Dn 87–91; NSM Bricket Wood *St Alb* 91–01; Chapl Garden Ho Hospice Letchworth 98–06; Befriending Co-ord Mencap 07–08; Soc worker 09–11; Chapl Nottm Univ Hosp NHS Trust 11–17; Hon C Chilwell *S'well* 15–17; P-in-c Allens Cross *Birm* from 17. *30 Lickey Square, Lickey, Birmingham B45 8HB* M: 07752-278987 E: laddanne@gmail.com or anne.stbs@gmail.com

LADD, Nicholas Mark. b 57. Ex Univ BA 78 Selw Coll Cam BA 81 MA 97 Anglia Ruskin Univ MA 03. Ridley Hall Cam 79.

d 82 p 83. C Aston SS Pet and Paul *Birm* 82–86; TV Bucknall and Bagnall *Lich* 86–91; V Bricket Wood *St Alb* 91–01; V Cambridge St Barn *Ely* 01–09; Dean and Lect St Jo Coll Nottm 09–17; Hon C Chilwell *S'well* 15–17; C Allens Cross *Birm* from 17. *30 Lickey Square, Rednal, Birmingham B45 8HB* T: 0121-445 4400 M: 07540-425381 E: nick.ladd57@gmail.com

LADDS, Alexander John. b 72. Univ of Wales (Abth) BD 94. LCTP 13. d 16 p 17. NSM Broughton, Marton and Thornton *Leeds* from 16. *Beck House, Raines Road, Giggleswick, Settle BD24 0DA* T: (01729) 893190 M: 07460-827764 E: ajladds@giggleswick.org.uk

✠**LADDS, The Rt Revd Robert Sidney.** b 41. Lon Univ BEd 71 LRSC 72. Cant Sch of Min 79. d 80 p 81 c 99. C Hythe *Cant* 80–83; R Bretherton *Blackb* 83–91; Chapl Bp Rawstorne Sch Preston 83–87; Bp's Chapl for Min and Adv Coun for Min *Blackb* 86–91; P-in-c Preston St Jo 91–96; R Preston St Jo and St Geo 96–97; Hon Can Blackb Cathl 93–97; Adn Lancaster 97–99; Suff Bp Whitby *York* 99–08; rtd 09; Hon Asst Bp Lon from 09; Hon C Hendon St Mary and Ch Ch 09–15; Hon C Lon Docks St Pet w Wapping St Jo from 15. *St Peter's Clergy House, Wapping Lane, London E1W 2RW* T: (020) 7488 3864 E: episcopus70@gmail.com

LADIPO, Canon Adeyemi Olalekan. b 37. Trin Coll Bris 63. d 66 p 76. C Bilston St Leon *Lich* 66–68; Nigeria 68–84; V Canonbury St Steph *Lon* 85–87; Sec for Internat Miss BCMS 87–90; Hon C Bromley SS Pet and Paul *Roch* 89–90; V Herne Hill *S'wark* 90–99; Hon Can Jos from 95; V S Malling *Chich* 99–02; rtd 02; PtO *Chich* from 03; *S'wark* from 07. *63 Elm Grove, London SE15 5DB* T: (020) 7639 8150 E: adeyemiladipo@hotmail.com

LAFFERTY, Miss Kim Elvin. b 62. RGN 85 RM 89. Wycliffe Hall Ox 10. d 12 p 13. C Horwich and Rivington *Man* 12–15; TV Farnworth, Kearsley and Stoneclough from 15. *The Vicarage, Stoneleigh Drive, Radcliffe, Manchester M26 1FZ* T: 01204 294831 M: 07703-417640 E: kelafferty@hotmail.co.uk

LAFFORD, Sylvia June. b 46. Middx Univ BA 04. NTMTC 01. d 04 p 05. NSM Hayes St Edm *Lon* 04–12; Asst Chapl Hillingdon Hosps NHS Foundn Trust 10–13; PtO *Lon* from 13; *Pet* from 13. *18 Blenheim Croft, Brackley NN13 7ET* T: (01280) 700122 E: sylvia.lafford@btinternet.com

LAIDLAW, Juliet. *See* MONTAGUE, Juliet

LAIN-PRIESTLEY, The Ven Rosemary Jane. b 67. Kent Univ BA 89 K Coll Lon MA 02. Carl Dioc Tr Course 92. d 96 p 97. C Scotforth *Blackb* 96–98; C St Martin-in-the-Fields *Lon* 98–06; Dean of Women's Min Two Cities Area 06–15; Adn Charing Cross 16–19; Bp's Adv on Policy and Strategy from 19. *15 Lisburne Road, London NW3 2NS* T: (020) 3837 5205 E: rosemary.lainpriestley@london.anglican.org

LAIRD, Alisdair Mark. b 60. Auckland Univ BA 84. Trin Coll Bris BA 92. d 92 p 93. C Linthorpe *York* 92–98; V Hull St Cuth 98–06; P-in-c Alne and Brafferton w Pilmoor, Myton-on-Swale etc 06–07; LtO 07–08; PtO 08–19; Chapl Hull and E Yorks Hosps NHS Trust from 09. *Hull Royal Infirmary, Anlaby Road, Hull HU3 2JZ* T: (01482) 875875 E: alisdair@trackways.net

LAIRD, Canon John Charles. b 32. Sheff Univ BA 53 MA 54 St Cath Coll Ox BA 58 MA 62 Lon Univ DipEd 70. Ripon Hall Ox 56. d 58 p 59. C Cheshunt *St Alb* 58–62; Chapl Bps' Coll Cheshunt 62–64; Vice-Prin 64–67; Prin 67–69; V Keysoe w Bolnhurst and Lt Staughton *St Alb* 69–01; Hon Can St Alb 87–02; LtO 01–15. *The College of St Barnabas, Blackberry Lane, Lingfield RH7 6NJ* T: (01342) 872838

LAIRD, Robert George (Robin). b 40. TCD Div Sch 58 Edin Th Coll 63. d 65 p 66. C Drumragh *D & R* 65–68; CF 68–93; QHC 91–93; Sen Chapl Sedbergh Sch 93–98; Lic to Offic *Bradf* 93–98; rtd 98; PtO *Sarum* from 98; *Ex* from 98. *Barrule, Hillside Road, Sidmouth EX10 8JD* T: (01395) 513948 E: robin@barrule.co.uk

LAIRD, Stephen Charles Edward. b 66. Oriel Coll Ox BA 88 MA 92 MSt 93 K Coll Lon MTh 91 Kent Univ PhD 06 FSA 14 FHEA 12. Wycliffe Hall Ox MPhil 96. d 94 p 95. C Ilfracombe, Lee, Woolacombe, Bittadon etc *Ex* 94–98; Chapl Kent Univ *Cant* 98–03; Dean of Chapl from 03; Hon Lect from 98; Chapl Kent Inst of Art and Design 98–02; Hon C Hackington *Cant* from 03; P-in-c Blean from 03. *24 Tyler Hill Road, Blean, Canterbury CT2 9HT* T: (01227) 763373 M: 07970-438840 E: s.c.e.laird@kent.ac.uk

LAKE, David Michael. b 57. St Mary's Sem Oscott 76. St Jo Coll Nottm BA 01. d 01 p 02. C Lilleshall, Muxton and Sheriffhales *Lich* 01–05; P-in-c Crick and Yelvertoft w Clay Coton and Lilbourne *Pet* 05–09; R from 09. *The Rectory,*

Main Road, Crick, Northampton NN6 7TU T: (01788) 822147
E: d.m.lake@btinternet.com

LAKE, Eileen Veronica. *See* CREMIN, Eileen Veronica

LAKE, Jeffrey Ronald. b 70. Univ of N Colorado MA 93
LSHTM MSc 06 Cov Univ PhD 98. SEITE 12. **d** 15 **p** 16. NSM
St Bride Fleet Street w Bridewell etc *Lon* from 15. *106 Florin
Court, 6-9 Charterhouse Square, London EC1M 6EY* T: (020)
7251   8173   E: jeffrey_r_lake@yahoo.com.sg   *or*
jeffrey.lake@btinternet.com

LAKE, Kevin William. b 57. St Mich Coll Llan 97. **d** 99 **p** 00.
C Penarth w Lavernock *Llan* 99–02; Chapl Marie Curie
Cen Holme Tower 02–04; P-in-c Cwm Ogwr *Llan* 04–06;
P-in-c Llandyfodwg and Cwm Ogwr 06–08; V Aberdare
St Fagan 08–12; V Caerleon and Llanfrechfa *Mon* 12–15;
P-in-c Barry All SS *Llan* 15–16; TV Barry from 16. *The
Rectory, 3 Park Road, Barry CF62 6NU* T: (01446) 701206
E: kevin.lake1@btinternet.com

LAKE, The Very Revd Stephen David. b 63. Southn
Univ BTh. Chich Th Coll 85. **d** 88 **p** 89. C Sherborne w
Castleton and Lillington *Sarum* 88–92; P-in-c Branksome
St Aldhelm 92–96; V 96–01; RD Poole 00–01; Can Res and
Sub-Dean St Alb 01–11; Dean Glouc from 11. *The Deanery,
1 Miller's Green, Gloucester GL1 2BP* T: (01452) 524167
E: dean@gloucestercathedral.org.uk

LAKE, Vivienne Elizabeth. b 38. Westcott Ho Cam 84. **dss** 86
d 87 **p** 94. Chesterton Gd Shep *Ely* 86–90; C 87–90; Ecum
Min K Hedges Ch Cen 87–90; NSM Bourn Deanery *Ely* 90–01;
NSM Papworth Everard 94–96; PtO from 01. *15 Storey's
House, Mount Pleasant, Cambridge CB3 0BZ* T: (01223)
369523 E: vel.camb@gmail.com

LAKEY, Michael John. b 70. Ches Coll of HE BA 98 MTh 01
St Jo Coll Dur PhD 08. St Steph Ho Ox 13. **d** 14 **p** 15. Lect
Ripon Coll Cuddesdon from 08; NSM Dorchester *Ox* 14–19;
V Chalgrove w Berrick Salome from 19. *58 Brinkinfield Road,
Chalgrove, Oxford OX44 7QX* T: (01865) 890392 M: 07534-
197280 E: revmichaellakey@gmail.com

LALL, Canon Julia Carole. b 56. Ch Ch Coll Cant CertEd 78
BEd 79. ERMC 07. **d** 10 **p** 11. C Bacton w Wyverstone,
Cotton and Old Newton etc *St E* 10–13; P-in-c S Hartismere
13–17; R from 17; Hon Can St E Cathl from 17; Spiritual
Dir Cursillo from 19. *The Rectory, Stanwell Green, Thorndon,
Eye   IP23 7JL*   T: (01379)   678064   M: 07837-785607
E: julia.lall@hotmail.co.uk

LAMB, Alison. *See* EARL, Alison

LAMB, Bruce. b 47. Keble Coll Ox BA 69 MA 73. Coll of Resurr
Mirfield 70. **d** 73 **p** 74. C Romford St Edw *Chelmsf* 73–76; C
Canning Town St Cedd 76–79; V New Brompton St Luke
Roch 79–83; Chapl RN 83–87; C Rugeley *Lich* 87–88; V Trent
Vale 88–92; Bereavement Cllr Cruse 94–99; Hon C Chorlton-
cum-Hardy St Clem *Man* 98–99; Asst Chapl N Man Health
Care NHS Trust 99–02; P-in-c Barton w Peel Green *Man*
02–14; rtd 14; PtO *Ches* from 14. *11 Kennet Drive, Congleton
CW12 3RH* T: (01260) 273707

LAMB, Canon Christopher Avon. b 39. Qu Coll Ox BA 61
MA 65 Birm Univ MA 78 PhD 87. Wycliffe Hall Ox BA 63.
d 63 **p** 64. C Enfield St Andr *Lon* 63–69; Pakistan 69–75;
Tutor Crowther Hall CMS Tr Coll Selly Oak 75–78; Co-
ord BCMS/CMS Other Faiths Th Project 78–87; Dioc
Community Relns Officer *Cov* 87–92; Can Th *Cov*
Cathl from 92; Sec Inter Faith Relns Bd of Miss 92–99; R
Warmington w Shotteswell and Radway w Ratley *Cov*
99–06; rtd 06; PtO *Cov* from 06. *8 Brookside Avenue,
Wellesbourne, Warwick CV35 9RZ* T: (01789) 842060
E: christopherlamb00@gmail.com

LAMB, David Andrew. b 60. Liv Inst of HE BA 94 Man Univ
MA 01 PhD 12. NOC 90. **d** 94 **p** 95. C Formby H Trin *Liv*
94–97; C St Helens St Matt Thatto Heath 97–98; C Halewood
98–01; Lect Liv Hope 99–00; V Birkenhead St Jas w St Bede
Ches 01–08; NSM Wallasey St Nic w All SS 08–12; V Ashton
Hayes 12–18; rtd 18. *Uwch-y-Llanw, Aber Place, Llandudno
LL30 3AR* E: david.a.lamb@btinternet.com

LAMB, Mrs Jean Evelyn. b 57. Reading Univ BA 79 Nottm
Univ MA 88. St Steph Ho Ox 81. **dss** 84 **d** 88 **p** 01. Leic H
Spirit 84–87; Asst Chapl Leic Poly 84–87; Par Dn Beeston
S'well 88–91; Hon C and Artist in Res Nottingham St Mary
and St Cath 92–95; Hon Par Dn Sneinton St Steph w St Alb
97–01; NSM Rolleston w Fiskerton, Morton and Upton
01–02; PtO 02–04; C Bilborough St Jo 04–11; C Bilborough
w Strelley 04–11; C Colwick 11–12; C Gedling from 12.
St Alban's House, 4 Dale Street, Nottingham NG2 4JX T: 0115-
958 5892 M: 07851-792552

LAMB, Mary. b 52. **d** 10 **p** 11. OLM Framlingham w
Saxtead *St E* 10–13; NSM 13–18; rtd 18; PtO *St E* from 18.
*2 The Coach House, The Square, Dennington, Woodbridge
IP13 8AB* T: (01728) 638897 E: marylamb1952@gmail.com

LAMB, Nicholas Henry. b 52. St Jo Coll Dur BA 74. St Jo Coll
Nottm 76. **d** 79 **p** 80. C Luton Lewsey St Hugh *St Alb* 79–84;
Bethany Fellowship 84–86; In Bapt Min 86–94; PtO *Chich*
97–99; C E Grinstead St Swithun 99–04; V Forest Row 04–13;
Asst Chapl Highgate Sch Lon 13–16; rtd 16. *Address temp
unknown* E: revnhlamb@hotmail.com

LAMB, Philip Richard James. b 42. Sarum & Wells Th
Coll. **d** 83 **p** 84. C Wotton-under-Edge w Ozleworth and
N Nibley *Glouc* 83–86; TV Worc SE 86–91; R Billingsley
w Sidbury, Middleton Scriven etc *Heref* 91–96; R
St Dominic, Landulph and St Mellion w Pillaton *Truro*
96–11; rtd 11; PtO *Truro* from 15. *3 Trelinnoe Gardens,
South Petherwin, Launceston PL15 7TH* T: (01566) 776805
E: p.lamb1571@btinternet.com

LAMB, Phillip. b 68. NEOC 00. **d** 03 **p** 04. C Bridlington Priory
York 03–06; V Hornsea w Atwick 06–16; V Hornsea, Atwick
and Skipsea 16–17; P-in-c Hull St Mary Sculcoates 17–18;
V from 18; P-in-c Sculcoates 17–18; V from 18. *St Paul's
Vicarage, 10 Bridlington Avenue, Hull HU2 0DU* M: 07803-
239611 E: imagine.peace9@yahoo.com

LAMB, Scott Innes. b 64. Edin Univ BSc 86 Fitzw Coll Cam
BA 92 Heythrop Coll Lon MA 15. Ridley Hall Cam 90. **d** 93
p 94. C E Ham w Upton Park and Forest Gate *Chelmsf* 93–97;
V W Holloway St Luke *Lon* 97–00; P-in-c Hammersmith
H Innocents 00–03; Chapl RN 03–09; V Bexley St Jo *Roch*
09–12; TR Bexley 12–18; R Guernsey Ste Marie du Castel
Win from 18; V Guernsey St Matt from 18. *The Rectory, La
Rue de la Lande, Castel, Guernsey GY5 7EJ* T: (01481) 256793
E: lambscott@sky.com

LAMB, William Robert Stuart. b 70. Ball Coll Ox BA 91 MA 95
Peterho Cam MPhil 94 Sheff Univ PhD 10 FHEA 07. Westcott
Ho Cam 92. **d** 95 **p** 96. C Halifax *Wakef* 95–98; TV Penistone
and Thurlstone 98–01; Chapl Sheff Univ 01–10; Can Res
Sheff Cathl 05–10; Vice-Prin Westcott Ho Cam 10–17; V Ox
St Mary V w St Cross and St Pet from 17. *9A Norham Gardens,
Oxford   OX2 6PS*   T: (01865)   279111   M: 07761-325449
E: william.lamb@oriel.ox.ac.uk

LAMBERT, David Francis. b 40. Oak Hill Th Coll 72. **d** 74
p 75. C Paignton St Paul Preston *Ex* 74–77; C Woking Ch
Ch *Guildf* 77–84; P-in-c Willesden Green St Gabr *Lon* 84–91;
P-in-c Cricklewood St Mich 85–91; V Cricklewood St Gabr
and St Mich 92–93; R Chenies and Lt Chalfont, Latimer
and Flaunden *Ox* 93–01; Chapl Izmir (Smyrna) w Bornova
Eur 01–03; TV Brixham w Churston Ferrers and Kingswear
Ex 03–05; rtd 05; PtO *Ex* from 12. *33 Singer Court, Manor
Crescent, Paignton TQ3 2BP*

LAMBERT, David Hardy. b 44. AKC 66. **d** 67 **p** 68. C Marske
in Cleveland *York* 67–72; V 85–09; V N Ormesby 73–85; RD
Guisborough 86–91; rtd 09; PtO *York* from 10. *13 Fell Briggs
Drive, Marske-by-the-Sea, Redcar TS11 6BU* T: (01642) 490235

LAMBERT, David Joseph. b 66. Coll of Resurr Mirfield 99. **d** 01
p 02. C Camberwell St Geo *S'wark* 01–04; C Walworth St Jo
04–06; V Stoke Newington St Faith, St Matthias and All SS
Lon from 06. *St Matthias Vicarage, Wordsworth Road, London
N16 8DD* T: (020) 7254 5063 E: frdavidlambert@aol.com

LAMBERT, David Nathaniel. b 34. Headingley Meth Coll 58
Linc Th Coll 66. **d** 66 **p** 67. In Methodist Ch 58–66; C
Canwick *Linc* 66–68; C-in-c Bracebridge Heath CD 68–69; R
Saltfleetby All SS w St Pet 69–73; R Saltfleetby St Clem 70–73;
V Skidbrooke 70–73; V Saltfleetby 73–80; R Theddlethorpe
74–80; RD Louthesk 76–82; R N Ormsby w Wyham 80; R
Fotherby 81–94; rtd 94; PtO *Linc* 94–03; *York* 03–05; *Ripon*
03–05; Dur 06–17. *Sandcroft, Market Place, Houghton-le-Spring
DH5 8AJ* T: 0191-584 1387 E: ruby.lambert@tiscali.co.uk

LAMBERT, John Connolly. b 61. Univ of Wales (Ban)
BTh 04. EAMTC 01. **d** 04 **p** 05. C Paris St Mich *Eur* 04–08;
C Preston-on-Tees and Longnewton *Dur* 08–10; P-in-c from
10. *The Vicarage, Quarry Road, Eaglescliffe, Stockton-on-Tees
TS16 9BD* T: (01642) 789814

LAMBERT, Malcolm Eric. b 58. Leic Univ BSc 80 Fitzw Coll
Cam BA 89 Nottm Univ MPhil 02 RMN 84. Ridley Hall
Cam 87. **d** 90 **p** 91. C Humberstone *Leic* 90–94; R S Croxton
Gp 94–99; V Birstall and Wanlip 99–05; TR Leic Resurr
05–07; RD Christianity N 05–07; Warden of Readers 97–05;
Dir Angl Th Inst Belize 08–09; TR Chigwell and Chigwell
Row *Chelmsf* 09–15; P-in-c Annesley w Newstead *S'well* 15; V
Annesley w Newstead and Kirkby Woodhouse 15–18; P-in-c
Crookes St Tim *Sheff* from 18. *St Timothy's Vicarage, 152 Slinn
Street, Sheffield S10 1NZ* E: malcolm.lambert@gmail.com

LAMBERT, Michael Roy. b 25. Univ Coll Dur BSc 49.
Cuddesdon Coll 52. **d** 52 **p** 53. C Middlesbrough St Oswald
York 52–56; C Romsey *Win* 56–59; C Cottingham *York*
59–64; Chapl Hull Univ 59–64; V Saltburn-by-the-Sea
64–72; P-in-c Shaftesbury H Trin *Sarum* 72–73; R Shaston
74–76; TR 76–78; R Corfe Mullen 78–91; rtd 91; PtO *Glouc*

91–17. *6 Capel Court, The Burgage, Prestbury, Cheltenham GL52 3EL* T: (01242) 300644

LAMBERT, Miss Olivia Jane. b 48. Matlock Coll of Educn BEd 70. Trin Coll Bris 84. **dss** 86 **d** 87 **p** 94. York St Luke 86–90; Par Dn 87–90; Chapl York Distr Hosp 86–90; Par Dn Huntington *York* 90–94; C 94–95; TV 95–00; TV Marfleet 00–07; C Harrogate St Mark *Ripon* 07–08; rtd 08; PtO *Leeds* from 17. *7 Almsford Place, Harrogate HG2 8EH* T: (01423) 202243

LAMBERT, Peter George. b 29. Coll of Resurr Mirfield 86. **d** 87 **p** 88. NSM Rothwell w Orton, Rushton w Glendon and Pipewell *Pet* 87–93; P-in-c Corby Epiphany w St Jo 93–96; rtd 96; PtO *Pet* from 96. *4 Cogan Crescent, Rothwell, Kettering NN14 6AS* T: (01536) 710692 E: pglambert@tiscali.co.uk

LAMBERT (née JOHNSON), Mrs Ruth Alice Edna. Leic Univ BA 80 PGCE 93 Nottm Univ MA 01 RGN 85 Birm Univ MPhil 08. EMMTC 98. **d** 01 **p** 02. C Mountsorrel Ch Ch and St Pet *Leic* 01–04; Chapl Univ Hosps Leic NHS Trust 04–07; P-in-c Belmopan St Ann Belize 08–09; Chapl Barking Havering and Redbridge Hosps NHS Trust 09–12; Sen Chapl Guy's and St Thos' NHS Foundn Trust 12–15; Lead Chaplain Sherwood Forest Hosps NHS Foundn Trust 15–18; Hd of Chaplaincy Sheff Teaching Hosps NHS Foundn Trust from 18. *A Floor Chapel, Sheffield Teaching Hospitals NHS Foundation Trust, Hallamshire Hospital, Glossop Road, Sheffield S10 2JF* T: 0114-226 1247 E: ruth.lambert@gmail.com *or* ruth.lambert7@nhs.uk

LAMBERT, Mrs Ruth Eleanor. b 52. ERMC. **d** 14 **p** 15. OLM Mile Cross *Nor* from 14. *22 Blomefield Road, Norwich NR3 2RA* T: (01603) 410565 E: ruthless52@hotmail.com

LAMBERT, William John. Man Univ BMus 81. St Mich Coll Llan. **d** 13 **p** 14. C Upper Ebbw Valleys *Mon* 13–16; P-in-c Kenmore w Brookfield Australia 16–18; P-in-c St Ishmael's w Llan-saint and Ferryside *St D* from 18. *The Vicarage, Water Street, Ferryside SA17 5RT* T: (01267) 267559 E: williamlambert314@hotmail.com

LAMBETH, Archdeacon of. *See* GATES, The Ven Simon Philip

LAMBOURN, David Malcolm. b 37. Lanc Univ BEd 76 Man Univ MEd 78 Warwick Univ PhD 01. Linc Th Coll 63. **d** 65 **p** 66. C Camberwell St Geo *S'wark* 65–67; C Mottingham St Andr w St Alban 67–70; rtd 03. *24 Frederick Road, Birmingham B15 1JN* T: 0121-242 3953 E: david.lambourn@blueyonder.co.uk

LAMDIN, Canon Keith Hamilton. b 47. Bris Univ BA 69. Ripon Coll Cuddesdon 86. **d** 86 **p** 87. Adult Educn Officer *Ox* 83–98; Team Ldr Par Resources Dept 88–94; Dioc Dir Tr 94–08; Prin Sarum Coll 08–15; NSM Cowley St Jo *Ox* 98–06; P-in-c Upper Kennet *Sarum* 08–10; Hon Can Ch Ch *Ox* 97–08; Hon Can Kimberley S Africa from 08; Can and Preb Sarum Cathl 09–15; PtO *Sarum* from 15. *2 Forge Close, West Overton, Marlborough SN8 4PG* T: (01672) 861550 E: khlamdin@gmail.com

LAMEY, Richard John. b 77. Keble Coll Ox BA 98 MA 02 Em Coll Cam BA 01 MA 05. Westcott Ho Cam 99. **d** 02 **p** 03. C Stockport SW *Ches* 02–05; P-in-c Newton in Mottram 05–11; P-in-c Newton in Mottram w Flowery Field 11–12; V Newton w Flowery Field 12; RD Mottram 08–12; R Wokingham St Paul *Ox* from 12; AD Sonning from 18. *St Paul's Rectory, Holt Lane, Wokingham RG41 1ED* T: 0118-327 9116 E: richardlamey@btinternet.com

LAMMAS, Miss Diane Beverley. b 47. Trin Coll Bris 76. **dss** 79 **d** 87 **p** 94. Lenton Abbey *S'well* 79–84; Wollaton Park 79–84; E Regional Co-ord and Sec for Voc and Min CPAS 84–89; Hon C Cambridge St Paul *Ely* 87–90; Voc and Min Adv CPAS 89–92; Sen Voc and Min Adv CPAS 92–95; R Hethersett w Canteloff w Lt and Gt Melton *Nor* 95–12; RD Humbleyard 98–03; rtd 12; PtO *Nor* from 13. *3 Turnberry Close, Lowestoft NR33 9JN* T: (01502) 218599 E: di.lammas@yahoo.co.uk

LAMMENS, Erwin Bernard Eddy. b 62. Catholic Univ Leuven BA 86 Gregorian Univ Rome MDiv 90. Grootseminarie Gent 84. **d** 87 **p** 88. In RC Ch 87–94; Asst Chapl Antwerp St Boniface *Eur* 98–05; TV Harwich Peninsula *Chelmsf* 05–10; R Wivenhoe from 10. *The Rectory, 44 Belle Vue Road, Wivenhoe, Colchester CO7 9LD* T: (01206) 822511 E: erwinlammens@btinternet.com

LAMMING, Sarah Rebecca. b 77. Middx Univ BA 02. Westcott Ho Cam 03 Yale Div Sch 05. **d** 06 **p** 07. C Handsworth St Jas *Birm* 06–09; USA from 09. *1000 Spa Road, Apt #202, Annapolis MD 21403, USA* E: fr.sarah@gmail.com

LAMOND, Stephen Paul. b 64. Trin Coll Bris BA 99. **d** 99 **p** 00. C Weston-super-Mare Ch Ch *B & W* 99–02; C Congresbury w Puxton and Hewish St Ann 02–03; Chapl RAF from 03. *Chaplaincy Services (RAF), HQ Air Command, RAF High Wycombe HP14 4UE* T: (01494) 496800

LAMONT, Charles John David. b 91. **d** 14 **p** 15. C Wisley w Pyrford *Guildf* 14–18; P-in-c S Wimbledon

St Andr *S'wark* from 18. *St Andrew's Vicarage, 105 Hartfield Road, London SW19 3TJ* M: 07786-265939 E: charlie@standrewswimbledon.com

LAMONT, Canon Euphemia Margaret (Fay). b 53. N Coll of Educn BA 98. TISEC 00. **d** 00 **p** 00. C Monifieth and Carnoustie *Bre* 00–07; P-in-c Dundee St Ninian from 07; Can St Paul's Cathl Dundee from 08. *St Ninian's Church House, Kingsway East, Dundee DD4 7RW* T: (01382) 453818 M: 07931-222092 E: flamont53@sky.com

LAMONT, Roger. b 37. Jes Coll Ox BA 60 MA 62 MBACP 00. St Steph Ho Ox 59. **d** 61 **p** 62. C Northampton St Alb *Pet* 61–66; V Mitcham St Olave *S'wark* 66–73; V N Sheen St Phil and All SS 73–85; P-in-c Richmond St Luke 82–85; Chapl St Lawr Hosp Caterham 85–93; Chapl Surrey Oaklands NHS Trust 94–01; rtd 01; PtO *S'wark* from 01. *36 Hillcroft Court, Chaldon Road, Caterham CR3 5XB* T: (01883) 340803 E: rmglamont@gmail.com

LAMONT, Ms Veronica Jane (Ronni). b 56. Bp Grosseteste Coll CertEd 77 Anglia Poly Univ MA 06. St Jo Coll Nottm 90. **d** 92 **p** 94. Par Dn St Alb St Pet 92–94; C 94–96; TV Hemel Hempstead 96–01; V Bexley St Jo *Roch* 01–08; PtO *Cant* from 08; *Roch* from 08; Dioc Faith and Nuture Adv *Cant* from 15. *86 Ufton Lane, Sittingbourne ME10 1EX* T: (01795) 553603 M: 07802-793910 E: ronni@lamonts.org.uk *or* rlamont@diocant.org

LAMPARD, Mrs Ruth Margaret. b 65. St Jo Coll Dur BA 87 Jes Coll Cam BA 99 MA 04 Heythrop Coll Lon MA 04. Westcott Ho Cam 97 Berkeley Div Sch 99. **d** 00 **p** 01. C Ealing St Pet Mt Park Lon 00–01; C Eastcote St Lawr 01–04; Hon C Norton St Alb 05–06; PtO *S'wark* 06–12; Chapl to Bp Kensington *Lon* 07–08; C W Brompton St Mary w St Peter and St Jude 08–13; Chapl Chapter 1 from 13; Hon C Waterloo St Jo w St Andr *S'wark* from 13. *St Barnabas' Vicarage, 146A Lavenham Road, London SW18 5EP* T: (020) 7835 1440 *or* 7593 0470 F: 7593 0478 M: 07712-321253 E: ruthlampard3@gmail.com

LANCASTER, Mrs Jennifer. b 48. NEOC 00. **d** 03 **p** 04. C Walker *Newc* 03–07; TV Jarrow *Dur* 07–12; rtd 12; PtO *Newc* from 12. *2 Heathdale Gardens, High Heaton, Newcastle upon Tyne NE7 7QR* E: jenny.lancaster@gmail.com

LANCASTER, John Rawson. b 47. BSc. NOC. **d** 82 **p** 83. C Bolton St Jas w St Chrys *Bradf* 82–86; V Barnoldswick w Bracewell 86–12; rtd 12; PtO *Bradf* 13–14; *Leeds* from 14. *Harold's Laithe, High Bradley Lane, Bradley, Keighley BD20 9ES* T: (01535) 634264

LANCASTER, Ronald. b 31. St Jo Coll Dur BA 53 MA 56 Hon MSc 09 FRSC 83 CChem 83. Cuddesdon Coll 55. **d** 57 **p** 58. C Morley St Pet w Churwell *Wakef* 57–60; C High Harrogate St Pet *Ripon* 60–63; LtO *Ely* 63–88; Chapl Kimbolton Sch 63–88; Asst Chapl 88–91; PtO *Ely* 88–16; rtd 96; PtO *St Alb* 13–18; *Ely* from 18. *7 High Street, Kimbolton, Huntingdon PE28 0HB* T: (01480) 860498 E: ronlancaster31@outlook.com

LANCASTER, Archdeacon of. Vacant

LANCASTER, Suffragan Bishop of. *See* DUFF, The Rt Revd Jillian Louise Calland

LANCHANTIN-PIGGOTT, Mrs Eve Line. b 51. Sorbonne Univ Paris BA 79 MA 80 MPhil 83. Protestant Inst of Th Paris BDiv 95 MDiv 99. **d** 07 **p** 08. C Ashford *Cant* 07–10; PtO 15–16; TV Ashford Town from 16. *212 Faversham Road, Kennington, Ashford TN24 9AF* M: 07949-349543 E: evelanchantin@gmail.com

LAND, Edward Charles. b 79. Trin Coll Bris 13. **d** 15 **p** 16. C Heigham St Thos *Nor* 15–17; C The Mitre Benefice from 17; P-in-c Costessey from 19. *The Vicarage, Folgate Lane, Costessey, Norwich NR8 5DP* M: 07917-285072 E: edward@costesseyparish.org

LAND, Michael Robert John. b 43. Ripon Hall Ox BA 72 MA. **d** 72 **p** 73. C Newbury St Nic *Ox* 72–73; C Newbury 73–75; TV Chigwell *Chelmsf* 75–80; V Walthamstow St Andr 80–08; rtd 08; PtO *Heref* 08–17. *20 St Mary's Lane, Burghill, Hereford HR4 7QL* T: (01432) 760452 E: mrland117@gmail.com

LANDALL, Allan Roy. b 55. Qu Coll Birm BA 98. **d** 98 **p** 99. C Thurnby w Stoughton *Leic* 98–02; R Walsoken *Ely* from 02. *The Rectory, Church Road, Wisbech PE13 3RA* T: (01945) 583740 E: arlandall@btinternet.com

LANDAU, Christopher David. b 80. Trin Coll Cam BA 01 MA 05 MPhil 02 Oriel Coll Ox DPhil 17. Ripon Coll Cuddesdon MPhil 12. **d** 13 **p** 14. C W Kilburn St Luke and Harrow Road Em *Lon* 13–17; NSM Ox St Aldate from 17. *39 York Road, Headington, Oxford OX3 8NR* T: (01865) 761852 M: 07703-958086 E: cdlandau@gmail.com *or* christopher.landau@staldates.org.uk

LANDER, Mrs Elizabeth Anne. b 69. St Andr Univ BSc 93 Ox Univ PGCE 94. Wycliffe Hall Ox 00. **d** 02 **p** 03. C Glascote and Stonydelph *Lich* 02–07; C Beckenham St Jo *Roch* 08–13; V 13–18; Chapl Alleyn's Sch Dulwich from 19; NSM Dulwich

St Barn *S'wark* from 19. *122 Woodwarde Road, London SE22 8UT* M: 07790-212302 E: landerliz@yahoo.co.uk

LANE, Alexander John. b 71. Leeds Univ BA 02. Coll of Resurr Mirfield 99. **d** 02 **p** 03. C Eastbourne St Andr *Chich* 02–06; C Littlehampton and Wick 06–08; V Hunslet w Cross Green *Ripon* 08–12; V Twickenham All SS *Lon* from 12; CMP from 08. *All Saints' House, Church View Road, Twickenham TW2 5BX* T: (020) 8894 3580 E: vicar.allsaintstwickenham@gmail.com

LANE, Mrs Amanda Mary. b 59. Hull Univ BA 82 Ch Ch Coll Cant PGCE 97. SEITE 13. **d** 16 **p** 17. NSM The Six *Cant* from 16. *Meadvale, Maidstone Road, Borden, Sittingbourne ME9 7QA* T: (01795) 842478 M: 07986-785659 E: amandamarylane@gmail.com

LANE, Andrew Harry John. b 49. Lanc Univ BA 71. Cuddesdon Coll 71. **d** 73 **p** 74. C Abingdon w Shippon *Ox* 73–78; Chapl Abingdon Sch 75–78; Chapl RAF 78–94; rtd 94; PtO *Nor* 94–01; Public Preacher from 01; RD Repps 02–05. *Society of St Luke, 32B Beeston Common, Sheringham NR26 8ES* T: (01263) 825623 F: 820334 E: superior@ssluke.org.uk *or* andrewssl@me.com

LANE, Anthony Richard. b 42. St Jo Coll Nottm 07. **d** 09 **p** 10. C Gtr Athens *Eur* 09–17. *Kefalas, Chania 73008, Crete, Greece* T: (0030) (282) 502 2345 M: 6944-131257 E: kritilanes@yahoo.co.uk

LANE, Canon Antony Kenneth. b 58. Ripon Coll Cuddesdon 84. **d** 87 **p** 88. C Crediton and Shobrooke *Ex* 87–90; C Amblecote *Worc* 90–94; C Sedgley All SS 94–95; TV 95–00; R Crayford Roch 00–17; AD Erith 09–14; P-in-c Gillingham St Aug from 17; Hon Can Roch Cathl from 09. *St Augustine's Vicarage, Rock Avenue, Gillingham ME7 5PW* T: (01634) 850288 M: 07928-769882 E: ak.lane@btinternet.com

LANE, Bernard Charles. b 59. Cam Coll of Art & Tech BA 81 Anglia Poly Univ MA 01. Trin Coll Bris BA 91 Ridley Hall Cam 99. **d** 01 **p** 02. C Sittingbourne St Mary and St Mich *Cant* 01–05; Chapl N Bris NHS Trust 10–16; TV Broadclyst, Clyst Honiton, Pinhoe, Rockbeare etc *Ex* from 16. *Rockbeare Vicarage, Rockbeare, Exeter EX5 2EG* M: 07756-797071 E: tvclystvalley@gmail.com

LANE, Christopher Paul. b 80. Regent's Park Coll Ox MA 01. St Mellitus Coll 17. **d** 19. C Walsall St Pet *Lich* from 19. *40 Princes Avenue, Walsall WS1 2DG* M: 07919-453413 E: revchrislane@gmail.com

⌖**LANE, The Rt Revd Elizabeth Jane Holden (Libby).** b 66. St Pet Coll Ox BA 89 MA 93. Cranmer Hall Dur 91. **d** 93 **p** 94 **c** 15. C Blackb St Jas 93–96; PtO *York* 96–99; Family Life Educn Officer *Ches* 00–02; TV Stockport 02–07; Asst Dir of Ords 05–07; V Hale and Ashley 07–15; Dean of Women in Min 10–15; Suff Bp Stockport 15–19; Bp Derby from 19. *The Bishop's House, 6 King Street, Duffield, Belper DE56 4EU* T: (01332) 840132

LANE, Gareth Ernest. b 71. Westmr Univ BSc 94 Univ of Wales MA 08. Wycliffe Hall Ox 08. **d** 10 **p** 11. C Bedgrove *Ox* 10–14; TV Aylesbury from 14. *28 Domino Way, Aylesbury HP18 0FZ* T: (01296) 328523 M: 07919-332859 E: garethlane@hotmail.com *or* gareth@churchonberryfields.org

LANE, George David Christopher. b 68. St Pet Coll Ox BA 89 MA 93. Cranmer Hall Dur 91. **d** 93 **p** 94. C Blackb St Jas 93–96; C Beverley Minster *York* 96–99; V Heald Green St Cath *Ches* 99–07; PtO from 07; *Man* 08–12; Chapl Man Airport from 12; Lic Preacher from 12. *Bishop's Lodge, Back Lane, Dunham Town, Altrincham WA14 4SG* T: 0161-489 2838 *or* 928 5611 E: george.lane@manairport.co.uk *or* george_dcl@yahoo.co.uk

LANE, Iain Robert. b 61. CCC Ox BA 83. Ripon Coll Cuddesdon BA 86 MA 88. **d** 87 **p** 88. C Rotherhithe St Mary w All SS *S'wark* 87–91; V Bierley *Bradf* 91–00; Can Res St Alb 00–08; Admin St Alb Cen for Chr Studies from 08; PtO *St Alb* from 08. *Hill House, Wild Hill, Hatfield AL9 6EB* T: (01707) 660485 E: iain.lane@christianstudies.org.uk *or* iain@iainlane.uk

LANE, Jennifer Mary. b 73. Leeds Univ BA 08 MA 12. NOC 05. **d** 08 **p** 09. C Crosland Moor and Linthwaite *Wakef* 08–11; P-in-c Crofton and Warmfield 11–14; Par Educn Adv 11–14; P-in-c E Richmond *Leeds* 14–16 and from 14; R Lower Swale from 19. *Address temp unknown* E: jennilane2013@btinternet.com

LANE, John Ernest. b 39. MBIM 76 Cranfield Info Tech Inst MSc 80. Handsworth Coll Birm 58. **d** 80 **p** 80. In Methodist Ch 62–80; Hon C Peckham St Jo w St Andr *S'wark* 80–95; Hon C Greenwich St Alfege 99–99; Dir St Mungo Housing Assn 80–94; Dir Corporate Affairs from 94; PtO *S'wark* 95–98; *Lich* 02–14. *2 Tregony Rise, Lichfield WS14 9SN* T: (01543) 415078

LANE, Libby. *See* LANE, Elizabeth Jane Holden

LANE, Mrs Lilian June. b 37. Stockwell Coll Lon TCert 59. **d** 02 **p** 03. OLM E Knoyle, Semley and Sedgehill *Sarum* 02–08; OLM St Bartholomew 08–09; Chapl St Mary's Sch Shaftesbury from 09. *Ashmede, Watery Lane, Donhead St Mary, Shaftesbury SP7 9DP* T: (01747) 828427 E: rev.jlane@icloud.com

LANE, Mrs Linda Mary. b 41. Lon Univ BD 87 ACIB 66. Gilmore Ho 67. **dss** 82 **d** 87 **p** 94. Hadlow *Roch* 82–94; Hon Par Dn 87–94; PtO 94–96; C Dartford H Trin 96–97; V Kensworth, Studham and Whipsnade *St Alb* 97–03; rtd 03; PtO *Wakef* 05–10. *Carey Cottage, The Green, Cleasby, Darlington DL2 2QZ* T: (01325) 464544

LANE, Malcolm Clifford George. b 48. ACIB. St D Coll Lamp. **d** 02 **p** 05. Par Dn Abergavenny St Mary w Llanwenarth Citra *Mon* 02–08; P-in-c Michaelston-y-Fedw 08–14; Asst Chapl Gwent Healthcare NHS Trust 02–14; rtd 14; PtO *Mon* from 15; *Heref* from 16. *14 Coed y Brenin, Llantilio Pertholey, Abergavenny NP7 6PY* T: (01873) 858464 E: st8711@msn.com

LANE, Canon Martin John. b 69. Open Univ BSc 03 Cardiff Univ LLM 08. Coll of Resurr Mirfield 92. **d** 95 **p** 96. C Liss *Portsm* 95–98; C Warren Park and Leigh Park 98–00; TV Littlehampton and Wick *Chich* 00–04; P-in-c Harting w Elsted and Treyford cum Didling 04–10; RD Midhurst 06–10; V Bosham from 10; RD Westbourne from 15; Can and Preb Chich Cathl from 18. *The Vicarage, Bosham Lane, Bosham, Chichester PO18 8HX* T: (01243) 573228 E: martinjlane@gmail.com

LANE, Robert David. b 66. St Steph Ho Ox 05. **d** 07 **p** 08. C Corringham *Chelmsf* 07–10; V Petts Wood *Roch* 10–17; P-in-c Borden *Cant* from 17. *The Vicarage, School Lane, Borden, Sittingbourne ME9 8JS* M: 07807-224748 E: robert.lane2@virgin.net

LANE, Ms Rosalind Anne. b 69. Trevelyan Coll Dur BA 91 Heythrop Coll Lon MTh 93 Man Univ MA 01 Ches Univ DProf 16. Westcott Ho Cam. **d** 95 **p** 96. C Huddersfield St Pet and All SS *Wakef* 95–99; Sub Chapl HM Pris and YOI New Hall 97–99; Asst Chapl HM Pris and YOI Doncaster 99–01; Chapl 01; Chapl HM Pris Wymott 01–05; Kirkham 05–08; Whitemoor 08–11; Ashwell 11; Chapl N Essex Partnership NHS Foundn Trust 11–12; Chapl Cambs and Pet NHS Foundn Trust 12–15; Chapl Peterborough and Stamford Hosps NHS Foundn Trust 12–15; Chapl K Ely from 15. *King's, Barton Road, Ely CB7 4EW* T: (01353) 660700 E: roslane@kingsely.org

LANE, Roy Albert. b 42. Bris Sch of Min 82. **d** 85 **p** 86. NSM Bedminster *Bris* 85–97; PtO 97–02; NSM Bishopsworth and Bedminster Down 02–12; rtd 12; PtO *Bris* from 12. *20 Ashton Drive, Bristol BS3 2PW* T: 0117-983 0747 M: 07701-002485 E: roypeg@blueyonder.co.uk

LANE, Simon. *See* DOUGLAS LANE, Charles Simon Pellew

LANE, Stuart Alexander Rhys. *See* LANE, Alexander John

LANE, Terry. b 50. STETS 94. **d** 97 **p** 98. NSM Freemantle *Win* 97–99; Chapl HM Pris Kingston (Portsm) 99–01; Chapl HM Pris Parkhurst 01–06; Co-ord Chapl HM Pris Win 06–10; rtd 10; PtO *Win* 10–16. *24 Claremont Crescent, Southampton SO15 4GS* E: samaritan1949@gmail.com

LANE, William Henry Howard. b 63. Bris Poly BA 85. Trin Coll Bris 00. **d** 02 **p** 03. C Frome H Trin *B & W* 02–06; P-in-c Woolavington w Cossington and Bawdrip 06–08; R 09–11; RD Sedgemoor 09–11; V Bridgwater H Trin and Durleigh from 11. *The New Vicarage, Hamp Avenue, Bridgwater TA6 6AN* T: (01278) 455022 E: reverend.lane@googlemail.com

LANG, William David. b 51. K Coll Lon BD 74 MA 94 AKC 74. St Aug Coll Cant 74. **d** 75 **p** 76. C Fleet *Guildf* 75–79; C Ewell St Fran 79–82; C W Ewell 79–82; V Holmwood 82–92; R Elstead 92–10; V Thursley 92–10; P-in-c Redhorn *Sarum* 10–12; P-in-c Bishop's Cannings, All Cannings etc 11–12; TR Cannings and Redhorn 12–16; rtd 16. *60 St Marys Gardens, Hilperton Marsh, Trowbridge BA14 7PQ* E: william@lang.net

LANGAN, Canon Eleanor Susan. b 56. Homerton Coll Cam BEd 78. Ripon Coll Cuddesdon 84. **d** 87 **p** 94. Hon Par Dn Grays Thurrock *Chelmsf* 87–89; LtO 89–94; NSM Creeksea w Althorne, Latchingdon and N Fambridge 94–95; NSM S Woodham Ferrers 95–99; NSM Overstrand, Northrepps, Sidestrand etc *Nor* 99–03; Chapl Norfolk and Nor Univ Hosps NHS Foundn Trust 00–10; Lead Chapl 10–19; V Nor St Helen from 19; Chapl Gt Hosp Nor from 19; Hon Can Nor Cathl from 18. *Calthorpe Lodge, Great Hospital, Bishopgate, Norwich NR1 4EL*

LANGDON, Ms Susan Mary. b 48. RN 69. Ripon Coll Cuddesdon 01. **d** 03 **p** 04. C Amesbury *Sarum* 03–06; Jt Ldr Pilgrimage Community of St Wite 06–19; Warden Pilsdon Community from 19; PtO *Sarum* from 16. *Pilsdon Manor, Pilsdon, Bridport DT6 5NZ* T: (01308) 868308 E: suelangdon@btinternet.com

LANGDON-DAVIES, Mrs Stella Mary. b 44. Bris Univ BSc 85 Nottm Univ MBA 97. St Jo Coll Nottm MTh 01. **d** 01 **p** 02. C Stamford All SS w St Jo *Linc* 01–04; V Herne *Cant* 04–06; P-in-c Saxonwell *Linc* 06–08; rtd 08; PtO *Leic* from 14; *Linc* 15–18. *5 Manor Paddock, Allington, Grantham NG32 2DL* T: (01400) 281395 M: 07976-380659 E: stellalangdondavies@btinternet.com

LANGDON-GRIFFITHS (née Erving), Christel Estelle Ann. b 79. Liv Univ BSc 01 St Jo Coll Dur BA 15. Cranmer Hall Dur 13. **d** 15 **p** 16. C Walton St Luke *Liv* 15–17; C Wavertree St Mary 17–18. *21 Chemin de Fonblanque, 81800 Rabastens, France* M: 07477-594790 E: christel.erving@outlook.com

LANGDON-GRIFFITHS, Daniel Steven. b 82. St Jo Coll Dur BA 14. Cranmer Hall Dur 11. **d** 14 **p** 15. C Sutton *Liv* 14–17; Chapl Midi-Pyrénées and Aude *Eur* from 18. *21 chemin de Fontblanque, 81800 Rabstens, France* T: (0033) 5 63 81 87 44 M: 07411-795237 E: dan.langdon.griffiths@gmail.com

LANGDON-SMITH, Thomas Robert. b 83. Liv Hope Univ BA 05. St Mellitus Coll 16. **d** 19. C Liv Ch Ch Norris Green from 19. *9 Kingsland Crescent, Liverpool L11 7AN* M: 07800-652662 E: tomlangdonsmith@gmail.com

LANGDOWN, Jennifer May. b 48. STETS 95. **d** 98 **p** 99. C S Petherton w The Seavingtons *B & W* 98–02; R Curry Rivel w Fivehead and Swell 02–12; rtd 12; PtO *B & W* from 15. *61 Vereland Road, Hutton, Weston-super-Mare BS24 9TH* T: (01934) 815499 M: 07850-245948 E: mrsvic7548@gmail.com

LANGERHUIZEN, Sandra Marilyn. b 45. **d** 11 **p** 12. NSM Birkenhead St Jas w St Bede *Ches* 11–15; rtd 15; PtO *Ches* from 15. *43 Shamrock Road, Birkenhead CH41 0EG* T: 0151-652 3109 E: w.langerhuizen@btinternet.com

LANGFORD, David Laurence. b 51. **d** 88 **p** 89. OLM Scotton w Northorpe *Linc* 88–16; OLM Messingham w E Butterwick, Scotter w E Ferry and Scotton w Northorpe from 16. *1 Westgate, Scotton, Gainsborough DN21 3QX* T: (01724) 763139

LANGFORD, Prof Michael John. b 31. New Coll Ox BA 54 MA 58 Cam Univ MA 59 Lon Univ PhD 66. Westcott Ho Cam 55. **d** 56 **p** 57. C Bris St Nath w St Kath 56–59; Chapl Qu Coll Cam 59–63; C Hampstead St Jo *Lon* 63–67; Philosophy Dept Memorial Univ Newfoundland 67–96; Prof Philosophy 82–96; Prof Medical Ethics 87–96; rtd 96; PtO *Ely* from 96. *19 High Street, Dry Drayton, Cambridge CB23 8BS* T: (01954) 789593 E: ml297@hermes.cam.ac.uk

LANGFORD, Peter Julian. b 33. Selw Coll Cam BA 58. Westcott Ho Cam 59. **d** 60 **p** 61. C E Ham St Mary *Chelmsf* 60–67; Hon C 67–68; Hon C E Ham w Upton Park 68–71; Hon C Beccles St Mich *St E* 71–76; Warden Ringsfield Hall Suffolk 71–87; P-in-c Ringsfield w Redisham *St E* 76–80; TV Seacroft *Ripon* 97–98; PtO *St E* from 99. *22 Alexander Road, Beccles NR34 9UD* T: (01502) 710034

LANGHAM, Paul Jonathan. b 60. Ex Univ BA 81 Fitzw Coll Cam BA 86 MA 91. Ridley Hall Cam 84. **d** 87 **p** 88. C Bath Weston All SS w N Stoke *B & W* 87–91; Chapl and Fell St Cath Coll Cam 91–96; V Combe Down w Monkton Combe and S Stoke *B & W* 96–10; P-in-c Clifton Ch Ch w Em *Bris* 10–15; V from 15. *Christ Church Clifton Church Office, Linden Gate, Clifton Down Road, Bristol BS8 4AH* T: 0117-973 6524 E: paul.langham@ccweb.org.uk

LANGILLE, Canon Melvin Owen. b 58. St Mary's Univ Halifax NS BA 79. Atlantic Sch of Th MDiv 82. **d** 82 **p** 83. Dn-in-c Falkland Canada 82; R Lockeport and Barrington 83–86; R French Village 87–90; R Cole Harbour St Andr 90–96; R Yarmouth H Trin 97–03; P-in-c Brora *Mor* 03–09; P-in-c Dornoch 03–09; R Arpafeelie from 09; R Cromarty from 09; R Fortrose from 09; Syn Clerk 07–12; Dioc Dir of Ords 08–14; Can St Andr Cathl Inverness 07–12 and from 13. *The Rectory, 1 Deans Road, Fortrose IV10 8TJ* T: (01381) 622241 M: 07780-512990 E: mel@sagart.me.uk

LANGLANDS, John Craig. Suffolk Coll BA 07. Qu Coll Birm 14. **d** 15 **p** 16. NSM Allesley Park and Whoberley *Cov* 15–18; C from 18. *52 Brookside Avenue, Coventry CV5 8AF* T: (024) 7667 5236 M: 07588-664962 E: jlanglands@sky.com

LANGLEY, Jean. *See* PHILLIPS, Jean

LANGLEY, Canon Myrtle Sarah. b 39. TCD BA 61 HDipEd 62 MA 67 Bris Univ PhD 76 Lon Univ BD 66 FRAI. Dalton Ho Bris 64. **d** 88 **p** 94. Dir Chr Development for Miss *Liv* 87–89; Dir Dioc Tr Inst *Carl* 90–98; Dioc Dir of Tr 90–98; Hon Can Carl Cathl 91–98; P-in-c Long Marton w Dufton and w Milburn 98–06; rtd 06; PtO *Carl* from 07. *Chena, 5 Farbrow Road, Carlisle CA1 3HW* T: (01228) 539291 E: canonmlangley@hotmail.com

LANGLEY, The Ven Robert. b 37. St Cath Soc Ox BA 61. St Steph Ho Ox. **d** 63 **p** 64. C Aston cum Aughton *Sheff* 63–68; Midl Area Sec Chr Educn Movement 68–71; HQ Sec

Chr Educn Movement 71–74; Prin Ian Ramsey Coll Brasted 74–77; Can Res St Alb and Dir St Alb Minl Tr Scheme 77–85; Can Res Newc Cathl 85–01; Dioc Missr 85–98; Dioc Dir of Min and Tr 98–01; Adn Lindisfarne 01–07; Local Min Development Officer 01–07; rtd 08; PtO *Newc* from 08; *York* 09–19. *1 Castle Farm Mews, Jesmond, Newcastle upon Tyne NE2 3RG* T: 0191-284 9526 E: r.langley648@btinternet.com

LANGMAN, Barry Edward. b 46. Master Mariner 73. Cant Sch of Min 87. **d** 90 **p** 91. NSM St Margarets-at-Cliffe w Westcliffe etc *Cant* 90–92; C Sandgate St Paul w Folkestone St Geo 92–95; P-in-c Headcorn 95–01; V 01–08; rtd 08; PtO *Cant* 08–14; *Ches* from 15. *23 Birkdale Close, Macclesfield SK10 2UA* T: (01625) 662287 E: barrylangman@yahoo.co.uk

✠**LANGRISH, The Rt Revd Michael Laurence.** b 46. Birm Univ BSocSc 67 Fitzw Coll Cam BA 73 MA 77 Ex Univ Hon DD 07. Ridley Hall Cam 71. **d** 73 **p** 74 **c** 93. C Stratford-on-Avon w Bishopton *Cov* 73–76; Chapl Rugby Sch 76–81; P-in-c Offchurch *Cov* 81–87; Dioc Dir of Ords 81–87; P-in-c Rugby 87–91; Hon Can Cov Cathl 90–93; TR Rugby 91–93; Suff Bp Birkenhead *Ches* 93–00; Bp Ex 00–13; rtd 13; Hon Asst Bp Chich from 13; Hon Asst Bp Eur from 18; PtO from 18. *39 The Meadows, Walberton, Arundel BN18 0PB* T: (01243) 551704 E: langrishm@btinternet.com

✠**LANGSTAFF, The Rt Revd James Henry.** b 56. St Cath Coll Ox BA 77 MA 81 Nottm Univ BA 80. St Jo Coll Nottm 78. **d** 81 **p** 82 **c** 04. C Farnborough *Guildf* 81–84 and 85–86; P-in-c 84–85; P-in-c Duddeston w Nechells *Birm* 86; V 87–96; RD Birm City 95–96; Bp's Dom Chapl 96–00; P-in-c Short Heath 98–00; R Sutton Coldfield H Trin 00–04; AD Sutton Coldfield 02–04; Suff Bp Lynn *Nor* 04–10; Bp Roch from 10; Bp HM Pris from 13. *Bishopscourt, 24 St Margaret's Street, Rochester ME1 1TS* T: (01634) 842712 E: bishopscourt@rochester.anglican.org *or* bishop.rochester@rochester.anglican.org

LANGTON, Robert. b 45. SAOMC 97. **d** 00 **p** 01. C Boyne Hill *Ox* 00–03; Chapl St Mich Hospice St Leonards-on-Sea 03–08; TV Cwmbran *Mon* 08–15; rtd 10; Hon C Cwmbran *Mon* 15–16; rtd 15. *4 Margetts Close, Kenilworth CV8 1EN* T: (01926) 259523 E: robertlangton.langton@gmail.com

LANHAM, Richard Paul White. b 42. Dur Univ BA 64. Wycliffe Hall Ox 65. **d** 67 **p** 68. C Gerrards Cross *Ox* 67–69; C Horwich H Trin *Man* 69–72; C Worsley 72–74; V Accrington St Andr *Blackb* 74–80; V Shillington *St Alb* 80–85; V Upper w Lower Gravenhurst 80–85; rtd 85; PtO *St Alb* from 85. *10 Alexander Close, Clifton, Shefford SG17 5RB* T: (01462) 813520

LANKESTER, Mrs Jane Elizabeth. b 53. Qu Mary Coll Lon BScEcon 74 SS Mark & Jo Univ Coll Plymouth MA 04. SWMTC 05. **d** 08 **p** 09. NSM Totnes w Bridgetown, Berry Pomeroy etc *Ex* 08–12; TV Honiton, Gittisham, Combe Raleigh, Monkton etc 12–18; rtd 18. *63 Cleeve Drive, Ivybridge PL21 9BP* E: jane.lankester@gmail.com

LANKSHEAR, Jane Frances. *See* MAINWARING, Jane Frances

LANNON, Joseph. b 61. QUB BD 83 PhD 02 Cranfield Univ MSc 85. SWMTC 15. **d** 17. C Newton Abbot *Ex* 17–18; C Newton Ferrers w Revelstoke from 18. *Church Hill House, Church Hill, Holbeton, Plymouth PL8 1LN* M: 07584-078985 E: lannonjoe@gmail.com

LANSDALE, Canon Charles Roderick. b 38. Leeds Univ BA 59. Coll of Resurr Mirfield 59. **d** 61 **p** 62. C Nunhead St Antony *S'wark* 61–65; Swaziland 65–71; V Benhilton *S'wark* 72–78; TR Catford (Southend) and Downham 78–87; TR Moulsecoomb *Chich* 87–97; V Eastbourne St Mary 97–08; Can and Preb Chich Cathl 98–08; rtd 08; PtO *Chich* from 08. *102 Channel View Road, Eastbourne BN22 7LJ* T: (01323) 646655

LANYON-HOGG, Mrs Anne Chester. b 49. St Anne's Coll Ox BA 71 MA 75 Worc Coll of Educn PGCE 92. WEMTC 01. **d** 04 **p** 05. NSM Colwall w Upper Colwall and Coddington *Heref* 04–19; NSM Malvern H Trin and St Jas *Worc* 07–14; PtO from 14; Bp's Adv for SSM *Heref* 15–19; rtd 19; PtO *Heref* from 19. *Address temp unknown* M: 07891-868676 E: stillannelh@gmail.com

LANYON JONES, Keith. b 49. Southn Univ BTh 79. Sarum & Wells Th Coll 74. **d** 77 **p** 78. C Charlton Kings St Mary *Glouc* 77–81; Sen Chapl Rugby Sch 81–99; LtO *Truro* 83–00; P-in-c St Cleer 00–15; C St Ive and Pensilva w Quethiock 02–15; Chapl Kelly Coll Tavistock 08–15; rtd 15. *The Old Forge, 17A St John Street, Wells BA5 1SW*

LAOTAN, Anthony Olanrewaju. b 77. Yorks Min Course 12. **d** 16 **p** 17. C Idle *Leeds* from 16. *33 Cavalier Drive, Apperley Bridge, Bradford BD10 0UF* E: olanonline@yahoo.com

LAPWOOD, Robin Rowland John. b 57. Selw Coll Cam MA. Ridley Hall Cam 80. **d** 82 **p** 83. C Bury St Edmunds St Mary *St E* 82–86; P-in-c Bentley w Tattingstone 86–93; P-in-c Copdock w Washbrook and Belstead 86–93; TV

High Wycombe *Ox* 93–96; P-in-c Marcham w Garford 96–02; Chapl Summer Fields Sch Ox 02–12; PtO *Ox* from 12. *Rose Cottage, Challow Road, Wantage OX12 9DN* E: robin.lapwood@gmail.com

LARCOMBE, Paul Richard. b 57. Portsm Poly BSc 79 CEng MIET. Trin Coll Bris 94. **d** 96 **p** 97. C Werrington *Pet* 96–98; C Longthorpe 98–00; V Pet St Paul 00–07; TR Worle *B & W* 07–16; PtO 16–18 and from 16. *55 Forest Drive, Weston-super-Mare BS23 2UG* T: (01934) 270470 E: plarcombe@mac.com

LARGE, Stephen James. b 48. All SS Cen for Miss & Min 15. **d** 17 **p** 18. NSM Burnley St Cuth *Blackb* from 17; NSM Brierfield from 17. *11 Sandiway Drive, Briercliffe, Burnley BB10 2JS*

LARGE, William Roy. b 40. Dur Univ BA DipEd Newc Univ MLitt 15. Edin Th Coll 82. **d** 84 **p** 85. C Leamington Priors All SS *Cov* 84–88; V Bishop's Tachbrook 88–99; Warden of Readers and Sen Tutor 88–99; TV N Tyne and Redesdale *Newc* 99–01; TR 01–05; rtd 05; PtO *Newc* from 05. *4 Osborne Court, Osborne Avenue, Newcastle upon Tyne NE2 1LE* T: 0191-281 1894 E: wr.large@btinternet.com

LARK, William Donald Starling. b 35. Keble Coll Ox BA 59 MA 63. Wells Th Coll 59. **d** 61 **p** 62. C Wyken *Cov* 61–64; C Christchurch *Win* 64–66; V Yeovil St Mich *B & W* 66–75; V Earley St Pet *Ox* 75–85; V Prittlewell *Chelmsf* 85–88; V Dawlish *Ex* 88–00; rtd 00; P-in-c Lanzarote *Eur* 00–05. *Las Alondras, 6 Cummings Court, Cummings Cross, Liverton, Newton Abbot TQ12 6HJ* T: (01626) 824966 E: lanzalarks@btinternet.com

LARKEY, Canon Deborah Frances. b 63. Univ of Wales (Abth) BA 85 Sarum Coll MA 17 Liv Inst of Educn PGCE 90. Dioc OLM tr scheme 95 NOC 03. **d** 98 **p** 99. OLM Toxteth St Cypr w Ch Ch *Liv* 98–01; OLM Edge Hill St Cypr w St Mary 01–04; C Netherton 04–07; TV Vale of Pewsey *Sarum* 07–11; TR from 11; Can and Preb Sarum Cathl from 17. *The Vicarage, Church Road, Woodborough, Pewsey SN9 5PH* T: (01672) 851746 E: deborahlarkey@btinternet.com

LARKIN, Andrew Brian. b 70. Warwick Univ BEng 92 PhD 95. Trin Coll Bris BA 06. **d** 06 **p** 07. C Littleover *Derby* 06–08; C Brailsford w Shirley, Osmaston w Edlaston etc 08–10; R Fenny Bentley, Thorpe, Tissington, Parwich etc 10–16; RD Ashbourne 12–16; P-in-c Wootton Wawen *Cov* from 16; P-in-c Claverdon w Preston Bagot from 16. *The Vicarage, Stratford Road, Wootton Wawen, Henley-in-Arden B95 6BD* T: (01564) 792870 M: 07758-704452 E: andy@larkin.me.uk *or* andy@churchesofarden.org.uk

LARKIN, Karen Maria. *See* GREENIDGE, Karen Maria

LARKIN, Lucy. b 66. Birm Univ BA 87 MPhil 91 PhD 01 Westmr Coll Ox PGCE 89. **d** 08 **p** 09. C Hawthorn Australia 08–10; C St Pet Cathl Adelaide 10–11; Tutor SWMTC from 13; PtO Truro 13–14; Public Preacher from 14. *3 The Cedars, Truro TR1 2FD* T: (01872) 241716 M: 07757-917473 E: lucylarkin@swmtc.org.uk

LARKIN, Canon Peter John. b 39. ALCD 62. **d** 62 **p** 63. C Liskeard w St Keyne *Truro* 62–65; C Rugby St Andr *Cov* 65–67; Sec Bp Cov Call to Miss 67–68; V Kea *Truro* 68–78; P-in-c Bromsgrove St Jo *Worc* 78–81; R Torquay St Matthias, St Mark and H Trin *Ex* 81–97; Can Sokoto Nigeria 91–98; Can Kaduna from 98; TR Plymouth Em, St Paul Efford and St Aug *Ex* 97–00; rtd 00; PtO *Ex* from 00; *Truro* from 08. *12 De Luci Park, Truro TR1 2FB* T/F: (01872) 859328 E: mollypeterlarkin@tiscali.co.uk

LARKIN, Mrs Susan Jane. b 52. Qu Foundn (Course) 10. **d** 12 **p** 13. NSM Garretts Green and Tile Cross *Birm* 12–18; NSM Garretts Green and Lea Hall from 18. *48 Horrell Road, Birmingham B26 2PD* T: 0121-574 3152 E: susanjlarkin@hotmail.co.uk

LARKIN, Mrs Treena Maud. b 72. Wolv Univ BSc 93 Keele Univ MSc 07. St Mellitus Coll BA 19. **d** 19. C Penn Fields *Lich* from 19. *131 Church Road, Bradmore, Wolverhampton WV3 7EN* T: (01902) 655485 M: 07971-049571 E: treenalarkin@hotmail.com

LASKEY, Cyril Edward. b 44. RMN 71 RGN 74. Llan Dioc Tr Scheme 85. **d** 88 **p** 89. NSM Troedrhiwgarth *Llan* 88–93; NSM Caerau St Cynfelin 94–01; P-in-c Glyncorrwg and Upper Afan Valley 01–10; rtd 10; PtO *Llan* from 11. *207 Bridgend Road, Maesteg CF34 0NL* T: (01656) 734639

LASLETT, Christopher John. b 42. Leeds Univ BA 64 Lon Univ PGCE 73. Lich Th Coll 64. **d** 66 **p** 67. C Bradf St Clem 66–69; C Upper Armley *Ripon* 69–70; PtO *Dur* 71–72; Hon C Stranton 77–88; PtO *Ripon* 87–88; rtd 07. *20 Richmond Street, Bridlington YO15 3DJ* T: (01262) 671527

LAST, Eric Cyril. b 50. Open Univ Th Coll 77. **d** 79 **p** 80. C Wandsworth All SS *S'wark* 79–83; V Earlsfield St Andr 83–88; V S Merstham 88–96; Asst RD Reigate 92–96; rtd 96; Hon C Upper Tean *Lich* 96–10; PtO 10–16. *16 Whitehaven Castle, Flatt Walks, Whitehaven CA28 7RA* T: (01946) 692716 M: 07594-668598 E: eric.last1@btinternet.com

LAST, Mrs Estella Ruth. b 76. Brunel Univ LLB 98. SEITE 11. **d** 14 **p** 15. C Herne *Cant* 14–18; P-in-c Bridge from 18; Bp's Adv for Women's Min from 19. *The Vicarage, 23 High Street, Bridge, Canterbury CT4 5JZ* M: 07951-607334 E: estellalast@gmail.com

LAST, Canon Michael Leonard Eric. b 60. St Jo Coll Nottm 92. **d** 94 **p** 95. C Tettenhall Wood *Lich* 94–98; V Pelsall 98–02; V Alton w Bradley-le-Moors and Oakamoor w Cotton 02–09; P-in-c Mayfield and Denstone w Ellastone and Stanton 06–09; I Saskatchewan Gateway Canada 09–11; R Adderley, Ash, Calverhall, Ightfield etc *Lich* 11–17; P-in-c Keith *Mor* from 17; P-in-c Huntly from 17; P-in-c Aberchirder from 17; P-in-c Fochabers from 17; P-in-c Dufftown from 18; Can St Andr Cathl Inverness from 19. *Holy Trinity Rectory, Seafield Avenue, Keith AB55 5BS* T: (01542) 882782 M: 07591-750575 E: rev.last@lastrose.uk

LATHAM, Christine Elizabeth. b 46. S'wark Ord Course 87. **d** 90 **p** 94. Par Dn Battersea St Pet and St Paul *S'wark* 90–94; Par Dn S'wark Ch Ch 94; C 94–97; C Merstham and Gatton 97–05; Chapl E Surrey Learning Disability NHS Trust 97–05; Chapl R Marsden NHS Foundn Trust 05–10; rtd 10; PtO *S'wark* from 10. *4 Bromley College, London Road, Bromley BR1 1PE* T: (020) 3489 7213 E: christine.latham@talktalk.net

LATHAM, Henry Nicholas Lomax. b 64. Reading Univ BA 86. Wycliffe Hall Ox BTh 93. **d** 93 **p** 94. C Aberystwyth *St D* 93–99; P-in-c Stoke Poges *Ox* 99–08; V 08–17; R Headley and Box Hill w Walton on the Hill *Guildf* from 17. *The Rectory, Breech Lane, Walton on the Hill, Tadworth KT20 7SD* T: (01737) 812105 E: isaiah61@uwclub.net

LATHAM, John Montgomery. b 37. Univ of NZ BA Cam Univ MA Cant Univ (NZ) MEd. Westcott Ho Cam 60. **d** 62 **p** 63. C Camberwell St Geo *S'wark* 62–65; Chapl Trin Coll Cam 65–70; Chapl Wanganui Colleg Sch New Zealand 71–79; Min Enabler New Brighton 96–01; V Christchurch St Luke 98–02; rtd 02. *43 Rugby Street, Christchurch 8014, New Zealand* T: (0064) (3) 355 6654 F: 355 6658 E: latham@xtra.co.nz

LATHAM, Robert Norman. b 53. Qu Coll Birm 82. **d** 85 **p** 86. C Tamworth *Lich* 85–89; TV Wordsley *Worc* 89–96; P-in-c Hallow 96–97; R Hallow and Grimley w Holt 97–18; rtd 19. *30 Elmdene Road, Kenilworth CV8 2BX* T: (01926) 716142 E: letsstartatthecross@gmail.com

LATHAM, Roger Allonby. b 69. Leic Univ BA 90 Warwick Univ MA 92 Leeds Univ PGCE 93 Nottm Univ PhD 07. St Jo Coll Nottm BTh 98. **d** 99 **p** 00. C Paston *Pet* 99–02; TV Cartmel Peninsula *Carl* 02–09; Officer for IME 4-7 08–18; Vice-Prin LCTP and C Beacon 09–16; Dir Cumbria Chr Learning 16–18; Dir Cuddesdon: Glouc and Heref from 18; Public Preacher *Heref* from 18. *12 College Green, Gloucester GL1 2LX* T: (01452) 874969 E: rogerlatham54@aol.com *or* roger.latham@rcc.ac.uk

LATHAM (*née* WEBSTER), Mrs Rosamond Mary. b 54. Coll of Ripon & York St Jo BEd 90 MA 00 Birm Univ MPhil 13. Westcott Ho Cam 00. **d** 02 **p** 03. C Frodingham *Linc* 02–05; TV Dur N 05–07; TV Dorchester *Ox* 07–13; P-in-c Alford w Rigsby *Linc* 13–18; P-in-c Bilsby w Farlesthorpe 13–18; P-in-c Hannah cum Hagnaby w Markby 13–18; P-in-c Saleby w Beesby and Maltby 13–18; P-in-c Well 13–18; P-in-c Willoughby 14–18; R Alford Gp from 18; RD Calcewaithe and Candleshoe from 17. *The Vicarage, 15 Bilsby Road, Alford LN13 9EW* T: (01507) 464859 M: 07779-784320

LATHAM, Trevor Martin. b 56. BD 84. Ripon Coll Cuddesdon 84. **d** 86 **p** 87. C Cantril Farm *Liv* 86–89; TV Croxteth Park 89–98; V 98–99; TR Walton-on-the-Hill 99–19; rtd 19. *The Walton Cornerstone, 2 Liston Street, Liverpool L4 5RT*

LATHE, Canon Anthony Charles Hudson. b 36. Jes Coll Ox BA 59 MA 64. Lich Th Coll 59. **d** 61 **p** 62. C Selby Abbey *York* 61–63; V Hempnall *Nor* 63–72; R Woodton w Bedingham 63–72; R Fritton w Morningthorpe w Shelton and Hardwick 63–72; R Topcroft 63–72; R Banham 72–76; TR Quidenham 76–83; P-in-c New Buckenham 78–79; V Heigham St Thos 83–94; Hon Can Nor Cathl 87–99; RD Nor S 90–94; P-in-c Sheringham 94–99; rtd 99; PtO *Nor* 99–06; *St Alb* from 07. *15A Kingsdale Road, Berkhamsted HP4 3BS* T: (01442) 863115

LATIMER, Andrew John. b 78. Qu Coll Cam MA 04 Lon Univ MB, BS 05. Oak Hill Th Coll BTh 10. **d** 10 **p** 11. C Limehouse *Lon* 10–19; LtO *S'wark* from 19. *49 Devonshire Drive, London SE10 8JZ* M: 07740-287545 E: andrew@thelatimers.net *or* andrew.latimer@gracechurchgreenwich.org.uk

LATIMER, Carol. b 45. Trent Park Coll of Educn CertEd 67 Stirling Univ BA 97 MLitt 04 MITI 14. TISEC 11. **d** 17. NSM Aberdour *St And* from 17; NSM Burntisland from 17; NSM Inverkeithing from 17. *35 Hawkcraig Road, Aberdour, Burntisland KY3 0XB* T: (01383) 860450 E: carollatimer98@gmail.com

LATIMER, Clifford James. b 45. City Univ BSc 68. **d** 99 **p** 00. OLM Burntwood *Lich* 99–10; rtd 10; PtO *Lich* 11–14 and from 15. *6 Bradwell Lane, Rugeley WS15 4RW* E: cliff.latimer@btinternet.com

LATTEY, Susan. See CUMMING-LATTEY, Susan Mary Ruth

LATTIMER, Nicholas William. b 84. Leeds Univ BA 08. Trin Coll Bris 12. **d** 15 **p** 16. C Woodside *Leeds* 15–19; C Burley from 19. *12 Beech Walk, Adel, Leeds LS16 8NY* T: 0113-281 7309 M: 07912-321377 E: nicklattimer@hotmail.com *or* nick.lattimer@leeds.anglican.org

LATTIMORE, Anthony Leigh. b 35. Dur Univ BA 57. Lich Th Coll 60. **d** 62 **p** 63. C Aylestone *Leic* 62–66; C-in-c Eyres Monsell CD 66–69; V Eyres Monsell 69–73; V Somerby, Burrough on the Hill and Pickwell 73–86; RD Goscote I 80–86; R Glenfield 86–95; rtd 95; PtO *Leic* 95–12; *Pet* 95–11. *28 Elizabeth Way, Uppingham, Oakham LE15 9PQ* T: (01572) 823193

LATTY, Howard James. b 54. SRCh 71. WEMTC 98. **d** 01 **p** 02. NSM Bath St Mich w St Paul *B & W* 01–08; NSM Chewton Mendip w Ston Easton, Litton etc from 08. *The Rectory, Lower Street, Chewton Mendip, Radstock BA3 4GP* T: (01761) 241189

LAU, Fung Ming. b 60. St Mellitus Coll BA 16. **d** 16 **p** 17. NSM Westminster St Jas the Less *Lon* from 16. *3 Strutton Court, 54 Great Peter Street, London SW1P 2HH* T: (020) 7233 4027 M: 07834-611610

LAU, Paul Chow Sing. b 49. Nat Chengchi Univ BA 74 Chinese Univ of Hong Kong MDiv 80. **d** 80 **p** 81. C Hong Kong H Trin Hong Kong 80–82; V Macao St Mark Macao 82–83; P-in-c Hong Kong Ch of Our Sav Hong Kong 83–94; V Angl Chinese Miss Ch Dio Westrnland New Zealand 94–01; Chapl Chinese Congregation *Lon* 01–19; rtd 19. *3 Strutton Court, 54 Great Peter Street, London SW1P 2HH* T: (020) 7233 4027 E: paul.lau@smitf.org

LAUCKNER, Averil Ann. b 55. Lanc Univ BSc 76. Ripon Coll Cuddesdon 03. **d** 04 **p** 05. C Royston *St Alb* 04–07; C Lich Ch Ch and Lich St Mich w St Mary and Wall 07–09; P-in-c Lich Ch Ch 09–11; P-in-c Hatfield Hyde *St Alb* 11–14; V from 14. *St Mary Magdalene Vicarage, Hollybush Lane, Welwyn Garden City AL7 4JS* T: (01707) 322313 E: averil.lauckner@btinternet.com

LAUENER (née MULLINER), Angela Margaret. b 54. Collingwood Coll Dur BSc 75 Sheff City Poly MSc 91 Sheff Hallam Univ PhD. Yorks Min Course 12. **d** 14 **p** 15. NSM Ranmoor *Sheff* 14–17; NSM Abbeydale and Millhouses from 17; Asst Bp's Adv in Spirituality from 15. *82 Pingle Road, Sheffield S7 2LL* T: 0114-236 2188 M: 07949-403992 E: angielauener@me.com *or* angela.lauener@sheffield.anglican.org

LAUNDON, Timothy James. b 83. CCC Cam MA 07 SS Coll Cam BTh 11. Westcott Ho Cam 09. **d** 12 **p** 13. C Wetherby *Leeds* 12–16; Chapl Hants Hosps NHS Foundn Trust 16–17; NSM New Windsor *Ox* 18–19; V Ludgershall and Tidworth *Sarum* from 19. *The Rectory, 10 St James's Street, Ludgershall, Andover SP11 9QF* T: (01264) 393026 E: revtimlaundon@gmail.com

LAURENCE, The Ven John Harvard Christopher. b 29. Trin Hall Cam BA 54 MA 57. Westcott Ho Cam 53. **d** 55 **p** 56. C Linc St Nic w St Jo Newport 55–59; V Crosby 59–74; Can and Preb Linc Cathl 74–79 and 85–94; Dioc Missr 74–79; Bp's Dir of Clergy Tr *Lon* 80–85; Adn Lindsey *Linc* 85–94; rtd 94; PtO *Linc* 94–97. *5 Haffenden Road, Lincoln LN2 1RP* T: (01522) 531444

LAURENCE, Preb Julian Bernard Vere. b 60. Kent Univ BA 82. St Steph Ho Ox 86. **d** 88 **p** 89. C Yeovil St Mich *B & W* 88–91; Chapl Yeovil Coll 90–91; Chapl Yeovil Distr Hosp 91; P-in-c Barwick *B & W* 91–94; V Taunton H Trin from 94; Dioc Adv in Deliverance Min from 14; Preb Wells Cathl from 17. *15 The Square, Hillyfields, Taunton TA1 2LU* T: (01823) 354800 E: frjulianssc@gmail.com

LAURIE, Canon Donovan Hugh. b 40. Man Univ MSc. Oak Hill NSM Course. **d** 82 **p** 83. NSM Cudham and Downe *Roch* 82–84; C Tunbridge Wells St Jas 84–88; P-in-c Ventnor St Cath *Portsm* 88–99; V 99–04; P-in-c Ventnor H Trin 88–99; V 99–04; P-in-c Bonchurch 00–03; R 03–04; Hon Chapl St Cath Sch Ventnor 88–04; Can Portsm Cathl 01–04; rtd 04; PtO *Roch* from 05. *39 Cleveland, Tunbridge Wells TN2 3NH* T: (01892) 539951 E: mail@dhl1525.plus.com

LAUT, Graham Peter. b 37. Chich Th Coll 63. **d** 67 **p** 68. C Corringham *Chelmsf* 67–68; C Leytonstone St Marg w St Columba 68–71; P-in-c Leytonstone St Andr 71–75; V 75–80; V Romford Ascension Collier Row 80–06; rtd 06; PtO *Chelmsf* from 07. *11 Archers Close, Billericay CM12 9YF* T: (01277) 630395 E: grahamlaut@rocketmail.com

LAUTENBACH, Edward Wayne. b 59. Univ Coll Ches BTh 04. St Paul's Coll Grahamstown 85. **d** 88 **p** 88. C Weltevredenpark St Mich S Africa 88–89; Asst P Florida St Gabr 89–91; Sen Asst P Bryanston St Mich 91–94; R Brakpan St Pet 94–99; P-in-c Grange St Andr *Ches* 99–04; P-in-c Runcorn H Trin 99–04; V Prenton 04–15; V Branksome St Aldhelm *Sarum* 15–16; Chapl R Berks NHS Foundn Trust 17; PtO *Ox* 17–18; P-in-c Hermitage 18–19; TR from 19. *The Vicarage, 8 Yew Tree Stables, Compton, Newbury RG20 6NG* M: 07828-534655 E: waynelautenbach@gmail.com

LAUTENBACH, Mrs Glynnis Valerie. b 59. Leeds Univ BA 08. NOC 05. **d** 08 **p** 09. C Oxton *Ches* 08–15; PtO *Sarum* 15–16; P-in-c Burghfield *Ox* 17–18; R from 18. *The Rectory, Hollybush Lane, Burghfield Common, Reading RG7 3JL* T: 0118-983 2115 E: glynn.laut@gmail.com

LAVARELLO-SMITH, Mrs Lorna Mary. b 64. Qu Coll Birm 10. **d** 13 **p** 14. C Billing *Pet* 13–16; S Africa from 16. *Address temp unknown* E: lavarellosmith@gmail.com

LAVELLE, Elizabeth Mary Nicola. b 63. ERMC. **d** 16 **p** 17. C Welwyn Garden City *St Alb* from 16; NSM 16–18. *24 Cheviots, Hatfield AL10 8JT* M: 07803-601162 E: lizlavelle01@googlemail.com

LAVENDER, Christopher Piers. b 61. Ridley Hall Cam 08. **d** 10 **p** 11. C Headcorn and The Suttons *Cant* 10–13; P-in-c Allington and Maidstone St Pet from 13; P-in-c Barming Heath from 13. *The Rectory, Poplar Grove, Maidstone ME16 0DE* T: (01622) 299715 M: 07910-442247 E: chris_piers@yahoo.com

LAVENDER, Mark Harley. b 70. Sheff Univ BSc 91 Univ Coll Lon PhD 95 Lon Inst of Educn PGCE 97. Ridley Hall Cam 14. **d** 16 **p** 17. C Crofton St Paul *Roch* from 16. *265A Crofton Road, Orpington BR6 8JF* M: 07816-668153 E: mark.lavender@stpaulscrofton.co.uk

LAVERTY, Walter Joseph Robert. b 49. CITC 70 Glouc Th Course 73. **d** 73 **p** 74. C Belfast St Donard *D & D* 73–77; C Ballymacarrett St Patr 77–82; I Kilwarlin Upper w Kilwarlin Lower 82–86; I Orangefield w Moneyreagh 86–14; Warden of Readers 96–14; Can Down Cathl 97–00; Preb Down Cathl 97–00; Treas Down Cathl 01–14; rtd 14. *6 Hanwood Heights, Dundonald, Belfast BT16 1XU* T: (028) 9573 8743 E: barbaralaverty58@hotmail.com

LAVERY, Edward Robinson. Lon Univ BA. St Aid Birkenhead 65. **d** 67 **p** 68. C Belfast Trin Coll Miss *Conn* 67–69; C Belfast St Mary Magd 69–71; CF (TA) 70–95; OCM from 75; I Belfast St Phil *Conn* 71–74; I Craigs w Dunaghy and Killagan 74–83; I Ballymoney w Finvoy and Rasharkin 83–05; Dioc Info Officer 83–05; Can Conn Cathl 96–05; Treas Conn Cathl 98–01; Chan Conn Cathl 01–05; rtd 05; P-in-c Ballyscullion *D & R* from 09. *11 Drummamallaght Park, Ballymoney BT53 7QZ* T: (028) 2766 9147 E: robin.lavery2@gmail.com

LAVIN, Alexandra Elizabeth. b 67. **d** 12 **p** 13. NSM Sheldon *Birm* 12–16; P-in-c 16–18; V Sheldon and Tile Cross from 18. *St Thomas's Vicarage, Rotherfield Road, Birmingham B26 2SH* T: 0121-384 5666 M: 07963-558242 E: alexpost@blueyonder.co.uk

LAW, Andrew Philip. b 61. BNC Ox BA 83 MA 93 G&C Coll Cam PGCE 86 Leic Univ MBA 04. WEMTC 90. **d** 93 **p** 94. C Tupsley w Hampton Bishop *Heref* 93–95; Chapl Heref Sixth Form Coll 94–95; Chapl City of Lon Freemen's Sch 95–97; LtO *Guildf* 95–97; Chapl and Hd RS Heref Cathl Sch 97–02; Chapl Malvern Coll 02–18; Ho Master 05–07; Fell Harris Manchester Coll Ox 13; PtO *Heref* from 02; *Worc* from 18. *1 The Moorlands, Malvern WR14 4PS* T: (01684) 563481 E: apl@malcol.org

LAW, David Richard. b 60. Keble Coll Ox BA 82 Wolfs Coll Ox MA 89 DPhil 89. NOC 98 Predigerseminar Preetz Germany 99. **d** 01 **p** 02. NSM Ashton-upon-Mersey St Martin *Ches* 01–09; NSM Timperley 09–14; NSM Altrincham from 14. *2 Winston Close, Sale M33 6UG* T: 0161-962 0297 E: david.r.law@manchester.ac.uk

LAW, Mrs Elizabeth Ann. b 49. Doncaster Coll of Educn CertEd 70 Loughb Univ MA 00. EAMTC 97. **d** 01 **p** 02. C Wickham Bishops w Lt Braxted *Chelmsf* 01–05; P-in-c Rattlesden w Thorpe Morieux, Brettenham etc *St E* 05–08; R 08–11; rtd 11; PtO *St E* 11–13; Hon C Gt Finborough w Onehouse, Harleston, Buxhall etc 13–15; Hon C Combs and Lt Finborough 13–15; Hon C Bildeston w Wattisham and Lindsey, Whatfield etc 15–17; Asst Dioc Dir of Ords 08–13. *15 Manor Road, Bildeston, Ipswich IP7 7BG* T: (01449) 740085 M: 07743-785282 E: rev.liz@btinternet.com

LAW, Jeremy Thomson. b 61. Univ of Wales (Abth) BSc 82 Southn Univ BTh 89 Ox Univ DPhil 00. Sarum & Wells Th Coll 84. **d** 87 **p** 88. C Wimborne Minster and Holt *Sarum* 87–90; C Highfield *Ox* 90–94; Chapl and Lect Ex Univ 94–03; Dean of Chpl Cant Ch Ch Univ from 03; PtO *Roch* from 13. *Canterbury Christ Church University, North Holmes Road, Canterbury CT1 1QU* T: (01227) 782747 E: jeremy.law@canterbury.ac.uk

LAW, John Francis. b 35. Bps' Coll Cheshunt 65. **d** 67 **p** 68. C Styvechale *Cov* 67–71; P-in-c Cov St Anne and All SS 71–73; TV Cov E 73–77; P-in-c Fillongley 77–82; P-in-c Corley 77–82; V Fillongley and Corley 82–00; RD Nuneaton 90–95; rtd 00; PtO *Cov* from 00. *10 Brodick Way, Nuneaton CV10 7LH* T: (024) 7632 5582 E: johnflaw@sky.com

LAW, Canon John Michael. b 43. Open Univ BA 79. Westcott Ho Cam 65. **d** 68 **p** 69. C Chapel Allerton *Ripon* 68–72; C Ryhope *Dur* 72–73; Mental Health Chapl Fulbourn Hosp Cam 74–04; Chapl Ida Darwin Hosp Cam 74–96; Hon Can Ely Cathl 04–05; rtd 04; PV Ely Cathl 06–08; PtO from 08. *2 Suffolk Close, Ely CB6 3EW* T: (01353) 659084

LAW, Nicholas Charles. b 58. Trin Coll Bris BA 89. **d** 89 **p** 90. C Goldington *St Alb* 89–92; C Teignmouth, Ideford w Luton, Ashcombe etc *Ex* 92–97; R Bere Ferrers from 97; RD Tavistock from 11. *The Rectory, Bere Alston, Yelverton PL20 7HH* T: (01822) 840229 E: nick123law@gmail.com

LAW, Peter James. b 46. Ridley Hall Cam 85. **d** 87 **p** 88. C Bournemouth St Jo w St Mich *Win* 87–91; V Chineham 91–96; V Luton Lewsey St Hugh *St Alb* 96–11; rtd 11; PtO *Portsm* from 13; *Guildf* from 16; *Win* from 16. *7 Anmore Drive, Waterlooville PO7 6DY* T: (023) 9226 8336 E: revpjl@btinternet.com

LAW, Richard Anthony Kelway. b 57. UWIST BEng 79. St Jo Coll Nottm MA(TS) 01 99. **d** 01 **p** 02. C Brundall w Braydeston and Postwick *Nor* 01–04; V Hollingworth w Tintwistle *Ches* 04–14; TV N Wingfield, Clay Cross and Pilsley *Derby* from 14. *The Vicarage, Stretton Road, Clay Cross, Chesterfield S45 9AQ* T: (01246) 250110 E: vicar@richardaklaw.plus.com

LAW, Canon Robert Frederick. b 43. St Aid Birkenhead 67. **d** 69 **p** 70. C Bengeo *St Alb* 69–72; C Sandy 72–76; P-in-c St Ippolyts 76–81; Chapl Jersey Gp of Hosps 81–84; V Crowan w Godolphin *Truro* 84–92; RD Kerrier 90–91; R St Columb Major w St Wenn 92–02; RD Pydar 95–02; P-in-c St Minver 02–05; Hon Can Truro Cathl 98–05; rtd 05; PtO *York* from 07; *Eur* from 06. *24 Parkfield, Stillington, York YO61 1JW* T: (01347) 810940 M: 07842-111525 E: robertlaw43@btinternet.com

LAW, Simon Anthony. b 55. Middx Univ BA 93 K Coll Lon MA 10. NTMTC 94. **d** 96 **p** 97. NSM Forest Gate St Mark *Chelmsf* 96–98; C Becontree W 98–99; TV 99–02; TR 02–07; V Becontree St Cedd 07–10; R Pitsea w Nevendon from 10. *The Rectory, Rectory Road, Pitsea, Basildon SS13 2AA* T: (01268) 556874 E: simon@revlaw.co.uk

LAW-JONES, Peter Deniston. b 55. Newc Univ BA 77 Nottm Univ BTh 87 Lanc Univ MA 03 Man Univ PGCE 81. Linc Th Coll 84. **d** 87 **p** 88. C Chorley St Laur *Blackb* 87–91; V Feniscliffe 91–96; V St Annes St Thos 96–13; AD Kirkham 09–13; Chapl Blackpool, Wyre and Fylde Community NHS Trust 97–04; TR Salter Street and Shirley *Birm* 13–17; V Shirley from 17. *The Rectory, 2 Bishopton Close, Shirley, Solihull B90 4AH* T: 0121-744 3123 or 293 7610 M: 07902-580237 E: pljx1000@gmail.com

LAWAL, Miss Basirat Adebanke Amope (Ade). b 67. Lon Bible Coll BTh 02. SAOMC 03. **d** 05 **p** 06. C Blurton *Lich* 05–09; V Wyther *Ripon* 09–13; Racial Justice Officer 10–14; *Leeds* 14–15; Chapl Leeds Teaching Hosps NHS Trust 13–15; P-in-c Gillingham St Mary *Roch* 15–17; C Roch St Justus from 17; PV Roch Cathl from 17. *82 Hathaway Court, Esplanade, Rochester ME1 1QY* E: baasiratlawal166@btinternet.com

LAWES, Geoffrey Hyland. b 37. St Jo Coll Dur BA 58 Hertf Coll Ox BA 60 MA 64 Newc Univ PGCE 76 MEd 79. Cranmer Hall Dur 61. **d** 63 **p** 64. C Millfield St Mark *Dur* 63–66; C Jarrow Grange 66–69; Hon C 69–86; LtO 86–90; V Collierley w Annfield Plain 90–05; rtd 05; Hon C Satley, Stanley and Tow Law *Dur* 05–06; PtO from 06. *Netherwood, St Mary's Avenue, Crook DL15 9HY* T: (01388) 766585 E: lawes@f2s.com

LAWES, Timothy Stanley. b 57. Nottm Univ BTh 88. Linc Th Coll 85. **d** 88 **p** 89. C Wymondham *Nor* 88–92; R Felmingham, Skeyton, Colby, Banningham etc 92–96; Sweden 96–12; Asst V Byske 98–09; TR Skelleftea Landsforsamling 11–12; V Swaffham and Sporle *Nor* 12–16; Sweden from 16. *Vintergatan 69A, 932 32 Skelleftehamn, Sweden* E: timothylawes@hotmail.com

LAWLESS, Mrs Patricia Elizabeth. b 36. Bris Univ BA 58 PGCE 59. S Dios Minl Tr Scheme 91. **d** 93 **p** 94. NSM Frome Ch Ch *B & W* 93–95; NSM Mells w Buckland Dinham, Elm, Whatley etc 96; NSM Frome St Jo and St Mary 96–00; Chapl Victoria Hosp Frome 96–98; rtd 00; PtO *B & W* from 00. *22 Braithwaite Way, Frome BA11 2XG* T: (01373) 466106

LAWLEY, Peter Gerald Fitch. b 52. Chich Th Coll 77. **d** 80 **p** 81. C Pet St Jo 80–83; C Daventry 83–87; P-in-c Syresham w Whitfield 87–90; TV Cen Telford *Lich* 90–98; V Priors Lee and St Georges' 98–12; rtd 12; PtO *Lich* from 13. *11 Kingsley Drive, Muxton, Telford TF2 8DH* T: (01952) 606160 E: peterlawley12@gmail.com

LAWLEY, Rosemary Ann. b 47. WMMTC 00. **d** 03 **p** 04. NSM Kinver and Enville *Lich* 03–07; TV Kidderminster St Mary and All SS w Trimpley etc *Worc* 07–15; TR Kidderminster Ismere 15–18; Ind Chapl 07–18; Hon Can Worc Cathl 15–18; rtd 18; PtO *Worc* from 19; *Heref* from 19. *Almain, Bridgnorth Road, Highley, Bridgnorth WV16 6HE* T: (01746) 862301 E: rosemarylawley@gmail.com

LAWLOR, Anne Louise. b 61. UEA BEd 83 Surrey Univ Roehampton BA 02 Lucy Cavendish Coll Cam BTh 12. Westcott Ho Cam 10. **d** 12 **p** 13. C Everton St Pet w St Chrys *Liv* 12–16; Chapl Liv Women's NHS Foundn Trust 16–17; TV Kirkby *Liv* from 17. *9 Redwood Way, Liverpool L33 4DU* T: 0151-548 0962 M: 07904-346101 E: annelawlor92@yahoo.co.uk

LAWLOR, Colin Robert. b 63. Lanc Univ BA 89 MPhil 97 St Martin's Coll Lanc PGCE 90. Chich Th Coll 90. **d** 93 **p** 94. C Moulsecoomb *Chich* 93–97; TV 97–99; Chapl Brighton Univ 99–18; P-in-c Stanmer w Falmer 13–18; V Waterlooville *Portsm* from 18. *The Vicarage, 5 Deanswood Drive, Waterlooville PO7 7RR* M: 07733-225263

LAWLOR, Paul. b 60. Nottm Univ BSc 82. St Jo Coll Nottm 06. **d** 08 **p** 09. C Warsop *S'well* 08–11; TV Redditch H Trin *Worc* from 11; RD Bromsgrove from 16. *The Vicarage, 219 St George's Road, Redditch B98 8EE* T: (01527) 62375 M: 07807-611090 E: paul@pjlawlor.me.uk

LAWRANCE, Robert William. b 63. Jes Coll Ox BA 85 MA 89 Man Univ MA 93. Ripon Coll Cuddesdon BA 87. **d** 88 **p** 89. C Astley *Man* 88–91; Lect Bolton St Pet 91–94; V Bury St Jo w St Mark 94–00; Chapl Bury Healthcare NHS Trust 95–00; Dir of Ords *Dur* 00–08; Chapl Hatf Coll Dur 00–05; Chapl Collingwood Coll Dur 05–08; TR Dur N 08–15; AD Dur 10–15; Hon Can Dur Cathl 10–15; Hon Chapl Dur and Darlington Fire and Rescue Brigade 09–15; V Newc St Fran from 15; AD Newc E from 17. *St Francis Vicarage, 66 Cleveland Gardens, Newcastle upon Tyne NE7 7QH* T: 0191-266 1071 E: robert.lawrance@newcastle.anglican.org

LAWRENCE, Mrs Anastasia Jane. b 63. Cam Coll of Art & Tech GMus 85 Kingston Poly PGCE 86. St Jo Coll Nottm 14. **d** 17 **p** 18. C Albrighton, Boningale and Donington *Lich* from 17. *2 Garridge Close, Albrighton, Wolverhampton WV7 3PZ* T: (01902) 373031 M: 07708-050310 E: revanalawrence@gmail.com

LAWRENCE, Charles Anthony Edwin. b 53. AKC 75. St Aug Coll Cant 75. **d** 76 **p** 77. C Mitcham St Mark *S'wark* 76–80; C Haslemere *Guildf* 80–82; P-in-c Ashton H Trin *Man* 82–84; V 84–93; AD Ashton-under-Lyne 91–93; V Saddleworth 93–97; V Effingham w Lt Bookham *Guildf* 97–05; Chapl Manor Ho Sch 97–05; R Shere, Albury and Chilworth *Guildf* 05–09; R Northfield *Birm* 09–15; rtd 15; PtO *Birm* from 15; *Heref* from 17. *The Heath, Munslow, Craven Arms SY7 9ET* T: (01584) 841862 E: fathercharles@hotmail.co.uk

LAWRENCE, Canon David Ian. b 48. Univ Coll Lon BSc 74 AIMLS 71 MRSB 76. Glouc Sch of Min 84 Sarum & Wells Th Coll 87. **d** 88 **p** 89. C Wotton St Mary *Glouc* 88–91; P-in-c Cheltenham St Mich 91–93; V 93–06; V Coleford, Staunton, Newland, Redbrook etc 06–11; Hon Can Glouc Cathl 06–11; rtd 12; PtO *Sarum* from 12. *14 Clappentail Park, Lyme Regis DT7 3NB* T: (01297) 442140 E: dandhlawrence@tiscali.co.uk

LAWRENCE, Isaac Sartaj. b 72. Peshawar Univ BSc 95 Philippine Chr Univ MBA 97. **d** 08 **p** 09. C Ripon H Trin 08–12; V Scotby and Cotehill w Cumwhinton *Carl* from 12. *The Vicarage, Lambley Bank, Scotby, Carlisle CA4 8BX* T: (01228) 513205 M: 07837-395770 E: revisaac.lawrence@gmail.com

LAWRENCE, James Andrew. b 87. Leeds Univ BA 05. Yorks Min Course 13. **d** 16 **p** 17. C Otley *Leeds* 16–19. *9 Bransdale Close, London NW6 4QH* M: 07545-211776 E: revjimmylawrence@gmail.com

LAWRENCE, James Conrad. b 62. St Jo Coll Dur BA 85. Ridley Hall Cam 85. **d** 87 **p** 88. Min Bar Hill LEP *Ely* 87–92; Min Bar Hill 92–93; Deanery Adv in Evang 90–93; CPAS Evang 93–98; PtO *Cov* from 93; Springboard Missr from 97; CPAS Dir Evang Projects from 99. *20 Cotton Mill Spinney, Cubbington, Leamington Spa CV32 7XH* T: (01926) 426761 or 334242 F: 337613 E: jlawrence@cpas.org.uk

LAWRENCE, John Graham Clive. b 47. ACIB. Trin Coll Bris. **d** 78 **p** 79. C Chatham St Phil and St Jas *Roch* 78–83; V Roch St Justus 83–97; Asst Chapl HM Pris Roch 83–97; UK Dir CMJ 97–00; Internat Co-ord Light to the Nations UK 00–10; Chapl Maidstone and Tunbridge Wells NHS Trust 03–04; Chapl W Kent NHS and Soc Care Trust 05–06; Chapl Kent & Medway NHS and Soc Care Partnership Trust 06–08; Chapl Team Ldr Bucks Healthcare NHS Trust 08–10;

rtd 10. *55 Elmshurst Gardens, Tonbridge TN10 3QT* T: (01732) 490549 M: 07984-951534 E: jgcl138@gmail.com

LAWRENCE, Mrs Judith Patricia. b 53. WEMTC 01. **d** 04 **p** 05. C Glastonbury w Meare *B & W* 04–09; PtO 09–11; Chapl Somerset Community Health NHS Trust 10–11; Chapl Somerset Partnership NHS Foundn Trust 10–11; Asst Chapl Taunton and Somerset NHS Foundn Trust 09–11; Chapl 11–18; rtd 18. *12 Glanvill Road, Street BA16 0TN* T: (01458) 445451 E: j.lawrence123@btinternet.com

LAWRENCE, Mrs Katherine Anne. b 75. Cranmer Hall Dur 14. **d** 16 **p** 17. C Win Cathl from 16. *18 Lynford Way, Winchester SO22 6BW* T: (01962) 857287 M: 07939-528714 E: katie@respectnature.com

LAWRENCE, Leslie. b 44. S'wark Ord Course 86. **d** 88 **p** 89. NSM Stanwell *Lon* 88–92; C Hounslow H Trin w St Paul 92–97; P-in-c Norwood St Mary 97–06; R 06–09; rtd 09; PtO *Lon* from 11. *22 Chestnut Road, Ashford TW15 1DG* T: (01784) 241773 E: leslielawrencestd@googlemail.com

LAWRENCE, Lorraine Margaret. b 58. Open Univ BA 08. SEITE 08. **d** 11 **p** 12. NSM Gravesend St Geo *Roch* 11–15; C Wye *Cant* from 15. *The Vicarage, Pilgrims Way, Hastingleigh, Ashford TN25 5HP* T: (01233) 750987 M: 07894-034409 E: lorraine_lawrence@btinternet.com

LAWRENCE, Canon Patrick Henry Andrew. b 51. TCD Div Test 79 BA 81. **d** 81 **p** 82. C Templemore *D & R* 81–84; C Kilkenny St Canice Cathl *C & O* 84–85; I Templebreedy w Tracton and Nohoval *C, C & R* 85–92; I Geashill w Killeigh and Ballycommon *M & K* 92–98; Can Kildare Cathl 92–09; Adn Kildare 93–09; Adn Meath 97–09; Warden of Readers 97–09; I Julianstown and Colpe w Drogheda and Duleek 98–09; I Monkstown *D & G* 09–15; Preb Monmohenock St Patr Cathl Dublin 00–12; Chan St Patr Cathl Dublin 12–15; Chapl St Vincent's Univ Hosp Dublin 15–17; rtd 17. *Sidebrook House, Rochfortbridge, Mullingar, Co Westmeath, N91 Y327, Republic of Ireland* T: (00353) (44) 922 2109 M: (00353) 86-056 2944 E: patricklawrence@eircom.net

LAWRENCE, Canon Peter Anthony. b 36. Lich Th Coll 67. **d** 69 **p** 70. C Oadby *Leic* 69–74; P-in-c Northmarston and Granborough *Ox* 74–81; P-in-c Hardwick St Mary 74–81; P-in-c Quainton 76–81; P-in-c Oving w Pitchcott 76–81; TR Schorne 81–91; RD Claydon 84–88; V Ivinghoe w Pitstone and Slapton 91–97; Hon Can Ch 97; rtd 97; PtO *Ox* 99–07; *Worc* from 01. *Hill House, Back Lane, Malvern WR14 2HJ* T: (01684) 564075 E: peter.molly2@waitrose.com

LAWRENCE (*née* MASON), Sarah Catherine. b 79. K Coll Lon BA 02 PGCE 03 Chu Coll Cam MPhil 06 Birm Univ PhD 17. Ridley Hall Cam 05. **d** 08 **p** 10. NSM Carr Dyke Gp *Linc* 08–10; C Shifnal and Sheriffhales *Lich* 10–13; C Tong 13–13; PtO *Linc* 16–19; Officer for IME from 18. *Address withheld by request* T: (01522) 729190 M: 07766-348170   E: revsarahlawrence@btinternet.com   *or* sarah.lawrence@lincoln.anglican.org

LAWRENCE, Canon Simon Peter. b 60. Nottm Univ BTh 88 MA 97 Indiana State Univ DMin 01. St Jo Coll Nottm 85. **d** 88 **p** 89. C Holbeach *Linc* 88–90; C Alford w Rigsby 90–91; R Rattlesden w Thorpe Morieux and Brettenham *St E* 91–93; V Churchdown *Glouc* 93; V Maenclochog w Henry's Moat and Mynachlogddu etc *St D* 93–94; R Overstrand, Northrepps, Sidestrand etc *Nor* 95–98; CF (TA) 89–05; CF (ACF) 90–05; PtO *Nor* 02–06; Public Preacher 06–07; R Stalham, E Ruston, Brunstead, Sutton and Ingham from 07; P-in-c Smallburgh w Dilham w Honing and Crostwight 16–18; R from 18; RD St Benet 12–19; Dioc Chapl MU 11–19; Hon Can Nor Cathl from 17. *The Rectory, Camping Field Lane, Stalham, Norwich NR12 9DT* T: (01692) 580250 E: simon.stalham@btinternet.com

LAWRENCE (*née* FOREMAN), Mrs Vanessa Jane. b 73. Ch Ch Coll Cant BA 95. Westcott Ho Cam. **d** 00 **p** 01. C N Stoneham *Win* 00–04; NSM Swaythling 04–07; NSM Chilworth w N Baddesley 07–10; NSM Ampfield 08–10; NSM Ampfield, Chilworth and N Baddesley from 10; Chapl Southern Health NHS Foundn Trust from 09. *164 Botley Road, North Baddesley, Southampton SO52 9EE* T: (023) 8073 6671 E: vanessalawrence@btconnect.com

LAWRENCE, Victor John. b 43. ACII. Oak Hill Th Coll. **d** 83 **p** 84. C Paddock Wood *Roch* 83–87; R Milton next Gravesend w Denton 87–09; RD Gravesend 05–09; rtd 09. *5 Riplingham, 44 Gaudick Road, Eastbourne BN20 7LW* E: victorjlaw@googlemail.com

LAWRENCE-MARCH, David Lawrence. b 61. Univ of Wales (Lamp) BA 83. Coll of Resurr Mirfield 83. **d** 85 **p** 86. C Pet St Jude 85–89; Chapl St Aug Sch Kilburn 89–92; C Kilburn St Aug w St Jo *Lon* 89–90; C Paddington St Mary 90–92; Chapl Bearwood Coll Wokingham 92–96; R Holt w High Kelling *Nor* 96–98; Sen Chapl Bedford Sch 98–09; Chapl Ardingly Coll 09–17; PtO *Lon* 14–17; P-in-c Shanklin

St Sav *Portsm* from 17; P-in-c Lake from 17. *The Vicarage, 46 Sandown Road, Sandown PO36 9JT* T: (01983) 407928 E: fatherdlm@icloud.com

LAWRENSON, Ronald David. b 41. CITC 68. **d** 71 **p** 72. C Seapatrick *D & D* 71–78; Min Can Down Cathl 78–79; V Choral Belf Cathl 79–86; Bp's C Tynan w Middletown and Aghavilly *Arm* 86–90 and 91–93; Hon V Choral Arm Cathl 87–02; Bp's C Tynan w Middletown 92–93; I Donaghmore w Upper Donaghmore 93–98; rtd 02. *Riverbrook Apartments, 5 Brooklands Drive, Whitehead, Carrickfergus BT38 9SL* T: (028) 9337 3625

LAWRINSON, Leslie Norman. b 35. IEng MCIPD 90 MCMI 84. **d** 99 **p** 00. OLM Onchan *S & M* 99–05; NSM Scarisbrick *Liv* 05–08; rtd 08; PtO *S & M* from 09. *8 Hillary Wharf Apartments, South Quay, Douglas, Isle of Man IM1 5BL* T: (01624) 627664 M: 07749-687469

LAWS, Clive Loudon. b 54. UEA BEd 76 Leeds Univ CertEd 75. Wycliffe Hall Ox 79. **d** 82 **p** 83. C Newcastle w Butterton *Lich* 82–85; C Gabalfa *Llan* 85–88; R Pendine w Llanmiloe and Eglwys Gymyn w Marros *St D* 89–94; CF 89–94; PtO *B & W* 95–96; C Portishead 96–02; TV 02–08; P-in-c High Laver w Magdalen Laver and Lt Laver etc *Chelmsf* 08–10; Chapl St Clare Hospice 08–10; rtd 10. *36 Alexandra Close, Illogan, Redruth TR16 4RS* T: (01209) 843117 E: clive_anne@yahoo.co.uk

LAWSON, Canon Alma Felicity. b 51. St Hugh's Coll Ox BA 73 MA 78. St Jo Coll Nottm. **d** 98 **p** 99. Dean of Min and Dir of Ords *Wakef* 93–00; Hon C Wakef Cathl 98–00; V Gildersome 00–14; *Leeds* 14–17; RD Birstall 10–14; P-in-c Drighlington 12–17; Hon Can Wakef Cathl 01–17; rtd 17. *23 Banks Bridge Close, Barnoldswick BB18 6YP* E: felicity.lawson@outlook.com

LAWSON, Anne. *See* LAWSON, Sarah Anne

LAWSON, Canon David McKenzie. b 47. Glas Univ MA 69 Edin Univ BD 76. Edin Th Coll 73. **d** 76 **p** 77. C Glas St Mary 76–82; V Keighley All SS *Bradf* 82–85; Chapl Asst Univ Coll Hosp Lon 85–91; Hon C St Pancras w St Jas and Ch Ch *Lon* 86–91; R Smithfield St Bart Gt 91–93; Hon C Paddington St Jas 94–00; TV Chambersbury *St Alb* 00–03; TR 03–09; TR Langelei 09–17; RD Hemel Hempstead 08–15; Hon Can St Alb 12–17; rtd 18; PtO *St Alb* from 18. *8 Nightingale Lodge, Cowper Road, Berkhamsted HP4 3ED* T: (01442) 872158 M: 07939-473717 E: davidmlawson@btinternet.com

LAWSON, Felicity. *See* LAWSON, Alma Felicity

LAWSON, Gary Austin. b 53. Man Univ BA 80. Ripon Coll Cuddesdon 80. **d** 82 **p** 83. C Nunhead St Antony *S'wark* 82–86; Hon C Reddish *Man* 86–87; Hon C Longsight St Jo w St Cypr 87–88; V Wythenshawe St Rich 88–98; Chapl Bolton Inst of F&HE 98–03; C Bolton St Pet 98–03; TR Westhoughton and Wingates 03–13; C Daisy Hill 11–13; TR Daisy Hill, Westhoughton and Wingates 13–14; rtd 14. *4 Brookfold Road, Stockport SK4 5EJ* T: 0161-442 7970 E: garyaustinlawson@btinternet.com

LAWSON, James Barry. b 68. Edin Univ MA 91 New Coll Ox DPhil 96. Coll of Resurr Mirfield 98. **d** 99 **p** 00. C Poplar *Lon* 99–02; Chapl CCC Cam 02–07; Bp's Sen Chapl *Sarum* 07–08; V Stoke Newington Common St Mich *Lon* 09–17; Vice-Prin St Steph Ho Ox from 17. *St Stephen's House, 16 Marston Street, Oxford OX4 1JX* T: (01865) 613500 E: james.lawson@ssho.ox.ac.uk

LAWSON, Canon John Alexander. b 62. Sheff Univ BA 84 Nottm Univ MA 97 PhD 06. St Jo Coll Nottm 85. **d** 87 **p** 88. C Wellington All SS w Eyton *Lich* 87–92; TV Dewsbury *Wakef* 92–98; P-in-c Birchencliffe 98–05; Dioc Vocations Adv and Asst Dir of Ords 02–05; Can Res Wakef Cathl 05–19; Dioc Dir Tr 05–16; Warden Wakef Min Scheme 06–08; Prin Mirfield Hub Leeds Sch of Min from 16; Hon Can Wakef Cathl *Leeds* from 19. *St Giles's Vicarage, 9 The Mount, Pontefract WF8 1NE* M: 07816-502014 E: john.lawson@leeds.anglican.org

LAWSON, Jonathan Halford. b 68. St Chad's Coll Dur BA 90 Heythrop Coll Lon MA 04. Westcott Ho Cam 91. **d** 93 **p** 94. C Sedgefield *Dur* 93–96; C Usworth 96–97; TV 97–00; TV Epping Distr *Chelmsf* 00–04; Chapl St Hild and St Bede Coll *Dur* 04–14; V Newc St Gabr from 14. *St Gabriel's Vicarage, 9 Holderness Road, Newcastle upon Tyne NE6 5RH* T: 0191-908 7835 E: vicarofheaton@gmail.com

LAWSON, Canon June Margaret. b 62. Birm Univ BA 83 Didsbury Coll of Educn PGCE 84 St Jo Coll York MA 02. NOC 00. **d** 02 **p** 03. C Huddersfield H Trin *Wakef* 02–05; Dir Adult Chr Educn Mirfield Cen 05–08; Dir Mirfield Cen 08–19; PV Wakef Cathl *Leeds* 05–19; Dean of Women's Min *Wakef* 09–14; *Leeds* 14–19; Clergy Development Officer Wakefield Area 17–19; Adv Wakef 17–19; V Pontefract from 19; Hon Can Wakef Cathl from 17. *St Giles's Vicarage, 9 The Mount, Pontefract WF8 1NE* E: june.lawson@leeds.anglican.org

LAWSON, Mrs Katherine Ellen. b 53. SEITE 11. **d** 14 **p** 15. NSM Hove All SS *Chich* 14–17; NSM Saltdean from 17. *Moray Cottage, 31 Oaklands Avenue, Saltdean, Brighton BN2 8LQ* T: (01273) 709330 M: 07878-959327 E: rev.kate.lawson@gmail.com

LAWSON, Matthew James. b 67. St Andr Univ MTheol 91 FRSA 02. Ripon Coll Cuddesdon MTh 94. **d** 94 **p** 95. C Bedford St Andr *St Alb* 94–97; Chapl and Hd RS St Jo Sch Leatherhead 97–07; Tutor Dioc Min Course *Guildf* 98; Chapl Hurstpierpoint Coll 07–10. *54 Hipwell Court, Olney MK46 5QB* M: 07768-515950 E: frlawson@aol.com

LAWSON, The Ven Michael Charles. b 52. Sussex Univ BA 75. Trin Coll Bris 75. **d** 78 **p** 79. C Horsham *Chich* 78–81; C St Marylebone All So w SS Pet and Jo *Lon* 81–87; V Bromley Ch Ch *Roch* 87–99; Adn Hampstead *Lon* 99–10; R Guildf St Sav 10–12; rtd 12; Chapl HM Pris Littlehey from 13; PtO *Ely* from 13. *HM Prison Littlehey, Perry, Huntingdon PE28 0SR* T: (01480) 335252 E: venmlawson@gmail.com *or* michael.lawson@justice.gov.uk

LAWSON, Miss Sarah Anne. b 66. Ches Coll of HE BA 87 Univ of Wales MA 12. Ridley Hall Cam. **d** 00 **p** 01. C Hollingworth w Tintwistle *Ches* 00–05; V Haslington w Crewe Green 05–14; V Acton and Worleston, Church Minshull etc from 14. *St Mary's Vicarage, Chester Road, Acton, Nantwich CW5 8LG* E: revanne@uwclub.net

LAWSON-JONES, Christopher Mark. b 68. Open Univ BA 98 Ripon Coll Cuddesdon MA 17. St Mich Coll Llan 98. **d** 00 **p** 01. C Risca *Mon* 00–03; Chapl Cross Keys Campus Coleg Gwent 00–03; TV Cyncoed 03–06; Dioc Soc Resp Officer 04–06; P-in-c Magor 06–09; TR 09–12; TR Cyncoed 12–17; AD Bassaleg 12–17; Chapl Miss to Seafarers S Wales Ports from 17. *55 William Belcher Drive, St Mellons, Cardiff CF3 0NZ* M: 07540-793653 E: marklawsonjones@gmail.com

LAWTON, Christopher. *See* LAWTON, Robin David Christopher

LAWTON, Donald John William. b 48. Huron Coll Ontario BMin 77. **d** 77 **p** 78. I Elsa Mayo Canada 77–80; C Ch Ch Cathl Whitehorse 80–13; C Eastling w Ospringe and Stalisfield w Otterden *Cant* 13–14; C Selling w Throwley, Sheldwich w Badlesmere etc 13–14; V High Downs 14–17; Co-Warden of Readers 14–17; rtd 17. *PO Box 612, Garibaldi Highlands, BC V0N 1TO, Canada* E: donaldjlawton@gmail.com

LAWTON, Robin David Christopher. b 73. St Jo Coll Dur BATM 14. Cranmer Hall Dur 12. **d** 14 **p** 15. C Leyburn w Bellerby *Leeds* 14–17; P-in-c Crakehall 17–18; P-in-c Hornby 17–18; P-in-c Patrick Brompton and Hunton 17–18; P-in-c Spennithorne w Finghall and Hauxwell 17–18; R Lower Wensleydale from 18. *The Vicarage, Patrick Brompton, Bedale DL8 1JN* T: (01677) 450920

LAWTON, Siân Lesley. b 77. St Jo Coll Dur BA 15. St Mellitus Coll MA 19. **d** 19. C Masham and Healey *Leeds* from 19; C W Tanfield and Well w Snape and N Stainley from 19. *The Vicarage, Patrick Brompton, Bedale DL8 1JN* T: (01677) 450920 M: 07583-874203 E: revsianlawton@gmail.com

LAXON, Canon Colin John. b 44. FRSA. Cant Sch of Min 86. **d** 89 **p** 90. C Folkestone St Mary and St Eanswythe *Cant* 89–94; P-in-c Barrow St Jas *Carl* 94–01; Soc Resp Officer 01–09; C Brampton and Farlam and Castle Carrock w Cumrew 01–02; TV Eden, Gelt and Irthing 02–06; C Carl St Cuth w St Mary 06–09; Hon Can Carl Cathl 06–09; rtd 09; PtO *Carl* 09–13. *15 Knowefield Avenue, Carlisle CA3 9BQ* T: (01228) 544215 E: c.laxon@btinternet.com

LAY, Mrs Alison Margaret. b 57. **d** 07 **p** 09. OLM Needham Market w Badley *St E* 07–08; OLM Combs and Lt Finborough 08–12. *The Hideaway, Park Road, Needham Market, Ipswich IP6 8BH* T: (01449) 721115 E: alidivineone@gmail.com

LAY, Geoffrey Arthur. b 54. Leic Poly BA 77 Man Univ MA 83 Lon Univ BD 88. Ridley Hall Cam 90. **d** 92 **p** 93. C St Neots *Ely* 92–95; P-in-c Long Stanton w St Mich 95–01; P-in-c Dry Drayton 95–97; R Chailey *Chich* 01–06; Chapl Chailey Heritage Hosp Lewes 01–06; rtd 06; PtO *Chich* 12–17. *77 Firle Road, Peacehaven BN10 7QH* T: (01273) 588048

LAYBOURNE, Teresa Margaret. *See* WALTON, Teresa Margaret

LAYNESMITH, Mark David. b 74. York Univ BA 97 MA 99. Ripon Coll Cuddesdon BA 01. **d** 02 **p** 03. C Tadcaster w Newton Kyme *York* 02–05; Chapl Reading Univ *Ox* from 05; PtO from 19. *30 Shinfield Road, Reading RG2 7BW* T: 0118-987 1495

LAYTON, Miss Norene. b 39. Trin Coll Bris 84. **dss** 86 **d** 87 **p** 94. Lindfield *Chich* 86–92; Par Dn 87–92; Par Dn Loughborough Em *Leic* 92–94; C Loughborough Em and St Mary in Charnwood 94–96; V Hengrove *Bris* 96–04; rtd 04; PtO *Leic* 14–18. *104 Outwoods Drive, Loughborough LE11 3LU* T: (01509) 218127

LAYZELL, Martyn Paul. b 75. Wycliffe Hall Ox 08. **d** 10 **p** 11. C Onslow Square and S Kensington St Aug *Lon* from 10. *139 Nightingale Lane, London SW12 8NE* M: 07891-015221 *or* 07702-968022 E: martyn.layzell@htb.org

LE BAS, Canon Jennifer Anne. b 60. Hull Univ BSc 81 Univ of Wales (Lamp) MA 06. S Dios Minl Tr Scheme 90. **d** 93 **p** 94. C Alverstoke *Portsm* 93–96; C Elson 97–01; P-in-c Gosport Ch Ch and Dioc FE Officer 01–04; PtO *Roch* 05–06; P-in-c Seal SS Pet and Paul 06–12; V from 12; Hon Can Roch Cathl from 19. *The Vicarage, Church Street, Seal, Sevenoaks TN15 0AR* T: (01732) 762955 E: annelebas@dsl.pipex.com

LE BILLON, Mrs Janet. b 42. STETS 99. **d** 02 **p** 03. NSM Guernsey St Jo *Win* 02–06; NSM Guernsey Ste Marie du Castel 06–09; NSM Guernsey St Matt 06–09; PtO from 09; Chapl Princess Eliz Hosp Guernsey 02–17. *Tranquillité, Clos des Quatre Vents, St Martin, Guernsey GY4 6SU* T: (01481) 234283 E: revjanleb@gmail.com

LE BRUN POWELL, Edward Llywelyn. Univ of Wales (Trin St Dav) BD 12 Cardiff Univ MTh 16. St Mich Coll Llan 13. **d** 16 **p** 17. C Milford Haven *St D* 16–17; C Llandaff *Llan* 17–19; C Eglwysilan and Caerphilly from 19. *St Andrew's House, Troed-y-Bryn, Caerphilly CF83 2PX* E: fatheredward.25@gmail.com

LE COUTEUR, Tracy. *See* BROMLEY, Tracy Le Couteur

LE GRYS, Alan Arthur. b 51. K Coll Lon BD 73 AKC 73 MTh 90. St Aug Coll Cant 73. **d** 74 **p** 75. C Harpenden St Jo *St Alb* 74–77; C Hampstead St Jo *Lon* 77–81; Chapl Westf Coll and Bedf Coll 81–83; V Stoneleigh *Guildf* 84–91; Lect Ripon Coll Cuddesdon 91–96; Prin SEITE 96–05; Hon PV Roch Cathl from 96; PtO from 06; *Chich* from 15. *2 Blenheim Avenue, Chatham ME4 6UU* T: (01634) 814298 M: 07958-547053 E: a.legrys@btinternet.com

LE ROSSIGNOL, Richard Lewis. b 52. Aston Univ BSc 75. Oak Hill Th Coll BA 79. **d** 79 **p** 80. C E Ham St Paul *Chelmsf* 79–81; C Willesborough w Hinxhill *Cant* 81–85; PtO 85–94; NSM Brabourne w Smeeth 94–01; NSM Mersham w Hinxhill and Sellindge 01–06; NSM Smeeth w Monks Horton and Stowting and Brabourne 06–07; P-in-c 07–14; P-in-c Mersham w Hinxhill and Sellindge 07–14; V A20 Benefice 14–17; rtd 17; PtO *Cant* from 18. *Stanelaw, Station Road, St Margarets-at-Cliffe, Dover CT15 6AY* E: rller@btinternet.com

LE SÈVE, Mrs Jane Hilary. b 63. SS Hild & Bede Coll Dur BA 86. EAMTC 01. **d** 04 **p** 05. NSM Brightlingsea *Chelmsf* 04–08; TV Greenstead w Colchester St Anne 08–15; P-in-c Wickham Bishops w Lt Braxted from 15; Asst Dir of Ords from 15. *The Rectory, 1 Church Road, Wickham Bishops, Witham CM8 3LA* E: revhilary@btinternet.com

LE VASSEUR, Mrs Linda Susan. b 48. Shenstone Coll of Educn CertEd 70. S Dios Minl Tr Scheme 92. **d** 95 **p** 96. NSM Guernsey Ste Marie du Castel and Guernsey St Matt *Win* 95–01; NSM Guernsey St Sav and Guernsey St Marguerite de la Foret 01–14; P-in-c Guernsey St Jo 14–16; Sen Chapl Princess Eliz Hosp Guernsey from 00. *Princess Elizabeth Hospital, Rue Mignot, St Martin, Guernsey GY4 6UU* T: (01481) 725241 ext 4699 E: linda@cugsy.nol

LE VAY, Clare Forbes Agard Bramhall Joanna. b 41. St Anne's Coll Ox BA 64 MA 66 Univ of Wales (Abth) MSc 72 PhD 86. Westcott Ho Cam 86. **d** 88 **p** 94. C Stamford Hill St Thos *Lon* 88–89; C Hackney 89–92; Asst Chapl Brook Gen Hosp Lon 92–95; Asst Chapl Greenwich Distr Hosp Lon 92–95; Chapl Greenwich Healthcare NHS Trust 95–01; PtO *S'wark* 02–06; rtd 04–06; *Glouc* 09–14. *Winton, Beards Lane, Stroud GL5 4HD* T: (01453) 767020 M: 07816-468112 E: clarelevay@yahoo.com

LE-WORTHY, Michael Raymond. b 50. **d** 98 **p** 99. OLM Glascote and Stonydelph *Lich* 98–12; NSM from 12; NSM Tamworth 12–15. *15 Abbey Road, Glascote, Tamworth B77 2QE* T: (01827) 55762 E: michael.leworthy1@btinternet.com

LEA, Canon Montague Brian. b 34. St Jo Coll Cam BA 55 Lon Univ BD 71. St Jo Coll Nottm 68. **d** 71 **p** 72. C Northwood Em *Lon* 71–74; Chapl Barcelona *Eur* 74–79; V Hove Bp Hannington Memorial Ch *Chich* 79–86; Adn N France *Eur* 86–94; Chapl Paris St Mich 86–94; Hon Can Gib Cathl from 95; R Chiddingly w E Hoathly *Chich* 94–96; Chapl The Hague *Eur* 96–00; rtd 01; PtO *Chich* from 01. *35 Summerdown Lane, East Dean, Eastbourne BN20 0LE* T: (01323) 423226 E: brian.lea@greenbee.net

LEA (née WETHERELL), Philippa Clare. b 80. Univ of Wales (Cardiff) BSc 02. Trin Coll Bris BA 08. **d** 09 **p** 10. C W Derby St Mary and St Jas *Liv* 09–13; TV Kirkby from 13. *The Rectory, Old Hall Lane, Kirkby, Liverpool L32 5TH* M: 07770-892639 E: philippaclea@yahoo.co.uk

LEA-WILSON, Nicholas Hugh. b 61. Man Poly BA 83 Univ Coll Ches BA 08 MLI 90. NOC 05. **d** 08 **p** 09. C Gateacre *Liv* 08–12; P-in-c Knowsley 12–14; TV 4Saints Team from 14.

The Vicarage, Tithebarn Road, Prescot L34 0JA T: 0151-546 4266 M: 07968-290553

LEACH, Alan Charles Graham. b 46. Univ Coll Ches BTh 04 Master Mariner 73. NOC 04. **d** 05 **p** 06. NSM Neston *Ches* 05–08; NSM Heswall 08–17; rtd 17; PtO *Ches* from 17. *8 Hill Top Lane, Ness, Neston CH64 4EL* T: 0151-336 5046 M: 07802-622143 E: alan.leach5@btinternet.com

LEACH, Andrew John Philip. b 54. Univ of Wales (Lamp) BA 77 Univ of Wales (Abth) PGCE 78. WEMTC 07. **d** 10 **p** 11. NSM Painswick, Sheepscombe, Cranham, The Edge etc *Glouc* from 10. *Melrose Cottage, Cheltenham Road, Painswick GL6 6SJ* T: (01452) 813609 M: 07564-448692 E: ajpleach@googlemail.com

LEACH, Miss Bethia Morag. b 62. Sheff Univ BA 84 Liv Inst of Educn PGCE 85. Ripon Coll Cuddesdon 95. **d** 97 **p** 98. C Stafford *Lich* 97–00; TV Bilston 00–07; V Pensnett *Worc* 07–10; rtd 10. *66 Lichfield Road, Walsall WS4 2DJ* T: (01922) 446956 E: bethialeach@virginmedia.com

LEACH, James Roger. b 66. Ball Coll Ox BA 89 MA 99. Wycliffe Hall Ox BA 98. **d** 99 **p** 00. C Knowle *Birm* 99–06; C Gerrards Cross and Fulmer Ox from 06. *3 The Uplands, Gerrards Cross SL9 7JQ* T: (01753) 886480 E: james.leach@saintjames.org.uk

LEACH, John. b 52. K Coll Lon BD 79 AKC 79 St Jo Coll Dur MA 83 Lambeth STh 02. **d** 81 **p** 82. C N Walsham w Antingham *Nor* 81–85; C Crookes St Thos *Sheff* 85–89; V Styvechale *Cov* 89–97; Dir Angl Renewal Min 97–02; R Jersey St Lawr *Win* 02–04; Par Development Adv *Mon* 04–09; V Folkestone St Jo *Cant* 09–13; PtO 13–14; Developing Discipleship Adv and Tr *Linc* 14–18; Growing Disciples Officer from 18. *105 Nettleham Road, Lincoln LN2 1RU* E: john.leach@lincoln.anglican.org

LEACH, Mrs Rebecca Mary. b 65. St Aid Coll Dur BA 87 Bris Univ PGCE 90. ERMC 05. **d** 08 **p** 09. C E Barnet *St Alb* 08–11; C Harpenden St Nic 11–16; V St Alb St Steph from 16. *St Stephen's Vicarage, 14 Watling STreet, St Albans AL1 2PX* T: (01727) 862598 E: vicar@ststephenandstjulian.org

LEACH, Samuel Mark. b 76. Westmr Coll Ox BEd 99. Ridley Hall Cam 05. **d** 08 **p** 09. C Walsall St Paul *Lich* 08–11; TV Wednesfield 11–18; R Upton *Ex* from 18. *Upton Rectory, Furzehill Road, Torquay TQ1 3JG* M: 07915-668714 E: vicar@stmags.org.uk

LEACH, Stephen Lance. b 42. St Steph Ho Ox 66. **d** 69 **p** 70. C Higham Ferrers w Chelveston *Pet* 69–72; TV Ilfracombe H Trin *Ex* 72; TV Ilfracombe, Lee and W Down 72–74; V Barnstaple St Mary 74–77; R Goodleigh 74–77; P-in-c Barnstaple St Pet w H Trin 76–77; P-in-c Landkey 77–79; TR Barnstaple and Goodleigh 77–79; TR Barnstaple, Goodleigh and Landkey 79–82; V Paignton St Jo 82–95; Chapl Paignton and Kings Ash Hosps 82–95; Gen Sec ACS 95–08; rtd 08; Public Preacher *Birm* 95–15; PtO *Ex* from 07. *16 Kings Avenue, Paignton TQ3 2AR* T: (01803) 552335

LEACH, Stephen Windsor. b 47. St Chad's Coll Dur BSc 70 Linacre Coll Ox BA 72 MA 76. Ripon Hall Ox 70. **d** 73 **p** 74. C Swinton St Pet *Man* 73–77; C Oldham St Chad Limeside 77–79; V Shaw 79–87; V St Just in Penwith *Truro* 87–14; V Sancreed 87–14; rtd 14. *Porthpean, 4 Bentham Avenue, Fleetwood FY7 8RH* T: (01253) 771624 E: windsorleach@aol.com

LEACH, Timothy Edmund. b 41. Dur Univ BA 63. Ridley Hall Cam 63. **d** 65 **p** 66. C Ecclesfield *Sheff* 65–68; C Stocksbridge 68–71; C-in-c W Bessacarr CD 71–80; V Goole and Hon Chapl Miss to Seamen 80–95; V Wath-upon-Dearne *Sheff* 95–08; rtd 08; PtO *Sheff* from 09. *6 Sawn Moor Avenue, Thurcroft, Rotherham S66 9DQ* T: (01709) 701263

LEADER, Miss Janette Patricia. b 46. EAMTC 94. **d** 97 **p** 98. C Desborough, Brampton Ash, Dingley and Braybrooke *Pet* 97–01; V Wellingborough St Barn 01–12; rtd 12; PtO *Pet* from 14. *15 Salisbury Road, Peterborough PE4 6NL* T: (01733) 685672 E: revjanleader@virginmedia.com

LEAF, Edward David Hugh. b 65. Oak Hill Th Coll BA 97. **d** 98 **p** 99. C Bath St Bart *B & W* 98–01; C Minehead 01–05; V Chadderton Em *Man* from 05. *Emmanuel Vicarage, 15 Chestnut Street, Chadderton, Oldham OL9 8HB* T: 0161-681 1310 E: stgeorgechadderton@icloud.com

LEAH, William Albert. b 34. K Coll Lon BA 56 AKC 57 K Coll Cam MA 63. Ripon Hall Ox 60. **d** 62 **p** 63. C Falmouth K Chas *Truro* 62–63; Chapl K Coll Cam 63–67; Min Can Westmr Abbey 67–74; V Hawkhurst *Cant* 74–83; Hon Min Can Cant Cathl 78–83; V St Ives *Truro* 83–94; rtd 98. *Trerice Cottage, Seaward Newbridge, Penzance TR20 8QR* T: (01736) 810987 E: w.leah1934@gmail.com

LEAHY, Canon David Adrian. b 56. Open Univ MA 90. Qu Coll Birm. **d** 85 **p** 86. C Tile Cross *Birm* 85–88; C Warley Woods 88–91; V Hobs Moat 91–07; AD Solihull 97–04; V Four Oaks from 07; AD Sutton Coldfield 13–19; Jt AD

Aston and Sutton Coldfield from 19; Hon Can Birm Cathl from 18. *The Vicarage, 26 All Saints Drive, Sutton Coldfield B74 4AG* T: 0121-308 5315 E: revaleahy@gmail.com

LEAK, Adrian Scudamore. b 38. Ch Ch Ox BA 60 MA 65 BD 89 FSA 17. Cuddesdon Coll 64. **d** 66 **p** 67. C Cov St Mark 66–69; C Dorchester Ox 69–73; V Badsey *Worc* 73–80; V Wickhamford 73–78; V Badsey w Aldington and Wickhamford 78–80; P-in-c Monkwearmouth St Pet *Dur* 80–81; V Choral and Archivist York Minster 81–86; Can Res and Prec Guildf Cathl 86–90; Hon C Guildf H Trin w St Mary 96–00; Hon C Worplesdon 00–06; P-in-c Withyham St Mich *Chich* 06–13; rtd 13; PtO *Guildf* from 14. *Flat 1, 10 Joseph's Road, Guildford GU1 1DW* T: (01483) 579503 E: adrian.leak@btinternet.com

LEAK, Harry Duncan. b 30. St Cath Coll Cam BA 53 MA 57. Ely Th Coll 53. **d** 54 **p** 55. S Africa 54–57; Portuguese E Africa 57–61; C Eccleshall *Lich* 62–64; V Normacot 64–66; C Stoke upon Trent 66–68; V Hanley All SS 68–71; R Swynnerton 71–80; PtO 80–03; rtd 92. *15 Sutherland Road, Tittensor, Stoke-on-Trent ST12 9JQ* T: (01782) 374341

✠**LEAKE, The Rt Revd David.** b 35. ALCD 59 LTh 74. **d** 59 **p** 60 **c** 69. C Watford *St Alb* 59–61; Lect 61–63; SAMS Argentina 63–69; Asst Bp Paraguay 69–73; Asst Bp N Argentina 69–80; Bp N Argentina 80–90; Bp Argentina 90–02; rtd 02; Hon Asst Bp Nor from 03; PtO from 03. *The Anchorage, Lower Common, East Runton, Cromer NR27 9PG* T: (01263) 513536 E: obispodavid@gmail.com

LEAKE, Duncan Burton. b 49. Leeds Univ BA 71 Leeds and Carnegie Coll PGCE 72 Keele Univ MA 85. Oak Hill Th Coll 90. **d** 92 **p** 93. C Stanwix *Carl* 92–97; C Chasetown *Lich* 97–00; V Chase Terrace 00–14; rtd 14; PtO *Lich* from 15. *12 Outwoods Close, Weston, Stafford ST18 0JR* E: revduncan@outlook.com or rev.dbl@googlemail.com

LEAKE, Roger Norman Simon. b 59. Dur Univ BSc 80 Coll of Ripon & York St Jo PGCE 81. Sarum Coll 16. **d** 19. NSM Chalke Valley *Sarum* from 19. *The Killick, Wylye Road, Hanging Langford, Salisbury SP3 4NW* T: (01722) 792862 E: revrleake@gmail.com

LEAKEY, Ian Raymond Arundell. b 24. K Coll Cam BA 47 MA 49. Ridley Hall Cam 48. **d** 50 **p** 51. C Litherland St Jo and St Jas *Liv* 50–53; Rwanda Miss 53–73; Can Burundi 66; V Cudham *Roch* 73–76; P-in-c Downe 76; V Cudham and Downe 76–89; rtd 89; PtO *Sarum* 89–11. *10 Francis Court, Spire View, Salisbury SP2 7GE* T: (01722) 329243 E: iandf.leakey@btinternet.com

LEAL, Mrs Clare Elizabeth. b 61. FCIH 97. Ripon Coll Cuddesdon 16. **d** 19. NSM Summertown *Ox* from 19. *19 Edgeway Road, Marston, Oxford OX3 0HD* E: curate@stmichaels-summertown.org.uk

LEAL, John Xavier. b 64. **d** 14. NSM Rock Ferry *Ches* 14–16; R Rossington *Sheff* 16–19; P-in-c New Rossington 16–19; R Coppenhall *Ches* from 19. *The Rectory, 198 Ford Lane, Crewe CW1 3TN* T: (01270) 215151 E: priestxman@gmail.com

LEAMY, Stuart Nigel. b 46. Pemb Coll Ox BA 68 MA 73 ACA 76 FCA 81. Sarum Th Coll 68. **d** 70 **p** 71. C Upholland *Liv* 70–78; LtO *Lon* 78–83 and 94–97; NSM Pimlico St Mary Bourne Street 97–16; PtO from 16. *92 Gloucester Road, Hampton TW12 2UJ* T: (020) 8979 9068 E: leamy@blueyonder.co.uk

LEAN, The Very Revd David Jonathan Rees. b 52. Coll of Resurr Mirfield 74. **d** 75 **p** 76. C Tenby *St D* 75–79; C Tenby w Gumfreston 80–81; V Llanrhian w Llanhywel and Carnhedryn etc 81–88; V Haverfordwest St Martin w Lambston 88–00; RD Roose 99–00; Can St D Cathl 00–17; TV Dewisland 01–09; TR 09–17; Dean St D 09–17; rtd 17; PtO *St D* from 17. *The Garth, Serpentine Road, Tenby SA70 8DD* T: (01834) 843341 E: jonathanlean1@gmail.com

LEAR, Peter Malcolm. b 45. FCMA. SEITE 95. **d** 98 **p** 99. NSM Ham St Andr *S'wark* 98–03; Chapl to Bp Kingston 98–99; NSM Wandsworth St Anne 03–04; NSM Upper Coquetdale *Newc* 04–11; rtd 11; PtO *York* from 11. *39 Farmanby Close, Thornton Dale, Pickering YO18 7TD* T: (01751) 470190 E: peterlear@learpm.com

LEARMONT, Oliver James. b 62. UEA BA 83 Wolv Univ LLM 96 SS Coll Cam BTh 07. Westcott Ho Cam 05. **d** 07 **p** 08. C Hitchin *St Alb* 07–11; P-in-c E Bridgford and Kneeton *S'well* 11–18; P-in-c Flintham 11–18; P-in-c Car Colston w Screveton 11–18; V N Bradley, Southwick, Heywood and Steeple Ashton *Sarum* from 18. *The Vicarage, 62 Church Lane, North Bradley, Trowbridge BA14 0TA* T: (01225) 774845 E: oliver.learmont@btinternet.com

LEARMOUTH, Michael Walter. b 50. FCA. Oak Hill Th Coll 84. **d** 84 **p** 85. C Harlow St Mary and St Hugh w St Jo the Bapt *Chelmsf* 84–89; V Hainault 89–97; TR Harlow Town Cen w Lt Parndon 97–00; TR Barnsbury *Lon* 00–19; AD Islington 08–14; rtd 19. *Address temp unknown*

LEARY, Thomas Glasbrook. b 42. AKC 66. **d** 67 **p** 68. C W Bromwich All SS *Lich* 67–70; TV Croydon St Jo *Cant* 70–75; C Limpsfield and Titsey *S'wark* 75–83; V Sutton New Town St Barn 83–92; V Merton St Mary 92–07; RD Merton 98–01; rtd 07; PtO *Heref* from 07; *S & B* 12–14. *Conduit Cottage, Livesey Road, Ludlow SY8 1EZ* T: (01584) 875619 E: glassbrook@msn.com

LEATHARD, Preb Brian. b 56. Sussex Univ BA Cam Univ MA Loughb Univ PhD 91. Westcott Ho Cam 79. **d** 82 **p** 83. C Seaford w Sutton *Chich* 82–85; Chapl Loughb Univ *Leic* 85–89; V Hampton Hill *Lon* 89–06; R Chelsea St Luke and Ch Ch from 06; Dir of Ords 99–09; Preb St Paul's Cathl from 05. *The Rectory, 64A Flood Street, London SW3 5TE* T: (020) 7352 6331 *or* 7351 7365 E: brianleathard@chelseaparish.org

LEATHARD, Prof Helen Louise. b 47. Chelsea Coll Lon BSc 70 K Coll Lon PhD 74 St Martin's Coll Lanc MA 06 FBPharmacolS 06. LCTP 12. **d** 13 **p** 14. NSM Slyne w Hest and Halton w Aughton *Blackb* 13–17; PtO from 17. *29 Coronation Way, Lancaster LA1 2TQ* T: (01524) 849495 E: helenleathard@btinternet.com

LEATHERBARROW, Andrew James Howard. b 68. All SS Cen for Miss & Min 12. **d** 15 **p** 16. C Rainhill *Liv* 15–18; P-in-c Stoneycroft All SS from 18. *The Vicarage, 7 Saints Close, Liverpool L13 4AT* T: 0151-228 3581 M: 07769-276734

LEATHERBARROW, Mrs Laura. b 70. **d** 14 **p** 15. C E Widnes *Liv* 14–18; P-in-c Croxteth Park from 18. *The Vicarage, 7 Saints Close, Liverpool L13 4AT*

LEATHERS, Preb Brian Stanley Peter. b 61. Nottm Univ BSc 83. Oak Hill Th Coll BA 89. **d** 89 **p** 90. C Watford St Alb 89–92; C Welwyn w Ayot St Peter 92–96; V Heacham *Nor* 96–99; P-in-c Stapenhill Immanuel *Derby* 99–00; V 00–09; V Alton w Bradley-le-Moors and Oakamoor w Cotton *Lich* 09–10; P-in-c Denstone w Ellastone and Stanton 09–10; P-in-c Mayfield 09–10; V Alton w Bradley-le-Moors and Denstone etc from 10; RD Uttoxeter from 11; Preb Lich Cathl from 18. *The New Vicarage, Limekiln Lane, Alton, Stoke-on-Trent ST10 4AR* T: (01538) 702469 E: briantopsey@googlemail.com

LEATHERS, Daniel Brian. b 88. Derby Univ BA 10 Trin Hall Cam BTh 15. Ridley Hall Cam 12. **d** 15 **p** 16. C Whitfield *Derby* 15–18; V Haydock St Mark *Liv* from 18. *2 Stanley Bank Road, St Helens WA11 0UW* M: 07526-660791 E: dan_leathers@hotmail.co.uk

LEATON, Martin John. b 46. Clifton Th Coll 68. **d** 71 **p** 72. C Kenilworth St Jo *Cov* 71–74; C Stratford-on-Avon w Bishopton 74–77; P-in-c Meriden 77–81; R Meriden w Packington 82–84; R Heanton Punchardon w Marwood *Ex* 84–87; PtO 95–97; P-in-c Rampton w Laneham, Treswell, Cottam and Stokeham *S'well* 97–06; P-in-c N and S Leverton 03–06; rtd 06; Hon C Tysoe w Oxhill and Whatcote *Cov* 06–17; PtO *Heref* from 17. *7 Centurian Way, Credenhill, Hereford HR4 7FF* T: (01432) 761374 E: martinjleaton@gmail.com

LEAVER, David Noel. b 63. Hatf Coll Dur BA 85. Wycliffe Hall Ox 89. **d** 91 **p** 92. C Blackheath Park St Mich *S'wark* 91–95; C Upton (Overchurch) *Ches* 95–98; C Wilmslow 98–99; PtO from 99. *42 Hill Top Avenue, Cheadle Hulme, Cheadle SK8 7HY* T: 0161-485 4302 E: davidleaver@btconnect.com

LEAVER, Mrs Janice Patricia. b 56. EAMTC 03. **d** 06 **p** 07. C Desborough, Brampton Ash, Dingley and Braybrooke *Pet* 06–09; TV Wilford Peninsula *St E* 09–18; rtd 18. *17 Elmhurst Court, Hamblin Road, Woodbridge IP12 1HB* M: 07913-977218 E: janpatleaver@gmail.com

LEAVER (née SMYTH), Mrs Lucinda Elizabeth Jane. b 67. New Hall Cam BA 88 MA 92. Wycliffe Hall Ox BTh 93. **d** 93 **p** 94. C Cambridge St Barn *Ely* 93–97; Chapl St Kath Hall Liv Hope 97–98; TV Stockport SW *Ches* 99–01; Chapl Stockport Gr Sch from 99; Chapl Univ Hosp of S Man NHS Foundn Trust 14–17; Chapl Man Univ NHS Foundn Trust 17–19; PtO *Eur* from 16; *Man* from 19. *42 Hill Top Avenue, Cheadle Hulme, Cheadle SK8 7HY* T: 0161-456 9000

LEAWORTHY, John Owen. b 40. Univ of Wales (Swansea) BSc 62. Oak Hill Th Coll 80. **d** 82 **p** 83. C Compton Gifford *Ex* 82–85; C Plymouth Em w Efford 85–86; P-in-c Marks Tey w Aldham and Lt Tey *Chelmsf* 86–88; R 88–89; Chapl HM Pris Full Sutton 89–91; NSM Portree *Arg* 96–04; rtd 05; PtO *Chelmsf* from 05. *46 Wilkin Drive, Tiptree, Colchester CO5 0QP* T: (01621) 810905 E: jleaworthy@btinternet.com

LECK, Stuart David. b 62. Cant Ch Ch Univ BA 11 ACIB 84. SEITE 03. **d** 06 **p** 07. NSM Brockley Hill St Sav *S'wark* 10–12; NSM Nunhead St Antony w St Silas 10–12; C Catford (Southend) and Downham 12–14; TV from 14. *St Barnabas' Vicarage, 1 Churchdown, Bromley BR1 5PS* T: (020) 8698 4851 M: 07811-384420 E: stuart.leck@btinternet.com

LECKEY, Paul Robert. b 61. QUB. Ripon Coll Cuddesdon Aston Tr Scheme. **d** 96 **p** 97. C Eastleigh *Win* 96–01; P-in-c Upton St Leonards *Glouc* 01–13; V Hall Green Ascension *Birm*

13–17; V Balsall Heath and Edgbaston SS Mary and Ambrose from 17. *15 Raglan Road, Birmingham B5 7RA* T: 0121-440 2196 E: rev.leckey@virginmedia.com

LECLÉZIO, Ms Marie Katryn. b 62. Natal Univ BA 83 All Nations Chr Coll MA 00. WEMTC 05. **d** 08 **p** 09. C Halas *Worc* 08–12; TV from 12; Deanery Miss Enabler from 12. *34 Beecher Road, Halesowen B63 2DJ* T: (01384) 411383 E: revkat@halasteam.org.uk

LEDGER, Mrs Margaret Phyllis. b 47. **d** 04 **p** 05. OLM Newburn *Newc* 04–17; rtd 17; PtO *Newc* from 17. *14 Woodside Avenue, Throckley, Newcastle upon Tyne NE15 9BE* T: 0191-267 2953 E: margaret.p.ledger@btinternet.com

LEDWARD, John Archibald. b 30. Lon Univ BD 58 Man Univ MA 81 FRSA 85. ALCD 57. **d** 58 **p** 59. C St Helens St Helen *Liv* 58–62; V Dearham *Carl* 62–66; V Mirehouse 66–71; V Daubhill *Man* 71–77; R Newcastle w Butterton *Lich* 77–88; R Rockland St Mary w Hellington, Bramerton etc *Nor* 88–94; P-in-c Kirby Bedon w Bixley and Whitlingham 92–94; R Rockland St Mary w Hellington, Bramerton etc 94–95; RD Loddon 92–95; rtd 95; PtO *Nor* from 95. *41 Lackford Close, Brundall, Norwich NR13 5NL* T: (01603) 714745 E: jledward@talktalk.net

LEE, Agnes Elizabeth. b 31. Open Univ BA 87 Whitelands Coll Lon TCert 51 ACP 76. NOC 97. **d** 98 **p** 99. NSM Dewsbury *Wakef* 98–02; rtd 02; PtO *Wakef* 02–14; *Leeds* from 14. *1 Moor Park Court, Dewsbury WF12 7AU* T: (01924) 467319

LEE, Andrew. *See* LEE, Sang Youn

LEE, Anne Louise. *See* WILKINS, Anne Louise

LEE, Anthony Maurice. b 35. Bps' Coll Cheshunt 62. **d** 65 **p** 66. C Pinner *Lon* 65–71; Asst Youth Chapl *Glouc* 71–72; V Childswyckham 72–73; R Aston Somerville 72–73; V Childswyckham w Aston Somerville 73–91; P-in-c Buckland 88–91; P-in-c Stanton w Snowshill 88–91; R Childswyckham w Aston Somerville, Buckland etc 91–94; RD Winchcombe 86–94; rtd 94. *Lysander House, 6 Lutyens Court, Upper Rissington, Cheltenham GL54 2RG*

LEE, Canon Brian. b 37. Linc Th Coll 78. **d** 80 **p** 81. C Duston *Pet* 80–84; P-in-c Spratton 84–89; V 89–06; Jt P-in-c Maidwell w Draughton, Lamport w Faxton 89–01; Jt P-in-c Cottesbrooke w Gt Creaton and Thornby 89–06; RD Brixworth 94–01; Can Pet Cathl 98–06; rtd 06; PtO *Pet* from 06. *1 Bishops Way, Corby NN18 0TJ* T: (01536) 747195 E: revbrianlee@gmail.com

LEE, Canon Brian Ernest. b 32. ACA 59 FCA 70. Linc Th Coll 60. **d** 62 **p** 63. C Birch St Jas *Man* 62–65; C Withington St Paul 65–66; R Abbey Hey 66–70; Hon C Gatley *Ches* 86–88; V Egremont St Jo 88–97; RD Wallasey 91–96; OGS from 92; Hon Can Ches Cathl 96–97; rtd 97; PtO *Nor* from 97. *St Fursey House, Convent of All Hallows, Ditchingham, Bungay NR35 2DZ* T: (01986) 892308 F: 894215 E: blee@ogs.net

LEE, Brian John. b 51. K Coll Lon BD 78 AKC 78. Coll of Resurr Mirfield 78. **d** 79 **p** 80. C Ham St Rich *S'wark* 79–82; C Surbiton St Andr and St Mark 82–85; V Shirley St Geo 85–93; V St Botolph Aldgate w H Trin Minories *Lon* 93–08; rtd 08. *6 Shore Cottages, Silverdale, Carnforth LA5 0TS*

LEE, Christopher James. b 52. FIBMS 77. St Mich Coll Llan 10. **d** 13 **p** 14. NSM Caerau w Ely *Llan* from 13. *10 Coronation Road, Cardiff CF14 4QY* T: (029) 2061 8054 M: 07831-500738

LEE, Christopher John Bodell. b 82. Kingston Univ BA 01 Cam Univ BTh 11. Ridley Hall Cam 08. **d** 07 **p** 11. C Onslow Square and S Kensington St Aug *Lon* 11–14; P-in-c Cobbold Road St Sav w St Mary 15–18; V from 18. *St Saviour's Vicarage, Cobbold Road, London W12 9LN* T: (020) 8743 4769 M: 07966-632161 E: revchris7@gmail.com

LEE, David Alexander. b 83. Imp Coll Lon MSci 05 PhD 10. Oak Hill Th Coll BA 14. **d** 14 **p** 15. C Fulham St Pet *Lon* from 14. *St Peter's Vicarage, St Peter's Terrace, London SW6 7JS* E: david.a.lee@gmail.com *or* david.lee@stpetersfulham.co.uk

LEE, The Ven David John. b 46. Bris Univ BSc 67 Fitzw Coll Cam BA 76 MA 79 Birm Univ PhD 96. Ridley Hall Cam 74. **d** 77 **p** 78. C Putney St Marg *S'wark* 77–80; Tutor Bp Tucker Th Coll Uganda 80–86; Tutor Crowther Hall CMS Tr Coll Selly Oak 86–91; P-in-c Wishaw and Middleton *Birm* 91–96; Can Res Birm Cathl 96–04; Dir Dioc Bd for Miss 96–04; Adn Bradf 04–15; rtd 15; Adn for Miss Resources 15–16; PtO *Birm* from 16; *Lich* from 17. *16 Tudor Hill, Sutton Coldfield B73 6BH* T: 0121-681 4347 M: 07711-671351 E: davidjlee@blueyonder.co.uk

LEE, The Ven David Stanley. b 30. Univ of Wales (Cardiff) BSc 51. St Mich Coll Llan 56. **d** 57 **p** 58. C Caerau w Ely *Llan* 57–60; C Port Talbot St Agnes 60–70; Ind Chapl 60–70; R Merthyr Tydfil 70–72; Chapl Merthyr Tydfil Hosp 70–91; R Merthyr Tydfil and Cyfarthfa *Llan* 72–91; RD Merthyr Tydfil 82–91; Can Llan Cathl 84–97; Adn Llan 91–97; R Llanfabon

91–97; rtd 97; PtO *Llan* from 97; *Mon* from 98. *2 Old Vicarage Close, Llanishen, Cardiff CF14 5UZ* T: (029) 2075 2431

LEE, David Wight Dunsmore. b 39. Wells Th Coll 61. **d** 63 **p** 64. C Middlesbrough St Oswald *York* 63–67; C Northallerton w Kirby Sigston 67–69; R Limbe W Thyolo and Mulanje Malawi 69–71; R S Highlands 71–75; V Newington Transfiguration *York* 76–81; P-in-c Sheriff Hutton 81–85; P-in-c Sheriff Hutton and Farlington 85–97; V Sheriff Hutton, Farlington, Stillington etc 97–04; rtd 04; PtO *York* from 04. *Kirkstone Cottage, Main Street, Oswaldkirk, York YO62 5XT* T: (01439) 788283 E: dwdlee@talk21.com *or* dawdle@dwdlee.plus.com

LEE, Edmund Hugh. b 53. Trin Coll Ox BA 75 MA 79 Goldsmiths' Coll Lon BMus 83 K Coll Lon MA 98. Ripon Coll Cuddesdon 93. **d** 95 **p** 96. C Malden St Jas *S'wark* 95–99; TV Mortlake w E Sheen 99–08. *67 North Worple Way, London SW14 8PP* T: (020) 8876 5270

LEE, Elizabeth. *See* LEE, Agnes Elizabeth

LEE, Franklin. *See* LEE, On Yip Franklin

LEE, Hugh. *See* LEE, John Charles Hugh Mellanby

LEE, Mrs Jane. b 71. Teesside Univ BA 96. St Mellitus Coll 16. **d** 19. C W Pendleside *Blackb* from 19. *19 Nab View, Whalley, Clitheroe BB7 9YG* M: 07769-951978 E: jane.lee1271@gmail.com

LEE, Mrs Janet. b 58. **d** 13 **p** 14. OLM Clifton Ch Ch w Em *Bris* from 13. *45 Alma Road, Clifton, Bristol BS8 2DE* E: janet.lee@ccweb.org.uk

LEE, Mrs Jayne Christine. b 53. Dundee Univ MA 75. **d** 06 **p** 07. OLM Roberttown w Hartshead *Wakef* 06–12; OLM Heckmondwike 06–12; OLM Liversedge w Hightown 06–12; OLM Heckmondwike (w Norristhorpe) and Liversedge 12–14; *Leeds* from 14; OLM Hartshead, Hightown, Roberttown and Scholes *Wakef* 12–14; *Leeds* from 14. *58 Prospect View, Liversedge WF15 8BD* T: (01924) 401264 E: jayneclee@hotmail.com

LEE, Jennifer. b 42. Westf Coll Lon BA 64 CQSW 78. NOC 01. **d** 03 **p** 04. NSM Millhouses H Trin *Sheff* 03–06; PtO 06–13; NSM Compton w Shackleford and Peper Harow *Guildf* 07–12; rtd 12; PtO *Guildf* from 12. *The Old Cottage Barn, Peper Harow Park, Peper Harow, Godalming GU8 6BQ* T: (01483) 424468 E: revjennylee@gmail.com

LEE, John Charles Hugh Mellanby. b 44. Trin Hall Cam BA 66 MA 69 Brunel Univ MTech 71. Ox NSM Course 78. **d** 81 **p** 82. NSM Amersham on the Hill *Ox* 81–88; NSM Ox St Aldate w St Matt 88–93; NSM Wheatley 93–95; Dioc Development Officer Miss in Work and Economic Life 95–02; P-in-c Ox St Mich w St Martin and All SS 02–09; LtO 09–13; NSM Wheatley 13–14; NSM Beckley, Forest Hill, Horton-cum-Studley and Stanton St John from 14. *64 Observatory Street, Oxford OX2 6EP* T: (01865) 316245 M: 07879-426625 E: hugh.lee@btinternet.com

LEE, John Michael Andrew. b 62. Leeds Univ BA 84. Trin Coll Bris 88. **d** 90 **p** 91. C Norbiton *S'wark* 90–94; C Leic H Trin w St Jo 94–02; R York St Paul 02–19; RD City of York 18–19; 20s-40s Team Ldr from 19; P-in-c York St Barn from 18. *42 East Mount Road, York YO24 1BD* E: johnmalee@btinternet.com *or* john.lee@yorkdiocese.org

LEE, John Samuel. b 47. Chich Th Coll 74. **d** 77 **p** 78. C Bramley *Ripon* 77–80; C Bideford *Ex* 81–84; TV Littleham w Exmouth 84–90; P-in-c Sidbury 90–91; TV Sidmouth, Woolbrook, Salcombe Regis, Sidbury etc 91–04; rtd 04; Hon C Torquay St Jo *Ex* 17–18; Hon C Torre and Torquay St Jo from 18. *Westward Ho!, Torpark Road, Torquay TQ2 5BQ* T: (01803) 293086 E: lee352@sky.com

LEE, Jonathan Wei Sing. Clare Coll Cam BA 09 MSci 09 MA 12. Oak Hill Th Coll BA 17. **d** 18 **p** 19. C Ashton-on-Ribble St Andr *Blackb* from 18. *Address withheld by request* E: jwslee2@gmail.com

LEE, Joseph Patrick. b 53. St Jos Coll Upholland 72 Ushaw Coll Dur 75. **d** 78 **p** 79. In RC Ch 78–99; NSM Charlton *S'wark* 99–09; NSM E Greenwich 09–17; NSM Charlton from 17. *11 Holly Court, School Square, London SE10 0BT* T: (020) 8465 5212 M: 07872-347058 E: joe@charlton.church

LEE, Mrs Judith Mary. b 44. Doncaster Coll of Educn TCert 65. **d** 06 **p** 07. OLM Frenchay and Winterbourne Down *Bris* 06–16; OLM Frenchay and Stapleton from 16. *8 Beaufort Road, Frampton Cotterell, Bristol BS36 2AD* T: (01454) 772381 E: jrplee@btinternet.com

LEE, Canon Kenneth Peter. b 45. Em Coll Cam BA 67 MA 71. Cuddesdon Coll 67. **d** 69 **p** 70. C Stoke Poges *Ox* 69–72; C Witton *Ches* 72–74; V Frankby w Greasby 74–92; R Christleton 92–10; Hon Can Ches Cathl 05–10; rtd 10; PtO *Ches* from 10. *16 Rookery Drive, Tattenhall, Chester CH3 9QS* T: (01829) 770292 E: leepf@btinternet.com

LEE, Luke Gun-Hong. b 37. Univ of Yon Sei BTh 62. St Jo Coll Morpeth 64. **d** 67 **p** 68. Lic to Offic Taejon Korea 67–79; C

Bloxwich *Lich* 79–83; TV Dunstable *St Alb* 83–90; V Croxley Green All SS 90–07; rtd 07; PtO *Ox* from 07; *Lon* from 08. *101 Lark Vale, Aylesbury HP19 0YP* T: (01296) 423133 E: luke.gh.lee@gmail.com

LEE, Mrs Margaret. b 48. Coll of Ripon & York St Jo BEd 71. NEOC 03. **d** 06 **p** 07. NSM Houghton le Spring *Dur* 06–19; rtd 19; PtO *Dur* from 19. *2 Rectory View, Shadforth, Durham DH6 1LF* T: 0191-372 0595 E: marglee372@outlook.com

LEE, Martin Paul. b 66. Leeds Univ BA 13 Teesside Univ MEd 15. Aston Tr Scheme 91 Linc Th Coll 93 St Steph Ho Ox 94. **d** 96 **p** 97. C Wells St Thos w Horrington *B & W* 96–00; P-in-c Brent Knoll, E Brent and Lympsham 00–01; R 01–08; RD Axbridge 03–08; V Long Benton *Newc* from 08; AD Newc E 12–17. *The Vicarage, 3 Station Road, Benton, Newcastle upon Tyne NE12 8AN* T: 0191-266 1921 E: martinlee903@btinternet.com

LEE, Mary Elizabeth. *See* DUNN, Mary Elizabeth

LEE, Michael. b 45. **d** 07 **p** 08. OLM Chickerell w Fleet *Sarum* 07–11; NSM 11–15; PtO from 15. *45 Lower Way, Chickerell, Weymouth DT3 4AR* T: (01305) 777031 E: michael.lynda@googlemail.com

LEE, Ms Michele Julie. b 57. Open Univ BSc 10. St Mellitus Coll BA 16. **d** 15 **p** 16. NSM Paddington St Steph w St Luke *Lon* from 15; NSM Bayswater from 15; Chapl Chelsea and Westmr Hosp NHS Foundn Trust from 15; Chapl Imp Coll Healthcare NHS Trust from 15. *37 Cumberland Mansions, Nutford Place, London W1H 5ZB* T: (020) 7262 7892 M: 07985-743650 E: m_lee157@sky.com *or* michele.lee@imperial.nhs.uk

LEE, Preb Nicholas Knyvett. b 54. Trin Coll Cam BA 76 MA 77. Cranmer Hall Dur 82. **d** 85 **p** 86. C Brompton H Trin w Onslow Square St Paul *Lon* 85–11; C Onslow Square and S Kensington St Aug from 11; Chapl R Brompton and Harefield NHS Trust 86–90; Chapl R Brompton and Harefield NHS Foundn Trust from 94; Preb St Paul's Cathl *Lon* from 16. *St Paul's Church House, Onslow Square, London SW7 3NX* T: 08456-447533 *or* (020) 7052 0324 E: nicky.lee@htb.org.uk

LEE, On Yip Franklin. b 82. York Univ BA 04 MA 06 Leeds Univ MA 07 Cam Univ BTh 12. Westcott Ho Cam 09. **d** 12 **p** 13. C Spalding St Mary and St Nic *Linc* 12–15; Min Can and Succ Windsor 15–18; Chapl St Geo Sch Windsor 15–18; Chapl St Jo Cathl Hong Kong from 18. *St John's Cathedral, 4-8 Garden Road, Central, Hong Kong* E: franklinleeuk@yahoo.co.uk

LEE, Peter. *See* LEE, Kenneth Peter

LEE, Peter Alexander. b 44. Hull Univ BSc(Econ) 65. Ex & Truro NSM Scheme 80. **d** 83 **p** 84. NSM Ex St Sidwell and St Matt 83–89; NSM Ex St Dav 90–98; C Paignton St Jo 98–01; PtO 01–03; Hon C Ex St Dav from 03. *Windyridge, Beech Avenue, Exeter EX4 6HF* T: (01392) 254118

LEE, Peter Kenneth. b 44. Selw Coll Cam BA 66 MA 69. Cuddesdon Coll 67. **d** 69 **p** 70. C Manston *Ripon* 69–72; C Bingley All SS *Bradf* 72–77; Chapl Bingley Coll of Educn 72–77; V Cross Roads cum Lees *Bradf* 77–90; V Auckland St Pet *Dur* 90–09; Tutor NEOC 91–09; rtd 09; Tutor NEITE 03–10; PtO *York* 10–18. *Mount Vale Care Home, The Mount, Yafforth Road, Northallerton DL7 8UE* T: (01609) 775444

LEE, Canon Raymond John. b 30. St Edm Hall Ox BA 53 MA 57. Tyndale Hall Bris 54. **d** 56 **p** 57. C Tooting Graveney St Nic *S'wark* 56–59; C Muswell Hill St Jas *Lon* 59–62; V Woking St Mary *Guildf* 62–70; V Gt Crosby St Luke *Liv* 70–82; Dioc Adv NSM 79–95; V Allerton 82–94; P-in-c Altcar 94–98; Hon Can Liv Cathl 89–95; rtd 95; PtO *Liv* from 98. *15 Barkfield Lane, Liverpool L37 1LY* T: (01704) 872670 E: rjlee@btinternet.com

LEE, Rebecca Susan. *See* HARRIS, Rebecca Susan

LEE, Richard. *See* LEE, Thomas Richard

LEE, Robert David. QUB BD 75. CITC 77. **d** 77 **p** 78. C Comber *D & D* 77–83; I Mt Merrion 83–87; CMS 89–92; Egypt 89–97; R Peebles *Edin* 97–11; P-in-c Innerleithen 97–11; rtd 11; LtO *Edin* from 11; PtO *Eur* from 17. *Flat 6, 32 Montgomery Street, Edinburgh EH7 5JS* T: 0131-623 1850 E: robindavidlee@gmail.com

LEE, Roderick James. b 50. Linc Th Coll 88. **d** 90 **p** 91. C Rushden w Newton Bromswold *Pet* 90–93; C Kingsthorpe w Northampton St Dav 93–94; TV 94–99; R Mears Ashby and Hardwick and Sywell etc 99–04; P-in-c Corby St Columba 04–12; RD Corby 07–12; rtd 12; Chapl Northants Fire and Rescue Service *Pet* 08–15. *79 Stanley Road, Northampton NN5 5EH* M: 07806-262822 E: revrjl@btinternet.com

LEE, Sang Youn (Andrew). b 65. Pontifical Gregorian Univ BPh 95 BTh 98 MTh 00. St Steph Ho Ox 10. **d** 98 **p** 99. In RC Ch 98–06; C Goldthorpe w Hickleton *Sheff* 12–14; P-in-c Dalton from 14; P-in-c Ryecroft St Nic from 14. *The Vicarage, 2 Vicarage Close, Rotherham S65 3QL* M: 07870-885705 E: frandrewlee@yahoo.co.kr

LEE, Steven Michael. b 56. Van Mildert Coll Dur BA 78. Trin Coll Bris 80. **d** 83 **p** 84. C Beckenham St Jo *Roch* 83–86; C Leic Martyrs 86–90; V Coalville and Bardon Hill 90–95; P-in-c Kibworth and Smeeton Westerby and Saddington 95–00; P-in-c Foxton w Gumley and Laughton 96–00; R Kibworth and Smeeton Westerby and Saddington 00–06; Chapl St Lawr Coll Ramsgate 06–08; R Newcastle w Butterton *Lich* 08–14; V Holmer w Huntington *Heref* from 14. *The New Vicarage, Holmer, Hereford HR4 9RG* T: (01432) 273200 E: revslee@btinternet.com

LEE, Stuart Graham. b 73. Roehampton Inst BA 94. St Steph Ho Ox BTh 00. **d** 00 **p** 01. C Eltham H Trin *S'wark* 00–03; TV Wimbledon 03–10; TV Mortlake w E Sheen 10–16; Chapl Richmond Charities' Almshouses from 16. *The Richmond Charities, 8 The Green, Richmond TW9 1PL* T: (020) 8948 4188 E: stuartlee73@blueyonder.co.uk

LEE, Stuart Michael. b 67. SEITE 06. **d** 09 **p** 10. NSM St Jo on Bethnal Green *Lon* 09–14; NSM Bethnal Green St Barn from 14. *29 Brierly Gardens, London E2 0TE* T: (020) 8980 1699 M: 07855-703766 E: stuartm.lee@virgin.net *or* stuartmlee@me.com

LEE, Thomas Richard. b 52. AKC 73 FRSA 03. St Aug Coll Cant 74. **d** 75 **p** 76. C Leam Lane CD *Dur* 75–80; Chapl RAF 80–09; Prin Armed Forces Chapl Cen Amport Ho 03–06; Hon C St Mary le Strand w St Clem Danes *Lon* 06–09; QHC 06–09; TR Egremont and Haile *Carl* 09–18; Regional Chapl (N) RAF Air Cadets 16–18; rtd 18. *20 Abbey Vale, St Bees CA27 0EF* M: 07841-398088 E: lee535877@aol.com

LEE, Veronica. b 47. Redland Coll of Educn TCert 68 Open Univ BA 84 Bris Poly MEd 89. STETS 02. **d** 05 **p** 06. NSM Bishopston and St Andrews *Bris* 05–17; P-in-c Bris Lockleaze St Mary Magd w St Fran 17–19; PtO from 19. *48 Chesterfield Road, Bristol BS6 5DL* T: 0117-949 8325 E: vronlee@hotmail.com

LEE, Young. b 75. Korea Univ BA 98. St Mellitus Coll BA 12. **d** 12 **p** 13. C Walthamstow *Chelmsf* 12–15; P-in-c Barking St Erkenwald from 15. *St Erkenwald Vicarage, Levett Road, Barking IG11 9JZ* T: (020) 8507 9017 M: 07800-969706

LEE-BARBER, Evelyn Mary. b 62. **d** 13 **p** 14. NSM Bath Abbey w St Jas *B & W* from 13. *6 Cranhill Road, Bath BA1 2YF* T: (01225) 421417 M: 07920-847322 E: evelyn@evelynleebarber.plus.com

LEE-PHILPOT, Derreck Anthony John. b 56. Ripon Coll Cuddesdon 08. **d** 11 **p** 12. NSM Cholsey and Moulsford *Ox* 11–16; C Seaford w Sutton *Chich* from 16. *St Luke's House, Seaford Road, Seaford BN25 3SP* T: (01323) 893391 E: derreck3147@gmail.com *or* dlp@seafordparish.org.uk

LEECE, Roderick Neil Stephen. b 59. Wadh Coll Ox BA 81 MA 85 Leeds Univ BA 84 ARCM 85. Coll of Resurr Mirfield 82. **d** 85 **p** 86. C Portsea St Mary *Portsm* 85–91; V Stamford Hill St Bart *Lon* 91–05; R Hanover Square St Geo from 05. *21A Down Street, London W1J 7AW* T: (020) 7629 0874 E: rleece@lineone.net *or* rector@stgeorgeshanoversquare.org

LEECH, Pieter-Jan Bosdin. b 73. K Alfred's Coll Win BA 96. St Jo Coll Nottm 08. **d** 10 **p** 11. C Stalham, E Ruston, Brunstead, Sutton and Ingham *Nor* 10–13; R Yare Valley from 13; Jt RD Blofield from 17. *The Rectory, 73 The Street, Brundall, Norwich NR13 5LZ* M: 07504-171311 E: peter.leech@live.co.uk

LEEDS, Archdeacon of. See AYERS, The Ven Paul Nicholas

LEEDS, Bishop of. See BAINES, The Rt Revd Nicholas

LEEKE, Charles Browne. b 39. Stranmillis Coll CertEd 62. CITC 80. **d** 83 **p** 84. C Ballymoney w Finvoy and Rasharkin *Conn* 83–86; I Faughanvale *D & R* 86–97; Chapl Port Londonderry Miss to Seamen 92–97; Bp's Dom Chapl *D & R* 92–96; Can Derry Cathl 96–00; I Drumragh w Mountfield 97–00; Reconciliation Development Officer *D & D* 00–06; Can Dromore Cathl 05–06; rtd 06; I Dromara w Garvaghy *D & D* 08–13. *41 Beechfield Lodge, Aghalee, Craigavon BT67 0GA* T: (028) 9265 0179 M: 07712-870799 E: charlieleeke@yahoo.co.uk

LEEKE, Canon Stephen Owen. b 50. EAMTC 82 Ridley Hall Cam 83. **d** 84 **p** 85. C Cherry Hinton St Andr *Ely* 84–87; P-in-c Warboys 87–91; P-in-c Bury 87–91; P-in-c Wistow 87–91; R Warboys w Broughton and Bury w Wistow 91–01; RD St Ives 92–01; V Cambridge St Martin 01–15; Hon Can Ely Cathl 05–15; rtd 15; PtO *Ely* from 15. *11 Sycamore Lane, Ely CB7 4TP* E: stephen.leeke9@gmail.com *or* stephen@leeke.me.uk

LEEMAN, Miss Penelope Anne. b 51. SNWTP 10. **d** 12 **p** 13. C Kirkdale St Athanaseus with St Mary *Liv* 12–16; C Maghull and Melling 17–19; rtd 19. *10 Garth Court, Haigh Road, Liverpool L22 3XL* E: pleeman22@gmail.com

LEEMING, Jack. b 34. Kelham Th Coll 56. **d** 61 **p** 62. C Sydenham St Phil *S'wark* 61–64; Chapl RAF 64–84; Chapl Salisbury Gen Infirmary 84–89; R Barford St Martin, Dinton, Baverstock etc *Sarum* 89–99; rtd 99; PtO *Sarum* 01–11.

8 Bower Gardens, Salisbury SP1 2RL T: (01722) 416800 E: leeming454@btinternet.com

LEES (née LESLIE), Mrs Amanda Louise Thornton. b 69. Univ Coll Dur BA 90. St Jo Coll Nottm MA 16. **d** 16 **p** 17. NSM Blidworth w Rainworth *S'well* 16–18; Bp's Dom Chapl from 18. *Wesley House, Forest Road, Oxton, Southwell NG25 0SZ* T: 0115-965 2946 M: 07809-279835 E: wesleyhouse@btinternet.com

LEES, Brian James. b 52. Lon Univ BA 74 Leeds Univ BA 00 Univ of Wales (Abth) PGCE 75. NOC 05. **d** 08 **p** 09. NSM Hutton Cranswick w Skerne, Watton and Beswick *York* 08–11; P-in-c 11–16; P-in-c Nafferton w Wansford 14–16; rtd 16. *The Old Post House, 20 Main Street, Beswick, Driffield YO25 9AS* T: (01377) 270806 E: brianjlees@tiscali.co.uk

LEES, Charles Alan. b 38. RGN TCert. WMMTC 78. **d** 81 **p** 82. NSM Yardley St Cypr Hay Mill *Birm* 81–84 and 86–87; Hon C Dorridge 84–86; Chapl E Birm Hosp 85–87; Hon C Leamington Spa H Trin and Old Milverton *Cov* 89–90; PtO *Birm* 95–01. *8 Fairlawn Close, Leamington Spa CV32 6EN*

LEES, Christopher John. b 58. Fitzw Coll Cam BA 80 Birkbeck Coll Lon MA 86 FCIPD. NOC 01. **d** 04 **p** 05. NSM Wilmslow *Ches* 04–14; Asst Dir of Ords 07–14; C Colyton, Musbury, Southleigh and Branscombe *Ex* from 15. *3 Vicarage Street, Colyton EX24 6LJ* T: (01297) 551351 E: info@johnleescareers.com

LEES, Jane. b 62. Ripon Coll Cuddesdon 05. **d** 07 **p** 08. NSM Ox St Matt from 07. *36 Canning Crescent, Oxford OX1 4XB* T: (01865) 250672 *or* 251616

LEES, John Raymond. b 57. Selw Coll Cam BA 78 MA 82. St Steph Ho Ox 89. **d** 91 **p** 92. C Eastbourne St Mary *Chich* 91–93; Min Can and Succ St Paul's Cathl *Lon* 93–98; TR Swindon New Town *Bris* 98–01; Asst to AD Swindon and C Highworth w Sevenhampton and Inglesham etc 01–02; PtO *Lon* 02–05; *Pet* 04–06; *Ely* 04–06; Can Res and Prec Wakef Cathl 06–09; rtd 09; PtO *Lich* 09–14; *Nor* from 14; Hon PV Nor Cathl from 15. *The Beeches, 58 Church Lane, Sprowston, Norwich NR7 8AZ*

LEES, Joshua Marcus. b 91. Staffs Univ BA 13 MA 16. Wycliffe Hall Ox MTh 19. **d** 19. C Onslow Square and S Kensington St Aug *Lon* from 19. *Address withheld by request* E: josh.lees@htb.org

LEES, Mrs Kathleen Marion. b 30. Birkbeck Coll Lon BA 60. S'wark Ord Course 77. dss 80 **d** 87 **p** 94. Epping St Jo *Chelmsf* 80–86; Hon C Hunstanton St Mary w Ringstead Parva, Holme etc *Nor* 87–88; PtO 88–94; Chapl King's Lynn and Wisbech Hosps NHS Trust 94–00; NSM Gaywood *Nor* 94–00; rtd 00; PtO *Nor* 00–16; *Chich* from 16. *24 Ramsay Hall, 9-13 Byron Road, Worthing BN11 3HN*

LEES, Peter John. b 39. St Jo Coll Nottm 91. **d** 95 **p** 96. NSM Buckie and Turriff *Ab* 95–00; P-in-c Fraserburgh 00–01; R 01–06; rtd 06; P-in-c Turriff *Ab* 08–09; LtO from 15. *7 Whitefield Court, Buckie AB56 1EY* T: (01542) 835011 M: 07929-668027

LEES, Stephen. b 55. St Jo Coll York CertEd 77 BEd 78 Nottm Univ MA 96. St Jo Coll Nottm 88. **d** 90 **p** 91. C Mansfield St Jo *S'well* 90–93; TV Bestwood 93–98; V Baxenden *Blackb* 98–08; P-in-c Halifax All SS *Wakef* 08–14; *Leeds* 14–18; V from 18. *All Saints' Vicarage, Arden Road, Halifax HX3 0LP* T: (01422) 251016 E: theleeslot@blueyonder.co.uk

LEES, Stephen David. b 63. Sheff City Poly BA 84 Bradf Coll of Educn PGCE 92 St Jo Coll Dur BA 09. Cranmer Hall Dur 07. **d** 09 **p** 10. C Frizinghall St Marg *Bradf* 09–13; C Wrose 13–14; C Bolton St Jas w St Chrys 13–14; V 14; *Leeds* from 14. *St James's Vicarage, 1056 Bolton Road, Bradford BD2 4LH* T: (01274) 772097 E: stelees51@gmail.com *or* steve.lees@leeds.anglican.org

LEES, Stuart Charles Roderick. b 62. Trin Coll Bris BA. **d** 89 **p** 90. C Woodford Wells *Chelmsf* 89–93; C Brompton H Trin w Onslow Square St Paul *Lon* 93–97; Chapl Stewards Trust 93–97; P-in-c Fulham Ch Ch *Lon* 97–03; V from 03. *Christ Church Vicarage, 40 Clancarty Road, London SW6 3AA* T: (020) 7736 4261 E: stuart@ccfulham.com

LEES-SMITH, Anthony James. b 77. Selw Coll Cam BA 99 MA 02 St Jo Coll Dur BA 08 MA 09 Westmr Inst of Educn PGCE 02. Cranmer Hall Dur 06. **d** 09 **p** 10. C Chesterton Gd Shep *Ely* 09–12; V Evington *Leic* from 12. *The Vicarage, Rectory Gardens, Leicester LE2 2FU* T: 0116-215 5500 M: 07967-353857 E: singers99@virginmedia.com

LEESE, Mrs Jane Elizabeth. b 50. Man Univ BA(Econ) 72 Avery Hill Coll PGCE 73. Sarum Th Coll 93. **d** 96 **p** 97. NSM Kempshott *Win* 96–01; NSM Herriard w Winslade and Long Sutton etc 01–08; NSM N Hants Downs 08–16; rtd 16; PtO *Win* from 16; Clergy Widows and Widowers Officer (Win Adnry) from 16. *15 Waverley Avenue, Basingstoke RG21 3JN* M: 07754-296994 E: reverendjane@hotmail.co.uk

LEESON, Bernard Alan. b 47. Bris Univ CertEd 68 Open Univ BA 75 Southn Univ MA 78 Sheff Univ PhD 97 FCollP 92 FRSA 92. EMMTC 84. **d** 87 **p** 88. Dep Hd Master Ripley Mill Hill Sch 80–91; NSM Breadsall *Derby* 87–91; Hd St Aid C of E Tech Coll Lancs 91–06; NSM Officer *Blackb* 92–96; Clergy Support and Development Officer 06–09; PtO 91–92; LtO 92–17; rtd 17; PtO *Blackb* from 17. *The Lodge, Daggers Lane, Preesall, Poulton-le-Fylde FY6 0QN* T: (01253) 811020 E: leeson@mail.org

LEFFLER, Christopher. b 33. Em Coll Cam BA 57 MA 61. Linc Th Coll. **d** 59 **p** 60. C Bermondsey St Mary w St Olave and St Jo *S'wark* 59–60; C Herne Hill St Paul 60–63; C-in-c Canley CD *Cov* 63–67; R Gt and Lt Glemham *St E* 67–72; R Badwell Ash w Gt Ashfield, Stowlangtoft etc 72–82; R Trimley 82–99; rtd 99; PtO *St E* from 99. *308 High Street, Felixstowe IP11 9QJ* T: (01394) 672279 M: 07765-785958 E: chrisleffler@uwclub.net

LEFFLER, Jeremy Paul (Jem). b 62. Westmr Coll Ox BEd 88. Wycliffe Hall Ox BTh 94. **d** 94 **p** 95. C Ormskirk *Liv* 94–97; C Much Woolton 97–00; P-in-c Widnes St Ambrose 00–03; V 03–12; P-in-c Birkdale St Jo from 12. *St John's Vicarage, 17 Kirkstall Road, Southport PR8 4RA* T: (01704) 568914 E: vicar@stjohnsbirkdale.co.uk

LEFROY, John Perceval. b 40. Trin Coll Cam BA 62. Cuddesdon Coll 64. **d** 66 **p** 67. C Maidstone St Martin *Cant* 66–69; C St Peter-in-Thanet 69–74; V Barming Heath 74–82; V Upchurch w Lower Halstow 82–05; P-in-c Iwade 95–05; rtd 05; PtO *Sarum* from 06. *23 Heather Avenue, Melksham SN12 6FX* T: (01225) 704012 E: jclefroy@tiscali.co.uk

LEFROY, Matthew William. b 62. Trin Coll Cam BA 84 Keele Univ PGCE 91. St Jo Coll Nottm MTh 02. **d** 02 **p** 03. C Portswood Ch Ch *Win* 02–06; TV Madeley *Heref* 06–13; RD Telford Severn Gorge 11–13; V Lilleshall and Muxton *Lich* from 13. *The Vicarage, 25 Church Road, Lilleshall, Newport TF10 9HE* T: (01952) 604281

LEFROY-OWEN, Neal. b 62. Bradf Univ BA 99. NOC 00. **d** 03 **p** 04. C Sandal St Cath *Wakef* 03–06; Asst Chapl HM Pris Hull 06–08; Chapl HM Pris Lindholme 08–12; Chapl HM Pris Wakef 12–14; P-in-c Warley *Leeds* 15–16; P-in-c Halifax St Hilda 15–16; V Warley and Halifax St Hilda 16–17. *2 Kitten Clough, Halifax HX2 0JJ* E: revneal.owen@gmail.com

LEGG, Adrian James. b 52. St Jo Coll Nottm BTh 82. **d** 82 **p** 83. C Haughton le Skerne *Dur* 82–85; C Lisnashen and Lisvane *Llan* 85–89; V Llanwddyn and Llanfihangel-yng-Nghwynfa etc *St As* 89–93; V Llansadwrn w Llanwrda and Manordeilo *St D* 93–10; Chapl Wadham Sch Crewkerne 11–15; C Yeovil St Mich *B & W* 12–14; PtO *S & B* from 15; *St D* from 17. *Llys Esgob, Abergwili, Carmarthen SA31 2JG* E: adrianlegg@btinternet.com

LEGG, Alison Grant. *See* MILBANK, Alison Grant

LEGG, Joanna Susan Penberthy. *See* PENBERTHY, Joanna Susan

LEGG, Margaret. b 50. SEITE. **d** 07 **p** 08. NSM Paddington St Jo w St Mich *Lon* from 07. *Flat 2, 134 Elgin Avenue, London W9 2NS* T: (020) 3536 9866 E: Margaret.rose.legg@gmail.com

LEGG, Richard. b 37. Selw Coll Cam BA 62 MA 66 Brunel Univ MPhil 77 NY Th Sem DMin 85. Coll of Resurr Mirfield 63. **d** 65 **p** 66. C Ealing St Pet Mt Park *Lon* 65–68; Chapl Brunel Univ 68–78; Wychcroft Ho (Dioc Retreat Cen) *S'wark* 78–81; C Chipping Barnet w Arkley *St Alb* 81–83; TV 83–85; R St Buryan, St Levan and Sennen *Truro* 85–93; Subwarden St Deiniol's Lib Hawarden 93; PtO *Ches* 93; TV Beaminster Area *Sarum* 93–97; P-in-c Veryan w Ruan Lanihorne *Truro* 97–00; rtd 01; PtO *Truro* 03–09; *B & W* 10–18. *27A Bath Road, Wells BA5 3HR* T: (01749) 670468 E: richardlegg@blue-earth.co.uk

LEGG, Roger Keith. b 35. Lich Th Coll 61. **d** 63 **p** 64. C Petersfield w Sheet *Portsm* 63–66; C Portsea St Mary 66–70; Rhodesia 70–75; V Clayton *Lich* 75–00; rtd 01; PtO *Lich* 01–14. *High Crest, Chapel Lane, Hookgate, Market Drayton TF9 4QP* T: (01630) 672766 E: rogjud@talktalk.net

LEGG, Miss Ruth Helen Margaret. b 52. Hull Univ BA 74 Homerton Coll Cam CertEd 75. Trin Coll Bris 86. **d** 88 **p** 94. C Clevedon St Andr and Ch Ch *B & W* 88–92; C Nailsea Ch Ch 92–96; C Nailsea Ch Ch w Tickenham 96–97; V Pill, Portbury and Easton-in-Gordano 97–16; rtd 16; PtO *Sarum* from 17. *Flat 11 Sunridge Shades, 11-15 Belle Vue Road, Poole BH14 8TW* E: ruthhmlegg@gmail.com

LEGG, Sandra Christine. *See* FACCINI, Sandra Christine

LEGGATE, Colin Archibald Gunson. b 44. Bris Sch of Min 86. **d** 88 **p** 89. NSM Brislington St Luke *Bris* 88–97; Asst Chapl Frenchay Healthcare NHS Foundation Bris 97–99; Asst Chapl N Bris NHS Trust 99–09; rtd 09; PtO *Heref* from 09. *5 Merrivale Crescent, Ross-on-Wye HR9 5JU* T: (01989) 564536 E: colin.leggate@tiscali.co.uk

LEGGE, Mrs Anne Christine. b 53. Ex Univ BA 73 BPhil 76 PGCE 94. Trin Coll Bris BA 10. **d** 10 **p** 11. C Newton Ferrers w Revelstoke *Ex* 10–13; P-in-c from 13; C Holbeton 11–13; P-in-c from 13; RD Ivybridge from 17. *The Rectory, 8 Court Road, Newton Ferrers, Plymouth PL8 1DL* T: (01752) 873192 M: 07929-153132 E: annelegge@live.com

LEGGE, Robert James. b 63. BSc 92. Ox Min Course. **d** 09 **p** 10. C Walton H Trin *Ox* 09–13; TV Kidderminster E *Worc* from 13. *38 Comberton Avenue, Kidderminster DY10 3EG* M: 07809-227660 E: rjlegge@live.co.uk

LEGGE, Trevor Raymond. b 42. Liv Univ BEng 63. **d** 11 **p** 12. NSM Oughtrington and Warburton *Ches* 11–16; PtO from 16. *17 Wychwood Avenue, Lymm WA13 0NE* T: (01925) 756872 E: trlegge@talktalk.net

LEGGETT, James Henry Aufrere. b 61. Oak Hill Th Coll 91. **d** 93 **p** 94. C Hensingham *Carl* 93–97; C-in-c Ryde St Jas Prop Chpl *Portsm* from 97. *84 Pellhurst Road, Ryde PO33 3BS* T: (01983) 565621 or 566381 E: james.leggett@stjamesryde.com

LEGGETT, Nicholas William Michael. b 62. Glos Univ BA 10. St Steph Ho Ox 00. **d** 02 **p** 04. C Clevedon St Jo *B & W* 02–06; P-in-c Bridgwater H Trin and Durleigh 06–07; V 07–10; V Tile Hill *Cov* 10–18; R Chenderit *Pet* from 18; Hon Chapl ATC from 04; CF(V) from 12. *Chenderit Rectory, 17 Astrop Road, Middleton Cheney, Banbury OX17 2PG* M: 07925-419068 E: leggett1uwe@yahoo.co.uk

LEGH, Mrs Jane Mary. b 52. Southn Univ BSc 73. Qu Coll Birm 08. **d** 09 **p** 10. NSM S Dales *Derby* from 09; NSM Boylestone, Church Broughton, Dalbury, etc from 09; P-in-c from 17. *Cubley Lodge, Cubley, Ashbourne DE6 2FB* T: (01335) 330297 E: jane.legh@cubleylodge.com

LEGOOD, Giles Leslie. b 67. K Coll Lon BD 88 AKC 88 Heythrop Coll Lon MTh 98 Derby Univ DMin 04. Ripon Coll Cuddesdon 90. **d** 92 **p** 93. C N Mymms *St Alb* 92–95; Chapl R Veterinary Coll Lon 95–07; Chapl R Free and Univ Coll Medical Sch 95–07; Chapl RAuxAF 04–07; Chapl RAF from 07; QHC from 18. *Chaplaincy Services (RAF), HQ Air Command, RAF High Wycombe HP14 4UE* T: (01494) 496800

LEHANEY, Frank George. b 44. MCIT 75 MILT 99 MIAM 78. **d** 99 **p** 00. OLM Brockham Green *S'wark* 99–07; NSM 07–14; OLM Leigh 99–07; NSM 07–14; Chapl Surrey and Sussex Healthcare NHS Trust 99–09; PtO *S'wark* from 14. *Twelve Trees, Small's Hill Road, Leigh, Reigate RH2 8PE* T: (01306) 611201

LEICESTER, Archdeacon of. *See* WORSFOLD, The Ven Richard Vernon

LEICESTER, Bishop of. *See* SNOW, The Rt Revd Martyn James

LEICESTER, Dean of. *See* MONTEITH, The Very Revd David Robert Malvern

LEIGH, Mrs Alison Margaret. b 40. CertEd 63 Goldsmiths' Coll Lon BEd 75. Sarum & Wells Th Coll 85. **d** 87 **p** 94. C Chessington *Guildf* 87–90; C Green Street Green *Roch* 90–92; Dn-in-c E Peckham and Nettlestead 92–94; P-in-c 94–95; R 95–01; rtd 01; PtO *Heref* from 02. *17 Orchard Green, Marden, Hereford HR1 3ED* T: (01432) 882032 E: alison.leigh@which.net

LEIGH, Mary Elizabeth. b 42. K Coll Lon BA 64 Univ of Wales (Lamp) MMin 06. Westcott Ho Cam 89. **d** 91 **p** 94. NSM Chesterfield St Mary and All SS *Derby* 91–92; C Hall Green Ascension *Birm* 92–94; Asst P Yardley St Edburgha 94–97; Chapl and Tutor NOC 97–08; rtd 08; PtO *Lich* 99–11; *Derby* from 14; *Lon* 16–19. *Downing Cottage, Jaggers Lane, Hathersage, Hope Valley S32 1AZ* T: (01433) 650567 M: 07796-980636 E: mel@leigh.me

LEIGH, Michael John. b 69. Leeds Univ BA 02 LWCMD 93. Coll of Resurr Mirfield 00. **d** 02 **p** 03. C N Hull St Mich *York* 02–06; P-in-c Newby 06–14; V from 14; V Cloughton and Burniston w Ravenscar etc from 14; RD Scarborough from 16. *St Mark's Vicarage, 77 Green Lane, Scarborough YO12 6HT* T: (01723) 363205 E: mike@singingvicar.co.uk

LEIGH, Nathan Daniel. b 90. Moorlands Coll BA 17. St Mellitus Coll MA 19. **d** 19. NSM Southampton (St Mary) *Win* from 19. *St Matthew's Vicarage, 12-14 Kings Park Road, Southampton SO15 2AT* M: 07434-958002 E: nathan.l2012la@gmail.com

LEIGH, Raymond. b 37. Lon Univ BEd 81. Clifton Th Coll 65. **d** 68 **p** 69. C Chadwell *Chelmsf* 68–71; Chapl RAF 71–77; Asst Teacher Swakeleys Sch Hillingdon 81–82; Hd RE 83–88; NSM Hillingdon St Jo *Lon* 87–88; C Rowley Regis *Birm* 88–90; V Londonderry 90–95; R Westbury w Turweston, Shalstone and Biddlesden *Ox* 95–99; CF (ACF) 95–02; rtd 99; PtO *Chich* 99–07; *Guildf* 07–14 and 16–18. *32 Wellington Court, 34-42 Waterloo Road, Epsom KT19 8EX* T: (01372) 436114 E: rayleigh093@gmail.com

LEIGH, Richenda Mary Celia. *See* WHEELER, Richenda Mary Celia

LEIGH-HUNT, Nicolas Adrian. b 46. MIEx 70. Qu Coll Birm 85. **d** 87 **p** 88. C Tilehurst St Geo *Ox* 87–91; TV

Wexcombe *Sarum* 91–99; TR 99–02; TR Savernake 02–11; RD Pewsey 97–10; rtd 11; PtO *Sarum* from 15. *Steeles Cottage, 22 Eastcourt, Burbage, Marlborough SN8 3AG* T: (01672) 810953 E: leighhunt@aol.com

LEIGHTON, Alan Granville Clyde. b 37. MInstM AMIDHE. S'wark Ord Course 73. **d** 76 **p** 77. C Silverhill St Matt *Chich* 76–79; C Eston *York* 79–82; V 82–84; TR Eston w Normanby 84–02; rtd 02; PtO *York* 02–15. *Priory Lodge, 86B Church Lane, Eston, Middlesbrough TS6 9QR* T: (01642) 504798 F: 283016

LEIGHTON, Anthony Robert. b 56. Trin Coll Bris BA 88. **d** 88 **p** 89. C Harrow Trin St Mich *Lon* 88–92; TV Ratby cum Groby *Leic* 92–94; TR Bradgate Team 94–00; P-in-c Newtown Linford 95–98; V Thorpe Acre w Dishley 00–08; NSM S Croxton Gp 08–14; Master Wyggeston's Hosp Leic from 14; NSM Leic H Apostles from 14. *The Master's House, Wyggeston's Hospital, 160 Hinckley Road, Leicester LE3 0UX* T: 0116-254 8682 E: tony0leighton@btinternet.com

LEIGHTON, Mrs Catherine Mary Alexandra. b 72. Surrey Univ BMus 93 Man Metrop Univ PGCE 08. Trin Coll Bris 16. **d** 18 **p** 19. C Tettenhall Regis *Lich* from 18. *12 Windmill Lane, Wolverhampton WV3 8HJ* M: 07903-164242 E: cmaleighton@icloud.com

LEIGHTON, Simon Andrew. b 90. Lon Sch of Th BA 13. Trin Coll Bris 16. **d** 18 **p** 19. C Lawrence Weston and Avonmouth *Bris* from 18. *11 Severn Road, Shirehampton, Bristol BS11 9TE* M: 07876-613629 E: revsimonleighton@gmail.com

LEIGHTON, Mrs Susan. b 58. Bretton Hall Coll BEd 80. Trin Coll Bris BA 89. **d** 89 **p** 94. Par Dn Harrow Weald All SS *Lon* 89–92; NSM Ratby cum Groby *Leic* 92–96; C Bradgate Team 96–00; Asst Warden of Readers 96–00; NSM Thorpe Acre w Dishley 00–08; TV S Croxton Gp 08–10; P-in-c 10–14; P-in-c Burrough Hill Pars 10–14; NSM Leic Martyrs 15–17; P-in-c Leic St Theodore from 17; Chapl for Deaf People from 15. *The Master's House, Wyggeston's Hospital, 160 Hinckley Road, Leicester LE3 0UX* T: 0116-254 8682 M: 07766-476490 E: susan.leighton2@btinternet.com

LEIPER, Nicholas Keith. b 34. SS Coll Cam BA 55 MB 58 BChir 58 MA 65. St Jo Coll Nottm LTh 82. **d** 84 **p** 85. C Bidston *Ches* 84–87; TV Gateacre *Liv* 87–92; P-in-c Bickerstaffe 92–94; P-in-c Melling 92–94; V Bickerstaffe and Melling 94–00; rtd 00; PtO *Liv* from 00. *31 Weldale House, Chase Close, Southport PR8 2DX* T: (01704) 566393

LEITCH, Peter William. b 36. FCA 58 ATII 59. Coll of Resurr Mirfield 83. **d** 85 **p** 86. C Newsome and Armitage Bridge *Wakef* 85–88; P-in-c Upper Hopton 88–91; P-in-c Mirfield Eastthorpe St Paul 88–91; Chapl Rouen Miss to Seamen *Eur* 92–94; Sen Chapl Rotterdam Miss to Seamen 94–97; Chapl Felixstowe Miss to Seafarers *St E* 97–01; rtd 01; PtO *St E* from 01. *104 St Andrew's Road, Felixstowe IP11 7ED* T: (01394) 285320

LEITHEAD, Mrs Lynette. b 54. Kent Univ BA 08. SEITE. **d** 08 **p** 09. NSM Kippington *Roch* 08–13 and from 17; NSM Sundridge w Ide Hill and Toys Hill 13–16; PtO 16–17. *45 Chipstead Park, Sevenoaks TN13 2SL* T: (01732) 742272 M: 07958-145959 E: lynetteleithead@hotmail.co.uk

LEMMEY, William Henry Michael. b 59. Jes Coll Cam BA 81 Jes Coll Ox PGCE 82. Westcott Ho Cam 03. **d** 05 **p** 06. C Milton *Win* 05–09; R Porlock and Porlock Weir w Stoke Pero etc *B & W* from 09. *The Rectory, Parsons Street, Porlock, Minehead TA24 8QL* T: (01643) 863135 E: billlemmey@yahoo.co.uk

LENG, Bruce Edgar. b 38. St Aid Birkenhead 68. **d** 69 **p** 70. C Sheff St Swithun 69–74; TV Yate New Town *Bris* 78–82; R Handsworth *Sheff* 82–95; R Thrybergh 95–05; Warden for Past Workers 96–05; rtd 05; PtO *Sheff* from 06. *41 Hall Close Avenue, Whiston, Rotherham S60 4AH* M: 07908-448337 E: brucelenguk@gmail.com

LENNOX, Joan Baxter. See LYON, Joan Baxter

LENNOX, Mark. Ulster Univ BA St Jo Coll Nottm MA. CITC. **d** 09 **p** 10. NSM Maghera w Killelagh *D & R* 09–12; NSM Camus-juxta-Mourne 12–15; Bp's C 15–18; I Killyman *Arm* from 18. *The Rectory, 85 Dungorman Road, Dungannon BT71 6SE* T: (028) 8772 2324 or 8772 2500 M: 07752-152991 E: mark.lennox6@btopenworld.com *or* killyman@armagh.anglican.org

LENOX-CONYNGHAM, Canon Andrew George. b 44. Magd Coll Ox BA 65 MA 73 CCC Cam PhD 73. Westcott Ho Cam 72. **d** 74 **p** 75. C Poplar *Lon* 74–77; TV 77–80; Chapl Heidelberg *Eur* 80–82; 91–95; Chapl R Marsden Hosp 95–96; Chapl Ch Coll Cam 82–86; Chapl and Fell St Cath Coll Cam 86–91; V Birm St Luke 91–94; AD Cen Birm 04–12; Hon Can Birm Cathl 14; rtd 14; PtO *Birm* from 14. *9 Hitches Lane, Birmingham B15 2LS* T: 0121-446 6783 E: lenox@birm.eclipse.co.uk

LENS VAN RIJN, Robert Adriaan. b 47. St Jo Coll Nottm 78. **d** 80 **p** 81. C Gt Baddow *Chelmsf* 80–83; C Edgware *Lon* 83–86;

C Derby St Pet and Ch Ch w H Trin 86–90; Chapl Eindhoven *Eur* 91–00; Chapl Burrswood Chr Cen 04–08; rtd 08; PtO *York* 09–18; Chapl Dove Ho Hospice Hull 09–18. *De Jongestraat 3, 4453 BP 's-Heerenhoek, The Netherlands* T: (0031) (113) 268763 E: rlvr@iae.nl

LENTHALL, Mrs Nicola Yvonne. b 73. Southn Univ BA 95. Westcott Ho Cam. **d** 99 **p** 00. C Leighton Buzzard w Eggington, Hockliffe etc *St Alb* 99–03; V Kensworth, Studham and Whipsnade from 03; RD Dunstable from 19. *The Vicarage, Clay Hall Road, Kensworth, Dunstable LU6 3RF* T: (01582) 872223

LENTON, John Robert. b 46. Ex Coll Ox BA 69 Harvard Univ MBA 74. Oak Hill Th Coll. **d** 00 **p** 02. NSM Muswell Hill St Jas w St Matt *Lon* 00–09; NSM Hampstead St Jo Downshire Hill Prop Chpl 09–10; NSM Bramley *Win* 10–14; NSM Sherfield-on-Loddon and Stratfield Saye etc from 14. *Bramley Vicarage, Silchester Road, Bramley, Tadley RG26 5DQ* T: (01256) 880570 M: 07714-237235 E: john.lenton@gmail.com

LENTON, Sarah Edwina. b 48. K Coll Lon BD 72. St Mellitus Coll 15. **d** 16 **p** 17. NSM Bedford Park *Lon* 16–18; NSM Covent Garden St Paul from 18; Chapl W End Theatres from 16. *10 Saltcoats Road, London W4 1AR* T: (020) 8994 1380 E: sarah.lenton@virgin.net

LENTON de DICKIN, Mrs Patricia Margarita. b 72. STETS MA 08. **d** 08 **p** 09. C Epsom Common Ch S *Guildf* 08–10; C Oxshott 10–12; P-in-c Mereworth w W Peckham *Roch* 12–19; R Mereworth, Wateringbury and W Peckham 19; TV S Gillingham from 19. *Address temp unknown*

LEON (née HOLLAND), Mrs Lesley Anne. b 52. Univ Coll Chich BA 04. STETS 04. **d** 07 **p** 08. NSM Northanger *Win* from 07; PtO *Portsm* from 11. *11A Tilmore Gardens, Petersfield GU32 2JQ* E: lesley.leon@ntlworld.com

LEONARD, Mrs Andrea Susan. b 60. SEITE 13. **d** 15 **p** 16. C Roch St Justus 15–19; P-in-c Luton Ch Ch from 19. *Address temp unknown* M: 07752-626644 E: andumiak@gmail.com *or* andrea@luton.church

LEONARD, Ms Ann Cressey. b 50. Open Univ BA 90 Lon Univ MA. S Dios Minl Tr Scheme 90. **d** 94 **p** 95. C Portsea St Cuth *Portsm* 94–96; C Farlington 96–00; Asst to RD Petersfield 00–03; Deanery Co-ord for Educn and Tr 00–03; V Hayling Is St Andr 03–15; V N Hayling St Pet 03–15; Dioc Ecum Officer 02–03; rtd 15; PtO *Portsm* from 15. *10 Trent Way, Lee-on-the-Solent PO13 8JF* T: (023) 9263 7673 E: anncleonard@gmail.com

LEONARD, John Francis. b 48. Lich Th Coll 69. **d** 72 **p** 73. C Chorley St Geo *Blackb* 72–75; C S Shore H Trin 75–80; V Marton Moss 81–89; V Kingskerswell w Coffinswell *Ex* 89–18; P-in-c Abbotskerswell 06–18; rtd 18. *Address temp unknown* E: john@w3church.co.uk

LEONARD, Canon John James. b 41. Southn Univ BSc 62. Sarum Th Coll 63. **d** 65 **p** 66. C Loughborough Em *Leic* 65–70; V New Humberstone 70–78; C-in-c Rushey Mead CD 78–85; V Leic St Theodore 85–05; Hon Can Leic Cathl 96–05; RD Christianity N 97–05; rtd 05; PtO *Leic* from 05. *1339 Melton Road, Syston, Leicester LE7 2EP* T: 0116-269 2691 E: j2.leonard@btinternet.com

LEONARD, Nicola Susan. See TERRY, Nicola Susan

LEONARD, The Ven Peter Philip. b 70. Trin Coll Bris BA 94. **d** 97 **p** 98. C Haslemere *Guildf* 97–00; C Haslemere and Grayswood 00–01; C Woodham 01–06; PtO 07–10; *Portsm* 12–14; Can Res Portsm Cathl 14–19; Adn Is of Wight from 19. *5 The Boltons, Wootton Bridge, Ryde PO33 4PB* T: (01983) 884432 M: 07817-722219 E: peterleonard200@gmail.com *or* peter.leonard@portsmouth.anglican.org

LEONARD-JOHNSON, Canon Philip Anthony. b 35. Selw Coll Cam BA 58 MA 60. Linc Th Coll 63. **d** 65 **p** 66. C Wymondham *Nor* 65–68; Zimbabwe 69–82; V Drayton in Hales *Lich* 82–92; R Adderley 82–92; P-in-c Moreton Say 88–92; S Africa 92–98; rtd 97; Hon Can Grahamstown from 97; PtO *Lich* 99–14. *Hillside, Mount Lane, Market Drayton TF9 1AG* T: (01630) 655480 E: philipandjohnson@hotmail.com

LEONARDI, Preb Jeffrey. b 49. Warwick Univ BA 71. Carl Dioc Tr Course 85. **d** 88 **p** 89. C Netherton *Carl* 88–91; V Cross Canonby 91–97; V Allonby 91–97; Bp's Adv for Past Care and Counselling *Lich* 97–14; C Colton, Colwich and Gt Haywood 97–10; C Abbots Bromley, Blithfield, Colton, Colwich etc 11–14; Preb Lich Cathl 12–14; rtd 14; PtO *St D* from 14. *Llwyncelyn, Cribyn, Lampeter SA48 7NH* T: (01570) 470526 E: jeff.leonardi@btinternet.com

LEPINE, Ayla Rowanna. b 83. Victoria Univ (BC) BA 03 Courtauld Inst of Art MA 05 PhD 11 Jes Coll Cam BA 17 MPhil 18. Westcott Ho Cam 15. **d** 18 **p** 19. C Hampstead St Jo *Lon* from 18. *10A Dennington Park Mansions, 267-279 West End Lane, London NW6 1QR* M: 07791-683042 E: ayla.lepine@gmail.com

LEPINE, The Very Revd Jeremy John. b 56. BA. St Jo Coll Nottm 82. **d** 84 **p** 85. C Harrow Trin St Mich *Lon* 84–88; TV Horley *S'wark* 88–95; Evang Adv Croydon Area Miss Team 95–02; Dioc Evang Adv and Hon Chapl S'wark Cathl 97–02; R Wollaton *S'well* 02–13; AD Nottm N 08–13; Hon Can S'well Minster 09–13; Dean Bradf 13–14; *Leeds* from 14. *The Deanery, 1 Cathedral Close, Bradford BD1 4EG* T: (01274) 777722 F: 777730 E: jerry.lepine@bradfordcathedral.org

LEPLEY, Mrs Kim Angela. b 60. St Mellitus Coll BA 12. **d** 12 **p** 13. C Takeley w Lt Canfield *Chelmsf* 12–15; C Gt Wakering w Foulness 15–17; P-in-c 17–19; C Barling w Lt Wakering 15–17; P-in-c 17–19; C Rochford and Sutton w Shopland 15–17; P-in-c 17–19; TR Roach Par from 19. *The Vicarage, 2 New Road, Great Wakering, Southend-on-Sea SS3 0AH* T: (01702) 216725 M: 07540-065837 E: revd.kim@outlook.com

LEPP, Miss Susan Elizabeth. b 76. Alberta Univ BSc 04 Nottm Univ MSc 09. Wycliffe Hall Ox 14. **d** 16 **p** 17. C Langley Marish *Ox* from 16. *21 Palmerston Avenue, Slough SL3 7PU* T: (01753) 901595 M: 07506-802922 E: sues.lepp@gmail.com

LEPPARD, Ms Heather Sian. b 85. Open Univ BA 09 Em Coll Cam BA 14. Westcott Ho Cam 12. **d** 15 **p** 16. C Harnham *Sarum* 15–19; V Old Basing and Lychpit *Win* from 19. *The Vicarage, Church Lane, Old Basing, Basingstoke RG24 7DJ* M: 07745-731729 E: curateheather@gmail.com

LEPPINGTON, Dian Marjorie. b 45. Leeds Univ BA 85. Cranmer Hall Dur 81. **dss** 83 **d** 87 **p** 94. Potternewton *Ripon* 83–85; Ind Chapl 85–97; Chapl Teesside Univ *York* 97–04; Can and Preb York Minster 03–04; Par Resources Adv *Man* 05–14; rtd 13; PtO *Man* 13–17; *York* from 14; *Eur* from 16. *39 Derwent Mews, York YO10 3DN* T: (01904) 500253 E: dleppington.shanks@gmail.com

LERRY, Keith Doyle. b 49. St Mich Coll Llan 69. **d** 72 **p** 73. C Caerau w Ely *Llan* 72–75; C Roath St Martin 75–84; V Glyntaff 84–11; rtd 11. *8 Wenvoe Terrace, Barry CF62 7AS*

LESITER, The Ven Malcolm Leslie. b 37. Selw Coll Cam BA 61 MA 65. Cuddesdon Coll 61. **d** 63 **p** 64. C Eastney *Portsm* 63–66; C Hemel Hempstead *St Alb* 66–71; TV 71–73; V Leavesden 73–88; RD Watford 81–88; V Radlett 88–93; Hon Can St Alb Abbey 90–93; Adn Bedford 93–03; rtd 03; PtO *Ely* 03–08; *Chelmsf* from 04. *349 Ipswich Road, Colchester CO4 0HN* T: (01206) 841479 E: mllesiter@hotmail.com

LESLIE, Christopher James. b 42. Open Univ BA 75. Wycliffe Hall Ox 97. **d** 05 **p** 06. NSM Loddon Reach Ox 05–18; PtO from 18. *Church Farm House, Church Lane, Shinfield, Reading RG2 9BY* T: 0118-988 8642 E: cj.leslie@btinternet.com

LESLIE, David Rodney. b 43. Liv Univ MEd 94 Birm Univ PhD 01 AKC 67. **d** 68 **p** 69. C Belmont *Lon* 68–71; C St Giles Cripplegate w St Bart Moor Lane etc 71–75; TV Kirkby *Liv* 76–84; TR Ditton St Mich 84–98; V Ditton St Mich w St Thos 98–03; V Croxteth Park 03–08; rtd 08; PtO *Ches* from 09. *10 Eversley Close, Frodsham WA6 6AZ* T: (01928) 732463 E: david.leslie3@gmail.com

LESLIE, Canon Richard Charles Alan. b 46. ACIB 71. St Alb Minl Tr Scheme 76. **d** 79 **p** 91. NSM Redbourn *St Alb* 79–88; NSM Newport Pagnell w Lathbury and Moulsoe *Ox* 88–94; Stewardship Adv St Alb Adnry 94–97; TV Borehamwood 97–05; TV Elstree and Borehamwood 05–15; Hon Can St Alb 14–15; rtd 15. *17 George Street, Hemel Hempstead HP2 5HJ* T: (01442) 769834 E: rcaleslie@idreamtime.com

LESTER, David Charles. b 46. BSc. **d** 99 **p** 00. NSM Trowell *S'well* 99–02; NSM Trowell, Awsworth and Cossall 02–06; rtd 06; PtO *York* from 07. *25 Ruby Street, Saltburn-by-the-Sea TS12 1EF* E: d.c.lester@hotmail.co.uk

LESTER, Stephanie Helen. *See* WARRELL, Stephanie Helen

LESTER, Canon Trevor Rashleigh. b 50. CITC 83. **d** 89 **p** 90. NSM Douglas Union w Frankfield *C, C & R* 89–93; Bp's V and Lib Kilkenny Cathl and C Kilkenny w Aghour and Kilmanagh *C & O* 93–95; I Abbeystrewry Union *C, C & R* 95–03; Dean Waterford *C & O* 03–11; I Waterford w Killea, Drumcannon and Dunhill 03–11; I Kilmoe Union *C, C & R* 11–17; Can Cork and Ross Cathls 14–17; rtd 17. *The Old White Farmhouse, Garrendruig, Kilbrittain, Co Cork, Republic of Ireland* M: (00353) 86-313 4617 E: lester@eircom.net

L'ESTRANGE, Timothy John Nicholas. b 67. Surrey Univ BA 90 FRSA 18. St Steph Ho Ox BA 92 MA 96. **d** 93 **p** 94. C Halesworth w Linstead, Chediston, Holton etc *St E* 93–96; Dom Chapl to Bp Horsham *Chich* 96–98; R Beeding and Bramber w Botolphs 98–08; R Monken Hadley *Lon* 08–11; V N Acton St Gabr from 11. *St Gabriel's Vicarage, 15 Balfour Road, London W3 0DG* T: (020) 8259 2138 M: 07845-211617 E: sacerdotal@gmail.com *or* vicar@saintgabrielacton.org

LETALL, Ronald Richard. b 29. ACII 76. Linc Th Coll 82. **d** 84 **p** 85. C Scarborough St Martin *York* 84–86; C Middlesbrough St Thos 86–88; R Kirby Misperton w Normanby, Edston and Salton 88–90; TV Louth *Linc* 90–94; rtd 94; PtO *Sheff* from 95; *Wakef* 95–97; *Chich* from 97. *6 Windlesham Court, Grand Avenue, Worthing BN11 5AE*

LETCHER, Canon David John. b 34. K Coll Lon 54. Chich Th Coll 56. **d** 58 **p** 59. C St Austell *Truro* 58–62; C Southbroom *Sarum* 62–64; R Odstock w Nunton and Bodenham 64–72; RD Alderbury 68–73 and 77–82; V Downton 72–85; Can and Preb Sarum Cathl 79–99; TV Dorchester 85–97; RD 89–95; rtd 97; PtO *Sarum* 97–15; CF 97–00; PtO *Ex* 12–15; *Truro* from 17. *15 Tregavethan View, Threemilestone, Truro TR3 6SS* T: (01872) 274615

LETHBRIDGE, Christopher David. b 43. NOC 90. **d** 93 **p** 94. NSM S Elmsall *Wakef* 93–95; C Knottingley 95–97; R Badsworth 97–01; P-in-c Bilham *Sheff* 01–13; Chapl HM YOI Hatfield 01–03; Chapl HM Pris Moorland 03–12; rtd 13; PtO *Sheff* from 13. *25 Mayfield, Scawthorpe, Doncaster DN5 7UA* T: (01302) 483084

LETHEREN, William Neils. b 37. St Aid Birkenhead 61. **d** 64 **p** 65. C Liv St Mich 64–67; V 71–75; C Kirkdale St Athanasius 67–69; C Walsall Wood *Lich* 69–71; V W Derby St Jas *Liv* 75–84; R Newton in Makerfield Em 84–88; V Garston 88–04; rtd 04; PtO *Liv* from 16. *24 Pitville Avenue, Liverpool L18 7JQ* T: 0151-724 5543

LETSCHKA, Mrs Alison Clare. b 58. Sussex Univ BA 79 Anglia Ruskin Univ BA 08. Westcott Ho Cam 06. **d** 08 **p** 09. C Haywards Heath St Wilfrid *Chich* 08–12; TV Bexley Peak 12–18; P-in-c W Grinstead *Chich* from 18. *Hookshole, Church Road, Partridge Green, Horsham RH13 8JS* M: 07950-152229 E: acletschka@yahoo.co.uk

LETSOM-CURD, Clifford John. *See* CURD, Clifford John Letsom

LEUNG, Peter. b 36. Trin Coll Singapore BTh 60 St Andr Univ PhD 73. SE Asia Sch of Th MTh 69. **d** 60 **p** 61. Singapore 60–62 and 65–76; Br N Borneo 62–63; Malaysia 63–65; Lect Congr Coll Man 76–77; USPG 77–83; PtO Roch 83–89; CCBI 83–90; CTBI from 90; PtO *S'wark* 88–94; Hon C Shortlands Roch 90–01; Regional Sec (S and E Asia) CMS 91–99; rtd 99. *35 Tufton Gardens, West Molesey KT8 1TD* T: (020) 8650 4157

LEVANWAY, William Douglas. b 85. Belmont Univ Nashville BA 07 Vanderbilt Univ (USA) MDiv 12 K Coll Lon PhD 17. St Steph Ho Ox 15. **d** 17 **p** 18. C Fulham All SS *Lon* from 17. *Parish Flat, 70A Fulham High Street, London SW6 3LG* M: 07568-342966 E: willlevanway@gmail.com

LEVASIER, Joanna Mary. b 68. Jes Coll Cam BA 89 MA 90. Wycliffe Hall Ox 07. **d** 09 **p** 10. C Ashtead *Guildf* 09–12; C Burpham from 12. *272 London Road, Guildford GU4 7LF* T: (01483) 853023 E: j.levasier@ntlworld.com *or* jo@burphamchurch.org.uk

LEVELL, Peter John. b 40. Bris Univ BA 62 CertEd 63. STETS 99. **d** 02 **p** 03. NSM Guildf St Sav 02–10; rtd 10; PtO *Guildf* from 11; *Lon* from 15. *23 Mountside, Guildford GU2 4JD* T: (01483) 871656 E: plevell@ntlworld.com

LEVERTON, Mrs Judith. b 55. Eaton Hall Coll of Educn CertEd 76. St Jo Coll Nottm 02. **d** 04 **p** 05. C Doncaster St Jas *Sheff* 04–07; TV Rivers Team 07–15; rtd 15; Chapl to Deaf People *Sheff* 09–15; PtO from 19. *35 Wayford Avenue, Bramley, Rotherham S66 2ST* M: 07960-573529 E: judy.leverton@yahoo.co.uk

LEVERTON, Canon Michael John. b 52. K Coll Lon BD 76 AKC 76 MTh 77. Cant Sch of Min 84. **d** 87 **p** 88. NSM Elham w Denton and Wootton *Cant* 87–92; C Yelverton, Meavy, Sheepstor and Walkhampton *Ex* 92–93; TV 93–98; C Tavistock and Gulworthy 98–00; P-in-c Stevenage All SS Pin Green *St Alb* 00–10; P-in-c Ardeley 10–12; P-in-c Benington w Walkern 10–12; P-in-c Cottered w Broadfield and Throcking 10–12; R Ardeley, Benington, Cottered w Throcking etc 12–19; RD Buntingford 18–19; Hon Can St Alb 14–19; rtd 19. *Address temp unknown* E: michael.leverton@btinternet.com

LEVETT, Julie. b 60. **d** 10 **p** 11. OLM Knaphill w Brookwood *Guildf* from 10. *7 Larks Way, Knaphill, Woking GU21 2LE* T: (01483) 850623 E: julie-levett@ntlworld.com *or* levtherev@knaphillchurch.co.uk

LEVINSOHN, Matthew James. b 79. Ex Univ BA 01 Bris Univ PGCE 04. Trin Coll Bris MA 14. **d** 17 **p** 18. C Salisbury St Fran and Stratford sub Castle *Sarum* from 17. *20 Thistlebarrow Road, Salisbury SP1 3RT* M: 07816-386623 E: matt.levinsohn@gmail.com

LEW, Henry. b 39. **d** 96 **p** 97. LtO *D & G* from 99; NSM Delgany from 10. *Lotts Cottage, Drummin West, The Downs, Delgany, Co Wicklow, Republic of Ireland* T: (00353) (1) 287 2957 M: 87-628 8049 E: healew@outlook.com

LEWER ALLEN, Mrs Patricia (Paddy). b 47. UNISA BA 79 HDipEd 85 Cape Town Univ BA 86 SRN 70. Th Ext Educn Coll 94. **d** 97 **p** 98. P-in-c Dunbar *Edin* 98–08; R Crieff *St And*

08–18; R Comrie 08–18; R Lochearnhead 08–18; Dioc Dir of Ords 10–18; rtd 18; PtO *Arg* from 19. *99 Alexandra Palace, Dunoon PA23 8AH* T: (01369) 705458 M: 07810-746121 E: paddyallen27@gmail.com

LEWES AND HASTINGS, Archdeacon of. *See* DOWLER, The Ven Robert Edward Mackenzie

LEWES, Area Bishop of. *See* JACKSON, The Rt Revd Richard Charles

LEWIS, Alaric Mark Edward. b 66. **d** 92 **p** 93. USA 92–14; PtO *Eur* 14–15; Chapl Costa del Sol E 15–18; V Nor Colegate and Tombland from 18; Dioc Voc Outreach Officer from 18. *8 Robert Gybson Way, Norwich NR3 3PH* T: (01603) 663757 E: st.george.alaric@gmail.com

LEWIS, Aled Wyn. b 77. St Jo Coll Dur LLB 98. St Mich Coll Llan 14. **d** 16 **p** 18. NSM Tregaron Gp *St D* from 16. *Afallon, Ystrad Meurig SY25 6AD* T: (01974) 831518 E: aled.lewis40@gmail.com

LEWIS, Prof Andrew Dominic Edwards. b 49. St Jo Coll Cam LLB 71 MA 74. SWMTC 04. **d** 07 **p** 08. NSM St Endellion w Port Isaac and St Kew *Truro* 07–12; NSM St Minver 07–12; NSM N Cornwall Cluster 12–19; Preb St Endellion 18–19; rtd 19. *Moorgate, Advent, Camelford PL32 9QH* T: (01840) 211161 E: a.d.e.lewis@ucl.ac.uk

LEWIS, Angela Jane. *See* HANNAFIN, Angela Jane

LEWIS, Ann Elizabeth. b 56. SWMTC 15. **d** 18. C Ilfracombe, Lee, Woolacombe, Bittadon etc *Ex* from 18. *Osborne House, West Down, Ilfracombe EX34 8NG* T: (01271) 865405 E: annlewis333@aol.com

LEWIS, Benjamin William Donald. b 78. Northumbria Univ BA 00. Ripon Coll Cuddesdon 12. **d** 14 **p** 15. C Goldington *St Alb* 14–17; V Wellingborough St Mark *Pet* from 17; Warden Lay Min Northn Adnry from 19. *St Mark's Vicarage, 142 Queensway, Wellingborough NN8 3SD* T: (01933) 673893 M: 07977-243197 E: ben.lewis33@live.co.uk

LEWIS, Miss Bethany Lynn. b 82. SOAS Lon BSc 03 PGCE 04. SEITE BA 16. **d** 16 **p** 17. C Bromley St Mark *Roch* from 16. *25 Heathfield Close, Bromley BR2 9DY* M: 07516-951540 E: bethlynnlewis@hotmail.com

LEWIS, Brian James. b 52. Cant Univ (NZ) BA 75. St Jo Coll Auckland 76. **d** 78 **p** 79. C Ashburton New Zealand 78–80; C Shrub End *Chelmsf* 80–82; P-in-c Colchester St Barn 82–84; V 84–88; P-in-c Romford St Andr 88–90; R 90–99; RD Havering 93–97; R Lt Ilford St Mich 99–18; rtd 18. *St Matthias' Vicarage, 48 Rushgrove Avenue, London NW9 6QY* E: brianlewis2014@btinternet.com

LEWIS, The Very Revd Christopher Andrew. b 44. Bris Univ BA 69 CCC Cam PhD 74. Westcott Ho Cam 71. **d** 73 **p** 74. C Barnard Castle *Dur* 73–76; Dir Ox Inst for Ch and Soc 76–79; Tutor Ripon Coll Cuddesdon 76–79; Sen Tutor 79–81; Vice-Prin 81–82; P-in-c Aston Rowant w Crowell *Ox* 78–81; V Spalding St Mary and St Nic *Linc* 82–87; Can Res Cant Cathl 87–94; Dir of Minl Tr 89–94; Dean St Alb 94–03; Dean Ch Ch *Ox* 03–14; rtd 14; PtO *St E* from 15. *The Old Brewery, 16 Victoria Road, Aldeburgh IP15 5ED* T: (01728) 454263 E: christopher.lewis@chch.ox.ac.uk

LEWIS, David Antony. b 48. Dur Univ BA 69 Nottm Univ MTh 84. St Jo Coll Nottm 81. **d** 83 **p** 84. C Gateacre *Liv* 83–86; V Toxteth St Cypr w Ch Ch 86–01; V Edge Hill St Cypr w St Mary 01–07; AD Liv N 94–03; Urban Development Adv 07–08; rtd 08. *48 Coulsdon Road, Sidmouth EX10 9JP* T: (01395) 516762 E: davenward@gmail.com

LEWIS, David Hugh. b 45. Oak Hill Th Coll 88. **d** 90 **p** 91. C Oakham, Hambleton, Egleton, Braunston and Brooke *Pet* 90–94; R Ewhurst *Guildf* 94–99; V Southway *Ex* 99–03; RD Plymouth Moorside 01–03; P-in-c Anglesey Gp *Ely* 03–04; V 04–11; rtd 11. *95 Myrtlebury Way, Exeter EX1 3XB* T: (01392) 467547 E: revdavidhlewis08@btinternet.com

LEWIS, David Tudor. b 61. Jes Coll Cam BA 83. Trin Coll Bris BA 88. **d** 88 **p** 89. C Tile Cross *Birm* 88–91; C Woking St Jo *Guildf* 91–95; TV Carl H Trin and St Barn 95–97; Chapl Carl Hosps NHS Trust 95–97; Asst Chapl Oslo w Bergen, Trondheim and Stavanger *Eur* 97–04; TV E Richmond *Ripon* 04–14; *Leeds* 14–16; R Wiske Benefice 16–18; R Elmley Castle w Bricklehampton and Combertons *Worc* from 18; C Overbury w Teddington, Alstone etc from 18. *The Rectory, 22 Parkwood, Elmley Castle, Pershore WR10 3HT* T: (01386) 710394 E: davidmlewis08@btinternet.com

LEWIS, Canon David Vaughan. b 36. Trin Coll Cam BA 60 MA 64. Ridley Hall Cam 60. **d** 62 **p** 63. C Rugby St Matt *Cov* 62–65; Asst Chapl K Edw Sch Witley 65–71; Hon C Rainham *Chelmsf* 71–76; V Stoke Hill *Guildf* 76–87; V Wallington *S'wark* 87–03; Hon Can S'wark Cathl 95–03; RD Sutton 97–00; rtd 03; PtO *Ely* from 03. *11 The Meadows, Haslingfield, Cambridge CB23 1JD* T: (01223) 874029 E: davidmargylewis@gmail.com

LEWIS, Canon David Watkin. b 40. Univ of Wales (Lamp) BA 61. Wycliffe Hall Ox 61. **d** 63 **p** 64. C Skewen *Llan* 63–66; Field Tr Officer Prov Youth Coun Ch in Wales 66–68; C Gabalfa *Llan* 68–71; P-in-c Marcross w Monknash and Wick 71–73; R 73–83; RD Llantwit Major and Cowbridge 81–83; V Baglan 83–10; Can Llan Cathl 00–10; Treas Llan Cathl 04–10; rtd 10; PtO *Llan* from 14. *23 St Illtyd's Close, Baglan, Port Talbot SA12 8BA* T: (01639) 821778 E: davidlewis322@btinternet.com

LEWIS, Edward John. b 58. Univ of Wales BEd 80 BA 82 Surrey Univ MA 07 FRSA 97 MInstD 01. Chich Th Coll 82. **d** 83 **p** 84. C Llangiwg *S & B* 83–85; Asst Chapl Morriston Hosp 85–87; V Tregaron w Ystrad Meurig and Strata Florida *St D* 87–89; Chapl Tregaron Hosp 87–89; Chapl Manor Hosp Walsall 89–92; Distr Co-ord Chapl Walsall Hosps 90–92; Sen Chapl Walsall Hosps NHS Trust 92–00; Chapl Walsall Community Health Trust 92–00; Chief Exec and Dir Tr Gen Syn Hosp Chapl Coun 00–10; PtO *St Alb* 02–10; P-in-c Watford St Jo 10–11; V Kenton *Lon* from 11; Visiting Lect St Mary's Univ Twickenham from 04; PV Westmr Abbey 07–12; Chapl to The Queen from 08; PtO *Lich* 00–16. *St Mary's Vicarage, 3 St Leonard's Avenue, Harrow HA3 8EJ* T: (020) 8907 2914 M: 07500-557953 E: fr@fredward.org.uk

LEWIS, Ella Pauline. b 41. SWMTC 94. **d** 98. NSM Paignton Ch Ch and Preston St Paul *Ex* 98–07; NSM Torquay St Luke 07–15; rtd 15; PtO *Ex* from 07. *Roselands, 5 Great Headland Road, Paignton TQ3 2DY* T: (01803) 555171 E: paulinelewis@eclipse.co.uk or eplewis@sky.com

LEWIS, Eric. b 47. NEOC 04. **d** 07 **p** 08. NSM Monkseaton St Mary *Newc* 07–11; P-in-c Ovingham 11–16; rtd 16; PtO *Newc* from 16. *1 Bideford Gardens, Whitley Bay NE26 1QW* E: e.lewis129@gmail.com

LEWIS, Gary. b 61. Lanc Univ BA 85. Ripon Coll Cuddesdon 86. **d** 89 **p** 90. C Blackb St Mich w St Jo and H Trin 89–92; C Altham w Clayton le Moors 92–95; V Lea 95–01; V Skerton St Luke 01–14; V Cockerham w Winmarleigh and Glasson from 14. *The Vicarage, 5 Lancaster Road, Cockerham, Lancaster LA2 0EB* T: (01524) 791390 E: garylewislewis@btinternet.com

LEWIS, Graham Rhys. b 54. Loughb Univ BTech 76 Cranfield Inst of Tech MBA 89. SEITE 95. **d** 98 **p** 99. NSM S Gillingham *Roch* 98–16; TV 12–16; NSM Burwash, Burwash Weald and Etchingham *Chich* from 16. *The Vicarage, Burwash Common, Etchingham TN19 7NA* M: 07508-882407 E: grahamstp@gmail.com

LEWIS, Gwynne. *See* LEWIS, Hywel Gwynne

LEWIS, Ms Hannah Margaret. b 71. CCC Cam BA 93 MA 96 Birm Univ PhD 03. Qu Coll Birm 95. **d** 97 **p** 98. C Cannock *Lich* 97–00; NSM Cen Telford 00–06; Team Ldr Past Services for Deaf Community *Liv* from 06. *9 Hougoumont Avenue, Liverpool L22 0LL* T: 0151-705 2130 E: hannah.lewis@liverpool.anglican.org

LEWIS, Hubert Godfrey. b 33. Univ of Wales (Lamp) BA 59. **d** 60 **p** 61. C Merthyr Tydfil *Llan* 60–64; C Caerphilly 64–66; PtO *S'wark* 66–76; *Cant* 76–82; Hon C Shirley St Jo *S'wark* 82–93; Hon C Whitchurch *Llan* from 94. *2 Heol Wernlas, Cardiff CF14 1RY* T: (029) 2061 3079

LEWIS, Hywel Gwynne. b 37. FCA 75. St D Dioc Tr Course 94. **d** 97 **p** 98. NSM Henfynyw w Aberaeron and Llanddewi Aberarth etc *St D* 97–07; rtd 07; PtO *St D* from 07. *Danycoed, Lampeter Road, Aberaeron SA46 0ED* T: (01545) 570577

LEWIS, Preb Ian Richard. b 54. Sheff Univ BA 76 Ox Univ BA 83 MA 87. Wycliffe Hall Ox 81. **d** 84 **p** 85. C Rusholme H Trin *Man* 84–88; C Sandal St Helen *Wakef* 88–91; V Bath St Bart *B & W* from 91; Preb Wells Cathl from 11. *St Bartholomew's Vicarage, 6A Oldfield Road, Bath BA2 3ND* T/F: (01225) 422070 E: ian.ir.lewis@btinternet.com or ianlewis@stbartsbath.org

LEWIS, James Michael. b 51. Trin Coll Carmarthen CertEd 73 Open Univ BA 86 MA 91. St Mich Coll Llan 98. **d** 02 **p** 03. NSM Laleston w Tythegston and Merthyr Mawr *Llan* 02–09; NSM Laleston and Merthyr Mawr 09–13; NSM Laleston and Merthyr Mawr w Penyfai 13–16; PtO from 16. *19 Austin Avenue, Laleston, Bridgend CF32 0LG* T: (01656) 660648 M: 07951-300206 E: mike.laleston@hotmail.co.uk

LEWIS, Jane Rosemary. b 59. **d** 13 **p** 14. OLM Southlake *Ox* 13–17; PtO 17–18; NSM Reading St Mark and All SS from 18. *Address withheld by request* M: 07703-266451 E: revdjanelewis@gmail.com

LEWIS, Mrs Jayne Lisa. b 63. Hull Univ BA 84 Leic Univ PGCE 99. Qu Coll Birm 12. **d** 15 **p** 16. C Market Harborough and The Transfiguration etc *Leic* 15–19; P-in-c Whatborough Gp from 19. *The Vicarage, Halstead Road, Tilton on the Hill, Leicester LE7 9LB* M: 07875-011924 E: jaynelewis28@sky.com

LEWIS, Mrs Jennifer Jane. b 56. Man Univ BA 78. All SS Cen for Miss & Min 12. **d** 15 **p** 16. OLM Eccles *Man* from 15. *4 Welbeck Road, Eccles, Manchester M30 9EH* T: 0161-707 6230 E: jennylewis@dsl.pipex.com

LEWIS, Jocelyn Vivien. b 49. Trevelyan Coll Dur BSc 70 Sheff Univ PhD 75. EMMTC 91. **d** 94 **p** 95. NSM Brimington *Derby* 94–99; P-in-c Whittington 99–09; Dioc Dir Reader Tr 99–09; P-in-c New Whittington 04–09; rtd 09. *13 Gower Crescent, Chesterfield S40 4LX* T: (01246) 229539 E: jocelyn@gandjlewis.plus.com

LEWIS, The Ven John Arthur. b 34. Jes Coll Ox BA 56 MA 60. Cuddesdon Coll 58. **d** 60 **p** 61. C Prestbury *Glouc* 60–63; C Wimborne Minster *Sarum* 63–66; R Eastington and Frocester *Glouc* 66–70; V Nailsworth 70–78; Chapl Memorial and Querns Hosp Cirencester 78–88; V Cirencester *Glouc* 78–88; RD 84–88; Hon Can Glouc Cathl 85–98; Adn Cheltenham 88–98; rtd 98. *5 Vilverie Mead, Bishop's Cleeve, Cheltenham GL52 7YY* T: (01242) 678425

LEWIS, John Herbert. b 42. Selw Coll Cam BA 64 MA 68. Westcott Ho Cam 64. **d** 66 **p** 67. C Wyken *Cov* 66–70; C Bedford St Andr *St Alb* 70–73; Lib Pusey Ho and Bp's Chapl for Graduates *Ox* 73–77; TV Woughton 78–82; TV Gt Chesham 82–88; P-in-c Newport Pagnell w Lathbury and Moulsoe 88–91; R 91–07; rtd 07; PtO *Ox* from 08. *54 Sparrows Way, Oxford OX4 7GE*

LEWIS, John Horatio George. b 47. Southn Univ BEd 72 MA 85. Ox NSM Course 86. **d** 89 **p** 90. NSM Newbury *Ox* 89–04; PtO *Win* 94–04; P-in-c Borden *Cant* 05–08; V 08–16; AD Sittingbourne 09–15; rtd 16; PtO *Lich* from 16. *Crossing Cottage, Shorthill, Lea Cross, Shrewsbury SY5 8JE* T: (01743) 860714 M: 07973-406622 E: jhgl240415@gmail

✠**LEWIS, The Rt Revd John Hubert Richard.** b 43. AKC 66. **d** 67 **p** 68 **c** 92. C Hexham *Newc* 67–70; Ind Chapl 70–77; Communications Officer *Dur* 77–82; Chapl for Agric *Heref* 82–87; Adn Ludlow 87–92; Suff Bp Taunton *B & W* 92–97; Bp St E 97–07; rtd 07. *Kenwater House, 14A Green Lane, Leominster HR6 8QJ* T: (01568) 613982 E: lewis310@btinternet.com

LEWIS, John Malcolm. b 41. Reading Univ BEd. Trin Coll Bris. **d** 82 **p** 83. C Kingswood *Bris* 82–85; TV Weston-super-Mare Cen Par *B & W* 85–91; Dioc Children's Adv *Nor* 91–97; TV Bishopsworth and Bedminster Down *Bris* 97–06; Hon Min Can Bris Cathl 04–06; rtd 06; PtO *Sarum* from 14. *35 Lodge Way, Weymouth DT4 9UU* T: (01305) 776560 E: monandjohn@btinternet.com

LEWIS, Canon John Pryce. b 65. Trin Coll Carmarthen BA 87. Wycliffe Hall Ox 92. **d** 94 **p** 95. C Carmarthen St Pet *St D* 94–97; V Nevern and Y Beifil w Eglwyswrw and Meline etc 97–07; V Henfynyw w Aberaeron and Llanddewi Aberarth etc from 07; Can St D Cathl from 14. *The Vicarage, Panteg Road, Aberaeron SA46 0EP* T: (01545) 570433 E: vicar@aberaeronparish.org.uk

LEWIS, Joycelyn Augusta. See LEWIS-GREGORY, Joycelyn Augusta

LEWIS, Kevin James. b 76. Nottm Univ BA 98. St Jo Coll Nottm MTh 04 MA(MM) 05. **d** 05 **p** 06. C Southgate *Chich* 05–09; C St Helier *S'wark* 09–17; V Carshalton Beeches from 17. *38 Beeches Avenue, Carshalton SM5 3LW* M: 07739-139389 E: kevinjlewis@btinternet.com

LEWIS, Leslie. b 28. LRAM 56. St Aid Birkenhead 61. **d** 63 **p** 64. C Eastham *Ches* 63–66; C St Kirby St Bridget 66–72; V Rainow w Saltersford 72–73; V Rainow w Saltersford and Forest 73–02; Dioc Clergy Widows and Retirement Officer 88–93; rtd 02; PtO *Ches* from 02. *25 Appleby Close, Macclesfield SK11 8XB* T: (01625) 616395

LEWIS, Marjorie Ann. See BROOKS, Marjorie Ann

LEWIS, Mark John. b 68. Ripon Coll Cuddesdon. **d** 16 **p** 17. C Whitewater *Win* from 16. *10 Canberra Close, Yateley GU46 7PZ* T: (01252) 650090 M: 07776-397617 E: mark@lewisonline.co.uk

LEWIS, Mrs Mary Carola Melton. b 51. LRAM 72 S Glam Inst HE CertEd 76 Lon Univ BD 93. St Mich Coll Llan 97. **d** 98 **p** 99. NSM Aberedw w Llandeilo Graban and Llanbadarn etc *S & B* 98–03; PtO *Arg* 13–18; rtd 18. *2C North Road, Wells BA5 2TJ* M: 07833-767273 E: mcmlewis@aol.com

LEWIS, Michael. See LEWIS, James Michael

✠**LEWIS, The Most Revd Michael Augustine Owen.** b 53. Mert Coll Ox BA 75 MA 79. Cuddesdon Coll 75. **d** 78 **p** 79 **c** 99. C Salfords *S'wark* 78–80; Chapl Thames Poly 80–84; V Welling 84–91; TR Worc SE 91–99; RD Worc E 93–99; Hon Can Worc Cathl 98–99; Suff Bp Middleton *Man* 99–07; Bp Cyprus and the Gulf from 07; Pres Bp Episc Ch Jerusalem and Middle E from 19. *PO Box 22075, CY 1517-Nicosia, Cyprus* T: (00357) (22) 671220 F: 674553 E: bishop@spidernet.com.cy *or* maolewis_2000@yahoo.com

LEWIS, Canon Michael David Bennett. b 41. Portsm Univ MA 01. St Mich Coll Llan 65. **d** 68 **p** 69. C Penarth w

Lavernock *Llan* 68–72; Chapl RAF 72–74; C Llanishen and Lisvane *Llan* 74–77; V Penyfai w Tondu 77–82; Chapl Ardingly Coll 82–90; R Merrow *Guildf* 90–95; RD Guildf 94–95; V Southsea H Spirit *Portsm* 95–11; RD Portsm 06–11; Hon Can Portsm Cathl 06–11; rtd 11; PtO *St D* from 11. *Stepping Stones, Reynalton, Kilgetty SA68 0PG* T: (01834) 891531 M: 07808-609912 E: jandmleiws@btinternet.com

LEWIS, Michael John. b 37. LLAM 86. St Aid Birkenhead 64. **d** 66 **p** 67. C Whitnash *Cov* 66–69; C Nuneaton St Nic 69–73; TV Basildon St Martin w H Cross and Laindon *Chelmsf* 73–79; V W Bromwich St Jas *Lich* 79–85; TV Buxton w Burbage and King Sterndale *Derby* 85–95; P-in-c Brampton St Mark 95–02; rtd 02; PtO *Lich* from 03. *15 Langley Street, Basford, Stoke-on-Trent ST4 6DX* T: (01782) 622762 E: michael.lewis@talktalk.net

LEWIS, Patrick Mansel. See MANSEL LEWIS, Patrick Charles Archibald

LEWIS, Pauline. See LEWIS, Ella Pauline

LEWIS, Peter. See LEWIS, Thomas Peter

LEWIS, Peter Andrew. b 67. Pemb Coll Ox MA PhD Univ of Wales (Abth) Bris Univ BA. Trin Coll Bris 92. **d** 96 **p** 97. C Cardigan w Mwnt and Y Ferwig *St D* 96–98; C Gabalfa *Llan* 98–01; V Aberpergwm and Blaengwrach 01–04; V Vale of Neath 04–12; AD Neath 10–12; V Pontypridd St Cath 12–15; TV Pontypridd from 15. *St Catherine's Vicarage, Gelliwastad Grove, Pontypridd CF37 2BS* T: (01443) 402021 E: revpeterlewis@gmail.com

LEWIS, Peter Richard. b 40. Dur Univ BA 62. Qu Coll Birm 62. **d** 64 **p** 65. C Moseley St Mary *Birm* 64–67; C Sherborne w Castleton and Lillington *Sarum* 67–71; P-in-c Bishopstone w Stratford Tony 72–80; V Amesbury 80–02; rtd 02; PtO *Sarum* from 02; *B & W* 05–19. *Rose Cottage, Silton Road, Bourton, Gillingham SP8 5DE*

LEWIS, The Very Revd Richard. b 35. Fitzw Ho Cam BA 78 MA 63. Ripon Hall Ox 58. **d** 60 **p** 61. C Hinckley St Mary *Leic* 60–63; C Sanderstead All SS *S'wark* 63–66; V S Merstham 67–72; V S Wimbledon H Trin 72–74; P-in-c S Wimbledon St Pet 72–74; V S Wimbledon H Trin and St Pet 74–79; V Dulwich St Barn 79–90; Chapl Alleyn's Foundn Dulwich 79–90; RD Dulwich *S'wark* 83–90; Hon Can S'wark Cathl 87–90; Dean Wells *B & W* 90–03; Warden of Readers 91–03; rtd 03; PtO *Worc* 03–08; *B & W* 08–19. *1 Monmouth Court, Union Street, Wells BA5 2PX* T: (01749) 672677 M: 07788-413525 E: dean.richard@btinternet.com

LEWIS, Richard. See LEWIS, John Hubert Richard

LEWIS, Canon Richard Charles. b 44. Univ of Wales (Lamp) MA 94 Sheff Univ MEd 96. ALCD 69. **d** 69 **p** 70. C Kendal H Trin *Carl* 69–72; C Chipping Barnet *St Alb* 72–76; V Watford Ch Ch 76–12; Chapl Abbot's Hill Sch Herts 81–96; Hon Can St Alb Abbey 90–12; Chapl from 12; Chapl Trin Hosp Retford from 12; PtO *S'well* from 12. *Rectory Farm, Rectory Road, Retford DN22 7AY* T: (01777) 719200 E: dick@ccwatford.u-net.com

LEWIS, Robert. b 38. St Pet Coll Ox BA 62 MA 66. Cuddesdon Coll 62. **d** 64 **p** 65. C Kirkby *Liv* 64–67 and 70–71; TV 71–75; Chapl St Boniface Coll Warminster 68–69; Tutor St Aug Coll Cant 69–70; Abp's Dom Chapl and Dir of Ords *York* 76–79; TR Thirsk 79–92; Chapl Oslo w Bergen, Trondheim, Stavanger etc *Eur* 93–96; P-in-c Danby *York* 96–98; V 98–04; RD Whitby 98–04; rtd 04; PtO *York* from 04. *17 Meadowfields, Chapel Street, Thirsk YO7 1TH* T: (01845) 523256 E: maureen240@btinternet.com

LEWIS, Canon Robert George. b 53. Lanc Univ BEd 76. Ripon Coll Cuddesdon. **d** 78 **p** 79. C Liv Our Lady and St Nic w St Anne 78–81; Asst Dir of Educn 81–88; P-in-c Newchurch 88–89; P-in-c Glazebury 88–89; R Newchurch and Glazebury 89–94; R Winwick 94–09; R Glazebury w Hollinfare 04–09; AD Winwick 01–09; Hon Can Liv Cathl from 01; Chapl Liv Univ from 09; Chapl Liv Jo Moores Univ from 09; Bp's Adv Sector Min from 11; P-in-c Toxteth St Marg from 14. *10 Ladychapel Close, Liverpool L1 7BZ* T: 0151-707 2988 E: thelewises@hotmail.com

LEWIS, Roger Gilbert. b 49. St Jo Coll Dur BA 70. Ripon Hall Ox 70. **d** 72 **p** 73. C Boldmere *Birm* 72–76; C Birm St Pet 76–77; TV Tettenhall Regis *Lich* 77–81; V Ward End *Birm* 81–91; rtd 91; PtO *Birm* 91–06. *8 Tudor Terrace, Ravenhurst Road, Birmingham B17 9SB*

LEWIS, Simon Wilford. b 66. Westmr Coll Ox BTh 94 Roehampton Inst PGCE 95. STETS 03. **d** 06 **p** 07. C Ventnor St Cath, Ventnor H Trin and Bonchurch *Portsm* 06–09; P-in-c Brent Knoll, E Brent and Lympsham *B & W* 09–18; R Blagdon w Compton Martin and Ubley from 18. *Easton House, Church Street, Blagdon, Bristol BS40 7SJ* E: rev.simonlewis@gmail.com

LEWIS, Thomas Peter. b 45. Selw Coll Cam BA 67 MA. Ripon Hall Ox 68. **d** 70 **p** 71. C Bp's Hatfield *St Alb* 70–74; C Boreham Wood All SS 74–78; Chapl Haileybury Coll 78–85; Chapl Abingdon Sch 86–03; R Narberth w Mounton w Roberston Wathen etc *St D* 03–14; rtd 14; PtO *St D* from 15. *Nantyfelin, Old St Clears Road, Johnstown, Carmarthen SA31 3HN* T: (01267) 234667 E: revtplewis@btinternet.com

LEWIS, Trevor Arnold. b 55. York St Jo Univ BA 12. NEOC 06. **d** 09 **p** 10. NSM Middlesbrough St Martin w St Cuth *York* 09–10; NSM Osmotherley w Harlsey and Ingleby Arncliffe 10–17; NSM Leake w Over and Nether Silton and Kepwick 10–17; NSM Felixkirk w Boltby 10–17; NSM Kirkby Knowle 10–17; NSM Cowesby 10–17; C Hurstbourne Tarrant, Faccombe, Vernham Dean etc *Win* from 17; RD Andover from 18. *The Vicarage, The Dene, Hurstbourne Tarrant, Andover SP11 0AH* T: (01264) 736565 E: revtrev02@gmail.com

LEWIS, Vera Elizabeth. b 45. Lon Univ BA 66 Univ of Wales (Abth) DipEd 67. St As Minl Tr Course 82. **d** 85 **p** 97. NSM Garthbeibio and Llanerfyl and Llangadfan *St As* 85–86; C 87–88; NSM Llanfair Caereinion w Llanllugan 85–86; C 87–88; Dn-in-c Llanrhaeadr-ym-Mochnant etc 88–96; Dn-in-c Llanddulas and Llysfaen 96–97; R 97–03; rtd 03; P-in-c Henllan and Llannefydd and Bylchau *St As* 12–15; NSM Caerwys and Bodfari 15–16. *Heulwen, Bronwylfa Square, St Asaph LL17 0BU* T: (01745) 584261 E: vera.lewis2@btinternet.com

LEWIS, Canon Walter Arnold. b 45. NUI BA 68 TCD MPhil 91. TCD Div Sch Div Test 71. **d** 71 **p** 72. C Belfast Whiterock *Conn* 71–73; C Belfast St Mark 73–80; Bp's C Belfast St Andr 80–84; I Belfast St Thos 84–12; Can Belf Cathl 97–12; rtd 12. *145 Mountsandel Road, Coleraine BT52 1TA* T: (028) 7034 0929 M: 07715-358127 E: waltera.lewis@btinternet.com

LEWIS, William George Rees. b 35. Hertf Coll Ox BA 59 MA 63. Tyndale Hall Bris 61. **d** 63 **p** 64. C Tenby w Gumfreston *St D* 63–66; C Llanelli St Paul 66–69; R Letterston 69–73; R Letterston w Llanfair Nantygof, Jordanston etc 73–84; R Jordanston w Llanstinan 73–78; R Letterston w Llanfair Nant-y-Gof etc 78–84; R Hubberston w Herbrandston and Hasguard etc 84–88; R Hubberston 89–90; Prov Officer for Evang and Adult Educn 90–94; V Gabalfa *Llan* 94–00; rtd 00; PtO *St D* from 00. *5 Westaway Drive, Hakin, Milford Haven SA73 3EG* T: (01646) 692280 E: billandchlorislewis@gmail.com

LEWIS, William Rhys. b 20. St Mich Coll Llan 53. **d** 55 **p** 56. C Ystrad Mynach *Llan* 55–58; C Bassaleg *Mon* 58–59; V Cwmtillery 59–62; V Newport St Andr 62–64; TR Ebbw Vale 64–73; R Llangattock and Llangynidr *S & B* 73–78; V Swansea St Luke 78–85; rtd 85; PtO *Llan* from 85. *6 Beech Avenue, Llantwit Major CF61 1RT* T: (01446) 796741

LEWIS-ANTHONY, Justin Griffith. b 64. LSE BA 86 Kent Univ PhD 12. Ripon Coll Cuddesdon BA 91 MA 97. **d** 92 **p** 93. C Cirencester *Glouc* 92–98; Prec Ch Ch *Ox* 98–03; R Hackington *Cant* 03–13; Assoc Dean of Students Virginia Th Sem USA 13–16; Research Fell Ripon Coll Cuddesdon 16–17; Dep Dir Angl Cen Rome from 18; PtO *Eur* from 18. *The Anglican Centre in Rome, Palazzo Doria Pamphilj, Piazza del Collegio Romano 2, 00186 Rome, Italy* T: (0039) (06) 678 0302 F: 678 0674 E: deputy.director@anglicancentre.it

LEWIS-GREGORY, Mrs Joycelyn Augusta. b 60. Qu Coll Birm. **d** 08 **p** 09. C Hall Green St Pet *Birm* 08–12; P-in-c Cotteridge 12; V 12–16; Bp's Adv for Minority Ethnic Angl from 12; PtO from 16. *28 Arton Croft, Birmingham B24 8RA* M: 07932-443769 E: revjoycelyn@gmail.com

LEWIS-MORRIS, Catherine Mary. *See* DAWKINS, Catherine Mary

LEWIS-NICHOLSON, Russell John. b 45. Oak Hill Th Coll 79. **d** 81 **p** 82. C Clayton *Bradf* 81–84; Australia from 84; rtd 10. *5 Rawlinson Street, Croydon Vic 3136, Australia* T: (0061) (3) 972 3653 M: 42-935 8490 E: dreamrider17@hotmail.com

LEWISHAM AND GREENWICH, Archdeacon of. *See* CUTTING, The Ven Alastair Murray

LEWORTHY, Graham Llewelyn. b 47. Reading Univ BA 69. S Dios Minl Tr Scheme 91. **d** 94 **p** 95. C Sark *Win* 94–11; rtd 11. *Summerland Nursing Home, Mount Durand, St Peter Port, Guernsey GY1 1DX*

LEWRY, Glyn Hugh Brendon. b 63. **d** 14 **p** 15. NSM Sampford Peverell, Uplowman, Holcombe Rogus etc *Ex* 14–18; TR from 18. *The Rectory, Blackdown View, Sampford Peverell, Tiverton EX16 7BE* T: (01884) 243727 E: revglyn01@gmail.com

LEYLAND, Derek James. b 34. Lon Univ BSc 55. Qu Coll Birm 58. **d** 60 **p** 61. C Ashton-on-Ribble St Andr *Blackb* 60–63; V 80–87; C Salesbury 63–65; V Preston St Oswald 65–67; V Pendleton 67–74; Dioc Youth Chapl 67–69; Ind Youth Chapl 70–74; R Brindle 74–80; V Garstang St Helen Churchtown 87–94; Sec SOSc 90–94; rtd 94; PtO *Blackb* from 94. *Greystocks, Goosnargh Lane, Goosnargh, Preston PR3 2BP* T: (01772) 865682

LEYLAND, Ty John. b 49. Aston Univ BSc 68. St Jo Coll Nottm 89. **d** 91 **p** 92. C Lich St Mary w St Mich 91–94; TV Willenhall H Trin 94–99; P-in-c The Ridwares and Kings

Bromley 99–08; R 08–18; rtd 18. *4 Ellsmore Meadow, Lichfield WS13 6NJ* E: ty.leyland@gmail.com

LEYSHON, Simon. b 63. Trin Coll Carmarthen BA 86 Southn Univ BTh 89. Sarum & Wells Th Coll. **d** 89 **p** 90. C Tenby *St D* 89–92; TV 92–96; Chapl and Hd RS Llandovery Coll 96–02; Chapl Lord Wandsworth Coll Hook 02–13; Hd Cransley Sch Northwich 13–16; PtO *Ches* 13–16; *S'wark* 17–18. *Emperor House, Burys Court School, Flanchford Road, Leigh, Reigate RH2 8RD* E: simonleyshon@yahoo.co.uk

LIBBY, Canon John Ralph. b 55. Trin Coll Cam BA 83. Ridley Hall Cam 89. **d** 91 **p** 92. C Enfield St Andr *Lon* 91–93; C Northwood Em 93–96; V Denton Holme *Carl* 96–14; RD Carl 04–10; Nat Dir Langham Partnership from 15; NSM Stanwix *Carl* from 16; Hon Can Carl Cathl from 08. *14 East Block, Shaddon Mill, Shaddongate, Carlisle CA2 5WD* E: john.libby@btinternet.com

LICARI, Luigi. b 49. St Jo Fisher Coll USA BA 71. **d** 96. C San Francisco St Aid USA 96–00; C San Francisco St Cypr 00–01; C New York St Jo in the Village 01–05; The Netherlands 05–11; C Toronto Transfiguration Canada 11–13; PtO *Lon* from 15. *17 Brookfield Court, Lionel Road, Bexhill-on-Sea TN40 1NT* T: (01424) 601497 M: 07946-576034 E: luigi_licari@yahoo.com

LICHFIELD, Archdeacon of. *See* WELLER, The Ven Susan Karen

LICHFIELD, Bishop of. *See* IPGRAVE, The Rt Revd Michael Geoffrey

LICHFIELD, Dean of. *See* DORBER, The Very Revd Adrian John

LICKESS, Canon David Frederick. b 37. St Chad's Coll Dur BA 63. **d** 65 **p** 66. C Howden *York* 65–70; V Rudby in Cleveland w Middleton 70–07; Can and Preb York Minster 90–07; RD Stokesley 93–00; rtd 07; PtO *York* from 07; *Leeds* from 17. *Bridge House, Snape, Bedale DL8 2SZ* T: (01677) 470077 E: davidlickess@gmail.com

LIDDELL, Mark. b 55. Birm Univ BA 00. Coll of Resurr Mirfield 96. **d** 98 **p** 99. C Wednesbury St Jas and St Jo *Lich* 98–00; C Walsall St Andr 00–01; P-in-c 01–05; V 06–08; V Nuneaton St Mary *Cov* 08–18; V Ocker Hill *Lich* from 18. *St Mark's Vicarage, Ocker Hill Road, Tipton DY4 0UT*

LIDDELL, Canon Peter Gregory. b 40. St Andr Univ MA 63 Linacre Ho Ox BA 65 MA 70 Andover Newton Th Sch DMin 75. Ripon Hall Ox 63. **d** 65 **p** 66. C Bp's Hatfield *St Alb* 65–71; USA 71–76; P-in-c Kimpton w Ayot St Lawrence *St Alb* 77–83; Dir of Past Counselling 80–05; Hon Can St Alb 99–05; rtd 05. *12 Old Hall Court, Horn Hill, Whitwell, Hitchin SG4 8AS* T: (01438) 832266 E: petermary.liddell@btinternet.com

LIDDELL, Roxane Harriet. b 68. City of Lon Poly BSc 90 Middx Univ PGCE 09. Westcott Ho Cam 16. **d** 18 **p** 19. C Stoke Newington St Mary *Lon* from 18. *Basement Flat, St Mary's Rectory, Stoke Newington Church Street, London N16 9ES* M: 07957-283238 E: roxaneliddell@hotmail.com

LIDDELOW, Peter William. b 33. Oak Hill NSM Course. **d** 82 **p** 83. NSM Finchley Ch Ch *Lon* 82–84; NSM S Mimms Ch Ch 84–11; PtO *St Alb* 95–18; Chapl Magic Circle 02–16; rtd 16. *23 King's Road, Barnet EN5 4EF* T: (020) 8441 2968 E: pliddelow@hotmail.co.uk

LIDDLE, George. b 48. NEOC 88. **d** 90 **p** 91. C Auckland St Andr and St Anne *Dur* 90–92; C Crook 92–94; C Stanley 92–94; P-in-c Evenwood 94–96; V 96–03; R Blackhall, Castle Eden and Monkhesleden 03–13; rtd 13; PtO *Dur* from 13. *3 Rush Park, Bishop Auckland DL14 6NR* E: george@liddle.co.uk

LIDGATE, Mrs Jacqueline Margaret. b 56. **d** 01 **p** 02. Hon C Milton Australia 01–02; C Indooroopilly 02–04; P-in-c Jimboomba 04–07; P-in-c Coolum 07–10; Chapl St Andr Angel Coll 08–10; PtO *S'well* 10–11; NSM Brampton St Thos *Derby* 11; PtO *S'well* 13–16; *Sheff* 15–16; P-in-c Firbeck w Letwell 16–18; PtO from 18. *4 Granary Court, Carlton-in-Lindrick, Worksop S81 9JZ* T: (01909) 733820 E: pandjlidgate@sky.com

LIDSTONE, Vernon Henry. b 43. SWMTC 89. **d** 92 **p** 93. NSM Bovey Tracey SS Pet, Paul and Thos w Hennock *Ex* 92–94; Sub-Chapl HM Pris Channings Wood 92–96; Asst Dioc Chr Stewardship Adv *Ex* 92–93; Dioc Chr Stewardship Adv 93–96; Dioc Officer for Par Development *Glouc* 96–97; Chapl HM Pris Lcyhill 97–03; rtd 03; PtO *Glouc* from 17. *The Pike House, Saul, Gloucester GL2 7JD* T: (01452) 741410 E: vernon@lidstone.net

LIEBERT, Ms Sarah Jane. b 66. Pemb Coll Ox BA 88 MA 14 Imp Coll Lon MSc 89 Fitzw Coll Cam BA 13. Westcott Ho Cam 11. **d** 14 **p** 15. C Upper Tooting H Trin w St Aug *S'wark* 14–19; V Stonebridge St Mich *Lon* from 19. *St Michael's Vicarage, Hillside, London NW10 8LB*

LIEVESLEY, Hannah Felicity. b 71. Univ of Cen England in Birm BA 93. St Jo Sch of Miss Nottm 14. **d** 16 **p** 17. C Farsley *Leeds* 16–19; TV Headingley from 19.

St Chad's Vicarage, Otley Road, Leeds LS16 5JT M: 07582-036290 E: hannah.lievesley@outlook.com or hannah.lievesley@leeds.anglican.org

LIEVESLEY, Mrs Joy Margaret. b 48. Lady Mabel Coll CertEd 69. Guildf Dioc Min Course 98. **d** 00 **p** 01. NSM Farnham Guildf 00–14; NSM Frimley 15–18; PtO from 18. 3 Kingfisher Close, Church Crookham, Fleet GU52 6JP T: (01252) 690223 E: joy.lievesley@ntlworld.com

LIGGINS, Andrew David. b 85. St Cath Coll Cam BA 06. Oak Hill Th Coll BA 16. **d** 17 **p** 18. C Southport SS Simon and Jude w All So Liv from 17. 1 Beacham Road, Southport PR8 6BA M: 07901-787586

LIGHT, Canon Madeline Margaret. b 54. Girton Coll Cam BA 77 MA 80 Lon Inst of Educn PGCE 78. EAMTC 96. **d** 99 **p** 00. C Eaton Nor 99–02; P-in-c Nor St Helen 02–09; Chapl Gt Hosp Nor 02–09; P-in-c Nor St Steph 09–16; V from 16; Hon Can Nor Cathl from 16. 12 The Crescent, Chapel Field Road, Norwich NR2 1SA T: (01603) 920598 E: madelinelight@gmail.com

LIGHT, Mrs Penelope Ann. b 46. Madeley Coll of Educn TCert 71 N Lon Poly BEd 81. WEMTC 06. **d** 09 **p** 10. NSM Cirencester Glouc 09–16; rtd 16. Toad Cottage, 22 Bingham Close, Cirencester GL7 1HJ T: (01285) 640125 E: jonpen22@tiscali.co.uk

LIGHTBOWN, Richard Andrew. b 66. Buckingham Univ MBA 07. Ripon Coll Cuddesdon MA 13. **d** 13 **p** 14. C Schorne Ox 13–16; R Winslow w Gt Horwood and Addington from 16. The Vicarage, Vicarage Road, Winslow, Buckingham MK18 3BJ T: (01296) 712564 M: 07711-234546 E: alightbown@hotmail.co.uk

LIGHTOWLER, Joseph Trevor. b 33. **d** 79 **p** 80. Hon C Leverstock Green St Alb 79–80; Hon C Chambersbury 80–84; C Woodmansterne S'wark 84–88; R Odell and Pavenham St Alb 88–97; rtd 97; PtO St Alb 97–18. 25 Yeats House, 2 Wordsworth Close, Kings Park, St Albans AL3 4GG T: (01727) 866906

LILBURN, Robert Irvine Terence. b 47. CITC 07. **d** 10 **p** 11. NSM Kilternan D & G 10–11; NSM Powerscourt w Kilbride from 11. 13 Churchfields, Dundrum Road, Milltown, Dublin 14, Republic of Ireland T: (00353) (1) 260 0003 M: 86-886 5361 E: terrylilburn@gmail.com

LILES, Malcolm David. b 48. Nottm Univ BA 69. St Steph Ho Ox 69. **d** 71 **p** 72. C Corby Epiphany w St Jo Pet 71–74; C New Cleethorpes Linc 74–76; TV Lt Coates 76–77; TV Gt and Lt Coates w Bradley 78–82; Soc Resp Sec 82–93; Hon C Gt Grimsby St Mary and St Jas 82–93; P-in-c Grimsby All SS 88–93; TV Dronfield w Holmesfield Derby 93–98; TR Crawley Chich 98–14; rtd 14; PtO Sheff from 15. 473 City Road, Sheffield S2 1GF T: 0114-453 7964 M: 07702-203273 E: malcolm.liles48@gmail.com

LILEY, The Ven Christopher Frank. b 47. Nottm Univ BEd 70. Linc Th Coll 72. **d** 74 **p** 75. C Kingswinford H Trin Lich 74–79; TV Stafford 79–84; V Norton St Alb 84–96; RD Hitchin 89–94; V Shrewsbury St Chad w St Mary Lich 96–01; P-in-c Shrewsbury St Alkmund 96–01; Adn Lich 01–13; Can Res and Treas Lich Cathl 01–13; rtd 13; PtO Worc from 14. 15 Holloway Drive, Pershore WR10 1JL T: (01386) 561608 E: lileyc@aol.com

LILEY, Peter James. b 60. Liv Univ BA 82 Westmr Coll Ox PGCE 83. Oak Hill Th Coll 91. **d** 93 **p** 94. C Exning St Martin w Landwade St E 93–96; V Acton w Gt Waldingfield 96–00; TV Bottesford w Ashby Linc 00–05; TR 05–12; Lic Preacher 12–14; R Mablethorpe w Trusthorpe from 14; R Sutton, Huttoft and Anderby from 14. The Vicarage, 7A Huttoft Road, Sutton-on-Sea, Mablethorpe LN12 2QZ T: (01507) 443948 E: rev.p.liley@btinternet.com

LILEY, Canon Stephen John. b 65. Liv Univ BA 87 MMus 88 ARCM 93. Wycliffe Hall Ox 97. **d** 99 **p** 00. C Throop Win 99–03; V Clapham St Alb from 03; RD Elstow 08–10; RD Sharnbrook from 15; Hon Can St Alb from 18. The Vicarage, Green Lane, Clapham, Bedford MK41 6ER T: (01234) 352814 E: the.lileys@ukgateway.net

LILLEY, Mrs Alexandra Mary. b 80. St Pet Coll Ox BA 01 MA 06. St Mellitus Coll BA 14. **d** 14 **p** 15. C Shadwell St Paul w Ratcliffe St Jas Lon 14–17; P-in-c Tufnell Park St Geo and All SS from 17. M: 07986-433658 E: alexandra_lilley@hotmail.com

LILLEY, Canon Christopher Howard. b 51. FCA 75 FTII 83. LNSM course 83 St Jo Coll Nottm 91. **d** 85 **p** 86. OLM Skegness and Winthorpe Linc 85–93; C Limber Magna w Brocklesby 93–96; PtO S'well 93–96; P-in-c Middle Rasen Gp Linc 96–97; R 97–02; V Scawby, Redbourne and Hibaldstow 02–10; P-in-c Bishop Norton, Waddingham and Snitterby 06–10; P-in-c Kirton in Lindsey w Manton 06–10; RD Yarborough 02–09; Hon C Mablethorpe w Trusthorpe from 10; Hon C Sutton, Huttoft and Anderby from 10; Can and

Preb Linc Cathl from 05. The Chrysalis, 12 Hillside Avenue, Sutton-on-Sea, Mablethorpe LN12 2JH T: (01507) 440039 E: c.lilley@btinternet.com

LILLEY, Ivan Ray. b 32. Bps' Coll Cheshunt 58. **d** 61 **p** 62. C Kettering SS Pet and Paul 61–64; C Gt Yarmouth Nor 64–75; P-in-c Tottenhill w Wormegay Ely 76–83; P-in-c Watlington 76–83; P-in-c Holme Runcton w S Runcton and Wallington 76–83; V Tysoe w Oxhill and Whatcote Cov 83–86; C Langold S'well 87–91; P-in-c 91–98; rtd 98; PtO Nor from 98. Linden Lea, 41 Cedar Drive, Attleborough NR17 2EY T: (01953) 452710 E: ivanlinlea@hotmail.co.uk

LILLEY, Thomas Robert. b 84. UEA BA 05 PGCE 06 Fitzw Coll Cam BTh 11. Westcott Ho Cam 08. **d** 11 **p** 12. C Attleborough w Besthorpe Nor 11–14; P-in-c Southchurch H Trin Chelmsf 14–17; Chapl Canon Slade Sch Bolton from 17. Canon Slade School, Bradshaw Brow, Bolton BL2 3BP T: (01204) 333343 M: 07984-181919 E: tom.lilley@gmail.com or contact@canon-slade.bolton.sch.uk

LILLICRAP, Peter Andrew. b 65. Hatf Poly BEng 87 CEng 93 MIMechE 93. Trin Coll Bris 00. **d** 02 **p** 03. C Kineton Cov 02–04; C Napton-on-the-Hill, Lower Shuckburgh etc 04–07; V Acton and Worleston, Church Minshull etc Ches 07–13; V Layton and Staining Blackb from 13; AD Blackpool from 19. St Mark's Vicarage, 163 Kingscote Drive, Blackpool FY3 8EH T: (01253) 392895 E: peterlillicrap@gmail.com

LILLICRAP, Canon Stephen Hunter. b 58. Newc Univ MB, BS 81 MRCGP 85. SEITE 00. **d** 03 **p** 04. C Wye w Brook and Hastingleigh etc Cant 03–08; C Stone Street Gp 06–08; C Mersham w Hinxhill and Sellindge 08; P-in-c Teynham w Lynsted and Kingsdown 08–14; P-in-c Norton 08–14; V Kingsdown and Creekside from 14; P-in-c High Downs from 19; AD Ospringe from 11; Hon Can Cant Cathl from 14. The Vicarage, 76 Station Road, Teynham, Sittingbourne ME9 9SN T: (01795) 522510 M: 07971-224094 E: steve.lillicrap@btopenworld.com

LILLIE, Judith Virginia. See THOMPSON, Judith Virginia

LILLINGTON (née POLLIT), Mrs Ruth Mary. b 65. SS Paul & Mary Coll Cheltenham BA 88. St Jo Coll Nottm 88. **d** 90 **p** 94. Par Dn Caverswall Lich 90–92; Par Dn Caverswall and Weston Coyney w Dilhorne 92–93; Par Dn Luton St Mary St Alb 93–94; C 94–97; Chapl Luton Univ 93–97; NSM Clifton Ch Ch w Em Bris from 16. 12 St Edyth's Road, Bristol BS9 2ES E: ruthy.lillington@ccweb.org.uk

LILLISTONE, Canon Brian David. b 38. SS Coll Cam BA 61 MA 65. St Steph Ho Ox 61. **d** 63 **p** 64. C Ipswich All Hallows St E 63–66; C Stokesay Heref 66–71; P-in-c Lyonshall w Titley 71–76; R Martlesham w Brightwell St E 76–03; Hon Can St E Cathl 98–03; rtd 03; PtO St E from 03. 23 Woodland Close, Risby, Bury St Edmunds IP28 6QN T: (01284) 811330 E: brianlillistone23@gmail.com

LIMA, Luiz Henrique. See DE ANDRADE LIMA, Luiz Henrique

LIMBERT, Crichton. b 57. Reading Univ BSc 79 St Jo Coll Cam PhD 87. St Mellitus Coll BA 12. **d** 12 **p** 13. C Ouzel Valley St Alb 12–15; V Southgate Ch Ch Lon from 15. Christchurch Vicarage, 1 The Green, London N14 7EG M: 07711-751501 E: frch138@btinternet.com

LIMBRICK, Gordon. b 36. Open Univ BA 88. St Jo Coll Nottm. **d** 87 **p** 91. Hon C Troon Glas 87–90; Hon C Yaxley Ely 90–97; Hon C Yaxley and Holme w Conington 97–04; rtd 04; PtO Pet 98–14 and from 15; Ely from 04. 271 Broadway, Yaxley, Peterborough PE7 3NR T: (01733) 243170 E: revgordonlimbrick@gmail.com

LIMERICK AND ARDFERT, Dean of. Vacant

LIMERICK, ARDFERT AND AGHADOE, Archdeacon of. See LUMBY, The Ven Simon John

LIMERICK, ARDFERT, AGHADOE, KILLALOE, KILFENORA, CLONFERT, KILMACDUAGH AND EMLY, Bishop of. See KEARON, The Rt Revd Kenneth Arthur

LINCOLN, Archdeacon of. See KIRK, The Ven Gavin John

LINCOLN, Bishop of. See LOWSON, The Rt Revd Christopher

LINCOLN, Dean of. See WILSON, The Very Revd Christine Louise

LIND, Jeremy Robert. b 55. ERMC 15. **d** 18 **p** 19. NSM Newmarket St Mary w Exning St Agnes St E from 18. Nutbeam, Ducksen Road, Mendlesham, Stowmarket IP14 5SE T: (01449) 766646 M: 07500-794303 E: lind05@btinternet.com

LIND-JACKSON, Peter Wilfrid. b 35. Leeds Univ BA 67. Linc Th Coll 67. **d** 68 **p** 69. C Heref St Martin 68–71; P-in-c Burghill 71–78; V 78–82; V Barnard Castle Dur 82–83; P-in-c Whorlton 82–83; V Barnard Castle w Whorlton 83–00; rtd 00; PtO Ripon 03–14; Leeds from 14. 5 Gill Lane, Barnard Castle DL12 9AS T: (01833) 630027 E: lindjacksons@googlemail.com

LINDECK, Peter Stephen. b 31. Oak Hill Th Coll 57. **d** 59 **p** 60. C Homerton St Luke Lon 59–62; C Salterhebble All SS Wakef 62–63; C Islington St Andr w St Thos and St Matthias Lon

64–67; PtO *Derby* 67–68; *St Alb* 67–68; V Toxteth Park St Bede *Liv* 68–74; V Kano St Geo Nigeria 74–76; C Netherton *Liv* 76–77; C Ollerton and Boughton *S'well* 77–80; V Whitgift w Adlingfleet and Eastoft *Sheff* 80–86; P-in-c Swinefleet 81–86; V Kilnhurst 86–94; Chapl Montagu Hosp Mexborough 86–94; rtd 94; PtO *Sheff* 94–06; *Leic* 14–19. *27 Stuart Court, High Street, Kibworth Beauchamp, Leicester LE8 0LR* T: 0116-279 6347 E: peter32.lindeck@gmail.com

LINDISFARNE, Archdeacon of. *See* ROBINSON, The Ven Peter John Alan

LINDLEY (*née* FLYNN), Mrs Anna Therese. b 42. Leeds Univ BSc 63 Surrey Univ MPhil 72 Westmr Coll Ox DipEd 64. Yorks Min Course 08. **d** 09 **p** 11. NSM York St Mich-le-Belfrey 09–12; NSM Skelton w Shipton and Newton on Ouse 12–16; rtd 16; PtO *York* from 17. *35 Manor Garth, Wigginton, York YO32 2WZ*

LINDLEY, Mrs Danie Maria. b 71. N Riding Coll of Educn BA(QTS) 93. Lindisfarne Regional Tr Partnership BA 16. **d** 15 **p** 16. NSM Chester le Street *Dur* 15–18; P-in-c Windy Nook St Alb from 18; P-in-c Gateshead Fell from 18. *The Vicarage, Coldwell Park Drive, Gateshead NE10 9BY* M: 07902-477474

LINDLEY, Graham William. b 47. CIPFA 77. **d** 97 **p** 98. OLM E Crompton *Man* 97–02; NSM Newhey 02–08; P-in-c 08–13; P-in-c Belfield 09–17; rtd 17; PtO *Man* from 17. *37 Jordan Avenue, Shaw, Oldham OL2 8DQ* T: (01706) 845677 E: g.lindley7@ntlworld.com

LINDLEY, Canon Richard Adrian. b 44. Hull Univ BA 65 Man Univ MA 79 Win Univ PhD 14. Cuddesdon Coll 66. **d** 68 **p** 69. C Ingrow w Hainworth *Bradf* 68–70; TV Ellesmere Port *Ches* 74–79; V Westborough *Guildf* 79–80; TR 80–84; Dir of Educn *Birm* 84–96; Hon Can Birm Cathl 96; Dir of Educn *Win* 96–04; Hon Can Win Cathl 03–04; rtd 04; PtO *Win* 04–13; NSM Win Cathl 13–16; PtO 16–17. *28 Denham Close, Winchester SO23 7BL* T: (01962) 621851 M: 07743-758639 E: richardlindley4@gmail.com

LINDNER, Christoph Walter. b 67. St Mellitus Coll BA 12. **d** 12 **p** 13. NSM Gerrards Cross and Fulmer *Ox* 12–16; R Denham from 16. *The Rectory, Ashmead Lane, Denham, Uxbridge UB9 5BB* M: 07905-530996 E: cwlindner@gmail.com

LINDOE, Jacqualine. b 56. St Mellitus Coll 12. **d** 16 **p** 17. OLM Prittlewell *Chelmsf* from 16. *18 Bridgwater Drive, Westcliff-on-Sea SS0 0DH* T: (01702) 308373 M: 07810-825694 E: jlindoe@blueyonder.co.uk

LINDOP, Andrew John. b 57. Cam Univ MA. Cranmer Hall Dur 80. **d** 82 **p** 83. C Brinsworth w Catcliffe *Sheff* 82–85; C S Shoebury *Chelmsf* 85–89; V Mosley Common *Man* 89–99; V Astley Bridge 99–11; AD Walmsley 02–10; TR Ramsbottom and Edenfield from 11. *St Andrew's Vicarage, 2 Henwick Hall Avenue, Ramsbottom, Bury BL0 9YH* T/F: (01706) 826482 E: andylindop95@tiscali.co.uk

LINDOP, Canon Kenneth. b 45. Linc Th Coll 71. **d** 74 **p** 75. C Leic St Phil 74–77; C Cov H Trin 77–80; P-in-c Cubbington 80–82; V 82–07; RD Warwick and Leamington 91–96; Jt P-in-c Leamington Spa H Trin and Old Milverton 03–07; Hon Can Cov Cathl 04–07; rtd 07; PtO *B & W* from 09. *2 Grove House, Blue Anchor, Minehead TA24 6JU* T: (01643) 821940 M: 07711-389551 E: rev.lindop@gmail.com

LINDSAY, Anne. *See* LINDSAY, Mary Jane Anne

LINDSAY, Anthony. b 38. Trin Coll Bris 92. **d** 89 **p** 90. CMS 76–92; Dioc Admin Bo Sierra Leone 89–92; C Rainham w Wennington *Chelmsf* 93–96; R Quendon w Rickling and Wicken Bonhunt etc 96–03; rtd 03; PtO *York* 03–07 and from 10; P-in-c Langtoft w Foxholes, Butterwick, Cottam etc 07–10; Rtd Clergy and Widows Officer (E Riding) from 12. *5 Bursary Court, Pickering YO18 8BF* T: (01751) 476849 M: 07398-038929 E: ptlindsay1@gmail.com

LINDSAY, Calum Oran. b 73. Edin Univ BEng 97. Ridley Hall Cam 09. **d** 11 **p** 12. C St Margaret's-on-Thames *Lon* 11–14; USA 14–16; PtO *Lon* from 15. *Dal-an-Eas, Kilmore, Oban PA34 4XU* E: revcalumlindsay@gmail.com

LINDSAY, David Macintyre. b 46. Trin Hall Cam BA 68 MA 72. Cuddesdon Coll 68. **d** 71 **p** 72. C Gosforth All SS *Newc* 71–74; C Keele *Lich* 74–78; PtO *St E* 79–80; Chapl Haberdashers' Aske's Sch Elstree 80–06; rtd 06; PtO *St Alb* 06–07; *Portsm* from 07; Co-ord Reader Tr from 10. *Kentmere, Ashling Close, Waterlooville PO7 6NQ* T: (023) 9225 7662 M: 07769-814165 E: lindsay_d46@hotmail.com

LINDSAY, Canon John Carruthers. b 50. Edin Univ MA 72 BD 82. Edin Th Coll 79. **d** 82 **p** 83. C Broughty Ferry *Bre* 82–84; C Edin St Hilda 84–85; TP 85–88; C Edin St Fillan 84–85; TP 85–88; R N Berwick 88–15; R Gullane 88–15; Can St Mary's Cathl 00–15; rtd 15; PtO *Eur* from 18. *2 West Meikle Pinkerton Cottages, Dunbar EH42 1RX* M: 07977-520277 E: canonjohnlindsay@icloud.com

LINDSAY (*née* CLEALL), Mrs Mary Jane Anne. b 54. Keele Univ BA 77 Herts Univ PGCE 92. SAOMC 00. **d** 03 **p** 04.

C Chipping Barnet *St Alb* 03–07; Chapl Portsm Hosps NHS Trust 07–17; rtd 17; PtO *Portsm* from 17. *Kentmere, Ashling Close, Waterlooville PO7 6NQ* T: (023) 9225 7662 E: annelindsay54@hotmail.com

LINDSAY, Richard John. b 46. Sarum & Wells Th Coll 74. **d** 78 **p** 79. C Aldwick *Chich* 78–81; C Almondbury w Farnley Tyas *Wakef* 81–84; V Mossley *Man* 84–15; rtd 15; PtO *Man* from 15; *Leeds* from 17. *Post Box Cottage, 15 Lindley Road, Elland HX5 0TE* T: (01422) 649250 E: lindsay.patricia@ymail.com

LINDSAY-SCOTT, Jonathan Mark. b 82. Bath Univ MEng 06. Ridley Hall Cam 11. **d** 14 **p** 15. C Romiley *Ches* 14–17; Min Wallington Springfield Ch *S'wark* from 17. *49 Stanley Park Road, Carshalton SM5 3HT* T: (020) 8404 6064 E: jon@springfieldchurch.org.uk

LINDSEY, John (Sami). b 73. Ch Ch Ox BA 95 Cranfield Univ MSc 97. Trin Coll Bris 11. **d** 13 **p** 14. C Leic H Trin w St Jo 13–16; C Emmaus Par Team 14–16; P-in-c from 16. *254 Kimberley Road, Leicester LE2 1LJ* M: 07850-326991 E: samilindsey@googlemail.com

LINDSEY, Judith Irene. b 50. **d** 19. NSM Huntington *York* from 19. *5 Lang Road, Huntington, York YO32 9SD* T: (01904) 274372 E: lindsey=j@sky.com

LINDSEY, Archdeacon of. *Vacant*

LINECAR, Rhian Wynn. b 52. Univ of Wales BMus 73 K Alfred's Coll Win CertEd 74. St Mich Coll Llan 13. **d** 15 **p** 16. NSM Cardiff City Par *Llan* from 15; NSM Cardiff Dewi Sant from 15. *Ty Llwyd, Drope Road, St George's-super-Ely, Cardiff CF5 6EP* T: (01446) 760007 M: 07545-425221 E: rlinecar@gmail.com

LINES, Graham Martin. b 55. St Jo Coll Nottm 97. **d** 99 **p** 00. C Crosby *Linc* 99–02; C Bottesford w Ashby 02–03; TV 03–14; V Crowle Gp from 14. *The Vicarage, Church Street, Crowle, Scunthorpe DN17 4LE* E: grahamlines62@gmail.com

LINES, Nicholas David John. b 64. York St Jo Univ MA 16. St Jo Coll Nottm 94. **d** 96 **p** 97. C Burton All SS w Ch Ch *Lich* 96–01; P-in-c Rodbourne Cheney *Bris* 01–02; R from 02. *St Mary's Rectory, 298 Cheney Manor Road, Swindon SN2 2PF* T: (01793) 522379 E: nick.lines1@gmail.com

LINFORD, Susan. b 51. STETS 10. **d** 13 **p** 14. OLM Bride Valley *Sarum* 13–16; NSM from 16. *North Hill Cottage, Shipton Lane, Burton Bradstock, Bridport DT6 4NQ* T: (01308) 897363 E: sue.linford@btopenworld.com

LING, Canon Adrian Roger. b 66. Goldsmiths' Coll Lon BA 89 Leeds Univ BA 02. Coll of Resurr Mirfield 00. **d** 02 **p** 03. C Mill End and Heronsgate w W Hyde *St Alb* 02–06; P-in-c Flegg Coastal Benefice *Nor* 06–08; R 08–12; R S Lynn from 12; PtO *Ely* from 17; Hon Can Nor Cathl from 18; CMP from 13. *All Saints' Rectory, 33 Goodwins Road, King's Lynn PE30 5QX* T: (01553) 771779 E: adrianrling@btinternet.com

LING, Timothy Charles. b 61. Ex Univ BA 85 Selw Coll Cam BA 91. Ridley Hall Cam 89. **d** 92 **p** 93. C Gerrards Cross and Fulmer *Ox* 92–96; C Woking St Pet *Guildf* 96–00; V Bathford *B & W* 00–09; PtO 10–18; NSM Bath St Bart from 18. *26 Mendip Gardens, Bath BA2 2UT* T: (01225) 722622 M: 07760-785829 E: tim@stbartsbath.org

LINGARD, Colin. b 36. Kelham Th Coll 58. **d** 63 **p** 64. C Middlesbrough St Martin *York* 63–66; C Stainton-in-Cleveland 66–71; V Eskdaleside w Ugglebarnby 71–77; P-in-c Redcar w Kirkleatham 77; V Kirkleatham 78–86; RD Guisborough 83–86; V Linc St Botolph 86–89; Dioc Dir of Readers 86–89; R Washington *Dur* 89–93; P-in-c Middleton St George 93–97; R 97–01; Chapl Teesside Airport 97–01; rtd 01; PtO *Dur* from 01. *29 Belgrave Terrace, Hurworth Place, Darlington DL2 2DW* M: 07752-179418 E: jlingard3@gmail.com

LINGARD, Jennifer Mary. *See* ALIDINA, Jennifer Mary

LINGS, Canon George William. b 49. Nottm Univ BTh 74 Ox Univ PGCE 75 Lambeth MLitt 93 Man Univ PhD 09. St Jo Coll Nottm 70. **d** 75 **p** 76. C Harold Wood *Chelmsf* 75–78; C Reigate St Mary *S'wark* 78–85; V Deal St Geo *Cant* 85–97; First Dir CA Sheff Cen for Ch Planting and Evang 97–17; NSM Norfolk Park St Leonard CD *Sheff* 97–03; NSM Arbourthorne and Norfolk Park 03–05; Hon Can Sheff Cathl 11–17; rtd 17; PtO *Sheff* from 17. *28 Norfolk Road, Sheffield S2 2SX* T: 0114-270 1780

LINGWOOD, Preb David Peter. b 51. Lon Univ BEd 73 Southn Univ BTh 80. Sarum & Wells Th Coll 75. **d** 78 **p** 79. C Ashford St Hilda *Lon* 78–81; TV Blakenall Heath, The Ridge *Worc* 81–86; TR Blakenall Heath *Lich* 86–96; V Rushall 96–04; RD Walsall 98–03; TR Stoke-upon-Trent 04–16; RD Stoke 07–14; Preb Lich Cathl 01–16; rtd 16; PtO *Worc* from 17. *32 Fairoak Drive, Bromsgrove B60 3PN* E: canonlingwood@gmail.com

LINN, Frederick Hugh. b 37. Em Coll Cam BA 61 MA 65. Ripon Hall Ox 61. **d** 63 **p** 64. C Bramhall *Ches* 63–68; V Liscard St Mary 68–71; V Liscard St Mary w St Columba 71–74; V Wybunbury 74–82; R Eccleston and Pulford 82–98;

rtd 98; PtO *Ches* from 98; *St As* from 09. *4 Stonewalls, Burton, Rossett, Wrexham LL12 0LG* T: (01244) 571942 *or* (01407) 810372 E: hugh.linn@btinternet.com

LINNEGAR, George Leonard. b 33. CGA. Kelham Th Coll 63. **d** 62 **p** 63. C Wellingborough St Mary *Pet* 62–65; LtO *Lich* 65–69; PtO *B & W* 69–80; Hon C Lewes All SS, St Anne, St Mich and St Thos *Chich* 80–86; C 87–99; rtd 99; PtO *Chich* from 99. *20 Morris Road, Lewes BN7 2AT* T: (01273) 478145

LINNEY, Barry James. b 64. Spurgeon's Coll BD 97 Anglia Poly Univ MA 02 Univ of Wales (Trin St Dav) MMin 14. Westcott Ho Cam 99. **d** 01 **p** 02. C Chingford SS Pet and Paul *Chelmsf* 01–04; V Cherry Hinton St Andr *Ely* 04–15; P-in-c Chatham St Steph *Roch* 15–17; V from 17. *St Stephen's Vicarage, 55 Pattens Lane, Chatham ME4 6JR* T: (01634) 305786 E: barryjameslinney@gmail.com

LINNEY, The Ven Gordon Charles Scott. b 39. CITC 66. **d** 69 **p** 70. C Agherton *Conn* 69–72; Min Can Down Cathl *D & D* 72–75; V Dublin St Cath w St Jas *D & G* 75–80; Preb Tipperkevin St Patr Cathl Dublin 77–80; I Glenageary *D & G* 80–04; Adn Dublin 88–04; Lect CITC 89–93; rtd 04. *208 Upper Glenageary Road, Glenageary, Co Dublin, Republic of Ireland* T: (00353) (1) 284 8503 M: 87-254 1775 E: glinney@eircom.net *or* linney.gordon@gmail.com

LINS, Hannah Melanie. b 78. St Mellitus Coll 14. **d** 17 **p** 18. C Bicton, Montford w Shrawardine and Fitz *Lich* from 17; C Leaton and Albrighton w Battlefield from 17. *41 Grange Road, Shrewsbury SY3 9DG* T: (01743) 232598 E: revhannahlins@gmail.com

LINTERN, John. b 61. Linc Th Coll BTh 93. **d** 93 **p** 94. C Preston on Tees *Dur* 93–96; Asst Dioc Youth Adv 96–99; P-in-c W Pelton 96–07; P-in-c Pelton 99–07; V Pelton and W Pelton from 07. *The Vicarage, West Pelton, Stanley DH9 6RT* T: 0191-370 2146 F: 07971-114359 E: john.lintern@durham.anglican.org

LINTERN, Robert George. b 43. **d** 10 **p** 11. OLM Codsall *Lich* 10–17; PtO from 17. *66 Ravenhill Drive, Codsall, Wolverhampton WV8 1BL* M: 07971-403157 E: lintern@gmail.com

LINTON, Mrs Angela Margaret. b 45. SAOMC 97. **d** 00 **p** 01. NSM Langtree *Ox* from 00. *10 Yew Tree Court, Goring, Reading RG8 9HF* T/F: (01491) 874236 M: 07884-346552 E: dormouse2@yahoo.co.uk

LINTON, The Ven Barry Ian. b 76. Glas Univ BSc 98 TCD BTh 04 MCIBS 01. CITC 01. **d** 04 **p** 05. C Enniskillen *Clogh* 04–08; I Drumcliffe w Lissadell and Munninane *K, E & A* 08–15; Adn Elphin and Ardagh 12–15; I Drumragh w Mountfield *D & R* from 15. *The Rectory, 8 Mullaghmenagh Avenue, Omagh BT78 5QH* M: 07931-600920

LINZEY, Prof Andrew. b 52. K Coll Lon BD 73 PhD 86 AKC 73 Lambeth DD 01. St Aug Coll Cant 75. **d** 75 **p** 76. C Charlton-in-Dover *Cant* 75–77; Chapl and Lect Th NE Surrey Coll of Tech 77–81; Chapl Essex Univ *Chelmsf* 81–92; Dir of Studies Cen for Study of Th 87–92; Sen Research Fell Mansf Coll Ox 92–00; Tutor Chr Ethics 93–00; Special Prof Th Nottm Univ 92–96; Special Prof St Xavier Univ Chicago from 96; Hon Prof Birm Univ 97–07; Sen Research Fell Blackfriars Hall Ox 00–06; Dir Ox Cen for Animal Ethics from 06; Hon Prof Win Univ from 07; Hon Res Fell St Steph Ho Ox from 08. *91 Iffley Road, Oxford OX4 1EG* T: (01865) 201565 E: andrewlinzey@aol.com *or* director@oxfordanimalethics.com

LION, Christopher Mark. b 84. St Mellitus Coll 12. **d** 15 **p** 16. C Gerrards Cross and Fulmer *Ox* 15–19; PtO from 19. *1 Manor House Mews, Oxford Road, Gerrards Cross SL9 7DW* M: 07796-115951 E: candclion@gmail.com *or* chris.lion@saintjames.org.uk

LIPOVSKY, Attila (Gregory). b 79. Pécs Th Coll Hungary BA 04 St Steph Ho Ox 16. **d** 03 **p** 03. PtO *Ox* 16–17; C Cambridge St Mary Less *Ely* 17–19; V Weymouth St Paul *Sarum* from 19. *Address temp unknown* M: 07796-963703 E: gregorio.hu@gmail.com

LIPPIATT, Michael Charles. b 39. Oak Hill Th Coll BD 71. **d** 71 **p** 72. C Ardsley *Sheff* 71–74; C Lenton *S'well* 74–78; V Jesmond H Trin *Newc* 78–96; rtd 96. *69 Lansdowne Crescent, Stanwix, Carlisle CA3 9ES* T: (01228) 537080

LIPPIETT, Canon Peter Vernon. b 47. Lon Univ MB, BS 73 MRCGP 80 Univ of Wales (Lamp) MA 08. Ripon Coll Cuddesdon 86. **d** 88 **p** 89. C Pinner *Lon* 88–91; V Twyford and Owslebury and Morestead *Win* 91–99; P-in-c Rydal *Carl* 99–03; Warden Rydal Hall and Ldr Rydal Hall Community 99–03; Dioc Spirituality Adv *Portsm* 03–10; Hon Can Portsm Cathl 10; rtd 11; PtO *Win* from 11. *Pax Lodge, Cox's Hill, Twyford, Winchester SO21 1PQ* T: (01962) 717438 E: peterlippiett@gmail.com

LIPSCOMB, Canon Timothy William. b 52. Chich Th Coll 82. **d** 85 **p** 86. C Sevenoaks St Jo *Roch* 85–89; C Stanningley

St Thos *Ripon* 89–92; V Armley w New Wortley 92–05; AD Armley 98–05; R Preston St Jo and St Geo *Blackb* 05–17; AD Preston 08–14; Hon Can Blackb Cathl 10–17; rtd 17. *Beach Lawn, 123 Peulwys Lane, Old Colwyn, Colwyn Bay LL29 8YF* T: (01492) 512759 M: 07855-396452 E: lavisherminegourmet@gmail.com

LIPSCOMBE, Brian. b 37. Bris Univ BA 62. Tyndale Hall Bris 62. **d** 64 **p** 65. C Eccleston Ch Ch *Liv* 64–66; C Halliwell St Pet *Man* 66–69; C Frogmore *St Alb* 69–72; V Richmond Ch Ch *S'wark* 72–75; TV Mortlake w E Sheen 76–80; P-in-c Streatham Vale H Redeemer 80–85; V 85–91; R Norris Bank *Man* 91–96; V Droylsden St Martin 96–02; PtO *Ripon* 02–14; *Bradf* 13–14; *Leeds* from 14. *15 St Anne's Drive, Leeds LS4 2SA* T: 0113-275 1893 M: 07743-168641

LISK, Canon Stewart. b 62. Regent's Park Coll Ox BA 84 MA 88. St Mich Coll Llan 86. **d** 88 **p** 89. C Glan Ely *Llan* 88–92; Chapl Cardiff Inst of HE 92–96; Chapl Welsh Coll of Music and Drama 92–96; Asst Chapl Univ of Wales (Cardiff) 92–96; V Glan Ely 96–06; AD Llan 04–06; V Roath from 06; AD Cardiff from 17; Can Llan Cathl from 14. *Roath Vicarage, Waterloo Road, Cardiff CF23 5AD* T: (029) 2048 4808 *or* 2048 7854 E: stewart.lisk@live.co.uk

LISSENDEN, Steven John. b 64. St Mellitus Coll 16. **d** 19. OLM Wickford and Runwell *Chelmsf* from 19. *102 Bruce Grove, Wickford SS11 8QH* T: (01268) 763670 M: 07944-959300 E: revsteveliss@gmail.com

LISTER, Mrs Jennifer Grace. b 44. Totley Hall Coll CertEd 65. NOC 87. **d** 92 **p** 94. C Cowgate *Newc* 92–95; C Wall and Lich St Mary w St Mich 95–96; P-in-c Yoxall and Asst P The Ridwares and Kings Bromley 96–07; rtd 07; PtO *Cov* from 09. *81 Kingsley Road, Bishops Tachbrook, Leamington Spa CV33 9RZ* T: (01926) 427922 E: jenny.lister@waitrose.com

LISTER (née AISBITT), Mrs Joanne. b 69. St Jo Coll Dur BA 91. St Steph Ho Ox 91. **d** 93. NSM Mill End and Heronsgate w W Hyde *St Alb* 93–96. *Via Maggio 16, Oltrarno, 50125 Firenze, Italy* T/F: (0039) (055) 294764 E: listerwilliam@hotmail.com

LISTER, Joseph Hugh. b 38. Tyndale Hall Bris 61. **d** 64 **p** 65. C Pemberton St Mark Newtown *Liv* 64–68; Hon C Braintree *Chelmsf* 68–71; C Darfield *Sheff* 71–73; P-in-c Sheff St Swithun 73–75; TV Sheff Manor 76–80; TR Winfarthing w Shelfanger *Nor* 80–81; P-in-c Burston 80–81; P-in-c Gissing 80–81; P-in-c Tivetshall 80–81; R Winfarthing w Shelfanger w Burston w Gissing etc 81–88; P-in-c Sandon, Wallington and Rushden w Clothall *St Alb* 88–89; R 89–93; R Nether and Over Seale *Derby* 93–96; V Lullington 93–96; R Seale and Lullington 96–98; Dean Ndola Repton 96–98; Zambia 99–02; rtd 02; Hon C Hartington, Biggin and Earl Sterndale *Derby* 02–04; C Stoke Canon, Poltimore w Huxham and Rewe etc *Ex* 05–06; PtO *Carl* 10–16. *Cliff Cottage, Thorpe, Ashbourne DE6 2AW* T: (01335) 350383 E: joeandgillie@gmail.com

LISTER, Miss Mary Phyllis. b 28. St Andr Ho Portsm 52. **dss** 80 **d** 87. Inkberrow w Cookhill and Kington w Dormston *Worc* 80–82; Ancaster *Linc* 82–87; C 87–88; rtd 88; PtO *Worc* 88–00; *Leic* from 15. *6 Stuart Court, High Street, Kibworth Beauchamp, Leicester LE8 0LR* T: 0116-279 3763

LISTER, Peter. b 42. Leeds Univ BA 64 Newc Univ PGCE 75. Coll of Resurr Mirfield 63. **d** 65 **p** 66. C Monkseaton St Pet *Newc* 65–68; C Cramlington 68–70; Hon C 71–78; C Morpeth 79–83; V Shilbottle 83–88; Asst Dioc Dir of Educn 83–88; Dir of Educn 88–95; Hon Can Newc Cathl 88–95; Dioc Dir of Educn *Lich* 95–06; rtd 07; PtO *Lich* 07–09; *Cov* from 09. *81 Kingsley Road, Bishops Tachbrook, Leamington Spa CV33 9RZ* T: (01926) 427922 E: peterlister@globalnet.co.uk

LISTER, Peter William Ryley. b 56. Linc Sch of Th and Min 08. **d** 10 **p** 11. OLM Bourne *Linc* from 10. *4 Linden Rise, Bourne PE10 9TD* T: (01778) 423730 E: pwr.lister@btinternet.com

LISTER, William Bernard. b 67. Keble Coll Ox BA 88 MA 92. St Steph Ho Ox BA 91. **d** 92 **p** 93. C Mill End and Heronsgate w W Hyde *St Alb* 92–96; CF 96–06; Sen CF 06–12; Chapl Florence w Siena *Eur* from 12. *Via Maggio 16, Oltrarno, 50125 Firenze, Italy* T: (0039) (055) 294764 M: (0039) 328-180 4196 E: chaplain@stmarksitaly.com

LISVANE, Lady (Constance Jane). b 51. Lanchester Poly Cov BA 73. WEMTC 10. **d** 13 **p** 14. C Cusop w Blakemere, Bredwardine w Brobury etc *Heref* 13–17; NSM from 17. *Blakemere House, Blakemere, Hereford HR2 9JZ* T: (01981) 500478 E: jane@blakemerehouse.myzen.co.uk

LITHERLAND, Terence. b 46. **d** 93 **p** 94. OLM Horwich and Rivington *Man* 93–16; OLM Blackrod 11–15; rtd 16. *61 Tomlinson Street, Horwich, Bolton BL6 5QR* T: (01204) 692201 M: 07436-019274 E: tlitherland36@gmail.com

LITTLE, Andrew. b 27. Open Univ BA 83 UEA BA 03. AKC 51. **d** 52 **p** 53. C Fulham All SS *Lon* 52–54; C Epsom St Barn *Guildf* 54–61; V Northwood *Lich* 61–72; V Stowe 72–85; P-in-c Hixon 72–85; V Hixon w Stowe-by-Chartley 86–89; rtd 89;

PtO *Nor* 89–09; Hon PV Nor Cathl 93–09. *4 Capel Court, The Burgage, Prestbury, Cheltenham GL52 3EL* T: (01242) 285800

LITTLE, Bryan Martin. b 80. Edin Univ MA 01. Cranmer Hall Dur 15. **d** 17 **p** 18. C E Clevedon w Clapton in Gordano etc *B & W* from 17. *Woodlands, 74 Walton Road, Clevedon BS21 6AN* M: 07816-955713

LITTLE, Ms Christine. b 60. Lanc Univ BA 83. St Jo Coll Nottm 88. **d** 91 **p** 94. Par Dn Meltham *Wakef* 91–94; C Hatcham St Jas *S'wark* 94–99; P-in-c 99–04; C Nottingham St Pet and All SS *S'well* 04–07; C Nottingham All SS, St Mary and St Pet 07–14; C Bestwood Em and St Mark w Rise Park from 14. *5 Hatton Close, Arnold, Nottingham NG5 9QG* T: 0115-840 7209 E: revchrissielittle@gmail.com

LITTLE, Derek Peter. b 50. St Jo Coll Dur BA 72. Trin Coll Bris. **d** 75 **p** 76. C Bradley *Wakef* 75–78; C Kidderminster St Geo *Worc* 78–82; V Lepton *Wakef* 82–85; E Regional Sec CPAS 85–88; V Canonbury St Steph *Lon* 88–96; R Bedhampton *Portsm* 96–99; rtd 99. *Sunnyside House, 14 Culimore Road, West Wittering, Chichester PO20 8HB* T: (01243) 671114 E: littlederek20@gmail.com

LITTLE, George Nelson. b 39. CITC 70. **d** 72 **p** 73. C Portadown St Mark *Arm* 72–76; I Newtownhamilton w Ballymoyer and Belleek 76–80; I Aghaderg w Donaghmore *D & D* 80–82; I Aghaderg w Donaghmore and Scarva 82–05; Can Dromore Cathl 93–05; Treas Dromore Cathl 93–05; Chan Dromore Cathl 03–05; rtd 05. *41 Carn Valley, Rathfriland, Newry BT34 5GA* T: (028) 4023 9102

LITTLE, Ian Dawtry Torrance. b 49. Keele Univ BEd 72. SWMTC 81. **d** 85 **p** 86. NSM St Stythians w Perranarworthal and Gwennap *Truro* 85–97; NSM Chacewater w St Day and Carharrack 97–06; PtO from 06. *Kernyk, Crellow Fields, Stithians, Truro TR3 7RE*

LITTLE, James Harry. b 57. York Univ BA 79. Qu Coll Birm 84. **d** 87 **p** 88. C Wollaton *S'well* 87–90; C N Wheatley, W Burton, Bole, Saundby, Sturton etc 90–93; R E Markham w Askham, Headon w Upton and Grove 93–06; P-in-c Dunham w Darlton, Ragnall, Fledborough etc 04–06; TR Howden *York* from 06; RD 10–15. *The Minster Rectory, Market Place, Howden, Goole DN14 7BL* T: (01430) 432056 E: revjlittle@aol.com

LITTLE, Martin. *See* LITTLE, Bryan Martin

LITTLE, Nigel James. b 73. Middx Univ BA 93. Oak Hill Th Coll 98. **d** 01 **p** 02. C Highgate St Mich *Lon* 01–07; TV Kirk Ella and Willerby *York* 07–12; Chapl Felsted Sch from 12. *Stavells, Braintree Road, Felsted, Dunmow CM6 3DR* T: (01371) 822600 E: nigel_little@yahoo.com

LITTLE, Canon Stephen Clifford. b 47. Man Univ MEd 81. AKC 72. **d** 72 **p** 73. C Grange St Andr *Ches* 72–73; C E Runcorn w Halton 73–75; P-in-c Newbold *Man* 75–77; P-in-c Broughton and Milton Keynes *Ox* 77–82; Sector Min Milton Keynes Chr Coun 77–84; TR Warwick *Cov* 84–93; R Harvington and Norton and Lenchwick *Worc* 93–96; R Harvington 96–98; Exec Officer Dioc Bd for Ch and Soc *Man* 98–05; Exec Officer Dioc Bd for Min and Soc 01–05; Hon Can Man Cathl 00–05; PtO from 05. *12 Redwood, Westhoughton, Bolton BL5 2RU* T: 0161-832 5253 M: 07795-821476 E: stephenlittle@essell.org.uk

LITTLEFORD, Peter John. b 40. St Mark & St Jo Coll Lon CertEd 63 ACP 65 Birkbeck Coll Lon BSc 70 Lon Inst of Educn DipEd 73 MA 76. SAOMC 96. **d** 99 **p** 00. Chapl De Montfort Univ *Leic* 99–01; NSM Bedf St Mark *St Alb* 99–01; NSM Bedford St Mich 01–04; NSM Elstow 04–10; rtd 10; PtO *St Alb* from 10. *1 Bindon Abbey, Bedford MK41 0AZ* T: (01234) 356645 E: peterlittleford@btinternet.com

LITTLEJOHN, Keith Douglas. b 59. Ripon Coll Cuddesdon BTh 03. **d** 03 **p** 04. C Horsham *Chich* 03–07; P-in-c Bolney 07–19; P-in-c Cowfold 07–19; V Goring-by-Sea from 19. *12 Compton Avenue, Goring-by-Sea, Worthing BN12 4UJ* T: (01903) 242525 M: 07905-544366 E: keithdlj@aol.com

LITTLER, Eric Raymond. b 36. AMIC 93. Roch Th Coll 65. **d** 68 **p** 69. C Hatfield Hyde *St Alb* 68–73; Chapl Welwyn Garden City Hosp 70–73; TV Pemberton St Jo *Liv* 73–78; Chapl Billinge Hosp Wigan 76–81; V Pemberton St Fran Kitt Green *Liv* 78–81; V White Notley, Faulkbourne and Cressing *Chelmsf* 81–88; V Westcliff St Andr 88–96; Chapl Westcliff Hosp 88–96; Chapl Southend HA 89–96; R E and W Tilbury and Linford *Chelmsf* 96–98; Chapl Orsett Hosp 96–98; RD Thurrock *Chelmsf* 96–98; R Gt Oakley w Wix and Wrabness 98–02; Chapl Essex Rivers Healthcare NHS Trust 98–02; rtd 02; PtO *Sarum* from 98; *Chelmsf* 02–19; *B & W* from 02; Chapl St Jo Hosp Heytesbury 03–08. *Minster Hall, 1 Pound Row, Warminster BA12 8NQ* T: (01985) 218818 E: ericandsuzette@uwclub.net

LITTLEWOOD, Alan James. b 51. Man Poly BEd 77. **d** 95 **p** 96. OLM Gosberton *Linc* 95–97; OLM Gosberton, Gosberton Clough and Quadring 97–01; C Bourne 01–03; P-in-c

Leasingham and Cranwell 03–08; P-in-c Ancaster Wilsford Gp 08–14; P-in-c Barkston and Hough Gp 11–14; rtd 15; PtO *Linc* from 16. *26 Alexander Road, Lincoln LN2 4FA* E: alanjlittlewood@gmail.com

LITTLEWOOD, Alistair David. b 68. St Cath Coll Ox BA 89. Qu Coll Birm 93. **d** 96 **p** 97. C Keyworth and Stanton-on-the-Wolds *S'well* 96–00; Chapl Birm Univ 00–05; P-in-c Edwinstowe *S'well* 05–10; P-in-c Perlethorpe 05–10; Hon C Mansfield Deanery 10–12; PtO *S'well* from 12. *24 The Heathers, Boughton, Newark NG22 9HE* E: 1alistairlittlewood@gmail.com

LITTLEWOOD, Miss Jacqueline Patricia. b 52. Linc Th Coll 77. **dss** 80 **d** 87 **p** 94. Crayford *Roch* 80–84; Gravesend H Family w Ifield 84–87; Par Dn 87–93; rtd 93; NSM Gravesend St Aid *Roch* from 93; NSM Milton next Gravesend Ch Ch from 06. *25 Beltana Drive, Gravesend DA12 4BT* T: (01474) 560106 E: jpl7skypilot@gmail.com

LITTLEWOOD, Mrs Penelope Anne. b 47. WEMTC 05. **d** 08 **p** 09. NSM Burghill *Heref* 08–12; P-in-c 12–17; NSM Pipe-cum-Lyde and Moreton-on-Lugg 08–12; P-in-c 12–17; NSM Stretton Sugwas 08–12; P-in-c 12–17; rtd 17; PtO *Heref* from 18. *Cobwebs, Burghill, Hereford HR4 7RL* T: (01432) 760835 M: 07734-347327 E: penny.cobwebs@virgin.net

LITTON, Alan. b 42. Ridley Hall Cam 66. **d** 69 **p** 70. C Bolton St Bede *Man* 69–71; C Ashton St Mich 71–73; V Haslingden St Jo Stonefold *Blackb* 73–77; Ind Chapl *York* 77–81; V Crewe All SS and St Paul *Ches* 81–84; Ind Chapl *Liv* 84–89; V Spotland *Man* 89–94; R Newchurch *Liv* 94–02; P-in-c Croft w Southworth 99–02; R Newchurch w Croft 02; rtd 02; PtO *Liv* 03–08; Hon C Burtonwood from 08. *3 Rosemary Close, Great Sankey, Warrington WA5 1TL* T: (01925) 222944 E: littonalan@gmail.com

LITZELL, Sven Anders. b 80. Wheaton Coll Illinois BA 03 Stockholm Univ MSc 04. Ridley Hall Cam 10. **d** 12 **p** 13. C Holborn St Geo w H Trin and St Bart *Lon* 12–15; Prior Community of St Anselm *Cant* 15–18; PtO *Lon* 18–18; R Westville St Eliz S Africa from 18. *St Elizabeth's Church, 45 Salisbury Avenue, Westville, Durban 3629, KwaZulu-Natal, South Africa* T: (0027) (31) 266 4325 E: rector@stelizabeths.co.za

LIVERPOOL, Archdeacon of. *See* MACGUIRE, The Ven Michael Joseph Patrick

LIVERPOOL, Bishop of. *See* BAYES, The Rt Revd Paul

LIVERPOOL, Dean of. *See* JONES, The Very Revd Susan Helen

LIVERSIDGE, Mrs Linda Sheila. b 48. Oak Hill Th Coll BA 98. **d** 98 **p** 99. C Kensal Rise St Mark and St Martin *Lon* 98–01; TV N Wingfield, Clay Cross and Pilsley *Derby* 01–11; P-in-c Willingham *Ely* 11–16; rtd 16; PtO *Lon* from 16. *2 Hatton Road, Cheshunt, Waltham Cross EN8 9QQ* T: (01992) 910398 M: 07941-667616 E: revlin@me.com

LIVESEY, Rachel Elizabeth. *See* DALE, Rachel Elizabeth

LIVESLEY, John. b 80. Magd Coll Ox BA 02 MSt 03 MA 07 Leeds Univ MA 07. Coll of Resurr Mirfield 04. **d** 07 **p** 08. C Swinton and Pendlebury *Man* 07–10; P-in-c Tudhoe Grange *Dur* 10–19; P-in-c Cassop cum Quarrington 10–19; V Spennymoor and Tudhoe Grange from 19. *St Andrew's Vicarage, St Andrew's Road, Spennymoor DL16 6NE* T: (01388) 814817 M: 07796-117568 E: johnlivesley1980@yahoo.co.uk

LIVINGSTONE, Jonathan David. b 84. St Andr Univ MA 06. Scottish Episc Inst 04. **d** 17 **p** 18. C Hamilton *Glas* from 17; C Uddingston from 17. *15 Chalmers Court, Main Street, Uddingston, Glasgow G71 7LR* T: (01698) 301577 M: 07545-303592 E: jdlivingstone@hotmail.com

LIYANAGE, Sylvester. b 78. Surrey Univ BEng 01 Surrey Univ MSc 03 Cam Univ BTh 08. Ridley Hall Cam 05. **d** 08 **p** 09. C Kingston Hill St Paul *S'wark* 08–12; TV Gt Chesham *Ox* 12–19. *Fabriksgatan 36C, 702 23 Orebro, Sweden* E: s.liyanage@btinternet.com

LLANDAFF, Archdeacon of. *See* JACKSON, The Ven Frances Anne

LLANDAFF, Bishop of. *See* OSBORNE, The Rt Revd June

LLANDAFF, Dean of. *See* CAPON, The Very Revd Gerwyn Huw

✠**LLEWELLIN, The Rt Revd John Richard Allan.** b 38. Fitzw Ho Cam BA 64 MA 78. Westcott Ho Cam 61. **d** 64 **p** 65 **c** 85. C Radlett *St Alb* 64–68; C Johannesburg Cathl S Africa 68–71; V Waltham Cross *St Alb* 71–79; R Harpenden St Nic 79–85; Hon Can Truro Cathl 85–92; Suff Bp St Germans 85–92; Suff Bp Dover *Cant* 92–99; Bp at Lambeth (Hd of Staff) 99–03; rtd 03; PtO *Truro* 04–07; Hon Asst Bp Cant from 08. *15A The Precincts, Canterbury CT1 2EL* T: (01227) 764645 M: 07850-185869 E: rllewellin@clara.co.uk

LLEWELLYN, Brian Michael. b 47. Univ of Wales (Cardiff) LLM 99 MRICS 73. Sarum & Wells Th Coll 78. **d** 80 **p** 81. C Farncombe *Guildf* 80–83; Chapl RAF 83–87; R Hethersett w Canteloff w Lt and Gt Melton *Nor* 87–95; RD Humbleyard 94–95; P-in-c Smallburgh w Dilham w Honing and Crostwight 95–98; R 98–00; P-in-c Folkestone St Sav *Cant*

00–07; rtd 07; P-in-c Ypres *Eur* 10–16; PtO *Chich* from 17. *19 James Avenue, Herstmonceux, Hailsham BN27 4PB* T: (01323) 832899 E: bllewy@gmail.com

LLEWELLYN, Canon Christine Ann. b 46. Univ of Wales (Ban) BA 69 DipEd 70. **d** 89 **p** 97. NSM Arthog w Fairbourne w Llangelynnin w Rhoslefain *Ban* 90–93; NSM Holyhead w Rhoscolyn w Llanfair-yn-Neubwll 93–94; C 94–95; C Holyhead 95–97; TV 97–04; TR 04–11; Hon Can Ban Cathl 03–07; Can Cursal Ban Cathl 07–11; rtd 12; PtO *Ban* from 12; AD Llifon and Talybolion 13–15. *The Old School, Rhoscolyn, Holyhead LL65 2RQ* T: (01407) 741593

LLEWELLYN, Neil Alexander. b 55. LWCMD 78. Westcott Ho Cam 79 Sarum & Wells Th Coll 83. **d** 84 **p** 85. C Heref St Martin 84–86; Chapl Rotterdam Miss to Seamen *Eur* 86–89; R Docking w The Birchams and Stanhoe w Barwick *Nor* 89–92; Chapl Ypres *Eur* 92–95; Toc H 92–95; CF 95–96; P-in-c Newport w Cilgwyn and Dinas w Llanllawer *St D* 06–07; V Newport w Cilgwyn and Nevern and Y Beifil etc 07–11; V Newport w Cilgwyn and Dinas w Llanllawer etc 11–18; P-in-c W Cemaes from 18. *The Rectory, Long Street, Newport SA42 0TJ* T: (01239) 820380

LLEWELLYN, Richard Morgan. b 37. FCMI 81. Sarum & Wells Th Coll 91. **d** 93 **p** 94. C Brecon St Mary and Battle w Llanddew *S & B* 93–95; Min Can Brecon Cathl 93–95; Chapl Ch Coll Brecon 95–14. *Field House, Llangattock, Crickhowell NP8 1HL* T: (01873) 810116 E: morgan.llewellyn@btinternet.com

LLEWELLYN-MACDUFF, Ms Lindsay. b 75. Kent Univ BA 97. St Mich Coll Llan 97. **d** 99 **p** 00. C Milton next Sittingbourne *Cant* 99–01; C Barham w Bishopsbourne and Kingston 01–03; C Margate All SS and Westgate St Sav 03–05; P-in-c Gt Finborough w Onehouse, Harleston, Buxhall etc *St E* 05–09; Chapl HM Pris Littlehey 10–14; Bp's Dom Chapl *Roch* from 14. *Bishopscourt, 24 St Margaret's Street, Rochester ME1 1TS* T: (01634) 814439 E: bishops.chaplain@rochester.anglican.org

LLEWELYN, Miss Gabrielle Jane. b 48. Trin Coll Bris 08. **d** 09 **p** 10. NSM Fair Oak *Win* 09–12; Chapl HM Pris Northd 12–15; PtO *Newc* from 12. *9 Acton Crescent, Felton, Morpeth NE65 9NF* M: 07817-731036 E: gabbyllewelyn@hotmail.com

LLOYD, Canon Bernard James. b 29. AKC 56. **d** 57 **p** 58. C Laindon w Basildon *Chelmsf* 57–65; V E Ham St Geo 65–82; RD Newham 76–82; Hon Can Chelmsf Cathl 82–94; R Danbury 82–94; P-in-c Woodham Ferrers 87–90; rtd 94; PtO *Chelmsf* from 94. *Chanterelle, 47 Seaview Avenue, West Mersea, Colchester CO5 8HE* T: (01206) 383892

LLOYD, The Ven Bertram Trevor. b 38. Hertf Coll Ox BA 60 MA 64. Clifton Th Coll 62. **d** 64 **p** 65. C S Mimms Ch Ch *Lon* 64–70; V Wealdstone H Trin 70–84; RD Harrow 77–82; P-in-c Harrow Weald St Mich 80–84; V Harrow Trin St Mich 84–89; Adn Barnstaple *Ex* 89–02; Preb Ex Cathl 91–02; rtd 02. *8 Pebbleridge Road, Westward Ho!, Bideford EX39 1HN* T: (01237) 424701 E: trevorlloyd152@outlook.com

LLOYD, Mrs Carole Barbara. b 53. Sheff Univ BA 74 Coll of Ripon & York St Jo MA 03 Leeds Metrop Univ PGCE 93. NOC 00. **d** 03 **p** 04. C Bolton St Jas w St Chrys *Bradf* 03–06; C Gt Aycliffe and Chilton *Dur* 06–07; TV Gt Aycliffe 07–09; P-in-c Chilton 09–11; P-in-c Kelloe and Coxhoe 08–11; P-in-c Swanwick and Pentrich *Derby* 11–12; V 12–15; rtd 15; PtO *Derby* 15–17; P-in-c Ilkeston St Mary 17–18; PtO *S'well* from 19. *1 Ascot Close, West Hallam, Ilkeston DE7 6LB* T: 0115-930 8316 M: 07948-836523 E: carole.lloyd@amnos.co.uk

LLOYD, David Edgar Charles. b 59. St Mich Coll Llan 97. **d** 99 **p** 00. C Newton Nottage *Llan* 99–03; V Newcastle from 03. *The Vicarage, 1 Walters Road, Bridgend CF31 4HE* T: (01656) 655999 E: frdavidlloyd@hotmail.com

LLOYD, David John. b 52. Lon Univ BD 82. Burgess Hall Lamp 73. **d** 76 **p** 77. C Pembroke St Mary w St Mich *St D* 76–77; C Llanelli 77–80; V Cil-y-Cwm and Ystrad-ffin w Rhandir-mwyn etc 80–82; Oman 82–84; R Llanllwchaearn and Llanina *St D* 84–88; V Llangennech and Hendy 88–90; PtO *St Alb* 91–95; V Bampton w Clanfield *Ox* 96–17; AD Witney 02–03; rtd 17; PtO *S & B* from 18. *26 Palace Avenue, Llanelli SA15 1NA* T: (01554) 228836 E: revdjlloyd@hotmail.co.uk

LLOYD, Dennis John. b 46. BSc 70 MSc 74 PhD 81. S Dios Minl Tr Scheme. **d** 90 **p** 91. C Hamworthy *Sarum* 90–92; Chapl UEA *Nor* 92–97; P-in-c Malvern St Andr *Worc* 97–99; V 99–01; Chapl Defence Evaluation Research Agency 97–01; RD Malvern *Worc* 98–01; P-in-c Rowlands Castle *Portsm* 01–11; Warden of Readers 01–11; rtd 11; PtO *Portsm* from 11. *24 Forest Hills, Newport PO30 5NQ* E: revdrdjlloyd@aol.com

LLOYD, Derek James. b 78. Birm Univ BA 00 Leeds Univ BA 03. Coll of Resurr Mirfield 02. **d** 04 **p** 05. C Burnley St Andr w St Marg and St Jas *Blackb* 04–07; C W Burnley

All SS 07–09; V Cross Heath *Lich* 09–17; V Newcastle St Paul 09–17; V Toxteth Park St Agnes and St Pancras *Liv* from 17; Catholic Miss Enabler from 17; CMP from 05. *St Agnes's Vicarage, 1 Buckingham Avenue, Liverpool L17 3BA* T: 0151-733 1742

LLOYD, Dyfrig Cennydd. b 80. K Coll Lon BA 01. Ripon Coll Cuddesdon 01. **d** 04 **p** 05. C Llandysul w Bangor Teifi and Llanfairollwyn etc *St D* 04–06; C Bro Teifi Sarn Helen 06–07; TV 07–11; V Cardiff Dewi Sant *Llan* from 11. *6 Rachel Close, Cardiff CF5 2SH* T: (029) 2056 6001

LLOYD, Edward Gareth. b 60. K Coll Cam BA 81 MA 85 Dur Univ PhD 98. Ridley Hall Cam 85. **d** 88 **p** 89. C Jarrow *Dur* 88–91; C Monkwearmouth St Pet 91–92; P-in-c 92–96; TV Monkwearmouth 97–99; V Birtley from 99. *6 Ruskin Road, Birtley, Chester le Street DH3 1AD* T: 0191-410 2115 E: gareth@dunelm.org.uk

LLOYD, Eileen. See TAVERNOR, Eileen

LLOYD, Canon Elizabeth Jane. b 52. GRIC 74 CChem MRIC 77. Linc Th Coll 77. **dss** 80 **d** 87 **p** 94. Linc St Nic w St Jo Newport 80–81; LtO *Sarum* 81–87; Hon Par Dn Lytchett Matravers 87–92; Chapl Poole Gen Hosp 85–94; Chapl Poole Hosp NHS Foundn Trust from 94; Pres Coll of Health Care Chapl 02–04; Can and Preb Sarum Cathl from 03. *23 Laurel Close, Corfe Mullen, Wimborne BH21 3TD* T: (01202) 699883 E: jane.lloyd@poole.nhs.uk *or* janelloyd52@gmail.com

LLOYD, Gareth. See LLOYD, Edward Gareth

LLOYD, Graham. b 36. Brasted Th Coll 62 St Aid Birkenhead 64 Glouc Sch of Min 86. **d** 89 **p** 90. NSM Churchstoke w Hyssington and Sarn *Heref* 89–97; NSM Lydbury N w Hopesay and Edgton 97–01; rtd 01; PtO *Heref* from 01. *74 Church Street, Bishop's Castle SY9 5AE* T: (01588) 630517

LLOYD, Harry James. b 22. Univ of Wales (Lamp) BA 50. **d** 51 **p** 52. C Hay *S & B* 51–55; C Llanigon 51–55; C Hillingdon St Jo *Lon* 55–56; C Marlborough *Sarum* 56–60; V Kingston and Worth Matravers 60–83; C Milton Abbas, Hilton w Cheselbourne etc 83–87; rtd 87; PtO *Sarum* 87–00. *Riverside Cottage, 35 Rockbridge Park, Presteigne LD8 2NF* T: (01547) 560115

LLOYD, Jane. See LLOYD, Elizabeth Jane

LLOYD, Jonathan Joseph Barrington. b 88. St Cuth Soc Dur BA 09 Clare Coll Cam BA 15 Dur Univ PGCE 10. Westcott Ho Cam 13. **d** 16 **p** 17. C Jarrow *Dur* 16–18; C Jarrow and Simonside 18–19; Prec and Min Can St Alb Abbey from 19. *1 Dean Moore Close, St Albans AL1 1DW* M: 07462-855550 E: jjblloyd@hotmail.co.uk *or* precentor@stalbanscathedral.org

LLOYD, Canon Jonathan Wilford. b 56. Surrey Univ & City of Lon Poly BSc 80 N Lon Poly MA 86 CQSW 82 DASS 82. S'wark Ord Course 87. **d** 90 **p** 91. NSM Sydenham St Bart *S'wark* 90–93; P-in-c 93–94; Dir of Soc Resp 91–95; Bp's Officer for Ch in Soc 95–97; Hon PV S'wark Cathl 91–97; Chapl Team Ldr Bath Univ *B & W* 97–04; P-in-c Charlcombe w Bath St Steph 04–09; Chapl Denmark *Eur* 09–14; Adn Germany and N Eur 10–14; Can Brussels Cathl 10–14; PtO from 14; P-in-c Bridge *Cant* 14–16; P-in-c Littlebourne and Ickham w Wickhambreaux etc 14–16; Asst Dir of Ords 15–16; R W Vancouver St Steph Canada from 16. *St Stephen's Anglican Church, 885 22nd Street, West Vancouver BC V7V 4C1, Canada* T: (001) (604) 926 4381 E: canonjonathanlloyd@gmail.com

LLOYD, Marc Andrew. b 78. LMH Ox BA 99 Middx Univ MA 02. Oak Hill Th Coll 04. **d** 07 **p** 08. C Eastbourne H Trin *Chich* 07–11; P-in-c Warbleton and Bodle Street Green 11–12; R Warbleton, Bodle Street Green and Dallington from 12; RD Dallington from 14. *Warbleton Rectory, Rookery Lane, Rushlake Green, Heathfield TN21 9QJ* T: (01435) 830421 M: 07812-054820 E: marc_lloyd@hotmail.com

LLOYD, Michael Francis. b 57. Down Coll Cam BA 79 MA 82 St Jo Coll Dur BA 83 Worc Coll Ox DPhil 97. Cranmer Hall Dur 81. **d** 84 **p** 85. C Locks Heath *Portsm* 84–87; Asst Chapl Worc Coll Ox 89–90; Chapl Ch Coll Cam 90–94; Chapl Fitzw Coll Cam 95–96; Hon C Westminster St Jas the Less *Lon* 96–03; Tutor St Steph Ho Ox 03–05; Tutor St Paul's Th Cen *Lon* 06–13; C St Andr Holborn 06–10; Chapl Qu Coll Ox 10–13; Prin Wycliffe Hall Ox from 13; LtO *Ox* from 19. *Wycliffe Hall, 54 Banbury Road, Oxford OX2 6PW* T: (01865) 274200 F: 274215 E: michael.lloyd@wycliffe.ox.ac.uk

LLOYD, Canon Nigel James Clifford. b 51. Nottm Univ BTh 81 Lambeth STh 90 Win Univ MA 10. Linc Th Coll 77. **d** 81 **p** 82. C Sherborne w Castleton and Lillington *Sarum* 81–84; R Lytchett Matravers 84–92; TR Parkstone St Pet w Branksea and St Osmund 92–02; R Parkstone St Pet and St Osmund w Branksea 02–12; Ecum Officer (Sherborne Area) 92–00; Dioc Ecum Officer 00–01; RD Poole 01–09; V Broadstone 12–17; Can and Preb Sarum Cathl 02–17; rtd 17; PtO *Sarum* from 18. *23 Laurel Close, Corfe Mullen,*

Wimborne BH21 3TD T: (01202) 699883 M: 07940-348776 E: canon.nigel@gmail.com

LLOYD, Rebecca Joanne. b 78. Univ of Wales (Ban) BA 00 K Coll Lon MMus 01 PhD 06 Cam Univ BA 13. Westcott Ho Cam 11. **d** 14 **p** 15. C S Dulwich St Steph *S'wark* 14–17; Bp's Dom Chapl *Lich* from 17; PV Lich Cathl from 17. *Bishop's House, 22 The Close, Lichfield WS13 7LG* T: (01543) 306000 E: rebecca.lloyd@lichfield.anglican.org

LLOYD, Richard Gary. b 75. Ex Coll Ox BA 98 St Jo Coll Dur MA 00. Cranmer Hall Dur 98. **d** 00 **p** 01. C Dibden *Win* 00–03; Asst Chapl Charterhouse Sch Godalming 04–11; C Claygate *Guildf* 11–13; C E Molesey 13–18; V E Molesey St Mary from 18; P-in-c W Molesey from 17. *25 Arnison Road, East Molesey KT8 9JF* M: 07753-835744 E: church.office@smem.org.uk or richard.lloyd@smem.org.uk

LLOYD, Robert Graham. b 42. St Jo Coll Nottm 82. **d** 84 **p** 85. C Tonyrefail *Llan* 84; C Tonyrefail w Gilfach Goch 85–87; V Martletwy w Lawrenny and Minwear and Yerbeston *St D* 87–91; V Monkton 91–96; V Cymmer and Porth *Llan* 96–07; AD Rhondda 04–06; rtd 07; PtO *St D* from 06. *7 Greenhill Park Drive, Haverfordwest SA61 1LS* T: (01437) 783682

LLOYD, Canon Ronald Henry. b 32. Univ of Wales (Lamp) BA 52 LTh 54. **d** 54 **p** 56. C Manselton *S & B* 54–56; C Sketty 56–59; C Swansea St Mary and H Trin 59–63; CF (TA) 59–65; V Elmley Castle w Netherton and Bricklehampton *Worc* 63–69; Chapl Dragon Sch Ox 69–82; Chapl St Hugh's Coll Ox 75–80; P-in-c Ox St Marg 75–76; Chapl Magd Coll Ox 75–82; Prec and Chapl Ch Ch Ox 82–87; R Alvescot w Black Bourton, Shilton, Holwell etc 87–95; P-in-c Broughton Poggs w Filkins, Broadwell etc 94–95; R Shill Valley and Broadshire 95–01; rtd 01; PtO *Glouc* from 02; *Ox* from 02. *3 The Lanes, Bampton OX18 2JG*

LLOYD, Mrs Sandra Edith. b 48. Sarum & Wells Th Coll 83. **dss** 86 **d** 87 **p** 94. Freshwater *Portsm* 86–87; C 87–89; C Whitwell 89–95; V 95–14; C Niton 89–95; P-in-c 95–96; R 96–14; R St Lawrence 96–04; rtd 14; PtO *Portsm* from 14. *St Kenelm, Guyers Road, Freshwater PO40 9QA* T: (01983) 756865 E: rhadegunde@aol.com

LLOYD, Sarah Jane. b 67. Leic Univ BA 88. Ripon Coll Cuddesdon MA 15. **d** 15 **p** 16. C Old Basing and Lychpit *Win* 15–19; V Shalford *Guildf* from 19. *The Vicarage, East Shalford Lane, Guildford GU4 8AE* E: vicar@stmary-shalford.org.uk

LLOYD, Simon David. b 58. Portsm Poly BA 79 RGN 91 RSCN 95. Wycliffe Hall Ox 80. **d** 83 **p** 84. C Cotmanhay *Derby* 83–85; Chapl Asst Nottm City Hosp 85–87; Chapl Basford Hosp Nottm 85–87; PtO *Birm* 91–97; TV Solihull 97–04; V Minehead *B & W* 04–10. *Yew Tree House, Yew Tree Lane, Bathpool, Taunton TA2 8BB* T: (01823) 322128 E: si_lloyd@btinternet.com

LLOYD, Stephen Russell. b 47. Worc Coll Ox BA 69 MA 77 CertEd. Oak Hill Th Coll 76. **d** 77 **p** 78. C Canonbury St Steph *Lon* 77–80; C Braintree *Chelmsf* 80–92; V Braintree St Paul 92–01; V Ipswich St Andr *St E* 01–14; rtd 14; PtO *St E* from 14; *Chelmsf* from 18. *26 Endsleigh Court, Colchester CO3 3QN* T: (01206) 560172 E: stephenrlloyd@btinternet.com

LLOYD, Canon Stuart George Errington. b 49. TCD BA 72. **d** 75 **p** 76. C Cloughfern *Conn* 75–79; C Cregagh *D & D* 79–82; I Eglantine *Conn* 82–89; I Ballymena w Ballyclug 89–15; Can Conn Cathl 97–15; Preb 97–01; Prec 01–15; rtd 15. *123 Knockan Road, Broughshane, Ballymena BT43 7JA* T: (028) 2586 2705 E: sgelloyd@btinternet.com

LLOYD, Trevor. *See* LLOYD, Brendan Trevor

LLOYD HUGHES, Gwilym. *See* HUGHES, Gwilym Lloyd

LLOYD-JAMES, Duncan Geraint. b 66. St Steph Ho Ox BTh 94. **d** 94 **p** 96. C St Leonards Ch Ch and St Mary *Chich* 94–96; C Rottingdean 96–99; R Brede w Udimore 99–07; rtd 07; PtO *Guildf* 08–10. *62 Richmond Street, Brighton BN2 9PE* T: (01273) 606550 M: 07511-772256 E: duncanlj@btinternet.com

LLOYD JONES, Ieuan. b 31. St Cath Coll Cam BA 51 MA 54 FBIM. Sarum & Wells Th Coll 80. **d** 83 **p** 84. NSM Claygate *Guildf* 83–89; PtO Ox 89–06; *Guildf* 07–17. *2C Aldersey Road, Guildford GU1 2ES* T: (01483) 449605 E: lloyd.jones4@ntlworld.com

LLOYD MORGAN, Richard Edward. b 48. Trin Coll Cam MA 70 Ox Univ DipEd 71. SEITE 95. **d** 98 **p** 99. NSM Clapham St Paul *S'wark* 98–03; Chapl K Coll Cam 03–15; rtd 15; PtO *Eur* from 15; *S'wark* from 17; *Lon* from 17. *111 Narbonne Avenue, London SW4 9LQ* T: (020) 8673 4149 E: richard.lloydmorgan@gmail.com

LLOYD-RICHARDS, David Robert. b 48. Open Univ BA 84 Hull Univ MA 87. St D Coll Lamp. **d** 71 **p** 72. C Skewen *Llan* 71–73; C Neath w Llantwit 73–76; Miss to Seamen 76–77; V Pontlottyn w Fochriw *Llan* 77–84; R Merthyr Dyfan 84–90; Chapl Barry Neale-Kent Hosp 84–90; Tutor

Open Univ 85–10; Sen Chapl Univ Hosp of Wales NHS Trust 90–95; Sen Chapl Univ Hosp of Wales and Llandough NHS Trust 95–00; Sen Chapl Manager Cardiff and Vale NHS Trust 00–08; rtd 08. *Jeantique, La Butte, La Trinité des Laitiers, Gace, 61230 Orne, France* T: (0033) (2) 33 36 11 15 E: robertlloydrichards@googlemail.com

LLOYD ROBERTS, Mrs Kathleen Ada May. b 49. Bordesley Coll of Educn CertEd 71. Qu Coll Birm 03. **d** 06 **p** 07. NSM Temple Balsall *Birm* 06–09; V from 09. *The Master's House, Temple Balsall, Knowle, Solihull B93 0AL* T: (01564) 772415 E: klloydroberts@leveson.org.uk

LLOYD WILLIAMS, The Ven Martin Clifford. b 65. Westmr Coll Lon BEd 87. Trin Coll Bris BA 93. **d** 93 **p** 94. C Bath Walcot *B & W* 93–97; R Bath St Mich w St Paul 97–14; R Bath St Mich Without 14–15; RD Bath 10–15; Adn Brighton and Lewes *Chich* from 15; R Ovingdean from 19. *12 Walsingham Road, Hove BN3 4FF* M: 07732-676273 E: archbandl@chichester.anglican.org

LO, Peter Kwan Ho. b 54. Chinese Univ of Hong Kong BD 84 Stirling Univ MBA 92 K Coll Lon LLB 99. **d** 84 **p** 85. Hong Kong 84–91; PtO *Chich* 02–03; C Uckfield 03–06; R Monterey Park USA from 07. *133 East Graves Avenue, Monterey Park CA 91755-3915, USA* T: (001) (626) 571 2714 E: peterkwanholo@hotmail.com

lo POLITO, Nicola. b 59. Catholic Th Union Chicago MDiv 85 MA(Theol) 87. Comboni Miss. **d** 85 **p** 86. In RC Ch 85–94; Egypt 86–88; Sudan 88–91; Italy 91–94; Asst Chapl Malta and Gozo *Eur* 94–98; C Castle Bromwich SS Mary and Marg *Birm* 98–01; TV Salter Street and Shirley 01–05; Chapl Birm Univ 05–13; P-in-c Highgate 13–16; Chapl St Alb Academy 13–16; V Potternewton w Lt London *Leeds* from 16. *St Martin's Vicarage, St Martin's View, Leeds LS7 3LB* T: 0113-262 4271 M: 07813-937756 E: nlopolito@hotmail.com

LOACH, Michael Graham. b 72. Bris Univ BA 94 Chelt & Glouc Coll of HE PGCE 95 Heythrop Coll Lon MA 03 St Jo Coll Dur MA 12. Cranmer Hall Dur 10. **d** 12 **p** 13. C W Kirby St Bridget *Ches* 12–15; V Higher Bebington from 15. *The Vicarage, King's Road, Bebington, Wirral CH63 8LX* M: 07878-338546 E: mgloach@gmail.com

LOADER, Michael John. b 43. Hull Univ BSc 64 Chelsea Coll Lon MSc 72. **d** 05 **p** 14. Asst Chapl Nicosia Cyprus *Cyprus* 05–12; NSM Tavistock and Gulworthy *Ex* 13–15; NSM Tavistock, Gulworthy and Brent Tor from 15. *20 Edgcumbe Drive, Tavistock PL19 0ET* T: (01822) 613231 M: 07799-766755 E: michaelloader@supanet.com

LOAT, Canon Andrew Graham. b 61. Aber Univ BD 83 Univ of Wales (Ban) MTh 00. St Jo Coll Nottm. **d** 87 **p** 88. C Llangynwyd w Maesteg *Llan* 87–90; C Llansamlet *S & B* 90–91; R Whitton and Pilleth and Cascob etc 91–98; R Llandrindod w Cefnllys and Disserth 98–09; R Lower Ithon Valley 09–14; V Upper Ithon Valley 09–14; Warden of Readers 02–08; AD Maelienydd 06–14; Can Res Brecon Cathl 03–14; P-in-c Llanbadarn Fawr and Elerch and Penrhyncoch etc *St D* from 14; Hon Can St D Cathl from 16. *The Vicarage, Llanbadarn Fawr, Aberystwyth SY23 3TT* T: (01970) 624638 E: vicarage.llanbadarn@gmail.com

LOBB, Edward Eric. b 51. Magd Coll Ox BA 74 MA 76. Wycliffe Hall Ox 73. **d** 76 **p** 77. C Haughton St Mary *Man* 76–80; C Rusholme H Trin 80–84; P-in-c Whitfield *Derby* 84–90; V 90–92; V Stapenhill w Cauldwell 92–03; rtd 03; PtO *Derby* 03–05. *Middleton House, Beith KA15 1HX* T: (01505) 500232

LOBB, Miss Josephine Mary. b 57. SRN 83. **d** 96 **p** 97. OLM St Germans *Truro* 96–06; NSM Saltash 06–12; TV 12–17; rtd 17. *19 Lowertown Close, Landrake, Saltash PL12 5DG* T: (01752) 851488 E: jolobb@btinternet.com

LOBSINGER, Eric John. b 78. Washington Univ AB 00 JD 03 Kyushu Univ Japan LLM 04 LLD 07. **d** 10 **p** 15. USA 10–13; Jun Chapl Mert Coll Ox 13–14; Jun Dean St Steph Ho Ox 13–14; C Hornsey H Innocents *Lon* 15–17; V Ruislip St Mary from 17. *9 The Fairway, Ruislip HA4 0SP* E: fr.eric.lobsinger@gmail.com

LOCK, Mrs Beverley. b 59. Loughb Univ BA 81 York St Jo Univ MA 12 Bris Univ PGCE 82. CBDTI 01. **d** 04 **p** 05. C Kendal St Geo *Carl* 04–07; C Beacon 07–08; P-in-c Orton and Tebay w Ravenstonedale etc 08–16; P-in-c Shap w Swindale and Bampton w Mardale 08–16; TR Loughrigg from 16. *The Vicarage, Millans Park, Ambleside LA22 9BW* T: (015394) 33205 E: reverend.beverley@gmail.com

LOCK, Mrs Jacqueline. b 43. **d** 08 **p** 09. OLM High Wycombe Ox from 08. *15 Kingsley Crescent, High Wycombe HP11 2UN* T: (01494) 532216 M: 07976-719909 E: jackie@thelocks.org.uk

LOCK, Nicholas George. b 62. **d** 06 **p** 07. OLM Melksham *Sarum* 06–10; OLM Atworth w Shaw and Whitley 07–10; OLM Broughton Gifford, Gt Chalfield and Holt 07–10. *4 Murray*

Walk, Melksham SN12 7AZ T: (01225) 353906 M: 100966 E: nicklock42@hotmail.com

LOCK, Paul Alan. b 65. St Chad's Coll Dur BA 86. Coll of Resurr Mirfield 87. **d** 89 **p** 90. C Upholland *Liv* 89–92; C Teddington SS Pet and Paul and Fulwell *Lon* 92–95; V 95–99; V Wigan St Anne *Liv* 99–04; Dioc Dir of Educn *Blackb* 13–14; C Dalton *Liv* 16–17; P-in-c from 17; C Upholland 16–17; P-in-c from 17. *The Rectory, 1A College Road, Upholland, Skelmersdale WN8 0PY* M: 07813-019863 E: paul.a_lock@btinternet.com

LOCK, The Ven Peter Harcourt D'Arcy. b 44. AKC 67. **d** 68 **p** 69. C Meopham *Roch* 68–72; C Wigmore w Hempstead 72; C S Gillingham 72–77; R Hartley 77–83; R Fawkham and Hartley 83–84; V Dartford H Trin 84–93; Hon Can Roch Cathl 90–01; V Bromley SS Pet and Paul 93–01; RD Bromley 96–01; Adn Roch and Can Res Roch Cathl 01–09; rtd 09; PtO *Cant* from 11; *Roch* from 11. *53 Preston Park, Faversham ME13 8LH* T: (01795) 529161 E: peter.lock123@btinternet.com

LOCK, Thomas. b 38. **d** 05 **p** 06. OLM N Poole Ecum Team *Sarum* 05–11; rtd 11; PtO *Sarum* from 11. *Smithy's Lodge, 75 Tatnam Road, Poole BH15 2DP* M: 07970-021768 E: thomaslock04@gmail.com

LOCKE, Mrs Jennifer Margaret. b 52. Edin Univ BEd 74. Ox Min Course 06. **d** 08 **p** 09. NSM Wexham *Ox* 08–11; TV Risborough 11–17; rtd 17; PtO *Ox* from 18. *7 Lynbury Place, 14 South Park Crescent, Gerrards Cross SL9 8HJ* T: (01753) 880546 E: revjmlocke@gmail.com

LOCKE, Nigel Richard. *See* HESFORD-LOCKE, Richard Nigel

LOCKE, Robert Andrew. b 62. St Steph Ho Ox 89. **d** 92 **p** 93. C Colchester St Jas, All SS, St Nic and St Runwald *Chelmsf* 92–95; CF 95–00; V Burnham *Chelmsf* 00–04. *5 Bellfield Terrace, Inverness IV2 4ST* M: 07545-320484 E: rablocke1603@gmail.com

LOCKE, Stephen John. b 60. St Chad's Coll Dur BA 82. Sarum & Wells Th Coll 84. **d** 86 **p** 87. C Blackb St Mich w St Jo and H Trin 86–89; C Oswaldtwistle Immanuel and All SS 89–92; V Blackb St Mich w St Jo and H Trin 92–98; Chapl to the Deaf 98–04; V Owton Manor *Dur* from 04. *The Vicarage, 18 Rossmere Way, Hartlepool TS25 5EF* T: (01429) 290278 E: frlockessc@ntlworld.com

LOCKETT, Preb Paul. b 48. Sarum & Wells Th Coll 73. **d** 76 **p** 77. C Horninglow *Lich* 76–78; C Tewkesbury w Walton Cardiff *Glouc* 78–81; P-in-c W Bromwich St Pet *Lich* 81–90; R Norton Canes 90–95; V Longton St Mary and St Chad 95–12; Dean's V Lich Cathl 91–12; Preb Lich Cathl 04–12; rtd 12; P-in-c Hempton and Pudding Norton *Nor* 12–16; Chantry P Shrine of Our Lady of Walsingham 12–16; P-in-c Shrewsbury All SS w St Mich *Lich* from 16; Chapl to The Queen 12–18. *5 Lingen Close, Shrewsbury SY1 2UN*

LOCKEY, Malcolm. b 45. Sunderland Poly BA 67 Newc Univ DipEd 68 FRSA 75. NEOC 87. **d** 90 **p** 91. NSM Yarm *York* 90–97; C 97–98; TV Whitby w Aislaby and Ruswarp 98–03; Hon Chapl Miss to Seafarers 98–03; Chapl RNLI 00–03; P-in-c Coldstream *Edin* 04–09; R Kelso 05–09; Offg Chapl RAF and Chapl ATC 02–03; rtd 09; PtO *Newc* 10–13; NSM Bilbrook and Coven *Lich* 13–14; V Coven 14–17; PtO from 17. *Ashtree House, Ashbrook Lane, Abbots Bromley, Rugeley WS15 3DW* T: (01283) 841947 M: 07710-467785 E: fr.mac1945@gmail.com

LOCKHART, Canon Clare Patricia Anne (Sister Clare). b 44. Bris Univ BA 74 Newc Univ MLitt 96. Cranmer Hall Dur 84. **d** 87 **p** 94. Sisters of Charity from 63; Chapl Asst Sunderland Distr Gen Hosp 84–89; Chapl 89–94; Chapl City Hosps Sunderland NHS Trust 94–95; NSM N Hylton St Marg Castletown *Dur* 87–95; P-in-c 95–99; NSM Eoropaidh *Arg* from 99; PtO *Dur* 02–14; Dioc Supernumerary *Arg* from 09; P-in-c Stornoway 11–12; Hon Can St Jo Cathl Oban from 17. *The Sisters of Charity, Carmel, 7A Gress, Isle of Lewis HS2 0NB* T: (01851) 820484 *or* 820734 E: srclarecarmel@btinternet.com

LOCKHART, David. b 68. QUB BSc 90 TCD BTh 93. CITC 90. **d** 93 **p** 94. C Belfast St Mary w H Redeemer *Conn* 93–96; I Belfast St Steph w St Luke 96–03; I Cloughfern 03–18; I Glynn w Raloo from 18; I Larne and Inver from 18. *The Rectory, 8 Lower Cairncastle Road, Larne BT40 1PQ* T: (028) 2827 2788 E: dandblockhart@btinternet.com

LOCKHART, Eileen Ann. b 52. Open Univ BA 93 ACII 74. EAMTC 95. **d** 98 **p** 99. NSM Shenfield *Chelmsf* 98–17; rtd 17. *6 Granary Meadow, Wyatts Green, Brentwood CM15 0QD* T/F: (01277) 822537 E: eileenlockhart@gmail.com

LOCKHART, Raymond William. b 37. Qu Coll Cam BA 58 MA 61 LLB 60. St Jo Coll Nottm 72. **d** 74 **p** 75. C Aspley *S'well* 74–76; V 81–88; R Knebworth *St Alb* 76–81; Warden Stella Carmel Haifa (CMJ) Israel 88–91; R Jerusalem Ch Ch 91–99; Dir CMJ 99–02; rtd 02; PtO *B & W* 03–16; *Chich*

from 16. *1 Selmeston Close, Hastings TN34 1TH* T: (01424) 437972 M: 07474-355944 E: raylockhart1@gmail.com

LOCKLEY, Miss Pauline Margaret. b 41. **d** 02. OLM Stoke-upon-Trent *Lich* 02–13; PtO from 13. *Highfields, 89 Tolkien Way, Stoke-on-Trent ST4 7SJ* T: (01782) 849806

LOCKLEY, Philip Jonathan. b 81. Newc Univ BA 02 St Hugh's Coll Ox MSt 04 New Coll Ox DPhil 10 St Jo Coll Dur MA 17. Cranmer Hall Dur 15. **d** 17 **p** 18. C Ox St Clem from 17. *12A Morrell Avenue, Oxford OX4 1NE* M: 07817-549099 E: pjlockley@gmail.com

LOCKYER, David Ralph George. b 41. Wells Th Coll 65. **d** 67 **p** 68. C Bottesford *Linc* 67–69; C Eling *Win* 69–72; C Eling, Testwood and Marchwood 72–73; TV 73–77; TR Speke St Aid *Liv* 77–84; V Halifax St Jude *Wakef* 84–96; Chapl Halifax RN Infirmary 84–96; V Banwell *B & W* 96–06; rtd 06. *The Old Quarry, Stour Provost, Gillingham SP8 5SB* T: (01747) 839970

LOCOCK (née MILES), Mrs Jillian Maud. b 33. Lon Univ BSc 55. NOC 81. **dss** 84 **d** 87 **p** 95. Didsbury Ch Ch *Man* 84–86; Chapl Asst Man R Infirmary 85–87; Chapl Asst Withington Hosp Man 86–88; Chapl Asst RN 88–93; NSM Dumbarton *Glas* 93–96; PtO *Ex* from 02. *Glebe Cottage, Dousland, Yelverton PL20 6LU* T: (01822) 854098 E: rjbirtles@aol.com

LODER, Sister Helen. b 43. S'wark Ord Course 91. **d** 94 **p** 95. Soc of St Marg from 70; Hon C S Hackney St Mich w Haggerston St Paul *Lon* 94–01; Hon C Bethnal Green St Matt w St Jas the Gt 02–10; PtO from 10. *St Saviour's Priory, 14 Queensbridge Road, London E2 8NS* T: (020) 7613 1464 E: helenloder@aol.com

LODGE, Prof Anne Elizabeth. NUI BEd PhD Man Univ MEd. CITI. **d** 16 **p** 18. Raheny w Coolock *D & G* 16–18; NSM Dublin Clontarf from 18. *70 Dunluce Road, Clontarf, Dublin 3, Republic of Ireland* M: (00353) 86-373 6995 E: anne.lodge454@gmail.com *or* lodgea@tcd.ie

LODGE, The Ven Michael John. b 53. Wycliffe Hall Ox 87. **d** 89 **p** 90. C Highworth w Sevenhampton and Inglesham etc *Bris* 89–93; P-in-c Cheltenham St Luke and St Jo *Glouc* 93–05; TR Rayleigh *Chelmsf* 05–17; RD Rochford 08–15; Adn Southend from 17; Hon Can Chelmsf Cathl from 12. *The Archdeacon's Lodge, 459 Rayleigh Road, Benfleet SS7 3TH* T: (01268) 779345 E: a.southend@chelmsford.anglican.org

LODGE, Petrina. b 18 **p** 19. C Llyn Safaddan *S & B* from 18. *Yr Hen Ffermdy, Llanywern, Brecon LD3 7UP* T: (01874) 658878

LODGE, Robin Paul. b 60. Bris Univ BA 82 Ch Ch Coll Cant PGCE 83. Chich Th Coll 88. **d** 90 **p** 91. C Calne and Blackland *Sarum* 90–94; Asst Chapl St Mary's Sch Calne 90–94; TV Wellington and Distr *B & W* 94–03; V Highbridge 03–09; V Taunton St Andr from 09; Warden of Readers Taunton Adnry from 17. *The Vicarage, 118 Kingston Road, Taunton TA2 7SR* T: (01823) 352471 M: 07772-567059 E: robin.lodge1@btinternet.com

LODGE, Roy Frederick. b 38. Lon Univ MB BTh DPhil 92. Tyndale Hall Bris 63. **d** 66 **p** 67. C Tardebigge *Worc* 66–67; Chapl and Warden Probation Hostel Redditch 67–69; Chapl RAF 69–75; C Kinson *Sarum* 76; LtO *Pet* 76–77; Asst Chapl HM Pris Stafford 77–78; Chapl HM Pris Ranby 78–84; Chapl HM Pris Long Lartin 84–93; Chapl HM Pris Service Coll 87–93; Chapl HM Pris Hewell Grange 93–98; Chapl HM Pris Brockhill 93–98; rtd 98; PtO *Cov* from 98; *Glouc* from 99; *St Alb* 12–17. *44 Eton Road, Stratford-upon-Avon CV37 7ER* T: (01789) 204850 E: lodgeconstantia1@btinternet.com

LODGE, Sally Nicole. b 61. Keele Univ BA 83 St Jo Coll Dur BA 09. Cranmer Hall Dur 07. **d** 09 **p** 10. C Halstead Area *Chelmsf* 09–12; P-in-c Witham 12–14; TR Witham and Villages 14–19; AD Witham 16–19; Hon Can Chelmsf Cathl 16–19; TR New Windsor *Ox* from 19. *Holy Trinity Vicarage, 73 Alma Road, Windsor SL4 3HD* M: 07747-612817 E: sally.lodge@btinternet.com

LODWICK, Canon Brian Martin. b 40. Leeds Univ BA 61 MPhil 76 Linacre Coll Ox BA 63 MA 67 Univ of Wales PhD 87 FSA 19. St Steph Ho Ox 61. **d** 64 **p** 65. C Aberaman *Llan* 64–66; C Newton Nottage 66–73; R Llansannor and Llanfrynach w Penllyn etc 73–94; R Llandough w Leckwith 94–04; RD Llantwit Major and Cowbridge 83–94; Warden of Readers 92–03; Chan Llan Cathl 92–02; Treas Llan Cathl 02–04; Chapl Llandough Hosp 94–99; Chapl Univ Hosp of Wales and Llandough NHS Trust 99–00; Chapl Cardiff and Vale NHS Trust 00–01; rtd 04; PtO *Llan* from 04. *26 New Road, Neath Abbey, Neath SA10 7NH*

LODWICK, Stephen Huw. b 64. Plymouth Poly BSc 85. St Mich Coll Llan. **d** 94 **p** 95. C Clydach *S & B* 94–95; Chapl St Woolos Cathl *Mon* 95–98; R Grosmont and Skenfrith and Llangattock etc 98–01; CF from 01. *c/o MOD Chaplains (Army)* T: (01264) 383430 F: 381824

LOEWE, The Very Revd Jost Andreas. b 73. St Pet Coll Ox BA 95 MA 99 MPhil 97 Selw Coll Cam PhD 01 FRHistS 11.

Westcott Ho Cam 97. **d** 01 **p** 02. C Upton cum Chalvey *Ox* 01–04; C Cambridge Gt St Mary w St Mich *Ely* 04–09; Chapl Trin Coll Melbourne Australia 09–12; Lect Th Trin Coll Th Sch 10–12; Dean Melbourne from 12. *St Paul's Cathedral, 209 Flinders Lane, Melbourne VIC 3000, Australia* T: (0061) (3) 9653 4333 F: 9653 4307 E: dean@stpaulscathedral.org.au

LOEWENDAHL, David Jacob (Jake). b 50. SS Coll Cam BA 74 MA 77. Ripon Coll Cuddesdon 75. **d** 77 **p** 78. C Walworth *S'wark* 77–80; Chapl St Alb Abbey 80–83; Chapl St Alb Sch 80–83; Team Ldr Community Service Volunteers 84–90; PtO *Lon* 83–90; R E and W Tilbury and Linford *Chelmsf* 90–95; V Menheniot *Truro* 95–98; RD W Wivelshire 97–98; rtd 98; PtO *Truro* from 98. *Bank Barn, Woodlands Farm, Sweetshouse, Bodmin PL30 5FE* T: (01208) 871384 M: 07816-430292

LOFT, Edmund Martin Boswell. b 25. St Jo Coll Cam BA 49 MA 55. Ely Th Coll 49. **d** 51 **p** 52. C Carl H Trin 51–54; C Barrow St Geo 54–56; V Allonby w Newton 56–62; V Fillongley *Cov* 62–77; V Earlsdon 77–90; rtd 90; PtO *Sheff* 90–09. *41 Brook Road, Sheffield S8 9FH* T: 0114-250 9979 E: martinloft@gmail.com

LOFTHOUSE, Canon Brenda. b 33. RGN 60 RM 62 RNT 69. NOC 84. **d** 87 **p** 94. Hon Par Dn Greengates *Bradf* 87–89; Par Dn Farsley 89–94; V Bolton St Jas w St Chrys 94–00; Hon Can Bradf Cathl 98–00; rtd 00; PtO *Bradf* 00–14; *Leeds* from 14. *33 Myrtle Court, Bingley BD16 2LP* T: (01274) 771476

LOFTHOUSE, Mrs Diane Lesley. b 66. Yorks Min Course 08. **d** 11 **p** 12. NSM Moor Allerton and Shadwell *Ripon* 11–14; *Leeds* 14–16; NSM Roundhay St Edm from 16; Chapl St Gemma's Hospice from 15. *33 Jackson Avenue, Leeds LS8 1NP* T: 0113-266 6495 E: dianelofthouse@virginmedia.com

LOFTS, Sally Anne. *See* BAYLIS, Sally Anne

LOFTUS, Francis. b 52. Newc Univ BA 73 St Andr Univ BPhil 76 York St Jo Coll PGCE 74 FRSA 94. NEOC 93. **d** 96 **p** 97. Hd Master Barlby High Sch 90–10; NSM Barlby and Riccall *York* 96–10; P-in-c 10–13; NSM Hemingbrough 06–10; P-in-c 10–13; V Riccall, Barlby and Hemingbrough 13–17; rtd 17; PtO *York* from 17; *St Alb* from 17. *13 Oak Crescent, Upper Caldecote, Biggleswade SG18 9DH* M: 07850-839419 E: francisloftus@btinternet.com

LOFTUS, John Michael. b 52. Sheff Univ BSc 74 Solicitor 77. **d** 00 **p** 01. OLM Hundred River *St E* 00–13; NSM Hundred River and Wainford from 13. *Keld House, Hulver Street, Henstead, Beccles NR34 7UE* T: (01502) 476257 F: 533001 E: jloftus@nortonpeskett.co.uk

LOGAN, Ms Alexandra Jane. b 73. Trin Coll Carmarthen BA 94. Ridley Hall Cam 99. **d** 02 **p** 03. C Penwortham St Mary *Blackb* 02–07; V Bethnal Green St Jas Less *Lon* 07–13; Chapl Co-ord Cumbria Univ *Blackb* from 14. *University of Cumbria, Bowerham Road, Lancaster LA1 3JD* E: alexandra.logan@cumbria.ac.uk

LOGAN, Ms Joanne. b 64. Ch Coll Cam BA 87 St Jo Coll Dur BA 04 MA 05 PhD 19. Cranmer Hall Dur 02. **d** 05 **p** 06. C Harrogate St Mark *Ripon* 05–09; PtO *Lich* 11–12; *St Alb* 12–17; *Dur* from 17; Tutor Lindisfarne Coll of Th from 18. *11 Beechways, Durham DH1 4LG* T: 0191-386 8346 *or* 270 4144 E: jo_logan@btopenworld.com *or* jo@lindisfarnect.org

LOGAN, Kevin. b 43. Oak Hill Th Coll. **d** 75 **p** 76. C Blackb Sav 75–78; C Leyland St Andr 78–82; V Gt Harwood St Jo 82–91; V Accrington Ch Ch 91–08; rtd 08; PtO *Blackb* from 08. *119 Kingsway, Church, Accrington BB5 5EL* T: (01254) 396139 M: 07776-007694 E: kevinlogan1@hotmail.com

LOGUE, Mrs Rosemary Christine. TCD BTh 93. CITC 90. **d** 93 **p** 94. C Clooney w Strathfoyle *D & R* 93–96; I Londonderry St Aug 96–03; I Tullyaughnish w Kilmacrennan and Killygarvan 03–05; I Sixmilecross w Termonmaguirke *Arm* 05–08; P-in-c Cambuslang and Uddingston *Glas* 08; I Kilskeery w Trillick *Clogh* 11–18; rtd 18. *17 Dunhugh Park, Londonderry BT47 2NL* T: (028) 7134 7480 E: r.logue@btinternet.com

LOH, Tom. b 79. UEA BSc 01. Wycliffe Hall Ox BTh 11. **d** 11 **p** 12. C Billericay and Lt Burstead *Chelmsf* 11–14; P-in-c Westcliff St Mich from 14; P-in-c Westcliff St Andr 16–19. *St Michael's Vicarage, 5 Mount Avenue, Westcliff-on-Sea SS0 8PS* T: (01702) 478462 M: 07905-743419 E: tomloh79@yahoo.co.uk

LOMAS, Anthony David. b 59. Cranfield Inst of Tech BSc 81. WEMTC 04. **d** 07 **p** 08. C Sevenhampton w Charlton Abbots, Hawling etc *Glouc* 07–11; R Redmarley D'Abitot, Bromesberrow, Pauntley etc 11–16; Chapl Aquitaine *Eur* from 16. *lieu-dit Labrande, 47800 Agnac, France* T: (0033) 6 72 31 72 87 E: revtonylomas@gmail.com

LOMAS, Mrs Catherine Mary. b 72. St Jo Coll Cam MA 93. STETS 07. **d** 10 **p** 11. C Wellingborough All SS *Pet* 10–11; C Cogenhoe and Gt and Lt Houghton w Brafield 11–14; LtO 15–16; V Irchester w Stanton Cross from 16. *The Vicarage, 19 Station Road, Irchester, Wellingborough NN29 7EH* T: (01933) 312674 E: revdcatherine@encircled.uk

LOMAX, Canon Barry Walter John. b 39. Lambeth STh Lon Coll of Div 63. **d** 66 **p** 67. C Sevenoaks St Nic *Roch* 66–71; C Southport Ch Ch *Liv* 71–73; V Bootle St Matt 73–78; P-in-c Litherland St Andr 76–78; V New Borough and Leigh *Sarum* 78–94; Can and Preb Sarum Cathl 91–02; R Blandford Forum and Langton Long 94–02; rtd 02; PtO *Sarum* from 03. *Shiloh, 2 Colborne Avenue, Wimborne BH21 2PZ* T: (01202) 856104 E: barry.lomax@talktalk.net

LOMAX, Eric John. b 64. St Jo Coll Dur BA 96 Leeds Univ PGCE 04. Cranmer Hall Dur 93. **d** 96 **p** 97. C Goodshaw and Crawshawbooth *Man* 96–00; V Copmanthorpe *York* 00–01; P-in-c Colsterworth Gp *Linc* 10–17; V Kempston All SS *St Alb* from 17; V Biddenham from 17. *The Vicarage, Church End, Kempston, Bedford MK43 8RH* E: ericjohnlomax64@aol.com

LOMAX, Mrs Kate Jane. b 73. RGN 96. St Jo Coll Nottm BA 02. **d** 02 **p** 03. C Luton St Mary *St Alb* 02–04; Asst Chapl Cam Univ Hosps NHS Foundn Trust 04–05; Chapl 05–07; NSM Penn Fields *Lich* 08–10; NSM Bayston Hill 10–16; PtO *St Alb* 17–18. *7 Corder Close, St Albans AL3 4NH* T: (01727) 758489 E: kate.lomax@virginmedia.com

LOMAX, Canon Timothy Michael. b 73. Derby Univ BEd 95 Nottm Univ MA 11. Ridley Hall Cam 05. **d** 07 **p** 08. C Penn Fields *Lich* 07–10; V Bayston Hill 10–16; Dir Miss *St Alb* from 16; Can Res St Alb from 16. *7 Corder Close, St Albans AL3 4NH* T: (01727) 758489 E: tim.lomax1@virginmedia.com

LONDON (St Paul's), Dean of. *See* ISON, The Very Revd David John

LONDON, Archdeacon of. *See* MILLER, The Ven Luke Jonathan

LONDON, Bishop of. *See* MULLALLY, The Rt Revd and Rt Hon Dame Sarah Elisabeth

LONEY, Mark William James. b 72. Cen Lancs Univ BSc 94 MA 97 TCD BTh 03. CITC 00. **d** 03 **p** 04. C Larne and Inver *Conn* 03–06; I Ahoghill w Portglenone 06–11; TV Digswell and Panshanger *St Alb* 12–15; I Dungiven w Bovevagh *D & R* from 15. *The Rectory, 14 Main Street, Dungiven, Londonderry BT47 4LB* T: (028) 7774 1394 *or* 7774 1226 E: rev.loney@btopenworld.com

LONG, Canon Anne Christine. b 33. Leic Univ BA 56 Ox Univ DipEd 57 Lon Univ BD 65 ALBC. **dss** 80 **d** 87 **p** 94. Lect St Jo Coll Nottm 73–84; Acorn Chr Healing Trust 85–98; Stanstead Abbots *St Alb* 85–92; Hon Par Dn 87–92; Hon Par Dn Camberley St Paul *Guildf* 92–94; Hon C 94–03; Hon Can Guildf Cathl 96–03; PtO *Sarum* from 06. *3 Chiselbury Grove, Salisbury SP2 8EP* T: (01722) 341488 E: annelong33@talktalk.net *or* anneclong33@gmail.com

LONG, Anthony Auguste. b 45. Linc Th Coll 79. **d** 81 **p** 82. C Kingswinford St Mary *Lich* 81–84; TV Ellesmere Port *Ches* 84–87; V Witton 87–97; P-in-c Wybunbury w Doddington 97–02; V 02–10; rtd 10; PtO *Ches* from 10. *23 Osborne Grove, Shavington, Crewe CW2 5BY* T: (01270) 561113 E: tojolong@hotmail.co.uk

LONG, Anthony Robert. b 48. SS Mark & Jo Coll Chelsea CertEd 70 Southn Univ BTh 93 UEA MA 96 Lambeth MA 04. Chich Th Coll 74. **d** 77 **p** 78. C Chiswick St Nic w St Mary *Lon* 77–80; C Earley St Pet *Ox* 80–85; P-in-c Worstead w Westwick and Sloley Nor 85–92; R Worstead, Westwick, Sloley, Swanton Abbot etc 92–16; P-in-c Tunstead w Sco' Ruston 85–16; Chapl Nor Cathl 85–16; rtd 16; PtO *Nor* from 17. *The Elms, The Street, Hemsby, Great Yarmouth NR29 4EU* T: (01493) 731727

LONG, The Ven Christopher William. b 47. Nottm Univ BTh 78 Open Univ BA 80. Linc Th Coll 75. **d** 78 **p** 79. C Shiregreen St Jas and St Chris *Sheff* 78–81; V 81–82; Chapl RAF 82–05; I Enniscorthy w Clone, Clonmore, Monart etc *C & O* 05–15; Adn Ferns 08–15; Adn Cashel, Waterford and Lismore 14–15; rtd 15. *20 Grange Mor Park, Grange Road, Rosslare, Co Wexford, Y35 X361, Republic of Ireland* T: (00353) (53) 913 2749 M: (00353) 87-695 0613 E: chriswlong1@eircom.net

LONG, David William. b 47. St Aug Coll Cant 70. **d** 72 **p** 73. C Stanley *Liv* 72–73; C W Derby St Luke 73–76; C Cantril Farm 76–79; V Warrington St Barn 79–81; V Westbrook St Jas 82–96; V Ince St Mary 96–12; AD Wigan E and Hon Can Liv Cathl 03–05; rtd 12; PtO *Blackb* from 14; *Liv* from 16. *25 Almond Brook Road, Standish, Wigan WN6 0TB* T: (01257) 400720 E: david@scars.org.uk

LONG, Mrs Frances Mary. b 58. SEITE 98. **d** 01 **p** 02. NSM Caterham *S'wark* 01–05; Chapl Surrey and Sussex Healthcare NHS Trust 01–03; C Riddlesdown *S'wark* 05–08; P-in-c Purley St Mark 08–12; P-in-c Purley St Swithun 08–12; PtO 12–14; NSM Caterham from 14. *56 Roffes Lane, Chaldon,*

Caterham CR3 5PT T: (01883) 340257 M: 07903-019620 E: franyb8@hotmail.com

LONG, Frederick Hugh. b 43. EMMTC 90. **d** 90 **p** 91. NSM Grantham *Linc* 90–00; C 00–01; TV 01–02; V Grantham St Anne New Somerby and Spitalgate 02–08; rtd 08; Hon C Drybrook, Lydbrook and Ruardean *Glouc* 08–13; PtO from 14. *2 Unlawater House, Unlawater Lane, Newnham GL14 1BJ* T: (01594) 510739

LONG, Geoffrey Lawrence. b 47. La Sainte Union Coll BTh 93 PGCE 94. Portsm Dioc Tr Course 88. **d** 89 **p** 98. NSM Whippingham w E Cowes *Portsm* 89–01; Chapl HM Pris Maidstone 01–12; rtd 12; PtO *Ely* from 13. *2 Fallowfield, Littleport, Ely CB6 1GY* T: (01353) 360702 E: geoffrey.long@outlook.com

LONG, Hermione Jane. *See* MORRIS, Hermione Jane

LONG, John. b 48. ACIB 72. Yorks Min Course 09. **d** 10 **p** 11. NSM Utley *Bradf* 10–14; *Leeds* 14–16; NSM Keighley from 16. *Rosslyn House, Cold Street, Haworth, Keighley BD22 8AY* T: (01535) 646592 E: haworthlongs@tiscali.co.uk

LONG, Canon John Sydney. b 25. Lon Univ BSc 49. Wycliffe Hall Ox 50. **d** 51 **p** 52. C Plaistow St Andr *Chelmsf* 51–54; C Keighley *Bradf* 54–57; C-in-c Horton Bank Top CD 57–59; V Buttershaw St Aid 59–64; V Barnoldswick w Bracewell 64–85; Hon Can Bradf Cathl 77–91; RD Skipton 83–90; R Broughton, Marton and Thornton 85–91; rtd 91. *1 Church Villa, Carleton, Skipton BD23 3DQ* T: (01756) 799095

LONG, Peter Ronald. b 48. Cuddesdon Coll 71. **d** 73 **p** 74. Chapl RAFVR 74–99; C Bodmin *Truro* 73–75; C Newquay 75–76; Asst Youth Chapl 75–76; Dioc Youth Chapl 76–79; PtO *Eur* 76 and 78–85 and 87–98; Public Preacher *Truro* 77; P-in-c Mawgan w St Martin-in-Meneage 79–82; Chapl Helston-Meneage Community and Geriatric Hosp 80–95; Miss to Seamen 80–98; P-in-c Cury w Gunwalloe *Truro* 80–82; R Cury and Gunwalloe w Mawgan 83–98; PtO *Ex* 82–93; Ecum Th in UK Rail Ind from 97; rtd 08. *26 Jubilee Street, Newquay TR7 1LA* T: (01637) 877060 M: 07780-976113 E: ipsn2009@yahoo.co.uk

LONG, Samuel Allen. b 48. EAMTC 03. **d** 05 **p** 06. NSM Barrow *St E* 05–08; NSM Pakenham w Norton and Tostock 08–10; P-in-c Badwell and Walsham 10–15; C Hepworth, Hinderclay, Wattisfield and Thelnetham 15; rtd 15; PtO *St E* from 15. *16 Drury Close, Rougham, Bury St Edmunds IP30 9JE* T: (01359) 271936 M: 07732-971925 E: samlong167@aol.com

LONGBOTTOM, Canon Frank. b 41. Birm Univ MA 15. Ripon Hall Ox 65. **d** 68 **p** 69. C Epsom St Martin *Guildf* 68–72; Chapl St Ebba's Hosp Epsom 68–72; Chapl Qu Mary's Hosp Carshalton 68–72; Chapl Henderson Hosp Sutton 68–72; Chapl Highcroft Hosp Birm 72–94; Chapl Northcroft Hosp Birm 74–94; Dioc Adv for Past Care of Clergy & Families *Birm* 89–94; Bp's Adv 94–06; Bp's Adv on Health and Soc Care *Birm* 01–06; P-in-c Middleton 99–00; Hon Can Birm Cathl 91–06; rtd 07; PtO *Birm* from 09. *46 Sunnybank Road, Sutton Coldfield B73 5RE* T/F: 0121-350 5823

LONGBOTTOM, Canon Paul Edward. b 44. Kent Univ MA 02 AKC 67. **d** 68 **p** 69. C Rainham *Roch* 68–71; C Riverhead 71–75; C Dunton Green 71–75; V Penge Lane H Trin 75–84; V Chatham St Wm 84–94; V Shorne and Dioc Dir of Ords 94–09; Hon Can Roch Cathl 96–09; rtd 09; PtO *Roch* from 09; *Cant* from 10. *30 Doubleday Drive, Bapchild, Sittingbourne ME9 9PJ* T: (01795) 428300 E: paul.longbottom@ymail.com

LONGDEN, Lee Paul. b 70. Peterho Cam BA 91 MA 95 Ches Coll of HE MTh 03 Birm Univ ThD 12 Huddersfield Univ MSc 13 FRCO 91 LLCM 93 ARCM 93 LRSM 96 FHEA 12 SFHEA 17 FInstLM 13. Qu Coll Birm 03. **d** 05 **p** 06. C Langley and Parkfield *Man* 05–08; V Ashton Ch Ch 08–15; Hon Assoc Dir of Ords 09–15; Vice Prin All SS Cen for Miss and Min 15–18; PtO *Man* 15–18; R Kersal Moor from 18; Extraordinary Sen Lect NW Univ S Africa from 13; Hon Research Fell Qu Foundn Birm from 18. *The Rectory, 1 Moorside Road, Salford M7 3PJ* T: 0161-792 5362 E: rectorofkersal@gmail.com

LONGDON, Anthony Robert James. b 44. STETS 00. **d** 03 **p** 04. OLM N Bradley, Southwick and Heywood *Sarum* 03–08; OLM N Bradley, Southwick, Heywood and Steeple Ashton 08 14; PtO from 14. *1A Holbrook Lane, Trowbridge BA14 0PP* T/F: (01225) 754771

LONGE, Canon David John Hastings. b 75. New Coll Edin BD 99. Ripon Coll Cuddesdon 07. **d** 09 **p** 10. C N Lambeth *S'wark* 09–15; Chapl to Abp in Jerusalem 15–18; R Matlaske *Nor* from 18. *The Rectory, The Street, Matlaske, Norfolk NR11 7AQ* T: (01263) 577252 M: 07881-950294 E: djhlonge@gmail.com

LONGE, James Robert. b 46. EAMTC 02. **d** 04 **p** 05. NSM Pakenham w Norton and Tostock *St E* 04–07; NSM St Edm Way 07–14; rtd 14; PtO *St E* from 14. *Bush House, Bradfield St Clare, Bury St Edmunds IP30 0EQ*

LONGFELLOW, Erica Denise. b 74. Duke Univ (USA) BA 97 Linc Coll Ox MSt 98 DPhil 01. SEITE 02. **d** 05 **p** 06. NSM Kew St Phil and All SS w St Luke *S'wark* 05–09; NSM Surbiton St Andr and St Mark 09–11; Chapl and Dean of Div New Coll Ox from 11. *New College, Holywell Street, Oxford OX1 3BN* T: (01865) 279555 E: chaplain@new.ox.ac.uk

LONGFOOT, Canon Richard. b 46. Oak Hill Th Coll 76. **d** 78 **p** 79. C Chaddesden St Mary *Derby* 78–81; C Cambridge St Martin *Ely* 81–83; R Folksworth w Morborne 83–89; R Stilton w Denton and Caldecote 83–89; R Stilton w Denton and Caldecote etc 90–11; RD Yaxley 02–07; Hon Can Ely Cathl 04–11; rtd 11; PtO *Ely* 11–16; *Pet* from 12. *5 Westfield Close, Yaxley, Peterborough PE7 3NW* T: (01733) 247700 E: richard.lfoot@lineone.net

LONGMAN, Edward. b 37. Hatf Coll Dur BSc 62 Fitzw Coll Cam BA 66 MA 70. Clifton Th Coll 62. **d** 66 **p** 67. C Lower Homerton St Paul *Lon* 66–72; C Parr *Liv* 72–73; TV 74–85; PtO 87–02; *Ches* from 96. *21 Canadian Avenue, Hoole, Chester CH2 3HG* T: (01244) 317544 F: 400450 M: 07779-650791 E: ted.longman@firstschool.org

LONGMAN, Edward George. b 35. St Pet Hall Ox BA 58 MA 62. Westcott Ho Cam 59. **d** 61 **p** 62. C Sheff St Mark Broomhall 61–65; V Brightside St Thos 65–74; V Yardley St Edburgha *Birm* 74–84; RD Yardley 77–84; Hon Can Birm Cathl 81–96; R Sutton Coldfield H Trin 84–96; RD Sutton Coldfield 94–96; Chapl Gd Hope Distr Gen Hosp Sutton Coldfield 84–90; P-in-c Cerne Abbas w Godmanstone and Minterne Magna *Sarum* 96–02; RD Dorchester 00–02; rtd 02; PtO *B & W* 04–14. *5 Old Wells Road, Shepton Mallet BA4 5XN* T: (01749) 343699 E: ted@roseted.co.uk *or* longmanrose@gmail.com

LONGUET-HIGGINS, John. b 62. Leeds Univ BA 85. St Jo Coll Nottm 88. **d** 91 **p** 92. C Kidlington w Hampton Poyle *Ox* 91–95; TV N Huddersfield *Wakef* 95–01; V Painswick, Sheepscombe, Cranham, The Edge etc *Glouc* 02–12; R Ashleworth, Corse, Hartpury, Hasfield etc from 12. *The Rectory, Over Old Road, Hartpury, Gloucester GL19 3BJ* T: (01452) 700965 E: vicar.westof7@gmail.com

LONSDALE, Mrs Gillian. b 36. Qu Mary Coll Lon BA 57 MA 59 Ex Univ MPhil 81 AIMSW 61. SWMTC 96. **d** 99 **p** 00. NSM Duloe, Herodsfoot, Morval and St Pinnock *Truro* 99–06; NSM Lansallos and Talland 01–03; RD W Wivelshire 03–06; rtd 06; PtO *Newc* from 11. *2 Garden Terrace, Whittingham, Alnwick NE66 4RD* T: (01665) 574907 E: lonsdale828@btinternet.com

LONSDALE, Ms Linda. b 49. SWMTC 08. **d** 10 **p** 11. NSM Alderley Edge *Ches* 10–13; P-in-c Beetham *Carl* 13–17; rtd 17; PtO *Ches* from 18. *The Woodlands, 13 Wood Lane, Goostrey, Crewe CW4 8NE* E: rev@jandll.plus.com

LOOKER, Clare Margaret. *See* FLEMING, Clare Margaret

LOOMES, Gaenor Mary. *See* HOCKEY, Gaenor Mary

LOPES, Marco Gonzaga. *See* FILIPE LOPES, Marco Gonzaga

LORD, Andrew Michael. b 66. Warwick Univ BSc 87 Birm Univ MA 99 PhD 10 Fitzw Coll Cam BA 02. Ridley Hall Cam 00. **d** 03 **p** 04. C Long Buckby w Watford *Pet* 03–06; C W Haddon w Winwick and Ravensthorpe 03–06; R Trowell, Awsworth and Cossall *S'well* 06–19; P-in-c Didcot All SS *Ox* from 19. *140 Lydalls Road, Didcot OX11 7EA* E: revandylord@gmail.com

LORD, Clive Gavin. b 69. St Martin's Coll Lanc BA. St Steph Ho Ox BTh. **d** 96 **p** 97. C Penwortham St Leon *Blackb* 96–98; C Blackpool St Mary 98–01; P-in-c 01–04; V 04–06; Chapl Blackpool, Fylde and Wyre Hosps NHS Trust from 06. *Chaplaincy Office, Victoria Hospital, Whinney Heys Road, Blackpool FY3 8NR* T: (01253) 306875

LORD, Mrs Deborah Alice. b 69. Reading Univ BSc 90 Univ of Wales (Swansea) PGCE 93. St Jo Coll Nottm 10. **d** 13 **p** 14. C Toton *S'well* 13–17; PtO *Ox* from 19; *S'well* from 17. *The Rectory, 140 Lydalls Road, Didcot OX11 7EA* E: debbie.lord@gmail.com *or* debbie.lord99@gmail.com

LORD, Mrs Sharon Ruth. b 68. Staffs Univ BSc 03 RGN 89 RM 92. Cranmer Hall Dur 13. **d** 15 **p** 16. C Burton All SS w Ch Ch *Lich* 15–17; C Branston and Burton All SS w Ch Ch 17–18; R Pakefield Nor from 18. *Pakefield Rectory, Causeway, Pakefield Street, Lowestoft NR33 0JZ* M: 07711-030203 E: rev@lord-family.com

LORDING, Miss Claire Ann. b 75. Roehampton Inst BA 96. Ripon Coll Cuddesdon BTh 96. **d** 99 **p** 00. C Ledbury *Heref* 99–02; TV Tenbury Wells 02–08; TR 08–10; P-in-c Clee Hill 09–10; TV Tenbury 10–15; RD Ludlow 10–15; P-in-c Pershore w Pinvin, Wick and Birlingham *Worc* from 15. *58 Three Springs Road, Pershore WR10 1HS* T: (01386) 300053 *or* 552071 E: vicar@pershoreabbey.org.uk

LORT-PHILLIPS, Mrs Elizabeth Priscilla. b 47. STETS 02. **d** 05 **p** 06. NSM Redhorn *Sarum* 05–12; NSM Cannings and Redhorn 12–15; rtd 15; PtO *St D* from 15. *Garron,*

Lawrenny, Kilgetty SA68 0PU T: (01834) 891634 E: e.lortphillips@btinternet.com

LOTHIAN, Iain Nigel Cunningham. b 59. Aber Univ MA 84 Bath Univ PGCE 86 Leeds Univ MA 05. NOC 02. **d** 05 **p** 06. C Sheff St Pet Abbeydale 05–09; C Sheff St Pet and St Oswald 09; PtO 09–17; P-in-c Crosspool from 17; C Lodge Moor St Luke from 17. *33 Gatefield Road, Sheffield S7 1RD* T: 0114-250 9736 E: if.lothian@blueyonder.co.uk

LOTT, Eric John. b 34. Lanc Univ MLitt 70 PhD 77. Richmond Th Coll BD 59. **d** 60 **p** 61. Miss Dornakal India 60–62; Lect Andhra Union Th Coll 62–64; Lect Andhra United Th Coll 65–75; Prof United Th Coll Bangalore 77–88; Wesley Hall Ch and Community Project Leics 88–94; rtd 94; PtO *Leic 94–15. 16 Main Road, Old Dalby, Melton Mowbray LE14 3LR* T: (01664) 822405 E: eric.lott@tiscali.co.uk

LOUDEN, Canon Terence Edmund. b 48. Ch Coll Cam BA 70 MA 74. Sarum & Wells Th Coll 72. **d** 75 **p** 76. C Portsea N End St Mark *Portsm* 75–78; C-in-c Leigh Park St Clare CD 78–81; R Chale 81–88; R Niton 81–88; P-in-c Whitwell 82–84; V Cosham 88–96; V E Meon 96–13; V Langrish 96–13; CME Officer 96–03; Hon Can Portsm Cathl 92–13; rtd 13; Hon Can Cape Coast Ghana from 12; PtO *Portsm* from 13. *34 Claire Gardens, Waterlooville PO8 0JH* T: (023) 9259 6525 M: 07711-319752 E: terrylouden@btinternet.com

LOUDON (née KING), Canon Ellen Francis. b 67. Liv Poly BA 90 Liv Univ MA 96 PhD 11. Trin Coll Bris 06. **d** 08 **p** 09. C Everton St Pet w St Chrys *Liv* 08–12; P-in-c Walton St Jo 14–15; P-in-c Walton St Luke 12–15; V 15–16; AD Walton 13–16; Hon Can Liv Cathl from 13. *3 Cathedral Close, Liverpool L1 7BR* M: 07718-806891 E: ellen@ellenloudon.com

LOUGHBOROUGH, Suffragan Bishop of. *See* FRANCIS DEHQANI, The Rt Revd Gulnar Eleanor

LOUIS, Ms Emma Christine. b 69. Trin Coll Bris 06. St Jo BA 92 St Jo Coll Dur BA 96. Cranmer Hall Dur 94. **d** 97 **p** 98. C Birm St Martin w Bordesley St Andr 97–00; Arts Development Officer 97–00; Asst Chapl Harrogate Health Care NHS Trust 00–02; Chapl Co-ord St Mich Hospice Harrogate 01–02; Asst Chapl Birm Heartlands and Solihull NHS Trust 02–04; Lead Chapl Black Country Partnership NHS Foundn Trust from 04; PtO *Birm* from 05; *Worc* from 14. *Black Country Partnership NHS Foundation Trust, Edward Street, West Bromwich B70 8NL* T: 0121-612 8067 M: 07817-564014 E: elouis@nhs.net

LOUIS, Canon Peter Anthony. b 41. St Cath Coll Ox BA 63 MA 77 Man Univ MPhil 85 Jes Coll Cam CertEd 64. Wells Th Coll 66. **d** 68 **p** 70. C E Grinstead St Mary *Chich* 68–75; C Radcliffe-on-Trent *S'well* 75–80; Hd Master Blue Coat Comp Sch Cov 80–85; V Welwyn Garden City *St Alb* 85–08; Chapl Oaklands Coll 93–95; Hon Can St Alb 04–08; rtd 08; PtO *Ox* from 08; *St Alb* 10–14. *27 Aylesbury Road, Wendover, Aylesbury HP22 6JG* T: (01296) 582683 E: plouis@ntlworld.com

LOVATT, Bernard James. b 31. Lich Th Coll 64. **d** 65 **p** 66. C Burford III w Lt Heref 65–67; C Cleobury Mortimer w Hopton Wafers 67–68; C Bradford-on-Avon H Trin *Sarum* 68–69; C Wootton Bassett 69–72; C Broad Town 69–72; R Bishopstrow and Boreham 72–79; P-in-c Brighton St Geo *Chich* 79–83; V Brighton St Anne 79–83; V Brighton St Geo and St Anne 83–86; P-in-c Kemp Town St Mark and St Matt 85–86; V Brighton St Geo w St Anne and St Mark 86–95; rtd 95; PtO *Ex* from 95. *7 Cambridge Terrace, Salcombe Road, Sidmouth EX10 8PL* T: (01395) 514154

LOVATT, Mrs Pamela. b 50. **d** 98 **p** 99. OLM Warrington St Ann *Liv* 98–14; OLM Warrington H Trin and St Ann from 14; Chapl 5 Boroughs Partnership NHS Foundn Trust from 99. *59 Amelia Street, Warrington WA2 7QD* T: (01925) 650849 *or* 655221 E: pam.lovatt@ntlworld.com

LOVATT, William Robert. b 54. SS Coll Cam MA 75 K Coll Lon PGCE 77 MA 78. Oak Hill Th Coll 85. **d** 87 **p** 88. C Devonport St Budeaux *Ex* 87–90; Asst Chapl Paris St Mich *Eur* 90–94; P-in-c Lenton *S'well* 94–00; V 00–04; V Eastbourne All SS *Chich* from 04; RD Eastbourne 06–09. *All Saints' Vicarage, 1A Jevington Gardens, Eastbourne BN21 4HR* T: (01323) 410033 M: 07815-138202 E: robertlovatt777@hotmail.com

LOVE, Mrs Alison Jane. b 63. Lanc Univ BA 84 Westmr Coll Ox PGCE 85 Win Univ BA 11. STETS 08. **d** 11 **p** 12. NSM Chippenham St Pet *Bris* 11–14; P-in-c Draycot 14–16; R from 16; AD N Wilts from 19. *Draycot Rectory, Seagry Road, Sutton Benger, Chippenham SN15 4RY* T: (01249) 720619 E: palove@tiscali.co.uk

LOVE, Ms Anette. b 53. Matlock Coll of Educn CertEd 74 Nottm Univ BEd 75. Cranmer Hall Dur 88. **d** 90 **p** 94. Par Dn Gresley *Derby* 90–92; C Heanor 92–94; C Loscoe 94–02; V Heath 02–15; rtd 15; PtO *Derby* from 15. *3 Chase View, Crich, Matlock DE4 5DZ* T: (01773) 852180 M: 07713-955249 E: anette.love@btinternet.com

LOVE, Joel Andrew. b 77. Birm Univ BA 99 MPhil 04 PhD 08 Cam Univ BA 11. Westcott Ho Cam 09. **d** 11 **p** 12. C Lancaster St Mary w St John and St Anne *Blackb* 11–15; V Roch from 15. *The Vicarage, 138 Delce Road, Rochester ME1 2EH* M: 07519-620889 E: joel.loves.trees@gmail.com

LOVE, Richard Angus. b 45. AKC 67. **d** 68 **p** 69. C Balham Hill Ascension *S'wark* 68–71; C Amersham *Ox* 71–73; R Scotter w E Ferry *Linc* 73–79; P-in-c Petham w Waltham and Lower Hardres w Nackington *Cant* 79–85; R Petham and Waltham w Lower Hardres etc 85–90; V Sittingbourne H Trin w Bobbing 90–02; P-in-c Aldington w Bonnington and Bilsington etc 02–10; rtd 10; PtO *Cant* from 10. *45 Greystones Road, Bearsted, Maidstone ME15 8PD* E: revralove@msn.com

LOVE, Robert. b 45. Bradf Univ BSc 68 PhD 74 NE Lon Poly PGCE 89. Trin Coll Bris. **d** 75 **p** 76. C Bowling St Jo *Bradf* 75–79; TV Forest Gate St Sav w W Ham St Matt *Chelmsf* 79–85; P-in-c Becontree St Elisabeth 85–96; V S Hornchurch St Jo and St Matt 96–10; AD Havering 08–10; rtd 10; PtO *Chelmsf* from 11. *7 Chelmer Drive, South Ockendon RM15 6EE* T: (01708) 530915 M: 07767-279598 E: revboblove@tiscali.co.uk

LOVEDAY, Mrs Jean Susan. b 47. Ex Univ BTh 10. SWMTC 09. **d** 11 **p** 16. NSM Braunton *Ex* 11–14; NSM Combe Martin, Berrynarbor, Lynton, Brendon etc 14–18; NSM Lynton, Brendon, Countisbury etc from 18. *Castle Garden, Castle Hill, Lynton EX35 6JA* T: (01598) 752699 E: jean.loveday35@gmail.com

LOVEDAY, Joseph Michael. b 54. AKC 75. St Aug Coll Cant 75. **d** 78 **p** 79. C Kettering SS Pet and Paul 78–81; C Upper Teddington SS Pet and Paul *Lon* 81–84; CF 84–09; rtd 09; PtO *Ox* from 13; *Pet* from 16. *6 Mansell Close, Towcester NN12 7AY*

LOVEDAY, Susan Mary. b 49. Sussex Univ BA 70 Surrey Univ MSc 81. STETS 94. **d** 97 **p** 98. NSM New Haw *Guildf* 97–03; NSM Egham Hythe 03–19; Ecum Co-ord Churches Together in Surrey 00–18; PtO from 19. *10 Abbey Gardens, Chertsey KT16 8RQ* T: (01932) 566920 E: sue.loveday.ctsurrey@lineone.net

LOVEGROVE, Anne Maureen. b 44. Oak Hill Th Coll 88. **d** 90 **p** 94. Par Dn Thorley *St Alb* 90–94; C 94–95; V Croxley Green St Oswald 95–02; V Letchworth St Paul w Willian 02–09; rtd 09; PtO *St Alb* from 09; *Ox* from 09. *24 Chenies Avenue, Amersham HP6 6PP* T: (01494) 763151 E: annelovegrove1@gmail.com

LOVEGROVE, Michael John Bennett. b 42. FCII FCIPD ACIArb. SEITE. **d** 00 **p** 01. NSM Saffron Walden w Wendens Ambo, Littlebury etc *Chelmsf* 00–08; TV 05–08; rtd 08; PtO *Chelmsf* from 09. *Craigside, 8 Beck Road, Saffron Walden CB11 4EH* T: (01799) 528232 M: 07980-103541 E: lovegrove8_@btinternet.com

LOVELESS, Martin Frank. b 46. N Bucks Coll of Educn CertEd 68. Wycliffe Hall Ox 72. **d** 75 **p** 76. C Caversham *Ox* 75–81; V Carterton 81–86; Chapl RAF 86–02; Chapl K Coll Taunton 02–04; PtO *Heref* 04–05 and from 07; P-in-c Glossop *Derby* 05–07. *Ridge Cottage, Staunton-on-Wye, Hereford HR4 7LP* T: (01981) 500311 M: 07810-002079 E: martinloveless@hotmail.com

LOVELESS, Mrs Natalie Louise. b 78. Southn Univ BA 01. SEITE 08. **d** 11 **p** 12. NSM Horsham *Chich* 11–14; TV from 14. *St Leonard's Vicarage, Cambridge Road, Horsham RH13 5ED* T: (01403) 243254 E: revnloveless@gmail.com

LOVELL, Mrs Cara Frances. b 79. Cant Ch Ch Univ Coll BSc 01 Sheff Hallam Univ MSc 10. St Mellitus Coll MA 18. **d** 18 **p** 19. NSM Hampton St Mary *Lon* from 18. *St Mary's Vicarage, 7 Church Street, Hampton TW12 2EB* M: 07879-404201 E: cara.lovell@hampton-church.org.uk

LOVELL, Charles Nelson. b 34. Oriel Coll Ox BA 57 MA 61. Wycliffe Hall Ox. **d** 59 **p** 60. C Walsall St Matt *Lich* 59–63; C St Giles-in-the-Fields *Lon* 63; Argentina 64–67; C Cambridge H Trin *Ely* 64; V Esh *Dur* 67–75; V Hamsteels 67–75; Chapl Winterton Hosp Sedgefield 75–83; R Stanhope *Dur* 83–86; Chapl Horn Hall Hosp Weardale 83–97; R Stanhope w Frosterley *Dur* 86–97; V Eastgate w Rookhope 86–97; RD Stanhope 87–97; rtd 97; PtO *Dur* 97–15. *10 Riverside, Wolsingham, Bishop Auckland DL13 3BP* T: (01388) 527038 E: charles@thefreeinternet.co.uk *or* charlesn@uklovell.co.uk

LOVELL, Mrs Gillian Jayne. b 58. Univ of Wales (Ban) BA 79 PGCE 80. Qu Coll Birm MA 04. **d** 04 **p** 05. C Burnham *Ox* 04–08; P-in-c Burghfield 08–10; R 10–16; R Sulhamstead Abbots and Bannister w Ufton Nervet 10–14; Par Development Adv (Bucks) from 16. *21 Seaward Avenue, Bournemouth BH6 3SJ*

LOVELL, Helen Sarah. *See* HOUSTON, Helen Sarah

LOVELL, Keith Michael Beard. b 43. K Coll Lon 67. **d** 68 **p** 69. C Romford St Edw *Chelmsf* 68–73; P-in-c Elmstead 73–79; V Tollesbury w Salcot Virley 79–09; rtd 09; PtO

Chelmsf from 09. *14 Brierley Avenue, West Mersea, Colchester CO5 8HG* T: (01206) 386626 E: keith@mary.freewire.co.uk

LOVELL, Kevin John. b 62. Salford Univ BSc 83 Leic Univ MSc 03. Ripon Coll Cuddesdon 18. **d** 19. C Prestwood and Gt Hampden *Ox* from 19. *28 Peters Close, Prestwood, Great Missenden HP16 9ET* T: (01494) 868845 E: kevin@htprestwood.org.uk

LOVELL (*née* STANTON), Mrs Kimberley Rebecca. b 88. Trin Coll Bris 14. **d** 17 **p** 18. C Plymouth St Jude *Ex* from 17. *120 Salisbury Road, Plymouth PL4 8TB* E: rev.k.lovell@gmail.com

LOVELUCK, Canon Graham David. b 34. Univ of Wales (Abth) BSc 55 PhD 58 CChem FRSC. St Deiniol's Hawarden 77. **d** 78 **p** 79. NSM Llanfair Mathafarn Eithaf w Llanbedrgoch *Ban* 78–87; NSM Llaneugrad w Llanallgo and Penrhosllugwy etc 87–96; P-in-c 96–03; R 03–04; Dioc Dir of Educn 92–03; Can Cursal Ban Cathl 00–04; rtd 04; PtO *Ban* from 11. *Gwenallt, Marianglas LL73 8PE* T: (01248) 853741 E: grahamloveluck@outlook.com

LOVEMAN, Mrs Ruth. b 45. STETS 01. **d** 04 **p** 05. NSM Portsea N End St Mark *Portsm* 04–09; NSM Cowplain 09–12; NSM Blendworth w Chalton w Idsworth 12–15; PtO from 15. *3 Cotwell Avenue, Waterlooville PO8 9AP* T: (023) 9259 1933 E: ruthlvm@googlemail.com

LOVERIDGE, Douglas Henry. b 52. Sarum & Wells Th Coll. **d** 84 **p** 85. C Earley St Pet *Ox* 84–88; V Hurst 88–03; Asst Chapl R Berks NHS Foundn Trust 03–07; Chapl Mid-Essex Hosp Services NHS Trust 07–09; Chapl W Herts Hosps NHS Trust 09–16; PtO *St Alb* from 16. *All Saints' Vicarage, Churchfields, Hertford SG13 8AE* T: (01992) 584899 *or* (01923) 217994 E: dhloveridge@hotmail.com *or* douglas.loveridge@whht.nhs.uk

LOVERIDGE, Emma Warren. b 65. St Jo Coll Cam BA 87 MA 90 PhD 01. **d** 99 **p** 00. NSM Highbury Ch Ch w St Jo and St Sav *Lon* 99–02; NSM Islington St Mary 03–05; Prin Adv to Abp York 06–07; PtO *Lon* from 14. *6 Prior Bolton Street, London N1 2NX* M: 07000-777977 E: eloveridge@rafanhouse.co.uk

LOVERIDGE (*née* RODEN), Canon Joan Margaretha Holland (Jo). b 57. K Coll Lon BD 78 AKC 78 Regent's Park Coll Ox MTh 98. SAOMC 95. **d** 97 **p** 98. NSM Caversham St Jo *Ox* 97–98; C Earley St Pet 98–03; P-in-c Burghfield 03–07; AD Bradfield 04–07; P-in-c Hertford All SS *St Alb* 07–08; TR Hertford from 08; Hon Can St Alb from 14; RD Hertford and Ware from 15. *All Saints' Vicarage, Churchfields, Hertford SG13 8AE* T: (01992) 584899 E: jonloveridge@hotmail.com

LOVERING, Mrs Jennifer Mary. b 39. Eastbourne Tr Coll CertEd 59. Wycliffe Hall Ox 81. **dss** 84 **d** 87 **p** 94. Abingdon w Shippon *Ox* 84–87; Par Dn Abingdon 87–94; C 94–97; rtd 98; PtO *Ox* 01–18. *5 Monksmead, Brightwell-cum-Sotwell, Wallingford OX10 0RL* T: (01491) 825329 E: jandmlovering@tiscali.co.uk

LOVERN, Mrs Sandra Elaine. b 48. Trin Coll Bris BA 07. **d** 07 **p** 08. NSM Chew Magna w Dundry, Norton Malreward etc *B & W* from 07. *Willow Lodge, Breach Hill Lane, Chew Stoke, Bristol BS40 8YA* T: (01275) 332657 M: 07515-031564 E: sandra_lovern@yahoo.com

LOVESEY, Katharine Patience Beresford. b 62. Trin Coll Bris 00. **d** 03 **p** 04. C Nor Lakenham St Jo and All SS and Tuckswood 03–08; C Stoke H Cross w Dunston, Arminghall etc 08–10; P-in-c Aldborough Hatch *Chelmsf* from 12; P-in-c Gt Ilford St Jo from 18. *Aldborough Hatch Vicarage, 89 St Peter's Close, Ilford IG2 7QN* T: (020) 8599 5413 E: revklovesey@gmail.com

LOVETT, Frances Mary Anderson. b 46. Plymouth Univ BA 92. NOC 00. **d** 03 **p** 04. Ind Chapl *Liv* 03–10; NSM Newton in Makerfield St Pet 03–05; Hon Chapl Liv Cathl 05–10; rtd 10; PtO *Liv* from 10. *11 Riverside Close, Bideford EX39 2RX* T: (01237) 471846 M: 07989-099483 E: fran.lovett@googlemail.com *or* fran.lovett@gmail.com

LOVETT, Francis Roland. b 25. Glouc Th Course. **d** 85 **p** 86. NSM Ludlow *Heref* 85–91; rtd 92; PtO *Heref* 96–05. *7 Poyner Road, Ludlow SY8 1QT* T: (01584) 872470

LOVETT, Ian Arthur. b 43. NE Lon Poly BSc 74. Linc Th Coll 85. **d** 87 **p** 88. C Uppingham w Ayston and Wardley w Belton *Pet* 87–91; R Polebrook and Lutton w Hemington and Luddington 91–04; Asst to RD Corby 05–08; rtd 08; PtO *Pet* from 09. *38 Northbrook, Corby NN18 9AX* T: (01536) 747644

LOVETT, Canon Ian James. b 49. CertEd 72 BTh 89 MA 92. S'wark Ord Course 73. **d** 76 **p** 77. NSM Gravesend St Geo *Roch* 76–77; NSM Willesborough w Hinxhill *Cant* 77–83; NSM Landcross, Littleham, Monkleigh etc *Ex* 83–85; C Compton Gifford 85–86; TV Plymouth Em w Efford 86–92; TV Plymouth Em, St Paul Efford and St Aug 93–97; Chapl Aintree Univ Hosp NHS Foundn Trust *Liv* 97–10; Bp's Adv for Hosp Chapl *Liv* 03–10; Hon Can Liv Cathl 08–10; TV Bideford, Northam, Westward Ho!, Appledore etc *Ex* 11–16;

rtd 16. *11 Riverside Close, Bideford EX39 2RX* T: (01237) 471846 M: 07989-085534

LOW, Prof Adrian Andrew. b 56. UEA BSc 77 Hull Univ MSc 78 Nottm Univ MA 10 CertEd 82 FBCS FIMA CEng CITP. EMMTC 08. **d** 10 **p** 11. NSM Alrewas *Lich* 10–14; NSM Wychnor 10–14; C Abbots Bromley, Blithfield, Colton, Colwich etc 14–15; P-in-c Costa del Sol W *Eur* from 15. *Calle Juan de Fuca 27, Beverly Hills, 29680 Estepona (Málaga), Spain* T: (0034) 952 808 605 E: a.a.low@staffs.ac.uk

LOW, Alastair Graham. b 43. Brunel Univ BSc 68 Reading Univ PhD 74. Ripon Coll Cuddesdon 90. **d** 92 **p** 93. C Brighton Gd Shep Preston *Chich* 92–96; TV Horsham 99–08; Chapl Surrey and Sussex Healthcare NHS Trust 02–08; rtd 08; PtO *Ox* from 08. *3 Sheepway Court, Iffley, Oxford OX4 4JL* T: (01865) 777257 E: glowpigs@gmail.com

LOW, Mrs Christine Mabel. b 48. Southlands Coll Lon CertEd 69 SS Mark & Jo Univ Coll Plymouth BEd 87. SWMTC. **d** 99 **p** 00. NSM Bideford, Northam, Westward Ho!, Appledore etc *Ex* 99–03; P-in-c Thornton in Lonsdale w Burton in Lonsdale *Bradf* 03–08; NSM Bingley All SS and Bingley H Trin 08–12; PtO *Sheff* from 12. *61 Woodburn Drive, Chapeltown, Sheffield S35 1YT* T: 0114-453 5199 M: 07717-096495 E: revchris.low@gmx.com

LOW, Canon David Michael. b 39. Cape Town Univ BA 60. Cuddesdon Coll 61. **d** 63 **p** 64. C Portsea St Cuth *Portsm* 63–65; S Africa 65–69; C Havant *Portsm* 69–72; V St Helens 72–88; V Sea View 81–88; V Sandown Ch Ch 88–95; V Lower Sandown St Jo 88–95; R Brading w Yaverland 95–01; Hon Can Portsm Cathl 00–01; rtd 01. *Copeland, Lane End Close, Bembridge PO35 5UF* T: (01983) 874306

LOW, Mrs Jennifer Anne. b 49. St Anne's Coll Ox MA 70 Nottm Univ PGCE 71. Trin Coll Bris 01. **d** 03 **p** 04. C Bris St Andr Hartcliffe 03–07; P-in-c Lawrence Weston and Avonmouth 07–14; Deanery Growth Officer Bris W 07–14; rtd 14; PtO *Bris* from 14. *4 Sheepwood Close, Henbury BS10 7BT* E: revjennylow@gmail.com

LOW, Robbie. See LOW, William Roberson

LOW, Terence John Gordon. b 37. Oak Hill Th Coll 75. **d** 77 **p** 78. C Kensal Rise St Martin *Lon* 77–79; C Longfleet *Sarum* 79–83; P-in-c Maiden Newton and Valleys 83–84; TV Melbury 84–88; TV Buckhurst Hill *Chelmsf* 88–92; R Gt Hallingbury and Lt Hallingbury 92–01; rtd 01; PtO *Sarum* 02–16. *37 Vicarage Lane, Charminster, Dorchester DT2 9QF* T: (01305) 260180 E: terrylow@talktalk.net

LOW, William Roberson (Robbie). b 50. Pemb Coll Cam BA 73 MA 77. Westcott Ho Cam 76. **d** 79 **p** 80. C Poplar *Lon* 79–83; Chapl St Alb Abbey 83–88; V Bushey Heath 88–03; rtd 10. *3 Trewince Lane, Bodmin Hill, Lostwithiel PL22 0AJ* T: (01208) 871517 E: robbielow2@hotmail.com

LOWATER, Canon Jennifer Blanche. b 34. Eastbourne Tr Coll TCert 54. Sarum & Wells Th Coll 82. **dss** 85 **d** 87 **p** 94. Locks Heath *Portsm* 85–88; Hon C 87–88; NSM Southsea St Pet 88–94; NSM Hook w Warsash 94–01; Asst Dir of Ords 91–99; Hon Can Portsm Cathl 95–97; rtd 97. *Lower Gubbles, Hook Lane, Warsash, Southampton SO31 9HH* T: (01489) 572156 F: 572252 E: jlowater@tiscali.co.uk

LOWDON, Christopher Ian. b 63. Plymouth Univ LLB 93 Barrister 94. Aston Tr Scheme 86 St Mich Coll Llan 04. **d** 06 **p** 07. C Chaddesden St Phil *Derby* 06–09; TV Buxton w Burbage and King Sterndale 09–13; P-in-c Maughold and S Ramsey *S & M* 13; V from 13. *The Vicarage, Walpole Drive, Ramsey, Isle of Man IM8 1NA* T: (01624) 812275 E: vicar@msr.im

LOWE, Anthony Richard. b 45. York Univ BA 66. Qu Coll Birm 66. **d** 69 **p** 70. C Greasbrough *Sheff* 69–71; C Thrybergh 71–75; P-in-c Sheff St Mary w St Simon w St Matthias 75; P-in-c Sheff St Barn and St Mary 75–78; V Shiregreen St Hilda 78–85; V Hoxne w Denham St Jo and Syleham *St E* 85–89; P-in-c Fressingfield w Weybread and Wingfield 86–89; R Hoxne w Denham, Syleham and Wingfield 90–05; rtd 06; PtO *Cant* from 16. *9 Alfred Road, Dover CT16 2AB* T: (01304) 214047

LOWE, Mrs Brenda June. b 53. Cranmer Hall Dur 75. **d** 88 **p** 94. Chapl to Families Trin Coll and Mortimer Ho Bris 86–91; NSM Clifton Ch Ch w Em *Bris* 88–91; Asst Chapl Southmead Health Services NHS Trust 86–91; NSM Marple All SS *Ches* 91–16; PtO *Man* 91–97; Asst Chapl Wythenshawe Hosp Man 94–96; Chapl Stockport Acute Services NHS Trust 96–98; Sen Chapl Stockport NHS Foundn Trust 98–16. *55 Woodlands Road, Handforth, Wilmslow SK9 3AU* T: 01625-525718 E: malowe@mail.com *or* brenda.lowe@stockport.nhs.uk *or* brendalowem@gmail.com

LOWE, Christopher Alan. b 75. Imp Coll Lon MEng 97. Oak Hill Th Coll MTh 08. **d** 08 **p** 09. C Cambridge St Andr Less Ely 08–13; C Chesterton Gd Shep from 13. *3 Iceni Way, Cambridge CB4 2NZ* T: (01223) 354207 M: 07962-060786

LOWE, Canon David Charles. b 43. Kelham Th Coll 62. **d** 67 **p** 68. C Wingerworth *Derby* 67–70; C Greenhill St Pet 70–73; TV Eckington 73–74; TV Eckington w Handley and Ridgeway 74–78; V Bury St Edmunds St Geo *St E* 78–86; V Leiston 86–98; RD Saxmundham 88–96; P-in-c Felixstowe St Jo 98–08; Hon Can St E Cathl 98–08; rtd 08; PtO *St E* from 08. *21 Firebrass Lane, Sutton Heath, Woodbridge IP12 3TS* T: (01394) 421722 E: davidlowe356@btinternet.com

LOWE, Donald. b 33. Lich Th Coll 57. **d** 60 **p** 61. C Horwich H Trin *Man* 60; C Wythenshawe St Martin CD 60–62; C Bury St Paul 62–65; S Africa 65–69; V Gannow *Blackb* 70–73; R Virginia St Alb S Africa 73–81; V Colne H Trin *Blackb* 81–89; TV Melbury *Sarum* 89–94; RD Beaminster 93–94; rtd 94; PtO *Bradf* 13–14; *Leeds* 14–16. *28 High Bank, Threshfield, Skipton BD23 5BU* T: (01756) 752344

LOWE, Mrs Elaine Mary. b 55. **d** 98 **p** 99. OLM Bardsley *Man* from 98. *5 Danisher Lane, Bardsley, Oldham OL8 3HU* T: 0161-633 4535 E: elaine@thelowes.f2s.com

LOWE, Mrs Heather Jocelyn. b 63. Bradf Univ BA 84. Ridley Hall Cam 12. **d** 14 **p** 15. C Harrington *Carl* 14–17; C Distington 14–17; R Brigstock w Stanion and Lowick and Sudborough *Pet* from 17. *14 Willow Lane, Stanion, Kettering NN14 1DT* M: 07587-172062 E: heatherlowe020@btinternet.com

LOWE, Mrs Janet Eleanor. b 56. Univ Coll Lon BSc 77. NTMTC 98. **d** 01 **p** 02. C Hendon St Paul Mill Hill *Lon* from 01. *12 Frobisher Road, London N8 0QS* T: (020) 8340 8764 E: janlowe@btinternet.com

LOWE, Canon Jonathan David. b 66. ACII 04. Trin Coll Bris 08. **d** 10 **p** 11. C Icknield Way Villages *Chelmsf* 10–13; P-in-c Steeple Bumpstead and Helions Bumpstead 13–15; P-in-c Ridgewell w Ashen, Birdbrook and Sturmer 14–15; R Two Rivers from 15; AD Hinckford from 15; Hon Can Chelmsf Cathl from 16. *The Vicarage, 3 Church Street, Steeple Bumpstead, Haverhill CB9 7DG* T: (01440) 731687 M: 07771-850705 E: vicar@2rivers.faith

LOWE, Keith Gregory. b 50. Sarum & Wells Th Coll 91. **d** 93 **p** 94. C Wallasey St Hilary *Ches* 93–94; C W Kirby St Bridget 94–98; V Sandbach Heath w Wheelock 98–01; V High Lane 01–04; Chapl Stockport NHS Trust 01–04; Asst Chapl Sheff Teaching Hosps NHS Trust 04–06; Chapl Sheff Teaching Hosps NHS Foundn Trust 06–15; rtd 15. *41 Ramsey Avenue, Bishopthorpe, York YO23 2SQ* T: (01904) 848894 E: brigidnkeith@talktalk.net

LOWE, Canon Michael Arthur. b 46. Lon Univ BD 67 Hull Univ MA 85. Cranmer Hall Dur 75. **d** 76 **p** 77. C Thorpe Edge *Bradf* 76–79; C N Ferriby *York* 79–84; TV 84–86; Dir Past Studies Trin Coll Bris 86–91; V Marple All SS *Ches* 91–00; RD Chadkirk 95–00; Dir of Miss and Unity 00–05; C Delamere 00–02; C Wilmslow 05–08; Hon Can Ches Cathl 00–08; rtd 08; Dioc Ecum Officer *Ches* 09–15; Hon C Cheadle 10–17; PtO from 17. *55 Woodlands Road, Handforth, Wilmslow SK9 3AU* T: (01625) 525718 E: malowe@mail.com

LOWE, Preb Stephen Arthur. b 49. Nottm Univ BSc 71. Cuddesdon Coll 71. **d** 74 **p** 75. C Mansfield St Mark *S'well* 74–77; Chapl Martyrs' Sch Papua New Guinea 77–78; P-in-c Nambaiyufa 79; V Kirkby Woodhouse *S'well* 80–86; V Beeston 86–99; St Wenlock *Heref* 99–14; RD Condover 06–11; Preb Heref Cathl 10–14; rtd 14. *Faith Cottage, West Lambrook, South Petherton TA13 5HA* T: (01460) 249447 E: stephen@slowe.eclipse.co.uk

✠**LOWE, The Rt Revd Stephen Richard.** b 44. Lon Univ BSc 66. Ripon Hall Ox 68. **d** 68 **p** 69 **c** 99. C Gospel Lane St Mich *Birm* 68–72; C-in-c Woodgate Valley CD 72–75; V E Ham w Upton Park *Chelmsf* 75–76; TR E Ham w Upton Park and Forest Gate 76–88; Hon Can Chelmsf Cathl 85–88; Adn Sheff 88–99; Can Res Sheff Cathl 88–99; Suff Bp Hulme *Man* 99–09; rtd 09; PtO *St As* 09–11 and 12–17; P-in-c Towyn 11–12; I Aled Miss Area 17–18; Hon Asst Bp Liv from 15. *2 Pen y Glyn, Bryn-y-Maen, Colwyn Bay LL28 5EW* T: (01492) 533510 M: 07801-505277 E: lowehulme@btinternet.com

LOWE, Ms Tessa Louise. b 71. SS Hild & Bede Coll Dur BA 92 Sir John Cass Coll Lon MBA 07. SWMTC 15. **d** 18 **p** 19. C Lann Pydar *Truro* from 18. *22 Stret Myghtern Arthur, Nansledan, Newquay TR8 4GJ* M: 07843-439102 E: tesslowe71@gmail.com

LOWELL, Ian Russell. b 53. AKC 75. St Aug Coll Cant 75. **d** 76 **p** 77. C Llwynderw *S & B* 76–79; C Swansea St Mary w H Trin and St Mark 79–81; Chapl Ox Hosps 81–83; TV Gt and Lt Coates w Bradley *Linc* 83–88; V Wellingborough St Mark *Pet* 88–02; V Northampton St Alb 02–13; Chapl Northants Ambulance Service 92–03; Officer for Major Emergencies 03–13; rtd 13; PtO *Truro* from 14. *24 Gwel Lewern, Eastern Green, Penzance TR18 3AX* T: (01736) 361924 E: ianlowell@btinternet.com

LOWEN, Mrs Anne Lois. b 60. Sarum Coll MA 17 DipCOT 82. ERMC 03. **d** 06 **p** 07. NSM Basle *Eur* from 06; Asst Chapl from 11. *The Anglican Church in Basel, St Johanns-Ring 92, 4056 Basel, Switzerland* T: (0041) (61) 731 1485 E: anne.lowen@anglicanbasel.ch

LOWER, David John. b 77. Huddersfield Univ BA 99. Wycliffe Hall Ox 08. **d** 10 **p** 11. C Sileby, Cossington and Seagrave *Leic* 10–14; P-in-c Clacton St Paul *Chelmsf* 14–19; V from 19; C Holland-on-Sea from 14. *St Paul's Vicarage, 7 St Albans Road, Clacton-on-Sea CO15 6BA* T: (01255) 475900 M: 07709-451681 E: david.lower@btinternet.com

LOWMAN, The Ven David Walter. b 48. K Coll Lon BD 73 AKC 73. St Aug Coll Cant 73. **d** 75 **p** 76. C Notting Hill *Lon* 75–78; C Kilburn St Aug w St Jo 78–81; Selection Sec and Voc Adv ACCM 81–86; TR Wickford and Runwell *Chelmsf* 86–93; Dioc Dir of Ords 93–01; C Chelmsf All SS 93–01; C Chelmsf Ascension 93–01; Hon Can Chelmsf Cathl 93–01; Adn Southend 01–13; Adn Chelmsf 13–16; rtd 16; PtO *Chelmsf* from 16. *16 Kelvin Court, Fourth Avenue, Frinton-on-Sea CO13 9DT* T: (01255) 676793 E: davidlowman@uwclub.net

LOWNDES, Harold John (Nobby). b 31. SAOMC 96. **d** 99 **p** 00. OLM Lamp *Ox* from 99. *98 Wolverton Road, Haversham, Milton Keynes MK19 7AB* T: (01908) 319939

LOWNDES, Canon Richard Owen Lewis. b 63. Univ of Wales (Ban) BD 86. Coll of Resurr Mirfield 87. **d** 89 **p** 90. C Milford Haven *St D* 89–91; C Roath St German *Llan* 91–94; Chapl Cardiff Royal Infirmary 91–94; V Tylorstown w Ynyshir *Llan* 94–96; Asst Chapl St Helier NHS Trust 96–98; Chapl Team Ldr W Middx Univ Hosp NHS Trust 98–03; Chapl Team Ldr Ealing Hosp NHS Trust 01–03; Chapl Team Ldr Univ Hosp Southn NHS Foundn Trust 03–11; Hon Can Win Cathl 11; Coaching and Lay Tr Officer *Llan* from 11. *28 Thornhill Road, Cardiff CF14 6PF* E: richardlowndes@churchinwales.org.uk

LOWRIE, David Andrew. b 81. **d** 14 **p** 15. C Gt Crosby St Luke *Liv* 14–18; NSM from 18. *17 Moor Coppice, Liverpool L23 2XJ* E: lowzie@yahoo.co.uk

LOWRIE, Ronald Malcolm. b 48. Bath Spa Univ MA 07. Ripon Hall Ox 70. **d** 72 **p** 73. C Knowle *Birm* 72–75; C Bourton-on-the-Water w Clapton *Glouc* 75–79; R Broadwell, Evenlode, Oddington and Adlestrop 79–81; TV Trowbridge H Trin *Sarum* 81–88; P-in-c Westwood and Wingfield 88–90; R 90–13; P-in-c Bradford-on-Avon Ch Ch 03–10; Chapl Wilts and Swindon Healthcare NHS Trust 88–05; rtd 13. *89 Thestfield Drive, Staverton, Trowbridge BA14 8TT* T: (01225) 768310 E: rmlowrie@btinternet.com

LOWRY, Canon Stephen Harold. b 58. QUB BSc 79 CertEd 80. CITC 82. **d** 85 **p** 86. C Coleraine *Conn* 85–88; I Greenisland 88–98; I Dromore Cathl *D & D* 98–13; Dean Dromore 02–13; I Killaney w Carryduff from 13; Can Belf Cathl from 13. *The Rectory, 700 Saintfield Road, Carryduff, Belfast BT8 8BU* T: (028) 9081 2342 or 9081 3489 M: 07834-584932 E: stephenlowry@me.com

✠**LOWSON, The Rt Revd Christopher.** b 53. Heythrop Coll Lon MTh 96 Univ of Wales (Cardiff) LLM 03 AKC 75. St Aug Coll Cant 76 Pacific Sch of Relig Berkeley STM 78. **d** 77 **p** 78 **c** 11. C Richmond St Mary w St Matthias *S'wark* 77–79; C Richmond St Mary w St Matthias and St Jo 79–82; P-in-c Burton H Trin 82–83; V 83–91; R Buriton *Portsm* 91–99; V Petersfield 91–99; RD 95–99; Adn Portsdown 99–06; Bp's Liaison Officer for Pris 00–03; Bp's Adv to Hosp Chapl 03–06; Dir Min Division Abps' Coun 06–11; PV Westmr Abbey 06–11; Bp Linc from 11. *Edward King House, The Old Palace, Lincoln LN2 1PU* T: (01522) 504090 E: bishop.lincoln@lincoln.anglican.org

LOWSON, Elizabeth Margaret. York Univ BA 04 MA 06 Surrey Univ PhD 10 St Jo Coll Cam BA 16. Westcott Ho Cam 14. **d** 17 **p** 18. C Gt Missenden w Ballinger and Lt Hampden *Ox* from 17. *2 Walnut Close, Great Missenden HP16 9AL* M: 07955-275338 E: curate.elizabeth@gmail.com

LOWTH, Miss Emma Patricia. Jes Coll Cam BA 08. Wycliffe Hall Ox BA 19. **d** 19. C Gipsy Hill Ch Ch *S'wark* from 19. *Address withheld by request* M: 07789-693520 E: revemmalowth@gmail.com

LOWTHER, Ms Kareen Anne. b 59. Loughb Univ BSc 81. WMMTC 98. **d** 01 **p** 02. C Lich St Mich w St Mary and Wall 01–04; TV Bloxwich 04–13; TV Penkridge 13–15; C Lt Aston 16–17; PtO from 18. *17 Leyfields, Lichfield WS13 7NJ* M: 07940-936033 E: kareenlowther@hotmail.com

LOWTHER, Peter Mark. b 56. GTCL 77. NTMTC BA 08. **d** 08 **p** 09. C Pimlico St Pet w Westmr Ch Ch *Lon* 08–15; P-in-c Aldeburgh w Hazlewood *St E* 15–17; P-in-c Whinlands 15–17; R Alde Sandlings from 17. *The Vicarage, Church Walk, Aldeburgh IP15 5DU* T: (01728) 452807 M: 07801-258503 E: mark@thelowthers.com

LOWTON, Nicholas Gerard. b 53. St Jo Coll Ox BA 76 FRSA 94. Glouc Sch of Min 86. **d** 89 **p** 90. NSM Prestbury *Glouc* 89–94; V Black Mountains Gp *Heref* from 10; RD Abbeydore from 14. *Forest Mill, Craswall, Hereford HR2 0PW* T: (01981) 510675 E: lowton.nicholas@virgin.net

LOXHAM, Edward. b 49. Lanc Univ BEd 78 Man Univ MEd 89. **d** 04 **p** 05. OLM Birkdale St Pet *Liv* 04–19; rtd 19; PtO *Liv* from 19. *34 Alma Road, Southport PR8 4AN* T: (01704) 568141

LOXHAM, Geoffrey Richard. b 40. Hull Univ BA 62. Cranmer Hall Dur. **d** 65 **p** 66. C Darwen St Barn *Blackb* 65–68; C Leyland St Andr 68–72; V Preston St Mark 72–79; V Edgeside *Man* 79–91; P-in-c Heapey and Withnell *Blackb* 91–92; V 92–99; V Grimsargh 99–10; rtd 10; PtO *Blackb* from 10. *63 Preston Road, Preston PR3 3AY* T: (01772) 780511 E: geoffreyloxham@gmail.com

LOXLEY, Harold. b 43. NOC 79. **d** 82 **p** 83. NSM Sheff St Cecilia Parson Cross 82–87; C Gleadless 87–90; V Sheff St Cath Richmond Road 90–14; rtd 14; PtO *Sheff* from 14. *508 Richmond Road, Sheffield S13 8NB* E: father.loxley@sky.com

LOXTON, John Sherwood. b 29. Bris Univ BSc 50 Birm Univ BA 53. Handsworth Coll Birm 50 Chich Th Coll 80. **d** 80 **p** 81. In Meth Ch 50–80; C Haywards Heath St Wilfrid *Chich* 80–82; TV 82–89; V Turners Hill 89–96; rtd 96; PtO *Chich* 96–10; *Win* 13–17. *2 Blackbird Court, Andover SP10 5PA* T: (01264) 358179 E: jsloxton@virgimedia.com

LOXTON, Canon Susan Ann. b 57. EAMTC 02. **d** 05 **p** 06. NSM Colchester, New Town and The Hythe *Chelmsf* 05–08; P-in-c Fressingfield, Mendham, Metfield, Weybread etc *St E* 08–13; C Hoxne w Denham, Syleham and Wingfield 08–13; R Sancroft from 13; RD Hoxne from 13; RD Hartismere from 14; Hon Can *St E* Cathl from 17. *The Rectory, Doctors Lane, Stradbroke, Eye IP21 5HU* T: (01379) 388493 E: revloxton@gmail.com

LUBBE, Linda Mary. b 61. Witwatersrand Univ BA 82 UNISA BTh 89 MTh 97 DTh 04. Rosebank Bible Coll 82. **d** 00 **p** 02. C Yeoville St Africa 00–05; C St Andrews 05–09; P-in-c 09–13; Adn Waterberg 14–18; Hon C Oxborough w Foulden and Caldecote *Nor* from 18; Hon C Hilborough w Bodney from 18; Hon C Mundford w Lynford from 18. *The Rectory, Elm Place, Gooderstone, King's Lynn PE33 9BX* T: (01366) 328921 M: 07724-783391 E: linda@senco.co.za

LUCAS, Anthony Stanley. b 41. Man Univ BA 62 K Coll Lon MA 99. Qu Coll Birm 63. **d** 65 **p** 66. C N Hammersmith St Kath *Lon* 65–69; C W Wimbledon Ch Ch *S'wark* 69–74; C Caterham 74–78; P-in-c Stockwell St Mich 78–86; V 86–91; R S'wark St Geo the Martyr w St Jude 91–94; P-in-c S'wark St Alphege 92–94; R S'wark St Geo w St Alphege and St Jude 95–06; rtd 06; PtO *S'wark* from 10. *23 Clements Road, London SE16 4DW* T: (020) 7064 9088 E: tonyslucas@btinternet.com

LUCAS, The Ven Brian Humphrey. b 40. FRSA 93 Univ of Wales (Lamp) BA 62. St Steph Ho Ox 62. **d** 64 **p** 65. C Llandaff w Capel Llanilltern *Llan* 64–67; C Neath w Llantwit 67–70; Chapl RAF 70–87; Asst Chapl-in-Chief RAF 87–91; Chapl-in-Chief RAF 91–95; QHC from 88; PtO *Llan* from 88; Can and Preb Linc Cathl 91–95; P-in-c Caythorpe 96–00; R 00–03. *Pen-y-Coed, 6 Arnhem Drive, Caythorpe, Grantham NG32 3DQ* T: (01400) 272085 E: brian@pen-y-coed.co.uk

LUCAS, Clive. b 52. St Mellitus Coll 15. **d** 16 **p** 17. OLM Westcliff St Andr *Chelmsf* from 16; OLM Westcliff St Mich from 16. *501 Woodgrange Drive, Southend-on-Sea SS1 3EQ* T: (01702) 585000 M: 07951-356143 E: lucasclive@gmail.com or lucasclive@gmail.com

LUCAS, Glyn Andrew. b 63. Oak Hill Th Coll. **d** 09 **p** 10. C Cheadle *Ches* 09–12; R Stanton-by-Dale w Dale Abbey and Risley *Derby* 12–18; V Woking St Jo *Guildf* from 18. *St John's Vicarage, St John's Hill Road, Woking GU21 7RQ* T: (01483) 726039

LUCAS, Mrs Jane Eleanor. b 49. SWMTC 00. **d** 03 **p** 04. NSM N Creedy *Ex* 03–07; NSM Burrington, Chawleigh, Cheldon, Chulmleigh etc 07–08; P-in-c Ashwater, Halwill, Beaworthy, Clawton etc 08–15; R 15–19; RD Holsworthy 17–19; rtd 19. *Mill House, Thorverton, Exeter EX5 5LX* E: therev.rectory62@gmail.com

LUCAS, John Kenneth. b 32. LNSM course 92. **d** 95 **p** 96. NSM Deptford St Nic and St Luke *S'wark* 95–97; PtO 97–00 and from 03. *4 The Colonnade, Grove Street, London SE8 3AY* T: (020) 8691 3161 E: johnl1932@johnl1932.plus.com

LUCAS, Julia Mary. *See* MYLES, Julia Mary

LUCAS, Lorna Yvonne. b 48. Bp Lonsdale Coll TCert 69. EMMTC 95. **d** 98 **p** 99. NSM Haxey and Owston *Linc* 98–00; NSM Scawby, Redbourne and Hibaldstow 00–04; NSM Lea Gp 05–16; PtO from 16. *4 Willingham Road, Lea, Gainsborough DN21 5EH* T: (01427) 811463

LUCAS, Mark Wesley. b 62. Man Univ BSc 83. Oak Hill Th Coll BA 94. **d** 94 **p** 95. C Harold Wood *Chelmsf* 94–98; Dir Oast Ho Retreat Cen *Chich* 98–00; Co-ord for Adult Educn (E Sussex Area) 98–00; V Polegate 00–10; R Barton Seagrave w Warkton *Pet* from 10. *The Rectory, St Botolph's Road, Kettering NN15 6SR* T: (01536) 628501 M: 07788-100757 E: rector@stbots.church

LUCAS, Ms Pamela Turnbull. b 68. Westmr Coll Ox BA 91 Glas Univ MSW 98 Edin Univ MTh 99 UNISA MTh 05. TISEC 98. **d** 00 **p** 01. C Easington, Easington Colliery and S Hetton *Dur* 00–04; CSC 04–06; Asst Chapl Basingstoke and N Hants NHS Foundn Trust 06–09; Chapl St Mich Hosp Toronto Canada from 09; Hon C Toronto St Monica 09–10; Hon C Toronto St Pet 11–14; Hon C Toronto St Leon 14–16; Hon C Toronto St Cypr from 16. *St Michael's Hospital, Spiritual Care, Room 3-018a, 30 Bond Street, Toronto ON M5B 1W8, Canada* T: (001) (647) 238 1499 E: lucas52727@gmail.com

LUCAS, Pauline Ada. b 60. SEITE 10. **d** 13 **p** 14. C Seaford w Sutton *Chich* 13–17; P-in-c Kirdford 17–18; V from 18. *The Vicarage, Kirdford, Billingshurst RH14 0LU* T: (01403) 820605

LUCAS, Preb Richard Charles. b 25. Trin Coll Cam BA 49 MA 57. Ridley Hall Cam. **d** 51 **p** 52. C Sevenoaks St Nic *Roch* 51–55; Cand Sec CPAS 55–61; Asst Sec 61–67; R St Helen Bishopsgate w St Martin Outwich *Lon* 61–80; P-in-c St Andr Undershaft w St Mary Axe 77–80; R St Helen Bishopsgate w St Andr Undershaft etc 80–98; Preb St Paul's Cathl 85–98; rtd 98. *16 Merrick Square, London SE1 4JB* T: (020) 7407 4164

LUCAS, Ronald James. b 38. St Aid Birkenhead 64. **d** 67 **p** 68. C Swindon Ch Ch *Bris* 67–71; C Knowle St Martin 71–74; V Swindon St Jo 74–77; TR Swindon St Jo and St Andr 77–81; V Wroughton 81–83; TV Liskeard w St Keyne, St Pinnock and Morval *Truro* 83–87; R St Ive w Quethiock 87–91; R St Ive and Pensilva w Quethiock 91–01; rtd 01; PtO *Truro* 01–17. *Ough's Folly, Castle Lane, Liskeard PL14 3AH* T: (01579) 345611 E: ronjulialucas@hotmail.com or mlcs2658@gmail.com

LUCAS, Ms Susan Catherine. b 59. City of Lon Poly BSc 90. STETS 97. **d** 00 **p** 01. C Streetly *Lich* 00–02; C Pheasey 02–04; Chapl HM Pris Albany 04–09; Chapl HM Pris Wandsworth 09–11; Chapl HM Pris High Down 11–15; Chapl HM YOI Aylesbury 15–18; PtO *St Alb* from 17; *Ox* from 18. *Address withheld by request*

LUCAS, Susan Joyce. b 61. Bedf Coll Lon BA 83 Univ of Wales (Swansea) PGCE 90 Birkbeck Coll Lon MPhil 05 PhD 07 Leeds Univ MA 08. **d** 08 **p** 09. NSM Anfield St Marg *Liv* 08–12; C Walton-on-the-Hill 12–14; P-in-c Gt Crosby St Faith and Waterloo Park St Mary 14–16; TR E Ham H Trin *Chelmsf* from 16. *The Vicarage, Navarre Road, London E6 3AQ* T: (020) 8586 7520 M: 07976-901389 E: revsue85@icloud.com

LUCKETT, Nicholas Frank. b 42. Univ of Wales BA 65 DipEd 66 MA 69. OLM course 95. **d** 98 **p** 99. Hd Master St Edw C of E Middle Sch Leek 94–00; OLM Ipstones w Berkhamsytch and Onecote w Bradnop *Lich* 98–02; NSM Siddington w Preston *Glouc* 02–07; NSM S Cerney w Cerney Wick, Siddington and Preston 07–08; rtd 08; PtO *Nor* from 09. *The Beeches, 10 Pauls Lane, Overstrand, Cromer NR27 0PE* T: (01263) 576895 E: nandeluckett@hotmail.com

LUCKETT, Virginia. b 67. **d** 11 **p** 12. NSM Isleworth All SS *Lon* 11–17; NSM Golden Cap Team *Sarum* from 18. *Abbott's Wootton Cottage, Wootton Fitzpaine, Bridport DT6 6NL* M: 07812-056564 E: virginia.luckett@gmail.com

LUCKING, Mrs Linda Pauline. b 61. St Jo Coll Nottm BA 10. **d** 10 **p** 11. C Caverswall and Weston Coyney w Dilhorne *Lich* from 10; Chapl N Staffs Combined Healthcare NHS Trust from 13. *5 Welsh Close, Lightwood Grange, Stoke-on-Trent ST3 4TQ* T: (01782) 321246 M: 07778-896584 E: linda.lucking.me@googlemail.com

LUCKING, Paul Anthony. b 58. Open Univ BA 94. Qu Foundn (Course) 17. **d** 19. NSM Chell *Lich* from 19. *5 Welsh Close, Stoke-on-Trent ST3 4TQ* M: 07775-898654 E: rev.paul.lucking@gmail.com

LUCKMAN, David Thomas William. b 71. Oak Hill Th Coll BA 95 K Coll Lon PGCE 96. CITC 98. **d** 00 **p** 01. C Portadown St Mark *Arm* 00–02; C Enniskillen *Clogh* 02–03; I Galloon w Drummully and Sallaghy 03–04; N Ireland Field Worker ICM 05–08; C Ardmore w Craigavon *D & D* 10–11; C Donaghcloney w Waringstown 12–13; Crosslinks Ireland Team Ldr from 15. *64 Dromore Road, Lurgan, Craigavon BT66 7JQ* T: (028) 3832 4936 M: 07742-513845 E: dluckman@crosslinks.org

LUCKRAFT, Christopher John. b 50. K Coll Lon BD 80 AKC 80. Ripon Coll Cuddesdon 80. **d** 81 **p** 82. C Sherborne w Castleton and Lillington *Sarum* 81–84; Bermuda 84–87; Chapl RN 87–07; R Merrow *Guildf* 07–16; rtd 16; PtO *Sarum* from 17. *10 Windy Ridge, Beaminster DT8 3SR* T: (01308) 862547 E: chrisluckraft@sky.com

LUDKIN, Miss Linda Elaine. b 50. NEOC 02. **d** 05 **p** 06. NSM Dunnington *York* 05–10; NSM Ireland Wood *Ripon* 10–14; *Leeds* 14–16; PtO *York* from 15; rtd 16; PtO *Leeds* from 17. *45 Guardian Mews, Lynwood Garth, Leeds LS12 4BN* T: 0113-263 5374 E: l.e.ludkin@btinternet.com

LUDLOW, Brian Peter. b 55. Lon Univ MB, BS 78 Birm Univ MMedSc 90 LRCP 78 MRCS 78 MRAeS 87 AFOM 90 MFOM 92 FFOM 01. WEMTC 01. **d** 04 **p** 05. NSM Winchcombe *Glouc* 04–06; NSM Cainscross w Selsley 06–09; NSM Rodborough 09–15; NSM The Stanleys 12–13; NSM The Stanleys w Selsley 13–15; C Gingin-Chittering Australia from 15; C Toodyay-Goomalling from 15. *The Rectory, 132 Stirling Terrace, Toodyay WA 6566, Australia* E: revdocbrian@gmail.com

LUDLOW, Miss Joy Elizabeth. b 90. Cardiff Univ BMus 12. Trin Coll Bris MA 17. **d** 17 **p** 18. C Thornbury and Oldbury-on-Severn w Shepperdine *Glouc* from 17. *13 Tilting Road, Thornbury, Bristol BS35 1EP* M: 07875-776089 E: joy_ludlow@hotmail.co.uk

LUDLOW, Mrs Lesley Elizabeth. b 43. SEITE 97 OLM course 04. **d** 06 **p** 07. NSM Allington and Maidstone St Pet *Cant* 06–10; NSM Bearsted w Thurnham 11–13; rtd 13; PtO *Cant* from 13. *37 Tudor Avenue, Maidstone ME14 5HJ* T: (01622) 673536 M: 07778-027031 E: lesley.ludlow@blueyonder.co.uk

LUDLOW, Prof Morwenna Ann. b 70. Trin Coll Ox BA 92 St Jo Coll Ox DPhil 97. SWMTC 13. **d** 15 **p** 16. C Ex Cathl from 15. *Address withheld by request* E: m.a.ludlow@exeter.ac.uk

LUDLOW, Archdeacon of. See MAGOWAN, The Rt Revd Alistair James

LUDLOW, Suffragan Bishop of. See MAGOWAN, The Rt Revd Alistair James

LUFF, Canon Alan Harold Frank. b 28. Univ Coll Ox MA 54 ARCM 77 Hon FGCM 93. Westcott Ho Cam 54. **d** 56 **p** 57. C Stretford St Matt 56–59; C Swinton St Pet 59–61; Prec Man Cathl 61–68; V Dwygyfylchi *Ban* 68–79; Prec and Sacr Westmr Abbey 79–86; Prec 86–92; Can Res Birm Cathl 92–96; rtd 96; PtO *Llan* 96–17. *12 Heol Ty'n-y-Cae, Cardiff CF14 6DJ* T/F: (029) 2061 6023

LUFF, Mrs Caroline Margaret Synia. b 44. St Hild Coll Dur BA 65 Bris Univ CertEd 66. SWMTC 87. **d** 90 **p** 94. NSM Teignmouth, Ideford w Luton, Ashcombe etc *Ex* 90–07; Chapl Trin Sch Teignmouth 97–11; C Diptford, N Huish, Harberton, Harbertonford etc *Ex* 07–16; C Ermington and Ugborough 11–16; rtd 16. *1 Elm Grove, Teignmouth TQ14 8SA* T: (01626) 778265 E: pgandcmsl@btinternet.com

LUFF, John Edward Deweer. b 46. STETS 04. **d** 07 **p** 08. NSM Guernsey St Peter Port *Win* 07–14; Chapl States of Guernsey Health and Soc Care 07–16; Chapl HM Pris Guernsey 12–16; PtO *Win* 15–16; P-in-c Sparkbrook St Agatha w Balsall Heath St Barn *Birm* from 16. *The Clergy House, 288A Ladypool Road, Birmingham B12 8JU* T: 0121-449 2790 E: fr.john46@saintagathas.org.uk

LUFF, Matthew John. b 70. Brighton Univ BA 95. Wycliffe Hall Ox 07. **d** 09 **p** 10. C Broadwater *Chich* 09–13; P-in-c Worthing H Trin 13–16; V Southbourne w W Thorney *Chich* from 16. *The Vicarage, 271 Main Road, Emsworth PO10 8JE* T: (01243) 375576 M: 07875-190203 E: matthewluff39@gmail.com

LUFF, Preb Philip Garth. b 42. St Chad's Coll Dur BA 63. **d** 65 **p** 66. C Sidmouth St Nic *Ex* 65–69; C Plymstock 69–71; Asst Chapl Warwick Coll Notts 71–74; V Gainsborough St Jo *Linc* 74–80; V E Teignmouth *Ex* 80–89; P-in-c W Teignmouth 85–89; TR Teignmouth, Ideford w Luton, Ashcombe etc 90–07; RD Kenn 01–05; Preb Ex Cathl 02–07; Chapl S Devon Healthcare NHS Trust 85–07; Chapl Trin Sch Teignmouth 88–97; rtd 07; PtO *Ex* from 07. *1 Elm Grove, Teignmouth TQ14 8SA* T: (01626) 778265 E: pgandcmsl@btinternet.com

LUGG, Donald Arthur. b 31. St Aid Birkenhead 56. **d** 59 **p** 60. C Folkestone H Trin w Ch Ch *Cant* 59–62; V Seasalter 62–66; Iran 67–73; V Cliftonville *Cant* 74–94; rtd 94; PtO *Cant* from 94. *Redcroft, Vulcan Close, Whitstable CT5 4LZ* T: (01227) 770434

LUKE, Anthony. b 58. Down Coll Cam BA 81 MA 85. Ridley Hall Cam 82. **d** 84 **p** 85. C Allestree *Derby* 84–87; C Oakham, Hambleton, Egleton, Braunston and Brooke *Pet* 87–88; V Allenton and Shelton Lock *Derby* 88–02; Dir Reader Tr 95–97; Warden of Readers *Derby* 97–00; R Aston on Trent, Elvaston, Weston on Trent etc from 02; RD Melbourne 07–18. *The Rectory, Rectory Gardens, Aston-on-Trent, Derby DE72 2AZ* T: (01332) 792658 E: theramsrev@gmail.com

LUMBY, Jonathan Bertram. b 39. Em Coll Cam BA 62 MA 66 Lon Univ PGCE 66. Ripon Hall Ox 62. **d** 64 **p** 65. C Moseley St Mary *Birm* 64–65; Asst Master Enfield Gr Sch 66–67; C Hall Green Ascension *Birm* 67–70; V Melling *Liv* 70–81; P-in-c Milverton w Halse and Fitzhead *B & W*

81–82; R 82–86; P-in-c Gisburn and Dioc Rural Adv *Bradf* 90–93; P-in-c Easton w Colton and Marlingford *Nor* 95–98; Dioc Missr 95–98; R Eccleston and Pulford *Ches* 98–05; rtd 05; Hon C Redmarley D'Abitot, Bromesberrow, Pauntley etc *Glouc* 05–08. *Valentines Cottage, Hollybush, Ledbury HR8 1ET* T: (01531) 650641 E: jonathanlumby@gmail.com

LUMBY, The Ven Simon John. b 56. Hull Univ BSc 80 Open Univ MTh 01. St Jo Coll Nottm 99. **d** 03 **p** 04. C Wirksworth *Derby* 01–06; R Clifton Campville w Edingale and Harlaston *Lich* 06–10; P-in-c Thorpe Constantine 06–10; P-in-c Elford 06–10; Chapl OHP 10–13; P-in-c Killarney w Aghadoe and Muckross *L & K* from 14; Adn Limerick, Ardfert and Aghadoe from 16. *The Rectory, Rookery Road, Ballycasheen, Killarney, Co Kerry, Republic of Ireland* T: (00353) (64) 663 1832 E: wl21011@outlook.com *or* rector@churchthesloes.ie

LUMGAIR, Michael Hugh Crawford. b 43. Lon Univ BD 71. Oak Hill Th Coll 66. **d** 71 **p** 72. C Chorleywood Ch Ch *St Alb* 71–74; C Prestonville St Luke *Chich* 74–75; C Attenborough *S'well* 75–80; R Tollerton 80–91; V Bexleyheath St Pet *Roch* 91–06; rtd 06; PtO *Roch* from 06. *11 Bromley College, London Road, Bromley BR1 1PE* T: (020) 8290 2011 E: michaellumgair@gmail.com

LUMMIS, Elizabeth Howieson. *See* McNAB, Elizabeth Howieson

LUND (née BEST), The Ven Karen Belinda. b 62. Qu Coll Birm 92. **d** 94 **p** 95. C Southall Green St Jo *Lon* 94–97; C Northolt Park St Barn 97–00; V Gillingham St Barn *Roch* 00–08; P-in-c Roxwell *Chelmsf* 08–14; Lay Discipleship Adv (Bradwell Area) 08–14; TV Turton Moorland *Man* 14–17; Adn Man from 17. *14 Moorgate Avenue, Manchester M20 1HE* T: 0161-448 1976 M: 07909-231280 E: archmanchester@manchester.anglican.org

LUNN, Preb Brooke Kingsmill. b 32. TCD BA 62 MA 66. Chich Th Coll 62. **d** 64 **p** 65. C Northolt Park St Barn *Lon* 64–66; C N St Pancras All Hallows 66–68; P-in-c Hornsey St Luke 68–79; V Stroud Green H Trin 79–02; AD W Haringey 90–95; Preb St Paul's Cathl 96–02; rtd 02; PtO *Lon* from 02. *The Charterhouse, Charterhouse Square, London EC1M 6AN* T: (020) 7251 5143

LUNN, David. b 47. Bris Univ BSc 69 St Jo Coll Dur BA 73. Cranmer Hall Dur. **d** 74 **p** 75. C Aigburth *Liv* 74–77; C Slough *Ox* 77–81; P-in-c Haversham w Lt Linford 81–84; R Haversham w Lt Linford, Tyringham w Filgrave 84–93; RD Newport 86–92; TR Walton Milton Keynes 93–12; Dioc Ecum Officer 00–10; rtd 12; Hon C Billing *Pet* from 13. *38 Riverwell, Northampton NN3 5EG* T: (01604) 784241 E: david@thelunns.vispa.com

✠**LUNN, The Rt Revd David Ramsay.** b 30. K Coll Cam BA 53 MA 57. Cuddesdon Coll 53. **d** 55 **p** 56 **c** 80. C Sugley *Newc* 55–59; C N Gosforth 59–63; Chapl Linc Th Coll 63–66; Sub-Warden 66–70; V Cullercoats St Geo *Newc* 71–72; TR 72–80; RD Tynemouth 75–80; Bp Sheff 80–97; rtd 97; PtO *York* 97–99; Hon Asst Bp York 99–14. *Rivendell, 28 Southfield Road, Wetwang, Driffield YO25 9XX* T: (01377) 236657 E: lunn48@gmail.com

LUNN, Graham Edward. b 86. Wycliffe Hall Ox BA 08 MA 12. St Steph Ho Ox MTh 11. **d** 11 **p** 12. C Reading St Mark and All SS *Ox* 11–15; Shrine P Shrine of Our Lady of Walsingham 15–16; C Beckenham St Jas w St Mich and St Aug *Roch* from 16. *St Michael's Vicarage, 120 Birkbeck Road, Beckenham BR3 4SS* E: frgrahamlunn@gmail.com

LUNN, Ms Helen Mary. b 61. Leic Univ BA 83 Newc Univ MA 99. Lindisfarne Regional Tr Partnership 14. **d** 17 **p** 18. NSM Byker St Mich w St Lawr *Newc* 17–19; NSM Byker St Martin from 19. *26 Copland Terrace, Newcastle upon Tyne NE2 1YB* T: 0191-670 4442 M: 07806-668580 E: lunnhelen@yahoo.co.uk

LUNN, Leonard Arthur. b 42. Culham Coll of Educn CertEd 64. Trin Coll Bris 69. **d** 72 **p** 73. C Walthamstow St Mary w St Steph *Chelmsf* 72–75; V Collier Row St Jas 75–85; V Collier Row St Jas and Havering-atte-Bower 86–87; Sen Chapl St Chris Hospice Sydenham *S'wark* 87–04; Hon C Redlynch and Morgan's Vale *Sarum* 04–06; Hon C Forest and Avon 06–09; PtO from 09. *Summerhayes, Whiteshoot, Redlynch, Salisbury SP5 2PR* T: (01725) 510322 E: len.lunn@btopenworld.com

LUNN, Mrs Lucy Ann (Lucie). b 71. Lanc Univ BA 93. Cranmer Hall Dur 11. **d** 13 **p** 14. C Binsey *Carl* 13–17; P-in-c Aldingham, Dendron, Rampside and Urswick from 18. *The Vicarage, Church Road, Great Urswick, Ulverston LA12 0TA* T: (01229) 587200 M: 07825-241366 E: revlucielunn@btinternet.com

LUNN, Maureen Susan. b 48. Middx Univ BSc 00. NTMTC BA 07. **d** 07 **p** 15. NSM Enfield St Jas *Lon* 07–10; NSM Enfield Chase St Mary 10–18; rtd 18; PtO *Lon* from 18. *62 First Avenue, Enfield EN1 1BN* T: (020)

8366   0592   E: mo@stmarymagdalene.church   *or* deacon@saintmarymagdalene.org.uk

LUNN, Mrs Rosemary Christine. b 51. Bris Univ BA 72. Trin Coll Bris 98. **d** 00 **p** 01. NSM Stoke Bishop *Bris* 00–01; C Chippenham St Pet 01–04; Hon Min Can Bris Cathl 02–04; P-in-c Wraxall *B & W* 04–09; R 09–12; P-in-c Evercreech w Chesterblade and Milton Clevedon 12–17; C Bruton and Distr 12–17; V Alham Vale 17–18; rtd 18; LtO *B & W* from 19. *357B Nore Road, Portishead, Bristol BS20 8EY* M: 07786-118762 E: rosemarylunn@btinternet.com

LUNN, Sarah Anne. b 63. Lanc Univ BMus 84 Man Metrop Univ MA 93. Cranmer Hall Dur 00. **d** 02 **p** 03. C Kirkby Lonsdale *Carl* 02–07; P-in-c Long Marton w Dufton and w Milburn 07–08; TV Heart of Eden 08–10; TR 10–17; R 17–18; P-in-c Kirkby Thore w Temple Sowerby and Newbiggin 11–17; C Brough w Stainmore, Musgrave and Warcop 15–17; Dioc Rural Officer 09–18; P-in-c Chollerton w Birtley and Thockrington *Newc* from 18; P-in-c St Oswald in Lee w Bingfield from 19; Jt Bp's Rural Affairs Adv from 19. *The Vicarage, Chollerton, Hexham NE46 4TF* T: (01434) 681721 E: sarahlunn63@gmail.com

LUNNON, Canon Robert Reginald. b 31. K Coll Lon BD 55 AKC 55 Kent Univ MA 99. St Boniface Warminster 55. **d** 56 **p** 57. C Maidstone St Mich *Cant* 56–58; C Deal St Leon 58–62; V Sturry 63–68; V Norbury St Steph 68–77; V Orpington All SS 77–79; RD Orpington 79–95; Hon Can Roch Cathl 96; rtd 96; PtO *Cant* from 96. *10 King Edward Road, Deal CT14 6QL* T: (01304) 364898 E: robert.lunnon@btinternet.com

LUNT, Colin Peter. b 54. York Univ BA 75 Bris Univ MA 02. Trin Coll Bris 95. **d** 97 **p** 98. C Westbury-on-Trym H Trin *Bris* 97–00; V Coalpit Heath from 00. *The Vicarage, Beesmoor Road, Coalpit Heath, Bristol BS36 2RP* T/F: (01454) 775129 E: colin@lunt.co.uk

LUNT, Margaret Joan. b 44. Leeds Univ MB, ChB 68. Cranmer Hall Dur 91. **d** 94 **p** 95. C Stanford-le-Hope w Mucking *Chelmsf* 94–97; C Rayleigh 97–00; TV 00–03; TV Rivers Team *Sheff* 03–10; rtd 10; Hon C Todwick *Sheff* 10–12; PtO from 14. *1 Rodwell Close, Treeton, Rotherham S60 5UF* T: 0114-269 4479 E: margaretlunt@yahoo.co.uk

LURIE, Miss Gillian Ruth. b 42. LRAM 62 GNSM 63. Gilmore Ho 68. **dss** 74 **d** 87 **p** 94. Camberwell St Phil and St Mark *S'wark* 74–76; Haddenham *Ely* 76–79; Dioc Lay Min Adv *Pet* 79–86; Longthorpe 79–81; Pet H Spirit Bretton 81–86; Bramley *Ripon* 86–93; C 87–88; Team Dn 88–93; P-in-c Methley w Mickletown 93–98; R 98–01; rtd 02; PtO *Cant* 02–17. *42A Cuthbert Road, Westgate-on-Sea CT8 8NR* T/F: (01843) 831698 E: gillandjean@hotmail.com

LURY, Anthony Patrick. b 49. K Coll Lon BD 71 AKC 71. St Aug Coll Cant 71. **d** 72 **p** 73. C Richmond St Mary w St Matthias *S'wark* 72–76; P-in-c Streatham Hill St Marg 76–81; V Salfords 81–90; V Emscote *Cov* 90–01; P-in-c Ascot Heath *Ox* 01–06; NSM The Churn 06–10; PtO *St E* from 11. *8 St Anthonys Crescent, Ipswich IP4 4SY* T: (01473) 273395 E: anthonylury@gmail.com

LUSCOMBE, John Nickels. b 45. Birm Univ BA 99. AKC 68. **d** 69 **p** 70. C Stoke Newington St Faith, St Matthias and All SS *Lon* 69–74; V Tottenham St Phil 74–81; Zimbabwe 82–96; V Queensbury All SS *Lon* 86–99; V Estover *Ex* 99–01; Dioc Ecum Officer 99–01; V Norton *St Alb* 01–10; RD Hitchin 02–07; rtd 10. *8 Manor Way, Totnes TQ9 5HP* T: (01803) 864514 E: jnluscombe@btinternet.com

✠LUSCOMBE, The Rt Revd Lawrence Edward (Ted). b 24. Dundee Univ LLD 87 MPhil 91 PhD 93 ACA 52 FSA 80 FRSA 87. K Coll Lon 63. **d** 63 **p** 64 **c** 75. C Glas St Marg 63–66; R Paisley St Barn 66–71; Provost St Paul's Cathl Dundee *Bre* 71–75; R Dundee St Paul 71–75; Bp Bre 75–90; Primus 85–90; rtd 90; PtO *Bre* 90–08; LtO *St And* from 05; LtO *Bre* from 08; LtO *Glas* from 08. *Woodville, Kirkton of Tealing, Dundee DD4 0RD* T: (01382) 380331

LUSTY, Tom Peter. b 71. Glas Univ BD 94 Leeds Univ MA 06. Coll of Resurr Mirfield 97. **d** 99 **p** 00. C Billingshurst *Chich* 99–02; Asst Chapl Leeds Teaching Hosps NHS Trust 02–06; Chapl Wheatfields Hospice 06–11; P-in-c Far Headingley St Chad *Ripon* 11–14; TV Headingley *Leeds* 14–19; V Bramhope from 19. *Ashbery House, 133 Leeds Road, Bramhope, Leeds LS16 9BL* E: tom.lusty@leeds.anglican.org

LUTHER, Canon Richard Grenville Litton. b 42. Lon Univ BD 64. Tyndale Hall Bris 66. **d** 68 **p** 69. C Preston St Mary *Blackb* 68–70; C Bishopsworth *Bris* 70–71; C Radipole *Sarum* 72–76; TV Radipole and Melcombe Regis 77–90; TR Hampreston 90–07; Can and Preb Sarum Cathl 00–07; rtd 07; PtO *Sarum* from 07. *49 North Street, Charminster, Dorchester DT2 9RN* T: (01305) 251547 E: rglluther@gmail.com

LYALL, Canon Graham. b 37. Univ of Wales (Lamp) BA 61. Qu Coll Birm 61. **d** 63 **p** 64. C Middlesbrough Ascension

York 63–67; C Kidderminster St Mary *Worc* 67–72; V Dudley St Aug Holly Hall 72–79; P-in-c Barbourne 79–81; V 81–93; RD Worc E 83–89; TR Malvern Link w Cowleigh 93–04; Hon Can Worc Cathl 85–04; rtd 04; PtO *Worc* from 04. *44 Victoria Street, Worcester WR3 7BD* T: (01905) 20511 E: lambourne43@hotmail.co.uk

LYDON, Mrs Barbara. b 34. Gilmore Ho 64. **dss** 72 **d** 87 **p** 94. Rastrick St Matt *Wakef* 72–85; Upper Hopton 85–87; Par Dn 87; Dn-in-c Kellington w Whitley 87–94; P-in-c 94–95; rtd 95; PtO *Wakef* 95–14; *Leeds* from 14. *17 Garlick Street, Brighouse HD6 3PW* T: (01484) 722704

LYES-WILSDON, Canon Patricia Mary. b 45. Open Univ BA 87 ALA 65. Glouc Sch of Min 84 Qu Coll Birm 86. **d** 87 **p** 94. C Thornbury *Glouc* 87–94; P-in-c Cromhall w Tortworth and Tytherington 94–03; Asst Dioc Dir of Ords 90–98; Dioc Voc Officer 94–01; RD Hawkesbury 98–04; R Cromhall, Tortworth, Tytherington, Falfield etc 02–09; Dioc Adv for Women's Min 01–09; Hon Can Glouc Cathl 02–09; rtd 09; PtO *Glouc* from 16. *24 Maple Avenue, Thornbury, Bristol BS35 2JW*

LYNAS, Mrs Angela. b 56. ERMC. **d** 14 **p** 15. NSM Cheshunt *St Alb* 14–18; NSM Beane Valley from 18. *8 Parkwood Close, Broxbourne EN10 7PF* E: clergy.angela@gmail.com

LYNAS, Preb Stephen Brian. b 52. St Jo Coll Nottm BTh 77. **d** 78 **p** 79. C Penn *Lich* 78–81; Relig Progr Org BBC Radio Stoke-on-Trent 81–84; C Hanley H Ev *Lich* 81–82; C Edensor 82–84; Relig Progr Producer BBC Bris 85–88; Relig Progr Sen Producer BBC S & W England 88–91; Hd Relig Progr TV South 91–92; Community (and Relig) Affairs Ed Westcountry TV 92–96; Abps' Officer for Millennium 96–01; Dioc Resources Adv *B & W* 01–07; Sen Chapl and Adv to Bps B & W and Taunton 07–17; Preb Wells Cathl from 07; rtd 17; Hon C Glastonbury *B & W* from 17. *Old Honeygar Cottage, Honeygar Lane, Westhay, Glastonbury BA6 9TS* T: (01458) 860763 E: stephen@lynas.org.uk

LYNCH, Canon Eithne Elizabeth Mary. b 45. TCD BTh. CITC 94. **d** 97 **p** 98. C Douglas Union w Frankfield *C, C & R* 97–01; I Kilmoe Union 01–10; I Mallow Union from 10; Min Can Cork Cathl 98–07; Bp's Dom Chapl from 99; Can Cork and Ross Cathls from 09. *The Rectory, Lower Bearforest, Mallow, Co Cork, Republic of Ireland* T: (00353) (22) 21473 M: 86-253 5002 E: eithnel@eircom.net *or* mallowunion@eircom.net

LYNCH, James. b 44. EAMTC 93. **d** 96 **p** 97. NSM High Oak *Nor* 96–97; NSM High Oak, Hingham and Scoulton w Wood Rising 97–99; Asst Chapl Norfolk Mental Health Care NHS Trust 99–03; P-in-c Nor St Steph 99–03; NSM Blanchland w Hunstanworth and Edmundbyers etc *Newc* 03–13; NSM Slaley 03–13; NSM Healey 03–13; NSM Whittonstall 03–13; rtd 13; PtO *Nor* from 13. *Beechenlea, 61 Church Lane, Wicklewood, Wymondham NR18 9QH* T: (01953) 798417 E: justjimlynch@hotmail.com

LYNCH, Michael Paul. b 54. Open Univ BA(Ed) 80 Birm Univ TCert 77. St Mellitus Coll 12. **d** 14 **p** 16. C St Marylebone All SS *Lon* 14–15; C Paddington St Jas 15–17; C St Giles-in-the-Fields 17–19; PtO from 19. *8 Dudley Mansions, 17 Hanson Street, London W1W 6TJ* T: (020) 7637 4062 E: reverend.michael.lynch@gmail.com

LYNCH, Ms Sally Margaret. b 60. St Jo Coll Dur BA 81 UEA MA 94 FRSA 96. Westcott Ho Cam 04. **d** 08 **p** 09. C Romford St Edw *Chelmsf* 08–11; V Maidenhead St Luke *Ox* from 11. *St Luke's Vicarage, 26 Norfolk Road, Maidenhead SL6 7AX* T: (01628) 783033 E: sally514@btinternet.com

LYNCH-WATSON, Graham Leslie. b 30. AKC 55. **d** 56 **p** 57. C New Eltham All SS *S'wark* 56–60; C W Brompton St Mary *Lon* 60–62; V Camberwell St Bart *S'wark* 62–66; V Purley St Barn 67–77; C Caversham *Ox* 77–81; C Caversham St Pet and Mapledurham etc 81–85; P-in-c Warwick St Paul *Cov* 85–86; V 86–92; rtd 92; PtO *Ox* 96–00. *11 Crouch Street, Banbury OX16 9PP* T: (01295) 263172

LYNES, Ann Louise. b 59. Moray Ho Edin BSc 01. Ripon Coll Cuddesdon BA 12. **d** 13 **p** 14. C Barnes *S'wark* 13–17; V Northwood H Trin *Lon* from 17. *Holy Trinity Vicarage, Gateway Close, Northwood HA6 2RP* T: (01923) 822990 E: annlynes@gmail.com

LYNESS, Nicholas Jonathan. b 55. Oak Hill Th Coll BA 97. **d** 97. C Reading Greyfriars *Ox* 97–99; PtO *St Alb* from 13. *2 Flint Cottages, Mill End, Sandon, Buntingford SG9 0RN* T: (01763) 288172 M: 07802-730485

LYNETT, Canon Anthony Martin. b 54. K Coll Lon BD 75 AKC 75 Darw Coll Cam PGCE 76. Sarum & Wells Th Coll 77. **d** 78 **p** 79. C Swindon Ch Ch *Bris* 78–81; C Leckhampton SS Phil and Jas w Cheltenham St Jas *Glouc* 81–83; Asst Chapl HM Pris Glouc 83–88; Chapl 91–98; V Coney Hill *Glouc* 83–88; Chapl HM YOI Deerbolt 88–91; P-in-c Glouc St Mark 91–99; P-in-c Glouc St Mary de Crypt w St Jo, Ch

Ch etc 98–99; Chapl HM Pris Wellingborough 99–01; V Wellingborough All SS *Pet* 01–19; P-in-c Wellingborough All Hallows 10–19; RD Wellingborough 07–15; Can Pet Cathl 12–19; rtd 19. *14 Thornbridge Close, Rushden NN10 9NJ* E: tartleknock@btinternet.com

LYNN, Anthony Hilton. b 44. Golds Coll Lon TCert 66 Open Univ BA 80. SAOMC 95. **d** 98 **p** 99. NSM Stanford in the Vale w Goosey and Hatford *Ox* 98–00; NSM Cherbury w Gainfield 00–03; TV Hermitage 03–13; rtd 13; PtO *Ox* from 13. *36 High Street, Stanford in the Vale, Faringdon SN7 8NQ* T: (01367) 718365 E: revtonylynn@btinternet.com

LYNN, Mrs Antonia Jane. b 59. Girton Coll Cam BA 80 MA 84. St Steph Ho Ox 82. dss 84 **d** 87. Portsm Cathl 84–87; Dn-in-c Camberwell St Mich w All So w Em *S'wark* 87–91; Par Dn Newington St Mary 87–91; PtO 91–94; Chapl Horton Hosp Epsom 91–94; Gen Sec Guild of Health from 94; Hon Par Dn Ewell *Guildf* 94–99. *7 Kingsmead Close, West Ewell, Epsom KT19 9RD* T: (020) 8786 8983 E: antonia.j.lynn@gmail.com

LYNN, Frank Trevor. b 36. Keble Coll Ox BA 61 MA 63. St Steph Ho Ox 62. **d** 63 **p** 64. C W Derby St Mary *Liv* 63–65; C Chorley *Ches* 65–68; V Altrincham St Jo 68–72; Chapl RN 72–88; Hon C Walworth St Jo *S'wark* 88–90; C Cheam 90–96; rtd 99. *7 Kingsmead Close, West Ewell, Epsom KT19 9RD* T: (020) 8786 8983 E: j.t.lynn@btinternet.com

LYNN, Peter Anthony. b 38. Keele Univ BA 62 St Jo Coll Cam BA 64 MA 68 PhD 72. Westcott Ho Cam 67. **d** 68 **p** 69. C Soham *Ely* 68–72; Min Can St Paul's Cathl *Lon* 72–78; PtO *St Alb* 78–86; Min Can and Sacr St Paul's Cathl *Lon* 86–88; C Westmr St Matt 89–91; V Glynde, W Firle and Beddingham *Chich* 91–03; rtd 03; PtO *Chich* from 16. *119 Stanford Avenue, Brighton BN1 6FA* T: (01273) 553361 E: lentteupal@gmail.com

LYNN, Trevor. *See* LYNN, Frank Trevor

LYNN, Archdeacon of. *See* BENTLEY, The Ven Ian Robert

LYNN, Suffragan Bishop of. *See* MEYRICK, The Rt Revd Cyril Jonathan

LYON, Adrian David. b 55. Coll of Resurr Mirfield 84. **d** 87 **p** 88. C Crewe St Andr *Ches* 87–90; C Altrincham St Geo 90–91; TV Accrington *Blackb* 91–00; TR Accrington Ch the King 00–10; P-in-c St Annes St Anne 10–11; V from 11; AD Kirkham from 17. *St Anne's Vicarage, 4 Oxford Road, Lytham St Annes FY8 2EA* T: (01253) 722725 E: david.lyon1955@googlemail.com

LYON, Miss Jane Madeline. b 50. Derby Univ MA 05. Ripon Coll Cuddesdon 07. **d** 09 **p** 10. NSM Derby St Andr w St Osmund 09–12; Asst Chapl Derby Hosps NHS Foundn Trust 12–14; C Marlpool *Derby* 14–16; rtd 16; PtO *Derby* 16–17; C Belper from 17. *19 John O'Gaunts Way, Belper DE56 0DA* T: (01773) 826884 M: 07974-806636 E: janelyon90@tiscali.co.uk

LYON, Joan Baxter. b 50. Strathclyde Univ BA 70. TISEC 94. **d** 96 **p** 00. NSM Glas E End 96–00; Asst Chapl Luxembourg *Eur* 05–11; TV Sole Bay *St E* 11–15; P-in-c Aberdeen St Ninian *Ab* from 15. *8 Seaton Stables, Don Street, Old Aberdeen, Aberdeen AB24 1XS* T: (01224) 740791 M: 07513-421700 E: joanblyon@gmail.com

LYON, John Forrester. b 39. Edin Th Coll CertEd 95. **d** 95 **p** 96. C Greenock *Glas* 95–98; C Gourock 95–98; Chapl Ardgowan Hospice 95–98; Chapl HM Pris Greenock

97–04; P-in-c Glas Gd Shep and Ascension 98–07; Chapl Rosshall Academy from 02; rtd 07; PtO *Bre* from 09. *28 Demondale Road, Arbroath DD11 1TR* T: (01241) 433601 E: lyon68@btinternet.com

LYON, John Harry. b 51. S Dios Minl Tr Scheme 86. **d** 89 **p** 90. NSM S Patcham *Chich* 89–91; C Chich St Paul and St Pet 91–94; R Earnley and E Wittering 94–04; V E Preston w Kingston 04–16; rtd 16; PtO *Chich* from 16. *58 Kendal Close, Littlehampton BN17 6SZ* T: (01903) 368650 E: frjohnlyon@gmail.com

LYON, Mark John. b 82. St Steph Ho Ox 08. **d** 11 **p** 12. C Brighton St Mich and St Paul *Chich* 11–15; C W Tarring 15–16; P-in-c 16–18; R Maybridge and W Tarring from 18. *West Tarring Rectory, Glebe Road, Worthing BN14 7PF* E: frmarklyon@gmail.com

LYONS, Bruce Twyford. b 37. K Alfred's Coll Win CertEd 61. Tyndale Hall Bris. **d** 70 **p** 71. C Virginia Water *Guildf* 70–73; Chapl Ostend w Knokke and Bruges *Eur* 73–78; V E Ham St Paul *Chelmsf* 78–85; V St Alb Ch Ch 85–91; Chapl Wellingborough Sch 92–95; P-in-c Stogumber w Nettlecombe and Monksilver *B & W* 96–98; P-in-c Ostend w Knokke and Bruges *Eur* 98–00; NSM Newbury Deanery Ox 01; Chapl Milton Abbey Sch Dorset 01–02; rtd 02; PtO *Sarum* 01–11; *Win* from 16; *B & W* from 18; *Eur* from 01. *Linhayes, West Street, Somerton TA11 6NB* E: bruce.lyons1@virgin.net

LYONS, Canon Edward Charles. b 44. Nottm Univ BTh 75 LTh. St Jo Coll Nottm 71. **d** 75 **p** 76. C Cambridge St Martin *Ely* 75–78; P-in-c Bestwood Park *S'well* 78–85; R W Hallam and Mapperley *Derby* 85–98; P-in-c Brownsover CD *Cov* 98–02; V Brownsover 02–06; V Clifton w Newton and Brownsover 07–09; RD Rugby 99–06; Dioc Ecum Officer 03–06; Hon Can Cov Cathl 07–09; rtd 09; PtO *Cov* from 10. *68 Juliet Drive, Rugby CV22 6LY* T: (01788) 333277 E: ted.lyons@virginmedia.com

LYONS, Margaret Rose Marie. b 47. **d** 89. OLM Gainsborough All SS *Linc* 89–91; Hon C Low Moor *Bradf* 04–05; Hon C Oakenshaw, Wyke and Low Moor 06–12; Hon C Wyke 12–14; *Leeds* from 14. *1C Common Road, Low Moor, Bradford BD12 0TN* M: 07940-558062

LYONS, Paul. b 67. Ulster Univ BA 91. TCD Div Sch BTh 98. **d** 98 **p** 99. C Seapatrick *D & D* 98–03; I Greenisland *Conn* 03–18; I Camus-juxta-Bann *D & R* from 18. *39 Belvedere Park, Castlerock, Coleraine BT51 4XW* T: (028) 7084 8774 *or* 7034 3918 M: 07791-472225 E: revpaul.lyons@btinternet.com *or* macosquin@derry.anglican.org

LYTHALL, Andrew Simon. b 86. Keele Univ BSc 07 St Jo Coll Dur BA 09 MA 11. Cranmer Hall Dur 07. **d** 10 **p** 11. C Stockport St Geo *Ches* 10–13; V Offerton St Alb and Stockport St Thos 13–17; Prec Birm Cathl 17–18; PtO *Lich* from 18. *St Martin's House, 17 Daffodil Road, Walsall WS5 3DQ* M: 07706-036425 E: aslythall@gmail.com *or* canonliturgist@birminghamcathedral.org

LYTHALL, Jennifer Elizabeth. *See* MAYO-LYTHALL, Jennifer Elizabeth

LYTTLE, Norma Irene. b 47. CITC. **d** 01 **p** 02. Aux Min Drumachose *D & R* 01–04; Aux Min Dungiven w Bovevagh 04–07; Bp's C Leckpatrick w Dunnalong 07–09; I 09–17; rtd 17. *Kurin House, 58 Kurin Road, Garvagh, Coleraine BT51 5NT* T: (028) 2955 7782 M: 07912-652714

M

MABBS, Miss Margaret Joyce. b 24. St Hilda's Coll Ox BA 45 MA 47 DipEd 46. S'wark Ord Course 79. dss 82 **d** 87 **p** 94. Eltham Park St Luke *S'wark* 82–05; NSM 87–05; PtO from 05. *70 Westmount Road, London SE9 1JE* T: (020) 8850 4621

MABEY, Mrs Johanna Stacey. b 65. ERMC 14. **d** 17 **p** 18. NSM Alde Sandlings *St E* from 17. *Regatta, 171-173 High Street, Aldeburgh IP15 5AN* T: (01728) 454417 M: 07729-795009 E: mabeyfamily@btinternet.com

MABUZA (née Morris), Catharine Mary. b 75. Regent's Park Coll Ox BA 96 MA 00. Ridley Hall Cam 99. **d** 01 **p** 02. C Malpas *Mon* 01–06; C Reading Greyfriars *Ox* 06–12; Par Development Adv (Berks) 12–17; V Warfield from 17. *The Vicarage, Church Lane, Warfield, Bracknell RG42 6EE* T: (01344) 884477 M: 07785-990208 E: vicar@warfield.org.uk *or* catharine.mabuza@warfield.org.uk

MAC BRUITHIN, Críostóir (Chris). **d** 15 **p** 16. Londonderry St Aug *D & R* 15–16; C Enniskillen *Clogh* 16–19; I Castlerock w Dunboe and Fermoyle *D & R* from 19. *The Rectory, 52 Main Street, Castlerock, Coleraine BT51 4RA* T: (028) 7055 6883 M: 07514-468730 E: criostoir316@gmail.com

McADAM, Gordon Paul. b 66. QUB BSc 88 TCD BTh 93. CITC 90. **d** 93 **p** 94. C Drumglass w Moygashel *Arm* 93–96; I Dungiven w Bovevagh *D & R* 96–02; I Loughgall w Grange *Arm* 02–17; I Aghalee *D & D* from 17. *The Rectory, 39 Soldierstown Road, Aghalee, Craigavon BT67 0ES* T: (028) 9209 0989 E: gpmcadam@sky.com *or* aghalee@dromore.anglican.org

McADAM, Ms Laura Elizabeth. b 85. Ripon Coll Cuddesdon BA 19. **d** 19. C Buckfastleigh, Dean Prior, Littlehempston etc *Ex* from 19. *The Vicarage, Week, Dartington, Totnes TQ9 6JL* E: dartcurate@gmail.com *or* laura.e.mcadam@gmail.com

McALISTER, Canon David. b 39. St Jo Coll Nottm 83. **d** 87 **p** 88. NSM Arpafeelie *Mor* 87–93; NSM Cromarty 87–93; NSM Fortrose 87–93; C Broughty Ferry *Bre* 93–95; P-in-c Nairn *Mor* 95–09; P-in-c Kishorn 08–09; P-in-c Lochalsh 08–09; P-in-c Poolewe 08–09; Chapl Inverness Airport 98–09; Can St Andr Cathl Inverness 01–09; OCM 03–09; rtd 09; LtO *Mor* from 10. *36 Feddon Hill, Fortrose IV10 8SP* T: (01381) 622530 E: feddmacon@gmail.com

McALISTER, Margaret Elizabeth Anne (Sister Margaret Anne). b 55. St Mary's Coll Dur BA 78 Ex Univ PGCE 79. Wycliffe Hall Ox 83 SAOMC 99. **d** 01 **p** 02. ASSP from 91; NSM Cowley St Jas Ox 01–04; NSM Cowley St Jo 04–09; NSM Ox St Mary Magd 09–11; Asst Chapl St Jo Home 11–14; PtO *Ox* from 11; *S'wark* from 15. *25 Orchard Road, Richmond TW9 4AQ* T: (020) 8876 5079 E: margaretanne@socallss.co.uk

McALLEN, James. b 38. Lon Univ BD 71. Oak Hill Th Coll 63. **d** 66 **p** 67. C Blackheath St Jo *S'wark* 66–69; C Edin St Thos 69–73; V Selby St Jas *York* 73–80; V Wistow 75–80; V Houghton *Carl* 80–91; Gen Sec Lon City Miss 92–03; Hon C Blackheath St Jo *S'wark* 94–04; rtd 04; PtO *Carl* from 04. *205 Brampton Road, Carlisle CA3 9AX* T: (01228) 540505 E: jmcallen@btinternet.com

McALLEN, Julian William. b 71. Lon Guildhall Univ BA 94 Avery Hill Coll PGCE 95. Wycliffe Hall Ox 11. **d** 13 **p** 14. C Epsom Common Ch Ch *Guildf* 13–17; C Finchampstead and California *Ox* from 17. *The Vicarage, Vicarage Close, Finchampstead, Wokingham RG40 4JW* M: 07817-745378 E: priestfinchampstead@gmail.com

McALLEN, Robert Roy. b 41. Bps' Coll Cheshunt 62. **d** 65 **p** 66. C Seagoe *D & D* 65–67; C Knockbreda 67–70; CF 70–96; Chapl R Memorial Chpl Sandhurst 87–92; Chapl Guards Chpl Lon 92–96; PtO *Guildf* 96–98; R Ockley, Okewood and Forest Green 98–06; rtd 06; PtO *Chich* 12–17. *Maranatha, Church Street, Rudgwick, Horsham RH12 3EG* T: (01403) 823172

McAN, Peter John Erdley. b 36. Bp Gray Coll Cape Town 58. **d** 60 **p** 61. C Matroosfontein S Africa 60–64; C Maitland Gd Shep 64–67; C S Lambeth St Ann *S'wark* 68–71; V Nunhead St Silas 72–81; P-in-c Clapham H Spirit 81–87; TV Clapham Team 87–90; V Dulwich St Clem w St Pet 90–02; rtd 02; PtO *S'wark* from 04; Retirement Officer Croydon Area from 08. *19 The Windings, South Croydon CR2 0HW* T: (020) 8657 1398 E: peter.macan@virgin.net

McARTHUR, Mrs Claire-Louise. b 70. Qu Coll Birm 13. **d** 16 **p** 17. C Walsgrave on Sowe *Cov* 16–19; TR Stoke St Mich, Coventry from 19. *9 Hulme Close, Binley, Coventry CV3 2XN* T: (024) 7705 4022 M: 07532-260027 E: clmcarthur70@gmail.com

McARTHUR, Duncan Walker. b 50. Strathclyde Univ BSc 73 Moore Th Coll Sydney ThL 80 Melbourne Univ BD 82 Newc Univ MA 94. **d** 82 **p** 82. C Hornsby Australia 82–85; Asst Chapl Barker Coll Hornsby 86–88; Asst Min 88–89; P-in-c Harraby *Carl* 90–93; R Hurstville Australia 93–95; Hon Asst P Wauchope St Matt from 99; Chapl St Columba Sch Port Macquarie from 02. *43 Narran River Road, Wauchope NSW 2446, Australia* T: (0061) (2) 6585 1147 or (2) 6583 6999 F: 6583 6982 M: 412-828341 E: dmcarthe@bigpond.net.au

MACARTHUR, Helen Anne. b 45. Ulster Univ BEd 90 QUB MSc 96. CITC 05. **d** 08 **p** 09. NSM Derriaghy w Colin *Conn* 08–11; P-in-c Ardclinis and Tickmacrevan w Layde and Cushendun from 11. *76 Largy Road, Carnlough, Ballymena BT44 0JJ* T: (028) 2888 5932 M: 07818-027040 E: helenmacar@btinternet.com

McARTHUR-EDWARDS, Mrs Judith Sarah. b 71. Westmr Coll Ox BTh 94. Cranmer Hall Dur 97. **d** 99 **p** 00. C Cradley *Worc* 99–02; C Quarry Bank 02–03; Asst Chapl Frimley Park Hosp NHS Foundn Trust 04–05; Asst Chapl R Surrey Co Hosp NHS Foundn Trust 05–16; Asst Chapl St Geo Univ Hosps NHS Foundn Trust from 16. *The Vicarage, 1 Garrison Lane, Chessington KT9 2LB* T: (020) 8397 3016 E: scott-edwards@btopenworld.com *or* judyedwards@nhs.net *or* judith.edwards@stgeorges.nhs.uk

MACARTNEY, Gerald Willam. b 52. TCD BTh 03. CITC. **d** 03 **p** 04. C Drumglass w Moygashel *Arm* 03–05; I Milltown 05–14; Dioc Communications Officer 09–10 and 11–14; I Drumgath w Drumgooland and Clonduff *D & D* from 14. *The Rectory, 29 Cross Road, Hilltown, Newry BT34 5TF* T: (028) 4063 1829 M: 07850-040027 E: drumgath@dromore.anglican.org

McATEER (née ROBINSON), Katharine Mary. b 51. NUU BA 73. CITC 03. **d** 06 **p** 07. NSM Conwal Union w Gartan *D & R* 06–08; NSM Londonderry Ch Ch, Culmore, Muff and Belmont from 08. *27 Northland Road, Londonderry*

BT48 7NF T: (028) 7137 4544 F: 7127 1991 M: 07813-885145 E: kmcateer51@gmail.com

MACAULAY, Jide. *See* MACAULAY, Rowland Ayoola Babajide

MACAULAY, John Roland. b 39. Man Univ BSc 61 Liv Inst of Educn PGCE 80. Wells Th Coll 61. **d** 63 **p** 64. C Padgate Ch Ch *Liv* 63–66; C Upholland 66–73; TV 73–75; V Hindley St Pet 75–81; Chapl Liv Coll 81–96; Sub-Chapl HM Pris Risley 85–96; R Lowton St Luke *Liv* 96–05; rtd 05; PtO *Liv* from 16. *83 Severn Road, Culcheth, Warrington WA3 5ED* T: (01925) 502639 E: macaulay.j@sky.com

MACAULAY, Kenneth Lionel. b 55. Edin Univ BD 78. Edin Th Coll 74. **d** 78 **p** 79. C Glas St Ninian 78–80; Dioc Youth Chapl 80–87; P-in-c Glas St Matt 80–87; R Glenrothes *St And* 87–89; Chapl St Mary's Cathl *Glas* 89–92; Min Glas St Mary 89–92; Min Glas St Serf 92–94; PtO 94–96; NSM Glas St Oswald 96–98; P-in-c 98–01; Chapl HM Pris Glas (Barlinnie) 99–00; P-in-c Dumbarton *Glas* 01–06; R 06–19; R Alexandria 14–19; rtd 19. *Address temp unknown* M: 07734-187250 E: frkenny@sky.com *or* frkenny@icloud.com

MACAULAY, Kenneth Russell. b 63. Strathclyde Univ BSc 85. TISEC 95. **d** 98 **p** 99. C Edin Old St Paul 98–01; C Edin St Pet 01–06; Dir Coracle Trust 01–09; Warden Epiphany Ho *Truro* 09–12; Public Preacher from 09. *Lismore, Perranuthnoe, Penzance TR20 9NF* E: kandbmacaulay@googlemail.com

McAULAY, Mark John Simon. b 71. Lanc Univ LLB 92 Leeds Univ BA 04 Heythrop Coll Lon MA 11 Barrister-at-Law (Inner Temple) 93. Coll of Resurr Mirfield 02. **d** 04 **p** 05. C Ruislip St Martin *Lon* 04–07; V New Southgate St Paul 07–18; V Eastbourne St Sav and St Pet *Chich* from 18. *St Saviour's Vicarage, Spencer Road, Eastbourne BN21 4PA* E: frmarkmcaulay@hotmail.com

MACAULAY, Rowland Ayoola Babajide. b 65. Thames Valley Univ LLB 96. Westcott Ho Cam 11. **d** 13. C E Ham w Upton Park and Forest Gate *Chelmsf* 13–14; C Leytonstone St Marg w St Columba from 18. *84 St James Road, London E15 1RN* M: 07521-130179 E: ramacaulay@gmail.com

McAUSLAND, Canon William James. b 36. Edin Th Coll 56. **d** 59 **p** 60. C Dundee St Mary Magd *Bre* 59–64; R 71–79; R Glas H Cross 64–71; Chapl St Marg Old People's Home 79–85; R Dundee St Marg *Bre* 79–01; Chapl St Mary's Sisterhood 82–87; Chapl Ninewells Hosp Dundee 85–01; Can St Paul's Cathl Dundee *Bre* 93–01; rtd 01; Hon Can from 01; NSM Monifieth *Bre* from 03. *18 Broadford Terrace, Broughty Ferry, Dundee DD5 3EF* T: (01382) 737721 E: billmcausland@talktalk.net

McAVOY, George Brian. b 41. TCD BA 61 MA 72. Div Test 63. **d** 63 **p** 65. C Cork St Luke w St Ann *C, C & R* 63–66; I Timoleague w Abbeymahon 66–68; Chapl RAF 68–88; Asst Chapl-in-Chief RAF 88–95; QHC 91–95; Chapl Fosse Health NHS Trust 95–98; Chapl Oakham Sch 98–03; rtd 03; PtO *Pet* 03–11 and from 18; *Leic* from 05; Past Care and Counselling Adv *Pet* 04–10. *1 The Leas, Cottesmore, Oakham LE15 7DG* T: (01572) 812404 M: 07967-967803 E: gbm825@outlook.com *or* brianmcavoy41@gmail.com

McAVOY, Philip George. b 63. Imp Coll Lon BSc 85 SS Coll Cam BA 90. Westcott Ho Cam 88. **d** 91 **p** 92. C W End *Win* 91–95; TV Swanage and Studland *Sarum* 95–00; P-in-c Littleton *Lon* 00–06; V Weston *Guildf* 06–10; PtO 10–13. *Four Acorns, Molesey Road, Walton-on-Thames KT12 3PP* T: (01932) 225098 E: pandk.mac@btinternet.com

MACBAIN, Patrick. b 77. G&C Coll Cam BA 99. Oak Hill Th Coll BTh 06. **d** 09 **p** 10. C Worksop St Anne *S'well* 09–13; V Danehill *Chich* from 13; RD Uckfield from 16. *The Vicarage, Lewes Road, Danehill, Haywards Heath RH17 7ER* T: (01825) 790269 E: pmacbain@hotmail.com

McBRIDE, Ms Catherine Sarah. b 64. Trent Poly BSc 87. Ridley Hall Cam 06. **d** 08 **p** 09. C Meole Brace *Lich* 08–12; C Busbridge and Hambledon *Guildf* 12–17; V Drayton in Hales *Lich* from 17. *The Vicarage, Mount Lane, Market Drayton TF9 1AQ* T: (01630) 653505 E: vicarofstmarys@gmail.com

McBRIDE, Mrs Katharine Alexandra. b 76. Bath Spa Univ BA 98 PGCE 99. St Hild Coll 17. **d** 19. C Strensall *York* from 19. *The Barn, Sycamore Farm, 72 The Village, Strensall, York YO32 5XA* E: revkmcbride@gmail.com

McBRIDE, The Ven Stephen Richard. b 61. QUB BSc 84 TCD BTh 89 MA 92 QUB PhD 96. CITC 84. **d** 87 **p** 88. C Antrim All SS *Conn* 87–90; I Belfast St Pet 90–95; Bp's Dom Chapl 94–02; I Antrim All SS from 95; Adn Conn from 02; Prec Belf Cathl from 02. *The Vicarage, 10 Vicarage Gardens, Antrim BT41 4JP* T/F: (028) 9446 2186 M: 07718-588191 E: archdeacon@connor.anglican.org

McCABE, Alan. b 37. Lon Univ BScEng 61. Ridley Hall Cam 61. **d** 63 **p** 64. C Bromley SS Pet and Paul *Roch* 63–67; PV Roch Cathl 67–70; V Bromley H Trin 70–77; V Westerham 77–88; V Eastbourne St Jo *Chich* 88–99; rtd 00; PtO *Chich* 00–14.

478

Dairy Cottage, Dunorlan Farm, Halls Hole Road, Tunbridge Wells TN2 4RE T: (01892) 458620 E: romymccabe@gmail.com

McCABE, Carol. b 49. **d** 03 **p** 04. OLM Blackrod *Man* 03–14; OLM Horwich and Rivington 11–14; PtO from 14. *1 Newlands Drive, Blackrod, Bolton BL6 5SD* T: (01204) 669775 E: carol.mccabe2@ntlworld.com

McCABE, John Hamilton. b 59. St Edm Hall Ox MA 82 PGCE 84 Ches Univ PhD 15. Trin Coll Bris MA 01. **d** 01 **p** 02. C Burpham *Guildf* 01–05; LtO 05–06; R Byfleet from 06; Dioc Adv for Sports Min from 17. *The Rectory, 81 Rectory Lane, Byfleet, West Byfleet KT14 7LX* T: (01932) 342374 M: 07710-094357 E: john.h.mccabe@btinternet.com

McCABE, The Ven John Trevor. b 33. Nottm Univ BA 55. Wycliffe Hall Ox 57. **d** 59 **p** 60. C Compton Gifford *Ex* 59–63; P-in-c Ex St Martin, St Steph, St Laur etc 63–66; Chapl RNR 63–03; Chapl Ex Sch 64–66; V Capel *Guildf* 66–71; V Scilly Is *Truro* 71–74; TR Is of Scilly 74–81; Can Res Bris Cathl 81–83; V Manaccan w St Anthony-in-Meneage and St Martin *Truro* 83–96; RD Kerrier 87–90 and 94–96; Chmn Cornwall NHS Trust for Mental Handicap 91–00; Hon Can Truro Cathl 93–96; Adn Cornwall 96–99; rtd 00; Non Exec Dir Cornwall Healthcare NHS Trust from 99; PtO *Truro* 99–09. *1 Sunhill, School Lane, Budock Water, Falmouth TR11 5DG* T: (01326) 378095

McCAFFERTY, Andrew. *See* McCAFFERTY, William Andrew

McCAFFERTY, Canon Christine Ann. b 43. FCA 76. Gilmore Course 76. **dss** 79 **d** 87 **p** 94. Writtle w Highwood *Chelmsf* 79–94; C 87–94; Chapl to Bp Bradwell 87–92; Dioc NSM Officer 87–94; TR Wickford and Runwell 94–00; Hon C Lt Baddow 00–09; Hon Can Chelmsf Cathl 91–09; rtd 09; PtO *Chelmsf* from 09. *68 Galleywood Road, Great Baddow, Chelmsford CM2 8DN* T: (01245) 690043 E: jcmccafferty@hotmail.co.uk

McCAFFERTY (née BACK), Mrs Esther Elaine. b 52. Saffron Walden Coll CertEd 74. Trin Coll Bris 79 Oak Hill Th Coll BA 81. **dss** 81 **d** 87 **p** 94. Collyhurst *Man* 81–84; Upton (Overchurch) *Ches* 84–88; Par Dn 87–88; Par Dn Upper Holloway St Pet w St Jo *Lon* 88–90; Min in charge 90–97; P-in-c Pitsea w Nevendon *Chelmsf* 97–02; R Basildon St Martin 02–18; RD Basildon 99–04; rtd 18. *58 Gwynne Park Avenue, Woodford Green IG8 8AB* T: (020) 8502 9790 E: emccafferty@talk21.com

McCAFFERTY, Keith Alexander. *See* DUCKETT, Keith Alexander

McCAFFERTY, William Andrew. b 49. Open Univ BA 93. SWMTC 94. **d** 97 **p** 98. NSM Lapford, Nymet Rowland and Coldridge *Ex* 97–00; CF 00–04; TR Crosslacon *Carl* 04–08; R Forfar *St And* 08–14; R Lunan Head 08–14; CF (TA) 09–14; rtd 14. *29 Willow Drive, Durrington, Salisbury SP4 8DE* T: (01980) 652584 M: 07891-119684 E: normandy08@btinternet.com

McCAGHREY, Mark Allan. b 66. Warwick Univ BSc 87. St Jo Coll Nottm BTh 93. **d** 94 **p** 95. C Byfleet *Guildf* 94–97; V Lowestoft St Andr *Nor* 97–12; R Mattishall and the Tudd Valley from 12; RD Dereham in Mitford from 16. *The Vicarage, Back Lane, Mattishall, Dereham NR20 3PU* T: (01362) 850971 E: mark.mccaghrey@matvchurch.uk

McCAMLEY, Gregor Alexander. b 42. TCD BA 64 MA 67. CITC 65. **d** 65 **p** 66. C Holywood *D & D* 65–68; C Bangor St Comgall 68–72; I Carnalea 72–80; I Knock 80–07; Stewardship Adv 89–07; Can Down Cathl 90–07; Dioc Registrar 90–95; Adn Down and Chan Belf Cathl 95–07; rtd 07. *1 Rocky Lane, Seaforde, Downpatrick BT30 8PW* T: (028) 4481 1111

McCAMMON, John Taylor. b 42. QUB BSc 65 Lon Univ BD 70. Clifton Th Coll 67. **d** 71 **p** 72. C Lurgan Ch the Redeemer *D & D* 71–75; I Kilkeel 75–82; I Lisburn Ch Ch Cathl *Conn* 82–98; Treas Lisburn Ch Ch Cathl 94–96; Prec Lisburn Ch Ch Cathl 96; Chan Lisburn Ch Ch Cathl 96–98; Can Conn Cathl 85–98; CMS Kenya 99–05; CMS Ireland 05–09; rtd 09; PtO *Eur* from 15. *9 Beechfield Park, Coleraine BT52 2HZ* T: (028) 7032 6046 E: jmmccammon@hotmail.com

McCANN, Alan. *See* McCANN, Thomas Alan George

McCANN, Michael Joseph. b 61. Man Univ BSc 82 TCD BTh 91 FCA. **d** 91 **p** 92. C Derryloran *Arm* 91–94; I Dunmurry *Conn* 94–99; I Kilroot and Templecorran from 99. *Kilroot Rectory, 29 Downshire Gardens, Carrickfergus BT38 7LW* T: (028) 9336 2387

McCANN, Roland Neil. b 39. Serampore Coll BD 73. Bp's Coll Calcutta. **d** 70 **p** 73. C Calcutta St Jas India 70–73; V Calcutta St Thos 73–74; C Earley St Bart *Ox* 74–77; C-in-c Harlington Ch Ch CD *Lon* 77–99; rtd 99; PtO *Lon* 02–13. *195 Park Road, Uxbridge UB8 1NP* T: (01895) 259265

McCANN, Stephen Thomas. b 60. Benedictine Coll Kansas BA 83 Boston Coll (USA) MA 89 Creighton Univ Nebraska MA 94. Pontifical Gregorian Univ 96. **d** 97 **p** 98. In RC

Ch 97–01; Rydal Hall *Carl* 02–05; C Kendal H Trin 05–10; I Ballydehob w Aghadown *C, C & R* from 10; Chapl Lay Min from 14. *The Rectory, Church Road, Ballydehob, Co Cork, Republic of Ireland* T: (00353) (28) 37117 E: ballydehobrector@gmail.com

McCANN, Thomas Alan George. b 66. Ulster Univ BA 90 TCD BTh 93 QUB MPhil 99. CITC 90. **d** 93 **p** 94. C Carrickfergus *Conn* 93–00; I Woodburn H Trin from 00. *20 Meadow Hill Close, Carrickfergus BT38 9RQ* T: (028) 9336 2126 E: rector@holytrinitycarrick.org.uk

McCARTAN, Mrs Audrey Doris. b 50. Keele Univ CertEd 71 BEd 72 Lanc Univ MA 74 Northumbria Univ MSc 99. NEOC 01. **d** 04 **p** 05. NSM Gosforth St Hugh *Newc* 04–07; P-in-c Heddon-on-the-Wall from 07. *St Andrew's Vicarage, The Towne Gate, Heddon-on-the-Wall, Newcastle upon Tyne NE15 0DT* T: (01661) 853142 E: audreymccartan@btinternet.com

McCARTER, Mrs Suzanne. b 63. Hull Univ BA 85 PGCE 86. CBDTI 04. **d** 07 **p** 08. C Standish *Blackb* 07–10; C Cullingworth *Bradf* 10–13; TV Harden and Wilsden, Cullingworth and Denholme 13–14; Leeds from 14; Area Missr S Craven Deanery *Bradf* 10–14; *Leeds* from 14. *The Vicarage, Halifax Road, Cullingworth, Bradford BD13 5DE* T: (01535) 270687 E: suzanne_mccarter@msn.com

McCARTHY, Christopher James. b 61. NEOC 04. **d** 06 **p** 07. C Bessingby *York* 06–08; C Bridlington Quay Ch Ch 06–08; V Bridlington Em 08–15; P-in-c Skipsea and Barmston w Fraisthorpe 08–12; V 12–15; P-in-c Doncaster St Jas *Sheff* from 15. *15 Grange View, Doncaster DN4 0XL* E: chrismbrid@aol.com

MacCARTHY, Denis Francis Anthony. b 60. St Patr Coll Maynooth BD 85 CITC 05. **d** 85 **p** 86. In RC Ch 85–05; C Bandon Union *C, C & R* 06–08; I from 10; I Mallow Union 08–10. *The Rectory, Castle Road, Bandon, Co Cork, Republic of Ireland* T: (00353) (23) 884 1259 E: noden1@eircom.net

McCARTHY, Lorraine Valmay. *See* REED, Lorraine Valmay

McCARTHY, Sandra Ellen. *See* MANLEY, Sandra Ellen

MacCARTHY, Stephen Samuel. b 49. ACII 81 Univ Coll Chich BA 02. **d** 01. NSM Burgess Hill St Edw *Chich* 01–10; NSM Albourne w Sayers Common and Twineham 10–17; NSM Burgess Hill St Jo from 17. *St Edward's House, 9 Coopers Close, Burgess Hill RH15 8AN* T: (01444) 248520 M: 07802-734903 E: ssmaccarthy@aol.com

McCARTNEY, Adrian Alexander. b 57. Stranmillis Coll BEd 79 TCD BTh 88. CITC 86. **d** 88 **p** 89. C Jordanstown w Monkstown *Conn* 88–91; Bp's C Monkstown 91–94; I 94–96; C Belvoir *D & D* 02–17; I from 17. *The Rectory, 86B Beechill Road, Belfast BT8 7QN* T: (028) 9064 3777 M: 07970-626384 E: adrian@boringwells.org

McCARTNEY, Ellis. b 47. Univ Coll Lon BSc 73 Lon Inst of Educn MA 82. NTMTC 94. **d** 97 **p** 98. NSM Tollington *Lon* 97–05. *6 Elfort Road, London N5 1AZ* T: (020) 7226 1533 E: macfour@btinternet.com

McCARTNEY, Robert Charles. CITC. **d** 85 **p** 85. C Portadown St Mark *Arm* 85–88; I Errigle Keerogue w Ballygawley and Killeshil 88–89; CF 89–04; I Belfast St Donard *D & D* 04–08; I Aghalee 08–15; rtd 15; P-in-c Clonfert Gp *L & K* from 17. *104 Breagh Hill, Portadown, Craigavon BT63 5QP* T: (028) 3833 0887 M: 07484-602420 E: dunroamin.mccartney@btopenworld.com

McCARTY, Colin Terence. b 46. Loughb Univ BTech 68 PhD 71 Lon Univ PGCE 73 FRSA 89. EAMTC 91. **d** 94 **p** 95. NSM Exning St Martin w Landwade *St E* 94–16; Bp's Officer for Self-Supporting Min 09–16; rtd 16; PtO *Ely* from 96; *St E* from 16. *1 Seymour Close, Newmarket CB8 8EL* T: (01638) 669400 *or* (01223) 552716 F: 553537 M: 07970-563166 E: test_and_eval@btinternet.com

MacCARTY, Paul Andrew. b 34. Sarum & Wells Th Coll 73. **d** 75 **p** 76. Ind Chapl *Win* 75–80; C Bournemouth St Andr 75–84; Hon C Christchurch 80–91; C 91–99; rtd 99; PtO *Win* from 01. *3 Douglas Avenue, Christchurch BH23 1JT* T: (01202) 483807 E: paulmaccarty@aol.com

McCAULAY, Stephen Thomas John. b 61. Leeds Univ BA 98 Cardiff Univ MTh 14. Coll of Resurr Mirfield 96. **d** 98 **p** 99. C Chaddesden St Phil *Derby* 98–02; V Mackworth St Fran 02–04; CF 04–16; R Lympne and Saltwood *Cant* 16–19; P-in-c Washburn and Mid-Wharfe *Leeds* from 19. *The Vicarage, Askwith, Otley LS21 2HX* E: stephen.mccaulay@leeds.anglican.org

McCAULEY, The Ven Craig William Leslie. b 72. Glam Univ BA 95 TCD BTh 98. CITC 96. **d** 99 **p** 00. C Seapatrick *D & D* 99–02; C Kill *D & G* 02–04; I Lurgan w Billis, Killinkere and Munterconnaught *K, E & A* from 04; Adn Kilmore from 10. *The Rectory, Virginia, Co Cavan, Republic of Ireland* T: (00353) (49) 854 8465 E: virginia@kilmore.anglican.org

McCAUSLAND, Norman. b 58. TCD BTh 89. CITC 89. d 89 p 90. C Portadown St Columba *Arm* 89–91; P-in-c Clonmel Union *C, C & R* 91–94; Miss to Seamen 91–94; CMS 94–95; Bp's V and Lib Ossory Cathl *C & O* 96; Chapl and Tutor CITC 96–00; PV Ch Ch Cathl Dublin *D & G* 96–00; CMS 00–01; LtO *D & G* 01–13; I Raheny w Coolock from 13. *The Rectory, 403 Howth Road, Raheny, Dublin 5, Republic of Ireland* T: (00353) (1) 831 3929 M: 86-837 0450 E: raheny@dublin.anglican.org

M'CAW, Stephen Aragorn. b 61. Magd Coll Cam BA 83 Lon Univ MB, BS 86 FRCS 90 MRCGP 92. Cranmer Hall Dur 97. d 99 p 00. C Thetford *Nor* 99–02; R Steeple Aston w N Aston and Tackley *Ox* 02–10; AD Woodstock 06–09; TR Keynsham *B & W* from 10; RD Chew Magna from 17. *68 Park Road, Keynsham, Bristol BS31 1DE* T: 0117-986 4437 E: samcaw@talk21.com

McCLAY, The Ven David Alexander. b 59. TCD MA 87. d 87 p 88. C Magheralin w Dollingstown *D & D* 87–90; I Kilkeel 90–01; I Willowfield from 01; P-in-c Mt Merrion from 07; Can Belf Cathl from 05; Adn Down *D & D* from 13. *Willowfield Rectory, 149 My Lady's Road, Belfast BT6 8FE* T: (028) 9046 0105 *or* 9045 7654 F: 9046 0105 M: 07854-395797 E: mcclayd@gmail.com

McCLEAN, Derek Alistair. b 69. Poly of Wales BA 92 QUB PGCE 94. Ridley Hall Cam 08. d 10 p 11. C Drayton *Nor* 10–13; R Hethersett w Canteloff w Lt and Gt Melton from 13. *The Rectory, 27 Norwich Road, Hethersett, Norwich NR9 3AR* M: 07889-284921 E: revdmac@gmail.com

McCLEAN, Dominic. d 89 p 11. NSM Leic St Aid 10–11; NSM Burbage w Aston Flamville 11–13; TR Bosworth and Sheepy Gp 13–15; Dir Voc *Ban* 15–16; Dir Voc and Discipleship from 16; PtO *Pet* from 12. *The Vicarage, Porthmadog LL49 9PA* E: dominicmcclean@cinw.org.uk

McCLEAN, Dominic Joseph James Albert Francis. b 59. Trin & All SS Coll Leeds BEd 82 De Montfort Univ MSc 07. Allen Hall Qu Coll Birm. d 89 p 11. NSM Leic St Aid 10–11; NSM Burbage w Aston Flamville 11–13; P-in-c Bosworth and Sheepy Gp 13–15; P-in-c Nailstone and Carlton w Shackerstone 13–15; Dioc Voc Dir *Ban* 15–16; Dioc Dir Discipleship and Voc from 16; C Bro Cyfeiliog and Mawddwy 15–16. *The Vicarage, Porthmadog LL49 9PA* T: (01766) 513187

McCLEAN, Lydia Margaret Sheelagh. See COOK, Lydia Margaret Sheelagh

McCLEAN, Robert Mervyn. b 38. Greenwich Univ BTh 91. Edgehill Th Coll Belf 57. d 85 p 88. NSM Seapatrick *D & D* 85–99; rtd 99. *2 Kiloanin Crescent, Banbridge BT32 4NU* T: (028) 4062 7419 E: rimmcclean1@gmail.com

McCLEAVE (formerly **WOODGATE**), **Mrs Elizabeth Mary.** b 66. W Sussex Inst of HE BEd 87. St Jo Coll Nottm MTh 02. d 02 p 04. C Crofton *Portsm* 02–03; C Lee-on-the-Solent 03–05; C Rowner and Bridgemary 05–07; NSM Kuwait 07–10; PtO *Portsm* 11–15; V Ringmer *Chich* from 15. *The Vicarage, Vicarage Way, Ringmer, Lewes BN8 5LA* T: (01273) 812243 E: revdbethmccleave@outlook.com

McCLEAVE, George. b 42. d 12 p 13. NSM Stokesley w Seamer *York* 12–15; rtd 15; PtO *York* from 15. *52 The Stripe, Middlesbrough TS9 5PU* T: (01642) 714254 E: gmccleave@btinternet.com

McCLELLAN, Andrew David. b 71. St Jo Coll Cam BA 93 MA 96. Oak Hill Th Coll BA 05. d 05. C Sevenoaks St Nic *Roch* 05–09; P-in-c Bromley St Jo 09–12; V from 12; Chapl St Olave's Gr Sch Orpington 09–15. *St John's Vicarage, 9 Orchard Road, Bromley BR1 2PR* T: (020) 8460 1844 M: 07931-731062 E: saintjohnsbromley@gmail.com

McCLELLAND (*née* **FARLEY**), **Mrs Claire Louise.** b 69. Man Univ BA 91 Heythrop Coll Lon MTh 99. Westcott Ho Cam 96. d 99 p 00. C Sherborne w Castleton and Lillington *Sarum* 99–00; C Weymouth H Trin 00–02; Chapl Barts and The Lon NHS Trust 02–03; Chapl Ealing Hosp NHS Trust 03–06; Chapl W Middx Univ Hosp NHS Trust 03–06; NSM S Lambeth St Anne and All SS *S'wark* 06–08; NSM Pimlico St Pet w Westmr Ch Ch *Lon* 08–12; NSM Charminster and Stinsford *Sarum* 12–16; TV Dorchester and the Winterbournes from 16. *The Vicarage, 38 Herrington Road, Dorchester DT1 2BS* T: (01305) 570733 E: clairemcclelland@icloud.com

McCLELLAND, Clifford Stanley. b 60. Trin Coll Bris BA 16. d 16 p 17. C Headbourne Worthy *Win* 16–18; C King's Worthy 16–18; C Upper Dever 16–18; Chapl HM Pris Win from 18. *HM Prison, Romsey Road, Winchester SO22 5DF* T: (01962) 723000 M: 07753-224078 E: cliff@cliffandsarah.co.uk

McCLELLAND, Sarah Perrée. b 68. St Andr Univ BSc 91 Qu Coll Cam MB, BChir 93 MRCP 96 MRCGP 99. Trin Coll Bris MA 16. d 16 p 17. C King's Worthy *Win* 16–18; C Headbourne Worthy 16–18; C Upper Dever 16–18; P-in-c Valley Park from 18. *35 Ragland Close, Chandler's Ford, Eastleigh SO53 4NH* M: 07753-224092 E: sarah@cliffandsarah.co.uk

McCLENAGHAN, John Mark. b 61. TCD BTh 05. CITC 02. d 05 p 06. C Portadown St Columba *Arm* 05–08; I Keady w Armaghbreague and Derrynoose 08–13; Hon V Choral Arm Cathl 07–13; I Aghalurcher w Tattykeeran, Cooneen etc *Clogh* from 13; Dioc Registrar from 17. *Colebrook Rectory, 8 Owenskerry Lane, Fivemiletown BT75 0SP* T: (028) 8953 1822 E: aghalurcher@clogher.anglican.org

MACCLESFIELD, Archdeacon of. See BISHOP, The Ven Ian Gregory

McCLINTOCK, Darren John. b 77. Hull Univ BA 98 Open Univ MA(TS) 00. St Jo Coll Nottm 98. d 01 p 02. C Drypool *York* 01–04; C Bilton *Ripon* 04–05; TV 05–15; Dioc Ecum Adv 08–09; Chapl Wakefield Hospice 15–18; Chapl Leeds Teaching Hosps NHS Trust from 18. *Leeds Teaching Hospitals NHS Trust, St James's University Hospital, Beckett Street, Leeds LS9 7TF* E: darrenjmcclintock1977@gmail.com

McCLURE, Mrs Catherine Abigail. b 63. Birm Univ BA 84 SS Hild & Bede Coll Dur PGCE 85. Ripon Coll Cuddesdon BTh 07. d 03 p 04. C Cirencester *Glouc* 03–07; Chapl Glos Hosps NHS Foundn Trust 07–13 and from 17; Chapl Cheltenham Ladies' Coll 13–16; Bp's Healthcare Chaplaincy Adv *Glouc* from 18. *Gloucestershire Hospitals NHS Foundation Trust, Cheltenham General Hospital, Sandford Road, Cheltenham GL53 7AN* T: 03004-224286 M: 07824-476505 E: katie.mcclure@glos.nhs.uk *or* mcclure.staverton@gmail.com

McCLURE, Jennifer Lynne. See MOBERLY, Jennifer Lynne

McCLURE, The Ven Timothy Elston. b 46. St Jo Coll Dur BA 68. Ridley Hall Cam 68. d 70 p 71. C Kirkheaton *Wakef* 70–73; C Chorlton upon Medlock *Man* 74–79; Chapl Man Poly 74–82; TR Man Whitworth 79–82; Gen Sec SCM 82–92; Bp's Soc and Ind Adv and Dir Chs' Coun for Ind and Soc Resp LEP *Bris* 92–99; Hon Can Bris Cathl 92–12; Hon C Cotham St Sav w St Mary 96; Chapl Lord Mayor's Chpl 96–99; Adn Bris 99–12; rtd 12. *Park House, Denton, Gilsland, Brampton CA8 7AG* E: tim@mcclure.me.uk

McCLUSKEY, Coralie Christine. b 52. Univ of Wales (Cardiff) BEd 74. SAOMC 98. d 01 p 02. C Welwyn w Ayot St Peter *St Alb* 01–04; P-in-c Datchworth 04–05; TV Welwyn 05–11; P-in-c Eaton Bray w Edlesborough 11–12; V 12–16; Agric Chapl for Herts 09–13; Agric Chapl for Beds 13–16; rtd 16. *Castle View, Oaklands, Builth Wells LD2 3ER* E: coralie_mccluskey@yahoo.co.uk

McCLUSKEY, James Terence. b 65. Coll of Resurr Mirfield 01. d 03 p 04. C Swanley St Mary *Roch* 03–06; V Prittlewell St Luke *Chelmsf* 06–18; R Colchester St Jas and St Paul w All SS etc from 18. *50B Priory Street, Colchester CO1 2QB* T: (01206) 860419 M: 07739-404082

McCOLLUM, The Ven Alastair Colston. b 69. Whitelands Coll Lon BA 91 Anglia Poly Univ MA 98. Westcott Ho Cam 95. d 96 p 97. C Hampton All SS *Lon* 96–98; C S Kensington St Aug 98–00; Chapl Imp Coll 98–00; TV Papworth *Ely* 00–08; V Kilmington, Stockland, Dalwood, Yarcombe etc *Ex* 08–13; R Victoria St Jo Canada from 13; Adn Tolmie from 14. *3896 Cadboro Bay Road, Victoria BC V8N 4G6, Canada* E: amccollum@bc.anglican.ca

McCOLLUM, Charles James. b 41. TCD BTh 89. CITC 85. d 89 p 90. C Larne and Inver *Conn* 89–91; Bp's C Belfast Whiterock 91–96; I Belfast St Pet and St Jas 96–08; I Dunleckney w Nurney, Lorum and Kiltennel *C & O* 08–12; Can Ossory Cathl 12; rtd 12. *Curragho, Cavan, Republic of Ireland* M: (00353) 87-288 5019 E: charlesjmccollum@gmail.com

McCONAGHIE, Colin Andrew. b 75. CITC MTh 12. d 11 p 12. C Drumglass w Moygashel *Arm* 11–14; C Dunboyne and Rathmolyon *M & K* 14–17; I Carrickmacross w Magheracloone *Clogh* from 17. *The Rectory, Drumconrath Road, Carrickmacross, Co Monaghan, Republic of Ireland* M: (00353) 87-346 6190 E: revcolinmcc@gmail.com

McCONNAUGHIE, Adrian William. b 66. Jes Coll Ox BA 89 MA 06 Lon Univ PhD 93 Cam Univ PGCE 96. Trin Coll Bris BA 08. d 08 p 09. C Bath Abbey w St Jas *B & W* 08–11; Chapl Mon Sch 11–13; Chapl Brentwood Sch from 13; C Warley Ch Ch and Gt Warley St Mary *Chelmsf* from 15. *Mitre House, 6 Shenfield Road, Brentwood CM15 8AA* T: (01277) 203280 E: awm@brentwood.essex.sch.uk

McCONNELL, Canon Brian Roy. b 46. St Paul's Coll Grahamstown. d 71 p 72. C Plumstead S Africa 71–74; C St Geo Cathl Cape Town 74–77; C Prestwich St Marg *Man* 77–79; R Sea Point S Africa 79–85; V Liscard St Mary w St Columba *Ches* 85–90; V Altrincham St Geo 90–06; RD Bowdon 95–13; Hon Can Ches Cathl 97–06; Can Res Carl Cathl 95–13; rtd 13; PtO *B & W* from 15. *30 Gunville Gardens, Milborne Port, Sherborne DT9 5FF* T: (01963) 251511 M: 07759-603583 E: brianles1@btinternet.com

McCORMACK, Alan William. b 68. Jes Coll Ox BA 90 MA 94 DPhil 94. CITC 93. d 96 p 97. C Knock *D & D* 96–98; Dean of

Res and Chapl TCD 98–07; Succ St Patr Cathl Dublin 98–06; Abp's Dom Chapl *D & G* 03–07; P-in-c St Botolph without Bishopgate *Lon* 07–15; P-in-c St Vedast w St Mich-le-Querne etc 07–15; Dean Goodenough Coll from 15; PtO *Lon* 15–17; NSM Hanover Square St Geo from 17; PtO *Eur* from 16. *Goodenough College, London House, Mecklenburgh Square, London WC1N 2AB* T: (020) 7837 8888 E: mccorma@gmail.com

McCORMACK, Colin. b 47. QUB BSc 70 DipEd 71. St Jo Coll Nottm BA 75. **d** 78 **p** 79. C Carl St Jo 78–81; C Ballynafeigh St Jude *D & D* 81–84; V Harraby *Carl* 84–89; NSM Carl H Trin and St Barn 95–99; Asst Chapl Costa Blanca *Eur* 00–04; Chapl Torrevieja 04–08; I Clonallon and Warrenpoint w Kilbroney *D & D* from 11. *Clonallon Rectory, 8 Donaghaguy Road, Warrenpoint, Newry BT34 3RZ* T: (028) 4175 3497 E: colinmccormack6@btinternet.com

McCORMACK, Canon David Eugene. b 34. Wells Th Coll 66. **d** 68 **p** 69. C Lillington *Cov* 68–71; C The Lickey *Birm* 71–75; V Highters Heath 75–82; V Four Oaks 82–00; Hon Can Birm Cathl 95–00; rtd 00; PtO *Linc* from 00; *Pet* from 00; *Birm* from 05. *27 Rockingham Close, Market Deeping, Peterborough PE6 8BY* T: (01778) 217043 E: jandmccormack@aol.com

McCORMACK, George Brash. b 32. ACIS 65 FCIS 75. S'wark Ord Course 82. **d** 85 **p** 86. Hon C Crofton St Paul *Roch* 85–89; C Crayford 89–91; R Fawkham and Hartley 91–97; rtd 97; PtO *Roch* from 98. *11 Turnpike Drive, Pratts Bottom, Orpington BR6 7SJ* E: geomacc@uwclub.net

McCORMACK, Ian Douglas. b 80. St Anne's Coll Ox BA 02 MA 06 MSt 03 Leeds Univ MA 10. Coll of Resurr Mirfield 07. **d** 10 **p** 11. C Horbury w Horbury Bridge *Wakef* 10–13; V Grimethorpe w Brierley 13–14; *Leeds* 14–18; P-in-c Nottingham St Geo w St Jo *S'well* from 18. *St George's Vicarage, Strome Close, Nottingham NG2 1HD* E: fatherianmccormack@hotmail.co.uk

McCORMACK, John Heddon. b 58. Chich Th Coll 85. **d** 88 **p** 89. C Cleobury Mortimer w Hopton Wafers *Heref* 88–90; C Lymington *Win* 90–92; C Portsea N End St Mark *Portsm* 92–95; Chapl St Barn Hospice Worthing 95–06. *10 Columbia Walk, Worthing BN13 2ST* T: (01903) 263700 M: 07974-603518 E: humanrites1@sky.com

McCORMACK, Canon Kevan Sean. b 50. Chich Th Coll 77. **d** 80 **p** 81. C Ross *Heref* 80–81; C Ross w Brampton Abbotts, Bridstow and Peterstow 81–83; C Leominster 83; TV 84–87; Chapl R Hosp Sch Holbrook 87–00; R Woodbridge St Mary *St E* from 00; Hon Can St E Cathl from 09; Chapl to The Queen from 14. *St Mary's Rectory, Church Street, Woodbridge IP12 1DS* T: (01394) 610424 E: rector@stmaryswoodbridge.org

McCORMACK, Canon Lesley Sharman. b 50. EAMTC. **d** 88 **p** 94. Hon Par Dn Chevington w Hargrave and Whepstead w Brockley *St E* 88–95; Asst Chapl W Suffolk Hosp Bury St Edm 88–95; Chapl Kettering Gen Hosp NHS Foundn Trust 95–09; Chapl Cransley Hospice 09–10; NSM Kettering SS Pet and Paul 09–18; Bp's Hosp Chapl Adv 00–12; Can Pet Cathl 03–18; rtd 18. *Barnbrook, Water Lane, Chelveston, Wellingborough NN9 6AP* T: (01933) 626636 E: mccormack26@outlook.com

MacCORMACK, Michael Ian. b 54. Kent Univ BA 77 Ch Ch Coll Cant MA 87 Bris Univ PGCE 78. STETS 02. **d** 05 **p** 06. NSM Martock w Kingsbury Episcopi and Ash *B & W* 05–19; PtO from 19; *Sarum* from 19. *2 Stourhead House, Stourton, Warminster BA12 6QH* M: 07717-878736 E: revmikemac@gmail.com

McCORMICK, Mrs Susan. b 60. NEOC 00. **d** 03 **p** 04. C Newburn *Newc* 03–07; P-in-c Fawdon 07–13; TR Willington from 13. *St Mary's Vicarage, 67 Churchill Street, Wallsend NE28 7TE* T: 0191-209 9995 M: 07452-35974 E: revsue14mack@gmail.com

McCORMICK, Mrs Anne Irene. b 67. Sheff Univ BA 89 Hull Univ PGCE 90 Cardiff Univ MTh 11. Ripon Coll Cuddesdon 90. **d** 92 **p** 94. C Spalding St Mary and St Nic *Linc* 92–96; C Gt Grimsby St Mary and St Jas 96–01; C Gt and Lt Coates w Bradley 98–16; TV from 16; Chapl Rotherham, Doncaster and S Humber NHS Foundn Trust 07–12; Chapl N Lincs and Goole NHS Foundn Trust 12–16. *Glebe House, 11 Church Lane, Limber, Grimsby DN37 8JN* T: (01469) 561082 M: 07903-749266

McCORMICK, David Mark. b 68. Univ of Wales (Ban) BD 89. Ripon Coll Cuddesdon 90. **d** 92 **p** 93. C Holbeach *Linc* 92–96; TV Gt Grimsby St Mary and St Jas 96–01; Prin Linc Min Tr Course 01–09; CME Officer 09–12; TV Gt and Lt Coates w Bradley 12–15; Chapl St Andr Hospice Grimsby 12–15; PtO *Linc* 17–19; TR Gt and Lt Coates w Bradley from 19. *St Nicolas' Vicarage, Great Coates Road, Great Coates, Grimsby DN37 9NS* E: david.mccormick@lincoln.anglican.org *or* rector@glcbchurches.org

McCOSH, Andrew James. b 58. **d** 14 **p** 15. NSM Shelfield and Heath Hayes *Lich* from 14. *4 Larch Close, Lichfield WS14 9UR* T: (01543) 256075 E: ajmccosh@tiscali.co.uk

McCOUBREY, William Arthur. b 36. CEng MIMechE. Sarum & Wells Th Coll 86. **d** 89 **p** 90. C Bedhampton *Portsm* 89–92; V Stokenham w Sherford *Ex* 92–96; R Stokenham w Sherford and Beesands, and Slapton 96–02; rtd 02; PtO *Portsm* from 02; *Chich* from 02. *19 Warblington Road, Emsworth PO10 7HE* T: (01243) 374011

McCOULOUGH, David. b 61. Man Univ BA 84 St Jo Coll Dur BA 88 Leeds Univ MA 01. Cranmer Hall Dur 86. **d** 89 **p** 90. C Man Apostles w Miles Platting 89–92; C Elton All SS 92–94; V Halliwell St Marg 94–98; Min Can Ripon Cathl 98–01; Chapl Univ Coll of Ripon and York St Jo 98–01; Ind Chapl *S'well* 01–07; Chapl Boots PLC 01–07; C Nottingham St Pet and St Jas 01–02; C Nottingham St Pet and All SS 02–07; Assoc Dir Partnerships 07–09; Dir from 09; P-in-c Edingley w Halam 07–14. *Jubilee House, Westgate, Southwell NG25 0JH* T: (01636) 817246 E: davidmcc@southwell.anglican.org

McCOULOUGH, Thomas Alexander. b 32. AKC 59. **d** 60 **p** 61. C Norton St Mich *Dur* 60–63; USPG India 63–67; P-in-c Derby St Jas 67–72; Ind Chapl *York* 72–82; P-in-c Sutton on the Forest 82–96; Dioc Sec for Local Min 82–89; Lay Tr Officer 89–96; rtd 96; PtO *Newc* from 96. *1 Horsley Gardens, Holywell, Whitley Bay NE25 0TU* T: 0191-298 0332 E: tg.mcc@hotmail.com

McCRACKEN, Victor John. b 61. **d** 19. NSM Athelington, Denham, Horham, Hoxne etc *St E* from 19. *Catlyn House, Wingfield, Diss IP21 5QZ* T: (01379) 388812

McCREA, Christina Elizabeth. b 53. **d** 08 **p** 09. NSM Glanogwen and Llanllechid w St Ann's and Pentir *Ban* 08–14; NSM Bro Ogwen from 14. *2 Bron-y-Waun, Rhiwlas, Bangor LL57 4EX* T: (01248) 372249 E: christinaemcc@aol.com

McCREADIE, Mrs Lesley Anne. b 51. Bp Otter Coll CertEd 73 Open Univ BA 93. STETS BA 10. **d** 10 **p** 11. NSM Sherborne w Castleton, Lillington and Longburton *Sarum* 10–16; TV from 16; Chapl St Antony's Leweston Sch Sherborne from 17. *5 Kings Close, Longburton, Sherborne DT9 5PW* T: (01963) 210548 E: revdlesley@aol.com

McCULLAGH, Danielle Susan. Northumbria Univ BA. **d** 16 **p** 17. Mallusk *Conn* 16–17; C Lisburn Ch Ch Cathl from 17. *82 Thornleigh Drive, Lisburn BT28 2DS* M: 07964-882269 E: danielle_199@hotmail.co.uk

McCULLAGH, Elspeth Jane Alexandra. *See* SAVILLE, Elspeth Jane Alexandra

McCULLAGH, Canon John Eric. b 46. TCD BA 68 BTh 88 QUB DipEd 70. **d** 88 **p** 89. C Stillorgan w Blackrock *D & G* 88–91; Chapl and Hd of RE Newpark Sch Dub 90–99; I Clondalkin w Rathcoole *D & G* 91–99; Sec Gen Syn Bd of Educn 99–08; I Rathdrum w Glenealy, Derralossary and Laragh *D & G* 08–14; Can Ch Ch Cathl Dublin 99–14; Treas Ch Ch Cathl Dublin 09–14; rtd 14. *Harcourt Villa, Kimberley Road, Greystones, Co Wicklow, Republic of Ireland* T: (00353) (1) 287 1408 M: 86-837 0384 E: jemccullagh@gmail.com

McCULLOCH, Alistair John. b 59. Univ of Wales (Lamp) BA 81 Leeds Univ BA 86 Lon Univ MA 07. Coll of Resurr Mirfield 84. **d** 87 **p** 88. C Portsm Cathl 87–90; C Portsea St Mary 90–94; V Reading St Matt *Ox* 94–95; PtO *S'wark* 99; Chapl King's Coll Hosp NHS Trust 00–04; Chapl R Marsden NHS Foundn Trust from 04; Bp's Adv for Hosp Chapl *S'wark* from 18. *The Royal Marsden Hospital, Fulham Road, London SW3 6JJ* T: (020) 7808 2818 M: 07929-965752 E: alistair.mcculloch@rmh.nhs.uk

McCULLOCH, Andrew Stewart. b 71. St Mellitus Coll 16. **d** 19. C Cogges and S Leigh *Ox* from 19. *1 Cherry Tree Court, Witney OX28 1GQ* E: andy@coggesparish.com

McCULLOCH, Mrs Celia Hume. b 53. Leeds Univ BA 08. NOC 05. **d** 08 **p** 09. C Cheetham *Man* 08–10; rtd 10; PtO *Man* 11–13; *Carl* 12–18. *Stonelea, 1 Heads Drive, Grange-over-Sands LA11 7DY* M: 07943-366331 E: cranfieldcmc@btinternet.com

MacCULLOCH, Prof Diarmaid Ninian John. b 51. Chu Coll Cam BA 72 MA 76 PhD 77 Ox Univ DD 01 FSA 78 FRHistS 81 FBA 01. Ripon Coll Cuddesdon 86. **d** 87. NSM Clifton All SS w St Jo *Bris* 87–88; Tutor Wesley Coll Bris 78–90; Fell St Cross Coll Ox from 95; Sen Tutor 96–00; Lect Th Ox Univ from 95; Prof Hist of Ch from 97. *St Cross College, St Giles, Oxford OX1 3LZ* T: (01865) 270794 F: 270795 E: diarmaid.macculloch@theology.ox.ac.uk

✠**McCULLOCH, The Rt Revd Nigel Simeon.** b 42. Selw Coll Cam BA 64 MA 69. Cuddesdon Coll 64. **d** 66 **p** 67 **c** 86. C Ellesmere Port *Ches* 66–70; Dir Th Studies Ch Coll Cam 70–75; Chapl 70–73; Dioc Missr *Nor* 73–78; P-in-c Salisbury St Thos and St Edm *Sarum* 78–81; R 81–86; Adn Sarum 79–86; Can and Preb Sarum Cathl 79–86; Suff Bp Taunton *B & W* 86–92; Preb Wells Cathl 86–92; Bp Wakef 92–02; Bp Man 02–13; Ld High Almoner 97–13; rtd 13; Hon Asst Bp Carl from 13. *Stonelea, 1 Heads Drive, Grange-over-Sands LA11 7DY* E: n.mcculloch374@btinternet.com

McCULLOCK, Patricia Ann. *See* FULLER, Patricia Ann

McCULLOUGH, Mrs Aphrodite Maria. b 47. Derby Univ MSc 95. EMMTC 97. **d** 00 **p** 01. NSM Kirby Muxloe *Leic* 00–04; TV 04–08; rtd 08; PtO *Leic* from 08. *33 Alton Road, Leicester LE2 8QB* T: 0116-283 7887 E: aphro.mccullough@btinternet.com

McCULLOUGH, Canon Roy. b 46. Brasted Th Coll 69 Linc Th Coll 70. **d** 73 **p** 74. Chapl Highfield Priory Sch Lancs 73–77; C Ashton-on-Ribble St Andr *Blackb* 73–77; V Rishton 77–86; V Burnley St Matt w H Trin 86–97; RD Burnley 91–97; Chapl Victoria Hosp Burnley 86–91; V Walton-le-Dale St Leon w Samlesbury St Leon *Blackb* 97–11; Hon Can Blackb Cathl 97–11; rtd 11; PtO *Blackb* from 11; *Carl* from 11. *Wescoe, Kirkby Thore, Penrith CA10 1XE* T: (01768) 361656 E: randjmcc@googlemail.com

McCURDY, The Ven Hugh Kyle. b 58. Portsm Poly BA Univ of Wales (Cardiff) PGCE. Trin Coll Bris. **d** 85 **p** 86. C Egham *Guildf* 85–88; C Woking St Jo 88–91; V Histon *Ely* 91–05; P-in-c Impington 98–05; RD N Stowe 94–05; Hon Can Ely Cathl 04–05; Adn Huntingdon and Wisbech from 05. *Whitgift House, The College, Ely CB7 4DL* T: (01353) 658404 *or* 652709 F: 652745 E: archdeacon.handw@elydiocese.org

McDERMOTT, Christopher Francis Patrick. b 54. Southeastern Coll USA BA 84 Wheaton Coll Illinois MA 87. EAMTC. **d** 95 **p** 96. C Gt Ilford St Clem and St Marg *Chelmsf* 95–99; PtO from 06; Chapl Sussex Univ *Chich* from 14. *The Chaplaincy, University of Sussex, Southern Ring Road, Falmer, Brighton BN1 9RH* T: (01273) 877123 M: 07952-700391 E: chrismcd54@aol.com *or* c.mcdermott@sussex.ac.uk

McDERMOTT, John Alexander James. b 52. Lon Univ BSc 74 MSc 77 K Coll Cam BA 80 MA 84 CertEd 75. Westcott Ho Cam 78. **d** 81 **p** 82. C Bethnal Green St Jo w St Bart *Lon* 81–84; P-in-c Walkern *St Alb* 84–86; R Benington w Walkern 86–87; PtO *Newc* 12–17; P-in-c Amble from 17. *The Vicarage, Straffen Court, Amble, Morpeth NE65 0HA* T: (01665) 713327 M: 07804-181543 E: johnmcdermott35@hotmail.co.uk

MacDERMOTT, Linda Karen. b 65. Ox Brookes Univ BA 12. Ripon Coll Cuddesdon 17. **d** 19. C Kington w Huntington, Old Radnor, Kinnerton etc *Heref* from 19. *5 Gravel Hill Drive, Kington HR5 3AE* M: 07546-259039 E: lindamacdermott@icloud.com

McDERMOTT, Mrs Stroma Gillian. b 65. York St Jo Univ BA 13. Yorks Min Course MA 16. **d** 16 **p** 17. C Wetherby *Leeds* 16–19; TV Knaresborough, Goldsborough, Nidd and Brearton from 19. *4 Greengate Drive, Knaresborough HG5 9EN* T: (01423) 860584 M: 07791-499036 E: stroma.mcdermott@ntlworld.com *or* stroma.mcdermott@leeds.anglican.org

MacDONALD, Preb Alan Hendry. b 49. St Steph Ho Ox 86. **d** 88 **p** 89. C Heavitree w Ex St Paul 88–91; C Withycombe Raleigh 91–92; TV 92–95; R Silverton, Butterleigh, Bickleigh and Cadeleigh 95–19; RD Tiverton 00–02 and 08–12; RD Cullompton 08–12; Preb Ex Cathl 10–19; rtd 19. *14 Applemede, Silverton, Exeter EX5 4JX* E: almac1@talktalk.net

MacDONALD, Alastair Robert. b 72. Edin Univ MA 94 MTh 03. TISEC. **d** 02 **p** 03. C Edin St Thos 02–06; Asst Chapl Amsterdam w Den Helder and Heiloo *Eur* 06–13; P-in-c Insch *Ab* from 13; P-in-c Fyvie from 13. *The Rectory, 17 South Road, Insch AB52 6XG* T: (01464) 820477 M: 07513-400081 E: macinsch@gmail.com

McDONALD, Barbara Joy. b 58. **d** 12 **p** 13. OLM Gt Bookham *Guildf* from 12. *3 Fiona Close, Great Bookham KT23 3JU* T: (01372) 454187 E: barbarajoymcdonald@gmail.com

McDONALD, Carollyn Elisabeth. b 54. Edin Univ BSc 76. EMMTC 07. **d** 09 **p** 10. C Sawley *Derby* 09–13; C Ashbourne St Oswald w Mapleton from 13; C Ashbourne St Jo from 13; C Clifton from 13; C Norbury w Snelston from 17; P-in-c Fenny Bentley, Thorpe, Tissington, Parwich etc from 17. *2A Windmill Lane, Ashbourne DE6 1EY* T: (01335) 664132 E: revcarollyn@peakfive.org

MACDONALD, Colin. b 47. St Jo Coll Nottm 87. **d** 89 **p** 90. C Limber Magna w Brocklesby *Linc* 89–92; P-in-c Barrow and Goxhill 92–97; V 97–99; R Hemingby 99–02; V Fulletby 99–02; R Belchford 99–02; TV Wilford Peninsula *St E* 02–09; rtd 09; P-in-c Siddal *Wakef* 09–12; PtO *Leeds* from 17. *2 Southdale Gardens, Ossett WF5 8BB* T: (01924) 276965

MACDONALD, Helen Maria. *See* BARTON, Helen Maria

McDONALD, Ian Henry. b 40. St Aid Birkenhead 65. **d** 68 **p** 69. C Kingston upon Hull H Trin *York* 68–70; C Drumglass *Arm* 70–73; I Eglish w Killylea 73–80; I Maghera w Killelagh *D & R* 80–91; I Killowen 91–98; I Errigal w Garvagh 98–05; Can Derry Cathl 94–00; Preb 00–05; CF (TAVR) 97–05; rtd 05. *7 Saintfield Road, Ballygowan, Newtownards BT23 6HN* T: (028) 9752 8861 M: 07740-708402

McDONALD, James Alexander. b 88. Leeds Univ BSc 10 Ox Brookes Univ MA 16. Ripon Coll Cuddesdon BA 14. **d** 14 **p** 15. C Brackley St Pet w St Jas *Pet* 14–17; C York St Lawr w St Nic 17–19; C York All SS Pavement w St Crux and St Mich 17–19; C York St Denys 17–19; C York St Helen w St Martin 17–19; C York St Olave w St Giles 17–19; C York H Trin Micklegate 17–19; TV Langelei *St Alb* from 19; CF (ACF) from 17. *The Vicarage, 1 The Glebe, Kings Langley WD4 9HY* M: 07981-429338 E: james.a.mcdonald@live.co.uk

McDONALD, Canon James Damian (Jack). b 66. Pemb Coll Cam BA 87 MA 91 K Coll Lon MA 96 SS Hild & Bede Coll Dur PGCE 88 Strasbourg Univ Dr Théol 07. Qu Coll Birm 90. **d** 92 **p** 93. C Camberwell St Geo *S'wark* 92–95; Chapl G&C Coll Cam 95–99; Fell and Dean 99–06; Sen Proctor Cam Univ 02–03; Headmaster Sancton Wood Sch 06–09; PtO *Eur* 09–12; P-in-c Leuven from 12; Can Th Brussels Cathl from 12. *Leeuwerikenstraat 57/0608, 3001 Heverlee, Belgium* T: (0032) (49) 737 9365 E: jackmcdonald@hotmail.be *or* chaplain@anglicanchurchleuven.be

MACDONALD, Mrs Janice Margaret. b 57. SCRTP 13. **d** 15 **p** 16. NSM Aldermaston and Woolhampton *Ox* 15–19; NSM Newbury St Nic and Speen from 19. *3 Heathland, Baughurst, Tadley RG26 5NF* T: 0118-981 3590 M: 07760-481854 E: macdonalds88@hotmail.co.uk *or* jmacdonald.awb@gmail.com

McDONALD, Lawrence Ronald. b 32. St Alb Minl Tr Scheme 84. **d** 87 **p** 88. NSM Sharnbrook and Knotting w Souldrop *St Alb* 87–90; C Bromham w Oakley and Stagsden 90–93; P-in-c Renhold 93–98; rtd 99; P-in-c Stevington *St Alb* 99–02; PtO from 02. *16 Townsend Road, Sharnbrook, Bedford MK44 1HY* T: (01234) 782849

MACDONALD, Malcolm Crawford. b 75. St Andr Univ MA 97 MLitt 98. Wycliffe Hall Ox BTh 05. **d** 05 **p** 06. C Kensington St Barn *Lon* 05–09; V Loughton St Mary *Chelmsf* from 09. *The Vicarage, 4 St Mary's Close, Loughton IG10 1BA* T: (020) 8508 7892 M: 07821-011435 E: malcolm@stmarysloughton.com

MACDONALD, Martin Stanley Harrison. b 51. Dur Univ BSc 72 ACA 75 FCA 82. SAOMC 98. **d** 01 **p** 02. NSM Tring *St Alb* 01–08; PtO *Wakef* 09–10; NSM Luddenden w Luddenden Foot 10–14; *Leeds* from 14; NSM Erringden *Wakef* 10–15; *Leeds* from 14; AD Calder Valley 15–17. *Broad Head End, Cragg Vale, Hebden Bridge HX7 5RT* T: (01422) 881543 M: 07777-691347 E: mshmacdonald@gmail.com

McDONALD, Robert William. b 72. Otago Univ BA 94 MA 96 Fitzw Coll Cam BA 06 MA 10 MPhil 07 PhD 12 LTCL 95. Ridley Hall Cam 04. **d** 10 **p** 11. C Shrewsbury St Geo w Greenfields *Lich* 10–13; Tutor Ridley Hall Cam from 13; Academic Dean from 18. *Ridley Hall, Ridley Hall Road, Cambridge CB3 9HG* T: (01223) 741068 F: 746581 E: rwm40@cam.ac.uk

McDONALD, Sarah Jane Futcher. b 90. Nottm Univ BA 12. St Mellitus Coll MA 16. **d** 16 **p** 17. C Hope Ch Islington *Lon* from 16. *59 Bride Street, London N7 8RN* M: 07957-669157 E: sarah.futchermcdonald@gmail.com

MACDONALD (formerly WIFFIN), Canon Susan Elizabeth. b 51. Edin Th Coll 93. **d** 96 **p** 97. NSM Jedburgh *Edin* 96–98; C Galashiels 98–01; P-in-c Fochabers and Dioc Miss Co-ord *Mor* 01–04; Can St Andr Cathl Inverness 03–04; Miss and Min Officer *Ab* 05–07; R Edin Ch Ch from 07; Dean Edin 12–16; Hon Can St Mary's Cathl from 17. *4 Morningside Road, Edinburgh EH10 4DD* T: 0131-229 6556 *or* 229 0090 E: susan@6a.org.uk

MACDONALD, Warren. b 54. Monash Univ Aus BEng Leeds Univ MPhil Gothenburg Univ PhD 00 CEng CPEng MIEAust. Trin Coll Bris 93. **d** 95 **p** 96. NSM Iford *Win* 95–98; PtO 98–12; *Sarum* from 15. *5 St James's Square, Bournemouth BH5 2BX* T: (01202) 422131 F: 422101 M: 07774-497872 E: warren@warrenmacdonald.com *or* w.macdonald@imperial.ac.uk

MACDONALD-MILNE, Canon Brian James. b 35. CCC Cam BA 58 MA 62 St Pet Coll Ox MA 81. Cuddesdon Coll 58. **d** 60 **p** 61. C Fleetwood St Pet *Blackb* 60–63; Solomon Is 64–78; Vanuatu 78–80; Acting Chapl Trin Coll Ox 81; Acting Chapl St Pet Coll Ox 81–82; Relief Chapl HM Pris Grendon and HM Pris Spring Hill 81–82; Research Fell Qu Coll Birm 82–83; Hon Asst P Bordesley SS Alb and Patr *Birm* 82–83; R Landbeach *Ely* 83–88; V Waterbeach 83–88; OCM 83–88; R Radwinter w Hempstead *Chelmsf* 88–97; RD Saffron Walden 91–97; P-in-c The Sampfords 95–97; rtd 97; PtO *Ely* from 97; *Chelmsf* from 02; Dioc Rep Melanesian Miss and Papua New Guinea Ch Partnership from 99; Chapl Ely Chapter Guild of Servants of the Sanctuary 00–15; Adv Melanesian Brotherhood 05–13; PtO Melanesia from 05; Can Honiara from 07. *39 Way Lane, Waterbeach, Cambridge CB25 9NQ* T: (01223) 861631 E: bj.macdonaldmilne@homecall.co.uk

MACDONNELL, The Very Revd David. b 80. TCD BEd 02 BTh 09 MA 09. CITC. **d** 09 **p** 10. C Dublin Ch Ch Cathl Gp *D & G* 09–14; Treas V St Patr Cathl Dublin 11–14; I Dunfanaghy, Raymunterdoney and Tullaghbegley *D & R* 14–18; Dean Ossory *C & O* from 18; I Kilkenny w Aghour and Kilmanagh from 18. *The Deanery, The Close, Coach Road, Kilkenny, R95 K2XC, Republic of Ireland* T: (00353) (56) 772 1516 E: ossorydean@gmail.com

McDONNELL, Mrs Mavis Marian. b 42. **d** 98 **p** 99. OLM Warrington St Ann *Liv* 98–12; rtd 12. *32 Shaws Avenue, Warrington WA2 8AX* T: (01925) 634408 E: mmavis@aol.com

McDONOUGH, David Sean. b 55. **d** 89 **p** 90. C Moseley St Mary *Birm* 89–92; TV Glascote and Stonydelph *Lich* 92–11; R Anstey and Thurcaston w Cropston *Leic* from 11. *The Rectory, 1 Hurd's Close, Anstey, Leicester LE7 7GH* T: 0116-236 2176 E: davidsmcdonough@outlook.com

McDONOUGH, Terence. b 57. St Jo Coll Nottm LTh 86. **d** 89 **p** 90. C Linthorpe *York* 89–94; TV Heworth H Trin 94–98; V Heworth Ch Ch 98–11; P-in-c York St Thos w St Maurice 06–09; V Fulford from 11; RD City of York from 12. *The Vicarage, 1 Fulford Park, Fulford, York YO10 4QE* T: (01904) 633261 E: vicar@stoswalds.church

McDOUGAL, John Anthony Phelps Standen. *See* STANDEN McDOUGAL, John Anthony Phelps

McDOUGALL, David Robin. b 61. Avery Hill Coll CertEd BEd 84. Ridley Hall Cam 85. **d** 87 **p** 88. C Bletchley *Ox* 87–91; C High Wycombe 91–93; C E Twickenham St Steph *Lon* 93–02; P-in-c Upper Sunbury St Sav 02–14; AD Spelthorne 10–14; R Bletchley *Ox* from 14. *The Rectory, 101 Whalley Drive, Bletchley, Milton Keynes MK3 6HX* T: (01908) 630305 *or* 366531

McDOUGALL, Mrs Denise Alma. b 48. Ban Coll TCert 69. NOC 00. **d** 03 **p** 04. NSM Waterloo Ch Ch and St Jo *Liv* 03–09; Chapl St Fran of Assisi City Academy Liv 05–09; NSM Gt Crosby St Faith and Waterloo Park St Mary *Liv* 09–13; rtd 13; PtO *Liv* from 16. *58 Hartley Crescent, Southport PR8 4SQ* T: (01704) 550590 E: revdenisemcdougall@gmail.com

MacDOUGALL, William Duncan. b 47. Anglia Ruskin Univ MA 04. St Jo Coll Nottm BTh 74 LTh 74. **d** 74 **p** 75. C Highbury New Park St Aug *Lon* 74–77; C Tunbridge Wells St Jo *Roch* 77–78; SAMS Argentina 78–82; V Rashcliffe and Lockwood *Wakef* 83–87; V Tonbridge St Steph *Roch* 87–03; RD Tonbridge 01–03; Dir Past and Evang Studies Trin Coll Bris 03–12; rtd 12; P-in-c Bradley Stoke N CD *Bris* 12–15; PtO *Roch* 16–19; C Chiddingstone w Chiddingstone Causeway from 19; C Penshurst and Fordcombe from 19. *The Rectgory, Chiddingstone, Edenbridge TN8 7AH* T: (01892) 870442 M: 07710-067239 E: williammacdougall0@gmail.com

McDOWALL, Julian Thomas. b 39. CCC Cam BA 62 MA 67 Barrister 61. Linc Th Coll 62. **d** 64 **p** 65. C Rugby St Andr *Cov* 64–70; C-in-c Stoke Hill CD *Guildf* 70–72; V Stoke Hill 72–76; R Elstead 76–91; V Thursley 82–91; TV Wellington and Distr *B & W* 91–93; C Lymington *Win* 93–04; rtd 04; PtO *Win* from 04. *Juniper Cottage, 20 Solent Avenue, Lymington SO41 3SD* T: (01590) 676750

McDOWALL, Robert Angus (Robin). b 39. AKC 66. **d** 67 **p** 68. C Bishopwearmouth St Mich w St Hilda *Dur* 67–69; CF 69–05; Sen CF 80–91; Asst Chapl Gen 91–94; QHC 93–05; rtd 05; PtO *York* from 05. *c/o Crockford, Church House, Great Smith Street, London SW1P 3AZ*

McDOWALL, Roger Ian. b 40. AKC 64. **d** 65 **p** 66. C Peterlee *Dur* 65–68; C Weaste *Man* 68–70; C Tonge Moor 70–73; V Whitworth St Bart 73–80; TV Torre *Ex* 80–88; V Torre All SS 88–00; Chapl S Devon Tech Coll Torbay 80–00; rtd 04. *51 Petitor Road, Torquay TQ1 4QF* T: (01803) 324223 E: roger@sagart.co.uk

⌖McDOWELL, The Rt Revd Francis John. b 56. QUB BA 78. CITC BTh 93. **d** 96 **p** 97 **c** 11. C Antrim *Conn* 96–99; I Ballyrashane w Kildollagh 99–02; I Dundela St Mark *D & D* 02–11; Bp Clogh from 11. *The See House, Ballagh Road, Fivemiletown BT75 0QP* T: (028) 8952 2461 E: bishop@clogher.anglican.org

McDOWELL, Canon Peter Kerr. b 69. QUB BA 91. CITC BTh 94. **d** 94 **p** 95. C Lisburn St Paul *Conn* 94–98; C Arm St Mark 98–99; I Belfast Upper Malone (Epiphany) *Conn* 99–05; I Ballywillan from 05; Can St Patr Cathl Dublin from 11. *The Rectory, 10 Coleraine Road, Portrush BT56 8EA* T: (028) 7082 4298 M: 07724-072944 E: revpetermcdowell@hotmail.co.uk

McDOWELL, Sheilah Rosamond Girgis. b 72. **d** 05. NSM Hammersmith H Innocents and St Jo *Lon* 05–13; PtO from

13. *36 Avenue Gardens, Teddington TW11 0BH* T: (020) 8943 9259 E: rosamond.mcdowell@btinternet.com

McDOWELL, William. b 61. Ox Min Course 12. **d** 15 **p** 16. C E Downland *Ox* from 15. *7 Paddock Road, Newbury RG14 7DL* T: (01635) 40810 M: 07877-358161 E: mcdowell@ntlworld.com

MACE, Alan Herbert. b 28. Lon Univ BA 49 Ex Inst of Educn TCert 50. Wycliffe Hall Ox 59. **d** 60 **p** 61. C Disley *Ches* 60–63; C Folkestone H Trin w Ch Ch *Cant* 63–67; LtO *Win* 67–93; rtd 93; Public Preacher *Win* 93–17. *15 Bassett Heath Avenue, Southampton SO16 7GP* T: (023) 8076 8161 E: alanh1978@hotmail.co.uk

McELHINNEY, Robert Stephen. b 70. Aston Univ BSc 91. CITC BTh 05. **d** 05 **p** 06. C Kill *D & G* 05–08; C Drumglass w Moygashel *Arm* 08–11; P-in-c Derryvolgie *Conn* 11–15; I 15–18; Miss Dir SAMS (Ireland) from 18. *SAMS Ireland, 1 Irwin Crescent, Lurgan, Craigavon BT66 7EZ* T: (028) 3831 0144 E: smcelh@gmail.com *or* stephen@samsireland.com

McENDOO, Canon Neil Gilbert. b 50. TCD BA 72. CITC 75. **d** 75 **p** 76. C Cregagh *D & D* 75–79; C Dublin St Ann *D & G* 79–82; I Dublin Rathmines w Harold's Cross 82–17; Can Ch Ch Cathl Dublin 92–02; Preb 02–05; Chan 05–15; Prec 15–17; rtd 17. *21 Derreen Drive, Harbour View, Wicklow Town, Co Wicklow, A67 NC86, Republic of Ireland* M: (00353) 87-989 3118 E: neil.mcendoo@gmail.com

McEUNE, Patrick John. b 55. Sarum Coll MA 12. **d** 04 **p** 05. NSM White Horse *Sarum* 04–12; TV 07–12; Liturg Chapl Bp Ramsbury 08–12; PtO *Nor* from 08; R Bradwell on Sea and St Lawrence *Chelmsf* 12–14; P-in-c Fingringhoe w E Donyland and Abberton etc 14–18; C W w E Mersea, Peldon, Gt and Lt Wigborough 15–18; R Binbrook Gp *Linc* from 18. *The Rectory, Louth Road, Binbrook, Market Rasen LN8 6BJ* M: 07411-761883 E: mceune@gmail.com

MACEY, Preb Anthony Keith Frank. b 46. St Steph Ho Ox 69. **d** 71 **p** 72. C Ex St Thos 71–76; V Wembury 76–88; RD Ivybridge 83–91; V Cockington 88–12; RD Torbay 98–03; Preb Ex Cathl 05–12; rtd 12; PtO *Ex* from 12. *28 All Saints Road, Torquay TQ1 3RD* T: (01803) 329540

MACEY, Michael David. b 81. Ex Univ BA 03 St Jo Coll Dur MATM 08. Cranmer Hall Dur 03. **d** 05 **p** 06. C Dartmouth and Dittisham *Ex* 05–08; Min Can and Prec Westmr Abbey 08–14; V Boxmoor St Jo *St Alb* from 14; PV Westmr Abbey from 14. *Boxmoor Vicarage, 10 Charles Street, Hemel Hempstead HP1 1JH* T: (01442) 243258 M: 07972-266881 E: vicar@stjohnsboxmoor.org.uk

McFADDEN, Canon Ronald Bayle. b 30. TCD BA 53 MA 55. **d** 54 **p** 55. C Drumglass *Arm* 54–58; S Africa 58–62; Bp's Dom Chapl *D & D* 62–64; C Dundela St Mark 62–64; V Pateley Bridge and Greenhow Hill *Ripon* 64–73; V Knaresborough St Jo 73–79; P-in-c Knaresborough H Trin 78–79; Can Res Ripon Cathl 79–90; rtd 90; Chapl Qu Mary's Sch Baldersby Park 90–00; PtO *Ripon* 90–14; *Leeds* 14–16; *York* 97–13. *12 Ure Bank Terrace, Ripon HG4 1JG* T: (01765) 604043

McFADYEN, Donald Colin Ross. b 63. Wolfs Coll Cam BTh 00 Peterho Cam MPhil 02 SS Coll Cam PhD 06. Ridley Hall Cam 97. **d** 01 **p** 02. NSM Haslingfield w Harlton and Gt and Lt Eversden *Ely* 01–05; P-in-c Bassingbourn 05–12; P-in-c Whaddon 05–12; Course Dir Ridley Hall Cam 05–08; V Orton Longueville w Bottlebridge *Ely* 12–14; P-in-c Orton Waterville 14; V The Ortons 14–16; P-in-c Sawtry and Glatton 16–17; RD Yaxley 14–16. *Thatch End Cottaage, 16 Main Street, Tansor, Peterborough PE8 5HS* M: 07595-539507 E: donald.mcfadyen@me.com

McFADYEN (formerly TALBOT), Canon Mair Josephine. b 59. Univ Coll Lon BA 84. Ridley Hall Cam 85. **d** 88 **p** 94. C Gt Yarmouth *Nor* 88–94; Sen Asst P Raveningham Gp 94–99; Chapl Norfolk Mental Health Care NHS Trust 94–02; Bp's Adv for Women's Min *Nor* 01–04; P-in-c Watton w Carbrooke and Ovington 02–06; Project Manager Magd Gp 06–10; Chapl Norfolk Community Health and Care NHS Trust 10–16; NSM Nor St Geo Colegate 14–17; Hon Can Nor Cathl 02–17; rtd 17; PtO *Nor* from 17. *Crow Hall Barn, Crow Hall Lane, Cawston, Norwich NR10 4TA* T: (01603) 872562 E: mair.mcfadyen@gmail.com

McFADYEN, Canon Phillip. b 44. K Coll Lon BD 69 AKC 69 MTh 70 ATD. St Aug Coll Cant 69. **d** 71 **p** 72. C Sheff St Mark Broomhall 71–74; Chapl Keswick Hall Coll of Educn 74–79; V Swardeston *Nor* 79–81; P-in-c E Carleton 79–81; P-in-c Intwood w Keswick 79–81; R Swardeston w E Carleton, Intwood, Keswick etc 81–90; R Ranworth w Panxworth, Woodbastwick etc 90–05; Dioc Clergy Tr Officer 90–98; P-in-c Nor St Geo Colegate 05–17; Relig Adv Anglia TV 01–17; Hon Can Nor Cathl 97–17; rtd 17; PtO *Nor* from 17; Bp's Officer for Visual Arts from 01. *Crow Hall Barn, Crow Hall Lane, Cawston, Norwich NR10 4TA* T: (01603) 872562 E: phillipmcfadyen@hotmail.com

McFARLAND, Darren William. b 71. QUB BA 93. CITC BTh 96. **d** 96 **p** 97. C Greystones *D & G* 96–98; PV Ch Ch Cathl Dublin 97–99; P-in-c Clydebank *Glas* 99–02; Asst Dioc Miss 21 Co-ord 99–02; R Paisley H Trin and St Barn 02–11; V Headington *Ox* from 11. *The Vicarage, 33 St Andrew's Road, Oxford OX3 9DL* T: (01865) 761094 M: 07773-772610 E: vicar.headington@gmail.com

McFARLAND, Jonathan Hamilton. CITI. **d** 16 **p** 17. Carnalea *D & D* 16–17; C Urney w Sion Mills *D & R* from 17. *112 Melmount Road, Sion Mills, Strabane BT82 9PY* T: (028) 8165 9309 M: 07866-583991 E: jhmcfarland1969@gmail.com

MACFARLANE, Elizabeth Clare. b 71. St Hugh's Coll Ox BA 92 MA 03 St Cross Coll Ox DPhil 12. Ripon Coll Cuddesdon BA 02. **d** 03 **p** 04. C Watford St Mich *St Alb* 03–06; TV Gt Marlow w Marlow Bottom, Lt Marlow and Bisham *Ox* 06–11; Chapl and Fell St Jo Coll Ox from 11. *St John's College, Oxford OX1 3JP* T: (01865) 277660 F: 277435 E: elizabeth.macfarlane@sjc.ox.ac.uk

MACFARLANE, Iain Philip. b 64. Essex Univ BSc 85 W Sussex Inst of HE PGCE 88. Trin Coll Bris BA 99. **d** 99 **p** 00. C Fishponds St Jo *Bris* 99–03; TV Yate from 03. *The Vicarage, 57 Brockworth, Bristol BS37 8SJ* T: (01454) 322921 E: imacfarlane@ukonline.co.uk

MACFARLANE, Iain Scott. b 70. St Jo Coll Nottm 02. **d** 04 **p** 05. C Malvern St Andr and Malvern Wells and Wyche *Worc* 04–07; V Taunton Lyngford *B & W* 07–14; P-in-c Boyatt Wood *Win* 14–19; V from 19. *St Peter's Church House, 53 Sovereign Way, Eastleigh SO50 4SA* T: (023) 8184 5032 M: 07834-191507 E: revmcfarlane@gmail.com

✠**McFARLANE, The Rt Revd Janet Elizabeth.** b 64. Sheff Univ BMedSci 87 St Jo Coll Dur BA 92. Cranmer Hall Dur 93. **d** 93 **p** 94 **c** 16. Par Dn Stafford *Lich* 93–94; C 94–96; Chapl and Min Can Ely Cathl 96–99; Dioc Communications Officer *Nor* 99–16; Hon PV Nor Cathl 00–09; Bp's Chapl 01–09; Adn Nor 09–16; Warden of Readers 15–16; Suff Bp Repton *Derby* from 16. *39 Hickton Road, Swanwick, Alfreton DE55 1AF* T: (01773) 608696 E: bishopofrepton@derby.anglican.org

MacFARLANE, Nigel Ian. b 56. Qu Foundn (Course) 13. **d** 18 **p** 19. NSM Drayton in Hales *Lich* from 18. *19 Pendrel Close, Buntingsdale, Market Drayton TF9 2ET* T: (01630) 638016 E: curateofsmarys@gmail.com

McGARRIGLE, John James Samuel (Don). b 51. QUB BSc 77 CEng 85 MIET 85. ERMC 12. **d** 14 **p** 15. C Ketton, Collyweston, Easton-on-the-Hill and Tinwell *Pet* 14–17; C Ketton and Tinwell 17–18; P-in-c Gt and Lt Casterton w Pickworth and Tickencote from 18. *48 Main Street, Greetham, Oakham LE15 7NL* T: (01572) 811343 M: 07802-401798 E: escapeenergy@btconnect.com

McGARVEY, Mrs Muriel Dorothy. b 51. SEITE 12. **d** 14 **p** 15. NSM Eynsford w Farningham and Lullingstone *Roch* from 14. *17 Tilmans Mead, Farningham, Dartford DA4 0BY* M: 07969-175768 E: eflcurate@gmail.com

McGEARY, Peter. b 59. K Coll Lon BD AKC. Chich Th Coll 84. **d** 86 **p** 87. C Brighton St Pet and St Nic w Chpl Royal *Chich* 86–90; C St Marylebone All SS *Lon* 90–95; P-in-c Hayes St Anselm 95–97; V 97–98; V St Geo-in-the-East St Mary from 98; PV Westmr Abbey from 00. *The Clergy House, All Saints Court, 68 Johnson Street, London E1 0BQ* T/F: (020) 7790 0973 E: mcgeary@pmcg.demon.co.uk

McGEENEY, Noel. b 59. St Patr Coll Maynooth 80. **d** 83 **p** 84. PtO *St Alb* 11–13; TV Ouzel Valley from 13. *The Vicarage, 2 Reach Lane, Heath and Reach, Leighton Buzzard LU7 0AL* T: (01525) 237633 M: 07401-782427 E: saggart@yahoo.com

MacGEOCH, David John Lamont. b 64. Bath Univ BSc 90 CQSW 90. Westcott Ho Cam 97. **d** 99 **p** 00. C Midsomer Norton w Clandown *B & W* 99–03; V Puriton and Pawlett 03–08; P-in-c Glastonbury w Meare 08–11; V from 11; RD Glastonbury from 11. *The Vicarage, 24 Wells Road, Glastonbury BA6 9DJ* T: (01458) 834281 E: vicarabbeyparish@btinternet.com

McGHIE, Clinton Adolphus. b 41. Univ of W Indies. **d** 78 **p** 79. Jamaica 78–96; PtO *Chelmsf* 96–97; P-in-c Highams Park All SS 97–02; V 02–11; rtd 11. *10 Sussex Way, Billericay CM12 0FA* T: (01277) 634389 E: clint1010@sky.com

MacGILLIVRAY, Jonathan Martin. b 53. Aber Univ MA 75. Coll of Resurr Mirfield. **d** 80 **p** 81. C Hulme Ascension *Man* 80–84; P-in-c Birch St Agnes 84–85; R 85–91; V Hurst 91–96; Chapl Tameside Gen Hosp 92–96; Dir of Ords and OLM Officer *Man* 96–02; V Carrington *S'well* 02–13; P-in-c Darton *Leeds* 13–16; P-in-c Cawthorne 13–16; V Darton w Staincross and Mapplewell 16–18; rtd 18. *Rosa Mystica, 31 Barnsley Road, Cawthorne, Barnsley S75 4HW* E: j.macg@virgin.net

McGINLEY, Canon Jack Francis. b 36. ALCD 65. **d** 65 **p** 66. C Erith St Paul *Roch* 65–70; C Morden *S'wark* 70–74; V New Catton Ch Ch *Nor* 74–94; RD Nor N 84–89; Hon Can Nor

Cathl 90–94; R Carlton-in-the-Willows *S'well* 94–02; R Colwick 96–02; rtd 02; PtO *Nor* 03–16; *Bris* 17–19. *82 Railton Jones Close, Stoke Gifford, Bristol BS34 8BF* T: 0117-979 3870 E: jack.mcginley14@btinternet.com

McGINLEY, Canon John Charles. b 69. Birm Univ BSocSc 90. Trin Coll Bris BA 96. **d** 96 **p** 97. C Hounslow H Trin w St Paul *Lon* 96–00; TV Hinckley H Trin *Leic* 00–04; TR 04–09; V Leic H Trin w St Jo from 09; P-in-c Emmaus Par Team 14–16; P-in-c Leic H Apostles from 17; Hon Can Leic Cathl from 18. *5 Ratcliffe Road, Leicester LE2 3JE* T: 0116-254 8981 E: office@holytrinityleicester.org *or* vicar@holytrinityleicester.org

McGINTY, Canon Nicola Jane. b 61. Bath Univ BSc 83 Warwick Univ MBA 06. Qu Coll Birm MA 09. **d** 09 **p** 10. NSM Barrow upon Soar w Walton le Wolds *Leic* 09–12; NSM Wymeswold and Prestwold w Hoton 09–12; PtO from 12; Hon Can Leic Cathl from 18. *5 Station Road, Rearsby, Leicester LE7 4YX* T: (01664) 424869 E: nicky@njmcginty.co.uk

McGIRR, Canon William Eric. b 43. CITC 68. **d** 71 **p** 72. C Carrickfergus *Conn* 71–74; C Mt Merrion *D & D* 74–77; I Donacavey w Barr *Clogh* 77–88; I Ballybeen *D & D* 88–94; I Magheraculmoney *Clogh* 94–10; Can Clogh Cathl 95–10; Chan Clogh Cathl 06–10; rtd 10. *11 Castle Manor, Kesh, Enniskillen BT93 1RT* T: (028) 6863 2221 E: eric@gallagh.com

McGIVERN, Ann Margaret. *See* SIMPSON, Ann Margaret

McGLADDERY, David John. b 62. Homerton Coll Cam BEd 85 Univ of Wales (Cardiff) MA 93 Ox Brookes Univ MA 17. St Mich Coll Llan 02. **d** 05 **p** 06. NSM Monmouth w Overmonnow etc *Mon* 05–09; V 09–18; AD Monmouth 13–18; Asst Chapl Mon Sch 05–18; Can St Woolos Cathl *Mon* 11–18; R Horfield H Trin *Bris* from 18. *The Rectory, 11 Audrey Walk, Bristol BS9 4SJ* T: 0117-401 3042 E: rector.horfield@gmail.com

McGLINCHEY, Patrick Gerard. b 59. NUU BA 82 Nottm Univ BTh 95 MA 06 QUB PhD 13. St Jo Coll Nottm 93. **d** 95 **p** 96. C Kettering Ch the King *Pet* 95–97; C Gorleston St Andr *Nor* 97–02; Assoc Min Cliff Park Community *Nor* 99–02; Chapl and Dean of Res QUB 03–09; TCD from 09; Lect Ch of Ireland Th Inst from 09. *40 Thorncliffe Park, Churchtown, Dublin 14, Republic of Ireland* T: (00353) (1) 405 5202 *or* (1) 499 7279 M: (00353) 89-475 3105 *or* 07500-464542 E: patrickmcglinchey@theologicalinstitute.ie

McGLYNN, Mrs Lesley Anne. b 59. St Mellitus Coll BA 16. **d** 15 **p** 16. OLM Canvey Is *Chelmsf* from 15. *3 Thorney Bay Road, Canvey Island SS8 0HG* T: (01268) 693218 M: 07795-844105 E: lesleymcglynn@hotmail.co.uk

McGOVERN, Leisa Caroline. *See* POTTER, Leisa Caroline

McGOWAN, Anthony Charles. b 57. Jes Coll Cam BA 79 MA 83. Coll of Resurr Mirfield 80. **d** 82 **p** 83. C Mildenhall Haven *St D* 82–85; C Penistone and Thurlstone *Wakef* 85–88; Asst Chapl Radcliffe Infirmary Ox 91–94; Chapl Radcliffe Infirmary NHS Trust 94–99; Chapl Ox Radcliffe Hosps NHS Trust 99–04; V Northampton H Trin and St Paul *Pet* from 05. *The Vicarage, 24 Edinburgh Road, Northampton NN2 6PH* T: (01604) 711468 E: anthony.mcgowan@tiscali.co.uk

McGOWAN, Daniel Richard Hugh. b 71. Oak Hill Th Coll. **d** 03 **p** 04. C Peterlee *Dur* 03–07; TV Morden *S'wark* 07–16; V Banbury St Paul *Ox* from 16. *St Paul's House, Bretch Hill, Banbury OX16 0LR*

McGOWAN, James. b 83. York St Jo Coll BA 04 St Jo Coll Dur BA 11 Ches Univ MA 17 St Hild Coll Dur PGCE 05. Cranmer Hall Dur 08. **d** 11 **p** 12. C St German's Cathl *S & M* 11–14; C W Coast 12–14; V Malew and Santan 14–19; V Fenham St Jas and St Basil *Newc* from 19; Chapl Dame Allan's Schs Newc from 19. *The Vicarage, Wingrove Road North, Newcastle upon Tyne NE4 9EJ* M: 07485-055178 E: revdjamesmcgowan@outlook.com

McGRATH, Gavin John. b 53. Marietta Coll (USA) BA 76 Trin Episc Sch for Min MDiv 81 Dur Univ PhD 90. **d** 81 **p** 82. USA 81–87 and 99–05; C Fulwood *Sheff* 87–95; Assoc Th Prof Trin Episc Sch for Min Ambridge 99–05; PtO *S'wark* 07–12; C Sevenoaks St Nic *Roch* from 12. *4 Braeside Close, Sevenoaks TN13 2JL* E: mcgrath.gavin@gmail.com

McGRATH, Joanna Ruth. *See* COLLICUTT McGRATH, Joanna Ruth

McGRATH, John. b 49. Salford Univ BSc 78 Univ of Wales (Lamp) MA 10 Man Poly CertEd 79. NOC 82. **d** 85 **p** 86. C Horwich *Man* 85–88; P-in-c Hillock 88–89; V 89–94; V York St Luke 94–97; V Hollinwood *Man* 97–02; P-in-c Oldham St Chad Limeside 97–02; V Hollinwood and Limeside 02–03; TV Turton Moorland 03–07; P-in-c Littleborough, Calderbrook and Shore 07–13; V Littleborough 13–14; rtd 14; PtO *Blackb* 15–17; Hon C Burnley St Pet and St Steph 17–19. *15 Hall Park Avenue, Burnley BB10 4JJ* T: (01282) 760256 E: johnbede@live.co.uk

McGREGOR, Alexander Scott. b 72. Ch Ch Ox BA 95 MA 00 Barrister 96. SAOMC 03. **d** 06 **p** 07. NSM Harrow St Mary *Lon* 06–09; NSM Pimlico St Mary Bourne Street 09–14; NSM Pimlico St Barn 09–15; NSM Clerkenwell H Redeemer from 15; Legal Adv Legal Office Nat Ch Inst 06–08; Dep Legal Adv Gen Syn and Abps' Coun 09–19; Chief Legal Adv from 19; Dep Solicitor Ch Commrs 16–19; Official Solicitor from 19; Dep Chan *Ox* 07–13; Chan from 13. *Church House, Great Smith Street, London SW1P 3AZ* T: (020) 7898 1748 E: asmcg@hotmail.com *or* alexander.mcgregor@churchofengland.org

McGREGOR, Donald Alexander Thomson. b 52. Loughb Univ BSc 75 Nottm Univ MA 97 Leic Univ CertEd 78. St Jo Coll Nottm 91. **d** 93 **p** 94. C Walmley *Birm* 93–96; C Braunstone *Leic* 96–97; TV 97–99; Chapl Loughb Univ 99–04; V Fishguard w Llanychar and Pontfaen w Morfil etc *St D* 04–13; P-in-c Llanrhian and Mathry w Grandstone etc 13–17; AD Dewisland and Fishguard 13–14; rtd 17; PtO *St D* from 19. *Amber Cottage, 1 Lower Moor, St Davids, Haverfordwest SA62 6RP* E: donmacg@live.co.uk

McGREGOR, Mrs Eileen. b 50. Ex Univ BA 71. STETS 07. **d** 10 **p** 11. NSM Fulham All SS *Lon* 10–16; NSM Chiswick St Nic w St Mary from 16. *44 Abinger Road, London W4 1EX* T: (020) 8994 2088 M: 07899-928785 E: mcgeileen@aol.com

McGREGOR, Mrs Lorraine Louise. b 59. Sarum Th Coll 02. **d** 05 **p** 06. OLM Colehill *Sarum* from 05. *Tapiola, Marianne Road, Wimborne BH21 2SQ* T: (01202) 886519 E: lorry886519@gmail.com

McGREGOR, Mrs Lynn. b 61. Ches Coll of HE BTh 00. NOC 97. **d** 00 **p** 01. C Colne and Villages *Blackb* 00–03; C Gt Harwood 03–06; P-in-c Wigan St Mich *Liv* 06–07; V 07–10; P-in-c Platt Bridge 10–17; rtd 17. *29 Moor Lane, Darwen BB3 0EJ*

MacGREGOR, Preb Neil. b 35. Keble Coll Ox BA 60 MA 80. Wells Th Coll. **d** 65 **p** 66. C Bath Bathwick St Mary w Woolley *B & W* 65–70; R Oare w Culbone 70–74; C Lynton, Brendon, Countisbury and Lynmouth *Ex* 70–74; P-in-c Kenn w Kingston Seymour *B & W* 74–76; R 76–80; R Wem and V Lee Brockhurst *Lich* 80–01; P-in-c Loppington w Newtown 95–01; RD Wem and Whitchurch 95–01; Preb Lich Cathl 97–01; rtd 01; PtO *Heref* from 01. *19 Castle View Terrace, Ludlow SY8 2NG* T: (01584) 872671 E: hatchment@talktalk.net

McGREGOR, Nigel Selwyn. b 47. FCA 69. Sarum & Wells Th Coll 87. **d** 89 **p** 90. C Charlton Kings St Mary *Glouc* 89–92; P-in-c Seale *Guildf* 92–95; P-in-c Puttenham and Wanborough 92–95; R Seale, Puttenham and Wanborough 95–04; R Barming *Roch* 04–12; rtd 12; PtO *York* from 12. *14 Chestnut Croft, Hemingbrough, Selby YO8 6UD* E: nigelmcgregor@ymail.com

McGREGOR, Stephen Paul. b 55. **d** 03 **p** 04. OLM Tonge Fold *Man* 03–10; OLM Leverhulme from 10. *32 Rawcliffe Avenue, Bolton BL2 6JX* T: (01204) 391205 E: steve.mcgregor@sky.com

McGUINNESS, Canon Gordon Baxter. b 57. St Andr Univ BSc 79 BNC Ox MSc 80. Oak Hill NSM Course 86. **d** 89 **p** 90. NSM Loudwater *Ox* 89–92; C Chilwell *S'well* 92–01; TR Ellesmere Port *Ches* 01–09; R from 09; Hon Can Ches Cathl from 14. *The Rectory, Vale Road, Whitby, Ellesmere Port CH65 9AY* T: 0151-356 8351 *or* 355 2516 E: revgordon@supanet.com *or* revgogs@icloud.com

McGURK, The Ven Michael Joseph Patrick. b 68. St Jo Coll Nottm 05. **d** 07 **p** 08. C Haughton St Mary *Man* 07–09; C Harpurhey 09–10; R 10–17; AD N Man 13–16; Adn Liv from 17. *445 Aigburth Road, Liverpool L19 3PA* M: 07811-360432 E: rev.mikemcgurk@hotmail.co.uk

MACHA, David. b 65. Keele Univ BA 88 CertEd 88 St Jo Coll Dur BA 97 Nottm Univ MA 03. Cranmer Hall Dur 94. **d** 97 **p** 98. C Loughborough Em and St Mary in Charnwood *Leic* 97–01; CMS Tanzania 02–09; R Linton in Craven *Bradf* 09–14; *Leeds* from 14; P-in-c Burnsall w Rylstone *Bradf* 09–14; *Leeds* from 14. *The Rectory, Hebden Road, Grassington, Skipton BD23 5LA* T: (01756) 752575 E: mchdmacha@gmail.com

McHAFFIE, Canon Alistair. b 57. Oak Hill Th Coll 92. **d** 94 **p** 95. C Braintree *Chelmsf* 94–98; R Falkland Is 98–03; V Leyland St Jo *Blackb* 03–18; AD Leyland 11–16; R Preston Risen Lord from 18; Hon Can Blackb Cathl from 17. *St Matthew's Vicarage, 20 Fishwick View, Preston PR1 4YA* E: alistair@mchaffie.com *or* alistairmchaffie@rocketmail.com

McHALE, John Michael. b 61. Ch Ch Coll Cant BA 84 Kingston Univ PGCE 89 Univ of Wales (Cardiff) BTh 08. St Mich Coll Llan 03. **d** 08 **p** 09. NSM Llandingat w Myddfai *St D* 08–10; Chapl Llandovery Coll 08–10; Chapl Lich Cathl Sch and Prec's V Lich Cathl 10–12; Chapl Wycliffe Coll Glos 12–19; V Berkeley w Wick, Breadstone, Newport, Stone etc *Glouc* from 19. *The Vicarage, Church Lane, Berkeley GL13 9BN* M: 07912-043374 E: john.mchale8@btinternet.com

MACHAM, Canon Anna. b 77. Trin Coll Ox BA 98 Cam Univ BA 02 MPhil 04. Ridley Hall Cam 00. **d** 04 **p** 05. C Cheshunt *St Alb* 04–07; Succ S'wark Cathl 07–13; Chapl K Coll Lon 07–13; P-in-c Camberwell St Phil and St Mark *S'wark* 13–19; Can Res Sarum Cathl from 19. *54 The Close, Salisbury SP1 2EL* E: a.macham@btinternet.com

McHARDY, David William. b 61. Edin Univ BD 88 BD 90 PhD 97 Aber Coll of Educn DCE 82. Edin Th Coll 85. **d** 88 **p** 03. C Dumfries *Glas* 88–89; Lect in World Religions Open Univ 97–08; Hon C Oldmeldrum *Ab* 99–08; P-in-c 08; Chapl Blue Coat Sch Reading 08–10; V Meir Heath and Normacot *Lich* from 10. *St Francis's Vicarage, Sandon Road, Stoke-on-Trent ST3 7LH* T: (01782) 398585 M: 07938-956755 E: david.mchardy@hotmail.co.uk

MACHELL, Georgina. b 59. Open Univ MEd 05 Mutare Coll Zimbabwe CertEd 81. Linc Sch of Th and Min 09. **d** 12 **p** 13. OLM Ruskington Gp *Linc* 12–13; OLM N Lafford Gp 13–17; R E Loveden from 17. *The Rectory, 117 Ermine Street, Ancaster, Grantham NG32 3QL* M: 07970-835611 E: rectoreastloveden19@gmail.com

McHENRY, Brian Edward. b 50. New Coll Ox BA 73 MA 77 Cant Ch Ch Univ BA 12 Barrister 76. SEITE 05. **d** 08 **p** 09. NSM Deptford St Paul *S'wark* 08–11; V Orpington All SS *Roch* 11–17; rtd 17; PtO *Cant* from 18. *14 Richmond Gardens, Canterbury CT2 8ES* T: (01227) 781899 M: 07780-308220 E: brian@mchenry.co.uk

MACHIN, Mrs Jacqueline June. b 62. STETS. **d** 10 **p** 11. C Romsey *Win* 10–14; R The Downs from 14. *c/o Crockford, Church House, Great Smith Street, London SW1P 3AZ* E: revdjax@downsbenefice.org.uk

MACHIN, Roy Anthony. b 38. BA 79. Oak Hill Th Coll 76. **d** 79 **p** 80. C Halliwell St Pet *Man* 79–83; V Eccleston St Luke *Liv* 83–91; V Kendal St Thos and Crook *Carl* 91–99; V Wigan St Barn Marsh Green *Liv* 99–03; rtd 03; PtO *Man* from 03. *56 Ferndown Road, Harwood, Bolton BL2 3NN* T/F: (01204) 362220 E: roy.machin@ntlworld.com

MACHIRIDZA, Douglas Tafara. b 71. Univ of Zimbabwe BSW 99 Birm Univ BPhil 07 St Edm Coll Cam BTh 10. Westcott Ho Cam 08. **d** 10 **p** 11. C Perry Barr and Perry Beeches *Birm* 10–14; V Handsworth St Andr from 14; P-in-c Handsworth St Jas from 18. *The Vicarage, 55 Laurel Road, Handsworth, Birmingham B21 9PB* T: 0121-551 2097 M: 07887-741029 E: dtmachiridza@yahoo.co.uk

McHUGH, Brian Robert. b 50. York Univ BA 72 Keele Univ CertEd 73 IEng 92 MIMA 98 CMath 98. S Dios Minl Tr Scheme 79. **d** 82 **p** 83. NSM Sarisbury *Portsm* 82–86; NSM Shedfield 86–06; NSM Shedfield and Wickham from 07; Perm to Offic Cyprus and the Gulf from 10. *28 Siskin Close, Bishops Waltham, Southampton SO32 1RQ* T: (01489) 896658 E: brian.mchugh@bcs.org.uk

McILROY (née NEWBY), Mrs Claire. b 77. UWE BSc 00 Ox Brookes Univ MA 09. Trin Coll Bris 12. **d** 14 **p** 15. C Antony w Sheviock and Torpoint Truro 14–18; Asst Chapl Univ of St Mark and St Jo from 18. *9 West Hill Road, Plymouth PL4 7LF* M: 07766-556321 E: revclairemcilroy@gmail.com

McILROY, Sister Honor Margaret. b 24. LRAM 44 GRSM 45. **d** 98 **p** 99. CSMV from 55; PtO *Ox* from 09. *St Mary's Convent, Denchworth Road, Wantage OX12 9AU* T: (01235) 763141

McINDOE, Darren Lee. b 76. Univ of Wales (Lamp) BA 97. Trin Coll Bris BA 05. **d** 06 **p** 07. C Stratford St Jo w Ch Ch and St Jas *Chelmsf* 06–09; C Forest Gate Em w Upton Cross 09–10; R Burslem *Lich* 10–19; TV Hanley H Ev 16–19; P-in-c Tye Green w Netteswell *Chelmsf* from 19; AD Epping Forest and Roding from 16. *The Rectory, Tawney Road, Harlow CM18 6QR* M: 07886-502307 E: rev.darren.mcindoe@gmail.com

MACINNES, Canon David Rennie. b 32. Jes Coll Cam BA 55 MA 59. Ridley Hall Cam 55. **d** 57 **p** 58. C Gillingham St Mark *Roch* 57–61; C St Helen Bishopsgate w St Martin Outwich *Lon* 61–67; Prec Birm Cathl 67–78; Angl Adv Cen TV 67–82 and 82–93; Dioc Missr *Birm* 79–87; Hon Can Birm Cathl 81–87; R Ox St Aldate w St Matt 87–94; R Ox St Aldate 95–02; Hon Can Ch Ch *Birm* 98–02; rtd 02. *Pear Tree Cottage, Milcombe, Banbury OX15 4RS* T: (01295) 721119 E: david@macinnes.org.uk

MacINNES, Harry Campbell. b 67. Nottm Poly BA 89. Wycliffe Hall Ox BTh 94. **d** 97 **p** 98. C E Twickenham St Steph *Lon* 97–00; P-in-c St Margaret's-on-Thames 00–04; R Shill Valley and Broadshire *Ox* from 04. *The Rectory, Church Lane, Shilton, Burford OX18 4AE* T: (01993) 845954 E: harrymacinnes@yahoo.co.uk

MacINNES (née HITCHEN), Mrs Lisa Jan. b 73. Linc Univ NZ BPR&TM 95 Graduate Sch of Educn Dip Teaching 01. Trin Coll Bris BA 09. **d** 09 **p** 10. C Brinnington w Portwood *Ches* 09–12; V Hallwood Ecum Par from 12. *The Vicarage, 6 Kirkstone Crescent, Beechwood, Runcorn WA7 3JQ* T: (01928) 713101 *or* 716050 M: 07769-800915

MACINTOSH, Andrew Alexander. b 36. St Jo Coll Cam BA 59 MA 63 BD 80 DD 97. Ridley Hall Cam 60. **d** 62 **p** 63. C S Ormsby Gp *Linc* 62–64; Lect St D Coll Lamp 64–67; LtO *Ely* 67–04; Chapl St Jo Coll Cam 67–69; Asst Dean 69–79; Dean 79–02; Lect Th from 70; Pres 95–99; PtO *Ely* from 14. *St John's College, Cambridge CB2 1TУ* T: (01223) 338709 E: aam1003@cus.cam.ac.uk *or* aam1003@cam.ac.uk

McINTOSH, Ian MacDonald. b 64. Jes Coll Cam BA 86. Trin Coll Bris BA 90. **d** 90 **p** 91. C Belmont *Lon* 90–92; C Pinner 92–95; Chapl Leic Univ 96–02; TV Leic H Spirit 96–02; Co-ord Reader Tr 00–02; Dir Cen for Course Studies Westcott Ho Cam 02–04; C Milton Ernest, Pavenham and Thurleigh *St Alb* 02–06; Hon C 06–08; RD Sharnbrook 04–06; Lect and Dir Studies ERMC *Ely* 06–07; Prin 07–15; PtO *St Alb* from 08; Hon Can St E Cathl 12–15; Hd Formation Min Division Abps' Coun from 15. *Church House, Great Smith Street, London SW1P 3AZ* T: (020) 7898 1897 E: ian.mcintosh@churchofengland.org

McINTOSH, Mrs Nicola Ann. b 60. Trin Coll Bris 87. **d** 90 **p** 94. Par Dn Queensbury All SS *Lon* 90–93; Par Dn Ruislip Manor St Paul 93–94; C 94–95; NSM Clarendon Park St Jo w Knighton St Mich *Leic* 96–02; Asst Dioc Dir of Ords 00–02; V Milton Ernest, Pavenham and Thurleigh *St Alb* 02–08; PtO 08–12; Lead Chapl Bedford Hosp NHS Trust from 12; Hon Can St Alb from 18. *22 Devon Road, Bedford MK40 3DJ* T: (01234) 302362 *or* 355122 ext 5901 E: nicola.mcintosh@bedfordhospital.nhs.uk

McINTYRE, Preb Robert Mark. b 69. Nottm Univ BA 91. Coll of Resurr Mirfield 92. **d** 94 **p** 95. C Wednesbury St Jas and St Jo *Lich* 94–97; TV Wolstanton 97–05; P-in-c Rickerscote 05–10; V 10–11; C Stafford 05–11; V Walsall St Gabr Fulbrook from 11; Preb Lich Cathl from 15; CMP from 97. *St Gabriel's Vicarage, Walstead Road, Walsall WS5 4LZ* T: (01922) 622583 E: stgabriels.frmark@gmail.com

MACIVER, Donald. b 46. Heriot-Watt Univ BSc 69 Nazarene Th Coll Man ThB 82 Lon Univ BD 82. **d** 08 **p** 09. OLM Heatons *Man* 08–14; NSM Cloughton and Burniston *York* 14–17; NSM Newby 14–17; NSM Hackness w Harwood Dale 14–17; NSM Ravenscar and Staintondale 14–17; NSM Scarborough St Luke 14–17; NSM Scalby 14–17; rtd 18; PtO *York* from 18. *38 Newlands Avenue, Scarborough YO12 6PS* E: dmaciver19@yahoo.com

McIVER, Lyn Cavell. b 56. SNWTP. **d** 10 **p** 11. C Toxteth Park Ch Ch and St Mich w St Andr *Liv* 10–13; TV E Widnes from 13. *St John's House, 134 Greenway Road, Widnes WA8 6HA* M: 07791-650911

MACK, Mrs Gillian Frances. b 50. SCM 72. Cant Sch of Min 84. **d** 87 **p** 94. NSM Deal St Geo *Cant* 87–88; NSM Deal St Leon and St Rich and Sholden 88–92; Par Dn 93–94; C 94–97; rtd 97; PtO *Cant* 97–06; Hon Chapl Cautley Ho Chr Cen 98–06; Pioneer Min Craven Adnry *Bradf* 08–11; Hon C Hurst Green and Mitton 06–07; P-in-c 07–13; V 13–14; V Hurst Green and Mitton *Blackb* 14–15; Hon C Waddington *Bradf* 06–14; Hon C Waddington *Blackb* 14–15; PtO from 15. *Halfpenny House, 7 Bowland Close, Longridge, Preston PR3 3TU* T: (01772) 783983 E: gfmack@talktalk.net

McKAE, William John. b 42. Liv Univ BSc 63 St Mark & St Jo Coll Lon PGCE 64. Wells Th Coll 68. **d** 71 **p** 72. C Tranmere St Paul w St Luke *Ches* 71–74; C Midsomer Norton *B & W* 74–75; TV Birkenhead Priory *Ches* 75–80; R Oughtrington 80–91; Chapl Asst Hope, Salford R and Ladywell Hosps Man 91–92; Lic Preacher *Man* 91–92; R Heaton Reddish 92–06; rtd 06; PtO *Ches* from 06. *3 Grantham Close, Wirral CH61 8SU* T: 0151-648 0858 E: john.g4ila@tiscali.co.uk

MACKARILL, Ian David. b 54. York St Jo Univ BA 09. NEOC 01. **d** 04 **p** 05. NSM Waggoners *York* 04–12; NSM Woldsburn 11–12; V Lesbury w Alnmouth *Newc* from 12; V Longhoughton w Howick from 12. *The Vicarage, Lesbury, Alnwick NE66 3AU* T: (01665) 830281 M: 07933-161419 E: rev@mackarill.co.uk

McKAY, Alastair James Mark. b 63. York Univ BA 85 Leeds Univ PGCE 87 E Mennonite Univ (USA) MA 99 Univ of Wales (Trin St Dav) DMin 14. St Mellitus Coll 12. **d** 15 **p** 16. C St Martin-in-the-Fields *Lon* 15–18; NSM Highgate All SS from 19. *26 Midhurst Avenue, London N10 3EN* T: (020) 8883 1336 M: 07999-492511 E: ajmmckay@gmail.com *or* alastair.mckay@smitf.org

MACKAY, Alison. See PHILLIPSON, Alison

MACKAY, James Hugh. b 57. Ridley Hall Cam. **d** 09 **p** 10. C Walesby *Linc* 09–13; R Stilton w Denton and Caldecote etc *Ely* 13–15; P-in-c Elton 13–15; PtO *Derby* 16–17; P-in-c Old Dalby, Nether Broughton, Saxelbye etc *Leic* from 17. *The Vicarage, 1 Church Lane, Old Dalby, Melton Mowbray LE14 3LB* T: (01664) 823475 M: 07946-895858 E: revjamiemackay@btinternet.com

McKAY, Jennifer Susan. UCD MVB 91 Cam Univ PhD 98 FRCPath 08 MRCVS 91. All SS Cen for Miss & Min 16. **d** 19. NSM Gt Budworth *Ches* from 19. *Address withheld by request* E: mckayjenny56@gmail.com

MACKAY, Miss Margaret. b 59. St Martin's Coll Lanc BEd 82. Lindisfarne Regional Tr Partnership 12. **d** 14 **p** 15. NSM High Spen and Rowlands Gill *Dur* 14–18; P-in-c Gateshead from 18. *48 Cedarway, Gateshead NE10 8LD* T: 0191-438 3808 M: 07910-697308 E: margaretmackay1@talktalk.net

McKAY, Margaret McLeish. See HALE, Margaret McLeish

MACKAY, Paul Douglas. b 60. Trin Coll Bris. **d** 00 **p** 01. C Becontree St Mary *Chelmsf* 00–03; V Mile Cross *Nor* 03–16; RD Nor N 10–16; P-in-c Prittlewell *Chelmsf* from 16. *Prittlewell Vicarage, 489 Victoria Avenue, Southend-on-Sea SS2 6NL* T: (01702) 343470 M: 07840-841972 E: revpaulstmarys@hotmail.com

MACKAY, Phyllis Marion. See BAINBRIDGE, Phyllis Marion

MACKAY, William James. b 61. QUB BTh 98. **d** 16 **p** 17. C Andreas, Ballaugh, Jurby and Sulby *S & M* from 16. *11 The Meadows, Kirk Michael, Isle of Man IM6 1EU* T: (01624) 815045 E: william.mackay@sodorandman.im

McKEARNEY, Andrew Richard. b 57. Selw Coll Cam MA. Edin Th Coll 81. **d** 82 **p** 83. Prec St Ninian's Cathl Perth *St And* 82–84; Chapl St Mary's Cathl *Edin* 84–88; R Hardwick and Toft w Caldecote and Childerley *Ely* 88–94; RD Bourn 92–94; V Chesterton Gd Shep 94–06; V Iffley *Ox* from 06. *The Rectory, Mill Lane, Iffley, Oxford OX4 4EJ* T: (01865) 773516 E: mckearney@windmillweb.net

McKEE, Nicholas John. b 71. Nottm Univ MEng 94. Ridley Hall Cam 05. **d** 08 **p** 09. C Didsbury St Jas and Em *Man* 08–11; V Astley Bridge 11–18; AD Walmsley 17–18; PtO from 18; Dir of Voc *Blackb* from 18. *Diocesan Offices, Clayton House, Walker Industrial Estate, Walker Road, Guide, Blackburn BB1 2QE* T: (01254) 503082 E: nick.mckee@blackburn.anglican.org

McKEE, Patrick Joseph. b 49. Ripon Coll Cuddesdon 92. **d** 94 **p** 95. C Oakham, Hambleton, Egleton, Braunston and Brooke *Pet* 94–97; V Ryhall w Essendine and Carlby 97–19; rtd 19. *Address temp unknown* E: revpaddymckee@aol.com

McKEE HANNA, Patricia Elizabeth. TCD BA HDipEd PhD 15 QUB BD NUU MA. **d** 99 **p** 00. NSM Nenagh *L & K* from 99; NSM Drumcliffe w Kilnasoolagh from 00; Chapl Limerick Univ 01–04. *Seafield Cottage, Baile an tSagart, Tromara West, Quilty, Co Clare, V95 Y0P4, Republic of Ireland* T: (00353) (65) 708 7965 M: (00353) 87-660 6003 E: hannape@tcd.ie

McKEGNEY, Canon John Wade. b 47. TCD BA 70 MA 81. CITC 70. **d** 72 **p** 73. C Ballynafeigh St Jude *D & D* 72–75; C Bangor St Comgall 75–80; I Drumgath w Drumgooland and Clonduff 80–83; I Gilnahirk 83–90; I Arm St Mark 90–13; Can Arm Cathl 01–13; rtd 13. *Tan y Bwlch, 2 Magheramenagh Gardens, Portrush BT56 8SU* T: (028) 7082 5019 M: 07801-866555 E: johnwmckegney@gmail.com

MacKEITH (*née* GODFREY), Mrs Ann Veronica. b 35. Bris Univ BSc 57 CertEd. Gilmore Course 78. **dss** 79 **d** 87 **p** 94. Bishopwearmouth Ch Ch *Dur* 79–83; Bishopwearmouth St Gabr 83–86; Ryhope 86–88; Par Dn 87–88; Par Dn Darlington H Trin 88–94; C 94–95; Family Life Officer 95–97; rtd 98; PtO *Chich* from 15. *26 Withdean Court, London Road, Brighton BN1 6RN* T: (01273) 552376 E: annmackeith@talktalk.net

McKELLEN, Pamela Joyce. b 47. Homerton Coll Cam TCert 69 BEd 70. Cranmer Hall Dur 01. **d** 02 **p** 03. C Ox St Matt 02–04; P-in-c Radley and Sunningwell 04–15; P-in-c Kennington 09–15; R Radley, Sunningwell and Kennington 15–16; AD Abingdon 07–12; rtd 16; PtO *Ox* from 16. *9 Hazels Paddock, Cold Ash, Thatcham RG18 9LD* T: (01635) 864274 E: pammckellen13@gmail.com

McKELVEY, Mrs Jane Lilian. b 48. Liv Inst of Educn BA 94. N Bapt Coll 94. **d** 97 **p** 98. C Aughton St Mich *Liv* 97–01; TV Gateacre 01–17; rtd 17. *Beth Abba, Wheathill Road, Liverpool L36 5US* E: revjanemc1@yahoo.co.uk

McKELVEY, The Very Revd Robert Samuel James Houston. b 42. QUB BA 65 MA(Ed) 88 Garrett-Evang Th Sem DMin 93. CITC 67. **d** 67 **p** 68. C Dunmurry *Conn* 67–70; CF (TAVR) 70–99; P-in-c Kilmakee *Conn* 70–77; I 77–81; Sec Gen Syn Bd of Educn (N Ireland) 81–01; Preb Newcastle St Patr Cathl Dublin 89–01; Dean Belf 01–11; rtd 11. *9 College Park, Coleraine BT51 3HE* T: (028) 7035 1621 M: 07802-207825 E: houston.mckelvey@btinternet.com

McKEMEY, Mrs Norma Edith. b 47. St Mary's Coll Chelt CertEd 71. STETS 04. **d** 10 **p** 11. NSM Swindon Ch Ch *Bris* 10–17; PtO from 17. *Bethany, Greens Lane, Wroughton, Swindon SN4 0RJ* T: (01793) 845917 M: 07760-457739 E: mckemeyn@talktalk.net

McKENDREY, Susan Margaret. b 55. **d** 02 **p** 03. NSM Allonby, Cross Canonby and Dearham *Carl* 02–08; TV Maryport,

Netherton, Flimby and Broughton Moor from 08. *The Vicarage, Church Street, Maryport CA15 6HE* T: (01900) 813077 E: s.mckendrey@btinternet.com

MACKENNA, Christopher. *See* MACKENNA, Robert Christopher Douglass

McKENNA, Edward Patrick. b 48. Liv Univ BTh 02. NOC 05. **d** 06 **p** 07. NSM Stretton and Appleton Thorn *Ches* 06–09; Asst Chapl HM Pris Risley 08–09; P-in-c Low Marple *Ches* 09–14; V from 14. *15 Brabyns Brow, Marple Bridge, Stockport SK6 5DT* T: 0161-427 2736 M: 07979-624271 E: ed1mckenna@aol.com

McKENNA, Lindsay Taylor Francis. b 62. Glas Univ MA 83 Aber Univ BD 86. Edin Th Coll 87. **d** 87 **p** 88. C Broughty Ferry *Bre* 87–90; C Wantage *Ox* 90–93; V Illingworth *Wakef* 93–99; Dir CARA 99–02; V Hanworth All SS *Lon* 02–08; Provost St Paul's Cathl Dundee *Bre* 08–09; R Dundee St Paul 08–09; PtO *Win* 09–10; P-in-c Catford St Andr *S'wark* 10–11; V from 11; Dir Ords Woolwich Area from 13. *St Andrew's Parsonage, 119 Torridon Road, London SE6 1RG* T: (020) 8697 2600 E: fatherlindsay@gmail.com

MACKENNA, Richard William. b 49. Pemb Coll Cam BA 71 MA 75. Ripon Coll Cuddesdon BA 77 MA 81. **d** 78 **p** 79. C Fulham St Dionis *Lon* 78–81; C Paddington St Jas 81–85; Tutor Westcott Ho Cam 85–89; V Kingston All SS w St Jo *S'wark* 90–91; PtO 94–01; *Nor* 99–04. *Flat 5, 11 Grassington Road, Eastbourne BN20 7BJ* T: (01323) 730477

MACKENNA, Robert Christopher Douglass. b 44. Oriel Coll Ox BA 72 MA 75 MBAP 85. Cuddesdon Coll 71. **d** 73 **p** 74. C Farncombe *Guildf* 73–77; C Tattenham Corner and Burgh Heath 77–80; P-in-c Hascombe 80–90; R 90–00; RD Godalming 91–96; Hon Can Guildf Cathl 99–00; Dir St Marylebone Healing and Counselling Cen from 00; NSM St Marylebone w H Trin *Lon* 00–14; PtO *Chelmsf* from 16. *17 Victory Road, London E11 1UL* T: (020) 8989 8551 E: chris_anne@aol.co.uk

MACKENZIE, Andrew John Kett. b 46. Southn Univ BA 68. Guildf Dioc Min Course 98. **d** 91 **p** 92. Fullbrook Sch New Haw 76–99; OLM Woodham *Guildf* 91–99; C Aldershot St Mich 99–05; V Effingham w Lt Bookham 05–15; rtd 15; Hon C Charminster and Stinsford *Sarum* 15–17; Hon C Bradford Peverell, Stratton, Frampton etc 15–17; PtO from 18. *8 Charlotte Close, Charminster, Dorchester DT2 9PY* T: (01305) 251532 M: 07511-756407 E: revandymac1@btinternet.com

MACKENZIE, Miss Ann. b 54. CertEd 76. Trin Coll Bris 82. **dss** 83 **d** 87 **p** 94. Normanton *Wakef* 86–90; Par Dn 87–90; Par Dn Bletchley *Ox* 90–94; C 94–98; TV W Swindon and the Lydiards *Bris* 98–04; P-in-c E Springfield *Chelmsf* 04–18; rtd 18; PtO *Cant* from 18. *3 Jacinth Drive, Sittingbourne ME10 5AP* E: ann.mackenzie@btinternet.com

McKENZIE, Mrs Ann Elizabeth. b 45. Leic Univ BA 67 PGCE 68. STETS 95. **d** 98 **p** 99. NSM Appleshaw, Kimpton, Thruxton, Fyfield etc *Win* 98–15; rtd 15; PtO *Win* from 15. *The Post House, Thruxton, Andover SP11 8LZ* T: (01264) 772788 M: 07733-112975 E: ann.mckenzie@waitrose.com

MACKENZIE, David Stuart. b 45. Open Univ BA 95 FRSA 00. Linc Th Coll 66. **d** 69 **p** 70. C Bishopwearmouth St Mary V w St Pet CD *Dur* 69–72; C Pontefract St Giles *Wakef* 72–74; Chapl RAF 74–02; Chapl OHP 02–08; RD Whitby *York* 04–08; QHC from 00; PtO *Ely* from 09. *57 London Road, Godmanchester, Huntingdon PE29 2HZ* T: (01480) 413120 E: dsm3557@gmail.com

McKENZIE, Ian Colin. b 31. CA 56. EMMTC 89. **d** 93. NSM Edin St Mark and Edin St Andr and St Aid 93–94; PtO *S'well* 01–06. *21 Crafts Way, Southwell NG25 0BL* T: (01636) 815755

MACKENZIE, Ian William. b 46. Trin Coll Bris 93. **d** 95 **p** 96. C Bideford *Ex* 95–96; C Bideford, Northam, Westward Ho!, Appledore etc 96–99; TV Littleham w Exmouth 99–11; rtd 11; PtO *Heref* from 13. *Ballavayre, New Street, Ledbury HR8 2EL* T: (01531) 579009 E: billandmaggiemackenzie@gmail.com

MACKENZIE, The Ven Janet. b 62. Westmr Coll Ox BEd 86 Anglia Ruskin Univ HA 08. Westcott Ho Cam 04. **d** 06 **p** 07. C Sandy *St Alb* 06–10; P-in-c Luton St Aug Limbury 10–14; V 14–16; AD Luton 12–16; Adn Hertford and Hon Can St Alb from 16. *Glebe House, St Mary's Lane, Hertingfordbury, Hertford SG14 2LE* T: (01727) 818159 E: archdherts@stalbans.anglican.org

McKENZIE, The Ven Jennifer Gaines. b 63. Auburn Univ Alabama BA 88. Virginia Th Sem MDiv 04. **d** 04 **p** 05. C Washington St Dav USA 04–07; C Alexandria Ch Ch 07–09; C Burke Gd Shep 11–12; P-in-c Oak Hill Episcopy 13; Adn Wigan and W Lancashire *Liv* from 15. *33 Elmers Green, Skelmersdale WN8 6RZ* T: (01695) 726472 *or* 0151-705 2154 M: 07464-548015 E: jennifer.mckenzie@liverpool.anglican.org

McKENZIE (née DOORES), Mrs Jennifer Mary. b 78. Hull Univ BA 99 St Jo Coll Dur BA 03. Cranmer Hall Dur 01.

d 04 **p** 05. C Old Swinford Stourbridge *Worc* 04–08; V Cam w Stinchcombe *Glouc* 08–17; V S Cerney w Cerney Wick, Siddington and Preston from 17. *The Vicarage, Silver Street, South Cerney, Cirencester GL7 5TP* T: (01285) 860221 E: mckenzie.jennifer@btinternet.com

MacKENZIE, John Christopher Newman. b 67. Trin Coll Bris 02. **d** 04 **p** 05. C Staplehurst *Cant* 04–07; P-in-c Willesborough 07–13; P-in-c Sevington 07–13; R Willesborough w Sevington 13–16; TR Ashford Town from 16; Jt AD Ashford from 18. *7 Augustine Drive, Finberry, Ashford TN25 7GH* E: mackthevicar@hotmail.com

MACKENZIE, Peter Sterling. b 65. Univ Coll Lon BSc 88. Oak Hill Th Coll BA 95. **d** 95 **p** 96. C Roxeth *Lon* 95–00; TV 00–08; V W Ealing St Jo w St Jas 08–18; V Hayes St Edm from 18. *The Vicarage, 1 Edmund's Close, Hayes UB4 0HA* M: 07780-562605

MACKENZIE, Canon Peter Thomas. b 44. Lon Univ LLB 67 Westmr Coll Ox MTh 97 Univ of E Lon MA 01. Cuddesdon Coll 68. **d** 70 **p** 71. C Leigh Park *Portsm* 70–75; P-in-c Sittingbourne St Mary *Cant* 75–82; V Folkestone St Sav 82–90; RD Elham 89–90; R Cant St Martin and St Paul 90–99; RD Cant 95–99; V Goudhurst w Kilndown 99–07; Hon Can Cant Cathl 97–07; AD Cranbrook 01–06; rtd 07; PtO *Cant* 09–11; P-in-c Turvey *St Alb* 11–14; P-in-c Stevington 11–14; PtO *Leic* from 15; *Pet* from 17; *Eur* from 16. *5 Madeline Close, Great Bowden, Market Harborough LE16 7HX* T: (01858) 440049 E: canonmack@talk21.com

McKENZIE, Robin Peter. b 61. Sheff Univ BEng 82 Birm Univ MSc(Eng) 87 Dur Univ BA 02 Warwick Univ EngD 02 CEng MIET. Cranmer Hall Dur 00. **d** 03 **p** 04. C Shrewsbury St Chad w St Mary *Lich* 03–07; P-in-c Hilton *Ely* 07–11; P-in-c Fenstanton 07–17; PtO from 18. *324 Trowell Road, Nottingham NG8 2DT* E: mckenzie_robin@hotmail.com

MACKENZIE, Simon Peter Munro. b 52. Univ Coll Ox BA 74. Coll of Resurr Mirfield 82. **d** 85 **p** 86. C Tipton St Jo *Lich* 85–91; V Perry Beeches *Birm* 91–13; P-in-c Lochgilphead *Arg* from 13; P-in-c Inveraray from 13; P-in-c Kilmartin from 13; P-in-c Is of Arran from 13. *Bishopton House, Bishopton Road, Lochgilphead PA31 8PY* E: dr.lachlan@zen.co.uk

McKENZIE, Stephen George. b 58. Leeds Univ BSc 80 Imp Coll Lon PhD 85. Oak Hill Th Coll 03. **d** 05 **p** 06. C Barton Seagrave w Warkton *Pet* 05–08; P-in-c Swynnerton and Tittensor *Lich* 08–09; C Broughton w Croxton and Cotes Heath w Standon 08–09; R Cotes Heath and Standon and Swynnerton etc from 09. *3 Rectory Gardens, Swynnerton, Stone ST15 0RT* T: (01782) 796564 M: 07986-558861 E: stephen_gill.swyn@btinternet.com

MACKENZIE, William. *See* MACKENZIE, Ian William

MACKENZIE MILLS, David Graham. b 75. Bris Univ BA 96 St Jo Coll Dur BA 01. Cranmer Hall Dur. **d** 01 **p** 02. C Glas St Marg 01–04; Chapl Trin Coll Cam 04–09; Min Can and Prec Cant Cathl 09–12; R Kinross *St And* from 13. *36 Manse Road, Milnathort, Kinross KY13 9YQ* T: (01577) 863795 E: frdavidkinross@gmail.com

McKEON, Linda Mary. b 64. **d** 09 **p** 10. OLM Gentleshaw *Lich* 09–16; P-in-c from 16; P-in-c Farewell from 16. *The Vicarage, Buds Road, Rugeley WS15 4NB* T: (01543) 670739 E: lynn.mckeon@btinternet.com

McKEOWN, Trevor James. b 53. Glos Univ BA 12. CITC 01. **d** 04 **p** 05. Aux Min Dromore Cathl *D & D* from 04. *39 Cedar Park, Portadown, Craigavon BT63 5LL* T: (028) 3832 1217 *or* 9269 3968 E: trevor.mckeown3@hotmail.com

McKERAN, James Orville. b 71. Kent Univ BA 94 K Coll Lon MA 06 Leeds Univ MA 08 Solicitor 98 ACIArb 08 FRGS 11 MCMI 13 FCMI 16 FZS 18. Coll of Resurr Mirfield 06. **d** 08 **p** 09. C Altrincham St Geo and Altrincham St Jo *Ches* 08–11; Chapl Trafford Coll 08–11; Tutor SSM Lesotho 11–12; Asst P Maseru St Jo and Maseru E 11–12; V Gen Botswana 12–15; Dean Gaborone 12–15; R Lobatse St Mark and Chapl Athlone Hosp 15–17; V Witley *Guildf* from 18. *Witley Vicarage, Petworth Road, Witley, Godalming GU8 5LT* T: (01428) 681867 M: 07493-695875 E: vicar@witleyallsaints.org.uk

MacKICHAN, Gillian Margaret. b 34. Cam Univ CertEd 56 CQSW 80. S Dios Minl Tr Scheme 90. **d** 93 **p** 94. NSM Upper Kennet *Sarum* 93–04; TV 95–04; RD Marlborough *Sarum* 02–04; rtd 04; PtO *Sarum* 04–08 and from 14. *West Bailey, Lockeridge, Marlborough SN8 4ED* T: (01672) 861629 E: g.mackichan@btinternet.com

MACKIE, Andrew. b 53. Glas Univ BSc 74 CEng MIET. SAOMC 03. **d** 00 **p** 01. OLM Purley *Ox* 00–18. *The Brambles, Stevenson Approach, Great Cornard, Sudbury CO10 0WD* M: 07900-213350 E: mackie.family@btinternet.com

MACKIE, Fiona Mary. *See* KOUBLE, Fiona Mary

McKILLOP, Mrs Caroline Annis. b 47. Glas Univ MB, ChB 72 PhD 77. TISEC 95. **d** 98 **p** 99. NSM Glas St Matt 98–01; Chapl Stobhill NHS Trust 99–00; NSM Glas St Mary 02–12; LtO from 12. *Flat 1, 6 Kirklee Gate, Glasgow G12 0SZ* T: 0141-339 7000 E: carolinemckillop@yahoo.co.uk

McKILLOP, Iain Malcolm. b 54. Man Univ BA 75 Man Poly PGCE 76 Kingston Univ MA 95. Guildf Dioc Min Course 07. **d** 10 **p** 11. NSM Effingham w Lt Bookham *Guildf* 10–15; NSM W Byfleet 15–18; PtO S'*wark* from 18. *10 Hopfield Avenue, Byfleet, West Byfleet KT14 7PE* T: (01932) 341687 E: imckillopi@aol.com

McKINLEY, Canon Arthur Horace Nelson. b 46. TCD BA 69 MA 79. CITC 70. **d** 70 **p** 71. C Taney Ch Ch *D & G* 71–76; I Dublin Whitechurch from 76; Preb Dunlavin St Patr Cathl Dublin from 91. *The Vicarage, Whitechurch Road, Rathfarnham, Dublin 16, Republic of Ireland* T: (00353) (1) 493 3953 *or* (1) 493 4972 E: whitechurchparish@eircom.net

✠**McKINNEL, The Rt Revd Nicholas Howard Paul.** b 54. Qu Coll Cam BA 75 MA 79. Wycliffe Hall Ox BA 79 MA 86. **d** 80 **p** 81 **c** 12. C Fulham St Mary N End *Lon* 80–83; Chapl Liv Univ 83–87; P-in-c Hatherleigh *Ex* 87–88; R Hatherleigh, Meeth, Exbourne and Jacobstowe 88–94; P-in-c Plymouth St Andr w St Paul and St Geo 94–95; TR Plymouth St Andr and Stonehouse 95–12; RD Plymouth Sutton 01–06; Preb Ex Cathl 02–12; Suff Bp Crediton 12–15; Suff Bp Plymouth from 15. *108 Molesworth Road, Stoke, Plymouth PL3 4AQ* T: (01752) 500059 E: bishop.of.plymouth@exeter.anglican.org

McKINNEY, Canon Mervyn Roy. b 48. St Jo Coll Nottm. **d** 81 **p** 82. C Tile Cross *Birm* 81–84; C Bickenhill w Elmdon 84–89; V Addiscombe St Mary S'*wark* 89–93; V Addiscombe St Mary Magd w St Martin 93–99; P-in-c W Wickham St Fran 99–02; V W Wickham St Fran and St Mary 02–14; AD Croydon Addington 04–11; Hon Can S'wark Cathl 05–14; rtd 14; PtO *Chelmsf* from 15. *12 Dedham Mill, Mill Lane, Dedham, Colchester CO7 6DJ* T: (01206) 323565 E: mervmckinney@btinternet.com

MacKINNON, Canon Karen Audrey. b 64. Ex Univ BA 85. Linc Th Coll 92. **d** 92 **p** 94. Par Dn Filton *Bris* 92–93; Par Dn Bris Lockleaze St Mary Magd w St Fran 93–94; C 94–96; P-in-c 96–98; V 98–00; Asst Chapl Southn Univ Hosps NHS Trust 00–02; Chapl 02–04; Dep Manager 04–11; Spiritual Care Manager Univ Hosp Southn NHS Foundn Trust from 11; Hon Can Win Cathl from 14. *Chaplaincy Department, MP 201, Univ Hospital Southampton NHS Trust, Tremona Road, Southampton SO16 6YD* T: (023) 8120 8517 E: karen.mackinnon@uhs.nhs.uk

McKINNON, Neil Alexander. b 46. Wycliffe Hall Ox 71. **d** 74 **p** 75. C Deptford St Nic w Ch Ch S'*wark* 74–76; C St Helier 76–79; Min W Dulwich All SS and Em 79–81; TV Thamesmead 87–95; R S'wark H Trin w St Matt 95–16; rtd 16. *7 The Quadrangle, Morden College, 19 St Germans Place, London SE3 0PW* T: 07745-287103 E: neilatelephant@yahoo.com

MACKINTOSH, Canon Robin Geoffrey James. b 46. Rhodes Univ BCom 71 Cranfield Inst of Tech MBA 78. Ripon Coll Cuddesdon BA 85 MA 91. **d** 86 **p** 87. C Cuddesdon *Ox* 86; C Cannock *Lich* 86–89; R Girton *Ely* 89–01; Exec Dir The Leadership Inst 01–06; PtO *Cant* from 03; Dir Min and Tr 06–14; rtd 14; Hon Can Cant Cathl 09–14. *4 Loop Court Mews, Sandwich CT13 9HF* E: robmackintosh@btinternet.com

McKITTRICK, The Ven Douglas Henry. b 53. St Steph Ho Ox 74. **d** 77 **p** 78. C Deptford St Paul S'*wark* 77–80; C W Derby St Jo *Liv* 80–81; TV St Luke in the City 81–89; V Toxteth Park St Agnes and St Pancras 89–97; V Brighton St Pet w Chpl Royal *Chich* 97–02; RD Brighton 98–02; Can and Preb Chich Cathl 98–02; Adn Chich 02–18; rtd 18. *3 Poplar Avenue, Kirkbymoorside, York YO62 6ES*

MACKLEY, Robert Michael. b 78. Ch Coll Cam BA 99 MA 03 Em Coll Cam PhD 16. Westcott Ho Cam 00. **d** 03 **p** 04. C Clerkenwell H Redeemer *Lon* 03–06; C Clerkenwell St Mark 03–06; C Liv Our Lady and St Nic 06–09; Asst Chapl Em Coll Cam 09–12; V Cambridge St Mary Less *Ely* from 12; RD Cambridge S from 16. *The Vicarage, 1B Summerfield, Cambridge CB3 9HE* T: (01223) 356641 *or* 366202 M: 07866-445877 E: vicar@lsm.org.uk

MACKNESS, The Ven Paul Robert. b 73. Univ of Wales (Lamp) BA 96 Univ of Wales (Cardiff) BA 01. St Mich Coll Llan 98. **d** 01 **p** 02. C Llanelli *St D* 01–04; P-in-c Maenordeifi and Capel Colman w Llanfihangel etc 04–05; R 05–07; R Maenordeifi Gp 07–10; AD Cemais and Sub-Aeron 08–10; V Haverfordwest 10–14; Bp's Chapl 14–18; Can St D Cathl from 14; Asst Dioc Warden Ords from 15; Adn St D from 18; P-in-c Jeffreyston w Reynoldston and Loveston etc from 18. *The Vicarage, 7 Churchill Park, Jeffreyston, Kilgetty SA68 0SD* T: (01267) 236597 E: archdeacon.stdavids@churchinwales.org.uk

MACKNIGHT, Glen. b 62. Lindisfarne Regional Tr Partnership 10. **d** 13 **p** 14. C Herrington, Penshaw and Shiney Row *Dur* 13–16; V Hillside from 16. *All Saints' Vicarage, Rowanwood Gardens, Gateshead NE11 0DP* M: 07983-572472 E: glenmacknight@mac.com *or* admin@hillsidechurch.co.uk

McKNIGHT, Thomas Raymond. b 48. QUB BEd 71. CITC 74. **d** 77 **p** 78. C Lisburn Ch Ch Cathl *Conn* 77–80; C Carrickfergus 80–82; I Kilcronaghan w Draperstown and Sixtowns *D & R* 82–86; I Magheragall *Conn* 86–91; CF 91–07; I Urney w Sion Mills *D & R* 07–11; rtd 11. *5 Pembury Mews, Brompton on Swale, Richmond DL10 7SG* T: (01748) 810348 E: raymcknight2003@hotmail.com

MACKRIELL, Peter John. b 64. Mansf Coll Ox BA 85 MA 93 Man Univ PGCE 87. St Jo Coll Nottm BTh 93 MA 94. **d** 94 **p** 95. C Hale and Ashley *Ches* 94–96; C Marple All SS 96–98; V Brandwood *Birm* 98–01; V Pontblyddyn *St As* 01–05; Chapl to Deaf People 01–11; Dioc Communications Officer 06–11; V Kelsall *Ches* 11–18; P-in-c Maelor Miss Area *St As* from 18; Dir Studies for Past Workers *Ches* from 15. *The Rectory, 4 Sundorne, Overton, Wrexham LL13 0EB* T: (01978) 710294 M: 07795-972325 E: revpeter@maelormissionarea.uk

MACKRILL, Mrs Deirdre Anne. b 49. ACIS 95. SAOMC 01. **d** 05 **p** 06. NSM Hemel Hempstead *St Alb* 05–09; NSM St Keverne *Truro* 11–16; NSM St Ruan w St Grade and Landewednack 11–16; NSM St Keverne, St Ruan w St Grade and Landewednack 17–19; rtd 19; PtO *Truro* from 19. *Rosenithon House, Rosenithon, St Keverne, Helston TR12 6QR* T: (01326) 281178 E: deirdre.mackrill@btinternet.com

MACKRILL, Robert John. b 51. Univ Coll Lon BSc 73 RIBA 79. EMMTC 92. **d** 93 **p** 94. NSM Stamford All SS w St Jo *Linc* 93–97; P-in-c Stamford Ch Ch 97–10; RD Aveland and Ness w Stamford 09–10; C Oakham, Hambleton, Egleton, Braunston and Brooke *Pet* 10; TV Oakham, Ashwell, Braunston, Brooke, Egleton etc 11; rtd 11; PtO *Pet* from 12; *Linc* 15–18. *8 St Lawrence Way, Tallington, Stamford PE9 4RH* T: (01780) 749283

McLACHLAN, Devin Shepard. b 73. Harvard Univ AB 96. Episc Div Sch (USA) MDiv 02. **d** 04 **p** 05. C St Mark's Cathl Seattle USA 04–07; R Newton Messiah 07–11; Asst Chapl Brent Ho Chicago Univ 11–14; Asst Chapl Jes Coll Cam 15–18; PtO *Ely* 14–16; C Cambridge Gt St Mary w St Mich from 16; Bp's Interfaith Adv from 18. *Great St Mary's Church, St Mary's Passage, Cambridge CB2 3PQ* T: (01223) 747277 M: 07478-646463 E: revmcdev@gmail.com *or* dm695@cam.ac.uk

MacLACHLAN (née GRIFFITHS), Mrs Margaret. b 44. Birm Poly CertEd 81 Open Univ BA 82 SRN 67. WMMTC 92. **d** 95 **p** 96. NSM Tile Cross *Birm* 95–08; NSM Garretts Green 07–08; NSM Garretts Green and Tile Cross 08–13; PtO from 13; Chapl Heart of England NHS Foundn Trust from 08. *Wayside, 17 Chester Road, Birmingham B36 9DA* T: 0121-747 2340 E: revmac@talktalk.net

MacLACHLAN, Michael Ronald Frederic. b 39. Wycliffe Hall Ox 75. **d** 75 **p** 76. C Mansfield SS Pet and Paul S'*well* 75–78; P-in-c Newark Ch Ch 78–80; TV Newark w Hawton, Cotham and Shelton 80–86; P-in-c Sparkhill St Jo *Birm* 86–90; P-in-c Sparkbrook Em 86–90; V Sparkhill w Greet and Sparkbrook 90–92; RD Bordesley 90–92; P-in-c Kugluktuk Canada 92–97; R Stoke-next-Guildf *Guildf* 97–05; rtd 05; Hon C Drayton Bassett *Lich* 05–12; Hon C Canwell 09–12; PtO *Birm* from 13; *Cov* from 13. *36A Grendon Road, Polesworth, Tamworth B78 1NU* T: (01827) 893109 E: michaelmcalachan@gmail.com

McLACHLAN, Canon Sheila Elizabeth. b 52. SRN 73 Kent Univ MA 89. Wycliffe Hall Ox 80. dss 83 **d** 87 **p** 94. Chapl Kent Univ *Cant* 83–94; Dep Master Rutherford Coll 87–94; Dn-in-c Kingsnorth w Shadoxhurst *Cant* 94; P-in-c Kingsnorth and Shadoxhurst 94–11; AD Ashford 03–09; Hon Can Cant Cathl 08–15; rtd 15 and 15; PtO *Cant* from 15. *33 Josephs Way, New Romney TN28 8AQ* T: (01797) 690461 M: 07751-691164 E: revsheila25@sky.com

MacLAREN, Canon Clare. b 67. Edin Univ LLB 88 Leeds Univ MA 14. Linc Th Coll BTh 95. **d** 95 **p** 96. C Benchill Man 95–98; C Bilton *Ripon* 98–03; TV Seacroft 03–10; P-in-c Heaton St Martin *Bradf* 10–14; *Leeds* 14–15; P-in-c Heaton St Barn *Bradf* 10–14; *Leeds* 14–15; Can Res Newc Cathl from 15. *55 Queens Terrace, Newcastle upon Tyne NE2 2PL* T: 0191-435 0834 M: 07952-760168 E: claremaclaren@gmail.com *or* clare.maclaren@stnicholascathedral.co.uk

MacLAREN, Duncan Arthur Spencer. b 69. Oriel Coll Ox BA 90 MA 96 K Coll Lon MA 97 PhD 03. Oak Hill Th Coll 92. **d** 94 **p** 95. C Ox St Clem 94–97; Chapl St Edm Hall Ox 97–04; Assoc R Edin St Paul and St Geo 04–09; R Edin St Jas 09–13; LtO from 13. *8 Keith Terrace, Edinburgh EH4 3NJ* T: 0131-467 8481

MacLAREN (née ALEXANDER), Mrs Jane Louise. b 69. LMH Ox BA 90 MA 96. Oak Hill Th Coll BA 95. **d** 95 **p** 96. C Ox St Clem 95–98; Chapl St Aug Sch 98–02; Chapl Ox Brookes Univ 02–04; Assoc R Edin St Paul and St Geo 04–09; NSM Edin St Jas from 09. *8 Keith Terrace, Edinburgh EH4 3NJ* T: 0131-467 8481 M: 07709-905528

McLAREN, Jessica Jean. b 83. Bournemouth Univ BA 06 Thames Valley Univ MA 10 St Jo Coll Dur BA 17. Cranmer Hall Dur 14. **d** 17 **p** 18. C Leagrave *St Alb* from 17. *39 Butely Road, Luton LU4 9EW* M: 07745-536237 E: jessica.j.mclaren@hotmail.com

McLAREN, Richard Francis. b 46. S'wark Ord Course 72. **d** 75 **p** 76. C Charlton St Luke w H Trin *S'wark* 75–78; C Kensington St Mary Abbots w St Geo *Lon* 78–81; Hon C St Marylebone w H Trin 82–96; P-in-c 96–97; Development Officer CUF 97; Chmn Art and Christianity Enquiry Trust 97–11; Hon C Regent's Park St Mark *Lon* 97–11; rtd 11; PtO *Lon* from 12. *The Chapter House, 2 East Wing, Stoneleigh Abbey, Kenilworth CV8 2LF* T: (01926) 851977 E: richardmclaren8@hotmail.co.uk

McLAREN, Canon Robert Ian. b 62. Bris Univ BSc 84 St Jo Coll Dur BA 87. Cranmer Hall Dur 85. **d** 88 **p** 89. C Birkenhead Ch Ch *Ches* 88–90; C Bebington 90–95; V Cheadle All Hallows 95–05; V Poynton from 05; RD Cheadle 09–16; Hon Can Ches Cathl from 14. *The Vicarage, 41 London Road North, Poynton, Stockport SK12 1AF* T: (01625) 850524 *or* 879277 E: poyntonvicar@talktalk.net

McLAREN-COOK, Paul Raymond. b 43. **d** 66 **p** 67. C Mt Lawley Australia 66–67; C Perth Cathl 67–69; R Carnarvon 69–72; V Seremban Malaysia 72–75; Warden Coll of Th 75–76; R Kensington 76–79; R Narrogin 79–84; P-in-c Wellington Australia 84–85; R Eugowra 85–86; P-in-c Berrigan 86–87; P-in-c Hay 87–88; P-in-c Yass 88; R Moruya 88–90; R Heywood 90–92; R Warracknabeal 92–95; Chapl Ballarat Base and St Jo of God Hosps 95–00; R Kansas City St Mary USA 00–03; R Stanway *Chelmsf* 03–13; rtd 13; PtO *Ox* from 14. *Ascot Priory, Priory Road, Ascot SL5 8RT* T: (01344) 882067 E: mclarencook@btinternet.com

McLARNON, Mrs Sylvia Caroline Millicent. b 45. S Dios Minl Tr Scheme 92. **d** 95 **p** 96. NSM Burgess Hill St Andr *Chich* 95–99; C 99–09; rtd 09; Asst Chapl St Pet and St Jas Hospice N Chailey from 05; PtO *Chich* from 14. *23 The Warren, Burgess Hill RH15 0DU* T: (01444) 233902

McLAUGHLIN, Adrian Robert. QUB BTh MTh PhD PGCE. **d** 07 **p** 08. C Bangor Abbey *D & D* 07–13; LtO 13–14; I Dunmurry *Conn* from 14. *The Rectory, 27 Church Avenue, Dunmurry, Belfast BT17 9RS* T: (028) 9061 0984 E: revadrian@btinternet.com *or* revdadrian@gmail.com

McLAUGHLIN, Hubert James Kenneth. b 45. CITC 85. **d** 88 **p** 89. NSM Donagheady *D & R* 88–89; NSM Glendermott 89–98; P-in-c Inver w Mountcharles, Killaghtee and Killybegs 98–02; I 02–10; rtd 10. *9 Cadogan Park, Londonderry BT47 5QW* T: (028) 7134 8916 E: kenandmart@yahoo.com

McLAUGHLIN, Capt Michael Anthony. b 48. **d** 97 **p** 98. C Gt Chart *Cant* 97–01; C-in-c Parkwood CD 01–11; rtd 11; PtO *Roch* from 12. *12 Medway Road, Gillingham ME7 1NH* M: 07977-051681 E: macl@blueyonder.co.uk

MACLAURIN, Ms Anne Fiona. b 62. St Andr Univ MA 84. Ridley Hall Cam. **d** 99 **p** 00. C Crookes St Thos *Sheff* 99–04; TV 04–05; Miss P Philadelphia St Thos 05–10; V Cambridge St Barn *Ely* from 10. *The Vicarage, 57 St Barnabas Road, Cambridge CB1 2BX*

MACLAY, Canon Christopher Willis. b 64. Stirling Univ BA 88 Reading Univ MA 92. Trin Coll Bris BA 01. **d** 01 **p** 02. C Bedhampton *Portsm* 01–05; P-in-c Ashington, Washington and Wiston w Buncton *Chich* 05–11; R 11–12; Chapl Versailles w Chevry *Eur* 12–15; V Bream *Glouc* from 15; AD Forest S from 16; Hon Can Glouc Cathl from 19. *St James's Vicarage, Coleford Road, Bream, Lydney GL15 6ES* T: (01594) 368558 E: chris.maclay@gmail.com

McLAY, The Ven Robert James. b 49. Cant Univ (NZ) BA 71. St Jo Coll Auckland. **d** 73 **p** 74. C Fendalton New Zealand 73–75; Hon C Yardley St Edburgha *Birm* 75–77; V Banks Peninsular New Zealand 77–80; V Marchwiel 80–83; V Huntly 83–89; Lect St Jo Coll 86–88; V Stokes Valley 89–93; V Pauatahanui 93–04; V Brooklyn 04–14; Can Wellington Cathl 96–00; Adn Wellington 07–13. *189 No 3 Line, Wanganui East, Wanganui 4500, New Zealand* T: (0064) (4) 343 2211 E: el.mclay@clear.net.nz *or* mclayrobert726@gmail.com

MACLEAN, Canon Allan Murray. b 50. Edin Univ MA 72. Cuddesdon Coll 72. **d** 76 **p** 77. Chapl St Mary's Cathl *Edin* 76–81; Tutor Edin Univ 77–80; R Dunoon *Arg* 81–86; R Tighnabruaich 84–86; Provost St Jo Cathl Oban 86–99; R Oban St Jo 86–99; R Ardbrecknish 86–99; R Ardchattan 89–99; Hon Can St Jo Cathl Oban from 99; LtO *Edin* from 00; PtO *Mor* from 00; P-in-c Ballachulish and St Vin from 15. *5 North Charlotte Street, Edinburgh EH2 4HR* T: 0131-225 8609 E: editoredge@aol.com

MacLEAN, Christopher Gavin. b 57. Kent Univ BA 85. SEITE 10. **d** 13 **p** 14. C Walmer *Cant* 13–17; P-in-c Brookland, Fairfield, Brenzett w Snargate etc from 17. *All Saints' Rectory, Park Street, Lydd, Romney Marsh TN29 9AY* E: busyonasunday@gmail.com

McLEAN, Donald Stewart. b 48. TCD BA 70. CITC 70. **d** 72 **p** 73. C Glendermott *D & R* 72–75; I Castledawson 75–87 and 03–12; I Londonderry Ch Ch 87–03; Dioc Dir of Ords 79–96; Adn Derry 96–12; Can Derry Cathl 91–12; rtd 12. *99 Oldtown Road, Castledawson, Magherafelt BT45 8BZ* T: (028) 7946 8656 M: 07710-387436 E: donaldmclean@btinternet.com

McLEAN, Mrs Eileen Mary. b 44. City Univ BSc 67. NOC 85. **d** 88 **p** 94. Par Dn Burley in Wharfedale *Bradf* 88–92; Par Dn Nottingham St Pet and St Jas *S'well* 92–94; C 94–02; AD Nottingham Cen 98–02; V Bamburgh *Newc* 02–08; V Ellingham 02–08; rtd 08; PtO *Ripon* 08–13; *Sarum* from 15. *8 Fordington Dairy, Athelstan Road, Dorchester DT1 1FD* T: (01305) 260126 E: eileen.mclean@btinternet.com

McLEAN, Mrs Elizabeth Mary. b 79. All SS Cen for Miss & Min 16. **d** 19. C Fulwood Ch Ch *Blackb* from 19. *3 The Turnpike, Fulwood, Preston PR2 3NT* E: emmclean@hotmail.co.uk

MacLEAN, Lawrence Alexander Charles. b 61. K Coll Lon BD 84 AKC 84. Chich Th Coll 86. **d** 88 **p** 89. C Cirencester *Glouc* 88–91; C Prestbury 91–96; PtO 01–02; Chapl Florence w Siena *Eur* 02–11; V Gt and Lt Torrington and Frithelstock *Ex* 11–14; RD Torrington 12–14; V Hove St Barn and St Agnes *Chich* 14–18; P-in-c Hove St Andr 14–18; Dioc Development Officer 14–18; Chapl Monte Carlo *Eur* from 18. *St Paul, 22 Avenue de Grande-Bretagne, MC 98000, Monaco* T: (00377) 9330 7106 E: lm61@live.co.uk *or* chaplain@stpaulsmonaco.com

McLEAN, Canon Margaret Anne. b 62. Birm Univ BA 91 Heythrop Coll Lon MA 99. Qu Coll Birm 88. **d** 91 **p** 94. Par Dn Bedford All SS *St Alb* 91–94; C 94; Chapl St Alb High Sch for Girls 94–98; Asst Soc Resp Officer *Derby* 98–99; Chapl Huddersfield Univ *Wakef* 99–02; P-in-c Scholes 02–09; P-in-c Cleckheaton St Luke and Whitechapel 02–09; P-in-c Battyeford 09–14; Dioc Tr Officer (Reader Formation) 09–14; *Leeds* from 14; V Battyeford from 14; Hon Can Wakef Cathl from 11. *Battyeford Vicarage, 107A Stocksbank Road, Mirfield WF14 9QT* T: (01924) 493277 M: 07777-673172 E: m.a.mclean@btinternet.com

McLEAN, Canon Robert Hedley. b 47. St Jo Coll Dur BA 69. Ripon Hall Ox 69. **d** 71 **p** 72. C Redhill St Jo *S'wark* 71–74; C S Beddington St Mich 74–77; C-in-c Raynes Park H Cross CD 77; P-in-c Motspur Park 77–80; V 80–84; V Tadworth 84–00; Asst RD Reigate 92–93; RD Reigate 93–00; R Morpeth *Newc* 00–12; AD 04–08; Chapl Northd Mental Health NHS Trust 00–09; Chapl Northumbria Healthcare NHS Foundn Trust 00–09; rtd 12; P-in-c Wylam *Newc* 12–16; Hon Can Newc Cathl from 11; Hon Can Asante Mampong Ghana from 15; PtO *Newc* from 16. *26 Dene Road, Wylam NE41 8HB* T: (01661) 852065 E: rhm47@hotmail.co.uk

McLEAN, Thomas Paul. b 86. Bath Univ BSc 08 Sarum Coll MA 16. Coll of Resurr Mirfield 15–16. **d** 17 **p** 18. C Higham Ferrers w Chelveston *Pet* from 17. *32 Coniston Close, Higham Ferrers, Rushden NN10 8NL* E: frtom.mclean@gmail.com

MacLEAY, Canon Angus Murdo. b 59. Univ Coll Ox BA 81 MA 86 Man Univ MPhil 92 Solicitor 83. Wycliffe Hall Ox 85. **d** 88 **p** 89. C Rusholme H Trin *Man* 88–92; V Houghton *Carl* 92–01; R Sevenoaks St Nic *Roch* from 01; Hon Can Roch Cathl from 15. *The Rectory, Rectory Lane, Sevenoaks TN13 1JA* T: (01732) 740340 F: 742810 E: angus.macleay@stnicholas-sevenoaks.org

MacLEOD, Alan Roderick Hugh (Roddie). b 33. St Edm Hall Ox BA 56 MA 61 Ox Univ DipEd 62. Wycliffe Hall Ox 56. **d** 58 **p** 59. C Bognor St Jo *Chich* 58–61; Chapl Wadh Coll Ox 62; Hd of RE Picardy Boys' Sch Erith 62–68; C Erith St Jo *Roch* 63–69; Dean Lonsdale Coll Lanc Univ 70–72; Hd of RE K Edw VI Sch Totnes 72–73; Dir of Resources St Helier Boys' Sch Jersey 73–84; V Shipton Bellinger *Win* 84–02; rtd 02; PtO *Win* 02–15. *Pippins Toft, Lashmar's Corner, East Preston, Littlehampton BN16 1EZ* T: (01903) 783523

McLEOD, David Leo Roderick. b 71. Westmr Coll Ox BA 92 DipCOT 96. **d** 05 **p** 06. OLM Coddenham w Gosbeck and Hemingstone w Henley *St E* 05–10; OLM Crowfield w Stonham Aspal and Mickfield 05–10; Chapl Team Co-ord Univ Campus Suffolk 07–10; Chapl Team Co-ord Suffolk New Coll 07–10; C Wokingham St Sebastian *Ox* 10–15; V Greenham from 15. *St Mary's Vicarage, New Road, Greenham, Thatcham RG19 8RZ* T: (01635) 41075 M: 07706-429805 E: davidmcleod01@btinternet.com

McLEOD, Everton William. b 57. Oak Hill Th Coll 89. **d** 91 **p** 92. C New Ferry *Ches* 91–93; C Moreton 93–98; Chapl R Liv Univ Hosp NHS Trust 98–01; R Weston-super-Mare St Nic w St Barn *B & W* 01–11; V Trentham *Lich* 11–16; V Hanford 11–16; TV Hampreston *Sarum* from 16. *19 Canford Bottom, Wimborne BH21 2HA*

MACLEOD, John Bain Maclennan. b 50. Aber Univ LLB 86 Solicitor 89. TISEC 03. **d** 06 **p** 08. NSM Hamilton *Glas* 06–12;

NSM Annan 12–18; NSM Eastriggs 12–18; NSM Gretna 12–18; NSM Lockerbie 12–18; NSM Moffat 12–18; rtd 18; LtO *Glas* from 18. *Greenrig Barn, Hawksland, Lesmahagow, Lanark ML11 9QB* T: (01555) 664866 M: 07826-163415 E: macleod.greenrig@btinternet.com

MacLEOD, John Malcolm (Jay). b 61. Harvard Univ AB 84 Pemb Coll Ox BA 87 MA 91. Linc Th Coll MDiv 93. **d** 93 **p** 94. C Chesterfield SS Aug *Derby* 93–96; C Stalybridge St Paul *Ches* 96–98; P-in-c Micklehurst 98–03; P-in-c Bedford All SS *St Alb* 03–13; Dioc Interfaith Adv 03–13; R New London USA from 13. *184 Shindagan Road, Wilmot Flat NH 03287, USA* E: jaymacleod@mac.com

McLEOD, Neil Raymond. b 61. Trin Coll Bris 06. **d** 08 **p** 09. C N w S Wootton *Nor* 08–12; P-in-c Newport and Widdington *Chelmsf* 12–13; V Newport w Widdington, Quendon and Rickling from 13. *The Vicarage, 5 Meadowford, Newport, Saffron Walden CB11 3QL* T: (01799) 540339

McLEOD, Paul Douglas. b 66. Cuddesdon Coll BTh 95. **d** 98 **p** 99. C Morpeth *Newc* 98–02; V Newbiggin Hall 02–10; R Silverstone and Abthorpe w Slapton etc *Pet* from 10; RD Towcester from 11. *The Vicarage, 24A High Street, Silverstone, Towcester NN12 8US* T: (01327) 858101 M: 07780-834099 E: revpaulmcleod@btinternet.com

McLEOD, Roderick. See MacLEOD, Alan Roderick Hugh

MacLEOD, Talisker Isobel. See TRACEY-MacLEOD, Talisker Isobel

McLOUGHLIN, Ian Livingstone. b 38. CEng MICE 64. Carl Dioc Tr Course 78. **d** 83 **p** 84. NSM Stanwix *Carl* 83–88; C Barrow St Geo w St Luke 88–90; R Kirkby Thore w Temple Sowerby and Newbiggin 90–01; rtd 01; PtO *Carl* from 01; *Bradf* 01–10. *29 Wordsworth Drive, Kendal LA9 7JW* T: (01539) 728209 E: nohastle@googlemail.com

McLOUGHLIN, John Robert. b 70. QUB BEng 92 Open Univ MSc 02. CITC BTh 09. **d** 09 **p** 10. C Arm St Mark 09–11; I Clonfeacle w Derrygortreavy 11–18; I Aghavea *Clogh* from 18. *256 Belfast Road, Lurgan, Brookeborough, Enniskillen BT94 4DS* T: (028) 8953 1210 M: 07488-371680 E: johnnymcloughlin@gmail.com

McLOUGHLIN, Ms Tracey. b 65. Liv Hope Univ Coll BA 05. SNWTP 09. **d** 12 **p** 13. C Skelmersdale St Paul *Liv* 12–16; TV Warrington E from 16. *The Vicarage, 1 Briers Close, Fearnhead, Warrington WA2 0DN* M: 07990-545489

McLUCKIE, Canon John Mark. b 67. St Andr Univ BD 89. Edin Th Coll MTh 91. **d** 91 **p** 92. C Perth St Ninian *St And* 91–94; Chapl K Coll Cam 94–96; TV Glas E End 96–00; Assoc R Edin St Jo 00–03; PtO from 08; Chapl Asst R Marsden NHS Foundn Trust 10–12; Vice Provost St Mary's Cathl *Edin* from 12. *33/1 Manor Place, Edinburgh EH3 7EB* M: 07967-711884 E: john.mcluckie@hotmail.com *or* international@dioceseofedinburgh.org

MACLURE, David Samuel. b 80. York Univ BA 02 MA 06. Oak Hill Th Coll BA 14. **d** 14 **p** 15. C Isleworth St Jo w St Mary *Lon* 14–17; V from 17. *The New Vicarage, St John's Road, Isleworth TW7 6NY* E: davidmaclure@gmail.com

MACLUSKIE, Canon Linda. b 55. Lanc Univ MA 99. CBDTI 95. **d** 98 **p** 99. NSM Halton w Aughton *Blackb* 98–02; NSM Bolton-le-Sands 02–10; P-in-c Sandylands 10–11; V from 11; P-in-c Overton 17–19; AD Lancaster and Morecambe 14–17; Hon Can Blackb Cathl from 18. *St John's Vicarage, 2 St John's Avenue, Morecambe LA3 1EU* T: (01524) 411039 M: 07827-923222 E: linda.macluskie@virgin.net

McMAHON, Stephen. b 66. Newc Univ BSc 87 MSc 89 Leeds Univ BA 03 Edin Univ MSc 17. Coll of Resurr Mirfield 01. **d** 03 **p** 04. C Lancaster St Mary w St John and St Anne *Blackb* 03–07; P-in-c Lowther and Askham and Clifton and Brougham *Carl* 07–10; P-in-c Kirkby Thore w Temple Sowerby and Newbiggin 07–10; Chapl Rossall Sch Fleetwood 10; NSM Lancaster St Mary w St John and St Anne *Blackb* 10–11; V Blyth St Cuth *Newc* 11–16; P-in-c Ipswich St Paul Australia 16–17; R Ipswich St Paul from 17. *11 Baystone Place, Raceview, Ipswich QLD 4305, Australia* E: steve1345.mcmahon@gmail.com

McMANN, Duncan. b 34. Jes Coll Ox BA 55 MA 60. Clifton Th Coll 55. **d** 58 **p** 59. C Newburn *Newc* 58–60; C Bishopwearmouth St Gabr *Dur* 60–62; N Area Sec BCMS 62–66; Midl and E Anglia Area Sec 66–92; Support Co-ord 84–92; LtO *Man* 62–66; LtO *Cov* 66–92; PtO *Birm* 79–92; P-in-c Awsworth w Cossall *S'well* 92–99; Chapl Notts Constabulary 93–99; rtd 99; PtO *Nor* 00–15; *York* from 15. *Dulverton Hall, Esplanade, Scarborough YO11 2AR*

McMANN, Canon Judith. b 46. Hull Univ BTh 96. EMMTC MA 98. **d** 98 **p** 99. NSM Gt Grimsby St Mary and St Jas *Linc* 98–08; NSM Caistor Gp 08–18; NSM Caistor from 18; Can and Preb Linc Cathl from 05. *23 Grasby Crescent, Grimsby DN37 9HE* T: (01472) 887523 E: mcmann@btopenworld.com

McMANUS, James Robert. b 33. Wycliffe Hall Ox 56. **d** 58 **p** 59. C Leic H Trin 58–60; C Aylestone 60–63; India 66–79; V Oldham St Barn *Man* 79–83; Asst Regional Sec CMS 83–85; V Wolverhampton St Matt *Lich* 85–93; V Lapley w Wheaton Aston 93–99; P-in-c Blymhill w Weston-under-Lizard 93–99; rtd 99; PtO *Lich* 99–15 and 17–18. *Delamere, McBean Road, Wolverhampton WV6 0JQ* T: (01902) 833436 F: 834170 E: jimandmavis.mcmanus@gmail.com

McMANUS-THOMPSON, Elizabeth Gray. See THOMPSON, Elizabeth Gray McManus

MACMATH, Terence Handley. See HANDLEY MACMATH, Terence

McMICHAEL, Andrew Hamilton. b 48. Univ of Wales (Ban) BA 77. Chich Th Coll 87. **d** 89 **p** 90. C Chorley St Geo *Blackb* 89–92; C Burnley St Andr w St Marg 92–94; Chapl Burnley Health Care NHS Trust 92–94; R Eccleston *Blackb* 94–99; V Lt Marsden w Nelson St Mary 99–04; P-in-c Tain, Lochinver and Invergordon St Ninian *Mor* 04–07; P-in-c Harrington *Carl* 07–09; R Port Glas 09–13; rtd 13. *11 Howard Court, 77 Albert Road, Southport PR9 9LN* E: andrew.mcmichael@tesco.net

MacMILLAN, Douglas Middleton. b 41. RCM DMus 13 St Thos Hosp Lon MB, BS 66 FRCS 70 FTCL 82 AMusLCM 80 FLCM 83. Guildf Dioc Min Course 96. **d** 00. NSM Guildf Cathl 00–02; PtO 02–04; NSM E and W Clandon 04–11; rtd 12; PtO *Guildf* from 12; *Lon* from 11. *Rivendell, 50 Speedwell Close, Guildford GU4 7HE* T: (01483) 533019 E: douglas.oriana@btinternet.com

McMULLEN (née Woodcock), Mrs Anne Caroline. b 63. Man Metrop Univ BA 97 Man Univ MA 07 RGN. SNWTP 08. **d** 10 **p** 11. C Newton in Mottram *Ches* 10–11; C Newton w Flowery Field 11–13; V 13–17; PtO *Man* from 16; *Ches* from 17; Chapl HM Pris Forest Bank from 17. *HM Prison Forest Bank, Pendlebury, Swinton, Manchester M27 8FB* T: 0161-925 7000

McMULLON, Andrew Brian. b 56. Sheff Univ BSc. St Jo Coll Nottm. **d** 83 **p** 84. C Stainforth *Sheff* 83–86; V Blackb Redeemer 86–90; Chapl RAF 90–13; V Sedbergh, Cautley and Garsdale *Carl* from 13; P-in-c Firbank, Howgill and Killington from 15. *20 Winfield Road, Sedbergh LA10 5AZ* T: (015396) 20018 E: andrew.mcmullon@outlook.com

McMURRAY, Matthew Paul. b 79. Trin Hall Cam BTh 11. Westcott Ho Cam 08. **d** 11 **p** 12. C Hawes Side and Marton Moss *Blackb* 11–14; C Fleetwood St Pet and St Dav 14–16; V Lostock Hall and Farington Moss from 16. *St James's Vicarage, 76A Brownedge Road, Lostock Hall, Preston PR5 5AD* T: (01772) 315404 E: frmatthew@cantab.net

McMURTARY, Simon Alexander. b 79. Wycliffe Hall Ox BA 00 MA 05. Ripon Coll Cuddesdon MTh 13. **d** 12 **p** 13. C Four Marks *Win* 12–15; Chapl Dur Sch from 15. *5 Monument Court, Durham DH1 4PD* T: 0191-386 0724 E: revsimontssf@gmail.com

McNAB (née LUMMIS), Mrs Elizabeth Howieson. b 44. Lon Univ BDS 68 LDS 68. St Jo Coll Nottm 85. **d** 88 **p** 95. NSM Lerwick *Ab* from 88; NSM Burravoe from 88. *Waters Edge, Bridge of Walls, Shetland ZE2 9NP* T: (01595) 809441 E: j.mcnab840@btinternet.com

McNAIR SCOTT, Benjamin Guthrie. b 76. K Coll Lon BA 98 MA 05. Ridley Hall Cam 05. **d** 07 **p** 08. NSM Guildf Ch Ch from 07; Chapl St Cath Sch Bramley from 12. *21 Lancaster Avenue, Guildford GU1 3JR* T: (01483) 455645 M: 07968-617084 E: benjaming@lycos.co.uk *or* benji@christchurchguildford.com

McNALLY, Paul. b 83. Wycliffe Hall Ox 15. **d** 17 **p** 18. C Accrington St Jas and St Paul *Blackb* 17–19; C Accrington Ch Ch from 19. *3 Bentcliffe Gardens, Accrington BB5 2NX* M: 07816-491522 E: revd.paul.mcnally@gmail.com

McNAMARA, Barbara. See SMITH, Barbara Mary

McNAUGHTAN-OWEN, James Thomas. b 48. Liv Univ MA 00. Linc Th Coll 77. **d** 80 **p** 81. C Palmers Green St Jo *Lon* 80–84; C Timperley *Ches* 84–87; C Bramhall 87–92; V Latchford St Jas 92–14; RD Gt Budworth 96–03; rtd 14. *9 Melton Road, Runcorn WA7 4AH*

MACNAUGHTON, Mrs Diana. b 54. St Hugh's Coll Ox BA 76 MA 90 Northumbria Univ MA 11 Dur Univ PGCE 78. NEOC 95. **d** 98 **p** 99. NSM Gosforth All SS *Newc* 98–01; C Willington 01–04; Chapl Team Ldr Northumbria Healthcare NHS Foundn Trust 04–11; P-in-c Byker St Silas *Newc* 11–16; V 16; rtd 16; PtO *Newc* 16–18; Hon C Tweedmouth from 18; Hon C Spittal from 18; Hon C Scremerston from 18. *St John's Vicarage, 129 Main Street, Spittal, Berwick-upon-Tweed TD15 1RP* M: 07950-627799 E: dmacnaughton@btinternet.com

McNAUGHTON, John. b 29. St Chad's Coll Dur BA 53. **d** 54 **p** 55. C Thorney Close CD *Dur* 54–58; C-in-c E Herrington St Chad CD 58–62; PC E Herrington 62–66; CF 66–94; V Hutton Cranswick w Skerne, Watton and Beswick *York*

94–99; rtd 99; PtO *York* from 99. *47 Southgate, Cranswick, Driffield YO25 9QX* T: (01377) 270869

MACNAUGHTON, Mrs Pamela Jean. b 63. Ox Min Course. **d** 08 **p** 09. NSM Bishopthorpe *York* from 08; NSM Acaster Malbis from 08; NSM Appleton Roebuck w Acaster Selby from 08; Dioc Adv for Pioneer Min 12–14; CPAS from 13. *64 Copmanthorpe Lane, Bishopthorpe, York YO23 2RS* T: (01904) 700141 E: workspacepjm@aol.com

MACNAUGHTON, Canon William <u>Malcolm</u>. b 57. Qu Coll Cam BA 80. Ridley Hall Cam 79. **d** 81 **p** 82. C Haughton le Skerne *Dur* 81–85; P-in-c Newton Hall 85–90; TV Shoreditch St Leon and Hoxton St Jo *Lon* 90–00; AD Hackney 94–99; V Hoxton St Jo w Ch Ch 00–02; R Hambleden Valley *Ox* 02–07; AD Wycombe 05–07; Chief of Staff to Abp York from 07; Can and Preb York Minster from 16. *The Palace, Bishopthorpe, York YO23 2GE* T: (01904) 772362 E: malcolm.macnaughton@archbishopofyork.org

MacNEANEY, Jonathan Niall Agnew. b 88. Oriel Coll Ox BA 09. Ripon Coll Cuddesdon MTh 13. **d** 13 **p** 14. C Hadleigh St Jas and Hadleigh St Barn *Chelmsf* 13–14; C Epping Distr 14–17; C Kensington St Mary Abbots *Lon* from 17. *Cottage 1, St Mary Abbots Vicarage, Vicarage Gate, London W8 4HW* E: macneaneyj@gmail.com

McNEE, Canon William Creighton. Ulster Univ MA NUU MA FCIPD. **d** 82 **p** 83. C Larne and Inver *Conn* 82–84; I Donagheady *D & R* 84–91; I Kilwaughter w Cairncastle and Craigy Hill *Conn* 91–93; I Ardstraw w Baronscourt, Badoney Lower etc *D & R* 93–04; P-in-c Londonderry Ch Ch 04–05; I 05–08; I Londonderry Ch Ch, Culmore, Muff and Belmont 08–09; Bp's Dom Chapl 96–07; Can Derry Cathl 00–09; rtd 09. *14 Tartnakilly Road, Limavady BT49 9NA* T: (028) 7727 8873 M: 07770-767737 E: billmcnee@usa.net

McNEICE, Kathleen Mary. b 51. SEITE. **d** 07 **p** 08. NSM Folkestone Trin *Cant* from 07. *2B Wear Bay Crescent, Folkestone CT19 6AX* T: (01303) 278791 M: 07786-365533 E: kate_mcneice@hotmail.com

McNEIL, Ann. *See* CAFFYN, Ann

McNEIL, Kyle Gillies. b 86. Univ Coll Dur BA 09. St Steph Ho Ox BA 14. **d** 14 **p** 15. C Cockerton *Dur* 14–17; P-in-c Horden from 17; P-in-c Blackhall, Castle Eden and Monkhesleden from 17. *St Mary's Vicarage, 4 Stapylton Drive, Horden, Peterlee SR8 4HY* E: kyle.g.mcneil@gmail.com

MACNEILL, Nicholas Terence. b 62. St Steph Ho Ox BTh 93. **d** 93 **p** 94. C Ex St Thos and Em 93–97; TV 97–98; V Cople, Moggerhanger and Willington *St Alb* 98–03; R Toddington and Chalgrave 03–06; rtd 07; PtO *Chich* 12–17. *20 Black Path, Polegate BN26 5AP* T: (01323) 485399 E: mogger12346@aol.com

McNELLY, Mrs Nicola. b 62. Cranmer Hall Dur 07. **d** 09 **p** 10. Chapl St Mary's Cathl *Edin* 09–10; C 10–12; Provost St Jo Cathl Oban *Arg* 12–17; R Ardbrecknish 12–17; Can Cumbrae 13–17; R Edin St Cuth from 17. *The Rectory, 6 Westgarth Avenue, Edinburgh EH13 0BD* T: 0131-441 7580 M: 07825-440580 E: stcuthbertsrector@gmail.com

McNICOL, Andrew <u>Keith</u>. b 45. Westmr Coll of Educn CertEd 69 Open Univ BA 79 Westmr Coll Ox MA 90. Westcott Ho Cam 92. **d** 92 **p** 93. C Whitstable *Cant* 92–95; V Ferring *Chich* 95–00; P-in-c Willesborough *Cant* 00–06; P-in-c Tunstall w Rodmersham 06–11; R Tunstall and Bredgar 11–14; rtd 14; PtO *Cant* from 15. *63 Shearwater Avenue, Whitstable CT5 4DY* T: (01227) 264592 E: kiththerector@gmail.com

McPHATE, The Very Revd Gordon Ferguson. b 50. Aber Univ MB, ChB 74 Fitzw Coll Cam BA 77 MA 81 MD 88 Surrey Univ MSc 86 Edin Univ MTh 94 FRCPEd 98. Westcott Ho Cam 75. **d** 78 **p** 79. NSM Sandstead All SS *S'wark* 78–81; Hon PV S'wark Cathl 81–86; Lect Lon Univ 81–86; Chapl St Andr Univ *St And* 86–02; Lect 86–93; Sen Lect 93–02; Dean Ches 02–17; rtd 17; PtO *Ban* from 18. *50 Llys Onnen, Llandudno Junction LL31 9EZ*

McPHEE, Mrs Margaret Theresa Maria. b 65. Nottm Univ BA 88 Anglia Ruskin Univ PGCE 97 FCIPD 04. ERMC 09. **d** 12 **p** 13. C Mile Cross *Nor* 12–13; C Stalham, E Ruston, Brunstead, Sutton and Ingham 13–16; R Horsford, Felthorpe and Hevingham from 16. *1B Gordon Godfrey Way, Horsford, Norwich NR10 3SG* M: 07759-913802 E: revmargaretmcphee@gmail.com

MACPHERSON, Aian Jonathan. b 84. BSc 07 St Jo Coll Dur BA 13. Cranmer Hall Dur 10. **d** 13 **p** 14. C Drypool *York* 13–17; TV Marfleet from 17. *107 Amethyst Road, Hull HU9 4JG* M: 07929-733555 E: aian.macpherson2012@gmail.com

McPHERSON, Canon Andrew Lindsay. b 58. St Jo Coll Dur BA 79 MCIPD 84. **d** 88 **p** 89. C Bitterne *Win* 88–92; V Weston 92–99; V Holdenhurst and Iford from 99; P-in-c Southbourne St Chris from 07; P-in-c Bournemouth H Epiphany 12–14;

AD Bournemouth 08–16; Hon Can Win Cathl from 16. *The Vicarage, 53A Holdenhurst Avenue, Bournemouth BH7 6RB* T: (01202) 425978 E: andy@stsaviours.net

MACPHERSON, Canon Anthony Stuart. b 56. Qu Coll Birm 77. **d** 80 **p** 81. C Morley St Pet w Churwell *Wakef* 80–84; C Penistone 84–85; P-in-c Thurlstone 85–86; TV Penistone and Thurlstone 86–88; V Grimethorpe 88–95; P-in-c Westgate Common 95–96; V 96–07; P-in-c Horbury Junction 02–07; RD Wakef 99–07; Hon Can Wakef Cathl 06–07; Can Missr Wakef 07–15; Can Pastor and Sub Dean Wakef *Leeds* 15–19; P-in-c Beadnell *Newc* from 19; P-in-c Ellingham from 19; P-in-c N Sunderland from 19. *The Vicarage, 155 Main Street, North Sunderland, Seahouses NE68 7TU* M: 07780-990354 E: canontonymac@gmail.com

MACPHERSON, Ms Catherine Annunciata. b 86. Univ of Wales (Lamp) BA 07 Em Coll Cam MPhil 10. Westcott Ho Cam 08. **d** 10 **p** 11. C Mirfield *Wakef* 10–14; P-in-c Fawdon *Newc* from 14. *St Mary's Vicarage, 7 Fawdon Lane, Newcastle upon Tyne NE3 2RR* T: 0191-285 6153 M: 07961-699486 E: revcatherinemac@gmail.com

MacPHERSON, David Alan John. b 42. Lon Univ BD 75 Open Univ BA 83 Hatf Poly MSc 89. Clifton Th Coll 69 Trin Coll Bris 72. **d** 72 **p** 73. C Drypool St Columba w St Andr and St Pet *York* 72–76; Asst Chapl HM Pris Hull 72–76; P-in-c Bessingby and Carnaby *York* 76–78; Chapl RAF 78–83; P-in-c Chedgrave w Hardley and Langley *Nor* 83–87; R 87–97; Chapl Langley Sch Nor 83–97; P-in-c Brington w Whilton and Norton *Pet* 97–98; R Brington w Whilton and Norton etc 98–02; rtd 02; PtO *Pet* 02–14 and from 18; Chapl to Retired Clergy and Clergy Widows' Officer 10–14. *24 Coldstream Close, Daventry NN11 9HL* T: (01327) 704500

MacPHERSON, Ewan Alexander. b 43. Toronto Univ BA 74. Wycliffe Coll Toronto MDiv 78. **d** 78 **p** 79. C Toronto St Cuth Canada 78–81; C Toronto Apostles 81–86; V Priddy and Westbury sub Mendip w Easton *B & W* 86–06; rtd 06. *20 Tuddington Gardens, Wells BA5 2EJ* T: (01749) 675876

MACPHERSON, Peter Sinclair. b 44. Lich Th Coll 68. **d** 71 **p** 72. C Honiton, Gittisham and Combe Raleigh *Ex* 71–72; C Bideford 72–74; C Devonport St Mark Ford 74–75; V Thorncombe *Sarum* 75–79; TV Dorchester 79–85; Chapl Jersey Gp of Hosps 85–90; Chapl Derriford Hosp Plymouth 90–98; rtd 98; PtO *Ex* 04–09. *Pump Cottage, 1 Rosemary Lane, Musbury, Axminster EX13 6AT* T: (01297) 552524

McQUAID, Mrs Jennifer Claire. b 79. Univ of Wales (Abth) BA 01. St Mellitus Coll BA 13 MA 14. **d** 14 **p** 15. NSM Hitchin *St Alb* 14–15; C 15–16; C Hitchin and St Paul's Walden 16–18; V Letchworth St Paul w Willian from 18. *177 Pixmore Way, Letchworth Garden City SG6 1QT* E: jennifercmcquaid@gmail.com

McQUILLEN, Brian Anthony. b 45. Ripon Hall Ox 73. **d** 75 **p** 76. C Northfield *Birm* 75–78; C Sutton Coldfield H Trin 78–80; V Bearwood 80–89; V Glouc St Geo w Whaddon 89–96; R St Martin w Looe *Truro* 96–11; RD W Wivelshire 98–03 and 06–08; rtd 11; PtO *Truro* from 14. *7 Bonython Drive, Grampound, Truro TR2 4RL* T: (01726) 883184 E: brianmcq.chap@btinternet.com

McREYNOLDS, Canon Kenneth Anthony. b 48. **d** 83 **p** 84. C Ballymena w Ballyclug *Conn* 83–86; I Rathcoole 86–90; I Lambeg 90–16; Can Conn Cathl 08–16; rtd 16. *35 Hazelgrove Avenue, Lurgan, Craigavon BT66 7TF* T: (028) 3815 2145 E: kenmcreynolds@hotmail.com

MacROBERT, Iain. b 49. Wolv Univ BA 80 PGCE 81 Birm Univ MA 85 PhD 89. **d** 00 **p** 00. NSM S Queensferry *Edin* from 00. *21 Long Crook, South Queensferry EH30 9XR* T: 0131-319 1558 *or* (01506) 600292 F: 0131-319 1558 E: iain0macrobert@aol.com

McROBERTS, Ms Tracey. b 68. QUB BTh 99 PGCE 00 Dub City Univ MA 09. CITC 08. **d** 09 **p** 10. C Belfast St Thos *Conn* 09–12; I Belfast St Matt from 12; Bp's Dom Chapl from 11. *Shankill Rectory, 51 Ballygomartin Road, Belfast BT13 3LA* T: (028) 9071 4325 M: 07718-490040 E: tracey.mcroberts@btinternet.com

McROSTIE, The Ven Lyn. b 50. Canberra Univ BA 77 Portsm Univ MA 03 MIInfSc 81. STETS 95. **d** 98 **p** 99. C Portsea St Cuth *Portsm* 98–02; P-in-c Shadwell St Paul w Ratcliffe St Jas *Lon* 02–04; Course Ldr NTMTC 04–06; P-in-c Northwood *Portsm* 06–07; R 07–11; P-in-c Gurnard 06–07; V 07–11; P-in-c Cowes St Faith 06–07; V 07–11; P-in-c Elizabeth Australia from 11; Ldr Angl Min Playford from 12; Adn The Para from 14. *13 Ashley Street, Elizabeth North SA 5113, Australia* T: (0061) (8) 8287 6722 E: lyn.mcrostie@mcrostie.com

MACROW-WOOD, The Ven Antony Charles. b 60. York Univ BA 82 Jes Coll Cam BA 91 ACA 86. Westcott Ho Cam 89. **d** 92 **p** 93. C Swindon St Jo and St Andr *Bris* 92–96; TV Preston w Sutton Poyntz, Littlemoor etc *Sarum* 96–04;

P-in-c N Poole Ecum Team 04–06; TR 06–15; Adn Dorset from 15; Can and Preb Sarum Cathl from 12. *28 Merriefield Drive, Broadstone BH18 8PB* E: amacrowwood@mac.com *or* addorset@salisbury.anglican.org

MacSWAIN, Robert Carroll. b 69. Liberty Univ USA BA 92 Princeton Th Sem MDiv 95 Edin Univ MTh 96 St Andr Univ PhD 10. Virginia Th Sem 99. **d** 01 **p** 02. C Kinston St Mary USA 01–04; Chapl and Fell St Chad's Coll Dur 05–08; Instructor Univ of the South USA 09–10; Asst Prof 10–15; Assoc Prof from 15. *The School of Theology, University of the South, Sewanee TN 37383-0001, USA* E: robert.macswain@sewanee.edu

McTEER, Canon Robert Ian. b 56. Chich Th Coll 90. **d** 92 **p** 93. C S Shields All SS *Dur* 92–95; P-in-c Auckland St Helen 95–97; V from 97; Chapl Bishop Auckland Hospitals NHS Trust 95–98; Chapl S Durham Healthcare NHS Trust 98–02; Hon Can Koforidua from 07. *The Vicarage, 8 Manor Road, St Helen Auckland, Bishop Auckland DL14 9EN* T: (01388) 604152 E: fr.r.mcteer@btinternet.com

McTERNAN, Ms Margaret Siobhan. b 70. Edin Univ LLB 92 Dundee Univ MSc 95 DipSW 95. **d** 11 **p** 12. C Glas St Marg from 11. *Flat 0/1, 9 Kennoway Drive, Glasgow G11 7UA* T: 0141-337 2604 M: 07738-054461 E: maggsmct@gmail.com

McTIGHE, Ann-Margaret. b 67. Brunel Univ BSc 97 PGCE 98. Trin Coll Bris BA 10. **d** 10 **p** 11. C Woodford St Mary w St Phil and St Jas *Chelmsf* 10–12; C Woodford Wells 12–14; Pioneer Min Olympic Park 14–19; C Stratford St Paul and St Jas *Chelmsf* 14–19; C Stratford St Jo w Ch Ch 15–19; Fresh Expressions Development Officer *St Alb* from 19; PtO *Lon* from 15. *Address temp unknown* M: 07940-892391 E: revanniemct@gmail.com *or* annie@churche20.org

MacVANE, Mrs Sara Ann Andrew. b 44. Wellesley Coll (USA) BA 66 Univ of Wales (Ban) BA 05. EAMTC 03. **d** 05 **p** 06. C Rome *Eur* 05–09; Asst Dir Angl Cen Rome 05–09; P-in-c Nord Pas de Calais *Eur* 09–11; Asst Chapl Zürich 11–14; PtO from 14. *60 rue Victor Hugo, 93170 Bagnolet, France* E: macvanesara@gmail.com

McVEAGH, Paul Stuart. b 56. Southn Univ BA 78. Oak Hill Th Coll BA 88. **d** 88 **p** 89. C Bebington *Ches* 88–92; Crosslinks Portugal 92–95; R High Halstow w All Hallows and Hoo St Mary *Roch* 95–02; V Westerham 02–15; P-in-c Ashburnham w Penhurst *Chich* 15–17; rtd 17. *91 Warrington Road, Paddock Wood, Tonbridge TN12 6JS* E: pmcveagh@aol.com

MACVEAN, Mrs Amanda Sharon. b 58. K Alfred's Coll Win BEd 80. STETS 09. **d** 12 **p** 13. C Banstead *Guildf* 12–16; V Effingham w Lt Bookham from 16. *The Rectory, 4 Leewood Way, Effingham, Leatherhead KT24 5JN* T: (01372) 458314 E: rev.mandymacvean@gmail.com

McVEETY, Canon Ian. b 46. NOC 82. **d** 85 **p** 86. C Langley and Parkfield *Man* 85–89; V Castleton Moor 89–99; AD Heywood and Middleton 95–99; V Baguley 99–12; AD Withington 06–12; Hon Can Man Cathl 07–12; rtd 12; PtO *Man* from 12. *873 Walmersley Road, Bury BL9 5LE* T: 0161-797 3575 E: imcveety22@btinternet.com

McVEIGH, Miss Dorothy Sara. b 67. QUB BA 89 TCD BTh 93. CITC 90. **d** 93 **p** 94. C Belfast St Matt *Conn* 93–96; C Carrickfergus 96–99; C Lurgan Ch the Redeemer *D & D* 99–04; I Annaghmore *Arm* from 04. *54 Moss Road, Portadown, Craigavon BT62 1NB* T: (028) 3885 2751 M: 07786-454346 E: mcveigh423@btinternet.com

McVEIGH, Canon Samuel. b 49. CITC 77. **d** 79 **p** 80. C Drumragh w Mountfield *D & R* 79–82; I Dromore *Clogh* 82–90; I Drumachose *D & R* from 90; Can Derry Cathl from 01; Can St Patr Cathl Dublin from 18. *49 Killane Road, Limavady BT49 0DJ* T: (028) 7776 2680 M: 07889-769412 E: mcveigh_family@yahoo.co.uk

McVEIGH, Sandra. *See* BARTON, Sandra

McWATT, Glenn Ellsworth. b 48. S'wark Ord Course 89. **d** 92 **p** 93. NSM Tulse Hill H Trin and St Matthias S'wark 92–99; C New Malden and Coombe 99–03; C Reigate St Mary 03–08; C Gillingham St Mark *Roch* 08–12; P-in-c Grain w Stoke 12–14; rtd 14. *16 Fittleworth Garden, Rustington, Littlehampton BN16 3EW* T: (01903) 774750 E: glennmcwatt@btinternet.com

McWHINNEY, Susan Elizabeth. b 59. Newnham Coll Cam BA 80 MB, BChir 83 MA 84 Sheff Univ BA 16. Yorks Min Course 13. **d** 16 **p** 17. NSM Baildon 16–17; NSM Calverley from 17. *54 Effingham Road, Harden, Bingley BD16 1LQ* E: sue.mcwhinney@gmail.com

McWHIRTER, James Angus. b 58. Portsm Poly BA 91 Trin Coll Carmarthen PGCE 93. St Steph Ho Ox 00. **d** 02 **p** 03. C Shifnal *Lich* 02–06; CF 07–18; Chapl RNR from 18. *29 Coniston Road, Edith Weston, Oakham LE15 8HP* E: revdjames.mcwh@btopenworld.com

McWHIRTER (née BELL), Canon Jennifer Kathryn. b 77. Harper Adams Univ Coll BSc 99. CITC BTh 04. **d** 04 **p** 05.

Asst Chapl R Gp of Hosps Health and Soc Services Trust 04–06; Asst Chapl Belfast City Hosp Health and Soc Services Trust 04–06; Chapl Belfast Health and Soc Care Trust 06–13; C Belfast St Anne *Conn* 04–06; C Belfast St Nic 06–08; I Templepatrick w Donegore 08–13; Bp's Dom Chapl 08–13; Dir CME Ch of Ireland Th Inst 13–16; Chapl Ch of Ireland Min to Deaf People from 13; P-in-c Killala w Dunfeeny, Crossmolina, Kilmoremoy etc *T, K & A* from 16; St Patr Cathl Dublin from 18. *St Michael's Rectory, Church Road, Ballina, Co Mayo, Republic of Ireland* T: (00353) (1) 499 7271 M: (00353) 85-877 8650 E: revjkmcwhirter@yahoo.co.uk

McWHIRTER, The Ven Stephen Joseph. b 64. Open Univ BA 02. St Jo Coll Nottm MTh 11. **d** 13. C Lisburn St Paul *Conn* 13–15; I Killala w Dunfeeny, Crossmolina, Kilmoremoy etc *T, K & A* from 15; Adn Killala and Achonry from 17; Adn Tuam from 18. *St Michael's Rectory, Church Road, Ballina, Co Mayo, Republic of Ireland* M: (00353) 85-877 8650 E: revsjmcwhirter@eircom.net

McWILLIAMS, Amelia. CITC. **d** 09 **p** 10. NSM Brackaville w Donaghendry and Ballyclog *Arm* 09–12; NSM Portadown St Mark from 12. *47 Alexander Avenue, Armagh BT61 7JD* T: (028) 3752 7456 E: amcwilliams861@btinternet.com

McWILLIAMS, Evan. *See* McWILLIAMS, Patrick Evan

McWILLIAMS, John Alan. b 46. Yorks Min Course 16. **d** 17. NSM S Holderness Deanery from 17. *5 Beechwood Views, Roos, Hull HU12 0HQ*

McWILLIAMS, Laura Jane. *See* HEWITT, Laura Jane

McWILLIAMS, Patrick Evan. b 86. Savannah Coll of Art and Design BFA 08 MA 09 York Univ PhD 16 St Jo Coll Dur BATM 18. Cranmer Hall Dur 15. **d** 18 **p** 19. C Spalding St Mary and St Nic *Linc* from 18. *6 Chambers Court, Spalding PE11 2QP* M: 07598-910722 E: evmcwil@gmail.com

MACY, Jonathan Edward Gordon. b 68. Oak Hill Th Coll BA 96 Heythrop Coll Lon MTh 98 K Coll Lon PhD 04. Wycliffe Hall Ox MTh 09. **d** 10 **p** 11. C Plumstead St Jo w St Jas and St Paul S'wark 10–14; TV Thamesmead from 14. *62-64 Battery Road, London SE28 0JT* T: (020) 8836 9069 M: 07910-988014 E: jegmacy@googlemail.com

MADDEN, Kenneth Usher. b 48. St Jo Coll Dur BA 70 Lon Inst of Educn PGCE 73. WEMTC 06. **d** 09 **p** 10. NSM Newent and Gorsley w Cliffords Mesne *Glouc* 09–13; NSM Bath St Mich Without *B & W* from 13; C Bath Abbey w St Jas from 18. *Odd Down Lodge, Upper Bloomfield Road, Bath BA2 2RU* T: (01225) 353071 M: 07894-208501 E: kenandlibby@virginmedia.com

MADDEN, Michael John. b 60. Lanc Univ BSc 81 Brunel Univ MBA 92 Open Univ MPhil 08 Lon Sch of Th MTh 12. St Mellitus Coll 17. **d** 19. NSM Hanborough and Freeland *Ox* from 19. *2 Hutchcombe Farm Close, Oxford OX2 9HG* T: (01865) 865743 M: 07768-450534 E: mmadden450@me.com

MADDISON, Simon Christopher. b 63. St Steph Ho Ox 10. **d** 12 **p** 13. C Salford The Alphage *Lon* 12–15; V Edmonton St Aldhelm 15–18; PtO from 19; V Cross Heath *Lich* from 19; V Newcastle St Paul from 19. *St Michael's Presbytery, Linden Grove, Newcastle ST5 9LJ* T: (01782) 614287 M: 07906-156932 E: fr.simon.ssc@outlook.com

MADDOCK, Claire Louise. *See* McCLELLAND, Claire Louise

MADDOCK, David John Newcomb. b 36. Qu Coll Cam BA 60 MA 64. Oak Hill Th Coll 60. **d** 62 **p** 63. C Bispham *Blackb* 62–65; R 82–93; RD Blackpool 90–93; Miss Payne Bay Canada 65–69; R Frobisher Bay 70; R Walsoken *Ely* 70–77; V Ore Ch Ch *Chich* 77–82; V Fowey *Truro* 93–02; Chapl Cornwall Healthcare NHS Trust 94–02; rtd 02; PtO *Chich* 14–19; *Blackb* from 19. *23 Fosbrooke House, 8 Clifton Drive, Lytham St Annes FY8 5RQ* E: david.maddock764@btinternet.com

MADDOCK, Nicholas Rokeby. b 47. ABSM 72 Birm Coll of Educn CertEd 73. Linc Th Coll 82. **d** 82 **p** 83. C Romford St Edw *Chelmsf* 82–87; V Sway *Win* 87–94; V Taunton St Mary *B & W* 94–04; R Wrington w Butcombe and Burrington 04–17; rtd 17; PtO *B & W* from 18. *3 Friary Close, Clevedon BS21 7QA* T: (01275) 870751 M: 07735-501659 E: nr.maddock@gmail.com

MADDOCK, Philip Arthur Louis. b 47. Open Univ BA 82 Lanc Univ MPhil 02. Oak Hill Th Coll 75. **d** 78 **p** 79. C New Ferry *Ches* 78–81; C Barnston 81–82; V Over St Jo 82–85; V Norley and Chapl to the Deaf 85–88; P-in-c Treales and Chapl to the Deaf *Blackb* 88–96; Chapl to the Deaf *Lich* 96–02; C Yoxall and The Ridwares and Kings Bromley 98–02; Adv for Deaf and Disabled People Min Div 03–12; rtd 13; NSM Alrewas and Wychnor *Lich* 03–13; PtO *Blackb* from 14. *35 Hampshire Crescent, Stoke-on-Trent ST3 4TR* E: pcmaddock@gmail.com

MADDOCK-LYON, John Frederick. b 38. K Coll Lon AKC 62 BD 64. **d** 64 **p** 65. C Woodchurch *Ches* 64–67; C Higher Bebington 67–70; V Sandbach Heath 70–80; V Egremont St Jo 80–88; Chapl Br Emb and Athens St Paul *Eur* 88–91;

rtd 99; PtO *Newc* from 05. *29 Robson's Way, Amble, Morpeth NE65 0GA* T: (01665) 711126 E: rivendel66@yahoo.co.uk

MADDOCKS, Alison Julie. b 63. Birm Univ BSc 84 Loughb Univ MBA 92. St Jo Coll Nottm MTh 03. **d** 03 **p** 04. C Wollaton *S'well* 03–06; Retail Chapl Birm City Cen 06–08; Ind Chapl *S'well* 08–11; C Nottingham All SS, St Mary and St Pet 08–11; P-in-c Breadsall *Derby* 11–17; Stewardship and Resources Officer *Worc* from 17. *The Old Palace, Deansway, Worcester WR1 2JE* T: (01905) 20537 E: amaddocks@cafe-worcestor.org.uk

MADDOX, Derek Adrian James. b 64. Kingston Poly BA 88. Trin Coll Bris 02. **d** 04 **p** 05. C Mitcham St Mark *S'wark* 04–07; P-in-c S Yardley St Mich *Birm* 07–08; V 08–13; P-in-c Withywood *Bris* from 13; P-in-c Bris St Andr Hartcliffe from 13. *St Oswald's Vicarage, Cheddar Grove, Bristol BS13 7EN* E: derekmaddox8@gmail.com

MADDOX, Hugh Inglis Monteath. b 37. CCC Cam BA 60. Westcott Ho Cam 61. **d** 63 **p** 64. C Attercliffe *Sheff* 63–66; C Maidstone All SS w St Phil *Cant* 66–67; C Folkestone St Mary and St Eanswythe 67–69; C St Martin-in-the-Fields *Lon* 69–73; R Sandwich *Cant* 73–81; V St Peter-in-Thanet 81–84; V Red Post *Sarum* 84–03; rtd 03; PtO *Sarum* from 03. *36 Corfe Road, Stoborough, Wareham BH20 5AD* T: (01929) 550872

MADDY, Kevin. b 58. Selw Coll Cam BA 83 MA 87 GRNCM 79 FRSA 96. Westcott Ho Cam 81. **d** 85 **p** 86. C St Peter-in-Thanet *Cant* 85–88; Chapl RAF 88–02; CF 02–07; Chapl Miss to Seafarers and R Yokohama Ch Ch 07–11; V Monk Bretton *Wakef* 11–14; *Leeds* 14; P-in-c Lundwood *Wakef* 11–14; *Leeds* 14; P-in-c Hackington *Cant* from 14; Chapl Abp's Sch Cant from 14; AD Cant from 17. *The Rectory, St Stephen's Green, Canterbury CT2 7JU* T: (01227) 477171 M: 07720-499403 E: revkmaddy@gmail.com

MADELEY, Mark Keith. b 68. AVCM 96. Oak Hill Th Coll BA 93. **d** 93 **p** 94. C Mickleover All SS *Derby* 93–96; C Charlesworth and Dinting Vale 96–99; Chapl Chr Tours (UK) Ltd 99–00; NSM Moldgreen and Rawthorpe *Wakef* 99–00; V Coley 00–11; R Weston-super-Mare St Nic w St Barn *B & W* from 12. *Uphill Rectory, 3 Old Church Road, Uphill, Weston-super-Mare BS23 4UH* T/F: (01934) 620156 M: 07947-159795 E: mark@mibtravel.co.uk

MADELEY, Timothy Philip. b 86. Derby Univ LLB 07 BPP Univ LLM 08. Ridley Hall Cam 13. **d** 16 **p** 17. C Bentham, Burton-in-Lonsdale, Chapel-le-Dale etc *Leeds* 16–19; V Bushmead *St Alb* from 19. *73 Hawkfields, Luton LU2 7NW* T: (01582) 487127 M: 07581-561042 E: timmadeley@icloud.com

MADGWICK, Mrs Philippa Jane. b 60. Magd Coll Ox BA 84 MA 88 DPhil 88 Anglia Ruskin Univ BA 09. SAOMC 04 ERMC 05. **d** 07 **p** 08. NSM St Alb St Steph 07–17; SSMs' Officer St Alb Adnry 14–17; R Empingham, Edith Weston, Lyndon, Manton etc *Pet* from 17. *19 Digby Drive, North Luffenham, Oakham LE15 8JS* T: (01780) 721286 E: rectorrwb@gmail.com

MADIN, Jacob Lloyd. b 92. Man Univ BA 14. Cranmer Hall Dur 14. **d** 16 **p** 17. C Walsall St Matt *Lich* 16–18; C York St Hilda from 18. *10 Cleveland Street, York YO24 4BS* M: 07403-271274

MADINDA, John Yohana. b 63. Ox Cen for Miss Studies MA 05. Lon Bible Coll BA 96. **d** 98 **p** 00. Lect St Phil Th Coll Tanzania 97–05; Prin 05–15; C Bunwell, Carleton Rode, Tibenham, Gt Moulton etc *Nor* 15–16; TV Long Stratton and Pilgrim TM from 16. *Old Church House, Chapel Road, Carleton Rode, Norwich NR16 1RN* T: (01953) 789240 M: 07486-352758 E: jymadinda@yahoo.com

MAFFEI, Andrea Jane. b 68. ERMC 16. **d** 18 **p** 19. C Flitwick *St Alb* from 18. *33 Shackleton Gardens, Flitwick, Bedford MK45 1GR* E: andrea@flitwickchurch.org

MAGEE, Keith Robert. b 60. Trin Coll Bris BA 95 Bris Univ PGCE 96. Westcott Ho Cam 99 Seabury-Western Th Sem 00. **d** 01 **p** 02. C S Woodham Ferrers *Chelmsf* 01–05; V Moulsham St Jo 05–12; V Knighton St Mary Magd *Leic* 12–16; V Braunstone Park from 16. *The Vicarage, Main Street, Leicester LE3 3AL* T: 0116-289 3377 M: 07766-645135 E: keith.magee@btinternet.com

MAGGS, Sophie Claire. *See* BANNISTER, Sophie Claire

MAGINNIS, Samuel Robert Henry. b 85. St Steph Ho Ox 17. **d** 19. C Loughton St Jo *Chelmsf* from 19. *12 The Greens Close, Loughton IG10 1QE* E: rev.smlt@gmail.com

MAGNESS, Anthony William John. b 37. New Coll Ox BA 62 MA 65 Ch Coll Liv PGCE 76. Coll of Resurr Mirfield 78. **d** 80 **p** 81. C Gt Crosby St Faith *Liv* 80–83; C Newc St Jo 83–85; P-in-c Newc St Luke 85–88; P-in-c Newc St Andr 88; V Newc St Andr and St Luke 89–99; Chapl Hunter's Moor Hosp 89–95; P-in-c Cambois *Newc* 99–00; C Sleekburn 99–00; V Cambois and Sleekburn 00–03; rtd 03; PtO *Newc* from 03. *59 Firtree Crescent, Newcastle upon Tyne NE12 7JU* T/F: 0191-268 4596

MAGNUSSON, Lisbet Maria. b 50. Mid-Sweden Univ BSc(Econ) 85 Uppsala Univ MDiv 93 ML 98. Past Inst Uppsala 93. **p** 94. In Ch of Sweden 94–98; C Crosby *Linc* 98–99; TV Gainsborough and Morton 99–04; P-in-c Swallow and Chapl Doncaster and S Humber Healthcare NHS Trust 04–06; Sweden from 06. *Haggkullevagen 26, 184 37 Akersberga, Stockholm, Sweden* T: (0046) (8) 5816 1478 *or* (0) 7 0340 3870 M: 70-638 9996 E: lisbet.magnusson@svenskakyrkan.se

MAGORRIAN, Brian Geoffrey. b 64. St Aid Coll Dur BSc 85 York Univ DPhil 89. St Jo Coll Nottm. **d** 01 **p** 02. C Bishopwearmouth St Gabr *Dur* 01–04; P-in-c Brough w Stainmore, Musgrave and Warcop *Carl* 04–10; C Whitfield *Derby* 10–14; V Walton St Jo 14–17. *41 New Hall Street, Macclesfield SK10 3AB* M: 07751-357194 E: brianmagorrian@tiscali.co.uk

✠**MAGOWAN, The Rt Revd Alistair James.** b 55. Leeds Univ BSc 77 Ox Univ MTh 02. Trin Coll Bris 78. **d** 81 **p** 82 **c** 09. C Owlerton *Sheff* 81–84; C Dur St Nic 84–89; Chapl St Aid Coll 85–89; V Egham *Guildf* 89–00; RD Runnymede 93–98; Adn Dorset *Sarum* 00–09; Can and Preb Sarum Cathl 00–09; Suff Bp Ludlow *Heref* from 09; Adn Ludlow from 09. *Bishop's House, Corvedale Road, Halford, Craven Arms SY7 9BT* T: (01588) 673571 E: alistair@bishopofludlow.co.uk

MAGOWAN, Harold Victor. b 34. QUB BA 55 BSc(Econ) 66 DipEd 69 ACII 69 FCII 73. TCD Div Sch Div Test 57. **d** 57 **p** 58. C Antrim All SS w Muckamore *Conn* 57–59. *6 Fold Mews, 22 Ballyholme Road, Bangor BT20 5JS* T: (028) 9146 5091

MAGOWAN, Ian Walter. b 51. St Paul's Coll Chelt CertEd 73 Ulster Poly BEd 82 TCD BTh 07. CITC 04. **d** 07 **p** 08. C Killowen *D & R* 07–10; I Connor w Antrim St Patr *Conn* from 10. *Connor Rectory, 50 Church Road, Kells, Ballymena BT42 3JU* T: (028) 2589 1254 M: 07810-636167 E: iwmagowan@hotmail.co.uk

MAGOWAN, Margaret Louise. b 57. SRN 77 SCM 80. WEMTC 11. **d** 14 **p** 15. NSM Church Stretton *Heref* from 14. *Bishop's House, Corvedale Road, Halford, Craven Arms SY7 9BT* T: (01588) 673810

MAGRATH, Richard David. b 84. Homerton Coll Cam BA 06 Jes Coll Cam BA 18. Ridley Hall Cam 16. **d** 19. C Finchley St Mary *Lon* from 19. *28 Hendon Lane, London N3 1TR* E: richard@richardmagrath.com

MAGUIRE, Alan. b 45. CBDTI 03. **d** 06 **p** 07. NSM Croglin and Holme Eden and Wetheral w Warwick *Carl* 06–09; NSM Carl H Trin and St Barn 09–12; P-in-c Lowther and Askham and Clifton and Brougham 12–17; rtd 17. *16 Harker Park Road, Harker Park, Carlisle CA6 4HS* T: (01228) 672891 E: alan.maguire2017@outlook.com

MAGUIRE, Canon Brian William. b 33. Hull Univ BTh 84 MA 88. Coll of Resurr Mirfield 70. **d** 72 **p** 73. C Guisborough *York* 72–76; TV Haxby w Wigginton 76–77; TR 78–89; V Huddersfield St Pet and All SS *Wakef* 89–00; Hon Can Wakef Cathl 94–00; rtd 00; PtO *Wakef* 00–14; *Leeds* 14–16; Bp's Dom Chapl *Wakef* 03–04; PtO *Lich* from 12. *33 Chapel Lane, Lichfield WS14 9BA* T: (01543) 305936 E: bwmaguire@virginmedia.com

MAGUIRE, Luke Karl. b 87. Warwick Univ BA 09 Leeds Univ BA 11. Coll of Resurr Mirfield 09. **d** 12 **p** 13. C Rochdale *Man* 12–13; C Salford All SS 13–15; P-in-c Stretford All SS 15–18; R from 18. *The Rectory, 233 Barton Road, Stretford, Manchester M32 9RB* T: 0161-865 1350 E: lukekarlmaguire@googlemail.com

MAGUIRE (formerly GRATTON), Canon Patricia Margaret. b 46. Leeds Univ BTh 94 MA 96 SRN 67 TCert 84 CertEd 88. EMMTC 89 NOC 96. **d** 97 **p** 98. NSM Shipley St Pet *Bradf* 97–99; C Brighouse and Clifton *Wakef* 99–00; Chapl Wakef Cathl Sch 00–05; P-in-c Lupset *Wakef* 05–11; P-in-c Thornes 00–11; RD Wakef 08–11; Hon Can Wakef Cathl 08–11; rtd 11; PtO *Lich* from 12. *33 Chapel Lane, Lichfield WS14 9BA* T: (01543) 305936 E: revmaguire@virginmedia.com

MAGUIRE, Sarah Alison. *See* EDMONDS, Sarah Alison

MAHER, David James. b 70. St Jo Coll Dur BA 01. Cranmer Hall Dur 98. **d** 01 **p** 02. C Hounslow H Trin w St Paul and St Mary *Lon* 01–04; C Staines 04–07; Chapl to Bp Kensington 04–07; V Chesterton Gd Shep *Ely* from 07; RD Cambridge N from 14. *The Good Shepherd Vicarage, 51 Highworth Avenue, Cambridge CB4 2BQ* T: (01223) 351844 *or* 312933 E: vicar@churchofthegoodshepherd.co.uk

MAHER, Capt Ian. b 58. Open Univ BA 97 MEd 01. CA Tr Coll 88 Yorks Min Course 11. **d** 12 **p** 13. Multifaith Chapl Co-ord Sheff Hallam Univ 06–18; rtd 18; Hon C Sheff Cathl 12–14; Min Can from 14. *3 Parsonage Street, Walkley, Sheffield S6 5BL* T: 0114-232 2330 *or* 225 4577 M: 07791-639820 E: ian.maher@sheffield.anglican.org

MAHILUM, Bello. b 60. **d** 10 **p** 11. NSM Notting Hill St Jo *Lon* 10–14; PtO 16–19; Chapl R Brompton and Harefield NHS Foundn Trust from 19. *5 Faith Court, Cooper's Road, London SE1 5HD* T: (020) 3731 7111 M: 07738-330861 E: blmahilum@gmail.com

MAHON, Stephanie Mary. *See* SOKOLOWSKI, Stephanie Mary

MAIDEN, Charles Alistair Kingsley. b 60. Trent Poly BSc 84. St Jo Coll Nottm LTh 88. **d** 89 **p** 90. C Porchester *S'well* 89–93; C Selston 93–96; P-in-c Huthwaite 96–11; V from 11. *The Vicarage, Blackwell Road, Huthwaite, Sutton-in-Ashfield   NG17 2QT   T: (01623)   555053* E: charliemaiden@hotmail.com

MAIDMENT, Ross James. b 90. Regent's Park Coll Ox BTh 15 Cardiff Univ MTh 17. St Padarn's Inst 16. **d** 17 **p** 18. C Rumney *Mon* from 17. *The Vicarage, Church Lane, Marshfield, Cardiff CF3 2UF* T: (01633) 680173 M: 07760-203078 E: rossjmaidment@gmail.com

MAIDMENT, Thomas John Louis. b 43. Lon Univ BSc 65. St Steph Ho Ox. **d** 67 **p** 68. C Westmr St Steph w St Jo *Lon* 67–73; P-in-c Twickenham Common H Trin 73–77; V 77–80; V Heston 80–98; V Bolton-le-Sands *Blackb* 98–08; P-in-c Tunstall w Melling and Leck 02–08; AD Tunstall 99–05; rtd 08; PtO *Blackb* from 08. *69 Aintree Road, Thornton-Cleveleys FY5 5HW* T: (01253) 829399 E: t.j.l.m@btinternet.com

MAIDSTONE, Archdeacon of. *See* TAYLOR, The Ven Stephen Ronald

MAIDSTONE, Suffragan Bishop. *See* THOMAS, The Rt Revd Roderick Charles Howell

MAIN, Clive Timothy. b 53. St Andr Univ MA 75 Cam Univ PGCE 76. Oak Hill Th Coll BA 94. **d** 96 **p** 97. C Alperton *Lon* 96–00; V Highbury New Park St Aug 00–12; TR Hackney Marsh from 12. *St Barnabas' Rectory, 111 Homerton High Street, London E9 6DL* T: (020) 8533 1156 E: clivemain@outlook.com

MAINES, Canon Trevor. b 40. Leeds Univ BSc 63. Ripon Hall Ox 63. **d** 65 **p** 66. C Speke All SS *Liv* 65–70; C Stevenage St Geo *St Alb* 70–73; V Dorridge *Birm* 73–78; Org Sec CECS Ex 79–80; Hon C Tiverton St Pet *Ex* 79–80; Org Sec (Wales) CECS 80–87; Hon C Newton Nottage *Llan* 81–83; PtO *Mon* 83–87; V Arlesey w Astwick *St Alb* 87–95; RD Shefford 91–95; V Goldington 95–05; RD Bedford 98–05; Hon Can St Alb 04–05; rtd 05; Hon C Beedon and Peasemore w W Ilsley and Farnborough *Ox* 05–07; Hon C Brightwalton w Catmore, Leckhampstead etc 05–07; PtO from 12. *1 Adlam Villas, Greenham Road, Newbury RG14 7HX* T: (01635) 551352 E: trevor.maines@ntlworld.com

MAINEY, Ian George. b 51. CertEd 73. Oak Hill Th Coll BA 87. **d** 87 **p** 88. C Denton Holme *Carl* 87–91; V Hensingham 91–02; RD Calder 01–02; TR Hackney Marsh *Man* 02–09; P-in-c Birkdale St Jas *Liv* 09–19; V from 19; P-in-c Birkdale St Pet from 09. *The Vicarage, 26 Lulworth Road, Southport PR8 2BQ* T: (01704) 566255 E: ian.mainey@gmail.com

MAINWARING (née LANKSHEAR), Canon Jane Frances. b 70. Leeds Univ BA 92 Trin Coll Carmarthen MPhil 97 PhD 99. EAMTC 98. **d** 00 **p** 01. C Sudbury and Chilton *St E* 00–03; TV Hitchin *St Alb* 03–16; TV Hitchin and St Paul's Walden from 16; RD Hitchin from 15; Hon Can St Alb from 19. *St Mark's Vicarage, St Mark's Close, Hitchin SG5 1UR* T: (01462) 434686 E: jane@stmarks-hitchin.org.uk

MAIRS, Canon Adrian Samuel. b 43. Oak Hill Th Coll 76. **d** 78 **p** 79. C Rugby St Matt *Cov* 78–82; P-in-c Mancetter 82–84; V 84–08; P-in-c Hartshill 97–01; Hon Can Cov Cathl 03–08; rtd 08; PtO *Blackb* from 14. *15 Salter Fell Road, Lancaster LA1 2PX* T: (01524) 382206 E: adrian.mairs@tesco.net

MAITLAND, The Hon Sydney Milivoje Patrick. b 51. Edin Univ BSc MRTPI. St Jo Coll Nottm. **d** 86 **p** 87. Hon C Glas St Geo 86–01; C Glas St Bride 03–11; P-in-c Glas All SS from 11. *14 Kersland Street, Glasgow G12 8BL* T: 0141-339 4573 E: sydneymaitland@btinternet.com

MAJOR, Richard James Edward. b 54. Trin Coll Bris 78. **d** 81 **p** 82. C Parr *Liv* 81–84; V Burton Fleming w Fordon *York* 84–85; V Grindale and Ergham 84–85; P-in-c Wold Newton 84–85; V Burton Fleming w Fordon, Grindale etc 85–91; V Bilton St Pet 91–15; R Woodhall Spa Gp *Linc* from 15. *The Vicarage, Alveston Avenue, Woodhall Spa LN10 6SN* E: revrichardmajor@gmail.com

MAJOR, Richard John Charles. b 63. Massey Univ (NZ) BA 85 Ex Coll Ox BA 91 MA 93 Magd Coll Ox DPhil 91. St Steph Ho Ox 92. **d** 94 **p** 95. C Truro Cathl 94–97; C Putney St Mary *S'wark* 97–98; Chapl Florence w Siena *Eur* 98–01; USA from 01. *Nansough Manor, Ladock, Truro TR2 4PB* T: (01726) 883315 *or* (001) (718) 442 1589 F: (718) 442 4555 E: email@richardmajor.com

MAK, Marcus Andreas. b 81. Ox Brookes Univ BA 10 St Jo Coll Dur BA 15. Cranmer Hall Dur 13. **d** 15 **p** 16. C N Poole

Ecum Team *Sarum* 15–16; C Creekmoor 17–19; V Felixstowe Ch Ch *St E* from 19. *Address temp unknown* M: 07978-588524 E: revmmak@gmail.com

MAKANJUOLA, Mrs Olufolake Oluyomi. b 60. New England Coll BA 84. St Aug Coll of Th 15. **d** 17 **p** 18. C Roch from 17. *5 The Street, Upper Halling, Rochester ME2 1HT* T: (01634) 243814 M: 07714-770769 E: lekkipen@gmail.com

MAKEL, Arthur. b 39. AKC 63. **d** 64 **p** 65. C Beamish *Dur* 64–68; Ind Chapl *York* 68–72; Ind Chapl and P-in-c Scotton w Northorpe *Linc* 72–81; R Epworth 81–89; P-in-c Wroot 81–89; R Epworth and Wroot 89–92; R Sigglesthorne and Rise w Nunkeeling and Bewholme *York* 92–04; P-in-c Aldbrough, Mappleton w Goxhill and Withernwick 98–04; rtd 04; PtO *York* 04–11. *43 Lowfield Road, Beverley HU17 9RF* T: (01482) 865798 E: arthur-makel@makelhouse.karoo.co.uk

MAKEPEACE, David Norman Harry. b 51. Magd Coll Ox BA 74. Trin Coll Bris 83. **d** 85 **p** 86. C Romford Gd Shep *Chelmsf* 85–88; Tanzania 88–89; C York St Paul 89–91; TV Radipole and Melcombe Regis *Sarum* 91–98; V Sandgate St Paul w Folkestone St Geo *Cant* 98–00; PtO from 01. *Flat 1, 33 Augusta Gardens, Folkestone CT20 2RT* T: (01303) 259342 E: dmakepeace51@gmail.com

MAKEPEACE, Preb James Dugard. b 40. Keble Coll Ox BA 63 MA 67. Cuddesdon Coll 63. **d** 65 **p** 66. C Cullercoats St Geo *Newc* 65–68; Lib Pusey Ho and Chapl Wadh Coll Ox 68–72; V Romford St Edw *Chelmsf* 72–79; V Tettenhall Regis *Lich* 79–80; TR 80–99; RD Trysull 87–97; Preb Lich Cathl 96–99; rtd 00; PtO *Lich* from 00; *Worc* from 17. *3 Shaw Lane, Albrighton, Wolverhampton WV7 3DS* T: (01902) 375472 E: jamesdugard@hotmail.com

✠**MAKHULU, The Most Revd Walter Paul Khotso.** b 35. Kent Univ Hon DD 88 Gen Th Sem NY Hon DD 99. St Pet Rosettenville Selly Oak Coll. **d** 57 **p** 58 **c** 79. S Africa 57–61; Bechuanaland 61–63; C Poplar All SS w St Frideswide *Lon* 64–66; C Pentonville St Silas w Barnsbury St Clem 66–68; V Battersea St Phil *S'wark* 68–72; V Battersea St Phil w St Bart 72–75; Bp Botswana 79–00; Abp Cen Africa 80–00; rtd 00; Hon Asst Bp Lon from 03. *16 Downside, 8-10 St John's Avenue, London SW15 2AE* T: (020) 8704 1220 E: makhulu@btinternet.com

MAKIN, Miss Pauline. b 45. Cranmer Hall Dur 75. **dss** 78 **d** 87 **p** 94. Ashton-in-Makerfield St Thos *Liv* 78–89; Par Dn 87–89; Par Dn Rainford 89–94; C 94–95; C Farnworth 95–10; Asst Dioc Chapl to the Deaf 89–10; rtd 10; PtO *Liv* from 16. *50 Farm Meadow Road, Orrell, Wigan WN5 8TE* T: (01695) 624995 E: paulinemakin@aol.com

MAKIN, Susan. b 65. **d** 13 **p** 14. NSM Hoxton St Anne w St Columba *Lon* 13–14; C St John-at-Hackney 14–17; V Hackney Wick St Mary of Eton w St Aug from 17. *The Vicarage, 95 Eastway, London E9 5JA* T: (020) 7018 2904 M: 07949-532978 E: sue.makin@london.anglican.org

MÄKIPÄÄ, Tuomas. b 78. Helsinki Univ 97. **d** 05 **p** 10. C Helsinki *Eur* 05–12; Chapl from 12. *Brysselinkatu 6 D 70, 00550 Helsinki, Finland* T: (00358) (50) 309 9132 E: tuomas.makipaa@anglican.fi

MAKOWER, Canon Malory. b 38. TCD BA 61 MA 68 St Jo Coll Ox MA 64 DPhil 64. Ridley Hall Cam 64. **d** 66 **p** 67. C Onslow Square St Paul *Lon* 66–69; Tutor Ridley Hall Cam 69–71; Sen Tutor 71–76; P-in-c Lode and Longmeadow *Ely* 76–84; Warden EAMTC 77–79; Prin 79–84; Dir of Post-Ord Tr for NSM *Nor* 84–90; C Gt Yarmouth 84–89; TV 89–95; Dioc NSM Officer 88–95; Hon Can Nor Cathl 94–97; Prin LNSM Tr Scheme 94–97; rtd 97; PtO *Nor* from 98. *114 Yarmouth Road, Lowestoft NR32 4AQ* T: (01502) 574769 E: m.makower@outlook.com

MAKUMBE, Tendai Puwai. b 72. Birm City Univ BSc 14. Bp Gaul Th Coll Harare 98. **d** 00 **p** 01. C Bonda Miss Zimbabwe 00–02; PtO *Birm* from 15. *30 Spring Road, Edgbaston,   Birmingham   B15 2HA   M: 07737-466697* E: t.papaya@yahoo.com

MALAM, Susan Mary. b 70. St Mellitus Coll BA 14. **d** 14 **p** 15. NSM Witham and Villages *Chelmsf* from 14; Chapl Mid-Essex Hosp Services NHS Trust from 18. *15 Ramsey Road, Halstead CO9 1EL* T: (01245) 515244 E: sue.malam18@gmail.com

MALAN, Victor Christian de Roubaix. b 39. Cape Town Univ BA 60 Linacre Coll Ox BA 63 MA 68. Wycliffe Hall Ox 61. **d** 63 **p** 64. C Springfield *Birm* 63–66; P-in-c 66–67; C New Windsor *Ox* 67–69; Chapl St Jo Coll Cam 69–74; V Northampton All SS w St Kath *Pet* 74–86; V Stockport St Geo *Ches* 86–89; R N Mundham w Hunston and Merston *Chich* 89–06; rtd 06; PtO *Cant* 07–15; *Chich* from 16. *2 The Hermitage, North Mundham, Chichester PO20 1LE* T: (01243) 781054

MALAY, Prof Jessica Lin. b 61. St Martin's Univ Washington (USA) BA 85 Warwick Univ MA 89 Kent Univ PhD 04 Dur Univ MA 18. St Hild Coll 15. **d** 18 **p** 19. NSM Almondbury w Farnley Tyas *Leeds* from 18. *88 Long Lane, Honley, Holmfirth HD9 6EB* T: (01484) 300963 M: 07541-941208 E: jlmalay@gmail.com *or* jessica.malay@leeds.anglican.org

MALBON, Canon John Allin. b 36. Oak Hill Th Coll 62. **d** 65 **p** 66. C Wolverhampton St Jude *Lich* 65–68; C Hoole *Ches* 68–71; P-in-c Crewe Ch Ch 71–75; V 75–79; V Plemstall w Guilden Sutton 79–01; Hon Can Ches Cathl 96–01; rtd 01; PtO *Ches* from 02. *22 Hawksey Drive, Nantwich CW5 7GF* T: (01270) 611584 E: janjon@hotmail.com

MALCOLM, Andrew Alexander. b 55. Open Univ BA 99 Leic Univ MSc 99 Leeds Univ BA 08 Man Metrop Univ MRes 11. NOC 05. **d** 08 **p** 09. NSM Salesbury *Blackb* 08–15; V Langho Billington 12–15; PtO from 15; *Ches* from 16. *32 Main Road, Higher Kinnerton, Chester CH4 9AJ* T: (01244) 661549 M: 07957-846428 E: andrew.malcolm34@btinternet.com

MALCOLM, Mercia Alana. *See* FLANAGAN, Mercia Alana

MALE, Canon David Edward. b 62. Southn Univ BA 83 St Jo Coll Dur BA 90. Cranmer Hall Dur 88. **d** 91 **p** 92. C Leic St Chris 91–94; C Kirkheaton *Wakef* 94–98; P Missr Huddersfield 99–06; Dioc Fresh Expressions Adv *Ely* 06–15; Tutor Ridley Hall Cam 06–15; Nat Adv for Pioneer Development Abps' Coun 15–18; Dir Evang and Discipleship from 18; Hon Can Ely Cathl from 14. *Church House, Great Smith Street, London SW1P 3AZ* T: (020) 7898 1398 M: 07469-855260 E: dave.male@churchofengland.org

MALEK, Mark Mayool. b 44. Khartoum Univ BSc 69 Salford Univ BSc 76 Bradf Coll of Educn PGCE 93. **d** 03 **p** 04. NSM Horton *Bradf* 03–04; NSM Bradf St Oswald Chapel Green 03–04; NSM Lt Horton 04–14; *Leeds* from 14. *26 Martlett Drive, Bradford BD5 8QG* T: (01274) 732712

MALES, Jeanne Margaret. b 49. Reading Univ BA 71 Lon Univ MPhil 73 Surrey Univ PhD 86 AFBPsS 75 CPsychol 88. S'wark Ord Course 93. **d** 96 **p** 97. NSM Caterham *S'wark* 96–00; C Addington 00–03; V 03–15; rtd 15; PtO *S'wark* from 15; *Cant* from 16. *Collingwood House, 53 High Street, Sandwich CT13 9EG* T: (01304) 275027 E: revjeanne2@gmail.com

MALINS, Mrs Judith. b 47. Bris Univ BA 69. STETS 97. **d** 00 **p** 01. NSM Wilton w Netherhampton and Fugglestone *Sarum* 00–04; P-in-c Kingston, Langton Matravers and Worth Matravers 04–10; P-in-c Wrington w Butcombe and Burrington *B & W* 10–12; rtd 12; PtO *B & W* from 12. *87 Knightcott Road, Banwell BS29 6HR* T: (01934) 824162 E: judith.malins@btinternet.com

MALKIN, Thomas Ross. Hertf Coll Ox BA 86. Trin Coll Bris BA 98 MPhil 00. **d** 99 **p** 00. C Old Trafford St Bride *Man* 99–03; P-in-c Firswood and Gorse Hill 03–10; R from 10. *The Rectory, 24 Canute Road, Stretford, Manchester M32 0RJ* T: 0161-865 1802

MALKINSON, Canon Christopher Mark. b 47. Chich Th Coll 84. **d** 86 **p** 87. C Stroud and Uplands w Slad *Glouc* 86–89; V Cam w Stinchcombe 89–00; P-in-c Tywardreath w Tregaminion *Truro* 00–02; P-in-c St Sampson 00–02; V Padstow 02–17; P-in-c St Merryn and St Issey w St Petroc Minor 16–17; R Padstow, St Merryn and St Issey w St Petroc Minor 17; RD Pydar 03–13; Hon Can Truro Cathl 07–17; rtd 17; Chapl Miss to Seafarers from 00. *101 Summercourt Way, Brixham TQ5 0RB* E: chrismalk@hotmail.com

MALKINSON, Michael Stephen. b 43. St Steph Ho Ox 65. **d** 68 **p** 69. C New Addington *Cant* 68–71; C Blackpool St Steph *Blackb* 71–74; V Wainfleet St Mary *Linc* 74–81; R Wainfleet All SS w St Thos 74–81; P-in-c Croft 80–81; V Lund *Blackb* 81–93; V Heyhouses on Sea 93–00; R Bamber Bridge Chich 00–09; P-in-c Staplefield Common 00–03; rtd 09; PtO *Worc* from 10. *8 Haines Avenue, Wyre Piddle, Pershore WR10 2RQ* T: (01386) 556102 E: malkinson@msn.com

MALLAS, Mrs Wendy Norris. b 42. Reading Univ MA 91 Cov Coll of Educn CertEd 63. STETS 00. **d** 03 **p** 04. NSM Liss *Portsm* 03–07; NSM Blackmoor and Whitehill 07–12; PtO 12–15; NSM Bordon *Guildf* 07–19; PtO *Portsm* from 19. *Mayfield, 45 Hogmoor Road, Whitehill, Bordon GU35 9ET* T: (01420) 478883 E: wendy.mallas@gmail.com *or* wendy.mallas@mayfieldjays.co.uk

MALLETT, John Christopher. b 44. EAMTC. **d** 82 **p** 83. NSM Hethersett w Canteloff *Nor* 82–85; NSM Hethersett w Canteloff w Lt and Gt Melton 85–90; Chapl Wayland Hosp Norfolk 88–94; Chapl Norwich Community Health Partnership NHS Trust 94–00; PtO *Nor* 00–03; NSM Hethersett w Canteloff w Lt and Gt Melton 03–10; rtd 10; PtO *Nor* from 10. *2 Bailey Close, Hethersett, Norwich NR9 3EU* T: (01603) 811010 E: christophersheila@tiscali.co.uk

MALLETT, Canon Marlene Rosemarie. b 59. Sussex Univ BA 81 Warwick Univ PhD 94. SEITE 01. **d** 04 **p** 05. C Brixton Road Ch Ch *S'wark* 04–07; P-in-c Angell Town St Jo 07–13; V from 13; Dir Ords Kingston Area from 13; Dioc Public Policy Adv from 15; Hon Can S'wark Cathl from 13. *St John's*

Vicarage, 49 Wiltshire Road, London SW9 7NE T: (020) 7733 0585 E: rosemarie.mallett@gmail.com

MALLINSON, Peter Albert. b 57. St Jo Coll Nottm 06 BA(ThM) 12. **d** 08 **p** 09. NSM Allestree St Edm and Darley Abbey *Derby* 08–12; TV Canvey Is *Chelmsf* 12–17; V Bury w Houghton and Coldwaltham and Hardham *Chich* from 17. *The Vicarage, Church Lane, Bury, Pulborough RH20 1PB* T: (01798) 839057 E: peter6hq@btinternet.com *or* vicar@arunchurches.com

MALLINSON, Canon Ralph Edward. b 40. Oriel Coll Ox BA 63 MA 66. St Steph Ho Ox 63. **d** 66 **p** 67. C Bolton St Pet *Man* 66–68; C Elton All SS 68–72; V Bury St Thos 72–76; V Bury Ch King 76–81; P-in-c Goodshaw 81–82; V 82–84; V Goodshaw and Crawshawbooth 84–93; AD Rossendale 83–93; V Unsworth 93–06; Hon Can Man Cathl 92–06; Vice Prin Dioc OLM Scheme 98–06; rtd 06; PtO *Man* from 06. *18 Woodgate Avenue, Bury BL9 7RU* T: 0161-797 2006 E: ralphmallinsonis@gmail.com

MALLON, Allister. b 61. Sheff Univ BA 83 TCD BTh 89 MA. CITC. **d** 87 **p** 88. C Ballymoney w Finvoy and Rasharkin *Conn* 87–90; C Belfast St Mary w H Redeemer 90–92; Bp's C Belfast St Mary Magd 92–00; Bp's C Stoneyford 00–11; Chapl R Gp of Hosps Health and Soc Services Trust 00–11; rtd 11. *64 Magheralave Meadows, Lisburn BT28 3NT* M: 07719-833034 E: bigal@talk21.com *or* allistersanna@gmail.com

MALMESBURY, Archdeacon of. *See* BRYAN, The Ven Christopher Paul

MALONE, Richard Patrick. b 66. Wycliffe Hall Ox BTh 03. **d** 03 **p** 04. C Fulham Ch Ch *Lon* 03–06; C Battersea St Pet and St Paul *S'wark* 06–12; P-in-c from 12. *The Vicarage, 43 Fowler Close, London SW11 2ES* T: (020) 7738 9943 M: 07973-104941

MALONEY, Ms Fiona Elizabeth. b 60. Bradf Univ BSc 82 St Jo Coll Dur BA 91. NOC 91. **d** 92 **p** 94. Par Dn Castleton Moor *Man* 92–94; C 94–96; C Pendlebury St Jo 96–99; C Fatfield *Dur* 99–03; NSM Harrow Trin St Mich *Lon* 03–05; NSM Wealdstone H Trin from 05. *The Vicarage, 39 Rusland Park Road, Harrow HA1 1UN* T: (020) 8863 5844 *or* 8863 6131 E: fiona@cofe.org.uk

MALONEY, Terence Mark. b 63. York Univ BSc 84 Dur Univ MA 09. Cranmer Hall Dur 88. **d** 91 **p** 92. C Blackley St Andr *Man* 91–96; P-in-c Pendlebury St Jo 96–99; P-in-c Fatfield *Dur* 99–03; P-in-c Harrow Trin St Mich *Lon* 03–05; V Wealdstone H Trin from 05. *The Vicarage, 39 Rusland Park Road, Harrow HA1 1UN* T: (020) 8863 5844 *or* 8863 6131 E: mark@cofe.org.uk

MALTBY, Canon Geoffrey. b 38. Leeds Univ BA 62. Wells Th Coll 68. **d** 70 **p** 71. C Mansfield St Mark *S'well* 70–73; V Skegby 73–78; V Carrington 78–87; C Rainworth 87–90; Chapl for People w Learning Disability (Mental Handicap) 90–03; Hon Can S'well Minster 99–03; rtd 03; PtO *S'well* from 03. *18 Beverley Close, Rainworth, Mansfield NG21 0LW* T: (01623) 474452

MALTBY, Canon Judith Diane. b 57. Univ of Illinois BA 79 Newnham Coll Cam PhD 92 FRHistS 99. S Dios Minl Tr Scheme 89. **d** 92 **p** 94. Tutor Sarum & Wells Th Coll 87–93; Hon Par Dn Wilton w Netherhampton and Fugglestone *Sarum* 92–93; Chapl and Fell CCC Ox from 93; Reader Ch Hist Ox Univ from 04; Can Th Leic Cathl from 04; Hon Can Ch Ch *Ox* from 06; Can Th Win Cathl 11–18. *Corpus Christi College, Oxford OX1 4JF* T: (01865) 276722 E: judith.maltby@ccc.ox.ac.uk

MALTON, William Peter Antony. b 33. K Coll Lon AKC 56. **d** 57 **p** 58. C N Hammersmith St Kath *Lon* 57–60; C-in-c Blackbird Leys CD *Ox* 60–65; R Pitsford *Pet* 65–66; Canada from 66; rtd 93. *97 Queen Street, PO Box 1433, Digby NS B0V 1A0, Canada* E: wnmurch@btinternet.com

MAMBU, Kutukenda Jules. b 64. Man Metrop Univ BA 08. **d** 92 **p** 94. C Prestwich St Mary *Man* 16; C Ashton 16–18; P-in-c Denton St Lawr from 18; C Haughton St Anne from 18. *131 Town Lane, Denton, Manchester M34 2DJ* M: 07897-697503 E: mambujules@hotmail.com

MAN, Archdeacon of the Isle of. *See* BROWN, The Ven Andrew

MANCHESTER, Canon John Charles. b 45. Lon Univ BD 69. ALCD 68. **d** 69 **p** 70. C Scarborough St Martin *York* 69–73; C Selby Abbey 73–76; P-in-c Old Malton 76–79; V 79–10; RD Bulmer and Malton 85–91; Can and Preb York Minster 05–10; rtd 10; PtO *York* from 10. *18 Castle Howard Road, Malton YO17 7AY* T: (01653) 690671 E: johncmanchester@gmail.com

MANCHESTER, Archdeacon of. *See* LUND, The Ven Karen Belinda

MANCHESTER, Bishop of. *See* WALKER, The Rt Revd David Stuart

MANCHESTER, Dean of. *See* GOVENDER, The Very Revd Rogers Morgan

MANCO, Gwenda Diane. b 54. NOC 97. **d** 99 **p** 00. NSM Rochdale *Man* 99–02; NSM Dearnley 02–04; Asst Chapl HM Pris Buckley Hall 99–03; Chapl HM Pris Styal 03; NSM Spotland *Man* 04–06; NSM Dearnley 06–13; NSM Littleborough 13–14. *5 Stansfield Hall, Littleborough OL15 9RH* T: (01706) 370264 M: 07966-217252 E: gwenda.manco@tesco.net

MANDER, Patricia Margaret. b 51. **d** 13 **p** 14. OLM Haddenham w Cuddington, Kingsey etc *Ox* 13–16; NSM Wychert Vale 16 and from 19; PtO 16–19. *7 Stockwell Furlong, Haddenham, Aylesbury HP17 8HD* T: (01844) 290985

MANDER, Peter John. b 52. Liv Univ BEd 75 Anglia Ruskin Univ MA 09. Sarum & Wells Th Coll 85. **d** 87 **p** 88. C Hale and Ashley *Ches* 87–90; TV Grantham *Linc* 90–00; P-in-c Quarrington w Old Sleaford 00–08; P-in-c Silk Willoughby 00–08; RD Lafford 03–07; Can and Preb Linc Cathl 05–08; R Ellon *Ab* 08–15; R Cruden Bay 08–15; TV N Tyne and Redesdale *Newc* 15–18; rtd 18; PtO *Newc* from 18. *181 Gloster Park, Amble, Morpeth NE65 0HQ* M: 07929-140425 E: peter.mander@gmail.com

MANDER, Canon Thomas Leonard Frederick. b 33. Roch Th Coll 59 Ely Th Coll 60. **d** 62 **p** 63. C Cov St Mary 62–66; V Bishop's Tachbrook 66–70; V Earlsdon 70–76; V Chesterton 76–83; R Lighthorne 76–83; V Newbold Pacey w Moreton Morrell 76–83; Hon Can Cov Cathl 80–92; P-in-c S Leamington St Jo 83–84; V 84–92; rtd 92; PtO *Cov* 92–15. *59 Murcott Road East, Whitnash, Leamington Spa CV31 2JJ* T: (01926) 339950

MANDERSON, Robert Dunlop (Leslie). b 35. LDS 59 FDS 65. Ox Min Course 92. **d** 94 **p** 95. NSM Maidenhead St Andr and St Mary *Ox* 94–00; PtO 00–02; NSM Chipping Norton 02–03; rtd 03; PtO *Ox* 03–04; *Ely* from 04. *14 Nursery Walk, Cambridge CB4 3PR* T: (01954) 782388 E: lesmanderson@gmail.com

MANHOOD, Phyllis. *See* DELVES, Phyllis

MANLEY, Mrs Gillian. b 59. St Martin's Coll Lanc BEd 80. St Jo Coll Nottm MA 00. **d** 00 **p** 01. C Eckington and Ridgeway *Derby* 00–04; TV Wirksworth 04–09; V Blackwell w Tibshelf from 09; C Pinxton from 14; RD Alfreton 16–18; AD Hardwick from 18. *The Vicarage, 67 High Street, Tibshelf, Alfreton DE55 5NU* T: (01773) 873305

MANLEY, Mrs Jane Elizabeth. b 58. Ox Min Course 05. **d** 08 **p** 09. C Bracknell *Ox* 08–11; C Crowthorne 11–12; V Ruislip Manor St Paul *Lon* 12–18; Dean of Women's Min Willesden Area 13–18; R Aldermaston and Woolhampton *Ox* from 18. *The Rectory, Wasing Lane, Aldermaston, Reading RG7 4LX* M: 07711-613057 E: jane.e.manley@btinternet.com

MANLEY, Canon Michael Alan. b 60. SS Hild & Bede Coll Dur BA 82. Trin Coll Bris. **d** 86 **p** 87. C Accrington St Jo w Huncoat *Blackb* 86–90; V Preston St Luke and St Oswald 90–96; V Blackpool St Jo 96–07; Can Res Carl Cathl from 07; RD Carl 10–16. *1 The Abbey, Carlisle CA3 8TZ* T: (01228) 542790 E: canonmissioner@carlislecathedral.org.uk

MANLEY, Pamela Mary. b 54. All SS Cen for Miss & Min 15. **d** 17 **p** 18. OLM Hope St Jas and Pendlebury St Jo *Man* from 17. *7 Hamilton Close, Prestwich, Manchester M25 9JS*

MANLEY (née McCARTHY), Canon Sandra Ellen. b 56. Man Univ MusB 77 Goldsmiths' Coll Lon PGCE 79 ARCM 75 FRCO 77 GRNCM 78. Aston Tr Scheme 86. **d** 95 **p** 96. C Beckenham St Geo *Roch* 95–99; V Heybridge w Langford *Chelmsf* 99–06; R Creeksea w Althorne, Latchingdon and N Fambridge 06–09; P-in-c Purleigh, Cold Norton and Stow Maries 08–09; V Althorne and Latchingdon w N Fambridge 09–16; V Cold Norton w Stow Maries from 09; RD Maldon and Dengie 11–17; Hon Can Chelmsf Cathl from 15. *The Vicarage, Fambridge Road, Althorne, Chelmsf CM3 6BZ* T: (01621) 742947 M: 07777-673096 E: sandra.manley@btinternet.com

MANLEY-COOPER, Simon James. b 46. S Dios Minl Tr Scheme 91. **d** 94 **p** 95. NSM Soho St Anne w St Thos and St Pet *Lon* 94–96; Ind Chapl 94–96; P-in-c Bedford St Mich *St Alb* 96–01; Ind Chapl 96–01; R Bramfield, Stapleford, Waterford etc 01–02; Chapl E and N Herts NHS Trust 03–11; rtd 11; PtO *St Alb* from 11. *19 Barnfield Road, Harpenden AL5 5TH* T: (01582) 460797 E: manleyc35@gmail.com

MANN, Alexandrina Elizabeth. b 67. Westmr Coll Ox BA 92 PGCE 93 Birm Univ MA 95 FGA 90. Trin Coll Bris 01. **d** 03 **p** 04. C Austrey and Warton *Birm* 03–06; V Hanbury, Newborough, Rangemore and Tutbury *Lich* 06–13; C Branston 13; C Cannock and Huntington from 13. *18 Queen Street, Cannock WS11 1AE* T: (01543) 577846 M: 07761-263849 E: alexandrina.shalom@virgin.net

MANN, Canon Charmion Anne Montgomery. b 36. Liv Univ BA 57 CertEd 62 AdDipEd 79 Univ of Wales (Lamp)

MA 06. Trin Coll Bris 80. **dss** 82 **d** 87 **p** 94. Bris St Nath w St Kath 82–84; Bris St Matt and St Nath 84–85; Asst Chapl Bris City Hosp 85–88; Chapl Bris Maternity Hosp 88–94; Chapl Bris R Hosp for Sick Children 88–94; Chapl Bris R Infirmary 88–94; Hon Can Bris Cathl 93–00; P-in-c Lacock w Bowden Hill 94–00; C Gtr Corsham 97–00; rtd 00; PtO *Bris* 00–06; *Sarum* 01–06; *Ex* from 07. *1 Gracey Court, Woodland Road, Broadclyst, Exeter EX5 3GA* T: (01392) 461451 E: charmion.mann@gmail.com

MANN, Christopher John. b 57. Glas Univ BSc 79. Westcott Ho Cam 83. **d** 86 **p** 87. C Worc SE 86–89; Min Can and Sacr St Paul's Cathl *Lon* 89–96; R Upminster *Chelmsf* 96–06; Chapl to Bp Bradwell 06–10; C Corringham 07–10; P-in-c Christchurch *Win* 10–14; Chapl Al Ain UAE 15–16; P-in-c Shenfield *Chelmsf* from 16. *The Rectory, 41 Worrin Road, Shenfield, Brentwood CM15 8DH* T: (01277) 220360 M: 07931-116897 E: fatherchris@domus.org.uk

MANN, David. b 57. St Jo Coll Dur BA 78. Ridley Hall Cam. **d** 82 **p** 83. C Monkwearmouth St Andr *Dur* 82–86; Chapl Sheff Cathl 86–87; C Leeds St Geo *Ripon* 87–94; V Ripon H Trin 94–06; Asst Dir of Ords 02–06; Nat Adv for Pre-Th Educn and Selection Sec Min Division 06–09; Dioc Voc Adv *York* from 09. *64 Strensall Road, Huntington, York YO32 9SH* T: (01904) 768668 E: david.mann@yorkdiocese.org

MANN, Ivan John. b 52. Brunel Univ BTech 74 Southn Univ BTh 80. Sarum & Wells Th Coll 75. **d** 78 **p** 79. C Hadleigh w Layham and Shelley *St E* 78–81; C Whitton and Thurleston w Akenham 81–83; V Leiston 83–86; PtO 86–89; R Aldringham w Thorpe, Knodishall w Buxlow etc 89–93; V Ipswich St Jo 93–96; Chapl St Mary's Convent Wantage 96–00; Asst Chapl R Berks and Battle Hosps NHS Trust 00; TV Gt Yarmouth *Nor* 00–03; Team Member Loyola Hall Jesuit Spirituality Cen Prescot 03–04; Prec and Hon Can Cumbrae *Arg* 04–06; Can St Jo Cathl Oban 04–06; rtd 06. *140 Somerleyton Gardens, Norwich NR2 2BS* T: (01603) 929591 E: ivan@ivanmann.f2s.com

MANN, Mrs Joan. b 40. **d** 98. NSM Eastbourne St Mary *Chich* 98–02; NSM The Hydneye 02–10; NSM Hampden Park and The Hydnye from 10. *39 Cherry Garden Road, Eastbourne BN20 8HF* T: (01323) 728259 E: joan.mann@hotmail.co.uk

MANN, John Owen. b 55. QUB BD 77 MTh 86 MPhil 98 Ulster Univ Hon DLitt 18. CITC 79. **d** 79 **p** 81. C Cloughfern *Conn* 79–82; C Knock *D & D* 82–85; I Ballyrashane w Kildollagh *Conn* 85–89; R Bentworth and Shalden and Lasham *Win* 89–93; RD Alton 92–93; I Cloughfern *Conn* 93–02; I Belfast Malone St Jo 02–11; Dean Belf 11–17; I Belfast St Anne *Conn* 11–17; Preb Clonmethan St Patr Cathl Dublin 99–17; TR Swanage and Studland *Sarum* from 17. *The Rectory, 12 Church Hill, Swanage BH19 1HU* T: (01929) 422916

MANN, Julia Corinne. b 52. Open Univ BA 92 Anglia Poly Univ BA 03 RGN 91. **d** 08 **p** 09. OLM Bury St Edmunds All SS w St Jo and St Geo *St E* 08–13; NSM from 13; NSM Lark Valley 14–19; NSM Lark Valley and N Bury from 19. *Orchard House, 13 Orchard Street, Bury St Edmunds IP33 1EH* T: (01284) 753984 E: jc.mann@btinternet.com

MANN, Julian Farrer Edgar. b 64. Peterho Cam MA 90. Oak Hill Th Coll BA 93. **d** 96 **p** 97. C Hoole *Ches* 96–00; V Oughtibridge *Sheff* from 00. *The Vicarage, Church Street, Oughtibridge, Sheffield S35 0FU* T: 0114-286 2317

MANN, Nicola Antoinette. b 70. Man Univ BA 92. SEITE 12. **d** 14 **p** 15. C Stamford All SS w St Jo *Linc* 14–17; P-in-c Raddesley Gp *Ely* from 17. *The Vicarage, 23 Stetchworth Road, Dullingham, Newmarket CB8 9UJ* T: (01638) 507980 M: 07738-266057 E: nikkimann40@hotmail.co.uk

MANN, Mrs Patricia Ann. b 62. STETS 08. **d** 11 **p** 12. C Havant *Portsm* 11–15; Chapl RN Coll Greenwich from 15; C Greenwich St Alfege *S'wark* from 15. *39 Burney Street, London SE10 8EX* T: (020) 8269 4750 M: 07890-304670 E: patmann17@yahoo.co.uk *or* pmann@ornc.org

MANN, Paul William. b 63. Leeds Univ BSc 84 CEng MIET. EAMTC 01. **d** 04 **p** 05. NSM Lawford *Chelmsf* 04–17; PtO 17–18; NSM Wormingford, Mt Bures and Lt Horkesley from 18; NSM Colchester St Mich Myland from 18; NSM Colchester St Luke from 18; NSM Langham w Boxted from 18; NSM W Bergholt and Gt Horkesley from 18. *8 Cherrywoods, Great Bentley, Colchester CO7 8QF* T: (01206) 252420 E: paul.mann@riffhams.co.uk

MANN, Peter Eric. b 51. St Jo Coll Dur BA 73. Westcott Ho Cam 73. **d** 75 **p** 76. C Barrow St Jo *Carl* 75–78; C Egremont 78–80; V Carl St Luke Morton 80–86; TR Egremont and Haile 86–93; P-in-c Barrow St Geo w St Luke 93–99; TR S Barrow 99–06; P-in-c Barrow St Jo 95–96; RD Furness 94–01; RD Barrow 01–06; Hon Can Carl Cathl 95–06; TR Harwich Peninsula *Chelmsf* 06–15; RD Harwich 09–14; rtd 15; PtO *Blackb* 16–17. *28 Church Hill Avenue, Warton, Carnforth LA5 9NU* T: (01524) 733763 E: cookbird@gmail.com

MANN, Canon Rachel. b 70. Qu Coll Birm 03. **d** 05 **p** 06. C Stretford St Matt *Man* 05–08; P-in-c Burnage St Nic 08–18; R from 18; C Ladybarn from 17; AD Withington from 19; Min Can Man Cathl 14–17; Hon Can Man Cathl from 17. *The Rectory, 408 Kingsway, Burnage, Manchester M19 1PL* T: 0161-432 7009 M: 07834-403195 E: rachelmann994@gmail.com

MANN, Robin. b 45. Fitzw Coll Cam BA 76 MA 80 MRTPI 73. Ridley Hall Cam 73. **d** 77 **p** 78. C Wetherby *Ripon* 77–80; V Hipswell 80–86; V Mamble w Bayton, Rock w Heightington etc *Worc* 86–96; V Avon Valley *Sarum* 96–02; R Selworthy, Timberscombe, Wootton Courtenay etc *B & W* 02–07; rtd 07; PtO *Glouc* from 14. *Hoarthorns Cottage, Malvern Way, Edge End, Coleford GL16 7DZ* T: (01594) 833576 E: hoarthorns@tiscali.co.uk

MANN, Samuel Andrew. b 93. Univ of S Wales BA 14. Ripon Coll Cuddesdon BA 17. **d** 17 **p** 18. C Coalbrookdale, Iron-Bridge and Lt Wenlock *Heref* from 17. *7 Mellor Close, Madeley, Telford TF7 5SS* M: 07554-063270 E: sam.mann.1993@gmail.com

MANN, Mrs Susan Mary. b 66. Coll of Ripon & York St Jo BA 89 Loughb Univ PGCE 90. St Mellitus Coll BA 12. **d** 12 **p** 13. C Wickford and Runwell *Chelmsf* 12–16; P-in-c Orsett and Bulphan and Horndon on the Hill 16–19; R from 19. *The Rectory, School Lane, Orsett, Grays RM16 3JS* T: (01375) 891254 E: suemann23@hotmail.com

MANN, Mrs Tessa Gillian. b 62. Nottm Univ BA 84. STETS 05. **d** 08 **p** 09. C Bourne Valley *Sarum* 08–17; C Salisbury St Fran and Stratford sub Castle 11–17; C N Bradford on Avon and Villages from 18. *Turleigh Cross, 24 Dane Rise, Winsley, Bradford-on-Avon BA15 2NB* T: (01225) 309374 M: 07588-533283 E: revtgm86@gmail.com

MANNERS, Jennifer Helen Edith. b 50. K Coll Lon MB, BS 73 AKC 73. **d** 06 **p** 07. OLM Bearsted w Thurnham *Cant* 06–13; PtO 13–14; *Portsm* from 15. *Address withheld by request* E: jhemanners@hotmail.com

MANNING, Adrian Peter. b 63. St Cath Coll Cam BA 84 MA 88 K Coll Lon PGCE 88. Ridley Hall Cam 92. **d** 95 **p** 96. C Oxhey All SS *St Alb* 95–97; Asst Chapl Bedford Sch 97–02; Chapl St Geo Sch Harpenden 02–15; V Ivinghoe w Pitstone and Slapton and Marsworth *Ox* from 15. *The Vicarage, 16 Station Road, Ivinghoe, Leighton Buzzard LU7 9EB* T: (01296) 668260 E: revadrianmanning@gmail.com

MANNING, Mrs Ann. b 42. Liv Univ CertEd 75. St Jo Coll Nottm 93 NOC 94. **d** 95 **p** 96. NSM Grasmere *Carl* 95–96; NSM Delamere *Ches* 96–99; C Middlewich w Byley 99–02; Chapl Mid Cheshire Hosps Trust 99–02; P-in-c Dunton w Wrestlingworth and Eyeworth *St Alb* 02–05; R 05–08; rtd 08; PtO *Ches* from 10. *27 Barley Croft, Great Boughton, Chester CH3 5SP* T: (01244) 316781 E: revmanning@hotmail.co.uk

MANNING, David Godfrey. b 47. Trin Coll Bris 73. **d** 76 **p** 77. C Richmond H Trin and Ch Ch *S'wark* 76–79; C Anston *Sheff* 79–83; V Blackpool St Mark *Blackb* 83–91; V Creech St Michael *B & W* 91–08; PtO 10–12 and 15–17. *163 Eaton Crescent, Taunton TA2 7UF* T: (01823) 253195 M: 07502-222875

MANNING, Mrs Jean Margaret. b 46. Oak Hill NSM Course 07. **d** 08 **p** 09. NSM Herstmonceux and Wartling *Chich* 08–13; PtO from 13. *Little Bathurst Farm, Cowbeech Road, Rushlake Green, Heathfield TN21 9QA* T/F: (01435) 831105 M: 07711-052131

MANNING, Neville Alexander. b 41. Lon Univ BD 68. ALCD 68. **d** 68 **p** 69. C Belvedere All SS *Roch* 68–71; C Hollington St Leon *Chich* 71–73; C Hersham *Guildf* 73–77; V Dawley St Jerome *Lon* 77–94; R Denton w S Heighton and Tarring Neville *Chich* 94–06; rtd 06; PtO *Chich* from 15. *7 Salvador Close, Eastbourne BN23 5TB* T: (01323) 479359 E: neville@roytown7.plus.com

MANNINGS, Andrew James. b 52. Trent Park Coll of Educn CertEd 73. St Jo Coll Nottm 90. **d** 92 **p** 94. C Over St Chad *Ches* 92–93; C Sale St Anne 93–96; C Timperley 96–98; P-in-c Egremont St Jo 98–04; P-in-c Liscard St Mary w St Columba 03–04; V Liscard Resurr 04–17; RD Wallasey 02–07; rtd 17; PtO *Ches* from 10. *Narrowboat - Lord Drinian, Preston Brook Marina, Preston Brook, Runcorn WA7 3AF* M: 07814-878175 E: frandrew2004@yahoo.co.uk

MANNINGS, Mrs Kimberley. b 89. Man Univ BA 11 Edge Hill Univ PGCE 12. St Mellitus Coll 15. **d** 18 **p** 19. C Prescot *Liv* from 18. *2 Spencer Close, Liverpool L36 0XT* M: 07969-731420 E: manningskimberley@gmail.com

MANNS, Edwin Ernest. b 30. Portsm Dioc Tr Course 84. **d** 85. C Paulsgrove *Portsm* 85–95; Chapl St Mary's Hosp Portsm 90–91; Team Chapl Portsm Hosps NHS Trust 91–95; rtd 95. *17 Kelvin Grove, Portchester, Fareham PO16 8LQ* T: (023) 9232 4818

MANOUCH, Miss Sarah Jane. b 65. SEITE 12. **d** 15 **p** 16. NSM W Wittering and Birdham w Itchenor *Chich* from 15. *9 Kent Road, Chichester PO19 7NH* T: (01243) 774841 M: 07833-914545 E: sarah035@btinternet.com

MANSEL LEWIS, Patrick Charles Archibald. b 53. Solicitor 79. St Mich Coll Llan 01. **d** 04 **p** 05. NSM Llandeilo Fawr and Taliaris *St D* 04–12; NSM Llanelli 12–17; NSM Bro Lliedi from 17. *Stradey Castle, Pwll, Llanelli SA15 4PL* T: (01554) 774626 M: 07792-921327 E: patmanlew@btconnect.com

MANSELL, Carol. b 52. Lon Bible Coll BA 75 Nottm Univ MA 86 CQSW 86 Leic Univ MBA 05 Anglia Ruskin Univ MA 11. ERMC 08. **d** 10 **p** 11. NSM Rattlesden w Thorpe Morieux, Brettenham etc *St E* 10–13; P-in-c Monks Eleigh w Chelsworth and Brent Eleigh etc 13–19; P-in-c Ipswich All Hallows from 19. *All Hallows Vicarage, Reynolds Road, Ipswich IP3 0JH* M: 07788-157147 E: carol.mansell@btinternet.com

MANSELL, The Ven Clive Neville Ross. b 53. Leic Univ LLB 74 Solicitor 77. **d** 82 **p** 83. C Gt Malvern St Mary *Worc* 82–85; Min Can Ripon Cathl 85–89; R Kirklington w Burneston and Wath and Pickhill 89–02; AD Wensley 98–02; Adn Tonbridge *Roch* 02–17; rtd 17; PtO *Leeds* from 17; Chapter Can Ripon Cathl from 18. *10 Watermill Lane, North Stainley, Ripon HG4 3LA*

MANSELL, Paul John. b 67. Staffs Univ MSc 05. Ripon Coll Cuddesdon 05. **d** 07 **p** 08. C Schorne *Ox* 07–10; V Forest Edge from 10. *The Vicarage, Mount Skippett, Ramsden, Chipping Norton OX7 3AP* T: (01993) 868687 M: 07983-707560

MANSFIELD, Alastair John Fraser. b 60. Ex Univ BA 82 Ch Coll Cam PGCE 84 City Univ MSc 92. SEITE. **d** 99 **p** 00. C Palmers Green St Jo *Lon* 99–02; P-in-c Enfield St Mich 02–07; Chapl RN from 08. *Royal Naval Chaplaincy Service, Mail Point 1-2, Leach Building, Whale Island, Portsmouth PO2 8BY* T: (023) 9262 5055 F: 9262 5134 E: alastair.mansfield@gmail.com

MANSFIELD, Ms Coralie Patricia. b 58. Nene Coll Northn BA 95. Ripon Coll Cuddesdon. **d** 13 **p** 14. NSM Olney *Ox* 13–17; P-in-c Sherington w Chicheley, N Crawley, Astwood etc from 17. *The Rectory, 21 School Lane, Sherington, Newport Pagnell MK16 9NF*

MANSFIELD, Glen Robert. b 76. St Jo Coll Ox BA 97. Oak Hill Th Coll BA 11. **d** 11 **p** 12. C Aldershot H Trin *Guildf* 11–15; C Rhyl w St Ann *St As* 15–16; C Aber-Morfa Miss Area 17–18; I from 18. *122 Rhuddlan Road, Rhyl LL18 2RD* T: (01745) 798864 E: tellspartans@yahoo.co.uk or glen@parishofrhyl.co.uk

MANSFIELD, Gordon Reginald. b 35. Lon Univ BA CertEd. Clifton Th Coll 58. **d** 63 **p** 64. C Carl St Jo 63–65; C Westcombe Park St Geo *S'wark* 65–68; C Rashcliffe *Wakef* 68–70; V Woodlands *Sheff* 70–80; V Steeple Bumpstead and Helions Bumpstead *Chelmsf* 80–02; PtO *Ely* 03–04 and from 13; *Heref* 04–13; *S & B* 04–13. *25 Rampton End, Willingham, Cambridge CB24 5JB* T: (01954) 261540

MANSFIELD, Julian Nicolas (Nick). b 59. K Coll Lon BD AKC. Edin Th Coll 83. **d** 85 **p** 86. C Kirkby *Liv* 85–89; TV Ditton St Mich 89–96; P-in-c Preston St Oswald *Blackb* 96–01; V Penwortham St Leon from 01. *St Leonard's Vicarage, Marshall's Brow, Penwortham, Preston PR1 9HY* T: (01772) 742367 E: nickthevic1@googlemail.com

MANSFIELD, Robert William. b 45. **d** 88 **p** 89. OLM Louth *Linc* from 88. *The Old Railway House, Stewton, Louth LN11 8SD* T: (01507) 327533

MANSFIELD, Simon David. b 55. Brunel Univ BSc 81 Lon Univ MA 94 Univ of Wales (Ban) MPhil 06 Glyndŵr Univ PhD 17. Ripon Coll Cuddesdon 88. **d** 90 **p** 91. C N Harrow St Alb *Lon* 90–93; C Birchington w Acol and Minnis Bay *Cant* 93–97; TV Accrington *Blackb* 97–00; TV Accrington Ch the King 00–05; P-in-c Wednesfield St Greg *Lich* 05–15; V Hockerill *St Alb* from 15. *Hockerill Vicarage, 4A All Saints Close, Bishop's Stortford CM23 2EA* T: (01279) 506542 E: smansfeeld@toucansurf.com

MANSFIELD, Canon Stephen McLaren. b 59. FGA. Cranmer Hall Dur 86. **d** 89 **p** 90. C Poynton *Ches* 89–92; C Bromborough 92–94; V Bidston 94–02; C Heswall 02–09; V Birkenhead St Jas w St Bede 09–18; P-in-c Backford and Capenhurst from 18; P-in-c Gt Saughall from 18; Hon Can Ches Cathl from 16. *Belmont Cottage, Church Road, Saughall, Chester CH1 6EP* E: steve.mansfield@mac.com

MANSHIP, Charmian Margaret. b 45. RCM BMus 68 ARCM 65 GRSM 67 FRCO 68. SAOMC 95. **d** 98 **p** 99. NSM Abingdon *Ox* 98–04; Succ and Min Can Worc Cathl 04–10; PtO from 11. *22 Stanmore Road, Worcester WR2 4PW* T: (01905) 421147 M: 07986-657110 E: charmian@manships.co.uk

MANSHIP, Canon David. b 27. ARCO Keble Coll Ox BA 52 MA 58. Qu Coll Birm 52. **d** 54 **p** 55. C Hackney St Jo *Lon* 54–58; C Preston Ascension 58–61; C St Andr Holborn 61–65; Members' Tr Officer C of E Youth Coun 65–68; Clergy Tr Officer 68–70; Dir of Educn *Win* 70–79; Hon Can Win Cathl 74–79; R Old Alresford 76–79; V Abingdon w Shippon *Ox* 79–89; TR Abingdon 89–93; V Shippon 89; RD Abingdon 87–90; rtd 93; PtO *Ox* 93–03; *Worc* from 04.

22 Stanmore Road, Worcester WR2 4PW T: (01905) 421147
E: david@manships.co.uk
MANSLEY, Caroline Anne Bimson. b 58. Bris Univ BA 80
TCD MTh 12. CITI 09. **d** 11 **p** 12. Par Dn Willowfield D & D
11–12; C Magheraculmoney Clogh 12–16; TV Ashford
Town Cant from 16; Jt AD Ashford from 18. The Rectory,
Church Hill, Kingsnorth, Ashford TN23 3EG T: (01233)
629279 M: 07580-634488 E: caroline@mansley.net
MANSLEY, Colin Edward. b 56. Edin Univ MA 80 BA 85.
Ripon Coll Cuddesdon 83. **d** 86 **p** 87. C Worle B & W
86–89; C Baguley Man 89–91; C Radcliffe St Mary 91; TV
Radcliffe 91–96; V Bartley Green Birm 96–08; R Trefnant
w Tremeirchion w Cefn St As 08–16; I Denbigh Miss Area
17–19; AD Denbigh 14–19; rtd 19. Address temp unknown
E: colin@archangel.clara.co.uk
MANSON-BRAILSFORD, Andrew Henry. b 64. NUU BA 86
Liv Univ MPhil 98 Sussex Univ DPhil 09. Ripon Coll
Cuddesdon 87. **d** 90 **p** 91. C Warrington St Elphin Liv 90–93;
C Torrisholme Blackb 93–96; V Brighton St Geo w St Anne
and St Mark Chich from 96; RD Brighton 10–15; Chapl
St Mary's Hall Brighton from 97. St George's House, 6 Sussex
Mews, Brighton BN2 1GZ T: (01273) 625538 or 279448
MANTLE, Michael. b 82. **d** 15 **p** 16. C St Helen Bishopsgate w
St Andr Undershaft etc Lon from 16. 15 Morgan Street, London
E3 5AA T: (020) 7283 2331 E: michaeljmantle@gmail.com
or m.mantle@st-helens.org.uk
MANTON, Paul Arthur. b 45. Oak Hill Th Coll BD 77. **d** 77
p 78. C Wolverhampton Lich 77–80; Ind Chapl Lon 80–87;
Hon C St Marylebone All So w SS Pet and Jo 80–87; PtO
03–18. 75 Homefield Gardens, London N2 0XL T: (020) 3224
3001 M: 07847-425946 E: paulikann@me.com
MANUEL, Paul. b 55. Univ of Wales (Ban) BA 76 Lon Sch of
Th MA 09 ACIS 79 FCIS 88. SAOMC 97. **d** 00 **p** 01. NSM
Luton St Paul St Alb 00–03; C Chorleywood Ch Ch 03–07;
P-in-c New Mill Coventry 10–14; V 10–15; AD Warwick and
Leamington 10–14; rtd 15; PtO St Alb from 19. 50 Roundwood
Lane, Harpenden AL5 3EP E: paul.manuel14@ntlworld.com
MAPES, David. Brunel Univ BSc 71 CEng 75 MIET 74
MIMechE 78 EurIng 89 FInstD 77 MBACP 99. NTMTC
BA 07. **d** 07 **p** 08. NSM Feltham Lon 07–10; P-in-c
Southampton St Mark Win 10–15; Hon C The Downs
15–17; PtO from 17. 5 Pigeonhouse Field, Sutton Scotney,
Winchester SO21 3NJ T: (01962) 761260 M: 07885-635378
E: davemapes@aol.com
MAPLE, David Charles. b 34. Sarum Th Coll 64. **d** 66 **p** 66.
C Buckland in Dover Cant 66–67; C St Laur in Thanet
67–71; Chapl RAF 71–75; P-in-c Ivychurch w Old Romney
and Midley Cant 75–76; P-in-c Newchurch 75–76; P-in-c
Burmarsh 75–78; P-in-c St Mary in the Marsh 75–76;
R Dymchurch 76–78; R Dymchurch w Burmarsh and
Newchurch 78–81; Hon Min Can Cant Cathl 79–18; Abp's
Dioc Chapl 81–91; Chapl St Jo Hosp Cant 91–95; rtd
95; PtO Cant 98–18. 1 Mount Pleasant, Blean, Canterbury
CT2 9EU T: (01227) 459044
MAPLE, John Philip. b 50. Chich Th Coll 71. **d** 74 **p** 79. C
Notting Hill St Mich and Ch Ch Lon 74–75; LtO 78–79;
C Barnsbury St Dav w St Clem 79–80; C Cotham St Sav w
St Mary Bris 80–83; TV St Marylebone Ch Ch Lon 83–91; R
St Marylebone St Paul 91–99; P-in-c Fulham St Alb w St Aug
99–04; P-in-c Fulham St Pet 99–02; Community Min Adv
04–15; rtd 15; PtO Lon from 15. 314 South Lambeth Road,
London SW8 1UQ T: (020) 7627 3575 M: 07736-546588
E: maplefoster@hotmail.co.uk
MAPLEY, Mrs Barbara Jean. b 46. Guy's Hosp Medical Sch
MCSP 69. Oak Hill NSM Course 86. **d** 89 **p** 94. NSM Kelvedon
Chelmsf 89–93; C Witham 93–94; TV 94–01; R Belbroughton
w Fairfield and Clent Worc 01–11; rtd 12; PtO Ox from 12. 2
Leamington Gate, Coxwell Road, Faringdon SN7 7FP T: (01367)
615009 E: barbaramapley@waitrose.com
MAPSTONE, Canon Trevor Anthony. b 63. Lanc Univ BSc 84
MA 96 K Coll Lon MA 16. St Jo Coll Nottm 86. **d** 89 **p** 90.
C Hoole Ches 89–92; C Lancaster St Thos Blackb 92–96;
V Harrow Trin St Mich Lon 96–03; Dir of Ords Willesden
Area 98–03; V S Croydon Em S'wark 03–19; AD Croydon
Cen 09–16; P-in-c Caterham from 19; Hon Can S'wark
Cathl from 14. The Rectory, 5 Whyteleafe Road, Caterham
CR3 5EG T: (01883) 373083
MARBUS, Alida Janny. See WHITTOCK, Alida Janny
MARCH, Alan Mervyn. b 48. Open Univ BA 91 CPFA 73.
EAMTC 00. **d** 03 **p** 04. NSM Northampton St Alb Pet 03–06;
NSM Northampton Ch Ch from 06; NSM Northampton
H Sepulchre w St Andr and St Lawr from 06; NSM
Northampton St Mich w St Edm from 06; NSM Northampton
H Trin and St Paul from 06. 236 Beech Avenue, Northampton
NN3 2LE T: (01604) 405722 E: march100@o2.co.uk or
alanmarch2016@outlook.com

MARCH, Andrew. b 81. UEA BA 03. St Jo Coll Nottm MA 09.
d 09 **p** 10. C Werrington and Wetley Rocks Lich 09–12; V
Allesley Park and Whoberley Cov from 12. St Christopher's
Vicarage, 99 Buckingham Rise, Coventry CV5 9HF M: 07816-
998642 E: revandymarch@gmail.com
MARCH, Charles Anthony Maclea (Tony). b 32. CCC
Cam BA 55 MA 70. Oak Hill Th Coll 55. **d** 57 **p** 58. C S
Croydon Em Cant 57–60; C Eastbourne H Trin Chich 60–63;
V Whitehall Park St Andr Hornsey Lane Lon 63–67; V
Tunbridge Wells H Trin w Ch Ch Roch 67–82; V Prestonville
St Luke Chich 82–97; rtd 97; PtO Roch 99–14. 17 Buckingham
Road, Oakham LE15 6RX T: (01572) 756113
MARCH, Gerald. b 44. Nottm Univ BA 75. Oak Hill Th Coll 92.
d 95 **p** 96. C Sandgate St Paul w Folkestone St Geo Cant
95–99; P-in-c Southampton St Mark Win 99–03; V 03–09; rtd
09; PtO Ox from 10; Cov 13–15. Dovetrees, 2B Curbridge Road,
Witney OX28 5JR E: rev.gerald@gmail.com
MARCH, Jonathan. b 79. Wycliffe Hall Ox. **d** 05 **p** 06. C
Brompton H Trin w Onslow Square St Paul Lon 05–11;
V Oseney Crescent St Luke from 11. 1 Bartholomew Road,
London NW5 2AH T: (020) 7916 0050 E: jon@slkt.org.uk
MARCH, Peter John. b 75. Cov Univ BA 97 Univ Coll Worc
PGCE 98. SWMTC 10. **d** 13 **p** 14. C Heavitree and St Mary
Steps Ex 13–16; P-in-c Torquay St Luke 16–18; V from 18;
P-in-c Torre All SS 16–18; V Torre and Torquay St Jo from 18.
All Saints' Vicarage, 45 Barton Road, Torquay TQ1 4DT
MARCHAND, Canon Rex Anthony Victor (Toby). b 47. K
Coll Lon BD 69 AKC 69. St Aug Coll Cant 69. **d** 70 **p** 71. C
Leigh Park Portsm 70–73; C Bp's Hatfield St Alb 73–80; R Deal
St Leon and St Rich and Sholden Cant 80–95; RD Sandwich
91–94; Hon Can Cant Cathl 94–95; V Bishop's Stortford
St Mich St Alb 95–12; RD Bishop's Stortford 03–06; Hon Can
St Alb 08–12; rtd 12; PtO Cant from 13. 12 Langton Close, Deal
CT14 6UL T: (01304) 371419 E: ravmarchand@gmail.com
MARCHANT, Canon Iain William. b 26. Wells Th Coll 59.
d 60 **p** 61. C Dalston Carl 60–63; V Hawkesbury Glouc 63–76;
R Newent 76–85; Hon Can Glouc Cathl 84–92; R Newent
and Gorsley w Cliffords Mesne 85–92; rtd 92; PtO Glouc from
92. 34 Parklands, Wotton-under-Edge GL12 7LT T: (01453)
844779 E: iwmarchant789@btinternet.com
MARCHANT (née ROWLAND), Sally Margaret. b 58. SEITE.
d 10 **p** 11. C Melton Mowbray Leic 10–13; TV Totton Win
from 13. The Vicarage, Cooks Lane, Calmore, Southampton
SO40 2RU E: revsallymarchant@gmail.com
MARCHMENT, Mrs Ethel Diane. b 53. Ridley Hall Cam.
d 11 **p** 12. NSM Douglas St Ninian S & M 11–14; NSM
W Coast 14–18. 181 Bowmans Close, Steyning BN44 3SR
E: revdimarchment@gmail.com
MARCUS, Mrs Candice Ann. b 52. FInstLEx 80. Trin Coll
Bris 05. **d** 07 **p** 08. C Timsbury and Priston B & W 07–10; C
Timsbury w Priston, Camerton and Dunkerton 10–11; TV
Whitton Sarum 11–18; rtd 18; PtO B & W from 19. Willow
Tree Cottage, Throop Road, Templecombe BA8 0HR M: 07788-
437063 E: revcandicemarcus@gmail.com
MARCUS, Sarah Caroline. See ROWLAND JONES, Sarah
Caroline
MARCUSSEN, Mrs Yolande Roberta. b 47. SEITE 98. **d** 01 **p** 02.
NSM Bromley Common St Aug Roch 01–03; NSM Orpington All
SS 03; Asst Chapl HM Pris Roch 01–03; Chapl 03–06; rtd 06; PtO
Roch from 09. 24 Lucerne Road, Orpington BR6 0EP T: (01689)
833599 E: yolande.marcussen@ntlworld.com
MARGAM, Archdeacon of. See KOMOR, The Ven Michael
MARGARET ANNE, Sister. See McALISTER, Margaret Elizabeth
Anne
MARGARET JOY, Sister. See HARRIS, Margaret Claire
MARIES, Phillip John. **d** 15 **p** 16. C Normanton Leeds 15–18;
C Cen Barnsley 18–19; C Barnsley St Geo 18–19; C Cen
Barnsley from 18. 186 Racecommon Road, Barnsley S70 6JY
E: philmaries@gmail.com
MARK, Catherine. See OKORONKWO, Catherine Chunyere
Mark
MARKBY, Ms Jane Elizabeth. b 67. Em Coll Cam BA 88
Homerton Coll Cam PGCE 89. Ridley Hall Cam 00.
d 02 **p** 03. NSM Edmonton All SS w St Mich Lon
02–06; Chapl Haberdashers' Aske's Sch Elstree 06–10;
Chapl Berkhamsted Sch Herts from 10. Adelbert House,
Mill Street, Berkamsted HP4 2BA T: (01442) 358095
E: jmarkby@berkhamstedschool.com
MARKBY, Peter John Jenner. b 38. Em Coll Cam BA 60.
Clifton Th Coll 62. **d** 64 **p** 65. C Tufnell Park St Geo Lon
64–68; C Crowborough Chich 68–73; C Polegate 73–77;
R Southover 77–02; rtd 02; PtO Chich from 02. 44 Warren
Drive, Lewes BN7 1HD T: (01273) 875724 M: 07944-
618340 E: petermarkby@gmail.com
MARKS, Canon Allan Willi. b 56. Cranmer Hall Dur 92. **d** 94
p 95. C Barnoldswick w Bracewell Bradf 94–96; C Willington

Newc 96–98; TV 98–02; V Newc H Cross 02–09; P-in-c Newc Ch Ch w St Ann 09–17; V Newc Ch Ch w St Anne from 17; AD Newc Cen 13–17; Hon Can Newc Cathl from 16. *St Ann's Vicarage, 11 Gibson Street, Newcastle upon Tyne NE1 6PY* T: 0191-232 0516 E: fatherallan@sky.com

MARKS, Dennis Ray. b 37. Lon Univ BSc 58 PhD 67 PGCE 59 Univ of Wales (Ban) BTh 04 CChem 85 MRSC 85. **d** 06 **p** 07. OLM Woking St Mary *Guildf* 06–12; PtO from 12. *Green Tiles, Shaftesbury Road, Woking GU22 7DU* T: (01483) 762030 E: ray.marks@mypostoffice.co.uk

MARKS, Timothy John. b 45. Man Univ BA 76 Anglia Poly Univ MA 96. **d** 88 **p** 89. NSM Burton and Sopley *Win* 88–91; R Croxton and Eltisley *Ely* 91–96; R Graveley w Papworth St Agnes w Yelling etc 91–96; Dir Network Counselling and Tr 96–05; Nat Adv for Personal/Spiritual Development YMCA 05–07. *102 Woodfarm Road, Malvern WR14 4PP* T: (01684) 564925 M: 07817-465213 E: tim@timmarksconsulting.com

MARL, David John. b 42. ARCA 67. **d** 01 **p** 02. OLM Okeford *Sarum* 01–12; PtO from 12. *St Probus, Marston Road, Sherborne DT9 4BL* T: (01935) 398673 E: burgoyne.marl@gmail.com

MARLEY, Alan Gordon. b 59. Birm Univ BA 89. Qu Coll Birm 87. **d** 89 **p** 90. C Blandford Forum and Langton Long *Sarum* 89–93; Chapl HM YOI Aylesbury 93–97; I Fermoy Union *C, C & R* 97–03; Bp's Dom Chapl 99–03; Dean Cloyne 03–18; I Cloyne Union 03–18; Dioc Dir of Ords 05–18; Chapl Univ Coll Cork from 18. *The Chaplaincy, Iona, University College Cork, College Road, Cork, T12 PY24, Republic of Ireland* T: (00353) (21) 490 2459 E: alan.marley@ucc.ie

MARLOW, Jonathan James. b 76. SS Hild & Bede Coll Dur MEng 99. Wycliffe Hall Ox BTh 06. **d** 06 **p** 07. C Elburton *Ex* 06–10; P-in-c Pennycross 10–15; V 15–18; Assoc Tutor Univ of St Mark and St Jo 10–15; Asst Dioc Dir of Ords 12–17; Miss and Min Development Team Ldr from 18. *The Old Deanery, The Cloisters, Exeter EX1 1HS* T: (01392) 294942 M: 07517-999935 E: jon.marlow@exeter.anglican.org

MARLOW *(née* **SIBBALD), Mrs Olwyn Eileen.** b 57. Aston Tr Scheme 85 Linc Th Coll 87. **d** 89 **p** 94. Par Dn Wythenshawe St Martin *Man* 89–93; Par Dn Baguley 93–94; C 94–95; Asst Chapl Cen Man Healthcare NHS Trust 95–00; NSM Newall Green St Fran *Man* 97–05; rtd 01; NSM Wythenshawe *Man* 01–05; PtO from 05; *Ches* from 05. *28 Arcadia Avenue, Sale M33 3SA* T: 0161-962 9292 E: olwynem@sky.com

MARLOW, Ms Tracy Margaret. b 64. St Mellitus Coll 12. **d** 15 **p** 16. C Rayleigh *Chelmsf* 15–19; TV from 19. *St Michael's House, 13 Sir Walter Raleigh Drive, Rayleigh SS6 9JB* M: 07886-442264 E: t-marlow@hotmail.co.uk *or* tracy.marlow@parishofrayleigh.org.uk

MARNHAM, Preb Charles Christopher. b 51. Jes Coll Cam BA 73 MA 77. Cranmer Hall Dur. **d** 77 **p** 78. C Brompton H Trin *Lon* 77–78; C Brompton H Trin w Onslow Square St Paul 78–80; C Linthorpe *York* 80–84; R Haughton le Skerne *Dur* 84–95; V Ches Square St Mich w St Phil *Lon* from 95; Preb St Paul's Cathl from 10. *St Michael's Vicarage, 4 Chester Square, London SW1W 9HH* T: (020) 7730 8889 F: 7730 0043 E: charles@stmichaelschurch.org.uk

MARNS, Canon Nigel Geoffrey. b 63. Univ of Wales (Abth) BSc(Econ) 85 Birm Univ BD 92 MA 10. Qu Coll Birm 90. **d** 93 **p** 94. C Addington *S'wark* 93–96; P-in-c W Bromwich Gd Shep w St Jo *Lich* 96–01; V Bromsgrove St Jo *Worc* 01–09; R Ludgvan, Marazion, St Hilary and Perranuthnoe *Truro* from 09; Hon Can Truro Cathl from 16. *The Rectory, Ludgvan, Penzance TR20 8EZ* T: (01736) 740784 E: canon@nigelmarns.plus.com

MARQUEZ, Edilberto. b 57. Bible Sem Alliance Peru BA 80 Westmr Coll Ox MTh 93 K Coll Lon DThM 04. St Steph Ho Ox 92. **d** 94 **p** 95. C Reading St Jo Ox 94–98; C New Malden and Coombe *S'wark* 98–01; P-in-c Bucklebury w Marlston Ox 01–08; P-in-c Bradfield and Stanford Dingley 04–08; P-in-c Woodley 08–09; V from 09. *6 Denmark Avenue, Woodley, Reading RG5 4RS* T: 0118-969 6540 E: vicar1992@hotmail.com

MARR *(née* **PARKER), Mrs Anne Elizabeth.** b 46. Hull Univ BSc 67 CertEd 68. NEOC 91. **d** 96 **p** 12. NSM Whorlton *Newc* 96–97; NSM Chapel House 97–14; Chapl Newc City Health NHS Trust 96–01; Chapl Newc Mental Health Unit 01–14; rtd 14; PtO *Newc* from 14. *26 The Chesters, Newcastle upon Tyne NE5 1AF* T: 0191-267 4808 E: marr1af@btinternet.com

MARR, Derek Paul. b 33. Dur Univ TCert 69. **d** 00 **p** 01. OLM Chapel House *Newc* 00–03; PtO from 03. *26 The Chesters, Newcastle upon Tyne NE5 1AF* T: 0191-267 4808

MARR, Canon Donald Radley. b 37. K Coll Lon 57. St Aid Birkenhead 61. **d** 64 **p** 65. C Macclesfield St Mich *Ches* 64–66; C Sale St Anne 66–67; V Marthall 67–72; C W Kirby St Bridget 72–76; R Waverton 76–83; R Nantwich 83–87; RD 86–87; RD Malpas 87–91; V Bunbury 87–91; rtd 91; Dioc Rural Officer *Ches* 91–07; Hon Can Ches

Cathl 91–92; PtO from 07. *St Boniface, 5 Hockenhull Crescent, Tarvin, Chester CH3 8LJ* T: (01829) 741302 E: revsdonaldandmargaret@btinternet.com

MARR, Mrs Margaret Rose. b 36. St Mary's Coll Ban TCert 56 Open Univ BA 00. Ripon Coll Cuddesdon 02. **d** 02 **p** 03. NSM Tarvin *Ches* 02–11; PtO from 11. *St Boniface, 5 Hockenhull Crescent, Tarvin, Chester CH3 8LJ* T: (01829) 741302 E: revsdonaldandmargaret@btinternet.com

MARRIAGE, Sophia Briony. b 71. Rob Coll Cam BA 93 Edin Univ PhD 98 Glas Univ MTh 05. TISEC 03. **d** 05 **p** 06. C Edin St Martin 05–11; R Edin St Mark from 11. *15 Viewforth Terrace, Edinburgh EH10 4LJ* T: 0131-229 8939 *or* 629 1219 E: sophia.marriage@stmarksportobello.org

MARRIOTT *(née* **REID), Mrs Amanda Joy.** b 63. Nottm Univ BTh 92. Linc Th Coll 89. **d** 92 **p** 96. Par Dn Rothwell *Ripon* 92–94; C 94–95; C Manston 95–97; C Wetherby 97–01; P-in-c Water Eaton *Ox* 01–06; AD Milton Keynes 05–06; P-in-c Sherington w Chicheley, N Crawley, Astwood etc 06–09; R 09–15; TR Duston and Upton *Pet* from 15. *The Rectory, 3 Main Road, Duston, Northampton NN5 6JB* T: (01908) 610521 E: aj.marriott123@gmail.com

MARRIOTT, Stanley Richard. b 36. AKC 60 Warwick Univ MA 92. **d** 61 **p** 62. C Coleshill *Birm* 61–64; C Maxstoke 61–64; V Ansley *Cov* 64–78; Org Sec (E Midl) CECS 79–83; P-in-c Baxterley w Hurley and Wood End and Merevale etc *Birm* 83–84; R 84–87; R Newton Regis w Seckington and Shuttington 87–97; rtd 97; PtO *B & W* from 97. *Dunkery Pleck, Wootton Courtenay, Minehead TA24 8RH* T: (01643) 841058

MARROW, David Edward Armfield. b 42. Nottm Univ BA 65 MA. Tyndale Hall Bris 65. **d** 67 **p** 68. C Clifton Ch Ch w Em *Bris* 67–70; BCMS Ethiopia 70–75; N Area Sec BCMS 75–77; C-in-c Ryde St Jas Prop Chpl *Portsm* 77–84; V Worthing St Geo *Chich* 84–07; rtd 07. *West View, 65 St Michael's Road, St Helens, Ryde PO33 1YJ* T: (01983) 872729 E: davidmarrow@btinternet.com

MARROW, John Willam. b 70. Wilson Carlile Coll 92 St Mellitus Coll BA 18. **d** 18 **p** 19. C Farnham *Guildf* from 18. *6 High Park Road, Farnham GU9 7JL* M: 07766-220884 E: johnwmarrow@hotmail.com

MARRY, Sarah Louise. **d** 11 **p** 12. C Douglas Union w Frankfield *C, C & R* 11–15; P-in-c Cork St Ann's Union 15–19; I Clonsast w Rathangan, Thomastown etc *M & K* from 19. *Address temp unknown* M: (00353) 86-171 3936

MARSDEN, Canon Andrew Philip. b 63. Keble Coll Ox BA 85 MA 90 Birm Univ MA 86. Wycliffe Hall Ox BA 90. **d** 91 **p** 92. C Newport St Jo *Portsm* 91–94; C Cowplain 94–97; V Wokingham St Sebastian *Ox* from 97; Hon Can Ch Ch from 15. *St Sebastian's Vicarage, Nine Mile Ride, Wokingham RG40 3AT* T: (01344) 761050 E: revamarsden@tiscali.co.uk

MARSDEN, Canon Carole. b 44. Avery Hill Coll TCert 65 Sheff Poly DipEd 87. NOC 88. **d** 91 **p** 94. NSM Saddleworth *Man* 91–92; Par Dn 92–94; C 94–95; P-in-c Oldham St Paul 95–02; C Werneth 98–02; P-in-c Shap w Swindale and Bampton w Mardale *Carl* 02–08; P-in-c Orton and Tebay w Ravenstonedale etc 07–08; rtd 08; PtO *Carl* 09–16; RD Appleby 09–13; P-in-c Kirkby Stephen w Mallerstang etc 16–18; Hon Can Carl Cathl 11–18; PtO *Blackb* from 13. *Fairfield, Faraday Road, Kirby Stephen CA17 4QL* T: (017683) 71279 M: 07866-006849 E: carole.sam@hotmail.com

MARSDEN, Faith Edith Mary. b 54. **d** 18 **p** 19. NSM Acton w Gt Waldingfield *St E* from 18. *4 Chapel Close, Great Waldingfield, Sudbury CO10 0UB* T: (01787) 312002 M: 07525-450444 E: femarsden@hotmail.com

MARSDEN, The Very Revd John Joseph. b 53. York Univ BA 74 Nottm Univ MTh 81 Kent Univ PhD 88. St Jo Coll Nottm 77. **d** 80 **p** 81. C Leigh St Mary *Man* 80–83; Hon C Chatham St Steph *Roch* 83–91; Ind Chapl 83–91; Lect Systematic Th CITC and TCD from 91; I Newbridge w Carnalway and Kilcullen *M & K* 97–16; I Kildare w Kilmeague and Curragh 06–16; Dean Kildare 06–16; rtd 16. *Firgrove House, Military Road, Killiney, Co Dublin, Republic of Ireland* T: (00353) (1) 211 5684 M: 87-949 9177 E: johnmarsden@eircom.net

MARSDEN, Robert. b 59. Ch Ch Ox BA 81 PGCE 82. Oak Hill Th Coll BA 92. **d** 92 **p** 93. C Sevenoaks St Nic *Roch* 92–95; Chapl Fettes Coll Edin 95–99; C-in-c Buxton Trin Prop Chpl *Derby* from 99. *37 Temple Road, Buxton SK17 9BA* T: (01298) 73656 E: bobinbuxton@sky.com

MARSDEN, Robert James. b 56. Ch Ch Coll Cant BEd 79. Oak Hill Th Coll 90. **d** 94 **p** 95. C Margate H Trin *Cant* 94–98; P-in-c Brinton, Briningham, Hunworth, Stody etc *Nor* 98–08; P-in-c Gressenhall w Longham w Wendling etc 08–16; RD Dereham in Mitford 13–15; P-in-c The Lulworths, Winfrith Newburgh and Chaldon *Sarum* from 16. *The Rectory, West Road, West Lulworth, Wareham BH20 5RY* T: (01929) 400741 E: revrobert.lulworth@camelhome.co.uk

MARSDEN, Samuel Edward. b 44. Keble Coll Ox BA 66 MA 85. Linc Th Coll 66. **d** 68 **p** 69. C Liskeard w St Keyne *Truro* 68–72; R Gerrans w St Anthony in Roseland 72–77; V Kowloon Ch Ch Hong Kong 77–81; P-in-c Ingrave *Chelmsf* 81–82; P-in-c Gt Warley w Childerditch 81–82; R Gt Warley w Childerditch and Ingrave 82–89; R Gilgandra Australia 89–93; R Kelso 94–00; Adn Wylde 00–01; R Parkes 01–07; Adn Bathurst 05–07; R Coffs Harbour 07–10; rtd 10; PtO *Ely* 10–12; *Truro* from 15. *7 Penmare Court, Hayle TR27 4RD* T: (01736) 756669 E: samuelmarsden@hotmail.com

MARSH, Anderson Jason. b 74. STETS 06. **d** 09. NSM Sheet *Portsm* from 09. *12 Rother Close, Petersfield GU31 4DN* T: (01730) 268156 E: amarsh@rotherbank.co.uk

MARSH, Carol Ann. *See* HATHORNE, Carol Ann

MARSH, Colin Arthur. b 54. Edin Univ PhD 02. St Jo Coll Nottm 79. **d** 82 **p** 83. C Kirkby *Liv* 82–86; TV St Luke in the City 86–91; P-in-c Chingola St Barn Zambia 91–95; PtO *Edin* 95–03; Tutor United Coll of Ascension Selly Oak 03–06; Ecum Development Officer Chs Together *Birm* from 06. *Birmingham Churches Together, The Jericho Building, 196-198 Edward Road, Balsall Heath, Birmingham B12 9LX* T: 0121-661 4273 E: office@birminghamchurches.org.uk

MARSH, David. b 32. St Jo Coll Dur BA 54. Cranmer Hall Dur. **d** 57 **p** 58. C Bilston St Leon *Lich* 57–62; Lic to Offic Dio Maseno Kenya 63–66; Chapl Scargill Ho 67–69; Adn S Maseno 70–72; V Meole Brace *Lich* 72–77; V Westlands St Andr 77–86; V Trentham 86–96; P-in-c Alstonfield, Butterton, Warslow w Elkstone etc 96–99; rtd 99; PtO *Ches* from 99; Chapl Mid Cheshire Hosps NHS Foundn Trust 02–16. *31 Spring Gardens, Nantwich CW5 5SH* T: (01270) 610079 E: dlmarsh@talktalk.net

MARSH, Mrs Deborah Lindsay. b 59. Westcott Ho Cam 13. **d** 15 **p** 16. C Hardingstone, Piddington w Horton and Quinton and Preston Deanery *Pet* 15–18; TV Oakham, Ashwell, Braunston, Brooke, Egleton etc from 18. *The Rectory, 3 Paddock Close, Whissendine, Oakham LE15 7HW* M: 07919-385314 E: debmarsh37@yahoo.com

MARSH, Mrs Elizabeth Alexandra (Sandra). b 60. QUB BA 94. St Aug Coll Cant 17. **d** 18 **p** 19. C Eastry and Woodnesborough *Cant* from 18. *The Vicarage, The Street, Woodnesborough, Sandwich CT13 0NG* M: 07788-715443 E: sam.marsh1@btopenworld.com

MARSH, Francis John. b 47. York Univ BA 69 DPhil 76 ATCL 65 ARCM 66 ARCO 71. Oak Hill Th Coll 72 Selw Coll Cam 73. **d** 75 **p** 76. C Cambridge St Matt *Ely* 75–78; C Pitsmoor w Wicker *Sheff* 79; C Pitsmoor w Ellesmere 79–81; C Crookes St Thos 81–85; V S Ossett *Wakef* 85–96; RD Dewsbury 93–96; Adn Blackb 96–01; Bp's Adv on Hosp Chapls 96–01; P-in-c Emley *Wakef* 11–14; Leeds 14–17; P-in-c Flockton cum Denby Grange *Wakef* 11–14; Leeds 14–17. *Bark House Mews, Bark Close, Shelley, Huddersfield HD8 8JR* T: (01484) 981530 E: john.marsh774@gmail.com

MARSH, John. b 53. Open Univ BSc 95 Open Unive MSc 04. Guildf Dioc Min Course 07. **d** 10 **p** 11. OLM Ockley, Okewood and Forest Green *Guildf* 10–18; OLM Ewhurst w Okewood and Forest Green from 18. *2 Chatsworth Row, Caburn Heights, Crawley RH11 8RT* T: (01293) 401639 E: home@john-marsh.co.uk

MARSH, Lawrence Allan. b 36. Sarum Th Coll 66. **d** 67 **p** 68. C Waterlooville *Portsm* 67–70; V Shedfield 70–76; R Fen Ditton *Ely* 76–01; P-in-c Horningsea 83–01; rtd 01; PtO *Ely* from 01. *The Old Bakery, 22 High Street, Bottisham, Cambridge CB25 9DA* T: (01223) 811314 E: l.marsh142@btinternet.com

MARSH, Leonard Stuart Alexander. b 55. Hull Univ BA 77 SOAS Lon MA 00. Linc Th Coll 77. **d** 79 **p** 80. C Eltham St Barn *S'wark* 79–81; C Camberwell St Giles 81–83; Hon C Clifton St Paul *Bris* 83–86; Asst Chapl Bris Univ 83–86; Area Sec (Dio S'wark) USPG 86–91; Chapl Guildhall Sch of Music and Drama *Lon* 91–97; Chapl City Univ 91–98; NSM Clerkenwell H Redeemer and St Mark 94–95; P-in-c Finsbury St Clem w St Barn and St Matt 95–01; P-in-c Upper Norwood All SS *S'wark* 01–08; V from 08; AD Croydon N 12–17. *The Vicarage, 49 Chevening Road, London SE19 3TD* T: (020) 8653 2820

MARSH, Canon Margaret Evaline. b 47. Univ of Wales (Lamp) MA 08. STETS 96. **d** 99 **p** 00. NSM Tattenham Corner and Burgh Heath *Guildf* 99–03; NSM Epsom St Martin 03–04; P-in-c Walton-on-the-Hill 04–15; Hon Can Guildf Cathl 10–15; PtO from 15. *9 Westways, Epsom KT19 0PH* T: (020) 8224 0607 M: 07894-302749 E: maggiemarsh17@gmail.com

MARSH, Michael John. b 47. Reading Univ BA 69 DipEd 70 York Univ MA 91 Leeds Univ BA 07. Coll of Resurr Mirfield 05. **d** 07 **p** 08. NSM Castleford *Wakef* 07–11; Knottingley and Kellington w Whitley *Leeds* from 11. *The Vicarage, 1*

Manor Farm Close, Kellington, Goole DN14 0PF T: (01977) 663553 M: 07884-952282 E: frmike.marsh@hotmail.com

MARSH, Peter Charles Ernest. b 57. Southn Univ CertEd 03 IEng 87. WEMTC 04. **d** 06 **p** 07. NSM Wotton-under-Edge w Ozleworth *Glouc* 06–09; PtO 14–15; NSM Tyndale from 15. *1 Pitt Court Villas, Pitt Court, North Nibley, Dursley GL11 6EB* T: (01453) 547521 E: pcemarsh@tiscali.co.uk

MARSH, Phillip Edward. b 73. Univ of Wales (Abth) BSc 94 Ch Ch Coll Cant PGCE 96. Wycliffe Hall Ox BTh 02. **d** 02 **p** 03. C Hubberston *St D* 02–05; C Werrington *Pet* 05–09; P-in-c Wilford *S'well* 09–11; R 11–19; PtO *Ely* from 19. *The Rectory, Main Street, Little Downham, Ely CB6 2ST* M: 07766-314957

MARSH, Robert Charles. b 58. Linc Univ BA 13. Linc Sch of Th and Min 09. **d** 13 **p** 14. NSM Whitwick, Thringstone and Swannington *Leic* 13–15; NSM Desford and Kirby Muxloe from 15. *43 Chevin Avenue, Leicester LE3 6PX* M: 07557-536926 E: ministry@family-marsh.uk

MARSH, Robert Christopher. b 53. Ex Univ BEd 76. St Steph Ho Ox 86. **d** 88 **p** 89. C St Leonards Ch Ch and St Mary *Chich* 88–91; TV Crawley 91–00; V Maybridge 00–02. *67 Hythe Crescent, Seaford BN25 3TZ* E: rmarsh6204@aol.com

MARSH, Roger Philip. b 44. K Coll Lon BD 72 AKC 72 Sussex Univ MA 95 K Alfred's Coll Win CertEd 66. St Aug Coll Cant 73. **d** 73 **p** 74. C Leagrave *St Alb* 73–76; Asst Youth Officer 76–77; Resources Officer 77–80; Chapl Marlborough Coll 80–86; Master Ardingly Coll Jun Sch Haywards Heath 86–95; Hd Master St Geo Sch Windsor 95–99; Chapl Lancing Coll 99–09; rtd 09; PtO *Cant* from 09; Chapl St Edm Sch Cant 10–11; Chapl Heathfield Sch Ascot 11–12; Acting Hd Master Lancing Coll Prep Sch Worthing 14; PtO *Chich* 14–19. *107 College Road, Deal CT14 6BU* T: (01304) 362851 E: rogermarsh573@gmail.com

MARSH, Sandra. *See* MARSH, Elizabeth Alexandra

MARSH, Mrs Shelley Ann. b 54. SRN 75 SCM 76. St Jo Coll Nottm 84. **d** 89 **p** 94. Hon C Glas Gd Shep and Ascension 89–96; P-in-c Johnstone and Renfrew 96–06; R Bishopbriggs 96–16; Chapl Paisley Univ 98–00; rtd 16. *9 Moredun Square, Perth PH2 0DE* T: (01738) 575040 E: revshelleymarsh@ntlworld.com

MARSH, Steven Philip. b 73. Lon Inst BA 96 Cov Univ MA 98 Lon Sch of Th BA 05. Ripon Coll Cuddesdon MA 13. **d** 13 **p** 14. C Crofton *Portsm* 13–17; TV Ouzel Valley *St Alb* from 17. *4 Warneford Way, Leighton Buzzard LU7 4PX* M: 07817-872163 E: s.p.marsh@hotmail.com or rev.steve.marsh@hotmail.com

MARSH, Susan Edith. b 42. Southn Univ BA 63 CertEd 64. SAOMC 01. **d** 01 **p** 02. NSM Bp's Hatfield *St Alb* 01–05; NSM Bp's Hatfield, Lemsford and N Mymms 05–15; rtd 15; PtO *St Alb* from 15. *141 Handside Lane, Welwyn Garden City AL8 6TA* T: (01707) 329744 E: susanianmarsh@ntlworld.com

MARSHALL, Alexander Robert. b 43. Glouc Sch of Min 84. **d** 87 **p** 88. NSM Newtown w Llanllwchaiarn w Aberhafesp *St As* 87–00; P-in-c Mochdre 00–06. *31 Bromley College, London Road, Bromley BR1 1PE* T: (020) 8464 9727 E: revalexandermarshall17@gmail.com

MARSHALL, Mrs Alison Mary. b 54. Middx Hosp MB, BS 79 MRCGP 82. SAOMC 98. **d** 01 **p** 02. NSM Reading St Jo Ox 01–14; PtO 14–19; Progr Co-ordinator Iona Community *Arg* 14–15. *79 Byrons Lane, Macclesfield SK11 7JS* T: (01625) 477171 M: 07740-944102 E: ali.m@rshall.org.uk

MARSHALL, Amanda Jane. b 64. Nottm Univ BA 86 Glam Univ MSc 04. Wycliffe Hall Ox 15. **d** 18 **p** 19. C Ashbourne St Oswald w Mapleton *Derby* from 18; C Ashbourne St Jo from 18; C Clifton from 18; C Norbury w Snelston from 18. *The New Vicarage, Clifton, Ashbourne DE6 2GL* T: (01335) 343009 M: 07557-567751 E: revamandamarshall@gmail.com

MARSHALL, Andrew Stephen. b 74. UNISA BTh 00. Coll of Resurr Mirfield 02. **d** 99 **p** 00. C Port Elizabeth St Hugh S Africa 00–02; C Port Elizabeth St Jo 02; C Easthampstead Ox 03–06; Sen Chapl Southn Solent Univ *Win* 06–09; Chapl Portsm Univ 09–17; Dioc Interfaith Adv 11–17; Chapl N Veterinary Coll *Lon* from 17. *Royal Veterinary College, 4 Royal College Street, London NW1 0TU* T: (020) 7468 5000 E: asmarshall@rvc.ac.uk

MARSHALL, Mrs Angela. b 48. Trin Coll Bris 74. **d** 88 **p** 96. Hon Par Dn Newcastle St Geo *Lich* 88–92; LtO *Eur* 92–94; Dn Versailles 94–96; Asst Chapl 96–04; PtO *St E* 04–07; Hon C Collier Row St Jas and Havering-atte-Bower *Chelmsf* 07–15; rtd 15; PtO *Eur* from 15. *Sous le Figuier, Hameau de Manieu, 32100 Condom, France* E: rev.ange@orange.fr

MARSHALL, Canon Bryan John. b 40. Chich Th Coll 63. **d** 65 **p** 66. C Poulton-le-Fylde *Blackb* 65–68; C S Shore H Trin 68–70; V Wesham 70–74; PV Chich Cathl 74–82;

V Boxgrove 82–91; P-in-c Tangmere 82–84; R 84–91; R Westbourne 91–95; V E Preston w Kingston 95–03; Can and Preb Chich Cathl 94–10; rtd 03. *11 Priory Close, Boxgrove, Chichester PO18 0EA* T: (01243) 536337 E: boxgrovebryan@yahoo.co.uk

MARSHALL, Mrs Christine Anne. b 40. Leeds Univ BSc 64. **d** 95 **p** 96. OLM Holbrook, Stutton, Freston, Woolverstone etc *St E* 95–05; PtO 05–06 and 09–13; *Truro* from 15. *8 Castle View Park, Mawnan Smith, Falmouth TR11 5HB* T: (01326) 250656 E: marshall616@btinternet.com

MARSHALL, Preb Christopher John Bickford. b 32. AKC 56. **d** 57 **p** 58. C Leatherhead *Guildf* 57–60; C Crewkerne *B & W* 60–63; V Long Sutton 63–72; V Long Sutton w Long Load 72–76; V Wiveliscombe 76–93; RD Tone 78–87; Preb Wells Cathl 88–96; P-in-c Chipstable w Huish Champflower and Clatworthy 93; R Wiveliscombe w Chipstable, Huish Champflower etc 93–96; rtd 96; PtO *B & W* from 96. *Tap Cottage, High Street, Milverton, Taunton TA4 1LL* T: (01823) 400419

MARSHALL, Craig Laurence. b 64. Southn Univ BEd 87 Open Univ MA 93. St Jo Coll Nottm MTh 01. **d** 01 **p** 02. C Staplegrove w Norton Fitzwarren *B & W* 01–04; Chapl K Coll Taunton 04–06; R Aisholt, Enmore, Goathurst, Nether Stowey etc *B & W* 06–14; RD Quantock 12–14; V Hurstbourne Priors, Longparish etc *Win* from 14; Dioc Rural Officer from 14; AD Whitchurch from 17. *The Vicarage, St Mary Bourne, Andover SP11 6AY* T: (01264) 738308 E: craig785@btinternet.com

MARSHALL, David Charles. b 52. St Chad's Coll Dur BA 73. Trin Coll Bris 74. **d** 76 **p** 77. C Meole Brace *Lich* 76–78; C W Teignmouth *Ex* 78–80; C Broadwater St Mary *Chich* 80–84; V Newcastle St Geo *Lich* 84–92; Chapl Versailles w Chevry *Eur* 92–04; Min Southgate LEP *St E* 04–07; P-in-c Collier Row St Jas and Havering-atte-Bower *Chelmsf* 07–15; V 15; AD Havering 10–14; rtd 15; PtO *Eur* from 15. *Sous le Figuier, Hameau de Manieu, 32100 Condom, France* E: dmrevdave6@gmail.com

MARSHALL, Canon David Evelyn. b 63. New Coll Ox BA 85 Birm Univ MA 88 PhD 96. Ridley Hall Cam 88. **d** 90 **p** 91. C Roundhay St Edm *Ripon* 90–92; Chapl Ex Coll Ox 95–98; Lect St Paul's United Th Coll Limuru Kenya 98–99; P-in-c Buckden and Hail Weston *Ely* 99–00; Abp's Dom Chapl Cant 00–05; Hon Can All SS Cathl Cairo from 02; PtO *S'wark* 05–09; *Carl* from 09; Assoc Prof Duke Div Sch USA 13–18; WCC from 18. *Jubiläumsplatz 2, 3005 Bern, Switzerland* E: revdem63@yahoo.co.uk

MARSHALL, Derek Stanley. b 53. All SS Cen for Miss & Min 11. **d** 14 **p** 15. NSM Tranmere St Cath *Ches* 14–18; Chapl YMCA Birkenhead 14–18; P-in-c Leasowe from 18. *70 Castleway North, Wirral CH46 1RW* M: 07746-943178 E: derekmarshall@yahoo.co.uk

MARSHALL, The Very Revd Geoffrey Osborne. b 48. St Jo Coll Dur BA 71. Coll of Resurr Mirfield 71. **d** 73 **p** 74. C Waltham Cross *St Alb* 73–76; C Digswell 76–78; P-in-c Belper Ch Ch and Milford *Derby* 78–86; V Spondon 86–93; Chapl Derby High Sch 87–01; RD Derby N 90–95; Can Res Derby Cathl 93–02; Dioc Dir of Ords 95–00; TR Wrexham *St As* 02–08; AD 02–08; Dean Brecon *S & B* 08–14; Warden of Readers 08–14; V Brecon St Mary w Llanddew 08–11; P-in-c Llanddew 11–14; rtd 14; PtO *Derby* 14–16; Hon C Morley and Smalley 16–18; PtO from 18. *36 Saundersfoot Way, Oakwood, Derby DE21 2RH* T: (01332) 280452 E: brecondeanery@btinternet.com

MARSHALL, Mrs Gillian Kathryn. b 54. Glouc Sch of Min 84. **d** 87 **p** 97. NSM Newtown w Llanllwchaiarn w Aberhafesp *St As* 87–98; P-in-c Betws Cedewain and Tregynon and Llanwyddelan 98–02; V 02–06. *31 Bromley College, London Road, Bromley BR1 1PE* T: (020) 8464 9727 E: revalexandermarshall17@gmail.com

MARSHALL, Graham George. b 38. Dur Univ BA 60 St Chad's Coll Dur. **d** 65 **p** 66. C Ashton-on-Ribble St Mich *Blackb* 65–67; C Lancaster St Mary 67–71; R Church Eaton *Lich* 71–75; Prec Man Cathl 75–78; R Reddish 78–85; V Chadderton St Luke 87–02; rtd 02; PtO *Man* from 02. *7 The Woods, Rochdale OL11 3NT* T: (01706) 642139 E: pizzicatoman@sky.com

MARSHALL (née CHADWICK), Mrs Helen Jane. b 63. UEA BA 84. St Jo Coll Nottm MTh 91. **d** 91 **p** 94. Par Dn Easton H Trin w St Gabr and St Lawr and St Jude *Bris* 91–94; C 94–95; PtO *Ox* 95–98; Lect St Paul's Th Coll Limuru Kenya 98–99; PtO *Ely* 99–00; Chapl K Coll Lon 01–05; P-in-c Addiscombe St Mildred *S'wark* 05–06; V 06–09; PtO *Carl* 09–13; NSM Keswick St Jo w Borrowdale 13–19; Asst Chapl Berne *Eur* from 19. *Jubiläumsplatz 2, 3005 Bern, Switzerland* E: helenmarshall2@yahoo.co.uk

MARSHALL, James Hudson. b 48. Sheff Univ CertEd 70 Open Univ BA 74 Cumbria Univ BA 08. LCTP 05. **d** 08 **p** 09.

NSM Lamplugh w Ennerdale *Carl* 08–13; P-in-c 11–13; rtd 14; PtO *Carl* from 14. *28 Arlecdon Road, Arlecdon, Frizington CA26 3UX* E: revjimmarshall@gmail.com

MARSHALL, Mrs Jean. b 36. SWMTC 84. **d** 87 **p** 94. NSM Stratton *Truro* 87–89; NSM Bodmin w Lanhydrock and Lanivet 89–94; P-in-c Lezant w Lawhitton and S Petherwin w Trewen 94–98; rtd 98; Hon C Bodmin w Lanhydrock and Lanivet *Truro* 00–06; PtO from 06. *10 Springwell View, Love Lane, Bodmin PL31 2QP* T: (01208) 79891

MARSHALL, John. b 37. Kelham Th Coll 53. **d** 62 **p** 63. C Winshill *Derby* 62–64; C Chaddesden St Phil 64–65; Chapl HM YOI Morton Hall 65–75; V Swinderby *Linc* 66–77; R Church Aston *Lich* 77–84; V Auckland St Andr and St Anne *Dur* 84–02; P-in-c Hunwick 88–90; Chapl Bishop Auckland Gen Hosp 84–94; Chapl Bishop Auckland Hospitals NHS Trust 94–98; Chapl S Durham Healthcare NHS Trust 98–00; rtd 02; PtO *Derby* 02–06 and 08–19; Hon C S Darley, Elton and Winster 06–08; Hon C Darley, S Darley and Winster 08; PtO *Dur* from 19. *11 Village Close, Newton Aycliffe DL5 4UD*

MARSHALL, John. b 50. St Luke's Coll Ex CertEd 74 W Lon Inst of HE DEHC 79. S'wark Ord Course 88. **d** 91 **p** 92. Hon C Brixton Hill St Sav *S'wark* 91–95; Hon C Clapham St Jas from 95. *57A Kingscourt Road, London SW16 1JA* T: (020) 8769 3665 M: 07873-712091 E: ajohn20002000@yahoo.co.uk

MARSHALL, John Linton. b 42. Worc Coll Ox BA 64 MA 68 Bris Univ MLitt 75. Wells Th Coll 66. **d** 68 **p** 69. C Bris St Mary Redcliffe w Temple etc 68–71; Tutor Sarum & Wells Th Coll 71–73; PtO *Pet* 74–77; LtO *S'wark* 77–81; V Choral S'well Minster 79–81; R Ordsall 81–88; P-in-c Grove 84–88; RD Retford 84–88; V Nottwoham *Wakef* 88–99; P-in-c Glouc St Mark and St Mary de Crypt w St Jo etc 99–00; R Glouc St Mary de Lode and St Mary de Crypt etc 00–09; rtd 09; PtO *Glouc* from 15. *166 Calton Road, Gloucester GL1 5ER*

MARSHALL, Mrs Judith Elizabeth. b 53. St Hild Coll Dur BEd 75. SCTEI 17. **d** 19. OLM Chipping Norton *Ox* from 19. *8 Church Street, Chipping Norton OX7 5NT* T: (01608) 643303 M: 07753-492654 E: joulesmarshall53@gmail.com

MARSHALL, Mrs Julie. b 62. **d** 08 **p** 09. OLM Bucknall *Lich* from 08. *27 Meadow Avenue, Wetley Rocks, Stoke-on-Trent ST9 0BD* T: (01782) 550993 E: julie.marshall@stokecoll.ac.uk

MARSHALL, Ms Karen Lesley. b 59. Coll of Ripon & York St Jo BA 82 Leeds Metrop Univ BSc 96 Huddersfield Univ MA 05. NEOC 04. **d** 07 **p** 08. C Horsforth *Ripon* 07–11; P-in-c Leeds All SS w Osmondthorpe 11–14; P-in-c Urmston *Man* 14–15; P-in-c Davyhulme Ch Ch 14–15; V Davyhulme Ch Ch and Urmston 15–19; P-in-c Hebden Bridge and Heptonstall *Leeds* from 19. *Address temp unknown* E: reverendkaren@btinternet.com

MARSHALL, Keith William. **d** 11 **p** 12. C Portadown St Mark *Arm* from 11. *4 Killycomain Drive, Portadown, Craigavon BT63 5JJ* E: keithmarshall777@yahoo.com

MARSHALL, Mrs Margaret Elizabeth. b 60. New Hall Cam BA 81 MA 84. EAMTC 01. **d** 04 **p** 05. C St Neots *Ely* 04–09; P-in-c Riversmeet *St Alb* 09–13; R 13–17; rtd 17; PtO *Ely* from 17; *St Alb* from 17. *80 Hardwick Road, Eynesbury, St Neots PE19 2SD*

MARSHALL, Melanie Kirsten. b 80. Ch Ch Ox BA 02 MSt 06 Toronto Univ MA 07 BNC Ox DPhil 11 Em Coll Cam MA 12. Westcott Ho Cam 10. **d** 13 **p** 14. C Bedford Park *Lon* 13–15; Chapl Linc Coll Ox from 15. *Lincoln College, Turl Street, Oxford OX1 3DR* M: 07967-762558 E: mthrmelanie@gmail.com *or* chaplain@lincoln.ox.ac.uk

MARSHALL, Michael David. b 51. BSc. Trin Coll Bris. **d** 84 **p** 85. C Kennington St Mark *S'wark* 84–88; V Streatham Park St Alb 88–96; RD Tooting 93–96; V Blackheath St Jo 96–06; RD Charlton 01–06; Chapl Bishop's Stortford Coll 06–11; V St Austell *Truro* 11–15; rtd 15; PtO *Nor* from 16. *12 Aspen Way, Cringleford, Norwich NR4 6UA* E: mikemarshall51@hotmail.com

✠**MARSHALL, The Rt Revd Michael Eric.** b 36. Ch Coll Cam BA 58 MA 60. Cuddesdon Coll 58. **d** 60 **p** 61 **c** 75. C Birm St Pet 60–62; Tutor Ely Th Coll 62–64; Min Can Ely Cathl 62–64; Chapl Lon Univ 64–69; V St Marylebone All SS 69–75; Suff Bp Woolwich *S'wark* 75–84; Episc Dir Angl Inst Missouri 84–92; Abps' Adv Springboard for Decade of Evang 92–97; Hon Asst Bp Lon 84–07; Hon Asst Bp Chich from 92; Can and Preb Chich Cathl 90–99; Bp in Res Upper Chelsea H Trin *Lon* 97–02; R 02–07; rtd 07; PtO *Eur* from 18. *Flat 18 Grosvenor Court, 99 Sloane Street, London SW1X 9PF* M: 07710-215131 E: awgust17est12345@gmail.com

MARSHALL, Mrs Michèle Jane. b 60. SEN 82. NTMTC 05. **d** 08 **p** 09. C Orsett and Bulphan and Horndon on the Hill *Chelmsf* 08–11; C Pitsea w Nevendon 11–13; C Woodham Ferrers and Bicknacre 13–19; C S Woodham Ferrers 13–19; P-in-c E and W Tilbury and Linford from 19; Lead Chapl (Essex) St Andr

Healthcare from 13. *The Rectory, 24 Somerset Road, Linford, Stanford-le-Hope SS17 0QA* E: mjmarshall@fastmail.co.uk

MARSHALL, Peter John Charles. b 35. Bris Univ BA 60. Ridley Hall Cam 60. **d** 62 **p** 63. C Lindfield *Chich* 62–65; Travelling Sec Scripture Union 65–83; Hon C Nottingham St Nic *S'well* 65–67; Hon C Cheadle Hulme St Andr *Ches* 67–83; V Ilkley All SS *Bradf* 83–98; RD Otley 92–97; rtd 98; PtO *Ches* 00–03; *St As* from 03; *Ban* 11–17. *Creuddyn Barn, Glanwydden, Llandudno Junction LL31 9JL* T: (01492) 547352 M: 07728-713175 E: revmarsh35@gmail.com

MARSHALL, Richard Arthur Howard. b 66. Regent's Park Coll Ox BA 88 MA 92 SS Coll Cam PGCE 89. Wycliffe Hall Ox BTh 99. **d** 98 **p** 99. C Broughton *Man* 98–02; Asst Chapl Sedbergh Sch 02–03; Sub Chapl HM Pris Man 02–04; V Blackb Redeemer from 04. *2 Kendall Close, Blackburn BB2 4FB* T: (01254) 51206 E: vicar@the-redeemer.org.uk

MARSHALL, Robert David. b 52. TCD BA 75 MA 00 Solicitor 77. CITC 99. **d** 02 **p** 03. NSM Stillorgan w Blackrock *D & G* from 02. *The Tontine, 84 The Rise, Mount Merrion, Co Dublin, Republic of Ireland* T: (00353) (1) 288 6170 *or* (1) 649 2137 F: 649 2649 M: 86-815 3089 E: curate@stillorgan.dublin.anglican.org

MARSHALL, Robert Paul. b 60. Sheff Univ BA 81 PhD 14 St Jo Coll Dur MA 85. Cranmer Hall Dur 81. **d** 83 **p** 84. C Kirkstall *Ripon* 83–85; C Otley *Bradf* 85–87; Dioc Communications Officer 87–91; P-in-c Embsay w Eastby 87–91; Dioc Communications Officer *Lon* 91–95; P-in-c S Kensington St Aug 95–00; Media Adv to Abp *York* 95–05; Communications Adv *Sheff* 04–13; Public Relns Adv Fresh Expressions from 05; Hd of Marketing St Mary's Univ Coll Twickenham *Lon* 05–07; Hon C Kensington St Mary Abbots w Ch Ch and St Phil 07–13; PtO *Ely* 08–13; *Derby* 08–13; *Sarum* 08–13; P-in-c E Ham w Upton Park and Forest Gate *Chelmsf* 13; TR 13–15; PtO *Lon* from 14; Min Digswell St Jo CD *St Alb* 15–16; P-in-c Digswell and Panshanger 16–18; R Digswell from 18. *The Rectory, 354 Knightsfield, Welwyn Garden City AL8 7NG* T: (01707) 592088 M: 07917-272833 E: robmarshalluk@gmail.com

MARSHALL, Sarah. b 75. E Lon Univ BA 97 Herts Univ MA 15 MCIPD 15. ERMC 16. **d** 19. C Tring *St Alb* from 19. *Address withheld by request*

MARSHALL, Simon Hardy. b 69. Bp Grosseteste Coll BA 92. St Jo Coll Nottm 00. **d** 02 **p** 03. C Bartley Green *Birm* 02–05; TV Solihull from 05. *Oak Cottage, Bryanston Road, Solihull B91 1BS* T: 0121-704 4730

MARSHALL, Mrs Sonia Margaret Cecilia. b 49. Westf Coll Lon BA 71 Nottm Univ MA 03. EMMTC 01. **d** 03 **p** 04. NSM Deeping St James *Linc* from 03; PtO *Pet* from 12. *135C Eastgate, Deeping St James, Peterborough PE6 8RB* T: (01778) 346420 E: curate@dsj.org.uk *or* sonia.marshall@btinternet.com

MARSHALL, Trevor. b 60. SEITE 08. **d** 11 **p** 12. C Bognor *Chich* 11–15; PtO 16–18; P-in-c Tangmere and Oving from 18. *St Andrew's Rectory, 21 Gibson Road, Tangmere, Chichester PO20 2JA* M: 07900-158982

MARSHALL, William John. b 35. TCD BA 57 BD 61 PhD 75. TCD Div Sch 59. **d** 59 **p** 60. C Ballyholme *D & D* 59–61; India 62–72; Asst Dean of Residence TCD 73–76; I Rathmichael *D & G* 76–92; Can Ch Ch Cathl Dublin 90–02; Chan Ch Ch Cathl Dublin 91–02; Vice-Prin CITC 92–02; rtd 02. *115 The Elms, Abberley, Killiney, Co Dublin, Republic of Ireland* T: (00353) (1) 239 0832 E: rail1948@eircom.net

MARSHMAN, Mrs Elizabeth Maryan. b 53. York St Jo Coll CertEd 74 Leeds Univ BEd 75. NEOC 03. **d** 06 **p** 07. C Clifton *York* 06–10; P-in-c Lockington and Lund and Scorborough w Leconfield 10–14; R 14–18; rtd 18; PtO *York* from 19. *36 Main Street, Kilnwick, Driffield YO25 9JD* E: emmarshman@yahoo.co.uk

MARSTON, Benjamin Charles. b 85. St Cuth Soc Dur BA 06. Wycliffe Hall Ox BA 19. **d** 19. C Retford Area *S'well* from 19. *25 Laurel Grove, Retford DN22 7WD* M: 07596-349882 E: benjamincmarston@gmail.com

MARSTON, David Howarth. b 48. St Jo Coll Dur BA 69. Edin Th Coll 69. **d** 71 **p** 72. C Kendal H Trin *Carl* 71–75; PtO *Glas* 75–78; NSM Barrow St Matt *Carl* 79–86; PtO *York* 86–91; Liv 91–93 and 99–00; NSM Southport All SS and All So 93–99; NSM Southport St Luke 00–09; PtO from 11. *33 Sandringham Road, Ainsdale, Southport PR8 2NY* T: (01704) 578303

MARSTON, James Duncan. b 75. Surrey Univ BSc 96 Anglia Ruskin Univ MA 19. Westcott Ho Cam 17. **d** 19. C Alde Sandlings *St E* from 19. *The Rectory, Aldeburgh Road, Friston, Saxmundham IP17 1NP* E: marstonjames@hotmail.com

MARSTON, William Thornton. b 59. Worc Coll Ox BA 81 MA 85 Cam Univ CertEd 83. St Steph Ho Ox BA 87. **d** 88 **p** 89. C Beckenham St Geo *Roch* 88–92; C-in-c Middleton-on-Sea CD *Chich* 97–99; V Middleton from 99. *The Vicarage, 106 Elmer Road, Middleton-on-Sea, Bognor Regis PO22 6LJ* T: (01243) 586348 E: w.marston@btinternet.com

MARSZALEK, Mrs Rachel Emma. b 74. St Jo Coll Nottm 08. **d** 11 **p** 12. C Belper *Derby* 11–14; V Ealing All SS *Lon* from 14. *All Saints' Vicarage, Elm Grove Road, London W5 3JH* T: (020) 8823 9160 M: 07906-632972 E: revrachelemma@gmail.com

MART, Terence Eugene. b 47. CertEd 76 BA 82. St Jo Coll Nottm LTh 87. **d** 87 **p** 88. C Prestatyn *St As* 87–91; Chapl Theatr Clwyd Mold 87–91; R Llangystennin *St As* 91–01; RD Llanrwst 96–00; V Llanfair DC, Derwen, Llanelidan and Efenechtyd 01–07. *31 Pengarth, Conwy LL32 8RW*

MARTELL, Samantha Tara. b 70. Girton Coll Cam BA 92. Ripon Coll Cuddesdon 14. **d** 17 **p** 18. C Meon Bridge *Portsm* from 17. *The Vicarage, Webbs Green, Soberton, Southampton SO32 3PY* T: (01489) 232041 E: revsamantha@alpha-omega.me

MARTIN, Mrs Adele Joan. b 51. BSc 74. Cranmer Hall Dur 05. **d** 07 **p** 08. C Seacroft *Ripon* 07–11; P-in-c Dinsdale w Sockburn *Dur* 11–16; P-in-c Hurworth 11–16; Chapl HM YOI Deerbolt 11–15; PtO *Leeds* from 17. *30 Darnborough Gate, Ripon HG4 2TF* E: adele.martin@leeds.anglican.org

MARTIN, Andrew Philip. b 78. **d** 14 **p** 15. C Selly Park St Steph and St Wulstan *Birm* from 14. *103 Bournbrook Road, Selly Park, Birmingham B29 7BY* T: 0121-247 6763 M: 07799-990179 E: andy.martin@sssw.org.uk

MARTIN, Angela Frances. b 66. SEITE 05. **d** 08 **p** 09. C Henfield w Shermanbury and Woodmancote *Chich* 08–12; C Worth, Pound Hill and Maidenbower 12–14; V Forest Row from 14; RD E Grinstead from 19. *The Vicarage, Ashdown Road, Forest Row RH18 5BW* T: (01342) 458263 E: revd.angelamartin@gmail.com

MARTIN, Angela Lee. b 61. EMMTC 00. **d** 03 **p** 04. NSM Derby St Barn 03–08; P-in-c Hatton 08–19; rtd 19. *9 Scarsdale Avenue, Allestree, Derby DE22 2LA* T: (01332) 552937 M: 07967-180531 E: hattonlee1968@yahoo.co.uk

MARTIN, Anne Elizabeth. b 61. Qu Foundn (Course) 15. **d** 18 **p** 19. OLM Oxley and Wednesfield St Greg *Lich* from 18. *30 Lodge Road, Wolverhampton WV10 6TH* T: (01902) 784917 M: 07709-616052 E: anneinwolves@blueyonder.co.uk

MARTIN, Brendan James. b 84. Oak Hill Th Coll. **d** 16 **p** 17. C Angmering *Chich* 16–19; R Frant w Eridge from 19. *The Rectory, Church Lane, Frant, Tunbridge Wells TN3 9DX* M: 07783-880257 E: revbjmartin@gmail.com

MARTIN, Canon Bryan Robert. b 71. TCD BTh 01. CITC 98. **d** 01 **p** 02. C Magheralin w Dollingstown *D & D* 01–04; C Knockbreda 04–07; I Dromore *Clogh* 07–10; I Donaghcloney w Waringstown *D & D* from 10; Can Dromore Cathl from 16. *The Rectory, 54 Banbridge Road, Waringstown, Craigavon BT66 7QD* T: (028) 3888 1218 E: brymrtn@aol.com *or* bryan.martin@btinternet.com

MARTIN, Canon Cameron Anthony Brian. b 56. Cape Town Univ BA 93 Cant Univ (NZ) MBA 02 MA 05. St Bede's Coll Umtata 82. **d** 84 **p** 85. C Nigel Ch the K S Africa 84–86; R Ennerdale St Nic 87–89; R Eldorado Park Transfiguration 89–90; P-in-c Kenwyn 90–95; R Woodlands 95–02; Adn Mitchell's Plain 98–02; Dioc Admin Kimberley and Kuruman 02–05; Can from 03; P-in-c Brumby *Linc* 05–07; TR from 07; RD Manlake from 14. *St Hugh's Rectory, 114 Ashby Road, Scunthorpe DN16 2AG* M: 07887-802784 E: cameron.martin@ntlworld.com *or* cameron.martin@lincoln.anglican.org

MARTIN, Caroline Evelyn. *See* BECKETT, Caroline Evelyn

MARTIN, Christopher Edward. b 70. Bris Poly BA 92 ACA 97. Trin Coll Bris 07. **d** 09 **p** 10. C Newton Flotman, Swainsthorpe, Tasburgh, etc *Nor* 09–12; C Whimple, Talaton and Clyst St Lawr *Ex* 12–13; P-in-c 13–16; R Whimple, Talaton, Clyst St Lawr and Clyst Hydon from 16; C Bradninch 13–17. *The Rectory, Grove Road, Whimple, Exeter EX5 2TP* T: (01404) 822427 E: cemartin70@gmail.com

MARTIN, Christopher John. b 45. Ball Coll Ox BA 67 MA 87 Aber Univ MTh 09. Wycliffe Hall Ox 86. **d** 88 **p** 89. C Edin St Thos 88–90; R Duns 90–00; Chapl Lyon *Eur* 00–13; rtd 13; PtO *Eur* from 16; *Edin* from 16. *10 Kirkhill Terrace, Edinburgh EH16 5DQ* E: revchris.martin@free.fr

MARTIN, David Howard. b 47. Worc Coll Ox BEd 79. AKC 70 St Aug Coll Cant 70. **d** 71 **p** 72. C Sedgley All SS *Lich* 71–75; Dioc Youth Chapl *Worc* 75–81; P-in-c Worc St Andr and All SS w St Helen 75–81; R Newland, Guarlford and Madresfield 81–91; R Alvechurch 91–13; rtd 13; PtO *Worc* from 13. *4 Denison Close, Malvern WR14 2EU* T: (01684) 577425 E: davidandlizmartin@gmail.com

MARTIN, David Raymond. **d** 14 **p** 15. Howth *D & G* 14–15; C Hillsborough *D & D* 15–18; Dir ICM from 18. *28 Bachelors Walk, Dublin 1, Republic of Ireland* M: (00353) 85-806 9659 E: drmartin79@gmail.com *or* david@irishchurchmissions.ie

MARTIN, Edward Eldred William. b 37. Cranfield Inst of Tech MSc 84 Herts Univ MA 88. S'wark Ord Course 65. **d** 68 **p** 69.

C Greenwich St Alfege w St Pet *S'wark* 68–71; C Kidbrooke St Jas 71–75; V Peckham St Jo 75–78; P-in-c Peckham St Andr w All SS 76–78; V Peckham St Jo w St Andr 78–81; Hon Chapl S'wark Cathl 81–02; Chapl Guy's Hosp Lon 81–88; rtd 02; PtO *S'wark* 02–03 and from 07; Hon C Lee St Marg 03–07. *4 Belmont Hill, London SE13 5BD*   T: (020) 8318 4957   M: 07956-204869 E: tedmartin2217@yahoo.co.uk

MARTIN, Edward James Russell. b 76. Hull Univ BA 98 Leeds Univ BA 02 MA 06. Coll of Resurr Mirfield 00. d 03 p 04. C Carrington *S'well* 03–06; P-in-c Chapel St Leonards w Hogsthorpe *Linc* 06–09; R Scartho 09–14; V Grimsby St Aug 14–19; V Gt Grimsby St Andr w St Luke and All SS 14–19; V Edenham w Witham on the Hill and Swinstead from 19. *The Rectory, 15 Hillview Road, South Witham, Grantham NG33 5QW*   M: 07736-711360 E: edward.martin@lincoln.anglican.org

MARTIN, Mrs Eileen. b 43. City of Portsm Coll of Educn TCert 65. d 03 p 15. OLM Queen Thorne *Sarum* 03–08; C Is of Scilly *Truro* 15–18; rtd 18. *Mellyns, Church Road, St Mary's, Isles of Scilly TR21 0NA*   T: (01720) 423660 E: rev_eileenm@yahoo.co.uk

MARTIN, Miss Eileen Susan Kirkland. b 45. LCST 66. Cranmer Hall Dur 77. dss 83 d 86. Kilmarnock *Glas* 84–86; Par Dn Heanor *Derby* 87–92; PtO 92–05. *1 Malin Court, Hardings Close, Hemel Hempstead HP3 9AQ*   T: (01442) 216768 E: eileen_martin8@yahoo.co.uk

MARTIN, Elizabeth Anne. See DADY, Elizabeth Anne

MARTIN, Glenn. b 52. Qu Coll Birm 84. d 86 p 87. C Chatham St Wm *Roch* 86–89; Chapl Pastures Hosp Derby 89–94; Chapl Kingsway Hosp Derby 89–94; Sen Chapl S Derbys Mental Health NHS Trust 94–97; Sen Chapl Community Health Sheff NHS Trust 97–01; Professional Development Officer for Chapl and Spiritual Healthcare 01–07; NSM Gilmorton, Peatling Parva, Kimcote etc *Leic* 04–07; NSM Guilsborough w Hollowell and Cold Ashby *Pet* 07–08; NSM Cottesbrooke w Gt Creaton and Thornby 07–08; NSM Spratton 07–08; NSM W Haddon w Winwick and Ravensthorpe 07–08; R Sutton Bonington w Normanton-on-Soar *S'well* 08–11; P-in-c Derby St Andr w St Osmund 11–13; P-in-c Allenton and Shelton Lock 11–13; rtd 13; PtO *Derby* 13–19; *Leic* from 14; *S'well* from 14. *27 Shields Crescent, Castle Donington, Derby DE74 2JS*   T: (01332) 818858 E: glenn.martinrev@btinternet.com

MARTIN, Graham Rowland. b 39. Liv Univ CertEd 58 Lon Univ BD 70 Bris Univ BEd 73 FRSA LCG 06. Wells Th Coll 71. d 71 p 72. Hon C Glouc St Cath 71–76; P-in-c Brookthorpe w Whaddon 76–78; PtO 78–80; Hon C Hucclecote 80–82; Hon C Tuffley 82–88; NSM Hardwicke, Quedgeley and Elmore w Longney 88–89; V Kemble, Poole Keynes, Somerford Keynes etc 89–96; P-in-c Bibury w Winson and Barnsley 96–04; Dioc Ecum Officer 96–04; rtd 04; PtO *Glouc* from 04; *Ox* from 16. *Wharf Cottage, Wharf Lane, Lechlade GL7 3AU*   T: (01367) 252825 E: graham.martin@appleinter.net

MARTIN, James Alwyn. b 47. St Paul's Coll Grahamstown 76. d 78 p 79. C Highlands St Mary Rhodesia 78–80; P-in-c Lowveld Zimbabwe 80–84; Adn Victoria 82–87; R Masvingo St Mich 84–87; R Borrowdale Ch Ch 87–98; Adn Harare S 96–98; Dean Bulawayo 98–04; V Aldershot St Mich *Guildf* 05–16; rtd 16; PtO *Cov* from 16. *11 Margetts Close, Kenilworth CV8 1EN*   T: (01926) 853120   M: 07749-770035 E: jamesmartin47@btinternet.com

MARTIN, Joan Jessica Heloise. b 63. Trin Hall Cam BA 86 PhD 93. EAMTC 00. d 03 p 04. NSM Trin Coll Cam 03–09; NSM Fen Ditton *Ely* 08–09; NSM Horningsea 08–09; NSM Teversham 08–09; P-in-c Duxford 10–16; P-in-c Hinxton 10–16; P-in-c Ickleton 10–16; P-in-c Whittlesford 15–16; Bp's Adv for Women's Min 14–16; Hon Can Ely Cathl 14–16; Can Res Ely Cathl from 16. *Powchers Hall, The College, Ely CB7 4DL*   M: 07780-704006 E: jessicamartin@virginmedia.com

MARTIN, John Eric Terence. b 75. SS Coll Cam MA 99 MEng 99. Wycliffe Hall Ox BTh 10. d 10 p 11. C Wolverhampton St Luke *Lich* 10–13. *18 Galileo Gardens, Cheltenham GL51 0GA*   M: 07941-978856 E: john@gracechurchcheltenham.org

MARTIN, John Henry. b 42. St Jo Coll Cam BA 63 MA 67. St Jo Coll Nottm BA 73. d 73 p 74. C Ecclesall *Sheff* 73–77; C Hednesford *Lich* 77–82; V Walsall Pleck and Bescot 82–92; V Whittington w Weeford 92–08; V Hints 05–08; rtd 08; PtO *Glouc* from 15. *2 Churn Close, South Cerney, Cirencester GL7 6HX*   T: (01285) 869585 E: john.h.martin642@gmail.com

MARTIN, John Hunter. b 42. AKC 64. d 65 p 66. C Mortlake w E Sheen *S'wark* 65–69; C-in-c Bermondsey St Hugh CD 69–72; V Bermondsey St Anne 72–78; P-in-c Lt Ouse *Ely* 78; V Littleport 78–89; V Attercliffe *Sheff* 89–90; P-in-c Darnall

89–90; TR Darnall-cum-Attercliffe 90–96; TR Attercliffe, Darnall and Tinsley 96; R Kirk Sandall and Edenthorpe 96–07; rtd 07; PtO *Glas* from 09. *Salara Haven, Sandgreen, Gatehouse of Fleet, Castle Douglas DG7 2DU*   T: (01557) 815068 E: vanessaandjohnmartin@gmail.com

MARTIN, Kevin. b 73. Surrey Univ BA 01 Heythrop Coll Lon MTh 03 Roehampton Univ MSc 10. Sarum Coll MA 18. d 17 p 18. C Shaftesbury *Sarum* 17–18; C St Bartholomew from 18. *The Rectory, Donhead St Andrew, Shaftesbury SP7 9DZ*   T: (01747) 828551   M: 07968-622585 E: curate@benofbart.org.uk

MARTIN, Lee. See MARTIN, Angela Lee

MARTIN (*née* BULLEN), Mrs Marilyn Patricia. b 46. Liv Hope Univ Coll BA(Theol) 00 MA 05. NOC 06. d 06 p 07. NSM Stretton and Appleton Thorn *Ches* 06–09; Asst Chapl HM YOI Thorn Cross 06–17; rtd 17; PtO *Ches* from 13; *Liv* from 17. *Address withheld by request* E: malmartin@btinternet.com

MARTIN, Nicholas Worsley. b 52. Sarum & Wells Th Coll 71. d 75 p 76. C Llandaff w Capel Llanilltern *Llan* 75–79; C Cardiff St Jo 79; C Caerphilly 79–83; TV Hemel Hempstead *St Alb* 83–93; Chapl Hemel Hempstead Gen Hosp 83–93; PtO *Chich* 94–98; *Truro* 98–99; NSM Penzance St Mary w St Paul 99–02; rtd 02; NSM Penzance St Mary w St Paul and St Jo *Truro* 02–07; PtO from 16. *1 Redinnick Gardens, Penzance TR18 4JF*   T: (01736) 350506

MARTIN, Canon Penelope Elizabeth. b 44. Cranmer Hall Dur 83. dss 86 d 87 p 94. Seaham w Seaham Harbour *Dur* 86–89; Par Dn 87–89; Par Dn Cassop cum Quarrington 89–93; Par Dn Sherburn w Pittington 93–94; C 94–95; V 95–02; R Shadforth 95–02; R Pittington, Shadforth and Sherburn 02–03; Hon Can Dur Cathl 01–03; rtd 03; PtO *Dur* from 03. *34A Rosemount, Durham DH1 5GA*   T: 0191-386 1742   E: penny.martin@durham.anglican.org   *or* penelizmartin@gmail.com

MARTIN, Preb Peter. b 50. MCIH 75. Linc Th Coll 82. d 84 p 85. C Taunton H Trin *B & W* 84–86; C Bath Bathwick 86–88; R Cannington, Otterhampton, Combwich and Stockland 88–15; RD Sedgemoor 00–06; Warden of Readers Taunton Adnry 06–14; Chapl Cannington Coll 89–15; Preb Wells Cathl *B & W* 09–15; rtd 15; PtO *B & W* from 15. *55 Irnham Road, Minehead TA24 5DW*   T: (01643) 706552 E: revd.petermartin@gmail.com

MARTIN, Philip James. b 58. Cam Univ BA. Coll of Resurr Mirfield. d 84 p 85. C Pontefract St Giles *Wakef* 84–88; C Wantage *Ox* 88–90; C Didcot All SS 90; V Alderholt *Sarum* 90–17; V Branksome St Aldhelm from 17. *The Vicarage, St Aldhelm's Road, Poole BH13 6BT*   T: (01202) 032193 E: frphilipmartin@gmail.com

MARTIN, Raymond William. b 32. Lon Univ BSc 66 MBIM. Glouc Th Course 73. d 76 p 76. NSM Glouc St Mary de Lode and St Nic 76–77; NSM Redmarley D'Abitot, Bromesberrow w Pauntley etc 77–84; R 84–91; P-in-c Falfield w Rockhampton 91–98; P-in-c Oldbury-on-Severn 91–98; Chapl HM YOI Eastwood Park 91–92; rtd 98; PtO *Glouc* 98–00 and 02–12; Clergy Widows' Officer (Glouc Adnry) 99–12; P-in-c Shipton Moyne w Westonbirt and Lasborough 00–02; PtO *Heref* 03–15; *Worc* 03–15. *Tree Tops, 35 Thirlstane Road, Malvern WR14 3PL*   T: (01684) 562714 E: rws.martin@btinternet.com

MARTIN, Richard. b 34. Rhodes Univ BA 54 Em Coll Cam BA 57 MA 58. Wells Th Coll 57. d 59 p 60. C Portsea St Mary *Portsm* 59–60; C Bloemfontein Cathl S Africa 60–62; R Wepener 62–64; R Odendaalsrus 64–67; R Newton Park St Hugh 67–76; Chapl St Bede's Coll Umtata 77–79; R Hillcrest 79–87; C Aldershot St Mich *Guildf* 87–94; R Wick *Mor* 94–99; P-in-c Thurso 94–99; rtd 99; Hon C Diptford, N Huish, Harberton, Harbertonford etc *Ex* 99–01; PtO 01–03; LtO *Mor* 03–19; PtO *Blackb* from 19. *16 Fosbrooke House, 8 Clifton Drive, Lytham St Annes FY8 5RQ* E: martin@chilledthames.co.uk

MARTIN, Richard Arthur. b 59. Leeds Univ BA 91 MA 97 Cant Ch Ch Univ Coll PGCE 03. SEITE 07. d 09 p 10. C Gravesend St Aid *Roch* 09–12; P-in-c Gravesend H Family w Ifield 12–19; R from 19; Bp's Adv for Inter-Faith Concerns from 15. *18 Brenchley Avenue, Gravesend DA11 7RQ*   T: (01474) 249792   M: 07593-092758 E: ramartin@talktalk.net

MARTIN, Richard Charles de Villeval. b 41. St Jo Coll Ox BA 63 MA 67. Ox Ord Course. d 84 p 85. NSM Ox St Thos w St Frideswide and Binsey 84–04; Asst Chapl Highgate Sch Lon 86–92; Asst Master Magd Coll Sch Ox 92–02; Chapl 94–02; rtd 04; LtO *Ox* 05–12; PtO 12–16. *1 Ritchie Court, 380 Banbury Road, Oxford OX2 7PW*   T: (01865) 510694 E: rickycmartin@icloud.com

✠**MARTIN, The Rt Revd Robert David Markland.** b 49. Trin Coll Cam BA 71 MA 74 FCA 80. Trin Coll Bris BA 91. d 91 p 92 c 08. C Kingswood *Bris* 91–95; V Frome H Trin *B & W* 95–08; RD Frome 03–08; Suff Bp Marsabit Kenya 08–11;

Bp 11–16; rtd 16; Hon Asst Bp B & W from 16; PtO *Eur* from 17. *Willowgate, 1 Egford Hill, Egford, Frome BA11 3JH* E: robandsuemartin@gmail.com

MARTIN, Robin. *See* MARTIN, Thomas Robin

MARTIN, Robin Hugh. b 35. Rhodes Univ BA 56. **d** 58 **p** 59. C Darnall *Sheff* 58–62; C-in-c Kimberworth Park 62–65; LtO 65–66; LtO *Newc* 67–71; PtO *Sheff* 65–66; *Newc* 67–71; *Man* 79–93; *Heref* 97–07; *Lich* 97–99 and from 11; P-in-c Maesbury 99–11. *Offa House, Treflach, Oswestry SY10 9HQ* T: (01691) 657090

MARTIN, Roger Allen. b 38. Westmr Coll Lon CertEd 59 Birkbeck Coll Lon BA 64 FRMetS 79. SAOMC 97. **d** 99 **p** 00. NSM Bramfield, Stapleford, Waterford etc *St Alb* 99–06; NSM Broxbourne w Wormley 06–10; rtd 10; PtO *St Alb* from 10. *41 The Avenue, Bengeo, Hertford SG14 3DS* T: (01992) 422441 E: roger.martin@ntlworld.com

MARTIN, Canon Roger Ivor. b 42. MCMI. Cant Sch of Min. **d** 85 **p** 86. NSM Saltwood *Cant* 85–90; P-in-c Crundale w Godmersham 90–01; Dioc Exec Officer for Adult Educn and Lay Tr 90–96; CME Officer 94–96; Chapl to Bp Maidstone *Cant* 96–01; R Saltwood 01–09; Hon Can Cant Cathl 09; rtd 09; PtO *Cant* from 09; Hon C Aldington w Bonnington and Bilsington etc 11–12; AD Elham 18–19. *Kwetu, 23 Tanners Hill Gardens, Hythe CT21 5HY* T: (01303) 237204 E: rogmartin@btinternet.com

MARTIN, Ronald Charles John Richard. b 61. Bris Univ BA 92. Wesley Coll Bris 88. **d** 15 **p** 15. Lead Chapl Dorset Co Hosp NHS Foundn Trust from 15; C Sherborne w Castleton, Lillington and Longburton *Sarum* from 15. *The Old Coach House, South Street, Sherborne DT9 3LZ* M: 07701-091627

MARTIN, Rosanna Stuart. *See* STUART-MARTIN, Rosanna

MARTIN, Rupert Gresley. b 57. Worc Coll Ox BA 78 Ox Univ MA 95. Trin Coll Bris 89. **d** 91 **p** 92. C Yateley *Win* 91–95; V Sandal St Helen *Wakef* 95–14; *Leeds* from 14. *The Vicarage, 333 Barnsley Road, Wakefield WF2 6EJ* T: (01924) 255441 E: sandalmagna@gmail.com

MARTIN, Steven Edward. b 81. Ex Univ BA 03 MA 04 Bris Univ PhD 10 LRSM 03. St Steph Ho Ox 13. **d** 15 **p** 16. C Tavistock, Gulworthy and Brent Tor *Ex* 15–19; R Colyton, Musbury, Southleigh and Branscombe from 19. *The Vicarage, Vicarage Street, Colyton EX24 6LJ* M: 07866-582519 E: stevenemartin@gmail.com

MARTIN, Mrs Susan Jane. b 69. SEITE BA 10. **d** 10 **p** 11. C Minster-in-Sheppey *Cant* 10–12; C W Sheppey 12–14; P-in-c Reculver and Herne Bay St Bart and Hoath from 14. *The Vicarage, 25 Dence Park, Herne Bay CT6 6BQ* T: (01227) 360948 E: revsuemartin@btinternet.com

MARTIN, Mrs Susan Mary. b 49. UEA BEd 94. ERMC 04. **d** 09 **p** 10. NSM Gayton, Gayton Thorpe, E Walton, E Winch etc *Nor* 09–13; Chapl Norfolk Hospice from 13; PtO *Ely* from 19. *The Old Dairy, 2 Church View Lane, Gayton, King's Lynn PE32 1PY* T: (01553) 636166 M: 07801-701677 E: revdsuemartin@gmail.com

MARTIN, Sylvia. b 43. Sarum Th Coll 94. **d** 97 **p** 98. NSM Locks Heath *Portsm* 97–02; PtO 02–04; NSM Fareham H Trin 04–07; Chapl Fareham Coll of F&HE 04–07; rtd 07; PtO *Portsm* from 07. *9 Harvester Drive, Fareham PO15 5NR* T: (01329) 312269

MARTIN, Thomas Robin. b 40. Bernard Gilpin Soc Dur 63 Bps' Coll Cheshunt 64. **d** 67 **p** 68. C Ripley *Derby* 67–70; C Ilkeston St Mary 70–74; V Chelmsley w Buxworth 74–83; V Knighton St Mich *Leic* 83–85; V Thurmaston 85–05; rtd 05; C Leic Resurr 08; C Braunstone Park 09; C Birstall and Wanlip 10–11; PtO from 14. *22 Sycamore Road, Birstall, Leicester LE4 4LT* T: 0116-267 1651 E: tr.martin@btinternet.com

MARTIN, William Harrison. b 38. Sarum & Wells Th Coll 91. **d** 87 **p** 88. NSM Rushen *S & M* 87–92; C German 92–97; V Lonan and Laxey 97–08; rtd 08; PtO *S & M* from 09. *Crossag Villa, Crossag Road, Ballasalla, Isle of Man IM9 3EF* T: (01624) 825982 E: billmartin@manx.net

MARTIN-DOYLE, Mrs Audrey Brenda. b 35. Cranmer Hall Dur 80. **dss** 82 **d** 87 **p** 95. The Lye and Stambermill *Worc* 82–86; Chapl Lee Abbey 86–88; Ldr Aston Cottage Community 88–93; C Cheltenham St Mary, St Matt, St Paul and H Trin *Glouc* 94–97; rtd 97; PtO *Glouc* from 97. *39 Moorend Street, Cheltenham GL53 0EH* T: (01242) 510352 E: amastindoyle@gmail.com

MARTINEAU, Canon David Richards Durani. b 36. AKC 59. **d** 60 **p** 61. C Ches St Jo 60–64; C St Mark's Cathl George S Africa 64; C Riversdale 64–66; R Beaufort W and Victoria W 66–69; C Jarrow St Paul *Dur* 69–72; TV 72–75; TR Jarrow 76–85; V Gildersome *Wakef* 85–00; Hon Can Wakef Cathl 94–00; rtd 00; PtO *Linc* from 00; Hon Asst Chapl Voorschoten *Eur* 02–03. *Harlough, St Chad, Barrow-upon-Humber DN19 7AU* T: (01469) 531475 E: davidmartineau@gmail.com

MARTINEAU, Canon Jeremy Fletcher. b 40. K Coll Lon BD 65 AKC 65. **d** 66 **p** 67. C Jarrow St Paul *Dur* 66–73; Bp's Ind

Adv 69–73; P-in-c Raughton Head w Gatesgill *Carl* 73–80; Chapl to Agric 73–80; Ind Chapl *Bris* 80–90; Nat Rural Officer Gen Syn Bd of Miss 88–03; Hon Can Cov Cathl 01–03; rtd 04; LtO *St D* from 05. *11 New Hill Villas, Goodwick SA64 0DT* T: (01348) 874886 E: jeremy.m@talktalk.net

MARTLEW, Andrew Charles. b 50. Nottm Univ BTh 76 Lanc Univ MA 80. Linc Th Coll 72. **d** 76 **p** 77. C Poulton-le-Fylde *Blackb* 76–79; Hon C Lancaster Ch Ch 79–80; Malaysia 81–83; V Golcar *Wakef* 83–89; Dioc Schs Officer 89–95; V Warmfield 89–95; Dioc Dir of Educn *York* 95–02; CF (TA) 87–02; CF 02–10; Chapl HM Pris Ranby 10–11; rtd 11; PtO *Wakef* 10–13; V Womersley 13–14; *Leeds* from 14; PtO *York* from 11. *Balne Moor Farm, Balne Moor Road, Balne, Goole DN14 0EN* T: (01405) 862484 E: andrew.martlew42@gmail.com

MARTLEW, Mrs Catherine Linda. b 54. Bolton Inst of Educn BSc 84 Lon Inst of Educn MSc 85. LCTP 09. **d** 12 **p** 15. NSM Chorley St Geo *Blackb* 12–17; NSM Standish from 17. *148 Appley Lane North, Appley Bridge, Wigan WN6 9DX* T: (01257) 253345 M: 07969-878655 E: smartlew@sky.com

MARWOOD, Canon Timothy John Edmonds. b 51. Whitelands Coll Lon CertEd 72 Open Univ BA 89 Lon Inst of Educn MA 91. S'wark Ord Course 92. **d** 95 **p** 96. NSM Putney St Mary *S'wark* 95–00; PtO *Ex* 00–07; P-in-c Petersham *S'wark* 07–11; V from 11; P-in-c Earlsfield St Jo 15–17; Chapl K Coll Sch Wimbledon 08–10; AD Richmond and Barnes *S'wark* 10–15; Hon Can S'wark Cathl from 08. *The Vicarage, Bute Avenue, Richmond TW10 7AX* T: (020) 8940 8435 M: 07973-518742 E: timmarwood@yahoo.co.uk

MASCALL, Mrs Margaret Ann. b 43. LRAM 64 Bris Univ CertEd 65 St Jo Coll Dur BA 71 MA 79. Cranmer Hall Dur 69. **dss** 76 **d** 87 **p** 94. Hertford St Andr *St Alb* 75–79; Herne Bay Ch Ch *Cant* 79–82; Seasalter 82–84; Whitstable 84–90; Par Dn 87–90; PtO 91–94; Hon C Hackington 94–95; V Newington w Hartlip and Stockbury 95–03; rtd 03; PtO *Cant* from 03. *48 Holmside Avenue, Minster on Sea, Sheerness ME12 3EY* T: (01795) 663095

MASCARENHAS, Felix Pedro Antonio. b 55. Bombay Univ BA 80 Pontifical Univ Rome JCD 88. Pilar Major Th Sem Goa BTh 81. **d** 82 **p** 82. In RC Ch 82–02; C Chich St Paul and Westhampnett 02–06; V Brighton Gd Shep Preston from 06. *The Vicarage, 272 Dyke Road, Brighton BN1 5AE* T: (01273) 882987 M: 07814-739312 E: felixmas@hotmail.com *or* vicar@goodshepherdbrighton.org.uk

MASEKO, Miss Lindiwe. b 72. Univ of Wales BTh 03 Roehampton Univ MA 07. Wycliffe Hall Ox MTh 17. **d** 17 **p** 18. C Deptford St Jo w H Trin and Ascension *S'wark* from 17. *3 Orchard Hill, London SE13 7QZ* M: 07817-283818 E: lindi98@hotmail.com

MASH, William Edward John. b 54. Imp Coll Lon BSc 75 Open Univ MA 00 ARCS. St Jo Coll Nottm 87. **d** 89 **p** 90. C Beverley Minster *York* 89–93; V Elloughton and Brough w Brantingham 93–01; P-in-c Newcastle St Geo *Lich* 01–08; V 08–10; P-in-c Knutton 06–08; V 08–10; Chapl Town Cen and Newcastle Coll 01–10; Team Ldr Black Country Urban Ind Miss *Lich* from 10; Dioc Officer for Miss in the Economy from 10; PtO *Worc* from 12. *20 Mahogany Drive, Stafford ST16 2TS* T: (01785) 509231 M: 07714-103007 E: william.e.j.mash@gmail.com

MASHEDER, Canon Peter Timothy Charles. b 49. AKC 71. St Aug Coll Cant 71. **d** 72 **p** 73. C Barkingside St Fran *Chelmsf* 72–75; C Chingford SS Pet and Paul 75–91; P-in-c High Laver w Magdalen Laver and Lt Laver etc 91–98; R 98–07; RD Ongar 98–04; R Ray Valley *Ox* 07–14; AD Bicester and Islip 08–13; Hon Can Ch Ch 13–14; rtd 14; Hon C Honiton, Gittisham, Combe Raleigh, Monkton etc *Ex* 14–15; P-in-c Bere Regis and Affpuddle w Turnerspuddle *Sarum* 15–19; PtO *Ex* from 19. *6 Higher Green, South Brent TQ10 9PL* E: chasmash@ic24.net

MASHITER, Mrs Marion. b 48. CBDTI 01. **d** 04 **p** 05. NSM Burnside *Carl* 04–07; NSM Beacon 07–10; NSM Natland from 10; NSM Old Hutton and New Hutton from 10. *The Maples, 5 Esthwaite Avenue, Kendal LA9 7NN* T: (01539) 731957 M: 07748-771836 E: revquackers5@gmail.com

MASIH, Emmanuel Nazir. *See* NAZIR MASIH, Emmanuel

MASIH, Wilson. b 49. **d** 11 **p** 12. NSM Hanwell St Mellitus w St Mark *Lon* 11–15; NSM Southall Ch Redeemer from 15. *37 West Avenue, Southall UB1 2AP* E: masih37@aol.com

MASKELL, John Michael. *See* MILLER-MASKELL, John Michael

MASKELL, Roland Wyndham (Wyn). **d** 17 **p** 18. NSM Carmarthen St Dav *St D* from 17. *Cwmgest, Talog, Carmarthen SA33 6NN* E: wynmaskell@btconnect.com

MASKELL, Miss Rosemary Helen. b 58. Ripon Coll Cuddesdon. **d** 00 **p** 01. C Goodrington *Ex* 00–04; V Littleport *Ely* 04–13; R Huntingdon St Barn and the Riptons 13–18; P-in-c Horsham St Faith, Spixworth and Crostwick *Nor* from

18; Chapl Norwich Internat Airport from 18. *The Rectory, Buxton Road, Spixworth, Norwich NR10 3PR* M: 07794-938501 E: rhmaskell@gmail.com

MASKREY, Mrs Susan Elizabeth. b 43. Cranmer Hall Dur IDC 70. **dss** 76 **d** 92 **p** 94. Littleover *Derby* 76–77; Sec to Publicity Manager CMS *Lon* 77–78; Stantonbury and Willen *Ox* 78–88; Billingham St Aid *Dur* 88–95; C 92–95; Asst Chapl HM Pris Holme Ho 94–95; Asst Chapl HM Pris Preston 95–01; Chapl HM Pris Kirkham 01–05; rtd 05; PtO *Blackb* from 05. *c/o the Bishop of Blackburn, Bishop's House, Ribchester Road, Blackburn BB1 9EF* E: maskreysue@hotmail.com

MASLEN, Mrs Linda Jane. b 62. Leeds Univ BA 83 Leic Univ MBA 95. Yorks Min Course 12. **d** 15 **p** 16. C Halifax St Aug and Mount Pellon *Leeds* 15–19; C Halifax w Siddal 17–19; C Inner Bradford and Outer Bradford Deaneries from 19. *The Rectory, 8 Redwing Drive, Bradford BD6 3YD* M: 07595-949153 E: linda_maslen@hotmail.com *or* linda.maslen@leeds.anglican.org

MASLEN (formerly CHILD), Mrs Margaret Mary. b 44. ALA 76 Open Univ BA 79. S Dios Minl Tr Scheme 89. **d** 92 **p** 94. C Portishead *B & W* 92–93; C Ilminster w Whitelackington 93–94; C Ilminster and Distr 94–96; C Tatworth 96–99; C Chaffcombe, Cricket Malherbie etc 99–00; TV Chard and Distr 00–05; Chapl Taunton and Somerset NHS Trust 97–05; rtd 05; Hon C Sherston Magna, Easton Grey, Luckington etc *Bris* 06–07; Hon C Hullavington, Norton and Stanton St Quintin 06–07; PtO from 07; *Glouc* from 14. *2 Woods Close, Sherston, Malmesbury SN16 0LF* T: (01666) 840387 E: maslens@tiscali.co.uk

MASLEN, Richard Ernest. b 34. S Dios Minl Tr Scheme 89. **d** 92 **p** 93. NSM Sherston Magna, Easton Grey, Luckington etc *Bris* 92–93; NSM Ilminster w Whitelackington *B & W* 93–94; NSM Ilminster and Distr 94–96; P-in-c Tatworth 96–99; TV Chard and Distr 99–00; rtd 00; PtO *B & W* 00–05; *Bris* from 05; *Glouc* from 14. *2 Woods Close, Sherston, Malmesbury SN16 0LF* T: (01666) 840387 E: maslens@tiscali.co.uk

MASLIN, Ian. b 65. Cranmer Hall Dur 14. **d** 16 **p** 17. C Cranleigh *Guildf* from 16. *22 Orchard Gardens, Cranleigh GU6 7LG* T: (01483) 379518 M: 07825-815170 E: ianmaslin831.im@gmail.com

MASON, Adrian Stanley. b 54. Hatf Poly BSc 77. Ripon Coll Cuddesdon 77. **d** 80 **p** 81. C Mill End and Heronsgate w W Hyde *St Alb* 80–83; TV Axminster, Chardstock, Combe Pyne and Rousdon *Ex* 83–87; TV Halesworth w Linstead, Chediston, Holton etc *St E* 87–88; R Brandon and Santon Downham 88–91; R Glemsford, Hartest w Boxted, Somerton etc 91–95; Min Can St E Cathl 95–97; R S Hartismere 06–11; P-in-c Stoke by Nayland w Leavenheath and Polstead 11–15; R Mid Elloe Gp *Linc* 15–19; rtd 19. *48 Queensway, Worksop S81 0AD* E: fr.adrian.mason@gmail.com

MASON, Ambrose. See MASON, Thomas Henry Ambrose

MASON, Andrew. b 73. **d** 10 **p** 11. NSM Chelsea St Jo w St Andr *Lon* from 10. *Flat 2, 465 Kings Road, London SW10 0LU* T: (020) 7351 1447 E: andymason73@yahoo.com *or* andy@stjohnchelsea.org

MASON, Miss Anna Louise. b 86. Glos Univ BEd 07. St Mellitus Coll MA 18. **d** 18 **p** 19. C Pentonville St Silas w All SS and St Jas *Lon* from 18. *260 Caledonian Road, London N1 0NG* M: 07793-277012 E: anna.mason@kxc.org.uk

✠**MASON, The Rt Revd Beverley Anne.** Trin Coll Bris BA 00. **d** 01 **p** 03 **c** 18. C Rusthall *Roch* 01–02; C Rainham 02–05; V Upper Norwood St Jo *S'wark* 05–12; AD Croydon N 10–12; P-in-c Bingley All SS *Bradf* 12–13; V 13–16; Adn Richmond and Craven *Leeds* 16–18; Suff Bp Warrington *Liv* from 18. *Bishop's House, 34 Central Avenue, Eccleston Park, Prescot L34 2QP* T: 0151-705 2140 E: revdbeverley@yahoo.co.uk *or* bishopofwarrington@liverpool.anglican.org

MASON, Charles Oliver. b 51. Jes Coll Cam BA 73 MA 99 St Jo Coll Dur BA 79. **d** 80 **p** 81. C Cheltenham St Mary, St Matt, St Paul and H Trin *Glouc* 80–84; C Enfield Ch Ch Trent Park *Lon* 84–88; P-in-c W Hampstead St Cuth 88–93; V 93–01; AD N Camden 98–01; V Braintree *Chelmsf* 01–16; rtd 16; P-in-c Waltham St Lawrence *Ox* from 16. *The Parsonage, School Road, Waltham St Lawrence, Reading RG10 0NU* T: 0118-934 1054 E: revdcom@btinternet.com

MASON, Christina Mary. b 42. Univ of Wales BMus 63 MA 67 BSc(Econ) 70 Dundee Univ PhD 84 Middx Univ MSc 02. St Jo Coll Nottm 81. **d** 83 **p** 10. LtO *Bre* 83–92; PtO *Nor* 09–10; NSM Gt and Lt Ellingham, Rockland and Shropham etc 10–18; P-in-c from 18. *9 Charles Avenue, Watton, Thetford IP25 6BY* T: (01953) 797622 E: ctrewartha@tiscali.co.uk

MASON, Damien David Robert. b 85. Edin Univ BD 11. St Steph Ho Ox MTh 15. **d** 15 **p** 16. C Hendon St Mary and Ch Ch *Lon* 15–18; V Brookfield St Mary from 18. *The Vicarage, 85 Darmouth Park Road, London NW5 1SL* T: (020) 7267 5941 M: 07505-723596 E: frdamienmason@gmail.com

MASON, David Gray. b 37. Birm Univ LDS 61 K Coll Lon MPhil 94. St Alb Minl Tr Scheme 83. **d** 95 **p** 95. NSM Biddenham *St Alb* 95–98; P-in-c Felmersham 98–05; NSM Sharnbrook, Felmersham and Knotting w Souldrop 05–12; RD Sharnbrook 06–12; PtO from 12. *2A Devon Road, Bedford MK40 3DF* T/F: (01234) 309737 E: david.mason93@ntlworld.com

MASON, Dawn Lavinia. b 53. Ripon Coll Cuddesdon 95. **d** 97 **p** 98. C Wisbech St Aug *Ely* 97–00; V Emneth and Marshland St James 00–09; P-in-c Elm and Friday Bridge w Coldham 04–09; V Fen Orchards from 09. *The Vicarage, 72 Church Road, Emneth, Wisbech PE14 8AF* T: (01945) 583089 E: dmason889@btinternet.com

MASON, Mrs Elizabeth Ann. b 42. Homerton Coll Cam TCert 64 Open Univ BA 90. Ox Min Course 91. **d** 94 **p** 95. NSM Worminghall w Ickford, Oakley and Shabbington *Ox* 94–95; NSM Swan 95–98; TV 98–05; PtO *Ox* from 06. *35 Common Road, North Leigh, Witney OX29 6RD* T: (01993) 883966

MASON, Francis Robert Anthony. b 56. Trin Coll Bris BA 90. **d** 90 **p** 91. C Denham *Ox* 90–94; P-in-c Jersey Grouville *Win* 94–98; R 98–04; R Tendring and Lt Bentley w Beaumont cum Moze *Chelmsf* 07–15; C Gt Oakley w Wix and Wrabness 13–15; R Fakenham w Alethorpe *Nor* from 15; P-in-c Fulmodeston w Croxton from 15. *The Rectory, 21 Gladstone Road, Fakenham NR21 9BZ* T: (01328) 862268 E: revmason@btinternet.com

MASON, John Evans. b 32. Linc Th Coll 57. **d** 59 **p** 60. C Putney St Mary *S'wark* 59–62; C Berry Pomeroy *Ex* 62–64; Chapl RN 64–68; V Hopton *Nor* 68–72; Chapl RNR 69–82; P-in-c Roydon St Remigius *Nor* 72–76; R Diss 72–80; Dir YMCA Cam 80–85; Prin YMCA Dunford Coll 85–88; PtO *Glouc* 88–97; *Ox* 89–99; rtd 96; PtO *Nor* 98–02; *Sarum* 02–04; *B & W* 05–08. *8 Nursteed Meadows, Nursteed, Devizes SN10 3HL* T: (01380) 728674

MASON, Jonathan Patrick. b 55. Univ of Wales (Trin St Dav) MA 12. Edin Th Coll 90. **d** 92 **p** 93. C Edin Ch Ch 92–94; C Edin Old St Paul 94–96; R St Andrews All SS *St And* 96–14; Chapl St Andr Univ 97–14; Dioc Dir of Ords 02–11; Can St Ninian's Cathl Perth 07–14; PtO *Newc* 15–16; P-in-c Kirkwhelpington, Kirkharle, Kirkheaton and Cambo from 16; P-in-c Bolam w Whalton and Hartburn w Meldon from 17; P-in-c Nether Witton from 17; Bp's Rural Affairs Adv from 16. *The Vicarage, Kirkwhelpington, Newcastle upon Tyne NE19 2RT* T: (01830) 540260 M: 07922-559854 E: j.mason@newcastle.anglican.org

MASON, Ms Josephine Margaret. b 41. Edin Univ BMus 64. WMMTC 88. **d** 93 **p** 94. Chapl Asst S Birm Mental Health NHS Trust 91–06; C Birm St Jo Ladywood 93–01; C Ladywood St Jo and St Pet 01–06; rtd 06; PtO *Birm* from 06. *340 Selly Oak Road, Birmingham B30 1HP* T: 0121-451 1412 E: jo.mason@freeuk.com *or* josephinemargaretmason@yahoo.co.uk

MASON, Julia Ann. b 43. St Jo Coll Nottm 89. **d** 91 **p** 95. NSM Troon *Glas* 91–93; NSM Ayr, Maybole and Girvan 93–95; LtO *Edin* from 08; PtO *Glas* from 08. *13/2 Rocheid Park, Edinburgh EH4 1RU* T: 0131-343 1165 E: revdjuliamason@btinternet.com

MASON, Canon Kenneth Staveley. b 31. ARCS 53 Lon Univ BSc 53 BD 64. Wells Th Coll 56. **d** 58 **p** 59. C Kingston upon Hull St Martin *York* 58–61; C Pocklington w Yapham-cum-Meltonby, Owsthorpe etc 61–63; C Millington w Gt Givendale 61–63; V Thornton w Allerthorpe 63–69; Sub-Warden St Aug Coll Cant 69–76; Abp's Adv in Past Min 76–77; Dir Cant Sch of Min 77–81; Prin 81–89; Sec to Dioc Bd of Min *Cant* 77–87; Six Preacher Cant Cathl 79–84; Hon Can Cant Cathl 84–89; Prin Edin Th Coll 89–94; Prin TISEC 95; Can St Mary's Cathl Edin 89–96; rtd 95; PtO *Ripon* 96–14; *Leeds* from 14. *2 Williamson Close, Ripon HG4 1AZ* T: (01765) 607041

MASON, Mrs Kimberley Sarah. b 82. Sheff Univ BA 04. **d** 18 **p** 19. C Harrogate St Mark *Leeds* from 18. *156 Pannal Ash Road, Harrogate HG2 9AJ* M: 07761-356464 E: kim.mason@leeds.anglican.org

MASON, Lesley Jane. b 55. Newnham Coll Cam BA 76 FInstD. St Jo Coll Nottm 04. **d** 07 **p** 08. NSM Busbridge and Hambledon *Guildf* 07–10; Chapl HM Pris Send from 10. *HM Prison Send, Ripley Road, Woking GU23 7LJ* T: (01483) 471000 E: ljmason@btinternet.com

MASON, Nigel Frederick. b 60. Wycliffe Hall Ox 93. **d** 95 **p** 96. C Highbury Ch Ch w St Jo and St Sav *Lon* 95–98; C Seaford w Sutton *Chich* 98–01; R Rotherfield w Mark Cross from 01. *The Rectory, Mayfield Road, Rotherfield, Crowborough TN6 3LU* T: (01892) 852536

MASON, Nigel James. b 56. Culham Coll of Educn BEd 78. St Steph Ho Ox 95. **d** 97 **p** 98. C Hove *Chich* 97–00; V Kemp

Town St Mary 00–07; Chapl St Mary's Hall Brighton 03–07; V Smethwick *Birm* 07–13; P-in-c Smethwick St Matt w St Chad 10–13; Chapl Ex Hospiscare 13–18; C Aylesbeare, Clyst St George, Clyst St Mary etc *Ex* from 18. *4 Velwell Road, Exeter EX4 4LE* T: (01392) 688000

MASON, Paul. b 51. Cranmer Hall Dur 93. **d** 93 **p** 94. C Handforth *Ches* 93–97; V Partington and Carrington 97–04; V Church Hulme 04–18; rtd 19; PtO *Ches* from 19. *10 Church Street, Sandbach CW11 1FX* E: paulandsuemason@tiscali.co.uk

MASON, Mrs Pauline. b 49. LCTP. **d** 08 **p** 09. NSM Chorley St Geo *Blackb* 08–12; V Wrightington 12–17; rtd 17; PtO *Cant* from 18. *3 Vicarage Lane, St Margarets-at-Cliffe, Dover CT15 6AB* E: revvypolly@btinternet.com

MASON, Peter Charles. b 45. K Coll Lon BD 72 AKC 72 Birm Univ PGCE 89. St Aug Coll Cant 72. **d** 73 **p** 74. C Ilkeston St Mary *Derby* 73–76; C Bridgnorth St Mary *Heref* 76–78; TV Bridgnorth, Tasley, Astley Abbotts, etc 78–88; RE Teacher from 89; rtd 10; PtO *Heref* 89–04; *St D* from 04; *St E* 19. *63 Nun Street, St Davids, Haverfordwest SA62 6NU* T: (01437) 721715 E: masonpeterc@gmail.com

MASON, Canon Peter Joseph. b 34. Lon Univ BA 58. Coll of Resurr Mirfield 58. **d** 60 **p** 61. C Belhus Park CD *Chelmsf* 60–63; LtO *Eur* 63–64; Asst Chapl Lon Univ 64–70; Chapl City Univ 66–70; R Stoke Newington St Mary 70–78; V Writtle *Chelmsf* 78–81; P-in-c Highwood 78–81; V Writtle w Highwood 81–86; R Shenfield 86–93; Hon Can Chelmsf Cathl 89–00; P-in-c Maldon All SS w St Pet 93–95; V 95–00; RD Maldon and Dengie 95–00; rtd 00; PtO *Chelmsf* from 00. *8 Canuden Road, Chelmsford CM1 2SX* T: (01245) 351465 E: petermason32@waitrose.com

MASON, Phillip Richard (Rolf). b 79. St Pet Coll Ox BA 00. Ripon Coll Cuddesdon 15. **d** 17 **p** 18. C Holbeck *Leeds* from 17. *St Peter's Vicarage, St Peter's Court, Leeds LS11 5NR* M: 07894-429214 E: revrolfmason@gmail.com

MASON, Robert Herbert George. b 48. ACII. Oak Hill Th Coll 82. **d** 84 **p** 85. C Ware Ch Ch *St Alb* 84–88; V Eastbourne All So *Chich* 88–98; P-in-c Poole *Sarum* 98–01; R 01–11; rtd 11; PtO *Portsm* from 11; Chapl Miss to Seafarers 98–11. *63 Tredegar Road, Southsea PO4 9BJ* T: (023) 928 24712 E: revbobmelmason@hotmail.com

MASON, Mrs Sally Lynne. b 52. EMMTC 05. **d** 08 **p** 09. NSM Alfreton *Derby* 08–12; NSM Blackwell w Tibshelf from 12; Spiritual Dir Derby Angl Cursillo 13–18. *27 Stretton Road, Morton, Alfreton DE55 6GW* T: (01773) 873508 E: spiritualdirector@derbycursillo.co.uk

MASON, Mrs Sally-Anne. b 55. Open Univ BA 86 C F Mott Coll of Educn CertEd 77. SNWTP 07. **d** 10 **p** 11. NSM Childwall St Dav *Liv* 10–19; NSM Stoneycroft All SS 10–19; NSM Mossley Hill from 19. *2 Reedale Road, Liverpool L18 5HL* T: 0151-724 1142 M: 07889-584885 E: revsallymason@hotmail.com

MASON, Sarah Catherine. *See* LAWRENCE, Sarah Catherine

MASON, Simon Ion Vincent. b 60. Birm Univ BA 82. Trin Coll Bris BA 00. **d** 00 **p** 01. C Nottingham St Nic *S'well* 00–05; P-in-c Newent and Gorsley w Cliffords Mesne *Glouc* 05–15; R from 15; AD Severn Vale from 16. *The Rectory, 43 Court Road, Newent GL18 1SY* T: (01531) 820248 E: simon@stmarysnewent.org

MASON, Stephen David. b 65. Univ of Wales (Lamp) BA 87. Ripon Coll Cuddesdon 89. **d** 92 **p** 93. C Gt Grimsby St Mary and St Jas *Linc* 92–97; V Southborough St Thos *Roch* 97–02; V Paddington St Jo w St Mich *Lon* from 02. *18 Somers Crescent, London W2 2PN* T: (020) 7262 1732 F: 7706 4475 E: parishadmin@stjohns-hydepark.com

MASON, Terry Mathew. b 56. Trin Coll Bris 94. **d** 96 **p** 97. C Bexleyheath Ch Ch *Roch* 96–99; P-in-c Stone 99–03; V Broadway w Wickhamford *Worc* 03–11; RD Evesham 05–10; P-in-c Wootton Wawen *Cov* 11–14; P-in-c Claverdon w Preston Bagot 11–14; AD Alcester 11–14; Deanery Missr 11–14; R Ditton Priors w Neenton, Burwarton etc *Heref* from 14. *The Vicarage, Ditton Priors, Bridgnorth WV16 6SQ* T: (01746) 712426 E: terrymason56@gmail.com

MASON, The Ven Thomas Henry Ambrose. b 51. Solicitor 75. Oak Hill Th Coll BA 86. **d** 86 **p** 87. C W Drayton *Lon* 86–89; Field Officer Oak Hill Ext Coll 89–94; Eur Sec ICS 94–95; Dir of Tr *Eur* 95–03; Dir Min and Dir of Ords 01–03; Can Brussels Cathl 00–03; Hon Can Brussels Cathl 03–07; R Grosmont and Skenfrith and Llangattock etc *Mon* 03–08; Dir Min from 06; Adn Mon from 13. *The Rectory, Gwernesney, Usk NP15 1HP* T: (01291) 672152

MASSEY, Alison June. b 63. **d** 13 **p** 14. C Stourdene Gp *Cov* 13–16; R Draycote Gp 16–19. *Address temp unknown* M: 07837-124509 E: reverendalimassey@gmail.com

MASSEY, Mrs Elizabeth Ann. b 53. N Staffs Poly BSc 75. STETS 04. **d** 07 **p** 08. C Whitton *Sarum* 07–10; TV

Marden Vale 10–17; rtd 17; PtO *Sarum* from 18. *Fairacre, Upavon Road, North Newnton, Pewsey SN9 6JT* T: (01980) 630256 M: 07777-800084 E: ea.massey@btinternet.com

MASSEY, George Douglas. b 44. St Jo Coll Nottm 91. **d** 93 **p** 94. C Higher Bebington *Ches* 93–98; V Messingham *Linc* 98–14; rtd 14. *12 Holme Lane, Messingham, Scunthorpe DN17 3SG* T: (01724) 762823

MASSEY, Mrs Kate Ishbel. b 77. Aber Univ MB, ChB 99. Qu Coll Birm 08. **d** 11 **p** 12. C Kenilworth St Nic *Cov* 11–13; C Meriden 13–15; V Stockingford from 15; Dean Women's Min from 15. *Stockingford Vicarage, 90 Church Road, Nuneaton CV10 8LG* T: (024) 7632 5359 E: revkatemassey@gmail.com

MASSEY, Keith John. b 46. Oak Hill Th Coll 69. **d** 72 **p** 73. C Bermondsey St Jas w Ch Ch *S'wark* 72–76; C Benchill *Man* 76–82; V Clifton Green 82–97; V Flixton St Jo 97–11; rtd 11; PtO *Man* from 11. *42 Curzon Road, Stockport SK2 5DH* T: 0161-285 3298 E: keithjmassey@yahoo.co.uk

MASSEY, Michelle Elaine. *See* WARD, Michelle Elaine

MASSEY, Peter. *See* MASSEY, William Peter

MASSEY, Peter William. b 45. St Mark & St Jo Coll Lon TCert 66 Open Univ BA 75. WMMTC 96. **d** 99 **p** 00. Lay Tr Officer *Heref* 97–09; NSM Holmer w Huntington 99–03; NSM Heref St Pet w St Owen and St Jas 03–15; PtO 15–17; *Blackb* from 17. *51 Copeland Drive, Standish, Wigan WN6 0XR* T: (01257) 427153 M: 07803-826728 E: pwmassey@btinternet.com

MASSEY, Shellie. *See* WARD, Michelle Elaine

MASSEY, Wayne Philip. b 74. Brunel Univ BSc 97. Wycliffe Hall Ox BA 05. **d** 06 **p** 07. C Clifton Ch Ch w Em *Bris* 06–12; TV Bishopston and St Andrews from 12. *8 Windsor Road, Bristol BS6 5BP*

MASSEY, Preb William Cyril. b 32. Lich Th Coll 58. **d** 61 **p** 62. C Heref St Martin 61–66; V Kimbolton w Middleton-on-the-Hill 66–75; V Alveley 75–83; P-in-c Quatt 81–83; R Alveley and Quatt 84–85; R Llangarron w Llangrove, Whitchurch and Ganarew 85–97; Preb Heref Cathl 92–97; rtd 97; PtO *Heref* from 97. *16 Siward James Close, Bodenham, Hereford HR1 3LS* T: (01568) 797520

MASSEY, William Peter. b 50. CITC 96. **d** 99 **p** 00. C Fermoy Union *C, C & R* 99–00; C Carrigrohane Union and Kinsale Union 00–03; PtO *Eur* 04–13; P-in-c Lorgues w Fayence 13–16 and from 17; PtO 16–17. *1801 chemin des Pailles, 83510 Lorgues, France* T: (0033) 4 94 73 93 37 *or* 4 94 99 40 74 E: peter@themasseys.fr

MASSHEDAR, Richard Eric. b 57. Nottm Univ BTh 86. Linc Th Coll 83. **d** 86 **p** 87. C Cassop cum Quarrington *Dur* 86–89; C Ferryhill 89–91; V Leam Lane 91–94; P-in-c Hartlepool St Paul 94–96; V from 96. *St Paul's Vicarage, 6 Hutton Avenue, Hartlepool TS26 9PN* T: (01429) 272934 E: masshedar@gmail.com

MASSIAH, Amrela Celeste. b 60. Westcott Ho Cam. **d** 07 **p** 08. C Lee St Marg *S'wark* 07–09; C Thamesmead 09–11; Asst Chapl RN Coll Greenwich 11–12; Hong Kong 12–16; P-in-c St Phil St Martin Barbados from 16. *Address temp unknown* T: (001) (246) 435 0634 E: acmassiah@yahoo.co.uk

MASSINGBERD-MUNDY, Roger William Burrell. b 36. Univ of Wales (Lamp) BA 59. Ridley Hall Cam 59. **d** 61 **p** 62. C Benwell St Jas *Newc* 61–64; C Whorlton 64–72; TV 73; P-in-c Healey 73–85; Dioc Stewardship Adv 73–85; Hon Can Newc Cathl 82–85; CF (TA) 63–68; CF (TAVR) 71–83; R S Ormsby w Ketsby, Calceby and Driby *Linc* 85–86; P-in-c Harrington w Brinkhill 85–86; P-in-c Haugh 85–86; P-in-c Oxcombe 85–86; P-in-c Ruckland w Farforth and Maidenwell 85–86; P-in-c Somersby w Bag Enderby 85–86; P-in-c Tetford and Salmonby 85–86; R S Ormsby Gp 86–96; RD Bolingbroke 88–96; rtd 96; Chapl Taverham Hall Sch 03–08; PtO *Nor* from 02. *The Old Post Office, West Raynham, Fakenham NR21 7AD* T: (01328) 838611 F: 838698 E: revmassingberd@gmail.com

MASSON, Canon Philip Roy. b 52. Hertf Coll Ox BA 75 Leeds Univ BA 77. Coll of Resurr Mirfield 75. **d** 78 **p** 79. C Port Talbot St Theodore *Llan* 78–82; V Penyfai w Tondu 82–92; Dioc Dir Post-Ord Tr 85–88; Warden of Ords 88–01; R Newton Nottage from 92; AD Margam 01–06 and 12–18; Can Llan Cathl from 02. *The Rectory, 64 Victoria Avenue, Porthcawl CF36 3HF* T: (01656) 782042 *or* 786899 E: philipmasson@hotmail.com *or* office@parishofporthcawl.org.uk

MASTERMAN, Malcolm. b 59. City Univ MSc 00. K Coll Lon 73 Chich Th Coll 76. **d** 77 **p** 78. C Peterlee *Dur* 77–80; Chapl Basingstoke Distr Hosp 80–85; Chapl Freeman Hosp Newc 85–95; Tr and Development Officer Hosp Chapl Coun 96–00; Sen Chapl N Dur Healthcare NHS Trust 00–02; Sen Chapl Co Durham and Darlington Acute Hosps NHS Trust 02–06; Lead Chapl S Tees Hosps NHS Foundn Trust 06–14; Bp's Adv on Hosp Chapl (Whitby Area) *York* from 06; PtO from 14; *Dur* from 14. *8 Fulthorpe Grove, Wynyard, Billingham TS22 5QZ* T: (01740) 644787 E: malhel49@btinternet.com

MASTERMAN, Miss Patricia Hope. b 28. St Mich Ho Ox 59. dss 79 **d** 87. Asst CF 79–90; rtd 90; PtO *Chich* from 90. *33 Sea Lane Gardens, Ferring, Worthing BN12 5EQ* T: (01903) 245231

MASTERS, Mrs Carol. b 61. SNWTP 11. **d** 13 **p** 14. OLM Denton Ch Ch *Man* from 13. *46 Ashbrook Avenue, Denton, Manchester M34 2GH* T: 0161-320 5485 M: 07759-130000 E: carol1masters@aol.com

MASTERS, Kenneth Leslie. b 44. Leeds Univ BA 68. Cuddesdon Coll 68. **d** 70 **p** 71. C Wednesbury St Paul Wood Green *Lich* 70–71; C Tettenhall Regis 71–75; TV Chelmsley Wood *Birm* 75–79; R Harting *Chich* 79–87; V Rustington 87–00; TR Beaminster Area *Sarum* 00–09; rtd 09; PtO *B & W* from 10; *Sarum* from 15. *9 Carrington Way, Wincanton BA9 9NX* T: (01963) 824209 E: k2masters4@btinternet.com

MASTERS, Rupert Paul Falla. b 52. Hull Univ BA 74 Ex Univ PGCE 75 Lon Inst of Educn MA 88. **d** 10 **p** 11. OLM Stoughton *Guildf* from 10. *32 Sheepfold Road, Guildford GU2 9TT* T: (01483) 573785 E: rupert.masters@talk21.com

MASTERS, Ms Vivien Claire. b 63. Yorks Min Course. **d** 14 **p** 15. C Kippax w Allerton Bywater *Leeds* 14–16 and from 14; TV Leverhulme *Man* from 18. *7 Alford Close, Bolton BL2 6NR* T: (01204) 285981 E: masters.vivien77@gmail.com

MASTIN, Brian Arthur. b 38. Peterho Cam BA 60 MA 63 BD 80 Mert Coll Ox MA 63 MSNTS 64 MSOTS 64 FHA 14. Ripon Hall Ox 62. **d** 63 **p** 64. Asst Lect Hebrew Univ Coll of N Wales (Ban) 63–65; Lect Hebrew 65–82; Sen Lect 82–98; Chapl Ban Cathl 63–65; LtO 65–98; rtd 98; PtO *Ely* 15–17. *2A Gurney Way, Cambridge CB4 2ED* T: (01223) 355078 E: brianarthurmastin@gmail.com

MATCHETT, Canon Christopher Jonathan. b 65. QUB BSSc TCD BTh 98. **d** 98 **p** 99. C Ballynafeigh St Jude *D & D* 98–01; C Holywood 01–04; I Magheracross *Clogh* 04–11; I Newtownards *D & D* from 11; Can Down Cathl from 17. *The Rectory, 36 Belfast Road, Newtownards BT23 4TT* T: (028) 9181 2527 *or* 9181 3193 M: 07875-179060 E: chris.matchett@btinternet.com

MATHER, David Jonathan. b 65. New Coll Ox BA 88 MA 95. St Steph Ho Ox BTh 95. **d** 95 **p** 96. C Pickering w Lockton and Levisham *York* 95–98; P-in-c Bridlington H Trin and Sewerby w Marton 98–99; V from 99. *Sewerby Vicarage, Cloverley Road, Bridlington YO16 5TX* T: (01262) 675725

MATHER, Mrs Elizabeth Ann. b 45. CertEd 66. Dalton Ho Bris IDC 70 St Jo Coll Nottm 92. **d** 94 **p** 95. NSM Littleover *Derby* 94–02; St Alb 02–05; rtd 05; PtO *York* 05–10. *Angel Court, 2 Rose Street, Fortrose IV10 8TN* T: (01381) 621745 E: revlibby@gmail.com

MATHER, James William. b 63. Sheff Univ BA 86. St Steph Ho Ox 88. **d** 91 **p** 92. C Doncaster St Leon and St Jude *Sheff* 91–94; C Cantley 94–95; V Lakenheath *St E* 95–01; P-in-c Downham Market w Bexwell *Ely* 01–02; P-in-c Crimplesham w Stradsett 01–02; R Downham Market and Crimplesham w Stradsett 02–19; R Downham Market and Stradsett from 19; RD Fincham and Feltwell 06–09. *The Rectory, King's Walk, Downham Market PE38 9LF* T: (01366) 382187

MATHER, William Bernard George. b 45. St Jo Coll Nottm 77. **d** 79 **p** 80. C St Leonards St Leon *Chich* 79–82; TR Netherthorpe *Sheff* 82–90; V Littleover *Derby* 90–02; Assoc Dir SOMA UK 02–05; TR Drypool *York* 05–10; rtd 10. *Angel Court, 2 Rose Street, Fortrose IV10 8TN* T: (01381) 621745 E: williammather@gmail.com

MATHERS, Alan Edward. b 36. Lon Univ BA FPhS. Oak Hill Th Coll 61. **d** 64 **p** 65. C Ox St Matt 64–66; C Bootle St Leon *Liv* 66–68; C Hampreston *Sarum* 68–70; P-in-c Damerham 70–71; V Queniborough *Leic* 71–76; USA 76–77; V Tipton St Matt *Lich* 77–86; P-in-c Tipton St Paul 77–84; V 85–86; V Sutton Ch Ch *S'wark* 86–95; Chapl Cannes *Eur* 95–98; rtd 98; PtO *Chich* from 98; *S'wark* from 98. *52 The Meadow, Copthorne, Crawley RH10 3RQ* T: (01342) 713325 E: alanandmuriel2@gmail.com

MATHERS, David Michael Brownlow. b 43. Em Coll Cam BA 65 MA 69. Clifton Th Coll 65. **d** 67 **p** 68. C Branksome St Clem *Sarum* 67–70; C Bromley Ch Ch *Roch* 70–73; V Bures *St E* 73–80; Brazil 80–82; P-in-c Old Newton w Stowupland *St E* 82–86; V 87–90; V Thurston 90–11; RD Ixworth 94–03; rtd 11; P-in-c Laughton w Ripe and Chalvington *Chich* 11–17; PtO *St E* from 17. *3 Bracken Row, Thurston, Bury St Edmunds IP31 3PT* T: (01359) 231734 E: lyndavidmathers@gmail.com

MATHERS, Derek. b 48. NOC 82. **d** 85 **p** 86. C Huddersfield St Jo *Wakef* 85–86; C N Huddersfield 86–88; TV Almondbury w Farnley Tyas 88–92; V Marsden 92–02; R Badsworth 02–12; rtd 12; PtO *Leeds* from 17. *17 Union Street, Slaithwaite, Huddersfield HD7 5ED* T: (01484) 846018 E: father.derek49@yahoo.com

MATHERS, Kenneth Ernest William. b 56. Trin Coll Bris 93. **d** 95 **p** 96. C Bournemouth St Jo w St Mich *Win* 95–99; NSM

Darenth *Roch* 99–04; Chapl Dartford and Gravesham NHS Trust 01–04; Chapl N Devon Healthcare NHS Trust 05–16. *42 Brynsworthy Park, Roundswell, Barnstaple EX31 3RB* T: (01271) 346293 E: revkmathers@btinternet.com

MATHERS (née STEWART), Mrs Kim Deborah. b 61. Southn Univ LLB 82. Trin Coll Bris 86. **d** 89 **p** 94. Par Dn Bitterne *Win* 89–93; NSM Stoke Bishop *Bris* 93–95; NSM Bournemouth St Jo w St Mich *Win* 95–99; P-in-c Darenth *Roch* 99–04; TR Newton Tracey, Horwood, Alverdiscott etc *Ex* 04–15; RD Torrington 09–12; Tutor SWMTC from 15. *42 Brynsworthy Park, Roundswell, Barnstaple EX31 3RB* T: (01271) 346293 E: revkmathers@btinternet.com

MATHEW, Mrs Alison Kate. b 65. Glas Coll of Tech BA 86 Glas Univ MPH 95 Kingston Univ BA 08. Ripon Coll Cuddesdon 10. **d** 12 **p** 13. C Spring Grove St Mary *Lon* 12–15; C Radley, Sunningwell and Kennington *Ox* from 15. *Kennington Vicarage, Ross Court, The Avenue, Kennington, Oxford OX1 5AD* M: 07980-262912 E: alisonmathew@gmail.com

MATHEW, Laurence Allen Stanfield. b 47. Sarum Th Coll 99. **d** 02 **p** 03. OLM Warminster Ch Ch *Sarum* 02–12; NSM Ross w Walford and Brampton Abbotts *Heref* 12–17; rtd 17; PtO *Sarum* from 17. *25 King Street, Warminster BA12 8DG* M: 07768-006245

MATHEW (née HOLLIS), Rebecca Catherine. b 78. St Martin's Coll Lanc BA 99. Ripon Coll Cuddesdon BTh 03. **d** 03 **p** 04. C Broughton *Blackb* 03–07; c Wharton Ch Ch Sri Lanka 07–08; Chapl St Thos Coll Mt Lavina 08–11; TV Bicester w Bucknell, Caversfield and Launton *Ox* 11–17; V Allestree St Nic *Derby* from 17; P-in-c Quarndon from 17. *St Nicholas' Vicarage, 4 Lawn Avenue, Allestree, Derby DE22 2PE* T: (01332) 550224 E: revdrebh@hotmail.com

MATHEW, Shemil. b 82. Mahatma Gandhi Univ Kerala BA 04 Madurai Univ MA 07 Glos Univ BA 07 MA 14 Ox Univ MTh 14. **d** 14 **p** 15. C Aynho and Croughton w Evenley etc *Pet* 14–17; Chapl Ox Brookes Univ from 17. *Brookes Chaplaincy, Oxford Brookes University, Gipsy Lane, Headington, Oxford OX3 0BP* T: (01865) 484690 M: 07388-872951 E: revshemil@gmail.com

MATHIAS, Steffan Idris Mano. b 87. K Coll Lon BA 08 MA 10 PhD 15 AKC 15. Coll of Resurr Mirfield 15. **d** 17 **p** 18. C Lewisham St Mary *S'wark* from 17. *36D Clarendon Rise, London SE13 5EY* M: 07811-981703 E: steffanmathias@gmail.com

MATHIAS-JONES, Edward Lloyd. b 71. Univ of Wales (Lamp) BA 93. St Mich Coll Llan BD 96. **d** 97 **p** 98. C Llanelli *St D* 97–00; C Milford Haven 00–04; V Newport St Steph and H Trin *Mon* 04–16; V Grangetown *York* from 16. *St Hilda's Vicarage, Clynes Road, Middlesbrough TS6 7LY* E: frmathias-jones@aol.com *or* frmathiasjones@aol.com

MATHOLE, Paul Mark. b 76. St Anne's Coll Ox BA 98 R Holloway Coll Lon MA 00 PhD 04. Oak Hill Th Coll 07. **d** 10 **p** 11. C Rusholme H Trin *Man* from 10. *3A Eileen Grove West, Manchester M14 5NW* T: 0161-224 1123 M: 07733-185670 E: paulmathole@gmail.com

MATLOCK, Miss Catherine Elizabeth. b 66. York Univ BSc 87 Ex Univ MA 15. Qu Foundn Birm 16. **d** 18 **p** 19. C Kings Norton *Birm* from 18. *53 Lanchester Road, Kings Norton B38 9AQ* M: 07443-475554 E: curate@kingsnorton.org.uk

MATLOOB, Canon Nazir Ahmad Barnabas. b 48. Punjab Univ BA 79. Gujranwala Th Sem BTh 77 BD 81 MDiv 85. **d** 78 **p** 78. Pakistan 78–93; PtO *Chelmsf* 94–97; C Forest Gate All SS 98–06; C Lt Ilford St Barn 06; Inter-Faith Worker Newham Deanery from 07; Hon Can Chelmsf Cathl from 12. *64 Henderson Road, London E7 8EF* T: (020) 8552 4280

MATSON de LAURIER, Mrs Sarah Kennerley. b 46. EMMTC 00. **d** 02 **p** 03. NSM Hilton w Marston-on-Dove *Derby* 02–14; PtO from 14. *1 Park Way, Etwall, Derby DE65 6HU* T: (01283) 732859 E: pskmdl@aol.com *or* peteandrev@gmail.com

MATTACKS, Mrs Lesley Anne. b 58. Birm Univ BA 79 K Coll Lon MA 86 Leeds Univ BA 07 W Lon Inst of HE PGCE 80. NOC 04. **d** 07 **p** 08. C Birkenshaw w Hunsworth *Wakef* 07–10; P-in-c Middlestown 10–14; *Leeds* 14–15; Dioc Tr Officer (Reader Formation) *Wakef* 10–14; *Leeds* 14–15; V Brownhill from 15. *St Saviour's Vicarage, 24 Intake Lane, Batley WF17 0BT* T: (01924) 471999 M: 07952-375176 E: revles.mattacks@hotmail.co.uk

MATTAPALLY, Sebastian Thomas. b 57. N Bengal Univ BA 77 Pontifical Salesian Univ BTh 84 Pontifical Gregorian Univ LTh 98 DTh 05. **d** 83 **p** 83. In RC Ch 83–00; PtO *Eur* 01–04; C Patcham *Chich* 05–07; P-in-c Kirdford 07–10; V Eastbourne St Mich 10–17; R Spring Line Gp *Linc* from 17. *The New Vicarage, Church Hill, Ingham, Lincoln LN1 2YE* T: (01522) 731793 E: smattapally@btinternet.com

MATTHEW, Peter. b 73. **d** 11 **p** 13. Kenya 11–12; C Woking St Jo *Guildf* 12–16; PtO *Ox* from 18. *6 Hunters Mews, Alma Road, Windsor SL4 3SL* T: (01753) 474462 M: 07919-577676

MATTHEWS, Canon Anna Ruth. b 78. Rob Coll Cam BA 99 MA 03 MPhil 03. Westcott Ho Cam 01. **d** 03 **p** 04. C Abbots Langley *St Alb* 03–06; Min Can St Alb Abbey 06–12; V Cambridge St Benedict *Ely* from 12; Dioc Dir of Ords 12–19; Hon Can Ely Cathl from 15. *61 St Bartholomew's Court, Riverside, Cambridge CB5 8HG* T: (01223) 321312 E: vicar@stbenetschurch.org

MATTHEWS, Brian. b 32. ARIC 55. Cranmer Hall Dur 59. **d** 62 **p** 63. C Belgrave St Pet *Leic* 62–65; C Whitwick St Jo the Bapt 65–69; C Kirby Muxloe 69–71; P-in-c Bardon Hill 71–78; V Thringstone St Andr 78–97; rtd 97; PtO *Leic* 97–05. *7 St Martin's Court, St Martin's Close, Sidmouth EX10 9JH*

MATTHEWS, Canon Campbell Thurlow. b 33. Lon Univ BA 56 Dur Univ DipEd 57. St Jo Coll Nottm 70. **d** 71 **p** 72. C Ryton *Dur* 71–74; Chapl R Victoria Infirmary Newc 74–82; V Greenside *Dur* 74–82; R Wetheral w Warwick *Carl* 82–93; RD Brampton 83–91; P-in-c Farlam and Nether Denton 87–93; P-in-c Gilsland 87–93; Hon Can Carl Cathl 87–00; P-in-c Thornthwaite cum Braithwaite and Newlands 93–00; P-in-c Borrowdale 97–00; rtd 00; PtO *Carl* from 00; *Newc* from 01. *Barn Croft, Applethwaite, Keswick CA12 4PN* T: (017687) 74899 E: ctm18@gmail.com

MATTHEWS, Celia Inger. b 30. St Chris Coll Blackheath 50. **d** 86 **p** 94. Dioc Missr *St And* from 86; rtd 95. *24 Barossa Place, Perth PH1 5HH* T: (01738) 623578 E: celia.matthews@icloud.com

MATTHEWS, Canon Colin John. b 44. Jes Coll Ox BA 67 MA 71 Fitzw Coll Cam BA 70 MA 74. Ridley Hall Cam 68. **d** 71 **p** 72. C Onslow Square St Paul *Lon* 71–74; C Leic H Apostles 74–78; Bible Use Sec Scripture Union 78–89; Dir Ch Cen Guildf St Sav 89–95; V Burpham 95–12; RD Guildf 01–06; Hon Can Guildf Cathl 02–12; rtd 12; PtO *Guildf* from 12. *Bargate, Little Tangley, Wonersh Common, Wonersh, Guildford GU5 0PW* T: (01483) 575334 M: 07787-575923 E: colinjmatthews@gmail.com

MATTHEWS, David John. b 90. Kent Univ BA 11. St Mellitus Coll 14. **d** 17 **p** 18. C Onslow Square and S Kensington St Aug *Lon* from 17. *23 Tonsley Road, London SW18 1BG* M: 07545-992620 E: dave.matthews@htb.org

MATTHEWS, David William. b 49. St Paul's Coll Grahamstown 88. **d** 90 **p** 91. C Port Eliz St Sav S Africa 90–91; C Port Eliz St Paul 91–94; R Zwartkops River Valley Par 94–00; Chapl Miss to Seafarers 00–03; R Boxford, Edwardstone, Groton etc *St E* 03–09; P-in-c Southampton St Anne Bermuda 09–16; PtO *Win* from 17. *148 Sullivan Road, Sholing, Southampton SO19 0HX* T: (023) 8032 4938 E: deltawhiskey5@gmail.com

MATTHEWS, David William Grover. b 73. Acadia Univ (NS) BA 93 Toronto Univ MDiv 98. Trin Coll Toronto 95. **d** 98 **p** 99. C Newport St Teilo *Mon* 98–00; NSM Cobbold Road St Sav w St Mary *Lon* 00–03; P-in-c Hammersmith H Innocents 03–05; P-in-c Hammersmith H Innocents and St Jo from 05. *35 Paddenswick Road, London W6 0UA* T: (020) 8741 6480 *or* 8748 2286 E: holyinnocentsw6@yahoo.com

MATTHEWS, Mrs Deborah Lynne. b 57. Southn Univ BTh 98 MCIPD 92. Ripon Coll Cuddesdon MTh 01. **d** 00 **p** 01. C Southampton (City Cen) *Win* 00–04; V Clapham St Paul *S'wark* 04–17; P-in-c Clapham H Spirit 12–13; Dir IME Kingston Area 13–17; AD Lambeth N 13–17; V Verwood *Sarum* from 17. *The Vicarage, 34 Dewlands Way, Verwood BH31 6JN* T: (01202) 823707

MATTHEWS, Mrs Diana Elizabeth Charlotte. b 43. MCSP 65. **d** 93 **p** 96. OLM Merrow *Guildf* 93–11; rtd 11; PtO *Guildf* from 11. *Avila, 13 Wells Road, Guildford GU4 7XQ* T: (01483) 839738 E: diana.matthews@ntlworld.com

MATTHEWS, Elis Alun. b 82. York Univ BA 04 Cam Univ BTh 15. Ridley Hall Cam 12. **d** 15 **p** 16. C E Ham St Paul *Chelmsf* 15–18; V Spring Grove St Mary *Lon* from 18. *St Mary's Vicarage, Osterley Road, Isleworth TW7 4PW* T: (020) 8569 7312 M: 07739-020288 E: rev.elis.matthews@gmail.com

MATTHEWS, Frederick Peter. b 45. Grey Coll Dur BA 66 MA 68 K Coll Lon PGCE 68 Lon Univ BSc(Econ) 75. Sarum & Wells Th Coll 70. **d** 72 **p** 73. C W Wickham St Jo *Cant* 72–74; C Sholing *Win* 74–77; LtO 78–79; V Woolston 79–03; P-in-c Over Wallop w Nether Wallop 03–07; Dioc Ecum Officer 03–07; rtd 07; PtO *Sarum* from 07; *Win* 07–14. *19 Berkshire Road, Salisbury SP2 8NY* T: (01722) 340508 E: fpetermatthews@hotmail.co.uk

MATTHEWS, George Charles Wallace. b 27. Sarum Th Coll 58. **d** 60 **p** 61. C Coppenhall St Paul *Ches* 60–63; C Lewes St Anne *Chich* 63–67; V Wheelock *Ches* 67–76; V Mossley 76–93; rtd 93; PtO *Ches* 93–14. *145 Primrose Avenue, Haslington, Crewe CW1 5QB* T: (01270) 587463

MATTHEWS, Gerald Lancelot. b 31. Bris Univ LLB 50. Ripon Hall Ox 55. **d** 57 **p** 58. C The Quinton *Birm* 57–60; C Olton

60–63; V Brent Tor *Ex* 63–72; P-in-c Lydford w Bridestowe and Sourton 70–72; TR Lydford, Brent Tor, Bridestowe and Sourton 72–78; P-in-c Black Torrington, Bradford w Cookbury etc 78–90; PtO from 90; rtd 94. *The Larches, Black Torrington, Beaworthy EX21 5PU* T: (01409) 231228

MATTHEWS, Harold James. b 46. Leeds Univ BSc 68 Fitzw Coll Cam BA 70 MA 74 Goldsmiths' Coll Lon PGCE 71. Westcott Ho Cam 68. **d** 71 **p** 72. C Mossley Hill St Matt and St Jas *Liv* 71–74; C Stanley 74–76; TV Hackney *Lon* 76–78; Chapl Forest Sch Snaresbrook 78–83; Hd Master Vernon Holme Sch Cant 83–88; Hd Master Heath Mt Sch Hertf 88–06; Chapl Roedean Sch Brighton 06–08; Chapl Kent Coll Pembury 10–16; PtO *Roch* 11–16; *Glouc* from 17; *Eur* from 10. *Flat 1, 12 Ashford Road, Cheltenham GL50 2EN* T: (01242) 231153 M: 07515-857110 E: hjmatth46@hotmail.co.uk

MATTHEWS, Hayley Deborah Yeshua. b 68. Ridley Hall Cam 05. **d** 07 **p** 08. C Lancaster St Mary w St John and St Anne *Blackb* 07–10; Chapl MediaCityUK *Man* 10–13; R Birch w Fallowfield 13–17; Dir Lay Tr *Leeds* from 17. *Diocese of Leeds, 17-19 York Place, Leeds LS1 2EX* T: 0113-353 0283 E: hayley.matthews@leeds.anglican.org

MATTHEWS, Canon Joan Muriel. b 53. NOC 89. **d** 92 **p** 94. C Aughton St Mich *Liv* 92–97; R Wavertree St Mary 97–06; AD Toxteth and Wavertree 04–06; Hon Can Liv Cathl 04–06 and 07–16; P-in-c Newton in Makerfield St Pet 06–07; P-in-c Earlestown 06–07; TR Newton 08–16; AD Winwick 09–16; rtd 16; PtO *Liv* from 17. *130 Belvedere Road, Newton-le-Willows WA12 0LG* T: (01925) 299668 E: revjoan@hotmail.com

MATTHEWS, John Goodman. b 77. Univ of Wales BTh 99. St Mich Coll Llan 99. **d** 02 **p** 03. C Lampeter and Llanddewibrefi Gp *St D* 02–05; P-in-c Aberporth w Tremain w Blaenporth and Betws Ifan 05–07; V 07–09; V Aberporth w Blaenporth w Betws Ifan 09; P-in-c Tregarth and Llandygai and Maes y Groes *Ban* 09–14; V Bro Ogwen from 14. *Pentir Vicarage, Pentir, Bangor LL57 4YB* T: (01248) 364991 E: fatherjohnmatthews@btinternet.com

MATTHEWS, Lewis William (Bill). b 29. St Jo Coll Dur BA 53 MSc 76. **d** 55 **p** 56. C Eston *York* 55–57; Ind Chapl *Sheff* 57–61; V Copt Oak *Leic* 61–64; R Braunstone 64–70; V Thornaby on Tees St Paul *York* 70–72; TR Thornaby on Tees 72–78; Dir Dioc Bd for Soc Resp *Lon* 79–84; PtO 84–94; Warden Durning Hall Chr Community Cen Forest Gate 84–94; rtd 94; Hon C Jersey Gouray St Martin *Win* 94–06; PtO from 06. *2 Malvern, La Ruelle es Ruaux, St Brelade, Jersey JE3 8BB* T: (01534) 498368 M: 07797-731143 E: revmatthews163@gmail.com

MATTHEWS, Canon Melvyn William. b 40. St Edm Hall Ox BA 63 MA 68. K Coll Lon BD 66 AKC 67. **d** 67 **p** 68. C Enfield St Andr *Lon* 67–70; Asst Chapl Southn Univ *Win* 70–72; Lect Univ of Nairobi Kenya 72–76; V Highgate All SS *Lon* 76–79; P-in-c Clifton St Paul *Bris* 79–87; Sen Chapl Bris Univ 79–87; Dir Ammerdown Cen for Study and Renewal 87–93; V Chew Magna w Dundry *B & W* 93–97; Can and Chan Wells Cathl 97–05; rtd 05; PtO *B & W* from 05. *36 Mondyes Court, Milton Lane, Wells BA5 2QX* T: (01749) 672068 M: 07791-875319 E: mwmatthews@onetel.com *or* melvyn.matthews@icloud.com

MATTHEWS, Michael Raymond. b 55. Huddersfield Univ MBA 96 Leeds Univ BA 04 CQSW 82. Coll of Resurr Mirfield 02. **d** 04 **p** 05. C Featherstone and Purston cum S Featherstone *Wakef* 04–07; P-in-c Haslingfield w Harlton and Gt and Lt Eversden *Ely* 07–10; TV Lordsbridge 10–13; RD Bourn 10–13; P-in-c Nassington w Yarwell and Woodnewton w Apethorpe *Pet* 13–15; V Nassington, Apethorpe, Thornhaugh etc 15; PtO 15–18; Chapl All SS C of E Primary Sch from 18. *8A Woodgate, Helpston, Peterborough PE6 7ED* T: (01733) 253768 E: frmichaelmatthews@btinternet.com

MATTHEWS, Paul. b 47. Brunel Univ BTech 70. S Dios Minl Tr Scheme 89. **d** 92 **p** 93. NSM Goring-by-Sea *Chich* 92–12; P-in-c Chidham 12–14; V 14–18; rtd 18. *7 Denton Close, Goring-by-Sea, Worthing BN12 4TZ* E: frpaulmatthews@btinternet.com

MATTHEWS, Peter. *See* MATTHEWS, Frederick Peter

MATTHEWS, Peter John. b 69. Leic Poly BEng 92. Wycliffe Hall Ox 07. **d** 09 **p** 10. C Catterick *Ripon* 09–13; Chapl St Fran Xavier Sch Richmond 09–13; P-in-c Old Trafford St Bride *Man* 13–18; R from 18; Young Adults Missr Man Adnry from 13. *St Bride's Rectory, 33 Shrewsbury Street, Manchester M16 9BB* T: 0161-226 1251 M: 07590-698333 E: peter@stbrides.org.uk

MATTHEWS, Canon Rodney Charles. b 36. Sarum Th Coll 62. **d** 64 **p** 65. C Gt Clacton *Chelmsf* 64–68; C Loughton St Mary 68–74; TV 74–76; V Goodmayes All SS 76–87; V Woodford Bridge 87–02; Hon Chapl Sail Tr Assn from 89; P-in-c Barkingside St Cedd *Chelmsf* 90–92; Hon Can Chelmsf Cathl 99–02; rtd 02; PtO *Chelmsf* from 03.

93 King's Head Hill, London E4 7JG T: (020) 8529 4372
E: canonrodney@ntlworld.com

MATTHEWS, Canon Roger Charles. b 54. Man Univ BSc 75 Nottm Univ MA 02 Fuller Th Sem California DMin 10 MBCS 82 CEng 90. Trin Coll Bris 87. **d** 89 **p** 90. C Gt Baddow *Chelmsf* 89–93; P-in-c Chigwell Row 93–94; TV Chigwell and Chigwell Row 94–96; Dioc Miss Officer 96–00; Millenium Ecum Officer 98–00; Bp's Adv for Miss and Min 01–12; Dean of Miss and Min from 12; Hon C Gt Baddow from 01; Hon Can Chelmsf Cathl from 00. *42 Riffhams Drive, Great Baddow, Chelmsford CM2 7DD* T: (01245) 478959 *or* 294455 E: rmatthews@chelmsford.anglican.org

MATTHEWS, Canon Roy Ian John. b 27. St Cath Soc Ox BA 52 MA 56. St Steph Ho Ox 52. **d** 54 **p** 55. C Barnsley St Mary *Wakef* 54–58; V Staincliffe 58–65; CF (TA) 58–92; V Penistone w Midhope *Wakef* 65–72; V Brighouse 72–84; Hon Can Wakef Cathl 76–92; V Darrington 84–92; Dioc Schs Officer 84–89; Dep Dir of Educn 85–89; rtd 92; PtO *Wakef* 92–14; *Leeds* 14–16; *York* 92–96 and from 17; P-in-c Selby Abbey 96–97. *14 Spring Walk, Brayton, Selby YO8 9DS* T: (01757) 707259

MATTHEWS, Canon Royston Peter. b 39. Univ of Wales (Lamp) BA 61. St Mich Coll Llan 61. **d** 64 **p** 65. C Fairwater CD *Llan* 64–67; C Cadoxton-juxta-Barry 67–71; V Bettws *Mon* 71–84; V Abergavenny H Trin 84–05; Hon Can St Woolos Cathl 05; rtd 05; PtO *Win* from 08; Clergy Widows and Widowers Officer (Bournemouth Adnry) from 18. *1 Hoburne Gardens, Christchurch BH23 4PP* T: (01425) 271216 E: roymatt1@aol.com

MATTHEWS, Simon David. b 64. Nottm Univ BA 91 Univ Coll Lon MPhil 93 Univ of Wales (Lamp) CertHE 10. Qu Foundn Birm MA 16. **d** 15 **p** 16. C Wistow *Leic* from 15. *4 Ensbury Gardens, Leicester LE5 6FB* T: 0116-243 2255 M: 07763-974419 E: simondmatthews@btinternet.com

MATTHEWS, Canon Stuart James. b 37. St Jo Coll Dur BA 60. Bps' Coll Cheshunt 60. **d** 62 **p** 63. C Horsham *Chich* 62–65; C Rednal *Birm* 65–67; Min Brandwood St Bede CD 67–68; C Northfield 68–73; V Thurcroft *Sheff* 73–82; RD Laughton 79–82; R Sprotbrough 82–00; RD Adwick 84–89; Hon Can Sheff Cathl 92–00; rtd 00; PtO *Sheff* from 00. *43 Dinnington Road, Woodsetts, Worksop S81 8RL* T: (01909) 560160

MATTHEWS, Timothy John. b 73. Univ of Wales (Cardiff) BScEcon 97 PhD 00 ACA 03. Wycliffe Hall Ox 06. **d** 08 **p** 09. C Brompton H Trin w Onslow Square St Paul *Lon* 08–11; C Onslow Square and S Kensington St Aug 11–14; C Bournemouth Town Cen *Win* 14–17; P-in-c Bournemouth St Clem from 17. *St Swithuns, 1 Gervis Road, Bournemouth BH1 3ED* T: (01202) 241077 E: tim@stswithuns.me

MATTHEWS, William. *See* MATTHEWS, Lewis William

MATTHEWS, William John Joseph. b 48. **d** 08 **p** 08. NSM Lee-on-the-Solent *Portsm* 08–10; TV St Helens Town Cen *Liv* 11–15; TV Wigan All SS 15–16; TR 16–18; rtd 18. *Belmont, 20 Kingsway, Waterloo, Liverpool L22 4RQ* T: 0151-281 4879 E: revbillmatthews@outlook.com

MATTHEWS-LOYDALL, Mrs Elaine. b 63. Bp Otter Coll BA 85. St Jo Coll Nottm LTh 89. **d** 90 **p** 94. Par Dn Nottingham All SS *S'well* 90–94; C 94–95; Asst Chapl to the Deaf 91–93; Chapl to the Deaf 93–99; Chapl for Deaf People *Leic* 99–10; TV Leic H Spirit 99–10. *Pumpkin Cottage, 54 Wilne Road, Long Eaton, Nottingham NG10 3AN* T: 0115-972 8943

MATTHIAE, Canon David. b 40. Fitzw Ho Cam BA 63 MA 69. Linc Th Coll 63. **d** 65 **p** 66. C New Addington *Cant* 65–70; C Charlton-by-Dover SS Pet and Paul 70–72; C Charlton-in-Dover 72–75; V Cant All SS 75–84; P-in-c Tunstall 84–87; R Tunstall w Rodmersham 87–05; RD Sittingbourne 88–94; Hon Can Cant Cathl 99–05; rtd 05; PtO *Ely* 06–16 and from 17. *7 Bustlers Rise, Duxford, Cambridge CB22 4QU* T: (01223) 835471 M: 07719-716240 E: david@matthiae.demon.co.uk

MATTHIAS, Canon John Rex. b 61. St Mich Coll Llan. **d** 94 **p** 95. C Llandrillo-yn-Rhos *St As* 94–98; R Llanfair Talhaearn and Llansannan etc 98–03; V Petryal 03–10; P-in-c Betws-yn-Rhos 03–10; Warden of Readers 09–10; P-in-c Newport St Julian *Mon* 10–12; V Mold *St As* 12–15; Can Prec St As Cathl from 15. *Cefn Coed, Upper Denbigh Road, St Asaph LL17 0RR* E: rexmatthias61@gmail.com

MATTHIAS, Paul. b 47. Philippa Fawcett Coll CertEd 75 Kent Univ DipEd 84. Cant Sch of Min 92. **d** 94 **p** 95. Head RE Hever Sch Maidstone 80–94; Chapl Ch Ch High Sch Ashford 94–07; NSM Gillingham St Aug *Roch* 94–10; P-in-c New Brompton St Luke 10–17; rtd 17; PtO *Roch* from 18; *Cant* from 18. *9 Pembroke Gardens, Rainham, Gillingham ME8 8TD* T: (01634) 267134 E: p.matthias@sky.com

MATTOCK, Colin Graham. b 38. Chich Th Coll. **d** 84 **p** 85. C Hove All SS *Chich* 84–87; C Bexhill St Pet 87–90; V Henlow *St Alb* 90–96; V Linslade *Ox* 96–00; P-in-c Pebworth w Dorsington and Honeybourne *Glouc* 00–02; R Pebworth, Dorsington, Honeybourne etc 02–10;

AD Campden 06–10; rtd 10; PtO *Glouc* from 17. *14 Mullings Court, Cirencester GL7 2AW* T: (01285) 653828 E: colin.mattock@btinternet.com

MATTOCKS, Mrs Margaret Muriel. b 61. **d** 06 **p** 07. C Tettenhall Regis *Lich* 06–09; V Burntwood 09–13; C Hammerwich 13–15; TR Burntwood, Chase Terrace etc 15–18; RD Lich 14–18; V Codsall from 18. *The Vicarage, 48 Church Road, Codsall, Wolverhampton WV8 1EH*

MATUMONA, Guy Diakiese. **d** 17 **p** 18. C The Hague *Eur* from 17. *St John and St Philip, Ary van der Spuyweg 1, 2585 HA The Hague, The Netherlands* T: (0031) (70) 355 5359 E: guydiakiese@gmail.com *or* guy@stjohn-stphilip.com

MAUCHAN, Andrew. b 44. Hertf Coll Ox BA 65 MA 69 Man Univ CertEd 66. Oak Hill Th Coll 88. **d** 90 **p** 91. C Bridlington Priory *York* 90–94; V Alverthorpe *Wakef* 94–01; R Wombwell *Sheff* 01–07; rtd 07; PtO *Leeds* from 17. *Hollins Barn, Top o' the Hill, Slaithwaite, Huddersfield HD7 5UA* T: (01484) 846371 E: andrew.mauchan@yahoo.co.uk

MAUDE, Gillian Hamer. b 53. St Anne's Coll Ox BA 75 MA 79 Edin Univ MSc 77. St Steph Ho Ox 99. **d** 01 **p** 02. C Hackney Wick St Mary of Eton w St Aug *Lon* 01–05; P-in-c Goodrington *Ex* 05–06; V 06–14; V Goodrington and Collaton St Mary 14–15; RD Torbay 09–13; P-in-c Jarrow *Dur* 15–18; R Jarrow and Simonside from 18. *St Peter's House, York Avenue, Jarrow NE32 5LP* T: 0191-483 3369 M: 07527-169016 E: revgilly.jarrow@gmail.com

MAUDLIN, David. b 39. EAMTC 92. **d** 95 **p** 96. NSM Bury St Edmunds St Jo *St E* 95–97; NSM Haverhill w Withersfield 97–98; P-in-c The Sampfords and Radwinter w Hempstead *Chelmsf* 98–04; RD Saffron Walden 00–04; rtd 04; PtO *Leic* 04–13; P-in-c Leic St Mary from 13; PtO *Pet* from 04; *Eur* from 04. *3 Goldfinch Road, Uppingham LE15 9UJ* T: (01572) 820181 E: dmaudlin@btinternet.com

MAUDSLEY, Canon George Lambert. b 27. St Jo Coll Nottm 74. **d** 75 **p** 76. C Binley *Cov* 75–77; Chapl Barn Fellowship Winterborne Whitechurch 77–83; V Salford Priors *Cov* 83–94; RD Alcester 87–92; Hon Can Cov Cathl 91–94; rtd 94; PtO *Cov* from 94. *12 Moorlands Lodge, Moorlands Avenue, Kenilworth CV8 1RT* T: (01926) 512206 E: lambert.maudsley@yahoo.co.uk

MAUDSLEY, Keith. b 51. York Univ BA 72. Ripon Hall Ox 72. **d** 75 **p** 76. C Rugby St Andr *Cov* 75–79; C Cambridge Gt St Mary w St Mich *Ely* 79–82; Chapl Girton Coll 79–82; P-in-c Binley *Cov* 82–89; RD Cov E 87–89; P-in-c Leek Wootton 89–91; Dioc Policy Development Adv 89–91; Dioc Adv on UPA *Liv* 91–97; Soc Resp Officer 91–97; R Lymm *Ches* 97–17; rtd 17; PtO *Ches* from 17. *21 Sandy Lane, Lymm WA13 9HJ* T: (01925) 759178 E: keith.maudsley@gmail.com

MAUDSLEY, Canon Michael Peter. b 38. St Andr Univ BSc 61. Oak Hill Th Coll 65. **d** 67 **p** 68. C Blackpool St Mark *Blackb* 67–70; C Hartford *Ches* 70–72; R Balerno *Edin* 72–82; V Stapenhill w Cauldwell *Derby* 82–91; Assoc R Edin St Paul and St Geo 91–95; C 00–03; R 95–00; rtd 03. *44 Buckstone Loan, Edinburgh EH10 6UG*

MAUDSLEY, Philip. b 73. St Martin's Coll Lanc BA(QTS) 96. St Jo Coll Nottm 13. **d** 15 **p** 16. C Fulwood Ch Ch *Blackb* 15–19; P-in-c Moston St Chad *Man* from 19; P-in-c Moston St Mary from 19. *The Rectory, 47 Nuthurst Road, Manchester M40 0EW* E: philmaudsley7@gmail.com

MAUDSLEY, Richard Leonard. b 55. Trent Park Coll of Educn BEd 76. NTMTC 04. **d** 07 **p** 08. NSM Clay Hill St Jo and St Luke *Lon* 07–09; NSM Silverton, Butterleigh, Bickleigh and Cadeleigh *Ex* 09–17; C Tiverton St Andr from 17. *The Parish Rooms, Bickleigh, Tiverton EX16 8RF* T: (01884) 855705 E: rlmaudsley@icloud.com

MAUGHAN, Angela. b 54. Newc Univ BA 93. NEOC 94. **d** 97 **p** 98. C Willington *Newc* 97–01; V Weetslade from 01. *Weetslade Vicarage, 59 Kirklands, Burradon, Cramlington NE23 7LE* T: 0191-268 9366 E: angmaughan@aol.com

MAUGHAN, Canon Geoffrey Nigel. b 48. CCC Cam BA 69 MA 73 Wycliffe Hall Ox MA 98. Oak Hill Th Coll 75. **d** 77 **p** 78. C New Malden and Coombe *S'wark* 77–81; C Abingdon w Shippon *Ox* 81–89; TV Abingdon 89–98; Dir of Min and Chapl Wycliffe Hall Ox 98–07; V Cumnor *Ox* 07–16; Hon Can Ch Ch 15–16; rtd 16; PtO *Ox* from 16. *1 The Old Workshop, North Green, West Hanney, Wantage OX12 0LU* T: (01235) 869160 E: geoff.maughan@btinternet.com

MAUND, Mrs Margaret Jennifer. b 42. RGN 64 RM 65. Llan Dioc Tr Scheme 89. **d** 94 **p** 97. NSM Cymmer and Porth *Llan* 94–97; NSM Pwllgwaun w Llanddewi Rhondda 97–04. *27 Mill Street, Tonyrefail, Porth CF39 8AB* T: (01443) 670085

MAUNDER, Alan John. b 52. UWIST BSc 74. Oak Hill Th Coll 88. **d** 90 **p** 91. C Birkenhead Ch Ch *Ches* 90–95; P-in-c Poulton 95–05; V Cwmaman *St D* 05–16; rtd 16; PtO *St D* 16–17; *Mon* from 17. *2 Newgale Row, Cwmbran NP44 3QJ* T: (01269) 822426 E: aljomau@tiscali.co.uk

MAUNDER, Miss Vicky Alexandra. b 73. Leeds Univ BA 95. Ripon Coll Cuddesdon BA 01. **d** 02 **p** 03. C Swaythling *Win* 02–05; C Pimlico St Pet w Westmr Ch Ch *Lon* 05–07; TV Kingston All SS w St Jo *S'wark* 07–12; TV Kingston 12–19; V W End *Win* from 19. *The Vicarage, Elizabeth Close, West End, Southampton SO30 3LT* M: 07762-673350 E: stjameswe.vicar@gmail.com

MAURICE, David Pierce. b 50. Pemb Coll Cam BA 72 MA 76 BChir 76. Dioc OLM tr scheme. **d** 01 **p** 02. OLM Marlborough *Sarum* from 01. *Isbury House, Kingsbury Street, Marlborough SN8 1JA* T: (01672)   514119 E: david_maurice2000@yahoo.com

✠**MAURICE, The Rt Revd Peter David.** b 51. St Chad's Coll Dur BA 72. Coll of Resurr Mirfield. **d** 75 **p** 76 **c** 06. C Wandsworth St Paul *S'wark* 75–79; TV Mortlake w E Sheen 79–85; V Rotherhithe H Trin 85–96; RD Bermondsey 91–96; V Tooting All SS 96–03; Adn Wells, Can Res and Preb Wells Cathl *B & W* 03–06; Suff Bp Taunton 06–15; rtd 15; PtO *Cant* from 16. *14 Saltwood Road, Maidstone ME15 6UY* E: pmaurice51@hotmail.co.uk

MAURITZ, Willem Jacobus. b 72. Fontys Univ Netherlands BA 98 Stoas Univ BSc 00 Surrey Univ MSc 04. St Mellitus Coll BA 14. **d** 14 **p** 15. C Tunbridge Wells St Jas *Roch* 14–18; V Copthorne *Chich* from 18. *Copthorne Vicarage, Church Road, Copthorne, Crawley RH10 3RD* M: 07799-076690 E: wim.mauritz@mail.com or vicar.copthorne@gmail.com

MAW, Mrs Jacqueline. b 59. Wycliffe Hall Ox 04. **d** 06 **p** 07. C Iwerne Valley *Sarum* 06–10; TV Wareham 10–16; C Aldershot H Trin *Guildf* from 16. *45 Scarletts Road, Wellesley, Aldershot GU11 4AE* M: 07747-561375 E: mawdiva@gmail.com

MAWBEY, Diane. *See* COUTURE, Diane

MAWDESLEY, Mrs Joy Maria. b 67. Keele Univ BA 90 CQSW 90. Ripon Coll Cuddesdon 14. **d** 16 **p** 17. C Newbury St Nic and Speen *Ox* from 16. *14 Strawberry Hill, Newbury RG14 1XJ* M: 07786-106636 E: joymawdesley@macace.net or joy@st-nics.org

MAWDITT, Stephen Donald Harvey. b 56. **d** 96 **p** 97. OLM Ashill w Saham Toney *Nor* 96–05; OLM Watton w Carbrooke and Ovington 00–05; Min Fountain of Life 05–17; Sen Min 17–19; rtd 19. *43 Cressingham Road, Ashill, Thetford IP25 7DG* T: (01760) 440363 E: themawditts@tiscali.co.uk or s.mawditt@folchurch.co.uk

MAWHINNEY, Alan Mark. b 67. Dur Univ BA 90 MA 00. St Steph Ho Ox 15. **d** 17 **p** 18. C Seaham and Dawdon *Dur* from 17. *Dawdon Vicarage, Melbury Street, Seaham SR7 7NF* E: curateseaham@gmail.com

MAWSON, Canon Arthur Cyril. b 35. St Pet Coll Ox BA 56 MA 61. Wycliffe Hall Ox 61. **d** 62 **p** 63. C Walsall *Lich* 62–66; V Millhouses H Trin *Sheff* 66–73; Selection Sec ACCM 73–79; Can Res and Treas Ris Cathl 79–98; Dioc Dir of Ords 81–87; rtd 99; PtO *Ox* from 08. *4 Woodlands Close, Headington, Oxford OX3 7RY* T: (01865) 764099 E: pandamaw@outlook.com

MAXFIELD-COOTE, Ms Olivia Constance. b 86. Kent Univ BA 09 Univ Coll Lon MA 10 Jes Coll Cam BTh 14. Westcott Ho Cam 12. **d** 15 **p** 16. C Black Notley, Gt Notley and Rayne Chelmsf 15–18; TV Epping Distr from 18. *9 Seymour Chase, Epping CM16 6FE* M: 07939-297048 E: o.maxfieldcoote@gmail.com

MAXIM, Claire Margaret Astrid. b 68. Birm Univ BEng 90 Reading Univ MBA 03 MIET 95. Qu Coll Birm 07. **d** 10 **p** 11. C Ampfield, Chilworth and N Baddesley *Win* 10–14; V Ludgershall and Faberstown *Sarum* 14–18; Chief Exec Officer Germinate from 18. *Germinate, The Arthur Rank Centre, 6th Street, Stoneleigh Park, Kenilworth CV8 2LG* T: (024) 7685 3060 *or* (01926) 817044 E: clairemaxim@btinternet.com

MAXTED, Neil Andrew. b 58. Aston Tr Scheme 88 Sarum & Wells Th Coll 90. **d** 92 **p** 93. C Folkestone St Sav *Cant* 92–96; CF 96–05; P-in-c Frome Ch Ch *B & W* 05–15; V Frome St Mary 11–15; V Frome Ch Ch w St Mary 15–18; rtd 19. *Address temp unknown*

MAXWELL, Christopher John Moore (Bill). b 31. Qu Coll Cam MA 75 MRCS 59 LRCP 59. Trin Coll Bris 74. **d** 75 **p** 76. SAMS Chile 75–81; Hon C Homerton St Luke *Lon* 81–94; Chapl Ibiza *Eur* 94–99; rtd 99; PtO *Chich* 99–08; *Win* from 08. *Willowbank, Sycamore Close, Milford on Sea, Lymington SO41 0RY* T: (01590) 643110 E: abmaxwell@btinternet.com

MAXWELL, Marcus Howard. b 54. Liv Univ BSc 76 Man Univ MPhil 89. St Jo Coll Nottm BA 79. **d** 80 **p** 81. C Chadderton St Matt *Man* 80–84; V Bircle 84–93; P-in-c Heaton Mersey 93–02; TR Heatons from 02; AD Heaton 98–04 and 13–18. *St John's Rectory, 15 Priestnall Road, Stockport SK4 3HR* T: 0161-442 1932 E: marcus.maxwell@ntlworld.com

MAY, Adrian. b 70. LSE BSc 94. Wycliffe Hall Ox 09. **d** 12 **p** 13. NSM Notting Hill St Pet *Lon* from 12. *15 Highlever Road, London W10 6PP* E: adrian@stpetersnottinghill.org.uk

MAY, Charles Henry. b 29. LTh 58. **d** 58 **p** 59. C Bethnal Green St Jas Less *Lon* 58–61; C Woking St Pet *Guildf* 61–64; Area Sec (W Midl) CPAS 64–67; V Homerton St Luke *Lon* 67–80; Home Sec SAMS 80–84; V Fulham Ch Ch *Lon* 84–94; rtd 94; PtO *Ely* 94–19; *Pet* from 94; *Linc* 95–15. *16 Kilverstone, Werrington, Peterborough PE4 5DX* T: (01733)   328108 E: clergy.c.may@gmail.com

MAY, Mrs Deborah Kim. b 60. Trin Coll Bris. **d** 01 **p** 02. C Haughley w Wetherden and Stowupland *St E* 01–04; R Ashwater, Halwill, Beaworthy, Clawton etc *Ex* 04–08; R Melville Australia from 08. *56 McLean Street, Melville WA 6156, Australia* T: (0061) (8) 9330 1550 F: 9317 4378 M: 41-817 8688 E: revd.debbie@gmail.com

MAY, Janet Isabel. b 51. Lon Univ CertEd 72. **d** 00 **p** 01. OLM Gt and Lt Ellingham, Rockland and Shropham etc *Nor* 00–05; PtO from 05. *The Mill House, 4 Church Street, Great Ellingham, Attleborough NR17 1LE* T: (01953) 452198 E: rev.may@btopenworld.com

MAY, Preb John Alexander Cyril. b 52. K Coll Lon BD 77 PhD 98 Ch Ch Ox PGCE 78. Linc Th Coll 79. **d** 80 **p** 81. C Tynemouth Ch Ch *Newc* 80–82; C Tynemouth Ch Ch w H Trin 82–85; C Tynemouth St Aug 82–85; TV Glendale Gp 85–90; V Wotton-under-Edge w Ozleworth, N Nibley etc *Glouc* 90–07; P-in-c St Endellion w Port Isaac and St Kew *Truro* 07–12; P-in-c St Minver 07–12; R N Cornwall Cluster 12–14; Preb St Endellion 07–14; rtd 14. *The Lawns, 31 St Peter Street, Tiverton EX16 6NW* T: (01208) 881041 E: johnmay187@hotmail.com

MAY, Peter Richard. b 43. St Jo Coll Cam BA 64 MA 68 MICE 70. Trin Coll Bris 77. **d** 79 **p** 80. C Lancaster St Thos *Blackb* 79–85; V Darwen St Barn 85–91; Chapl Lyon w Grenoble *Eur* 91–92; Chapl Lyon 92–94; PtO *S'wark* 94–95; TR Horley 95–02; rtd 03; PtO *Chich* 04–11. *North Lodge, Exminster, Exeter EX6 8AT* T: (01392)· 823047 E: openhearts.2@btinternet.com

MAY, Roger Austin. b 45. SWMTC 07. **d** 10 **p** 11. NSM Bodmin w Lanhydrock and Lanivet *Truro* 10–15; rtd 15; PtO *Truro* from 15. *12 Hanson Road, Liskeard PL14 3NT* T: (01579) 342924 M: 07779-349257 E: rev_bluejeans@me.com

MAY, Preb Simon George. b 47. Ex Univ BA 69 Univ of Wales (Ban) CertEd 72 FCA 77. Sarum & Wells Th Coll 86. **d** 88 **p** 89. C Tamworth *Lich* 88–92; V Whitchurch *Ex* 92–07; Warden of Readers (Plymouth Adnry) 00–07; RD Tavistock 02–07; C Barnstaple 07–17; Preb Ex Cathl 09–17; rtd 17; P-in-c Upton *Ex* 17–18. *10 Rogers Close, Tiverton EX16 6UW* T: (01884) 259470 E: simon@sgmay.me.uk

MAY, Toby Sebastian. b 67. Bris Univ BEng 89. St Jo Coll Nottm MTh 02. **d** 02 **p** 03. C Kendal St Thos *Carl* 02–06; V Alsager Ch Ch *Ches* 06–18; V Whitfield *Derby* from 18. *16 Scotty Brook Crescent, Glossop SK13 8UG* E: toby@mays-in-grace.co.uk

MAYBEE, Christine. *See* DALE, Christine

MAYBURY, Doreen Lorna. b 33. RGN 54 SCM 56. Edin Th Coll 76. dss 81 **d** 95 **p** 95. Jedburgh *Edin* 81–84; Warden Whitchester Conf Cen 84–91; Duns *Edin* 84–91; Hawick 91–97; NSM 95–97; rtd 97; Chapl Borders Gen Hosp NHS Trust 98–04. *c/o 55 Howdenbank, Hawick TD9 7JY* T: (01450) 375750 M: 07801-354134

MAYBURY, Canon John Montague. b 30. G&C Coll Cam BA 53 MA 57. Ridley Hall Cam 53. **d** 55 **p** 56. C Allerton *Liv* 55–59; C Rowner *Portsm* 59–62; V Wroxall 62–67; V Southsea St Simon 67–78; V Crofton 78–91; Hon Can Portsm Cathl 81–95; C Locks Heath 91–95; rtd 95; PtO *Portsm* from 95. *19 Netley Road, Titchfield Common, Fareham PO14 4PE* T: (01489) 584168 E: jandbmaybury@talktalk.net

MAYBURY, Canon Paul Dorian. b 58. Trin Coll Bris 93. **d** 95 **p** 96. C Spondon *Derby* 95–99; V Gawthorpe and Chickenley Heath *Wakef* 99–02; P-in-c Ossett cum Gawthorpe 01–02; V Ossett and Gawthorpe 02–13; RD Dewsbury 08–13; Hon Can Wakef Cathl 13; Spirituality Co-ord and Bp's Missr SE Cyprus 13–16; Can Res Bradf Cathl *Leeds* from 16. *3 Cathedral Close, Bradford BD1 4EG* T: (01274) 777720 E: pauldmaybury@gmail.com

MAYCOCK, Ms Jane Ellen. b 66. Somerville Coll Ox BA 90 MA 95 Glas Univ MPhil 98. Cranmer Hall Dur 90. **d** 92 **p** 94. Par Dn Harrow Trin St Mich *Lon* 92–94; C 94–95; C Kendal H Trin *Carl* 95–99; Dir of Ords 01–07. *The Rectory, Longlands Road, Bowness-on-Windermere, Windermere LA23 3AS* T: (015394) 43063 E: j.e.maycock@btinternet.com

MAYELL, Howard John. b 50. Bris Sch of Min 81. **d** 84 **p** 88. NSM Patchway *Bris* 84–86; NSM Weston-super-Mare Cen Par *B & W* 87–88; C N Stoneham *Win* 88–91; P-in-c Black Torrington, Bradford w Cookbury etc *Ex* 91–97; C Ledbury w Eastnor *Heref* 97–98; TV Ledbury 98–17; V Cider Churches 17–18; rtd 18. *2 Shepherds Close, Ledbury HR8 2XF* T: (01531) 631530

MAYER, Alan John. b 46. AKC 70. St Aug Coll Cant 70. **d** 71 **p** 72. C Stanningley St Thos *Ripon* 71–74; C St Helier *S'wark* 74–79; TV Wimbledon 79–85; V Reigate St Luke S Park 85–00; R Oxted and Tandridge 00–11; rtd 11; PtO *S'wark* 11–14. *17 Saxon Crescent, Horsham RH12 2HX* E: aandkmayer@gmail.com

MAYER, Graham Keith. b 46. St Cath Coll Ox BA 68 Nottm Univ PGCE 69 Ex Univ MA 93. Linc Th Coll 78. **d** 80 **p** 81. C Paignton St Jo *Ex* 80–93; PtO 93–96; P-in-c Christow, Ashton and Bridford 96–10; P-in-c Dunchideock 97–10; V Christow, Ashton, Bridford, Dunchideock etc 10–18; RD Kenn 05–10; P-in-c Colbury *Win* from 18. *The Vicarage, Deerleap Lane, Totton, Southampton SO40 7EH* E: rivertide@btinternet.com *or* teignway@gmail.com

MAYER-JONES, Miss Fiona Ruth. b 70. Westcott Ho Cam 08. **d** 10 **p** 11. C Beverley Minster *York* 10–14; V Northallerton w Kirby Sigston from 14; RD Mowbray from 17. *27 Mowbray Road, Northallerton DL6 1QT* E: revdfmj@gmail.com

MAYES, Miss Alexier Olwen. St Mich Coll Llan 08. **d** 11 **p** 12. C Bistre *St As* 11–14; V Kerry, Llanmerewig, Dolfor and Mochdre 14–16; TV Cedewain Miss Area 17–18; P-in-c Borderlands Miss Area from 18. *The New Vicarage, Mold Road, Connah's Quay, Deeside CH5 4QL* E: rev.alex@btinternet.com

MAYES, Canon Andrew Dennis. b 56. K Coll Lon BD 79 AKC 79 Man Univ MA 97. Armenian Orthodox Sem Jerusalem 79 St Steph Ho Ox 80. **d** 81 **p** 82. C Hendon St Alphage *Lon* 81–84; C Hockley *Chelmsf* 84–87; V Kingstanding St Mark *Birm* 87–92; V Saltdean *Chich* 92–01; P-in-c Ovingdean 01–09; CME Officer 01–09; Course Dir St Geo Coll and C St Geo Cathl Jerusalem 09–11; R E Blatchington and Bishopstone *Chich* 11–16; Chapl Limassol St Barn Cyprus from 18; Hon Can Niger Delta from 96. *St Barnabas Church House, PO Box 51494, 3506 Limassol, Cyprus* T: (00357) (25) 362713 E: andrew.mayes@gmail.com

MAYES, Aonghus William Alun. **d** 05 **p** 06. C Cregagh *D & D* 05–10; I Moy w Charlemont *Arm* from 10; Dioc Communications Officer 10–11. *The Rectory, 37 The Square, Moy, Dungannon BT71 7SG* T: (028) 8778 4312 M: 07748-710148 E: aonghusmayes@yahoo.ie

MAYES, John Charles Dougan. b 44. Bps' Coll Cheshunt 63. **d** 67 **p** 68. C Portadown St Mark *Arm* 67–74; I Aghadowey w Kilrea *D & R* 74–86; USPG Area Sec 77–94; I Clooney w Strathfoyle *D & R* 86–07; Can Derry Cathl 92–96; Preb 96–07; rtd 07. *10 Ebrington Park, Londonderry BT47 6JE* T: (028) 7131 2973

✠**MAYES, The Rt Revd Michael Hugh Gunton.** b 41. TCD BA 62 Lon Univ BD 85. TCD Div Sch Div Test 64. **d** 64 **p** 65 **c** 93. I Portadown St Columba *Arm* 64–68; USPG Kobe Japan 68-69; Tokyo 69-70; Yokkaichi 70–74; Area Sec USPG *C & O, C, C & R, L & K* and *T, K & A* 75–93; I Cork St Mich Union *C, C & R* 75–86; Adn Cork, Cloyne and Ross 86–93; I Moviddy Union 86–88; I Rathcooney Union 88–93; Bp K, E & A 93–00; Can Elphin Cathl 93–00; Bp L & K 00–08; rtd 08. *5 Rockfield Crescent, Church Road, Blackrock, Cork, Republic of Ireland T12 R9X3* T: (00353) (21) 496 7688 E: mhg.mayes@gmail.com

MAYES, Canon Stephen Thomas. b 47. St Jo Coll Nottm 67. **d** 71 **p** 72. C Cullompton *Ex* 71–75; C Cheltenham St Mark *Glouc* 76–84; P-in-c Water Orton *Birm* 84–91; V 91–12; AD Coleshill 99–05; Hon Can Birm Cathl 05–12; rtd 12; P-in-c Barston *Birm* 12–14; PtO from 14; *Lich* from 19. *47 Yew Tree Lane, Solihull B91 2NX* T: 0121-704 1356 E: stmayes@yahoo.co.uk

✠**MAYFIELD, The Rt Revd Christopher John.** b 35. G&C Coll Cam BA 57 MA 61 Cranfield Inst of Tech MSc 83. Wycliffe Hall Ox 61. **d** 63 **p** 64 **c** 85. C Birm St Martin 63–67; Lect 67–71; V Luton St Mary *St Alb* 71–80; RD Luton 74–80; Adn Bedford 80–85; Suff Bp Wolverhampton *Lich* 85–92; Area Bp Wolverhampton 92–93; Bp Man 93–02; rtd 02; Hon Asst Bp Worc from 02. *23 Petunia Close, Worcester WR5 3RT* T: (01905) 764822 E: christophermayfield54@gmail.com

MAYFIELD, Timothy James Edward. b 60. LMH Ox BA 82. Trin Coll Bris BA 88. **d** 88 **p** 89. C Ovenden *Wakef* 88–92; V Mount Pellon 92–03; V Cheltenham Ch Ch *Glouc* 03–19; V Earsdon and Backworth *Newc* from 19; AD Tynemouth from 19. *The Vicarage, 5 Front Street, Earsdon, Whitley Bay NE25 9JU* T: 0191-252 9393

MAYHEW, The Hon David Francis. b 51. Ch Ch Ox BA 72 MA 76 Wycliffe Hall Ox BA 75. NEOC 89. **d** 91 **p** 92. NSM High Elswick St Paul *Newc* 91–94; Toc H 91–94; V Mitford *Newc* 94–09; C Longhorsley and Hebron 07–09; Chapl Northgate and Prudhoe NHS Trust 94–09; V Cov H Trin 09–16; rtd 16; PtO *Cov* from 18. *119 Cannon Hill Road, Coventry CV4 7DF* M: 07720-964586 E: davidfmayhew@gmail.com

MAYHEW (née GURNEY), Jean Elizabeth. b 39. New Hall Cam BA 61 MA 65 K Coll Lon BD 84 AKC 84 PGCE 85 Ulster Univ

Hon DUniv 98 FKC 00. SEITE 02. **d** 05 **p** 06. NSM Maidstone St Paul *Cant* 05–10; PtO from 11. *Pump Hill, Kilndown, Cranbrook TN17 2SG* T: (01580) 211820 F: 212232 M: 07773-404554 E: jean@jmayhew.free-online.co.uk *or* mayhew.jean@gmail.com

MAYLAND, Mrs Jean Mary. b 36. LMH Ox BA 58 MA 61 TCert 60. St Deiniol's Hawarden 91. **d** 91 **p** 94. NSM York Minster 91–93; Lect and Tutor NOC 91–93; Lect NEOC 93–96; Dioc Ecum Officer *Dur* 93–96; Local Unity Officer Dur Ecum Relns Gp 93–96; Assoc Sec CCBI 96–99; Co-ord Sec for Ch Life CTBI 99–03; Asst Gen Sec 99–03; PtO *Lon* 97–03; *S'wark* 97–00; *Chelmsf* 00–03; rtd 03; PtO *York* 03–09; *Newc* from 04. *5 Hackwood Glade, Hexham NE46 1AL* T: (01434) 600339 E: jeanmayland@btinternet.com

MAYLAND, Canon Ralph. b 27. Ripon Hall Ox 57. **d** 59 **p** 60. C Lambeth St Andr w St Thos *S'wark* 59–62; Chapl RNR 61–94; C-in-c Worksop St Paul CD *S'well* 62–68; V Brightside St Marg *Sheff* 68–72; Ind Chapl 68–81; V Ecclesfield 72–81; Can Res and Treas York Minster 82–94; rtd 94; Hon C Brancepeth *Dur* 94–96; PtO *York* 96–15; *Chelmsf* 01–03. *5 Hackwood Glade, Hexham NE46 1AL* T: (01434) 600339

MAYLES, Helena Rosemary Laura. *See* ROULSTON, Helena Rosemary Laura

MAYLOR, David Charles. b 59. Lanc Univ BSc 80 Edge Hill Coll of HE PGCE 81. St Jo Coll Nottm 89. **d** 91 **p** 92. C Hindley All SS *Liv* 91–94; P-in-c Spalding St Paul *Linc* 94–07; Chapl United Lincs Hosps NHS Trust 99–07; Lic Gen Preacher *Linc* 07–12; Music Dir Stamford St Geo w St Paul 07–12; P-in-c Barnack w Ufford and Bainton *Pet* 12–16; V Barnack w Ufford, Bainton, Helpston and Wittering from 16. *The Rectory, Millstone Lane, Barnack, Stamford PE9 3ET* T: (01780) 740234 E: dmaylor@btinternet.com

MAYNARD, Gay Caroline. b 50. Sarum Coll 13. **d** 16 **p** 17. C Warminster St Denys and Upton Scudamore *Sarum* 16–17; C River Were 17–19; C Cley Hill Villages from 19. *Stone Cottage, 32 Huntenhull Green, Corsley, Warminster BA12 7QB* T: (01373) 832490 M: 07941-623446 E: gcmstonecottage@yahoo.co.uk

MAYNARD, John William. b 37. Lon Univ BSc 58. Ripon Hall Ox 60. **d** 62 **p** 63. C St Laur in Thanet *Cant* 62–67; C S Ashford Ch Ch 67–70; V Pagham *Chich* 70–00; rtd 00. *2 West Checkstone, 2 Douglas Avenue, Exmouth EX8 2AU* T: (01395) 222675

MAYNARD, Jonathan Mark (Josh). b 80. Ex Univ BA 02. Trin Coll Bris BA 09. **d** 10 **p** 11. C Woodchester and Brimscombe *Glouc* 10–15; V Styvechale *Cov* from 15. *Styvechale Vicarage, 16 Armorial Road, Coventry CV3 6GJ* T: (024) 7641 6074 M: 07825-795257 E: jmaynard1044@googlemail.com

MAYNARD, Canon Richard Edward Buller. b 42. AKC 66. **d** 67 **p** 68. C St Ives *Truro* 67–71; C Falmouth K Chas 71–74; V St Germans 74–85; RD E Wivelshire 81–85; TR Saltash 85–08; Hon Can Truro Cathl 82–08; Chapl St Barn Hosp Saltash 90–93; Chapl Cornwall Healthcare NHS Trust 93–02; Chapl N and E Cornwall Primary Care Trust 02–06; Chapl Cornwall and Is of Scilly Primary Care Trust 06–08; rtd 08; C Altarnon w Bolventor, Laneast and St Clether *Truro* 11–12; PtO from 15. *Harewood, Dunheved Road, Launceston PL15 9JJ* T: (01566) 779135 E: canonrichardmaynard@btinternet.com *or* rebmaynard@btinternet.com

MAYNE, Canon Brian John. b 52. Univ of Wales (Cardiff) BA 73 LTCL 75 MRICS 81. NEOC 82 Coll of Resurr Mirfield 84. **d** 85 **p** 86. C Stainton-in-Cleveland *York* 85–89; P-in-c Rounton w Welbury 89–96; Chapl HM YOI Northallerton 89–96; Chapl HM YOI Lanc Farms 96–10; Chapl HM Pris Kirkham 10–17; Hon Can Blackb Cathl 09–17; rtd 17; PtO *Blackb* from 17. *Address withheld by request* E: brianmayne@tiscali.co.uk

MAYO, Christopher Paul. b 68. Heythrop Coll Lon BD 91 Birm Univ PGCE 96. Qu Coll Birm 91. **d** 93 **p** 94. C Wednesfield *Lich* 93–94; C Bilston 94–95; Miss P E Sutherland *Mor* 10–17; P-in-c Tain 12–17; P-in-c Thurso 17–19; P-in-c Wick 17–19; P-in-c Brora 17–19; Dioc Miss Officer 17–19. *9 Academy Street, Brora KW9 6QP* T: (01408) 600818 M: 07860-333892 E: frchrismayo@gmail.com *or* chris.mayo@theauldkirk.org

MAYO, Deborah Ann. *See* MURPHY, Deborah Ann

MAYO, Inglis John. b 46. FCA. Ripon Hall Ox 74. **d** 77 **p** 78. C Bitterne Park *Win* 77–81; C Christchurch 81–86; P-in-c Sturminster Marshall *Sarum* 86–89; P-in-c Kingston Lacy and Shapwick 86–89; V Sturminster Marshall, Kingston Lacy and Shapwick 89–00; P-in-c Lilliput 00–06; V 06–08; rtd 08; PtO *Sarum* 08–18; *Win* from 08. *49B St Catherine's Road, Bournemouth BH6 4AQ* T: (01202) 424971 E: inglis.mayo@btinternet.com

MAYO, Robert William. b 61. Keble Coll Ox BA 83 Trin Coll Carmarthen PhD 00. Cranmer Hall Dur 85. **d** 87 **p** 88. C Luton Lewsey St Hugh *St Alb* 87–90; Hd Cam Univ Miss and NSM Bermondsey St Jas w Ch Ch *S'wark* 90–95; Chapl S Bank Univ 95–98; Dir Youth Work Tr Ridley Hall Cam 98–05;

V Shepherd's Bush St Steph w St Thos *Lon* 05–19; Chapl HM YOI Roch from 19. *HM Prison Rochester, 1 Fort Road, Rochester ME1 3QS* T: (01634) 803100 M: 07977-003227 E: bobmayo43@gmail.com

MAYO, Mrs Susan. b 53. Didsbury Coll Man BEd 78. St Jo Coll Nottm 08. **d** 10 **p** 11. NSM Edgeley and Cheadle Heath *Ches* 10–15; NSM Cheadle All Hallows 15–17; Chapl Stockport Academy 11–15; TV Penkridge *Lich* from 17. *3 Bitham Close, Penkridge, Stafford ST19 5HT* T: (01785) 715605 E: mayos32@btinternet.com

MAYO-LYTHALL, Ms Jennifer Elizabeth. b 83. St Jo Coll Dur BA 10. Cranmer Hall Dur 07. **d** 10 **p** 11. C Norbury *Ches* 10–14; Transforming Lives Together Development Officer 14–16; NSM Offerton St Alb and Stockport St Thos 14–17; V Walsall St Martin *Lich* from 17. *St Martin's House, 17 Daffodil Road, Walsall WS5 3DQ* T: (01922) 277695 or 635217 M: 07749-949830 E: jmayo-lythall@hotmail.com

MAYO-SMITH, Peter. b 49. Open Univ BA 80. Ridley Hall Cam 05. **d** 06 **p** 07. C Greengates *Bradf* 06–09; C Idle 06–09; C Cottingley 08–09; P-in-c Haworth 09–14; *Leeds* 14–15; R Haworth and Cross Roads cum Lees 15–17; P-in-c Oxenhope *Bradf* 10–13; C Bingley All SS *Leeds* from 17. *Winston Grange, Otley Road, Bingley BD16 3EQ* M: 07880-866222 E: peter@mayo-smith.net

MAYOR, Henry William. b 39. Oriel Coll Ox BA 62. Westcott Ho Cam 62. **d** 64 **p** 65. C The Quinton *Birm* 64–66; C Dudley St Thos and St Luke *Worc* 67–71; R Birch St Agnes *Man* 71–83; Community Chapl Aylesbury *Ox* 83–89; Community Chapl Aylesbury w Bierton and Hulcott 89; R Cheetham St Luke and Lower Crumpsall St Thos *Man* 89–96; R Cheetham and Lower Crumpsall 97–01; rtd 01; PtO *Man* from 01. *18 Sycamore Close, Heaton Road, Manchester M20 4PH* M: 07958-639967 E: henrywmayor@hotmail.com

MAYOR, Janet Hilary. *See* TAYLOR, Janet Hilary

MAYOSS, Anthony (Aidan). b 31. Leeds Univ BA 55. Coll of Resurr Mirfield 55. **d** 57 **p** 58. C Meir *Lich* 57–62; Lic to Offic *Wakef* 62–72 and 78–14; CR from 64; S Africa 73–75; Asst Chapl Lon Univ 76–78; Bursar CR 84–90; rtd 98; PtO *Lon* 98–07; LtO *Leeds* from 14. *House of the Resurrection, Stocks Bank Road, Mirfield WF14 0BN* T: (01924) 483330 E: amayoss@mirfield.org.uk

MAYOSS-HURD, Canon Susan Patricia. b 59. Lanc Univ BA 81. Cranmer Hall Dur 82. **dss** 84 **d** 87 **p** 94. Ribbesford w Bewdley *Worc* 84–88; Par Dn 87–88; Chapl W Heath Hosp 88–96; C W Heath *Birm* 88–96; V 96–03; V Peachland St Marg Canada from 03. *6146 Turner Avenue, Peachland BC V0H 1X4, Canada* T: (001) (250) 767 9682 E: revsuemh@shaw.ca

MAZUR, Mrs Ann Carol. b 47. St Mich Coll Sarum CertEd 69. TISEC 01. **d** 04 **p** 05. NSM St Ninian's Cathl Perth *St And* 04–07; Prec 07–12; Chapl Craigclowan Sch Perth 04–07; rtd 12; PtO *Linc* from 16. *Fairmead, Langton-by-Wragby, Market Rasen LN8 5PX* T: (01673) 857720 E: ann@mazur.org.uk

MBANUDE, Chidiebere. p 16. NSM Croydon St Andr *S'wark* from 16. *61A Church Street, Croydon CR0 1RH* M: 07448-478236 E: chychyltd@gmail.com

MDUMULLA, Jonas Habel. b 50. Nairobi Univ Hull Univ BTh 87 MA 89. St Phil Coll Kongwa. **d** 74 **p** 75. Tanzania 74–82; C Sutton St Jas and Wawne *York* 82–96; P-in-c Carlton and Drax 96–15; Ind Chapl 96–15; rtd 15; PtO *York* from 16. *26 Riverside Court, Rawcliffe, Goole DN14 8TD* T: (01405) 839327 E: mdumulla@btinternet.com

MEAD, Arthur Hugh. b 39. K Coll Cam BA 60 MA 64 New Coll Ox BLitt 66. St Steph Ho Ox 61. **d** 80 **p** 80. NSM Hammersmith St Jo *Lon* 80–05; NSM Hammersmith H Innocents and St Jo 05–09; Chapl St Paul's Sch Barnes 82–97; Dep P in O 85–90 and 95–09; P in O 90–95; Reader of The Temple 95–15; PtO *Lon* from 18. *11 Dungarvan Avenue, London SW15 5QU* T: (020) 8876 5833

MEAD, Elveen. b 67. Trin Coll Bris 15. **d** 17 **p** 18. C Gauzebrook *Bris* from 17. *3 Garth Close, Chippenham SN14 6XF* E: elveen@me.com

MEAD, Mrs Lynda Roberta. b 44. Open Univ BA 91. STETS. **d** 99 **p** 00. NSM Hythe *Win* 99–04; PtO 04–09; NSM Boldre w S Baddesley 09–16; rtd 17; PtO *Win* from 17. *22 Furzedale Park, Hythe, Southampton SO45 3HW* T: (023) 8084 8901

MEAD, Nicholas Charles. b 50. Newc Univ BEd 73 Reading Univ MA 76. Ridley Hall Cam 83. **d** 85 **p** 86. C Bilton *Cov* 85–88; C Whittlesey *Ely* 88–89; Hd RS Neale-Wade Community Coll March 89–97; Fell Farmington Inst for Chr Studies Ox from 96; Sen Lect RE Westmr Coll Ox 97–00; Sen Lect RE Ox Brookes Univ 00–13. *9 Yarnells Road, Oxford OX2 0JY* T: (01865) 240865 E: nmead@brookes.ac.uk

MEAD, Peter Tony. b 63. St Jo Coll Dur BA 08. Cranmer Hall Dur 06. **d** 08 **p** 09. C Yeovil H Trin w Barwick *B & W* 08–12; Chapl Yeovil Distr Hosp NHS Foundn Trust 08–10;

R St Leonards St Ethelburga and St Leon *Chich* 12–16; R Arbroath *Bre* from 16; R Auchmithie from 16; Chapl NHS Tayside from 16. *St Mary's Rectory, 2 Springfield Terrace, Arbroath DD11 1EL* T: (01241) 873392 M: 07791-642598 E: pete.mead@sky.com

MEADEN, Philip George William. b 40. Open Univ BA 75. Lich Th Coll 63. **d** 66 **p** 67. C Aston SS Pet and Paul *Birm* 66–70; V Lozells St Paul 70–76; Asst Chapl HM Pris Brixton 76–77; Chapl HM Pris Lewes 77–84; Chapl HM Pris Aylesbury 84–88; Chapl HM Pris Wandsworth 88–01; rtd 01; PtO *St E* 01–05. *2 Waterloo Lane, Fairford GL7 4BP* T: (01285) 713917

MEADER, Jennifer Lindsay. b 68. UEA BA 89. Westcott Ho Cam. **d** 01 **p** 02. C Teversham and Cherry Hinton St Andr *Ely* 01–05; C Westmr St Jas *Lon* from 05. *St James's Church, 197 Piccadilly, London W1J 9LL* T: (020) 7734 4511 E: revlindsaym@gmail.com

MEADOWS, Mrs Freda Angela. b 46. CertEd 68. Oak Hill Th Coll 93. **d** 96 **p** 97. NSM N Wembley St Cuth *Lon* 96–01; NSM Roxeth 01–07; rtd 07; PtO *Lon* 07–12; *B & W* from 12. *38 Maple Rise, Radstock BA3 3LH* T: (01761) 435320 M: 07887-484497 E: fred@famead.net

MEADOWS, Philip Michael. b 71. Univ of Wales (Lamp) BA 95. St Steph Ho Ox BTh 01. **d** 01 **p** 03. C W Bromwich St Fran *Lich* 01; C Leeds Belle Is St Jo and St Barn *Ripon* 02–06; PtO *Ches* from 06; *Man* from 17; CMP from 04. *13 Naburn Close, Stockport SK5 8JQ* T: 0161-494 8073 M: 07971-035513 E: frmeadows@hotmail.co.uk

MEADWAY, Prof Jeanette Valerie. b 47. Edin Univ MB, ChB 69 FRCP 87 FRCPEd 87. Oak Hill NSM Course 89. **d** 93 **p** 94. NSM Stratford St Jo w Ch Ch and St Jas *Chelmsf* 93–14; NSM Stratford St Paul and St Jas 14–19; V Plaistow St Martin from 19; PtO *Lon* 99–03; Hon Prof Gulu Univ Uganda from 09; Can Mbale Cathl from 09. *4 Glebe Avenue, Woodford Green IG8 9HB* T: (020) 8504 1958 E: revjeanettem16@gmail.com

MEAKIN, Canon Anthony John. b 28. Down Coll Cam BA 52 MA 56. Westcott Ho Cam 52. **d** 54 **p** 55. C Gosforth All SS *Newc* 54–60; V Alnwick St Paul 60–71; V Edlingham 62–71; CF (TA) 63–83; R Whickham *Dur* 71–88; RD Gateshead W 78–88; Hon Can Dur Cathl 83–93; Bp's Sen Chapl and Exec Officer for Dioc Affairs 88–93; rtd 93; PtO *Dur* from 94. *73 Oakfields, Burnopfield, Newcastle upon Tyne NE16 6PQ* T: (01207) 270429 E: a.meakin2@homecall.co.uk

MEAKIN, David John. b 61. Hull Univ BA 82 Dur Univ MA 96 Hughes Hall Cam PGCE 83 Lambeth STh 88. Westcott Ho Cam 86. **d** 88 **p** 89. C Upminster *Chelmsf* 88–92; Prec and Sacr Dur Cathl 92–97; V Ryhope 97–04; P-in-c Schorne *Ox* 04–11; TR from 11; AD Claydon from 11. *The Rectory, 1 Green Acres Close, Whitchurch, Aylesbury HP22 4JP* T: (01296) 641606 E: d.meakin@btinternet.com

MEARA, The Ven David Gwynne. b 47. Oriel Coll Ox BA 70 MA 73. Lambeth STh 76 Cuddesdon Coll 71. **d** 73 **p** 74. C Whitley Ch Ch Ox 73–77; Chapl Reading Univ 77–82; V Basildon 82–87; P-in-c Aldworth and Ashampstead 85–87; V Basildon w Aldworth and Ashampstead 87–94; RD Bradfield 90–94; V Buckingham w Radclive cum Chackmore 94–97; P-in-c Nash w Thornton, Beachampton and Thornborough 96–97; R Buckingham 97–00; RD 95–00; Hon Can Ch Ch 98–00; R St Bride Fleet Street w Bridewell etc *Lon* 00–14; Adn Lon 09–14; P-in-c St Mary Aldermary 10–12; rtd 14; PtO *Ox* from 14. *Stonewalls Barn, 10 The Closes, Kidlington OX5 2DP* T: (01865) 803729 E: david.meara14@gmail.com

MEARDON, Canon Brian Henry. b 44. Reading Univ BSc 66 PhD 71. Oak Hill Th Coll MPhil 84. **d** 79 **p** 80. C Reading St Jo *Ox* 79–82; V Warfield 82–09; Hon Can Ch Ch 03–09; rtd 09; Hon C Bemerton *Sarum* 10–12; PtO from 12. *382 Devizes Road, Salisbury SP2 9LY* T: (01722) 501300 E: brian.meardon@googlemail.com

MEARDON, Mark James. b 73. Southn Univ BSc 94. Trin Th Coll Singapore MTS 07 St Jo Coll Nottm MA 09. **d** 09 **p** 10. C Hazlemere *Ox* 09–17; V from 17; Chapl Pipers Corner Sch from 18. *17 Southcote Way, Penn, High Wycombe HP10 8JG* T: (01494) 812748 M: 07905-887125 E: mark.meardon@gmail.com or mark.hazlemere@gmail.com

MEARDON, Trevor John. b 78. **d** 16 **p** 17. C Southmead *Bris* 16–18; C Patchway from 18. *2 Applegate, Bristol BS10 6QJ* M: 07947-610169 E: trev.meardon@gmail.com

MEARS, Mrs Hannah Marie. b 80. St Cuth Soc Dur BA 02 St Mary's Ho Dur MA 03. Trin Coll Bris 06. **d** 08 **p** 09. NSM Henbury *Bris* 08–09; C St Austell *Truro* 09–13; V Rugby W *Cov* 13–17; Dioc Voc Adv *Ex* from 19. *The Rectory, 27 West End Road, Bradninch, Exeter EX5 4QS* T: (01392) 881733 E: revhannahmears@hotmail.com

MEARS, Oliver Harry John. b 80. Ball Coll Ox BA 02. Trin Coll Bris BA 08. **d** 09 **p** 10. C St Austell *Truro* 09–13; NSM

Rugby W *Cov* 13–14; V 14–17; P-in-c Bradninch *Ex* from 17; C Cullompton from 17. *The Rectory, 27 West End Road, Bradninch, Exeter EX5 4QS* T: (01392) 881733 M: 07806-420473

MEARS, Phillip David. b 40. Dur Univ BA 62. **d** 65 **p** 66. C Sandylands *Blackb* 65–68; C Chorley St Geo 68–71; V Leyland St Ambrose 71–81; Chapl Warrington Distr Gen Hosp 81–00; PtO *Ches* 81–06; Hon C Schorne *Ox* 06–15. *4 Newell Close, Bedgrove, Aylesbury HP21 7FE* T: (01296) 655237

MEATH AND KILDARE, Bishop of. See STOREY, The Most Revd Patricia Louise

MEATHREL, Timothy James. b 78. Ox Brookes Univ BSc 99. Wycliffe Hall Ox BTh 07. **d** 08 **p** 09. C Harborne Heath *Birm* 08–13; C Clifton Ch Ch w Em *Bris* 13–17; V Northwood Em *Lon* from 17. *Emmanuel Vicarage, 3 Gatehill Road, Northwood HA6 3QB* M: 07818-401372 E: tim.meathrel@ecn.org.uk

MEATS, Canon Alan John. b 41. Univ of Wales (Cardiff) BA 62 DipEd 63 Lon Univ BD 70 Trin Coll Carmarthen MTh 00. St Mich Coll Llan 68. **d** 70 **p** 71. C Pontypridd St Cath *Llan* 70–73; TV Ystradyfodwg 73–75; Dioc Inspector of Schs 73–75 and 83–89; V Llandeilo Tal-y-bont *S & B* 75–83; RD Llwchwr 81–83; V Aberdare St Fagan *Llan* 83–89; V Felin-foel *St D* 89–01; Asst Dioc Dir of Educn 89–92; Dioc Dir of Educn 92–97; V Pen-bre 01–07; Can St Cathl *Llan* 94–07; rtd 07; PtO *S & B* from 12. *45A Capel Road, Llanelli SA14 8SL* T: (01554) 229427

MECHANIC, Mrs Bridget Elisheva. b 54. Cape Town Univ TDip 74 Nazarene Th Coll Man BA 08 Anglia Ruskin Univ MA 10. Ridley Hall Cam 08. **d** 10 **p** 11. C Ipswich St Jo *St E* 10–13; rtd 13; Academic Supervisor Africa Sch of Miss S Africa 13–14; P-in-c Escomb *Dur* from 14; P-in-c Etherley from 14; P-in-c Witton Park from 14; P-in-c Hamsterley and Witton-le-Wear from 14. *1 Vicarage Court, Howden le Wear, Crook DL15 8RB* T: (01388) 768898 E: elishevamechanic@gmail.com

MECHANIC, Rodney Ian (Roni). b 48. Man Univ MA(Theol) 00. **d** 78 **p** 78. S Africa 78–98; P-in-c Shebbear, Buckland Filleigh, Sheepwash etc *Ex* 98–01; Australia 01–02; TV Heatons *Man* 02–08; TV Mildenhall *St E* 08–13; rtd 13; Tr Dir Africa Sch of Miss S Africa 13–14; Hon C Escomb *Dur* 14–19; Hon C Etherley 14–19; Hon C Witton Park 14–19; Hon C Hamsterley and Witton-le-Wear 14–19; PtO from 19. *1 Vicarage Court, Howden le Wear, Crook DL15 8RB* T: (01388) 768898 E: ronimechanic@gmail.com

MECREDY, Ruth. b 60. STETS 09. **d** 12 **p** 13. NSM Broughton Gifford, Gt Chalfield and Holt *Sarum* from 12. *9 Little Parks, Holt, Trowbridge BA14 6QR* T: (01225) 783197 E: rmecredy@gmail.com

MEDFORTH, Allan Hargreaves. b 27. Qu Coll Cam BA 48 MA 52. Westcott Ho Cam 50. **d** 51 **p** 52. C Hexham *Newc* 51–55; PV S'well Minster 55–59; V Farnsfield 59–72; RD S'well 66–72; V St Alb St Pet 72–95; RD St Alb 74–84; rtd 95; PtO *St Alb* from 95. *62 Cuckmans Drive, St Albans AL2 3AF* T: (01727) 836437 E: allan.medforth@talktalk.net

MEDHURST, Mrs June. b 44. St Hild Coll Dur TCert 66. NOC 99. **d** 02 **p** 03. C Silsden *Bradf* 02–06; P-in-c Oxenhope 06–10; Chapl Manorlands Hospice Keighley 04–09; PtO *Bradf* 10–14; *Leeds* from 14. *100 Langley Lane, Baildon, Shipley BD17 6TD* T: (01274) 599177 E: medjune@tiscali.co.uk

MEDHURST, Prof Kenneth Noel. b 38. Edin Univ MA 61 Man Univ PhD 69. **d** 91 **p** 93. NSM Baildon *Bradf* 91–06; NSM Oxenhope 06–09; Can Th Bradf Cathl *Leeds* from 00; PtO *Bradf* 10–14; *Leeds* from 14. *100 Langley Lane, Baildon, Shipley BD17 6TD* T: (01274) 599177

MEDLEY, Steven Thomas. b 70. Moorlands Coll BA 02. Qu Foundn Birm 14. **d** 15 **p** 16. C Chilvers Coton w Astley *Cov* 15–19; C Cov Cathl from 19. *4 St Christian's Croft, Coventry CV3 5GY* T: (024) 7667 2268 M: 07751-384297 E: steve.medley42@gmail.com

MEDWAY, Daron. b 72. Univ of N Lon BA 98. Wycliffe Hall Ox BTh 04. **d** 04 **p** 05. C Crofton *Portsm* 04–08; V Penge St Jo *Roch* 08–13; P-in-c Weston *Win* from 13. *Weston Vicarage, Weston Lane, Southampton SO19 9HG* T: (023) 8044 8421 M: 07900-574691 E: d.medway@mac.com

MEE, Colin Henry. b 36. Reading Univ BSc 58. Bris Sch of Min 83. **d** 85 **p** 86. NSM Stanton St Quintin, Hullavington, Grittleton etc *Bris* 85–87; C Swindon Ch Ch 88–90; TV Washfield, Stoodleigh, Withleigh etc *Ex* 90–95; TR 95–99; Chapl Marie Curie Foundn (Tidcombe Hall) 95–99; rtd 99; PtO *B & W* 02–19. *Rickstones, Burgundy Road, Minehead TA24 5QJ* T: (01643) 706048 E: mee.mavcol@talktalk.net

MEE, Gerard Henry. b 72. St Mary's Coll Twickenham BA 13. Sarum Coll 13. **d** 16 **p** 17. NSM Thorpe *Guildf* from 16. *229 Albert Drive, Woking GU21 5RD* T: (01932) 336462 M: 07746-915418 E: gerardmee@yahoo.com

MEEK, Anthony William. b 45. ACIB. Ox NSM Course 80. **d** 83 **p** 84. NSM Gt Chesham *Ox* 83–01; PtO *Ex* from 01; Clergy Widow(er)s Officer 02–12. *The Willows, Orley Road, Ipplepen, Newton Abbot TQ12 5SA* T: (01803) 814370 E: frtonymeek@aol.com

MEERING, Laurence Piers Ralph. b 48. Man Univ BSc 70. Trin Coll Bris 79. **d** 81 **p** 82. C Downend *Bris* 81–84; C Crofton *Portsm* 84–87; V Witheridge, Thelbridge, Creacombe, Meshaw etc *Ex* 87–94; TV Southgate *Chich* 94–02; TV Walton H Trin *Ox* 02–07; P-in-c Bedgrove 02–07; P-in-c Newton Longville and Mursley w Swanbourne etc 07–08; R 08–09; V Newton Longville, Mursley, Swanbourne etc 09–14; AD Mursley 11–14; rtd 14; PtO *B & W* from 15. *21 St Michael's Gardens, South Petherton TA13 5BD* T: (01460) 242653 E: laurencemeering@yahoo.co.uk

MEESAM, Melanie Louise. b 77. St Hild Coll 17. **d** 19. NSM Hull St Cuth *York* from 19. *31 Sutton Road, Hull HU6 7DR*

MEESE, Dudley Noel. b 63. Leic Univ BA 86 Nottm Univ PGCE 87. Ridley Hall Cam 99. **d** 01 **p** 02. C Sheff St Jo 01–05; Chapl Lee Abbey 05–13. *1 Borrowdale Close, Nottingham NG2 6PD* E: dnmeese@gmail.com

MEESON, Andrew Scott. b 86. Man Univ MB, ChB 09. Oak Hill Th Coll MTheol 15. **d** 15 **p** 16. C Whittle-le-Woods *Blackb* 15–18; V Leyland St Jo from 18. *St John's Vicarage, Leyland Lane, Leyland PR25 1XB* M: 07532-271740 E: andyandamymeeson@aol.co.uk

MEGARRELL, Miss Joanne Myrtle. b 70. QUB BA 93 PGCE 94. CITC BTh 03. **d** 03 **p** 04. C Moira *D & D* 03–12; I from 12. *1 Main Street, Moira, Craigavon BT67 0LE* T: (028) 9261 3359 E: joanne@moiraparish.org.uk

✠**MEHAFFEY, The Rt Revd James.** b 31. TCD BA 52 MA 56 BD 56 QUB PhD 75 Ulster Univ Hon DLitt 99. **d** 54 **p** 55 **c** 80. C Ballymacarrett St Patr *D & D* 54–56; C Deptford St Jo *S'wark* 56–58; C Down Cathl *D & D* 58–60; C-in-c Ballymacarrett St Chris 60–62; I Kilkeel 62–66; I Cregagh 66–80; Bp's Private Chapl 72–76; Preb Down Cathl 76–80; Dioc Missr 76–80; Bp D & R 80–02; rtd 02. *10 Clearwater, Londonderry BT47 6BE* T: (028) 7134 2624 E: james.mehaffey@btinternet.com

MEHEN, Donald Wilfrid. b 44. Birkbeck Coll Lon BSc 72 CertEd 66. **d** 00 **p** 01. OLM Sproughton w Burstall, Copdock w Washbrook etc *St E* 00–13; NSM 13–14; rtd 14; PtO *St E* from 14; RD Samford 13–15. *19 The Link, Bentley, Ipswich IP9 2DJ* T: (01473) 310383 E: donmehen@gmail.com

MEIGHEN, Alan Hugh. b 54. **d** 15 **p** 16. NSM Killingworth *Newc* from 15. *4 Hazelwood, Killingworth, Newcastle upon Tyne NE12 6FF* T: 0191-268 1953 M: 07709-647892 E: alanmeighen@btinternet.com

MEIKLE, Ross Alexander. b 90. St Jo Coll Dur BA 17. Cranmer Hall Dur 14. **d** 17 **p** 18. C Witney *Ox* from 17. *9 Oakfield Place, Witney OX28 4NH* E: ross@witneyparish.org.uk

MEIN, The Very Revd James Adlington. b 38. Nottm Univ BA 60. Westcott Ho Cam 61. **d** 63 **p** 64. C Edin St Columba 63–67; Bp's Dom Chapl 65–67; Malawi 67–72; R Grangemouth *Edin* 72–82; P-in-c Bo'ness 76–82; TV Livingston LEP 82–90; R Edin Ch Ch 90–04; Can St Mary's Cathl 90–01; Syn Clerk 00–01; Dean Edin 01–04; rtd 04. *Cardhu, Bridgend, Linlithgow EH49 6NH* T: (01506) 834317 E: jim@meins.plus.com

MEIRIONNYDD, Archdeacon of. See JONES, The Ven Andrew

MELANIPHY, Miss Angela Ellen. b 55. SRN 79. Cranmer Hall Dur 87. **d** 90 **p** 94. Par Dn Leytonstone St Jo *Chelmsf* 90–94; C 94–95; TV Harlow Town Cen w Lt Parndon 95–06; TV Hackney Marsh *Lon* 06–15; R Fowlmere, Foxton, Shepreth and Thriplow *Ely* from 15. *The Rectory, High Street, Fowlmere, Royston SG8 7SU* E: rector@thefourchurchbenefice.org

MELCHOR, Stuart Floyd. b 64. St Mellitus Coll 14. **d** 17 **p** 18. C Northolt St Jos *Lon* from 17. *8 Wells Close, Northolt UB5 6JD* E: curate@josephtheworker.org

MELDRUM, Andrew John Bruce. b 66. Univ of Wales (Abth) LLB 89 Lon Univ MA 98. Westcott Ho Cam 91. **d** 94 **p** 95. C Paddington St Jas *Lon* 94–99; P-in-c Brookfield St Anne, Highgate Rise 99–02; V from 02; Communications Adv to Bp Edmonton from 00; AD S Camden 08–16. *St Anne's Vicarage, 106 Highgate West Hill, London N6 6AP* T/F: (020) 8340 5190 E: javintner@aol.com

MELLARS, Paul David. b 72. York St Jo Univ BA 15. Yorks Min Course 12. **d** 15 **p** 16. C Clifton St Jas *Sheff* 15–17; C Hoyland 17–18; C Stainforth 18–19; C Fishlake w Sykehouse and Kirk Bramwith etc 18–19; TV Dronfield w Holmesfield *Derby* from 19. *11 Rothay Close, Dronfield Woodhouse, Dronfield S18 8PR*

MELLERUP, Miss Eiler Mary. b 37. Saffron Walden Coll CertEd 58. **d** 96 **p** 97. OLM Happisburgh, Walcott, Hempstead w Eccles etc *Nor* 96–08; PtO from 08. *Channings, The Crescent, Walcott, Norwich NR12 0NH* T: (01692) 651393

MELLESS, Miss Claire Louise. b 75. Nottm Trent Univ BA 10. Cranmer Hall Dur 17. **d** 19. C Ravenshead *S'well* from 19. *1 Cromford Court, Ravenshead, Nottingham NG15 9GG* M: 07709-315065 E: claire.melless@yahoo.com

MELLOR, Canon Kenneth Paul. b 49. Southn Univ BA 71 Leeds Univ MA 72. Cuddesdon Coll 72. **d** 73 **p** 74. C Cottingham *York* 73–76; C Ascot Heath *Ox* 76–80; V Tilehurst St Mary 80–85; V Menheniot *Truro* 85–94; Hon Can Truro Cathl 90–94; Can Res and Treas Truro Cathl 94–03; RD W Wivelshire 88–96; R Guernsey St Peter Port *Win* 03–14; P-in-c Sark 03–14; Dean Guernsey 03–14; Hon Can Win Cathl 03–14; rtd 14; PtO *Win* from 14; Master St Nic Hosp Salisbury from 16; PtO *Sarum* from 16. *The Master's House, St Nicholas Hospital, 5 St Nicholas Road, Salisbury SP1 2SW* T: (01722) 340369 M: 07720-506863 E: kpaulmellor@cwgsy.net

MELLOR, Roy. b 52. Lanc Univ BA 92. Cuddesdon Coll 94. **d** 96 **p** 97. C Oakdale *Sarum* 96–00; TV Kingsthorpe w Northampton St Dav *Pet* 00–03; R Blisworth and Stoke Bruerne w Grafton Regis etc 03–10; P-in-c Collingtree w Courteenhall and Milton Malsor 09–10; rtd 10; PtO *Dur* 11–15; *Ox* from 15; *Eur* from 16. *7 Honeysuckle Way, Ambrosden, Bicester OX25 2AN* M: 07914-767191 E: roy_mellor2002@yahoo.co.uk

MELLORS, Derek George. b 38. Bris Univ CertEd 60 Lon Univ BSc 71 Nottm Univ DipEd 74 Liv Univ MEd 83. NOC 81. **d** 84 **p** 85. NSM Eccleston Ch Ch *Liv* 84–92; C Lowton St Mary 92–93; V Ashton-in-Makerfield St Thos 93–99; rtd 99; PtO *Liv* from 00. *20 Millbrook Lane, Eccleston, St Helens WA10 4QU* T: (01744) 28424

MELLUISH, Preb Mark Peter. b 59. Oak Hill Th Coll. **d** 89 **p** 90. C Ashtead *Guildf* 89–93; V Ealing St Paul *Lon* from 93; P-in-c Hanwell St Mellitus w St Mark from 14; P-in-c W Ealing St Jo w St Jas from 19; Preb St Paul's Cathl from 13. *St Paul's Vicarage, 102 Elers Road, London W13 9QE* T: (020) 8567 4628 or 8799 3779 F: 8567 4628 E: mark@stpaulsealing.com

MELOT, Mrs Sheila Mary. b 48. Bris Univ BA 69 MLitt 76. Trin Coll Bris 15. **d** 17 **p** 18. OLM Bishopston and St Andrews *Bris* 17–19. *34 Downs Park West, Bristol BS6 7QL* M: 07818-001119 E: sheilamelot@gmail.com

MELTON, Anne. b 44. N Riding Coll of Educn CertEd 65. Cranmer Hall Dur 80. **dss** 83 **d** 87 **p** 94. Newton Aycliffe *Dur* 83–88; Par Dn 87–88; Par Dn Shildon w Eldon 88–94; Asst Dir of Ords 88–94; P-in-c Usworth 94–96; TR 96–06; rtd 06; PtO *Dur* from 07. *4 Lindisfarne, High Shincliffe, Durham DH1 2PH* T: 0191-374 0823

MELVIN, Gordon Thomas. b 55. BA 86. Sarum & Wells Th Coll 86. **d** 88 **p** 89. C Linc St Faith and St Martin w St Pet 88–91; TV Horsham *Chich* 91–94; Chapl Horsham Gen Hosp 91–94; Chapl Ipswich Hosp NHS Trust 94–00; Sen Chapl 00–04; Chapl Local Health Partnerships NHS Trust 94–00; Sen Chapl 00–04; Retreat Ldr from 04; PtO *St E* from 04. *50 Constable Road, Ipswich IP4 2UZ* T: (01473) 233517 E: gordon.melvin@keme.co.uk

MENDEL, Canon Thomas Oliver. b 57. Down Coll Cam BA 79 MA 82. Cranmer Hall Dur 79. **d** 81 **p** 82. Chapl Down Coll Cam 81–86; Fell 84–86; Hon C Cambridge St Mary Less *Ely* 81–86; V Minsterley *Heref* 86–92; R Habberley 86–92; Chapl Shrewsbury Sch 93–95; Chapl Milan w Genoa and Varese *Eur* 95–96; Chapl Copenhagen w Aarhus 96–04; Sen Chapl Malta and Gozo 04–08; Can and Chan Malta Cathl 04–08; V Eastbourne St Mary *Chich* from 08. *St Mary's Vicarage, 2 Glebe Close, Eastbourne BN20 8AW* T: (01323) 720420

MENDHAM, Vivien Evelyn. b 44. **d** 18 **p** 19. OLM Lexden *Chelmsf* from 18. *Address withheld by request* E: viv@stleonardslexden.org.uk

✠**MENIN, The Rt Revd Malcolm James.** b 32. Univ Coll Ox BA 55 MA 59. Cuddesdon Coll 55. **d** 57 **p** 58 **c** 86. C Southsea H Spirit *Portsm* 57–59; C Fareham SS Pet and Paul 59–62; V Nor St Jas w Pockthorpe 62–72; P-in-c Nor St Martin 62–74; P-in-c Nor St Mary Magd 68–72; V Nor St Mary Magd w St Jas 72–86; RD Nor E 81–86; Hon Can Nor Cathl 82–86; Suff Bp Knaresborough *Ripon* 86–97; rtd 97; PtO *Nor* 97–04; Hon Asst Bp Nor from 00; PtO from 16. *32C Bracondale, Norwich NR1 2AN* T: (01603) 627987

MENNIE, Joel John. b 83. Ox Brookes Univ BA 06. Trin Coll Bris BA 16. **d** 16 **p** 17. C Bath Twerton-on-Avon *B & W* from 16. *20A Bellotts Road, Bath BA2 3RT* M: 07527-545692 E: joel.mennie@mac.com

MENNISS, Canon Andrew Philip. b 49. Univ of Wales (Swansea) BSc 73. Sarum & Wells Th Coll 83. **d** 85 **p** 86. C Horsell *Guildf* 85–89; V Bembridge *Portsm* 89–14; RD E Wight 95–00; Hon Can Portsm Cathl 09–14; rtd 14; PtO *Birm* from 14. *102 Sunnybank Road, Sutton Coldfield B73 5RL* M: 07762-228629 E: andrewpm49@gmail.com

MENON, Nicholas Anthony Thotekat. b 39. Mert Coll Ox BA 61 MA 65. St Steph Ho Ox 61. **d** 63 **p** 64. C Paddington Ch Ch *Lon* 63–66; Hon C 66–70; V Thorpe *Guildf* 70–76; V Ox SS Phil and Jas w St Marg 76–79; Chapl Surrey Univ *Guildf* 79–82; Chapl and Ho Master Cranleigh Sch Surrey 82–00; Asst Chapl Malvern Coll 00–06; rtd 04; PtO *Worc* from 05; *Heref* from 06. *Pilgrim Cottage, 187 West Malvern Road, Malvern WR14 4BB* T: (01684) 577189 E: nicholasmenon159@btinternet.com

MENON, Suresh Vijayan. b 64. Man Poly BA 88. Oak Hill Th Coll 96. **d** 98 **p** 99. C Braintree *Chelmsf* 98–02; C Leic H Trin w St Jo 02–05; C Ox St Ebbe w H Trin and St Pet 10–14; PtO *Guildf* from 18. *7 Berkeley Crescent, Frimley, Camberley GU16 8YN* T: (01252) 835956 E: mail2suresh.menon@gmail.com

MENSINGH, Gregg Richard. b 69. Portsm Univ BSc 94. Westcott Ho Cam 95. **d** 97 **p** 98. C Birchfield *Birm* 97–01; V Gravelly Hill 01–12; R Botley *Portsm* from 12; V Curdridge from 12; R Durley from 12; AD Bishop's Waltham 14–19. *The Rectory, 46 High Street, Botley, Southampton SO30 2EA* T: (01489) 780994 E: gregg.mensingh@gmail.com

MENTZEL, Kevin David. b 60. Reading Univ BSc 82 Down Coll Cam BA 87 MA 91 QUB MTh 04 Heythrop Coll Lon MA 09. Ridley Hall Cam 85. **d** 88 **p** 89. C Ditton *Roch* 88–91; Asst Chapl Eton Coll 91–93; Asst Chapl R Hosp Sch Holbrook 93–94; Sen C Fulham St Dionis *Lon* 94–97; CF from 97. *c/o MOD Chaplains (Army)* T: (01264) 383430 F: 381824 E: kdmentzel@gmail.com

MENZIES, Stanley Hay. b 33. Edin Univ MA 55 BD 58. New Coll Edin 55. **d** 02 **p** 03. NSM Boston Spa *York* 02–10; rtd 10; PtO *York* from 10. *Cairn Croft, 2 Crag Gardens, Bramham, Wetherby LS23 6RP* T/F: (01937) 541047

MEON, Archdeacon of the. See COLLINS, The Ven Gavin Andrew

MEPHAM, Ali Henry. b 75. Trin Coll Bris BA 07. **d** 07 **p** 08. C Warminster Ch Ch *Sarum* 07–10; TV The Lytchetts and Upton 10–16; V Fair Oak *Win* from 16. *The Vicarage, Fair Oak Court, Fair Oak, Eastleigh SO50 7BG* T: (023) 8178 3018 M: 07546-170008 E: ali@sttoms.co.uk

MEPHAM, Alistair Gregory Simon. See MEPHAM, Ali Henry

MEPHAM, Mrs Kathryn Mary. b 75. Sarum Coll. **d** 17 **p** 18. C Bishopstoke *Win* from 17; C Fair Oak from 17. *The Vicarage, Fair Oak Court, Fair Oak, Eastleigh SO50 7BG* T: (023) 8129 0975 M: 07512-222635 E: kat@sttoms.co.uk

MEPHAM, Kevin Aubrey. b 55. Sarum & Wells Th Coll 85. **d** 88 **p** 89. NSM Sidley *Chich* 88–90; C Hollington St Leon 90–94; V Horam 94–99; P-in-c Hastings All So 99–03; V Alkham w Capel le Ferne and Hougham *Cant* 03–05; P-in-c Sedlescombe w Whatlington *Chich* from 12. *The Rectory, Church Hill, Sedlescombe, Battle TN33 0QP* E: mephamka@aol.com

MERCER, Jacob Laurence Charles. b 88. Peterho Cam BA 11. Wycliffe Hall Ox BA 18. **d** 18 **p** 19. C Bermondsey St Jas and St Anne *S'wark* from 18. *161 Lynton Road, London SE1 5QX* M: 07833-462066

MERCER, James John. b 56. Bp Otter Coll Chich BEd 79 Lon Inst of Educn MA 85. Ridley Hall Cam 00. **d** 02 **p** 03. C Heref St Pet w St Owen and St Jas 02–07; V Harrow Weald All SS *Lon* 07–18; Lic Lay Min Tr Officer Willesden Area 08–14; Warden Lay Min 16–18; C St Aldhelm *Sarum* from 18. *The Rectory, St George's Close, Langton Matravers, Swanage BH19 3HZ* T: (01929) 422454 M: 07713-236709 E: james_staldhelm@icloud.com

MERCER, Jarred Austin. b 86. SE Coll (USA) BA 09 St Andr Univ MLitt 10 Qu Coll Ox DPhil 15. St Steph Ho Ox 13. **d** 15 **p** 16. C Ox St Mary Magd from 15; Jun Chapl Mert Coll Ox 15–17; Asst Chapl from 17. *67 Iffley Road, Oxford OX4 1EF* M: 07583-503796 E: jarred.mercer@gmail.com

MERCER, Lt Col Nicholas Justin. b 62. St Andr Univ BD 85 Cardiff Univ LLM 99 Ox Univ MTh 14 Solicitor 91. Ripon Coll Cuddesdon 08. **d** 11 **p** 12. C Gillingham and Milton-on-Stour *Sarum* 11–14; Asst Chapl Sherborne Sch 14–17; R Ch Ch Cathl and the Falkland Is 18–19; R Bolton Abbey *Leeds* from 19. *The Old Rectory, Bolton Abbey, Skipton BD23 6AL* M: 07912-619533 E: mercer-family@hotmail.com

MERCER, The Ven Nicholas Stanley. b 49. Selw Coll Cam BA 72 MA 76 PGCE 73 Spurgeon's Coll BA 78 Lon Bible Coll MPhil 86. Cranmer Hall Dur 95. **d** 95 **p** 95. C Northwood Hills St Edm *Lon* 95–98; C Pimlico St Mary Bourne Street 98–03; Dir of Min 03–07; V Gen Lon Coll of Bps 07–17; Dir of Ords 03–17; Lic Preacher 03–17; Hon C Wilton Place St Paul from 04; Adn Lon 15–16; P-in-c St Botolph without Bishopsgate 15–16; Preb St Paul's Cathl 08–17; rtd 17; PtO *Lon* from 17; *Eur* from 18. *42 Broomhouse Road, London SW6 3QX* M: 07782-250377 E: frnick@gmail.com

MERCER, Canon Timothy James. b 54. Fitzw Coll Cam BA 76 MA 80. Westcott Ho Cam 78. **d** 81 **p** 82. C Bromley SS

Pet and Paul *Roch* 81–85; R Swanscombe 85–96; Chapl Bromley Hosps NHS Trust 96–09; Chapl S Lon Healthcare NHS Trust 09–14; Hon Can Roch Cathl from 10; Dep Hd of Chapl King's Coll Hosp NHS Foundn Trust 14–18. *75 Tintagel Road, Orpington BR5 4LH* E: mercer180@btinternet.com

MERCERON, Daniel John. b 58. Lon Univ BA 81. Westcott Ho Cam 88. **d** 90 **p** 91. C Clevedon St Jo *B & W* 90–94; CF 94–14; P-in-c Alfriston w Lullington, Litlington and W Dean *Chich* 14–15; R Alfriston w Lullington, Litlington, W Dean and Folkington 15–17; Chapl Wellington Coll Berks 17–18; Chapl Eastbourne Coll from 19. *The Chaplaincy, Eastbourne College, Old Wish Road, Eastbourne BN21 4JY* E: djmerceron@eastbourne-college.co.uk

MERCHANT, Robert Ian. b 73. Keele Univ BA 98. Wycliffe Hall Ox BA 00 MA 05. **d** 01 **p** 02. C Harborne Heath *Birm* 01–04; Prin Lect Spirituality and Health Staffs Univ *Lich* 05–09; Dep Dir Cen for Ageing and Mental Health 05–09; NSM Cheltenham St Mark *Glouc* 05–06; C Cheltenham St Mich and Cheltenham St Luke and St Jo 06–10; R Ashleworth, Corse, Hartpury, Hasfield etc 10–12; Dir Dispersed Learning St Mellitus Coll 12–16; Dir St Mellitus Coll Chelmsf from 16; PtO *Lon* 12–13; NSM Hornsey Rise from 13; Public Preacher *Chelmsf* from 17. *3 Highcroft Road, London N19 3AQ* T: (020) 7281 1459

MERCHANT, Mrs Tamsin Laetitia Rachel. b 70. Wycliffe Hall Ox BTh 01. **d** 01 **p** 02. C Harborne Heath *Birm* 01–04; Sen Chapl Glos Univ 04–12; V Hornsey Rise from 12. *3 Highcroft Road, London N19 3AQ* T: (020) 7281 1459 E: revtamsinmerchant@gmail.com

MERCURIO, Canon Frank James Charles. b 46. Webster Univ (USA) BA 73 MA 75. St Alb Minl Tr Scheme 87. **d** 89 **p** 90. C Cheshunt *St Alb* 89–93; TV Hitchin 93–00; RD 94–00; TR Tring 00–07; P-in-c Alfreton *Derby* 07–16; P-in-c Riddings and Ironville 08–16; Hon Can Derby Cathl 15–16; rtd 16. *81 Queen Street, Eckington, Sheffield S21 4FD* E: frankmercurio@dialstart.net

MEREDITH, Ian. b 53. Univ of Wales BA 85 K Coll Lon MTh 89 Edin Univ MTh 96 Dur Univ PhD 07. K Coll Lon 86. **d** 02 **p** 03. Assoc Min Dumfries *Glas* 02–06; NSM Annan 06–07; NSM Eastriggs 06–07; NSM Gretna 06–07; NSM Lockerbie 06–07; NSM Moffat 06–07; R Ayr 07–13; R Girvan 07–13; R Maybole 07–13; P-in-c Portchester *Portsm* 13–17; V from 17; AD Fareham from 17. *The Vicarage, 164 Castle Street, Portchester, Fareham PO16 9QH* T: (023) 9237 5422 E: irev@ymail.com

MEREDITH, Canon Roland Evan. b 32. Trin Coll Cam BA 55 MA 59. Cuddesdon Coll 55. **d** 57 **p** 58. C Bishopwearmouth St Mich *Dur* 57–59; Dioc Chapl *Birm* 59–60; C Kirkby *Liv* 60–63; V Hitchin St Mary *St Alb* 63–72; TR Preston St Jo *Blackb* 72–76 and 76–79; RD Preston 72–79; Hon Can Blackb Cathl 77–79; TR Witney *Ox* 79–94; P-in-c Hailey w Crawley 79–82; RD Witney 89–97; Hon Can Ch Ch 92–97; rtd 94; PtO *Ox* from 97; *Eur* from 98. *37 Otters Court, Priory Mill Lane, Witney OX28 1GJ* T: (01993) 703698 M: 07971-370647 E: roland@canonmeredith.free-online.co.uk

MERIVALE, Charles Christian Robert. b 44. Cranmer Hall Dur 76. **d** 78 **p** 79. C Highbury Ch Ch w St Jo *Lon* 78–81; P-in-c Hawes *Ripon* 81–82; P-in-c Hardrow and St Jo w Lunds 81–82; V Hawes and Hardraw 82–84; Chapl R Cornwall Hosps Trust 85–92; PtO *B & W* 92–00; *Ex* 00–02; TV Shebbear, Buckland Filleigh, Sheepwash etc 02–08; rtd 08; PtO *B & W* 10–19. *The Cider House, Coxs Close, North Cadbury, Yeovil BA22 7DY* T: (01963) 440917 M: 07934-780766 E: christianandjane@hotmail.co.uk

MERRICK, Caroline Jane. b 65. SCRTP 14. **d** 17 **p** 18. C Walton-on-Thames *Guildf* from 17. *Parish Office, St Mary's Church Hall, Church Street, Walton-on-Thames KT12 2QS* E: caroline@waltonparish.org.uk

MERRICK, Richard Christopher. b 57. Qu Coll Birm 08. **d** 11 **p** 12. C Bushbury *Lich* 11–14; V Heath Town from 14. *Holy Trinity Vicarage, Bushbury Road, Wolverhampton WV10 0LY* T: (01902) 772840 E: revrichht@gmail.com

MERRIMAN, Stephen Richard. b 74. Leeds Univ BA 02. Coll of Resurr Mirfield 99. **d** 02 **p** 03. C Littlehampton and Wick *Chich* 02–06; TV 08–16; C Brighton St Matthias 06–08; V Chich St Wilfrid 16–17; C Arundel w Tortington and S Stoke from 17. *St James's Vicarage, 12 Cornwall Road, Littlehampton BN17 6EE* T: (01903) 724311 E: fr-smerriman@sky.com

MERRINGTON, Bill. b 55. Sheff Hallam Univ BSc 78 Birm Univ MPhil 95 Warwick Univ PhD 03. Cranmer Hall Dur 80. **d** 83 **p** 84. C Harborne Heath *Birm* 83–88; V Leamington Priors St Paul *Cov* 88–99; RD Warwick and Leamington 97–99; R Ilmington w Stretton-on-Fosse etc 99–07; R Tredington and Darlingscott 05–07; RD Shipston 99–03; Hon Can Cov

Cathl 01–07; Sen Chapl Bournemouth Univ *Sarum* 07–18; PtO *Win* 09–17; *York* 18; Chapl HM Pris Full Sutton from 18. *HM Prison Full Sutton, York YO41 1PS* T: (01759) 475100 E: bmerrington@bournemouth.ac.uk

MERRINGTON, Mrs Hilary. b 47. **d** 14 **p** 15. NSM Norley, Crowton and Kingsley *Ches* from 14. *Cartref, Ball Lane, Kingsley, Frodsham WA6 8HP* T: (01928) 788087 E: hilary.merrington@btinternet.com

MERRIOTT, Pamela Ann. b 51. SNTS. **d** 12 **p** 13. OLM Abbots Bromley, Blithfield, Colton, Colwich etc *Lich* from 12. *The Oaklands, 1 Billington Avenue, Little Haywood, Stafford ST18 0UZ* T: (01889) 881030 M: 07967-717181 E: davidmerriott@btinternet.com

MERRY, Philip John. b 58. ERMC 11. **d** 14 **p** 15. NSM Gt and Lt Bealings w Playford and Culpho *St E* 14–17; P-in-c Badwell and Walsham 17–18; V from 18. *The Rectory, The Causeway, Walsham-le Willows, Bury St Edmunds IP31 3AB* T: (01359) 258806 M: 07900-058418 E: philipmerry@hotmail.co.uk

MERRY, Rex Edwin. b 38. AKC 67. **d** 68 **p** 69. C Spalding St Jo *Linc* 68–73; C Boxmoor St Jo *St Alb* 73–83; TV Hemel Hempstead 83–95; V Farley Hill St Jo 95–06; rtd 06; PtO *St Alb* 06–18. *4 Wellcroft, Hemel Hempstead HP1 3EG* T: (01442) 401122 E: rex.merry@yahoo.co.uk

MERRY, Tommy Philip. b 85. UEA BA 08 Sheff Univ BA 13. Coll of Resurr Mirfield 10. **d** 13 **p** 14. C Hanley H Ev *Lich* 13–16; TV Stoke-upon-Trent and Fenton from 16; P-in-c Fenton 16. *10 Fenton Hall Close, Stoke-on-Trent ST4 4PU* T: (01782) 846087 M: 07585-954122 E: frtommymerry@gmail.com

MERRYWEATHER, Mrs Rosalynd. b 50. Hull Coll of Educn CertEd 72. NEOC. **d** 00 **p** 01. NSM Beverley St Nic *York* 00–12; PtO from 12. *10 West Close, Beverley HU17 7JJ* T: (01482) 867958 E: rmerryweather@rmerryweather.karoo.co.uk

MESLEY-SPONG, Terence John. b 32. Roch Th Coll 63. **d** 66 **p** 67. C Forton *Portsm* 66–68; Rhodesia 68–80; Zimbabwe 80–84; R Christow, Ashton, Trusham and Bridford *Ex* 84–86; Chapl Puerto de la Cruz Tenerife *Eur* 86–93; Miss to Seamen 86–93; rtd 93; PtO *Win* 93–13; Chapl R Bournemouth and Christchurch Hosps NHS Trust 97–98. *14B Stuart Road, Highcliffe, Christchurch BH23 5JS* T: (01425) 277833

MESSAM, Paul James. b 65. Lon Coll of Printing BA 87. Cranmer Hall Dur 01. **d** 03 **p** 04. C Market Harborough and The Transfiguration etc *Leic* 03–07; P-in-c Bulkington *Cov* 07–16; Lead Chapl Cov Blue Coat C of E Sch 07–15; P-in-c Elstow *St Alb* from 16. *Abbey Vicarage, Church End, Elstow, Bedford MK42 9XT* T: (01243) 261477 M: 07711-098209 E: paul@mahoose.co.uk

MESSENGER, Paul. b 38. Univ of Wales (Lamp) BA 63. Coll of Resurr Mirfield 63. **d** 65 **p** 66. C Battersea St Luke *S'wark* 65–69; C Ainsdale *Liv* 69–71; V Wigan St Steph 71–74; Asst Chapl St Marg Convent E Grinstead 74–76; Chapl Kingsley St Mich Sch W Sussex 74–76; P-in-c Southwater *Chich* 76–81; V 81–97; R Sullington and Thakeham w Warminghurst 97–07; rtd 07; PtO *Chich* 12–17. *122 Ninfield Road, Bexhill-on-Sea TN39 5BB* T: (01424) 220044 E: paulmessenger@uwclub.net

MESSER, David Harry. b 61. MCIH 93. EAMTC 01. **d** 04 **p** 05. C Stanton, Hopton, Market Weston, Barningham etc *St E* 04–07; R 07–17; C Hepworth, Hinderclay, Wattisfield and Thelnetham 15–17; RD Ixworth 14–17; R Walkington, Bishop Burton, Rowley etc *York* from 17. *The Rectory, 2 Little Weighton Road, Walkington, Beverley HU17 8SP* E: davidharrymesser93@gmail.com

MESSHAM, Canon Barbara Lynn. b 52. Bretton Hall Coll CertEd 75. STETS 96. **d** 99 **p** 00. C The Bourne and Tilford *Guildf* 99–03; V Guildf All SS 03–13; RD Guildf 06–11; Hon Can Guildf Cathl 10–13; P-in-c Deerhurst and Apperley w Forthampton etc *Glouc* 13–18; C Tewkesbury w Walton Cardiff and Twyning 13–18; rtd 18; PtO *Glouc* from 19. *Waysmeet, Innerstone Lane, Redmarley, Gloucester GL19 3JH* M: 07932-615132 E: barbara@messhams.co.uk *or* barbaramessham@gmail.com

MESSINGER, Jacqueline Violet. b 51. St Mellitus Coll 16. **d** 19. OLM Lexden *Chelmsf* from 19. *3 Baines Close, Colchester CO3 4AL* T: (01206) 760742 M: 07886-468596 E: jacquie@stleonardslexden.org.uk

METCALF, Preb Michael Ralph. b 37. Clare Coll Cam BA 61 MA 65 Birm Univ MA 80. Ridley Hall Cam 63. **d** 64 **p** 65. C Downend *Bris* 64–67; PtO *Birm* 68–78; *Lich* 72–81; Lect W Midl Coll of Educn 72–77; Sen Lect 77–81; Dioc Dir of Educn *Lich* 83–94; V Stafford St Paul Forebridge 94–05; Preb Lich Cathl 91–05; RD Stafford 00–05; rtd 05; PtO *Heref* from 87; *Lich* from 05. *196 Stone Road, Stafford ST16 1NT* T/F: (01785) 600260 E: prebmetcalf@hotmail.com *or* berylm@ntlworld.com

METCALFE, Alistair Andrew. b 77. Warwick Univ BA 99 St Jo Coll Dur BA 18. Cranmer Hall Dur 16. **d** 18 **p** 19. C Bebington *Ches* from 18. *8 Rolleston Drive, Bebington,*

Wirral   CH63 3DB   E: alistairmetcalfe@gmail.com   or curate@standrewsbebington.org.uk

METCALFE, Bernard. See METCALFE, William Bernard

METCALFE, Canon Ronald. b 41. BA. Edin Th Coll 67. **d** 69 **p** 70. C Saltburn-by-the-Sea York 69–72; P-in-c Crathorne 73–77; Youth Officer 73–77; Dioc Adult Tr Officer 78–88; Can Res York Minster 88–00; Sec for Miss and Min 88–00; V Kendal H Trin Carl 00–07; rtd 07; PtO Dur from 08. 50 Carlton Moor Crescent, Darlington DL1 4RF   T: (01325) 367219 E: ronaldmetcalfe100@outlook.com

METCALFE, Canon William Bernard. b 47. St Jo Coll Cam BA 69 MA 73 Ball Coll Ox BA 71. Ripon Hall Ox 70. **d** 72 **p** 73. C Caversham Ox 72–75; C Aylesbury 75–79; Ind Chapl 75–79; TV Thamesmead S'wark 79–84; TR Totton Win 84–94; R Gt Bentley and Frating w Thorrington Chelmsf 94–10; V Gt Bentley 10–12; RD St Osyth 99–07; Hon Can Chelmsf Cathl 06–12; rtd 12; PtO Ox from 13. 60 Elmhurst Road, Reading RG1 5HY   T: 0118-975 6586 E: bernard.metcalfe@btinternet.com

METHUEN, Canon Charlotte Mary. b 64. Girton Coll Cam BA 85 MA 89 New Coll Edin BD 91 PhD 95. Edin Th Coll 87. **d** 98 **p** 99. C E Netherlands Eur 98–01; C Bonn w Cologne 01–03; Hon Asst Chapl 03–05; Dioc Dir of Tr 03–05; Hon C Offenbach (Old Catholic Ch) 05–07; Hon C Bottrop (Old Catholic Ch) from 08; Lect Ecclesiastical Hist Ox Univ 05–11; Dioc Can Th Glouc 07–13; Lect Ripon Coll Cuddesdon 09–11; Lect Ch History Glas Univ from 11. 2/1, 34 Keir Street, Glasgow G41 2NW   T: 0141-429 4716 E: charlotte.methuen@glasgow.ac.uk

METIVIER, Canon Robert John. b 31. Lon Univ BA 68. Lambeth STh 61 Ch Div Sch of the Pacific (USA) BD 66 MDiv 69 Codrington Coll Barbados 56. **d** 60 **p** 61. Trinidad and Tobago 61–64 and 68–78; USPG 66–67; C Gt Berkhamsted St Alb 78–82; V Goff's Oak St Jas 82–90; V Tokyngton St Mich Lon 90–01; Hon Can Trinidad from 98; rtd 01; PtO Lon from 02. 17 Willowcourt Avenue, Kenton, Harrow HA3 8ET   T: (020) 8909 1371 E: ej.metivier@googlemail.com

METZ, Susanna. b 50. Immaculata Univ (USA) BA 72 W Chester State Coll (USA) MA 82 Univ of the S (USA) MDiv 96 DMin 03. **d** 96 **p** 97. C Battle Creek St Jo USA 96–07; R 07–11; TV Shebbear, Buckland Filleigh, Sheepwash etc Ex from 11; RD Torrington from 15. The Rectory, Petrockstow, Okehampton EX20 3HQ   T: (01837) 810621 E: petrockstowevicaris@gmail.com

METZNER (née JEFFREY), Mrs Katrina. b 73. St Jo Coll Ox BA 96 MA 01. St Steph Ho Ox 97. **d** 99 **p** 00. C Glouc St Geo w Whaddon 99–00; C Parkstone St Pet and St Osmund w Branksea Sarum 00–04; PtO S'wark 05–16; Edin from 18. The Rectory, 2 May Terrace, North Berwick EH39 4BA   T: (01620) 892154 E: katemetzner@sky.com

METZNER, Simon David. b 64. Magd Coll Ox BA 85 K Coll Lon MA 95 St Luke's Coll Ex PGCE 93. St Steph Ho Ox 98. **d** 00 **p** 01. C Branksome St Aldhelm Sarum 00–04; V Tooting All SS S'wark 04–16; R N Berwick Edin from 16; R Gullane from 16. The Rectory, 2 May Terrace, North Berwick EH39 4BA   T: (01620) 892154 E: simonmetzner@sky.com

MEWIS, Canon David William. b 47. Leeds Inst of Educn CertEd 68 Leeds Poly BEd 83. NOC 87. **d** 90 **p** 91. C Skipton Ch Ch Bradf 90–92; R Bolton by Bowland w Grindleton 92–12; C Waddington, Hurst Green and Mitton 05–12; RD Bowland 99–08; Hon Can Bradf Cathl 00–12; rtd 12; PtO Bradf 13–14; Leeds from 14. 23 Darkwood Crescent, Chatburn, Clitheroe BB7 4AL   T: (01200) 440335 E: dwm.dmewis@gmail.com

MEYER, Jonathan Peter. b 55. Keble Coll Ox BA 76 MA 95. SAOMC 03. **d** 05 **p** 06. NSM Kintbury w Avington Ox 05–08; NSM W Woodhay w Enborne, Hampstead Marshall etc 05–09; P-in-c Ewelme, Brightwell Baldwin, Cuxham w Easington 09–17; Hon C Benson w Ewelme 17–18; R Winchelsea and Icklesham Chich from 18. The Rectory, St Thomas Street, Winchelsea TN36 4EB   T: (01797) 226254 E: revdjonathan@btinternet.com

MEYER, William John. b 46. ACIB. Cranmer Hall Dur 83. **d** 85 **p** 86. C Merrow Guildf 85–89; V Grayshott 89–98; R Binfield Ox 98–11; rtd 11. 27A Oxford Drive, Bognor Regis PO21 5QU E: bill.meyer@hotmail.com

MEYNELL, Canon Andrew Francis. b 43. Westcott Ho Cam 70. **d** 73 **p** 74. C Cowley St Jas Ox 73–79; TV 79–81; P-in-c Halton 81–95; V Wendover 81–95; P-in-c Monks Risborough 95–98; TV Risborough 98–08; Dir Ords Bucks Adnry 95–08; Hon Can Ch Ch 01–08; rtd 08; PtO Ox from 09. Pettits House, The Green, Great Milton, Oxford OX44 7NT   T: (01844) 277912 E: andrew.meynell@oxford.anglican.org

MEYNELL, Mrs Honor Mary. b 37. EMMTC 84. **d** 87 **p** 94. NSM Kirk Langley Derby 87–03; NSM Mackworth All SS 87–03; NSM Mugginton and Kedleston 87–03; rtd 04; PtO Derby 04–18. The Coachman's Cottage, Meynell Langley, Kirk Langley, Ashbourne DE6 4NT   T: (01332) 824207

MEYNELL, Mark John Henrik. b 70. New Coll Ox MA 93. Ridley Hall Cam MA 97. **d** 97 **p** 98. C Fulwood Sheff 97–01; Dean Kampala Evang Sch of Th Uganda 01–05; C Langham Place All So Lon 05–14; Hon C from 14; PtO Ox from 18. 29 Raymond Road, Maidenhead SL6 6DF   T: (01628) 780776   M: 07725-048617 E: mark.meynell@langham.org

✠**MEYRICK, The Rt Revd Cyril Jonathan.** b 52. St Jo Coll Ox BA 73 MA 77. Sarum & Wells Th Coll 74. **d** 76 **p** 77 **c** 11. C Bicester Ox 76–78; Bp's Dom Chapl 78–81; Tutor Codrington Coll Barbados 81–84; TV Burnham w Dropmore, Hitcham and Taplow Ox 84–90; TR Tisbury Sarum 90–98; Link Officer Black Angl Concerns 90–98; RD Chalke 97–98; Can Res Roch Cathl 98–05; Dean Ex 05–11; P-in-c Cen Ex 06–11; Suff Bp Lynn Nor from 11; Provost Woodard Corp (S Division) from 17. The Old Vicarage, Priory Road, Castle Acre, King's Lynn PE32 2AA   T: (01760) 755553   F: 755085 E: bishop.lynn@dioceseofnorwich.org

MEYRICK, Thomas Henry Corfe. b 67. Magd Coll Ox BA 88 MA 92 Leeds Univ PhD 05. St Steph Ho Ox BA 94. **d** 95 **p** 96. C Bierley Bradf 95–99; Chapl Oriel Coll Ox 99–04; P-in-c Ox St Thos w St Frideswide and Binsey 04–05; P-in-c Newbold de Verdun and Kirkby Mallory Leic 05–10; P-in-c Barlestone 09–10; R Newbold de Verdun, Barlestone and Kirkby Mallory 10–17; AD Sparkenhoe W 08–15; P-in-c Peckleton 16–17; R Keyworth and Stanton-on-the-Wolds and Bunny etc S'well from 17. The Rectory, Nottingham Road, Keyworth, Nottingham NG12 5FD   E: thomas.meyrick@gmail.com   or rector@ksbb.org.uk

MIALL, Mrs Hazel Henrietta. b 49. Open Univ BSc 97 DipCOT 70. St Mellitus Coll BA 12. **d** 12. NSM Southgate Ch Ch Lon from 12. 85 Conway Road, London N14 7BD   T: (020) 8882 6738   M: 07980-740587 E: hazelhmiall@btinternet.com

MICHAEL, Canon Ian MacRae. b 40. Aber Univ MA 62 Hertf Coll Ox DPhil 66. Westcott Ho Cam 77. **d** 79 **p** 80. C Kings Heath Birm 79–82; Vice-Provost St Paul's Cathl Dundee Bre 82–88; V Harborne St Faith and St Laur Birm 88–03; RD Edgbaston 91–98; Hon Can Birm Cathl 00–03; rtd 03; PtO Birm 03–13; Lect St And from 04; NSM St Andrews All SS from 05. 46 Argyle Court, St Andrews KY16 9BW   T: (01334) 473901

MICHAEL, Stephen David. b 71. Ripon Coll Cuddesdon 01. **d** 03 **p** 04. C St Blazey Truro 03–07; C Tywardreath w Tregaminion 03–07; C Lanlivery w Luxulyan 03–07; P-in-c Treverbyn 07–13; P-in-c Boscoppa 07–13. Berry Narbor, 96 Truro Road, St Austell PL25 5HH   T: (01726) 61154 E: sdm.554@gmail.com

MICHAELS, David Albert Emmanuel. b 49. Bede Coll Dur BA 72 Barrister-at-Law (Inner Temple) 73. Westcott Ho Cam 86. **d** 88 **p** 89. C Hampstead St Jo Lon 88–91; TV Wolvercote w Summertown Ox 91–04; P-in-c Launceston Truro 04–13; rtd 13; PtO Ox from 15. 5 Northmoor Place, Northmoor Road, Oxford OX2 6XB   T: (01865) 558035 E: david.michaels@dunelm.org.uk

MICHAUX, Mrs Teresa Mary. b 56. STETS 09. **d** 12 **p** 13. NSM Swindon St Jo and St Andr Bris 12–18; TV Marden Vale Sarum from 18. 7 Richmond Road, Calne SN11 9UW   M: 07963-399645 E: tmx256@hotmail.co.uk

MICHELL, Philip Leonard. b 69. Trin Coll Bris 08. **d** 10 **p** 11. C Brailsford w Shirley, Osmaston w Edlaston etc Derby 10–13; R Hulland, Atlow, Kniveton, Bradley and Hognaston from 13. The Rectory, 16 Eaton Close, Hulland Ward, Ashbourne DE6 3EX   T: (01335) 371947   M: 07815-940409 E: phil.michell@live.co.uk

MICKLEFIELD, Andrew Mark. b 71. K Alfred's Coll Win BEd 93. Ridley Hall Cam 04. **d** 06 **p** 07. C Alton Win 06–10; R Itchen Valley 10–14; V Alton from 14. St Lawrence Vicarage, Church Street, Alton GU34 2BW   T: (01420) 88794   M: 07749-483407 E: andrewmicklefield@gmail.com

MICKLETHWAITE, Andrew Quentin. b 67. Univ Coll Dur BA 89. Trin Coll Bris BA 94. **d** 94 **p** 95. C Abington Pet 94–97; TV Duston 97–04; V Castle Donington and Lockington cum Hemington Leic 04–18; PtO from 18. The Rectory, Wigston Road, Blaby, Leicester LE8 4FU   E: revandrew67@yahoo.co.uk

MICKLETHWAITE, Jane Catherine. b 56. Lanc Univ BSc 78. Trin Coll Bris 92. **d** 95 **p** 96. C Kings Heath Pet 95–99; Chapl Nene Coll of HE Northn 97–98; PtO Pet 98–01; NSM Kings Heath 01–04; PtO Leic 04–06; Chapl E Midl Airport 06–15; NSM Loughborough All SS w H Trin 13–15; Chapl to Internat Students Leic Univ 15–18; P-in-c Blaby from 18. The Rectory, Wigston Road, Blaby, Leicester LE8 4FU E: j.micklethwaite@yahoo.co.uk

MIDDLEBROOK, The Ven David John. b 61. Newc Univ BSc 83 Cranfield Inst of Tech MSc 85. Trin Coll Bris BA 98.

d 98 **p** 99. C Chorleywood Ch Ch *St Alb* 98–02; TV Hemel Hempstead 02–08; P-in-c Watford St Luke 08–12; V 12–19; RD Watford 09–19; Hon Can St Alb 13–19; Adn Bedford from 19. *17 Lansdowne Road, Luton LU3 1EE*

MIDDLEDITCH, Terry Gordon. b 30. Univ of Wales (Lamp) BA 62 St Martin's Coll Lanc PGCE 68. St D Coll Lamp 59. **d** 63 **p** 64. C Poulton-le-Fylde *Blackb* 63–65; C-in-c Heysham 65–67; Sch Master 68–88; Hon C Cheltenham St Pet *Glouc* 75–87; Hon C Badgeworth w Shurdington 75–87; Hon C Up Hatherley 75–87; C Poulton-le-Sands w Morecambe St Laur *Blackb* 88–91; V Stalmine 91–00; rtd 00; PtO *Blackb* from 00. *93 Thornton Road, Morecambe LA4 5PG* T: (01524) 413378 M: 07879-426173 E: terry.middleditch@gmail.com

MIDDLEMISS, Fritha Leonora. b 47. Man Univ BA 68 CertEd 68. Glouc Sch of Min 86. **d** 89 **p** 94. NSM Bengeworth *Worc* 89–94; NSM Stoulton w Drake's Broughton and Pirton etc 94–96; Chapl Malvern Girls' Coll 96–03; Asst Chapl HM Pris Long Lartin 03–08. *5 Orchard Close, Bidford-on-Avon, Alcester B50 4BT* T: (01789) 490701 E: frithamiddlemiss@hotmail.com

MIDDLESEX, Archdeacon of. See WELCH, The Ven Stephan John

MIDDLETON, Alan Derek. b 46. St Jo Coll Dur BA 68 MA 85 Bris Univ PGCE 70 Sheff Univ MMin 00. Qu Coll Birm. **d** 72 **p** 73. C Cannock *Lich* 72–76; Warden St Helen's Youth and Community Cen Bp Auckd 76–79; V Darlington St Jo *Dur* 79–89; TR E Darlington 89–90; V Upper Norwood All SS *S'wark* 90–99; TR Warlingham w Chelsham and Farleigh 99–11; Bp's Ecum Adv 96–11; AD Caterham 05–11; rtd 11; PtO *Dur* from 11. *21 Boste Crescent, Durham DH1 5US* T: 0191-386 4467 E: alan.middleton21@btinternet.com

MIDDLETON, Mrs Alison Jayne. b 71. Leic Univ BA 92. Ripon Coll Cuddesdon 13. **d** 16 **p** 17. C Gleneagles *Pet* from 16. *18 Landseer Close, Wellingborough NN8 4HF* M: 07891-608612 E: rev.ali.j.middleton@gmail.com

MIDDLETON, Arthur. See MIDDLETON, Thomas Arthur

MIDDLETON, Barry Glen. b 41. Lich Th Coll 68. **d** 70 **p** 71. C Westhoughton *Man* 70–73; C Prestwich St Marg 73–74; TV Buxton w Burbage and King Sterndale *Derby* 74–77; Chapl Worc R Infirmary 77–83; Chapl Fairfield Hosp Hitchin 83–85; P-in-c Erpingham w Calthorpe *Nor* 85–86; R Erpingham w Calthorpe, Ingworth, Aldborough etc 86–92; R Badingham w Bruisyard, Cransford and Dennington *St E* 92–96; V Sidcup St Jo *Roch* 96–98; V Gt and Lt Bardfield w Gt and Lt Saling *Chelmsf* 98–00; rtd 00; PtO *St E* 00–18. *20 Lynwood Avenue, Felixstowe IP11 9HS* T: (01394) 286506 E: bgm.jfm@btinternet.com

MIDDLETON, David Jeremy. b 68. Ex Univ BSc 90. Wycliffe Hall Ox 01. **d** 03 **p** 04. C Ipswich St Jo *St E* 03–06; Hon C Wimbledon Park St Luke *S'wark* 06–09; C Fulwood *Sheff* 09–11; C Heeley and Gleadless Valley 11–12; V Gleadless Valley from 12. *The Vicarage, 5 Blackstock Close, Sheffield S14 1AE* T: 0114-239 3808 E: djm.middleton@googlemail.com

MIDDLETON, Hugh Charles. b 50. Nottm Univ BTh 77. Linc Th Coll 74. **d** 77 **p** 78. C New Sleaford *Linc* 77–81; C Grantham 81; TV 81–83; R Caythorpe 83–95; P-in-c Bracebridge Heath 97–00; V 00–15; P-in-c Bracebridge 07–15; rtd 15. *3 Roman Close, Navenby, Lincoln LN5 0GW* T: (01522) 415494

MIDDLETON, Miss Jennifer Ann. b 82. St Jo Coll Dur BA 03. St Jo Coll Nottm 06. **d** 08 **p** 09. C Fatfield *Dur* 08–12; NE Regional Dir Urban Saints 12–15; PtO *Dur* 14–15; C Aldridge *Lich* from 16. *6 Linley Close, Aldridge, Walsall WS9 0ES* M: 07775-330935 E: jenpuddleduck@hotmail.com

MIDDLETON, Canon Michael John. b 40. Dur Univ BSc 62 Fitzw Ho Cam BA 66 MA 70. Westcott Ho Cam 63. **d** 66 **p** 67. C Newc St Geo 66–69; V 77–85; Chapl St Geo Gr Sch Cape Town S Africa 69–72; Chapl Sch Tynemouth 72–77; R Hexham *Newc* 85–92; Hon Can Newc Cathl 90–92; Adn Swindon *Bris* 92–97; Can and Treas Westmr Abbey 97–04; rtd 04; PtO *Carl* 05–19. *2 Cleveland Mews, Cleveland Road, Chichester PO19 7AD* T: (01243) 530580

MIDDLETON, Canon Rodney. b 54. St Andr Univ BD 80. St Steph Ho Ox 80. **d** 82 **p** 83. C Walton St Mary *Liv* 82–87; C-in-c Kew St Fran CD 87–94; V Kew 94–95; Chapl Southport and Formby Distr Gen Hosp 87–95; V Haydock St Jas *Liv* 95–17; Asst Chapl Costa Blanca *Eur* from 17; Hon Can Wiawso Ghana from 13. *Urb El Aspre, Carrer Les Fonts 19, 03792 Orba, Alicante, Spain* T: (0034) 678 318 688 E: rodmid169@yahoo.co.uk

MIDDLETON, Canon Thomas Arthur. b 36. Dur Univ MLitt 95 FRHistS 04. K Coll Lon AKC 61 St Boniface Warminster 61. **d** 62 **p** 63. C Sunderland *Dur* 62–63; C Auckland St Helen 63–67; C Winlaton 67–70; C-in-c Pennywell St Thos and Grindon St Oswald CD 70–79; Chapl Grindon Hall Hosp 73–79; R Boldon *Dur* 79–03; Adv in Stewardship Dur Adnry

87–92; Tutor St Chad's Coll Dur 93–07; Acting Prin 96–97; Hon Fell from 07; Hon Can Dur Cathl 98–03; rtd 03; PtO *Dur* 03–15. *24 Peregrine Drive, Chelmsford CM2 8XY* T: (01245) 901634 E: tamiddleton@talktalk.net

MIDDLETON, Wendy Josephine. b 59. LMH Ox BA 80 MA 85 Birm Univ MSc 81. Ox Min Course 14. **d** 17 **p** 18. C Goring and Streatley w S Stoke *Ox* from 17. *1 Milldown Avenue, Goring, Reading RG8 0AG* T: (01491) 875435 E: wendy.middleton@tiscali.co.uk

MIDDLETON, Suffragan Bishop of. See DAVIES, The Rt Revd Mark

MIDDLETON-DANSKY, Serge Wladimir. b 45. Cuddesdon Coll 74. **d** 77 **p** 78. C Wisbech SS Pet and Paul *Ely* 77–79; LtO Adnry Riviera *Eur* from 80; C Ox St Giles and SS Phil and Jas w St Marg 83–86; PtO 86–88; *Truro* 88–90; P-in-c Zennor and Towednack 90–96; PtO 97–99; LtO from 99. *The Old Vicarage, Zennor, St Ives TR26 3BY* T: (01736) 796955

MIDDLEWICK, Robert James. b 44. Lon Univ BD 76 K Alfred's Coll Win CertEd 67. Ripon Coll Cuddesdon 75. **d** 77 **p** 78. C Bromley SS Pet and Paul *Roch* 77–81; C Belvedere All SS 81–84; P-in-c Lamberhurst 85–88; P-in-c Matfield 85–88; V Lamberhurst and Matfield 88–99; rtd 09. *4 St James Court, Wood Street, Tunbridge Wells TN1 2QS* E: middlewick@btinternet.com

MIDGLEY, Stephen Nicholas. b 60. Jes Coll Cam BA 83 MA 86 Lon Hosp MB, BS 86. Wycliffe Hall Ox. **d** 97 **p** 98. C Hove Bp Hannington Memorial Ch *Chich* 97–01; C Cambridge H Sepulchre *Ely* 01–04; P-in-c Cambridge St Andr Less 04–09; V from 09. *St Andrew the Less Vicarage, 21 Parsonage Street, Cambridge CB5 8DN* T: (01223) 353794 or 750450 E: steve.midgley@christchurchcambridge.org.uk

MIDLANE, Colin John. b 50. Qu Mary Coll Lon BA 72. Westcott Ho Cam 73 Sarum & Wells Th Coll 77. **d** 78 **p** 79. C Bethnal Green St Pet w St Thos *Lon* 78–82; P-in-c Haggerston All SS 82–88; Chapl Hengrave Hall Ecum Cen 88–89; P Cllr St Botolph Aldgate *Lon* 89–94; C St Botolph Aldgate w H Trin Minories 93–94; TV Haywards Heath St Wilfrid *Chich* 94–97; C Brighton St Geo w St Anne and St Mark 97–01; Chapl Brighton and Sussex Univ Hosps NHS Trust 01–03; 03; PtO *Lon* from 04. *30 Damien Court, Damien Street, London E1 2HL* T: (020) 7791 0001

MIDWINTER, Sister Josie Isabel. b 46. Open Univ BA 84 Univ of Wales (Lamp) MA 98. CA Tr Coll IDC 71. **d** 87 **p** 99. CA from 71; CMS 84–93; Uganda 85–91; Kenya 92–96; C Didcot All SS *Ox* 98–05; P-in-c Drayton St Pet (Abingdon) 05–10; rtd 06; PtO *Ox* from 10. *32 Barnes Close, Didcot OX11 8JN* T: (01235) 759398 E: josie.midwinter@lineone.net

MIDWOOD, Canon Peter Stanley. b 47. CertEd 69. Linc Th Coll 80. **d** 82 **p** 83. C Garforth *Ripon* 82–85; C-in-c Grinton w Arkengarthdale, Downholme and Marske 85–86; C-in-c Melbecks and Muker 85–86; V Swaledale 86–97; R Romaldkirk w Laithkirk 97–08; AD Richmond 97–08; R Walkingham Hill 08–13; Hon Can Ripon Cathl 05–13; rtd 13; PtO *Nor* from 14. *4 Larch Crescent, Holt NR25 6TU* E: ps.midwood@gmail.com

MIELL, David Keith. b 57. Lanc Univ BSc 78 PhD 81 Trin Coll Cam BA 85. Westcott Ho Cam 83. **d** 86 **p** 87. C Blackbird Leys CD *Ox* 86–88; C Blackbird Leys 88–89; C Walton Milton Keynes 89–90; TV Wo Milton Keynes 93–95; TR Upton cum Chalvey 96–05; AD Burnham and Slough 02–05; PtO 05–08; *Sarum* 10–11; P-in-c Ringwood *Win* 11–16; rtd 16; PtO Win from 16. *73 Barton Drive, Barton on Sea, New Milton BH25 7JH* T: (01425) 615633 E: dkmiell@gmail.com

MIER, Miss Catherine Elizabeth. b 60. Bris Univ BSc 81 Chelsea Coll Lon MSc 84 Dur Univ BA 95. Cranmer Hall Dur 93. **d** 96 **p** 97. C Royston *St Alb* 96–00; C Bilton *Cov* 00–04; P-in-c Wellesbourne 04–14; V 14–17; P-in-c Walton d'Eiville 04–14; R 14–17; AD Fosse 11–17; R Arden Marches from 18. *The Vicarage, 3 Manor Mews, Studley B80 7PR* T: (01527) 852830 E: kate.mier1@gmail.com

MIGHALL, Robert. b 33. St Pet Coll Ox BA 57 MA 61. Wycliffe Hall Ox 57. **d** 58 **p** 59. C Stoke *Cov* 58–62; C Rugby St Andr 62–64; V Newbold on Avon 64–76; V Combroke w Compton Verney 76–96; V Kineton 76–96; rtd 96. *40 Rempstone Road, Wimborne BH21 1RP* T: (01202) 883522

MIHILL, Dennis George. b 31. St Alb Minl Tr Scheme 78. **d** 81 **p** 82. NSM Harpenden St Nic *St Alb* 81–86; C Sawbridgeworth 86–89; V Motspur Park *S'wark* 89–96; rtd 96; PtO *St Alb* 96–98 and 01–08; Hon C Biddenham 98–01; PtO *Roch* from 06. *7 Bourchier Close, Sevenoaks TN13 1PD* T: (01732) 459760 E: d.mihill@sky.com

MILBANK (née LEGG), Alison Grant. b 54. Girton Coll Cam BA 78 MA 81 PGCE 79 Lanc Univ PhD 88. EMMTC 05. **d** 06 **p** 07. NSM Lambley *S'well* 06–09; PV S'well Minster from 09. *Burgage Hill Cottage, Burgage, Southwell NG25 0EP* T: (01636) 819224 E: alison.milbank@nottingham.ac.uk

MILBANK, Arabella Mary. *See* ROBINSON, Arabella Mary Milbank

MILBANK, Arabella Mary. *See* ROBINSON, Arabella Mary

MILES, Mrs Beverley Anne. b 54. d 09 p 15. NSM Findon Valley *Chich* 09–15; P-in-c from 15; Chapl Care for Veterans Worthing from 14. *The Vicarage, 29 Central Avenue, Worthing BN14 0DS* T: (01903) 873732 M: 07786-924942 E: beverley_miles@hotmail.com

MILES, Damian Stewart. b 76. Fitzw Coll Cam BTh 02. Westcott Ho Cam 99. d 02 p 03. C Willingdon *Chich* 02–06; P-in-c Nork *Guildf* 06–11; P-in-c Thorpe 11–15; V from 15. *The Vicarage, Church Approach, Egham TW20 8TQ* T: (01932) 565986 M: 07815-848735 E: damomiles@btinternet.com

MILES, Daniel James. b 85. York St Jo Coll BA 06 York St Jo Univ MA 12 PGCE 08 Dur Univ BA 19. Ridley Hall Cam 16. d 19. C Erringden *Leeds* from 19. *12 Phoenix Court, Todmorden OL14 5SJ* M: 07547-242855 E: daniel.miles@leeds.anglican.org

MILES, Gerald Christopher Morgan. b 36. Peterho Cam BA 57 MA 72 Cranfield Inst of Tech MSc 72 CEng MIET. Wycliffe Hall Ox 74. d 76 p 77. C Tunbridge Wells St Jas *Roch* 76–80; V Leigh 80–90; R Addington w Trottiscliffe 90–91; P-in-c Ryarsh w Birling 90–91; R Birling, Addington, Ryarsh and Trottiscliffe 91–00; Chapl ATC 80–11; rtd 00; PtO *Roch* from 00. *2 Spa Close, Hadlow, Tonbridge TN11 0JX* T/F: (01732) 852323 E: gcmmiles@btinternet.com

MILES (née HOARE), Ms Janet Francis Mary. b 48. St Aid Coll Dur BA 70 Bris Univ MEd 84. Sarum & Wells Th Coll 91. d 93 p 94. C Bruton and Distr *B & W* 93–98; P-in-c Llangarron w Llangrove, Whitchurch and Ganarew *Heref* 98–04; P-in-c Dixton 02–04; P-in-c Chewton Mendip w Ston Easton, Litton etc *B & W* 04–08; Dir Studies WEMTC 04–07; rtd 11; PtO *B & W* 11–15; *Ex* from 12. *The Sanctuary, Bridford, Exeter EX6 7HS* T: (01647) 252750 E: jfm2@btinternet.com

MILES, Jillian Maud. *See* LOCOCK, Jillian Maud

MILES, Ms Patricia Ellen. b 56. RGN 79. STETS 00. d 03 p 04. NSM Verwood *Sarum* from 03. *4 Firs Glen Road, Verwood BH31 6JB* T: (01202) 824211 E: pe.miles@btinternet.com *or* pem654@gmail.com

MILES, Miss Sharon Elizabeth Ann. b 66. Westcott Ho Cam 00. d 02 p 03. C Shrub End *Chelmsf* 02–05; P-in-c Rivenhall 05–10; P-in-c St Osyth 10–15; V St Osyth and Great Bentley from 15; Adv for Ordained Women's Min (Colchester Area) from 07. *The Vicarage, The Bury, St Osyth, Clacton-on-Sea CO16 8NX* T: (01255) 822055 E: revdsmiles@hotmail.com

MILES, Stephen John. b 44. Monash Univ Aus BA 66 Worc Coll Ox DipEd 68 Univ Coll Lon MA 75 California Univ PhD 80. Melbourne Coll of Div BTheol 86. d 87 p 88. C E Malvern St Jo Australia 87; C Clifton Hill St Andr 87–89; Chapl Co-ord and Angl Chapl Monash Med Cen 89–97; Asst Chapl Bonn w Cologne *Eur* 97–00; Chapl 00–03; Perm to Offic Melbourne Australia from 03. *67 Caroline Street, South Yarra VIC, Australia* T: (0061) (3) 9866 1463 E: stephenmiles@iprimus.com.au

MILES, Mrs Susan. b 63. LTCL 85. STETS 10. d 13 p 14. C White Horse *Sarum* 13–16; Chapl S Warks Gen Hosps NHS Trust from 16. T: (01926) 495321 M: 07545-497254 E: reverendsusanmiles@btinternet.com

MILFORD, Canon Catherine Helena. b 39. LMH Ox BA 61 MA 65 FRSA 92. Gilmore Course 81. dss 82 d 87 p 94. Heaton St Barn *Bradf* 82–88; Par Dn 87–88; Adult Educn Adv *Win* 88–96; TR Barnham Broom *Nor* 96–00; P-in-c Reymerston w Cranworth, Letton, Southburgh etc 96–00; TR Barnham Broom and Upper Yare 00–04; Hon Can Nor Cathl 00–04; rtd 04; PtO *Bradf* 05–14; *Leeds* from 14. *6 Leylands Grove, Bradford BD9 5QP* E: cthmilfordb@gmail.com

MILFORD, Graham Alan. b 57. Trin Coll Bris 00. d 02 p 03. C Wolborough and Ogwell *Ex* 02–08; P-in-c Newburgh w Westhead *Liv* 08–10; V 10–16; C Maghull and Melling 17–18; TV Sutton from 18. *Allerton Vicarage, Harthill Road, Liverpool L18 3HU* T: 0151-724 1561 M: 07508-818634 E: grahammilford@btinternet.com

MILFORD, Mrs Nicola Claire. b 75. Liv Univ BTh 03. Trin Coll Bris 00 NOC 02. d 04 p 05. C Alphington, Shillingford St George and Ide *Ex* 04–08; Dioc Adv NSM *Liv* from 11; P-in-c Sefton 13–16; TV Mossley Hill from 16; AD Liv S from 19. *Allerton Vicarage, Harthill Road, Liverpool L18 3HU* T: 0151-724 1561 M: 07816-567598 E: nicola.milford@liverpool.anglican.org *or* nicola@allhallowsallerton.org.uk

MILLAR, Alexander. *See* MILLAR, John Alexander Kirkpatrick

MILLAR, Andrew Charles. b 48. Hull Univ BSc 69. Cuddesdon Coll 71. d 73 p 74. C Rushmere *St E* 73–76; C Ipswich All Hallows 76–79; Dioc Youth Chapl *Sheff* 79–83; Youth Chapl *Win* 83–92; V Colden 92–08; V Twyford and Owslebury and Morestead etc 08–10; rtd 10; PtO *St As* from 13.

22 Fford Bryn Estyn, Mold CH7 1TJ T: (01352) 754745 E: acmillar@btinternet.com

MILLAR, Christine. *See* WHEELER, Christine

MILLAR, David Glassell. b 43. Dur Univ BSc 64 St Cath Coll Cam BA 66 MA 71 Birkbeck Coll Lon BSc 78 Leeds Univ MSc 80. Cuddesdon Coll 66. d 68 p 69. C Pershore w Wick *Worc* 68–72; C Malden St Jas *S'wark* 72–73; V W Dean *Chich* 73–75; rtd 08. *5 Beacon Hill, London N7 9LY* T/F: (020) 7607 3809 E: davidgmillar@hotmail.com

MILLAR, Gary. b 67. St Mich Coll Llan 88. d 91 p 92. C Tonyrefail w Gilfach Goch *Llan* 91–93; C Barry All SS 93–95; TV Cowbridge 95–97; I Dromara w Garvaghy *D & D* 97–01; I Kilkeel 01–08; I Belfast St Paul w St Barn *Conn* 08–12; I Ahoghill w Portglenone 12–18; I Kilrea, Tamlaght O'Crilly Upper and Lower *D & R* from 18. *2 Moneygran Road, Kilrea, Coleraine BT51 5SJ* T: (028) 2954 0257 M: 07817-968357 E: revgarymillar@btinternet.com

✠**MILLAR, The Rt Revd John Alexander Kirkpatrick (Sandy).** b 39. Trin Coll Cam BA 62 MA 66. Cranmer Hall Dur 74. d 76 p 77 c 05. C Brompton H Trin w Onslow Square St Paul *Lon* 76–85; V 85–05; Hon C 05–11; Hon C Onslow Square and S Kensington St Aug from 11; P-in-c Tollington 03–10; AD Chelsea 89–94; Preb St Paul's Cathl from 97; Asst Bp Uganda from 05; Hon Asst Bp Lon from 06; Hon Asst Bp St E from 12. *Fairlawn, 37 Alde Lane, Aldeburgh IP15 3DZ* T: (01728) 452926 E: sandy.millar@techademic.net

MILLAR, Canon Sandra Doreen. b 57. Univ of Wales (Cardiff) BA 79 Warwick Univ MA 94 PhD 99. Ripon Coll Cuddesdon 98. d 00 p 01. C Chipping Barnet w Arkley St Alb 00–03; TV Dorchester *Ox* 03–07; Dioc Children's Officer *Glouc* 07–13; Hd of Projects and Development Abps' Coun from 13; Public Preacher *Glouc* from 13; Hon Can Glouc Cathl from 14. *Church House, Great Smith Street, London SW1P 3AZ* T: (020) 7898 1458 M: 07976-823986 E: sandra.millar@churchofengland.org *or* revdocsand@gmail.com

MILLARD, Malcolm Edoric. b 38. Lon Univ BA 60 AKC 60 Lon Inst of Educn PGCE 61. St Jo Coll Nottm 80. d 77 p 81. Dn Banjul Cathl The Gambia 77–79; Dn Lamin St Andr 79–81; P-in-c 81–82; P-in-c Fajara St Paul 82–88; V Gen 86–88; 89–95; C S Shoebury *Chelmsf* 95–97; C Rainham w Wennington 97–02; P-in-c N Ockendon 02–08; PtO *Sarum* 08–18. *29 Moorcombe Drive, Preston, Weymouth DT3 6NP* T: (01305) 834060 E: weeksmary@gmail.com

MILLARD, Paul Richard. b 77. York St Jo Coll BSc 99 MCIMA 08. Cranmer Hall Dur 14. d 16 p 17. C Clifton *York* from 16. *2 Doe Park, York YO30 4UQ* T: (01904) 340981 E: prmillard@gmail.com

MILLER, Adrian David. b 74. Open Univ BSc 02. St Jo Coll Nottm MTh 06. d 06 p 07. C Newton Flotman, Swainsthorpe, Tasburgh, etc *Nor* 06–09; TV 09–14; R Mulbarton w Bracon Ash, Hethel and Flordon from 14. *The Rectory, The Common, Mulbarton, Norwich NR14 8JS* T: (01508) 571167 M: 07871-085013 E: aidymiller@i12.com *or* adrian@mulbchurch.org.uk

MILLER, Andrew. *See* MILLER, Ronald Andrew John

MILLER, Andrew Philip. b 72. Liv Univ BSc 94 PhD 98. Cranmer Hall Dur 09. d 11 p 12. C Barnard Castle w Whorlton *Dur* 11–15; V Tanfield w Burnopfield and Dipton from 15. *The Vicarage, Bryans Leap, Burnopfield, Newcastle upon Tyne NE16 6HQ* T: (01207) 270261 M: 07747-191989 E: andrew.miller@durham.anglican.org

MILLER, Mrs Annette. b 53. W Midl Coll of Educn BEd 83. LCTP 07 Cranmer Hall Dur 12. d 13 p 14. NSM Levens *Carl* 13–17; PtO 17–18; NSM Arnside from 18. *Airton, Eden Park Road, Grange-over-Sands LA11 6BW* T: (015395) 33840 E: miller3637@btinternet.com

MILLER, Anthony. *See* MILLER, Ronald Anthony

MILLER, Charles. *See* MILLER, Ernest Charles

MILLER, Charles Irvine. b 35. Nottm Univ BEd 76. Bps' Coll Cheshunt 61. d 63 p 64. C Anlaby Common St Mark *York* 63–66; C Whitby 66–68; R Ingoldmells w Addlethorpe *Linc* 68–72; P-in-c Bishop Norton 72–76; V Scunthorpe St Jo 76–83; Chapl Manor Hosp Walsall 83–89; rtd 89; PtO *Ely* 89–98 and 99–18; P-in-c Isleham 98–99. *The Old Studio, 6 Chapel Street, Duxford, Cambridge CB22 4RJ*

MILLER, The Ven Darren Noel. b 67. Birm Univ BSocSc 89. Chich Th Coll BTh 95 Coll of Resurr Mirfield 94. d 95 p 96. C Weoley Castle *Birm* 95–98; C Shard End 98–00; V Castle Vale St Cuth 00–06; AD Sutton Coldfield 04–06; TR Cheam *S'wark* 06–18; AD Sutton 13–18; Hon Can S'wark Cathl 16–18; Adn Ashford *Cant* from 18. *The Archdeaconry, Pett Lane, Charing, Ashford TN27 0DL* T: (01233) 712649 M: 07548-232377 E: darren.miller@archdeacashford.org

MILLER, Canon David George. b 54. Oriel Coll Ox BA 76 MA 80 BD 06 Ex Univ PhD 13. Ripon Coll Cuddesdon 78. d 81 p 82. C Henfield w Shermanbury and Woodmancote

Chich 81–84; C Monk Bretton *Wakef* 84–87; V Rastrick St Jo 87–93; TR Helston and Wendron *Truro* from 93; RD Kerrier from 17; Chapl R Cornwall Hosps Trust 95–01; Chapl W of Cornwall Primary Care Trust 01–06; Hon Can Truro Cathl from 06. *St Michael's Rectory, Church Lane, Helston TR13 8PF* T: (01326) 572516 E: millerourrectory@gmail.com

MILLER, David James Tringham. b 45. AKC 70. Sarum & Wells Th Coll 76. **d** 77 **p** 78. C Abington *Pet* 77–80; TV Corby SS Pet and Andr w Gt and Lt Oakley 80–83; V Kettering All SS 83–94; RD Kettering 87–94; V Pet All SS 94–09; rtd 09; C Penrith w Newton Reigny and Plumpton Wall *Carl* 10–11; PtO 11–16. *27 Drovers Terrace, Penrith CA11 9EN* T: (01768) 840406 E: djtmiller@o2.co.uk

MILLER, David Robert. b 47. Middx Univ BA 98. ERMC 94. **d** 08 **p** 09. C Eaton Socon *St Alb* 08–12; rtd 12; PtO *St Alb* from 12. *32 Cornwall Court, Eaton Socon, St Neots PE19 8PR* T: (01480) 471132 E: davidmiller.rev@gmail.com

MILLER, Ernest Charles. b 56. Franklin & Marshall Coll (USA) BA 78 Univ of Michigan MA 79 Keble Coll Ox DPhil 90. Nashotah Ho MDiv 82. **d** 82 **p** 83. C Dallas St Andr USA 82–84; Warden Ho of SS Greg and Macrina 84–90; Asst Chapl Keble Coll Ox 84–88; P-in-c New Marston *Ox* 91–96; Ramsey Prof Th Nashotah Ho Wisconsin USA 96–00; R New York Transfiguration USA 00–04; Adjunct Prof Ch Hist Gen Th Sem 02–04; TR Abingdon *Ox* from 06. *The Rectory, St Helen's Court, Abingdon OX14 5BS* T: (01235) 532722 M: 07726-743924 E: rector@sthelens-abingdon.org.uk

MILLER, Gareth. *See* MILLER, John Gareth

MILLER, The Very Revd Geoffrey Vincent. b 56. Dur Univ BEd 78 Newc Univ MA 94. St Jo Coll Nottm 81. **d** 83 **p** 84. C Jarrow *Dur* 83–86; TV Billingham St Aid 86–92; Dioc Urban Development Officer 91–97; Community Chapl Stockton-on-Tees 92–94; P-in-c Darlington St Cuth 94–96; V 96–99; Soc Resp Officer 97–99; Can Res Newc Cathl 99–05; Dioc Urban Officer 99–05; Adn Northd and Can Res Newc Cathl 05–18; Dean Newc from 18. *26 Mitchell Avenue, Newcastle upon Tyne NE2 3LA* T: 0191-232 1939 E: g.miller@newcastle.anglican.org *or* dean@stnicholascathedral.co.uk

MILLER, Graham William. b 71. St Andr Univ BD 94 Dur Univ MA 98. Westcott Ho Cam 99. **d** 01 **p** 02. C Ex St Dav 01–03; C Sunderland St Mary and St Pet and Sunderland Pennywell St Thos *Dur* 03–07; C Paddington St Jas *Lon* 07–14; R Greenford H Cross from 14. *The Rectory, 75 Oldfield Lane South, Greenford UB6 9JT* T: (020) 8575 5402 M: 07851-013457 E: graham.miller@london.anglican.org

✠**MILLER, The Rt Revd Harold Creeth.** b 50. TCD BA 73 MA 78. St Jo Coll Nottm BA 75. **d** 76 **p** 77 **c** 97. C Carrickfergus *Conn* 76–79; Dir Ext Studies St Jo Coll Nottm 79–84; Chapl QUB 84–89; I Carrigrohane Union *C, C & R* 89–97; Bp's Dom Chapl 91–97; Can Cork and Cloyne Cathls 94–96; Treas Cork Cathl 96–97; Can Cork Cathl 96–97; Preb Tymothan St Patr Cathl Dublin 96–97; Bp D & D 97–19; rtd 19. *Address temp unknown*

MILLER, Ian Daukes Douglas. St Hugh's Coll Ox BA 96 MA 97. Called to the Bar (Gray's Inn) 99. Oak Hill Th Coll 17. **d** 19. C Maidenhead St Andr and St Mary *Ox* from 19. *Address withheld by request*

MILLER (née BLUNDEN), Mrs Jacqueline Ann. b 63. Leic Univ BA 86 SS Coll Cam BA 90. Ridley Hall Cam 88. **d** 91 **p** 19. Par Dn Bedford St Paul *St Alb* 91–94; C 94–95; PtO *Lon* 05–18; Hon C St Andr-by-the-Wardrobe w St Ann, Blackfriars and St Martin Ludgate from 16. *The Rectory, St Andrew's House, 35 St Andrew's Hill, London EC4V 5DE* M: 07742-104065 E: jacqui.miller7@btinternet.com

MILLER, Canon John David. b 50. Nottm Univ BTh 73 Lanc Univ CertEd 74 Newc Univ MA 93. Kelham Th Coll 68. **d** 74 **p** 75. C Horden *Dur* 74–79; C Billingham St Aid 79–80; TV 80–84; TR S Shields All SS 84–10; Hon Can Dur Cathl 04–10; rtd 10; PtO *Dur* from 10. *6 Tynedale Road, South Shields NE34 6EX* T: 0191-455 6911

MILLER, John David. b 76. Ch Ch Ox BA 98 MA 07. Oak Hill Th Coll BA 10. **d** 10 **p** 11. C Bath St Bart *B & W* 10–13; NSM Ox St Ebbe w H Trin and St Pet 16–18. *33A Bushmead Avenue, Bedford MK40 3QH* M: 07821-180901 E: johnmiller.jdm@gmail.com

MILLER, John Gareth. b 57. St Jo Coll Dur BA 78 Hull Univ MA 11. Ridley Hall Cam 79 Ven English Coll Rome 80. **d** 81 **p** 82. C Addiscombe St Mary *Cant* 81–84; TV Melbury *Sarum* 84–88; TR 88–91; V Leamington Priors All SS *Cov* 91–94; PtO *Ox* 15–17; R Akeman from 17; AD Bicester and Islip from 18. *The Rectory, Troy Lane, Kirtlington, Kidlington OX5 3HA* T: (01869) 350224 E: jgarethmiller@gmail.com

MILLER (née Donaldson), Mrs Katherine. b 90. St Jo Coll Dur BA 12 St Cath Coll Ox PGCE 14. St Mellitus Coll MA 18. **d** 19. C Fulham St Matt *Lon* from 19. *2A Clancarty Road, London SW6 3AB* M: 07403-674406 E: katherine@stmf.org.uk

MILLER, Kathryn Rebecca. b 63. Ex Univ BSc 84 Abth Univ MSc 86 UEA PhD 10 Wolfs Coll Cam BTh 15. Ridley Hall Cam 13. **d** 15 **p** 16. C Speke St Aid w All SS *Liv* 15–18; V Becontree St Mary *Chelmsf* from 18. *The Vicarage, 191 Valance Wood Road, Dagenham RM8 3AH* T: (020) 8592 2822 M: 07914-529310 E: katie.miller.063@gmail.com

MILLER, The Ven Luke Jonathan. b 66. SS Coll Cam BA 87 MA 91. St Steph Ho Ox BA 90. **d** 91 **p** 92. C Oxhey St Matt *St Alb* 91–94; C Tottenham St Mary *Lon* 94–95; V 95–10; AD E Haringey 05–10; Adn Hampstead 10–15; P-in-c Winchmore Hill H Trin 11–12; P-in-c St Andr-by-the-Wardrobe w St Ann, Blackfriars 15–17; R St Andr-by-the-Wardrobe w St Ann, Blackfriars and St Martin Ludgate from 17; Adn Lon from 16; P-in-c St Botolph without Bishopgate 16–18. *The Rectory, St Andrew's House, 35 St Andrew's Hill, London EC4V 5DE* T: (020) 3837 5204 E: archdeacon.london@london.anglican.org

MILLER, Mark George. b 69. Cranmer Hall Dur 10. **d** 12 **p** 13. C Stockton *Dur* 12–16; P-in-c Stockton Par Ch from 16. *Stockton Parish Church, High Street, Stockton-on-Tees TS18 1SP* T: (01642) 611734 E: mark@stocktonparishchurch.org.uk

MILLER, Martin Michael. b 55. St Jo Coll Dur BSc 78. Trin Coll Bris 94. **d** 96 **p** 97. C Leamington Priors St Paul *Cov* 96–99; C Bermondsey St Anne and St Aug *S'wark* 99–05; R Newhaven *Chich* from 05. *The Rectory, 36 Second Avenue, Newhaven BN9 9HN* T: (01273) 515251 E: southcoastmillers@gmail.com

MILLER, Michael Andrew. b 58. Ripon Coll Cuddesdon 03. **d** 05 **p** 06. C Hockerill *St Alb* 05–08; P-in-c Kensal Town St Thos w St Andr and St Phil *Lon* 08–12; V 12–16; V Northwood Hills St Edm from 16. *St Edmund's Vicarage, 2 Pinner Road, Northwood HA6 1QS* T: (020) 8866 9230 M: 07778-617482 E: mmiller832@btinternet.com

MILLER, Michael Daukes. b 46. Qu Coll Cam MA 71 Lon Univ BCh 70 MB 71 MRCGP 74. Glouc Th Course 82. **d** 85 **p** 94. NSM Lydney w Aylburton *Glouc* 85–95; NSM Lydney 95–06; Asst Chapl HM Pris Ex from 07; PtO *Ex* from 07. *HM Prison, 30 New North Road, Exeter EX4 4EX* T: (01392) 415650 E: mmiller@btinternet.com

MILLER, Patrick Figgis. b 33. Ch Coll Cam BA 56 MA 60 Surrey Univ PhD 95. Cuddesdon Coll 56. **d** 58 **p** 59. C Portsea St Cuth *Portsm* 58–61; C Cambridge Gt St Mary w St Mich *Ely* 61–63; Chapl SCM 61–63; Hd RS Man Gr Sch 63–69; Can Res and Lib S'wark Cathl 69–72; Dir of Soc Studies Qu Mary's Coll Basingstoke 72–79; Prin Sunbury Coll 79–80; Prin Esher Coll 81–98; Project Dir Learning for Living 00–05; Chapl London Flotilla from 00; PtO *Guildf* from 01. *9 Fairfax Avenue, Epsom KT17 2QN* T: (020) 8394 0970 M: 07740-909414 E: patrickmiller@ntlworld.com

MILLER, Canon Paul. b 49. Oak Hill Th Coll 71. **d** 74 **p** 75. C Upton *Ex* 74–77; C Farnborough *Guildf* 77–78; P-in-c Torquay St Luke *Ex* 78–81; V 81–86; V Green Street Green *Roch* 86–94; V Green Street Green and Pratts Bottom 94–01; RD Orpington 96–01; V Shortlands 01–12; Hon Can Roch Cathl 00–12; AD Beckenham 09–12; Chapl Is of Scilly *Truro* 12–15; rtd 15; Chapl to The Queen from 05; PtO *Cant* from 16; *Roch* from 16. *11 Bishopswood, Kingsnorth, Ashford TN23 3RD* T: (01233) 365176 M: 07940-582040 E: paulmiller@roundisland.net

MILLER, Canon Philip Harry. b 58. Leeds Univ BA 79. Chich Th Coll 80. **d** 82 **p** 83. C Reddish *Man* 82–86; R Lower Broughton Ascension 86–94; P-in-c Cheetwood St Alb 91–94; P-in-c Langley and Parkfield 95–00; TR 00–10; V Langley from 10; AD Heywood and Middleton 10–15; Hon Can Man Cathl from 07. *The Rectory, Wood Street, Middleton, Manchester M24 5GL* T: 0161-643 5013 E: canonphil@hotmail.co.uk

MILLER, Philip Howard. b 40. Tyndale Hall Bris 67. **d** 72 **p** 73. Argentina 72–73; C Rusholme H Trin *Man* 73–74; SAMS Paraguay 74–77; C Toxteth St Cypr w Ch Ch *Liv* 78–80; V Burscough Bridge 80–85; V Woodbridge St Jo *St E* 85–91; P-in-c Combs 91–92 and 93–96; Chapl Burrswood Chr Cen 92–93; V Yoxford and Peasenhall w Sibton *St E* 96–01; rtd 01; PtO *St E* 07–17. *Salta, 54 Orchard Close, Melton, Woodbridge IP12 1LD* T: (01394) 388615 E: phm914@lineone.net

MILLER, Richard Bracebridge. b 45. Wycliffe Hall Ox 68. **d** 70 **p** 71. C Lee Gd Shep w St Pet *S'wark* 70–74; C Roehampton H Trin 74–77; C Earley St Pet *Ox* 77–80; V Aldermaston w Wasing and Brimpton 80–96; C Newbury 96–01; PtO 03–18. *28 Golden Court, Isleworth TW7 4EQ* T: (020) 8847 2179 M: 07870-555474 E: richard.b.miller@btinternet.com

MILLER, The Ven Robert Stephen. b 71. QUB BSc 92. CITC BTh 95. **d** 95 **p** 96. C Lurgan Ch the Redeemer *D & D* 95–99; I Tullylish 99–03; I Maghera w Killelagh *D & R* 03–10; I Londonderry Ch Ch, Culmore, Muff and Belmont from 10; Adn Derry from 12. *The Rectory, 1B*

Heathfield, Londonderry BT48 8JD   T: (028) 7135 2396 *or* 7135 8925   M: 07711-748406   E: rector@cccmsp.org *or* archdeacon@derry.anglican.org

MILLER, Ronald <u>Andrew</u> John. b 46. **d** 96 **p** 97. OLM Heywood *Man* 96–09; PtO *St As* from 12; *Ban* 16–18. *16 Bryn Morfa, Bodelwyddan, Rhyl LL18 5TP*   T: (01745) 530055   E: rajlinmiller@btinternet.com

MILLER, Ronald Anthony. b 41. City Univ BSc 63 CEng CPA MRAeS. S'wark Ord Course 69. **d** 72 **p** 80. NSM Crookham *Guildf* 72–73 and 80–85; NSM New Haw 85–95; NSM Effingham w Lt Bookham 95–04; PtO 05–09; NSM Nork 09–11; rtd 11. *190 Gossops Drive, Crawley RH11 8LD*   M: 07710-294786   E: ramiller@sky.com

MILLER, Rosamund Joy. See SEAL, Rosamund Joy

MILLER, Miss Sarah Lydia. b 65. St Andr Univ BD 90 Hughes Hall Cam PGCE 91. EAMTC 98. **d** 01 **p** 02. NSM Nor St Pet Mancroft w St Jo Maddermarket 01–03; C Wythenshawe *Man* 03–07; C Tewkesbury w Walton Cardiff and Twyning *Glouc* 07–11; V Newbiggin Hall *Newc* 11–18. *c/o 16 Hungerford Road, Bath BA1 3BU* E: sarahmiller1413@gmail.com

MILLER, Stuart William. b 71. Univ of Wales (Cardiff) BA 92. Trin Coll Bris BA 97. **d** 97 **p** 98. C Fordingbridge *Win* 97–98; C Bursledon 98–02; V W Moors *Sarum* 02–05; Chapl Bournemouth and Poole Coll of FE *Win* 05–10; C Bournemouth Town Cen 05–10; V Moordown 10–16; V Winton, Moordown and Charminster 16–17. *53 Victoria Road, Bournemouth BH1 4RT*

MILLER, Canon Thomas Paul. b 49. **d** 90. Asst R NY St Mich USA 90–94; P-in-c Woodstock St Greg 94–03; Can Lit and the Arts NY 03–13; P-in-c Stromness *Ab* from 15. *Quarrybrae, Hillside Road, Stromness KW16 3HR*   T: (01856) 850691   E: tmiller.stromness@btinternet.com

MILLER, Timothy Ian. b 85. Ustinov Coll Dur MA 09 St Jo Coll Dur MATM 14. Cranmer Hall Dur 12. **d** 14 **p** 15. C Primrose Hill St Mary w Avenue Road St Paul *Lon* 14–17; P-in-c Highgate All SS from 17. *56 North Hill, London N6 4RH*   M: 07588-644217   E: believethesescars@gmail.com

MILLER, William David. b 45. Man Univ BA 66. Linc Th Coll 69. **d** 71 **p** 72. C Newc St Geo 71–74; C Corbridge w Halton 74–77; C N Gosforth 77–81; TV Whorlton 81–90; Chapl K Sch Tynemouth 90–09; rtd 09; PtO *Newc* from 09; *Dur* from 15. *7 Strawberry Terrace, Hazlerigg, Newcastle upon Tyne NE13 7AR*   T: 0191-236 5024   E: millers@talktalk.net

MILLER-MASKELL, John Michael. b 45. Sarum & Wells Th Coll 86. **d** 88 **p** 89. C Swanborough *Sarum* 88–91; Chapl RAF 91–95; P-in-c Ollerton w Boughton *S'well* 95–97; P-in-c Capel *Guildf* 97–02; TV Walton H Trin *Ox* 02–03; Healing Co-ord Acorn Chr Foundn 03–04; rtd 04; PtO *Chich* 04–10; P-in-c Chailey 10–18. *Valley Farm Cottage, Danehill Lane, Horsted Keynse, Haywards Heath RH17 7BP*   T: (01825) 790186   M: 07852-741515

MILLEST, Daniel John. b 86. St Mellitus Coll. **d** 13 **p** 14. C Onslow Square and S Kensington St Aug *Lon* 13–14; Malaysia from 14. *C-20-6, The Capers, Jalan Enam, 51000, Kuala Lumpur, Malaysia* E: dan.millest@htbb.org

MILLGATE, Victor Frederick. b 44. St Mich Coll Llan 81. **d** 83 **p** 84. C Pembroke St Mary w St Mich *St D* 83–85; V Manorbier and St Florence w Redberth 85–04; TR Carew 04–09; AD Castlemartin 03–09; rtd 09. *3 Grove Drive, Pembroke SA71 5QB*   T: (01646) 621683

MILLIER, Gordon. b 28. St Aid Birkenhead 63. **d** 65 **p** 66. C Congresbury *B & W* 65–69; P-in-c Badgworth w Biddisham 69–76; R Weare w Badgworth and Biddisham 76–84; R Pilton w Croscombe, N Wootton and Dinder 84–93; rtd 93; PtO *Ex* from 93. *28 Withy Close, Canal Hill, Tiverton EX16 4HZ*   T: (01884) 253128

MILLIGAN, Peter John. b 52. **d** 01 **p** 02. NSM Putney St Marg S'wark 01–06; NSM Angell Town St Jo from 06. *39 Stapleton Road, London SW17 8BA*   T: (020) 8767 3497   M: 07811-395662   E: peter.j.milligan@btinternet.com

MILLINCHIP (*née* DAVENPORT), **Susan Jane.** b 56. Somerville Coll Ox MA 79. All SS Cen for Miss & Min 10. **d** 14 **p** 15. NSM Witton *Ches* from 14. *2 Manor Grove, Northwich CW8 1JE*   T: (01606) 784042   M: 07591-942297   E: revjanemillinchip@outlook.com

MILLINGTON, Stuart. b 45. Lich Th Coll 67. **d** 70 **p** 71. C Boulton *Derby* 70–73; C Moseley St Mary *Birm* 73–76; TV Staveley and Barrow Hill *Derby* 76–82; R Wingerworth 82–99; RD Chesterfield 91–97; P-in-c Elton All SS *Man* 99–09; P-in-c Woolfold 07–09; V Kirklees Valley 09–10; AD Bury 05–10; rtd 10; PtO *Man* 10–12; *Wakef* 10–14; *Leeds* from 14. *33 Westways, Wrenthorpe, Wakefield WF2 0TE*   T: (01924) 375996   E: stumillington@btinternet.com

MILLS, Alexandra. b 56. Univ of Wales (Abth) BMus 78 CertEd 79. Ripon Coll Cuddesdon 88. **d** 90 **p** 94. Par Dn Earlsfield St Andr *S'wark* 90–94; C Kingston All SS w

St Jo 94–99; C Brixton Road Ch Ch 99–00; PtO from 05. *121A Tranmere Road, London SW18 3QP*   T: (020) 8944 1641   M: 07900-543068 E: perfidafalerina@yahoo.co.uk

MILLS, Anne. See MILLS, Leslie Anne

MILLS, Anthony James. b 55. Nottm Univ BA. Linc Th Coll. **d** 84 **p** 85. C Mexborough *Sheff* 84–86; C Howden *York* 86–89; V Fylingdales and Hawsker cum Stainsacre 89–95; V Scarborough St Sav w All SS 95–09; P-in-c Scarborough St Martin 02–05; V 05–09; R Failsworth H Family *Man* 09–17; rtd 17; PtO *Leeds* from 17. *2 Kaye Hill, Cullingworth, Bradford BD13 5HT*   T: (01535) 270553 E: aj.mills@hotmail.com

MILLS, David Francis. b 51. Oak Hill Th Coll 76. **d** 79 **p** 80. C Rodbourne Cheney *Bris* 79–82; C Wolverhampton St Matt *Lich* 82–85; CF 85–88; TV Braunstone *Leic* 88–95; Past Asst to Adn Leic 95–97; C Barkestone w Plungar, Redmile and Stathern 97–99; C Bottesford and Muston 97–99; C Harby, Long Clawson and Hose 97–99; C Vale of Belvoir 00–02; R Winfarthing w Shelfanger w Burston w Gissing etc *Nor* from 02. *The Rectory, Church Lane, Winfarthing, Diss IP22 2EA*   T: (01379) 643646 E: revdfmills1812@gmail.com

MILLS, David Graham Mackenzie. See MACKENZIE MILLS, David Graham

MILLS, Mrs Elizabeth Frances Margaret. b 56. Westhill Coll Birm BEd 78. Qu Foundn (Course) 15. **d** 17 **p** 18. NSM Wigginton *Lich* from 17. *The Vicarage, 90 Briar, Tamworth B77 4DZ*   T: (01827) 769413 E: firstclassliz999@gmail.com

MILLS, Canon Geoffrey Charles Malcolm. b 33. Wycliffe Hall Ox 59. **d** 61 **p** 62. C Buckhurst Hill *Chelmsf* 61–65; C Ecclesall *Sheff* 65–69; V Endcliffe 69–78; R Whiston 78–99; Hon Can Sheff Cathl 96–99; rtd 99; PtO *Sheff* from 99. *8 Hall Road, Rotherham S60 2BP*   T: (01709) 373863 E: gcmills@blueyonder.co.uk

MILLS, Gordon Derek. b 35. Lich Th Coll 60. **d** 63 **p** 64. C W Derby St Mary *Liv* 63–65; C Clifton w Glapton *S'well* 65–67; V N Wilford St Faith 67–72; V Farnsfield 72–82; P-in-c Kirklington w Hockerton 77–82; P-in-c Brindle and Asst Dir of Educn *Blackb* 82–86; V Gt Budworth *Ches* 86–88; P-in-c Antrobus 87–88; V Gt Budworth and Antrobus 88–92; V Gt Budworth 92–00; rtd 00; PtO *Blackb* 01–04; *York* from 04; *Bradf* 04–07; *Dur* 04–15; *Leeds* from 17. *Holmelands House, Raby Lane, East Cowton, Northallerton DL7 0BW*   T: (01325) 378798 E: derek.mills77@gmail.com

MILLS, Canon Hubert Cecil. b 44. TCD BA 66 MA 71 HDipEd 73. CITC 67. **d** 67 **p** 68. C Dublin Rathfarnham *D & G* 67–72; C Dublin St Steph and St Ann 72–77; I Holmpatrick w Balbriggan and Kenure 77–86; I Killiney H Trin 86–11; Min Can St Patr Cathl Dublin 69–92; Succ St Patr Cathl Dublin 77–92; Preb Rathmichael St Patr Cathl Dublin 92–01; Treas St Patr Cathl Dublin 01–11; rtd 11. *2 Verona, Queens Park, Monkstown, Co Dublin, Republic of Ireland*   T: (00353) (1) 214 3689   M: 87-286 8743 E: cecil.mills@alterum.com

MILLS, Jennifer Clare. See TOMLINSON, Jennifer Clare

MILLS, Mrs Leslie Anne. b 44. K Alfred's Coll Win CertEd 65. SWMTC 99. **d** 02 **p** 03. NSM Kilmington, Stockland, Dalwood, Yarcombe etc *Ex* 02–16; rtd 16; PtO *Ex* from 16. *2 Church Lane, Feniton, Honiton EX14 3BY*   T: (01404) 850923

MILLS, Martin. b 58. **d** 14 **p** 15. NSM Bolney *Chich* from 14; NSM Cowfold from 14. *19 Honeywood Road, Horsham RH13 6AE*   T: (01403) 267284

MILLS, Michael Henry. b 51. AKC 73. St Aug Coll Cant. **d** 74 **p** 75. C Newton Aycliffe *Dur* 74–78; C Padgate *Liv* 78–79; TV 79–95; V Frodsham *Ches* 95–19; rtd 19. *4 Grove Terrace, Helsby, Frodsham WA6 0QG* E: mikehmills@mac.com

MILLS, Michael John. b 52. St Andr Univ BSc 75 Cam Univ PGCE 76. Cranmer Hall Dur 97. **d** 99 **p** 00. C Brockmoor *Worc* 99–03; P-in-c St Leonards St Ethelburga *Chich* 04–09; P-in-c St Leonards St Leon 04–09; R St Leonards St Ethelburga and St Leon 09–11; TV Glascote and Stonydelph *Lich* 11–18; Resource Min Tamworth Deanery from 18. *The Vicarage, 90 Briar, Tamworth B77 4DZ*   M: 07789-913013   E: michael_mills@talktalk.net

MILLS, Peter James. b 32. Univ Coll Lon LLB 58. **d** 99 **p** 00. NSM Woodchurch *Ches* 99–03; rtd 03; PtO *Ches* from 03. *6 West Heath Court, Gerard Road, West Kirby, Wirral CH48 4ES*   T: 0151-625 3314   M: 07989-374499   E: pjmills@uwclub.net *or* rev.peter@holycrosswoodchurch.uk

MILLS, Mrs Philippa Jane. b 63. Rob Coll Cam MA 86 Open Univ PGCE 96. STETS 06. **d** 09 **p** 10. NSM Hook w Warsash *Portsm* 09–12; C Whiteley CD 12–13; C-in-c from 13. *20 Sheridan Gardens, Whiteley, Fareham PO15 7DY*   M: 07760-771667 E: revpjmills@gmail.com

MILLS, Roger Conrad. b 58. Selw Coll Cam BA 79 MA 83. Sarum Th Coll Nottm 83. **d** 85 **p** 86. C Jesmond H Trin *Newc* 85–88; C Alnwick 88–91; Chapl Newc Univ 91–00; P-in-c Newc St Barn and St Jude 95–97; V Kingston Park 00–18;

rtd 18; PtO *Newc* from 19. *4 The Grove, Morpeth NE61 1HY* E: rogermills123@yahoo.co.uk

MILLS, Stephen Paul. b 70. Sheff Univ BA 00 Brighton Univ PGCE 09. St Steph Ho Ox MTh 18. **d** 17 **p** 18. C Preston St Jo w Brighton St Aug and St Sav *Chich* 17–18; C Steyning from 18; C Ashurst from 18. *New House, Tanyard Lane, Steyning BN44 3RN* E: revstephenmills@hotmail.com

MILLSON, Brian Douglas. b 53. Univ of W Ontario BA 76 Huron Coll MDiv 84 Open Univ BSc 10. Westcott Ho Cam 82. **d** 83 **p** 84. C Walton-on-Thames *Guildf* 83–86; R Par of the Six Nations Canada 86–89; Canadian Forces Chapl 89–98; CF 98–12; Miss to Seafarers from 12. *Hoevenesbaan 253, 2950 Kapellen, Belgium* T: (0032) (3) 294 5922 M: 46-815 5522 E: brianmillson@gmail.com

MILLSON, Mrs Margaret Lily. b 41. CertEd 61. EMMTC 83. **dss** 86 **d** 87 **p** 94. NSM Bottesford w Ashby *Linc* 86–01; P-in-c St Tudy w St Mabyn and Michaelstow *Truro* 01–10; rtd 10; PtO *Truro* from 16. *Winterbourne, 2 Gwelmeneth Park, St Cleer, Liskeard PL14 5HU* T: (01579) 346338 E: mlmillson@aol.com

MILLWOOD, Stephen Grant. b 44. Sheff City Coll of Educn CertEd 77 Open Univ BA 92. St Jo Coll Nottm 92. **d** 94 **p** 95. C Anston *Sheff* 94–98; V Kimberworth Park 98–09; Bp's Urban Adv 05–09; rtd 09; PtO *Sheff* from 09. *6 Quarryfield Drive, Sheffield S9 5AG* T: 0114-243 4948 E: steveandjanetm@mac.com

MILMINE, Canon Neil Edward Douglas. b 46. Kent Univ BSc 70. Wycliffe Hall Ox 80. **d** 82 **p** 83. C Hailsham *Chich* 82–86; C Horsham 86; TV 86–93; V Patcham 93–11; Can and Preb Chich Cathl 00–11; RD Brighton 02–09; rtd 11; PtO *Chich* from 12; *S'wark* 12–14. *8 The Willows, Barcombe, Lewes BN8 5FJ* T/F: (01273) 401521 E: n.milmine@yahoo.co.uk

MILNE, Alan. b 54. RMN SRN TCert. Cranmer Hall Dur 89. **d** 91 **p** 92. C Hartlepool St Luke *Dur* 91–94; P-in-c Dalton le Dale 94–00; V 00–05; P-in-c Hawthorn 94–00; R 00–05; R Hawthorn and Murton 05–17; AD Easington 03–15; rtd 17; PtO *Dur* from 18. *5 Park Lane, Murton, Seaham SR7 9QS*

MILNE, Miss Christine Helen. b 48. LTCL 71. S'wark Ord Course 83. **dss** 86 **d** 87 **p** 90. NSM S Lambeth St Steph *S'wark* 86–89; Par Dn 87–89; C Wainuiomata New Zealand 89–92; C Eastbourne 93; Chapl Nga Tawa Sch Marton 94–02; Chapl Palmerston North Hosp 04–13; Chapl Auckland City Hosp 13–17; PtO from 17. *7 Hobson Street, Levin 5510, New Zealand* T: (0064) (6) 367 3233 *or* 21-2617045 M: (0064) 21-261 7045 E: hmilne@xtra.co.nz

MILNE, Canon James Harley. b 73. Univ of Wales (Lamp) BD 94 New Coll Edin MTh 96. TISEC 95. **d** 98 **p** 99. C Dundee St Mary Magd *Bre* 98–01; Chapl St Marg Res Home Dundee 98–01; R Dundee St Marg *Bre* 01–09; Chapl Ninewells Hosp Dundee 01–09; R Glas St Bride 09–15; Can St Paul's Cathl Dundee *Bre* 08–09; Hon Can St Paul's Cathl Dundee 09–15; Min Can and Sacr St Paul's Cathl *Lon* 15–19; Can Res and Prec St Paul's Cathl from 19. *6 Amen Court, London EC4M 7BU* T: (020) 7246 8331

MILNE SMITH, Christopher. *See* SMITH, Christopher Milne

MILNER, David. b 38. St Aid Birkenhead 63. **d** 66 **p** 67. C Ulverston H Trin *Carl* 66; C Ulverston St Mary w H Trin 66–68; C Mickleover All SS *Derby* 68–71; C Mickleover St Jo 68–71; V 71–82; P-in-c Sandiacre 82–86; P-in-c Doveridge 86–97; P-in-c Sudbury and Somersal Herbert 92–97; R Doveridge, Scropton, Sudbury etc 98–03; RD Longford 86–96 and 01–03; rtd 03; PtO *Lich* 04–08 and 17–18. *21 Greenwood Park, Hednesford WS12 4DQ* T: (01543) 428972

✠**MILNER, The Rt Revd Ronald James.** b 27. Pemb Coll Cam BA 49 MA 52. Wycliffe Hall Ox 51. **d** 53 **p** 54 **c** 88. Succ Sheff Cathl 53–58; V Westwood *Cov* 58–64; V Fletchamstead 64–70; R Southampton St Mary w H Trin *Win* 70–72; P-in-c Southampton St Matt 70–72; LtO 72–73; TR Southampton (City Cen) 73–83; Hon Can Win Cathl 75–83; Adn Linc 83–88; Can and Preb Linc Cathl 83–88; Suff Bp Burnley *Blackb* 88–93; rtd 93; Hon Asst Bp S'well and Nottm from 94. *7 Crafts Way, Southwell NG25 0BL* T: (01636) 816256

MILNER, William David. b 52. St Jo Coll Nottm. **d** 93 **p** 94. C Wollaton *S'well* 93–97; P-in-c Daybrook 97; C W Bridgford 98–99; TV Clifton 99–04; P-in-c Collingham w S Scarle and Besthorpe and Girton 04–10; P-in-c E Trent 10–11; P-in-c Farndon w Thorpe, Hawton and Cotham 11–17; AD Newark and S'well 12–17; rtd 17; PtO *Leic* from 19; *S'well* from 17. *Mill Pond, Old Forge Lane, Granby, Nottingham NG13 9PS* T: (01949) 850504

MILNES, David Ian. b 45. Chich Th Coll 74. **d** 76 **p** 77. C Walthamstow St Sav *Chelmsf* 76–80; C Chingford SS Pet and Paul 80–83; P-in-c Gt Ilford St Alb 83–87; V 87–09; rtd 09; PtO *Chich* from 15. *Walsingham House, Main Road, Hadlow Down, Uckfield TN22 4ES* T: (01825) 830076 E: frmilnes@aol.com

MILSON, Julian James. b 70. De Montfort Univ BEd 96. Oak Hill Th Coll BA 04. **d** 04 **p** 05. C Bramcote *S'well* 04–07; C Hove Bp Hannington Memorial Ch *Chich* 07–18; Crosslinks from 18. *Calle de los Centelles 54, 8-27, 46006 Valencia, Spain* E: joolsm@mac.com

MILTON, Miss Angela Daphne. b 50. FInstLEx 79. Oak Hill Th Coll 84. **d** 87 **p** 94. NSM Watford *St Alb* 87–95; NSM St Alb St Mary Marshalswick 95–97; C Stevenage St Mary Shephall w Aston 97–02; P-in-c E Molesey St Paul *Guildf* 02–05; V E Molesey 05–10; rtd 10; PtO *St Alb* from 10. *75 Furtherfield, Abbots Langley WD5 0PN* T: (01923) 519453 E: angelamilton@msn.com

MILTON-THOMPSON, Jonathan Patrick. b 51. Nottm Univ BA 76. Oak Hill Th Coll 86. **d** 88 **p** 89. C Bispham *Blackb* 88–92; C Darfield *Sheff* 92; C-in-c Gt Houghton CD 92–03; P-in-c Livesey *Blackb* 03–11; V from 11; P-in-c Blackb St Barn 10–14; V from 14. *St Andrew's Vicarage, 112 Full View, Blackburn BB2 4QB* T: (01254) 59422 E: jarpmt51@hotmail.co.uk

MILVERTON, The Revd and Rt Hon Lord (Fraser Arthur Richard Richards). b 30. Bps' Coll Cheshunt. **d** 57 **p** 58. C Beckenham St Geo *Roch* 57–59; C Sevenoaks St Jo 59–60; C Gt Bookham *Guildf* 60–63; V Okewood 63–67; R Christian Malford w Sutton Benger etc *Bris* 67–93; Public Preacher 93–95; rtd 95; PtO *Sarum* from 96. *7 Betjeman Road, Marlborough SN8 1TL* T: (01672) 514068

MILVERTON, Mrs Ruth Erica. b 32. Open Univ BA 78 Southn Univ MA 82. Sarum Th Coll 83. **dss** 86 **d** 87 **p** 95. Weymouth H Trin *Sarum* 86–87; Hon Par Dn 87–95; NSM 95–02; Dioc NSM Officer 89–97; rtd 02; PtO *Sarum* from 02. *4 Compass South, Rodwell Road, Weymouth DT4 8QT* T: (01305) 788930 E: rev.milv.compass@care4free.net

MILWAIN, James Callum. b 90. UCL BSc 11. Ripon Coll Cuddesdon BA 19. **d** 19. C Chesterfield St Mary and All SS *Derby* from 19. *8 Birkdale Drive, Chesterfield S40 3JL* M: 07735-303185 E: milwain@gmail.com

MINALL, Peter. b 26. Lon Univ BSc 47. Bps' Coll Cheshunt 51. **d** 53 **p** 54. C Bishop's Stortford St Mich *St Alb* 53–57; C Luton w E Hyde 57–63; C Tuffley *Glouc* 63–65; Asst Youth Chapl 65–69; V Stroud 69–78; RD Bisley 78–84; P-in-c Barnwood 84–91; rtd 91; Chapl Coney Hill Hosp Glouc 86–95; Chapl Severn NHS Trust 95–05; Chapl Glos Primary Care Trust 05–06; PtO *Glouc* 06–15. *29 Queen Anne Court, Quedgeley, Gloucester GL2 4JY* T: (01452) 886811 E: peter.minall@btinternet.com

MINAY, Francis Arthur Rodney. b 44. Westcott Ho Cam 66. **d** 68 **p** 69. C Edenbridge *Roch* 68–73; C Bromley St Mark 73–75; V Tudeley w Capel 75–79; TV Littleham w Exmouth *Ex* 79–82; P-in-c Bolton Percy and Asst Chapl to Arts and Recreation in the NE *York* 82–06; rtd 06; LtO *Mor* 07–14; PtO from 14. *Rosedyke, Achintee, Strathcarron IV54 8YX* T: (01520) 722144 E: francisandjaney@btinternet.com

MINCHIN, Anthony John. b 35. St Cath Coll Cam BA 59 MA. Wells Th Coll 59. **d** 61 **p** 62. C Cheltenham St Pet *Glouc* 61–64; C Bushey *St Alb* 64–67; V Cheltenham St Mich *Glouc* 67–74; V Lower Cam 74–82; V Tuffley 82–92; R Huntley and Longhope 92–00; rtd 00; PtO *Glouc* from 00. *2 Melbourne Drive, Stonehouse GL10 2PJ* T: (01453) 828899

MINCHIN, Charles Scott. b 51. Trin Coll Cam BA 72 MA 75. Linc Th Coll 73. **d** 75 **p** 76. C Gt Wyrley *Lich* 75–78; TV Wilnecote 78–82; C Tamworth 82–84; C-in-c Glascote CD 84–88; R Brierley Hill *Worc* 88–03; P-in-c Stonehouse *Glouc* 03–16; TV Stroudwater Team 16–18; rtd 18. *278 Linden Road, Gloucester GL1 5DU* T: (01452) 901262 E: cminchin@talktalk.net

MINCHIN, Christopher David. b 88. Newc Univ BA 11 RCA(Lon) MA 14. Coll of Resurr Mirfield 16. **d** 18 **p** 19. C Benwell and Scotswood *Newc* from 18. *14 Bentinck Road, Newcastle upon Tyne NE4 6UU* E: revd@chrisminchin.com

MINETT STEVENS, Mrs Christina Noelle. b 68. Hull Univ BSc 92 Sheff Univ BA 14. Coll of Resurr Mirfield 12. **d** 14 **p** 15. C Scarborough St Mary w Ch Ch and H Apostles *York* 14–17; V Hornsea, Atwick and Skipsea from 17. *The Vicarage, 9 Newbegin, Hornsea HU18 1AB* E: vicar@hornseabenefice.org

MINION, Canon Arthur. b 65. TCD BTh 92. CITC 89. **d** 92 **p** 93. C Bandon Union *C, C & R* 92–95; I Taunagh w Kilmactranny, Ballysumaghan etc *K, E & A* 95–99; I Shinrone w Aghancon etc *L & K* 99–08; I Crosspatrick Gp *C & O* 08–12; I Wexford and Kilscoran Union from 12; Can Ferns Cathl from 14. *The Rectory, Park, Co Wexford, Y35 X2T4, Republic of Ireland* T: (00353) (53) 914 0652 M: 86-825 1065 E: minionarthur@gmail.com

MINION, Hazel Elizabeth Alice. b 47. TCD BA 68 HDipEd 69. CITC 00. **d** 03 **p** 04. Aux Min Templebreedy w Tracton and Nohoval *C, C & R* 03–04; Aux Min Carrigaline Union from 04; Chapl Ashton Sch Cork 03–07. *22 Inchvale Drive,*

Shamrock Lawn, Douglas, Cork, Republic of Ireland T: (00353) (21) 436 1924 E: hminion22@hotmail.com

MINKKINEN, Mrs Janet Mary. b 63. Ox Brookes Univ BA 12. **d** 10 **p** 12. NSM Cippenham *Ox* 10–14; V from 14. *St Andrew's House, Washington Drive, Slough SL1 5RE* T: (01628) 661994 M: 07856-047960 E: janetminkkinen@hotmail.co.uk

MINNS, David Andrew. b 59. St Jo Coll Nottm 95. **d** 97 **p** 98. C Burpham *Guildf* 97–00; C Knaphill w Brookwood 00–04; R Ewhurst 04–17; R Churn Valley *Glouc* from 17. *The Rectory, Gloucester Road, Stratton, Cirencester GL7 2LJ* T: (01285) 655199 E: dlkminns@gmail.com

MINNS, Canon John Charles. b 42. EAMTC. **d** 85 **p** 86. NSM Heigham St Barn w St Bart *Nor* 85–91; P-in-c Nor St Geo Tombland 91–18; Asst Chapl Norfolk and Nor Health Care NHS Trust 92–95; Chapl Nor Sch of Art and Design 99–03; Hon Can Nor Cathl 05–18; rtd 18; PtO *Nor* from 19. *43 Bridgemaster Court, Wherry Road, Norwich NR7 1XG* T: (01603) 617736 M: 07951-434485 E: j.c.minns1942@gmail.com

MINTER, Miss Julie Louise. b 82. Ripon Coll Cuddesdon 15. **d** 18 **p** 19. C Cowplain *Portsm* from 18. *24 Wincanton Way, Waterlooville PO7 8NW* M: 07732-699448 E: julie_minter@hotmail.com

MINTERN, Mrs Juliette Melinda. b 55. Homerton Coll Cam CertEd 76 UEA BEd 77. Ripon Coll Cuddesdon 13. **d** 16 **p** 17. C Wokingham St Paul *Ox* 16–19; V Lambourn Valley from 19. *The Vicarage, 4 Newbury Street, Lambourn, Hungerford RG17 8PD* M: 07749-844600 E: julieuk98@aol.com *or* revjulie.mintern@lambournvalley.org

MINTON, Bernard John. b 68. St Chad's Coll Dur BA 89 Sheff Univ PhD 14 MRICS 00. Coll of Resurr Mirfield 00. **d** 04 **p** 05. C Lancing w Coombes *Chich* 04–08; TV Ouzel Valley *St Alb* from 08; RD Dunstable 14–19. *St Barnabas' Vicarage, Vicarage Road, Leighton Buzzard LU7 2LP* T: (01525) 372149 E: bernardminton@aol.com

MIR, Amene Rahman. b 58. Man Univ BA 81 PhD 93. Coll of Resurr Mirfield 81. **d** 83 **p** 84. C Walton St Mary *Liv* 83–87; Chapl Walton Hosp Liv 83–87; PtO *Man* 87–90; Asst Chapl Salford Mental Health Unit 90–94; Chapl Salford Mental Health Services NHS Trust 94–96; Chapl R Marsden NHS Trust 96–04; LtO *Lon* 96–04; PtO *S'wark* 96–04. *9 Mylne Close, Upper Mall, London W6 9TE* T: (020) 8741 7961 E: amenemir@ymail.com

MIRZANIA, Ms Bassirat Bibi. b 43. Tehran Univ MS 74 Thames Valley Coll of HE BSc 83. **d** 04 **p** 05. Chapl Persian Community UK and NSM Guildf Ch Ch w St Martha-on-the-Hill 04–13; rtd 13; PtO *Guildf* from 13. *Shiraz, 11 Nelson Gardens, Guildford GU1 2NZ* T: (01483) 569316 E: bassi.mirzania@btinternet.com

MITCHELL, Alec Silas. b 52. Man Univ BA 75 MPhil 95. N Bapt Coll 77 Coll of Resurr Mirfield 98. **d** 99 **p** 99. C Ashton *Man* 99–05; TV 05–07; P-in-c Haughton St Anne 07–18; Dioc Officer for Racial Justice 02–18; Borough Dean Tameside 10–18; C Denton Ch Ch 13–18; C Denton St Lawr 13–18; C Audenshaw St Steph 13–18; rtd 18. *Address temp unknown* M: 07436-589604

MITCHELL, Alison Jane. b 68. All SS Cen for Miss & Min. **d** 16 **p** 17. NSM Reddish *Man* from 16. *19 Finsbury Road, Stockport SK5 6EZ* T: 0161-442 3226 M: 07540-792409 E: alison@alisonmitchell.org.uk

MITCHELL, Andrew Patrick (Paddy). b 37. English Coll Valladolid 59 Ripon Coll Cuddesdon 84. **d** 64 **p** 65. In RC Ch 64–85; C Woolwich St Mary w St Mich *S'wark* 85–87; V E Wickham 87–94; P-in-c Walsall St Andr *Lich* 94–00; TV Sedgley All SS *Worc* 00–03; rtd 03; PtO *Birm* 03–04 and 05–07. *714 Pershore Road, Selly Oak, Birmingham B29 7NR* T: 0121-415 5828 E: paddy3739@hotmail.co.uk

MITCHELL, Anne-Marie. b 57. **d** 13 **p** 14. NSM Camberley St Mich Yorktown *Guildf* from 13. *13 Verran Road, Camberley GU15 2ND* T: (01276) 682802

MITCHELL, Anthony. b 54. St Jo Coll Nottm 05. **d** 07 **p** 08. C Plas Newton w Ches Ch Ch 07–10; P-in-c Halton from 10. *27 Halton Brow, Halton, Runcorn WA7 2EH* T: (01928) 563636 E: vicar@haltonparish.org.uk

MITCHELL, Ashley. *See* MITCHELL, Christopher Ashley

MITCHELL, Mrs Brenda Margaret. b 53. Leeds Univ BA 06. NOC 03. **d** 06 **p** 07. C Golcar *Wakef* 06–10; P-in-c Oldham Moorside *Man* 10–16; rtd 16. *20 Oakfield Drive, Baildon, Shipley BD17 6AW* T: (01274) 596202 E: brenda_m_mitchell@hotmail.com

MITCHELL, Christian Strang. b 72. Ripon Coll Cuddesdon 12. **d** 14 **p** 15. C Uckfield *Chich* 14–17; V Heathfield from 17. *Heathfield Vicarage, Hailsham Road, Heathfield TN21 8AF* T: (01435) 862744 M: 07796-008426 E: revchristianmitchell@gmail.com

MITCHELL, Christopher Allan. b 51. Newc Univ BA 72. Oak Hill Th Coll 82. **d** 84 **p** 85. C Guisborough *York* 84–87; C Thornaby on Tees 87–88; TV 88–92; V Dent w Cowgill *Bradf* 92–98; R Barney, Fulmodeston w Croxton, Hindringham etc *Nor* 98–03; R Hulland, Atlow, Kniveton, Bradley and Hognaston *Derby* 03–11; RD Ashbourne 09–11; rtd 11; PtO *York* from 12. *42 Melton Avenue, York YO30 5QG* T: (01904) 623872 E: pennychris51@btinternet.com

MITCHELL, Christopher Ashley. b 69. Leeds Univ BA(Econ) 91. Ridley Hall Cam 92. **d** 95 **p** 96. Min Can St As Cathl 95–98; CF 98–02; Chapl RAF from 02. *Chaplaincy Services (RAF), HQ Air Command, RAF High Wycombe HP14 4UE* T: (01494) 496800 E: ashley.mitchell258@mod.uk

MITCHELL, Canon David George. b 35. QUB BA 56. Sarum Th Coll 59. **d** 61 **p** 62. C Westbury-on-Trym H Trin *Bris* 61–64; C Cricklade w Latton 64–68; V Fishponds St Jo 68–77; RD Stapleton 76–77; TR E Bris 77–87; R Syston 87–94; V Warmley 87–94; P-in-c Bitton 87–94; R Warmley, Syston and Bitton 94–01; RD Bitton 87–93; Hon Can Bris Cathl 87–01; rtd 01; P-in-c Chedworth, Yanworth and Stowell, Coln Rogers etc *Glouc* 01–09; AD Northleach 04–09; PtO *Bris* from 01; *Glouc* from 15. *32 Flower Way, Longlevens, Gloucester GL2 9JD* T: (01452) 500119 E: canongeorgemitchell@btinternet.com

MITCHELL, Preb David Norman. b 35. Tyndale Hall Bris 64. **d** 67 **p** 68. C Marple All SS *Ches* 67–70; C St Helens St Helen *Liv* 70–72; V S Lambeth St Steph *S'wark* 72–78; P-in-c Brixton Road Ch Ch 73–75; SE Area Sec CPAS 78–81; R Uphill *B & W* 81–92; TR 92–01; Chapl Weston Area Health NHS Trust 86–01; Preb Wells Cathl *B & W* 90–10; rtd 01; PtO *B & W* from 02. *3 Pizey Close, Clevedon BS21 7TP* T: (01275) 349176 E: davidnmitchell@talktalk.net

MITCHELL, Canon Edwin. b 44. St Jo Coll Nottm BTh 74. **d** 74 **p** 75. C Worksop St Jo *S'well* 74–77; C Waltham Abbey *Chelmsf* 77–80; V Whiston *Liv* 80–91; R Rowmarsh Sheff 91–99; V Mortomley St Sav High Green 99–11; P-in-c Stocksbridge 06–07; AD Ecclesfield 01–07; Hon Can Sheff Cathl 07–11; rtd 11; PtO *Bradf* 12–14; *Leeds* from 14. *3 North View, Lothersdale, Keighley BD20 8EX* T: (01535) 631837 E: theedmitchell@gmail.com

MITCHELL, Elizabeth Edgar. b 43. **d** 14. NSM S Cheltenham *Glouc* from 14. *1 Coach House Mews, Commercial Street, Cheltenham GL50 2AU* T: (01242) 241311

MITCHELL, Elizabeth Jane. b 17. C Bath Abbey w St Jas *B & W* 16–19; V Sway *Win* from 19. *The Vicarage, Station Road, Sway, Lymington SO41 6BA*

MITCHELL, Geoffrey. b 36. SS Coll Cam BA 60 MA 64 Nottm Univ BA 97 CEng 66 FIMechE 76 FCIT 92. EMMTC 88. **d** 91 **p** 92. NSM Oaks in Charnwood and Copt Oak *Leic* 91–94; NSM Loughborough All SS w H Trin 94–00; P-in-c Oaks in Charnwood and Copt Oak 00–03; NSM Shepshed and Oaks in Charnwood 03–04; Dioc NSM Officer 98–02; rtd 04; PtO *Leic* from 04. *36 Brick Kiln Lane, Shepshed, Loughborough LE12 9EL* T: (01509) 502280 E: mitchell.household@talk21.com

MITCHELL, Geoffrey Peter. b 30. Liv Univ BEng 57 Man Univ MSc 68. Wells Th Coll 57. **d** 59 **p** 60. C Bradford cum Beswick *Man* 59–61; R Man St Pet Oldham Road w St Jas 61–64; LtO 64–68; Hon C Unsworth 68–86; V Woolfold 86–95; rtd 95; PtO *Man* from 95. *14 Redfearn Wood, Rochdale OL12 7GA* T: (01706) 638180 E: geoffrey@geoffreymitchell.plus.com

MITCHELL, George. *See* MITCHELL, David George

MITCHELL, Geraint Owain. b 71. Lincs & Humberside Univ BA 96 Leeds Univ BA. Coll of Resurr Mirfield 99. **d** 02 **p** 03. C Bridlington Em *York* 02–05; V Brigg, Wrawby and Cadney cum Howsham *Linc* from 05; V Bonby from 10; V Worlaby from 10. *The Vicarage, 10 Glanford Road, Brigg DN20 8DJ* T: (01652) 653989 E: briggvicarage@btinternet.com

MITCHELL, Gordon Frank Henry. b 26. FIFireE. Sarum & Wells Th Coll 74. **d** 77 **p** 78. NSM Alderbury and W Grimstead *Sarum* 77–91; NSM Alderbury Team 91–96; PtO 96–07 and from 14. *Seefeld, Southampton Road, Whaddon, Salisbury SP5 3EB* T: (01722) 710516 E: rev.mitchell@btinternet.com

MITCHELL, Mrs Helen Miranda. b 55. **d** 10 **p** 11. NSM Sudbury and Chilton *St E* 10–17; NSM Petersfield *Portsm* from 18. *9 Monks Orchard, Petersfield GU32 2JJ* T: (01730) 710682 E: helenoldvic@hotmail.com

MITCHELL, Ian. *See* MITCHELL, Stuart Ian

MITCHELL, Jane. *See* MITCHELL, Elizabeth Jane

MITCHELL, Karen Irene. b 68. Westcott Ho Cam 07. **d** 09 **p** 10. C Cheshunt *St Alb* 09–13; P-in-c Bridgemary *Portsm* 13–17; V from 17; P-in-c Elson 13–17; V from 17; AD Gosport from 16. *St Matthew's Vicarage, 7 Duncton Way, Gosport PO13 0FD* T: (01329) 829883 M: 07834-322943 E: karen.mitchell@talktalk.net

MITCHELL, Kevin. b 49. Newc Univ BSc 71 Ox Univ BA 83. Ripon Coll Cuddesdon 81. **d** 83 **p** 84. C Cantril Farm *Liv* 83–86; Chapl N Middx Hosp 86–90; C Gt Cambridge Road St Jo and St Jas *Lon* 86–90; P-in-c Cricklewood St Pet 90–96; V Whetstone St Jo 96–10; rtd 10. *32 Guildford Street, Brighton BN1 3LS* T: (01273) 203429 E: kevin.mitchell.49@googlemail.com

MITCHELL, Mrs Lisa Jane. b 71. Qu Foundn Birm 17. **d** 19. C W Bromwich All SS *Lich* from 19. *3 Tiverton Drive, West Bromwich B71 1DA* E: lisajmitchell26@outlook.com

MITCHELL, Owain. *See* MITCHELL, Geraint Owain

MITCHELL, Paddy. *See* MITCHELL, Andrew Patrick

MITCHELL, Rachel Elizabeth. b 60. St Jo Sch of Miss Nottm 14. **d** 17 **p** 18. C Radcliffe-on-Trent and Shelford *S'well* from 17. *2 Rockley Avenue, Radcliffe-on-Trent, Nottingham NG12 1AR* M: 07944-992178 E: revdremitchell@gmail.com

MITCHELL, Canon Richard John Anthony. b 64. St Martin's Coll Lanc 83 PGCE 86. Sarum & Wells Th Coll 88. **d** 91 **p** 92. C Kendal H Trin *Carl* 91–95; TV Kirkby Lonsdale 95–04; P-in-c Badgeworth, Shurdington and Witcombe w Bentham *Glouc* 04–09; R 09–16; AD Glouc N 04–09; AD Severn Vale 09–16; Hon Can Glouc Cathl 10–16; Can Res Glouc Cathl from 16. *4A Millers Green, Gloucester GL1 2BN* E: richard.mitchell@talk21.com

MITCHELL, Robert Hugh. b 53. Ripon Coll Cuddesdon. **d** 82 **p** 83. C E Dulwich St Jo *S'wark* 82–86; C Cambridge Gt St Mary w St Mich *Ely* 86–90; Chapl Girton Coll Cam 86–90; Asst Chapl Win Coll 90–91; Asst Chapl Addenbrooke's NHS Trust 91–93; Chapl Portsm Hosps NHS Trust 93–95; Chapl Mental Health Chapl Portsm Health Care NHS Trust 93–95; Chapl R Free London NHS Foundn Trust 95–14; PtO *Lon* from 14. *The Undercroft, Stoneleigh Abbey, Kenilworth CV8 2LF* E: roberthughmitchell@mac.com

MITCHELL, Robert McFarlane. b 50. Man Univ BA 72 Lambeth STh 92. Wycliffe Hall Ox 73. **d** 75 **p** 76. C Tonbridge SS Pet and Paul *Roch* 75–80; CF 80–08; P-in-c Tillington *Chich* 08–17; P-in-c Duncton 08–17; P-in-c Upwaltham 08–17; rtd 17. *11 Cross Bank, Skipton BD23 6AH* M: 07530-852896 E: bobandjillmitchell@gmail.com

MITCHELL, Mrs Sally. b 58. St Aug Coll of Th. **d** 19. NSM W Grinstead *Chich* from 19. *26 Little Bridges Close, Southwater, Horsham RH13 9HH*

MITCHELL, Sarah Rachel. *See* TAN, Sarah Rachel

MITCHELL, Stephen Andrew John. b 56. Ch Ch Coll Cant CertEd 78 K Coll Lon AKC 77 BD 80 MA 02 Lambeth STh 90 Heythrop Coll Lon MTh 05 PhD 10. Coll of Resurr Mirfield 80. **d** 82 **p** 83. C Chatham St Steph *Roch* 82–87; C Edenbridge 87–91; V from 91; P-in-c Crockham Hill H Trin 91–14; Chapl Invicta Community Care NHS Trust 91–06; Chapl Kent & Medway NHS and Soc Care Partnership Trust from 06. *The Vicarage, Mill Hill, Edenbridge TN8 5DA* T: (01732) 862258 F: 864335 E: ssppvicarage@hotmail.com

MITCHELL, Canon Stephen John. b 51. Ex Univ BA 73 Fitzw Coll Cam BA 78 MA. Ridley Hall Cam 76. **d** 79 **p** 80. C Gt Malvern St Mary *Worc* 79–81; Prec Leic Cathl 82–85; R Barrow upon Soar w Walton le Wolds 85–02; P-in-c Gazeley w Dalham, Moulton and Kentford *St E* 02–04; V Dalham, Gazeley, Higham, Kentford and Moulton 05–16; P-in-c Mildenhall 14–16; RD Mildenhall 14–16; Min Can St E Cathl 05–10; Hon Can St E Cathl 10–16; rtd 16. *93 Bantocks Road, Great Waldingfield, Sudbury CO10 0XT* T: (01787) 370416 E: smitch4517@aol.com

MITCHELL, Stuart Ian. b 50. Wadh Coll Ox BA 71 DPhil 74. S'wark Ord Course 81. **d** 85 **p** 87. NSM Charlton St Luke w H Trin *S'wark* 85–86; NSM Kidbrooke St Jas 86–88; NSM Newbold w Dunston *Derby* 88–94; C 94–96; C Newbold and Gt Barlow 96–97; P-in-c Matlock Bank 97–03; RD Wirksworth 98–03; P-in-c Mackworth All SS 03–10; P-in-c Mugginton and Kedleston 03–10; P-in-c Kirk Langley 03–10; rtd 10; PtO *Derby* 10–18. *Old Stores, 138 Church Street, Braintree CM7 5LA* M: 07989-147158 E: sianmitchell050787@yahoo.com

MITCHELL, Wendy Mary. b 47. Glas Univ MA 70 Callendar Park Coll of Educn Falkirk PGCE 71. Trin Coll Bris 99. **d** 01 **p** 02. C Yatton Moor *B & W* 01–07; TV Parkham, Alwington, Buckland Brewer etc *Ex* 07–17; rtd 17; PtO *B & W* from 18; Dioc Chapl MU from 19. *25 St Michael's Gardens, South Petherton TA13 5BD* T: (01460) 249027 E: wendymarym@aol.com

MITCHELL-INNES, Canon Charles William. b 47. Pemb Coll Cam BA 69 MA 73. Sarum Th Coll 83. **d** 86 **p** 87. Asst Chapl Sherborne Sch 86–89; Chapl Milton Abbey Sch Dorset 90–96; Conduct Eton Coll 96–07; rtd 07; V of the Close Sarum Cathl 07–14; PtO from 14; Can and Preb Sarum Cathl from 13. *South Bank, South Street, Sherborne DT9 3LZ* T: (01935) 812656 E: charlesm-i@hotmail.com

MITCHELL-INNES, James Alexander. b 39. Ch Ch Ox BA 64 MA 66. Lon Coll of Div 65. **d** 67 **p** 68. C Cullompton *Ex* 67–71; Nigeria 71–75; P-in-c Puddletown w Athelhampton and Burleston *Sarum* 75–78; R Puddletown and Tolpuddle 78–82; V Win Ch Ch 82–92; V Titchfield *Portsm* 92–98; rtd 98; PtO *Win* from 99. *115 Battery Hill, Winchester SO22 4BH* T: (01962) 859039 E: jmitchellinnes@gmail.com

MITCHINSON, Canon Ronald. b 35. Westmr Coll Ox MA 91. Linc Th Coll 66. **d** 68 **p** 69. C Heworth St Mary *Dur* 68–72; C Banbury *Ox* 72–73; TV 73–76; New Zealand 76–82; TR Banbury *Ox* 82–86; RD Deddington 84–86; Ind Chapl 86–92; Hon Can Ch Ch 90–92; TV Brayton *York* 92–96; Sen Chapl Selby Coalfield Ind Chapl 92–96; rtd 96; PtO *York* 04–11. *2 The Cottages, The Green, Stillington, York YO61 1JY* T: (01347) 810064 E: ronmitchinson@mac.com

MITFORD, Bertram William Jeremy (Bill). b 27. Wells Th Coll 62. **d** 64 **p** 65. C Hollinwood *Man* 64–67; C Atherton 67–68; C Frome St Jo *B & W* 68–71; V Cleeve 72–74; V Cleeve w Chelvey and Brockley 74–79; Chapl HM Pris Shepton Mallet 79–92; C Shepton Mallet *B & W* 79–84; C Shepton Mallet w Doulting 84–92; rtd 92. *21 Monkton Road, Honiton EX14 1PZ* T: (01404) 42632

MITRA, Avijit (Munna). b 53. Keble Coll Ox BA 76. Ox NSM Course 84. **d** 88 **p** 89. NSM Abingdon *Ox* 88–96; Asst Chapl Abingdon Sch 88–96; Sen Chapl Ch Hosp Horsham 96–09; Asst Chapl and Hd Classics K Sch Roch 09–14; C S Gillingham *Roch* from 14. *26 Pear Tree Lane, Hempstead, Gillingham ME7 3PT* T: (01634) 375869 M: 07713-727708 E: avijit@mitra1953.plus.com

MITRA, Mrs Nicola Jane. b 54. St Hugh's Coll Ox BA 76 MA 81 PGCE 77. Ox Min Course 92. **d** 94 **p** 95. NSM Abingdon *Ox* 94–96; Asst Chapl Ch Hosp Horsham 96–08; Chapl Maidstone and Tunbridge Wells NHS Trust from 08; PtO *Roch* from 10. *26 Pear Tree Lane, Hempstead, Gillingham ME7 3PT* T: (01622) 224569 E: nicolamitra@nhs.net

MITSON, Mrs Carol Mae. b 46. SRN SCM. Oak Hill NSM Course 89. **d** 93 **p** 94. NSM Lawford *Chelmsf* 93–96; NSM Elmstead 96–98; NSM Harwich 96–98; NSM Dedham 98–00; PtO from 01. *Drift Cottage, The Drift, Dedham, Colchester CO7 6AH* T/F: (01206) 323116 E: johnandcarolmitson@talktalk.net

MITSON, Miss Joyce. b 37. Man Univ CertEd 64. Trin Coll Bris 77. **dss** 79 **d** 87 **p** 94. Wellington w Eyton *Lich* 79–85; Farnworth *Liv* 85–91; Par Dn 87–91; Team Dn Bilston *Lich* 91–94; TV 94; Lich Local Min Adv 91–94; C W Bromwich St Jas 94–97; C W Bromwich St Jas w St Paul 97–98; rtd 98; PtO *Man* 00–12. *13 Birkenhills Drive, Bolton BL3 4TX* T: (01204) 655081

MITTON, Canon Michael Simon. b 53. Ex Univ BA 75. St Jo Coll Nottm 76. **d** 78 **p** 79. C High Wycombe *Ox* 78–82; TV Kidderminster St Geo *Worc* 82–89; Dir Angl Renewal Min 89–97; Dep Dir Acorn Chr Foundn 97–03; Renewing Min Project Officer *Derby* 03–06; Miss and Min Development Adv 06–09; Dioc Fresh Expressions Adv 09–13; Fresh Expressions Officer 13–17; P-in-c Derby St Paul 09–19; Hon Can Derby Cathl 11–19; rtd 19. *264 Broadway, Derby DE22 1BN* T: (01332) 552448 E: michaelmitton@btinternet.com

MOAT, Terry. b 61. Nottm Univ BTh 92. Aston Tr Scheme 86 Linc Th Coll 88. **d** 92 **p** 93. C Caterham *S'wark* 92–96; Hon C Tynemouth Priory *Newc* 04–06; C Morpeth 06–09; V Choppington from 09. *The Vicarage, Scotland Gate, Choppington NE62 5SX* T: (01670) 822216

MOATE, Gerard Grigglestone. b 54. BA 82 Essex Univ PhD 14 FRSA 01. Oak Hill Th Coll 79. **d** 82 **p** 83. C Mildmay Grove St Jude and St Paul *Lon* 82–85; C Hampstead St Jo 85–88; P-in-c Pinxton *Derby* 88; V Charlesworth and Dinting Vale 88–95; V Dedham *Chelmsf* 95–15; RD Dedham and Tey 98–03; Chapl Bloxham Sch 15–17; PtO *Ox* from 15; *Lon* from 17; *Glouc* from 19. *27 Great Barrington, Burford OX18 4UR* M: 07906-357707 E: gerard@moate.org

MOATE, Phillip. b 47. RGN 70 RNT 75. NOC 87. **d** 90 **p** 91. NSM Upper Holme Valley *Wakef* 90–92; NSM Almondbury Deanery 92–94; NSM Honley *Wakef* 94–95; P-in-c Roos and Garton w Tunstall, Grimston and Hilston *York* 95–02; R Lockington and Lund and Scorborough w Leconfield 02–09; rtd 09; PtO *York* from 09. *58 Pilmar Lane, Roos, Hull HU12 0HN* T: (01964) 671321 E: phillipmoate@btinternet.com

MOATT, Canon Richard Albert. b 54. K Coll Lon BD 76 AKC 76. Linc Th Coll 80. **d** 81 **p** 82. C Egremont and Haile *Carl* 81–85; V Addingham, Edenhall, Langwathby and Culgaith 85–04; P-in-c Skirwith, Ousby and Melmerby w Kirkland 98–04; V Cross Fell Gp 04–13; RD Penrith 09–13; Hon Can Carl Cathl 10–13; R Lewes St Anne and St Mich and St Thos etc *Chich* from 13. *St Anne's Rectory,*

57 St Anne's Crescent, Lewes BN7 1SD T: (01273) 472545
E: moatt@btinternet.com

MOBBERLEY, Keith John. b 56. BA. Westcott Ho Cam. **d** 84 **p** 85. C Coventry Caludon *Cov* 84–87; C Kenilworth St Nic 87–92; V Keresley and Coundon 92–98; P-in-c Hatton w Haseley, Rowington w Lowsonford etc 98–00; R from 00. *North Ferncumbe Rectory, Hatton Green, Hatton, Warwick CV35 7LA* T: (01926) 484332

MOBBERLEY, Mrs Susan. b 57. Kent Univ BA 79. Westcott Ho Cam 81. **dss** 84 **d** 90 **p** 94. Coventry Caludon *Cov* 84–87; LtO 87–92; NSM Keresley and Coundon 92–98; NSM Hatton w Haseley, Rowington w Lowsonford etc from 98. *North Ferncumbe Rectory, Hatton Green, Hatton, Warwick CV35 7LA* T: (01926) 484332 E: sumob@tiscali.co.uk

MOBERLY (née McCLURE), Mrs Jennifer Lynne. b 62. Ball State Univ (USA) BSc 84. Cranmer Hall Dur 98. **d** 01 **p** 02. C Belmont *Dur* 01–07; C Belmont and Pittington 07–08; Chapl St Mary's Coll Dur from 09. *St Mary's College, Elvet Hill Road, Durham DH1 3LR* E: j.l.moberly@durham.ac.uk

MOBERLY, Richard Hamilton. b 30. Trin Hall Cam BA 53 MA 57. Cuddesdon Coll 53. **d** 55 **p** 56. C Walton St Mary *Liv* 55–59; C Kensington St Mary Abbots w St Geo *Lon* 59–63; R Chingola Zambia 63–66; V Kennington Cross St Anselm *S'wark* 67–73; TV N Lambeth 74–80; Ind Chapl 80–95; rtd 95; PtO *S'wark* 95–18. *Flat 2, 1 Chester Way, London SE11 4UT* T: (020) 7735 2233 E: richard@richardmoberly.org.uk

MOBERLY, Robert Walter Lambert. b 52. New Coll Ox MA 77 Selw Coll Cam MA 80 Trin Coll Cam PhD 81. Ridley Hall Cam 74. **d** 81 **p** 82. C Knowle *Birm* 81–85; Lect Dur Univ from 85; PtO *Dur* from 85. *Department of Theology, Abbey House, Palace Green, Durham DH1 3RS* T: 0191-334 3953 E: r.w.l.moberly@durham.ac.uk

MOBEY, Jonathan Lee. b 73. Pemb Coll Cam MA 95 St Edm Hall Ox BM, BCh 98 MRCGP 02. Wycliffe Hall Ox BA 07. **d** 08 **p** 09. NSM Ox St Andr 08–11; R Harwell w Chilton from 11. *The Rectory, Church Lane, Harwell, Didcot OX11 0EZ* T: (01235) 799376 E: rectora@harwellandchiltonchurches.org.uk

MOBSBY, Ian Jonathan. b 68. Leeds Univ BHSc 93 Anglia Ruskin Univ MA 06 SROT 93. EAMTC 00. **d** 04 **p** 05. C Westmr St Matt *Lon* 04–11; C St Mary Aldermary 11–12; P-in-c 12–15; P-in-c Camberwell St Luke *S'wark* from 15; Par Miss Enabler Woolwich Area from 15. *St Luke's Church, Chandler Way, London SE15 6DT* T: (020) 7703 4913 E: ian.mobsby@southwark.anglican.org

MOCK, David Lawrence. b 64. Whitman Coll Washington BA 86 Heythrop Coll Lon MTh 01. Trin Coll Bris BA 98. **d** 98 **p** 99. C Tadworth *S'wark* 98–01; P-in-c Sutton St Geo *Ches* 01–02; C Macclesfield Team 01–02; TV 02–17; P-in-c Barnton from 17; P-in-c Northwich St Luke from 18. *The Vicarage, Church Road, Barnton, Northwich CW8 4JH* T: (01606) 74358 E: revdavem@gmail.com

MOCK, Mrs Ruth Elizabeth. b 66. York Univ BA 87 Lon Inst of Educn MA 98. All SS Cen for Miss & Min 14. **d** 17 **p** 18. C Stretton and Appleton Thorn *Ches* from 17. *The Vicarage, Church Road, Barnton, Northwich CW8 4JH* T: (01606) 74358 E: mockvicar@gmail.com

MOCKFORD (née WATKINS), Mrs Betty Anne. b 45. Leeds Univ BA 66 Nottm Univ CertEd 67. EAMTC 94. **d** 97 **p** 98. C Ipswich St Aug *St E* 97–00; P-in-c Charsfield w Debach, Monewden, Hoo etc 01–06; rtd 06; PtO *St E* from 06. *Mirembe, 10 Castle Brooks, Framlingham, Woodbridge IP13 9SF* T: (01728) 724193 M: 07890-110741

MODY, Rohintan Keki. b 63. New Coll Ox BA 85 MA 88 Fitzw Coll Cam MPhil 05 Aber Univ PhD 08. Oak Hill Th Coll BA 00. **d** 00 **p** 01. C Wolverhampton St Luke *Lich* 00–03; C Virginia Water *Guildf* 08–11; P-in-c Throop *Win* 11–16; Lect Evang Th Coll of Asia from 17. *5 Hume Avenue, Parc Palais #03-04, Singapore 598753, Republic of Singapore* E: romody@hotmail.com

MOFFAT, Canon George. b 46. Edin Univ BD 77 Open Univ BA 87 Bradf Univ MA 04. Edin Th Coll 67. **d** 72 **p** 73. C Falkirk *Edin* 73–76; C Edin St Pet 76–81; Chapl Edin Univ 77–81; C Heston *Lon* 81–84; V S Elmsall *Wakef* 84–93; TR Manningham *Bradf* 93–07; R Bolton Abbey 07–12; Hon Can Bradf Cathl 02–12; rtd 12; Chapl to The Queen 00–16; PtO *Glouc* from 16. *Fir Cottage, The Stenders, Mitcheldean GL17 0JE* T: (01594) 543668 E: rev.g.moffat@gmail.com

MOFFAT, Richard Bruce. b 65. All SS Cen for Miss & Min 15. **d** 18 **p** 19. OLM Tottington *Man* from 18. *110 Summerseat Lane, Ramsbottom, Bury BL0 9TP*

MOFFATT, Joseph Barnaby. b 72. Fitzw Coll Cam BA 96 MA 99. Ripon Coll Cuddesdon MTh 99. **d** 99 **p** 00. C Cen Wolverhampton *Lich* 99–03; C Chelsea St Luke and Ch Ch *Lon* 03–09; V Teddington St Mary w St Alb from 09; P-in-c Teddington SS Pet and Paul from 16; AD Hampton from 14. *The Vicarage, 11 Twickenham Road, Teddington TW11 8AQ* T: (020) 8977 2767

MOFFATT, Ms Lorraine Susan. b 56. LCTP 12. **d** 15 **p** 16. NSM Sandylands *Blackb* 15–16; C 16–19; C Overton 17–19; V from 19. *St Helen's Vicarage, Chapel Lane, Overton, Morecambe LA3 3HU* T: (01524) 858234 E: lozmof55@gmail.com

MOFFATT, Canon Neil Thomas. b 46. Fitzw Coll Cam BA 68 MA 72. Qu Coll Birm 69. **d** 71 **p** 72. C Charlton St Luke w St Paul *S'wark* 71–74; C Walworth St Pet 74–75; C Walworth 75–77; V Dormansland 77–86; TR Padgate *Liv* 86–96; V 96–98; TR Thatcham *Ox* 98–10; AD Newbury 02–10; S Africa 10–11; Hon Can Ch Ch *Ox* 10–11; rtd 11; PtO *Ox* 11–18; *Cov* from 11. *7 Jeffs Close, Upper Tysoe, Warwick CV35 0TQ* T: (01295) 688030 E: revd.tom.moffatt@googlemail.com

MOFFETT-LEVY, Joanna. b 45. **d** 11 **p** 12. NSM Ox St Mich w St Martin and All SS 11–15; NSM Osney from 15. *15 Third Acre Rise, Oxford OX2 9DA* T: (01865) 862715 M: 07765-175164 E: jo.moffett-levy@virginmedia.com

MOGER, Canon Peter John. b 64. Mert Coll Ox BA 85 BMus 86 MA 89 St Jo Coll Dur BA 93 ARSCM 08 Hon FGCM 10. Cranmer Hall Dur 89. **d** 93 **p** 94. C Whitby *York* 93–95; Prec, Sacr and Min Can Ely Cathl 95–01; V Godmanchester 01–05; Nat Worship Development Officer Abps' Coun 05–10; PtO *Ely* 05–10; Sec Liturg Commn 09–10; Can Res and Prec York Minster 10–19; P-in-c Eoropaidh *Arg* from 19; P-in-c Stornoway from 19. *St Peter's House, 19 Churchill Drive, Stornoway HS1 2NP* M: 07970-694021 E: petermoger.stpeterstornoway@gmail.com

MOGHAL, Dominic Jacob. See MUGHAL, Dominic Jacob

MOGRIDGE, Christopher James. b 31. Culham Coll of Educn CertEd 62 LCP 70 FCollP 86. St Steph Ho Ox 93. **d** 94 **p** 95. NSM Wellingborough St Andr *Pet* 94–98; NSM Ecton 98–02; rtd 02; PtO *Pet* from 02. *April Cottage, Little Harrowden, Wellingborough NN9 5BB* T: (01933) 678412

MOIR, Canon Nicholas Ian. b 61. G&C Coll Cam BA 82 MA 86 Ox Univ BA 86 MA 91 Lon Univ MTh 92. Wycliffe Hall Ox 84. **d** 87 **p** 88. C Enfield St Andr *Lon* 87–91; Bp's Dom Chapl *St Alb* 91–94; Chapl St Jo Coll Cam 94–98; V Waterbeach and R Landbeach *Ely* 98–07; RD N Stowe 05–07; V Chesterton St Andr from 07; P-in-c Cambridge St Clem from 14; RD Cambridge N 11–14; Hon Can Ely Cathl from 12. *The Vicarage, 10 Lynfield Lane, Cambridge CB4 1DR* T: (01223) 303469 E: nicholas.moir@standrews-chesterton.org

MOLE, David Eric Harton. b 33. Em Coll Cam BA 54 MA 58 PhD 62. Ridley Hall Cam 55. **d** 59 **p** 59. C Selly Hill St Steph *Birm* 59–62; Tutor St Aid Birkenhead 62–63; Chapl Peterho Cam 63–69; Ghana 69–72; Lect Qu Coll Birm 72–76; Tutor USPG Coll of the Ascension Selly Oak 76–87; C Burton *Lich* 87–93; Chapl Burton Gen Hosp 90–93; Chapl Ostend w Knokke and Bruges *Eur* 93–98; rtd 98; PtO *Birm* from 99. *48 Green Meadow Road, Selly Oak, Birmingham B29 4DE* T: 0121-475 1589 E: susananddavidmole@yahoo.com

MOLE, Jonathan Roger. b 67. Jes Coll Cam BA 91 MA 94 Lon Univ MB, BS 94 MRCP 98 FRCA 00. St Mellitus Coll 17. **d** 19. C Gamston and Bridgford *S'well* from 19. *21 Melton Road, West Bridgford, Nottingham NG2 7NW*

0**MOLL, Christopher David Edward.** b 67. St Cath Coll Cam BA 89 MA 93 Covenant Th Sem St Louis DMin 17. Ridley Hall Cam 94. **d** 98 **p** 99. C Byker St Mark and Walkergate St Oswald *Newc* 98–02; C Eastrop *Win* 02–06; V Wembdon *B & W* from 07. *The Vicarage, 12 Greenacre, Wembdon, Bridgwater TA6 7RD* T: (01278) 423647 E: ed@sgw.org.uk

MOLL, Nicola. b 47. Bedf Coll Lon BA 69. TISEC 99. **d** 03 **p** 04. C Edin Gd Shep 03–17; C Edin St Salvador 03–06; TV 06–08; P-in-c 08–17; rtd 17; PtO *Edin* from 18. *9/3 Forth Street, Edinburgh EH1 3JX* T: 0131-558 3729 E: nicolamjmoll3@gmail.com

MOLL, Randell Tabrum. b 41. Lon Univ BD 65. Wycliffe Hall Ox 62. **d** 66 **p** 67. C Drypool St Columba w St Andr and St Pet *York* 66–70; Asst Chapl HM Pris Hull 66–70; Asst Master Hull Gr Sch 66–70; C Netherton *Liv* 70–74; C Sefton 70–72; Ind Chapl 70–74 and 92–99; Belgium 75–76; P-in-c Brockmoor *Lich* 76–81; Team Ldr Black Country Urban Ind Miss 76–81; Dir Chilworth Home Services 81–84; Asst Master Bp Reindorp Sch Guildf 84–90; France and Iraq 91; Chapl Sedbergh Sch 92; Sen Chapl Miss in the Economy (Merseyside) 92–99; Hon Can Liv Cathl 97–99; Chapl Campsfield Ho Immigration and Detention Cen 00–02; Sen Chapl Immigration Detention Services 01–02; Team Ldr Workplace Min *St Alb* 03–07; rtd 08; PtO *St Alb* from 08; *Ox* from 17. *Penn Cottage, Green End, Granborough, Buckingham MK18 3NT* T/F: (01296) 670970 E: randellmoll@yahoo.co.uk

MOLLAN, Patricia Ann Fairbanks. b 44. QUB BSc 67 PhD 70 BD 97. **d** 97 **p** 98. Aux Min *D & D* from 97; Aux Min Lecale Gp 02–04; Dep Dir Ch's Min of Healing from 04. *Echo Sound,*

69 Killyleagh Road, Downpatrick BT30 9BN T: (028) 4482 1620 F: 9073 8665 E: pat@mollan.net

MOLLAN, Prof Raymond Alexander Boyce. b 43. QUB MB, BCh 69 BAO 69 MD 84 FRCS. CITC 97. **d** 97 **p** 98. Aux Min *D & D* from 97; NSM Comber 02–10; NSM Orangefield w Moneyreagh from 10. *Echo Sound, 69 Killyleagh Road, Downpatrick BT30 9BN* T: (028) 4482 1620 E: rab@mollan.net

MOLLER, George Brian. b 35. TCD BA 60 MA 64 Div Test 61 Lon Univ BD 84. **d** 61 **p** 62. C Belfast St Pet *Conn* 61–64; C Larne and Inver 64–68; P-in-c Rathcoole 68–69; I 69–86; Dioc Dir Ords 82–92; I Belfast St Bart 86–01; Chapl Stranmillis Univ Coll Belf 88–01; Preb Conn Cathl 90–96; Treas Conn Cathl 96; Prec Conn Cathl 96–98; Dean Conn 98–01; rtd 01. *Deneholme, 7 Sunningdale Park, Bangor BT20 4UU* T: (028) 9145 5903 E: gb@moller2.plus.com

MOLLOY, Mrs Heather. b 54. Bradf Univ BTech 76. **d** 95 **p** 96. OLM Harwood *Man* from 95; AD Walmsley 15–17. *7 Fellside, Bolton BL2 4HB* T: (01204) 520395 E: randhmolloy@hotmail.com

MOLONEY, Francis Deogratias. b 94. Staffs Univ BA 16. St Mellitus Coll 16. **d** 19. C Redditch H Trin *Worc* from 19. *120 Carthorse Lane, Redditch B97 6SZ* M: 07916-637923 E: francisdeogratiasmoloney@gmail.com

MOLONY, Canon Nicholas John. b 43. St Jo Coll Dur BA 67 Birm Univ MA 78 Fuller Th Sem California DMin 06. Qu Coll Birm 67. **d** 70 **p** 71. C Beaconsfield *Ox* 70–75; P-in-c Chesham Ch Ch 75–80; TV Gt Chesham 80–81; P-in-c Weston Turville 81–90; P-in-c Stoke Mandeville 87–89; P-in-c Gt Marlow 90–93; P-in-c Bisham 90–93; TR Gt Marlow w Marlow Bottom, Lt Marlow and Bisham 93–10; rtd 10; Hon Can Kimberley and Kuruman from 08; PtO *Ox* from 11. *9 Culverton Hill, Princes Risborough HP27 0DZ* T: (01844) 273895 E: nick.molony@btopenworld.com

MOLUDY, Omid. b 81. All SS Cen for Miss & Min. **d** 14 **p** 14. NSM Heatons *Man* from 14; Miss Support P for Cultural Diversity from 15. *12 Neston Way, Handforth, Wilmslow SK9 3BX* M: 07590-363221 E: omidmoludy@gmail.com *or* omid.moludy@manchester.anglican.org

MOLYNEUX, Ms Tina Mercedes. b 68. Ox Min Course 07. **d** 10 **p** 11. NSM Burchetts Green *Ox* from 10. *1 Littlewick Place, Coronation Road, Littlewick Green, Maidenhead SL6 3RA* T: (01628) 822813 E: tina.molyneux@btconnect.com

MONAGHAN, Mrs Hilary Alice. b 78. Edin Univ MA 01 Cam Univ BA 04. Ridley Hall Cam 02. **d** 06 **p** 07. C Gerrards Cross and Fulmer *Ox* 06–10; NSM Clifton Ch Ch w Em *Bris* 12–13; NSM Malmesbury w Westport and Brokenborough 13–16; NSM Gt Somerford, Lt Somerford, Seagry, Corston etc 13–16; NSM Malmesbury and Upper Avon 16–17; Chapl Westonbirt Sch from 13; Asst Dioc Dir of Ords *Bris* from 12; PtO from 17. *St Edyth's Vicarage, Avonleaze, Bristol BS9 2HU* T: (01666) 881382 E: alicemon7@gmail.com

MONAGHAN, John Emanuel. b 80. Carlow Coll BSc 02 UEA MSc 06. Trin Coll Bris 10. **d** 13 **p** 14. C Malmesbury w Westport and Brokenborough *Bris* 13–16; C Gt Somerford, Lt Somerford, Seagry, Corston etc 13–16; C Malmesbury and Upper Avon 16–17; V Sea Mills from 17. *St Edyth's Vicarage, Avonleaze, Bristol BS9 2HU* T: 0117-968 6965 M: 07791-684160

MONBERG, Canon Ulla Stefan. b 52. Copenhagen Univ BA 79. Westcott Ho Cam 88. **d** 90 **p** 94. C Westmr St Jas *Lon* 90–94; Dean Women's Min and Area Dir of Ords Cen Lon 94–99; Dean Women's Min Kensington 94–99; C Paddington St Jo w St Mich *Lon* 96–98; P-in-c S Kensington H Trin w All SS 98–02; Dir of Ords Two Cities Area 99–02; Denmark from 02; Dioc Adv for Women's Min *Eur* 04–05; Dioc Dir of Tr 05–16; Dioc Dir Minl Development from 16; Can Brussels Cathl *Eur* from 10. *Borgmester Jensens Alle 9, 2th, DK-2100 Copenhagen 0, Denmark* T: (0045) 3526 0660 E: ulla.monberg@churchofengland.org

MONDON, Simon Charles. b 57. WEMTC. **d** 02 **p** 03. OLM Worfield *Heref* 02–09; V Goodrich, Marstow, Welsh Bicknor, Llangarron etc 09–15; V Clun Valley from 15. *The Vicarage, Vicarage Road, Clun, Craven Arms SY7 8JG* M: 07805-784859 E: revsimon@btinternet.com

MONDS, Canon Anthony John Beatty. b 53. **d** 97 **p** 00. OLM Queen Thorne *Sarum* 97–04; C Sherborne w Castleton, Lillington and Longburton 04–06; V Piddle Valley, Hilton, Cheselbourne etc 06–15; Bp's Dom Chapl from 15; Can and Preb Sarum Cathl from 18. *25 Lime Kiln Way, Salisbury SP2 8RN* T: (01722) 334031 *or* 420942 E: bishops.chaplain@salisbury.anglican.org

MONEME, Dozie Chukwubulkem. b 79. W Africa Th Sem Lagos BA 10. **d** 08 **p** 10. Nigeria 08–11; PtO S'wark 11–13; C Orpington Ch Ch *Roch* 14–16; TV Eccleston Team *Liv* from 16. *St John's Vicarage, Crossley Road, St Helens WA10 3ND* M: 07915-530670 E: chuu200@yahoo.com

MONEY, John Charles. b 69. Wycliffe Hall Ox 01. **d** 03 **p** 04. C Porchester *S'well* 03–06; TV Plymouth St Andr and Stonehouse *Ex* 06–13; Chapl RN from 13. *Royal Naval Chaplaincy Service, Mail Point 1.2, Leach Building, Whale Island, Portsmouth PO2 8BY* T: (023) 9262 5055 F: 9262 5134 M: 07711-285217

MONEY, Mrs Lynn Astrid. b 59. St Martin's Coll Lanc BEd 80. WEMTC 03. **d** 06 **p** 07. C Letton w Staunton, Byford, Mansel Gamage etc *Heref* 06–09; R Bredenbury 09–14; TV Dunstable *St Alb* 14–18; R The Ashfords *Heref* from 18. *St Mary's House, Donkey Lane, Ashford Carbonel, Ludlow SY8 4DA* M: 07791-349406 E: revlynnmoney@gmail.com

MONGER, Paul James. b 54. Reading Univ BEd 77 Greenwich Univ MSc 99. NTMTC 07. **d** 10 **p** 11. NSM Chingford St Edm *Chelmsf* 10–15; PtO from 15. *64 Trinity Street, Shrewsbury SY3 7PD* M: 07739-905363 E: hampshireboy@ymail.com

MONIE, Rachel Jane. b 70. Sheff Univ BA 92 Chu Coll Cam BTh 17. Ridley Hall Cam 15. **d** 17 **p** 18. C Perranzabuloe and Crantock w Cubert *Truro* from 17; C St Agnes and Mount Hawke w Mithian from 17. *The Vicarage, 6 Penwinnick Parc, St Agnes TR5 0UQ* M: 07507-673575 E: rachel.monie@gmail.com

MONK, Carol Lorna. b 57. STETS 08. **d** 11 **p** 12. NSM Ash *Guildf* 11–15 and from 17; PtO 15–17. *The Hawthorns, 2 Rowhill Avenue, Aldershot GU11 3LU* T: (01252) 313239 E: carol.monk159@btinternet.com

MONK, Mrs Mary. b 38. CertEd 58. S'wark Ord Course 85. **d** 88 **p** 94. NSM Lee Gd Shep w St Pet *S'wark* 88–99; NSM Harpenden St Jo *St Alb* 99–07; rtd 07; PtO *St Alb* 07–19. *3 Hawthorn Close, Harpenden AL5 1HN* T: (01582) 462057

MONK, Paul Malcolm Spenser. b 65. Ex Univ BSc 86 PhD 90 Leeds Univ MA 07 CChem MRSC. NOC 05. **d** 07 **p** 08. C Oldham *Man* 07–09; TV Medlock Head 09–17; V Clarksfield and Waterhead from 17. *St Barnabas Vicarage, 1 Arundel Street, Oldham OL4 1NL* T: 0161-624 7708 M: 07854-776410 E: paul_and_jo_monk@yahoo.co.uk

MONK, Simon William Andrew. b 80. **d** 16 **p** 17. C Churchdown St Jo and Innsworth *Glouc* 16–19. *47 Elmbridge Road, Gloucester GL2 0NX* T: (01452) 526364 E: simonmonk47@gmail.com

MONK, Stephen David. b 74. Leuven Univ Belgium STB 03. Qu Coll Birm 05. **d** 00 **p** 01. C Knighton St Mary Magd *Leic* 06–08; C Wigston Magna 08–11; P-in-c Darley *Derby* 11–12; C S Darley, Elton and Winster 11–12; R Darley, S Darley and Winster from 12. *10 Normanhurst Park, Darley Dale, Matlock DE4 3BQ* T: (01629) 734257 E: rev.stephenmonk@btinternet.com

MONKHOUSE, William Stanley. b 50. Qu Coll Cam BA 72 MA 76 MB, BChir 75 Nottm Univ PhD 85 MA 06. EMMTC 04. **d** 06 **p** 07. C Wirksworth *Derby* 06–08; P-in-c Old Brampton 08–09; P-in-c Gt Barlow 08–09; P-in-c Old Brampton and Great Barlow 09–11; R 11; P-in-c Loundsley Green 09–11; Asst Dir of Ords 09–11; I Maryborough w Dysart Enos and Ballyfin *C & O* 11–14; Chapl Midlands and Portlaoise Pris 11–14; Chapl Midland Regional Hosp Portlaoise 11–14; V Burton St Aid and St Paul *Lich* from 14; V Burton St Modwen from 14. *The Vicarage, Rangemore Street, Burton-on-Trent DE14 2ED* T: (01283) 565570 E: wsmonkhouse@gmail.com

MONKS, Ian Kay. b 36. K Coll Lon BA 60 Lon Inst of Educn PGCE 61. Oak Hill NSM Course 90. **d** 93 **p** 94. NSM Woodford Bridge *Chelmsf* 93–06; PtO from 06. *46 Summit Drive, Woodford Green IG8 8QP* T: (020) 8550 2390 E: irquemonachi@hotmail.co.uk

MONMOUTH, Archdeacon of. See MASON, The Ven Thomas Henry Ambrose

MONMOUTH, Bishop of. See VANN, Cherry Elizabeth

MONMOUTH, Dean of. See TONGE, The Very Revd Lister

MONRO, Alexander James. b 55. Oriel Coll Ox BA 77 Lon Hosp MB, BS 80 MRCP 86 MRCGP 88. STETS 09. **d** 12 **p** 13. NSM Hunstanton St Mary w Ringstead Parva etc *Nor* 12–16; NSM Hunstanton St Edm w Ringstead from 16. *Manor Cottage, Church Place, Docking, King's Lynn PE31 8LW* T: (01485) 518342 E: alexander.monro@btinternet.com

MONTAGUE (née LAIDLAW), Mrs Juliet. b 52. Nottm Univ BTh 82. Linc Th Coll 78. **dss** 82 **d** 87 **p** 94. Gainsborough All SS *Linc* 82–86; Chapl Linc Cathl and Linc Colls of FE 86–92; Dn-in-c Gedney Hill and Whaplode Drove *Linc* 92–94; P-in-c 94–99; P-in-c Crawley and Littleton and Sparsholt w Lainston *Win* 99–03; R 03–08; R The Downs 08–13; Hon C Shedfield and Wickham *Portsm* from 13. *The Vicarage, 52 Brooklynn Close, Waltham Chase, Southampton SO32 2RZ* T: (01489) 895012 E: revdjuliet@gmail.com

MONTEITH, The Very Revd David Robert Malvern. b 68. St Jo Coll Dur BSc 89 Nottm Univ BTh 92 MA 93 Leic Univ Hon LLD 16. St Jo Coll Nottm 90. **d** 93 **p** 94. C Kings Heath *Birm*

93–97; C St Martin-in-the-Fields *Lon* 97–02; P-in-c S Wimbledon H Trin and St Pet *S'wark* 02–09; TR Merton Priory 09; AD Merton 04–09; Can Res and Chan Leic Cathl 09–13; Dean Leic from 13. *The Deanery, 23 St Martins, Leicester LE1 5DE* T: 0116-261 5356 M: 07952-238291 E: david.monteith@leccofe.org

MONTGOMERIE, Canon Alexander (Sandy). b 47. St Jo Coll Nottm 89. **d** 94 **p** 96. NSM Irvine St Andr LEP *Glas* from 94; NSM Ardrossan from 94; Dioc Ecum Relns Co-ord from 05; Can St Mary's Cathl from 16. *105 Sharphill Road, Saltcoats KA21 5QU* T/F: (01294) 465193 E: sandy.montgomerie@btinternet.com

MONTGOMERIE, Andrew Simon. b 60. Keble Coll Ox BA 82. Ridley Hall Cam 83. **d** 85 **p** 86. C Childwall All SS *Liv* 85–87; C Yardley St Edburgha *Birm* 87–90; TV Solihull 90–96; V Balsall Common 96–05; P-in-c Eyam *Derby* 05–11; C Baslow w Curbar and Stoney Middleton 06–11; R Baslow and Eyam 11–12; RD Bakewell and Eyam 07–12; R Iver Heath *Ox* from 12. *The Rectory, 2 Pinewood Close, Iver SL0 0QS* T: (01753) 654470 M: 07545-385629 E: asmontgomerie@hotmail.co.uk

MONTGOMERY, Canon Ian David. b 44. St Andr Univ LLB 66 Univ of the South (USA) DMin 02 FCA 69. Wycliffe Hall Ox 71. **d** 75 **p** 76. C Fulham St Dionis *Lon* 75–78; Chapl Amherst Coll USA 78–83; R New Orleans St Phil 83–93; R Nashville St Bart 92–97; R Menasha St Thos 97–09; rtd 09; SAMS Peru from 09; Can from 10. *Iglesia Anglicana del Perú, Calle Doña Maria 141, Surco, Lima 13, Peru* T: (001) (802) 428 4762 *or* (802) 463 2175 E: frianm@aol.com

MONTGOMERY (née YOUATT), Canon Jennifer Alison. b 49. St Aid Coll Dur BSc 70 Homerton Coll Cam PGCE 71. NOC 89. **d** 92 **p** 94. NSM Ripon H Trin 92–14; *Leeds* from 14; Warden of Readers from 99; Dioc Adv on Women's Min from 10; Hon Can Ripon Cathl 10–16. *12 Clotherholme Road, Ripon HG4 2DA* E: littlethorpe@btinternet.com

MONTGOMERY, Jennifer Susan. b 54. QUB MB, BCh 77 Leeds Univ MA 05. NOC 02. **d** 05 **p** 06. NSM Ackworth *Wakef* 05–10; P-in-c Goodshaw and Crawshawbooth *Man* 10–18; rtd 18; PtO *D & D* from 18. *15 Ballygelagh Road, Ardkeen, Newtownards BT22 1JQ* T: (028) 4273 8079 M: 07780-764233 E: jsm1954@hotmail.com

MONTGOMERY, Rachel. *See* TREWEEK, Rachel

MONTGOMERY, Timothy Robert. b 59. Hull Univ BA 82 Cam Univ PGCE 83. EAMTC 90. **d** 93 **p** 94. Dir Romsey Mill Community Cen *Ely* 93–94; NSM Cambridge St Phil 93–96; Chief Exec Kepplewray Cen Broughton-in-Furness 96–00; NSM Kendal St Thos *Carl* 96–00; V 00–13; Bp's Leadership and Strategy Adv 11–15; Hon Can Carl Cathl 06–15; Dir Miss Wigan *Liv* from 15. *Transforming Wigan, Wigan Investment Centre, Waterside Drive, Wigan WN3 5BA* T: (01942) 705260 M: 07985-290493 E: tim.montgomery@liverpool.anglican.org

MONTGOMERY, Archdeacon of. *See* WILSON, The Ven Barry Frank

MOODY, Canon Christopher John Everard. b 51. New Coll Ox BA 72 Lon Univ MSc 90. Cuddesdon Coll BA 74. **d** 75 **p** 76. C Fulham All SS *Lon* 75–79; C Surbiton St Andr and St Mark *S'wark* 79–82; Chapl K Coll Lon 82–87; V S Lambeth St Anne and All SS *S'wark* 87–95; RD Lambeth 90–95; P-in-c Market Harborough *Leic* 95–97; P-in-c Market Harborough Transfiguration 95–97; V Market Harborough and The Transfiguration etc 97–05; Hon Can Leic Cathl 04–05; V Greenwich St Alfege *S'wark* 05–19; Hon Can S'wark Cathl 18–19; rtd 19. *Address temp unknown* E: chrisjemoody@btinternet.com

MOODY, George Richard. b 65. Clare Coll Cam BA 88 MA 91 Ox Brookes Univ MA 14. Ripon Coll Cuddesdon 11. **d** 14 **p** 15. NSM Vale *Ox* 14–18; TV Three Valleys *Sarum* from 18. *The Rectory, Church Street, Yetminster, Sherborne DT9 6LG* T: (01935) 873214 E: revgeorgemoody@gmail.com

MOODY, Canon Ivor Robert. b 57. K Coll Lon BD 80 AKC Anglia Ruskin Univ MA 03. Coll of Resurr Mirfield. **d** 82 **p** 83. C Leytonstone St Marg w St Columba *Chelmsf* 82–85; C Leigh-on-Sea St Marg 85–88; V Tilbury Docks 88–96; Chapl Anglia Ruskin Univ 96–10; Hon Can Chelmsf Cathl 09–10; Vice-Dean and Can Res Chelmsf Cathl from 10. *83 Ridgewell Avenue, Chelmsford CM1 2GF* T: (01245) 267773 *or* 294493 E: vicedean@chelmsfordcathedral.org.uk *or* ivor.moody@chelmsfordcathedral.org.uk

MOODY, John Kelvin. b 30. St Fran Coll Brisbane ThL 55. **d** 56 **p** 57. C Warwick Australia 56–57; C Southport 57–58; C Dalby 58–61; C Earl's Court St Cuth w St Matthias *Lon* 61–64; Chapl Ankara *Eur* 64–69; Chapl Istanbul 64–66; Chapl Palma 69–75; Chapl Tangier 75–79; Can Gib Cathl 74–79; Hon Can Gib Cathl from 79; Australia from 79; rtd 01. *1 Short Street, Watsons Bay NSW 2030, Australia* T: (0061) (2) 9337 2871 E: jm986672@bigpond.net.au

MOOKERJI, Michael Manoje. b 45. Baring Union Coll Punjab BSc 69. Ridley Hall Cam 83. **d** 85 **p** 86. C Heanor *Derby* 85–92; V Codnor and Loscoe 92–93; V Codnor 93–02; V Winshill 02–15; C Hartshorne and Bretby 13–15; rtd 15; PtO *Derby* from 15; Retirement Chapl from 15. *1 Plymouth Walk, Church Gresley, Swadlincote DE11 9GU* T: (01283) 335582 M: 07481-765018 E: michael.mookerji@live.co.uk

MOON, John Charles. b 23. Sarum Th Coll 49. **d** 51 **p** 52. C Bottesford *Linc* 51–54; C Habrough 54–55; V Immingham 55–61; V Weaste *Man* 61–67; V Spalding St Jo *Linc* 67–82; V Spalding St Jo w Deeping St Nicholas 82–86; rtd 86; PtO *Linc* 87–02. *14 Harrox Road, Moulton, Spalding PE12 6PR* T: (01406) 370111

MOON, Nicola Jane. b 71. Bradf Univ BSc 94 Sheff Univ PhD 99. Ox Min Course 13. **d** 15 **p** 16. C Harbury and Ladbroke *Cov* 15–18; C Stoneleigh w Ashow 18–19; P-in-c from 19. *Forge Cottage, Hockley Lane, Ettington, Stratford-upon-Avon CV37 7SS* T: (024) 7641 5506 M: 07891-012660 E: njmoon@outlook.com

MOON, Preb Philip. b 59. CCC Ox BA 80 Warwick Univ PhD 92. Wycliffe Hall Ox BTh 01. **d** 01 **p** 02. C Otley *Bradf* 01–05; V Lt Aston *Lich* 05–16; V Bishopswood from 16; V Brewood from 16; Preb Lich Cathl from 18. *Brewood Vicarage, 15 Sandy Lane, Brewood, Stafford ST19 9ET* E: familyofmoon@aol.com

MOON, Canon Philip Russell. b 56. Em Coll Cam BA 78 MA 81 Reading Univ PGCE 79. Wycliffe Hall Ox BA 82. **d** 85 **p** 86. C Crowborough *Chich* 85–87; Hd of CYFA (CPAS) 87–94; V Lowestoft Ch Ch *Nor* 94–04; P-in-c Hove Bp Hannington Memorial Ch *Chich* 04–06; V from 06; RD Hove 05–08; Can and Preb Chich Cathl from 15. *82 Holmes Avenue, Hove BN3 7LD* T: (01273) 985219 E: phil@moons.org.uk

MOON, Sarah Ann. b 70. Huddersfield Univ BSc 93 Newc Univ PhD 97 PGCE 98. Lindisfarne Regional Tr Partnership 13. **d** 16 **p** 17. C Killingworth *Newc* from 16. *27 Mount Close, Killingworth, Newcastle upon Tyne NE12 6GE* M: 07762-111862 E: sarah@lleuad.co.uk

MOONEY, Mrs Julie. b 66. Cranmer Hall Dur 11. **d** 13 **p** 14. C Newc H Cross 13–16; TV Willington from 16. *Battle Hill Vicarage, Berwick Drive, Wallsend NE28 9ED* M: 07443-410781 E: m-jmooney@hotmail.com

MOONEY, The Very Revd Paul Gerard. b 58. St Patr Coll Maynooth BD 84 Asian Cen for Th Studies and Miss Seoul ThM 92 Protestant Th Faculty Brussels DrTheol 02. **d** 84 **p** 85. In RC Ch 84–90; Chapl Miss to Seamen Korea 90–94; Hon Can Pusan from 94; Asst Chapl Antwerp St Boniface *Eur* 94–97; C Galway w Kilcummin *T, K & A* 97–98; I New w Old Ross, Whitechurch, Fethard etc *C & O* 98–07; Hon Chapl New Ross and Waterford Miss to Seamen 98–07; Prec Ferns Cathl *C & O* 01–07; Adn Ferns 02–07; Chapl Seoul Cathl Korea 07–11; Dean Ferns *C & O* from 11; I Ferns w Kilbride, Toombe, Kilcormack etc from 11; Prec Ossory Cathl from 11; Prec Leighlin Cathl from 14. *The Deanery, Ferns, Enniscorthy, Co Wexford, Republic of Ireland* T: (00353) (53) 936 6124 E: pgmoon@hotmail.com

MOOR, Canon Simon Alan. b 65. Nottm Univ BTh 93. Linc Th Coll 90. **d** 93 **p** 94. C Skegness and Winthorpe *Linc* 93–96; C Airedale w Fryston *Wakef* 96–98; V Hoylandswaine and Silkstone w Stainborough 98–11; Bp's Adv for Ecum Affairs 08–11; V Huddersfield St Pet *Leeds* 11–19; Hon Can Wakef Cathl from 11; AD Huddersfield 17–19; Jt AD Kirkburton 18–19; R Bedale and Leeming and Thornton Watlass from 19. *The Rectory, North End, Bedale DL8 1AF* E: simoor@talktalk.net *or* simon.moor@leeds.anglican.org

MOORE, Albert William. b 47. WMMTC 91. **d** 94 **p** 95. C Hobs Moat *Birm* 94–98; V Dosthill 98–06; V Hill 06–13; rtd 13; PtO *Birm* from 13; *Derby* from 14; *Lich* from 19. *40 Main Street, Walton-on-Trent, Swadlincote DE12 8LZ* E: bill@fammoore.plus.com *or* billmoore313@gmail.com

MOORE, Anna. b 77. SEITE 14. **d** 16 **p** 17. C Reigate St Mark *S'wark* 16–19; R Betchworth and Buckland from 19. *Address temp unknown* M: 07939-388607

MOORE, Anthony Michael. b 71. Ex Univ BA 94 Leeds Univ BA 98 MA 99 PhD 10 Cam Univ MA 10. Coll of Resurr Mirfield 96. **d** 99 **p** 00. C Carnforth *Blackb* 99–03; Fell and Past Tutor Coll of Resurr Mirfield 03–04; C Wilton Place St Paul *Lon* 04–07; Chapl R Academy of Music 04–07; Chapl and Fell St Cath Coll Cam 07–12; Dean of Chpl 12; Can Res Lich Cathl 13–17; Vice-Dean 14–17; V Rottingdean *Chich* from 17. *The Vicarage, Steyning Road, Rottingdean, Brighton BN2 7GA* T: (01273) 281302 E: fr.anthony@stmargaret.org.uk

MOORE, Anthony Richmond. b 36. Clare Coll Cam BA 59 MA 63. Linc Th Coll 59. **d** 61 **p** 62. C Roehampton H Trin *S'wark* 61–66; C New Eltham All SS 66–70; P Missr Blackbird

Leys CD *Ox* 70–81; Dioc Ecum Officer 80–98; TV Dorchester 81–93; R Enstone and Heythrop 93–01; rtd 01; PtO *Ox* 01–14. *13 Cobden Crescent, Oxford OX1 4LJ* T: (01865) 244673 E: moore.t@which.net

MOORE, Arlene. b 64. Dundee Univ BSc 87 N Coll of Educn PGCE 90 TCD BTh 95. CITC 92. **d** 95 **p** 96. C Portadown St Mark *Arm* 95–99; PtO *Sheff* 99–02 and 03–09; C Crookes St Thos 02–03; Chapl Belfast Health and Soc Care Trust 09–10; P-in-c Monkstown *Conn* 09–16; P-in-c Rathcoole from 16. *25 Lindara Park, Larne BT40 2GD* T: (028) 2827 2082 M: 07450-284484 E: sendmyemails2me@yahoo.com

MOORE, Canon Bernard Geoffrey. b 27. New Coll Ox BA 47 MA 52. Ely Th Coll 49. **d** 51 **p** 52. C Chorley St Pet *Blackb* 51–54; Bp's Dom Chapl 54–55; C-in-c Blackpool St Mich CD 55–67; Chapl Victoria Hosp Blackpool 58–67; V Morecambe St Barn *Blackb* 67–81; R Standish 81–88; Hon Can Blackb Cathl 86–92; RD Chorley 86–92; V Charnock Richard 88–92; rtd 92; PtO *Ex* 92–00; *Carl* 01–10; *Win* 00–12. *16 Calgarth Park, Ambleside Road, Troutbeck Bridge, Windermere LA23 1LF* E: anammoore@hotmail.com

MOORE, Bernard George. b 32. Qu Coll Birm 57. **d** 60 **p** 62. C Middlesbrough St Columba *York* 60–62; C Kimberley Cathl S Africa 62–64; R Kimberley St Matt 64–69; Chapl RN 70–74; C Milton *Portsm* 74–76; V Glenfield New Zealand 76–80; V Kaitala 80–84; V Gisborne 84–86; rtd 92. *45 Feasegate Street, Manurewa 2102, New Zealand* T: (0064) (9) 267 6924 E: freesaxon2000@yahoo.com

✠**MOORE, The Rt Revd Bruce Macgregor.** b 31. Univ of NZ BA 55. Coll of Resurr Mirfield. **d** 57 **p** 58 **c** 92. C Blackpool St Steph *Blackb* 57–61; New Zealand from 61; Hon Can Auckland 78–96; Adn Manukau 81–90; Asst Bp Auckland 92–97. *5 Pokaka Crescent, Taupo 3330, New Zealand* T: (0064) (7) 378 4849 E: brucemoore@xtra.co.nz

MOORE, Caroline Judith. *See* FALKINGHAM, Caroline Judith

MOORE, Miss Catherine Joy. b 63. Bretton Hall Coll BEd 85 Anglia Poly Univ MEd 94. St Mellitus Coll BA 10. **d** 10 **p** 11. NSM Springfield All SS *Chelmsf* 10–13; NSM Chelmsf Cathl from 13. *33 Church Street, Witham CM8 2JP* T: (01376) 501128 M: 07860-459465 E: katejmoore@aol.com

MOORE, Charles David. b 59. Dundee Univ BSc 82 BArch 85 Open Univ MA 96 RIBA 86. St Jo Coll Nottm 91. **d** 93 **p** 94. C Deane *Man* 93–97; Crosslinks 98–02; R and Sub Dean Mutare Zimbabwe 98–02; R Bermondsey St Mary w St Olave, St Jo etc *S'wark* from 02. *The Rectory, 193 Bermondsey Street, London SE1 3UW* T: (020) 7357 0984

MOORE, Christopher Baden. b 58. **d** 12 **p** 13. NSM Stretton and Appleton Thorn *Ches* 12–14; C Stockport St Geo 14–15; V Over St Chad from 15. *The Vicarage, 1 Over Hall Drive, Winsford CW7 1EY* E: chrismoore58@aol.com

MOORE, Christopher John. b 73. Stirling Univ BA 95 K Coll Lon MA 98 PGCE 99 Anglia Ruskin Univ MA 13. Westcott Ho Cam 11. **d** 13 **p** 14. C Croydon St Jo *S'wark* 13–17; R Man Clayton St Cross w St Paul from 17. *The Rectory, 54 Clayton Hall Road, Manchester M11 4WH* M: 07793-144841 E: christophermoore100@hotmail.com

MOORE, Christopher Kevin William. b 69. Ox Brookes Univ BSc 92 Bris Univ BA 01 Trin Coll Bris PhD 10 MRICS 95. Bris Bapt Coll 98. **d** 09 **p** 10. C Tenbury *Heref* 09–11; P-in-c Fownhope w Mordiford, Brockhampton etc 11–13; R from 13; RD Heref 16–18. *The Rectory, Fownhope, Hereford HR1 4PS* T: (01432) 860365 E: chris@fownhoperectory.com

MOORE, Canon Colin Frederick. b 49. CITC 69. **d** 72 **p** 73. C Drumglass w Moygashel *Arm* 72–80; I Newtownhamilton w Ballymoyer and Belleek 80–15; Hon V Choral Arm Cathl 85–96; Can and Preb Arm Cathl 97–15; rtd 15; Asst Dioc and Prov Registrar *Arm* 96–09; Dioc and Prov Registrar from 09. *8 Willow Dean, Markethill, Armagh BT60 1QG* T: (028) 3755 1992 E: cf.moore@btinternet.com

MOORE, Darren Lee. b 73. Kingston Univ BEng 95. Oak Hill Th Coll BA 01. **d** 01 **p** 02. C Camberwell All SS *S'wark* 01–04; P-in-c Tranmere St Cath *Ches* 04–07; V 07–12. *104 St Fabian's Drive, Chelmsford CM1 2PR*

MOORE, Darren Richard. b 70. Univ of Wales (Abth) BD 91 Hull Univ PGCE 97 St Jo Coll York MA(Ed) 03 Leeds Univ MA 04. Coll of Resurr Mirfield 02. **d** 04 **p** 05. C Scarborough St Martin *York* 04–07; R Brayton 07–09; Chapl Ranby Ho Sch Retford 09–11; Asst Dir of Ords *Ripon* 12–14; *Leeds* 14–15; P-in-c Leeds Halton St Wilfrid 11–15; Chapl Barnard Castle Sch from 15. *Barnard Castle School, Newgate, Barnard Castle DL12 8UN* T: (01833) 696071 *or* 696043 M: 07545-657154 E: drm@barneyschool.org.uk

MOORE, David James Paton. b 60. Sheff Univ BSc 82. Cranmer Hall Dur 88. **d** 91 **p** 92. C Pemberton St Mark Newtown *Liv* 91–94; C St Helens St Helen 94–97; V Canonbury St Steph *Lon* 97–07; NSM Easton H Trin w St Gabr and St Lawr and

St Jude *Bris* 08–17; P-in-c from 17. *65 Chelsea Park, Bristol BS5 6AH* M: 07557-932304

MOORE, David Metcalfe. b 41. Hull Univ BA 64 PhD 69. Trin Coll Bris 76. **d** 78 **p** 79. C Marple All SS *Ches* 78–82; V Loudwater *Ox* 82–90; V Chilwell *S'well* 90–93; rtd 93; PtO *Ely* 05–16. *12 Rhugarve Gardens, Linton, Cambridge CB21 4LX* T: (01223) 894315 E: davidmmoore@mypostoffice.co.uk

MOORE, David Roy. b 39. Clare Coll Cam BA 61. Ripon Hall Ox 61. **d** 63 **p** 64. C Melton Mowbray w Thorpe Arnold *Leic* 63–66; C St Steph Walbrook and St Swithun etc *Lon* 66–72; Dep Dir The Samaritans 66–72; Public Preacher *S'well* 72–77; C Daybrook 77–80; V 80–87; V Ham St Andr *S'wark* 87–99; P-in-c Rothbury *Newc* 99–04; rtd 04; P-in-c Kneesall w Laxton and Wellow *S'well* 04–07. *Lily Cottage, Far Back Lane, Farnsfield, Newark NG22 8JX*

MOORE, Douglas Gregory. b 49. Bris Univ BA 71 CertEd 72. Coll of Resurr Mirfield 87. **d** 89 **p** 90. C Hessle York 89–93; P-in-c Micklefield w Aberford 93–95; V Aberford w Micklefield 95–04; P-in-c Darwen St Cuth w Tockholes St Steph *Blackb* 04–14; rtd 14; PtO *York* from 15. *53 Saxon Road, Whitby YO21 3NU* T: (01947) 602329 E: douglasgmoore@yahoo.co.uk

MOORE, David. b 51. Poly Cen Lon BA 73. ERMC 04. **d** 07 **p** 08. NSM Brackley St Pet w St Jas *Pet* 07–11; NSM Aston-le-Walls, Byfield, Boddington, Eydon etc from 11. *The New Vicarage, Parsons Street, Woodford Halse, Daventry NN11 3RE* T: (01327) 264927 E: geoff@ccvp.co.uk

MOORE, Geoffrey Robert. b 46. WEMTC 03. **d** 06 **p** 07. NSM Upton-on-Severn, Ripple, Earls Croome etc *Worc* from 06. *12 Hillview Gardens, Ryall, Upton-upon-Severn, Worcester WR8 0QJ* M: 07961-505871 E: moores.moorings@btinternet.com

MOORE, Gillian Mary. *See* MORGAN, Gillian Mary

MOORE, Mrs Hannah Térèse. b 74. UNISA BA 95 Rand Afrikaans Univ TDip 98. St Mellitus Coll BA 16. **d** 16 **p** 17. C Badshot Lea and Hale *Guildf* from 16. *195 Eton Place, Farnham GU9 0EG* T: (01252) 612414 M: 07748-983525 E: revd.hannah@gmail.com

MOORE, Henry James William. b 33. TCD BA 55 MA 70. **d** 56 **p** 57. C Mullabrack *Arm* 56–61; C Drumglass 61–63; I Clogherney 63–81; I Ballinderry, Tamlaght and Arboe 81–08; Can Arm Cathl 90–08; Chan 98–01; Prec 01–08; rtd 08. *20 Laragh Road, Beragh, Omagh BT79 0TH* T: (028) 8075 7384

✠**MOORE, The Rt Revd Henry Wylie.** b 23. Liv Univ BCom 50 Leeds Univ MA 72. Wycliffe Hall Ox 50. **d** 52 **p** 53 **c** 83. C Farnworth *Liv* 52–54; C Middleton *Man* 54–56; CMS 56–60; Iran 57–60; R Burnage St Marg *Man* 60–63; R Middleton 60–74; Home Sec CMS 74–80; Exec Sec CMS 80–83; Bp Cyprus and the Gulf 83–86; Gen Sec CMS 86–90; rtd 90; Asst Bp Dur 90–94; PtO *Heref* 94–16. *17 Fosbrooke House, 8 Clifton Drive, Lytham St Annes FY8 5RQ*

MOORE, Preb Hugh Desmond. b 37. St Cath Soc Ox BA 58 MA 64. St Steph Ho Ox 58. **d** 61 **p** 62. C Kingston St Luke *S'wark* 61–68; Asst Chapl Lon Univ 68–70; Chapl Edgware Community Hosp 70–92; Chapl Barnet and Chase Farm Hosps NHS Trust 92–99; V Hendon St Alphage *Lon* from 70; AD W Barnet 85–90; Preb St Paul's Cathl from 95. *The Vicarage, Montrose Avenue, Edgware HA8 0DN* T: (020) 8952 4611 E: hugh.moore@tesco.net

MOORE, Canon James Kenneth. b 37. AKC 62. St Boniface Warminster 62. **d** 63 **p** 64. C W Hartlepool St Oswald *Dur* 63–66; C-in-c Manor Park CD *Sheff* 66–76; TV Sheff Manor 76–78; R Frecheville and Hackenthorpe 78–87; V Bilham 87–91; V Sheff St Oswald 91–02; Hon Can Sheff Cathl 93–02; rtd 02; PtO *Sheff* from 02. *115 Greenhill Main Road, Sheffield S8 7RG* T: 0114-283 9634

MOORE (formerly BEVAN), Ms Janet Mary. b 46. Bris Poly CertEd 86. WMMTC. **d** 98 **p** 99. C Bishop's Cleeve *Glouc* 98–02; V Overbury w Teddington, Alstone etc *Worc* 02–08; Faith Co-ord Surrey Police *Guildf* 08–11; rtd 11; PtO *Glouc* from 15. *8 St John's Close, Cirencester GL7 2JA* T: (01285) 640077 E: therevjan@gmail.com

MOORE, Janis. b 47. **d** 05 **p** 06. OLM Bridport *Sarum* 05–17; PtO from 17. *61 North Allington, Bridport DT6 5DZ* T: (01305) 425644 E: janis@bridport-team-ministry.org

MOORE, John Arthur. b 33. Cuddesdon Coll 70. **d** 71 **p** 72. Hon C Gt Burstead *Chelmsf* 71–74; Chapl Barnard Castle Sch 74–97; rtd 97; PtO *Dur* from 96; *Ripon* 02–14; *Leeds* 14–16. *39 Woodside, Barnard Castle DL12 8DY* T: (01833) 690947 E: j.d.mooremoore@btinternet.com

MOORE, John Bishop. b 53. Haverford Coll (USA) BA 75 Columbia Univ MBA 78 Sheff Univ MA 18. ERMC. **d** 08 **p** 09. C Paris St Mich *Eur* 08–12; Asst Chapl 12–15; V Guernsey St Steph *Win* from 15. *St Stephen's Vicarage, Les Gravées, St Peter Port, Guernsey GY1 1RN* T: (01481) 720268 E: frjohnbishopmoore@gmail.com

MOORE, John Cecil. b 37. TCD BA 61 MA 67 BD 69. CITC 62. **d** 62 **p** 63. C Belfast St Matt *Conn* 62–65; C Holywood *D & D* 65–70; I Ballyphilip w Ardquin 70–77; I Mt Merrion 77–79; I Donaghcloney w Waringstown 79–02; Treas Dromore Cathl 90–93; Chan Dromore Cathl 93–02; rtd 02. *22 Kensington Court, Dollingstown, Craigavon BT66 7HU* T: (028) 3832 1606 E: canonjohnmoore@gmail.com

MOORE, John Henry. b 35. Nottm Univ BMus 56 CertEd 57 MA 61. EMMTC 87. **d** 90 **p** 91. NSM Gotham *S'well* 90–95; NSM Kingston and Ratcliffe-on-Soar 90–95; NSM Bunny w Bradmore 95–00; P-in-c 97–00; rtd 00. *19 Hall Drive, Gotham, Nottingham NG11 0JT* T: 0115-983 0670 E: revjhm@btinternet.com

MOORE, John Michael. b 48. Em Coll Cam BA 70 MA 73. Cuddesdon Coll 72. **d** 74 **p** 75. C Almondbury *Wakef* 74–78; TV Basingstoke *Win* 78–88; P-in-c Southampton St Alb 88–91; V Swaythling 91–99; rtd 99; Chapl St Jo Win Charity 99–11. *13 Priors Way, Winchester SO22 4HQ* T: (01962) 862341 *or* 854226 F: 840602 E: office@stjohnswinchester.co.uk

MOORE, Canon John Richard. b 45. Linc Th Coll 80. **d** 82 **p** 83. C Gt Grimsby St Mary and St Jas *Linc* 82–86; V Skirbeck Quarter 86–95; P-in-c Coningsby w Tattershall 95–99; R 99–06; R Bain Valley Gp 06–10; Can and Preb Linc Cathl 09–10; rtd 11; PtO *Linc* 15–18. *23 Church Lane, Hutton, Alford LN13 9RD* T: (01507) 490246 E: moorejr1605@btinternet.com

MOORE, Canon John Richard. b 35. Lambeth MA 01. St Jo Coll Nottm 56. **d** 59 **p** 60. C Northwood Em *Lon* 59–63; V Burton Dassett *Cov* 63–66; Dioc Youth Chapl 63–71; Dir Lindley Lodge Educn Trust Nuneaton 71–82; TR Kinson *Sarum* 82–88; Gen Dir CPAS 88–96; Hon Can Cov Cathl 95–01; Internat Dir ICS 96–01; rtd 01; PtO *Cov* 01–18. *2 Milligan Court, Merlin Way, Warwick CV34 6UG* T: (01926) 429299 E: moore.fam@tiscali.co.uk

MOORE, Joseph Andrew. b 92. K Coll Lon BA 15 St Jo Coll Dur BA 19. Cranmer Hall Dur 16. **d** 19. C Croydon St Jo *S'wark* from 19. *37 Alton Road, Croydon CR0 4LZ* M: 07984-277979 E: joe.moore@hotmail.com

MOORE, Canon Joyce. b 48. TCD BA 70 HDipEd 71 ARIAM 68. CITC 98. **d** 01 **p** 02. NSM Camlough w Mullaglass *Arm* 01–07; NSM Drogheda w Ardee, Collon and Termonfeckin from 07; Hon V Choral Arm Cathl 07–16; Can Arm Cathl from 16. *Dundalk Road, Dunleer, Co Louth, Republic of Ireland* T: (00353) (41) 685 1327 E: am.drogheda@armagh.anglican.org

MOORE, Margaret Louise. b 62. DipОТ 85. SAOMC 04. **d** 06 **p** 07. C Bp's Hatfield, Lemsford and N Mymms *St Alb* 06–10; C Letchworth St Paul w Willian 10–17; Chapl Garden Ho Hospice Letchworth 09–17; TR Sutton *Liv* from 17. *Sutton Rectory, 225 Gartons Lane, Clock Face, St Helens WA9 4RB* T: (01744) 602871 M: 07729-385830 E: louisemoore85@btinternet.com *or* suttonparish@btconnect.com

MOORE, Matthew Edward George. b 38. Oak Hill Th Coll 77. **d** 77 **p** 78. C Larne and Inver *Conn* 77–80; I Desertmartin w Termoneeny *D & R* 80–84; I Milltown *Arm* 84–96; I Culmore w Muff and Belmont *D & R* 96–06; Dioc Warden for Min of Healing 97–06; Can Derry Cathl 04–06; rtd 06. *90 Baronscourt Road, Newtownstewart, Omagh BT78 4EZ* M: 07598-840976 E: matt-audreymoore@hotmail.co.uk

MOORE, Canon Michael Mervlyn Hamond. b 35. Pemb Coll Ox BA 60 MA 63. Wells Th Coll 60. **d** 62 **p** 63. C Bethnal Green St Matt *Lon* 62–66; Chapl Bucharest w Sofia and Belgrade *Eur* 66–67; Asst Gen Sec C of E Coun on Foreign Relns 67–70; Gen Sec 70–72; Abp's Chapl on Foreign Relns *Cant* 72–82; Hon C Walworth St Pet *S'wark* 67–75; Hon C Walworth 75–80; Hon Can Cant Cathl 74–90; Chapl Chpl Royal Hampton Court Palace 82–99; Dep P in O 92–99; rtd 99. *The College of St Barnabas, Blackberry Lane, Lingfield RH7 6NJ* T: (01342) 872859 E: mmhm@collegeofstbarnabas.com

MOORE, Michael Peter John. b 60. Qu Coll Birm 05. **d** 08 **p** 09. C Pet St Mary Boongate 08–11; V from 11. *St Mary's Vicarage, 214 Eastfield Road, Peterborough PE1 4BD* T: (01733) 554815 E: revmichael@tiscali.co.uk

MOORE, Nicholas James. b 84. Magd Coll Ox BA 07 MSt 08 Keble Coll Ox DPhil 15. Wycliffe Hall Ox 09. **d** 14 **p** 15. C Stranton *Dur* 14–17; Tutor Cranmer Hall Dur from 17. *St John's College, 3 South Bailey, Durham DH1 3RJ* T: 0191-334 3894 M: 07969-393031 E: njmoore121@gmail.com *or* nicholas.j.moore@durham.ac.uk

MOORE, The Ven Paul Henry. b 59. Ball Coll Ox BA 82 DPhil 86. Wycliffe Hall Ox 87. **d** 89 **p** 90. C Ox St Andr 89–93; V Kildwick *Bradf* 93–01; V Cowplain *Portsm* 01–14; RD Havant 04–09; Hon Can Portsm Cathl 13–14; Adn for Miss Development *Win* from 14; Hon Can Win Cathl from

14. *2 Maldon Close, Eastleigh SO50 6BD* T: (023) 8065 0824 *or* (01962) 710964 E: paul.moore@winchester.anglican.org

MOORE, Philip. b 49. York Univ MA 71 Leeds Univ MA 05 PGCE 72. NOC 02. **d** 05 **p** 06. NSM Heworth Ch Ch *York* 05–09; P-in-c York St Thos w St Maurice 09–14; PtO from 14. *14 Whitby Avenue, York YO31 1ET* T: (01904) 425250 E: phil.moore@stthomaswithstmaurice.org.uk

MOORE, Raymond. b 47. QUB BSc 70. **d** 87 **p** 88. Aux Min Belfast All SS *Conn* 87–95; NSM 95–96; Aux Min Kilmakee 96–04; P-in-c Drung w Castleterra, Larah and Lavey etc *K, E & A* 04–09; NSM Albert Park Australia 09–12; P-in-c Belfast St Simon w St Phil *Conn* from 13. *21 Kilwarlin Avenue, Hillsborough BT26 6LQ* T/F: (028) 9268 2789 M: 07746-583471 E: rev.raymond.moore@gmail.com

MOORE, Canon Richard Norman Theobald. b 39. St Andr Univ BSc 62 Lon Univ BD 66. Clifton Th Coll. **d** 66 **p** 67. C Stowmarket *St E* 66–69; C New Humberstone *Leic* 69–72; P-in-c Leic Martyrs 73; V 73–84; Chapl Manor Hosp Epsom 84–94; Chapl Surrey Oaklands NHS Trust 94–00; rtd 00; PtO *Guildf* 02–07; *St E* from 07; *Eur* 06–16; Can Dornakal India from 04. *9 Cranmer Cliff Gardens, Felixstowe IP11 7NH* T: (01394) 273889

MOORE, Richard William Robert. b 39. UCD BA 70 TCD HDipEd 71. CITC 98. **d** 01 **p** 02. Aux Min Drogheda w Ardee, Collon and Termonfeckin *Arm* 01–05; Aux Min Dundalk w Heynestown from 05; Aux Min Ballymascanlan w Creggan and Rathcor from 05. *Dundalk Road, Dunleer, Co Louth, Republic of Ireland* T: (00353) (41) 685 1327 E: richwmoore@yahoo.ie

MOORE, Robert Allen. b 32. Univ of the Pacific BA 54 Boston Univ STB 58 STM 59. **d** 63 **p** 63. USA 63–80; V Farington *Blackb* 80–83; TV Preston St Jo 83–85; P-in-c Fleetwood St Pet 85–87; V Leyland St Jas 87–97; rtd 97; PtO *Blackb* from 97. *19 Lea Road, Whittle-le-Woods, Chorley PR6 7PF* T: (01257) 265701

MOORE, Mrs Roberta. b 46. CITC 03. **d** 06 **p** 07. Aux Min Drung w Castleterra, Larah and Lavey etc *K, E & A* 06–09; NSM Albert Park Australia 09–12; P-in-c Belfast St Aid *Conn* from 13. *21 Kilwarlin Avenue, Hillsborough BT26 6LQ* T/F: (028) 9268 2789 M: 07746-583470 E: bobbiemoore1@gmail.com

MOORE, Robin Alan. b 42. Lon Univ BA 71 Garnett Coll Lon CertEd 75. S Dios Minl Tr Scheme 91. **d** 94 **p** 95. NSM Barcombe *Chich* 94–06; PtO from 07; *Portsm* from 18. *The Moorings, 6 Foxes Close, Sandown PO36 9AF* E: robin@starfish5.plus.com

MOORE, Robin Hugh. b 52. CertEd BEd QUB BD. **d** 84 **p** 85. C Derryloran *Arm* 84–86; C Knock *D & D* 86–89; Bp's C Belfast St Steph w St Luke *Conn* 89–94; I 94–96; I Whitehouse 96–03; Bp's C Belfast St Mary Magd 03–07; I Belfast St Mark from 07; P-in-c Belfast St Mary w H Redeemer from 12. *9 Sycamore Park, Newtownabbey BT37 0NR* T: (028) 9086 9569 E: moorerobin@sky.com

MOORE, Shaun Christopher. b 52. Open Univ BA 92 NE Lon Poly CertEd 75 K Coll Lon MA 10. NTMTC BA 08. **d** 08 **p** 09. NSM Leyton St Mary w St Edw and St Luke *Chelmsf* 08–11; TV Walthamstow 11–12; PtO 12–14; V Harold Hill St Geo from 14. *St George's Vicarage, Chippenham Road, Romford RM3 8HX* E: shaunmoore@freeola.com

MOORE, Simon Quentin. b 61. Sheff Univ BA 83 PGCE 84. St Jo Coll Nottm MA 99. **d** 00 **p** 01. C St Alb St Paul 00–03; TV Digswell and Panshanger 03–10; P-in-c Letchworth St Paul w Willian 10–13; V 13–17; C Sutton *Liv* from 17. *Sutton Rectory, 225 Gartons Lane, Clock Face, St Helens WA9 4RB* E: sqmoore@btinternet.com

MOORE, Thomas Sydney. b 50. St Paul's Coll Grahamstown 77. **d** 79 **p** 80. C Rondebosch St Thos S Africa 79–82; 83–84; C Bredasdorp 82–83; R Green Pt 84–88; C Bushey *St Alb* 97–08; C Aldershot St Mich *Guildf* 08–19; rtd 19. *3 College Court, Old Sticklepath Hill, Sticklepath, Barnstaple EX31 2BG* E: ts.moore@virgin.net

MOORE, William. *See* MOORE, Albert William

MOORE-BICK, Miss Elizabeth Mary. b 77. Qu Coll Cam BA 99 MA 03 Anglia Poly Univ BA 04 Brighton Univ PGCE. Westcott Ho Cam 02. **d** 05 **p** 06. C Hillingdon St Jo *Lon* 05–09; TV Clarendon *Sarum* 09–15; Chapl Salisbury Cathl Sch 15. *The Gore, West End, Herstmonceux, Hailsham BN27 4NZ* M: 07803-044217 E: lizmoore_bick@yahoo.co.uk

MOORE BROOKS, Dorothy Anne. b 66. York Univ BA 87 Hughes Hall Cam PGCE 88. Ridley Hall Cam 96. **d** 98 **p** 99. C S Kensington St Jude *Lon* 98–01; PtO 02–08; Chapl Gt Ormond Street Hosp for Children NHS Trust 02–08; NSM Hoddesdon *St Alb* 01–10; Chapl Isabel Hospice 08–10; Chapl Gt Ormond Street Hosp NHS Foundn Trust from 10; LtO Amersham Deanery 10–17; PtO *Lon* 14–18; *Ox* from 17. *Great Ormond*

Street Hospital, Great Ormond Street, London WC1N 3JH T: (020) 7813 8232 *or* (01494) 730876 E: moorebrooks@sky.com *or* dorothy.moorebrooks@gosh.nhs.uk

MOORES, Jonathan Ian. b 75. Glos Univ BA 10. Trin Coll Bris MA 12. **d** 12 **p** 13. C Denton Holme *Carl* 12–16; TV Atherton and Hindsford w Howe Bridge *Man* 16–19; TV New Bury w Gt Lever from 19. *Howe Bridge Rectory, Leigh Road, Atherton, Manchester M46 0PH* M: 07753-427329 E: youthmissioner@googlemail.com

MOORES, Samantha Jane. *See* DUDDLES, Samantha Jane

MOORHEAD, Preb Michael David. b 52. BSc BA. St Steph Ho Ox. **d** 83 **p** 84. C Kilburn St Aug w St Jo *Lon* 83–87; C Kenton 87–89; Chapl Cen Middx Hosp NHS Trust from 89; V Harlesden All So *Lon* from 89; P-in-c Willesden St Matt 92–02; Preb St Paul's Cathl from 13. *All Souls' Vicarage, 3 Station Road, London NW10 4UJ* T/F: (020) 8965 4988 E: frmichaelmoorhead@gmail.com

MOORHOUSE, Peter. b 42. Liv Univ BSc 64 Hull Univ CertEd. Linc Th Coll 79. **d** 81 **p** 82. C Horsforth *Ripon* 81–85; R Ackworth *Wakef* 85–96; Dep Chapl HM Pris Leeds 96–97; Chapl HM Pris Stocken 97–98; Chapl HM Pris Everthorpe 98–07; rtd 07; PtO *York* from 07. *65 Eastfield Lane, Dunnington, York YO19 5ND* T: (01904) 481055

MOORSOM, Canon Christopher Arthur Robert. b 55. Ox Univ BA. Sarum & Wells Th Coll 79. **d** 82 **p** 83. C Bradford-on-Avon H Trin *Sarum* 82–85; R Broad Town, Clyffe Pypard and Tockenham 85–89; V Banwell *B & W* 89–96; R Upper Stour *Sarum* 96–14; Prec and Can Res Derby Cathl 14–18; PtO *B & W* from 19. *31 Castle Street, Stogursey, Bridgwater TA5 1TG* E: chris@moorsom.co.uk

MORAN, Patricia Margaret. b 54. Dur Univ BA 77 PGCE 81 Loyola Univ MA 99 Newc Univ PhD 10. Lindisfarne Regional Tr Partnership 12. **d** 14 **p** 15. NSM Monkseaton St Mary *Newc* 14–18; P-in-c Bywell and Mickley from 18. *Bywell Vicarage, 9 Meadowfield Road, Stocksfield NE43 7PY* T: (01661) 842272 E: patmoran54@gmail.com

MORAY, Shena Alison. b 61. St Hild Coll 17. **d** 18 **p** 19. C Newby *York* from 18. *9 Green Lane, Scarborough YO12 6HL* M: 07576-443765 E: revmoray@gmail.com

MORAY, ROSS AND CAITHNESS, Bishop of. *See* STRANGE, The Most Revd Mark Jeremy

MORAY, ROSS AND CAITHNESS, Dean of. *See* SIMPSON, The Very Revd Alison Jane

MORBY, Preb Helen Mary. b 62. Wolv Univ BA 99. Ripon Coll Cuddesdon 99. **d** 01 **p** 02. C Lich St Chad 01–04; V Farnworth *Liv* 04–12; AD Widnes 05–07; Hon Can Liv Cathl 05–12; P-in-c Kinnerley w Melverley and Knockin w Maesbrook *Lich* 12–16; P-in-c Maesbury 12–16; R Kinnerley w Melverley, Knockin w Maesbrook and Maesbury 16–18; R Edgmond w Kynnersley and Preston Wealdmoors from 18; R Tibberton w Bolas Magna and Waters Upton from 18; Preb Lich Cathl from 18. *The Rectory, High Street, Edgmond, Newport TF10 8JR* E: rectory.kinnerley@btinternet.com

MORDECAI, Mrs Betty. b 27. Birm Univ BA 48 Cam Univ CertEd 49. Wycliffe Hall Ox 85. **dss** 86 **d** 87 **p** 94. Leamington Priors All SS *Cov* 86–89; Hon Par Dn 87–89; C Worc City St Paul and Old St Martin etc 89–94; rtd 94; PtO *Cov* from 00. *8 Swain Crofts, Leamington Spa CV31 1YW* T: (01926) 882001 E: bettyhoward@btinternet.com

MORDECAI, Thomas Huw. b 59. Bris Univ BA 81 St Jo Coll Dur BA 86 MA 92. Cranmer Hall Dur 83. **d** 87 **p** 88. C Gillingham St Mary *Roch* 87–90; Chapl Warw Sch 90–96; Chapl Giggleswick Sch 96–98; Chapl Westmr Sch and PV Westmr Abbey 98–01; Chapl Geelong Gr Sch Australia 02–04; Chapl Malvern Coll 05–07; Chapl K Wm's Coll Is of Man 07–12; PtO *Ox* 13–16; C Winkfield and Cranbourne 16–19; V from 19. *The Vicarage, Winkfield Street, Winkfield, Windsor SL4 4SW* M: 07961-430556 E: huwmordecai@hotmail.com *or* beneficeminister@gmail.com

MORE, Ajay Yohan. b 68. **d** 14 **p** 15. C Alperton *Lon* 14–17; C Ealing St Steph Castle Hill 17–18; C Greenhill St Jo from 18. *56 Devon Close, Perivale, Greenford UB6 7DR* T: (020) 7912 9173 M: 07868-662703 E: ajay_kavita@hotmail.com

MORE, Canon Richard David Antrobus. b 48. St Jo Coll Dur BA 70. Cranmer Hall Dur 70. **d** 72 **p** 73. C Macclesfield St Mich *Ches* 72–77; Chapl Lee Abbey 77–82; V Porchester *S'well* 82–96; RD Gedling 90–96; Bp's Dom Chapl *Chelmsf* 96–01; Dioc Dir of Ords 01–13; Dioc NSM Officer 01–13; Hon Can Chelmsf Cathl 96–13; rtd 13; PtO *Chich* from 14. *16 Russell Street, Chichester PO19 7EL*

MORELAND, Andrew John. b 64. St Jo Coll Nottm 09. **d** 11 **p** 12. C Bridlington Priory *York* 11–14; V Seamer w East Ayton 14–17; V Seamer, E Ayton and Cayton from 17. *The Vicarage, 3 Stockhill, Seamer, Scarborough YO12 4QG* T: (01723) 866284 M: 07784-020848 E: andrew.moreland@btinternet.com

MORETON, Harley. *See* MORETON, Philip Norman Harley

MORETON, Preb Mark. b 39. Jes Coll Cam BA 64 MA 68. Westcott Ho Cam 63. **d** 65 **p** 66. C Portsea All SS *Portsm* 65–70; C St Martin-in-the-Fields *Lon* 70–72; Chapl Jes Coll Cam 72–77; R Stafford St Mary and St Chad *Lich* 77–79; P-in-c Stafford Ch Ch 77–79; TR Stafford 79–91; P-in-c Marston w Whitgreave 77–79; V W Bromwich All SS 91–04; Preb Lich Cathl 99–04; rtd 04; PtO *Worc* from 05. *Rosemont, Dry Mill Lane, Bewdley DY12 2BL* T: (01299) 401965 E: moreton@fatbeehive.com

MORETON, Philip Norman Harley. b 28. Linc Th Coll. **d** 57 **p** 58. C Howden *York* 57–60; C Bottesford *Linc* 60–65; V Linc St Giles 65–70; V Bracebridge Heath 71–77; V Seasalter *Cant* 77–84; TV Whitstable 84–88; rtd 88; PtO *York* 96–06; *Linc* 15–18. *112 Grantham Road, Bracebridge Heath, Lincoln LN4 2QF* T: (01522) 534672 M: 07851-717891 E: moretonjosie@googlemail.com

MOREY, Miss Lydia Mary. b 66. Down Coll Cam BA 89 MA 92 Dur Univ BA 17 Lon Inst of Educn PGCE 90. Ridley Hall Cam 15 Trin Th Coll Singapore 16 Ox Min Course 17. **d** 18 **p** 19. NSM Swindon St Jo and St Andr *Bris* from 18. *10 Lion Mews, Newbury Street, Lambourn, Hungerford RG17 8YY* T: (01488) 724790 M: 07967-135403 E: moreylydiam@gmail.com

MORFILL, Mrs Mary Joanna. b 46. Seaford Coll of Educn TCert 67. STETS 01. **d** 04 **p** 08. NSM Swanmore St Barn *Portsm* 04–14; PtO from 14; Chapl MU from 12. *Whistlers, New Road, Swanmore, Southampton SO32 2PF* T: (01489) 878227 M: 07906-755145 E: mary@swanmore.net

MORGAN, Adrian. b 85. Univ of Wales (Abth) BA 06 MPhil 08 PhD 12 Peterho Cam BA 13 MA 18. Ridley Hall Cam 11. **d** 14 **p** 15. C Gorseinon *S & B* 14–17; P-in-c from 17; Chapl Gower Coll Swansea from 14; Dioc Ecum Officer *S & B* from 15. *The Vicarage, 40 Princess Street, Gorseinon, Swansea SA4 4US* T: (01792) 892849 E: adrian@stcath.org.uk

MORGAN, Mrs Adrienne Elizabeth. b 58. Liv Univ BA 80 PGCE 81. All SS Cen for Miss & Min 16. **d** 18 **p** 19. OLM Harwood *Man* from 18. *13 Fossgill Avenue, Bolton BL2 3FR* T: (01204) 598337 M: 07917-652955 E: aem13@btinternet.com

MORGAN, Alison Jean. b 59. Girton Coll Cam BA 82 MA 85 Darw Coll Cam PhD 86. EMMTC 93. **d** 96 **p** 97. NSM Oadby *Leic* 96–97; NSM Leic H Trin w St Jo 97–08; Dir Rooted in Jesus from 02; Thinker and Writer ReSource 04–16; Assoc Mathetes Trust from 17; PtO *B & W* from 08. *10 Dairy Close, Wells BA5 2ND* E: ajm@alisonmorgan.co.uk

MORGAN, Andrew Paul. b 80. **d** 14 **p** 15. C Trentham *Lich* 14–17; V Heref St Pet w St Owen and St Jas from 17. *The Vicarage, 102 Green Street, Hereford HR1 2QW* M: 07880-730295 E: vicar@spsj.org.uk

✠**MORGAN, The Rt Revd Barry Cennydd.** b 47. Lon Univ BA 69 Selw Coll Cam BA 72 MA 74 Univ of Wales PhD 86. Westcott Ho Cam 70. **d** 72 **p** 73 **c** 93. Chapl Bryn-y-Don Community Sch 72–75; C St Andrews Major w Michaelston-le-Pit *Llan* 72–75; Ed *Welsh Churchman* 75–82; Lect Th Univ of Wales (Cardiff) 75–77; Chapl and Lect St Mich Coll Llan 75–77; Warden Ch Hostel Ban 77–84; Chapl and Lect Th Univ of Wales (Ban) 77–84; In-Service Tr Adv *Ban* 78–84; Dir of Ords 82–84; Can Ban Cathl 83–84; TR Wrexham *St As* 84–86; Adn Meirionnydd *Ban* 86–93; R Criccieth w Treflys 86–93; Bp Ban 93–99; Bp Llan 99–17; Abp Wales 03–17; rtd 17. *Crud yr Allt, Westbourne Crescent, Cardiff CF14 2BL* T: (029) 2061 8458

✠**MORGAN, The Rt Revd Christopher Heudebourck.** b 47. Lanc Univ BA 73 Heythrop Coll Lon MTh 91. Kelham Th Coll 66. **d** 73 **p** 74 **c** 01. C Birstall *Leic* 73–76; Asst Chapl Brussels *Eur* 76–80; P-in-c Redditch St Geo *Worc* 80–81; TV Redditch, The Ridge 81–85; V Sonning *Ox* 85–96; Prin Berks Chr Tr Scheme 85–89; Dir Past Studies Ox Min Course 92–96; Dioc Can Res Glouc Cathl and Officer for Min 96–01; Area Bp Colchester *Chelmsf* 01–13; rtd 13; Hon Asst Bp Chich from 14. *6 Wellington Court, Grand Avenue, Worthing BN11 5AB* T: (01903) 246184 E: chrishmorgan47@gmail.com

MORGAN, Christopher Laurence John. b 66. **d** 12 **p** 13. NSM Stepney St Dunstan and All SS *Lon* 12–16; PtO 16–17; NSM Stoke Newington St Andr from 17; PtO *S'wark* from 16. *13 Ursula Court, 146 Brownfield Street, London E14 6NF* M: 07894-099039

MORGAN, David Bramwell. b 82. Open Univ BA 08. Ripon Coll Cuddesdon BA 15. **d** 17 **p** 18. C Havant *Portsm* 17–19; V Soberton, Newtown and Hambledon from 19; C Meon Bridge from 19. *The Vicarage, Church Lane, Hambledon, Waterlooville PO7 4RT* M: 07590-008964 E: david.morgan@oxon.org

MORGAN, David Farnon Charles. b 43. Leeds Univ BA 68. Coll of Resurr Mirfield 68. **d** 70 **p** 71. C Swinton

St Pet *Man* 70–73; C Langley All SS and Martyrs 73–75; R Salford St Clem w St Cypr Ordsall 75–76; R Salford Ordsall St Clem 76–86; V Adlington *Blackb* 86–11; AD Chorley 98–04; rtd 11. *1 Holly Close, Farishes Lane, South Ferriby, Barton-upon-Humber DN18 6HG* T: (01652) 408500 E: morgyvic@talktalk.com

MORGAN, David Joseph. b 47. Bp Burgess Hall Lamp 66 St Deiniol's Hawarden 74. **d** 74 **p** 75. C Pembroke Dock *St D* 74–77; C Burry Port and Pwll 77–80; Miss to Seafarers 80–12; Sen Chapl and Sec Welsh Coun 85–12; rtd 12. *19 Clos Bevan, Gowerton, Swansea SA4 3GY* T: (01792) 923368

MORGAN, Canon Enid Morris Roberts. b 40. St Anne's Coll Ox BA 61 Univ of Wales (Ban) MA 73. United Th Coll Abth BD 81. **d** 84 **p** 97. C Llanfihangel w Llanafan and Llanwnnws etc *St D* 84–86; Dn-in-c 86–93; Dir Bd of Miss Ch in Wales 93–00; V Llangynwyd w Maesteg *Llan* 00–05; Hon Can Llan Cathl 02–05; rtd 05; PtO *St D* from 11. *Rhiwlas, Cliff Terrace, Aberystwyth SY23 2DN* T: (01970) 624648

MORGAN, Gareth Morison Kilby. b 33. Bris Univ BA 56. Cuddesdon Coll 57 Bangalore Th Coll. **d** 61 **p** 62. C St Helier *S'wark* 61–65; Chapl Scargill Ho 65–70; Dir RE *Linc* 71–74; Dioc Dir of Educn *St E* 74–81; TR Hanley H Ev *Lich* 81–89; TR Cen Telford 89–92; Warden Glenfall Ho *Glouc* 92–98; rtd 98; Chapl Hants Partnership NHS Trust 08–11; PtO *Win* 00–11; *Ely* from 12. *102 Lambs Lane, Cottenham, Cambridge CB24 8TA* T: (01954) 201696 E: morgan3341@virginmedia.com

MORGAN, Geoffrey. See MORGAN, James Geoffrey Selwyn

MORGAN, Gerwyn. See MORGAN, William Charles Gerwyn

MORGAN (formerly MOORE), Mrs Gillian Mary. b 70. NTMTC. **d** 09 **p** 10. NSM Harwich Peninsula *Chelmsf* 09–13; Chapl St Helena Hospice Colchester 13–19; NSM Lawford *Chelmsf* 15–17; NSM Lawford, Lt Bentley and The Bromleys 17–19; TV N Hinckford from 19. *The Vicarage, Gages Road, Belchamp St Paul, Sudbury CO10 7BT* T: (01787) 584993 M: 07875-982456 E: revgillmorgan@outlook.com

MORGAN, Glyn. b 33. Univ of Wales (Ban) BA 55 MA 69. Coll of Resurr Mirfield 55. **d** 57 **p** 58. C Dolgellau *Ban* 57–60; C Conway 60–63; V Corris 63–68; Hd of RE Friars' Sch Ban 69–70; LtO *Ban* 70–71; Hd of RE Oswestry Boys' Modern Sch 70–74; Hd of RE Oswestry High Sch for Girls 74–79; Hon C Oswestry H Trin *Lich* 71–79; Hd of RE Fitzalan Sch Oswestry 79–88; V Meifod and Llangynyw *St As* 88–01; RD Caereinion 89–01; rtd 01; PtO *St As* from 08. *Crib y Gwynt Annexe, Trefnanney, Meifod SY22 6XX* T: (01691) 828797

MORGAN, Graham. b 47. S'wark Ord Course. **d** 83 **p** 84. NSM S Kensington St Steph *Lon* 83–90; NSM Hammersmith H Innocents 90–02; NSM Bedford Park from 02. *24 Charleville Court, Charleville Road, London W14 9JG* T: (020) 7381 3211 E: grahammorgan1@btinternet.com

MORGAN, Henry. b 45. Hertf Coll Ox BA 68. Westcott Ho Cam 68. **d** 70 **p** 71. C Lee St Marg *S'wark* 70–73; C Newington St Paul 73–76; V Camberwell St Mich w All So w Em 76–84; V Kingswood 84–93; PtO 93–03; *Sheff* 03–11; *Worc* from 11. *2 Brook Cottage, Eckington Road, Birlingham, Pershore WR10 3DA* M: 07714-569375 E: henry.morgan10@btinternet.com

MORGAN, Ian Stephen. b 50. Open Univ BA 88. Sarum & Wells Th Coll 86. **d** 88 **p** 89. C Baldock w Bygrave *St Alb* 88–91; C S Elmham and Ilketshall *St E* 91–95; V Bungay H Trin w St Mary 95–05; R Lt Barningham, Blickling, Edgefield etc *Nor* 05–10; rtd 10. *Plessey Cottage, Oulton, Norwich NR11 6NX* T: (01263) 587535 M: 07808-451350 E: smorganciho@yahoo.co.uk

MORGAN, James Geoffrey Selwyn. b 59. Ex Univ BA 81 PGCE 82 Open Univ MPhil 97 K Coll Lon PhD 14. Cranmer Hall Dur 88. **d** 91 **p** 92. C Reading St Agnes w St Paul *Ox* 91–93; C Bromham w Oakley and Stagsden *St Alb* 94–95; PtO *Pet* 95–98; C Epsom St Martin *Guildf* 98–01; Tutor Ox Cen for Miss Studies 01–05; Lic Preacher *Ox* 01–05; PtO *Guildf* 01–17; Chapl Imp Coll Healthcare NHS Trust 11–13; Lead Chapl 13–16; Chapl N Middx Univ Hosp NHS Trust from 16. *North Middlesex University Hospital NHS Trust, North Middlesex Hospital, Sterling Way, London N18 1QX* T: (020) 8887 2000 M: 07796-315334 E: jgs_morgan@talktalk.net

MORGAN, Mrs Jane Elizabeth. b 60. Keele Univ MA 96. SNWTP 11. **d** 14 **p** 15. NSM Southport H Trin *Liv* 14–17; NSM Halsall, Lydiate and Downholland 17–18; P-in-c Newburgh w Westhead from 18. *19 Massams Lane, Formby, Liverpool L37 7BD* E: revjanemorgan@hotmail.com

MORGAN, John Laurence. b 41. Melbourne Univ BA 62 Oriel Coll Ox BA 69 MA 73 DPhil 76. **d** 68 **p** 69. Acting Chapl Oriel Coll Ox 69; and Chapl 70–76; USA 77–78; Australia 78–13; PtO *Ely* from 13; *Eur* from 14. *PO Box 918, Moe, VIC 3825, Australia* T: (0061) (3) 5127 3091 E: john.morgan@uq.edu.au

MORGAN, John William. b 51. **d** 15 **p** 16. NSM Tenby *St D* from 15. *Avalon, 80 Upper Hill Park, Tenby SA70 8JG* T: (01834) 843625 E: jmorg410@aol.com

MORGAN, John William Miller. b 34. Lon Univ BSc 56. Wycliffe Hall Ox 61. **d** 63 **p** 64. C St Alb Ch Ch 63–68; V Luton St Matt High Town 68–79; V Mangotsfield *Bris* 79–90; P-in-c Stanton St Quintin, Hullavington, Grittleton etc 90–95; R Hullavington, Norton and Stanton St Quintin 95–99; rtd 99; PtO *Bris* from 00. *3 Bouverie Park, Stanton St Quintin, Chippenham SN14 6EE* T: (01666) 837670 E: morganssq@tiscali.co.uk

MORGAN, Joseph. See MORGAN, David Joseph

MORGAN, Kathleen Irene. b 52. St Martin's Coll Lanc CertEd 74. WEMTC 93. **d** 96 **p** 97. NSM Barnwood *Glouc* 96–99; C Coney Hill 99–02; V Churchdown St Jo and Innsworth 02–14; rtd 14; PtO *Worc* from 15; *Glouc* from 14. *12 Pyke Road, Tewkesbury GL20 8DX* T: (01684) 298988 E: revkaty@aol.com

MORGAN, Linda Marianne. b 48. Bris Univ BSc 69 Surrey Univ MSc 72 Lon Univ PhD 77 FRCPath 01. STETS 99. **d** 02 **p** 03. NSM Claygate *Guildf* 02–18; PtO from 18. *8 Melbury Close, Claygate KT10 0EX* T: (01372) 462911 E: lindamorgan@holytrinityclaygate.org.uk

MORGAN, Mrs Marian Kathleen Eleanor. b 38. Birm Univ MA 94 FCMI 82. WEMTC. **d** 00 **p** 01. NSM Cusop w Blakemere, Bredwardine w Brobury etc *Heref* 00–03; P-in-c New Radnor and Llanfihangel Nantmelan etc *S & B* 03–07; rtd 08; Hon C Aberedw w Llandeilo Graban and Llanbadarn etc *S & B* 10–13; Hon C Bryngwyn and Newchurch and Llanbedr etc 10–13; PtO 13–16. *Carob Tree House, 4 Koukkoulas Street, Nata, 8525 Paphos, Cyprus* E: mkemorgan@btinternet.com

MORGAN, Mark Anthony. b 58. LLB. Chich Th Coll. **d** 84 **p** 85. C Thorpe St Andr *Nor* 84–87; C Eaton 87–90; V Southtown 90–92; PtO from 92. *Nethergate End, The Street, Saxlingham Nethergate, Norwich NR15 1AJ* T: (01508) 498003

MORGAN, Mark Steven Glyn. b 60. Essex Univ BSc 83 RGN 86. Ridley Hall Cam 95. **d** 97 **p** 99. C Herne Bay Ch Ch *Cant* 97–02; TV Ipswich St Mary at Stoke w St Pet and St Fran *St E* 02–18; rtd 18. *72 Cemetery Road, Ipswich IP4 2HZ*

MORGAN, Martin Paul. b 46. St Steph Ho Ox 71. **d** 73 **p** 74. C Kettering St Mary *Pet* 73–76; C Fareham SS Pet and Paul *Portsm* 76–80; V Portsea Ascension 80–94; V Rottingdean *Chich* 94–15; rtd 15; PtO *Chich* from 16. *116 The Welkin, Lindfield, Haywards Heath RH16 2PL*

MORGAN, Nicholas John. b 69. Surrey Univ MBus 91 Sheff Univ BA 15. Yorks Min Course 13. **d** 15 **p** 16. C Masham and Healey *Leeds* 15–18; P-in-c Bramham *York* from 18. *The Vicarage, Church Causeway, Thorp Arch, Wetherby LS23 7AE* T: (01937) 849471 or 844402 M: 07387-728009 E: revnjmorgan@gmail.com

MORGAN, Canon Nicholas John. b 50. K Coll Lon BD 71 AKC 71 CertEd. St Aug Coll Cant 72. **d** 73 **p** 74. C Wythenshawe Wm Temple Ch *Man* 73–76; C Southam w Stockton *Cov* 76–79; V Brailes 79–16; R Sutton under Brailes 79–16; P-in-c Tysoe w Oxhill and Whatcote 06–16; RD Shipston 90–98; Hon Can Cov Cathl 03–16; rtd 16. *21 Marshall Avenue, Shipston-on-Stour CV36 4HN*

MORGAN, Nicola. b 64. Nottm Univ BA 86. Linc Th Coll BTh 95. **d** 95 **p** 96. C Lillington *Cov* 95–98; C Gospel Lane St Mich *Birm* 98–01; P-in-c Gt Paxton *Ely* 01–05; P-in-c Lt Paxton 01–05; P-in-c Diddington 01–05; V The Paxtons w Diddington 05; PtO *Pet* 06–08; P-in-c Hallaton and Allexton, w Horninghold, Tugby etc *Leic* 08–12; R Quantock Coast *B & W* from 12. *The Rectory, High Street, Stogursey, Bridgwater TA5 1PL* T: (01278) 732873 E: nickymorgan25@btinternet.com

MORGAN, Philip. b 51. Lon Univ BSc 75 Univ of Wales (Cardiff) BD 78. St Mich Coll Llan 75. **d** 78 **p** 79. C Swansea St Nic *S & B* 78–81; C Morriston 81–83; C Swansea St Mary w H Trin 83–84; USA from 84. *17476 Hawthorne Avenue, Culpeper VA 22701-8003, USA* E: padre4u@hotmail.com

MORGAN, Canon Philip Brendan. b 35. G&C Coll Cam BA 59 MA 63. Wells Th Coll 59. **d** 61 **p** 62. C Paddington Ch Ch *Lon* 61–66; C Trunch w Swafield *Nor* 66–68; P-in-c Nor St Steph 68–72; Sacr Nor Cathl 72–74; Can Res and Sub-Dean St Alb 74–81; Hon Can St Alb 81–94; R Bushey 81–94; RD Aldenham 91–94; Can Res and Treas Win Cathl 94–01; rtd 01; PtO *Win* from 01. *9 Clifton Hill, Winchester SO22 5BL* T: (01962) 867549

MORGAN, Canon Reginald Graham. b 25. St D Coll Lamp BA 46 LTh 48. **d** 48 **p** 49. C Chirk *St As* 48–50; C Llangollen and Trevor 50–55; R Llanwyddelan w Manafon 55–66; V Rhuddlan 66–94; RD St As 78–94; Hon Can St As Cathl 83–89; Can St As Cathl from 89; rtd 94; PtO *St As* 10–13. *Manafon, 49 Ffordd Ffynnon, Rhuddlan, Rhyl LL18 2SP* T: (01745) 591036

MORGAN, Rhys Bryn. b 65. E Lon Univ BA 94. St Mich Coll Llan 00. **d** 02 **p** 03. C Carmarthen St Pet *St D* 02–05; P-in-c Cil-y-Cwm and Ystrad-ffin w Rhandir-mwyn etc 05–09; PtO *Birm* from 18. *9 Homecroft Road, Birmingham B25 8XN* M: 07393-327094 E: rhysbmorgan@gmail.com

MORGAN, Canon Richard Mervyn. b 50. Wadh Coll Ox BA 73 MA 75 K Alfred's Coll Win PGCE 74. **d** 92 **p** 93. CMS 85–94; Kenya 88–94; PtO *S'wark* 95–96; R Therfield w Kelshall *St Alb* 96–18; RD Buntingford 11–16; Tutor ERMC 99–11; Hon Can St Alb 14–18; rtd 18; PtO *Glouc* from 19. *9 Five Acres, Dursley GL11 4JP* T: (01453) 549062 E: therfieldrectory1@btinternet.com

MORGAN, Richard Thomas. b 70. Peterho Cam BA 91 MA 95. Wycliffe Hall Ox 94. **d** 96 **p** 97. C Bath Twerton-on-Avon *B & W* 96–99; Chapl Lee Abbey 99–01; R Marks Tey and Aldham *Chelmsf* 01–08; C Fisherton Anger *Sarum* 08–12; R Paoli USA from 12. *212 West Lancaster Avenue, Paoli PA 19301, USA* T: (001) (610) 644 4040 E: revrichardmorgan@googlemail.com

MORGAN, Robert Chowen. b 40. St Cath Coll Cam BA 63 MA 67. St Chad's Coll Dur 64. **d** 66 **p** 67. C Lancaster St Mary *Blackb* 66–76; Lect Th Lanc Univ 67–76; Fell Linacre Coll Ox from 76; Lect Th Ox Univ 76–97; Reader from 97; P-in-c Sandford-on-Thames Ox from 87. *Lower Farm, Sandford-on-Thames, Oxford OX4 4YR* T: (01865) 748848 E: robert.morgan@theology.ox.ac.uk

MORGAN, Roger William. b 40. Mert Coll Ox BA 62 Cam Univ MA 67. Ridley Hall Cam 80. **d** 81 **p** 82. NSM Cambridge St Paul *Ely* 81–84; V Corby St Columba *Pet* 84–90; V Leic H Trin w St Jo 90–08; C-in-c Leic St Leon CD 01–08; Hon Can Leic Cathl 06–08; Missr ReSource 08–16; Dir Mathetes Trust from 16; PtO *B & W* from 15. *10 Dairy Close, Wells BA5 2ND* T: (01749) 679865 E: rogerwmorgan@outlook.com

MORGAN, Russell Dean. b 80. R Agric Coll MSc 08. Ridley Hall Cam 15. **d** 17 **p** 18. C Cullompton *Ex* 17–19. *Postfach 11 29, 35001 Marburg, Germany* M: 07710-538111 E: russell.d.morgan@gmail.com

MORGAN, Stephen. *See* MORGAN, Ian Stephen

MORGAN, Stephen John. b 67. UEA BA 89 SS Coll Cam BA 02. Westcott Ho Cam 99. **d** 02 **p** 03. C Pitlochry and Kilmaveonaig *St And* 02–04; P-in-c E Knoyle, Semley and Sedgehill *Sarum* 05–08; P-in-c St Bartholomew 08–09; R 09–15; RD Chalke 12–15; Chapl RN 15–18; P-in-c Liskeard and St Keyne *Truro* 17; V from 17; RD W Wivelshire from 18. *The Rectory, Church Street, Liskeard PL14 3AQ* T: (01579) 347411 E: stevethevicar@gmail.com

MORGAN, Stephen Roy David. b 62. Qu Foundn (Course) 17. **d** 19. NSM Burntwood, Chase Terrace etc *Lich* from 19. *54 Lichfield Road, Walsall WS4 2DJ* M: 07305-852152 E: s.morgan12@virginmedia.com

MORGAN, Canon Steve Shelley. b 48. St Mich Coll Llan 67. **d** 71 **p** 72. C Llanharan w Peterston-super-Montem *Llan* 71; C Llandaff w Capel Llanilltern 71–74; C Neath w Llantwit 74–77; TV Merthyr Tydfil and Cyfarthfa 77–91; V Merthyr Tydfil Ch Ch 91–13; RD Merthyr Tydfil 93–04; Can Llan Cathl 98–13; rtd 13; PtO *Llan* from 14. *33 Parc Cwm Pant Bach, Merthyr Tydfil CF48 1TQ* T: (01685) 268571 M: 07870-241681 E: smorgan842@yahoo.com

MORGAN, Mrs Susan Dianne. b 53. Univ of Wales (Lamp) BA 74 Westmr Coll Ox PGCE 75. NOC 03. **d** 05 **p** 06. C Droylsden St Martin *Man* 05–07; P-in-c Kirkholt 08–13; rtd 13; PtO *Man* 13–14; Hon C Langley 14–15; NSM Rochdale 15–17; NSM Langley from 17. *Address withheld by request* M: 07837-706037 E: sue_morgan14@hotmail.com

MORGAN, Teresa Jean. b 68. Clare Coll Cam BA 90 MA 94 PhD 95 Oriel Coll Ox MA 98 BA 01 LRAM 91. SAOMC 00. **d** 02 **p** 03. NSM Littlemore *Ox* from 02. *Oriel College, Oxford OX1 4EW* T: (01865) 728807 E: teresa.morgan@oriel.ox.ac.uk

MORGAN, Mrs Victoria Louise. b 78. Ripon Coll Cuddesdon BA 16. **d** 17 **p** 18. C Havant *Portsm* 17–19; P-in-c Blendworth w Chalton w Idsworth from 19; P-in-c Rowlands Castle from 19. *The Vicarage, Church Lane, Hambledon, Waterlooville PO7 4RT* M: 07429-187233 E: vickiemorgan78@gmail.com

MORGAN, William Charles Gerwyn. b 30. Univ of Wales (Lamp) BA 52. St Mich Coll Llan 52. **d** 56 **p** 57. C Hubberston *St D* 56–62; V Ambleston w St Dogwells 62–68; Miss to Seamen 68–93; V Fishguard w Llanychar *St D* 68–84; V Fishguard w Llanychar and Pontfaen w Morfil etc 85–93; Can St D Cathl 85–93; Chan St D Cathl 91–93; rtd 93; PtO *St D* from 12. *Wrth y Llan, Pontycleifion, Cardigan SA43 1DW* T: (01239) 613943

MORGAN-GUY, John Richard. b 44. St D Coll Lamp BA 65 Univ of Wales PhD 85 Univ of Wales (Trin St Dav) DD 09 ARHistS 80 FRHistS 05 FRSM 81 FSA 18. St Steph Ho Ox 65.

d 67 **p** 68. C Canton St Cath *Llan* 67–68; C Roath St Sav 68–70; Chapl Llandough Hosp 70–71; C Machen and Rudry *Mon* 71–74; R Wolvesnewton w Kilgwrrwg and Devauden 74–80; PtO *B & W* 80–93; V Betws Cedewain and Tregynon and Llanwyddelan *St As* 93–97; RD Cedewain 97; Lect Univ of Wales (Lamp) 98–03 and 07–08; Research Fell 04–07; Research Fell Cen for Adv Welsh & Celtic Studies 99–04; Tutor Welsh Nat Cen for Ecum Studies Carmarthen 00–09; Hon Research Fell Univ of Wales (Trin St Dav) from 03; Chapl 13–15; PtO *St D* 10–16; Visiting Fell Ox Brookes Univ 10. *Tyngors, Silian, Lampeter SA48 8AS* T: (01570) 422710 E: j.morgan-guy@uwtsd.ac.uk or j.morgan-guy@uwstd.ac.uk

MORGAN-JONES, Canon Christopher John. b 43. Bris Univ BA 66 Chicago Univ MBA 68 McMaster Univ Ontario MA 69. Cuddesdon Coll 70. **d** 73 **p** 74. C Folkestone St Sav *Cant* 73–76; P-in-c Swalecliffe 76–82; V Addington 82–84; V Addington *S'wark* 85–92; RD Croydon Addington 85–90; V Maidstone All SS and St Phil w Tovil *Cant* 92–14; Hon Can Cant Cathl 99–14; rtd 14; PtO *Cant* from 14. *35 Shearwater Avenue, Whitstable CT5 4DX* T: (01227) 271172 E: cmorganjones1@gmail.com

MORGAN LUNDIE, Ben Robert. b 71. Univ Coll Lon BSc 93. Wycliffe Hall Ox 16. **d** 18 **p** 19. C Budock *Truro* from 18. *The Rectory, Old Church Road, Mawnan Smith, Falmouth TR11 5HY*

MORGANNWG, Archdeacon of. *See* SMITH, The Ven Christopher Blake Walters

MORGANS, Ms Jenny Louise. b 84. Birm Univ BA 05 Edin Univ MSc 09. Qu Coll Birm 12. **d** 16 **p** 17. C N Lambeth *S'wark* from 16. *12 Moat Place, London SW9 0TA* T: (020) 7095 1739 M: 07817-493336 E: jenny.morgans@gmail.com

MORIARTY, Patrick John. b 66. St Jo Coll Ox MA 88 K Coll Lon MA 95 PGCE 89 FRSA 16. ERMC 14. **d** 17 **p** 18. NSM E Barnet *St Alb* 17–18; NSM St Alb St Steph from 18. *73 Oxhey Avenue, Watford WD19 4HB* T: (01923) 816885 M: 07990-836956 E: father.patrick@myphone.coop

MORIARTY, Mrs Susan Margaret. b 43. Cartrefle Coll of Educn TCert 65. St As Minl Tr Course. **d** 02 **p** 09. Par Dn Gorsedd w Brynford, Ysgeifiog and Whitford *St As* 02–15; rtd 16; PtO *St As* from 16. *7 St Michael's Drive, Caerwys, Mold CH7 5BS* T: (01352) 720874 E: reverendsuecaerwys@hotmail.co.uk

MORING, Sally Margaret. b 61. St Martin's Coll Lanc BEd 84 Middx Univ BA 06. NTMTC 03. **d** 06 **p** 07. NSM Northolt St Mary *Lon* 06–09; V Hayes St Edm 09–17; R Wendover and Halton *Ox* from 17. *The Vicarage, 34A Dobbins Lane, Wendover, Aylesbury HP22 6DH* T: (01296) 696136 E: vicar@stmarywendover.org

MORISON, John Donald. b 34. ALCD 60. **d** 61 **p** 62. C Rayleigh *Chelmsf* 61–64; C St Austell *Truro* 64–67; V Meltham Mills *Wakef* 67–71; Youth Chapl *Cov* 71–76; S Africa 76–82; Can Port Elizabeth 80–82; Bardsley Missr 82–86; LtO *S'wark* 82–86; Dioc Missr *Derby* 86–99; V Quarndon 86–99; rtd 99; PtO *Sarum* 01–13. *Flat 1, Canford Place, 59 Cliff Drive, Canford Cliffs, Poole BH13 7JX* T: (01202) 709377 E: kayandjohn@waitrose.com

MORITZ, Michael Andreas Peter. b 82. Portsm Univ BSc 03 K Coll Lon PGCE 05. St Mellitus Coll BA 19. **d** 19. C Locks Heath *Portsm* from 19. *11 Laurel Road, Locks Heath, Southampton SO31 6QG* M: 07865-091517 E: mikemoritz82@gmail.com

MORLEY, Alison Ruth. b 67. Sarum Coll MA 13. STETS 05 Ripon Coll Cuddesdon 13. **d** 13 **p** 14. C Devizes St Jo w St Mary *Sarum* 13–15; P-in-c Upper Wylye Valley 15–18; R Seaview, St Helens, Brading and Yaverland *Portsm* from 18. *The Vicarage, Eddington Road, Seaview PO34 5EF* M: 07500-007437

MORLEY, Andrew John. b 69. Liv Jo Moores Univ BA 92. St Mellitus Coll BA 17. **d** 17 **p** 18. NSM Onslow Square and S Kensington St Aug *Lon* from 17; Pres World Vision Internat from 19. *The Dormer Cottage, Bridle Lane, Loudwater, Rickmansworth WD3 4JG* M: 07738-808999 E: andrewmorley0@gmail.com

MORLEY, Georgina Laura (George). b 63. Dur Univ BA 84 Nottm Univ MTh 95 PhD 99. Cranmer Hall Dur. **d** 03 **p** 03. Dir Studies NEOC 99–04; NSM Osmotherley w Harlsey and Ingleby Arncliffe *York* 03–08; Lect Cranmer Hall Dur 07–10; rtd 10. *Beacon Hill, High Street, Low Pittington, Durham DH6 1BE* T: 0191-372 0385

MORLEY, John. b 43. AKC 67. St Deiniol's Hawarden 67. **d** 68 **p** 69. C Newbold on Avon *Cov* 69–73; C Solihull *Birm* 73–77; C-in-c Elmdon Heath CD 76–77; Chapl RAF 77–93; TR Wallingford *Ox* 93–99; RD 95–99; Dean St Paul's Cathl and Chapl Nicosia 99–02; V Henlow and Langford *St Alb* 02–08; RD Shefford 06–08; rtd 08; PtO *Leic* 08–11 and from 13; *Pet* from 08; Chpln 11–13; P-in-c Gaulby *Leic* 11–12; Spiritual Dir Leic Angl Cursillo from 13. *31 Walcot Road, Market Harborough LE16 9DL* T: (01858) 419714 M: 07900-892566 E: revjmorley@talktalk.net

MORLEY, Keith. b 44. St Chad's Coll Dur BA 66 Open Univ BSc 93. **d** 67 **p** 68. C S Yardley St Mich *Birm* 67–70; C Solihull 70–73; V Shaw Hill 73–77; P-in-c Burton Coggles *Linc* 77–79; P-in-c Boothby Pagnell 77–79; V Lenton w Ingoldsby 77–79; P-in-c Bassingthorpe w Bitchfield 77–79; R Ingoldsby 79–87; RD Beltisloe 84–87; P-in-c Old Dalby and Nether Broughton *Leic* 87–94; RD Framland 88–90; rtd 04; PtO *Linc* 03–13. *10 Gracey Court, Woodland Road, Broadclyst, Exeter EX5 3GA*

MORLEY, Canon Leslie James. b 45. K Coll Lon BD 67 AKC 67 MTh 68. St Boniface Warminster 68. **d** 69 **p** 70. C Birm St Pet 69–72; C W Brompton St Mary *Lon* 72; C W Brompton St Mary w St Pet 73–74; Chapl Nottm Univ *S'well* 74–80; Dir Post-Ord Tr 80–85; Can Res and Vice-Provost S'well Minster 80–85; Hon Can S'well Minster 85–99; Chapl Bluecoat Sch Nottm 85–90; R Nottingham St Pet and St Jas *S'well* 85–99; AD Nottingham Cen 90–93; Dioc Rural Officer *Ripon* 99–10; Hon Chapl Yorks Agric Soc *York* from 09; rtd 10; PtO *Dur* from 13. *Beacon Hill, High Street, Low Pittington, Durham DH6 1BE*   T: 0191-372 0385   M: 07879-470752   E: leslie@lesliemorley.plus.com

MORLEY, Stephen Raymond. b 55. Birm Univ LLB 76. STETS 07. **d** 10 **p** 11. C Aisholt, Enmore, Goathurst, Nether Stowey etc *B & W* 10–14; V Bures w Assington and Lt Cornard *St E* from 14; RD Sudbury from 19. *The Vicarage, Church Square, Bures, Sudbury CO8 5AA*   M: 07723-786688   E: steve.morley@btinternet.com

MORLEY, Terence Martin Simon. b 49. SS Hild & Bede Coll Dur CertEd 78. St Steph Ho Ox 71. **d** 74 **p** 75. C Kingston upon Hull St Alb *York* 74–76; C Middlesbrough All SS 76–77; PtO *Dur* 77–78; Hon C Worthing St Andr *Chich* 78–80; C Brighton Ch 80–82; C Hove St Patr 80–82; C Ayr *Glas* 83–86; C Maybole 83–84; P-in-c Coatbridge 86–88; R 88–92; P-in-c 92; V Plymouth St Jas Ham *Ex* 93–09; Chapl Plymouth Community Services NHS Trust 96–98; rtd 09. *37 Great College Street, Brighton BN2 1HJ*

MORLEY, Trevor. b 39. Man Univ BSc 62 MPS 62 MRSPH 84. Ripon Hall Ox 65. **d** 67 **p** 68. C Compton Gifford *Ex* 67–70; Chapl Hammersmith Hosp Lon 70–83; Hon C N Hammersmith St Kath *Lon* 70–83; Chapl Univ Coll Hosp Lon 83–94; Chapl Univ Coll Lon Hosps NHS Trust 94–99; Chapl St Luke's Hosp for the Clergy 89–99; V Linthwaite *Wakef* 99–06; rtd 06; PtO *Sheff* from 06. *19 Queenswood Road, Sheffield S6 1RR*   T: 0114-232 5232   E: tmqwr@tiscali.co.uk

MORLEY-BUNKER, John Arthur. b 27. Wells Th Coll 67. **d** 68 **p** 69. C Horfield H Trin *Bris* 68–71; P-in-c Easton All Hallows 71–75; V 75–82; RD Bris City 74–79; V Horfield St Greg 82–93; rtd 93; PtO *Bris* 93–11. *1 Knoll Court, Knoll Hill, Bristol BS9 1QX*   T: 0117-968 5837

MORLEY-JONES, Anthony Roger. St Mich Coll Llan. **d** 04 **p** 05. NSM Cydweli and Llandyfaelog *St D* 04–12; P-in-c 12–15; rtd 15; PtO *St D* from 15. *11 Westhill Crescent, Cydweli SA17 4US*   T: (01554) 890458

MORPHY, George David. b 49. Birm Univ BEd 71 Lon Univ BA 75 Warwick Univ MA 90. WMMTC. **d** 89 **p** 90. NSM Ribbesford w Bewdley *Worc* 89–06; NSM Barbourne from 06; Dioc Dir of Educn 99–11. *41 Hallow Road, Worcester WR2 6BX*   T: (01905) 422007   M: 07867-525779   E: morphy611@btinternet.com

MORRALL, Heather Lynne. See COOKE, Heather Lynne

MORRELL, Mrs Jennifer Mary. b 48. NOC 84. **d** 87 **p** 94. Par Dn Crewe All SS and St Paul *Ches* 87–90; Par Dn Padgate *Liv* 90–94; C 94–95; TV Kirkby 95–00; V Croxteth Park 00–02; PtO *Arg* from 13; Welcome Cen Co-ord Iona Community 13–15. *5 Mellendean Farm Cottage, Kelso TD5 8HF*   M: 07880-757607   E: shazandjen@gmail.com

MORRELL, Paul Rodney. b 49. SRN 70. SWMTC 91. **d** 93 **p** 94. C Heavitree w St Paul 93–02; C Heavitree and St Mary Steps 02–05; TV 05–16; rtd 16. *9 Coburg Place, Cullompton EX15 1XN*

MORRELL, His Honour Peter Richard. b 44. Univ Coll Ox MA 71 Solicitor 70 Barrister-at-Law (Gray's Inn) 74. ERMC 06. **d** 08 **p** 09. NSM Uppingham w Ayston and Wardley w Belton *Pet* 08–10; NSM Nassington w Yarwell and Woodnewton w Apethorpe 10–12; PtO from 12. *New Sulehay Lodge, Nassington, Peterborough PE8 6QT*   T/F: (01780) 782281   M: 07860-573597   E: pmorrell@btinternet.com or petermorrell@sulehay.co.uk

MORRELL, Mrs Susan Marjorie. b 46. Open Univ BA 94. SEITE 93. **d** 96 **p** 97. NSM E Peckham and Nettlestead *Roch* from 96; Chapl Kent Coll Pembury 99–00. *7 Pippin Road, East Peckham, Tonbridge TN12 5BT*   T: (01622) 871150

MORRIS, Miss Alison Mary. b 58. W Midl Coll of Educn BEd 81 Wolv Univ PGCE 00 MA 02. Qu Coll Birm 06. **d** 09 **p** 10. NSM Pelsall *Lich* from 09. *32 Chestnut Road, Leamore, Walsall WS3 1BD*   T: (01922) 477734   M: 07837-649756

MORRIS, Mrs Ann. b 52. N Co Coll Newc CertEd 73. WEMTC 00. **d** 03 **p** 04. C Churchdown St Jo and Innsworth *Glouc* 03–07; P-in-c Barnwood 07–17; rtd 17. *5 Chaceley Close, Quedgeley, Gloucester GL2 4WW*

MORRIS (née SHAW), Mrs Anne. b 47. LMH Ox BA 69 MA 72 Lon Univ BD 82. NOC 01. **d** 03 **p** 04. NSM Leamington Priors All SS *Cov* 03–18; NSM Leamington Spa H Trin 03–18; rtd 18; PtO *Cov* from 18. *20 Hayle Avenue, Warwick CV34 5TW*   T: (01926) 403512 E: am.gm@hotmail.co.uk

MORRIS, Anne. See MORRIS, Margaret Anne

MORRIS, Anthony David. b 61. Aston Univ BSc 83. Qu Coll Birm 06. **d** 09 **p** 10. NSM Droitwich Spa *Worc* 09–13; NSM Stoke Prior, Wychbold and Upton Warren 13–14; P-in-c Bowbrook N from 14; P-in-c Bowbrook S from 14; NSM Stoke Prior, Wychbold and Upton Warren from 14. *The Parsonage, Church Lane, Tibberton, Droitwich WR9 7NW*   T: (01905) 345169   M: 07891-837194 E: revdm777@gmail.com

MORRIS, Beti Elin. b 36. CertEd 57. Sarum & Wells Th Coll 87. **d** 89 **p** 97. C Llangeitho and Blaenpennal w Betws Leucu etc *St D* 89–92; C-in-c Pencarreg and Llanycrwys 92–97; V 97–05; rtd 05. *Bro Mihangel, Maes y Tren, Felinfach, Lampeter SA48 8AH* E: betimorris345@btinternet.com

MORRIS, Catharine Mary. See MABUZA, Catharine Mary

MORRIS, Canon Christopher John. b 45. K Coll Lon AKC 67 BD 68. **d** 68 **p** 69. C W Bromwich All SS *Lich* 68–72; C Porthill 72–74; Min Can Carl Cathl 74–77; Ecum Liaison Officer BBC Radio Carl 74–77; Dioc Communications Officer *Carl* 77–83; V Thursby 77–83; Angl Adv Border TV from 82; V Upperby St Jo *Carl* 83–91; P-in-c Lanercost w Kirkcambeck and Walton 91–99; P-in-c Gilsland w Nether Denton 96–99; R Lanercost, Walton, Gilsland and Nether Denton 99–10; RD Brampton 98–05; Hon Can Carl Cathl 98–10; rtd 10; PtO *Carl* from 10. *15 Nook Lane Close, Dalston, Carlisle CA5 7JA*   T: (01228) 711872 E: chrisandmarjorie.morris@btinternet.com

MORRIS, David. See MORRIS, Anthony David

MORRIS, Preb David Meeson. b 35. Trin Coll Ox BA 56 MA 60. Chich Th Coll 57. **d** 60 **p** 61. C Westmr St Steph w St Jo *Lon* 60–65; Lib Pusey Ho 65–68; Chapl Wadh Coll Ox 67–68; C Sheff St Leon Norwood 68–69; Ind Chapl 68–72; C Brightside St Marg 69–72; R Adderley *Lich* 72–82; V Drayton in Hales 72–82; RD Tutbury 82–95; Chapl Burton Gen Hosp 82–90; P-in-c Burton St Modwen *Lich* 82; V Burton 82–99; Preb Lich Cathl 93–99; P-in-c Shobnall 94–99; rtd 99; PtO *Lich* 99–16; *Heref* from 99. *Watling House, All Stretton, Church Stretton SY6 6HH*   T: (01694) 722243

MORRIS, David Michael. b 59. Ox Univ MA 84 Cam Univ PGCE 91. Sarum & Wells Th Coll 82. **d** 84 **p** 85. C Angell Town St Jo *S'wark* 84–87; C Mitcham SS Pet and Paul *S'wark* 87–90; V Llandygwydd and Cenarth w Cilrhedyn etc *St D* 90–98; Lect Th St D Coll Lamp from 90; Hd RE Lampeter Comp Sch from 98. *Bronant, Rhydargaeau, Carmarthen SA32 7DR*

MORRIS, Canon David Pryce. b 39. St Mich Coll Llan 62. **d** 63 **p** 64. C Colwyn Bay *St As* 63–70; R St George 70–76; Dioc Children's Adv 75–87; V Bodelwyddan and St George 76–79; V Connah's Quay 79–95; St As Dioc Adult Lay Tr Team 88–06; Ed *St Asaph Diocesan News* from 89; Dioc Communications Officer *St As* 90–06; V Shotton 95–06; Hon Can St As Cathl 96–00; Can Cursal St As Cathl 00–06; rtd 07; PtO *St As* from 09. *7 Rhuddlan Road, Buckley CH7 3QA*   T: (01244) 540779   M: 07711-519752   E: daviddandpmorris@talktalk.net

MORRIS, David Thomas. Ban Univ BTh 07 Cardiff Univ MTh 10. St Mich Coll Llan. **d** 09 **p** 10. C Merthyr Tydfil St Dav and Abercanaid *Llan* 09–12; C Cardiff St Mary w St Dyfrig and St Samson 12–16; P-in-c Grangetown w Cardiff St Dyfrig and St Sansom from 16; Voc Adv from 13. *St Paul's Vicarage, Llannaes Street, Cardiff CF11 7LR*   T: (029) 2221 2177 E: dtmorris@sky.com

MORRIS, Dennis Gordon. b 41. ALCM 58. St D Coll Lamp. **d** 67 **p** 68. C Neath w Llantwit *Llan* 67–92; V Troedrhiwgarth 92–10; rtd 10. *12 Cwrt yr Hen Ysgol, Tondu, Bridgend CF32 9GE*

MORRIS, Mrs Elizabeth Anne. b 59. BA 05. **d** 00 **p** 01. OLM Darsham and Westleton w Dunwich *St E* 00–04; C Hadleigh, Layham and Shelley 04–06; C Yoxmere 08–09; Asst Chapl Aquitaine *Eur* from 10. *Maison Neuve, Plaisance, 24560 Issigeac, France*   T: (0033) 5 53 23 40 51   E: cookingcurate@gmail.com

MORRIS, Geoffrey. See MORRIS, Martin Geoffrey Roger

MORRIS, Geoffrey David. b 43. Fitzw Coll Cam BA 65 MA 69 Westmr Coll Ox DipEd 67. NOC. **d** 82 **p** 83. C Man Clayton St Cross w St Paul 82–85; V Lower Kersal 85–03; P-in-c Priors Hardwick, Priors Marston and Wormleighton *Cov* 03–08; Asst Chapl HM Pris Rye Hill 03–07; rtd 08; PtO *Cov* from 08. *20 Hayle Avenue, Warwick CV34 5TW*   T: (01926) 403512 E: am.gm@hotmail.co.uk

MORRIS, Hayley Jayne. b 64. **d** 16 **p** 17. OLM Gt Ilford St Andr *Chelmsf* from 16. *15 Mistley Thorn, 5 Cranbrook Rise, Ilford IG1 3QP* E: hayleyjaym@yahoo.co.uk

MORRIS, Preb Henry James. b 47. Lon Univ BSc 69. Wycliffe Hall Ox MA. **d** 79 **p** 80. C Woodford Wells *Chelmsf* 79–82; C Gt Baddow 82–87; R Siddington w Preston *Glouc* 87–01; RD Cirencester 97–01; TR Madeley *Heref* 01–12; Preb Heref Cathl 09–12; rtd 12; PtO *Lich* from 12. *2 Waveney Avenue, Perton, Wolverhampton WV6 7RA* T: (01902) 757797 E: henrym@dircon.co.uk

MORRIS (née LONG), Hermione Jane. b 66. Univ of Wales (Swansea) BSc 97 RGN 88. St Mich Coll Llan 05. **d** 07 **p** 08. C Bassaleg *Mon* 07–11; R Llanfyllin, Bwlchycibau and Llanwddyn *St As* 11–14; R Llanfyllin w Llanwddyn and Bwlchycibau 14–16; I Vyrnwy Miss Area from 17. *The Rectory, Coed Llan Lane, Llanfyllin SY22 5BW* T: (01691) 648306

MORRIS, Miss Jane Elizabeth. b 50. York Univ BA 71 CertEd 72 MSc 80. NEOC 92. **d** 92 **p** 94. NSM York St Mich-le-Belfrey 92–95; C Leeds St Geo *Ripon* 95–05; V Cricklewood St Gabr and St Mich *Lon* 05–19; rtd 19; PtO *Lon* from 19. *50A Mattock Lane, London W13 9NS* M: 07702-301328 E: jane.morris100@gmail.com

MORRIS, Canon Jeremy Nigel. b 60. Ball Coll Ox MA 81 DPhil 86 Clare Coll Cam BA 92. Westcott Ho Cam 90. **d** 93 **p** 94. C Battersea St Mary *S'wark* 93–96; Dir Studies Westcott Ho Cam 96–01; Vice-Prin 97–01; Dean and Chapl Trin Hall Cam 01–10; Dean K Coll Cam 10–14; Trin Hall Cam from 14; Hon Can Ely Cathl from 19. *Trinity Hall, Cambridge CB2 1TJ* T: (01223) 332500 E: jnm20@cam.ac.uk or jnm20@trinhall.cam.ac.uk

MORRIS, Mrs Joanna Elizabeth. b 60. N Riding Coll of Educn CertEd 81. Qu Coll Birm 07. **d** 09 **p** 10. C Riddings and Ironville *Derby* 09–13; R Whittington from 13. *The Rectory, 84 Church Street North, Old Whittington, Chesterfield S41 9QP* E: jomorris17@gmail.com

MORRIS, John Douglas. b 37. Cam Univ BA 58 Lon Inst of Educn PGCE 60 Univ of E Africa MEd 67 Ex Univ PhD 87. S Dios Minl Tr Scheme 94. **d** 95 **p** 96. NSM Twyford and Owslebury and Morestead *Win* 95–01; PtO from 01; Chapl Twyford Sch Win 95–05. *9 Parkside Gardens, Winchester SO22 5NA* T: (01962) 852033 E: johnmarymorris@btopenworld.com

MORRIS, John Dudley. b 33. Ball Coll Ox BA 57 MA 61. Wycliffe Hall Ox 58. **d** 60 **p** 61. C Tonbridge SS Pet and Paul *Roch* 60–65; C Enfield Ch Ch Trent Park *Lon* 65–69; Chapl Elstree Sch Woolhampton 70–74; Hd Master Handcross Park Sch W Sussex 74–89; V Rudgwick *Chich* 89–98; RD Horsham 93–98; rtd 98; PtO *Chich* from 98. *13 Hoadlands, Handcross, Haywards Heath RH17 6HB* T: (01444) 400184

MORRIS, John Owen. b 56. Nottm Univ BA 82 Ex Univ MA 06. Linc Th Coll 79. **d** 82 **p** 83. C Morriston *S & B* 82–84; C Kingstone w Clehonger and Eaton Bishop *Heref* 84–87; P-in-c Lugwardine w Bartestree and Weston Beggard 87–92; Chapl RN 92–13; Chapl Lord Wandsworth Coll Hook 13–15; PtO *Ex* 15–17; V The Bourne and Tilford *Guildf* from 17. *The Vicarage, 2 Middle Avenue, Farnham GU9 8JL* T: (01252) 820771 M: 07970-667219 E: johnowenmorris@me.com

MORRIS, Kevin John. b 63. Univ of Wales (Ban) BMus 84 Lon Univ MA 12. Westcott Ho Cam 85. **d** 88 **p** 89. C Roath *Llan* 88–91; C Holborn St Alb w Saffron Hill St Pet *Lon* 91–96; V Bedford Park from 96; P-in-c Acton Green 15–16; V from 16; Dir Post-Ord Tr 99–10. *The Vicarage, Priory Gardens, London W4 1TT* T: (020) 8994 0139 or 8994 1380 E: stpetersactongreen@gmail.com or parishoffice@smaaa.org.uk

MORRIS, Kirsteen Helen Grace. b 44. STETS 99. **d** 01 **p** 03. NSM Cowes H Trin and St Mary *Portsm* 02–12; rtd 12; PtO *Portsm* from 12. *Meda, Medham Farm Lane, Cowes PO31 8PH* T: (01983) 289585 F: 292919

MORRIS, Mrs Lynne. b 48. STETS 07. **d** 10 **p** 11. NSM Horton, Chalbury, Hinton Martel and Holt St Jas *Sarum* 10–14; NSM Witchampton, Stanbridge and Long Crichel etc 11–14; PtO 14–15; NSM W Moors from 15. *2 Garth Close, St Leonards, Ringwood BH24 2RG* E: lynnemorrislp@btinternet.com

MORRIS, Mrs Lynne Margaret. b 53. SEN. WMMTC 95. **d** 98 **p** 99. NSM Wrockwardine Wood *Lich* 98–01; Chapl Birm Community Healthcare NHS Foundn Trust 01–17; rtd 17; PtO *Lich* from 17. *5 Kingston Road, Trench, Telford TF2 7HT* T: (01952) 618158 E: revlynne.morris@yahoo.co.uk

MORRIS, Margaret Anne. b 61. Man Univ BA 82 MA 91 Ches Univ DProf 16. NOC 04. **d** 96 **p** 97. C Bury St Pet *Man* 96–98; C Accrington St Jo w Huncoat *Blackb* 98–01; V Knuzden from 01. *St Oswald's Vicarage, 68 Bank Lane, Blackburn BB1 2AP* T: (01254) 698321 E: revannemorris@gmail.com

MORRIS, Canon Margaret Jane. Ox Univ MTh 96 Leic Univ Hon LLM 96. EMMTC 86. **d** 89 **p** 94. NSM Quorndon

Leic 89–96; Chapl for People affected by HIV 94–05; NSM Loughborough All SS w H Trin 96–98; Chapl Asst Leic R Infirmary NHS Trust 98–00; Chapl Asst Univ Hosps Leic NHS Trust 00–10; Hon Can Leic Cathl 97–10; rtd 10; PtO *Leic* 10–13; *Derby* from 18. *2 Chatsworth Close, Sandiacre, Nottingham NG10 5PF* T: 0115-949 7997 E: margaretmorris.147@gmail.com

MORRIS, Martin Geoffrey Roger. b 41. Trin Coll Cam BA 63 MA 67. St D Coll Lamp 63. **d** 66 **p** 67. C Newport St Paul *Mon* 66–72; R Lampeter Velfrey *St D* 72–74; R Lampeter Velfrey and Llanddewi Velfrey 74–08; RD St Clears 83–98; Can St D Cathl 92–08; Chan St D Cathl 03–08; rtd 08; PtO *St D* from 08. *Greenfield Cottage, Gilfach Hill, Lampeter Velfrey, Narberth SA67 8UL* T: (01834) 831241

MORRIS, Ms Mary. b 27. Birm Univ BA 49 CertEd 50 MA 56. dss 68 **d** 87 **p** 94. Kinver *Lich* 83–87; Kinver and Enville 87; Hon Par Dn 87–94; Hon C 94–11; PtO 11–12. *12 Pavilion End, Prestwood, Stourbridge DY7 5PF* T: (01384) 877245

MORRIS, Michael. *See* MORRIS, David Michael

MORRIS, Michael Alan. b 46. Jes Coll Cam BA 70 MA 74. Coll of Resurr Mirfield 79. **d** 81 **p** 82. C Leamington Priors All SS *Cov* 81–83; C Milton *Portsm* 83–88; R Petworth *Chich* 88–90; R Egdean 88–90; Chapl St Pet Hosp Chertsey 90–95; Hon C Thorpe *Guildf* 90–95; P-in-c Harbledown *Cant* 95–97; R 97–16; Chapl St Nic Hosp Cant 95–00; rtd 16. *Hopbine, 4 The Oast Paddock, Durlock Road, Staple, Canterbury CT3 1JX* T: (01304) 714096 E: michael@themorrises.co.uk

MORRIS, Michael James. b 70. Univ of Wales (Abth) BScEcon 92. Qu Coll Birm BA. **d** 00 **p** 01. C Tupsley w Hampton Bishop *Heref* 00–04; TV Watling Valley *Ox* 04–12; TR from 12. *21 Edzell Crescent, Westcroft, Milton Keynes MK4 4EU* T: (01908) 507123 E: mike.morris@wvep.org

MORRIS (née ROBERTS), Canon Nia Wyn. b 64. Univ of Wales (Ban) BA 86 PGCE 87 CQSW 90 Anglia Poly Univ MA 00. Westcott Ho Cam 98. **d** 00 **p** 01. C Rhyl w St Ann *St As* 00–03; R Bala 03–14; AD Penllyn and Edeirnion 12–13; R Llanllwchaiarn and Newtown w Aberhafesp 14–16; I Cedewain Miss Area from 17; AD Cedewain from 14; Can Cursal St As Cathl from 15. *The Rectory, 3 Old Barn Lane, Newtown SY16 2PT* T: (01686) 951395 M: 07833-302312 E: niawyn1000@yahoo.com

MORRIS, Preb Norman Foster Maxwell. b 46. Ex Univ BA 68 MA 71 K Coll Lon MTh 85 Univ of Wales (Cardiff) MA 91 Cheltenham & Glouc Coll of HE MA 98 Leic Univ PGCE 69. S'wark Ord Course 75. **d** 78 **p** 79. C Hackbridge and N Beddington *S'wark* 78–81; Chapl Tonbridge Sch 81–85; Chapl Mon Sch 85–00; Asst Warden Jones Almshouses Mon 89–00; R Wentnor w Ratlinghope, Myndtown, Norbury etc *Heref* 00–16; P-in-c Churchstoke w Hyssington 04–16; RD Clun Forest 11–16; Preb Heref Cathl 11–16; CF (ACF) 02–12; rtd 16; TV Cedewain Miss Area *St As* from 16. *6 Penymaes, Adfa, Newtown SY16 3BQ* T: (01938) 810198 M: 07974-771069 E: revnormmorris@gmail.com

MORRIS, Canon Paul David. b 56. St Jo Coll Nottm BTh 79. **d** 80 **p** 81. C Billericay and Lt Burstead *Chelmsf* 80–84; C Luton Lewsey St Hugh *St Alb* 84–89; Dioc Adv on Evang *S'well* 89–00; Dioc Millennium Officer 97–01; Min Tommy's (ch for the unchurched) 96–01; C Barton in Fabis 01–02; C Gotham 01–02; C Thrumpton 01–02; C Kingston and Ratcliffe-on-Soar 01–02; C Sutton Bonington w Normanton-on-Soar 01–02; Dir Evang Chr Associates Internat 02–04; Assoc Eur Dir 04–06; Eur Dir 06–08; Brussels Team 08–09; P-in-c Derby St Pet and Ch Ch w H Trin 09–16; V from 16; Prin Chapl Derby City Cen from 12; Prin Chapl Workplace Chapl in Derbyshire from 12; Bp's Appts Officer 15–17; Hon Can Derby Cathl from 12. *St Peter's Vicarage, 16 Farley Road, Derby DE23 6BX* T: (01332) 204686 E: paul@stpetersderby.org.uk

MORRIS, Peter. b 45. Leeds Univ CertEd 66. Tyndale Hall Bris 68. **d** 71 **p** 72. C Southport SS Simon and Jude *Liv* 71–74; Min-in-c Ch Ch Netherley LEP 74–76; V Bryn *Liv* 76–91; R Redenhall, Harleston, Wortwell and Needham *Nor* 91–05; rtd 05; PtO *Roch* from 15. *9 Bromley College, London Road, Bromley BR1 1PE* T: (020) 8460 3455 E: petermorris203@btinternet.com

MORRIS, The Ven Philip Gregory. b 50. Leeds Univ BA 71 MPhil 74. Coll of Resurr Mirfield 71. **d** 73 **p** 74. C Aberdare *Llan* 74–77; C Neath w Llantwit 77–80; V Cymmer and Porth 80–88; TV Llantwit Major 88–01; Dioc Missr 88–99; Can Res Llan Cathl 00–01; Adn Margam 02–15; TV Aberavon 02; P-in-c Kenfig Hill 02–05; P-in-c Ewenny w St Brides Major 05–15; rtd 15; PtO *Llan* from 15. *12 Groeswen, Llantwit Major CF61 2UA* T: (01446) 796459

MORRIS, Philip John. b 50. FCIPD 96. St Mich Coll Llan 97. **d** 99 **p** 00. NSM Builth and Llanddewi'r Cwm w Llangynog etc *S & B* 99–04; NSM Aberedw w Llandeilo Graban and Llanbadarn etc 04–13; LtO from 14. *Lochaber,*

22 North Road, Builth Wells LD2 3BU T: (01982) 552390 E: pip@pipmorris.plus.com

MORRIS, Canon Raymond. b 48. Open Univ BA 88. NOC 80. **d** 83 **p** 84. C Tonge w Alkrington *Man* 83–86; R Blackley St Paul 86–91; V Heyside 91–14; AD Tandle 02–09; C Royton St Anne 12–14; Hon Can Man Cathl 07–14; rtd 14; PtO *Man* from 14. *46 Penthorpe Drive, Royton, Oldham OL2 6JL* T: (01706) 842192

MORRIS, Raymond Arthur. b 42. Trin Coll Ox BA 64 MA 66 Lon Univ LLB 71 CQSW 72. Clifton Th Coll 66. **d** 67 **p** 91. C Greenstead *Chelmsf* 67–68; PtO *York* 69–91; NSM Linthorpe 91–12; PtO from 12. *3 Medina Gardens, Middlesbrough TS5 8BN* T: (01642) 593726 E: morris101@btinternet.com

MORRIS, Canon Robert John. b 45. Leeds Univ BA 67. Coll of Resurr Mirfield 74. **d** 76 **p** 77. C Beeston Hill St Luke *Ripon* 76; C Holbeck 76–78; C Moseley St Mary *Birm* 78–83; P-in-c Handsworth St Jas 83–88; V 88–99; P-in-c Handsworth St Mich 86–87; AD Handsworth 92–99; TR Kings Norton 99–15; Hon Can Birm Cathl 97–15; rtd 15; PtO *Birm* from 15; Dioc Retirement Officer from 17. *61 Oxford Street, Stirchley, Birmingham B30 2LH* T: 0121-247 0355 M: 07973-389427 E: morrisrob4@aol.com

✠**MORRIS, The Rt Revd Roger Anthony Brett.** b 68. Imp Coll Lon BSc 89 Trin Coll Cam BA 92 MA 08 ARCS 89. Ridley Hall Cam 90. **d** 93 **p** 94 **c** 14. C Northleach w Hampnett and Farmington etc *Glouc* 93–96; P-in-c Sevenhampton w Charlton Abbotts and Hawling etc 96–00; P-in-c Dowdeswell and Andoversford w the Shiptons etc 96–00; R Sevenhampton w Charlton Abbots, Hawling etc 00–03; Dioc Dir Par Development and Evang *Cov* 03–08; Adn Worc 08–14; Area Bp Colchester *Chelmsf* from 14. *1 Fitzwalter Road, Colchester CO3 3SS* T: (01206) 576648 M: 07590-696212 E: b.colchester@chelmsford.anglican.org

MORRIS, Mrs Sally Jane. b 69. Imp Coll Lon BSc 91. Qu Coll Birm 07. **d** 10 **p** 11. NSM Bowbrook S *Worc* 10–13; NSM Chipping Campden w Ebrington *Glouc* 13–14; NSM Vale and Cotswold Edge 14–15; NSM Lawford *Chelmsf* 15–17; NSM Lawford, Lt Bentley and The Bromleys from 17. *1 Fitzwalter Road, Colchester CO3 3SS* T: (01206) 576648 M: 07920-588994 E: sjmorris@mypostoffice.co.uk

MORRIS (*née* GILES), **Preb Sarah Jayne.** b 76. Aston Univ BSc 98. St Jo Coll Nottm MTh 07. **d** 06 **p** 07. C Cen Telford *Lich* 06–10; Chapl HM YOI Stoke Heath 10–17; Chapl HM Pris Drake Hall from 17; PtO *Lich* 10–16; Dioc Co-ord Chapl for Pris from 16; Preb Lich Cathl from 18. *HM Prison and Young Offender Institution, Drake Hall, Eccleshall, Stafford ST21 6LQ* T: (01785) 774100 E: sarah.morris@justice.gov.uk

MORRIS, Shaun Anthony. b 64. Keele Univ BSocSc 85. Oak Hill Th Coll 04. **d** 06 **p** 07. C Westlands St Andr *Lich* 06–10; C Hanford 10–17; P-in-c from 17; C Trentham 10–17; RD Stoke-on-Trent from 18. *Hanford Vicarage, 76 Church Lane, Stoke-on-Trent ST4 4QD* T: (01782) 657848 E: morris.shaun@btinternet.com

MORRIS, Simon John. b 83. St Jo Coll Dur BA 05. St Steph Ho Ox BA 07. **d** 08 **p** 09. C Tottenham St Mary *Lon* 08–11; V from 11. *St Mary's Vicarage, Lansdowne Road, London N17 9XE* E: fr.morris@hotmail.com

MORRIS, Stanley James. b 35. Keble Coll Ox BA 58 MA 63. Chich Th Coll 59. **d** 61 **p** 62. C Tunstall Ch Ch *Lich* 61–64; C W Bromwich All SS 64–67; V Wilnecote 67–88; V Alrewas and Wychnor 88–00; rtd 01; PtO *Derby* 01–18. *44 Pinfold Close, Repton, Derby DE65 6FR* T: (01283) 703453

MORRIS, Stephanie Ruth. b 72. All SS Cen for Miss & Min 16. **d** 19. NSM Sutton, Wincle, Wildboarclough and Bosley *Ches* from 19. *St James' Vicarage, Church Lane, Sutton, Macclesfield SK11 0DS* M: 07703-578003 E: stephmorris1106@btinternet.com

MORRIS, Stephen Bryan. b 54. Linc Th Coll 88. **d** 90 **p** 91. C Glouc St Geo w Whaddon 90–94; C Glouc St Mark and St Mary de Crypt w St Jo etc 94–02; C Barnwood 02–03; Chapl for the Deaf 94–13; Dioc Chapl among Deaf and Adv on Disability 13–15; Chapl among Deaf from 15. *5 Chaceley Close, Quedgeley, Gloucester GL2 4WW* T: (01452) 610450

MORRIS, Stephen Francis. b 52. St Jo Coll Nottm BTh 79. **d** 79 **p** 80. C N Hinksey *Ox* 79–82; C Leic H Apostles 82–85; TV Shenley and Loughton *Ox* 85–88; TV Watling Valley 88–95; V Chatham St Wm *Roch* 95–98; TR S Chatham H Trin 98–00; Lect Nottingham St Mary and St Cath *S'well* 00–07; Lect Nottingham All SS, St Mary and St Pet 07–14; AD Nottingham Cen 02–08; Dioc Ecum Officer 10–14; P-in-c Newark w Coddington 14–17; rtd 17; C Newark w Coddington *S'well* 17; C Nottingham St Mary Lace Market 17–18; PtO from 19. *21 Private Road, Sherwood, Nottingham NG5 4DD*

MORRIS, Steven Ralph. b 62. UEA BA 84 MA 85. Wycliffe Hall Ox 08. **d** 10 **p** 11. C Ealing St Steph Castle Hill *Lon*

10–13; C Neasden St Cath w St Paul 13–15; V N Wembley St Cuth from 15. *St Cuthbert's Vicarage, 214 Carlton Avenue West, Wembley HA0 3QY* T: (020) 8904 1457 E: steve_stcuthberts@hotmail.com

MORRIS, Canon Stuart Collard. b 43. AKC 66. St Boniface Warminster 66. **d** 67 **p** 68. C Hanham *Bris* 67–71; C Whitchurch 71–74; P-in-c Westerleigh and Wapley w Codrington and Doddington 74–77; P-in-c Holdgate w Tugford *Heref* 77–82; P-in-c Abdon w Clee St Margaret 77–82; R Diddlebury w Bouldon and Munslow 77–82; P-in-c Sotterley, Willingham, Shadingfield, Ellough etc *St E* 82–87; RD Beccles and S Elmham 83–94; P-in-c Westhall w Brampton and Stoven 86–88; P-in-c Flixton w Homersfield and S Elmham 86–92; Hon Can St E Cathl 87–99; V Bungay H Trin w St Mary 87–94; P-in-c Hadleigh w Layham and Shelley 94–96; R Hadleigh 96–99; Dean Bocking 94–99; RD Hadleigh 94–98; rtd 99; PtO *Ely* 07–14; Hon C Tottenhill w Wormegay 14–16; Hon C Watlington 14–16; Hon C Holme Runcton w S Runcton and Wallington 14–16; PtO *Derby* 16–18; *Man* from 18. *St Edmund's Vicarage, Sinfin Avenue, Derby DE24 9JA* E: stuartmorris20@gmail.com

MORRIS, Canon Timothy David. b 48. Lon Univ BSc 69. Trin Coll Bris. **d** 75 **p** 76. C Edin St Thos 75–77; R Edin St Jas 77–83; R Troon *Glas* 83–85; R Galashiels *Edin* 85–02; R Edin Gd Shep 02–08; Dean Edin 92–01; Hon Can St Mary's Cathl from 01; rtd 08; Canada 08–10; LtO *Edin* from 10. *2 The Firs, Foulden Newton, Berwick-upon-Tweed TD15 1UL* T: (01289) 386615 M: 07979-196824 E: tim@foulden.org.uk

MORRIS, Mrs Tracey. b 78. Bradf Univ BSc 00 Sheff Univ BA 16. St Hild Coll 16. **d** 19. NSM Lodge Moor St Luke *Sheff* from 19. *19 Cardoness Road, Sheffield S10 5RT* M: 07882-589685 E: tracey.mozza@hotmail.com

MORRIS, Mrs Trudie Elizabeth. b 53. UEA BA 91 PGCE 92 Leic Univ MBA 04 Cam Univ BTh 12 Anglia Ruskin Univ PhD 19. Westcott Ho Cam 10. **d** 12 **p** 13. C Fowlmere, Foxton, Shepreth and Thriplow *Ely* 12–15; P-in-c Derby St Andr w St Osmund 15–16; V Pride Park, Wilmorton, Allenton and Shelton Lock 15–16; P-in-c Allenton and Shelton Lock 16–18; R Stand *Man* from 18. *Stand Rectory, 32 Church Lane, Whitefield, Manchester M45 7NF* M: 07710-494871 E: revtrudie@gmail.com

MORRIS, Mrs Valerie Ruth. b 46. St Hugh's Coll Ox BA 68 MA 72. Gilmore Course 76. **dss** 78 **d** 87 **p** 05. Drayton in Hales *Lich* 78–82; Burton 82–90; Par Dn 87–91; PtO *Heref* 04–05; Hon C Church Stretton from 05. *Watling House, All Stretton, Church Stretton SY6 6HH* T: (01694) 722243 E: valerieanddavid@talktalk.net

MORRIS, Victor Bernard. b 50. **d** 14 **p** 15. OLM Wigginton *Lich* from 14. *14 Wentworth Drive, Lichfield WS14 9HN* E: vicbmorris@yahoo.co.uk

MORRIS, Vincent Sidney. **d** 18 **p** 19. C Bro Tysilio *Ban* from 18. *The Vicarage, Tan y Ffordd, Llansadwrn, Menai Bridge LL59 5SH* T: (01248) 811342

MORRIS, William Hazlitt. b 62. Trin Coll Cam BA 84 MA 88 Virginia Univ LLM 89 Solicitor 88. NTMTC BA 09. **d** 09 **p** 10. NSM St Martin-in-the-Fields *Lon* from 09. *St Martin-in-the-Fields, 6 St Martin's Place, London WC2N 4JH* T: (020) 7766 1100 E: william.morris@smitf.org

MORRISON, Ailsa. See SPACKMAN, Ailsa

MORRISON, Barry John. b 44. Pemb Coll Cam BA 66 MA 70. ALCD 69. **d** 69 **p** 70. C Stoke Bishop *Bris* 69–72; C Edgware *Lon* 72–76; Chapl Poly Cen Lon 76–83; Hon C Langham Place All So 76–83; P-in-c W Hampstead St Luke 83–88; V 88–98; Chapl Westf Coll 84–92; R Rushden St Mary w Newton Bromswold *Pet* 98–08; rtd 08; PtO *Pet* from 09. *11 Lytham Park, Oundle, Peterborough PE8 4FB* T: (01832) 274242 E: gandbmorrison@btinternet.com

MORRISON, Bryony Clare. b 47. Lon Univ CertEd 67 Brentwood Coll of Educn BEd 86. NTMTC 96. **d** 99 **p** 00. C Epping Distr *Chelmsf* 99–05; TV 05–17; Chapl Epping Forest Primary Care Trust 02–05; rtd 17; PtO *Sarum* from 18. *Dibley House, 562 Ringwood Road, Poole BH12 4LY* T: (01202) 461360 M: 07850-876304 E: revmorry@gmail.com

MORRISON, Diana Mary (Sister Diana). b 43. St Kath Coll Liv CertEd 64. EAMTC 02. **d** 05 **p** 06. NSM Breadsall *Derby* 05–13; PtO from 13; *Man* 14–18. *Convent of the Holy Name, Morley Road, Oakwood, Derby DE21 4TB* E: dianachn@tiscali.co.uk

MORRISON, Edward John Scott. b 89. York Univ BA 10. St Steph Ho Ox BA 14. **d** 15 **p** 16. C Cantley *Sheff* 15–18; P-in-c Mexborough from 18. *The Vicarage, Church Street, Mexborough S64 0ER* E: esmorrison@hotmail.com

MORRISON, Iain Edward. b 36. St Steph Ho Ox 76. **d** 78 **p** 79. C Brighton St Aug and St Sav *Chich* 78–81; C Felpham w Middleton 81–83; P-in-c Barnham and Eastergate 83–85; R Aldingbourne, Barnham and Eastergate 85–91; V Jarvis Brook 91–98; R Hastings St Clem and All SS 98–03; rtd 03;

P-in-c Arlington, Folkington and Wilmington *Chich* 03–10; PtO from 15. *2 Priory Close, Hastings TN34 1UJ* T: (01424) 420499 E: ian.iona@gmail.com *or* iain.iona@gmail.com

MORRISON, Preb James Wilson Rennie. b 42. Aber Univ MA 65. Linc Th Coll 76. **d** 78 **p** 79. C Whitley Ch Ch *Ox* 78–81; R Burghfield 81–87; CF 87–97; P-in-c Burghill *Heref* 97–03; V 03–11; P-in-c Stretton Sugwas 97–03; R 03–11; P-in-c Pipe-cum-Lyde 97–03; P-in-c Pipe-cum-Lyde and Moreton-on-Lugg *Heref* 03–11; Preb Heref Cathl 08–11; rtd 11; PtO *Heref* from 13. *Brambles, 8 Dernside Close, Wellington, Hereford HR4 8BP* T: (01432) 830911 E: jimmy67@btinternet.com

MORRISON, The Ven John Anthony. b 38. Jes Coll Cam BA 60 MA 64 Linc Coll Ox MA 68. Chich Th Coll 61. **d** 64 **p** 65. C Birm St Pet 64–68; C Ox St Mich 68–71; Chapl Linc Coll Ox 68–74; C Ox St Mich w St Martin and All SS 71–74; V Basildon 74–82; RD Bradfield 78–82; V Aylesbury 82–89; RD 85–89; TR 89–90; Adn Buckingham 90–98; P-in-c Princes Risborough w Ilmer 96–97; Adn Ox and Can Res Ch Ch 98–05; rtd 05; PtO *Ox* from 05. *39 Crown Road, Wheatley, Oxford OX33 1UJ* T: (01865) 876625 E: morrison039@btinternet.com

MORRISON, Keith Charles. b 63. Wycliffe Hall Ox 99. **d** 01 **p** 02. C Ipswich St Aug *St E* 01–04; Asst Chapl Cam Univ Hosps NHS Foundn Trust 04–13; Chapl Arthur Rank Ho Brookfields Hosp Cam 13–16; Chapl Arthur Rank Hospice Cam from 16; LtO *Ely* from 05. *Arthur Rank Hospice, Cherry Hinton Road, Shelford Bottom, Cambridge CB22 3FB* T: (01223) 675771 M: 07798-865651 E: keith.morrison@arhc.org.uk

MORRISON, Myrtle. b 46. Wilson Carlile Coll 84 CITI 16. **d** 17 **p** 18. Ardmore w Craigavon *D & D* from 17. *23 Mandeville Manor, Portadown, Craigavon BT62 3UP* T: (028) 3833 4307 M: 07774-565914 E: myrtlechurcharmy@btinternet.com

MORRISON, Richard James. b 55. Sarum & Wells Th Coll 87. **d** 89 **p** 90. C Boston *Linc* 89–93; P-in-c Digby 93–99; V Whaplode Drove 99–16; V Gedney Hill 99–16; P-in-c Whaplode 10–14; P-in-c Holbeach Fen 10–14; V Elloe Fen Gp 17; rtd 17. *35 Danestream Court, Sea Road, Milford on Sea, Lymington SO41 0DA*

MORRISON, Canon Robin Victor Adair. b 45. Nottm Univ BA 67. Bucharest Th Inst 67 Ripon Hall Ox 68. **d** 70 **p** 71. C Hackney St Jo *Lon* 70–73; Chapl Newc Univ 73–76; P-in-c Teversal *S'well* 76–78; Chapl Sutton Cen 76–78; Asst Hd Deans Community Sch Livingston *Edin* 78–80; R Edin St Columba 80–81; Chapl Birm Univ 81–88; Prin Soc Resp Officer *Derby* 88–96; TV Southampton (City Cen) *Win* 96–01; Ind Chapl 96–01; Non Exec Dir Southampton and SW Hants HA 00–01; Officer for Ch and Soc Ch in Wales Prov Coun 01–11; Hon Can Llan Cathl 09–11; rtd 11; PtO *Lon* from 18. *Headley, The Broadway, Laleham, Staines-upon-Thames TW18 1RZ* E: revrobinmorrison@gmail.com

MORRISS (formerly HEYN), Lucinda Jane. b 68. Ripon Coll Cuddesdon 07. **d** 10 **p** 11. C Goring and Streatley w S Stoke *Ox* 10–14; TV Hermitage 14–18; Bp's Adv for Women in Ord Min 14–18; P-in-c Cusop w Blakemere, Bredwardine w Brobury etc *Heref* from 18. *The Rectory, Cusop, Hay-on-Wye, Hereford HR3 5RF* T: (01497) 821877 E: luci.borderlinkbenefice@outlook.com

MORROW, David. b 63. NUU BSc 86 TCD BTh 89. CITC 86. **d** 89 **p** 90. C Portadown St Mark *Arm* 89–91; C Ballymena w Ballyclug *Conn* 91–94; I Tempo and Clabby *Clogh* 94–01; I Kilcronaghan w Draperstown and Sixtowns *D & R* 01–11; Bp's Dom Chapl 07–11; rtd 11. *Address temp unknown* M: 07540-134601 E: davidmorrow763@btinternet.com

MORROW, Canon Joseph John. b 54. Edin Univ BD 79 Dundee Univ LLB 92 NY Th Sem DMin 87. Edin Th Coll 76. **d** 79 **p** 80. Chapl St Paul's Cathl Dundee *Bre* 79–82; P-in-c Dundee St Martin 82–85; R 85–90; P-in-c Dundee St Jo 85–08; P-in-c Dundee St Ninian 02–07; Can St Paul's Cathl Dundee 00–08; Hon Can St Paul's Cathl Dundee from 08; Dioc Chan 08–14; PtO from 09. *Miltonhaugh, Tealing, Dundee DD4 0QZ* T: (01382) 380501 E: j.jmorrow@btinternet.com

MORROW, Keri Anne. b 72. R Cen Sch Speech & Drama BSC 95. ERMC 16. **d** 19. NSM Pet St Mary Boongate from 19. *21 College Park, Peterborough PE1 4AW* T: (01733) 253272 M: 07528-690010 E: revkerimorrow@gmail.com

MORROW, Nigel Patrick. b 68. Dur Univ BA 94 TCD MPhil 02 Anglia Ruskin Univ MA 05. Westcott Ho Cam 03. **d** 05 **p** 06. C Linc St Botolph and Linc St Pet-at-Gowts and St Andr 05–08; C Camberwell St Giles w St Matt *S'wark* 08–10; Chapl K Coll Lon 08–10; Chapl and Inter Faith Adv Brunel Univ 11–12; PtO 12–13; *S'wark* 13–14; C Lt Ilford St Mich *Chelmsf* from 14; Chapl Camden and Islington NHS Foundn Trust 14–19; Sen Chapl HM Pris Chelmsf from 19. *HM Prison, 200 Springfield Road, Chelmsford CM2 6LQ* T: (01245) 552212 E: patrick.morrow@justice.gov.uk

MORSE, Mrs Elisabeth Ann. b 51. New Hall Cam MA 73 Qu Eliz Coll Lon MSc 74 Heythrop Coll Lon MA 97. S'wark Ord Course 91. **d** 94 **p** 95. C Wimbledon *S'wark* 94–99; C Fulham All SS *Lon* 99–08; V Battersea St Luke *S'wark* 08–16; rtd 16; PtO *S'wark* from 16. *31 Elm Bank Gardens, London SW13 0NU* E: morseelisabeth@yahoo.co.uk

MORSE, Ms Gita. b 55. Wolv Univ CertEd 10. Qu Coll Birm 10. **d** 13 **p** 14. NSM Sparkhill St Jo *Birm* 13–16; NSM Harborne St Faith and St Laur 16–17. *54 Park Hill Road, Harborne, Birmingham B17 9HJ* M: 07716-496154 E: gmorse@mypostoffice.co.uk

MORSON, Mrs Eleanor. b 42. CA Tr Coll 63 TISEC 95. **d** 96 **p** 96. NSM Kirkwall *Ab* 96–01; R Edin St Mark 01–05. *4 Broadshaw Mews, Leazes Parkway, Newcastle upon Tyne NE15 9QL* T: 0191-264 6885

MORSON, John. b 41. CA Tr Coll 62. **d** 88 **p** 92. NSM Duns *Edin* 88–89; CF 89–92; R Kirkwall *Ab* 92–01; R Stromness 92–01; NSM Edin St Mark 01–05; rtd 06. *4 Broadshaw Mews, Leazes Parkway, Newcastle upon Tyne NE15 9QL* T: 0191-264 6885

MORT, Alister. b 52. BSc BA. Oak Hill Th Coll. **d** 82 **p** 83. C Cheadle Hulme St Andr *Ches* 82–85; C Rodbourne Cheney *Bris* 86–87; TV 87–90; V New Milverton *Cov* 90–05; PtO 05–09; TR Bilton *Ripon* 09–14; rtd 14; Tutor Johannesburg Bible Coll S Africa from 14. *c/o J Mort Esq, 168 Tachbrook Road, Leamington Spa CV31 3EF* E: alister9mort@gmail.com

MORTER, Canon Ian Charles. b 54. AKC 77. Coll of Resurr Mirfield 77. **d** 78 **p** 79. C Colchester St Jas, All SS, St Nic and St Runwald *Chelmsf* 78–82; C Brixham w Churston Ferrers *Ex* 82–83; TV 84–86; TV Sidmouth, Woolbrook, Salcombe Regis, Sidbury etc 86–95; P-in-c Exminster and Kenn 95–00; TR Littleham w Exmouth 00–10; RD Aylesbeare 07–10; Preb Ex Cathl 08–10; Can Res Ex Cathl 10–17; rtd 17; Hon PV Ex Cathl from 18. *17 Bapton Lane, Exmouth EX8 3JS* E: ian.morter@talktalk.net

MORTIBOYS, John William. b 45. K Coll Lon BD 69 AKC 69. Sarum Th Coll 71. **d** 71 **p** 72. C Reading All SS *Ox* 71–95; PtO *Portsm* from 97. *13 Oyster Street, Portsmouth PO1 2HZ* T: (023) 9275 6676 F: 9266 2626 E: johnmortiboys@gmail.com

MORTIMER, Aileen Jane. b 46. Edin Univ MA 67 CQSW 69. ERMC 05. **d** 08 **p** 09. NSM E Bergholt and Brantham *St E* 08–13; rtd 13; PtO *St E* from 13. *20 Leggatt Drive, Bramford, Ipswich IP8 4ET* T: (01473) 747419 E: ajmortimer@hotmail.co.uk

MORTIMER, Anthony John. b 42. Sarum & Wells Th Coll 68. **d** 71 **p** 72. C Heref St Martin 71–79; V Kingstone 79–85; P-in-c Clehonger and Eaton Bishop 80–85; TR Pinhoe and Broadclyst *Ex* 85–05; rtd 05. *97 Egremont Road, Exmouth EX8 1SA* T: (01395) 271390 E: themortimers@totalise.co.uk

MORTIMER, Elizabeth Anne. *See* DUDLEY, Elizabeth Anne

MORTIMER, Jonathan Michael. b 60. Bris Univ BA 83. Oak Hill Th Coll BA 92. **d** 92 **p** 93. C Rugby St Matt *Cov* 92–96; C Southgate *Chich* 96–98; TR 98–07; Through Faith Miss Ev 07–11; V Peckham All SS *S'wark* from 11. *78 Talford Road, London SE15 5NZ* T: (020) 7252 7549 E: mortimerj@btinternet.com

MORTIMER, Canon Lawrence George. b 45. St Edm Hall Ox BA 67 MA 71. St Chad's Coll Dur. **d** 70 **p** 71. C Rugby St Andr *Cov* 70–75; V Styvechale 75–89; Dioc Broadcasting Officer 80–89; Dioc Communications Officer 80–03; P-in-c Wootton Wawen 95–10; P-in-c Claverdon w Preston Bagot 03–10; Hon Can Cov Cathl 98–10; rtd 10; PtO *Lich* from 11. *3 Top Street, Whittington, Oswestry SY11 4DR* T: (01691) 657986 E: l.mortimer@btinternet.com

MORTIMER, Canon Peter Jackson. b 41. St Jo Coll York CertEd 63 Essex Univ MA 71 DUniv 09 UEA DUniv 09 FRSA 97 Hon GCM 07. EAMTC 97. **d** 98 **p** 99. NSM Needham Market w Badley *St E* 98–02; NSM Ringshall w Battisford, Barking w Darmsden etc 98–02; Bp's Ecum Adv 02–16; Chapl to Suffolk Fire Service from 03; Hon Can *St E* Cathl 06–11; Hon Fell UEA *Nor* from 07; PtO *St E* from 11. *20 Leggatt Drive, Bramford, Ipswich IP8 4ET* T: (01473) 747419 E: petermortimer@hotmail.co.uk

MORTIMORE, David Jack. b 42. Master Mariner 69. St Mich Coll Llan 90. **d** 91 **p** 92. C Pembroke St Mary w St Mich *St D* 91–92; C Bargoed and Deri w Brithdir *Llan* 92–97; PtO 98–02; P-in-c Llangeinor 02–04; P-in-c Llangeinor and the Garw Valley 04–12; rtd 12; PtO *St D* from 13. *10 Lawrenny Street, Neyland, Milford Haven SA73 1TB* T: (01646) 602555 E: cleddau39@gmail.com

MORTIMORE, Robert Edward. b 39. Kelham Th Coll 61 Wells Th Coll 66. **d** 69 **p** 70. C Byfleet *Guildf* 69–72; C Fitzroy New Zealand 72–77; C Remuera 76–77; Min Bell Block 77–79; V Te Kuiti 79–85; Offic Min Auckland 86–89; Sen Asst P Whangarei 89–92; V Avondale 92–98; V Milford 98–04; Offic Min from 04. *69 Crawford Crescent, Kamo,*

Whangarei 0112, New Zealand T/F: (0064) (9) 435 1285
E: b.jmortimore@xtra.co.nz

MORTIMORE, Robin Malcolm. b 46. **d** 11 **p** 12. NSM Yardley
St Edburgha *Birm* 11–15; PtO from 15. *33 Stonebow Avenue,
Solihull B91 3UP* T: 0121-705 9116 M: 07812-728526
E: robinmortimore@hotmail.com

MORTIS, Lorna Anne. b 54. Moray Ho Coll of Educn
DipEd 76 Open Univ BA 88. TISEC 95. **d** 98 **p** 99. NSM
Gullane and N Berwick *Edin* 98–02; P-in-c Edin St Marg
02–08; NSM Prestonpans and Musselburgh 08–10; R Airdrie
Glas 10–14; Bp's Dom Chapl 11–14; rtd 14; LtO *Edin*
from 15. *Rosebank, 2 School Cottages, Athelstaneford, North
Berwick EH39 5BE* T: (01620) 880505 M: 07779-553807
E: lorna.mortis@btinternet.com

MORTON, Adrian Ian. b 65. Brighton Poly BSc 87 Brunel
Univ MSc 93. Ridley Hall Cam 98. **d** 00 **p** 01. C Kettering Ch
the King *Pet* 00–04; P-in-c Bozeat w Easton Maudit 04–06;
P-in-c Wollaston and Strixton 04–06; V Wollaston w Strixton
and Bozeat etc from 06. *The Vicarage, 81 Irchester Road,
Wollaston, Wellingborough NN29 7RW* T: (01933) 664256
E: adrianmorton762@btinternet.com

MORTON, Albert George. b 34. Saskatchewan Univ BA 61
McGill Univ Montreal MA 73. Em Coll Saskatoon 56. **d** 61
p 61. Canada 61–65; C Stanford-le-Hope *Chelmsf* 66–69; V
Linc St Geo Swallowbeck 69–82; R Lt Munden w Sacombe
St Alb 82–89; R The Mundens w Sacombe 89–96; rtd 96; PtO
Sarum from 00. *10 Church Green, Bishop's Caundle, Sherborne
DT9 5NN* T: (01963) 23383 E: amorton1@waitrose.com

MORTON, Christine Marjorie. b 60. **d** 13 **p** 14. NSM Marton
Blackb 13–18; NSM Treales from 18. *7 Trinity Gardens,
Thornton-Cleveleys FY5 2UA* T: (01253) 824657

MORTON, Mrs Christine Mary. b 39. Linc Th Coll 78. **dss** 80
d 87 **p** 94. Ore St Helen and St Barn *Chich* 80–84; Southwick
St Mich 84–85; Winchmore Hill St Paul *Lon* 85–87; Par Dn
87–94; C 94–99; Hon C 00–02; rtd 00; PtO *Lon* from 02. *122
Bourne Hill, London N13 4BD* T: (020) 8886 3157

MORTON, Clive Frederick. b 47. Lon Univ BA 70 Birm Univ
MA 98. Cranmer Hall Dur 78. **d** 80 **p** 81. C Countesthorpe
w Foston *Leic* 80–83; C Glen Parva and S Wigston 83–86;
Asst Chapl HM Youth Cust Cen Glen Parva 83–86; V Birm
St Pet 86–98; Miss Partner CMS 99–02; Chapl St Petersburg
Eur 99–02; Lect St Petersburg Th Academy and Sem 99–02;
V Kingsbury H Innocents *Lon* 02–12; rtd 13; PtO *Truro* from
16. *14 Penmare Court, Hayle TR27 4RD* M: 07947-883559
E: cfmpam@gmail.com

MORTON, Howard Knyvett. b 30. St Jo Coll Cam BA 51
MA 61. Linc Th Coll 55. **d** 57 **p** 58. C Hatfield Hyde *St Alb*
57–60; Hd RE Heaton Gr Sch Newc 60–66; 72–75; CMS
66–72; Regional Org Oxfam 88–91; Grainger Gr Sch Newc
91–94; LtO *Newc* 73–93; Dioc World Development Officer
94–95; rtd 95; PtO *Dur* 95–98; *Newc* from 96. *17 Cragside
View, Rothbury, Morpeth NE65 7YU*

MORTON, Mrs Jacqueline Mavis. b 46. UEA BSc 67 York
Univ BSc 82. EMMTC 97. **d** 00 **p** 01. NSM Sibsey w Frithville
Linc 00–14; NSM Alford w Rigsby 14–18; NSM Well 14–18;
NSM Saleby w Beesby and Maltby 14–18; NSM Bilsby w
Farlesthorpe 14–18; NSM Hannah cum Hagnaby w Markby
14–18; NSM Willoughby 14–18; NSM Alford Gp from
18. *13 Tothby Lane, Alford LN13 0AQ* T: (01507) 622639
E: jacqui.morton@talktalk.net

MORTON, Jennifer. b 50. Bedf Coll Lon BA 72 Leic Univ
PGCE 73. EMMTC 87. **d** 90 **p** 94. C New Mills *Derby* 90–94;
Chapl Asst Nottm City Hosp NHS Trust 94–98; Chapl
Basford Hosp Nottm 94–98; Chapl S Derbyshire Acute Hosps
NHS Trust 98–02; Vice Prin EMMTC *S'well* 02–10; rtd 10; PtO
S'well from 10. *5 Fellbarrow Close, West Bridgford, Nottingham
NG2 6QQ* T: 0115-981 2616

MORTON, Jennifer Pam. b 49. **d** 15 **p** 16. NSM Dorchester
Ox from 15. *8 Toot Baldon, Oxford OX44 9NG* T: (01865)
343302

MORTON, Philip John. b 79. Birm Univ BA 05 St Jo Coll
Dur BATM 11 Dur Univ MA 12. Cranmer Hall Dur 09.
d 12 **p** 13. C Maney *Birm* 12–16; P-in-c Badsey w
Aldington and Offenham and Bretforton *Worc* 16–18;
P-in-c Cleeve Prior and The Littletons 16–18; V E Vale
and Avon Villages from 18. *The Vicarage, 33 High
Street, Badsey, Evesham WR11 7EJ* T: (01386) 832599
E: revphilipmorton@gmail.com

MORTON, Rex Gerald. b 61. St Jo Coll Nottm 96. **d** 98 **p** 99.
C Bury St Edmunds All SS *St E* 98–01; C Woodside Park
St Barn *Lon* 01–07; V Golders Green from 07. *The Vicarage,
3 St Alban's Close, London NW11 7RA* T: (020) 8455
4525 M: 07968-088714 E: rex@gp-pc.co.uk

MORTON, Sister Rita. b 34. Wilson Carlile Coll. **dss** 85 **d** 87
p 94. CA from 76; Par Dn Harlow New Town w Lt Parndon
Chelmsf 87–89; C Harold Hill St Geo 89–94; rtd 94; NSM

Elm Park St Nic Hornchurch *Chelmsf* 94–05; PtO from
05. *38 Havering Court Care Home, Havering Road, Romford
RM1 4YW* T: (01708) 874820

MORTON, Rosemary Jane. b 79. LRAM 02 Lon Univ BMus 03.
Westcott Ho Cam 07. **d** 10 **p** 11. C Coggeshall w Markshall
Chelmsf 10–14; Min Can and Succ St Paul's Cathl *Lon* from
14. *7A Amen Court, London EC4M 7BU* T: (020) 7246 8338
E: rjmorton@cantab.net

MORTON, Mrs Sheila. b 44. Leeds Univ. Sarum & Wells Th
Coll 79. **dss** 84 **d** 87 **p** 94. HM Forces Düsseldorf 84–86;
Cov St Mary 86–89; Par Dn 87–89; Par Dn Boston Spa *York*
89–92; C Flitwick *St Alb* 93–00; R Wilden w Colmworth and
Ravensden 00–14; rtd 14; PtO *St Alb* from 14; *Ely* from 15.
11 Roundhouse Drive, Perry, Huntingdon PE28 0DJ T: (01480)
810363 E: revsheila827@gmail.com

MORTON, Mrs Susan Ann. b 58. Ex Univ BA 80 Warwick
Univ PGCE 84. Ripon Coll Cuddesdon 10. **d** 12 **p** 13.
NSM Hambleden Valley *Ox* from 12. *The Vicarage,
Turville, Henley-on-Thames RG9 6QU* M: 07808-517347
E: suemorton131@gmail.com

MOSEDALE, Jonathan Ralph. b 69. Imp Coll Lon BSc 90
York Univ MSc 91 Trin Coll Ox DPhil 95. Protestant Th Inst
Montpellier Lic 99 Ripon Coll Cuddesdon 07. **d** 09 **p** 10. C
St Endellion w Port Isaac and St Kew *Truro* 09–12; C St Minver
09–12; C N Cornwall Cluster 12–13; PtO from 16. *The Flat,
43-45 Molesworth Street, Wadebridge PL27 7DR* M: 07760-
275087 E: mosedale@metanoa.net

MOSELEY, Canon Hugh Martin. b 47. St Jo Coll Dur BA 70.
Westcott Ho Cam 71. **d** 73 **p** 74. C Hythe *Cant* 73–77; P-in-c
Eythorne w Waldershare 77–83; V Ringmer *Chich* 83–99;
RD Lewes and Seaford 93–97; P-in-c E Dean w Friston and
Jevington 99–00; R 00–03; TR Rye 03–09; RD 03–09; Can and
Preb Chich Cathl 07–09; rtd 09; PtO *Cant* from 11; *Chich*
from 15; Hon C Winchelsea and Icklesham 11–15. *Rushey
Green Mill, Rushey Green, Ringmer, Lewes BN8 5JB* T: (01273)
813260 E: annabelle.moseley@btinternet.com

MOSELEY, Michael. b 45. Oak Hill Th Coll 02. **d** 04 **p** 05.
NSM Forty Hill Jes Ch *Lon* 04–07; P-in-c Murston w
Bapchild and Tonge *Cant* 07–12; rtd 12; PtO *Cant* from 12.
56 Park Drive, Sittingbourne ME10 1RD T: (01795) 556258
E: michaelmoseley07@googlemail.com

MOSELEY, Roger Henry. b 38. Edin Th Coll 60. **d** 63 **p** 64.
C Friern Barnet All SS *Lon* 63–66; C Grantham St Wulfram
Linc 66–69; P-in-c Swaton w Spanby 69–73; P-in-c Horbling
69–73; V Soberton w Newtown *Portsm* 73–80; V Sarisbury
80–03; rtd 03; PtO *Portsm* from 03. *1 Birchdale Close, Warsash,
Southampton SO31 9PT* E: rhmoseley29@gmail.com

MOSELING, Canon Peter. b 48. WMMTC 92. **d** 95 **p** 96.
C Daventry, Ashby St Ledgers, Braunston etc *Pet* 95–97;
P-in-c Northampton H Trin 97–99; P-in-c Northampton
St Paul 98–99; V Northampton H Trin and St Paul 99–05;
Chapl Univ Coll Northn 99–05; P-in-c Bletchingley *S'wark*
05–06; R Bletchingley and Nutfield 06; AD Godstone 12–16;
Hon Can S'wark Cathl 14–06; rtd 16; PtO *Leic* from 17. *48
Wymondham Way, Melton Mowbray LE13 1HX* T: (01664)
669283 E: frp.moseling@tiscali.co.uk

MOSES, The Very Revd John Henry. b 38. Nottm Univ BA 59
PhD 65. Linc Th Coll 62. **d** 64 **p** 65. C Bedford St Andr *St Alb*
64–70; P-in-c Cov St Pet 70; P-in-c Cov St Mark 71–73; TR Cov
E 73–77; RD 73–77; Adn Southend *Chelmsf* 77–82; Provost
Chelmsf 82–96; Chmn Coun of Cen for Th Study Essex Univ
87–96; Dean St Paul's *Lon* 96–06; rtd 06; PtO *S'well* from 17.
Chestnut House, Burgage, Southwell NG25 0EP T: (01636)
814880 E: johnmoses.southwell@gmail.com

MOSES, Preb Leslie Alan. b 44. Hull Univ BA 71 Edin Univ
BD 76. Edin Th Coll 73. **d** 76 **p** 77. C Edin Old St Paul
76–79; R Leven *St And* 79–85; R Edin Old St Paul 85–95;
P-in-c Edin St Marg 86–92; V St Marylebone All SS *Lon*
from 95; AD Westmr St Marylebone from 01; Preb St Paul's
Cathl from 10. *All Saints' Vicarage, 7 Margaret Street, London
W1W 8JG* T: (020) 7636 1788 or 7636 9961 F: 7436 4470
E: alan@moses.org.uk or alanmoses111@gmail.com

MOSFORD, Canon Denzil Huw Erasmus. b 56. Florida State
Univ MTh 04 AKC 78. St D Coll Lamp 74 Sarum & Wells
Th Coll 77. **d** 79 **p** 80. C Clydach *S & B* 79–82; V 87–97;
Jamaica 82–85; V Ystalyfera *S & B* 85–87; Dioc World Miss
Officer 91–10; RD Cwmtawe 93–97; V Gorseinon 97–10;
AD Llwchwr 00–10; Hon Can Brecon Cathl 01–04; Can Res
Brecon Cathl 04–10; Dir of Min Miss to Seafarers 10–14;
P-in-c Dafen *St D* from 14; P-in-c Llanelli 16–17; P-in-c Bro
Lliedi from 17; AD from 17; Dioc Ecum Officer from 14; Can
St D Cathl from 18. *The Vicarage, 1 Cysgod Y Llan, Llanelli
SA15 3HD* T: (01554) 746034 E: huw.mosford@gmail.com

MOSLEY, Edward Peter. b 38. Clifton Th Coll 62. **d** 67 **p** 68.
C Mirehouse *Carl* 67–69; C Newbarns w Hawcoat 69–72;
R Aikton and Orton St Giles 72–77; V Silloth 77–78; CF

78–94; Hon C Rothiemurchus and Grantown-on-Spey *Mor* 94–95; rtd 98; P-in-c Strathnairn St Paul *Mor* 03–09. *52 Castle Heather Crescent, Inverness IV2 4BF* T: (01463) 232552 E: epmos@onetel.com *or* petermosley@gmail.com

MOSLEY, Robin Howarth. b 46. Birm Univ LLB 67 Leeds Univ BA 09 Solicitor 71. NOC 06. **d** 09 **p** 10. NSM Ches St Mary 09–11; V Brereton 11–17; rtd 17; PtO *Ches* from 17. *Brookside, Sandy Lane, Higher Kinnerton, Chester CH4 9BJ* T: (01244) 660341 M: 07818-568017 E: rev.robinmosley@gmail.com

MOSS, Alan Charles. b 81. St Mellitus Coll 16. **d** 18 **p** 19. C Collier Row St Jas and Havering-atte-Bower *Chelmsf* from 18. *9 Irons Way, Romford RM5 3RJ* M: 07928-770220 E: alanmoss1981@gmail.com

MOSS, Canon Barbara Penelope. b 46. St Anne's Coll Ox BA 66 MA 70 Lon Univ BD 97 Middx Univ MA 00. EAMTC 95. **d** 97 **p** 98. NSM Leytonstone H Trin and St Aug Harrow Green *Chelmsf* 97–00; C Cambridge Gt St Mary w St Mich *Ely* 00–05; P-in-c Gothenburg w Halmstad, Jönköping etc *Eur* 05–16; Chapl Gothenburg Univ and Chalmers Univ of Tech 05–16; Hon Can *Eur* 12–16; rtd 16; PtO *S'wark* from 17; *Eur* from 16. *327 Holly Court, Greenroof Way, London SE10 0BP* M: 07492-232453 E: barmoss.bm@gmail.com

MOSS, Bernard Roger. b 44. Ex Univ BA 65 Mansf Coll Ox BA 67 Man Univ MA 85 Staffs Univ PhD 11. **d** 15 **p** 16. NSM Odd Rode *Ches* 15–17; NSM Nantwich from 17. *34 Leicester Avenue, Alsager, Stoke-on-Trent ST7 2BS* T: (01270) 882238 M: 07917-543356 E: profbernard23@gmail.com

MOSS, Catherine. b 53. ERMC. **d** 09 **p** 10. NSM Guilsborough and Hollowell and Cold Ashby etc *Pet* from 09. *Saxon Spires Practice, West Haddon Road, Guilsborough, Northampton NN6 8QE* T: (01604) 740210 F: 740869 M: 07779-000897 E: cattimoss@aol.com

MOSS, Christopher Ashley. b 52. Ex Univ BA 73 Southn Univ DASS 78 CQSW 78. Wycliffe Hall Ox 89. **d** 91 **p** 92. C Malvern H Trin and St Jas *Worc* 91–96; V Longdon, Castlemorton, Bushley, Queenhill etc from 96; RD Upton from 11. *The Vicarage, Longdon, Tewkesbury GL20 6AT* T/F: (01684) 833256 E: cmoss@holyplace.feeserve.co.uk *or* cmoss.lcbq@gmail.com

MOSS, David. b 60. WEMTC 12. **d** 15 **p** 16. NSM Gt Hanwood and Longden and Annscroft etc *Heref* 15–19; R Westbury, Worthen and Yockleton from 19. *The Rectory, Westbury, Shrewsbury SY5 9QX* E: david.moss@sanctuary-housing.co.uk

MOSS, David Sefton. b 59. Sunderland Poly BSc 80 Anglia Poly Univ MA 05 MRPharmS 81. Ridley Hall Cam 91. **d** 93 **p** 94. C Highworth w Sevenhampton and Inglesham etc *Bris* 93–97; V Bedminster St Mich 97–17; P-in-c Alveston and Littleton-on-Severn w Elberton from 17; C Almondsbury and Olveston from 17. *St Helen's Vicarage, Gloucester Road, Alveston, Bristol BS35 3QT* T: (01454) 415190 M: 07890-262334 E: mossds@gmail.com

MOSS, Canon Denis. b 32. St Jo Coll Auckland LTh 83. **d** 74 **p** 75. New Zealand 74–92; Chapl Budapest *Eur* 92–10; Hon Can Malta Cathl 01–10; PtO from 16. *8353 Zalaszántó, Zrinyi M utca 39, Hungary* T: (0036) (83) 572003 F: 572004 E: denismoss@t-online.hu

MOSS, The Ven Leonard Godfrey. b 32. K Coll Lon BD 59 AKC 59. **d** 60 **p** 61. C Putney St Marg *S'wark* 60–63; C Cheam 63–67; R Much Dewchurch w Llanwarne and Llandinabo *Heref* 67–72; Dioc Ecum Officer 69–83; V Marden w Amberley 72–78; V Marden w Amberley and Wisteston 78–84; P-in-c 92–94; Preb Heref Cathl 79–97; Can Heref Cathl 84–91; Dioc Soc Resp Officer 84–91; Adn Heref 91–97; rtd 97; PtO *Heref* from 97. *10 Saxon Way, Ledbury HR8 2QY* T: (01531) 631195

MOSS, Miss Lucy Margaret. b 85. Cant Ch Ch Univ BA 07. St Jo Coll Nottm MTh 15. **d** 15 **p** 16. C Spennymoor and Whitworth *Dur* 15–18; C Easington and Easington Colliery from 18. *The Rectory, 5 Tudor Grange, Easington Village, Peterlee SR8 3DF* M: 07891-491386 E: lucymoss1@hotmail.com

MOSS, Mrs Nelva Elizabeth. b 44. Bp Grosseteste Coll TCert 66 Sussex Univ BEd 73. S Dios Minl Tr Scheme 90. **d** 93 **p** 94. NSM Bincombe w Broadwey, Upwey and Buckland Ripers *Sarum* 93–96; NSM Langtree *Ox* 96–98; TV 98–09; rtd 09; PtO *Sarum* from 11. *5 Wynnes Rise, Sherborne DT9 6DH* T: (01935) 814329 E: nelvamoss@hotmail.com

MOSS, Peter Hextall. b 34. Clare Coll Cam BA 59 MA 62. Linc Th Coll 59. **d** 61 **p** 62. C Easington Colliery *Dur* 61–63; C Whickham 63–65; C-in-c Town End Farm CD 65–72; TV Mattishall *Nor* 72–75; P-in-c Welborne 75–84; P-in-c Mattishall w Mattishall Burgh 75–84; P-in-c Yaxham 80–84; TR Hempnall 84–89. *High House Cottage, Gunn Street, Foulsham, Dereham NR20 5RN* T: (01362) 683823 E: pandgmoss@gmail.com

MOSSE, Mrs Barbara Ann. b 51. CertEd 73 Open Univ BA 77 Univ of Wales (Lamp) MA 99 Lambeth STh 83. CA Tr Coll IDC 81. **d** 90 **p** 95. CA 81–91; NSM Southbourne w W Thorney *Chich* 90–93; Community Mental Health

Chapl Fareham/Gosport 94–97; NSM Purbrook *Portsm* 95–03; Team Chapl Portsm Hosps NHS Trust 01–09; Asst Dioc Spirituality Adv *Portsm* 05–09; PtO 03–15. *Drogo, 1 Grenfield Court, Emsworth PO10 7SA* T: (01243) 376155 E: barbaramosse@btinternet.com

MOSSMAN, Mrs Margaret. b 46. NOC 97. **d** 00 **p** 01. NSM Beighton *Sheff* 00–02; C 02–04; V Owston 04–12; rtd 12; PtO *Pet* from 12. *32 Tennyson Road, Rothwell, Kettering NN14 6JH* T: (01536) 660928 E: mmossman@hotmail.co.uk

MOSSOP, Patrick John. b 48. St Jo Coll Cam MA LLB Solicitor. Linc Th Coll BTh 93. **d** 93 **p** 94. C Halstead St Andr w H Trin and Greenstead Green *Chelmsf* 93–97; Assoc Chapl Essex Univ 97–99; Chapl 99–04; V Forest Gate Em w Upton Cross 04–09; TR Plaistow and N Canning Town 09–14; rtd 14; PtO *Chelmsf* 15–18; Hon C Wanstead H Trin Hermon Hill from 18. *18 Aileen Walk, London E15 4BB* M: 07908-688078 E: patmossop2@gmail.com

MOSTON, William Howard. b 47. **d** 10 **p** 11. OLM E Crompton *Man* from 10. *36 Clough Road, Shaw, Oldham OL2 8QD* T: (01706) 847940 M: 07440-947328 E: whmoston@hotmail.com

MOTE, Gregory Justin. b 60. Oak Hill Th Coll BA 83. **d** 86 **p** 87. C W Ealing St Jo w St Jas *Lon* 86–90; C St Helen Bishopsgate w St Andr Undershaft etc 90–95; V Poulton Lancelyn H Trin *Ches* 96–04; PtO *Blackb* from 04. *22 Evergreen Avenue, Leyland PR25 3AW* E: gjmote@aol.com

MOTHERSOLE, Hugh Robert. b 43. Essex Univ BA 70 MSc 73. **d** 11 **p** 12. OLM Halstead Area *Chelmsf* 11–15; NSM 15–18; rtd 18; PtO *Chelmsf* from 18. *10 Park Lane, Earls Colne, Colchester CO6 2RJ* T: (01787) 222211 M: 07803-699268 E: hrmsteam@btinternet.com

MOTHERSOLE, John Robert. b 25. Lon Univ MA 99. Chich Th Coll. **d** 84 **p** 85. NSM Hayes St Anselm *Lon* 84–93; NSM Hayes St Edm 93–98; P-in-c St Mary Aldermary 98–10; rtd 10; PtO *Lon* 10–18. *116 Nestles Avenue, Hayes UB3 4QD* T: (020) 8848 0626 E: jm014t1045@blueyonder.co.uk

MOTT, Mrs Marjorie. b 51. Westf Coll Lon BSc 72 Univ Coll Lon PhD 78. **d** 15 **p** 16. NSM Greenhill St Jo *Lon* 15–18; PtO from 18. *51 Brook Drive, Harrow HA1 4RT* T: (020) 8930 9119 M: 07976-609287 E: marjorie.mott@gmail.com

MOTT, Peter John. b 49. Ch Coll Cam BA 70 MA 75 Dundee Univ PhD 73. St Jo Coll Nottm BA 79. **d** 80 **p** 81. C Hull St Jo Newland *York* 80–83; C Selly Park St Steph and St Wulstan *Birm* 83–87; C Mosborough *Sheff* 87–92; R Colne St Bart *Blackb* 92–98; TV Colne and Villages 98–01; P-in-c Keighley St Andr *Bradf* 01–14; *Leeds* 14; Dioc Ecum Officer *Bradf* 04–14; *Leeds* 14; rtd 14; PtO *York* from 14. *Cornerways, 13 Hall Park, Heslington, York YO10 5DT* T: (01904) 206958 E: petermott57@gmail.com

MOTT, Wendy Sandra. b 59. St Mellitus Coll 16. **d** 18 **p** 19. OLM Corringham and Fobbing *Chelmsf* from 18. *Ambleside, 35 Conrad Road, Stanford-le-Hope SS17 0AT* T: (01375) 642017 E: revwendy@ubocaf.org.uk

✠**MOTTAHEDEH, The Rt Revd Iraj Kalimi.** b 32. United Th Coll Bangalore 56. **d** 59 **p** 60 **c** 86. C Isfahan St Luke Iran 59–62; V Shiraz St Simon 62–66; V Tehran St Paul 67–75; V Isfahan St Luke 75–83; Adn Iran 83–86; Asst Bp Iran 86–90; Bp Iran 90–02; Pres Bp Episc Ch Jerusalem and Middle E 00–02; rtd 02; Interim Bp Iran 02–04; Hon Asst Bp Birm and Lich from 05. *2 Highland Road, Newport TF10 7QE* T: (01952) 813615 E: bishraj@btinternet.com

MOTTERSHEAD, Derek. b 39. Open Univ BA 74 BEd. Chich Th Coll 65. **d** 69 **p** 70. C Walthamstow St Barn and St Jas Gt *Chelmsf* 69–72; C Chelmsf All SS 72–77; P-in-c Cold Norton w Stow Maries 77–80; V Leytonstone St Andr 80–92; V Eastbourne St Sav and St Pet *Chich* 92–04; Miss to Seafarers 92–04; rtd 04; PtO *Cant* 05–06 and from 11; Hon C Preston next Faversham, Goodnestone and Graveney 06–10. *Sherwood, 25B The Paddock, Spring Lane, Canterbury CT1 1SX* T: (01227) 453118 E: dmottershead11@btinternet.com

MOTTERSHEAD, Nicholas John Leigh. b 66. Reading Univ BSc 88 Cant Ch Ch Univ BA 15 FCA 91. SEITE 12. **d** 15 **p** 16. NSM St Olave Hart Street w All Hallows Staining etc *Lon* from 15; PtO *Roch* from 16. *47 Barnmead Road, Beckenham BR3 1JF* T: (020) 8289 3858 M: 07950-010640 E: nickmottershead@btinternet.com

MOTTRAM, Andrew Peter. b 53. AKC 77. Ripon Coll Cuddesdon 77. **d** 78 **p** 79. C E Bedfont *Lon* 78–81; C Bp's Hatfield *St Alb* 81–84; V Milton Ernest 84–91; V Thurleigh 84–91; P-in-c Heref All SS 91–06; RD Heref City 02–03; Ch Buildings Officer *Worc* from 09; PtO *Heref* from 06; *Worc* from 09. *Mulberry Dock, Pencombe, Bromyard HR7 4SH* M: 07960-726717 E: andrew.mottram@btinternet.com

MOTYER, Stephen. b 50. Pemb Coll Cam BA 73 MA 77 Bris Univ MLitt 79 K Coll Lon PhD 93. Trin Coll Bris 73.

d 76 **p** 77. Lect Oak Hill Th Coll 76–83; C Braughing, Lt Hadham, Albury, Furneux Pelham etc *St Alb* 83–87; Lect Lon Sch of Th from 87; PtO *Lon* 87–13; *St Alb* from 87. *7 Hangar Ruding, Watford WD19 5BH* T: (020) 8386 6829 *or* (01923) 826061 E: s.motyer@londonbiblecollege.ac.uk *or* s.mothyer@ntlworld.com

MOUGHTIN, Ross. b 48. St Cath Coll Cam BA 70 St Jo Coll Dur BA 75. **d** 76 **p** 77. C Litherland St Paul Hatton Hill *Liv* 76–79; C Heswall *Ches* 79–84; Chapl Edw Unit Rochdale Infirmary 83–92; V Thornham w Gravel Hole *Man* 84–92; V Aughton Ch Ch *Liv* 92–18; Chapl W Lancashire NHS Trust 94–11; rtd 18; PtO *Liv* from 19. *Christ Church Vicarage, 22 Long Lane, Aughton, Ormskirk L39 5AT* T: (01695) 422175 E: ross.moughtin@gmail.com

MOUGHTIN-MUMBY, Andrew Denis Paul. b 78. Birm Univ BA 00 SS Coll Cam BA 05 MA 09. Westcott Ho Cam 03. **d** 06 **p** 07. C Walworth St Chris *S'wark* 06–10; R Walworth St Pet from 10; AD S'wark and Newington from 14; PV Westmr Abbey from 14. *St Peter's Rectory, 12 Villa Street, London SE17 2EJ* T: (020) 7703 3139 E: rector@stpeterswalworth.org

MOUGHTIN-MUMBY, Sharon. b 76. St Jo Coll Dur BA 97 MA 98 Worc Coll Ox DPhil 04. Westcott Ho Cam 05. **d** 06 **p** 07. C Walworth St Pet *S'wark* 06–10; Dioc Miss Th Angl Communion 10–11; Hon C S'wark St Geo w St Alphege and St Jude 10–15; Hon C Walworth St Pet from 15. *St Peter's Rectory, 12 Villa Street, London SE17 2EJ* M: 07980-611347 E: sharon.mm@btinternet.com

MOUK, Mae Elizabeth. See CHRISTIE, Mae Elizabeth

MOUL, Russell Derek. b 56. Reading Univ BA 83. Oak Hill Th Coll 97. **d** 99 **p** 00. C Harold Wood *Chelmsf* 99–02; C Harold Hill St Paul 02–03; V from 03. *St Paul's Vicarage, Redcar Road, Romford RM3 9PT* T: (01708) 341225 E: russell@stpaulsharoldhill.org.uk

MOULAND, Norman Francis. b 38. OLM course 98. **d** 99 **p** 00. OLM Verwood *Sarum* 99–18; PtO from 18. *13 Park Drive, Verwood BH31 7PE* T: (01202) 825320

MOULD, Mrs Jacqueline. b 66. QUB BD 88. CITC BTh 91. **d** 91 **p** 92. C Belfast St Aid *Conn* 91–94; C Drumragh w Mountfield *D & R* 94–96; NSM Kinson *Sarum* 97–00; C Belvoir *D & D* from 03. *10A Ballyclough Road, Lisburn BT28 3UY* T: (028) 9264 7912 *or* 9049 1436 E: jacmould@gmail.com

MOULD, Jeremy James. b 63. Nottm Univ BA 85 TCD BTh 91. CITC 88. **d** 91 **p** 92. C Mossley *Conn* 91–94; C Drumragh w Mountfield *D & R* 94–96; C Kinson *Sarum* 97–00; I Templepatrick w Donegore *Conn* from 19. *10A Ballyclough Road, Lisburn BT28 3UY* T: (028) 9264 7912 E: jermould@gmail.com

MOULDEN, David Ivor. b 52. Cant Ch Ch Univ BA 02. SEITE 05. **d** 08 **p** 09. C Madeley *Heref* 08–12; V Canonry *Cant* from 12. *The Vicarage, Queen's Road, Ash, Canterbury CT3 2BG* E: davidmoulden@hotmail.com

MOULDER, Kenneth. b 53. Lon Univ BEd 75. Ridley Hall Cam 78. **d** 81 **p** 82. C Harold Wood *Chelmsf* 81–84; C Darfield *Sheff* 84–88; V Walkergate *Newc* 88–92; P-in-c Byker St Mark 90–92; V Byker St Mark and Walkergate St Oswald from 92. *St Oswald's Parsonage, Woodhead Road, Newcastle upon Tyne NE6 4RX* T: 0191-263 6249

MOULES-JONES, Roy Llewellyn. **d** 17 **p** 18. C Bro Deiniol *Ban* 17–18; C Bro Cwyfan from 18. *Bridin, Gaerwen LL60 6AS* T: (01248) 715349 E: llewmoules-jones@esgobaethbangor.net

MOULT, Jane Elizabeth Kate. b 61. Trin Coll Bris 91. **d** 94 **p** 95. C St Jo in Bedwardine *Worc* 94–97; NSM Bilton *Cov* 97–99; Chapl Staunton Harold Hosp 00–01; Sen Chapl Leics Partnership NHS Trust 01–07; PtO *Leic* 07–14. *17 The Leascroft, Ravenstone, Coalville LE67 2BL* T: (01530) 833160

MOULT, Simon Paul. b 66. Trin Coll Bris BA 94. **d** 94 **p** 95. C St Jo in Bedwardine *Worc* 94–97; C Bilton *Cov* 97–99; P-in-c Thringstone St Andr *Leic* 99–05; RD Akeley S 03–05; Chapl Cov and Warks Partnership NHS Trust from 05; Chapl Geo Eliot Hosp NHS Trust Nuneaton from 05. *The Chaplaincy, George Eliot Hospital, College Street, Nuneaton CV10 7DJ* T: (024) 7686 5046 *or* 7635 1351 E: simon.moult@covwarkpt.nhs.uk

MOUNCER, David Peter. b 65. Univ of Wales (Abth) BA 86. Oak Hill Th Coll BA 94. **d** 94 **p** 95. C Folkestone St Jo *Cant* 94–98; Min Grove Green LEP 98–03; R Brampton St Thos *Derby* 03–07; C Chesterfield Deanery 07–16; C Old Brampton and Great Barlow *Derby* from 16; C Loundsley Green from 16. *5 Foxbrook Drive, Chesterfield S40 3JR* T: (01246) 551313 E: therevdp@tiscali.co.uk

MOUNSEY, William Lawrence Fraser. b 51. St Andr Univ BD 75. Edin Th Coll 76. **d** 78 **p** 79. C Edin St Mark 78–81; Chapl RAF 81–90 and 96–06; R Dalmahoy and Chapl Heriot-Watt Univ *Edin* 90–96; PtO *Eur* from 06; C Roslin (Rosslyn Chpl) *Edin* 06–11; C Edin St Vin from 11. *9 Upper*

Coltbridge Terrace, Edinburgh EH12 6AD M: 07967-322651 E: wlfm@hotmail.co.uk

⌖**MOUNSTEPHEN, The Rt Revd Philip Ian.** b 59. Southn Univ BA 80 Magd Coll Ox MA 87 PGCE. Wycliffe Hall Ox 85. **d** 88 **p** 89 **c** 18. C Gerrards Cross and Fulmer *Ox* 88–92; V W Streatham St Jas *S'wark* 92–98; Hd Pathfinders CPAS 98–02; Dir CY Network 01–02; Hd Min 02–07; Dep Gen Dir 04–07; Chapl Paris St Mich *Eur* 07–12; Exec Ldr CMS 12–18; Hon Can *Eur* from 12; Bp Truro from 18. *Lis Escop, Feock, Truro TR3 6QQ* T: (01872) 862657 M: 07775-528556 E: bishop@truro.anglican.org

MOUNT, Canon Judith Mary. b 35. Bedf Coll Lon BA 56 Lon Univ CertEd 57. Ripon Coll Cuddesdon 81. **dss** 83 **d** 87 **p** 94. Carterton *Ox* 83–85; Charlton on Otmoor and Oddington 85–87; Dioc Lay Min Adv and Asst Dir of Ords 86–89; Par Dn Islip w Charlton on Otmoor, Oddington, Noke etc 87–94; C 94–95; Assoc Dioc Dir Ords and Adv for Women in Ord Min 89–95; Hon Can Ch Ch 92–95; rtd 95; PtO *Ox* 95–10; *Glouc* from 99. *Lathams, Bell Lane, Poulton, Cirencester GL7 5JF* T: (01285) 850242 E: jmount315@gmail.com

MOUNTAIN, John Raymond. b 46. LCTP 11. **d** 12 **p** 13. NSM Appley Bridge and Parbold *Blackb* 12–16; PtO 16–17. *50 The Common, Parbold, Wigan WN8 7EA* T: (01257) 463919 M: 07542-000996 E: john_mountain@talktalk.net

MOUNTFORD, Canon Brian Wakling. b 45. Newc Univ BA 66 Cam Univ MA 73 Ox Univ MA 90. Westcott Ho Cam 66. **d** 68 **p** 69. C Westmr St Steph w St Jo *Lon* 68–69; C Paddington Ch Ch 69–73; Chapl SS Coll Cam 73–78; V Southgate Ch Ch *Lon* 78–86; V Ox St Mary V w St Cross and St Pet 86–16; Chapl St Hilda's Coll Ox 89–16; Hon Can Ch Ch *Ox* 98–16; rtd 16; PtO *Ox* from 16. *The Old Barn, Mill Street, Islip, Kidlington OX5 2SY* T: (01865) 515778 *or* 279111 E: brian.mountford@oriel.ox.ac.uk

MOURANT, Julia Caroline. b 58. Sheff Univ BA 79. St Jo Coll Nottm 82. **dss** 84 **d** 92 **p** 94. Cropwell Bishop w Colston Bassett, Granby etc *S'well* 84–86; Marple All SS *Ches* 86–89; Harlow St Mary and St Hugh w St Jo the Bapt *Chelmsf* 89–92; NSM 92–04; Asst Dir of Min 98–04; CME Officer 00–02; PtO *Win* 04–05; Lay Tr Officer 05–07; Voc, Recruitment and Selection Officer 07–15; PtO from 15; *Sarum* from 18. *The Rectory, Church Lane, Ellisfield, Basingstoke RG25 2QR* T: (01256) 381217 E: julia.caroline@btinternet.com

MOURANT, Sidney Eric. b 39. Lon Univ BD 73. Oak Hill Th Coll. **d** 89 **p** 90. C Oxton *Ches* 89–92; V Douglas All SS and St Thos *S & M* 92–96; I Rathkeale w Askeaton, Kilcornan and Kilnaughtin *L & K* 96–00; I Nenagh 00–04; rtd 04. *12 Breezemount, Hamiltonsbawn, Armagh BT61 9SB* T: (028) 3887 2203 M: (00353) 87-239 9785

MOURANT, Stephen Philip Edward. b 54. St Jo Coll Nottm BTh 83. **d** 83 **p** 84. C Cropwell Bishop w Colston Bassett, Granby etc *S'well* 83–86; C Marple All SS *Ches* 86–89; P-in-c Harlow St Mary and St Hugh w St Jo the Bapt *Chelmsf* 89–90; V 90–04; P-in-c Bitterne *Win* 04–08; C Fair Oak 08–11; C Farleigh, Candover and Wield from 11. *The Rectory, Church Lane, Ellisfield, Basingstoke RG25 2QR* T: (01256) 381217 E: stephen.mourant@btinternet.com *or* stevemourant@btinternet.com

MOUSIR-HARRISON, Stuart Nicholas. b 68. SW Poly Plymouth BSc 89 Nottm Univ MSc 92 St Martin's Coll Lanc PhD 99 St Jo Coll Dur BA 99. Cranmer Hall Dur. **d** 00 **p** 01. C Oadby *Leic* 00–03; C W Malling w Offham *Roch* 03–07; C Mereworth w W Peckham 03–07; P-in-c Dallington *Pet* 07–12; Chapl Northn Univ from 07. *125 Kingsley Road, Northampton NN2 7BT* T: (01604) 892468

MOWBRAY, David. b 38. Fitzw Ho Cam BA 60 MA 64 Lon Univ BD 62. Clifton Th Coll. **d** 63 **p** 64. C Northampton St Giles *Pet* 63–66; Lect Watford St Mary *St Alb* 66–70; V Broxbourne 70–77; R Broxbourne w Wormley 77–84; V Hertford All SS 84–91; V Darley Abbey *Derby* 91–03; Asst Chapl Derby R Infirmary 94–99; Chapl Derbyshire Mental Health Services NHS Trust 99–03; rtd 03; PtO *Linc* from 17. *4 Marigold Close, Lincoln LN2 4SZ* T: (01522) 546753 E: davidanddiana@hotmail.com

MOWBRAY, Ms Jill Valerie. b 54. Sussex Univ BEd 76 Lon Inst of Educn MA 86 Anglia Poly Univ MA 01. Ridley Hall Cam 99. **d** 01 **p** 02. C Tufnell Park St Geo and All SS Low 01–04; V Whitton SS Phil and Jas 04–09; CME Adv *Chelmsf* from 09; C Walthamstow from 16. *41 Fraser Road, London E17 9DD* T: (020) 8520 9740 E: revjillmowbray@googlemail.com

MOWFORTH, Mark. b 64. Reading Univ BSc 86. Trin Coll Bris 93. **d** 96 **p** 97. C Buckingham *Ox* 96–98; C High Wycombe 98–03; P-in-c Prestwood and Gt Hampden 03–07. *Flat 2, 118 Totteridge Road, High Wycombe HP13 6EX* T: (01494) 521097

MOWLL, John William Rutley. b 42. Sarum Th Coll 63. **d** 66 **p** 67. C Oughtibridge *Sheff* 66–69; C Hill *Birm*

69–73; Ind Chapl and V Upper Arley *Worc* 73–78; P-in-c Upton Snodsbury and Broughton Hackett etc 78–81; R 81–83; V Boughton under Blean w Dunkirk *Cant* 83–89; V Boughton under Blean w Dunkirk and Hernhill 89–07; RD Ospringe 95–01; Hon Min Can Cant Cathl 96–07; rtd 07; Chapl to The Queen 00–12; PtO *Cant* 07–16. *Holly Cottage, Water Lane, Ospringe, Faversham ME13 8TS* T: (01795) 597597

MOXLEY, Mrs Elizabeth Jane. b 52. St Jo Coll Nottm. d 05 p 06. C Aston Clinton w Buckland and Drayton Beauchamp *Ox* 05–08; R 08–17; rtd 17; PtO *Portsm* from 18. *34 Granville Road, Cowes PO31 7JF* E: elizabethmoxley@hotmail.com

MOY, Miss Elizabeth. b 55. Leeds and Carnegie Coll CertEd 76. LCTP 07. d 10 p 13. NSM Harden and Wilsden, Cullingworth and Denholme *Bradf* 10–14; *Leeds* from 14. *3 Parkside Court, Cross Roads, Keighley BD22 9DS* T: (01535) 645991 *or* 650552 F: 650550

MOY (née PLUMB), Mrs Nicola Louise. b 80. Birm Univ BA 01 Bris Univ MA 03 PGCE 04. St Jo Coll Nottm 06. d 08 p 09. C Wolverhampton St Jude *Lich* 08–12; C Turnham Green Ch Ch *Lon* from 13. *The Vicarage, 2 Wellesley Road, London W4 4BL* T: (020) 8996 0366 M: 07595-082918 E: nicolalouisemoy@gmail.com *or* nicola.moy@christchurchw4.com

MOY, Richard John. b 78. St Cath Coll Cam BA 99. Trin Coll Bris MA 03. d 04 p 05. C Wolverhampton St Jude *Lich* 04–07; Pioneer Min Wolv City Cen 07–10; Fresh Expressions Adv 10–12; V Turnham Green Ch Ch *Lon* from 12. *The Vicarage, 2 Wellesley Road, London W4 4BL* T: (020) 8996 0366 E: notintheratrace@yahoo.co.uk *or* richard.moy@christchurchw4.com

MOYES (née WATSON), Mrs Stephanie Abigail. b 61. Heriot-Watt Univ BA 84. Cranmer Hall Dur 86. d 90 p 94. C Bishop's Castle w Mainstone *Heref* 90–93; Dep Chapl HM Pris Dur 93–95; Chapl HM Rem Cen Low Newton 95–98; V Chilton and Cornforth *Dur* 98–02; Chapl Wrekin Coll Telford 02–04; PtO *Worc* from 04; Sub-Chapl HM YOI Hewell Grange from 14; Sub-Chapl HM Rem Cen Brockhill from 14. *7 Birchanger Green, Worcester WR4 0DW* T: (01905) 619181 E: revd.stephanie.watson@hotmail.com

MOYNAGH, Michael Digby. b 50. Southn Univ BA 73 Lon Univ MA 74 Aus Nat Univ PhD 78 Bris Univ MA 85. Trin Coll Bris. d 85 p 86. C Northwood Em *Lon* 85–89; P-in-c Wilton *B & W* 89–90; TR 90–96; Dir Cen for Futures Studies St Jo Coll Nottm 96–04; Co-Dir Tomorrow Project 04–14; Fresh Expressions Team *Ox* from 05. *14 Dale Close, Oxford OX1 1TU* T: (01865) 722551 E: michael.moynagh@wycliffe.ox.ac.uk

MOYNAN, Canon David George. b 53. d 86 p 87. C Seagoe *D & D* 86–88; C Taney *D & G* 88–89; I Arklow w Inch and Kilbride 89–94; Dioc Stewardship Adv 92–15; Dioc Ch of Ireland Bps' Appeal Rep 92–15; I Kilternan 94–15; Dioc Dir Decade of Evang 96–15; Can Ch Ch Cathl Dublin 97–15; New Zealand from 15. *250 Annesbrooke Drive, Wakatu, Nelson 7011, New Zealand* M: (0064) 21-0826 6278 E: moynandg.nz@gmail.com

MOYO (née Hudghton), Deborah Elizabeth. b 92. Nottm Univ BA 13. St Mellitus Coll 16. d 18 p 19. C Carlton *S'well* from 18; C Colwick from 18. *5 Langton Close, Colwick, Nottingham NG4 2BW*

MUBARAK, Riaz. b 70. d 01. Pakistan 01–14; P-in-c W Winch w Setchey, N Runcton and Middleton *Nor* 14–15; R Middlewinch from 15; Chapl Norfolk Constabulary from 18. *The New Rectory, Rectory Lane, West Winch, King's Lynn PE33 0NR* T: (01553) 841519 E: rev.riaz.mubarak@gmail.com

MUCKLE, Andrew Philip. b 69. Bris Univ BVSc 93 Middx Univ MSc 04. Coll of Resurr Mirfield BA 16. d 16 p 17. C Gillingham and Milton-on-Stour *Sarum* 16–19; V W Moors from 19. *Address temp unknown* M: 07505-007498 E: andymuckle@outlook.com

MUDD, Mrs Linda Anne. b 59. WMMTC 00. d 03 p 04. C Exhall *Cov* 03–07; Chapl Geo Eliot Hosp NHS Trust Nuneaton 07–11; TV Coventry Caludon *Cov* 11–19; V Mancetter from 19. *The Vicarage, Quarry Lane, Atherstone CV9 1NL* E: linda.mudd@btinternet.com

MUDGE, Frederick Alfred George. b 31. Leeds Univ BSc 58 Univ of Wales BD 67. St Mich Coll Llan 58. d 61 p 62. C Cwmavon *Llan* 61–64; PV Llan Cathl 64–70; R Llandough w Leckwith 70–88; V Penarth All SS 88–96; rtd 96; PtO *Llan* from 07. *Pathways, 6 Fairwater Road, Llandaff, Cardiff CF5 2LD*

MUDIE, Martin Bruce. b 54. Goldsmiths' Coll Lon BA 76. Sarum & Wells Th Coll 92. d 92 p 93. C Bromley St Mark *Roch* 92–95; rtd 95; PtO *B & W* 02–03; Hon C Glastonbury w Meare 03–10; PtO from 10. *20 Oriel Road, Street BA16 0JL* T: (01458) 448034 E: mmudie5@gmail.com

MUFFETT, Mrs Sarah Susan. b 53. STETS 02. d 05 p 06. NSM Okeford *Sarum* 05–13; rtd 13; PtO *Sarum* from 13. *Highlands, High Street, Child Okeford, Blandford Forum DT11 8EH* T: (01258) 860010 E: sarahmuffett@btopenworld.com

MUGAN, Canon Miriam Ruth. b 56. RNMH 77. Oak Hill Th Coll 93. d 96 p 97. NSM St Alb St Sav 96–07; P-in-c Croxley Green All SS 07–12; V from 12; Hon Can St Alb from 19. *All Saints' Vicarage, The Green, Croxley Green, Rickmansworth WD3 3HJ* T: (01923) 772109 E: miriam.mugan@btopenworld.com

MUGGE, Martijn. b 69. Oak Hill Th Coll BA 12. d 12 p 13. C Wombwell *Sheff* 12–15; P-in-c Conisbrough from 15. *The Vicarage, 8 Castle Avenue, Conisbrough, Doncaster DN12 3BT* M: 07732-492998 E: mugge@onetel.com *or* martijn.mugge@sheffield.anglican.org

MUGGERIDGE, Ms Sara Ann (Sally). b 49. Westf Coll Lon BA 73 Reading Univ MBA 92 Cant Ch Ch Univ BA 13. d 15 p 16. C St Steph Walbrook and St Swithun etc *Lon* 15–17; PtO *Cant* from 18. *8 Hayfield House, 11-15 Hayfield Passage, London E1 3LQ* T: (01304) 831964 M: 07770-381911 E: revdsallymuggeridge@gmail.com

MUGGLETON, James. b 55. Bris Univ BA 80. Chich Th Coll 81 EAMTC 99. d 01 p 02. NSM E Leightonstone *Ely* 01–03; C 03–04; C Buckworth and Alconbury cum Weston 04; R Barney, Fulmodeston w Croxton, Hindringham etc *Nor* 04–15; R Barney, Hindringham, Thursford, Great Snoring, Little Snoring and Kettlestone and Pensthorpe from 15. *The Rectory, The Street, Hindringham, Fakenham NR21 0AA* T: (01328) 878159 E: jamie@muggs.myzen.co.uk

MUGHAL, Dominic Jacob. b 59. Asian Soc Inst Manila MSc 88 Edin Univ MTh 93 Leeds Univ MPhil 04. St Jo Coll Nottm 05. d 07 p 08. C Fairweather Green *Bradf* 07–09; Community Outreach P 09–13; C Thornbury 09–13; C Woodhall 09–13; C Bradf St Aug Undercliffe 09–13; C Bradf St Clem 09–13; Pakistan Miss Partner CMS 13–15; C Tong and Laisterdyke *Leeds* 15–16; TV Seacroft from 16. *St James's Vicarage, 47 St James Approach, Leeds LS14 6JJ* M: 07821-246891 E: dominic_moghal@hotmail.com

MUGRIDGE, Mrs Gloria Janet. b 45. R Holloway Coll Lon BA 66. S Dios Mini Tr Scheme 92. d 95 p 96. NSM Dorchester *Sarum* 95–97; Asst Chapl Weymouth Coll 95–97; Chapl 97–04; NSM Melbury *Sarum* 97–02; NSM Stour Vale 04–06; PtO from 12. *27 St John's Priory, 1 Shaftesbury Road, Wilton, Salisbury SP2 0JN* T: (01722) 742386 E: janetmug@aol.com

MUIR, David Murray. b 49. Glas Univ MA 70. St Jo Coll Nottm BA 72. d 76 p 77. C Fulham St Mary N End *Lon* 76–80; C Aspley *S'well* 80; India 81–85; Dir Ext Studies St Jo Coll Nottm 85–02; C Upton (Overchurch) *Ches* 02–04; Adult Educn and Par Development Adv *Ex* 04–08; Pioneer Min Okehampton Deanery 08–14; rtd 14. *265 Milton Road, Weston-super-Mare BS22 8JA* T: (01934) 622036 M: 07854-845067 E: davidandjunemuir@gmail.com

MUIR, David Trevor. b 49. TCD MA MLitt 93. CITC 75. d 78 p 79. C Dublin Clontarf *D & G* 78–80; C Monkstown St Mary 80–83; I Kilternan 83–94; I Delgany 94–97; Can Ch Ch Cathl Dublin 95–97; Chapl to Ch of Ireland Assn of Deaf People 97–15; rtd 15. *Luogh North, Doolin, Co Clare, Republic of Ireland* T: (00353) (65) 707 4778 F: 707 4871 M: 87-921 1501 E: muirdt@gmail.com

MUIR, Peter Robert James. b 49. Ex Univ BSc 71. d 09 p 10. OLM Thursley *Guildf* 09–13; NSM 13–19; OLM Elstead 09–13; NSM 13–19; PtO from 19. *Yew Cottage, Thursley, Godalming GU8 6QA* T: (01252) 702360 *or* 703857 M: 07747-793253 E: vicar@thursleychurch.org.uk *or* petermuir@cellarworld.co.uk

MUKHERJEE, Supriyo. b 42. Calcutta Univ BA 70 Serampore Th Coll BD 76 Derby Univ MA 97. Bp's Coll Calcutta 70. d 75 p 76. India 75–91; C Crook *Dur* 91–92; V Nelson in Lt Marsden *Blackb* 92–95; Dioc Community Relns Officer *Cov* 95–02; TV Cov E 95–02; rtd 02; PtO *Cov* 02–04. *30 Ulverscroft Road, Coventry CV3 5EZ* T: (024) 7650 1559

MUKHOLI, Patrick John Eshuchi. b 60. Nairobi Univ BSc 86 Aber Univ MTh 09. Nairobi Evang Graduate Sch of Th MDiv 98. d 98 p 99. Dioc Youth Adv and C Ukunda St Steph Kenya 98–02; Dioc Miss and Communications Officer 99–02; Chapl St Aug Prep Sch 99–02; NSM Blackbird Leys *Ox* 02–08; Youth Worker 03–09; Prin Bp Hannington Th Coll Mombasa Kenya 10–12; NSM Penhill *Bris* 13–17; NSM Upper Stratton 13–17; C Wokingham St Paul *Ox* from 17. *23 Sheridan Way, Wokingham RG41 3AP* T: 0118-977 3397 M: 07448-794154 E: pmukholi@yahoo.com *or* patrick.mukholi@spauls.org.uk

MUKUNGA, James. b 74. Univ of Zimbabwe BA 00. Bp Gaul Th Coll Harare 95. d 97 p 99. Zimbabwe 97–04; R Kadoma All SS 01–02; R Mabelreign St Pet and Lect Bp Gaul Coll 02–04; PtO *Ox* 04–06; C High Wycombe

06–07; C Peckham St Sav *S'wark* 07–10; PtO 11–12. *7 Neville Close, London SE15 5UE* M: 07886-235698 E: james_mukunga@yahoo.com

MULCAHY, Richard Patrick. b 67. SW Poly Plymouth BSc 90. St Mich Coll Llan 02. **d** 05 **p** 06. NSM Bassaleg *Mon* 05–16; NSM Bedwas w Machen w Michaelston-y-Fedw w Rudry from 16. *9 High Cross Drive, Rogerstone, Newport NP10 9AB* M: 07940-997741 E: richard-mulcahy@ntlworld.com

MULFORD, Robert. b 57. Middx Poly CertEd 79 Open Univ BA 87 MA 93 Oak Hill Th Coll BA 03. ERMC 05. **d** 07 **p** 08. C Billing *Pet* 07–11; PtO 11–12; V Westfield and Guestling *Chich* 12–19; rtd 19. *9 Moor View Close, Sidmouth EX10 9UP* M: 07768-960896

MULHALL, Canon James Gerard. b 60. NUI DipSW 92 CQSW 92. Carlow Coll BA 95. **d** 86 **p** 87. C Clonmel w Innislounagh, Tullaghmelan etc *C & O* 09–10; C Lismore w Cappoquin, Kilwatermoy, Dungarvan etc 11–17; P-in-c Kells Gp from 17; Can Kilkenny Cathl from 18. *The Priory, Kells, Co Kilkenny, Republic of Ireland* M: (00353) 87-240 1913 E: jamesgmulhall@gmail.com

MULHOLLAND, Canon Nicholas Christopher John. b 44. Chich Th Coll 77. **d** 79 **p** 80. C Thornbury *Glouc* 79–83; R Boxwell, Leighterton, Didmarton, Oldbury etc 83–11; RD Tetbury 00–03; Hon Can Glouc Cathl 06–11; rtd 11; PtO *Bris* from 11; *Glouc* from 15. *Little Badminton Farmhouse, Little Badminton, Badminton GL9 1AB* T: (01454) 218427 E: revmulholland@btinternet.com

✠**MULLALLY, The Rt Revd and Rt Hon Dame Sarah Elisabeth.** b 62. S Bank Univ BSc 84 MSc 92 Bournemouth Univ Hon DSc 01 Wolv Univ Hon DSc 04 Herts Univ Hon DSc 05 RGN 84. SEITE 98. **d** 01 **p** 02 **c** 15. C Battersea Fields *S'wark* 01–06; TR Sutton 06–12; Can Res and Treas Sarum Cathl 12–15; Suff Bp Crediton *Ex* 15–18; Bp Lon from 18. *The Old Deanery, Dean's Court, London EC4V 5AA* T: (020) 3837 5200 E: bishop.london@london.anglican.org

MULLANEY, Daniel Robert John. b 83. Warwick Univ BSc 04 Keble Coll Ox MPhil 17. Wycliffe Hall Ox BA 15. **d** 19. C Higher Openshaw *Man* from 19. *10 Redacre Road, Manchester M18 8RU* T: (01612) 308363 E: daniel@stclementschurchmanchester.org

MULLANEY, Mrs Jane Megan. b 48. Kingston Poly BA 72. **d** 04 **p** 05. OLM Kenilworth St Jo *Cov* 04–15; rtd 15; PtO *Cov* from 15. *5 Knightlow Close, Kenilworth CV8 2PX* T: (01926) 850723 E: jane_m_mullaney536@btinternet.com

MULLEN, Canon Charles William. b 64. CITC BTh 92. **d** 92 **p** 93. C Lecale Gp *D & D* 92–95; I Gorey w Kilnahue, Leskinfere and Ballycanew *C & O* 95–00; Dean's V St Patr Cathl Dublin from 00; Preb Rathmichael St Patr Cathl Dublin from 08. *35A Kevin Street Upper, Dublin 8, Republic of Ireland* T: (00353) (1) 453 9472 M: 87-261 8878 E: deans.vicar@stpatrickscathedral.ie

MULLEN, Peter John. b 42. Liv Univ BA 70 Middx Univ PhD 00. St Aid Birkenhead 66. **d** 70 **p** 71. C Manston *Ripon* 70–72; C Stretford All SS *Man* 72–73; C Oldham St Mary w St Pet 73–74; LtO 74–77; V Tockwith and Bilton w Bickerton *York* 77–89; PtO 97–98; P-in-c St Mich Cornhill w St Pet le Poer etc *Lon* 98–03; R 03–12; P-in-c St Sepulchre w Ch Ch Greyfriars etc 98–12; Chapl City Inst Stock Exchange 98–12; rtd 12; PtO *Chich* from 14. *3 Naomi Close, Eastbourne BN20 7UU* E: rpetermullen@gmail.com

MÜLLER, Anton Michael. b 61. Grey Coll Dur BA 83 MA 91 Grey Coll Cur PGCE 84. Trin Coll Bris 97. **d** 99 **p** 00. C Sandgate St Paul w Folkestone St Geo *Cant* 99–03; TV Penrith w Newton Reigny and Plumpton Wall *Carl* 03–04; P-in-c Dacre 03–04; Chapl N Cumbria Mental Health NHS Trust 03–04; Chapl Eden Valley Hospice Carl 05–08; PtO *Carl* from 08; Tutor Cumbria Chr Learning from 09; PtO *Blackb* 13–15; V Scorton and Barnacre and Calder Vale from 15. *St Peter's Vicarage, Snowhill Lane, Scorton, Preston PR3 1AY* T: (01524) 791229 M: 07525-395923 E: antonandsue@gmail.com

MULLETT, Janette Constance. b 58. SWMTC 17. **d** 19. NSM Highertown and Baldhu *Truro* from 19. *Epiphany House, Kenwyn Church Road, Truro TR1 3DR* E: manager@epiphanyhouse.co.uk

MULLEY, Mrs Margery Ann Oclanis. b 38. **d** 07 **p** 08. OLM Iwerne Valley *Sarum* 07–12; NSM 12; PtO *Cov* from 13. *17 South Parade, Harbury, Leamington Spa CV33 9HZ*

MULLIGAN, Ronald Leslie. b 53. LCTP. **d** 08 **p** 09. NSM Haslingden w Grane and Stonefold *Blackb* 08–11; NSM Blackb St Thos w St Jude 11–13; NSM Blackb St Mich w St Jo and H Trin 11–13; NSM N and E Blackb 13–14; Chapl Airedale NHS Foundn Trust from 14. *3 Chatburn Close, Rossendale BB4 8UT* T: (01706) 220749 E: ronmulligan@talktalk.net

MULLIN, Horace Boies (Dan). b 44. **d** 00 **p** 01. OLM Mildenhall *St E* 00–13; rtd 13; PtO *St E* from 13. *47 Oak Drive,*

Beck Row, Bury St Edmunds IP28 8UA T: (01638) 718200 E: dan.marthan@btinternet.com

MULLINER, Angela Margaret. *See* LAUENER, Angela Margaret

MULLINER, Canon Denis Ratliffe. b 40. BNC Ox BA 62 MA 66. Linc Th Coll 70. **d** 72 **p** 73. C Sandhurst *Ox* 72–76; Chapl Bradfield Coll Berks 76–00; Chapl Chpl Royal Hampton Court Palace 00–15; Can 10–15; Dep P in O 00–15; rtd 15; PtO *Nor* from 15. *The Patch, Hillington, King's Lynn PE31 6DN*

MULLINER, Eliska Fiona Jo. b 71. Bp Otter Coll BA 94 W Sussex Inst of HE PGCE 98. Ridley Hall Cam 12. **d** 14 **p** 15. C Lymington *Win* 14–17; TV Redruth w Lanner and Treleigh *Truro* 17–19; R Bridge of Allan *St And* from 19; Chapl Stirling Univ from 19. *The Rectory, 21 Fountain Road, Bridge of Allan, Stirling FK9 4AT* T: (01786) 357603 M: 07493-657187 E: jomulliner@cantab.net

MULLINGS, Paulette Patricia Yvonne. b 53. **d** 07 **p** 08. NSM Cobbold Road St Sav w St Mary *Lon* 07–17; NSM Hammersmith H Innocents and St Jo from 17. *53A Melina Road, London W12 9HY* T: (020) 7386 1262 M: 07751-374857 E: pmullings@aol.com *or* paulette.mullings@london.anglican.org

MULLINS, Caroline Anne. b 56. Ex Univ BA 78 St Anne's Coll Ox CertEd 79. SEITE 04. **d** 07 **p** 08. NSM Wandsworth St Paul *S'wark* 07–11; NSM Hinchley Wood *Guildf* from 11. *1 Chesterfield Drive, Esher KT10 0AH* T: (020) 8224 3334 E: rev.carolinemullins@gmail.com

MULLINS, Mrs Margaret. b 49. Southn Univ CertEd 70. Sarum & Wells Th Coll 94. **d** 94 **p** 95. C Bishopstoke *Win* 94–98; TV Bicester w Bucknell, Caversfield and Launton *Ox* 98–10; rtd 10. *5 Hardings Lane, Fair Oak, Eastleigh SO50 8GL*

MULLINS, Peter Matthew. b 60. Ch Ch Ox BA 82 MA 86 Irish Sch of Ecum MPhil 90. Qu Coll Birm 82. **d** 84 **p** 85. C Caversham St Pet and Mapledurham etc *Ox* 84–88; PtO *D & G* 88–89; TV Old Brumby *Linc* 89–94; Clergy Tr Adv 94–99; TR Gt and Lt Coates w Bradley 99–17; Can and Preb Linc Cathl 02–17; RD Grimsby and Cleethorpes 05–10; R Haworth and Cross Roads cum Lees *Leeds* from 17. *78 Prince Street, Haworth, Keighley BD22 8JD* E: p.m.mullins@virgin.net

MULLINS, Timothy Dougal. b 59. St Jo Coll Dur BA 81. Wycliffe Hall Ox 83. **d** 85 **p** 86. C Reading Greyfriars *Ox* 85–89; C Haughton le Skerne *Dur* 89–95; Chapl Eton Coll 95–05; Chapl Radley Coll 05–12; C Ches Square St Mich w St Phil *Lon* 12–17; Chapl Stowe Sch from 17. *Stowe School, Buckingham MK18 5EH* T: (01280) 818000 E: timmullins1010@gmail.com

MULLINS, Mrs Yvonne Beryl. b 69. Witwatersrand Univ BPrimEd 90 BEd 93. Ripon Coll Cuddesdon 16. **d** 19. C Shelswell *Ox* from 19. *10C St Michael's Close, Fringford, Bicester OX27 8DW* M: 07545-299517 E: y.mullins@outlook.com

MULLIS, Robert Owen. b 49. Open Univ BA 77 Glam Univ MSc 00 St Paul's Coll Chelt CertEd 71. St Mich Coll Llan 90. **d** 93 **p** 94. NSM Llangenni and Llanbedr Ystrad Yw w Patricio *S & B* 93–03; NSM Llantilio Pertholey w Bettws Chpl etc *Mon* 03–06; PtO *Heref* 06–19; NSM Eardisley w Bollingham, Willersley, Brilley etc from 19. *Church Gate, Almeley, Hereford HR3 6LB* T: (01544) 327801 E: bob.mullis@hotmail.co.uk

MULRENAN, David John. b 57. **d** 18 **p** 19. NSM Four Rivers *St E* from 18. *4 Sunnyside Cottages, The Thorofare, Brundish, Woodbridge IP13 8BB* T: (01728) 628063 M: 07881-481745 E: djmulrenan@gmail.com

MULRYNE, Thomas Mark. b 70. St Cath Coll Cam BA 91 MA 95 Lon Inst of Educn PGCE 93. Oak Hill Th Coll BA 02. **d** 02 **p** 03. C W Streatham St Jas *S'wark* 02–06; C Gt Clacton *Chelmsf* 06–19; V from 19. *112 Woodlands Close, Clacton-on-Sea CO15 4RU* T: (01255) 425159 E: mark_and_caroline_mulryne@hotmail.com

MULVANEY, James Eric John. b 89. Melbourne Univ BA 10 K Coll Lon MA 13. St Mellitus Coll BA 16. **d** 16 **p** 17. C Onslow Square and S Kensington St Aug *Lon* 16–17; C Clapham H Trin *S'wark* from 17. *Trinity House Clapham, 31–33 Bromell's Road, London SW4 0BN* M: 07867-499599 E: jamie.mulvaney@holytrinityclapham.org

MUMBY, Andrew. *See* MOUGHTIN-MUMBY, Andrew Denis Paul

MUMFORD, Prof David Bardwell. b 49. St Cath Coll Cam BA 71 MA 75 Bris Univ MB, ChB 81 MD 92 Edin Univ MPhil 89 MRCPsych 86. Bp's Coll Calcutta 71 Cuddesdon Coll 73. **d** 75. C Bris St Mary Redcliffe w Temple etc 75–76; NSM 76–82; NSM Edin St Columba 82–86; NSM Calverley *Bradf* 86–92; PtO *B & W* 92–06 and 11–14 and from 14. *14 Clifton Vale, Clifton, Bristol BS8 4PT* T: 0117-927 2221 M: 07501-134525 E: david.mumford@bristol.ac.uk

MUMFORD, David Christopher. b 47. Mert Coll Ox BA 68 MA 74 York Univ MSW CQSW 81. Linc Th Coll 84. **d** 86 **p** 87. C Shiremoor *Newc* 86–89; C N Shields 89–91; V Byker St Ant 91–97; RD Newc E 96–97; V Cowgate 97–02;

Internat Co-ord Internat Fellowship of Reconciliation 02–07; R Brechin *Bre* 07–15; R Tarfside 07–15; Dean Bre 08–12; rtd 15; LtO *Edin* from 16. *10 Temple Mains Steading, Innerwick, Dunbar EH42 1EF*   T: (01368) 840361 E: dmumford@phonecoop.coop

MUMFORD, Geoffrey Robert. b 70. York Univ BSc 92 St Jo Coll Nottm MA 00. **d** 00 **p** 01. C Rowley Regis *Birm* 00–03; TV Darwen St Pet w Hoddlesden *Blackb* 03–08; P-in-c Copmanthorpe *York* 08–09; V from 09; P-in-c Askham Bryan 08–09; V from 09; P-in-c Bolton Percy 08–09; R from 09; RD New Ainsty from 16. *The Vicarage, 17 Sutor Close, Copmanthorpe, York YO23 3TX*   T: (01904) 707716   M: 07980-569450 E: gmumford@btinternet.com *or* vicar@stgileschurchcopmanthorpe.org

MUMFORD, Grenville Alan. b 34. Richmond Th Coll. **d** 78 **p** 78. C Witham *Chelmsf* 78–81; C-in-c Gt Ilford St Marg CD 81–85; V Gt Ilford St Marg 85–87; P-in-c Everton and Mattersey w Clayworth *S'well* 87–89; R 89–96; RD Bawtry 93–96; rtd 96; PtO *Ches* from 96. *146 Audlem Road, Nantwich CW5 7EB*   T: (01270) 610221 E: mumford7eb@btinternet.com

MUMFORD, Canon Hugh Raymond. b 24. Oak Hill Th Coll 50. **d** 53 **p** 54. C Bethnal Green St Jas Less *Lon* 53–57; C Watford St Mary *St Alb* 57–59; R Thetford St Pet w St Nic *Nor* 59–69; RD Thetford 68–69; V Nether Cerne *Sarum* 69–71; R Godmanstone 69–71; V Cerne Abbas w Upcerne 69–71; R Minterne Magna 69–71; V Cerne Abbas w Godmanstone and Minterne Magna 71–89; RD Dorchester 75–79; Can and Preb Sarum Cathl 77–89; rtd 89; PtO *Sarum* 89–10. *10 South Walks Road, Dorchester DT1 1ED*   T: (01305) 264971 E: hughmumford@me.com

MUMFORD, Lesley Anne. *See* CHEETHAM, Lesley Anne

MUMFORD, Thomas James. b 90. York Univ BA 15 Peterho Cam BA 18. Westcott Ho Cam 16. **d** 19. C Sudbury and Chilton *St E* from 19. *5 Clermont Avenue, Sudbury CO10 1ZJ* E: rev.tommumford@outlook.com

MUNBY, Canon David Philip James. b 52. Pemb Coll Ox BA 75 MA 80. St Jo Coll Nottm 76. **d** 78 **p** 79. C Gipsy Hill Ch Ch *S'wark* 78–82; C-in-c W Dulwich Em CD 82–88; V Barnsley St Geo *Wakef* 88–14; Leeds 14–18; Asst Dioc Ecum Officer *Wakef* 99–01; Can Bungoma from 04; rtd 18. *7 Park Close, Royston, Barnsley S71 4TE* E: david.munby@blueyonder.co.uk

MUNCEY, William. b 49. Oak Hill Th Coll BA 80. **d** 80 **p** 81. C Wandsworth St Mich *S'wark* 80–84; C Morden 84–88; TV 88–01; RD Merton 00–01; P-in-c Croydon Ch Ch 01–04; V 04–12; NSM Shelswell *Ox* 12–18. *12 Church Street, Histon, Cambridge CB24 9EP* E: munceybill@gmail.com

MUNCH, Philip Douglas. b 55. Witwatersrand Univ BMus. Cranmer Hall Dur. **d** 88 **p** 89. C Wlvis Bay Namibia 88–89; P-in-c 89–92; Warden Ho of Prayer Luderitz 92–99; Prec Port Elizabeth S Africa 99–02; Warden Emmaus Ho of Prayer Northampton from 02; NSM Northampton St Mich w St Edm *Pet* from 02. *Emmaus House of Prayer, St Michael's Church, Perry Street, Northampton NN1 4HL*   T: (01604) 627669   F: 230316 E: pdmunch@gmail.com

MUNCHIN, David Leighfield. b 67. Imp Coll Lon BSc 88 K Coll Lon MA 00 Heythrop Coll Lon PhD 09. Ripon Coll Cuddesdon 89. **d** 92 **p** 93. C Golders Green *Lon* 92–96; Prec and Min Can St Alb Abbey 96–02; P-in-c Hatfield Hyde 02–10; TR Welwyn from 10. *The Rectory, 2 Ottway Walk, Welwyn AL6 9AS*   T: (01438) 714150   M: 07787-567747 E: rector@welwyn.org.uk *or* davidmunchin@outlook.com

MUNCHIN, Ysmena Rachael. *See* PENTELOW, Ysmena Rachael

MUNDAY, Clive Ian. b 57. BNC Ox BA 78 MA 85. St Mellitus Coll BA 17. **d** 17 **p** 18. C Bridgnorth and Morville Par *Heref* from 17. *41 Innage Lane, Bridgnorth WV16 4HS*   T: (01746) 766197   M: 07763-177152 E: clive_munday@btinternet.com

MUNDAY, Elaine Jeanette. b 56. SWMTC. **d** 10 **p** 11. NSM Bodmin w Lanhydrock and Lanivet *Truro* 10–17; TV Bodmin from 17. *70 St Mary's Crescent, Bodmin PL31 1NP*   T: (01208) 77945 E: elaine.munday@bodminway.org

MUNDAY, Nicholas John. b 54. Jes Coll Cam BA 76 PGCE 77 MA 97. Ripon Coll Cuddesdon BTh 13. **d** 11 **p** 12. C Monmouth w Overmonnow etc *Mon* 11–14; R S Lafford *Linc* 14–19; Discipleship Development Adv 14–19; rtd 19. *1 Tithebarn, Felmersham, Bedford MK43 7JF*   T: (01234) 782800 E: n.j.munday@btinternet.com

MUNDAY, Mrs Sandra Anne. b 61. St Jo Sem Wonersh BTh 89 Ripon Coll Cuddesdon 97. **d** 99 **p** 00. C Esher *Guildf* 99–02; Team Chapl R United Hosp Bath NHS Trust 02–03; PtO *B & W* 03–17; Hon C Chew Stoke w Nempnett Thrubwell from 17. *1 Home Orchard, Chew Stoke, Bristol BS40 8UZ* E: csntchurches@fastblue.net

MUNDEN, Alan Frederick. b 43. Nottm Univ BTh 74 Birm Univ MLitt 80 Dur Univ PhD 87. St Jo Coll Nottm. **d** 74 **p** 75. C Cheltenham St Mary *Glouc* 74–76; C Cheltenham St Mary, St Matt, St Paul and H Trin 76; Hon C Jesmond Clayton Memorial *Newc* 76–80; C 80–83; V Cheylesmore *Cov* 83–01; R Weddington and Caldecote 01–03; rtd 03; Hon C Jesmond Clayton Memorial *Newc* from 03; PtO *Dur* from 11. *11 The Crescent, Benton, Newcastle upon Tyne NE7 7ST*   T: 0191-266 1227 E: alan.munden@church.org.uk

MUNDY, David Hugh. b 58. Lon Univ BSc 80 Newc Univ PhD 88 Sheff Univ MA 16. Yorks Min Course 12. **d** 15 **p** 16. NSM Chapel-en-le-Frith *Derby* 15–16; NSM Bakewell, Ashford w Sheldon and Rowsley 16–17; NSM Dinting Vale 17–18; NSM Glossop from 17; P-in-c from 18; Asst Dir of Ords *Derby* from 18. *103 Station Road, Hadfield, Glossop SK13 1AR*   T: (01457) 856554 E: dhmundy@btinternet.com

MUNDY, Kay. b 67. **d** 14 **p** 15. C Deerhurst and Apperley w Forthampton etc *Glouc* from 14; Chapl to Bp Tewksbury from 18. *2 College Green, Gloucester GL1 2LY*   T: (01452) 835563 E: kmundy@glosdioc.org.uk

MUNDY, Paul Kevin. b 68. Westcott Ho Cam 11. **d** 13 **p** 14. C Barcombe *Chich* 13–17; C Newick from 17. *The Rectory, 36A Allington Road, Newick, Lewes BN8 4NB*   T: (01825) 723186   M: 07717-000281 E: paul@barcombe.net *or* church.newick@gmail.com

MUNEZA, Steve b 80. Redcliffe Coll Glouc MA 10. **d** 14 **p** 16. Youth Min Bujumbura Burundi 14–15; NSM Dur N 15–19; Dir Minl Formation and Mixed Mode Tr Cranmer Hall Dur from 19. *25 Barnard Close, Durham DH1 5XN*   T: 0191-384 5954 E: stevemuneza@gmail.com

MUNGAVIN, Canon Gerald Clarence. b 27. Edin Th Coll 51. **d** 54 **p** 55. C Dunfermline *St And* 54–55; C Glas Gd Shep 55–57; CF 57–60; C Stanwix *Carl* 60–62; Chapl RAF 62–75; R Turriff *Ab* 75–81; R Cuminestown 75–81; R Banff 75–81; R Banchory 81–92; R Kincardine O'Neil 81–92; Can St Andr Cathl 89–92; Hon Can St Andr Cathl from 92; rtd 92. *5 Lade Court, Lochwinnoch PA12 4BT*   T: (01505) 843972 E: mungavin@hotmail.com

MUNNS, Ms Alice Wiliemhina (Mina). b 78. York Univ BA 99 St Jo Coll Dur BA 15 Derby Univ PGCE 00. Cranmer Hall Dur 13. **d** 15 **p** 16. C Selston *S'well* 15–18; P-in-c Cresswell and Lynemouth *Newc* from 18. *33 Till Grove, Ellington, Morpeth NE61 5ER*   M: 07960-250497 E: minamunns90@gmail.com

MUNNS, Stuart Millington. b 36. St Cath Coll Cam BA 58 MA 62 MCIPD 91. Cuddesdon Coll 58. **d** 60 **p** 61. C Allenton and Shelton Lock *Derby* 60–63; C Brampton St Thos 63–65; C-in-c Loundsley Green Ascension CD 65–66; Bp's Youth Chapl 66–72; Nat Dir of Community Industry 72–77; Hon C Hornsey Ch Ch *Lon* 72–77; Dioc Missr *Liv* 77–82; V Knowsley 77–82; P-in-c Stramshall *Lich* 82–88; V Uttoxeter w Bramshall 82–88; RD Uttoxeter 82–87; P-in-c Kingstone w Gratwich 84–88; P-in-c Marchington w Marchington Woodlands 84–88; P-in-c Checkley 86–88; PtO *B & W* 88–90; NSM Wells St Thos w Horrington 90–94; P-in-c Fosse Trinity 94–02; rtd 02; Dioc Pre-Th Educn Co-ord *B & W* 02–06; PtO from 03; *Eur* from 07. *Applewood House, Ham Street, Baltonsborough, Glastonbury BA6 8PX*   T: (01458) 851443   M: 07791-111904 E: munns@cantab.net

MUÑOZ-TRIVIÑO, Daniel. b 75. Hatf Coll Dur BA 99 Madrid Univ PhD 16. Wycliffe Hall Ox MTh 01. **d** 01 **p** 02. C Hazlemere *Ox* 01–04; TV Gt Marlow w Marlow Bottom, Lt Marlow and Bisham 04–09; Chapl Los Olivos Retreat Cen Spain from 09; PtO *Ox* 13–16; LtO from 16. *Hacienda los Olivos, Haza Llana, Sierra de Mondújar, 18656 Lecrín (Granada), Spain*   T: (0034) 958 068 001 E: daniel.munoz@facultadseut.org

MUNRO, Alexander Ian. b 78. Leic Univ LLB. St Mellitus Coll BA 17. **d** 17 **p** 18. C W Molesey *Guildf* from 17. *The Vicarage, 518 Walton Road, West Molesey KT8 2QF*   M: 07889-456266 E: alex.munro@spwm.org.uk

MUNRO, Duncan John Studd. b 50. Magd Coll Ox BA 72 MA 76 Warwick Univ MBA 96 CDir 05. Wycliffe Hall Ox 73. **d** 76 **p** 77. C Ecclesall *Sheff* 76–77; C Sheff St Barn and St Mary 78–80; LtO 80–86; PtO 97–05; LtO *Edin* 06–17; PtO *Glouc* 13–15; Public Preacher from 15. *Hosanna House, 43 Cudnall Street, Charlton Kings, Cheltenham GL53 8HL*   T: (01242) 321712   M: 07802-871156 E: duncan.munro@munrostrategic.co.uk *or* dmunro@glosdioc.org.uk

MUNRO, Ingrid Phyllis. b 51. Herts Univ BEd 80. St Jo Coll Nottm MA 96 St Alb Minl Tr Scheme 83. **d** 98 **p** 99. NSM Walbrook Epiphany *Derby* 98–01 and 05–09; NSM Alvaston from 09. *40 Brisbane Road, Mickleover, Derby DE3 9JZ*

MUNRO, Robert. b 40. Leeds Univ BA 62 Bris Univ PGCE 63. SWMTC 95. **d** 98 **p** 99. NSM Saltash *Truro* 98–03; NSM Calstock 03–11; PtO from 14. *15 Valley Road,*

Saltash PL12 4BT T: (01752) 844731 M: 07729-907889 E: munrobob88@gmail.com

MUNRO, Robert Speight. b 63. Bris Univ BSc 84 Reformed Th Sem (USA) DMin 08 Man Univ PGCE 87. Oak Hill Th Coll BA 93. **d** 93 **p** 94. C Hartford *Ches* 93–97; R Davenham 97–03; R Cheadle from 03; RD from 16. *The Rectory, 1 Depleach Road, Cheadle SK8 1DZ* T: 0161-428 3440 *or* 428 8050 E: rob@munro.org.uk

MUNRO-SMITH, Alison Jean. *See* WATERS, Alison Jean

MUNT, Mrs Linda Christine. b 55. NEOC 92. **d** 95 **p** 96. C Beverley St Nic *York* 95–98; Chapl E Yorkshire Hosps NHS Trust 97–99; V Bridlington Em *York* 99–03; P-in-c Skipsea w Ulrome and Barmston w Fraisthorpe 02–03; Chapl Martin House Hospice for Children Boston Spa 03–05; Hon C Boston Spa, Thorp Arch w Walton etc 03–05; V Market Weighton *York* 05–10; V Sancton 05–10; R Goodmanham 05–10; PtO 10–12; V Attercliffe and Darnall *Sheff* 12–15; PtO *York* 16–18; P-in-c Garrowby Hill 18–19; R from 19. *Foxfields, Worsendale Road, Bishop Wilton, York YO42 1ST* M: 07888-668663 E: garrowbyvicar@gmail.com

MURDOCH, Alexander Edward Duncan. b 37. Oak Hill Th Coll 68. **d** 71 **p** 72. C Kensington St Helen w H Trin *Lon* 71–72; C Kensington St Barn 73–74; CF 74–78; C W Kirby St Bridget *Ches* 78–84; V N Shoebury *Chelmsf* 84–87; V W Poldens *B & W* 87–96; R Gayhurst w Ravenstone, Stoke Goldington etc *Ox* 96–07; rtd 07. *Hopp House, Back Lane, Old Bolingbroke, Spilsby PE23 4EU* T: (01790) 763603

MURDOCH, David John. b 58. Birm Univ BSocSc 81 Leeds Univ MA 03. Ripon Coll Cuddesdon 81. **d** 84 **p** 85. C Penwortham St Leon *Blackb* 84–87; C Wirksworth w Alderwasley, Carsington etc *Derby* 87–89; R Shirland 89–97; Dioc World Development Officer 96–00; P-in-c New Mills 97–01; V 01–05; RD Glossop 04–05; TR Wilford Peninsula *St E* 05–19; rtd 19; P-in-c Horsted Keynes *Chich* from 19. *The Rectory, Station Road, Horsted Keynes, Haywards Heath RH17 7ED* E: revdave@timicomail.co.uk

MURDOCH, Canon Lucy Eleanor. b 41. STETS BTh 99. **d** 99 **p** 00. NSM Mapledon and Bodle Street Green *Chich* 99–02; NSM Rye 02–12; TV 03–12; RD 10–11; P-in-c Fletching 12–16; Can and Preb Chich Cathl 10–16; rtd 16. *Cottenham, Tubwell Lane, Maynards Green, Heathfield TN21 0BY* M: 07508-931198 E: dog.home@uwclub.net

MURFET, Edward David. b 36. Qu Coll Cam BA 59 MA 63. Chich Th Coll 59. **d** 61 **p** 62. C Croydon St Mich *Cant* 61–64; C Hunslet St Mary and Stourton *Ripon* 64–65; C Hackney Wick St Mary of Eton w St Aug *Lon* 65–69; Chapl Berne *Eur* 69–71; Chapl Naples 71–74; Chapl Rome 74–77; LtO *Bris* 78–81; Gen Sec CEMS 81–86; C Leeds St Pet *Ripon* 87–89; P-in-c 89–90; C Leeds City 91–93; Min Can Ripon Cathl 93–03; rtd 03; PtO *Ripon* from 14. *3 Old Deanery Close, St Marygate, Ripon HG4 1LZ* T: (01765) 608422

MURFET, Gwyn. b 44. Linc Th Coll 71. **d** 74 **p** 75. C Scalby w Ravenscar and Staintondale *York* 74–77; P-in-c S Milford 77–83; R 83–84; V Kirkby Ireleth *Carl* 84–05; rtd 05; PtO *Carl* 11–14. *75 Portsmouth Street, Walney, Barrow-in-Furness LA14 3AJ* T: (01229) 471157

MURLEY, Anthony James Raymond. b 82. Univ Coll Lon BA 04. St Steph Ho Ox 12. **d** 14 **p** 15. C Small Heath *Birm* 14–18; P-in-c Brighton Annunciation *Chich* from 18. *Annunciation Vicarage, 89 Washington Street, Brighton BN2 9SR* M: 07738-252676 E: anthony.murley@ssho.ox.ac.uk *or* anthony.murley@me.com

MURPHIE, Andrew Graham. b 65. Reading Univ BA 86. St Jo Coll Nottm BTh 91 MA 92. **d** 92 **p** 93. C Boulton *Derby* 92–96; C Marston on Dove w Scropton 96–97; V Hilton w Marston-on-Dove 98–18; RD Longford 04–15; P-in-c Crosthwaite Keswick *Carl* from 18. *Crosthwaite Vicarage, Vicarage Hill, Keswick CA12 5QB* E: andymurphie@btinternet.com

MURPHY, Andrew John. b 46. Edin Univ LLB 67 MA 68. Ox Min Course 14. **d** 95 **p** 16. NSM Aberdeen St Marg *Ab* 95–98; NSM Fraserburgh 98–01; Hon Asst C Bridge of Don St Luke's Miss 01–06; NSM Finchley St Mary *Lon* 16–17. *Flat 2, 50B Birdhurst Road, South Croydon CR2 7EB* M: 07920-596990 E: andrew.murphy@advocates.org.uk

MURPHY, Anthony Michael. b 11. **d** 11 **p** 12. NSM Moviddy Union *C, C & R* 11–12; NSM Carrigaline Union from 12. *9 Riverside, Church Road, Carrigaline, Co Cork, Republic of Ireland* M: (00353) 87-832 7347 E: tmurphy@tmahr.com

MURPHY, Christopher Campbell. b 84. Hatf Coll Dur BA 06. Wycliffe Hall Ox 09. **d** 12 **p** 13. C Bovey Tracey SS Pet, Paul and Thos w Hennock *Ex* 12–16; C Barnston *Ches* from 16. *8 Antons Road, Wirral CH61 9PT* T: 0151-648 9440 M: 07595-742970 E: christopher.c.murphy@gmail.com

MURPHY, Mrs Deborah Ann. b 67. Newc Univ BA 89. Qu Coll Birm BD 92. **d** 93 **p** 94. C Bloxwich *Lich* 93–97; TV Gt Grimsby St Mary and St Jas *Linc* 97–00; Chapl N Lincs

and Goole Hosps NHS Trust 99–00; PtO *St Alb* 01–05; Asst Chapl Walsall Healthcare NHS Trust 05–08; TV Blakenall Heath *Lich* 08–10; Chapl Heart of England NHS Foundn Trust 10–12; Chapl Walsall Healthcare NHS Trust 12–14; C Pheasey *Lich* 12–13; PtO 14–18. *84 Gainsborough Crescent, Birmingham B43 7LB* T: 0121-360 2122 E: deborahamurphy8@gmail.com

MURPHY, Jack. b 27. NOC 83. **d** 86 **p** 87. C Armley w New Wortley *Ripon* 86–90; C Hawksworth Wood 90–94; rtd 94; PtO *York* from 96. *24 Dulverton Hall, Esplanade, Scarborough YO11 2AR*

MURPHY, Ms Julia Mary. b 58. Essex Univ BA 81 Lon Bible Coll BTh 00. Wycliffe Hall Ox MTh 07. **d** 07 **p** 08. C Thetford *Nor* 07–11; TV Forest Gate St Sav w W Ham St Matt *Chelmsf* 11–12; Chapl Essex Univ from 12. *Mariners, Rectory Hill, Wivenhoe, Colchester CO7 9LB* T: (01206) 683676 M: 07779-266034 E: revjuliamurphy@gmail.com

MURPHY, Keith Anthony. b 72. St Jo Coll Nottm 10. **d** 12 **p** 13. C Ware Ch Ch *St Alb* 12–16; C Cheshunt 16–17; C Eggbuckland w Estover *Ex* from 17. *The Vicarage, 70 Inchkeith Road, Plymouth PL6 6EJ* M: 07980-745437 E: keithmurphymusic@gmail.com

MURPHY, Owen. b 52. Open Univ BA 85 Liv Univ MA 04. Chich Th Coll 92. **d** 94 **p** 95. C Oxhey St Matt *St Alb* 94–96; C Watford St Mich 96–98; P-in-c Shinfield *Ox* 98–05; V Barnehurst *Roch* 05–07; Dir St Columba's Retreat and Conf Cen 07–12; PtO *Guildf* 12–13; P-in-c Yealmpton and Brixton *Ex* 13–19; TV Withycombe Raleigh from 19. *All Saints' Vicarage, 2 Church Road, Exmouth EX8 1RZ* E: owen.murphy52@btconnect.com

MURPHY, Peter Frederick. b 40. AKC 65. **d** 67 **p** 68. C Paddington St Jo w St Mich *Lon* 67–72; P-in-c Basingstoke *Win* 72–76; TV 76–81; V Hythe 81–92; V Lyndhurst and Emery Down 92–99; P-in-c Copythorne and Minstead 95–99; V Lyndhurst and Emery Down and Minstead 99–05; rtd 05; Hon C Fordingbridge and Breamore and Hale etc *Win* 05–10; PtO from 10. *11 Watton Road, Holbury, Southampton SO45 2LW* T: (02380) 893243 M: 07815-050096 E: petermurf@gmail.com

MURPHY, Rosalyn Frances Thomas. b 55. Marquette Univ (USA) BA 85 Ustinov Coll Dur MTh 00 Union Th Sem West Virginia MDiv 99 St Jo Coll Dur PhD 05. Cranmer Hall Dur 04. **d** 05 **p** 06. C Dur St Nic 05–08; P-in-c Blackpool St Thos *Blackb* 08–12; V 12–18; Prior Community of St Anselm *Cant* from 18. *Lambeth Palace, London SE1 7JU* T: (020) 7898 1200 E: rosalyn.murphy@lambethpalace.org.uk

MURPHY, Shirley. b 18 **p** 19. C Narberth w Mounton w Robeston Wathen etc *St D* from 18. *16 Redstone Court, Narberth SA67 7EU* E: revshirleymurphy@gmail.com

MURPHY, Stephen Charles James. b 55. All SS Cen for Miss & Min 17. **d** 19. NSM Prestbury *Ches* from 19. *12-14 Silver Street, Bollington, Macclesfield SK10 5QL* M: 07976-728721

MURPHY, Wendy Susan. b 54. St Jo Coll Nottm 12. **d** 13 **p** 14. NSM Carlton-in-the-Willows *S'well* from 13. *The Rectory, Church Street, Carlton, Nottingham NG4 1BJ* M: 07905-868230 E: rev.wendy@hotmail.co.uk

MURPHY, William Albert. b 43. Lon Univ BD 73 QUB MTh 78. **d** 73 **p** 74. C Lisburn Ch Ch *Conn* 73–79; Supt and Chapl Ulster Inst for the Deaf 79–98; Chapl HM Pris The Maze 82–00; Dioc Dir Ords *Conn* 92–13; Chapl Ch of Ireland Min to Deaf People 98–13; Can Belf Cathl 04–13; rtd 13. *2 Maghaberry Manor, Moira, Craigavon BT67 0JZ* T: (028) 9261 9140 E: murphy43@btinternet.com

MURPHY, Mrs Yvonne Letita. b 52. Brunel Univ BA 90 PGCE 91. SEITE 95. **d** 98 **p** 99. NSM Hampton St Mary *Lon* 98–01; NSM Staines St Mary and St Pet 01–04; Chapl Bp Wand Sch Sunbury-on-Thames 98–04; P-in-c Kennington Cant 04–09; TV High Wycombe *Ox* 09–12; rtd 12; PtO *Guildf* from 12. *41 Jersey Close, Chertsey KT16 9PA* T: (01932) 429288 E: ylm.bwm@virgin.net

MURRAY, Alan. b 61. St Jo Coll Nottm BTh 92. **d** 92 **p** 93. C Wombwell *Sheff* 92–95; C Mortomley St Sav High Green 95–99; P-in-c Doncaster St Jas 99–01; V 01–13; V Normanton *Wakef* 13–14; Leeds from 14. *All Saints' Vicarage, 140 High Street, Normanton WF6 1NR* T: (01924) 893100 E: vicarofallsaints@gmail.com

MURRAY, Andrew James. b 72. Loughb Univ BEng 95 PhD 01. Trin Coll Bris 10. **d** 12 **p** 13. C Clifton Ch Ch w Em *Bris* 12–15; P-in-c Lawrence Weston and Avonmouth from 15. *The Vicarage, 335 Long Cross, Lawrence Weston, Bristol BS11 0NN* T: 0117-325 8722

MURRAY, Anne. b 53. MCSP 75. NOC 03. **d** 06 **p** 07. NSM Fairfield *Liv* 06–10; NSM Liv All SS from 11. *11 Elstree Road, Liverpool L6 8NU* T: 0151-428 2254 E: anne.allsaintsliverpool@gmail.com

MURRAY, David McIlveen. b 36. ALCD 61. **d** 61 **p** 62. C Mortlake w E Sheen *S'wark* 61–64; C Lyncombe *B & W* 64–67; C Horsham *Chich* 67–73; V Devonport St Bart *Ex* 73–79; R Chalfont St Peter *Ox* 79–95; RD Amersham 86–89; R Lower Windrush 95–03; rtd 03; PtO *Glouc* from 03. *Collum End Farm, 88 Church Road, Leckhampton, Cheltenham GL53 0PD* T: (01242) 528008

MURRAY, Elaine Mary Edel. b 58. TCD BTh 05 MICS 97. CITC 02. **d** 05 **p** 06. Bp's V and Lib Kilkenny Cathl *C & O* 05–11; C Kilkenny w Aghour and Kilmanagh 05–08; V 08–11; I Carrigaline Union *C, C & R* from 11. *The Rectory, Church Road, Carrigaline, Co Cork, Republic of Ireland* T: (00353) (21) 437 2224 M: 87-236 3100 E: emit@eircom.net

MURRAY, Elizabeth. b 57. **d** 10 **p** 11. NSM Eastwood and Brinsley w Underwood *S'well* 10–13; P-in-c Elston w Elston Chapelry from 13; P-in-c E Stoke w Syerston from 13; P-in-c Kilvington from 13; P-in-c Shelton from 13; P-in-c Sibthorpe from 13; P-in-c Staunton w Flawborough from 13; P-in-c Farndon w Thorpe, Hawton and Cotham from 18. *The Rectory, Top Street, Elston, Newark NG23 5NP* T: (01636) 525417 E: reveimurray24@gmail.com

MURRAY, Elizabeth <u>Ruth</u>. **d** 03 **p** 04. C Antrim All SS *Conn* 03–06; I Woodschapel w Gracefield *Arm* from 06. *The Rectory, 140 Ballyronan Road, Magherafelt BT45 6HU* T: (028) 7941 8311 E: eruthmurray@gmail.com

MURRAY, Gordon John. b 33. St Cath Coll Cam BA 57 MA 61. Clifton Th Coll 57. **d** 59 **p** 60. C Heref St Jas 59–61; C Uphill *B & W* 62–65; C-in-c Reading St Mary Castle Street Prop Chpl *Ox* 65–68; Ed *English Churchman* 65–71; Prin Kensit Coll Finchley 68–75; Hd of RE Sandown High Sch 76–78; rtd 98. *18 Longcroft, Felixstowe IP11 9QH* T: (01394) 273372

MURRAY, Canon Heather. b 62. RGN 82. NEOC 04. **d** 07 **p** 08. NSM Burnopfield *Dur* 07–12; P-in-c Harelaw and Annfield Plain 12–18; AD Lanchester 14–18; P-in-c Belmont and Pittington from 18; AD Dur from 18; Hon Can Dur Cathl from 16. *Belmont Vicarage, Broomside Lane, Durham DH1 2QW* T: 0191-386 1545 E: revheather@btinternet.com *or* heather.murray@durham.anglican.org

MURRAY, Preb Ian Hargraves. b 48. Man Univ BSc 71. St Jo Coll Nottm 79. **d** 81 **p** 82. C Erith St Paul *Roch* 81–84; C Willenhall H Trin *Lich* 84–87; TV 87–92; P-in-c Moxley 92–00; C Darlaston St Lawr 99–00; TR Glascote and Stonydelph 00–14; RD Tamworth 04–09; Preb Lich Cathl 11–14; rtd 14; PtO *S'well* from 15. *9 Winlock Drive, Hucknall, Nottingham NG15 8HX* T: rockin.rev@ntlworld.com

MURRAY, John Grainger. b 45. CITC 67. **d** 70 **p** 71. C Carlow Union *C & O* 70–72; C Limerick City *L & K* 72–77; I Rathdowney w Castlefleming, Donaghmore etc *C & O* 77–14; Can Leighlin Cathl 83–88; Preb Ossory Cathl 83–88; Treas Ossory and Leighlin Cathls 88–89; Chan Ossory and Leighlin Cathls 89–90; Prec Ossory and Leighlin Cathls 90–92; Adn Ossory and Leighlin 92–14; Adn Cashel, Waterford and Lismore 94–14; rtd 14. *Vicarstown, Stradbally, Co Laois, Republic of Ireland* T: (00353) (57) 864 1686 M: 87-248 8241 E: venjgm@gmail.com

MURRAY, Mrs Kim Margaret. b 58. **d** 07 **p** 09. OLM Camberley St Mich Yorktown *Guildf* 07–18; OLM Camberley St Martin Old Dean from 18. *9 Dorchester Court, 283 London Road, Camberley GU15 3JJ* T: (01276) 23354 E: k.murray208@btinternet.com

MURRAY, Mrs Margaret Janice. b 46. Carl Dioc Tr Course. dss 86 **d** 87 **p** 94. Walney Is *Carl* 86–87; Hon Par Dn 87–89; Par Dn Carl H Trin and St Barn 89–94; Chapl Cumberland Infirmary 90–94; C Harraby *Carl* 94–97; P-in-c 97–00; V 00–02; Chapl to the Deaf and Hard of Hearing 94–02; rtd 02; PtO *Carl* from 02. *6 Follyskye Cottages, Tindale Fell, Brampton CA8 2QB* T: (016977) 46400

MURRAY, Paul Ridsdale. b 55. BEd. St Steph Ho Ox 80. **d** 83 **p** 84. C Hartlepool St Oswald *Dur* 83–86; C S Shields All SS 86–88; V Sacriston and Kimblesworth 88–94; P-in-c Waterhouses 94–98; P-in-c Chopwell from 98; PtO *Newc* from 99. *St John's Vicarage, Derwent View, Chopwell, Newcastle upon Tyne NE17 7AN* T: (01207) 561248 F: 563850 M: 07803-906727 E: p.r.murray@durham.anglican.org

MURRAY, Philip. b 88. CCC Cam BA 10 MA 14 PhD 13. Westcott Ho Cam 15. **d** 18 **p** 19. C Stockton St Pet *Dur* from 18; C Elton from 18. *2 Overton Way, Stockton-on-Tees TS18 3AP* T: (01642) 616985 M: 07825-331119 E: frphilipmurray@gmail.com

MURRAY, Rachel Eleanor. b 70. Univ of Wales (Swansea) BA 92. Westcott Ho Cam 16. **d** 18 **p** 19. C Winchcombe *Glouc* from 18. *22 Delavale Road, Winchcombe, Cheltenham GL54 5HN* E: revrachel@winchcombeparish.org.uk

MURRAY, Roy John. b 47. Open Univ BA 92 Wolv Poly CertEd 89 RGN 75 RMN 77. WMMTC 01. **d** 04 **p** 05. NSM Solihull *Birm* 04–08; C Torquay St Jo and Ellacombe *Ex*

08–11; P-in-c Torquay St Jo 11–13; rtd 13; NSM Solihull *Birm* 13–18; NSM Upminster *Chelmsf* from 18. *6 Gaynes Park Road, Upminster RM14 2HH* T: (01708) 225374 M: 07768-436363 E: roy.murray@upminsterparish.co.uk

MURRAY, Ruth. *See* MURRAY, Elizabeth Ruth

MURRAY, The Very Revd Sarah Elisabeth. b 70. Aber Univ BTh 12. TISEC 10. **d** 13 **p** 14. Dioc C *Mor* 13–16; Vice-Provost St Andr Cathl Inverness 16–17; Provost from 17. *15 Ardross Street, Inverness IV3 5NS* T: (01463) 233535 M: 07794-532052 E: revsarahmurray@gmail.com

MURRAY, Mrs Sheila Elizabeth. b 53. Ripon Coll Cuddesdon 10. **d** 11 **p** 12. NSM Taunton St Mary *B & W* 11–14; NSM Taunton St Mary and St Jo 14–17; PtO 17; NSM Ripon Cathl *Leeds* from 17. *The Vicarage, Knaresborough Road, Bishop Monkton, Harrogate HG3 3QQ* E: revsmurray@btinternet.com

MURRAY, Stephen Michael. b 74. Windsor Univ Ontario BA 97. Trin Coll Toronto MDiv 03. **d** 03 **p** 04. C Dundas St Jas Canada 03–06; R Hamilton Resurr 06–11; P-in-c Ghent *Eur* from 11; P-in-c Knokke 11–16. *Begijnhoflaan 29, B-9000 Ghent, Belgium* T: (0032) (9) 336 4722 M: (4) 9745 1809 E: stephenmurray92@gmail.com

MURRAY (*née* GOULD), **Mrs Susan Judith.** b 61. Poly of Wales BSc 83 Open Univ MA 95. St Jo Coll Nottm 90. **d** 91 **p** 94. Par Dn Stokesley *York* 91–94; CMS 94–95; Argentina 95–03; P-in-c Haddlesey w Hambleton and Birkin *York* 03–09; TV Crawley *Chich* 09–17; V Three Bridges 17–18; V Bisley, Chalford, France Lynch, and Oakridge etc *Glouc* from 18. *The Vicarage, Manor Street, Bisley, Stroud GL6 7BJ* T: (01452) 770897 E: vicar@bisleybenefice.org.uk

MURRAY, Thomas Christopher. b 87. St Luke's Coll Ex BSc 09. Trin Coll Bris BA 19. **d** 19. C Ox St Andr from 19. *St Andrew's Church, Linton Road, Oxford OX2 6UG* M: 07851-600778 E: tcm202@gmail.com

MURRAY, Canon William Robert Craufurd. b 44. St Chad's Coll Dur BA 66. **d** 68 **p** 69. C Workington St Mich *Carl* 68–71; C Harrogate St Wilfrid *Ripon* 71–74; P-in-c Sawley 74; V Winksley cum Grantley and Aldfield w Studley 74; R Fountains 75–81; V Hutt New Zealand 81–87; V Fendalton and Chapl Medbury Sch 87–00; V Merivale 00–09; Can Christchurch Cathl 91–09; rtd 09. *92 Tauhina Avenue, Lincoln 7608, New Zealand* T: (0064) (3) 325 2196 E: craufurd@xtra.co.nz

MURRAY, Bishop of The. *See* FORD, John Frank

MURRAY-LESLIE, Adrian John Gervase. b 46. Lich Th Coll 67. **d** 69 **p** 70. C Sheff St Cuth 69–73; C Mosborough 73–75; C-in-c Mosborough CD 75–80; P-in-c Edale and Warden The Peak Cen 80–11; rtd 11. *Woodside House, New Road, Barlborough, Chesterfield S43 4HY* T: (01246) 819021 E: adrian@murray-leslie.org.uk

MURRAY-PETERS, Mrs Nancy Susan. b 48. WEMTC 09. **d** 11 **p** 12. NSM Worc St Barn w Ch Ch 11–14; NSM Peopleton and White Ladies Aston w Churchill etc 14–18; rtd 18. *Wee Wee Cottage, Worcester Road, Wyre Piddle, Pershore WR10 2HR* T: (01386) 553286 E: nmp.murraypeters@btinternet.com

MURRELL, Canon John Edmund. b 28. Westcott Ho Cam. **d** 66 **p** 67. C Ivychurch w Old Romney and Midley *Cant* 66–70; R Bardwell *St E* 70–75; PtO *Ely* 75–77; V Wenhaston w Thorington and Bramfield w Walpole *St E* 77–86; V Thorington w Wenhaston and Bramfield 86–92; P-in-c Walberswick w Blythburgh 86–92; V Thorington w Wenhaston, Bramfield etc 92–93; RD Halesworth 85–90; Hon Can St E Cathl 89–93; rtd 93; PtO *St E* 93–16. *Strickland Cottage, 12 Lorne Road, Southwold IP18 6EP* T: (01502) 722074

MURRILLS, Mrs Rosemary Jill. b 62. Cam Coll of Art & Tech BSc 84 Brunel Univ MSc 93. ERMC 09. **d** 12 **p** 13. NSM Hartford and Houghton w Wyton *Ely* 12–15; NSM Upper St Leonards St Jo *Chich* 15–17; rtd 17. *4 Hobart Court, 5 Ellenslea Road, St Leonards-on-Sea TN37 6HX* M: 07525-186205 E: rev.murrills@btinternet.com

MURRIN, Robert Staddon. b 42. Reading Univ BA 68 Open Univ MA 96. WMMTC 90. **d** 93 **p** 95. NSM Peterchurch w Vowchurch, Turnastone and Dorstone *Heref* 93–95; NSM Tupsley w Hampton Bishop 95–97; Chapl Kemp Hospice Kidderminster 97–05; PtO *Heref* 06–18. *Albion Cottage, Peterchurch, Hereford HR2 0RP* T: (01981) 550656 *or* 550467 F: 550432

✠**MURSELL, The Rt Revd Alfred <u>Gordon</u>.** b 49. BNC Ox BA 70 MA 73 BD 87 Birm Univ Hon DD 05 ARCM 74. Cuddesdon Coll 71. **d** 73 **p** 74 **c** 05. C Walton St Mary *Liv* 73–77; V E Dulwich St Jo *S'wark* 77–86; Tutor Sarum & Wells Th Coll 87–91; TR Stafford *Lich* 91–99; Dean Birm 99–02 and 02–05; Area Bp Stafford *Lich* 05–10; rtd 10; Can Th Leic Cathl from 10; LtO *Glas* from 10. *The Old*

Manse, Borgue, Kirkcudbright DG6 4SH T: (01557) 870307
E: gordon.mursell@btinternet.com

MURTHEN, Mark Anthony. b 77. UEA BA 99 MA 00. Oak Hill Th Coll BA 14. **d** 14 **p** 15. C Deane *Man* 14–17; C Muswell Hill St Jas w St Matt *Lon* from 17. *St James Church, St James Lane, London N10 3DB* T: (020) 8883 6277 E: markmurthen@gmail.com

MUSINDI, Mrs Beatrice Nambuya Balibali. b 64. Birm Univ MA 94. Bp Tucker Coll Mukono BD 90. **d** 03 **p** 04. C Caerleon w Llanhennock *Mon* 03–07; C Malpas 07–08; PtO *Cant* 09–14; Chapl Dover Immigration Removal Cen 14; Chapl HM YOI Roch from 14. *HM Young Offender Institution, 1 Fort Road, Rochester ME1 3QS* T: (01634) 803100 M: 07989-469938 E: beatrice.musindi@hotmail.co.uk

MUSINDI, Philip. b 63. Bp Tucker Coll Mukono BD 91 Univ of Wales (Cardiff) MA 94. **d** 87 **p** 90. C and Sch Chapl Naigana Uganda 87–89; C Builth and Llanddewi'r Cwm w Llangynog etc *S & B* 92–94; C Newport St Teilo *Mon* 94–97; P-in-c Newport St Matt 97–04; V Newport St Andr 04–09; Min Thanet St Andr CD *Cant* 09–11; V Reading Street from 11. *St Andrew's House, 29 Reading Street, Broadstairs CT10 3AZ* T: (01843) 579945 E: philip.musindi@hotmail.co.uk

MUSIWACHO, Taurayi Theresa. b 69. Seke Teachers' Coll Zimbabwe TDip 95. ERMC 13. **d** 16 **p** 17. C Royston *St Alb* from 16. *12 Prince Andrew's Close, Royston SG8 9DZ* T: (01763) 662199 E: revtmusi@gmail.com

✠**MUSK, The Rt Revd Bill Andrew.** b 49. Ox Univ BA 70 MA 75 Fuller Th Sem California ThM 80 UNISA D Litt et Phil 84. Trin Coll Bris. **d** 81 **p** 82 **c** 08. Egypt 81–86; CMS 88–89; TV Maghull *Liv* 89–97; V Tulse Hill H Trin and St Matthias *S'wark* 97–08; Hon Can S'wark Cathl 07–08; Area Bp N Africa and R Tunis St Geo 08–15; rtd 15; PtO *Chich* from 15. *38 Falaise, West Quay, Newhaven BN9 9GG* T: (01273) 612430 E: billamusk@gmail.com

MUSKER, Mrs Hilary. b 56. St Mellitus Coll 15. **d** 15 **p** 16. NSM Barkingside St Laur *Chelmsf* 15–18; NSM Chingford SS Pet and Paul from 18. *13 Deacon Way, Woodford Bridge IG8 8DF* E: hilary.musker@parishofchingford.org.uk

MUSSER, Ms Christine. b 55. Ex Univ 96. **d** 00 **p** 01. C Torpoint *Truro* 00–03; P-in-c Boscastle w Davidstow 03–07; P-in-c Pirbright *Guildf* 07–17; V 17–19; rtd 19. *Address temp unknown* E: revdchrismusser@aol.com

MUSSON, David John. b 46. Open Univ BA 86 Univ of Wales (Lamp) MPhil 96 Univ of Wales (Ban) PhD 00. Linc Th Coll 70. **d** 73 **p** 74. C New Sleaford *Linc* 73–76; C Morton 76–80; P-in-c Thurlby 80–86; R Quarrington w Old Sleaford 86–99; P-in-c Silk Willoughby 86–87; R 87–99; PtO *Chich* from 01. *Flat 9, Regency Court 4-5, South Cliff, Eastbourne BN20 7AE* T: (01323) 723345

MUSSON, Mrs Joanne Chatterley. b 60. Qu Coll Birm 07. **d** 09 **p** 10. C Redditch Ch the K *Worc* 09–13; P-in-c Claines St Jo from 13; C Worc City 13–14; P-in-c Worc St Geo w St Mary Magd from 14. *The Vicarage, Claines Lane, Worcester WR3 7RN* M: 07590-514115

MUSSON, John Keith. b 39. Nottm Univ BSc 61 PhD 66 CEng MIMechE. St As Minl Tr Course 85. **d** 88 **p** 89. Assoc Prin NE Wales Inst of HE 80–93; NSM Holywell *St As* 88–93; C 93–95; R Caerwys and Bodfari 95–02; rtd 02; PtO *Lich* from 02; *St As* from 09. *4 Hayes View, Oswestry SY11 1TP* T: (01691) 656212 E: musson908@btinternet.com

MUSSON, William John. b 58. UMIST BSc 80 Open Univ MA 02. St Jo Coll Nottm 88. **d** 91 **p** 92. C Nantwich *Ches* 91–94; C Finchley Ch Ch *Lon* 94–97; V Lynchmere and Camelsdale *Chich* 97–10; V Cudham and Downe *Roch* from 10; AD Orpington from 18. *The Boundary, Hangrove Hill, Downe, Orpington BR6 7LQ* T: (01959) 540012 E: stpandp@googlemail.com

MUST, Albert Henry. b 27. Clifton Th Coll 61. **d** 63 **p** 64. C Becontree St Mary *Chelmsf* 63–68; V Highbury Vale St Jo *Lon* 68–78; V Highbury New Park St Aug 78–84; V Walthamstow St Jo *Chelmsf* 84–93; rtd 93; PtO *Cant* 93–16. *24 Nightingale Avenue, Whitstable CT5 4TR* T/F: (01227) 772160

MUST, Mrs Shirley Ann. b 35. St Mich Ho Ox 61. **dss** 82 **d** 87 **p** 94. Highbury New Park St Aug *Lon* 82–84; Walthamstow St Jo *Chelmsf* 84–93; Hon Par Dn 87–93; PtO *Cant* 93–94; Hon C Herne Bay Ch Ch 94–05; PtO 05–12. *24 Nightingale Avenue, Whitstable CT5 4TR* T/F: (01227) 772160

MUSTARD, Canon James Edmond Alexander. b 74. Ex Univ BA 95 Clare Coll Cam BA 04 MA 08 K Coll Lon MA 13. Westcott Ho Cam 02 Berkeley Div Sch 04. **d** 05 **p** 06. C Nor St Pet Mancroft w St Jo Maddermarket 05–08; C Pimlico St Pet w Westmr Ch Ch *Lon* 08–12; R E Barnet *St Alb* 12–18; AD Barnet 16–18; Can Res and Prec Ex Cathl from 18. *6 Cathedral Close, Exeter EX1 1EZ* M: 07763-973647 E: james.mustard@exeter-cathedral.org.uk

MUSTOE, Canon Alan Andrew. b 52. Man Univ BA 74. Qu Coll Birm. **d** 78 **p** 79. C Chatham St Wm *Roch* 78–82; R Burham and Wouldham 82–88; Dioc Info Officer 83–88; V Strood St Nic w St Mary 88–99; V Orpington All SS 99–10; AD Orpington 05–10; R Chislehurst St Nic from 10; Hon Can Roch Cathl from 16. *The Rectory, 2 Cardinal Close, Chislehurst BR7 6SA* T: (020) 8467 4405 M: 07725-909733 E: alan.mustoe@akmustoe.co.uk *or* alan.mustoe@alanmustoe.co.uk

MUTCH, Canon Sylvia Edna. b 36. St Mich Ho Ox 57. **dss** 79 **d** 87 **p** 94. Clifton *York* 79–95; Par Dn 87–94; C 94–95; Chapl Clifton Hosp York 81–94; R Elvington w Sutton on Derwent and E Cottingwith *York* 95–01; Can and Preb York Minster 98–01; rtd 01; PtO *York* 01–18. *18 Waite Close, Pocklington, York YO42 2YU* T: (01759) 307894

MUTEMWAKWENDA, Jones Chibuye. b 63. Trin Coll Bris BA 05. Mindolo Th Coll Zambia 89. **d** 92 **p** 93. C Lusaka Cathl Zambia 93–95; Chapl Univ Teaching Hosp Lusaka 93–94; P-in-c Choma 95–98; Adn Lusaka 96–98; V Gen 99–02; PtO *B & W* 03–06; *Bris* 08–14; P-in-c Easton All Hallows 15–19; V from 19. *All Hallows Church, All Hallows Road, Easton, Bristol BS5 0HH* T: 0117-909 9545 *or* 955 1804 E: jonesgladys99@hotmail.com

MUTETE, Lameck. b 61. Bp Gaul Th Coll Harare 94. **d** 96 **p** 97. C Harare St Luke Zimbabwe 96–97; Asst P Harare Cathl 97–01; P-in-c 01; Adn Harare E 01; Can Harare 01–04; PtO *Bradf* 04; P-in-c Tattenhall and Handley *Ches* 04–10; R 10–11; R Tattenhall w Burwardsley and Handley from 11; PtO *Birm* from 14. *The Rectory, Chester Road, Gatesheath, Tattenhall, Chester CH3 9AH* T: (01829) 770245 M: 07940-512748 E: lameckmutete@yahoo.co.uk

MUTHALALY, Varghese Malayil Lukose (Saju). b 79. S Asia Bible Coll Bangalore BTh 01. Wycliffe Hall Ox BTh 08. **d** 08 **p** 09. C Lancaster St Thos *Blackb* 08–11; C Kendal St Thos and Crook *Carl* 11–15; P-in-c Gillingham St Mark *Roch* 15–19; V from 19. *St Mark's Vicarage, 173 Canterbury Street, Gillingham ME7 5TU* T: 01634 570489 E: sajudoj@yahoo.com

MUTHUVELOE, Samuel Rajakumar. b 50. Colombo Univ MB, BS 76 MRCGP 91 DRCOG 84. Ripon Coll Cuddesdon 13. **d** 16 **p** 17. OLM Bletchley *Ox* 16–19; OLM Stantonbury and Willen from 19; PtO *St Alb* from 17. *21 Lower Stonehayes, Great Linford, Milton Keynes MK14 5ES* T: (01908) 668829 M: 07854-745669 E: sam.muthuveloe@gmail.com

MUTIKANI, Mrs Martha Tsungayi Zivito. b 66. SEITE 12. **d** 15 **p** 16. NSM Reigate St Luke *S'wark* 15–17; NSM S Beddington and Roundshaw 17–19; NSM Horley from 19; PtO *Win* from 19. *68 Middlefield, Horley RH6 9XP* T: (01293) 773991 M: 07901-568549 E: mtzmutikani20@hotmail.com

MUTTER, Richard Douglas. b 73. **d** 14 **p** 15. C Cleobury Mortimer w Hopton Wafers etc *Heref* 14–17; R Arden Valley *Cov* from 17. *The Vicarage, Church Road, Snitterfield, Stratford-upon-Avon CV37 0LN* E: richard_mutter@hotmail.com

MUTUKU, Norbert. *See* CHUMU MUTUKU, Norbert

MUXLOW, Judy Ann. b 47. Univ of Wales (Cardiff) BSc 69 St Luke's Coll Ex CertEd 73. SEITE. **d** 00 **p** 01. Chapl Ch Ch High Sch Ashford 00–03; Bp's Officer for NSM *Cant* 03–07; NSM Biddenden and Smarden 00–06; NSM Appledore w Brookland, Fairfield, Brenzett etc 06–08; NSM Wittersham w Stone and Ebony 06–08; NSM Woodchurch 06–08; PtO *Roch* 00–12; *Cant* 09–19. *29 The Meadows, Biddenden, Ashford TN27 8AW* T: (01580) 291016 E: judy@mucat.eclipse.co.uk

✠**MWAMBA, The Rt Revd Musonda Trevor Selwyn.** b 58. LLB 81 Ox Univ BA 83 MA 88 MPhil 98. St Steph Ho Ox 81. **d** 84 **p** 85 **c** 05. C Notting Hill All SS w St Columb *Lon* 84; R Luanshya and Voc Dir Cen Zambia 85–86; Prov Sec Cen Africa and Dioc Sec Botswana 87–96; Asst Chapl Keble Coll Ox 96–98; NSM Wolvercote w Summertown *Ox* 97–99; NSM Botswana 99–02; V Gen 02–05; Bp Botswana 05–13; TR Barking *Chelmsf* 13–16; TR Barking St Marg from 17; Hon Asst Bp Chelmsf from 13. *20 Sandringham Road, Barking IG11 9AB* T: (020) 8594 4513 E: stmags@tiscali.co.uk *or* musondamuwamba@gmail.com

MWANDIA, Nicholas Kyalo. b 64. Anglia Ruskin Univ BA 09 K Coll Lon MA 10. ERMC 16. **d** 14 **p** 16. PtO *St Alb* 17; C Luton St Mary from 17; C Luton St Matt High Town from 17. *St Matthew's Vicarage, 85 Wenlock Street, Luton LU2 0NN* T: (01582) 516944 E: nickmwandia@stmarysluton.org

MYATT, Francis Eric. b 60. St Jo Coll Nottm 89. **d** 92 **p** 93. C W Derby St Luke *Liv* 92–95; TV Sutton 95–98; V Liv St Chris Norris Green 98–01; CF 01–13; C Walton St Jo *Liv* 13–15; V from 15. *66 Roseworth Avenue, Liverpool L9 8HF*

MYCOCK, Malcolm George Robert. b 71. Wycliffe Hall Ox 15. **d** 17 **p** 18. C Bucknall *Lich* from 17. *The Vicarage, 161A Dawlish Drive, Stoke-on-Trent ST2 0ET* T: (01782) 915813 M: 07908-200782 E: malcolm1cor13.13@gmail.com

MYERS, Canon Alison Margaret. b 66. Bris Univ BSc 88. SEITE 04. d 07 p 08. NSM Cambourne *Ely* 07–10; TV Lordsbridge 10–17; TR from 17; Hon Can Ely Cathl from 19. *The Rectory, 50 Main Street, Hardwick, Cambridge CB3 7QS* T: (01954) 212815 M: 07884-370933 E: alisonmyers@lordsbridge.org

MYERS, Duncan Frank. b 57. Warwick Univ BSc. St Jo Coll Nottm 81. d 84 p 85. C Upton cum Chalvey *Ox* 84–86; C Farnborough *Guildf* 86–90; Chapl Nottm Poly *S'well* 90–92; Chapl Nottm Trent Univ 92–95; Sen Past Adv 95–02; Hon Min Can Dur Cathl 04–08; Chapl Hatf Coll Dur 06–08; Chapl Salford Univ *Man* 08–12; Chapl Lon S Bank Univ *S'wark* 12–14; Nat Adv for HE Abps' Coun 14–15; Hon Min Can S'wark Cathl from 13. *7 Temple West Mews, West Square, London SE11 4TJ* T: (020) 7582 4442

MYERS, Canon Gillian Mary. b 57. Warwick Univ BSc 78 Nottm Univ MA 96. St Jo Coll Nottm 83. d 95 p 97. NSM Nottingham St Jude *S'well* 95–97; NSM Gedling 97–00; P-in-c Nottingham All SS 00–02; Succ, Sacr and Min Can Dur Cathl 02–08; Can Res Man Cathl 08–12; Can Res and Prec S'wark Cathl from 12. *7 Temple West Mews, West Square, London SE11 4TJ* T: (020) 7582 4442 E: gilly@myers.uk.net

MYERS, Paul Henry. b 49. ALA 72. Qu Coll Birm 74. d 77 p 78. C Baildon *Bradf* 77–80; C W Bromwich All SS *Lich* 80–83; Chapl RAF 83–86; V Milton *Lich* 87–92; C Baswich 96–99; C Hixon w Stowe-by-Chartley 99–02; TV Mid Trent 02–05; TR Blakenall Heath 05–14; rtd 14. *110 Buxton Road, Leek ST13 6EJ* E: rev.paulmyers@btinternet.com

MYERS, Robert William John. b 57. Aus Nat Univ BSc 80 Newc Univ Aus DipEd 82. Trin Coll Bris 93. d 95 p 96. C Addiscombe St Mary Magd w St Martin *S'wark* 95–98; C Surbiton St Matt 98–03; P-in-c Blayney Australia 04–10; I Bellarine from 10. *PO Box 365, Drysdale VIC 3222, Australia* T: (0061) (3) 5251 2571 M: 48-857 4855 E: rwj127@hotmail.com

MYERS, Sally Ann. b 65. Leic Univ BA 86 Nottm Univ MA 06 Cam Univ PhD 14. EMMTC 02. d 06 p 07. C Grantham St Wulfram *Linc* 06–08; Vice-Prin Dioc Min Tr Course 08–09; Dir of Studies Dioc Min Tr Course from 09; Prin Linc Sch of Th from 14. *15 Wain Well Mews, Lincoln LN2 4BF* T: (01522) 567804 *or* 504083 M: 07495-315402 E: sally.myers@lincoln.anglican.org

MYLES (*née* LUCAS), Mrs Julia Mary. b 63. Westhill Coll Birm BEd 85 Birm Univ MA 92. Lindisfarne Regional Tr Partnership 10. d 13 p 14. C Alnwick *Newc* 13–17; P-in-c Arle Valley *Win* from 17. *The Rectory, 37 Jacklyns Lane, Alresford SO24 9LF* T: (01962) 732105 M: 07716-771164 E: juliamyles@btinternet.com

MYLNE, Mrs Christine. b 44. Open Univ BA 76 Univ of Wales (Lamp) MA 03. St Alb Minl Tr Scheme 89 NEOC 04. d 04 p 05. NSM Norham and Duddo *Newc* 04–06; NSM Cornhill w Carham 04–06; NSM Branxton 04–06; P-in-c Challoch *Glas* 06–11; rtd 11; P-in-c Glenurquhart *Mor* 11–17; LtO from 18. *2 Wester Moniack Cottages, Kirkhill, Inverness IV5 7PQ* T: (01463) 831668 E: christinemylne@gmail.com *or* christine.mylne@btinternet.com

MYNORS, Canon James Baskerville. b 49. Peterho Cam BA 70 MA 74. Ridley Hall Cam 70 St Jo Coll Nottm 77. d 78 p 80. Hon C Leic H Apostles 78–79; C Virginia Water *Guildf* 79–83; C Patcham *Chich* 83–88; P-in-c Fowlmere and Thriplow *Ely* 88–01; Sen Tutor EAMTC 88–90; Vice-Prin 90–97; P-in-c Gt w Lt Abington 01–07; P-in-c Hildersham 01–07; Dioc Rural Miss Officer 04–07; R Aldwincle, Clopton, Pilton, Stoke Doyle etc *Pet* 07–17; Can Pet Cathl 13–17; rtd 17; PtO *Ox* from 17. *58 Coxwell Road, Faringdon SN7 7JX* T: (01367) 243219 E: jim@mynors.me.uk

MYRES, Peter John Lukis. b 67. Trin Coll Bris 16. d 18 p 19. C Malvern Chase *Worc* from 18. *17 Whitborn Close, Malvern WR14 2SP* E: peter.myres1@btinternet.com *or* curate@chaseteam.org

N

NADARAJAH (*née* GOODDEN), Mrs Stephanie Anne. b 81. Fitzw Coll Cam MA 04. Ripon Coll Cuddesdon MTh 10. d 10 p 11. C Caterham *S'wark* 10–15; V Worcester Park Ch Ch w St Phil from 15. *9 Avon Close, Worcester Park KT4 7AQ* E: stephnadarajah@gmail.com

NADEN, Anthony Joshua. b 38. Jes Coll Ox BA 62 MA 64 SOAS Lon PhD 73. Wycliffe Hall Ox 60. d 62 p 63. C Rowner *Portsm* 62–66; C Fisherton Anger *Sarum* 69–72; Ghana 72–10; PtO *Ox* from 10. *Lost Marbles, 31 Reading Road, Pangbourne, Reading RG8 7HY* T: 0118-984 2368 E: lostmarbles31@gmail.com

NADIN, Dennis Lloyd. b 37. St D Coll Lamp BA 60 Man Univ MEd 81. Ridley Hall Cam 60. d 64 p 65. C Childwall All SS *Liv* 64–67; P-in-c Seacroft *Ripon* 67–69; Project Officer Grubb Inst 69–70; Lect CA Tr Coll Blackheath 70–72; Community Educn Essex Co Coun 73–80; Public Preacher *Chelmsf* from 73; PtO *St Alb* 01–03. *The Hermitage, 201 Willowfield, Harlow CM18 6RZ* T: (01279) 325904 E: nadennadinsociety@yahoo.co.uk

NAGEL, Canon Lawson Chase Joseph. b 49. Univ of Michigan BA 71 K Coll Lon PhD 82 ARHistS 75. Sarum & Wells Th Coll 81. d 83 p 84. C Chiswick St Nic w St Mary *Lon* 83–86; C Horsham *Chich* 86; TV 86–91; V Aldwick 91–19; rtd 19; Sec Gen Confraternity of the Blessed Sacrament 85–10; Hon Can Popondota from 05; PtO *Eur* from 07. *22 Bishopsgate Walk, Chichester PO19 6FG* T: (01243) 537831 E: fatherlawson@gmail.com

NAGEL, Lucy Mary. See WEBB, Lucy Mary

NAHABEDIAN, Canon Harold Joseph. b 39. Toronto Univ BA 63 MA 66. Trin Coll Toronto STB 70 Armenian Orthodox Sem Jerusalem 70. d 73 p 74. C Vancouver St Jas Canada 73–76; Chapl Trin Coll Toronto 76–81; V Toronto St Thos 81–83; P-in-c Toronto St Mary Magd 83–88; R 88–09; Hon Can Toronto from 93; rtd 09; P-in-c Strasbourg *Eur* 10–13; Hon C Toronto St Martin-in-the-Fields Canada from 14. *33 Amroth Avenue, Toronto ON M4C 4H3, Canada* E: hj.nahabedian@gmail.com

NAIRN, Canon Stuart Robert. b 51. K Coll Lon BD 75 AKC 75 Univ of Wales (Lamp) MTh 04 FRSA 01. St Aug Coll Cant 75. d 76 p 77. C E Dereham *Nor* 76–80; TV Hempnall 80–88; V Narborough w Narford 88–99; R Pentney St Mary Magd w W Bilney 88–99; R Narborough w Narford and Pentney 99–10; P-in-c Castleacre, Newton, Westacre and Southacre 97–10; R Nar Valley from 11; RD Lynn 91–99; RD Breckland 06–17; Hon Can Nor Cathl from 03. *The Rectory, Main Road, Narborough, King's Lynn PE32 1TE* T: (01760) 338552 *or* 338562 E: nairn.nvgrectory@btinternet.com

NAIRN-BRIGGS, The Very Revd George Peter. b 45. AKC 69. St Aug Coll Cant 69. d 70 p 71. C Catford St Laur *S'wark* 70–73; C Raynes Park St Sav 73–75; V Salfords 75–81; V St Helier 81–87; Dioc Soc Resp Adv *Wakef* 87–97; Can Res Wakef Cathl 92–97; Provost Wakef 97–00; Dean Wakef 00–07; rtd 07; PtO *Wakef* 09–14; *Leeds* from 14. *Abbey House, 2 St James Court, Park Avenue, Wakefield WF2 8DN* T: (01924) 291029 M: 07770-636840 E: nairnbriggs@btinternet.com

NAISH, Miss Annie Claire. b 65. St Jo Coll Dur BA 04 MA 08. Cranmer Hall Dur. d 05 p 06. C Gorleston St Andr *Nor* 05–09; Dioc Ecum Miss Enabler *B & W* 09–11; Missr Lee Abbey Movement 11–16; Bp's Enabler of Miss *Edin* from 16. *21A Grosvenor Crescent, Edinburgh EH12 5EL* T: 0131-538 7033 E: mission@dioceseofedinburgh.org

NAISH, Mrs Joanna Mary. b 60. Bris Univ BA 81 Southn Univ MA 92 Sheff Univ PGCE 82. STETS 06. d 09 p 10. NSM Woodford Valley w Archers Gate *Sarum* 09–17; NSM Amesbury 13–17; NSM Nadder Valley from 17. *Coombe Warren, Hindon Lane, Tisbury, Salisbury SP3 6QQ* T: (01747) 871820 M: 07810-810231 E: joanna.naish44@gmail.com

NAISH, Canon Timothy James Neville. b 57. St Jo Coll Ox BA 80 MA 88 Bris Univ PhD 05. WMMTC 86. d 87 p 88. CMS 81–00; C Cov H Trin 87; Dir Th Formation Dio Shaba Zaïre 88–91; Research Fell, Tutor, and Lect Qu Coll Birm 92–93; Tutor and Lect Bp Tucker Th Coll Uganda 93–00; R Hanborough and Freeland *Ox* 00–06; Dir Studies Ox Min Course 06–09; Dean 09–18; Lect Ripon Coll Cuddesdon 06–18; Asst Chapl Campsfield Ho Immigration Removal Cen 07–15; Can Res and Lib Cant Cathl from 18. *19 The Precincts, Canterbury CT1 2EP* T: (01227) 762862 E: tim.naish@canterbury-cathedral.org

NALL, Sheila Ann. b 48. Univ of Wales (Ban) BA 69. WMMTC 00. d 03 p 04. NSM Worc St Wulstan 03–07; Chapl HM Pris Hewell 07–09; PtO *Worc* from 15. *108 Ombersley Road, Worcester WR3 7EZ* T: (01905) 26284 E: nall.mail@tiscali.co.uk

NANCARROW, Mrs Rachel Mary. b 38. Cam Inst of Educn TCert 59. EAMTC 87. **d** 90 **p** 94. NSM Girton *Ely* 90–95; P-in-c Foxton 95–01; P-in-c Shepreth 98–01; C Fulbourn and Gt and Lt Wilbraham 01–03; rtd 03; PtO *Pet* from 04. *Thimble Cottage, 11 Geeston, Ketton, Stamford PE9 3RH* T: (01780) 729382

NANKIVELL, Christopher Robert Trevelyan. b 33. Jes Coll Ox BA 55 MA 63 Birm Univ MSocSc 79. Linc Th Coll 56. **d** 58 **p** 59. C Bloxwich *Lich* 58–60; C Stafford St Mary 60–64; P-in-c Malins Lee 64–72; Soc Welfare Sector Min to Milton Keynes Chr Coun 73–76; Tutor Qu Coll Birm 76–81; rtd 96. *77 Pereira Road, Birmingham B17 9JA* T: 0121-427 1197

NAPIER, Graeme Stewart Patrick Columbanus. b 66. Magd Coll Ox BA MA MPhil LRSM. St Steph Ho Ox. **d** 95 **p** 96. C Inverness St Andr *Mor* 95–98; Asst P St Laurence Ch Ch Australia 98–02; Min Can and Succ Westmr Abbey 02–10; Prec St Geo Cathl Perth Australia 10–16; PtO *Ox* 16–18; R New York St Jo in the Village USA from 18. *St John's in the Village, 224 Waverly Place, New York, NY 10014-2405, USA* T: (001) (212) 243 6192 M: (001) (972) 822 0099 E: rector@stjvny.org

NAPIER, Jennifer Beryl. *See* BLACK, Jennifer Beryl

NASH, David. b 25. K Coll Lon BD 51 AKC 51. **d** 52 **p** 53. C Buckhurst Hill *Chelmsf* 52–58; Min St Cedd CD Westcliff 58–66; R Rivenhall *Chelmsf* 66–83; P-in-c Boscastle w Davidstow *Truro* 83–85; TR 85–90; rtd 90; PtO *Truro* 90–14. *9 Boscundle Avenue, Falmouth TR11 5BU* E: revdavid@btinternet.com

NASH, Preb David John. b 41. Pemb Coll Ox BA 64 MA 70. Wells Th Coll 65. **d** 67 **p** 68. C Preston Ascension *Lon* 67–70; TV Hackney 70–75; TV Clifton *S'well* 76–82; V Winchmore Hill St Paul *Lon* 82–98; AD Enfield 87–91; R Monken Hadley 98–08; AD Cen Barnet 00–04; Preb St Paul's Cathl 96–08; rtd 08; PtO *Lon* from 08; *St Alb* from 10. *36 Birkbeck Road, Enfield EN2 0DX* T: (020) 8367 6873 E: prebdjnash@yahoo.co.uk

NASH (formerly **HORSFALL**), **Mrs Deborah.** b 66. Sheff Univ BA 14. Yorks Min Course 11. **d** 14 **p** 15. C S Ossett *Leeds* 14–18; R Thornhill and Whitley Lower from 18. *51 Frank Lane, Dewsbury WF12 0JW* M: 07834-788618 E: revdhorsfall@gmail.com

NASH, Mrs Ingrid. b 36. SRN 57 RNT 80 BEd 78. S'wark Ord Course 91. **d** 94 **p** 95. NSM Eltham Park St Luke *S'wark* 94–06; PtO *Roch* 97–17; *S'wark* from 06. *13 Crookston Road, London SE9 1YH* T: (020) 8850 0750

NASH, Canon James Alexander. b 56. St Jo Coll Nottm BA 94. **d** 97 **p** 98. C Trunch *Nor* 97–01; R Stratton St Mary w Stratton St Michael etc 01–10; R The Ch in the Woottons from 10; RD Lynn from 13; Hon Can Nor Cathl from 15. *The Rectory, 47 Castle Rising Road, South Wootton, King's Lynn PE30 3JA* T: (01553) 671381 E: jamesnash8@talktalk.net

NASH, James David Gifford. b 76. New Coll Ox MEng 98. Wycliffe Hall Ox BTh 03. **d** 03 **p** 04. C Plymouth St Andr and Stonehouse *Ex* 03–07; Hon C Preston All SS *Blackb* 07–11; C W Preston 11–16; V Ashton-on-Ribble St Andr from 17. *The Vicarage, 240 Tulketh Road, Ashton-on-Ribble, Preston PR2 1ES* T: (01772) 726848 M: 07889-424907 E: jdgnash@gmail.com

NASH, Mrs Jane. b 58. ERMC 05. **d** 08 **p** 09. C Kempston All SS and Biddenham *St Alb* 08–11; V Chadsmoor *Lich* 11–17; rtd 17; PtO *Ox* from 18. *8 Weston Court, Weston Road, Aston Clinton, Aylesbury HP22 5YT*

NASH, Paul. b 59. Liv Univ MA 03 Glos Univ MA 14. WMMTC 94. **d** 97 **p** 98. C Aston SS Pet and Paul *Birm* 97–02; Asst Chapl Birm Children's Hosp NHS Trust 02–04; Sen Chapl Birm Children's Hosp NHS Foundn Trust 05–18; Chapl and Spiritual Care Team Ldr Birm Women's NHS Foundn Trust from 18; Tutor St Jo Coll Nottm from 02. *13 Jaffray Road, Birmingham B24 8AZ* T: 0121-384 6034 *or* 333 8526 F: 333 8527 E: paulandsal@msn.com

NASH, Penelope Jane. b 71. Trin Coll Bris 04. **d** 06 **p** 07. C Downend *Bris* 06–09; TV Gt Berkhamsted, Gt and Lt Gaddesden etc *St Alb* 09–18; Chapl Wycombe Abbey Sch from 18. *Wycombe Abbey School, Abbey Way, High Wycombe HP11 1PE* T: (01494) 520381 E: vicarpenny@icloud.cpom

NASH, Robin Louis. b 51. Open Univ BA 87. Aston Tr Scheme 80 Chich Th Coll 82. **d** 84 **p** 85. C Lymington *Win* 84–86; C Andover w Foxcott 86–90; R Kegworth *Leic* 90–01; P-in-c Bournemouth St Alb *Win* 01–10; V 10–14; V Bournemouth St Luke 10–14; rtd 14; PtO *Win* from 14; *Eur* from 14. *6 Shreen Way, Gillingham SP8 4EL* T: (01747) 823183 E: my_quarters@yahoo.co.uk

NASH, Sally Ann. b 57. Sussex Univ BA 78 Sheff Univ DMinTh 03 Ox Brookes Univ MA 10 Birmingham Univ PhD 16 PGCE 79. Qu Coll Birm 10. **d** 12 **p** 13. Dir Midl Inst for Children, Youth and Miss St Jo Coll Nottm from 99; Team Ldr from 18; NSM Hodge Hill *Birm* from

12. *Wellman, 13 Jaffray Road, Erdington, Birmingham B24 8AZ* T: 0121-384 6034 *or* 0115-968 3222 M: 07824-542104 E: revsally12@gmail.com

NASH, Thomas James. b 82. SS Hild & Bede Coll Dur BA 03 MA 04. Wycliffe Hall Ox 07. **d** 09 **p** 10. C St Helen Bishopsgate w St Andr Undershaft etc *Lon* 09–14; C Sevenoaks St Nic *Roch* from 14. *26 Woodside Road, Sevenoaks TN13 3HE* E: thomas.nash@stnicholas-sevenoaks.org

NASH-WILLIAMS, Mark Christian Victor. b 64. Trin Hall Cam BA 86 MA 90 PGCE 87. Qu Coll Birm BD 01. **d** 02 **p** 03. C Edgmond w Kynnersley and Preston Wealdmoors *Lich* 02–06; P-in-c Stamfordham w Matfen *Newc* 06–14; R Alston Moor from 14; Bp's Adv for Environment from 19. *Parsonage House, Brampton Road, Alston CA9 3AA* T: (01434) 382558 E: vicar@alstonmoorcofe.org.uk

NASH-WILLIAMS, Canon Piers le Sor Victor. b 35. Trin Hall Cam BA 57 MA 61. Cuddesdon Coll 59. **d** 61 **p** 62. C Milton Win 61–64; Asst Chapl Eton Coll 64–66; PtO *Chich* 66–68; C Furze Platt *Ox* 69–72; V Newbury St Geo Wash Common 72–73; TV Newbury 73–91; R Ascot Heath 91–01; Hon Can Ch Ch 01; rtd 01; PtO *Ox* from 02. *18 Chiltern Close, Newbury RG14 6SZ* T: (01635) 31762

NASHASHIBI, Pauline. b 48. **d** 11 **p** 12. NSM Finsbury Park St Thos *Lon* 11–15; NSM Hornsey St Mary w St Geo 15–16; PtO from 16. *36A Woodstock Road, London N4 3EX* T: (020) 7263 8268 E: prnashashibi89@gmail.com

NASON, Canon Thomas David. b 44. Open Univ BA 92 ACA 68 FCA 78. Ripon Coll Cuddesdon 84. **d** 86 **p** 87. C Banstead *Guildf* 86–89; Chapl Prebendal Sch *Chich* 89–14; PV Chich Cathl 89–14; Can and Preb Chich Cathl 06–14; PtO from 14. *The Gables, Hambrook Hill South, Hambrook, Chichester PO18 8UJ* T: (01243) 573716 M: 07732-114279 E: d.nason@tesco.net

NASSAR, Nadim. b 64. Near E Sch of Th BTh 88. **d** 03 **p** 04. Prin Trin Foundn for Christianity and Culture 03–05; Dir Awareness Foundn from 05; Hon C Upper Chelsea H Trin *Lon* 03–11; Hon C Upper Chelsea H Trin and St Sav from 11; PtO *S'wark* 13–16 and from 17. *Awareness Foundation, Lodge House, 69 Beaufort Street, London SW3 5AH* T: (020) 7730 8830 M: 07961-968193 E: director@awareness-foundation.com

NATHANAEL, Martin Moses. b 43. Lon Univ BEd 73 K Coll Lon MTh 77. Ripon Coll Cuddesdon 77. **d** 79 **p** 80. C Hampton All SS *Lon* 79–82; P-in-c Kensal Town St Thos w St Andr and St Phil 82–83; Hd Div Bp Stopford Sch Lon 83–91; TV Tring *St Alb* 91–00; rtd 00. *43 Morehall Close, York YO30 4WA* T: (01904) 691201 E: matrtin.nathanael@btinternet.com

NATHANIAL. b 82. BA 04 MA 15. BD 09. **d** 10 **p** 12. P Kasauli Ch Ch India 12–15; PtO *Eur* 17–18; Chapl Prague from 18. *Pat'anka 2614/11A, 16000 Praha 6 - Dejvice, Czech Republic* T: (00420) 233 310 266 M: 737 039 082 E: nathanialbm@gmail.com

NATHANIEL, Canon Garth Edwin Peter. b 61. Brunel Univ BTh 99. Lon Bible Coll 96. **d** 98 **p** 99. NSM Hanwell St Mary w St Chris *Lon* 98–99; C Lt Stanmore St Lawr 99–01; P-in-c Brockmoor *Worc* 02–07; TV Brierley Hill 07–10; RD Kingswinford 08–10; TR Ipsley from 10; RD Bromsgrove 15–16; Hon Can Worc Cathl from 15. *The Rectory, Icknield Street, Ipsley, Redditch B98 0AN* T: (01527) 522847 M: 07949-490265 E: g.nathaniel@btinternet.com

NATNAEL, Daniel. b 66. Wycliffe Hall Ox 10. **d** 12 **p** 13. C Goldsworth Park *Guildf* 12–15; Chapl Twyford C of E Academies Trust 15–17; C Camberley St Paul *Guildf* from 17. *24 London Road, Camberley GU15 3UZ* T: (01276) 504023 M: 07815-137714 E: rev.dnatnael@gmail.com *or* dnatnael@yahoo.co.uk

NATTRASS, Elizabeth Jane. b 59. CBDTI 97. **d** 00 **p** 01. C Dalston w Cumdivock, Raughton Head and Wreay *Carl* 00–03; TV S Barrow 03–08; P-in-c 08; TR 08–10; P-in-c York St Olave w St Giles from 10; P-in-c York St Helen w St Martin from 10; P-in-c York All SS Pavement w St Crux and St Mich from 10; P-in-c York St Denys from 10; P-in-c York H Trin Micklegate from 13; P-in-c York St Lawr w St Nic from 15. *St Olave's Vicarage, 52 Bootham, York YO30 7BZ* T: (01904) 623559 E: nattrassjane@aol.com

NATTRASS, Michael Stuart. b 41. Man Univ BA 62. Cuddesdon Coll 62. **d** 64 **p** 65. C Easington Colliery *Dur* 64–65; C Silksworth 65–68; PtO *S'well* 68–72; LtO *Dur* 72–76; PtO *Lon* 76–78 and from 05; Hon C Pinner 78–05; rtd 05; PtO *Eur* from 18. *28 Waxwell Lane, Pinner HA5 3EN* T: (020) 8866 0217 F: 8930 0622

NAUDÉ, John Donald. b 62. Ridley Hall Cam 95. **d** 97 **p** 98. C Kettering Ch the King *Pet* 97–00; C Wellingborough All Hallows 00–06; Dioc Disability Adv 05–06; V Crookhorn *Portsm* 06–12; Dean Liwonde Bible Coll Malawi 12–16; C

Hurstpierpoint *Chich* from 16; Dioc Disability Adv from 16. *The Presentation Vicarage, 1 Marylands, New England Road, Haywards Heath RH16 3JZ* T: (01444) 616291 M: 07534-554587 E: john@naudeuk.com

NAUMANN, Canon David Sydney. b 26. Ripon Hall Ox 54. **d** 55 **p** 56. C Herne Bay Ch Ch *Cant* 55–58; Asst Chapl United Sheff Hosps 58–60; V Reculver *Cant* 60–64; Dioc Youth Chapl 63–70; R Eastwell w Boughton Aluph 65–67; V Westwell 65–67; Warden St Gabr Retreat Ho Westgate 68–70; V Littlebourne *Cant* 70–82; RD E Bridge 78–82; Hon Can Cant Cathl 81–00; R Sandwich 82–91; RD 85–90; rtd 91; PtO *Cant* from 91. *2 The Forrens, The Precincts, Canterbury CT1 2ER* T: (01227) 458939

NAUNTON, Hugh Raymond. b 38. Whitelands Coll Lon CertEd 69 Open Univ BA 75 Roehampton Univ Hon BEd 17. Bernard Gilpin Soc Dur 59 Chich Th Coll 60. **d** 63 **p** 64. C Stanground *Ely* 63–66; NSM Woolwich St Mary w H Trin *S'wark* 66–67; NSM Wandsworth St Anne 67–69 and 71–73; NSM Paddington St Sav *Lon* 69–71; NSM Cuddington *Guildf* 73–78; Hd RE Raynes Park High Sch 69–76; Hd RE Paddington Sch 76–78; Sen Teacher and Hd RE Ch Sch Richmond 79–93; Hon C Cheam Common St Phil *S'wark* 79–95; C Cheam 95–02; TV Selsdon St Jo w St Fran 02–03; PtO *Guildf* 73–18; *S'wark* from 66. *35 Farm Way, Worcester Park KT4 8RZ* T: (020) 8337 6685 M: 07581-412607 E: h.naunton@hotmail.com

NAWROCKYI, Nicholas Daniel. b 85. Dur Univ BA 06 MA 07 Leeds Univ BA 10. Coll of Resurr Mirfield 09. **d** 12 **p** 13. C Gt Grimsby St Mary and St Jas *Linc* 12–16; Min Cleethorpes St Fran CD from 16; V Cleethorpes St Aid from 19; V Clee from 19. *St Nicolas' Vicarage, Great Coates Road, Great Coates, Grimsby DN37 9NS* T: (01472) 459218 M: 07912-681092 E: nick.nawrockyi@lincoln.anglican.org

NAYLOR, Alison Louise. See CHESWORTH, Alison Louise

NAYLOR, Anne-Marie. b 66. St Andr Univ BSc 88 Nazarene Th Coll Man MA 16. Cranmer Hall Dur 16. **d** 18 **p** 19. C Marton, Siddington w Capesthorne etc *Ches* from 18. *The Burrow, 42 Willowmead Drive, Prestbury, Macclesfield SK10 4DD* T: (01625) 820468 M: 07799-112204

NAYLOR, Barry. See NAYLOR, James Barry

NAYLOR, Fiona. b 68. CQSW 93. St Jo Coll Nottm 02. **d** 05 **p** 08. C Len Valley *Cant* 05–06; Hon C Lower Darwen St Jas *Blackb* 07–10; P-in-c Lea 10–12; PtO 12–14 and from 18. *82 Pear Tree Avenue, Coppull, Chorley PR7 4NL* T: (01257) 793283 E: revfionanaylor@sky.com

NAYLOR, Canon Frank. b 36. Lon Univ BA 58 Liv Univ MA 63. NW Ord Course 75. **d** 75 **p** 76. NSM Eccleston Ch Ch *Liv* 75–92; Asst Dioc Chapl to the Deaf 92–94; Sen Chapl from 94; Hon Can Liv Cathl from 01. *27 Daresbury Road, Eccleston, St Helens WA10 5DR* T: (01744) 757034

NAYLOR, Grant Lambert. b 87. Univ of Wales (Lamp) BA 09. St Steph Ho Ox MTh 11. **d** 11 **p** 12. C Auckland St Helen *Dur* 11–15; P-in-c Sheff St Matt 15–17; V from 17; Miss Development Adv from 15. *St Matthew's Vicarage, 9 Ashdell Road, Sheffield S10 3DA* T: 0114-266 5681 E: father.naylor@gmail.com

NAYLOR, Ian Stuart. b 63. Wycliffe Hall Ox. **d** 01 **p** 02. C Ipswich St Marg St E 01–04; P-in-c Martlesham w Brightwell 04–11; P-in-c Coalbrookdale, Iron-Bridge and Lt Wenlock *Heref* from 11; RD Telford Severn Gorge from 13. *The Rector's House, Paradise, Coalbrookdale, Telford TF8 7NR* T: (01952) 433248 M: 07712-309848 E: iandjnaylor@hotmail.co.uk

NAYLOR, Canon James Barry. b 50. Lon Univ BSc 71 St Benet's Hall Ox BA 75. Wycliffe Hall Ox 72. **d** 76 **p** 76. C Catford (Southend) and Downham *S'wark* 76–79; TV 79–82; P-in-c Lewisham St Swithun 82–87; V E Dulwich St Jo 87–97; RD Dulwich 90–97; P-in-c Blythburgh w Reydon *St E* 97–99; P-in-c Wrentham w Benacre, Covehithe, Frostenden etc 97–99; P-in-c Southwold 97–99; P-in-c Uggeshall w Sotherton, Wangford and Henham 97–99; TR Sole Bay 99–02; Chapl Supervisor St Felix Sch Southwold 99–02; Can Res Leic Cathl 02–15; C The Abbey Leic 02–15; C St Stythians w Perranarworthal and Gwennap 10–13; C Devoran 10–13; C Feock 10–13; PtO from 13. *11 Adelaide Street, Camborne TR14 8HH* T: (01209) 712733 E: steamerneal@talktalk.net

NAYLOR, Miss Jean. b 29. Linc Th Coll 77. **dss** 79 **d** 87. Charlton St Luke w H Trin *S'wark* 79–84; Crofton Park St Hilda w St Cypr 84–89; Par Dn 87–89; rtd 89; PtO *Wakef* 89–14; *Leeds* from 14. *12 Winter Terrace, Barnsley S75 2ES* T: (01226) 204767

NAYLOR, Martin. b 72. Leeds Univ BA 10 Darw Coll Cam PhD 98 Hertf Coll Ox BA 94 ALCM 90. Coll of Resurr Mirfield 08. **d** 10 **p** 11. C Bedford All SS *St Alb* 10–14; P-in-c Batley All SS and Purlwell *Leeds* 14–16; P-in-c Hanging Heaton 14–16; V Batley from 16. *The Vicarage, Churchfield Street, Batley WF17 5DL* T: (01924) 473049 E: martin.mna@gmail.com

NAYLOR, Canon Peter Aubrey. b 33. Kelham Th Coll 54 Ely Th Coll 57. **d** 58 **p** 59. C Shepherd's Bush St Steph *Lon* 58–62; C Portsea N End St Mark *Portsm* 62–66; Chapl HM Borstal Portsm 64–66; V Foley Park *Worc* 66–74; V Maidstone All SS w St Phil and H Trin *Cant* 74–81; P-in-c Tovil 79–81; V Maidstone All SS and St Phil w Tovil 81–91; Hon Can Cant Cathl 79–93; RD Sutton 80–86; R Biddenden and Smarden 91–93; P-in-c Leic St Marg and All SS 93–96; P-in-c Leic St Aug 93–96; TR The Abbey Leic 96; rtd 98; PtO *Chich* 98–02; P-in-c Crowborough St Jo 02–09; PtO from 15. *1 Hobart Quay, Eastbourne BN23 5PB*

NAYLOR, Peter Henry. b 41. MIMechE. Chich Th Coll 64. **d** 67 **p** 68. C Filton *Bris* 67–70; C Brixham *Ex* 70–72; C Leckhampton St Pet *Glouc* 72–76; V Brockworth 76–94; P-in-c Gt Witcombe 91–94; RD Glouc N 91–94; P-in-c The Ampneys w Driffield and Poulton 94–95; R 95–99; P-in-c Cheltenham Em w St Steph 99–07; rtd 07; PtO *Glouc* from 16. *20 Glebe Farm Court, Up Hatherley, Cheltenham GL51 3EB*

NAYLOR, Russell Stephen. b 45. Leeds Univ BA 70. St Chad's Coll Dur 70. **d** 72 **p** 73. C Chapel Allerton *Ripon* 72–75; Ind Chapl *Liv* 75–81; P-in-c Burtonwood 81–83; V 83–05; rtd 05; PtO *Ches* from 05; *St As* from 16. *6 Hillside Avenue, Runcorn WA7 4BW* T: (01928) 835139 E: russnaylor@ntlworld.com

✠**NAZIR-ALI, The Rt Revd Michael James.** b 49. Karachi Univ BA 70 St Edm Hall Ox BLitt 74 MLitt 81 Fitzw Coll Cam MLitt 77 ACT ThD 85 Lambeth DD 05 Bath Univ Hon DLitt 03 Greenwich Univ Hon DLitt 03 Kent Univ Hon DD 04 Westmr Coll Penn (USA) DHumLit 04 Nashotah Ho Wisconsin Hon DD 10. Ridley Hall Cam 70. **d** 74 **p** 76 **c** 84. C Cambridge H Sepulchre w All SS *Ely* 74–76; Tutorial Supervisor Th Cam Univ 74–76; Sen Tutor Karachi Th Coll Pakistan 76–81; Provost Lahore 81–84; Bp Raiwind 84–86; Asst to Abp Cant 86–89; Co-ord of Studies and Ed Lambeth Conf 86–89; Hon C Ox St Giles and SS Phil and Jas w St Marg 86–89; Gen Sec CMS 89–94; Asst Bp S'wark 89–94; Hon C Limpsfield and Titsey 89–94; Can Th Leic Cathl 92–94; Bp Roch 94–09; President Ox Cen for Tr Research Advocacy and Dialogue from 09; Visiting Prof Th and RS Univ of Greenwich from 96; Hon Fell St Edm Hall Ox from 99; Hon Fell Fitzw Coll Cam from 06; Hon Asst Bp Roch from 11. *70 Wimpole Street, London W1G 8AX* T: (020) 3327 1139 E: oxtrad@gmail.com

NAZIR MASIH, Emmanuel. b 72. Westcott Ho Cam 14. **d** 00 **p** 01. PtO *Ely* 14–17; C Milton *Portsm* 16–19; P-in-c Middlesbrough Ascension *York* from 19. *Ascension Vicarage, Penrith Road, Middlesbrough TS3 7JR* M: 07949-817487 E: naziremmanuel@yahoo.com

NDEGWA, Timothy. b 81. **d** 04 **p** 05. Kenya 04–11; PtO *S'wark* 11–14 and 16; NSM Lee Gd Shep w St Pet from 16. *St Alban's Parsonage, 132 William Barefoot Drive, London SE9 3BP* M: 07504-829190 E: timobet@gmail.com

NDUKU, Chika Felix. b 71. Ridley Hall Cam 15. **d** 17 **p** 18. C Chadwell Heath *Chelmsf* from 17. *St Peter's Vicarage, 29 Warrington Road, Dagenham RM8 3JH* M: 07799-565754

NEAL, Alan. b 27. Trin Coll Bris 82. **d** 84 **p** 85. Hon C Broughty Ferry *Bre* 84–85; P-in-c Dundee St Ninian 85–86; R Lockerbie and Annan *Glas* 86–94; rtd 94. *c/o Mr and Mrs Graham Rew, 3 Vallance Drive, Lockerbie DG11 2DU*

NEAL, Canon Anthony Terrence. b 42. Open Univ BA 84 Leeds Univ CertEd 73 Univ of Wales MPhil 12. Chich Th Coll 65. **d** 68 **p** 69. C Cross Green St Sav and St Hilda *Ripon* 68–73; NSM Hawksworth Wood 73–78; Asst Chapl and Hd RE Abbey Grange High Sch 73–81; NSM Farnley *Ripon* 78–81; Dioc Adv in RE *Truro* 81–85; Children's Officer 85–87; Stewardship Adv *Truro* 87–88; P-in-c St Erth 81–84; V 84–96; P-in-c Phillack w Gwithian and Gwinear 94–96; P-in-c Hayle 94–96; TR Godrevy 96–06; Hon Can Truro Cathl 94–06; C Chacewater w St Day and Carharrack 10–13; C St Stythians w Perranarworthal and Gwennap 10–13; C Devoran 10–13; C Feock 10–13; PtO from 13. *11 Adelaide Street, Camborne TR14 8HH* T: (01209) 712733 E: steamerneal@talktalk.net

NEAL, James Frederick Charles. b 87. Nottm Univ BA 08. Trin Coll Bris 12. **d** 14 **p** 15. C Ashton-upon-Mersey St Mary Magd *Ches* 14–16; C Cambridge St Barn *Ely* from 16. *80 St Barnabas Road, Cambridge CB1 2DE* T: (01223) 519526 M: 07734-360421 E: jamesfcneal@gmail.com *or* james.neal@stbs.org.uk

NEAL, Stephen Charles. b 44. K Coll Lon BSc 66 MCMI 76. NOC 90. **d** 93 **p** 94. C Walmsley *Man* 93–96; P-in-c Bolton St Matt w St Barn 96–98; TV Halliwell 98–02; Chapl Bolton Hospice 02–05; PtO *Man* 05–08; *Derby* from 08; *Eur* from 08; rtd 09; Asst Chapl Derby Teaching Hosps NHS Foundn Trust from 09. *21 Utah Close, Hilton, Derby DE65 5JA* T: (01283) 480450 M: 07775-794890 E: stephencneal@yahoo.co.uk

NEALE, Andrew Jackson. b 58. Oak Hill Th Coll 97. **d** 99 **p** 00. C Harold Hill St Geo *Chelmsf* 99–02; C Bentley

Common, Kelvedon Hatch and Navestock 02–03; TV Chigwell and Chigwell Row 03–10; PtO 10–17; C High Ongar w Norton Mandeville 17–19. *12 Barker Way, Acres Avenue, Ongar CM5 0FJ* M: 07787-802085 E: andy.neale2pray@btopenworld.com

NEALE, Canon David. b 50. Lanchester Poly Cov BSc 72. St Mich Coll Llan BD 83. **d** 83 **p** 84. Min Can St Woolos Cathl *Mon* 83–87; Chapl St Woolos Hosp Newport 85–87; R Blaina and Nantyglo *Mon* 87–91; Video and Tech Officer Bd of Miss 91–01; TV Cyncoed *Mon* 99–01; Creative Resources Officer 01–03; V Maindee Newport *Mon* 03–16; AD Newport 09–16; Can St Woolos Cathl 12–16; rtd 16. *4 Legion Row, Navigation Street, Trethomas, Caerphilly CF83 8JA* T: (029) 2140 6670 E: revdneale@googlemail.com

NEALE, Edward. *See* NEALE, James Edward McKenzie

NEALE, Geoffrey Arthur. b 41. Brasted Th Coll 61 St Aid Birkenhead 63. **d** 65 **p** 66. C Stoke *Cov* 65–68; C Fareham H Trin *Portsm* 68–71; TV 71–72; R Binstead 72–77; TR Bottesford w Ashby *Linc* 77–80; V Horncastle w Low Toynton 80–90; V Brigg 90–95; V Blockley w Aston Magna and Bourton on the Hill *Glouc* 95–01; Local Min Officer 95–01; V Heath and Reach *St Alb* 01–05; TV Billington, Egginton, Hockliffe etc 06; RD Dunstable 02–04; rtd 06; PtO *Cant* from 06. *46 Cavendish Road, Herne Bay CT6 5BB* T: (01227) 360717 M: 07703-174761 E: revd.geoffn@gmail.com

NEALE, Hannah. b 40. SEITE. **d** 99 **p** 00. NSM Mitcham St Mark *S'wark* 99–00; NSM Merton St Jo 00–09; NSM Merton Priory 09; PtO from 09. *55 Boyd Road, London SW19 2DF* T: (020) 8648 5405

NEALE, Canon James Edward McKenzie (Eddie). b 38. Selw Coll Cam BA 61 Nottm Trent Univ Hon DLitt 00 Nottm Univ Hon DD 03. Clifton Th Coll 61. **d** 63 **p** 64. C Everton St Ambrose w St Tim *Liv* 63–72; Relig Adv BBC Radio Merseyside 72–76; V Bestwood St Matt *S'well* 76–86; Dioc Urban Officer 86–91; V Nottingham St Mary and St Cath 91–03; Hon Can *S'well* Minster 91–03; rtd 03; PtO *S'well* from 03. *Church Cottage, Church Lane, Maplebeck, Nottingham NG22 0BS* T: (01636) 636559

NEALE, Mrs Jan Celia. b 42. EMMTC 92. **d** 92 **p** 94. C Gt and Lt Coates w Bradley *Linc* 92–96; TV 96–01; TV Chambersbury *St Alb* 01–07; rtd 07; PtO *St Alb* 08–19. *1 Dickens Close, St Albans AL3 5PP* T: (01727) 853936

✠**NEALE, The Rt Revd John Robert Geoffrey.** b 26. AKC 54 St Boniface Warminster 54. **d** 55 **p** 56 **c** 74. C St Helier *S'wark* 55–58; Chapl Ardingly Coll 58–62; Recruitment Sec CACTM 63–66; ACCM 66–68; R Hascombe *Guildf* 68–74; Can Missr and Dir Post-Ord Tr 68–74; Hon Can Guildf Cathl 68–74; Adn Wilts *Sarum* 74–80; Area Bp Ramsbury 74–81 and 81–88; Can and Preb Sarum Cathl 74–88; Sec Partnership for World Miss 89–91; Hon Asst Bp Lon and S'wark 89–91; rtd 91; Hon Asst Bp B & W 91–08; Bris 92–15; Glouc from 94. *Shockerwick House, Lower Shockerwick, Bath BA1 7LL* T: (01225) 743636 ext 1417

NEALE, Paul Edward. b 46. Portsm Coll of Tech BSc 68. **d** 07 **p** 08. OLM Cromer *Nor* 07–16; rtd 16; PtO *Nor* from 16. *30 Fulcher Avenue, Cromer NR27 9SG* T: (01263) 513563 E: paulneale127@btinternet.com

NEALE, Mrs Sandra Anne. b 50. Yorks Min Course 12. **d** 13 **p** 14. NSM Lt Horton *Bradf* 13–14; *Leeds* 14–17; NSM Queensbury from 17. *4 Foxcroft Close, Queensbury, Bradford BD13 2DG* T: (01274) 816168 M: 07729-338618 E: sandineale@hotmail.co.uk

NEALE-STEVENS, Mrs Harriet Anna. b 82. R Holloway Coll Lon BMus 03 Goldsmiths' Coll Lon MA 04 Cam Univ BTh 17. Westcott Ho Cam 15. **d** 17 **p** 18. C Henfield w Shermanbury and Woodmancote *Chich* from 17. *41 Furners Mead, Henfield BN5 9JA* M: 07816-970605

NEARY (*née* TAYLOR), Mrs Joanna Beatrice. b 74. Warwick Univ BA 96 Homerton Coll Cam PGCE 97. St Jo Coll Nottm 04. **d** 06 **p** 07. C Northolt St Jos *Lon* 06–09; NSM Charminster and Stinsford *Sarum* 10–12; TV Beaminster Area from 12. *The Vicarage, Orchard Mead, Broadwindsor, Beaminster DT8 3RA* T: (01308) 867816 M: 07939-062409 E: revneary@gmail.com

NEAUM, Canon Andrew David Irwin. b 45. Lon Univ BA 67 PGCE 68. St Paul's Coll Grahamstown 72. **d** 74 **p** 75. C Salisbury Rhodesia 74–77; R Gatooma Zimbabwe 77–82; V St Helena 82–85; Adn 84–85; R Skipton Australia 85–89; R Ararat 89–95; Can Ballarat 93–95; R Wodonga 95–03; R Shepparton 03–13; Can Wangaratta 02–13; Hon C Boldre w S Baddesley *Win* 13–19. *Address temp unknown* E: andrew.neaum@gmail.com

NEAUM, David Andrew. b 79. Trin Coll Melbourne BA 01 SS Coll Cam BA 06 Em Coll Cam MPhil 08 PhD 16. Westcott Ho Cam 04 Yale Div Sch 06. **d** 07 **p** 08. NSM Cambridge St Mary Less *Ely* 07–08; C Marnhull *Sarum* 08–11; C Ox

St Mary V w St Cross and St Pet 11–13; Asst Chapl Keble Coll Ox 11–12; Chapl and Fell St Cath Coll Cam 13–19; Dean 16–19; PtO *Guildf* from 19. *The Rectory, Coxcombe Lane, Chiddingfold, Godalming GU8 4QA* M: 07411-675157 E: david.neaum@gmail.com

NEAVE, Garry Reginald. b 51. Leic Univ BA 72 MA 73 PGCE 74 MCMI. S'wark Ord Course. **d** 82 **p** 83. NSM Harlow St Mary Magd *Chelmsf* 82–87 and from 92; NSM St Mary-at-Latton 87–92; Chapl and Asst Prin Harlow Tertiary Coll 84–99; Dir Student Services and Admin W Herts Coll 99–04; Educn Dir Girls' Day Sch Trust 04–10; Nat FE 16-19 Adv Abps' Coun from 11. *35 Perry Spring, Harlow CM17 9DQ* T: (01279) 411775 E: garry.neave@churchofengland.org

NEED, Canon Philip Alan. b 54. AKC 75. Chich Th Coll 76. **d** 77 **p** 78. C Clapham Ch Ch and St Jo *S'wark* 77–79; C Luton All SS w St Pet *St Alb* 80–83; V Harlow St Mary Magd *Chelmsf* 83–89; P-in-c Chaddesden St Phil *Derby* 89–91; Bp's Dom Chapl *Chelmsf* 91–96; R Bocking St Mary 96–13; Dean Bocking 96–13; RD Braintree 00–06 and 09–13; Dioc Dir of Ords from 13; Hon Can Chelmsf Cathl from 07. *25 The Lintons, Sandon, Chelmsford CM2 7UA* T: (01245) 472212 or 294421 E: ddo@chelmsford.anglican.org

NEED, Stephen William. b 57. K Coll Lon BD 79 MTh 83 PhD 93 AKC 79 FRSA 95. **d** 08 **p** 08. Dean St Geo Coll Jerusalem 05–11; C St Geo Cathl 08–11; P-in-c Stock Harvard *Chelmsf* from 11; P-in-c W Hanningfield from 11. *The Rectory, 61 High Street, Stock, Ingatestone CM4 9BN* T: (01277) 840442

NEEDHAM, Mrs Marian Ruth. b 52. Birm Univ BMus 74 City Univ MA 96. NOC 06. **d** 08 **p** 09. NSM Ches H Trin 08–12; NSM Dodleston 12–15; NSM Chase Ox 15–17; rtd 18; PtO Ox from 18. *September House, 58B Mill Street, Kidlington OX5 2EF* M: 07804-032938 E: marianrnmailbox-rev@yahoo.co.uk

NEEDHAM, Peter Douglas. b 56. Chich Th Coll 86. **d** 88 **p** 88. SSF 76–00; C S Moor *Dur* 88–90; Chapl RN 91–93; LtO *Newc* 91–96; LtO *Lon* 97–99; C Ealing Ch the Sav 99–02; P-in-c Grimethorpe *Wakef* 02–05; V Grimethorpe w Brierley 05–12; Chapl Barnsley Hosp NHS Foundn Trust 12–19; V Athersley and Carlton *Leeds* from 19. *The Vicarage, 27 Laithes Lane, Barnsley S71 3AF* T: (01226) 245361 E: needham278@aol.com

NEEDLE, Paul Robert. b 45. Oak Hill Th Coll 67. **d** 70 **p** 71. C Gt Horton *Bradf* 70–74; C Pudsey St Lawr 74–77; Hon C Horton and Chapl St Luke's Hosp Bradf 78–80; NSM Irthlingborough *Pet* 87–90; NSM Gt w Lt Addington 90–94; NSM Gt w Lt Addington and Woodford 94–98; Bp's Media Adv 94–02; NSM Higham Ferrers w Chelveston 02–06; Bp's Communications Officer *Eur* 05–17; P-in-c Costa Azahar 07–12; PtO 05–07 and from 12; *Pet* 07–13 and from 15; Hon C Higham Ferrers w Chelveston 13–15. *2 Swallow Drive, Rushden NN10 6EG* M: 07712-463806 E: paulneedle@aol.com

NEEDS, Michael John. b 42. Open Univ BA 82 Univ of Wales (Swansea) MSc 84 PhD 87. Wycliffe Hall Ox 91. **d** 93 **p** 94. C Aberystwyth *St D* 93–96; R Llanllwchaearn and Llanina 96–06; rtd 06; P-in-c Martletwy w Lawrenny and Minwear etc *St D* 07–09. *Flat 10, Chartley, 22 The Avenue, Sneyd Park, Bristol BS9 1PE* E: mneeds@talktalk.net

NEIL, Prof Peter Sydney. b 62. Edin Univ MA 83 MEd 86 QUB PhD 95 MDiv 03 Cardiff Univ MPhil 10 Univ of Wales DMin 13 FHEA FRSA. **d** 08 **p** 09. NSM Elerch w Penrhyncoch w Capel Bangor and Goginan *St D* 08–09; NSM Ayr *Glas* 09–13; Vice Chan Bp Grosseteste Univ from 13; Gen Preacher *Linc* from 13; Can and Preb Linc Cathl from 13. *Vice Chancellor's House, Bishop Grosseteste University, Longdales Road, Lincoln LN1 3DY* T: (01522) 523166 M: 07816-953859 E: vicechancellor@bishopg.ac.uk

NEILL, Barbara June. b 39. St Jo Coll Nottm. **d** 00 **p** 01. NSM Bestwood Park w Rise Park *S'well* 00–09; rtd 09; PtO *S'well* from 10. *17 Harvest Close, Nottingham NG5 9BW* T: 0115-975 3378 E: barbjn@live.co.uk

✠**NEILL, The Rt Revd John Robert Winder.** b 45. TCD BA 66 MA 69 Jes Coll Cam BA 68 MA 72 NUI Hon LLD 03. Ridley Hall Cam 67. **d** 69 **p** 70 **c** 86. C Glenageary *D & G* 69–71; Lect CITC 70–71 and 82–84; Dioc Registrar (Ossory, Ferns and Leighlin) *C & O* 71–74; Bp's V, Lib and Registrar Kilkenny Cathl 71–74; I Abbeystrewry *C, C & R* 74–78; I Dublin St Bart w Leeson Park *D & G* 78–84; Chapl Community of St Jo the Ev 78–84; Dean Waterford *C & O* 84–86; Prec Lismore Cathl 84–86; Adn Waterford 84–86; I Waterford w Killea, Drumcannon and Dunhill 84–86; Bp T, K & A 86–97; Bp C & O 97–02; Abp Dublin *D & G* 02–11; Preb Cualaun St Patr Cathl Dublin 02–11; rtd 11. *3 Whitegate Lawn, Freshford Road, Kilkenny, Co Kilkenny, R95 P92N, Republic of Ireland* T: (00353) (56) 771 5449 E: jrwneill@eircom.net

NEILL, Richard Walter. b 67. Wadh Coll Ox BA 89 Em Coll Cam BA 92. Westcott Ho Cam 90. **d** 93 **p** 94. C Abbots Langley *St Alb* 93–97; C Wisley w Pyrford *Guildf* 97–00; V Winkfield and Cranbourne *Ox* 00–08; V Isle of Wedmore *B & W* from 08; P-in-c Chapel Allerton from 14. *The Vicarage, Manor Lane, Wedmore BS28 4EL* T: (01934) 713566 E: richardneill1967@sky.com

NEILL, Canon Robert Chapman. b 51. Lon Univ BD 82. CITC 77. **d** 77 **p** 78. C Lurgan Ch the Redeemer *D & D* 77–82; I Tullylish 82–88; I Mt Merrion 88–98; I Drumbo 98–16; Can Down Cathl 07–16; rtd 16. *149 Coopers Mill Avenue, Dundonald, Belfast BT16 1WR* T: (028) 9041 0832 E: r4cneill@btinternet.com

NEILL, William Barnett. b 30. TCD BA 61. **d** 63 **p** 64. C Belfast St Clem *D & D* 63–66; C Dundonald 66–72; I Drumgath 72–80; I Drumgooland 76–80; I Mt Merrion 80–83; I Dromore Cathl 83–97; adn Dromore 85–97; rtd 97. *10 Cairnshill Court, Saintfield Road, Belfast BT8 4TX* T: (028) 9079 2969

NEILL, William Benjamin Alan. b 46. Open Univ BA 76. CITC 68. **d** 71 **p** 72. C Dunmurry *Conn* 71–74; C Coleraine 75–77; C Dublin St Ann w St Steph *D & G* 77–78; I Convoy w Monellan and Donaghmore *D & R* 78–81; I Faughanvale 81–86; I Waterford w Killea, Drumcannon and Dunhill *C & O* 86–97; Dean Waterford 86–97; Prec Lismore Cathl 86–97; Prec Cashel Cathl 87–97; Can Ossory and Leighlin Cathls 96–97; I Dalkey St Patr *D & G* 97–12; Can Ch Ch Cathl Dublin 04–12; rtd 12. *Cleevaun, 77 Ballinclea Heights, Killiney, Co Dublin, Republic of Ireland* T: (00353) (1) 202 4849 E: neillben77@gmail.com

NEILL, William George. b 45. Edin Univ MA 67 BD 70 Open Univ BA 97 Jordanhill Coll Glas PGCE 00. **d** 15 **p** 16. C Broughty Ferry *Bre* 15–19; PtO from 19. *Roseheath Cottage, 2 Malt Row, Pitlessie, Cupar KY15 7SY* T: (01337) 830910 M: 07732-367252 E: neill.pitlessie@btinternet.com

NELLIST, Canon Valerie Ann. b 48. SRN 69 SCM 71. St And Dioc Tr Course 87. **d** 90 **p** 94. NSM All Souls Fife *St And* 90–99; R Aberdour 99–13; R Burntisland 99–13; R Inverkeithing 99–13; Hon Can St Ninian's Cathl Perth 97–13; rtd 13; PtO *St And* from 13. *28 Glamis Gardens, Dalgety Bay, Dunfermline KY11 9TD* T: (01383) 824066 E: valnellist@btinternet.com

NELMES, Mrs Christine. b 41. St Mary's Coll Chelt Dip Teaching 63 UWE BA 97. S Dios Minl Tr Scheme 92. **d** 95 **p** 96. NSM Winscombe *B & W* 95–99; PtO 00–03; P-in-c Mark w Allerton 03–08; rtd 08; PtO *B & W* from 09. *Yarrow Farm, Yarrow Road, Mark, Highbridge TA9 4LW* T: (01278) 641650 E: revcnelmes@googlemail.com

NELSON, Hugh Edmund. b 72. Worc Coll Ox BA 94. Ripon Coll Cuddesdon 07. **d** 09 **p** 10. C Newington w Hartlip and Stockbury *Cant* 09–12; C Iwade 09–12; C Upchurch w Lower Halstow 09–12; V Goudhurst w Kilndown from 12. *The Vicarage, Back Lane, Goudhurst, Cranbrook TN17 1AN* T: (01580) 211739 E: hugh.nelson@ymail.com

NELSON, Jane. b 42. **d** 94 **p** 99. Par Dn Muchalls *Bre* 94–99; C 99–04; Asst Chapl Grampian Healthcare NHS Trust 93–97; NSM Brechin *Bre* 04–14; NSM Tarfside from 05; P-in-c from 15. *4 St Michael's Road, Newtonhill, Stonehaven AB39 3RW* T: (01569) 730967 E: nelson.jane1@btinternet.com

NELSON, Mrs Julie. b 52. St Aid Coll Dur BA 73 Ex Univ MA 95. SWMTC 92. **d** 95 **p** 96. NSM Tavistock and Gulworthy *Ex* 95–01; Germany 01–04; P-in-c Kirklington w Burneston and Wath and Pickhill *Ripon* 04–10; AD Wensley 08–10; Dioc Adv on Women's Min 08–10; R Panfield and Rayne *Chelmsf* 10–15; Dioc Rural Officer 10–15; rtd 15; PtO *Carl* from 16. *41 Blencathra Street, Keswick CA12 4HX* E: rev.julienelson@googlemail.com

NELSON, Marcus John Reginald. b 81. QUB LLB 03. Wycliffe Hall Ox BA 11. **d** 11 **p** 12. C Plymouth St Andr and Stonehouse *Ex* 11–15; V Bris St Matt and St Nath 15–18; V Gabalfa *Llan* from 18; P-in-c Tremorfa St Phil CD from 18. *St Mark's Vicarage, North Road, Cardiff CF14 3BL* M: 07731-424874 E: marcusjrnelson@gmail.com

NELSON, Mark. b 72. Ripon Coll Cuddesdon 16. **d** 19. C Winslow w Gt Horwood and Addington *Ox* from 19. *16 Station Road, Winslow, Buckingham MK18 3ES* T: (01296) 291493 M: 07414-633450 E: revmarknelson@outlook.com

NELSON, Michael Andrew Kahrs. b 82. Univ of Wales (Ban) BSc 06. Ripon Coll Cuddesdon BA 16. **d** 16 **p** 17. C Horsham *Chich* 16; C Holbrook 16–19; C Gravesend St Geo *Roch* from 19. *28 The Sandpipers, Gravesend DA12 5QB* M: 07590-260570 E: mike.n82@gmail.com

NELSON, Sister Norma Margaret. b 34. Liv Univ DASS 77 CQSW 82. CA Tr Coll IDC 60. **d** 93 **p** 94. Team Dn Kirkby *Liv* 93–94; TV 94–95; rtd 95; PtO *Liv* from 95. *15 Pateley Close, Kirkby, Liverpool L32 4UT* T: 0151-292 0255

NELSON, Canon Paul John. b 52. Nottm Univ BCombStuds 84. Linc Th Coll 81. **d** 84 **p** 85. C Waltham Cross *St Alb* 84–87; C Sandridge 87–90; V 90–98; R Hundred River *St E* 98–13; C Wainford 06–13; R Hundred River and Wainford 13–15; RD Beccles and S Elmham 03–11; Hon Can St E Cathl 08–15; rtd 15; PtO *St E* from 16. *7 Queens Road, Beccles NR34 9DU* T: (01502) 713392 E: hedgeparson@btinternet.com

NELSON, Peter Joseph. b 46. Nottm Poly BSc 73. N Bapt Coll 82 NEOC 99. **d** 99 **p** 99. In Bapt Min 85–99; Chapl R Hull Hosps NHS Trust 94–99; Chapl Hull and E Yorks Hosps NHS Trust 99–02; Sen Chapl 02–11; NSM Sutton St Mich *York* 99–06; rtd 11; PtO *York* from 11. *Cobblestones, 1 Low Street, Sancton, York YO43 4QZ* T: (01430) 828779 E: peternelson46@live.co.uk

NELSON, Ralph Archbold. b 27. St Cuth Soc Dur BA 50. Bps' Coll Cheshunt 50. **d** 52 **p** 53. C Penwortham St Mary *Blackb* 52–57; C Eglingham *Newc* 57–58; V Featherstone *Wakef* 58–80; V Kirkham *Blackb* 80–92; RD 88–91; rtd 92; PtO *Blackb* 92–11. *6 Blundell Lane, Penwortham, Preston PR1 0EA* T: (01772) 742573

NELSON, Robert Towers. b 43. Liv Coll of Tech BSc 65 MSOSc. NW Ord Course 76. **d** 79 **p** 80. NSM Liv Our Lady and St Nic w St Anne 79–83; NSM Liscard St Thos *Ches* 83–87; P-in-c 87–12; V from 12; Ind Missr from 87; Asst Sec SOSc from 89; PtO *Liv* 89–98; Chapl Wirral and W Cheshire Community NHS Trust 98–03. *5 Sedbergh Road, Wallasey CH44 2BR* T: 0151-630 2830 E: rtnelson43@googlemail.com

NELSON, Warren David. b 38. TCD BA 67. **d** 68 **p** 69. C Belfast St Mich *Conn* 68–70; I Kilcooley w Littleton, Crohane, Killenaule etc *C & O* 70–76; Chapl Coalbrook Fellowship Hosp Ho Thurles 76–94; PtO (Cashel, Waterford and Lismore) *C & O* 93–94; I Lurgan w Billis, Killinkere and Munterconnaught *K, E & A* 94–98; rtd 98. *6 Mucklagh, Tullamore, Co Offaly, Republic of Ireland* T: (00353) (57) 932 4218 E: wnelson@eircom.net

NELSON, William. b 38. Oak Hill Th Coll 74. **d** 76 **p** 77. C Hensingham *Carl* 76–81; V Widnes St Paul *Liv* 81–89; R Higher Openshaw *Man* 89–03; AD Ardwick 96–00; rtd 03; PtO *S'well* from 03. *215 Stapleford Road, Trowell, Nottingham NG9 3QE* T: 0115-932 2910 E: revwilliamnelson@gmail.com

NENER, Canon Thomas Paul Edgar. b 42. Liv Univ MB, ChB FRCSEd 71 FRCS 71. Coll of Resurr Mirfield 78. **d** 80 **p** 81. C Warrington St Elphin *Liv* 80–83; V Haydock St Jas 83–95; V W Derby St Jo 95–10; Hon Can Liv Cathl 95–10; rtd 10; PtO *Lich* 16–17; *Liv* from 16. *16 Princes Park Mansions, Croxteth Road, Liverpool L8 3SA* T: 0151-726 7003

NENO, David Edward. b 62. SS Mark & Jo Univ Coll Plymouth BA 85. Ripon Coll Cuddesdon 85. **d** 88 **p** 89. C Chapel Allerton *Ripon* 88–91; C Acton St Mary *Lon* 91–94; V Kingsbury H Innocents 94–02; R Brondesbury Ch Ch and St Laur 02–12; V Ealing St Pet Mt Park from 12. *St Peter's Vicarage, 56 Mount Park Road, London W5 2RU* T: (020) 8997 1620 M: 07976-905294 E: david.neno@virginmedia.com

NESBITT, Heather Hastings. b 48. S'wark Ord Course 88. **d** 90 **p** 94. Par Dn Camberwell St Luke *S'wark* 90–94; C Addiscombe St Mary Magd w St Martin 94–01; TV Sutton St Jas and Wawne *York* 01–10; rtd 10; PtO *Linc* from 17. *21 Glengarry Way, Greylees, Sleaford NG34 8XU* T: (01529) 419298 E: h.nesbitt@yahoo.co.uk

NESBITT, Patrick Joseph. b 72. St Martin's Coll Lanc BA 96. St Jo Coll Nottm 00. **d** 03 **p** 04. C Blackpool St Thos *Blackb* 03–07; TV Kinson and W Howe *Sarum* 07–13; C Canford Magna from 16. *16 Croft Road, Ringwood BH24 1TA* M: 07879-660100 E: patricknesbitt72@hotmail.com

NESBITT, Canon Ronald. b 58. Sheff Univ LLB. CITC 82. **d** 85 **p** 86. C Ballymena w Ballyclug *Conn* 85–88; C Holywood *D & D* 88–90; I Helen's Bay 90–96; I Bangor Abbey from 96; Can Belf Cathl from 04. *The Abbey Rectory, 5 Downshire Road, Bangor BT20 3TW* T: (028) 9146 0173 *or* 9145 1087 E: ronnienesbitt@aol.com *or* bangorabbeyparish@gmail.com

NESBITT, Mrs Sarah Joy. b 62. Bath Univ BSc 84. Ox Min Course 15. **d** 18 **p** 19. C Shiplake w Dunsden and Harpsden *Ox* from 18. *The Ashes, 112 The Street, Crowmarsh Gifford, Wallingford OX10 8EJ* M: 07770-930756 E: revsarahjoy@icloud.com

NESBITT, Miss Wilhelmina. b 65. Qu Coll Birm 98. **d** 00 **p** 01. C Bridgnorth, Tasley, Astley Abbotts, etc *Heref* 00–04; TV Saddleworth *Man* 04–08; I Fanlobbus Union *C, C & R* 08–13; R Greenock *Glas* from 17. *St John's Rectory, 96 Finnart Street, Greenock PA16 8HL* T: (01475) 732441

NETHERWAY, Diana Margaret. b 47. Bp Otter Coll 94. **d** 96. NSM Northwood *Portsm* from 96; NSM Gurnard 96–14; Asst Chapl Isle of Wight NHS Trust from 09; NSM Gurnard w Cowes St Faith *Portsm* from 14. *138 Bellevue Road, Cowes PO31 7LD* T: (01983) 298505 E: dnetherway1@gmail.com

NETHERWOOD, Mrs Anne Christine. b 43. Liv Univ BArch 66 Lon Univ BD 92 ARIBA 68. St Deiniol's Hawarden 88. **d** 91 **p** 94. NSM Ellesmere and Welsh Frankton *Lich* 91–94; C Dudleston 94–97; C Criftins 94–97; C Criftins w Dudleston and Welsh Frankton 97; P-in-c 97–10; rtd 10; PtO *Lich* 10–12 and from 17; Hon C Pradoe 12–16. *11 Cottage Fields, St Martins, Oswestry SY11 3EJ* T: (01691) 778495 E: anne@annenetherwood.co.uk

NEVELL, Simeon Zvi Benjamin. b 84. York Univ BSc 06 Cant Ch Ch Univ PGCE 07. Cranmer Hall Dur 17. **d** 19. C The Six *Cant* from 19. *15 Oak Lane, Upchurch, Sittingbourne ME9 7AT* M: 07552-231908 E: simeonnevell@gmail.com

NEVILL, James Michael. b 50. Cranmer Hall Dur 84. **d** 86 **p** 87. C Sowerby Bridge w Norland *Wakef* 86–91; CF 91–94; TV Broadwater *Chich* 94–99; Chapl St Mich Hospice Hereford 99–05; Spiritual Care Co-ord St Cath Hospice Crawley 05–15; rtd 15; PtO *Chich* from 15. *Teviotdale, Ivy Close, Ashington, Pulborough RH20 3LW* E: mikenevill1509@sky.com

NEVILL, Mavis Hetty. b 45. Bradf Univ BEd 95. NOC 92. **d** 95 **p** 96. NSM Mount Pellon *Wakef* 95–99; P-in-c Mixenden 99–04; Hon C Harden and Wilsden *Bradf* 06–07; P-in-c Steeton 07–11; rtd 11; PtO *Bradf* 11–14; *Leeds* from 14. *1 Willow Bank Close, Allerton, Bradford BD15 7YL* T: (01274) 813584 E: mh.nevill@btinternet.com

NEVILLE, Michael Robert John. b 56. Hatf Coll Dur BA 80 Hughes Hall Cam PGCE 81. Wycliffe Hall Ox 82. **d** 85 **p** 86. C E Twickenham St Steph *Lon* 85–88; Asst Dir Proclamation Trust 88–93; R Fordham *Chelmsf* 93–11; P-in-c Upper Chelsea St Sav and St Simon *Lon* 11; V Upper Chelsea St Simon from 11; PtO *Eur* from 16. *St Simon Zelotes Vicarage, 34 Milner Street, London SW3 2QF* T: (020) 7589 8999 E: mike.neville@btinternet.com

NEW, David John. b 37. Lon Univ BScEng 58. Chich Th Coll 65. **d** 67 **p** 68. C Folkestone St Mary and St Eanswythe *Cant* 67–72; C Kings Heath *Birm* 72–74; V S Yardley St Mich 74–83; V Moseley St Agnes 83–00; rtd 00; PtO *Worc* from 00. *6 Falmouth, Worcester WR4 0TE* T: (01905) 458084 E: davidnew@talktalk.net

NEW, Canon Thomas Stephen. b 30. K Coll Cam BA 52 MA 56. Cuddesdon Coll 52. **d** 54 **p** 55. C Greenford H Cross *Lon* 54–55; C Old St Pancras w Bedford New Town St Matt 55–58; C Woodham *Guildf* 58–64; V Guildf All SS 64–72; V Banstead 72–93; RD Epsom 76–80; Hon Can Guildf Cathl 79–93; Sub-Chapl HM Pris Downview 88–93; rtd 93; PtO *Ex* from 94. *St Katharine's, North Street, Denbury, Newton Abbot TQ12 6DJ* T: (01803) 813775 E: tomrev@btinternet.com

NEWALL, Arthur William. b 24. Univ of Wales (Lamp) BA 49. Chich Th Coll 49. **d** 51 **p** 52. C Hulme St Phil *Man* 51–53; C Fallowfield 53–55; V Oldham St Barn 55–60; V Aspull *Liv* 60–68; R Foots Cray *Roch* 68–78; V Henlow *St Alb* 78–89; rtd 89; PtO *Liv* from 89. *38 Fairhaven Road, Southport PR9 9UH* T: (01704) 26045

NEWALL, Richard Lucas. b 43. K Coll Lon AKC 66. **d** 66 **p** 67. C Roby *Liv* 66–69; C Douglas St Geo and St Barn *S & M* 69–71; LtO *Man* 72–75; C Ban St Mary 75–77; R Newborough w Llangeinwen w Llangaffo etc 77–97; R Newborough w Llanidan and Llangeinwen etc 98–07; AD Tindaethwy and Menai 03–07; V Llanilar w Rhostie and Llangwyryfon etc *St D* 07–09; rtd 09; PtO *St D* from 09. *Himmelbjerg, 18 Maesydderwen, Cardigan SA43 1PE* T: (01239) 623816

NEWARK, Archdeacon of. See PICKEN, The Ven David Anthony

NEWBOLD, Mrs Caroline Sarah. b 62. K Alfred's Coll Win BA 83 Homerton Coll Cam PGCE 85. St Mellitus Coll BA 10. **d** 10 **p** 11. C Yiewsley *Lon* 10–13; Chapl Lady Margaret Sch from 13; Hon C Ealing St Steph Castle Hill *Lon* from 13. *St Stephen's Vicarage, Sherborne Gardens, London W13 8AQ* T: (020) 7736 7138 M: 07958-073583 E: chaplain@ladymargaret.lbhf.sch.uk

NEWBOLD, Stephen Mark. b 60. Trin Coll Bris 01. **d** 03 **p** 04. C Roxeth *Lon* 03–09; V Ealing St Steph Castle Hill from 09; AD Ealing from 15. *St Stephen's Vicarage, Sherborne Gardens, London W13 8AQ* T: (020) 8810 4929

NEWBON, Michael Charles. b 59. Oak Hill Th Coll 92. **d** 94 **p** 95. C Bedford St Jo and St Leon *St Alb* 94–99; V Luton St Fran 99–11; P-in-c Georgeham *Ex* 11–15; R from 15. *The Rectory, Newberry Road, Georgeham, Braunton EX33 1JS* T: (01271) 890616 E: mikenewbon@aol.com

NEWBORN, Carol Margaret. b 45. **d** 05 **p** 06. OLM Styvechale *Cov* 05–17; NSM Napton-on-the-Hill, Lower Shuckburgh etc from 17; NSM Priors Hardwick, Priors Marston and Wormleighton from 17. *76 The Park Paling, Coventry CV3 5LL* T: (024) 7650 3707 E: carol_newborn@hotmail.co.uk

NEWBY, Canon Ailsa Ballantyne. b 56. Collingwood Coll Dur BA 78 Heythrop Coll Lon MA 09. St Steph Ho Ox 98. **d** 98 **p** 99. C Streatham Ch Ch *S'wark* 98–01; V S Lambeth St Anne and All SS 01–10; Dir IME Kingston Area 04–10; TR Putney St Mary 10–17; Hon Can S'wark Cathl 15–17; Can Res Ripon Cathl *Leeds* from 17. *St Peter's House, Minster Close, Ripon HG4 1QP* T: (01765) 604108 E: canonailsa@riponcathedral.org.uk

NEWBY, Claire. See McILROY, Claire

NEWBY, Mrs Susan. b 48. Lady Spencer Chu Coll of Educn CertEd 70 BEd 71. **d** 04 **p** 05. OLM Adderbury w Milton *Ox* 04–10; NSM Banbury 10–16; rtd 16; PtO *Arg* from 18. *Tigh na Baigh, Bayhead, Isle of North Uist HS6 5DS* M: 07824-470877 E: revnewby@hotmail.co.uk

NEWCASTLE, Bishop of. See HARDMAN, The Rt Revd Christine Elizabeth

NEWCASTLE, Dean of. See MILLER, The Very Revd Geoffrey Vincent

NEWCOMBE, Andrew Charles. b 70. Melbourne Univ BA 92 BMus 92 Ox Univ BTh 09 Monash Univ Aus DipEd 96 LTCL 93. St Steph Ho Ox 03. **d** 05 **p** 06. C Tottenham St Mary *Lon* 05–08; C Edmonton St Alphege and Ponders End St Matt 08–11; V Hoxton H Trin w St Mary from 11. *Holy Trinity Vicarage, 3 Bletchley Street, London N1 7QG* T: (020) 7253 4796 M: 07931-700675 E: andrewnewcombe@yahoo.co.uk

NEWCOMBE, John Adrian. b 61. Univ of Wales (Lamp) BA 83 SS Paul & Mary Coll Cheltenham PGCE 85. Ripon Coll Cuddesdon 90. **d** 92 **p** 93. C Stroud and Uplands w Slad *Glouc* 92–96; C Nailsworth 96–01; P-in-c Childswyckham w Aston Somerville, Buckland etc 01–05; TV Winchcombe from 05. *New Vicarage, Buckland Road, Childswickham, Broadway WR12 7HH* T: (01386) 853824

NEWCOMBE, Jonathan Charles Dymoke. b 75. St Anne's Coll Ox BA 97 MA 09 Fitzw Coll Cam BA 04 MA 09. Ridley Hall Cam 02. **d** 07 **p** 08. NSM Wimbledon Em Ridgway Prop Chpl *S'wark* 07–10; Asst Chapl Tervuren *Eur* 10–14; C Cambridge H Sepulchre *Ely* 14–18; C Huntingdon All SS w St Jo St Mary etc from 18. *36 Claytons Way, Huntingdon PE29 1UT* M: 07535-501110 E: revcharlienewc@gmail.com

NEWCOMBE, Canon Timothy James Grahame. b 47. AKC 75. St Aug Coll Cant 75. **d** 76 **p** 77. C Heref St Martin 76–79; C Hitchin *St Alb* 79–85; R Croft and Stoney Stanton *Leic* 85–91; P-in-c Launceston *Truro* 91–92; V 92–97; TR 97–03; Hon Can Truro Cathl 01–03; Chapl Cornwall Healthcare NHS Trust 96–03; V Wotton St Mary *Glouc* 03–12; rtd 12. *18 Kempley Road, Okehampton EX20 1DS* T: (01837) 52901 E: tnewco@btinternet.com

✠**NEWCOME, The Rt Revd James William Scobie.** b 53. Trin Coll Ox BA 74 MA 78 Selw Coll Cam BA 77 MA 81. Ridley Hall Cam 75. **d** 78 **p** 79 **c** 02. C Leavesden *St Alb* 78–82; P-in-c Bar Hill LEP *Ely* 82–92; V Bar Hill 92–94; Tutor Ridley Hall Cam 83–88; P-in-c Dry Drayton *Ely* 89–94; RD N Stowe 93–94; Can Res Ches Cathl and Dioc Dir of Ords 94–02; Dir of Educn and Tr 96–02; Suff Bp Penrith *Carl* 02–09; Bp Carl from 09; Clerk of the Closet from 15. *Bishop's House, Ambleside Road, Keswick CA12 4DD* T: (01768) 773430 E: bishop.carlisle@carlislediocese.org.uk

NEWELL, Christopher David. b 53. Ex Univ MA 03 Win Univ PhD 15. S'wark Ord Course 84. **d** 87 **p** 88. C Stockwell St Mich *S'wark* 87–90; Asst Chapl R Lon Hosp (Whitechapel) 90–92; Asst Chapl R Lon Hosp (Mile End) 90–92; R Birch St Agnes *Man* 92–96; P-in-c Longsight St Jo w St Cypr 94–96; R Birch St Agnes w Longsight St Jo w St Cypr 97; R Lansallos and T Talland *Truro* 97–98; Asst P Liskeard and St Keyne 00–02; C Duloe, Herodsfoot, Morval and St Pinnock 02–03; P-in-c 03–05; C Lansallos and Talland 02–03; Chapl Cornwall Partnership NHS Foundn Trust 02–16; P-in-c St Goran w Caerhays *Truro* 14–17; rtd 17. *5 The Old School Mews, Bices Court, Kenwyn Street, Truro TR1 3DU* T: (01872) 496086 E: christophernewell@talk21.com

NEWELL, David Walter. b 37. Nottm Univ BSc 57. WEMTC 01. **d** 03 **p** 04. OLM Painswick, Sheepscombe, Cranham, The Edge etc *Glouc* from 03. *Firle Cottage, Blakewell Mead, Painswick GL6 6UR* T: (01452) 812083 E: d.newell083@btinternet.com

NEWELL, Canon Edmund John. b 61. Univ Coll Lon BSc 83 Nuff Coll Ox DPhil 88 MA 89 FRHistS 98 FRSA 08. Ox Min Course 89 Ripon Coll Cuddesdon 92. **d** 94 **p** 95. C Deddington w Barford, Clifton and Hempton *Ox* 94–98; Bp's Dom Chapl 98–01; Chapl Headington Sch 98–01; Can Res St Paul's Cathl *Lon* 01–08; Chan St Paul's Cathl 03–08; Can Res and Sub-Dean Ch Ch Ox 08–13; Prin Cumberland Lodge Windsor from 13; PtO *Ox* from 13; Hon Can Ch Ch from 14. *Cumberland Lodge, The Great Park, Windsor SL4 2HP* T: (01784) 497786 F: 497799 E: enewell@cumberlandlodge.ac.uk

NEWELL, Samuel James. b 28. TCD BA 53 MA 63. TCD Div Sch Div Test 54. **d** 54 **p** 55. C Belfast St Mary *Conn* 54–57;

C Derriaghy 57–60; C Reading St Mary V *Ox* 60–63; V Chesham Ch Ch 63–74; P-in-c Wraysbury 74–78; TV Riverside 78–94; rtd 94; PtO *Ox* 97–10. *41 Redford Road, Windsor SL4 5ST* T: (01753) 862300

NEWEY, Canon Edmund James. b 71. Linc Coll Ox BA 95 MA 97 Em Coll Cam BA 99 Man Univ PhD 08. Westcott Ho Cam 97. **d** 00 **p** 01. C Birch w Fallowfield *Man* 00–03; R Newmarket St Mary w Exning St Agnes *St E* 03–07; V Handsworth St Andr *Birm* 07–13; AD Handsworth 11–13; Can Res and Sub-Dean Ch Ch *Ox* from 13. *Christ Church, St Aldates, Oxford OX1 1DP* T: (01865) 276278 M: 07986-530511 E: subdean@chch.ox.ac.uk *or* ejnewey@phonecoop.coop

NEWHAM, Simon Frank Eric. b 65. Sheff Univ BSc 87 MSc 89. Trin Coll Bris BA 00. **d** 00 **p** 01. C Horsham *Chich* 00–04; P-in-c Wisborough Green 04–09; V 09–10; RD Petworth 06–09; TR Ifield 10–17; R 17–19; V Brockenhurst *Win* from 19; V Boldre w S Baddesley from 19. *The Vicarage, Meerut Road, Brockenhurst SO42 7TD* T: (01590) 624163

NEWING, Peter. b 33. Birm Univ CertEd 55 Dur Univ BA 63 Bris Univ BEd 76 State Univ NY BSc 85 EdD 88 Worc Univ BA 12 FRSA 60 FSAScot 59 ACP 67 MCollP 86 FCollT 95 APhS 63 FVCM 01. Cranmer Hall Dur 63. **d** 65 **p** 66. C Blockley w Aston Magna *Glouc* 65–69; P-in-c Taynton 69–75; P-in-c Tibberton 69–75; R Brimpsfield w Elkstone and Syde 75–83; R Brimpsfield, Cranham, Elkstone and Syde 83–97; P-in-c Daglingworth w the Duntisbournes and Winstone 95–97; R Brimpsfield w Birdlip, Syde, Daglingworth etc 97–01; C Redmarley D'Abitot, Bromesberrow, Pauntley etc 01–02; NSM 02–10; rtd 02; PtO *Heref* 02–17; *Worc* from 04; *Glouc* from 10. T: (01453) 790766 E: profnewing@btinternet.com

NEWITT, Mark Julian. b 76. Bradf Univ BSc 97 St Jo Coll Dur BA 02. Cranmer Hall Dur 00. **d** 03 **p** 04. C Billing *Pet* 03–06; Asst Chapl Sheff Teaching Hosps NHS Foundn Trust from 06. *Chaplaincy Services, Royal Hallamshire Hospital, Glossop Road, Sheffield S10 2JF* T: 0114-271 1900 E: mark.newitt@sth.nhs.uk

NEWLAND, Mrs Patricia Frances. b 35. Edin Univ MA 56. EAMTC 96. **d** 97 **p** 98. NSM Duxford *Ely* 97–02; NSM Hinxton 97–02; NSM Ickleton 97–02; rtd 02; PtO *Ely* 02–07. *Ickelton Lodge, 14 Frogge Street, Ickleton, Saffron Walden CB10 1SH* T: (01799) 530268 F: 531146 E: patricia.newland@googlemail.com

NEWLANDS, Canon Christopher William. b 57. Bris Univ BA 79. Westcott Ho Cam 81. **d** 84 **p** 85. C Bishop's Waltham *Portsm* 84–87; Hon C Upham 85–87; Prec, Sacr and Min Can Dur Cathl 87–92; Chapl Bucharest w Sofia *Eur* 92–95; V Shrub End *Chelmsf* 96–04; Bp's Chapl 04–10; P-in-c Lancaster St Mary w St John and St Anne *Blackb* 10–11; V from 11; Hon Can Blackb Cathl from 18. *The Vicarage, Priory Close, Lancaster LA1 1YZ* T: (01524) 63200 E: cnewlands@gmail.com

NEWLANDS, Prof George McLeod. b 41. Edin Univ MA 63 DLitt 05 Heidelberg Univ BD 66 PhD 70 Ch Coll Cam MA 73 FRSE 08. **d** 82 **p** 82. Lect Cam Univ 73–86; Fell and Dean Trin Hall Cam 82–86; Prof Div Glas Univ 86–08; PtO *Glas* from 86; Hon Fell New Coll Edin Univ from 10. *12 Jamaica Street Lane, Edinburgh EH3 6HQ, or 49 Highsett, Cambridge CB2 1NZ* T: 0131-225 2545 *or* (01223) 569984 M: 07979-691966 E: newlands71@hotmail.com

NEWLYN, Canon Edwin. b 39. AKC 64. **d** 65 **p** 66. C Belgrave St Mich *Leic* 65–68; Miss to Seamen 68–81; Chapl Santos Brazil 68–69; Asst Chapl Glas and C Glas St Gabr 69–73; Chapl E Lon S Africa 73–76; R W Bank St Pet 75–76; V Fylingdales *York* 81; P-in-c Fylingdales and Hawsker cum Stainsacre 81; V 81–88; RD Whitby 85–92; Sec Dioc Adv Cttee for Care of Chs 87–01; P-in-c Goathland 88–99; Can and Preb York Minster 90–08; rtd 01; PtO *York* from 01. *The Garden Flat, 12 Royal Crescent, Whitby YO21 3EJ* T: (01947) 604533 *or* 606578 F: 602798 E: edwin.newlyn@talktalk.net

✠**NEWMAN, The Rt Revd Adrian.** b 58. Bris Univ BSc 80 MPhil 89. Trin Coll Bris 82. **d** 85 **p** 86 **c** 11. C Forest Gate St Mark *Chelmsf* 85–89; V Hillsborough and Wadsley Bridge *Sheff* 89–96; RD Hallam 94–96; R Birm St Martin w Bordesley St Andr 96–05; Hon Can Birm Cathl 01–05; Dean Roch 05–11; Area Bp Stepney *Lon* 11–18. *Priory Mews, The Street, Little Dunmow, Dunmow CM6 3HT* E: adriannewman145@gmail.com

NEWMAN, Mrs Alison Myra. b 55. K Coll Lon BD 77. SEITE 99. **d** 02 **p** 03. C Bromley SS Pet and Paul *Roch* 02–06; C Shortlands 06–08; C Farnborough 08–15; V Biggin Hill from 15. *Church House, 10 Church Road, Biggin Hill, Westerham TN16 3LB* T: (01959) 540482 E: vicar@movingchurch.org

NEWMAN, Christopher David. *See* NEWMAN-DAY, Christopher David

NEWMAN, David. *See* NEWMAN, Richard David

NEWMAN, The Ven David Maurice Frederick. b 54. Hertf Coll Ox BA 75 MA 79. St Jo Coll Nottm. **d** 79 **p** 80. C Orpington Ch Ch *Roch* 79–83; C Bushbury *Lich* 83–86; V Ockbrook *Derby* 86–97; TR Loughborough Em and St Mary in Charnwood *Leic* 97–09; RD Akeley E 99–06; Hon Can Leic Cathl 06–09; Adn Loughborough 09–17; Warden Launde Abbey from 17; PtO *Pet* from 17. *The Warden's House, Launde Road, Launde, Leicester LE7 9XB* T: (01572) 717254 M: 07817-664189 E: warden@launde.org.uk

NEWMAN, Mrs Diana Joan. b 43. Sarum Th Coll 81. **dss** 84 **d** 87 **p** 94. Parkstone St Pet and St Osmund w Branksea *Sarum* 84–13; NSM 87–13; TV 96–02; PtO *Sarum* from 14. *62 Vale Road, Poole BH14 9AU* T/F: (01202) 745136 E: diana.n@sky.com

NEWMAN, Elizabeth Margot. b 50. Reading Univ BA 92. Ox Min Course 09. **d** 12 **p** 13. NSM Earley St Nic *Ox* from 12. *37 Sevenoaks Road, Earley, Reading RG6 7NT* T: 0118-926 5557 E: revlibby.newman@yahoo.co.uk

NEWMAN, Gillian Ann. b 60. St Mellitus Coll 15. **d** 17. NSM S Hackney St Jo w Ch Ch *Lon* from 17; Chapl Guy's and St Thos' NHS Foundn Trust from 18; Chapl Princess Alexandra Hosp NHS Trust from 18. *63 Coborn Road, London E3 2DB* T: (020) 8981 2323 E: gillie09ann@live.co.uk

NEWMAN, Canon Helen Margaret. b 58. York Univ BA 80 Nottm Univ MA 02. EMMTC 99. **d** 02 **p** 03. NSM Thorpe Acre w Dishley *Leic* 02–05; NSM Loughborough Em and St Mary in Charnwood 05–09; Chapl LOROS Hospice 09–17; Chapl Launde Abbey *Leic* from 17; PtO *Pet* from 17; Hon Can Leic Cathl from 16. *The Warden's House, Launde Road, Launde, Leicester LE7 9XB* T: (01572) 717254 M: 07814-444538 E: helen.newman@launde.org.uk

NEWMAN, James Edwin Michael. b 59. Nottm Univ BA 80 Ox Univ BA 90. Wycliffe Hall Ox 88. **d** 91 **p** 92. C Bidston *Ches* 91–95; C Cheadle from 95. *4 Cuthbert Road, Cheadle SK8 2DT* T: 0161-428 3983 E: mike@thenewmanfamily.org

NEWMAN, Ms Jennifer Margaret. b 73. K Alfred's Coll Win BEd 95. St Mellitus Coll 16. **d** 19. C Derby St Alkmund and St Werburgh from 19. *27 Wheeldon Avenue, Derby DE22 1HP* M: 07717-807237 E: jenny.newman@stwderby.org *or* jenmnewman73@hotmail.com

NEWMAN, Kevin Richard. b 74. Warwick Univ BSc 95 PGCE 96. Oak Hill Th Coll BA 06. **d** 06 **p** 07. C Crowborough *Chich* 06–10; C Bromley Ch Ch *Roch* 10–14. *Christ Church, 150 High Street, Banstead SM7 2NZ* M: 07920-843385 E: kev@kevandfran.co.uk

NEWMAN, Mrs Lynda Elizabeth. b 61. Univ of Wales (Swansea) DipEd 81 BEd 83 MEd 93. St Mich Coll Llan 07. **d** 10 **p** 11. NSM Neath *Llan* 10–13; TV 13–19; C Llansawel, Briton Ferry 16–19; TV Neath from 19; Asst Dioc Children's Officer from 12. *The Rectory, London Road, Neath SA11 1LE* T: (01639) 633354 E: lenewman@hotmail.co.uk

NEWMAN, Michael Alan. b 40. Chich Th Coll 67. **d** 70 **p** 71. C Kilburn St Aug *Lon* 70–73; C St Geo-in-the-East St Mary 75–78; rtd 78. *April Cottage, Georges Lane, Storrington, Pulborough RH20 3JH* T: (01903) 744354 E: tcepriest@tiscali.co.uk *or* michael.newman@talktalk.net

NEWMAN, Preb Michael John. b 50. Leic Univ BA 72 MA 75. Cuddesdon Coll 73. **d** 75 **p** 76. C Tettenhall Regis *Lich* 75–79; C Uttoxeter w Bramshall 79–82; R Norton Canes 82–89; TR Rugeley 89–06; TR Brereton and Rugeley 06–15; RD Rugeley 07–15; Preb Lich Cathl 02–15; rtd 15; PtO *Lich* from 16. *2 Firs Close, Weeping Cross, Stafford ST17 0DW* T: (01785) 660158 E: eileenandmichael@outlook.com

NEWMAN, Paul Anthony. b 48. Lon Univ BSc 70 Sarum Coll MA 18 Win Univ MA 18. Coll of Resurr Mirfield 73. **d** 76 **p** 77. C Catford St Laur *S'wark* 76–81; TV Grays All SS and Lt Thurrock St Mary *Chelmsf* 81–83; Youth Chapl W Ham Adnry 83–87; P-in-c Forest Gate All SS 83–89; V 89–91; Dep Chapl HM Pris Wormwood Scrubs 91–92; Chapl HM Pris Downview and Asst Chapl HM Pris High Down 92–02; Chapl HM Pris Win 02–07; Chapl HM Pris Kingston (Portsm) 07–13; rtd 13; PtO *Win* 07–13. *5 Cranworth House, Cranworth Road, Winchester SO22 6EJ* T: (01962) 863138 E: paulnewman603@yahoo.com

NEWMAN, Richard David. b 38. BNC Ox BA 60 MA 63. Lich Th Coll 60. **d** 62 **p** 63. C Grinstead St Swithun *Chich* 62–66; C Gt Grimsby St Jas *Linc* 66–69; C Gt Grimsby St Mary and St Jas 69–73; TV 73–74; V St Nicholas at Wade w Sarre *Cant* 74–75; P-in-c Chislet w Hoath 74–75; V St Nicholas at Wade w Sarre and Chislet w Hoath 75–81; V S Norwood H Innocents 81–84; *S'wark* 85–04; rtd 04; PtO *B & W* from 04. *10 Hardy Court, Lang Road, Crewkerne TA18 8JE* T: (01460) 271496 E: david.newman123@btinternet.com

NEWMAN-DAY, Christopher David. b 81. Bath Univ BSc 02 Anglia Ruskin Univ BA 10. Ridley Hall Cam 07. **d** 11 **p** 12.

C Canonbury St Steph *Lon* 11–14; V Bethnal Green St Jas Less from 14. *St James the Less Vicarage, St James's Avenue, London E2 9JD* T: (020) 8980 1612 M: 07921-505744 E: revnewmanday@gmail.com

NEWMARCH, Christine Anne. b 54. St Mellitus Coll 15. **d** 17 **p** 18. C Witham and Villages *Chelmsf* from 17. *Hobbits, 159 High Street, Kelvedon, Colchester CO5 9JA* T: (01376) 571623 E: christinenewmarch@hotmail.co.uk

NEWNES, Steven William. b 61. **d** 14 **p** 15. C Brockworth *Glouc* 14–18; NSM 18; Chapl HM Pris Long Lartin from 18; PtO *Glouc* from 18. *HM Prison, South Littleton, Evesham WR11 8TZ* T: (01386) 295100 E: bullincs17@sky.com

NEWNHAM, Carol Ann. St Mellitus Coll. **d** 15 **p** 16. OLM Becontree St Thos *Chelmsf* 15–18; NSM Theydon Par from 18. *Theydon Garnon Vicarage, Fiddlers Hamlet, Epping CM16 7PQ*

NEWNHAM, Eric Robert. b 43. FCA. Sarum & Wells Th Coll 70. **d** 75 **p** 76. C Blackheath Ascension *S'wark* 75–06; NSM Deptford St Jo w H Trin and Ascension 06–13; PtO 13–17. *27 Morden Hill, London SE13 7NN* T: (020) 8692 6507 *or* 8691 6559 E: e.n@btopenworld.com

NEWNHAM, Osmond James. b 31. Leeds Univ BA 55. Coll of Resurr Mirfield 55. **d** 57 **p** 58. C Salisbury St Mark *Sarum* 57–60; CF (R of O) 59–71; C Pewsey *Sarum* 60–62; R Chickerell w Fleet 62–94; CF (TA) 71–86; rtd 96. *32 Woodpecker Drive, Poole, Dorset BH17 7SY* T: (01202) 658386

NEWPORT, Prof Kenneth George Charles. b 57. Columbia Union Coll (USA) BA 83 Andrews Univ (USA) MA 84 Linacre Coll Ox MSt 85 St Hugh's Coll Ox DPhil 88. NOC 98. **d** 00 **p** 01. Reader Chr Thought Liv Hope 99–01; Prof Th and RS Liv Hope Univ from 01; Asst Vice Chan from 05; Hon Research Fell Man Univ from 98; NSM Bolton St Pet 00–11; NSM Bolton St Pet w St Phil from 11; PtO *Liv* from 00; Hon Can Man Cathl from 16. *Theology and Religious Studies, Liverpool Hope, Hope Park, Taggart Avenue, Liverpool L16 9JD* T: 0151-291 3510 F: 291 3772 E: knewport@hope.ac.uk

NEWPORT, Archdeacon of. *See* WILLIAMS, The Ven Jonathan Simon

NEWSOME, Preb David Ellis. b 55. St Jo Coll Dur BA 77. Westcott Ho Cam 80. **d** 82 **p** 83. C Finchley St Mary *Lon* 82–85; C Fulham All SS 85–87; Bp's Dom Chapl *Birm* 87–91; V Gravelly Hill 91–00; P-in-c Stockland Green 93–96; AD Aston 95–00; TR Tettenhall Regis *Lich* 00–08; Dioc Dir of Ords 08–15; Preb Lich Cathl 15; rtd 16; PtO *Lich* from 16; *Heref* from 16; *Birm* from 19. *36 Highbridge Road, Sutton Coldfield B73 5QB* T: 0121-354 9203 E: davidenewsome@gmail.com

NEWSOME, Monica Jane. b 55. WMMTC 96. **d** 99 **p** 00. NSM Kingshurst *Birm* 99–00; Asst Chapl HM YOI Stoke Heath 00–10; Chapl HM Pris Swinfen Hall 10–15; rtd 15; PtO *Heref* from 17; *Lich* from 17; *Birm* from 19. *36 Highbridge Road, Sutton Coldfield B73 5QB* T: 0121-354 9203 E: m.j.newsome2@gmail.com

NEWSON, Julie. b 60. Southn Univ BA 97. Bp Otter Coll 00. **d** 03. NSM Brighton St Pet w Chpl Royal *Chich* 03–09; NSM Brighton Chpl Royal 09–10; C Brighton St Luke Queen's Park from 10. *St Luke's Vicarage, Queen's Park Terrace, Brighton BN2 9YA* T: (01273) 570978 M: 07803-750147 E: julie.newson@btinternet.com

NEWSTEAD, Dominic Gerald Bruno. b 65. Wycliffe Hall Ox BTh 95. **d** 95 **p** 96. C Windlesham *Guildf* 95–00; Asst Chapl Fontainebleau *Eur* 00–05; V Southwater *Chich* 05–09; C Bebington *Ches* 09–16; V Lt Heath *St Alb* from 16. *The Vicarage, Thornton Road, Potters Bar EN6 1JJ* T: (01707) 643119 E: dominic@cclh.org.uk

NEWSUM, Alfred Turner Paul. b 28. Coll of Resurr Mirfield 52. **d** 53 **p** 54. C Roath St German *Llan* 53–59; C Westmr St Matt *Lon* 59–60; C Washwood Heath *Birm* 60–68; P-in-c Small Heath St Greg 68–78; V Birm St Aid Small Heath 72–80; V Stockland Green 80–93; rtd 93; PtO *Llan* 93–16; *Mon* 93–16. *Nazareth House, Colum Road, Cardiff CF10 3UN*

NEWTON, Angela Margaret. b 48. RGN 70. Ripon Coll Cuddesdon 06. **d** 07 **p** 08. NSM Luton St Aug Limbury *St Alb* 07–12; PtO from 12; NSM Christchurch *Win* from 12; Chapl R Bournemouth and Christchurch Hosps NHS Foundn Trust from 14. *23 Regency Crescent, Christchurch BH23 2UF* T: (01202) 950010 M: 07940-824206 E: angelanewton48@gmail.com

NEWTON, Barrie Arthur. b 38. Dur Univ BA 61. Wells Th Coll 61. **d** 63 **p** 64. C Walton St Mary *Liv* 63–67; C N Lynn w St Marg and St Nic *Nor* 67–69; Chapl Asst The Lon Hosp (Whitechapel) 69–71; Chapl K Coll Hosp Lon 72–77; P-in-c Bishops Sutton w Stowey *B & W* 77–81; P-in-c Compton Martin w Ubley 79–81; P-in-c Bridgwater St Jo w Chedzoy 81–83; Chapl St Mary's Hosp Praed Street Lon 83–94; Chapl St Mary's NHS Trust Paddington 94–99; rtd 00; PtO *Lon* from 04. *10 Brondesbury Park Mansions, 132 Salusbury Road, London NW6 6PD* T/F: (020) 7328 0397 E: newrie@btinternet.com

NEWTON, Brian Karl. b 30. Keble Coll Ox BA 55 MA 59. Wells Th Coll 56. **d** 58 **p** 59. C Barrow St Geo *Carl* 58–61; Trinidad and Tobago 61–69 and 71–77; Gen Ed USPG 69–71; P-in-c Gt Coates *Linc* 77; TV Gt and Lt Coates w Bradley 78–88; V Burgh le Marsh 88–94; R Bratoft w Irby-in-the-Marsh 88–94; V Orby 88–94; R Welton-le-Marsh w Gunby 88–94; rtd 94; PtO *Linc* 94–97 and from 18. *17 Stuart Court, High Street, Kibworth Beauchamp, Leicester LE8 0LR* T: 0116-279 6242

NEWTON, David. *See* NEWTON, Michael David

NEWTON, David. *See* NEWTON, Raymond David

NEWTON, David Ernest. b 42. Sarum & Wells Th Coll 72. **d** 74 **p** 75. C Wigan All SS *Liv* 74–80; V Choral York Minster 80–85; R Ampleforth w Oswaldkirk 85–86; P-in-c E Gilling 85–86; R Ampleforth and Oswaldkirk and Gilling E 86–97; V Ampleforth w Oswaldkirk, Gilling E etc 98–01; RD Helmsley 94–99; P-in-c Overton *Blackb* 01–10. *4 Lunesdale Court, Derwent Road, Lancaster LA1 3ET* T: (01524) 599101 E: davidnoot@aol.com

NEWTON, Derek. b 50. NEOC 89. **d** 92 **p** 93. NSM Houghton le Spring *Dur* 92–96; C 06–09; NSM Deanery of Houghton 97–06; P-in-c Chilton Moor from 09. *1 Fields View, East Rainton, Houghton le Spring DH5 9GA*

NEWTON, Canon Fiona Olive. b 46. GTCL 67. WMMTC 96. **d** 99 **p** 00. C Southam and Ufton *Cov* 99–03; P-in-c Laxfield, Cratfield, Wilby and Brundish *St E* 03–04; R 04–13; C Hoxne w Denham, Syleham and Wingfield 06–13; R Worlingworth, Southolt, Tannington, Bedfield etc 12–13; R Bedfield, Brundish, Cratfield, Laxfield etc 13; RD Hoxne 07–13; RD Hartismere 08–10; Hon Can St E Cathl 11–13; rtd 13; PtO *Nor* from 14; LtO *Mor* from 15. T: (01328) 830947 *or* (01599) 544345 E: fionanewton46@gmail.com

NEWTON, Canon George Peter Howgill. b 62. Pemb Coll Cam BA 84 MA 88. Oak Hill Th Coll BA 93. **d** 93 **p** 94. C Blackpool St Thos *Blackb* 93–99; P-in-c Aldershot H Trin *Guildf* 99–03; V from 03; AD Aldershot 11–18; Chapl Farnborough Coll of Tech from 00; Hon Can Guildf Cathl from 18. *2 Cranmore Lane, Aldershot GU11 3AS* T: (01252) 320618 E: g@gjsk.prestel.co.uk

NEWTON, Canon Graham Hayden. b 47. AKC 69. St Aug Coll Cant 70. **d** 70 **p** 71. C St Mary-at-Lambeth *S'wark* 70–73; TV Catford (Southend) and Downham 73–78; P-in-c Porthill *Lich* 78–79; TV Wolstanton 79–86; V Stevenage H Trin *St Alb* 86–96; TR Dunstable 96–04; RD 96–02; R Barton-le-Cley w Higham Gobion and Hexton 04–12; Hon Can St Alb 04–12; rtd 12; PtO *St Alb* 12–15; *Win* from 12. *23 Regency Crescent, Christchurch BH23 2UF* T: (01202) 950010 E: revdghnewton@gmail.com

NEWTON, John. b 39. AKC 65. **d** 66 **p** 67. C Whipton *Ex* 66–68; C Plympton St Mary 68–74; V Broadwoodwidger 74–81; R Kelly w Bradstone 74–81; R Lifton 74–81; Chapl All Hallows Sch Rousdon 81–94; LtO *Ex* 81–94; rtd 99. *Flat 2, 5 Eyewell Green, Seaton EX12 2BN* T: (01297) 625887 E: lyinclight@live.co.uk

NEWTON, Louis Kalbfleisch. b 44. N Texas State Univ BA 73. Westcott Ho Cam 90. **d** 93 **p** 94. C Walthamstow St Pet *Chelmsf* 93–97; USA from 97; rtd 09. *265 Fell Street, Apt 207, San Francisco CA 94102-5151, USA* M: (415) 621 3409 E: louisknewton@yahoo.com

NEWTON, Michael David. b 89. Trin Hall Cam BA 11 MA 15 PGCE 12. Cranmer Hall Dur 13. **d** 15 **p** 16. C Ely 15–17; TV Lordsbridge from 17. *The Vicarage, 92 Swaynes Lane, Comberton, Cambridge CB23 7EF* E: mdavidn16@gmail.com

NEWTON, Canon Nigel Ernest Hartley. b 38. St Jo Coll Nottm 87. **d** 89 **p** 90. C Largs *Glas* 89–92; Angl Chapl Ashbourne Home Largs 89–92; P-in-c Eyemouth *Edin* 92–95; Chapl Miss to Seamen 92–95; P-in-c Challoch *Glas* 95–04; R 04–06; Can St Mary's Cathl 04–06; Hon Can St Mary's Cathl from 06; rtd 06; P-in-c Stranraer *Glas* 10–13. *Glenairlie, 7 Wigtown Road, Newton Stewart DG8 6JZ* T: (01671) 401228 M: 07885-436892 E: glenairlie@btinternet.com

NEWTON, Peter. b 39. St Jo Coll Nottm 73. **d** 75 **p** 76. C Porchester *S'well* 75–79; R Wilford 79–99; rtd 99. Warden Advent Ho Healing Min Birmingham USA 99–12; PtO *Leic* from 00. *20 Main Street, Eaton, Grantham NG32 1SE* T: (01476) 870024 E: newtonji@hotmail.com

NEWTON, Raymond David. b 43. K Coll Lon BSc 65. Linc Th Coll 65. **d** 67 **p** 68. C Ipswich St Matt *St E* 67–71; C E w W Barkwith *Linc* 71–74; R Chelmondiston w Harkstead *St E* 74–78; R Chelmondiston w Harkstead and Shotley w Erwarton 78–91; R Chelmondiston and Erwarton w Harkstead 91–04; rtd 04. *Langley Cottage, 4 Church Road, Chelmondiston, Ipswich IP9 1HS* T: (01473) 780117 M: 07718-808970 E: david.newton@stedmundsbury.anglican.org

NEWTON, Richard. b 47. Trin Coll Bris 72. **d** 73 **p** 74. C Fareham St Jo *Portsm* 73–76; C Cheltenham St Mark *Glouc* 76–83; P-in-c Malvern St Andr *Worc* 83–95; TR Kingswood

Bris 95–99; Master St Jo Hosp Bath 00–07; rtd 07; PtO *Worc* from 08. *61 Columbia Drive, Worcester WR2 4DB* T: (01905) 426702 E: 2antiques41@talktalk.net

NEWTON, Richard John Christopher. b 60. Bris Univ BSc 81. Qu Coll Birm 85. **d** 88 **p** 89. C Bris Ch the Servant Stockwood 88–92; C Dorking w Ranmore *Guildf* 92–96; P-in-c Hagley *Worc* 96–00; R from 00; Hon C Belbroughton w Fairfield and Clent from 15. *The Rectory, 6 Middlefield Lane, Hagley, Stourbridge DY9 0PX* T: (01562) 882442 E: richardn.kathy@gmail.com

NEWTON, Ruth Elizabeth. b 71. Cen Lancs Univ BA 93 Huddersfield Univ PGCE 13. St Jo Coll Nottm MTh 01. **d** 02 **p** 03. C Caldbeck, Castle Sowerby and Sebergham *Carl* 02–06; V Hutton Cranswick w Skerne, Watton and Beswick *York* 06–11; RD Harthill 10–11; P-in-c Kirklington w Burneston and Wath and Pickhill *Ripon* 11–14; *Leeds* 14–15; Can Evang Ripon Cathl from 15; C Ripon Cathl *Leeds* from 17; Lay Tr Officer Ripon Area 17–18. *St Peter's House, Minster Close, Ripon HG4 1QP* T: (01765) 604108 E: ruthhind@gmail.com

NEWTON, Ruth Katherine. b 58. **d** 10 **p** 11. NSM Rowley w Skidby *York* 10–15; NSM Walkington, Bishop Burton, Rowley etc 15–18; rtd 18; PtO *York* from 18. *6 Manor Barns, Little Weighton, Cottingham HU20 3UA* T: (01482) 841875 E: newtonr@newtonrk.karoo.co.uk

NEWTON, Mrs Sonya Teresa. b 74. Trin Coll Bris 17. **d** 19. C Coney Hill *Glouc* from 19. *29 Windfall Way, Gloucester GL2 0RP* E: howdoyoulikeyours@hotmail.com

NGOY, Lusa. *See* NSENGA-NGOY, Lusa

NICE, Canon John Edmund. b 51. Univ of Wales (Ban) BA 73. Coll of Resurr Mirfield 74. **d** 76 **p** 77. C Oxton *Ches* 76–79; C Liscard St Mary w St Columba 79–82; V Latchford St Jas 82–92; TR Holyhead w Rhoscolyn w Llanfair-yn-Neubwll *Ban* 92–95; TR Holyhead 95–04; RD Llifon and Talybolion 97–01; AD 01–04; R Llandudno 04–17; Can Cursal Ban Cathl 02–04; Can and Preb Ban Cathl 04–17; AD Archllechwedd 10–15; rtd 17; PtO *St As* from 14; *Ban* from 17. *61 The Dale, Abergele LL22 7DT* E: john.nice2@btopenworld.com

NICHOL, Canon William David. b 58. Hull Univ BA 84. Ridley Hall Cam 84. **d** 87 **p** 88. C Hull St Jo Newland *York* 87–90; C Kirk Ella 90–92; TV 92–98; P-in-c Powick *Worc* 98–99; R Powick and Guarlford and Madresfield w Newland 99–05; V Malvern H Trin and St Jas from 05; RD Malvern 07–13 and from 17; Hon Can Worc Cathl from 17. *Holy Trinity Vicarage, 2 North Malvern Road, Malvern WR14 4LR* T: (01684) 561126 E: davidnichol1958@gmail.com

NICHOLAS, Jonathan. b 78. Cranmer Hall Dur 08. **d** 10 **p** 11. C Lt Horton *Bradf* 10–14; C Oldbury, Langley and Londonderry *Birm* 14–15; V Sutton Coldfield St Chad from 15. *The Vicarage, 41 Hollyfield Road, Sutton Coldfield B75 7SN* T: 0121-329 2995 E: vicar@stchadsc.org.uk

NICHOLAS, Malcolm Keith. b 46. Open Univ BA 79 FIBMS 71. S Dios Minl Tr Scheme 81. **d** 84 **p** 85. NSM Gatcombe *Portsm* 84–92; NSM Shorwell w Kingston 88–92; C Hartley Wintney, Elvetham, Winchfield etc *Win* 92–96; TV Grantham *Linc* 96–02; V Grantham, Harrowby w Londonthorpe 02–03; V Carr Dyke Gp 03–11; rtd 11; PtO *Nor* from 12. *20 Marrams Avenue, Cromer NR27 9BB* T: (01263) 514036 E: malnic46@gmail.com

NICHOLAS, Paul James. b 51. Univ of Wales (Lamp) BA. Coll of Resurr Mirfield 73. **d** 74 **p** 75. C Llanelli *St D* 74–78; C Roath *Llan* 78–84; P-in-c Leic St Pet 84–87; V Shard End *Birm* 87–96; rtd 96; PtO *Birm* from 96. *50 Delrene Road, Shirley, Solihull B90 2HJ* T: 0121-745 7339

NICHOLAS, Peter John. b 78. BNC Ox MA 00 MSc 02. Wycliffe Hall Ox 10. **d** 12 **p** 13. C Langham Place All So *Lon* from 12; P-in-c Clerkenwell St Jas and St Jo w St Pet from 18. *14 Steadman Court, 165 Old Street, London EC1V 9ND* T: (020) 7251 1190 E: pete@inspirelondon.org

NICHOLAS ALAN, Brother. *See* WORSSAM, Nicholas Alan

NICHOLAS-LETCH, Carol. **d** 19 **p** 19. C Wissey Valley *Ely* from 19. *Address temp unknown* E: carolnl53@hotmail.com

NICHOLLS (née HUMPHRIES), Mrs Catherine Elizabeth. b 53. Anglia Poly Univ MA 97. Trin Coll Bris BA 87. **d** 87 **p** 94. C Bath Twerton-on-Avon *B & W* 87–90; Personnel Manager and Tr Officer TEAR Fund 90–95; Hon C Norbiton *S'wark* 91–95; PtO *Ely* 95–97; Dir Past Studies EAMTC 97–03; Vice Prin 01–03; Hon Min Can Ch Ch Cathl 97–03; PtO *Nor* 03–05 and from 10; Dioc Dir CME 05–10. *North Cottage, King John's Thorn, Hethel, Norwich NR14 8HE* T: (01508) 570557 E: cathynicholls@allbelievers.org

NICHOLLS (née TOVAR), Mrs Gillian Elaine. b 48. Sussex Univ CertEd 69. Trin Coll Bris BA 86. dss 86 **d** 87 **p** 94. Tonbridge SS Pet and Paul *Roch* 86–00; Par Dn 87–94; C 94–00; V Gillingham H Trin 00–10; rtd 10; PtO *Ox* from 11. *29 The Gables, Haddenham, Aylesbury HP17 8AD* T: (01844) 291993 E: gilltovar2008@gmail.com

NICHOLLS, Helen. **d** 18 **p** 19. NSM Bro Lliedi *St D* from 18. *The Ridge, 6 Trosserch Road, Llangennech, Llandeilo SA14 8AQ* E: hnicholls28@googlemail.com

NICHOLLS, Irene Elizabeth. b 41. **d** 09 **p** 10. OLM Penkridge *Lich* 09–14; PtO 14–19. *79 Croydon Drive, Penkridge, Stafford ST19 5DW* T: (01785) 714686 E: irenenichollz@gmail.com

NICHOLLS, Mrs Janet Elizabeth. b 64. Southlands Coll Lon BEd 86. ERMC 09. **d** 12 **p** 13. NSM Panfield and Rayne *Chelmsf* 12–15; NSM Finchingfield and Cornish Hall End etc 12–15; Dioc Rural Officer from 15. *Park House, Braintree Road, Shalford, Braintree CM7 5HQ* T: (01371) 851317 E: jnicholls@chelmsford.anglican.org

✠**NICHOLLS, The Rt Revd John.** b 43. AKC 66. **d** 67 **p** 68 **c** 90. C Salford St Clem Ordsall *Man* 67–69; C Langley All SS and Martyrs 69–72; V 72–78; Dir Past Th Coll of Resurr Mirfield 78–83; Can Res Man Cathl 83–90; Suff Bp Lancaster *Blackb* 90–97; Bp Sheff 97–08; rtd 08; Hon Asst Bp Derby from 09; Hon Asst Bp Man from 12. *75 Rowarth Grange Road, Chapel-en-le-Frith, High Peak SK23 0LD* T: (01298) 938249 M: 07773-244946 E: jnseraphim@gmx.com

NICHOLLS, Keith Barclay. b 57. Nottm Univ BA 78. Wycliffe Hall Ox 03. **d** 05 **p** 06. C Bisley and W End *Guildf* 05–09; V Burchetts Green *Ox* from 09. *The Vicarage, Burchetts Green Road, Burchetts Green, Maidenhead SL6 6QS* T: (01628) 828822 E: kbnicholls@hotmail.com

NICHOLLS, Canon Mark Richard. b 60. LSE BSc(Econ) 82 Leeds Univ BA 88. Coll of Resurr Mirfield 86. **d** 89 **p** 90. C Warrington St Elphin *Liv* 89–92; V Wigan St Andr 92–96; R North End St Marg Zimbabwe 96–00; Shrine P Shrine of Our Lady of Walsingham 00–02; V Mill End and Heronsgate w W Hyde *St Alb* 02–07; P-in-c Rotherhithe St Mary w All SS *S'wark* 07–10; R from 10; P-in-c Bermondsey St Kath w St Bart from 14; AD Bermondsey 13–18; Hon Can Manicaland Zimbabwe from 14. *St Mary's Rectory, 72A St Marychurch Street, London SE16 2JE* M: 07909-546659 E: mmarini2001@aol.com

NICHOLLS, Robert Graham. b 56. Sheff Univ BEng 77 CEng MIET 07. STETS 05. **d** 08 **p** 09. NSM Fair Oak *Win* from 08. *20 The Spinney, Eastleigh SO50 8PF* T: (023) 8069 3716 M: 07837-804366 E: bob.nicholls@dsl.pipex.com

NICHOLLS, Roger Frank. b 43. Ox Univ MA Cam Univ DipEd. **d** 01 **p** 02. OLM Kenwyn w St Allen *Truro* 01–04; NSM Truro St Paul and St Clem 04–08; NSM Truro St Geo and St Jo 04–08; P-in-c Mylor w Flushing 08–13; rtd 13; PtO *Truro* from 16. *8 Truro Vean Terrace, Truro TR1 1HA* T: (01872) 275753 E: rognicholls@tesco.net

NICHOLLS, Simon James. b 53. Anglia Ruskin Univ MA 08 Trent Park Coll of Educn CertEd 76. Ridley Hall Cam. **d** 00 **p** 01. C Nuneaton St Nic *Cov* 00–04; R Markfield, Thornton, Bagworth and Stanton etc *Leic* from 04. *The Rectory, 3A The Nook, Markfield LE67 9WE* T: (01530) 242844 E: markfield.rector@gmail.com

NICHOLS, Barry Edward. b 40. ACA 63 FCA 73. S'wark Ord Course 66. **d** 69 **p** 70. NSM Surbiton St Andr and St Mark *S'wark* 69–92; Dean for MSE Kingston Area 90–92; Hon Can S'wark Cathl 90–92; PtO 99–01; NSM Upper Tooting H Trin 01–04; NSM Upper Tooting H Trin w St Aug 04–12; rtd 12; PtO *S'wark* from 12. *19 Arterberry Road, London SW20 8AF* T/F: (020) 8879 0154 M: 07740-152309 E: barrynichols@btinternet.com

NICHOLS, Mrs Elizabeth Margaret. b 45. WEMTC 00. **d** 02 **p** 03. NSM Ledbury *Heref* 02–05; NSM Boxwell, Leighterton, Didmarton, Oldbury etc *Glouc* 05–10; rtd 10; PtO *Glouc* from 16. *27 Noverton Lane, Prestbury, Cheltenham GL52 5DD* T: (01242) 572249

NICHOLS, Frank Bernard. b 43. Kelham Th Coll 64. **d** 68 **p** 69. C Luton St Andr *St Alb* 68–72; C Cheshunt 72–76; C-in-c Marsh Farm CD 76–81; PtO Brisbane Australia 08–10; PtO *Nor* from 10. *15A Wells Road, Walsingham NR22 6DL* T: (01328) 821459 M: 07503-932804 E: lyngateman@hotmail.co.uk

NICHOLS, Howard Keith. b 54. CCC Ox BA 64 MA 68 CEng 86 FIEE 92 EurIng 94. WEMTC 98. **d** 01 **p** 02. NSM Ledbury *Heref* 01–04; NSM Boxwell, Leighterton, Didmarton, Oldbury etc *Glouc* 04–10; PtO from 16. *27 Noverton Lane, Prestbury, Cheltenham GL52 5DD* T: (01242) 572249

NICHOLS, Mark Steven. b 68. Lon Bible Coll BA 94 Ridley Hall Cam 95. **d** 97 **p** 98. C Balham Hill Ascension *S'wark* 97–99. *16 Beckside Close, Rossendale BB4 9DE* M: 07875-636737 E: markn1968uk@yahoo.co.uk

NICHOLS, Robert Warren. b 54. Biola Univ (USA) BA 77 Fuller Th Sem California MA 81. SAOMC 93. **d** 96 **p** 97. C Headington Quarry *Ox* 96–00; Sen Asst P Wymondham *Nor* 00–05; Lect 01–05; R Caston, Griston, Merton, Thompson etc *Nor* 05–16; rtd 16; PtO *Nor* from 17. *The Old Rectory, Station Road, Hillington, King's Lynn PE31 6DE* T: (01485) 609294 E: revbobnichols@gmail.com

NICHOLS, Stephen Robert Chamberlain. b 73. Ch Coll Cam BA 96 MA 00 SOAS Lon MA 98 Bris Univ PhD 11. Wycliffe Hall Ox BA 06. **d** 09 **p** 10. C Plymouth St Andr and Stonehouse *Ex* 09–14; C Langham Place All So *Lon* from 14. *All Souls' Church, 2 All Souls' Place, London W1B 3DA* T: (020) 7580 3522 M: 07960-063174 E: srcnichols@gmail.com

NICHOLSON, Mrs Barbara Ruth. b 39. Nor City Coll TCert 59. **d** 02 **p** 03. OLM Reculver and Herne Bay St Bart *Cant* 02–11; PtO from 11. *34 Cliff Avenue, Herne Bay CT6 6LZ* T: (01227) 364606 F: 365384 E: barbaranicholson@me.com

NICHOLSON, Brian Warburton. b 44. ALCD 73 LTh 74. St Jo Coll Nottm 70. **d** 73 **p** 74. C Canford Magna *Sarum* 73–77; C E Twickenham St Steph *Lon* 77–80; V Colchester St Jo *Chelmsf* 80–96; R Oakley w Wootton St Lawrence *Win* 96–09; rtd 09; PtO *Win* from 09. *Nuthatches, 16 St Vigor Way, Colden Common, Winchester SO21 1UU* T: (01962) 713433 E: brian.nic@talktalk.net

NICHOLSON, Christina Olive. b 59. **d** 08 **p** 09. OLM Mossley Hill *Liv* 08–12; C Ince Ch Ch w Wigan St Cath 12–15; C Hindley Green 15–16; TV Wigan All SS from 16. *St Andrew's Vicarage, 3A Mort Street, Wigan WN6 7AU* E: tina2nic@sky.com

NICHOLSON, David. b 57. Sarum & Wells Th Coll 80. **d** 83 **p** 84. C Trevethin *Mon* 83–85; C Ebbw Vale 85–87; V Newport St Steph and H Trin 87–95; V Abertillery w Cwmtillery w Six Bells 95–97; Hon Chapl Miss to Seamen 87–97; P-in-c Cudworth *Wakef* 97–98; P-in-c Lundwood 01–04; V Cudworth 98–14; *Leeds* from 14; Dioc Urban Officer *Wakef* 08–14; *Leeds* from 14; Chapl to The Queen from 14. *The Vicarage, St John's Road, Cudworth, Barnsley S72 8DE* T: (01226) 710279 E: frnicholson@aol.com

NICHOLSON, Dorothy Ann. b 40. Surrey Univ Roehampton MSc 04. S'wark Ord Course 81. **dss** 84 **d** 87 **p** 94. Carshalton Beeches *S'wark* 84–88; Par Dn 87–88; Par Dn Brixton Road Ch Ch 88–89; C Malden St Jo 89–95; V Balham St Mary and St Jo 95–05; rtd 05; PtO *Pet* 16–18. *7 Bromley College, London Road, Bromley BR1 1PE* T: (020) 3754 9987 E: nichoda@uwclub.net

NICHOLSON, Gary. b 62. Open Univ BA 89. Cranmer Hall Dur 91 NEOC 92. **d** 95 **p** 96. NSM Whitworth w Spennymoor *Dur* 95–97; NSM Spennymoor, Whitworth and Merrington 97–00; C Coundon and Eldon 00–02; P-in-c from 02. *St James's Vicarage, 2A Collingwood Street, Coundon, Bishop Auckland DL14 8LG* E: frgary@hotmail.com

NICHOLSON, Mary. *See* NICHOLSON, Yuet-Yee Mary

NICHOLSON, Canon Nigel Patrick. b 46. Sarum & Wells Th Coll 72. **d** 75 **p** 76. C Farnham *Guildf* 75–78; C Worplesdon 78–81; CF (ACF) from 80; P-in-c Compton *Guildf* 81–85; R Compton w Shackleford and Peper Harow 85–89; R Cranleigh 89–12; RD 95–00; Hon Can Guildf Cathl 01–12; rtd 12; PtO *Chich* from 12; *Guildf* from 12; *Portsm* from 12. *Banford House, 25 Portsmouth Road, Liphook GU30 7DJ* T: (01428) 724979 E: nicholson.banford@outlook.com

NICHOLSON, Paul Shannon. b 52. York Univ BA 74 Middx Univ BA 02 Heythrop Coll Lon MA 07 ARCO 74 ARCM 75. NTMTC 99. **d** 02 **p** 03. C Primrose Hill St Mary w Avenue Road St Paul *Lon* 02–06; P-in-c S Hampstead St Sav from 06; P-in-c Belsize Park from 06. *St Saviour's Vicarage, 30 Eton Villas, London NW3 4SQ* T: (020) 7586 6522 M: 07971-223764 E: paul.nicholson@london.anglican.org

NICHOLSON, Canon Peter Charles. b 25. Lambeth MA 89. Chich Th Coll 57. **d** 59 **p** 60. C Sawbridgeworth *St Alb* 59–62; Min Can, Prec and Sacr Pet Cathl 62–67; V Wroxham w Hoveton *Nor* 67–74; V Lyme Regis *Sarum* 74–80; Gen Sec St Luke's Hosp for the Clergy 80–93; NSM Harlington *Lon* 80–87; Min Can Ch Ch Ox from 87; Can and Preb Chich Cathl 89–93; rtd 93. *St Luke's Cottage, 13 Brearley Close, Uxbridge UB8 1JJ* T: (01895) 233522

NICHOLSON, Peter Charles. b 44. Oak Hill Th Coll 74. **d** 76 **p** 77. C Croydon Ch Ch Broad Green *Cant* 76–80; C Gt Baddow *Chelmsf* 80–88; TV 88–96; V Westcliff St Mich 96–13; rtd 13; PtO *Chelmsf* from 14. *Kiononia, 25 Eastwood Park Drive, Leigh-on-Sea SS9 5RP* T: (01702) 527444 E: pedinic@yahoo.co.uk

NICHOLSON, Canon Rodney. b 45. Mert Coll Ox BA 68 MA 71. Ridley Hall Cam 69. **d** 72 **p** 73. C Colne St Bart *Blackb* 72–75; C Blackpool St Jo 75–78; V Ewood 78–90; V Clitheroe St Paul Low Moor 90–14; P-in-c Chatburn and Downham 03–14; Hon Can Blackb Cathl 06–14; rtd 14; PtO *York* from 15; RD S Wold 17–19. *96 Shipman Road, Market Weighton, York YO43 3RB* T: (01430) 650271 E: rodnic03@gmail.com

NICHOLSON, Roland. b 40. Sarum & Wells Th Coll 72. **d** 74 **p** 75. C Morecambe St Barn *Blackb* 74–78; V Feniscliffe 78–90; V Sabden and Pendleton 90–02; C Poulton-le-Fylde 02–04; C Poulton Carleton and Singleton 04–07; rtd 08; PtO *Blackb* from 08. *25 St Mary's Court, Church Lane, Mellor, Blackburn BB2 7JE*

NICHOLSON, Miss Velda Christine. b 44. Charlotte Mason Coll of Educn TCert 65. Cranmer Hall Dur 81. **dss** 82 **d** 87 **p** 94. Gt and Lt Driffield *York* 82–86; Newby 86–88; Par Dn 87–88; Team Dn Cramlington *Newc* 88–94; TV 94–96; PtO from 96; rtd 04. *24 Glendale, Amble, Morpeth NE65 0RG* T: (01665) 713796

NICHOLSON, Yuet-Yee Mary. b 60. Man Univ MB, ChB 91 MRCGP 96 Win Univ PGCE 11. Sarum Coll 13. **d** 16 **p** 17. C Brockenhurst *Win* 16–19; C Southampton St Mark from 19. *Pikes Post, Chapel Lane, Burley, Ringwood BH24 4DJ* T: (01425) 404155 M: 07799-811888 E: pikespost@tiscali.co.uk

NICKLAS-CARTER, Derath May. *See* DURKIN, Derath May

NICKOLS, James Alexander. b 75. Regent's Park Coll Ox BA 96. Ridley Hall Cam 98. **d** 00 **p** 01. C Plymouth St Jude *Ex* 00–04; C Camberwell All SS *S'wark* 04–08; Hon C Camberwell Ch Ch 09–18; PtO *Ox* 13–16; NSM Chich St Pancras and St Jo from 18. *Martlet Cottage, Itchenor Green, Itchenor, Chichester PO20 7DA* M: 07968-062339 E: jamesnkls@aol.com or james@thefillingstation.org.uk

NICKOLS-RAWLE, Peter John. b 44. St Luke's Coll Ex CertEd 73. Sarum & Wells Th Coll 76. **d** 78 **p** 79. C Ex St Thos 78–80; Old and New Shoreham *Chich* 80–86; P-in-c Donnington 86–90; Chapl RAF 90–92; TV Ottery St Mary, Alfington, W Hill, Tipton etc *Ex* 92–97; V Breage w Germoe and Godolphin *Truro* 98–01; rtd 01; PtO *Truro* 01–05. *14 The Copse, Exmouth EX8 4EY* T: (01395) 270068

NICKSON, Canon Ann Louise. b 58. New Hall Cam BA 80 Fitzw Coll Cam BA 95 Solicitor 81. Ridley Hall Cam PhD 98. **d** 98 **p** 99. C Sanderstead All SS *S'wark* 98–01; P-in-c Norbury St Steph and Thornton Heath 01–05; V 05–10; AD Croydon N 06–10; TR Mortlake w E Sheen from 10; Hon Can S'wark Cathl from 10. *The Rectory, 170 Sheen Lane, London SW14 8LZ* T: (020) 8876 4816 E: annnickson@aol.com

NICOL, David Christopher. b 56. Westmr Coll Ox BEd 84 Ox Univ Inst of Educn 91. SAOMC 95. **d** 98 **p** 99. NSM Deddington w Barford, Clifton and Hempton *Ox* 98–01; V Longnor, Quarnford and Sheen *Lich* 01–08; P-in-c Woore and Norton in Hales 09–12; Local Par Development Adv Shrewsbury Area 10–12; R Empingham, Edith Weston, Lyndon, Manton etc *Pet* 12–15; TV Leek and Meerbrook *Lich* from 15. *6 Hill View, Leek ST13 5TA* T: (01538) 528545 E: fr.david@tinyworld.co.uk or allsaints.leek@outlook.com

NICOL, Harvie Thomas. b 61. Aston Tr Scheme 95 St Jo Coll Nottm 97. **d** 99 **p** 00. C Balderstone *Man* 99; C S Rochdale 00–03; TV Ashton 03–08; P-in-c Ashton St Pet 03–08; V Formby St Luke *Liv* from 08. *St Luke's Vicarage, St Luke's Church Road, Liverpool L37 2DF* T: (01704) 877655

NICOL, Stephen Trevor. b 52. Oak Hill Th Coll BA 82. **d** 82 **p** 83. C Harold Hill St Geo *Chelmsf* 82–85; C Greenstead 85–88. *Les Fosses, 87330 Nouic, France* T: (0033) 6 37 39 01 82 E: nicolnouic@orange.fr

NICOLE, Bruce. b 54. K Coll Lon MA 96 ACIB. Wycliffe Hall Ox 89. **d** 91 **p** 92. C Headley All SS *Guildf* 91–95; V Camberley St Mich Yorktown from 95; RD Surrey Heath 02–06. *The Vicarage, 286 London Road, Camberley GU15 3JP* T: (01276) 23602 E: revbrucenicole@gmail.com

NICOLL, Alexander Charles Fiennes Jack. b 34. Lon Coll of Div 66. **d** 68 **p** 69. C Trentham *Lich* 68–71; C Hednesford 72–74; P-in-c Quarnford 74–84; V Longnor 74–84; P-in-c Sheen 80–84; V Longnor, Quarnford and Sheen 85–00; RD Alstonfield 96–00; rtd 00; PtO *Lich* 00–11. *110 Stone Road, Uttoxeter ST14 7QW* T: (01889) 569361 E: alexandernicoll@hotmail.com

NICOLL, Miss Angela Olive Woods. b 50. Linc Th Coll 77. **dss** 79 **d** 87 **p** 94. Catford St Laur *S'wark* 79–83; Peckham St Jo w St Andr 83–88; Par Dn 87–88; Par Dn New Addington 88–94; C 94–02; S Africa 02–06; PtO *Ely* 06–10; *Nor* from 14. *15 Manor Park, Watton, Thetford IP25 6HH* T: (01953) 889074

NICOLSON, Paul Roderick. b 32. Cuddesdon Coll 65. **d** 67 **p** 68. C Farnham Royal *Ox* 67–68; LtO *St Alb* 69–82; C Hambleden Valley *Ox* 82–99; rtd 99. *93 Campbell Road, London N17 0AX* T: (020) 8376 5455 F: 8376 5319 M: 07961-177889 E: paul@nicolson.com

NIECHCIAL, Stephen Alexander. b 53. St Chad's Coll Dur BA 74 CQSW 85. St Steph Ho Ox 12. **d** 14 **p** 15. C Sidcup St Jo *Roch* 14–18; C Beckenham St Jas w St Mich and St Aug 16–17; V Petts Wood from 18. *St Francis's Vicarage, 60 Willett Way, Petts Wood, Orpington BR5 1QE* T: (01689) 829971 M: 07976-011494 E: sjniechcial@hotmail.com

NIEMIEC, Paul Kevin. b 56. EAMTC 03. **d** 05 **p** 06. Youth Officer *Pet* 97–08; NSM Thrapston, Denford and Islip 05–08; TV Barnstaple *Ex* 08–11; TV Ouzel Valley *St Alb* 11–17; TV Heacham and Snettisham *Nor* 17–18; RD Heacham and Rising 17–18; rtd 18. *52 Culloden Drive, Kettering NN15 5DF* E: pkniemiec@gmail.com

NIGHTINGALE, Canon John Brodie. b 42. Pemb Coll Ox BA 64 Qu Coll Cam BA 67. Westcott Ho Cam 65. **d** 67 **p** 68. C Wythenshawe St Martin *Man* 67–70; Nigeria 70–76; P-in-c Amberley w N Stoke *Chich* 76–79; Adult Educn Adv 76–79; Asst Home Sec Gen Syn Bd for Miss and Unity 80–84; Miss Sec 84–87; P-in-c Wolverton w Norton Lindsey and Langley *Cov* 87–95; Dioc Miss Adv 87–95; V Rowley Regis *Birm* 95–07; Hon Can Birm Cathl 01–07; Warden of Readers 03–07; rtd 07; PtO *Birm* from 07; *Lich* from 15. *19 Berberry Close, Birmingham B30 1TB* T: 0121-458 6182 M: 07811-128831

NIGHTINGALE, Philip James. b 82. Birm Univ BA 05. Wycliffe Hall Ox BA 17. **d** 18 **p** 19. C Rushden St Mary w Newton Bromswold *Pet* from 18. *36 Meadow Sweet Road, Rushden NN10 0GA* M: 07815-095964 E: philnightingale@hotmail.com

NIGHTINGALE, Susan Kay. b 44. Keele Univ BA 66 Seabury-Western Th Sem DMin 99. S'wark Ord Course 90. **d** 93 **p** 94. NSM St Giles Cripplegate w St Bart Moor Lane etc *Lon* 93–99; PtO *York* 93–99; Asst Chapl H Trin Geneva *Eur* 99–02; P-in-c Sutton on the Forest *York* 03–06; NSM Forest of Galtres 06–12; rtd 12; PtO *York* from 12. *27 East Mount Road, York YO24 1BD* T: (01904) 689742 E: suenightingale3@gmail.com

NIMMO, Canon Alexander Emsley. b 53. Aber Univ BD 76 PhD 97 Edin Univ MPhil 83 FSAScot 93. Edin Th Coll 76. **d** 78 **p** 79. Prec St Andr Cathl Inverness *Mor* 78–81; P-in-c Stornoway *Arg* 81–83; R 84; R Edin St Mich and All SS 84–90; Chapl HM Pris Saughton 87–90; R Aberdeen St Marg *Ab* from 90; Can St Andr Cathl from 96; Syn Clerk 01–08; Dean Ab 08–17. *St Margaret's Clergy House, Gallowgate, Aberdeen AB25 1EA* T: (01224) 644969 F: 630767 E: alexander306@btinternet.com

NIND, Robert William Hampden. b 31. Ball Coll Ox BA 54 MA 60. Cuddesdon Coll 54. **d** 56 **p** 57. C Spalding St Mary and St Nic *Linc* 56–60; Jamaica 60–67; P-in-c Battersea St Bart *S'wark* 67–70; V Brixton St Matt 70–82; LtO 82–84; Ind Chapl 84–89; Ind Chapl *Ox* 89–95; rtd 95; PtO *Ox* 15–18. *19 Binswood Avenue, Headington, Oxford OX3 8NY* T: (01865) 766604 E: b467@btinternet.com

NISBECK, Peter. b 51. SOAS Lon BA 73 Aston Univ MSc 94. NOC 03. **d** 06 **p** 07. NSM Newcastle w Butterton *Lich* from 06. *The Village Farmhouse, Clayton Road, Newcastle ST5 4AB* T: (01782) 662379 E: peternisbeck@hotmail.com

NISBET, Tessa Jane. b 66. **d** 14 **p** 15. C Heatherlands St Jo *Sarum* 14–18; R Hamworthy from 18. *St Michael's Rectory, 1 St Michael's Close, Poole BH15 4QT* T: (01202) 674878 M: 07789-602682 E: tessafuhri@gmail.com

NISSEN, Peter Edlef. b 76. Copenhagen Univ BA 99 MA 05 and 11. St Steph Ho Ox 14. **d** 16 **p** 17. C Alyn Miss Area *St As* 16–18. *19 Acacia Court, Llay, Wrexham LL12 0TX* T: (01978) 448902 M: 07805-921053 E: revd.peter.nissen@gmail.com

NIXON, Mrs Annette Rose. b 37. K Coll Lon BD 58 Newc Univ CertEd 73. **d** 88 **p** 94. Dioc Youth Officer *Ox* 84–90; Par Dn Earley St Pet 88–93; Par Dn Olney w Emberton 93–94; C 94–96; P-in-c Worminghall w Ickford, Oakley and Shabbington 96–00; rtd 00; PtO *Liv* from 16. *3 Harington Close, Liverpool L37 1XP* T: (01704) 872245 E: annette.nixon@sky.com

NIXON, David John. b 59. St Chad's Coll Dur BA 81 Ex Univ PhD 02. St Steph Ho Ox 88. **d** 91 **p** 92. C Plymouth St Pet *Ex* 91–94; Chapl Ex Univ 94–03; P-in-c Stoke Damerel 03–09; P-in-c Devonport St Aubyn 03–09; R Stoke Damerel and Devonport St Aubyn 09–13; RD Plymouth Devonport 11–13; Dean of Studies SWMTC 13–18; PtO *Ex* 13–18; TR Ex St Thos and Em from 18; RD Christianity from 18; Public Preacher *Truro* from 14. *Emmanuel Vicarage, 49 Okehampton Road, Exeter EX4 1EL* E: rev.dave@virgin.net

NIXON, Frances (Isobel). b 34. TCD BA 62. **d** 94 **p** 95. NSM Rossorry *Clogh* from 94. *59 Granshagh Road, Enniskillen BT92 2BL* T: (028) 6634 8723 M: 07710-307263 E: agfin@btinternet.com

NIXON, Ms Naomi Jane. b 75. Keele Univ BA 97. St Jo Coll Nottm MA 00. **d** 01 **p** 02. C Ludlow, Ludford, Ashford Carbonell etc *Heref* 01–04; Chapl N Warks and Hinckley Coll of FE 04–12; Dioc Learning Adv for Minl Development *Cov* from 12; NSM Lillington and Old Milverton 10–17; C St Clare in Cov Cathl from 17; Gen LtO from 18. *Cathedral and Diocesan Offices, 1 Hill Top, Coventry CV1 5AB* T: (024) 7652 1304 E: naomi.nixon@covcofe.org

NIXON, Canon Phillip Edward. b 48. Ch Ch Ox MA 73 DPhil 73 Trin Coll Cam BA 80 K Coll Lon MA 00. Westcott Ho Cam 78. **d** 81 **p** 82. C Leeds Halton St Wilfrid *Ripon* 81–84; V Goring *Ox* 84; V Goring w S Stoke 84–03; RD Henley 94–02; Hon Can Ch Ch 00–03; P-in-c Northampton St Jas *Pet* 03–13; Warden of Readers 05–12; rtd 13; PtO *Ox* from 13. *32 Cedar Road, Oxford OX2 9EB* T: (01865) 241385 E: phillipn@btinternet.com

NIXON, Mrs Tonya. b 69. Plymouth Univ BSc 93 St Mark & St Jo Coll Lon PGCE 94. Qu Coll Birm 06. **d** 09 **p** 10. C Farmborough, Marksbury and Stanton Prior *B & W* 09–13; P-in-c Huntspill 13–18; P-in-c Mark w Allerton 13–18; R The Huntspills and Mark 18–19; C Highbridge 13–19; R Braydon Brook *Bris* from 19. *The Rectory, 1 Days Court, Crudwell, Malmesbury SN16 9HG* E: tonya39n@btinternet.com or vicarbraydon@gmail.com

NIXON, William Samuel. Reading Univ BSc 94 TCD BTh 00. **d** 00 **p** 01. C Lisburn St Paul *Conn* 00–02; C Hillsborough *D & D* 02–06; P-in-c Edin Clermiston Em 06–08; I Killaney w Carryduff *D & D* 08–12; I Drumbeg from 12; Warden of Readers from 08; Chapl HM Pris Hydebank Wood 08–17. *The Rectory, 64 Drumbeg Road, Dunmurry, Belfast BT17 9LE* T: (028) 9543 6592 M: 07764-277771 E: cazza_willie@hotmail.com

NIXON, Rosemary Clare. *See* WARD, Rosemary Clare

NJENGA, Lukas. b 68. Natal Univ BTh 97 MTh 98 Birm Univ PhD. Trin Coll Nairobi. **d** 92 **p** 93. V Kitengela Kenya 92–96; R Sobantu S Africa 96–01; Lect Carlile Coll Nairobi 01–02; R Glas St Geo 02–05; Chapl Glas Caledonian Univ 05–11; Chapl York St Jo Univ 11–14; Chief Exec Officer Heart for the City from 14. *Heart for the City, Purpose Centre, 582 London Road, Glasgow G40 1DZ* T: 0141-258 1060 M: 07534-719450 E: admin@heartforthecity.co.uk

NJOKA, Stanley. b 80. Middx Univ BA 09. St Andr Coll Kabare 01. **d** 04 **p** 05. Kenya 04–06; PtO *Lon* 06–07; S'wark 08–10; NSM Peckham St Jo w St Andr 10–11; NSM Camberwell St Giles w St Matt 11–19; Chapl King's Coll Hosp NHS Foundn Trust 10–19; Lead Chapl Surrey and Sussex Healthcare NHS Trust from 19. *Surrey and Sussex Healthcare NHS Trust, East Surrey Hospital, Canada Avenue, Redhill RH1 5RH* T: (01737) 768511 M: 07846-759133 E: stanley.njoka@nhs.net

NJOKU, Canon Chinenye Ngozi. b 63. Trin Coll Bris. **d** 09 **p** 10. C Goldington *St Alb* 09–13; I Garrison w Slavin and Belleek *Clogh* from 13; Preb Clogh Cathl from 19. *Garrison Rectory, 39 Brollagh Road, Kockarevan, Garrison, Enniskillen BT93 4AE* T: (028) 6865 8699 M: 07515-171579 E: gozy78@hotmail.com or garrison@clogher.anglican.org

NJOROGE, John Kibe Mwangi. b 47. **d** 79 **p** 79. C Llantwit Major *Llan* 07–10; Chapl HM Pris Elmley from 11. *HM Prison Elmley, Church Road, Eastchurch, Sheerness ME12 4DZ* T: (01795) 882130 E: john.njoroge@justice.gov.uk

NJUE, James Mbugua. b 86. CA Tr Coll Nairobi 06. **d** 10 **p** 11. C Mbeere Cathl Kenya 09–12; Bp's Chapl 11–12; V St Phil Rwika 12–13; Dioc Communications Dir 09–17; Dioc Sec 13–17; PtO *S'wark* 17–18; C Addington from 18. *56 Viney Bank, Court Wood Lane, Croydon CR0 9JT* M: 07508-182583 E: mbugua.james@hotmail.com

NJUGUNA, Daniel Cahira. b 73. St Jo Coll Nottm BA 04. **d** 00 **p** 01. Kenya 00–03; C Balderton and Barnby-in-the-Willows *S'well* 04–06; TV Hucknall Torkard 06–11; V Wednesbury St Paul Wood Green *Lich* from 11. *St Paul's Vicarage, 68 Wood Green Road, Wednesbury WS10 9QT* M: 07817-577436 E: daniel.njuguna@btinternet.com or vicar@paulandluke.co.uk

NOBBS, Canon Charles Henry ffrench. b 67. Hatf Coll Dur BSc 89 St Jo Coll Dur BA 99 CEng 96. Cranmer Hall Dur 97. **d** 99 **p** 00. C Northampton St Giles *Pet* 99–02; C Collingtree w Courteenhall and Milton Malsor 02–11; Min Grange Park LEP 11–16; Police Chapl Co-ord from 03; Pioneer and Ch Planting Enabler 13–16; Pioneer and New Initiatives Tr Officer 16–19; Dir Miss *Pet* from 19; Can Pet Cathl from 15. *Bouverie Court, 6 The Lakes, Bedford Road, Northampton NN4 7YD* T: (01604) 887000 M: 07742-013599 E: charlie@dunelm.org.uk or charlie.nobbs@peterborough-diocese.org.uk

NOBEL, Johannes. b 81. Evang Th Faculty Leuven BA 03 Utrecht Univ MA 05 St Jo Coll Dur MA 08. Cranmer Hall Dur 06. **d** 08 **p** 09. C Norton St Mary *Dur* 08–12; C Stockton St Chad 08–12; V Heslington York from 12. *The Vicarage, School Lane, Heslington, York YO10 5EE* T: (01904) 870814 or 412300 E: johannes.nobel@gmail.com or jan.nobel@gmail.com

NOBES, Mrs Gillian Mary. b 65. Lon Univ BA 90. Ripon Coll Cuddesdon MA 12. **d** 12 **p** 13. C Broughton, Bossington, Houghton and Mottisfont *Win* 12–16; P-in-c Highcliffe 16–19; V from 19. *33 Nea Road, Christchurch BH23 4NB* E: nobes@guernsey.net

NOBLE, Ann Carol. *See* PHILP, Ann Carol

NOBLE, Anne Valerie. b 60. Univ Coll Ox BA 82 Toronto Univ MSc 84 PhD 91. St Jo Coll Nottm 04. **d** 07 **p** 08. C Wollaton *S'well* 07–11; TV Clifton 11–17; NSM Abbots Bromley, Blithfield, Colton, Colwich etc *Lich* from 17. *The New Rectory, Bellamour Way, Colton, Rugeley WS15 3JW* T: (01889) 576449 E: anoblerev@gmail.com

NOBLE, Christopher John Lancelot. b 58. Oak Hill Th Coll 88. d 90 p 91. C Tonbridge SS Pet and Paul Roch 90–95; P-in-c Stansted w Fairseat and Vigo 95–98; R from 98. The Rectory, 9 The Coach Drive, Meopham, Gravesend DA13 0SZ T: (01732) 822494

NOBLE, Canon Eileen Joan. b 45. NEOC 90. d 93 p 94. C Gosforth All SS Newc 93–96; C Cramlington 96–97; TV 97–01; V Ashington 01–06; rtd 06; Hon C Monkseaton St Mary Newc 07–15; Hon Can Newc Cathl from 12; PtO from 14. 34 Gorsedene Road, Whitley Bay NE26 4AH E: revnoble2000@yahoo.com

NOBLE, Jack Michael. b 89. Bris Univ BA 12 Sheff Univ BA 14 MA 15. Coll of Resurr Mirfield 12. d 15 p 16. C Ruislip St Martin Lon 15–18; C St Marylebone w H Trin from 18; Chapl St Marylebone C of E Sch from 18; Chapl Univ of Westmr from 18. Flat 5, 38 Nottingham Place, London W1U 5NU M: 07765-771547 E: frjacknoble@gmail.com

NOBLE, Canon Paul Vincent. b 54. Leeds Univ BA 75 PGCE 76 Ox Univ BA 81 MA 85. St Steph Ho Ox 79. d 82 p 83. C Prestbury Glouc 82–85; P-in-c Avening w Cherington 85–90; R The Suttons w Tydd Linc 90–98; R Skirbeck St Nic 98–19; RD Holland 15–19; V Linc All SS from 19; Can and Preb Linc Cathl from 18. 17 Gerald's Close, Lincoln LN2 4AL E: frpnoble@gmail.com

NOBLE, Canon Philip David. b 46. Glas Univ BSc 67 Edin Univ BD 70. Edin Th Coll 67. d 70 p 71. C Edin Ch Ch 70–72; C Port Moresby Papua New Guinea 72–73; P-in-c Sakarina 73–75; R Cambuslang Glas 76–83; R Uddingston 76–83; Ev Prestwick 83–85; R 85–11; Can St Mary's Cathl 99–11; rtd 11; LtO Mor from 12. 28 Duncraig Street, Inverness IV3 5DJ T: (01463) 233612 E: philipdnoble@btopenworld.com

NOBLE, Robert. b 43. TCD BA 66 BD 73. d 68 p 69. C Holywood D & D 68–71; Chapl RAF 71–98; Chapl Holmewood Ho Sch Tunbridge Wells 98–04; PtO Chich 01–08; Heref from 08. Temperance Cottage, Weston under Penyard, Ross-on-Wye HR9 7NX T: (01989) 566748 E: rjnobles@tiscali.co.uk

NOBLET, David. b 62. Cranmer Hall Dur 97. d 99 p 00. C Standish Blackb 99–03; P-in-c Langho Billington 03–11; LtO from 11; Chapl HM Pris Kirkham from 08; Chapl HM Pris Lanc Farms from 12. HM Prison Kirkham, Freckleton Road, Kirkham, Preston PR4 2RN T: (01772) 675625 E: davidnoblet@aol.com

NOBLETT, The Ven William Alexander. b 53. Southn Univ BTh 78 Westmr Coll Ox MTh 99. Sarum & Wells Th Coll 74. d 78 p 79. C Sholing Win 78–80; I Ardamine w Kiltennel, Glascarrig etc C & O 80–82; Chapl RAF 82–84; V Middlesbrough St Thos York 84–87; Dep Chapl HM Pris Wakef 87–89; Chapl 89–92; Chapl HM Pris Nor 92–97; Chapl HM Pris Full Sutton 97–01; Chapl Gen of Pris and Adn to HM Pris 01–12; Can and Preb Nor Minster 01–12; Hon Can Liv Cathl 09–12; rtd 12; PtO York 12–17; Eur from 12; Pet from 15; Ely from 16; Chapl to The Queen from 05. Address withheld by request E: williamnoblett@hotmail.com

NOCK, Roland George William. b 62. St Andr Univ BSc 84 BD 89. Edin Th Coll 91. d 91 p 92. C Dunfermline St And 91–93; C W Fife Team Min 91–93; R Cupar 93–96; CF 96–99. 46 Heol y Parc, Cefneithin, Llanelli SA14 7DL T: (01269) 845847

NODDER, Marcus Charles Colmore. b 67. Pemb Coll Cam BA 89 PGCE 90. Oak Hill Th Coll BA 01. d 01 p 02. C Denton Holme Carl 01–04; C Limehouse Lon from 04; P-in-c St Pet Barge from 12. St Peter's Barge, Hertsmere Road, London E14 4AL T: (020) 7515 7947 M: 07727-713744 E: mnodder@googlemail.com or m.nodder@stpetersbarge.org

NODDINGS, John Henry. b 29. Chich Th Coll 80. d 81 p 82. C Southborough St Pet w Ch Ch and St Matt Roch 81–83; C Prittlewell Chelmsf 83–86; V Clay Hill St Jo Lon 86–88; V Clay Hill St Jo and St Luke 88–02; Chapl Chase Farm Hosp Enfield 88–94; Chapl Chase Farm Hosps NHS Trust 94–95; P-in-c Gt Coxwell w Buscot, Coleshill etc Ox 03–10; rtd 03; PtO Sarum 10–11. 9 Fisherton Island, Salisbury SP2 7TG T: (01722) 320177 E: johnnoddings@btinternet.com

NODDINGS, John Michael. b 69. Oak Hill Th Coll BA 97 Catholic Univ Leuven STB 02 Heythrop Coll Lon MTh 04. Allen Hall Westcott Ho Cam 16. d 02 p 19. In RC Ch 02–14; C Corringham and Fobbing Chelmsf from 18. The Glebe House, High Road, Fobbing, Stanford-le-Hope SS17 9JH T: (01375) 466811 E: jmnoddings@icloud.com

NOEL, Rachel Naomi. b 75. BSc MBA MA. STETS. d 14 p 15. C Fordingbridge and Hyde and Breamore etc Win 14–18; P-in-c Pennington from 18. 29 Ramley Road, Lymington SO41 8HF M: 07773-717813 E: rachel@noels.org.uk

NOGHIU, Bernard. b 74. Pontifical Lateran Univ 94. d 99 p 00. NSM Leyton Em Chelmsf 18–19; C Prittlewell from 19. 2 Redstock Road, Southend-on-Sea SS2 5DJ M: 07417-407910 E: bernardnoghiu@gmail.com

NOKE, Christopher. b 48. Ex Coll Ox BA 69 MA 79 LSE MSc 78 ACA 72 FCA 79. SEITE 03. d 06 p 07. NSM Raynes Park St Sav and S Wimbledon All SS S'wark 06–16; P-in-c S Wimbedon All SS from 17. Cedar Lodge, Church Road, Ham, Richmond TW10 5HG T: (020) 8948 7986 E: c.noke@lse.ac.uk

NOKES, Michael David Patrick. b 44. York St Jo Coll MA 05. d 02 p 03. CA from 88; NSM Heworth Ch Ch York 02–08; PtO Bradf 02–11; Ripon 03–14; Leeds 14–16; York from 08; rtd 10. 5 Fox Covert, York YO31 9EN T: (01904) 674879 M: 07776-252440 E: michaelanddi@talktalk.net or mdpnokes@gmail.com

NOKES, Canon Peter Warwick. b 48. Leic Univ BA 71. Westcott Ho Cam 79. d 81 p 82. C Northfield Birm 81–84; C Ludlow Heref 84–87; P-in-c Writtle w Highwood Chelmsf 87–91; V 91–92; P-in-c Epping St Jo 92–95; P-in-c Coopersale 93–95; TR Epping Distr 95–99; R Nor St Pet Mancroft w St Jo Maddermarket 99–15; Hon Can Nor Cathl 10–15; rtd 15; Chapl Beauchamp Community 15–18. 23 Cockshot Road, Malvern WR14 2TT M: 07711-384009 E: pwnokes@gmail.com

NOKES, Robert Harvey. b 39. Keble Coll Ox BA 61 MA 65. Qu Coll Birm 61. d 63 p 64. C Totteridge St Alb 63–67; C Dunstable 67–73; V Langford 73–90; R Braughing w Furneux Pelham and Stocking Pelham 90–04; PtO Ox from 04. 92 Western Drive, Hanslope, Milton Keynes MK19 7LE T: (01908) 337939 E: r.nokes@easykey.com

NOLAN, James Charles William. b 44. Chich Th Coll 75. d 77 p 78. C Crewe St Andr Ches 77–79; C Sale St Anne 79–83; R Holme Runcton w S Runcton and Wallington Ely 83–14; V Tottenhill w Wormegay 83–14; R Watlington 83–14; rtd 14; PtO Nor from 14. 26 Holt Road, Langham, Holt NR25 7BX

NOLAN, Marcus. b 54. Bris Univ BEd. Ridley Hall Cam. d 83 p 84. C Dagenham Chelmsf 83–86; C Finchley St Paul and St Luke Lon 86–90; V W Hampstead Trin 90–98; rtd 99; PtO Derby 00–06 and 14–19. 16 Cartwright Close, Melbourne, Derby DE73 8LA

NOLES, Jeremy Andrew. b 67. St Jo Coll Nottm 02. d 04 p 05. C Southchurch Ch Ch Chelmsf 04–07; C Colchester St Jo 07–12; V Colchester St Luke 12–16; Chapl HM Pris Highpoint 16–18; Chapl HM Pris Chelmsf 18–19; Grants Officer Allchurches Trust Ltd 16–19; Grants and Relationships Manager from 19. Allchurches Trust Ltd, Beaufort House, Brunswick Road, Gloucester GL1 1JZ M: 07748-761191 E: jeremy.noles@allchurches.co.uk

NOLLAND, John Leslie. b 47. New England Univ (NSW) BSc 67 Clare Coll Cam PhD 78. Moore Th Coll Sydney ThL 70 BD 71. d 71 p 72. Res Min Cabramatta Australia 71–74; Asst Prof NT Studies Regent Coll Vancouver Canada 78–86; Tutor Trin Coll Bris from 86; Vice Prin 91-97 and 06–07. 6 Phoenix Grove, Bristol BS6 7XY T: 0117-924 4896 E: john.nolland@cantab.net

NOPPEN, Ms Chantal Mary. b 83. Newc Univ BMus 06 Clare Coll Cam BTh 12. Westcott Ho Cam 10. d 13 p 14. C Byker St Martin Newc 13–17; C Byker St Mich w St Lawr 13–17; TV N Wearside Dur from 17. The Team Rectory, 28 Rotherham Road, Sunderland SR5 5QS E: c.noppen+revd@gmail.com

NORBURN, Christopher Richard. b 62. Cov Poly BSc 85. Aston Tr Scheme 92 Ridley Hall Cam 94. d 96 p 97. C Exning St Martin w Landwade St E 96–99; P-in-c Redgrave cum Botesdale w Rickinghall 99–01; R from 01. The Rectory, Bury Road, Rickinghall, Diss IP22 1HA T: (01379) 898685 E: chris.norburn@breathemail.net

NORBURN, Mrs Lesley Jane. b 62. d 19. NSM Blackbourne St E from 19. 9 Orchard Close, Great Livermere, Bury St Edmunds IP31 1JN T: (01359) 269570 E: lesley.norburn@btinternet.com

NORBURY, Robert John. b 60. Southn Univ BA 83 Univ of Wales (Ban) BTh 07. S'wark Ord Course 01. d 04 p 05. NSM Eltham Park St Luke S'wark 04–07; PtO Chich 07–08; NSM Crowborough St Jo 08–12; P-in-c 09–13; V 13–15; V Brighton St Mich and St Paul from 15; Chapl Wandsworth Primary Care Trust 09–10; Dir of Ords Croydon Area S'wark 10–12. The Vicarage, 6 Montpelier Villas, Brighton BN1 3DH T: (01273) 727362 M: 07715-595828 E: frrobnorbury@aol.com

NORBY, Dean Luverne. d 11 p 12. C Edin St Paul and St Geo 11–14; P-in-c Aberdour St And from 14; P-in-c Burntisland from 14; P-in-c Inverkeithing from 14. The Rectory, Inverkeithing Road, Aberdour, Burntisland KY3 0RS T: (01383) 861000 M: 07821-712500 E: dean@allsoulsfife.org.uk

NORFIELD, David Jonathan. b 67. Humberside Univ BA 89. Linc Th Coll MA 94 Westcott Ho Cam 95. d 97 p 98. C Halstead St Andr w H Trin and Greenstead Green Chelmsf 97–01; V Moulsham St Jo 01–04; Chapl RAF from 04. Chaplaincy Services (RAF), HQ Air Command, RAF High Wycombe HP14 4UE T: (01494) 496800 E: davidnorfield@hotmail.com

NORFOLK, Kirsten. b 85. **d** 16 **p** 17. C Ludgvan, Marazion, St Hilary and Perranuthnoe *Truro* from 16. *2 Bankfield, Trevennar Lane, Marazion TR17 0BL*

NORFOLK, Archdeacon of. *See* BETTS, The Ven Steven James

NORKETT, Alan. b 45. Sarum & Wells Th Coll 85. **d** 87 **p** 88. C Shrewsbury St Giles w Sutton and Atcham *Lich* 87–90; V Mow Cop 90–94; NSM Astbury and Smallwood *Ches* 96–97; NSM Sandbach Heath w Wheelock 97–98; C Castleford All SS and Whitwood *Wakef* 98–01; C Glass Houghton 98–01; R Shrawley, Witley, Astley and Abberley *Worc* 01–10; rtd 10; PtO *Worc* from 11. *15 New Road, Far Forest, Kidderminster DY14 9TQ* T: (01299) 269355 E: vicaralan@btinternet.com

NORMAN, Andrew Bryan. b 90. Selwyn Coll Cam BA 11 MA 15. Ripon Coll Cuddesdon BA 14. **d** 15 **p** 16. C Cartmel Peninsula *Carl* 15–19; P-in-c Arnside from 19; P-in-c Beetham from 19. *The Parsonage, Stanley Street, Beetham, Milnthorpe LA7 7AS* E: revdabn@gmail.com

NORMAN, Canon Andrew Herbert. b 54. K Coll Lon BD 77 AKC 77 Lon Univ PhD 88. St Steph Ho Ox 77. **d** 78 **p** 79. C Deal St Leon w Sholden *Cant* 78–81; C Maidstone All SS and St Phil w Tovil 81–84; V Tenterden St Mich 84–93; Chapl Benenden Hosp 86–91; Dir Post-Ord Tr *Cant* 91–93; R Guildf St Nic from 93; Hon Can Guildf Cathl from 05. *The Rectory, 3 Flower Walk, Guildford GU2 4EP* T: (01483) 504895 E: ahnorman14@gmail.com

NORMAN, Canon Andrew Robert. b 63. Univ Coll Ox BA 84 MA 99 Selw Coll Cam BA 94 MA 99 Birm Univ MPhil 08 AIL 89. Ridley Hall Cam 92. **d** 95 **p** 96. Asst Chapl Paris St Mich *Eur* 95–00; C Clifton Ch Ch w Em *Bris* 00–02; Abp's Asst Sec for Ecum and Angl Affairs *Cant* 02–05; Abp's Prin Sec for Internat, Ecum and Angl Communion Affairs 05–08; Prin Ridley Hall Cam 08–17; Dir Min and Miss *Leeds* from 17; Hon Prov Can Cant Cathl from 06; Hon Can Ely Cathl 12–17; Hon Can Wakef Cathl *Leeds* from 17. *Church House, 17-19 York Place, Leeds LS1 2EX* T: 0113-353 0280 F: 249 1129 E: andrew.norman@leeds.anglican.org

NORMAN, Ann. *See* NORMAN, Margaret Ann

NORMAN, Catherine. b 51. Nottm Univ BSc 73 N Counties Coll Newc CertEd 74. Linc Th Coll 95. **d** 95 **p** 96. C Scartho *Linc* 95–99; V Ulceby Gp 99–02; TV Guiseley w Esholt *Bradf* 02–08; P-in-c Rawdon 08–13; V 13–14; *Leeds* 14; RD Otley *Bradf* 09–14; AD Ilkley *Leeds* 14; rtd 14; PtO *Leeds* from 17. *3 Borrowdale Croft, Yeadon, Leeds LS19 7FN* E: caytenorman@aol.com

NORMAN, Mrs Elizabeth Ann. b 43. SAOMC 95. **d** 98 **p** 99. OLM Amersham *Ox* 98–04; PtO *Ex* from 04. *Lamorna, Main Road, Bickington, Barnstaple EX31 2NA* T: (01271) 859314 E: liz.norman4@btinternet.com

NORMAN, The Ven Garth. b 38. St Chad's Coll Dur BA 62 MA 68 UEA MEd 84 Cam Inst of Educn PGCE 68. **d** 63 **p** 64. C Wandsworth St Anne *S'wark* 63–66; C Trunch w Swafield *Nor* 66–71; R Gimingham 71–77; TR Trunch 77–83; RD Repps 75–83; Prin Chiltern Chr Tr Course *Ox* 83–87; C W Wycombe w Bledlow Ridge, Bradenham and Radnage 83–87; Dir of Tr *Roch* 88–94; Adn Bromley and Bexley 94–03; Hon Can Roch Cathl 91–03; rtd 03; PtO *S'well* 03–09; Chapl to Rtd Clergy 04–09; PtO *Ely* 10–16. *12 Scotsdowne Road, Trumpington, Cambridge CB2 9HU* T: (01223) 844303

NORMAN, Gary. b 64. Newc Univ BA 87. Ripon Coll Cuddesdon 02. **d** 04 **p** 05. C Spennymoor and Whitworth *Dur* 04–09; P-in-c Croxdale and Tudhoe 08–16; P-in-c Merrington 09–16; V Cornforth and Ferryhill from 16. *St Luke's Vicarage, Church Lane, Ferryhill DL17 8LT* T: (01695) 580262

NORMAN, Jillianne Elizabeth. b 59. Ridley Hall Cam 85. **d** 88 **p** 94. Par Dn Fishponds St Jo *Bris* 88–92; PtO 92–94; Hon C Warmley, Syston and Bitton from 94; Chapl Univ Hosps Bris NHS Foundn Trust from 02. *74 Blackhorse Road, Mangotsfield, Bristol BS16 9AY* T: 0117-956 1551 F: 904 6894 E: jilliannenorman@blueyonder.co.uk

NORMAN, Linda Mary. b 48. Man Univ BSc 69 CertEd 70 St Jo Coll Dur BA 82. **dss** 83 **d** 87. York St Mich-le-Belfrey 83–88; Par Dn 87–88; rtd 88. *23 Ainsty Avenue, Dringhouses, York YO24 1HH* T: (01904) 706152

NORMAN, Lynette Dianne. b 52. Sussex Univ CertEd 73 Univ of Wales (Ban) BEd 89. Ripon Coll Cuddesdon 00. **d** 02 **p** 03. C Welshpool w Castle Caereinion *St As* 02–04; R Llanrwst 04–11; C Llanrhaeadr ym Mochnant etc 11–15; V 15–16; I Tanat Valley Miss Area from 17. *The Vicarage, Llanrhaedr ym Mochnant, Oswestry SY10 0JZ* T: (01691) 780341 M: 07889-184517

NORMAN, Margaret Ann. b 48. N Lon Poly CertEd 76 ALA 73. SEITE 09. **d** 11. NSM Erith St Paul *Roch* 11–13; NSM Erith Ch Ch 13–18; rtd 18. *27 Kempton Close, Erith DA8 3SR* T: (01322) 340902 E: ann.norman@hotmail.com

NORMAN, Michael John. b 61. St Jo Coll Ox BSc 83 Univ Coll Lon MSc 84. Aston Tr Scheme 89 St Jo Coll Nottm 91. **d** 93 **p** 94. C Haughton le Skerne *Dur* 93–97; R Sapcote and Sharnford w Wigston Parva *Leic* from 97; RD Sparkenhoe W 02–07. *The Rectory, 4 Sharnford Road, Sapcote, Leicester LE9 4JN* T: (01455) 272215 M: 07895-320985 E: micknorman@msn.com

NORMAN, Michael John. b 59. Southn Univ LLB 82. Wycliffe Hall Ox 82. **d** 85 **p** 86. C Woodley St Jo the Ev *Ox* 85–89; C Uphill *B & W* 89–92; TV 92–98; R Bath St Sav w Swainswick and Woolley from 98. *St Saviour's Rectory, Claremont Road, Bath BA1 6LX* T: (01225) 311637 E: michael@stsaviours.org.uk

NORMAN, Peter John. b 42. Culham Coll of Educn TCert 66 Lon Inst of Educn DipEd 83 MA 86. STETS 95. **d** 98 **p** 99. NSM Bath Weston All SS w N Stoke and Langridge *B & W* 98–13; PtO 14–18. *5 Rockliffe Avenue, Bathwick, Bath BA2 6QP* T: (01225) 463348 E: peterjnorman@sky.com

NORMAN, Richard Jonathan. b 88. Ch Ch Ox BA 10 Leeds Univ MA 11. Coll of Resurr Mirfield 09. **d** 11 **p** 12. C Rotherhithe St Mary w All SS *S'wark* 11–15; V Bickley *Roch* from 15. *St George's Vicarage, Bickley Park Road, Bromley BR1 2BE* T: (020) 8467 3809 *or* 8295 6411 M: 07752-732324 E: rjnorman@hotmail.co.uk

NORMAN, Timothy. b 68. Jes Coll Cam BA 91 Univ Coll Lon PhD 95. Spurgeon's Coll 95 Wycliffe Hall Ox BA 00. **d** 01 **p** 02. C Chipping Norton *Ox* 01–04; Asst Chapl Paris St Mich *Eur* 04–06; PtO 06–08; C Rugby W *Cov* 09–14; PtO from 15; *Ox* from 15; *Lich* 18. *Fir Lodge, Forest Road, Hayley Green, Warfield, Bracknell RG42 6DB* M: 07545-564918 E: tim@theminster.org

NORMAN, Canon William Beadon. b 26. Trin Coll Cam BA 49 MA 55. Ridley Hall Cam 52. **d** 52 **p** 53. C Beckenham St Jo *Roch* 52–54; CMS Miss and Tutor Buwalasi Th Coll Uganda 55–65; Hon Can Mbale 63–65; V Alne *York* 65–74; RD Warley *Birm* 74–79; V Blackheath 74–79; Hon Can Birm Cathl 78–91; TR Kings Norton 79–91; RD 82–87; Warden Dioc Readers Bd 84–91; rtd 91; PtO *S'wark* from 91; Preacher Lincoln's Inn 94–06. *37 Cloudesdale Road, London SW17 8ET* T: (020) 8673 9134 F: 8675 6890 E: bbnorman@hotmail.com

NORMAN-WALKER, Anna Elizabeth. b 67. RGN 89. St Jo Coll Nottm BA 03. **d** 03 **p** 04. C Cullompton, Willand, Uffculme, Kentisbeare etc *Ex* 03–06; TV 06–10; Chapl Stover Sch Newton Abbot 06–08; RD Cullompton *Ex* 09–10; Can Res Ex Cathl 10–17; Dioc Missr 10–14; Chan 14–17; R Streatham St Leon *S'wark* from 17. *1 Becmead Avenue, London SW16 1UH* T: (020) 8769 4366 M: 07557-053567 E: rectorstleonards@btinternet.com

NORMAND, Stephen Joseph William. b 48. N Texas State Univ BSEd 80. Sarum & Wells Th Coll 90. **d** 92 **p** 93. C Norton St Alb 92–94; C St Alb St Pet 95–97; Chapl Oaklands Coll 95–97; TV Horsham *Chich* 97–01; R Wimbotsham w Stow Bardolph and Stow Bridge etc *Ely* 01–04; rtd 04; PtO *Ely* 05–09; *S'wark* 13–16; *Chich* from 19. *The Alms Houses, 14 St Mary's House, Normandy, Horsham RH12 1JL* T: (01403) 210824 M: 07854-493883 E: snormand4@gmail.com

NORRINGTON, Canon Paul Richard. b 57. Brighton Poly BSc 80. Trin Coll Bris 96. **d** 98 **p** 99. C Prittlewell St Pet w Westcliff St Cedd *Chelmsf* 98–02; R Colchester Ch Ch w St Mary V from 02; AD Colchester from 14; Hon Can Chelmsf Cathl from 15. *The Rectory, 21 Cambridge Road, Colchester CO3 3NS* T: (01206) 563478 E: paul.nozzer@btinternet.com

NORRIS, Alexander Frederick. b 74. Westmr Coll Ox BTh 96. St Aug Coll of Th MA 19. **d** 19. NSM St Giles Cripplegate w St Bart Moor Lane etc *Lon* from 19. *307 Duncan House, Dolphin Square, London SW1V 3PW* M: 07786-257047 E: curate@stgileschurch.com

NORRIS, Preb Alison. b 55. St Andr Univ MTheol 77 Dur Univ PGCE 78. Cant Sch of Min 80. **dss** 82 **d** 87 **p** 94. Warlingham w Chelsham and Farleigh *S'wark* 82–85; Willingham *Ely* 85–90; Hon Par Dn 87–90; Hon Par Dn Worle *B & W* 90–94; NSM Milverton w Halse and Fitzhead 94–02; P-in-c Deane Vale 02–10; R 10–19; Preb Wells Cathl 14–19; rtd 19. *26 Palmers Mead, Wellington TA21 8FG* E: revalison@revsnorris.co.uk

NORRIS, Allan Edward. b 43. St Jo Coll Dur BA 72. Cranmer Hall Dur 69. **d** 73 **p** 74. C Plumstead St Jo w St Jas and St Paul *S'wark* 73–78; C Battersea Park St Sav 78–82; C Battersea St Geo w St Andr 78–82; V Grain w Stoke *Roch* 82–92; R Sissinghurst w Frittenden *Cant* 92–12; rtd 12; PtO *Cant* from 13. *17 Abbots Road, Faversham ME13 8DD* T: (01795) 227927 E: allannorris@talktalk.net

NORRIS, Andrew David. b 54. St Andr Univ BSc 78 Lon Univ MPhil 80 CPsychol. EAMTC 87. **d** 90 **p** 91. C Worle *B & W* 90–94; R Milverton w Halse and Fitzhead 94–08; RD Tone 01–07; Nat Chapl Adv Methodist Homes for the Aged 08–14; St Monica Trust Westbury Fields from 14; PtO *B & W* from

14. *St Monica Trust, Cote Lane, Bristol BS9 3UN* T: 0117-949 4000 M: 07812-061761 E: revandrew@revsnorris.co.uk

NORRIS, James Arthur Anson. b 86. Sheff Univ MMath 08. Trin Coll Bris 15. **d** 18 **p** 19. C Woodseats St Chad *Sheff* from 18. *13 Meadow Head, Sheffield S8 7UA* M: 07796-652988 E: jamesaanorris@hotmail.co.uk

NORRIS, Julie Mary. b 63. Westmr Coll Ox BA 84 Fitzw Coll Cam MPhil 88 Birm Univ PhD 03. Wesley Ho Cam 86. **d** 06 **p** 06. C Orwell Gp *Ely* 06–09; P-in-c Gt w Lt Abington 09–16; P-in-c Hildersham 09–16; P-in-c Balsham, Weston Colville, W Wickham etc 10–16; RD Granta 11–16; PtO from 16. *67 High Street, Barrington, Cambridge CB22 7QX* T: (01223) 870120 E: revjulienorris@gmail.com

NORRIS, Mark. b 68. Brunel Univ BEng 90. Oak Hill Th Coll BA 93. **d** 93 **p** 94. C Roby *Liv* 93–97; C St Helens St Helen 97–00; TV Gateacre 00–09; Asst Dioc Dir of Ords 05–09; Leadership Development Adv (Voc) CPAS 09–12; V Keresley and Coundon *Cov* from 12. *Keresley Vicarage, 34 Tamworth Road, Coventry CV6 2EL* T: (024) 7633 2717 E: vicar@keresley.church

NORRIS, Paul. b 48. **d** 10 **p** 11. OLM Woughton *Ox* from 10. *20 Thirsk Gardens, Bletchley, Milton Keynes MK3 5LH* T: (01908) 371824 M: 07840-296676 E: paul88547@gmail.com

NORTH, Andrew James. b 80. Open Univ BA 10 Nottm Trent Univ PGCE 11. St Jo Coll Nottm MA 16. **d** 16 **p** 17. C Mulbarton w Bracon Ash, Hethel and Flordon *Nor* from 16. *4 Minnow Way, Mulbarton, Norwich NR14 8FP* M: 07866-691296 E: rev.north@btinternet.com

NORTH, Christopher David. b 69. Trin Coll Bris BA 01. **d** 01 **p** 02. C Bathampton w Claverton *B & W* 01–05; P-in-c Chilcompton w Downside and Stratton on the Fosse 05–17; RD Midsomer Norton 12–17; Dioc Dir of Ords *Bris* from 17. *Bristol Diocesan Board of Finance, Hillside House, Bristol Parkway North, Newbrick Road, Stoke Gifford, Bristol BS34 8YU* T: 0117-906 0100 E: c.north123@btinternet.com

NORTH, Preb David Roland. b 45. Lich Th Coll 70 Qu Coll Birm 72. **d** 73 **p** 74. C Salesbury *Blackb* 73–76; C Marton 76–79; V Penwortham St Leon 79–87; R Whittington St Jo *Lich* 87–10; P-in-c W Felton 96–10; RD Oswestry 02–09; Chapl Robert Jones/Agnes Hunt Orthopaedic NHS Trust 00–01; Preb Lich Cathl 07–10; rtd 11; PtO *Lich* from 11; *St As* 11–16. *Honeycroft, Daisy Lane, Whittington, Oswestry SY11 4EA* T: (01691) 676130

NORTH, Canon Mark Richard. b 71. St Steph Ho Ox 03. **d** 05 **p** 06. C Sevenoaks St Jo *Roch* 05–09; V Burnham *Chelmsf* 09–18; RD Maldon and Dengie 17–18; P-in-c Brentwood St Thos from 18; Hon Can Chelmsf Cathl from 17. *The Vicarage, 91 Queens Road, Brentwood CM14 4EY* M: 07776-231681 E: frmarknorth@btinternet.com

NORTH, Michael Henry. b 50. SWMTC 11. **d** 13. NSM Stokenham, Slapton, Charleton w Buckland etc *Ex* 13–17; NSM Willand, Uffculme, Kentisbeare etc 17–18; P-in-c Meneage *Truro* from 18. *The Rectory, St Martin, Helston TR12 6BU* M: 07590-648121 E: northrnm@btinternet.com

NORTH, Paul Anthony. b 73. All SS Cen for Miss & Min 17. **d** 19. C Wistaston *Ches* from 19. *St Mary the Virgin, Church Lane, Wistaston, Crewe CW2 8HA* E: revd.paul@stmaryswistaston.org.uk

✠**NORTH, The Rt Revd Philip John.** b 66. York Univ BA 88. St Steph Ho Ox BA 91 MA 01. **d** 92 **p** 93 **c** 15. C Sunderland St Mary and St Pet *Dur* 92–96; V Hartlepool H Trin 96–02; AD Hartlepool 00–02; P Admin Shrine of Our Lady of Walsingham 02–08; P-in-c Hempton and Pudding Norton *Nor* 04–07; TR Old St Pancras *Lon* 08–15; Suff Bp Burnley *Blackb* from 15; Can Res Blackb Cathl from 16; P-in-c Burnley St Mark from 19; CMP from 97. *Diocesan Offices, Clayton House, Walker Industrial Estate, Walker Road, Guide, Blackburn BB1 2QE* T: (01254) 503087 M: 07919-180788 E: bishop.burnley@blackburn.anglican.org

NORTH, Preb Robert. b 54. Lon Univ BSc 77. Ripon Coll Cuddesdon 78. **d** 81 **p** 82. C Leominster *Heref* 81–86; TV Heref St Martin w St Fran, Dewsall etc 86–92; P-in-c Heref St Nic 92–97; TR W Heref from 97; Dir of Ords 92–00; Preb Heref Cathl from 94; Dioc Chapl MU from 05. *St Nicholas's Rectory, 76 Breinton Road, Hereford HR4 0JY* T: (01432) 273810

NORTH, William Walter. b 77. Ox Brookes Univ BA 03. St Jo Coll Nottm 07. **d** 09 **p** 10. C N Farnborough *Guildf* 09–13; R Barming *Roch* from 13; RD Malling from 19. *The Rectory, Church Lane, Barming, Maidstone ME16 9HA* T: (01622) 726263 M: 07766-560793 E: revwilnorth@hotmail.co.uk

NORTH WEST EUROPE, Archdeacon of. See VROLIJK, The Ven Paul Dick

NORTHALL, Linda Barbara. See ISIORHO, Linda Barbara

NORTHALL, Ms Sarah Elizabeth. b 69. Ex Univ BA 91 PGCE 92. Ox Min Course 09. **d** 12 **p** 13. C Iffley *Ox* 12–16;

P-in-c Wollescote *Worc* 16–18; P-in-c Pedmore 16–18; V Worc St Wulstan from 19. *St Wulstan's Vicarage, Cranham Drive, Worcester WR4 9PA* E: revsarahnorthall@gmail.com

NORTHAM, Cavell Herbert James Cavell. See CAVELL-NORTHAM, Cavell Herbert James

NORTHAM, Mrs Susan Jillian. b 36. Oak Hill Th Coll 87. **d** 89. NSM Enfield Ch Ch Trent Park *Lon* 89–91; Par Dn 91–94; C 94–97; rtd 97; PtO *Lon* from 02. *5 Beech Hill Avenue, Barnet EN4 0LW* T/F: (020) 8440 2723

NORTHAMPTON, Archdeacon of. See ORMSTON, The Ven Richard Jeremy

NORTHERN, Elaine Joy. See TIPP, Elaine Joy

NORTHEY, Edward Alexander Anson. b 81. Trin Coll Bris BA 08. Wycliffe Hall Ox 09. **d** 11 **p** 12. C Barrow St Mark *Carl* 11–14; Chapl Univ Hosps of Morecambe Bay NHS Foundn Trust 14–17; Chapl RN from 17. *Royal Naval Chaplaincy Service, Mail Point 1-2, Leach Building, Whale Island, Portsmouth PO2 8BY* T: (023) 9262 5055 M: 07952-938797 E: edwardnorthey@gmail.com

NORTHEY (née GANT), Canon Joanna Elizabeth. b 75. Dur Univ BSc 96 Ox Univ PGCE 97. Trin Coll Bris BA 09. **d** 09 **p** 10. C Swindon Ch Ch *Bris* 09–11; C Barrow St Mark *Carl* 11–14; TV S Barrow 14–17; PtO *Portsm* 18; C Warblington w Emsworth from 18; Hon Can Mampong Ghana from 15. *1 Godwin Close, Emsworth PO10 7XT* M: 07807-188912 E: revjonorthey@gmail.com

NORTHFIELD, Stephen Richmond. b 55. Lon Univ BSc 77 Southn Univ BTh 84. Sarum & Wells Th Coll 79. **d** 82 **p** 83. C Colchester St Jas, All SS, St Nic and St Runwald *Chelmsf* 82–85; C Chelmsf All SS 85–89; V Ramsey w Lt Oakley and Wrabness 89–95; V Hatfield Peverel w Ulting from 95. *The Vicarage, Church Road, Hatfield Peverel, Chelmsf CM3 2LE* T: (01245) 380958 E: srnorthfield@aol.com

NORTHING, Ross. b 58. St Steph Ho Ox 92. **d** 94 **p** 95. CA from 87; C Up Hatherley *Glouc* 94–98; C Cheltenham St Steph 94–95; C Cheltenham Em w St Steph 95–98; V Stony Stratford *Ox* 98–11; R Calverton 98–11; R Stony Stratford w Calverton from 12. *St Mary and St Giles Vicarage, 14 Willow Lane, Stony Stratford, Milton Keynes MK11 1FG* T: (01908) 562148 F: 565132 E: r.northing@btinternet.com

NORTHOLT, Archdeacon of. See GREEN, The Ven Duncan Jamie

NORTHOVER, Kevin Charles. b 57. Coll of Resurr Mirfield 89. **d** 91 **p** 92. C Kingston upon Hull St Alb *York* 91–94; V Moorends *Sheff* 94–00; R Guernsey St Michel du Valle *Win* 00–16; Vice-Dean Guernsey 07–13; Sen Vice-Dean 13–16; Chapl HM Pris Guernsey 00–16; rtd 16; CMP 99–09. *Ker Maria, 73 River Holme View, Brockholes, Holmfirth HD9 7BP* E: revkevnorthover@gmail.com

NORTHUMBERLAND, Archdeacon of. See WROE, The Ven Mark

NORTON, Anthony Bernard. b 40. Man Univ BA 62. Linc Th Coll 63. **d** 65 **p** 66. C Westbury-on-Trym H Trin *Bris* 65–68; C Bris St Agnes w St Simon 68–70; P-in-c Bris St Werburgh 70–72; TV Bris St Agnes and St Simon w St Werburgh 72–77; V Lakenham St Alb *Nor* 77–85; TV Trunch 85–93; TV Halesworth w Linstead, Chediston, Holton etc *St E* 93–99; TV Blyth Valley 99–05; RD Halesworth 98–01; rtd 05; PtO *St E* 06–08; P-in-c Heveningham 12–16. *6 Bramblewood Way, Halesworth IP19 8JT* T: (01986) 875374 E: anthonynorton@btinternet.com

NORTON, Benjamin James. b 80. Hull Univ BTh 05 Nottm Univ MTh 13. St Jo Coll Nottm 06. **d** 07 **p** 08. C Bridlington Em *York* 07–12; C Marton-in-Cleveland 12–15; C Wawne 15–18; C Sutton Park and Wawne from 18. *1 Richmond Lane, Kingswood, Hull HU7 3AE* M: 07780-606314 E: thepartycanstart@yahoo.co.uk

NORTON, Howard John. b 41. Fitzw Coll Cam BA 64 MA 68. S'wark Ord Course 78 St Jo Coll Nottm 79. **d** 80 **p** 81. C Sutton Ch Ch *S'wark* 80–82; C Morden 82–84; V Motspur Park 84–88; PtO *Chich* from 03. *Rye View, The Strand, Winchelsea TN36 4JY* T: (01797) 226524 E: howard@ryeview.net

NORTON, Michael Clive Harcourt. b 34. Selw Coll Cam BA 58 MA 60 Union Th Sem (NY) STM 69 Univ of NSW MCom 81 MACE 84. Wells Th Coll 56 Bossey Ecum Inst Geneva 57. **d** 58 **p** 59. C Gt Ilford St Jo *Chelmsf* 58–62; NSW Sec Aus Coun Chs Australia 62–68; C Manhattan St Steph USA 68–69; C-in-c Mortdale Australia 69–77; R Mortdale 77–79; Assoc Chapl and Hd RS Cranbrook Sch Sydney 79–85; R Hunter's Hill 85–00; rtd 00. *7 Dulwich Road, Chatswood NSW 2067, Australia* T: (0061) (2) 9411 8606 F: 9410 2069 M: 417-041779 E: chnorton@bigpond.com

NORTON, Michael James Murfin. b 42. Lich Th Coll 66. **d** 67 **p** 68. C W Bromwich St Fran *Lich* 67–70; C Wellington Ch Ch 70–72; C Norwood All SS *Cant* 72–76; V Elstow *St Alb* 76–82; Asst Chapl HM Pris Wakef 82–83; Chapl

HM Pris Camp Hill 83–86; Parkhurst 86-88; Win 88–93; V Somborne w Ashley *Win* 93–03; rtd 03; PtO *Win* from 17. *20 Cloverbank, Kings Worthy, Winchester SO23 7TP* T: (01962) 621621 E: mandjnorton@gmail.com

NORTON, Paul James. b 55. Oak Hill Th Coll BA 86. **d** 86 **p** 87. C Luton St Fran *St Alb* 86–89; C Bedworth *Cov* 89–95; TV Hitchin *St Alb* 95–02; V Portsdown *Portsm* 03–07; rtd 07; PtO *Portsm* from 11. *23 Oxford Road, Southsea PO5 1NP*

NORTON, Canon Peter Eric Pepler. b 38. TCD BA 61 G&C Coll Cam PhD 64. Cranmer Hall Dur 78. **d** 80 **p** 81. C Ulverston St Mary w H Trin *Carl* 80–83; P-in-c Warcop, Musgrave, Soulby and Crosby Garrett 83–84; R 84–90; OCM 83–90; V Appleby and R Ormside *Carl* 90–04; P-in-c Kirkby Thore w Temple Sowerby and Newbiggin 01–04; RD Appleby and Hon Can Carl Cathl 00–04; rtd 04; PtO *Nor* 05–08. *Ard na Cree, Church Hill, Wicklow, Co Wicklow, Republic of Ireland* T: (00353) (404) 62648 M: 07802-334575 E: pepnorton@gmail.com

NORTON, Sam Charles. b 70. Trin Coll Ox BA 92 MA 99 Heythrop Coll Lon MA 00. Westcott Ho Cam 97. **d** 99 **p** 00. C Stepney St Dunstan and All SS *Lon* 99–02; R W w E Mersea *Chelmsf* 03–10; P-in-c Peldon w Gt and Lt Wigborough 03–10; R W w E Mersea, Peldon, Gt and Lt Wigborough 10–18; C Fingringhoe w E Donyland and Abberton etc 15–18; V Parkend and Viney Hill *Glouc* from 18; Assoc Dioc Dir of Ords and Voc Adv from 18. *The Vicarage, Lower Road, Yorkley, Lydney GL15 4TN* M: 07771-349319 E: revsamnorton@gmail.com

NORTON (née FISHER), Mrs Susan Alexandra. b 54. Man Univ BA 75 Hughes Hall Cam PGCE 76. NEOC 01. **d** 04 **p** 05. NSM York St Olave w St Giles and York St Helen w St Martin 04–09. *21 Wentworth Road, York YO24 1DG* T: (01904) 634911 E: e.norton@tinyworld.co.uk

NORWICH, Archdeacon of. *See* HUTCHINSON, The Ven Karen Elizabeth

NORWICH, Bishop of. *See* USHER, The Rt Revd Graham Barham

NORWICH, Dean of. *See* HEDGES, The Very Revd Jane Barbara

NORWOOD, Andrew David. b 65. Lon Bible Coll BA 91. Cranmer Hall Dur 92. **d** 94 **p** 95. C Headingley *Ripon* 94–97; C Handsworth St Mary *Birm* 97–00; PtO *Lon* 01–02; Chapl Univ of the Arts 02–12; PtO *S'wark* 06–13; *Lon* 12–17; NSM Pimlico St Mary Bourne Street from 17; Chapl Univ Coll 18. *30 Bourne Street, London SW1W 8JJ* M: 07411-737224 E: adn272@yahoo.co.uk

NORWOOD, David John. b 40. SS Paul & Mary Coll Cheltenham BEd 82. Linc Th Coll 65. **d** 68 **p** 69. C Hitchin St Mary *St Alb* 68–71; P-in-c Luanshya Zambia 72–76; C Littlehampton St Jas *Chich* 76–77; P-in-c Chacewater *Truro* 77–79; Chapl R Cornwall Hosp Treliske 77–79; Hd RE Red Maids Sch Bris 82–85; Appeals Organiser Children's Soc 86–94; P-in-c Clarkston *Glas* 94–96; R 96–99; R Dalbeattie 99–05; rtd 05; PtO *St D* 13. *Dove Cottage, Wellfield Terrace, Ferryside SA17 5SD* T: (01267) 267125 E: norwood794@btinternet.com

NORWOOD, Paul James. b 71. **d** 08 **p** 09. OLM S Lynn *Nor* 08–19; OLM Hempton and Pudding Norton from 19. *46 Tennyson Avenue, King's Lynn PE30 2QJ* T: (01553) 777455 M: 07720-806318

NORWOOD, Canon Philip Geoffrey Frank. b 39. Em Coll Cam BA 62 MA 66. Cuddesdon Coll 63. **d** 65 **p** 66. C New Addington *Cant* 65–69; Abp's Dom Chapl 69–72; V Hollingbourne 72–78; P-in-c Wormshill and Huckinge 74–78; V St Laur in Thanet *Cant* 78–88; RD Thanet 86–88; V Spalding St Mary and St Nic *Linc* 88–98; RD Elloe W 96–98; R Blakeney w Cley, Wiveton, Glandford etc *Nor* 98–05; RD Holt 02–05; Hon Can Nor Cathl 03–05; rtd 05; PtO *Leic* from 14. *30 Home Close Road, Houghton-on-the-Hill, Leicester LE7 9GT* T: 0116-241 0255 E: pandanorwood@hotmail.com

NOTHHELFER-BATTEN, Sibylle Eva. *See* BATTEN, Sibylle

NOTT, Canon George Thomas Michael. b 34. Ex Coll Ox BA 58 MA 62 Birm Univ MEd 88 Cov Univ PhD 95. Coll of Resurr Mirfield. **d** 60 **p** 61. C Solihull *Birm* 60–69; Chapl K Sch Worc and Min Can Worc Cathl 69–77; P-in-c Worc St Nic and Children's Officer 77–87; P-in-c Worc St Andr and All SS w St Helen 82–84; Droitwich Spa 87–89; V Broadheath, Crown East and Rushwick 89–04; Chapl Worc Coll of HE 89–96; RD Martley and Worc W 95–03; Hon Can Worc Cathl 99–04; P-in-c Worc St Mich 00–01; rtd 04; PtO *Worc* from 06. *17 Wirlpiece Avenue, Worcester WR4 0NF* T: (01905) 729494 E: mnott17@btinternet.com

NOTT, Philip James. b 69. Nottm Trent Univ BA 92. Ridley Hall Cam 95. **d** 98 **p** 99. C Kersal Moor *Man* 98–01; C Ealing St Mary *Lon* 01–04; Chapl Thames Valley Univ 01–04; P-in-c Broxtowe *S'well* 04–06; P-in-c Easton H Trin w St Gabr and St Lawr and St Jude *Bris* 06–16; Min Inner City Partnership 06–16; V Aston and Nechells *Birm* from 16. *Aston Vicarage, Sycamore Road, Aston, Birmingham B6 5UH* M: 07863-086143 E: revphilipjnott@gmail.com

NOTTINGHAM, Archdeacon of. *See* WILLIAMS, The Ven Philip Andrew

NOVIS, Timothy Wellington George. b 70. Trin Coll Toronto BA 93 MDiv 96. **d** 96 **p** 96. C Guelph St Geo Canada 96–98; R Hornby St Steph 98–05; Chapl Ridley Coll 05–08; Chapl Wellington Coll Berks 08–17; Chapl Marlborough Coll from 17. *Marlborough College, Marlborough SN8 1PA* T: (01672) 892200 E: twgn@marlboroughcollege.org

NOWELL, Canon John David. b 44. AKC 67. **d** 68 **p** 69. C Lindley *Wakef* 68–70; C Lightcliffe 70–72; V Wyke *Bradf* 72–80; V Silsden 80–92; V Baildon 92–14; *Leeds* 14; rtd 14; Hon Can Bradf Cathl 00–14; PtO *Leeds* from 17. *Fairview, Carlisle Road, Pudsey LS28 8LW* E: john@johnnowell.com

NOWÉN, Lars Fredrik. b 71. Summit Pacific Coll BC BTh 93 Regent Coll Vancouver MCS 98. **d** 98 **p** 99. Dn Halifax St Geo Canada 98–99; P-in-c Meadow Lake and Loon Lake 99–04; C Pelton and W Pelton *Dur* 04–07; P-in-c St Bees *Carl* 07–10; Chapl St Bees Sch Cumbria 07–10; Chapl Chelsea Academy 11–12; Sen Chapl Algarve *Eur* 13–15; P-in-c Edmonton Ch the K Canada from 15. *8804 160 St NW, Edmonton AB T5R 2H7, Canada* T: (001) (780) 807 3136 E: revlfnowen@gmail.com

NOY, Rufus William. b 63. St Mich Coll Llan 11. **d** 13 **p** 14. C Blaenavon w Capel Newydd *Mon* 13–16; P-in-c 16–17; P-in-c Upper Torfaen from 17. *The Vicarage, Vicarage Lane, Abersychan, Pontypool NP4 8PX* T: (01495) 524599 E: reverend.noy@gmail.com

NOYCE, Colin Martley. b 45. Brasted Th Coll 73 Ridley Hall Cam 74. **d** 76 **p** 77. C Cambridge St Jas *Ely* 76–78; Chapl RN 78–82; R Mistley w Manningtree *Chelmsf* 82–86; Miss to Seamen Kenya 86–89; Trinidad and Tobago 89–90; V Four Marks *Win* 90–99; Chapl Pilgrims Hospices E Kent 99–01; Chapl and Dir Ch Ch and Ras Morbat Clinics Yemen 01–03; Chapl Limassol St Barn and Miss to Seafarers 03–05; rtd 05; PtO *Chelmsf* 06–09; *Portsm* from 08. *64 Whitwell Road, Southsea PO4 0QS* T: (023) 9275 3517 E: candinoyce@sky.com

NOYCE, Preb Graham Peter. b 62. Bedf Coll Lon BSc 84. Trin Coll Bris BA 92. **d** 92 **p** 93. C Sketty *S & B* 92–94; C Swansea St Jas 94–96; C Kensal Rise St Mark and St Martin *Lon* 96–04; TV 04–11; V Kensal Rise St Martin from 11; AD Brent 13–18; Preb St Paul's Cathl from 17. *26 Ashburnham Road, London NW10 5SD* T: (020) 8960 6211 M: 07515-702862 E: graham@noycefamily.co.uk

NOYES, Gary Robert. b 50. Ripon Coll Cuddesdon. **d** 14 **p** 14. C Ipsley *Worc* 14–15; P-in-c Abberton, The Flyfords, Naunton Beauchamp etc from 15; P-in-c Peopleton and White Ladies Aston w Churchill etc from 15; C Fladbury, Hill and Moor, Wyre Piddle etc from 15; C Stoulton w Drake's Broughton and Pirton etc from 17. *The Rectory, Peopleton, Pershore WR10 2EE* T: (01905) 841563 E: granoyes@gmail.com

NSENGA-NGOY, Canon Lusa. b 77. Cranmer Hall Dur. **d** 08 **p** 09. C Staplehurst *Cant* 08–12; V Gravesend St Aid *Roch* 12–17; Black, Asian and Minority Ethnic Miss and Min Enabler *Leic* from 17; Hon Can Leic Cathl from 17. *St Martin's House, 7 Peacock Lane, Leicester LE1 5PZ* T: 0116-261 5200 E: lusansenga@gmail.com

✠**NTAHOTURI, The Most Revd Bernard.** b 48. St Jo Coll Cam MA. Bp Tucker Coll Mukono 68. **d** 73 **c** 97. Burundi 73–17; Bp Matana 97–17; Abp Burundi 05–16; Dir Angl Cen Rome 17–18. *Address temp unknown*

NTEGE, Nathan Kasolo. b 59. **d** 87 **p** 89. C St Paul's Cathl Namirembe Uganda 87–91; Bp Tucker Coll Mukono 91–94; V Luzira and Kabowa 94–96; PtO *S'wark* 97–02; P-in-c Thornton Heath St Jude w St Aid 02–07; V from 07. *St Jude's Vicarage, 11 Dunheved Road North, Thornton Heath CR7 6AH* T: (020) 8665 5564 M: 07904-197329

NTOYIMONDO, Samuel. b 54. All Nations Chr Coll BA 02 Wolv Univ BA 05 Qu Foundn for Ecum Th Educn MA 11. Butare Th Sch Rwanda 80. **d** 84 **p** 87. Pastor Mutunda Rwanda 84–87; Pastor Butare 87–92; Dioc Sec Kigeme 92–94; Germany 96–99; PtO *Birm* 08–11; Chapl HM Pris Wellingborough 11–12; Chapl HM Pris Nottm 13–15; Chapl HM Pris Stocken 13–15; Chapl HM YOI Glen Parva 15–17; Chapl HM Pris Swinfen Hall from 17. *HM Prison Swinfen Hall, Swinfen, Lichfield WS14 9QS* T: (01543) 484000 E: samuel.ntoyimondo@justice.gov.uk

NUGENT, Canon Alan Hubert. b 42. Dur Univ BA 65 MA 78. Wycliffe Hall Ox 65 United Th Coll Bangalore 66. **d** 67 **p** 68. C Mossley Hill St Matt and St Jas *Liv* 67–71; C Bridgnorth St Mary *Heref* 71–72; Chapl Dur Univ 72–78; P-in-c Bishopwearmouth Ch Ch 78–85; P-in-c Brancepeth 85–94;

Dioc Dir of Educn 85–97; Hon Can Dur Cathl 86–97; Dir of Miss and Tr Development Forum *Linc* 97–03; Can and Preb Linc Cathl 98–03; Can Res and Subdean Linc Cathl 03–11; rtd 11; PtO *Linc* from 17. *2 The Link, Wellingore, Lincoln LN5 0BJ*

NUGENT, David Richard. b 54. MInstPS 84 Liv Poly BA 87. Oak Hill Th Coll BA 95. **d** 95 **p** 96. C Birkenhead St Jas w St Bede *Ches* 95–99; V Blundellsands St Mich *Liv* 99–02; Asst Chapl Wirral and W Cheshire Community NHS Trust 02–03; Asst Chapl Cheshire and Wirral Partnership NHS Foundn Trust 03–16; P-in-c Gt Saughall *Ches* 13–16; rtd 16; PtO *Ches* from 18. *92 Easton Road, Wirral CH62 1DS* E: david.jan.nugent@gmail.com

NUGENT, Mary Patricia. *See* JEPP, Mary Patricia

NUNN, Ms Alice Candida. b 52. Ripon Coll Cuddesdon 95. **d** 97 **p** 98. C Margate St Jo *Cant* 97–01; V Winterton Gp *Linc* from 01. *The Vicarage, High Street, Winterton, Scunthorpe DN15 9PU* T: (01724) 732262

NUNN, The Very Revd Andrew Peter. b 57. Leic Poly BA 79 Leeds Univ BA 82. Coll of Resurr Mirfield 80. **d** 83 **p** 84. C Manston *Ripon* 83–87; C Leeds Richmond Hill 87–91; Chapl Agnes Stewart C of E High Sch Leeds 87–95; V Leeds Richmond Hill *Ripon* 91–95; Personal Asst to Bp S'wark 95–99; Hon PV S'wark Cathl 95–99; Sub-Dean, Prec and Can Res S'wark Cathl 99–12; Dean S'wark from 12; Dioc Warden of Readers from 01. *51 Bankside, London SE1 9JE* T: (020) 7928 3336 M: 07961-332051 E: andrew.nunn@southwark.anglican.org

NUNN, Mrs Christine Jane. b 47. **d** 05 **p** 06. OLM Kesgrave *St E* 05–13; NSM 13–17; rtd 17; PtO *St E* from 17. *37 Bracken Avenue, Kesgrave, Ipswich IP5 2PP* T: (01473) 622363

NUNN, Peter Rawling. b 51. St Cath Coll Ox BA 73 Sheff Univ MSc 74. Oak Hill Th Coll BA 85. **d** 85 **p** 86. C Bispham *Blackb* 85–87; C-in-c Anchorsholme 87–89; V 89–08; P-in-c Preston Risen Lord 08–17; rtd 17; PtO *Blackb* from 17. *13 Meadows Avenue, Thornton-Cleveleys FY5 2TN* E: peter.r.nunn51@gmail.com

NUNNERLEY, William John Arthur. b 27. Univ of Wales (Lamp) BA 54. St Chad's Coll Dur. **d** 56 **p** 57. C Tredegar St Geo *Mon* 56–60; Chapl RN 60–81; QHC from 79; R Barnoldby le Beck *Linc* 81–92; R Waltham 81–92; rtd 92; PtO *B & W* 00–14. *Juniper Cottage, 82B Lower Street, Merriott TA16 5NW* T: (01460) 76049

NUNNEY, Sheila Frances. b 49. SRN 74 RSCN 74 SCM 75. Oak Hill Th Coll BA 92. **d** 92 **p** 94. C Swaffham *Nor* 92–96; Chapl Asst Norfolk and Nor Health Care NHS Trust 96–00; Chapl 00–01; Chapl Norfolk Primary Care Trust 01–09; Chapl Norfolk & Waveney Mental Health NHS Foundn Trust 03–09; rtd 09; PtO *Nor* from 09. *9 Coralie Court, Westfield View, Norwich NR4 7FJ* T: (01603) 504655 E: sfn60@btinternet.com

NURSER, Canon John Shelley. b 29. Peterho Cam BA 50 MA 54 PhD 58. Wells Th Coll 58. **d** 58 **p** 59. C Tankersley *Sheff* 58–61; Dean Trin Hall Cam 61–68; Australia 68–74; R Freckenham w Worlington *St E* 74–76; Can Res and Chan Linc Cathl 76–92; Can and Preb Linc Cathl 92–94; P-in-c Shudy Camps *Ely* 92–94; rtd 94; PtO *St E* from 94; *Ely* 00–10. *68 Friars Street, Sudbury CO10 2AG* T: (01787) 378595 E: jsnurser@btinternet.com

NURSEY (née HYLTON), Mrs Jane Lois. b 56. Leeds Univ BA 78. **d** 07 **p** 08. OLM Dereham and Distr *Nor* from 07; Chapl Norfolk and Nor Univ Hosps NHS Foundn Trust from 11. *Chaplaincy Department, Norfolk and Norwich University Hospital, Colney Lane, Norwich NR4 7UY* T: (01603) 287470 E: nursey1@btinternet.com

NUTH, Stephen William. b 55. St Jo Coll Nottm 93. **d** 95 **p** 96. C Wadhurst and Stonegate *Chich* 95–99; R Marks Tey and Aldham *Chelmsf* 99–01; PtO *St E* 01–04; P-in-c Woburn w Eversholt, Milton Bryan, Battlesden etc *St Alb* 04–08; V from 08. *The Vicarage, Park Street, Woburn, Milton Keynes MK17 9PG* T: (01525) 290225 E: stephen.nuth@googlemail.com

NUTT, Angela Karen. b 66. Homerton Coll Cam BEd 89. STETS 08. **d** 11 **p** 12. C Totton *Win* 11–15; C Copythorne 11–15; P-in-c Freemantle 15–18; Asst Dioc Dir of Ords and

IME Adv from 18; PtO *Win* from 19. *The Diocesan Office, Old Alresford Place, Old Alresford, Alresford SO24 9DH* T: (01962) 737300 M: 07740-424143 E: revdangi@gmail.com

NUTT, Susan Mary. b 45. **d** 99 **p** 00. OLM Blackbourne *St E* 99–13; NSM 13–15; rtd 15; PtO *St E* from 15; Hon Chapl St Nic Hospice Care Bury St Edmunds from 08. *Portelet, Blacksmith Lane, Barnham, Thetford IP24 2NE* T: (01842) 890409 E: suenutt@hotmail.co.uk

NUTTALL, Michael John Berkeley. b 36. K Coll Lon AKC 60. St Boniface Warminster 61. **d** 61 **p** 62. C Chapel Allerton *Ripon* 61–64; C Stanningley St Thos 64–68; V Leeds Gipton Epiphany 68–76; P-in-c Stainby w Gunby *Linc* 76–83; R N Witham 76–83; R S Witham 76–83; TV Bottesford w Ashby 83–88; I Adare w Kilpeacon and Croom *L & K* 88–94; I Adare and Kilmallock w Kilpeacon, Croom etc 94–01; Chapl Limerick Univ 88–95; Adn Limerick 92–01; rtd 01; PtO *York* 12–17. *29 Dulverton Hall, Esplanade, Scarborough YO11 2AR* T: (01723) 340129 E: adnmichaelnuttall@yahoo.com

NUTTER, Ms Tracy Jane. b 58. NTMTC. **d** 10 **p** 11. NSM Prittlewell St Steph *Chelmsf* 10–14; NSM Rayleigh from 14. *8 Ailsa Road, Westcliff-on-Sea SS0 8BL* T: (01702) 342470 E: t.nutter@virgin.net *or* tracy.nutter@parishofrayleigh.org.uk

NUZUM, Daniel Robert. b 73. TCD BTh 99 UCC PhD 16 RGN 94. **d** 99 **p** 00. C Bandon Union *C, C & R* 99–01; I Templebreedy w Tracton and Nohoval 02–09; Chapl Cork Univ Hosp from 09; Can Cork Cathl *C, C & R* from 14; Can Cloyne Cathl from 14. *Cork University Hospital, Wilton, Cork, Republic of Ireland* T: (00353) (21) 454 6400

NWAEKWE, Augustine Ugochukwu. b 75. Leuven Univ Belgium MA 07. St Paul's Univ Coll Awka Nigeria 95. **d** 98 **p** 00. LtO Dio Mbaise Nigeria 98–04; Asst Chapl Brussels *Eur* 06–13; Chapl Ostend from 13; P-in-c Bruges from 13; P-in-c Knokke from 16. *Torhoutsesteenweg 132, 8200 Sint Andries, Belgium* T: (0032) (47) 320 9763 M: (0032) 48-499 5790 E: stpetersbrugge@skynet.be

NWOGBE, David Nwabueze. *See* PETERSON, David Nwabueze Nwogbe

NWOGU, Okwunna Nketa. b 66. Uyo Univ Nigeria LLB 02 BL 02 Sunderland Univ LLM 12. Trin Coll Umuahia Nigeria 91. **d** 94 **p** 95. Can Aba Cathl Nigeria 02–08; Adn from 08; Chapl Law Sch Enugu 05–06; PtO *Dur* 12–13; NSM The Boldons 13–17; USA from 17. *Address temp unknown* E: revdokwunnanwogu@gmail.com

NYAONGO, Jairo Omondi. b 73. **d** 14 **p** 15. C Mill End and Heronsgate w W Hyde *St Alb* 14–17; V Luton St Aug Limbury from 17. *St Augustine's Vicarage, 215 Icknield Way, Luton LU3 2JR* M: 07763-104640 E: jnyaongo@hotmail.com

NYATSANZA, Petros Hamutendi. b 69. Redcliffe Coll Glouc BA 04. Bp Gaul Th Coll Harare 95. **d** 95 **p** 96. R Greendale St Luke Zimbabwe 95–96; C Highfields St Paul 96–97; R Mufakose St Luke 97–01; PtO *Glouc* 02–04; P-in-c Rounds Green *Birm* 04–08; V Goodmayes All SS *Chelmsf* 08–18; Kenya from 18. *Address temp unknown* E: petrosnyatsanza@yahoo.co.uk

NYE, Canon David Charles. b 39. K Coll Lon BD 65 Glos Univ MA 01. **d** 63 **p** 64. C Charlton Kings St Mary *Glouc* 63–67; C Yeovil St Jo w Preston Plucknett *B & W* 67–70; V Lower Cam *Glouc* 70–74; Min Can Glouc Cathl 74–79; Dir of Ords 74–79; Prin Glouc Th Course 74–79; V Glouc St Mary de Lode and St Nic 74–76; V Maisemore 76–79; Chapl Grenville Coll Bideford 79–81; V Leckhampton SS Phil and Jas w Cheltenham St Jas *Glouc* 81–95; Hon Can Glouc Cathl 88–04; RD Cheltenham 89–95; P-in-c Northleach w Hampnett and Farmington 95–00; P-in-c Cold Aston w Notgrove and Turkdean 95–00; R Northleach w Hampnett and Farmington etc 00–04; RD Northleach 99–04; rtd 04. *3 Blackberry Field, Prestbury, Cheltenham GL52 5LT* T: (01242) 268964 E: dcnye@btinternet.com

NYIRONGO, David. b 79. Wycliffe Hall Ox. **d** 11 **p** 12. C Penketh *Liv* 11–14; C Warrington W 14–15; TV Pontypridd *Llan* 15–18; TV Tolworth, Hook and Surbiton *S'wark* from 18. *Address withheld by request* E: nyirongodavy@gmail.com

O

OADES, Michael Anthony John. b 45. Brasted Th Coll 69 Sarum & Wells Th Coll 71. **d** 73 **p** 74. C Eltham Park St Luke *S'wark* 73–78; C Coulsdon St Andr 78–81; P-in-c Merton St Jas 81–86; V 86–87; V Benhilton 87–10; rtd 10; PtO *Truro* from 14. *Cranleigh, Penbothidno, Constantine, Falmouth TR11 5AU* T: (01326) 341304 E: michaelandsylvia@btinternet.com

OAKDEN, David Ian. b 60. **d** 10 **p** 11. OLM Shere, Albury and Chilworth *Guildf* from 10. *102 New Road, Chilworth, Guildford GU4 8LU* T: (01483) 578230 E: david.oakden@yahoo.co.uk

OAKE, Canon Barry Richard. b 47. MRICS 71. Ripon Coll Cuddesdon 83. **d** 85 **p** 86. C Wantage *Ox* 85–88; C Warlingham w Chelsham and Farleigh *S'wark* 88–91; R N w S Wootton *Nor* 91–05; R Thorpe St Andr 05–15; rtd 15; V Nor St Helen 15–18; Chapl Gt Hosp Nor 15–18; Chapl among Deaf and Hearing-Impaired People *Nor* 01–18; Hon Can Nor Cathl 07–18; PtO from 19. *2A Cliff Road, Cromer NR27 0BU* T: (01263) 514192 E: barryoake@gmail.com

OAKES, Graham. b 42. Chich Th Coll 68. **d** 70 **p** 71. C Hulme Ascension *Man* 70–74; C Clifton All SS w Tyndalls Park *Bris* 74–76; P-in-c Chadderton St Mark *Man* 76–78; V 78–82; V King Cross *Wakef* 82–95; R Bath H Trin *B & W* 95–07; Chapl R United Hosp Bath NHS Trust 99–07; rtd 07; PtO *Worc* from 13. *St Christophers, Newland, Malvern WR13 5AX* T: (01684) 576654 E: oakes551@btinternet.com

OAKES, Miss Jennifer May. b 43. Trin Coll Bris 78. **dss** 82 **d** 87 **p** 94. Wilnecote *Lich* 82–85; Stoneydelph St Martin CD 82–85; Bentley 85–89; Par Dn 87–89; Par Dn Hixon w Stowe-by-Chartley 89–94; C 94–98; Par Dn Fradswell, Gayton, Milwich and Weston 93–94; C 94–98; P-in-c Standon and Cotes Heath 98–00; rtd 03; Hon C Alfrick, Lulsley, Suckley, Leigh and Bransford *Worc* 03–04; PtO *Lich* 05–17. *Willow Rise, Ashbourne Road, Whiston, Stoke-on-Trent ST10 2JE* T: (01538) 260013

OAKES, Canon Jeremy Charles. b 51. ACA 75 FCA 81. Westcott Ho Cam 75. **d** 78 **p** 79. C Evington *Leic* 78–81; C Ringwood *Win* 81–84; P-in-c Thurnby Lodge *Leic* 84–89; TV Oakdale Sarum 89–95; P-in-c Canford Cliffs and Sandbanks 95–03; V 03–14; rtd 14; Can and Preb Sarum Cathl from 03; PtO from 16. *5 Townsend Road, Corfe Castle, Wareham BH20 5ET* T: (01929) 480181 E: oakesjeremyc@gmail.com

OAKES, John Cyril. b 49. AKC 71. St Aug Coll Cant 71. **d** 72 **p** 73. C Broseley w Benthall *Heref* 72–76; C Cannock *Lich* 76–79; TV 79–83; V Rough Hills 83–09; P-in-c Wolverhampton St Steph 94–09; rtd 09; PtO *Lich* from 09; *Worc* from 10. *Glendower, Bull Street, Gornal Wood, Dudley DY3 2NQ* T: (01384) 232097 M: 07821-199122 E: classfortyseven@hotmail.co.uk

OAKES, Canon Leslie John. b 28. AKC 53. **d** 54 **p** 55. C Bedford Leigh *Man* 54–58; C Walsall St Matt *Lich* 58–60; Chapl Selly Oak Hosp Birm 60–64; V Longbridge *Birm* 64–93; Hon Can Birm Cathl 84–93; rtd 93; PtO *Birm* 93–18. *108 Hole Lane, Birmingham B31 2DF* T: 0121-476 8514 E: joakes123@talktalk.net

OAKES, Robert. b 47. Chan Sch Truro 79. **d** 82 **p** 83. NSM Probus, Ladock and Grampound w Creed and St Erme *Truro* 82–84; TV Bodmin w Lanhydrock and Lanivet 85–88; R S Hill w Callington 88–03; RD E Wivelshire 95–00; Bp's Adv on Healing Min 98–03; Hon Can Truro Cathl 01–03; C Calstock 06–14; C St Dominic, Landulph and St Mellion w Pillaton 12–14; Chapl Cornwall and Is of Scilly Primary Care Trust 09–13; rtd 14; PtO *Truro* from 14. *Kernick House, 11 Trelawney Rise, Callington PL17 7PT* T: (01579) 389109 M: 07890-099248 E: oakesrobert@hotmail.co.uk

OAKES, Simon Paul. b 77. SS Coll Cam BA 00 MA 03 PhD 06. Coll of Resurr Mirfield 11. **d** 13 **p** 14. C Walsall St Gabr Fulbrook *Lich* 13–16; V Holbrooks *Cov* from 16. *St Luke's Vicarage, Rotherham Road, Coventry CV6 4FE* T: (024) 7668 8604 E: frsimonoakes@outlook.com

OAKEY-JONES, Ms Angela Jean. b 71. Keele Univ BA 93. NTMTC BA 08. **d** 08 **p** 09. C Rushmere *St E* 08–11; P-in-c Ipswich All Hallows 11–16; R Cheriton w Newington *Cant* 16–19; Spiritual Care Worker St Eliz Hospice Ipswich from 19. *18 Chatsworth Drive, Rushmere St Andrew, Ipswich IP4 5XA* T: (01473) 325828 M: 07930-141091 E: revangelaoj@gmail.com

OAKHAM, Archdeacon of. *See* STEELE, The Ven Gordon John

OAKLAND, Mrs Sarah Marie. b 54. UEA BEd 85. EAMTC 99. **d** 02 **p** 03. C Diss *Nor* 02–06; V Chessington *Guildf* 06–11; R E w W Harling, Bridgham w Roudham, Larling etc *Nor*

11–15; rtd 15. *Sea Holly, Fearns Close, Cromer NR27 0DZ* E: sarahoakland@hotmail.com

OAKLEY, Hilary Robert Mark. b 53. Univ of Wales (Ban) BSc 75 Ox Univ BA 78 MA 81 MCIPD 91. Ripon Coll Cuddesdon 76. **d** 79 **p** 80. C Birm St Pet 79–82; C Cambridge Gt St Mary w St Mich *Ely* 82–86; Chapl Girton Coll Cam 82–86; Chapl Zürich w St Gallen and Winterthur *Eur* 86–88; NSM Lon 88–92; PtO *St Alb* 92–13; NSM Hitchin and St Paul's Walden 13–19; rtd 19. *55 Southdown Road, Harpenden AL5 1PQ* T: (01582) 761514 E: hilaryoakley@hotmail.com

OAKLEY, James Robert. b 75. St Edm Hall Ox BA 96. Oak Hill Th Coll BA 05. **d** 05 **p** 06. C Audley *Lich* 05–09; P-in-c Kemsing and Woodlands *Roch* from 09. *Sunnybank Cottage, West End, Kemsing, Sevenoaks TN15 6PX* T: (01732) 762556 E: ccd@c3.oakleys.org

OAKLEY, Jeremy Steven. b 52. Birm Univ BA 99. Trin Coll Bris 95. **d** 97 **p** 98. C Walsall *Lich* 97–02; V Penn Fields 02–16; P-in-c W Bromwich St Jas w St Paul 16–18; rtd 18. *Guildwood, Old Weston Road, Bishops Wood, Stafford ST19 9AG*

OAKLEY, Mark David. b 68. K Coll Lon BD 90 AKC 90. St Steph Ho Ox 90. **d** 93 **p** 94. C St John's Wood *Lon* 93–96; Bp's Chapl 96–00; P-in-c Covent Garden St Paul 00–03; R 03–05; AD Westmr St Marg 04–05; Chapl RADA 03–05; Chapl Copenhagen and Adn Germany and N Eur 05–08; P-in-c Grosvenor Chpl *Lon* 08–10; Can Res St Paul's Cathl 10–18; Fell and Dean St Jo Coll Cam from 18; Dep P in O from 96; PtO *Eur* from 18. *St John's College, Cambridge CB2 1TP* T: (01223) 338600 E: mdo26@camac.uk

OAKLEY, Robert Paul. b 51. Sheff Univ BScTech 72 PGCE 74 Open Univ MA(Theol) 97. St Jo Coll Nottm 87. **d** 89 **p** 90. C Heatherlands St Jo *Sarum* 89–92; V Burton All SS w Ch Ch *Lich* 92–99; V Gt Wyrley 99–07; Tutor Wilson Carlile Coll of Evang 07–12; V Totley *Sheff* 12–16; rtd 16. *34 James Clarke Road, Willington, Derby DE65 6RD* M: 07971-325222

OAKLEY, Stephen Alfred. b 66. **d** 13 **p** 14. NSM Lundwood *Wakef* 13–14; *Leeds* 14–19; NSM Cen Barnsley from 19. *9 Parkland View, Barnsley S71 5LG* T: (01226) 781797 E: stephenoakley66@googlemail.com

OAKLEY, Susan Mary. *See* HENWOOD, Susan Mary

OAKLEY, Timothy Crispin. b 45. Qu Coll Cam BA 66 MA 70 Bris Univ PGCE 69. St Jo Coll Nottm 73. **d** 76 **p** 77. C Bromley Common St Aug *Roch* 76–79; C Fairfield *Liv* 79–81; CMS Kenya 82–90; P-in-c Beaford, Roborough and St Giles in the Wood *Ex* 91–96; Chapl St Andr Sch Turi Kenya 96–98; V Woodford Halse w Eydon *Pet* 99–10; RD Brackley 03–05; rtd 10; PtO *Heref* from 12. *Sunny Bank, Clive Avenue, Church Stretton SY6 7BL* T: (01694) 724225 E: tim@taitaoakleys.co.uk

OATES, Alan. b 32. S'wark Ord Course 79. **d** 80 **p** 81. NSM Rayleigh *Chelmsf* 80–87; TV Jarrow *Dur* 87–92; P-in-c Stella 92–95; R 95–97; rtd 97; PtO *Dur* 98–14; from 00. *1 The Haven, North Shields NE29 6YH* T: 0191-258 6984

OATES, Alexander John. b 38. Clifton Th Coll 63. **d** 67 **p** 68. C Brixton Hill St Sav *S'wark* 67–68; C Westcombe Park St Geo 68–71; C Stechford *Birm* 71–74; R Greenhithe St Mary *Roch* 74–77; Soc worker 77–02; rtd 03. *1 Fairlight Villas, North Road, Havering-atte-Bower, Romford RM4 1PP* T: (01708) 760252

OATES, Douglas. b 39. Bolton Coll of Educn CertEd 74 Ches Coll of HE BTh 97. NOC 94. **d** 97 **p** 98. NSM Balderstone *Man* 97–01; NSM Oldham St Barn 01–06; P-in-c 03–06; P-in-c Waterhead 05–06; TV Medlock Head 06–09; rtd 09; PtO *Man* from 09. *43 Devonport Crescent, Royton, Oldham OL2 6JX* T: (01706) 849929 M: 07743-993381

OATES, Canon John. b 30. Kelham Th Coll 53. **d** 57 **p** 58. C Hackney Wick St Mary of Eton w St Aug *Lon* 57–60; Development Officer C of E Youth Coun 60–64; Sec C of E Coun Commonwealth Settlement 64–65; Gen Sec 65–72; Sec C of E Cttee on Migration & Internat Affairs 68–72; Hon Can Bunbury from 69; V Richmond St Mary w St Matthias *S'wark* 70–79; P-in-c Richmond St Jo 76–79; V Richmond St Mary w St Matthias and St Jo 79–84; RD Richmond and Barnes 79–84; R St Bride Fleet Street w Bridewell etc *Lon* 84–00; AD The City 97–00; Preb St Paul's Cathl 97–00; rtd 00; PtO *S'wark* 03–18; *Lon* from 01. *27 York Court, Albany Park Road, Kingston upon Thames KT2 5ST* E: john.oates@blueyonder.co.uk

OATES, Michael Graham. b 62. Leic Poly BSc 84. Aston Tr Scheme 87 Cranmer Hall Dur 89. **d** 92 **p** 93. C Enfield St Andr *Lon* 92–96; TV N Poole Ecum Team *Sarum* 96–07; PtO 07–08; Chapl Dorset HealthCare University NHS Foundn Trust from 14. *51 Ringwood Road, Poole BH14 0RE* T: (01202) 731389 E: oates@madasafish.com *or* michael.oates@dhuft.nhs.uk

OATES (*née* **ADAMS**), **Canon Ruth.** b 47. Bris Univ BSc 69. SEITE 97. **d** 00 **p** 01. C Rainham *Roch* 00–03; V Gravesend St Mary 03–13; RD Gravesend 09–13; P-in-c Ash 13–17; P-in-c Ridley 13–17; Hon Can Roch Cathl 11–17; rtd 17; PtO *Ex* from 18. *19 Fluder Crescent, Kingskerswell, Newton Abbot TQ12 5JE*

OATRIDGE, Andrew Philip. b 77. Sheff Univ MMath 00. Oak Hill Th Coll MTh 10. **d** 10 **p** 11. C Chapeltown *Sheff* 10–13; Crosslinks Hungary from 13. *Zsigmond király utca 17, 2051 Biatorbágy, Hungary* E: andyzsofi@gmail.com

OBAN, Provost of. *See* CAMPBELL, The Very Revd Margaret Ruth

OBEDOZA, William. b 58. NTMTC 05. **d** 08 **p** 09. C Walthamstow St Sav *Chelmsf* 08–12; V Woodford St Barn from 12. *St Barnabas' Vicarage, 127 Snakes Lane East, Woodford Green IG8 7HX* T: (020) 3659 4023 M: 07916-281227 E: fatherobedoza@gmail.com

O'BENEY, Robin Mervyn. b 35. Ely Th Coll 61. **d** 64 **p** 65. C Liss *Portsm* 64–65; C Portsea St Cuth 65–68; Hon C Wymondham *Nor* 74–76; R Swainsthorpe w Newton Flotman 76–80; NSM Sparkenhoe Deanery *Leic* 87–90; V Billesdon and Skeffington 90–91; rtd 95; PtO *Heref* 10–15. *19 Bridge Street, Kington HR5 3DL* T: (01544) 230416 E: roobeney@gmail.com

OBIN, Raymond Clive. b 63. Girton Coll Cam BA 85 MA 89. Wycliffe Hall Ox BTh 07. **d** 04 **p** 05. NSM Bucklebury w Marlston *Ox* 04–12; NSM Bradfield and Stanford Dingley 04–12; Asst Dir of Ords (Berks) from 12; PtO *Win* from 13; LtO *Ox* from 15. *Solfonn, Enborne Row, Wash Water, Newbury RG20 0LY* T: (01635) 38212 E: raymond@obin.org.uk

OBIORA, Arthur Cuenyem. b 42. **d** 95 **p** 95. NSM Hatcham St Cath *S'wark* 95–12; PtO from 12. *126 Perry Hill, London SE6 4EY* T: (020) 8699 3845

OBORNE, Mrs Martine Amelia. b 57. St Hilda's Coll Ox MA 80. SEITE BA 09. **d** 09 **p** 10. C Islington St Mary *Lon* 09–12; P-in-c Chiswick St Mich 12–15; V from 15. *St Michael's Vicarage, 60 Elmwood Road, London W4 3DZ* T: (020) 8994 3173 M: 07842-199556 E: maoborne@hotmail.com *or* vicar@stmichael-suttoncourt.org.uk

O'BOYLE, Liam Patrick Butler. b 66. Nottm Univ BA 90 MA 98. EMMTC 98. **d** 01 **p** 02. C Cinderhill *S'well* 01–06; TV Clifton 06–10; Dioc Partnerships Officer from 10; C Chilwell from 11; C Lenton Abbey from 11. *23 Fellows Road, Beeston, Nottingham NG9 1AQ* T: 0115-943 1032 E: liam.oboyle@ntlworld.com *or* liam.o'boyle@southwell.anglican.org

O'BRIEN, Andrew Peter. b 81. Jes Coll Cam BA 03. Wycliffe Hall Ox BTh 14. **d** 14 **p** 15. C Wimbledon Park St Luke *S'wark* from 14. *37 Lucien Road, London SW19 8EL*

O'BRIEN, David. b 62. Moorlands Th Coll BA 99. CBDTI 01. **d** 04 **p** 05. C Bispham *Blackb* 04–08; C S Shore H Trin 08–10; P-in-c Shelton and Oxon *Lich* 10–18; V 18–19; Uplands Nursing Home 15–17; V Blackpool St Thos *Blackb* from 19. *St Thomas's Vicarage, 80 Devonshire Road, Blackpool FY3 8AE*

O'BRIEN, Capt David. b 48. Wilson Carlile Coll 87. **d** 16 **p** 17. NSM Upton Ascension *Ches* from 16. *1 Caldy Close, Chester CH2 2BZ* T: (01244) 375782 M: 07828-206090 E: daveobrienca@hotmail.com

O'BRIEN, Mrs Elaine. b 55. CITC 94. **d** 97 **p** 98. Aux Min Killyman *Arm* 97–00; Aux Min Gilnahirk *D & D* 00–06; Bp's C Clogherny w Seskinore and Drumnakilly *Arm* 06–08; R 08–11; I Whitehouse *Conn* from 11. *The Rectory, 283 Shore Road, Newtownabbey BT37 9SR* T: (028) 9036 9955 M: 07703-618119 E: elaineobrien1@btinternet.com

O'BRIEN, George Edward. b 32. Clifton Th Coll 61. **d** 64 **p** 65. C Denton Holme *Carl* 64–68; V Castle Town *Lich* 68–88; Chapl St Geo Hosp Stafford 88–94; Chapl Kingsmead Hosp Stafford 88–94; Chapl Foundation NHS Trust Stafford 94–99; rtd 99; PtO *Lich* 99–17. *Abily, 185 Tixall Road, Stafford ST16 3XJ* T: (01785) 244261 E: georgemary18@tiscali.co.uk

O'BRIEN, Kevin Michael. b 60. Herts Univ BA 82. St Steph Ho Ox BTh 05. **d** 01 **p** 02. C Uppingham w Ayston and Wardley w Belton *Pet* 01–04; Asst Chapl Wellington Coll Berks 04–06; Bp's Chapl and Office Manager *Eur* 06–10; V Burgess Hill St Jo *Chich* from 10; RD Hurst 11–18. *St John's Rectory, 48 Park Road, Burgess Hill RH15 8HG* T: (01444) 232582

O'BRIEN, Thomas Anthony. b 72. Open Univ BSc 09 TCD MSc 10 MTh 18. TCD Div Sch 12. **d** 16 **p** 18. Howth *D & G* 16–18; NSM Holmpatrick w Balbriggan and Kenure from 18. *75 Trimleston, Hamlet Lane, Balbriggan, Co Dublin, Republic of Ireland* (00353) 87-650 2504 E: revtobrien@gmail.com

O'BRIEN, Mary Veronica. *See* GUBBINS, Mary Veronica

O'BRIEN, Shelagh Ann. *See* STACEY, Shelagh Ann

O'CALLAGHAN, Regan Robert Rehe. b 67. Brunel Univ BA 97 K Coll Lon MA 98 Anglia Poly Univ MA 01. Westcott Ho Cam 99. **d** 01 **p** 02. C Whitton St Aug *Lon* 01–03; C St Jo on Bethnal Green 03–04; NSM 04–14; PtO from 14. *Emmanuel Vicarage, Lyncroft Gardens, London NW6 1JU* T: (020) 7419 8384 E: reganocallaghan@googlemail.com

OCHOLA, George Otieno. b 58. Lon Sch of Th BTh 02. St Jo Sch of Miss Kokise. **d** 88 **p** 89. Kenya 88–99; PtO *Lon* 00–08; NSM Watford St Mich *St Alb* 08–10; Chapl W Herts Hosps NHS Trust from 10. *Foundation Trust Office, Watford General Hospital, 60 Vicarage Road, Watford WD18 0HB* T: (01923) 436280 M: 07866-359120 E: georgeochola@hotmail.com

OCKFORD, Paul Philip. b 46. St Chad's Coll Dur BA 67. St Steph Ho Ox 68. **d** 70 **p** 71. C Streatham St Pet *S'wark* 70–74; C Cheam 74–77; P-in-c Eastrington *York* 77–79; TV Howden 80–83; R Sherburn and W and E Heslerton w Yedingham 83–92; V Bampton, Morebath, Clayhanger and Petton *Ex* 92–98; R Goodmanham *York* 98–04; V Market Weighton 98–04; V Sancton 98–04; rtd 04. *78 Wold Road, Pocklington, York YO42 2QG* E: rocktord@msn.com

O'CONNELL, Peter David. b 69. St Edm Hall Ox BA 91 MA 97 Cant Ch Ch Univ BA 12. SEITE 09. **d** 12 **p** 13. C Henfield w Shermanbury and Woodmancote *Chich* 12–16; R Godstone and Blindley Heath *S'wark* from 16. *The Rectory, 17 Ivy Mill Lane, Godstone RH9 8NH* T: (01883) 741945 E: peter.oconnell@cheerful.com

O'CONNELL, William Anthony. b 61. STETS. **d** 10 **p** 11. C Milton *Win* 10–13; P-in-c Lyddington and Wanborough and Bishopstone etc *Bris* from 13. *The Vicarage, 19 Church Road, Wanborough, Swindon SN4 0BZ* T: (01793) 791359 E: villagevicar@hotmail.co.uk

O'CONNOR, Canon Brian Michael McDougal. b 42. St Cath Coll Cam BA 67 MA 69. Cuddesdon Coll 67. **d** 69 **p** 70. C Headington *Ox* 69–71; Sec Dioc Past and Redundant Chs Uses Cttees 72–79; P-in-c Merton 72–76; V Rainham *Roch* 79–97; RD Gillingham 81–88; Hon Can Roch Cathl 89–97; Dean Auckland New Zealand 97–00; Hon Can from 00; PtO *Ox* 00–02 and 04–16; P-in-c Lt Missenden 02–04; rtd 04. *The Lawn, 64 Fore Street, Otterton, Budleigh Salterton EX9 7HB* T: (01395) 488898 M: 07740-702161 E: canonmichaeloc@aol.com

O'CONNOR, Canon Daniel. b 33. Univ Coll Dur BA 54 MA 67 St Andr Univ PhD 81. Cuddesdon Coll 56. **d** 58 **p** 59. C Stockton St Pet *Dur* 58–62; C W Hartlepool St Aid 62–63; Cam Miss to Delhi 63–70; USPG India 70–72; Chapl St Andr Univ *St And* 72–77; R Edin Gd Shep 77–82; Prin Coll of Ascension Selly Oak 82–90; Dir Scottish Chs Ho (Chs Together in Scotland) 90–93; Can Res Wakef Cathl 93–96; Bp's Adv on Inter-Faith Issues 93–96; rtd 96; Hon C Cupar *St And* 12–13; PtO from 13. *15 School Road, Balmullo, St Andrews KY16 0BA* T: (01334) 871326 E: danoconnor@btinternet.com

O'CONNOR, Martin John. b 48. UCD BComm 73. **d** 11 **p** 12. NSM Dublin St Ann and St Steph *D & G* from 11. *137 Braemor Road, Churchtown, Dublin, D14 YE92, Republic of Ireland* T: (00353) (1) 298 8900 M: 87-207 0907 E: m.oconnor91@upcmail.ie

O'CONNOR, Stephen James. b 62. K Coll Lon BSc 93 MSc 01 Lanc Univ PhD 08. Ripon Coll Cuddesdon BA 19. **d** 19. C Walmer and Cornilo *Cant* from 19. *35 Church Path, Deal CT14 9TH* M: 07921-313869 E: sjoconnor@hotmail.co.uk

O'CONNOR, Michael. *See* O'CONNOR, Brian Michael McDougal

ODDY, Joan Winifred. b 34. **d** 97 **p** 98. OLM Kessingland w Gisleham *Nor* 97–99; OLM Kessingland, Gisleham and Rushmere 99–04; rtd 04; PtO *Nor* from 04. *3 The Paddocks, Kessingland, Lowestoft NR33 7SE* T: (01502) 742001

ODDY-BATES, Mrs Julie Louise. b 61. SRN 82 SCM 85. Ridley Hall Cam 04. **d** 06 **p** 07. C Watton w Carbrooke and Ovington *Nor* 06–07; C Ashill, Carbrooke, Ovington and Saham Toney 07–09; P-in-c Gillingham w Geldeston, Stockton, Ellingham etc 09–18; C Loddon, Sisland, Chedgrave, Hardley and Langley 09–16; rtd 18. *Old Chapel House, Priory Lane, Grimoldby, Louth LN11 8SP* E: jlo32@tiscali.co.uk

ODLING-SMEE, George William. b 35. K Coll Dur MB, BS 59 FRCS 68 FRCSI 86. **d** 77 **p** 78. NSM Belfast St Thos *Conn* 77–90; NSM Belfast St Geo 90–02. *The Boathouse, 24 Rossglass Road South, Killough, Downpatrick BT30 7RA* T: (028) 4484 1868 F: 4484 1143 E: wodlingsmee@gmail.com

ODOEMENA, Prince Doms. b 88. Oak Hill Th Coll BA 17. **d** 11 **p** 12. C Walthamstow St Barn and St Jas Gt *Chelmsf* 17–19; C Forest Gate Em w Upton Cross from 19. *10 Masterman House, Elmington Estate, London SE5 7HU* M: 07529-989241 E: princedoms@me.com *or* podoemena@chelmsford.anglican.org

O'DONNELL, Mrs Mollie. b 39. Portsm Poly BA 91. STETS 97. **d** 00 **p** 03. NSM Calbourne w Newtown and Shalfleet *Portsm* 00–09; rtd 09; PtO *Portsm* 09–15. *36 Medina Court, Old Westminster Lane, Newport PO30 5PW*

O'DONNELL, Paula Ella. *See* CHALLEN, Paula Ella

O'DONOGHUE, Mark Ronald. b 69. St Aid Coll Dur BA 91 Solicitor 93. Oak Hill Th Coll BA 04. **d** 04 **p** 05. C St Helen

Bishopsgate w St Andr Undershaft etc *Lon* 04–11; C Kensington St Mary Abbots w Ch Ch and St Phil 11–16; V Kensington Ch Ch from 17; AD Kensington from 16. *20 South End Row, London W8 5BZ* T: (020) 7795 6330 E: mark@christchurchkensington.com

O'DONOGHUE, Mrs Sarah Helen. b 75. Ches Coll of HE BA 96 Liv Hope PGCE 97. St Mellitus Coll 13. **d** 15 **p** 16. C Aughton Ch Ch *Liv* 15–19; V from 19. *22 Long Lane, Aughton, Ormskirk L39 5AT* M: 07847-931323 E: revsarahodonoghue@gmail.com

O'DONOVAN, Canon Oliver Michael Timothy. b 45. Ball Coll Ox BA 68 MA 71 DPhil 75. Wycliffe Hall Ox 68. **d** 72 **p** 73. Tutor Wycliffe Hall Ox 72–77; Prof Systematic Th Wycliffe Coll Toronto 77–82; Regius Prof Moral and Past Th Ox Univ 82–06; Can Res Ch Ch *Ox* 82–06; Prof Chr Ethics Edin Univ 06–12; Hon Prof St Andr Univ *St And* from 13; Can Prov and Can Th York Minster from 15; PtO from 15. *6A Comely Park, Dunfermline KY12 7HU* E: oliver.odonovan@ed.ac.uk

O'DOWD-SMYTH, Christine. CITC. **d** 09 **p** 10. NSM Lismore w Cappoquin, Kilwatermoy, Dungarvan etc *C & O* 09–14; P-in-c Fiddown w Clonegam, Guilcagh and Kilmeaden 14; Dioc Spokesperson for Healing Min from 14. *Eldon, 16 John's Hill, Waterford, Republic of Ireland* T: (00353) (51) 304423 M: 87-293 3461 E: odowdsmythchristine@gmail.com

OEHRING, Alexander James. b 81. Hull Univ BA 02. Cranmer Hall Dur 16. **d** 18 **p** 19. C Walton-on-Thames *Guildf* from 18. *1 Egmont Road, Walton-on-Thames KT12 2NW* M: 07920-098867 E: alexanderoehring@hotmail.com

OEHRING, Anthony Charles. b 56. Sheff City Poly BA 79 CQSW 79 Kent Univ MA 02. Ridley Hall Cam 86. **d** 88 **p** 89. C Gillingham *Sarum* 88–91; TV S Gillingham *Roch* 91–00; P-in-c Faversham *Cant* 00–12; C Preston next Faversham, Goodnestone and Graveney 02–12; P-in-c The Brents and Davington w Oare and Luddenham 03–06; AD Ospringe 02–11; Co-ord Chapl HM Pris E Sutton Park 12–13; Co-ord Chapl HM Pris Blantyre Ho 12–13; Hon Can Cant Cathl 06–13; Managing Chapl HM Pris Ford from 13; PtO *Sarum* from 13. *HM Prison Ford, Ford Road, Ford, Arundel BN18 0BX* T: (01903) 663085 E: anthony.oehring@justice.gov.uk

OEPPEN, Canon John Gerard David. b 44. St D Coll Lamp. **d** 67 **p** 68. C-in-c Cwmmer w Abercregan CD *Llan* 67–70; TV Glyncorrwg w Afan Vale and Cymmer Afan 70–71; C Whitchurch 71–74; V Aberavon H Trin 74–78; V Bargoed and Deri w Brithdir 78–86; R Barry All SS 86–08; Can Llan Cathl 04–08; rtd 08; PtO *Llan* from 08. *6 Heol Fioled, Barry CF63 1HB*

OESTREICHER, Canon Paul. b 31. Univ of NZ BA 53 MA 56 Cov Poly Hon DLitt 91 Sussex Univ Hon LLD 05 Lambeth DD 08 Otago Univ Hon DD 09. Linc Th Coll 56. **d** 59 **p** 60. C Dalston H Trin w St Phil *Lon* 59–61; C S Mymms K Chas 61–68; Asst in Relig Broadcasting BBC 61–64; Assoc Sec Internat Affairs Dept BCC 64–69; V Blackheath Ascension *S'wark* 68–81; Dir of Tr 69–72; Hon Can S'wark Cathl 78–81; Asst Gen Sec BCC 81–86; Can Res Cov Cathl 86–97; Dir of Internat Min 86–97; Humboldt Fell Inst of Th Free Univ of Berlin 92–93; rtd 98; PtO *Cov* 98–10; *Chich* 03–17; Hon Chapl Sussex Univ 04–09. *97 Furze Croft, Furze Hill, Hove BN3 1PE* T: (01273) 728033 E: paul.oestreicher.nz@gmail.com

O'FARRELL, Anne Marie. **d** 08 **p** 09. NSM Dublin Sandford w Milltown *D & G* from 08. *138 Meadow Grove, Dundrum, Dublin 14, Republic of Ireland* T: (00353) (1) 296 6222 E: amofharp@gmail.com

O'FERRALL, Patrick Charles Kenneth. b 34. New Coll Ox BA 58 MA 60. **d** 00 **p** 01. OLM Godalming *Guildf* 00–04; PtO from 04. *Pear Tree House, 66 Firgrove Hill, Farnham GU9 8LW* T: (01252) 724498 E: patrickoferrall@gmail.com

OFFER, The Ven Clifford Jocelyn. b 43. Ex Univ BA 67 FRSA 97. Westcott Ho Cam 67. **d** 69 **p** 70. C Bromley SS Pet and Paul *Roch* 69–74; TV Southampton (City Cen) *Win* 74–83; TR Hitchin *St Alb* 83–94; Adn Nor and Can Res Nor Cathl 94–08; rtd 08; PtO *Heref* from 09. *Chase House, Peterstow, Ross-on-Wye HR9 6JX* T: (01989) 567874

OFFORD, Mrs Judith Anne. b 50. **d** 19. NSM Sudbury w Ballingdon and Brundon *St E* from 19; NSM Sudbury and Chilton from 19. *98 Melford Road, Sudbury CO10 1JY* T: (01787) 315689 E: judithofford@btinternet.com

O'FLAHERTY, Mrs Sheila Mary. b 53. Huddersfield Univ MA 08 Man Univ CertEd 00. SNWTP 11. **d** 13 **p** 14. NSM Heatons *Man* 13–15; NSM Coldhurst and Oldham St Steph 15–18; P-in-c Newton w Flowery Field *Ches* from 18; PtO *Man* from 18. *St Mary's Vicarage, 39 Bradley Green Road, Hyde SK14 4NA* T: 0161-368 1489 M: 07803-084442 E: revsheila@oflaherty.co.uk

OGBEDE, Ms Olufunke Oladunni. b 48. Lon Inst of Educn MA 81. **d** 05 **p** 06. OLM S Lambeth St Anne and All SS *S'wark* 05–13; NSM Stockwell St Andr and St Mich 13–18; PtO from 18. *Flat 11, 2 Allingham Road, London SW4 8EG* M: 07944-424931 E: fundunni@aol.com

OGILVIE, The Ven Gordon. b 42. Glas Univ MA 64 Lon Univ BD 67. ALCD 66. **d** 67 **p** 68. C Ashtead *Guildf* 67–72; V New Barnet St Jas *St Alb* 72–80; Dir Past Studies Wycliffe Hall Ox 80–87; P-in-c Harlow New Town w Lt Parndon *Chelmsf* 87–89; R 89–94; TR Harlow Town Cen w Lt Parndon 94–96; Hon Can Chelmsf Cathl 94–96; Chapl Princess Alexandra Hosp Harlow 88–96; Adn Nottingham *S'well* 96–06; rtd 07; LtO *St And* from 07. *49 Argyle Street, St Andrews KY16 9BX* T: (01334) 470185 E: gordon.ogilvie@virgin.net

OGILVIE, Ian Douglas. b 37. Em Coll Cam BA 59 MA 63. Linc Th Coll 59. **d** 61 **p** 62. C Clapham H Trin *S'wark* 61–63; C Cambridge Gt St Mary w St Mich *Ely* 63–66; Chapl Sevenoaks Sch 66–77; Hon C Sevenoaks St Nic *Roch* 67–77; Chapl Malvern Coll 77–84; Hd Master St Geo Sch Harpenden 84–87; LtO *St Alb* 84–87; Bp's Dom Chapl 87–89; P-in-c Aldenham 87–91; Appeals Dir Mind 89–91; Fund Raising Dir Br Deaf Assn 91–94; NSM Tring *St Alb* 92–94; PtO from 94; Fund Raising Dir R Nat Miss to Deep Sea Fishermen from 94; PtO *Ox* from 11; *Eur* from 17. *The White House, 19 Lower Icknield Way, Marsworth, Tring HP23 4LN* T: (01296) 661479 E: ia.ogilve@gmail.com

OGILVIE, Pamela. b 56. Brunel Univ MA 89 CQSW 82. Qu Coll Birm 01. **d** 03 **p** 04. C Hill *Birm* 03–07; V Billesley Common 07–15; rtd 15; PtO *Birm* from 15; *Lich* from 16. *Address withheld by request* E: pamelaogilvie@outlook.com

OGILVIE THOMPSON, Christopher William. b 58. Witwatersrand Univ BSc 83. Ox Min Course 14. **d** 16 **p** 17. NSM Bentley, Binsted and Froyle *Win* from 16. *Mill Court House, Mill Court, Upper Froyle, Alton GU34 4JF* T: (01420) 23125 M: 07776-178690 E: christopherot@me.com

OGLE, The Very Revd Catherine. b 61. Leeds Univ BA 82 MPhil 85 MA 91 Fitzw Coll Cam BA 87. Westcott Ho Cam 85. **d** 88 **p** 94. C Middleton St Mary *Ripon* 88–91; Relig Progr Ed BBC Radio Leeds 91–95; NSM Leeds St Marg and All Hallows 91–95; P-in-c Woolley *Wakef* 95–01; P-in-c Huddersfield St Pet and All SS 01–03; V Huddersfield St Pet 03–10; RD Huddersfield 09–10; Chapl Huddersfield Univ 03–06; Hon Can Wakef Cathl 08–10; Dean Birm 10–17; Dean Win from 17. *The Deanery, The Close, Winchester SO23 9LS* E: dean@winchester-cathedral.org.uk

OGLESBY, Ms Elizabeth Jane. b 73. Roehampton Inst BA 95 Man Univ MPhil 98. Westcott Ho Cam 00. **d** 03 **p** 04. C S Dulwich St Steph *S'wark* 03–06; P-in-c Camberwell St Mich w All So w Em 06–07; V 07–14; AD S'wark and Newington 13–14; V Eltham Park St Luke from 14. *St Luke's Vicarage, 107 Westmount Road, London SE9 1XX* T: (020) 8850 3030 M: 07790-219725

OGLESBY, Canon Leslie Ellis. b 46. Univ Coll Ox BA 69 MA 73 City Univ MPhil 73 Fitzw Coll Cam BA 73 MA 77 Lambeth PhD 12. Ripon Coll Cuddesdon 77. **d** 78 **p** 79. C Stevenage St Mary Shephall *St Alb* 78–80; Dir St Alb Minl Tr Scheme 80–87; V Markyate Street *St Alb* 80–87; Dir CME 87–94; Hon Can St Alb 93–01; TR Hitchin 94–01; Adult Educn and Tr Officer *Ely* 01–04; Dioc Dir Minl and Adult Learning 04–12; Dir Min 12; Hon Can Ely Cathl 04–12; rtd 12; PtO *Ely* from 12; *St Alb* from 12. *55 Swansholme Gardens, Sandy SG19 1HN* E: oglesbyles75@yahoo.com

O'GRADY, Anthony Donald. b 87. RNMH 11 Sheff Univ BA 15. Coll of Resurr Mirfield 12. **d** 15 **p** 16. C Newc Ch Ch w St Anne 15–18; V Woodhorn w Newbiggin from 18. *34A Front Street, Newbiggin-by-the-Sea NE64 6PS* M: 07519-683355 E: fr.aogrady@hotmail.com

OGRAM, Mrs Ann. b 44. WEMTC 04. **d** 06 **p** 07. NSM Clun w Bettws-y-Crwyn and Newcastle *Heref* 06–14; NSM Clun Valley 14–15; PtO *B & W* from 15. *21 Orchard Drive, Sandford, Winscombe BS25 5RD* M: 07970-072836 E: ann@ogram.com or revron@btinternet.com

OGUGUO, Barnabas Ahuna. b 47. Rome Univ BA 70 BD 74 Glas Univ MTh 84 PhD 90 Strathclyde Univ PGCE 93. **d** 73 **p** 74. Nigeria 73–93; RE Teacher Lenzie Academy *Glas* 93–96; Bearsden Academy from 96; Hon C Lenzie 95–05; P-in-c Glas St Matt 05–07; P-in-c Cumbernauld 07–09; R 09–13; rtd 13; LtO *Glas* from 14. *32 Carron Crescent, Lenzie, Glasgow G66 5PJ* T: 0141-578 9802 M: 07757-502054 E: bahunog01@yahoo.co.uk

OGUNYEMI, Dele Johnson. b 56. Obafemi Awolowo Univ BA 90. SEITE 04. **d** 07 **p** 08. NSM Plumstead All SS *S'wark* 07–11; C Nunhead St Antony w St Silas 11–14; P-in-c 14–15; V from 15. *St Antony with St Silas Vicarage, Athenlay Road, London SE15 3EP* T: (020) 7639 4261 M: 07958-396118 E: djogunyemi@tiscali.co.uk

OGUNYINKA, Olasupo. b 59. ACMA 96. Yorks Min Course 13. **d** 15 **p** 16. NSM Beeston *Leeds* from 15. *36 Holmwood Avenue, Leeds LS6 4NJ* T: 0113-275 7574 M: 07780-806010 E: olasupo.ogunyinka@ntlworld.com

OH, Abraham (Taemin). b 75. St Steph Ho Ox 08. **d** 11 **p** 12. C Colchester St Jas and St Paul w All SS etc *Chelmsf* 11–14; P-in-c Enfield St Geo *Lon* 14–18; V from 18. *St George's Vicarage, 706 Hertford Road, Enfield EN3 6NR* M: 07737-161317 E: taemin.oh@gmail.com

O'HARE, Phelim Sean. b 71. QUB BA 94 Gregorian Univ Rome STB 97 St Thos Aquinas Pontifical Univ Rome MA 98 St Mary's Coll Twickenham PGCE 02. **d** 97 **p** 98. In RC Ch 97–12; Chapl Llan Cathl Sch 12–14; NSM Canton Cardiff *Llan* 12–14; TV 14–17; P-in-c Cardiff St German w St Sav from 17. *48 Scholars Drive, Penylan, Cardiff CF23 9FE* T: (029) 2241 1229 E: phelimohare@gmail.com

OHEN, John Chuks. b 42. **d** 06 **p** 07. NSM Clapham St Jas *S'wark* 06–12; PtO from 12. *47 Kirkstall Gardens, London SW2 4HR* T: (020) 8671 0028 M: 07758-935906 E: revjohn.ohen@gmail.com

OHLSSON, Nicolas Hilding. See HILDING OHLSSON, Nicolas

OKEKE, Christian Chukwudi. b 71. Strathclyde Univ MSc 09. United Th Coll Harare BTheol 04. **d** 05 **p** 06. C Avondale Zimbabwe 05; C Glas St Silas 05–08; P-in-c Glas Gd Shep and Ascension 08–15; Chapl Strathclyde Univ 08–15; Chapl Princess Alexandra Hosp NHS Trust from 15; Hon C Tye Green w Netteswell *Chelmsf* from 16; P-in-c Staple Tye from 19. *The Rectory, Perry Road, Harlow CM18 7NP* T: (01279) 424064 M: 07748-590407 E: bishopc7@yahoo.com

OKEKE, Ifeanyichukwu Ernest. b 68. Pontifical Univ Rome LTh 17. ERMC 13. **d** 17 **p** 18. C Elmswell *St E* from 17. *14 Loch Rannoch Close, Elmswell, Bury St Edmunds IP30 9FA* T: (01359) 241624 M: 07717-158500 E: elmswellcurate1@gmail.com

✠**OKEKE, The Rt Revd Ken Sandy Edozie.** b 41. Nigeria Univ BSc 67 Man Univ MA 94. Igbaja Sem Nigeria. **d** 76 **p** 76 **c** 00. Nigeria 76–80 and 87–89; Chapl to Nigerians in UK and Irish Republic 80–87; Hon Can Kwara from 85; Hon Adn from 98; C Man Whitworth 89–95; Chapl Inst of Higher Learning Man 89–95; CMS 95–01; PtO *S'wark* 96–02; Bp on the Niger 00–11; Hon Asst Bp Roch from 16. *50 Essex Road, Longfield DA3 7QL* T: (01474) 709627 E: kengozi8@yahoo.com

OKELLO, Modicum. b 53. Trin Coll Bris BA 90. St Paul's Coll Limuru 76 Wycliffe Hall Ox 86. **d** 78 **p** 79. Kenya 78–80; Uganda 80–86; NSM Goodmayes All SS *Chelmsf* 91–92; C Barking St Marg w St Patr 92–96; C Stratford St Jo and Ch Ch w Forest Gate St Jas 96–99; TV Forest Gate St Sav w W Ham St Matt 99–10; P-in-c Hall Green St Mich *Birm* 10–14; PtO *Chelmsf* from 18. *217 Abbeville Apartments, 37 London Road, Barking IG11 8FW* E: modicum@btinternet.com

O'KELLY, Ruth Julia. **d** 14 **p** 15. Mullingar, Portnashangan, Moyliscar, Kilbixy etc *M & K* 14–15; C Dublin Rathfarnham *D & G* from 15. *15 Woodlawn Park Grove, Dublin 24, Republic of Ireland* T: (00353) (1) 452 7153 M: 86-081 3126 E: revruthokelly@gmail.com

OKORONKWO, Catherine Chunyere Mark. b 71. **d** 16 **p** 17. C Streetly *Lich* from 16. *11 Icknield Close, Sutton Coldfield B74 3NN* M: 07879-989577 E: cathymarko@yahoo.co.uk

OKPALA, Chibuzor Kenechukwu. b 86. Greenwich Univ BSc 07. **d** 16. NSM Harmondsworth *Lon* from 17. *69 Bentinck Road, West Drayton UB7 7RG* M: 07916-347570 E: chiokpala08@gmail.com

OLADIPO, Jesutosin (Tosin). b 79. Reading Univ BA 00. St Mellitus Coll BA 18. **d** 18 **p** 19. C St John-at-Hackney *Lon* 18–19; C Hackney from 19. *21 Sutton Place, London E9 6EH* M: 07895-916007 E: tosin.oladipo@gmail.com

OLADUJI, Christopher Temitayo. b 57. Awosika Th Coll Nigeria 84. **d** 87 **p** 88. C Ilutitun Ebenezer Nigeria 87; Asst P Ondo Cathl 88; NSM W Ham *Chelmsf* 89–93; NSM Peckham St Jo w St Andr *S'wark* 97–98; NSM E Ham St Geo *Chelmsf* 99–01; NSM Hackney Wick St Mary of Eton w St Aug *Lon* 02–04; NSM Smithfield St Bart Gt 04–13; NSM Plaistow and N Canning Town *Chelmsf* 13–17; NSM Plaistow SS Phil and Jas and St Mary from 17; NSM Plaistow St Martin from 17; Chapl Barts Health NHS Trust from 15. *103 Browning Road, London E12 6RB* T: (020) 8472 6506 M: 07985-465401 E: coladuji@yahoo.com

OLADUNJOYE, Oluwayemi Abiodun. b 82. Fed Univ of Tech Akure BTech 10 UWE MSc 14. Immanuel Coll Ibadan 10. **d** 11 **p** 12. C Lafiaji Nigeria 11–15; C Lagos Cathl 15–17; PtO *Birm* 17–18; LtO 18–19; PtO from 19. *15 Gower Croft, Oldbury B69 2GH* M: 07958-530375 E: yemmyola2@yahoo.com

OLANCZUK, Jonathan Paul Tadeusz. b 49. EAMTC 94. **d** 96 **p** 97. C Haverhill w Withersfield *St E* 96–00; P-in-c Badingham w Bruisyard, Cransford and Dennington 00–04; P-in-c Rendham w Sweffling 00–04; R Upper Alde 04–17; rtd 17; PtO *St E* from 17; *Nor* from 17. *82 Park Drive, Worlingham,*

Beccles NR34 7DL T: (01502) 470079 M: 07766-953558 *or* 07944-186526 E: olanczuk@me.com

OLD, Arthur Anthony George (Tony). b 36. Clifton Th Coll 69. **d** 71 **p** 72. C Clitheroe St Jas *Blackb* 71–73; C Bispham 73–77; V Haslingden St Jo Stonefold 77–81; TV Lowestoft and Kirkley *Nor* 81–83; Chapl to the Deaf *Cant* 83–01; P-in-c Hernhill 83–85; C Preston next Faversham, Goodnestone and Graveney 85–01; rtd 01; PtO *Cant* 01–15. *62 Knaves Acre, Headcorn, Ashford TN27 9TJ* T: (01622) 891498

OLDFIELD, Jonathan Thomas. b 54. Bede Coll Dur TCert 76. NEOC 04. **d** 07 **p** 08. NSM Crakehall *Leeds* 07–16; NSM Hornby 07–16; NSM Patrick Brompton and Hunton 07–16; NSM Spennithorne w Finghall and Hauxwell 12–16; P-in-c Slaidburn w Tosside from 16. *The Rectory, Church Street, Slaidburn, Clitheroe BB7 3ER* T: (01200) 446478 E: joldfield12@btinternet.com

OLDFIELD, Canon Roger Fielden. b 45. Qu Coll Cam BA 67 MA 71 Lon Univ BD 75. Trin Coll Bris 75. **d** 75 **p** 76. C Halliwell St Pet *Man* 75–80 and 03–10; V Bolton St Bede 93–02; Hon Can Man Cathl 00–10; rtd 10; PtO *Man* from 11. *70 Eastgrove Avenue, Bolton BL1 7HA* T: (01204) 305228 E: rogerandruth@googlemail.com

OLDHAM, Susan Yvonne. b 60. SWMTC BTh 14. **d** 10 **p** 11. NSM Georgeham *Ex* 10–14; P-in-c Dolton 14–15; P-in-c Monkokehampton 14–15; P-in-c Iddesleigh w Dowland 14–15; R Dolton, Dowland, Iddesleigh etc from 15. *The Rectory, Cleave Hill, Dolton, Winkleigh EX19 8QT* T: (01805) 804264 E: susan.oldham7@btinternet.com

OLDROYD, David Christopher Leslie. b 42. FRICS. S Dios Minl Tr Scheme. **d** 85 **p** 86. NSM Four Marks *Win* 85–90; PtO *Portsm* from 06; *Guildf* from 08; *Chich* from 12. *18 Rozeldene, Grayshott, Hindhead GU26 6TW* T: (01428) 606620 E: chrisoldroyd@live.co.uk

OLDROYD, Mrs Sheila Margaret. b 40. Liv Univ BSc 63. St Steph Ho Ox 98. **d** 99 **p** 00. NSM Cotgrave *S'well* 99–03; NSM Keyworth and Stanton-on-the-Wolds and Bunny etc 03–08; rtd 08; PtO *S'well* from 08. *27 Lowlands Drive, Keyworth, Nottingham NG12 5HG* T: 0115-937 6344 E: revdmargaret@gmail.com

OLEY, Mrs Carolyn Joan Macdonald. b 44. Ox Min Course 05. **d** 08 **p** 09. NSM Lambfold *Pet* 08–12; R 12–16; Hon C Chenderit from 18. *10 The Green, Evenley, Brackley NN13 5SQ* T: (01280) 701311 M: 07483-851425 E: carolyn.oley@btinternet.com

OLHAUSEN, William Paul. b 67. Wycliffe Hall Ox BA 97. **d** 98 **p** 99. C Reading Greyfriars *Ox* 98–01; Sub Chapl HM YOI Reading 98–01; C Cambridge H Trin *Ely* 01–04; I Carrigrohane Union *C, C & R* 04–08; Chapl Monkton Combe Sch Bath 08–11; I Killiney Ballybrack *D & G* from 11. *The Rectory, Killiney Avenue, Killiney, Co Dublin, Republic of Ireland* T: (00353) (1) 285 2228 M: 87-166 0356 E: wolhausen@googlemail.com

OLISA, Tagbo Brown Ikechukwu. b 63. St Mellitus Coll 11. **d** 12 **p** 13. NSM Harmondsworth *Lon* from 17. *140 Burlington Road, Thornton Heath CR7 8PH* T: (020) 8771 5743 M: 07740-101419 E: brown.olisa@btinternet.com

OLIVER, David Leath. b 41. **d** 96. Old Catholic Ch Germany 96–01; PtO *Eur* 10–11; Asst Chapl Helsinki from 11. *Ajurinkatu 5 A 1, 65100 Vaasa, Finland* M: (00358) 407-325250 E: tuulandavid@yahoo.com

OLIVER, Canon David Ryland. b 34. Univ of Wales (Lamp) BA 56 St Cath Coll Ox BA 58 MA 62. Wycliffe Hall Ox 56. **d** 58 **p** 59. C Carmarthen St Pet *St D* 58–61; C Llangyfelach *S & B* 61–63; R Aberedw w Llandeilo Graban etc 63–66; R Llanbadarn Fawr, Llandegley and Llanfihangel etc 66–67; LtO *Llan* 68–70; LtO *Ban* 70–73; V Nefyn w Pistyll w Tudweiliog w Llandudwen etc 73–74; V Abercraf and Callwen *S & B* 74–77; V Llangyfelach 77–79; R Llanllwchaearn and Llanina *St D* 79–83; V Cwmaman 83–94; Can *St D* Cathl from 90; RD Dyffryn Aman 93–94; V Cynwyl Gaeo w Llansawel and Talley 94–99; rtd 99; PtO *St D* 05–17. *Maes y Gelynen, 40 Heol Bryngwili, Cross Hands, Llanelli SA14 6LR* T: (01269) 840146 *or* 843157 E: drylandoliver@yahoo.co.uk

OLIVER, Diane Margaret. b 49. **d** 14 **p** 15. OLM Cheddleton, Horton, Longsdon and Rushton Spencer *Lich* 14–19; PtO from 19. *17 Cauldon Close, Leek ST13 5SH* T: (01538) 373800 E: dmoliver@btinternet.com

OLIVER, Gordon. See OLIVER, Thomas Gordon

✠**OLIVER, The Rt Revd John Keith.** b 35. G&C Coll Cam BA 59 MA 63 MLitt 65. Westcott Ho Cam 59. **d** 64 **p** 65 **c** 90. C Hilborough w Bodney *Nor* 64–68; Chapl Eton Coll 68–72; R N Molton w Nymet St George *Ex* 73–75; P-in-c Filleigh w E Buckland 73–75; P-in-c Warkleigh w Satterleigh and Chittlehamholt 73–75; P-in-c High Bray w Charles 73–75; TR S Molton, Nymet St George, High Bray etc 75–82;

P-in-c N Molton w Twitchen 77–79; RD S Molton 74–80; TR Cen Ex 82–85; Adn Sherborne *Sarum* 85–90; P-in-c W Stafford w Frome Billet 85–90; Can Res Sarum Cathl 85–90; Bp Heref 90–03; rtd 03; Hon Asst Bp S & B from 04; PTO *Heref* from 05. *The Old Vicarage, Glascwm, Llandrindod Wells LD1 5SE* T/F: (01982) 570771

OLIVER, John Kenneth. b 47. Brunel Univ MA 92 ALBC 70. EAMTC 98. **d** 00 **p** 01. C E Ham St Paul *Chelmsf* 00–03; V Stratford New Town St Paul 03–05; TV Totton *Win* 05–12; rtd 12; PTO *Win* from 12. *91B Wentworth Avenue, Bournemouth BH5 2EH* T: (01202) 417666 E: revjohnoliver@btinternet.com

OLIVER, The Ven John Michael. b 39. Univ of Wales (Lamp) BA 62. Ripon Hall Ox 62. **d** 64 **p** 65. C High Harrogate St Pet *Ripon* 64–67; C Bramley 67–72; V Low Harrogate St Mary 72–78; V Beeston 78–92; RD Armley 86–92; Adn Leeds 92–05; Hon Can Ripon Cathl 87–05; rtd 05; PTO *Ripon* 05–14; *Leeds* from 14. *42A Chapel Lane, Barwick in Elmet, Leeds LS15 4EJ* T: 0113-393 5019

OLIVER, Jonathan Andrew. b 79. Cam Univ MPhil 11. Ridley Hall Cam 08. **d** 11 **p** 12. C Sholing *Win* from 11. *Peartree Vicarage, 65 Peartree Avenue, Southampton SO19 7JN* T: (023) 8178 2238 E: jon@sholingchurch.com

OLIVER, (née TROMANS), Judith Anne. b 54. Liv Univ BSc 76 Lanc Univ PGCE 77 Birm Univ MA 07. WMMTC. **d** 96 **p** 97. C Old Swinford Stourbridge *Worc* 96–99; C Pensnett 99–01; Asst to Suff Bp Dudley 99–01; P-in-c Dudley Wood 01–08; V 08–10; TV Dudley 10–15; Hon Can Worc Cathl 11–15; rtd 15; PTO *Worc* from 15; Sub-dean rtd clergy from 16. *37 Haden Park Road, Cradley Heath B64 7HF* T: (01384) 832095 M: 07903-104862 E: juditholiver@blueyonder.co.uk

OLIVER, Mark Leonard. b 61. **d** 14 **p** 15. OLM New Haw *Guildf* from 14. *39 Kingston Rise, New Haw, Addlestone KT15 3EX* T: (01932) 910355 E: markthechurch@gmail.com

OLIVER, Canon Philip Maule. b 38. Birm Univ LLB 59. Wells Th Coll 62. **d** 64 **p** 65. C Chesterton *Lich* 64–67; C Tettenhall Wood 67–71; V Milton 71–78; V Ixworth and Bardwell *St E* 78–92; P-in-c Honington w Sapiston and Troston 81–92; TR Blackbourne 92–08; RD Ixworth 85–94; Hon Can St E Cathl 00–08; rtd 08; PTO *St E* from 08. *25 Millfield Road, Barningham, Bury St Edmunds IP31 1DX*

OLIVER, Ryland. *See* OLIVER, David Ryland

OLIVER, Prof Simon Andrew. b 71. Mansf Coll Ox BA 93 MA 98 Peterho Cam BA 97 MA 00. Westcott Ho Cam 95. **d** 98 **p** 99. NSM Teversham *Ely* 98–01; NSM Cherry Hinton St Andr 98–01; Chapl Hertf Coll Ox 01–05; Lect Univ of Wales (Lamp) St D 05; Sen Lect 06–09; Assoc Prof Nottm Univ *S'well* 09–15; Can Th S'well Minster 11–15; Van Mildert Prof Div Dur Univ from 15; Can Res Dur Cathl from 15. *University of Durham, Department of Theology, Abbey House, Palace Green, Durham DH1 3RS* T: 0191-334 3293 E: simon.oliver@durham.ac.uk

✠**OLIVER, The Rt Revd Stephen John.** b 48. AKC 69. St Aug Coll Cant 70. **d** 71 **p** 72 **c** 03. C Clifton *S'well* 71–75; P-in-c Newark Ch Ch 75–79; R Plumtree 79–85; Sen Producer BBC Relig Broadcasting Dept Lon 85–87; Chief Producer 87–91; TR Leeds City *Ripon* 91–97; Can Res and Prec St Paul's Cathl *Lon* 97–03; Area Bp Stepney 03–10; rtd 10. *Garden Cottage, Church Lane, Averham, Newark NG23 5RB* T: (01636) 673861 E: stepoliver7@gmail.com

OLIVER, Canon Susan Jacqueline. b 54. Univ Coll Lon LLB 78 CQSW 86. Qu Coll Birm 03. **d** 05 **p** 06. C Fladbury w Wyre Piddle and Moor etc *Worc* 05–09; TV Louth *Linc* 09–12; P-in-c Pensnett *Worc* 12–17; V 17–18; P-in-c Churchill-in-Halfshire w Blakedown and Broome from 18; C Belbroughton w Fairfield and Clent from 18; Dioc Warden of Readers from 17; Hon Can Worc Cathl from 17. *The Rectory, 5 Mill Lane, Blakedown, Kidderminster DY10 3ND* M: 07843-750451 E: sueoliver778@gmail.com

OLIVER, Suzanne Marie. *See* PATTLE, Suzanne Marie

OLIVER, Canon Thomas Gordon. b 48. Nottm Univ BTh 72 DipAdEd 80 Lon Univ MA 15 ALCD 72. St Jo Coll Nottm 68. **d** 72 **p** 73. C Thorpe Edge *Bradf* 72–76; C Woodthorpe *S'well* 76–80; V Huthwaite 80–85; Dir Past Studies St Jo Coll Nottm 85–94; Dir of Min and Tr *Roch* 94–09; R Meopham w Nurstead 09–13; Hon Can Roch Cathl 95–13; rtd 13; PTO *Roch* from 13. *112 Bush Road, Cuxton, Rochester ME2 1HA* T: (01634) 735137 E: canongordon.oliver@gmail.com

OLIVER, Mrs Trudi. b 65. Brighton Univ BA 09. Trin Coll Bris BA 11. **d** 11 **p** 12. C Southampton Lord's Hill and Lord's Wood *Win* 11–14; P-in-c Gravesend St Mary *Roch* 14–18; V from 18; Chapl St Geo Sch Gravesend from 14. *The Vicarage, 57 New House Lane, Gravesend DA11 7HJ* T: (01474) 353612 M: 07432-131079 E: revtrudi@gmail.com

OLIVER, Canon Wendy Louise. b 54. Aston Tr Scheme 93 Oak Hill Th Coll 94. **d** 96 **p** 97. C Walmsley *Man* 96–99; P-in-c

Goodshaw and Crawshawbooth 99–08; AD Rossendale 04–08; V Harwood from 08; AD Walmsley 10–14; Hon Can Man Cathl from 11. *The Vicarage, Stitch Mi Lane, Bolton BL2 4HU* T: (01204) 525196 E: wendyloliver@gmail.com

OLIVIER, The Very Revd Bertrand Maurice Daniel. b 62. Ecole des Cadres Paris BA 84. S'wark Ord Course 93. **d** 96 **p** 97. C Walworth St Jo *S'wark* 96–00; V Southfields St Barn 00–05; RD Wandsworth 03–05; V All Hallows by the Tower etc *Lon* 05–18; Dean Montreal Canada from 18; Hon Can St Paul's Cathl Nicosia from 18; PTO *Eur* from 16. *The Cathedral Office, 1444 Union Avenue, Montreal QC H3A 2B8, Canada* T: (001) (514) 843 6577 E: bertrand.olivier@montrealcathedral.ca

OLLIER, Canon Timothy John Douglas. b 44. Trin Hall Cam BA 66 MA 69. Cuddesdon Coll 66. **d** 68 **p** 69. C Silksworth *Dur* 68–71; C St Marylebone w H Trin *Lon* 71–74; C Winlaton *Dur* 74–77; R Redmarshall and V Bishopton w Gt Stainton 77–88; P-in-c Grindon and Stillington 83–88; V Gainford and R Winston 88–00; AD Barnard Castle 88–00; P-in-c Egglescliffe 00–03; R 03–13; AD Stockton 01–07; Hon Can Dur Cathl 94–13; rtd 13; PTO *Dur* from 14. *14 Low Coniscliffe, Darlington DL2 2JY* T: (01325) 495458 E: timdollie3@gmail.com

OLLIFF, Roland. b 61. Leeds Univ BTh 95 Ex Coll Ox MA 00. Coll of Resurr Mirfield 93. **d** 95 **p** 96. C Bickleigh and Shaugh Prior *Ex* 95–98; CF 98–07; Sen CF 07–10; V Crookham *Guildf* from 15; Dir of Ords 09–15; V Crookham *Guildf* 15–17; Bp's Chapl from 17. *59 Brookside, Jacob's Well, Guildford GU4 7NS* M: 07956-028128 E: roland.olliff@gmail.com

OLLIVE, Preb Patricia Ann. b 55. St Luke's Coll Ex BA 91. Ripon Coll Cuddesdon BTh 05. **d** 05 **p** 06. C Backwell w Chelvey and Brockley *B & W* 05–09; P-in-c Shapwick w Ashcott and Burtle 09–11; P-in-c W Poldens 09–11; V Polden Wheel 11–15; V Bridgwater St Mary and Chilton Trinity from 15; Preb Wells Cathl from 18. *11 Vickery Close, Bridgwater TA6 7JU* T: (01278) 323302 M: 07840-387121 E: ollivetrish@hotmail.co.uk

OLLMAN, Mrs Elaine Margaret. b 45. SNWTP 07. **d** 10 **p** 11. NSM Frankby w Greasby *Ches* 10–12; P-in-c Delamere 12–14; R 14–19; rtd 19; PTO *Ches* from 19. *5 Leslie Avenue, Wirral CH49 1RS* M: 07599-511887 E: revemollman@btinternet.com

OLNEY, Dorian Frederick. b 50. Kingston Poly BA 71 Anglia Poly Univ MA 03 MIL 88 MCIPD 88. Ridley Hall Cam 96. **d** 98 **p** 99. C Glenfield *Leic* 98–02; Chapl ATC 99–01; TV Newark *S'well* 02–07; P-in-c Shenstone *Lich* 07–09; P-in-c Stonnall 07–09; V Shenstone and Stonnall 09–13; R Sissinghurst w Frittenden *Cant* 13–19; rtd 19. *61 Tiverton Road, Loughborough LE11 2RU* E: fred.olney01@gmail.com

OLOKOSE, Folorunso Oladosu. b 70. Lyon Univ MA 08. Trin Coll Bris 11. **d** 13 **p** 14. C Cobham and Stoke D'Abernon *Guildf* 13–17; V Oatlands from 17. *5 Beechwood Avenue, Weybridge KT13 9TE* E: folo.olokose@gmail.com

O'LOUGHLIN, Mrs Kathryn. b 60. Man Univ BSc 81 Win Univ MA 08. STETS 96. **d** 99 **p** 00. NSM Basing *Win* 99–03; PTO 03–08; C N Hants Downs 08–16; Tutor STETS 08–11; PTO *Win* from 17; *Portsm* from 18. *4 South Downs Close, Swanmore, Southampton SO32 2FR* T: (01489) 890515 E: kathy.oloughlin@gmail.com

OLSEN, Arthur Barry. b 37. Univ of NZ BA 61 Melbourne Coll of Div BD 73. ACT ThL 64. **d** 64 **p** 64. C Nelson All SS New Zealand 64–67; V Ahuara 67–69; V Motupiko 69–70; V Amuri 70–73; Maori Miss and C Dunedin St Matt 73–76; V Brooklyn 77–81; C Hersham *Guildf* 81–84; P-in-c Botleys and Lyne 84–95; V 95–03; P-in-c Long Cross 84–95; V 95–03; Chapl NW Surrey Mental Health Partnership NHS Trust 85–03; rtd 03; Hon C Rotherfield Peppard and Kidmore End etc *Ox* 03–12; PTO from 13; *St Alb* 13–18. *29 Sandhill Way, Aylesbury HP19 8GU* E: barry.o22@virgin.net

OLSWORTH-PETER, Edward James. b 77. UWE BA 99. Wycliffe Hall Ox BTh 04. **d** 04 **p** 05. C Guildf Ch Ch w St Martha-on-the-Hill 04–07; C Upper Chelsea St Sav and St Simon *Lon* 07–10; V Sydenham H Trin and St Aug *S'wark* 10–15; Dioc Fresh Expressions Adv *Ely* 15–18; Nat Adv for Pioneer Development Abps' Coun from 18. *Ministry Division, Church House, Great Smith Street, London SW1P 3AZ* T: (020) 7898 1000 E: revedop@gmail.com *or* edward.olsworth-peter@churchofengland.org

OLUKANMI, Miss Stella Grace Oluwafunmilayo Olanrewaju. b 57. St Jo Coll Nottm BTh 95 LTh 92. **d** 96 **p** 97. C Gt Ilford St Jo *Chelmsf* 96–01; V Barkingside St Cedd 01–15; P-in-c Walthamstow St Andr from 15. *St Andrew's Vicarage, 37 Sutton Road, London E17 5QA* T: (020) 8527 3969 E: revdsolukanmi@btinternet.com *or* stella.sta@btinternet.com

OLUMUYIWA, Olubunmi Taiwo. b 67. Ibadan Univ Nigeria BA 93 Birm Univ MPhil 07 PhD 11. Immanuel Coll

Ibadan 88. **d** 93 **p** 94. C Owo St Patr Nigeria 93–94; C Somolu St Paul 94–95; C Ch Ch Cathl Lagos 95–97; Chapl Owo Dioc Angl Gr Sch 97–99; V Orisunmibare-Bodija Ch Ch 99–05; PtO *Birm* 05–18; Asst Chapl Univ Hosp Birm NHS Foundn Trust 16–18; Chapl HM Pris Oakwood from 18. *HM Prison Oakwood, Oaks Drive, Featherstone, Wolverhampton WV10 7QD* T: (01902) 799700 M: 07534-270120 E: olumuyiwataiwo37@gmail.com *or* taiwo.olumuyiwa@uk.g4s.com

O'MALLEY, Canon Brian Denis Brendan. b 40. Univ of Wales (Lamp) MA 97 MHCIMA 60. Oscott Coll (RC) 74 Coll of Resurr Mirfield 82. **d** 77 **p** 83. In RC Ch 77–81; Warden St Greg Retreat Rhandirmwyn *St D* 80–83; Chapl and Min Can St D Cathl 83–85; V Wiston w Ambleston, St Dogwells, Walton E etc 85–88; V Wiston w Clarbeston and Walton E 89; R Walton W w Talbenny and Haroldston W 89–98; Chapl Pembrokeshire Coll of FE 93–98; Chapl St D Coll Lamp 98–07; Can St D Cathl 01–07; rtd 07; PtO *St D* from 07. *Millbank, North Road, Lampeter SA48 7HZ* T: (01570) 422148

O'MAOIL MHEANA, Patrick John. b 66. Coll of Resurr Mirfield 12. **d** 14 **p** 15. C Paulsgrove *Portsm* 14–17; R Airdrie *Glas* from 17. *The Rectory, 44 Gartmore Road, Airdrie ML6 9BH* E: paji65@hotmail.com

OMOBUDE, Boyle Osaro. b 69. Ushaw Coll Dur 07. **d** 11 **p** 15. In RC Ch 11–14; NSM Fenham St Jas and St Basil *Newc* from 15; Chapl Tees, Esk and Wear Valleys NHS Foundn Trust from 16; PtO *York* from 17. *St Margaret's Vicarage, 14 Heighley Street, Newcastle upon Tyne NE15 6AR* E: omobude@btinternet.com

OMOLE, Oluremi Richard. b 63. **d** 05 **p** 07. NSM Dur N 05–14; Chapl City Hosps Sunderland NHS Foundn Trust from 14. *7 Frensham Way, Meadowfield, Durham DH7 8UR* T: 0191-378 9756 E: romole@sky.com

✠**OMUKU, The Rt Revd Precious Sotonye.** b 47. Ibadan Univ Nigeria BSc 73. Lagos Angl Dioc Sem 00. **d** 02 **p** 03 **c** 16. V Ikoyi Nativity Nigeria 02–06; LtO *Lon* 07–08; PtO *S'wark* 07–08; Hon C Morden from 08; Hon Asst Bp S'wark from 16. *4 Litchfield Avenue, Morden SM4 5QS* T: (020) 8640 7311 M: 07790-593392 E: precious.omuku@yahoo.com

O'NEILL, Gary. b 57. K Coll Lon BD 79 AKC 79 Liv Univ MA 06. Westcott Ho Cam 80. **d** 81 **p** 82. C Oldham *Man* 81–84; C Birch w Fallowfield 84–87; R Moston St Chad 87–97; Can Res Birm Cathl 97–07; Dir Studies for Ords *Ches* from 07; Bp's Adv for Minl Development Review from 15. *10 Neston Close, Helsby, Frodsham WA6 0FH* T: (01928) 723327 M: 07976-729449 E: gary.oneill@chester.anglican.org

O'NEILL, Mrs Gillian. b 73. Westmr Coll Ox BTh 95. Ripon Coll Cuddesdon MTh 12. **d** 12 **p** 13. C W Dulwich All SS *S'wark* 12–16; V E Dulwich St Jo from 16. *St John's Parish Office, Goose Green Community Centre, 62A East Dulwich Road, London SE22 9AT* T: (020) 8693 3897 E: gill_oneilluk@hotmail.com

O'NEILL, Victoria Elaine. *See* BRYSON, Victoria Elaine

ONGYERTH, Michael George. b 50. **d** 13 **p** 14. OLM Crowland *Linc* 13–19; V Elloe Fen Gp from 19. *22 North Street, Crowland, Peterborough PE6 0EF*

ONIONS, Mrs Angela Ann. b 33. STETS 01. **d** 02. NSM Bradford-on-Avon H Trin *Sarum* 02–08; PtO from 08; *B & W* from 14. *27 Berryfield Road, Bradford-on-Avon BA15 1SX* T: (01225) 309001 M: 07719-726461 E: r.a.onions@btinternet.com

ONUIGBO, Maria Helena. b 73. Westcott Ho Cam. **d** 10 **p** 15. NSM Brockley Hill St Sav *S'wark* 11–14; C S Beddington and Roundshaw 14–18; R Manchester Gd Shep and St Barn *Man* from 18. *St Barnabas' Rectory, South Street, Openshaw, Manchester M11 2EY* M: 07898-311943 E: mariaobafemi@hotmail.com

ONUNWA, The Ven Udobata Rufus. b 47. Univ of Nigeria BA 78 MA 82 PhD 85. Trin Coll Umuahia 72. **d** 74 **p** 75. Chapl Owerri Cathl Nigeria 74–75; Chapl Univ of Nigeria 75–78 and 82–84; Chapl to Abp Nigeria 78–79; P-in-c Okebola St Paul 78–79; Lect Trin Th Coll Umuahia 79–81; Hon Can Okigwe-Orlu 84–89; Can Res Calabar 90–91; V St Jude 92–96; Adn 94–96; Tutor Crowther Hall CMS Tr Coll Selly Oak 97–02; NW Regional Dir Crosslinks 03–05; P-in-c Grange St Andr *Ches* 05–09; rtd 09. *76 Firedrake Croft, Coventry CV1 2DR* M: 07766-724510 E: uonunwa@yahoo.co.uk

ONWUKA, Mrs Kechinyere Chimuemelulau. b 47. 18. NSM Enfield St Jas *Lon* from 17. *48 Clydesdale, Enfield EN3 4RJ*

ONYEKWELU, Mrs Ada. b 54. Ibadan Univ Nigeria BSc 83 SEN 98. **d** 07 **p** 08. NSM Selsdon St Fran CD *S'wark* 07–16; NSM S Croydon St Pet and St Aug from 16. *80 Tedder Road, South Croydon CR2 8AQ* T: (020) 8657 4018 E: a_onye@yahoo.co.uk

OOSTERHOF, Canon Liesbeth. b 61. Ripon Coll Cuddesdon 02. **d** 04 **p** 05. C E Bergholt and Brantham *St E* 04–07; R Shoreline from 07; Dioc Adv for Women's Min 11–16; Dean of Women's Min 16–18; RD Samford from 15; Hon Can St E Cathl from 16. *The Rectory, Rectory Field, Chelmondiston, Ipswich IP9 1HY* T: (01473) 781902 E: l.oosterhof@btinternet.com

OPALA, Robert. b 62. Catholic Univ of Lublin BTh 87 MTh 88 Chr Th Academy Warsaw PhD 99. Milltown Inst Dub MA 06 STL 08. **d** 10 **p** 11. In RC Ch 10–16; PtO *York* 16–17; NSM Crathorne from 17; NSM Kirklevington w Picton, and High and Low Worsall from 17; NSM Rudby in Cleveland w Middleton from 17; NSM Whorlton w Carlton and Faceby from 18. *2 Langbaurgh Road, Hutton Rudby, Yarm TS15 0HL* M: 07729-661764 E: robertopala62@yahoo.co.uk

OPENSHAW, Steven Paul. b 62. Open Univ BA 91 Birm Univ MSc 01. All SS Cen for Miss & Min 09. **d** 12 **p** 13. C Ramsbottom and Edenfield *Man* 12–16; P-in-c Elton St Steph 16–18; P-in-c Walshaw Ch Ch from 16. *37 Gisburn Drive, Bury BL8 3DH* T: 0161-797 5121 M: 07963-100345 E: steve_openshaw@hotmail.com

OPIE, Steven Philip. b 86. Ridley Hall Cam 16. **d** 19. C Loughton St Mary *Chelmsf* from 19. *22 The Lindens, Loughton IG10 3HS* E: steve@stmarysloughton.com

OPPERMAN, Graham William. b 40. Th Ext Educn Coll 98. **d** 00 **p** 03. C Linden St Thos S Africa 00–04; NSM Aberdour *St And* 04; NSM Burntisland 04; NSM Inverkeithing 04; TV Jarrow *Dur* 05–10; rtd 10; Hon C Cwmbran *Mon* 10–15; Hon C Usk Min Area from 15. *The Rectory, Parc Road, Llangybi, Usk NP15 1NL* T: (01633) 450811 M: 07792-451622 E: graham@deanery.info

OPPERMAN, Mrs Jennifer Catharine. b 57. ERMC 09. **d** 12 **p** 13. NSM Pet Cathl 12–16; Lay Voc Officer from 16. *Littleworth Mission, Main Road, Deeping St Nicholas, Spalding PE11 3EN* T: (01775) 630497 M: 07912-380464 E: jenny@littleworthmission.com

ORAM, Anthony. b 63. York St Jo Univ BA 08 Hull Univ PGCE 09. St Jo Coll Nottm 12. **d** 15 **p** 16. C Kingston upon Hull St Aid Southcoates *York* 15–19; V Cottesmore and Burley, Clipsham, Exton etc *Pet* from 19. *The Rectory, 38 Main Street, Cottesmore, Oakham LE15 7DJ* M: 07740-257173 E: anthony@theorams.com

ORAM, Roland Martin David. b 45. Trin Coll Cam BA 68 ARCM 70. Cranmer Hall Dur. **d** 78 **p** 79. C Aspley *S'well* 78–81; Chapl Alleyn's Sch Dulwich 81–88; Chapl Versailles w Grandchamp and Chevry *Eur* 88–92; Chapl Denstone Coll Uttoxeter 92–01; C Hanford and Trentham Lich 02–10; rtd 10; PtO *Lich* 10–18; *Ches* from 10. *12 Ash Grove, Rode Heath, Stoke-on-Trent ST7 3TD* T: (01270) 747271 E: orams45@btinternet.com

ORAM, Stephen John. b 58. **d** 84 **p** 85. C Kidderminster St Jo *Worc* 84–88; Chapl RAF 88–92; P-in-c Brislington St Anne *Bris* 92–97; V Cricklade w Latton 97–04; Co-ord Chapl N Bris NHS Trust 04–16; Chapl Univ Hosps Bris NHS Foundn Trust 16–18; rtd 18; PtO *Bris* 16–19; Hon C Alveston and Littleton-on-Severn w Elberton from 19; PtO *Mon* from 18. *9 Cutter Close, Newport NP19 7LN* E: stephen.oram@blueyonder.co.uk

ORAMS, Ronald Thomas. b 49. ACMA 80. **d** 08 **p** 09. NSM Laxfield, Cratfield, Wilby and Brundish *St E* 08–13; NSM Four Rivers 13–19; PtO from 19. *Crane Lodge, Bickers Hill, Laxfield, Woodbridge IP12 8DP* T: (01986) 798901 M: 07721-682183 E: ron.orams@btinternet.com

ORCHARD, Canon George Richard. b 41. Ex Coll Ox BA 62 BA 64 MA 66. Ripon Hall Ox 62. **d** 65 **p** 66. C Greenhill St Pet *Derby* 65–70; Member Ecum Team Min Sinfin Moor 70–78; V Sinfin Moor *Derby* 76–78; TR Dronfield 78–86; Can Res Derby Cathl 86–92; Hon Can Derby Cathl 92–06; P-in-c Baslow 92–93; P-in-c Curbar and Stoney Middleton 92–93; V Baslow w Curbar and Stoney Middleton 93–06; rtd 06; PtO *Cant* from 07; *Chich* from 07. *7 Love Lane, Rye TN31 7NE* T: (01797) 225916 E: richardorchard41@yahoo.co.uk

ORCHARD, Helen Claire. b 65. Sheff Univ BA 87 PhD 96 Em Coll Cam MPhil 02 Ox Univ MA 06 Heythrop Coll Lon MA 18. Westcott Ho Cam 01. **d** 03 **p** 04. C Merrow Guildf 03–06; Chapl and Fell Ex Coll Ox 06–11; TV Wimbledon *S'wark* from 11. *St Matthew's House, 10 Coombe Gardens, London SW20 0QU* T: (020) 8286 4584 E: orchard.helen@gmail.com

ORCHARD, Nigel John. b 56. CertEd 78. St Steph Ho Ox 82. **d** 85 **p** 86. C Tottenham St Paul *Lon* 85–89; C Is of Dogs Ch Ch and St Jo w St Luke 89–90; TV 90–92; P-in-c Southall Ch Redeemer 92–99; V from 99. *Christ the Redeemer Vicarage, 299 Allenby Road, Southall UB1 2HE* T: (020) 8578 2711 E: nigel.orchard1@btinternet.com

ORCHARD, Richard. *See* ORCHARD, George Richard

O'REILLY, Brian. **d** 07 **p** 08. C Seagoe D & D 07–10; I Cobh and Glanmire *C, C & R* 10–14; I Rathcooney Union from 10. *The Rectory, Rathdrum, Co Wicklow, Republic of Ireland* T: (00353) (404) 43814 M: 86-223 0271 E: brianor@eircom.net

O'REILLY, Clare Maria. *See* KING, Clare Maria

O'REILLY, Canon Philip Jonathon. b 66. Portsm Poly BSc 87 Kent Univ MA 97 MRICS. Westcott Ho Cam 93. **d** 93 **p** 94. C Selsdon St Jo w St Fran *S'wark* 93–96; TV Staveley and Barrow Hill *Derby* 96–01; V Wistow *Leic* from 01; Hon Can Leic Cathl from 10. *The Vicarage, 12 Saddington Road, Fleckney, Leicester LE8 8AW* T: 0116-240 2215 E: philiporeilly@leicester.anglican.org

O'REILLY, William Anthony. b 62. St Mellitus Coll 12. **d** 15 **p** 16. NSM Bow w Bromley St Leon *Lon* from 15. *48 Ridgdale Street, London E3 2TW* M: 07798-914298

ORFORD, Barry Antony. b 49. Univ of Wales (Ban) BA 71 MTh 97 PhD 01. St Steph Ho Ox 71. **d** 73 **p** 74. C Monmouth *Mon* 73–77; V Choral St As Cathl 77–81; CR 83–96; PtO *St As* 97–99; Hon Asst Chapl Univ of Wales (Ban) *Ban* 99–01; Lib Pusey Ho 01–14; PtO *Lon* 14–18; P-in-c St Dunstan in the West 16–19; PtO from 19. *8 Hampstead Square, London NW3 1AB* E: barry.orford@stx.ox.ac.uk

ORFORD, Canon Keith John. b 40. FCIT. EMMTC 76. **d** 79 **p** 80. NSM Matlock Bank *Derby* 79–99; NSM Wirksworth from 99; Hon Can Derby Cathl 00–10. *27 Lums Hill Rise, Matlock DE4 3FX* T/F: (01629) 55349 E: keith.orford@btinternet.com

ORGAN, Mrs Alma. b 45. Bordesley Coll of Educn CertEd 66. WEMTC 08. **d** 09 **p** 10. NSM Worc St Barn w Ch Ch 09–12; NSM Pershore w Pinvin, Wick and Birlingham 12–15; PtO from 15. *14 Ongrils Close, Pershore WR10 1QE* T: (01386) 554248 M: 07531-461810 E: piglet1723@btinternet.com

ORGAN, Peter. b 73. K Coll Lon BA 97 Birm Univ MA 01. Qu Coll Birm 99. **d** 01 **p** 02. C E Wickham *S'wark* 01–05; TV Thamesmead 05–11; V E Wickham from 11. *St Michael's Vicarage, Upper Wickham Lane, Welling DA16 3AP* T: (020) 8304 1214 E: revpeterorgan@gmail.com

ORME, Christopher Malcolm. b 60. City Univ BSc 83. Wycliffe Hall Ox 03. **d** 05 **p** 06. C Shrewsbury H Cross *Lich* 05–08; P-in-c Meanwood *Ripon* 08–12; V 12–15; R Thorley *St Alb* 15–18; rtd 19; PtO *B & W* from 19. *9 Abbey View Gardens, Bath BA2 6DQ* E: rev.chris.orme@gmail.com

ORME, Mrs Delia. b 57. STETS 01. **d** 08 **p** 09. NSM Haslemere and Grayswood *Guildf* 08–12; NSM Seale, Puttenham and Wanborough 12–19; NSM Elstead from 19; NSM Thursley from 19. *Nightingale Cottage, Peat Common, Elstead, Godalming GU8 6DX* T: (01252) 702217 E: delia.orme@btinternet.com

ORME, Edward John Gilbert. b 42. Man Univ BSc 64. Ox Min Course 04. **d** 07 **p** 08. NSM Reading St Agnes w St Paul and St Barn *Ox* 07–12; rtd 12; PtO *Ox* 12–15. *191 Carr Lane, Dronfield Woodhouse, Dronfield S18 8XF* M: 07901-528971 E: eddie.orme@yahoo.co.uk

ORME, Sydney. b 27. Oak Hill Th Coll 54. **d** 58 **p** 59. C Halliwell St Pet *Man* 58–61; V Friarmere 61–73; V Knypersley *Lich* 73–92; rtd 92; PtO *Ches* 92–14. *c/o Mrs M Ellis, 27A Woodhouse Lane, Biddulph, Stoke-on-Trent ST8 7DR* T: (01270) 759233

ORMEROD, Henry Lawrence. b 35. Pemb Coll Cam BA 58 MA 63. Qu Coll Birm. **d** 60 **p** 61. C Chigwell *Chelmsf* 60–64; C Thundersley 64–68; C Canvey Is 68–72; V Stanground *Ely* 72–77; TR Stanground and Farcet 77–81; TR Swindon St Jo and St Andr *Bris* 81–90; TR N Wingfield, Clay Cross and Pilsley *Derby* 90–97; rtd 97; Hon C Ironstone *Ox* 98–03; PtO 03–19. *5 Waterloo Drive, Banbury OX16 3QN* T: (01295) 278483 E: henryplusp@yahoo.co.uk

ORMROD, Jonathan Robert. b 63. Open Univ BSc 04. Wycliffe Hall Ox 06 Ripon Coll Cuddesdon 09. **d** 11 **p** 12. C Llantrisant *Llan* 11–14; P-in-c Sully from 14; P-in-c Wenvoe and St Lythans from 14; C St Andrews Major w Michaelston-le-Pit from 14. *The Rectory, Port Road, Wenvoe, Cardiff CF5 6DF* T: (029) 2059 5347 E: jonormrod@yahoo.co.uk

ORMROD, Canon Paul William. b 57. Liv Univ BA 80 MTh 08. Westcott Ho Cam 80. **d** 83 **p** 84. C Prescot *Liv* 83–86; TV Padgate 86–95; V Formby St Pet 95–13; Chapl Madrid *Eur* 13–18; Chapl Montreux w Villars from 19; Hon Can from 18. *St John's Church House, avenue de Chillon, 92 CH-1820 Montreux-Territet, Switzerland* T: (0041) (21) 963 4354 E: paul.ormrod1@gmail.com

ORMSTON, Derek. b 43. St D Coll Lamp. **d** 67 **p** 68. C Ogley Hay *Lich* 67–70; C Tettenhall Regis 70–74; P-in-c Leek All SS 74–79; TV Leek and Meerbrook 79–83; Youth Chapl *Bris* 83–87; R Brinkworth w Dauntsey 87–12; Chapl New Coll Swindon 87–12; rtd 12; PtO *Sarum* from 13. *49 Lime Kiln, Royal Wootton Bassett, Swindon SN4 7HF* T: (01793) 852779

ORMSTON, The Ven Richard Jeremy. b 61. Southlands Coll Lon BA 83 Brunel Univ MTh 98. Oak Hill Th Coll BA 87. **d** 87 **p** 88. C Rodbourne Cheney *Bris* 87–91; R Collingtree w Courteenhall and Milton Malsor *Pet* 91–01; RD Wootton 96–01; R Oundle w Ashton and Benefield w Glapthorn 01–14; RD Oundle 03–13; Can

Pet Cathl from 03; Adn Northn from 14. *Westbrook, 11 The Drive, Northampton NN1 4RZ* T: (01604) 714015 E: archdeacon.northampton@peterborough-diocese.org.uk

O'ROURKE, Canon Brian Joseph Gerard. b 58. TCD BA 82 HDipEd 83. CITC 89. **d** 92 **p** 93. Chapl E Glendalough Sch 90–96; C Newcastle w Newtownmountkennedy and Calary *D & G* 92–96; Bp's C 96–98; I 98–00; I Cork St Ann's Union *C, C & R* 00–15; I Maryborough w Dysart Enos and Ballyfin *C & O* 15–17; Bp's C Lismore w Cappoquin, Kilwatermoy, Dungarvan etc 17–19; I Tullow w Shillelagh, Aghold and Mullinacuff from 19; Can Ossory Cathl from 17; Can Kilkenny Cathl from 18; Hon Chapl Miss to Seafarers from 00. *The Rectory, Barrack Street, Tullow, Co Carlow, R93 X722, Republic of Ireland* M: (00353) 86-807 9452 E: bjgorourke@gmail.com

O'ROURKE, Shaun. b 58. NOC 02. **d** 05 **p** 06. C Gorton and Abbey Hey *Man* 05–08; P-in-c Heaton Reddish 08–12; Borough Dean Stockport 10–12; P-in-c Swimbridge, W Buckland, Landkey, and E Buckland *Ex* from 12; RD Shirwell 12–18. *The Rectory, Barnstaple Hill, Swimbridge, Barnstaple EX32 0PH* T: (01271) 830950 M: 07914-361905 E: revd.shaun@gmail.com

ORPIN, Mrs Gillian. b 32. SRN 53. Oak Hill Th Coll 82. **d** 87 **p** 95. Par Dn Passenham *Pet* 87–92; rtd 92; NSM Oban St Jo *Arg* 92–95; Dioc Chapl 95–98; PtO *St Alb* from 98. *11 Berwick Way, Sandy SG19 1TR* T: (01767) 680629 E: gillian.orpin@talktalk.net

ORR, Andrew Dermot Harman. b 66. Sheff Univ BSc 89. CITC BTh 92. **d** 92 **p** 93. C Ballymacash *Conn* 92–95; I Castlecomer w Colliery Ch, Mothel and Bilboa *C & O* 95–00; I Castleknock and Mulhuddart w Clonsilla *D & G* 00–09; I Tullow w Shillelagh, Aghold and Mullinacuff *C & O* 09–18; Dioc Registrar 95–00 and 12–18; Adn Ossory and Leighlin 14–18; P-in-c Youghal Union *C, C & R* from 18. *13 The Pinnacles, Midleton, Co Cork, Republic of Ireland* T: (00353) (24) 92350 M: 87-419 6051 E: andreworr1234@gmail.com

ORR, David Cecil. b 33. TCD BA 56 MA 68. **d** 57 **p** 58. C Drumragh *D & R* 57–60; I Convoy 60–70; I Maghera w Killelagh 70–80; I Drumragh w Mountfield 80–84; Dean Derry 84–97; I Templemore 84–97; Miss to Seamen 84–97; rtd 97. *Kilrory, 11 Broomhill Court, Londonderry BT47 6WP* T: (028) 7134 8183 E: dcecilorr@btopenworld.com

ORR, Mark. b 61. St Jo Coll Nottm BA 14. **d** 14 **p** 15. C Clifton *S'well* 14–17; R Carlton-in-Lindrick and Langold w Oldcotes from 17. *The Rectory, 21 Grange Close, Carlton-in-Lindrick, Worksop S81 9DX* M: 07568-585638 E: odman01@yahoo.co.uk

ORR, Robert Vernon. b 50. Westmr Univ 80 MIQA 89. Wycliffe Hall Ox 96. **d** 98 **p** 99. C Cowley St Jo *Ox* 98–01; P-in-c Reading St Agnes w St Paul 01–02; R Reading St Agnes w St Paul and St Barn 02–18; rtd 18. *17 East Street, Oxford OX2 0AU* E: vernon.orr@gmail.com

ORR, William James Craig. TCD BTh 01. CITC 98. **d** 01 **p** 02. C Lurgan Ch the Redeemer *D & D* 01–07; I Muckamore *Conn* 07–16; I Killead w Gartree 07–16; I Portadown St Mark *Arm* from 16. *The Rectory, 56 Brownstown Road, Portadown, Craigavon BT62 3PY* T: (028) 3815 6771 M: 07850-156942 *or* 07806-882783 E: william-orr@sky.com

ORR-EWING, Canon Francis Ian Lance (Frog). b 75. Regent's Park Coll Ox BA 97. Wycliffe Hall Ox MTh 00. **d** 00 **p** 01. C Ox St Aldate 00–03; V Camberwell All SS *S'wark* 03–10; PtO *Ox* 10–13; NSM Amersham Deanery from 13; PtO *Lich* from 17; Can Th Win Cathl from 18; Research Fell Win Univ from 18. *Applebarn, Bull Lane, Chalfont St Peter, Gerrards Cross SL9 8RH* T: (01753) 886540 M: 07712-175851 E: rector@latimerminster.org

ORRIDGE, Harriet Grace. b 72. St Jo Coll Nottm. **d** 09 **p** 10. C Ironstone Villages *Leic* 09–13; P-in-c Saxonwell *Linc* from 13. *Saxonwell Vicarage, Church Street, Long Bennington, Newark NG23 5ES* T: (01400) 281281 E: vicar.saxonwell@gmail.com

ORTON, Giles Anthony Christopher. b 59. Qu Coll Ox MA 82. St Steph Ho Ox 12. **d** 16 **p** 17. NSM Long Eaton St Laur *Derby* from 16; NSM Ilkeston H Trin from 16. *Brun Meadows, Brun Lane, Kirk Langley, Ashbourne DE6 4LU* T: (01332) 824233 M: 07768-827101 E: gilesorton@fastmail.fm

ORTON, Peter Joseph. b 57. **d** 03 **p** 04. OLM Burton St Chad *Lich* 03–10; NSM Burton St Aid and St Paul 10–17; NSM Burton 15–17; P-in-c Stevenage All SS Pin Green *St Alb* 17–19; V from 19. *All Saints' Vicarage, 100 Derby Way, Stevenage SG1 5TJ* M: 07837-387412 E: pete.orton@outlook.com

ORTON, Canon Richard. b 33. Keble Coll Ox BA 56 MA 60 Leeds Univ. Lich Th Coll 60. **d** 61 **p** 64. C Penistone w Midhope *Wakef* 61–66; Hon C Meltham 62–69; Hon C Horsforth *Ripon* 69–72; C Far Headingley St Chad 72–75; V Hellifield *Bradf* 75–80; RD Bowland 78–80; R Hutton *Chelmsf* 80–87; R Wallasey St Hilary *Ches* 87–00; Dioc Ecum

Officer 92–99; RD Wallasey 96–99; Hon Can Ches Cathl 97–00; rtd 00; C Gt Sutton *Ches* 01–05; PtO from 05. *137 Brimstage Road, Barnston, Wirral CH60 1XF* T: 0151-348 4911 E: rokeblox@gmail.com

O'RYAN, Mrs Elizabeth Ann. b 63. Birm Univ BA 84 Glas Univ MTh 11 Roehampton Inst PGCE 85. TISEC 09. **d** 11 **p** 12. NSM Greenock *Glas* 11–14; C Dumbarton 14–19; C Alexandria 14–19; R Haddington *Edin* from 19. *6 Church Street, Haddington EH41 3EX* T: (01620) 826667 M: 07949-667135 E: lizoryan@talktalk.net

OSBORN, Charlotte Elizabeth. b 56. Birm Univ BA 77 Trin Hall Cam CertEd 78 Cardiff Univ MTh 14. ERMC 15. **d** 17 **p** 18. C Oakham, Ashwell, Braunston, Brooke, Egleton etc *Pet* from 17. *2 Wensum Close, Oakham LE15 6FU* T: (01572) 724198 M: 07957-367457 E: charlotte@oakhamteam.org.uk

OSBORN, Canon David Ronald. b 42. Bris Univ BA 66 Leeds Univ CertEd 77 Bath Univ MEd 80. Clifton Th Coll 62. **d** 66 **p** 67. C Farndon *S'well* 66–69; P-in-c W Bridgford 69–72; Asst Dioc Dir Educn *Carl* 72–77; P-in-c Kirkandrews-on-Eden w Beaumont and Grinsdale 72–77; Hd RE and Chapl Dauntsey's Sch Devizes 77–83; V Southbroom *Sarum* 83–86; Hd RE Bexhill High Sch 86–93; TV Langtree *Ox* 93–95; TR 95–97; TR Bracknell 97–06; rtd 06; P-in-c Llantilio Crossenny w Penrhos, Llanvetherine etc *Mon* 06–14; AD Abergavenny 11–14; Can St Woolos Cathl from 12; PtO from 14. *51 Cornpoppy Avenue, Monmouth NP25 5SD* M: 07803-618464 E: d.osborn42@btinternet.com

OSBORN, David Thomas. b 58. K Coll Lon BD 79 AKC 79 PGCE 80. Linc Th Coll 82. **d** 83 **p** 84. C Bearsted w Thurnham *Cant* 83–86; Chapl RAF 86–90; R Bassingham *Linc* 90–91; V Aubourn w Haddington 90–91; V Carlton-le-Moorland w Stapleford 90–91; R Thurlby w Norton Disney 90–91; Chapl RAF from 91. *Chaplaincy Services (RAF), HQ Air Command, RAF High Wycombe HP14 4UE* T: (01494) 496800

OSBORNE, Canon Brian Charles. b 38. St Andr Univ MA 61. Clifton Th Coll 61. **d** 63 **p** 64. C Skirbeck H Trin *Linc* 63–68; V 80–03; P-in-c New Clee 68–71; V 71–75; V Derby St Aug 75–80; Chapl Pilgrim Hosp Boston 84–88; RD Holland E *Linc* 85–95; Can and Preb Linc Cathl 92–03; rtd 03; Chapl to The Queen 97–08; PtO *Linc* 15–18. *3 Newlands Road, Haconby, Bourne PE10 0UT* T: (01778) 570818 E: revbrianosborne@ukonline.co.uk *or* brian_ruh.osorne@hotmail.co.uk

OSBORNE, Preb David Robert. b 50. Birm Univ BSc 71 MEd 86 Bris Univ PGCE 73. Cranmer Hall Dur 78. **d** 80 **p** 81. C Penkridge w Stretton *Lich* 80–85; R Longdon-upon-Tern, Rodington, Uppington etc 85–94; R Pilton w Croscombe, N Wootton and Dinder *B & W* 94–13; RD Shepton Mallet 01–07; Sub-Dean Wells Cathl 11–13; rtd 13; PtO *B & W* from 14; Preb Wells Cathl from 11. *10 Millbrook Gardens, Castle Cary BA7 7EF* T: (01963) 351275 M: 07719-391485 E: drosborne@btinternet.com

OSBORNE, David Victor. b 36. Dur Univ BA 59 Univ of Wales MA 99. Cranmer Hall Dur. **d** 62 **p** 63. C Kennington Cross St Anselm *S'wark* 62–66; C Sandal St Helen *Wakef* 66–67; R Ancoats *Man* 67–73; V Claremont H Angels 73–80; R Breedon cum Isley Walton and Worthington *Leic* 80–87; V Beaumont Leys 87–92; V Billesdon and Skeffington 92–01; rtd 01; PtO *Leic* 02–17; *Pet* from 02. *Rose Cottage, 12 Barlows Lane, Wilbarston, Market Harborough LE16 8QB* T: (01536) 770400

OSBORNE, Canon Derek James. b 32. Tyndale Hall Bris 53. **d** 57 **p** 58. C Weymouth St Mary *Sarum* 57–60; C Southgate *Chich* 60–63; V Croydon Ch Ch Broad Green *Cant* 63–71; V Cromer *Nor* 71–83; P-in-c Gresham w Bessingham 71–83; Hon Can Nor Cathl 77–83; V Northwood Em *Lon* 83–94; Chapl Lee Abbey 94–97; rtd 97; PtO *Nor* from 97. *50 Clifton Park, Cromer NR27 9BG* T: (01263) 511272 E: derek.and.hilary.osborne@gmail.com

OSBORNE, Mrs Elizabeth Rachel. b 85. Goldsmiths' Coll Lon MA 10 St Cath Coll Cam MA 11 BTh 17. Ridley Hall Cam 15. **d** 19. C Oseney Crescent St Luke *Lon* from 19. *30A Hadley Street, London NW1 8SS* M: 07877-186450 E: osborne.lizzie@gmail.com

OSBORNE, Canon Gerald Edward Richard. b 63. Ch Ch Ox MA 85 Wye Coll Lon MSc 86. **d** 99 **p** 00. OLM Pewsey and Swanborough *Sarum* 99–10; OLM Vale of Pewsey from 10; RD Pewsey from 12; Can and Preb Sarum Cathl from 14. *Lower Farm House, Milton Lilbourne, Pewsey SN9 5LQ* T: (01672) 563459 F: 564271 M: 07747-603795 E: gerald.osborne@lawnfarm.co.uk

OSBORNE, Graham Daking. b 51. Univ of Wales MPhil 13 City Univ ACII 74 FCII 77. Ripon Coll Cuddesdon 94. **d** 96 **p** 97. C Cirencester *Glouc* 96–00; V Glouc St Cath 00–09; AD Glouc City 03–08; R Leatherhead and Mickleham

Guildf from 09. *The Rectory, 3 St Mary's Road, Leatherhead KT22 8EZ* T: (01372) 372313 E: revgdo@gmail.com

OSBORNE, The Ven Hayward John. b 48. New Coll Ox BA 70 MA 73. Westcott Ho Cam 71. **d** 73 **p** 74. C Bromley SS Pet and Paul *Roch* 73–77; C Halesowen *Worc* 77–80; TV 80–83; TR Worc St Barn w Ch Ch 83–88; V Moseley St Mary *Birm* 88–01; AD Moseley 94–01; Hon Can Birm Cathl 00–01; Adn Birm 01–18; P-in-c Allens Cross 08–09; rtd 18; PtO *Birm* from 18; *Worc* from 19. *30A Roden Avenue, Kidderminster DY10 2RE* T: (01562) 745638 M: 07752-091371 E: hs.osborne@btinternet.com

OSBORNE, Iain George. b 69. Qu Coll Ox BA 92 Man Univ MA 93 Cam Univ BTh 17. Ridley Hall Cam 15. **d** 17 **p** 18. C Oakham, Ashwell, Braunston, Brooke, Egleton etc *Pet* from 17. *The Vicarage, 67 Church Street, Langham, Oakham LE15 7JE* T: (01572) 723978 M: 07935-549947 E: iaingosborne@gmail.com *or* iain@oakhamteam.org.uk

OSBORNE, Preb Jonathan Lloyd. b 62. Ripon Coll Cuddesdon 95. **d** 97 **p** 98. C Mill End and Heronsgate w W Hyde *St Alb* 97–00; Asst Chapl Ealing Hosp NHS Trust 00–03; Chapl Team Ldr 03–10; Asst Chapl W Middx Univ Hosp NHS Trust 00–03; Chapl Team Ldr 03–10; Chapl Team Ldr Meadow House Hospice 03–10; Chapl W Lon Mental Health NHS Trust 03–10; Sen Chapl Metrop Police *Lon* from 10; PtO *St Alb* from 10; Hon Min Can S'wark Cathl from 03; PtO *Roch* from 10; PV Westmr Abbey from 12; Preb St Paul's Cathl *Lon* from 13; Hon C St Andr-by-the-Wardrobe w St Ann, Blackfriars and St Martin Ludgate from 16; Dep P in O from 17. *Senior Chaplain Metropolitan Police Service, Room 7 New Scotland Yard , Victoria Embankment, London SW1A 2JL* T: (020) 7928 9203

OSBORNE, Julian Marcus. b 60. Loughb Univ BSc 82 Lancs Poly MBA 91. St Mellitus Coll 18. **d** 19. NSM Tarporley *Ches* from 19. *3 Dingle Way, Cuddington, Northwich CW8 2UW* T: (01606) 888392 M: 07421-323699 E: jcrcosborne@gmail.com

✠**OSBORNE, The Rt Revd June.** b 53. Man Univ BA 74. Wycliffe Hall Ox 78. **dss** 80 **d** 87 **p** 94 **c** 17. Birm St Martin 80–84; Old Ford St Paul and St Mark *Lon* 84–95; Par Dn Old Ford St Paul w St Steph and St Mark 87–94; P-in-c Old Ford St Paul and St Mark 94–95; Can Res and Treas Sarum Cathl 95–04; Bp's Dom Chapl 95–97; Dean Sarum 04–17; Bp Llan from 17. *Llys Esgob, The Cathedral Green, Llandaff, Cardiff CF5 2YE* T: (029) 2056 2400 F: 2057 7129 E: bishop.llandaff@churchinwales.org.uk

OSBORNE, Malcolm Eric (Max). b 64. EN(G) 87 RMN 92. St Jo Coll Nottm 94. **d** 96 **p** 97. C Walton *St E* 96–99; C Ipswich St Matt 99–02; Soc Resp Adv 99–02; V Newmarket All SS from 02; Asst Dioc Dir of Ords from 16. *All Saints' Vicarage, 32 Warrington Street, Newmarket CB8 8BA* T: (01638) 662514 E: max9@btinternet.com

OSBORNE, Mrs Marianne Lily-May. St Mich Coll Llan. **d** 09 **p** 10. C Tenby *St D* 09–11; P-in-c Burton and Rosemarket 11–14; P-in-c St Issell's and Amroth w Crunwere and Marros 14–17; Children and Youth Development Chapl 11–17; P-in-c Prendergast w Rudbaxton from 17; Dioc Min Area Development Officer from 17. *54 Glenfields Road, Haverfordwest SA61 1EB* T: (01437) 214612 E: marianneosbor@aol.com

OSBORNE, Mark Alexander. b 68. Univ of Wales (Swansea) BA 95. Ridley Hall Cam 16. **d** 18 **p** 19. C Chesterton Gd Shep *Ely* from 18. *48 Metcalfe Road, Cambridge CB4 2DD* M: 07900-552377 E: markosborne8@gmail.com

OSBORNE, Mark William. b 67. Univ of Wales BA 89 Lon Univ MTh 06. Coll of Resurr Mirfield 94. **d** 94 **p** 95. C Goldthorpe w Hickleton *Sheff* 94–97; C-in-c Southey Green St Bernard CD 97–01; P-in-c Walham Green St Jo w St Jas *Lon* 01–12; V 12–18; Chapl Paris St Geo *Eur* from 18. *St George, 7 rue Auguste-Vacquerie, 75116 Paris, France* T: (0033) 1 47 20 22 51 E: mark.osborne5@btinternet.com *or* office@stgeorgesparis.com

OSBORNE, Norma Roberta. b 36. **d** 97 **p** 03. NSM Upper Tooting H Trin *S'wark* 02–03; NSM Tooting St Aug 02–03; NSM Wandsworth St Mich 03–06; NSM Wandsworth St Mich w St Steph 06–07; PtO 07–14 and from 17. *7 Riverside Drive, Richmond TW10 7QA* T: (020) 8255 0280

OSBORNE, Ralph. b 38. Bernard Gilpin Soc Dur 62 Clifton Th Coll 63. **d** 66 **p** 67. C Harpurhey Ch Ch *Man* 66–68; C Chorlton on Medlock St Sav 68–71; C Wilmington *Roch* 71–74; V St Mary Cray and St Paul's Cray 74–85; P-in-c Bath St Steph *B & W* 85–88; P-in-c Charlcombe 86–88; R Charlcombe w Bath St Steph 88–03; rtd 03; PtO *B & W* 09–14. *406 Bath Road, Saltford, Bristol BS31 3DH* T: (01225) 872536

OSBOURNE, Canon David John. b 56. Linc Th Coll 78. **d** 79 **p** 80. C Houghton le Spring *Dur* 79–82; C Spalding

St Jo *Linc* 82–83; C Spalding St Jo w Deeping St Nicholas 83–84; V Swineshead 84–94; RD Holland W 86–92; P-in-c Boultham 94–01; R from 01; RD Christianity 08–17; Can and Preb Linc Cathl from 12. *The Rectory, 2A St Helen's Avenue, Lincoln LN6 7RA* T/F: (01522) 682026 E: david.osbourne@hotmail.co.uk

OSBOURNE, Steven John. b 59. St Jo Coll Nottm 92. **d** 94 **p** 95. C Bushbury *Lich* 94–98; C Tamworth 98–03; V Caverswall and Weston Coyney w Dilhorne 03–17; RD Cheadle 07–14; rtd 17. *8 Vicarage Crescent, Caverswall, Stoke-on-Trent ST11 9EW* T: (01782) 312570 *or* 388037 E: steve.osbourne@btopenworld.com

OSGOOD (*née* **Shipton), Mrs Eileen Kay.** b 81. Cardiff Univ BMus 03. St Mellitus Coll 12. **d** 15 **p** 16. C Chertsey, Lyne and Longcross *Guildf* 15–19; C New Malden and Coombe *S'wark* from 19. *Address temp unknown* M: 07891-953164

OSGOOD, Graham Dean. b 39. Lon Univ BSc 62 ALCD 71. St Jo Coll Nottm 71. **d** 71 **p** 72. C Bebington *Ches* 71–76; V Gee Cross 76–05; rtd 05; PtO *Ox* from 08. *4 Lower Close, Bodicote, Banbury OX15 4DZ* T: (01295) 266848 E: grahamosgood55@yahoo.co.uk

O'SHAUGHNESSY, Mrs Janice Florence. b 51. STETS 95. **d** 98 **p** 99. NSM Bembridge *Portsm* 98–02; Asst Chapl Isle of Wight Healthcare NHS Trust 99–02; C Catherington and Clanfield *Portsm* 02–07; P-in-c Arreton 07–09; V from 09; P-in-c Newchurch 07–09; V from 09; P-in-c Gatcombe 07–09. *The Vicarage, High Street, Newchurch, Sandown PO36 0NN* T: (01983) 865504 E: colleenaluinn@aol.com

OSISIOGU, Lawrence Eberendu. b 60. Qu Foundn Birm 16. **d** 14 **p** 16. PtO *Birm* from 18. *107 Pitfield Road, Birmingham B33 0NY* T: 0121-572 3855 M: 07507-706332 E: eberelaw@yahoo.com

OSMAN, Canon David Thomas. b 49. Bradf Univ BTech 72 Newc Univ MA 93. Trin Coll Bris 75. **d** 78 **p** 79. C Stranton *Dur* 78–81; C Denton Holme *Carl* 81–84; V Preston on Tees *Dur* 84–97; P-in-c Hebburn St Jo 97–18; P-in-c Jarrow Grange 00–18; rtd 18; PtO *Dur* from 18; Hon Can Owo Nigeria from 07. *5 Scotts Court, Gateshead NE10 8JG*

OSMAN, Stephen William. b 53. Matlock Coll of Educn CertEd 74 Teesside Poly CQSW 80. Cranmer Hall Dur 88. **d** 90 **p** 91. C Newbarns w Hawcoat *Carl* 90–93; TV Marfleet *York* 93–00; P-in-c Gotham *S'well* 00–10; P-in-c Barton in Fabis 02–10; P-in-c Thrumpton 02–10; P-in-c Kingston and Ratcliffe-on-Soar 02–10; P-in-c Herrington, Penshaw and Shiney Row *Dur* 10–14; R from 14. *23 Barnwell View, Herrington Burn, Houghton le Spring DH4 7FB* T: 0191-584 5657

OSMASTON, Canon Amiel Mary Ellinor. b 51. Ex Univ BA 73 St Jo Coll Dur BA 84. Cranmer Hall Dur 82. **dss** 84 **d** 87 **p** 94. Chester le Street *Dur* 84–88; Par Dn 87–88; Dir Miss and Past Studies Ridley Hall Cam 89–96; Min Development Officer *Ches* 96–03; C Lache cum Saltney 00–03; Min Development Officer *Carl* 03–16; C Penrith w Newton Reigny and Plumpton Wall 03–16; Hon Can Carl Cathl 05–16; rtd 16; PtO *Carl* from 18. *The Rock, Charney Well Lane, Grange-over-Sands LA11 6DB*

OSMOND, Andrew Mark. b 62. Leeds Univ LLB 85. Wycliffe Hall Ox 02. **d** 02 **p** 09. C Cheltenham St Mary, St Matt, St Paul and H Trin *Glouc* 02–03; NSM Cheltenham St Mark 09–11; Chapl Gloucs Docks Mariners' Ch from 12. *11 Sandhurst Road, Gloucester GL1 2SE* T: (01452) 699552 M: 07906-314463 E: andy@marinersgloucester.org.uk

OSMOND, David Methuen. b 38. Qu Coll Birm 75. **d** 77 **p** 78. C Yardley St Edburgha *Birm* 77–80; V Withall 80–89; R W Coker w Hardington Mandeville, E Chinnock etc *B & W* 89–95; PtO 96–98; rtd 98; Hon C Castle Town *Lich* 01–03; PtO *Blackb* 05–10; *Heref* 14–16; *Lich* 17–18. *56 Essex Road, Church Stretton SY6 6AY* T: (01694) 328329 E: dandhosmond@hotmail.co.uk

OSMOND, Mrs Heather Christine. b 44. ABSM 64 ARCM 65 Birm Poly CertEd 65. Qu Coll Birm 83. **dss** 84 **d** 87 **p** 97. Brandwood *Birm* 84–85; Withall 85–89; Par Dn 87–89; PtO *B & W* 89–01; P-in-c Castle Town *Lich* 01–03; rtd 04; PtO *Blackb* 05–09; *Heref* 14–16; *Lich* from 17. *56 Essex Road, Church Stretton SY6 6AY* T: (01694) 328329 E: dandhosmond@hotmail.co.uk

OSMOND, Tobias Charles. b 74. Plymouth Univ BSc 96. Ripon Coll Cuddesdon BTh 99. **d** 99 **p** 00. C Wilton *B & W* 99–02; C Bath Abbey w St Jas 02–05; I Craighurst, Midhurst and Minesing Canada 05–11; P-in-c Wells St Thos w Horrington *B & W* 11–17; V from 17; P-in-c Chewton Mendip w Ston Easton, Litton etc from 11; RD Shepton Mallet from 16. *The Vicarage, 94 St Thomas Street, Wells BA5 2UZ* T: (01749) 672193 E: vicar@stthomaswells.co.uk

OSSORY AND LEIGHLIN, Archdeacon of. *See* ELMES, The Ven Ruth Katherine

OSSORY, Dean of. *See* MACDONNELL, The Very Revd David

OSTLER, Mrs Christine Anne. b 46. Bp Otter Coll CertEd 68. Westcott Ho Cam 07. **d** 09 **p** 10. NSM Gt w Lt Harrowden and Orlingbury and Isham etc *Pet* 09–12; P-in-c Wellingborough St Barn 12–17; rtd 17; Hon C Wellingborough All Hallows *Pet* from 18; Hon C Wellingborough All SS from 18. *19B Castle Street, Wellingborough NN8 1LW* T: (01933) 226730 E: c.ostler@btinternet.com

OSTLI-EAST (formerly **EAST), Peter Alan.** b 61. Southn Univ LLB 82. Cranmer Hall Dur 90. **d** 93 **p** 94. C Combe Down w Monkton Combe and S Stoke *B & W* 93–97; PtO *Bris* 06–09; TV Bourne Valley *Sarum* 09–15; P-in-c from 15. *The Vicarage, Winterbourne Earls, Salisbury SP4 6HA* T: (01980) 611350 M: 07805-581269 E: ostlieast@gmail.com

O'SULLIVAN, Mrs Hazel. b 50. Open Univ BA 16. S Dios Minl Tr Scheme 91. **d** 94 **p** 95. C Cove St Jo *Guildf* 94–98; TV Headley All SS 98–02; V Bordon 02–04; Chapl Whiteley Village 04–11; rtd 11; PtO *Win* 12–15; *Portsm* 15–19; C Alverstoke from 19. *3 The Avenue, Gosport PO12 2JS* T: (023) 9252 6664 E: hosull@hotmail.co.uk

O'SULLIVAN, Mrs Hazel May. b 64. Surrey Univ BSc 86 ACA 90. SEITE 09. **d** 12 **p** 13. C Reigate St Mary *S'wark* 12–15; P-in-c W Wickham St Fran and St Mary 15–19; V from 19. *St Mary's Vicarage, The Avenue, West Wickham BR4 0DX* M: 07810-698906 E: osullivan_hazel@yahoo.co.uk

O'SULLIVAN, Miss Helen. b 72. Homerton Coll Cam BEd 00. Trin Coll Bris 16. **d** 18 **p** 19. C N Hants Downs *Win* from 18. *The Rectory, Greywell Road, Up Nately, Hook RG27 9PL* M: 07596-749950 E: osullivan.helen333@gmail.com

O'SULLIVAN, Helen Louise. b 68. Westmr Coll Ox BTh 96. St Steph Ho Ox 06. **d** 08 **p** 09. C Chinnor, Sydenham, Aston Rowant and Crowell *Ox* 08–11; P-in-c Brighstone and Brooke w Mottistone *Portsm* 11–13; R 13–16; P-in-c Shorwell w Kingston 11–13; V 13–16; P-in-c Chale 11–13; R 13–15; Chapl St Paul's Cathl *Lon* 16–19; P-in-c Warkworth and Acklington *Newc* from 19; P-in-c Shilbottle from 19. *The Vicarage, 11 Dial Place, Warkworth, Morpeth NE65 0UR* E: aswvicarage@gmail.com

O'SULLIVAN, Kate. b 67. Coll of Resurr Mirfield 14 Qu Foundn Birm 16. **d** 17 **p** 18. C Reddish *Man* from 17. *5 Tytherington Drive, Manchester M19 3TD* M: 07854-598269 E: revdkateosullivan@gmail.com

O'SULLIVAN, Richard Norton. b 59. Glas Coll of Tech BSc 80. Gregorian Univ Rome PhB 85 STB 88 STL 90. **d** 89 **p** 90. In RC Ch 89–96; NSM Clarkston *Glas* 00–02; P-in-c Glas St Oswald 02–06; P-in-c Peterhead *Ab* 06–09; R from 09; R Longside from 09; R Old Deer from 09. *The Rectory, 19 York Street, Peterhead AB42 1SN* T: (01779) 472217 E: richardosullivan01@talktalk.net

OSUNSANMI, Sunkanmi Ebunoluwa. b 71. Univ of Benin MB, BS 97 K Coll Lon MSc 13 MRCPsych 07. Trin Coll Bris 15. **d** 15 **p** 16. PtO *Birm* 15–17; *Glouc* from 17. *Tangley House, Pamington, Tewkesbury GL20 8LX* M: 07785-785647 E: osunsanmi@doctors.org.uk *or* orsunky@yahoo.com

OSWALD, John Edward Guy. b 39. Qu Coll Cam BA 63 MA 67. Ridley Hall Cam. **d** 68 **p** 69. C Chippenham St Paul w Langley Burrell *Bris* 68–72; C Hengrove 72–75; P-in-c Hardenhuish 75–79; P-in-c Kington St Michael 75–79; TV Chippenham St Paul w Hardenhuish etc 79–82; P-in-c Gt w Lt Somerford and Seagry 82–86; P-in-c Corston w Rodbourne 84–86; R Gt Somerford, Lt Somerford, Seagry, Corston etc 86–09; rtd 09; PtO *Bris* from 09; *Sarum* from 15. *Chauffeur Cottage, 26 Draycot Cerne, Chippenham SN15 5LG* T: (01249) 720182

OSWIN, Frank Anthony (Tony). b 43. Chich Th Coll 69. **d** 71 **p** 72. C Radford *Cov* 71–74; C Shrub End *Chelmsf* 74–76; V Layer de la Haye 76–80; V Eastwood St Dav 80–93; TR Withycombe Raleigh *Ex* 93–10; rtd 10. *39 West Cliff Park Drive, Dawlish EX7 9ER* T: (01626) 888897

OTTER, Martin John. b 65. Liv Poly BSc 87 Leeds Univ BA 11. Yorks Min Course 08. **d** 11 **p** 12. C Sherburn in Elmet w Saxton *York* 11–18; C Aberford w Micklefield 15–18; V Marston Moor from 18; Chapl Stockton Hall Hosp from 15. *The Vicarage, Wetherby Road, Rufforth, York YO23 3QF* M: 07842-106044 E: martin@theottersholt.plus.com

OTTEY, Canon John Leonard. b 34. AKC 60 Nottm Univ BA 70. **d** 61 **p** 62. C Grantham St Wulfram *Linc* 61–64; R Keyworth *S'well* 70–85; P-in-c Stanton-on-the-Wolds 71–85; P-in-c E Retford 85–87; V 87–99; P-in-c W Retford 85–87; R 87–99; Hon Can S'well Minster 93–99; rtd 99; PtO *Linc* from 00; *S'well* 04–11. *1 The Orchards, Grantham NG31 9GW* T: (01476) 578762

OTTLEY, David Ronald. b 57. Lanc Univ BA 78. Sarum & Wells Th Coll 79. **d** 81 **p** 82. C Urmston *Man* 81–85; Lect Bolton St Pet 85–87; P-in-c Halliwell St Thos 87–88; V Bolton St Thos 88–98; TR Halliwell 98–03; P-in-c Goostrey

Ches 03–05; V Goostrey w Swettenham 05–09; rtd 09; PtO *Ches* from 10; *Man* from 10; Chapl HM Pris Forest Bank from 16. *HM Prison Forest Bank, Pendlebury, Swinton, Manchester M27 8FB* T: 0161-925 7000 E: ottley696@btinternet.com

OTTO, Andrew Samuel. b 63. St Pet Coll Ox BA 86 MA 90 Bris Univ BA 01. Trin Coll Bris 99. **d** 01 **p** 02. C Trowbridge H Trin *Sarum* 01–05. *37 Timor Road, Westbury BA13 2GA* T: (01373) 858357

OTTO, Mrs Melanie. b 67. Whitelands Coll Lon BSc 89. Sarum Coll BA 16. **d** 16 **p** 18. C N Bradford on Avon and Villages *Sarum* 16–17; C White Horse from 17. *37 Timor Road, Westbury BA13 2GA* T: (01373) 858357 M: 07948-598558 E: melanievotto@gmail.com

OTULE, Robert Samuel. b 66. Univ of E Lon BA 01. St Mellitus Coll 10. **d** 18 **p** 19. C Stratford St Jo w Ch Ch *Chelmsf* from 18. *29 Maryland Park, London E15 1HB* M: 07507-211481

OTUO-ACHEAMPONG, Gilbert Duah. b 79. Cape Coast Univ Ghana BSc 05 Roehampton Univ MA 18. St Nic Th Coll Ghana 08. **d** 09 **p** 10. P-in-c Abonkoso St Thos Ghana 11–12; Chapl St Monica Coll 11–18; C Kumawu St Pet 15; C Nsuta St Jos 15–18; Dioc Evang Dir Mampong 15–18; PtO *S'wark* from 18. *St Anselm's Vicarage, 286 Kennington Road, London SE11 5DU* M: 07594-154483 E: archiedag@yahoo.co.uk

OUGH, John Christopher. b 51. Lon Univ CertEd 74 Open Univ BA 82. SWMTC 91. **d** 94 **p** 95. C Plymouth Em, St Paul Efford and St Aug *Ex* 94–97; P-in-c Diptford, N Huish, Harberton and Harbertonford 97–01; P-in-c Halwell w Moreleigh 97–01; R Diptford, N Huish, Harberton, Harbertonford etc 01–14; C Ermington and Ugborough 10–14; rtd 14; PtO *Truro* from 15. *Carndu, Rosenithon, St Keverne, Helston TR12 6QR* T: (01326) 281079 E: johnoughrev@gmail.com

OULD, Julian Charles. b 57. MHCIMA 77. Coll of Resurr Mirfield 80. **d** 83 **p** 84. C Hebburn St Cuth *Dur* 83–86; C Pet H Spirit Bretton 86–90; R Peakirk w Glinton 90–95; R Peakirk w Glinton and Northborough 95–96; TR Is of Scilly *Truro* 96–98; R 98–06; TR Totnes w Bridgetown, Berry Pomeroy etc *Ex* from 06; RD Totnes 06–18. *The Rectory, Northgate, Totnes TQ9 5NX* T: (01803) 865615 E: julian@totnesrectory.co.uk

OULD, Peter. b 74. Man Univ BA 96. Wycliffe Hall Ox BTh 05. **d** 05 **p** 06. C Ware Ch Ch *St Alb* 05–11; PtO *Cant* from 12. *3 Goudhurst Close, Canterbury CT2 7TZ* T: (01227) 456209 E: mail@peter-ould.net

OUTEN (née BAILEY), Mrs Joyce Mary Josephine. b 33. St Gabr Coll Lon CertEd 69. S'wark Ord Course 80. **dss** 83 **d** 87 **p** 94. Par Dn Woolwich St Mary w St Mich *S'wark* 87–89; Par Dn Rusthall *Roch* 89–94; C 94–97; rtd 97; Asst Chapl Kent and Cant Hosps NHS Trust 97–99; Asst Chapl E Kent Hosps NHS Trust 99–00; TV Whitstable *Cant* 00–07; PtO from 07. *10 Foxgrove Road, Whitstable CT5 1PB* T: (01227) 273643 E: joyceouten@talktalk.net

OVENDEN, Canon John Anthony. b 45. Open Univ BA 80 BA 93 K Coll Lon MA 96. Sarum & Wells Th Coll 71. **d** 74 **p** 75. C Handsworth *Sheff* 74–77; C Isfield *Chich* 77–80; C Uckfield 77–80; P-in-c Stuntney *Ely* 80–85; Min Can, Prec and Sacr Ely Cathl 80–85; V Primrose Hill St Mary w Avenue Road St Paul *Lon* 85–98; Can Windsor and Chapl in Windsor Gt Park 98–12; rtd 12; Dean of Chpl and Fell Harris Manchester Coll Ox from 12; Dir English Hymnal Co 93–00; Chapl to The Queen 02–15; PtO *Glouc* from 17. *Little Croft, Great Rissington, Cheltenham GL54 2LN* E: johnovenden@btinternet.com

OVEREND, Alan. b 53. Sheff Univ BA 75. Oak Hill Th Coll 84. **d** 86 **p** 87. C Aughton St Mich *Liv* 86–89; P-in-c Eccleston Park 89–92; V 92–99; V Ainsdale 99–07; V Billinge 07–17; rtd 17; PtO *Ches* from 18. *4 Hazelwood Road, Barnton, Northwich CW8 4SJ*

OVEREND, Barry Malcolm. b 49. K Coll Lon BD 71 AKC 71. St Aug Coll Cant 71. **d** 72 **p** 73. C Nailsworth *Glouc* 72–74; C High Harrogate Ch Ch *Ripon* 75–78; V Collingham w Harewood 78–87; V Far Headingley St Chad 87–10; rtd 10; PtO *Bradf* 10–14; *Leeds* from 14. *46 Langford Lane, Burley in Wharfedale, Ilkley LS29 7EJ* T: (01943) 968248 E: barry.sue.overend@gmail.com

OVEREND, Canon Paul. b 66. Coll of Ripon & York St Jo BA 88 Hull Univ MA 96 Univ of Wales (Cardiff) PhD 04. Coll of Resurr Mirfield 88. **d** 93 **p** 94. C Cayton w Eastfield *York* 93–96; Asst Chapl Univ of Wales (Cardiff) *Llan* 96; Sen Chapl 97–03; Tutor 03–04; Tutor St Mich Coll Llan 03–04; Teaching Fell Liv Hope Univ 04–05; Dir Initial Minl Formation *Sarum* 05–06; Vice Prin Sarum OLM Scheme 05–06; Prin OLM 06–08; Tutor STETS and Co-ord for Locally Deployable Ord Min 08–09; Tutor STETS 11–12; C Wymondham *Nor* 12–13; Lay Development Officer 14–18; Asst Dir of Ords 15–18; Hon PV Nor Cathl 16–18; Can Res and Chan Linc Cathl from 18.

3A Vicars Court, Lincoln LN2 1PT E: paul.overend@gmail.com *or* chancellor@lincolncathedral.com

OVERINGTON, Canon David Vernon. b 34. ALCD 60. **d** 60 **p** 61. C Penge Ch Ch w H Trin *Roch* 60–62; C Lenton *S'well* 62–65; PC Brackenfield w Wessington *Derby* 65–71; P-in-c Cubley w Marston Montgomery 71–76; R Bridgetown Australia 76–79; Par P Denmark 79–85; Can Bunbury 84–85; R E Fremantle w Palmyra Australia 85–90; Field Officer Angl Dept of Educn 90–93; R Wembley 93–99; Hon Can Perth from 96; rtd 99; P-in-c Longside *Ab* 99–03; P-in-c New Pitsligo 99–03; P-in-c Old Deer 99–03; P-in-c Strichen 99–03; PtO *Roch* from 04; *Guildf* from 17. *7 Kingsmead, 98 Foley Road, Claygate, Esher KT10 0NB* E: overington@talktalk.net

OVERTHROW, Royston John. b 45. Southn Univ BTh 94. Portsm Dioc Tr Course 84. **d** 85. NSM Portsm Cathl 85–91; PtO 91–94; Bp's Dom Chapl *Sarum* 94–02; NSM Marlborough 02–04; rtd 04; PtO *Sarum* from 04. *19 Bratton Avenue, Devizes SN10 5BA* T: (01380) 722404 E: roy.overthrow@btinternet.com

OVERTON, Charles Henry. b 51. CCC Ox BA 74 MA 77 Fitzw Coll Cam PGCE 75 BA 79 MA 85. Ridley Hall Cam 77. **d** 80 **p** 81. C Tonbridge SS Pet and Paul *Roch* 80–84; Asst Chapl St Lawr Coll Ramsgate 84–87; P-in-c Aythorpe w High and Leaden Roding *Chelmsf* 88–95; P-in-c Hughenden *Ox* 95–01; P-in-c Chalfont St Peter 05–08; R 08–16; rtd 16; PtO *Heref* from 17. *The Vallets, Letton, Hereford HR3 6DN* T: (01544) 327912 E: charlesoverton@hotmail.com

OVERTON, John Michael. b 48. CCC Ox BA 71 MA 74 CPA 77 MRSC 01. Ripon Coll Cuddesdon 11. **d** 12 **p** 13. NSM New Mills *Derby* 12–16; NSM Buxton w Burbage and King Sterndale from 16. *6 Brown Edge Close, Buxton SK17 7AS* T: (01298) 24845 E: jm.overton@btinternet.com

OWEN, Mrs Carole Janice. b 55. **d** 01 **p** 02. NSM Cley Hill Warminster *Sarum* 01–07; NSM Warminster St Denys and Upton Scudamore 07–17; PtO from 17; Chapl Gt Western Hosps NHS Foundn Trust from 14. *11 Stuart Green, Warminster BA12 9NU* T: (01985) 214849 E: richardowen50@hotmail.com

OWEN, Caroline Ann. b 59. Univ of Wales (Abth) BA 80 PGCE 81. St Mich Coll Llan 03. **d** 05 **p** 06. NSM Bangor *Ban* 05–09; V Cadoxton-juxta-Neath and Tonna *Llan* 09–12; V Dan yr Eppynt *S & B* 12–16; P-in-c Dowlais and Penydarren *Llan* from 16. *The Rectory, Gwernllwyn Uchaf, Dowlais, Merthyr Tydfil CF48 3NA* T: (01685) 558660 E: calowen18@gmail.com

OWEN, Christine Rose. b 62. Univ of Wales (Ban) BA 83 PGCE 84. Qu Coll Birm 86. **d** 88 **p** 94. C Ynyscynhaearn w Penmorfa and Porthmadog *Ban* 88–90; Asst Chapl Lon Univ 90–96; Hon C St Marylebone w H Trin 94–96; Min Can and Prec Worc Cathl 96–00; R Llansantffraid Glan Conwy and Eglwysbach *St As* 00–12; AD Llanrwst 09–12; V Colwyn Bay w Brynymaen 12–16; TV Aled Miss Area from 17. *The Vicarage, 27 Walshaw Avenue, Colwyn Bay LL29 7UY* T: (01492) 539522 E: revdchristine@btinternet.com

OWEN, Christopher David. b 73. Trin Coll Bris 10. **d** 12 **p** 13. C Walton-on-Thames *Guildf* 12–16; TV High Wycombe *Ox* from 16. *70 Marlow Road, High Wycombe HP11 1TH* M: 07890-422357 E: cdowen1973@gmail.com

OWEN, Clifford. *See* OWEN, Phillip Clifford

OWEN, Daniel James. b 71. Anglia Poly Univ BSc 94 TCD BTh 00. CITC 97. **d** 00 **p** 01. C Belfast St Donard *D & D* 00–03; I Rathcooney Union *C, C & R* 03–09; I Kilgariffe Union 09–15; Chapl St Columba's Coll Dub from 15. *8 Hurley Lane, St Columba's College, Kilmashogue Lane, Rathfarnham, Dublin 16, Republic of Ireland* T: (00353) (1) 493 2219 E: danielsonja@gmail.com

OWEN, David Cadwaladr. b 56. Grey Coll Dur BSc 77 Univ Coll Worc PGCE 99. WEMTC 00. **d** 03 **p** 04. NSM Pershore w Pinvin, Wick and Birlingham *Worc* 03–07; TV Droitwich Spa 07–14; P-in-c Salwarpe and Hindlip w Martin Hussingtree 10–14; V Loddon, Sisland, Chedgrave, Hardley and Langley *Nor* from 14; RD Loddon from 16. *The Vicarage, 4 Market Place, Loddon, Norwich NR14 6EY* M: 07837-800009 E: david.chetvalley@gmail.com

OWEN, Canon David William. b 31. Down Coll Cam BA 55 MA 58. Linc Th Coll 55. **d** 57 **p** 58. C Salford St Phil w St Steph *Man* 57–61; C Grantham St Wulfram *Linc* 61–65; V Messingham 65–70; V Spilsby w Hundleby 70–77; R Aswardby w Sausthorpe 71–77; R Langton w Sutterby 71–77; R Halton Holgate 73–77; P-in-c Firsby w Gt Steeping 75–77; P-in-c Lt Steeping 75–77; TR Louth 77–92; Chapl Louth Co Hosp 77–92; RD Louthesk *Linc* 82–89; Can and Preb Linc Cathl 85–92; TR Swan *Ox* 92–97; RD Claydon 94–96; rtd 97; PtO *Ox* 10–19. *19 Stephen Road, Headington, Oxford OX3 9AY* T: (01865) 766585 E: davidowen9@sky.com

OWEN, Miss Denise. b 65. Warwick Univ BA 87 Westmr Coll of Educn PGCE 92. Coll of Resurr Mirfield 12. **d** 14 **p** 15. C Spotland and Oakenrod *Man* 14–17; P-in-c Oldham Moorside 17–18; V from 18; C Clarksfield and Waterhead from 17. *1 Glebe Lane, Oldham OL1 4SJ* T: 0161-652 0292 E: therevd.dowen@yahoo.co.uk

OWEN, Edgar. b 26. WMMTC. **d** 82 **p** 83. NSM Garretts Green *Birm* 82–88; NSM Stechford 88–94; rtd 94; PtO *Birm* from 94. *36 Colbourne Court, 116 Frederick Road, Stechford, Birmingham B33 8AE* T: 0121-783 5603 E: edgar.owen78@gmail.com

OWEN, Gary John. b 72. City Univ BSc 93 Fitzw Coll Cam BA 97 MA 01. Ridley Hall Cam 95. **d** 98 **p** 99. C Welshpool w Castle Caereinion *St As* 98–01; TV Wrexham 01–10; R Eynsford w Farningham and Lullingstone *Roch* 10–19; TR Newton Tracey, Horwood, Alverdiscott etc *Ex* from 19. *The Rectory, High Bickington, Umberleigh EX37 9AY* M: 07947-358050

OWEN, Geoffrey Neill. b 55. Chich Th Coll. **d** 85 **p** 86. C Streatham St Pet *S'wark* 85–89; C Battersea Ch Ch and St Steph 89–91; TV Surbiton St Andr and St Mark 91–97; V Merton St Jas 97–08; V Battersea Ch Ch and St Steph from 08; RD Battersea 10–16. *Christ Church Vicarage, Candahar Road, London SW11 2PU* T: (020) 7228 1225 E: geoffreyowen1956@gmail.com

OWEN, Glyn John. b 56. Open Univ BA 91 Nottm Univ MSc 93 St Jo Coll Dur BA 05. Cranmer Hall Dur 01. **d** 03 **p** 04. C Whiston *Sheff* 03–07; V Rudston w Boynton, Carnaby and Kilham *York* 07–15; P-in-c Burton Fleming w Fordon, Grindale etc 07–15; V Rudston, Boynton, Carnaby etc from 15; RD Bridlington 12–17. *The Vicarage, Rudston, Driffield YO25 4XA* T: (01262) 420313 E: revglynowen@btinternet.com

OWEN, Graham Anthony. b 54. Birm Univ BA 77. Trin Coll Bris 92. **d** 94 **p** 95. C Wiveliscombe w Chipstable, Huish Champflower etc *B & W* 94–98; R Frome w Frome H Trin from 99; RD Frome from 17. *Holy Trinity Vicarage, Orchard Street, Frome BA11 3BX* T: (01373) 462586 E: graham-owen@hotmail.co.uk

OWEN, Miss Hannah Mair. b 72. **d** 13 **p** 14. NSM Carmarthen St Pet and Abergwili etc *St D* 13–16; C Cwmaman 16; C Catheiniog 16–18; P-in-c Llandybie from 18. *The Vicarage, 77 King's Road, Llandybie, Ammanford SA18 2TL* E: revmair@gmail.com

OWEN, Harry Dennis. b 47. Oak Hill Th Coll 73. **d** 76 **p** 77. C Fulham Ch Ch *Lon* 76–81; V Byker St Mark *Newc* 81–89; V Plumstead All SS *S'wark* 89–14; RD Plumstead 03–14; rtd 14. *13 Ratton Road, Eastbourne BN21 2LU* T: (01323) 419425 E: h.d.owen@talk21.com

OWEN, James Thomas. *See* McNAUGHTAN-OWEN, James Thomas

OWEN, Canon John Edward. b 52. Middx Poly BA 75. Sarum & Wells Th Coll BTh 81. **d** 81 **p** 82. C S Ashford Ch Ch *Cant* 81–85; TV Bemerton *Sarum* 85–91; V St Leonards and St Ives *Win* 91–95; R N Stoneham 95–09; V Steep and Froxfield w Privett *Portsm* from 09; Hon Can Portsm Cathl from 18. *The Vicarage, 77 Church Road, Steep, Petersfield GU32 2DF* T: (01730) 264282 E: revjohnowen@gmail.com

OWEN, Karen. *See* HOPWOOD OWEN, Karen

OWEN, Kenneth Phillip. b 56. Liv Univ BA 77 PGCE 78. NOC 92. **d** 95 **p** 96. C Heswall *Ches* 95–01; V Frankby w Greasby from 01. *The Vicarage, 14 Arrowe Road, Greasby, Wirral CH49 1RA* T: 0151-678 6155 E: kennethpowen@gmail.com

OWEN, Mair. *See* OWEN, Hannah Mair

OWEN, Mark. b 63. RMN. St Mich Coll Llan 03. **d** 05 **p** 06. C Tredegar *Mon* 05–08; V Rhymney 08–14; P-in-c Mynyddislwyn 14–18; P-in-c Blackwood w Fleur-de-Lis 15–18; TR Upper Islwyn from 18; AD Bedwellty from 15. *The Vicarage, Commercial Street, Pengam, Blackwood NP12 3UA* T: (01443) 836805 E: fathermarkowen12@gmail.com

OWEN, Paul Jonathan. b 59. S Bank Poly BSc 81 Anglia Poly Univ MA 03. Ridley Hall Cam 00. **d** 02 **p** 03. C Seaford w Sutton *Chich* 02–06; R Denton w S Heighton and Tarring Neville 06–11; V Seaford w Sutton from 11. *The Vicarage, 46 Sutton Road, Seaford BN25 1SH* T: (01323) 893508 E: revpowen@gmail.com

OWEN, Phillip Clifford. b 42. G&C Coll Cam BA 65 MA 69 Birm Univ PhD 07. Ridley Hall Cam 71. **d** 73 **p** 74. C Stowmarket *St E* 73–76; C Headley All SS *Guildf* 76–81; TV 81–89; P-in-c Clifton-on-Teme, Lower Sapey and the Shelsleys *Worc* 89–97; R 97–02; Dioc Ecum Officer 98–02; P-in-c Corfu *Eur* 03–08; P-in-c Ostend 08–12; rtd 12; PtO *Ely* from 13; *Eur* from 18. *147 Sapley Road, Hartford, Huntingdon PE29 1YH* T: (01480) 435488 M: 07887-745632 E: cliffordret@gmail.com

OWEN, Mrs Phyllis Elizabeth. b 48. NTMTC. **d** 05 **p** 06. NSM Southend *Chelmsf* from 05. *42 Harcourt Avenue, Southend-on-Sea SS2 6HU* T: (01702) 353049 E: thephiz@blueyonder.co.uk

OWEN, Raymond Philip. b 37. Man Univ BScTech 60 AMCST 60. Chich Th Coll 65. **d** 67 **p** 68. C Elland *Wakef* 67–70; C Lindley 70–73; V Bradshaw 73–80; Ind Chapl *Dur* 80–91; TR Hanley H Ev *Lich* 91–99; Bp Stafford's Past Aux 03–04; rtd 04; PtO *Lich* 04–07; C Alton w Bradley-le-Moors and Denstone etc 07–17; PtO from 17. *Dove House, Bridge Hill, Mayfield, Ashbourne DE6 2HN* M: 07747-601379 E: revrayowen@hotmail.com

OWEN, Canon Richard Llewelyn. b 27. Univ of Wales (Lamp) BA 51. St Mich Coll Llan 51. **d** 53 **p** 54. C Holyhead w Rhoscolyn w Llanfair-yn-Neubwll *Ban* 53–57; C Porthmadog 57–59; R Llanfechell w Bodewryd, Rhosbeirio etc 59–67; Youth Chapl 66–67; V Penrhyndeudraeth and Llanfrothen 67–77; R Llangefni w Tregaean and Llangristiolus etc 77–89; Can Ban Cathl 82–93; Hon Can Ban Cathl from 93; Treas Ban Cathl 86–93; Can Missr and V Ban Cathl 89–93; RD Arfon 92–93; rtd 93; PtO *Ban* from 93. *Bodowen, Great Orme's Road, Llandudno LL30 2BF* T: (01492) 872765

OWEN, Richard Matthew. b 49. Sheff Univ BA 70 Leeds Univ CertEd 73. NOC 84. **d** 87 **p** 88. NSM Chorlton-cum-Hardy St Werburgh *Man* 87–89; C N Reddish 89–91; PtO *York* 91–96 and 97–03; NSM York St Olave w St Giles 96–97; PtO *Cant* from 12. *17 Mill Lane, St Radigunds, Canterbury CT1 2AW* T: (01227) 784430 M: 07789-923516 E: richardowen100@gmail.com

OWEN, Ronald Alfred. b 44. Wilson Carlile Coll 73 Sarum & Wells Th Coll 80. **d** 81 **p** 82. C Wotton St Mary *Glouc* 81–83; CF 83–97; P-in-c Salcombe *Ex* 97–02; V Salcombe and Malborough w S Huish 02–06; RD Woodleigh 00–03; rtd 07; PtO *B & W* from 07. *9 Reedmoor Gardens, Bridgwater TA6 3SL* T: (01278) 433801 M: 07540-102030 E: owenrarev@gmail.com

OWEN, Sally Ann. *See* ROBERTSON, Sally Ann

OWEN, Stuart James. b 68. Sunderland Poly BA 91. Ripon Coll Cuddesdon BTh 00. **d** 00 **p** 01. C Hendon St Mary and Ch Ch *Lon* 00–04; P Missr Edmonton St Mary w St Jo 04–08; V Edmonton All SS w St Mich from 08; AD Enfield from 16. *All Saints' Vicarage, 43 All Saints' Close, London N9 9AT* T: (020) 8803 9199 E: fr.stuart@gmail.com

OWEN, Susan Elizabeth. *See* WYATT, Susan Elizabeth

OWEN-JONES, Mrs Ingrid. b 41. **d** 11 **p** 12. OLM W Hallam and Mapperley w Stanley *Derby* 11–19; PtO *Win* from 19. *Bron Erw, 1 Harfield Crescent, Medstead, Alton GU34 5TE* M: 07977-808041 E: ingrid@ipoj.co.uk

OWEN-JONES, Peter Charles. b 57. Ridley Hall Cam 92. **d** 94 **p** 95. C Leverington and Wisbech St Mary *Ely* 94–97; R Haslingfield w Harlton and Gt and Lt Eversden 97–05; P-in-c Glynde, W Firle and Beddingham *Chich* from 05. *The Vicarage, The Street, Firle, Lewes BN8 6NP* T: (01273) 858005 M: 07973-265953

OWEN-JONES, Peter John. b 47. RMCS BScEng 68 CEng 84 MIMechE 84 MBIM 87 FPWI 89. EMMTC 85. **d** 88 **p** 89. NSM Holbrook and Lt Eaton *Derby* 88–00; NSM W Hallam and Mapperley w Stanley 01–13; RD Erewash 12–13; MSE Officer 11–13; rtd 13; PtO *Derby* 13–19; *Win* from 19. *Bron Erw, 1 Harfield Crescent, Medstead, Alton GU34 5TE* M: 07771-828018 E: peter@ipoj.co.uk

OWENS, Christopher Lee. b 42. SS Mark & Jo Coll Chelsea 61 Lon Inst of Educn TCert. Linc Th Coll 66. **d** 69 **p** 70. C Dalston H Trin w St Phil *Lon* 69–72; C Portsea N End St Mark *Portsm* 72–81; TV E Ham w Upton Park and Forest Gate *Chelmsf* 81–92; C Is of Dogs Ch Ch and St Jo w St Luke *Lon* 92–98; P-in-c Chingford St Edm *Chelmsf* 98–02; V 02–07; rtd 07; PtO *Chelmsf* from 08. *67 Disraeli Road, London E7 9JU* T: (020) 8555 6337 E: owenseaster@gmail.com

OWENS, Mrs Janet. b 49. Liv Univ MEd 99. NOC 90. **d** 13 **p** 14. NSM Stockport St Sav *Ches* 13–14; NSM Offerton St Alb and Stockport St Thos 14–18; rtd 18; PtO *Ches* from 18. *6 Chelworth Manor, 37 Manor Road, Bramhall, Stockport SK7 3LX* T: 0161-312 4683 M: 07990-570778 E: revandrog@gmail.com

OWENS, Mrs Margaret Jean. b 49. Man Univ BSc 70 Birm Univ MSc 72. St Jo Coll Nottm BA(ThM) 03. **d** 01 **p** 02. NSM Hurdsfield *Ches* 01–07; V Disley 07–18; rtd 18; PtO *Ches* from 19. *7 Ridge View, Macclesfield SK11 8DB* T: (01625) 501242 M: 07775-801613 E: mowens44@btinternet.com

OWENS, Canon Patricia Margaret. **d** 07 **p** 08. NSM Buckley *St As* 07–16; NSM Ruabon and Rhosymedre 10–16; NSM Offa Miss Area from 17; Hon Can St As Cathl from 14. *The Clappers, Pont-y-Capel Lane, Gresford, Wrexham LL12 8RS* T: (01978) 854855

OWENS, Stephen Graham Frank. b 49. Ch Coll Cam BA 71 MA 75 CertEd 72. Qu Coll Birm 73. **d** 75 **p** 76. C Stourbridge St Mich Norton *Worc* 75–80; Tanzania 80–88; V Dudley Wood

Worc 88–99; P-in-c Mamble w Bayton, Rock w Heightington etc 99–02; V 02–14; rtd 14; PtO *Worc* from 15. *9 Waterlaide Road, Hartlebury, Kidderminster DY11 7TP* T: (01299) 251176

OWERS, Ian Humphrey. b 46. Em Coll Cam BA 68 MA 72. Westcott Ho Cam 71. **d** 73 **p** 74. C Champion Hill St Sav *S'wark* 73–77; V Peckham St Sav 77–82; P-in-c E Greenwich Ch Ch w St Andr and St Mich 82–83; V 83–94; P-in-c Westcombe Park St Geo 85–94; RD Greenwich 92–94; PtO *St E* 01–07; *Bradf* 03–10; *Sheff* from 10. *St Aidan's Vicarage, 4 Manor Lane, Sheffield S2 1UF* T: 0114-272 4676 M: 07808-613252

OXBORROW, Alison Louise. b 68. Nottm Univ BA 90 Lon Sch of Th BA 04 Solicitor 92. St Jo Coll Nottm 08. **d** 11 **p** 12. C Didsbury St Jas and Em *Man* 11–14; PtO 14–15; Chapl Springhill Hospice from 15. *15 Grotton Hollow, Grotton, Oldham OL4 4LN* M: 07870-917710

OXBROW, Canon Mark. b 51. Reading Univ BSc 72 Fitzw Ho Cam BA 75 MA 79. Ridley Hall Cam 73. **d** 76 **p** 77. C Luton Ch Ch *Roch* 76–80; TV Newc Epiphany 80–88; Chapl Newc Mental Health Unit 80–88; Regional Sec Eur CMS 88–01; Communication Resources Sec 94–97; Internat Miss Dir 01–03; Asst Gen Sec 03–08; Internat Co-ord Faith2Share Network 08–18; Dir Guided Study Progr Ox Cen for Miss Studies from 18; Hon Can Brussels Cathl *Eur* from 98; PtO from 19. *Oxford Centre for Mission Studies, St Philip and St James Church, Woodstock Road, Oxford OX2 6HR* M: 07984-631816 E: moxbrow@ocms.ac.uk

OXENFORTH, Colin Bryan. b 45. St Chad's Coll Dur BA 67. **d** 69 **p** 70. C Bromley St Andr *Roch* 69–72; C Nunhead St Antony *S'wark* 72–76; V Toxteth St Marg *Liv* 76–89; V Brixton St Matt *S'wark* 89–00; V Pemberton St Jo *Liv* 00–10; rtd 10; PtO *Liv* from 10. *Flat 3, 5 Walmer Road, Liverpool L22 5NL* T: 0151-721 2018 E: crosbyboy@sky.com

OXFORD (Christ Church), Dean of. *See* PERCY, The Very Revd Prof Martyn William

OXFORD, Archdeacon of. *See* GORICK, The Ven Martin Charles William

OXFORD, Bishop of. *See* CROFT, The Rt Revd Steven John Lindsey

OXLEY, Canon Christopher Robert. b 51. Sheff Univ BA 73 PGCE 74. Wycliffe Hall Ox BA 78 MA 83. **d** 79 **p** 80. C Greasbrough *Sheff* 79–82; C Doncaster St Leon and St Jude 82–84; Asst Chapl Brussels *Eur* 84–87; V Humberstone *Leic* 87–93; V Beaumont Leys 93–05; RD Christianity S 98–01; P-in-c Leic St Anne 05–09; P-in-c Leic St Paul and St Aug 05–09; V Leic St Anne, St Paul w St Aug 09–11; P-in-c Avon-Swift 11–17; Dir Post-Ord Tr 04–09; Hon Can Leic Cathl 10–17; Cathedral Chaplain Leic Cathl from 15; rtd 17; PtO *Leic* from 18. *The Vicarage, Vicarage Drive, Foxton, Market Harborough LE16 7RJ* M: 07803-878879 E: chrisandpaula@canonoxley.co.uk

OXLEY, Ms Helen Mary. b 64. TCD BA 88 HDipEd 89 Univ of Wales (Trin St Dav) MMin 11. **d** 11 **p** 12. NSM Dunleckney w Nurney, Lorum and Kiltennel *C & O* from 11. *11 Ashbrook, Tullow Hill, Tullow, Co Carlow, Republic of Ireland* T: (00353) (59) 918 0975 M: 86-378 6980 E: revheleno@gmail.com

OXLEY, Mrs Paula Jane. b 51. Sheff Univ BA 74 Nottm Univ MA 00 PGCE 75. EMMTC 93. **d** 93 **p** 94. NSM Birstall and Wanlip *Leic* 93–95; C Beaumont Leys 95–05; NSM Leic St Anne, St Paul w St Aug 05–14; PtO *Cov* from 13; *Leic* 14–17; P-in-c Foxton w Gumley and Laughton from 17. *The Vicarage, Vicarage Road, Foxton, Market Harborough LE16 7RJ* T: (01858) 540439 E: oxleypj@btinternet.com

OXTOBY, David Antony. b 72. Huddersfield Univ BSc 98. Ridley Hall Cam 08. **d** 10 **p** 11. C Stamford St Geo w St Paul *Linc* 10–13; P-in-c Sutton Bridge 13–14; C The Suttons w Tydd 13–14; V Sutton Bridge and Tydd St Mary 14–18; TR Rayleigh *Chelmsf* from 18. *The Rectory, Hockley Road, Rayleigh SS6 8BA* M: 07595-387652 E: david@oxtobyhome.co.uk

P

PACEY, Graham John. b 52. Open Univ BA 81 Leeds Univ CertEd 74 Teesside Poly AdDipEd 85. NEOC 90. **d** 93 **p** 94. C Kirkleatham *York* 93–96; V Middlesbrough St Agnes 96–00; R Skelton w Upleatham 00–09; V Boosbeck and Lingdale 07–09; R Guisborough 09–13; RD 11–13; rtd 13; PtO *York* from 14. *16 Exeter Street, Saltburn-by-the-Sea TS12 1BN* T: (01287) 280883 E: g.pacey@ntlworld.com

PACEY, James Stewart. b 84. Nottm Trent Univ 07 Cam Univ BTh 15. Westcott Ho Cam 12. **d** 15 **p** 16. C Hucknall Torkard *S'well* 15–18; V Carrington from 18. *Carrington Vicarage, 6 Watcombe Circus, Nottingham NG5 2DT* M: 07595-035342 E: revjamespacey@gmail.com

PACK, Barbara Denise. b 62. Lanc Univ BEd 86 Dur Univ PGCE 18. All SS Cen for Miss & Min 15. **d** 18 **p** 19. NSM Blackb St Aid, St Luke, St Mark and St Phil from 18. *41 Pendle Road, Leyland PR25 5TU* T: (01772) 304201 E: barcarr@sky.com

PACKER, Catherine Ruth. *See* PICKFORD, Catherine Ruth

✠**PACKER, The Rt Revd John Richard.** b 46. Keble Coll Ox BA 67 MA. Ripon Hall Ox 67. **d** 70 **p** 71 **c** 96. C St Helier *S'wark* 70–73; Chapl Abingdon St Nic *Ox* 73–77; Tutor Ripon Hall Ox 73–75; Tutor Ripon Coll Cuddesdon 75–77; V Wath-upon-Dearne w Adwick-upon-Dearne *Sheff* 77–86; RD Wath 83–86; TR Sheff Manor 86–91; RD Attercliffe 90–91; Adn W Cumberland *Carl* 91–96; P-in-c Bridekirk 95–96; Suff Bp Warrington *Liv* 96–00; Bp Ripon and Leeds 00–14; rtd 14; Hon Asst Bp Newc from 14. *Devonshire House, Alma Place, Whitley Bay NE26 2EQ* T: 0191-253 4321 E: bppacker@googlemail.com

PACKER, Peter Aelred. b 48. St Jo Coll Dur BA 70 St Chad's Coll Dur PhD 79 Strathclyde Univ MBA 00. Ven English Coll Rome 95. **d** 96 **p** 97. SSM 91–98; Hon C S Lambeth St Anne and All SS *S'wark* 96–98; OSB and LtO *Ox* 98–99; Bp's Adv in Miss and Resources *Glas* 99–00; PtO *S'wark* 08–09; Hon C Deptford St Paul 09–10; P-in-c Peckham St Jo w St Andr 10–18; rtd 18. *Address withheld by request* M: 07932-648034 E: packerpunch@gmail.com

PACKER, Preb Roger Ernest John. b 37. ARCO 59 Pemb Coll Cam BA 60 MA 64. Cuddesdon Coll 60. **d** 62 **p** 63. C Chippenham St Andr w Tytherton Lucas *Bris* 62–65; C Caversham *Ox* 65–70; R Sandhurst 70–91; V Bridgwater St Mary, Chilton Trinity and Durleigh *B & W* 91–00; RD Bridgwater 94–00; Preb Wells Cathl 96–00; rtd 00; PtO *Chelmsf* from 00. *3 Kreswell Grove, Harwich CO12 3SZ* T: (01255) 502239 E: roger.packer44@gmail.com

PACKMAN, James Morley. b 76. SS Hild & Bede Coll Dur MSci 99. Oak Hill Th Coll BA 04. **d** 04 **p** 05. C Eastbourne All SS *Chich* 04–08; R Frant w Eridge 08–18; RD Rotherfield 15–18; R Nailsea H Trin *B & W* from 18. *10 Ilminster Close, Nailsea, Bristol BS48 4YU* T: (01275) 853227

PADDICK, Graham. b 47. S'wark Ord Course. **d** 89 **p** 90. C St Helier *S'wark* 89–93; P-in-c Thornton Heath St Paul 93–96; V Dormansland 98–14; Chapl MU 03–08; AD Godstone *S'wark* 08–12; Dir Ords Croydon Area 96–14; rtd 14; PtO *S'wark* 14–16. *14 Went Hill Gardens, Eastbourne BN22 0QP* T: (01323) 502970 M: 07866-820547 E: graham.paddick@gmail.com

PADDISON, Mrs Jennifer Sheila. b 70. Cranmer Hall Dur. **d** 07 **p** 08. C Newc H Cross 07–11; Chapl Nottm Trent Univ *S'well* 12–18; PtO *Ely* from 19; *Leic* from 11. *The Vicarage, 2 Bardolph Way, Alconbury Weald, Huntingdon PE28 4BP* T: (01480) 454114 E: jenny.paddison@outlook.com

PADDISON, Canon Michael David William. b 41. Oak Hill Th Coll 75. **d** 77 **p** 78. C Gt Warley Ch Ch *Chelmsf* 77–80; C Rayleigh 80–83; R Scole, Brockdish, Billingford, Thorpe Abbots etc *Nor* 83–95; RD Redenhall 89–94; R Reepham, Hackford w Whitwell, Kerdiston etc 95–06; RD Sparham 00–05; Hon Can Nor Cathl 02–06; rtd 06; PtO *Nor* from 06. *4 North Street, Castle Acre, King's Lynn PE32 2BA* T: (01760) 755648 E: m.s.paddison@gmail.com

PADDISON, Robert Michael. b 70. Cranmer Hall Dur. **d** 07 **p** 08. C Whorlton *Newc* 07–11; P-in-c Barrow upon Soar w Walton le Wolds *Leic* 11–18; P-in-c Wymeswold and Prestwold w Hoton 11–18; Pioneer Min *Ely* from 18. *The Vicarage, 2 Bardolph Way, Alconbury Weald, Huntingdon PE28 4BP* T: (01480) 454114 M: 07905-136836 E: rev.paddison@outlook.com

PADDOCK, The Very Revd John Allan Barnes. b 51. Liv Univ BA 74 MA 91 Ox Univ BA 77 MA 81 Glas Univ PhD 05 Cardiff Univ LLM 08 Man Univ PGCE 75 FRSA 94. St Steph Ho Ox 75. **d** 80 **p** 81. C Matson *Glouc* 80–82; Asst Chapl Madrid *Eur* 82–83; Chapl R Gr Sch Lanc 83–86; Hon C Blackb Ch Ch w St Matt 83–86; Chapl RAF 86–91; OCM 92–94; Chapl St Olave's Gr Sch Orpington 91–94; PtO *Blackb* 94–97; Chapl R Russell Sch Croydon 97–00; Hon C Bickley *Roch* 97–00; V Folkestone St Pet *Cant* 00–03; Hon Min Can Cant Cathl 01–03; V Glouc St Geo w Whaddon 03–08; Dean Gib *Eur* 08–17; rtd 17. *Address withheld by request*

PADFIELD, Stephen James. b 68. Ex Univ BA 90 Univ Coll Dur PGCE 92. Trin Coll Bris BA 00 MA 01. **d** 01 **p** 02. C Luton Ch Ch *Roch* 01–05; Chapl R Russell Sch Croydon 05–12; Chapl Dulwich Coll 12–15; Hon C Dulwich St Barn *S'wark* 12–15; Chapl K Sch Roch from 15. *Deanery Lodge, Kings Orchard, Rochester ME1 1TG* M: 07747-775385 E: padfieldstephen@gmail.com *or* spadfield@kings-rochester.co.uk

PADLEY, Kenneth Peter Joseph. b 78. Ex Coll Ox BA 00 MA 04 CCC Ox DPhil 16. Ripon Coll Cuddesdon BA 03 MSt 04. **d** 04 **p** 05. C Cen Swansea *S & B* 04–07; Warden of Ch Hostel and Chapl Ban Univ 07–12; Dir of Ords 11–12; V St Alb St Mich from 12. *St Michael's Vicarage, St Michael's Street, St Albans AL3 4SL* T: (01727) 835037 E: kennethpadley@gmail.com

PADMORE, Lynn Beverley. b 51. EMMTC. **d** 06 **p** 07. NSM Beaumont Leys *Leic* 06–09; TV Ascension TM 09–14; rtd 14; PtO *Nor* from 14. *Brightmore, 13 Clifton Way, Overstrand, Cromer NR27 0NG* T: (01263) 576720 E: lynn.padmore@hotmail.co.uk

PAGAN, Canon Keith Vivian. b 37. St Jo Coll Dur BA 60 MA 66. Chich Th Coll 60. **d** 62 **p** 63. C Clacton St Jas *Chelmsf* 62–64; C Wymondham *Nor* 64–70; P-in-c Guestwick 70–80; P-in-c Kettlestone 70–79; V Hindolveston 70–80; R Islay *Arg* 80–98; R Campbeltown 80–98; Miss to Seamen 80–98; Can St Jo Cathl Oban *Arg* 85–98; Can Cumbrae 85–98; Hon Can Cumbrae from 99; rtd 98; LtO *Arg* from 04. *Mariefield, Southend, Campbeltown PA28 6RW* T: (01586) 830310

PAGDEN, Wendy Jane. b 59. St Mellitus Coll MA 16. **d** 16 **p** 17. NSM Marks Tey and Aldham *Chelmsf* from 16. *5 Rockingham Close, Colchester CO4 0NJ* E: pagdenfamily@virginmedia.com

PAGE, David. b 48. Bris Univ BA 70 Leic Univ MA 74 Southn Univ PGCE 74. St Jo Coll Nottm 81. **d** 83 **p** 84. C Morden *S'wark* 83–86; V Wimbledon St Luke 86–91; P-in-c Clapham Common St Barn 91–92; V 92–08; rtd 08; PtO *Chich* from 13. *Rye View, The Strand, Winchelsea TN36 4JY* T: (01797) 226524 E: david@ryeview.net

PAGE, Canon David James. b 62. Liv Univ BSc 83 Qu Coll Ox DPhil 87. Trin Coll Bris BA 93 MA 95. **d** 96 **p** 97. C Knutsford St Jo and Toft *Ches* 96–99; R Elworth and Warmingham 99–11; V Elworth from 11; RD Congleton 13–18; Hon Can Ches Cathl from 19. *The Rectory, 2 Taxmere Close, Sandbach CW11 1WT* T: (01270) 762415 E: vicar@stpeters-elworth.org.uk

PAGE, Mrs Gill Lydia. b 53. Bp Grosseteste Coll PGCE 91 Derby Lonsdale Coll BCombStuds 85 Sheff Univ BA 12 MA 18. Yorks Min Course 10. **d** 12 **p** 13. NSM Todmorden w Cornholme and Walsden *Leeds* 12–15; NSM Clifton 15–16; NSM Clifton 16–19; rtd 19. *2 Pierson Street, Newark NG24 4JG* M: 07974-704374 E: gillpagetod@yahoo.co.uk

PAGE, Gillian Fiona. b 55. Hull Coll of Educn CertEd 76. Cranmer Hall Dur 08. **d** 10 **p** 11. C W Bolton *Man* 10–13; TV Walkden and Lt Hulton from 13. *St Paul's Vicarage, 10 Old Vicarage Gardens, Worsley, Manchester M28 3JR* M: 07866-936323 E: gill91@btopenworld.com

PAGE, Mrs Heather. b 54. **d** 13 **p** 14. NSM Hadley and Wellington Ch Ch *Lich* 13–16; NSM Oakengates, Priors Lee and Wrockwardine Wood 16–17; NSM Cen Telford from 17. *46 Appledore Gardens, Wellington, Telford TF1 1RR* T: (01952) 249165 E: h.page@blueyonder.co.uk

PAGE, John Jeremy. b 56. Keble Coll Ox BA 79 MA 82 New Coll Edin BD 86. Edin Th Coll 83. **d** 86 **p** 87. C Wetherby *Ripon* 86–89; TV Wrexham *St As* 89–92; Chapl Hymers Coll Hull 92–98; Chapl Charterhouse Sch Godalming 98–03; TR Hale w Badshot Lea *Guildf* 03–10; R Elstead 10–19; V Thursley 10–19; rtd 19. *Address temp unknown*

PAGE, Jonathan Michael. b 58. Ripon Coll Cuddesdon 97. **d** 99 **p** 00. C Littlemore *Ox* 99–02; V Chaddesden St Phil *Derby* 02–09; P-in-c Derby St Mark 07–09; V Chaddesden St Phil w Derby St Mark 09–10; RD Derby N 06–10; P-in-c Belper Ch Ch w Turnditch 10–13; V from 13; C Ambergate and Heage 10–12; RD Duffield 10–18; PtO *Eur* from 17. *Christ Church Vicarage, Bridge Street, Belper DE56 1BA* T: (01773) 824974 E: vicar@christchurchbelper.co.uk

PAGE, Judy. b 42. Keele Univ DipEd 63 BA 63 Westmr Coll Ox BTh 02. TISEC 03. **d** 05 **p** 06. C Paisley H Trin and St Barn *Glas* 05–13; PtO *Win* from 14. *109B Priory Road, Southampton SO17 2JS* T: (023) 8032 1241 E: revjudypage@live.co.uk

PAGE, Lynda Christina. b 55. STETS 04. **d** 07 **p** 08. NSM Blackmoor and Whitehill *Portsm* 07–14; P-in-c Lyng, Sparham, Elsing, Bylaugh, Bawdeswell etc *Nor* 14–16; PtO from 17. *The Sycamores, 28 King's Lynn Road, Hunstanton PE36 5HT* T: (01485) 534605 M: 07790-494296 E: lyn.page@willow-bank.co.uk

PAGE, Canon Michael John. b 42. K Coll Lon BD 66 AKC 66. **d** 67 **p** 68. C Rawmarsh w Parkgate *Sheff* 67–72; C-in-c Gleadless Valley CD 72–74; TR Gleadless Valley 74–77; V

Lechlade *Glouc* 77–86; RD Fairford 81–86; V Winchcombe, Gretton, Sudeley Manor etc 86–02; Hon Can Glouc Cathl 91–02; RD Winchcombe 94–99; Chapl E Glos NHS Trust 94–02; rtd 02; PtO *Sheff* from 03. *18 Brocco Bank, Sheffield S11 8RR* T: 0114-266 3798 E: michael278@me.com

PAGE, Owen Richard. b 53. FIBMS 83. Linc Th Coll 89. **d** 91 **p** 92. C Gt Bookham *Guildf* 91–94; V Kings Heath *Pet* 94–99; TR Daventry, Ashby St Ledgers, Braunston etc 99–07; RD Daventry 00–07; ACUPA Link Officer 00–07; CUF Project Officer 00–05; Can Pet Cathl 07; V Todmorden *Wakef* 07–13; P-in-c Cornholme and Walsden 12–13; V Todmorden w Cornholme and Walsden *Leeds* 13–15; Asst Dir of Ords 09–15; AD Calder Valley 13–15; TR Clifton *S'well* 15–19; rtd 19. *2 Pierson Street, Newark NG24 4JG* M: 07980-639631 E: ramblingrector@virginmedia.com

PAGE, Canon Thomas William. b 57. Sarum & Wells Th Coll 84. **d** 87 **p** 88. C Caterham *S'wark* 87–91; C Cheam 91–95; P-in-c Cranham *Chelmsf* 95–04; R Chingford SS Pet and Paul 04–12; V Chelmsf Ascension 12–14; P-in-c Chelmsf All SS 14; V Chelmsf Ascension from 14; AD Chelmsf N 15–18; Dioc NSM Officer from 99; Hon Can Chelmsf Cathl from 15. *Ascension Vicarage, 57 Maltese Road, Chelmsford CM1 2PB* T: (01245) 269906 E: frtom1@priest.com

PAGE, Canon Trevor Melvyn. b 41. Dur Univ BA 63 Fitzw Coll Cam BA 67 MA 72. Westcott Ho Cam 64. **d** 67 **p** 68. C Millhouses H Trin *Sheff* 67–69; Chapl Sheff Univ 69–74; V Doncaster Intake 74–82; Can Res Sheff Cathl 82–00; Dioc Dir of In-Service Tr 82–95; Dioc Dir of Ords and Post-Ord Tr 82–00; R Bradfield 00–06; Hon Can Sheff Cathl 01–06; rtd 06; PtO *Sheff* 06–18. *39 Benty Lane, Sheffield S10 5NF* T: 0114-268 3879

PAGE, William George. b 42. Linc Th Coll 83. **d** 85 **p** 86. C Boston *Linc* 85–89; V Sibsey w Frithville 89–07; RD Holland E 95–97; rtd 07; PtO *York* from 08. *20 Marshall Drive, Pickering YO18 7JT* T: (01751) 476915 E: dunvicaring@btinternet.com

PAGE-CLARK, Howard David. b 53. Fitzw Coll Cam MA 77. **d** 97 **p** 98. OLM Lytchett Minster *Sarum* 97–10; OLM The Lytchetts and Upton from 10. *37 Gorse Lane, Poole BH16 5RR* T: (01202) 620239 E: hdpc@talktalk.net

PAGE DAVIES, David John. b 36. St Cath Soc Ox BA 58 MA 62. St D Coll Lamp 58. **d** 60 **p** 61. C Rhosddu *St As* 60–68; Chr Aid Area Sec (Glos, Herefords and Worcs) 68–85; Midl Regional Co-ord 78–85; Area Co-ord (Devon and Cornwall) 86–01; LtO *Truro* 86–01; PtO 01–09; rtd 01. *3 Chyenhal Cottages, Buryas Bridge, Penzance TR19 6AN* T: (01736) 732466 E: johnp-d@tiscali.co.uk

PAGE-TURNER, Canon Edward <u>Gregory</u> **Ambrose Wilford.** b 31. Qu Coll Birm 57. **d** 60 **p** 61. C Helmsley *York* 60–64; C Kensington St Phil Earl's Court *Lon* 64–67; C Walton-on-Thames *Guildf* 67–70; V Seend *Sarum* 70–71; V Seend and Bulkington 71–79; R Bladon w Woodstock *Ox* 79–87; P-in-c Begbroke 80–86; P-in-c Shipton-on-Cherwell 80–86; P-in-c Hampton Gay 80–85; RD Woodstock 84–87; P-in-c Wootton by Woodstock 85–87; R Patterdale *Carl* 87–89; R Askerswell, Loders and Powerstock *Sarum* 89–01; RD Lyme Bay 92–98; RD Beaminster 94–97; Can and Preb Sarum Cathl 99–01; rtd 01; PtO *Sarum* 01–18; B & W 02–05; *Eur* 02–06. *The Old School House, 9 School House Close, Beaminster DT8 3AH* T: (01308) 861410 E: canon.pageturner@btinternet.com

PAGET, Robert James Innes. b 35. AKC 59. **d** 60 **p** 61. C Attenborough w Bramcote *S'well* 60–63; C Cheltenham St Mark *Glouc* 63–72; P-in-c Pilsley *Derby* 72–73; TV N Wingfield, Pilsley and Tupton 73–89; R Pinxton 89–97; P-in-c Ambergate and Heage 97–05; rtd 06; PtO *Derby* from 06. *1A Jeffries Lane, Crich, Matlock DE4 5DT* T: (01773) 852072 E: bob@locksunart.plus.com

PAGET-WILKES, The Ven Michael Jocelyn James. b 41. ALCD 69. **d** 69 **p** 70. C Wandsworth All SS *S'wark* 69–74; V Hatcham St Jas 74–82; V Rugby St Matt *Cov* 82–90; Adn Warwick 90–09; rtd 09; PtO *Glouc* from 16. *64 Tarlton, Cirencester GL7 6PA* T: (01285) 770553 E: michael.pw@btinternet.com

PAILING, Canon Crispin Alexander. b 75. Qu Coll Ox BA 98 MA 01 Birm Univ PhD 08. Ripon Coll Cuddesdon BA 02. **d** 03 **p** 04. C Four Oaks *Birm* 03–06; P-in-c Perry Barr 06–10; V 10–14; AD Handsworth 13–14; R Liv Our Lady and St Nic from 14; Hon Can Liv Cathl from 19. *St Nicholas' House, 71 Woodlands Road, Aigburth, Liverpool L17 0AL* T: 0151-727 4872 E: crispin.pailing@queens.oxon.org *or* rector@livpc.co.uk

PAILING, Canon Rowena Fay. b 77. Qu Coll Ox BA 99 MA 02 Birm Univ PhD 08. Ripon Coll Cuddesdon BA 02. **d** 03 **p** 04. C Four Oaks *Birm* 03–04; C Gravelly Hill 04–07; P-in-c Handsworth St Mich 07–12; Dir Past Studies Coll of Resurr Mirfield 12–18; PtO *Birm* 12–15; *Liv* from 14; Can Res

Blackb Cathl from 18. *1 Cathedral Close, Blackburn BB1 5AA* E: missioner@blackburncathedral.co.uk

PAIN, Isaac Timothy. b 86. Southn Univ BA 09 PGCE 10. Oak Hill Th Coll BA 17. **d** 17 **p** 18. C Burgess Hill St Andr *Chich* from 17. *9 Pendean, Burgess Hill RH15 0DW* M: 07738-301996 E: isaacpain@hotmail.com

✠**PAIN, The Rt Revd Richard Edward.** b 56. Bris Univ BA 79 Univ of Wales (Cardiff) BD 84. St Mich Coll Llan 81. **d** 84 **p** 85 **c** 13. C Caldicot *Mon* 84–86; P-in-c Cwmtillery 86–88; V 88–91; V Six Bells 88–91; V Risca 91–98; V Overmonnow w Wonastow and Michel Troy 98–03; V Monmouth w Overmonnow etc 03–08; Adn Mon 08–13; P-in-c Mamhilad w Monkswood and Glascoed Chapel 08–13; Warden of Ords 01–06; Can St Woolos Cathl 03–13; Bp Mon 13–19; rtd 19. *Address temp unknown*

PAINE, Alasdair David MacConnell. b 60. Trin Coll Cam BA 82 MA 86 MSc 84. Wycliffe Hall Ox 94. **d** 96 **p** 97. C Ex St Leon w H Trin 96–01; V Westbourne Ch Ch Chpl *Win* 02–11; V Cambridge H Sepulchre *Ely* from 11. *The Round Church Vicarage, Manor Street, Cambridge CB1 1LQ* T: (01223) 518218 E: alasdair.paine@stag.org

PAINE, Peter Stanley. b 46. K Coll Lon BD 69 AKC 69. Cuddesdon Coll 69. **d** 71 **p** 72. C Leeds St Aid *Ripon* 71–74; C Harrogate St Wilfrid 74–78; V Beeston Hill S Spirit 78–82; TV Seacroft 82–90; V Martham w Repps w Bastwick *Nor* 90–94; V Martham and Repps w Bastwick, Thurne etc 94–04; P-in-c Foremark and Repton w Newton Solney *Derby* 04–08; V 08–11; rtd 11; PtO *Liv* from 16. *Beachway House, 27 Stratford Close, Southport PR8 2RT* E: peterspaine@gmail.com

PAINE, Canon William Barry. b 58. CITC. **d** 84 **p** 85. C Glendermott *D & R* 84–86; C Lurgan St Jo *D & R* 86–88; I Kilbarron w Rossnowlagh and Drumholm *D & R* 88–91; CF 91–00; I Tynan w Middletown and Aghavilly *Arm* 00–09; I Ballinderry, Tamlaght and Arboe from 09; Can Arm Cathl from 17. *The Rectory, 10 Brookmount Road, Cookstown BT80 0BB* T: (028) 7941 8500 E: bpaine.888@hotmail.co.uk

PAINTER, Christopher Mark. b 65. Cranmer Hall Dur. **d** 00 **p** 01. C Melksham *Sarum* 00–03; Chapl Wilts and Swindon Healthcare NHS Trust 02–03; TV Eccles *Man* 03–07; PtO *Ches* 13–14; NSM Hale Barns w Ringway 14–15; P-in-c Calstock *Truro* 15–17; P-in-c St Dominic, Landulph and St Mellion w Pillaton 15–17; R Tamar Valley from 17; RD E Wivelshire from 17. *Oaklands House, Albaston, Gunnislake PL18 9EZ* E: revchrispainter@gmail.com

PAINTER, The Ven David Scott. b 44. Worc Coll Ox BA 68 MA 72 LTCL 65. Cuddesdon Coll 68. **d** 70 **p** 71. C Plymouth St Andr w St Paul and St Geo *Ex* 70–73; Chapl Plymouth Poly 71–73; C St Marylebone All SS *Lon* 73–76; Abp's Dom Chapl and Dir of Ords *Cant* 76–80; V Roehampton H Trin *S'wark* 80–91; RD Wandsworth 85–90; PV Westmr Abbey 81–91; Can Res and Treas S'wark Cathl 91–00; Dioc Dir of Ords 91–00; Adn Oakham and Can Res Pet Cathl 00–11; rtd 11; Hon C Towcester Deanery 11–17; R Brington w Whilton and Norton etc *Pet* 17–19. *3 Meeting Lane, Towcester NN12 6JX* T: (01327) 438392 M: 07976-687059

PAINTING, Stephen Nigel. b 60. Trin Coll Bris 01. **d** 03 **p** 04. C Heanton Punchardon w Marwood *Ex* 03–08; TV Beaconsfield *Ox* 08–11; Chapl Lee Abbey 11–14; TV Wellington and Distr *B & W* 14–16; PtO *Ex* 17–18; P-in-c Heanton Punchardon, Marwood and W Down from 18. *The Rectory, Heanton, Barnstaple EX31 4DG* T: (01271) 812605

PAIRMAN, David Drummond. b 47. GGSM CertEd. Chich Th Coll 82. **d** 84 **p** 85. C Cowes St Mary *Portsm* 84–87; C Marshwood Vale *Sarum* 87–88; C Hawkchurch 87–88; C Marshwood Vale 88–95; rtd 95. *Chestnut Cottage, Old Pinn Lane, Exeter EX1 3RF* T: (01392) 464488

PAISEY, Gerald Herbert John. b 31. Wm Booth Memorial Coll 51 Lanc Univ CertEd 62 Nottm Univ DipAdEd 70 MPhil 77 Lanc Univ MA 78 K Coll Lon PhD 91. St Alb Minl Tr Scheme 80. **d** 88 **p** 90. NSM Montrose *Bre* 88–90; NSM Inverbervie 88–90; Lect Robert Gordon Univ *Ab* 89–97; P-in-c Stonehaven and Catterline *Bre* 90–01; rtd 01; Tutor Open Univ 90–05; PtO *Bre* 03–07; LtO *Edin* from 08. *40 South Middleton, Uphall, Broxburn EH52 5GB* T: (01506) 865937

PAISEY, Canon Jeremy Mark. b 58. Aber Univ LLB 81 Solicitor 83. Coates Hall Edin 92. **d** 94 **p** 95. C Turriff *Ab* 94–97; C Buckie 94–97; C Banff 94–97; C Cuminestown 94–97; C Portsoy 94–97; P-in-c Buckie from 97; P-in-c Portsoy from 97; P-in-c Banff from 98; Can St Andr Cathl from 08. *All Saints' Rectory, 14 Cluny Square, Buckie AB56 1HA* T: (01542) 832312 M: 07817-261435 E: jpaisey@aol.com

PAISLEY, Canon Samuel Robinson (Robin). b 51. Man Univ BSc 72. Edin Th Coll BD 91. **d** 91 **p** 92. C St Mary's Cathl *Glas* 91–95; P-in-c Bishopbriggs 95–06; Teaching Consultant Glas Univ 95–99; Chapl Stobhill NHS Trust 95–99; Bp's Adv in Min *Glas* 99–07; R Dumfries 06–16; Chapl NHS Dumfries

and Galloway 06–16; Can St Mary's Cathl *Glas* 06–16; rtd 16; Hon Can St Mary's Cathl *Glas* from 16; PtO from 16. *30 Grampian Way, Bearsden, Glasgow G61 4RW* M: 07464-234308 E: essrpg@gmail.com

PAKENHAM, Kia Louise. b 73. RGN 95. SCRTP 15. **d** 18 **p** 19. NSM Wonersh w Blackheath *Guildf* from 18. *Goblins, Elmbridge Road, Cranleigh GU6 8NW* T: (01483) 277919 M: 07971-077664 E: kiapakenham@icloud.com

PALAIRET, Agnes Ka Yee. b 84. Aber Univ BSc 06 MSc 07. Trin Coll Bris 17. **d** 19. C Bris St Mary Redcliffe w Temple etc from 19. *1A Colston Parade, Bristol BS1 6RA* M: 07727-275157 E: aggypal@gmail.com

PALK, Deirdre Elizabeth Pauline. b 41. Reading Univ BA 63 Lon Univ MA 94 Leic Univ PhD 02 AIL 77 FIOSH 96 FRHistS 06. S'wark Ord Course 81. **dss** 84 **d** 87. Wanstead H Trin Hermon Hill *Chelmsf* 84–88; Hon Par Dn 87–88; Hon Par Dn Walthamstow St Pet 88–93; Hon Chapl UPA Projects 97; Tutor NTMTC 97–01; rtd 01. *3 Ashdon Close, Woodford Green IG8 0EF* T: (020) 8498 0649

PALLANT, Canon Roger Frank. b 35. Trin Coll Cam BA 57 MA 61. Wells Th Coll 57. **d** 59 **p** 60. C Stafford St Mary *Lich* 59–62; C Ipswich St Mary le Tower *St E* 62–65; Dioc Youth Chapl 62–65; Development Officer C of E Youth Coun 65–70; Hon C Putney St Mary *S'wark* 66–71; Org Sec New Syn Gp 70–71; R Hintlesham w Chattisham *St E* 71–80; V Ipswich All Hallows 80–88; Hon Can St Cathl 85–00; P-in-c Sproughton w Burstall 88–00; Dioc Officer for OLM 88–00; RD Samford 93–99; rtd 00; PtO *St E* from 00. *163 Fircroft Road, Ipswich IP1 6PT* T: (01473) 461148

PALLENT, Ian. b 70. Newc Poly BA 91. Ridley Hall Cam 05. **d** 07 **p** 08. C Bayston Hill *Lich* 07–10; R Jersey St Ouen w St Geo *Win* from 10. *The Rectory, La Route du Marais, St Ouen, Jersey JE3 2GG* T: (01534) 481800 *or* 485686 M: 07870-630433 E: ianpallent@hotmail.com

PALLETT, Canon Ian Nigel. b 59. Leeds Univ BA 80. Linc Th Coll 81. **d** 84 **p** 85. C Halesowen *Worc* 84–88; C Mansfield Woodhouse *S'well* 88–91; R Morton and Stonebroom *Derby* 91–98; P-in-c Heanor 98–01; V 01–03; P-in-c Dingwall *Mor* 03–11; P-in-c Strathpeffer 03–11; R Dingwall 11–16; R Strathpeffer 11–16; P-in-c Invergordon St Ninian 15–16; Chapl NHS Grampian from 16; Can St Andr Cathl Inverness *Mor* from 09. *23 Stuart Street, Ardersier, Inverness IV2 7RS* T: 03454-566000 *or* (01667) 460030 E: pallett3000@btinternet.com

PALLIS, Mrs Maria. b 60. NOC 96. **d** 99 **p** 00. C Chapel Allerton *Ripon* 99–03; P-in-c Collingham w Harewood 03–11; P-in-c Spofforth w Kirk Deighton 07–11; V Banstead *Guildf* from 11; RD Epsom 14. *The Vicarage, 21 Court Road, Banstead SM7 2NQ* T: (01737) 351134 E: mariapallis@hotmail.com

PALMER, Abigail Louise. b 79. Leeds Univ BA 01 PGCE 02. St Hild Coll 15. **d** 17 **p** 18. C Pannal w Beckwithshaw *Leeds* from 17. *80 Beckwith Crescent, Harrogate HG2 0BH* T: (01423) 543478 E: curate@strobertschurch.co.uk

PALMER, Alister Gordon. b 46. Univ of Tasmania BA 73 DipEd 74. Trin Coll Bris 76 Ridley Hall Cam 78. **d** 80 **p** 81. C Patchway Bris 80–83; C Bushbury *Lich* 83–86; V Wednesfield Heath 86–93; NSM Independent Ch Community Work 93–98; Dioc Officer for Min Tas Australia 98–02; Dir Angl Miss 99–02; C Smestow Vale *Lich* 02–03; V Knowle St Barn Bris 03–07; P-in-c Inns Court H Cross 05–07; V Filwood Park 07–13; rtd 13; PtO *Bris* from 18. *4 Rowberrow, Bristol BS14 0AD* T: (01275) 832208 E: agpal46@hotmail.co.uk

PALMER, Andrew Richmond. b 84. St Chad's Coll Dur BA 06. Oak Hill Th Coll MA 14. **d** 14 **p** 15. C Hampstead St Jo Downshire Hill Prop Chpl *Lon* 14–18; PtO *S'wark* from 18. *Christ Church Balham, 15 Chestnut Grove, London SW12 8JA* T: (020) 3302 6640 M: 07866-584293 E: andy.palmer@live.com

PALMER, Angus Douglas. b 40. St Chad's Coll Dur BA 62. **d** 63 **p** 64. C Wallsend St Pet *Newc* 63–66; C Newc H Cross 66–69; C Bottesford *Linc* 69–70; R Penicuik *Edin* 70–84; R W Linton 77–84. *6 Hackworth Gardens, Wylam NE41 8EJ* T: (01661) 853786 E: angusandjanet@gmail.com

PALMER, Canon Christopher John Ingamells. b 71. **d** 98 **p** 99. C Emscote *Cov* 98–02; TV Mortlake w E Sheen *S'wark* 02–10; AD Richmond and Barnes 05–10; TR Merton Priory 10–18; Can Res and Chan Ex Cathl from 18. *Exeter Cathedral Office, 1 The Cloisters, Exeter EX1 1HS* T: (01392) 255573 E: chris.palmer@exetercathedral.org.uk

PALMER, David Edward. See HAGAN-PALMER, David Edward

PALMER, David Michael. b 53. QUB BA 95 MSc. CITC 95. **d** 97 **p** 98. C Glenageary *D & G* 97–99; C Agherton *Conn* 99–00; I Ramoan w Ballycastle and Culfeightrin 00–10; I Magherally w Annaclone *D & D* from 10. *Magherally Rectory, 46 Kilmacrew Road, Banbridge BT32 4EP* T: (028) 4062 5625 M: 07591-382599 E: david.palmer@cantab.net

PALMER, Derek James. b 54. Man Univ BA 77. Qu Coll Birm 77. **d** 79 **p** 80. C Leek *Lich* 79–83; CF 83–92; R Riviera Beach St Geo USA 92–95; C S Ockendon and Belhus Park *Chelmsf* 95–98; V Walthamstow St Mich 98–00; Chapl Salford Univ *Man* 00–06; AD Salford 02–03; P-in-c Droylsden St Andr 06–09; TR Oldham 09–11; V Oldham St Mary w St Pet from 11; Bp's Adv on New Relig Movements from 02. *The Rectory, Prince Charlie Street, Oldham OL1 4HJ* T: 0161-633 1560 M: 07979-121635 E: vicarofoldham@gmail.com

PALMER, Elizabeth. *See* BLATCHLEY, Elizabeth

PALMER, Graham. b 31. Em Coll Cam BA 53 MA 57. Qu Coll Birm 56. **d** 58 **p** 59. C Camberwell St Giles *S'wark* 58–61; C Kilburn St Aug *Lon* 61–67; P-in-c Fulham St Alb 67–73; V 73–92; V Fulham St Alb w St Aug 92–97; rtd 97; PtO *Lon* 97–13. *7 Wellington Court, 116 Knightsbridge, London SW1X 7PL* T: (020) 7584 4036

PALMER, Hugh. b 50. Pemb Coll Cam BA 72 MA 76. Ridley Hall Cam 73. **d** 76 **p** 77. C Heigham H Trin *Nor* 76–80; Bp's Chapl for Tr and Miss 80–84; C St Helen Bishopsgate w St Andr Undershaft etc *Lon* 85–95; C Fulwood *Sheff* 95–97; V 97–05; Hon Can Sheff Cathl 01–05; R Langham Place All So *Lon* from 05; Chapl to The Queen from 12. *12 Weymouth Street, London W1W 5BY* T: (020) 7580 3522 E: ramona.ramsahadeo@allsouls.org

✠**PALMER, The Rt Revd Ian Stanley.** b 50. K Coll Lon BD 71. Cranmer Hall Dur 73. **d** 75 **p** 76 **c** 13. C Huyton St Mich *Liv* 75–78; Chapl Dur Univ 78–83; V Collierley w Annfield Plain 83–90; Dir Evang Newc Australia 90–92; R Belmont N and Redhead 93–00; Adn Upper Hunter and R Muswellbrook 00–05; R Queanbeyan 05–13; Adn Chapl 09–13; Adn S Canberra and Queanbeyan 09–13; Bp Bathurst 13–19; rtd 19. *PO Box 1001, North Melbourne VIC 3051, Australia* M: (0061) 41-124 2596 E: palmeris50@fastmail.fm

PALMER, Mrs Jane Alexandra. b 83. Univ of Wales (Ban) BA 05 Homerton Coll Cam PGCE 06. St Jo Sch of Miss Nottm MA 16. **d** 16 **p** 17. C Trowbridge St Jas and Keevil *Sarum* 16–19; V Atworth w Shaw and Whitley from 19. *The Vicarage, Corsham Road, Shaw, Melksham SN12 8EH* M: 07530-513243 E: janepalmer042013@gmail.com

PALMER, John Richard Henry. b 29. AKC 52. **d** 53 **p** 54. C Englefield Green *Guildf* 53–57; P-in-c Brewarrina Australia 57–62; C Wareham w Arne *Sarum* 62–63; PC Derby St Jo 63–66; Chapl Holloway Sanatorium Virginia Water 66–70; Chapl Brookwood Hosp Woking 70–94; rtd 94; PtO *Truro* from 94. *Lightning Ridge, Pentreath Road, The Lizard, Helston TR12 7NY* T: (01326) 290654

PALMER, Judith Angela. b 47. Bris Univ MB, ChB 71. NOC 02. **d** 05 **p** 06. NSM Strensall *York* 05–14; PtO from 14. *6 Portisham Place, Strensall, York YO32 5AZ* T: (01904) 613356 E: j.palmer@phonecoop.coop

PALMER, Mrs Julia Elizabeth. b 57. Hull Univ BA 80. St Jo Coll Nottm MA 98. **d** 99 **p** 00. C Snodland All SS w Ch Ch *Roch* 99–03; P-in-c Sutton Bonington w Normanton-on-Soar *S'well* 03–08; P-in-c Sutton in Ashfield St Mary 08–11; PtO *Lon* 18–19; V W Acton St Martin from 19. *St Martin's Vicarage, 25 Birch Grove, London W3 9SP* M: 07939-043959 E: juliapalmer12@gmail.com

PALMER, Mrs June Ann. b 42. **d** 11 **p** 12. OLM Elmton and Whitwell *Derby* 11–14; OLM E Scarsdale from 14. *22 Field Drive, Shirebrook, Mansfield NG20 8BN* T: (01623) 744835

PALMER, Mrs Kathleen. b 50. **d** 19. NSM Brandon *St E* from 19. *Address temp unknown* E: palm427@aol.com

PALMER, Kevin Anthony. b 59. St Steph Ho Ox. **d** 01 **p** 02. C Tunstall *Lich* 01–04; R Wednesbury St Jas and St Jo 04–13; V Longton St Mary and St Chad from 13; CMP from 02. *St Mary and St Chad's Presbytery, 269 Anchor Road, Stoke-on-Trent ST3 5DN* T: (01782) 313142 E: frkevinpalmer@live.co.uk

PALMER, Marc Richard. b 72. St Jo Coll Dur BA 96. Cranmer Hall Dur 93. **d** 98 **p** 99. C Chester le Street *Dur* 98–03; TV Bensham 03–08; V Bensham and Teams 08–10; V Nor St Mary Magd w St Jas 10–18; P-in-c Drayton from 18. *The Rectory, 46 School Road, Drayton, Norwich NR8 6EF*

PALMER, Marion Denise. b 42. Open Univ BA 82 SRN 64 SCM 66. Linc Th Coll 84. **dss** 86 **d** 87 **p** 94. Poplar *Lon* 86–90; Par Dn 87–90; Par Dn Gillingham St Mary *Roch* 90–94; C 94–96; C Farnborough 96–02; rtd 02; PtO *St E* from 04. *14 Prestwick Avenue, Felixstowe IP11 9LF* T: (01394) 671588

PALMER, Canon Maureen Florence. b 38. Qu Eliz Coll Lon BSc 60 PhD 64. Ripon Coll Cuddesdon. **dss** 85 **d** 87 **p** 94. Tupsley *Heref* 85–88; C 87–88; Par Dn Talbot Village *Sarum* 88–91; Chapl Birm Cathl 91–96; Can Pastor and Can Res Guildf Cathl 96–06; Sub-Dean 99–06; rtd 06; PtO *Heref* from 06. *28A Green Street, Hereford HR1 2QG* T: (01432) 353771 E: palmer349@btinternet.com

PALMER, Michael Christopher. b 43. AKC 67 CQSW 76. **d** 68 **p** 69. C Easthampstead *Ox* 68–71; Miss to Seamen 71–73;

Hong Kong 73; LtO *Ox* 76–79; LtO *Truro* 79–83; Dioc Soc Resp Adv 83–98; Bp's Dom Chapl 85–87; V Devoran 87–98; rtd 98; PtO *Truro* 98–08; *Ox* 08–10; *Chich* from 10. *5 Little Drove, Singleton, Chichester PO18 0HD* M: 07717-222385

PALMER, Nigel Shaun. b 50. Ch Ch Ox BA 71 MA 84. St Steph Ho Ox BA 15. **d** 17 **p** 18. NSM Kentish Town *Lon* from 17. *The Manor House, 13 Park Vista, London SE10 9LZ* M: 07710-423790 E: nigel1palmer@btinternet.com

PALMER, Mrs Patricia. b 51. STETS. **d** 09 **p** 10. NSM Basingstoke *Win* from 09. *97 Packenham Road, Basingstoke RG21 8YA* T: (01256) 412986 E: pat.palmer@ntlworld.com

PALMER, Steven Roy. b 51. Birm Univ BSc 71. WMMTC 91. **d** 94 **p** 95. C Sheldon *Birm* 94–97; P-in-c Duddeston w Nechells 97–99; V Nechells 99–03; R Billing *Pet* 03–16; RD Northn 06–07; rtd 16; PtO *Birm* from 16. *63 Steyning Road, Birmingham B26 1JE* T: 0121-707 4677 E: stevenpalmer951@btinternet.com

PAMMENT, Derek. b 55. Staffs Univ MBA 98. Qu Foundn (Course) 16. **d** 19. NSM Trentham *Lich* from 19. *Stag Villa, Milwich, Stafford ST18 0EG* T: (01889) 505190 M: 07977-022558 E: modernisation@btopenworld.com

PAMPHILON-GREEN, Sister Phaedra Kay. b 64. Anglia Ruskin Univ MA 12. St Mellitus Coll 12. **d** 14 **p** 15. C Gainsborough and Morton *Linc* 14–17; R Bletchingley and Nutfield *S'wark* from 17. *The Rectory, Outwood Lane, Bletchingley, Redhill RH1 4LR* M: 07775-954144 E: pamphilon@gmail.com

PAMPLIN, Canon Richard Lawrence. b 46. Lon Univ BScEng 68 Dur Univ BA 75 NY Th Sem DMin 85. Wycliffe Hall Ox 75. **d** 77 **p** 78. C Greenside *Dur* 77–80; C Sheff St Barn and St Mary 80–84; R Wombwell 84–90; P-in-c Madeley *Heref* 90–91; TR 91–01; Chapl Berne w Neuchâtel *Eur* 01–07; Can Gib Cathl 04–07; Chapl Viña del Mar w Valparaiso Chile 07–12; rtd 12; PtO *Cant* from 12; *Eur* from 18. *126 Downs Road, Folkestone CT19 5PX* T: (01303) 779126 E: richard.l.pamplin@gmail.com

PAMPLIN, Samantha Jane. *See* FERGUSON, Samantha Jane

PANG, Wing-On. b 43. Manitoba Univ BA 67 SOAS Lon MA 70. Oak Hill Th Coll 85. **d** 87 **p** 88. C Pennycross *Ex* 87–91; TV Mildenhall *St E* 91–96; Assoc P Kowloon St Andr Hong Kong 96–08; rtd 08; PtO *Ches* from 09. *20 Oakland Drive, Wirral CH49 6JL* T: 0151-677 2690 E: wingonheather@gmail.com *or* wingon@stm-upton.org.uk

PANGBOURNE, John Godfrey. b 36. Ridley Hall Cam 82. **d** 84 **p** 85. C Ashtead *Guildf* 84–88; V Ore Ch Ch *Chich* 88–03; rtd 03; PtO *Ex* 04–06; Hon C Ottery St Mary, Alfington, W Hill, Tipton etc from 06. *Meon Croft, Toadpit Lane, West Hill, Ottery St Mary EX11 1TR* T: (01404) 812139

PANKHURST, Ian Charles. b 50. Trin Coll Cam BA 72 Lon Inst of Educn PGCE 88. SAOMC 01. **d** 04 **p** 05. C Watford St Luke *St Alb* 04–10; P-in-c Watford St Andr 10–13; V from 13. *2 Albert Road North, Watford WD17 1QE* T: (01923) 249139 E: ian_pankhurst@btinternet.com

PANTER, The Ven Richard James Graham. b 48. Oak Hill Th Coll 73. **d** 76 **p** 77. C Rusholme H Trin *Man* 76–80; C Toxteth St Cypr w Ch Ch *Liv* 80–85; V Clubmoor 85–96; P-in-c Litherland St Jo and St Jas 96–02; AD Bootle 99–02; V Orrell Hey St Jo and St Jas 02–11; Adn Liv 02–17; rtd 17. *115 Papillon Drive, Liverpool L9 9HL* T: 0151-705 2154

PANTING, Nigel Roger. b 47. St Pet Coll Ox BA 69 PGCE 70. Local Minl Tr Course 06. **d** 11. NSM Ruskington Gp *Linc* 11–13; NSM N Lafford Gp from 13. *The Cottage, Roxholm, Sleaford NG34 8NE* T: (01526) 832020 M: 07866-808737 E: nigelpanting@yahoo.co.uk

PANTLING, Rosemary Caroline. b 60. Ex Coll Ox BA 83 MA 89 Anglia Poly Univ MA 03 Birm Univ PGCE 84. EAMTC 98. **d** 01 **p** 02. NSM Bishop's Tachbrook *Cov* 01–08; P-in-c Cubbington 08–10; PtO 10–16; NSM Lillington and Old Milverton from 16; Chapl S Warks Gen Hosps NHS Trust from 16. *22 Touchstone Road, Heathcote, Warwick CV34 6EE* M: 07846-220974 E: revrosyp@gmail.com

PANTON, Alan Edward. b 45. K Coll Lon BD 67 AKC 67. **d** 68 **p** 69. C Eltham St Jo *S'wark* 68–73; C Horley 73–78; V Dallington *Pet* 78–07; rtd 07; PtO *Pet* from 09. *12B The Avenue, Dallington, Northampton NN5 7AN*

PANTRY, John Richard. b 46. Oak Hill NSM Course 90. **d** 93 **p** 94. NSM Alresford *Chelmsf* 93–04; NSM W w E Mersea 04–10; NSM W w E Mersea, Peldon, Gt and Lt Wigborough 10–18; PtO from 18. *48 Empress Avenue, West Mersea, Colchester CO5 8EX* T/F: (01206) 386910 E: johnpantry@outlook.com

PAPADOPULOS, The Very Revd Nicholas Charles. b 66. G&C Coll Cam BA 88 MA 92 Barrister-at-Law (Middle Temple) 90. Ripon Coll Cuddesdon. **d** 99 **p** 00. C Portsea N End St Mark *Portsm* 99–02; Bp's Dom Chapl *Sarum* 02–07; Hon Chapl 07–10; V Pimlico St Pet w Westmr Ch Ch *Lon* 07–13; Can Res Cant Cathl 13–18; Dir IME 4-7 13–18; Dean Sarum from

18. *The Deanery, 7 The Close, Salisbury SP1 2EF* T: (01722) 555110 M: 07903-620018 E: n.papadopulos@salcath.co.uk

PAPE, David. b 54. **d** 98 **p** 99. OLM S'wark St Geo w St Alphege and St Jude from 98; OLM Waterloo St Jo w St Andr from 98. *10 Stopher House, Webber Street, London SE1 0RE* T: (020) 7928 3503 M: 07986-099959 E: revpape@hotmail.co.uk

PAPWORTH, Daniel John. b 69. Plymouth Poly BSc 90. Trin Coll Bris BA 98 MA 00. **d** 99 **p** 00. C Gabalfa *Llan* 99–02; PtO *B & W* 03–04; Asst Chapl Dudley Gp of Hosps NHS Trust 04–07; Chapl R Devon and Ex NHS Foundn Trust 07–08; TV N Cheltenham *Glouc* 08–13; PtO from 13; *Worc* 14–17; *Bris* from 15. *7 Campden Road, Cheltenham GL51 6AA* T: (01242) 575649 E: papworth@gmail.com

PAPWORTH, Miss Shirley Marjorie. b 33. CA Tr Coll. **d** 88 **p** 94. Par Dn Hornchurch H Cross *Chelmsf* 88–93; rtd 93; Chapl Havering Primary Care Trust 93–08; NSM Hornchurch St Andr *Chelmsf* 93–08; PtO from 08. *14 Paines Brook Court, 14 Paines Brook Way, Romford RM3 9JN* T: (01708) 370177

PARBURY, Mrs Heather Christina Winifred. b 56. **d** 01 **p** 02. C Long Compton, Whichford and Barton-on-the-heath *Cov* 01–05; C Barcheston 01–05; C Cherington w Stourton 01–05; C Wolford w Burmington 01–05; TV Cherwell Valley *Ox* 05–08; P-in-c Pangbourne w Tidmarsh and Sulham 08–10; R from 10; AD Bradfield from 17; Chapl MU from 10. *The Rectory, St James's Close, Pangbourne, Reading RG8 7AP* T: 0118-984 2928 E: parbury@btinternet.com

PARES, John. b 57. Bedf Coll Lon BA 79. Westcott Ho Cam 08. **d** 10 **p** 11. C Diss *Nor* 10–14; P-in-c Pokesdown St Jas *Win* from 14. *St James's Vicarage, 12 Harewood Avenue, Bournemouth BH7 6NQ* T: (01202) 434460 M: 07972-075459 E: j.pares@virginmedia.com

PARFFETT, Allan John. b 51. Open Univ BA 97 CQSW 76. Qu Coll Birm MA 00. **d** 98 **p** 99. C Hall Green Ascension *Birm* 98–00; Soc Worker 00–09; rtd 09. *20 Kiln Close, Corfe Mullen, Wimborne BH21 3UR* T: (01202) 690164

PARFITT, Anthony Colin. b 44. Ox Univ Inst of Educn CertEd 66 Open Univ BA 71 Plymouth Poly MPhil 84. SWMTC 93. **d** 96 **p** 97. NSM Langport Area *B & W* 96–00; NSM Bruton and Distr 01–06; PtO 07–18; *Sarum* from 16. *Woodside, 13 Ashton Rise, Hilperton, Trowbridge BA14 7QZ* T: (01225) 356193 M: 07930-144522 E: tonyparfitt1@gmail.com

PARFITT, Brian John. b 49. Ex Coll Ox BA 71 MA 76. Wycliffe Hall Ox 71. **d** 74 **p** 75. C Newport St Mark *Mon* 74–78; R Blaina 78–83; R Blaina and Nantyglo 83–86; Chapl Blaina and Distr Hosp Gwent 83–86; Regional Consultant (W Midlands and Wales) CPAS 86–95; TR Magor 98–06; Local Min Officer *Glouc* 06–14; P-in-c Highnam, Lassington, Rudford, Tibberton etc 14–15; rtd 15; PtO *Win* from 16. *11 Eynham Avenue, Southampton SO19 5LA* T: (023) 8044 7962 M: 07847-359062 E: brianparfitt@btinternet.com

PARFITT, David George. b 65. De Montfort Univ Leic BA 87 Bris Univ MA 12. Wycliffe Hall Ox BTh 95. **d** 95 **p** 96. C Malpas *Mon* 95–98; C Bassaleg 98–00; TV 00–01; V Malpas 01–16; rtd 16. *c/o Crockford, Church House, Great Smith Street, London SW1P 3AZ*

PARFITT, George Rudolf William. b 54. WMMTC 96. **d** 99 **p** 00. OLM Highnam, Lassington, Rudford, Tibberton etc *Glouc* 99–08; NSM Hardwicke and Elmore w Longney from 08. *66 Holbeach Drive, Kingsway, Quedgeley, Gloucester GL2 2BF* T: (01452) 728180 E: george.parfitt@btinternet.com

PARFITT, Mrs Janet Lesley. b 49. St Hilda's Coll Ox BA 70 MA 73. WEMTC 12. **d** 16. NSM Bitterne *Win* from 16. *11 Eynham Avenue, Southampton SO19 5LA* T: (023) 8044 7962 E: janetparfitt1@btinternet.com

PARFITT, Preb John Hubert. b 29. Southn Univ MA 72 BPhil. Qu Coll Birm 78. **d** 80 **p** 81. C Fladbury, Wyre Piddle and Moor *Worc* 80–82; C Malvern Link w Cowleigh 82; V Hanley Castle, Hanley Swan and Welland 82–83; Dir RE *B & W* 84–93; Preb Wells Cathl 85–05; rtd 93; PtO *B & W* 93–14; *Sarum* 06–17; Master Hugh Sexey's Hosp Bruton 95–05; PtO *B & W* 15–18. *3 Willow Farm Cottages, Brister End, Yetminster, Sherborne DT9 6NH* T: (01935) 873260

PARFITT, Susan Mary. b 42. Bris Univ BA 63 CertEd 68. Bris Minl Tr Scheme 82. **dss** 84 **d** 87 **p** 94. Assoc Dir of Ords *Bris* 84–86; CME Officer 87–91; Dir Past Care and Counselling S'wark 91–01; rtd 01; PtO *Bris* from 02. *Garden Cottage, Rectory Gardens, Bristol BS10 7AQ* E: sue.parfitt@slg.org.uk

PARISH, Mrs Mary Eileen. b 48. Nottm Univ BA 70. STETS BTh 98. **d** 98 **p** 99. NSM Worthing Ch the King *Chich* 98–08; NSM Worthing St Matt 08–16; rtd 16; PtO *Chich* from 16. *The Heritage, 10 Winchester Road, Worthing BN11 4DJ* T: (01903) 236909 E: frmary@hotmail.co.uk

PARISH, Nicholas Anthony. b 58. Oak Hill Th Coll BA 84 Kingston Univ MA 97. Ridley Hall Cam 84. **d** 86 **p** 87.

C Eltham H Trin *S'wark* 86–89; C Barnes St Mary 89–91; V Streatham St Paul 91–96; Ind Chapl *Ox* 96–07; P-in-c Bracknell 07–14; AD 04–12; Hon Can Ch Ch 08–14; P-in-c Epsom St Martin *Guildf* 14–16; V from 16. *35 Burgh Heath Road, Epsom KT17 4LP* E: nick.parish@ntlworld.com

PARISH, Canon Stephen Richard. b 49. Liv Univ MTh 05. Oak Hill Th Coll 74. **d** 77 **p** 78. C Chadderton Ch Ch *Man* 77–81; C Chell *Lich* 81–82; TV 82–88; V Warrington St Ann *Liv* 88–14; P-in-c Warrington H Trin 06–14; V Warrington H Trin and St Ann 14–15; Hon Can Liv Cathl 14–15; rtd 15; PtO *Liv* from 16. *26 Leamington Close, Warrington WA5 3PY* T: (01925) 711830 E: bloovee@outlook.com

PARK, Christopher John. b 62. Sheff Poly BA 83. Cranmer Hall Dur 00. **d** 02 **p** 03. C Didsbury St Jas and Em *Man* 02–08; P-in-c Alne *York* 08–17; P-in-c Brafferton w Pilmoor, Myton-on-Swale etc 08–17; C Huntington from 17. *402 Huntington Road, York YO31 9HU* E: pastaparko@parkfamily.me.uk

PARK, Canon John Charles. b 55. St Pet Coll Ox BA 77 St Mary's Coll Newc PGCE 81. Cranmer Hall Dur 00. **d** 02 **p** 03. C Morpeth *Newc* 02–06; R Bothal and Pegswood w Longhirst from 06; AD Morpeth from 13; Hon Can Newc Cathl from 17. *Bothal Rectory, Longhirst Road, Pegswood, Morpeth NE61 6XF* T: (01670) 510793 E: johnp2910@gmx.co.uk

PARK, Tarjei Erling Alan. b 64. W Lon Inst of HE BA 88 Lanc Univ MA 89 Pemb Coll Ox DPhil 96. Ripon Coll Cuddesdon 92. **d** 94 **p** 95. C Lancaster St Mary w St John and St Anne *Blackb* 94–98; V Enfield St Mich *Lon* 98–01; Asst Dir Post-Ord Tr 98–03; V Golders Green 01–06; C St Pancras w St Jas and Ch Ch 06–08; rtd 09; PtO *Lon* 12–18. *22 Colman Court, Christchurch Avenue, London N12 0DT* T: (020) 8445 7985 M: 07929-465991 E: tarjei.park@pmb.oxon.org

PARK, Trevor. b 38. Lon Univ BA 64 Open Univ PhD 90 Lambeth STh 81. Linc Th Coll 64. **d** 66 **p** 67. C Crosthwaite Keswick *Carl* 66–68; Asst Chapl Solihull Sch 69–71; Chapl St Bees Sch and V St Bees *Carl* 71–77; V Dalton-in-Furness 77–84; V Natland *Carl* 84–89; Hon Can Carl Cathl 86–97; RD Kendal 89–94; Sen Chapl Oslo w Bergen, Trondheim and Stavanger *Eur* 97–05; rtd 05; P-in-c St Petersburg *Eur* 06–07; PtO *Carl* 09–19. *20 Seacroft Drive, St Bees CA27 0AF*

PARKER, Angus Michael Macdonald. b 53. Bris Univ BSc 74. St Jo Coll Nottm 80. **d** 83 **p** 84. C Northampton St Giles *Pet* 83–86; C Attenborough *S'well* 86–96; V Pennycross *Ex* 96–09; P-in-c Bitterne *Win* 09–18; rtd 18. *6 Cotehele Close, Callington PL17 7TP* E: angusmpparker@gmail.com

PARKER, Miss Anika Lois. b 74. BMus *Birm*. **d** 06 **p** 07. NSM Redland *Bris* 06–10; PtO *Ox* from 15. *5 Belle Avenue, Reading RG6 7BL* M: 07935-225844 E: anikaparker@gmail.com

PARKER, Mrs Ann Jacqueline. b 41. Dur Inst of Educn TCert 63 Sunderland Poly TCert 65 Open Univ BA 82. WEMTC 91. **d** 95 **p** 96. NSM Pilning w Compton Greenfield *Bris* 95–98; NSM Almondsbury and Olveston 98–03; Asst Chapl N Bris NHS Trust from 98; PtO *Bris* from 11. *Address temp unknown* E: annatdibley@btinternet.com

PARKER, Anne Elizabeth. *See* MARR, Anne Elizabeth

PARKER, Anne Margaret. *See* HINDLE, Anne Margaret

PARKER, Mrs Brenda. b 36. **d** 00 **p** 01. OLM Eccleston Ch Ch *Liv* 00–06; rtd 06; PtO *Liv* from 16. *22 Selkirk Drive, Eccleston, St Helens WA10 5PE* T: (01744) 757495

PARKER, Carole Maureen. *See* PROUSE, Carole Maureen

PARKER, David Anthony. b 38. St Chad's Coll Dur BA 62. **d** 64 **p** 65. C Palmers Green St Jo *Lon* 64–65; C Kenton 65–71; C W Hyde St Thos *St Alb* 71–75; P-in-c Brinksway *Ches* 76–80; V 80–83; V Weston 83–92; NSM Cheadle Hulme All SS 97–98; C Offerton 98–00; V Crosslacon *Carl* 00–02; rtd 02; C Cheadle Hulme All SS *Ches* 02–12; PtO from 12; *Ely* from 18. *36A St Mary's Street, Ely CB7 4ES*

PARKER, David Charles. b 53. St Andr Univ MTheol 75 Leiden Univ DTh 90 FSA 09 FBA 12. Ridley Hall Cam 75. **d** 77 **p** 78. C Hendon St Paul Mill Hill *Lon* 77–80; C Bladon w Woodstock *Ox* 80–85; C-in-c Shipton-on-Cherwell 80–85; C-in-c Begbroke 80–85; C-in-c Hampton Gay 80–85; Lect Qu Coll Birm 85–93; Sen Angl Tutor 89–93; Lect Birm Univ 93–96; Sen Lect 96–98; Reader in NT Textual Criticism and Palaeography from 98; Prof Th from 02; Dir Inst Textual Scholarship and Electronic Editing from 15; PtO *Heref* 03–17. *Dumbleton Cottage, 24 Church Street, Bromyard HR7 4DP* T: 0121-415 2415 E: d.c.parker@bham.ac.uk

PARKER, David John. b 57. Em Coll Cam BA 79 MA 83 Qu Coll Ox DPhil 84. Qu Coll Birm 12. **d** 15 **p** 16. NSM Selly Oak St Mary *Birm* from 15. *1 Spirehouse Lane, Blackwell, Bromsgrove B60 1QE* T: 0121-445 1901 E: davidparker124@btinternet.com

PARKER, Canon David Louis. b 47. Lon Univ LLB 70. Wycliffe Hall Ox BA 79 MA 82. **d** 80 **p** 81. C Broadwater St Mary *Chich* 80–84; TR Ifield 84–97; R Lavant 97–12; RD Chich

01–06; Can and Preb Chich Cathl 03–12; rtd 12; PtO *Chich* 12–17. *6 Queens Gate, 1 Osborne Road, Southsea PO5 3LX*

PARKER, (*née* JOHNSON), Mrs Emma Louise. b 82. St Mary's Coll Dur BA 05 MA 06. Ridley Hall Cam 07. d 09 p 10. C Cockfield *Dur* 09–12; C Lynesack 09–12; C Evenwood 09–12; C Easington and Easington Colliery 12–14; P-in-c 14–18; Dep Warden Cranmer Hall Dur from 18. *Cranmer Hall, St John's College, 3 South Bailey, Durham DH1 3RJ* T: 0191-334 3851 E: cran.depwarden@durham.ac.uk

PARKER, Canon Janet Elizabeth. b 54. Cranmer Hall Dur 05. d 07 p 08. C Sale St Anne *Ches* 07–10; V High Lane from 10; RD Chadkirk 11–18; Hon Can Ches Cathl from 16. *The Vicarage, 2 Vicarage Close, High Lane, Stockport SK6 8DL* T: (01663) 764519 E: revjanetparker@btinternet.com

PARKER, Mrs Joanna Caroline. b 63. UEA BA 95 Leeds Univ MA 07 RGN 85 RM 92. NOC 04. d 07 p 08. C Pocklington Wold *York* 07–11; V Hyde St Geo *Ches* 11–17; V New Milverton *Cov* from 17. *The Vicarage, 2 St Mark's Road, Leamington Spa CV32 6DL* T: (01926) 421004 E: vicar@st-marks.net

PARKER, Mrs Joanne Clare. b 76. St Hild Coll 17. d 19. C Eastfield *York* from 19. *7 Malling Avenue, Eastfield, Scarborough YO11 3FA* M: 07988-973219 E: jopkr76@gmail.com

PARKER, John David. b 61. Ridley Hall Cam 00. d 02 p 03. C Aston cum Aughton w Swallownest and Ulley *Sheff* 02–06; TV Rugby *Cov* 06–12; V Newbold Pacey w Moreton Morrell 12–18; R Lighthorne 12–18; V Chesterton 12–18; V Wath-upon-Dearne *Sheff* from 18. *The Vicarage, Church Street, Wath-upon-Dearne, Rotherham S63 7RD* E: parkersuk@aol.com

PARKER, Jonathan Edward. d 17 p 18. C Fishguard w Llanychar and Pontfaen w Morfil etc *St D* 17–18; C Llanwnda, Goodwick w Manorowen and Llanstinan 17–18; C W Cemaes from 18. *5 Hillside Close, Goodwick SA64 0AX* T: (01348) 871868 E: jpfishguard@gmail.com

PARKER, Justin Trevelyan. b 71. Reading Univ LLB 92. WEMTC 11. d 12 p 13. NSM Cleobury Mortimer w Hopton Wafers etc *Heref* 12–19; R Bromfield from 19. *The Vicarage, Bromfield, Ludlow SY8 2JP* M: 07932-606420

PARKER, Canon Lynn. b 54. SS Mark & Jo Univ Coll Plymouth BEd 94. SWMTC 04. d 07 p 08. NSM S Hill w Callington *Truro* 07–10; P-in-c Antony w Sheviock 10–15; P-in-c Torpoint 10–15; C Maker w Rame and St John w Millbrook 12–15; V Antony w Sheviock and Torpoint 15–19; V St Germans w Antony and Sheviock from 19; Hon Can Truro Cathl from 15. *The New Vicarage, 17 Quay Road, St Germans, Saltash PL12 5LY* E: parker30@hotmail.com

PARKER, Margaret Grace. *See* TORDOFF, Margaret Grace

PARKER, The Ven Matthew John. b 63. Man Univ BA 85 SS Coll Cam BA 88. Ridley Hall Cam 85. d 88 p 89. C Twickenham St Mary *Lon* 88–91; Chapl Stockport Gr Sch 91–94; C Stockport St Geo *Ches* 91–93; P-in-c Stockport St Mark 93–94; TV Stockport SW 94–00; TR Leek and Meerbrook *Lich* 00–13; RD Leek 07–13; Adn Stoke-upon-Trent from 13. *39 The Brackens, Newcastle ST5 4JL* T: (01782) 663066 E: archdeacon.stoke@lichfield.anglican.org

PARKER, Michael. b 54. d 07. C Ebbw Vale *Mon* 07–09; Hon C Llanhilleth w Six Bells 09–10; Hon C Abertillery w Cwmtillery w Llanhilleth etc 10–17; P-in-c from 17. *St Michael's Vicarage, Church Street, Abertillery NP13 1DA* T: (01495) 212883 E: mikeparker54@gmail.com

PARKER, Canon Michael Alan. b 70. St Jo Coll Dur BA 91. CITC BTh 93. d 96 p 97. C Dundela St Mark *D & D* 96–00; I Carnalea from 00; Can Belf Cathl from 15. *St Gall's Rectory, 171 Crawfordsburn Road, Bangor BT19 1BT* T: (028) 9185 3366 *or* 9185 3810 E: carnalea@down.anglican.org *or* stgalloffice@btconnect.com

PARKER, Michael John. b 54. Cam Coll of Art and Tech BA 76 Lon Univ BD 85. Trin Coll Bris 82. d 85 p 86. C Leic H Trin w St Jo 85–88; P-in-c Edin Clermiston Em 88–90; I Edin St Thos 90–03; Can St Mary's Cathl 94–03; NSM Edin St Paul and St Geo 03–06; Gen Sec Evang Alliance Scotland 03–06; Middle E Dir Middle E Chr Outreach 06–09; Internat Dir from 13; Sen Min All SS Cathl Cairo 09–13; Hon Can from 09; PtO *Edin* 06–14. *4 Liberton Place, Edinburgh EH16 6NA* E: canonmikep@gmail.com

PARKER, Canon Michael John. b 57. BSc Nottm Univ MA 04. Wycliffe Hall Ox 80. d 83 p 84. C Heigham H Trin *Nor* 83–86; C Muswell Hill St Jas w St Matt *Lon* 86–90; R Bedford St Jo and St Leon *St Alb* 90–98; V Knowle *Birm* 98–18; AD Solihull 04–09; Hon Can Birm Cathl 05–18. *82 Wilsdon Way, Kidlington OX5 1TX*

PARKER, Nicolas. *See* PARKER, Robert Nicolas

PARKER, Nigel Howard. b 69. St Jo Coll Dur BSc 90. CITC BTh 97. d 97 p 98. C Holywood *D & D* 97–00; Outreach Development Officer Think Again 00–04; I Bangor St Comgall from 04. *1A Maxwell Road, Bangor BT20 3RA* T: (028) 9146 0712 E: nigel@parkers123.plus.com *or* nigel@bangorparishchurch.org.uk

PARKER, Philip Vernon. b 60. Birm Univ BSc 82 PGCE 83 Heythrop Coll Lon MA 09. Wycliffe Hall Ox BA 89. d 90 p 91. C Walkergate *Newc* 90–93; Chapl Shiplake Coll Henley 93–96; C Lindfield *Chich* 97–99; Team Ldr Titus Trust 99–04; Chapl Cranleigh Sch Surrey 04–12; CF (TA) 97–05; P-in-c Frimley Green and Mytchett *Guildf* 13–19; Chapl Loretto Sch Musselburgh from 19. *Loretto School, 1-7 Linkfield Road, Musselburgh EH21 7RE* T: 0131-653 4455

PARKER, Canon Richard Bryan. b 64. Sheff Poly BA 87. Coll of Resurr Mirfield 92. d 95 p 96. C Norton *Sheff* 95–98; C Hoyland 98–00; V Moorends 00–08; V Hoyland from 08; Dioc Warden of Readers 10–13; Hon Can Sheff Cathl from 10. *The Vicarage, 104 Hawshaw Lane, Hoyland, Barnsley S74 0HH* T: (01226) 749231 E: r.b.parker@btinternet.com

PARKER, Richard Frederick. b 36. Oak Hill Th Coll 72. d 74 p 75. C Wootton *St Alb* 74–76; C Hove Bp Hannington Memorial Ch *Chich* 76–81; R Northwood *Portsm* 81–88; V W Cowes H Trin 81–88; V Aldershot H Trin *Guildf* 88–98; R Spaxton w Charlynch, Goathurst, Enmore etc *B & W* 98–03; rtd 03. *47 Banneson Road, Nether Stowey, Bridgwater TA5 1NS* T: (01278) 733883 E: ricktherec@hotmail.com

PARKER, Robert Lawrence. b 34. ALCD 59. d 59 p 60. C Chippenham St Paul *Bris* 59–61; C Swindon Ch Ch 61–63; C Epsom St Andr New Zealand 63–64; V Glen Eden 64–71; V Nether Stowey *B & W* 71–73; V Nether Stowey w Over Stowey 73–93; RD Quantock 87–93; V Pitminster w Corfe 93–99; rtd 99; PtO *B & W* 00–18. *Oratia, 9 Brookfield Way, Street BA16 0UE* T: (01458) 442906 E: bvparker@uwclub.net

PARKER, Robert Nicolas. b 71. Nottm Univ BA 93 PGCE 95. Ridley Hall Cam 95. d 98 p 99. C Yardley St Edburgha *Birm* 98–02; Asst P Eugene St Mary USA 02–05; P-in-c Coleshill *Birm* 05–08; V from 08; P-in-c Maxstoke 05–08; V from 11; Bp's Ecum Adv from 12. *The Vicarage, High Street, Coleshill, Birmingham B46 3BP* T: (01675) 462188 E: nickthevicarparker@btinternet.com

PARKER, Roger Thomas Donaldson. b 55. Simon Fraser Univ BC BA 80 Univ of Wales (Cardiff) LLB 84 Univ Coll Lon LLM 85. Coll of Resurr Mirfield 85. d 95 p 96. C Swinton and Pendlebury *Man* 95–02; V Burnley St Cath w St Alb and St Paul *Blackb* from 02. *St Catherine's Parsonage, 156 Todmorden Road, Burnley BB11 3ER* T: (01282) 424587 F: 458579 M: 07977-291166 E: frrogerparker@aol.com

PARKER, Roland John Graham. b 48. AKC 72 Hull Univ BA(Ed) 83. St Aug Coll Cant 71. d 74 p 75. C Linc St Faith and St Martin w St Pet 74–78; V Appleby 78–84; Ind Chapl 78–84; V N Kelsey 84–92; V Cadney 84–92; P-in-c Waddington 92–97; R 97–11; rtd 11. *29 Castle Street, Kirkcudbright DG6 4JD* T: (01557) 330317 E: rolapark2@btinternet.com

PARKER, Stephen. b 88. Ches Univ BA 09. St Steph Ho Ox BA 12. d 13 p 14. C Worksop Priory *S'well* 13–16; V S Leamington St Jo *Cov* from 16; AD Warwick and Leamington from 18. *St John's Vicarage, Tachbrook Street, Leamington Spa CV31 3BN* E: stephen.parker88@gmail.com *or* priest@stjohnsleamingtonspa.org.uk

PARKER, Prof Stephen George. b 65. Birm Univ BEd 89 MA 97 PhD 03 FRHistS. Qu Coll Birm 96. d 98. Teaching Asst Westhill Coll of HE Birm 98–01; Sen Lect Th Univ Coll Ches 01–04; Hd RS Cadbury Sixth Form Coll 04–08; Hd Postgraduate Studies in Educn Worc Univ 08–12; Prof Hist of Relig and Educn 13–17. *University of Worcester, Henwick Grove, Worcester WR2 6AJ* T: (01905) 542165 E: s.parker@worc.ac.uk

PARKER, Canon Thomas Richard. b 52. Imp Coll Lon BScEng 73 Keele Univ MEd 83. Cranmer Hall Dur. d 94 p 95. C Chadkirk *Ches* 94–08; RD Ch 08; P-in-c Stalybridge H Trin and Ch Ch 08–11; V 11–17; Hon Can Ches Cathl 13–17; rtd 18. *Naze View, Lesser Lane, Combs, High Peak SK23 9UZ* E: tomparker121@gmail.com

PARKER, Timothy Percy. b 58. Man Univ BA. St Jo Coll Nottm. d 85 p 86. C Pitsmoor Ch Ch *Sheff* 85–87; C Kimberworth 87–89; C Brightside w Wincobank 89–91; C Upper Armley *Ripon* 91–95; TV Billingham St Aid *Dur* 95–97; V Billingham St Luke 97–12; Chapl Harrogate and Distr NHS Foundn Trust 12–16; P-in-c Hunmanby w Muston *York* 16–18; R Hertford from 18. *The Vicarage, 6 Northgate, Hunmanby, Filey YO14 0NT* T: (01723) 448351 E: timparker17@gmail.com

PARKER-McGEE, Robert Thomas. b 78. Leeds Univ BA 10 Dur Univ MA 17. Coll of Resurr Mirfield 07. d 10 p 11. C Gornal and Sedgley *Worc* 10–14; P-in-c Geddington w Weekley *Pet* 14–18; V Orpington All SS *Roch* 18–19; R Boxford, Edwardstone, Groton etc *St E* from 19. *The Rectory, School Hill, Boxford, Sudbury CO10 5JT* M: 07588-801593 E: rparkermcgee@gmail.com

PARKERSON, Trevor Richard. b 46. Qu Coll Birm 06. d 08 p 09. NSM Ashby-de-la-Zouch and Breedon on the Hill *Leic* 08–15; PtO *Lich* from 14; *Leic* from 15. *36 Ashby*

Road, Woodville, Swadlincote DE11 7BY T: (01283) 225408
E: trp@gofast.co.uk

PARKES, Arthur Burnham. b 42. Univ of Wales MSc 72 PhD 76 FIBiol 94 LTCL 82. St Mich Coll Llan 11. **d** 12 **p** 13. NSM Cyncoed *Mon* 12–16; NSM Bedwas w Machen w Michaelston-y-Fedw w Rudry from 16. *17 Bramshill Drive, Pontprennau, Cardiff CF23 8NX* T: (029) 2048 1970 M: 07950-454926 E: arthur.b.parkes@virginmedia.com

PARKES, Mrs Celia Anne. b 50. STETS 06. **d** 09 **p** 10. NSM Bursledon *Win* 09–11; NSM Southampton (City Cen) 11–15; NSM Margaretting w Mountnessing and Buttsbury *Chelmsf* 15–17; NSM Ingatestone w Fryerning 15–17; NSM Napton-on-the-Hill, Lower Shuckburgh etc *Cov* from 17; NSM Priors Hardwick, Priors Marston and Wormleighton from 17. *The Vicarage, Vicarage Lane, Priors Marston, Southam CV47 7RT* M: 07842-151387 E: m.parkes345@btinternet.com

PARKES, Edward Patrick. b 58. Crewe & Alsager Coll BEd 80 Ban Univ MTh 11. SWMTC 10. **d** 11 **p** 12. Dioc Miss Resources Adv *Ex* from 11; NSM Dawlish 11–12; NSM Ex Cathl 12–14; C Yelverton, Meavy, Sheepstor and Walkhampton 14–16; C Sampford Spiney w Horrabridge 14–16; P-in-c Wolborough and Ogwell 16; TR Newton Abbot from 17; RD Newton Abbot and Ipplepen from 18; Tutor SWMTC from 14. *The Rectory, 5 Coach Place, Newton Abbot TQ12 1ES* T: (01626) 681498 M: 07960-102001 E: epp@sky.com

PARKES, Jack Christopher. b 53. Leeds Univ BA 81 Hughes Hall Cam PGCE 82. Yorks Min Course 14. **d** 15 **p** 16. NSM Cleckheaton *Leeds* from 15. *29 Huntington Crescent, Leeds LS16 5RT* T: 0113-443 7383 M: 07890-724223 E: fr.jack@outlook.com

PARKES, Kevin. b 62. Trent Poly BA 84. Sarum & Wells Th Coll BTh 90. **d** 88 **p** 89. C Wandsworth St Anne *S'wark* 88–92; USPG 92–95; Trinidad and Tobago 93–95; Kingston Area Miss Team *S'wark* 95–01; V Wandsworth Common St Mary 01–09; AD Tooting 07–09; Chapl Univ Coll Lon Hosps NHS Foundn Trust 09–13; Chapl Hillingdon Hosps NHS Foundn Trust 13–14; Chapl King's Coll Hosp NHS Foundn Trust 14–15; Chapl Lewisham and Greenwich NHS Trust from 15. *University Hospital Lewisham, Lewisham High Street, London SE13 6LH* T: (020) 8333 3000 E: bloomsbury1@hotmail.com *or* kevinparkes@nhs.net

PARKES, Patrick. *See* PARKES, Edward Patrick

PARKHILL, Alan John. b 43. TCD BA 66. CITC 68. **d** 67 **p** 68. C Knockbreda *D & D* 67–70; Asst Warden Elswick Lodge Newc 71–72; C Bangor St Comgall *D & D* 73–78; Bp's C Kilmore 78–81; I Kilmore and Inch 82–86; I Clonfeacle w Derrygortreavy *Arm* 86–09; rtd 09. *1 Rodney Park, Bangor BT19 6FN* T/F: (028) 9147 3916 E: aparkhill1@btinternet.com

PARKIN, Christopher. *See* PARKIN, Melvyn Christopher

PARKIN, George David. b 37. Cranmer Hall Dur BA 60. **d** 62 **p** 63. C Balderstone *Man* 62–65; C Tunstead 65–67; C Gateshead Fell *Dur* 69–73; CMS Nigeria 74–76; V Walton Breck *Liv* 80–92; V Rawtenstall St Mary *Man* 92–07; P-in-c Constable Lee 02–07; rtd 07; PtO *Man* 08 and from 16. *174 Bury Road, Rawtenstall, Rossendale BB4 6DJ* E: pamandco@googlemail.com

PARKIN, Gillian Elizabeth. b 48. Heref Coll of Educn CertEd 69. Trin Coll Bris. **d** 13 **p** 14. OLM By Brook *Bris* from 13; OLM Colerne w N Wraxall from 13. *4 Kents Bottom, Yatton Keynell, Chippenham SN14 7BW* T: (01249) 782165 E: gillianparkin4@gmail.com

PARKIN, Mrs Jennifer Anne. b 47. Nene Coll Northn BEd 85. WMMTC 95. **d** 98 **p** 99. C Northampton St Alb *Pet* 98–02; P-in-c Ecton 02–07; P-in-c Wootton w Quinton and Preston Deanery 07–12; Chapl Cynthia Spencer Hospice 02–07; Warden of Past Assts *Pet* 06–10; rtd 12; Lay Voc Officer *Pet* 12–13; PtO from 13. *40 Pinewood Road, Northampton NN3 2RB* T: (01604) 244549 E: parkinjen@btinternet.com *or* jenny.johnparkin@gmail.com

PARKIN, John Anthony. b 37. CBDTI 06. **d** 07 **p** 08. NSM Otley *Bradf* 07–11; PtO 11–14; *Leeds* from 14. *1 Pearsons Buildings, Otley LS21 3BQ* T: (01943) 466895 E: jamparkin@talktalk.net

PARKIN, Canon John Edmund. b 44. Open Univ BA 73. St Jo Coll Nottm 83. **d** 85 **p** 86. C Aberavon *Llan* 85–90; R Eglwysilan 90–01; P Missr Merthyr Tydfil Ch Ch 01–09; Hon Can Llan Cathl 09; rtd 09; PtO *Llan* from 12; *S & B* from 15. *2 Mount Pleasant, Penderyn Road, Hirwaun, Aberdare CF44 9RT*

PARKIN, Jonathan Samuel. b 73. La Sainte Union Coll BTh 95 Birm Univ MA 97. Qu Coll Birm 98. **d** 98 **p** 99. C Skegness and Winthorpe *Linc* 98–01; Chapl Leic Coll of FE 01–03; Chapl De Montfort Univ 04–07; Chapl Leic Cathl 01–07; TV Market Harborough and The Transfiguration etc 07–11;

P-in-c Welham, Glooston and Cranoe and Stonton Wyville 07–11; C Branston w Nocton and Potterhanworth *Linc* 11–16; C Metheringham w Blankney and Dunston 11–16; Dioc Fresh Expressions Enabler 16; C S Grantham from 18; PtO *Ely* from 16. *The Vicarage, 4 Station Road East, Grantham NG31 6HX* E: jonnie.parkin@gmail.com

PARKIN, Melvyn Christopher. b 57. NEOC 99. **d** 02 **p** 03. NSM Boston Spa *York* 02–03; C Elvington w Sutton on Derwent and E Cottingwith 03–06; R Howardian Gp 06–11; V Gt and Lt Ouseburn w Marton cum Grafton etc *Leeds* 11–17; rtd 17; PtO *Leeds* from 17. *20 Forest Grove, Harrogate HG2 7JU* E: chrisandlindaparkin@yahoo.com

PARKINSON, Alan. *See* PARKINSON, Thomas Alan

PARKINSON, Alec. b 60. All SS Cen for Miss & Min 14. **d** 16 **p** 17. NSM Pemberton St Jo *Liv* from 16. *28 Townfields, Ashton-in-Makerfield, Wigan WN4 9LJ* T: (01942) 272838 E: alecp28@hotmail.co.uk

PARKINSON, David Thomas. b 42. Linc Th Coll 77. **d** 79 **p** 80. C Yate New Town *Bris* 79–82; TV Keynsham *B & W* 82–88; R Bleadon 88–07; rtd 07; PtO *B & W* from 08. *Sherwell Court, 48 Old Church Road, Uphill, Weston-super-Mare BS23 4UP* T: (01934) 708125 M: 07951-239778 E: dtparkinson@talktalk.net

PARKINSON, Francis Wilson. b 37. Open Univ BA 80. St Aid Birkenhead 59. **d** 62 **p** 63. C Monkwearmouth St Andr *Dur* 62–64; C Speke All SS *Liv* 64–67; CF 67–92; PtO *Ox* from 92. *9 Priory Mead, Longcot, Faringdon SN7 7TJ* T: (01793) 784406

PARKINSON, Canon Ian Richard. b 58. Dur Univ BA 79 Lon Univ BD 84. Wycliffe Hall Ox 80. **d** 83 **p** 84. C Hull St Jo Newland *York* 83–86; C Linthorpe 86–92; V Saltburn-by-the-Sea 92–01; V Marple All SS *Ches* 01–15; Hon Can Ches Cathl 12–15; Leadership Specialist CPAS from 16; PtO *Sheff* from 16. CPAS, *Unit 3, Sovereign Court 1, Sir William Lyons Road, University of Warwick Science Park, Coventry CV4 7EZ* E: iparkinson@cpas.org.uk

PARKINSON, John Reginald. b 32. Qu Coll Birm 79. **d** 81 **p** 82. NSM Catshill and Dodford *Worc* 81–85; C Knightwick w Doddenham, Broadwas and Cotheridge 85–88; C Martley and Wichenford 85–88; P-in-c Berrow w Pendock and Eldersfield 88–89; R Berrow w Pendock, Eldersfield, Hollybush etc 89–97; RD Upton 95–97; rtd 97; PtO *Glouc* from 97; *Worc* 97–08. *8 Glebe Close, Stow on the Wold, Cheltenham GL54 1DJ* T: (01451) 830822

PARKINSON, Nicholas John. b 46. FCCA 75 Cranfield Inst of Tech MBA 85. St Alb Minl Tr Scheme 92. **d** 95 **p** 96. NSM Woburn Sands *St Alb* 95–98; NSM Westoning w Tingrith 98–01; NSM Woburn Sands 01–15; rtd 15; PtO *St Alb* from 15. *Thornbank House, 7 Church Road, Woburn Sands, Milton Keynes MK17 8TE* T: (01908) 583397 E: nickp@thornbank.com

PARKINSON, Richard Duncan. b 51. UMIST BSc 72 S Bank Univ MA 01 Nottm Trent Univ PGCE. ERMC 04. **d** 07 **p** 08. NSM Leverington, Newton and Tydd St Giles *Ely* 07–11; NSM Wisbech St Mary and Guyhirn w Ring's End etc from 11; P-in-c from 17. *Colegate House, 166 Leverington Common, Leverington, Wisbech PE13 5BP* T: (01945) 465818 E: rykparkinson@btinternet.com

PARKINSON, Richard Francis. b 76. Cranmer Hall Dur. **d** 10 **p** 11. C Ilkley All SS *Bradf* 10–13; R Cherry Burton *York* from 13; C Etton w Dalton Holme 13–19; P-in-c from 19; Chapl Bp Burton Coll York from 13; RD Beverley *York* from 17. *The Rectory, Main Street, Cherry Burton, Beverley HU17 7RF* T: (01964) 503036 E: richard@poiema.co.uk *or* rector@stmichaelscherryburton.org.uk

PARKINSON, Mrs Sarah Kathryn Rachel. b 80. Trin Coll Ox MMath 02. Ripon Coll Cuddesdon BA 06. **d** 07 **p** 08. NSM Steeple Aston w N Aston and Tackley *Ox* 07–10; Chapl HM Pris Bullingdon 05–08; Manager Relig Affairs Campsfield Ho Immigration Removal Cen 08–12; PtO *Carl* 12–16; *Ripon* 13–14; *Leeds* 14–16; Chapl HM YOI Deerbolt 16–17; Chapl HM Pris Low Newton from 17. *HM Prison Low Newton, Finchale Avenue, Brasside, Durham DH1 5YA* T: 0191-386 1141 E: sarah.parkinson@justice.gov.uk

PARKINSON, Thomas Alan. b 40. St Jo Coll York CertEd 61. NW Ord Course 75. **d** 78 **p** 79. NSM Sheff St Cecilia Parson Cross 78–82; NSM Goldthorpe w Hickleton 82–90; C Cantley 90–01; Dioc RE and Worship Adv 93–04; V Ryecroft St Nic 02–10; rtd 10; PtO *Sheff* from 10; CMP from 00. *40 South Street, Rawmarsh, Rotherham S62 5RG* T: (01709) 525654

PARKMAN, Christopher Charles. b 67. Selw Coll Cam MA 88 Birm Univ MSc 92. Wycliffe Hall Ox 14. **d** 16 **p** 17. C Bris St Steph w St Jas and St Jo w St Mich etc 16–19. *Address temp unknown* E: rev.chris.parkman@gmail.com

PARKMAN, Mrs Michelle Joy. b 77. SS Mark & Jo Univ Coll Plymouth BA 00. Trin Coll Bris BA 08. **d** 08 **p** 09. C Nailsea H Trin *B & W* 08–13; PtO *Truro* from 16; Chapl Univ of

St Mark and St Jo from 19. *16 Home Park Road, Saltash PL12 6BH* M: 07740-366597 E: mparkman@hotmail.co.uk

PARMENTER, Canon Deirdre Joy. b 45. EAMTC 91. **d** 94 **p** 95. C Ipswich St Aug *St E* 94–97; P-in-c Haughley w Wetherden 97–00; V Haughley w Wetherden and Stowupland 00–07; RD Stowmarket 99–05; Bp's Chapl 07–10; Dioc Adv for Women's Min 08–10; Hon Can St E Cathl 03–10; rtd 10; PtO *St E* from 10; Dioc Warden of Readers 10–13; RD Loes 14–15. *Avalon, Marlesford Road, Campsea Ashe, Woodbridge IP13 0QG* T: (01728) 748145 E: deirdre@stedmundsbury.anglican.org *or* deirdreparmenter@gmail.com

PARNELL, Bryan Donald. b 38. DipEd 88. Chich Th Coll 66. **d** 69 **p** 70. C Lewisham St Jo Southend *S'wark* 69–72; Asst Chapl Cooleg Sch of St Pet Australia 72–76; R Angaston 76–78; Chapl RAN 78–88; R Edwardstown 89–02; rtd 02. *PO Box 2131, Unit 19, Manson Towers, 13 Moseley Street, Glenelg SA 2035, Australia* M: (0061) 41-469 2340 E: trinitas@senet.com.au

PARNELL, Michael Gordon. b 61. Yorks Min Course 15. **d** 17. NSM Doncaster St Jas *Sheff* from 17. *25 Bramworth Road, Doncaster DN4 0HZ* T: (01302) 855475 E: mikegp2003@yahoo.co.uk

PARR, Mrs Anne Patricia. b 38. Nottm Univ CertEd 59. **d** 07 **p** 08. OLM Penistone and Thurlstone *Wakef* 07–14; OLM Penistone and Thurlstone 14–15; PtO from 15. *7 Rydal Close, Penistone, Sheffield S36 8HN* T: (01226) 764490 M: 07971-513301 E: mail@anneparr.co.uk

PARR, Clive William. b 41. FCIS FHA. WEMTC 02. **d** 03 **p** 04. NSM Evesham w Norton and Lenchwick *Worc* 03–07; NSM Hampton w Sedgeberrow and Hinton-on-the-Green 07–14; Bp's Health Service Adv 08–12; PtO 14–19; *Heref* from 19. *Nimrod, Church Lane, Bridgnorth WV16 4NW* T: (01746) 767023 M: 07801-820006 E: cw.parr@btinternet.com

PARR, Frank. b 35. Nottm Univ BCombStuds 82 Lanc Univ MA 86. Linc Th Coll 79. **d** 82 **p** 83. C Padiham *Blackb* 82–85; P-in-c Accrington St Andr 85–88; V Oswaldtwistle Immanuel and All SS 88–96; V Tunstall w Melling and Leck 96–01; rtd 01; PtO *Blackb* from 01; *Bradf* 02–14; *Leeds* from 14. *1 Bank View, Burton Road, Lower Bentham, Lancaster LA2 7DZ* T: (015242) 61159 E: f.parr207@btinternet.com

PARR, Jeffrey John. b 48. FCA 73. EMMTC 03. **d** 06 **p** 07. NSM Bassingham Gp *Linc* 06–09; NSM Claypole 09–10; LtO from 10. *3 Manor Paddocks, Bassingham, Lincoln LN5 9GW* T: (01522) 789869 M: 07785-281215 E: jparr@chesapeake.co.uk

PARR, Canon John. b 53. St Edm Hall Ox BA 74 MA 87 Lon Univ BD 79 Sheff Univ PhD 90. Trin Coll Bris 75. **d** 79 **p** 80. C Gt Crosby St Luke *Liv* 79–82; C Walton St Mary 82–84; V Ince St Mary 84–87; Tutor and Lect Ridley Hall Cam 87–95; Chapl 87–93; Dir Studies 93–95; CME Officer *Ely* 95–99; P-in-c Harston w Hauxton 95–99; P-in-c Newton 97–99; Can Res and CME Officer *St E* 99–00; PtO 06–09; TR Bury St Edmunds All SS w St Jo and St Geo 09–12; Dir Min Educn and Tr 12–16; C Hadleigh, Layham and Shelley 16–18; Min Formation Adv 18–19; Hon Can St E Cathl 15–19; rtd 19. *18 Victoria Street, Bury St Edmunds IP33 3BB* E: parishpriest53@gmail.com

PARR, Mabel Ann. b 37. CBDTI 07. **d** 07 **p** 08. NSM Bentham *Bradf* 07–10; PtO *Blackb* from 10; *Bradf* 12–14; *Leeds* from 14. *1 Bank View, Burton Road, Lower Bentham, Lancaster LA2 7DZ* T: (015242) 61159 E: f.parr207@btinternet.com

PARR, Vanessa Caroline. See CONANT, Vanessa Caroline

PARRATT, Dennis James. b 53. Glos Coll of Art & Design BA 74. St Steph Ho Ox 82. **d** 84 **p** 85. C Cainscross w Selsley *Glouc* 84–88; C Old Shoreham and New Shoreham *Chich* 88–91; PtO *Glouc* 01–08. *11 Millbrook Gardens, Cheltenham GL50 3RQ* T: (01242) 525730 E: djparratt@hotmail.co.uk

PARRETT, Mrs Mary Margaret. b 42. Shenstone Coll of Educn DipEd 63. St Alb Minl Tr Scheme 86. **d** 98 **p** 99. NSM Barton-le-Cley w Higham Gobion and Hexton *St Alb* 98–06; PtO from 06; NSM Officer Bedford Adnry 10–14. *49 Manor Road, Barton-le-Clay, Bedford MK45 4NP* T: (01582) 883089 E: mary.parrett@btinternet.com

PARRETT, Mrs Rosalind Virginia. b 43. Ox Brookes Univ MTh 02. Cant Sch of Min 84. **d** 87 **p** 94. NSM Selling w Throwley, Sheldwich w Badlesmere etc *Cant* 87–91; Asst Chapl Cant Hosp 87–91; Par Dn Stantonbury and Willen *Ox* 91–94; TV 94–96; P-in-c Owlsmoor 96–98; V 98–03; rtd 03; PtO *Cant* 03–04; Hon C Faversham 04–11; Hon C Preston next Faversham, Goodnestone and Graveney 04–10; PtO from 11. *16 Hilton Close, Faversham ME13 8NN* T: (01795) 530380 M: 07881-788155 E: revros@talktalk.net

PARRETT, Stephen. b 65. Cant Ch Ch Univ Coll BA 96. **d** 07 **p** 08. OLM Herne Bay Ch Ch *Cant* 07–14; NSM 14–19; NSM Reculver and Herne Bay St Bart and Hoath from 19. *1 Birkdale Gardens, Herne Bay CT6 7TS* T: (01227) 360139 M: 07742-439563 E: stephenparrett@lycos.co.uk

PARRIS, Mrs Alison Louise. b 54. **d** 14 **p** 15. NSM Camelot Par *B & W* from 14. *76 Combe Park, Yeovil BA21 3BE* T: (01935) 476412 M: 07710-539855

PARRISH, Ian Robert. b 62. SEITE 05. **d** 09 **p** 10. C Kingsnorth and Shadoxhurst *Cant* 09–10; C Maidstone St Paul 11–14; P-in-c Maidstone All SS and St Phil w Tovil from 14. *The Vicarage, Priory Road, Maidstone ME15 6NL* T: (01622) 756002 E: vicar.allsaintsmaidstone@gmail.com

PARRISH, Robert Carey. b 57. St Steph Ho Ox 89. **d** 91 **p** 92. C Abington *Pet* 91–94; C Leckhampton SS Phil and Jas w Cheltenham St Jas *Glouc* 94–97; PV Llan Cathl 97–02; R Merthyr Dyfan 02–16; TV Barry from 16. *9 Glas y Llwyn, Barry CF63 1DD* T: (01446) 748527

PARROTT, David Wesley. b 58. Univ of Wales (Cardiff) LLM 01. Oak Hill Th Coll BA. **d** 84 **p** 85. C Thundersley *Chelmsf* 84–87; C Rainham 87–89; P-in-c Heydon w Gt and Lt Chishill 89–90; P-in-c Chrishall 89–90; P-in-c Elmdon w Wendon Lofts and Strethall 89–90; R Heydon, Gt and Lt Chishill, Chrishall etc 91–96; R Rayleigh 96–00; TR 00–04; RD Rochford 02–04; Barking Area CME Adv 04–09; C Hornchurch St Andr 05–09; Hon Can Chelmsf Cathl 07–09; V St Lawr Jewry *Lon* from 09. *St Lawrence Jewry Vicarage, Guildhall Yard, London EC2V 5AA* T: (020) 7600 9478 E: dwparrott01@aol.com

PARROTT, George. b 37. Leeds Univ BA 61. Bps' Coll Cheshunt 61. **d** 63 **p** 64. C Lower Mitton *Worc* 63–65; C-in-c Fairfield St Rich CD 65–68; Zambia 68–70; C Cleethorpes *Linc* 70–75; R Withern 75–80; P-in-c Gayton le Marsh 76–80; P-in-c Strubby 76–80; P-in-c Authorpe 76–80; P-in-c Belleau w Aby and Claythorpe 76–80; P-in-c N and S Reston 76–80; P-in-c Swaby w S Thoresby 76–80; R Withern 80–90; V Reston 80–90; V Messingham 90–93; P-in-c Fincham *Ely* 95–02; P-in-c Marham 95–02; P-in-c Shouldham 95–02; P-in-c Shouldham Thorpe 95–02; rtd 02; PtO *Linc* from 03. *8 Anson Close, Skellingthorpe, Lincoln LN6 5TH* T: (01522) 694417 E: george.parrott15@gmail.com

PARROTT, Canon Gerald Arthur. b 32. St Cath Coll Cam BA 56 MA 60. Chich Th Coll. **d** 58 **p** 59. C Ashington *Newc* 58–61; C Brighton St Pet *Chich* 61–63; V Leeds St Wilfrid *Ripon* 63–68; R Lewisham St Jo Southend *S'wark* 69–73; TR Catford (Southend) and Downham 73–77; RD E Lewisham 75–77; Can Res and Prec S'wark Cathl 77–88; TR Wimbledon 88–95; rtd 95; PtO *Chich* from 95. *10 Palings Way, Fernhurst, Haslemere GU27 3HJ* T: (01428) 641533

PARROTT, Martin William. b 57. Keele Univ BA 79 K Coll Lon MA 93 W Lon Inst of HE PGCE 80. Ripon Coll Cuddesdon 82. **d** 85 **p** 86. C Birchfield *Birm* 85–88; Chapl Univ Coll Medical Sch *Lon* 88–93; Chapl SOAS 88–93; P-in-c Univ Ch Ch the K 90–93; V Hebden Bridge *Wakef* 93–01; Asst Chapl Pinderfields and Pontefract Hosps NHS Trust 01–02; Chapl Calderdale and Huddersfield NHS Trust 02–11; V Crosland Moor and Linthwaite *Wakef* 11–12; rtd 12; P-in-c Todmorden w Cornholme and Walsden *Leeds* 16–19. *16 Upper Bell Hall, Halifax HX1 3EQ* T: (01422) 363386 M: 07905-444872 E: martinwilliamparrott@gmail.com

PARRY, Canon Alfred Charles Ascough. b 37. Natal Univ BA 58. Westcott Ho Cam 59. **d** 61 **p** 62. C E Ham w Upton Park *Chelmsf* 61–63; C Durban N St Martin S Africa 63–64; R Newcastle H Trin 64–70; Dir Chr Educn Kloof 70–76; Sub Dean Pietermaritzburg 76–81; R Estcourt S Africa 81; Adn N Natal 81–85; R Kloof S Africa 86–93; R Berea 93–98; Hon Can Pietermaritzburg from 86; Sen Asst Min Hornchurch St Andr *Chelmsf* 99–04; C Furze Platt *Ox* 04–05; Hon C 05–07; rtd 05; PtO *St Alb* 08–18. *16 Capel Court, The Burgage, Prestbury, Cheltenham GL52 3EL* T: (01242) 352992

PARRY, Andrew Martyn. b 61. Witwatersrand Univ BA 81 MBA 91 Open Univ BSc 04 Birkbeck Coll Lon MSc 16. Ox Min Course 06. **d** 09 **p** 10. NSM Horton and Wraysbury *Ox* 09–12; NSM Stoke Poges 12–19; P-in-c Wexham from 19. *2 Pennylets Green, Stoke Poges, Slough SL2 4BT* M: 07972-142073 E: andrewmparry@icloud.com

PARRY, Benjamin. See PARRY, Owen Benjamin

PARRY, Canon Bryan Horace. b 33. St Mich Coll Llan 65. **d** 67 **p** 68. C Holyhead w Rhoscolyn w Llanfair-yn-Neubwll *Ban* 67–71; TV 71–73; P-in-c Small Heath St Greg *Birm* 73–78; V 78–80; V Perry Barr 80–94; RD Handsworth 83–91; P-in-c Kingstanding St Luke 86–92; Hon Can Birm Cathl 87–94; rtd 94; PtO *Nor* from 94. *St Seiriol, Old Crown Yard, Walsingham NR22 6BU* T: (01328) 820019

PARRY, Charles. See PARRY, Alfred Charles Ascough

PARRY, David Allan. b 62. Bris Univ BSc 83 Univ of Wales (Cardiff) CQSW 88. Trin Coll Bris. **d** 94 **p** 95. C Withywood *Bris* 94–98; P-in-c Litherland St Phil *Liv* 98–02; V 02–06; Hon Chapl to the Deaf 00–05; AD Bootle 02–05; Dioc

Dir of Ords 05–16; V Toxteth Park Ch Ch and St Mich w St Andr 06–16; Hon Can Liv Cathl 03–05 and 12–16; V Bro Celynnin *Ban* from 16. *The Vicarage, Rose Hill Street, Conwy LL32 8LD* T: (01492) 593402 M: 07403-635510 E: davidparry@esgobaethbangor.net

PARRY, David Thomas Newton. b 45. Selw Coll Cam BA 67 MA 71 Victoria Univ Man MPhil 91 Linacre Coll Ox MSt 07 Linc Coll Ox DPhil 15. Lambeth STh 76 Cuddesdon Coll 67. **d** 69 **p** 70. C Oldham St Mary w St Pet *Man* 69–73; C Baguley 73–74; Tutor Sarum & Wells Th Coll 74–78; V Westleigh St Pet *Man* 78–88; TR E Farnworth and Kearsley 88–97; TR Chambersbury *St Alb* 97–03; V Blackbird Leys *Ox* 03–11; rtd 11; PtO *Llan* from 11. *32 Barry Road, Pontypridd CF37 1HY* T: (01443) 650549 E: david@parsonage.org.uk

PARRY, Denis. b 34. Sarum & Wells Th Coll 83. **d** 85 **p** 86. C Hubberston w Herbrandston and Hasguard *etc St D* 85–88; C Herbrandston and Hasguard w St Ishmael's 89; P-in-c 89–90; R 90–99; Dioc RE Adv 89–99; rtd 99; PtO *Heref* from 99; *St D* 10–17. *Mayfield, 33 Mill Street, Kington HR5 3AL* T: (01544) 230550

PARRY, Canon Dennis John. b 38. Univ of Wales (Lamp) BA 60. St Mich Coll Llan 60. **d** 62 **p** 63. C Caerphilly *Llan* 62–64; C Aberdare St Fagan 64–67; Miss at Povungnituk Canada 67–69; R Gelligaer *Llan* 69–75; V Llanwnnog and Caersws w Carno *Ban* 75–89; V Llanidloes w Llangurig 89–01; RD Arwystli 89–01; Hon Can Ban Cathl 90–01; Can Cursal Ban Cathl 97–01; rtd 02; PtO *Ban* 02–17. *Lock Cottage, Groesffordd, Brecon LD3 7UY* T: (01874) 665400 E: djs19@btinternet.com

PARRY, Derek Nugent Goulding. b 32. Ely Th Coll 60. **d** 63 **p** 64. C Fareham SS Pet and Paul *Portsm* 63–67; C Portsea N End St Mark 67–74; P-in-c Piddletrenthide w Plush, Alton Pancras etc *Sarum* 74–92; rtd 92; PtO *Sarum* 92–15. *Farthing Cottage, 12 Fordington Green, Dorchester DT1 1LU* T: (01305) 269794

PARRY, Gordon Martyn Winn. b 47. Down Coll Cam BA 68 MA 70 Univ Coll Chich MA 02. **d** 04 **p** 05. NSM Turners Hill *Chich* 04–07; NSM E Grinstead St Swithun from 07. *31A Mount Close, Crawley RH10 7EF* M: 07802-432398 E: gordonmwparry@btinternet.com

PARRY, Canon Kenneth Charles. b 34. Ripon Hall Ox 56. **d** 58 **p** 59. C Stoke Cov 58–61; Chapl RN 61–65; V Cradley *Worc* 65–70; V Gt Malvern H Trin 70–83; RD Malvern 74–83; Hon Can Worc Cathl 80–83; V Budleigh Salterton *Ex* 83–91; Can Res and Prec Ex Cathl 91–00; rtd 00. *Brook Cottage, Pye Corner, Kennford, Exeter EX6 7TB* T: (01392) 832767 E: kc.parry@btinternet.com

PARRY, Lily Jacqueline Nicola. b 58. All SS Cen for Miss & Min 15. **d** 17 **p** 18. C Gt Crosby St Luke *Liv* from 17; Chapl Liv Women's NHS Foundn Trust from 18; Chapl Wirral Univ Teaching Hosp NHS Foundn Trust from 19. *Liverpool Women's NHS Foundation Trust, Crown Street, Liverpool L8 7SS* T: 0151-708 9988

PARRY, Manon Ceridwen. *See* JAMES, Manon Ceridwen

PARRY, Canon Marilyn Marie. b 46. W Coll Ohio BA 68 Man Univ MA 77 PhD 00. Episc Th Sch Cam Mass 68 Gilmore Ho 76. **dss** 79 **d** 87 **p** 94. Westleigh St Pet *Man* 78–85; Chapl Asst N Man Gen Hosp 85–90; Tutor NOC 90–97; Dir Studies 91–97; Lic Preacher *Man* 78–85; C E Farnworth and Kearsley 94–97; Nat Adv for Pre-Th Educn and Selection Sec Min Division Abps' Coun 97–01; Public Preacher *St Alb* 98–01; Can Res Ch Ch *Ox* 01–10; Vice Dir of Ords 01–10; IME Officer 10–11; rtd 11; PtO *Llan* from 11. *32 Barry Road, Pontypridd CF37 1HY* T: (01443) 650549 M: 07952-309667 E: marilyn@parsonage.org.uk

PARRY, Mrs Olwen Margaret. b 45. Cardiff Coll of Educn CertEd 67. Llan Dioc Tr Scheme 88. **d** 92 **p** 97. NSM Newcastle *Llan* 92–04; NSM Llansantffraid, Bettws and Aberkenfig 04–15; rtd 15; PtO *Llan* from 15. *17 Wernlys Road, Bridgend CF31 4NS* T: (01656) 721860

PARRY, Owen Benjamin. b 42. St As Minl Tr Course 99. **d** 01 **p** 02. C Llangollen w Trevor and Llantysilio *St As* 01–07; rtd 07; C-in-c Pradoe *Lich* 09–11; PtO *St As* from 09; *Lich* from 14. *Fairways, Halton, Chirk, Wrexham LL14 5BD* T: (01691) 778484

PARRY, Peter John. b 42. Westmr Coll Ox BTh 99 Sarum Coll MA 14. EAMTC 99. **d** 01 **p** 02. NSM Montreux w Gstaad *Eur* 01–06; PtO *Pet* from 05. *Forge House, Church Road, Hargrave, Wellingborough NN9 6BQ* E: phwparry@btinternet.com

PARRY, Robin Allinson. b 69. Qu Foundn (Course) 17. **d** 18 **p** 19. NSM Worc SE from 18. *12 Whitewood Way, Worcester WR5 2LN*

PARRY, Miss Violet Margaret. b 30. Selly Oak Coll 53. **dss** 82 **d** 87. W Kilburn St Luke w St Simon and St Jude *Lon* 82–83; St Marylebone St Mary 83–86; Stamford All SS w St Jo *Linc* 86–90; C 87–90; rtd 90; PtO *Linc* 90–01; *Leic* 03–16.

2 Stuart Court, High Street, Kibworth Beauchamp, Leicester LE8 0LR T: 0116-279 6858

PARRY-JENNINGS, Christopher William. b 34. Lon Coll of Div 57. **d** 60 **p** 62. C Claughton cum Grange *Ches* 60–63; C Folkestone H Trin w Ch Ch *Cant* 63–67; V Lincoln New Zealand 67–72; Chapl Cant Univ 68–72; V Riccarton St Jas 72–88; V Heathcote Mt Pleasant 88–96; First Gen Sec SPCK (NZ) 89–90; P Asst Upper Riccarton St Pet New Zealand from 96. *22 Ambleside Drive, Burnside, Christchurch 8053, New Zealand* T/F: (0064) (3) 358 9304 E: chpj@globe.net.nz

PARRY JONES, Dylan Caradog. **d** 18 **p** 19. C Dyffryn Clwyd Miss Area *St As* from 18. *7 Maes Celyn, Llanbedr Dyffryn Clwyd, Ruthin LL15 1YR* E: dcparryjones@gmail.com

PARRY-JONES, Leonard. b 29. Univ of Wales (Ban) BA 52. St Mich Coll Llan 52. **d** 54 **p** 55. C Newtown w Llanllwchaiarn w Aberhafesp *St As* 54–58; C Abergele 58–60; V Pennant, Hirnant and Llangynog 60–65; V Llanynys w Llanychan 65–71; V Brynymaen w Trofarth 71–94; RD Rhos 77–94; rtd 94; PtO *Lich* 15. *29 Pengwern Court, Longden Road, Shrewsbury SY3 7JE*

PARSELLE, Stephen Paul. b 53. Univ of Wales (Cardiff) MTh 06. St Jo Coll Nottm. **d** 82 **p** 83. C Boscombe St Jo *Win* 82–86; CF 86–05; Dir of Ords 02–05; Chapl RN 05–08; PtO *Win* from 09. *11 Southbourne Overcliff Drive, Bournemouth BH6 3TE* T: (01202) 433858 M: 07711-017282 E: parselle@aol.com

PARSONAGE, Robert Hugh. b 55. Nottm Trent Univ BSc 78. Trin Coll Bris BA 97. **d** 97 **p** 98. C Chell *Lich* 97–01; R Poringland *Nor* from 01; RD Loddon from 10. *The Rectory, Rectory Lane, Poringland, Norwich NR14 7SL* T: (01508) 492215 E: rector@poringland-benefice.org.uk

PARSONS, Andrew David. b 53. UEA BA 74 Fitzw Coll Cam BA 77 MA 81. Westcott Ho Cam 75. **d** 78 **p** 79. C Hellesdon *Nor* 78–82; C Eaton 82–85; P-in-c Burnham Thorpe w Burnham Overy 85–87; R Burnham Sutton w Burnham Ulph etc 85–87; R Burnham Gp of Par 87–93; P-in-c Wroxham w Hoveton and Belaugh 93; R 93–07; RD St Benet 99–07; V Old Catton from 07. *St Margaret's Vicarage, 1 Parkside Drive, Norwich NR6 7DP* T: (01603) 425615

PARSONS, Canon Christopher Kelly. b 75. Simon Fraser Univ BC BA 99. Vancouver Sch of Th MDiv 03. **d** 03 **p** 04. C Ch Ch Cathl Victoria Canada 04–05; R Victoria St Martin in the Fields and St Columba 06–11; C Victoria Three Saints 10–12; R Cordova Bay and Lakehill 12–15; P-in-c Freiburg-im-Breisau *Eur* from 15. *Schlossbergstrasse 8, 79189 Bad Krotzingen, Germany* E: freiburganglican.pastor@gmail.com

PARSONS, Christopher Paul. b 58. EAMTC 01. **d** 04 **p** 05. C Pakefield *Nor* 04–08; P-in-c Kenwyn w St Allen *Truro* 08–16; R from 16. *The Vicarage, Kenwyn Church Road, Truro TR1 3DR* T: (01872) 263015 E: vicarkenstallen@gmail.com

PARSONS, David Norman. b 39. FCIB 83. Trin Coll Bris 92. **d** 94 **p** 95. NSM Swindon Dorcan *Bris* 94–03; PtO *Glouc* 03–15; Carl from 15. *24 Helme Lodge, Natland, Kendal LA9 7QA* T: (01539) 727183 E: davidnparsons39@btinternet.com

PARSONS, Mrs Deborah Anne. b 66. Surrey Univ BA 87. STETS 04. **d** 07. C Goodrington *Ex* 07–11; TV Totnes w Bridgetown, Berry Pomeroy etc from 11; RD Totnes from 18. *St John's Vicarage, Crosspark, Totnes TQ9 5BQ* T: (01803) 840113 E: d.a.parsons@btinternet.com

PARSONS, Geoffrey Fairbanks. b 35. Trin Coll Cam BA 58 MA 68. Ridley Hall Cam 59. **d** 61 **p** 62. C Over St Chad *Ches* 61–64; C Heswall 64–69; V Congleton St Steph 69–75; V Weaverham 75–94; P-in-c Backford and Capenhurst 94–00; R 00–01; rtd 01; PtO *Ches* from 02. *28 Springcroft, Parkgate, South Wirral CH64 6SE* T: 0151-336 3354

PARSONS, George Horace Norman. b 19. S'wark Ord Course 65. **d** 68 **p** 69. C Hatcham St Cath *S'wark* 68–72; C Horley 72–76; P-in-c S Wimbledon All SS 76–78; P-in-c Caterham 78–81; C Caterham and Chapl St Lawr Hosp Caterham 82–84; rtd 85; PtO *S'wark* 85–13. *Address temp unknown*

PARSONS, Canon Jennifer Anne. b 53. Univ of Wales (Lamp) BA 76 MA 78 Jes Coll Cam PhD 90. Westcott Ho Cam 92. **d** 94 **p** 95. C Halesowen *Worc* 94–97; TV Worc St Barn w Ch Ch 97–04; R Matson *Glouc* 04–12; Hon Can Glouc Cathl 07–12; Asst Dean of Women Clergy 09–11; rtd 12; PtO *St D* from 12; Dioc Officer for Soc Resp 15–16. *Lan Fach, Cefnypant, Whitland SA34 0TS* T: (01994) 419808 E: jeniparsons7@gmail.com

PARSONS, Jeremy Douglas Adam. b 64. Ox Univ MA. Ridley Hall Cam. **d** 09 **p** 11. NSM Cambridge St Martin *Ely* 09–13; PtO *S'well* 13–14; TV Saffron Walden and Villages *Chelmsf* 14–17; R St Edm Way *St E* from 17. *The Rectory, Harrow Green, Lawshall, Bury St Edmunds IP29 4PB* M: 07980-016974 E: rector@stedmundway.uk

580

PARSONS, Canon John Banham. b 43. Selw Coll Cam BA 65 MA 68. Ridley Hall Cam 65. **d** 67 **p** 68. C Downend *Bris* 67–71; Public Preacher Withywood LEP 71–77; P-in-c Hengrove 77–78; V 78–85; V Letchworth St Paul w Willian *St Alb* 85–94; P-in-c Barking St Marg w St Patr *Chelmsf* 94–98; TR 98–04; RD Barking and Dagenham 00–04; P-in-c Hornchurch H Cross 04–09; RD Havering 04–08; Hon Can Chelmsf Cathl 01–09; rtd 09; PtO *St Alb* from 09. *8 Pound Close, Upper Caldecote, Biggleswade SG18 9AU* T: (01767) 315285 E: j.parsons986@btinternet.com

PARSONS, Canon Marlene Beatrice. b 43. Wilson Carlile Coll. **dss** 76 **d** 87 **p** 94. Coulsdon St Jo *S'wark* 76–79; Hill *Birm* 79–86; Dioc Lay Min Adv 80–90; Vice Prin WMMTC 86–90; Dioc Dir of Ords *Birm* 90–04; Dean of Women's Min 90–04; Hon Can Birm Cathl 89–04; rtd 04; PtO *Birm* 04–18. *20 Copperbeech Close, Birmingham B32 2HT* T: 0121-427 2632

PARSONS, Michael. b 46. Open Univ BA 84. SWMTC 05. **d** 08 **p** 09. NSM Boscastle w Davidstow *Truro* 08–15; NSM Boscastle and Tintagel Gp 15–16; rtd 16; PtO *Truro* from 16. *2 Penally Terrace, Boscastle PL35 0HA* T: (01840) 250625 E: mike@2penally.co.uk

PARSONS, Canon Michael William Semper. b 47. St Cath Coll Ox BA 69 MA 74 DPhil 74 Selw Coll Cam BA 77 MA 81. Ridley Hall Cam 75. **d** 78 **p** 79. C Edmonton All SS *Lon* 78–81; SPCK Research Fell Dur Univ 81–84; Hon Lect Th 84–85; SPCK Fell N of England Inst for Chr Educn 84–85; P-in-c Derby St Aug 85–95; TR Walbrook Epiphany 95–96; Dioc Voc Adv 86–96; P-in-c Hempsted *Glouc* 96–00; Dir of Ords 96–04; Dir Curates' Tr 00–04; Prin WEMTC *Glouc* 04–11; Prin Lect Glos Univ 09–11; P-in-c Coney Hill 11–15; rtd 15; PtO *Glouc* from 15; Clergy Retirement Officer from 17; Hon Can Glouc Cathl from 03. *6 Spa Villas, Montpellier, Gloucester GL1 1LB* T: (01452) 308227 E: mwsp@btinternet.com

PARSONS, Canon Robert Martin. b 43. Qu Coll Cam BA 65 MA 69. ALCD 68. **d** 68 **p** 69. C Chapeltown *Sheff* 68–71; C Sheff St Jo 71–75; V Swadlincote *Derby* 75–91; RD Repton 81–91; P-in-c Gresley 82–86; R Etwall w Egginton 91–93; Can Res Derby Cathl 93–98; Hon Can Derby Cathl 98–09; P-in-c Belper 98–03; V 03–09; Jt P-in-c Ambergate and Heage 06–09; rtd 09; Hon C Bicton, Montford w Shrawardine and Fitz *Lich* 09–18; Hon C Leaton and Albrighton w Battlefield 09–18; PtO from 18. *43 Steepside, Shrewsbury SY3 6DS* T: (01743) 365845 E: canonparsons@btinternet.com

PARSONS, Mrs Samantha Jayne. b 69. Aber Univ MA 93 N Coll of Educn PGCE 95 St Jo Coll Dur BATM 16. Cranmer Hall Dur 14. **d** 16 **p** 17. C Horncastle Gp *Linc* 16–19; V Grantham, Harrowby w Londonthorpe from 19. *The Vicarage, 2 Millstone Close, Horncastle LN9 5SU* E: rev.samparsons@gmail.com

PARSONS, Stephen Christopher. b 45. Keble Coll Ox BA 67 MA 72 BLitt 78. Cuddesdon Coll 68. **d** 70 **p** 71. C Whitstable All SS *Cant* 70–71; C Croydon St Sav 71–74; PtO *Ox* 74–76; C St Laur in Thanet *Cant* 76–79; V Lugwardine w Bartestree and Weston Beggard *Heref* 79–87; V Lechlade *Glouc* 87–03; R Edin St Cuth 03–10; rtd 10; PtO *Carl* 12–19; *Newc* from 16. *3 Church Road, Greystoke, Penrith CA11 0TW* T: (01768) 483221 E: parsvic2@gmail.com

PARSONS, Stephen Drury. b 54. Qu Mary Coll Lon BSc 76 CCC Cam MSc 79. Westcott Ho Cam 79. **d** 82 **p** 83. C Stretford All SS *Man* 82–85; C Newton Heath All SS 85–86; V Ashton St Jas 86–90; PtO 90–13; TR Turton Moorland 13–19; rtd 19. *Address temp unknown*

PARSONS, Mrs Susan Catherine. b 60. SWMTC 06 ERMC 08. **d** 09 **p** 10. NSM Oakham, Ashwell, Braunston, Brooke, Egleton etc *Pet* 09–11; NSM Polden Wheel *B & W* 12–14; PtO from 14. *Greystones, Broadway, Chilton Polden, Bridgwater TA7 9DJ* T: (01278) 723885 E: susie.parsons@hotmail.co.uk

PARSONS, Thomas James. b 74. K Coll Lon BMus 97 LRAM 96. Oak Hill Th Coll BA 06. **d** 06 **p** 07. C Hensingham *Carl* 06–10; V Sidcup Ch Ch *Roch* from 10. *The Vicarage, 16 Christchurch Road, Sidcup DA15 7HE* T: (020) 8308 0835 M: 07960-944287 E: tjparsons@tiscali.co.uk

PARTINGTON, The Ven Brian Harold. b 36. St Aid Birkenhead 60. **d** 63 **p** 64. C Barlow Moor *Man* 63–66; C Deane 66–68; V Patrick *S & M* 68–96; Bp's Youth Chapl 68–77; RD Peel 76–96; P-in-c German St Jo 77–78; V 78–96; P-in-c Foxdale 77–78; V 78–96; Can St German's Cathl 85–96; Adn of Man 96–05; V Douglas St Geo 96–04; rtd 04. *Brambles, Patrick Village, Peel, Isle of Man IM5 3AH* T: (01624) 844173 E: bpartington@mcb.net *or* mjt16@hotmail.co.uk

PARTINGTON, John. See PARTINGTON, Peter John

PARTINGTON, Canon Kevin. b 51. Huddersfield Poly BA 73. St Jo Coll Nottm 91. **d** 93 **p** 94. C Salt-erhebble All SS *Wakef* 93–96; V Pontefract All SS 96–03; TR Dewsbury 03–14; *Leeds* 14–15; Hon Can Wakef Cathl 07–15; RD Dewsbury *Wakef*

13–14; AD *Leeds* 14–15; rtd 15; PtO *Leeds* from 15. *46 Larch Road, Huddersfield HD1 4JG* T: (01484) 614767 M: 07563-513632 E: kevin.partington@aol.co.uk

PARTINGTON, Peter John. b 57. Peterho Cam MA. St Jo Coll Nottm 79. **d** 81 **p** 82. C Cov H Trin 81–85; C Woking St Jo *Guildf* 85–87 and 94–99; R Busbridge 87–94; Dir of Ords 94–03; P-in-c Winchcombe, Gretton, Sudeley Manor etc *Glouc* 03–05; TR Winchcombe 05–15; TV S Cotswolds 15–19; rtd 19. *32 The Slade, Charlbury, Chipping Norton OX7 3SJ* E: john@pjohnp.me.uk

PARTON, Mrs Michelle Elizabeth. b 82. Univ of Wales (Abth) BA 05 Newman Univ BA(Theol) 17. Qu Coll Birm 12. **d** 15 **p** 16. C Wythall *Birm* from 15. *247 Alcester Road, Hollywood, Birmingham B47 5HG* T: 0121-246 5482 E: michelleparton@hotmail.co.uk

PARTRIDGE, Alan Christopher. b 55. Thames Poly BA 77 Ex Univ PGCE 78. St Jo Coll Nottm MA 00. **d** 00 **p** 01. C Woking St Jo *Guildf* 00–03; C Ely 03–08; TV 08–09; P-in-c Sawston 09–18; V from 19; P-in-c Babraham 09–18; V from 19. *The Vicarage, Church Lane, Sawston, Cambridge CB2 3JR* T: (01223) 832248 E: a.partridge7@ntlworld.com

PARTRIDGE, Mrs Bryony Gail. b 51. St Anne's Coll Ox BA 72 MA 76 Ox Univ PGCE 73 Leeds Univ BA 11. Yorks Min Course 09. **d** 11 **p** 12. NSM Oakworth *Bradf* 11–14; *Leeds* from 14. *New House Farm, Oakworth, Keighley BD22 7JW* T: (01535) 643206 E: geraldandbryony@hotmail.com

PARTRIDGE, Ian Starr. b 36. Linc Th Coll 87. **d** 89 **p** 90. C Barton upon Humber *Linc* 89–92; P-in-c Barkwith Gp 92–97; R 97–02; rtd 02; PtO *Linc* from 02; RD Calcewaithe and Candleshoe 03–05. *Altair, 4 Thames Street, Louth LN11 7AD* T: (01507) 600398 E: ian@altair.org.uk

PARTRIDGE, Preb Michael John. b 61. St Edm Hall Ox BA 83 MA 89 St Jo Coll Dur BA 86. Cranmer Hall Dur 84. **d** 87 **p** 88. C Amington *Birm* 87–90; C Sutton Coldfield H Trin 90–93; P-in-c W Exe *Ex* 93–01; RD Tiverton 96–00; V Tiverton St Geo and St Paul 01–06; P-in-c Pinhoe and Broadclyst 06–13; P-in-c Aylesbeare, Rockbeare, Farringdon etc 06–13; TR Broadclyst, Clyst Honiton, Pinhoe, Rockbeare etc 13–17; R Alphington, Shillingford St George and Ide from 17; Preb Ex Cathl from 12. *The Rectory, 6 Lovelace Gardens, Exeter EX2 8XQ* T: (01392) 491476 M: 07751-725306 E: rev.mike.partridge@gmail.com

PARTRIDGE, Richard Bruce. b 65. Kingston Poly BA 87. STETS 10. **d** 12 **p** 13. NSM Christchurch *Win* 12–16; C from 16. *The Paddocks, Holly Lane, Walkford, Christchurch BH23 5QQ* T: (01425) 279043 E: richardpartridge310@btinternet.com

PARTRIDGE, Ronald Malcolm. b 49. Bris Bapt Coll LTh 74 Cuddesdon Coll 74. **d** 75 **p** 76. C Bris St Andr Hartcliffe 75–78; C E Bris 78–82; V Easton All Hallows 82–85; TV Brighton St Pet w Chpl Royal and St Jo *Chich* 85–86; TV Brighton St Pet and St Nic w Chpl Royal 86–88; C-in-c Bermondsey St Hugh CD *S'wark* 88–90; Asst Chapl Gt Ormond Street Hosp for Children NHS Trust 91–97; PtO *Chich* 13–17. *29 All Saints Street, Hastings TN34 3BJ* T: (01424) 715219

PARTRIDGE, Ronald William. b 42. Shimer Coll Illinois BA 64. Cant Sch of Min 93. **d** 96 **p** 97. NSM Upchurch w Lower Halstow *Cant* 96–12; PtO *Roch* from 10; *Cant* from 12. *4 The Green, Lower Halstow, Sittingbourne ME9 7DT* T: (01795) 842007 M: 07779-789039

PARTRIDGE, Canon Sarah Mercy. b 59. SEITE 04. **d** 07 **p** 08. NSM Tunbridge Wells K Chas *Roch* from 07; Hon Can Roch Cathl from 18. *Long Hedges, Station Road, Rotherfield, Crowborough TN6 3HP* T: (01892) 853451 E: sm.partridge@outlook.com

PARTRIDGE, Stephen Hugh. b 70. Bath Univ BSc 91 Univ of Wales (Swansea) PGCE 92. St Jo Coll Nottm MTh 13. **d** 13 **p** 14. C Canford Magna *Sarum* 13–16; TV The Lytchetts and Upton from 16. *The Rectory, Jennys Lane, Lytchett Matravers, Poole BH16 6BP* E: revspartridge@gmail.com

PARTRIDGE, Timothy David. b 85. Bath Univ BSc 07. Oak Hill Th Coll BA 18. **d** 18. C Plymouth St Andr and Stonehouse *Ex* from 18. *The Rectory, 6 Underhill Road, Plymouth PL3 4BP* M: 07709-491261 E: timothydpartridge@gmail.com

PARTRIDGE, Canon Timothy Reeve. b 39. Lon Univ BSc 60 AKC 60. Wells Th Coll 60. **d** 62 **p** 63. C Glouc St Cath 62–65; C Sutton St Nicholas *Linc* 65–74; R Bugbrooke *Pet* 74–95; R Bugbrooke w Rothersthorpe 95–04; RD Daventry 81–88; Can Pet Cathl 83–04; Warden of Par Ev 96–02; rtd 04; PtO *Ox* from 06. *54 Thorney Leys, Witney OX28 5LS* T: (01993) 864926 E: tim.partridge39@tiscali.co.uk

PASCHAL, Brother. See WORTON, David Reginald Paschal

PASCOE, Preb Caroline Elizabeth Alice. b 62. **d** 08 **p** 09. NSM Ewenny w St Brides Major *Llan* 08–10; NSM Ross w Walford and Brampton Abbotts *Heref* from 15; Lay

Development Officer from 10; Preb Heref Cathl from 17. *Diocese of Hereford, Unit 8-9, The Business Quarter, Eco Park Road, Ludlow SY8 1FD* T: (01584) 871086 E: c.pascoe@hereford.anglican.org

PASCOE, Lorraine Eve. *See* SUMMERS, Lorraine Eve

PASCOE, Michael Lewis. b 43. **d** 99 **p** 00. OLM Crowan and Treslothan *Truro* 99–02; C 02–13; OLM Penponds 01–02; C 02–13; P-in-c 13–14; rtd 14; PtO *Truro* from 14. *Genesis, Bosparva Lane, Leedstown, Hayle TR27 6DN* T: (01736) 850425 E: revdmike@supanet.com

PASHLEY, Howard Thomas. b 47. Kent Univ MSc 85 Keele Univ PGCE 71 ARIC 70. **d** 06 **p** 07. OLM Sandwich *Cant* 06–12; OLM Sandwich and Worth 12–17; rtd 17; PtO *Cant* from 18. *56 New Street, Sandwich CT13 9BB* T: (01304) 612018

PASK, Howard. b 54. St Jo Coll Nottm. **d** 99 **p** 00. C Todmorden *Wakef* 99–02; P-in-c Hebden Bridge 02–03; P-in-c Heptonstall 02–03; V Hebden Bridge and Heptonstall 03–14; *Leeds* 14–18; rtd 18. *11 Southfield, Heptonstall, Hebden Bridge HX7 7LS* M: 07779-243176 E: howardpask@btinternet.com

PASK (*formerly* THURTELL), **Canon Victoria Ann.** b 59. St Jo Coll Dur BSc 82 Univ of Wales (Lamp) BA 11 PGCE 96. STETS 02. **d** 05 **p** 06. C Chickerell w Fleet *Sarum* 05–08; TV Dorchester 08–14; TV Dorchester and the Winterbournes 14–15; Can Res and Prec Ex Cathl 15–17; PtO from 17; *Lon* from 19. *12 Victoria Park Road, Exeter EX2 4NT* M: 07813-859825 E: paskvictoria@gmail.com

PASKETT, Ms Margaret Anne. b 45. Northd Coll of Educn CertEd 67 York Univ BSc 81 Leeds Univ MEd 83. NEOC 84. **d** 87 **p** 94. Par Dn Marske in Cleveland *York* 87–91; C 92–96; Dioc Adv for Diaconal Mins 92–96; P-in-c Hemingbrough and Tr Officer (York Adnry) 96–05; rtd 06; PtO *York* from 07. *15 Hubert Street, York YO23 1EF* T: (01904) 626521 E: annepaskett62@gmail.com

PASKINS, David James. b 52. Univ of Wales (Lamp) BA 73 Trin Hall Cam BA 76 MA 81. Westcott Ho Cam 74. **d** 77 **p** 78. C St Peter-in-Thanet *Cant* 77–80; C Swanage *Sarum* 80–82; R Waldron *Chich* 82–92; R Bere Ferrers *Ex* 92–96; V Lockerley and E Dean w E and W Tytherley *Win* 96–03; R Cranborne w Boveridge, Edmondsham etc *Sarum* 03–15; rtd 15; PtO *Nor* from 16. *28 Renwick Park East, West Runton, Cromer NR27 9LY* T: (01263) 838926 E: david@paskins.eclipse.co.uk

PASTERFIELD, Laura Sophia. *See* FERGUSON, Laura Sophia

PATCH, Simon John. b 63. Aus Nat Univ BA 88 Southn Univ BTh 95 Univ of S Qld MEd 15. Chich Th Coll 92 Westcott Ho Cam 94. **d** 95 **p** 96. C Ifield *Chich* 95–99; C Stepney St Dunstan and All SS *Lon* 03–06; Hong Kong from 07. *6 San Francisco Avenue, Royal Palms, Phase B, Wo Shang Wai, Yuen Long, NT, Hong Kong, China* E: simon_patch@yahoo.com.au

PATCHELL, Miss Gwendoline Rosa. b 49. Goldsmiths' Coll Lon BA 69 TCert 70. Trin Coll Bris 90. **d** 92 **p** 94. C Ashton-upon-Mersey St Mary Magd *Ches* 92–98; TV Hemel Hempstead *St Alb* 98–06; P-in-c Kirkby in Ashfield *S'well* 06–11; R 11–14; rtd 14; PtO *S'well* from 16. *21 Leivers Close, East Leake, Loughborough LE12 6PQ* E: revdwendypatchell@gmail.com

PATCHING, Julian Francis. b 65. Colchester Inst BA 87 Liv Inst of HE PGCE 88. Ushaw Coll Dur 88. **d** 93 **p** 94. In RC Ch 93–09; C Langdon Hills *Chelmsf* 13–19; P-in-c Hornchurch H Cross from 19. *Holy Cross Vicarage, 260 Hornchurch Road, Hornchurch RM11 1PX* M: 07860-119450 E: jfp65@hotmail.co.uk *or* holycrosschurch1409@gmail.com

PATE, Barry Emile Charles. b 50. NE Lon Poly BA 80 CQSW 80. S'wark Ord Course 85. **d** 88 **p** 89. NSM E Dulwich St Jo *S'wark* 88–92; C Farnborough *Roch* 92–94; C Broxbourne w Wormley *St Alb* 94–00; V Wilbury 00–19; rtd 19. *31 Greengarth, St Ives PE27 5QS* E: b.pate@ntlworld.com

PATEL, Jitesh Krisnakant. b 82. Jes Coll Ox MPhys 04 Kellogg Coll Ox PGCE 06. Wycliffe Hall Ox BA 09 MA 09. **d** 10 **p** 11. C Abingdon *Ox* 10–13; C N Abingdon 13–15; C Southsea St Jude *Portsm* 15–18; C Leic H Trin w St Jo from 18; Asst Dir St Mellitus E Midl from 19. *46 Brading Road, Leicester LE3 9BG* T: 0116-254 8981 E: jit@cca.uk.net

PATEMAN, Miles Thomas. b 89. Swansea Univ BA 12 Sheff Univ MA 19. Coll of Resurr Mirfield BA 17. **d** 18 **p** 19. C Stanground and Farcet *Ely* 18–19; C Fulbourn from 19; C Lt Wilbraham from 19; C Gt Wilbraham from 19. *18 Beech Drive, Trumpington, Cambridge CB2 9PR* M: 07557-351806 E: rev.miles@outlook.com

PATERNOSTER, Canon Michael Cosgrove. b 35. Pemb Coll Cam BA 59 MA 63. Cuddesdon Coll 59. **d** 61 **p** 62. C Surbiton St Andr *S'wark* 61–63; Chapl Qu Coll Dundee 63–68; Dioc Supernumerary *Bre* 63–68; Chapl Dundee Univ 67–68; Sec Fellowship of SS Alb and Sergius 68–71; R Dollar *St And* 71–75; R Stonehaven *Bre* 75–90; Hon Can St Paul's Cathl Dundee 81–12; R Aberdeen St Jas *Ab* 90–00; rtd 00; PtO *B & W* from 00. *12 Priest Row, Wells BA5 2PY*

PATERSON, Canon Alan Michael. b 64. **d** 06 **p** 07. SSF 87–11; NSM Bartley Green *Birm* 06–10; V Cowgate *Newc* from 10; P-in-c Newbiggin Hall from 18; Hon Can Newc Cathl from 19. *St Peter's Vicarage, Druridge Drive, Newcastle upon Tyne NE5 3LP* T: 0191-286 9913 E: fatheralan64@btinternet.com

PATERSON (*née* SOAR), **Mrs Angela Margaret.** b 59. Aston Univ MSc 81 MCIPD 82. SAOMC 97. **d** 00 **p** 01. NSM Icknield *Ox* from 00. *86 Hill Road, Watlington OX49 5AF* T: (01491) 614033 E: angie.paterson@btinternet.com

PATERSON, Douglas Monro. b 30. Em Coll Cam BA 54 MA 57. Tyndale Hall Bris 55. **d** 57 **p** 58. C Walcot *B & W* 57–60; C Portman Square St Paul *Lon* 60–62; Lect Oak Hill Th Coll 60–62; Min Hampstead St Jo Downshire Hill Prop Chpl *Lon* 62–65; Lect All Nations Chr Coll Ware 62–65; Rwanda 67–73; C Edin St Thos 73–75; Lect Northumbria Bible Coll 73–94; PtO *Edin* 75–94; LtO *Newc* 76–94; rtd 94; PtO *Ox* 94–10; *York* from 10. *8 Dulverton Hall, Esplanade, Scarborough YO11 2AR* T: (01723) 340108

PATERSON, Geoffrey Gordon. b 45. Cant Univ (NZ) LTh 69. **d** 69 **p** 70. C Linwood New Zealand 69–71; C Belfast-Redwood 71–76; V Mayfield Mt Somers 76–78; P-in-c Astwood Bank w Crabbs Cross *Worc* 78–80; V Halswell-Prebbleton New Zealand 80–87; Chapl Sunnyside Hosp 87–95. *19 Ridder Place, Christchurch 8025, New Zealand* T: (0064) (3) 322 7787 *or* (3) 365 3211 E: geoffpat@xtra.co.nz

PATERSON, Mrs Jennifer Ann. b 49. Brooklands Tech Coll 69. S Dios Minl Tr Scheme 85. **d** 88 **p** 95. C Hale *Guildf* 88–92; PtO 94–95; NSM Seale, Puttenham and Wanborough 95–01; rtd 01; PtO *Guildf* 01–16. *4 St George's Close, Badshot Lea, Farnham GU9 9LZ* T: (01252) 316775 E: ja.paterson@btinternet.com

PATERSON, Michael Séan. b 61. Heythrop Coll Lon BD 89 MA 95 Univ of Wales (Lamp) MMin 04. **d** 04 **p** 05. C Stonehaven *Bre* 04–05; C Arbroath 05–06; C Edin Ch Ch 06–08; Chapl St Andr Hospice Airdrie 08–09; Chapl St Columba's Hospice 09–13; Dir Inst Past Supervision and Reflective Practice from 08. *8 Greenmount Road North, Burntisland KY3 9JQ* E: michael@ipsrp.org.uk

PATERSON, Paul Philip. b 49. St Jo Coll Dur BA 11 MA 13. Cranmer Hall Dur. **d** 18 **p** 19. NSM Hawthorn and Murton *Dur* from 18. *The Old Rectory, The Village, Hawthorn, Seaham SR7 8SG* T: 0191-527 1908 M: 07834-348580 E: p@ulpaterson.net

✠**PATERSON, The Rt Revd Robert Mar Erskine.** b 49. St Jo Coll Dur BA 71 MA 82. Cranmer Hall Dur. **d** 72 **p** 73 **c** 08. C Harpurhey St Steph and Harpurhey Ch Ch *Man* 72–73; C Sketty *S & B* 73–78; R Llangattock and Llangynidr 78–83; V Gabalfa *Llan* 83–94; TR Cowbridge 94–00; Prin Officer Ch in Wales Coun for Miss and Min 00–06; Metrop Can 04–08; Abp's Chapl and Researcher *York* 06–08; Bp S & M 08–16; rtd 16; Hon Asst Bp Worc from 17; Hon Asst Bp Heref from 17. *Cedar House, 63 Greenhill, Evesham WR11 4LX* T: (01386) 247105 M: 07979-600627 E: mar.erskine@me.com

PATERSON, Robin Fergus (Robert). b 32. Moore Th Coll Sydney 83. **d** 87 **p** 89. Singapore 87–88; NSM Crieff *St And* 88–92; NSM Comrie 88–92; R Dunkeld 93–98; R Strathtay 93–98; rtd 98; LtO *St And* from 98; LtO *Eur* from 98; PtO from 98. *1 Corsiehill House, Corsiehill, Perth PH2 7BN* T: (01738) 446621 E: robinatcorsie@talktalk.net

PATERSON, Robin Lennox Andrew. b 43. NOC 84. **d** 87 **p** 88. C Manston *Ripon* 87–91; P-in-c Leeds All So 91–95; V 95–98; V Middleton St Mary 98–08; rtd 08; PtO *Leeds* from 17; *York* from 18. *22 Manston Way, Leeds LS15 8BR* M: 07778-860178 E: rlap@mypostoffice.co.uk

PATERSON, Mrs Shirley Anne. b 56. Reading Univ BA 78 Ex Univ PGCE 79. SWMTC 11. **d** 14 **p** 15. NSM Barnstaple *Ex* 14–17; NSM Barnstaple H Trin and Goodleigh from 17. *Elm Cottage, Ladywell, Barnstaple EX31 1QS* T: (01271) 346095 M: 07971-251707 E: shirley.p@live.co.uk

PATERSON, Mrs Susan Ann. b 57. St Hilda's Coll Ox MA 84. EMMTC 92. **d** 95 **p** 96. NSM Evington *Leic* 95–98; C Humberstone 98–03; TV Melton Mowbray 03–09; P-in-c Ab Kettleby and Holwell w Asfordby 09–15; V Deeping St James *Linc* 15–18; R Whippingham w E Cowes *Portsm* from 18. *The Rectory, 69 Victoria Grove, East Cowes PO32 6DL* E: revspaterson@gmail.com

PATMORE, Hector Michael. b 81. Trevelyan Coll Dur BA 03 MA 05 St Jo Coll Dur PhD 08. Westcott Ho Cam 13 Ripon Coll Cuddesdon 14. **d** 16. NSM Lisvane *Llan* 16; Dir Studies St Geo Coll Jerusalem from 16. *St George's College, PO Box 1248, Jerusalem 91000, Israel* T: (00972) (2) 626 4704 E: hec_uk@yahoo.co.uk

✠**PATON, The Rt Revd Ian James.** b 59. Jes Coll Cam MA 78 PGCE 79 Edin Univ MTh 07. Westcott Ho Cam MA 81. **d** 82 **p** 83 **c** 18. C Whitley Ch Ch *Ox* 82–84; Bp's Dom Chapl 84–86; Chapl Wadh Coll Ox 86–90; C Ox St Mary V w

St Cross and St Pet 86–90; Can and Vice Provost St Mary's Cathl Edin 90–94; R Edin St Mary 90–94; R Haddington and Dunbar 94–97; R Edin Old St Paul 97–18; Can St Mary's Cathl 04–18; Hon Chapl Edin Univ 11–18; Bp St And from 18. *28A Balhousie Street, Perth PH1 5HJ* T: (01738) 580426 M: 07751-510594 E: bishop@standrews.anglican.org

PATON, Canon John William Scholar. b 52. Mert Coll Ox BA 74 MA 95. St Steph Ho Ox 93. **d** 95 **p** 96. C Sherborne w Castleton and Lillington *Sarum* 95–98; Succ S'wark Cathl 98–01; Chapl Medical and Dental Students K Coll Lon 98–01; P-in-c Purley St Mark *S'wark* 01–07; P-in-c Purley St Swithun 05–07; Prec Ch Ch Ox 07–17; P-in-c Sulhamstead Abbots and Bannister w Ufton Nervet *Ox* from 17; Hon Can Ch Ch from 18. *The Rectory, Sulhamstead Road, Ufton Nervet, Reading RG7 4DH* M: 07790-498175 E: sunrector@outlook.com

PATON-WILLIAMS, David Graham. b 58. Warwick Univ BA 81 Selw Coll Cam BA 86 MA 90 Newc Univ MA 92. Ridley Hall Cam 84. **d** 87 **p** 88. C S Westoe *Dur* 87–90; C Newton Aycliffe 90–91; TV 91–93; Chapl Univ Coll of Ripon and York St Jo 93–98; Min Can Ripon Cathl 93–98; R Bedale 98–02; P-in-c Leeming 98–02; R Bedale and Leeming 03–08; P-in-c Thornton Watlass 07–08; R Bedale and Leeming and Thornton Watlass 08; AD Wensley 05–08; V Roundhay St Edm 08–14; *Leeds* 14–16; Hon Can Ripon Cathl 11–16; R Edin St Columba from 16. *28 Castle Terrace, Edinburgh EH1 2EL*

PATRICIA, Sister. See PERKINS, Patricia Doris

PATRICK, Andrew. b 83. Hull Univ BA 06. St Jo Coll Nottm 09. **d** 12 **p** 13. C Harrogate St Mark *Leeds* 12–16; TV Bilton from 16. *8 Pecketts Way, Harrogate HG1 3EW* M: 07966-360437 E: mrandrewpatrick@gmail.com

PATRICK, Charles. See PATRICK, Peter Charles

PATRICK, Hugh Joseph. b 37. TCD BA 62 MA 66. **d** 63 **p** 64. C Dromore Cathl *D & D* 63–66; C Lurgan Ch the Redeemer 66–70; C Rothwell *Ripon* 70–73; V Thurnscoe St Hilda *Sheff* 73–78; W Wales 78–02; P-in-c Thorpe Salvin 78–82; RD Laughton 93–98; rtd 02; PtO *Sheff* 02–10. *5 Fairfax Avenue, Worksop S81 7RH* T: (01909) 477622 E: hughpatrick@sky.com

PATRICK, Canon John Andrew. b 62. St Jo Coll Dur BA 84. Ripon Coll Cuddesdon 87. **d** 89 **p** 90. C Frankby w Greasby *Ches* 89–92; Lect Boston *Linc* 92–95; P-in-c Graffoe Gp 95–97; R 97–02; P-in-c New Sleaford 02–12; P-in-c Kirkby Laythorpe 10–12; RD Lafford 08–12; Can and Preb Linc Cathl 07–12; Can Res and Subdean Linc Cathl from 12. *The Subdeanery, 18 Minster Yard, Lincoln LN2 1PX* T: (01522) 561600 E: japatrick1@btinternet.com *or* subdean@lincolncathedral.com

PATRICK, Canon Peter Charles. b 64. Leeds Univ BA 86 Fitzw Coll Cam BA 91 MA 95. Ridley Hall Cam 89. **d** 92 **p** 93. C Barton upon Humber *Linc* 92–96; TV Gt Grimsby St Mary and St Jas 96–03; RD Grimsby and Cleethorpes 99–03; R Middle Rasen Gp 03–15; P-in-c Barkwith Gp 07–15; R Horncastle Gp from 15; Can and Preb Linc Cathl from 18. *9 Langton Drive, Horncastle LN9 5AJ*

PATTEN (née STARNS), Mrs Helen Edna. b 43. St Hilda's Coll Ox BA 65 Maria Grey Coll Lon CertEd 70. Trin Coll Bris 73 Oak Hill Th Coll 81. **dss** 82 **d** 87 **p** 94. Tunbridge Wells St Jo *Roch* 82–86; Patcham *Chich* 86–91; Par Dn 87–91; Par Dn Eckington w Handley and Ridgeway *Derby* 91–94; C 94–95; TV 95–98; Chapl St Mich Hospice St Leonards-on-Sea 98–03; rtd 03; Hon C Fairlight and Pett *Chich* from 04. *Holyoak, Workhouse Lane, Westfield, Hastings TN35 4QJ* T: (01424) 752052

PATTEN, The Ven Ruth Janet. b 72. Roehampton Inst BA 94 Goldsmiths' Coll Lon MMus 98. Westcott Ho Cam 08. **d** 10 **p** 11. C Witham *Chelmsf* 10–14; P-in-c Gt Dunmow and Barnston 14–19; Adn Colchester from 19. *63 Powers Hall End, Witham CM8 1NH* T: (01376) 513130 E: a.colchester@chelmsford.anglican.org

PATTENDEN, Mrs Alison Margaret. b 53. Eastbourne Tr Coll CertEd 75 Sussex Univ BEd 76. St Steph Ho Ox 04. **d** 06 **p** 07. C Goring-by-Sea *Chich* 06–10; P-in-c Amberley w N Stoke and Parham, Wiggonholt etc 10–14; V 14–16; rtd 16. *16 Crowborough Court, Elverlands Close, Ferring, Worthing BN12 5QF* E: revpattenden@btinternet.com

PATTERSON, Alfred Percy. **d** 85 **p** 87. NSM Aghalee *D & D* 85–91; C Gilford 91–93; Bp's C 93–95; I 95–00; rtd 00. *Brookdale, 723 Upper Newtownards Road, Belfast BT4 3NU* T: (028) 9029 4741 E: revap.patterson@ntlworld.com

PATTERSON, Andrew John. b 56. Master Mariner 85. Qu Coll Birm 85. **d** 88 **p** 89. C Newc St Phil and St Aug 88–92; Chapl Hunter's Moor Hosp 91–92; Asst Chapl R Victoria Infirmary Newc 92–96; V Whitley *Newc* from 96; Chapl Hexham Gen Hosp from 96. *The Vicarage, Whitley, Hexham NE46 2LA* T: (01434) 673379 E: revdocpatt@doctors.org.uk

PATTERSON, Anthony. b 43. Moore Th Coll Sydney BTh 82. **d** 83 **p** 83. Australia 83–91; C Darfield *Sheff* 91–94; TR Marfleet *York* 94–99; TV Heeley and Gleadless Valley *Sheff* 99–04; TR 04–10; AD Attercliffe 04–10; rtd 11; PtO *York* 11–13; P-in-c Bempton w Flamborough, Reighton w Speeton 13–17. *Address temp unknown* E: tonypatterson1@gmail.com

PATTERSON, Colin Hugh. b 52. St Pet Coll Ox MA 77 Univ of Wales (Cardiff) MPhil 90 CertEd 75. Trin Coll Bris. **d** 87 **p** 88. C Blackb Sav 87–90; C Haughton le Skerne *Dur* 90–93; Adult Educn Adv 93–05; Asst Dir Bridge Builders Min 05–17; NSM Dur St Nic 05–17; rtd 17; PtO *Dur* from 18. *24 Monks Crescent, Durham DH1 1HD*

PATTERSON, Colin Peter Matthew. b 62. Newc Poly BA 84. St Steph Ho Ox 92. **d** 94 **p** 95. C Cullercoats St Geo *Newc* 94–97; Shrine P Shrine of Our Lady of Walsingham 97–99; P-in-c Harlow St Mary Magd *Chelmsf* 99–00; V 00–09; V Willesden Green St Andr and St Fran *Lon* from 09; CMP from 97. *The Clergy House, 4 St Andrew's Road, London NW10 2QS* T: (020) 8459 2670

PATTERSON, Mrs Diane Rosemary. b 46. WMMTC 88. **d** 91 **p** 94. C Hill *Birm* 91–95; PtO 95–96; C Shottery St Andr *Cov* 96–01; C Hunningham 01–13; C Wappenbury w Weston under Wetherley 01–13; C Long Itchington and Marton 01–13; C Offchurch 01–13; RD Southam 02–08; rtd 13; PtO *Cov* from 13. *169A Clopton Road, Stratford-upon-Avon CV37 6TF* T: (01789) 266453 E: revdianepatterson@yahoo.co.uk

PATTERSON, Hugh John. b 38. Southn Univ MPhil 76. AKC 63. **d** 64 **p** 65. C Epsom St Martin *Guildf* 64–65; Chapl Ewell Coll 65–68; Asst Chapl and Lect Bp Otter Coll Chich 68–71; Lect Dudley Coll of Educn 71–77; Lect Wolv Poly 77–92; Wolv Univ 92–00; Chapl 89–00; rtd 01; Hon C Morville w Aston Eyre *Heref* 82–16; Hon C Upton Cressett w Monk Hopton 82–16; Hon C Acton Round 82–16; Hon C Bridgnorth and Morville Par from 16. *6 Victoria Road, Bridgnorth WV16 4LA* T: (01746) 765298

PATTERSON, John. See PATTERSON, Norman John

PATTERSON, Marjorie Jean. See BROWN, Marjorie Jean

PATTERSON, Neil Sydney. b 79. BNC Ox BA 00 MA 04. Ripon Coll Cuddesdon BA 03 BD 17. **d** 04 **p** 05. C Cleobury Mortimer w Hopton Wafers etc *Heref* 04–08; TV Ross 08; R Ariconium 08–15; Dioc Dir Voc and Dir of Ords from 15; RD Heref from 18. *Diocese of Hereford (Ludlow), 8-9 The Business Quarter, Eco Park Road, Ludlow SY8 1FD* E: pattersonneil@hotmail.com *or* ddvo@hereford.anglican.org

PATTERSON, Norman John. b 47. Peterho Cam BA 69 ALCD. St Jo Coll Nottm 70. **d** 73 **p** 74. C Everton St Ambrose w St Tim *Liv* 73–74; C Everton St Pet 74–78; TV 79–84; C Aigburth and Dioc Adv for Past Care and Counselling 84–92; V Gt Crosby All SS 92–04; Crosslinks Uganda 05–09; rtd 12; PtO *Ches* from 11. *6 Brookside, Great Boughton, Chester CH3 5TL* T: (01244) 314613 E: johnpatterson6098@yahoo.com

PATTERSON, Scott Robert. b 71. GTCL 92. Oak Hill Th Coll 07. **d** 09 **p** 10. C Newton Tracey, Horwood, Alverdiscott etc *Ex* 09–13; P-in-c Curry Rivel w Fivehead and Swell *B & W* 13–18; R from 18. *The Rectory, Church Street, Curry Rivel, Langport TA10 0HQ* M: 07973-139092 E: scottr.patterson@btinternet.com

PATTERSON, Susan Margaret. b 48. Otago Univ BA 71 BD 89 PhD 92. Knox Coll Dunedin 84. **d** 88 **p** 89. C Dunedin St Martin New Zealand 88–91; Tutor Otago Univ and Knox Coll 89–91; USA 91–92; Assoc P Hawke's Bay New Zealand 92–96; Lect Trin Coll Bris 97–00; I Kildallon w Newtowngore and Corrawallen *K, E & A* 00–04; I Killala w Dunfeeny, Crossmolina, Kilmoremoy etc *T, K & A* 04–10; Dean Killala 05–10; Sen Lect and Registrar Bishopdale Th Coll New Zealand from 10. *Bishop Eaton House, 30 Vanguard Street, PO Box 100, Nelson 7040, New Zealand* T: (0064) (3) 548 8785 E: sue.patterson@bishopdale.ac.nz

PATTIMORE, Daniel James. b 64. Nottm Univ MEng 88 Lon Bible Coll BA 94. Wycliffe Hall Ox 97. **d** 99 **p** 00. C Charlesworth and Dinting Vale *Derby* 99–03; NSM Norley, Crowton and Kingsley *Ches* 03–04; P-in-c Heanor *Derby* 04–14; P-in-c Langley Mill and Aldercar 07–14; NSM Kirkby Thore w Temple Sowerby and Newbiggin *Carl* 14–17; NSM Heart of Eden from 14. *The Rectory, Kirkby Thore, Penrith CA10 1UR* T: (017683) 62655 M: 07973-406022 E: danpattimore@gmail.com

PATTIMORE (née GORDON), Mrs Kristy. b 72. Leeds Univ BA 94 Newc Univ PGCE 95. Wycliffe Hall Ox 98. **d** 01 **p** 02. C Hallwood *Ches* 01–04; NSM Heanor *Derby* 04–14; NSM Kirkby Thore w Temple Sowerby and Newbiggin *Carl* 14–17; NSM Heart of Eden from 14. *The Rectory, Kirkby Thore, Penrith CA10 1UR* T: (017683) 62655 E: kristy@pattimore.com

PATTINSON, Christine Brodie. b 43. Darlington Tr Coll CertEd 64. **d** 06 **p** 07. OLM Chertsey, Lyne and Longcross

Guildf 06–13; PtO from 13. *32 Twynersh Avenue, Chertsey KT16 9DE* E: cbpattinson@btinternet.com

PATTINSON, Rhobert James. St Mich Coll Llan. **d** 04 **p** 05. C Llanelli *St D* 04–07; TV Dewisland 07–10; V Llanegwad w Llanfihangel Uwch Gwili from 10; Min Can St D Cathl from 07. *Y Ficerdy, Clos y Myrtwydd, Nantgaredig, Carmarthen SA32 7LT* T: (01267) 290142

PATTINSON, Richard Clive. b 46. Keble Coll Ox BA 68 MA 84. CBDTI 98. **d** 00 **p** 01. C Hesket-in-the-Forest and Armathwaite *Carl* 00–04; C Inglewood Gp 04–05; P-in-c Dacre 05–12; TV Penrith w Newton Reigny and Plumpton Wall 05–12; TV Gd Shep TM 10–12; rtd 12; PtO *Carl* 12–16; *Bris* from 17. *Hall Floor, South Parade Mansions, 47 Oakfield Road, Bristol BS8 2BA* T: 0117-973 1947 E: clivepattinson@btinternet.com

PATTISON, Prof George Linsley. b 50. Edin Univ MA 72 BD 77 Dur Univ PhD 83 DD 04. Edin Th Coll 74. **d** 77 **p** 78. C Benwell St Jas *Newc* 77–80; P-in-c Kimblesworth *Dur* 80–83; R Badwell Ash w Gt Ashfield, Stowlangtoft etc *St E* 83–91; Dean of Chpl K Coll Cam 91–01; Lect Aarhus Univ Denmark 01–04; Lady Marg Prof Div Ox Univ 04–13; Can Res Ch Ch *Ox* 04–13; Prof Div Glas Univ from 13. *School of Divinity, University of Glasgow, University Avenue, Glasgow G12 8QQ*

PATTISON, Stephen Bewley. b 53. Selw Coll Cam BA 76. Edin Th Coll 76. **d** 78 **p** 80. C Gosforth All SS *Newc* 78–79; NSM St Nic Hosp Newc 78–82; Hon C Newc St Thos Prop Chpl 80–82; Chapl Edin Th Coll 82–83; Lect Past Studies Birm Univ 83–88; PtO *Birm* 83–86 and 87–00 and from 17; Hon C Moseley St Mary 86–87. *11A Salisbury Road, Moseley, Birmingham B13 8JS* M: 07951-145989 E: stephenbpattison@gmail.com

PATTLE (née OLIVER), Mrs Suzanne Marie. b 66. LMH Ox BA 88 SSEES Lon MA 91. Trin Coll Bris BTS 03. **d** 03 **p** 04. C Rainham *Roch* 03–07; P-in-c Gillingham St Mary 07–14; V Colehill *Sarum* from 14. *The Vicarage, Smugglers Lane, Colehill, Wimborne BH21 2RY* T: (01202) 883721 M: 07971-073093 E: suzanne.pattle@btinternet.com

PAUL, Ian Benjamin. b 62. St Jo Coll Ox BA 84 MA 88 Southn Univ MSc 85 Nottm Univ BTh 91 PhD 98. St Jo Coll Nottm 89. **d** 96 **p** 97. C Longfleet *Sarum* 96–00; NSM 00–04; Visiting Lect Trin Coll Bris 00–01; Th Adv Dioc Bd of Min *Sarum* 00–04; Tutor Sarum OLM Scheme 00–04; Visiting Lect STETS 00–04; Dir Partnership Development St Jo Coll Nottm 04–05; Dean of Studies 05–13; NSM Nottingham St Nic *S'well* from 13. *102 Cator Lane, Beeston, Nottingham NG9 4BB* T: 0115-752 5422 E: editor@grovebooks.co.uk

PAUL, John Matthew. b 61. K Coll Lon BA 82 Fitzw Coll Cam BA 88 MA 92 FRSA 06. Westcott Ho Cam 86. **d** 89 **p** 90. C Writtle w Highwood *Chelmsf* 89–94; Min Can and Chapl St Paul's Cathl *Lon* 94–96; Min Can and Sacr St Paul's Cathl 96–99; V Winchmore Hill St Paul 99–09; AD Enfield 04–09; PtO from 09; *Portsm* from 18. *4 Woodcroft Mews, Station Road, Petersfield GU32 3FE* M: 07800-606555 E: jm.paul@virgin.net *or* john.paul@london.anglican.org

PAUL, Naunihal Chand (Nihal). b 40. Allahabad Univ MA. Bangalore Th Coll BD. **d** 69 **p** 70. C Simla Ch Ch India 69–70; V Kangra w Dharamsala 70–74; C Urmston *Man* 75–77; P-in-c Farnworth St Pet 77–80; TV E Farnworth and Kearsley 80–83; TV Laindon St Martin and St Nic w Nevendon *Chelmsf* 83–90; R Laindon w Dunton 90–05; rtd 05; PtO *Chelmsf* from 06. *3 Wellstye Green, Basildon SS14 2SR* T: (01268) 293965 E: nihalpaul@live.co.uk

PAUL, Roger Philip. b 53. Clare Coll Cam BA 74 MA 88 CertEd 76 Open Univ PhD 98. Westcott Ho Cam 78. **d** 81 **p** 82. C Coventry Caludon *Cov* 81–85; R Warmington w Shotteswell and Radway w Ratley 85–98; R Kirkby Stephen w Mallerstang etc *Carl* 98–08; Nat Adv (Unity in Miss) Coun for Chr Unity 08–17; rtd 17; PtO *Ox* 11–19; *Lich* from 18. *3 Farm Lane, Tetchill, Ellesmere SY12 9AT* T: (01961) 623066

PAUL, Canon Rosalind Miranda. b 53. Man Univ BA 74 Bris Univ PGCE 77 Paris Univ LèsL 86 Open Univ MBA 95. Ripon Coll Cuddesdon 05. **d** 07 **p** 08. C Budock *Truro* 07–09; C Mawnan 07–09; R Higham, Holton St Mary, Raydon and Stratford *St E* 09–18; Can Res Wells Cathl *B & W* from 18; PtO *Chelmsf* from 13. *2 The Liberty, Wells BA5 2SU* E: rosalind.paul@yahoo.co.uk

PAVEY, Canon Angela Mary. b 55. Hull Univ BA 77 Nottm Univ BCombStuds 84 Univ of Wales (Lamp) MA 06. Linc Th Coll 81. **dss** 84 **d** 87 **p** 94. Linc St Faith and St Martin w St Pet 84–86; Chapl Boston Coll of FE 87–95; Asst Min Officer *Linc* 89–95; C Birchwood 95–97; Dioc Dir of Ords 97–07; P-in-c Linc St Faith and St Martin w St Pet 07–13; Chapl Lincs Partnership NHS Foundn Trust from 07; Can and Preb Linc Cathl from 00. *The Gatehouse, Long Leys Road, Lincoln LN1 1EJ* T: 01522 518500 E: Angela.Pavey@LPFT.nhs.uk

PAVLOU, Michael. b 55. St Jo Coll Nottm BA. **d** 06 **p** 07. C Woodside Park St Barn *Lon* 06–10 and from 12; C Wandsworth St Mich w St Steph *S'wark* 10–12. *53 Gallants Farm Road, East Barnet, Barnet EN4 8ER* M: 07956-573217 E: mikepavlou@stbarnabas.co.uk

PAVLOU, Paul Christopher. b 87. Brunel Univ BA 08 Middx Univ PGCE 10 Dur Univ BA 18. Ridley Hall Cam 15. **d** 18 **p** 19. C Bletchley *Ox* from 18. *1 Ashburnham Close, Bletchley, Milton Keynes MK3 7TR* M: 07525-534250 E: paulpav2@gmail.com

PAVYER, Jennifer Elizabeth. *See* FENNELL, Jennifer Elizabeth

PAWSON (née ROYLE), Mrs Gillian Mary. b 57. Kingston Univ BA 79 Roehampton Inst PGCE 82. SEITE 99. **d** 02 **p** 03. C Bursledon *Win* 02–06; P-in-c Merton St Jo 06–09; P-in-c Colliers Wood Ch Ch 06–09; TV Merton Priory 09; PtO 10–12; C Putney St Mary 12–14; PtO *Eur* from 18. *20 Beaumont Gardens, Poulton-le-Fylde FY6 7NX* E: gillypawson@gmail.com

PAWSON, John. b 66. Moorlands Th Coll BA 00. Wycliffe Hall Ox. **d** 02 **p** 03. C Bursledon *Win* 02–06; P-in-c Sway 06–12; V 12–18; P-in-c Bursledon from 18. *The Vicarage, School Road, Bursledon, Southampton SO31 8BW* M: 07762-246947 E: john.pawson@bursledonparish.org

PAWSON, Preb John Walker. b 38. Kelham Th Coll 58. **d** 63 **p** 64. C N Hull St Mich *York* 63–67; C Lower Gornal *Lich* 67–70; V Tipton St Jo 70–78; V Meir Heath 78–03; RD Stoke 88–98; Preb Lich Cathl 93–03; rtd 03; PtO *Nor* from 03. *39 Runton Road, Cromer NR27 9AT* T: (01263) 511715 E: pawson.meirton@btinternet.com

PAXON, Robin Michael Cuninghame. b 46. St Jo Coll Dur BA 69. Westcott Ho Cam 69. **d** 71 **p** 72. C Croydon St Pet S End *Cant* 71–77; C Saffron Walden w Wendens Ambo and Littlebury *Chelmsf* 77–80; P-in-c Plaistow St Mary 80–83; TV Plaistow 83–89; TV Dovercourt and Parkeston 90–95; rtd 95. *20 Park Road, Harwich CO12 3BJ* T: (01255) 551139 E: r.paxon@btinternet.com

PAXTON, Elizabeth Glynis. b 53. Salford Univ BSc 74. St Mellitus Coll BA 12. **d** 13 **p** 14. NSM Sible Hedingham w Castle Hedingham *Chelmsf* 13–16; C Upper Colne 16–17; C Sible Hedingham w Castle Hedingham 16–17; C The Hedinghams and Upper Colne 17–18; R from 18. *The Old Stables, The Street, Stoke by Clare, Sudbury CO10 8HP* T: (01787) 277270 M: 07932-160594 E: liz@paxtonconsulting.co.uk

PAXTON, John Ernest. b 49. Ex Univ BA 71. Westcott Ho Cam 74. **d** 74 **p** 75. C Redditch St Steph *Worc* 74–77; UAE 77–81; C Bolton St Pet *Man* 81–91; Ind Missr 81–91; TV Southampton (City Cen) *Win* 91–96; R S'wark Ch Ch 96–03; Sen Chapl S Lon Ind Miss 96–03; Adv to Bd of Soc Resp *Worc* 03–11; Miss Development Officer 11–13; rtd 13; PtO *Chich* from 15. *8 Bridge Road, Chichester PO19 7NW* T: (01243) 931318 E: johnpaxton@talktalk.net

PAXTON, William Neil. b 60. Brunel Univ BSc 88 MA 90. Ripon Coll Cuddesdon 02. **d** 04 **p** 05. C Camberwell St Geo *S'wark* 04–08; TV Southend *Chelmsf* from 08. *All Saints' Vicarage, 1 Sutton Road, Southend-on-Sea SS2 5PA* E: neil.paxton@blueyonder.co.uk

PAY, Norman John. b 50. St Jo Coll Dur BA 72. Cranmer Hall Dur. **d** 74 **p** 75. C S Moor *Dur* 74–78; C Rawmarsh w Parkgate *Sheff* 78–80; C-in-c New Cantley CD 80–82; V New Cantley 82–89; V Doncaster St Leon and St Jude 89–17; P-in-c Moorends 11–17; Asst Clergy In-Service Tr Officer 90–93; rtd 17; PtO *Sheff* from 17. *13 Market Street, Goldthorpe, Rotherham S63 9HB* E: njpay@btinternet.com

PAYNE, Alan. *See* PAYNE, Kenneth Alan

PAYNE, Mrs Anne Margaret. b 52. Bris Univ BA 73 Southn Univ PGCE 74. STETS 11. **d** 14 **p** 15. NSM Worplesdon *Guildf* 14–18; PtO from 18. *Address temp unknown* M: 07796-420382

PAYNE, Arthur Edwin. b 37. K Alfred's Coll Win TCert 59. St Mich Coll Llan 86. **d** 87 **p** 88. C Swansea St Gabr *S & B* 87–90; Chapl Univ of Wales (Swansea) 87–90; V Brynmawr 90–91; TV Wickford and Runwell *Chelmsf* 91–94; Chapl Runwell Hosp Wickford 91–94; P-in-c Wraxall *B & W* 94–95; PtO 95–97; V Rhymney *Mon* 97–98; rtd 98; PtO *B & W* from 99. *4 Villa Rosa, Shrubbery Road, Weston-super-Mare BS23 2JB* T: (01934) 615522 E: aepayne630@btinternet.com

PAYNE, David Charles. b 62. Univ of Wales (Abth) BLib 84. St Jo Coll Nottm MA 93. **d** 95 **p** 96. C Horncastle w Low Toynton *Linc* 95–99; V Metheringham w Blankney and Dunston 99–04; Chapl Sherwood Forest Hosps NHS Trust 04–06; R Standon and The Mundens w Sacombe *St Alb* 06–14; C Vale *Ox* 14–15; TV Vale of Belvoir *Leic* from 15. *4 Rutland Lane, Bottesford, Nottingham NG13 0DG* M: 07985-922553 E: revdpayne24@gmail.com

PAYNE, Mrs Joanna Nicola. b 72. Liv Univ BA 93 Homerton Coll Cam PGCE 95. Trin Coll Bris BA 00 MA 01. **d** 01 **p** 02. C

Chislehurst St Nic *Roch* 01–06; C The Mitre Benefice *Nor* from 17. *15 Nursery Lane, Costessey, Norwich NR8 5BU* T: (01603) 745792 M: 07958-598145 E: joanna.payne@hotmail.com

PAYNE, John. b 58. Glas Univ BSc 80 Edin Univ BD 84. Edin Th Coll 81. **d** 90 **p** 90. C Dur St Nic 90–94; Australia from 94; Chapl Toorak Coll Melbourne from 02. *11 Feathertop Chase, Burwood East, Melbourne Vic 3151, Australia* T: (0061) (3) 9887 8748 E: johnpayne@rabbit.com.au

PAYNE, John Rogan. b 44. Episc Th Coll São Paulo. **d** 78 **p** 79. Brazil 78–86; C Ilkley All SS *Bradf* 86–88; R Elvington w Sutton on Derwent and E Cottingwith *York* 88–94. *Manor Farm House, East Flotmanby Road, Muston, Filey YO14 0HX* T: (01723) 513969

PAYNE, Julia Kathleen. *See* PEATY, Julia Kathleen

PAYNE, Canon Kenneth Alan. b 45. Pemb Coll Ox BA 68 MA 71. Qu Coll Birm 71. **d** 74 **p** 74. Hon C Perry Barr *Birm* 74–78; Hon C Ruislip Manor St Paul *Lon* 78–79; C Hawksworth Wood *Ripon* 79–84; R Stanningley St Thos 84–94; TR Kippax w Allerton Bywater 94–00; AD Whitkirk 95–00; P-in-c Lambley and Dioc Min Development Adv *S'well* 00–09; Dioc Dir of Min 02–09; Hon Can S'well Minster 06–09; rtd 10; PtO *York* from 10. *Fern Cottage, 2 Gladstone Terrace, Thornton Dale, Pickering YO18 7SS* T: (01751) 476243 E: alanlambley@mac.com

PAYNE, Leonard John. b 49. St Jo Coll Nottm 93. **d** 95 **p** 96. C Trimley *St E* 95–98; TV Sole Bay 98–09; P-in-c Wrentham, Covehithe w Benacre etc 09–15; V 15–16; rtd 16. *3 Chartwell Avenue, Wingerworth, Chesterfield S42 6SR* M: 07777-636808 E: rev.leonard.payne@gmail.com

PAYNE, Mark David. b 73. Univ of Wales (Ban) BD 95. All SS Cen for Miss & Min 15. **d** 17 **p** 18. C Bocking St Mary and Panfield *Chelmsf* 17–19; TV Halstead Area from 19. *20 Swallow Field, Earls Colne, Colchester CO6 2RW* E: markdpayne@outlook.com

PAYNE, Matthew Charles. b 62. Ex Univ LLB 85 All Nations Chr Coll BA 95 Solicitor 89. Oak Hill Th Coll 99. **d** 01 **p** 02. C Angmering *Chich* 01–05; V Lowestoft Ch Ch *Nor* from 05. *The Vicarage, 16 Corton Road, Lowestoft NR32 4PL* T: (01502) 572444 E: revmattpayne@gmail.com

PAYNE, Michael Frederick. b 49. St Jo Coll Nottm 81. **d** 83 **p** 84. C Hyson Green *S'well* 83–86; P-in-c Peckham St Mary Magd *S'wark* 86–90; V 90–05; Hon C Chenies and Lt Chalfont, Latimer and Flaunden *Ox* 05–09; P-in-c Tollerton *S'well* 09–11; R 11–14; rtd 14; PtO *S'well* from 15. *100 Denison Street, Beeston, Nottingham NG9 1DQ* T: 0115-808 6506 M: 07961-515840 E: mikefpayne@hotmail.com

PAYNE, Michael Jeffrey. b 75. Hull Univ MA 00 Cant Ch Ch Univ MA 08 Open Univ PGCE 09. St Steph Ho Ox 13. **d** 15 **p** 16. C Northfleet and Rosherville *Roch* 15–18; C Perry Street 15–18; V Gravesend St Aid from 18. *The Vicarage, St Gregory's Crescent, Gravesend DA12 4JL* E: frmichael.anglican@gmail.com *or* vicar.staidans@gmail.com

PAYNE, Mrs Norma. b 48. Bris Univ BA 70 Homerton Coll Cam PGCE 71. STETS 98. **d** 01 **p** 02. NSM Cley Hill Warminster *Sarum* 01–04; TV 04–07; R Cley Hill Villages 07–13; rtd 13; PtO *Sarum* from 13. *2 The Mews, Newport, Warminster BA12 8BX* E: revnpayne@btinternet.com

PAYNE, Mrs Penelope Kenward. b 42. LGSM 64. Bp Otter Coll 94. **d** 94 **p** 98. NSM Portsea N End St Mark *Portsm* 94–05; NSM S Hayling 05–12; rtd 12; PtO *Portsm* from 12. *38 Allcot Road, Portsmouth PO3 5DF* E: pennie@ppayne.f9.co.uk

PAYNE, Philip John. b 56. Warwick Univ BA 77 UMIST MSc 94. Westcott Ho Cam 09. **d** 11 **p** 12. C Bury St Edmunds All SS w St Jo and St Geo *St E* 11–14; P-in-c Coddenham w Gosbeck and Hemingstone w Henley 14–19; P-in-c Crowfield w Stonham Aspal and Mickfield 14–19; P-in-c The Creetings and Earl Stonham w Stonham Parva 14–19; R N Bosmere from 19. *The Rectory, The Street, Stonham Aspal, Stowmarket IP14 6AQ* T: (01449) 711684 E: revphilippayne@btinternet.com

PAYNE, Mrs Priscilla Mary. b 40. **d** 04 **p** 05. NSM Ditton *Roch* 04–15; PtO from 15; *Leeds* 15–16. *4 Station Road, Ditton, Aylesford ME20 6AX* T: (01732) 841257 E: priscillapayne@outlook.com

PAYNE, Robert Harold Vincent. b 44. St Jo Coll York CertEd 69. St Jo Coll Nottm 77. **d** 79 **p** 80. C Didsbury St Jas *Man* 79–80; C Didsbury St Jas and Em 80–83; V Southchurch Ch Ch *Chelmsf* 83–90; P-in-c Charles w Plymouth St Matthias *Ex* 90–94; Warden Lee Abbey 94–02; R Thorley *St Alb* 02–14; rtd 14; PtO *Sarum* from 14. *131 Stour View Gardens, Corfe Mullen, Wimborne BH21 3TN*

PAYNE, Robert Sandon. b 48. Reading Univ BSc 69 MRICS 72. Ripon Coll Cuddesdon 77. **d** 80 **p** 81. C Bridgnorth, Tasley, Astley Abbotts and Oldbury *Heref* 80–83; P-in-c Wistanstow 83–92; P-in-c Acton Scott 86–92; P-in-c

Dorrington 92–94; P-in-c Leebotwood w Longnor 92–94; P-in-c Smethcott w Woolstaston 92–94; P-in-c Stapleton 92–94; R Dorrington w Leebotwood, Longnor, Stapleton etc 94–11; rtd 11; PtO *Heref* from 11. *6 Clun Road, Aston-on-Clun, Craven Arms SY7 8EW* T: (01588) 661008 E: robert.payne48@btinternet.com

PAYNE, Mrs Trudy. b 48. K Coll Lon BA 66 Lon Inst of Educn PGCE 73. **d** 04 **p** 05. OLM Clapham Park St Steph *S'wark* 04–06; NSM Telford Park 06–09; NSM Mitcham St Barn 09–18; PtO from 18. *6 Clarence Road, Croydon CR0 2EN* T: (020) 8689 5857 E: paynetrudy@hotmail.com

PAYNTER, Stephen Denis. b 59. Bath Univ BSc 82 CertEd 82. Trin Coll Bris BA 89. **d** 89 **p** 90. C Nailsea Ch Ch *B & W* 89–92; C Farnborough *Guildf* 92–97; TV N Farnborough 97–98; V Ealing St Mary *Lon* from 98. *11 Church Place, London W5 4HN* T: (020) 8567 0414 *or* 8579 7134 F: 8840 4534 E: steve.paynter@stmarysealing.org.uk

PAYTON, Paul John. b 59. Middx Poly MA 90 LRAM 79 GRSM 80. Ripon Coll Cuddesdon. **d** 05 **p** 06. C Lancaster St Mary w St John and St Anne *Blackb* 05–08; P-in-c Leeds Gipton Epiphany *Ripon* 08–13; TR Leeds All So and St Aid 13–14 and 14–15; rtd 15; PtO *Blackb* 15–19; V Briercliffe from 19. *Address withheld by request*

PEABODY, Anthony John. b 43. St Cuth Soc Dur BSc 64 MSc 67 Surrey Univ PhD 82 Huddersfield Univ MA 18 CBiol 82 MRSB 82. Cuddesdon Coll 08. **d** 08. NSM Sulhamstead Abbots and Bannister w Ufton Nervet *Ox* 08–14; PtO from 14; *Eur* from 14. *Blackberries, 29 Woodlands Avenue, Burghfield Common, Reading RG7 3HU* T: 0118-983 2491 E: pisumcorporum@gmail.com

PEACE, Brian. b 38. St Jo Coll Nottm 90. **d** 92 **p** 93. C Huddersfield H Trin *Wakef* 92–95; R Cheswardine, Childs Ercall, Hales, Hinstock etc *Lich* 95–00; TR 00–03; RD Hodnet 00–03; rtd 03; PtO *Ches* from 03. *2 Mouldsworth Close, Northwich CW9 8FT* T: (01606) 333013

PEACE, Stuart Vaughan. b 47. **d** 04 **p** 05. OLM Dorking w Ranmore *Guildf* 04–14; rtd 14; PtO *Guildf* from 14. *95 Ashcombe Road, Dorking RH4 1LW* T: (01306) 883002 E: revdstuartpeace01@gmail.com

PEACH, Malcolm Thompson. b 31. St Chad's Coll Dur BA 56. Sarum Th Coll 56. **d** 58 **p** 59. C Beamish *Dur* 58–61; Chapl Dur Univ 61–65; NE England Sec SCM 61–65; C-in-c Stockton St Mark CD *Dur* 65–72; P-in-c Bishopwearmouth St Nic 72–81; V 81–85; V S Shields St Hilda w St Thos 85–95; Hon Chapl Miss to Seamen 85–95; P-in-c S Shields St Aid w St Steph *Dur* 92–95; rtd 95; PtO *Dur* from 95. *116 Mount Road, Sunderland SR4 7QD* T: 0191-522 6216 E: peachestwo20@hotmail.co.uk

PEACHEY, Elizabeth Ann. b 70. St Mellitus Coll 14. **d** 17 **p** 18. C Knowle *Birm* from 17. *1717 High Street, Knowle, Solihull B93 0LN* E: ann.peachey@kpc.org.uk

PEACOCK, Canon David. b 39. Liv Univ BA 61 Lanc Univ MA 71 Univ of the South (USA) Hon DD 00 FRSA 95. Westcott Ho Cam 84. **d** 84 **p** 85. Prin Lect St Martin's Coll Lanc 81–85; Hon C Lancaster St Mary *Blackb* 84–85; Prin Whitelands Coll *S'wark* 85–00; Pro Rector Surrey Univ *Guildf* 93–00; Hon C Roehampton H Trin *S'wark* 85–92; Hon C Putney St Mary 92–00; Hon Can S'wark Cathl 97–00; PtO *Blackb* from 00. *Orchard House, 11 Parsonage Fold, Beetham, Milnthorpe LA7 7RJ* T: (15395) 63032 E: keersidecowshed@aol.com

PEACOCK, Mrs Kate Rebecca. b 78. Hatf Coll Dur BA 00. Westcott Ho Cam 01. **d** 03 **p** 04. C Cambridge Ascension *Ely* 03–07; C Three Rivers Gp 07–12; P-in-c Hormead, Wyddial, Anstey, Brent Pelham etc *St Alb* 12–13; V 13–18; RD Buntingford 16–18; Dean of Women's Min 17–18; Ch Growth Officer from 18. *Address withheld by request* E: kate.peacock@btopenworld.com

PEAL, Jacqueline. b 46. MCSP 70. Cant Sch of Min 88. **d** 91 **p** 94. NSM Bexley St Jo *Roch* 91–97; NSM Crayford 91–94; C 94–97 and 00–01; C Dartford H Trin 97–00; Hon C Ash 01–11; Asst Chapl Thames Gateway NHS Trust 01–11; Chapl Wisdom Hospice 04–11; rtd 11; PtO *Chich* from 17. *9 Crescent Rise, Thakeham, Pulborough RH20 3NB* T: (01903) 743286 E: peal@btinternet.com

PEAL, John Arthur. b 46. K Coll Lon BD 70 AKC. **d** 71 **p** 72. C Portsea All SS w St Jo Rudmore *Portsm* 71–74; C Westbury *Sarum* 74–77; V Borstal *Roch* 77–82; Chapl HM Pris Cookham Wood 78–82; V Erith Ch Ch *Roch* 82–91; P-in-c Erith St Jo 86–91; V Bexley St Jo 91–00; Chapl Erith and Distr Hosp 82–90; R Ash *Roch* 00–11; R Ridley 00–11; RD Cobham 08–11; rtd 11; PtO *Roch* from 11; *Chich* from 17. *9 Crescent Rise, Thakeham, Pulborough RH20 3NB* T: (01903) 743083 M: 07919-410438 E: peal@btinternet.com

PEALL, Mrs Linda Grace. b 66. Westmr Coll Ox BEd 88. EAMTC 99. **d** 02 **p** 03. NSM Blackwell All SS and Salutation *Dur* 02–04; C Darlington H Trin 04–07; Chapl

Co Durham and Darlington NHS Foundn Trust 05–10; Chapl Basildon & Thurrock Univ Hosps NHS Foundn Trust from 10. *Basildon University Hospital, Nethermayne, Basildon SS16 5NL* T: (01268) 524900 *or* 08451-553111 E: linda.peall@btopenworld.com *or* linda.peall@btuh.nhs.uk

PEARCE, Adrian Francis. b 55. Westmr Coll Ox BTh 05. S Dios Minl Tr Scheme 92. **d** 95 **p** 96. NSM Jersey St Luke w St Jas *Win* 95–13; NSM Jersey St Mary 01–13; P-in-c Bournemouth St Ambrose from 13; NSM Bournemouth St Fran 13–16. *72A West Cliff Road, Bournemouth BH4 8BE* T: (01202) 911569 E: afpear2@gmail.com

PEARCE, Mrs Angela Elizabeth. b 36. K Coll Lon BSc 58 CertEd 59 BD 79 AKC 79. **dss** 79 **d** 87. Chapl Raines Foundn Sch Tower Hamlets Lon 79–97; Homerton St Barn w St Paul *Lon* 79–85; Upper Chelsea St Simon 85–89; Hon Par Dn 87–89; Hon Par Dn Limehouse 89–97; PtO *St E* 97–17. *41 Cross Penny Court, Cotton Lane, Bury St Edmunds IP33 1XY* T: (01284) 760016

PEARCE, Canon Brian Edward. b 39. Kelham Th Coll 59. **d** 64 **p** 65. C Smethwick St Matt *Birm* 64–68; C Kings Norton 68–72; TV 73–80; TR Swindon Dorcan *Bris* 80–91; Min Withywood CD 91–94; V Withywood 94–98; V Fishponds All SS 98–05; RD Bedminster 92–98; Hon Can Bris Cathl 97–05; rtd 05; PtO *Heref* from 09; *Mon* from 15. *32 Brook Estate, Monmouth NP25 5AW* T: (01600) 716057 E: brianpearce777@btinternet.com

PEARCE, Daniel. *See* PEARCE, William Philip Daniel

PEARCE, Mrs Janet Elizabeth. b 49. Somerville Coll Ox BA 72 MA 76 CertEd 74. NOC 85. **d** 88 **p** 94. Par Dn Helsby and Dunham-on-the-Hill *Ches* 88–94; C 94–96; C Norley, Crowton and Kingsley 96–06; Dioc Adv in Spirituality 02–06; R Llanfair Mathafarn Eithaf w Llanerchymedd *Ban* 06–11; TR Bangor 11–13; rtd 13; PtO *Ban* 13–16; *Roch* from 15. *2 Egdean Walk, Sevenoaks TN13 3UQ* T: (01732) 464598

PEARCE, Jonathan. b 55. St Jo Coll Nottm BTh 85. **d** 85 **p** 86. C Gt Chesham *Ox* 85–89; C Newport Pagnell w Lathbury and Moulsoe 89–93; TV Waltham H Cross *Chelmsf* 93–07; R Gt Totham and Lt Totham w Goldhanger 07–17; rtd 17; PtO *Chelmsf* 18–19. *15 Mill Close, Roxwell, Chelmsford CM1 4PG* E: revdjpearce@aol.com

PEARCE, Neville John Lewis. b 33. CBIM 88 Leeds Univ LLB 53 LLM 54. Trin Coll Bris 90. **d** 91 **p** 92. NSM Bath Walcot *B & W* 91–93; P-in-c Bath St Sav w Swainswick and Woolley 93–98; PtO from 98. *Penshurst, Weston Lane, Bath BA1 4AB* T: (01225) 426925 E: nevillepearce@tiscali.co.uk

PEARCE, Robert John. b 47. GLCM LLCM 72 Birm Univ PGCE 73. Ripon Coll Cuddesdon 79. **d** 82 **p** 83. C Broseley w Benthall *Heref* 82–83; C Kington w Huntington, Old Radnor, Kinnerton etc 83–85; R Westbury 85–94; R Yockleton 85–94; V Gt Wollaston 85–94; V Gwersyllt *St As* 94–99; V Northop 99–03; P-in-c Cerrigydrudion w Llanfihangel Glyn Myfyr etc 08–15; Hon C Henllan and Llannefydd and Bylchau 15–17; rtd 17; PtO *St As* from 17. *14 Trinity Avenue, Llandudno LL30 2SJ* T: (01492) 874340

PEARCE, Sacha John Tremain. b 64. Reading Univ BA 92 Ches Univ DProf 18 RGN 86. Ripon Coll Cuddesdon. **d** 00 **p** 01. C Tisbury *Sarum* 00–01; C Nadder Valley 01–04; V Seend, Bulkington and Poulshot 04–09; Chapl Plymouth Hosps NHS Trust from 09; LtO *Ex* from 09; PtO *Truro* from 14. *Derriford Hospital, Derriford Road, Plymouth PL6 8DH* T: (01752) 792022 E: sacha.pearce@nhs.net *or* sjtpearce@gmail.com

PEARCE, Shirley May. b 60. St Mellitus Coll BA 18. **d** 18 **p** 19. C Basildon St Andr w H Cross *Chelmsf* from 18. *12 Holden Gardens, Basildon SS14 3LF* T: (01268) 984913 E: revshirleym@gmail.com

PEARCE, Simon David. b 81. Univ of E Lon BSc 07. St Mellitus Coll BA 18. **d** 18 **p** 19. C Springfield All SS *Chelmsf* from 18. *12 Matfield Close, Chelmsford CM1 7TP* M: 07544-126990 E: revdsimonpearce@outlook.com

PEARCE, Mrs Susan Elizabeth. b 44. NEOC 03. **d** 06 **p** 07. NSM Pannal w Beckwithshaw *Ripon* 06–11; NSM High Harrogate St Pet 11–14; *Leeds* 14–17; PtO from 17. *8 Wheatlands Grove, Harrogate HG2 8JH* E: sue.pearce56@btopenworld.com

PEARCE, Trevor John. b 27. FSR 57. Roch Th Coll 65. **d** 67 **p** 68. C Cheriton Street *Cant* 67–69; C Willesborough w Hinxhill 69–73; V Devonport St Barn *Ex* 73–79; Chapl N Devon Healthcare NHS Trust 79–83; V Derby St Andr w St Osmund 83–84; Chapl Derbyshire R Infirmary 83–92; LtO *Derby* 84–92; rtd 92; PtO *Derby* 92–13. *47 Marsh Lane, Belper DE56 1GS*

PEARCE, Valerie Olive. b 46. Whitelands Coll Lon CertEd 67. SEITE 96. **d** 97 **p** 98. CSC 77–04; LtO *S'wark* 97–04; PtO from 09; Cant 15–18. *10 Bromley College, London Road, Bromley BR1 1PE* T: (020) 8290 6662 E: revdval@gmail.com

PEARCE, William Philip Daniel. b 26. Stanford Univ BA 48 Leeds Univ CertEd 64 MA 75. Cuddesdon Coll 54.

d 56 **p** 57. USA 56–60; CR 60–84; C St Geo-in-the-East w St Paul *Lon* 84–86; USA from 86; rtd 02. *1037 Olympic Lane, Seaside CA 93955-6226, USA* T: (001) (831) 393 2176 E: danielp@mbay.net

PEARKES, Nicholas Robin Clement. b 49. Ex Univ BA. Linc Th Coll. **d** 82 **p** 83. C Plymstock *Ex* 82–85; P-in-c Weston Mill 85–86; TV Devonport St Boniface and St Phil 86–99; R Broadhempston, Woodland, Staverton etc 99–14; rtd 14; PtO *Ex* from 14. *The Old Post Office, 128-130 Fore Street, Barton, Torquay TQ2 8DP* E: nicholaspearkes1@yahoo.com

PEARL, Mrs Sandra Ruth. b 47. SRN 69. LCTP 15. **d** 16. NSM N Westmorland *Carl* from 16. *Upper Orchard, Morland, Penrith CA10 3AX* T: (01931) 714564 E: sandra.pearl@btinternet.com

PEARMAIN, Brian Albert John. b 34. Lon Univ BD 68. Roch Th Coll 63. **d** 66 **p** 67. C Shirley St Jo *Cant* 66–69; C Selsdon St Jo w St Fran 69–73; P-in-c Louth H Trin *Linc* 73–75; TV Louth 75–79; R Scartho 79–97; RD Grimsby and Cleethorpes 89–94; Can and Preb Linc Cathl 94–97; rtd 97; PtO *Linc* 00–07; *Bradf* 07–14; *Leeds* from 14. *11 Ivy Garth, Church Lane, Chapel Allerton, Leeds LS7 4LY* M: 07944-675321

PEARMAN, Mrs Barbara Elizabeth Anne. b 48. RGN 69 RHV 72. ERMC 07. **d** 09 **p** 10. NSM E Marshland *Ely* 09–18; PtO from 18. *Rambles, 8 School Road, Tilney All Saints, King's Lynn PE34 4RS* T: (01553) 828808 M: 07946-348744 E: barbarapearman@hotmail.com

PEARSE, Andrew George. b 46. Wycliffe Hall Ox 71. **d** 74 **p** 75. C Homerton St Luke *Lon* 74–77; C Chadderton Em *Man* 77–81; R Collyhurst 81–89; Area Sec (NE, E Midl and Scotland) SAMS 89–03; rtd 03; Chapl Co-ord St Leon Hospice York 03–11; PtO *York* 11–16; Hon C Knaresborough *Leeds* 14–18. *39 Birkdale Avenue, Knaresborough HG5 0LS* T: (01423) 797033 E: tarvethecurkey@yahoo.co.uk

PEARSE, Christopher George. b 84. Surrey Univ BA 06 Spurgeon's Coll Lon MA 14. Ridley Hall Cam 14. **d** 16 **p** 17. C Wollaton *S'well* 16–19; P-in-c Farnsfield from 19; P-in-c Kirklington w Hockerton from 19; P-in-c Maplebeck from 19; P-in-c Winkburn from 19. *The Vicarage, Beck Lane, Farnsfield, Newark NG22 8ER* M: 07866-196282 E: chrispearse@email.com

PEARSE, Jeffery Alun. **d** 16 **p** 17. C Abergavenny St Mary w Llanwenarth Citra *Mon* from 16; C Abergavenny H Trin from 16. *St Mary's Priory Church, Monk Street, Abergavenny NP7 5ND* M: 07985-241700 E: jeff.pearse@hotmail.com

PEARSE, Ronald Thomas Hennessy. b 26. AKC 52. **d** 53 **p** 54. C Leic St Pet 53–55; C Hanwell St Thos *Lon* 55–58; R Asfordby *Leic* 58–84; P-in-c Scalford w Wycombe and Chadwell 75–76; R Thurcaston 84–89; rtd 89; PtO *Leic* 89–90. *142A Harestone Hill, Caterham CR3 6DH* E: ronald.pearse@myphone.coop

PEARSON, Andrew John. b 59. Westcott Ho Cam 86. **d** 89 **p** 90. C Knaresborough *Ripon* 89–92; C Wetherby 92–94; P-in-c Hunslet Moor St Pet and St Cuth 94–96; V 96–01; V Hawksworth Wood 01–06; Dioc Environment Officer 97–06; P-in-c Oulton w Woodlesford and Methley w Mickletown 06–13; P-in-c Wyther 13–14; *Leeds* from 14. *Beeston Vicarage, 16 Town Street, Beeston, Leeds LS11 8PN* T: 0113-272 3337 E: revajp@btinternet.com

PEARSON, Andrew Michael. b 54. Univ of Wales (Ban) BTh 10. Solicitor 77. **d** 07 **p** 08. OLM Shere, Albury and Chilworth *Guildf* 07–12; C 12–16. *The Forge, The Street, Albury, Guildford GU5 9AG* M: 07815-049950 E: rev.a.m.pearson@btinternet.com

PEARSON, Mrs Béatrice Levasseur. b 53. Sorbonne Univ Paris LèsL 74 MèsL 75 Lon Inst of Educn PGCE 76. Ripon Coll Cuddesdon 01. **d** 03 **p** 04. C Easthampstead *Ox* 03–06; TV Loddon Reach 06–13; rtd 13. *1 Northanger Court, Grove Street, Bath BA2 6PE* T: (01225) 571344 M: 07981-462145

PEARSON, Ms Brenda Elizabeth Frances (Brandy). b 51. SEITE 00. **d** 03 **p** 04. NSM Finsbury Park St Thos *Lon* 03–07; C Acton Green 07–15; NSM W Acton St Martin from 15. *St Martin's Cottage, Hale Gardens, London W3 9SQ* T: (020) 8992 9557 E: therevvedbee@hotmail.co.uk

PEARSON, Canon Brian William. b 49. Brighton Poly BSc 71 City Univ MSc 80 Westmr Coll Ox MTh 94 FHSM. S'wark Ord Course & Clapham Ord Scheme 76. **d** 79 **p** 80. Hon C Plumstead All SS *S'wark* 79–81; PtO *Chich* 81–83; Hon C Broadwater St Mary 83–88; Bp's Research and Dioc Communications Officer *B & W* 88–90; Dioc Missr 91; Abp's Officer for Miss and Evang and Tait Missr *Cant* 91–97; Abp's Dioc Chapl 91–97; Hon Prov Can Cant Cathl 91–97; Gen Dir CPAS 97–00; P-in-c Leek Wootton and Dioc Officer for OLM *Cov* 00–06; Assoc Dir of Voc *B & W* from 11; PtO from 18. *Woodspring, Northfield, Somerton TA11 6SL* T: (01458) 274360 E: brian@vividclouds.com

PEARSON, Christopher John. b 49. GRSM LRAM ARCM. Oak Hill NSM Course 81. **d** 84 **p** 85. NSM Barton Seagrave w

Warkton *Pet* 84–86; C Kettering St Andr 86–88; V Nassington w Yarwell and Woodnewton 88–91; V Pet St Mark 91–03; P-in-c Gt Doddington and Wilby 03–12; P-in-c Ecton 07–12; R Gt Doddington and Wilby and Ecton 12–15; rtd 15; PtO *Pet* from 15; *Eur* from 17. *10 Ashley Way, Weston, Northampton NN3 3DZ* T: (01604) 947861 E: c.pearson1@homecall.co.uk

PEARSON, Christopher William. b 56. Univ Coll Ox MA. St Jo Coll Nottm 07. **d** 09 **p** 10. C Norton St Mary and Stockton St Chad *Dur* 09–11; P-in-c Easington and Easington Colliery 11–14; TR Gt Aycliffe 14–16; rtd 16; PtO *Leeds* from 17. *1 The Paddock, Appleton Wiske, Northallerton DL6 2BE* T: (01609) 881872 E: revcwpearson@gmail.com

PEARSON, David. *See* PEARSON, James David

PEARSON, Fergus Thomas. b 58. Middx Poly BA 81 Moore Th Coll Sydney MA 98. Oak Hill Th Coll BA 95. **d** 92 **p** 93. C Mildmay Grove St Jude and St Paul *Lon* 92–95; Australia 96–98; C Heatherlands St Jo *Sarum* 98–03; V Hensingham *Carl* from 03; C Mirehouse from 19. *St John's Vicarage, Egremont Road, Hensingham, Whitehaven CA28 8QW* T: (01946) 692822 E: fpe@rson.justbrowsing.com *or* fergus@stjohnshensingham.org.uk

PEARSON, Geoffrey Charles. b 49. Imp Coll Lon BSc 70 ARCS. Oak Hill Th Coll 80. **d** 82 **p** 83. C Folkestone St Jo *Cant* 82–86; V Ramsgate St Luke 86–93; Chapl to People at Work in Cam *Ely* 93–01; Co-ord Chapl HM Pris Chelmsf 01–07; rtd 07; PtO *Cant* from 08. *30 Tannery Way North, Canterbury CT1 2FH* M: 07890-808739 E: pearsongeoff@hotmail.co.uk

✠**PEARSON, The Rt Revd Geoffrey Seagrave.** b 51. St Jo Coll Dur BA 72. Cranmer Hall Dur 72. **d** 74 **p** 75 **c** 06. C Kirkheaton *Wakef* 74–77; C-in-c Blackb Redeemer 77–82; V 82–85; Asst Home Sec Gen Syn Bd for Miss and Unity 85–89; Hon C Forty Hill Jes Ch *Lon* 85–89; Exec Sec BCC Evang Cttee 86–89; V Roby *Liv* 89–06; AD Huyton 02–06; Hon Can Liv Cathl 03–06; Suff Bp Lancaster *Blackb* 06–17; C Ellel w Shireshead 08–16; C Shireshead 16–17; rtd 17. *10 Elderswood, Rainhill, Prescot L35 4QY* M: 07809-618385 E: geoff.s.pearson@outlook.com

PEARSON, Canon Henry Gervis. b 47. Mansf Coll Ox BA 72 MA 76. St Jo Coll Nottm 72. **d** 74 **p** 75. C Southgate *Chich* 74–76; TV 76–82; V Debenham w Aspall and Kenton *St E* 82–91; Chapl to Suffolk Fire Service 88–91; RD Loes 89–91; TR Marlborough *Sarum* 91–02; RD 94–02; R Queen Thorne 02–12; P-in-c Gifle Valley 10–12; RD Sherborne 04–11; Chapl Savernake Hosp Marlborough 91–94; Chapl E Wilts Health Care NHS Trust 94–99; Chapl Wilts and Swindon Healthcare NHS Trust 99–12; Can and Preb Sarum Cathl 99–12; rtd 12; PtO *Sarum* from 12. *1 Morris Road, Marlborough SN8 1TJ* T: (01672) 511788 E: henryandjudith@btinternet.com

PEARSON, Ian. b 49. Liv Univ BA 71. S'wark Ord Course 79. **d** 82 **p** 83. Archivist USPG 82–85; Archivist Nat Soc 85–91; NSM Lavender Hill Ascension *S'wark* 82–84; LtO *Lon* 84–86 and 88–90; NSM Westmr St Matt 86–88; PtO *S'wark* 85–90; *St Alb* 90–91; C Chesterfield St Mary and All SS *Derby* 91–95; R Bengeo *St Alb* 95–04; P-in-c Worc City St Paul and Old St Martin etc 04–06; R Worc City 06–10; rtd 10; PtO *B & W* from 10; *Sarum* from 16. *7 Rosedale Walk, Frome BA11 2JH* T: (01373) 469739 E: ianandlizpearson@waitrose.com

PEARSON, Miss Jacqueline Susan. b 86. Univ of Wales (Abth) BSc 08 Lucy Cavendish Coll Cam BTh 18. Ridley Hall Cam 16. **d** 19. C Boreham *Chelmsf* from 19. *Ladyhope House, Mill Lane, Broomfield, Chelmsford CM1 7BQ* M: 07734-375938 E: jacqui.pearson07@hotmail.co.uk

PEARSON, James David. b 51. Cape Town Univ BSocSc 74. St Paul's Coll Grahamstown 76. **d** 78 **p** 79. C St Geo Cathl Cape Town S Africa 78–80; R Caledon H Trin 80–84; R Tristan da Cunha St Mary 84–86; R Camps Bay St Pet 86–89; R Kuruman St Mary-le-Bourne w Wrenchville 89–91; R Amalinda Ch Ch 92–96; Asst P Cambridge St Mark 96–98; Asst P-in-c Kidds Beach St Mary & St Andr 99; C Prittlewell St Steph *Chelmsf* 00–04; TV Barking St Marg w St Patr 04–09; P-in-c Hornchurch H Cross 09–18; rtd 18. *28 Victory Lane, Rochford SS4 3AN* E: revdavidpearson@outlook.com

PEARSON, Joanna Ruth. *See* SEABOURNE, Joanna Ruth

PEARSON, Mrs Katherine Elizabeth. b 77. Birm Univ LLB 99 MSc 08. Qu Coll Birm. **d** 12 **p** 13. C Brandwood *Birm* 12–15; C Brandwood and Weoley Castle 12–15; Chapl Warw Univ *Cov* from 15. *92 De Montfort Way, Coventry CV4 7DT* T: (024) 7641 9666 M: 07890-648008 E: kate.e.pearson@me.com

✠**PEARSON, The Rt Revd Kevin.** b 54. Leeds Univ BA 75 Edin Univ BD 79. Edin Th Coll 76. **d** 79 **p** 80 **c** 11. C Horden *Dur* 79–81; Chapl Leeds Univ *Ripon* 81–87; R Edin St Salvador 87–93; Chapl Edin Napier Univ 88–92 and 92–94; Dioc Dir of Ords 90–95; Prov Dir of Ords 91–11; Assoc R Edin Old St Paul 93–94; P-in-c Linlithgow *Edin* 94–95; R Edin St Mich and All

SS 95–11; Can St Mary's Cathl 03–11; Dean Edin 04–10; Bp Arg from 11; Provost Cumbrae Cathl from 11. *St Moluag's Diocesan Centre, Croft Avenue, Oban PA34 5JJ* T: (01631) 570870 *or* 562617 E: bishop@argyll.anglican.org

PEARSON, Lewis Nicholas. b 82. Sarum Coll 14. **d** 17 **p** 18. C Poole *Sarum* from 17. *14 Colborne Close, Poole BH15 1US* M: 07922-137348 E: revlewispearson@gmail.com

PEARSON, Mrs Lindsey Carole. b 61. Cov Poly BA 86 CQSW 86. Westcott Ho Cam 86. **d** 89 **p** 94. Par Dn High Harrogate St Pet *Ripon* 89–93; C Moor Allerton 93–96; Chapl St Gemma's Hospice 94–96; TV Seacroft *Ripon* 96–04; World Development Officer 97–04; Area Co-ord (N and W Yorks) Chr Aid 04–07; PtO *Ripon* 04–07; P-in-c Swillington 07–13; NSM Kippax w Allerton Bywater 12–13; P-in-c Beeston 13–14; *Leeds* from 14. *Beeston Vicarage, 16 Town Street, Beeston, Leeds LS11 8PN* T: 0113-272 3337 M: 07961-016052 E: revlcp@btinternet.com

PEARSON, Nigel Hetley Allan. b 45. Fitzw Coll Cam BA 67 MA 87. EMMTC 04. **d** 06 **p** 07. NSM Papworth *Ely* 06–15; PtO from 15. *The House behind the Hedge, 71 Caxton End, Bourne, Cambridge CB23 2SS* T: (01954) 719351 M: 07713-639928 E: njfarm@gmail.com

PEARSON, Pauline Hilary. b 54. BA 77 PhD 88 RN 77 RHV 79. NEOC 02. **d** 05 **p** 06. NSM Denton *Newc* 05–10; NSM Newc St Geo and St Hilda from 10. *3 Belle Grove Place, Newcastle upon Tyne NE2 4LH* T: 0191-232 5980 M: 07753-744349 E: pauline.pearson@northumbria.ac.uk

PEARSON, Mrs Priscilla Dawn. b 45. Oak Hill Th Coll BA 90. **d** 90 **p** 94. Par Dn Stanford-le-Hope w Mucking *Chelmsf* 90–94; C 94; C Colchester St Jo 94–96; Hon C Woking St Jo *Guildf* 03–05; rtd 10. *Talywain Cottage, Shop Road, Cwmavon, Pontypool NP4 7RU* T: (01495) 774132 E: priscillapearson@btinternet.com

PEARSON, Raymond Joseph. b 44. AKC 71. St Aug Coll Cant 71. **d** 72 **p** 73. C Wetherby *Ripon* 72–75; C Goring-by-Sea *Chich* 75–77; C Bramley *Ripon* 77–82; V Patrick Brompton and Hunton 82–94; V Crakehall 82–94; V Hornby 82–94; World Miss Officer 88–94; RD Wensley 92–94; V Bardsey 94–09; rtd 09; PtO *York* from 09. *7 St George's Croft, Bridlington YO16 7RW* T: (01262) 424332 E: r.pearson121@btinternet.com

PEARSON, Robert James Stephen. b 52. Cov Poly BA 74. St Steph Ho Ox 85. **d** 87 **p** 88. C Stoke Newington St Mary *Lon* 87–90; C Haggerston All SS 90–97; C Dalston H Trin w St Phil and Haggerston All SS 97–98; Chapl HM Pris Wandsworth 98–02; Chapl HM Pris Pentonville 02–07; PtO *Lon* from 07. *St Martin's Cottage, Hale Gardens, London W3 9SQ* T: (020) 8992 9557 E: ahjay@hotmail.co.uk

PEARSON, Robert Lyon. b 57. St Jo Coll Nottm 90. **d** 92 **p** 93. C Netherton *Liv* 92–96; V Woolston 96–02; V Highfield 02–19; C E Widnes from 19. *St Matthew's Vicarage, Billinge Road, Wigan WN3 6BL* T: (01942) 222121 F: 211332

PEARSON, Preb Roy Barthram. b 35. K Coll Lon 56. **d** 60 **p** 61. C Brookfield St Mary *Lon* 60–64; C St Marylebone St Cypr 64–70; V Tottenham All Hallows from 70; AD E Haringey 95–00; Preb St Paul's Cathl from 96. *The Priory, Church Lane, London N17 7AA* T: (020) 8808 2470

PEARSON-GEE, William Oliver Clinton. b 61. Wycliffe Hall Ox 04. **d** 06 **p** 07. C Ox St Andr 06–10; R Buckingham from 10. *The Rectory, 8 Aris Way, Buckingham MK18 1FX* T: (01280) 830221 E: rector@buckinghambenefice.org.uk

PEARSON-HICKS, John Michael. b 67. Crewe & Alsager Coll BA 89 K Coll Lon MA 01 K Alfred's Coll Win PGCE 90. NTMTC 02. **d** 05 **p** 06. NSM Grosvenor Chpl *Lon* 05–09; NSM Westmr St Steph w St Jo 09–15; P-in-c Pimlico St Barn from 15. *167 John Ruskin Street, London SE5 0PQ* T: (020) 7641 5930 M: 07971-670092 E: frhicks@me.com *or* john.hicks@sjsp.islington.sch.uk

PEARSON-SMITH, Mrs Danielle Alanna. b 82. SEITE BA 15. **d** 16 **p** 17. C Welling *Roch* 16–19; R Snodland All SS w Ch Ch from 19. *The Rectory, 11 St Katherine's Lane, Snodland ME6 5EH* E: sjwcurate2@gmail.com

PEART, John Graham. b 36. Bps' Coll Cheshunt 65. **d** 68 **p** 69. C Cheshunt *St Alb* 68–70; C St Alb St Pet 70–73; R Hunsdon 73–76; R Widford 73–76; Ind Chapl 76–82; Chapl St Geo Hosp Stafford 82–87; Chapl Stafford Distr Gen Hosp 82–87; Chapl Qu Eliz Hosp Gateshead 87–89; Chapl Bensham Hosp Gateshead 87–89; Chapl Garlands Hosp 89–94; P-in-c Irthington and Cumwhinton *Carl* 89–94; V Irthington, Crosby-on-Eden and Scaleby 94–98; rtd 98; Chapl Douglas MacMillan Hospice Stoke-on-Trent 98–01; P-in-c Salt and Sandon w Burston 01–07; PtO *Lich* 04–07; *Eur* 07–13; *Lich* 15–16; *St E* from 17. *Skinners End, Skinners Lane, Metfield, Harleston IP20 0LH* T: (01379) 586089 E: johnpeart@hotmail.co.uk

PEASE, Alexander Michael. b 56. Mansf Coll Ox MA. St Mellitus Coll BA 12. **d** 12 **p** 13. NSM Itchen Valley *Win* 12–18; P-in-c from 18. *Chilland Ford, Lower Chilland Lane, Martyr Worthy, Winchester SO21 1EB* T: (01962) 791010 M: 07931-380321 E: rev@ampease.co.uk

PEAT, Mrs Ann Kathleen. b 40. TCert 60. **d** 98 **p** 99. OLM Brumby *Linc* 98–14; PtO *Newc* from 15. *Ashgrove, Church Lane, Longframlington, Morpeth NE65 8HR* T: (01665) 570564

PEAT, David William. b 37. Clare Coll Cam MA 59 PhD 62 FRAS 63. Westcott Ho Cam 72. **d** 75 **p** 76. C Chesterton St Andr *Ely* 75–77; Chapl Univ Coll of Ripon and York St Jo 77–83; V E Ardsley *Wakef* 83–87; Prin Willesden Min Tr Scheme 87–94; NSM Headingley *Ripon* 94–14; P-in-c 06–12; Research Lect Leeds Univ 94–12; rtd 12; PtO *Leeds* from 12. *12 North Grange Mews, Headingley, Leeds LS6 2EW* T: 0113-275 3179 E: dw.peat@btinternet.com

PEAT, Canon Matthew. b 71. Bradf and Ilkley Coll BA 97. Ripon Coll Cuddesdon BTh 03. **d** 03 **p** 04. C Walney Is *Carl* 03–06; C Barrow St Matt 06–08; TR 08–10; TR N Barrow 10–13; RD Barrow 11–12; P-in-c Whitkirk *Leeds* 13–18; V from 18; AD from 18; Hon Can Ripon Cathl from 19. *Whitkirk Vicarage, 386 Selby Road, Leeds LS15 0AA* T: 0113-264 5790 M: 07772-560014 E: matthewpeat@talktalk.net *or* vicar@whitkirkchurch.org.uk

PEATMAN, Michael Robert. b 61. Keble Coll Ox BA 85 MA 89 St Jo Coll Dur BA 89 Lanc Univ MA 06. Cranmer Hall Dur 87. **d** 90 **p** 91. C Greasley *S'well* 90–94; C Whitley *Cov* 94–02; Dio Stewardship Adv 94–02; Sen Chapl St Martin's Coll *Blackb* 02–07; Sen Chapl Cumbria Univ 07–09; P-in-c Poulton-le-Sands w Morecambe St Laur 09–11; R 11–18; AD Lancaster and Morecambe 10–14; V Beverley St Nic *York* from 18. *St Nicholas' Vicarage, 72 Grovehill Road, Beverley HU17 0ER* T: (01482) 881458 E: mikepeatman@gmail.com

PEATTIE, The Ven Colin Hulme Reid. b 39. Natal Univ BSc 59. Ripon Hall Ox 61. **d** 63 **p** 64. C Belmont *Lon* 63–65; R Durban St Columba S Africa 65–69; R Dundee St Jas 69–72; Chapl St Andr Sch Bloemfontein 72–76; R Pietermaritzburg St Alphege 76–83; V S Ossett *Wakef* 83–85; R York-cum-Ravensworth S Africa 85–93; R Stranger All SS 93–96; R Umhlali All So from 96; Adn N Coast from 01. *PO Box 222, Salt Rock, 4391 South Africa* T/F: (0027) (32) 947 2001 M: 82-413 8650 E: cpeattie@absamail.co.za

PEATY, Canon Julia Kathleen. b 53. Salford Univ BSc 75 Glos Univ BA 07. STETS 96. **d** 99 **p** 00. NSM E Grinstead St Swithun *Chich* from 99; RD E Grinstead 10–19; Dean of Women's Min 13–17; Dean of Self-Supporting Min from 18; Can and Preb Chich Cathl from 10. *15 Overton Shaw, East Grinstead RH19 1EN* T: (01342) 322386 E: julia@peaty.net

PEBERDY (née GARNETT), Mrs Alyson Susan. b 48. Trevelyan Coll Dur BA 69 Reading Univ MA 75. Ox Min Course 95. **d** 96 **p** 97. C New Windsor Ox 96–99; V Brockley Hill St Sav *S'wark* 99–18; P-in-c Perry Hill St Geo 00–01; P-in-c Forest Hill St Aug 00–02; Adv Women's Min Woolwich Area 10–18; Dean of Women's Min 12–17; rtd 18; PtO Ox from 18. *77 Lonsdale Road, Oxford OX2 7ES* M: 07552-958257 E: aspeberdy@aol.com

PECK, Christopher Wallace. b 49. UEA BA 72 Lon Bible Coll BA 75 Ches Coll of HE MTh 96. Ripon Coll Cuddesdon 10. **d** 11 **p** 12. C Abington *Pet* 11–15; R Guilsborough and Hollowell and Cold Ashby etc from 15. *The Vicarage, 15 Church Mount, Guilsborough, Northampton NN6 8QA* T: (01604) 743734 M: 07505-253096 E: revchrispeck@hotmail.co.uk

PECK, Kay Margaret. b 51. Milton Keynes Coll of Ed BEd 76. Ox Min Course 04. **d** 07 **p** 08. NSM Swan *Ox* 07–09; NSM The Claydons and Swan 09–10; NSM Lenborough 11–17; PtO from 17. *21 Beamish Way, Winslow, Buckingham MK18 3EU* T: (01296) 714253 E: kmpeck@btinternet.com

PECKHAM, Richard Graham. b 51. Sarum & Wells Th Coll 84. **d** 86 **p** 87. C Bishop's Cleeve *Glouc* 86–89; TV Ilfracombe, Lee, Woolacombe, Bittadon etc *Ex* 89–96; TV Sidmouth, Woolbrook, Salcombe Regis, Sidbury etc 96–12; RD Ottery 98–02; P-in-c Dunkeswell, Luppitt, Sheldon and Upottery 12–16; C Broadhembury, Payhembury and Plymtree 12–16; R Broadhembury, Dunkeswell, Luppitt, Plymtree, Sheldon, and Upottery 17; Hon Chapl ATC 98–17; rtd 17; PtO *B & W* from 17. *Ossory, Silvermead, Minehead TA24 6AP* E: rikpeckham@btinternet.com

PEDLAR, Canon John Glanville. b 43. Ex Univ BA 68 De Montfort Univ Hon MA 06. St Steph Ho Ox 68. **d** 70 **p** 71. C Tavistock and Gulworthy *Ex* 70–73; Prec Portsm Cathl 74–77; Prec St Alb Abbey 77–81; V Redbourn 81–98; V Bedford St Paul 98–13; PV Westmr Abbey 87–04; Hon Can St Alb 06–13; rtd 13; P-in-c Bris Ch Ch w St Ewen, All SS and St Geo from 16. *1 Priory Dene, Bristol BS9 3EG* E: johnpedlar@btinternet.com

PEDLEY, Canon Betty. b 49. Ripon Coll of Educn CertEd 70 Leeds Univ BEd 71 ALCM 78. NOC 85. **d** 88 **p** 03. Par Dn Sowerby *Wakef* 88–92; Par Educn Adv and Youth Chapl 92–03; P-in-c Luddenden w Luddenden Foot 03–08; P-in-c Norland 06–08; Hon Can Wakef Cathl 00–08; rtd 08; PtO *Wakef* 08–14; *Leeds* from 14. *7 Ogden View Close, Halifax HX2 9LY* T: (01422) 252014 E: bettypedley@aol.com

✠**PEDLEY, The Rt Revd Geoffrey Stephen.** b 40. Qu Coll Cam BA 64 MA 67. Cuddesdon Coll 64. **d** 66 **p** 67 **c** 98. C Liv Our Lady and St Nic 66–69; C Cov H Trin 69–71; P-in-c Kitwe Zambia 71–77; P-in-c Stockton H Trin *Dur* 77–83; V Stockton St Pet 77–88; Chapl to The Queen 84–98; R Whickham *Dur* 88–93; Can Res Dur Cathl 93–98; Suff Bp Lancaster *Blackb* 98–05; Hon Can Blackb Cathl 98–05; rtd 05. *The Blue House, Newbrough, Hexham NE47 5AN* T: (01434) 674238

PEDLEY, Nicholas Charles. b 48. DipSW 75. Qu Coll Birm 88. **d** 90 **p** 91. C Stafford St Jo and Tixall w Ingestre *Lich* 90–93; C Kingswinford St Mary *Worc* 93–96; TV 96–97; C Cheswardine, Childs Ercall, Hales, Hinstock etc *Lich* 97–99; Chapl HM YOI Stoke Heath 97–99; rtd 99; PtO *Worc* from 00; *Lich* from 15. *1 Brindley Heath Cottages, Enville Road, Kinver, Stourbridge DY7 5LU* T: (01384) 877219 E: nickpedley48@gmail.com

PEDLEY, Simon David. b 76. Imp Coll Lon BSc 98 ARCS 98. Oak Hill Th Coll BA 10. **d** 10 **p** 11. C St Helen Bishopsgate w St Andr Undershaft etc *Lon* 10–14; C Teddington SS Pet and Paul from 18. *106 Fulwell Road, Teddington TW11 0RQ* T: (020) 8241 0761 M: 07713-897991 E: simon@stmichaelsfulwell.co.uk

PEDLOW, Henry Noel. b 37. QUB BA 59. **d** 61 **p** 62. C Belfast St Phil *Conn* 61–66; C Belfast St Nic 66–70; I Eglantine 70–82; I Kilkeel *D & D* 82–89; I Belfast St Donard 89–03; rtd 03. *8 Old Mill Dale, Dundonald, Belfast BT16 1WG* T: (028) 9048 5416

PEEBLES, David Thomas. b 64. Bris Univ BA 85 St Chad's Coll Dur PGCE 86 Man Univ MA 94 Heythrop Coll Lon MA 04 K Coll Lon DThMin 17. Coll of Resurr Mirfield 90. **d** 90 **p** 91. C Crewe St Andr *Ches* 90–93; Lect and Asst Dir Studies Mirfield 93–95; Chapl Qu Mary Univ of Lon 95–00; P-in-c Bethnal Green St Matt w St Jas the Gt 97–99; Chapl LSE 00–10; R Bloomsbury St Geo w Woburn Square Ch Ch from 10; Bp's Adv on New Relig Movements from 01. *The Rectory, 6 Gower Street, London WC1E 6DP* T: (020) 7580 4010 M: 07838-388074 E: rector@stgb.org.uk

PEEK, Alan Nicholas. b 65. Ridley Hall Cam 02. **d** 04 **p** 05. C Much Woolton *Liv* 04–08; I Derg w Termonamongan *D & R* 08–14; I Movilla *D & D* from 14. *The Rectory, 34 Hollymount Road, Newtownards BT23 7DL* T: (028) 9181 0787 *or* 9181 9794 E: rev.al@sky.com

PEEK, John Richard. b 51. Bris Univ BSc 72 Nottm Univ BA 75. St Jo Coll Nottm. **d** 76 **p** 77. C Hebburn St Jo *Dur* 76–78; C Dunston 78–81; R Armthorpe *Sheff* 81–86; RE Teacher K Edw VI Sch Southn 87–88; Chapl and Hd RE Casterton Sch Lancs 89; Teacher Furze Platt Comp Sch Berks 89–90; Chapl Bearwood Coll Wokingham 96–97; Teacher K Manor Sch Guildf 97–98; Teacher Stowford Coll Sutton 98–08; Teacher Ryde Sch w Upper Chine 08–09; PtO *Portsm* 08–11. *41 North Road, Shanklin PO37 6DE* T: (01983) 719631

PEEL, Mrs Christine Mary. b 44. Whitelands Coll Lon CertEd 66. Portsm Dioc Tr Course. **d** 90. NSM Sheet *Portsm* 90–03; PtO *York* from 03. *11 Whiteoak Avenue, Easingwold, York YO61 3GB* T: (01347) 823548 E: peel3gb@btinternet.com

PEEL, Canon David Charles. b 41. AKC 75. St Aug Coll Cant 75. **d** 76 **p** 77. C Tynemouth Cullercoats St Paul *Newc* 76–79; C Tynemouth St Jo 79–84; Ldr Cedarwood Project 84–88 and 91–11; Warden Communicare Ho 89–91; Min Killingworth 89–91; Hon Can Newc Cathl 08–11; rtd 11; PtO *Newc* from 11. *116 Grey Street, North Shields NE30 2EG* T: 0191-272 8743 E: peeldc524@gmail.com

PEEL, Derrick. b 50. Open Univ BA 82. Linc Th Coll 75. **d** 78 **p** 79. C Otley *Bradf* 78–82; V Shelf 82–94; P-in-c Buttershaw St Aid 89–94; TR Shelf w Buttershaw St Aid 94–95; V E Crompton *Man* 95–05; V Ware St Mary *St Alb* 05–15; rtd 15; PtO *Chelmsf* from 15. *10 Thornwood Close, West Mersea, Colchester CO5 8BU*

PEELING, Mrs Pamela Mary Alberta. b 44. Oak Hill Th Coll 83. dss 86 **d** 87 **p** 94. NSM Moulsham St Luke *Chelmsf* 86–88; NSM N Springfield 88–95; C Basildon St Martin 95–97; TV Grays Thurrock 97–05; rtd 05; PtO *St E* from 05. *4 Heron Road, Saxmundham IP17 1WR* T: (01728) 604584 E: ppeeling@freebie.net

PEER, Charles Scott. b 69. Bris Univ BSc 91 PGCE 94 Ex Univ MA 05. Trin Coll Bris BA 02. **d** 02 **p** 03. C Dawlish *Ex* 02–05; P-in-c Kea *Truro* 05–12; Miss Development Officer *Portsm* 12–16; Strategic Progr Manager *B & W* from 16. *Diocesan Office, The Old Deanery, Wells BA5 2UG* E: charliepeer@gmail.com

PEERS, Esther Louise. b 76. St Mellitus Coll 15. **d** 18 **p** 19. C Leamington Spa H Trin *Cov* from 18. *18 Arlington Avenue, Leamington Spa CV32 5UD*

PEERS, Michael John. b 65. SS Paul & Mary Coll Cheltenham BA 86. Ripon Coll Cuddesdon 88. **d** 91 **p** 92. C Birstall and Wanlip *Leic* 91–94; C Leic St Marg and All SS 94–96; TV The Abbey *Leic* 96–00; P-in-c Langley Park *Dur* 00–01; V from 01; P-in-c Esh 00–01; V 01–11; P-in-c Hamsteels 00–01; V 01–11; V Esh and Hamsteels from 11; P-in-c Waterhouses 00–01; V from 01. *The Vicarage, Church Street, Langley Park, Durham DH7 9TZ* T: 0191-373 3110 E: mjpeers@aol.com

PEERS, Richard Charles. b 65. K Alfred's Coll Win BEd 88 Lon Inst of Educn MA 05. Chich Th Coll BTh 93. **d** 93 **p** 94. C Grangetown *York* 93–95; C Portsea St Mary *Portsm* 95–97; Dep Hd Emsworth Primary Sch 97–01; Hon Chapl Portsm Cathl 01–03; Chapl St Luke's Sch Southsea 01–03; Dep Hd Ch Sch Richmond 03–06; Chapl Abp Tenison's Sch Kennington 06–08; Headmaster Trin Sch Lewisham 08–16; Hon C Earlsfield St Andr *S'wark* 06–11; Hon C Blackheath All SS 11–13; Hon C Lewisham St Mary 13–16; Dir Educn *Liv* from 16; Lic Preacher from 16; PtO *Lich* from 16. *St James House, 20 St James House, Liverpool L1 7BY* E: richard.peers@liverpool.anglican.org *or* richard.peers1@btopenworld.com

PEET, John Christopher. b 56. Oriel Coll Ox BA 80 MA 83 Clare Coll Cam BA 82 MA 87. Ridley Hall Cam 80. **d** 83 **p** 84. C Menston w Woodhead *Bradf* 83–86; C Prenton *Ches* 86–89; V Harden and Wilsden *Bradf* 89–97; V Cononley w Bradley 97–14; *Leeds* 14–17; rtd 17; PtO *Leeds* from 17. *Highfield, 19 Main Street, Cononley, Keighley BD20 8LR* T: (01535) 634369

PEET, Ruth Marie. b 59. **d** 15 **p** 16. C Plaistow St Mary *Roch* 15–19; V Aylesford from 19. *The Vicarage, Vicarage Close, Aylesford ME20 7BB* T: (01622) 717434 E: ruthmpeet@gmail.com

PEETERS, Erik Christian. b 75. Pretoria Univ BA 98 Leeds Univ MA 04 PhD 07. St Hild Coll 15. **d** 17 **p** 18. C Lupset *Leeds* from 17; C Thornes from 17. *2 Elm Grove, Horbury, Wakefield WF4 5EP* M: 07761-919564 E: erik.c.peeters@gmail.com

PEGG, Danny Lee. b 89. Kent Univ BA 11 Cam Univ BTh 17 MPhil 18. Westcott Ho Cam 15. **d** 18 **p** 19. C Stone Cross St Luke w N Langney *Chich* from 18. *Address withheld by request* T: 07939-497002 E: revdpegg@gmail.com

PEGG, Josephine Anne. See ROBERTSON, Josephine Anne

PEGLER, Mrs Eve Charlotte. b 73. Cheltenham & Glouc Coll of HE BSc 95. Ridley Hall Cam 05. **d** 07 **p** 08. C Hullavington, Norton and Stanton St Quintin *Bris* 07–10; C Sherston Magna, Easton Grey, Luckington etc 07–10; TV Shaftesbury *Sarum* 10–14; Chapl Port Regis Sch 10–14; C Gillingham and Milton-on-Stour *Sarum* 14–19; C Gillingham, Milton-on-Stour and Silton from 19. *The Vicarage, 49 Fern Brook Lane, Gillingham SP8 4FL* T: (01747) 851442 E: evepegler@gmail.com

PEIRCE, John. b 35. Worc Coll Ox BA 59 MA 64 Kent Univ MA 96. Wycliffe Hall Ox 59. **d** 61 **p** 62. C Brompton H Trin *Lon* 61–64; C Wareham w Arne *Sarum* 64–68; V Sturminster Newton and Hinton St Mary 68–74; V Kingswood *Bris* 74–79; Dir Coun Chr Care *Ex* 79–89; Public Preacher 89–92; NSM Hackney *Lon* 90–94; NSM St Botolph Aldgate w H Trin Minories 94–02; Co-ord Ch Action on Disability 90–98; PtO *Ex* 92–98. *3 Mile End Place, London E1 4BH* T: (020) 7790 9418 E: peircejohn@aol.com

PEIRCE, Canon John Martin. b 36. Jes Coll Cam BA 59 MA 65. Westcott Ho Cam 65. **d** 66 **p** 67. C Croydon St Jo *Cant* 66–70; C Fareham H Trin *Portsm* 70–71; TV 71–76; TR Langley Marish 76–85; RD Burnham 78–82; Dir of Ords and Post-Ord Tr 85–01; Can Res Ch Ch *Ox* 87–01; rtd 01; PtO *Ox* from 08. *8 Burwell Meadow, Witney, Oxford OX28 5JQ*

PELHAM, Thomas John. b 87. Bris Univ BA 09 MA 11. Ripon Coll Cuddesdon BA 18. **d** 18 **p** 19. C Canford Cliffs and Sandbanks *Sarum* from 18. *4 Haven Heights, 22 Birchwood Road, Parkstone, Poole BH14 9ND* M: 07922-849982 E: revthomaspelham@gmail.com

PELLY, Mrs Elizabeth Wigram (Lulu). b 52. Bris Univ BA 73. ERMC 05. **d** 08 **p** 09. C Towcester w Caldecote and Easton Neston etc *Pet* from 08. *Pear Tree Cottage, Spring Lane, Alderton, Towcester NN12 7LW* T: (01327) 811488 M: 07723-604316 E: lulupelly@yahoo.com

PELLY, Margaret Helen. b 50. ERMC. **d** 11 **p** 12. OLM Stebbing and Lindsell w Gt and Lt Saling *Chelmsf* from 11. *Purples Farmhouse, Bardfield Saling, Braintree CM7 5EJ* T: (01371) 810369

PEMBERTON, Anthony Thomas Christie (Chris). b 57. BA. Cranmer Hall Dur 82. **d** 84 **p** 85. C Maidstone St Luke *Cant* 84–88; Chapl Ox Pastorate 88–98; V Cant St Mary Bredin 98–09; Tr Dir New Wine 09–16; PtO *Chelmsf* from 13; Tutor Ridley Hall Cam from 16; PtO *Eur* from 18. *Newhouse Farm,*

Walden Road, Radwinter, Saffron Walden CB10 2SP T: 03000-406205 E: chrisp@nwtp.org.uk

PEMBERTON, Crispin Mark Rugman. b 59. St Andr Univ MTheol 83. St Steph Ho Ox 84. **d** 86 **p** 87. C Acton Green *Lon* 86–90; C Leckhampton SS Phil and Jas w Cheltenham St Jas *Glouc* 90–93; V Tuffley 93–97; RE Teacher Cheltenham Coll Jun Sch 97–00; PtO *Heref* 13–16; P-in-c Brampton 16–17; V StowCaple from 17. *Jenny Penny Whites, Little Dewchurch, Hereford HR2 6PR* M: 07824-444655 E: crispinpemberton@yahoo.co.uk

PEMBERTON FORD, Carrie Mary. b 55. St Hilda's Coll Ox BA 78 Cam Univ PGCE 82 Leeds Univ MA 92 Newnham Coll Cam PhD 98. Cranmer Hall Dur 83 NEOC 84. **dss** 86 **d** 87 **p** 94. NSM Leeds St Geo *Ripon* 86–87; Miss Partner CMS and Dir Women's Studies Angl Th Inst Zaïre 87–91; PtO *Pet* 92–94; NSM Bourn and Kingston w Caxton and Longstowe *Ely* 94–99; TV Elsworth w Knapwell 99; Min Cambourne LEP 00–01; PtO 01–07; Relig Manager Yarlswood Immigration and Detention Cen 01–03; Chief Exec CHASTE 04–08; Chief Exec Officer and Founding Dir Cam Cen for Applied Research in Human Trafficking from 07; PtO *Ely* from 16. *Rectory Farm, Hildersham, Cambridge CB21 6DD* T: (01223) 891765 E: carrie@ccarht.org *or* carrieford@cantab.net

✠**PENBERTHY, The Rt Revd Joanna Susan.** b 60. Newnham Coll Cam BA 81 MA 85 St Jo Coll Nottm MTh 84. Cranmer Hall Dur 83. **dss** 84 **d** 87 **p** 97 **c** 16. Haughton le Skerne *Dur* 84–85; Llanishen and Lisvane *Llan* 85–89; NSM 87–89; NSM Llanwddyn and Llanfihangel-yng-Nghwynfa etc *St As* 89–93; NSM Llansadwrn w Llanwrda and Manordeilo *St D* 93–95; Prov Officer Div for Par Development Ch in Wales 94–99; P-in-c Cynwyl Gaeo w Llansawel and Talley *St D* 99–01; V 01–10; Dioc Adult Educn Officer 01–02; Warden of Readers 02–10; Can St D Cathl 07–10; P-in-c Charlton Musgrove, Cucklington and Stoke Trister *B & W* 10–11; R 11–15; R Glan Ithon *S & B* 15–16; Bp St D from 16. *Llys Esgob, Abergwili, Carmarthen SA31 2JG* T: (01267) 236597

PENDENQUE, Mrs Susan Mary. b 68. Nottm Poly BEd 90. St Hild Coll 17. **d** 19. C Sherwood *S'well* from 19. *152 Perry Road, Nottingham NG5 1GL* M: 07932-242398 E: sue.pendenque@gmail.com

PENDLEBURY, Richard Norman. **d** 16 **p** 17. OLM Bris St Matt and St Nath from 16. *27 Stanley Avenue, Bishopston, Bristol BS7 9AH*

PENDLEBURY, Stephen Thomas. b 50. Southn Univ BSc 73 ACA 78. Ridley Hall Cam 86. **d** 88 **p** 89. C Birkenhead St Jas w St Bede *Ches* 88–91; V 91–00; V Ches St Paul 00–16; P-in-c Huntington 12–16; rtd 16; PtO *Ches* from 16; Hon C Cornerstone *Sheff* from 18. *The Vicarage, Stone Moor Road, Bolsterstone, Sheffield S36 3ZN* T: 0114-283 1238 E: stpendleby@aol.com

PENDORF, Canon James Gordon. b 45. Drew Univ New Jersey BA 67. Episc Th Sch Cam Mass STB 71. **d** 71 **p** 71. V Newark St Greg USA 71–76; V Colne H Trin *Blackb* 76–80; Sen Dioc Stewardship Adv *Chelmsf* 80–83; Dioc Sec *Birm* 83–95; P-in-c Highgate 95–97; V 97–04; Dioc Stewardship Adv 95–04; AD Birm City Cen 96–02; Hon Can Birm Cathl 90–04; Par Resources Adv and Chapl St Nic Ch Cen *St E* 04–13; NSM Holbrook, Stutton, Freston, Woolverstone etc 05–13; P-in-c Capel St Mary w Lt and Gt Wenham 13–19. *10 Joseph Close, Hadleigh, Ipswich IP7 5FH* M: 07973-265037 E: canonpendorf@aol.com

PENFOLD, Brian Robert. b 54. Lon Univ BSc 75 Bris Univ PGCE 77. Oak Hill Th Coll BA 84. **d** 84 **p** 85. C Norwood St Luke *S'wark* 84–88; C Rayleigh *Chelmsf* 88–92; V New Barnet St Jas *St Alb* 92–08; V Worthing St Geo *Chich* 08–19; rtd 19. *Haversham House, 12 Nevill Avenue, Eastbourne BN22 9PU* M: 07753-680839

PENFOLD, Colin Richard. b 52. St Pet Coll Ox BA 74 MA 78. Ridley Hall Cam 81. **d** 84 **p** 85. C Buckhurst Hill *Chelmsf* 84–87; C Greenside *Dur* 87–90; V Cononley w Bradley *Bradf* 90–97; P-in-c Shipley St Paul and Frizinghall 97; V Shipley St Paul 98–08; P-in-c Gt Harwood *Blackb* 08–12; V 12–18; AD Whalley 17–18; rtd 18. *10 Parkwood Road, Shipley BD18 4SS* M: 07753-255419 E: colinpenfold45@gmail.com

PENFOLD, Julian Oliver Kevin. b 56. Cliff Coll MA 13. All SS Cen for Miss & Min. **d** 15 **p** 16. NSM Alfreton *Derby* from 15; NSM Riddings and Ironville from 15; NSM Somercotes from 19. *Shirland Park Farm, Park Lane, Shirland, Alfreton DE55 6AX* T: (01773) 833242 M: 07932-564888 E: jokpenfold@aol.com

PENFOLD, Marion Jean. b 49. NEOC 96. **d** 99 **p** 00. NSM Lesbury w Alnmouth *Newc* 99–02; C 02–03; NSM Longhoughton w Howick 99–02; C 02–03; TV N Tyne and Redesdale 03–11; TV Glendale Gp 11–17; V Chatton w Chillingham, Eglingham and S Charlton and Ingram 17–19;

rtd 19. *16 Meadow Lands, Tweedmouth, Berwick-upon-Tweed TD15 2FW* E: marion.penfold@btinternet.com

PENFOLD, Canon Susan Irene. b 52. York Univ BA 73 Bris Univ PhD 77 Selw Coll Cam BA 83 MA 87. Ridley Hall Cam 81. **dss** 84 **d** 87 **p** 94. Buckhurst Hill *Chelmsf* 84–87; Hon C Greenside *Dur* 87–90; Hon C Cononley w Bradley *Bradf* 90–97; Assoc Dioc Dir of Ords 96–01; Hon C Shipley St Paul 97–00; PtO 00–08; Dir of Ords and CME Officer *Wakef* 01–03; Dir of Ords and Dean of Min 03–08; Hon Can Wakef Cathl 04–08; Can Res Blackb Cathl 08–15; Dir of Min 08–18; rtd 18. *10 Parkwood Road, Shipley BD18 4SS* M: 07753-987977 E: sue.penfold@gmail.com

PENGELLY, Canon Geoffrey. b 50. Oak Hill Th Coll 86. **d** 88 **p** 89. C Redruth w Lanner and Treleigh *Truro* 88–91; TV Bolventor 91–92; V Egloskerry, N Petherwin, Tremaine, Tresmere etc from 92; RD Trigg Major 04–10; Hon Can Truro Cathl from 03. *The Vicarage, Egloskerry, Launceston PL15 8RX* T: (01566) 785365

PENISTAN, Richard Luke. *See* PENNYSTAN, Richard Luke

PENMAN, Robert George. b 42. St Jo Coll Auckland LTh 66. **d** 65 **p** 66. C Mt Roskill New Zealand 65–68; C Henderson 69–70; V Glen Innes 71–72; C Alverstoke *Portsm* 73–74; CF 74–77; C Bridgwater St Mary w Chilton Trinity *B & W* 77–80; P-in-c Haselbury Plucknett w N Perrott 80–81; P-in-c Misterton 80–81; V Haselbury Plucknett, Misterton and N Perrott 81–89; P-in-c Appleton *Ox* 89–07; P-in-c Besselsleigh w Dry Sandford 89–00; P-in-c Besselsleigh 00–07; rtd 07; PtO *Ox* from 07. *31 High Street, Sherington, Newport Pagnell MK16 9NU* T: (01908) 611838 E: penman298@btinternet.com

PENN, Barry Edwin. b 46. Univ of Wales (Swansea) BA 72 Trin Coll Bris MA 04. St Jo Coll Nottm 77. **d** 79 **p** 80. C New Barnet St Jas *St Alb* 79–83; TV Preston St Jo *Blackb* 83–92; V Patchway *Bris* 92–01; PtO 01–17. *50 Eastfield Road, Westbury-on-Trym, Bristol BS9 4AG* T: 0117-962 2862 E: barrypenn@aol.com

PENN, Christopher Francis. b 34. ACII 63. Wells Th Coll 68. **d** 70 **p** 71. C Andover w Foxcott *Win* 70–72; C Odiham w S Warnborough 72–75; C Keynsham *B & W* 75–76; TV 76–82; R Chilcompton w Downside and Stratton on the Fosse 82–87; RD Midsomer Norton 84–86; V Bathford 87–90; V Avonmouth St Andr *Bris* 90–96; Ind Chapl 90–96; rtd 96; PtO *B & W* from 96; *Bris* 96–01. *53 Caernarvon Road, Keynsham, Bristol BS31 2PF* T: 0117-986 6831 E: c.s.penn@talktalk.net

PENN, Christopher Wilson. b 60. Cranmer Hall Dur 98. **d** 00 **p** 01. C Wrockwardine Deanery *Lich* 00–03; P-in-c Llanyblodwel and Trefonen 03–07; P-in-c Llanymynech 03–07; P-in-c Morton 03–07; R Llanyblodwel, Llanymynech, Morton and Trefonen 07–13; Rural Officer (Salop Adnry) 08–13; P-in-c Holsworthy w Hollacombe and Milton Damerel *Ex* 13–15; R Holsworthy, Hollacombe, Pyworthy etc 15–17; RD Holsworthy 15–17; P-in-c Broseley w Benthall, Jackfield, Linley etc *Heref* 17–19; R from 19. *All Saints' Rectory, Church Street, Broseley TF12 5DA* T: (01952) 882647 M: 07941-735318 E: crispy50@hotmail.co.uk *or* rector@broseleyparishes.org.uk

PENN, Ms Jane Rachel. b 52. ERMC 07. **d** 10 **p** 11. NSM Orton Longueville w Bottlebridge *Ely* 10–13; NSM Tadley w Pamber Heath and Silchester *Win* 13–17; P-in-c Worlingham w Barnby and N Cove *St E* from 17. *The Rectory, 27 Lowestoft Road, Worlingham, Beccles NR34 7DZ* T: (01502) 716210 M: 07792-220156 E: janepenn@hotmail.co.uk

PENN, Mrs Jennifer Anne. b 61. Imp Coll Lon BEng 84 Leeds Univ BA 07. NOC 04. **d** 07 **p** 08. C Halliwell St Pet *Man* 07–10; TV New Bury w Gt Lever 10–14; P-in-c Reigate St Phil *S'wark* 14–18; V from 18; Chapl St Bede's Sch Reigate from 14. *The Parsonage, 102A Nutley Lane, Reigate RH2 9HA* T: (01737) 244542 E: jenpenn@virginmedia.com

PENN, Mrs Sarah Jane. b 56. City Univ BSc 83 Chelsea Coll Lon PGCE 84 Dur Univ BA 18. Lindisfarne Regional Tr Partnership 10. **d** 14 **p** 15. OLM St John Lee *Newc* 14–18; OLM Warden w Newbrough 14–18; P-in-c Bempton w Flamborough, Reighton w Speeton *York* from 18. *The Vicarage, Church Street, Flamborough, Bridlington YO15 1PE* M: 07747-865747 E: janepenn11@gmail.com

PENN-ALLISON, Mrs Nicola Alison. b 69. Man Univ BSc 99 Open Univ MBA 11 St Jo Coll Dur BA 14 Ox Brookes Univ PGCE 04. Cranmer Hall Dur. **d** 14 **p** 15. C Redcar *York* 14–17; P-in-c Saxilby Gp *Linc* from 17; P-in-c Stow Gp from 17. *The Vicarage, 69 Mill Lane, Saxilby, Lincoln LN1 2HN* T: (01522) 702427 M: 07918-941656 E: nicky.allison@outlook.com

PENNAL, David Bernard. b 37. Ripon Hall Ox 64. **d** 67 **p** 68. C Moseley St Mary *Birm* 67–71; C Bridgwater St Mary w Chilton Trinity *B & W* 71–73; P-in-c Hilton w Cheselbourne and Melcombe Horsey *Sarum* 73–76; R Milton Abbas, Hilton w Cheselbourne etc 76–78; P-in-c Spetisbury w Charlton

Marshall 78–88; R Spetisbury w Charlton Marshall etc 89–00; rtd 00. *11 High Street, Wicken, Ely CB7 5XR* T: (01353) 624295 M: 07778-120668 E: dbipennall1@gmail.com

PENNANT, David Falconer. b 51. Trin Coll Cam MA 73. Trin Coll Bris BD 84 PhD 88. **d** 86 **p** 87. C Bramcote *S'well* 86–88; C Woking St Jo *Guildf* 88–93. *30 Oriental Road, Woking GU22 7AW* T: (01483) 768055 E: df.pennant@ntlworld.com

PENNANT, Rachel Elizabeth Burrows. b 74. Ex Univ BA 95 Sheff Univ PhD 01. Trin Coll Bris MA 12. **d** 12 **p** 13. C Biggleswade *St Alb* 12–16; V Hoddesdon from 16. *The Vicarage, 11 Oxenden Drive, Hoddesdon EN11 8QF* T: (01992) 462627 M: 07811-774192 E: rpennant@btinternet.com

PENNELL, Ms Pamela. EAMTC 94. **d** 97 **p** 98. NSM Moulsham St Luke *Chelmsf* 97–98; NSM Writtle w Highwood 98–00; PtO 01–04; NSM St Waltham w Ford End 04–06; PtO 06–08; P-in-c Sandon 08–10; P-in-c E Hanningfield 08–13; rtd 13; PtO *Chelmsf* from 14. *Address withheld by request*

PENNELLS, David Malcolm Benedict. b 56. Leeds Univ BA 11 CQSW 80. Coll of Resurr Mirfield 09. **d** 11 **p** 12. C Kennington St Jo w St Jas *S'wark* 11–15; V Mitcham SS Pet and Paul from 15. *The Vicarage, 11 Vicarage Gardens, Mitcham CR4 3BL* T: (020) 8646 0066 E: fatherdavid@btinternet.com

PENNEY, David Richard John. b 39. St Jo Coll Dur BA 63. Cranmer Hall Dur 63. **d** 67 **p** 68. C Chilvers Coton w Astley *Cov* 67–70; C Styvechale 70–72; P-in-c Shilton w Ansty 72–77; P-in-c Withybrook w Copston Magna 74–77; R Easington w Liverton *York* 77–85; Dir Soc Resp *Sarum* 85–93; PtO *Blackb* 93–02; rtd 01; PtO *Blackb* 16–17. *Noyna House, 2 Noyna Street, Colne BB8 0PE* T: (01282) 870076 M: 07966-157697 E: davepenney75@gmail.com

PENNEY, William Affleck. b 41. MBIM 75 FRSA 91. K Coll Lon BD 63 AKC 63 St Boniface Warminster 65. **d** 66 **p** 67. C Chatham St Steph *Roch* 66–70; Ind Chapl 70–77; P-in-c Bredhurst 70–72; Hon C S Gillingham 72–74; Hon C Eynsford w Farningham and Lullingstone 74–77; Bp's Dom Chapl 74–88; Hon Ind Chapl 77–88; Hon C Balham St Mary and St Jo *S'wark* 89–91; PtO *St Alb* 91–94; Hon C Bushey 94–05; rtd 05. *3 Byron Close, Abingdon OX14 5PA* T: (01235) 206366 E: wpenney@btconnect.com

PENNIE, Mrs Fiona Clare. b 64. All SS Cen for Miss & Min 12. **d** 15 **p** 16. NSM Liv All So Springwood 15–18; P-in-c Descroof 18–19; PtO from 19. *Address temp unknown* M: 07941-652488 E: revpennie@gmail.com

PENNIECOOKE, Dorothy Victoria. b 45. Dioc OLM tr scheme 97. **d** 00 **p** 01. NSM Balham Hill Ascension *S'wark* 00–15; PtO from 15. *56 Lysias Road, London SW12 8BP* T: (020) 8673 0037 E: dotty.pcooke@gmail.com

PENNINGTON, Edward Francis Quentin. b 76. G&C Coll Cam BA 97 MA 01 Birm Univ MSc 98. Oak Hill Th Coll BTh 04. **d** 04 **p** 05. C Moulton *Pet* 04–07; C Fulwood *Sheff* 07–18; LtO from 18. *237 Bannerdale Road, Sheffield S11 9FD* T: 0114-221 9393 M: 07743-942931 E: efqpennington@hotmail.com *or* ed@endcliffechurch.co.uk *or* ed.pennington@sheffield.anglican.org

PENNINGTON, Canon Emma Louise. b 71. Ex Univ BA 92 Kent Univ MA 96 Ox Univ DPhil 14. Ripon Coll Cuddesdon BA 00. **d** 00 **p** 01. C Shepperton *Lon* 00–03; Chapl Worc Coll Ox 03–08; TV Wheatley *Ox* 08–14; V Garsington, Cuddesdon and Horspath 14–19; AD Aston and Cuddesdon 18–19; Can Res Cant Cathl from 19. *15 The Precincts, Canterbury CT1 2EL* E: emmapennington153@gmail.com

PENNINGTON, James Edward. b 78. Essex Univ BA 00. St Jo Coll Nottm 12. **d** 14 **p** 15. C Nailsea H Trin *B & W* 14–18; R Passenham *Pet* from 18. *The Rectory, Wicken Road, Deanshanger, Milton Keynes MK19 6JP* T: (01908) 262371 M: 07736-299889 E: jepennington@hotmail.com

PENNINGTON, Ms Nicola Gail. b 67. Nottm Univ BA 88 Leic Univ MA 93 Cumbria Univ MA 18 CQSW 93. LCTP 10. **d** 13 **p** 14. C Maryport, Netherton and Flimby *Carl* 13–17; Team Ldr Cumbria Chr Learning 17–18; P-in-c Crosslacon *Carl* from 19. *Limetree House, Broughton Cross, Cockermouth CA13 0TY* M: 07462-194549 E: revnickipennington@gmail.com

PENNOCK, Canon Christine. b 48. Bp Grosseteste Coll BEd 71 Leeds Univ PGCE 94 Teesside Univ PGDE 95. NEOC 98. **d** 01 **p** 02. C Crowland *Linc* 01–05; P-in-c Ruskington Gp 05–13; P-in-c Leasingham 09–13; P-in-c Cranwell 11–13; R N Lafford Gp 13–19; RD Lafford 12–19; Can and Preb Linc Cathl 15–19; rtd 19. *6 Hilda Close, Quarrington, Sleaford NG34 8UW* T: (01529) 415897 M: 07813-954043 E: revpennock77@btinternet.com

PENNY, Alexander Stuart Egerton. b 52. Wolv Art Coll BA 75. Ridley Hall Cam MA 00. **d** 00 **p** 01. C Uttoxeter Area *Lich* 00–03; V Crosthwaite Keswick *Carl* 03–17; RD Derwent 16–17; rtd 17; PtO *Lich* from 17; *Eur* from 18. *51 Armoury Gardens, Shrewsbury SY2 6PJ*

PENNY, David Roy. b 67. Wilson Carlile Coll 89 NOC 00. d 03 p 04. C Hey and Waterhead *Man* 03–05; V Chadderton St Matt w St Luke from 05; AD Oldham W 09–17. *St Matthew's Vicarage, Mill Brow, Chadderton, Oldham OL1 2RT* T: 0161-624 8600 E: revdpenny@btinternet.com

PENNY, Diana Eleanor. b 51. Open Univ BA 87 MSc 13 Birm Univ DipEd 96. Nor Ord Course 87. d 89 p 94. NSM Gillingham w Geldeston, Stockton, Ellingham etc *Nor* 89–93; NSM Upton St Leonards *Glouc* 93–97; NSM Stiffkey and Cockthorpe w Morston, Langham etc *Nor* 97–03; NSM Stiffkey and Bale 03–04; C Lowestoft St Marg 04–06; V E Marshland *Ely* 06–10; rtd 10; PtO *Ely* 10–16 and from 18; Hon C Blanchland w Hunstanworth and Edmundbyers etc *Newc* 16–18. *Hibiscus, 33 Church Drove, Outwell, Wisbech PE14 8RH* E: dep451@btinternet.com

PENNY, Edwin John. b 43. Leeds Univ BA 64. Coll of Resurr Mirfield 64. d 66 p 67. C Acocks Green *Birm* 66–69; C Wombourne *Lich* 69–71; C Wednesbury St Paul Wood Green 71–74; V Kingshurst *Birm* 74–79; Chapl All Hallows Convent Norfolk 79–82; Hon Chapl Overgate Hospice Yorkshire 82–84; Hon C Raveningham *Nor* 84–90; All Hallows Hosp Nor Past Team 90–93; P-in-c Upton St Leonards *Glouc* 93–97; Dioc Communications Officer 93–97; P-in-c Stiffkey and Cockthorpe w Morston, Langham etc *Nor* 97–03; P-in-c Gunthorpe w Bale w Field Dalling, Saxlingham etc 99–03; R Stiffkey and Bale 03–04; rtd 04; PtO *Nor* from 04; *Ely* 08–16 and from 18; RD Wisbech Lynn Marshland 09–11; PtO *Dur* from 17. *Hibiscus, 33 Church Drove, Outwell, Wisbech PE14 8RH* E: noakhillpupil@dialstart.net

PENNY, Michael John. b 36. Linc Th Coll 78. d 80 p 81. C Knighton St Mary Magd *Leic* 80–83; TV Leic Resurr 83–85; V Blackfordby 85–95; V Blackfordby and Woodville 95–00; RD Akeley W 88–93; rtd 00; PtO *Nor* from 00. *15 Sarah's Road, Hunstanton PE36 5PA* T: (01485) 534957

PENNY, Stuart. See PENNY, Alexander Stuart Egerton

PENNYSTAN, Richard Luke. b 74. Newc Univ BA 97 St Jo Coll Cam BA 02. Ridley Hall Cam 00. d 03 p 04. C E Twickenham St Steph *Lon* 03–06; C Fulham Ch Ch 06–11; V Romiley *Ches* from 11. *18 Chadkirk Road, Romiley, Stockport SK6 3JY* T: 0161-285 7748 M: 07971-663129 E: vicar@stchadsromiley.co.uk

PENRITH, Suffragan Bishop of. See INESON, The Rt Revd Emma Gwynneth

PENTELOW, Mrs Ysmena Rachael. b 73. St Andr Univ BD 96 MLitt 99. EAMTC 01. d 03 p 04. C Stevenage H Trin *St Alb* 03–06; P-in-c Langleybury St Paul 06–13; V 13–16; Dioc CME Officer 06–16; V Ware St Mary from 16. *The Vicarage, 31 Thunder Court, Ware SG12 0PT* T: (01920) 464817 M: 07798-654194 E: vicar@stmarysware.co.uk

PENTLAND, The Ven Raymond Jackson. b 57. Wm Booth Memorial Coll CertEd 79 Open Univ BA 90 Westmr Coll Ox MTh 02. St Jo Coll Nottm 86. d 88 p 89. C Nottingham St Jude *S'well* 88–90; Chapl RAF 90–05; Command Chapl RAF 05–06; Adn RAF 06–14; Chapl-in-Chief RAF 09–14; QHC 06–14; Can and Preb Linc Cathl 06–14; rtd 14; PtO *Ox* 14–19; *Lon* 14–19; NSM Walton H Trin *Ox* from 19. *16 Nicholas Charles Crescent, Aylesbury HP18 0GU* E: ray.pentland@htaylesbury.org

PEOPLES, Mervyn Thomas Edwards. b 53. Open Univ BA 88. CITC 03. d 06 p 07. NSM Raphoe w Raymochy and Clonleigh *D & R* 06–09; NSM Clooney w Strathfoyle from 09. *29 Dunnalong Road, Magheramason, Londonderry BT47 2RU* T: (028) 7184 1416 E: mervynpeoples@hotmail.com

PEPPER, David Reginald. b 50. Lon Bible Coll. St Alb Minl Tr Scheme 89. d 92 p 93. NSM Cheshunt *St Alb* 92–95; NSM Bengeo 06–08; NSM Hertford from 08. *Bramley Cottage, 414 Ware Road, Hertford SG13 7EW* E: davidpepper2@yahoo.co.uk

PEPPER, Leonard Edwin. b 44. Ex Univ BA 71. Ripon Hall Ox 71. d 73 p 74. C Cottingham *York* 73–76; C Kingshurst *Birm* 76–79; Dir Past Studies St Steph Ho Ox 80–89; TV Aylesbury *Ox* 89–91; TV High Wycombe 91–96; rtd 96. *19 Gardiner Street, Oxford OX3 7AW* T: (01865) 66191

PEPPIATT, Martin Guy. b 33. Trin Coll Ox BA 57 MA 60. Wycliffe Hall Ox 57. d 59 p 60. C St Marylebone All So w SS Pet and Jo *Lon* 59–63; Kenya 65–69; V E Twickenham St Steph *Lon* 69–96; rtd 96; PtO *Ox* from 06. *Pipers Cottage, East End, North Leigh, Witney OX29 8ND* T: (01993) 883001 E: mcpeppiatt@hotmail.com

PERCIVAL, Darren James. b 70. Yorks Min Course 09. d 12 p 13. NSM Dodworth *Wakef* 12–14; *Leeds* 14–16; C W Barnsley 16–17; P-in-c Hunslet w Cross Green 17–18; P-in-c Cross Green from 18. *8 High Keep Fold, Hall Green, Wakefield WF4 3QL* T: (01924) 253045 M: 07960-555609 E: percivalfamily1@gmail.com

PERCIVAL, James Frederick. b 74. New Coll Ox BA 96 MA 01 Barrister-at-Law (Middle Temple) 99. Ripon Coll Cuddesdon MA 02. d 03 p 04. C Redhill St Matt *S'wark* 03–06; TV Sanderstead 06–13; TR Limpsfield and Tatsfield from 13. *The Rectory, High Street, Limpsfield, Oxted RH8 0DG* T: (01883) 722351 E: james.percival7@gmail.com

PERCIVAL, Joanna Vera. b 52. Univ of San Francisco BA 87. Ch Div Sch of Pacific MDiv 94. d 94 p 94. Asst R Almaden USA 94–95; NSM Ockham w Hatchford *Guildf* 95–96; C Cobham 96–00; Dioc Spirituality Adv 00–02; V Weston 02–06; PtO *Lon* 06–07; *S'wark* 06–07; *S & B* 07–08; Chapl Univ Hosp Southn NHS Foundn Trust 08–16; Chapl R Surrey Co Hosp NHS Foundn Trust 16–18; rtd 18; PtO *Sarum* from 19. *74 Hamilton Road, Salisbury SP1 3TQ* E: joanna.percival@btinternet.com

PERCIVAL, John Harry. b 83. Pemb Coll Cam MA 08. Wycliffe Hall Ox BA 10 Oak Hill Th Coll MA 12. d 12 p 13. C Eastbourne All So *Chich* 12–16; PtO *Ely* from 16. *58 Montague Road, Cambridge CB4 1BX* M: 07818-028494 E: john.percival@cantab.net

PERCIVAL, Mrs Kathryn Janet. b 74. St Hilda's Coll Ox BA 95 MA 01 ARCM 89 Barrister-at-Law (Lincoln's Inn) 98. Ripon Coll Cuddesdon 08. d 10 p 11. C Purley St Mark and Purley St Swithun *S'wark* 10–13; P-in-c Lingfield and Crowhurst 13–15; C Dormansland 13–15; V Lingfield and Dormansland from 15; AD Tandridge from 16. *The Rectory, High Street, Limpsfield, Oxted RH8 0DG* T: (01883) 724501 M: 07985-272437 E: lingfieldppchurch@btinternet.com *or* kathrynpercival@btinternet.com

PERCIVAL, Martin Eric. b 45. Lon Univ BSc 66 Linacre Coll Ox BA 70 MA 74. Wycliffe Hall Ox 67. d 70 p 71. C Anfield St Marg *Liv* 70–73; C Witney *Ox* 73–74; TV Bottesford w Ashby *Linc* 74–76; TV Grantham 76–80; R Coningsby w Tattershall 80–82; P-in-c Coleford w Holcombe *B & W* 82–83; V 83–84; Chapl Rossall Sch Fleetwood 84–88; Chapl Woodbridge Sch 88–02; R Downham w S Hanningfield *Chelmsf* 02–05; P-in-c Ramsden Crays w Ramsden Bellhouse 02–05; P-in-c Leiston *St E* 05–13; rtd 13; PtO *St E* 13–18; P-in-c Upper Alde from 18. *18 Culcutt Close, Yoxford, Saxmundham IP17 3GZ* T: (01728) 668537 E: revmepercival@gmail.com

PERCIVAL, Patricia Anne. b 52. SEITE 03. d 06 p 07. NSM Footscray w N Cray *Roch* 06–10; NSM Blendon from 10. *31 Collindale Avenue, Sidcup DA15 9DN* T: (020) 8302 9754 E: mppercival@gmail.com

PERCY, Brian. b 34. d 93 p 94. OLM Walton *St E* 93–00; OLM Walton and Trimley 00–04; rtd 04; PtO *St E* from 04. *16 Lynwood Avenue, Felixstowe IP11 9HS* T: (01394) 286782

PERCY, Christopher. See HEBER PERCY, Christopher John

PERCY, Canon Emma Margaret. b 63. Jes Coll Cam BA 85 MA 89 St Jo Coll Dur BA 89 Nottm Univ PhD 12. Cranmer Hall Dur 87. d 90 p 94. C Bedford St Andr *St Alb* 90–94; Chapl Anglia Poly Univ *Ely* 94–97; P-in-c Millhouses H Trin *Sheff* 97–03; V 03–04; Chapl Trin Coll Ox from 05; Hon Can Ch Ch *Ox* from 17. *The Deanery, Christ Church, St Aldates, Oxford OX1 1DP* T: (01865) 276162 E: emma.percy@trinity.ox.ac.uk

PERCY, Gordon Reid. b 46. St Jo Coll Dur BA 68. Cranmer Hall Dur 69. d 71 p 72. C Flixton St Jo *Man* 71–76; C Charlesworth *Derby* 76–77; P-in-c 77–87; P-in-c Dinting Vale 80–87; V Long Eaton St Jo 87–98; RD Ilkeston 92–98; R Torquay St Matthias, St Mark and H Trin *Ex* 98–12; rtd 12; PtO *Ex* from 13. *13 Wembury Drive, Torquay TQ2 8DT* E: gordonpercy@minister.com

PERCY, The Very Revd Prof Martyn William. b 62. Bris Univ BA 84 K Coll Lon PhD 92 Sheff Univ MEd. Cranmer Hall Dur 88. d 90 p 91. C Bedford St Andr *St Alb* 90–94; Chapl and Dir Th and RS Ch Coll Cam 94–97; Dir Th and RS SS Coll Cam 95–97; Dir Linc Th Inst Man Univ 97–04; Hon C Millhouses H Trin *Sheff* 97–04; Hon Can Sheff Cathl 97–04; Can Th Sheff Cathl 04–10; Sen Lect Relig and Soc Sheff Univ 97–00; Reader 00–02; Reader Man Univ 02–04; Prof Th and Min Hartford Sem Connecticut USA 02–07; Prin Ripon Coll Cuddesdon 04–14; Prin Ox Min Course 06–14; Dean Ch Ch *Ox* from 14; Prof Th Educn K Coll Lon from 04; Can and Preb Sarum Cathl 09–14; PtO *Ox* from 18. *The Deanery, Christ Church, St Aldates, Oxford OX1 1DP* T: (01865) 276161 E: sarah.hope@chch.ox.ac.uk

PERCY, Mrs Pauline. b 62. Sheff City Poly BSc 84 Sheff Univ BA 14. Yorks Min Course 11. d 14 p 15. NSM Crathorne *York* 14–18; NSM Kirklevington w Picton, and High and Low Worsall 14–18; NSM Rudby in Cleveland w Middleton 14–18; NSM Sowerby from 18; NSM Sessay from 18; NSM Thirkleby w Kilburn and Bagby from 18; Chapl Qu Mary's Sch Baldersby Park from 19. *The Vicarage, Kilburn, York YO61 4AH* E: non.pauline.percy@gmail.com

PEREIRA, Alwyn Antonio Basilio. b 63. Trin Coll Bris. d 11 p 12. C Sea Mills *Bris* 11–15; NSM Abbots Leigh w Leigh Woods 17; V Aldershot St Mich *Guildf* from 18. *The Vicarage,*

120 Church Lane East, Aldershot GU11 3SS M: 07767-702094
E: alwynper@googlemail.com

PEREIRA, Melvyn Christopher. b 52. Oak Hill Th Coll BA 04. **d** 04 **p** 05. C Kettering Ch the King *Pet* 04–07; Min Gleneagles CD 07–13; V Gleneagles from 13; Warden of Par Ev 10–18. *20 Ribble Close, Wellingborough NN8 5XJ* T: (01933) 673437 M: 07810-816744 E: melvyn.pereira@gleneagleschurch.co.uk

PERERA, Ms Chandrika Kumudhini. b 61. Qu Coll Birm. **d** 03 **p** 04. C Luton All SS w St Pet *St Alb* 03–07; TV Hemel Hempstead 07–14; V Stevenage St Hugh and St Jo from 14. *St Hugh's House, 4 Mobbsbury Way, Stevenage SG2 0HL* T: (01438) 727577 E: chandy.perera@btinternet.com

PERERA, George Anthony. b 51. Edin Univ BD 74. Linc Th Coll 74. **d** 76 **p** 77. Chapl Mabel Fletcher Tech Coll Liv 76–79; C Wavertree H Trin *Liv* 76–79; TV Maghull 79–94; V Hunts Cross 94–04; Chapl Park Lane Hosp Maghull 79–89; Asst Chapl Ashworth Hosp Maghull 89–04; Chapl R Liverpool and Broadgreen Univ Hosps NHS Trust from 05; CF (TA) 06–11; CF (ACF) from 12. *Broadgreen Hospital, Thomas Drive, Liverpool L14 3LB* T: 0151-425 4001 M: 07803-129501 E: padre.yacf@gmail.com

PERKIN, Canon Jonathan Guy. b 52. Westmr Coll Ox BEd 76. Trin Coll Bris 89. **d** 91 **p** 92. C Cullompton *Ex* 91–96; C Ashtead *Guildf* 96–01; V Egham 01–05; V Churchdown *Glouc* from 05; Hon Can Glouc Cathl from 17. *The Vicarage, 5 Vicarage Close, Churchdown, Gloucester GL3 2NE* T: (01452) 712154 or 548437 E: jjperkin@btconnect.com or vicar@standrewschurchdown.org.uk

PERKIN, Paul John Stanley. b 50. Ch Ch Ox BA 71 MA 75 CertEd. Wycliffe Hall Ox 78. **d** 80 **p** 81. C Gillingham St Mark *Roch* 80–84; C Brompton H Trin w Onslow Square St Paul *Lon* 84–87; P-in-c Battersea Rise St Mark *S'wark* 87–92; V from 92; P-in-c Battersea St Pet and St Paul 00–12. *St Mark's Vicarage, 7 Elsynge Road, London SW18 2HW* T: (020) 8874 6023 *or* 7223 6188 E: mark.mail@ukonline.co.uk *or* paul.perkin@smbr.org.uk

PERKINS, Barnaby Charles Rudolf. b 80. Peterho Cam BA 08 MPhil 10. Ridley Hall Cam 06. **d** 10 **p** 11. C Guildf St Nic 10–13; R E and W Clandon from 13. *The Rectory, The Street, West Clandon, Guildford GU4 7RG* T: (01483) 222573 E: barnaby.perkins@cantab.net

PERKINS, Colin Blackmore. b 35. FCII 65. Lon Coll of Div 68. **d** 70 **p** 71. C Hyson Green *S'well* 70–73; V Clarborough w Hayton 73–79; P-in-c Cropwell Bishop 79–84; P-in-c Colston Bassett 79–84; P-in-c Granby w Elton 79–84; P-in-c Langar 79–84; V Tithby w Cropwell Butler 79–84; R Cropwell Bishop w Colston Bassett, Granby etc 84–94; P-in-c Sutton Bonington w Normanton-on-Soar 94–01; rtd 01; PtO *Newc* from 01. *6 Ravensmede, Alnwick NE66 2PX* T: (01665) 510445 E: cperk68836@aol.com

PERKINS, Canon David. b 51. Sarum & Wells Th Coll. **d** 87 **p** 88. C New Mills *Derby* 87–90; V Marlpool 90–95; P-in-c Turnditch 95–02; Min in charge Belper Ch Ch and Milford 95–02; V Belper Ch Ch w Turnditch 02–09; Jt P-in-c Ambergate and Heage 06–09; RD Duffield 97–09; Chapl Derbyshire Mental Health Services NHS Trust 95–09; Can Res Derby Cathl 09–13; rtd 13; P-in-c Beeley and Edensor *Derby* 13–15; V from 15. *The Vicarage, Edensor, Bakewell DE45 1PH* T: (01246) 386385 E: revdaveperkins@aol.com

PERKINS, David John Elmslie. b 45. Dur Univ BA 66 ATII 75. Cranmer Hall Dur 66. **d** 69 **p** 70. C Wadsley *Sheff* 69–71; C Shortlands *Roch* 71–73; PtO *Lon* 76–78; *B & W* 78–80 and from 02; LtO 80–02; rtd 02. *Rainbow's End, Montacute Road, Stoke-sub-Hamdon TA14 6UQ* T: (01935) 823314 M: 07840-598220 E: perkinsdavid@talktalk.net

PERKINS, John Everard. b 47. SEITE 04. **d** 06 **p** 07. NSM Speldhurst w Groombridge and Ashurst *Roch* 06–10; NSM Tonbridge St Steph 10–18; rtd 18; PtO *Roch* from 18. *25 Northfields, Speldhurst, Tunbridge Wells TN3 0PN* T: (01892) 863239 E: revjohnp@outlook.com

PERKINS, Miss Julia Margaret. b 49. Linc Th Coll 85. **d** 87 **p** 94. Par Dn Owton Manor *Dur* 87–89; Par Dn Leam Lane 89–94; C 94; C Stockton St Chad 94–96; V 96–00; C Eppleton and Hetton le Hole 00–06; C Heworth St Mary 06–11; rtd 11; PtO *Pet* from 14. *12 Portman Close, Peterborough PE3 9RJ* T: (01733) 262240

PERKINS, Julian John. b 67. Southn Univ BSc 90 MSc 92. Trin Coll Bris BA 00 MPhil 03. **d** 01 **p** 02. C Thornbury *Glouc* 01–02; C Thornbury and Oldbury-on-Severn w Shepperdine 02–04; C Tewkesbury w Walton Cardiff and Twyning 04–07; P-in-c Crosland Moor *Wakef* 07–08; P-in-c Linthwaite 07–08; V Crosland Moor and Linthwaite 08–10; Chapl Sheff Teaching Hosps NHS Foundn Trust 11–17; Chapl Waikato Hosp New Zealand from 17. *47 Edgeview Crescent, Fitzroy, Hamilton 3206, New Zealand* M: (0064)

204-124 6555 E: julianjperkins@gmail.com *or* julianperkins@rocketmail.com

PERKINS, Kenneth Ronald. b 57. **d** 16 **p** 17. NSM Gidea Park *Chelmsf* 16–19; NSM Cranham Park from 19. *7 Laburnham Gardens, Upminster RM14 1HU* E: kenperkins28@gmail.com

PERKINS, Patricia Doris (Sister Patricia). b 29. Gilmore Ho 60. **dss** 73 **d** 87. CSA from 71; Sherston Magna w Easton Grey *Bris* 73–75; Cant St Martin and St Paul 76–78; Kilburn St Aug w St Jo *Lon* 80–84; Abbey Ho Malmesbury 84–87; Hon Par Dn Bayswater *Lon* 87–94; Chapl St Mary's Hosp Praed Street Lon 88–89; Chapl St Chas Hosp Ladbroke Grove 88–89; Dean of Women's Min *Lon* from 89; Dioc Dir of Ords 90–94; Hon Par Dn St Olave Hart Street w All Hallows Staining etc 94–01. *St Mary's Convent and Nursing Home, Burlington Lane, London W4 2QF*

PERKINTON, Keith Glyn. b 61. Humberside Poly BA 83 Leeds Univ BA 92. Coll of Resurr Mirfield 93. **d** 93 **p** 94. C Knowle H Nativity *Bris* 93–97; TV Brighton Resurr *Chich* 97–05; P-in-c Hangleton 05–07; V from 07; RD Hove 10. *The Vicarage, 127 Hangleton Way, Hove BN3 8ER* T: (01273) 413044

PERKS, David Leonard Irving. b 38. Avery Hill Coll TCert 61 Sussex Univ MA 76. S Dios Minl Tr Scheme 84. **d** 87 **p** 88. NSM Lewes All SS, St Anne, St Mich and St Thos *Chich* 87–91; Chapl HM Pris Lewes 91–94; NSM Deanery of Lewes and Seaford *Chich* 94–96; C Peacehaven and Telscombe Cliffs 96–00; rtd 00; Hon C Lewes and Seaford *Chich* from 00; Asst to RD S Downs Health NHS Trust from 01; PtO *Eur* from 05. *45 Fitzjohns Road, Lewes BN7 1PR* T: (01273) 478719 E: danddperks@btopenworld.com

PERREAU, Mrs Deborah. b 57. **d** 16 **p** 17. NSM Ilminster and Whitelackington *B & W* from 16. *Croft House, Combe St Nicholas, Chard TA20 3NA* T: (01460) 67168 E: deborah@perreau.co

PERRETT, David Thomas. b 48. Cranmer Hall Dur 80. **d** 82 **p** 83. C Stapleford *S'well* 82–86; V Ollerton 86–87; P-in-c Boughton 86–87; V Ollerton w Boughton 87–93; V Winklebury *Win* 93–05; P-in-c Gresley *Derby* 05–10; V 10–13; RD Repton 11–13; rtd 13; PtO *Pet* from 14. *14 Dunbar Court, Kettering NN15 5DN* T: (01536) 659065 E: davdotp2405@sky.com

PERRETT (formerly ROWE), Canon Vanda Sheila. b 63. STETS 95. **d** 98 **p** 99. C Marlborough *Sarum* 98–01; TV Pewsey and Swanborough 01–06; TR Bourne Valley 06–14; C Salisbury St Fran and Stratford sub Castle 09–14; RD Alderbury 06–14; Can and Preb Sarum Cathl 12–14; P-in-c St Buryan, St Levan and Sennen *Truro* 14–15; R from 15; RD Penwith 17–19. *The Rectory, Rectory Road, St Buryan, Penzance TR19 6BB* T: (01736) 810216 E: canonvanda@gmail.com

PERRICONE, Vincent James. b 50. Connecticut Univ BA 74 Pontifical Univ Rome STB 88 STL 90 Glas Univ PhD 98. **d** 90 **p** 90. In RC Ch 89–94; C Glas St Mary 94–95; P-in-c Glas All SS and Glas H Cross 95–03; USA 03–04; PtO *Eur* 04–08; Asst Chapl Florence w Siena 08–09; LtO *Ab* from 10; C Kincardine O'Neil 10–12; Chapl Grampian Univ Hosp NHS Trust 10–12; P-in-c Devizes St Pet *Sarum* 14–15; V 15–16; Chapl Hants Hosps NHS Foundn Trust from 16. *Basingstoke and North Hampshire Hospital, Aldermaston Road, Basingstoke RG24 9NA* T: (01256) 473202 M: 07733-740372 E: vjperricone@googlemail.com

PERRIN, Andrew. **d** 12 **p** 13. C Morriston *S & B* 12–14; C Upper Ithon Valley 14–15; P-in-c 16–17; C Lower Ithon Valley 14–15; P-in-c 16–17; P-in-c Ithon Valley 17; R Glan Ithon from 17. *7 Rock House Court, Llandrindod Wells LD1 6AX* T: (01597) 829356 E: revperrin@btinternet.com

PERRIN, Bruce Alexander. b 72. Birm Univ BSc 94 MSc 96. St Jo Coll Nottm 08. **d** 09 **p** 10. C Marple All SS *Ches* 09–12; V Hollingworth w Tintwistle from 15. *6 Taylor Street, Hollingworth, Hyde SK14 8PB* M: 07914-211376 E: rev.bruce.perrin@gmail.com

PERRINS, Christopher Neville. b 68. St Steph Ho Ox 01. **d** 03 **p** 04. C Warrington St Elphin *Liv* 03–08; TV Walton-on-the-Hill 08–12; C Rainhill 12–15; PtO from 17. *1 Wesley Place, Liverpool L15 8JB* T: 0151-733 7930 E: revdcnperrins@btinternet.com

PERRIS, Preb Anthony. b 48. Univ of Wales (Abth) BSc 69 Selw Coll Cam BA 76 MA 79. Ridley Hall Cam 74. **d** 77 **p** 78. C Sandal St Helen *Wakef* 77–80; C Plymouth St Andr w St Paul and St Geo *Ex* 80–87; TV Yeovil *B & W* 87–88; V Preston Plucknett 88–16; RD Yeovil 06–16; Preb Wells Cathl 11–16; rtd 16; PtO *Ox* from 19. *Meadow Cottage, Meadow Lane, Shipton-under-Wychwood, Chipping Norton OX7 6BW* E: antonyperris@yahoo.com

PERRIS, Mrs Jocelyn Clare. b 69. Surrey Univ BSc 91. ERMC 08. **d** 11 **p** 12. C St Alb St Pet 11–17; Chapl Aldenham Sch Herts from 17. *Aldenham School, Aldenham*

Road, Elstree, Borehamwood WD6 3AJ M: 07979-590480 E: josperris@aol.com

PERRIS, John Martin. b 44. Liv Univ BSc 66. Trin Coll Bris 69. **d** 72 **p** 73. C Sevenoaks St Nic *Roch* 72–76; C Bebington *Ches* 76–79; V Redland *Bris* 79–97; RD Horfield 91–97; R Barton Seagrave w Warkton *Pet* 97–09; rtd 09; PtO *Carl* from 11. *3 Old Myse, Storth, Milnthorpe LA7 7HQ* T: (01539) 564446 E: martin.perris@hotmail.co.uk

PERRY, Alan David. b 64. Greenwich Univ BA 86 Lon Inst of Educn PGCE 87 Greenwich Univ MA 99. NTMTC 01. **d** 03 **p** 04. NSM Romford St Edw *Chelmsf* 03–08; Hd Teacher St Edw C of E Sch Havering 08–16; Public Preacher *Chelmsf* 08–16; TV Sole Bay *St E* from 16. *The Vicarage, 45A Wangford Road, Reydon, Southwold IP18 6PZ* T: (01502) 453624 M: 07946-730291 E: adperry64@gmail.com

PERRY, Andrew John. b 65. St Steph Ho Ox BTh 00. **d** 00 **p** 01. C Southwick St Mich *Chich* 00–03; P-in-c Upper St Leonards St Jo 03; R 03–13; P-in-c Portslade St Nic and St Andr and Mile Oak 13–16; V 16–17; V E Preston w Kingston from 17. *The Vicarage, 33 Vicarage Lane, East Preston, Littlehampton BN16 2SP* T: (01903) 783318 M: 07900-981345 E: revajperry@btinternet.com

PERRY, Canon Andrew Nicholas. b 62. Westmr Coll Ox BA 86. Trin Coll Bris MA 91. **d** 91 **p** 92. C Bath Weston All SS w N Stoke *B & W* 91–93; C Bath Weston All SS w N Stoke and Langridge 93–95; P-in-c Longfleet *Sarum* 95–00; V from 00; Can and Preb Sarum Cathl from 12. *The Vicarage, 2 Twemlow Avenue, Poole BH14 8AN* T: (01202) 253527 *or* 338720 F: 253527 E: andrew@smlpoole.org.uk

PERRY, Andrew William. b 44. MRAC 65. WMMTC 91. **d** 94 **p** 95. NSM Redmarley D'Abitot, Bromesberrow, Pauntley etc *Glouc* 94–14; PtO *Heref* 05–12; rtd 14; PtO *Glouc* from 14; *Heref* from 17. *Rye Cottage, Broomsgreen, Dymock GL18 2DP* T: (01531) 890489 E: aperry9381@aol.com

PERRY, Anthony Henry. b 54. Leic Univ BA 76. Aston Tr Scheme 89 Linc Th Coll 93. **d** 93 **p** 94. C Bartley Green *Birm* 93–97; V Bearwood from 97; AD Warley 06–13. *St Mary's Vicarage, 27 Poplar Avenue, Birmingham B17 8EG* T: 0121-429 2165 E: trinity20@hotmail.co.uk

PERRY, David. b 62. Newman Coll Birm BEd 86. Sarum Coll 15. **d** 18 **p** 19. NSM Clarendon *Sarum* from 18. *11 St Lawrence Close, Stratford sub Castle, Salisbury SP1 3LW* T: (01722) 328342 M: 07749-199453 E: bumbledp@gmail.com

PERRY, Edward John. b 35. AKC 62. **d** 63 **p** 64. C Honicknowle *Ex* 63–65; C Ashburton w Buckland-in-the-Moor 65–70; V Cornwood 70–92; Asst Dir of Educn 71–92; Chapl Moorhaven Hosp 81–92; V Ermington and Ugborough *Ex* 92–00; rtd 00; PtO *Ex* from 01. *32 Finches Close, Elburton, Plymouth PL9 8DP* T: (01752) 405364 E: perry.retvie@blueyonder.co.uk

PERRY, James Marcus. b 71. Ridley Hall Cam 02. **d** 04 **p** 05. C Cen Wolverhampton *Lich* 04–07; TV Tettenhall Regis 07–19; V Sydenham St Bart *S'wark* from 19. *The Vicarage, 4 Westwood Hill, London SE26 6QR* T: (020) 8776 5722 E: revjimperry@gmail.com

✠**PERRY, The Rt Revd John Freeman.** b 35. Lon Coll of Div MPhil 86 ALCD 59. **d** 59 **p** 60 **c** 89. C Woking Ch Ch *Guildf* 59–62; C Chorleywood Ch Ch *St Alb* 62; Min Chorleywood St Andr 63–66; V 66–77; RD Rickmansworth 72–77; Warden Lee Abbey 77–89; RD Shirwell *Ex* 80–84; Hon Can Win Cathl 89–96; Suff Bp Southampton 89–96; Bp Chelmsf 96–03; rtd 03; Hon Asst Bp B & W from 11; PtO from 19. *The Firs, Bath BA2 5ED* T: (01225) 833987 E: jperry8@btinternet.com

PERRY, John Walton Beauchamp. b 43. Ex Coll Ox BA 64 Sussex Univ MA 67. EAMTC 82 Westcott Ho Cam 84. **d** 85 **p** 86. C Shrewsbury St Chad w St Mary *Lich* 85–89; V Batheaston w St Cath *B & W* 89–99; V Milborne Port w Goathill 99–07; P-in-c Charlton Horethorne w Stowell 06–07; V Milborne Port w Goathill etc 07–09; rtd 09; PtO *Heref* from 10. *67 Steventon New Road, Ludlow SY8 1JY* T: (01584) 873755 E: jwbperry@gmail.com

PERRY, Lesley Anne. b 52. K Coll Lon BA 73 MIPR 99. SEITE 96. **d** 99 **p** 00. NSM Fulham All SS *Lon* 99–07; NSM Kensington St Mary Abbots w Ch Ch and St Phil 07–16; NSM Earl's Court Road St Phil from 17. *39A Gunter Grove, London SW10 0UN* T: (020) 7938 1357 E: lesley.perry@specr.org

PERRY, Canon Lynne Janice. b 48. **d** 90 **p** 97. NSM Llanfair Mathafarn Eithaf w Llanbedrgoch *Ban* 90–97; C Bangor 97–99; TV 99–05; V Tregarth 04–05; V Tregarth and Llandygai and Maes y Groes 05–09; AD Ogwen 02–07; C Ogwen Deanery 09–10; Hon Chapl Ban Cathl 10–12; Hon Can 11–12; rtd 12; PtO *B & W* from 15. *32 Adams Road, Highbridge TA9 3DX* M: 07817-518337 E: lynne.pcc@btinternet.com

PERRY, Mark Colin. b 71. K Alfred's Coll Win BA 97 Homerton Coll Cam PGCE FRSA 14 FCollT 15 FCMI 15. Regent's Park Coll Ox 02 Ripon Coll Cuddesdon 09. **d** 10 **p** 11. In Bapt Min

05–09; C Bourne Valley *Sarum* 10–11; C Iwerne Valley 11–13; Asst Chapl Shaftesbury Sch 11–13; Res Chapl Port Regis Sch 13–15; CF (ACF) 12–15; Chapl RAF from 15; P Assoc Shrine of Our Lady of Walsingham from 11; Hon Chapl Sarum Cathl 13–17; Bp's Ecum Officer (Dorset) 13–15; Hon Chapl Cottesmore Sch Crawley from 15. *Chaplaincy Services (RAF), HQ Air Command, RAF High Wycombe HP14 4UE* T: (01494) 496800 E: mark.perry725@mod.gov.uk

PERRY, Michael James Matthew. b 66. Bris Univ BSc 87 MSc 89 PhD 93. Trin Coll Bris BA 99. **d** 99 **p** 00. C Keynsham *B & W* 99–03; R Cam Vale 03–13; V Woodford Valley w Archers Gate *Sarum* from 13. *The Vicarage, Middle Woodford, Salisbury SP4 6NR* T: (01722) 782310 E: mikepqc@gmail.com

PERRY, Michael Leonard. b 47. Univ of W Ontario BA 68 Wilfred Laurier Univ MA 90 Ottawa Univ PhD 00. Huron Coll Ontario MDiv 82. **d** 82 **p** 83. C London St Steph Canada 82–83; R Tyrconnell 83–84; R Dorchester 84–88; R Point Edward 90–93; P-in-c Quebec 93–95; R Ottawa All SS 95–97; P-in-c Hull St Jas 97–00; R Capreol and Garson 01–04; P-in-c Menton *Eur* 09. *701-99 Holland Avenue, Ottawa ON K1Y 0Y1, Canada* E: michaelperry47@gmail.com

PERRY, Nicholas Charles. **d** 07 **p** 08. NSM Ebbw Vale *Mon* 07–10; R Blaina and Nantyglo 10–13; TR Upper Ebbw Valleys 13–18; V Cwmbran from 18. *The Rectory, Clomendy Road, Cwmbran NP44 3LS* E: nick.perry1@btinternet.com

PERRY, Timothy Richard. b 64. Ox Brookes Univ LLM 17. Trin Coll Bris BA 93. **d** 93 **p** 95. C Abingdon *Ox* 93–97; New Life Outreach/Fit Lives 97–01; Mountaintop Life Coaching Canada 01–09; Chapl Cothill Ho Sch 10–17; Chapl Cothill Trust 11–17; Hon C Wootton and Dry Sandford *Ox* 11–17; V Dry Sandford 17; Chapl Cothill Ho Sch from 19; PtO *Ox* from 19. *29 St Peter's Road, Abingdon OX14 3SJ* E: perry.tim@sky.com

PERRY, Valerie Evelyn. b 39. Southn Univ CertEd 59. S'wark Ord Course 82. **dss** 85 **d** 87 **p** 94. NSM Romford St Edw *Chelmsf* 85–89; Par Dn 89–91; Asst Chapl Middx Hosp Lon 92–93; Asst Chapl Univ Coll Lon Hosps NHS Trust 94; Chapl S Kent Hosps NHS Trust 94–98; Hon C Aylesham w Adisham *Cant* 98–00; Hon C Nonington w Wymynswold and Goodnestone etc 98–00; rtd 99; PtO *Truro* from 01. *115 Century Close, St Austell PL25 3UZ* T: (01726) 68075 E: vep10@hotmail.com

PERRY, Canon William Francis Pitfield. b 61. Keble Coll Ox BA 84 MA 87. Ripon Coll Cuddesdon 94. **d** 96 **p** 97. C Brockworth *Glouc* 96–01; P-in-c Millbrook *Win* 01–18; V Hawley H Trin *Guildf* from 18; V Minley from 18; Can Ruvuma Tanzania from 14. *Hawley Vicarage, Fernhill Road, Blackwater, Camberley GU17 9BN* E: fr.will@icxc.org

PERRYMAN, Preb David Francis. b 42. Brunel Univ BSc 64. Oak Hill Th Coll 74. **d** 76 **p** 77. C Margate H Trin *Cant* 76–80; R Ardingly *Chich* 80–90; V Bath St Luke *B & W* 90–07; RD Bath 96–03; Preb Wells Cathl 01–07; rtd 07; PtO *Win* from 08. *Treetops, Upper Froyle, Alton GU34 4JH* T: (01420) 520647 E: david.perrypeople@gmail.com

PERRYMAN, Graham Frederick. b 56. Southn Univ BA 78 Reading Univ PGCE 80. Aston Tr Scheme 90 Trin Coll Bris 92. **d** 94 **p** 95. C Hamworthy *Sarum* 94–98; P-in-c Moreton and Woodsford w Tincleton 98–02; R 02–04; TV Melbury 04–06; TV Sherborne 12–14; P-in-c Upper Stour 15–19; rtd 19. *42 Combe Park, Yeovil BA21 3BD* E: revgfp@btopenworld.com

PERRYMAN, James Edward. b 56. Lon Bible Coll BA 85. Oak Hill Th Coll 86. **d** 88 **p** 89. C Gidea Park *Chelmsf* 88–91; C Becontree St Mary 91–94; Chapl Lyon *Eur* 94–00; R Allington and Maidstone St Pet *Cant* 00–08; Dioc Ecum Officer 02–08; P-in-c Leek Wootton *Cov* from 08; P-in-c Stoneleigh w Ashow 08–13; PtO *Eur* from 16. *The Vicarage, 4 Hill Wootton Road, Leek Wootton, Warwick CV35 7QL* T/F: (01926) 850610 E: jim@me16.com *or* vicar@leekwoottonchurch.org.uk

PERRYMAN, Canon John Frederick Charles. b 49. Mert Coll Ox BA 71 MA 74 MInstGA 98. Ridley Hall Cam 72. **d** 74 **p** 75. C Shortlands *Roch* 74–78; Asst Chapl St Geo Hosp Lon 78–82; Chapl Withington Hosp Man 83–94; Chapl Univ Hosp of S Man NHS Foundn Trust 94–09; Hon Can Man Cathl 00–09; rtd 09; PtO *Man* from 09. *50 Maudlin Drive, Teignmouth TQ14 8SB* T: (01626) 439109 E: jd_perryman@lineone.net

PERSSON, Matthew Stephen. b 60. Dundee Univ BSc 82 Bris Univ MA 98. Wycliffe Hall Ox 88. **d** 91 **p** 92. C Bath Twerton-on-Avon *B & W* 91–94; Chapl HM Pris Shepton Mallet 94–97; PtO *B & W* 97–98; C Shepton Mallet w Doulting 98–00. *Grange Farm, Fair Place, West Lydford, Somerton TA11 7DN* T: (01963) 240024

PERTH, Provost of. *See* FARQUHARSON, The Very Revd Hunter Buchanan

✠**PERUMBALATH, The Rt Revd John.** b 66. Calicut Univ BA 86 Union Bibl Sem Pune BD 90 Osmania Univ Hyderabad MA 93

NW Univ S Africa PhD 07. Serampore Th Coll MTh 93. **d** 94 **p** 95 **c** 18. C Calcutta St Jo India 94–95; V Calcutta St Jas 95–00; V Calcutta St Thos 00–01; C Beckenham St Geo *Roch* 02–05; TV Northfleet and Rosherville 05–08; V Perry Street 08–13; Dioc CUF Link Officer 08–13; Adn Barking *Chelmsf* 13–18; Area Bp Bradwell from 18. *Bishop's House, Orsett Road, Horndon-on-the-Hill, Stanford-le-Hope SS17 8NS* T: (01375) 673806 E: b.bradwell@chelmsford.anglican.org

PESCE, Fabrizio. b 73. Universidad del Salvador Buenos Aires BA MA 03 MD 09. St Steph Ho Ox 14. **d** 02 **p** 03. In RC Ch 02–09; C Bedford Park *Lon* from 15; C Acton Green St Pet from 15. *206 St Albans Avenue, London W4 5JU* M: 07713-444382

PESCOD, John Gordon. b 44. Leeds Univ BSc 70. Qu Coll Birm. **d** 72 **p** 73. C Camberwell St Geo *S'wark* 72–75; Chapl R Philanthropic Soc Sch Redhill 75–80; P-in-c Nunney w Wanstrow and Cloford *B & W* 80–84; R Nunney and Witham Friary, Marston Bigot etc 84–87; R Milverton w Halse and Fitzhead 87–93; V Frome St Jo and St Mary 93–00; V Frome St Jo 01; V Woodlands 93–01; RD Frome 97–01; V Castle Cary w Ansford 01; rtd 09. *32 Churchfield Drive, Castle Cary BA7 7LA* E: jjpescod@tiscali.co.uk

PESKETT, Richard Howard. b 42. Selw Coll Cam BA 64 MA 67. Ridley Hall Cam 64. **d** 68 **p** 69. C Jesmond H Trin *Newc* 68–71; Lect Discipleship Tr Cen Singapore 71–76; Dean 76–86; Lect Coll of SS Paul and Mary Cheltenham 86–87; Research Dir OMF 88–91; Tutor Trin Coll Bris 91–06; Vice-Prin 98–06; Scholars Dir Langham Partnership 06–08; rtd 07; PtO *Truro* 06–08; Hon C Penzance St Mary w St Paul and St Jo 08–13; RD Penwith 08–13; PtO from 16. *7 North Parade, Penzance TR18 4SH* T: (01736) 362913 E: howard.peskett@btinternet.com

PESKETT, Canon Timothy Lewis. b 64. St Kath Coll Liv BA 86. Chich Th Coll BTh 90. **d** 90 **p** 91. C Verwood *Sarum* 90–91; C Southsea H Spirit *Portsm* 91–95; TV Burgess Hill St Jo w St Edw *Chich* 95–00; V Burgess Hill St Edw 00–05; R Felpham 05–14; R Whyke w Rumboldswhyke and Portfield from 14; Can and Preb Chich Cathl from 15. *The Rectory, 199 Whyke Road, Chichester PO19 7AQ* T: (01243) 774595 E: tpeskett@gmail.com

PESTELL, Miss Josephine Frances. b 72. Leeds Univ BSc 93 Bris Univ MPhil 17. Trin Coll Bris BA 14. **d** 16 **p** 17. C S Cheltenham *Glouc* 16–19; V Glouc St Cath from 19. *The Vicarage, 5 Kenilworth Avenue, Gloucester GL2 0QJ* T: (01452) 502673 E: jpestell@stcatharine.org.uk

PESTELL, Robert Carlyle. b 54. Aston Tr Scheme 89 Linc Th Coll 91. **d** 93 **p** 94. C Matson *Glouc* 93–97; P-in-c Charfield 97–01; R Charfield and Kingswood 02–06; P-in-c Cheltenham St Mich 06–13; P-in-c Cheltenham St Luke and St Jo 06–12; Chapl Leckhampton Court Hospice from 13. *Leckhampton Court Hospice, Church Road, Leckhampton, Cheltenham GL53 0QJ* T: (01242) 246290

PESTELL, Mrs Susan Beryl. b 56. Hull Coll of Educn CertEd 77. **d** 19. OLM The Guitings, Cutsdean, Farmcote etc *Glouc* from 19. *135 Gretton Road, Winchcombe, Cheltenham GL54 5EL* T: (01242) 609223 E: susan.pestell@gmail.com

PETCH, Canon Douglas Rodger. b 57. Nottm Univ BSc 79. St Jo Coll Nottm MA 96. **d** 94 **p** 94. C Vom Nigeria 94–95; C Pendleton *Man* 96–98; P-in-c Werneth and C Oldham St Paul 98–03; CMS Nigeria 03–07; Hon Can Jos from 05; TV Halliwell *Man* 07–11; TV W Bolton from 11; AD Bolton 10–15. *101 Cloister Street, Bolton BL1 3HA* T: (01204) 842627 M: 07837-423501 E: rodgerpetch@yahoo.co.uk

PETCH, Michelle Diane. b 68. Leeds Univ BA 89 Dur Univ BA 17. St Hild Coll 15. **d** 17 **p** 18. C Halifax H Trin and St Jude *Leeds* from 17. *27 Central Park, Halifax HX1 2BT* T: (01422) 362220 E: michelle.petch2@btinternet.com

PETER, Christopher Javed. b 51. Peshawar Univ BA 75. Qu Coll Birm 94. **d** 96 **p** 97. C Darwen St Pet w Hoddlesden *Blackb* 96–98; C Accrington 98–99; C Burnley St Andr w St Marg and St Jas 99–05; Chapl R Liverpool and Broadgreen Univ Hosps NHS Trust from 05. *Royal Liverpool University Hospital, Prescot Street, Liverpool L7 8XP* T: 0151-706 2826 E: christopher.peter@rlbuht.nhs.uk

PETER DOUGLAS, Brother. See NEEDHAM, Peter Douglas

PETERBOROUGH, Bishop of. See ALLISTER, The Rt Revd Donald Spargo

PETERBOROUGH, Dean of. See DALLISTON, The Very Revd Christopher Charles

PETERS, Ann Margaret. See PETERS-WOTHERSPOON, Ann Margaret

PETERS, Carl Richard. b 62. Ripon Coll Cuddesdon 95. **d** 97 **p** 98. C Coventry Caludon *Cov* 97–01; V Gt Grimsby St Andr w St Luke and All SS *Linc* 01–02; TV Leek and Meerbrook *Lich* 02–14; P-in-c Brandon and Ushaw Moor *Dur* from 14. *The Clergy House, Sawmills Lane, Brandon, Durham DH7 8NS* T: 0191-378 0845 E: revpeters28@gmail.com

PETERS, Miss Carole Jean. b 61. Ripon Coll Cuddesdon 07. **d** 09 **p** 10. C Ivinghoe w Pitstone and Slapton and Marsworth *Ox* 09–11; C Aston Clinton w Buckland and Drayton Beauchamp 12–13; R Astwell Gp *Pet* 13–18; Dioc Dir Communications *Sarum* from 18; LtO from 19. *Church House, Crane Street, Salisbury SP1 2QB* M: 07710-128859 E: carolepeters@aol.com

PETERS, David. b 62. Reading Univ BSc 83. Wycliffe Hall Ox 11. **d** 14 **p** 15. NSM Wonersh w Blackheath *Guildf* from 14. *Rushtons, 15 Longdown Road, Guildford GU4 8PP* T: (01483) 575906 E: david.peters@knightfrank.com

PETERS, David Alexander. b 72. K Coll Lon BA 94. St Steph Ho Ox BA 98 MA 08. **d** 99 **p** 00. C Paddington St Jas *Lon* 99–03; PV Westmr Abbey 01–13; V Reading H Trin and Reading St Mark *Ox* 03–08; Asst Chapl Tonbridge Sch 08–11; Sen Chapl from 11. *Tonbridge School, High Street, Tonbridge TN9 1JP* T: (01732) 365555 E: dap@tonbridge-school.org

PETERS, Diane Rosemary. b 48. Ox Brookes Univ BA 18 Southn Univ CertEd 70. **d** 16 **p** 17. OLM Westborough *Guildf* from 16. *10 Weston Road, Guildford GU2 8AS* T: (01483) 532796 E: dianerpeters@netscape.net

PETERS, Heather. b 63. St Aug Coll of Th 15. **d** 17 **p** 18. NSM Brixton St Paul w St Sav *S'wark* 17–18; NSM Herne Hill from 18. *53 Stambourne Way, London SE19 2PY* M: 07885-569464 E: heather-peters@hotmail.co.uk

PETERS, Mrs Helen Elizabeth. b 67. Qu Marg Coll Edin BSc 88. Ox Min Course 08. **d** 11 **p** 12. NSM Hughenden *Ox* from 11. *Boundary House, Missenden Road, Great Kingshill, High Wycombe HP15 6EB* T: (01494) 716772 E: helen.peters@peters-research.com

PETERS, Mrs Jane Elisabeth. b 48. Kent Univ BA 08. **d** 08 **p** 09. NSM Shortlands *Roch* from 08. *27 The Gardens, Beckenham BR3 5PH* T: (020) 8650 5986 E: revjane@virginmedia.com

PETERS, John Peter Thomas. b 63. Keble Coll Ox BL 85. Wycliffe Hall Ox BA 91. **d** 95 **p** 96. C Brompton H Trin w Onslow Square St Paul *Lon* 95–99; P-in-c Bryanston Square St Mary w St Marylebone St Mark 00–04; R from 04. *13 Chomeley Crescent, London N6 5EZ* T: (020) 7258 5042

PETERS, John Thomas. b 58. Connecticut Univ BA 80. St Jo Coll Nottm 84. **d** 87 **p** 88. C Virginia Water *Guildf* 87–93; R Grand Rapids Ch Ch USA 93–00; R Eden Prairie St Alb from 00. *14434 Fairway Drive, Eden Prairie MN 557344-1904, USA* E: johnpeters@isd.net

PETERS, Canon Kenneth. b 54. Newport Univ Tokyo MBA 88 Greenwich Univ MA 02 MIW 96 FNI 11. St Mich Coll Llan 74. **d** 77 **p** 78. C Mountain Ash *Llan* 77–80; Asst Chapl Mersey Miss to Seamen 80–82; Chapl Miss to Seamen Japan 82–89; Hon Can Kobe from 85; Chapl Supt Mersey Miss to Seamen 89–93; Justice and Welfare Sec 94–09; Dir Justice and Public Affairs 09–17; Tutor UN Internat Tr Cen Turin 12–17; rtd 17; PtO *Lon* from 17. *82 Old Church Lane, Stanmore HA7 2RR* T: (020) 8357 4326 M: 07767-202087 E: kenpeters54@gmail.com or ken@formin.org

PETERS, Malcolm John. b 71. Leic Univ BA 92. Oak Hill Th Coll BA 03. **d** 03 **p** 04. C Braintree *Chelmsf* 03–06; C Hull St Jo Newland *York* 06–09; P-in-c High Ongar w Norton Mandeville *Chelmsf* 09–18; PtO 18–19. *49 Kettlebury Way, Ongar CM5 9HA* E: malcolm.peters892@btinternet.com

PETERS, Preb Marilyn Ann. b 49. Open Univ BA 90. Qu Coll Birm 96. **d** 98 **p** 99. C Blakenall Heath *Lich* 98–01; TV Cen Telford 01–05; TR 05–13; Preb Lich Cathl 09–13; rtd 13; PtO *Lich* 15–16; Hon C Mease Valley 16–17; Hon C Yoxall 17–18; Hon C Kings Bromley, The Ridwares and Yoxall 18–19; PtO from 19. *40 Campion Way, Uttoxeter ST14 7TB* T: (01889) 624127 M: 07889-372275 E: marilynpeters@talktalk.net

PETERS, Canon Michael. b 41. Chich Th Coll 75. **d** 77 **p** 78. C Redruth *Truro* 77–79; TV 79–80; TV Redruth w Lanner 80–82; R St Mawgan w St Ervan and St Eval 82–86; Chapl HM Pris Liv 86–87; Chapl HM Pris Bris 87–01; Hon Can Bris Cathl 96–01; P-in-c Middlezoy and Othery and Moorlinch *B & W* 01–08; rtd 08; PtO *B & W* from 08. *Archway House, North Lane, Othery, Bridgwater TA7 0QG* T: (01823) 690208 E: archwaymike@gmail.com

PETERS, Muriel. b 50. Lindisfarne Regional Tr Partnership. **d** 16 **p** 17. NSM Haswell and Shotton *Dur* from 16. *1 Tudor Court, Shotton Colliery, Durham DH6 2RE* T: 0191-526 1671 M: 07971-577715 E: muriel-at.the.lodge@live.co.uk

PETERS, Rebecca Ann. b 76. St Hilda's Coll Ox MPhys 98 St Cross Coll Ox PGCE 99. Wycliffe Hall Ox 06. **d** 08 **p** 09. C Roxeth *Lon* 08–11; P-in-c Drayton St Pet (Abingdon) *Ox* 11–16; LtO from 16; Min Peachcroft Chr Cen LEP from 16. *14 Boxhill Road, Abingdon OX14 2EU* T: (01235) 530227 M: 07821-710285 E: rebecca.a.peters@gmail.com or minister@peachcroftcc.org

PETERS, Samuel Benjamin Stuart. b 92. St Pet Coll Ox BA 14. Westcott Ho Cam 16. **d** 18 **p** 19. C Loughton St Jo *Chelmsf*

from 18. *2 Doubleday Road, Loughton IG10 2AT* M: 07930-676260 E: revdpeters@outlook.com

PETERS-WOTHERSPOON, Ann Margaret. b 48. Lon Univ BD 84 Open Univ MA 95 UEA EdD 05 Anglia Ruskin Univ MA 09. ERMC 05. **d** 07 **p** 08. NSM Somersham w Pidley and Oldhurst and Woodhurst *Ely* 07–11; NSM Tweedmouth *Newc* 11–16; NSM Spittal 11–16; NSM Scremerston 11–16; NSM Upper Coquetdale from 16. *Burleigh House Maisonette, High Street, Rothbury, Morpeth NE65 7TB* E: ann_m_peters@hotmail.com

PETERSEN, Jennifer Elizabeth. b 55. Aus Nat Univ BA 78. Moore Th Coll Sydney BTh 82 Wycliffe Hall Ox 92. **d** 94 **p** 95. C Elloughton and Brough w Brantingham *York* 94–96; C Ealing St Mary *Lon* 96–00; Chapl Thames Valley Univ 96–00; Chapl Qu Mary Univ of Lon 00–15; PV Westmr Abbey 16–17; Min Can and Chapl from 17; PtO *Lon* 17–19. *The Chapter Office, 20 Dean's Yard, London SW1P 3PA* T: (020) 7654 4850 M: 07976-312089 E: jennifer.petersen@westminster-abbey.org

PETERSON, David Gilbert. b 44. Sydney Univ BA 65 MA 74 Lon Univ BD 68 Man Univ PhD 78. Moore Th Coll Sydney ThL 68. **d** 68 **p** 69. C Manly St Matt Australia 68–70; Lect Moore Th Coll 71–75; C Cheadle *Ches* 75–78; Sen Can and R Wollongong Cathl Australia 80–84; Lect Moore Th Coll 84–96; Prin Oak Hill Th Coll 96–07; PtO *Lon* 96–07; *St Alb* 96–07; Research Fell Moore Th Coll Australia from 07; rtd 09. *1 Vista Street, Belrose NSW 2085, Australia* E: davidandlesleypeterson@gmail.com

PETERSON, David Nwabueze Nwogbe. b 87. **d** 12 **p** 17. NSM Harlesden All So *Lon* 15–19; TV Grays Thurrock *Chelmsf* from 19. *Wendover Vicarage, College Avenue, Grays RM17 5UW* M: 07985-647897 E: david.3000@hotmail.co.uk

PETERSON, Ms Elise Michelle. b 70. San Jose State Univ BA 93 W Sem MA 12 St Jo Coll Dur MA 18. Cranmer Hall Dur 16. **d** 17 **p** 18. NSM Chigwell and Chigwell Row *Chelmsf* 17–18; C 18–19; C Vale of Roding from 19. *The Rectory, 66 High Road, Chigwell IG7 6QB* T: (020) 3648 5482 E: revelisepeterson@outlook.com

PETERSON, Paul John. b 67. Trin Coll Bris 94. **d** 97 **p** 98. C Burney Lane *Birm* 97–01; C-in-c Bradley Stoke N CD *Bris* 01–10; C Downend from 10. *15 Glendale, Bristol BS16 6EQ* T: 0117-330 7673 E: paulpeterson@blueyonder.co.uk

PETFIELD, Bruce Le Gay. b 34. FHA. NEOC 76. **d** 79 **p** 80. NSM Morpeth *Newc* 79–86; C Knaresborough *Ripon* 86–87; V Flamborough *York* 87–94; V Bempton 87–94; rtd 94; PtO *York* from 94. *36 Maple Road, Bridlington YO16 6TE* T: (01262) 676028 E: bruce.petfield@talktalk.net

PETHERAM, Louise Anne Miranda. b 62. Nottm Univ BSc 84 PGCE 85. Qu Coll Birm 09. **d** 12 **p** 13. NSM Upper Soar *Leic* 12–15; PtO *Derby* 15–17; P-in-c Youlgreave, Middleton, Stanton-in-Peak etc from 17. *34 Grove Place, Youlgrave, Bakewell DE45 1UU* T: (01629) 636814 E: rev.louise.p@gmail.com

PETHERICK, Mrs Karen Elizabeth. b 64. Victoria Univ Man BSc 85. Qu Foundn Birm 12. **d** 14 **p** 15. OLM Hanley H Ev *Lich* 14–18; C Bradwell and Porthill from 18. *80 Birches Head Road, Stoke-on-Trent ST1 6LQ* T: (01782) 865240 M: 07941-725459 E: karenpetherick@ntlworld.com

PETIT, Andrew Michael. b 53. Em Coll Cam MA 78. Trin Coll Bris. **d** 83 **p** 84. C Stoughton *Guildf* 83–87; C Shirley *Win* 87–92; V Cholsey *Ox* 92–04; C Streatley w Moulsford 03–04; V Cholsey and Moulsford from 04; Chapl W Berks Priority Care Services NHS Trust 92–03. *The Vicarage, Church Road, Cholsey, Wallingford OX10 9PP* T: (01491) 651216 M: 07986-005618 E: andrewpetit@virginmedia.com

PETITT, Mrs Lydia Ann. b 81. St Mellitus Coll BA 16. **d** 16 **p** 17. C Loughton St Mary *Chelmsf* 16–19; V Loughton St Mich from 19. *St Michael's House, Roding Road, Loughton IG10 3EJ* M: 07769-694907 E: lydia@stmichaelsloughton.com

PETITT, Mark Peter. b 81. Trin Coll Bris BA 12. **d** 12 **p** 13. C Langdon Hills *Chelmsf* 12–16; PtO 16–19; NSM Loughton St Mich from 19. *St Michael's House, Roding Road, Loughton IG10 3EJ* M: 07900-466373 E: mark@stmichaelsloughton.com

PETRIE, Alistair Philip. b 50. Fuller Th Sem California DMin 99. Oak Hill Th Coll 76. **d** 76 **p** 77. C Eston *York* 76–79; P-in-c Prestwick *Glas* 79–81; R 81–82; Canada from 82. *PO Box 25103, Kelowna BC V1W 3Y7, Canada* T: (001) (250) 764 8590 F: 656 3298 E: alistair@partnershipministries.org

PETRIE, Ian Robert (Eric). b 53. Avery Hill Coll PGCE 84 Oak Hill Th Coll BA 83. Qu Coll Birm 93. **d** 95 **p** 96. C Sedgley All SS *Worc* 95–98; P-in-c Salwarpe and Hindlip w Martin Hussingtree 98–08; Co-ord Chapl W Mercia Police 98–08; rtd 08; PtO *B & W* from 12. *100 Highbridge Road, Burnham-on-Sea TA8 1LW* T: (01278) 787402 E: revdericpetrie@outlook.com

PETRIE, Ms Jane Margaret. b 85. LMH Ox MA 10 St Jo Coll Dur BA 15 MA 17. Cranmer Hall Dur 13. **d** 16 **p** 17. C Wallington Springfield Ch *S'wark* from 16. *Flat 2, 40 North Street, Carshalton SM5 2JD* M: 07488-599786 E: petrie.jane@icloud.com *or* jane@springfieldchurch.org.uk

PETRINE, Andrei Anatolievich. b 73. St Jo Coll Dur BA 05. Cranmer Hall Dur 02. **d** 05 **p** 06. C Hounslow H Trin w St Paul and St Mary *Lon* 05–08; PtO 08–09; P-in-c Greensted-juxta-Ongar w Stanford Rivers etc *Chelmsf* 09–15; Chapl Russian Community *Lon* 09–14; P-in-c Laindon w Dunton *Chelmsf* from 15. *38 Claremont Road, Basildon SS15 5PZ* M: 07723-026925 E: a.petrine@mac.com

PETTENGELL, Ernest Terence. b 43. Ex Univ MA 98. K Coll Lon 65. **d** 69 **p** 70. C Chesham St Mary *Ox* 69–72; C Farnborough *Guildf* 72–75; Asst Master K Alfred Sch Burnham-on-Sea 75–78; C Bishop's Cleeve *Glouc* 78–80; Chapl Westonbirt Sch 80–85; P-in-c Shipton Moyne w Westonbirt and Lasborough *Glouc* 80–85; V Berkeley w Wick, Breadstone and Newport 85–92; TV Weston-super-Mare Cen Par *B & W* 92–95; P-in-c Weston super Mare Em 96–99; Chapl Staffs Univ *Lich* 99–03; V Douglas All SS and St Thos *S & M* 03–07; rtd 07; PtO *Ox* from 09; Ld Chapl Ripon Coll Cuddesdon from 15. *3 Rushall Road, Thame OX9 3TR* T: (01844) 216298 E: ernest.pettengell@gmail.com

PETTER, Oliver Robert Hugh. b 80. St Edm Hall Ox BA 05. St Steph Ho Ox 11. **d** 14 **p** 15. C Old St Pancras *Lon* 14–17; C Ox St Barn and St Paul w St Thos 17–18; Chapl Missr Pusey Ho 17–18; V Yarnton w Begbroke and Shipton-on-Cherwell *Ox* from 18. *The Rectory, 26 Church Lane, Yarnton, Kidlington OX5 1PY* E: oliver.petter@gmail.com

PETTERSEN, Canon Alvyn Lorang. b 51. TCD BA 73 Dur Univ BA 75 PhD 81. Sarum & Wells Th Coll 78. **d** 81 **p** 82. Chapl Clare Coll Cam 81–85; Fell and Chapl Ex Coll Ox 85–92; Research Fell Linc Coll Ox 92–93; V Frensham *Guildf* 93–02; Can Res Worc Cathl 02–18; rtd 19; PtO *Ox* from 19. *1 Plantation Road, Oxford OX2 6JD*

PETTET, Christopher Farley. b 54. Ox Univ BEd 78. St Jo Coll Nottm 87. **d** 90 **p** 91. C Luton St Mary *St Alb* 90–93; C Fawley *Win* 93–97; P-in-c Amport, Grateley, Monxton and Quarley 97–09; TV Portway and Danebury 09–12; V E w W Wellow and Sherfield English from 12. *Wellow Vicarage, 1 The Beeches, West Wellow, Romsey SO51 6RN* T: (01794) 323562 E: cpettet@btinternet.com

PETTIFER, Bryan George Ernest. b 32. Qu Coll Cam BA 55 MA 59 Bris Univ MEd 74. Wm Temple Coll Rugby 56 Ridley Hall Cam 57. **d** 59 **p** 60. C Attercliffe w Carbrook *Sheff* 59–61; C Ecclesall 61–65; Chapl City of Bath Tech Coll 65–74; Adult Educn Officer *Bris* 75–80; Dir Past Th Sarum & Wells Th Coll 80–85; Can Res St Alb 85–92; Prin St Alb Minl Tr Scheme 85–92; Prin Ox Area Chr Tr Scheme 92–94; PtO 94–98; Min and Deployment Officer/Selection Sec ABM 94–97; rtd 97; PtO *Bris* from 98; *Glouc* 98–00; *Sarum* from 98; *B & W* 02–05; Rtd Clergy Officer Malmesbury Adnry *Bris* from 04. *23 Curlew Drive, Chippenham SN14 6YG* T: (01249) 659823

PETTIFOR, Mrs Anne Elizabeth. b 64. Man Univ BSc 85 FIA 99. LCTP 10. **d** 14 **p** 15. NSM Kirkby Lonsdale *Carl* 14–18; TV from 18; RD Kendal from 18. *Stonebeck, Fairbank, Kirkby Lonsdale, Carnforth LA6 2DU* T: (015242) 73530 M: 07973-869475 E: anne.pettifor@btinternet.com

PETTIFOR, Canon David Thomas. b 42. Ripon Coll Cuddesdon 78. **d** 81 **p** 82. C Binley *Cov* 81–84; P-in-c Wood End 84–88; V 88–92; V Finham 92–98; TV Coventry Caludon 98–07; Hon Can Cov Cathl 04–07; rtd 07; PtO *Cov* from 08. *8 Austin Edwards Drive, Warwick CV34 5GW* T: (01926) 498736 E: davidtpettifor@yahoo.co.uk

PETTINGELL, Hubert. b 32. ACA 54 FCA 65 AKC 58. **d** 59 **p** 60. C Mansfield SS Pet and Paul *S'well* 59–61; CMS Iran 61–66; C Wellington w W Buckland and Nynehead *B & W* 67–68; Warden Student Movement Ho Lon 68–69; R Holywell w Needingworth *Ely* 69–71; Dir Finance WCC 80–96; PtO *Eur* from 94; rtd 97. *chemin du Pommier 22, CH-1218 Le Grand Saconnex, Geneva, Switzerland* T: (0041) (22) 798 8586 E: hpettingell@hotmail.com

PETTIT, James Lee. b 78. Lon Bible Coll BA 01 MA 03. Ox Min Course 07. **d** 09 **p** 10. C Faversham *Cant* 09–13; TV Sittingbourne w Bobbing 13–17; PtO *S'wark* from 17. *17 Martingales Close, Richmond TW10 7JJ* E: jamesthemonk@gmail.com

PETTITT, Canon Robin Adrian. b 50. Newc Univ BA 77 MRTPI 79. St Steph Ho Ox 81. **d** 83 **p** 84. C Warrington St Elphin *Liv* 83–87; C Torrisholme *Blackb* 87–93; P-in-c Charnock Richard 93–00; Dioc Par Development Officer 93–98; Sec Dioc Adv Cttee for the Care of Chs 98–99; C Broughton 00–01; rtd 01; PtO *Liv* from 03; *Eur* from 17; Hon Can Wiawso Ghana from 13. *Urb El Aspre, Carrer Les*

Fonts 19, 03790 Orba (Alicante), Spain T: (0034) 965 583 447 M: 677 638 449

PETTMAN, Mrs Hilary Susan. b 45. STETS 99. **d** 02 **p** 03. NSM Shottermill *Guildf* 02–08; PtO from 08. *Stacey's Farm Cottage, Thursley Road, Elstead, Godalming GU8 6DG* T: (01252) 703217 E: hilarypettman@btinternet.com

PETTS, Mrs Anna Carolyn. b 44. St Mich Coll Sarum CertEd 65. STETS 00. **d** 03 **p** 04. NSM Hordle *Win* 03–11; NSM NW Hants 11–15; rtd 15; PtO *Win* from 16. *8 Woodland Way, New Milton BH25 5RT* E: carolynpetts@tiscali.co.uk

PETTY, Alicia Christina Margaret. *See* DRING, Alicia Christina Margaret

PETTY, Brian. b 34. Man Univ BA 90. St Aid Birkenhead 59. **d** 62 **p** 63. C Meole Brace *Lich* 62–65; Chapl RAF 65–69; Australia 70–75; P-in-c Kimbolton w Middleton-on-the-Hill *Heref* 76–79; P-in-c Pudleston-cum-Whyle w Hatfield, Docklow etc 76–79; P-in-c Haddenham *Ely* 79–80; V 80–84; V Fairfield *Derby* 84–90; Chapl St Geo Sch Ascot 90–93; TR Sampford Peverell, Uplowman, Holcombe Rogus etc *Ex* 93–99; RD Cullompton 95–99; rtd 99; PtO *Ex* 99–02; Hon C Diptford, N Huish, Harberton, Harbertonford etc 02–13. *23 Gracey Court, Woodland Road, Broadclyst, Exeter EX5 3GA* E: petty245@btinternet.com

PETTY, Duncan. *See* PETTY, William Duncan

PETTY, Capt Stuart. b 56. Chich Th Coll 91. **d** 93 **p** 94. CA from 88; C W Bromwich St Andr w Ch Ch *Lich* 93–96; Asst Chapl Walsall Hosps NHS Trust 96–00; Sen Chapl Walsall Healthcare NHS Trust 00–03; Chapl Team Ldr R Wolv Hosps NHS Trust 03–08; Sen Chapl York Hosps NHS Foundn Trust 08–14; Asst Chapl R Wolv NHS Trust 14–19; Chapl from 19. *New Cross Hospital, Wolverhampton Road, Heath Town, Wolverhampton WV10 0QP* T: (01902) 307999

PETTY, William Duncan. b 55. Ex Univ BSc 76 Leic Univ PGCE 77. Oak Hill Th Coll 97. **d** 99 **p** 00. C Burscough Bridge *Liv* 99–04; Min Tanhouse The Oaks CD from 04; AD Ormskirk from 16. *181 Ennerdale, Skelmersdale WN8 6AH* T: (01704) 892444

PETZER, Garth Stephen. Rhodes Univ BTh 95. St Paul's Coll Grahamstown. **d** 88 **p** 91. C Queenstown St Mich S Africa 88–89; C E London St Sav 90–93; R E London St Martin 93–95; Chapl RN 96–03 and 04–07; CF 03–04; rtd 07; PtO *Nor* 04–07. *43 Damask Way, Warminster BA12 9PP* M: 07803-436897 E: petzeggs@hotmail.com

PETZSCH, Hugo Max David. b 57. Edin Univ MA 79 BD 83 PhD 95 FSAScot 91. Edin Th Coll 80. **d** 83 **p** 84. C Dollar *St And* 83–86; New Zealand 86–90; P-in-c Alyth, Blairgowrie and Coupar Angus *St And* 90–91; Chapl Glenalmond Coll 91–98; Dep Headmaster Benenden Sch 99–12; rtd 12. *45 Portland Street, Leamington Spa CV32 5EY*

PEVERELL, Canon Paul Harrison. b 57. Hull Univ BA 80. Ripon Coll Cuddesdon. **d** 82 **p** 83. C Cottingham *York* 82–85; V Middlesbrough St Martin 85–93; V Gt Ayton w Easby and Newton under Roseberry from 93; P-in-c Nunthorpe 17–18; Hon Can Ho Ghana from 04. *The Vicarage, Low Green, Great Ayton, Middlesbrough TS9 6NN* T: (01642) 722333 E: pevepv@btinternet.com

✠**PEYTON, The Rt Revd Nigel.** b 51. Edin Univ MA 73 BD 76 Lanc Univ PhD 09. Union Th Sem (NY) STM 77 Edin Th Coll 73. **d** 76 **p** 77 **c** 11. Chapl St Paul's Cathl Dundee *Bre* 76–82; Dioc Youth Chapl 76–85; Chapl Invergowrie 79–82; P-in-c 82–85; Chapl Univ Hosp Dundee 82–85; V Nottingham All SS *S'well* 85–91; P-in-c Lambley 91–99; Chapl Bluecoat Sch Nottm 90–92; Dioc Min Development Adv *S'well* 91–99; Adn Newark 99–11; Bp Bre 11–17; Bp Miss to Seafarers Scotland 13–17; rtd 17; Hon Teaching Fell Lanc Univ *Blackb* 10–18; Hon Scholar Liv Univ from 18; Hon Can Iowa USA from 12; Hon Asst Bp Linc from 17; PtO *S'well* from 18. *8 Bishops Place, Welton, Lincoln LN2 3FR* T: (01673) 862174 M: 07974-402449 E: nigel@peytons.org

PEYTON JONES, Mrs Dorothy Helen. b 58. LMH Ox BA 79 MPhil 80 DipSW 02. Trin Coll Bris 84. dss 86 **d** 87 **p** 94. W Holloway St Luke *Lon* 86–89; Par Dn 87–89; C Glas St Oswald 89–92; NSM Drumchapel 92–98; PtO *Ely* 98–03; NSM Chesterton St Andr from 03; Ind Chapl 09–12. *71 Humberstone Road, Cambridge CB4 1JD* T: (01223) 523485 *or* 311727 M: 07503-746520 E: dorothypj@ntlworld.com *or* dorothy@peytonjones.org

PHARAOH, Carol Helen. b 63. Preston Poly BTech 84. Cranmer Hall Dur 96. **d** 98 **p** 99. C Heaton Ch Ch *Man* 98–02; TV Walkden and Lt Hulton 02–09; P-in-c E Farnworth and Kearsley 09–10; TR Farnworth, Kearsley and Stoneclough 10–19; TR Blackrod, Daisy Hill, Westhoughton and Wingates from 19. *The Rectory, Market Street, Westhoughton, Bolton BL5 3AZ* T: (01942) 859251 E: carol.pharaoh@gmail.com

PHEELY, William Rattray. b 35. EN(M) 88. Edin Th Coll 57. **d** 60 **p** 61. C Glas St Mary 60–63; C Salisbury St Martin

Sarum 63–66; Guyana 66–82; V Bordesley St Oswald *Birm* 82–86; PtO from 00; *Ex* 00–05; Flat 2, 16 Westcliffe Road, Birkdale, Southport PR8 2BN T: (01704) 563346

PHELPS, Canon Arthur Charles. b 26. St Cath Coll Cam BA 50 MA 55. Ridley Hall Cam 51. **d** 53 **p** 54. C Kirkdale St Lawr *Liv* 53–56; C Rainham *Chelmsf* 56–60; Min Collier Row St Jas CD 60–65; V Collier Row St Jas 65–75; R Thorpe Morieux w Preston and Brettenham *St E* 75–84; R Rattlesden w Thorpe Morieux and Brettenham 84–90; Hon Can St E Cathl 89–90; rtd 90; PtO *Truro* 90–00; *St E* from 01. *8 Northfield Court, Aldeburgh IP15 5LU* T: (01728) 454772

PHELPS, Ian Ronald. b 28. Lon Univ BSc 53 PhD 57 FLS 58. Chich Th Coll 57. **d** 59 **p** 60. C Brighton Gd Shep Preston *Chich* 59–61; C Sullington 62–64; C Storrington 62–64; R Newtimber w Pyecombe 64–68; V Brighton St Luke 68–74; TV Brighton Resurr 74–76; V Peacehaven 76–94; rtd 94; PtO *Chich* from 94. *2 Kingston Green, Seaford BN25 4NB* T: (01323) 899511 E: prescote1849@outlook.com *or* prescote1849@outlook.com

PHENNA, Timothy Peter. b 69. Ridley Hall Cam BTh 01. **d** 01 **p** 02. C Woodseats St Chad *Sheff* 01–04; USA from 04. *965 Colorow Road, Golden CO 80401, USA* E: timphenna@yahoo.co.uk

PHILBRICK, Craig Edward. b 86. Win Univ BA 11 Dur Univ BA 19. Wycliffe Hall Ox 16. **d** 19. C N Stoneham and Bassett *Win* from 19. *24 Butterfield Road, Southampton SO16 7EE* M: 07539-408004 E: craig@nsab.org.uk

PHILBRICK, Canon Gary James. b 57. Southn Univ BA 78 K Alfred's Coll Win CertEd 79 MA(Theol) 00 Edin Univ BD 86. Edin Th Coll 83. **d** 86 **p** 87. C Southampton Maybush St Pet *Win* 86–90; R Fawley 90–00; P-in-c Swaythling 00–04; V 04–13; AD Southampton 07–13; P-in-c Fordingbridge and Breamore and Hale etc 13–17; R Fordingbridge and Hyde and Breamore etc from 17; AD Christchurch from 13; Hon Can Win Cathl from 09. *The Rectory, 71 Church Street, Fordingbridge SP6 1BB* T: (01425) 839622 E: gary.philbrick@dsl.pipex.com

PHILIP, Mathew. b 54. Leeds Univ BSc 77 MSc 78 PhD 83 Surrey Univ BA 05. STETS 02. **d** 05 **p** 06. NSM Patcham *Chich* from 05. *Hillside Lodge, 76 Redhill Drive, Brighton BN1 5FL* T: (01273) 883726 M: 07756-005331 E: m.philip1968r@gmail.com

PHILIP, Peter Wells. b 35. Ridley Hall Cam 64. **d** 67 **p** 68. C Tollington Park St Mark w St Anne *Lon* 67–70; C Battersea St Pet *S'wark* 70–72; Hon C Kennington St Mark 72–73; V Titirangi New Zealand 74–80; Hon C Blockhouse Bay 80–92; Past Dir Chr Advance Min 80–84; Dir Evang Fellowship of NZ 87–90; C Finchley Ch Ch *Lon* 92–93; V Frankton New Zealand 94–00; rtd 00. *608 Rototuna Street, Thames 3500, New Zealand* T: (0064) (7) 868 5028 E: peterp@xnet.co.nz

PHILIP BARTHOLOMEW, Brother. *See* KENNEDY, Philip Bartholomew

PHILLIP, Ms Gail Ann. b 72. Trevelyan Coll Dur BA 95 Sheff Univ MA 09. St Jo Coll Nottm 14. **d** 16 **p** 17. C Kenilworth St Jo *Cov* 16–19; V Exhall from 19. *16 St Giles Road, Coventry CV7 9HA* M: 07794-643335 E: revgailphillip@outlook.com

PHILLIP, Isaiah Ezekiel. b 59. Univ of W Indies BA 88. Codrington Coll Barbados 85. **d** 88 **p** 89. C St Jo Cathl Antigua 88–91; R St Geo Dominica 91–96; R All SS Antigua 96–01; P-in-c Handsworth St Mich *Birm* 02–05; V Basseterre St Kitts-Nevis from 05. *St Peter's Rectory, PO Box 702, Basseterre, St Kitts, West Indies* T: (001869) (465) 2774 E: phillipisaiah@hotmail.com

PHILLIPS, Mrs Adele. b 59. Newc Univ LLB 84. NEOC 04. **d** 07 **p** 08. NSM Gateshead *Dur* from 07; PtO *Newc* from 15. *47 Blackstone Court, Blaydon NE21 4HH* T: 0191-414 0955 M: 07752-325736 E: revadele@googlemail.com

PHILLIPS, Alison Claire. b 72. St Edm Hall Ox BA 93 Univ Coll Lon MA 99. St Mellitus Coll 15. **d** 18 **p** 19. NSM Edmonton All SS w St Mich *Lon* from 18. *33 Orpington Road, London N21 3PD* T: (020) 8882 8874 M: 07910-315918 E: alisonphillips2@gmail.com

PHILLIPS, Anne Jacqueline. b 53. **d** 17 **p** 17. NSM Matlock Bank and Tansley *Derby* from 17. *Tagg Hill Cottage, 43 Church Street, Matlock DE4 3BY* T: (01629) 583281 E: annejphillips@icloud.com

PHILLIPS, Canon Anthony Charles Julian. b 36. Lon Univ BD 63 AKC 63 G&C Coll Cam PhD 67 St Jo Coll Ox MA 75 DPhil 80. Coll of Resurr Mirfield 66. **d** 66 **p** 67. C-in-c Chesterton Gd Shep CD *Ely* 66–69; Dean, Chapl and Fell Trin Hall Cam 69–74; Hon Bp's Chapl *Nor* 70–71; Chapl and Fell St Jo Coll Ox 75–86; Lect Th Jes Coll Ox 75–86; Lect Th Hertf Coll Ox 84–86; Hd Master K Sch Cant 86–96; Hon Can Cant Cathl 87–96; Can Th Truro Cathl 86–02; PtO 02–10; rtd 01. *47 Warwick Street, Oxford OX4 1SZ* T: (01865) 244871 E: a.phillips920@btinternet.com

PHILLIPS, Benjamin Lambert Meyrick. b 64. K Coll Cam BA 86 MA 90. Ridley Hall Cam 87. **d** 90 **p** 91. C Wareham *Sarum* 90–94; C Chipping Barnet w Arkley *St Alb* 94–96; V Bodicote *Ox* 96–12; AD Deddington 05–10; V Towcester w Caldecote and Easton Neston etc *Pet* 12–19; V Goring and Streatley w S Stoke *Ox* from 19. *The Vicarage, Manor Road, Goring, Reading RG8 9DR* E: vicarofgsandss@yahoo.com

PHILLIPS, Beryl. *See* PHILLIPS, Elizabeth Beryl

PHILLIPS, Mrs Brenda. b 41. St Hugh's Coll Ox BA 63 MA 68. **d** 04 **p** 05. OLM Sherborne w Castleton, Lillington and Longburton *Sarum* 04–11; rtd 11; PtO *Sarum* from 11. *5 Earls Close, Sherborne DT9 3RS* E: revd.brenda@btinternet.com

PHILLIPS, Brian Edward Dorian William. b 36. Bris Univ BA 58. Ripon Hall Ox 58. **d** 60 **p** 61. C Ross *Heref* 60–64; Chapl RAF 64–68; Hon C Fringford w Hethe and Newton Purcell *Ox* 68–73; Chapl Howell's Sch Denbigh 73–76; C Cleobury Mortimer w Hopton Wafers *Heref* 76–80; V Dixton 80–02; rtd 02; PtO *Heref* from 02. *37 Duxmere Drive, Ross-on-Wye HR9 5UW* T: (01989) 562993 M: 07712-071558 E: pastorprint@gmx.co.uk

PHILLIPS, Mrs Caroline Jill. b 80. Nottm Univ BA 02 Man Univ MA 04. Qu Coll Birm 07. **d** 10 **p** 11. C Ollerton w Boughton *S'well* 10–13; P-in-c Mansfield St Aug 13–15; P-in-c Pleasley Hill 13–15; V Mansfield St Aug and Pleasley Hill 15–19; V Mansfield St Mark from 19; V Mansfield SS Pet and Paul from 19. *The Vicarage, Lindhurst Lane, Mansfield NG18 4JE* E: revcarolinephillips@gmail.com

PHILLIPS, Christopher Peter. b 82. St Jo Coll Dur BA 00. Ripon Coll Cuddesdon BA 12. **d** 13 **p** 14. C Ilkley St Marg *Leeds* 13–16; V Willesden St Mary *Lon* from 16. *110 Ellesmere Road, London NW10 1JS* M: 07917-798285 E: frchrisphillips@gmail.com

PHILLIPS, David Arthur. b 36. S Dios Minl Tr Scheme 90. **d** 94 **p** 95. NSM Canford Magna *Sarum* 94–06; rtd 06; PtO *Sarum* from 14. *32 Lynwood Drive, Wimborne BH21 1UG* T: (01202) 880262 E: d.phillips581@btinternet.com

PHILLIPS, David Gordon. b 60. Toronto Univ BASc 82. Wycliffe Coll Toronto MDiv 95. **d** 94 **p** 95. R Kawawachikamach Canada 94–99; Exec Adn Prince Albert 99–03; R Petite Riviere and New Dublin 04–09; P-in-c Palermo w Taormina *Eur* 10–13; Chapl Utrecht w Zwolle from 13. *Van Hogendorpstraat 26, 3581 KE Utrecht, The Netherlands* T: (0031) (06) 1241 0431 E: revdgphillips@hotmail.com *or* chaplain@holytrinityutrecht.nl

PHILLIPS, David Keith. b 61. New Coll Ox MA 90 St Jo Coll Dur BA 90. Cranmer Hall Dur 88. **d** 91 **p** 92. C Denton Holme *Carl* 91–94; C Chadderton Ch Ch *Man* 94–98; Gen Sec Sec Ch Soc 98–11; Public Preacher *St Alb* 98–11; V Chorley St Jas *Blackb* from 11. *St James's Vicarage, St James's Place, Chorley PR6 0NA* T: (01257) 233714 E: vicar@stjameschorley.org

PHILLIPS, David Thomas. b 47. NEOC 03. **d** 05 **p** 06. NSM Gt and Lt Driffield *York* 05–06; C Elloughton and Brough w Brantingham 06–10; rtd 11; P-in-c Vernet-les-Bains *Eur* from 11. *Lot 22, Cams de Baille, 66360 Olette, France* E: dphill9590@yahoo.co.uk

PHILLIPS, Eldon. b 50. Univ of Wales (Cardiff) BEd 85 MEd 92. St Mich Coll Llan. **d** 90 **p** 91. NSM Merthyr Cynog and Dyffryn Honddu etc *S & B* 90–94; LtO *St D* 94–99; NSM Ystradgynlais *S & B* 95–99; Chapl Trin Coll Carmarthen 95–99; P-in-c Llanrhidian w Llanmadoc and Cheriton *S & B* 99–05; Dioc Press Officer from 02; NSM Burry Port and Pwll *St D* 07–15; PtO *S & B* from 13; St D from 15. *2 Gerddi Glasfryn, Llanelli SA15 3LL* T: (01554) 744770 E: reveldon@btinternet.com

PHILLIPS, Mrs Elizabeth Beryl. b 34. **d** 94 **p** 95. C N Farnborough *Guildf* 94–99; rtd 99; PtO *Sarum* from 00. *8 Byron Road, Wimborne BH21 1NX* T: (01202) 883328 E: eberylp@talktalk.net

PHILLIPS, Mrs Emma Catharine. b 62. St Anne's Coll Ox BA 84. Trin Coll Bris BA 99. **d** 99 **p** 00. C Shawbury *Lich* 99–01; C Moreton Corbet 99–01; C Stanton on Hine Heath 99–01; C Cen Telford 01–02; TV 03–07; PtO 07–09; NSM Cen Telford 09–13; Chapl Severn Hospice from 09; PtO *Lich* 14–16; *Heref* from 16. *The Rectory, Plealy Lane, Longden, Shrewsbury SY5 8ET* T: (01743) 861003

PHILLIPS (née PULLEN), Frances Jill. b 54. Birm Univ MB, ChB 76. WEMTC 10. **d** 13 **p** 14. NSM St Weonards *Heref* from 13. *New House, Garway Hill, Hereford HR2 8EZ* T: (01981) 240032 E: franjphillips@gmail.com·

PHILLIPS, Ms Gillian. b 44. EMMTC 07. **d** 10 **p** 12. NSM Old Brampton and Great Barlow and Loundsley Green *Derby* 10–11; NSM Wrockwardine Deanery *Lich* 12–14; rtd 14. *78 Lawley Gate, Telford TF4 2NZ* T: (01952) 506038

PHILLIPS, Graham Donald. b 57. Magd Coll Cam BA 79 MA 83 Goldsmiths' Coll Lon PGCE 90. Qu Coll Birm 08. **d** 12 **p** 13. C Madeley *Heref* 12–15; R Gt Hanwood and Longden and Annscroft etc from 15. *The Rectory, Plealy Lane, Longden, Shrewsbury SY5 8ET* T: (01743) 861003 E: revgrahamphillips@gmail.com

PHILLIPS, Ivor Lyn. b 44. Leeds Univ BA 70. Cuddesdon Coll 69. **d** 71 **p** 72. C Bedlinog *Llan* 71–73; C Roath 73–77; TV Wolverhampton All SS *Lich* 77–78; TV Wolverhampton 78–81; Chapl Charing Cross Hosp Lon 81–91; Chapl Milan w Genoa and Lugano *Eur* 91–94; C Hampstead St Jo *Lon* 95–00; V Whitton St Aug 00–09; rtd 09; PtO *S'wark* 10–11; *Newc* from 12; *Eur* from 18. *10 Northumberland Avenue, Berwick-upon-Tweed TD15 1JZ* T: (01289) 305075 E: ly.phillipsuk@gmail.com

PHILLIPS, Jason Paul Benedict Blezard. b 73. Man Metrop Univ BA 95 CertEd 95 PhD 05 FCollT 09. Ripon Coll Cuddesdon MA 09. **d** 09 **p** 10. C Mid Trent *Lich* 09–14; C Stafford St Mary and Marston 14–15; C Blakenall Heath 15; V Whittington w Weeford from 15; Dioc Voc Adv from 14. *The Vicarage, 5 Bramley Way, Whittington, Lichfield WS14 9SB* E: revdjason@fastmail.co.uk

PHILLIPS (née LANGLEY), Mrs Jean. b 52. St Mary's Coll Chelt CertEd 73. WEMTC 03. **d** 06 **p** 07. NSM Bishop's Cleeve *Glouc* 06–08; NSM Bishop's Cleeve and Woolstone w Gotherington etc 08–13; rtd 13. *3 St Nicholas Drive, Cheltenham GL50 4RY* T: (01242) 673612

PHILLIPS, John. b 50. ACIB 74. NOC 01. **d** 04. NSM Wavertree H Trin *Liv* 04–18; rtd 18. *12 Montclair Drive, Liverpool L18 0HA* T: 0151-722 2542 E: jpipps@hotmail.com

PHILLIPS, John David. b 29. G&C Coll Cam BA 50 MA 54 CertEd 69. SWMTC 85. **d** 87 **p** 88. NSM St Martin w E and W Looe *Truro* 87–88; NSM St Merryn 88–94; rtd 94; PtO *Truro* from 94. *Restings, Plaidy, Looe PL13 1LF* T: (01503) 262121

PHILLIPS, John Eldon. b 50. Univ of Wales (Cardiff) BEd 85 MEd 92. St Mich Coll Llan. **d** 90 **p** 91. NSM Merthyr Cynog and Dyffryn Honddu etc *S & B* 90–94; LtO *St D* 94–99; NSM Ystradgynlais *S & B* 95–99; Chapl Trin Coll Carmarthen 95–99; P-in-c Llanrhidian w Llanmadoc and Cheriton *S & B* 99–05; Dioc Press Officer from 02; NSM Burry Port and Pwll *St D* 07–15; PtO *S & B* from 13; *St D* from 15. *2 Gerddi Glasfryn, Llanelli SA15 3LL* T: (01554) 744770 E: reveldon@btinternet.com

PHILLIPS, Jonathan Richard. b 79. Liv Univ BA 01 Cam Univ BTh 13. Ridley Hall Cam 10. **d** 13 **p** 14. C Lache cum Saltney *Ches* 13–17; P-in-c Chester St Pet from 17. *20 Lime Wood Close, Chester CH2 2HD* T: (01244) 403634 M: 07813-709035 E: pioneerministerpic@chesterstpeter.org.uk

PHILLIPS, Lamont Wellington Sanderson. b 33. S'wark Ord Course 73. **d** 76 **p** 78. NSM Tottenham St Paul *Lon* 76–83; P-in-c Upper Clapton St Matt 83–88; V 88–97; rtd 98. *24 Berkshire Gardens, London N18 2LF* T: (020) 8807 7025

PHILLIPS, Mrs Lena. b 61. STETS 12. **d** 15. NSM Shirley *Win* from 15. *11 Clifton Road, Southampton SO15 4GU* T: (023) 8077 4307 E: lena@stjamesbythepark.org

PHILLIPS, Lyn. *See* PHILLIPS, Ivor Lyn

PHILLIPS, Mark. b 66. STETS 10. **d** 13 **p** 14. C Portland *Sarum* 13–16; V Charminster and Stinsford 16–17; P-in-c Bradford Peverell, Stratton, Frampton etc 16–17; R Charminster, Stinsford and the Chalk Stream villages from 17. *The Vicarage, Mill Lane, Charminster, Dorchester DT2 9QP* E: revdmarkphillips@outlook.com

PHILLIPS, Mary Alice. *See* ILSLEY, Mary Alice

PHILLIPS, Matthew Paul. b 89. Trin Coll Cam BA 11 BTh 17 MPhil 18. Ridley Hall Cam 15. **d** 18 **p** 19. C Ely from 18. *8 Hertford Close, Ely CB6 3QS* T: (01353) 666759 M: 07533-677822 E: matt.phillips89@gmail.com

PHILLIPS, Michael John. b 54. Trent Poly BA 77. Sarum & Wells Th Coll 78. **d** 81 **p** 82. C Killay *S & B* 81–83; C Treboeth 83–85; Hong Kong 85–88; Japan 88–91; TR Is of Scilly *Truro* 91–95; TR Cwmbran *Mon* 95–15; AD Pontypool 12–15; R Jersey St Pet *Win* from 15. *The Rectory, La Rue du Presbytere, St Peter, Jersey JE3 7ZH* T: (01534) 481805 E: mj-phillips1@hotmail.co.uk

PHILLIPS, Michael Thomas. b 46. CQSW 81. Linc Th Coll 89. **d** 90 **p** 91. C Hyson Green *S'well* 90–91; C Basford w Hyson Green 91–99; Chapl HM Pris Gartree 93–99; Chapl HM Pris Nottm 99–08; rtd 08; Hon C Radford All So and St Pet *S'well* 08–12; PtO from 12. *12 Edgbaston Gardens, Aspley, Nottingham NG8 5AY* T: 0115-929 7029 E: bigviola@hotmail.com

PHILLIPS, Noel William. b 70. Lanc Univ BSc 92 PhD 99 St Martin's Coll Lanc PGCE 97. Ox Min Couse 14. **d** 17 **p** 18. C Stoke St Mich, Coventry *Cov* from 17. *50 Amelia Crescent, Coventry CV3 1NA* M: 07779-244174 E: n.w.phillips@live.com

PHILLIPS, Mrs Patricia. b 45. Glouc Sch of Min 83. **dss** 86 **d** 87 **p** 94. Newent and Gorsley w Cliffords Mesne *Glouc* 86–95; C 87–95; P-in-c Childswyckham w Aston Somerville, Buckland etc 95–97; R 97–00; R Redmarley D'Abitot,

Bromesberrow, Pauntley etc 00–10; rtd 10; PtO *Glouc* from 14. *5 Freemans Orchard, Newent GL18 1TX* T: (01531) 828444 E: revpp@tesco.net

PHILLIPS, Miss Pauline. b 54. **d** 96 **p** 97. OLM Mossley *Man* 96–16; rtd 16. *82 Waterton Lane, Mossley, Ashton-under-Lyne OL5 0NQ* T: (01457) 832151 M: 07484-838332 E: pauline.phillips2015@gmail.com

PHILLIPS, Peter Miles Lucas. b 44. Reading Univ BA 66 QUB DipEd 69 Univ of Wales (Cardiff) MEd 88 Bris Univ MA 07 Cardiff Univ PhD 14. St Mich Coll Llan 90. **d** 92 **p** 93. Dep Hd Teacher Dynevor Sch 82–96; NSM Llangyfelach *S & B* 92–96; Dep Chapl HM Pris Liv 96–97; Chapl HM Pris Usk and Prescoed 97–01; Chapl HM Pris Bris 01–04; rtd 04; PtO *Bris* 04–12; Chapl Wesley Coll Bris 08–11. *Gwalia, Felindre, Swansea SA5 7PQ* T: (01792) 772523 E: revdpeterphillips@yahoo.co.uk

PHILLIPS, Canon Rachel Susan. b 64. Newnham Coll Cam BA 86 MA 90 Nottm Univ MPhil 11 Solicitor 89. St Jo Coll Nottm 04. **d** 07 **p** 08. C Eastcote St Lawr *Lon* 07–10; P-in-c Northaw and Cuffley *St Alb* 10–13; V 13–17; RD Cheshunt 12–17; Can Res Roch Cathl 17–19; TR Dunstable *St Alb* from 19. *8 Furness Avenue, Dunstable LU6 3BN*

PHILLIPS, Richard Paul. b 76. Man Univ BA 08. Trin Coll Bris 09. **d** 11 **p** 12. C Kingston upon Hull St Aid Southcoates *York* 11–14; V from 14. *St Aidan's Vicarage, 139 Southcoates Avenue, Hull HU9 3HF* M: 07944-541968 E: rich.phillips76@gmail.com

PHILLIPS, Robert Gareth. b 82. Bris Univ BSc 04. Oak Hill Th Coll BA 16. **d** 17 **p** 18. C Eastrop *Win* from 17. *15 Camwood Close, Basingstoke RG21 3BL* T: (01256) 357745 M: 07807-907661 E: rob_phil1@hotmail.com *or* rob.phillips@stmarys-basingstoke.org.uk

PHILLIPS, Robin Michael. b 33. AKC 58. **d** 59 **p** 60. C Hanwell St Mellitus *Lon* 59–61; C St Margaret's-on-Thames 61–64; C Hangleton *Chich* 64–68; V Mellor *Derby* 68–95; RD Glossop 89–93; rtd 95; Hon C Bridekirk *Carl* 95–96. *27 Calgarth Park, Troutbeck Bridge, Windermere LA23 1LF* T: (015394) 88841

PHILLIPS, Timothy Leo. b 72. Bris Univ BSc 95 PhD 99. Trin Coll Bris BA 01 MA 02. **d** 02 **p** 03. C Leic H Trin w St Jo 02–05; TV Ashby-de-la-Zouch and Breedon on the Hill from 05. *Holy Trinity Vicarage, 1 Trinity Close, Ashby-de-la-Zouch LE65 2GQ* T: (01530) 412339

PHILLIPS, Wayne. b 45. **d** 10 **p** 11. NSM Pontefract All SS *Wakef* 10–14; Leeds 14–19; NSM Pontefract from 19. *16 Maple Walk, Knottingley WF11 0PU* T: (01977) 678024 E: wayne.phillips16@btinternet.com

PHILLIPSON (née MACKAY), Alison. b 62. Teesside Univ BA 00. NEOC 01. **d** 04 **p** 05. C Stokesley w Seamer *York* 04–08; P-in-c Cosby *Leic* 08–09; P-in-c Whetstone 08–09; V Coatham and Dormanstown *York* 09–14; R Guisborough from 14. *The Rectory, Church Street, Guisborough TS14 6BS* E: alisonphillipson@aol.com

PHILLIPSON-MASTERS, Miss Susan Patricia. b 52. Sussex Univ CertEd 73 K Alfred's Coll Win BEd 81 Leeds Univ MA 04 Glos Univ MA 09 FISt 76 ACP 80. Trin Coll Bris 86. **d** 89 **p** 95. C Saltford w Corston and Newton St Loe *B & W* 89–94; C Uphill 94–97; C Nailsea Ch Ch w Tickenham 97–98; P-in-c Tredington and Darlingscott w Newbold on Stour *Cov* 98–00; P-in-c The Stanleys *Glouc* 00–11; Chapl Wycliffe Prep Sch 07–11; rtd 11; PtO *Glouc* from 11; Hon C Cromhall, Tortworth, Tytherington, Falfield etc from 19. *Recsretreat, 1 Oakleaze Road, Thornbury, Bristol BS35 2LG* T: (01454) 600674 E: suepm@sky.com

PHILLPOT, Donald John. b 27. St Jo Coll Dur BA 53. **d** 55 **p** 56. C Southmead *Bris* 55–60; C Brislington St Luke 60–63; R Stapleton *Heref* 63–68; V Dorrington 63–68; P-in-c Astley Abbotts 68–78; R Bridgnorth w Tasley 68–78; V Lillington *Cov* 78–92; rtd 92; PtO *Glouc* from 92. *22 Williams Orchard, Highnam, Gloucester GL2 8EL* T: (01452) 386844

PHILP (née NOBLE), Canon Ann Carol. b 42. Sarum Dioc Tr Coll CertEd 63 Southn Univ MA(Ed) 89 MCIPD. S Dios Minl Tr Scheme 93. **d** 95 **p** 96. Dir Sarum Chr Cen 93–98; Chapl Sarum Cathl 95–02; Dioc NSM Officer 98–02; P-in-c Woodford Valley w Archers Gate 02–12; Dioc Dir of Ords 02–07; Bp's Dom Chapl 07–12; Can and Preb Sarum Cathl 05–12; rtd 12; PtO *Sarum* from 12. *55 The Close, Salisbury SP1 2EL* T: (01722) 555178 E: acphilp55@virginmedia.com

PHILPOT, Barbara May. See WILKINSON, Barbara May

PHILPOT, Canon John David. b 43. Leic Univ BA 64. Trin Coll Bris 69. **d** 72 **p** 73. C Knutsford St Jo and Toft *Ches* 72–75; C Bickenhill w Elmdon *Birm* 75–79; V Birm St Luke 79–91; RD Birm City 83–88; Hon Can Birm Cathl 89–91; V Chilvers Coton w Astley *Cov* 91–00; RD Nuneaton 95–00; Hon Can Cov Cathl 96–00; P-in-c Prague *Eur* 00–08; rtd 08; PtO *Eur* from 08; Ex from 09; *Birm* from 17. *2 Portland Court,*

1 Portland Avenue, Exmouth EX8 2DJ T: (01395) 225044 E: jamphilpott@yahoo.com

PHILPOTT, Jonathan Mark. b 76. Chelt & Glouc Coll of HE BA 98. Trin Coll Bris BA 06 MA 10. **d** 07 **p** 08. C Lydney *Glouc* 07–10; P-in-c By Brook *Bris* 10–16; P-in-c Colerne w N Wraxall 10–11; C 11–16; P-in-c Berrow and Breane *B & W* from 16. *1 Manor Way, Berrow, Burnham-on-Sea TA8 2RG* T: (01278) 751806 E: rev.jonathanphilpott@gmail.com

PHILPOTT, Preb Samuel. b 41. Kelham Th Coll 60. **d** 65 **p** 66. C Swindon New Town *Bris* 65–70; C Torquay St Martin Barton *Ex* 70–73; TV Withycombe Raleigh 73–76; V Shaldon 76–78; P-in-c Plymouth St Pet 78–80; V 80–09; RD Plymouth Devonport 86–93 and 95–01; Preb Ex Cathl 91–09; rtd 09; P-in-c Plymouth St Pet and H Apostles Ex 09–13; PtO from 15; Truro from 16. *21 Plaistow Crescent, Plymouth PL5 2EA* T: (01752) 298502 E: prebphilpott@gmail.com

PHILPOTT-HOWARD, John Nigel. b 54. Univ of Wales Coll of Medicine MB, BCh 77 FRCPath 83. SEITE 99. **d** 02 **p** 03. NSM Shooters Hill Ch Ch *S'wark* 02–11; PtO 11–15; NSM E Greenwich from 15. *80 Charlton Road, London SE7 7EY* T: (020) 8858 4692 M: 07789-985415 E: philpotthoward@aol.com

PHILPS, Mark Seymour. b 51. Worc Coll Ox BA 73 MA 78 Lon Univ MA 75 Nottm Univ BA 79. St Jo Coll Nottm 77. **d** 80 **p** 81. C Chadwell Heath *Chelmsf* 80–83; C Woodford Wells 83–87; V Tipton St Matt *Lich* 87–02; TV Roxeth *Lon* 02–03; TR 03–11; V 11–15; rtd 15; PtO *Sarum* from 16. *1 White Horse Road, Marlborough SN8 2FE* E: marksphilps@gmail.com

PHIPPS, David John. b 46. Bris Univ BSc 68 Ex Univ PhD 94 Nottm Univ PGCE 69. Trin Coll Bris 75. **d** 78 **p** 79. C Madron w Morvah *Truro* 78–80; C Kenilworth St Jo *Cov* 80–83; TV Barnstaple *Ex* 83–95; I Abercraf w Callwen w Capel Coelbren *S & B* 95–02; P-in-c Gulval and Madron *Truro* 02–05; rtd 05. *11 Walton Way, Barnstaple EX32 8AE* T: (01271) 349746

PHIPPS, Mathew Jamie David. b 76. Univ of Wales (Abth) LLB 98 All Nations Chr Coll BA 08 Barrister 99 Solicitor 04. ERMC 13. **d** 15 **p** 17. C Madrid *Eur* 15–16; Bp's Dom Chapl *Win* from 16; Dep Registrar from 19. *Wolvesey, Winchester SO23 9ND* T: (01962) 897082 E: mat.phipps@winchester.anglican.org

PHIZACKERLEY, The Ven Gerald Robert. b 29. Univ Coll Ox BA 52 MA 56. Wells Th Coll 52. **d** 54 **p** 55. C Carl St Barn 54–57; Chapl Abingdon Sch 57–64; R Gaywood, Bawsey and Mintlyn *Nor* 64–78; RD Lynn 68–78; Hon Can Nor Cathl 75–78; Hon Can Derby Cathl 78–96; P-in-c Ashford w Sheldon 78–90; Adn Chesterfield 78–96; rtd 96; PtO *Derby* 96–18; *Cov* from 96. *Archway Cottage, Hall Road, Leamington Spa CV32 5RA* T: (01926) 332740 E: phizleam@yahoo.co.uk

PHOEBE, Sister. See HANMER, Phoebe Margaret

PHYPERS, David John. b 39. Leic Univ BA 60 CertEd 61 Lon Univ BD 65. Linc Th Coll 76. **d** 78 **p** 79. NSM Normanton *Derby* 78–80; NSM Sinfin 80–87; LtO 87–88; P-in-c Denby and Horsley Woodhouse 88–00; P-in-c Wormhill, Peak Forest w Peak Dale and Dove Holes 00–07; Adv for Chr Giving 00–07; rtd 07; PtO *Derby* from 07. *15 Albert Road, Chaddesden, Derby DE21 6SL* T: (01332) 239134 E: david@phypers.co.uk

PICKARD, Mrs Patricia Anne. b 44. **d** 04 **p** 05. NSM Ovenden *Wakef* 04–14; Leeds 14; rtd 14; PtO *Leeds* from 14. *8 Chapel Lane, Oakworth, Keighley BD22 7HY*

✠**PICKARD, The Rt Revd Stephen Kim.** b 52. Newc Univ Aus BCom 74 Van Mildert Coll Dur PhD 90. Melbourne Coll of Div BD 79 St Jo Coll Morpeth 77. **d** 80 **p** 80 **c** 07. Singleton Australia 80–82; C Dur St Cuth 82–84; Chapl Van Mildert Coll Dur 84–90; Chapl Trev Coll Dur 84–90; Lect United Th Coll Sydney Australia 91–97; Dir St Mark's Nat Th Cen 98–06; Assoc Prof and Hd Th Chas Sturt Univ 99–06; Asst Bp Adelaide 07–10; Adn The Port Australia 07–09; Visiting Fell Ripon Coll Cuddesdon 10–11; Dir Ox Cen for Ecclesiology and Practical Th 10–11; Six Preacher Cant Cathl 11–12; Chief Exec Anglicare NSW Australia from 12. *Anglicare, PO Box 427, Parramatta NSW 2124, Australia* T: (0061) (2) 9895 8000 F: 9633 4620 E: s.k.pickard@gmail.com

PICKEN, The Ven David Anthony. b 63. Lon Univ BA 84 Kent Univ PGCE 85 Nottm Univ MA 96. Linc Th Coll 87. **d** 90 **p** 91. C Worth *Chich* 90–93; TV Wordsley *Worc* 93–97; TR 97–04; RD Kingswinford 01–04; TR High Wycombe *Ox* 04–12; AD Wycombe 07–11; Hon Can Ch Ch 11–12; Adn Newark *S'well* from 12. *22 Rufford Road, Edwinstowe, Mansfield NG21 9HY* T: (01623) 238957 E: archdeacon-newark@southwell.anglican.org

PICKERING, David Arthur Ashley. b 67. G&C Coll Cam BA 89. Wycliffe Hall Ox BTh 06. **d** 06 **p** 07. C Hornchurch H Cross *Chelmsf* 06–09; P-in-c Fyfield w Tubney and Kingston Bagpuize *Ox* 09–16; V from 16. *1 Oxford Road, Kingston Bagpuize, Abingdon OX13 5FZ* T: (01865) 820451 E: vicar.kbsft@gmail.com

PICKERING, Canon David Colville. b 41. Kelham Th Coll 61. **d** 66 **p** 67. C Chaddesden St Phil *Derby* 66–70; C New Mills 70–72; C Buxton 72–74; V Chesterfield SS Aug 74–90; R Whittington 90–99; P-in-c Hathersage 99; P-in-c Bamford 99; R Hathersage w Bamford and Derwent 00–06; Hon Can Derby Cathl 05–06; rtd 06; PtO *Derby* 06–18. *Les Chênes Verts, Chemin de St Laurent, Le Rang, 84750 Viens, France* T: (0033) 4 90 74 68 55 M: 6 33 84 95 86 E: pickport@gmail.com

PICKERING, John Alexander. b 41. TCD BA 63 MA 66. CITC 65. **d** 65 **p** 66. C Magheralin *D & D* 65–67; C-in-c Outeragh *K, E & A* 67–68; I 68–71; Deputation Sec Hibernian Bible Soc 71–74; C-in-c Drumgoon w Dernakesh, Ashfield etc *K, E & A* 74–80; I Keady w Armaghbreague and Derrynoose *Arm* 80–83; I Portadown *Arm* 83–07. rtd 07. *25 Twinem Court, Portadown, Craigavon BT63 5FH* M: 07752-339558

PICKERING, Malcolm. b 37. Sarum Th Coll 65. **d** 68 **p** 69. C Milton *Portsm* 68–70; C Stanmer w Falmer and Moulsecoomb *Chich* 70–75; Chapl Brighton Coll of Educn 71–75; V Hooe and R Ninfield *Chich* 75–80; V Ventnor H Trin and Ventnor St Cath *Portsm* 80–88; Chapl St Cath Sch Ventnor 87–88; V Marton *Blackb* 88–97; P-in-c Badingham w Bruisyard, Cransford and Dennington *St E* 97–99; V Leiston 99–04; rtd 04; PtO *B & W* 04–07; Hon C Drybrook, Lydbrook and Ruardean *Glouc* 07–08; PtO *Cant* 16–17; *Chich* from 17. *51 Lydd Road, Camber, Rye TN31 7RJ* T: (01797) 458516 E: malpic@btinternet.com

PICKERING, Mark Penrhyn. b 36. Liv Univ BA 59 St Cath Coll Ox BA 62 MA 67. Wycliffe Hall Ox 60. **d** 63 **p** 64. C Claughton cum Grange *Ches* 63–67; C Newland St Jo *York* 67–72; TV Marfleet 72–76; V Kingston upon Hull St Nic 76–85; V Elloughton and Brough w Brantingham 85–88; Chapl R Hull Hosps NHS Trust 88–99; Chapl Hull and E Yorks Hosps NHS Trust 99–01; PtO *York* from 01. *43 Lowerdale, Elloughton, Brough HU15 1SD* T: (01482) 662102

PICKERING, Mrs Maureen Anne. b 46. Man Univ CertEd 67 Open Univ BA 88 MA 93 Leeds Univ MA 07. NOC 04. **d** 07 **p** 08. NSM Ches St Mary 07–15; PtO from 15. *Curzon Cottage, 2A Curzon Park South, Chester CH4 8AB* T: (01244) 677352 M: 07966-409404 E: mapickering@btinternet.com

PICKERING, Sally Ann. b 64. St Hild Coll 16. **d** 19. C Starbeck *Leeds* from 19. *6 Florin Drive, Knaresborough HG5 0WG* E: sally.pickering@leeds.anglican.org

PICKERSGILL, James Richard. b 74. Brunel Univ BA 96. Trin Coll Bris 11. **d** 13 **p** 14. C Winchcombe *Glouc* 13–17; C Market Harborough and The Transfiguration etc *Leic* from 17. *Ashtree House, 38 Alvington Way, Market Harborough LE16 7NF* T: (01858) 465876 E: james@harborough-anglican.org.uk

PICKETT, Brian Laurence. b 48. Reading Univ BA 70 Qu Coll Birm BA 73 MA 77. Ripon Coll Cuddesdon. **d** 88 **p** 88. C Highcliffe w Hinton Admiral *Win* 88–91; P-in-c Colbury 91–01; P-in-c W End 01–04; V 04–12; rtd 12; PtO *Win* from 12. *6 Woodlands Gardens, Romsey SO51 7TE* T: (01794) 523463

PICKETT, Ms Joanna Elizabeth. b 53. Leic Univ BA 74 MA 80 Lon Univ MTh 95. Wycliffe Hall Ox 87. **d** 89 **p** 94. Chapl Southn Univ *Win* 89–94; C N Stoneham 94–95; NSM Colbury 97–01; NSM W End 01–12; PtO from 12. *6 Woodlands Gardens, Romsey SO51 7TE* T: (01794) 523463 E: liz.pickett@btinternet.com

PICKETT, Mark William Leslie. b 60. Westhill Coll Birm BEd 84. Trin Coll Bris 93. **d** 95 **p** 96. C Hellesdon *Nor* 95–98; TV Thetford 98–03; R Clitheroe St Jas *Blackb* from 03; P-in-c Clitheroe St Paul Low Moor 15–17. *The Rectory, Woone Lane, Clitheroe BB7 1BJ* T: (01200) 423608 E: rector@stjamesclitheroe.co.uk

PICKETT, Peter Leslie. b 28. Guy's Hosp Medical Sch LDS 52. S Dios Minl Tr Scheme 83. **d** 86 **p** 87. NSM Eastbourne H Trin *Chich* 86–88; P-in-c Danehill 88–93; rtd 93; PtO *Chich* from 93. *Springfield, 76 Meads Road, Eastbourne BN20 7QJ* T: (01323) 731709 M: 07733-090957 E: pjpickett@btinternet.com

PICKFORD (née PACKER), Mrs Catherine Ruth. b 76. Nottm Univ BA 97 Anglia Poly Univ MA 00. Westcott Ho Cam MA 00. **d** 00 **p** 01. C Gosforth All SS *Newc* 00–04; TV Benwell 04–09; TR 09–15; TR Benwell and Scotswood 15; P-in-c Stannington from 15; Dioc CMD Officer from 15. *The Vicarage, Stannington, Morpeth NE61 6HL* T: (01670) 789025 E: catherine_pickford@hotmail.co.uk

PICKLES, Julia Clare. *See* BALDWIN, Julia Clare

PICKSTONE, Canon Charles Faulkner. b 55. BNC Ox BA 77 MA 81 Leeds Univ BA 80. Coll of Resurr Mirfield 78. **d** 81 **p** 82. C Birkenhead Priory *Ches* 81–84; Chapl Paris St Geo *Eur* 84; C Camberwell St Giles w St Matt *S'wark* 84–89; V Catford St Laur from 89; Asst RD E Lewisham 92–99; Hon Can S'wark Cathl from 13. *St Laurence's Vicarage, 31 Bromley Road, London SE6 2TS* T: (020) 8698 2871 *or* 8698 9706 E: st.laurence@btconnect.com

PIDOUX, Ian George. b 32. Univ Coll Ox BA 55 MA 60. Coll of Resurr Mirfield 54. **d** 57 **p** 58. C Middlesbrough All SS *York* 57–60; C Haggerston St Aug w St Steph *Lon* 60–62; C Aylesford *Roch* 80–81; TV Rye *Chich* 81–84; P-in-c Bridgwater St Jo w B & W 84–86; V 86–98; Chapl Bridgwater Hosp 91–98; rtd 98; PtO *B & W* 98–15; *St Alb* from 15. *21 Hollybush Avenue, St Albans AL2 3AE* M: 07746-615854 E: igsepidoux@btinternet.com

PIDSLEY, Preb Christopher Thomas. b 36. ALCD 61. **d** 61 **p** 62. C Enfield Ch Ch Trent Park *Lon* 61–66; C Rainham *Chelmsf* 66–70; V Chudleigh *Ex* 70–98; RD Moreton 86–91; Preb Ex Cathl 92–98; rtd 98. *Bellever, Shillingford Abbot, Exeter EX2 9QF* T: (01392) 833588

PIERCE, Alan. b 46. St Mark & St Jo Coll Lon TCert 68 Southlands Coll Lon BEd 75 K Coll Lon MA 85. NOC 89. **d** 92 **p** 93. NSM Bolton St Thos *Man* 92–98; NSM Halliwell 98–00; NSM Bolton Breightmet St Jas 00–06; NSM Leverhulme 06–15; rtd 15; PtO *Man* from 15. *3 Astley Road, Bolton BL2 4BR* T: (01204) 300071 F: 401556 E: alan_pierce@hotmail.co.uk

✠**PIERCE, The Rt Revd Anthony Edward.** b 41. Univ of Wales (Swansea) BA 63 Linacre Coll Ox BA 65 MA 71. Ripon Hall Ox 63. **d** 65 **p** 66 **c** 99. C Swansea St Pet *S & B* 65–67; C Swansea St Mary and H Trin 67–74; Chapl Univ of Wales (Swansea) 71–74; V Llwynderw 74–92; P-in-c Swansea St Barn 92–96; Dioc Dir of Educn 93–96; Can Brecon Cathl 93–99; Adn Gower 95–99; V Swansea St Mary w H Trin 96–99; Bp S & B 99–08; rtd 08. *2 Coed Ceirios, Swansea Vale, Swansea SA7 0NU* T: (01792) 790258

PIERCE, Bruce Andrew. b 58. TCD BBS 80 BTh 89 Dub City Univ MA 99 MA 02. CITC 86. **d** 89 **p** 90. C Raheny w Coolock *D & G* 89–92; C Taney 92–93; I Lucan w Leixlip 93–98; Chapl Adelaide and Meath Hosp Dublin 98–02; C Haarlem *Eur* 02–03; Chapl Toronto Gen Hosp Canada 03–04; Chapl Princess Marg Hosp Toronto 04–05; Supervisor (Assoc) Kerry Gen Hosp 06–08; Dir Educn St Luke's Home Mahon *C, C & R* from 08. *Aquila, Church Road, Blackrock, Cork, Republic of Ireland* T: (00353) (21) 435 8914 *or* 435 9444 ext 507 F: 435 9450 E: bruapierce@hotmail.com *or* bruce.pierce@stlukeshome.ie

PIERCE, Christopher Douglas. b 61. Middle Tennessee State Univ BSc 95 Covenant Th Sem St Louis MA 96. Asbury Th Sem Kentucky 92. **d** 08 **p** 09. C St Jo Cathl Antigua 08–10; I Clondehorkey w Cashel *D & R* from 10. *Ballymore Rectory, Port-na-Blagh, Letterkenny, Co Donegal, Republic of Ireland* T: (00353) (74) 913 6185 E: revcdp@gmail.com

PIERCE, Daniel Charles. b 78. Redcliffe Coll Glouc BA 01 St Jo Coll Dur MA 12. Cranmer Hall Dur 10. **d** 12 **p** 13. C Stockton St Jas *Dur* 12–15; C Stockton St Jo 12–15; TV Billericay and Lt Burstead *Chelmsf* 15–18; C Boreham from 18; C Broomfield from 18; C The Chignals w Mashbury from 18; C Gt and Lt Leighs and Lt Waltham from 18; C Gt Waltham w Ford End from 18; C Pleshey from 18; C Springfield All SS from 18; C N Springfield from 18. *2 Fairway Drive, Chelmsford CM3 3FH* M: 07790-558579 E: todanpierce@yahoo.co.uk

PIERCE, David. *See* PIERCE, Thomas David Benjamin

PIERCE, David Richard. b 49. **d** 15 **p** 16. OLM Prittlewell St Pet w Westcliff St Cedd *Chelmsf* 15–18; OLM Prittlewell St Steph 16–18; PtO from 18. *7 Holmsdale Close, Westcliff-on-Sea SS0 0QW* E: david@revdavidpierce.net

PIERCE, Jeffrey Hyam. b 29. Chelsea Coll Lon BSc 51 FBIM 80. Ox NSM Course 86. **d** 88 **p** 89. NSM Gt Missenden w Ballinger and Lt Hampden *Ox* 88–93; NSM Penn 93–97; rtd 97; PtO *Ox* 97–15. *Glebe Cottage, Manor Road, Penn, High Wycombe HP10 8HY* T: (01494) 817179 E: jeff@revjeff.co.uk

PIERCE, Roderick Martin. b 52. ACIB 74. **d** 06 **p** 07. OLM Guildf H Trin w St Mary from 06. *Appledore, 18 Blackwell Avenue, Guildford GU2 8LU* T: (01483) 505816 E: ann.rodpierce@ntlworld.com

PIERCE, Thomas David Benjamin. b 67. Ulster Univ BA 88. Oak Hill Th Coll BA 94. **d** 94 **p** 95. C Cromer *Nor* 94–97; C Belfast St Donard *D & D* 97–99; C Holywood 99–00; I Kilwarlin Upper w Kilwarlin Lower 00–17; rtd 18. *2 Broomhill Grove, Magheralin, Craigavon BT67 0GY* T: (028) 3834 7242 M: 07787-741254

PIERCE-JONES, Alan. b 74. Coll of Ripon & York St Jo BA 98. St Mich Coll Llan 98. **d** 00 **p** 01. C Port Talbot St Theodore *Llan* 00–02; TV Neath 02–05; V Lt Marsden w Nelson St Mary and Nelson St Bede *Blackb* 05–10; C W Burnley All SS 10; C Burnley St Mark 10; Chapl HM YOI Lanc Farms and HM Pris Lanc Castle 10–11; Chapl HM Pris Kennet 11–17; Chapl HM Pris Liv 13–14; Chapl HM Pris Berwyn from 17; PtO *Man* 14–17. *HM Prison Berwyn, Bridge Road, Wrexham Industrial Estate, Wrexham LL13 9QE* E: alan.pierce-jones@justice.gov.uk

PIERCY, Elizabeth Claire. *See* FRANCE, Elizabeth Claire

PIERPOINT, The Ven David Alfred. b 56. d 86 p 88. NSM Athboy w Ballivor and Killallon *M & K* 86–88; NSM Killiney Ballybrack *D & G* 88–89; NSM Narraghmore and Timolin w Castledermot etc 89–91; Chan V St Patr Cathl Dublin 90–96; C Dublin St Patr Cathl Gp *D & G* 92–95; V Dublin Ch Ch Cathl Gp from 95; Can Ch Ch Cathl Dublin from 95; Adn Dublin from 04. *The Vicarage, 30 Phibsborough Road, Dublin 7, Republic of Ireland* T: (00353) (1) 830 4601 M: 87-263 0402 E: pierpoint.david@gmail.com

PIERPOINT, Nigel John. TCD MTh 16. CITC 12. d 15 p 16. Taney *D & G* 15–16; C from 16. *Church Lodge, 21 Taney Road, Dundrum, Dublin 14, Republic of Ireland* T: (00353) (1) 295 1895 M: 87-638 8238 E: nigel.pierpoint@gmail.com

PIERSSENÉ, Frances Jane. *See* GRIEVE, Frances Jane

PIGGOT, Alan Robert Lennox. b 62. Peterho Cam BA 84 MA 88 Ox Univ DPhil 04. Westcott Ho Cam 00. d 02 p 03. C Dalston H Trin w St Phil and Haggerston All SS *Lon* 02–04; C Stoke Newington St Mary 04–05; P-in-c Hackney Wick St Mary of Eton w St Aug 05–10; PtO 14–16; NSM Grosvenor Chpl from 16; NSM Hanover Square St Geo from 16. *20 Ascott Road, Aylesbury HP20 1HX* E: alan.piggot@btinternet.com

PIGGOTT, The Ven Andrew John. b 51. Qu Mary Coll Lon BSc(Econ) 72. St Jo Coll Nottm 83. d 86 p 87. C Dorridge *Birm* 86–89; TV Kidderminster St Geo *Worc* 89–94; V Biddulph *Lich* 94–99; Min and Voc Adv CPAS 99–01; Patr Sec 01–05; Adn Bath and Preb Wells Cathl *B & W* 05–17; rtd 17. *19 Sheraton Drive, Kidderminster DY10 3QR*

PIGGOTT, Clive. b 47. St Luke's Coll Ex CertEd 69. d 96 p 97. OLM Malden St Jas *S'wark* 96–18; PtO from 18. *84 Manor Drive North, New Malden KT3 5PA* T: (020) 8337 0801 E: cliveoldmalden@aol.com

PIGOTT, Graham John. b 44. Lon Bible Coll BD 73 Nottm Univ MPhil 84 MEd 94 Lon Inst of Educn PGCE 74. St Jo Coll Nottm 79. d 81 p 82. C Beeston *S'well* 81–84; P-in-c W Bridgford 84–88; V Wilford Hill 88–09; AD W Bingham 97–04; Hon Can S'well Minster 04–09; rtd 09; PtO *Derby* from 09; Sheff from 15. *Tanner's House, 5A Goatscliff Cottages, Grindleford, Hope Valley S32 2HG* T: (01433) 639641 E: graham.pigott@btinternet.com

PIGOTT, Nicholas John Capel. b 48. Qu Coll Birm 75. d 78 p 79. C Belmont *Dur* 78–79; C Folkestone St Sav *Cant* 79–82; C Birm St Geo 82–85; V Stevenage St Hugh and St Jo *St Alb* 85–91; TV Totnes w Bridgetown, Berry Pomeroy etc *Ex* 91–02; Asst P 02–04; rtd 04. *27 Croft Road, Ipplepen, Newton Abbot TQ12 5SS* T: (01803) 813664

PIGREM, Terence John (Tim). b 39. Middx Univ BA 97 MA 01. Oak Hill Th Coll 66. d 69 p 70. C Islington St Andr w St Thos and St Matthias *Lon* 69–73; C Barking St Marg w St Patr *Chelmsf* 73–75; TV 75–76; C W Holloway St Luke *Lon* 76–79; V 79–95; P-in-c Abbess Roding, Beauchamp Roding and White Roding *Chelmsf* 95–96; R S Rodings 96–07; RD Dunmow 97–02; rtd 07; PtO *Chelmsf* from 08. *96 Vicarage Lane, Great Baddow, Chelmsford CM2 8JB* T: (01245) 471878 E: pigrem@btinternet.com

PIIR, The Very Revd Gustav Peeter. b 61. St Olaf Coll Minnesota BA 83 Saskatchewan Univ MDiv 86. d 88. Asst Toronto St Pet Canada 88–92; Asst Chas Ch Tallinn Estonia 92–95; R Tallinn H Spirit from 95; Dean Tallinn from 99; P-in-c Tallinn SS Tim and Titus *Eur* from 00. *Pühavaimu 2, Tallinn 10123, Estonia* T: (00372) 646 4430 F: 644 1487 M: 51-76159 E: praost@hot.ee

PIKE, Mrs Amanda Shirley Jane. b 69. Cranmer Hall Dur 99. d 01 p 02. C Boston Spa *York* 01–03; C Elloughton and Brough w Brantingham 03–05; P-in-c Eggleston and Middleton-in-Teesdale w Forest and Frith *Dur* 05–08; TV Bosworth and Sheepy Gp *Leic* 08–11; C Nailstone and Carlton w Shackerstone 08–11; P-in-c Elmton and Whitwell *Derby* 11–13; P-in-c Cheddleton *Lich* 13–14; P-in-c Horton, Lonsdon and Rushton Spencer 13–14; V Cheddleton, Horton, Longsdon and Rushton Spencer from 14. *The Vicarage, Hollow Lane, Cheddleton, Leek ST13 7HP* T: (01538) 360226 M: 07968-543569 E: amanda@ichthos.me.uk

PIKE, David Frank. b 35. BA Lon Univ TCert CEng MIMechE. S Dios Minl Tr Scheme 82. d 85 p 86. NSM Lancing w Coombes *Chich* 85–88; R Albourne w Sayers Common and Twineham 88–94; V Wisborough Green 94–04; rtd 04; PtO *Chich* from 15. *42 Greenoaks, Lancing BN15 0HE* T: (01903) 766209 E: davidf.pike@outlook.com

PIKE, Nicholas Keith. b 52. Warwick Univ BA 74 Brunel Univ MA 80 Cardiff Univ DSW 13 CQSW 80. Ox NSM Course 10. d 12 p 13. NSM Cogges and S Leigh *Ox* from 12; NSM N Leigh from 12. *The Old Nursery, 29 Bridge Street, Witney OX28 1DA* T: (01993) 200843 M: 07962-623310 E: nick.pike@coggesparish.com

PIKE, Paul Alfred. b 38. Bognor Regis Coll of Educn CertEd 58 MIL 88. Wycliffe Hall Ox 83. d 84 p 85. C Penn Fields *Lich* 84–89; OMF Internat Japan 89–03; rtd 03; PtO *Bris* 03–11; *B & W* from 09. *18 Silverlow Road, Nailsea, Bristol BS48 2AD* T: (01275) 856270 E: papike@btinternet.com

PIKE, Timothy David. b 68. Collingwood Coll Dur BA 90 Leeds Univ BA 94. Coll of Resurr Mirfield 92. d 95 p 96. C Owton Manor *Dur* 95–98; C Old St Pancras w Bedford New Town St Matt *Lon* 98–03; CR 03–04; P-in-c Hornsey H Innocents *Lon* 04–07; V 07–16; C Stroud Green H Trin 04–16; P-in-c Harringay St Paul 10–16; AD W Haringey 06–11; V Croydon St Mich w St Jas *S'wark* from 16; CMP from 98; Warden 05–12. *St Michael's Vicarage, 39 Oakfield Road, Croydon CR0 2UX* T: (020) 8680 2848 E: fathertimpike@hotmail.com *or* michaels.church@btinternet.com

PILAVACHI, Canon Michael. b 58. St Mellitus Coll. d 12 p 13. Soul Survivor Watford St Pet *St Alb* from 12; Hon Can St Alb from 16. *37 Maytree Crescent, Watford WD24 5NJ*

PILCHER, Mrs Jennifer. b 42. d 04 p 05. OLM Eastry and Northbourne w Tilmanstone etc *Cant* 04–12; PtO from 12. *1 Long Drive, Church Street, Eastry, Sandwich CT13 0HN* T: (01304) 611472 E: jenniferpilcher@btinternet.com

PILGRIM, Canon Colin Mark. b 56. BA 77. Westcott Ho Cam 81. d 84 p 85. C Chorlton-cum-Hardy St Clem *Man* 84–87; C Whitchurch *Bris* 87–89; V Bedminster Down 89–95; Dioc Youth Officer 95–01; Hon C Stoke Bishop 96–01; V Henleaze from 01; AD Bris W 06–16; Hon Can Bris Cathl from 09. *St Peter's Vicarage, 17 The Drive, Henleaze, Bristol BS9 4LD* T: 0117-962 0636 *or* 962 3196 E: markpilgrimis@aol.com

PILGRIM, Ms Judith Mary. b 44. Westcott Ho Cam 88. d 90 p 94. C Probus, Ladock and Grampound w Creed and St Erme *Truro* 90–94; C Nottingham All SS *S'well* 94–97; Asst Chapl to the Deaf 94–97; PtO 97–00; Ox 00–01; P-in-c Zennor and Towednack *Truro* 02–06; rtd 06. *356 Bennett Street, Long Eaton, Nottingham NG10 4JD* T: 0115-972 5805

PILGRIM, Kenneth George. b 49. Lon Univ BEd 77 Kent Univ MA 94. d 01 p 02. OLM Alkham w Capel le Ferne and Hougham *Cant* 01–03; PtO *Nor* 04–05; NSM E Dereham and Scarning 05–06; NSM Swanton Morley w Beetley w E Bilney and Hoe 05–06; NSM Dereham and Distr from 06; Bp's Officer for Wholeness and Healing from 10. *Sunny Oak, 27 Fakenham Road, Beetley, Dereham NR20 4BT* T: (01362) 861265 E: kenpilgrim@btinternet.com

PILGRIM, Mark. *See* PILGRIM, Colin Mark

PILKINGTON, Miss Anne. b 57. Aston Tr Scheme 88 NOC 90. d 93 p 94. C Wythenshawe Wm Temple Ch *Man* 93–96; P-in-c 96–99; TV Wythenshawe 99–06; P-in-c Didsbury Ch Ch 06; P-in-c Withington St Chris 06; R W Didsbury and Withington St Chris from 06. *Christ Church Rectory, 35 Darley Avenue, Manchester M20 2ZD* T: 0161-445 4152 E: anne@christchurchdidsbury.org.uk

PILKINGTON, David Stuart. b 70. St Mellitus Coll 17. d 19. C Old Ford St Paul and St Mark *Lon* from 19. *58 Chisenhale Road, London E3 5QZ* M: 07491-956861 E: dave@stpauloldford.com

PILKINGTON, Canon Timothy William. b 54. Nottm Univ BA 85 Univ of Wales (Lamp) MA 09. Linc Th Coll 82. d 85 p 86. C Newquay *Truro* 85–88; C Cockington *Ex* 88–91; R St John w Millbrook *Truro* 91–97; V Northampton St Matt *Pet* 97–02; TR Solihull *Birm* 02–14; AD 09–13; Hon Can Birm Cathl 06–14; TR Gt Berkhamsted, Gt and Lt Gaddesden etc *St Alb* from 14. *The Rectory, Rectory Lane, Berkhamsted HP4 2DH* T: (01442) 879739 E: rector@greatberkhamsted.org.uk

PIMENTA, Valmor Alves. b 78. d 03 p 03. USA 01–13; NSM Harlesden All So *Lon* 14–16; C Bedford St Martin *St Alb* 16–18; V from 18; PtO *Lon* from 16. *St Martin's Vicarage, 76 Clapham Road, Bedford MK41 7PN* T: (012343) 57862 M: 07950-897771 E: pr.valmor@hotmail.com

PIMM, Robert John. b 57. Bris Univ BA 78 ACIB 82. Trin Coll Bris 92. d 94 p 95. C Long Benton *Newc* 94–98; TV Bath Twerton-on-Avon *B & W* from 98. *Ascension Vicarage, 35A Claude Avenue, Bath BA2 1AG* T: (01225) 405354 M: 07505-470815 E: robertjpimm@gmail.com

PINCHBECK, Caroline Rosamund. b 70. Hatf Coll Dur BA 93. Wesley Ho Cam MA 00. d 02 p 03. C Mawnan *Truro* 02–06; C Budock 03–06; P-in-c Eastling w Ospringe and Stalisfield w Otterden *Cant* 06–11; Communities and Partnership Exec Officer 11–19; Rural Life Adv 06–19; Rural Life Adv *Roch* 06–11; C Blean *Cant* 12–19; Hon Can Cant Cathl 11–19; R Goodmanham *York* from 19; V Market Weighton from 19; V Sancton from 19; RD S Wold from 19. *38 Cliffe Road, Market Weighton, York YO43 3BN* T: (01430) 879996 E: caroline.pinchbeck575@btinternet.com

PINDER, Mrs Christine Alison. b 61. Birm Univ BSc 83 MSc 84. d 18 p 19. NSM Martlesham w Brightwell *St E* from 18. *3*

Mayfields, Martlesham Heath, Ipswich IP5 3TU M: 07555-748345 E: christine.pinder@btinternet.com

PINDER, Canon John Ridout. b 43. Peterho Cam BA 65 MA 69. Cuddesdon Coll 65. **d** 73 **p** 74. C Leavesden *St Alb* 73–76; Gen Sec Melanesian Miss 77–89; P-in-c Harpsden *Ox* 82–89; R Farlington *Portsm* 89–02; R Liss 02–09; RD Portsm 96–01; Hon Can Portsm Cathl 01–09; rtd 09; P-in-c Stapleford *Ely* 09–15; PtO from 15. *12A Granta Road, Sawston, Cambridge CB22 3HT* T: (01223) 502450 E: johnpinder@waitrose.com

PINDER-PACKARD, John. b 47. Lon Univ BSc. NOC 81. **d** 84 **p** 85. NSM Mosborough *Sheff* 84–85; C Norton 85–88; V New Whittington *Derby* 88–04; P-in-c Newbold and Gt Barlow 99–00; Chapl Whittington Hall Hosp 88–04; R Barlborough and Renishaw *Derby* 04–09; P-in-c Clowne 05–09; rtd 09; PtO *Leeds* from 17. *1 Great Common Close, Barlborough, Chesterfield S43 4SY* E: packards@tiscali.co.uk

PINE, David Michael. b 41. Lich Th Coll 68. **d** 71 **p** 72. C Northam *Ex* 71–74; R Toft w Caldecote and Childerley *Ely* 74–80; R Hardwick 74–80; V Ipswich St Andr *St E* 80–84; P-in-c Hazelbury Bryan w Stoke Wake etc *Sarum* 84–91; R Hazelbury Bryan and the Hillside Par 91–93; V Steep and Froxfield w Privett *Portsm* 93–00; rtd 00; PtO *Portsm* 07–11. *62 Carisbrooke Road, Newport PO30 1BW* T: (01983) 872939 E: davidmpine@hotmail.co.uk

PINFIELD, Leslie Arthur. b 57. Birm Univ BMus 79. St Steph Ho *Ox* 92. **d** 94 **p** 95. C Bath Bathwick *B & W* 94–98; TV Swindon New Town *Bris* 98–07; P-in-c Huddersfield All SS and St Thos *Wakef* 07–14; *Leeds* 14–15; V from 15; Bp's Adv on Inter-Faith Issues *Wakef* 07–14; *Leeds* from 14. *The Vicarage, 17 Cross Church Street, Paddock, Huddersfield HD1 4SN* T: (01484) 428253 E: frleslie@btopenworld.com

PINNEGAR, Alan Edward. b 58. SEITE 09. **d** 12 **p** 13. C Bearsted w Thurnham *Cant* 12–15; R Tunstall and Bredgar from 15. *The Rectory, Tunstall, Sittingbourne ME9 8DU* T: (01795) 471483 M: 07402-717325 E: aepinnegar@gmail.com

PINNELL *(formerly* **ALLEN), Ms Beverley Carole.** b 52. Ch Ch Coll Cant CertEd 74 Open Univ BA 91. Sarum Th Coll 93. **d** 96 **p** 97. NSM Ruislip Manor St Paul *Lon* 96–12; PtO 12–16; *Ox* 14–17; *Chich* from 16. *10 Shipley Mill Close, Stone Cross, Pevensey BN24 5PY* T: (01323) 740283 E: revbev@tiscali.co.uk

PINNELL, George. b 39. NTMTC 96. **d** 99 **p** 00. NSM Hillingdon St Jo *Lon* 99–16; Chapl Heathrow Airport 08–16; PtO *Chich* from 16. *10 Shipley Mill Close, Stone Cross, Pevensey BN24 5PY* T: (01323) 740283 M: 07951-124976 E: pinneg@tiscali.co.uk

PINNER, Mrs Cheri Lee. b 36. Marietta Coll (USA) BA 59. **d** 07 **p** 08. C Greytown New Zealand 07–10; P-in-c Whaley Bridge *Ches* 10–12; rtd 12. *The Maple, Westend, Wickwar, Wotton-under-Edge GL12 8LB* M: 07889-796020 E: cheri.pinner@mac.com

PINNER, John Philip. b 37. K Coll Lon BA 59 AKC 59 Lon Inst of Educn PGCE 60. Westcott Ho Cam 69. **d** 71 **p** 72. C Dover St Mary *Cant* 71–74; Chapl Felsted Sch 74–81; Chapl Rathkeale Coll New Zealand 81–02; P-in-c Greytown St Luke 04–08; rtd 10; Hon C Whaley Bridge *Ches* 10–12. *The Maple, Westend, Wickwar, Wotton-under-Edge GL12 8LB* E: johnpinner1@icloud.com

PINNER, Canon Terence Malcolm William. b 35. Southn Univ MA 59. AKC 59. **d** 60 **p** 61. C Eltham St Barn *S'wark* 60–64; C Grahamstown Cathl S Africa 64–67; USPG 67–69; R King William's Town S Africa 69–72; R Beacon Bay 72–74; Sec for Home Affairs Conf of Br Miss Socs 74–76; P-in-c Hinstock *Lich* 76–79; Adult Educn Officer 76–79; Adult RE Officer 79–83; Chapl Southn Univ *Win* 83–88; Dioc Dir of Ords 88–98; Tutor S Dios Minl Tr Scheme 88–92; P-in-c Old Alresford and Bighton *Win* 93–00; Dir Old Alresford Place 93–00; Hon Can Win Cathl 92–00; rtd 00; PtO *Win* from 00. *11 Sorrell Way, Highcliffe, Christchurch BH23 4LY* M: 07889-177203

PINNINGTON, Mrs Gillian. b 59. St Kath Coll Liv BEd 81 Ches Coll of HE BTh 02. NOC 99. **d** 02 **p** 03. C Roby *Liv* 02–06; TV Speke St Aid 06–17; R Speke St Aid w All SS 17–18; V Coalville w Bardon Hill and Ravenstone *Leic* from 18. *Christ Church Vicarage, 28 London Road, Coalville LE67 3JA* T: (01530) 810655 E: pinny@supanet.com

PINNINGTON, The Ven Suzanne Jane. b 66. Trevelyan Coll Dur BA 89. St Steph Ho *Ox* 95. **d** 97 **p** 98. C Oakham, Hambleton, Egleton, Braunston and Brooke *Pet* 97–00; V Cottingley *Bradf* 00–08; Hon Can Bradf Cathl 04–08; R Houghton le Spring *Dur* 08–18; Adn Gwent Valleys *Mon* from 18; Dioc Dir of Miss from 18. *The Vicarage, Twyn Road, Abercarn, Newport NP11 5GU* T: (01495) 449946 E: archdeacon.gwentvalleys@cinw.org.uk

PINNOCK, Martyn Elliott. b 47. Linc Th Coll 91. **d** 93 **p** 94. C Fordingbridge *Win* 93–97; V St Minver *Truro* 97–01;

P-in-c Luray Ch Ch USA 01–02; V Steeton *Bradf* 02–05; P-in-c Scottsville USA 05–08; rtd 09; P-in-c Tregony w St Cuby and Cornelly *Truro* 13–14; PtO from 14; Chapl Cornwall Partnership NHS Foundn Trust from 15. *Neyth Golvan, 149 Treffry Road, Truro TR1 1WE* T: (01872) 264578 E: martyn.pinnock@nhs.net

PINSENT, Ewen Macpherson. b 30. Edin Th Coll 67. **d** 69 **p** 70. C Holt *Nor* 69–72; R Kelso *Edin* 72–82; R Blendworth w Chalton w Idsworth etc *Portsm* 82–90; R Blendworth w Chalton w Idsworth 90–92; rtd 92; PtO *Sarum* from 94. *The Cross House, The Cross, Child Okeford, Blandford Forum DT11 8ED* T: (01258) 860803 E: ewenandjean@gmail.com

PINTO, James Neil. b 82. Ex Univ BA 04 UEA PGCE 06. Oak Hill Th Coll BA 19. **d** 19. C Heigham H Trin *Nor* from 19. *14 Trinity Street, Norwich NR2 2BQ* M: 07739-582349 E: jamesnpinto@gmail.com *or* jamesnpinto@hotmail.com

PIPER, Canon Andrew. b 58. Magd Coll Ox BA 79 MA 83. Chich Th Coll 80. **d** 83 **p** 84. C Eastbourne St Mary *Chich* 83–88; TV Lewes All SS, St Anne, St Mich and St Thos 88–93; TR Worth 93–03; Can Res and Prec Heref Cathl from 03. *1 The Close, Hereford HR1 2NG* T: (01432) 266193 F: 374220 E: precentor@herefordcathedral.org

PIPER, Calum Lewis. b 91. Ches Univ BTh 12. St Jo Coll Nottm 12. **d** 14 **p** 15. C Wallasey St Hilary *Ches* 14–18; C Cheadle Deanery 18–19; V Bramhall *Ches* from 19. *66 St Michael's Avenue, Bramhall, Stockport SK7 2PG* M: 07890-977064 E: calum.piper14@gmail.com *or* calum.piper@bramhall.church

PIPER, Canon Clifford John. b 53. Moray Ord Course 91. **d** 93 **p** 94. C Invergordon St Ninian *Mor* 93–96; P-in-c 00–03; NSM Tain 96–98; P-in-c 98–03; P-in-c Forres 03–09; R 09–16; Can St Andr Cathl Inverness 00–09; Dean Mor 09–14; rtd 16; Hon Can St Andr Cathl Inverness *Mor* from 14. *17 Craig Crescent, Tain IV19 1JW* T: (01862) 892593 M: 07895-105104

PIPER, Gary Quentin David. b 42. Nottm Coll of Educn TCert 65 Maria Grey Coll Lon DipEd 71. Oak Hill Th Coll 75. **d** 78 **p** 79. NSM Fulham St Matt *Lon* 78–85; V 85–13; AD Hammersmith 86–92; AD Hammersmith and Fulham 06–12; rtd 13; PtO *Lon* from 13. *The Flat, St Saviour's Church, Walton Street, London SW3 1SA* T: (020) 7823 8979 E: revgarypiper@hotmail.com

PIPER, Graham. b 58. Southn Univ BTh 91. Chich Th Coll 88. **d** 91 **p** 92. C Horsham *Chich* 91–94; TV Haywards Heath St Wilfrid 94–99; Dioc Voc Adv 96–99; V Bamber Bridge St Aid *Blackb* 99–04; V Hawes Side and Marton Moss 04–17; rtd 17; PtO *Blackb* 17–18; Hon C Accrington St Andr, St Mary and St Pet and Church Kirk 18–19; P-in-c Mitcham St Olave *S'wark* from 19. *All Saints' Vicarage, 10 Deburgh Road, London SW19 1DX* M: 07816-525843 E: fathergraham@live.co.uk

PIPER, Jessica Ann. b 92. Ches Univ BTh 13. St Mellitus Coll 15. **d** 17 **p** 18. C Bowdon Ches from 17. *66 St Michael's Avenue, Bramhall, Stockport SK7 2PG* M: 07854-185860 E: jessica.a.piper@outlook.com *or* jess@bowdonchurch.com

PIPPEN, Canon Brian Roy. b 50. St D Coll Lamp. **d** 73 **p** 74. C Maindee Newport *Mon* 73–77; TV Cwmbran 77–84; V Newport Ch Ch 84–90; R Pontypool 90–17; AD 98–08; Can St Woolos Cathl 01–17; rtd 17; PtO *Mon* from 17. *37 Thistle Court, Ty Canol, Cwmbran NP44 6JD* T: (01633) 869303

PIRET, Michael John. b 57. State Univ NY BA 79 Univ of Michigan MA 80 PhD 91 Mert Coll Ox MLitt 89. Edin Th Coll 90. **d** 92 **p** 93. C St Andr Cathl Inverness *Mor* 92–94; Dean of Div and Chapl Magd Coll Ox 94–16; R Oyster Bay USA from 16. *65 East Main Street, Oyster Bay NY 11771, USA* E: rector@christchoysterbay.org

PITCHER, Canon David John. b 33. Ely Th Coll 55. **d** 58 **p** 59. C Kingswinford St Mary *Lich* 58–61; C Kirkby *Liv* 61–66; R Ingham w Sutton *Nor* 66–72; V Lakenham St Jo 72–76; R Framlingham w Saxtead *St E* 76–91; RD Loes 82–89; Hon Can St E Cathl 85–99; R Woodbridge St Mary 91–99; rtd 99; PtO *St E* from 00. *25 Coucy Close, Framlingham, Woodbridge IP13 9AX* T: (01728) 621580

PITCHER, George Martell. b 55. Birm Univ BA 77 Middx Univ MA 05. NTMTC 02. **d** 05 **p** 06. NSM St Bride Fleet Street w Bridewell etc *Lon* 05–13; P-in-c Waldron *Chich* from 13. *Culverwood, Little London Road, Cross in Hand, Heathfield TN21 0AX* T: (01435) 865376 M: 07778-917182 E: mail@georgepitcher.com

PITCHER, Canon Simon John. b 63. Reading Univ BA 85. Ridley Hall Cam 00. **d** 02 **p** 03. C Lightcliffe *Wakef* 02–05; P-in-c Heckmondwike 05–10; C Liversedge w Hightown 05–10; C Roberttown w Hartshead 05–10; RD Birstall 08–10; TR Sole Bay *St E* from 10; RD Waveney and Blyth from 11; Hon Can St E Cathl from 16. *The Vicarage, Gardner Road, Southwold IP18 6HJ* T: (01502) 725424 E: revsimon@talktalk.net

PITE, Sheila Reinhardt. *See* SWARBRICK, Sheila Reinhardt

PITHERS, Canon Brian Hoyle. b 34. Chich Th Coll 63. **d** 66 **p** 67. C Wisbech SS Pet and Paul *Ely* 66–70; V Fenstanton 70–75; V Hilton 70–75; V Habergham Eaves St Matt *Blackb* 75–85; P-in-c Habergham Eaves H Trin 78–85; V Burnley St Matt w H Trin 85–86; TR Ribbleton 86–92; V Torrisholme 92–00; Hon Can Blackb Cathl 97–00; rtd 01; PtO *Blackb* from 01. *37 Dallam Avenue, Morecambe LA4 5BB* T: (01524) 424786 E: brianpithers@talktalk.net

PITKETHLY (*née* CHEVILL), Elizabeth Jane. b 65. Colchester Inst of Educn BA 86 K Coll Lon MMus 87 PhD 93 Warwick Univ BPhil 00 AKC 89 Lon Inst of Educn PGCE 91. Wycliffe Hall Ox MSt 04 MLitt 08. **d** 08 **p** 09. C Blackheath St Jo *S'wark* 08–11; PtO *Ox* 11–12; NSM Ox St Andr from 12; Chapl St Pet Coll Ox from 14. *24 Thorncliffe Road, Oxford OX2 7BB* T: (01865) 552571 M: 07952-024571 E: ejpitkethly@btinternet.com

PITKIN, James Mark. b 62. Man Univ BSc 83 Glos Univ BA(Theol) 03 MRAeS 90 CEng 90. STETS. **d** 99 **p** 00. C Chilworth w N Baddesley *Win* 99–03; V Lockerley and E Dean w E and W Tytherley from 03; P-in-c Somborne w Ashley from 19; AD Romsey from 17; Corps Chapl ATC from 15. *The Vicarage, The Street, Lockerley, Romsey SO51 0JF* T: (01794) 340635 F: 08701-674691 M: 07931-736166 E: jamespitkin@priest.com

PITKIN, Mrs Susan Margaret. b 60. Man Univ BA 84 Surrey Univ BA 03. STETS 00. **d** 03 **p** 04. C Southampton Maybush St Pet *Win* 03–06; C Maybush and Southampton St Jude 06–09; Asst Chapl Southn Univ Hosps NHS Trust 09–10; Trust Chapl Univ Hosp Southn NHS Foundn Trust from 10. *The Vicarage, The Street, Lockerley, Romsey SO51 0JF* T: (01794) 340635 M: 07906-027042 E: suepitkin@minister.com

PITMAN, Mrs Janet Elizabeth. b 67. Salford Univ BEng 90 Open Univ BA 99. All SS Cen for Miss & Min 12. **d** 15 **p** 16. C Oldham St Paul and Werneth *Man* 15–19; V Milnrow and New Hey from 19. *St Thomas's Vicarage, Church Street, Newhey, Rochdale OL16 3QS* M: 07985-971022 E: hildaofwhitby67@gmail.com

PITMAN, Jessica. b 62. Newton Park Coll Bath BEd 85. STETS 07. **d** 10 **p** 11. C Langport Area *B & W* 10–17; R Aller, High w Low Ham and Huish Episcopi cum Langport from 17. *Vicarage, Huish Episcopi, Langport TA10 9QR* T: (010458) 251489 E: jessicapitman@aol.com

PITMAN, Roger Thomas. b 64. St Mich Coll Llan BTh 00. **d** 00 **p** 01. C Caerphilly *Llan* 00–02; C Coity w Nolton 02–07; P-in-c Llanharry 07–12; P-in-c Llangeinor and the Garw Valley from 12; Chapl Pontypridd and Rhondda NHS Trust 07–10. *The Vicarage, 2 Waun Wen, Bettws Road, Llangeinor, Bridgend CF32 8PH* T: (01656) 870280 E: vicar@the-vicarage.net

PITT, George. b 52. QUB BD 79 MTh 88. CITC 81. **d** 81 **p** 82. C Belfast St Mary *Conn* 81–86; CMS 86–92; Zaïre 88–92; V Penycae *St As* 92–98; I Killesher *K, E & A* 98–01; Eucan Adv Ch of Ireland Bps' Appeal 01–03; PtO *Bradf* 04–06; Chapl HM Pris Moorland 06–13; rtd 13. *20 Thornsbank, Sedbergh LA10 5LF* T: (01539) 622095

PITT, Karen Lesley Finella. *See* TIMMIS, Karen Lesley Finella

PITT, Canon Trevor. b 45. Hull Univ BA 66 MA 69 Open Univ DipEd 91. Linc Th Coll 68 Union Th Sem (NY) STM 70. **d** 70 **p** 71. C Sheff St Geo 70–74; TV Gleadless Valley 74–78; TR 78–79; P-in-c Elham *Cant* 79–82; V Elham w Denton and Wootton 82–91; Vice Prin Cant Sch of Min 81–91; Six Preacher Cant Cathl 85–91; Prin NEOC *Newc* 91–10; Hon Can Newc Cathl 91–10; PtO *York* from 91; *Ripon* 91–14; *Leeds* 14–16; rtd 10; PtO *Newc* from 10; Hon C Escomb *Dur* 12–15; Hon C Etherley 12–15; Hon C Witton Park 12–15; Hon C Hamsterley and Witton-le-Wear 12–15; PtO from 15. *Green View House, Hamsterley, Bishop Auckland DL13 3QF* T: (01388) 488898 E: trevorpitt@aol.com

PITT, Mrs Valerie. b 55. Liv Univ BA 77. STETS 02. **d** 05 **p** 06. NSM Oxshott *Guildf* 05–09; NSM Meole Brace *Lich* from 09. *4 Meole Hall Gardens, Shrewsbury SY3 9JS* T: (01743) 270102 E: valerie.pitt@trinitychurches.org

PITTARIDES, Renos. b 62. Surrey Univ BA 85. **d** 07 **p** 08. OLM Cobham and Stoke D'Abernon *Guildf* 07–15; P-in-c E Horsley 15–17; R from 17. *The Rectory, Ockham Road South, East Horsley, Leatherhead KT24 6RL* E: renosp@gmail.com

PITTIS, Canon Stephen Charles. b 52. Sheff Univ MA 01. Oak Hill Th Coll. **d** 76 **p** 77. C Win Ch Ch 76–79; Chapl Dorset Inst of HE and Bournemouth and Poole Coll of FE *Sarum* 79–84; V Woking St Paul *Guildf* 84–97; Dir of Faith Development *Win* 97–09; Dioc Missr and Can Res *Win* Cathl 09–11; R Michelmersh and Awbridge and Braishfield etc from 11; Hon Can Win Cathl from 13. *The Rectory, Braishfield Road, Braishfield, Romsey SO51 0PR* T: (01794) 368335 E: pittisinc@gmail.com

PITTMAN, Louisa. b 76. Coll of Charleston (USA) BSc 06 Bris Univ MA 09 PhD 15 Cam Univ BTh 18. Westcott Ho Cam 16. **d** 18 **p** 19. C Wymondham *Nor* 18–19; C Barnham Broom and Upper Yare from 19. *The Vicarage, Honingham Road, Barnham Broom, Norwich NR9 4DB*

PITTS, Canon Evadne Ione (<u>Eve</u>). b 50. Qu Coll Birm. **d** 89 **p** 94. C Bartley Green *Birm* 89–93; Team Dn Kings Norton 93–94; TV 94–98; P-in-c Highters Heath 98–00; V 00–09; P-in-c Birchfield 09–14; V from 14; Hon Can Birm Cathl from 05. *Holy Trinity Vicarage, 213 Birchfield Road, Birmingham B20 3DG* T: 0121-356 4241 E: blackuhru@aol.com

PITTS, The Very Revd Michael James. b 44. Worc Coll Ox BA 66 Worc Coll of Educn MA 69. Qu Coll Birm 67. **d** 69 **p** 70. C Pennywell St Thos and Grindon St Oswald CD *Dur* 69–72; C Darlington H Trin 72–74; Chapl Dunkerque w Lille Arras etc Miss to Seamen *Eur* 74–79; V Tudhoe *Dur* 79–81; Chapl Helsinki w Moscow *Eur* 81–85; Chapl Stockholm 85–88; Hon Can Brussels Cathl 87–88; Hon Chapl Miss to Seafarers Canada from 88; R Montreal St Cuth 88–91; Dean Ch Ch Cathl Montreal 91–09; P-in-c Montreal St Ignatius from 09; rtd 09. *3279 rue Gariepy RR4, Sainte Julienne QC J0K 2T0, Canada* T: (001) (450) 834 2956 E: michael.pitts@worc.oxon.org

PIX, Stephen James. b 42. Ex Coll Ox BA 64 MA 68 Univ of Wales (Cardiff) LLM 97. Clifton Th Coll 66. **d** 68 **p** 69. C St Helens St Helen *Liv* 68–71; LtO *S'wark* 71–76; Hon C Wallington 76–84; V Osmotherley w E Harlsey and Ingleby Arncliffe *York* 84–89; V Ox St Mich w St Martin and All SS 89–01; rtd 01; PtO St E 01–07; Ox from 07. *10 Cadogan Park, Woodstock OX20 1UW* T: (01993) 812473

PIZZEY, Canon Lawrence Roger. b 42. Dur Univ BA 64. Westcott Ho Cam 65. **d** 67 **p** 68. C Bramford *St E* 67–71; Tutor Woodbridge Abbey 71–77; Asst Chapl Woodbridge Sch 71–77; P-in-c Flempton w Hengrave and Lackford *St E* 77–85; R Culford, W Stow and Wordwell 77–85; P-in-c Acton w Gt Waldingfield 85–89; V 89–95; P-in-c Sudbury and Chilton 95–98; R 98–07; RD Sudbury 96–06; Hon Can St E Cathl 00–07; rtd 07; PtO *St E* from 07. *9 Constable Road, Bury St Edmunds IP33 3UQ* T: (01284) 762863 E: lrp.sudbury@virgin.net

PLACE, Rodger Goodson. b 37. St Chad's Coll Dur BA 60. **d** 62 **p** 63. C Pontesbury I and II *Heref* 62–65; C Heref St Martin 65–68; V Ditton Priors 68–75; R Neenton 68–75; P-in-c Aston Botterell w Wheathill and Loughton 69–75; P-in-c Burwarton w N Cleobury 69–75; P-in-c Dacre w Hartwith *Ripon* 75–76; V 76–82; V Wyther 82–92; P-in-c Roundhay St Jo 92–97; V 97–00; rtd 00; PtO *York* from 00. *72 Field Lane, Thorpe Willoughby, Selby YO8 9FL* T: (01757) 703174

PLAISTER, Keith Robin. b 43. K Coll Lon BD 65 AKC 65. **d** 66 **p** 67. C Laindon w Basildon *Chelmsf* 66–71; V Gt Wakering 71–78; V Gt Wakering w Foulness 78–90; C Witham 91–94; V 94–99; P-in-c Sandon and E Hanningfield 99–08; rtd 08; PtO *Chelmsf* from 10. *118 Maldon Road, Great Baddow, Chelmsford CM2 7DH* T: (01245) 473135 E: keithplaister@hotmail.com

PLANT, Miss Elizabeth Bowers. b 48. Westf Coll Lon BA 70 Man Univ PGCE 71. **d** 08 **p** 09. OLM Deane *Man* 08–18; rtd 18; PtO *Man* from 18. *25 Kintyre Drive, Bolton BL3 4PE* T: (01204) 63730 E: eplant@supanet.com or eplant225@gmail.com

PLANT, Mrs Glenys. b 49. ALA 71. EMMTC 95. **d** 98 **p** 99. C Allestree *Derby* 98–01; rtd 01; PtO *Derby* from 01. *3 Stoodley Pike Gardens, Allestree, Derby DE22 2TN* T: (01332) 552697

PLANT, Katharine Jill. b 66. Leeds Univ BA 88 Bradf and Ilkley Coll PGCE 94. Coll of Resurr Mirfield 14. **d** 16 **p** 17. C Holbeach *Linc* 16–19; P-in-c Breadsall *Derby* from 19; P-in-c Morley and Smalley from 19. *The Rectory, 57 Rectory Lane, Breadsall, Derby DE21 5LL* M: 07975-774170 E: kateplant2610@gmail.com

PLANT, Michael Ian. b 47. Man Univ MEd 85 GNSM 68. St Jo Coll Nottm 97. **d** 99 **p** 00. NSM St D Cathl 99–01; NSM Dewisland 01–18; NSM Gtr Dewisland from 18. *Pencnwc Cottages, 1 Spring Gardens, Castle Morris, Haverfordwest SA62 5ER* T: (01348) 841390 E: mikeandvalplant@btinternet.com

PLANT, Nicholas. b 58. Sarum Coll MA 15 MAAT 87. SAOMC 95. **d** 98 **p** 99. OLM W Slough *Ox* 98–04; OLM Burnham w Dropmore, Hitcham and Taplow 04–08; NSM Taplow and Dropmore 08–09; C The Cookhams 09–14; V from 14. *The Vicarage, Churchgate, Sutton Road, Cookham, Maidenhead SL6 9SP* T: (01628) 529183 E: fr.nick@ymail.com

PLANT, Nicholas. *See* PLANT, Richard George Nicholas

PLANT, Richard. b 41. Open Univ BSc 93. Qu Coll Birm 88. **d** 90 **p** 91. C Skelmersdale St Paul *Liv* 90–93; R Golborne 93–00; R Hesketh w Becconsall *Blackb* 00–07; rtd 07; PtO

Blackb from 07. *12 Granville Avenue, Hesketh Bank, Preston PR4 6AH* T: (01772) 815257 E: richard.plant1@yahoo.com

PLANT, Richard George Nicholas. b 45. Man Univ BA 67. Coll of Resurr Mirfield 68. **d** 71 **p** 72. C Cleckheaton St Jo *Wakef* 71–74; P-in-c Adel *Ripon* 74–78; V Ireland Wood 78–82; V Armley w New Wortley 82–92; R Garforth 92–08; rtd 08; PtO *York* from 08. *3 Holman Avenue, Garforth, Leeds LS25 1HU* T: 0113-287 6064 E: nick.plant@tiscali.co.uk

PLANT, Stephen John. b 64. Birm Univ BA 86 Fitzw Coll Cam PhD 93. ERMC 10. **d** 11 **p** 11. Dean Trin Hall Cam from 10; NSM Cambridge St Jas *Ely* from 11. *Trinity Hall, Cambridge CB2 1TJ* T: (01223) 241169 *or* 332548 M: 07824-835199 E: sjp27@cam.ac.uk

PLANT, Thomas Richard. b 79. St Andr Univ MA 01 Bris Univ MPhil 05 Selw Coll Cam PhD 13. Westcott Ho Cam 08. **d** 12 **p** 13. C Gt Berkhamsted, Gt and Lt Gaddesden etc *St Alb* 12–16; TV Old St Pancras *Lon* 16–17; Chapl Lich Cathl Sch from 17; PV and Subchanter Lich Cath from 17; CF(V) from 14. *2 Rudge Street, Streethay, Lichfield WS13 8FZ* T: (01543) 306170 M: 07766-283546 E: tomplant@mac.com

PLATT, Anne Cecilia. *See* HOLMES, Anne Cecilia

PLATT, Damian Edward. b 82. Ox Brookes Univ BA 04. Oak Hill Th Coll BA 12. **d** 12 **p** 13. C Bispham *Blackb* 12–15; V Thornton-le-Fylde from 15. *Christ Church Vicarage, Meadows Avenue, Thornton-Cleveleys FY5 2TW* T: (01253) 855099 M: 07875-311929 E: damian@theplattfamily.org

PLATT, David. *See* PLATT, William David

PLATT, Mrs Jane Marie. b 54. Westhill Coll Birm CertEd 76 Open Univ BA 90. Qu Coll Birm 05. **d** 08 **p** 09. NSM Quinton Road W St Boniface *Birm* 08–15; PtO 15–18; P-in-c Frankley from 18. *39 Richmond Road, Rubery, Rednal, Birmingham B45 9UN* T: 0121-453 3035 E: janeplatt@onetel.com

PLATT, John Emerson. b 36. Pemb Coll Ox BA 59 MA 65 DPhil 77 Hull Univ MTh 72. Cuddesdon Coll 59. **d** 61 **p** 62. C Adlington *Blackb* 61–64; C Sutton St Mich *York* 64–68; C Ox St Giles 68–71; Asst Chapl Pemb Coll Ox 68–69; Chapl 69–02; rtd 02. *Apple Tree Cottage, 2 Church Road, Wilmcote, Stratford-upon-Avon CV37 9XD* T: (01789) 770127 E: johnplatt567@gmail.com

PLATT, William David. b 31. St Chad's Coll Dur BA 54. Coll of Resurr Mirfield 54. **d** 56 **p** 57. C Bethnal Green St Jo w St Simon *Lon* 56–60; C Pinner 60–65; V N Hammersmith St Kath 65–72; V Woodham *Guildf* 72–88; Chapl Community of St Mary V Wantage 88–96; rtd 96; NSM Blewbury, Hagbourne and Upton *Ox* 96–03. *Wyndham Hall, Skimmingdish Lane, Launton, Bicester OX26 5AF* T: (01869) 722767

PLATTEN, Canon Aidan Stephen George. b 76. Ripon Coll Cuddesdon BTh 03. **d** 03 **p** 04. C Woodbridge St Mary *St E* 03–06; Bp's Chapl *Glouc* 06–11; Hon Min Can Glouc Cathl 09–11; V St Marylebone St Mark Hamilton Terrace *Lon* 11–17; Prec and Can Res Nor Cathl from 17. *33 The Close, Norwich NR1 4DZ* T: (01603) 218314 E: canonprecentor@cathedral.org.uk

PLATTEN, Gregory Austin David. b 78. Worc Coll Ox BA 00 MA 08 Ox Univ MTh 05 Linc Coll Ox DPhil 13. Ripon Coll Cuddesdon 01. **d** 03 **p** 04. C St John's Wood *Lon* 03–07; Chapl Linc Coll and Hon C Ox St Mich w St Martin and All SS 07–13; V Friern Barnet All SS *Lon* from 13; AD Cen Barnet from 16; AD W Barnet from 18. *14 Oakleigh Park South, London N20 9JU* T: (020) 8445 0015 M: 07891-124478 E: gregory@priest.com

✠**PLATTEN, The Rt Revd Stephen George.** b 47. Lon Univ BEd 72 Trin Coll Ox BD 03 UEA Hon DLitt 03 Huddersfield Univ Hon DUniv 12 Hon FGCM 12. Cuddesdon Coll 72. **d** 75 **p** 76 **c** 03. C Headington *Ox* 75–78; Chapl and Tutor Linc Th Coll 78–83; Can Res Portms Cathl and Dir of Ords *Portsm* 83–89; Abp's Sec for Ecum Affairs *Cant* 90–95; Hon Can Cant Cathl 90–95; Dean Nor 95–03; Bp Wakef 03–14; rtd 14; R St Mich Cornhill w St Pet le Poer etc *Lon* 14–16; Hon Asst Bp Lon from 14; Hon Asst Bp Newc from 14; Asst Bp S'wark from 14; Hon Can Musoma from 08. *73A Gloucester Place, London W1U 8JW* E: stephen.platten@icloud.com

PLATTIN, Miss Darleen Joy. b 63. Oak Hill Th Coll BA 94. ERMC 04. **d** 07 **p** 08. C Barnham Broom and Upper Yare *Nor* 07–10; P-in-c Easton, Colton, Marlingford and Bawburgh 10–14; P-in-c Gt and Lt Plumstead w Thorpe End and Witton 14–18; P-in-c Rackheath and Salhouse 18; R Gt and Lt Plumstead, Rackheath w Salhouse and Witton from 18. *The Rectory, 56 Green Lane West, Rackheath, Norwich NR13 6PG* E: darleenplattin@btinternet.com

PLATTS, Anthony Russell. b 41. Qu Coll Birm. **d** 08 **p** 09. NSM Hill *Birm* 08–11; PtO from 11; *Lich* from 16. *14 Wheatcroft Close, Four Oaks, Sutton Coldfield B75 5SU* M: 07984-817564 E: a_platts1@sky.com

PLATTS, Mrs Hilary Anne Norrie. b 60. K Coll Lon BD 85 AKC 85 SRN 81. Ripon Coll Cuddesdon 86. **d** 88 **p** 94. C Moulsham St Jo *Chelmsf* 88–90; Chapl Reading Univ *Ox* 90–99; C Calcot 90–92; NSM Reading Deanery 99–00; PtO *Birm* 00–07; Chapl Birm Community Healthcare NHS Foundn Trust 01–07; Chapl Cov and Warks Partnership NHS Trust 03–07; PtO *Chelmsf* 07–09; Adv for Women's Min (Colchester Area) from 08; Chapl Colchester Hosp Univ NHS Foundn Trust 09–18; Chapl E Suffolk and N Essex NHS Foundn Trust from 18. *The Rectory, 7 Merlin End, Colchester CO4 3FW* T: (01206) 866145 E: hilaryplatts@googlemail.com

PLATTS, Timothy Caradoc. b 61. LMH Ox BA 83 MA 88 St Cross Coll Ox DPhil 88. Ripon Coll Cuddesdon 87. **d** 89 **p** 90. C Whitley Ch Ch *Ox* 89–95; P-in-c Earley St Nic 95–98; V 98–00; V Four Oaks *Birm* 00–07; P-in-c Elmstead *Chelmsf* 07–14; Chapl to Bp Colchester 07–14; P-in-c Greenstead w Colchester St Anne from 14. *The Rectory, 7 Merlin End, Colchester CO4 3FW* E: dogwalker2512@gmail.com

PLAYER, Leslie Mark. b 65. Ridley Hall Cam 92. **d** 95 **p** 96. C Belper *Derby* 95–98; C Hamworthy *Sarum* 98–03; R W Downland from 03. *The Rectory, 97 Mill End, Damerham, Fordingbridge SP6 3HU* T: (01725) 518642 E: leslieplayer@hotmail.com

PLAYLE, Ms Merrin Laura. b 58. Univ of Wales (Swansea) BSc 79. Ridley Hall Cam 99. **d** 01 **p** 02. C Haslemere and Grayswood *Guildf* 01–05; V E Ham St Paul *Chelmsf* from 05. *St Paul's Vicarage, 227 Burges Road, London E6 2EU* T: (020) 8472 5531 E: merrin.playle@btopenworld.com

PLEDGER, Mrs Nicola. b 55. Lon Bible Coll BA 94. SAOMC 99. **d** 01 **p** 02. C Ware Ch Ch *St Alb* 01–05; PtO 05–11; V Hitcham *Ox* 11–16; rtd 16; PtO *Ox* from 16; *St Alb* from 17. *132 Quickley Lane, Chorleywood, Rickmansworth WD3 5PQ* T: (01923) 283200 E: npledger77@gmail.com

PLIMLEY, Canon William. b 17. St Aid Birkenhead 50. **d** 52 **p** 53. C Norbury *Ches* 52–55; V Laisterdyke *Bradf* 55–83; RD Calverley 65–78; Hon Can Bradf Cathl 67–83; rtd 83; PtO *Bradf* 83–14; *Leeds* from 14. *18 Holden Grange, 31 Holden Lane, Baildon, Shipley BD17 6JF*

PLIMMER, Wayne Robert. b 64. St Chad's Coll Dur BA 85 Leeds Univ MA 07. St Steph Ho Ox 86. **d** 88 **p** 89. C Cockerton *Dur* 88–91; C Poulton-le-Fylde *Blackb* 91–93; V Darton *Wakef* 93–06; P-in-c Cawthorne 04–06; V Beeston *S'well* from 06. *The Vicarage, Middle Street, Beeston, Nottingham NG9 1GA* T: 0115-925 4571 E: wplimmer@tiscali.co.uk

PLOWMAN, Richard Robert Bindon. b 38. Solicitor 61. Ridley Hall Cam 76. **d** 78 **p** 79. C Combe Down w Monkton Combe *B & W* 78–81; C Combe Down w Monkton Combe and S Stoke 81–83; V Coxley w Godney, Henton and Wookey 83–03; RD Shepton Mallet 95–01; rtd 03; PtO *B & W* from 04. *Hyland House, Lower Rudge, Frome BA11 2QE* T: (01373) 831316

PLOWS, Jonathan. b 57. Warwick Univ BA 79 Homerton Coll Cam PGCE 80 Birkbeck Coll Lon MSc 85. STETS BA 07. **d** 07 **p** 08. NSM Salisbury St Thos and St Edm *Sarum* 07–19; P-in-c Wylye and Till Valley from 19. *The Rectory, Duck Street, Steeple Langford, Salisbury SP3 4NH* E: jonplows@aol.com

PLUMB, Gordon Alan. b 42. Leeds Univ BA 64. Sarum & Wells Th Coll. **d** 82 **p** 83. C Biggleswade *St Alb* 82–86; TV Grantham *Linc* 86–95; P-in-c Saxby All Saints 95–97; R 97–07; P-in-c Bonby 95–97; V 97–07; P-in-c Horkstow 95–97; V 97–07; P-in-c S Ferriby 95–97; R 97–07; P-in-c Worlaby 95–97; V 97–07; rtd 07; PtO *Linc* from 08. *Ingham House, 45A Dam Road, Barton-upon-Humber DN18 5BT* T: (01652) 636445 E: gplumb2000@aol.com

PLUMB, Nicola Louise. *See* MOY, Nicola Louise

PLUMB, Capt Stephen Paul. b 59. Wilson Carlile Coll. **d** 15 **p** 17. C The Six *Cant* 15–18; NSM Hackney Marsh *Lon* from 18. *All Souls' Vicarage, 44 Overbury Street, London E5 0AJ* M: 07905-040119 E: revcaptainplumby@hotmail.com

PLUMB, Stuart Peter. b 81. Ox Brookes Univ BA 04. Trin Coll Bris MA 14. **d** 14 **p** 15. C Kingston Hill St Paul *S'wark* 14–17; C Ealing St Paul *Lon* from 17; C Hanwell St Mellitus w St Mark from 17. *St Mellitus' Vicarage, 1 Church Road, London W7 3BA* M: 07598-335324 E: stuplumb@gmail.com *or* stu@stmellitushanwell.com

PLUMB, Miss Valerie Isabelle Dawn Frances. b 69. Ripon Coll Cuddesdon BTh 02. **d** 01 **p** 02. C Newport St Andr *Mon* 01–03; C Monmouth w Overmonnow etc 03–06; TV By Brook and Colerne w N Wraxall *Bris* 06–09; OCM 06–09; R Quantock Towers *B & W* 09–15; Area Dean for Rural Miss and Development Buckm Adnry *Ox* from 15. *Westfields, Church Lane, Ludgershall, Aylesbury HP18 9NU* T: (01844) 239347 M: 07825-877722 E: val.plumb@oxford.anglican.org

PLUMLEY, Paul Jonathan. b 42. St Jo Coll Nottm 71. **d** 74 **p** 75. C Mile Cross *Nor* 74–77; P-in-c Wickham Skeith *St E* 77–79; P-in-c Stoke Ash, Thwaite and Wetheringsett 77–79; Assoc Min Woodbridge St Jo 80–81; Chapl RAF 81–86; PtO *Roch* 86–95; R Hever, Four Elms and Mark Beech 95–00; Sen Chapl Maidstone and Tunbridge Wells NHS Trust 00–07; rtd 07; PtO *Roch* from 08; PV Roch Cathl from 12. *4 Cedar Ridge, Tunbridge Wells TN2 3NX* T: (01892) 514499 M: 07925-615601 E: pauljplumley@gmail.com *or* paulplumley@btinternet.com

PLUMMER, Angela. b 59. Linc Sch of Th and Min. **d** 13 **p** 14. C Melbourne, Ticknall, Smisby and Stanton *Derby* 13–17; P-in-c Kenton Ascension *Newc* from 17. *The Vicarage, Creighton Avenue, Newcastle upon Tyne NE3 4UN* T: 0191-285 7803 M: 07721-023339 E: aplummer@live.co.uk

PLUMMER, Miss Anne Frances. b 36. Bedf Coll Lon BA 57. S'wark Ord Course 79. **dss** 82 **d** 87 **p** 94. NSM Salfords *S'wark* 82–06; Dean MSE (Croydon) 97–02; PtO from 06. *50 Park View Road, Salfords, Redhill RH1 5DN* T: (01293) 785852

PLUMMER, Canon Deborah Ann. b 49. St Hugh's Coll Ox BA 71 MA 75. St Alb Minl Tr Scheme 82. **dss** 85 **d** 87 **p** 94. Ickenham *Lon* 85–88; Par Dn 87–88; C Northolt St Mary 88–92; Chapl Lee Abbey 92–95; P-in-c Kintbury w Avington *Ox* 95–01; Lect Bolton St Pet *Man* 01–07; P-in-c Prestwich St Marg 07–14; C Prestwich St Gabr 10–14; AD Radcliffe and Prestwich 09–13; Hon Can Man Cathl 12–14; rtd 14; PtO *Man* from 15; *Leeds* from 17. *Meadow View, 7 Church Terrace, Berry Brow, Huddersfield HD4 7NB* T: (01484) 667661 M: 07593-837343 E: debberry@mail.com

PLUMPTON, Paul. b 50. Keble Coll Ox BA 72 MA 76. St Steph Ho Ox 72. **d** 74 **p** 75. C Tonge Moor *Man* 74–76; C Atherton 76–79; V Oldham St Jas 79–99; V Oldham St Jas w St Ambrose 99–17; rtd 17. *6 Hallet Court, Hughes Hallet Street, Sliema SLM 3142, Malta GC* T: (00356) 2783 6339 E: theplookes@gmail.com

PLUNKETT, Michael Edward. b 38. Leeds Univ BSc 61. Ely Th Coll 61. **d** 63 **p** 64. C Kirkby *Liv* 63–68; Lect Stockton-on-Tees 68–72; LtO *Dur* 72–73; TV Stockton 73–75; V Cantril Farm *Liv* 75–81; Soc Resp Officer 81–89; V Melling 81–91; TR Speke St Aid 91–04; rtd 04; PtO *Heref* from 04. *1 The Ridge, Bishops Castle SY9 5AB* T: (01588) 630018 E: m.plunkettzzl@btinternet.com

PLUNKETT, Canon Peter William. b 30. Oak Hill Th Coll. **d** 61 **p** 62. C Fazakerley Em *Liv* 61–64; C St Helens St Mark 64–68; V Kirkdale St Paul N Shore 68–79; P-in-c Bootle St Mary w St Jo 77–79; V Bootle St Mary w St Paul 79–81; V Goose Green 81–89; V W Derby St Jas 89–98; Hon Can Liv Cathl 97–98; rtd 98. *50 Trinity Crescent, West Shore, Llandudno LL30 2PQ* T: (01492) 872109

PLYMING, Philip James John. b 74. Rob Coll Cam BA 96 St Jo Coll Dur BA 00 Edin Univ PhD 08. Cranmer Hall Dur 98. **d** 01 **p** 02. C Chineham *Win* 01–06; V Claygate *Guildf* 06–17; AD Emly 12–17; Warden Cranmer Hall Dur from 17. *St John's College, 3 South Bailey, Durham DH1 3RJ* T: 0191-334 3894 E: cranmer.warden@durham.ac.uk

PLYMOUTH, Archdeacon of. See SHUTT, The Ven Nicholas Stephen

PLYMOUTH, Suffragan Bishop of. See MACKINNEL, The Rt Revd Nicholas Howard Paul

PNEMATICATOS, Nicholas Peter Anthony. b 59. N Lon Univ BA 92 Lon Univ MA 93. Ripon Coll Cuddesdon 93. **d** 95 **p** 96. C Yeovil St Mich *B & W* 95–98; Chapl Yeovil Coll 95–96; Chapl RN 98–02; Chapl RAF 02–08; P-in-c Mill End and Heronsgate w W Hyde *St Alb* 08–10; rtd 16. *c/o Crockford, Church House, Great Smith Street, London SW1P 3AZ* M: 07703-566787 E: delvillewood@aol.com

POARCH, Canon John Chilton. b 30. Bris Univ BA 54. Ridley Hall Cam 54. **d** 56 **p** 57. C Swindon Ch Ch *Bris* 56–59; C Corsham 59–61; R Praslin Seychelles 61–63; V Brislington St Cuth *Bris* 63–69; Adn Seychelles 69–72; R St Paul's Cathl Mahé 69–72; V Warmley *Bris* 72–86; R Syston 72–86; RD Bitton 79–85; P-in-c 80–86; Hon Can Bris Cathl 82–95; P-in-c Langley Fitzurse 86–94; Dioc Convenor Rtd Clergy Assn from 01. *16 Norley Road, Bristol BS7 0HP* T: 0117-329 4496

POCOCK, Mrs Gillian Margaret. b 35. Nottm Univ BA 57. Cranmer Hall Dur 82. **dss** 83 **d** 87 **p** 94. Bearpark *Dur* 83–88; Hon Par Dn 87–88; Par Dn S Hetton w Haswell 88; Asst RD Dur 89–90; Chapl St Aid Coll Dur 89–93; Par Dn Esh *Dur* 90–92; P-in-c 92–99; P-in-c Hamsteels 97–99; P-in-c Langley Park 98–99; rtd 99; PtO *Dur* from 04. *11 Cooke's Wood, Broom Park, Durham DH7 7RL* T: 0191-386 1140 E: gillian.pocock@lineone.net

POCOCK, Lynn Elizabeth. b 48. Coll of Wooster Ohio BA 69 CertEd 71. Qu Coll Birm 73. **dss** 82 **d** 87 **p** 94. Gleadless *Sheff* 82–85; Thorpe Hesley 85–92; Par Dn 87–92; NSM Ribbesford w Bewdley *Worc* 92–03; PtO 03–15; *Sheff* from 15. *149 Crimicar Lane, Sheffield S10 4FD* M: 07985-160470 E: lynn_pocock@yahoo.com

POCOCK, Canon Nigel John. b 47. Lon Univ BSc 68 Birm Univ MA 83 Lambeth STh 78 Univ of Wales (Lamp) MMin 11. Oak Hill Th Coll 69. **d** 72 **p** 73. C Tunbridge Wells St Jas *Roch* 72–75; C Heatherlands St Jo *Sarum* 75–78; V Leic St Chris 78–83; R Camborne *Truro* 83–97; RD Carnmarth N 91–96; Hon Can Truro Cathl 92–97; V Old Windsor *Ox* 97–09; rtd 09; PtO *Liv* from 17. *19 Epping Drive, Woolston, Warrington WA1 4QL* T: (01925) 555996 E: njpoc@tiscali.co.uk

PODGER, Richard Philip Champeney. b 38. K Coll Cam BA 61 MA 66. Cuddesdon Coll 62. **d** 64 **p** 65. C Doncaster St Geo *Sheff* 64–68; C Orpington All SS *Roch* 68–74; W Germany 76–88; Chapl Kassel *Eur* 83–88; TV Whitstable *Cant* 88–94; PtO 95–12; Chapl E Kent NHS and Soc Care Partnership Trust 02–06; Chapl Kent & Medway NHS and Soc Care Partnership Trust 06–10; PtO *S & B* from 12. *Dros y Sir, Pen Cantref, Cantref, Brecon LD3 8LT* T: (01874) 622160 E: podger38@gmail.com

✠**POGGO, The Rt Revd Anthony Dangasuic.** b 64. Univ of Juba BSc 88 Nairobi Internat Sch of Th MA 94 Ox Brookes Univ MBA 01. **d** 95 **p** 96 **c** 07. C Moyo Town Uganda 95–96; C Nairobi St Luke Kenya 96–07; Bp Kajo-Keji S Sudan 07–16; Abp's Adv for Angl Communion Affairs *Cant* from 16; Hon Asst Bp Lon from 17; Hon Asst Bp S'wark from 17. *Lambeth Palace, London SE1 7JU* T: (020) 7898 1218 M: 07765-090963 E: anthony.poggo@lambethpalace.org.uk

POGMORE, Canon Edward Clement. b 52. Sarum & Wells Th Coll 76. **d** 79 **p** 80. C Calne and Blackland *Sarum* 79–82; TV Oakdale 82–89; Min Creekmoor LEP 82–89; Chapl Geo Eliot Hosp Nuneaton 89–94; Chapl Nuneaton Hosps 89–94; Chapl Geo Eliot Hosp NHS Trust Nuneaton 94–14; Chapl Co-ord for N Warks 94–14; PtO *Leic* from 91; Hon Can Cov Cathl 00–14; rtd 14; Chapl Abbeyfield Binley from 14. *1 Bowman Green, Burbage, Hinckley LE10 2QY* T: (01455) 611492 M: 07721-510221 E: edpog@hotmail.com

POINTS, John David. b 43. Qu Coll Birm 78. **d** 80 **p** 81. C Wednesbury St Paul Wood Green *Lich* 80–85; V 93–01; V Sedgley St Mary 85–93; TR Wednesfield 01–08; AD Wolverhampton 03–08; rtd 08; PtO *St As* from 09. *13 Oldcastle Avenue, Guilsfield, Welshpool SY21 9PA* T: (01938) 552092 E: jd.spoints@gmail.com

POLASHEK, Miss Stella Christine. b 44. Leic Poly MA 85. EMMTC 92. **d** 95 **p** 96. NSM Appleby Gp *Leic* 95–08; NSM Woodfield 08–10; Chapl Leic Gen Hosp NHS Trust 99–00; Chapl Univ Hosps Leic NHS Trust 00–10; rtd 10; PtO *Leic* from 11. *85 Parkfield Crescent, Appleby Magna, Swadlincote DE12 7BW* T: (01530) 272707 E: stella.85@btinternet.com

POLE, David John. b 46. Bath Academy of Art BA 72. Trin Coll Bris 84. **d** 86 **p** 87. C Bris St Mary Redcliffe w Temple etc 86–90; V Alveston 90–98; V Alveston and Littleton-on-Severn w Elberton 98–15; C Pilning w Compton Greenfield 11–15; rtd 15. *18 Nelson House, Nelson Place West, Bath BA1 2TL* T: (01225) 333427 E: davepole@gmail.com

POLE, Francis John Michael. b 42. FRSA 64 MInstTA 00 CQSW 74 MCMI 99. St Jo Sem Wonersh 62. **d** 67 **p** 68. In RC Ch 67–75; NSM Walthamstow St Pet *Chelmsf* 75; NSM Penge Lane H Trin *Roch* 76–77; NSM Shirley St Jo *Cant* 77–79; Assoc Chapl The Hague *Eur* 79–83; V Norbury St Steph and Thornton Heath *Cant* 83–94; S'wark 85–00; Sen Dioc Police Chapl 95–00; Sen Chapl Sussex Police 00–03; Nat Co-ord Police Chapl 00–04; Sen Chapl Sussex Ambulance Service 04–06; Co-ord Chapl SE Coast Ambulance Service 06–12; TV Crawley *Chich* 00–12; Chapl to People at Work 00–12; Sen Chapl SE Coast Ambulance Service NHS Foundn Trust from 12; PtO *Chich* from 13. *35 Turnpike Place, Crawley RH11 7UA* T: (01293) 513264 M: 07764-752608 E: francis.pole@virgin.net

POLHILL, Mrs Christine. b 46. Nottm Coll of Educn CertEd 67 Qu Coll Birm BA 00. St Alb Minl Tr Scheme 81. **dss** 84 **d** 87 **p** 94. St Alb St Mary Marshalswick 84–94; Hon Par Dn 87–94; C Cottered w Broadfield and Throcking 94–96; P-in-c 96–99; C Ardeley 94–96; P-in-c 96–99; C Weston 94–96; PtO *Lich* 99–00; C Lich St Mich w St Mary and Wall 00–06; rtd 06; LtO *Lich* 06–12; PtO 12–13; Hon C Hints 13–14; PtO from 16. *Address withheld by request*

POLITT, Robert William. b 47. ARCM LGSM 68. Oak Hill Th Coll 73. **d** 76 **p** 77. C Bexleyheath St Pet *Roch* 76–82; TV Southgate *Chich* 82–90; Chapl N Foreland Lodge Sch Basingstoke 90–98; R Sherfield-on-Loddon and Stratfield Saye etc *Win* 98–13; P-in-c Bramley 10–13; rtd 13; PtO

Ely from 15. *53 Somerset Road, Histon, Cambridge CB24 9JS*
E: bobpolitt@btinternet.com

POLKINGHORNE, Canon John Charlton. b 30. Trin Coll Cam BA 52 PhD 55 MA 56 ScD 74 FRS 74. Westcott Ho Cam 79. **d** 81 **p** 82. NSM Chesterton St Andr *Ely* 81–82; C Bedminster St Mich *Bris* 82–84; V Blean *Cant* 84–86; Dean Trin Hall Cam 86–89; Pres Qu Coll Cam 89–96; Can Th Liv Cathl from 94; rtd 95; Six Preacher Cant Cathl 96–00; PtO *Ely* 96–15. *74 Hurst Park Avenue, Cambridge CB4 2AF* T: (01223) 360743

POLKINHORN, Mrs Judith Edith Elizabeth. b 47. Wolv Univ MBA 04. ERMC 13. **d** 14 **p** 15. NSM Lordsbridge *Ely* 14–16; PtO from 16; *Carl* from 16. *Robridding, Kaber, Kirkby Stephen CA17 4ER* E: judypolkinhorn@gmail.com

POLL, Canon Martin George. b 61. Kent Univ BA 83. Ripon Coll Cuddesdon 84. **d** 87 **p** 88. C Mill Hill Jo Keble Ch *Lon* 87–90; Chapl RN 90–10; Prin Angl Chapl and Adn for the RN 10–12; QHC 10–12; Hon Can Portsm Cathl 11–12; Can Windsor and Chapl in Windsor St Park from 12. *1 The Cloisters, Windsor Castle, Windsor SL4 1NJ* T: (01753) 848713 E: martin.poll@stgeorges-windsor.org

POLLARD, Adrian. *See* POLLARD, James Adrian Hunter

POLLARD, Mrs Christine Beryl. b 45. NOC 86. **d** 89 **p** 94. Par Dn Ingrow w Hainworth *Bradf* 89–94; C Nuneaton St Nic *Cov* 94–98; P-in-c Bourton w Frankton and Stretton on Dunsmore etc 98–07; C Leam Valley 06–07; rtd 07; PtO *Cov* 08–18. *9 Overberry Orchard, Leamington Spa CV33 9SJ* T: (01926) 832053 E: cbpollard@talktalk.net

POLLARD, David John Athey. b 44. ACP 74 Culham Coll Ox CertEd 69. St Jo Coll Nottm LTh 88. **d** 88 **p** 89. C Illogan *Truro* 88–91; R Roche and Withiel 91–95; TV Maidstone St Martin *Cant* 95–97; C Parkwood CD 95–97; R Lanreath *Truro* 97–99; V Pelynt 97–99; R Lanreath, Pelynt and Bradoc 99–03; rtd 03; PtO *Truro* from 14. *Melyn Brea, 11 Mill Hill, Lostwithiel PL22 0HB* T: (01208) 871541 E: dave@melynbrea.co.uk

POLLARD, Eric John. b 43. Chich Th Coll 83. **d** 85 **p** 86. C Brighton St Matthias *Chich* 85–90; C E Grinstead St Swithun 90–96; C Hove 96–00; P-in-c Brighton St Matthias 00–13; rtd 13; PtO *Chich* 14–17. *30 Pondsyde Court, Sutton Drove, Seaford BN25 3ET* E: eric.pollard@btinternet.com

POLLARD, James Adrian Hunter. b 48. St Jo Coll Nottm BTh 78. **d** 78 **p** 79. C Much Woolton *Liv* 78–81; CMS 81–84; V Toxteth Park Ch Ch *Liv* 85–90; CF 90–09; rtd 09; PtO *Sarum* 09–12; Hon C Upper Wylye Valley 12–14; PtO from 14. *Horwood House, 80 Boreham Road, Warminster BA12 9JW* E: ade.pollard@gmail.com

POLLARD, Mrs Judith Mary. b 56. Westcott Ho Cam 09. **d** 11 **p** 12. C Newark w Coddington *S'well* 11–14; C Gayton, Gayton Thorpe, E Walton, E Winch etc *Nor* 14–15; TV Ashwicken w Leziate, Bawsey etc from 15. *The Rectory, Watery Lane, Grimston, King's Lynn PE32 1BQ* M: 07852-257734 E: wotzpollard@aol.com

POLLARD, Matthew Rupert. b 66. Qu Coll Ox BA 88 MA 92. St Jo Coll Nottm. **d** 03 **p** 04. C Huddersfield St Pet *Wakef* 03–07; Asst Chapl Huddersfield Univ 03–07; P-in-c Rastrick St Matt 07–08; P-in-c Rastrick St Jo 07–08; V Rastrick 08–13; R Bridlington Priory *York* from 13; RD Bridlington from 17. *The Rectory, Church Green, Bridlington YO16 7JX* T: (01262) 672221 E: matthewrpollard@btinternet.com

POLLARD, Stephen. b 59. Coll of Resurr Mirfield 96. **d** 98 **p** 99. C Lt Lever *Man* 98–02; P-in-c Westleigh St Pet 02–10; P-in-c Westleigh St Paul 08–10; P-in-c Rosebud w McCrae Australia from 10. *120 Fifth Avenue, Rosebud, Victoria 3939, Australia* E: fatherstephenpollard@googlemail.com

POLLARD (née RAMSBOTTOM), Mrs Susan Elizabeth. b 56. Trin Coll Bris BD 79. Qu Coll Birm 06. **d** 09 **p** 10. NSM Warndon St Nic *Worc* 09–16; NSM Bowbrook N 16–18; NSM Bowbrook S 16–18; NSM Stoke Prior, Wychbold and Upton Warren 16–18; NSM Claines St Jo from 18; NSM Worc St Geo w St Mary Magd from 18. *5 Falmouth, Worcester WR4 0TE* T: (01905) 759214 E: suepollard2610@hotmail.com

POLLINGER (née WHITFORD), Canon Judith. b 41. Ex Univ TCert 78 BEd 79. SWMTC 92. **d** 95 **p** 96. NSM St Endellion w Port Isaac and St Kew *Truro* 95–12; NSM St Minver 07–12; NSM N Cornwall Cluster 12–15; Convenor Bp's Gp for Min of Healing 04–11; Hon Can Truro Cathl 10–18; Preb St Endellion 12–18; rtd 15; PtO *Truro* from 15. *4 Marshalls Way, Trelights, Port Isaac PL29 3TE* T: (01208) 880181 E: rev.judith@btinternet.com

POLLINGTON, Miss Ann Elizabeth Jane. b 56. Univ Coll Chich BA 00. Ripon Coll Cuddesdon 00. **d** 02 **p** 03. C Honiton, Gittisham, Combe Raleigh, Monkton etc *Ex* 02–07; P-in-c St Ippolyts *St Alb* 07–10; P-in-c and Lt Wymondley 07–10; R St Ippolyts w Gt and Lt Wymondley 10–15; RD Hitchin 11–15; V Cranbrook *Cant* from 15; AD Weald from 17. *The*

Vicarage, Waterloo Road, Cranbrook TN17 3JQ T: (01580) 388173 E: ann.pollington@btinternet.com

POLLIT, Preb Michael. b 30. Worc Coll Ox BA 54 MA 58. Wells Th Coll 54. **d** 56 **p** 57. C Cannock *Lich* 56–59; C Codsall 59–62; V W Bromwich St Pet 62–67; R Norton in the Moors 67–76; RD Leek 72–76; V Shrewsbury St Chad 76–87; V Shrewsbury St Chad w St Mary 87–95; Preb Lich Cathl 81–95; P-in-c Shrewsbury St Alkmund 91–95; rtd 95; PtO *Heref* from 96. *Pentreheyling House, Churchstoke, Montgomery SY15 6HU* T: (01588) 620273

POLLIT, Ruth Mary. *See* LILLINGTON, Ruth Mary

POLLITT, Graham Anthony. b 48. BA 79. Oak Hill Th Coll 76. **d** 79 **p** 80. C Rusholme H Trin *Man* 79–82; TV Southgate *Chich* 82–83; C Burgess Hill St Andr 83–86; Chapl St Martin's Coll of Educn *Blackb* 86–90; Chapl Cheltenham and Glouc Coll of HE 90–98; PtO *Glouc* 98–99; C Bispham *Blackb* 99–04; P-in-c Caton w Littledale 04–17; rtd 17; PtO *Blackb* from 18. *12 Haydock Road, Lancaster LA1 4NB* E: grahamapollitt@gmail.com

POLLOCK, Christopher John. b 62. TCD BTh 89 QUB BD. CITC 86. **d** 89 **p** 90. C Agherton *Conn* 89–91; C Ballymoney w Finvoy and Rasharkin 91–93; I Derryvolgie 93–03; I Saintfield *D & D* from 03. *The Vicarage, 11 Lisburn Road, Saintfield, Ballynahinch BT24 7AL* T: (028) 9751 0286 E: chris.pollock3@btinternet.com

POLLOCK, Duncan James Morrison. b 54. Nottm Univ BCombStuds 83. Linc Th Coll 80. **d** 83 **p** 84. C Folkestone St Mary and St Eanswythe *Cant* 83–85; CF 85–98; R Broughton, Bossington, Houghton and Mottisfont *Win* 98–00; I Groomsport *D & D* from 00. *22 Sandringham Drive, Bangor BT20 5NA* T: (028) 9146 4476 E: duncanjmpollock@btinternet.com

POLLOCK, James Colin Graeme. b 53. St Chad's Coll Dur BA 76. Ripon Coll Cuddesdon 77. **d** 78 **p** 79. C Hartlepool St Oswald *Dur* 78–81; C Hartlepool St Aid 81–84; V Dawdon 84–05; V Seaham Harbour 03–05; TV S Shields All SS 05–13; rtd 13; PtO *Dur* from 13. *25 Knocklofty Court, Belfast BT4 3NF* E: graeme.pollock@hotmail.co.uk

POND, Canon Geraldine Phyllis. b 53. SRN 74 HVCert 75. St Jo Coll Nottm MA 97. **d** 97 **p** 98. C Ancaster Wilsford Gp *Linc* 97–01; P-in-c Harlaxton Gp 01–07; Chapl Linc Distr Healthcare NHS Trust 01–07; P-in-c Ashbourne St Oswald w Mapleton *Derby* 07–14; V 14–15; P-in-c Ashbourne St Jo 07–15; P-in-c Clifton 07–15; P-in-c Norbury w Snelston 09–15; Asst Dir of Ords 08–09; Dioc Dir of Ords 09–15; Hon Can Derby Cathl 10–19; Dioc Voc Dir 15–19; Warden of Readers 17–19; rtd 19; Chapl to The Queen from 18. *Address temp unknown* M: 07736-196323

POND, Nigel Peter Hamilton. b 40. AKC 65. **d** 66 **p** 67. C E Dereham w Hoe *Nor* 66–69; C Chapl RN 69–85; TR Woughton *Ox* 85–93; Chapl Milton Keynes Gen Hosp 85–93; RD Milton Keynes *Ox* 90–93; R Olney w Emberton 93–97; R Olney 97–03; rtd 03. *11 Gippingstone Road, Bramford, Ipswich IP8 4DR* T: (01473) 741887 E: nigelphpond@talktalk.net

PONSONBY, Simon Charles Reuben. b 66. Bris Univ MLitt 96. Trin Coll Bris BA 94. **d** 95 **p** 96. C Thorpe Edge *Bradf* 95–98; Pastorate Chapl Ox St Aldate 98–05; C from 05. *St Aldate's Parish Centre, 40 Pembroke Street, Oxford OX1 1BP* T: (01865) 254800 F: 201543 E: simon.ponsonby@staldates.org.uk

PONTEFRACT, Archdeacon of. *See* TOWNLEY, The Ven Peter Kenneth

PONTER, John Arthur. b 37. Univ of Wales (Abth) BA 61 Linacre Coll Ox BA 63 MA 68 UEA PhD 81. Wycliffe Hall Ox 61. **d** 63 **p** 64. C Gidea Park *Chelmsf* 63–67; C-in-c Colchester St Anne CD 67–69; V Colchester St Anne 69–72; Chapl UEA *Nor* 72–78; Chapl Chelmsf Cathl 78–79; Chapl Chelmsf Cathl Cen 78–84; V Moulsham St Jo *Chelmsf* 79–85; Dir Man Chr Inst and Chr Leadership Course 85–92; Educn Officer N Federation for Tr in Min 85–92; TR Stantonbury and Willen *Ox* 92–02; rtd 02; PtO *Sarum* from 07. *3 The Croft, 43A East Street, Wareham BH20 4NW* T: (01929) 558286 E: john@ponter.net

POOLE, Clifford George. b 36. Keble Coll Ox BA 61 MA 65 Lon Univ PGCE 75. S'wark Ord Course 83. **d** 86 **p** 87. C W Dulwich All SS and Em *S'wark* 86–90; Chapl Luxembourg *Eur* 90–02; rtd 02; P-in-c Alderton, Gt Washbourne, Dumbleton etc *Glouc* 02–05; TV Winchcombe 05–08; PtO *S'wark* from 09; *Truro* from 15; *Lon* from 17; *Eur* from 09. *11 Berwyn Road, London SE24 9BD* T: (020) 8674 3369 E: poole_clifford@yahoo.co.uk

POOLE, Canon Denise June. b 49. Leic Univ BSc 70 Bradf and Ilkley Coll DipAdEd 85. NOC 90. **d** 93 **p** 94. C Horton and Bradf St Oswald Chapel Green 93–97; Chapl Co-ord Bradf Hosps NHS Trust 97–00; V Bradf St Aug Undercliffe 00–06; Dioc Dir of Ords 01–06; Bp's Dom Chapl 06–14; Min and Miss Officer 14–16; Hon Can Bradf Cathl 07–16; rtd

16; Hon C Heaton St Barn *Leeds* 17–18; Hon C Girlington, Heaton and Manningham from 18. *23 Leylands Lane, Bradford BD9 5PX* T: (01274) 401679 *or* 545414 F: 544831 E: denise.poole@leeds.anglican.org

POOLE, Edward John. b 53. Hull Univ BA 81 Heythrop Coll Lon MA 04. St Steph Ho Ox 81. **d** 83 **p** 84. C Stevenage St Andr and St Geo *St Alb* 83–86; Tutor St Paul's Th Coll Madagascar 86–88; V Weston and P-in-c Ardeley *St Alb* 88–96; P-in-c Cottered w Broadfield and Throcking 94–96; Chapl Bucharest w Sofia *Eur* 96–98; Chapl HM Pris Lewes 98–03; Chapl HM Pris Featherstone 03–09; R York, Beverley w Brookton and Quairading Australia 09–12; PtO *Heref* 12–16; *Lon* 13–16; P-in-c Tenerife Sur *Eur* from 16. *Residencial Sonia 17, Calle El Mojon, Callao Salvaje, 38678 Adeje, Santa Cruz de Tenerife, Spain* T: (0034) 922 742 045 E: john_poole_uk@yahoo.co.uk

POOLE, Helen Margaret. b 39. SRN. SWMTC. **d** 94 **p** 95. NSM Ludgvan *Truro* 94–97; NSM Paul 97–02; NSM St Buryan, St Levan and Sennen 02–04; rtd 04; PtO *Truro* 05–08; *Guildf* from 12. *12 Lansdown, Guildford GU1 2LY* T: (01483) 546234 E: helenbob@stlevan.eclipse.co.uk

POOLE, Ian Richard Morley. b 62. Birm Univ MB, ChB 85 MRCGP 90. St Jo Coll Nottm MTh 02. **d** 02 **p** 03. C Willenhall H Trin *Lich* 02–06; TV Bushbury 06–17; TR from 17. *St Mary's Vicarage, Bushbury Lane, Wolverhampton WV10 8JP* T: (01902) 788151 E: woodchipper@btinternet.com

POOLE, James Christopher. b 73. Peterho Cam BA 94 MA 98. Aston Tr Scheme 96 Wycliffe Hall Ox 97. **d** 00 **p** 01. C Wimbledon Park St Luke *S'wark* 00–04; Miss Partner Crosslinks 04–07; Kenya 05–07; C Cambridge H Sepulchre *Ely* 07–14; Exec Dir Wycliffe Bible Translators from 14; PtO *Ox* 14–15; NSM Ox St Ebbe w H Trin and St Pet from 15. *28 Horseman Close, Headington, Oxford OX3 0NT* T: (01865) 513268 E: james@poolehouse.org

POOLE, Miss Joan Wendy. b 37. Sarum Dioc Teacher Tr Coll CertEd 57 Trin Coll Bris 86. **d** 87 **p** 94. Par Dn Longfleet *Sarum* 87–89; Par Dn Hamworthy 89–94; C 94–97; rtd 97; PtO *Sarum* from 97. *35 Borley Road, Poole BH17 7DT* T: (01202) 256377 E: jwendypoole@virginmedia.com

POOLE, John. *See* POOLE, Edward John

POOLE, Martin Bryce. b 53. Reading Univ BSc 80. St Jo Coll Nottm 81. **d** 87 **p** 88. NSM Tulse Hill H Trin and St Matthias *S'wark* 87–99; NSM Hove *Chich* 00–01; PtO 01–10; P-in-c Prestonville St Luke 10–13; V from 13. *St Luke's Vicarage, 64A Old Shoreham Road, Brighton BN1 5DD* T/F: (01273) 557772 E: martin@stlukesonline.co.uk

POOLE, Martin Ronald. b 59. Aston Univ BSc 81 Leeds Univ BA 86. Coll of Resurr Mirfield 84. **d** 87 **p** 88. C Sheff St Cath Richmond Road 87–90; C W Hampstead St Jas *Lon* 90–94; V Colindale St Matthias 94–06; V Munster Square Ch Ch and St Mary Magd 06–16; rtd 16; PtO *Lon* from 16. *17B Brodie Road, Enfield EN2 0EU* T: (020) 7388 3095 E: martin@martlondon.plus.com

POOLE, Nigel John Graydon. b 53. **d** 15 **p** 16. C Penge St Jo *Roch* 15–17; P-in-c from 17. *37 Groveland Road, Beckenham BR3 3PU* T: (020) 8663 1344 M: 07849-609486 E: nigel_poole@hotmail.co.uk *or* nigel@penge-anglicans.org

POOLE, Peter William. b 35. St Pet Hall Ox BA 59 MA 63. Wells Th Coll 59. **d** 61 **p** 62. C Cheriton Street *Cant* 61–64; C Birchington w Acol 64–67; V Newington 67–73; P-in-c Lower Halstow 72–73; V Bearsted 73–76; V Lane End w Cadmore End *Ox* 84–89; R Chalfont St Giles 89–99; rtd 99; PtO *Guildf* from 99. *Primrose Cottage, St Nicholas Avenue, Cranleigh GU6 7AQ* T: (01483) 272703

POOLE, Stuart. b 33. Lon Univ BScEng 55 Man Univ MSc 76 CEng 65 FIEE 85. **d** 91 **p** 92. NSM Cheadle *Ches* 91–03; PtO from 03. *1 Dene House, 3 Green Pastures, Stockport SK4 3RB* T/F: 0161-432 6426 E: stuart.poole33@tiscali.co.uk

POOLE, Wendy. *See* POOLE, Joan Wendy

POOLEY, Clifford Russell. b 48. Glos Univ BA 03. WEMTC 08. **d** 09 **p** 10. NSM Coberley, Cowley, Colesbourne and Elkstone *Glouc* 09–14; NSM Churn Valley from 14. *8A Salterley Grange, Leckhampton Hill, Cheltenham GL53 9QW* T: (01242) 243981 E: cliff.pooley@btinternet.com

POOLEY, Clive Nicholas. b 51. Lon Univ BEd 74. NTMTC 96. **d** 99 **p** 00. C Barking St Marg w St Patr *Chelmsf* 99–02; V Barking St Erkenwald 02–14; rtd 14; PtO *Chelmsf* from 14. *Bethel, 68 Tolkien Road, Eastbourne BN23 7AQ* M: 07986-451671 E: clive.n.pooley@gmail.com

POOLMAN, Alfred John. b 46. K Coll Lon BD 69 AKC 69. St Aug Coll Cant 69. **d** 70 **p** 71. C Headingley *Ripon* 70–74; C Moor Allerton 75–78; C Monk Bretton *Wakef* 78–80; V Copley and Chapl Halifax Gen Hosp 80–90; R Llanfynydd *St As* 90–06; P-in-c 06–10; rtd 11; PtO *St As* from 14. *The Rectory, Llanfynydd, Wrexham LL11 5HH* T: (01978) 762304 E: johnpoolman@btinternet.com

POOLMAN, Mrs Carole Margaret. b 53. St As & Ban Minl Tr Course 98. **d** 01 **p** 02. NSM Pontblyddyn *St As* 01–06; P-in-c 06–16; P-in-c Llanfynydd 10–14; P-in-c Treuddyn w Nercwys 15–16; I Mold Miss Area from 17. *The Rectory, Llanfynydd, Wrexham LL11 5HH* T: (01978) 762304 E: cc.sm@btinternet.com

POOLTON, Martin Ronald. b 60. Kingston Poly BSc 81 Salford Univ MSc 83 Bp Grosseteste Coll PGCE 85 FRGS 81. Ripon Coll Cuddesdon 95. **d** 97 **p** 98. C Penzance St Mary w St Paul *Truro* 97–99; C Northampton St Matt *Pet* 99–01; R Jersey St Pet *Win* 01–15. *Address withheld by request* E: poolton2608@gmail.com

POON, Michael Nai-Chiu. b 53. Univ of BC BSc 75 MSc 77. Wycliffe Coll Toronto MDiv 80 DPhil 84. **d** 86 **p** 87. C St Steph Hong Kong Hong Kong 86–90; V Macau St Mark 90–99; P-in-c Morrison Chpl 90–04; Dir Cen for Story of Christianity Singapore Singapore 04–14; Hon Can Singapore from 07; PtO *Lon* from 14. *5 Avalon Close, London W13 0BJ* T: (020) 8998 4525 M: 07779-537601 E: mncpoon@gmail.com

POPE, Preb Charles Guy. b 48. AKC 70. St Aug Coll Cant 70. **d** 71 **p** 72. C Southgate Ch Ch *Lon* 71–74; C N St Pancras All Hallows 74–77; C Hampstead St Steph 74–77; V New Southgate St Paul 77–86; V Brookfield St Mary 86–17; P-in-c Brookfield St Anne, Highgate Rise 88–99; AD S Camden 95–00; Preb St Paul's Cathl 04–17; rtd 17; PtO *Lon* 17–18. *6 Horsham Avenue, London N12 9BE* M: 07770-693435 E: guypope@blueyonder.co.uk

POPE, Miss Elizabeth Mercy. b 51. Man Univ BSc 73 Ex Univ PGCE 74. Trin Coll Bris 99. **d** 01 **p** 02. C Bardsley *Man* 01–05; P-in-c Oldham St Paul 05–08; P-in-c Denton St Lawr 08–17; C Audenshaw St Steph 13–17; C Denton Ch Ch 13–17; C Haughton St Anne 13–17; rtd 17; PtO *Ban* from 17. *33 Lon Gardener, Valley, Holyhead LL65 3DN* T: (01407) 740972 M: 07754-059364 E: elizabeth@mpope.plus.com

POPE, Guy. *See* POPE, Charles Guy

POPE, Michael John. b 37. Sarum Th Coll 62. **d** 65 **p** 66. C Broseley w Benthall *Heref* 65–68; C Shrewsbury St Giles *Lich* 68–71; P-in-c Shrewsbury St Geo 71–75; V 75–79; V Gnosall 79–00; RD Eccleshall 92–00; rtd 00; PtO *Lich* 01–14; *Heref* from 10. *Rivendell, 2 Dark Lane, Broseley TF12 5LH* T: (01952) 883960

POPE, Stephen Paul. b 49. Liv Univ MB, ChB 73 FRCA. Yorks Min Course 15. **d** 16 **p** 17. NSM Coxwold and Husthwaite *York* from 16; NSM Crayke w Brandsby and Yearsley from 16; NSM Alne from 17; NSM Brafferton w Pilmoor, Myton-on-Swale etc from 17; NSM Easingwold w Raskelf from 17; NSM Skelton w Shipton and Newton on Ouse from 17; NSM Strensall from 17; NSM Forest of Galtres from 17. *Bishop's Cottage, Church Hill, Crayke, York YO61 4TA* M: 07816-168735 E: stephenrevdoc@gmail.com

POPHAM, Neil Andrew. b 69. Trin Coll Ox BA 91 DPhil 96 MA 05 St Jo Coll Dur BA 05. Cranmer Hall Dur 03. **d** 05 **p** 06. C Quarry Bank *Worc* 05–07; C Brierley Hill 07–09; P-in-c Kirkby in Ashfield St Thos *S'well* 09–11; V 11–19; P-in-c Kirkby in Ashfield 15–19; TV Stantonbury and Willen *Ox* from 19. *Church House, 1A Atterbrook, Bradwell, Milton Keynes MK13 9EY* E: thepophams@talktalk.net *or* revneilpopham.mk@gmail.com

POPP, Miss Julia Alice Gisela. b 45. Univ of BC BA 71. St Jo Coll Nottm 78. **dss** 81 **d** 87 **p** 94. Woking St Mary *Guildf* 81–83; Hornsey Rise St Mary w St Steph *Lon* 83–87; Par Dn Hornsey Rise Whitehall Park Team 87–91; Par Dn Sutton St Nic *S'wark* 91–94; C 94–98; Missr Sutton Town Cen 91–98; TV Hackney Marsh *Lon* 98–05; rtd 05; PtO *Ely* from 06. *32 Regatta Court, Oyster Row, Cambridge CB5 8NS* T: (01223) 350164 E: juliapopp16@gmail.com

POPPE, Andrew Nils. b 60. NE Lon Poly BSc 83. STETS 08. **d** 11 **p** 12. C Clarendon *Sarum* 11–15; V Cowes H Trin and St Mary *Portsm* from 15. *The Vicarage, Church Road, Cowes PO31 8HA* T: (01983) 292509 M: 07729-322616 E: stmarysvicarage@outlook.com

POPPLETON, Julian George. b 63. St Chad's Coll Dur BA 85 PGCE 86 Surrey Univ BA 02. STETS 99. **d** 02 **p** 03. NSM Harnham *Sarum* from 02; Chapl K Edw VI Sch Southn from 02. *19 Thompson Close, Salisbury SP2 8QU* T: (01722) 334272 *or* (023) 8070 4561 E: julianpoppleton@gmail.com

POPPLEWELL, Andrew Frederick. b 53. St Jo Coll Dur BA 75. Wycliffe Hall Ox 76. **d** 78 **p** 79. C Clifton *York* 78–81; C Lich St Chad 82–84; V Laisterdyke *Bradf* 84–99. *Clifton, 210A Leeds Road, Eccleshill, Bradford BD2 3JU* T: (01274) 637651

PORT, Mrs Betty Anne. b 50. Univ of W Indies BA 71 Open Univ MA 93. STETS BA 10. **d** 10 **p** 11. NSM Preston w Sutton Poyntz, Littlemoor etc *Sarum* 10–14; NSM Wyke Regis from 14. *68 Mellstock Avenue, Dorchester DT1 2BQ* T: (01305) 263058 E: betty.port@which.net

PORTER, Andrew William. b 69. Bris Univ BSc 91 BA 01 PGCE 94. Trin Coll Bris 98. **d** 01 **p** 02. C Ipsley *Worc* 01–04; V Fairfield *Liv* 04–10; P-in-c Liv St Phil w St Dav 08–10; V Liv All SS 11–13; V S'well H Trin from 13. *Holy Trinity Vicarage, Westhorpe, Southwell NG25 0NB* E: awporter9@gmail.com

✠**PORTER, The Rt Revd Anthony.** b 52. Hertf Coll Ox BA 74 MA 78 Fitzw Ho Cam BA 76 MA 80. Ridley Hall Cam 74. **d** 77 **p** 78. C Edgware *Lon* 77–80; C Haughton St Mary *Man* 80–83; P-in-c Bacup Ch Ch 83–87; V 87–91; R Rusholme H Trin 91–06; Hon Can Man Cathl 04–06; Suff Bp Sherwood *S'well* from 06. *Jubilee House, Westgate, Southwell NG25 0JH* T: (01636) 819133 F: 819085 E: bishopsherwood@southwell.anglican.org

PORTER, Anthony. *See* PORTER, David Anthony

PORTER, Anthony David. b 79. Univ of Wales (Swansea) BS 03 BSc 04. St Mich Coll Llan 14. **d** 16 **p** 17. NSM Morriston *S & B* 16–17; C Llangyfelach from 17. *The Vicarage, 8 Maes y Dderwen, Llangyfelach, Swansea SA6 6ET* T: (01792) 790606 M: 07989-572837 E: a-porter38@sky.com

PORTER, Barbara Judith. *See* JEAPES, Barbara Judith

PORTER, Brian Meredith. b 39. Monash Univ Aus BA 66 Trin Hall Cam BA 75 MA 79 New England Univ NSW BLitt 79 MLitt 85 ACT ThD 01. Cuddesdon Coll 68. **d** 68 **p** 71. C Kew Australia 68–69; K Sch Parramatta 70–73; Chapl Canberra Gr Sch 75–82; Chapl Ivanhoe Gr Sch 83–97; Sen Chapl Melbourne Gr Sch 98–05; Chapl Brighton Gr Sch from 05. *4 Fairholme Grove, Camberwell Vic 3124, Australia* T: (0061) (3) 9882 8740 E: bmporter@comcen.com.au

PORTER (née RICHARDSON), Mrs Catherine Elisabeth. b 75. Edge Hill Coll of HE BA 96 Trin Coll Bris BA 99 MA 01. SNWTP 07. **d** 08 **p** 09. NSM Fairfield *Liv* 08–10; NSM Liv All SS 11–13; PtO S'well from 13. *Holy Trinity Vicarage, Westhorpe, Southwell NG25 0NB* E: cathy.porter@bigfoot.com

PORTER, Damian Michael. b 66. Linc Th Coll BTh 92. **d** 92 **p** 93. C Pelsall *Lich* 92–96; V Greenlands *Blackb* 96–00; V St Annes St Anne 00–09; AD Kirkham 06–09; P-in-c Warton St Oswald w Yealand Conyers 09–11; V 11–17; AD Tunstall 14–16; V Torrisholme from 17. *The Vicarage, 63 Michaelson Avenue, Morecambe LA4 6SF* T: (01524) 732946 E: fatherd@btinternet.com

PORTER, Canon David Anthony (Tony). b 34. Wycliffe Hall Ox 73. **d** 75 **p** 76. C Watford St Luke *St Alb* 75–78; C Worting *Win* 78–81; V Snettisham *Nor* 81–82; P-in-c Ingoldisthorpe 81–82; C Fring 81–82; R Snettisham w Ingoldisthorpe and Fring 82–84; Chapl Asst Colchester Gen Hosp 87–88; Chapl Maidstone Hosp 88–94; Chapl Mid Kent Healthcare NHS Trust 94–98; Hon Can Cant Cathl 97–98; rtd 98; PtO *Nor* from 98; *Ely* from 98. *The Greys, 12 Hawthorn Close, Watlington, King's Lynn PE33 0HD* T: (01553) 811301 E: daporter7985@btinternet.com

PORTER, David Michael. b 37. Coll of Ripon & York St Jo BA 88. Ely Th Coll 61. **d** 64 **p** 65. C Clun w Chapel Lawn *Heref* 64–67; C Scarborough St Mary w Ch Ch, St Paul and St Thos *York* 67–69; C Fulford 69–71; V Strensall 71–78; Chapl Claypenny and St Monica's Hosps 78–91; V Easingwold w Raskelfe *York* 78–91; TR York All SS Pavement w St Crux and St Martin etc 91–97; R York All SS Pavement w St Crux and St Mich 97–02; rtd 02; PtO *York* from 02. *10 Hall Rise, Haxby, York YO32 3LP* T: (01904) 769823

PORTER, David Rowland Shelley. b 46. City of Liv Coll of HE CertEd 69. STETS 00. **d** 03 **p** 04. NSM Whitehawk *Chich* 03–16; rtd 16; PtO *Chich* from 16. *33 Warleigh Road, Brighton BN1 4NT* T: (01273) 703499 M: 07733-418755 E: porter@davejanera.co.uk

PORTER, Howard. b 56. S Glam Inst HE CertEd 78. St Mich Coll Llan 99. **d** 01 **p** 02. C Maindee Newport *Mon* 01–05; TV Aberystwyth *St D* 05–09. *21 Gwalch y Penwaig, Barry CF62 5AG*

PORTER, James Richard. b 73. Lon Univ BMedSci 97 MB, BS 98. Oak Hill Th Coll MTh 05. **d** 05 **p** 06. C Cromer *Nor* 05–09; R W Horsley *Guildf* 09–15; V Cromer *Nor* from 15. *42 Cromwell Road, Cromer NR27 0BE* T: (01263) 512000 E: jamestherector@yahoo.co.uk *or* james.porter@cromer-church.com

PORTER, Joanna Kathryn. b 73. Open Univ BA 10. Cranmer Hall Dur 15. **d** 17 **p** 18. C Ashington *Newc* 17–19; C Cannings and Redhorn *Sarum* from 19. *The Vicarage, The Street, Bishop's Cannings, Devizes SN10 2LD* M: 07943-239700

PORTER, John Dudley Dowell. b 33. St Edm Hall Ox BA 60 MA 61. Qu Coll Birm 57. **d** 59 **p** 60. C Londonderry *Birm* 59–62; C Tettenhall Regis *Lich* 62–65; Chapl RAF 65–69; V Wombourne *Lich* 69–75; V Rickerscote 75–81; P-in-c Chapel Chorlton 81–85; P-in-c Maer 81–85; P-in-c Whitmore 81–85; R Chapel Chorlton, Maer and Whitmore 85–92; TR Wednesfield 92–00; rtd 00; P-in-c Haughton St Anne *Man* 00–03; P-in-c Nord Pas de Calais *Eur* 04–06. *10 Pear Tree Drive, Madeley, Crewe CW3 9EN* T: (01782) 750485 E: porterjdd@gmail.com

PORTER, Mrs Linda Mary. b 55. St Mellitus Coll BA 13. **d** 13 **p** 14. NSM Walton le Soken *Chelmsf* 13–16; NSM Harwich Peninsula 16–17; PtO from 17; *Portsm* 18–19; NSM W Wight from 19. *Sarum House, Moortown Lane, Brighstone, Newport PO30 4AN* M: 07854-156077 E: lindamporter@yahoo.co.uk

PORTER, Malcolm Derek. b 53. BSc. NTMTC. **d** 05 **p** 06. C Woodford Wells *Chelmsf* 05–09; NSM from 10; V Highams Park All SS from 19. *The Vicarage, All Saints' Church, Castle Avenue, London E4 9QD* T: (020) 8531 5107 M: 07779-146892 E: thoseporters@aol.com *or* malcolm@asww.org.uk

PORTER, Matthew James. b 69. Nottm Univ BA 90. Wycliffe Hall Ox BTh 93. **d** 96 **p** 97. C Dore *Sheff* 96–00; V Woodseats St Chad 00–09; C York St Mich-le-Belfrey 09–10; V from 10. *St Barnabas' Vicarage, Jubilee Terrace, York YO26 4YZ* T: (01904) 412057 M: 07985-645844 E: matthew.porter@belfrey.org

PORTER, Canon Michael Edward. b 44. Trin Coll Bris 75. **d** 77 **p** 78. C Corby St Columba *Pet* 77–81; C Rainham *Chelmsf* 81–82; TV 82–92; P-in-c S Hornchurch St Jo and St Matt 92–95; V Anerley *Roch* 95–09; TR 09; AD Beckenham 05–09; Hon Can Roch Cathl 09; rtd 09; PtO *Nor* from 10. *20 Park Lane, Wymondham NR18 9BG* T: (01953) 602708 E: mike@porterfamily.freeuk.com

PORTER, Nigel Jonathan. b 58. Sunderland Univ BEd 90 Portsm Univ MPhil 99 PhD 05. STETS MA 10. **d** 10 **p** 11. C Lower Sandown St Jo *Portsm* 10–14; PtO 14–15; P-in-c Whitwell 15–16; V from 16; P-in-c Niton 15–16; R from 16; P-in-c St Lawrence 15–16; R from 16; P-in-c Chale 15–16; R from 16. *Niton Rectory, Pan Lane, Niton, Ventnor PO38 2BT* M: 07533-394043 E: nigel.porter6@btinternet.com

PORTER, Raymond John. b 43. Worc Coll Ox BA 66 MA 70 Wycliffe Hall Ox MPhil 93 FRAS 93. **d** 06 **p** 07. Dir World Miss Studies Oak Hill Th Coll 06–13; Visiting Lect Oak Hill Coll from 13; PtO *St Alb* from 07; *Ely* from 11; *Ox* from 16. *24 Bevington Way, Eynesbury, St Neots PE19 2HQ* T: (01480) 211839 *or* (020) 8449 0467 M: 07976-753822 E: porterray@me.com *or* rayp@oakhll.ac.uk

PORTER-BABBAGE, Michelle Louise. b 64. EN(G) 86 RGN 04. Ridley Hall Cam 12. **d** 14 **p** 15. C Bourton-on-the-Water w Clapton etc *Glouc* 14–18; PtO 18–19; C Warfield *Ox* from 19. *Glen Lossie, Gough's Lane, Bracknell RG12 2PL* M: 07387-912920 E: michelle.porter-babbage@warfield.org.uk

PORTER-PRYCE, Preb Julia Frances. b 57. Man Univ BA 78 Leic Univ MPhil 94. NTMTC 93. **d** 96 **p** 97. C Stoke Newington Common St Mich *Lon* 96–99; C Is of Dogs Ch Ch and St Jo w St Luke 99–02; V De Beauvoir Town St Pet from 02; AD Hackney 09–14; Preb St Paul's Cathl from 17. *St Peter's Vicarage, 86 De Beauvoir Road, London N1 5AT* T: (020) 7254 5670 E: juliap@freeuk.com

PORTEUS, Canon James Michael. b 31. Worc Coll Ox BA 55 MA 58. Cuddesdon Coll. **d** 57 **p** 58. C Fleetwood St Pet *Blackb* 57–60; C Ox St Mary V 60–62; Staff Sec SCM Ox 60–62; Chapl Chicago Univ USA 62–65; Chapl Bryn Mawr, Haverford and Swarthmore Colls 62–65; Chapl Lon Univ 69–74; V Hampstead Garden Suburb 74–86; Chapl Arizona Univ USA 86–91; Min Livingston LEP *Edin* 91–96; rtd 96; P-in-c Portree *Arg* 96–05; Hon Can Cumbrae from 06; PtO *Truro* from 09. *Triskele, Rinsey, Ashton, Helston TR13 9TS* T: (01736) 761870

PORTEUS, Canon Robert John Norman. b 50. TCD BA 72 MA 76. CITC 75. **d** 75 **p** 76. C Portadown St Mark *Arm* 75–79; I Ardtrea w Desertcreat 79–83; I Annaghmore 83–98; I Derryloran from 98; Can Arm Cathl from 98; Preb from 01. *Derryloran Rectory, 13 Loy Street, Cookstown BT80 8PZ* T/F: (028) 8676 2261 E: rector@derryloran.com

PORTHOUSE, Roger Gordon Hargreaves. b 39. Tyndale Hall Bris 66. **d** 69 **p** 70. C Wellington w Eyton *Lich* 69–71; C Cheadle *Ches* 71–75; R Frettenham w Stanninghall *Nor* 75–81; R Spixworth w Crostwick 75–81; V Hailsham *Chich* 81–04; RD Dallington 96–03; rtd 05. *19 Cornmill Gardens, Polegate BN26 5NJ* T: (01323) 487372 E: ghporthouse@hotmail.com

PORTLOCK, John Anthony. b 37. RIBA. WMMTC 96. **d** 99 **p** 00. NSM Lyddington w Stoke Dry and Seaton etc *Pet* 99–07; NSM Bulwick, Blatherwycke w Harringworth and Laxton 05–07; rtd 07; PtO *Pet* 08–19. *7 Chestnut Close, Uppingham, Oakham LE15 9TQ* T: (01572) 823225 E: jandmportlock@gmail.com

PORTSDOWN, Archdeacon of. *Vacant*

PORTSMOUTH, Bishop of. *See* FOSTER, The Rt Revd Christopher Richard James

PORTSMOUTH, Dean of. *See* CANE, The Very Revd Anthony William Nicholas Strephon

POSKITT, Mark Sylvester. b 63. Loughb Univ BSc 84. St Jo Coll Nottm MA 95. **d** 97 **p** 98. C Brigg, Wrawby and

Cadney cum Howsham *Linc* 97–00; TV Howden *York* 00–09; P-in-c Barnsley St Edw *Wakef* 09–14; *Leeds* 14–16; P-in-c Gawber *Wakef* 09–14; *Leeds* 14–16; P-in-c Bosworth and Sheepy Gp *Leic* from 16. *The Rectory, Park Street, Market Bosworth, Nuneaton CV13 0LL* T: (01455) 291152 E: rev.markp63@talktalk.net

POSS, Steven Keith. b 78. St Mellitus Coll BA 13. **d** 13 **p** 14. NSM Leigh-on-Sea St Aid *Chelmsf* 13–16; C 16–17; P-in-c Bradwell on Sea and St Lawrence from 17; P-in-c Tillingham from 17; P-in-c Dengie w Asheldham from 17. *6 Bakery Close, Tillingham, Southminster CM0 7TT* M: 07830-150713 E: stevenposs@hotmail.com

POST, David Charles William. b 39. Jes Coll Cam BA 61 MA 65. Oak Hill Th Coll 61. **d** 63 **p** 64. C Orpington Ch Ch *Roch* 63–66; C Fulwood *Sheff* 66–68; V Lathom *Liv* 68–75; V Poughill *Truro* 75–78; V Braddan and Santan *S & M* 78–79; Dioc Missr 78–79; V Sherburn in Elmet *York* 79–91; P-in-c Kirk Fenton 84–85; V Thornthwaite cum Braithwaite and Newlands *Carl* 91–93; R Wheldrake w Thorganby *York* 93–04; P-in-c Elvington w Sutton on Derwent and E Cottingwith 03–04; rtd 04; PtO *Linc* 15–18. *Cheviot, 5 Mayfield Crescent, Middle Rasen, Market Rasen LN8 3UA* T: (01673) 843388 E: davidcwpost@googlemail.com

POST, Oswald Julian. b 48. Derby Lonsdale Coll BEd 79. EMMTC. **d** 84 **p** 85. Travelling Sec Ruanda Miss 79–89; Hon C Hulland, Atlow, Bradley and Hognaston *Derby* 84–89; V Wormhill, Peak Forest w Peak Dale and Dove Holes 89–99; P-in-c Youlgreave, Middleton, Stanton-in-Peak etc 99–09; rtd 09; UK Ambassador AE Evangelisoc Enterprise Ltd from 10; PtO *Lich* from 13. *Rose Cottage, Hulland Village, Ashbourne DE6 3EP* T: (01335) 370285 E: ossiepost@icloud.com

POSTILL, John Edward. b 35. Oak Hill Th Coll 64. **d** 67 **p** 68. C Southgate *Chich* 67–70; C Bowling St Jo *Bradf* 70–74; TV Winfarthing w Shelfanger *Nor* 74–79; R Slaugham *Chich* 79–97; C Busbridge and Hambledon *Guildf* 97–03; rtd 03; PtO *Guildf* from 04. *Dora Cottage, Beech Hill, Hambledon, Godalming GU8 4HL* T: (01428) 687968 E: j.epostill@gmail.com

POSTILL, Canon Richard Halliday. b 37. Hull Univ BSc 59. Westcott Ho Cam 66. **d** 68 **p** 69. C Wylde Green *Birm* 68–72; C Kingswinford St Mary *Lich* 72–76; V Yardley Wood *Birm* 76–86; V Acocks Green 86–02; AD Yardley 93–00; Hon Can Birm Cathl 99–02; rtd 02; PtO *Birm* from 03. *32 Longmore Road, Shirley, Solihull B90 3DY* T: 0121-744 6217

POSTON, Jonathan David. b 59. Ches Coll of HE MTh 05. NOC 01. **d** 04 **p** 05. C Prestwich St Marg *Man* 04–10; PtO 10–14; NSM Matlock Bank and Tansley and Dethick, Lea and Holloway *Derby* 10–12; NSM Spondon 12–14; R Wingerworth from 14. *The Rectory, Longedge Lane, Wingerworth, Chesterfield S42 6PU* T: (01246) 279932 M: 07754-517797 E: jont.post@gmail.com

POTE, Thomas Gerald Edward. b 90. R Holloway Coll Lon BA 15 MA 17 CCC Cam BA 18. Westcott Ho Cam 16. **d** 19. C Guildf H Trin w St Mary from 19. *27 Pewley Way, Guildford GU1 3PX* M: 07578-502420 E: tom_pote@hotmail.co.uk

POTTAGE, Timothy Lindsay. b 65. **d** 15 **p** 16. C Galmington *B & W* from 15. *Midfields, Comeytrowe Lane, Taunton TA1 5BJ* T: (01823) 256152 M: 07971-010710 E: timpottage@hotmail.com

POTTEN, Rosemary Elizabeth. b 48. **d** 13 **p** 14. OLM Barkingside H Trin *Chelmsf* 13–17; NSM from 17. *51 Greenleafe Drive, Barkingside, Ilford IG6 1LH* T: (020) 8551 2011 E: rosemaryp@hotmail.co.uk

POTTER, Mrs Anne Mary. b 57. Open Univ BA 92 Chich Coll PGCE 96. Qu Coll Birm 09. **d** 11 **p** 12. C Badsey w Aldington and Offenham and Bretforton *Worc* 11–15; TV Worcs W Rural from 15; C Worc Dines Green St Mich and Crown E, Rushwick from 15; RD Martley and Worc W from 19. *The Rectory, Leigh, Worcester WR6 5LE* M: 07783-711665 E: revannepotter@gmail.com

POTTER, The Ven Christopher Nicholas Lynden. b 49. Leeds Univ BA 71. St As Minl Tr Course 90. **d** 93 **p** 94. C Flint *St As* 93–96; V Llanfair DC, Derwen, Llanelidan and Efenechtyd 96–01; Dean and Lib St As Cathl 01–11; V St As 01–13; TR 03–11; R Caerwys and Bodfari 11–14; Adn St As 11–14; rtd 14; PtO *St As* from 14. *Bryn Celyn, Willow Street, Llangollen LL20 8HH* T: (01978) 861831

POTTER, Clive Geoffrey. b 55. Aston Tr Scheme 88 Sarum & Wells Th Coll 90. **d** 92 **p** 93. C Epsom Common Ch Ch *Guildf* 92–97; TV Westborough 97–98; TR 98–07; V Milford from 07; AD Godalming 12–19. *The New Vicarage, Milford Heath, Milford, Godalming GU8 5BX* T: (01483) 414710 E: milfordvicarage@gmail.com

POTTER, Harry Drummond. b 54. Em Coll Cam BA 76 MA 79 MPhil 81 LLB 92 Barrister 93. Westcott Ho Cam 79. **d** 81 **p** 82. C Deptford St Paul *S'wark* 81–84; Chapl Selw Coll Cam

84–87; Chapl Newnham Coll Cam 84–87; Chapl HM Pris Wormwood Scrubs 87–88; Chapl HM YOI Aylesbury 88–93; NSM Camberwell St Giles w St Matt *S'wark* 93–03; PtO 03–07. *19 Dobell Road, London SE9 1HE* T: (020) 7067 1500 E: tuahousis@hotmail.com

POTTER, John Dennis. b 39. Ealing Tech Coll. S Dios Minl Tr Scheme 92. **d** 94 **p** 95. NSM Box w Hazlebury and Ditteridge *Bris* 94–98; PtO *B & W* 06–19. *87A Southdown Road, Bath BA2 1HL* T: (01225) 316656 M: 07745-873759 E: johndpotter@talktalk.net

POTTER, Mrs Judith Anne. b 46. Rolle Coll CertEd 68. **d** 05 **p** 06. OLM Shere, Albury and Chilworth *Guildf* 05–12; NSM 12–16; Chapl Birtley Ho Bramley 08–12; PtO from 16. *3 Bank Terrace, Gomshall Lane, Shere, Guildford GU5 9HB* T: (01483) 203352 F: 202077 E: judyp@btopenworld.com

POTTER, Mrs Leisa Caroline. b 69. Plymouth Univ BSc 92. SWMTC. **d** 14 **p** 15. C Ottery St Mary, Alfington, W Hill, Tipton etc *Ex* 14–18; P-in-c Brighstone and Brooke w Mottistone *Portsm* 18–19; P-in-c Shorwell w Kingston 18–19; P-in-c Calbourne w Newtown 18–19; P-in-c Shalfleet 18–19; P-in-c Thorley 18–19; P-in-c Freshwater 18–19; P-in-c Yarmouth 18–19; P-in-c Totland Bay 18–19; TV W Wight from 19. *The Rectory, 1 The Nurseries, Freshwater PO40 9FG* T: (01983) 753078 M: 07732-120233 E: revleisa@btinternet.com

POTTER, Mrs Linda. b 47. Cranmer Hall Dur 92. **d** 94 **p** 95. C Shildon w Eldon *Dur* 94–98; P-in-c Castleside 98–04; TR Gt Aycliffe 04–12; rtd 12; PtO *Ripon* 14; *Leeds* from 14. *32 Knaresborough Road, Harrogate HG2 7LU*

POTTER, Malcolm Emmerson. b 48. Bedf Coll Lon BSc 70. St Jo Coll Nottm. **d** 75 **p** 76. C Upton (Overchurch) *Ches* 76–78; CPAS Staff 78–84; Development Officer St Jo Coll Nottm 84–86; P-in-c Wellington All SS w Eyton *Lich* 86–95; V 95–06; Preb Lich Cathl 99–06; Membership Development Manager Age Concern 06–07; Chapl Shropshire Co Primary Care Trust 07–12; rtd 12. *2 Barns Green, Shrewsbury SY3 9QB* T: (01743) 235430 E: malcolm@kerameus.co.uk

POTTER, Mark Richard Anthony. b 77. Sheff Univ BA 99 Sheff Hallam Univ PGCE 00. St Mellitus Coll MA 19. **d** 19. C Wisley w Pyrford *Guildf* from 19. *Church House, Coldharbour Road, Woking GU22 8SP* M: 07776-341648 E: markpotter@btinternet.com

POTTER, Neil John. b 63. **d** 12 **p** 13. NSM Redruth w Lanner and Treleigh *Truro* 12–15; NSM Camborne and Tuckingmill 15–16; NSM Penponds 15–16; NSM Camborne, Tuckingmill and Penponds from 16. *Strawberry Bank, 2 Dam Bungalows, Carn, Stithians, Truro TR3 7AW* M: 07539-593684 E: neilpotter@talktalk.net

POTTER, Phillip. b 54. Stirling Univ BA 75. Trin Coll Bris 82. **d** 84 **p** 85. C Yateley *Win* 84–88; V Haydock St Mark *Liv* 88–07; Dir Pioneer Min 07–14; C Haydock St Mark 07–09; P-in-c Southport St Phil and St Paul 12–14; Hon Can Liv Cathl 03–14; Abps' Missr and Team Ldr Fresh Expressions Cant from 14; NSM Bowdon *Ches* 15–19; PtO from 19. *Chapel House, Chester Road, Tabley, Knutsford WA16 0HN* T: (01565) 634327 E: phil.potter@freshexpressions.org.uk

POTTER, Miss Sharon Jane. b 63. UEA BSc 96 K Coll Lon MSc 00 RGN 91. Dioc OLM tr scheme 00. **d** 04 **p** 05. OLM Ipswich All Hallows *St E* 04–06; OLM Ipswich St Helen, H Trin, and St Luke 07–12; R Bradfield St Clare, Bradfield St George etc from 12. *The Rectory, Howe Lane, Cockfield, Bury St Edmunds IP30 0HA* T: (01284) 828599 M: 07825-086063 E: revsharon@btinternet.com

POTTER, Simon Jonathan. b 76. Southn Univ BA 98 Ex Univ PGCE 99. Trin Coll Bris MA 14. **d** 14 **p** 15. C Ox St Andr 14–18; C Stoke Bishop *Bris* from 18. *3 Hollybush Lane, Bristol BS9 1BH* M: 07837-843229 E: potterjsimon@gmail.com

POTTER, Stephen Michael. b 55. Oak Hill Th Coll 93. **d** 95 **p** 96. C Chesterfield H Trin and Ch Ch *Derby* 95–99; P-in-c S Normanton 99–01; R from 01. *The Rectory, Church Street, South Normanton, Alfreton DE55 2BT* T: (01773) 811273 E: stephen.potter55@gmail.com

POTTER, Timothy John. b 49. Bris Univ BSc 71. Oak Hill Th Coll 73. **d** 76 **p** 77. C Wallington *S'wark* 76–79; C Hampreston *Sarum* 79–81; TV Stratton St Margaret w S Marston etc *Bris* 81–87; P-in-c Hatfield Heath *Chelmsf* 87–89; P-in-c Sheering 87–89; R Hatfield Heath and Sheering 90–09; P-in-c Gt Hallingbury and Lt Hallingbury 06–09; RD Harlow 07–09; Hon Can Chelmsf Cathl 02–09; rtd 09. *Redcot, 91 High Street, Dunmow CM6 1AF* E: tim.potter1@btinternet.com

POTTERTON, David Steven. b 59. Ox Min Course 13. **d** 15 **p** 16. C Romsey *Win* 15–18; P-in-c Lyndhurst and Emery Down and Minstead from 18. *The Vicarage, Forest Gardens, Lyndhurst SO43 7AF* M: 07827-994083 E: david.potterton@btinternet.com

POTTINGER, Justin Charles Edward. b 82. Keble Coll Ox BA 03 Ox Brookes Univ PGCE 04. STETS 05 Ripon Coll Cuddesdon 07. **d** 08 **p** 09. C Devizes St Jo w St Mary *Sarum* 08–11; Chapl Clayesmore Sch Blandford 11–14; V Red Post *Sarum* from 15. *The Vicarage, East Morden, Wareham BH20 7DW* T: (01929) 459244 E: redpostbenefice@gmail.com

POTTS, Heather Dawn. *See* BUTCHER, Heather Dawn

POTTS, James. b 30. K Coll Lon BD 56 AKC 56. **d** 57 **p** 58. C Brighouse *Wakef* 57–59; Tanganyika 59–64; Tanzania 64–71; C-in-c Athersley and New Lodge CD *Wakef* 71–73; V Athersley 73–77; V Madeley *Lich* 77–85; V Baswich 85–93; RD Stafford 88–95; rtd 93; PtO *Lich* from 05. *16A Christchurch Lane, Lichfield WS13 8BA* T: (01543) 418808

POTTS, Mrs Jill. b 46. Open Univ BA 89. STETS 02. **d** 05 **p** 06. NSM Corfe Mullen *Sarum* 05–07; NSM Grantham, Manthorpe *Linc* 07–13; rtd 13; PtO *Linc* from 13. *18 Dallygate, Great Ponton, Grantham NG33 5DP* T: (01476) 530361 E: jill@dallygate.uk

POTTS, Mrs Susan Pamela. b 54. Huddersfield Poly BA 76 Lanc Univ PGCE 77. ERMC 09. **d** 12 **p** 13. NSM Raddesley Gp *Ely* 12–14; NSM Three Rivers Gp from 14. *The Vicarage, High Street, Chippenham, Ely CB7 5PP* M: 07851-184295 E: susan.potts@scherzando.org *or* revd.sue@icloud.com

POULARD, Christopher. b 39. FCA 64. Ridley Hall Cam 82. **d** 84 **p** 85. C N Walsham w Antingham *Nor* 84–86; C Oulton Broad 86–90; TV Raveningham 90–94; R Raveningham Gp 94–99; RD Loddon 98–99; PtO *Chelmsf* from 99; rtd 04. *Cuddington, Colam Lane, Little Baddow, Chelmsford CM3 4SY* T: (01245) 224221 F: 221394 E: chris@poulard.org.uk

POULSON, Anna Louise. b 73. Univ Coll Dur BA 94 K Coll Lon MA 97 PhD 06. Ridley Hall Cam 98. **d** 02 **p** 03. C Ealing St Mary *Lon* 02–06; C Southall Green St Jo 11–14; V from 15. *St John's Vicarage, Church Avenue, Southall UB2 4DH* T: (020) 8571 3027 M: 07795-595915 E: annapoulson@btinternet.com

POULSON, Canon Mark Alban. b 63. Bath Coll of HE BEd 86 Anglia Poly Univ MA 03. Ridley Hall Cam. **d** 00 **p** 01. C Alperton *Lon* 00–03; P-in-c Southall Green St Jo 03–06; V 06–14; Adv for Inter Faith Matters 14–18; Abp's Sec for Inter-Relig Affairs *Cant* 15–18; Dioc Co-ord for Presence and Engagement *Lon* from 18; Can for Interfaith Relns St Paul's Cathl from 18; Hon Can Bradf Cathl *Leeds* from 17. *St John's Vicarage, Church Avenue, Southall UB2 4DH* T: (020) 8571 9877 E: mpoulson@btinternet.com

POULTNEY, Andrew Timothy. b 68. K Coll Lon MA 03. St Paul's Th Cen Lon 06. **d** 08 **p** 09. C Collier Row Sheff St Jas and Havering-atte-Bower *Chelmsf* 08–17; P-in-c Sheff St Paul from 18; C Sheff St Cecilia Parson Cross from 18; C Sheff St Leon Norwood from 18. *98 Chaucer Close, Sheffield S5 9QE* M: 07903-112599 E: andypoultneypxpioneerminister@gmail.com

POULTNEY, Ann Josephina. b 76. Southn Univ BSc 97. St Mellitus Coll BA 17. **d** 17 **p** 18. C Aldenham, Radlett and Shenley *St Alb* 17–18; C Attleborough *Cov* from 18. *2 Bryony Close, Bedworth CV12 0GF* T: (024) 7636 4961

POULTNEY, David Elis. b 73. Loughb Univ BEng 96 CEng 97. Trin Coll Bris 07. **d** 09 **p** 10. C Luton Lewsey St Hugh *St Alb* 09–13; C Bushey 13–18; TR Bedworth *Cov* from 18. *2 Bryony Close, Bedworth CV12 0GF* T: (024) 7631 0688 E: dave.poultney@outlook.com

POULTON, Arthur Leslie. b 28. K Coll Lon BA 53 AKC 53 BD 60 Leic Univ MA 85. Tyndale Hall Bris 53. **d** 55 **p** 56. C New Catton St Luke *Nor* 55–56; C Earlham St Anne 56–58; C Chorleywood Ch Ch *St Alb* 58–61; R E Barnet 61–64; Ches Coll of HE 64–87; Chapl 64–84; Sen Lect 66–87; Dir of Studies Course in Chr Studies *Chelmsf* 87–94; P-in-c Gt Canfield 87–94; rtd 94; PtO *Ches* 96–08. *16 Adlington House, Abbey Road, Rhos on Sea, Colwyn Bay LL28 4PU* T: (01492) 549473

POULTON, Neville John. b 48. STETS. **d** 02. NSM Portsea St Cuth *Portsm* 02–07. *18 Belgravia Road, Portsmouth PO2 0DX* T: (023) 9236 1104 M: 07768-661796 E: moandnev@ntlworld.com

POUNCEY, Christopher Michael Godwin. b 52. Reading Univ BSc 74 Wycliffe Hall Ox BA 77 MA. SWMTC 03. **d** 04 **p** 05. NSM S Molton w Nymet St George, High Bray etc *Ex* 04–16; NSM S Molton w Nymet St George, Chittlehamholt etc from 16. *Brightley Barton, Umberleigh EX37 9AL* T: (01769) 540405 M: 07977-930045

POUND, Canon Keith Salisbury. b 33. St Cath Coll Cam BA 54 MA 58. Cuddesdon Coll 55. **d** 57 **p** 58. C St Helier S'wark 57–61; Tr Officer Hollowford Tr and Conf Cen Sheff 61–64; Warden 64–67; R S'wark H Trin 68–74; P-in-c Newington St Matt 68–74; R S'wark H Trin w St Matt 74–78;

RD S'wark and Newington 73–78; TR Thamesmead 78–86; Sub-Dean Woolwich 84–86; RD Greenwich 85–86; Hon Can S'wark Cathl 85–86; Chapl Gen of Pris 86–93; Chapl to The Queen 88–03; Chapl HM Pris Grendon and HM Pris Spring Hill 93–98; rtd 98; PtO *Chich* from 99. *1 Sinnock Square, Hastings TN34 3HQ* T: (01424) 428330

POUNTAIN, Thomas Iain. b 86. Ex Univ BA 07. Moore Th Coll Sydney BTh 17. **d** 18 **p** 19. C W Hampstead St Luke *Lon* from 18. *40 Ingham Road, London NW6 1DE* M: 07484-716281 E: t.pountain@gmail.com

POUT, John Robert. b 61. Salford Univ BA 83. WEMTC 09. **d** 12 **p** 14. NSM Moreton-in-Marsh w Batsford, Todenham etc *Glouc* 12–16; C 16–17; V Paignton Ch Ch and Preston St Paul *Ex* from 17. *The Vicarage, Locarno Avenue, Paignton TQ3 2DH* M: 07739-500913 E: johnpout@icloud.com

POVEY, William Peter. b 36. Man Univ MSc 82 MRCS 61 LRCP 61 FFPH 79 FRIPH HonFChS. NOC 90. **d** 93 **p** 94. Dioc Drug Liaison Officer *Ches* 93–01; NSM Latchford Ch Ch 93–00; NSM Daresbury 00–03; rtd 03; PtO *Ches* from 03; *Ex* from 04. *Applebrook House, 4 Trinnicks Orchard, Ugborough, Ivybridge PL21 0NX* T: (01752) 691654 E: povey.peter@googlemail.com

POWDRILL, Penelope Anne. b 47. Lon Univ BSc 69 PGCE 71 Birm Univ MEd 77. WEMTC 10. **d** 11 **p** 12. OLM Wye Brooks Benefice *Heref* 11–19; OLM Wye Reaches Gp 11–19; rtd 19. *Homebush, Lower Prospect Road, Osbaston, Monmouth NP25 3HS* T: (01600) 714096 E: pennypowdrill@btinternet.com

POWELL, Canon Anthony James. b 51. Sarum & Wells Th Coll 78. **d** 79 **p** 80. C Larkfield *Roch* 79–83; C Leybourne 79–83; V Borough Green 83–16; Hon Can Roch Cathl 04–16; rtd 16. *Address withheld by request*

POWELL, Charles David. b 38. St Pet Coll Saltley CertEd 61 ACP 74. SAOMC 96. **d** 99 **p** 00. NSM Ampthill w Millbrook and Steppingley *St Alb* 99–04; PtO from 05; RD Ampthill 03–08. *33 Putnoe Heights, Bedford MK41 8EB* T: (01234) 345020 M: 07811-260675 E: rev.davidpowell@btinternet.com

POWELL, Christopher John. b 71. K Coll Lon BA 94 AKC 94. Coll of Resurr Mirfield 95. **d** 97 **p** 98. C Botley *Portsm* 97–01; C Portsea N End St Mark 01–05; P-in-c Clayton w Keymer *Chich* 05–13; R 13–16; V Wivelsfield from 16. *The Vicarage, Church Lane, Wivelsfield, Haywards Heath RH17 7RD* E: christopher.powell123@btinternet.com

POWELL, Colin Arthur. b 32. Hatf Coll Dur BA 53. Oak Hill Th Coll 56. **d** 58 **p** 59. C Leyland St Andr *Blackb* 58–61; C Lancaster St Thos 61–64; C Tranmere St Cath *Ches* 64–65; R Cheetham Hill *Man* 65–81; TV Oldham 81–86; TV Rochdale 86–97; Chapl Rochdale Healthcare NHS Trust 94–97; rtd 97; PtO *Man* from 97. *103 Parsonage Road, Withington, Manchester M20 4NU* T: 0161-434 2409

POWELL, David. *See* POWELL, Charles David

POWELL, Mrs Diane. b 41. SWMTC 85. **d** 88 **p** 94. Hon C St Merryn *Truro* 88–92; Dn-in-c Gerrans w St Anthony in Roseland 92–94; P-in-c 94–00; Asst Chapl R Cornwall Hosps Trust 00–05; rtd 05; PtO *Truro* from 05. *Pendower, 15 Fairfield, St Merryn, Padstow PL28 8FQ* T: (01841) 521610 E: dianepowell389@gmail.com

POWELL, Dudley John. b 44. Tyndale Hall Bris 65. **d** 69 **p** 70. C Blackb Sav 69–71; C Rodbourne Cheney *Bris* 71–74; P-in-c Kingsdown 74 79; V 79–80; V Stoke Gifford 80–90; TR 90–91; Ancient World Outreach Albania 91–03; PtO *Bris* 91–03; *Win* 03–13; rtd 09. *30 Homechurch House, 31 Purewell, Christchurch BH23 1EH* T: (01202) 481379

POWELL, Eleanor Ann. b 55. Univ of Wales BA 82 Leeds Univ MA 06 Gwent Coll Newport CertEd 76. Qu Coll Birm 82. **d** 83 **p** 94. C Caereithin *S & B* 83–86; C Bishopston 86–88; Dioc Children's Officer *Glouc* 88–94; Dioc Adv for Women's Min 94–01; P-in-c The Edge, Pitchcombe, Harescombe and Brookthorpe 94–00; V Churchdown St Jo 00–01; Hon Can Glouc Cathl 94–01; Chapl Univ Hosps Bris NHS Foundn Trust 01–06; Lead Chapl Cwm Taf Univ Health Bd 06–18; PtO *Llan* from 18. *Park Farm Lodge, The Legar, Langattock, Crickhowell NP8 1HH* T: (01873) 811355 E: epowell97@gmail.com

POWELL, Preb Frank. b 29. AKC 52. **d** 53 **p** 54. C Stockingford *Cov* 53–56; C Netherton St Andr *Worc* 56–60; P-in-c W Bromwich St Jo *Lich* 60–66; C W Bromwich Gd Shep w St Jo 60–66; V 66–69; V Bilston St Leon 69–76; P-in-c Hanbury 76–82; V Hanbury w Newborough 83–86; V Basford 86–92; Preb Lich Cathl 87–92; rtd 92; PtO *Ches* from 92. *39 Wright Court, London Road, Nantwich CW5 6SE* T: (01270) 618679 E: fjpowell1@gmail.com

POWELL, Jason Corrin. b 79. St Mellitus Coll. **d** 16 **p** 17. C Middleton w Thornham *Man* from 16. *6 Westbrook Close, Rochdale OL11 2XY* T: (01706) 631050 M: 07968-482058 E: jasoncorrinpowell@gmail.com

POWELL, John. b 44. St Luke's Coll Ex CertEd 66 Univ of Wales (Lamp) MA 02. Glouc Sch of Min 81. **d** 84 **p** 85. NSM Stroud and Uplands w Slad *Glouc* 84–89; Chapl Eliz Coll Guernsey 89–92; C Llandudno *Ban* 92–93; TV 94–96; V Dwygyfylchi 96–02; V Cardigan w Mwnt and Y Ferwig w Llangoedmor *St D* 02–10; rtd 10; P-in-c Llangrannog w Llandysiliogogo w Penbryn *St D* 10–11; PtO 11–12; P-in-c Maenordeifi Gp 12–14; PtO from 14. *Crud yr Haul, 12 Maes y Dderwen, Cardigan SA43 1PE* T: (01239) 621512 E: parchjohnpowell@btinternet.com

POWELL, John Keith Lytton. b 52. S Dios Minl Tr Scheme 91. **d** 94 **p** 95. NSM Bridgwater H Trin *B & W* 94–97; P-in-c Hatch Beauchamp w Beercrocombe, Curry Mallet etc 97–02; P-in-c Staple Fitzpaine, Orchard Portman, Thurlbear etc 97–02; R Beercrocombe w Curry Mallet, Hatch Beauchamp etc 02–05; P-in-c Exford, Exmoor, Hawkridge and Withypool 05–09; P-in-c Middlezoy and Othery and Moorlinch 09–11; P-in-c Greinton 09–11; R Middlezoy w Othery, Moorlinch and Greinton 11–17; Dioc Renewal Adv from 06. *Honeywood, East Lyng, Taunton TA3 5AU* E: jill.powell3@googlemail.com

POWELL, Kelvin. b 49. Wycliffe Hall Ox 71. **d** 74 **p** 75. C Prescot *Liv* 74–77; C Ainsdale 77–79; V Bickershaw 79–85; R Hesketh w Becconsall *Blackb* 85–99; rtd 14; PtO *Leic* 14–19. *17 Fosbrooke House, 8 Clifton Drive, Lytham St Annes FY8 5RG*

POWELL, Laurence James. b 86. Win Univ BA 08. Ripon Coll Cuddesdon 10. **d** 13 **p** 14. C Strood St Nic w St Mary *Roch* 13–16; V Tunbridge Wells K Chas from 16; P-in-c Tunbridge Wells St Mark from 19. *The Vicarage, Rodmell Road, Tunbridge Wells TN2 5ST* T: (01892) 525455

POWELL, Canon Mark. b 57. Bath Univ BSc 78 PhD 81. Ripon Coll Cuddesdon BA 84 MA 88. **d** 85 **p** 86. C Evesham *Worc* 85–88; V Exhall *Cov* 88–96; V Leavesden St Alb 96–00; V Ealing St Pet Mt Park *Lon* 00–11; V Melbourne, Ticknall, Smisby and Stanton *Derby* 11–16; Can Windsor from 16. *6 The Cloisters, Windsor Castle, Windsor SL4 1NJ* T: (01753) 848709 E: mark.powell@stgeorges-windsor.org

POWELL, Martin. b 71. St Steph Ho Ox BTh 00. **d** 00 **p** 01. C Caterham *S'wark* 00–03; V New Addington 03–14; R Aldingbourne, Barnham and Eastergate *Chich* 14–18; P-in-c Moulsecoomb from 18. *St Andrew's Vicarage, Hillside, Brighton BN2 4TA* E: frmartinpowell@gmail.com

POWELL, Canon Pamela. b 56. Univ of Wales BEd 79 Goldsmiths' Coll Lon MA 82. St As Minl Tr Course 00. **d** 03 **p** 04. C Wrexham *St As* 03–06; P-in-c Llansantffraid-ym-Mechain and Llanfechain 06–08; V 08–15; AD Llanfyllin 11–12; AD Caereinion and Llanfyllin 12–14; V Brymbo w Bwlchgwyn 15–16; Dir Lay Min from 10; P-in-c Borderlands Miss Area from 18; Dir Lay Min from 10; Chan St As Cathl from 14. *The Vicarage, 8 Whiteoaks, Bwlchgwyn, Wrexham LL11 5UJ* T: (01978) 721083 M: 07711-053565 E: pampowell@microplusmail.co.uk

POWELL, Patricia Mary. b 46. STETS. **d** 03 **p** 04. NSM Woodford Valley *Sarum* 03–09; NSM Tidworth, Ludgershall and Faberstown 09–12; NSM Woodford Valley w Archers Gate 13–16; NSM Amesbury 13–16; rtd 16; PtO *Sarum* 16–18. *Hawthorne Cottage, Great Durnford, Salisbury SP4 6AZ* T: (01722) 782546 E: p.powell22@btinternet.com

POWELL, Peter John. b 57. G&C Coll Cam MA 80 MB, BChir 83. Coll of Resurr Mirfield 17. **d** 18 **p** 19. C Workington St Mich *Carl* from 18. *St Michael's Rectory, Dora Crescent, Workington CA14 2EZ* M: 07952-372435 E: ppowellhome@gmail.com *or* stmichaelsworkington@btinternet.com

POWELL, Canon Ralph Dover. b 49. ARMCM 70. Chich Th Coll 71. **d** 74 **p** 75. C Coppenhall *Ches* 74–77; C Heref H Trin 77–80; V Crewe St Barn from 80; Hon Can Ches Cathl from 14. *St Barnabas' Vicarage, West Street, Crewe CW1 3AX* T: (01270) 212418 E: stbarnabascrewe@outlook.com

POWELL, Richard Graham. b 88. Glos Univ BA 11. Oak Hill Th Coll BA 19. **d** 19. C Kensington Ch Ch *Lon* from 19. *Flat 1, 94 Warwick Gardens, London W14 8PR* M: 07854-550778 E: richpowell938@gmail.com

POWELL, Robert John. b 65. Trin Coll Bris BA 92. **d** 92 **p** 93. C Biggin Hill *Roch* 92–95; C Edgware *Lon* 95–01; Area Sec SAMS (NW England and N Wales) 01–04; TV Upper Holloway *Lon* 04–12; V Whitehall Park 12–13; TR Furzedown *S'wark* from 13. *St James's Rectory, 236 Mitcham Lane, London SW16 6NT*

POWELL, Roger Roy. b 68. Thames Poly BSc 91. Ripon Coll Cuddesdon BTh 94. **d** 94 **p** 95. C Leic St Jas 94–98; C The Abbey Leic 98–00; TV 00–05; P-in-c Leic St Paul 01–05; Youth Chapl 98–05; P-in-c Ridgeway *Sarum* 05–10; R from 10; RD Marlborough from 18. *The Rectory, 3 Butts Road, Chiseldon, Swindon SN4 0NN* T: (01793) 740369 E: revd.rpowell@btopenworld.com

POWELL, Stuart William. b 58. K Coll Lon BD 80 AKC 80. Ripon Coll Cuddesdon 86. **d** 88 **p** 89. C Horden *Dur*

88–90; C Northolt Park St Barn *Lon* 90–93; V Castle Vale St Cuth *Birm* 93–00; V Stockland Green 00–11; P-in-c Rough Hills *Lich* 11–15; P-in-c Wolverhampton St Steph 11–15; V Wolverhampton St Martin and St Steph 15–19; PtO from 19; CF(V) from 08. *16 Belvidere Road, Walsall WS1 3AU* M: 07889-887358   Pager: 07336-734456 E: spowell.t21@btinternet.com

POWER, Canon David Michael. b 56. BA 81 BEd. Oak Hill Th Coll. **d** 81 **p** 82. C Warblington w Emsworth *Portsm* 81–84; C-in-c Hartplain CD 84–88; V Hartplain 88–91; Adv in Evang 91–97; V Portsea St Cuth 97–18; Hon Can Portsm Cathl 13–18; rtd 18; Hon Can Ho Ghana from 19. *22 Ashling Park Road, Denmead, Waterlooville PO7 6EH* E: davidmpower@ntlworld.com

POWER, James Edward. b 58. Nottm Univ BSc 81 Leeds Univ BA 85. Coll of Resurr Mirfield 83. **d** 86 **p** 87. C Cadoxton-juxta-Barry *Llan* 86–89; Chapl Harrow Sch from 89; V Harrow St Mary *Lon* from 15; PtO *C & R* from 18. *35 West Street, Harrow HA1 3EG* T: (020) 8872 8234 *or* 8423 4014 E: jep@harrowschool.org.uk

POWER, Canon Jeanette. b 57. Oak Hill Th Coll BA 81. **dss** 82 **d** 87 **p** 94. Warblington w Emsworth *Portsm* 84–86; Hartplain CD 84–87; Hon C Hartplain 87–91; Community Mental Health Chapl Havant and Petersfield from 91; NSM Wickham 93–97; NSM Portsea St Cuth 97–18; PtO from 18; Team Chapl Portsm Hosps NHS Trust from 01; Hon Can Ho Ghana from 19. *22 Ashling Park Road, Denmead, Waterlooville PO7 6EH* T: (023) 9234 2044 E: jeanettepower1@virginmedia.com

POWER, Mrs Lynn Diane. b 59. K Coll Lon BA 81 PGCE 82 AKC 81. STETS 10. **d** 13 **p** 14. NSM N Hants Downs *Win* 13–16; NSM Alton from 16; Chapl Treloar Coll Alton from 16. *1 Alton Road, South Warnborough, Hook RG29 1RT* T: (01256) 861433 M: 07850-232995

POWER, Canon Michael Andrew. b 61. Westcott Ho Cam. **d** 12 **p** 13. C Romford St Edw *Chelmsf* 12–15; V from 15; P-in-c Romford Ascension Collier Row from 19; AD Havering from 18; Hon Can Chelmsf Cathl from 19. *St Edward's Vicarage, 15 Oaklands Avenue, Romford RM1 4DB* T: (01708) 731180 M: 07793-463640 E: mikeapower@aol.com

POWER, Richard Victor John. b 80. Oak Hill Th Coll 13. **d** 15 **p** 16. C Banbury St Paul *Ox* 15–19; C Harold Wood *Chelmsf* from 19. *8 Archibald Road, Romford RM3 0RH* T: (01708) 348406 M: 07925-394122 E: rvjpower@gmail.com

POWIS, Amy Victoria. See ADENIRAN, Amy Victoria

POWIS, Michael Ralph. b 63. St Jo Coll Nottm BTh 95. **d** 95 **p** 96. C Dibden *Win* 95–00; V Hedge End St Luke 00–09; Adult Discipleship and Evang Tr Officer 09–11; P-in-c Bournemouth St Clem 11–17; P-in-c Pokesdown All SS 11–18; V from 18. *All Saints' Vicarage, 14 Stourwood Road, Bournemouth BH6 3QP* T: (01202) 423747 E: mikepowischurch@gmail.com

POWLES, Charles Anthony. b 39. EAMTC. **d** 88 **p** 89. NSM Hemsby *Nor* 88–93; NSM Bradwell 01–07; PtO from 07. *94 Winifred Way, Caister-on-Sea, Great Yarmouth NR30 5PE* T: (01493) 720096 E: charles.powles@btinternet.com

POWLES, Michael Charles. b 34. Reading Univ BSc 56 Lon Univ PGCE 83. Qu Coll Birm. **d** 60 **p** 61. C Goodmayes All SS *Chelmsf* 60–65; C Surbiton St Matt *S'wark* 65–78; Lect Woolwich Coll 79–99; rtd 99. *Spring Cottage, 3 Rushett Close, Thames Ditton KT7 0UR* T: (020) 8398 9654

POWLEY, Miss Julia Hodgson. b 55. St Andr Univ MA 77 Anglia Ruskin Univ MA 10 FCA 80. Ridley Hall Cam 07. **d** 09 **p** 10. C Carl H Trin and St Barn 09–12; P-in-c Harrington 12–18; P-in-c Distington 12–18; R Harrington and Distington from 18. *The Rectory, Rectory Close, Harrington, Workington CA14 5PN* T: (01946) 830215 M: 07765-217335 E: julia@powley.plus.com

POWLEY, Canon Mark Thomas. b 75. Nottm Univ BA 96 Birm Univ PGCE 98. Wycliffe Hall Ox 01. **d** 03 **p** 04. C Addiscombe St Mary Magd w St Martin *S'wark* 03–06; C Hammersmith St Paul *Lon* 06–09; TV Leeds St Geo *Ripon* 10–14 and 14–15; Prin Yorks Min Course from 15; Prin St Hild Coll from 17; Hon Can Ripon Cathl *Leeds* from 17. *11 Brookfield Road, Leeds LS6 4EJ* E: principal@ymc.org.uk

POWLEY, Canon Robert Mallinson. b 39. Fitzw Coll Cam MA 65. Ridley Hall Cam 61. **d** 63 **p** 64. C Bermondsey St Mary w St Olave, St Jo etc *S'wark* 63–67; C Moseley St Anne *Birm* 67–69; LtO *Man* 72–77; Hon C Walshaw Ch Ch 77–88; V Prestwich St Gabr *Man* 88–94; Bp's Dom Chapl 88–94; P-in-c Hargrave *Ches* 94–05; Exec Officer Bd for Soc Resp 94–05; Hon Can Ches Cathl 00–05; rtd 05; PtO *Ban* 05–12; *Leeds* from 17. *39A Bentley Lane, Leeds LS6 4AJ* T: 0113-275 9876 E: powley915@btinternet.com

POWNALL, Lydia Margaret. See HURLE, Lydia Margaret

POWNALL-JONES, Timothy William. b 79. Univ of Wales (Cardiff) BD 00 MTh 02. Trin Coll Bris 04. **d** 06 **p** 07. C Newark w Coddington *S'well* 06–10; Chapl Farndon Unit 08–10; Chapl N Notts Coll of FE *S'well* 10–11; Hon C Bassetlaw and Bawtry Deanery from 10; Tutor All SS Cen for Miss and Min 12–18; Chapl Notts Healthcare NHS Foundn Trust from 15; Chapl Sherwood Forest Hosps NHS Foundn Trust 17–18. *Rampton Hospital, Retford DN22 0PD* M: 07837-630005 E: t_pownall_jones@hotmail.com

POYNER, David Roy. b 61. WEMTC 15. **d** 18 **p** 19. NSM Highley w Billingsley, Glazeley etc *Heref* from 18. *136 Hoo Road, Kidderminster DY10 1LP* T: (01562) 686638 E: d.r.poyner@aston.ac.uk

POYNTZ, Jocelin Georgina Massey. b 58. Ridley Hall Cam. **d** 13 **p** 14. C Stanford-le-Hope w Mucking *Chelmsf* 13–17; TV Harlow Town Cen w Lt Parndon from 17. *4A The Drive, Harlow CM20 3QD* M: 07743-124181 E: rev.jokey.poyntz@gmail.com

PRAGNELL, Michael John. b 40. Down Coll Cam BA 62 PhD 65 MA 66 FIQA 81 MRSC CChem MSOSc 88. Ox NSM Course 81. **d** 84 **p** 85. NSM High Wycombe *Ox* 84–98; C Beercrocombe w Curry Mallet, Hatch Beauchamp etc *B & W* 98–05; rtd 05; PtO *B & W* from 05. *2 Listers Court, Listers Hill, Ilminster TA19 0DP* T: (01460) 54212 E: curatemjp@waitrose.com

PRAGNELL, Sandra Ann. b 53. Hull Univ BA 75 TCD BTh 01 Dub City Univ MA 04. CITC 98. **d** 01 **p** 02. C Castleknock and Mulhuddart w Clonsilla *D & G* 01–05; PV Ch Ch Cathl Dublin 03–05; I Dundalk w Heynestown *Arm* 05–12; I Ballymascanlan w Creggan and Rathcor 05–12; Dean Limerick and Ardfert *L & K* 12–17; I Limerick City 12–17; rtd 17. *c/o Robbins, Drynachan, Invergarry PH35 4HL* E: sandrapragnell@eircom.net or revsandrapragnell@gmail.com

PRANCE, Robert Penrose. b 47. Southn Univ BTh 73. Sarum & Wells Th Coll 69. **d** 72 **p** 73. C Gillingham and Fifehead Magdalen *Sarum* 72–76; P-in-c Edmondsham 76–80; P-in-c Woodlands 76–80; P-in-c Wimborne St Giles 76–80; P-in-c Cranborne 77–80; R Cranborne w Boveridge, Edmondsham etc 80–83; Chapl Sherborne Sch 83–93; Asst Dir of Ords *Sarum* 76–86; V Stoke Gabriel and Collaton *Ex* 93–99; Dep PV Ex Cathl 95–99; Chapl Shiplake Coll Henley 99–09; Chapl St Edm Sch Cant 09–10; rtd 10; PtO *Ox* 09–12; *Sarum* from 11. *Sedgehill House, 9 Wyndham Road, Salisbury SP1 3AA* T: (01722) 329289 E: robertprance@live.co.uk

PRATT, Basil David. b 38. Westmr Coll of Educn TCert 59. Ripon Hall Ox 64. **d** 67 **p** 68. C Lewisham St Jo Southend *S'wark* 67–68; C Caterham Valley 68–70; CF 70–93; PtO *Glas* from 08. *St Michael's, Bankend Road, Dumfries DG1 4AL* T: (01387) 267933

PRATT, Edward Andrew. b 39. Clare Coll Cam BA 61 MA 65. Clifton Th Coll 63. **d** 66 **p** 67. C Southall Green St Jo *Lon* 66–69; C Drypool St Columba w St Andr and St Pet *York* 69–71; P-in-c Radbourne *Derby* 71–74; R Kirk Langley 71–78; V Mackworth All SS 71–78; V Southsea St Simon *Portsm* 78–97; rtd 97; PtO *Sarum* from 97. *7 Bay Close, Swanage BH19 1RE*

PRATT, Mrs Janet Margaret. b 40. Herts Coll BEd 78. St Alb Minl Tr Scheme 78. **dss** 81 **d** 87 **p** 94. High Wych and Gilston w Eastwick *St Alb* 81–89; Hon Par Dn 87–89; Par Dn Histon *Ely* 89–94; C 94–97; Par Dn Impington 89–94; C 94–97; R Bardney *Linc* 97–07; rtd 07; PtO *Ely* 08–18; *St Alb* from 08. *26 Stamford Avenue, Royston SG8 7DD* T: (01763) 243508 E: janetmpratt99@yahoo.com

PRATT, Michael. *See* HARRIS, Michael

PRATT, The Ven Richard David. b 55. Linc Coll Ox BA 77 MA 81 Birm Univ PhD 01 Nottm Univ BCombStuds 84. Linc Th Coll 81. **d** 84 **p** 85. C Wellingborough All Hallows *Pet* 84–87; TV Kingsthorpe w Northampton St Dav 87–92; V Northampton St Benedict 92–97; Dioc Communications Officer *Carl* from 97; P-in-c Carl St Cuth w St Mary 97–08; Adn W Cumberland from 09; Hon Can Carl Cathl from 02. *50 Stainburn Road, Stainburn, Workington CA14 1SN* T: (01900) 66190 E: archdeacon.west@carlislediocese.org.uk

PRATT, Stephen Samuel. b 67. Univ Coll Ches BA 88 Keele Univ PGCE 89. Oak Hill Th Coll BA 00. **d** 00 **p** 01. C Goodmayes All SS *Chelmsf* 00–03; TV Chell *Lich* 03–07; P-in-c 07–08; V 08–15; CF(V) 05–15; CF from 15. *c/o MOD Chaplains (Army)* T: (01264) 383430 F: 381824 E: stephen_pratt@sky.com

PRATTEN, Miss Susan Avarina. b 60. Birm Univ BA 81 Univ Coll of Swansea PGCE 82. St Mich Coll Llan 10. **d** 12 **p** 13. C Caerphilly *Llan* 12–15; C Eglwysilan and Caerphilly 15–18; V Caerleon and Llanfrechfa *Mon* from 18. *The Vicarage, High Street, Caerleon, Newport NP18 1AZ* T: (01633) 421485 M: 07979-742198 E: s.pratten@btinternet.com

PRECIOUS, Christopher. b 78. Open Univ BSc 01. Cranmer Hall Dur 14. **d** 16 **p** 17. C Alrewas *Lich* 16–19; C Wychnor 16–19; R Kinnerley w Melverley, Knockin w Maesbrook and Maesbury from 19. *The Rectory, Vicarage Lane, Kinnerley, Oswestry SY10 8DE* M: 07867-367627 E: chrismrgpreciousclm@gmail.com

PRECIOUS, Sally Joanne. *See* WRIGHT, Sally Joanne

PREECE, Barry Leslie. b 48. Lich Th Coll 68. **d** 71 **p** 72. C Ewell *Guildf* 71–74; C York Town St Mich 75–77; P-in-c Ripley 77–81; Chapl HM Det Cen Send 77–81; V Cuddington *Guildf* 81–88; V Cobham 88–03; R E and W Clandon 03–13; rtd 13; PtO *Cant* from 13. *43 Paxton Avenue, Hawkinge, Folkestone CT18 7GW* T: (01303) 894304 E: rev.preece@btinternet.com

PREECE, Canon Colin George. b 51. Bernard Gilpin Soc Dur 71 Chich Th Coll 72. **d** 75 **p** 76. C Upper Gornal *Lich* 75–78; C Wednesbury St Paul Wood Green 78–81; V Oxley 81–89; V Kennington *Cant* 89–03; RD E Charing 92–98; P-in-c Ashford 03–15; Hon Can Cant Cathl 08–15; rtd 15; PtO *Ex* from 15; Hon Can Toliara Madagascar from 13. *Bowood House, 2 Bishop Court, Colyton EX24 6RQ* T: (01297) 552154 E: colinpreece@btinternet.com

PREECE, David Nathan. b 87. Ox Brookes Univ BA 11 K Coll Lon PGCE 12. Trin Coll Bris MA 17. **d** 17 **p** 18. C Busbridge *Guildf* from 17. *2 South Hill, Godalming GU7 1JT* M: 07716-313519 E: dnpreece@hotmail.co.uk

PREECE, Mrs Jill Annette. b 58. Bp Otter Coll BEd 79. SEITE 08. **d** 11 **p** 12. NSM Eastbourne St Elisabeth *Chich* 11–15; NSM Eastbourne St Jo from 15. *17 Rowsley Road, Eastbourne BN20 7XS* T: (01323) 638020 M: 07742-655986 E: jill@stjm.org.uk

PREECE, Canon Mark Richard. b 61. St Paul's Coll Chelt BA 85. Linc Th Coll 85. **d** 87 **p** 88. C Coity w Nolton *Llan* 87–89; C Penarth w Lavernock 89–92; V Ewenny w St Brides Major 92–99; V Canton St Luke 99–02; TR Canton Cardiff from 02; AD Cardiff 08–13; Can Llan Cathl from 14. *Canton Rectory, 12 Thompson Avenue, Cardiff CF5 1EY* T/F: (029) 2056 2022

PREECE, Roger Martin Howell. b 64. Imp Coll Lon BSc 86 FRSA 96. St Steph Ho Ox BA 05 MA 10. **d** 06 **p** 07. C Marple All SS *Ches* 06–08; V Bowdon 08–15; Adn St Helens and Warrington *Liv* 15–19; Master R Foundn of St Kath in Ratcliffe from 19. *The Royal Foundation of St Katharine, 2 Butcher Row, London E14 8DS* T: (020) 7790 3540 E: roger.preece@gmail.com or master@rfsk.org.uk

PRENDERGAST, Mrs Sally Elizabeth. b 67. Portsm Univ BA 05. SCTEI 16. **d** 19. NSM Wendover and Halton *Ox* from 19. *Wylderne, Bridge Street, Great Kimble, Aylesbury HP17 9TW* T: (01844) 761206 M: 07876-515098 E: sallyprendergast22@gmail.com

PRENTICE, Mrs Heike. b 58. St Mellitus Coll BA 18. **d** 18 **p** 19. C Hammersmith St Pet *Lon* from 18. *44 Leamore Street, London W6 0JZ* M: 07752-308048

PRENTIS, Calvert Clayton. b 62. St Jo Coll Nottm 95. **d** 97 **p** 98. C Wood End *Cov* 97–00; TV Leeds St Geo *Ripon* 00–05; Asst Dioc Dir of Ords 02–05; P-in-c Huddersfield H Trin *Wakef* 05–07; V 07–12; Asst Dioc Dir of Ords 09–12; TR Horley *S'wark* 12–15; Asst Dir of Ords Croydon Area 13–15; Dioc Minority Ethnic Voc Champion 14–15; P-in-c Gt Ilford St Jo *Chelmsf* 15–18; Asst Dioc Dir of Ords 15–18; Dioc Dir of Ords and Voc Development *Birm* from 18. *Diocesan Office, 1 Colmore Row, Birmingham B3 2BJ* T: 0121-426 0400 M: 07505-036602 E: calvertprentis93@gmail.com

PRENTIS, Sharon Teresa. b 64. Cov Univ BA 93 Keele Univ MSc 97 Leeds Univ PhD 05 Sheff Univ MA 13. Yorks Min Course 10. **d** 13 **p** 14. NSM Redhill St Matt *S'wark* 13–15; NSM Gt Ilford St Jo *Chelmsf* 15–18; Lect St Mellitus Coll 15–18; Intercultural Miss Enabler and Dean of Black, Asian and Minority Ethnic Affairs *Birm* from 18; PtO from 18. *Diocesan Office, 1 Colmore Row, Birmingham B3 2BJ* E: sharonp@cofebirmingham.org

PRESCOTT, David Anthony. b 62. Univ of Wales (Lamp) BA 84 Coll of Ripon & York St Jo PGCE 85. Ripon Coll Cuddesdon MTh 07. **d** 07 **p** 08. C W Heref 07–10; TV Burrington, Chawleigh, Cheldon, Chulmleigh etc *Ex* 10–12; Chapl Warminster Sch 12–18; Hon C River Were *Sarum* 17–19; Chapl Wycliffe Coll Glos from 19. *Wycliffe College, Bath Road, Stonehouse GL10 2JQ* M: 07779-588619 E: revd.david.prescott@gmail.com

PRESCOTT, David John. b 51. St Kath Coll Liv BEd 73. NOC 00. **d** 03 **p** 04. C Southport Em *Liv* 03–07; P-in-c Birchwood 07–11; rtd 11. *90 Halsall Lane, Ormskirk L39 3AX* T: (01695) 574602 M: 07762-943138 E: prezzy@hotmail.co.uk

PRESCOTT, Thomas Robert. b 41. St Mich Coll Llan 93. **d** 95 **p** 96. C Abertillery w Cwmtillery w Six Bells *Mon* 95–99; V Llanhilleth 99–03; rtd 03. *70 Glandwr Street, Abertillery NP13 1TZ* T: (01495) 216782

PRESCOTT, William Allan. b 57. ACIS 87. Sarum & Wells Th Coll 91. d 93 p 94. C Horsell *Guildf* 93–98; R Guernsey St Sav *Win* 98–08; P-in-c Guernsey St Marguerite de la Foret 98–08; Chapl Guernsey Airport 08; R Compton, Hursley, and Otterbourne *Win* from 08. *The Rectory, Kiln Lane, Otterbourne, Winchester SO21 2EJ* T: (01962) 714551

PRESS, Richard James. b 45. Southn Univ CertEd 67. Sarum & Wells Th Coll 92. d 92 p 93. C Bradford-on-Avon H Trin *Sarum* 92–95; P-in-c Rowde and Poulshot 95–98; R Rowde and Bromham 98–01; Chapl Wilts and Swindon Healthcare NHS Trust 98–00; P-in-c Chickerell w Fleet *Sarum* 01–07; R 07–11; P-in-c Abbotsbury, Portesham and Langton Herring 09–11; rtd 11; PtO *Sarum* from 12. *10 Carrick Close, Dorchester DT1 2SB* T: (01305) 262130 E: rjpress@gmail.com

PRESS, William John. b 72. QUB MEng 94 BTh. d 99 p 00. C Knockbreda *D & D* 99–03; C Dundonald 03–05; I Annalong 05–14; I Knockbreda from 14. *Knockbreda Rectory, 69 Church Road, Newtownbreda, Belfast BT8 7AN* T: (028) 9064 1493 E: billclaire.press@gmail.com

PREST, Hilary Irene. b 58. p 16. NSM Bassaleg *Mon* 15–18; NSM Magor from 18. *6 Silure Way, Langstone, Newport NP18 2NU* T: (01633) 412803 E: hilprest@aol.com

PRESTIDGE, Colin Robert. b 58. W Sussex Inst of HE BEd 86 Open Univ BA 01. STETS 01. d 04 p 05. NSM Crofton *Portsm* from 04; Asst Chapl E Hants Primary Care Trust 04–08. *96 Titchfield Road, Stubbington, Fareham PO14 2JB* T: (01329) 664375 E: colin@prestidge.org.uk

PRESTNEY, Canon Patricia Christine Margaret. b 49. UEA BEd 94. Oak Hill Th Coll 84. d 87 p 94. NSM Lawford *Chelmsf* 87–95; Chapl Benenden Sch 95–97; Chapl St Jo Coll Ipswich 97–00; R Lawford *Chelmsf* 00–10; Hon Can Chelmsf Cathl 09–10; rtd 10; PtO *Chelmsf* 11–13; P-in-c Gt Bentley 13–15; PtO 15–16; Hon C Colchester Ch Ch w St Mary V from 16. *36 Inglis Road, Colchester CO3 3HU* T: (01206) 574287 M: 07825-222780 E: patprestney@yahoo.com

PRESTON, David Francis. b 50. BNC Ox BA 72 MA 78. St Steph Ho Ox 72. d 74 p 75. C Beckenham St Jas *Roch* 74–79; C Hockley *Chelmsf* 81–83; C Lamorbey H Redeemer *Roch* 83–89; V Gillingham St Barn 89–00; PtO 00–11. *103 High Street, Kirkcudbright DG6 4JG* T: (01557) 330650 E: d.preston.347@btinternet.com

PRESTON, Mrs Deborah Anne. b 46. GTCL 67. CBDTI 01. d 04 p 06. OLM Kirkby Lonsdale *Carl* 04–06; NSM Old Hutton and New Hutton and Crosscrake 06–10; NSM Kirkby Lonsdale 10–16; rtd 16; PtO *Carl* from 16. *The Old Schoolhouse, Kirkby Lonsdale, Carnforth LA6 2DX* T: (015242) 72509 M: 07799-246380 E: deborahpreston@gmail.com

PRESTON, James Martin. b 31. Trin Coll Cam MA 55 Ch Ch Ox MA 57. Virginia Th Sem 57 S'wark Ord Course 87. d 88 p 88. NSM Blackheath Ascension *S'wark* 88–95; NSM Lewisham St Mary 95–97; NSM Catford St Laur 97–99; PtO *Chich* 99–08; S'wark 08–13 and 16–17. *14 Curness Street, London SE13 6JY* T: (020) 8690 0993

PRESTON, John Michael. b 40. K Coll Lon BD 63 AKC 63 Lon Univ BA 81 Southn Univ PhD 91 Univ of Wales (Lamp) MA 09. St Boniface Warminster. d 65 p 66. C Heston *Lon* 65–67; C Northolt St Mary 67–72; Trinidad and Tobago 72–74; P-in-c Aveley *Chelmsf* 74–78; V 78–82; C Eastleigh *Win* 82–84; C-in-c Boyatt Wood CD 84–87; V W End 87–00; P-in-c Newton Valence, Selborne and E Tisted w Colemore 00–03; rtd 03; Chapl SSB from 03; PtO *Portsm* from 03; *Win* from 09. *10 Trent Way, Lee-on-the-Solent PO13 8JF* T: (023) 9263 7673 M: 07801-553233 E: john.preston1508@gmail.com

PRESTON, Martin. See PRESTON, James Martin

PRESTON, Michael Christopher. b 47. Hatf Coll Dur BA 68. Ripon Coll Cuddesdon 75. d 78 p 79. C Epsom St Martin *Guildf* 78–82; C Guildf H Trin w St Mary 82–86; V Epsom St Barn 86–14; rtd 14. *1 Madeira Court, Clifton Crescent, Folkestone CT20 2ER* T: (01303) 211605 E: rev.retired@m-c-preston.org.uk

PRESTON, Oliver Robert. b 88. Ox Brookes Univ BA 10 St Jo Coll Dur BA 17. Cranmer Hall Dur 14. d 17 p 18. C Halliwell St Pet *Man* from 17. *29 Tattersall Avenue, Bolton BL1 5TE* M: 07912-622646 E: oli@stpetersparish.info

PRESTON, Mrs Paula Ann. b 65. St Jo Coll Nottm 10. d 12 p 13. C Cambridge St Martin *Ely* 12–16; TV Chigwell and Chigwell Row *Chelmsf* 16–19; TV Vale of Roding from 19. *All Saints' Vicarage, Romford Road, Chigwell IG7 4QD* T: (020) 8508 1145 E: revpaulapreston@gmail.com

PRESTON, Reuben James. b 65. York Univ BSc 86 MEng 87 Univ of Cen England in Birm MA 05 Birm Univ PGCE 97. Westcott Ho Cam 88. d 91 p 92. C Weoley Castle *Birm* 91–94; TV Malvern Link w Cowleigh *Worc* 94–96; PtO *Birm* 96–99; C Bordesley St Benedict 99–07; PtO *Portsm* 07–08; Hon C Portsea St Sav and Portsea St Alb 08; P-in-c Bridgemary and Chapl Bridgemary Community Sports Coll

08–11; Chapl HM Pris Kingston (Portsm) 08–11; V Hackney Wick St Mary of Eton w St Aug *Lon* 11–16; R Sharnbrook, Felmersham and Knotting w Souldrop *St Alb* 16–18; R Johnstone *Glas* from 18; R Renfrew from 18. *29 Gleniffer Road, Renfew PA4 0RD* T: 0141-885 1398 M: 07971-895897 E: rjp@reubenjamespreston.co.uk

PRESTWOOD, James Anthony. b 78. York Univ BSc 99 K Coll Lon MA 03. St Mellitus Coll BA 11. d 11 p 12. C Tollington *Lon* 11–14; P-in-c Linc St Swithin 14–18; V from 18. *41 Mercer Drive, Lincoln LN1 1AG* E: jimprestwood@me.com

PRESTWOOD, Ms Jayne Marie. b 64. Man Univ BA 86 Nottm Univ MA 93. Linc Th Coll MA 94. d 94 p 95. C Reddish *Man* 94–98; Dioc Drugs Misuse Project Worker 98–00; P-in-c N Reddish 00–04; P-in-c Haughton St Anne 04–06; Tr Officer for Reader Tr 04–06; Vice Prin Dioc Reader and OLM Schemes 06–12; Chapl Man Univ 12–16; Chapl Man Metrop Univ 12–16; Chapl RNCM 12–16; Dioc Officer for Lay Voc and Min *Chich* from 17. *Church House, 211 New Church Road, Hove BN3 4ED* T: (01273) 421021 E: jayne.prestwood@chichester.anglican.org or jprestwood@sky.com

PRETT, Alan. b 39. d 05 p 06. OLM Styvechale *Cov* 05–12; PtO 12–13; St And from 13. *Meikleour Lodge, Meikleour, Perth PH2 6DY* T: (01250) 883304 E: alanprett@btinternet.com

PRETTY, John Leslie. b 51. d 10 p 11. OLM Draycott-le-Moors w Forsbrook *Lich* 10–15; OLM Walsall Wood 16–18; PtO from 18. *14 Shire Ridge, Walsall Wood, Walsall WS9 9RB* T: (01543) 820194

PREUSS-HIGHAM, Mrs Margaret. b 56. STETS 07. d 10 p 11. NSM Bridport *Sarum* 10–15; NSM Abbotsbury, Portesham and Langton Herring from 15. *The Rectory, Church Lane, Portesham, Weymouth DT3 4HB* T: (01305) 873978 E: margaret.preusshigham@gmail.com

PREVETT, Mark Norman. b 59. Univ of Wales (Cardiff) BD 88. St Mich Coll Llan 85. d 88 p 89. C Brynmawr *S & B* 89–90; C Bassaleg *Mon* 90–92; R Blaina and Nantyglo 92–97; TV Halas *Worc* 97–04; RD Dudley 00–04; TR Totton *Win* 04–13; P-in-c Merthyr Tydfil St Dav and Abercanaid *Llan* from 13; P-in-c Merthyr Tydfil Ch Ch from 18. *6 Llwyncelyn Lane, Merthyr Tydfil CF48 1AL* T: (01685) 553529 E: prevtherev@sky.com

PREWER, Dennis. b 30. Kelham Th Coll 50. d 54 p 55. C Stockport St Thos *Ches* 54–58; C Gt Grimsby St Mary and St Jas *Linc* 58–62; V Gt Harwood St Jo *Blackb* 62–64; V Scarcliffe *Derby* 64–70; Org Sec CECS 70–92; Dios Liv, Ban and St As 70–78; Dio Man 78–92; LtO *Ches* 70–92; PtO *Man* 78–96; rtd 92; PtO *Ches* 92–10. *10 Langton Close, Grimsby DN33 1HG*

PRICE, Alan John. b 48. Wilson Carlile Coll 69. d 08 p 08. P-in-c Charlesworth and Dinting Vale *Derby* 08–11; rtd 11; LtO *Mor* 12–17. *28 Manor Road, Belper DE56 1NT* M: 07785-723952 E: alan@alanprice.me.uk

PRICE, Alison Jane. See DOBELL, Alison Jane

PRICE, Alison Jean. b 50. Man Univ BSc 71 Open Univ MA 93 Kellogg Coll Ox DPhil 01 PGCE 89. Ox Min Course 05. d 08 p 09. NSM Marston w Elsfield *Ox* 08–16; rtd 16; PtO *Ox* from 17. *33 Holliers Close, Thame OX9 2EN* T: (01844) 214942 M: 07792-460923 E: alisonjeanprice@gmail.com

PRICE, Mrs Alison Mary. b 48. K Alfred's Coll Win CertEd 69. d 01. Par Dn Magor *Mon* 01–11; PtO 11–12; rtd 13. *103 Bawnmore Road, Bilton, Rugby CV22 6EJ* T: (01788) 879738 E: alisonprice@talktalk.net

PRICE, Alun Huw. b 47. St D Coll Lamp. d 70 p 71. C Carmarthen St Dav *St D* 70–73; V Betws Ifan 73–77; CF 77–03; PtO *St D* from 02. *Bryn Seion, Llyn y Fran Road, Llandysul SA44 4JW* T: (01559) 363954 E: alun47@sky.com

PRICE, Anthony Ronald. b 49. Linc Coll Ox BA 71 MA 83 St Jo Coll Dur BA 78. d 79 p 80. C St Alb St Paul 79–81; C Wootton 81–85; C Lydiard Millicent w Lydiard Tregoz *Bris* 85–86; TV The Lydiards 86–91; V Marston *Ox* 91–95; V Marston w Elsfield 95–16; RD Cowley 97–02; rtd 16; PtO *Ox* from 17. *33 Holliers Close, Thame OX9 2EN* T: (01844) 214942 M: 07584-492225 E: tonyprice01@gmail.com

PRICE, Carol Ann. b 46. St Jo Coll Nottm 02. d 03 p 04. NSM Derby St Alkmund and St Werburgh 03–04; NSM Charlesworth and Dinting Vale 04–11; rtd 11; LtO *Mor* 12–17. *28 Manor Raod, Belper DE56 1NT* M: 07787-522127 E: carol@carolprice.me.uk

PRICE, Mrs Christine Janice. b 45. Sarum & Wells Th Coll 83. dss 86 d 87 p 94. Roxbourne St Andr *Lon* 86–90; NSM 87–90; NSM Roxeth Ch Ch and Harrow St Pet 90–93; C Roxeth 93–96; C Costessey *Nor* 96–98; rtd 98; PtO *Nor* 98–05; *Ox* 06–16. *49 Turner Road, Marple, Stockport SK6 7NJ* M: 07702-818256 E: chrisjpri@aol.com

PRICE, Canon Clive Stanley. b 42. ALCD 69. d 69 p 70. C Chenies and Lt Chalfont *Ox* 69–75; R Upper Stour *Sarum* 75–79; C-in-c Panshanger CD *St Alb* 79–82; TV Digswell and Panshanger 82–86; P-in-c St Oswald in Lee w Bingfield *Newc* 86–07; Dioc Ecum Officer 86–07; Hon Can Newc Cathl 97–07; AD Bellingham 00–06; rtd 07; PtO *Newc* from 07. *24 Castlegate Court, Berwick-upon-Tweed TD15 1BU*

PRICE, David. b 27. Wycliffe Hall Ox 61. **d** 63 **p** 64. C Bucknall and Bagnall *Lich* 63–67; C Abingdon w Shippon *Ox* 67–76; Warden Stella Carmel Conf Cen Haifa Israel 76–80; Dir Israel Trust of the Angl Ch and R Jerusalem 80–84; V S Kensington St Luke *Lon* 84–92; P-in-c S Kensington St Jude 88–92; rtd 92; Hon C Hordle *Win* 92–97; PtO 97–98; *Worc* 98–07. *16 Masefield Avenue, Ledbury HR8 1BW* T: (01531) 634831

PRICE, David Gareth Michael. b 64. Ex Univ BA 86 Kent Univ MA 87 FSS. Wycliffe Hall Ox BTh 94. **d** 97 **p** 98. C Godalming *Guildf* 97–00; Min Elvetham Heath LEP 00–12; V Heatherlands St Jo *Sarum* from 12. *St John's Vicarage, 21 Crescent Road, Poole BH14 9AS* T: (01202) 740235 E: mail@pricefamilypoole.plus.com

PRICE, Canon David Rea. b 39. St Aid Birkenhead 61. **d** 63 **p** 64. C Green Street Green *Roch* 63–66; C Gillingham St Mary 66–69; C New Windsor St Jo *Ox* 69–72; V Winkfield 72–80; RD Bracknell 78–86; V Sunningdale 80–86; TR Wimborne Minster and Holt *Sarum* 86–96; R Wimborne Minster 96–01; RD Wimborne 88–98; Can and Preb Sarum Cathl 92–01; P-in-c Witchampton, Stanbridge and Long Crichel etc 00–01; Chapl Wimborne Hosp 86–01; rtd 01; PtO *Ex* 01–14; RD Aylesbeare 11–13; PtO *Sarum* from 14. *161 Sopwith Crescent, Wimborne BH21 1SR* T: (01202) 885488 E: rea@14broadway.eclipse.co.uk

PRICE, Canon David Trevor William. b 43. Keble Coll Ox BA 65 MA 69 Univ of Wales (Trin St Dav) Hon DD 18 MEHS 79 FRHistS 79 FSA 95. Sarum & Wells Th Coll 72. **d** 72 **p** 73. Lect Univ of Wales (Lamp) *St D* 70–87; Sen Lect 87–97; Chapl 79–80; Dean of Chpl 90–91; Public Preacher 72–86; Dioc Archivist 82–98; P-in-c Betws Bledrws 86–97; Hon Can St D Cathl 90–92; Can St D Cathl 92–00; V Cydweli and Llandyfaelog 97–00; P-in-c Myddle and Broughton *Lich* 00–08; P-in-c Loppington w Newtown 02–08; rtd 08; PtO *St As* 01–17; *Lich* from 08; RD Wem and Whitchurch 14–15; Can St Helena from 18. *57 Kynaston Drive, Wem, Shrewsbury SY4 5DE* T: (01939) 234777 M: 07811-712911 E: williamprice@talktalk.net

PRICE, Derek Henry. b 51. Trin Coll Bris BA 98. **d** 98 **p** 99. C Bayston Hill *Lich* 98–02; R Barrow St Paul *Carl* 02–18; rtd 18. *15 Langford Drive, Boldon Colliery NE35 9LJ* E: dh.price@virgin.net

PRICE, Canon Derek William. b 27. St Pet Hall Ox BA 51 MA 55. Qu Coll Birm 51. **d** 53 **p** 54. C St Marylebone St Mark w St Luke *Lon* 53–57; C Stevenage *St Alb* 57–63; Jamaica 63–67; R Bridgham and Roudham *Nor* 67–80; R E w W Harling 69–80; Hon Can Nor Cathl 75–92; RD Thetford and Rockland 76–86; P-in-c Kilverstone 80–87; P-in-c Croxton 80–87; TR Thetford 80–87; R Castleacre w Newton, Rougham and Southacre 87–92; PtO 92–99 and from 00; P-in-c Easton w Colton and Marlingford 99–00. *Fourways, King's Road, Dereham NR19 2AG* T: (01362) 691660 E: pricefourways@Gmail.com

PRICE, Canon Edward Glyn. b 35. Univ of Wales (Lamp) BA 55. Ch Div Sch of the Pacific (USA) BD 58. **d** 58 **p** 59. C Denbigh *St As* 58–65; V Llanasa 65–76; V Buckley 76–91; Dioc RE Adv 77–88; RD Mold 86–91; Can St As Cathl from 87; Preb and Sacr from 95; V Llandrillo-yn-Rhos 91–00; rtd 00; PtO *St As* from 09. *7 Rhodfa Criccieth, Bodelwyddan, Rhyl LL18 5WL* T: (01745) 571286 or 582912 E: glynandfreda@gmail.com

PRICE, Elizabeth Anne. b 49. **d** 17. OLM Loughton St Mich *Chelmsf* from 17. *6 The Plains, 3 Crescent Road, London E4 6AU*

PRICE, Frederick Leslie. b 30. Oak Hill Th Coll 59. **d** 61 **p** 62. C Hougham in Dover Ch Ch *Cant* 61–64; R Plumbland and Gilcrux *Carl* 64–95; rtd 95; PtO *Carl* 98–14. *29 Cumwhinton Road, Carlisle CA1 3LA* T: (01228) 596445 E: flprice@btinternet.com

PRICE, Glyn. *See* PRICE, Edward Glyn

PRICE, Gregory Philip. b 54. Cranmer Hall Dur. **d** 83 **p** 84. C Gt Crosby St Luke *Liv* 83–86; PtO *Derby* 12–13; *S'well* 12–15; V Tuxford w Weston, Markham Clinton etc from 15. *The Vicarage, 30 Lincoln Road, Newark NG22 0HP* T: (01777) 872917 M: 07850-182951 E: gregory.price1@btinternet.com

PRICE, Janine Susan Grace. b 51. **d** 18 **p** 19. NSM Pakenham w Norton, Tostock etc *St E* from 18. *Honeysuckle Cottage, Bobby Hill, Wattisfield, Diss IP22 1NL* T: (01359) 251268 E: jsgprice@aol.com

PRICE, Mrs Katherine Ann Magdalene. b 83. Mert Coll Ox BA 04 MA MSt 05 Sheff Univ BA 13. Coll of Resurr Mirfield 11. **d** 14 **p** 15. C Gt Grimsby St Mary and St Jas *Linc* 14–17; Chapl Qu Coll Ox from 17. *The Queen's College, High Street, Oxford OX1 4AW* E: katherine.price@queens.ox.ac.uk

PRICE, Laurence Martin. b 81. Ex Coll Ox BA 03 Cam Univ BTh 16. Westcott Ho Cam 14. **d** 16 **p** 17. C Waltham Go *Linc* 16–19; Chapl Qu Coll Ox 19. *24B Leopold Street, Oxford OX4 1PS* M: 07753-466761

PRICE, Preb Lawrence Robert. b 43. LICeram 71. Cranmer Hall Dur 76. **d** 78 **p** 79. C Harlescott *Lich* 78–80; C Cheddleton 80–83; P-in-c Calton, Cauldon, Grindon and Waterfall 83–88; R 85–88; P-in-c Kingsley 95–00; R Kingsley and Foxt-w-Whiston 01–07; P-in-c 00–01; C Alton w Bradley-le-Moors and Oakamoor w Cotton 06–07; RD Cheadle 98–07; Preb Lich Cathl 00–08; rtd 08; P-in-c Cheddleton *Lich* 07–13; PtO 13–16; Hon C Alstonfield, Ilam and Wetton from 16; RD Cheadle from 16. *3 Beech Close, Leek ST13 7AF* E: preblrprice@btinternet.com

PRICE, Leslie. *See* PRICE, Frederick Leslie

PRICE, Canon Mari Josephine. b 43. St Hugh's Coll Ox BA 65 Ox Univ MA 69 DipEd 66. Llan Dioc Tr Scheme 93. **d** 97 **p** 98. NSM Lisvane *Llan* 97–02; NSM Roath 02–03; Hon Chapl Llan Cathl 03–14; Hon Can Llan Cathl 11–14. *23 Ty Draw Road, Roath, Cardiff CF23 5HB* T: (029) 2045 6757 M: 07850-019883 E: mari.price23@gmail.com

PRICE, Martin Randall Connop. b 45. Lon Univ BSc 71 Fitzw Coll Cam BA 75 MA 79 Univ of Wales (Swansea) PhD 02. Ridley Hall Cam 73. **d** 76 **p** 77. C Keynsham *B & W* 76–79; Ind Chapl *Sheff* 79–83; V Wortley 79–83; R Hook Norton w Gt Rollright, Swerford etc *Ox* 83–91; V Shiplake w Dunsden 91–03; P-in-c Harpsden 02–03; R Shiplake w Dunsden and Harpsden 03–09; rtd 09; PtO *Heref* 10–19. *Address withheld by request* E: martinconnopprice@btinternet.com

PRICE (née ALDERTON), Mrs Mary Louise. b 54. Nottm Univ BSc 75 IPFA 87. EAMTC 02. **d** 05 **p** 06. NSM Melbourn *Ely* from 05; NSM Meldreth from 05. *4 Barrons Green, Shepreth, Royston SG8 6QN* T: (01763) 261569 E: maryprice9486@gmail.com

PRICE, Matthew James. b 78. Selw Coll Cam BA 99 MA 03. Wycliffe Hall Ox 14. **d** 16 **p** 17. C Bradwell *Nor* 16–18; P-in-c Gorleston St Mary 18–19; V from 19. *The Vicarage, 41 Nuffield Crescent, Gorleston, Great Yarmouth NR31 7LL* M: 07746-498574 E: revmatthewprice@gmail.com

PRICE, Michael Graham. b 62. Ex Coll Ox BA 84. Linc Th Coll 84. **d** 86 **p** 87. C Salford St Phil w St Steph *Man* 86–90; R Man Gd Shep 90–95; V Netherton St Andr *Worc* 95–99; Chapl Bloxham Sch 00–14; Dep Hd from 14; PtO *Ox* from 14. *Bloxham School, Bloxham, Banbury OX15 4PQ* T: (01295) 720222

PRICE, Morris John. b 39. **d** 03 **p** 04. OLM Gt Wyrley *Lich* 03–19; PtO 19. *42 Huthill Lane, Walsall WS6 6PB* T: (01922) 412846

PRICE, Norman. *See* PRICE, William Norman

✠**PRICE, The Rt Revd Peter Bryan.** b 44. Redland Coll of Educn CertEd 66. Oak Hill Th Coll 72. **d** 74 **p** 75 **c** 97. C Portsdown *Portsm* 74–78; Chapl Scargill Ho 78–80; P-in-c Addiscombe St Mary *Cant* 80–81; V 81–84; V Addiscombe St Mary *S'wark* 85–88; Can Res and Chan S'wark Cathl 88–92; Gen Sec USPG 92–97; Area Bp Kingston *S'wark* 97–02; Bp B w W 02–13; rtd 13; Hon Asst Bp S'wark 16–18. *86 Whitgift House, 76 Brighton Road, South Croydon CR2 6AB* E: peter@peterlongways.myzen.co.uk

PRICE, Philip Huw. b 84. Essex Univ BA 05 Dur Univ BA 18. Ridley Hall Cam 15. **d** 18 **p** 19. C Earley St Pet *Ox* from 18. *33 Clevedon Drive, Earley, Reading RG6 5XF* M: 07960-947068 E: curate@earleystpeters.org.uk

PRICE, Rachel Anne. *See* JACKSON, Rachel Anne

PRICE, Ramon Philip. *See* PRICE, Gregory Philip

PRICE, Raymond Francklin. b 30. Wycliffe Hall Ox 61. **d** 62 **p** 63. C Bilston St Leon *Lich* 62–67; C Keighley *Bradf* 67–70; V Mangotsfield *Bris* 70–79; Ind Chapl *Birm* 79–86; C Birm St Martin 84–85; C Birm St Martin w Bordesley St Andr 85–86; V Edgbaston St Aug 86–99; rtd 99; PtO *Birm* 00–12. *35 Middle Park Road, Selly Oak, Birmingham B29 4BH* T: 0121-475 4458 E: raymondprice@virginmedia.com

PRICE, Stanley George. b 32. FRICS 69. Trin Coll Bris 84. **d** 85 **p** 86. C Newport w Longford and Chetwynd *Lich* 85–88; V Ipstones w Berkhamsytch and Onecote w Bradnop 88–97; rtd 98; PtO *B & W* 98–03 and 08–19; P-in-c Rodney Stoke w Draycott 03–08. *St Aidan, Rectory Way, Lympsham, Weston-super-Mare BS24 0EN* T: (01934) 750323

PRICE, Steven Albert. b 68. Brunel Univ BSc 90 CEng 95. Oak Hill Th Coll BTh 06. **d** 06 **p** 07. C New Borough and Leigh *Sarum* 06–09; C Loose *Cant* 09–11; P-in-c 11–14; V from 14. *The Vicarage, 17 Linton Road, Loose, Maidstone ME15 0AG* T: (01622) 745882 E: steveandhelenprice@btinternet.com

PRICE, Timothy Fry. b 51. CQSW. St Jo Coll Nottm 85. **d** 87 **p** 88. C Church Stretton *Heref* 87–91; V Sinfin *Derby* 91–00; Regional Adv (SW) CMJ 00–03; Nat Field Co-ord 03–05; PtO *Glouc* 01–05; *B & W* 01–05; *Bris* 01–05; V Chaffcombe, Cricket Malherbie etc *B & W* 06–16; PtO *Ex* 06–09; rtd 16; Dioc Ecum Miss Enabler *B & W* from 17; PtO from 17. *65 Herne Rise, Ilminster TA19 0HH* T: (01460) 929282 E: pricetf@aol.com

PRICE, Victor John. b 35. Oak Hill Th Coll 62. **d** 65 **p** 66. C Rainham *Chelmsf* 65–70; V Dover St Martin *Cant* 70–78; V Madeley *Heref* 78–90; P-in-c Derby St Pet and Ch Ch w H Trin 90–91; V 91–96; P-in-c Morley 96–00; P-in-c Smalley 96–00; rtd 00; PtO *S'well* from 00. *4 Holmefield, Farndon, Newark NG24 3TZ* T: (01636) 611708

PRICE, William. See PRICE, David Trevor William

PRICE, William Norman. b 52. GRNCM 73. NOC 86. **d** 89 **p** 90. C Lower Broughton *Man* 89–91; Min Can and Succ St E *Cathl* 92–96; Prec 94–96; V Par *Truro* 96–00; V Musbury *Blackb* 00–06; rtd 06; PtO *Man* 06–16; *Liv* from 14. *5 Lower Drake Fold, Westhoughton, Bolton BL5 2RE* T: 07071-299999 E: golfsierra999@rcsb.co.uk

PRIDDIN, Emma. See YOUNG, Emma

PRIDDIN, Mrs Maureen Anne. b 46. Leeds Univ BA 67 Nottm Univ DipEd 68. EMMTC 82. **dss** 85 **d** 87 **p** 94. Mickleover St Jo *Derby* 85–11; Hon Par Dn 87–94; Hon C 94–06; P-in-c 06–11; Hon C Mickleover All SS 06–11; Dioc World Development Officer 87–90; rtd 11. *7 Portland Close, Mickleover, Derby DE3 9BZ* T: (01332) 513672 E: mpriddin@ntlworld.com

✠**PRIDDIS, The Rt Revd Anthony Martin.** b 48. CCC Cam BA 69 MA 73 New Coll Ox MA 75. Cuddesdon Coll 69. **d** 72 **p** 73 **c** 96. C New Addington *Cant* 72–75; Chapl Ch Ch Ox 75–80; TV High Wycombe *Ox* 80–86; P-in-c Amersham 86–90; R 90–96; RD 92–96; Hon Can Ch Ch 95–96; Suff Bp Warw and Hon Can Cov Cathl 96–04; Bp Heref 04–13; rtd 13; Hon Asst Bp Worc from 13; Hon Asst Bp Glouc from 14; PtO *Heref* from 15. *Round Oak Cottage, Bridstow, Ross-on-Wye HR9 6QJ* T: (01989) 218503 E: anthony@priddis.me

PRIDEAUX, Humphrey Grevile. b 36. CCC Ox BA 59 MA 63 Birm Univ CertEd 66 Lon Univ DipEd 73 Open Univ BA 87. Linc Th Coll 59. **d** 61 **p** 62. C Northampton St Matt *Pet* 61–62; C Milton *Portsm* 62–65; PtO *Birm* 65–66; Hd of RE Qu Mary's Gr Sch Walsall 66–69; Lect St Martin's Coll Lanc 69–80; PtO *Portsm* 80–86; Hon C Fareham H Trin 86–87; Hon C Bishop's Waltham 87–94; NSM P-in-c W Meon and Warnford 94–03. *6 Rectory Close, Alverstoke, Gosport PO12 2HT* T: (023) 9251 1794

PRIDIE, William Raleigh. b 49. Bris Univ BEd 72 ACP 82 FCollP 83. SWMTC 90. **d** 93 **p** 94. C Kingstone w Clehonger, Eaton Bishop etc *Heref* 93–96; P-in-c Kimbolton w Hamnish and Middleton-on-the-Hill 96–97; P-in-c Bockleton w Leysters 96–97; CME Officer 96–00; TV Leominster 97–00; R Fownhope w Mordiford, Brockhampton etc 00–10; rtd 11; PtO *Heref* from 11. *64 Bargates, Leominster HR6 8EY* E: wpridie365@waitrose.com

PRIDMORE, John Stuart. b 36. Nottm Univ BA 62 MA 67 Lon Inst of Educn PhD 00. Ridley Hall Cam 62. **d** 65 **p** 66. C Camborne *Truro* 65–67; Tutor Ridley Hall Cam 67–68; Chapl 68–71; Asst Chapl K Edw Sch Witley 71–75; Chapl 75–86; Tanzania 86–88; Angl Chapl Hengrave Hall Cen 88–89; C St Martin-in-the-Fields *Lon* 89–95; TR Hackney 95–03; R St John-at-Hackney 03–06; rtd 06. *Flat 2, 3 Palmeira Square, Hove BN3 2JA*

PRIEST, Richard Philip. b 52. WEMTC 08. **d** 10 **p** 11. NSM Frome Valley *Heref* 10–17; V Stour Vale *Sarum* from 17. *The Vicarage, Kington Magna, Gillingham SP8 5EW* T: (01747) 838494 M: 07717-132896 E: richard@allegro.co.uk

PRIESTLEY, Adam James. b 80. Wolv Univ BA 11. St Jo Coll Nottm MTh 15. **d** 14 **p** 15. C W Bessacarr *Sheff* 14–16; C Doncaster St Geo 16–17; C Doncaster St Mary and St Paul from 17. *278 Thorne Road, Doncaster DN2 5AJ* M: 07883-851700   E: adampriestley@hotmail.co.uk   or adam.priestley@sheffield.anglican.org

PRIESTLEY, Richard Allan. b 63. Ridley Hall Cam 07. **d** 09 **p** 10. C Broughton w Loddington and Cransley etc *Pet* 09–12; PtO 13; P-in-c Beacon Trinity *B & W* from 13; C Shepton Mallet w Doulting from 13. *The Rectory, Fosse Road, Oakhill, Radstock BA3 5HU* T: (01749) 840239 E: rpriestley@me.com

PRIESTLEY, Rosemary Jane. See LAIN-PRIESTLEY, Rosemary Jane

PRIESTNER, Hugh. b 45. Nottm Univ BTh 75. Linc Th Coll 71. **d** 75 **p** 76. C Seaton Hirst *Newc* 75–78; C Longbenton St Bart 78–81; P-in-c Glendale Gp 81–82; TV 83–88; Chapl Stafford Acute Hosps 88–89; Tr Co-ord W Cumberland Hosp 89–92; Chapl Fair Havens Hospice 94–98; Chapl Walsgrave Hosps NHS Trust 98–00; Chapl Team Ldr Univ Hosps Cov and Warks NHS Trust 00–17; PtO *Cov* 10–17; V Offchurch Gp from 17. *The Vicarage, School Lane, Hunningham, Leamington Spa CV33 9DS* M: 07568-166910 E: hugh.priestner@btinternet.com

PRIGG, Patrick John. b 53. K Coll Lon BD 82. Sarum & Wells Th Coll 89. **d** 92 **p** 93. C Wavertree St Mary *Liv* 92–96; Chapl Sandown Coll 92–96; P-in-c Glemsford, Hartest w Boxted, Somerton etc *St E* 96–99; R from 99. *The Rectory, 6 Lion Road, Glemsford, Sudbury CO10 7RF* T: (01787) 282164 E: revpatrick@btinternet.com

PRIME, David Alan. b 54. Chelt & Glouc Coll of HE BEd 98. Wesley Coll Bris 82. **d** 12. NSM Trellech and Penallt *Mon* 12–15; PtO 15–17. *Address temp unknown* M: 07870-216995 E: prime.family@yahoo.com

PRIME, Mrs Kathryn Rhian. d 12. NSM Trellech and Penallt *Mon* 12–15; PtO 15–17; TV Llantwit Major *Llan* 17–18; TV Glamorgan Heritage Coast from 18. *The Rectory, 1 Rectory Drive, St Athan, Barry CF62 4PD* T: (01446) 750273 E: rhianprime1960@gmail.com

PRIMROSE, David Edward Snodgrass. b 55. St Jo Coll Cam MA 80. Trin Coll Bris BA 92. **d** 87 **p** 92. Pakistan 87–89; C Glouc St Paul 92–96; R Badgeworth, Shurdington and Witcombe w Bentham 96–03; V Thornbury and Oldbury-on-Severn w Shepperdine 03–10; AD Hawkesbury 04–09; Dir Transforming Communities *Lich* from 10. *Hill House, Vicarage Lane, Bednall, Stafford ST17 0SE* E: david.primrose@lichfield.anglican.org

PRINCE, Alastair. b 76. Nottm Univ BSc 99 SS Coll Cam BTh 06. Westcott Ho Cam 03. **d** 06 **p** 07. C Toxteth Park Ch Ch and St Mich w St Andr *Liv* 06–09; V Croxteth Park 09–17; Voc and Strategy Development Adv *Dur* from 17. *20 Murphy Close, Crook DL15 9GL* M: 07732-489424   E: alastairprince@hotmail.com   or alastair.prince@durham.anglican.org

PRINCE (née RUMBLE), Mrs Alison Merle. b 49. Surrey Univ BSc 71. Trin Coll Bris BA 89. **d** 89 **p** 94. Par Dn Willesden Green St Gabr *Lon* 89–91; Par Dn Cricklewood St Gabr and St Mich 92; Par Dn Herne Hill *S'wark* 92–94; C 94–95; Chapl Greenwich Healthcare NHS Trust 95–96; TV Sanderstead All SS *S'wark* 97–03; TV Kegworth, Hathern, Long Whatton, Diseworth etc *Leic* 04–09; rtd 09; PtO *Leic* from 13. *23 Grangefields Drive, Rothley, Leicester LE7 7ND*

PRINCE, Mrs Melanie Amanda. b 71. St D Coll Lamp BA 92 Univ of Wales (Cardiff) MPhil 93. St Mich Coll Llan 96. **d** 98 **p** 99. C Aberavon *Llan* 98–01; C Gabalfa 01–08; TV Llantwit Major 08–13; P-in-c Porthkerry and Rhoose from 13; Voc Adv from 13. *The Vicarage, 6 Milburn Close, Rhoose, Barry CF62 3EJ* T: (01446) 719734 E: maprince77@gmail.com

PRINCE, Penelope Ann. b 46. SWMTC 96. **d** 99 **p** 00. NSM Halsetown *Truro* 99–02; P-in-c Breage w Godolphin and Germoe 02–12; rtd 12; Hon C Is of Scilly *Truro* 13–16; PtO from 16; *Ex* from 17. *1 Angel Place, Coinagehall Street, Helston TR13 8EF* T: (01326) 574924 M: 07535-202855 E: revpenp@googlemail.com

PRINCE, Roderick Hubert. b 63. All SS Cen for Miss & Min 17. **d** 18 **p** 19. NSM Wirksworth *Derby* from 18. *Red Lion House, Red Lion Hill, Brassington, Matlock DE4 4HA* T: (01629) 540475

PRING, Althon Kerrigan. b 34. AKC 58. **d** 59 **p** 60. C Limehouse St Anne *Lon* 59–61; C Lt Stanmore St Lawr 61–64; C Langley Marish *Ox* 64–68; P-in-c Radnage 68–72; P-in-c Ravenstone w Weston Underwood 72–75; P-in-c Stoke Goldington w Gayhurst 72–75; R Gayhurst w Ravenstone, Stoke Goldington etc 75–85; P-in-c 85–86; RD Newport 78–80; TV Woughton 86–90; P-in-c Nash w Thornton, Beachampton and Thornborough 90–94; R 94–96; rtd 96; PtO *Ox* 99–07. *Kingsmead, 9 Malting Close, Stoke Goldington, Newport Pagnell MK16 8NX* T: (01908) 551345 E: kerriganpring@btinternet.com

PRINGLE, The Ven Cecil Thomas. b 43. TCD BA 65. CITC 66. **d** 66 **p** 67. C Belfast St Donard *D & D* 66–69; I Cleenish Clogh 69–80; I Cleenish w Mullaghdun 78–80; I Rossorry 80–08; Bp's C Drumkeeran w Templecarne and Muckross 08–18; Preb Clogh Cathl 86–89; Adn Clogh 89–14; rtd 18. *35 Station Road, Derryscobe, Letterbreen, Enniskillen BT74 9FB* M: 07742-516188 E: cecilpringle@hotmail.com

PRINGLE, Graeme Lindsley. b 59. St Cath Coll Cam BA 81 MA 85. St Jo Coll Nottm 92. **d** 94 **p** 95. C Binley *Cov* 94–99; V Allesley Park and Whoberley 99–11; Dioc Projects and Communications Officer from 11; PtO 11–16; Hon

C Leamington Priors St Paul from 16; Gen LtO from 18. *The Rectory, Ryton Road, Bubbenhall, Coventry CV8 3BL* E: graeme.pringle@covcofe.org

PRINGLE, Margaret Brenda. b 49. CITC. **d** 05 **p** 06. NSM Clogh w Errigal Portclare 05–13; NSM Carrickmacross w Magheracloone 13–15; NSM Ematris w Rockcorry, Aghabog and Aughnamullan from 15. *Rawdeer Park, Clones, Co Monaghan, Republic of Ireland* T: (00353) (47) 51439 E: margaretpringle14@gmail.com

PRINGLE, Richard John. b 55. Lon Univ AKC 76 CertEd 77 Open Univ BA 84. Chich Th Coll 78. **d** 78 **p** 79. C Northampton St Matt *Pet* 78–81; C Delaval *Newc* 81–84; V Newsham 84–18; RD Bedlington 93–98; rtd 18; PtO *Newc* from 18. *72 Goschen Street, Blyth NE24 1NL* T: (01670) 797736 E: father.pringle@blythchurches.co.uk

PRINT, Michael Guy. b 81. Sheff Univ BA 02. Wycliffe Hall Ox BTh 15. **d** 15 **p** 16. C Padiham w Hapton and Padiham Green *Blackb* 15–19; V Chorley St Geo from 19. *St George's Vicarage, Letchworth Place, Chorley PR7 7HJ* E: michael.padihamparish@gmail.com

PRIOR, Adam Phillip. b 72. Cen Lancs Univ BA 94 K Coll Lon MA 05. Ridley Hall Cam. **d** 08 **p** 09. NSM Watford St Pet *St Alb* from 08. *31 Harefield, Stevenage SG2 9NG* M: 07931-896750

PRIOR, Carla. *See* VICENCIO PRIOR, Carla Alexandra Torres Lopes

PRIOR, David Clement Lyndon. b 40. Trin Coll Ox BA 63 MA 66. Ridley Hall Cam 65. **d** 67 **p** 68. C Reigate St Mary *S'wark* 67–72; C Kenilworth Ch Ch S Africa 72–76; R Wynberg 76–79; Can Cape Town 76–79; C Ox St Aldate w H Trin 79–82; C Ox St Aldate w St Matt 82–84; USA 84–85; V Ches Square St Mich w St Phil *Lon* 85–95; P-in-c Mayfair Ch Ch 85–95; Public Preacher 95–97; P-in-c St Botolph without Aldersgate 97–00; rtd 05; PtO *Chich* from 05. *2 North Lane, Wiston, Steyning BN44 3DQ* T: (01903) 893566 E: dclraprior@hotmail.com

PRIOR (née CHIUMBU), Esther Tamisa. b 73. Univ of Zimbabwe BSc 95. Trin Coll Bris BA 02 MA 07. **d** 03 **p** 04. NSM Redland *Bris* 03–05; C Deptford St Jo w H Trin and Ascension *S'wark* 05–08; Chapl Blackheath Bluecoat C of E Sch 08–09; Chapl HM Pris Cookham Wood 10–11; TV Cove St Jo *Guildf* 11–18; V Egham from 18. *Mauley Cottage, 13 Manorcrofts Road, Egham TW20 9LU* T: (01784) 432066 E: esthertj@yahoo.com

PRIOR, Gregory Stephen. b 68. Geo Whitefield Coll S Africa BTh 90. **d** 95 **p** 96. In C of E in S Africa 95–01; Min for Miss Muswell Hill St Jas w St Matt *Lon* 01–04; P-in-c Wandsworth All SS *S'wark* 04–06; V from 06; AD Wandsworth 13–18. *Wandsworth Vicarage, 11 Rusholme Road, London SW15 3JX* T: (020) 8788 7400

PRIOR, Canon Ian Graham. b 44. Lon Univ BSc(Econ) 71. Oak Hill Th Coll 78. **d** 80 **p** 81. C Luton Ch Ch *Roch* 80–83; TV Southgate *Chich* 83–93; V Burgess Hill St Andr 93–09; RD Hurst 98–04; Can and Preb Chich Cathl 03–09; rtd 09; PtO *Chich* from 14. *5 Chestnut Walk, Worthing BN13 3QL* T: (01903) 830127 E: ian3gl@btinternet.com

PRIOR, Ian Roger Lyndon. b 46. St Jo Coll Dur BA 68. Lon Coll of Div 68. **d** 70 **p** 71. C S Croydon Em *Cant* 70–73; PtO *S'wark* 73–85; Dir Overseas Personnel TEAR Fund 73–79; Dep Dir 79–83; Fin and Admin Dir CARE Trust and CARE Campaigns 85–92; Dir Careforce 92–12; NSM New Malden and Coombe *S'wark* 85–12; rtd 12; PtO *S'wark* from 12. *39 Cambridge Avenue, New Malden KT3 4LD* T: (020) 8949 0912 E: ianrlprior@gmail.com

PRIOR, James Murray. b 39. Edin Univ BCom 64. St And Dioc Tr Course 85. **d** 90 **p** 91. NSM Kirriemuir *St And* 90–02; NSM Forfar 90–02; NSM Dundee St Jo and Dundee St Ninian *Bre* 02–10; rtd 10. *Naughton Lodge, Balmerino, Newport-on-Tay DD6 8RN* T: (01382) 330132 E: ham.prior@tiscali.co.uk

PRIOR, Jonathan Roger Lyndon. b 74. Trin Coll Ox BA 95 MA 99 K Coll Lon PGCE 96. Wycliffe Hall Ox 07. **d** 09 **p** 10. C Elworth and Warmingham *Ches* 09–11; C Elworth 11–12; Chapl City of Lon Freemen's Sch from 12; C Ashtead *Guildf* 12–16. *15 Post House Lane, Bookham, Leatherhead KT23 3EA* M: 07957-220650 E: prior.jon@gmail.com

PRIOR, Matthew Thomas. b 74. Rob Coll Cam BA 97 MA 00. Trin Coll Bris BA 04 MA 05. **d** 05 **p** 06. C Deptford St Jo w H Trin and Ascension *S'wark* 05–08; P-in-c Borstal *Roch* 08–11; PtO *Guildf* 11–13; NSM Cove St Jo 13–18; Chapl Abp Tenison's C of E High Sch Croydon 13–14; Adult Discipleship and Learning Adv *Guildf* from 15 and from 15. *Mauley Cottage, 13 Manorcroft Road, Egham TW20 9LU* T: (01784) 432066 E: mprior36@gmail.com *or* matt.prior@cofeguildford.org

PRIOR, Nigel John. b 56. Bris Univ BA 78 Chich Univ MA 09. Westcott Ho Cam 79. **d** 81 **p** 82. C Langley All SS and Martyrs *Man* 81–82; C Langley and Parkfield 82–84; C Bury

St Jo w St Mark 84–87; R Man Clayton St Cross w St Paul 87–99; P-in-c Mark Cross *Chich* 99–00; V Mayfield from 99. *The Vicarage, High Street, Mayfield TN20 6AB* T: (01435) 873180 E: stdunstan@tiscali.co.uk

PRIOR, Mrs Rachel Elizabeth. b 93. Ch Coll Cam BA 14. Trin Coll Bris 15. **d** 17 **p** 18. C Saffron Walden and Villages *Chelmsf* from 17. *42 De Vigier Avenue, Saffron Walden CB10 2BN* E: rachel-prior@outlook.com

PRIOR, Canon Stephen Kenneth. b 55. Rhode Is Coll (USA) BA 78. Wycliffe Hall Ox 79. **d** 82 **p** 83. C Aberavon *Llan* 82–85; P-in-c New Radnor and Llanfihangel Nantmelan etc *S & B* 85–86; R 86–90; V Llansamlet 90–94; P-in-c Chester le Street *Dur* 94–96; R 96–01; R Caldbeck, Castle Sowerby and Sebergham *Carl* 01–09; Dir of Ords 04–08; R Rushden St Mary w Newton Bromswold *Pet* from 09; RD Higham from 14; Can Pet Cathl from 16. *The Rectory, Rectory Road, Rushden NN10 0HA* T: (01933) 312554 E: sprior@toucansurf.com

PRIORY, Barry Edwin. b 44. Open Univ BA 81 FCIS. Qu Coll Birm 84. **d** 86 **p** 87. C Boldmere *Birm* 86–89; C Somerton w Compton Dundon, the Charltons etc *B & W* 89–93; R Porlock and Porlock Weir w Stoke Pero etc 93–08; RD Exmoor 97–03; rtd 08; PtO *B & W* from 08; Chapl Somerset Partnership NHS Foundn Trust from 09. *Dove Cottage, Moor Road, Minehead TA24 5RX* T: (01643) 706808 M: 07811-092416 E: barry.priory@btinternet.com

PRITCHARD, Andrew James Dunn. *See* PRITCHARD-KEENS, Andrew James Dunn

PRITCHARD, Antony Robin. b 53. Van Mildert Coll Dur BSc 74 SS Paul & Mary Coll Cheltenham CertEd 75. St Jo Coll Nottm. **d** 84 **p** 85. C Desborough *Pet* 84–87; C Rushden w Newton Bromswold 87–91; R Oulton St Mich *Nor* 91–17; rtd 17; PtO *Nor* from 19. *17 West End Avenue, Costessey, Norwich NR8 5BA* T: (01603) 748903 E: robinpritchard925@btinternet.com

PRITCHARD, Brian James. Open Univ BA 05 ACIS 85. SAOMC 99. **d** 01 **p** 02. NSM Newbury *Ox* 01–06; V Billingshurst *Chich* 06–16; rtd 16; PtO *St D* from 05; *Win* from 16; AD Alton from 17. *15 Blackberry Lane, Four Marks, Alton GU34 5BN* T: (01420) 561394 E: brianpritchard15@gmail.com

PRITCHARD, Brian James Pallister. b 27. CCC Cam BA 51 MA 66. Westcott Ho Cam 51. **d** 53 **p** 54. C Attercliffe w Carbrook *Sheff* 53–58; V New Bentley 58–60; Chapl Park Hill Flats Sheff 60–67; P-in-c Sheff St Swithun 67–72; V Welton *Linc* 72–92; RD Lawres 86–92; rtd 92; PtO *Derby* 92–16. *21 London Court, 9-13 London Road, Headington, Oxford OX3 7SL* T: (01865) 766204

PRITCHARD, Mrs Carol Sandra. b 52. St Aid Coll Dur BA 74 Bris Univ PGCE 75. EAMTC 96. **d** 99 **p** 00. NSM Oulton St Mich *Nor* 99–17; rtd 17; PtO *Nor* from 18. *17 West End Avenue, Costessey, Norwich NR8 5BA* T: (01603) 748903 E: carolpritchard3@btinternet.com

PRITCHARD, Colin Wentworth. b 38. K Coll Lon 59 St Boniface Warminster 59. **d** 63 **p** 64. C Putney St Marg *S'wark* 63–67; C Brixton St Matt 67–70; C Milton *Portsm* 70–74; V Mitcham St Mark *S'wark* 74–82; R Long Ditton 82–94; V Earlsfield St Andr 94–03; RD Wandsworth 98–03; rtd 03; PtO *Chich* from 03. *38 Hartfield Road, Seaford BN25 4PW* T: (01323) 894899 E: colin.pritchard@gmx.co.uk

PRITCHARD, Canon David Paul. b 47. Newc Univ BA 68 Em Coll Cam PGCE 69 LTCL 70 FRCO 72. Wycliffe Hall Ox 80. **d** 82 **p** 83. C Kidlington *Ox* 82–84; P-in-c Marcham w Garford 84–85; V 86–96; RD Abingdon 91–96; R Henley w Remenham 96–04; Can Res and Pastor Ely Cathl 04–14; Vice Dean 08–14; Acting Dean 11–12; Rtd Clergy Officer *Ely* from 13; rtd 15; PtO *Ely* from 14. *2 Chapel Lane, Little Downham, Ely CB6 2TN* T: (01353) 698831 M: 07470-072322 E: dpp123@cantab.net

PRITCHARD, John Anthony. b 74. Ripon Coll Cuddesdon BTh 07. **d** 07 **p** 08. C Gt Berkhamsted, Gt and Lt Gaddesden etc *St Alb* 07–11; C St Marylebone All SS *Lon* 11–13; P-in-c Upper Norwood St Jo *S'wark* 13–17; V from 17. *The Vicarage, 2 Sylvan Road, London SE19 2RX* T: (020) 8771 6686

✠**PRITCHARD, The Rt Revd John Lawrence.** b 48. St Pet Coll Ox BA 70 MA 73 Dur Univ MLitt 93. Ridley Hall Cam 70. **d** 72 **p** 73 **c** 02. C Birm St Martin 72–76; Asst Dir RE *B & W* 76–80; Youth Chapl 76–80; P-in-c Wilton 80–88; Dir Past Studies Cranmer Hall Dur 89–93; Warden 93–96; Adn Cant and Can Res Cant Cathl 96–02; Suff Bp Jarrow *Dur* 02–07; Bp Ox 07–14; rtd 14; Hon Asst Bp Dur from 15; Hon Asst Bp Leeds from 15. *42 Bolton Avenue, Richmond DL10 4BA* T: (01748) 850854 E: johnlpritchard@btinternet.com

PRITCHARD, Jonathan Llewelyn. b 64. Edin Univ MA 87 Leeds Univ MA 89 PhD 99. Ripon Coll Cuddesdon 98. **d** 00 **p** 01. C Skipton H Trin *Bradf* 00–04; P-in-c Keighley All SS 04–14; *Leeds* 14–16; P-in-c Thwaites Brow *Bradf* 06–14;

Leeds 14–16; TV Keighley from 16. *All Saints' Vicarage, 21 View Road, Keighley BD20 6JN* T: (01535) 665312 E: jon@thans.info *or* jon@thans.work

PRITCHARD, Kathryn Anne. b 60. St Cath Coll Ox MA K Coll Lon MA 10 Win Univ PhD. Cranmer Hall Dur. d 87. Par Dn Addiscombe St Mary *S'wark* 87–90; CPAS Staff 90–92; PtO *Cov* 92–95; Producer Worship Progr BBC Relig Broadcasting 94–99; Publicity Manager Hodder & Stoughton Relig Books 99–01; Commissioning and Product Development Manager Ch Ho Publishing 01–09; Project Manager and Research Fell Templeton Project Abps' Coun from 15. *Mission and Public Affairs, Church House, Great Smith Street, London SW1P 3AZ* E: kathryn.pritchard@churchofengland.org *or* k.pritchard410@btinternet.com

PRITCHARD, Kenneth John. b 30. Liv Univ BEng 51. NW Ord Course 72. d 74 p 75. C Ches 74–78; Miss to Seamen 78–84; V Runcorn St Jo Weston *Ches* 78–84; V Gt Meols 84–98; rtd 98; PtO *Ches* 99–14; *Liv* from 99. *13 Fieldlands, Scarisbrick, Southport PR8 5HQ* T: (01704) 514600 E: kennethpritchard@btinternet.com

PRITCHARD, Malcolm John. b 55. Bradf Univ BA 85 CQSW 85. St Jo Coll Nottm 86. d 88 p 89. C Peckham St Mary Magd *S'wark* 88–93; V Luton St Matt High Town *St Alb* 93–16; PtO from 17; CMS Uganda from 17. *Church Mission Society, Watlington Road, Cowley, Oxford OX4 6BZ* E: malcolmpritchard@outlook.com

PRITCHARD, Martin Dale. d 16 p 17. C Bro Deiniol *Ban* 16–17; C Bro Celynnin 17–18; C Llandudno from 18. *The Vicarage, 9 Morfa Road, Llandudno LL30 2BS* T: (01492) 478686

PRITCHARD, Michael Owen. b 49. Trin Coll Carmarthen CertEd 71. St Mich Coll Llan 71. d 73 p 74. C Conwy w Gyffin *Ban* 73–76; TV Dolgellau w Llanfachreth and Brithdir etc 76–78; Dioc Children's Officer 77–86; V Betws y Coed and Capel Curig 78–83; V Betws-y-Coed and Capel Curig w Penmachno etc 83–86; CF (TAVR) from 79; Chapl Claybury Hosp Woodford Bridge 86–96; Chapl Team Leader Forest Healthcare NHS Trust Lon 96–01; Chapl Team Leader NE Lon Foundn Trust 01–12; rtd 12. *1 St James Court, 71 Aldersbrook Road, London E12 5DL* T: (020) 8989 3813 M: 07852-194967 E: mopritchard@hotmail.com

PRITCHARD, Paul John. b 74. Wycliffe Hall Ox 16. d 18 p 19. C Barnton *Ches* from 18; C Northwich St Luke from 18. *77 Townfield Lane, Barnton, Northwich CW8 4QJ* T: (01606) 215216 M: 07810-264764 E: revpaulpritchard@protonmail.com

PRITCHARD, Paul Martin. b 46. d 13 p 14. OLM Mickleover All SS *Derby* 13–14; OLM Mickleover St Jo 13–14; OLM Mickleover from 14. *11 Gisborne Close, Mickleover, Derby DE3 9LU* T: (01332) 512530

PRITCHARD, Peter Benson. b 30. FPhS 60 LCP 68 Univ of Wales (Lamp) BA 51 Lon Univ PGCE 68 DipEd 70 Liv Univ MEd 74 PhD 81. Ripon Hall Ox 55. d 58 p 59. C Wavertree H Trin *Liv* 58–60; C Sefton 60–61; C-in-c Thornton CD 61–64; Chapl Liv Coll Boys' Sch 64–70; Hon C Wavertree St Bridget *Liv* 70–89; Lect CF Mott Coll of Educn 70–76; Sen Lect Liv Coll of HE 76–83; Liv Poly 83–87; PtO *Liv* 90–96; *Ches* 90–10; Chapl St Jo Hospice Wirral from 93; Tutor Open Univ 90–95; rtd 95. *68 Gleggside, West Kirby, Wirral CH48 6EA* T: 0151-625 8093

PRITCHARD, Peter Humphrey. b 47. Univ of Wales (Ban) BA 70 MA 98 Liv Univ PGCE 73. Qu Coll Birm 85. d 87 p 88. C Llanbeblig w Caernarfon and Betws Garmon etc *Ban* 87–90; R Llanberis w Llanrug 90–94; R Llanfaethlu w Llanfwrog and Llanrhuddlad etc 94–99; R Llanfair Mathafarn Eithaf w Llanbedrgoch 99–05; rtd 05. *4 Penlon Gardens, Bangor LL57 1AQ*

PRITCHARD, Robin. *See* PRITCHARD, Antony Robin

PRITCHARD, Simon Geraint. b 61. Coll of Ripon & York St Jo BA 85 Ex Univ PGCE 88. Cranmer Hall Dur 98. d 00 p 01. C Heysham *Blackb* 00–01; C Morecambe St Barn 01–03; C Standish 03–06; V Haigh and Aspull *Liv* 06–15; TV Wigan All SS 15–19; R Stamford Bridge Gp *York* from 19. *The Rectory, 8 Viking Road, Stamford Bridge, York YO41 1BR* E: s.pritchard41@btinternet.com

PRITCHARD, Thomas James Benbow. b 47. St Paul's Coll Chelt CertEd 69 Univ of Wales (Cardiff) BEd 79 MSc 85 Ex Univ BTh 08. SWMTC 96. d 99 p 00. NSM St Enoder *Truro* 99–01; P-in-c Roche and Withiel 01–05; V Llangollen w Trevor and Llantysilio *St As* 05–06; P-in-c Mylor w Flushing *Truro* 06–07; rtd 07; PtO *Truro* from 15. *Suncot, Short Cross Road, Mount Hawke, Truro TR4 8DU* T: (01209) 891766 E: thms_pritchard@yahoo.co.uk

PRITCHARD, The Ven Thomas William. b 33. Keele Univ BA 55 DipEd 55 Univ of Wales (Cardiff) LLM 94. St Mich Coll Llan 55. d 57 p 58. C Holywell *St As* 57–61; C Ruabon 61–63; V 77–87; R Pontfadog 63–71; V Llanferres, Nercwys

and Eryrys 71–77; Dioc Archivist 76–98; Can St As Cathl 84–98; RD Llangollen 86–87; Adn Montgomery 87–98; V Berriew and Manafon 87–98; rtd 98; PtO *St As* from 09. *32B Glynne Way, Hawarden, Deeside CH5 3NL* T: (01244) 538381

PRITCHARD-KEENS, Andrew James Dunn. b 57. Van Mildert Coll Dur BSc 79 Ch Ch Ox PGCE 80. Wycliffe Hall Ox 07. d 09 p 10. C Cogges and S Leigh *Ox* 09–12; C N Leigh 09–12; TV Wheatley 12–14; V Beckley, Forest Hill, Horton-cum-Studley and Stanton St John 14–18; R Olney from 18; Chapl Thames Valley Police from 12. *The Rectory, 9 Orchard Rise, Olney MK46 5HB* M: 07944-522098 E: andrewjdp@yahoo.co.uk

PRITCHETT, Antony Milner. b 63. Kent Univ BA 86 York Univ MA 15. Westcott Ho Cam 96. d 98 p 99. C Broughton Astley and Croft w Stoney Stanton *Leic* 98–02; V Gawber *Wakef* 02–08; Chapl Barnsley Hospice 02–08; P-in-c Pickering w Lockton and Levisham *York* 08–12; V 12–19; rtd 19. *Address temp unknown*

PRITCHETT, Mrs Beryl Ivy. b 48. Worc Coll of Educn TCert 69. WMMTC 02. d 05 p 06. NSM Brockmoor *Worc* 05–07; NSM Brierley Hill from 07. *7 Muirville Close, Wordsley, Stourbridge DY8 5NR* T: (01384) 271470 M: 07790-563479 E: berylpritchett@hotmail.co.uk

PRITCHETT, Edward Robert. b 87. Cant Ch Ch Univ BA 09 Wolfs Coll Cam BTh 16. Westcott Ho Cam 14. d 17 p 18. C Beckenham St Geo *Roch* 17–18; C Beckenham St Geo and St Barn from 18. *37 Rectory Road, Beckenham BR3 1HL* T: (020) 8663 6996 E: edward.pritchett@cantab.net *or* revedwardpritchett@outlook.com

PRIVETT, Peter John. b 48. Qu Coll Birm 75. d 78 p 79. C Moseley St Agnes *Birm* 78–81; V Kingsbury 81–87; P-in-c Dilwyn and Stretford *Heref* 87–90; Dioc Children's Adv 87–01; TV Leominster 90–98; NSM 98–05; Dioc Millennium Officer 98–01; PtO 05–07; *Cov* 07–09; C Rugby 09–13; C Rugby St Andr w St Pet and St John 13–17; rtd 18. *166 Lower Hillmorton Road, Rugby CV21 3TJ* T: (01788) 570332 E: peter.privett@yahoo.co.uk

PROBERT, Beverley Stuart. b 42. d 01 p 02. OLM Canford Magna *Sarum* 01–12; rtd 13; PtO *Sarum* from 13. *Blaenafon, 102 Knights Road, Bournemouth BH11 9SY* T: (01202) 571731 E: bevprobert@tiscali.co.uk

PROBERT, Christopher John Dixon. b 54. Univ of Wales (Ban) BTh 95 MTh 97. St Mich Coll Llan 74. d 78 p 79. C Aberdare St Fagan *Llan* 78–79; C Cadoxton-juxta-Barry 79–81; R Llanfynydd *St As* 81–84; V Gosberton Clough and Quadring *Linc* 84–86; TV Coventry Caludon *Cov* 86–88; V Llanrhian w Llanhywel and Llanrheithan *St D* 88–91; V Tregaron w Ystrad Meurig and Strata Florida 91–93; Chapl and Tutor St D NSM Course Tregaron Hosp 91–93; V Betws-y-Coed and Capel Curig w Penmachno etc *Ban* 93–98; Warden of Readers 96–98; V Lt Drayton *Lich* 98–04; P-in-c North Hill and Lewannick *Truro* 04–10; C Lezant w Lawhitton and S Petherwin w Trewen 04–10; R Three Rivers 10–11; rtd 11. *La Haudaidière, 50640 Heusse, France* T: (0033) (2) 33 61 35 82 E: cjdprobert@gmail.com

PROBERT, Canon Edward Cleasby. b 58. St Cath Coll Cam BA 80 MA 84. Ripon Coll Cuddesdon BA 84. d 85 p 86. C Esher *Guildf* 85–89; V Earlsfield St Andr *S'wark* 89–94; V Belmont 94–04; Can Res and Chan Sarum Cathl from 04. *24 The Close, Salisbury SP1 2EH* T: (01722) 555193 E: chancellor@salcath.co.uk

PROCTER, Andrew David. b 52. St Jo Coll Ox BA 74 MA 86. Trin Coll Bris 74. d 77 p 78. C Barnoldswick w Bracewell *Bradf* 77–80; P-in-c Kelbrook 80–82; V 82–87; V Heaton St Barn 87–93; V Swanley St Paul *Roch* 93–07; V Shipbourne w Plaxtol 07–16; rtd 16. *6 Grange Road, Platt, Sevenoaks TN15 8NF* M: 07963-943524 *or* 07872-597953 E: a.procter@live.co.uk

PROCTER, Nicholas Jonathan. b 59. Liv Univ BVSc 84 MRCVS 84. LCTP 06. d 09 p 10. NSM Leyland St Jo *Blackb* 09–14; PtO 14–15; NSM Bamber Bridge St Aid from 15; NSM Walton-le-Dale St Leon from 15. *23 Regents Way, Euxton, Chorley PR7 6PG* T: (01257) 241927 E: n.r.procter@btinternet.com

PROCTOR, Canon Michael Thomas. b 41. Ch Ch Ox BA 65 MA 67. Westcott Ho Cam 63. d 65 p 66. C Monkseaton St Mary *Newc* 65–69; Pakistan 69–72; C Willington *Newc* 72–77; TV 77–79; Ed Sec Nat Soc 79–84; P-in-c Roxwell *Chelmsf* 79–84; Bp's Ecum Officer 85–00; Dir of Miss and Unity 85–94; P-in-c Gt Waltham w Ford End 94–00; Hon Can Chelmsf Cathl 85–00; rtd 00; Dir Chelmsf Counselling Foundn from 00. *Claremont, South Street, Great Waltham, Chelmsford CM3 1DP* E: mtproctor@lineone.net

PROCTOR, Nicholas Jonathan. *See* PROCTER, Nicholas Jonathan

PROCTOR, Canon Noel. b 30. St Aid Birkenhead 62. **d** 64 **p** 65. C Haughton le Skerne *Dur* 64–67; R Byers Green 67–70; Chapl HM Pris Eastchurch 70–74; Chapl HM Pris Dartmoor 74–79; Chapl HM Pris Man 79–95; Hon Can Man Cathl 91–95; rtd 95; PtO *Man* from 95. *Mizpah, 64 Barton Road, Swinton, Manchester M27 5LP* T: 0161-794 6040 E: berylproctor@talktalk.net

PROSSER, Jean. b 40. Open Univ BA 84 Surrey Univ PhD 94. **d** 02 **p** 05. NSM Grosmont and Skenfrith and Llangattock etc *Mon* 02–16; P-in-c 09–16. *Yew Tree Farm, Llangattock Lingoed, Abergavenny NP7 8NS* T: (01873) 821405 E: revjean.prosser@btinternet.com

PROTHERO, Brian Douglas. b 52. St Andr Univ MTheol 75 Dundee Univ CertEd 77. Linc Th Coll 84. **d** 86 **p** 87. C Thornbury *Glouc* 86–89; V Goodrington *Ex* 89–04; R Weybridge *Guildf* from 04; Chapl Sam Beare Hospice from 06. *The Rectory, 3 Churchfields Avenue, Weybridge KT13 9YA* T: (01932) 842566 M: 07715-364389 E: brian.prothero@talktalk.net

PROTHERO, John Martin. b 32. Oak Hill Th Coll 64. **d** 66 **p** 67. C Tipton St Martin *Lich* 66–69; C Wednesfield Heath 69–72; Distr Sec BFBS 72–85; LtO *S'well* 73–86; Hon C Gedling 73; R Willoughby-on-the-Wolds w Wysall and Widmerpool 86–98; rtd 98. *The Elms, Vicarage Hill, Aberaeron SA46 0DY* T: (01545) 570568

PROTHEROE, Canon Rhys Illtyd. b 50. St D Coll Lamp. **d** 74 **p** 75. C Pen-bre *St D* 74–76; C Carmarthen St Dav 76–78; V Llanegwad 78–79; V Llanegwad w Llanfynydd 79–82; V Gors-las 82–95; RD Dyffryn Aman 94–95; V Llan-llwch w Llangain and Llangynog 95–15; Hon Can St D Cathl 13–15; rtd 15; PtO *St D* from 15. *69 Meysydd y Coleg, Carmarthen SA31 3GR* T: (01267) 232427 E: parch.rhys@gmail.com

PROTHEROE, Canon Robin Philip. b 33. St Chad's Coll Dur BA 54 MA 60 Nottm Univ MPhil 75 Ox Univ DipEd 62. **d** 57 **p** 58. C Roath *Llan* 57–60; Asst Chapl Culham Coll Abingdon 60–64; Sen Lect RS Trent (Nottm) Poly *S'well* 64–84; PtO 64–66; LtO 66–84; P-in-c Barton in Fabis 70–73; P-in-c Thrumpton 70–73; Dir of Educn *Bris* 84–98; Hon Can Bris Cathl 85–98; Capitular Can Bris Cathl 01–07; PtO 98–10; *Chich* from 10. *58 Stroudley Road, Brighton BN1 4BH* T: (01273) 687822 E: rpprotheroe@gmail.com

✠**PROUD, The Rt Revd Andrew John.** b 54. K Coll Lon BD 79 AKC 79 SOAS Lon MA 01. Linc Th Coll 79. **d** 80 **p** 81 **c** 07. C Stansted Mountfitchet *Chelmsf* 80–83; TV Borehamwood *St Alb* 83–90; C Bp's Hatfield 90–92; R E Barnet 92–01; Chapl Adis Ababa St Matt Ethiopia 02–07; Area Bp Ethiopia and Horn of Africa 07–11; Area Bp Reading *Ox* 11–19; rtd 19. *21 Clarence Avenue, Northampton NN2 6NX*

PROUD, David John. b 56. Leeds Univ BA 77 Dur Univ CertEd 78. Ridley Hall Cam 85. **d** 88 **p** 89. C Lindfield *Chich* 88–91; TV Horsham 91–97; V Ware Ch *St Alb* 97–10; RD Hertford and Ware 04–10; Chapl E Herts NHS Trust 97–00; Chapl E and N Herts NHS Trust 00–06; R Bedhampton *Portsm* 10–18; rtd 18; PtO *Portsm* from 18. *33 Pine Road, Bishop's Waltham, Southampton SO32 1EJ*

PROUDFOOT (née BLACKBURN), Mrs Jane Elizabeth. b 66. Lanc Univ BA 88 St Martin's Coll Lanc PGCE 93 Leeds Univ BA 09. NOC 06. **d** 09 **p** 10. C Stockton Heath *Ches* 09–12; R Grappenhall from 12. *The Rectory, 17 Hill Top Road, Stockton Heath, Warrington WA4 2ED* T: (01925) 661546 E: revdproudfoot@hotmail.co.uk

PROUDLEY, Sister Anne. b 38. Edin Univ BSc 60. SAOMC 97. **d** 00 **p** 01. CSJB from 00; NSM Blackbird Leys *Ox* 00–04; LtO 04–11; Chapl to the Homeless 05–11; NSM Blenheim 11–12; PtO from 12. *Harriet Monsell House, Ripon College, Cuddesdon, Oxford OX44 9EX* E: annecsjb@csjb.org.uk

PROUDLOVE, Lee Jason. b 70. Lon Bible Coll BA 94. Trin Coll Bris MA 01. **d** 01 **p** 02. C Morden *S'wark* 01–04; CMS Philippines 05–08; P-in-c W Bridgford *S'well* 08–11; R from 11. *The Rectory, 86 Bridgford Road, West Bridgford, Nottingham NG2 6AX* T: 0115-981 1112 E: rector@stgilesparish.com

PROUDLOVE, Stephen. b 81. SS Coll Cam BA 02 MA 05. Ridley Hall Cam 12. **d** 14 **p** 15. C Ilkley All SS *Leeds* 14–17; V Menston w Woodhead from 17; Asst Dir of Ords from 17. *The Vicarage, 12 Fairfax Gardens, Menston, Ilkley LS29 6ET* T: (01943) 872433 M: 07794-678268 E: stephen.proudlove@leeds.anglican.org or vicar@stjohnmenston.org.uk

PROUSE, Ms Carole Maureen. b 45. NOC. **dss** 86 **d** 87 **p** 95. NSM Coalville and Bardon Hill *Leic* 87–90; PtO 90–95; NSM Thorpe Acre w Dishley 95–96; P-in-c Packington w Normanton-le-Heath 96–01; Chapl HM Pris Low Newton 01–04; Asst Chapl 04–10; rtd 10; PtO *Nor* from 13. *1 Acacia Grove, Sheringham NR26 8PA* T: (01263) 479781 E: carole.prouse@btinternet.com

PROVOST, Ian Keith. b 47. CA Tr Coll IDC 73 Ridley Hall Cam 91. **d** 93 **p** 94. C Verwood *Sarum* 93–97; P-in-c

Redlynch and Morgan's Vale 97–02; TV Plymstock and Hooe *Ex* 02–10; rtd 10; PtO *Ex* from 10. *8 Larkhall Rise, Plymouth PL3 6LY* T: (01752) 319528 E: ian.provost17@gmail.com

PROWSE, Mrs Barbara Bridgette Christmas. b 41. R Holloway Coll Lon BA 62. **d** 91 **p** 94. C Kingsthorpe w Northampton St Dav *Pet* 91–97; V Northampton St Jas 97–02; rtd 02; PtO *Truro* from 02. *36 Carn Basavern, St Just, Penzance TR19 7QX* T: (01736) 787994 E: vicarette.prowse@btinternet.com

PRUDOM, William Haigh. b 26. STh 79 APhS 81 Hull Univ MPhil 88. St D Coll Lamp 60. **d** 62 **p** 63. C Aylesford *Roch* 62–63; C Margate St Jo *Cant* 63–66; V Long Preston *Bradf* 66–73; C Darlington St Cuth *Dur* 73–75; V Ticehurst *Chich* 75–79; P-in-c Flimwell 78–79; V Ticehurst and Flimwell 79–81; R Spennithorne w Finghall and Hauxwell *Ripon* 81–91; rtd 91; PtO *Ripon* 91–14; *Leeds* 14–16. *9 Sydall's Way, Catterick Village, Richmond DL10 7ND* T: (01748) 818604

PRUEN, Canon Edward Binney. b 56. K Coll Lon BD 77 AKC 77. St Jo Coll Nottm 78. **d** 79 **p** 80. C Kidderminster St Mary *Worc* 79–82; C Woking St Jo *Guildf* 82–84; Chapl Asst R Marsden Hosp 84–86; C Stapleford *S'well* 86–88; Min Winklebury CD *Win* 88; V Winklebury 88–93; Chapl Ld Mayor Treloar Coll Alton 93–09; Hon Can Win Cathl 05–09; Can Res S'well Minster 09–12; P-in-c St Columb Major *Truro* 12–16; P-in-c St Mawgan w St Ervan and St Eval 12–16; R Lann Pydar 16; P-in-c Bentworth, Lasham, Medstead and Shalden *Win* from 16. *The Rectory, Trinity Hill, Medstead, Alton GU34 5LT* T: (01420) 561154 M: 07752-569794 E: edpruen@gmail.com

PRYCE, Donald Keith. b 35. Man Univ BSc. Linc Th Coll 69. **d** 71 **p** 72. C Heywood St Jas *Man* 71–74; P-in-c 74–75; V 75–86; R Ladybarn 86–06; Chapl S Man Coll 87–06; Chapl Christie Hosp NHS Trust Man 93–06; rtd 06; PtO *Ches* from 06; *Man* from 06. *62 Belmont Road, Gatley, Cheadle SK8 4AQ* T: 0161-286 9985 E: donaldpryce@hotmail.com

PRYCE, Canon Robin Mark. b 60. Sussex Univ BA 82 Cam Univ MA 94 Birm Univ DPT 15. Westcott Ho Cam 84 United Th Coll Bangalore 85. **d** 87 **p** 88. C W Bromwich All SS *Lich* 87–90; Chapl Sandwell Distr Gen Hosp 90; Chapl and Fell CCC Cam 90–02; Tutor 92–02; Dean of Chpl 96–02; V Smethwick *Birm* 02–06; Bp's Adv for Clergy CME from 06; Dir Min from 17; Hon Can Birm Cathl from 11; Chapl to The Queen from 17. *1 Colmore Row, Birmingham B3 2BJ* T: 0121-426 0430 E: markp@cofebirmingham.com

PRYCE, Mrs Yvonne. **d** 16 **p** 17. NSM Alyn Miss Area *St As* from 16. *Hazeldene, King Street, Acrefair, Wrexham LL14 3RH* T: (01978) 824891 E: yvonnepryce2@aol.com

PRYKE, Jonathan Justin Speaight. b 59. Trin Coll Cam BA 80 MA 85. Trin Coll Bris BD 85. **d** 85 **p** 86. C Corby St Columba *Pet* 85–88; C Jesmond Clayton Memorial *Newc* from 88. *15 Lily Avenue, Newcastle upon Tyne NE2 2SQ* T: 0191-281 9854

PRYOR, William Lister Archibald. b 39. Trin Coll Cam BA 67 MA 69 DipEd 68. Ox NSM Course 72. **d** 75 **p** 90. NSM Summertown *Ox* from 75; PtO *Nor* 93–04 and from 09. *23 Harbord Road, Oxford OX2 8LH* T: (01865) 515102

PRYS, Deiniol. b 53. Univ of Wales (Ban) BTh 91. St Mich Coll Llan 82. **d** 83 **p** 84. C Llanbeblig w Caernarfon and Betws Garmon etc *Ban* 83–86; TV Amlwch 86–88; V Llanerch-y-medd 89–92; R Llansadwrn w Llanddona and Llaniestyn etc 92–11; LtO from 11. *Bryn Celyn, Llansadwrn, Menai Bridge LL59 5SL* T: (01248) 810534 M: 07740-541316

PRYSE, Preb Hugh Henry David. b 58. St Chad's Coll Dur BA 81 SS Coll Cam PGCE 82 K Coll Lon MA 96. St Steph Ho Ox 94. **d** 96 **p** 97. C Branksome St Aldhelm *Sarum* 96–00; Chapl St Edw Sch Poole 98–00; TV Hove *Chich* 00–05; R Ex St Jas from 05; Asst Dioc Dir of Ords from 09; Preb Ex Cathl from 17. *The Rectory, 45 Thornton Hill, Exeter EX4 4NR* T: (01392) 431297 or 420407 E: henry.pryse@blueyonder.co.uk

PRYSOR-JONES, John Glynne. b 47. Heythrop Coll Lon MA 94 Leeds Metrop Univ BSc 05 CQSW 73 FRSA 13. Westcott Ho Cam 88. **d** 90 **p** 91. C Mitcham St Mark *S'wark* 90–93; V Dudley St Fran *Worc* 93–99; R Woodchurch *Ches* 99–01; Hd Past Care Services Chorley and S Ribble NHS Trust and Preston Acute Hosps NHS Trust 01–02; Hd Past Care Services Lancs Teaching Hosps NHS Trust 02–06; PtO *Ban* from 16. *Bryn-y-Mor, St John's Park, Penmaenmawr LL34 6NE* T: (01492) 622515

PRZESLAWSKI, Maria Christina. b 50. Nottm Univ MA 91. EMMTC 08. **d** 10 **p** 11. NSM Wilne and Draycott w Breaston *Derby* 10–17; rtd 17; PtO *Derby* from 17. *9 Holmes Road, Breaston, Derby DE72 3BT* T: (01332) 874480 E: maria.9@btinternet.com

PRZYWALA, Karl Andrzej. b 63. Univ Coll Dur BA 85 Chas Sturt Univ NSW BTh 04. St Mark's Nat Th Cen Canberra 01. **d** 04 **p** 05. C Houghton le Spring *Dur* 04–05; C Chester le Street 05–07; P-in-c Whatton w Aslockton, Hawksworth, Scarrington etc *S'well* 07–11; V 11–14; R

Vancouver H Trin Canada from 14. *908 - 1755 West 14th Avenue, Vancouver V6J 2J6, Canada* T: (001) (604) 731 3221 E: karl_sydney@yahoo.co.uk

PUCKRIN, Christopher. b 47. Oak Hill Th Coll. **d** 82 **p** 83. C Heworth H Trin *York* 82–84; C Sherburn in Elmet 84–85; P-in-c Kirk Fenton 85–86; P-in-c Kirkby Wharfe 85–86; V Kirk Fenton w Kirkby Wharfe and Ulleskelfe 86–87; C York St Mich-le-Belfrey 87–94; P-in-c Barnstaple *Ex* 94–97; TV 97–00; V Woodside *Ripon* 00–07; C Holbeck 07–09; V Bardsey 09–12; P-in-c 12–13; rtd 12. *Flat 23, 9 Fink Hill, Horsforth, Leeds LS18 5DY* T: 0113-267 8584

PUDGE, Mark Samuel. b 67. K Coll Lon BD 90 AKC 90 Heythrop Coll Lon MA 99. Ripon Coll Cuddesdon 91. **d** 93 **p** 94. C Thorpe Bay *Chelmsf* 93–96; TV Wickford and Runwell 97–00; Management Consultant Citizens' Advice Bureau 00–04; Consultant Legal Services Commn 04–06; Dir Voluntary Action Westmr 06–10; Hon C Paddington St Jo w St Mich *Lon* 03–10; PtO *Eur* from 13. *Finca La Maroma, Cerro Panadero s/n, 29715 Sedella (Málaga), Spain* E: markpudge@hotmail.com

PUDNEY, Malcolm Lloyd. b 48. SEITE 99. **d** 01 **p** 02. NSM S Nutfield w Outwood *S'wark* 01–06; P-in-c Woodham Mortimer w Hazeleigh and Woodham Walter *Chelmsf* 06–10; P-in-c Lurgashall and N Chapel w Ebernoe *Chich* 10–13; rtd 13; PtO *Chich* from 14. *26 Cuckfield Crescent, Worthing BN13 2ED* M: 07860-464836 E: yenduptoo@madasafish.com

PUGH, Harry. b 48. K Coll Lon BD 70 AKC 71 Lanc Univ MA 89. **d** 72 **p** 73. C Milnrow *Man* 72–75; P-in-c Rochdale Gd Shep 75–78; TV Rochdale 78–79; PtO *Liv* 79–82; C Darwen St Cuth *Blackb* 82–85; C Darwen St Cuth w Tockholes St Steph 85–86; V Burnley St Steph 86–93; R Hoole 93–01; P-in-c Porthleven w Sithney *Truro* 01–13; rtd 13; PtO *Blackb* from 16. *17 Cavendish Road, Blackpool FY2 9JR* T: (01253) 594016

PUGH, Lynda. b 49. Man Univ BSocSc 93 MA 96 PhD 04. Ripon Coll Cuddesdon 07. **d** 09 **p** 10. C Glen Gp *Linc* 09–12; P-in-c Ringstone in Aveland Gp 12–17; rtd 17; PtO *Ches* from 18. *8 Patch Lane, Bramhall, Stockport SK7 1JB* M: 07775-660081 E: dr.lynda.pugh@gmail.com

PUGH, Stephen Gregory. Southn Univ BEd 77. Linc Th Coll 85. **d** 87 **p** 88. C Harpenden St Nic *St Alb* 87–90; C Stevenage All SS Pin Green 90–93; V Stotfold and Radwell 93–00; V Gt Ilford St Marg and St Clem *Chelmsf* from 00. *The Vicarage, 70 Brisbane Road, Ilford IG1 4SL* T: (020) 8554 7542 M: 07910-395925 E: stephenpugh@waitrose.com

PUGH, Miss Wendy Kathleen. b 48. Newnham Coll Cam BA 69 MA 75. Trin Coll Bris 93. **d** 95 **p** 96. C Hailsham *Chich* 95–99; C Frimley *Guildf* 99–07; Hon C Chertsey, Lyne and Longcross 07–12; rtd 13; PtO *Sarum* from 14. *6 Friars Orchard, Salisbury SP1 2SY* T: (01722) 501443 E: wkpugh@aol.com

PUGMIRE, Canon Alan. b 37. Tyndale Hall Bris 61. **d** 64 **p** 65. C Islington St Steph w St Bart and St Matt *Lon* 64–66; C St Helens St Mark *Liv* 66–71; R Stretford St Bride *Man* 71–82; R Burnage St Marg 82–02; AD Heaton 88–98; Hon Can Man Cathl 98–02; rtd 02; PtO *Man* from 02. *20 Shortland Crescent, Manchester M19 1SZ* T/F: 0161-431 3476 E: alan.pugmire@tiscali.co.uk

PUGSLEY, Anthony John. b 39. ACIB. Oak Hill Th Coll 89. **d** 90 **p** 91. C Chadwell *Chelmsf* 90–94; P-in-c Gt Warley Ch Ch 94–01; V Warley Ch Ch and Gt Warley St Mary 01–04; rtd 04; PtO *Chelmsf* from 07. *3 Southcliffe Court, Southview Drive, Walton on the Naze CO14 8EP* T: (01255) 850967 E: revtonp@aol.com

PULESTON, Mervyn Pedley. b 35. K Coll Lon BD 60 AKC 60. **d** 61 **p** 62. C Gt Marlow *Ox* 61–65; P Missr Blackbird Leys CD 65–70; V Kidlington 70–85; R Hampton Poyle 70–85; TR Kidlington w Hampton Poyle 85–86; Chapl Geneva *Eur* 86–92; TV Dorchester *Ox* 92–00; rtd 00; PtO *Ox* from 00. *55 Benmead Road, Kidlington OX5 2DB* T: (01865) 372360 E: mpuleston@aol.com

PULFORD, John Shirley Walter. b 31. Jes Coll Cam BA 55 MA 59. Cuddesdon Coll 55. **d** 57 **p** 58. C Blackpool St Steph *Blackb* 57–60; N Rhodesia 60–63; V Newington St Paul *S'wark* 63–68; C Seacroft *Ripon* 68–70; Chapl HM Pris Liv 70–72; Chapl HM Pris Linc 72–73; Student Cllr Linc Colls of Art and Tech 73–79; Cam Univ Counselling Service 79–96; Dir 82–96; rtd 96. *59 Cromer Road, North Walsham NR28 0HB* T: (01692) 404320 E: jpulford@btinternet.com

PULKO, Susan Helen. b 55. Imp Coll Lon BSc 77 Nottm Univ PhD 81 Sheff Univ BA 14 CEng 88. Yorks Min Course 11. **d** 14 **p** 15. NSM Market Weighton *York* 14–18; NSM Goodmanham 14–18; NSM Sancton 14–18; P-in-c Hedon, Paull, Sproatley and Preston from 18. *The Vicarage, Staithes Road, Preston, Hull HU12 8TD* E: s.h.pulko@hull.ac.uk

PULLEN, Adam William. b 73. Univ of Wales (Abth) BSc 97. St Jo Coll Nottm 03. **d** 06 **p** 07. C Swansea St Pet *S & B* 06–09; C Swansea St Thos and Kilvey 09–10; I Ballisodare

w Collooney and Emlaghfad *T, K & A* 10–15; Dom Chapl to Bp Tuam 12–15; I Stranorlar w Meenglas and Kilteevogue *D & R* from 15. *The Rectory, The Glebe, Stranorlar, Co Donegal, F93 C8Y8, Republic of Ireland* M: (00353) 87-682 9627 E: adam.pullen@googlemail.com

PULLEN, Frances Jill. *See* PHILLIPS, Frances Jill

PULLEN, Roger Christopher. b 43. Lon Univ BSc 65 PGCE 90. Wells Th Coll 65. **d** 67 **p** 68. C S w N Hayling *Portsm* 67–69; C Farlington 69–73; V Farington *Blackb* 73–80; V Chorley All SS 80–83; V Kingsley *Ches* 83–92; R Cilcain and Nannerch and Rhydymwyn *St As* 92–99; Dioc MU Admin *Guildf* 99–02; Hon C Bramley and Grafham 99–00; PtO 00–02; *Chich* from 03. *16 East Way, Selsey, Chichester PO20 0SL* T: (01243) 603425 M: 07909-954772 E: rogerselsey@icloud.com

PULLEN, Timothy John. b 61. BNC Ox BA 84 St Jo Coll Dur MA 96. Cranmer Hall Dur 93. **d** 96 **p** 97. C Allesley *Cov* 96–00; V Wolston and Church Lawford 00–08; Can Res Cov Cathl 08–13; Sub-Dean 10–13; R Wollaton *S'well* from 13. *St Leonard's Rectory, 143 Russell Drive, Nottingham NG8 2BD* T: 0115-928 9963 M: 07974-007665 E: pullen1961@gmail.com

PULLIN, Andrew Eric. b 47. Kelham Th Coll 67 Linc Th Coll 71. **d** 73 **p** 74. C Pershore w Pinvin, Wick and Birlingham *Worc* 73–77; TV Droitwich 77–80; V Woburn Sands *St Alb* 80–85; PtO *B & W* 85–87. *85 Weymouth Road, Frome BA11 1HJ* T: (01373) 472170 E: a.pullin@talktalk.net

PULLIN, Canon Christopher. b 56. St Chad's Coll Dur BA 77 Heythrop Coll Lon MA 04. Ripon Coll Cuddesdon 78 Ch Div Sch of Pacific 79. **d** 80 **p** 81. C Tooting All SS *S'wark* 80–85; V New Eltham All SS 85–92; V St Jo in Bedwardine *Worc* 92–08; RD Martley and Worc W 03–08; Hon Can Worc Cathl 07–08; Can Res and Chan Heref Cathl from 08. *2 Cathedral Close, Hereford HR1 2NG* T: (01432) 374273 F: 374220 E: chancellor@herefordcathedral.org

PULLIN, Rebecca. *See* CLARKE, Kathleen Jean Rebecca

PULLIN, Canon Stephen James. b 66. S Bank Univ BEng 89 Open Univ MBA 98. Trin Coll Bris BA 04. **d** 04 **p** 05. C Soundwell *Bris* 04–07; P-in-c Stapleton 07–14; C Frenchay and Winterbourne Down 07–14; Bp's Adv for Deliverance Min 10–14; P-in-c Reading St Mary the Virgin *Ox* 14–15; V from 15; AD Reading 14–17; Hon Can Ch Ch from 19. *344 Wokingham Road, Reading RG6 7DE* T: 0118-966 9165 M: 07866-700881 E: vicar@readingminster.org.uk *or* stephen.pullin@oxford.anglican.org

PULLINGER, Mrs Catherine Ann. b 54. York Univ BA 76. Oak Hill Th Coll 91. **d** 93 **p** 97. NSM Luton St Paul *St Alb* 93–99; NSM Luton Lewsey St Hugh 99–11; P-in-c Woodside 11–17; V from 17. *St Andrew's Vicarage, Church Road, Slip End, Luton LU1 4BJ* T: (01582) 480391 E: cathy@pullinger.net

PULLINGER, Ian Austin. b 61. Oak Hill Th Coll. **d** 96 **p** 97. C Weston *Win* 96–00; TV The Ortons, Alwalton and Chesterton *Ely* 00–10; TV Alwalton and Chesterton 10–12; C-in-c Orton Goldhay CD 12–13; V Corby St Columba *Pet* from 13; RD Corby from 13. *St Columba's Vicarage, 157 Studfall Avenue, Corby NN17 1LG* T: (01536) 400225 E: ianpullinger@btinternet.com

PULLINGER, Peter Mark. b 53. Heythrop Coll Lon MA 97. Ridley Hall Cam 01. **d** 03 **p** 04. C Clapham Park St Steph *S'wark* 03–06; C Telford Park 06–07; TV Sutton 07–15; P-in-c Merstham, S Merstham and Gatton 15–16; TR from 16. *The Rectory, Battlebridge Lane, Merstham, Redhill RH1 3LH* T: (01737) 642647 E: mark@pullinger.net *or* mplarksong@aol.co.uk *or* rector.mgteam@btinternet.com

PULMAN, John. b 34. EMMTC 78. **d** 81 **p** 82. NSM Mansfield SS Pet and Paul *S'well* 81–83; C Mansfield Woodhouse 83–86; V Flintham 86–99; R Car Colston w Screveton 86–99; Chapl HM YOI Whatton 87–90; Chapl HM Pris Whatton 90–99; rtd 99; PtO *S'well* from 99; *Derby* 00–18. *101 Ling Forest Road, Mansfield NG18 3NQ* T: (01623) 474707

PUMFREY (née CERRATTI), Canon Christa Elisabeth. b 54. Wycliffe Hall Ox 94. **d** 97 **p** 98. C Chipping Norton *Ox* 97–00; P-in-c Lavendon w Cold Brayfield, Clifton Reynes etc 00–08; R from 08; R Gayhurst w Ravenstone, Stoke Goldington etc from 08; Deanery Youth Co-ord from 00; AD Newport 06–12; Hon Can Ch Ch from 11. *The New Rectory, 7A Northampton Road, Lavendon, Olney MK46 4EY* T: (01234) 240013 E: christin.pumfrey@btinternet.com

PUNSHON, Carol Mary. *See* BRENNAND, Carol Mary

PUNSHON, Canon Keith. b 48. Jes Coll Cam BA 69 MA 73 Birm Univ MA 77. Qu Coll Birm 71. **d** 73 **p** 74. C Yardley St Edburgha *Birm* 73–76; Chapl Eton Coll 76–79; V Hill *Birm* 79–86; CF (TA) from 79; V S Yardley St Mich *Birm* 86–96; Can Res Ripon Cathl 96–14; *Leeds* 14; rtd 14. *4 Willow Bridge Lane, Dalton, Thirsk YO7 3QQ*

PURDY, Canon John David. b 44. Leeds Univ BA 65 MPhil 76. Coll of Resurr Mirfield 72. **d** 75 **p** 76. C Marske in Cleveland *York* 75–78; C Marton-in-Cleveland 78–80; V Newby 80–87; V Kirkleatham 87–95; V Kirkbymoorside w Gillamoor, Farndale etc 95–09; RD Helmsley 99–09; rtd 09; P-in-c Fylingdales and Hawsker cum Stainsacre *York* 10–12; Can and Preb York Minster 98–17; PtO from 12. *Drewann, Westfields, Kirkbymoorside, York YO62 6AG* T: (01751) 431809 M: 07504-428713 E: david.purdy@virgin.net

PURLE, Joanne Louise. b 70. Surrey Univ BSc 92. Trin Coll Bris 14. **d** 17 **p** 18. C Folkestone St Jo *Cant* from 17. *2 Chalk Close, Folkestone CT19 5TD* M: 07790-342718 E: purleyjo@gmail.com

PURNELL, Mrs Laura Louise. b 75. Southn Univ BA 96. Ridley Hall Cam 16. **d** 18 **p** 19. C Gaywood *Nor* from 18. *170 Wootton Road, Gaywood, King's Lynn PE30 4BU* M: 07787-975408 E: laurapurnell@hotmail.co.uk

PURNELL, Marcus John. b 75. Ridley Hall Cam 07. **d** 09 **p** 10. C Northampton St Benedict *Pet* 09–12; V Cottesmore and Burley, Clipsham, Exton etc 12–18; TV March *Ely* from 18. *The Vicarage, 177 Station Road, March PE15 8NG* M: 07535-639915 E: revmarcuspurnell@gmail.com

PURSER, Alec. d 10 **p** 11. NSM Abbeyleix w Ballyroan etc *C & O* 10–14; P-in-c Stradbally w Ballintubbert, Coraclone etc from 14. *The Rectory, Main Street, Stradbally, Co Laois, Republic of Ireland* T: (00353) (57) 862 5173 M: (00353) 87-923 2694 E: alecpurser@gmail.com

PURVEY-TYRER, Neil. b 66. Leeds Univ BA 87 MA 88. Westcott Ho Cam 88. **d** 90 **p** 91. C Denbigh and Nantglyn *St As* 90–92; Chapl Asst Basingstoke Distr Hosp 92–95; TV Cannock *Lich* 95–99; V Northampton H Sepulchre w St Andr and St Lawr *Pet* 99–02; Dioc Co-ord for Soc Resp 99–03; TR Duston 02–08; Chapl St Andr Hosp Northn 08–12; Hd of Chapl 12–19; Past Care and Counselling Adv *Pet* 10–13; Chapl Kettering Gen Hosp NHS Foundn Trust from 19; Bp's Adv for Healthcare Chapl *Pet* from 19. *Kettering General Hospital NHS Trust, Rothwell Road, Kettering NN16 8UZ* T: (01536) 492000

PURVIS, Sandra Anne. *See* TAUSON, Sandra Anne

PURVIS, Canon Stephen. b 48. AKC 70. **d** 71 **p** 72. C Peterlee *Dur* 71–75; Dioc Recruitment Officer 75–79; V Stevenage All SS Pin Green *St Alb* 79–88; TR Borehamwood 88–00; RD Aldenham 94–98; V Leagrave 00–13; RD Luton 07–12; Hon Can St Alb 02–13; rtd 13; PtO *St Alb* from 13; *Bris* from 14. *23 Almeda Road, Bristol BS5 8RY* T: 0117-967 0507 E: stephen.purvis48@gmail.com

PURVIS-LEE, Lynn. b 58. St Jo Coll Dur BA 97. Cranmer Hall Dur 94. **d** 98 **p** 99. C Gt Aycliffe *Dur* 98–02; Chapl N Tees and Hartlepool NHS Foundn Trust 02–14; R Penhill *Leeds* 14–18 and from 14. *10 Church Bank, Eggleston, Barnard Castle DL12 0AH* E: lynnhome28@gmail.com

PUSEY, Canon Ian John. b 39. Sarum Th Coll 69. **d** 71 **p** 72. C Waltham Abbey *Chelmsf* 71–75; TV Stantonbury *Ox* 75–80; P-in-c Bletchley 80–84; R 84–00; RD Milton Keynes 96–00; P-in-c Lamp 00–06; AD Newport 04–06; Hon Can Ch Ch 06; rtd 06. *16 Gussiford Lane, Exmouth EX8 2SF* T: (01395) 275549 E: ian.pusey@btinternet.com

PUTNAM, Mrs Gillian. b 43. WEMTC 00. **d** 02 **p** 03. NSM Milton *B & W* 02–09; NSM Milton and Kewstoke 09–13; PtO 13–18. *c/o All Saints' Vicarage, Tresawls Road, Truro TR1 3LD* E: revgillputnam@gmail.com

PUTNAM, Jeremy James. b 76. Ripon Coll Cuddesdon 09. **d** 11 **p** 12. C Portishead *B & W* 11–15; P-in-c Highertown and Baldhu *Truro* from 15. *All Saints' Vicarage, Tresawis Road, Truro TR1 3LD* M: 07477-921397 E: jeremyjputnam@gmail.com

PUTT, Thomas David. b 83. Loughb Univ BEng 05. Oak Hill Th Coll BA 11. **d** 11 **p** 12. C Kirk Ella and Willerby *York* 11–15; Chapl Yeovil Coll *B & W* 15–19; C Yeovil w Kingston Pitney 15–19; V Burford w Fulbrook, Taynton, Asthall etc *Ox* from 19. *The Vicarage, Church Lane, Burford OX18 4SD* E: tomputt@burfordchurch.org

✠**PWAISIHO, The Rt Revd William Alaha.** b 48. Bp Patteson Th Coll (Solomon Is) 71. **d** 74 **p** 75 **c** 81. Solomon Is 74–76; New Zealand 78–79; Solomon Is 79–95; Dean Honiara 80–81; Bp Malaita 81–89; C Sale St Anne *Ches* 97–99; R Gawsworth 99–14; R Gawsworth w North Rode 14–19; Hon Asst Bp Ches 97–19; rtd 19; PtO *Ches* from 19. *1 Williams Way, Henbury, Macclesfield SK11 9NR* M: 07711-241625 E: bishop.gawsworth@hotmail.co.uk

PYBUS, Antony Frederick. b 54. Birm Univ BA 77. Cranmer Hall Dur 78. **d** 81 **p** 82. C Ches H Trin 81–84; C W Hampstead St Jas *Lon* 84–89; V Alexandra Park St Andr 89–93; V Alexandra Park from 93. *The Vicarage, 34 Alexandra Park Road, London N10 2AB* T: (020) 8883 3181 *or* 8444 6898 E: office@alexandrapark.org *or* vicar@alexandrapark.org

PYE, Alexander Frederick. b 61. St Mich Coll Llan 93. **d** 95 **p** 96. C Griffithstown *Mon* 95–97; P-in-c Bistre *St As* 97–99; P-in-c Penmaen and Crumlin *Mon* 99–00; V 00–02; R Govilon w Llanfoist w Llanelen 02–09; V Beguildy and

Heyope and Llangynllo and Bleddfa *S & B* 09–12; V Swansea St Pet 12–17; P-in-c Gowerton from 17. *The Vicarage, 14 Church Street, Gowerton, Swansea SA4 3EA* T: (01792) 927158 E: aok13@btinternet.com

PYE, Canon Allan Stephen. b 56. Univ of Wales (Lamp) BA 78 Lanc Univ MPhil 86. Westcott Ho Cam 79. **d** 81 **p** 82. C Scotforth *Blackb* 81–85; C Oswaldtwistle All SS 85–87; V Wrightington 87–91; P-in-c Hayton St Mary *Carl* 91–93; V Hayton w Cumwhitton 93–98; RD Brampton 95–98; P-in-c Hawkshead and Low Wray w Sawrey 98–03; V Hawkshead and Low Wray w Sawrey and Rusland etc 03–06; V Keswick St Jo 06–15; P-in-c Cross Fell Gp 15–18; V from 18; C Kirkoswald, Renwick w Croglin, Gt Salkeld etc from 18; Hon Can Carl Cathl from 97. *1 Low Farm, Langwathby, Penrith CA10 1NH* T: (01768) 881212 E: stephen.pye@virgin.net

PYE, Mrs Gay Elizabeth. b 46. RN 67 RM 68. Trin Coll Bris BD 73. **d** 96 **p** 96. NSM Castle Church *Lich* 96–00; Asst Chapl HM Pris Stafford 96–97; Chapl HM Pris Shrewsbury 97–00; Regional Manager Bible Soc 00–06; NSM Upper Derwent *Carl* 06–15; rtd 15; PtO *Lich* from 16. *5 Thorneyfields Lane, Stafford ST17 9YS* T: (01768) 777238 M: 07901-837813 E: gay.pye@gmail.com

PYE, James Timothy. b 58. Oak Hill Th Coll BA 90. **d** 90 **p** 91. C Normanton *Derby* 90–94; R Talke *Lich* 94–04; R Knebworth *St Alb* from 04. *The Rectory, 15 St Martin's Road, Knebworth SG3 6ER* T: (01438) 817396 E: revpye@gmail.com

PYE, Joseph Terence Hardwidge. b 41. MRICS 64. Trin Coll Bris 70. **d** 73 **p** 74. C Blackb Ch Ch 73–76; OMF 77–90; Korea 77–90; V Castle Church *Lich* 90–06; rtd 06; PtO *Carl* 07–15; *Lich* from 16. *5 Thorneyfields Lane, Stafford ST17 9YS* T: (01768) 777238 E: terry.pye@gmail.com

PYE, Michael Francis. b 53. New Coll Ox BA 75 MA 78 DPhil 79. STETS 97. **d** 00 **p** 01. C Fareham H Trin *Portsm* 00–07; V Portsea All SS 07–18; rtd 18; PtO *Portsm* from 19. *22 Harvey Crescent, Warsash, Southampton SO31 9TA* E: revmikepye@btinternet.com

PYE, Nicholas Richard. b 62. Univ Coll Lon BA 84 Man Univ PGCE 87 Anglia Poly Univ MA 03. Ridley Hall Cam 95. **d** 98 **p** 99. C Epsom Common Ch Ch *Guildf* 98–01; C Harrow Trin St Mich *Lon* 01–03; V Finchley St Paul and St Luke from 03. *St Paul's Vicarage, 50 Long Lane, London N3 2PU* T: (020) 8346 8729 *or* 8349 3792 E: vicar@stpaulsfinchley.org.uk *or* revpye1@gmail.com

PYE, Robin. b 63. Clare Coll Cam BA 86 Man Univ PGCE 97. All SS Cen for Miss & Min 12. **d** 15 **p** 16. C Hale and Ashley *Ches* 15–17; V Alderley Edge from 17. *The Vicarage, Church Lane, Alderley Edge SK9 7UZ* M: 07794-122602 E: revrobinpye@gmail.com

PYE, Sandra Anne. *See* ELLISON, Sandra Anne

PYE, Stephen. *See* PYE, Allan Stephen

PYKE, Alan. b 37. Trin Coll Bris BA 87. **d** 87 **p** 88. CA 58–87; C Ipswich St Mary at Stoke w St Pet *St E* 87–90; R The Creetings and Earl Stonham w Stonham Parva 90–98; C S Trin Broads 98–02; rtd 03; PtO *Nor* 03–08; *Leic* from 14. *29 Stuart Court, High Street, Kibworth Beauchamp, Leicester LE8 0LR* T: 0116-279 0113 E: alan.pyke@o2.co.uk

PYKE, Canon Barry John. b 62. Qu Mary Coll Lon BSc 83 Southn Univ BTh 94 Open Univ BA 96 FGS 84. Sarum & Wells Th Coll 91. **d** 94 **p** 95. C Bengeworth *Worc* 94–96; C Worc City St Paul and Old St Martin etc 96–99; R Chipping Ongar w Shelley *Chelmsf* 99–06; RD Ongar 04–06; R Hinderwell, Roxby and Staithes etc *York* 06–16; RD Whitby 13–16; Can Res Ripon Cathl *Leeds* from 16; AD Ripon 16–17. *16 Primrose Drive, Ripon HG4 1EY* T: (01765) 603462 *or* 600427 E: canonbarry@riponcathedral.org.uk

PYKE, Canon Richard Ernest. b 50. Sarum & Wells Th Coll. **d** 82 **p** 83. C Bushey *St Alb* 82–85; C Gt Berkhamsted 85–89; V St Alb St Mary Marshalswick 89–00; TR Bp's Hatfield 00–05; TR Bp's Hatfield, Lemsford and N Mymms 05–16; RD Welwyn Hatfield 03–16; Hon Can St Alb 12–16; rtd 16; PtO *St Alb* from 16. *The Rectory, 135 High Street, Barkway, Royston SG8 8ED* T: (01763) 848756 E: richard50pyke@tiscali.co.uk

PYKE, Canon Ruth Cheryl. b 56. Bath Coll of HE BA 78 W Lon Inst of HE PGCE 80. SAOMC 95. **d** 98 **p** 99. C Leavesden *St Alb* 98–02; C St Alb St Steph 02–06; P-in-c Caddington 06–12; Bedfordshire Area Children's Work Adv 06–12; Dioc Children's Work Adv 12–15; R Barkway, Barley, Reed and Buckland from 15; Hon Can St Alb from 18. *The Rectory, 135 High Street, Barkway, Royston SG8 8ED* T: (01763) 848756 M: 07787-112376 E: ruth.pyke@tesco.net

PYKE, Thomas Fortune. b 62. St Chad's Coll Dur BA 85 Fitzw Coll Cam BA 88. Ridley Hall Cam 86. **d** 89 **p** 90. C Hitchin *St Alb* 89–94; Chapl Aston Univ *Birm* 94–99; V Birm St Paul 99–06; Ind Chapl 01–06; Th Ecum Officer Birm Bd for Miss 01–06; V Is of Dogs Ch Ch and St Jo w St Luke *Lon* from 06. *Christ Church Vicarage, Manchester Road,*

London E14 3BN T: (020) 7538 1766 M: 07753-616499 E: tom.pyke@parishiod.org.uk

PYM, David Pitfield. b 45. Nottm Univ BA 65 Ex Coll Ox DPhil 68. Ripon Hall Ox 66. **d** 68 **p** 69. C Nottingham St Mary *S'well* 68–72; Chapl RN 72–76 and 79–84; Chapl Worksop Coll Notts 76–79; R Avon Dassett w Farnborough and Fenny Compton *Cov* 84–07; rtd 07; PtO *Ox* from 07; *Cov* from 08. *Sunrise, Bury Court Lane, Shotteswell, Banbury OX17 1JA* T: (01295) 738948 E: davidpym@lineone.net

PYMBLE, Adam Oliver James. b 79. **d** 11 **p** 12. C Lindfield *Chich* 11–14; C Clerkenwell St Mark *Lon* 14–15; C Hornsey Ch Ch 15–19; V from 19. *157 Park Road, London N8 8JJ* T: (020) 8340 1445 E: adam@christchurchn8.org.uk

PYNE-BAILEY, Mrs Sarian Iyamide Remilekun. b 40. Sierra Leone Th Hall 99. **d** 03 **p** 05. Sierra Leone 06–10; PtO *Chelmsf* from 11. *10 Hibiscus Lodge, 1A Glenavon Road, London E15 4DT* T: (020) 8279 4221 M: 07415-995370 E: iyamidepb@ymail.com

PYNN, Catherine. b 45. Reading Univ BSc 67. SAOMC 93. **d** 96 **p** 97. NSM Caversham St Pet and Mapledurham etc *Ox* 96–03; NSM Aldermaston w Wasing and Brimpton 03–06; NSM Woolhampton w Midgham and Beenham Valance 05–06; Chapl Bradfield Coll Berks 00–06; NSM Kintbury w Avington *Ox* 06–11; NSM W Woodhay w Enborne, Hampstead Marshall etc 06–11; NSM Walbury Beacon 11–13; PtO from 13; *Win* from 13. *27 Silchester Road, Pamber Heath, Tadley RG26 3ED* T: 0118-970 1007 M: 07863-968624 E: cathy.pynn@btinternet.com

PYNN, David Christopher. b 47. Trin Coll Cam MA 70 Cam Inst of Educn CertEd 69. NOC 06. **d** 08 **p** 09. NSM Scalby *York* 08–17; NSM Scarborough St Luke 08–17; RD Scarborough 11–16; NSM Hackness w Harwood Dale 14–17; NSM Ravenscar and Staintondale 14–17; PtO from 17. *6 Stepney Drive, Scarborough YO12 5DH* T: (01723) 369687 M: 07980-922208 E: davidpynn12@aol.com

PYRKE, Adam Lee Julien. b 79. St Mellitus Coll 17. **d** 19. C Roch St Justus from 19. *18 Kings Avenue, Rochester ME1 3DS* M: 07419-901676 E: aljpyrke@hotmail.com

✠**PYTCHES, The Rt Revd George Edward David.** b 31. Bris Univ BA 54 Nottm Univ MPhil 84. Tyndale Hall Bris 51. **d** 55 **p** 56 **c** 70. C Ox St Ebbe 55–58; C Wallington *S'wark* 58–59; Chile 59–77; Suff Bp Valparaiso 70–72; Bp Chile, Bolivia and Peru 72–77; V Chorleywood St Andr *St Alb* 77–96; rtd 96; PtO *St Alb* 96–19. *5 Churleswood Court, Shire Lane, Chorleywood, Rickmansworth WD3 5NH*

PYTCHES, Preb Peter Norman Lambert. b 32. Lon Univ BD 57 Bris Univ MLitt 67 Southn Univ PhD 81 K Coll Lon MA 00 Potchefstroom Univ MTh 03 Open Univ MPhil 06 Lambeth STh 74. Tyndale Hall Bris 53. **d** 57 **p** 58. C Heatherlands St Jo *Sarum* 57–61; C Cromer *Nor* 61–63; V Plymouth St Jude *Ex* 63–71; V Heatherlands St Jo *Sarum* 71–76; Dir Past Tr Oak Hill Th Coll and Registrar Oak Hill NSM Course 76–81; V Finchley Ch Ch *Lon* 81–91; AD Cen Barnet 86–91; V Forty Hill Jes Ch 91–97; Preb St Paul's Cathl 92–97; rtd 97; PtO *Lon* from 98. *25 Weardale Gardens, Enfield EN2 0BA* T/F: (020) 8366 5126 E: peterpytches@gmail.com

Q

QUAK-WINSLOW, Mrs Kimberley. b 82. Huddersfield Univ BSc 09. Trin Coll Bris MA 17. **d** 17 **p** 18. C Sutton, Wincle, Wildboarclough and Bosley *Ches* 17–19; Youth Chapl and Min Can St Alb from 19. *The Abbey, Sumpter Yard, Holywell Hill, St Albans AL1 1BY* T: (01727) 890210 E: chaplain@stalbanscathedral.org

QUANTRILL, Mrs Sarah Ellen. b 67. Newnham Coll Cam BA 90 MA 93 UEA PGCE 92. Westcott Ho Cam 13. **d** 15 **p** 16. C Oulton Broad *Nor* 15–18; P-in-c New Catton St Luke w St Aug from 18. *St Luke's Vicarage, 61 Aylsham Road, Norwich NR3 2HF* E: sarah.quantrill@cantab.net

QUARMBY, David John. b 43. St Jo Coll Dur BA 64 Lon Univ CertEd 70 Man Univ MEd 89 Sheff Univ MA 99. Ridley Hall Cam 65. **d** 67 **p** 68. C Bournville *Birm* 67–71; V Erdington St Chad 71–73; LtO *Blackb* 73–83; PtO *Man* 83–90; C Oldham St Paul 90–98; Hon C 98–14; Hon C Oldham St Paul and Werneth from 14; Cllr Huddersfield Poly 90–92; Huddersfield Univ 92–01; Prin Adult Psychotherapist Hyndburn Community Mental Health Team from 00; Sen Cllr Blackb and Darwen Primary Care Trust 01–08. *6 Windy Bank, Port Sunlight, Wirral CH62 5EA* T: 0161-626 2771 E: david.quarmby@zen.co.uk

QUARTON, Robert Edward. b 43. Wilson Carlile Coll 64 EMMTC 84. **d** 87 **p** 88. C Gresley *Derby* 87–88; C Clay Cross 88–90; C N Wingfield, Clay Cross and Pilsley 90–91; R Darley 91–10; P-in-c S Darley, Elton and Winster 03–10; RD Wirksworth 03–08; rtd 10. *12 Blenheim Avenue, Swanwick, Alfreton DE55 1PQ* T: (01773) 605766 E: robertquarton@uwclub.net

QUASH, Canon Jonathan Ben. b 68. Peterho Cam BA 90 MA 94 PhD 99. Westcott Ho Cam 91. **d** 95 **p** 96. NSM Cambridge St Mary Less *Ely* 95–96; Asst Chapl Peterho Cam 95–96; Chapl Fitzw Coll Cam 96–99; Fell 98–99; Tutor Wesley Ho Cam 96–99; Fell and Dean Peterho Cam 99–07; Prof K Coll Lon from 07; Can Th Cov Cathl from 04; Can Th Bradf Cathl 13–14; *Leeds* from 14. *King's College London, Strand, London WC2R 2LS* T: (020) 7848 2336 F: 7848 2255 E: ben.quash@kcl.ac.uk

QUAYLE, Margaret Grace. b 28. Gipsy Hill Coll of Educn TCert 48 Lon Univ BA 53 Liv Univ MPhil 78. **d** 98 **p** 99. OLM Gt Crosby St Luke *Liv* 98–03; PtO from 03. *Clwyd, 9 Myers Road West, Liverpool L23 0RS* T: 0151-924 1659

QUAYLE, Martin Stuart. b 60. Lon Hosp BDS 82 Birkbeck Coll Lon BA 98 Leeds Univ BA 08 Open Univ MA 11. Coll of Resurr Mirfield 06. **d** 08 **p** 09. C Basingstoke *Win* 08–11; PtO *Heref* 12–14; NSM Diddlebury w Munslow, Holdgate and Tugford 14–17; PtO 17–19; NSM Cleobury Mortimer w Hopton Wafers etc from 19. *3 Stanway Barns, Stanway, Rushbury, Church Stretton SY6 7EF* T: (01584) 841840 M: 07976-664872 E: martinsq@btinternet.com

QUIBELL, Mrs Susan Elizabeth. b 50. **d** 03 **p** 04. OLM Aldridge *Lich* from 03. *20 Summer Lane, Walsall WS4 1DS* T: (01922) 744205 E: s.quibell@googlemail.com

QUICK, John Michael. b 46. N Counties Coll Newc TCert 68 Birkbeck Coll Lon BSc 73 FRGS 70. SAOMC 97. **d** 00 **p** 01. OLM New Windsor *Ox* 00–16; PtO from 16. *White Roses, 45 York Road, Windsor SL4 3PA* T: (01753) 865557 M: 07977-754822 E: littlefrquick@aol.com

QUICK, Roger Aelfred Melvin Tricquet. b 55. Leeds Univ BA 79 BA 96 PGCE 81. Coll of Resurr Mirfield 94. **d** 96 **p** 97. C Chapel Allerton *Ripon* 96–00; C Ireland Wood 00–04; Chapl Strathallan Sch 04–11; R Pitlochry *St And* 11–13; R Kilmaveonaig 11–13; R Kinloch Rannoch 11–13; Chapl St Geo Crypt Leeds from 13. *17 Wensleydale Court, Stainbeck Lane, Leeds LS7 3SA* T: 0113-245 9061 M: 07762-159047 E: father@priest.com

QUIGLEY, Adam. b 80. **d** 03 **p** 04. NSM Castlerock w Dunboe and Fermoyle *D & R* from 03. *41 Queens Park, Coleraine BT51 3JS* T: (028) 7035 5191 E: adam.quigley@hotmail.co.uk

QUIGLEY, Donna Maree. b 40. Ulster Univ BEd BTh. **d** 01 **p** 02. C Portadown St Columba *Arm* 01–03; I Derryvolgie *Conn* 04–09. *284 Tennent Street, Belfast BT13 3GG* E: donna_quigley@yahoo.co.uk

QUIGLEY, John Christopher. b 41. Pontifical Lateran Univ STL 68. **d** 67 **p** 68. P-in-c N Bersted *Chich* 03–08; rtd 08; P-in-c Lyminster *Chich* 11–15; PtO from 16. *West House, 6 Hillview Crescent, East Preston, Littlehampton BN16 1RD* T: (01903) 417501 M: 07792-718875 E: quigs41@sky.com

QUILL, Andrew Thomas Edward. b 67. Heriot-Watt Univ BArch 91. Uganda Chr Univ 05. **d** 05 **p** 07. Dioc Co-ord Community Health Empowerment Uganda 05–06; C Drumragh w Mountfield *D & R* 06–09; I Kinawley w H Trin *K, E & A* 09–16; Dioc Communications Officer 10–16; I Dromore *Clogh* from 16. *The Rectory, 19 Galbally Road, Dromore, Omagh BT78 3EE* T: (028) 8289 8246 M: 07738-960707 E: quills155@btinternet.com

QUILL, John Stephen. b 51. Linc Th Coll 76. **d** 79 **p** 80. C Sawbridgeworth *St Alb* 79–81; C Watford Ch Ch 81–85; Dioc Soc Services Adv *Worc* 85–90; Adv to Bd of Soc Resp 90–95; PtO *St Alb* 07–14; Chapl R Masonic Sch for Girls Rickmansworth from 14; PtO *S & B* from 13. *35 Kingfisher Drive, Hemel Hempstead HP3 9DD* T: (01442) 266369 *or* 266369 *or* 773168 E: johnsquill@btopenworld.com

QUILL, Walter Paterson. b 35. **d** 60 **p** 61. C Glendermott *D & R* 60–63; I Kilbarron 63–66; I Kilcronaghan w Ballynascreen 66–81; I Derg w Termonamongan 81–07; Can Derry Cathl 89–07; Preb Howth St Patr Cathl Dublin 94–07; rtd 07; P-in-c Clondevaddock w Portsalon and Leatbeg *D & R* 09–11. *1 University Gardens, Coleraine BT52 1JT* T: (028) 7035 2114 E: wquill@btinternet.com

QUIN, David Christopher. b 42. SAOMC 97. d 00 p 01. NSM Blunham, Gt Barford, Roxton and Tempsford etc *St Alb* 00–06; rtd 06; PtO *Glouc* from 15. *16 Beceshore Close, Moreton-in-Marsh GL56 9NB* T: (01608) 651571 M: 07867-664924 E: davidcquin@aol.com

QUIN, John James Neil. b 31. Ox Univ MA DipEd 53. Qu Coll Birm 61. d 63 p 64. C Cannock *Lich* 63–68; V Sneyd Green 68–78; V Stafford St Paul Forebridge 78–90; TV Tettenhall Regis 90–98; rtd 98; PtO *Ex* from 00. *Watcombe House, 28 Barnpark Road, Teignmouth TQ14 8PN* T: (01626) 772525

QUINE, Christopher Andrew. b 38. St Aid Birkenhead 61. d 64 p 65. C Hunts Cross *Liv* 64–67; C Farnworth and C-in-c Widnes St Jo 67–71; V Clubmoor 71–78; V Formby H Trin 78–99; V Arbory and Santan *S & M* 99–03; rtd 03; PtO *Liv* from 16. *31 Trinity Lodge, 103 Lonsdale Road, Formby, Liverpool L37 3AA* M: 07963-588332 E: chris.quine@googlemail.com

QUINN, Canon Arthur Hamilton Riddel. b 37. TCD BA 60 MA 64 BD 67. d 61 p 62. C Belfast H Trin *Conn* 61–63; C Belfast St Mary Magd 63–64; Chapl Hull Univ *York* 64–69; Chapl Keele Univ *Lich* 69–74; P-in-c Keele 72–74; V Shirley St Jo *Cant* 74–84; V Shirley St Jo *S'wark* 85–06; RD Croydon Addington 95–04; Hon Can S'wark Cathl 03–06; rtd 06; PtO *S'wark* from 06. *23 Eden Road, Croydon CR0 1BB* T: (020) 8680 3049 E: quinncanon@btinternet.com

QUINN, John James. b 46. TCD BA 70 PhD 76. St Jo Coll Nottm. d 81 p 82. C Gorleston St Andr *Nor* 81–84; R Belton 84–90; R Burgh Castle 84–90; R Belton and Burgh Castle 90–10; rtd 10; PtO *Nor* from 10. *23 Wren Drive, Bradwell, Great Yarmouth NR31 8JW* T: (01493) 718634 E: johnjquinn@lineone.net

QUINN, Naomi Caroline. d 11 p 12. C Derg w Termonamongan *D & R* from 11. *44 Strabane Road, Castlederg BT81 7HZ* T: (028) 8167 1440 E: revnaomi@outlook.com

QUINNELL, Peter Francis. b 48. St Steph Ho Ox 93. d 95 p 96. C Tewkesbury w Walton Cardiff *Glouc* 95–99; R Stratton, N Cerney, Baunton and Bagendon 99–08; AD Cirencester 06–08; R Whitewater *Win* 08–14; rtd 14; Hon C Tetbury, Beverston, Long Newnton etc *Glouc* 14–15; Hon C Avening w Cherington 14–15; TV Stroud Team 15–17; Hon C S Cheltenham from 17. *4 Foxgrove Drive, Cheltenham GL52 6TQ* T: (01242) 227112 M: 07752-341916 E: quinnell708@btinternet.com

QUINT, Mrs Patricia Mary. b 51. Milton Keynes Coll of Ed CertEd 76 Open Univ BA 77 Lon Univ MA 99. St Alb Minl Tr Scheme 90. d 93 p 94. C Hertford St Andr *St Alb* 93–96; C Bromham w Oakley and Stagsden 96–00; V Stotfold and Radwell 00–14; rtd 14; PtO *St E* from 15. *Upper Church Cottage, Church Hill, Walpole, Halesworth IP19 9AX* T: (01986) 784565 E: rev.quint@btinternet.com

QUINTON, Mrs Jane. b 63. Ridley Hall Cam 15. d 17 p 18. C Chipping Ongar w Shelley etc *Chelmsf* from 17. *49 Kettlebury Way, Ongar CM5 9HA* M: 07973-295492 E: janequinton@hotmail.com

QUINTON, Rosemary Ruth. *See* BRABY, Rosemary Ruth

QUIREY, Mrs Edith. b 56. CITC 98. d 01 p 02. Aux Min Belfast St Mich *Conn* 01–05; P-in-c Belfast St Steph w St Luke 05–07; Bp's C 07–09; I 09–15; P-in-c Hodnet *Lich* from 15; P-in-c Moreton Corbet 16–17; P-in-c Shawbury 16–17; P-in-c Stanton on Hine Heath 16–17; C Edstaston, Fauls, Prees, Tilstock and Whixall from 18. *The Rectory, Abbots Way, Hodnet, Market Drayton TF9 3NQ* T: (01630) 685491 E: e.quirey@btinternet.com

QUIST, Ms Frances Buckurel. NTMTC BA 09. d 09 p 10. C E Ham w Upton Park and Forest Gate *Chelmsf* 09–12; P-in-c Matson *Glouc* 12–18. *Address withheld by request* M: 07734-711929 E: francesquist@btinternet.com

R

RAAFF, Trevor Howard. b 74. Cape Town Univ BBS 97. Ridley Hall Cam 10. d 12 p 13. C Biddulph *Lich* 12–16; P-in-c Linby w Papplewick *S'well* from 16. *The Rectory, Main Street, Linby, Nottingham NG15 8AE* T: 0115-963 2346 M: 07847-660618 E: revraaff@gmail.com

RABJOHNS, Alan. b 40. Leeds Univ BA 62. Coll of Resurr Mirfield 62. d 64 p 65. C Ashington *Newc* 64–67; C Upton cum Chalvey *Ox* 67–76; V Roath St Sav *Llan* 76–08; AD Cardiff 03–08; rtd 08. *40 Cwmgelli Close, Treboeth, Swansea SA5 9BY* T: (01792) 561157

RABJOHNS, Benjamin Thomas. b 86. Ex Univ BA 07 Cardiff Univ BA 11. St Mich Coll Llan 08. d 11 p 12. C Aberavon *Llan* 11–14; TV 14–16; P-in-c Penrhiwceiber, Matthewstown and Ynysboeth from 16. *The Vicarage, Winifred Street, Mountain Ash CF45 3YF* T: (01443) 473716 E: b.t.rabjohns@gmail.com

RABY, Malcolm Ernest. b 47. St Jo Coll York BEd 73. NOC 81. d 84 p 85. NSM Chadkirk *Ches* 84–88; Consultant E England CPAS 88–94; C Ely 94–96; TV 96–98; Dioc Adv in Miss and Evang 98–13; P-in-c Over 98–13; P-in-c Long Stanton w St Mich 02–13; rtd 13; Hon C Leatherhead and Mickleham *Guildf* 13–17; PtO 17. *3 Greenbank Court, Sherwood Way, Epsom KT19 8LQ* T: (01372) 729757 E: rm.raby007@btinternet.com

RACE, Alan. b 51. Bradf Univ BTech 73 Birm Univ MA 82. Ripon Coll Cuddesdon 73. d 76 p 77. C Tupsley *Heref* 76–79; Asst Chapl Kent Univ *Cant* 79–84; Dir Studies S'wark Ord Course 84–94; R Aylestone St Andr w St Jas *Leic* 94–07; P-in-c Leic St Phil 07–11; Hon Can Leic Cathl 07–11; R Lee St Marg *S'wark* 11–17; rtd 17. *14 Nelson Street, Market Harborough LE16 9AY* E: alan2race@gmail.com

RACE, Andrew James. b 68. Birm Univ BA 92 MA 93. Ripon Coll Cuddesdon MTh 15. d 15 p 16. C Littleover *Derby* 15–19; V Castle Donington and Lockington cum Hemington *Leic* from 19. *The Vicarage, 6 Delven Lane, Castle Donington, Derby DE74 2LJ* T: (01332) 810364

RACE, Christopher Keith. b 43. St Paul's Coll Grahamstown 76. d 78 p 80. Angl Chapl Stellenbosch Univ S Africa 79–81; R Kalk Bay 81–83; P-in-c E Kalahari, Dioc Admin Botswana and Personal Asst to Abp Cen Africa 83–86; V Tanworth St Patr Salter Street *Birm* 86–96; P-in-c Rothiemurchus *Mor* 96–01; PtO *Glouc* 02–03; P-in-c Kemble, Poole Keynes, Somerford Keynes etc 03–04; R 04–06; Prin Tutor and Lect Cant Ch Ch Univ 06–08; rtd 08. *c/o the Revd S P Race, 22 Elmwood Way, Barnsley S75 1EY* M: 07866-585973 E: ck.race@gmail.com

RACE, Canon Stephen Peter. b 69. SS Hild & Bede Coll Dur BA 93. St Steph Ho Ox MTh 03. d 02 p 03. C Wigton *Carl* 02–05; V Dodworth *Wakef* 05–14; P-in-c Barnsley St Mary *Leeds* 14–18; P-in-c Barnsley St Edw 17–18; P-in-c Gawber 17–18; R Cen Barnsley 18–19; P-in-c Barnsley St Geo 18–19; R Cen Barnsley from 19; Asst Dioc Dir of Ords *Wakef* 05–09; Dir from 09; AD Barnsley *Leeds* from 09; Hon Can Wakef Cathl from 11. *22 Elmwood Way, Barnsley S75 1EY* M: 07549-876505 E: stephen.race@leeds.anglican.org

RACKLYEFT, Emma Joy. b 79. Univ Coll Chich BA 01. Wycliffe Hall Ox BTh 13. d 13 p 14. C Thame *Ox* 13–17; V Denmead *Portsm* from 17. *The Vicarage, Ludcombe, Denmead, Waterlooville PO7 6TL* M: 07837-845420 E: emma@theracklyefts.co.uk

RACTLIFFE, Dudley John. b 38. Man Univ BA 62. Ridley Hall Cam 63. d 66 p 67. C Radford *Cov* 66–68; C Haslemere *Guildf* 69–73; V Perry Beeches *Birm* 73–78; V Worle *B & W* 78–88; Dioc Ecum Officer and R Dowlishwake w Kingstone, Chillington etc 88–93; TR Swanage and Studland *Sarum* 93–01; rtd 01; PtO *B & W* 02–19. *12 Sid Lane, Sidmouth EX10 9AN* T: (01395) 579712

RADCLIFFE, Canon Albert Edward. b 34. Lon Univ BD 63. St Aid Birkenhead Ch Div Sch of the Pacific (USA) 61. d 62 p 63. C Knotty Ash St Jo *Liv* 62–64; C Blundellsands St Nic 64–66; Chapl Haifa St Luke Israel 66–69; V Tonge w Alkrington *Man* 69–77; R Ashton St Mich 77–91; AD Ashton-under-Lyne 87–91; Can Res Man Cathl 91–00; rtd 00; PtO *Man* from 01. *26 St Chad's Road, Withington, Manchester M20 4WH* T: 0161-445 1327 E: albertradcliffe34@gmail.com

RADCLIFFE, David Jeffrey. b 52. Linc Th Coll 77. d 79 p 80. C Poulton-le-Fylde *Blackb* 79–84; V Ingol 84–88; R Lowther and Askham *Carl* 88–96; R Lowther and Askham and Clifton and Brougham 96–06; R Upton-on-Severn, Ripple, Earls Croome etc *Worc* 06–11; P-in-c W Preston *Blackb* 11–15; rtd 15; PtO *Blackb* 16–17. *Flat 2, 10 Lancaster Road, Southport PR8 2LE* M: 07791-922411 E: revjeffradcliffe@hotmail.co.uk

RADCLIFFE, Eileen Rose. b 54. Carl Dioc Tr Inst 92. **d** 95 **p** 96. NSM Gt Salkeld w Lazonby *Carl* 95–96; NSM Dacre 99–02; PtO 02–06; *Worc* 06–08; NSM Upton-on-Severn, Ripple, Earls Croome etc 08–11; PtO *Blackb* from 11. *39 Naze Lane, Freckleton, Preston PR4 1RH* T: (01772) 726157 E: rosieradcliffe@hotmail.com

RADCLIFFE, James Scotson. b 75. Rob Coll Cam MA 98. Oak Hill Th Coll BA 08. **d** 08 **p** 09. C Hove Bp Hannington Memorial Ch *Chich* 08–13; R Lavant 13–15; C Linc St Pet in Eastgate from 15. *45 Blackfriars Road, Lincoln LN2 4WS* M: 07941-248213 E: jamesradcliffe@gmail.com *or* james@stpeterineastgate.org.uk

RADCLIFFE, John Frederick. b 39. **d** 01 **p** 02. OLM Meltham *Wakef* 01–14; *Leeds* from 14. *13 Orchard Close, Meltham, Huddersfield HD9 4EG* T: (01484) 348806 E: johnandenid@yahoo.com

RADCLIFFE, Robert Mark. b 63. St Jo Coll Dur BA 08. Cranmer Hall Dur 05. **d** 08 **p** 09. C Welling *Roch* 08–11; P-in-c Erith St Jo 11–12; V from 12. *St John's Church House, 100 Park Crescent, Erith DA8 3DZ* T: (01322) 332555 E: markradcliffe@msn.com

RADCLIFFE, Mrs Rosemary. b 45. SWMTC 87. **d** 90 **p** 94. NSM Devoran *Truro* 90–93; Dn-in-c N Newton w St Michaelchurch, Thurloxton etc *B & W* 93–94; P-in-c 94–00; Chapl to the Deaf 93–96; P-in-c Whipton *Ex* 00–01; rtd 01; PtO *Truro* from 03. *76 Upland Crescent, Truro TR1 1NE* T: (01872) 273906

RADCLIFFE, Rosie. *See* RADCLIFFE, Eileen Rose

RADFORD, Andrew James. b 67. St Mellitus Coll BA 16. **d** 16 **p** 17. C Much Woolton *Liv* from 16. *25 Linkside Road, Liverpool L25 9NX* M: 07966-033648 E: radfordandy67@gmail.com

RADFORD, Blair William. St Steph Ho *Ox* 15. **d** 18 **p** 19. C Monk Bretton *Leeds* from 18. *24 Kirkland Gardens, Barnsley S71 2GD* M: 07973-478867 E: blair.radford@leeds.anglican.org

RADFORD, Georgina Margaret. b 55. R Free Hosp Sch of Medicine MB, BS 79 FFPH 97 FRCP 02. ERMC 14. **d** 16 **p** 17. NSM Anglesey Gp *Ely* 16–19; TV Buckfastleigh, Dean Prior, Littlehempston etc *Ex* from 19. *The Vicarage, Hillside, South Brent TQ10 9AN* E: gina.radford@btinternet.com

RADFORD, Mrs Janet. b 58. Chelt & Glouc Coll of HE BSc 00 RN 79. Ripon Coll Cuddesdon 11. **d** 14 **p** 15. NSM Harwell w Chilton *Ox* from 14; Chapl Ox Univ Hosps NHS Foundn Trust from 14. *1 The Croft, Marcham, Abingdon OX13 6NF* T: (01865) 391282 M: 07956-448011 E: janradford58@yahoo.com

RADFORD, Vincent Arthur. b 45. Ches Coll of HE CertEd 69. **d** 05 **p** 06. OLM Westhoughton and Wingates *Man* 05–13; OLM Daisy Hill, Westhoughton and Wingates 13–15; rtd 15; PtO *Man* from 16. *64 Molyneux Road, Westhoughton, Bolton BL5 3EU* T: (01942) 790091 E: revrad1@virginmedia.com

RADLEY, Richard Brian. b 68. St Jo Coll Nottm 02. **d** 04 **p** 05. C Utley *Bradf* 04–08; P-in-c Doncaster St Mary *Sheff* 09–10; P-in-c Wheatley Park 09–10; V Doncaster St Mary and St Paul 10–15; TV Billingham *Dur* from 15. *68 Wolviston Road, Billingham TS22 5ET* E: revrichardr@gmail.com

RADMALL, Andre. **d** 07 **p** 08. NSM Woodside Park St Barn *Lon* 07–17; PtO 17–18; *St Alb* 17–18; NSM St Alb St Paul from 18. *11 Kenerne Drive, Barnet EN5 2NW* T: (020) 8440 2138 E: andreradwriter@gmail.com

RAE, Stephen Gordon. b 65. AGSM 87. Oak Hill Th Coll BA 09. **d** 09 **p** 10. C Danehill *Chich* 09–13; V Westgate St Jas *Cant* from 13. *The Vicarage, Orchard Gardens, Margate CT9 5JT* T: (01843) 446832 E: stephenrae@stjameswestgate.church

RAE SMITH, Tristram Geoffrey. b 57. Clare Coll Cam BA 79 MA 83 St Jo Coll Dur BA 04. Cranmer Hall Dur 02. **d** 04 **p** 05. C Bradford-on-Avon Ch Ch *Sarum* 04–08; C Westwood and Wingfield 04–08; R Camelot Par *B & W* from 08; C Bruton and Distr 08–12. *The Rectory, 6 The Close, North Cadbury, Yeovil BA22 7DX* T: (01963) 440585 M: 07751-306272 E: tristrangthesmith@gmail.com

RAFFAY, Marie Josephine. b 63. Nottm Univ MA 85. All SS Cen for Miss & Min 16. **d** 18 **p** 19. C Mossley Hill *Liv* from 18. *1 Greenhill Road, Mossley Hill, Liverpool L18 6JJ* M: 07853-796270 E: marie.allhallows@outlook.com

RAGAN, Mrs Jennifer Mary. b 39. Linc Th Coll 71. **dss** 80 **d** 87 **p** 94. Hackney *Lon* 80–84; Hornchurch St Andr *Chelmsf* 84–88; Par Dn 87–88; Par Dn Ingrave St Steph CD 88–90; Par Dn Gt Parndon 90–94; C 94–99; TV 99–07; rtd 07; PtO *Chelmsf* 07–13; *St E* from 07. *18 Holme Oaks Court, 50 Cliff Lane, Ipswich IP3 0PE* T: (01473) 213577 E: revjenniferragan@btinternet.com

RAGGETT, Anita Jane. b 56. NOC. **d** 07 **p** 08. C Gomersal *Wakef* 07–10; C Cleckheaton St Jo 08–10; P-in-c Lepton 10–14; *Leeds* 14–16; Chapl Huddersfield Univ 10–16; P-in-c Walton

Ches from 16. *13 Hillfoot Crescent, Stockton Heath, Warrington WA4 6SB* T: (01925) 262939 E: anitaraggett138@gmail.com

RAIKES, Miss Gwynneth Marian Napier. b 51. Somerville Coll Ox MA 72 Lon Univ BD 81. Trin Coll Bris 79. **dss** 81 **d** 98 **p** 98. Asst Chapl Bris Poly 81–86; Beckenham Ch Ch *Roch* 86–00; C 98–00; Dean of Women and Oak Hill Th Coll 00–13; 14; PtO *Lon* 03–13; *Ely* from 07. *28 Pilgrims Way, Ely CB6 3DL* E: gmnrpilgrim@gmail.com

RAIKES, Canon Peter. b 37. St Mich Coll Llan 78. **d** 80 **p** 81. C Roath *Llan* 80–82; V Resolven 82–86; V Resolven w Tonna 86–92; RD Neath 89–01; V Skewen 92–02; Can Llan Cathl 97–02; rtd 02; PtO *Llan* 04–18. *2 Kennedy Drive, Pencoed, Bridgend CF35 6TW* T: (01656) 862317

RAIKES, Robert Laybourne. b 32. Wells Th Coll 59. **d** 61 **p** 62. C Poplar All SS w St Frideswide *Lon* 61–66; C Grendon Underwood w Edgcott *Ox* 66–68; C Swan 68–71; V Whitchurch Canonicorum w Wootton Fitzpaine etc *Sarum* 71–81; P-in-c Bransome St Aldhelm 81–82; V 82–91; V Pitminster w Corfe *B & W* 91–92; rtd 92; Chapl Madeira *Eur* 93–95; PtO *Glouc* 95–98; Hon C Broadwell, Evenlode, Oddington, Adlestrop etc 98–01; LtO *Eur* 02–19; PtO *Chelmsf* 09–13; S'wark 10–19. *The College of St Barnabas, Blackberry Lane, Lingfield RH7 6NJ* T: (01342) 872826

RAILTON, David James. b 66. Bradf Univ BPharm 89. EMMTC 06. **d** 08 **p** 09. C Melbourne, Ticknall, Smisby and Stanton *Derby* 08–11; V Hazelwood, Holbrook and Milford 11–15; Bp's Asst Chapl 11–15; V Blackwell All SS and Salutation *Dur* 15–19; AD Darlington 17–19; R Dunoon *Arg* from 19; R Rothesay from 19. *The Rectory, Kilbride Road, Dunoon PA23 7LN* T: (01369) 702444 E: davidrailton@gmail.com *or* dunoonrector@gmail.com

RAILTON, John Robert Henry. b 45. Reading Univ BSc 68 PhD 82 FCIB 79. S Dios Minl Tr Scheme 82. **d** 85 **p** 86. NSM Wickham *Portsm* 85–89; C Bridgemary 89–90; V 90–96; TR Ridgeway *Sarum* 96–02; TR Whitton 02–08; rtd 08; P-in-c Purton *Bris* 11–12; PtO 13–18 and from 19; *Ox* 16–19; *Sarum* from 16. *20 Baileys Way, Wroughton, Swindon SN4 9AH* T: (01793) 814162 E: john.railton@btinternet.com

RAILTON, Malcolm. b 60. Lindisfarne Regional Tr Partnership 17. **d** 19. NSM Tynemouth Priory *Newc* from 19. *St Peter's Old Rectory, North Terrace, Wallsend NE28 6PY* M: 07880-945095 E: railtontownfield@btinternet.com

RAILTON, Ray. b 44. ERMC 13. **d** 15 **p** 16. NSM Wellingborough St Barn *Pet* 15–18; NSM Wellingborough St Andr and St Barn from 18. *Saltbox Cottage, 10 Buckwell End, Wellingborough NN8 4LR* M: 07502-510545 E: ray.railton@btinternet.com

RAILTON, Sandra. b 46. S Dios Minl Tr Scheme 82. **dss** 85 **d** 87 **p** 94. Catherington and Clanfield *Portsm* 85–86; Lee-on-the-Solent 86–89; C 87–89; Par Dn Burnham w Dropmore, Hitcham and Taplow *Ox* 89–94; TV Wallingford w Crowmarsh Gifford etc 94–98; TV Wallingford 98; Dioc Dir Ords (OLM) *Berks* 96–99; TV Ridgeway *Sarum* 98–02; Dioc Voc Adv 99–02; TV Whitton 02–08; RD Marlborough 04–08; rtd 08; PtO *Bris* from 10; *Ox* from 16; *Sarum* from 16. *20 Baileys Way, Wroughton, Swindon SN4 9AH* T: (01793) 814162 E: sandyrailton@btinternet.com

RAILTON-CROWDER, Mrs Mary. b 51. Luton Univ BA 96 RN 72 RM 91 MIOSH 93. SAOMC 98. **d** 01 **p** 02. NSM Elstow *St Alb* 01–04; Chapl De Montfort Univ 02–04; C Douglas All SS and St Thos *S & M* 04–07; P-in-c Birchencliffe *Wakef* 07–08; V Birkby and Birchencliffe 08–14; *Leeds* 14–16; AD Huddersfield 10–15; rtd 16; PtO *Ches* from 16. *Thorn Villa, 36 Newton Park Road, Wirral CH48 9XF* T: 0151-384 2482 E: revmrc@yahoo.com

RAINBIRD, Ms Ruth Patricia. b 40. SRN 62. **d** 01 **p** 02. OLM Limpsfield and Titsey *S'wark* 01–10; PtO from 10. *73 Stoneleigh Road, Oxted RH8 0TP* T: (01883) 713683 E: ruthrainbird@btinternet.com

RAINE, Alan. b 49. NEOC 92. **d** 95 **p** 96. NSM Jarrow *Dur* 95–05; Chapl S Tyneside Coll 95–05; V Leam Lane *Dur* from 05. *St Andrew's Vicarage, Whinbrooke, Gateshead NE10 8HR* T: 0191-489 3042 E: alanraine@virginmedia.com

RAINE, David. b 58. Dur Univ MBA 96 Open Univ BSc 96 MCIM 99 MCIPD 03. NEOC 01. **d** 04 **p** 05. NSM N Wearside *Dur* 04–06; NSM Millfield St Mary 06–17; NSM Bishopwearmouth Gd Shep 06–17; V Grangetown from 17. *St Aidan's Vicarage, Ryhope Road, Sunderland SR2 9RS* E: davidraine@dunelm.org.uk *or* farvad@sky.com

RAINE, Stephen James. b 49. Sheff Poly BA 80. NOC 85. **d** 86 **p** 87. C Cottingham *York* 86–90; V Dunscroft Ch Ch *Sheff* 90–92; V Dunscroft St Edwin 92–96; V Kettering St Mary *Pet* 96–08; P-in-c Ipswich St Mary at the Elms *St E* 08–14; Chapl Ipswich Hosp NHS Trust 08–14; rtd 14. *20 rue du Château, 16190 Montmoreau-St-Cybard, France* T: (0033) 5 45 61 74 43 E: evangelist24@hotmail.com

RAINER, John Charles. b 54. Ex Univ BA 76 CertEd 78 Hull Univ MBA 02. St Jo Coll Nottm 86. **d** 88 **p** 89. C Fletchamstead *Cov* 88–94; V Leic H Apostles 94–03; V Shipley St Pet *Bradf* 03–14; *Leeds* from 14. *The Vicarage, 2 Glenhurst Road, Shipley BD18 4DZ* T: (01274) 584488 *or* 400381 E: john.rainer@leeds.anglican.org *or* johnrainer@btinternet.com

RAINES, Mrs Gisela Rolanda. b 58. Groningen Univ Kandidaats 80. K Coll Lon BD 83. **dss** 84 **d** 87 **p** 94. Charlton St Luke w H Trin *S'wark* 84–87; Par Dn 87; Chapl Imp Coll *Lon* 87–91; Hon C Birch w Fallowfield *Man* 94–95; P-in-c Withington St Chris 95–03; C Man St Ann 03–10; R Withington St Paul 10–18; rtd 18; PtO *Blackb* from 18. *15 Powis Road, Ashton-on-Ribble, Preston PR2 1AD* E: revgisela@btinternet.com

RAINES, William Guy. b 46. Lon Univ BSc 69 MSc 70 Ox Univ BA 80. Ripon Coll Cuddesdon 78. **d** 81 **p** 82. C W Drayton *Lon* 81–84; C Charlton St Luke w H Trin *S'wark* 84–87; Chapl K Coll Lon 87–94; Chapl Imp Coll 91–94; P-in-c Birch w Fallowfield *Man* 94–95; R 95–12; rtd 12; PtO *Man* from 13; *Blackb* from 18. *15 Powis Road, Ashton-on-Ribble, Preston PR2 1AD* M: 07908-758804 E: wraines@btinternet.com

RAINFORD, Robert Graham. b 55. Lanc Univ CertEd 76 BEd 77. St Steph Ho Ox 81. **d** 83 **p** 84. C Burnley St Cath w St Alb and St Paul *Blackb* 83–86; C-in-c Hawes Side St Chris CD 86–89; V Hawes Side 89–03; P-in-c Marton Moss 01–03; AD Blackpool 00–03; Hon Can Blackb Cathl 00–03; Sen Chapl to Bp Dover *Cant* 03–05; P Admin Upper Chelsea H Trin *Lon* 05–08; PtO 08–11; Hon C Upper Chelsea H Trin and St Sav 11–15; PtO from 15; Hd RS Sussex Ho Sch from 15. *Sussex House School, 68 Cadogan Square, London SW1X 0EA* E: gr@sussexhouseschool.co.uk

RAINSFORD, Peter John. b 31. FCP 72. Qu Coll Birm 75. **d** 77 **p** 78. Hon C Lich St Chad 77–81; C 82; C Coseley Ch Ch 82–84; V Wednesbury St Bart 84–91; Chapl Sandwell Distr Gen Hosp 89–91; rtd 91; PtO *Lich* 91–18. *34 Pegasus Court, 155 Chester Road, Streetly, Sutton Coldfield B74 3NW* E: ppr157@hotmail.co.uk

RAISTRICK, Brian. b 38. St Paul's Coll Chelt TCert 60 Ex Univ AdDipEd 68 Newc Univ MEd 76 UEA PhD 86. Westcott Ho Cam 92. **d** 93 **p** 94. C Haverhill w Withersfield, the Wrattings etc *St E* 93–95; P-in-c Horringer cum Ickworth 95–02; P-in-c Risby w Gt and Lt Saxham and Westley 99–02; P-in-c Chevington w Hargrave and Whepstead w Brockley 00–02; R Horringer 02; RD Thingoe 99–01; rtd 03; PtO *St E* from 03. *Greenways, Westwood, Great Barton, Bury St Edmunds IP31 2SF* T: (01284) 787372 *or* 747372 E: braistrick@btinternet.com

RAISTRICK, Mrs Tracey Ann. b 65. Coll of Resurr Mirfield 13. **d** 15 **p** 16. C Utley *Leeds* 15–16; C Keighley from 16; P-in-c Ingrow w Hainworth from 19. *St John's Vicarage, Oakfield Road, Keighley BD21 1BT* M: 07850-940079 E: rev.tracey@outlook.com

RAISTRICK, Tulo Dirk. b 69. Jes Coll Ox BA 91. SEITE 08. **d** 11 **p** 12. C Telford Park *S'wark* 11–14; V Earlsdon *Cov* from 14. *St Barbara's Vicarage, 24 Rochester Road, Coventry CV5 6AG* T: (024) 7501 7889 M: 07552-948068 E: tulo@raistricks.com

RAITT, Derek. b 41. K Coll Lon BD 63 AKC 63. **d** 64 **p** 65. C Blackb St Jas 64–67; C Burnley St Pet 67–69; V Foulridge 69–74; V Euxton 74–91; V Penwortham St Mary 91–00; P-in-c Halton w Aughton 00–06; rtd 06; PtO *Blackb* from 06. *84 Lymm Avenue, Lancaster LA1 5HR* E: draitt@wightcablenorth.net

RAITT, Hannah Elizabeth. b 92. Homerton Coll Cam BA 13 MA 17 St Jo Coll Dur BA 17 MA 18. Cranmer Hall Dur 15. **d** 18 **p** 19. C Bankfoot and Bowling St Steph *Leeds* from 18. *1 Arnside Road, Bradford BD5 8DP* E: hannah.e.raitt@gmail.com

RAJ-SINGH, Reji. b 52. Sidney Webb Coll of Educn CertEd 79 N Lon Poly BEd 90 Heythrop Coll Lon MA 02. SAOMC 02. **d** 05 **p** 06. NSM Paddington St Jas *Lon* 05–11; NSM Paddington St Mary Magd and St Pet 11–17; rtd 17; PtO *Lon* from 17; *Sarum* from 18. *29 Peverell Avenue East, Poundbury, Dorchester DT1 3RH* M: 07983-430050 E: reji4@btinternet.com

RAJA, Canon John Christopher Joshva. b 65. Serampore Coll MTh 93 Leic Univ MA 96. **d** 93 **p** 94. India 93–95; Hon C Leic H Spirit 95–96; Hon C Edin H Cross 96–99; Tutor Qu Foundn Birm 00–12; R Curdworth, Middleton and Wishaw *Birm* 12–18; Hon Can Birm Cathl 18; Academic Co-ord Barnabas Fund from 18; NSM Wellsprings *Sarum* from 18. *The Vicarage, High Street, Seend, Melksham SN12 6NR* E: joshvajohn@yahoo.co.uk

RAJKOVIC, Michael. b 52. Sheff Univ BMet 74 MMet 75 PhD 79 St Jo Coll Nottm MA 95 Lon Bible Coll MPhil 03. Cranmer Hall Dur 93. **d** 95 **p** 96. C Harrow Weald All SS *Lon* 95–98; C Woodford Wells *Chelmsf* 98–02; V Bricket Wood *St Alb* 02–15; TR Maltby *Sheff* from 15; P-in-c Thurcroft from 15; P-in-c Laughton-en-le-Morthen and Throapham from 18. *The Rectory, 69 Blyth Road, Maltby, Rotherham S66 7LF* T: (01709) 814914 E: mikerajkovic@btinternet.com

RAKE, David John. b 47. Nottm Univ BA 68 PhD 73. Wycliffe Hall Ox 73. **d** 74 **p** 75. C Radcliffe-on-Trent *S'well* 74–77; P-in-c Upwell St Pet *Ely* 77–79; P-in-c Outwell 77–79; Chapl Warw Univ *Cov* 79–86; V Kenilworth St Nic 86–98; P-in-c Tintagel *Truro* 98–08; Bp's Adv on Spiritual Formation 98–03; Dioc Adv 03–08; rtd 08; PtO *Truro* from 09. *The Old Vicarage, Zennor, St Ives TR26 3BY* T: (01736) 796955

RALPH, Brian Charles. b 66. St Steph Ho Ox 89. **d** 92 **p** 93. C Yeovil St Mich *B & W* 92–95; TV St Jo on Bethnal Green *Lon* 95–01; P-in-c Bethnal Green St Barn 01–03; V from 03. *12 Chisenhale Road, London E3 5TG* T: (020) 7247 1448 *or* 8983 3426 *or* 8806 4130 E: brianralph@btinternet.com *or* frbrianralph@gmail.com

RALPH, Ms Caroline Susan. b 60. Birm Univ BA 81 UWE LLM 98. Westcott Ho Cam 04. **d** 06 **p** 07. C Crediton, Shobrooke and Sandford etc *Ex* 06–10; V Harborne St Pet *Birm* 10–13; R Dunster, Carhampton, Withycombe w Rodhuish etc *B & W* from 13; RD Exmoor from 17. *The Rectory, Church Lane, Carhampton, Minehead TA24 6NT* E: caroline@249ralph.eclipse.co.uk

RALPH, Canon Nicholas Robert. b 63. Lanc Univ BSc 85 Trin Coll Cam BA 91. Westcott Ho Cam 89. **d** 92 **p** 93. C Fareham H Trin *Portsm* 92–95; C Portsea St Cuth 95–96; V Hayling Is St Andr 96–03; V N Hayling St Pet 96–03; Soc Resp Adv 03–06; Hd Miss and Soc from 06; Hon Can Portsm Cathl 06–09; Can Res Portsm Cathl from 09. *101 St Thomas's Street, Portsmouth PO1 2HE* T: (023) 9289 9674 E: nick@ralphy.org *or* nick.ralph@portsmouth.anglican.org

RALPH, Richard Gale. b 51. Pemb Coll Ox BA 73 MA 78 DPhil 78 FRSA 90. S Dios Minl Tr Scheme 84. **d** 87 **p** 88. NSM St Leonards Ch Ch and St Mary etc *Chich* from 87; NSM St Pancras H Cross w St Jude and St Pet *Lon* 87–94; Prin Westmr Coll Ox 96–00. *St Alban, 11 The Mount, St Leonards-on-Sea TN38 0HR* T: (01424) 422722 E: rgale@nildram.co.uk

RALPHS, Sharon Ann. *See* SIMPSON, Sharon Ann

RAMPTON, Paul Michael. b 47. St Jo Coll Dur BA 69 MA 73 K Coll Lon PhD 85 Westmr Coll Ox MTh 99. Wycliffe Hall Ox 72. **d** 73 **p** 74. C Folkestone H Trin w Ch Ch *Cant* 73–77; P-in-c Ringwould w Oxney 77–79; P-in-c Kingsdown 77–79; R Ringwould w Kingsdown 79–83; V Maidstone St Paul 83–88; V Maidstone St Martin 88–95; V Steyning *Chich* 95–12; R Ashurst 95–12; RD Storrington 99–03; rtd 12; Dioc Warden of Readers *Chich* from 12. *54 Greenacres, Shoreham-by-Sea BN43 5WY* T: (01273) 271488

RAMPTON, Canon Valerie Edith. b 41. Nottm Univ BSc 63 MSc 66 BA 79. Gilmore Course 78. **dss** 82 **d** 87 **p** 94. Sneinton St Chris w St Phil *S'well* 80–87; Par Dn 87–88; Par Dn Stapleford 88–93; Dioc Adv on Women in Min 90–01; Dn-in-c Kneesall w Laxton and Wellow 93–94; V 94–02; Hon Can S'well Minster 97–02; rtd 02; PtO *Linc* from 02; *S'well* from 02. *Tansy Cottage, Hillside, Beckingham, Lincoln LN5 0RQ* T: (01636) 626665 E: valerie.rampton@waitrose.com

RAMSARAN, Susan Mira. b 49. K Coll Lon BA 70 Univ Coll Lon MA 72 PhD 78. Ripon Coll Cuddesdon BA 92. **d** 93 **p** 94. C Selling w Throwley, Sheldwich w Badlesmere etc *Cant* 93–97; P-in-c Shipbourne *Roch* 97–99; P-in-c Plaxtol 97–99; R Shipbourne w Plaxtol 99–06; R Shoreham 01–06; TR N Tyne and Redesdale *Newc* from 06; AD Bellingham 06–16. *The Rectory, Bellingham, Hexham NE48 2JS* T: (01434) 220019 E: smramsaran@aol.com

RAMSAY, Canon Alan Burnett. b 34. AKC 62. **d** 63 **p** 64. C Clapham H Trin *S'wark* 63–67; C Warlingham w Chelsham and Farleigh 67–71; P-in-c Stockwell St Mich 71–78; V Lingfield 78–85; P-in-c Crowhurst 83–85; V Lingfield and Crowhurst 85–92; RD Godstone 88–92; V Mitcham St Mark 92–00; Hon Can S'wark Cathl 93–00; rtd 00; PtO *Cant* from 00; *S & B* from 10. *Kent House, 9 Scotton Street, Wye, Ashford TN25 5BU* T: (01233) 813730 E: aramsay@talktalk.net

RAMSAY, Preb Carl Anthoney St Aubyn. b 55. WMMTC 88. **d** 90 **p** 91. C Wednesfield Heath *Lich* 90–94; V Willenhall St Anne 94–03; V Pelsall from 03; RD Walsall from 15; Preb Lich Cathl from 04. *The Vicarage, 39 Hall Lane, Pelsall, Walsall WS3 4JN* T: (01922) 682098 E: spreeboy@talk21.com

RAMSAY, Christopher. b 68. St Jo Coll Dur BA 90. Wycliffe Hall Ox BTh 94. **d** 97 **p** 98. C Cricklewood St Gabr and St Mich *Lon* 97–01; P-in-c Southall St Geo 01–06; V from 06; AD Ealing 10–15. *1 Lancaster Road, Southall UB1 1NP* T: (020) 8574 1876 E: christopher.ramsay@btinternet.com

RAMSAY, James Anthony. b 52. Wadh Coll Ox BA 75 MA. **d** 86 **p** 87. C Olney w Emberton *Ox* 86–89; V Blackbird Leys 89–02; Chapl Bucharest w Sofia *Eur* 02–05; P-in-c Lt Ilford

St Barn *Chelmsf* 05–10; V 10–17; Chapl E Lon Univ 05–17; rtd 17; PtO *Nor* from 17. *Lawn Cottage, Edgefield Road, Briston, Melton Constable NR24 2HX* T: (01263) 502309 M: 07985-993191 E: ramsay.jas@gmail.com

RAMSAY, Kerry. *See* TUCKER, Kerry

RAMSAY, Max Roy MacGregor. b 34. Ball Coll Ox MA 58. Qu Coll Birm 82. d 84 p 85. C Hale *Ches* 84–86; C Nantwich 87; V Haslington w Crewe Green 87–91; P-in-c Dunham Massey St Marg and St Mark 92–95; rtd 95; PtO *Ches* 95–14. *6 Comber Way, Knutsford WA16 9BT* T: (01565) 632362 E: mrm.ramsay@ntlworld.com *or* maxtmramsay@gmail.com

RAMSBOTTOM, David James. b 48. d 12 p 13. NSM Crowthorne *Ox* 12–18; PtO from 18. *The Rectory, The Village, Finchampstead, Wokingham RG40 4JX* T: 0118-973 6374 M: 07986-852970 E: d.j.ramsbottom@btinternet.com

RAMSBOTTOM, Canon Julie Frances. b 54. Trevelyan Coll Dur BA 76. S'wark Ord Course 88. d 91 p 94. Par Dn Bray and Braywood *Ox* 91–94; C 94–97; R W Woodhay w Enborne, Hampstead Marshall etc 97–11; P-in-c Kintbury w Avington 05–11; R Finchampstead and California from 11; AD Sonning 13–18; Hon Can Ch Ch from 16. *The Rectory, The Village, Finchampstead, Wokingham RG40 4JX* T: 0118-973 6374 E: julie.ramsbottom@talk21.com

RAMSBOTTOM, Susan Elizabeth. *See* POLLARD, Susan Elizabeth

RAMSBURY, Area Bishop of. *See* RUMSEY, The Rt Revd Andrew Paul

✠**RAMSDEN, The Rt Revd Peter Stockton.** b 51. Univ Coll Lon BSc 74 Leeds Univ MA 92. Coll of Resurr Mirfield 74. d 77 p 78 c 07. C Houghton le Spring *Dur* 77–80; C S Shields All SS 80–83; Papua New Guinea 83–90 and 93–96; P-in-c Micklefield *York* 90–93; V Long Benton *Newc* 96–07; Bp Port Moresby 07–14; rtd 14; Hon Asst Bp Carl from 15. *Brampton Fell Cottage, Tarn Road, Brampton CA8 1HN* T: (016977) 41851 E: bishopramsden@gmail.com

RAMSDEN, Raymond Leslie. b 49. Open Univ BA 86. d 78 p 79. C Greenhill St Jo *Lon* 78–85; C Staines St Mary and St Pet 85–90; V Hounslow St Steph 90–19; rtd 19; PtO *St E* from 19. *58 Castle Brooks, Framlingham, Woodbridge IP13 9SF*

RAMSEY, Christopher John. b 76. St Jo Coll Nottm BA 07. d 07 p 08. C Saxmundham w Kelsale cum Carlton *St E* 07–10; V Gt Cornard from 10. *The Vicarage, 95 Bures Road, Great Cornard, Sudbury CO10 0JE* T: (01787) 376293 E: revchrisramsey@gmail.com

RAMSEY, Victoria Claire. b 71. d 11 p 12. C Ex St Mark, St Sidwell and St Matt 11–18. *Address temp unknown* E: toria@ramseys.org.uk

RAMSEY-HARDY, Stuart John Andrew. b 46. St Jo Coll Dur BA 69. Wycliffe Hall Ox 69. d 74 p 75. C Stoke Newington St Mary *Lon* 74–77; C Hersham *Guildf* 78–79; Hon C Thames Ditton 79–83; rtd 11. *Villa Tristana, 83040 Guardia dei Lombardi AV, Italy* T: (0039) (389) 486 2681 E: ramsey.hardy@gmail.com

RANCE, Mrs Eleanor Jane. b 72. K Coll Lon BA 93 AKC 93 St Jo Coll Dur MA 96. Cranmer Hall Dur 94. d 96 p 97. C Barnes *S'wark* 96–99; Chapl RAF 99–10; PtO *Blackb* 10–13; P-in-c Wylye and Till Valley *Sarum* 13; V Salisbury Plain from 14; RD Stonehenge from 15. *The Rectory, Chapel Lane, Shrewton, Salisbury SP3 4BX* T: (01980) 620580 E: reveleanorrance@gmail.com

RAND, Stacey Elizabeth. b 82. Qu Coll Cam BA 04 MA 08. SEITE 13. d 16 p 17. NSM Hackington *Cant* 16–19; NSM Herne from 19; NSM Kent Univ from 19. *Address withheld by request* E: staceyelizabethrand@hotmail.com

RANDALL, Benjamin Thomas. b 84. St Andr Univ MA 06 Bradf Univ MA 08. Ridley Hall Cam 11. d 14 p 15. C Pudsey St Lawr and St Paul *Leeds* 14–17; V McMinnville St Matt USA from 17. *105 Edgewood Avenue, McMinnville TN 37110, USA* T: (001) (931) 473 8233 E: benjamin.t.randall@hotmail.com

RANDALL, Bernard Charles. b 72. St Andr Univ MA 95 Edin Univ MSc 97 Man Univ PhD 00. St Steph Ho Ox BA 06. d 06 p 07. C Bury St Mary *Man* 06–07; C Atherton and Hindsford w Howe Bridge 07–09; C Sale St Paul *Ches* 09–11; Chapl Ch Coll Cam 11–15; Chapl Trent Coll Nottm from 15. *Trent College, Derby Road, Long Eaton, Nottingham NG10 4AD* T: 0115-849 4949 E: bernard.randall@hotmail.co.uk

RANDALL, Colin Antony. b 57. St Jo Coll Nottm 78. d 80 p 81. C Denton Holme *Carl* 84–87; C Brampton RD 87–90; R Hanborough and Freeland *Ox* 90–99; P-in-c Croglin *Carl* 99–09; P-in-c Holme Eden 99–05; P-in-c Wetheral w Warwick 99–05; R Holme Eden and Wetheral w Warwick 05–09; RD Brampton 05–09; Hon Can Carl Cathl 08–09; P-in-c Barrow *Ches* 09–10; R 10–14; Dioc Worship Adv 09–14; P-in-c Sevenhampton w Charlton Abbots, Hawling etc *Glouc* 14–16; R from 16. *The Rectory, Station Road, Andoversford, Cheltenham GL54 4LA* T: (01242) 820631 E: colinrandall@mac.com

RANDALL, Preb Colin Michael Sebastian. b 50. Aston Univ BSc 72. Qu Coll Birm 72. d 75 p 76. C Tonge w Alkrington *Man* 75–78; C Elton All SS 78–82; P-in-c Bridgwater H Trin *B & W* 82–86; V 86–90; V Bishops Hull 90–00; TR Wellington and Distr 00–12; Preb Wells Cathl 05–12; rtd 12. *16 The Rosemullion, Cliff Road, Budleigh Salterton EX9 6LA* E: colin.randall@outlook.com

RANDALL, Elizabeth Nicola. *See* BILLETT, Elizabeth Nicola

RANDALL, Evelyn. b 49. d 10 p 11. NSM Dormansland S'wark 10–15; NSM Lingfield and Dormansland 15–16; NSM Godstone and Blindley Heath 16–17; PtO from 17. *58 Hickmans Close, Godstone RH9 8EB* T: (01883) 742751

RANDALL, Gordon Charles. b 58. STETS BA 11. d 11 p 12. NSM Chineham *Win* 11–19; C Alton from 19. *The Vicarage, 7 Church Lane, Holybourne, Alton GU34 4HD* M: 07913-742208

RANDALL, Ian Neville. b 39. Oriel Coll Ox BA 62 MA 65. St Steph Ho Ox 62. d 65 p 66. C Perivale *Lon* 65–68; C Fulham St Jo Walham Green 68–73; C Cowley St Jas *Ox* 73–79; TV 79–82; V Didcot St Pet 82–93; P-in-c Clewer St Andr 93–04; rtd 04. *12 Westmead Road, Fakenham NR21 8BL* T: (01328) 862443 E: iandfrandall@tiscali.co.uk

RANDALL, Canon John Terence. b 29. St Cath Coll Cam BA 52 MA 59. Ely Th Coll 52. d 54 p 55. C Luton Ch St Alb 54; C Dunstable 54–57; C Ely 57–60; C March St Jo 60–62; Area Sec (S Midl) UMCA 62–64; Area Sec USPG Birm and Cov 65–76; P-in-c Avon Dassett w Farnborough *Cov* 76–78; P-in-c Fenny Compton 76–78; R Avon Dassett w Farnborough and Fenny Compton 78–84; V New Bilton 84–94; RD Rugby 89–94; Hon Can Cov Cathl 93–94; rtd 94; PtO *Cov* from 94; *Pet* from 94; *Leic* from 96. *52 Cymbeline Way, Rugby CV22 6LA* T: (01788) 816659 E: fatherjohnrandall@gmail.com

RANDALL, Jonathan Aubrey. b 64. Bris Univ BSc 85. Ridley Hall Cam 04. d 06 p 07. C Hemingford Abbots and Hemingford Grey *Ely* 06–09; V Yaxley and Holme w Conington 09–18; P-in-c Farcet Hampton 09–12; Jt RD Yaxley 16–18; C Huntingdon St Barn and the Riptons 18–19; C Huntingdon All SS w St Jo St Mary etc 18–19; R Huntingdon from 19. *St Barnabas' Vicarage, Coneygear Road, Huntingdon PE29 1RQ* E: huntingdon.vicar@gmail.com

RANDALL, Julian Adrian. b 45. Open Univ BA 78 Stirling Univ MSc 94 St Andr Univ PhD 01 MCIPD. St Jo Sem Wonersh 68. d 70 p 71. Asst P Mortlake w E Sheen *S'wark* 71–72; Asst P Welling 72–74; Asst P Tunbridge Wells H Trin w Ch Ch *Roch* 74–79; NSM Dunfermline *St And* 96–98; P-in-c Elie and Earlsferry 98–03; P-in-c Pittenweem 98–03; Asst P St Andrews *St And* 03–05; Dir Progr Business Sch St Andr Univ 03–10; Sen Lect Aber Univ *Ab* from 05. *Flat D, 10 Shearwater Crescent, Dunfermline KY11 8JX* T: (01224) 273571 E: drjulianrandall@gmail.com

RANDALL, Kelvin John. b 49. K Coll Lon BD 71 AKC 71 Birm Univ PGCE 72 Trin Coll Carmarthen MPhil 97 Univ of Wales (Ban) PhD 00. St Jo Coll Nottm 73. d 74 p 75. C Peckham St Mary Magd *S'wark* 74–78; C Portsdown *Portsm* 78–81; C-in-c Crookhorn Ch Cen CD 81–82; R Bedhampton 82–90; Bp's Chapl for Post-Ord Tr 84–89; RD Havant 87–89; P-in-c Bournemouth St Jo w St Mich *Win* 90–94; V 94–97; Chapl Talbot Heath Sch Bournemouth 90–94; Research Fell Trin Coll Carmarthen 97–00; C Portswood St Denys *Win* 00–02; P-in-c 02–15; rtd 15; Visiting Research Fell Glyndŵr Univ from 10; PtO *Win* from 15. *28 Ravenshall, 19-21 West Cliff Road, Bournemouth BH4 8AT* T: (01202) 244818 E: k.randall@glyndwr.ac.uk *or* kelvinjohnrandall@gmail.com

RANDALL, Mrs Lynda Lorraine. b 44. Sarum & Wells Th Coll 89. d 91 p 94. Par Dn Chesterton St Andr *Ely* 91–94; C 94–95; C Linton 95–96; TV 96–99; R Byfield w Boddington and Aston le Walls *Pet* 99–10; rtd 10; PtO *Pet* from 12; *Ox* from 16. *14 Smithland Court, Greens Norton, Towcester NN12 8DA* T: (01327) 350203 E: lynda@chrislyn.demon.co.uk

RANDALL, Miss Marian Sally. b 49. Trin Coll Bris 75. dss 80 d 87 p 94. Peckham St Mary Magd *S'wark* 80–83; Sutton Ch Ch 83–97; Par Dn 87–94; C 94–97; P-in-c S Merstham 97–08; rtd 08; PtO *Cant* 09–12; *S'wark* from 14. *4 Vision Place, 8 Oxford Road, Redhill RH1 1QE* T: (01737) 764169 E: marian.randall@btinternet.com

RANDALL, Martin Trevor. b 51. St Jo Coll Dur BA 74. Trin Coll Bris 74. d 77 p 78. C Ashton-upon-Mersey St Mary Magd *Ches* 77–80; C Everton St Sav w St Cuth *Liv* 80–82; V W Derby Gd Shep 82–91; P-in-c Toxteth Park Ch Ch 91–94; P-in-c Toxteth Park St Bede 91–94; V Toxteth Park Ch Ch w St Bede 95–97; Chapl HM Pris Altcourse 97–07; PtO *Liv* 07–18; *Ab* from 19. *7 Greenwell, Gott, Shetland ZE2 9UL* T: (01595) 840784 M: 07717-845518 E: martinrandall51@gmail.com

RANDLE-BISSELL, Alexander Paul. b 71. **d** 12 **p** 13. C E Green *Cov* 12–15; P-in-c Pastrow *Win* from 15. *The Rectory, Chalkcroft Lane, Penton Mewsey, Andover SP11 0RD* M: 07717-778853 E: revdalex@me.com

RANDOLPH-HORN, David Henry. b 47. Nottm Univ BA 69 CQSW 71 Leeds Beckett Univ PhD 15. Qu Coll Birm 80. **d** 82 **p** 83. C Hamstead St Paul *Birm* 82–84; V Aston St Jas 84–94; Hon C Leytonstone H Trin and St Aug Harrow Green *Chelmsf* 93–99; Sec Inner Cities Relig Coun 94–99; Assoc Dir Leeds Ch Inst 99–07; P-in-c Heptonstall *Wakef* 99–02; Hon C Farnley *Ripon* 03; Leeds St Marg and All Hallows 07–18. *23 Spencer Place, Leeds LS7 4DQ* T: 0113-229 7546 E: davidhrh23@outlook.com

RANGER, Keith Brian. b 34. Down Coll Cam BA 58 MA 63. Glas NSM Course 58. **d** 81 **p** 82. OMF Internat 81–99; Ethnic Min Co-ord 90–99; Hong Kong 81–89; PtO *Ches* 89–93; *Man* 93–99; rtd 99; PtO *Ches* 99–02 and 06–17; Hon C Macclesfield Team 02–06; PtO *York* from 17. *12 Dulverton Hall, Esplanade, Scarborough YO11 2AR* T: (01723) 350307 M: 07779-528997 E: keithranger73@gmail.com

RANKIN, John. *See* RANKIN, William John Alexander

RANKIN, Stephen Brian. b 65. Salford Univ BSc 88. Trin Coll Bris 95. **d** 97 **p** 98. C Ashton-upon-Mersey St Mary Magd *Ches* 97–06; V from 06. *St Mary's Vicarage, 20 Beeston Road, Sale M33 5AG* T: 0161-973 5118 E: srankin@uk2.net

RANKIN, Canon William John Alexander. b 45. Van Mildert Coll Dur BA 68 Fitzw Coll Cam BA 73 MA 77. Westcott Ho Cam 71. **d** 74 **p** 75. C St John's Wood *Lon* 74–78; Chapl Clifton Coll Bris 78–86; P-in-c The Claydons *Ox* 86–91; R 91–93; R Clare w Poslingford, Cavendish etc *St E* 93–04; R Stour Valley 04–10; Hon Can St E Cathl 05–10; rtd 10; PtO *St E* from 10; *Pet* from 11. *12 Hawthorn Drive, Uppingham, Oakham LE15 9TA* T: (01572) 822180 E: therankins123@gmail.com

RANKINE, Christopher Barry. b 66. Portsm Poly BA 88. Linc Th Coll BTh 93. **d** 93 **p** 95. C Farlington *Portsm* 93–96; C Alverstoke 96–98; C Romsey *Win* 98–00; P-in-c W Andover 00–09; TR Portway and Danebury 09–13; V Eastcote St Lawr *Lon* from 13. *The Vicarage, 2 Bridle Road, Pinner HA5 2SJ* T: (020) 3665 2029 M: 07766-475743 E: chris-eastcote@sky.com

RANSLEY, Steven Edward. b 82. Cardiff Univ LLB 03. Oak Hill Th Coll BA 15. **d** 16 **p** 17. C Cornerstone Team *Leic* 16–19; TV from 19. *59 Somerby Road, Thurnby, Leicester LE7 9PR* T: 0116-241 6895 M: 07977-298838 E: steve@thurnbychurch.com

RANSOM, Adam John. b 85. Chich Univ BA 07 Sheff Univ MA 15. Coll of Resurr Mirfield 13. **d** 15 **p** 16. C Eastbourne Ch Ch and St Phil *Chich* 15–18; P-in-c Hampden Park and The Hydnye from 18. *60 Brassey Avenue, Eastbourne BN22 9QH* T: (01323) 502738 E: adamjransom@outlook.com

RANSOM, Nigel Lester. b 60. Leeds Univ BA 81. Wycliffe Hall Ox 83 SE Asia Sch of Th MTh 83. **d** 85 **p** 86. C Gidea Park *Chelmsf* 85–88; C Widford 88–91; V Eastwood 91–10; PtO *Nor* from 10; *St E* from 10; *Ely* from 16. *86 Nunnery Drive, Thetford IP24 3EP* T: (01842) 820922 E: nlran@btinternet.com

RANSON, Canon Arthur Frankland. b 50. St Jo Coll Dur BA 73. Wycliffe Hall Ox 73. **d** 75 **p** 76. C Bare *Blackb* 75–78; C Scotforth 78–81; V Leyland St Ambrose 81–02; AD Leyland 96–02; P-in-c Blackb St Silas 02–15; Hon Can Blackb Cathl 00–15; rtd 15; PtO *Blackb* from 15. *6 Hazlewood, Silverdale, Carnforth LA5 0TQ* T: (01524) 702959 E: arthur.ranson@ntlworld.com

RANYARD, Michael Taylor. b 43. Nottm Univ BTh 74. Linc Th Coll 71. **d** 74 **p** 75. C Sutton in Ashfield St Mary *S'well* 74–76; Hon C Lewisham St Mary *S'wark* 76–77; C Rushmere *St E* 77–79; R Hopton, Market Weston, Barningham etc 79–83; Chr Educn and Resources Adv *Dur* 83–93; Prin Adv to Dioc Bd of Educn *Blackb* 93–98; Asst P Blackb Cathl 98–99; rtd 99; PtO *Heref* from 99. *72 Wyedean Rise, Belmont, Hereford HR2 7XZ* T/F: (01432) 355452 E: sm@ranyard.plus.com

RAO, Norma Ruoman. b 63. Westmr Coll Ox BTh 97 Anglia Ruskin Univ MA 05. Westcott Ho Cam 99. **d** 01 **p** 02. C Endcliffe *Sheff* 01–04; C Rotherham 04–08; R Rossington 08–15; V W Acklam *York* from 15. *The Vicarage, 50 Church Lane, Middlesbrough TS5 7EB* E: norma.rao@btinternet.com

RAPHOE, Archdeacon of. *See* HUSS, The Ven David Ian

RAPHOE, Dean of. *See* BARRETT, The Very Revd Kenneth Arthur Lambart

RAPLEY, Mrs Joy Naomi. b 41. Portsm Poly CertEd 63 Open Univ BA 79. Sarum & Wells Th Coll 87. **d** 89 **p** 94. Par Dn Welwyn Garden City *St Alb* 89–92; Chapl S Beds Community Healthcare Trust 92–98; C Wilbury *St Alb* 94–95; NSM St Mary's Bay w St Mary-in-the-Marsh etc *Cant* 98–02; NSM New Romney w Old Romney and Midley 98–02; Asst

Chapl E Kent NHS and Soc Care Partnership Trust 99–02; P-in-c Clopton w Otley, Swilland and Ashbocking *St E* 02–08; PtO 08–17; *Cant* from 18. *20 Rogersmead, Tenterden TN30 6LF* T: (01580) 762391 E: revraps@aol.com

RAPSEY, Preb Peter Nigel. b 46. K Coll Lon BD 68 AKC 68. St Boniface Warminster. **d** 69 **p** 70. C Walton-on-Thames *Guildf* 69–73; C Fleet 73–77; P-in-c The Collingbournes and Everleigh *Sarum* 77–79; TV Wexcombe 79–84; R Wokingham St Paul *Ox* 84–93; Chapl Warminster Sch 93–96; V Frome Ch Ch *B & W* 96–04; P-in-c Evercreech w Chesterblade and Milton Clevedon 04–11; RD Frome 01–03; Dir of Ords 03–11; Preb Wells Cathl 04–11; rtd 11; PtO *Ex* from 12. *3A Saxon Close, Crediton EX17 3DS* T: (01363) 774068 E: peter.rapsey@btinternet.com

RAPSON, Jonathan David. b 95. Wycliffe Hall Ox 16. **d** 19. C Gt Stanmore *Lon* from 19. *Church House Cottage, Old Church Lane, Stanmore HA7 2QX* M: 07557-808527 E: jonny.rapson@hotmail.com

RAPSON, Tina Angela. b 62. **d** 16 **p** 17. NSM Uxbridge *Lon* from 16. *30 Station Road, Uxbridge UB8 3AA* T: (01895) 813923 M: 07867-557472 E: tina.rapson247@hotmail.co.uk

RATCLIFF, Canon David William. b 37. Edin Th Coll 59. **d** 62 **p** 63. C Croydon St Aug *Cant* 62–65; C Selsdon St Jo w St Fran 65–69; V Milton Regis St Mary 69–75; Hon Min Can Cant Cathl 75–91; Asst Dir of Educn 75–91; Dioc Adv in Adult Educn and Lay Tr 75–91; Hon Pres Protestant Assn for Adult Educn in Eur 82–88; Chapl Frankfurt-am-Main 91–98; Adn Scandinavia *Eur* 96–05; Chapl Stockholm w Gävle and Västerås 98–02; rtd 05; PtO *Cant* from 02; *Eur* from 19. *9 The Orchards, Elham, Canterbury CT4 6TR* T: (01303) 840624 F: 840871 E: archdeacon.david@zen.co.uk

RATCLIFF, Paul Ronald. b 62. Univ Coll Lon BSc 83 Leic Univ MSc 84 PhD 89 FRAS MInstP. SEITE 05. **d** 09 **p** 10. C Cant St Martin and St Paul 09–12; R King's Wood 12–19; AD W Bridge 14–19; P-in-c Stonegate *Chich* from 19; P-in-c Tidebrook from 19; P-in-c Wadhurst from 19. *The Vicarage, High Street, Wadhurst TN5 6AA* E: pr.ratcliff@gmail.com

RATCLIFFE, Elizabeth Clare. b 65. Leeds Univ BSc 87 York Univ DPhil 91. Ox Min Course 12. **d** 15 **p** 16. C Reading Ch Ch *Ox* 15–18; R Tilehurst St Mich from 18. *Tilehurst Rectory, Routh Lane, Tilehurst, Reading RG30 4JY* M: 07752-388707 E: liz-ratcliffe@live.co.uk *or* office@stmichaelstilehurst.org.uk

RATCLIFFE, Canon Michael David. b 43. Lon Univ BSc 65 Southn Univ PGCE 67 Lon Univ BA 75 Lanc Univ MA 84. Cranmer Hall Dur 75. **d** 77 **p** 78. C Blackpool St Thos *Blackb* 77–81; V Oswaldtwistle St Paul 81–10; RD Accrington 97–03; Hon Can Blackb Cathl 00–10; rtd 10; PtO *Blackb* from 10. *8 Stanhill Road, Oswaldtwistle, Accrington BB5 4PP* E: mratossy@tiscali.co.uk

RATCLIFFE, Peter Graham Bruce. St Mich Coll Llan. **d** 08 **p** 09. C Carmarthen St Pet *St D* 08–09; C E Carmarthen 09–10; P-in-c Llanpumsaint w Llanllawddog 10–15; P-in-c Cilgerran w Bridell and Llantwyd and Eglwyswrw 15–18; P-in-c Bro Teifi from 18. *The Rectory, Penllyn, Cilgerran, Cardigan SA43 2RZ* T: (01239) 612511 E: peter@revpeter.plus.com

RATE, Susan. *See* LEIGHTON, Susan

RATHBAND, The Very Revd Kenneth William. b 60. Edin Univ BD 86. Edin Th Coll 82. **d** 86 **p** 87. C Dundee St Paul *Bre* 86–88; TV Dundee St Martin 88–89; C Edin SS Phil and Jas 90–91; R Alyth *St And* 91–18; R Blairgowrie 91–18; R Coupar Angus 91–18; R Dunfermline from 18; R Lunan Head from 18; Can St Ninian's Cathl Perth from 05; Dean St Andr from 07. *10 Rosemount Park, Blairgowrie PH10 6TZ* T: (01250) 872431 *or* 874583 E: krathband@btinternet.com *or* abcsaints@btinternet.com

RATHBONE, Mrs Isobel. b 48. Girton Coll Cam MA 70 Leeds Univ MA 02 Solicitor 81. NEOC 02. **d** 05 **p** 06. NSM Moor Allerton *Ripon* 05–08; NSM Hooe and Ninfield *Chich* 08–09; NSM Guiseley w Esholt *Bradf* 10–13; P-in-c Batheaston w St Cath *B & W* 13–18; rtd 18; PtO *B & W* from 18. *Meadowcroft House, Draughton, Skipton BD23 6EB* M: 07775-656257 E: isobel.rathbone@lmh.ox.ac.uk *or* isobel.rathbone@gmail.com

RATHBONE, Paul. b 36. BNC Ox BA 58 MA 62. Wycliffe Hall Ox 58. **d** 60 **p** 61. C Carl St Jo 60–63; C Heworth w Peasholme St Cuth *York* 63–68; V Thorganby w Skipwith and N Duffield 68–83; V Bishopthorpe and Acaster Malbis 83–01; rtd 01; PtO *York* from 01. *12 Whitelass Close, Thirsk YO7 1FG* T: (01845) 523347 E: paul2rathbone@btinternet.com

RATHBONE, Stephen Derek. b 61. Wycliffe Hall Ox. **d** 00 **p** 01. C W Kirby St Bridget *Ches* 00–03; P-in-c Rainow w Saltersford and Forest 03–10; V from 10. *The Vicarage, Pedley Hill, Rainow, Macclesfield SK10 5TZ* T: (01625) 572013

RATTENBERRY, Christopher James. b 59. York Univ BA 80 Solicitor. St Jo Coll Nottm 91. **d** 93 **p** 94. C Porchester *S'well* 93–98; P-in-c Daybrook 98–04; V 04–06; AD Nottm N 01–05;

P-in-c Ravenshead 06–11; V 11–17; rtd 17; P-in-c Danby w Castleton and Commondale *York* 18–19; P-in-c Moorsholm 18–19; P-in-c Westerdale 18–19. *Sherwin, Butt Lane, Robin Hood's Bay, Whitby YO22 4PF* E: revdcjr@aol.com

✠**RATTERAY, The Rt Revd Alexander Ewen.** b 42. Codrington Coll Barbados 61. **d** 65 **p** 66 **c** 96. C S Kirkby *Wakef* 66–68; C Sowerby St Geo 68–71; V Airedale w Fryston 71–80; Bermuda 80–08; Adn Bermuda 94–96; Bp Bermuda 96–08; rtd 08; PtO *York* from 09. *PO Box HM 2021, Hamilton HM CX, Bermuda* E: bishopratteray@ibl.bm

RATTIGAN, Canon Paul Damian. b 61. Reading Univ BSc 87 Liv Hope MA 00 Sussex Univ PGCE 88. Qu Coll Birm 93. **d** 95 **p** 96. C Parr *Liv* 95–99; P-in-c St Helens St Matt Thatto Heath 99–01; V 01–05; P-in-c Boldmere *Birm* 05–08; V 08–13; Can Res Liv Cathl 13–19; Can Res and Chan Leic Cathl from 19; Dir of Ords from 19. *Leicester Cathedral, St Martin's House, 7 Peacock Lane, Leicester LE1 5PZ* T: 0116-261 5200

RATTUE, James. b 69. Ball Coll Ox BA 91 MA 04 Leic Univ MA 93. St Steph Ho Ox 03. **d** 05 **p** 06. C Weybridge *Guildf* 05–08 and 09; C Englefield Green 08–09; R Farncombe from 09. *The Rectory, 38 Farncombe Hill, Godalming GU7 2AU* T: (01483) 860709 M: 07952-615499 E: jamesrattue@hotmail.com

RAVALDE, Canon Geoffrey Paul. b 54. St Cuth Soc Dur BA 76 SS Coll Cam BA 86 MA 90 Lon Univ MTh 91 Barrister 78. Westcott Ho Cam 84. **d** 87 **p** 88. C Spalding St Mary and St Nic *Linc* 87–91; P-in-c Wigton *Carl* 91–92; V from 92; P-in-c Thursby from 10; RD Carl 95–00; Hon Can Carl Cathl from 96; Chapl to The Queen from 14. *The Vicarage, Longthwaite Road, Wigton CA7 9JR* T: (016973) 42337 E: gpravalde@yahoo.co.uk

RAVEN, Ann. *See* GURNER, Margaret Ann

RAVEN, Canon Barry. b 48. Sarum & Wells Th Coll 69. **d** 72 **p** 73. C Henbury *Bris* 72–76; P-in-c S Marston w Stanton Fitzwarren 76–78; TV Stratton St Margaret w S Marston etc 78–80; P-in-c Coalpit Heath 80–84; V 84–91; R Ashley, Crudwell, Hankerton and Oaksey 91–13; P-in-c Ashton Keynes, Leigh and Minety 07–13; RD N Wilts 99–06; Hon Can Bris Cathl 12–13; rtd 13; PtO *Bris* from 14; *Glouc* from 14. *10 Springfields, Tetbury GL8 8EN* T: (01666) 505616 E: barry@deanery.org.uk

RAVEN, Canon Charles Frank. b 58. Magd Coll Ox BA 80 MA 86 St Jo Coll Dur BA 87 ACIB 84. Cranmer Hall Dur 85. **d** 88 **p** 89. C Heckmondwike *Wakef* 88–92; TV Kidderminster St Jo and H Innocents *Worc* 92–02; Abp's Officer for Angl Communion Affairs Kenya from 12; Hon Can All SS Cathl Nairobi from 16; PtO *Dur* from 13. *Anglican Church of Kenya, PO Box 40502-00100, Nairobi, Kenya* T: (00254) (20) 271 4755 M: 00254-716-835315 *or* 07789-934836 E: charlesraven@gafcon.org

RAVEN, Margaret Ann. *See* GURNER, Margaret Ann

RAVEN, Margaret Hilary. b 45. Dur Univ BA 67 Man Univ MEd 73. Wesley Th Sem Washington MDiv 95. **d** 96 **p** 97. USA 96–01; Asst R Martinsburg Trin Ch 96–99; Assoc R Toms River Ch Ch 99–00; PtO *Edin* 02–06 and from 14; NSM Edin Ch Ch 06–12. *4 Warrender Crescent, Dunbar EH42 1LU* T: (01368) 860524 E: margaret0545raven@hotmail.com

RAVEN, Tony. b 39. Garnett Coll Lon CertEd 65. SAOMC 94. **d** 97 **p** 98. NSM Lt Berkhamsted and Bayford, Essendon etc *St Alb* 97–01; P-in-c Lt Hadham w Albury 01–05; rtd 05; Hon C Hazelbury Bryan and the Hillside Par *Sarum* 07–11; PtO *Ex* from 11. *33 Liberty Way, Exeter EX2 7AS* T: (01392) 875150 E: tony@theravens.org *or* tonyraven39@john-lewis.com

RAVENSCROFT, The Ven Raymond Lockwood. b 31. Leeds Univ BA 53. Coll of Resurr Mirfield 54. **d** 55 **p** 56. C Goodwood S Africa 55–57; C St Jo Cathl Bulawayo S Rhodesia 57–59; R Francistown Bechuanaland 59–62; C St Ives *Truro* 62–64; V Falmouth All SS 64–68; V St Stephens by Launceston 68–73; P-in-c Launceston St Thos 68–73; V Launceston St Steph w St Thos 73–74; TR Probus, Ladock and Grampound w Creed and St Erme 74–88; RD Powder 77–81; Hon Can Truro Cathl 82–88; P-in-c St Erme 84–85; Adn Cornwall and Can Lib Truro Cathl 88–96; rtd 96; PtO *Ex* from 00. *14 Treviglas Rise, Probus, Truro TR2 4LJ* E: rlravenscroft@btinternet.com

RAWDING, Andrew. b 70. Cranmer Hall Dur 00. **d** 02 **p** 03. C Enfield St Andr *Lon* 02–05; Hon C Arm St Mark 05–07; Chapl RN 08–11; I Brackaville w Donaghendry and Ballyclog *Arm* from 11. *Holy Trinity Rectory, 82 Dungannon Road, Coalisland, Dungannon BT71 4HT* T: (028) 8774 0243 M: 07771-851838 E: andrewrawding@gmail.com *or* rector@coalisland.gmail.com

RAWDON-MOGG, Timothy David. b 45. St Jo Coll Dur BA 76. Cuddesdon Coll 75. **d** 77 **p** 78. C Wotton St Mary *Glouc* 77–80; C Ascot Heath *Ox* 80–82; V Woodford Halse w Eydon *Pet* 82–88; V Shrivenham w Watchfield and Bourton

Ox 88–00; R Horsted Keynes *Chich* 00–08; rtd 08; PtO *Heref* from 12; *Lich* from 13. *Stone Cottage, The Bog, Minsterley, Shrewsbury SY5 0NJ* T: (01743) 792073 E: timrm@mail.com

RAWLING, Miss Jane Elizabeth. b 51. Birm Univ BSc 73 St Jo Coll York CertEd 75. St Jo Coll Nottm 81. **dss** 84 **d** 87 **p** 94. Southsea St Jude *Portsm* 84–88; C 87–88; C St Paul's Cray St Barn *Roch* 88–91; Hon C from 91; SE Regional Co-ord BCMS Crosslinks 91–01; Sec for Bps' Selection Conf and CME Sec Min Division 01–07. *89 Beddington Road, Orpington BR5 2TE* T: (020) 8309 2987 E: j.rawling@outlook.com

RAWLINGS, Elizabeth. b 66. Nottm Univ BSc 96 RGN 87. St Jo Coll Nottm 04. **d** 06 **p** 07. C Derby St Alkmund and St Werburgh 06–07; C Walbrook Epiphany 07–10; Min Hamilton CD *Leic* from 10; Warden Past Assts 11–14; AD City of Leic from 18. *2 Cransley Close, Hamilton, Leicester LE5 1QQ* T: 0116-274 2088 E: lizrawlings@btinternet.com

RAWLINGS, The Ven John Edmund Frank. b 47. AKC 69. St Aug Coll Cant 69. **d** 70 **p** 71. C Rainham *Roch* 70–73; C Tattenham Corner and Burgh Heath *Guildf* 73–76; Chapl RN 76–92; V Tavistock and Gulworthy *Ex* 92–05; Chapl Kelly Coll Tavistock 93–02; RD Tavistock *Ex* 97–02; Preb Ex Cathl 99–14; Adn Totnes 06–14; PtO from 05. *9 Rosemount Lane, Honiton EX14 1RJ* T: (01404) 43404 E: rawlings1@btinternet.com

RAWLINGS, Canon Philip John. b 53. St Jo Coll Nottm BTh 83. **d** 83 **p** 84. C Blackley St Andr *Man* 83–87; C Halliwell St Pet 87–93; R Old Trafford St Bride 93–11; AD Stretford 98–05; Borough Dean Trafford 10–11; Interfaith Officer Oldham from 11; Hon Can Man Cathl from 04. *68 Dudley Road, Manchester M16 8DE* T: 0161-232 0413 E: philjr053@gmail.com

RAWLINS, Mrs Nicola Jane Phillips. b 60. Newc Poly BA 86 Cant Ch Ch Univ BSc 10. St Aug Coll of Th BA 18. **d** 18. NSM Gillingham St Aug *Roch* from 18. *3 Marble Close, Gillingham ME7 2EP* T: (01634) 787660 E: nicky.rawlins@hotmail.co.uk

RAWLINSON, Curwen. b 32. Leeds Univ CertEd 55 Man Univ DipEd 56 Open Univ BA 80. Sarum Th Coll 59. **d** 61 **p** 62. C Wigan St Mich *Liv* 61–63; CF 63–78; Dep Asst Chapl Gen 78–80; Asst Chapl Gen 80–85; QHC 83–98; R Uley w Owlpen and Nympsfield *Glouc* 85–98; RD Dursley 89–96; rtd 98; PtO *Glouc* from 98; Sub Chapl HM Pris Glouc 02–13. *Cark House, 6 Groves Place, Fairford GL7 4BJ* T: (01285) 711009

RAWLINSON, Preb James Nigel. b 56. Em Coll Cam BA 77 MB, BCh 80 FRCSE 86 FFAEM 98. WMMTC 95. **d** 98 **p** 99. NSM Bath Weston All SS w N Stoke and Langridge *B & W* 98–16; Chapl Bath Univ from 16; PtO *Bris* from 98; Consultant Bris R Infirmary from 99; Preb Wells Cathl *B & W* from 15. *The Chaplain's House, The Avenue, Claverton Down, Bath BA2 7AX* T: (01225) 386458 M: 07722-005452 E: email@nigelrawlinson.co.uk

RAWSON, Canon Michael Graeme. b 62. York Univ BA 84. St Steph Ho Ox BA 88. **d** 89 **p** 90. C Brighouse St Martin *Wakef* 89–92; C Brighouse and Clifton 92–93; V Gomersal 93–04; Bp's Dom Chapl and Publicity Officer 04–07; Can Res Wakef Cathl 07–14; Can Res S'wark Cathl from 14; Vice Dean S'wark from 14; Min Bermondsey St Hugh CD from 14. *73 St George's Road, London SE1 6ER* E: michael.rawson@southwark.anglican.org

RAY, Mrs Joanna Zorina. b 55. K Coll Lon BSc 77 Garnett Coll Lon PGCE 80 Lon Inst of Educn MA 92 MIBMS 10. S'wark Ord Course 84. **d** 87 **p** 94. NSM Carshalton S'wark 87–91; NSM Sutton New Town St Barn 91–93; NSM Knighton St Mary Magd *Leic* 93–94; C Leic H Spirit 94–98; Chapl for Deaf People 94–98; Chapl St Andr Hosp Northn 99–03; PtO *S'well* 04–12; S'wark 12–15; rtd 15. *27 Sunningdale Gardens, Bognor Regis PO22 9LE* T: (01243) 866082 M: 07879-033031 E: revdjoannaray@gmail.com

RAY, John Mead. b 28. St Andr Univ MA 50 DipEd 51. CMS Tr Coll Chislehurst 60. **d** 70 **p** 71. Miss Partner CMS 70–95; C Sparkhill St Jo *Birm* 87–90; C Sparkbrook Em 87–90; C Sparkhill w Greet and Sparkbrook 90; Deanery Missr 90–95; rtd 95; PtO *Birm* 95–14; *Sheff* from 15. *2 Birchfield, Hook, Goole DN14 5NJ* T: (01405) 475238 M: 07506-563239 E: hardyraycj@gmail.com

RAY, Robin John. b 44. Sarum & Wells Th Coll 72. **d** 74 **p** 75. C Bourne Valley *Sarum* 74–78; P-in-c Dilton's-Marsh 78–82; V 82–87; V Taunton Lyngford *B & W* 87–93; R Exford, Exmoor, Hawkridge and Withypool 93–04; ACORA Link Officer and Rural Affairs Officer 93–04; rtd 04; PtO *B & W* from 04; RD Glastonbury 09–11. *Leigholt Farm, Somerton Road, Street BA16 0SU* T: (01458) 841281 M: 07772-563597 E: robinray@btinternet.com

RAYBOULD, James Clive Ransford. b 37. Wolv Univ BSc 62 Anglia Poly Univ MBA 94 PhD 01. Cranmer Hall Dur 81. **d** 83 **p** 84. C Cannock *Lich* 83–86; P-in-c Leek Wootton *Cov* 86–89; Dioc Tr Adv 86–89; TV Cannock *Lich* 89; Assoc Lect

Anglia Ruskin Univ *Chelmsf* from 90; rtd 00. *29 Greystones, Bromham, Chippenham SN15 2JT* T: (01380) 859623

✠**RAYFIELD, The Rt Revd Lee Stephen.** b 55. Southn Univ BSc 78 Lon Univ PhD 81 SOSc 95. Ridley Hall Cam 93. **d** 93 **p** 94 **c** 05. C Woodford Wells *Chelmsf* 93–97; P-in-c Furze Platt *Ox* 97–05; AD Maidenhead and Windsor 00–05; Suff Bp Swindon *Bris* from 05. *Mark House, Field Rise, Swindon SN1 4HP* T: (01793) 538654 F: 525181 E: bishop.swindon@bristoldiocese.org

RAYMENT, Alexander Louis. b 88. Ox Brookes Univ BA 10. St Mellitus Coll 14. **d** 17 **p** 18. C Onslow Square and S Kensington St Aug *Lon* from 17. *48 Nelson Road, London SW19 1HT* M: 07530-861537 E: alexlrayment@gmail.com

RAYMENT, Andrew David. b 45. Univ of Wales (Lamp) BA 68 Univ of Wales (Abth) MA 70 Nottm Univ PhD 06. Ridley Hall Cam 78. **d** 80 **p** 81. C Costessey *Nor* 80–83; C Earlham St Anne 83–90; V Old Catton 90–96; PtO *Pet* 00–11; Min Partnership Development Officer 04–11; Adult Educn Officer (CME and Min Partnership) 05–11; rtd 11; P-in-c Ketton, Collyweston, Easton-the-Hill and Tinwell *Pet* 11–17; P-in-c Ketton and Tinwell 17–18. *Address temp unknown* M: 07752-648537 E: andrew-rayment2010@hotmail.co.uk

RAYMER, Victoria Elizabeth. b 46. Wellesley Coll (USA) BA 68 Harvard Univ MA 69 JD 78 PhD 81. St Steph Ho Ox BA 86 Qu Coll Birm 88. **d** 89 **p** 94. Par Dn Bushey *St Alb* 89–94; C Eaton Socon 94–98; V Milton Ernest, Pavenham and Thurleigh 98–01; Tutor Westcott Ho Cam from 01; Dir Studies 01–14; PtO *St Alb* from 08; *Ely* from 16. *Westcott House, Jesus Lane, Cambridge CB5 8BP* T: (01223) 272967 E: ver21@cam.ac.uk

RAYMOND, The Very Revd Walter Harvey. b 49. **d** 92 **p** 93. OGS from 93; C Willowdale All So Canada 92–94; Chapl H Trin Sch Toronto 94–99; Dean and R H Trin Cathl Quebec 99–07; Chapl Monte Carlo *Eur* 08–17; rtd 17; PtO *Eur* from 17. *25 rue Saint Louis, Standon QC G0R 4L0, Canada* T: (001) (418) 951 3307 E: wraymond@ogs.net

RAYMONT, Philip Richard. b 56. Univ of Qld BA 79 BEdSt 86 Melbourne Univ MEd 00 Cam Univ PhD 05 MACE. **d** 04 **p** 09. Asst Chapl Selw Coll Cam 04–07; PtO *Ely* 07–09; Sen Chapl Guildford Gr Sch Australia from 09. *Guildford Grammar, 11 Terrace Road, Guildford WA 6935, Australia* T: (0061) (8) 9377 9245 E: praymont@ggs.wa.edu.au

RAYNER, Angela Claire. Rob Coll Cam BA 02 MPhil 03 MA 06 Heythrop Coll Lon MTh 04. Westcott Ho Cam 16. **d** 18 **p** 19. C Hayley's Lynn St Marg w St Nic *Nor* from 18. *Pilot Hoy, 10 Pilot Street, King's Lynn PE30 1QL* M: 07480-051148 E: fr.angela.rayner@gmail.com

RAYNER, Canon George Charles. b 26. Bps' Coll Cheshunt 50. **d** 52 **p** 53. C Rowbarton *B & W* 52–56; V Taunton H Trin 56–63; Chapl Taunton and Somerset Hosp 60–63; V Lower Sandown St Jo *Portsm* 63–69; R Wootton 69–89; Hon Can Portsm Cathl 84–89; rtd 89; PtO *B & W* 89–92; *Portsm* 98–15; P-in-c Six Pilgrims *B & W* 93–02. *The Bungalow, 1 Alresford Road, Shanklin PO37 6HX* T: (01983) 867304 E: rennergc@hotmail.com

RAYNER, Michael John. b 55. Magd Coll Ox BA 78 DPhil 85. Ox Min Course 04. **d** 07 **p** 08. Dir Br Heart Foundn Health Promotion Research Gp from 94; NSM Ox St Matt from 07. *198 Marlborough Road, Oxford OX1 4LT* T: (01865) 289244 M: 07871-758745 E: mike.rayner@dph.ox.ac.uk

RAYNER, Paul Anthony George. b 39. Dur Univ BA 60 Lon Univ BD 68 Cape Town Univ MA 79. Lon Coll of Div 65. **d** 68 **p** 69. C Crookes St Thos *Sheff* 68–72; P-in-c Diep River St Luke S Africa 72–79; P-in-c S Shoebury *Chelmsf* 80–84; R 84–97; V Loughton St Mich 97–04; rtd 04; PtO *Chelmsf* from 04; *Eur* from 08. *36 Amberley Road, Buckhurst Hill IG9 5QW* T: (020) 8504 7434 E: prayner@globalnet.co.uk

RAYNER, Miss Rosemary Jane. b 54. ERMC 12. **d** 15 **p** 16. NSM Nor Lakenham St Jo and All SS and Tuckswood from 15. *7 St Andrew's Close, Poringland, Norwich NR14 7TB* T: (01508) 495650 E: rosemaryrayner@btinternet.com

RAYNER, Mrs Shirley Christine. b 54. SEITE BA 08. **d** 05 **p** 06. C S Croydon St Pet and St Aug *S'wark* 05–09; C Carew *St D* 09–11; TV 11–14; P-in-c Carew and Cosheston and Nash and Redberth 14; Dioc Lay Development Officer 11–14; rtd 14; PtO *St D* 14–15 and 17–18 and from 19; Hon C St Issell's and Amroth w Crunwere and Marros 15–17; Hon C Begelly w Ludchurch and E Williamston 18–19. *Address withheld by request*

RAYNER, Stewart Leslie. b 39. St Jo Coll Dur BA 61 MA 73. Cranmer Hall Dur. **d** 67 **p** 68. C Whiston *Sheff* 67–70; C Doncaster St Geo 70–74; Chapl Doncaster R Infirmary 70–74; R Adwick-le-Street *Sheff* 74–85; V Totley 85–91; Asst Chapl Pastures Hosp Derby 91–94; Asst Chapl Kingsway Hosp Derby 91–94; Asst Chapl S Derby Mental Health Services 91–94; P-in-c Etwall w Egginton *Derby*

94–99; R 99–08; RD Longford 96–01; rtd 09. *26 Lawn Avenue, Etwall, Derby DE65 6JB* T: (01283) 736079 E: stewart.rayner37@googlemail.com

RAYNER-WILLIAMS, Gareth Wynn. b 67. St D Coll Lamp BA 88 Hull Univ MA 89 Trin Coll Carmarthen PGCE 06. Westcott Ho Cam 89. **d** 91 **p** 92. C Mold *St As* 91–93; TV Hawarden 93–95; Ecum Chapl Glam Univ *Llan* 95–99; Lect Cardiff Univ from 99; Dir Academic Studies St Mich Coll Llan 99–04; Vice-Prin 02–04; V Roath *Llan* 04–05; PtO from 05; Hd RS Hawthorn Comp Sch Pontypridd 06–08; Chapl Bp of Llan High Sch 08–18; Hd RE 12–18; Asst Hd Teacher 15–18; Sen Teacher St Teilo's High Sch Cardiff from 19. *12 Fairwater Grove West, Llandaff, Cardiff CF5 2JQ* T: (029) 2056 9581 E: garethrw@icloud.com

RAYNES, Canon Andrew. b 60. R Holloway Coll Lon BA 83. Wycliffe Hall Ox 93. **d** 95 **p** 96. C Crowborough *Chich* 95–99; V Blackb Ch Ch w St Matt from 99; AD Blackb and Darwen 03–16; Hon Can Blackb Cathl from 10. *The Vicarage, Brandy House Brow, Blackburn BB2 3EY* T: (01254) 56292 E: andrewraynes@btopenworld.com

RAYNHAM, Mrs Penelope Anne. b 44. SWMTC 97. **d** 00 **p** 01. OLM S Hill w Callington *Truro* 00–15; rtd 15. *Bramblings, Honicombe Corner, Harrowbarrow, Callington PL17 8JN* T: (01822) 833065 E: penny@bramvista.co.uk

RAYNOR, Duncan Hope. b 58. Ex Coll Ox MA 80 MA 82 Birm Univ PGCE 88 MLitt 93. Qu Coll Birm 82. **d** 84 **p** 85. C Kings Heath *Birm* 84–87; PtO 87–94; Hd of RE Alderbrook Sch Solihull 88–94; Chapl K Edw Sch Birm 94–18; rtd 18. *29 Edenhall Road, Quinton, Birmingham B32 1DA* T: 0121-684 3407

RAYNOR, Lynn Mary. b 52. HCIMA 00. St Jo Coll Nottm 12. **d** 13 **p** 14. NSM Ravenshead *S'well* 13–16; NSM Epperstone, Gonalston, Oxton and Woodborough from 17; Chapl Nottm Univ Hosp NHS Trust from 16. *18 Park Drive, Hucknall, Nottingham NG15 7LQ* T: 0115-953 5949 M: 07855-648410 E: rev.raynorshine@virginmedia.com

RAYNOR, Michael. b 53. Lanc Univ BA 74 MSc 75. Ripon Coll Cuddesdon BA 84 MA 99. **d** 85 **p** 86. C Gt Crosby St Faith *Liv* 85–88; V Warrington St Barn 88–97; V Orford St Andr from 97; AD Warrington 99–05; Hon Can Liv Cathl 03–05. *St Andrew's Vicarage, Poplars Avenue, Orford, Warrington WA2 9UE* T: (01925) 631903 E: mjraynor@care4free.net

RAZZALL, Charles Humphrey. b 55. Worc Coll Ox BA 76 MA 81 Qu Coll Cam BA 78. Westcott Ho Cam 76. **d** 79 **p** 80. C Catford (Southend) and Downham *S'wark* 79–83; V Crofton Park St Hilda w St Cypr 83–87; UPA Officer 87–92; TV Oldham *Man* 87–01; AD 92–99; Hon Can Man Cathl 98–01; R Coppenhall *Ches* 01–19; V N Thornaby *York* from 19. *St Paul's Vicarage, 60 Lanehouse Road, Thornaby, Stockton-on-Tees TS17 8EA* T: (01642) 868086 E: razzall@angelfields.eclipse.co.uk

REA, Simon William John. b 60. G&C Coll Cam MA Victoria Univ Wellington MA Liv Univ BTh 07 Univ of Wales (Ban) PGCE. Ridley Hall Cam 02. **d** 04 **p** 05. C Moreton *Ches* 04–08; C Edgware *Lon* from 08. *9 Lacey Drive, Edgware HA8 8GH* T: (020) 8958 6939 M: 07905-699185 E: simonrea@gmx.net *or* simon.rea@london.anglican.org

READ, Barbara Ann. b 50. **d** 16 **p** 17. OLM Loughton St Jo *Chelmsf* from 16. *20 Theydon Bower, Bower Hill, Epping CM16 7AB* E: barb_and_dave@talktalk.net *or* barbara@loughtonchurch.org.uk

READ, Benjamin Stanley. b 85. Univ of Wales (Cardiff) BA 07. St Mich Coll Llan BTh 12. **d** 12 **p** 13. C Carmarthen St Pet *St D* 12–14; C Carmarthen St Pet and Abergwili etc 14–16; V Kingsclere and Ashford Hill w Headley *Win* from 16. *The Vicarage, Fox's Lane, Kingsclere, Newbury RG20 5SL* T: (01635) 298471 E: readben@hotmail.com

READ, Charles William. b 60. Man Univ BA 81 MPhil 95 Man Poly PGCE 82. St Jo Coll Nottm 86. **d** 88 **p** 89. C Oldham *Man* 88–90; C Urmston 90–94; P-in-c Broughton St Jas w St Clem and St Matthias 94–96; TV Broughton 96–99; Lect Cranmer Hall Dur 99–06; Dir Studies 00–06; Teacher Dur Sch 06–07; Vice-Prin and Dir Studies Nor Dioc Min Course 07–13; Reader Tr Co-ord from 13; Dir Liturgy and Worship ERMC from 13; Dep Warden of Readers *Nor* from 14. *42 Heigham Road, Norwich NR2 3AU* T: (01603) 660824 *or* 632041 E: charles.read@dioceseofnorwich.org

READ, Geoffrey Philip. b 61. Bris Univ LLB 82 Spurgeon's Coll MTh 04. Wycliffe Hall Ox 85. **d** 88 **p** 89. C Dorking St Paul *Guildf* 88–92; TV Westborough 92–97; TR 97–98; Chapl Basle *Eur* 98–13; P-in-c Freiburg-im-Breisau 98–01; CMD Adv Colchester Area *Chelmsf* 13–18; Public Preacher 13–16; C Colchester St Jo 16–18; Chapl Luxembourg *Eur* from 18. *5 In der Acht, Steinsel, 7302 Luxembourg* T: (00352) 621 199 242 E: chaplain@anglican.lu

READ, James Arthur. b 51. Nottm Coll of Educn BEd 74. EMMTC 84. **d** 87 **p** 88. C Weoley Castle *Birm* 87–91; C W Smethwick 91–92; TV Atherton *Man* 92–97; P-in-c Facit 97–00; V Whitworth w Facit 00–08; P-in-c Royton St Anne 08–15; C Heyside 12–15; V Heyside and Royton from 15. *St Anne's Vicarage, St Anne's Avenue, Royton, Oldham OL2 5AD* T: 0161-652 3090

READ, Mrs Julie Margaret. b 61. Keble Coll Ox BA 82 Univ of Wales (Ban) PGCE 83. WEMTC 97. **d** 00 **p** 01. C Bishop's Castle w Mainstone, Lydbury N etc *Heref* 00–03; R Pembridge w Moor Court, Shobdon, Staunton etc 03–11; PtO 11–12; C Bredenbury 12–13; C Kingsland w Eardisland, Aymestrey etc 13; P-in-c from 13. *The Rectory, Kingsland, Leominster HR6 9QW* T: (01568) 708255 E: rev.julie@btinternet.com

READ, Maureen Elizabeth. b 52. Man Metrop Univ BEd 93 Ches Coll of HE BTh 99. NOC 95. **d** 98 **p** 99. NSM Leesfield *Man* 98–99; C 99–02; TV Heywood 02–09; V Meltham *Wakef* 09–14; *Leeds* 14–17; P-in-c Petton w Cockshutt, Welshampton and Lyneal etc *Lich* from 17. *The Rectory, Cockshutt, Ellesmere SY12 0JQ* E: maureen.read09@btinternet.com

READ, Michael Antony. b 75. Lanc Univ BA 99 St Jo Coll Dur BA 01. Cranmer Hall Dur 99. **d** 02 **p** 03. C Stanley *Liv* 02–05; P-in-c Lowton St Luke 05–11; TV Leigh w Sudden and Heywood All So *Man* 11–16; V from 16. *St Aidan's Vicarage, 41 Harold Lees Road, Heywood OL10 4DW* T: (01706) 360693 E: revmikeread@yahoo.co.uk

READ, Canon Nicholas George. b 51. Chelsea Coll Lon BSc 72 PhD 81. SEITE 97. **d** 00 **p** 01. NSM Beckenham St Jo *Roch* 00–03; P-in-c Penge Lane H Trin 03–09; V from 09; Hon Can Roch Cathl from 18. *Holy Trinity Vicarage, 64 Lennard Road, London SE20 7LX* T: (020) 8778 8113 M: 07904-317488 E: hancompro@aol.com

READ, Canon Robert Edgar. b 47. Kelham Th Coll 66. **d** 70 **p** 71. C Harton Colliery *Dur* 70–75; C Wilmslow *Ches* 76–80; V Gatley 80–92; V Offerton 92–06; RD Stockport 00–05; V Newton 06–07; P-in-c Gatley 07–10; V 10–14; Hon Can Ches Cathl 03–14; rtd 14; PtO *Ches* from 14; *Cov* 17–19. *16 Windsor Avenue, Gatley, Cheadle SK8 4DU* E: reread@btinternet.com

✠**READE, The Rt Revd Nicholas Stewart.** b 46. Leeds Univ BA 70. Coll of Resurr Mirfield 70. **d** 73 **p** 74 **c** 04. C Coseley St Chad *Lich* 73–75; C Codsall 75–78; V Upper Gornal 78–82; V Mayfield *Chich* 82–88; RD Dallington 82–88; V Eastbourne St Mary 88–97; RD Eastbourne 88–97; Can and Preb Chich Cathl 90–97; Min The Hydneye CD 91–93; Adn Lewes and Hastings 97–04; Bp Blackb 04–12; rtd 12; Hon Asst Bp Eur from 13; Hon Asst Bp Chich from 13. *5 Warnham Gardens, Bexhill-on-Sea TN39 3SP* E: nicholas.reade@btinternet.com

READE, Richard Barton. b 66. Wolv Poly BA 88. Ripon Coll Cuddesdon BA 91 MA 97. **d** 92 **p** 93. C Wilnecote *Lich* 92–96; C Penkridge 96–98; P-in-c Basford 98–04; P-in-c Matlock Bank *Derby* 04–11; V Matlock Bank and Tansley from 11. *2 Portway Drive, Matlock DE4 3TS* T: (01629) 581233 E: richardreade@btinternet.com

READER, John. b 53. Trin Coll Ox BA 75 MA 79 Man Univ MPhil 87 Univ of Wales (Ban) PhD 02. Ripon Coll Cuddesdon 76. **d** 78 **p** 79. C Ely 78–80; C Baguley *Man* 80–83; TV Kirkby Lonsdale *Carl* 83–86; V Lydbury N *Heref* 86–89; P-in-c Hopesay w Edgton 86–89; R Lydbury N w Hopesay and Edgton 89–90; Tutor Glouc Sch for Min 86–88; Vice-Prin 88–90; Dir Past Th Sarum & Wells Th Coll 90–92; P-in-c Elmley Lovett w Hampton Lovett and Elmbridge etc *Worc* 92–07; Assoc Tr and Educn Officer 92–02; Ind Chapl 01–07; P-in-c Chelford w Lower Withington and Dioc Rural Officer *Ches* 07–09; R Ironstone *Ox* from 09. *The Rectory, Church Street, Wroxton, Banbury OX15 6QE* T: (01295) 730344 E: drjohnreader@hotmail.com.uk

READER, The Ven Trevor Alan John. b 46. Lon Univ BSc 68 MSc 70 Portsm Poly PhD 72. S Dios Minl Tr Scheme 83. **d** 86 **p** 87. C Alverstoke *Portsm* 86–89; P-in-c Hook w Warsash 89–95; V 95–98; P-in-c Blendworth w Chalton w Idsworth 98–03; Dioc Dir NSM 98–03; Adn Is of Wight 03–06; Adn Portsdown 06–13; Bp's Liaison Officer for Pris 03–06; Bp's Liaison Officer for Hosps 06–13; rtd 13; PtO *Portsm* from 13. *54 David Newberry Drive, Lee-on-the-Solent PO13 8FE* M: 07826-846133 E: trevor.reader@hotmail.co.uk

READING, Glenn Thomas. b 76. Staffs Univ BSc 98. Ripon Coll Cuddesdon 07. **d** 09 **p** 10. C Horninglow *Lich* 09–13; TV Redditch Ch the K *Worc* from 13. *The Vicarage, 16 Church Road, Astwood Bank, Redditch B96 6EH* T: (01527) 894436 M: 07964-282278 E: glenn.reading@gmail.com

READING, Lesley Jean. *See* ARMSTRONG, Lesley Jean

READING, Michael Dudley. b 66. Coll of Ripon & York St Jo BEd 90 Nottm Trent Univ MA 98. Wycliffe Hall Ox 15. **d** 17 **p** 18. C Thame *Ox* from 17. *8 Victoria Mead, Thame OX9 3HY* M: 07808-548807 E: michael.reading.mr@gmail.com

READING, Area Bishop of. *See* GRAHAM, The Rt Revd Olivia Josephine

REAGON, Darrol Franklin. b 46. St Mich Coll Llan 74. **d** 76 **p** 77. C Llandrillo-yn-Rhos *St As* 76–78; C Hawarden 78–81; V Northwich St Luke and H Trin *Ches* 81–85; V Moulton *Linc* 85–91; V Scunthorpe Resurr 91–92; P-in-c Branston 92–94; R Branston w Nocton and Potterhanworth 94–07; rtd 07; PtO *Win* from 09. *17 Wessex Avenue, New Milton BH25 6NG* T: (01425) 613622 E: revddarrol@btinternet.com

REAKES, Richard Frank. b 68. STETS 02. **d** 05 **p** 06. NSM Shepton Mallet w Doulting *B & W* 05–09; NSM Evercreech w Chesterblade and Milton Clevedon 09–14; TV Bishop's Cleeve and Woolstone w Gotherington etc *Glouc* from 14. *The Rectory, 67 Malleson Road, Gotherington, Cheltenham GL52 9EX* E: reakes4@aol.com

REAKES-WILLIAMS, Canon Gordon Martin. b 63. St Cath Coll Cam BA 86 MA 89 St Jo Coll Dur BA 90. Cranmer Hall Dur. **d** 91 **p** 92. C Harold Wood *Chelmsf* 91–94; Chapl Leipzig *Eur* from 95; Hon Can from 17. *Shakespearestrasse 53, 04107 Leipzig, Germany* T: (0049) (341) 302 7951 M: 177-240 4207 E: pastor@leipzig-english-church.de

REANEY, Mrs Beverly Jane. b 58. Nottm Univ BA 81. S Wales Ord Course 00. **d** 03 **p** 04. NSM Llanharry *Llan* 03–11; NSM Llangynwyd w Maesteg 11–13; P-in-c Glyncorrwg and the Upper Afan Valley etc from 13. *12 Cwrt y Fedwen, Maesteg CF34 9GH* T: (01656) 734142 E: bevreaney11@btinternet.com

REANEY, Christopher Thomas. b 60. Univ of Wales (Lamp) BA 82. St Mich Coll Llan. **d** 85 **p** 86. C Maindee Newport *Mon* 85–87; C Griffithstown 88–89; V Treherbert w Treorchy *Llan* 89–99; V Treorchy and Treherbert 99–02; R Llanfabon 02–11; V Troedrhiwgarth from 11. *12 Cwrt y Fedwen, Maesteg CF34 9GH* T: (01656) 734142 E: c.reaney350@btinternet.com

REAST, Eileen Joan. *See* BANGAY, Eileen Joan

REAVLEY, Cedric. b 51. Lon Univ BPharm 73. **d** 05 **p** 06. OLM Burford w Fulbrook, Taynton, Asthall etc *Ox* from 05. *124 High Street, Burford OX18 4QR* T: (01993) 823957 F: 824887 E: cedric_reavley@lineone.net

REBOKS, Guntars. b 87. Univ of Latvia BA 09 MTheol 12. **p** 15. PtO *Eur* 15–16; C Sherborne w Castleton, Lillington and Longburton *Sarum* from 16. *69 Granville Way, Sherborne DT9 4AT* M: (00371) 2208 5148 E: guntarsreboks@gmail.com

RECORD, John. b 47. St Chad's Coll Dur BA 71. Westcott Ho Cam 71. **d** 73 **p** 74. C Paddington St Jo w St Mich *Lon* 73–75; C Witney *Ox* 75–78; P-in-c Lt Compton and Chastleton 78–80; R Lt Compton w Chastleton, Cornwell etc 80–83; V Hawkhurst *Cant* 83–97; RD W Charing 89–95; Hon Can Cant Cathl 96–97; P-in-c Devizes St Jo w St Mary *Sarum* 97–07; P-in-c Devizes St Pet 00–04; RD Devizes 98–07; Can and Preb Sarum Cathl 02–07; V Hammersmith St Pet *Lon* 07–14; rtd 15; PtO *Lon* from 15. *135 Watchfield Court, Sutton Court Road, London W4 4NE* M: 07802-716630 E: jrecord47@gmail.com

REDDIN, Mrs Christine Emily. b 46. Essex Univ BA 67. STETS 01. **d** 04 **p** 05. NSM Burpham *Guildf* 04–10; rtd 11; PtO *Guildf* from 11. *1 New Cottages, Sutton Green Road, Sutton Green, Guildford GU4 7QD* T: (01483) 714708 M: 07764-677898 E: c.reddin@sky.com

REDDING, Roger Charles. b 45. Chich Th Coll 87. **d** 89 **p** 90. C Yeovil St Mich *B & W* 89–93; P-in-c Salisbury St Mark *Sarum* 93–94; LtO 94–96; TV Chalke Valley 96–12; Chapl to Travelling People 02–12; rtd 12; PtO *Bris* 02–14; *B & W* from 03; *Win* 12–16. *46 Queen Street, Tintinhull, Yeovil BA22 8PQ* T: (01935) 825057 E: mail@rogerredding.co.uk

REDDINGTON, Gerald Alfred. b 34. S'wark Ord Course 76. **d** 79 **p** 79. NSM St Vedast w St Mich-le-Querne etc *Lon* 79–85; Dir Past Support Gp Scheme 83–86; Hon C St Marylebone All SS 85–90; PtO *Portsm* 88–15; V Ealing St Barn *Lon* 90–99; rtd 99; PtO *Lon* from 02. *The Orange Tree, Madeira Road, Seaview PO34 5BA* T: (01983) 617026 E: rev.redd@btinternet.com

REDEYOFF, Neil Martyn. b 69. St Jo Coll Nottm BA 01. **d** 01 **p** 02. C Grange St Andr and Runcorn H Trin *Ches* 01–04; R Darfield *Sheff* 04–08; P-in-c Finningley w Auckley 08–10; R from 10; AD W Doncaster 11–15. *The Rectory, Rectory Lane, Finningley, Doncaster DN9 3DA* T: (01302) 770240 E: neilredeyoff1@btinternet.com

REDFEARN, Michael. b 42. Open Univ BA 78 Hull Univ MA 84 BA 86. St Aid Birkenhead 64. **d** 68 **p** 69. C Bury St Pet *Man* 68–71; C Swinton St Pet 71–74; Ind Chapl *Bris* 74–79 and 80–81; Ind Chapl Australia 79–80; Ind Chapl *York* 81–86; V Southill and Course Dir St Alb Minl Tr Scheme 86–93; Dep Chapl HM Pris Wandsworth 94; Chapl HM YOI and Rem Cen Feltham 94–97; Chapl HM YOI Aylesbury 97–02; rtd 02; Asst Chapl Palma de Mallorca *Eur* 04–10. *26 Chardwar*

Gardens, Bourton-on-the-Water, Cheltenham GL54 2BL E: mandsfearn42@gmail.com

REDFERN, Lisa. b 67. Man Univ MB, ChB 94 Salford Univ MA 10. All SS Cen for Miss & Min 12. **d** 15 **p** 16. NSM Broadheath *Ches* from 15. *St Alban's Church Office, Lindsell Road, West Timperley, Altrincham WA14 5NX*

REDFERN, Paul. b 48. Ulster Univ BA 88. CITC BTh 94. **d** 94 **p** 95. C Belfast St Aid *Conn* 94–97; I Belfast St Mark 97–03; I Kilbride 03–16; rtd 16. *25 Beechview, Ballyclare BT39 9XT* T: (028) 9332 2895

REDGERS, Brian. b 42. St Jo Coll Dur BA 65 Keswick Hall Coll PGCE 75. Westcott Ho Cam 65. **d** 67 **p** 68. C Rushmere *St E* 67–73; LtO 73–15; PtO *Ely* from 15. *Two Acres, Downham Road, Salters Lode, Downham Market PE38 0AY* T: (01366) 387666 E: revredgers@live.co.uk

REDGRAVE, Christine Howick. b 50. AIAT 73. Trin Coll Bris 75. dss 78 **d** 87 **p** 94. Watford *St Alb* 78–83; Maidenhead St Andr and St Mary *Ox* 83–85; Bracknell 85–96; Par Dn 87–94; TV 94–96; P-in-c Woolhampton w Midgham and Beenham Valance 96–04; Asst Dir of Ords 95–04; Dir of Ords (Reading and Dorchester) 04–10; Hon Can Ch Ch 00–10; C Yoxmere *St E* 10–14; V from 14; RD Saxmundham 12–16. *The Rectory, The Street, Darsham, Saxmundham IP17 3QA* T: (01728) 667095 E: redgrave460@btinternet.com

REDHOUSE, Mark David. b 67. Oak Hill Th Coll BA 94. **d** 94 **p** 95. C Fulham St Mary N End *Lon* 94–96; C Hove Bp Hannington Memorial Ch *Chich* 96–01; V Horam 01–10; RD Dallington 04–07; V Eastbourne All So from 10. *All Souls Vicarage, 53 Susans Road, Eastbourne BN21 3TH* T: (01323) 727033

REDMAN, Anthony James. b 51. Reading Univ BSc 72 Anglia Ruskin Univ MA 05 FRICS 95. EAMTC 01. **d** 03 **p** 04. NSM Bury St Edmunds All SS w St Jo and St Geo *St E* 03–06; NSM Blackbourne from 06; Bp's Officer for Self-Supporting Min from 16; Asst Dioc Dir of Ords from 17. *The Cottage, Great Livermere, Bury St Edmunds IP31 1JG* T: (01359) 269335 F: (01284) 704734 E: tony@theredmans.co.uk

REDMAN, Julia Elizabeth Hithersay. *See* WHITE, Julia Elizabeth Hithersay

REDMAN, Michael John. b 52. St Jo Coll Ox BA 76 MA 80 Heythrop Coll Lon MA 13 Solicitor 86. NTMTC 04. **d** 06 **p** 07. NSM St Marylebone St Paul *Lon* 06–19; rtd 19; PtO *Lon* from 19. *8 Bryanston Mews West, London W1H 2DD* T: (020) 7723 7407 E: redman.michaelj@gmail.com

REDPARTH, Paul Robert. b 58. Open Univ BSc 97 K Coll Lon PhD 01. Westcott Ho Cam 04. **d** 06 **p** 07. C Roughey *Chich* 06–09; C Forest Row 09–11; P-in-c Kirdford 11–16; P-in-c Crowborough St Jo 16–17; V from 17. *St John's Vicarage, St John's Road, Crowborough TN6 1RZ* T: (01892) 668188

REDPATH, Mrs Grace. b 53. TISEC 12. **d** 15 **p** 16. C Duns *Edin* 15–18; C Kelso from 18. *12 Bowmont Court, Heiton, Kelso TD5 8JY* T: (01573) 450752 M: 07768-456671 E: grace.redpath@btconnect.com

REDSHAW, Mrs Alison Janet. b 58. EMMTC 08. **d** 10 **p** 11. NSM Crich and S Wingfield *Derby* 10–13; C and Missr for Retirement Communities Repton 13–16; C Swadlincote *Derby* from 16; C Hartshorne and Bretby from 16. *107 Ashby Road, Burton-on-Trent DE15 0NX* M: 07986-527293 E: revalisonr@gmail.com

REECE, Donald Malcolm Hayden. b 36. CCC Cam BA 58 MA 62. Cuddesdon Coll 58. **d** 60 **p** 61. C Llandrindod *Ches* 60–63; C Matlock and Tansley *Derby* 63–67; C-in-c Hackenthorpe Ch Ch CD 67–70; C Salisbury Cathl Rhodesia 70–73; V Leic St Pet 74–82; V Putney St Marg *S'wark* 82–91; Home Sec Coun for Chr Unity 92–97; Hon C Wandsworth St Anne *S'wark* 94–97; V Shepherd's Bush St Steph w St Thos *Lon* 97–04; rtd 04; PtO *Ox* from 05. *8 Lamarsh Road, Oxford OX2 0LD* T: (01865) 792678 E: dmh.reeve@gmail.com

REECE, Paul Michael. b 60. Southn Univ BA 81. Coll of Resurr Mirfield 83. **d** 85 **p** 86. C Borehamwood *St Alb* 85–89; C Potters Bar 89–92; R Lt Stanmore St Lawr *Lon* from 92; AD Harrow 97–02. *Whitchurch Rectory, St Lawrence Close, Edgware HA8 6RB* T: (020) 8952 0019 F: 8537 0547 M: 07860-690503 E: paul.reece@london.anglican.org

REECE, Roger Walton Arden. b 56. **d** 00 **p** 01. OLM Chadderton St Luke *Man* 00–04; OLM Chadderton St Matt w St Luke 04–08; NSM 08–09; C Ashton 09–16; PtO from 16; Chapl HM Pris Buckley Hall from 08; PtO *Leeds* from 17. *HM Prison Buckley Hall, Buckley Hall Road, Rochdale OL12 9DP* T: (01706) 514300 M: 07904-078901 E: roger.reece@ntlworld.com

REED, Adam Michael Frederick. b 73. Humberside Univ BA 95. Cranmer Hall Dur 96. **d** 99 **p** 00. C Northallerton w Kirby Sigston *York* 99–03; R Middleton, Newton and Sinnington 03–11; V Saltburn-by-the-Sea from 11; V New

Marske from 14. The Vicarage, Greta Street, Saltburn-by-the-Sea TS12 1LS T: (01287) 622007 E: bilpop@btinternet.com

REED, Canon Annette Susan. b 54. Birm Univ BA 76 CQSW 78. Qu Coll Birm 84. **d** 87 **p** 94. C Churchover w Willey *Cov* 89–92; C Clifton upon Dunsmore and Newton 89–92; C Walsgrave on Sowe 92–95; C Cov E 92–95; C Burbage w Aston Flamville *Leic* 95–98; C Hinckley St Mary 95–98; C The Sheepy Gp 98–00; TV Bosworth and Sheepy Gp 00–06; V The Paxtons w Diddington *Ely* 06–15; V The Paxtons w Diddington and Southoe from 15; RD St Neots 07–19; Hon Can Ely Cathl from 14. *The Vicarage, 24 St James's Road, Little Paxton, St Neots PE19 6QW* T: (01480) 211048 E: canonannettereed@gmail.com

REED, Brian. b 43. Bris Univ BSc 65. Linc Th Coll 73. **d** 76 **p** 77. C S Ashford Ch Ch *Cant* 76–78; C Spring Park 78–83; V Barming Heath 83–13; rtd 13; PtO *Cant* from 14. *8 The Thatchers, Maidstone ME16 0XA* T: (01622) 298164 M: 07759-620502

REED, Christopher John. b 42. Selw Coll Cam BA 64 MA 68. Cranmer Hall Dur 64. **d** 67 **p** 68. C Gt Ilford St Andr *Chelmsf* 67–70; P-in-c Bordesley St Andr *Birm* 70–72; V 72–80; V Crofton St Paul *Roch* 80–98; V Yalding w Collier Street 98–08; RD Paddock Wood 01–06; rtd 08; PtO *Roch* from 09. *66 Willow Park, Otford, Sevenoaks TN14 5NG* T: (01959) 523439 E: rev.chris.reed@sky.com

REED, Colin. *See* REED, Matthew Colin

REED, Colin Bryher. b 58. York Univ BA 80 RGN 86. Ridley Hall Cam 93. **d** 95 **p** 96. C Grays North *Chelmsf* 95–99; Chapl Plymouth Hosps NHS Trust 99–02; Hd Chapl Services Norfolk and Nor Univ Hosps NHS Foundn Trust 02–09; Asst RD Ingworth *Nor* 10–11; TR High Oak, Hingham and Scoulton w Wood Rising 11–16; R from 16; RD Humbleyard from 18. *The Rectory, Attleborough Road, Hingham, Norwich NR9 4HP* T: (01953) 853154 M: 07825-559132 E: rev-colinreed@btconnect.com

REED, David. *See* REED, Richard David

REED, Mrs Elizabeth Christine. b 43. Lon Bible Coll Lon Univ BD 65. WMMTC 95. **d** 97 **p** 98. NSM Ledbury *Heref* 97–17; Chapl Bromsgrove Sch 99–06; PtO *Heref* from 17. *The Old Barn, Perrystone Hill, Ross-on-Wye HR9 7QX* T: (01989) 780439 E: 34831@oldbarnperrystone.co.uk

REED, Ethel Patricia Ivy. *See* WESTBROOK, Ethel Patricia Ivy

REED, Harvey. *See* REED, William Harvey

REED, The Ven John Peter Cyril. b 51. BD 78 AKC 78. Ripon Coll Cuddesdon 78. **d** 79 **p** 80. C Croydon St Jo *Cant* 79–82; Prec St Alb Abbey 82–86; R Timsbury and Priston *B & W* 86–93; Chapl Rural Affairs Bath Adnry 87–93; P-in-c Ilminster w Whitelackington 93–94; TR Ilminster and Distr 94–99; Adn Taunton 99–16; rtd 16; PtO *Truro* from 17. *11 Morwellham, Tavistock PL19 8JL* T: (01822) 834105 E: john.morwellham@hotmail.com

REED, John William. b 57. Sussex Univ BSc 79. NOC 95. **d** 97 **p** 98. C Padgate *Liv* 97–99; C Orford St Marg 99–01; V 01–08; P-in-c Golborne 08–13; TV Lowton and Golborne 13–17; P-in-c Gt Crosby St Faith and Waterloo Park St Mary from 17. *St Faith's Vicarage, Milton Road, Waterloo, Liverpool L22 4RE* E: reed926@btinternet.com

REED (née McCARTHY), Mrs Lorraine Valmay. b 52. Birm Univ CertEd 73 Univ of Wales (Ban) BA 95 MTh 97 LGSM 82. SNWTP 09. **d** 11 **p** 12. NSM Middlewich w Byley *Ches* from 11; Asst Dir of Ords from 14. *1 Douglas Close, Hartford, Northwich CW8 1SH* T: (01606) 781071 M: 07711-379339 E: revlvreed@gmail.com

REED, Malcolm Edward. b 45. Graduate Soc Dur MSc 75. Yorks Min Course 08. **d** 10 **p** 11. NSM Hoylandswaine and Silkstone w Stainborough *Wakef* 10–14; NSM Ryhill 14; *Leeds* 14–17; Bp's Hon Asst Chapl *Wakef* 11–14; *Leeds* 14–17; rtd 17; PtO *Leeds* from 18. *Clough Cottage, Cathill, Hoylandswaine, Sheffield S36 7JB* T: (01226) 767328 M: 07803-031199 E: cathillreed@btinternet.com

REED, Matthew Colin. b 50. Edin Univ BD 82. Edin Th Coll 72. **d** 84 **p** 85. C Edin St Pet 84–87; P-in-c Linlithgow 87–94; P-in-c Bathgate 87–91; Chapl HM YOI Polmont 91–94; R Motherwell *Glas* 94–97; R Wishaw 94–97; Hon Asst P Edin St Fillan 00–14; Chapl HM Pris Edin 02–13; Hon C Edin Old St Paul from 14; P-in-c Edin St Marg from 14. *48 Braeside Road South, Gorebridge EH23 4DL* T: (01875) 823169 M: 07713-775435 E: colinmcreed@aol.com

REED, Canon Pamela Kathleen. b 38. EMMTC. dss 84 **d** 87 **p** 94. Cambridge Ascension *Ely* 84–88; Par Dn 87–88; Par Dn Cherry Hinton St Andr 88–90; C 91–95; C Teversham 91–95; V Chesterton St Geo 95–04; Hon Can Ely Cathl 00–04; rtd 04; PtO *Ely* from 04. *14 Woodland Road, Sawston, Cambridge CB22 3DT* T: (01223) 832571 E: pamkreed@hotmail.com

REED, Richard David. b 32. K Alfred's Coll Win CertEd 54 Ex Univ MA 02. Trin Coll Carmarthen. **d** 91 **p** 92. NSM Dale and

St Brides w Marloes *St D* 91–96; P-in-c Blisland w St Breward *Truro* 96–99; rtd 99; PtO *Truro* 99–16; *St D* from 02. *7 Fairsea Close, Hakin, Milford Haven SA73 3RL* T: (01646) 663819 E: dr663819@gmail.com

REED, Simon John. b 63. Trin Coll Ox BA 86 MA 90 K Coll Lon MPhil 05. Wycliffe Hall Ox BA 90. **d** 91 **p** 92. C Walton H Trin *Ox* 91–96; P-in-c Hanger Hill Ascension and W Twyford St Mary *Lon* 96–01; V from 01. *The Ascension Vicarage, Beaufort Road, London W5 3EB* T/F: (020) 8566 9920 E: simonreed@ascensionealing.org

REED, William Harvey. b 47. K Coll Lon BD 69 AKC 69. St Aug Coll Cant 69. **d** 70 **p** 71. C Stockton St Mark CD *Dur* 70–72; C Billingham St Cuth 72–76; C S Westoe 76–79; V Chilton Moor 79–87; R Hutton *Chelmsf* 87–95; V Hullbridge 95–10; C Rawreth w Rettendon 06–10; V Rettendon and Hullbridge 10–12; rtd 12; PtO *Nor* from 12. *117 Lloyds Avenue, Kessingland, Lowestoft NR33 7TT* T: (01502) 741881 E: whreed@btinternet.com

REEDER, Michael William Peter. b 58. Wilson Carlile Coll 84. **d** 09 **p** 10. Chapl St Luke's Hospice Sheff from 07; Hon C Sheff Cathl 09–12; Min Can from 12; Liturg Chapl to Bp Doncaster from 12. *St Luke's Hospice, Little Common Lane, Sheffield S11 9NE* T: 0114-236 9911 M: 07947-706256 E: m.reeder@hospicesheffield.co.uk

REES, Anthony John. b 49. St Jo Coll Dur BA 72 MA 77 Man Univ MEd 89 MPhil 07. **d** 74 **p** 75. C Smethwick St Matt w St Chad *Birm* 74–77; C Bolton St Pet *Man* 77–80; R Cheetham St Mark 80–88; V Mottram in Longdendale w Woodhead *Ches* 88–93; V Mottram in Longdendale 93–02; V Chirk *St As* 02–14; rtd 14; PtO *Blackb* from 14. *31 Redhills Road, Arnside, Carnforth LA5 0AR* T: (01524) 761478 E: tonyandmary75@btinternet.com

REES, Canon Brian Allison. b 48. McGill Univ Montreal BA 74 St Andr Univ BD 76 PhD 80. Montreal Dioc Th Coll 76. **d** 80 **p** 81. C Montreal St Jas and Chapl Concordia Univ Canada 80–82; R Rawdon Ch Ch 82–85; Chapl Bedford Sch 85–92; Hd Master Bedford Prep Sch 92–97; Hd Master Pilgrims' Sch 97–11; rtd 11; Hon Can Win Cathl from 11. *39 Grange Close, Winchester SO23 9RS* T: (01962) 853508 E: brianarees@aol.com

REES, Celia Pamela. b 48. St D Coll Lamp BA 70. **d** 98 **p** 99. OLM Leominster *Heref* 98–18; rtd 19; PtO *Heref* from 19. *Rivendell, 50 Oldfields Close, Leominster HR6 8TL* T: (01568) 616581 *or* 612124

REES, Mrs Christine Deryn Irving. b 57. Nottm Univ BSc Sheff Univ MA. Qu Coll Birm. **d** 00 **p** 01. NSM Astwood Bank *Worc* 00–01; C 01–03; TV Dronfield w Holmesfield *Derby* 03–11; PtO 11–18; *Sheff* 16–19; NSM Gleadless from 19; NSM Hackenthorpe from 19; NSM Woodhouse St Jas from 19. *54 Wake Road, Sheffield S7 1HG* T: 0114-250 7619 E: revdchristine.rees@btopenworld.com

REES, Christopher John. b 40. Dur Univ BA 62. Ridley Hall Cam 62. **d** 64 **p** 65. C Wilmslow *Ches* 64–70; C Birkenhead St Pet w St Matt 70–74; V Lostock Gralam 75–83; R Davenham 83–96; P-in-c Aldford and Bruera 96–05; rtd 05; PtO *Ches* from 05. *15 Chapel Close, Comberbach, Northwich CW9 6BA* T: (01606) 891366 E: christopherrees954@btinternet.com

REES, David Richard. b 60. St Mich Coll Llan. **d** 84 **p** 85. C Llanstadwel *St D* 84–86; C Carmarthen St Dav 86–91; V Llanrhian w Llanhywel and Carnhedryn etc 91–99; V Spittal w Trefgarn and Ambleston w St Dogwells from 99. *The Vicarage, Spittal, Haverfordwest SA62 5QP* T: (01437) 741505 E: rev.rees@btinternet.com

REES, Ms Diane Eluned. b 61. Univ of Wales (Ban) BSc 82 Univ of Wales (Swansea) MEd 87 K Coll Lon DThMin 13 Em Coll Cam PGCE 83 CPsychol 87 AFBPsS 84. St Jo Coll Nottm BTh 95 MA 96. **d** 96 **p** 97. C Hall Green St Pet *Birm* 96–00; P-in-c Bozeat w Easton Maudit *Pet* 00–03; C Putney St Mary *S'wark* 03–04; TV 04–05; Asst Dir of Min and Tr *Roch* 06–09; PtO 09–15; V Shoreham from 15; Chapl St Mich Sch Otford from 15. *The Vicarage, Station Road, Shoreham, Sevenoaks TN14 7SA* T: (01959) 522363 M: 07764-678661 E: revdrdi@outlook.com

REES, Emma Louise. *See* REES-KENNY, Emma Louise

REES, Canon Ian Kendall. b 66. St Mich Coll Llan 98. **d** 00 **p** 01. C Barry All SS *Llan* 00–03; Assoc P Grangetown 03–05; P-in-c Pyle w Kenfig 05–10; R Llandrindod w Cefnllys and Disserth *S & B* 10–13; V Gowerton 13–16; V Cen Swansea from 16; Bp's Officer for Lay Min 14–18; Dioc Dir for Ords and Voc from 18; Hon Can Brecon Cathl from 16. *50 St Catherine's Court, Maritime Quarter, Swansea SA1 1SD* T: (01792) 472760 E: ianrees66@gmail.com

REES, Jane Elizabeth. b 70. K Coll Lon BD 92. Westcott Ho Cam 12 ERMC 13. **d** 14 **p** 15. NSM Wisbech St Mary and Guyhirn w Ring's End etc *Ely* 14–17; NSM March from 17. *49 Gresley Way, March PE15 8QA* E: revjanerees@gmail.com

REES, Jennifer Mary. *See* MORRELL, Jennifer Mary

REES, Joanna Mary. *See* STOKER, Joanna Mary

REES, John. *See* REES, Vivian John Howard

REES, John Nigel. b 58. Derby Lonsdale Coll BCombStuds 79 Coll of Ripon & York St Jo PGCE 80. STETS 03. **d** 06 **p** 07. NSM Broad Blunsdon and Highworth w Sevenhampton and Inglesham etc *Bris* 06–10; P-in-c Rowde and Bromham *Sarum* 10–16; R Canalside Benefice from 16; Chapl Wilts Air Ambulance from 18. *The Rectory, 22 Warren Road, Staverton, Trowbridge BA14 8UZ* M: 07912-503267 E: canalsidebeneficerector@gmail.com

REES, Canon John Philip Walford. b 41. St D Coll Lamp BA 62 Linacre Coll Ox BA 64 MA 69 Univ of Wales (Cardiff) BD 72. Wycliffe Hall Ox 62. **d** 64 **p** 65. C Reading St Jo *Ox* 64–67; V Patrick *S & M* 67–68; C Pontypool *Mon* 68–70; Area Sec CMS Glouc, Heref and Worc 70–75; V Bream *Glouc* 75–91; Team Ldr Ichthus Chr Fellowship 91–96; TV Glyncorrwg w Afan Vale and Cymmer Afan *Llan* 96–99; R Llandogo and Tintern *Mon* 99–00; R Llandogo w Whitebrook Chpl and Tintern Parva 00–07; AD Monmouth 02–06; Hon Can St Woolos Cathl 05–07; rtd 07; PtO *Glouc* from 15. *Sparrow Cottage, The Narth, Monmouth NP25 4QG* T: (01600) 869194

REES, Canon Judith Margaret. b 39. Southn Univ BTh 89. dss 86 **d** 87 **p** 94. Sanderstead All SS *S'wark* 86–87; Par Dn 87; Dir Cottesloe Chr Tr Progr *Ox* 89–99; Par Dn Gt Horwood 89–91; Par Dn Winslow w Gt Horwood and Addington 91–94; C 94–99; RD Claydon 96–99; Hon Can Ch Ch 97–99; rtd 99; PtO *Sarum* from 01. *10 Hadrians Close, Salisbury SP2 9NN* T: (01722) 410050 E: sidcot@btinternet.com

REES, Leslie. b 49. Leeds Univ LLB 72. NOC 03. **d** 06 **p** 07. NSM Swinton H Rood *Man* 06–08; NSM Eccles 08–09; NSM Hanbury, Newborough, Rangemore and Tutbury *Lich* 09–14; P-in-c 14–18; C Rolleston 14–18; C Anslow 14–18; V Hanbury, Newborough and Rangemoor from 18. *The New Vicarage, Church Lane, Hanbury, Burton-on-Trent DE13 8TF* T: (01283) 813357 E: leslie.rees@virgin.net

REES, Canon Michael Lloyd. b 51. St D Coll Lamp. **d** 74 **p** 75. C Cardigan w Mwnt and Y Ferwig *St D* 74–77; Min Can St D Cathl 77–81; TV Aberystwyth 81–83; Dioc Children's Adv 83–92; V Pen-boyr 83–88; V Henfynyw w Aberaeron and Llanddewi Aberarth 88–99; RD Glyn Aeron 95–99; V Gors-las 99–13; V Betws w Ammanford 13–15; AD Dyffryn Aman 07–14; Can St D Cathl 95–14; rtd 15; PtO *St D* from 15; *Ban* from 18; *Eur* from 18. *3 Clôs Y Drindod, Buarth Road, Aberystwyth SY23 1LR* T: (01970) 627593 M: 07972-602620 E: michaelrees2013@outlook.com *or* mlr1@hotmail.co.uk

REES (née CURREY), Mrs Pauline Carol. b 46. WMMTC 94. **d** 98 **p** 99. OLM Leominster *Heref* 98–16; rtd 17; PtO *Heref* from 17. *Crossways Cottage, Leysters, Leominster HR6 0HR* T: (01568) 750300 *or* 612124 E: rees.crossways@btinternet.com

REES, Philip. *See* REES, John Philip Walford

REES, Canon Richard John Edward Williams. b 36. Univ of Wales (Lamp) BA 58. St Mich Coll Llan 58. **d** 60 **p** 61. C St Issells *St D* 60–64; C Llanedy 64–67; V Whitchurch w Solva and St Elvis 67–77; V Whitchurch w Solva and St Elvis w Brawdy etc 77–01; RD Dewisland and Fishguard 73–01; Can St D Cathl 87–01; Treas St D Cathl 97–01; rtd 01; PtO *St D* from 05. *The Smithy, Cheriton, Stackpole, Pembroke SA71 5BZ* T: (01646) 672235 E: richardrees396@btinternet.com

REES, Mrs Sally Elizabeth. b 14. NSM Crickhowell *S & B* 14–15; NSM Gtr Brecon from 16; Bp's Officer for Min to Older People from 18. *Curlews, Tretower, Crickhowell, NP8 1RG* T: (01873) 811332 E: sallyrees50@gmail.com

REES, Stephen Philip. b 70. St Luke's Coll Ex BA. Oak Hill Th Coll BA 03. **d** 03 **p** 04. C Moreton-in-Marsh w Batsford, Todenham etc *Glouc* 03–06; P-in-c Lt Heath *St Alb* 06–12; V 12–16; V Crowborough *Chich* from 16. *All Saints Vicarage, Church Road, Crowborough TN6 1ED* T: (01892) 652081 M: 07970-619469 E: zipyzac@globalnet.com *or* steve@allsaintscrowborough.org

REES, Miss Susan Mary. b 61. Univ of Wales (Cardiff) BSc 82 Ox Univ BTh 05. Ripon Coll Cuddesdon 00. **d** 02 **p** 03. C Penarth All SS *Llan* 02–05; C Roath 05–08; P-in-c Eglwysilan 08–14; P-in-c Pontyclun w Talygarn 14–19; P-in-c Llanharry 14–19. *Address temp unknown* E: susanmrees@hotmail.com

REES, Vivian John Howard. b 51. Southn Univ LLB 72 Ox Univ BA 79 MA 84 Leeds Univ MPhil 84. Wycliffe Hall Ox 76. **d** 79 **p** 80. C Moor Allerton *Ripon* 79–82; Sierra Leone 82–86; Lct Ox from 86; Jt Dioc Reg from 98; Dep Prov Reg 98–00; Prov Reg from 00; Legal Adv ACC from 98; Hon Prov Can Cant Cathl from 01; Hon Can Ch Ch *Ox* from 17; Chapl to The Queen from 14. *Oxford Diocesan Registry,*

2 Chawley Park, Cumnor Hill, Oxford OX2 9GG T: (01865) 297214 F: 726274 E: jrees@wslaw.co.uk

REES-JONES, Mrs Diana Mary. b 58. St Jo Coll Dur BA 80 Anglia Ruskin Univ MA 07 Hughes Hall Cam PGCE 81. Ridley Hall Cam 04. **d** 07 **p** 08. C Ness Gp *Linc* 07–09; Asst Chapl Oundle Sch 09–13; PtO *Pet* 13–14; C Northampton St Giles 14–19; rtd 19. *Address temp unknown*

REESE, Preb John David. b 49. Cuddesdon Coll 73. **d** 76 **p** 77. C Kidderminster St Mary *Worc* 76–81; Malaysia 81–85; V Bishop's Castle w Mainstone *Heref* 85–91; RD Clun Forest 87–91; V Tupsley 91–93; P-in-c Hampton Bishop and Mordiford w Dormington 91–93; V Tupsley w Hampton Bishop 93–98; RD Heref City 96–02; TR Heref S Wye 08–14; Preb Heref Cathl 96–14; rtd 14; PtO *Cov* from 15. *32 Burns Road, Leamington Spa CV32 7EL* T: (01926) 833389

REES-KENNY, Mrs Emma Louise. b 79. Univ of Wales (Abth) BTh 01. St Mich Coll Llan MTh 11. **d** 11 **p** 12. C Barry All SS *Llan* 11–15; V Llansantffraid-yn-Mechain and Llanfechain *St As* 15–16; TV Vyrnwy Miss Area 17–18; TV Canton Cardiff *Llan* from 18. *The New Rectory, 3A Romilly Road, Canton, Cardiff CF5 1FH* T: (01691) 829307 E: reverendemma@gmail.com

REEVE, Canon Brian Charles. b 36. Lon Univ BSc 57 BD 60. Tyndale Hall Bris 58. **d** 61 **p** 62. C Eccleston St Luke *Liv* 61–63; C Upton (Overchurch) *Ches* 63–65; C Pemberton St Mark Newtown *Liv* 65–68; V Macclesfield Ch Ch *Ches* 68–74; V Stone Ch Ch *Lich* 74–84; RD Trentham 77–84; V Hoole *Ches* 84–94; Chapl Ches City Hosp 84–91; P-in-c Alderley *Ches* 94–01; Dioc Warden of Readers 94–00; Hon Can Ches Cathl 94–01; rtd 01; PtO *Ches* 02–14; *Lich* from 09. *18 Mount Crescent, Stone ST15 8LR* T: (01785) 749178 E: reeveinleek@talktalk.net

REEVE, David Michael. b 44. St Cath Coll Cam BA 67 MA 71. Coll of Resurr Mirfield 68. **d** 70 **p** 71. C Willingdon *Chich* 70–73; C Hove All SS 73–76; C Moulsecoomb 76–80; R Singleton and V E and W Dean 80–90; R Hurstpierpoint 90–99; R Kingston Buci 99–05; rtd 05; PtO *Cant* from 06; Clergy Widows Officer Cant Adnry from 09. *11 Wells Avenue, Canterbury CT1 3YB* T: (01227) 478446

REEVE, Kenneth John. b 42. Sarum & Wells Th Coll 91. **d** 93 **p** 94. C Thorpe St Matt *Nor* 93–96; P-in-c S Lynn 96–99; PtO 03–04; P-in-c Gt and Lt Ellingham, Rockland and Shropham etc 04–11; RD Thetford and Rockland 09–11; rtd 11; PtO *Nor* from 11. *Anglebeck, Heath Road, Kenninghall, Norwich NR16 2DS* T: (01953) 887582 E: kenreeve@btinternet.com

REEVE, Michael. *See* REEVE, David Michael

REEVE, Richard Malcolm. b 64. Reading Univ BSc 85. Trin Coll Bris BA 92. **d** 92 **p** 93. C Northolt St Mary *Lon* 92–95; C Acton Green 95–98; V Hayes St Edm 98–08; TR Tettenhall Regis *Lich* from 08. *The Rectory, 2 Lloyd Road, Tettenhall, Wolverhampton WV6 9AU* T: (01902) 742801 E: richardmreeve@aol.com

REEVE, Preb Roger Patrick. b 42. Fitzw Coll Cam BA 65 MA 68. Coll of Resurr Mirfield. **d** 67 **p** 68. C Barnstaple St Pet w H Trin *Ex* 67–74; V Ernesettle 74–78; V Braunton 78–05; RD Barnstaple 85–93 and 01–03; Preb Ex Cathl from 92; rtd 05. *27 Westacott Meadow, Barnstaple EX32 8QX* T: (01271) 326927 E: rogerreeve@cwcom.net

REEVE, Sally Ann. *See* EPPS, Sally Ann

REEVES, David Eric. b 46. Sarum Th Coll 68. **d** 71 **p** 72. C Guildf H Trin w St Mary 71–74; C Warmsworth *Sheff* 74–78; V Herringthorpe 78–90; V Cleveleys *Blackb* 90–12; RD Poulton 94–00; rtd 12; PtO *Blackb* from 12. *443 North Drive, Thornton-Cleveleys FY5 3AP* T: (01253) 864636

REEVES, Donald St John. b 34. Qu Coll Cam BA 57 MA 61 Lambeth MLitt 03. Cuddesdon Coll 62. **d** 63 **p** 64. C Maidstone All SS w St Phil *Cant* 63–65; Bp's Dom Chapl *S'wark* 65–68; V St Helier 69–80; R Westmr St Jas *Lon* 80–98; Dir Soul of Eur Project from 98; rtd 98; PtO *Ex* from 00. *The Coach House, Church Street, Crediton EX17 2AQ* T: (01363) 775100 F: 773911 E: donalreeve@aol.com *or* donaldnunn34@gmail.com

REEVES, Elizabeth Anne. *See* THOMAS, Elizabeth Anne

REEVES, George Edward Charles. b 70. Dundee Univ MA 92. St Jo Coll Nottm 11. **d** 13 **p** 14. C Ashton *Man* 13–17; R Levenshulme from 17. *1 Windmill Lane, Denton, Manchester M34 3RN* T: 0161-335 9675 M: 07484-310276 E: revgeorgereeves@outlook.com

REEVES, Gillian Patricia. b 46. S'wark Ord Course 87. **d** 90 **p** 94. Par Dn Shirley St Geo *S'wark* 90–94; C 94–96; C Caterham 96–98; TV 98–12; rtd 12. *3 Kynaston Court, Underwood Road, Caterham CR3 6BB* E: revgill99@hotmail.com

REEVES, Graham. b 65. Southn Univ BTh 94 Univ Coll Chich MA 04. Chich Th Coll 94. **d** 94 **p** 95. C Cardiff St Mary and St Steph w St Dyfrig etc *Llan* 94–95; C Roath 95–98; Chapl Sussex Weald and Downs NHS Trust 98–02; Chapl W

Sussex Health and Soc Care NHS Trust 02–08; Chapl Sussex Partnership NHS Foundn Trust from 08; NSM Aldingbourne, Barnham and Eastergate *Chich* from 18; OSB from 11. *2 Abbottsbury, Bognor Regis PO21 4RX* T: (01243) 265209 E: graham.reeves@sussexpartnership.nhs.uk

REEVES, Helen Marie. b 68. SEITE BA 15. **d** 15 **p** 16. NSM Gravesend St Geo *Roch* 15–18; R Ash from 18; R Ridley from 18. *The Rectory, 11 Lambardes, New Ash Green, Longfield DA3 8HX* T: (01474) 872209 E: ashandridleyrector@gmail.com

REEVES, John Graham. b 44. Kelham Th Coll 64. **d** 69 **p** 71. C Aston cum Aughton *Sheff* 69–71; C Ribbleton *Blackb* 72–74; C Cleveleys 74–75; P-in-c Huncoat 75–77; V 77–82; V Knuzden 82–92; V Sandylands 92–09; rtd 09; PtO *Blackb* from 09. *51 Parkfield Drive, Lancaster LA1 4BT* T: (01524) 411299 E: revjgr961@btinternet.com

REEVES, Kenneth William. b 38. TCD 67. **d** 69 **p** 70. C Killowen *D & R* 69–70; I Ardara 70–75; TV Quidenham *Nor* 76–81; V Swaffham 81–86; Chapl Nor City Coll of F&HE 86–91; P-in-c Lakenham St Alb 86–91; rtd 92; PtO *Nor* 92–98 and from 05; P-in-c Trowse 99–03; P-in-c Nerja and Almuñécar *Eur* 03–04. *Address temp unknown* E: revkenn@btinternet.com

REEVES, Maria Elizabeth Ann. *See* COULTER, Maria Elizabeth Ann

REEVES, Nicholas John Harding. b 44. Glos Univ BA 99 Nottm Univ MA 02 Dur Univ DThM 14. ALCD 69. **d** 69 **p** 70. C Upton (Overchurch) *Ches* 69–72; C Woodlands *Sheff* 72–74; C-in-c Cranham Park CD *Chelmsf* 74–79; V Cranham Park 79–88; R Aldridge *Lich* 88–02; Dioc Officer for Evang *Carl* 03–10; rtd 09; V Dacre *Carl* 12–16; PtO *Lich* from 17. *Trefonen Cottage, Trefonen, Oswestry SY10 9DZ* T: (01691) 590172 M: 07400-340668 E: the7reeves@aol.com

REEVES, Pamela Lindsay. b 49. Ridley Hall Cam 06. **d** 07 **p** 08. C Immingham, Habrough Gp and Keelby Gp *Linc* 07–09; C Scawby, Redbourne and Hibaldstow 09–10; C Bishop Norton, Waddingham and Snitterby 09–10; C Kirton in Lindsey w Manton 09–10; C Grayingham 09–10; S Wolds Community Chapl from 10; C Wolds Gateway Group from 17. *Maple Cottage, Aylesby, Grimsby DN37 7AW* M: 07756-852907 E: pamcostin@yahoo.co.uk

REGAN, Brian. b 46. MBIM 80. WMMTC 88. **d** 91 **p** 92. C Cov St Jo 91–94; V Tile Hill 94–09; PtO *Cov* from 09. *160 Ansley Road, Nuneaton CV10 8NU* T: (024) 7673 4240 M: 07766-721837 E: brianregan32@hotmail.com

REGAN, Canon Noel Henry Likely. b 49. **d** 99 **p** 00. Aux Min Cloonclare w Killasnett, Lurganboy and Drumlease *K, E & A* 99–06; Dioc C and P-in-c Garrison w Slavin and Belleek *Clogh* 06–11; I Clogh w Errigal Portclare 11–16; Prec Clogh Cathl 11–16; rtd 16; P-in-c Skreen w Kilmacshalgan and Dromard *T, K & A* from 18. *Gurteen Farm, Cliffoney, Co Sligo, Republic of Ireland* T: (00353) (71) 916 6253 M: 86-887 5714

REGAN, Paul John. b 67. Southn Univ BA 88 PhD 96 St Jo Coll Dur BA 98. Cranmer Hall Dur 96. **d** 99 **p** 00. C St Alb St Pet 99–03; TV Smestow Vale *Lich* 03–09; Chapl Trevelyan Coll *Dur* 09–14; Chapl Dur Univ 09–14; C Dur St Oswald and Shincliffe 09–14; Tutor Cranmer Hall Dur from 14. *Cranmer Hall, St John's College, 3 South Bailey, Durham DH1 3RJ* T: 0191-334 3893 E: cran.udos@durham.ac.uk

REICH, Joachim. b 66. ERMC 18. **d** 96 **p** 99. NSM Berlin *Eur* from 19. *St George's Anglican Church, Preussenallee 17-19, 14052 Berlin, Germany* T: (0049) (30) 304 1280 E: reich.joachim@email.de

REID, Alison Margaret. *See* WADSWORTH, Alison Margaret

REID, Amanda Joy. *See* MARRIOTT, Amanda Joy

REID, Andrew John. b 47. Birm Univ BEd 70 Man Univ MEd 76. S'wark Ord Course 88. **d** 88 **p** 89. NSM Westerham *Roch* 88–90; Chapl Abp Tenison's Sch Kennington 90–05; PtO *Roch* from 05. *12 Westways, Westerham TN16 1TT* T: (01959) 561428

REID, Andrew John. b 58. Thames Poly BA 90. Trin Coll Bris 09. **d** 11 **p** 12. C Chorleywood St Andr *St Alb* 11–15; R Musselburgh *Edin* from 15. *12 Windsor Gardens, Musselburgh EH21 7LP* T: 0131-653 4809 *or* 665 3585 M: 07854-049875 E: revreidserving@gmail.com

REID, Andrew Kieran. b 67. Coll of SS Mark and Jo Plymouth BA 90. Trin Coll Bris 10. **d** 12 **p** 13. C Addlestone *Guildf* 12–15; C Woking Ch Ch 15–19; V New Haw from 19. *The Vicarage, 149 Woodham Lane, New Haw, Addlestone KT15 3NJ* M: 07799-883412 E: andykreid@outlook.com *or* newhawvicar@gmail.com

REID, Angus David Ingvar. b 77. K Coll Lon LLB 99 Nottm Univ MA 14. Westcott Ho Cam 14. **d** 18 **p** 19. C Hove All SS *Chich* from 18. *28 Lyndhurst Road, Hove BN3 6FA* T: (01273) 959158 M: 07884-207270 E: angusreid40@hotmail.com

REID, Catherine Elizabeth. b 79. Hull Univ BA 00 MA 02 St Petersburg State Univ PhD 07. Coll of Resurr

Mirfield MA 14. **d** 14 **p** 15. C Ingleby Barwick *York* 14–17; V Ampleforth w Oswaldkirk, Gilling E etc from 17. *The Vicarage, West End, Ampleforth, York YO62 4DU* E: crcatherinereid@gmail.com

REID, Christopher Jason. b 69. Glos Univ BA 08. Trin Coll Bris 01. **d** 03 **p** 04. C Woodley *Ox* 03–07; V Selby St Jas *York* from 07. *St James's Vicarage, 14 Leeds Road, Selby YO8 4HX* T: (01757) 702861 E: cjasonreid@hotmail.com

REID, Canon Colin Guthrie. b 30. **d** 56 **p** 57. C Kendal St Thos *Carl* 56–59; C Crosthwaite Keswick 59–60; R Caldbeck w Castle Sowerby 60–76; RD Wigton 69–70; P-in-c Sebergham 75; R Caldbeck, Castle Sowerby and Sebergham 76–93; Hon Can Carl Cathl 88–93; rtd 93; PtO *Carl* from 93. *Mellbreak, Longthwaite Road, Wigton CA7 9JR* T: (016973) 45625

REID, David Graham. b 78. Hatf Coll Dur BSc 00. Wycliffe Hall Ox BTh 09. **d** 09 **p** 10. C Ox St Ebbe w H Trin and St Pet 09–18; PtO from 18. *50 Ramsay Road, Headington, Oxford OX3 8AY* T: (01865) 430965 E: davereid78@gmail.com

REID, Mrs Diane Mary. b 73. Lanc Univ BMus 94 Huddersfield Univ PGCE 98. Trin Coll Bris BA 04. **d** 04 **p** 05. C Reading St Agnes w St Paul and St Barn *Ox* 04–07; PtO *York* 11–12; Hon C Selby St Jas from 12. *St James's Vicarage, 14 Leeds Road, Selby YO8 4HX* T: (01757) 702861 E: dianereid2003@hotmail.com

REID, Donald. b 58. Glas Univ LLB 79 Pemb Coll Ox MPhil 81 Edin Univ BD 85. Edin Th Coll 82. **d** 85 **p** 86. C Greenock *Glas* 85–88; C Baillieston 88–91; R 91–95; C Glas St Serf 88–91; R 91–95; Chapl Glas Univ 89–00; Chapl Glas Caledonian Univ 89–00; Chapl Strathclyde Univ 89–00; TP Glas St Mary 95–00; Assoc P 00–04; C Edin St Jo 04–13; Chapl St Columba's Hospice Edin 13–16; PtO *Edin* 15–17. *Address temp unknown* E: dreid212@me.com

REID, Eileen. b 54. **d** 12 **p** 13. NSM Westward, Rosley-w-Woodside and Welton *Carl* 12–18; P-in-c from 18; NSM Caldbeck, Castle Sowerby and Sebergham 12–18; P-in-c from 18. *Ceardach, Brackenthwaite, Wigton CA7 8AS* T: (01697) 343089 E: ereid2002@yahoo.co.uk

REID, Gareth McEwan. b 82. Univ of Wales (Abth) BA 03. St Mich Coll Llan BTh 10. **d** 10 **p** 11. C Dewisland *St D* 10–13; P-in-c Llandysul w Bangor Teifi and Llanfairollwyn etc from 13; Dioc Warden Ords 14–15. *The Vicarage, Tanyfron, Well Street, Llandysul SA44 4DR* T: (01559) 363874 E: garethmreid@googlemail.com

✠**REID, The Rt Revd Gavin Hunter.** b 34. K Coll Lon BA 56. Oak Hill Th Coll 56. **d** 60 **p** 61 **c** 92. C E Ham St Paul *Chelmsf* 60–63; C Rainham 63–66; Publications Sec CPAS 66–71; Hon C St Paul's Cray St Barn *Roch* 68–71; Ed Sec USCL 71–74; Hon C Woking St Jo *Guildf* 72–92; Sec for Evang CPAS 74–92; Consultant Missr CPAS and BMU Adv 90–92; Suff Bp Maidstone *Cant* 92–00; Six Preacher Cant Cathl 92–97; rtd 00; PtO *Nor* from 00; *St E* from 00; Hon Asst Bp St E from 08. *Furzefield, 17 Richard Crampton Road, Beccles NR34 9HN* T: (01502) 717042 F: 710739 M: 07941-770549 E: gavin@reids.org

REID, Geraldine Felicity (Jo). b 47. RGN 69. EMMTC 95. **d** 98 **p** 99. NSM Skellingthorpe w Doddington *Linc* 98–02; NSM Hykeham from 02. *Tol Peden, Monson Park, Skellingthorpe, Lincoln LN6 5UE* T: (01522) 828402 or 828403 E: tolpedn@ntlworld.com

REID, James. b 46. Strathclyde Univ BSc 69. WMMTC 88. **d** 91 **p** 92. C Attleborough *Cov* 91–95; V Walsall Pleck and Bescot *Lich* 95–99; TR Cheddleton Grange 99–04; rtd 06; PtO *Cov* from 08. *22 St Ives Way, Nuneaton CV11 6FR* T: (024) 7634 2264 E: jimoreid@gmail.com

REID, Jason. *See* REID, Christopher Jason

REID, Jo. *See* REID, Geraldine Felicity

REID, Joanne. b 68. St Mich Coll Llan 08. **d** 10 **p** 11. C Brize Norton and Carterton *Ox* 10–14; TV Savernake *Sarum* from 14. *The Vicarage, Church Street, Collingbourne Ducis, Marlborough SN8 3EL* T: (01264) 850385 E: jo.reid185@btinternet.com

REID, Miss Margaret Patricia. b 41. Hull Univ BSc 62 Leeds Univ MA 07. Yorks Min Course 09. **d** 10 **p** 11. NSM Ilkley All SS *Bradf* 10–14; *Leeds* from 14. *1 Chestnut Close, Ilkley LS29 8PX* T: (01943) 609232 E: pat.reid29@btinternet.com

REID, Mrs Pauline Ann. b 57. Anglia Ruskin Univ MA 10. EAMTC 00. **d** 03 **p** 04. C Silverstone and Abthorpe w Slapton etc *Pet* 03–07; P-in-c Raddesley Gp *Ely* 07–14; P-in-c Cley Hill Villages *Sarum* 14–19; R from 19; RD Heytesbury from 15. *The Rectory, 6 Homefields, Longbridge Deverill, Warminster BA12 7DQ* T: (01985) 841290 M: 07586-358162 E: revpauline@btinternet.com

REID, Roderick Andrew Montgomery. b 80. Brunel Univ BSc 01 Trin Hall Cam BTh 10. Westcott Ho Cam 08. **d** 11 **p** 12. C Waltham H Cross *Chelmsf* 11–14; C Bocking St Mary 14–16; C Panfield and Rayne 16; P-in-c Bocking St Mary and Panfield from 16. *The Deanery, Deanery Hill,*

Braintree CM7 5SR T: (01376) 324887 M: 07799-734898 E: rod.a.reid@gmail.com

REID, Stewart Thomas. b 45. Liv Hope MA 01. Oak Hill Th Coll 66. **d** 70 **p** 71. C Normanton *Derby* 70–73; C Leyland St Andr *Blackb* 73–78; V Halliwell St Luke *Man* 78–95; V Southport Ch Ch *Liv* 95–16; rtd 16; PtO *Liv* from 16. *1 Sanderling Drive, Banks, Southport PR9 8RY* T: (01704) 226400 E: stewartreid1945@icloud.com

REID, Stuart Alexander. York Univ MEng. CITI. **d** 17. Faughanvale *D & R* from 17. *41 Millburn Road, Coleraine BT52 1QT* M: 07951-723619 E: streid@tcd.ie

REIDE, Susannah Louise Court. b 69. Clare Coll Cam BA 91. Trin Coll Bris BA 04. **d** 04 **p** 05. C Marlborough *Sarum* 04–08; TV Cowley St Jas *Ox* 08–11; PtO 11–18; Chapl Harris Manchester Coll Ox from 18. *96 Cricket Close, Oxford OX4 3DJ* T: (01865) 401439 E: sr@reide.plus.com

REIGATE, Archdeacon of. *See* ASTIN, The Ven Moira Anne Elizabeth

REILLY, Thomas Gerard. b 38. **d** 64 **p** 64. In RC Ch 64–73; Hon C Clapton Park All So *Lon* 73–76; Hon C Haggerston All SS 76–78; Hon C Walthamstow St Sav *Chelmsf* 79–85; P-in-c Forest Gate Em w Upton Cross 85–89; V 89–92; V Chaddesden St Phil *Derby* 92–01; RD Derby N 95–00; rtd 01; PtO *B & W* 01–12 and from 17; *Eur* from 17. *High Beech, East Street, Crewkerne TA18 7AG* T: (01460) 76246 E: grryreilly@yahoo.co.uk

REILY, Jacqueline Estelle. b 61. Oak Hill Th Coll BA 84. ERMC 08. **d** 11 **p** 12. C Rayleigh *Chelmsf* 11–14; Chapl Scargill Ho from 14. *Scargill House, Kettlewell, Skipton BD23 5HU* T: (01756) 761236 M: 07580-114641 E: admin@scargillmovement.org or jackie@reily.co.uk or jackie.reily@scargillmorement.org

REILY, Paul Alan. b 59. UEA BA 81. St Jo Coll Nottm MA 92. **d** 92 **p** 93. C Westcliff St Mich *Chelmsf* 92–96; P-in-c Barkingside St Cedd 96–98; V 98–01; V Leyton St Cath and St Paul 01–11; AD Waltham Forest 04–07; PtO 11–14; *Leeds* from 17. *Scargill House, Kettlewell, Skipton BD23 5HU* T: (01756) 761236 M: 07967-977115 E: paul@reily.co.uk

REINDORP, David Peter Edington. b 52. Trin Coll Cam BA 82 MA 86 CQSW 77. Westcott Ho Cam 79. **d** 83 **p** 84. C Chesterton Gd Shep *Ely* 83–85; C Hitchin *St Alb* 85–88; R Landbeach and V Waterbeach *Ely* 88–97; OCM 88–97; CF(V) 92–12; RD Quy *Ely* 94–97; V Cherry Hinton St Jo 97–06; RD Cambridge 04–06; Hon Can Ely Cathl 05–06; V Chelsea All SS *Lon* from 06; AD Chelsea 11–17. *2 Old Church Street, London SW3 5DQ* T: (020) 7352 5627 E: david.reindorp@talk21.com

REINDORP, Canon Michael Christopher Julian. b 44. Trin Coll Cam BA 67 MA 70 K Coll Lon MA 99. Cuddesdon Coll 67 United Th Coll Bangalore 68. **d** 69 **p** 70. C Poplar *Lon* 69–74; V Chatham St Wm *Roch* 74–84; R Stantonbury *Ox* 84–87; TR Stantonbury and Willen 87–92; P-in-c Richmond St Mary w St Matthias and St Jo *S'wark* 92–95; TR 96–09; Hon Can S'wark Cathl 03–09; rtd 09; PtO *Lon* from 10; *S'wark* from 11. *10 Alpha Road, Teddington TW11 0QG* T: (020) 8614 6800 E: julianreindorp@hotmail.co.uk

REISS, Prof Michael Jonathan. b 58. Trin Coll Cam BA 78 MA 82 PhD 82 PGCE 83 FIBiol 90 Open Univ MBA 02. EAMTC 87. **d** 90 **p** 91. Lect Cam Univ 88–94; Reader 94–00; NSM Comberton *Ely* 90–94; NSM Deanery of Bourn 94–96; NSM 99–00; P-in-c Boxworth and Elsworth w Knapwell 96–99; PtO 99–03; Prof Science Educn Inst of Educn Lon Univ from 01; NSM Toft w Caldecote and Childerley *Ely* 03–10; NSM Lordsbridge from 10. *Institute of Education, University of London, 20 Bedford Way, London WC1H 0AL* T: (020) 7947 9522 E: m.reiss@ucl.ac.uk

REISS, Canon Peter Henry. b 62. Hertf Coll Ox BA 85 MA 91 Natal Univ MA 95. St Jo Coll Nottm 95. **d** 95 **p** 96. C Sherwood *S'well* 95–00; TV Bestwood 00–03; V Bestwood Park w Rise Park 03–04; Tr Officer CME and Laity Development *Man* 04–06; Dir Discipleship and Min Tr from 06; Hon Can Man Cathl from 11. *Discipleship and Ministry Training, 5th Floor, Church House, 90 Deansgate, Manchester M3 2GJ* T: 0161-828 1455 F: 828 1485 E: preiss@manchester.anglican.org

REISS, Canon Robert Paul. b 43. Trin Coll Cam BA 67 MA 71 Lambeth PhD 12. Westcott Ho Cam 67. **d** 69 **p** 70. C St John's Wood *Lon* 69–73; Bangladesh 73; Chapl Trin Coll Cam 73–78; Selection Sec ACCM 78–85; Sen Selection Sec 83; TR Grantham *Linc* 86–96; RD 92–96; Adn Surrey and Hon Can Guildf Cathl 96–05; Can Westmr Abbey 05–13; rtd 13; Min and Tr Consultant *S'wark* from 13; PtO from 13. *35 Addington Square, London SE5 7LB* M: 07545-178192 E: bobreiss@hotmail.com

REITH, Robert Michael. b 55. Oak Hill Th Coll BA 83. **d** 83 **p** 84. C Kendal St Thos *Carl* 83–87; C Leyland St Andr *Blackb* 87–92; V Leyland St Jo 92–94; TR Dagenham *Chelmsf*

94–03; V 03–14; rtd 14. *155 Woodward Road, Dagenham RM9 4SU* M: 07595-303023 E: mikereith@me.com

RENAUT, Vanessa Anne. See HERRICK, Vanessa Anne

RENDALL, Canon John Albert. b 43. Hull Univ BTh 84 MA 89. Ripon Hall Ox 65. **d** 68 **p** 69. C Southsea St Simon *Portsm* 68–71; C Wallington *S'wark* 71–77; P-in-c Rufforth w Moor Monkton and Hessay *York* 77–79; R 79–08; P-in-c Long Marston 77–79; R 79–08; RD New Ainsty 85–97; P-in-c Healaugh w Wighill, Bilbrough and Askham Richard 02–08; P-in-c Tockwith and Bilton w Bickerton 03–08; Can and Preb York Minster 94–08; Chapl Purey Cust Nuffield Hosp 82–04; rtd 08; PtO *York* from 09. *5 Wains Road, York YO24 2TP* T: (01904) 778764 E: canjohnrendall@aol.com

RENDALL, Richard John. b 54. Wadh Coll Ox BA 76 LLB 76 MA 92 Solicitor 78. Wycliffe Hall Ox 90. **d** 92 **p** 93. C Heswall *Ches* 92–98; R High Ongar w Norton Mandeville *Chelmsf* 98–04; R Broadwell, Evenlode, Oddington, Adlestrop etc *Glouc* from 04. *The Rectory, Broadwell, Moreton-in-Marsh GL56 0TU* T: (01451) 831866 E: rendalls@talk21.com

RENDALL, Mrs Susan. b 49. Northumbria Univ MA 94. Lindisfarne Regional Tr Partnership 13. **d** 13 **p** 14. NSM Kenton Ascension *Newc* 13–18; NSM Weetslade from 18. *5 Fawdon Walk, Brunton Bridge, Newcastle upon Tyne NE13 7AW* T: 0191-286 5090 E: irendall@btinternet.com

RENDELL, Jason. b 68. **d** 05 **p** 09. Chapl to Bp Stepney *Lon* 05–07; NSM Clerkenwell H Redeemer 06–07; NSM Clerkenwell St Mark 06–07; Min Can and Succ St Paul's Cathl 07–09; Min Can and Sacr St Paul's Cathl 09–13; Chapl to Bp Chich 13–14; V Kingsbury St Andr *Lon* from 14. *St Andrew's Vicarage, 28 Old Church Lane, London NW9 8RZ* T: (020) 8205 7447

RENDLE, Graham Barton. b 40. **d** 99 **p** 00. OLM Rougham, Beyton w Hessett and Rushbrooke *St E* 99–10; rtd 10; PtO *St E* 10–16. *Appletrees, Bury Road, Beyton, Bury St Edmunds IP30 9AB* T: (01359) 270924 E: graham.rendle@tiscali.co.uk

RENDLE, Lesley Joy. **d** 17 **p** 18. NSM Bro Tysilio *Ban* from 17. *Hafod Rhug, Llandonna, Beaumaris LL58 8UR* T: (01248) 810965 E: lesley.rendle@gmail.com

RENFREY, Edward Donald John-Baptist. b 53. ACT. **d** 76 **p** 77. C Naracoorte Australia 76–77; P-in-c Kingston w Robe 78–81; R 81–84; Chapl RN 84–00; Chapl R Aus Navy Australia 00–10; rtd 10. *4 Coconut Grove, Kuranda QLD 4872, Australia* T: (0061) (7) 4093 7296 M: 45-893 7222 E: edwardrenfrey@hotmail.com

RENGERT, Mrs Helen Caroline. b 70. Open Univ BSc 97 Anglia Ruskin Univ MA 14 RGN 92. ERMC 10. **d** 13 **p** 14. C Thorpe St Matt *Nor* 13–17; C Reepham and Wensum Valley 17–18; TV from 18. *The Rectory, Station Road, Reepham, Norwich NR10 4LJ* T: (01603) 871263 *or* 879275 E: revdhelen@yahoo.co.uk *or* helen.rengert@dioceseofnorwich.org

RENGERT, Keith Alan Francis. b 67. RGN 92. Ripon Coll Cuddesdon 07. **d** 09 **p** 10. C N Walsham and Edingthorpe *Nor* 09–12; R Horsham St Faith, Spixworth and Crostwick 12–17; TR Reepham and Wensum Valley from 17; Hon PV Nor Cathl from 14. *The Rectory, Station Road, Reepham, Norwich NR10 4LJ* T: (01603) 879275 M: 07796-607649 E: revdkeith@gmail.com

RENISON, Simon James. b 88. St Mellitus Coll BA 18. **d** 18 **p** 19. C Southport Ch Ch *Liv* from 18. *St Peter's Vicarage, 2 St Peter's Road, Southport PR8 4BY* M: 07891-323291 E: renison.s@hotmail.com

RENNARD, Edward Lionel. b 51. CertEd 72 Nottm Univ BTh 80. Linc Th Coll 76. **d** 80 **p** 81. C Old Brumby *Linc* 80–82; C-in-c Gt Grimsby St Matt Fairfield CD 82–86; V Fairfield St Matt 86–88; V Hykeham 88–91; TR 91–00; TR Blyth Valley *St E* from 00. *The Rectory, Highfield Road, Halesworth IP19 8SJ* T: (01986) 872602 M: 07958-191975 E: edward.rennard@btinternet.com

RENNARD, Margaret Rose. b 49. CertEd 75. Linc Th Coll 76. **dss** 80 **d** 87 **p** 94. C Fairfield St Matt *Linc* 87–88; C Hykeham 88–00; Chapl HM Pris Morton Hall 91–00; Asst Chapl HM Pris Blundeston 00–01; Asst Chapl HM Pris Hollesley Bay from 01; Chapl Allington NHS Trust 00–01; PtO *St E* from 00. *The Rectory, Highfield Road, Halesworth IP19 8SJ* T: (01986) 872602 E: edward.rennard@btinternet.com

RENNIE, Iain Hugh. b 43. Ripon Coll Cuddesdon 88. **d** 90 **p** 91. C Poulton-le-Sands w Morecambe St Laur *Blackb* 90–94; V Hornby w Claughton 94–02; V Hornby w Claughton and Whittington etc 02–11; rtd 11; PtO *Blackb* from 11. *65 Ashton Drive, Lancaster LA1 2LQ* T: (01524) 382926 E: iain.rennie@btinternet.com

RENNIE, John Aubery. b 47. Lon Univ MB, BS 70 FRCS 75. SEITE 04. **d** 06 **p** 07. NSM Melbury *Sarum* 06–10; NSM Sherborne w Castleton, Lillington and Longburton 10–12; Deanery Missr Sherborne 12–16; rtd 16; P-in-c Upper Dever

Win from 19. *10 Pigeonhouse Field, Sutton Scotney, Winchester SO21 3NJ* M: 07552-034225 E: johnrennie40@hotmail.com

RENNIX, Raymond Latham. b 37. QUB BTh 02. CITC 00. **d** 03 **p** 04. NSM Killaney w Carryduff *D & D* 03–08; NSM Glencraig 08–12; rtd 12. *5 Brompton Court, Dromara, Dromore BT25 2DQ* T: (028) 9753 3167 M: 07777-584053 E: r.rennix@btinternet.com

RENSHAW, Mrs Anne-Marie Louise. b 71. St Hilda's Coll Ox MA 96 Fitzw Coll Cam BA 97. Ridley Hall Cam 95. **d** 98 **p** 99. C Norton *St Alb* 98–02; TV Borehamwood 02–05; TV Elstree and Borehamwood 05–11; P-in-c Tolleshunt Knights w Tiptree and Gt Braxted *Chelmsf* 11–13; TR Thurstable and Winstree from 13. *The Rectory, Rectory Road, Tiptree, Colchester CO5 0SX* T: (01621) 815260 E: amlrenshaw@btinternet.com

RENSHAW, Mrs Claire Louise. b 80. Yorks Min Course 12. **d** 15 **p** 16. C Knaresborough *Leeds* 15–18; P-in-c Walkingham Hill 18–19; R from 19. *The Rectory, Main Sreet, Staveley, Knaresborough HG5 9LD* T: (01423) 341957 M: 07912-104442 E: claire.renshaw@sky.com *or* claire.renshaw@leeds.anglican.org

RENSHAW, David William. b 59. Oak Hill Th Coll BA 85. **d** 85 **p** 86. C Shawbury *Lich* 85–88; V Childs Ercall and R Stoke upon Tern 88–92; V Stoneleigh *Guildf* 92–97; RD Epsom 95–97; Chapl Scarborough and NE Yorks Healthcare NHS Trust 97–99; Chapl St Cath Hospice Scarborough 97–99; R Meppershall w Campton and Stondon *St Alb* 99–01; C Bedford St Andr 02; PtO *Chich* 05–06; Hon C Bexhill St Pet 06; TV Rye 09–11; P-in-c Lynch w Iping Marsh and Milland 11–12; R 12–14; PtO 16–18; P-in-c Worthing Ch Ch from 18. *102 Wallace Avenue, Worthing BN11 5QA* T: (01903) 244283 E: renshaw221@btinternet.com

RENSHAW, Canon Susan Kathryn. b 55. Shenstone Coll of Educn CertEd 77. WMMTC 99. **d** 02 **p** 03. C Sedgley All SS *Worc* 02–05; C Gornal and Sedgley 05–06; V Eckington 06–18; V Defford w Besford 06–18; C Overbury w Teddington, Alstone etc 09–18; RD Pershore 11–18; Hon Can Worc Cathl 15–18; rtd 18. *Tangnefedd, 2 Church Walk, Meifod SY22 6BZ* T: (01938) 500967 E: canonsusan@btinternet.com

RENYARD, Paul Holmwood. b 42. K Coll Lon BD 65 AKC 65. **d** 66 **p** 67. C Croydon St Aug *Cant* 66–69; C Farnham *Guildf* 69–72; V Capel 72–78; Asst Dir RE 72–78; Asst Dir RE *Roch* 78–83; Hon C Roch 78–83; V Holdenhurst *Win* 83–95; V Pennington 95–07; rtd 07; PtO *Win* from 07; *Sarum* from 07. *53 Scarf Road, Poole BH17 8QJ* T: (01202) 682460 E: vandprenyard@gmail.com

RENZ, Thomas. b 69. Freie Theologische Akademie Giessen MA 93 Chelt & Glouc Coll of HE PhD 97. Coll of Resurr Mirfield 08. **d** 09 **p** 10. C Highgate St Mich *Lon* 09–12; R Monken Hadley from 12. *The Rectory, Hadley Common, Barnet EN5 5QD* T: (020) 8449 9441 M: 07933-073692 E: thomas.renz@gmail.com

REPATH, John Richard. b 48. St Mich Coll Llan 72. **d** 75 **p** 76. C Canton St Jo *Llan* 75–79; C Burghclere w Newtown and Ecchinswell w Sydmonton *Win* 80–83; R Bewcastle and Stapleton *Carl* 83–88; P-in-c Kirklinton w Hethersgill and Scaleby 86–88; R Bewcastle, Stapleton and Kirklinton etc 88–97; P-in-c New Galloway *Glas* 97–18; rtd 18. *9 The Meads, Kington HR5 3DQ* T: (01544) 239245 E: johnrepath@btinternet.com

REPTON, Suffragan Bishop of. See MACFARLANE, The Rt Revd Janet Elizabeth

RESCH, Colin Ernst. b 67. Trin Coll Bris 04. **d** 06 **p** 07. C Highley w Billingsley, Glazeley etc *Heref* 06–10; P-in-c Stottesdon w Farlow, Cleeton St Mary etc 10–14; P-in-c Mountsorrel Ch Ch and St Pet *Leic* from 14. *Christ Church Vicarage, 4 Rothley Road, Mountsorrel, Loughborough LE12 7JU* E: colin@godstuff.org.uk

RESCH, Mrs Elizabeth Barbara. b 66. Edge Hill Coll of HE BEd 88 Cant Ch Ch Univ BA 16. SEITE 10. **d** 13 **p** 14. C Sittingbourne w Bobbing *Cant* from 13. *88 Albany Road, Sittingbourne ME10 1EL* T: (01795) 473393 M: 07454-242679 E: lizresch@me.com

RESCH, Michael Johann. b 63. NTMTC 96. **d** 99 **p** 00. C Cullompton, Willand, Uffculme, Kentisbeare etc *Ex* 99–03; P-in-c Sittingbourne H Trin w Bobbing *Cant* 03–12; TR Sittingbourne w Bobbing from 12; AD Sittingbourne from 15. *88 Albany Road, Sittingbourne ME10 1EL* T: (01795) 473393 M: 07967-771231 E: mikeresch@me.com

RESTALL, Miss Susan Roberta. b 45. MSc. Sarum & Wells Th Coll 79. **dss** 82 **d** 87 **p** 94. Dorchester *Sarum* 82–84; Portland All SS w St Pet 84–87; Par Dn 87; Team Dn Yate New Town *Bris* 87–94; TV 94–95; Chapl Birm Heartlands and Solihull NHS Trust 95–01; rtd 01; PtO *Birm* from 03. *45 Fentham Road, Hampton-in-Arden, Solihull B92 0AY* E: suerestall@gmail.com

REUSS, Nathanael. b 76. Ballarat Univ BSc 98. St Jo Coll Nottm MA(MM) 12. **d** 11 **p** 12. C Ripley *Derby* 11–13; C Brailsford w Shirley, Osmaston w Edlaston etc 13–14; C Launceston St Jo Australia 15–17; P-in-c Onkaparinga Valley from 17. *The Rectory, 10 Junction Road, Balhannah SA 5242, Australia* M: (0061) 44-829 7863 E: nathanaelreuss@gmail.com

REVELEY, James Stewart. b 69. Goldsmiths' Coll Lon BMus 92. Ch Div Sch of the Pacific (USA) 95 Ripon Coll Cuddesdon BA 97. **d** 96 **p** 97. C Goldington *St Alb* 96–00; C Harpenden St Nic 00–04; V Boxmoor St Jo 04–13; V Bedford St Andr from 13. *St Andrew's Vicarage, 1 St Edmond Road, Bedford MK40 2NQ* T: (01234) 254234 E: revjumble@aol.com

REVELL, Roger Lawson. b 82. Wycliffe Hall Ox BTh 11. Vancouver Sch of Th MTh 16. **d** 15 **p** 15. PtO *Ely* from 18. *Selwyn College, Cambridge CB3 9DQ* E: roger.revell@theology.oxon.org

REW, Eric Malcolm. b 63. UEA BSc 84 PGCE 89. Qu Coll Birm 98. **d** 00 **p** 01. C Shepshed *Leic* 00–04; TV Kingsthorpe *Pet* 04–16; Chapl HM Pris 07–16; Chapl HM Pris Gartree 16–18; PtO *Leic* from 18. *14 Brampton Way, Brixworth, Northampton NN6 9BD* E: revrew@rewfamily.plus.com

REY, Joshua Barnabas. b 65. Ball Coll Ox BA 03 MA 10. Ripon Coll Cuddesdon BA 11 MSt 12. **d** 12 **p** 13. C Streatham St Leon *S'wark* 12–16; Bp's Chapl from 16; Hon Min Can S'wark Cathl from 16. *Bishop's House, 38 Tooting Bec Gardens, London SW16 1QZ* T: (020) 8769 3256 M: 07525-421681 E: mail@joshuarey.com

REYNISH, David Stuart. b 52. Nottm Univ BEd 75. Linc Th Coll 72. **d** 77 **p** 78. C Boston *Linc* 77–80; C Chalfont St Peter *Ox* 80–84; V Thursby *Carl* 84–88; R Iver Heath *Ox* 88–03; V Kelvedon and Feering *Chelmsf* 03–13; TR Bexhill St Pet *Chich* from 13. *The Rectory, Church Street, Bexhill-on-Sea TN40 2HE* T: (01424) 217203

REYNOLDS, Alan Thomas William. b 43. Lon Univ BSc 64. Linc Th Coll 64. **d** 66 **p** 67. C Leic St Pet 66–70; C Huntington *York* 70–72; R Darliston Jamaica 72–76; V Stechford *Birm* 76–83; Chapl E Birm Hosp 76–83; P-in-c Hampton in Arden *Birm* 83–86; V 87–93; Chapl Parkway Hosp Solihull 83–93; V Moseley St Anne *Birm* 93–02; Chapl Moseley Hall Hosp Birm 93; Chapl Birm Community Healthcare NHS Foundn Trust 94–02; V Kerry, Llanmerewig, Dolfor and Mochdre *St As* 02–08; AD Cedewain 03–08; rtd 08; PtO *Lich* from 08; *St As* from 09. *49 Gittin Street, Oswestry SY11 1DU* T: (01691) 680416 E: robbie.reynolds1@btinternet.com

REYNOLDS, Mrs Angela Heather. b 44. Wye Coll Lon BSc 66 Birm Univ CertEd 67. EAMTC 94. **d** 97 **p** 98. NSM Barnham Broom *Nor* 97–99; C Easton w Colton and Marlingford 99–00; P-in-c Easton, Colton, Marlingford and Bawburgh 00–09; rtd 09; PtO *Nor* from 09; Hon PV Nor Cathl from 14. *26 Clickers Road, Norwich NR3 2DD* T: (01603) 402688 E: angord@btinternet.com

REYNOLDS, David James. b 48. St Jo Coll Dur BA 72 Lanc Univ MA 85. Cranmer Hall Dur 69. **d** 73 **p** 74. C Formby H Trin *Liv* 73–77; P-in-c Widnes St Paul 77–80; V Southport St Paul 80–87; P-in-c Mawdesley *Blackb* 87–91; R 91–14; P-in-c Croston and Bretherton 06–13; R 13–14; Chapl Derian Ho Children's Hospice 93–97; rtd 14; PtO *Blackb* from 14; *Liv* from 16. *Holy Mount, Rufford Road, Bispham, Ormskirk L40 3SA* T: (01704) 821684 E: rectordavid@hotmail.co.uk

REYNOLDS, Mrs Emily Jane. b 84. Lanc Univ BA 05. Westcott Ho Cam 11. **d** 15 **p** 16. C Walsall St Paul *Lich* 15–19; V Walsall Pleck and Bescot from 19. *St John's Vicarage, Vicarage Terrace, Walsall WS2 9HB* M: 07964-598760

REYNOLDS, Gordon. b 42. Sarum & Wells Th Coll 71. **d** 72 **p** 73. C Tunstall *Lich* 72–74; USPG Zambia 75–88; C Southmead *Bris* 88–90; rtd 07. *78 William Bentley Court, Graiseley Lane, Wolverhampton WV11 1QW* T: (01902) 730381

REYNOLDS, Hannah Claire. b 67. Kingston Univ MBA 95. St Steph Ho Ox BTh 09. **d** 06 **p** 07. C Twickenham All Hallows *Lon* 06–09; P-in-c Hanworth All SS 09–13; P-in-c Didcot St Pet *Ox* from 13. *The Vicarage, 47A Newlands Avenue, Didcot OX11 8QA* T: (01235) 812114 M: 07981-981493 E: hcreynolds@hotmail.co.uk

REYNOLDS, Canon John Lionel. b 34. Westmr Coll Ox MTh 00. Chich Th Coll 58. **d** 61 **p** 62. C Whitkirk *Ripon* 61–64; C Tong *Bradf* 64–68; V Chisledon and Draycot Foliatt *Sarum* 68–74; TR Ridgeway 74–76; RD Marlborough 74–76; V Calne and Blackland 76–89; RD Calne 77–84; Can and Preb Sarum Cathl 80–02; V Woodford Valley 89–02; rtd 02; PtO *Sarum* from 02; *Win* from 03. *St Edmund, 21 New Road, Romsey SO51 7LL* T: (01794) 516349 E: carolannreynolds@aol.com

REYNOLDS, Mandy Elizabeth. b 59. NTMTC 99. **d** 02 **p** 03. NSM Wembley St Jo *Lon* 02–04; CF 04–15; R Alde River *St E* 15–16; Chapl Ipswich Hosp NHS Trust 16–18; Chapl E Suffolk and N Essex NHS Foundn Trust 18–19; TV Wilford Peninsula *St E* from 19; PtO *Chelmsf* from 18. *The Vicarage, 11 Walnut Tree Avenue, Rendlesham, Woodbridge IP12 2GG* T: (01394) 420129 E: mandyreynoldsuk@yahoo.co.uk

REYNOLDS, Marion. b 49. Chelmer Inst of HE CertEd 84. STETS 04. **d** 06 **p** 07. NSM Quantock Towers *B & W* 06–07; NSM Shelswell *Ox* 07–11; P-in-c Pattishall w Cold Higham and Gayton w Tiffield *Pet* 12–16; R 16–17; V Fulford w Hilderstone *Lich* from 17. *The Vicarage, 20 Tudor Hollow, Fulford, Stoke-on-Trent ST11 9NP* M: 07834-062268 E: marion.reynolds2@btopenworld.com

REYNOLDS, Michael. *See* REYNOLDS, Richard Michael

REYNOLDS, Mrs Michelle Angela. b 70. Ridley Hall Cam 02. **d** 04 **p** 05. C Hoddesdon *St Alb* 04–07; TV Grays Thurrock *Chelmsf* 07–18; rtd 18. *3B Bower Grove, West Mersea, Colchester CO5 8GJ* M: 07854-055660 E: michellea_reynolds@hotmail.com

REYNOLDS, Paul Andrew. b 57. BA 86. Trin Coll Bris 83. **d** 86 **p** 87. C Reading St Jo *Ox* 86–90; C Dorridge *Birm* 90–95; TV Riverside *Ox* 95–06; R Beercrocombe w Curry Mallet, Hatch Beauchamp etc *B & W* 06–18; rtd 18. *Nutshell Cottage, South Knighton, Newton Abbot, TQ12 6NT*

REYNOLDS, Paul Frederick. b 56. St Jo Coll Nottm 90. **d** 92 **p** 93. C Hyde St Geo *Ches* 92–96; P-in-c Delamere 96–00; Asst Dir Par Support and Development 96–98; Acting Dir 98–00; V Handforth *Ches* 00–07; P-in-c Bramcote *S'well* 07–11; V from 11. *The Vicarage, Moss Drive, Bramcote, Beeston NG9 3NF* T: 0115-922 9600 E: vicar@bramcoteparishchurch.com

REYNOLDS, Philip Delamere. b 53. Leeds Univ CertEd 74 Nottm Univ BCombStuds 82. Linc Th Coll 79. **d** 82 **p** 83. C Huddersfield St Jo *Wakef* 82–85; C Barkisland w W Scammonden 85–87; P-in-c Skelmanthorpe 87–14; Leeds 14–18; V 18–19; rtd 19. *St Aidan's Vicarage, Radcliffe Street, Skelmanthorpe, Huddersfield HD8 9AF* T: (01484) 863232

REYNOLDS, Raymond Ernest. b 29. Nottm Univ MPhil 89. Lambeth STh 84 CA Tr Coll 50 Chich Th Coll 58. **d** 60 **p** 61. C Leeds St Marg *Ripon* 60–62; C Beeston *S'well* 62–64; R Farnley *Ripon* 64–76; R Higham-on-the-Hill w Fenny Drayton *Leic* 76–81; R Higham-on-the-Hill w Fenny Drayton and Witherley 81–90; V Sutton *Ely* 90–94; R Witcham w Mepal 90–94; rtd 94; C Nantwich *Ches* 94–96; PtO 96–14. *4 St Alban's Drive, Nantwich CW5 7DW* T: (01270) 623483 E: syl.rayreynolds@gmail.com

REYNOLDS, Richard Michael. b 42. St Steph Ho Ox 65. **d** 67 **p** 68. C Kidderminster St Mary *Worc* 67–70; Guyana 70–73; TV N Creedy *Ex* 73–80; R Holsworthy w Hollacombe 80–86; R Holsworthy w Hollacombe and Milton Damerel 86–12; Chapl N Devon Healthcare NHS Trust 94–12; rtd 12. *Blagrove, Germansweek, Beaworthy EX21 5BH* T: (01837) 871226 E: michaelreynolds64@hotmail.co.uk

REYNOLDS, Roderick Bredon (Rory). b 58. Man Univ BA 80. Ripon Coll Cuddesdon 93. **d** 95 **p** 96. C Hitchin *St Alb* 95–98; C Stevenage St Andr and St Geo 98–00; P-in-c High Wych and Gilston w Eastwick 00–06; TV Plaistow and N Canning Town *Chelmsf* 06–10; Chapl S Lon and Maudsley NHS Foundn Trust 10–12; Chapl SW Lon and St George's Mental Health NHS Trust 12–13; Chapl St Geo Healthcare NHS Trust Lon from 13; PtO *S'wark* from 16. *77 Tulsemere Road, London SE27 9EH* M: 07515-353456 E: roryreynolds@mac.com

REYNOLDS, Mrs Rosemary Joan. b 46. WMMTC 00. **d** 03 **p** 04. NSM Brandwood *Birm* 03–16; rtd 16. *23 Chanston Avenue, Birmingham B14 5BD* T: 0121-444 7015 E: rosemary560@btinternet.com

REYNOLDS, Stephen Paul. b 52. **d** 08 **p** 09. NSM Cannock *Lich* 08–09; NSM Heath Hayes 09–16; NSM Cannock and Huntington 13–18; NSM Hatherton 16–18; rtd 19; PtO *Lich* from 19. *4 Harebell Close, Cannock WS12 3XA* T: (01543) 270940

RHOADES, Andrew Craig. b 56. Hatf Poly BSc 79 CEng 84 MIEE 84. St Jo Coll Nottm MTh 09. **d** 09 **p** 10. C Hexagon *Leic* 09–12; P-in-c Broom Leys 12–17; V 17–19; rtd 19. *Address temp unknown* M: 07531-121145 E: acrhoades@cheerful.com

RHODES, Mrs Abigail Louise. b 75. St Pet Coll Ox BA 98 MA 03 FLCM 05. St Mellitus Coll 17. **d** 19. C Finham *Cov* from 19. *St Martin-in-the-Fields Church, 136 Green Lane, Coventry CV3 6EA* T: (024) 7669 2358 E: revabbyrhodes@gmail.com

RHODES, Canon Adrian Michael. b 48. K Coll Lon BD 71 AKC 71. Qu Coll Birm 71. **d** 72 **p** 73. C Bury St Jo *Man* 73–75; Chapl N Man Gen Hosp 75–77; C Crumpsall *Man* 75–77; Chapl Walsall Manor and Bloxwich Hosps 77–83; Chapl Walsall Gen Hosp 81–83; Chapl Man R Infirmary 83–94; Chapl St Mary's Hosp Man 83–94; Chapl Man R Eye Hosp 83–94; Chapl Cen Man Healthcare NHS Trust 94–00; PtO *Man* 00–08; Hon Can Man Cathl from 08; PtO from 18. *58*

Errwood Road, Burnage, Manchester M19 2QH T: 0161-224 1739 M: 07753-677422 E: adrian@rhodes.net

RHODES, Mrs Amanda Louise. b 63. Leeds Univ BA 07. NOC 04. **d** 07 **p** 08. C Kippax w Allerton Bywater *Ripon* 07–11; P-in-c Lofthouse 11–14; *Leeds* 14–15; TV Rothwell, Lofthouse, Methley etc from 15. *The Vicarage, 8 Church Farm Close, Lofthouse, Wakefield WF3 3SA* T: (01924) 823286 M: 07971-998621 E: revmac63@googlemail.com

RHODES, Ann. b 56. **d** 13 **p** 14. NSM Hackenthorpe *Sheff* 13–17; NSM Gleadless from 17. *1 Ormes Meadow, Owlthorpe, Sheffield S20 6TE* T: 0114-247 8749 E: treble20jr@hotmail.com *or* ann.rhodes@sheffield.anglican.org

RHODES, Anthony John. b 27. Mert Coll Ox BA 50 MA 53. St Steph Ho Ox 52. **d** 54 **p** 55. C Northampton St Alb *Pet* 54–57; C Oakham 57–60; P-in-c S Queensferry *Edin* 60–74; V Mitcham St Olave *S'wark* 74–81; V Owston *Linc* 81–92; V W Butterwick 81–92; rtd 92; PtO *Leic* 14–17. *12 Stuart Court, High Street, Kibworth Beauchamp, Leicester LE8 0LR* T: 0116-279 3674

RHODES, Arthur. b 31. Dur Univ BA 58. Cranmer Hall Dur 57. **d** 59 **p** 60. C Kirkdale St Lawr *Liv* 59–61; C Litherland St Phil 61–64; V St Helens St Matt Thatto Heath 64–67; V Samlesbury *Blackb* 67–79; LtO 80–01; PtO from 01. *76 The Pennines, Fulwood, Preston PR2 9GB* T: (01772) 712212 E: ajbrhodes@hotmail.co.uk

RHODES, Benjamin. b 71. Portsm Univ BSc 93 Heythrop Coll Lon MA 10. Westcott Ho Cam 94. **d** 97 **p** 98. C Upminster *Chelmsf* 97–01; Asst Chapl Lewisham Hosp NHS Trust 01–05; Sen Chapl Barts and The Lon NHS Trust 05–08; Lead Chapl 08–10; Lead Chapl Tower Hamlets Primary Care Trust 08–10; Spiritual Care Lead and Chapl Team Ldr King's Coll Hosp NHS Foundn Trust 10–18; Hd Chapl Services Leeds Teaching Hosps NHS Trust from 18; NSM St Bart Less *Lon* 05–07; Bp's Adv for Healthcare Chapl Stepney Area 08–10; Bp's Adv for Hosp Chapl *S'wark* 15–18; Hon Can S'wark Cathl 15–18; Bp's Adv for Healthcare Chapl *Leeds* from 18. *The Chaplaincy, Leeds Teaching Hospitals NHS Trust, St James's University Hospital, Beckett Street, Leeds LS9 7TF* T: 0113-206 4658 M: 07786-510292 E: benrhodes@nhs.net

RHODES, Mrs Caroline Laura. b 66. Bath Univ BPharm 87 K Coll Lon MSc 91. Ripon Coll Cuddesdon 08. **d** 10 **p** 11. C Allestree St Edm and Darley Abbey *Derby* 10–14; C Wirksworth 14–15; P-in-c Pool Miss Area from 18. *The Vicarage, Guilsfield, Welshpool SY21 9NF* T: (01938) 554245 E: revcarolinerhodes@me.com

RHODES, Christine. *See* RHODES, Lois Christine

RHODES, David George. b 45. Univ of Wales (Abth) BA 66. Trin Coll Bris 83. **d** 85 **p** 86. C Brinsworth w Catcliffe *Sheff* 85–89; V Mortomley St Sav 89–90; V Mortomley St Sav High Green 90–99; V Totley 99–11; rtd 11; PtO *Sheff* from 11; rtd 11. *12 Sheards Close, Dronfield Woodhouse, Dronfield S18 8NJ* T: (01246) 767838 E: drhodes@toucansurf.com

RHODES, David Grant. b 43. Ex Univ BA 66 Leeds Univ DipAdEd 75. Sarum & Wells Th Coll 69. **d** 72 **p** 73. C Mirfield *Wakef* 72–75; V Batley St Thos 75–80; Dioc Adult Educn Officer 76–80; Hon C Huddersfield St Jo 85–86; Dir BRF 86–87; V Robert Town *Wakef* 87–94; Project Worker 'Faith in Leeds' 94–99; Hon C Potternewton *Ripon* 95–99; Chapl Missr Children's Soc 99–03; Hon C Leeds City *Ripon* 99–03; rtd 03; PtO *York* 00–08. *2 Moorland Road, York YO10 4HF* T: (01904) 651749 M: 07712-006930 E: rhodes@freeuk.com

RHODES, John. *See* RHODES, Anthony John

RHODES, Jonathan Peter. b 69. Coll of Ripon & York St Jo BA 96. NOC 01. **d** 04 **p** 05. C High Harrogate Ch Ch *Ripon* 04–08; P-in-c Hartlepool St Aid and St Columba *Dur* 08–11; R Brotton Parva *York* from 11. *St Margaret's Rectory, 9 Crispin Court, Brotton, Saltburn-by-the-Sea TS12 2XL* T: (01287) 201961

RHODES, Mrs Laura Clare. b 82. Ripon Coll Cuddesdon 13. **d** 15 **p** 16. C Wilmslow *Ches* 15–17; NSM Ches St Mary from 17; Chapl Ches Univ from 18. *78 Ringway, Waverton, Chester CH3 7NR* M: 07875-657784 E: lauracrhodes@gmail.com

RHODES, Lois Christine. b 34. Lon Univ BSc 61. Glouc Sch of Min 84. **d** 87 **p** 94. NSM Weobley w Sarnesfield and Norton Canon *Heref* 87–92; NSM Letton w Staunton, Byford, Mansel Gamage etc 87–92; Chapl Asst Wye Valley NHS Trust from 93. *Bellbrook, Bell Square, Weobley, Hereford HR4 8SE* T: (01544) 318410 *or* (01432) 355444

RHODES, Matthew Ivan. b 66. Bris Univ BA 89 Birm Univ MPhil 95 PhD 05. Qu Coll Birm BD 93. **d** 94 **p** 95. C Willenhall H Trin *Lich* 94–97; Chapl Maadi St Jo Egypt 97–00; P-in-c Middleton *Birm* 00–07; P-in-c Wishaw 00–07; P-in-c Curdworth 05–07; R Curdworth, Middleton and Wishaw 07–11; P-in-c Maney 11; V 11–18; AD Sutton Coldfield 06–13; Dioc Chapl MU 11–18; Hon Can Birm

Cathl 16–18; V Ranmoor *Sheff* from 18; AD Hallam from 18. *The Vicarage, 389A Fulwood Road, Sheffield S10 3GA*

RHODES, Robert George. b 41. Man Univ BSc 62. Ripon Hall Ox 72. **d** 74 **p** 75. C Banbury *Ox* 74–77; TV 77–81; P-in-c Long Horsley and Adult Educn Adv *Newc* 81–86; TR Wolverton *Ox* 86–97; P-in-c Bledlow w Saunderton and Horsenden 97–98; TV Risborough 98–02; Warden of Readers 97–02; USPG Miss Belize 02–06; rtd 06; PtO *Derby* from 07. *3 China House Yard, St Mary's Gate, Wirksworth, Matlock DE4 4DQ* T: (01629) 823623 E: bandjrhodes@hotmail.com

RHYDDERCH, David Huw. b 48. St Mich Coll Llan 70. **d** 73 **p** 74. C Gelligaer *Llan* 73–76; C Penarth All SS 76–78; V Resolven 78–81; V Ystrad Rhondda w Ynyscynon 81–93; RD Rhondda 89–93; St Andrews Major w Michaelston-le-Pit 93–13; rtd 13; PtO *Llan* from 13. *34 Holly Road, Cardiff CF5 3HJ* T: (029) 2055 5597

RICE, David. b 57. Nottm Univ BA 79. Ripon Coll Cuddesdon 80. **d** 82 **p** 83. C Cirencester *Glouc* 82–86; R Theale and Englefield *Ox* 86–00; TR Wallingford from 00; AD from 17. *The Rectory, 22 Castle Street, Wallingford OX10 8DW* T: (01491) 202188

RICE, John Leslie Hale. b 38. Lon Univ BScEng 60 BD 68 FCMI. EMMTC 73. **d** 76 **p** 77. NSM Allestree St Nic *Derby* 76–90; LtO 90–08; PtO 08–18. *14 Gisborne Crescent, Allestree, Derby DE22 2FL* T: (01332) 557222 E: j.rice.t21@btinternet.com

RICE-OXLEY, John Richard. b 44. Keble Coll Ox BA 66 MA 69 Dur Univ MA 85. Lon Coll of Div 68. **d** 70 **p** 71. C Eastwood *S'well* 70–73; Youth Adv CMS 73–78; V Mansfield St Jo *S'well* 78–82; P-in-c Thornley *Dur* 82–85; P-in-c Darlington St Matt and St Luke 85–87; V 87–98; V Hornsea w Atwick *York* 98–06; P-in-c Aldbrough, Mappleton w Goxhill and Withernwick 05–06; rtd 06; PtO *York* 07–17; *Linc* from 16. *3 Bertie Close, Swinstead, Grantham NG33 4PW* E: richardriceoxley@gmail.com

RICE-OXLEY, Mrs Sylvia Jeanette Kathleen. b 48. **d** 08 **p** 09. C Aldbrough, Mappleton w Goxhill and Withernwick *York* 08–11; P-in-c 11–13; rtd 13; PtO *Linc* from 16. *3 Bertie Close, Swinstead, Grantham NG33 4PW* E: sylviariceoxley@gmail.com

RICH, Brian John. b 49. Reading Univ BSc 70. Guildf Dioc Min Course 94. **d** 97 **p** 98. OLM Stoke Hill *Guildf* 97–12; PtO *Win* 12–15. *2 Boon Way, Oakley, Basingstoke RG23 7BS* T: (01256) 783111 E: btrich@talktalk.net

RICH, Paul Michael. b 36. Sarum Th Coll 62. **d** 65 **p** 66. C Woodbridge St Mary *St E* 65–68; C W Wycombe *Ox* 68–70; CF 70–88; LtO *S & B* 88–90; V Crondall and Ewshot *Guildf* 91–05; rtd 05; PtO *Win* 08–13. *The Firs, The Street, Binsted, Alton GU34 4PF* T: (01420) 525302 E: padrerich@btinternet.com

RICH, Peter Geoffrey. b 45. Oak Hill Th Coll 74. **d** 77 **p** 78. C Blackheath St Jo *S'wark* 77–80; C Surbiton St Matt 80–87; V St Alb St Luke 87–98; V Gravesend St Aid *Roch* 98–10; rtd 11; P-in-c Stone w Dinton and Hartwell *Ox* 11–16; PtO from 16. *8 Broadmarsh Close, Grove, Wantage OX12 0NH* E: angela_richuk@yahoo.co.uk

RICHARDS, Anne. b 69. **d** 10 **p** 11. NSM Hull St Mich *York* 10–15; Chapl Abp Sentamu Academy Hull from 14; PtO *York* from 18. *42 Riplingham Road, Kirk Ella, Hull HU10 7TP* M: 07947-160455 E: richards.a1@sentamuacademy.org *or* personal@anne-richards.com

RICHARDS, Mrs Anne Maria. b 54. Wolv Poly CertEd 88 HCIMA 83. Qu Coll Birm 08. **d** 11 **p** 12. OLM Fletchamstead *Cov* 11–18; P-in-c Whitley from 18; Chapl Cov Univ from 18. *2 Farthing Walk, Coventry CV4 8GR* T: (024) 7646 8660 M: 07769-943019 E: anne.richards_uk@yahoo.co.uk

RICHARDS, Mrs April Deborah. b 42. Man Univ BSc 63. S Dios Minl Tr Scheme 82. **dss** 85 **d** 87 **p** 94. Catherington and Clanfield *Portsm* 85–89; C 87–89; C E Meon and Langrish 89–95; Chapl Portsm Hosps NHS Trust 92–95; P-in-c Blackmoor and Whitehill *Portsm* 95–98; V 98–05; RD Petersfield 99–04; rtd 05; PtO *Pet* 06–08; Hon C Brington w Whilton and Norton etc 08–12; PtO from 12. *6 Burrows Vale, Brixworth, Northampton NN6 9US* T: (01604) 882230 E: aprilrichards@btinternet.com

RICHARDS, Christopher Mordaunt. b 40. New Coll Ox BA 63 MA 72 Bris Univ MB, ChB 72. Cuddesdon Coll 63. **d** 65 **p** 81. C Bris St Mary Redcliffe w Temple etc 65–66; PtO 66–72; Hon C Keynsham *B & W* 81–90; PtO 90–93; *Bris* from 04. *4 St Ronans Avenue, Bristol BS6 6EP* T: 0117-974 4062

RICHARDS, Daniel James. b 40. St D Coll Lamp. **d** 66 **p** 67. C Kingswinford H Trin *Lich* 66–69; C Banbury *Ox* 69–71; C Aylesbury 71–73; C-in-c Stoke Poges St Jo Manor Park CD 73–78; R W Slough 78–80; R Ilchester w Northover, Limington, Yeovilton etc *B & W* 80–90; RD Ilchester 81–91; RD Martock 89–91; TR Bruton and Distr 90–97; R Axbridge w Shipham and Rowberrow 97–04; rtd 04; PtO *B & W* from 05; Co-ord Clergy Retirement and Widows' Officer 06–14.

29 Sexey's Hospital, Bruton BA10 0AS M: 07762-189958
E: revdanrich@btinternet.com

RICHARDS, David Arnold. b 56. Wycliffe Hall Ox 76. d 81 p 82. C Skewen *Llan* 81–84; C Barking St Marg w St Patr *Chelmsf* 84–85; TV 85–90; Chapl Barking Hosp 87–88; P-in-c Stratford St Jo and Ch Ch w Forest Gate St Jas *Chelmsf* 90–97; V Stratford St Jo w Ch Ch from 97; P-in-c W Ham St Matt 13–15; C from 15. *Stratford Vicarage, 20 Deanery Road, London E15 4LP* T: (020) 8534 8388 *or* 8503 1913 E: david.richards@stjohnse15.co.uk

RICHARDS, David Gareth. b 60. Hull Univ BA 83. Qu Coll Birm 89. d 92 p 93. C Knowle *Birm* 92–96; Assoc R Edin St Paul and St Geo 96–00; R from 00. *10 Broughton Street, Edinburgh EH1 3RH* T: 0131-332 3904 *or* 556 1355 F: 556 0492 E: dave@pandgchurch.org.uk

RICHARDS, Mrs Delyth Anne. b 63. d 13 p 14. NSM Carmarthen St Dav *St D* 13–18; C from 18; Dioc Schools Officer from 18. *36 Meysydd y Coleg, Carmarthen SA31 3GU* T: (01267) 229134 E: delyth.richards@icloud.com

RICHARDS, Mrs Glenys Heather. b 51. SEN 73. d 06 p 07. OLM Heatons *Man* 06–16; PtO from 16. *32 Lomas Close, Manchester M19 1TE* T: 0161-282 7831

RICHARDS, James Johnston. b 59. Solicitor 84 Lon Bible Coll BA 90 Dur Univ MA 97. Cranmer Hall Dur 90. d 92 p 93. C Harrow Trin St Mich *Lon* 92–95; C Kendal H Trin *Carl* 95–99; R Windermere from 99; RD 10–16. *The Rectory, Longlands Road, Bowness-on-Windermere, Windermere LA23 3AS* T: (015394) 43063 E: rector@stmartin.org.uk

RICHARDS, Mrs Jane Susan. b 64. Univ of E Lon MSc 03. St Mellitus Coll BA 14. d 14 p 15. NSM S Woodham Ferrers *Chelmsf* 14–17; NSM Woodham Ferrers and Bicknacre 14–17; Asst Chapl Mid-Essex Hosp Services NHS Trust 15–17; V Basildon St Andr w H Cross *Chelmsf* from 17. *St Andrew's Vicarage, 3 The Fremnells, Basildon SS14 2QX* T: (01268) 520516 M: 07702-808408 E: revjanerichards2@gmail.com

RICHARDS, Mrs Jane Valerie. b 43. Westf Coll Lon BA 64 Birm Univ CertEd 65. S Dios Minl Tr Scheme 84. d 87 p 94. NSM Locks Heath *Portsm* 87–90; Chapl Qu Alexandra Hosp Portsm 90–92; Chapl Portsm Hosps NHS Trust 92–95; Asst to RD Fareham *Portsm* 95–96; C Locks Heath 95–96; Chapl Southn Univ Hosps NHS Trust 96–03; rtd 03; PtO *Portsm* from 97; *Win* 03–06. *16 Lodge Road, Locks Heath, Southampton SO31 6QY* T: (01489) 573891 E: revjane.richards@btinternet.com

RICHARDS, Mrs Joanna Sue. b 67. Univ Coll Lon MSc 96. SEITE 11. d 14 p 15. C Cant St Martin and St Paul 14–18; R Cant St Dunstan, St Mildred and St Pet from 18. *St Dunstan's Vicarage, 5 Harkness Drive, Canterbury CT2 7RW* M: 07932-656876 E: jorichards123@btinternet.com *or* rev.jo.richards@gmail.com

RICHARDS, Preb John Francis. b 37. Dur Univ BA 61. Wells Th Coll 61. d 63 p 64. C Sherwood *S'well* 63–67; C Bishopwearmouth St Mich *Dur* 67–69; C Egg Buckland *Ex* 69–75; CF (ACF) 72–02; V Plymouth St Jas Ham *Ex* 75–83; V Plympton St Mary 83–02; RD Plymouth Moorside 88–93 and 96–01; Preb Ex Cathl 91–07; rtd 02; Clergy Widow(er)s Officer *Ex* from 02. *24 Trewithy Drive, Plymouth PL6 5TY* T: (01752) 214442 E: jfr-sjr@blueyonder.co.uk

RICHARDS, John George. b 48. Qu Coll Birm 87. d 89 p 90. C Acocks Green *Birm* 89–92; TV Shirley 92–96; P-in-c Yardley Wood 96–00; V 00–13; rtd 13; PtO *Birm* from 13; Dioc Retirement Officer 16. *60 Alderney Gardens, Birmingham B38 8YW* T: 0121-603 0801 E: rev.johnrichards@virginmedia.com

RICHARDS, John Michael. b 53. Univ of Ripon & York St Jo TCert 76 Open Univ BA 81. Cranmer Hall Dur 93. d 93 p 94. C Wath-upon-Dearne *Sheff* 93–95; R Warmsworth 95–01; R Sprotbrough 01–10; P-in-c Barningham w Hutton Magna and Wycliffe *Ripon* 10–14; *Leeds* 14–15; P-in-c Gilling and Kirkby Ravensworth *Ripon* 10–14; *Leeds* 14–15; AD Richmond *Ripon* 12–14; *Leeds* 14–15; rtd 15; PtO *Leeds* from 17. *Peep-o-Day, Low Row, Richmond DL11 6PH* T: (01748) 886246 E: johnmr1953@talk21.com

RICHARDS *(née* WOOLLEY*),* **Ms Justine Clare.** b 73. Plymouth Univ BSc 95 SS Mark & Jo Coll Chelsea PGCE 98. Cranmer Hall Dur 03. d 05 p 06. C Dulverton and Brushford *B & W* 05–10; PtO 10–16; Chapl Wellington Sch Somerset 16–19; V Galmington *B & W* from 19. *1 Comeytrowe Lane, Taunton TA1 5PA* M: 07821-536460 E: rev.justine.richards@gmail.com

RICHARDS, Keith David. b 50. Didsbury Coll of Educn CertEd 72. S'wark Ord Course 79. d 82 p 83. NSM Walworth *S'wark* 82–85; Chapl Derbyshire Coll of HE 85–87; V Rottingdean *Chich* 87–93; TR Crawley 93–97; V Arundel w Tortington and S Stoke 97–07; RD Arundel and Bognor 04–07; Can and Preb Chich Cathl 07; V Selby Abbey *York*

07–10; P-in-c Hove St Barn and St Agnes *Chich* 10–13; RD Hove 11–13; rtd 13; P-in-c Durrington *Chich* 14–15; P-in-c Worthing St Andr 16; PtO *Nor* from 15; *Chich* 17–19; R Balcombe from 19. *The Rectory, Haywards Heath Road, Balcombe, Haywards Heath PO19 7PE* T: (01444) 811249 E: keithdrichards2@btinternet.com

RICHARDS, Kelvin. b 58. Univ of Wales (Abth) BSc 80 MA 88. Ripon Coll Cuddesdon BA 82. d 83 p 84. C Killay *S & B* 83–86; C Morriston 86–89; R Llangattock and Llangyndir 89–15; P-in-c The Beacons from 15; P-in-c Llyn Safaddan from 15; AD Crickhowell 02–14. *The Rectory, Talybont-on-Usk, Brecon LD3 7UX* T: (01874) 676146 E: kelvin.richards@btinternet.com *or* kelvin@beaconssafaddan.plus.com

RICHARDS, Mrs Mary Edith. b 33. SWMTC 85. d 87 p 94. NSM Kea *Truro* 87–88; Asst Chapl Bris Poly 88–91; C E Clevedon and Walton w Weston w Clapton *B & W* 91–96; rtd 96; Hon C Probus, Ladock and Grampound w Creed and St Erme *Truro* from 97; Mental Health Chapl Cornwall Healthcare NHS Trust 97–01; PtO *Truro* from 16. *62 Midway Drive, Uplands Park, Truro TR1 1NQ* T: (01872) 277556 E: revdmary@hotmail.co.uk

RICHARDS, Poppy. *See* THORPE, Eleanor Poppy

RICHARDS, Rebecca Mary. b 66. d 14 p 15. C Stafford St Jo and Tixall w Ingestre *Lich* 14–18; TR Cheswardine, Childs Ercall, Hales, Hinstock etc from 18. *3 High Street, Cheswardine, Market Drayton TF9 2RS* T: (01630) 661204 M: 07905-891869 E: beckyrichards@hotmail.co.uk

RICHARDS, Robert Graham. b 42. St Jo Coll Nottm 77. d 80 p 81. C Radipole and Melcombe Regis *Sarum* 80–83; TV Billericay and Lt Burstead *Chelmsf* 84–91; UK Dir CMJ 91–95; Chief Exec Nat Bibl Heritage Cen Ltd Trust 95–97; C Chorleywood St Andr *St Alb* 97–00; Chapl Lee Abbey 02–05; rtd 05; PtO *Sarum* from 05. *33 Stowell Crescent, Wareham BH20 4PT* T: (01929) 552174 E: rev_rob_richards@yahoo.co.uk

RICHARDS, Simon Granston. b 47. St Jo Coll Nottm BTh 72 ALCD 72. d 72 p 73. C Waltham Abbey *Chelmsf* 72–77; TV Basildon St Martin w H Cross and Laindon etc 77–80; V Grayshott *Guildf* 80–88; V Eccleston Ch Ch *Liv* 88–92; V Berkeley w Wick, Breadstone and Newport *Glouc* 92–02; P-in-c Stone w Woodford and Hill 99–02; V Berkeley w Wick, Breadstone, Newport, Stone etc 02–05; RD Dursley 96–02; Chapl Severn NHS Trust 94–05; V Bisley, Chalford, France Lynch, and Oakridge *Glouc* 05–12; AD Bisley 06–08; rtd 12; PtO *Heref* from 14. *1 Wynyard Close, Leominster HR6 8HH* T: (01568) 616602 E: simon@granstonrichards.co.uk

RICHARDS, Stephen. b 51. Bris Univ BSc 72 Maria Grey Coll Lon PGCE 73 Birm Univ MEd 77. STETS 07. d 10 p 11. NSM Corfe Mullen *Sarum* 10–16. *Longacre, Buzzacott Lane, Combe Martin, Ilfracombe EX34 0LB* T: (01271) 883566 M: 07767-066321 E: richards.steve@btinternet.com

RICHARDS, Stuart Anthony. b 70. K Coll Lon BA 92 AKC 92 Keble Coll Ox BA 97 MA 02. St Steph Ho Ox MTh 02. d 99 p 00. C Reading All SS *Ox* 99–02; C Solihull *Birm* 02–06; Deanery P Handsworth 06–07; CF from 07. *c/o MOD Chaplains (Army)* T: (01264) 383430 F: 381824

RICHARDS, Terence David. b 43. Trin Coll Carmarthen DipEd 64 Open Univ BA 73 Magd Coll Ox MSc 83. Ox Min Course 04. d 07 p 08. NSM Chenderit *Pet* 07–13; rtd 13; PtO *Pet* from 13; *Ox* from 15. *11 Portway Drive, Croughton, Brackley NN13 5NA* T: (01869) 811251 E: tasker1@btinternet.com

RICHARDS, Canon Thomas John Wynzie. b 25. St D Coll Lamp BA 49. d 51 p 52. C Llandybie *St D* 51–53; V 71–87; C Llandegai *Ban* 53–56; R Llanymawddwy 56–57; Chapl Nat Nautical Sch Portishead 57–71; RD Dyffryn Aman *St D* 78–85; Can St D Cathl 83–92; Treas St D Cathl 89–92; V Pencarreg and Llanycrwys 87–92; rtd 92; PtO *St D* from 05. *Maes Teifi, Cwmann, Lampeter SA48 8DT* T: (01570) 423354

RICHARDS, Tony Benjamin. b 48. STETS. d 09 p 10. NSM Sandown Ch Ch *Portsm* from 09; NSM Lower Sandown St Jo from 09. *Abbotsford Lodge, Cliff Bridge, Shanklin PO37 6QJ* T: (01983) 863607

RICHARDS, Canon William Hughes. b 37. St D Coll Lamp BA 58. d 60 p 61. C Llandysul *St D* 60–63; C Llanelli 63–65; V Llanddewi Brefi w Llanbadarn Odwyn 65–73; V Penbre 73–83; V Llangunnor w Cwmffrwd 83–88; V Cardigan w Mwnt and Y Ferwig 88–99; V Cardigan w Mwnt and Y Ferwig w Llangoedmor 99–01; Can St D Cathl 89–01; Treas St D Cathl 01; rtd 01; PtO *St D* 05–17. *Hafan Godbaith, 6 Cwrt y Gloch, Peniel, Carmarthen SA32 7HW* T: (01267) 235995

RICHARDS, Canon William Neal. b 38. ALCD 63. d 63 p 64. C Otley *Bradf* 63–65; C Leamington Priors St Mary *Cov* 65–67; CMS 67–69; Kenya 69–74; Asst Provost and Can Res Nairobi 70–74; V Gt Malvern St Mary *Worc* 74–86; Chapl

Kidderminster Health Distr 86–91; RD Kidderminster *Worc* 89–91; R Martley and Wichenford, Knightwick etc 91–01; rtd 01; PtO *Worc* from 01. *Bay Tree Cottage, 32 Pump Street, Malvern WR14 4LU* T: (01684) 569658

RICHARDSON, Ms Alison Mary. b 63. Leic Univ BSc 84 St Jo Coll Dur BA 09. Cranmer Hall Dur 07. **d** 09 **p** 10. C Spennymoor and Whitworth *Dur* 09–11; C Upper Skerne 11–13; P-in-c Blackhall, Castle Eden and Monkhesleden 13–16; C Peterlee 13–16; P-in-c Kelloe and Coxhoe 16–19; P-in-c Chilton 16–19; Chapl Tudor Hall Sch from 19. *Tudor Hall School, Wykham Lane, Banbury OX16 9UR* T: (01295) 263434 M: 07873-596164 E: arichardson@btinternet.com

RICHARDSON, Andrew Edward John. b 75. St Andr Univ BD 97. TISEC 04. **d** 06 **p** 07. C Dundee St Mary Magd *Bre* 06–09; Hon Chapl Dundee Univ 07–09; TR Glas E End 09–15; Chapl St Botolph Aldgate w H Trin Minories *Lon* from 15. *8A Amen Court, London EC4M 7BU* T: (020) 7248 6115 E: aejrichardson@hotmail.com or chaplain@stbotolphs.org.uk

RICHARDSON, Miss Ann. b 72. Leeds Univ BA 94. Trin Coll Bris BA 10. **d** 10 **p** 11. C Bromley St Mark *Roch* 10–14; V Gillingham H Trin from 14; P-in-c Gillingham St Barn 16–19; RD Gillingham from 15. *Holy Trinity Vicarage, 2 Waltham Road, Gillingham ME8 6XQ* T: (01634) 231690 M: 07710-160972 E: ann_r@btinternet.com

RICHARDSON, Anne Charlotte. b 84. Warwick Univ BA 05. St Mellitus Coll BA 18. **d** 18 **p** 19. C Styvechale *Cov* from 18. *23 Mary Herbert Street, Coventry CV3 5ER* M: 07973-221635 E: talktoanne@gmail.com

RICHARDSON, Carol Margaret. b 47. Leeds Univ BA 07. NOC 04. **d** 07 **p** 08. Sub Chapl HM Pris Stafford 03–17; NSM Upper Tean *Lich* 07–11; R Kingsley and Foxt-w-Whiston and Oakamoor etc 11–17; rtd 17; PtO *Lich* from 17. *The Woodlands, Spicerstone Estate, Leek ST13 7DS* T: (01538) 372082 E: crichardson@spicerstone.plus.com

RICHARDSON, Catherine Elisabeth. *See* PORTER, Catherine Elisabeth

RICHARDSON, Christopher Edward. b 72. STETS 12. **d** 15 **p** 16. C Alverstoke *Portsm* 15–19; V Camberley St Martin Old Dean *Guildf* from 19. *Address temp unknown* M: 07584-308877

RICHARDSON, David. b 71. Edin Univ MA 93 Stranmillis Coll PGCE 94 QUB PhD 98. CITC BTh 02. **d** 02 **p** 03. C Coleraine *Conn* 02–06; Chapl RAF from 06. *Chaplaincy Services (RAF), HQ Air Command, RAF High Wycombe HP14 4UE* T: (01494) 496800

RICHARDSON, David John. b 50. MA LLB FCIArb. S'wark Ord Course. **d** 85 **p** 86. NSM S Croydon Em *S'wark* 85–06; PtO 06–13. *20 Hurst View Road, South Croydon CR2 7AG* T: (020) 8688 4947 or 8688 6676 E: richardsonhome@blueyonder.co.uk

RICHARDSON, Edward John. b 39. Westmr Coll Ox MTh 98 Chich Univ PhD 17. Lich Th Coll 62. **d** 65 **p** 66. C Chessington *Guildf* 65–70; TV Trunch *Nor* 70–75; V Stoneleigh *Guildf* 75–79; PtO *S'wark* 92–94; Hon C Kingston All SS w St Jo 94–99; C 99–04; rtd 04; PtO *S'wark* from 04; P-in-c Burpham *Chich* 05–09; PtO *Guildf* from 09. *3 Westways, Epsom KT19 0PH* T: (020) 8393 3648 E: revdejr@gmail.com

RICHARDSON, (née WOOD), Elaine Mary. b 51. SRN 74. SEITE 00. **d** 03 **p** 04. C Hythe *Cant* 03–06; C Folkestone Trin 06–07; V Herne 07–16; Jt AD Reculver 12–16; rtd 16. *Kenora, St Arvans, Chepstow NP16 6EZ* T: (01291) 622300 E: elaine.longview@virgin.net or elaine.kenora@gmail.com

RICHARDSON, Mrs Elizabeth Rosalind. b 54. STETS 05. **d** 08 **p** 09. NSM Ewell St Fran *Guildf* 08–11; TV Surrey Weald from 11. *54 The Street, Capel, Dorking RH5 5LE* T: (01306) 711260 E: liz@hostmyserver.co.uk or vicar@stjohnthebaptistcapel.org.uk

RICHARDSON, Geoffrey Stewart. b 47. St Jo Coll Ox BA 69 MA 73. St Steph Ho Ox 70. **d** 72 **p** 73. C Roxbourne St Andr *Lon* 72–75; C Woodford St Barn *Chelmsf* 76–80; V Goodmayes St Paul 80–87; R Stow in Lindsey *Linc* 87–92; P-in-c Coates 87–92; P-in-c Willingham 87–92; R Stow Gp 92–01; RD Corringham 93–00; R Shaldon, Stokeinteignhead, Combeinteignhead etc *Ex* 01–12; rtd 12; PtO *Ex* from 12. *167 Westhill Road, Torquay TQ1 4NS*

RICHARDSON, Graeme James. b 75. Oriel Coll Ox BA 97. Ripon Coll Cuddesdon MPhil 02. **d** 04 **p** 04. C Hatfield Hyde *St Alb* 03–06; Chapl BNC Ox 06–14; V Harborne St Pet *Birm* 14–19. *Frauenplan 8, 99423 Weimar, Germany*

RICHARDSON, Mrs Jacqueline Ann. b 61. Ox Brookes Univ BA 14. **d** 10 **p** 11. OLM Walton-on-Thames *Guildf* 10–16; C Weston 16–19; V Hersham from 19. *The Vicarage, 5 Burwood Road, Hersham, Walton-on-Thames KT12 4AA* M: 07787-445272 E: jackier6161@gmail.com or vicar@stpetershersham.com

RICHARDSON, Canon James John. b 41. Hull Univ BA 63 Sheff Univ DipEd 64 FRSA 91. Cuddesdon Coll 66. **d** 69 **p** 70. C Wolverhampton St Pet *Lich* 69–72; P-in-c Hanley All SS 72–75; R Nantwich *Ches* 75–82; Hon Can Ripon Cathl 82–88; V Leeds St Pet 82–88; Exec Dir Coun of Chrs and Jews 88–92; P-in-c Brington w Whilton and Norton *Pet* 93–96; P-in-c Brington w Whilton and Norton and Brockhall 96; P-in-c Church Brampton, Chapel Brampton, Harleston etc 94–96; TR Bournemouth St Pet w St Swithun, H Trin etc *Win* 96–08; P-in-c Bournemouth St Aug 01–08; rtd 09; Hon C Sherborne w Castleton, Lillington and Longburton *Sarum* 09–14; PtO *B & W* 14–18; *Sarum* from 14. *6 St John's Almshouse, Half Moon Street, Sherborne DT9 3LJ* T: (01935) 814984 E: canonrichardson@btinternet.com

RICHARDSON, John. b 47. Linc Th Coll 78. **d** 80 **p** 81. C Keighley St Andr *Bradf* 80–83; V Hugglescote w Donington *Leic* 83–84; V Hugglescote w Donington-le-Heath and Ellistown 84–86; TR Hugglescote w Donington, Ellistown and Snibston 86–97; RD Akeley S 87–96; Chapl ATC 84–97; R Hallaton w Horninghold, Allexton, Tugby etc *Leic* 97–00; Rural Officer (Leic Adnry) 97–00; rtd 00; PtO *Pet* 04–05; P-in-c Fylingdales and Hawsker cum Stainsacre *York* 05–09; C Alton w Bradley-le-Moors and Denstone etc *Lich* 09–17. *All Saints House, 10 Bennion Grove, Denstone, Uttoxeter ST14 5EZ* T: (01889) 590266 E: allsaints2012@btinternet.com

RICHARDSON, John. b 41. Qu Coll Birm 69. **d** 72 **p** 73. C Ormskirk *Liv* 72–74; C Doncaster St Geo *Sheff* 74–77; R Hemsworth *Wakef* 77–79; V Penallt *Mon* 79–85; R Amotherby w Appleton and Barton-le-Street *York* 85–89; P-in-c Hovingham 86–89; P-in-c Slingsby 86–89; TR Street 89–90; R Skelton w Shipton and Newton on Ouse 90–93; V Alsager St Mary *Ches* 93–96; V Grangetown *York* 96–00; V E Coatham 00–02; V Coatham and Dormanstown 02–04; P-in-c York St Lawr w St Nic 04–06; rtd 06; Chapl Castle Howard 06–13; PtO *York* from 06. *27 Park Road, Norton, Malton YO17 9DZ* T: (01653) 690146 E: johnrichardson841@btinternet.com

RICHARDSON, John. b 55. Lon Univ BEd BD Kent Univ MA. St Steph Ho Ox. **d** 83 **p** 84. C Thornbury *Glouc* 83–86; C Sheff St Cecilia Parson Cross 86–87; C Clacton St Jas *Chelmsf* 87–90; R Gt and Lt Tey w Wakes Colne and Chappel from 90. *The Rectory, Brook Road, Great Tey, Colchester CO6 1JF* T: (01206) 211481

RICHARDSON, John. *See* RICHARDSON, Edward John

✠**RICHARDSON, The Rt Revd John Henry.** b 37. Trin Hall Cam BA 61 MA 65. Cuddesdon Coll 61. **d** 63 **p** 64 **c** 94. C Stevenage *St Alb* 63–66; C Eastbourne St Mary *Chich* 66–68; V Chipperfield St Paul *St Alb* 68–75; V Rickmansworth 75–86; RD 77–86; V Bishop's Stortford St Mich 86–94; Hon Can St Alb 87–94; Suff Bp Bedford 94–02; rtd 02; Hon Asst Bp Carl from 03; Hon Asst Bp Newc from 03. *The Old Rectory, Bewcastle, Carlisle CA6 6PS* T: (01697) 748389

RICHARDSON, John Humphrey. b 33. Dur Univ BA 57. Chich Th Coll 57. **d** 59 **p** 60. C Bexhill St Barn *Chich* 59–61; C Stanmer w Falmer and Moulsecoomb 61–64; C Ifield 64–70; R Earnley and E Wittering 70–79; V Stamford All SS w St Pet *Linc* 79–81; R Stamford St Jo w St Clem 79–81; V Stamford All SS w St Jo 81–92; RD Aveland and News w Stamford 80–87; P-in-c Metheringham w Blankney 92–94; V Metheringham w Blankney and Dunston 94–98; rtd 98; PtO *Chich* from 99. *68 Bishopsgate Walk, Chichester PO19 6FQ* T: (01243) 536864

RICHARDSON, John Malcolm. b 39. Glas Univ MA 60 BD 63 Andover Newton Th Coll STM 65. Edin Th Coll 84. **d** 84 **p** 85. C Edin Old St Paul 84–86; R Leven *St And* 86–90; R Newport-on-Tay 90–96; R Tayport 90–96; R Forfar 96–07; Can St Ninian's Cathl Perth 93–07; rtd 07; LtO *St And* from 07; LtO *Edin* from 13. *14 Chewton Road, Thornton, Kirkcaldy KY1 4AZ* T/F: (01592) 775133 E: audrey.richardson@tesco.net

RICHARDSON, John Stephen. b 50. Southn Univ BA 71. St Jo Coll Nottm 72. **d** 74 **p** 75. C Bramcote *S'well* 74–77; C Radipole and Melcombe Regis *Sarum* 77–80; P-in-c Stinsford, Winterborne Came w Whitcombe etc 80–83; Asst Dioc Missr 80–83; V Nailsea Ch Ch *B & W* 83–90; Adv on Evang 86–90; Provost Bradf 90–00; Dean Bradf 00–01; V Wye w Brook and Hastingleigh etc *Cant* 01–09; P-in-c 04–09; C Mersham w Hinxhill and Sellindge 08–09; AD W Bridge 03–09; Chapl Wye Coll Kent *Lon* 01–09; P-in-c Margate H Trin *Cant* 09–13; V 13–16; rtd 16; C Romney Marsh *Cant* from 16. *135 Hight Street, Dymchurch, Romney Marsh TN29 0LD* E: vicarjohnsrichardson@googlemail.com

RICHARDSON, Canon John Stuart. b 46. Trin Coll Ox BA 68 MA 71 DPhil 73 FRSE 96. **d** 79 **p** 80. NSM St Andrews St Andr *St And* 79–87; Chapl St Andr Univ 80–87; Prof Classics Edin Univ 87–02; TV Edin St Columba 87–16; PtO from 16; Hon

Can St Mary's Cathl from 00. *Marketgate Farmhouse, Main Street, Ormiston, Tranent EH35 5HT* E: j.richardson@ed.ac.uk

RICHARDSON, John Thandule. b 49. Bradf and Ilkley Coll BSc 80 Lanc Univ MA 97. CBDTI 94. **d** 97 **p** 98. NSM Lea *Blackb* 97–02; NSM Broughton 02–04; NSM Lanercost, Walton, Gilsland and Nether Denton *Carl* 04–05; PtO *Blackb* 06–09; C Preston Risen Lord 09–12; Chapl Preston Coll 09–11; TV Costa Blanca *Eur* 12–13; PtO *Leeds* 15–16; NSM Guiseley w Esholt from 16. *17 Queens Terrace, Otley LS21 3JE* T: (01943) 969402 M: 07769-716861 E: johntr123@aol.com

RICHARDSON, Katherine Ruth. b 50. **d** 15 **p** 16. NSM Cirencester *Glouc* from 15. *1 Chesterton Terrace, 16 Watermoor Road, Cirencester GL7 1JW* T: (01285) 652576 E: revkatie@cirenparish.co.uk

RICHARDSON, Canon Laurence Leigh. b 71. Trin Coll Carmarthen BA 92 PGCE 93 Univ of Wales (Cardiff) BTh 97 FGMS 04. St Mich Coll Llan 94. **d** 97 **p** 98. C Carmarthen St Pet *St D* 97–01; Chapl Carmarthenshire Coll 99–01; P-in-c Abergwili w Llanfihangel-uwch-Gwili etc *St D* 01–03; V 03–09; TV E Carmarthen 09–10; TR 10–12; P-in-c Carmarthen St Pet 12–14; P-in-c Carmarthen St Pet and Abergwili etc 14–18; AD Carmarthen 09–18; Dioc Warden Ords 15–18; Can St D Cathl from 15; Sub Dean from 18; CF(V) from 01. *Brecon House, The Close, St Davids , Haverfordwest SA62 6PE* T: (01437) 720456 E: landcat10a@aol.com *or* subdean@stdavidscathedral.org.uk

RICHARDSON, Malcolm. *See* RICHARDSON, John Malcolm

RICHARDSON, Preb Neil. b 46. Southn Univ BTh 83. Sarum & Wells Th Coll 71. **d** 74 **p** 75. C Oldham St Mary w St Pet *Man* 74–77; C-in-c Holts CD 77–82; R Greenford H Cross *Lon* 82–13; Preb St Paul's Cathl 02–13; rtd 13; PtO *Chelmsf* from 14. *27 Hatchfields, Great Waltham, Chelmsford CM3 1AJ* E: neilandmarion49@btinternet.com

RICHARDSON, Canon Paul. b 58. Univ of Wales (Cardiff) BSc 80. Ridley Hall Cam 81. **d** 84 **p** 85. C Stanwix *Carl* 84–87; Ind Chapl 87–89; Staff P Dalton-in-Furness 87–89; V Marton Moss *Blackb* 89–95; P-in-c Prestwich St Gabr *Man* 95–00; Bp's Dom Chapl 95–00; V Westbury *Sarum* 00–02; TR White Horse 02–07; RD Heytesbury 04–07; R Devizes St Jo w St Mary from 07; Can and Preb Sarum Cathl from 07; RD Devizes 10–11 and from 15; PtO *Eur* from 18. *The Rectory, Brandon House, Potterne Road, Devizes SN10 5DD* T: (01380) 829616 E: paul.richardson8@btinternet.com

RICHARDSON, Pauline Kate. *See* JENKINS, Pauline Kate

RICHARDSON, Philip David. b 82. Reading Univ BA 04. St Mellitus Coll BA 17. **d** 17 **p** 18. C E Green *Cov* from 17. *23 Mary Herbert Street, Coventry CV3 5ER* M: 07747-776230 E: philrichardson@gmail.com *or* revphilrichardson@gmail.com

RICHARDSON, Simon Kay Caoimhin. b 74. St Jo Coll Dur BA 96 Cant Ch Ch Univ MA 10 QUB MTh 13. Wycliffe Hall Ox 01. **d** 03 **p** 04. C Folkestone Trin *Cant* 03–06; C Hillsborough *D & D* 06–08; I 08–11; C Holywood 11–14; I Glencraig 14–18; Min Can Belf Cathl 15–18; V Kempston Transfiguration *St Alb* from 18. *The Vicarage, Cleveland Street, Kempston, Bedford MK42 8DW* T: (01234) 635721 M: 07875-514431 E: simonkcr@gmail.com

RICHARDSON, Miss Susan. b 58. Cranmer Hall Dur. **d** 87 **p** 94. Par Dn Stokesley *York* 87–91; Par Dn Beverley St Nic 91–94; P-in-c Cloughton 94–97; V Cloughton and Burniston w Ravenscar etc 97–99; V Middlesbrough St Oswald 99–10; P-in-c Middlesbrough St Chad 09–10; V Middlesbrough St Oswald and St Chad from 10; Tr Officer E Riding from 94. *St Oswald's Vicarage, Lambton Road, Middlesbrough TS4 2RG* T: (01642) 816156 E: sue.richardson3@btinternet.com

RICHBOROUGH, Suffragan Bishop of (Provincial Episcopal Visitor). *See* BANKS, The Rt Revd Norman

RICHERBY, Canon Glynn. b 51. K Coll Lon BD 73 AKC 73. St Aug Coll Cant 73. **d** 74 **p** 75. C Weston Favell *Pet* 74–78; Prec Leic Cathl 78–81; V Glen Parva and S Wigston 81–93; V Leic St Jas 93–16; Dir Post-Ord Tr 86–95; Dir CME 95–16; Hon Can Leic Cathl 98–16; rtd 17. *115 Bath Road, Worcester WR5 3AF* T: (01905) 355757

RICHES, Malcolm Leslie. b 46. St Jo Coll Nottm 92. **d** 94 **p** 95. C Swaythling *Win* 94–97; P-in-c Boldre w S Baddesley 97–01; V 01–03; V Ellingham and Harbridge and Hyde w Ibsley 03–11; rtd 11; Hon C Caldbeck, Castle Sowerby and Sebergham *Carl* 11–16; PtO from 16. *13 Edmondson Close, Brampton CA8 1GH* M: 07968-139851 E: malcolm.l.riches@gmail.com

RICHEUX, Marc Stephen. b 66. Man Univ BA 89. Trin Coll Bris BA 00. **d** 00 **p** 01. C Plumstead St Jo w St Jas and St Paul S'wark 00–04; V Streatham Park St Alb 04–12; TV Furzedown from 12. *St Alban's Vicarage, 5 Fayland Avenue, London SW16 1SR* T: (020) 8677 4521 *or* 8769 5415 E: mricheux@clara.co.uk

RICHMOND, Patrick Henry. b 69. Ball Coll Ox BA 90 Green Coll Ox MA 94 DPhil 94. Wycliffe Hall Ox BA 96. **d** 97 **p** 98. C Leic Martyrs 97–01; Chapl and Fell St Cath Coll Cam 01–07; Dean of Chpl 06–07; V Eaton Ch Ch *Nor* from 07; RD Nor S from 19. *161 Newmarket Road, Norwich NR4 6SY* T: (01603) 250844 E: phr@eatonparish.com

RICHMOND, Peter James. b 54. Cant Ch Ch Univ MSc 07 Ex Univ PGCE 95. St Jo Coll Nottm. **d** 80 **p** 81. C Ogley Hay *Lich* 80–83; C Trentham 83–85; P-in-c Wolverhampton St Jo 85–89; P-in-c Loppington w Newtown 89–93; P-in-c Edstaston 89–93; PtO *Ex* 94–95; P-in-c Weston Zoyland w Chedzoy *B & W* 95–03; Chapl Somerset Partnership NHS and Soc Care Trust 97–03; Lead Chapl E Kent NHS and Soc Care Partnership Trust 03–06; Lead Chapl Kent & Medway NHS and Soc Care Partnership Trust 06–13; Hon C St Nicholas at Wade w Sarre and Chislet w Hoath *Cant* 04–10; rtd 13; PtO *Cant* 13–16. *41 The Rope Walk, Canterbury CT1 2FY* T: (01227) 379229

RICHMOND AND CRAVEN, Archdeacon of. *See* GOUGH, The Ven Jonathan Robin Blanning

RICHMOND TULLOCH, Yvonne Lorraine. *See* TULLOCH, Yvonne Lorraine

RICHMOND, Suffragan Bishop of. *See* SLATER, The Rt Revd Paul John

RICKETTS, Mrs Diane. b 54. NTMTC 98. **d** 01 **p** 02. NSM Nazeing and Roydon *Chelmsf* 01–06; R Laindon w Dunton 06–14; rtd 14. *8 Tots Gardens, Barrow Hill, Acton, Sudbury CO10 0DJ*

RICKETTS, Canon Kathleen Mary. b 39. Southlands Coll Lon TCert 59 Univ of W Aus BA 79. Westcott Ho Cam 81. **dss** 83 **d** 87 **p** 94. All Hallows by the Tower etc *Lon* 83–88; C 87–88; C Hall Green Ascension *Birm* 88–91; Chapl Birm Children's Hosp 91–94; Chapl Birm Children's Hosp NHS Trust 94–99; Hon Can Birm Cathl 96–99; rtd 99; PtO *Birm* from 00. *22 Holly Drive, Birmingham B27 7NF* T: 0121-706 1087

RICKETTS, Mrs Linda Elizabeth. b 52. RNMH 85. EAMTC 98. **d** 01 **p** 02. C Loddon, Sisland, Chedgrave, Hardley and Langley *Nor* 01–05; V Gorleston St Mary 05–17; rtd 17; PtO *Nor* from 19. *17 Muriel Kenny Court, Hethersett, Norwich NR9 3EZ* T: (01603) 814964 E: l.ricketts787@btinternet.com

RICKETTS, Theresa Lesley. b 76. Greyfriars Ox BA 00 Kingston Univ PGCE 07 Cam Univ BTh 14. Westcott Ho Cam 12. **d** 14 **p** 15. C Weybridge *Guildf* 14–17; P-in-c Cuddington from 17. *St Mary's Vicarage, St Mary's Road, Worcester Park KT4 7JL* M: 07949-769580 E: theresaricketts@hotmail.co.uk

RIDDEL, Robert John. b 37. CITC 65. **d** 68 **p** 69. C Derryloran *Arm* 68–74; I Keady w Armaghbreague and Derrynoose 74–80; I Cleenish w Mullaghdun *Clogh* 80–84; I Cleenish 80–84; I Fivemiletown 84–05; Can Clogh Cathl 91–05; Preb Donaghmore St Patr Cathl Dublin 95–05; rtd 05. *9 Coolcrannel Square, Maguiresbridge, Enniskillen BT94 4RE* T: (028) 6772 3199 E: riddel.r.j@btinternet.com

RIDDING, George. b 24. Oriel Coll Ox BA 50 MA 57. Wells Th Coll 60. **d** 61 **p** 62. C Wear *Ex* 61–62; Chapl Ex Sch 62–64; India 64–68; Hd Master W Buckland Sch Barnstaple 68–78; USPG 78–82; P-in-c Broadhembury w Payhembury *Ex* 82–83; P-in-c Plymtree 82–83; R Broadhembury, Payhembury and Plymtree 83–89; rtd 89; PtO *Sarum* 89–09. *The College of St Barnabas, Blackberry Lane, Lingfield RH7 6NJ* T: (01342) 872821 E: georgridding@gmail.com

RIDDLESTONE, Mrs Jennifer Jane. b 83. Warwick Univ BSc 05 St Jo Coll Dur BATM 15. Cranmer Hall Dur 12. **d** 15 **p** 16. C Egham *Guildf* 15–19; V Shottermill from 19. *The Vicarage, Vicarage Lane, Haslemere GU27 1LQ* E: jenn.riddlestone@gmail.com

RIDER, Andrew. b 62. Nottm Univ BTh 90 K Coll Lon MA 96 RMN 85. Aston Tr Scheme 85 St Jo Coll Nottm 87. **d** 90 **p** 91. C Luton Ch Ch *Roch* 90–93; C w resp for Clubhouse Langham Place All So *Lon* 93–03; P-in-c Spitalfields Ch Ch w All SS 03–04; R from 04; AD Tower Hamlets from 12. *The Rectory, 2 Fournier Street, London E1 6QE* T: (020) 7247 0790 *or* 7247 7202 F: 7247 5921 E: andy.rider@ccspits.org

RIDER, Canon Dennis William Austin. b 34. St Aid Birkenhead 58. **d** 61 **p** 62. C Derby St Aug 61–64; C Sutton Liv 64–67; R Stiffkey w Morston, Langham Episcopi etc *Nor* 67–71; V Buxton w Oxnead 71–79; R Lammas w Lt Hautbois 72–79; R Gaywood, Bawsey and Mintlyn 79–91; RD Lynn 89–91; Hon Can Nor Cathl 90–99; R E Dereham and Scarning 91–98; TR 98–99; RD Dereham in Mitford 95–98; rtd 99; PtO *Nor* 01–08; C Litcham w Kempston, E and W Lexham, Mileham etc 08–09; C Gt and Lt Dunham w Gt and Lt Fransham and Sporle 08–09; C Foulsham, Guestwick, Stibbard, Themelthorpe etc 10–11; PtO from 15. *37A Holt Road, Fakenham NR21 8BW* T: (01328) 856018 E: dandprider@btinternet.com

RIDER, Geoffrey Malcolm. b 29. Selw Coll Cam BA 53 MA 56 Lon Inst of Educn PGCE 68. Coll of Resurr Mirfield 53. **d** 55 **p** 56. C S Elmsall *Wakef* 55–60; C Barnsley St Mary 60–63; V Cleckheaton St Jo 63–67; Public Preacher *S'wark* 67–92; rtd 92; Succ Kimberley Cathl S Africa 92–95; PtO *S'wark* 95–03; Chapl and Hon Min Can Ripon Cathl 04–14; *Leeds* from 14. *26 Riverside House, Williamson Close, Ripon HG4 1AZ* T: (01765) 690517   E: geoffrey.rider2016@gmail.com   or geoffreyr547@gmail.com

RIDER, Paul Gill. b 57. Univ of Arkansas BA 81 MA 85. Nashotah Ho MDiv 89. **d** 89 **p** 90. R Fourche and Sturgis USA 89–93; R Minot 93–00; Can Minneapolis Cathl 00–02; R Mankato 02–17; P-in-c Nor Lakenham St Jo and All SS and Tuckswood from 18. *Old Lakenham Vicarage, Harwood Road, Norwich NR1 2NG* M: 07745-846770 E: prider57@mac.com

RIDGE, The Ven James Scott. b 77. Ex Univ BSc 99 Selw Coll Cam BTh 05. Westcott Ho Cam 02. **d** 05 **p** 06. C Halstead Area *Chelmsf* 05–09; C Bocking St Pet 09; Chapl HM Pris Chelmsf 09–16; Chapl HM Pris Wayland 16–18; Chapl Gen of Pris and Adn to HM Pris from 18. *HMPPS Chaplaincy HQ, Post Point 8.34, Ministry of Justice, 102 Petty France, London SW1H 9AJ* M: 07394-715223 E: james.ridge@justice.gov.uk

RIDGE, Jennifer Karen. b 64. Yorks Min Course 14. **d** 17 **p** 18. NSM Leic H Trin w St Jo 17–19; C from 19; NSM Leic H Apostles 17–19; C from 19. *96 Highway Road, Leicester LE5 5RF*

RIDGEWAY, David. b 59. St Chad's Coll Dur BSc 80 Cam Univ CertEd 81. Ripon Coll Cuddesdon 84. **d** 87 **p** 88. C Kempston Transfiguration *St Alb* 87–90; C Radlett 90–95; P-in-c Heath and Reach 95–98; V St Alb St Steph 01–15; RD St Alb 05–15; R Castor w Upton and Stibbington etc *Pet* from 15. *The Rectory, 5 Church Hill, Castor, Peterborough PE5 7AU* T: (01733) 380244   F: 07092-109111 E: davidridgeway@btinternet.com

RIDGEWELL, Miss Mary Jean. b 54. Dur Univ BA 76 PGCE 77. Ridley Hall Cam 89. **d** 91 **p** 94. Par Dn Trowbridge St Jas *Sarum* 91–94; C 94–95; Chapl Lee Abbey 95–96; NSM Bradford Peverell, Stratton, Frampton etc *Sarum* 96–97; Chapl HM Pris and YOI Guys Marsh 97–12; rtd 12; PtO *Sarum* from 12. *11 Gower Road, Shaftesbury SP7 8RU* E: rewarmedgilly@gmail.com

RIDGWAY, Mrs Janet Elizabeth Knight. b 40. St Alb Minl Tr Scheme 83. **dss** 86 **d** 87 **p** 94. Tring *St Alb* 86–87; Hon Par Dn 87–94; Hon C 94–05; rtd 05; PtO *St Alb* from 06. *Barleycombe, Trooper Road, Aldbury, Tring HP23 5RW* T: (01442) 851303 E: rev.j.ridgway@breathe.com

RIDGWELL, Graham Edgar Charles. b 46. LGSM 71 Open Univ BA 82 Leeds Univ MA 04. **d** 02 **p** 03. NSM Whitby w Aislaby and Ruswarp *York* 02–05; Hon TV Linton *Ely* 05–15; PtO *Chelmsf* from 15; *Ely* from 15. *76 Swan Street, Sible Hedingham, Halstead CO9 3HT* T: (01799) 584545 E: gecridgwell@googlemail.com or ridgwell@onetel.com

RIDING, Pauline Alison. See BICKNELL, Pauline Alison

RIDINGS, Neil Arthur. b 66. Man Poly BEd 90. St Jo Coll Nottm 01. **d** 01 **p** 02. C Holyhead *Ban* 01–05; TV 05–07; R Valley w Llechylched and Caergeiliog 07–14; R Bro Cwyfan 14–18; C Bro Cybi from 18. *Y Ficerdy, Trearddur House Mews, Lon St Ffraid, Trearddur Bay, Holyhead LL65 2UD* T: (01407) 861663 E: revridings@aol.com

RIDLEY, Alfred Forbes. b 34. Bps' Coll Cheshunt 62. **d** 65 **p** 66. C Prittlewell St Mary *Chelmsf* 65–69; R Paulerspury *Pet* 69–73; P-in-c Wicken 71–73; V W Haddon w Winwick 73–83; RD Brixworth 80–83; R Guernsey St Philippe de Torteval *Win* 83–92; R Guernsey St Pierre du Bois 83–92; R Blakesley w Adstone and Maidford etc *Pet* 92–99; rtd 99; PtO *Pet* 99–07. *36 Verona Court, Yeo Vale Road, Barnstaple EX32 7EN* T: (01271) 327850

RIDLEY, Andrew Roy. b 55. St Pet Coll Ox BA 77. Ripon Coll Cuddesdon 78. **d** 79 **p** 80. C Bollington St Jo *Ches* 79–83; V Runcorn St Mich 83–94; Dioc Chapl MU 92–98; RD Frodsham 94–98; V Helsby and Dunham-on-the-Hill 94–98; P-in-c Alvanley 94–98; R Whitchurch *Lich* 98–11; RD Wem and Whitchurch 01–06; V Barton under Needwood w Dunstall and Tatenhill from 11. *The Vicarage, 3 Church Lane, Barton under Needwood, Burton-on-Trent DE13 8HU* T: (01283) 712359 E: arceridley@btinternet.com

RIDLEY, David Gerhard. b 60. Southn Univ BSc 82 Bath Univ PGCE 83. Qu Coll Birm 91. **d** 93 **p** 94. C Faversham *Cant* 93–97; Min Folkestone St Aug CD 97–01; V Dover St Mary 01–13; P-in-c Whitfield w Guston 02–12; P-in-c Guston 13; AD Dover 06–11; R Eastry and Woodnesborough from 13. *The Rectory, Brook Street, Eastry, Sandwich CT13 0HR* M: 07887-880272 E: davidridley@btopenworld.com

RIDLEY, Derek. b 40. Newc Univ BSc 74. Cranmer Hall Dur 75. **d** 78 **p** 79. C Upperby St Jo *Carl* 78–81; C Penrith w Newton Reigny 81; C Penrith w Newton Reigny and Plumpton Wall 81–82; TV 82–86; V Cadishead *Man* 86–99; R Asfordby and P-in-c Ab Kettleby Gp *Leic* 99–02; P-in-c Old Dalby and Nether Broughton 99–01; rtd 02; PtO *Carl* from 08. *32 Carleton Place, Penrith CA11 8LW* T: (01768) 890676 E: lesley.ridley@me.com

RIDLEY, Jay. b 41. Birm Univ BA 63. St Steph Ho Ox 63. **d** 65 **p** 66. C Woodford St Mary *Chelmsf* 65–67; C Prittlewell St Mary 67–70; C-in-c Dunscroft CD *Sheff* 70–74; Asst Chapl HM Pris Wormwood Scrubs 75–77; Chapl HM Rem Cen Ashford 77–84; Chapl HM YOI Feltham 84–91; Chapl HM Pris Ashwell 91–00; C Oakham, Hambleton, Egleton, Braunston and Brooke *Pet* 00; rtd 11; PtO *Chich* from 16. *11 Ramsay Hall, 9-13 Byron Road, Worthing BN11 3HN* T: (01903) 210224 E: jay.ridley@hotmail.co.uk

RIDLEY, Mrs Jennifer Mary. b 62. **d** 14 **p** 15. NSM Sudbury w Ballingdon and Brundon *St E* 14–17; NSM Gt Cornard from 17. *67 Acton Lane, Sudbury CO10 1QW* T: (01787) 375974 E: jennie67mr@gmail.com

RIDLEY, Mrs Lesley. b 46. Cranmer Hall Dur 75. **dss** 78 **d** 87 **p** 94. Upperby St Jo *Carl* 78–81; Penrith w Newton Reigny and Plumpton Wall 81–86; Cadishead *Man* 86–99; Par Dn 87–94; C 94–99; C Asfordby and Ab Kettleby Gp *Leic* 99–02; rtd 02; PtO *Carl* from 08. *32 Carleton Place, Penrith CA11 8LW* T: (01768) 890676 E: lesley.ridley@me.com

RIDLEY, Michael Laurence. b 59. BA 81. Ripon Coll Cuddesdon 81. **d** 83 **p** 84. C Bollington St Jo *Ches* 83–88; V Thelwall 88–95; V Weaverham 95–05; RD Middlewich 99–05; V Stockton Heath from 05; P-in-c Latchford St Jas from 19. *12 Milne Avenue, Walton, Warrington WA4 6PQ* T: (01925) 261396 E: stocktonheathvicar@tiscali.co.uk

RIDLEY, Peter John. b 39. Keble Coll Ox BA 61. Tyndale Hall Bris 61. **d** 63 **p** 64. C Clifton Ch Ch w Em *Bris* 63–67; C Lambeth St Andr w St Thos *S'wark* 67–69; V W Hampstead St Cuth *Lon* 69–77; V Eynsham *Ox* 77–85; RD Woodstock 82–84; V Nicholforest and Kirkandrews on Esk *Carl* 85–96; P-in-c E Knoyle, Semley and Sedgehill *Sarum* 96–04; rtd 04; PtO *Carl* from 05. *The Castle, Castle Street, Hilton, Appleby-in-Westmorland CA16 6LX* T/F: (017683) 51682 E: peterandsally.ridley@btinternet.com

RIDLEY, Stewart Gordon. b 47. K Coll Lon AKC 72. St Aug Coll Cant 72. **d** 73 **p** 74. C Armley w New Wortley *Ripon* 73–77; C Hawksworth Wood 77–79; C Rothwell w Lofthouse 79–81; R Whitwood *Wakef* 81–87; R Ingoldmells w Addlethorpe *Linc* 87–92; RD Calcewaithe and Candleshoe 89–92; V Settle *Bradf* 92–05; C Bolton by Bowland w Grindleton 05–07; P-in-c Hurst Green and Mitton 05–07; P-in-c Waddington 05–07; rtd 07; PtO *York* 09–14; Chapl S Tees Hosps NHS Foundn Trust 11–14; PtO *Leeds* from 14. *18 Brough Meadows, Catterick, Richmond DL10 7LQ* T: (01748) 519359   M: 07952-584138 E: stewartridley@uwclub.net

RIDLEY, Vic. See RIDLEY, David Gerhard

RIDOUT, Canon Christopher John. b 33. K Coll Lon BD 57 AKC 57 MA 92. **d** 58 **p** 59. C Roxeth Ch Ch *Lon* 58–62; CMS 62–63; Kenya 63–75; C Gt Malvern St Mary *Worc* 75–79; R Bredon w Bredon's Norton 79–98; RD Pershore 91–97; Hon Can Worc Cathl 92–98; rtd 98; PtO *Glouc* from 98. *5 Belworth Drive, Hatherley, Cheltenham GL51 6EL* T: (01242) 231765 E: shirleyjohn@tiscali.co.uk

RIDPATH, Ms Vivienne Elizabeth Theresa. b 54. Aber Univ BSc 77 UEA PGCE 94. ERMC 16. **d** 19. OLM Belton and Burgh Castle *Nor* from 19. *30 North Denes Road, Great Yarmouth NR30 4LU* M: 07523-717810 E: vivridpath@aol.com

RIEM, Canon Roland Gerardus Anthony. b 60. St Chad's Coll Dur BSc 82 Kent Univ PhD 86 Heythrop Coll Lon MA 99. St Jo Coll Nottm 86. **d** 89 **p** 90. C Deal St Leon and St Rich and Sholden *Cant* 89–92; Sen Chapl Nottm Univ *S'well* 92–98; Dir Min STETS 98–05; Can Res Win Cathl from 05. *5A The Close, Winchester SO23 9LS* T: (01962) 857216 or 857239 F: 857201 E: roland.riem@winchester-cathedral.org.uk

RIENSTRA, Bruce Elliot. b 59. Ohio Univ (USA) BA 83 Ches Univ MA 18. St Jo Coll Nottm 11. **d** 13 **p** 14. C Warsop *S'well* 13–16; R Inkberrow w Cookhill and Kington w Dormston *Worc* from 16. *The Vicarage, High Street, Inkberrow, Worcester WR7 4DU* T: (01386) 792222   M: 07742-172333 E: b.e.rienstra@gmail.com

RIESS, Trevor William. b 54. Down Coll Cam MA 76 CertEd 77. St Jo Coll Nottm 84. **d** 86 **p** 87. C Stainforth *Sheff* 86–88; Chapl St Jas Choir Sch Grimsby 89; C Lowestoft and Kirkley *Nor* 89–90; TV 90–94; TV Lowestoft St Marg 94–95; Chapl Lothingland Hosp 90–95; V Gorleston St Mary *Nor* 95–05; P-in-c Scole, Brockdish, Billingford, Thorpe Abbots etc 05–11; P-in-c Scole 11–19; rtd 20. *26 Bellflower Road, Grimsby DN33 3AZ* E: trevorriess@btinternet.com

RIGBY, Harold. b 34. Nottm Univ BA 56 St Cath Soc Ox BA 58 MA 62 Man Poly PGCE 77. Ripon Hall Ox 56. **d** 58 **p** 59.

C Didsbury St Jas and Em *Man* 58–61; C Bury St Jo 61–64; P-in-c Lostock St Thos and St Jo 64–76; Hon C Davyhulme St Mary 76–79; Lic Preacher 79–10; PtO 10–17. *17 Atwood Road, Didsbury, Manchester M20 0TA* T: 0161-445 7454 E: haroldr172@gmail.com

RIGBY, Joseph. b 37. Open Univ BA 72. Ox NSM Course. d 78 p 79. NSM Earley St Pet *Ox* 78–80; C Penzance St Mary w St Paul *Truro* 80–82; V Mevagissey 82–83; P-in-c St Ewe 83; R Mevagissey and St Ewe 83–90; rtd 90; PtO *Truro* 90–09; *Guildf* 10–16. *Flat 5, Manormead, Tilford Road, Hindhead GU26 6RA* T: (01428) 601505 E: josephrigbyba112@yahoo.com

RIGBY, William. b 51. Leic Univ BSc(Econ) 72 Newc Poly BSc 82. Cranmer Hall Dur 86. d 88 p 89. C Morpeth *Newc* 88–92; R St John Lee 92–00; Chapl to the Deaf 92–08; P-in-c Chapel House 00–08; V Bywell and Mickley 08–16; rtd 16; PtO *Dur* from 16. *1 Bromley Close, High Shincliffe, Durham DH1 7TZ* M: 07734-068668 E: bill.rigby1@btopenworld.com

RIGELSFORD, Mrs Anne Catharina (Ank). b 44. EAMTC 99. d 02 p 03. NSM Cambridge H Cross *Ely* 02–06; NSM Cambridge Ascension 06–15; PtO from 15. *19 Clare Street, Cambridge CB4 3BY* T: (01223) 368150 M: 07932-846395 E: ank1@btinternet.com

RIGLIN, Ms Jacqueline Anne. b 57. ERMC 13. d 16 p 17. C Chesterton St Geo *Ely* from 16. *30 Lavender Road, Cambridge CB4 2PU* T: (01223) 660144 M: 07513-331783 E: jackie.riglin@gmail.com

RIGLIN, Keith Graham. b 57. Lon Inst of Educn BEd 80 Regent's Park Coll Ox BA 83 MA 86 Heythrop Coll Lon MTh 85 Birm Univ ThD 08 FRSA 09 AKC 16. Westcott Ho Cam 06. d 08 p 08. In Bapt Union 83-96; in URC 97–08; C Notting Dale St Clem w St Mark and St Jas *Lon* 08–11; PtO 12–16; *S'wark* 12–13; *Arg* from 12; Chapl K Coll Lon from 12; Visiting Lect from 16; Asst Dean from 17; NSM Soho St Anne w St Thos and St Pet from 16; NSM St Mary le Strand w St Clem Danes from 17; Dir of Ords Two Cities Area from 19. *49 City Road, London EC1Y 1AU* M: 07946-871850 E: kgr23@cam.ac.uk *or* keith.riglin@kcl.ac.uk

RILEY, Alison Mary. b 70. Warwick Univ BSc 91 St Martin's Coll Lanc PGCE 98. St Mellitus Coll 15. d 17 p 18. C Whitehaven *Carl* from 17. *8 Spruce Grove, Whitehaven CA28 6NP* T: (01946) 65451 M: 07787-508391 E: alidunnuk@yahoo.co.uk

RILEY, David Leo. b 57. S Bank Univ MSc 95. Dioc OLM tr scheme 97. d 00 p 01. NSM Bellingham St Dunstan *S'wark* from 00. *117 Whitefoot Lane, Bromley BR1 5SB* T: (020) 8516 4544 E: driley3020@aol.com

RILEY, John Graeme. b 55. St Jo Coll Dur BA 78. Trin Coll Bris 79. d 81 p 82. C Hensingham *Carl* 81–84; C Preston St Cuth *Blackb* 84–87; V Blackb Ch Ch w St Matt 87–98; Chapl Qu Park Hosp Blackb 87–94; V Shevington *Blackb* 98–04; V Euxton 04–14; P-in-c Gosforth w Nether Wasdale and Wasdale Head *Carl* 14–17; P-in-c Beckermet St Jo and St Bridget w Ponsonby 14–17; R Seatallan from 17. *The Rectory, Gosforth, Seascale CA20 1AZ* T: (01946) 725251 E: lesleyjohn.riley@gmail.com

RILEY, The Very Revd Kenneth Joseph. b 40. Univ of Wales BA 61 Linacre Ho Ox BA 64 MA 68. Wycliffe Hall Ox 61. d 64 p 65. C Fazakerley Em *Liv* 64–66; Chapl Brasted Place Coll Westerham 66–69; Chapl Oundle Sch 69–74; Chapl Liv Cathl 74–75; Chapl Liv Univ 74–93; V Mossley Hill St Matt and St Jas 75–83; RD Childwall 82–83; Can Res and Treas Liv Cathl 83–87; Can Res and Prec Liv Cathl 87–93; Dean Man 93–05; rtd 05. *4 Lindisfarne Road, Alnwick NE66 1AU*

RILEY, Mrs Lesley Anne. b 54. Totley Thornbridge Coll TCert 75. Trin Coll Bris. d 86 p 87 p 98. Hensingham *Carl* 81–84; Preston St Cuth *Blackb* 84–87; Hon Par Dn Blackb Ch Ch w St Matt 87–98; Asst Dir of Ords 96–00; Dir of Ords and Dir IME 4-7 00–05; Hon C Shevington 98–04; Hon C Whittle-le-Woods 06–07; Resources Co-ord Dioc Bd of Educn 07–14; NSM Gosforth w Nether Wasdale and Wasdale Head *Carl* 14–17; NSM Beckermet St Jo and St Bridget w Ponsonby 14–17; NSM Seatallan 17–19; PtO from 19. *The Rectory, Gosforth, Seascale CA20 1AZ* T: (01946) 725251 E: lesley.riley@uwclub.net

RILEY, Linda. *See* RILEY-DAWKIN, Linda

RILEY, Martin Shaw. b 47. Selw Coll Cam BA 71 MA 75 Cam Univ CertEd 72. Sarum & Wells Th Coll 85. d 87 p 88. C Tuffley *Glouc* 87–91; Hon Min Can Glouc Cathl from 88; P-in-c Barnwood 91–94; V 94–99; P-in-c Highnam, Lassington, Rudford, Tibberton etc 99–04; R 04–06; Chapl Glos Hosps NHS Foundn Trust 06–12; rtd 12; PtO *Eur* from 17. *61 Kingsholm Road, Gloucester GL1 3BA* T: (01452) 417337

RILEY, Michael Charles. b 57. Ball Coll Ox BA 79 MA 83 Ex Univ CertEd 80. Edin Th Coll 84. d 86 p 87. C Newc St Geo 86–89; C Chiswick St Nic w St Mary *Lon* 89–90; V Chiswick St Paul Grove Park from 90. *St Paul's Vicarage, 64 Grove Park Road, London W4 3SB* T: (020) 8987 0312 E: michaelc.riley@virgin.com

RILEY, Preb Patrick John. b 39. Leeds Univ BA 62. Coll of Resurr Mirfield 62. d 64 p 65. C Rowbarton *B & W* 64–72; P-in-c Farleigh Hungerford w Tellisford 72–73; P-in-c Rode Major 72–73; R 73–85; RD Frome 78–85; V Glastonbury w Meare and W Pennard 85–01; Preb Wells Cathl 90–01; rtd 01; PtO *Sarum* from 02. *30 St James Street, Shaftesbury SP7 8HE* T: (01747) 850361 E: andy.blows@phonecoop.coop

RILEY-BRALEY, Robert James. b 57. Ch Ch Ox BA 82 MA 82 Down Coll Cam BA 83 MA 87 K Coll Lon MA 98 Surrey Univ PGCE 92. Ridley Hall Cam 81. d 84 p 85. C Thames Ditton *Guildf* 84–87; C Gravesend St Geo *Roch* 87–91; PtO *Lon* 91–92; *Blackb* 92–95; *S'wark* 95–00; C Stevenage St Mary Shephall w Aston *St Alb* 02–08; P-in-c Croxley Green St Oswald 08–12; V from 12. *St Oswald's Vicarage, 159 Baldwins Lane, Croxley Green, Rickmansworth WD3 3LL* T: (01923) 332244

RILEY-DAWKIN, Mrs Linda. b 67. St Jo Coll Nottm BA 00. d 00 p 01. C Ince Ch Ch *Liv* 00–06; Chapl Knowsley Community Coll 06–08; V Ditton St Mich w St Thos *Liv* from 08. *339 Ditchfield Road, Widnes WA8 8XR* T: 0151-420 4963 M: 07932-038443 E: revlin.riley@btinternet.com

RIMMER, Alan Howard. b 88. Ch Ch Ox MA 10. St Steph Ho Ox BA 18. d 19. C Tottenham St Mary *Lon* from 19. *The Mission House, Mitchley Road, London N17 9HG* M: 07582-399967 E: alanhowardrimmer@gmail.com

RIMMER, Andrew Malcolm. b 62. Magd Coll Cam BA 84 MA 88. Wycliffe Hall Ox 86. d 88 p 89. C Romford Gd Shep *Chelmsf* 88–92; C Hazlemere *Ox* 92–97; V Crookhorn *Portsm* 97–05; TV Canford Magna *Sarum* 05–17; V S Mimms Ch Ch *Lon* from 17. *Christ Church Vicarage, St Albans Road, Barnet EN5 4LA* E: andy@rimmerteam.com *or* vicar@ccbarnet.org.uk

RIMMER, Canon David Henry. b 36. Ex Coll Ox BA 60 MA 65. Linc Th Coll 62. d 64 p 65. C Liv Our Lady and St Nic 64–66; C Daybrook *S'well* 66–69; Chapl St Mary's Cathl *Edin* 69–71; R Kirkcaldy *St And* 71–78; R Haddington *Edin* 78–83; R Dunbar 79–83; R Edin Gd Shep 83–01; Hon Can St Mary's Cathl 98–01; rtd 01; LtO *Edin* from 01. *28/25 Roseburn Place, Edinburgh EH12 5NX* T: 0131-237 3070 E: ehhdhome@icloud.com

RIMMER, Mrs Margaret. b 55. St Jo Coll Dur BA 05 SRN 77 SCM 78. Cranmer Hall Dur 00. d 02 p 03. C Aysgarth and Bolton cum Redmire *Ripon* 02–06; V Gt and Lt Ouseburn w Marton cum Grafton etc 06–10; P-in-c Lostock Hall and Farington Moss *Blackb* 10–12; V 12–16; rtd 16; PtO *Blackb* from 16. *28 Hampson Avenue, Leyland PR25 5TH* T: (01772) 512109 E: margaretrimmer.rev@gmail.com

RINDL, Antony William. b 64. St Jo Coll Nottm 97. d 99 p 00. C Syston *Leic* 99–03; TV Colne and Villages *Blackb* 03–08; TR 08–13; P-in-c Brierfield 10–13; AD Pendle 05–13; V Watford *St Alb* from 13. *The Vicarage, 14 Cassiobury Drive, Watford WD17 3AB* T: (01923) 819152 E: tony.rindl@googlemail.com

RINGER, Philip James. b 47. Ox Min Course 88. d 91 p 92. NSM Chalfont St Peter *Ox* 91–95; P-in-c Lynton, Brendon, Countisbury, Lynmouth etc *Ex* 95–96; TV Combe Martin, Berrynarbor, Lynton, Brendon etc 96–03; Chapl Devon and Cornwall Constabulary 00–03; R Wriggle Valley *Sarum* 03–08; rtd 08; PtO *Sarum* from 08; Chapl SW Dorset Primary Care Trust from 08; Chapl Dorset Police from 10. *7 Wanderwell Farm Lane, Bridport DT6 4JW* T: (01308) 425774 E: philipringer@aol.com

RINGLAND, Tom Laurence. b 61. SS Hild & Bede Coll Dur BSc 83. Trin Coll Bris BA 89. d 89 p 90. C Southgate *Chich* 89–92; C Polegate 92–96; P-in-c Coalville and Bardon Hill *Leic* 96–98; V 98–06; TR Kirby Muxloe 06–15; C Desford and Peckleton w Tooley 13–15; R Desford and Kirby Muxloe from 15; AD Sparkenhoe E from 16. *The Rectory, 6 Station Road, Kirby Muxloe, Leicester LE9 2EJ* T: 0116-238 6822 *or* 238 6811 E: tringland@aol.com

RINGROSE, The Ven Hedley Sidney. b 42. Open Univ BA 79. Sarum Th Coll 65. d 68 p 69. C Bishopston *Bris* 68–71; C Easthampstead *Ox* 71–75; V Glouc St Geo w Whaddon 75–88; RD Glouc City 83–88; Hon Can Glouc Cathl 86–09; V Cirencester 88–98; RD 89–97; Adn Cheltenham 98–09; rtd 10; Acting Adn Malmesbury *Bris* 10–11; Acting Adn Ox 11–13; PtO *Sarum* from 10; *Bris* from 12. *131 North Street, Calne SN11 0HL* T: (01249) 821215 E: hedleyringrose@gmail.com

RINK, Caroline Natalie. b 82. Ex Univ BA 06. Coll of Resurr Mirfield BA 19. d 19. C Kilburn St Mary w All So and W Hampstead St Jas *Lon* from 19. *3 St James's*

House, Sherriff Road, London NW6 2AP M: 07740-336829 E: rev.caroline.rink@gmail.com

RINK, Pamela Rosemary. b 56. Kent Univ BA 05. SEITE 08. d 10 p 12. NSM E Malling, Wateringbury and Teston *Roch* 10–16; Guardian Pilsdon at Malling Community 11–15; TV Shaftesbury *Sarum* from 16. *The Vicarage, Bittles Green, Motcombe, Shaftesbury SP7 9NX* T: (01747) 590712 M: 07881-786526 E: pam.rink@gmail.com

RIOCH, Mrs Wenda Jean. b 35. Sarum & Wells Th Coll 84. d 87 p 94. Par Dn Basingstoke *Win* 87–91; Par Dn Catshill and Dodford *Worc* 91–94; C 94–98; TV Ottery St Mary, Alfington, W Hill, Tipton etc *Ex* 98–05; rtd 05; PtO *Win* from 08; *Sarum* from 09. *76 Gardeners Green, Shipton Bellinger, Tidworth SP9 7TA* T: (01980) 842334 E: wrioch123@aol.com

RIPLEY, Gordon. b 48. SWMTC 03. d 06 p 07. NSM Torquay St Matthias, St Mark and H Trin *Ex* 06–10; NSM Timsbury w Priston, Camerton and Dunkerton *B & W* 10–17; rtd 17. *42 Ampney Drive Kingsway, Quedgeley, Gloucester GL2 2HR* E: gordon.ripley364@btinternet.com

RIPON, Dean of. *See* DOBSON, The Very Revd John Richard

RIPON, Suffragan Bishop of. *See* HARTLEY, The Rt Revd Helen-Ann Macleod

RISBRIDGER, Jeffrey Edward. b 58. K Alfred's Coll Win BA 80 PGCE 81. Ripon Coll Cuddesdon 12. d 14 p 15. C Waterloo St Jo w St Andr *S'wark* 14–18; C Ludgvan, Marazion, St Hilary and Perranuthnoe *Truro* from 18; RD Penwith from 19. *The Vicarage, 7A North Road, Goldsithney, Penzance TR20 9JY* M: 07711-019590 E: fatherjeffrey@icloud.com

RISBY, John. b 40. Lambeth STh 82. Oak Hill Th Coll 64. d 67 p 68. C Fulham Ch Ch *Lon* 67–68; C Ealing St Mary 68–70; C Chitts Hill St Cuth 70–73; C Hove Bp Hannington Memorial Ch *Chich* 73–76; V Islington St Jude Mildmay Park *Lon* 76–82; P-in-c Islington St Paul Ball's Pond 78–82; V Mildmay Grove St Jude and St Paul 82–84; R Hunsdon w Widford and Wareside *St Alb* 84–05; RD Hertford 91–96; rtd 05; PtO *St Alb* from 06; *Chelmsf* from 06. *1 Pilgrim Close, Great Chesterford, Saffron Walden CB10 1QG* T: (01799) 530232

RISDON, Mrs Caroline Louise. b 79. Cape Town Univ BSocSc 01 Univ Coll Lon MA 11 Chu Coll Cam BTh 14. Westcott Ho Cam 12. d 14 p 15. C Greenwich St Alfege *S'wark* from 14. *88 Ashburnham Grove, London SE10 8UJ* M: 07899-916089 E: caroline.risdon@st-alfege.org.uk

RISDON, John Alexander. b 42. Clifton Th Coll 66. d 68 p 69. C Ealing Dean St Jo *Lon* 68–72; C Heref St Pet w St Owen 72–74; Ord Cand Sec CPAS and Hon C Bromley Ch Ch *Roch* 74–77; TV Cheltenham St Mary, St Matt, St Paul and H Trin *Glouc* 77–86; R Stapleton *Bris* 86–00; R Bedhampton *Portsm* 00–09; rtd 09; PtO *Glouc* from 10. *10 St Margarets Road, Gloucester GL3 3BP* T: (01452) 372702 M: 07719-460991 E: john.risdon65@btinternet.com

RISHTON, Mrs Tracy Jane. b 67. St Jo Coll Nottm 01. d 04 p 05. C Earby *Bradf* 04–07; C Kelbrook 04–07; C Cross Roads cum Lees 07–09; Area Missr S Craven Deanery 07–09. *Hovland, 4389 Vikesa, Norway* E: tracy@rishton.info

RITCHIE, Canon Angus William Mark. b 74. Magd Coll Ox BA 94 BPhil 96 MA 98. Westcott Ho Cam 96. d 98 p 99. C Plaistow and N Canning Town *Chelmsf* 98–02; TV 02–04; Dir Contextual Th Cen R Foundn of St Kath in Ratcliffe 05–16; Fells' Chapl Magd Coll Ox from 05; Hon C Gt Ilford St Luke *Chelmsf* 05–08; Chapl E Lon Univ 08–11; Asst Chapl Keble Coll Ox 11–12; Hon C Bethnal Green St Pet w St Thos *Lon* 12–15; NSM St Geo-in-the-East w St Paul from 15; P-in-c 15–18; Hon Can Worc Cathl from 15. *St George-in-the-East Church, 14 Cannon Street Road, London E1 0BH* T: (020) 7481 1345 M: 07841-362786 E: angus@stgeorgeintheeast.org *or* director@theology-centre.org

RITCHIE, David John Rose. b 48. St Jo Coll Dur BA 72. Cranmer Hall Dur. d 74 p 75. C Harold Wood *Chelmsf* 74–79; TV Ipsley *Worc* 79–84; Chapl Vevey w Château d'Oex and Villars *Eur* 84–93; V Stoke Bishop *Bris* 93–13; rtd 13; PtO *Worc* from 15. *The Old Stores, Forty Green, Lowbands, Redmarley, Gloucester GL19 3SL* E: davidritchie@live.co.uk

RITCHIE, Canon David Philip. b 60. Hatf Coll Dur BA 85. Wycliffe Hall Ox 85. d 87 p 88. C Chadwell *Chelmsf* 87–90; C Waltham H Cross 90–94; TV Becontree W 94–98; TR 98–01; Lay Tr Officer 01–11; C Lt Waltham 02–05; C Gt and Lt Leighs and Lt Waltham 05–11; Dir Lay Min Studies NTMTC 06–11; TR Gt Baddow *Chelmsf* from 11; Hon Can Chelmsf Cathl from 09. *The Rectory, 12 Church Street, Great Baddow, Chelmsford CM2 7HZ* E: dpritchie1@gmail.com

RITCHIE, Miss Jean. b 30. Lon Univ CertEd 51. Trin Coll Bris 77. dss 79 d 87 p 94. Ox St Ebbe w H Trin and St Pet 79–87; Par Dn 87–91; rtd 91; PtO *B & W* 91–94 and 96–18; NSM Clevedon St Andr and Ch Ch 94–96. *63 Holland Road, Clevedon BS21 7YJ* T: (01275) 871762 E: jean.ritch@o2.co.uk

RITCHIE, June. *See* FAULKNER, June

RITCHIE, Philip. *See* RITCHIE, David Philip

RITCHIE, Philip Simon James. b 68. Man Univ BA 90 Sussex Univ MA 98 Leeds Univ MA 01 Man Metrop Univ PGCE 92. Coll of Resurr Mirfield 99. d 01 p 02. C Brighton St Nic *Chich* 01–04; P-in-c Chich St Wilfrid 04–08; P-in-c Hove 08–10; V Hove All SS 10–15; V Cowley St Jo *Ox* from 15. *Redwood House, 276A Cowley Road, Oxford OX4 1UR* E: philipsj68@gmail.com *or* philipsj@gmail.com

RITCHIE, William James. b 62. TCD MA 84. CITC. d 86 p 87. C Enniscorthy w Clone, Clonmore, Monart etc *C & O* 86–89; Asst Chapl Alexandria Egypt 89–91; Bp's C Kells Gp *C & O* 91–92; I Kells Union *M & K* 92–99; Warden of Readers 93–97; Dioc Ecum Officer 97–99; Min Can St Patr Cathl Dublin 97–99; I Clondehorkey w Cashel *D & R* 99–00; I Dublin St Bart w Leeson Park *D & G* 00–04; I Tullow w Shillelagh, Aghold and Mullinacuff *C & O* 04–08; Warden of Readers 05–08; PtO *Lon* 08–12; P-in-c Newport All SS *Mon* 12–15; P-in-c Abertillery w Cwmtillery w Llanhilleth etc 15–16. *73 Cae'r Wern, Merthyr Tydfil CF48 1AF* E: duwillo@yahoo.co.uk

RITSON, Canon Gerald Richard Stanley (Bill). b 35. CCC Cam BA 59 MA 63. Linc Th Coll 59. d 61 p 62. C Harpenden St Jo *St Alb* 61–65; C Goldington 65–69; R Clifton 69–76; Sec to Dioc Past Cttee and P-in-c Aldenham 76–87; Hon Can St Alb 80–87; Can Res St Alb 87–00; rtd 00; PtO *S'wark* 00–16; *Lon* 04–09. *Terry's Cross House, Brighton Road, Woodmancote, Henfield BN5 9SX* T: (01273) 494215

RITTMAN, Mrs Margaret. b 52. C F Mott Coll of Educn CertEd 73 Trent Poly BEd 80. Ripon Coll Cuddesdon MA 11. d 11 p 12. NSM Knight's Enham and Smannell w Enham Alamein *Win* 11–13; NSM Martlesham w Brightwell *St E* from 13. *Woodlea, The Street, Martlesham, Woodbridge IP12 4RG* M: 07914-771061 E: mgtritt@me.com

RIVETT, Canon Peter John. b 42. St Jo Coll Dur BA 71. Cranmer Hall Dur 68. d 72 p 73. C Newland St Jo *York* 72–76; TV Marfleet 76–82; V Oxhey All SS *St Alb* 82–93; TR Swanborough *Sarum* 93–98; TV Pewsey and Swanborough 98–01; USPG Zambia 01–07; Adn S Zambia 08–10; Hon Can Lusaka 10; rtd 10; PtO *Sheff* from 14. *16 Birks Lane, Millhouse Green, Sheffield S36 9NB* T: (01226) 765829

RIVIERE, Canon Jonathan Byam Valentine. b 54. Cuddesdon Coll. d 83 p 84. C Wymondham *Nor* 83–88; TV Quidenham 88–94; P-in-c Somerleyton w Ashby, Fritton and Herringfleet 94; R Somerleyton, Ashby, Fritton, Herringfleet etc 95–03; R Sandringham w W Newton and Appleton etc from 03; P-in-c Castle Rising 03–11; R from 11; P-in-c Hillington 03–11; R from 11; RD Heacham and Rising 13–17; Dom Chapl to The Queen from 03; Chapl to The Queen from 07; Hon Can Nor Cathl from 14. *The Rectory, Sandringham PE35 6EH* T: (01485) 540587 E: rector.sandringham@gmail.com

RIZZELLO, Karen Margaret. b 56. d 16 p 17. C Whitton *Sarum* from 16. *Brindley House, Vastern Wharf, Royal Wootton Bassett, Swindon SN4 7PD* T: (01793) 850945 E: karen@rizzello.co.uk

ROACH, Jason O'Neale. b 77. Guy's Hosp Medical Sch BSc 99 K Coll Lon MB, BS 02 St Mary's Coll Twickenham MA 05. Oak Hill Th Coll MTh 10. d 10 p 11. C Mayfair Ch Ch *Lon* from 10; Bp's Adv on Policy and Strategy from 19. *15 Manor Court, 180 Battersea Bridge Road, London SW11 3AH* T: (020) 7223 0273 M: 07957-473507 E: revdrjroach@gmail.com

ROACHE, Anthony. b 60. Nazarene Th Coll Man BA 98. Qu Coll Birm 98. d 99 p 00. C Bury St Mary *Man* 99–02; P-in-c Ringley w Prestolee 02–06; Voc Adv 04–06; CF(V) 03–06; CF 06–19; P-in-c Darlington St Hilda and St Columba *Dur* from 19; P-in-c Darlington St Jo from 19. *104 Blackwell Lane, Darlington DL3 8QQ*

ROAKE, Anthony Richard Garrard. b 52. Keble Coll Ox BA 75 MA 80. Wycliffe Hall Ox 75. d 77 p 78. C Clifton *S'well* 77–80; V Lapley w Wheaton Aston *Lich* 80–86; V Bournemouth St Andr *Win* 86–98; V Fernhurst *Chich* 98–07; Chapl The Hague *Eur* 07–12; R Nailsea Ch Ch w Tickenham *B & W* 12–19; NSM Timsbury w Priston, Camerton and Dunkerton from 19. *The Rectory, Skinners Hill, Camerton, Bath BA2 0PU* E: tonyrgr@gmail.com

ROAN, Canon William Forster. b 21. St Chad's Coll Dur BA 47. d 49 p 50. C Barrow St Jas *Carl* 49–52; C-in-c Westf St Mary CD 52–57; V Westfield St Mary 58–61; R Greystoke 61–69; V Workington St Jo 70–86; Hon Can Carl Cathl 72–86; RD Solway 77–84; rtd 86; PtO *Carl* 86–16. *41 Chiswick Street, Carlisle CA1 1HJ* T: (01228) 521756

ROBARTS, Mrs Freda Margaret. b 43. Open Univ BA 86. St As Minl Tr Course 98. d 04 p 06. NSM Berriew *St As* 04–06; P-in-c Llansilin w Llangadwaladr and Llangedwyn 06–09; rtd 09; PtO *St As* 09–16. *23 Fordwich Close, St Arvans, Chepstow NP16 6EL*

ROBB, Ian Archibald. b 48. K Coll Lon 68. d 72 p 73. C E Ham w Upton Park *Chelmsf* 72–74; C Leckhampton SS Phil and Jas w Cheltenham St Jas *Glouc* 74–79; P-in-c Cheltenham

St Mich 79–90; V Lower Cam w Coaley 90–14; rtd 14; PtO *Glouc* from 14. *19 Pear Tree Close, Hardwicke, Gloucester GL2 4TL* T: (01452) 676059 E: ia_jdr@lineone.net

ROBB, Timothy Simon. b 72. Cant Univ (NZ) BMus 94 LTCL 94 Lon Bible Coll BTh 98. Trin Coll Bris MA 03. **d** 03 **p** 04. C Bedford Ch Ch *St Alb* 03–07; Chapl De Montford Univ 05–07; V Eaton Socon from 07. *St Mary's Vicarage, 34 Drake Road, Eaton Socon, St Neots PE19 8HS* T: (01480) 212219 E: vicar@eatonsocon.org

ROBBIE, James Neil. b 68. Strathclyde Univ BEng 90. Oak Hill Th Coll BTh 02. **d** 05 **p** 06. C Wolverhampton St Luke *Lich* 05–09; V W Bromwich H Trin from 09. *Holy Trinity Vicarage, 1 Burlington Road, West Bromwich B70 6LF* T: 0121-525 3595 E: rev.robbie@btinternet.com

ROBBINS, Angela Mary. *See* TOWNSHEND, Angela Mary

ROBBINS, David Ronald Walter. b 47. Sarum & Wells Th Coll 85. **d** 87 **p** 88. C Meir Heath *Lich* 87–89; C Collier Row St Jas and Havering-atte-Bower *Chelmsf* 89–93; C Tamworth *Lich* 93–97; P-in-c Hulland, Atlow, Kniveton, Bradley and Hognaston *Derby* 97–98; R 98–02; R Widford *Chelmsf* 02–12; rtd 12; PtO *Lich* from 18. *65 The Lawns, Rollston-on-Dove, Burton-on-Trent DE13 9DD* T: (01283) 814051 E: dave@therobbinsfamily.co.uk

ROBBINS, Mrs Janet Carey. b 41. LMH Ox BA 63 MA 95 Nôtre Dame Coll Bearsden PGCE 81. St D Dioc Tr Course 96. **d** 98 **p** 99. NSM Llanfihangel Ystrad and Cilcennin w Trefilan etc *St D* 98–01; NSM Quantock Towers *B & W* 02–03; rtd 03; Hon C Bro Teifi Sarn Helen *St D* 08–11; PtO 11–14; *Worc* from 14. *Gothic House, 48 Bridge Street, Pershore WR10 1AT* T: (01386) 555709 E: revdjcr@gmail.com

ROBBINS, The Ven Stephen. b 53. K Coll Lon BD 74 AKC 74. St Aug Coll Cant 75. **d** 76 **p** 77. C Tudhoe Grange *Dur* 76–80; C-in-c Harlow Green CD 80–84; V Gateshead Harlow Green 84–87; CF 87–97; Sen CF 97–01; Chapl R Memorial Chpl Sandhurst 01–02; Asst Chapl Gen 02–07; Dep Chapl Gen 07–09; Chapl Gen 08–11; Adn for the Army 04–11; QHC 05–11; Can and Preb Sarum Cathl 07–11; PtO 11–16; Bp's Chapl 12–15; Bp's Adv for Deliverance Min from 15; PtO *Newc* from 12. *Mill Leat, Gomeldon, Salisbury SP4 6JY* E: venstephen@gmail.com

ROBBINS, Walter. b 35. **d** 72 **p** 73. Argentina 73–82; Adn N Argentina 80–82; C Southborough St Pet w Ch Ch and St Matt *Roch* 82–86; V Sidcup St Andr 86–95; V Grain w Stoke 95–00; rtd 00; PtO *Roch* 00–13; *Cant* 01–09. *Mariners, Imperial Avenue, Minster on Sea, Sheerness ME12 2HG* T: (01795) 876588

ROBERT, Brother. *See* ATWELL, Robert Ronald

ROBERTS, Alan Moss. b 39. CEng 68 MIMechE 68 MIMarEST 68. St Jo Coll Nottm 77. **d** 79 **p** 80. C Bromsgrove St Jo *Worc* 79–83; C Edgbaston St Germain *Birm* 83–89; R Broadhembury, Payhembury and Plymtree *Ex* 89–06; rtd 06. *8 Oakleigh, Sheldon, Honiton EX14 4QT* T: (01404) 841358

ROBERTS, Mrs Alison Jane. b 51. Luton Univ MSc 97. Ripon Coll Cuddesdon 13. **d** 16 **p** 17. OLM Aston Clinton w Buckland and Drayton Beauchamp *Ox* from 16. *Dormers, Buckland, Aylesbury HP22 5HY* T: (01296) 630256 M: 07702-268157 E: alisonroberts999@btinternet.com

ROBERTS, Allen. b 47. Trin Coll Ox MA 72 Warwick Univ MA 74 PhD 79 Wolv Univ LLM 99. Qu Coll Birm 06. **d** 07 **p** 09. NSM Tettenhall Regis *Lich* 07–19; PtO from 19. *11 Grosvenor Court, Lime Tree Avenue, Wolverhampton WV6 8HB* T: (01902) 765741 M: 07885-341540 E: allen.roberts1@btinternet.com

ROBERTS, Mrs Andrea Joan. b 46. Liv Poly ALA 68 St Jo Coll Dur BA 73 PGCE 74. Cranmer Hall Dur 70 CBDTI 03. **d** 04 **p** 05. NSM Garstang St Thos *Blackb* 04–13; PtO from 16. *35 Worcester Avenue, Garstang PR3 1FJ* T: (01995) 603787 E: andrea.j.roberts@btinternet.com

ROBERTS, Preb Andrew Alexander. b 49. Open Univ BA 75. Bp Otter Coll CertEd 70 Sarum & Wells Th Coll 76. **d** 80 **p** 81. NSM Dorchester *Sarum* 80–85; C Swanage and Studland 85–87; TV 87–94; TR Bridgnorth, Tasley, Astley Abbotts, etc *Heref* 94–09; P-in-c Morville w Aston Eyre 08–09; P-in-c Acton Round 08–09; P-in-c Upton Cressett w Monk Hopton 08–09; RD Bridgnorth 05–09; Preb Heref Cathl 03–09; rtd 09; PtO *Sarum* from 11. *Quayway Cottage, 2 Cliff Place, Swanage BH19 2PL* T: (01929) 424324 E: andyaroberts@talk21.com

ROBERTS, Anne Judith. b 44. CertEd 65 DipEd 78 Open Univ BA 82. S Dios Minl Tr Scheme 86. **d** 89 **p** 94. Hon Par Dn S Kensington H Trin w All SS *Lon* 89–92; NSM Barnes *S'wark* 92–14; S'wark OLM Scheme 98–04; PtO *S'wark* from 14. *5 Avenue Gardens, London SW14 8BP* T: (020) 8878 5642 M: 07115-041212 E: revjr@blueyonder.co.uk

ROBERTS, Anne Marie. b 55. York Univ BA 77. St Jo Coll Nottm 80 WMMTC 93. **d** 96 **p** 97. NSM Meole Brace *Lich* 96–08; Chapl Robert Jones/Agnes Hunt Orthopaedic NHS

Trust 98–00; Chapl Prestfelde Sch Shrewsbury 99–08; Dioc Healing Adv *Carl* 09–13; Dioc Dir of Ords 10–11; Chapl N Cumbria Univ Hosps NHS Trust 11–16; Palace Pastor B & W 16–18; PtO *Lich* from 19. *9 Bickerton Grove, Telford TF3 5JL* M: 07470-400301 E: revsroberts55@gmail.com

ROBERTS, Anthony. *See* ROBERTS, John Anthony Duckworth

ROBERTS, Barrie Moelwyn Antony. b 43. RN Coll Dartmouth 63 Trin Coll Carmarthen CertEd 70 Birm Poly BA 83. Qu Coll Birm 00. **d** 04 **p** 05. NSM Bartley Green *Birm* 04–12; NSM Rowley Regis 12–13; PtO from 13. *34 Wheats Avenue, Harborne, Birmingham B17 0RJ* T: 0121-426 2501 E: b.roberts@lineone.net

ROBERTS, Barry. *See* ROBERTS, Ronald Barry

ROBERTS, Brian David. b 44. Ball Coll Ox BA 66 Univ of Wales (Ban) BTh 06 FRSA 00. **d** 03 **p** 04. OLM Guildf H Trin w St Mary 03–14; PtO from 14. *Risby, Upper Guildown Road, Guildford GU2 4EZ* T: (01483) 570556 F: (020) 7631 6224 M: 07979-766471 E: brianroberts2012@gmail.com

ROBERTS, Bryan Richard. b 55. Univ of Wales (Cardiff) BD 80. St Mich Coll Llan 78. **d** 80 **p** 81. C Finham *Cov* 80–83; Asst Youth Officer *Nor* 83–86; R N and S Creake w Waterden 86–91; P-in-c E w N and W Barsham 86–91; Chapl Epsom Coll 91–01; Chapl Gresham's Sch Holt from 01. *10 Kelling Road, Holt NR25 6RT* T: (01263) 713234

ROBERTS, Carol Susan Butler. b 63. Univ of Wales (Ban) BA 84 MTh 99 MPhil 02 PhD 05. Ban Ord Course 06. **d** 07 **p** 08. NSM Bangor *Ban* 07–10; C 10–11; P-in-c Llanberis, Llanrug and Llandinorwig 11–15; V Bro Eryri 15–18; PtO from 18; P-in-c Penedeyrn Miss Area *St As* from 18. *The Rectory, Bala LL23 7YA* E: parchcarolroberts@yahoo.co.uk

ROBERTS, Charles Richard Meyrick. b 53. Huddersfield Poly BA 75 ARCM 75. St Paul's Coll Grahamstown 89. **d** 92 **p** 92. C Lansdowne St Aidan S Africa 92–93; C Claremont St Sav 93–94; C Bath Abbey w St Jas *B & W* 94–98; P-in-c Chew Magna w Dundry 98–00; R Chew Magna w Dundry and Norton Malreward 00–10; R Chew Magna w Dundry, Norton Malreward etc from 10; P-in-c Chew Stoke w Nempnett Thrubwell from 03. *The Rectory, Tunbridge Close, Chew Magna, Bristol BS40 8SU* T: (01275) 332199 M: 07876-451376 E: chewrector@gmail.com

ROBERTS, Christopher Michael. b 39. Man Univ DipAE 79. Qu Coll Birm 62. **d** 64 **p** 65. C Milton next Gravesend Ch Ch *Roch* 64–68; C Thirsk w S Kilvington *York* 68–69; V Castleton *Derby* 69–75; TV Buxton w Burbage and King Sterndale 75–79; PtO 84–87; NSM Marple All SS *Ches* 87–90; Chapl Asst St Helens Hosp Liv 90–91; Chapl Asst Whiston Co Hosp Prescot 90–91; Chapl R United Hosp Bath 91–94; Chapl R United Hosp Bath NHS Trust 94–99; Sen Chapl Birm Children's Hosp NHS Trust 99–04; rtd 04; PtO *Birm* 04–12. *6 Myring Drive, Sutton Coldfield B75 7RZ* T: 0121-329 2547

ROBERTS, Canon Cyril. b 41. St Deiniol's Hawarden. **d** 84 **p** 85. C Maltby *Sheff* 84–86; TR Gt Snaith 86–12; AD Snaith and Hatfield 03–11; Hon Can Sheff Cathl 05–12; rtd 12; PtO *Sheff* from 12; *York* from 13. *28 Broadacres, Carlton, Goole DN14 9NF* T: (01405) 947328 M: 07979-949485 E: cyrilroberts@hotmail.co.uk

ROBERTS, David Alan. b 38. Open Univ BA 82. Ripon Hall Ox 71. **d** 73 **p** 74. C W Bridgford *S'well* 73–77; V Awsworth w Cossall 77–82; V Oxclose *Dur* 82–94; P-in-c New Seaham 94–04; rtd 04; PtO *Dur* 13–16. *8 Hazel Road, Gateshead NE8 2EP* T: 0191-460 9919

ROBERTS, Preb David Henry. b 38. St Chad's Coll Dur BA 60. Qu Coll Birm. **d** 62 **p** 63. C Stonehouse *Glouc* 62–65; C Hemsworth *Wakef* 65–69; V Newsome 69–76; R Pontesbury I and II *Heref* 76–03; RD Pontesbury 83–93; Preb Heref Cathl from 85; rtd 03; PtO *Heref* from 03. *14 Beaconsfield Park, Ludlow SY8 4LY* T: (01584) 878568 E: dhroberts38@gmail.com

ROBERTS, Canon David John. b 36. Man Univ BSc 58. St D Coll Lamp 65. **d** 67 **p** 68. C Rhosllannerchrugog *St As* 67–70; R Cerrigydrudion w Llanfihangel Glyn Myfyr etc 70–75; R Llanrwst and Llanddoget 75–76; R LLanrwst 76–77; R Llanrwst and Llanddoget and Capel Garmon 77–84; RD Llanrwst 77–84; V Abergele 84–01; RD Rhos 94–01; Hon Can St As Cathl 95–96; Can Cursal St As Cathl 96–01; rtd 01; PtO *St As* from 09. *21 Lowther Court, Bodelwyddan, Rhyl LL18 5YG* T: (01745) 798604 E: david.roberts608@uwclub.net

ROBERTS, Dean Aaron. b 91. Cardiff Univ BA 12. Trin Coll Bris MA 17. **d** 16 **p** 17. C Bedwas w Machen w Michaelston-y-Fedw w Rudry *Mon* from 16. *The Rectory, Michaelston-y-Fedw, Cardiff CF3 6XS* T: (01633) 309691 E: rev.roberts@vicar.email

ROBERTS, Mrs Deryn Anne. b 49. Nottm Univ TCert 70 BEd 71. SWMTC 04. **d** 07 **p** 08. C St Teath and Lanteglos by

Camelford w Advent *Truro* 07–12; PtO 12–14; P-in-c Altarnon w Bolventor, Laneast and St Clether 14–15; C Boscastle w Davidstow 14–15; R Moorland Gp 15–19; rtd 19. *11 Cambeak Close, Crackington Haven, Bude EX23 0PE* M: 07977-318589 E: stnonnas@gmail.com

ROBERTS, Canon Dewi James Llewelyn. b 63. United Th Coll Abth 83. **d** 96 **p** 97. C Llandudno *Ban* 96–02; C Bodedern w Llanfaethlu 99–02 and 99–02; V Newcastle Emlyn and Llandyfriog etc *St D* from 02; AD Emlyn from 12; Can St D Cathl from 13. *The Vicarage, Terra Cotta, Station Road, Newcastle Emlyn SA38 9BX* T: (01239) 710154 E: dewi44@googlemail.com

ROBERTS, Diane. b 45. Bris Univ CertEd 66 BEd 82. STETS 02. **d** 05 **p** 06. NSM Kinson and W Howe *Sarum* 05–13; NSM Salisbury St Mark and Laverstock 13–15; rtd 15; PtO *Sarum* from 15. *6 Herbert Road, Woodfalls, Salisbury SP5 2LF* T: (01725) 510894 E: robertsdiane1@aol.com

ROBERTS, Canon Edward Owen. b 38. K Coll Lon BD 63 AKC 63. **d** 64 **p** 65. C Auckland St Andr and St Anne *Dur* 64–67; C Cheltenham St Paul *Glouc* 67–68; Asst Master Colne Valley High Sch Linthwaite 69–71; V Meltham Mills *Wakef* 71–75; R Emley 75–88; RD Kirkburton 80–88; V Huddersfield H Trin 88–04; RD Huddersfield 89–99; Hon Can Wakef Cathl 92–04; rtd 04; PtO *York* from 04. *2B Queen Street, Filey YO14 9HB* T: (01723) 515535

ROBERTS, Garry Peter. b 77. Ripon Coll Cuddesdon 12. **d** 14 **p** 15. C Fareham H Trin *Portsm* 14–18; C Chandler's Ford *Win* from 18. *45 Pantheon Road, Chandler's Ford, Eastleigh SO53 2PD* M: 07554-142729 E: garryroberts@parishcf.church or revdgarryroberts@virginmedia.com

ROBERTS, Gillian Susan. b 54. **d** 13 **p** 14. C Napton-on-the-Hill, Lower Shuckburgh etc *Cov* 13–16; P-in-c from 16; C Priors Hardwick, Priors Marston and Wormleighton 13–16; P-in-c from 16. *Sycamore Lodge, Church Street, Stockton, Southam CV47 8JG* T: (01926) 815831 E: gillian@thebridgesgroup.org.uk

ROBERTS, Graham Miles. b 59. Open Univ BA 95. Trin Coll Bris 90. **d** 92 **p** 93. C Charles w Plymouth St Matthias *Ex* 92–96; Chapl Plymouth Univ 92–94; TV Liskeard, St Keyne, St Pinnock, Morval etc *Truro* 96–99; P-in-c Bournemouth St Andr *Win* 99–04; V from 04. *St Andrew's Vicarage, 53 Bennett Road, Bournemouth BH8 8QQ* T: (01202) 396022 E: grahamrobert@talktalk.net

ROBERTS, Gregory Stephen. b 64. St Chad's Coll Dur BSc 86 PGCE 87 CPhys 95. Ripon Coll Cuddesdon 08. **d** 10 **p** 11. C Kettering SS Pet and Paul 10–14; Asst Chapl St Andr Healthcare 12–13; P-in-c Pet All SS 14–16; V from 16. *All Saints' Vicarage, 208 Park Road, Peterborough PE1 2UJ* E: gregroberts81@hotmail.com

ROBERTS, Gwyneth. *See* WATKINS, Gwyneth

ROBERTS, Jane Elizabeth. b 53. SEITE 98. **d** 01 **p** 02. NSM Mitcham Ascension *S'wark* 01–17; PtO from 17. *23 Downsview Drive, Midhurst GU29 9LW* M: 07790-703710 E: janeroberts@nasuwt.net or janeroberts40@gmail.com

ROBERTS, Canon Janet Lynne. b 56. Trin Coll Bris 76. **dss** 82 **d** 87 **p** 94. Dagenham *Chelmsf* 82–86; Huyton St Mich *Liv* 86–91; Par Dn 87–91; C Aughton Ch Ch 91–98; TV Parr 98–05; TR 05–13; P-in-c Blundellsands St Nic 13–19; V 19; Hon Can Liv Cathl 13–19; rtd 19. *Address temp unknown* E: rovingrector@btinternet.com

ROBERTS, Mrs Jasmine Cynthia. b 46. Cant Sch of Min 88. **d** 91. NSM Sandwich *Cant* 91–13; Asst Dir of Ords 02–09; PtO from 14. *The Rectory, Knightrider Street, Sandwich CT13 9ER* T/F: (01304) 613138

ROBERTS, Jennifer. *See* GRAY, Jennifer

ROBERTS, John Anthony Duckworth. b 43. K Coll Lon BD 65 AKC 65. St Boniface Warminster 65. **d** 66 **p** 67. C Wythenshawe Wm Temple Ch CD *Man* 66–69; C Bradford-on-Avon H Trin *Sarum* 69–72; Chapl Dauntsey's Sch Devizes 72–73; CF 73–77; P-in-c Verwood *Sarum* 77–81; V 81–86; V Clitheroe St Mary *Blackb* 86–97; R Paget St Paul Bermuda 97–03; rtd 03; PtO *Glouc* from 14; *Win* from 17. *The Old Coach House, Forwood, Minchinhampton, Stroud GL6 9AB* T: (01453) 835811 E: anthilr@hotmail.com

ROBERTS, John Charles Welch. b 39. UMIST BSc 60. Oak Hill NSM Course 91 SWMTC 92. **d** 94 **p** 95. NSM Washfield, Stoodleigh, Withleigh etc *Ex* from 94. *East Sidborough, Loxbeare, Tiverton EX16 8DA* T/F: (01884) 256302 E: john@sidborough.eclipse.co.uk

ROBERTS, Canon John Hugh. b 42. K Alfred's Coll Win CertEd 72 Open Univ BA 75. Wells Th Coll 65. **d** 67 **p** 68. C Wareham w Arne *Sarum* 67–70; C Twyford *Win* 70–72; Asst Teacher Rawlins Sch Leics 72–74; V Nassington w Yarwell *Pet* 74–77; Asst Teacher Sponne Sch Towcester 78–92; RD Brackley *Pet* 94–03; P-in-c Helmdon w Stuchbury

and Radstone etc 93–03; P-in-c Weedon Lois w Plumpton and Moreton Pinkney etc 02–03; R Astwell Gp 03–05; Can Pet Cathl 01–05; rtd 05; PtO *Pet* from 05; Chapl to Retired Clergy and Clergy Widows' Officer 08–10. *Pimlico House, Pimlico, Brackley NN13 5TN* T: (01280) 850378 E: rev.roberts@virgin.net or johnpimlicohouse@gmail.com

ROBERTS, Canon John Mark Arnott. b 54. AKC 75 CertEd 76. Chich Th Coll 77. **d** 77 **p** 78. C Ashford *Cant* 77–82; V St Mary's Bay w St Mary-in-the-Marsh etc 82–91; R Sandwich 91–12; P-in-c Woodnesborough w Worth and Staple 04–12; P-in-c Eastry and Northbourne w Tilmanstone etc 10–12; R Sandwich and Worth from 12; AD Sandwich 00–06; Hon Can Cant Cathl from 03. *The Rectory, Knightrider Street, Sandwich CT13 9ER* T/F: (01304) 613138 E: revdmarkroberts@supanet.com

ROBERTS, Canon John Victor. b 34. St Edm Hall Ox BA 58 MA 62. Tyndale Hall Bris 58. **d** 60 **p** 61. C Southport Ch Ch *Liv* 60–62; C Pemberton St Mark Newtown 62–65; V Blackb Sav 65–71; Chapl Blackb and Lancs R Infirmary and Park Lee Hosp 65–71; V Parr *Liv* 71–73; TR 73–80; R Much Woolton 80–02; RD Childwall 84–89; AD Liv S 89–00; Hon Can Liv Cathl 95–02; rtd 02; PtO *Liv* from 02; Hon Chapl Liv Cathl from 04. *8 Cherry Vale, Liverpool L25 5PX* T/F: 0151-428 8290 E: canonjvr@hotmail.com

ROBERTS, John Victor. b 40. GIPE 61. Qu Coll Birm 83. **d** 85 **p** 86. C Ludlow *Heref* 85–89 and 92–93; P-in-c Coreley w Doddington 89–92; P-in-c Knowbury 89–92; TV Ludlow, Ludford, Ashford Carbonell etc 93–02; rtd 02; PtO *Heref* from 02. *Carwood, 16 Stretton Farm Road, Church Stretton SY6 6DX* T: (01694) 723164

ROBERTS, Jonathan Christopher. b 82. Reading Univ BA 09. Ripon Coll Cuddesdon BA 15. **d** 15 **p** 16. C Dorchester *Ox* from 15. *39 The Motte, Abingdon OX14 3NZ* M: 07980-929302 E: revjonroberts@gmail.com

ROBERTS, Jonathan George Alfred. b 60. Lon Univ BD 82 Dur Univ MA 93. Qu Coll Birm. **d** 84 **p** 85. C Shepshed *Leic* 84–86; C Braunstone 86–87; Dioc Youth Adv *Dur* 88–92; Nat Youth Officer Gen Syn Bd of Educn 92–94; P-in-c Washington *Dur* 94–95; R 95–99; Regional Co-ord for Community Work Assessment Consortium for the NE 99–03; Sen Lect Teesside Univ *York* 03–14; PtO *Dur* 99–14; *Newc* 01–14; Par Development Adv Woolwich Area *S'wark* from 14; Chapl Ark All SS Academy Camberwell from 14; PtO *S'wark* 14–15; P-in-c Camberwell St Mich w All So w Em from 15. *128 Bethwin Road, London SE5 0YY* T: (020) 7701 2231 M: 07530-003368 E: jonathan.roberts@southwark.anglican.org

ROBERTS, Jonathan Peter Higham. b 76. St Jo Coll Dur BA 97 PGCE 98. St Jo Coll Nottm 09. **d** 12 **p** 13. C Cotes Heath and Standon and Swynnerton etc *Lich* 12–15; R Draycott-le-Moors w Forsbrook from 15. *The Rectory, Cheadle Road, Blythe Bridge, Stoke-on-Trent ST11 9PW* T: (01782) 437600 E: jonathanroberts@talktalk.net

ROBERTS, Joseph Samuel. b 86. Birm Univ BA 16 Anglia Ruskin Univ MA 16. Westcott Ho Cam 14. **d** 16 **p** 17. C Marston Green *Birm* from 16. *11 St Leonard's Close, Birmingham B37 7DJ* M: 07966-175803 E: josephroberts11@hotmail.com or revjoeroberts@hotmail.com

ROBERTS, Judith. *See* ABBOTT, Judith

ROBERTS, Judith. *See* ROBERTS, Anne Judith

ROBERTS, Preb Kathleen Marie. b 50. Th Ext Educn Coll 94. **d** 00 **p** 01. S Africa 00–02; C Crediton, Shobrooke and Sandford etc *Ex* 03–05; P-in-c Black Torrington, Bradford w Cookbury etc 05–15; R 15–19; RD Holsworthy 11–15; Dean of Women's Min 15–19; Preb Ex Cathl 15–19; rtd 19. *Mill House, Thorverton, Exeter EX5 5LX* E: robertskm8@aol.com

ROBERTS, Keith Mervyn. b 55. St Pet Coll Birm CertEd 76 LGSM 78 GMus 78. Qu Coll Birm 89. **d** 91 **p** 92. C Hall Green St Pet *Birm* 91–95; TV Warwick *Cov* 95–00; P-in-c Bishop's Tachbrook 00–09; Dir Communications 03–04 and 04–09; Relig Affairs Correspondent BBC W Midl 95–01; Presenter/Producer 01–09; Hon Can Cov Cathl 07–09; TR Godalming *Guildf* 09–16. *15 Anderson Avenue, Rugby CV22 5PE* E: mervynrob@aol.com or revmervyn@gmail.com

ROBERTS, The Ven Kevin Thomas. b 55. Qu Coll Cam BA 78 MA 82 Nottm Univ BA 82. St Jo Coll Nottm 80. **d** 83 **p** 84. C Beverley Minster *York* 83–86; C Woodley St Jo the Ev *Ox* 86–91; V Meole Brace *Lich* 91–09; RD Shrewsbury 98–08; Preb Lich Cathl 02–08; Adn Carl and Can Res Carl Cathl 09–16; Can Res Carl Cathl 09–16; RD Brampton 15–16; Dir ReSource from 16; Adn Wells *B & W* 16–17; Public Preacher 16–19; Public Preacher *Lich* from 19. *9 Bickerton Grove, Telford TF3 5JL* T: (01952) 371300 M: 07880-762868 E: revsroberts55@gmail.com or kevinroberts@resource-arm.net

ROBERTS, Canon Leanne Kelly. b 74. St Hilda's Coll Ox BA 95 MA 02 Em Coll Cam BA 01 MA 05 Hertf Coll Ox MSt 08. Westcott Ho Cam 99. **d** 02 **p** 03. C Hampton All SS *Lon* 02–05; Chapl Hertf Coll Ox 05–11; Voc Adv *Ox* 07–11; Chapl Ox and Bucks Mental Health Trust 10–11; Can Res and Treas S'wark Cathl from 11; Dioc Dir of Ords from 11. *Trinity House, 4 Chapel Court, London SE1 1HW* T: (020) 7939 9400 F: 7939 9468 E: leanne.roberts@southwark.anglican.org

ROBERTS, Mark. See ROBERTS, John Mark Arnott

ROBERTS, Martin Vincent. b 53. Birm Univ BA 76 MA 77 PhD 82 LRAM 72. Ripon Coll Cuddesdon 76. **d** 78 **p** 79. C Perry Barr *Birm* 78–81; Sen Chapl and Lect W Sussex Inst of HE 81–86; Leic Poly 86–92; Sen Chapl De Montfort Univ 92–95; TV Leic H Spirit 86–89; TR 89–95; V Baswich *Lich* 95–01; V Selly Oak St Mary *Birm* 01–08; rtd 08; PtO *Birm* 08–18. *14 Hartley Place, Vicarage Road, Edgbaston, Birmingham B15 3HS* T: 0121-454 5180

ROBERTS, Mervyn. See ROBERTS, Keith Mervyn

ROBERTS, Michael Brian. b 46. Oriel Coll Ox BA 68 MA 72 St Jo Coll Dur BA 73. Cranmer Hall Dur 71. **d** 74 **p** 75. C St Helens St Helen *Liv* 74–76; C Goose Green 76–78; C Blundellsands St Nic 78–80; V Fazakerley St Nath 80–87; V Chirk *St As* 87–01; V Cockerham w Winmarleigh and Glasson *Blackb* 01–13; rtd 13; PtO *Blackb* 13–16; P-in-c Woodplumpton 16–19. *35 Worcester Avenue, Garstang PR3 1FJ* T: (01995) 603787 E: michaelroberts@btinternet.com

ROBERTS, Michael Frederick. b 46. Sarum Th Coll 86. **d** 88 **p** 89. C Reading St Matt *Ox* 88–91; NSM Douglas St Geo and St Barn *S & M* 91–93; V Malew 93–11; rtd 11. *Rose Cottage, St Mary's Road, Port Erin, Isle of Man IM9 6JL* E: revroberts@manx.net

ROBERTS, Neil Charles. b 72. K Coll Lon BA 94 AKC 94 Kent Univ BA(Theol) 10 Cant Ch Ch Univ MA 14 Homerton Coll Cam PGCE 95 FGMS 01. SEITE. **d** 10 **p** 11. C Bletchingley and Nutfield *S'wark* 10–14; V Steyning *Chich* 14–16; R Ashurst 14–16; Boarders' Chapl Steyning Gr Sch 14–16; Chapl Repton Sch Derby from 16. *Repton School, Willington Road, Repton DE65 6FH* T: (01283) 559360 E: ncr@repton.org.uk

ROBERTS, Nia Wyn. See MORRIS, Nia Wyn

ROBERTS, Nicholas John. b 47. Lon Univ BD 70 AKC 70 MTh 78 Surrey Univ MSc 93 K Coll Lon PhD 15. St Aug Coll Cant 70. **d** 71 **p** 72. C Tividale *Lich* 71–74; St Pancras H Cross w St Jude and St Pet *Lon* 74–76; C Camberwell St Giles *S'wark* 76–78; Chapl Ch Coll Cam 78–82; V Kingstanding St Luke *Birm* 82–85; Chapl St Chas Hosp Ladbroke Grove 85–96; Chapl Princess Louise Hosp Lon 85–96; Chapl Paddington Community Hosp 85–96; Chapl Cen Middx Hosp NHS Trust 96–99; Chapl St Mary's NHS Trust Paddington 99–04; Chapl CSC 04–10; rtd 10; PtO *S'wark* from 10; *Lon* from 14. *183 Dukes Avenue, Richmond TW10 7YH* T: (020) 8940 5504 M: 07946-243660 E: n.roberts7@homecall.co.uk

ROBERTS, Mrs Patricia Frances. b 62. Roehampton Inst BEd 85. Trin Coll Bris 93. **d** 96 **p** 97. NSM Buckhurst Hill *Chelmsf* 96–99; NSM Gt Baddow 99–07; NSM W Swindon and the Lydiards *Bris* 11–18; NSM NW Swindon and Lydiard Millicent from 18. *The Vicarage, The Butts, Lydiard Millicent, Swindon SN5 3LR* T: (01793) 772417 E: tricia.f.roberts@gmail.com

ROBERTS, Paul Carlton. b 57. Worc Coll Ox BA 78 MA 86 CertEd. St Jo Coll Nottm 84. **d** 87 **p** 88. C Hazlemere *Ox* 87–91; C Woodley St Jo the Ev 91–92; TV Woodley 92–03; R Coulsdon St Jo *S'wark* from 03; RD Croydon S from 16. *The Rectory, 232 Coulsdon Road, Coulsdon CR5 1EA* T/F: (01737) 552152 E: rev.paul.c.roberts@gmail.com

ROBERTS, Paul John. b 60. Man Univ BA 82 PhD 91 Man Poly PGCE 83. St Jo Coll Nottm 83. **d** 85 **p** 86. C Burnage St Marg *Man* 85–88; Tutor Trin Coll Bris 88–00; V Cotham St Sav w St Mary and Clifton St Paul *Bris* 00–08; Hon Can Bris Cathl 06–08; Dean Non-Res Tr St Mich Coll Llan 09–10; Dir Angl Formation and Tutor Trin Coll Bris from 10. *Trinity College, Stoke Hill, Bristol BS9 1JP* T: 0117-968 0267 E: p.roberts@trinitycollegebristol.ac.uk

ROBERTS, Paul Matthew. b 78. Leeds Univ BA 00 UWE MA 07. Ripon Coll Cuddesdon. **d** 15 **p** 16. C Bartestree Cross *Heref* 15–18; R Maund Gp from 18. *The Vicarage, Bodenham, Hereford HR1 3JX* M: 07735-430335 E: revdpaulroberts@gmail.com

ROBERTS, Peter Francis. b 59. N Illinois Univ BSc 81 Leeds Univ BA 87. Coll of Resurr Mirfield 85. **d** 88 **p** 89. C Leeds All So *Ripon* 88–92; Asst Dioc Youth Chapl 91–92; USPG Belize 92–94; V Collingham w Harewood *Ripon* 95–01; World Miss Officer 95–01; Chapl Dubai and Sharjah w N Emirates 01–03; R Merritt Is USA 03–19; R Monk Fryston and S Milford *York* from 19. *The Rectory, Main Street, Hillam, Leeds LS25 5HH* E: frpeterroberts@gmail.com

ROBERTS, Peter Reece. b 43. Chich Th Coll 73. **d** 75 **p** 76. C Cadoxton-juxta-Barry *Llan* 75–79; C Brixham w Churston Ferrers *Ex* 79–81; C Bexhill St Pet *Chich* 81–84; R Heene 84–14; RD Worthing 89–97; rtd 14; PtO *Chich* from 14. *7 Mayfair Court, 21 Parchment Street, Chichester PO19 3RA* T: (01243) 778543 E: revp.roberts@btinternet.com

ROBERTS, Philip Anthony. b 50. St Jo Coll Dur BA 73. Wycliffe Hall Ox 75. **d** 77 **p** 78. C Roby *Liv* 77–79; C Ainsdale 79–80; C Pershore w Pinvin, Wick and Birlingham *Worc* 80–83; Chapl Asst Radcliffe Infirmary Ox 83–88; John Radcliffe and Littlemore Hosps Ox 83–88; Chapl R Victoria Hosp Bournemouth 88–91; Chapl R Bournemouth Gen Hosp 88–91; Chapl Heref Co Hosp 91–94; Chapl Wye Valley NHS Trust 94–12; rtd 12. *More House, More, Bishop's Castle SY9 5HH* E: philipandsueroberts@gmail.com

ROBERTS, Mrs Rebecca Helena. b 80. Salford Univ BA 01. Trin Coll Bris BA 12. **d** 12 **p** 13. C Penwortham St Mary *Blackb* 12–16; TV Warrington E *Liv* from 16. *The Vicarage, 20 Warren Lane, Woolston, Warrington WA1 4ES* M: 07511-142197 E: revrebecca@hotmail.com

ROBERTS, Miss Rebecca Mary. b 71. Glam Univ BA 92 Chelt & Glouc Coll of HE PGCE 93. Qu Coll Birm BA 02 MA 03. **d** 03 **p** 04. C Greenstead w Colchester St Anne *Chelmsf* 03–06; PtO *Win* 06–10; NSM Southampton (City Cen) 10–13; V Harnham *Sarum* from 13. *The Vicarage, Old Blandford Road, Salisbury SP2 8DQ* M: 07727-154234 E: reverendbecky@gmail.com

ROBERTS, Ronald Barry. b 40. S Dios Minl Tr Scheme 80. **d** 83 **p** 85. NSM Wedmore w Theale and Blackford *B & W* 83–85; C Odd Rode *Ches* 85–87; V Eaton and Hulme Walfield 87–04; rtd 04; PtO *Ches* from 04. *Iona, 8 Belmont Avenue, Sandbach CW11 1BX* T: (01270) 766124 E: barryroberts@uwclub.net

ROBERTS, Mrs Rosamunde Mair. b 58. RN 80. STETS 98. **d** 01 **p** 02. C Farnham *Guildf* 01–04; C Fleet 04–08; V Lenborough *Ox* from 08; AD Buckingham from 17. *The Vicarage, Thornborough Road, Padbury, Buckingham MK18 2AH* T: (01280) 813162 E: lenborough.vicar@gmail.com

ROBERTS, Mrs Rosanne Elizabeth. b 51. Glouc Sch of Min 85. **d** 88 **p** 94. NSM Charlton Kings St Mary *Glouc* 88–93; C Leckhampton SS Phil and Jas w Cheltenham St Jas 93–96; R Ashchurch 96–08; R Ashchurch and Kemerton 08–13; rtd 13; PtO *Glouc* from 16. *25 Buckles Close, Charlton Kings, Cheltenham GL53 8QT* T: (01242) 248194 E: rosanne.roberts@btinternet.com

ROBERTS, Mrs Sharon. b 56. **d** 11 **p** 12. OLM Amersham on the Hill *Ox* 11–18; NSM Beaconsfield 18–19; TV from 19. *St Michael's Parsonage, 3 St Michael's Green, Beaconsfield HP9 2BN* E: sharon.roberts433@gmail.com

ROBERTS, Stephen Bradley. b 66. K Coll Lon BD 90 Heythrop Coll Lon MA 03 PhD 11. Wycliffe Hall Ox 89. **d** 91 **p** 92. C W Hampstead St Jas *Lon* 91–94; TV Uxbridge 94–98; Chapl Brunel Univ 98–04; Vice Prin St Mich Coll Llan 04–12; PtO *Llan* from 12. *122 Pwllmelin Road, Cardiff CF5 3NA* E: drsbroberts@gmail.com

ROBERTS, Canon Stephen John. b 58. K Coll Lon BD 81 Heythrop Coll Lon MTh 99. Westcott Ho Cam. **d** 83 **p** 84. C Riverhead w Dunton Green *Roch* 83–86; C St Martin-in-the-Fields *Lon* 86–89; Warden Trin Coll Cen Camberwell 89–99; V Camberwell St Geo *S'wark* 89–99; RD Camberwell 97–99; Treas and Can Res S'wark Cathl 00–05; Sen Dioc Dir of Ords 00–05; Adn Wandsworth 05–15; P-in-c Upper Tooting H Trin w St Aug 10–11; Dep Dioc Sec from 15; Bp's Officer for Non-Stipendiary Clergy from 15; Public Preacher from 15; Hon Can S'wark Cathl from 15. *2 Alma Road, London SW18 1AB* T: (020) 8874 8567 E: stephen.roberts@southwark.anglican.org

ROBERTS, Preb Susan Emma. b 60. La Sainte Union Coll BTh 93. St Steph Ho Ox 94. **d** 96 **p** 97. C Petersfield *Portsm* 96–00; P-in-c Ashprington, Cornworthy and Dittisham *Ex* 00–04; TV Totnes w Bridgetown, Berry Pomeroy etc 04–06; RD Totnes 03–06; TR Honiton, Gittisham, Combe Raleigh, Monkton etc from 06; RD Honiton 07–13; Preb Ex Cathl from 06. *The Rectory, Rookwood Close, Honiton EX14 1BH* T: (01404) 42925 E: sue41260@gmail.com

ROBERTS, Mrs Sylvia Ann. b 40. Stockwell Coll Lon TCert 60. S Dios Minl Tr Scheme 81. **dss** 84 **d** 87 **p** 94. Crookhorn *Portsm* 84–88; Hon Par Dn Bedhampton 88–89; Par Dn Southampton (City Cen) *Win* 89–91; Team Dn 91–94; TV 94–96; V Merton St Jo *S'wark* 96–06; P-in-c Colliers Wood Ch Ch 01–06; rtd 06; PtO *Portsm* from 07. *16 Bramble Road, Petersfield GU31 4HL* T: (01730) 301501 E: annarobb40@hotmail.com

ROBERTS, Terry Harvie. b 45. Sarum & Wells Th Coll 87. **d** 89 **p** 90. C Weymouth H Trin *Sarum* 89–93; TV Basingstoke *Win* 93–98; P-in-c Win St Barn 98–10; rtd 10;

PtO *Win* from 10; *Sarum* from 16. *1 Poulner Park, Ringwood BH24 1TZ* T: (01425) 470232

ROBERTS, Timothy Frank. b 85. Univ of Wales BA 11. St Jo Coll Nottm MTh 16. **d** 16 **p** 17. C Clayton *Leeds* 16–19; C Preston St Jo *Blackb* from 19. *8 Kings Drive, Fulwood, Preston PR2 3HN* M: 07825-542312 E: 1rev.roberts@gmail.com

ROBERTS, Tudor Vaughan. b 58. Newc Univ BA 81. All Nations Chr Coll 91 Trin Coll Bris BA 94. **d** 96 **p** 97. C Buckhurst Hill *Chelmsf* 96–99; TV Gt Baddow 99–07; TV W Swindon and the Lydiards *Bris* 07–18; V NW Swindon and Lydiard Millicent from 18. *The Vicarage, The Butts, Lydiard Millicent, Swindon SN5 3LR* T: (01793) 722417 E: tudorandtricia@btinternet.com

ROBERTS, Tunde. *See* ROBERTS, Vincent Akintunde

ROBERTS, Canon Vaughan Edward. b 65. Selw Coll Cam BA 88 MA 91. Wycliffe Hall Ox 89. **d** 91 **p** 92. C Ox St Ebbe w H Trin and St Pet 91–95; Student Pastor 95–98; R from 98; Hon Can Ch Ch from 16. *St Ebbe's Rectory, 2 Roger Bacon Lane, Oxford OX1 1QE* T: (01865) 240438 E: vroberts@stebbes.org.uk

ROBERTS, Vaughan Simon. b 59. Univ of Wales (Ban) BA 80 Bath Univ PhD 99. McCormick Th Sem Chicago MA 82 Westcott Ho Cam 83. **d** 85 **p** 86. C Bourne *Guildf* 85–89; Chapl Phyllis Tuckwell Hospice Farnham 88–89; Chapl Bath Univ *B & W* 89–96; NSM Bath Ch Ch Prop Chpl 90–96; P-in-c 92–96; P-in-c Chewton Mendip w Ston Easton, Litton etc 96–03; Dioc Voc Adv 96–99; Dir of Ords 99–03; TR Warwick *Cov* from 03. *St Mary's Vicarage, The Butts, Warwick CV34 4SS* T/F: (01926) 492909 E: vaughan.roberts@btinternet.com

ROBERTS, Preb Vincent Akintunde (Tunde). b 55. Kingston Poly BA(Econ) 81. S'wark Ord Course. **d** 91 **p** 92. Hon C Brixton Road Ch Ch *S'wark* 91–96; C Mitcham St Barn 96–99; P-in-c Stoke Newington St Olave *Lon* 99–03; V from 03; P-in-c Stoke Newington St Andr 06–12; P-in-c Upper Clapton St Matt 08–12; Preb St Paul's Cathl from 07. *St Olave's Vicarage, Woodberry Down, London N4 2TW* T/F: (020) 8800 1374

ROBERTS, Vivian Phillip. b 35. Univ of Wales BD 78. St D Coll Lamp 57. **d** 60 **p** 61. C Cwmaman *St D* 60–64; R Puncheston, Lt Newcastle and Castle Bythe 64–72; V Brynamman 72–77; V Brynaman w Cwmllynfell 77–83; V Pen-bre 83–00; rtd 00. *40 New Road, Llanelli SA15 3DR* T: (01554) 755506

ROBERTSHAW, Mrs Eleanor Elizabeth Mary. b 77. Univ of Wales (Ban) BA 98 MTh 00 Leeds Univ MA 10 PGCE 99. Yorks Min Course 08. **d** 10 **p** 11. C Stainforth *Sheff* 10–13; TR Gt Snaith from 13. *The Orchard, Pontefract Road, Snaith, Goole DN14 9JS* T: (01405) 860866 M: 07718-123138 E: eleanor.robertshaw@sheffield.anglican.org

ROBERTSHAW, Canon John Sean. b 66. York St Jo Coll BA 12 Cardiff Univ MTh 17. Cranmer Hall Dur 90. **d** 93 **p** 94. C Morley St Pet w Churwell *Wakef* 93–96; TV Upper Holme Valley 96–01; TR 01–14; *Leeds* from 14; CF (TA) from 98; Hon Can Wakef Cathl *Leeds* from 11. *The Vicarage, Kirkroyds Lane, New Mill, Holmfirth HD9 1LS* T/F: (01484) 683375 M: 07980-289727 E: revsean@tiscali.co.uk

ROBERTSHAW, Mrs Kina Perrira Njamba. b 75. Anglia Ruskin Univ BA 13. Ridley Hall Cam 10. **d** 16 **p** 17. C Bromyard and Stoke Lacy *Heref* from 16. *12 Lower Thorn, Bromyard HR7 4AZ* M: 07917-664182 E: robertshawkina@yahoo.com

ROBERTSHAW, Sean. *See* ROBERTSHAW, John Sean

ROBERTSON, Ms Beverley Ann. b 57. Qu Coll Birm 98. **d** 01 **p** 02. C Sutton Coldfield H Trin *Birm* 01–05; C Portsea N End St Mark *Portsm* 05–06; TV 06–10; P-in-c Bromsgrove All SS *Worc* 10–12; C Catshill and Dodford 10–12; TV Bromsgrove from 12. *20 Burcot Lane, Bromsgrove B60 1AE* T: (01527) 578297 E: bevrobertson.church@gmail.com

ROBERTSON, Brian Ainsley. b 50. Warwick Univ BSc 72. St Jo Coll Nottm 94. **d** 94 **p** 95. C Leic Martyrs 94–97; C Oadby 97–98; TV 98–02; P-in-c Ashby-de-la-Zouch St Helen w Coleorton 02–05; P-in-c Breedon cum Isley Walton and Worthington 03–05; TR Ashby-de-la-Zouch and Breedon on the Hill 05–14; RD NW Leics 07–11; rtd 14; PtO *Leic* from 14. *84 Highway Road, Leicester LE5 5RF* T: 0116-319 5676 E: barobertson105@gmail.com

ROBERTSON, Charles Peter. b 57. Aston Tr Scheme 92 Linc Th Coll 94. **d** 96 **p** 97. C Holbeach *Linc* 96–99; C S Lafford 01–03; P-in-c 03–13; P-in-c Bicker 13–14; P-in-c Donington 13–14; P-in-c Swineshead 13–14; P-in-c Sutterton and Wigtoft 13–14; V Haven Fen from 14. *The Rectory, Church Lane, Swineshead, Boston PE20 3JA* T: (01205) 820223

ROBERTSON, Mrs Claire Mary. b 63. Ridley Hall Cam 15. **d** 17 **p** 18. C Two Rivers *Chelmsf* from 17. *18 St Mary's Walk, Steeple Bumpstead, Haverhill CB9 7EX* E: claire.cann@yahoo.co.uk *or* curate@2rivers.faith

ROBERTSON, David John. b 54. Sheff Univ BA 76. Ridley Hall Cam 77. **d** 79 **p** 80. C Downend *Bris* 79–83; C Yate New Town 83–85; TV 85–87; TV High Wycombe *Ox* 87–97; RD Wycombe 91–97; P-in-c Haley Hill *Wakef* 97–99; V Ovenden 97–11; V S Ossett 11–14; *Leeds* from 14. *South Ossett Vicarage, 36 Manor Road, Ossett WF5 0AU* T: (01924) 263311 E: rev.d.robertson@gmail.com

ROBERTSON, Douglas Laurence. b 52. St Edm Hall Ox MA 75. SEITE 04. **d** 07 **p** 08. C Roch 07–11; V Pembury 11–18; rtd 18. *3 Damson Avenue, Malton YO17 7FR* E: dlrobertson@btinternet.com

ROBERTSON, Mrs Elizabeth Mary. b 60. Cam Univ BA 82 MA 86 ACA 85 FCA 95. SEITE 03. **d** 06 **p** 07. NSM Fawkham and Hartley *Roch* 06–13; NSM Ash from 13; NSM Ridley from 13. *58 Redhill Wood, New Ash Green, Longfield DA3 8QP* T: (01474) 874144 E: robertem@supanet.com

ROBERTSON, Fiona Jane. *See* GREGSON, Fiona Jane Robertson

ROBERTSON, Iain Michael. b 67. Trin Coll Bris 03. **d** 05 **p** 06. C E Clevedon w Clapton in Gordano etc *B & W* 05–09; TV Salter Street and Shirley *Birm* 09–11; P-in-c Heanton Punchardon w Marwood *Ex* 11–15; R Heanton Punchardon, Marwood and W Down 15–16; P-in-c Southway 16–17; TV Tamerton Foliot and Southway from 17. *16 Southway Lane, Plymouth PL6 7DH* E: reviain@hotmail.co.uk

ROBERTSON, Canon James Alexander. b 46. Ox Univ MTh 99. Sarum & Wells Th Coll 72. **d** 75 **p** 76. C Monkseaton St Pet *Newc* 75–78; C Prudhoe 78–79; TV Brayton *York* 79–84; V Redcar 84–93; V Selby Abbey 93–96; V Monkseaton St Pet *Newc* 96–11; AD Tynemouth 98–09; V Whittingham and Edlingham w Bolton Chapel 11–15; AD Alnwick 11–15; Hon Can Newc Cathl 05–15; rtd 15; PtO *Newc* from 15. *4 Greenrigg Place, Shiremoor, Newcastle upon Tyne NE27 0GA* T: 0191-253 7637 E: canjamesrobertson@outlook.com

ROBERTSON, James Macaulay. b 51. St Jo Coll Dur BA 73. Oak Hill Th Coll. **d** 00 **p** 01. C Holdenhurst and Iford *Win* 00–04; V Marden *Cant* 04–11; R Holwell, Ickleford and Pirton *St Alb* 11–16; rtd 16; PtO *Win* from 17. *23 Wick Point Mews, Christchurch BH23 1NZ* E: jmrobertson91@gmail.com

ROBERTSON, Mrs Jane Elizabeth. b 58. Bp Grosseteste Coll BA 04. Linc Sch of Th and Min 13. **d** 16 **p** 17. C Boston *Linc* 16–19; TV from 19. *The Vicarage, Church Lane, Swineshead, Boston PE20 3JA* T: (01205) 820223 E: janeyrob@btopenworld.com

ROBERTSON, Jane Lesley. *See* TRENHOLME, Jane Lesley

ROBERTSON, Canon John Charles. b 61. St Pet Coll Ox BA 81 Trin Coll Cam BA 89. Ridley Hall Cam 87. **d** 90 **p** 91. C Kenilworth St Jo *Cov* 90–94; Chapl York Univ 94–00; V Grove *Ox* 00–12; RD Wantage 09–12; Dir Ecum Miss Milton Keynes from 12; Hon Can Ch Ch from 11. *16 Clover Close, Loughton, Milton Keynes MK5 8HA* T: (01908) 660338 E: jcrdem@gmail.com

ROBERTSON (née PEGG), Mrs Josephine Anne. b 51. Lon Univ CertEd 72 Ch Ch Coll Cant BSc 91. **d** 02 **p** 03. OLM Folkestone H Trin w Ch Ch *Cant* 02–06; Chapl Dover Coll 02–05; C Sandgate St Paul w Folkestone St Geo *Cant* 05–06; C Folkestone Trin 06–10; C Wingham w Elmstone and Preston w Stourmouth 10–12; C Canonry 12–15; PtO 15–19; P-in-c Cheriton w Newington from 19. *100 Surrenden Road, Folkestone CT19 4AQ* T: (01303) 277330 M: 07905-954504 E: jo.robertson@ntlworld.com

ROBERTSON, Kathryn. b 58. Leeds Univ BA 05. NOC 02. **d** 05 **p** 06. C Dewsbury *Wakef* 05–08; TV 08–14; *Leeds* 14–17; C Wakef St Andr and St Mary 17–18; C Wakefield St Andr and St Mary and Belle Vue from 18. *St Andrew's Vicarage, Johnston Street, Wakefield WF1 4DZ* M: 07967-909560 E: revkathyrob@gmail.com

ROBERTSON, Mrs Linda Margaret. b 51. Somerville Coll Ox BA 71 MA 76 Aber Univ MSc 73. STETS 00. **d** 03 **p** 04. NSM Ampfield *Win* 03–08; NSM Totton 08–15; TV 10–15; R Cocking w W Lavington, Bepton and Heyshott *Chich* from 15. *Cocking Rectory, Mill Lane, Cocking, Midhurst GU29 0HJ* T: (01730) 814275 M: 07802-955133 E: revlindarob@yahoo.co.uk

ROBERTSON, Neil Matthew John. b 78. Bournemouth Univ BSc 10. Trin Coll Bris BA 17. **d** 17 **p** 18. C Blandford Forum and Langton Long *Sarum* from 17. *4 Gurkha Road, Blandford Forum DT11 7FL* M: 07809-149606 E: neilmjr@btqa.co.uk

ROBERTSON, Canon Paul Struan. b 45. St Jo Coll Dur BA 73 Newc Univ Aus BEdSt 79 MA 95. **d** 72 **p** 73. C Chester le Street *Dur* 72–73; C Hamilton Australia 73–77; C Cessnock 77–79; R Scone 79–88; V Collierley w Annfield Plain *Dur* 88–89; R New Lambton Australia 89–10; AD Newc W 96–10; Lect St Jo Coll Morpeth 97–06; Can Newc Cathl 01–10; rtd 10. *40 Cromwell Street, New Lambton NSW 2305, Australia* T: (0061) (2) 4957 2795 E: paulstruanrobertson@gmail.com

ROBERTSON, Philip Stuart. b 55. Newc Univ BA 77 BArch 80. Oak Hill Th Coll BA 07. **d** 07 **p** 08. C Woking St Jo *Guildf* 07–11; V Wolverhampton St Jude *Lich* from 11; P-in-c Wolverhampton St Andr 15–18. *St Jude's Vicarage, St Jude's Road, Wolverhampton WV6 0EB* T: (01902) 827214 E: philipsrobertson@virginmedia.com

ROBERTSON, Rachel Heather. b 75. Dur Univ BA 96. Trin Coll Bris MA 18. **d** 17 **p** 18. C Tupsley w Hampton Bishop *Heref* from 17; Asst Dir of Ords from 19. *St Paul's Church, 107 Church Road, Hereford HR1 1RT* E: rachel.robertson@stpaulshereford.org.uk

ROBERTSON (née OWEN), Mrs Sally Ann. b 68. New Hall Cam BA 89. Ox Min Course 07. **d** 10 **p** 11. NSM Purley *Ox* 10–13; NSM Haydon Wick *Bris* 13–17; P-in-c N Swindon St Andr from 17. *15 Rackham Close, Tadpole Garden Village, Swindon SN25 2QT* M: 07588-594410 E: sally.robertson@btinternet.com

ROBERTSON, Canon Scott. b 64. Edin Univ BD 90 Open Univ MA 02 Glas Univ PhD 08. Edin Th Coll 86. **d** 90 **p** 91. C Glas Gd Shep and Ascension 90–92; P-in-c 92–97; P-in-c Ardrossan 97–10; P-in-c Dalry 97–10; P-in-c Irvine St Andr LEP 97–10; R Glas St Marg from 10; Can St Mary's Cathl from 12. *The Rectory, 22 Monreith Road, Glasgow G43 2NY* T: 0141-632 3292 *or* 636 1131 E: revscottrobertson@gmail.com

ROBERTSON, Stuart Lang. b 40. Glas Univ MA 63 Edin Univ MTh 97. St Jo Coll Nottm 72. **d** 75 **p** 76. C Litherland St Jo and St Jas *Liv* 75–78; C Edin St Thos 78–81; Chapl Edn Univ and C Edin St Pet 81–83; R Edin St Jas 83–91; Miss to Seamen 83–91; Crosslinks 91–05; Hon Chapl St Petersburg *Eur* 93–98; Chapl Warsaw 98–04; Asst Chapl Barcelona 04–05; rtd 05. *3 Pentland Villas, Juniper Green EH14 5EQ* T: 0131-453 4755 E: langs.robertson2@gmail.com

ROBILLIARD (née DE GARIS), Mrs Juliette Elizabeth Charmaine. b 58. STETS 11. **d** 13 **p** 14. NSM Guernsey Ste Marie du Castel *Win* 13–16; NSM Guernsey St Matt 13–16; NSM Guernsey St Andr from 16; Chapl Guernsey Financial Services Commn from 18. *Le Petit Gree, Torteval, Guernsey GY8 0RD* T: (01481) 264344 E: revrob151@gmail.com

ROBINS, Christopher Charles. b 41. St Mich Coll Llan 66. **d** 68 **p** 69. C Bideford *Ex* 68–71; C Dawlish 71–74; V Laira 74–81; P-in-c Dodbrooke 81–83; P-in-c Churchstow w Kingsbridge 81–83; R Kingsbridge and Dodbrooke 83–06; rtd 07; PtO *Ex* from 17. *26 Brownings Walk, Ogwell, Newton Abbot TQ12 6YR* T: (01626) 331366

ROBINS, Canon Douglas Geoffrey. b 45. Open Univ BA 90. Ex & Truro NSM Scheme. **d** 81 **p** 83. NSM Kenwyn *Truro* 81–84; Public Preacher 84–00; NSM Truro St Paul and St Clem 00–04; P-in-c Gerrans w St Anthony-in-Roseland and Philleigh 04–08; P-in-c Veryan w Ruan Lanihorne 08–16; Hon Can Truro Cathl 09–16; rtd 16; PtO *Truro* from 16. *Caladrick Barn, Veryan Green, Truro TR2 5QQ* T: (01872) 501788 E: fatherdougrobins@outlook.com

ROBINS, Ian Donald Hal. b 28. K Coll Lon BD 51 AKC 51 Lanc Univ MA 74. **d** 52 **p** 53. C Heyhouses on Sea *Blackb* 52–55; C Clitheroe St Mary 55–57; V Trawden 57–66; Hd of RE St Chris C of E Sch Accrington 67–75; P-in-c Hugill *Carl* 75–82; Asst Adv for Educn 75–82; Chapl St Martin's Coll of Educn *Blackb* 82–86; V St Annes St Marg 86–91; rtd 91; PtO *Blackb* from 91; *Bradf* 05–14; *Leeds* 14–16. *33 Manorfields, Whalley, Clitheroe BB7 9UD* T: (01254) 824930

ROBINS, Canon Wendy Sheridan. b 56. Lanc Univ BA 77. EAMTC 93. **d** 93 **p** 94. Dir Communications and Resources S'wark from 92; NSM Walthamstow St Pet *Chelmsf* 93–02; Hon C S'wark Cathl from 02; Hon Can S'wark Cathl from 08. T: (020) 8523 0016 *or* 7403 8686 F: 7403 4770 E: wendy.s.robins@southwark.anglican.org

ROBINSON, Alison Jane. b 55. WEMTC 99. **d** 02 **p** 03. C Bishop's Cleeve *Glouc* 02–06; P-in-c Meysey Hampton w Marston Meysey and Castle Eaton 06–08; TV Fairford Deanery 09–10; rtd 10. *19 Marsh Drive, Cheltenham GL51 9LN* T: (01242) 698759 M: 07773-721238 E: alicesonrobinson@virginmedia.com

ROBINSON, Andrew David. b 61. St Cath Coll Ox BA 84 MA 01 RMN 89. Trin Coll Bris 97. **d** 02 **p** 08. C Southmead *Bris* 02–03; C Kington St Michael and Chippenham St Paul w Hardenhuish etc 03–04; NSM Barlby and Riccall *York* 05–10; P-in-c Ledsham w Fairburn from 10. *The Vicarage, 11 Main Street, Ledston, Castleford WF10 2AA* T: (01977) 553591 M: 07896-506321 E: andrewrobinson9@hotmail.com

ROBINSON, Canon Andrew Nesbitt. b 43. AKC 67. **d** 68 **p** 69. C Balsall Heath St Paul *Birm* 68–71; C Westmr St Steph w St Jo *Lon* 71–75; Chapl Sussex Univ *Chich* 75–12; Chapl Brighton Poly 75–92; Chapl Brighton Univ 92–93; P-in-c Stanmer w Falmer 80–12; Can and Preb Chich Cathl 98–12; rtd 12; PtO *Chich* 12–17. *Appleberry Cottage,*

Newhaven Road, Kingston, Lewes BN7 3NE T: (01273) 757797 E: goretti_uk@yahoo.co.uk

⚓**ROBINSON, The Rt Revd Anthony William.** b 56. CertEd. Sarum & Wells Th Coll. **d** 82 **p** 83 **c** 02. C Tottenham St Paul *Lon* 82–85; TV Leic Resurr 85–89; TR 89–97; RD Christianity N 92–97; P-in-c Belgrave St Pet 94–95; Hon Can Leic Cathl 94–97; Adn Pontefract *Wakef* 97–03; Suff Bp Pontefract 02–15; Suff Bp Wakef *Leeds* from 15; Can Res Wakef Cathl 05–13. *Pontefract House, 181A Manygates Lane, Sandal, Wakefield WF2 7DR* T: (01924) 250781 E: bishop.tony@leeds.anglican.org

ROBINSON, Mrs Arabella Mary Milbank. b 87. New Coll Ox BA 10 MSt 11 Em Coll Cam PhD 18 MPhil 19. Westcott Ho Cam 17. **d** 18 **p** 19. C Louth *Linc* from 18. *The Rectory, Church Lane, Legbourne, Louth LN11 8LN* M: 07734-871159

ROBINSON, Arthur Robert Basil. b 32. ACP 67 St Jo Coll Dur BA 56 Bradf Univ MA 84. Wycliffe Hall Ox 56. **d** 58 **p** 59. C Pemberton St Mark Newtown *Liv* 58–62; CF 62–65; Asst Master Colne Valley High Sch Linthwaite 65–69; Asst Chapl HM Pris Man 69; Chapl HM Borstal Roch 69–74; Peru 74–77; V Golcar *Wakef* 77–83; Admin Sheff Fam Conciliation Service 84–91; Warden St Sampson's Cen York 91–00; rtd 00. *Morangie, 2A Brecksfield, Skelton, York YO30 1YD* T: (01904) 470558

ROBINSON, Arthur William. b 35. Dur Univ BSc 60. Clifton Th Coll 60. **d** 62 **p** 63. C Ox St Clem 62–65; Chile 65–77; V Hoxton St Jo w Ch Ch *Lon* 78–88; TV Gateacre *Liv* 88–00; rtd 00; PtO *Liv* from 00. *86 Kingsthorne Park, Liverpool L25 0QS* T: 0151-486 2588 E: arthelrob@frasani.com

ROBINSON, Mrs Christine. b 50. Nottm Univ BA 71. EAMTC 01. **d** 04 **p** 05. NSM Prittlewell St Pet w Westcliff St Cedd *Chelmsf* 04–13; NSM Hadleigh St Jas from 13; NSM Hadleigh St Barn from 13. *Pasadena, St John's Road, Benfleet SS7 2PT* T: (01702) 557000 E: crrob75@aol.com

ROBINSON (née KILCOOLEY), Mrs Christine Margaret Anne. b 59. K Coll Lon BA 05. SEITE 06. **d** 07 **p** 08. C Notting Hill St Pet *Lon* 07–10; V Belmont from 10. *St Anselm's Vicarage, Ventnor Avenue, Stanmore HA7 2HU* T: (020) 8907 3186 E: xtinerob@googlemail.com

ROBINSON, Christopher Gordon. b 49. Ridley Hall Cam. **d** 82 **p** 83. C Stanton *St E* 82–85; C Lawshall 85–86; P-in-c Lawshall w Shimplingthorne and Alpheton 86–89; TV Oakdale *Sarum* 89–99; V Easton H Trin w St Gabr and St Lawr and St Jude Bris 99–05; C S Molton w Nymet St George, High Bray etc *Ex* 05–12; C Shirwell, Loxhore, Kentisbury, Arlington, etc 12–14; rtd 14. *22 John Street, Bargoed CF81 8PG*

ROBINSON, Christopher James. b 52. St Pet Coll Birm CertEd 74. OLM course 97. **d** 99 **p** 00. OLM Wilnecote *Lich* 99–16; PtO from 16. *55 Sycamore, Wilnecote, Tamworth B77 5HB* T: (01827) 282331 E: chrisrobinson55@hotmail.co.uk

ROBINSON, Christopher Mark Scott. b 83. Warwick Univ BSc 04. Ridley Hall Cam 06. **d** 09 **p** 10. C S Hartismere *St E* 09–12; R Rattlesden w Thorpe Morieux, Brettenham etc from 12; RD Lavenham from 17. *The Rectory, High Street, Rattlesden, Bury St Edmunds IP30 0RA* T: (01449) 737197 M: 07789-772024 E: tifferrobinson@gmail.com

ROBINSON, Daffyd Charles. b 48. Qu Coll Birm 77. **d** 80 **p** 85. C Abington *Pet* 80–82; C Immingham *Linc* 85–90; R Willoughby 90–13; rtd 13; PtO *Linc* from 17. *57 Weelsby Avenue, Grimsby DN32 0AU* T: (01472) 753862 E: d_m@post.com

ROBINSON, Mrs Danielle Georgette Odette. b 47. SEITE 98. **d** 01 **p** 02. NSM Reigate St Mary *S'wark* 01–17; Chapl Surrey and Sussex Healthcare NHS Trust 01–15; PtO *Chich* from 01; *S'wark* from 17. *1 Chandler Way, Dorking RH5 4GA* T: (01306) 883947 *or* (01293) 600300 ext 3141 E: daniellerobinson@uwclub.net

ROBINSON, David. b 42. Sarum & Wells Th Coll. **d** 82 **p** 83. C Billingham St Cuth *Dur* 82–86; V Longwood *Wakef* 86–94; C Athersley 94–97; P-in-c Brotherton 97–02; rtd 02; PtO *York* 03–13. *5 High Street, Stanhope, Bishop Auckland DL13 2UP*

ROBINSON, David. See ROBINSON, Roy David

ROBINSON, Canon David Hugh. b 47. Linc Th Coll 76. **d** 79 **p** 80. C Bulkington *Cov* 79–82; C Whitley 82–87; Chapl Whitley, Gulson & Cov and Warks Hosp 82–87; Chapl Walsgrave Hosp Cov 87–97; Hon Can Cov Cathl 92–98; Succ 00–05; PtO *Cov* 97–00 and 05–07; P-in-c Cov St Mary 07–10; rtd 10; PtO *Ex* 11–16. *23A Crockwells Road, Exminster, Exeter EX6 8DH* T: (01392) 833135 M: 07947-023888

ROBINSON, David Mark. b 55. Univ Coll Dur BSc 76 Leic Univ MA 80 CQSW 80. Cranmer Hall Dur 86. **d** 88 **p** 89. C Shipley St Pet *Bradf* 88–92; P-in-c Ingrow w Hainworth 92–97; V Bramhope *Ripon* 97–05; V Chapel Allerton 05–14; *Leeds* from 14. *The Vicarage, Wood Lane, Chapel Allerton, Leeds LS7 3QF* T: 0113-268 3072

ROBINSON, David Michael Wood. *See* WOOD-ROBINSON, David Michael

ROBINSON, Denis Hugh. b 53. SS Mark & Jo Univ Coll Plymouth CertEd 75. S Dios Minl Tr Scheme 88. **d** 91 **p** 92. NSM Bisley and W End *Guildf* 91–18; Hd RS Gordon's Sch Woking 80–12; Asst Chapl 91–94; Chapl 94–17; rtd 17; C Sparkwell *Ex* from 18. *Mistledown, Dousland, Yelverton PL20 6NA* E: steviedenrob@aol.com

ROBINSON, Dennis Winston. b 42. QUB BScEng 68. CITC. **d** 88 **p** 89. NSM Mullavilly *Arm* 88–92; NSM Arm St Mark 92–95; C Portadown St Mark 95–98; I Aghavea *Clogh* 98–10; Preb Clogh Cathl 06–10; rtd 10. *Oakridge, 31 Snowhill Road, Beagho, Lisbellaw, Enniskillen BT94 5FY* T: (028) 6638 5858 E: dw.robinson@btopenworld.com

ROBINSON, Derek Charles. b 43. S'wark Ord Course 91. **d** 94 **p** 95. NSM Abbey Wood *S'wark* 94–13; PtO from 13. *19 Silverdale Road, Bexleyheath DA7 5AB* T: (01322) 523870

ROBINSON, Dorothy Ann. b 50. Cranmer Hall Dur 05. **d** 07 **p** 08. NSM Tynemouth Priory *Newc* 07–17; NSM N Shields from 17. *57 Millview Drive, North Shields NE30 2QD* T/F: 0191-257 0980 E: dottirobinson@hotmail.com

ROBINSON, Elizabeth Carole Lesley. b 67. CITC 99. **d** 02 **p** 03. Aux Min Clonfert Gp *L & K* 02–06; Aux Min Roscrea w Kyle, Bourney and Corbally 06–11; Dioc C 11–13; I Dublin Clontarf *D & G* from 13. *The Rectory, 15 Seafield Road West, Clontarf, Dublin 3, Republic of Ireland* T: (00353) (1) 833 1181 M: 87-909 1561 E: clontarf@dublin.anglican.org

ROBINSON, Eric Charles. b 47. Lon Univ BD 71 Lanc Univ MA 97. CBDTI 94. **d** 97 **p** 98. NSM Carl St Cuth w St Mary 97–99; C Kendal H Trin 99–01; P-in-c Arthuret 01–07; P-in-c Nicholforest and Kirkandrews on Esk 01–07; R Arthuret w Kirkandrews-on-Esk and Nicholforest 07–08; P-in-c Kendal H Trin 08–10; rtd 10; PtO *Carl* 10–13; C York H Trin Micklegate 14–18; P-in-c Erpingham w Calthorpe, Ingworth, Aldborough etc *Nor* from 19. *The Rectory, School Road, Erpingham, Norwich NR11 7QY* M: 07964-061810 E: revecrobinson@aol.com

ROBINSON, Fiona. b 69. Yorks Min Course 15. **d** 17 **p** 18. NSM Sutton Park *York* 17–18; NSM Wawne 17–18; NSM Sutton Park and Wawne from 18. *13 Wivern Road, Hull HU9 4HS* T: (01482) 703038 M: 07561-847972 E: revd-robinson@outlook.com

ROBINSON, Fiona Heather Anne. b 61. SNWTP 14. **d** 17 **p** 18. NSM Chelford and Lower Withington w Marthall *Ches* from 17. *1 Drumble Field, Chelford, Macclesfield SK11 9BT* T: (01625) 860679 E: fionarobinson61@btinternet.com

ROBINSON, Frank. *See* ROBINSON, John Francis Napier

ROBINSON, Gareth James. b 74. Sheff Univ BA 95 Sheff Hallam Univ PGCE 96 K Coll Lon MA 13. St Mellitus Coll 13. **d** 13 **p** 14. C Marple All SS *Ches* 13–16; V Salford St Phil w St Steph *Man* from 16. *6 Encombe Place, Salford M3 6FJ* T: 0161-839 9709 M: 07825-413430 E: gareth.r@saintphilips.org.uk

ROBINSON, Mrs Hazel. b 61. RGN 83 RSCN 83. St Jo Coll Nottm 02. **d** 04 **p** 05. C Toton *S'well* 04–09; P-in-c Blidworth w Rainworth 09–11; V 11–19; P-in-c Annesley w Newstead and Kirkby Woodhouse from 19. *The Vicarage, Annesley Cutting, Annesley, Nottingham NG15 0AJ* E: haze.rob@btopenworld.com

ROBINSON, Canon Ian. b 57. Nottm Univ BTh 87 MA 97. Linc Th Coll 84. **d** 87 **p** 88. C Bottesford w Ashby *Linc* 87–90; TV 90–95; P-in-c Caistor w Clixby 95–00; P-in-c Grasby 95–00; P-in-c Searby w Owmby 95–00; V Caistor Gp 00–18; V Caistor from 18; RD W Wold 01–17; Can and Preb Linc Cathl from 07. *3 Spa Top, Caistor, Market Rasen LN7 6RB* T: (01472) 851339 E: revianrobinson@tiscali.co.uk

ROBINSON, Ian Morgan. b 53. Lanc Univ BA 08 CEng 86 MCIBSE 86. CBDTI 05. **d** 08 **p** 09. NSM Askrigg w Stallingbusk *Ripon* 08–12; NSM Hawes and Hardraw 09–12; R Bedale and Leeming and Thornton Watlass 12–14; *Leeds* 14–18; rtd 18. *High Dalby House, Dalby, Pickering YO18 7LP* M: 07801-657988 E: revrobbo@btinternet.com

ROBINSON, James Edward. b 85. Univ of Wales (Swansea) BA 09 Linc Coll Ox MSt 10 St Jo Coll Cam BA 14. Westcott Ho Cam 12. **d** 15 **p** 16. C Grantham St Wulfram *Linc* 15–18; C Grantham, Manthorpe 15–18; V Legbourne and Wold Marsh from 18. *The Rectory, Church Lane, Legbourne, Louth LN11 8LN* T: (01507) 603008 M: 07500-829413 E: jrobinson@stwulframs.com *or* jrobinson7980@gmail.com

ROBINSON, Mrs Jane Hippisley. b 41. Somerville Coll Ox MA 66 K Coll Lon PGCE. S Dios Minl Tr Scheme 88. **d** 91. NSM Ealing St Pet Mt Park *Lon* 91–96; NSM N Acton St Gabr 96–00; PtO from 00. *40 Brentham Way, London W5 1BE* T: (020) 8991 0206

ROBINSON, Mrs Janet. b 34. Milton Keynes Coll of Ed CertEd 77. Open Univ BA 78. WMMTC 89. **d** 92 **p** 94.

NSM Roade and Ashton w Hartwell *Pet* 92–94; NSM Potterspury, Furtho, Yardley Gobion and Cosgrove 94–99; rtd 99; PtO *Pet* 99–14. *73 Eastfield Crescent, Yardley Gobion, Towcester NN12 7TT* T: (01908) 542331 E: revjandrewrobinson@btinternet.com

ROBINSON, Jean. *See* CLARK, Jean Robinson

ROBINSON, Mrs Jean Anne. b 50. Lon Univ BPharm 72 MRPharmS 73 Southn Univ BTh 98. STETS 95. **d** 98 **p** 99. NSM Frimley *Guildf* 98–03; NSM Worplesdon 03–05; NSM Egham Hythe 05–07; C Woodham 07–14; Chapl Surrey and Borders Partnership NHS Foundn Trust 05–14; Chapl Alpha Hosp Woking 06–14; NSM E Clevedon w Clapton in Gordano etc *B & W* 14–17; PtO *Guildf* from 17. *8 Westfield Avenue, Woking GU22 9PH* E: revjar95@yahoo.co.uk

ROBINSON, Jennifer Elizabeth. b 53. Sheff Hallam Univ BA 96. NOC 01. **d** 04 **p** 06. NSM Fishlake w Sykehouse and Kirk Bramwith etc *Sheff* 04–08; PtO 08–11; Chapl Rotherham, Doncaster and S Humber NHS Foundn Trust 13–19; rtd 19. *14 Thorncliffe Drive, Stainforth, Doncaster DN7 5PX* E: jerobinson@hotmail.co.uk

ROBINSON, Joan. b 62. **d** 13 **p** 14. NSM Blaydon and Swalwell *Dur* 13–16; Chapl Gateshead Health NHS Foundn Trust from 16. *9 Rose Avenue, Whickham, Newcastle upon Tyne NE16 4NA* T: 0191-420 1572 E: jrdallas@btinternet.com

ROBINSON, John Francis Napier (Frank). b 42. St Edm Hall Ox BA 64 MA 68. Clifton Th Coll 65. **d** 68 **p** 69. C Southport Ch Ch *Liv* 68–71; C Coleraine *Conn* 71–74; Deputation Sec (Ireland) BCMS 74–76; TV Marfleet *York* 76–81; V Yeadon St Jo *Bradf* 81–95; P-in-c Rounds Green *Birm* 95–00; V 00–02; rtd 02; PtO *S'well* from 03; *Derby* from 03. *61 Clumber Avenue, Beeston, Nottingham NG9 4BH* T: 0115-922 1704

ROBINSON, The Very Revd John Kenneth. b 36. K Coll Lon BD 61 AKC 61. **d** 62 **p** 63. C Poulton-le-Fylde *Blackb* 62–65; C Lancaster St Mary 65–66; Chapl HM Pris Lanc 65–66; Chapl St Jo Sch Singapore 66–68; V Colne H Trin *Blackb* 68–71; Dir Educn Windward Is 71–74; V Skerton St Luke *Blackb* 74–81; Area Sec (E Anglia) USPG 81–91; Hon Min Can St E Cathl 82–91; Chapl Gtr Lisbon *Eur* 91–00; Adn Gib 94–02; Can Gib Cathl 94–00; Dean Gib 00–03; rtd 03; PtO *Blackb* from 03; *Eur* from 03. *9 Poplar Drive, Coppull, Chorley PR7 4LS* T: (01257) 470042

ROBINSON, Judith Lee Hughes. b 83. NW Univ Illinois BA 05 Wycliffe Hall Ox MTh 16. St Mellitus Coll 16. **d** 18 **p** 19. C W Hampstead Trin *Lon* 18–19. *46 Aberdare Gardens, London NW6 3QA* M: 07895-820540 E: judy.lh.robinson@gmail.com

ROBINSON, Katharine Mary. *See* McATEER, Katharine Mary

ROBINSON, Kathryn Elizabeth. b 55. Hull Univ BA 76 K Coll Lon MSc 86 St Hilda's Coll Ox PGCE 77. NTMTC 03. **d** 05 **p** 06. NSM Leytonstone St Jo *Chelmsf* 05–12; PtO from 12. *80 Carr Road, London E17 5EN* M: 07956-658450 E: krobinsonrev14@gmail.com

ROBINSON, Kenneth. *See* ROBINSON, John Kenneth

ROBINSON, Kenneth Borwell. b 37. Lon Univ BA 62. Ridley Hall Cam 68. **d** 70 **p** 71. C Walthamstow St Jo *Chelmsf* 70–74; P-in-c Becontree St Alb 74–78; P-in-c Heybridge w Langford 78–84; TV Horley *S'wark* 84–98; C Oxted and Tandridge 98–02; rtd 02; PtO *Portsm* 03–15; *S'wark* from 16. *8 Master Close, Oxted RH8 9NA* E: kennethrobinson@hotmail.co.uk

ROBINSON, Kevan John. b 63. Chich Univ BA 09. SEITE 08. **d** 10 **p** 11. NSM Southbourne w W Thorney *Chich* 10–14; P-in-c E Dean, Singleton, and W Dean 14–19; Chapl Chich Coll from 14; P-in-c Bexhill St Steph *Chich* from 19. *St Stephen's Vicarage, Woodsgate Park, Bexhill-on-Sea TN39 4DL* T: (01424) 211186 M: 07757-122446 E: k.robinson275@btinternet.com

ROBINSON, Lesley. *See* ROBINSON, Elizabeth Carole Lesley

ROBINSON, Leslie. b 31. St Aid Birkenhead 56. **d** 59 **p** 60. C Hugglescote w Donington *Leic* 59–61; C Greenside *Dur* 61–63; C-in-c New Cantley CD *Sheff* 63–66; V Choral Heref Cathl 66–67; R Easton-on-the-Hill *Pet* 67–69; Hon Min Can Pet Cathl 68–69; C Weston-super-Mare St Jo *B & W* 69–70; V Winkleigh *Ex* 70–72; V Thorpe Acre w Dishley *Leic* 72–78; V Cloughton *York* 78–79; V Hedon w Paull 79–81; V Bywell *Newc* 81–86; V Wymeswold and Prestwold w Hoton *Leic* 86–97; rtd 97; PtO *Pet* 97–98. *16 Victoria Road, Oundle, Peterborough PE8 4AY* T: (01832) 275048

ROBINSON, Linda Ann. b 53. **d** 12 **p** 13. NSM Newington w Hull St Andr *York* 12–18; PtO from 18. *153 Boothferry Road, Hessle HU13 9BA* E: robinson.linda28@yahoo.co.uk

ROBINSON, Linda Anne. b 54. Westf Coll Lon BA 75 Man Univ MEd 05 Ches Univ DProf 15. Yorks Min Course. **d** 14 **p** 15. NSM Bedale and Leeming and Thornton Watlass *Leeds* 14–18 and from 14. *High Dalby House, Dalby, Pickering YO18 7LP* M: 07736-771216 E: lindarobinson@talk21.com

ROBINSON, Matthew Jamie. b 72. St Steph Ho Ox 13. **d** 15 **p** 16. C Sevenoaks St Jo *Roch* 15–19; V King's Sutton and Newbottle and Charlton *Pet* from 19. *The Vicarage, Church Avenue, King's Sutton, Banbury OX17 3RJ* T: (01295) 811364

ROBINSON, Michael Thomas Edward. b 87. Magd Coll Cam BA 08 MA 12. Westcott Ho Cam 13. **d** 16 **p** 17. C Walworth St Pet *S'wark* from 16. *9 Arments Court, 392 Albany Road, London SE5 0DF* E: michael.robinson@cantab.net

ROBINSON, Monica Dorothy. b 40. SAOMC 99. **d** 01 **p** 02. NSM Bedford St Andr *St Alb* 01–10; PtO from 10. *Shoyswell, Radwell Road, Milton Ernest, Bedford MK44 1RY* T: (01234) 824366 E: mdrobinson@btopenworld.com

ROBINSON, Neil. b 66. Trin Coll Bris 13. **d** 16 **p** 17. C Bemerton *Sarum* 16–19; Chapl to the Deaf from 16. *28 Queen Mary Road, Salisbury SP2 9LD* M: 07717-055219 E: coolie66smiley@gmail.com

ROBINSON, Mrs Norma Georgina. b 57. Edge Hill Coll of HE BEd 78 RGN 03. SNWTP 10. **d** 12 **p** 13. NSM Hyde St Geo *Ches* 12–14; NSM Macclesfield St Jo w Henbury from 14. *St John's Vicarage, 25 Wilwick Lane, Macclesfield SK11 8RS* T: (01625) 424185 or 425510

ROBINSON, Oliver Patrick Kilcooley. b 88. Heythrop Coll Lon BA 10 MA 11. Wycliffe Hall Ox MTh 15. **d** 15 **p** 17. C Cricklewood St Gabr and St Mich *Lon* 15–16; C W Hampstead Trin 16–19; PtO from 19. *Ground Floor Flat, 46 Aberdare Gardens, London NW6 3QA* M: 07904-531036 E: opk.robinson@gmail.com

ROBINSON, Mrs Patricia May. b 51. Man Poly BEd 92 St Jo Coll Nottm MA 16. All SS Cen for Miss & Min 15. **d** 16 **p** 17. NSM Rostherne w Bollington *Ches* from 16; NSM High Legh from 16; NSM Over Tabley from 16. *The Vicarage, Rostherne Lane, Rostherne Village, Knutsford WA16 6RZ* T: (01565) 830595 M: 07854-418488 E: pmrobinson51@gmail.com

ROBINSON, Capt Paul Andrew. b 68. Hull Univ MBA 09. **d** 09 **p** 10. OLM Royton St Anne *Man* 09–12; NSM Medlock Head 12–17; CF (R of O) from 13. *19 Dorchester Drive, Royton, Oldham OL2 5AU* T: 0161-628 9019 M: 07984-938393 E: paul@nomoreproblems.co.uk

ROBINSON, Paul Leslie. b 65. St Steph Ho Ox 95. **d** 97 **p** 98. C Upholland *Liv* 97–01; V Lydiate and Downholland 01–08; P-in-c Halsall 04–08; R Halsall, Lydiate and Downholland from 08. *The Vicarage, Church Lane, Lydiate, Liverpool L31 4HL* T: 0151-526 0512 E: frpaul.robinson@btopenworld.com or paulrobinson407@gmail.com

ROBINSON, Canon Paul Leslie. b 46. Dur Univ BA 67. Linc Th Coll 71. **d** 74 **p** 75. C Poynton *Ches* 74–76; C Prenton 76–78; V Seacombe 78–88; V Stalybridge St Paul 88–00; P-in-c Wallasey St Hilary 00–04; R 04–10; Urban Min Officer 96–00; Hon Can Ches Cathl 98–10; P-in-c E and W Tilbury and Linford *Chelmsf* 10–16; R 16; PtO from 16. *37 Clyde Crescent, Rayleigh SS6 7SX* T: (01268) 963911 E: canonrobinson@outlook.com

ROBINSON, Paula Patricia. b 50. Man Univ MEd 83 TCD BTh 94. **d** 94 **p** 95. C Killala w Dunfeeny, Crossmolina, Kilmoremoy etc *T, K & A* 94–97; I Crosspatrick Gp *C & O* 97–00; R Leonardtown St Andr USA 00–09; P-in-c Tockwith and Bilton w Bickerton *York* 09–11; P-in-c Rufforth w Moor Monkton and Hessay 09–11; P-in-c Healaugh w Wighill, Bilbrough and Askham Richard 09–11; PtO *Man* 12–15; NSM Heaton Reddish 15–16; NSM N Reddish 15–16; rtd 16; PtO *Man* from 16. *3 Lea Court, Heaton Moor Road, Stockport SK4 4PZ* T: 0161-975 0986 E: revpaularobinson@gmail.com

ROBINSON, Peter Charles. b 53. Open Univ BA 83. Oak Hill Th Coll 85. **d** 87 **p** 88. C Nottingham St Ann w Em *S'well* 87–89; C Worksop St Anne 89–92; V S Ramsey St Paul *S & M* 92–99; Can St German's Cathl 98–99; P-in-c Goostrey and Dioc Dir of Ords *Ches* 99–03; P-in-c Aldeburgh w Hazlewood *St E* 03–04; C Arbory *S & M* 05–06; V 06–13; C Santan 05–06; V 06–13; C Castletown 05–06; V 06–13; RD Castletown and Peel 08–12; Hon Can St German's Cathl 09–12; Can and Bp's Chapl 12–13; V Malton and Old Malton *York* 13–18; rtd 18; PtO *York* from 19. *1 Shaftesbury Avenue, Hornsea HU18 1LX*

ROBINSON, The Ven Peter John Alan. b 61. St Jo Coll Cam BA 83 MA 87 St Jo Coll Dur BA 92 PhD 97. Cranmer Hall Dur 90. **d** 95 **p** 96. C N Shields *Newc* 95–99; P-in-c Byker St Martin 99–08; P-in-c Byker St Mich w St Lawr 01–08; Hon Can Newc Cathl 07–08; Adn Lindisfarne from 08. *4 Acomb Close, Morpeth NE61 2YH* T: (01670) 503810 F: 510469 E: p.robinson@newcastle.anglican.org

ROBINSON, Philip. b 38. S Dios Minl Tr Scheme 88. **d** 91 **p** 92. NSM Ickenham *Lon* 91–95; P-in-c 95–04; P-in-c Hayes St Anselm 98–99; P-in-c Harlington 98–00; AD Hillingdon 97–03; rtd 04; PtO *Eur* from 04; *Lon* from 04. *5 Preston Court,*

4 Fairfield Road, Uxbridge UB8 1DQ T: (01895) 200303 or (0033) (4) 93 04 75 11 E: philiprobinson208@gmail.com

ROBINSON, Philip John. b 50. St Luke's Coll Ex CertEd 71 Leeds Univ BA 07. NOC 04. **d** 06 **p** 07. NSM Macclesfield Team *Ches* 06–09; P-in-c Rostherne w Bollington 09–13; V from 13; P-in-c High Legh from 15; P-in-c Over Tabley from 15. *The Vicarage, Rostherne Lane, Rostherne Village, Knutsford WA16 6RZ* T: (01565) 830595 E: robinsonpj50@gmail.com

ROBINSON, Raymonde Robin. b 43. St Jo Coll Dur BA 66. Chich Th Coll 67. **d** 70 **p** 71. C Ealing St Barn *Lon* 70–72; C Pinner 72–75; C Clerkenwell H Redeemer w St Phil 75–80; TV Kingsthorpe w Northampton St Dav *Pet* 80–89; R Letchworth *St Alb* 89–95; V Noel Park St Mark *Lon* 95–06; rtd 06; PtO *Chich* 12–17. *12 West Hill Street, Brighton BN1 3RR* T: (01273) 728778

ROBINSON, Robert James. **d** 14 **p** 15. Drumglass w Moygashel *Arm* 14–15; C Drumragh w Mountfield *D & R* from 15. *12 Crevenagh Road, Omagh BT79 0JE* T: (028) 8216 0883 E: robertjamesrobinson3@gmail.com

ROBINSON, Roy David. b 35. AKC 59. **d** 60 **p** 61. C Acocks Green *Birm* 60–62; C Shirley 62–65; C Haslemere *Guildf* 65–70; R Headley w Box Hill 70–85; V Hinchley Wood 85–00; rtd 00; PtO *Guildf* from 02. *1 Park Road, Slinfold, Horsham RH13 0SD* T: (01403) 791640

ROBINSON, Prof Simon John. b 51. Edin Univ MA 72 PhD 89 Ox Univ BA 77. Wycliffe Hall Ox 75. **d** 78 **p** 79. C Haughton le Skerne *Dur* 78–81; Chapl Asst N Tees Hosp Stockton-on-Tees 81–83; C Norton St Mary *Dur* 81–83; Chapl Heriot-Watt Univ *Edin* 83–90; R Dalmahoy 83–90; Chapl Leeds Univ *Ripon* 90–04; P-in-c Leeds Em 90–04; Prof Ethics Leeds Metrop Univ 04–14; NSM Leeds City 05–14 and from 14; Prof Ethics Leeds Beckett Univ from 14. *42 Woodside Avenue, Meanwood, Leeds LS7 2UL* T: 0113-283 7440 M: 07931-916381 E: s.j.robinson@leedsmet.ac.uk or s.j.robinson@leedsbeckett.ac.uk

ROBINSON, Simon Joseph. b 67. Warwick Univ BA 89. STETS. **d** 12 **p** 13. C Freshford, Limpley Stoke and Hinton Charterhouse *B & W* 12–15; V Minehead from 15. *7 Paganel Road, Minehead TA24 5ET* M: 07825-925243 E: sijorobinson@me.com

ROBINSON, Steven Paul. b 65. Roehampton Univ BEd 89 Oak Hill Th Coll BA 05. St Mellitus Coll MA 13. **d** 10 **p** 11. C Perranzabuloe and Crantock w Cubert *Truro* 10–13; R St Illogan from 13. *The Rectory, Robartes Terrace, Illogan, Redruth TR16 4RX* T: (01209) 843938 M: 07813-324148

ROBINSON, Canon Teresa Jane. b 56. SAOMC 98. **d** 01 **p** 02. OLM The Cookhams *Ox* 01–08; NSM Maidenhead St Luke from 08; Angl Communion Office from 14; Hon Can Ch Ch *Ox* from 18. *7 Golden Ball Lane, Maidenhead SL6 6NW* T: (01628) 634107 E: terrie.robinson@anglicancommunion.org

ROBINSON, Tiffer. *See* ROBINSON, Christopher Mark Scott

ROBINSON, Timothy. b 56. Hull Univ BSc 78 Liv Univ PhD 83 St Jo Coll Dur BA 07 FGA 86. Cranmer Hall Dur 05. **d** 07 **p** 08. C Nantwich *Ches* 07–10; V Stalybridge St Paul 10–14; V Macclesfield St Jo w Henbury from 14. *St John's Vicarage, 25 Wilwick Lane, Macclesfield SK11 8RS* T: (01625) 424185 or 612511 or 425510 M: 07981-108779 E: trtimrobinson@gmail.com

ROBINSON, Timothy James. b 59. Middx Poly BA 84 Coll of Ripon & York St Jo PGCE 00 Open Univ MA 14. St Steph Ho Ox 88. **d** 91 **p** 92. C W Acklam *York* 91–95; P-in-c N Ormesby 95–96; V 96–99; Teacher Hall Garth Sch Middlesbrough 00–10; PtO *Ripon* 99–02; Tutor NEOC 02–09; P-in-c Helmsley *York* 10–11; V from 11; P-in-c Upper Ryedale 10–11; R from 11; AD N Ryedale from 11. *The Vicarage, Baxtons Road, Helmsley, York YO62 5HT* T: (01439) 770983 E: tim.robinson123@btinternet.com

ROBOTTOM, David Leonard Douglas. b 40. Qu Coll Birm 80 Sarum & Wells Th Coll 81. **d** 83 **p** 84. C Uppingham w Ayston and Wardley w Belton *Pet* 83–87; TV Sidmouth, Woolbrook and Salcombe Regis *Ex* 87–91; TV Sidmouth, Woolbrook, Salcombe Regis, Sidbury etc 91–95; R Bradninch and Clyst Hydon 95–10; RD Cullompton 03–08; rtd 10. *2 Bridge Meadow Close, Lapford, Crediton EX17 6FH* T: (01363) 884495 E: su2312@eclipse.co.uk

ROBSON, Claire English. b 62. Middx Poly BEd 88. Westcott Ho Cam 96. **d** 99 **p** 00. C Dorchester *Sarum* 99–02; C Kilburn St Mary w All So and W Hampstead St Jas *Lon* 02–04; Min Can and Chapl St Paul's Cathl 04–09; C Bath Abbey w St Jas *B & W* 09–18; Dioc Dir of Ords *Newc* from 18; NSM Hexham from 18. *20 Chesters Meadow, Humshaugh, Hexham NE46 4BF* E: clairerobson@clara.net

ROBSON, Howard. *See* ROBSON, John Howard

ROBSON, Preb Ian Leonard. b 32. K Coll Lon MA 00. Bps' Coll Cheshunt 61. **d** 63 **p** 64. C Croxley Green All SS *St Alb* 63–65; C Harpenden St Nic 65–68; V Redbourn 68–72; V

Ashford St Matt *Lon* 72–77; V Kensington St Mary Abbots w St Geo 77–97; AD Kensington 94–97; Preb St Paul's Cathl 96–97; rtd 97; PtO *Chich* from 97. *Wepham Lodge, Wepham, Arundel BN18 9RA* T: (01903) 884667

ROBSON, James Edward. b 65. Pemb Coll Ox BA 88 Middx Univ PhD 05. Wycliffe Hall Ox 91. **d** 94 **p** 95. C Enfield Ch Ch Trent Park *Lon* 94–98; C Oakwood St Thos 98–00; Tutor Oak Hill Th Coll 00–09; Tutor Wycliffe Hall Ox 09–10; Sen Tutor 10–17; Min Dir Keswick Min from 17. *Keswick Ministries, Skiddaw Street, Keswick CA12 4BY* T: (017687) 80075 M: 07454-865670 E: james.robson@keswickministries.org

ROBSON, John Howard. b 60. Newc Univ BA 81 ACIB 87. Cranmer Hall Dur 98. **d** 00 **p** 01. C Hethersett w Canteloff w Lt and Gt Melton *Nor* 00–04; R Brooke, Kirstead, Mundham w Seething and Thwaite 04–13; V Littleport *Ely* from 13; RD Ely from 14. *St George's Vicarage, 30 Church Lane, Littleport, Ely CB6 1PS* T: (01353) 864695 E: therevhoward@btinternet.com

ROBSON, John Phillips. b 32. St Edm Hall Ox. AKC 58. **d** 59 **p** 60. C Huddersfield SS Pet and Paul *Wakef* 59–62; Asst Chapl Ch Hosp Horsham 62–65; Chapl 65–80; Sen Chapl Wellington Coll Berks 80–89; Chapl to RVO and Qu Chpl of the Savoy 89–02; Chapl to The Queen 93–02; rtd 02; Extra Chapl to The Queen from 02. *Charterhouse, Charterhouse Square, London EC1M 6AN* T: (020) 7253 1591 E: johnrevolt@gmail.com

ROBSON, Mrs Julie. b 52. **d** 12 **p** 13. NSM Corbridge w Halton and Newton Hall *Newc* 12–17; rtd 17; PtO *Newc* from 18. *Whinburn, 9 Alexandra Crescent, Hexham NE46 3AA* T: (01434) 603958 E: j-r@talktalk.net

ROBSON, Martin Douglas. b 62. St Andr Univ MTheol 85 Cam Univ PGCE 88 Edin Univ MTh 94. Edin Th Coll 92. **d** 94 **p** 95. C Perth St Ninian *St And* 94–97; P-in-c Lockerbie *Glas* 97–01; P-in-c Moffat 97–01; R Edin St Hilda 01–06; R Edin St Fillan 01–14; R Edin St Mich and All SS from 14. *203 Gilmore Place, Edinburgh EH3 9PN* T: 0131-923 1179 E: rector@stmichaelandallsaints.org

ROBSON, Nolan Daniel Rhyl. b 77. Bath Univ BSc 99 Sheff Univ DipArch 02. Oak Hill Th Coll BA 13. **d** 13 **p** 14. C Kilnhurst *Sheff* 13–16; R Thrapston, Denford and Islip *Pet* from 16. *The Rectory, 48 Oundle Road, Thrapston, Kettering NN14 4PD* T: (01932) 734614 M: 07740-700899 E: nolanrobson@me.com

ROBSON, Pamela Jean. b 44. STETS 94. **d** 97 **p** 98. NSM W Ewell *Guildf* 97–01; P-in-c Wotton and Holmbury St Mary 02–14; rtd 14; PtO *St E* from 15. *Old Guildhall, The Street, Badwell Ash, Bury St Edmunds IP31 3DP* T: (01359) 258939 E: robsonpam@btinternet.com

ROBSON, Canon Patricia Anne. b 40. CertEd 60. SWMTC 85. **d** 87 **p** 94. Dioc Youth Officer *Truro* 87–92; Hon C Paul 87–92; Hon C Kenwyn St Geo 88–92; Dn-in-c St Enoder 92–94; P-in-c Newlyn St Newlyn 03–05; Hon Can Truro Cathl 98–05; RD Pydar 02–03; rtd 05; P-in-c St Goran w Caerhays *Truro* 06–09; PtO from 16. *Mill Cottage, Mill Lane, Grampound, Truro TR2 4RU* T: (01726) 882366 E: intercelt@aol.com

ROBSON, Paul Coutt. b 37. Leeds Univ BA 60. Coll of Resurr Mirfield 63. **d** 64 **p** 65. C Stokesay *Heref* 64–66; C St Geo Cathl Cape Town S Africa 66–68; R Roodebloem All SS 68–70; Chapl HM Pris Man 70–71; Chapl HM Borstal Feltham 71–74; Chapl HM Borstal Hollesley Bay 74–78; Chapl HM Pris Grendon and HM Pris Spring Hill 78–85; Chapl HM Pris Nor 85–92; Chapl HM YOI and Remand Cen Brinsford 92–99; rtd 99; PtO *Heref* 00–01 and from 04; P-in-c Wistanstow 01–04. *Pilgrims, Henley Common, Church Stretton SY6 6RS* T: (01694) 781221 E: robson718@btinternet.com

ROBSON, Peter. b 58. Leeds Univ BEd 80. Cranmer Hall Dur 05. **d** 07 **p** 08. C Bishopwearmouth St Gabr *Dur* 07–11; PtO 16–18; Hon C Shildon from 18. *1 Broad Oak, Bishop Middleham, Ferryhill DL17 9BW* E: peterpoprobson@aol.co.uk

ROBSON, Thomas Iain. b 83. Ridley Hall Cam 10. **d** 13 **p** 14. C Angmering *Chich* 13–16; P-in-c Lyminster and Wick 16–17; V from 17. *The Vicarage, 40 Beaconsfield Road, Wick, Littlehampton BN17 6LN* T: (01903) 714838 E: tom.robson@allsaintswick.org.uk

ROBSON, William. b 34. FCIS 66 FCCA 80. Sarum & Wells Th Coll 77. **d** 79 **p** 80. C Lymington *Win* 79–81; CF 81–93; V Barton Stacey and Bullington etc *Win* 93–98; rtd 98; Hon C Knaresborough *Ripon* 98–01; PtO *Newc* 03–04; Hon C Barrow upon Soar w Walton le Wolds *Leic* 04–07; Hon C Wymeswold and Prestwold w Hoton 04–07; PtO *Linc* 11–14. *15 Capel Court, The Burgage, Prestbury, Cheltenham GL52 3EL* T: (01242) 226001 M: 07914-829885 E: camble@greenbee.net

ROBUS, Keith Adrian. b 59. Heythrop Coll Lon MA 01 MHCIMA 82. Chich Th Coll 85. **d** 88 **p** 89. C Greenhill St Jo *Lon* 88–92; C Willesden St Matt 92–02; V N Acton St Gabr 02–09; Chapl RN 09–19; P-in-c Stoke Damerel and Devonport St Aubyn *Ex* 19; R Stoke Damerel from 19. *The Rectory, 6 Underhill Road, Plymouth PL3 4BP* T: (01752) 509724 M: 07801-069997 E: keith.robus@btinternet.com

ROBY, Richard James. b 33. Imp Coll Lon BSc 54 Lon Inst of Educn PGCE 55. St Alb Minl Tr Scheme 82. **d** 85 **p** 86. NSM Bushey *St Alb* 85–92; NSM Wootton 92–00; rtd 00; PtO *St Alb* 00–16. *53 Kingsfield Road, WATFORD WD19 4PP* T: 01923 444323 E: richard.roby@ntlworld.com

ROCHDALE, Archdeacon of. See VANN, The Ven Cherry Elizabeth

ROCHE, Miss Alison Mary. b 70. Man Univ BSc 91 Nottm Univ PGCE 94. St Jo Coll Nottm MA 00. **d** 01 **p** 02. C Leic Martyrs 01–05; P-in-c Leic St Chris 05–09; V 09–16; PtO from 18. *Knighton Vicarage, 5 Church Lane, Leicester LE2 3WG* T: 0116-270 4268 M: 07901-621250

ROCHE, Barry Robert Francis. b 40. Lon Univ BD 66 Ox Univ MTh 93. Clifton Th Coll 63. **d** 68 **p** 69. C Beckenham Ch Ch *Roch* 68–72; C Chester le Street *Dur* 72–74; C-in-c N Bletchley CD *Ox* 74–78; R Luton Ch Ch *Roch* 78–92; Chapl All SS Hosp Chatham 78–92; TR Glascote and Stonydelph *Lich* 92–99; RD Tamworth 95–99; V Oulton Broad *Nor* 99–05; rtd 05; PtO *S & B* from 06. *24 Lakeside Close, Nantyglo, Ebbw Vale NP23 4EG* T: (01495) 311048 E: roche440@btinternet.com

ROCHE, David Michael. b 71. Redcliffe Coll Glouc MA 14. **d** 16 **p** 16. P-in-c Beirut All SS Lebanon 16–18; P-in-c Whitchurch w Tufton and Litchfield *Win* from 18. *The Vicarage, Church Street, Whitchurch RG28 7AS* M: 07783-506944 E: david.roche@hotmail.com

ROCHE, Philip Edmund. b 70. SCRTP 14. **d** 17 **p** 18. C Milford *Guildf* 17–18; C Seale, Puttenham and Wanborough from 18. *130 Ockford Road, Godalming GU7 1RG* E: rev.phil@outlook.com

ROCHELL, Stephen Peter. b 56. Open Univ MA 95 Sheff Univ BA 14. Yorks Min Course 11. **d** 14 **p** 15. NSM Hartshead, Hightown, Roberttown and Scholes *Leeds* from 14. *55 Greenside Road, Mirfield WF14 0AU* T: (01924) 521121 M: 07707-763689 E: stephen.rochell@ntlworld.com

ROCHESTER, Archdeacon of. See WOODING JONES, The Ven Andrew David

ROCHESTER, Bishop of. See LANGSTAFF, The Rt Revd James Henry

ROCHESTER, Dean of. See HESKETH, The Very Revd Philip John

ROCK, Mrs Jean. b 37. Gilmore Course 76. dss 79 **d** 87 **p** 97. Douglas St Matt *S & M* 79–81; Marown 81–83; Chapl Asst Oswestry and Distr Hosp 83–87; Oswestry St Oswald *Lich* 83–90; Par Dn 87–90; C-in-c Pont Robert and Pont Dolanog *St As* 90–97; V 97; rtd 97; PtO *Lich* 99–13; *St As* from 09. *Burnet Cottage, Church Lane, St Martins, Oswestry SY11 3AP* T: (01691) 773766

ROCKEY, Antony Nicolas. b 65. Kingston Poly BEng 89 Cumbria Univ MA 12. CBDTI 02. **d** 05 **p** 06. C Bournemouth Area *Carl* 05–09; P-in-c Fernhurst *Chich* 09–11; PtO *Ex* 15–16; TR Burrington, Chawleigh, Cheldon, Chulmleigh etc from 16. *The Rectory, Chulmleigh EX18 7BY* T: (01769) 581712 E: rev.tony@rockey5.net

ROCKS, James Anthony. b 82. Trin Coll Bris BA 10. **d** 11 **p** 12. C Stoke Gifford *Bris* 11–15. *8 Somerset Crescent, Stoke Gifford, Bristol BS34 8PP* M: 07786-034993 E: jimmy@st-michaels-church.org.uk

RODD, Philip Rankilor. b 60. Ex Univ BA 79 K Coll Lon PGCE 85. Ridley Hall Cam 03. **d** 05 **p** 06. C Heigham H Trin *Nor* 05–08; V Eaton St Andr from 08. *The Vicarage, 210 Newmarket Road, Norwich NR4 7LA* T: (01603) 455778

RODDAM, Helen Margaret. See BAILEY, Helen Margaret

RODDY, Keith Anthony. b 67. Leic Univ BA 89. Oak Hill Th Coll BA 09. **d** 09 **p** 10. C Chesterton *Lich* 09–12; V Springfield H Trin *Chelmsf* from 12. *The Vicarage, 61 Hill Road, Chelmsford CM2 6HW* T: (01245) 359299 M: 07986-903110 E: keitharoddy@googlemail.com

RODEL, Mark Neil. b 71. Southn Univ BA 96. STETS 02. **d** 05 **p** 06. C Southsea St Jude *Portsm* 05–08; C Portsea St Luke 08–12; V Lady Bay w Holme Pierrepont and Adbolton *S'well* 12–19; Tutor St Jo Coll Nottm 12–19; Dioc Fresh Expressions Adv *Ely* from 19. *Ely Diocesan Office, Bishop Woodford House, Barton Road, Ely CB7 4DX* T: (01353) 652701

RODEN, Jo. See LOVERIDGE, Joan Margaretha Holland

RODEN, John Michael. b 37. St Jo Coll York CertEd 64 Open Univ BA 82 MA 92 York Univ DPhil 96. Ripon Hall Ox 71. **d** 73 **p** 74. C Saltburn-by-the-Sea *York* 73–77; Chapl St Pet Sch York 77–82; Warden Marrick Priory *Ripon* 83; Hon C Appleton Roebuck w Acaster Selby *York* 84–85; P-in-c

86–03; Youth Officer 86–91; Sen Chapl Selby Coalfield Ind Chapl 96–03; rtd 03; PtO *York* from 03; *Eur* from 10. *Ebor Cottage, 8 Copmanthorpe Grange, Copmanthorpe, York YO23 3TN* T: (01904) 744826 E: j.m.roden@btinternet.com

RODEN, Canon Michael Adrian Holland. b 60. Birm Univ MA 03. Ripon Coll Cuddesdon 82. **d** 85 **p** 86. C S Lambeth St Anne and All SS *S'wark* 85–88; C Wandsworth St Paul 88–90; C Ox St Mary V w St Cross and St Pet 90–94; Chapl Wadh Coll Ox 90–94; R Steeple Aston w N Aston and Tackley *Ox* 94–02; TR Hitchin *St Alb* 02–16; P-in-c St Paul's Walden 10–16; TR Hitchin and St Paul's Walden 16–19; RD Hitchin 07–15; Hon Can St Alb 14–19; Can Res Bris Cathl from 19. *Bristol Cathedral, College Green, Bristol BS1 5TJ* T: 0117-926 4879 E: michaelroden@btinternet.com

RODERICK, Philip David. b 49. Univ of Wales (Swansea) BA 70 Univ of Wales (Abth) BD 77 Lon Univ CertEd 71. Linc Th Coll 80. **d** 80 **p** 81. C Llanfair-is-gaer and Llanddeiniolen *Ban* 80–82; TV Holyhead w Rhoscolyn w Llanfair-yn-Neubwll 82–84; Chapl and Lect Th Univ of Wales (Ban) 84–88; Warden Angl Chapl Cen 84–88; Prin Bucks Chr Tr Scheme *Ox* 88–94; Dir Chiltern Chr Tr Progr 88–94; Dir Quiet Garden Trust from 92; Dir The Well Inst from 96; V Amersham on the Hill *Ox* 96–04; Ldr Contemplative Fire from 04; Bp's Adv in Spirituality *Sheff* 10–16; Chapl Whirlow Grange Conf Cen Sheff 10–15; rtd 16. *16 Chorley Avenue, Saltdean, Brighton BN2 8AQ* T: (01273) 275352 E: philip@contemplativefire.org

RODGER, Canon Raymond. b 39. Westmr Coll Ox MTh 93. Bps' Coll Cheshunt 62. **d** 63 **p** 64. C Frodingham *Linc* 63–66; Asst Chapl St Geo Hosp Lon 66–69; C Waltham *Linc* 69–73; V Nocton 73–86; P-in-c Potter Hanworth 74–86; P-in-c Dunston 77–86; RD Graffoe 81–92; Can and Preb Linc Cathl from 85; V Nocton w Dunston and Potterhanworth 86–92; Bp's Dom Chapl 92–05; Gen Preacher 92–05; rtd 05. *13 Lupin Road, Lincoln LN2 4GB* T: (01522) 536723 M: 07803-123975 E: canrod@hotmail.com

RODGERS, Alasdair Martin. b 75. Lon Bible Coll BA 96 Ches Univ PhD 19. St Jo Coll Nottm 13. **d** 15 **p** 16. C Bebington *Ches* from 15. *22 Woodhey Road, Wirral CH63 8PD* T: 0151-645 8375 M: 07790-270060 E: al@kateandal.com or al@standrewsbebington.org.uk

RODGERS, Eamonn Joseph. b 41. QUB BA 63 PhD 70. TISEC 04. **d** 05 **p** 06. NSM Glas St Ninian 05–12; LtO from 12. *4 Albert Drive, Glasgow G73 3RT* T: 0141-583 6949 M: 07586-302613 E: er8907@ntlworld.com

RODGERS, Preb Frank Ernest. b 46. Tyndale Hall Bris 68. **d** 71 **p** 72. C Madeley *Heref* 71–74; C Littleover *Derby* 74–77; V Clodock and Longtown w Craswell and Llanveyno *Heref* 77–79; P-in-c St Margaret's w Michaelchurch Eskley and Newton 77–79; V Clodock and Longtown w Craswall, Llanveynoe etc 79–10; RD Abbeydore 90–96; Preb Heref Cathl 96–10; rtd 10; PtO *Heref* from 10. *Thorneyglatt Cottage, Didley, Hereford HR2 9DA* T: (01981) 570629

RODGERS, Matthew. b 87. Cliff Coll BA 13. St Mellitus Coll 16. **d** 19. C Linc St Swithin from 19. *6 Ross Close, Lincoln LN2 4WQ* T: (01522) 540180 M: 07476-950414 E: mattrodgers@stswithins.org.uk or matt.rodgers@stswithins.org.uk

RODGERS, Richard Thomas Boycott. b 47. Lon Univ MB, BS 70 FRCS 81. St Jo Coll Nottm. **d** 77 **p** 78. C Littleover *Derby* 77–80; Lect Birm St Martin w Bordesley St Andr 89–90; PtO from 90; rtd 12. *63 Meadow Brook Road, Birmingham B31 1ND* T: 0121-476 0789 E: dick@rodgers.org.uk

RODHAM, The Ven Morris. b 59. Hatf Coll Dur BA 81 St Jo Coll Dur PGCE 85. Trin Coll Bris MA 93. **d** 93 **p** 94. C New Milverton *Cov* 93–97; V Leamington Priors St Mary 97–10; RD Warwick and Leamington 06–09; Adn Missr 10–19; Adn Warwick 10–19; P-in-c Patterdale *Carl* from 19. *The Rectory, Patterdale, Penrith CA11 0NL* M: 07929-861233

RODLEY, Ian Tony. b 48. Open Univ BA 08. Qu Coll Birm 77. **d** 80 **p** 81. C Baildon and Dioc Children's Adv *Bradf* 80–85; V Bradf St Wilfrid Lidget Green 85–90; Chapl to the Deaf 88–90; V Otley 90–98; C Wolverton *Ox* 98–03; TR Bramley *Ripon* 03–13; rtd 13. *4 Beadon Avenue, Huddersfield HD5 8QZ* E: ianrod@clara.co.uk

RODLEY, James William Eric. b 66. SS Hild & Bede Coll Dur BA 86 ACA 89. St Steph Ho Ox BTh 11. **d** 09 **p** 10. C Pokesdown All SS and Bournemouth St Clem *Win* 09–13; P-in-c Harlow St Mary Magd *Chelmsf* 13–18; V from 18; P-in-c N Weald Bassett 13–18. *The Vicarage, 3 Oaklands Drive, Harlow CM17 9BE* T: (01279) 451065 E: jwerodley@yahoo.co.uk

RODRIGUEZ, Luis Mario. b 64. Occidental Coll (USA) BA 86 S California Univ MA 93. St Steph Ho Ox MTh 99. **d** 98 **p** 99. C Battersea Ch Ch and St Steph *S'wark* 98–02; C Pimlico St Pet w Westmr Ch Ch *Lon* 02–05; PtO *S'wark* 07–08; R Hanford USA from 08. *510 N Douty Street, Hanford*

CA 93230, USA T: (001) (559) 584 7706 F: 584 7710 E: luis@smeltern.com

RODRIGUEZ, Miguel. *See* SANCHEZ RODRIGUEZ, Miguel

RODRIGUEZ-VEGLIO, Francis Bonny. b 33. Sarum Th Coll 62. **d** 64 **p** 65. C Alnwick St Paul *Newc* 64–68; V Horton w Piddington *Pet* 68–79; P-in-c Preston Deanery 68–72; P-in-c Wootton w Quinton and Preston Deanery 72–79; CF (ACF) 75–82; TV Is of Scilly *Truro* 79–82; Hon Chapl Miss to Seamen 79–82; PtO *Pet* 86–88; C Leic Ch Sav 88–91; V Kirkwhelpington, Kirkharle, Kirkheaton and Cambo *Newc* 91–95. *Gemacq Cottage, 14 Daventry Road, Norton, Daventry NN11 2ND* T: (01327) 872030 E: francis.andree@tiscali.co.uk or andree@gemacq.co.uk

RODWELL, Barry John. b 39. Birm Univ CertEd 59 Cam Univ DipAdEd 77. Ridley Hall Cam 67. **d** 70 **p** 71. C Sudbury St Greg and St Pet *St E* 70–73; Hd RE Hedingham Sch 73–80; R Sible Hedingham *Chelmsf* 80–85; RE Adv 85–93; V Gt Burstead 93–00; rtd 00; PtO *Nor* 00–07 and from 15. *The Nutshell, 11 Filbert Road, Loddon, Norwich NR14 6LW* T: (01508) 522949

RODWELL, Mrs Helen. b 70. WEMTC. **d** 09 **p** 10. NSM Forest of Dean Ch Ch w English Bicknor *Glouc* 09–16. *The Other House, English Bicknor, Coleford GL16 7PD* T: (01594) 860205 E: rev.rodwell@icloud.com

RODWELL (née VINCENT), Mrs Jacqueline Margaret. b 59. Glos Univ BA 04. WEMTC 01. **d** 04 **p** 05. NSM Cheltenham St Mark *Glouc* 04–08; NSM Cheltenham Em w St Steph 08–09; NSM S Cheltenham 10–14; PtO from 14. *7 Winchester House, Malvern Road, Cheltenham GL50 2NN* E: the.rodwells@blueyonder.co.uk

RODWELL, Canon John Stanley. b 46. Leeds Univ BSc 68 Southn Univ PhD 74. Cuddesdon Coll 71. **d** 74 **p** 75. Hon C Horfield H Trin *Bris* 74–75; Hon C Skerton St Luke *Blackb* 75–77; LtO 77–16; Hon Can Blackb Cathl 03–16; rtd 16; PtO *Blackb* 16–17. *7 Derwent Road, Lancaster LA1 3ES* T: (01524) 62726 E: johnrodwell@tiscali.co.uk

ROE, Mrs Caroline Ruth. b 57. Birm Univ BA 80 PGCE 93. Wycliffe Hall Ox 84. **dss** 84 **d** 87 **p** 96. Olveston *Bris* 84–87; Par Dn 87; NSM Alveley and Quatt *Heref* 87–94; Bp's Voc Officer 90–94; Hon C Loughborough Em and St Mary in Charnwood *Leic* 97–98; C Hathern, Long Whatton and Diseworth w Belton etc 98–00; PtO 01–04; Chapl Univ Hosps Leic NHS Trust 04–07; Lead Chapl 07–13. *4 John's Lee Close, Loughborough LE11 3LN* T: (01509) 260217 or 0116-258 5487 E: roe_caroline@hotmail.com

ROE, Daniel Cameron. b 84. Ball Coll Ox BA 05. Oak Hill Th Coll MTh 10. **d** 10 **p** 11. C Clifton *York* 10–15; PtO from 17. *Shincliffe Hall, Hall Lane, Shincliffe, Durham DH1 2SY* M: 07778-572928 E: daniel.roe@balliol.oxon.org or daniel.c.roe@gmail.com

ROE, Canon Joseph Thorley. b 22. AKC 49 DipAdEd Hull Univ PhD 90. K Coll Lon 46. **d** 50 **p** 51. C Methley *Ripon* 50–53; C Richmond 53–55; V Leeds Gipton Epiphany 55–60; C of E Youth Coun Tr Officer 60–64; Sec Youth Dept BCC 64–67; Prin Lect Bretton Hall Coll Wakef 67–74; Sec for Miss and Unity *Ripon* 74–78; Dioc Missr and Bp's Dom Chapl 75–78; Can Res Carl Cathl 78–82; Dioc Dir of Tr 78–82; Dioc Adult Educn Officer *Wakef* 82–88; Hon Can Wakef Cathl 83–88; Dir Educn 85–88; rtd 88; PtO *Wakef* 88–08. *2 Fosbrook House, 8 Clifton Drive, Lytham St Annes FY8 5RQ* T: (01253) 667032

ROE, Peter Harold. b 37. K Coll Lon BD 62 AKC 62. **d** 63 **p** 64. C Knowle St Barn *Bris* 63–65; C Leckhampton St Pet *Glouc* 65–68; V Shaw Hill *Birm* 68–73; V Hobs Moat 73–90; V Packwood w Hockley Heath 90–99; rtd 99; PtO *Blackb* from 99. *14 Worcester Avenue, Garstang, Preston PR3 1EJ* T: (01995) 605775

ROE, Thorley. *See* ROE, Joseph Thorley

ROEMMELE, Canon Michael Patrick. b 49. TCD BA 72 MA 76. **d** 73 **p** 74. C Portadown St Columba *Arm* 73–77; C Drumachose *D & R* 77–80; Bahrain 79–83; Cyprus 79–83; Chapl RAF 83–00; CF 00–07; I Camus-juxta-Bann *D & R* 07–17; Can Derry Cathl 14–17; rtd 18. *30 Drumrane Road, Limavady BT49 9LB* T: (028) 7776 3554 M: 07977-239863 E: mproemmele@gmail.com

ROESCHLAUB, Robert Friedrich. b 39. Purdue Univ BSc 63. Berkeley Div Sch MDiv 66. **d** 66 **p** 66. USA 66–77; Hon C Tilehurst St Cath *Ox* 78–79; Hon C Tilehurst St Mich 79–82; P-in-c Millom H Trin w Thwaites *Carl* 82–85; P-in-c Millom 85–89; R Dunstall w Rangemore and Tatenhill *Lich* 89–93; rtd 94; PtO *Carl* from 98; *Lich* 02–16. *20 Pannatt Hill, Millom LA18 5DB* T: (01229) 772185 E: hoosier@btconnect.com

ROEST, Wilma. b 62. Utrecht Univ MA 88 Roehampton Inst PGCE 92. SEITE 96. **d** 99 **p** 00. C Merton St Mary *S'wark* 99–02; TV N Lambeth 02–06; P-in-c Balham St Mary and St Jo 06–10; V 10–16; AD Tooting 09–16; TR Richmond

St Mary w St Matthias and St Jo from 16. *The Vicarage, Ormond Road, Richmond TW10 6TH*   T: (020) 8940 0362 E: rector@richmondteamministry.org

ROFF, Andrew Martin. b 42. Bede Coll Dur BSc 65. Westcott Ho Cam 65. **d** 70 **p** 71. C Ches St Mary 70–73; Min Can Blackb Cathl 73–76; P-in-c Blackb St Jo 74–75; V Longton 76–81; Chapl Trin Coll Glenalmond 82–83; R Allendale w Whitfield *Newc* 83–92; V Gosforth St Nic 92–97; Dioc Supernumerary *Mor* 01–07; LtO from 08. *Rowan Glen, Upper Braefindon, Culbokie, Dingwall IV7 8GY*   T: (01349) 877762 E: martin@roff-rowanglen.co.uk

ROFF, Canon John Michael. b 47. St Chad's Coll Dur BSc 69. Westcott Ho Cam 70. **d** 72 **p** 73. C Lancaster St Mary *Blackb* 72–75; C Dronfield *Derby* 75–76; TV 76–80; TR N Wingfield, Pilsley and Tupton 80–85; V Ilkeston St Mary 85–90; V Stockport St Geo *Ches* 90–94; TR Stockport SW 94–00; RD Stockport 95–00; Dioc Ecum Officer 92–99; Hon Can Ches Cathl 98–00; Can Res Ches Cathl 00–04; rtd 04; PtO *Ches* 05–06; *Blackb* from 05. *12 Westbourne Road, Lancaster LA1 5DB*   T: (01524) 841621 E: roff@roff.org.uk

ROGAN, Canon John. b 28. St Jo Coll Dur BA 49 MA 51 Open Univ BPhil 81. **d** 54 **p** 55. C Ashton St Mich *Man* 54–57; C Sharrow St Andr *Sheff* 57–61; Ind Chapl 57–61; Sec C of E Ind Cttee 61–66; V Leigh St Mary *Man* 66–78; RD Leigh 71–78; Hon Can Man Cathl 75–78; Provost St Paul's Cathl Dundee *Bre* 78–83; R Dundee St Paul 78–83; Soc Resp Adv *Bris* 83–93; Can Res Bris Cathl 83–93; rtd 93; PtO *Bris* from 93. *84 Concorde Drive, Bristol BS10 6PX*   T: 0117-950 5803 E: john.j.rogan@btinternet.com

ROGERS, Anne Frances. *See* ILSLEY, Anne Frances

ROGERS, Brian Victor. b 50. Trin Coll Bris 75. **d** 78 **p** 79. C Plumstead St Jo w St Jas and St Paul *S'wark* 78–83; P-in-c Gayton *Nor* 83–85; P-in-c Gayton Thorpe w E Walton 83–85; P-in-c Westacre 83–85; P-in-c Ashwicken w Leziate 83–85; R Gayton Gp of Par 85–91; R Rackheath and Salhouse 91–96; P-in-c Warmington, Tansor, Cotterstock and Fotheringhay *Pet* 96–97; V Warmington, Tansor and Cotterstock etc 97–15; rtd 15. *Gortatlea, Mastergeehy, Killarney, Kerry, Republic of Ireland* E: bvictorr@hotmail.co.uk

ROGERS, Christopher Antony. b 47. NOC 79. **d** 81 **p** 82. C Chesterfield SS Aug *Derby* 81–84; C Chaddesden St Phil 84–86; R Whitwell 86–95; V W Burnley All SS *Blackb* 95–01; V Ashford St Hilda *Lon* 01–17; rtd 17; PtO *Lon* from 17; *St Alb* from 17. *17 Lochnell Road, Northchurch, Berkhamsted HP4 3QD*   M: 07931-685100 E: chris1947rogers@gmail.com

ROGERS, Christopher Ian. b 79. Trin Coll Bris BA 01. K Coll Lon MA 05. **d** 07 **p** 08. NSM Roxeth *Lon* 07–10; C Shadwell St Paul w Ratcliffe St Jas from 10; C Bromley by Bow All Hallows 10–14; P-in-c 14–15; R from 15. *All Hallows' Rectory, Devons Road, London E3 3PN*   T: (020) 7538 9756   M: 07974-371418 E: revcrisrogers@me.com

ROGERS, Christopher Thomas Augustine. b 80. CCC Cam MA 06 K Coll Lon MA 13 Barrister-at-Law 04. Westcott Ho Cam 15. **d** 18 **p** 19. Dep Chan *Ox* from 16; C Catford (Southend) and Downham *S'wark* from 18. *59 Southend Lane, London SE6 3AA*   M: 07720-912410 E: frchristopherrogers@outlook.com

ROGERS, Clive Trevor Thorne. b 49. SAOMC 02. **d** 05 **p** 06. NSM Beaconsfield *Ox* 05–10; PtO *Ex* from 11. *Leeward House, West Charleton, Kingsbridge TQ7 2AB* E: clive_rogers@btinternet.com

ROGERS, Canon Clive William. b 62. Selw Coll Cam BA 83 MA 87 MEng 83 Southn Univ BTh 90. Chich Th Coll 87. **d** 90 **p** 91. C Leic St Aid 90–93; P-in-c Ryhall w Essendine *Pet* 93–94; LtO *Ely* 94–03; PtO 03–04; LtO *Sarum* 04–06; Hon C Forest and Avon from 06; Can and Preb Sarum Cathl from 17. *4 The Sidings, Downton, Salisbury SP5 3QZ*   T: (01725) 512141 E: bill@billrogers.info

ROGERS, Cyril David. b 55. Birm Univ BA 76 BTheol. Sarum & Wells Th Coll 80. **d** 83 **p** 84. C Leagrave *St Alb* 83–87; TV Langtree *Ox* 87–97; R Ballaugh *S & M* 97–12; V Michael 97–12; R Andreas, Ballaugh, Jurby and Sulby 12–16; RD Ramsey 12; Hon Can St German's Cathl 12–16; rtd 16; PtO *Win* from 17. *23 Chantry Mews, Basingstoke RG22 4UE*   T: (01256) 359827 E: cdr851392@gmail.com

ROGERS, Damon. b 66. Cov Univ BEng 92 Wolv Univ PGCE 94 Warwick Univ BPhil 02. Cranmer Hall Dur 01. **d** 03 **p** 04. C Heigham St Thos *Nor* 03–06; R Freethorpe, Wickhampton, Halvergate etc 06–13; V Lowestoft St Andr from 13; Jt RD Lothingland from 18. *51 Beresford Road, Lowestoft NR32 2NQ*   T: (01502) 511521 E: damon.rogers@romanhill.org.uk

ROGERS, David Alan. b 55. City of Lon Poly BA 77 MCIT 82. Linc Th Coll 88. **d** 90 **p** 91. C Kingston upon Hull St Nic *York* 90–93; P-in-c Kingston upon Hull St Mary 93–96; N Humberside Ind Chapl 93–02; Dir Leeds Ch Inst *Ripon*

02–04; Chief Officer Hull Coun for Voluntary Service 04–12; TR Marfleet *York* from 12. *33 Carden Avenue, Hull HU9 4RT*

ROGERS, The Ven David Arthur. b 21. Ch Coll Cam BA 47 MA 52. Ridley Hall Cam 47. **d** 49 **p** 50. C Stockport St Geo *Ches* 49–53; R Levenshulme St Pet *Man* 53–59; V Sedbergh *Bradf* 59–74; P-in-c Cautley w Dowbiggin 59–60; V 60–74; P-in-c Garsdale 59–60; V 60–74; V Sedbergh, Cautley and Garsdale 74–79; P-in-c Firbank, Howgill and Killington 73–77; RD Sedbergh 59–73; RD Ewecross 73–77; Hon Can Bradf Cathl 67–77; Adn Craven 77–86; rtd 86; Lic to Offic *Bradf* 86–06; PtO *Blackb* 87–06; *Carl* 89–06; *St Alb* from 07. *18 Sharnbrook House, High Street, Sharnbrook, Bedford MK44 1PB*   T: (01234) 782650

ROGERS, David Barrie. b 46. S Dios Minl Tr Scheme 89. **d** 93. NSM Old Alresford and Bighton *Win* 93–96; Dep Warden Dioc Retreat Ho (Holland Ho) Cropthorne *Worc* 96–98; Warden Stacklands Retreat Ho W Kingsdown 98–03; Hon C Kingsdown *Roch* 98–03; Warden St Pet Bourne Cen 03–13; rtd 13. *16 Quay Road, Newton Abbott TQ12 2BU* E: adecon.dr@gmail.com

ROGERS, Mrs Gail. b 77. Qu Foundn Birm 16. **d** 18 **p** 19. C Bournville *Birm* from 18. *117 Sellywood Road, Birmingham B30 1XA*   T: 0121-243 2199   M: 07941-765727 E: gailrogers26@outlook.com

ROGERS, Canon George Hutchinson. b 51. Windsor Univ Ontario BSW 75. Wycliffe Coll Toronto MDiv 78. **d** 78 **p** 78. C Victoria St Matthias Canada 78–81; R Cobble Hill and Cowichan Station 81–86; I Vancouver St Matthias 86–97; Hon C Vancouver St Helen 97–98; C Tonbridge SS Pet and Paul *Roch* 99–03; V Werrington *Pet* from 03; Can Pet Cathl from 18. *The Vicarage, 51 The Green, Werrington, Peterborough PE4 6RT*   T: (01733) 571649 E: george@revgeorgerogers.plus.com

ROGERS, George Michael Andrew. b 69. Yale Div Sch MDiv 95. **d** 99 **p** 99. C Brant Lake St Paul USA 99–00; C New York St Thos 00–03; C Pelham Ch Ch 03–10; C Staines *Lon* 10–13; P-in-c Milton next Sittingbourne *Cant* 13–16; P-in-c Murston w Bapchild and Tonge 13–16; V Milton Regis w Murston, Bapchild and Tonge from 16. *The Vicarage, Vicarage Road, Sittingbourne ME10 2BL*   T: (01795) 472016   M: 07527-746060 E: george.rogers3@gmail.com

ROGERS, Jane. *See* LISVANE, Constance Jane

ROGERS, John. b 61. St Jo Coll Nottm 03. **d** 05 **p** 06. C Otley *Bradf* 05–08; V Oakworth 08–14; *Leeds* 14–19; V Meanwood from 19. *15 Parkside Green, Leeds LS6 4NY* E: john.rogers@leeds.anglican.org

ROGERS, John Arthur. b 47. MBIM. Edin Dioc NSM Course 90. **d** 92. C Middlesbrough St Martin *York* 92–93; NSM The Trimdons *Dur* 00–05; NSM Upper Skerne 05–07; R Tilehurst St Mich *Ox* 07–17; rtd 17; PtO *B & W* from 18. *Bow Cottage, Selworthy Green, Selworthy, Minehead TA24 8TP*   T: (01643) 863100 E: rogj8@aol.com

ROGERS, John Howard. b 47. Ripon Coll Cuddesdon. **d** 09 **p** 09. NSM Southgate Ch Ch *Lon* 09–12; NSM Highgate All SS from 12; NSM Highgate St Mich from 12. *48 Twisden Road, London NW5 1DN*   T: (020) 7485 6376 E: hrogers442@aol.com

ROGERS, John Robin. b 36. St Alb Minl Tr Scheme 78. **d** 81 **p** 82. NSM Digswell and Panshanger *St Alb* 81–84; C Welwyn w Ayot St Peter 85–92; R Wilden w Colmworth and Ravensden 92–99; rtd 99; PtO *St Alb* 99–02; *Heref* from 03. *37 The Birches, Shobdon, Leominster HR6 9NG*   T: (01568) 708903

ROGERS, Canon Kathleen. b 56. Open Univ BA 93 Leeds Univ BA 07. NOC 04. **d** 07 **p** 08. Sen Resources Officer *Liv* 93–09; NSM Formby H Trin 07–09; C 09–12; P-in-c Thornton and Crosby 12–13; V from 13; Hon Can Liv Cathl from 19. *The Rectory, Water Street, Thornton, Liverpool L23 1TB*   T: 0151-931 4676

ROGERS, Canon Kathleen Anne. b 54. **d** 08 **p** 09. C Machynlleth w Llanwrin and Penegoes *Ban* 08–11; P-in-c 11–12; P-in-c Machynlleth w Corris w Llanwrin and Penegoes 12–14; P-in-c Bro Cyfeiliog and Mawddwy 14–18; rtd 18; PtO *Ban* from 18. *30 Tregarth, Machynlleth SY20 8HU*   T: (01654) 702961 E: kathleenrogers@hotmail.co.uk

ROGERS, Kevin. b 62. Ridley Hall Cam 13. **d** 15 **p** 16. C Parkstone St Luke *Sarum* 15–19; R Abbas and Templecombe, Henstridge and Horsington *B & W* from 19. *The Vicarage, Church Street, Henstridge, Templecombe BA8 0QE*   M: 07979-932241 E: revkrogers@gmail.com

ROGERS, Leon James. b 83. St Andr Univ MTheol 06. Qu Coll Birm MA 09. **d** 09 **p** 10. C E Darlington *Dur* 09–12; P-in-c Hartlepool St Aid and St Columba 12–17; R Creston Ch Ch Canada from 17. *430 7th Avenue North, Creston BC V0B 1G4, Canada*   T: (001) (250) 428 4248   M: 07714-354771 E: lnrgrs@gmail.com

ROGERS, Canon Llewelyn. Univ of Wales (Lamp) BA 59. St Mich Coll Llan. **d** 61 **p** 62. C Holywell *St As* 61–64; C Hawarden 64–70; R Bodfari 70–73; V Rhosymedre 73–78; V Llansantffraid-ym-Mechain 77–83; V Llansantffraid-ym-Mechain and Llanfechain 83–98; RD Llanfyllin 84–88; V Pont Robert, Pont Dolanog, Garthbeibio etc 98–01; Can St As Cathl 98–01; rtd 01; PtO *Lich* from 02; *St As* from 09. *17 Orchard Green, Llanymynech SY22 6PJ* T: (01691) 839920

ROGERS, Mrs Lynne Rosemary. b 49. CITC 00. **d** 03 **p** 04. Aux Min Ferns w Kilbride, Toombe, Kilcormack etc *C & O* 03–06; Aux Min Gorey w Kilnahue, Leskinfere and Ballycanew 06–07; P-in-c New w Old Ross, Whitechurch, Fethard etc 07–11; NSM Chartham *Cant* 11–14; NSM Stone Street Gp 11–14; C Chartham and Upper Hardres w Stelling 14–16; rtd 16; PtO *Sarum* from 17. *1 Boyte Road, Pimperne, Blandford Forum DT11 8UY* T: (01258) 456202 E: lynnerogers123@gmail.com

ROGERS, Malcolm Dawson. b 63. SS Hild & Bede Coll Dur BA 84 Selw Coll Cam BA 88. Ridley Hall Cam 86. **d** 89 **p** 90. C Ipswich St Jo *St E* 89–93; CMS Russia 93–95; C Holloway St Mary Magd *Lon* 95–97; V 97–05; V Bury St Edmunds St Mary *St E* 05–17; Hon Can St E Cathl 13–17; Chapl Moscow *Eur* from 17. *8/5 Voznesensky Pereulok, Moscow 125009, Russia* T: (007) (495) 629 0990 E: malcolm.d.rogers@gmail.com

ROGERS, Canon Malcolm Kenneth. b 72. Liv Inst of Educn BA 93. St Jo Coll Nottm MA 95 LTh 96. **d** 96 **p** 97. C W Derby St Luke *Liv* 96–00; V Huyton Quarry from 00; AD Huyton from 18; Hon Can Liv Cathl from 13. *St Gabriel's Vicarage, 2 St Agnes Road, Huyton, Liverpool L36 5TA* T: 0151-489 2688 E: malcolm.rogers@huytondeanery.org

ROGERS, Mark James. b 64. Univ of Wales (Lamp) BA. Qu Coll Birm. **d** 89 **p** 90. C Dudley St Aug Holly Hall *Worc* 89–93; C Worc St Barn w Ch Ch 93–94; TV 94–97; USPG Belize 97–00; R Montreal St Columba Canada from 00. *4020 Hingston Avenue, Montreal QC H4A 2J7, Canada* T: (001) (514) 486 1753 E: mrogers@montreal.anglican.ca

ROGERS, Martin Brian. b 53. **d** 92 **p** 93. OLM Collyhurst *Man* from 92. *8 Greenford Road, Crumpsall, Manchester M8 0NW* T: 0161-740 4614 E: m.rogers17@ntlworld.com

ROGERS, Michael Andrew. b 47. FRAeS 96. Ripon Coll Cuddesdon. **d** 01 **p** 02. C Bromsgrove St Jo *Worc* 01–04; R Berrow w Pendock, Eldersfield, Hollybush etc 04–13; rtd 13; PtO *Ches* from 14. *York House, Wyche Lane, Bunbury, Tarporley CW6 9PD* T: (01829) 261682 E: mandmrogers@btinternet.com

ROGERS, Michael Ernest. b 34. Sarum & Wells Th Coll 83. **d** 85 **p** 86. C Roehampton H Trin *S'wark* 85–88; V Ryhill *Wakef* 88–94; V S Elmsall 94–00; rtd 00; PtO *Derby* from 00. *The Willows, 49 Main Street, Weston-on-Trent, Derby DE72 2BL* T: (01332) 706654 E: michaelrogers1398@gmail.com

ROGERS, Michael Hugh Walton. b 52. K Coll Lon BD 73 AKC 73. St Aug Coll Cant 74. **d** 75 **p** 76. C Eastbourne St Andr *Chich* 75–78; C Uppingham w Ayston *Pet* 78–82; V Eye 82–90; R Cottesmore and Barrow w Ashwell and Burley 90–04; C 04–09; C Greetham and Thistleton w Stretton and Clipsham 01–05; P-in-c 05–09; C Empingham and Exton w Horn w Whitwell 06–09; RD Rutland 95–00; Can Pet Cathl 01–09; Bp's Adv for Min of Healing 05–09; P-in-c Ilfracombe SS Phil and Jas w W Down *Ex* 09–15; R Ilfracombe SS Phil and Jas 15–18; rtd 18. *7 Meadow Park, Molland, South Molton EX36 3ND* E: mhwrogers76@gmail.com

ROGERS, Mrs Patricia Anne. b 54. Lon Univ BD. Trin Coll Bris. **d** 87 **p** 94. Hon C Gayton Gp of Par *Nor* 87–91; Hon C Rackheath and Salhouse 91–96; Chapl to the Deaf 91–96; Chapl to the Deaf *Pet* 96–00; Visual Communications 00–11; TR Binsey *Carl* 11–19; Disability Adv from 19; C Beacon from 19. *Church House, 19-24 Friargate, Penrith CA11 7XR* T: (01768) 807777

ROGERS, Patricia Gladys Sylvia. b 48. **d** 13 **p** 14. NSM Llanrhian and Mathry w Grandstone etc *St D* 13–14; NSM Letterston w Llanfair Nant-y-Gof etc 14–18. Crud *yr Awel, Wolfscastle, Haverfordwest SA62 5LT* T: (01437) 741338 E: raprogers@btinternet.com *or* parishoffice@stgileslet.plus.com

ROGERS, Pauline Ann. See GODFREY, Pauline Ann

ROGERS, Philip John. b 52. Univ of Wales CertEd 74 Nottm Univ BTh 79. St Jo Coll Nottm 76. **d** 79 **p** 80. C Stretford St Bride *Man* 79–84; P-in-c Plumstead St Jo w St Jas and St Paul *S'wark* 84–85; V from 85. *St John's Vicarage, 176 Griffin Road, London SE18 7QA* T: (020) 8855 1827 E: philipjrogers@ukonline.co.uk

ROGERS (née GOLDER), Mrs Rebecca Marie (Beki). b 71. Brunel Univ BA 94. Trin Coll Bris BA 02. **d** 02 **p** 03. C Short Heath *Birm* 02–05; Dir Faith Willesden Area *Lon* from 05;

NSM Roxeth 05–10; NSM Bromley by Bow All Hallows from 10; Prin St Edm Course from 18; Dir Lon Cen for Spiritual Direction from 19. *All Hallows' Rectory, Devons Road, London E3 3PN* T: (020) 7538 9756 E: bekirogers@gmail.com *or* beki.rogers@london.anglican.org

ROGERS, Richard Anthony. b 46. Ex Coll Ox BA 69. Qu Coll Birm 70. **d** 71 **p** 72. C Shirley *Birm* 71–74; Chapl Solihull Sch 74–78; Hon C Cotteridge *Birm* 78–84; Hon C Hill 84–93; Hd RE Kings Norton Girls' Sch 93–05; rtd 05; PtO *Birm* 93–07. *4 Byron House, Belwell Place, Sutton Coldfield B74 4AY* T: 0121-308 0310

ROGERS, Canon Robert. b 42. Bernard Gilpin Soc Dur 66 St Aid Birkenhead 67 Ridley Hall Cam 69. **d** 70 **p** 71. C Childwall St Dav *Liv* 70–73; C Huntington *York* 73–76; TR Brayton 76–89; RD Selby 84–89; V New Malton 89–98; RD Bulmer and Malton 97–98; Asst Chapl York Health Services NHS Trust 98–99; Sen Chapl York Hosps NHS Foundn Trust 99–08; Can and Preb York Minster 03–08; rtd 08; PtO *York* from 08. *Tabgha, 9 Middlecave Drive, Malton YO17 7BB* T: (01653) 699469 E: bob.jacqui@btinternet.com

ROGERS, Robert Charles. b 55. St Pet Coll Birm CertEd 77 Warwick Univ MA 99. St Jo Coll Nottm 87. **d** 89 **p** 90. C Wellesbourne *Cov* 89–93; R Bourton w Frankton and Stretton on Dunsmore etc 93–97; Behaviour Support Teacher Warks LEA from 98; LtO *Cov* 98–07; NSM Rugby 07–13; NSM Rugby St Andr from 13. *18 Waring Way, Dunchurch, Rugby CV22 6PH* T: (01788) 817361 E: rob.rogers@talktalk.net

ROGERS, Robin. See ROGERS, John Robin

ROGERS, Ryder Rondeau. b 44. Lon Bible Coll 62. **d** 08 **p** 08. In Bapt Min 68–04; NSM Bride Valley *Sarum* 08–16; PtO from 16. *Stonehaven, 25 Bindbarrow Road, Burton Bradstock, Bridport DT6 4RG* T: (01308) 897780

ROGERS, Ms Sally Jean. b 54. Univ of Wales (Lamp) BA 77 Nottm Univ BTh 87. Linc Th Coll 84. **d** 87 **p** 94. Par Dn Bris St Mary Redcliffe w Temple etc 87–90; Par Dn Greenford H Cross *Lon* 90–94; C 94–96; TV Hemel Hempstead *St Alb* 96–02; Development Worker Changing Attitude 03–06; Chapl R Holloway and Bedf New Coll *Guildf* 06–10; R Petryal and Betws yn Rhos *St As* 10–16; TV Aled Miss Area 17–18; rtd 18. *1 Warren Road, Deganwy, Conwy LL31 9SU*

ROGERS, Sarah Ann. b 73. York Univ BSc 94 Univ of Wales (Cardiff) PhD 98. St Mich Coll Llan BA 09. **d** 09 **p** 10. C Caerphilly *Llan* 09–12; P-in-c Abercynon 12–17; Dom Chapl Bp Llan from 17. *The Maisonette, Pendinas, The Cathedral Green, Cardiff CF5 2EB* T: (029) 2056 2400 E: sarahrogers@churchinwales.org.uk

ROGERS, Timothy Harold. b 73. SS Hild & Bede Coll Dur BSc 95. Ridley Hall Cam 14. **d** 16 **p** 17. NSM Redenhall w Scole *Nor* from 16. *50 Harvest Way, Harleston IP20 9GD* M: 07887-352564 E: timrogers197@gmail.com

ROGERS, Canon Valentine Hilary. b 48. UCD BA 68. St Columban's Coll Navan 65. **d** 71 **p** 72. C Dandenong Australia 88–89; P-in-c Eltham 89–92; I 92–96; C Dublin Ch Ch Cathl Gp and PV Ch Ch Cathl Dublin *D & G* 96–97; I Armadale H Advent Australia 98–09; I Aughaval w Achill, Knappagh, Dugort etc *T, K & A* from 09; Can Tuam Cathl from 14; Can Killala Cathl from 14. *The Rectory, Newport Road, Westport, Co Mayo, Republic of Ireland* T: (00353) (98) 25127 M: 87-147 5597 E: valandjorogers@gmail.com

ROGERS, William. See ROGERS, Clive William

ROGERSON, Anthony Carroll. b 37. Trin Coll Ox BA 59 MA 63 MCIPD 92. SAOMC 96. **d** 98 **p** 99. NSM Radley and Sunningwell *Ox* 98–02; PtO from 02. *9 Selwyn Crescent, Radley, Abingdon OX14 3AW* T: (01235) 550214 E: tonylrogerson@gmail.com

✠**ROGERSON, The Rt Revd Barry.** b 36. Leeds Univ BA 60 Bris Univ Hon LLD 93. Wells Th Coll 60. **d** 62 **p** 63 **c** 79. C S Shields St Hilda w St Thos *Dur* 62–65; C Bishopwearmouth St Nic 65–67; Lect Lich Th Coll 67–71; Vice-Prin 71–72; Lect Sarum & Wells Th Coll 72–74; V Wednesfield St Thos *Lich* 75–79; TR Wednesfield 79; Suff Bp Wolverhampton 79–85; Bp Bris 85–02; rtd 02; Hon Asst Bp B & W from 03. *Flat 2, 30 Albert Road, Clevedon BS21 7RR* T: (01275) 541964 E: barry.rogerson@blueyonder.co.uk

ROGERSON, Colin Scott. b 30. St Andr Univ MA 55. Edin Th Coll. **d** 57 **p** 58. C Byker St Ant *Newc* 57–59; C Newc St Geo 59–63; C Wooler 63–67; V Tynemouth St Aug 67–75; C Dur St Marg 75–88; P-in-c Hebburn St Jo 88–95; rtd 95; PtO *Dur* 95–17. *6 Edlingham Road, Durham DH1 5YS* T: 0191-386 1956

ROGERSON, Canon Ian Matthew. b 45. Bede Coll Dur CertEd 67 Open Univ BA 76. Oak Hill Th Coll. **d** 83 **p** 84. C Haughton St Mary *Man* 83–86; V Ramsbottom St Andr 86–05; P-in-c Edenfield and Stubbins 04–05; TR Ramsbottom and Edenfield 05–10; AD Bury 96–05; Hon Can Man Cathl 04–10; rtd 10; PtO *Man* 10–14; *St D* from 10; *Llan* from

17. *16 Heol Erwin, Cardiff CF14 6QP* T: (029) 2062 1849
E: ian@rogerson.org.uk

ROLAND, Andrew Osborne. b 45. Mert Coll Ox BA 66 St Jo Coll Dur BA 84. Cranmer Hall Dur. **d** 84 **p** 85. C Streatham St Leon *S'wark* 84–87; C Kingston All SS w St Jo 87–94; P-in-c Hackbridge and Beddington Corner 94–06; V 06–15; rtd 15; PtO *Lon* from 16. *Flat 2, 100 Philbeach Gardens, London SW5 9ET* T: (020) 7370 7431 E: aoroland@gmail.com

ROLES, John William. b 54. Middx Poly BA 76 Whitelands Coll Lon PGCE 77. Ripon Coll Cuddesdon 11. **d** 12 **p** 13. NSM Ilfracombe, Lee, Woolacombe, Bittadon etc *Ex* 12–16; P-in-c from 16. *The New Vicarage, St Brannock's Road, Ilfracombe EX34 8EG* E: johnroles@talk21.com

ROLFE, Charles Edward. b 34. Wells Th Coll 68. **d** 70 **p** 71. C Bath Twerton-on-Avon *B & W* 70–79; TV Wellington and Distr 79–85; P-in-c Frome Ch Ch 85–89; V 89–94; Chapl Victoria Hosp Frome 85–94; Chapl St Adhelm's Hosp Frome 88–94; rtd 94; NSM Fordingbridge and Breamore and Hale etc *Win* 95–05; PtO 05–19; *Sarum* from 14. *29 Ayleswade Road, Salisbury SP2 8DW* T: (01722) 335601 E: chas.rolfe34@yahoo.com

ROLFE, Joseph William. b 37. Qu Coll Birm 78. **d** 81 **p** 82. NSM Tredington and Darlingscott w Newbold on Stour *Cov* 81–91; NSM Brailes from 91; NSM Sutton under Brailes from 91; NSM Shipston Deanery from 98. *35 Manor Lane, Shipston-on-Stour CV36 4EF* T: (01608) 661737

ROLFE, Paul Douglas. b 46. MIBC 90. NOC 90. **d** 93 **p** 94. C Urmston *Man* 93–96; V Lawton Moor 96–03; P-in-c Burnage St Nic 03–07; Sen Chapl Costa Blanca *Eur* 07–08; P-in-c Mellor *Blackb* 09–11; P-in-c Balderstone 09–11; rtd 12; PtO *Leeds* from 17. *51A Westfield Lane, Scholes, Cleckheaton BD19 6DR* T: (01274) 690476 E: paul.d.rolfe@btinternet.com

ROLFE, Mrs Susan Margaret. b 58. Man Univ BA 81. ERMC 05. **d** 08 **p** 09. NSM Pet Ch Carpenter 08–11; NSM Paston 11–12; NSM Pet St Paul 13; rtd 13; Hon C Wellingborough St Mark *Pet* 15–17; PtO from 17. *1 Woodfield Road, Peterborough PE3 6HD* T: (01733) 567509 E: susan.m.rolfe@btinternet.com

ROLLETT, Robert Henry. b 39. Leeds Univ BA 61 Leic Univ CertEd 62. Linc Th Coll 77. **d** 79 **p** 80. C Littleport *Ely* 79–82; P-in-c Manea 82–83; V 83–85; P-in-c Wimblington 82–83; R 83–85; V Thorney Abbey 85–93; P-in-c The Ramseys and Upwood 93–94; TR 94–99; rtd 99; P-in-c Scalford w Goadby Marwood and Wycombe etc *Leic* 99–00; PtO *Pet* 01–05. *2 Stockerston Crescent, Uppingham, Oakham LE15 9UB* T: (01572) 823685 E: r.rollett@btinternet.com

ROLLINGS, Mrs Tina Petula. b 51. St Mellitus Coll 12. **d** 13 **p** 14. OLM Chingford SS Pet and Paul *Chelmsf* 13–17; PtO 17–18; Ox from 18. *29 Lavender View, Witney OX28 1EH* T: (01993) 210054 E: tinaprollings@aol.com

ROLLINS, David. b 65. De Montfort Univ BA 98. St Steph Ho Ox 99. **d** 01 **p** 02. C Leic St Aid 01–05; P-in-c Corringham *Chelmsf* 05–10; P-in-c Fobbing 05–10; R Corringham and Fobbing from 10. *The Rectory, Church Road, Corringham, Stanford-le-Hope SS17 9AP* T: (01375) 673074 E: drollins@btinternet.com

ROLLINS, Deborah Mary Rollins. See FLACH, Deborah Mary Rollins

ROLLS (née Jobling), Mary. b 77. Aachen University BPharm 99 Derby Univ MSc 03. Cranmer Hall Dur 13. **d** 15 **p** 16. C Cayton w Eastfield *York* 15–17; C Eastfield 17–19; 20s-40s Team Ldr from 19. *6 Turkhan Close, Thirsk YO7 1GA* E: maryjobling@hotmail.com

ROLLS, Miss Pamela Margaret. b 59. **d** 10 **p** 11. OLM Harwell w Chilton *Ox* from 10. *15 Elderfield Crescent, Chilton, Didcot OX11 0RY* T: (01235) 834475 E: pamrolls@tiscali.co.uk

ROLLS, Peter. b 40. Leeds Inst of Educn CertEd. NOC 80. **d** 83 **p** 84. NSM Meltham *Wakef* 83–14; *Leeds* from 14. *14 Heather Road, Meltham, Huddersfield HD7 3EY* T: (01484) 340342 E: p.c.rolls@hotmail.com

ROLT (formerly SHARPLES), Mrs Jean. b 37. Padgate Coll of Educn TCert 58. **d** 04 **p** 05. NSM Gerrans w St Anthony-in-Roseland and Philleigh *Truro* 04–08; NSM St Just-in-Roseland and St Mawes 05–08; rtd 08; PtO *Truro* from 14. *Tregear Vean Farmhouse, St Mawes, Truro TR2 5AB* T: (01326) 270954 M: 07840-567933 E: revjeanrolt@mac.com

ROLTON, Patrick Hugh. b 49. Sarum & Wells Th Coll 72. **d** 74 **p** 75. C Roch 74–79; C Edenbridge 79–81; R N Cray 81–97; rtd 97. *71 The Grove, Sidcup DA14 5NG* E: pcrolton@virginmedia.com

ROMANIS, Adam John Aidan. b 57. Pemb Coll Ox BA 78 MA 83. Westcott Ho Cam 81. **d** 84 **p** 85. C Northfield *Birm* 84–88; TV Seaton Hirst *Newc* 88–93; V Newc Ch Ch w St Ann 93–99; V Cowley St Jo *Ox* 99–14; V Perry Beeches *Birm* from 14. *St Matthew's Vicarage, 313*

Beeches Road, Birmingham B42 2QR* T: 0121-360 2100 E: adam.romanis@btinternet.com

RONCHETTI, Quentin Marcus. b 56. Ripon Coll Cuddesdon 79. **d** 80 **p** 81. C Eastbourne St Mary *Chich* 80–83; C Moulsecoomb 83–85; TV 85–90; V Findon Valley 90–97; V Shoreham Beach 97–07; V Midhurst 07–12; Chapl Costa Blanca *Eur* 12–15; Sen Chapl from 15. *Partida Cuxarret 20C, 03710 Calpe (Alicante), Spain* T: (0034) 965 874 166 *or* 603 259 769 E: marcusronchetti@yahoo.co.uk

ROOKE, James Templeman. b 43. Saltley Tr Coll Birm CertEd 65. EMMTC 79. **d** 84 **p** 85. NSM Bassingham *Linc* 84–89; NSM Hykeham 89–94; Sub Chapl HM Pris Morton Hall 94; P-in-c Borrowdale *Carl* 94–97; Chapl Keswick Sch 94–95; NSM Hykeham *Linc* 97–02; Sub Chapl HM Pris Morton Hall 97–00; CF (ACF) 00–08; NSM Swinderby *Linc* from 02. *The Chestnuts, Main Street, Norton Disney, Lincoln LN6 9JU* T: (01522) 788315 E: jim.rooke@lincoln.anglican.org

✠**ROOKE, The Rt Revd Patrick William.** b 55. Open Univ BA 85 TCD MPhil 04. Sarum & Wells Th Coll 75. **d** 78 **p** 79 **c** 11. C Mossley *Conn* 78–81; C Ballywillan 81–83; I Craigs w Dunaghy and Killagan 83–88; I Ballymore *Arm* 88–94; Asst Prov and Dioc Registrar 92–94; Hon V Choral Arm Cathl 93–94; I Agherton *Conn* 94–06; Preb and Can Conn Cathl 01–06; Adn Dalriada 05–06; Dean Arm and Keeper of Public Lib 06–11; Bp T, K & A from 11. *Bishop's House, Breaffy Woods, Castlebar, Co Mayo , Republic of Ireland* T: (00353) (94) 903 5703 E: bishop@tuam.anglican.org *or* rooke59@hotmail.com

ROOKWOOD (née TASH), Elizabeth. b 82. Leeds Univ BA 05. Cranmer Hall Dur 12. **d** 15 **p** 16. C Morpeth *Newc* 15–19; Bp's Adv for Pioneer Min from 19. *1 Barns Farm, Netherwitton, Morpeth NE61 4NW* M: 07793-964392

ROOMS (née JONES), Canon Karen Sheila Frances. b 61. Bris Univ BA 82. St Jo Coll Nottm MTh 06. **d** 06 **p** 07. C Hyson Green and Forest Fields *S'well* 06–09; P-in-c Nottingham St Ann w Em 09–11; V 11–16; AD Nottm S 13–16; Can Res Leic Cathl from 16; C Leic H Spirit from 16; Women's Min Enabler from 19. *St Andrew's Church Vicarage, 53B Jarrom Street, Leicester LE2 7DH* T: 0116-261 5389 M: 07906-899611 E: roomskaren@gmail.com *or* karen.rooms@leccofe.org

ROOMS, Canon Nigel James. b 60. Leeds Univ BSc 81 Nottm Univ MA 95 Birm Univ ThD 08 CEng 86 MIChemE 86. St Jo Coll Nottm 87. **d** 90 **p** 91. C Chell *Lich* 90–94; Min Moshi St Marg Tanzania 94–01; Dir Th Educn by Ext 94–01; Hon Can Arusha from 01; Dioc Dir of Tr *S'well* 02–07; Assoc Dir Practical Th 07–10; P-in-c Basford St Leodegarius 07–09; Dir Min and Miss 10–16; C Bestwood Park w Rise Park 10–16; Ldr Partnership for Missional Ch UK CMS from 16; NSM Braunstone Park *Leic* from 16. *St Andrew's Church Vicarage, 53B Jarrom Street, Leicester LE2 7DH* M: 07920-292956 E: nigel.rooms@churchmissionsociety.org

ROONEY, Andrew John. b 59. Univ Coll Ox MA 81. St Mellitus Coll BA 15. **d** 15 **p** 16. NSM Hammersmith H Innocents and St Jo *Lon* 15–19; NSM White City from 19. *123 Duke Road, London W4 2BX* T: (020) 8994 3216 M: 07788-414408 E: andy@rooneyw4.net

ROOSE-EVANS, James Humphrey. b 27. St Benet's Hall Ox BA 52 MA 56. **d** 81 **p** 81. NSM Kington and Weobley *Heref* 81–05; NSM Primrose Hill St Mary w Avenue Road St Paul *Lon* 82–97; PtO *Heref* 05–13; *S & B* 07–13; *Lon* from 97. *26B Upper Park Road, London NW3 2UT* T: (020) 7586 6507 E: j.rooseevans@btinternet.com

ROOT, Preb John Brereton. b 41. Lon Univ BA 64 Em Coll Cam BA 66 MA. Ridley Hall Cam 64. **d** 68 **p** 69. C Harlesden St Mark *Lon* 68–73; C Lower Homerton St Paul 73–76; Chapl Ridley Hall Cam 76; Vice-Prin 76–79; V Alperton *Lon* 79–11; AD Brent 95–00; Preb St Paul's Cathl 01–11; rtd 11; Licensed Preacher Under Seal Lic Preacher *Lon* from 12. *42 Newlyn Road, London N17 6RX* M: 07723-033831 E: stjames.john@gmail.com

ROOTES, William Brian. b 44. St And NSM Tr Scheme 88. **d** 91. NSM Auchterarder *St And* 91–97; NSM Muthill 91–97; Dioc Sec 98–00; Treas Action of Chs Together in Scotland 01–06; LtO *St And* from 06. *The School House, Fowlis Wester, Crieff PH7 3NL* T: (01764) 683772 E: w.rootes77@btinternet.com

ROOTHAM, Gerald Raymond. b 47. **d** 02 **p** 03. OLM Mattishall and the Tudd Valley *Nor* 02–10; C 10–14; rtd 15; PtO *Nor* from 15; *Eur* from 18. *8 Burgh Lane, Mattishall, Dereham NR20 3QW* T: (01362) 858533 E: geraldrootham@outlook.com

ROPER, David John. b 53. St Steph Ho Ox 93. **d** 95 **p** 96. C Hunstanton St Mary w Ringstead Parva etc *Nor* 95–98; TV E Dereham and Scarning 98–00; R Barham w Bishopsbourne and Kingston *Cant* 00–08; C Nonington w Wymynswold and Goodnestone etc 00–08; AD E Bridge 01–08; P-in-c

Broadstairs 08–11; R 11–14; AD Thanet 08–09; P-in-c St Peter-in-Thanet 10–11; Hon Min Can Cant Cathl 03–08; Hon Can Cant Cathl 08–14; R Falkland Is 14–15; R Poppyland *Nor* 15–18; Hon PV Nor Cathl 16–18; rtd 18; PtO *Nor* from 19. *11 George Close, Drayton, Norwich NR8 6EA* M: 07464-693701 E: davidjroper53@gmail.com

ROPER, Glenn. b 51. York Univ MA 91 Caerleon Coll of Educn CertEd 73. **d** 04 **p** 05. NSM Ovenden *Wakef* 04–14; *Leeds* from 14. *113 Meadow Drive, Halifax HX3 5JZ* T: (01422) 368086 E: glennroperhfx@gmail.com

ROPER, Mrs Joan. b 49. **d** 10 **p** 11. NSM Newport w Longford, and Chetwynd *Lich* 10–12; NSM Tong, Shifnal and Sheriffhales 12–13; NSM Gt and Lt Ouseburn w Marton cum Grafton etc *Leeds* from 13. *11 Back Lane, Whixley, York YO26 8BG* T: (01423) 331661 E: revjoanroper@outlook.com

ROPER, Michael Darwin Alston. b 66. Leeds Univ BA 03. Coll of Resurr Mirfield 01. **d** 03 **p** 04. C Mortlake w E Sheen *S'wark* 03–07; P-in-c Egham Hythe *Guildf* 07–16; P-in-c Epsom St Barn from 16. *St Barnabas' Vicarage, Hook Road, Epsom KT19 8TU* E: gore_lodge@yahoo.co.uk

ROSAMOND, Derek William. b 49. Linc Th Coll 87. **d** 89 **p** 90. C Coventry Caludon *Cov* 89–93; Urban Regeneration Chapl S Tyneside *Dur* 93–96; TV Sunderland 96–04; P-in-c Stockton St Paul 04–15; Community P SW Stockton 04–15; rtd 15. *28 Stoneybrough Lane, Thirsk YO7 2LS* E: derekrosamond@hotmail.com

ROSBOROUGH, Mrs Rachel Claire. b 76. Anglia Poly Univ BA 00 Ches Univ MA 14. St Jo Coll Nottm 06. **d** 08 **p** 09. C Charlton Kings H Apostles *Glouc* 08–11; R Bourton-on-the-Water w Clapton etc 11–17; P-in-c Cambridge St Mark *Ely* from 17; P-in-c Grantchester from 17; Chapl Wolfs Coll Cam from 17. *The Vicarage, 44 High Street, Grantchester, Cambridge CB3 9NF* T: (01223) 845634 E: rachelrosborough@hotmail.com

ROSE, Anthony James. b 47. Trin Coll Bris BD 72. **d** 73 **p** 74. C Halliwell St Pet *Man* 73–76; CF 76 94; R Colchester Ch Ch w St Mary V *Chelmsf* 94–01; RD Colchester 98–01; P-in-c Boreham 01–06; rtd 06; PtO *Chelmsf* from 06. *30 The Mill Apartments, East Street, Colchester CO1 2QT* T: (01206) 616739 E: aj.rose@talktalk.net

ROSE, Anthony John. b 53. Birm Univ BA 79. Trin Coll Bris 84. **d** 86 **p** 87. C The Quinton *Birm* 86–90; R Abbas and Templecombe w Horsington *B & W* 90–98; V New Thundersley *Chelmsf* 98–19; rtd 19. *1 Freeman Road, Devizes SN10 3FF*

ROSE, Canon Bernard Frederick. b 47. **d** 91 **p** 92. OLM Ipswich St Thos *St E* 91–09; P-in-c Somersham w Flowton and Offton w Willisham 09–15; P-in-c Ringshall w Battisford, Barking w Darmsden etc 09–15; Hon Can St E Cathl from 05; rtd 15; PtO *St E* from 15. *84 Chesterfield Drive, Ipswich IP1 6DN* T: (01473) 462390 E: holy-rose@supanet.com

ROSE, Christopher John. b 66. Edin Univ BSc 88. EAMTC 97. **d** 00 **p** 01. NSM Cambridge St Paul *Ely* from 00; NSM All Hallows Lon Wall 07–14; P-in-c St Clem Eastcheap w St Martin Orgar 14–19. *6 Montreal Road, Cambridge CB1 3NP* T: (01223) 511241 M: 07758-650512 E: chris@amostrust.org

ROSE, Miss Geraldine Susan. b 47. Trin Coll Bris BD 78. dss 78 **d** 87 **p** 94. Tonbridge St Steph *Roch* 78–80; Littleover *Derby* 80–88; Par Dn 87–88; Par Dn Wombwell *Sheff* 88–94; C 94–96; rtd 96; PtO *Sheff* from 96. *5 Wheatcroft, Conisbrough, Doncaster DN12 2BL* T: (01709) 867761

ROSE, Harry. See ROSE, Lionel Stafford Harry

ROSE, Ms Helen Anita. b 63. STETS 09. **d** 12 **p** 13. C Shoreham Beach *Chich* 12–14; C New Shoreham and Shoreham Beach 14–16; C Chich St Paul and Westhampnett 16–17; P-in-c Woodingdean 17–19; V from 19. *The Vicarage, 2 Downsway, Brighton BN2 6BD* M: 07971-779284 E: revrosyrosy@gmail.com

ROSE, Ingrid Elizabeth. b 57. Univ of Wales (Abth) BA 78 DipEd 79. Trin Coll Carmarthen 84. **d** 87 **p** 01. NSM Ysbyty Cynfyn w Llantrisant and Eglwys Newydd *St D* 87–90 and 92–95; NSM to Adn Cardigan 00–03; NSM Grwp Bro Ystwyth a Mynach 03–13; PtO from 13. *Ystwyth Villa, Pontrhydygroes, Ystrad Meurig SY25 6DS* T: (01974) 282728 E: ingridrose@btinternet.com

ROSE, John Clement Wansey. b 46. New Coll Ox BA 71 MA 72. Ripon Hall Ox 70. **d** 72 **p** 73. C Harborne St Pet *Birm* 72–76; TV Kings Norton 76–81; V Maney 81–02; R Condover w Frodesley, Acton Burnell etc *Heref* 02–12; rtd 12; PtO *Lich* from 13. *32 Park Lane, High Ercall, Telford TF6 6AY* T: (01952) 770243

ROSE, Jonathan Graham. b 47. Leeds Univ BA 72 Birm Univ MEd 83 Ex Univ MA 08 Bris Univ MPhil 17 FRSA 97 MCIPD 03. STETS 10. **d** 11 **p** 12. NSM Quantock Towers *B & W* 11–17; RD Quantock 15–17; PtO from 17; *Ex* from 19.

Rosemount, Cottington Mead, Sidmouth EX10 8HB T: (01395) 512094 M: 07969-008091 E: revjonrose@gmail.com

ROSE, Judith Barbara. b 51. TCert 72. SAOMC 96. **d** 99 **p** 00. OLM Stantonbury and Willen *Ox* 99–11; PtO from 11. *16 Runnymede, Giffard Park, Milton Keynes MK14 5QL* T/F: (01908) 618634

ROSE, The Ven Kathleen Judith. b 37. Lon Bible Coll BD 73 St Mich Ho Ox 64. dss 76 **d** 87 **p** 94. Leeds St Geo *Ripon* 76–81; Bradf Cathl 81–85; S Gillingham *Roch* 85–87; Par Dn 87–90; RD Gillingham 88–90; Bp's Dom Chapl 90–95; Asst Dir of Ords 90–95; Hon Can Roch Cathl 93–02; Acting Adn Tonbridge 95–96; Adn Tonbridge 96–02; rtd 02; PtO *B & W* from 03 and from 17. *47 Hill Lea Gardens, Cheddar BS27 3JH* T: (01934) 744871 M: 07719-670954 E: rose.gwyer@btinternet.com

ROSE, Lionel Stafford Harry. b 38. Wells Th Coll 69. **d** 71 **p** 72. C Minchinhampton *Glouc* 71–73; C Thornbury 73–75; R Ruardean 75–80; V Whiteshill 80–84; CF 84–93; Chapl HM Pris Kirkham 93–95; Chapl HM Pris Wymott 95–01; Chapl HM Pris Rye Hill 01; rtd 01; PtO *Ely* 02–17. *4 Samian Close, Highfield, Caldecote, Cambridge CB23 7GP* E: revdrose@gmail.com

ROSE, Mrs Lynda Kathryn. b 51. Ex Univ BA 73 Barrister-at-Law (Gray's Inn) 81. Wycliffe Hall Ox BA 86. **d** 87 **p** 94. C Highfield *Ox* 87–88; C Ox St Clem 89–93; Dir Anastasis Min 93–99; NSM Ambrosden w Merton and Piddington *Ox* 94–99. *14 Scholar Mews, Marston Ferry Road, Oxford OX2 7GY* T: (01865) 554421 E: lyndarose2000@yahoo.co.uk

ROSE, Michael Mark. b 63. Hull Univ BA 04. Westcott Ho Cam 07. **d** 09 **p** 10. C Linc St Nic w St Jo Newport 09–10; C Boultham 10–12; V Carr Dyke Gp 12–18; PtO from 18. *5 Irby Street, Boston PE21 8SA* M: 07846-601141 E: mikeredrose63@hotmail.com

ROSE, Mrs Nadine Jayne. b 64. Ripon Coll Cuddesdon 13. **d** 16 **p** 17. C Wychert Vale *Ox* from 16. *Church Bungalow, 2 Church Close, Cuddington, Aylesbury HP18 0AT* M: 07834-771008 E: nadinerose1987@outlook.com

ROSE, Mrs Pamela Inneen. b 49. Hull Univ BSc 71 Moray Ho Coll of Educn PGCE 72. **d** 06 **p** 07. OLM Stow Gp *Linc* 06–16; PtO from 17. *Daisy Cottage, 16-18 Grange Lane, Willingham by Stow, Gainsborough DN21 5LB* T: (01427) 787578 E: pam.i.rose@hotmail.co.uk

ROSE, Robert Alec Lewis. b 41. Man Univ BSc 64. Wycliffe Hall Ox 85. **d** 87 **p** 88. C Vange *Chelmsf* 87–91; C Langdon Hills 91–94; P-in-c Bentley Common 94–00; P-in-c Kelvedon Hatch 94–00; P-in-c Navestock 94–00; R Bentley Common, Kelvedon Hatch and Navestock 00–08; rtd 08; PtO *St E* from 09. *47 High Street, Wickham Market, Woodbridge IP13 0HE* T: (01728) 748199 E: robdaphnerose@btinternet.com

ROSE, Susan. See ROSE, Geraldine Susan

ROSE, Preb Susan Margaret. b 59. Westmr Coll of Educn BEd 81. SAOMC 95. **d** 98 **p** 99. C N Petherton w Northmoor Green *B & W* 98–01; P-in-c 01–03; P-in-c N Newton w St Michaelchurch, Thurloxton etc 01–03; R Alfred Jewel 03–09; RD Sedgemoor 06–09; P-in-c Cheddar 09–11; P-in-c Rodney Stoke w Draycott 09–11; R Cheddar, Draycott and Rodney Stoke 11–15; RD Axbridge 14–15; Dir of Voc from 15; Dir IME 4-7 from 15; Preb Wells Cathl from 17. *25 Wood Close, Wells BA5 2GA* T: (01749) 938449 E: rev.suerose@virgin.net

ROSE, Miss Susan Mary. b 36. TCert 56. Dalton Ho Bris 68 Trin Coll Bris 74. dss 81 **d** 87 **p** 94. Brinsworth w Catcliffe *Sheff* 75–77; Scargill Ho 77–83; Netherthorpe *Sheff* 83–87; Tutor Trin Coll Bris 87–96; V Normanton *Wakef* 96–01; rtd 01; PtO *Sheff* from 01. *23 Kendal Vale, Worsborough Bridge, Barnsley S70 5NL* T: (01226) 771590 E: s.rose2012@icloud.com

ROSE, Suzanne Elaine. b 59. Cant Ch Ch Univ MA 00. Westcott Ho Cam 15 Sewanee Sch of Th 16. **d** 17 **p** 18. C Boston *Linc* from 17. *5 Irby Street, Boston PE21 8SA* M: 07748-982128 E: sue.rose@parishofboston.co.uk or revsuerose@outlook.com

ROSE, Timothy Edward Francis. b 72. Univ of Wales (Cardiff) BD 93 MA 95 K Coll Lon PhD 98. Wycliffe Hall Ox MTh 03. **d** 01 **p** 02. C Jesmond H Trin and Newc St Barn and St Jude 01–04; Chapl R Holloway and Bedf New Coll *Lon* 04–06; C Farnham *Guildf* 06–09; P-in-c Stanford in the Vale w Goosey and Hatford *Ox* 09–13. *13 Nea Road, Christchurch BH23 4NA* M: 07709-722325 E: tefrose@gmail.com

ROSE, Timothy Mark. b 77. Luton Univ BA 98. St Mellitus Coll BA 10. **d** 10 **p** 11. C Upper Sunbury St Sav *Lon* 10–13; C Shepperton and Littleton from 13. *Littleton Rectory, Rectory Close, Shepperton TW17 0QE* T: (01932) 562249 M: 07966-031432 E: tm_rose@hotmail.co.uk

ROSE-CASEMORE, Claire Pamela. b 63. St Paul's Coll Chelt BA 84 St Luke's Coll Ex PGCE 85 Anglia Poly Univ MA 02.

Ridley Hall Cam 95. **d** 97 **p** 98. Par Dn Kingsthorpe w Northampton St Dav *Pet* 97–98; C 98–01; TV Daventry, Ashby St Ledgers, Braunston etc 01–10; P-in-c Bideford, Northam, Westward Ho!, Appledore etc *Ex* 10–17; TR Bideford, Landcross, Littleham etc from 17. *The Rectory, Abbotsham Road, Bideford EX39 3AB* T: (01237) 475765 E: clairerc@btopenworld.com

ROSE-CASEMORE, John. b 27. Chich Th Coll. **d** 55 **p** 56. C Epsom Common Ch Ch *Guildf* 55–58; C Hednesford *Lich* 58–60; V Dawley 60–65; R Puttenham and Wanborough *Guildf* 65–72; R Frimley 72–83; RD Surrey Heath 76–81; R Ludgershall and Faberstown *Sarum* 83–86; R Tidworth, Ludgershall and Faberstown 86–92; rtd 92; PtO *Ex* 93–14. *5 Culvery Close, Woodbury, Exeter EX5 1LZ* T: (01395) 233426 E: pamjohnrc@gmail.com

ROSE-CASEMORE, Canon Penelope Jane. b 56. Bris Univ CertEd 77 BEd 78. Westcott Ho Cam 83. **dss** 85 **d** 87 **p** 94. Waterloo St Jo w St Andr *S'wark* 85–87; Par Dn 87–88; Asst Chapl Gt Ormond Street Hosp for Sick Children Lon 88–90; Par Dn Balham St Mary and St Jo *S'wark* 90–94; C 94–96; Par Dn Upper Tooting H Trin 90–94; C 94–96; TV Clapham Team 96–01; V Clapham Ch Ch and St Jo from 02; AD Lambeth N 05–10; Dir Ords Kingston Area from 13; Hon Can S'wark Cathl from 17. *Christchurch Vicarage, 39 Union Grove, London SW8 2QJ* T/F: (020) 7622 3552 E: penny@christchurchstjohn.com

ROSEDALE, John Richard. b 54. Leeds Univ BA 05. NOC 02. **d** 05 **p** 06. NSM Hadfield *Derby* 05–10; TV Saddleworth *Man* from 10. *Friarmere Vicarage, 1 Coblers Hill, Delph, Oldham OL3 5HT* T: (01457) 874209

ROSENTHAL, Canon James Milton. b 51. **d** 07 **p** 09. Dir Communications Angl Communion Office 89–09; NSM All Hallows by the Tower etc Lon 07–12; C Wantsum Gp *Cant* 12–16; P-in-c Merton St Jas *S'wark* 16–19; V from 19. *St James's Vicarage, Beaford Grove, London SW20 9LB* T: (020) 8715 4353 M: 07742-856149 E: james.rosenthal@gmail.com *or* sjtgpic@gmail.com

ROSENTHAL, Sheila. b 57. Warwick Univ BA 81 MA 95. Ripon Coll Cuddesdon 04. **d** 06 **p** 07. C Worc SE 06–09; Asst Chapl St Richard's Hospice Worc from 09; Chapl Mancrs Primary Care Trust from 10; PtO *Glouc* from 16. *Springwood Cottage, Bourton on the Hill, Moreton-in-Marsh GL56 9AE* T: (01386) 700530

ROSIE, James Robert. b 78. Leeds Univ BA 08. Coll of Resurr Mirfield 08. **d** 10 **p** 11. C Kingston upon Hull St Alb *York* 10–14; R Cheadle w Freehay *Lich* 14–17; TV Dereham and Distr *Nor* from 17. *The Vicarage, Woodgate Lane, Swanton Morley, Dereham NR20 4NS* M: 07931-120897 E: jamesrosie952@gmail.com

ROSINGH, Anna Clara Abena. *See* THOMASSON-ROSINGH, Anna Clara Abena

ROSKELLY, James Hereward Emmanuel. b 57. BSc ACSM 80. Cranmer Hall Dur 83. **d** 86 **p** 87. C Dunster, Carhampton and Withycombe w Rodhuish *B & W* 86–90; C Ealing St Mary *Lon* 90–93; Chapl R Marsden Hosp 93–95; CF 95–03; TV Rayleigh *Chelmsf* 03–10; R Dickleburgh and The Pulhams *Nor* 10–16. *Address withheld by request* M: 07989-442434 E: jamesroskelly@btinternet.com

ROSKILLY, John Noel. b 33. Man Univ MB, ChB 58 MRCGP 68. St Deiniol's Hawarden 74. **d** 75 **p** 76. NSM Bramhall *Ches* 75–86; V Capesthorne w Siddington and Marton 86–91; Dioc Dir of Counselling 84–93; Bp's Officer for NSM 87–93; NSM Macclesfield St Paul 92–93; rtd 93; PtO *Ches* from 93. *North View, Hawkins Lane, Rainow, Macclesfield SK10 5TL* T: (01625) 501014 E: johnliz.roskilly@gmail.com

ROSS, Alexander. *See* ROSS, David Alexander

ROSS, Alexander John. b 84. Melbourne Univ BEd 08 BA 09 Melbourne Coll of Div BTh 10 Aus Catholic Univ MA 11 Ox Univ MTh 13 Em Coll Cam PhD 18. Trin Coll Melbourne 09 Ripon Coll Cuddesdon 11. **d** 13 **p** 13. C S Yarra Ch Ch Australia 13–15; Asst Chapl Em Coll Cam 15–18; Assoc Dean and Bye-Fell from 18; Tutor Westcott Ho Cam from 18; NSM Cambridge St Clem *Ely* from 18. *Emmanuel College, St Andrews Street, Cambridge CB2 3AP* E: ajr211@cam.ac.uk

ROSS, Canon Anthony McPherson. b 38. Univ of Wales (Lamp) BA 60 Lon Univ BD 63. St Mich Coll Llan 60. **d** 61 **p** 62. C Gabalfa *Llan* 61–65; Chapl RN 65–93; QHC 89–93; P-in-c Coln St Aldwyns, Hatherop, Quenington etc *Glouc* 93–95; V 95–08; RD Fairford 96–04; rtd 08; Bp's Adv on Deliverance Min *Glouc* from 08; Hon Can Glouc Cathl from 02. *Rowan Tree Cottage, Ampney Crucis, Cirencester GL7 5RY* T: (01285) 851410 E: tonyrosstssf468@gmail.com

ROSS (née BENSON), Ashley Dawn. b 85. **d** 14 **p** 15. C Everton St Geo *Liv* 14–17; PtO from 17. *St Paul's Vicarage, Victoria Square, Widnes WA8 7QU* T: 0151-260 7397

ROSS, Daniel James. b 87. Bath Univ BSc 09 Open Univ BA 12. Ridley Hall Cam 14. **d** 17 **p** 18. C Upper Armley *Leeds* from 17. *27 Hough End Lane, Leeds LS13 4EY* T: 0113-255 7679 M: 07410-411453 E: revdanross@gmail.com

ROSS, David Alexander. b 46. Oak Hill Th Coll 73. **d** 75 **p** 76. C Northwood Em *Lon* 75–80; R Eastrop *Win* 80–86; V Hove Bp Hannington Memorial Ch *Chich* 86–93; V Muswell Hill St Jas w St Matt *Lon* 93–07; rtd 07; Hon C S Tottenham St Ann *Lon* 07–11; PtO *Ox* from 11. *4 Glissard Way, Bradwell Village, Burford OX18 4XD* T: (01993) 824871 E: alexlynne.ross@googlemail.com

ROSS, Douglas. b 58. SEITE 12. **d** 15 **p** 16. NSM Salfords *S'wark* from 15. *40 Brockham Lane, Brockham, Betchworth RH3 7EH* M: 07717-665007 E: revdoug@squarepeg.com

ROSS, Preb Duncan Gilbert. b 48. Lon Univ BSc 70. Westcott Ho Cam 75. **d** 78 **p** 79. C Stepney St Dunstan and All SS *Lon* 78–84; V Hackney Wick St Mary of Eton w St Aug 84–95; P-in-c Bow Common 95–03; V 03–13; Preb St Paul's Cathl 95–13; rtd 13; PtO *Lon* from 14. *37 Aberavon Road, London E3 5AR* M: 07957-235078 E: duncan.ross5@btopenworld.com

ROSS, Frederic Ian. b 34. Man Univ BSc 56. Westcott Ho Cam 58. **d** 62 **p** 63. C Oldham *Man* 62–65; Sec Th Colls Dept SCM 65–69; Teacher Man Gr Sch 69–84; V Shrewsbury H Cross *Lich* 84–02; rtd 02; PtO *Heref* from 02; *Lich* 02–13. *The Paddock, Plealey Road, Annscroft, Shrewsbury SY5 8AN* T: (01743) 860327 E: mail@fiross.plus.com

ROSS, Mrs Helen Jane. b 61. Moray Ho Coll of Educn PGCE 87 St Andr Univ BSc 84 Aber Univ DipEd 90 MTh 12 SOSc 10. TISEC DipTheol 09. **d** 09 **p** 10. C Aberdeen St Clem *Ab* 09–12; P-in-c 12; R Prestwick *Glas* from 12; Can St Mary's Cathl from 18. *St Ninian's Rectory, 56 Ayr Road, Prestwick KA9 1RR* T: (01292) 479582 E: rector@stniniansprestwick.org.uk

ROSS, John. b 41. Wells Th Coll 66. **d** 69 **p** 70. C Newc St Gabr 69–71; C Prudhoe 71–75; Hon C Shotley 75–87; Hon C Whittonstall 75–87; P-in-c Wallsend St Pet 93–94. *20 Holburn Gardens, Ryton NE40 3DZ* E: rossj41@blueyonder.co.uk

ROSS, John Colin. b 50. Oak Hill Th Coll 84. **d** 86 **p** 87. C Stowmarket *St E* 86–89; C Wakef St Andr and St Mary 89–91; R Gt and Lt Whelnetham w Bradfield St George *St E* 91–94; V Newmarket All SS 94–02; V Erith St Paul *Roch* 02–04; P-in-c Combs and Lt Finborough *St E* 04–13; rtd 13; PtO *St E* from 14. *23 Pinner's Way, Bury St Edmunds IP33 3JN* T: (01284) 706776 M: 07904-124227 E: john@johnross.org

ROSS, Mrs Kirsty Leanne. b 88. Trin Coll Melbourne BTh 10 Qu Coll Ox PGCE 13. Ripon Coll Cuddesdon 11. **d** 13 **p** 13. C Toorak Australia 13–15; Chapl Trin Coll Cam from 15. *M6 Blue Boar, Trinity College, Cambridge CB2 1TQ* M: 07482-341010 E: kirstylross@hotmail.com *or* kr421@cam.ac.uk

ROSS, Malcolm Hargrave. b 37. Dur Univ BSc 58. Westcott Ho Cam 63. **d** 64 **p** 65. C Armley St Bart *Ripon* 64–67; USPG 67–71; Trinidad and Tobago 67–71; V New Rossington *Sheff* 71–75; Bp's Missr in E Lon 75–82; P-in-c Haggerston All SS 75–82; V Bedford Leigh *Man* 82–85; Area Sec USPG Bris and Glouc 85–90; Bp's Officer for Miss and Evang *Bris* 90–94; P-in-c Lacock w Bowden Hill 90–94; V Sherston Magna, Easton Grey, Luckington etc 94–06; rtd 06; PtO *Truro* from 16. *36 Haddon Way, Carlyon Bay, St Austell PL25 3QG* T: (01726) 813576 E: m-eross@tiscali.co.uk

ROSS, Oliver Charles Milligan. b 58. SOAS Lon BA 80 St Edm Ho Cam BA 86 K Coll Lon MA 17 Whitelands Coll Lon PGCE 81. Ridley Hall Cam 84. **d** 87 **p** 88. C Preston St Cuth *Blackb* 87–90; C Paddington St Jo w St Mich *Lon* 90–95; V Hounslow H Trin w St Paul and St Mary 95–06; P-in-c Isleworth St Mary 01–02; R St Olave Hart Street w All Hallows Staining etc 06–18; P-in-c St Kath Cree 06–18; P-in-c St Clem Eastcheap w St Martin Orgar 12–14; P-in-c St Marg Pattens 14–18; AD The City 09–18; V Malmesbury and Upper Avon *Bris* from 18. *The Vicarage, Holloway, Malmesbury SN16 9BA* M: 07879-490139 E: ocmross@me.com

ROSS, Ms Rachel Anne. b 64. York Univ BSc 85 SS Coll Cam PGCE 86 Sheff Univ MA 97 Coll of Ripon & York St Jo MA 00. NOC 97. **d** 00 **p** 01. C Pendleton *Man* 00–04; P-in-c Salford Ordsall St Clem 03–04; P-in-c Salford St Ignatius and Stowell Memorial 03–04; R Ordsall and Salford Quays 04–07; P-in-c Loughborough All SS w H Trin *Leic* 07–08; R 08–14; Bp's NSM Officer 10–13; Chapl Qu Anne's Sch Caversham from 15; NSM Caversham Thameside and Mapledurham *Ox* from 15. *The Rectory, 20 Church Road, Caversham, Reading RG4 7AD* T: 0118-947 9505 M: 07884-371688 E: rachelross@tiscali.co.uk

ROSS (née FAIRWEATHER), Mrs Sally Helen. b 69. St Hilda's Coll Ox BA 91. Cranmer Hall Dur 94. **d** 97 **p** 98. C Illingworth *Wakef* 97–01; Warden H Rood Ho and C Thirsk *York* 01–02; Chapl Northallerton Health Services NHS Trust 01–02;

C Sheff St Mark Broomhill 02–04; Mental Health Chapl Sheff Care Trust 04–08; Mental Health Chapl Sheff Health and Social Care NHS Foundn Trust from 08. *40 Bents Drive, Sheffield S11 9RP* T: 0114-235 1652 E: sh.ross@tiscali.co.uk *or* sally.ross@shsc.nhs.uk

ROSS, The Ven Vernon. b 57. Portsm Poly BSc 79 RGN 86 York St Jo Univ MA 13. Trin Coll Bris 89. d 91 p 92. C Fareham St Jo *Portsm* 91–94; P-in-c Witheridge, Thelbridge, Creacombe, Meshaw etc *Ex* 94–00; TR Barnstaple 00–08; P-in-c Fyfield, Moreton w Bobbingworth etc *Chelmsf* 08–16; NSM Chigwell and Chigwell Row 16–17; Miss Min Adv Barking Area 12–17; Adn Westmorland and Furness *Carl* from 17. *The Vicarage, Windermere Road, Lindale, Grange-over-Sands LA11 6LB* T: (01539) 534717 E: archdeacon.south@carlislediocese.org.uk

ROSS-McCABE, Mrs Philippa Mary Seton. b 63. Natal Univ BA 83 HDipEd 86 Bris Univ BA 01. Trin Coll Bris 99. d 01 p 02. C Burpham *Guildf* 01–05; LtO 05–06; C Wisley w Pyrford 06–08; Tutor Local Min Progr from 06; Hon C Byfleet from 09. *The Rectory, 81 Rectory Lane, Byfleet, West Byfleet KT14 7LX* T: (01932) 342374 E: p.rossmccabe@btinternet.com

⳾**ROSSDALE, The Rt Revd David Douglas James.** b 53. Westmr Coll Ox MA 91 Surrey Univ MSc 01 K Coll Lon MSc 10. Chich Th Coll 80. d 81 p 82 c 00. C Upminster *Chelmsf* 81–86; V Moulsham St Luke 86–90; V Cookham *Ox* 90–00; RD Maidenhead 94–00; Hon Can Ch 99–00; Suff Bp Grimsby *Linc* 00–13; rtd 13; Can and Preb Linc Cathl from 00; Hon Asst Bp Linc from 13. *Home Farm, Fen Lane, East Keal, Spilsby PE23 4AY* T: (01790) 752163 E: rossdale@btinternet.com

ROSSETER, Miss Susan Mary. b 46. Man Univ BA 67 Edin Univ DASS 71. St Jo Coll Nottm LTh 84. d 87 p 94. Par Dn Bromley Common St Aug *Roch* 87–88; C Pudsey St Lawr and St Paul *Bradf* 88–95; C Haughton le Skerne *Dur* 95–00; C Wilnecote *Lich* 00–11; rtd 11. *14 Meadowsway, Upton, Chester CH2 1HZ* E: sue.rosseter@btinternet.com

ROSSITER, Canon Gillian Alice. b 56. SRN 75 RSCN 75. NOC 98. d 01 p 02. C Neston Ches 01–06; P-in-c Gt Meols 06–09; V from 09; RD Wirral N 08–15; Hon Can Ches Cathl from 15. *The Vicarage, 1 Stanley Road, Hoylake, Wirral CH47 1HL* T: 0151-632 3897 E: stjohnthebaptist@uwclub.net

ROSSITER, Paul Albert. b 55. Leeds Univ BA 06. NOC 03. d 06 p 07. NSM Wallasey St Nic w All SS *Ches* 06–12; V Hoylake from 12. *The Vicarage, 1 Stanley Road, Hoylake, Wirral CH47 1HL* T: 0151-632 3897 E: p.a.rossiter@uwclub.net

ROSSLYN SMITH, Mrs Katherine Dorothy Nevill. b 40. STETS 97. d 00 p 01. NSM Tisbury *Sarum* 00–01; NSM Nadder Valley 01–03; NSM Chalke Valley 03–06; rtd 06; PtO *Sarum* 06–16 and from 18. *The Old School House, Church Street, Bowerchalke, Salisbury SP5 5BE* T: (01722) 780011 E: katersinthevalley@gmail.com

ROSSLYN-SMITH, Mrs Kirsten Louise. b 73. Nottm Trent Univ BA 96. St Jo Coll Nottm MTh 05. d 05 p 06. C Tunbridge Wells St Jas *Roch* 05–10; V Stoke Hill *Guildf* from 10. *St Peter's Church House, 37 Hazel Avenue, Guildford GU1 1NP* T: (01483) 451908

ROSTILL, Brian. b 50. K Alfred's Coll Win BTh 00. Cranmer Hall Dur 01. d 03 p 04. C Knight's Enham and Smannell w Enham Alamein *Win* 03–07; P-in-c Boyatt Wood 07–09; V 09–12; Hon C Jersey St Mary 12–13; R 13–18; NSM Tamworth *Lich* from 18. *The Parsonage, Church Drive, Hopwas, Tamworth B78 3AL* T: (01827) 311750 E: brianrostill@gmail.com

ROSTRON, Derek. b 34. St Mich Coll Llan 65. d 67 p 68. C Morecambe St Barn *Blackb* 67–70; C Ribbleton 70–72; V Chorley All SS 72–79; C Woodchurch *Ches* 79–80; V Audlem 80–83; RD Nantwich 87–97; rtd 04; PtO *Lich* 04–06; *Ches* 04–06. *30 St Matthew's Drive, Derrington, Stafford ST18 9LU* T: (01785) 246349 E: fr.derek@btinternet.com

ROTH, Jill Marie. b 61. Ox Min Course 07. d 10 p 11. NSM Flackwell Heath *Ox* 10–16; NSM Gerrards Cross and Fulmer from 16. *White Cottage, Hay Lane, Fulmer, Slough SL3 6HJ* T: (01753) 663181 M: 07985-945990 E: jillroth@btinternet.com

ROTHERHAM, Eric. b 36. Clifton Th Coll 63. d 67 p 68. C Gt Crosby St Luke *Liv* 67–69; C Sutton 69–71; V Warrington St Paul 72–79; LtO 79–80; PtO from 80; *Ches* 80–10. *7 Paul Street, Warrington WA2 7LE* T: (01925) 633048

ROTHERY, Robert Frederick (Fred). b 34. Lon Coll of Div 67. d 69 p 70. C Burscough Bridge *Liv* 69–72; C Chipping Campden *Glouc* 72–75; P-in-c Didmarton w Oldbury-on-the-Hill and Sopworth 75–77; R Boxwell, Leighterton, Didmarton, Oldbury etc 77–83; R Stow on the Wold 83–90; RD Stow 90–99; rtd 00; PtO *Sarum* 06–18. *12 Phillips Road,*

Marnhull, Sturminster Newton DT10 1LF T: (01258) 820668 E: woodyperson@gmail.com

ROTHWELL, Canon Bryan. b 60. St Edm Hall Ox BA 81 MA 85. Trin Coll Bris. d 85 p 86. C Carl St Jo 85–88; C Ulverston St Mary w Trin 88–90; P-in-c Preston St Mary *Blackb* 90–96; P-in-c St John's in the Vale w Wythburn *Carl* 96–99; R St John's-in-the-Vale, Threlkeld and Wythburn 99–11; Warden Dioc Youth Cen 96–11; RD Derwent 05–10; TR Solway Plain 11–18; R from 18; Hon Can Carl Cathl from 08. *The Vicarage, Wigton Road, Silloth, Wigton CA7 4NJ* T: (016973) 31413 E: bryan@therothwells.co.uk

ROTHWELL, Steven. b 68. Roehampton Inst BA 99 Cam Univ MA 02. Westcott Ho Cam 00. d 02 p 03. C Chesterton Gd Shep *Ely* 02–06; R Gamlingay and Everton 06–16; P-in-c Cambridge St Jas from 16. *St James's Vicarage, 110 Wulfstan Way, Cambridge CB1 8QJ* E: s.rothwell3@btinternet.com

ROTHWELL-JACKSON, Christopher Patrick. b 32. St Cath Soc Ox BA 58 MA 61 Bris Univ PGCE 66. St Steph Ho Ox 55. d 59 p 60. C E Clevedon All SS *B & W* 59–62; C Midsomer Norton 62–65; Asst Teacher St Pet Primary Sch Portishead 66–68; Clevedon Junior Sch 68–72; Dep Hd Clevedon All SS Primary Sch 72–75; Hd Master Bp Pursglove Sch Tideswell 75–90; rtd 90; PtO *Ex* 95–13. *Rosedale, Hookway, Crediton EX17 3PU* T: (01363) 772039 E: crothwelljackson@gmail.com

ROUCH, David Vaughan. b 36. Oak Hill Th Coll 67. d 69 p 70. C Denton Holme *Carl* 69–74; V Litherland St Jo and St Jas *Liv* 74–95; V Pemberton St Mark Newtown 95–06; P-in-c Wigan St Barn Marsh Green 03–06; rtd 06; PtO *Lich* 07–18. *16 Parrs Lane, Bayston Hill, Shrewsbury SY3 0JS* T: (01743) 873800 E: drouch@sky.com

ROUCH, The Ven Peter Bradford. b 66. BNC Ox MA 87 Peterho Cam MA 99 Man Univ PhD 05. Westcott Ho Cam 96. d 99 p 00. C E Dulwich St Jo *S'wark* 99–02; Jun Research Fell St Steph Ho Ox 02–04; Chapl St Jo Coll Ox 03–04; P-in-c Man Apostles w Miles Platting 05–11; Hon Research Fell Man Univ 07–11; Adn Bournemouth *Win* from 11. *Glebe House, 22 Bellflower Way, Chandler's Ford, Eastleigh SO53 4HN* T/F: (023) 8026 0955 E: peter.rouch@winchester.anglican.org

ROULSTON (née MAYLES), Helena Rosemary Laura. b 84. Nottm Univ BA 06. Westcott Ho Cam 12. d 14 p 15. C Over St Chad *Ches* 14–17; Chapl Sheff Hallam Univ from 18. *20 Rydal Road, Sheffield S8 0US* T: 0114-225 3153 E: h.roulston@shu.ac.uk

ROULSTON, Joseph Ernest. b 52. BNC Ox BA 74 MA 78 Lon Univ PhD 81 FRSC 86 FLS 94 FIBiol 01 FRCPath 01 CSci 04. Edin Dioc NSM Course 83. d 86 p 87. C Edin St Hilda 86–88; C Edin St Fillan 86–88; NSM Edin St Mich and All SS 88–97; Dioc Chapl Gen from 96; Assoc P Roslin (Rosslyn Chpl) 99–07; P-in-c from 07. *16 Summerside Street, Edinburgh EH6 4NU* T: 0131-554 6382 *or* 242 9225 M: 07903-969698 E: revjoeroulston@gmail.com

ROUND, Canon Malcolm John Harrison. b 56. Lon Univ BSc 77 BA 81. Oak Hill Th Coll. d 81 p 82. C Guildf St Sav w Stoke-next-Guildford 81–85; C Hawkwell *Chelmsf* 85–88; R Balerno *Edin* from 88; Hon Chapl Heriot-Watt Univ from 12; Can St Mary's Cathl from 10. *St Mungo's Ministry Centre, 46B Bavelaw Road, Balerno EH14 7AE* T: 0131-449 9907 E: malcolm.round@stmungos.org

ROUNDHILL, The Ven Andrew (John). b 65. CCC Cam BA 87. Ripon Coll Cuddesdon BTh 93. d 94. C Lancaster Ch Ch w St Jo and St Anne *Blackb* 93–97; Chapl Loretto Sch Musselburgh 97–02; Chapl Hong Kong Cathl 02–04; Sub-Dean 04–06; R Aspley w Albany Creek Australia 06–07; AD Brisbane NW 07–08; Adn Lilley from 08. *30 Ridley Road, Bridgeman Downs QLD 4035, Australia* T: (0061) (7) 3263 9254 *or* (7) 3263 3518

ROUNDTREE, James Clabern (Clay). b 75. Oklahoma Univ BFA 98 York Univ MA 00. St Steph Ho Ox BA 02. d 03 p 04. C Yarm *York* 03–07; V Ingleby Barwick from 07. *St Francis's House, Barwick Way, Ingleby Barwick, Stockton-on-Tees TS17 0WD* T: (01642) 760171 E: clayroundtree@hotmail.com

ROUNTREE, Richard Benjamin. b 52. NUI BA 73. CITC 76. d 76 p 77. C Orangefield *D & D* 76–80; C Dublin Zion Ch *D & G* 80–83; I Dalkey St Patr 83–97; I Powerscourt w Kilbride 97–18; Dioc Dir Decade of Evang 90–96; Can Ch Ch Cathl Dublin 92–18; Treas Ch Ch Cathl Dublin 04–09; Dioc Dir Lay Min 05–09; Adn Glendalough 09–18; rtd 18. *8 Blacklion Manor, Greystones, Co Wicklow, Republic of Ireland* M: (00353) 87-276 7564 E: rbrountree@gmail.com

ROUSE, Graham. b 58. Sheff City Coll of Educn CertEd 79 Leic Univ DipEd 84. Cranmer Hall Dur 90. d 92 p 93. C Longridge *Blackb* 92–96; P-in-c Fairhaven 96–97; V 97–07; P-in-c Blackpool St Mary 07–10; P-in-c S Shore St Pet 07–10;

P-in-c S Shore H Trin 08–10; PtO from 10. *36 Canterbury Street, Chorley PR6 0LN* T: (01257) 265996

ROUSELL, Ian Douglas. b 64. Trin Coll Bris 11. **d** 13 **p** 14. C Keynsham *B & W* 13–17; P-in-c Westfield from 17. *85 Beauchamp Avenue, Midsomer Norton, Radstock BA3 4FW* M: 07896-598830 E: rev.ian.stpeters@gmail.com

ROUT, Thomas. b 78. Univ Coll Lon BA 02. Wycliffe Hall Ox BA 10. **d** 11 **p** 12. C Rothley *Leic* 11–15; P-in-c Ipswich St Helen, H Trin, and St Luke *St E* from 15; Chapl Suffolk New Coll from 15. *The Rectory, 42 Clapgate Lane, Ipswich IP3 0RD* M: 07791-122331 E: tom@ipswichwaterfrontchurches.co.uk

ROUTH, Canon Eileen Rosemary. b 41. Cant Sch of Min 82. **dss** 85 **d** 87 **p** 94. Folkestone St Sav *Cant* 85–90; Par Dn 87–90; Par Dn Woodnesborough w Worth and Staple 90–91; Dn-in-c 91–94; V 94–96; V Maidstone St Martin 96–99; Hon Can Cant Cathl 99; rtd 99; PtO *Cant* from 00. *4C St John's Hospital, Northgate, Canterbury CT1 1BG* T: (01227) 464052

ROUTH, William John. b 60. Magd Coll Ox BA 81 MA 92. Ripon Coll Cuddesdon 93. **d** 95 **p** 96. C Longton *Blackb* 95–99; V Sutton Coldfield St Chad *Birm* 99–06; P-in-c 06–11; P-in-c Sutton Coldfield H Trin 06–11; R from 11. *Holy Trinity Rectory, 5 Broome Gardens, Sutton Coldfield B75 7JE* T: 0121-311 0474 E: john.routh@btinternet.com or john.routh.htsc@gmail.com

ROUTLEDGE, Christopher Joseph. b 78. Keele Univ BSc 99 SS Mark & Jo Univ Coll Plymouth PGCE 01. Oak Hill Th Coll BA 08. **d** 08 **p** 09. C Tiverton St Geo and St Paul *Ex* 08–12; P-in-c Egg Buckland 12–17; C Estover 12–17; V Eggbuckland w Estover from 17; C Plymouth Crownhill Ascension from 12; C Bickleigh and Shaugh Prior from 12. *The Vicarage, 100 Church Hill, Eggbuckland, Plymouth PL6 5RD* T: (01752) 781564 E: chrisroutledge829@btinternet.com

ROUTLEDGE, Christopher Simon Bruce. b 73. Southn Univ BA 94. Ripon Coll Cuddesdon BTh 12. **d** 11 **p** 12. C Northfleet and Rosherville *Roch* 11–15; V Bradwell and Porthill *Lich* from 15; Chapl Staffs and Stoke on Trent Partnership NHS Trust 15–16; Chapl Univ Hosps of N Midl NHS Trust from 16. *St Barnabas' Vicarage, Oldcastle Avenue, Newcastle ST5 8QG* T: (01782) 929216 M: 07837-177571 E: rev.chrisr73@gmail.com

ROWAN, Canon Nicholas Edward. b 76. Essex Univ BA. Trin Coll Bris. **d** 06 **p** 07. C Rayleigh *Chelmsf* 06–10; TV 10–18; P-in-c Hawkwell from 18; AD Rochford from 18; Hon Can Chelmsf Cathl from 19. *The Rectory, 53 Hawkwell Road, Hockley SS5 4DE* M: 07795-245212 E: nickrowan@btinternet.com or nick.rowan@hawkwellparishchurch.org

ROWBERRY, Christopher Michael. b 58. Univ of Wales (Lamp) MA 04 CQSW 85. Qu Coll Birm 94. **d** 96 **p** 97. C Lytchett Minster *Sarum* 96–00; TV Totton *Win* 00–10; V Hedge End St Jo from 10. *The Vicarage, Vicarage Drive, Hedge End, Southampton SO30 4DU* T: (01489) 789578 E: chrisrow@btopenworld.com

ROWBERRY, Michael James. b 46. Sussex Univ BA 74. Edin Th Coll 85. **d** 87 **p** 92. C Wolvercote w Summertown *Ox* 87–88; NSM Cov St Fran N Radford 91–95; PtO 95–98; C Doncaster Intake and Doncaster H Trin *Sheff* 98–00; C-in-c St Edm Anchorage Lane CD 00–06; C Doncaster St Geo 06–12; rtd 12; PtO *Leic* from 16. *5 Thorntree Close, Leicester LE3 9QS* T: 0116-319 5469 E: microbert@talktalk.net

ROWBORY, Simon Michael. b 84. Grey Coll Dur BSc 06. Westcott Ho Cam 10. **d** 13 **p** 14. C Leic Martyrs 13–16; P-in-c Mill Hill Jo Keble Ch *Lon* from 16. *1A Church Close, Edgware HA8 9NS* M: 07799-300771 E: simon.rowbory@gmail.com

ROWE, Andrew Robert. b 64. Westmr Coll Ox BA 85 PGCE 86. Ridley Hall Cam 93. **d** 95 **p** 96. C Broadheath *Ches* 95–99; V E Ardsley *Wakef* 99–06; Chapl HM Pris Wakef 06–13; Chapl HM YOI Wetherby from 13. *HM Young Offender Institution, York Road, Wetherby LS22 5ED* T: (01937) 544200 E: andyrowe@uwclub.net

ROWE, Canon Bryan. b 50. Carl Dioc Tr Course 87. **d** 90 **p** 91. C Kells *Carl* 90–93; P-in-c Aspatria w Hayton 93–02; R Workington St Mich 02–15; P-in-c Distington 06–08; P-in-c Westfield St Mary 10–12; RD Solway 99–08 and 11–15; Hon Can Carl Cathl 99–15; rtd 15. *7 Berwick Street, Workington CA14 3EN* E: bryan.rowe50@yahoo.com

ROWE, Christine Elizabeth. b 55. Southn Univ BEd 77. Ripon Coll Cuddesdon 83. **dss** 86 **d** 87 **p** 94. Denham *Ox* 86–87; Par Dn 87–89; Par Dn Aylesbury 89 and 89–93; NSM Caversham St Jo 93–99; Chapl HM Pris Reading 93–98; Chapl MU 95–00; Chapl R Berks and Battle Hosps NHS Trust 96–00; P-in-c Vancouver St Thos Canada 00–01; R 01–04; Adn Burrard 04–06; R N Vancouver St Cath from 06. *1062 Ridgewood Drive, North Vancouver BC V7R 1H8, Canada* T: (001) (604) 987 6307 or (604) 985 0666 F: 980 3868 E: stcatherinecr@aol.com

ROWE, The Very Revd David Brian. b 58. Trin Coll Bris 80. **d** 83 **p** 84. C Radipole and Melcombe Regis *Sarum* 83–86; C Cranham Park *Chelmsf* 86–88; Assoc Min and Par Missr Eastrop *Win* 88–92; P-in-c Arborfield w Barkham *Ox* 92–97; Asst Dioc Adv in Evang *S'well* 97–02; P-in-c Wilford 00–06; R 06–08; Warden Lee Abbey 08–15; P-in-c Win Ch Ch 15–18; V 18; Dean Wellington New Zealand from 18. *Wellington Cathedral of St Paul, PO Box 12-044, Thorndon, Wellington 6144, New Zealand* T: (0064) (4) 472 0286 M: 07787-522307 E: davidrowe3@sky.com or admin@wellingtoncathedral.org.nz

ROWE, Geoffrey Lewis. b 44. Univ of Wales (Lamp) BA. Ripon Coll Cuddesdon 80. **d** 82 **p** 83. C Milber *Ex* 82–84; TV Withycombe Raleigh 84–90; R Clyst St Mary, Clyst St George etc 90–08; rtd 08. *33 Sandringham Drive, Preston, Paignton TQ3 1HU*

ROWE, George William. b 36. K Alfred's Coll Win CertEd 64 BEd 82 Win Univ Hon BA 15. **d** 07 **p** 08. NSM Week St Mary Circle of Par *Truro* 07–11; PtO 11–15; *Guildf* from 15. *Tanglewood, 5 Crofts Close, Chiddingfold, Godalming GU8 4SG* T: (01428) 288078 M: 07970-186038 E: jwellar05@gmail.com

ROWE, Miss Joan Patricia. b 54. Trin Coll Bris BA 87. **d** 88 **p** 94. C Radstock w Writhlington *B & W* 88–92; C Nailsea H Trin 92–96; P-in-c Shapwick w Ashcott and Burtle 96–07; Master St Jo Hosp Bath 07–09; PtO *Liv* 10–11; P-in-c Westbury *Heref* 11–13; P-in-c Worthen 11–13; P-in-c Yockleton 11–13; R Westbury, Worthen and Yockleton 13–17; rtd 17; PtO *B & W* from 18. *14 Waverley Road, Backwell, Bristol BS48 3LP* T: (01275) 463214 E: j.rowe91@btinternet.com

ROWE, Jonathan. b 67. Bath Univ BSc 89 Open Univ BA 96 MA 97 St Andr Univ PhD 09. **d** 19. Dir Min and Miss Resources *Truro* from 17; Jt Prin SWMTC from 17; NSM Chacewater w St Day and Carharrack *Truro* from 19; NSM Devoran from 19; NSM Feock from 19; NSM St Stythians w Perranarworthal and Gwennap from 19. *Address withheld by request*

ROWE, Mrs Pauline Frances. b 58. **d** 13 **p** 14. NSM Wigan All SS and St Geo *Liv* 13–15; C Wigan All SS 15–16; TV Parr from 16. *St Peter's Vicarage, Broad Oak Road, St Helens WA9 2DZ* T: (01744) 751553 M: 07960-102862 E: pauline.rowe2@btinternet.com

ROWE, Philip William. b 57. Southn Univ BSc 78 Lambeth STh 86. Trin Coll Bris 82. **d** 85 **p** 86. C Tooting Graveney St Nic *S'wark* 85–89; V Abbots Leigh w Leigh Woods *Bris* 89–96; V Almondsbury 96–98; P-in-c Littleton on Severn w Elberton 96–98; V Almondsbury and Olveston from 98; C Pilning w Compton Greenfield 10–18; P-in-c from 18; AD Bris W 00–06. *The Vicarage, 3 Sundays Hill, Almondsbury, Bristol BS32 4DS* T: (01454) 613223 E: office@stmarysevernside.org.uk

ROWE, Shiela. See JOHNSON, Shiela

ROWE, Stephen Mark Buckingham. b 59. SS Mark & Jo Univ Coll Plymouth BA 81. Ripon Coll Cuddesdon 83. **d** 86 **p** 87. C Denham *Ox* 86–89; C Aylesbury 89–90; TV 90–93; V Caversham St Jo 93–00; Canada from 00; Sen Chapl Miss to Seafarers 00–01; P-in-c Surrey Epiphany Canada 01–02; R from 02; Adn Fraser 07–17. *962 29th Street East, North Vancouver BC V7K 1B8, Canada* T: (001) (604) 987 6307 or (604) 588 4511 F: (604) 588 4511 E: rowesmb@aol.com

ROWE, Vanda Sheila. See PERRETT, Vanda Sheila

ROWELL, Canon Alan. b 50. Lon Univ BSc 71 AKC 71. Trin Coll Bris. **d** 75 **p** 76. C W Hampstead St Cuth *Lon* 75–78; C Camborne *Truro* 78–81; V Pendeen 81–84; V Pendeen w Morvah 85–15; Hon Can Truro Cathl 03–15; rtd 15. *34 Penhaligon Court, Truro TR1 1YB* E: canonrowell@outlook.com

ROWELL, Mrs Gillian Margaret. b 56. Lon Bible Coll BA 96. SAOMC 97. **d** 99 **p** 00. NSM The Lee *Ox* 99–04; NSM Hawridge w Cholesbury and St Leonard 99–04; TV Cottesloe 13–18; V Tilehurst St Cath and Calcot from 18. *The Vicarage, Wittenham Avenue, Tilehurst, Reading RG31 5LN* T: 0118-942 7786 E: gillrowell@tiscali.co.uk

ROWELL, William Kevin. b 51. Reading Univ BSc 71. Linc Th Coll 78. **d** 80 **p** 81. C Cannock *Lich* 80–83; Ind Chapl 83–86; C Ketley and Oakengates 83–86; R Norton in the Moors 86–93; RD Leek 91–93; P-in-c Minsterley and Habberley *Heref* 93–01; RD Pontesbury 99–01; Miss Adv USPG Heref, Worc and Glouc 01–03; NSM Wenlock *Heref* 02–03; R Llandysilio and Penrhos and Llandrinio etc *St As* 04–08; R Welshpool, Castle Caereinion and Pool Quay 08–11; Can Cursal St As Cathl 08–11; rtd 11; PtO *Heref* from 15. *17 Croft Road, Welshpool SY21 7QD* T: (01938) 552064 M: 07714-509952 E: wkrowell@btinternet.com

ROWETT, Canon David Peter. b 55. Univ Coll Dur BA 76. Ripon Coll Cuddesdon 82. **d** 84 **p** 85. C Yeovil *B & W* 84–88; C Yeovil St Mich 88–89; V Fairfield St Matt *Linc*

89–05; P-in-c Barton upon Humber 05–10; V from 10; R Saxby All Saints from 10; V Horkstow from 10; R S Ferriby from 10; RD Yarborough from 11; Can and Preb Linc Cathl from 18. *The Vicarage, Beck Hill, Barton-upon-Humber DN18 5EY* T: (01652) 632202

ROWLAND, Andrew John William. b 60. STETS 98. **d** 01 **p** 02. C Verwood *Sarum* 01–06; V W Moors 06–18; R Wimborne Minster and the N Villages from 18; RD Wimborne from 16. *The Rectory, 17 King Street, Wimborne BH21 1DZ* E: ajwrowland@tiscali.co.uk

ROWLAND, Prof Christopher Charles. b 47. Ch Coll Cam BA 69 MA 73 PhD 75. Ridley Hall Cam 72. **d** 75 **p** 76. Lect RS Newc Univ 74–79; Hon C Benwell St Jas 75–78; Hon C Gosforth All SS 78–79; Dean Jes Coll Cam 79–91; Asst Lect Div Cam Univ 83–85; Lect Div 85–91; LtO *Ely* 79–91; Prof of Exegesis of H Scripture Ox Univ 91–14; Fell Qu Coll Ox from 91; LtO *Ox* 91–12; Can Th Liv Cathl 05–14. *Queen's College, Oxford OX1 4AW* T: (01865) 279120

ROWLAND, Ms Dawn Jeannette. b 38. RSCN 61 RGN 63. S'wark Ord Course 81. **dss** 84 **d** 87 **p** 94. Par Dn Croydon H Sav *S'wark* 84–89; NSM Riddlesdown 89–08; PtO from 08. *18 Le Personne Road, Caterham CR3 5SU*

ROWLAND, Jennifer Norah. b 48. Worc Coll of Educn CertEd 70 Open Univ BA 83 Worc Univ Hon BA 12 ACIB. WMMTC 96. **d** 99 **p** 00. C Stratford-upon-Avon, Luddington etc *Cov* 99–03; P-in-c Ditton Priors w Neenton, Burwarton etc *Heref* 03–12; R 12–14; rtd 14; PtO *Cov* from 15. *19 Farnell Drive, Stratford-upon-Avon CV37 9DJ* T: (01789) 415548 E: jennyrowlandsoa@gmail.com

ROWLAND, Mrs June Mary. b 46. SRN 67. EMMTC 03. **d** 05 **p** 06. NSM Grantham St Wulfram *Linc* from 05; Chapl United Lincs Hosps NHS Trust from 06. *73 Harlaxton Road, Grantham NG31 7AE* M: 07710-455379 E: junerowlandhome@aol.com

ROWLAND, Matthew John. b 80. UWE BA 02 Bris Univ PGCE 03. Wycliffe Hall Ox 11. **d** 14 **p** 15. C Ex St Leon w H Trin 14–18; R Modbury, Bigbury, Ringmore etc from 18. *The Vicarage, Church Lane, Modbury, Ivybridge PL21 0QN* M: 07818-422449 E: m.rowland@oxon.org

ROWLAND, Canon Robert William. b 51. Birm Univ BA 72. St Mich Coll Llan 72. **d** 74 **p** 75. C Connah's Quay *St As* 74; C Shotton 74–76; C Llanrhos 76–81; V Dyserth and Trelawnyd and Cwm 81–17; P-in-c Bryn a Mor Miss Area from 18; AD St As 94–10; Hon Can St As Cathl 08–11; Can Cursal St As Cathl from 11. *The Vicarage, Dyserth, Rhyl LL18 6DB* T: (01745) 570750

ROWLAND, Sally Margaret. *See* MARCHANT, Sally Margaret

ROWLAND JONES, The Very Revd Sarah Caroline. b 59. Newnham Coll Cam BA 80 MA 84. St Jo Coll Nottm BTh 98. **d** 99 **p** 00. C Wrexham *St As* 99–02; S Africa 02–13; P-in-c Cardiff City Par *Llan* 13–18; Dean St D from 18. *The Deanery, The Pebbles, St David's, Haverfordwest SA62 6RD* T: (01437) 720202 E: dean@stdavidscathedral.org.uk

ROWLANDS, Alun Geoffrey. b 51. Open Univ MBA 02. **d** 12 **p** 13. OLM Mickleover All SS *Derby* 12–14; OLM Mickleover St Jo 12–14; OLM Mickleover 14–16; NSM from 16. *117 Western Road, Mickleover, Derby DE3 9GR* T: (01332) 517964 E: alunrowlands@btinternet.com

ROWLANDS, The Ven Emyr Wyn. b 42. St Mich Coll Llan 69. **d** 70 **p** 71. C Holyhead w Rhoscolyn *Ban* 70–71; C Holyhead w Rhoscolyn w Llanfair-yn-Neubwll 71–74; V Bodedern w Llechgynfarwy and Llechylched etc 74–88; R Machynlleth and Llanwrin 88–97; R Machynlleth w Llanwrin and Penegoes 97–10; AD Cyfeiliog and Mawddwy 96–10; Can Ban Cathl 97–03; Can and Preb Ban Cathl 03–10; Adn Meirionnydd 04–10; rtd 10; PtO *Ban* from 10. *2 Ffordd Meillion, Llangristiolus, Bodorgan LL62 5DQ* T: (01248) 750148

ROWLANDS, Preb Graeme Charles. b 53. K Coll Lon BD 74 AKC 74. St Aug Coll Cant 75. **d** 76 **p** 77. C Higham Ferrers w Chelveston *Pet* 76–79; C Gorton Our Lady and St Thos *Man* 79–81; J Reading H Trin *Ox* 81–89; P-in-c Kentish Town St Silas *Lon* 89–92; V 92–98; P-in-c Haverstock Hill H Trin w Kentish Town St Barn 93–98; V Kentish Town St Silas and H Trin w St Barn from 98; Preb St Paul's Cathl from 16. *St Silas's House, 11 St Silas's Place, London NW5 3QP* T: (020) 7485 3727 E: ssmktw@gmail.com

ROWLANDS, Mrs Jacqueline Adèle. b 43. Golds Coll Lon CertEd 65 BEd 72 Heythrop Coll Lon MA 05. St Alb Minl Tr Scheme 82. **dss** 85 **d** 87 **p** 05. Bromham w Oakley *St Alb* 85–88; Par Dn 87–88; Par Dn Bromham w Oakley and Stagsden 88–89; PtO 04–05 and from 11; Hon C Bedford St Andr 05–11. *20 Anvil Close, Portslade, Brighton BN41 2HT* M: 07793-045203 E: sienajar@hotmail.com

ROWLANDS, Canon John Henry Lewis. b 47. Univ of Wales (Lamp) BA 68 Magd Coll Cam BA 70 MA 74 Dur Univ

MLitt 86. Westcott Ho Cam 70. **d** 72 **p** 73. C Aberystwyth *St D* 72–76; Chapl Univ of Wales (Lamp) 76–79; Youth Chapl 76–79; Dir Academic Studies St Mich Coll Llan 79–84; Sub-Warden 84–88; Warden 88–97; Lect Univ of Wales (Cardiff) *Llan* 79–97; Asst Dean 81–83; Dean 93–97; Dean of Div 91–95; Dir of Ords 85–88; V Whitchurch 97–02; TR 02–17; Hon Can Llan Cathl 90–97; Can Llan Cathl 97–02; Chan Llan Cathl 02–17; Chapl Cardiff and Vale Univ Health Bd 97–17; Fell Woodard Corp 89–17; Hon Fell from 17; rtd 17. *Llys y Coed, Bwlch Gwynt, New Quay SA45 9QS* T: (01545) 560143 M: 07343-579466 E: johnrowlands1915@outlook.com

ROWLANDS, Marc Alun. b 62. Univ of Wales (Abth) BSc 84 St D Coll Lamp MPhil 89 PhD 95. Wycliffe Hall Ox 97. **d** 99 **p** 00. C Betws w Ammanford *St D* 99–01; C Carmarthen St Pet 01–02; P-in-c Llanpumsaint w Llanllawddog 02–05; TV Cwm Gwendraeth 06–10; TR Trisant 10–18; P-in-c Lampeter w Maestir and Silian and Llangybi and Betws Bledrws from 18. *The Vicarage, Maesllan, Lampeter SA48 7EN* E: revdocrock@yahoo.com

ROWLANDS, Robert. b 31. Roch Th Coll. **d** 68 **p** 69. C Hooton *Ches* 68–71; V Stretton 71–88; P-in-c Appleton Thorn and Antrobus 87–88; V Stretton and Appleton Thorn 88–00; rtd 00; PtO *Carl* from 01. *Uplands, Redhills Road, Arnside, Carnforth LA5 0AS* T: (01524) 761612

ROWLANDS, Simon David. b 66. **d** 99 **p** 00. C St Peter-in-Thanet *Cant* 99–03; Chapl Cant Ch Ch Univ 03–06; V Bridge *Cant* 07–13; P-in-c Faversham 13–17; C The Brents and Davington w Oare and Luddenham 13–14; C Eastling w Ospringe and Stalisfield w Otterden 13–14; P-in-c The Brents and Davington 14–17; P-in-c Ospringe 14–17; P-in-c Preston-next-Faversham 16–17; V Faversham from 17. *The Vicarage, 16 Newton Road, Faversham ME13 8DY* T: (01795) 532592

ROWLANDS, Mrs Valerie Christine. b 54. St As Minl Tr Course 99. **d** 02 **p** 03. NSM Llanbedr DC w Llangynhafal, Llanychan etc *St As* 02–04; Chapl St As Cathl 04–14; TV St As 06–14; V Llanrhaeadr-yng-Nghinmeirch and Prion w Nantglyn 14–16; TV Denbigh Miss Area from 17. *The Rectory, Llandyrnog, Denbigh LL16 4LT* T: (01824) 790777

ROWLANDSON, Diana Mary. b 56. Ox Min Course 10. **d** 13 **p** 14. NSM Gerrards Cross and Fulmer *Ox* 13–18; R Earlham *Nor* from 18; C The Mitre Benefice from 18. *The Vicarage, Bluebell Road, Norwich NR4 7LP* T: (01603) 501713 M: 07831-265806 E: earlhamparish@gmail.com *or* di.rowlandson@earlhamparish.org

ROWLEY, Ms Anne Christine. b 50. Lanc Univ BA 96 Leeds Univ MA 10 Huddersfield Univ PGCE 99. Yorks Min Course 07. **d** 10 **p** 11. NSM Dunnington *York* 10–12; Chapl York Hosps NHS Foundn Trust from 12; NSM Rural E York 12–14; NSM York All SS Pavement w St Crux and St Mich 14; NSM York St Olave w St Giles 14; NSM York St Helen w St Martin 14; NSM York St Denys 14; Chapl York Hosps NHS Foundn Trust from 14. *2 Lady Hewley's Cottages, St Saviourgate, York YO1 8NW* T: (01904) 651189 *or* 876606 E: a.rowley@yorksj.ac.uk

ROWLEY, Preb Christopher Francis Elmes. b 48. St Jo Coll Dur BA 70 St Luke's Coll Ex PGCE 71. St Steph Ho Ox 76. **d** 78 **p** 79. C Parkstone St Pet w Branksea and St Osmund *Sarum* 78–81; TV 82–85; P-in-c Chard Gd Shep Furnham *B & W* 85–89; P-in-c Dowlishwake w Chaffcombe, Knowle St Giles etc 88–89; R Chard, Furnham w Chaffcombe, Knowle St Giles etc 89–91; V Stoke St Gregory w Burrowbridge and Lyng 91–04; RD Taunton 01–04; TV Wellington and Distr 04–13; RD Tone 07–12; Preb Wells Cathl 09–13; rtd 13; Chapl Wellington Hosps from 14; PtO *B & W* from 13. *39 Cornlands, Sampford Peverell, Tiverton EX16 7UA* T: (01884) 799011 E: christopherrowley@uwclub.net

ROWLEY, David Michael. b 39. NOC 87. **d** 90 **p** 91. C Stainland *Wakef* 90–93; V Hayfield *Derby* 93–99; P-in-c Chinley w Buxworth 98–99; V Glossop 99–04; RD 96–04; rtd 04; PtO *Derby* 04–18. *8 Weavers Close, Belper DE56 0HZ* T: (01773) 882690

ROWLEY, Jennifer Jane Elisabeth. b 61. LMH Ox BA 84 MA 92. EAMTC 99. **d** 02 **p** 03. C Kingsthorpe w Northampton St Dav *Pet* 02–04; C Kettering SS Pet and Paul 04–06; P-in-c Nettleham *Linc* 06–13; P-in-c Welton and Dunholme w Scothern 10–13; R Selsdon St Jo w St Fran *S'wark* from 13; AD Croydon Addington from 15. *St John's Rectory, Upper Selsdon Road, South Croydon CR2 8DD* T: 0208 657 2343 E: jennyrowley@waitrose.com

ROWLEY, Mrs Susan. b 49. **d** 01 **p** 02. OLM Fazeley *Lich* 01–11; rtd 11; PtO *Lich* from 12. *137 Reindeer Road, Fazeley, Tamworth B78 3SP* T: (01827) 250431 *or* 289414 E: s.rowley2@sky.com

ROWLEY-BROOKE, Marie Gordon. b 46. ARIAM 69. Ripon Coll Cuddesdon 00. **d** 02 **p** 03. C Leckhampton SS Phil and Jas w Cheltenham St Jas *Glouc* 02–05; I Nenagh *L & K* 05–15; Can Limerick Cathl 10–15; Treas Limerick Cathl 14–15; Treas 14–15; rtd 15; PtO *L & K* from 15. *Holly Cottage, Sallypark, Latteragh, Nenagh, Co Tipperary, Republic of Ireland* M: (00353) 85-147 4792 E: canonmarie@me.com

ROWLING, Canon Catherine. b 55. Man Poly BEd 77. Westcott Ho Cam 83 NEOC 85. **dss** 86 **d** 87 **p** 94. Gt Ayton w Easby and Newton-in-Cleveland *York* 86–89; Par Dn 87–89; Chapl Teesside Poly 89–92; Chapl Teesside Univ 92–96; Dean of Women's Min 96–08; Co Dir of Ords 96–05; Dioc Dir of Ords 05–09; Dioc Moderator Reader Tr 99–04; Dir Reader Studies 05–09; Can and Preb York Minster 01–09; Prin Lindisfarne Regional Tr Partnership 09–17; PtO *York* 09–15. *Address withheld by request* M: 07714-052282 E: cathyrowling0408@gmail.com

ROWNTREE, Peter. b 47. St D Coll Lamp BA 68 Univ of Wales (Cardiff) MA 70. St Steph Ho Ox 70. **d** 72 **p** 73. C Stanwell *Lon* 72–75; C Northolt St Mary 75–79; Chapl Ealing Gen Hosp 79–83; Chapl Cherry Knowle Hosp Sunderland 83–87; Chapl Ryhope Hosp Sunderland 83–87; Chapl Ealing Gen Hosp 87–90; Chapl Ealing Hosp NHS Trust 91–94 and 94–99; Chapl W Lon Healthcare NHS Trust 94–99; Sen Co-ord Chapl Univ Coll Lon Hosps NHS Foundn Trust 99–08; rtd 08; PtO *Nor* from 08. *Address withheld by request*

✠**ROWTHORN, The Rt Revd Jeffery William.** b 34. Ch Coll Cam BA 57 MA 62 Union Th Sem (NY) BD 61 Oriel Coll Ox BLitt 72 Berkeley Div Sch DD 87. Cuddesdon Coll 61. **d** 62 **p** 63 **c** 87. C Woolwich St Mary w H Trin *S'wark* 62–65; R Garsington *Ox* 65–68; Chapl and Dean Union Th Sem NY USA 68–73; Assoc Prof Past Th Yale and Berkeley Div 73–87; Suff Bp Connecticut 87–93; Bp in Charge Convocation of American Chs in Eur 94–01; Asst Bp Eur 95–01; Asst Bp Spain 97–01; Asst Bp Portugal 97–01; rtd 01. *17 Woodland Drive, Salem CT 06420-4023, USA* T: (001) (860) 859 3377 E: jefferyrowthorn@yahoo.com

ROXBY, Gordon George. b 39. Lon Univ BSc 61. Coll of Resurr Mirfield 61. **d** 63 **p** 64. C Fleetwood St Pet *Blackb* 63–66; C Kirkham 66–68; V Runcorn St Jo Weston *Ches* 68–78; R Moston St Chad *Man* 78–86; V Bury St Pet 86–99; AD Bury 86–96; Hon Can Man Cathl 97–99; V Sandiway *Ches* 99–05; Initial Minl Tr Officer 99–04; rtd 05; PtO *Ches* from 05. *16 St Joseph's Way, Nantwich CW5 6TE* T: (01270) 619898 E: gordon@roxbylife.org.uk

ROY, Jennifer Pearl. *See* DREW, Jennifer Pearl

ROYDEN, Canon Charles. b 60. Wycliffe Hall Ox BA 86 MA 91. **d** 87 **p** 88. C Bidston *Ches* 87–91; V N Brickhill and Putnoe *St Alb* 91–92; V Bedf St Mark from 93; Hon Can St Alb from 13. *The Vicarage, Calder Rise, Bedford MK41 7UY* T: (01234) 309175 F: 342613 M: 07973-113861 E: vicar@thisischurch.com

ROYDEN, Eric Ramsay. b 29. St Deiniol's Hawarden 75. **d** 77 **p** 78. Hon C Tranmere St Paul w St Luke *Ches* 77–81; C Eastham 81; V New Brighton All SS 81–95; P-in-c 95–97; rtd 95; PtO *Ches* 97–07; *St Alb* from 07. *84 Asgard Drive, Bedford MK41 0UT* T: (01234) 294496 E: eroyden@googlemail.com

ROYDEN, Ross Eric. b 55. Lon Bible Coll BA 77 Nottm Univ MTh 82. Wycliffe Hall Ox 79. **d** 81 **p** 82. C Moreton *Ches* 81–84; Chapl and Tutor Bedf Coll of HE *St Alb* 84–93; R Banchory *Ab* 93–00; R Kincardine O'Neil 93–00; V Kowloon Tong Ch Ch Hong Kong from 00. *Christ Church Vicarage, 2 Derby Road, Kowloon Tong, Kowloon, Hong Kong* T: (00852) 2338 4433 F: 2338 8422 E: rossroyden@gmail.com

ROYLANCE, Mrs Margaret. b 47. St Mary's Coll Chelt CertEd 68. Cant Sch of Min 93. **d** 96 **p** 97. Chapl Ashford Sch 96–10; NSM Tenterden and Smallhythe *Cant* 96–16; NSM Rother and Oxney 13–16; NSM Tenterden, Rother and Oxney 16–17; rtd 17; PtO *Cant* from 17. *5 Southgate Road, Tenterden TN30 7BS* T: (01580) 762332 F: 765267 E: johnsroylance@gmail.com

ROYLE, Antony Kevan. b 50. Lon Univ BSc 71 FIA 76. Trin Coll Bris 76. **d** 79 **p** 80. C Chell *Lich* 79–82; C Leyland St Andr *Blackb* 82–86; V Blackb Sav 86–95; Chapl Blackb R Infirmary and Park Lee Hosp 86–95; Chapl E Lancs Hospice 86–95; TR Walton H Trin *Ox* 95–01; NSM Wendover Deanery 01–17; PtO *B & W* from 17. *20 Earlesfield, Nailsea, Bristol BS48 4SF* M: 07796-143905 E: kevanroyle@gmail.com

ROYLE, Gillian Mary. *See* PAWSON, Gillian Mary

ROYLE, Canon Peter Sydney George. b 34. K Coll Lon BD 57 AKC 57. **d** 58 **p** 59. C St Helier *S'wark* 58–62; C Alice Springs Australia 62–63; R 63–68; Can Darwin 68; P-in-c Sydenham St Phil *S'wark* 69–72; V Leigh Park *Portsm* 72–85; RD Havant 77–82; V S w N Hayling 85–96; V S Hayling 96–97; Hon Can Portsm Cathl 95–97; rtd 97; PtO *Ex* 97–06; *Sarum* from 06. *The Lodge, Easton Farm, Bishop's Canning, Devizes SN10 2LR* T: (01380) 862900 E: george.royle.1@btinternet.com

ROYLE, Canon Roger Michael. b 39. AKC 61 Lambeth MA 90. **d** 62 **p** 63. C Portsea St Mary *Portsm* 62–65; C St Helier *S'wark* 65–68; Succ S'wark Cathl 68–71; Warden Eton Coll Dorney Par Project *Ox* 71–74; Conduct Eton Coll 74–79; LtO *S'wark* 79–90; Chapl Ld Mayor Treloar Coll Alton 90–92; Hon C Froyle and Holybourne *Win* 90–92; Hon Can and Chapl S'wark Cathl 93–99; PtO from 99; rtd 04. *Address withheld by request*

ROYSTON, Virginia Helen. b 53. Bris Univ BSc 76 MB, ChB 79. STETS 09. **d** 12 **p** 13. NSM Cotham St Sav w St Mary and Clifton St Paul *Bris* from 12. *14 Grove Avenue, Coombe Dingle, Bristol BS9 2RP* T: 0117-968 6622 M: 07813-692852

RUBIE, William Edward. b 80. Ox Univ BA 03 Oak Hill Th Coll BA 12. St Mellitus Coll 18. **d** 19. C Heatons *Man* from 19. *112 Crescent Park, Stockport SK4 2JE* E: will@stms.org.uk

RUDALL, Mark Edward. b 53. Regent's Park Coll Ox BA 80 MA 84. Ripon Coll Cuddesdon 00. **d** 01 **p** 02. In Bapt Min 80–00; C Wallingford *Ox* 01–03; Dioc Dir Communications *Guildf* 04–13; rtd 13; PtO *Win* 11–14; *Guildf* from 13. *108 Prospect Road, Farnborough GU14 8NS* T: (01252) 645486 M: 07779-654975 E: mark.rudall@ntlworld.com

RUDD, Carl Nigel. b 71. Salford Univ BSc 93 PhD 97. Trin Coll Bris BA 06. **d** 06 **p** 07. C Whitstable *Cant* 06–10; C Penn Fields *Lich* 10–18; V Stafford St Jo and Tixall w Ingestre from 18. *The Rectory, Westhead Avenue, Stafford ST16 3RP* T: (01785) 253493 E: carl.rudd@gmail.com

RUDD, Colin Richard. b 41. AKC 64. **d** 65 **p** 66. C N Stoneham *Win* 65–70; V Rotherwick, Hook and Greywell 70–74; R Hook w Greywell 74–78; Toc H 78–89; V Buckland *Ox* 89–98; V Littleworth 89–98; R Pusey 89–98; R Gainfield 98–99; RD Vale of White Horse 96–99; rtd 99; PtO *B & W* from 06. *Alcudia, Bilbrook, Minehead TA24 6HE* T: (01984) 640021 E: colinrudd70@gmail.com

RUDD, Robert Arthur. b 33. ALCD 60. **d** 60 **p** 61. C Blackb Sav 60–63; C Huyton St Geo *Liv* 63–65; V Bickershaw 65–72; Asst Chapl HM Pris Liv 72–73; Birm 73–78; Parkhurst 78–86; Camp Hill 86–92; Chapl St Mary's Hosp Newport 92–95; rtd 95; PtO *Portsm* from 95. *The Elms, 13 Horsebridge Hill, Newport PO30 5TJ* T: (01983) 524415

RUDD, Mrs Sonia Winifred. b 44. Nottm Univ BSc 66 Leeds Univ MSc 68. Ox Min Course 92. **d** 94 **p** 95. NSM Ox St Andr 94–96; C Buckland 96–99; PtO *B & W* from 06. *Alcudia, Bilbrook, Minehead TA24 6HE* T: (01984) 640021 M: 07886-451743 E: soniarudd67@googlemail.com

RUDDICK, David Mark. b 76. Pemb Coll Cam BA 98 Homerton Coll Cam PGCE 99. Oak Hill Th Coll BA 09. **d** 09 **p** 10. C Elmswell *St E* 09–12; TV Morden *S'wark* from 12. *140 Stonecot Hill, Sutton SM3 9HQ* T: (020) 8330 6566 M: 07761-320736 E: davidruddick09@gmail.com

RUDDLE, Canon Donald Arthur. b 31. Linc Th Coll 64. **d** 66 **p** 67. C Kettering SS Pet and Paul 66–70; V Earlham St Anne *Nor* 70–79; V E Malling *Roch* 79–95; RD Malling 84–93; Hon Can Roch Cathl 88–95; Chapl Nord Pas de Calais *Eur* 95–98; rtd 98; PtO *Eur* from 98; *Cant* from 05. *Sycamore Lodge, 5 Windmill Lane, Faversham ME13 7GT* T: (01795) 533461 E: don.ruddle@talktalk.net

RUDDOCK, Brian John. b 45. Dur Univ BA 66 Nottm Univ MEd 91. Westcott Ho Cam 67. **d** 69 **p** 70. C Ross *Heref* 69–72; C Kettering SS Pet and Paul 72–75; P-in-c Colchester St Steph *Chelmsf* 75–77; TR Colchester St Leon, St Mary Magd and St Steph 77–84; R March St Pet *Ely* 84–89; R March St Mary 84–89; RD March 87–89; Bp's Officer for Unemployment *Sheff* 89–94; Resource and Development Officer Chs Community Work Alliance 96–02; LtO *Sheff* from 96; PtO *Sarum* 07–15; rtd 09. *10 Holly Drive, Wick, Littlehampton BN17 6LB* T: (01903) 721467 E: brianjruddock@btinternet.com

RUDDOCK, Bruce. *See* RUDDOCK, Reginald Bruce

RUDDOCK, Canon Edgar Chapman. b 48. St Jo Coll Dur BA 70 MA 76. Cranmer Hall Dur 70. **d** 74 **p** 75. C Birm St Geo 74–78; R 78–83; Dir Tr Dio St Jo S Africa 83–86; P-in-c Mandini 86–87; Prov Dir Tr 88–91; Hon Can Zululand from 95; TR Stoke-upon-Trent *Lich* 91–02; Dir Internat Relns United Soc 03–14; Dep Gen Sec 05–14; rtd 14; PtO *Guildf* 04–14; *Win* from 15. *2 Talbot Road, Dibden Purlieu, Southampton SO45 4PP* T: (023) 8194 4047 E: edgar.ruddock@gmail.com

RUDDOCK, Kenneth Edward. b 30. TCD BA 52 QUB MTh 79. CITC 53 TCD Div Sch Div Test. **d** 53 **p** 54. C Ballymena *Conn* 53–56; C Belfast St Thos 56–60; I Tomregan w Drumlane *K, E & A* 60–68; I Belfast St Luke *Conn* 68–80; Miss to Seamen 80–96; I Whitehead and Islandmagee *Conn* 80–96; Can Lisburn Ch Ch Cathl 90–96; Dioc Info Officer from 90; Chan Conn Cathl 96; rtd 96; Dioc C *Conn* 98–18. *24 Fourtowns Manor, Ahoghill, Ballymena BT42 1RS* T: (028) 2587 8966

RUDDOCK, Canon Leonard William. b 58. CITC 90. **d** 94 **p** 95. NSM Roscrea w Kyle, Bourney and Corbally *L & K*

94–06; C Stillorgan w Blackrock *D & G* 06–08; I Blessington w Kilbride, Ballymore Eustace etc from 08; Can Ch Ch Cathl Dublin from 18. *The Rectory, 13 Ashton, Blessington, Co Wicklow, Republic of Ireland* T: (00353) (45) 865178 M: 87-764 3296 E: leonardruddock@gmail.com

RUDDOCK, Canon Reginald Bruce. b 55. AGSM 77. Chich Th Coll 80. **d** 83 **p** 84. C Felpham w Middleton *Chich* 83–86; C Portsea St Mary *Portsm* 86–88; P-in-c Barnes St Mich *S'wark* 88–95; Dir Angl Cen Rome 95–99; Hon Can American Cathl Paris from 96; Can Res Worc Cathl 99–04; Can Res Pet Cathl 04–17; Liturg Officer 04–12; rtd 17; Chapl Chich Cathl from 18; Custos St Mary's Hosp Chich from 18; Chapl to The Queen from 08. *6 Priory Road, Chichester PO19 1NS* E: rbruddock@outlook.com

RUDGE, Colin. b 48. Open Univ BA 04. Wilson Carlile Coll 96 SEITE 08. **d** 10 **p** 11. C Hollington St Jo *Chich* 10–12; C Seaford w Sutton 12–16; rtd 16; PtO *Chich* from 16. *10 Harrow Close, Seaford BN25 3PE* T: (01323) 898739 M: 07967 778765 E: colin.rudge@gmail.com

RUDGE, Susannah Mary. *See* BRASIER, Susannah Mary

RUDKIN, Simon David. b 51. Bradf Univ BA 74 K Coll Lon BD 77 AKC 77. Coll of Resurr Mirfield 77. **d** 78 **p** 79. C Flixton St Mich *Man* 78–81; C Atherton 81–84; V Lever Bridge 84–91; P-in-c Pennington w Lindal and Marton *Carl* 91–96; P-in-c Pennington and Lindal w Marton and Bardsea 96–00; R Morland, Thrimby, Gt Strickland and Cliburn 00–09; P-in-c Kirkby Thore w Temple Sowerby and Newbiggin 04–07; P-in-c Bolton and Crosby Ravensworth 05–09; R Bedale and Leeming and Thornton Watlass *Ripon* 09–11; V The Thorntons and The Otteringtons *York* 11–16; Chapl N Yorks Police 11–16; rtd 16. *4 Templars Court, Temple Sowerby, Penrith CA10 1SR* T: (01768) 362059 E: sd.rudkin@btinternet.com

RUDMAN, Preb David Walter Thomas. b 48. Oak Hill Th Coll BD 72. **d** 72 **p** 73. C Plymouth St Jude *Ex* 72–75; C Radipole *Sarum* 76; C Radipole and Melcombe Regis 77; Warden St Geo Ho Braunton 77–03; R Georgeham *Ex* 88–03; Dioc Adv in Adult Tr 97–03; TV S Molton w Nymet St George, High Bray etc 03–13; Dioc Adv in OLM 03–13; Preb Ex Cathl 09–13; rtd 13. *Greendale Farm, Pill Lane, Barnstaple EX32 9EQ* E: rudman1604@gmail.com

RUDMAN, Thomas Peter William. b 22. Oak Hill Th Coll 60. **d** 62 **p** 63. C St Paul's Cray St Barn CD *Roch* 62–65; C Morden *S'wark* 65–67; V Lowestoft Ch Ch *Nor* 67–73; V Stapenhill w Cauldwell *Derby* 73–81; V Sutton le Marsh *Linc* 81–87; RD Calcewaithe and Candleshoe 85–87; rtd 87; PtO *Win* 87–96; *Ex* 96–09. *27 Gracey Court, Broadclyst, Exeter EX5 3GA* T: (01392) 466436

RUE, Kenneth Gordon. TCD BBS 75. **d** 10 **p** 11. NSM Powerscourt w Kilbride *D & G* 10–11; NSM Wicklow w Killiskey from 11; OLM Co-ord Ch of Ireland from 19. *Shancarrig, Cronroe, Ashford, Co Wicklow, Republic of Ireland* M: 87-276 6590 E: krue@eircom.net

RUEHORN, Eric Arthur. b 33. St Aid Birkenhead 58. **d** 61 **p** 62. C Harpurhey Ch Ch *Man* 61–65; V Roughtown 65–74; V Hawkshaw Lane 74–99; rtd 99; PtO *Man* from 00. *101 Bankhouse Road, Bury BL8 1DZ* T: 0161-761 3983 E: e.ruehorn@btopenworld.com

RUFF, Brian Chisholm. b 36. Lon Univ BD 66 ACA 60 FCA 70. Oak Hill Th Coll 63. **d** 67 **p** 68. C Cheadle *Ches* 67–72; Educn and Youth Sec CPAS 72–76; V New Milverton *Cov* 76–90; V Westbourne Ch Ch Chpl *Win* 90–01; rtd 02; PtO *Win* from 02; *Sarum* 03–18. *19 Hardy Road, West Moors, Wimborne BH22 0EX* T: (01202) 868733 E: bandjruff@yahoo.co.uk

RUFF, Michael Ronald. b 49. K Coll Lon BD 72 AKC 72 Ch Ch Coll Cant PGCE 77. St Aug Coll Cant 72. **d** 73 **p** 74. C Old Shoreham *Chich* 73–76; Chapl Ellesmere Coll 77–81; Chapl Grenville Coll Bideford 81–87; Chapl Stamford Sch 87–06; P-in-c Stamford St Mary and St Martin *Linc* 06–13; rtd 11; PtO *Linc* from 17; *Pet* from 17. *3 Baxters Lane, Easton on the Hill, Stamford PE9 3NH* T: (01780) 766567 E: michael.ruff342@btinternet.com

RUFFLE, Preb John Leslie. b 43. ALCD 66. **d** 66 **p** 67. C Eastwood *S'well* 66–70; C Keynsham w Queen Charlton *B & W* 70–75; P-in-c Weston-super-Mare Em 75; TV Weston-super-Mare Cen Par 75–84; V Yatton Moor 84–91; TR 91–98; P-in-c Chew Stoke w Nempnett Thrubwell 98–03; Dioc Adv in Past Care and Counselling 03–06; rtd 06; Preb Wells Cathl *B & W* 97–13; PtO 06–14. *52 Highbridge Road, Burnham-on-Sea TA8 1LN* T: (01278) 788322 E: john.ruffle01@btinternet.com

RUFFLE, Wendy Ann. b 56. **d** 10 **p** 11. C Tewkesbury w Walton Cardiff and Twyning *Glouc* from 10. *High Bank, Gambles Lane, Cleeve Hill, Cheltenham GL52 3QA* T: (01242) 674103 E: rev.wendy@me.com

RUGEN, Peter. b 60. Crewe & Alsager Coll BEd 86. Trin Coll Bris MA 00. **d** 00 **p** 01. C Shipley St Pet *Bradf* 00–04; P-in-c Riddlesden and Morton St Luke 04–08; P-in-c Norley, Crowton and Kingsley *Ches* 08–11; V 11–18; RD Frodsham 11–18; V Plas Newton from 18. *St Michael's Vicarage, 22 Plas Newton Lane, Chester CH2 1PA* T: (01244) 319677 E: peterugen@gmail.com

RUGG, Andrew Philip. b 47. Kent Univ BA 82. Sarum & Wells Th Coll 83. **d** 85 **p** 86. C Harlesden All So *Lon* 85–90; TV Benwell *Newc* 90–97; V Weetslade 97–00; rtd 00; PtO *York* 00–12. *2 Ellen Wilson Cottages, Lawrence Street, York YO10 3WP* M: 07980-390051

RUGG, Christopher James McTeer. b 75. St Jo Coll Dur BSc 97. Trin Coll Bris 06. **d** 08 **p** 09. C Week St Mary Circle of Par *Truro* 08–11; USA from 11. *4104 Tiffany Lane, Redding CA 96002, USA* T: (001) (503) 233 3833

RUGMAN, Mrs Hazel. b 47. R Holloway Coll Lon BA 68 ACIS 89. NOC 01. **d** 03 **p** 04. NSM Sandbach *Ches* 03–06; NSM Crewe St Andr w St Jo 06–17; NSM Crewe Ch Ch 07–13; rtd 18; PtO *Ches* from 18. *High Trees, 157 Sandbach Road North, Alsager, Stoke-on-Trent ST7 2AX* T: (01270) 876386 F: 883737 M: 07762-706120 E: hazelrugman@btinternet.com

RUITERS, Ivan John. b 61. Coll of Transfiguration Grahamstown 94. **d** 96 **p** 97. C Berea S Africa 96–00; R Maidstone 00–01; R Newlands 02–07; I Killesher *K, E & A* 07–16; Can Kilmore Cathl 14–16; V Milnrow and New Hey *Man* 16–18; S Africa from 18. *Address temp unknown* E: ivanruiters@yahoo.com

✠**RUMALSHAH, The Rt Revd Munawar Kenneth (Mano).** b 41. Punjab Univ BSc 60 Serampore Coll BD 65 Karachi Univ MA 68 Homerton Coll Cam PGCE 88. Bp's Coll Calcutta 62. **d** 65 **p** 66 **c** 94. C H Trin Cathl Karachi Pakistan 65–69; C Roundhay St Edm *Ripon* 70–73; Area Sec and Asst Home Sec CMS 73–78; Educn Sec BCC 78–81; P-in-c Southall St Geo *Lon* 81–88; Lect Edwardes Coll Peshawar Pakistan 89–94; Bp Peshawar 94–99 and 03–07; Gen Sec USPG and Hon Asst Bp S'wark 99–03; rtd 07. *81 Bantry Road, Slough SL1 5FD*

RUMBALL, William Michael. b 41. Surrey Univ BSc 63 Hon BUniv 11 Birm Univ PhD 66 MA 11 Open Univ BA 75 MIM 66 MINucE 73 FIMMM 03. Wycliffe Hall Ox 78. **d** 80 **p** 81. C S Molton, Nymet St George, High Bray etc *Ex* 80–83; V S Hetton w Haswell *Dur* 83–90; V S Wingfield and Wessington *Derby* 90–99; rtd 99; Hon C Brailsford w Shirley and Osmaston w Edlaston *Derby* 01–03; PtO 03–10; *Lich* 08–10; *B & W* 10–14; *Glouc* 14–19. *21 Capel Court, The Burgage, Prestbury, Cheltenham GL52 3EL* E: wm.rumball@gmail.com

RUMBLE, Alison Merle. *See* PRINCE, Alison Merle

RUMBLE, Sarah Victoria. b 74. Newc Univ BA 96 St Martin's Coll Lanc PGCE 97. SCTEI 17. **d** 19. C Portswood St Denys *Win* from 19. *The Vicarage, 54 Whitworth Crescent, Southampton SO18 1GD* M: 07818-857239 E: serarumble@gmail.com

RUMENS, Ms Katharine Mary. b 53. UEA BEd 76. Westcott Ho Cam 90. **d** 92 **p** 94. Par Dn E Ham w Upton Park and Forest Gate *Chelmsf* 92–94; C 94–95; C Waterloo St Jo w St Andr *S'wark* 95–00; Chapl S Bank Cen and Chapl Lon Weekend TV 95–00; R St Giles Cripplegate w St Bart Moor Lane etc *Lon* from 00. *The Rectory, 4 The Postern, Wood Street, London EC2Y 8BJ* T: (020) 7588 3013 *or* 7638 1997 F: 7588 3013 E: rumens@stgileschurch.com

✠**RUMSEY, The Rt Revd Andrew Paul.** b 68. Reading Univ BA 89 K Coll Lon DThMin 16. Ridley Hall Cam MA 98. **d** 97 **p** 98 **c** 19. C Harrow Trin St Mich *Lon* 97–01; V Gipsy Hill Ch Ch *S'wark* 01–11; R Oxted and Tandridge 11–14; TR Oxted 14–19; Area Bp Ramsbury *Sarum* from 19. *Ramsbury House, Bath Road, Marlborough SN8 4HS* E: andrew.rumsey@icloud.com

RUMSEY, Ian Mark. b 58. Van Mildert Coll Dur BSc 79 St Jo Coll Dur BA 89. Cranmer Hall Dur 87. **d** 90 **p** 91. C Dalston *Carl* 90–94; C Wreay 92–94; TV Cockermouth w Embleton and Wythop 94–04; Adv for Post-Ord Tr 97–00; V Hurdsfield *Ches* 04–12; Par Development Officer 12–16; V Bowdon from 16. *The Vicarage, Church Brow, Bowdon, Altrincham WA14 2SG* T: 0161-928 2468

RUNCORN, David Charles. b 54. BA 77. St Jo Coll Nottm 77. **d** 79 **p** 80. C Wealdstone H Trin *Lon* 79–82; Chapl Lee Abbey 82–87; C Ealing St Steph Castle Hill *Lon* 89–90; V 90–96; Dir Past and Evang Studies Trin Coll Bris 96–03; Dir Min Development *Lich* 03–08; Tutor St Jo Coll Nottm 08–12; Public Preacher *Glouc* from 12; Assoc Dioc Dir of Ords 15–19; Warden of Readers 15–19. *32 The Avenue, Tiverton EX16 4HW* M: 07870-331537 E: davidruncorn@mac.com

RUNCORN, Jacqueline Ann. *See* SEARLE, Jacqueline Ann

RUNDELL, Gerard Kenneth Bate. b 85. Goldsmiths' Coll Lon BMus 08 RCM MPerf 11 St Jo Coll Dur BA 18. Cranmer Hall Dur 15. **d** 18 **p** 19. C Alnwick *Newc* from 18. *10 Allerburn Lea, Alnwick NE66 2NJ* M: 07891-612791 E: gerard.rundell@gmail.com

RUNDELL, Simon Philip. b 67. Univ of N Lon BSc 95 Leeds Univ BA 01 RGN 90. Coll of Resurr Mirfield 99. **d** 01 **p** 02. C Southsea H Spirit *Portsm* 01–04; P-in-c Elson 04–09; V 09–12; P-in-c Bickleigh and Shaugh Prior *Ex* from 12; C Egg Buckland 12–17; C Estover 12–17; C Eggbuckland w Estover from 17; C Plymouth Crownhill Ascension from 12. *33 Leat Walk, Roborough, Plymouth PL6 7AT* E: simon@rundell.org.uk

RUNDELL-EVANS, Benjamin Oscar. b 94. Ripon Coll Cuddesdon 13. **d** 16 **p** 17. C Devizes St Jo w St Mary *Sarum* from 16. *52 Queen's Road, Devizes SN10 5HW* M: 07503-777172 E: rev.ben.rundell-evans@outlook.com

RUNDLE, Mrs Beryl Rosemary. b 28. Bris Univ BA 49 CertEd 50. S Dios Minl Tr Scheme 83. **dss** 86 **d** 87. Tangmere *Chich* 86–87; Hon Par Dn 87–92; Boxgrove 86–87; Hon Par Dn 87–92; Hon Par Dn Eastbourne St Sav and St Pet 92–98; PtO *Portsm* from 98. *22 Sovereign Drive, Southsea PO4 8XX* T: (01705) 826859

RUNDLE, Hilary. See WONG, Hilary

RUOFF, Mark Frederick John. b 76. K Coll Lon BA 98. St Mellitus Coll BA 15. **d** 15 **p** 16. C Onslow Square and S Kensington St Aug *Lon* 15–17; C Hammersmith St Paul from 17. *147 Lavenham Road, London SW18 5EP* M: 07919-403853 E: markfjruoff@gmail.com *or* mark.ruoff@sph.org

RUSCOE, Canon John Ernest. b 32. Dur Univ BA 57. Qu Coll Birm 57. **d** 59 **p** 60. C Jarrow St Paul *Dur* 59–63; C Whitburn 63–65; V S Hylton 65–10; Hon Can Dur Cathl 85–10; rtd 10; PtO *Dur* from 10. *17 Marina Avenue, Sunderland SR6 9AL* T: 0191-549 8371

RUSDELL-WILSON, Arthur Neville. b 43. Lon Univ BScEng 65 Linacre Coll Ox BA 70 MA 74. St Steph Ho Ox 68. **d** 71 **p** 72. C Whitton St Aug *Lon* 71–73; C Chiswick St Nic w St Mary 73–76; C Littlehampton St Jas *Chich* 76–81; C Littlehampton St Mary 76–81; C Wick 76–81; V Whitworth St Bart *Man* 81–88; V Shaw 88–98; rtd 03. *21 Fairview Avenue, Goring-by-Sea, Worthing BN12 4HT* T: (01903) 242561 E: arthur@go-forward.co.uk

RUSH, Paul Andrew. b 57. Lon Bible Coll BA 79 Anglia Poly Univ MA 01. Ridley Hall Cam 98. **d** 00 **p** 01. C Bar Hill *Ely* 00–03; Dioc Evang Officer *Leic* 03–06; Adv in Evang and Par Development *Bris* 06–13; C W Sheppey *Cant* from 13. *2 St Peter's Close, Minster on Sea, Sheerness ME12 3DD* T: (01795) 663661 M: 07906-118810 E: revdpaulrush@gmail.com

RUSH, Miss Shan Elizabeth. b 64. RGN 86 RSCN 86. Yorks Min Course 07. **d** 10 **p** 12. NSM Sheff St Mark Broomhill from 10; Chapl Bluebell Wood Children's Hospice 14–16. *28 Rivelin Street, Sheffield S6 5DL* M: 07598-156817 E: shan.rush@sheffield.anglican.org

RUSHFORTH, Colin Stephen. b 53. Chich Th Coll 74. **d** 77 **p** 78. C Moulsecoomb *Chich* 77–79; C Rumboldswyke 79–81; C Whyke w Rumboldswhyke and Portfield 81–82; V Friskney *Linc* 82–84; P-in-c Thorpe St Peter 82–84; TV Leic H Spirit 84–87; Chapl Leic R Infirmary 87–94; Chapl Leic R Infirmary NHS Trust 94–98; PtO *Leic* 08–12; P-in-c Sneinton St Steph w St Matthias *S'well* 12–16; P-in-c Nottingham St Geo w St Jo 12–16; rtd 16. *24 Holly Tree Avenue, Birstall, Leicester LE4 4LF* M: 07960-649191 E: colinrushforth@hotmail.co.uk

RUSHFORTH, Richard Hamblin. b 40. Keble Coll Ox BA 62 MA 71. Chich Th Coll 62. **d** 64 **p** 65. C St Leonards Ch Ch *Chich* 64–79; Org Sec Fellowship of St Nic 79–81; V Portslade St Nic and St Andr *Chich* 81–12; Min Portslade Gd Shep CD 88–89; rtd 12; PtO *Chich* 12–17. *12 Upper Church Road, St Leonards-on-Sea TN37 7AT* E: rhrushforth@btinternet.com

RUSHOLME, Susan. b 53. Leeds Univ BA 10. Yorks Min Course 07. **d** 10 **p** 11. NSM Chapel Allerton *Ripon* 10–14; *Leeds* from 14. *71 Eaton Hill, Leeds LS16 6SE* T: 0113-261 2913 M: 07504-880199 E: revsue.rusholme@virginmedia.com

RUSHTON, Charlotte Louise. **d** 17 **p** 18. C Merthyr Tydfil St Dav and Abercanaid *Llan* from 17. *Address withheld by request* T: (01685) 385884 E: rev.rushton@gmail.com

RUSHTON, Christopher John. b 54. LBIPP 93. Qu Coll Birm 10. **d** 11 **p** 12. OLM Hartshill, Penkhull and Trent Vale *Lich* 11–14; NSM 14–15; R from 15; Dioc Lay Min Adv from 12. *The School House, Vicarage Road, Hartshill, Stoke-on-Trent ST4 7NL* T: (01782) 410011 E: church@chrisrushton.co.uk

RUSHTON, David William. b 70. St Chad's Coll Dur BA 96 Cardiff Univ MTh 19. St Steph Ho Ox. **d** 98 **p** 99. C Hornsey St Mary w St Geo *Lon* 98–01; C Thameshead *S'wark* 01–02; Asst Chapl King's Coll Hosp NHS Trust 02–04; Chapl King's Coll Hosp NHS Foundn Trust 04–10;

Lead Chapl and Hospitaller Barts and The Lon NHS Trust 10–14; Lead Chapl R Free London NHS Foundn Trust 14–17; Chapl St Chad's Coll *Dur* from 17. *St Chad's College, 18 North Bailey, Durham DH1 3RH* T: 0191-334 3352 E: david.rushton@durham.ac.uk

RUSHTON, Gavin Michael. b 77. St Jo Coll Nottm 14. **d** 16 **p** 17. C Kendal St Thos *Carl* 16–19; P-in-c Oxclose *Dur* from 19. *Address temp unknown* M: 07976-701454 E: gavin.rushton@yahoo.co.uk

RUSHTON, Canon James David. b 39. Dur Univ BA 61. Cranmer Hall Dur. **d** 64 **p** 65. C Upper Armley *Ripon* 64–67; C Blackpool Ch Ch *Blackb* 67–70; V Preston St Cuth 70–79; V Denton Holme *Carl* 79–96; P-in-c Preston All SS *Blackb* 96–00; V 00–04; AD Preston 98–03; Hon Can Blackb Cathl 00–04; rtd 04; PtO *Blackb* from 04. *1 Stable Mews, Fleetwood Road, Thornton-Cleveleys FY5 1SQ* T: (01253) 820402

RUSHTON, Ms Janet Maureen. b 46. Keele Univ BA 68 Leic Univ PGCE 69. Wycliffe Hall Ox BTh 94. **d** 94 **p** 95. C Harrow St Mary *Lon* 94–98; C Putney St Mary *S'wark* 98–02; P-in-c Wolvercote w Summertown *Ox* 02–07; P-in-c Summertown 07–11; rtd 11; PtO *Lon* from 11. *20 Harvard Court, Honeybourne Road, London NW6 1HJ* T: (020) 7431 4606 E: jan.rushton5@gmail.com

RUSHTON, Canon Matthew John. b 75. St Anne's Coll Ox BA 96 MA 01 Linc Univ MA 13 Solicitor 01. Ripon Coll Cuddesdon 07. **d** 09 **p** 10. C Nettleham *Linc* 09–12; Hon PV Linc Cathl 11–12; Abp's Chapl *Cant* 12–13; Chapl to Bp Dover 12–13; C Cant St Dunstan w H Cross and Cant St Pet w St Alphege and St Marg etc 12–13; Prec Cant Cathl 13–17; Can Res Roch Cathl from 17. *East Canonry, 2 Kings Orchard, Rochester ME1 1TG* E: matthew.rushton@rochestercathedral.org

RUSHTON, Patricia Mary. See DUFFETT-SMITH, Patricia Mary

RUSHTON, The Ven Samantha Jayne. b 65. St Hilda's Coll Ox MA 87. Trin Coll Bris BA 05. **d** 05 **p** 06. C Highworth w Sevenhampton and Inglesham etc *Bris* 05–08; C Broad Blunsdon 05–08; Dioc Adv for Lic Min 08–15; C Chippenham St Paul w Hardenhuish etc 08–15; C Kington St Michael 08–15; Warden of Readers 11–15; AD Chippenham 13–15; Adn Cleveland *York* from 15. *48 Langbaurgh Road, Hutton Rudby, Yarm TS15 0HL* T: (01642) 706095 M: 07906-376036 E: adcl@yorkdiocese.org

RUSHTON, Mrs Susan Elizabeth. b 44. Univ of Wales (Cardiff) BA 65. Bris Sch of Min 83. **dss** 86 **d** 87 **p** 94. Westbury-on-Trym H Trin *Bris* 86–91; Hon Par Dn 87–91; C Wotton St Mary *Glouc* 91–94; P-in-c Frampton Cotterell *Bris* 94–07; Chapl United Bris Healthcare NHS Trust 94–98; P-in-c Iron Acton *Bris* 98–07; rtd 07; PtO *York* from 08. *9 Lime Avenue, Heworth, York YO31 1BT* T: (01904) 410363 E: rushton.sue.e@gmail.com

RUSHTON, Mrs Valerie Elizabeth Wendy. b 40. Birm Univ BSocSc 62. WMMTC 86. **d** 89 **p** 94. C Nuneaton St Nic *Cov* 89–93; C Stockingford 93–96; TV Watling Valley *Ox* 96–01; rtd 02; PtO *Ox* from 02. *106 Moreton Road, Buckingham MK18 1PW* T: (01280) 824942

RUSS, Canon Timothy John. b 41. AKC 64. Sarum Th Coll 66. **d** 66 **p** 67. C Walthamstow St Pet *Chelmsf* 66–70; C Epping St Jo 70–73; C Stepney St Dunstan and All SS *Lon* 73–75; Youth Officer 75–79; Tutor YMCA Nat Coll Walthamstow 79–84; Hon C St Botolph Aldgate w H Trin Minories *Lon* 82–89; Selection Sec ACCM 84–89; Dir St Marylebone Healing and Counselling Cen 89–92; Gen Sec Inst of Relig and Medicine 89–92; Hon C Hoxton St Anne w St Columba *Lon* 90–92; P-in-c St Dennis *Truro* 92–06; Par Development Adv 92–99; Dioc Dir Minl Tr 99–06; Hon Can Truro Cathl 01–06; rtd 06. *7 The Cedars, Truro TR1 2FD* T: (01872) 272286 E: timruss@tesco.net

RUSSELL, Adrian Camper. b 45. Chich Th Coll 79. **d** 81 **p** 82. C Marton *Blackb* 81–84; C Haslemere *Guildf* 84–85; V Hartlepool H Trin *Dur* 85–89; P-in-c Cornforth 89–94; R Auchterarder and Muthill *St And* 94–97; P-in-c Kenton Ascension *Newc* 97–07; rtd 07; PtO *Newc* from 17. *23 Lambley Avenue, North Shields NE30 3SL* T: 0191-280 9552 E: acr26682@blueyonder.co.uk

RUSSELL, Andrea. b 64. K Coll Lon LLB 86 Nottm Univ BA 04 MA 05 PhD 10. EMMTC 08. **d** 10 **p** 11. C Sherwood *S'well* 10–12; Dir of Studies St Jo Coll Nottm 12–14; Tutor Qu Foundn Birm from 14; PtO *Birm* from 16. *Queen's College, Somerset Road, Edgbaston, Birmingham B15 2QH* T: 0121-452 2668 E: russella@queens.ac.uk

✠**RUSSELL, The Rt Revd Anthony John.** b 43. St Chad's Coll Dur BA 65 Trin Coll Ox DPhil 71. Cuddesdon Coll 65. **d** 70 **p** 71 **c** 88. C Hilborough w Bodney *Nor* 70–73; P-in-c Preston-on-Stour w Whitchurch *Cov* 73–76; P-in-c Atherston on Stour 73–76; V Preston on Stour and Whitchurch w Atherstone 77–88; Can Th Cov Cathl 77–88;

Chapl Arthur Rank Cen 73-82; Dir 83–88; Chapl to The Queen 83–88; Area Bp Dorchester *Ox* 88–00; Bp Ely 00–10; rtd 10; Hon Asst Bp Ox 11–18. *Lye Hill House, Holton, Oxford OX33 1QF* T: (01865) 876415

RUSSELL, The Ven Brian Kenneth. b 50. Trin Hall Cam BA 73 MA 76 Birm Univ MA 77 PhD 83. Cuddesdon Coll 74. **d** 76 **p** 77. C Redhill St Matt *S'wark* 76–79; Dir Studies NEOC 79–83; P-in-c Merrington *Dur* 79–83; Dir of Studies and Lect Linc Th Coll 83–86; Selection Sec and Sec Cttee for Th Educn ABM 86–93; Bp's Dir for Min *Birm* 93–05; Adn Aston 05–14; Hon Can Birm Cathl from 99; Sen Chapl Oslo w Bergen, Trondheim and Stavanger *Eur* 14–17; PtO *Birm* from 14; *Eur* from 17. *1 Plover Close, Stratford-upon-Avon CV37 9EN* T: (01789) 299923 E: b-russell5@sky.com

RUSSELL, Clive Phillip. b 61. Ridley Hall Cam 04. **d** 06 **p** 07. C High Ongar w Norton Mandeville *Chelmsf* 06–09; V Grays North from 09. *St John's Vicarage, 8A Victoria Avenue, Grays RM16 2RP* T: (01375) 372101 E: russell-mail@tiscali.co.uk

RUSSELL, Canon David John. b 57. Sarum & Wells Th Coll BTh 94. **d** 94 **p** 95. C Glouc St Geo w Whaddon 94–98; P-in-c Wickwar w Rangeworthy 98–01; R Wickwar, Rangeworthy and Hillesley 02–11; R Charfield and Kingswood w Wickwar etc from 11; AD Wotton from 15; Hon Can Glouc Cathl from 17. *The Rectory, 75 High Street, Wickwar, Wotton-under-Edge GL12 8NP* T: (01454) 294267 E: davidrussell@gmx.com

RUSSELL, David John Timothy. b 75. Oak Hill Th Coll. **d** 09 **p** 10. C Padiham w Hapton and Padiham Green *Blackb* 09–13; V Woodford *Ches* from 13. *The Vicarage, 531 Chester Road, Woodford, Stockport SK7 1PR* T: 0161-439 2286 E: revdavidrussell@yahoo.com

RUSSELL, Canon Derek John. b 30. St Pet Hall Ox BA 54 MA 58. Qu Coll Birm 54. **d** 56 **p** 57. C Boxley *Cant* 56–59; C Whitstable All SS 59–63; Chapl HM Pris Wormwood Scrubs 63–65; Chapl HM Pris Stafford 65–69; Chapl HM Pris Pentonville 70; Chapl HM Pris Wormwood Scrubs 71–89; SE Regional Chapl 74–81; Chapl HM Rem Cen Latchmere Ho 74–77; Asst Chapl Gen of Pris 81–83; Dep 83–90; Hon Can Cant Cathl 86–90; rtd 90; PtO *Cant* 90–16. *25 Pier Avenue, Whitstable CT5 2HQ* T: (01227) 276654 E: derekandlizrussell@tiscali.co.uk

RUSSELL, Ms Elizabeth Marilyn Vivia. b 50. LRAM 70 GRSM 72. Westcott Ho Cam 95. **d** 97 **p** 98. C Alton St Lawr *Win* 97–01; C St Martin-in-the-Fields *Lon* 01–08; P-in-c S Kensington St Jude w All SS from 08; Dir of Cdos Two Cities Area from 08. *5 Aldwyn House, Davidson Gardens, London SW8 2HX* T: (020) 7498 5623 E: erussell101@btinternet.com

RUSSELL, Eric Watson. b 39. FCA 76. Clifton Th Coll 66. **d** 69 **p** 70. C Kinson *Sarum* 69–73; C Peckham St Mary Magd *S'wark* 73–77; TV Barking St Marg w St Patr *Chelmsf* 77–82; V Lozells St Paul and St Silas *Birm* 82–95; RD Aston 89–94; P-in-c Barston and C Knowle 95–04; I Kells Union *M & K* 04–09; rtd 09; PtO *St E* from 15. *Address temp unknown* E: ericandjoan@uwclub.net

RUSSELL, Gary William Algernon. b 64. Ripon Coll Cuddesdon 04. **d** 06 **p** 07. C Harpenden St Nic *St Alb* 06–09; P-in-c St Alb St Mary Marshalswick 09–14; Hon Chapl ATC from 07; rtd 14. *33 Suffolk House, 31-33 Suffolk Road, Bournemouth BH2 6AT* E: moreteavicar@hotmail.co.uk

RUSSELL, Ms Isoline Lucilda (Lyn). b 41. **d** 03 **p** 04. OLM Camberwell St Giles w St Matt *S'wark* 03–11; PtO from 11. *124 Hindman's Road, London SE22 9NH* T: (020) 8299 4431

RUSSELL, James Anthony Tomkins. *See* TOMKINS-RUSSELL, James Anthony

RUSSELL, Canon Janet Mary. b 53. Univ of Wales BSc 74 BArch 76. Ox Min Course 91. **d** 94 **p** 95. C Watlington w Pyrton and Shirburn *Ox* 94–97; C Icknield 97–98; TV Wallingford 98–05; Par Development Adv (Berks) 05–11; Dir Miss *S & B* 11–16; Hon Can Brecon Cathl 12–15; Can Res Brecon Cathl 15–16; PtO *Heref* from 17. *Meadow Breeze, Llanddew, Brecon LD3 9ST* M: 07894-821828 E: janetrussell@churchinwales.org.uk

RUSSELL, John Bruce. b 56. Ripon Coll Cuddesdon. **d** 95 **p** 96. C Newport Pagnell w Lathbury and Moulsoe *Ox* 95–98; P-in-c Wing w Grove 98–02; AD Mursley 02–03; PtO *St Alb* 08–10; TV Gt Berkhamsted, Gt and Lt Gaddesden etc from 10. *St John's Vicarage, Pipers Hill, Great Gaddesden, Hemel Hempstead HO1 3BY* T: (01442) 214898 E: john_russell@live.co.uk

RUSSELL, John Graham. b 35. G&C Coll Cam BA 58 MA 62. Westcott Ho Cam 59. **d** 61 **p** 62. C Durleigh *B & W* 61–66; C Bridgwater St Mary w Chilton Trinity 61–66; C Far Headingley St Chad *Ripon* 66–72; P-in-c Leeds St Matt Lt London 72–79; V Rowley Regis *Birm* 79–84; V Hall Green Ascension 84–95; Deanery P Warley Deanery 95–00; rtd 01; PtO *Birm* from 01. *1 Stapylton Avenue, Harborne, Birmingham B17 0BA* T: 0121-426 4529

RUSSELL, John Richard. b 53. Westmr Coll Ox MTh 01 FRSA 02. Spurgeon's Coll 77 Ripon Coll Cuddesdon 01. **d** 01 **p** 02. Hon C St Mary le Strand w St Clem Danes *Lon* 01–02; Chapl RAF 02–08; PtO *Chelmsf* from 09. *32 Feeches Road, Southend-on-Sea SS2 6TD* T: (01702) 300978 E: revjohnrussell@virginmedia.com

RUSSELL, Canon Jonathan Vincent Harman. b 43. K Coll Lon 68. **d** 69 **p** 70. C Addington *Cant* 69–73; C Buckland in Dover w Buckland Valley 73–76; P-in-c Selling 76–85; P-in-c Throwley w Stalisfield and Otterden 79–85; R Selling w Throwley, Sheldwich w Badlesmere etc 85–95; Hon Min Can Cant Cathl 83–94; RD Ospringe 90–95; P-in-c Elham w Denton and Wootton 95–01; V 01–08; Hon Can Cant Cathl 94–08; rtd 08; PtO *Cant* from 08. *Kirkella, Goodwin Road, St Margaret's Bay, Dover CT15 6ED* T: (01304) 852811 M: 07702-314865 E: jvhrussell@btinternet.com

RUSSELL, Jonathan Wingate. b 55. Newc Univ BSc 76. St Jo Coll Nottm BA 83. **d** 84 **p** 85. C Southsea St Jude *Portsm* 84–87; P-in-c Shorwell w Kingston 87–92; V 92–06; P-in-c Gatcombe 87–92; R 92–06; P-in-c Chale 89–92; R 92–06; RD W Wight 96–01; R Allendale w Whitfield *Newc* from 06; AD Hexham 11–16. *The Rectory, 16 Forstersteads, Allendale, Hexham NE47 9AS* T/F: (01434) 618607   E: rector@allendalechurch.co.uk   or cuthbertallendale@gmail.com

RUSSELL, Lyn. *See* RUSSELL, Isoline Lucilda

RUSSELL, Madeleine. b 41. Pargau Teacher Tr Coll Switzerland TDip 62. **d** 04 **p** 05. NSM Halifax H Trin and St Jude *Wakef* 04–13; rtd 13; PtO *Leeds* from 13. *Hillcroft, 12 Westborough Drive, Halifax HX2 7QN*

RUSSELL, Canon Marion Elisabeth. b 54. Glas Univ BEd 75 Jordanhill Coll Glas TCert 75. CBDTI 03. **d** 06 **p** 07. NSM Altham w Clayton le Moors *Blackb* 06–10; Chapl Trin Academy Halifax 10–12; C Huddersfield St Pet *Wakef* 12–14; V Rastrick *Leeds* from 14; AD Brighouse and Elland from 16; Jt AD Calder Valley from 18; Hon Can Ripon Cathl from 19. *1 Vicarage Gardens, Rastrick, Brighouse HD6 3HD* T: (01484) 713386 E: revd.marion@gmail.com

RUSSELL, Martin Christopher. b 48. St Jo Coll Dur BA 70. Coll of Resurr Mirfield 72. **d** 74 **p** 75. C Huddersfield St Pet *Wakef* 74–77; Trinidad and Tobago 78–85; V S Crosland *Wakef* 86–00; P-in-c Helme 86–00; P-in-c Halifax H Trin 00–02; P-in-c Halifax St Jude 00–02; V Halifax H Trin and St Jude 02–13; rtd 13; PtO *Leeds* from 17. *Hillcroft, 12 Westborough Drive, Halifax HX2 7QN*

RUSSELL, Canon Neil. b 47. EMMTC 78. **d** 81 **p** 82. NSM Wyberton *Linc* 81–84; C 84–85; V Frampton 85–93; Agric Chapl and Countryside Officer 88–93; P-in-c Stamford All SS w St Jo 93–97; V 97–08; RD Aveland and Ness w Stamford 00–06; Warden Sacrista Prebend Retreat Ho *S'well* 08–10; Can and Preb Linc Cathl 02–10; rtd 10; PtO *Dur* 11–17. *Clare Cottage, 4 The Paddocks, Gainford, Darlington DL2 3GA* T: (01325) 733140 M: 07730-403630 E: canonneilrussell@yahoo.co.uk

RUSSELL, Mrs Noreen Margaret. b 39. Man Univ BA 60 Lon Univ PGCE 61 BD 66. WMMTC 90. **d** 91 **p** 94. NSM Swynnerton and Tittensor *Lich* 91–97; C Draycott-le-Moors w Forsbrook 97–06; rtd 06; PtO *Lich* from 06. *40 Old Road, Barlaston, Stoke-on-Trent ST12 9EQ* T: (01782) 372992 E: norrenbungalow40@gmail.com

RUSSELL, The Ven Norman Atkinson. b 43. Chu Coll Cam BA 65 MA 69 Lon Univ BD 70. Lon Coll of Div 67. **d** 70 **p** 71. C Clifton Ch Ch w Em *Bris* 70–74; C Enfield Ch Ch Trent Park *Lon* 74–77; R Harwell w Chilton *Ox* 77–84; P-in-c Gerrards Cross 84–88; P-in-c Fulmer 85–88; R Gerrards Cross and Fulmer 88–98; Hon Can Ch Ch 95–98; RD Amersham 96–98; Adn Berks 98–13; rtd 13; PtO *Ox* from 13; *Guildf* from 14. *47A Theobalds Way, Frimley, Camberley GU16 9RF* E: ven.narussell@gmail.com

RUSSELL, Paul Selwyn. b 38. ALCD 61. **d** 61 **p** 62. C Gillingham St Mark *Roch* 61–64; SAMS 64–84; Chile, Peru and Bolivia 64–84; V Brinsworth w Catcliffe *Sheff* 84–91; R Brinklow *Cov* 91–04; R Harborough Magna 91–04; V Monks Kirby w Pailton and Stretton-under-Fosse 91–04; rtd 04. *19 Larchfields, Wolston, Coventry CV8 3JL* T: (024) 7654 3906 E: paul.russell024@yahoo.com

RUSSELL, Peter Richard. b 60. Ch Ch Coll Cant BA 99. SEITE 02. **d** 05 **p** 06. NSM Margate All SS and Westgate St Sav *Cant* 05–08; Chapl St Lawr Coll Ramsgate 09–19; rtd 19; PtO *Cant* from 19. *40 Dane Road, Birchington CT7 9PT* E: minnisbay@hotmail.com

RUSSELL, Richard Alexander. b 44. Univ of Wales (Abth) BA 65 McMaster Univ Ontario MA 67 Bris Univ MA 73 PGCE 74 MEd 76. Trin Coll Bris 79. **d** 82 **p** 83. C Hartlepool St Paul *Dur* 82–85; P-in-c Bath Widcombe *B & W* 85–88; V 88–00; rtd 00; PtO *B & W* from 09. *76*

Waterside Way, Radstock, Bath BA3 3YQ T: (01761) 433217
E: therealrichardrussell@gmail.com

RUSSELL, Roger Geoffrey. b 47. Worc Coll Ox BA 69 MA 73. Cuddesdon Coll 70. **d** 72 **p** 73. C Anlaby Common St Mark *York* 72–75; C Wilton Place St Paul *Lon* 75–86; R Lancing w Coombes *Chich* 86–12; RD Worthing 97–05; rtd 13; PtO *Chich* 13–17. *32 Lime Grove, Angmering, Littlehampton BN16 4HA*

RUSSELL, Canon William Warren. b 52. QUB BSocSc 74. CITC 74. **d** 77 **p** 78. C Agherton *Conn* 77–79; C Lisburn Ch Ch Cathl 79–83; I Magheradroll *D & D* from 83; Treas Dromore Cathl from 08; Dioc C from 11. *The Rectory, 18 Church Road, Ballynahinch BT24 8LP* T: (028) 9756 2289 M: 07810-222906 E: rev_wwrussell@hotmail.com *or* revwrussell@gmail.com

RUSSELL GRANT, Julia Rosalind. b 45. **d** 11 **p** 12. OLM Layer de la Haye and Layer Breton w Birch etc *Chelmsf* 11–13; OLM Thurstable and Winstree 13–15; NSM 15–18; rtd 18; PtO *Chelmsf* from 18. *8 Heath House, Crayes Green, Layer Breton, Colchester CO2 0PN* T: (01206) 330235 E: church@hatfield-broad-oak.net *or* julia@bretonheath.me.uk

RUSSELL-SMITH, Mark Raymond. b 46. New Coll Edin MTh 91 St Jo Coll Dur BA 71. Cranmer Hall Dur. **d** 72 **p** 73. C Upton (Overchurch) *Ches* 72–75; C Deane *Man* 75–77; UCCF Travelling Sec 77–80; LtO *York* 81–88; BCMS Kenya 81–92; P-in-c Slaidburn *Bradf* 92–11; P-in-c Long Preston w Tosside 97–11; rtd 11; PtO *York* from 12. *11 Osprey Close, York YO24 2YE* T: (01904) 792154 E: mars4654@uwclub.net

RUST, Mrs Alison Theresa (Tessa). Auckland Univ BA 76. St Mellitus Coll BA 11. **d** 11 **p** 12. C W Ealing St Jo w St Jas *Lon* 11–14; Chapl Heathrow Airport from 14. *The Chapel of St George, Central Terminal Area, London Heathrow Airport, Hounslow TW6 1BP* M: 07979-627714 E: tessa.rust@london.anglican.org

RUST, Jonathan Kenneth. b 62. Reading Univ BSc 84 St Mellitus Coll MA 14. Ridley Hall Cam. **d** 00 **p** 01. C Holloway St Mary Magd *Lon* 00–16; Dir Miss Development Kensington Area from 16; Public Preacher from 16. *10 Eversley Crescent, Isleworth TW7 4LS* E: jonathan.rust@london.anglican.org

RUSTED, Mrs Mary Elizabeth. b 44. **d** 00 **p** 01. OLM Mildenhall *St E* 00–10; rtd 10; PtO *St E* from 10. *3 Ford Close, West Row, Bury St Edmunds IP28 8NR* T: (01638) 715054 E: maryrusted@hotmail.com

RUSTELL, Canon Anthony Christopher. b 77. Ch Ch Ox BA 98 MSt 01 MA 02 Keble Coll Ox DPhil 07. St Steph Ho Ox 98. **d** 01 **p** 02. NSM Ox St Barn and St Paul 01–04; P-in-c N Hinksey and Wytham 04–10; P-in-c Ox St Frideswide w Binsey 09–10; R Osney 10–11; Dir Minl Tr *Llan* 11–14; P-in-c Tongwynlais 11–14; Can Res Portsm Cathl from 14; Hd Miss, Discipleship and Min from 14. *1 Pembroke Close, Portsmouth PO1 2NX* T: (023) 9282 3300 E: acrustell@btinternet.com

RUTHERFORD, Anthony Richard. b 37. Culham Coll Ox TCert 62 Sussex Univ MA 77. S'wark Ord Course 83. **d** 86 **p** 87. Hon C Tunbridge Wells St Luke *Roch* 86–88; C Bromley SS Pet and Paul 88–90; V Wragby *Linc* 90–94; Asst Min Officer 90–94; V Penge Lane H Trin *Roch* 94–02; rtd 02; PtO *Roch* from 03; *Chich* from 16; *Eur* from 16. *6 Ashley Gardens, Tunbridge Wells TN4 8TY* T: (01892) 541009 E: tony.rutherford37@icloud.com

RUTHERFORD, Daniel Fergus Peter. b 65. Hatf Coll Dur BA 86 CertEd 87. Ridley Hall Cam 88. **d** 90 **p** 91. C Harold Wood *Chelmsf* 90–94; C Hove Bp Hannington Memorial Ch *Chich* 94–97; Chapl City of Lon Freemen's Sch 97–11; Chapl Strathallan Sch 12–15; Asst Hd (Past) Dulwich Prep Sch Cranbrook from 15; PtO *Cant* from 16. *Dulwich Preparatory School, Coursehorn, Golford Road, Cranbrook TN17 3NP* T: (01580) 712179 E: drutherford@dcpskent.org

RUTHERFORD, Emma Catherine. Ulster Univ BA. St Jo Coll Nottm MTh. **d** 11 **p** 12. C Coleraine *Conn* 12–13; Dioc C 13–17; I Stormont *D & D* from 17. *St Molua's Rectory, 3 Rosepark, Belfast BT5 7RG* T: (028) 9048 2292 M: 07753-117838 E: revecr@gmail.com

✠**RUTHERFORD, The Rt Revd Graeme Stanley.** b 43. Cranmer Hall Dur BA 77 MA 78 ACT 66. **d** 66 **p** 67 **c** 00. C Bendigo Cathl Australia 66–70; V Pyramid Hill 70–73; C Holborn St Geo w H Trin and St Bart *Lon* 73–74; C Dur St Nic 74–77; R Kyabram Australia 77–82; I Malvern 82–87; I Camberwell St Jo 87–00; Can Melbourne Cathl 91–00; Asst Bp Newcastle 00–08; rtd 08. *3/68 Campbell Road, Hawthorn East VIC 3123, Australia* T: (0061) (3) 9813 4185 M: 40-837 4847 E: gcruth@bigpond.com

RUTHERFORD, Ian William. b 46. Univ of Wales (Lamp) BA 68. Cuddesdon Coll 68. **d** 70 **p** 71. C Gosforth All SS *Newc* 70–72; C Prestbury *Glouc* 73–76; Chapl RN 76–93; TV

Redruth w Lanner and Treleigh *Truro* 93–94; V Paulsgrove *Portsm* 94–99; V Leeds Belle Is St Jo and St Barn *Ripon* 99–11; rtd 11; CMP from 93; PtO *Portsm* from 11; *Eur* from 15. *Flat 12, 27-29 St Simons Road, Southsea PO5 2QE* E: fatherian@onetel.com

RUTHERFORD, Janet Elizabeth. b 37. S'wark Ord Course 86. **d** 89. NSM Plaistow St Mary *Roch* 89–90; NSM Linc St Botolph 91–93. *6 Ashley Gardens, Tunbridge Wells TN4 8TY* T: (01892) 541009

RUTHERFORD, Peter Marshall. b 57. St Andr Univ MTheol 81 Ulster Univ MA 96. CITC 83. **d** 83 **p** 84. C Stormont *D & D* 83–85; CF 85–01; Asst Chapl Gen 01–02; Asst Chapl Milan w Genoa and Varese *Eur* 03–04; I Castlepollard and Oldcastle w Loughcrew etc *M & K* 04–10; I Julianstown and Colpe w Drogheda and Duleek 10–15; Dioc Dir of Ords 05–15; Warden of Readers 12–15; I Kinsale Union *C, C & R* from 15. *The Rectory, 3 Abbeycourt, Kinsale, Co Cork, Republic of Ireland* T: (00353) (21) 477 2220 E: peterrutherford@me.com

RUTHERFORD (née ERREY), Ms Rosalind Elisabeth. b 52. St Hugh's Coll Ox BA 74 Surrey Univ BA 02 Goldsmiths' Coll Lon PGCE 78. STETS 99. **d** 02 **p** 03. C Earley St Pet *Ox* 02–06; TV Basingstoke *Win* 06–18; rtd 18; PtO *Ox* from 18. *7 Godwyn Close, Abingdon OX14 1BU* E: revrosalind@btinternet.com

RUTLEDGE, Canon Christopher John Francis. b 44. Lon Univ BSc 67 Univ of Wales MPhil 94 PhD 99 Glyndŵr Univ MSc 15 TCert 80. Sarum Th Coll 67. **d** 70 **p** 71. C Birm St Pet 70–73; C Calne and Blackland *Sarum* 73–76; P-in-c Derry Hill 76–78; V 78–81; P-in-c Talbot Village 81–82; V 82–10; Can and Preb Sarum Cathl 95–10; Chapl Talbot Heath Sch Bournemouth 04–09; rtd 10; PtO *Sarum* from 10. *48 Wollaton Road, Ferndown BH22 8QY* T: (01202) 895116 E: christopher.rutledge@talktalk.net

RUTT, Mrs Celia Mary Avril. b 43. Cranmer Hall Dur. **d** 02 **p** 03. NSM Heworth H Trin *York* 02–05; NSM Acomb St Steph and St Aid 05–09; NSM Clifton 09–11; rtd 11; PtO *York* from 11. *226 Shipton Road, York YO30 5RZ* T: (01904) 627384 E: celiarutt7@gmail.com

RUTTER, Canon Allen Edward Henry (Claude). b 28. Qu Coll Cam BA 52 MA 56. Cranmer Hall Dur. **d** 59 **p** 60. C Bath Abbey w St Jas *B & W* 59–60; C E Dereham w Hoe *Nor* 60–64; R Cawston 64–69; Chapl Cawston Coll 64–69; P-in-c Felthorpe w Haveringland *Nor* 64–69; R Gingindhlovu S Africa 69–73; P-in-c Over and Nether Compton, Trent etc *Sarum* 73–80; RD Sherborne 77–87; P-in-c Oborne w Poyntington 79–80; P-in-c Queen Thorne 80–96; Can and Preb Sarum Cathl 86–96; rtd 96; PtO *B & W* 98–99 and from 00; P-in-c Thorncombe w Winsham and Cricket St Thomas 99; C Chard and Distr 99–00. *Home Farm, Chilson, South Chard, Chard TA20 2NX* T: (01460) 221368

RUTTER, Graham Piers. b 77. St Jo Coll Dur BSc 98 PhD 03 Liv Univ MSc 99. St Jo Coll Nottm 06. **d** 08 **p** 09. C Wellington All SS w Eyton *Lich* 08–12; P-in-c Swadlincote *Derby* from 12; C Hartshorne and Bretby from 13; RD Repton 13–18; AD Mercia from 18. *The Vicarage, Church Street, Swadlincote DE11 8LF* T: (01283) 214583 E: gprutter@gmail.com

RUTTER, John Edmund Charles. b 53. Qu Coll Cam MA 76. St Jo Coll Nottm MA 93. **d** 93 **p** 94. C Penge St Jo *Roch* 93–97; Bp's Chapl Bangor Primacy *D & D* 97–04; I Glenavy w Tunny and Crumlin *Conn* from 04. *The Vicarage, 30 Crumlin Road, Glenavy, Crumlin BT29 4LG* T: (028) 9442 2361 E: jec.rutter@gmail.com

RUTTER, Preb Martin Charles. b 54. Wolv Poly BSc 75 Southn Univ BTh 81. Sarum & Wells Th Coll 76. **d** 79 **p** 80. C Cannock *Lich* 79–82; C Uttoxeter w Bramshall 82–86; V W Bromwich St Jas 86–97; P-in-c W Bromwich St Paul 89–97; W Bromwich St Jas w St Paul 97–02; RD W Bromwich 94–02; V Gt Barr from 02; RD Walsall 10–15; Preb Lich Cathl from 16. *St Margaret's Vicarage, Chapel Lane, Great Barr, Birmingham B43 7BD* T: 0121-357 1390 E: martincrutter@gmail.com

RYALL, Michael Richard. b 36. TCD BA 58 MA 65 HDipEd 66. TCD Div Sch Div Test 58. **d** 58 **p** 59. C Dublin St Geo and St Thos, Finglas and Free Ch *D & G* 58–62; Chapl Mountjoy Pris 58–62; CF 62–65 and 68–90; CF (TAVR) 67–68; C Dublin Rathmines *D & G* 65–66; R Yardley Hastings, Denton and Grendon etc *Pet* 90–01; Chapl HM Pris Wellingborough 92–93; rtd 01; PtO *St D* from 07; P-in-c Mayland *Chelmsf* 08–12. *62 Waterloo Road, Hakin, Milford Haven SA73 3PD* T: (01646) 695274 M: 07968-111258 E: michaelryall36@michaelryall36.plus.com

RYALLS, Craig James. b 74. Bris Univ BA 96 Peterho Cam BA 01. Ridley Hall Cam 99. **d** 02 **p** 03. C Bearsted w Thurnham *Cant* 02–06; C Woking Ch Ch *Guildf* 06–14; R Fisherton Anger *Sarum* from 14. *St Paul's Church Centre, Fisherton Street, Salisbury SP2 7QW* T: (01722) 334005 E: craig@wearestpauls.church

RYAN, Mrs Barbara. b 56. d 12 p 13. NSM Hessle *York* 12–16; NSM Bilton St Pet 16–18; NSM Sutton St Mich 16–18; NSM Spofforth w Kirk Deighton *Leeds* from 18. *The Rectory, Church Lane, Spofforth, Harrogate HG3 1AF* E: revbryan@hotmail.com

RYAN, David Peter. b 64. Aston Univ BSc 86. Linc Th Coll BTh 94. d 94 p 95. C Horsforth *Ripon* 94–97; C Bedale 97–98; P-in-c Startforth and Bowes and Rokeby w Brignall 98–00; V 00–04; P-in-c Warndon St Nic *Worc* 04–13; Chapl Worcs Acute Hosps NHS Trust from 13; Dioc Ecum Officer *Worc* from 04. *The Alexandra Hospital, Woodrow Drive, Redditch B98 7UB* T: (01527) 503030 E: david.ryan@cofe-worcester.org.uk *or* david.ryan5@nhs.net

RYAN, Mrs Diane Thérèse Hazel. b 69. Lanc Univ BA 90. St Hild Coll 14. d 17 p 18. C Gt Snaith *Sheff* from 17. *1 Church View, Hensall, Goole DN14 0UU* T: (01977) 663488 M: 07501-271754 E: diane_ryan@btinternet.com *or* diane.ryan@greatsnaith.org.uk

RYAN, Graham William Robert (Gregg). b 51. CITC 90. d 93 p 94. NSM Clonsast w Rathangan, Thomastown etc *M & K* 93–97; Dioc Communications Officer 96–97; Press Officer from 97; Dioc C *M & K* 97–16; P-in-c Clane w Donadea and Coolcarrigan 16–18; rtd 18. *Millicent Hall, Millicent South, Sallins, Naas, Co Kildare, Republic of Ireland* T: (00353) (45) 879464 F: 875173 E: gwr.ryan@gmail.com

RYAN, James Francis. b 47. Surrey Univ BSc. St Jo Coll Nottm. d 83 p 84. C Littleover *Derby* 83–86; C Chipping Sodbury and Old Sodbury *Glouc* 86–89; V Pype Hayes *Birm* 89–99; R W Winch w Setchey, N Runcton and Middleton *Nor* 99–12; rtd 12; PtO *Chich* from 13. *30 Rook Way, Horsham RH12 5FR*

RYAN, Maureen Sheila. d 98 p 99. NSM Tuam w Cong and Aasleagh *T, K & A* 98–16; Preb Kilmactalway St Patr Cathl Dublin 01–09; Can Tuam Cathl *T, K & A* 05–16; Provost Tuam 14–16; Can Killala Cathl 13–16; rtd 16. *Marshal's Park, Rinville, Oranmore, Galway, Republic of Ireland* T/F: (00353) (91) 794599 E: ryans@iol.ie

RYAN, Robert Lloyd. b 65. Warwick Univ BA 87. SEITE 05. d 08 p 09. C Roch Cathl 08–12; NSM Gillingham St Mark 12–15; TV E Greenwich *S'wark* 15–18; Chapl Ch Ch and St Mary Magd Primary Schs 15–18; P-in-c Lt Ilford St Barn *Chelmsf* from 18. *St Barnabas' Vicarage, 153C Browning Road, London E12 6PB* T: (020) 8472 2777 M: 07595-354067 E: rob.ryan@mac.com *or* stbarnabasmanorpark@gmail.com

RYAN, Roger John. b 47. Lon Bible Coll BA 79 Surrey Univ MA 00 St Pet Coll Ox DPhil 06 Univ Coll Lon MA 09. Oak Hill Th Coll 79. d 80 p 81. C Luton St Fran *St Alb* 80–83; R Laceby *Linc* 83–88; V Summerstown *S'wark* 88–17; rtd 17; PtO *S'wark* from 18. *7 Beechwood Court, West Street Lane, Carshalton SM5 2PZ* T: (020) 3802 8978 E: rogerryan307@hotmail.com

RYAN, Mrs Saffron Mandy. b 77. Surrey Univ BA 99. St Mellitus Coll BA 17. d 17 p 18. C Hornchurch St Andr *Chelmsf* from 17. *70 Swanbourne Drive, Hornchurch RM12 6RE* M: 07557-309979 E: saffron@jjssp.co.uk

RYAN, Canon Stephen John. b 49. Univ of Wales (Swansea) BA 70. Sarum & Wells Th Coll 70. d 73 p 74. C Llantrisant *Llan* 73–77; V Treherbert w Treorchy 77–89; Youth Chapl 80–85; RD Rhondda 84–89; V Aberdare St Fagan 89–02; RD Cynon Valley 97–02; TR Neath 02–18; P-in-c Llansawel, Briton Ferry 16–18; AD Neath 04–10 and 15–17; Can Llan Cathl 02–18; rtd 18. *43 Mayals Avenue, Blackpill, Swansea SA3 5DB* T: (01792) 406062 E: ryanstephen1949@gmail.com

RYCRAFT, Andrew George. b 48. Ox Brookes Univ BA 12 FRICS 94. Wycliffe Hall Ox 02 SAOMC 04. d 06 p 07. NSM Ray Valley *Ox* 06–07 and 09–15; P-in-c Exning St Martin w Landwade *St E* 15–18; rtd 18; PtO *St E* from 18. *19 Cardigan Street, Newmarket CB8 8HZ* E: andrew.rycraft@gmail.com

RYCRAFT, Mrs Rosemary Ives Stewart. b 49. Westmr Coll Ox BTh 00 SRN 72 SCM 74. SAOMC 00. d 03 p 04. NSM New Marston *Ox* 03–07; TV Aylesbury 07–11; PtO 11–12; C Mildenhall *St E* 12–17; P-in-c Dalham, Gazeley, Higham, Kentford and Moulton from 17; RD Mildenhall from 19. *The Vicarage, The Street, Gazeley, Newmarket CB8 8RB* E: rosemaryrycraft121@gmail.com

RYDEN, Huw Deiniol. b 73. Cardiff Univ BTh 17. St Mich Coll Llan 15. d 17 p 18. C Littleham-cum-Exmouth w Lympstone *Ex* from 17. *24 Humphries Park, Exmouth EX8 4DX* T: (01395) 708783 M: 07594-284038

RYDER, Elaine Lesley. b 52. Lindisfarne Regional Tr Partnership 16. d 18 p 19. NSM N Tyne and Redesdale *Newc* from 18. *The Vicarage, Otterburn, Newcastle upon Tyne NE19 1NP* T: (01830) 520212 E: revelaine212@gmail.com

RYDER, John Merrick. b 55. Natal Univ BA 75 BA 77. St Pet Coll Natal 81. d 82 p 83. S Africa 84–88; St Helena 88–91; C Havant *Portsm* 91–95; P-in-c Godshill 95–99; V from 99; P-in-c Wroxall 99–02. *The Vicarage, Church Hill, Godshill, Ventnor PO38 3HY* T: (01983) 300421 E: johnryder@mac.com

RYDER, Judith Ruth. b 76. St Jo Coll Ox BA 98 MPhil 02 DPhil 06 FRHistS 12. Ripon Coll Cuddesdon 13. d 16 p 17. C Caversham Thameside and Mapledurham *Ox* from 16. *51 Galsworthy Drive, Caversham, Reading RG4 6PR* T: 0118-947 3783 M: 07890-114456 E: judith.ryder@wolfson.ox.ac.uk

RYDER, Lisle Robert Dudley. b 43. Selw Coll Cam BA 68 MA 72. Sarum Th Coll 69. d 71 p 72. C Lowestoft St Marg *Nor* 71–75; Chapl Asst Oxon Area HA 76–79; C Littlehampton St Jas *Chich* 79–85; C Littlehampton St Mary 79–85; C Wick 79–85; Chapl Worc R Infirmary 85–94; Chapl Worc R Infirmary NHS Trust 94–00; Chapl Worcs Acute Hosps NHS Trust 00–03; Hon Can Worc Cathl 89–04; P-in-c Pyworthy, Pancrasweek and Bridgerule *Ex* 04–08; rtd 08; PtO *Leeds* from 17. *Little Appleton, 3 Lumley Terrace, Newton le Willows, Bedale DL8 1SS* T: (01677) 450180 E: lislryder@gmail.com

RYDER, Oliver Hugh Dudley. b 74. UEA BA 98. Ridley Hall Cam 05. d 07 p 08. C Tollington *Lon* 07–10; C Kensal Rise St Mark and St Martin 10–11; V Kensal Rise St Mark 11–16; P-in-c Charles w Plymouth St Matthias *Ex* from 16. *St Matthias Vicarage, 6 St Lawrence Road, Plymouth PL4 6HN* M: 07963-580242 E: oliver.ryder@gmail.com

RYDINGS, Donald. b 33. Jes Coll Ox BA 57 MA 61. Linc Th Coll 57. d 59 p 60. C Poulton-le-Fylde *Blackb* 59–62; C Ox St Mary V 62–66; Staff Sec SCM 62–66; C-in-c Bourne End St Mark CD *Ox* 66–74; R Hedsor and Bourne End 74–76; P-in-c Gt Missenden w Ballinger and Lt Hampden 76–93; RD Wendover 79–89; V Gt Missenden w Ballinger and Lt Hampden 93–02; rtd 02; PtO *Ox* from 02. *16 Marroway, Weston Turville, Aylesbury HP22 5TQ* T: (01296) 612281

RYELAND, John. b 58. K Coll Lon BD 80 AKC 80 Lon Sch of Th MA 09. Linc Th Coll 80. d 81 p 82. C Enfield St Jas *Lon* 81–84; C Coulsdon St Andr *S'wark* 84–87; C-in-c Ingrave St Steph CD *Chelmsf* 87–97; Dir Chr Healing Miss from 97. *8 Cambridge Court, 210 Shepherd's Bush Road, London W6 7NJ* T: (020) 7603 8118 F: 7603 5224 E: chm@healingmission.org

RYLANCE, Wendy Sheila. b 52. Lon Univ MB, BS 78 MRCGP 82 DRCOG 89. WEMTC 14. d 13 p 14. NSM Highley w Billingsley, Glazeley etc *Heref* 13–18; rtd 19; PtO *Heref* from 19. *Roughton Farmhouse, Roughton, Bridgnorth WV15 5HE* T: (01746) 716399 M: 07523-352210 E: wendyrylance@aol.com

RYLANDS, Preb Amanda Craig. b 52. Homerton Coll Cam CertEd 75. Trin Coll Bris 83. dss 85 d 87 p 94. Chippenham St Andr w Tytherton Lucas *Bris* 85–87; Par Dn Stockport St Geo *Ches* 87–91; Par Dn Acton and Worleston, Church Minshull etc 91–94; C 94–97; Dioc Adv for Min Among Children 95–97; NSM Langport Area *B & W* 97–98 and 99–01; TV 98–99; Asst Dioc Voc Adv 00–01; PtO *Ex* 02–03; C Tedburn St Mary, Whitestone, Oldridge etc 04–05; Dioc Dir of Ords 05–09; Bp's Adv for Women in Min 06–09; Preb Ex Cathl 08–09; PtO *Lich* 10–13; NSM Shrewsbury St Chad, St Mary and St Alkmund 13–17; Rep for Women in Min Shrewsbury Area 13–17; SSM Officer 13–17; rtd 17; PtO *Lich* 17–18; *Ex* 18–19; RD Moreton from 19. *The Rectory, Copperwood Close, Ashburton, Newton Abbot TQ13 7JQ* T: (01364) 716309 E: rylandsamanda@gmail.com

⊞**RYLANDS, The Rt Revd Mark James.** b 61. SS Hild & Bede Coll Dur BA 83 Sheff Univ MA 06. Trin Coll Bris BA 87. d 87 p 88 c 09. C Stockport St Geo *Ches* 87–91; V Acton and Worleston, Church Minshull etc 91–97; TR Langport Area *B & W* 97–02; Dioc Missr and Can Res Ex Cathl 02–09; Area Bp Shrewsbury *Lich* 09–18; P-in-c Ashburton, Bickington, Buckland in the Moor etc *Ex* from 18; Asst Bp *Ex* from 18. *The Rectory, Copperwood Close, Ashburton, Newton Abbot TQ13 7JQ* T: (01364) 716309 E: mark.rylands@mmuk.net

RYLETT, Adam Geoffrey. b 78. Southn Univ MEng 00 Ox Brookes Univ BA 04. Trin Coll Bris 10. d 12 p 13. C S Croydon Em *S'wark* 12–15; C Barnes 15–18; V Kingston Hill St Paul from 18. *St Paul's Vicarage, 33 Queens Road, Kingston upon Thames KT2 7SF* T: (020) 8549 8597 *or* 8549 5444 M: 07595-345480 E: adam@rylett.co.uk *or* adam.rylett@stpaulskingston.org.uk

RYLEY, Canon Patrick Macpherson. b 30. Pemb Coll Ox BA 54 Lon Univ BD 56. Clifton Th Coll 54. d 56 p 57. C Ox St Clem 56–59; Burma 60–66; Kenya 68–75; V Lynn St Jo *Nor* 76–92; V King's Lynn St Jo the Ev 92–95; RD Lynn 78–83; Hon Can Nor Cathl 90–95; rtd 95; PtO *Bradf* 95–11. *12 Green End, Denton, Manchester M34 7PU*

RYLEY, Timothy Patrick. b 64. Man Univ BA 86. St Jo Coll Nottm MA 93. d 93 p 94. C Pendlebury St Jo *Man* 93–97; P-in-c Norris Bank 97–01; Age Concern from 01; PtO *Man* from 09. *12 Green End, Denton, Manchester M34 7PU*

RYRIE, Alexander Crawford. b 30. Edin Univ MA 52 BD 55 Glas Univ MLitt 75. New Coll Edin 52 Union Th Sem (NY) STM 56. d 83 p 83. Hon C Edin St Mary 83–85; R Jedburgh 85–95; rtd 95. *Boisils, Bowden, Melrose TD6 0ST* T: (01835) 823226 E: sandyryrie@googlemail.com

S

SABELL, Michael Harold. b 42. Open Univ BA 78 Surrey Univ MSc 84 Cam Univ MA 05. Sarum & Wells Th Coll 77. **d** 80 **p** 81. NSM Shirley *Win* 80–82; NSM Finham *Cov* 82–85; Chapl to the Deaf *Win* 81–82; PtO *Cov* 82–85; *Sheff* 85–89; Chapl to the Deaf 85–89; PtO *Lich* 89–96; Sen Chapl to the Deaf 89–96; PtO *St Alb* 96–01; Chapl to the Deaf 96–01; P-in-c Gt and Lt Wymondley 96–01; R Ingoldsby *Linc* 01–04; R Old Somerby 01–04; R Ropsley 01–04; R Sapperton w Braceby 01–04; rtd 04; PtO *Lich* 05–08 and 10–12; P-in-c Muchalls *Bre* 08–10; PtO *S & B* 12–18; *Leeds* from 18. *Halwyn Lodge, 32 Church Avenue, Dacre Banks, Harrogate HG3 4EB* M: 07935-776656 (text only) E: sabell42117@gmail.com

SABEY-CORKINDALE, Charmaine Clare. b 58. SROT 87. SAOMC. **d** 02 **p** 03. NSM St Ippolyts *St Alb* 02–03; C Hitchin 03–05; TV 05–13; PtO 16–18 and from 18. *5 Lavender Way, Hitchin SG5 2LU* T: (01462) 435497 E: c.sabeycorkindale@btinternet.com

SABINE WILLIS, Anthony Charles. *See* WILLIS, Anthony Charles Sabine

SACKLEY (*née* WITT), Mrs Caroline Elizabeth. b 51. Surrey Univ BSc 04. STETS 02. **d** 05 **p** 06. C Graffoe Gp *Linc* 05–08; P-in-c W Meon and Warnford *Portsm* 08–12; rtd 12; P-in-c The Vendée *Eur* 13–16; Hon C E Clevedon w Clapton in Gordano etc *B & W* from 17. *5 Chestnut Grove, Clevedon BS21 7LA* E: revcarosack1@gmail.com

SACRE, Phillip Daniel. b 83. Essex Univ BSc 04. Oak Hill Th Coll BA 14. **d** 14 **p** 15. C Gt Clacton *Chelmsf* 14–19. *Address temp unknown* E: phillip.sacre@gmail.com

SADDINGTON, Mrs Jean. b 53. Bournemouth Univ BSc 02 Cant Ch Ch Univ PGCE 04. STETS 05. **d** 08 **p** 12. NSM Dorchester *Sarum* 08–14; NSM Dorchester and the Winterbournes from 14. *The Rectory, Martinstown, Dorchester DT2 9JZ* E: jean.saddington@hotmail.co.uk

SADGROVE, The Very Revd Michael. b 50. Ball Coll Ox BA 71 MA 75. Trin Coll Bris 72. **d** 75 **p** 76. LtO *Ox* 75–77; Tutor Sarum & Wells Th Coll 77–82; Vice-Prin 80–82; V Alnwick *Newc* 82–87; Vice-Provost, Can Res and Prec *Cov* Cathl 87–95; Provost Sheff 95–00; Dean Sheff 00–03; Dean Dur 03–15; rtd 16; PtO *Newc* from 16. *Burswell House, 27 Church Street, Haydon Bridge, Hexham NE47 6JG* T: (01434) 688675 M: 07828-516198 E: sadgrove@outlook.com

SADLER, Ann Penrith. *See* IRVINE, Ann Penrith

SADLER, Michael Stuart. b 57. Wycliffe Hall Ox 78. **d** 81 **p** 82. C Henfynyw w Aberaeron and Llanddewi Aberarth *St D* 81–88; V Llanddewi Rhydderch w Llangattock-juxta-Usk etc *Mon* 88–09; V Llandeilo Fawr and Taliaris *St D* from 09. *The New Vicarage, Thomas Terrace, Llandeilo SA19 6NN* T: (01558) 823862 E: mssadler@macunlimited.net

SAGE, Canon Andrew George. b 58. Univ Coll Chich BA 99. Chich Th Coll 83. **d** 85 **p** 86. C Rawmarsh w Parkgate *Sheff* 85–87; C Fareham SS Pet and Paul *Portsm* 87–89; C Southsea H Spirit 89–91; P-in-c Nuthurst *Chich* 91–93; R 93–95; V Hangleton 95–04; Chapl Worthing and Southlands Hosps NHS Trust 01–02; Chapl W Sussex Health and Soc Care NHS Trust 02–04; V Blackpool St Steph *Blackb* from 04; Warden Whalley Abbey 08–10; Hon Can Blackb Cathl from 08. *The Vicarage, St Stephen's Avenue, Blackpool FY2 9RB* T: (01253) 351484 E: andrewsage@aol.com *or* vicarststephens@aol.com

SAGOVSKY, Canon Nicholas. b 47. CCC Ox BA 69 St Edm Ho Cam PhD 81. St Jo Coll Nottm BA 73. **d** 74 **p** 75. C Newc St Gabr 74–77; C Cambridge Gt St Mary w St Mich *Ely* 81; Vice-Prin Edin Th Coll 82–86; Dean of Chpl Clare Coll Cam 86–97; Wm Leech Prof Fell Newc Univ 97–02; Liv Hope Univ Coll 02–04; Can Westmr Abbey 04–11; rtd 11; PtO *Newc* from 11; *S'wark* 12–17; *Lon* from 16. *92 Tyndale Mansions, Upper Street, London N1 2XG* T: (020) 7682 3287 E: nsagovsky@gmail.com

SAID, Yazid. b 75. Hebrew Univ Jerusalem BA 96 CCC Cam BA 99 MA 03 MPhil 05 PhD 10. Westcott Ho Cam 97. **d** 99 **p** 01. Chapl Ch Ch Sch Nazareth Israel 99–00; Chapl to Bp Jerusalem 00–02; C St Geo Cathl 00–04; Acting Dean 02–04; Asst Chapl CCC Cam 04–09; PtO *Ely* 08–11; Research Fell McGill Univ Canada 10–11; Israel 11–12; Lect Dublin City Univ *D & G* 13–14; Lect Free Univ Berlin from 15; Research Fell Tübingen Univ 15–16; Lect Liv Hope Univ from 16; PtO *Liv* from 16. *Liverpool Hope University College, Hope Park, Taggart Avenue, Liverpool L16 9JD* E: yazeed.said@gmx.net

SAINSBURY, Peter Donald. b 67. K Coll Lon MA 04. Ridley Hall Cam 98. **d** 00 **p** 01. C Longfleet *Sarum* 00–04; Chapl Glos Univ 04–08; V Summerfield *Birm* 08–19; PtO from 19. *64 Selwyn Road, Birmingham B16 0SW* M: 07717-414787 E: revpetesainsbury@gmail.com

✠**SAINSBURY, The Rt Revd Roger Frederick.** b 36. Jes Coll Cam BA 58 MA 62. Clifton Th Coll. **d** 60 **p** 61 **c** 91. C Spitalfields Ch Ch w All SS *Lon* 60–63; Missr Shrewsbury Ho Everton *Liv* 63–74; P-in-c Everton St Ambrose w St Tim 67–74; Warden Mayflower Family Cen Canning Town *Chelmsf* 74–81; P-in-c Victoria Docks St Luke 78–81; V Walsall *Lich* 81–87; TR 87–88; Adn W Ham *Chelmsf* 88–91; Area Bp Barking 91–02; Moderator Ch's Commn for Racial Justice 99–02; rtd 02; Hon Asst Bp B & W from 03. *Abbey Lodge, Battery Lane, Portishead, Bristol BS20 7JD* T: (01275) 847082 E: bishopsroger@talktalk.net

SAINT, Richard John. b 85. Edin Univ BSc 07 Qu Coll Cam PhD 13. Wycliffe Hall Ox 16. **d** 19. C Southbroom *Sarum* from 19. *14 Stockwell Road, Devizes SN10 2DP* M: 07773-028907 E: richardjsaint@gmail.com

ST ALBANS, Archdeacon of. *See* SMITH, The Ven Jonathan Peter

ST ALBANS, Bishop of. *See* SMITH, The Rt Revd Alan Gregory Clayton

ST ALBANS, Dean of. *See* JOHN, The Very Revd Jeffrey Philip Hywel

ST ANDREWS, DUNKELD AND DUNBLANE, Bishop of. *See* PATON, The Rt Revd Ian James

ST ANDREWS, DUNKELD AND DUNBLANE, Dean of. *See* RATHBAND, The Very Revd Kenneth William

ST ASAPH, Bishop of. *See* CAMERON, The Rt Revd Gregory Kenneth

ST ASAPH, Dean of. *See* WILLIAMS, The Very Revd Nigel Howard

ST DAVIDS, Archdeacon of. *See* MACKNESS, The Ven Paul Robert

ST DAVIDS, Bishop of. *See* PENBERTHY, The Rt Revd Joanna Susan

ST DAVIDS, Dean of. *See* ROWLAND JONES, The Very Revd Sarah Caroline

ST EDMUNDSBURY AND IPSWICH, Bishop of. *See* SEELEY, The Rt Revd Martin Alan

ST GERMANS, Suffragan Bishop of. *Vacant*

ST JOHN, Christopher George. b 66. Open Univ BA 98 MA 02 MA 05 Hull Univ MEd 05 Ulster Univ PhD 14. CITI 14. **d** 16 **p** 17. Woodburn H Trin *Conn* 16–17; C Dundela St Mark *D & D* from 17. *17 Dalchoolin, Holywood BT18 0HR* T: (028) 9042 7513 M: 07463-745105 E: christopher.stjohn@btinternet.com *or* curate.dundela@down.anglican.org

ST JOHN NICOLLE, Jason Paul. b 66. Mert Coll Ox BA 88 Called to the Bar (Inner Temple) 95. Ripon Coll Cuddesdon 01. **d** 04 **p** 05. C Kidlington w Hampton Poyle *Ox* 04–08; R The Churn from 08; AD Wallingford 12–17; AD Wantage from 13; AD Vale of White Horse from 18. *The Rectory, Church End, Blewbury, Didcot OX11 9QH* T: (01235) 850267 E: office@churnchurches.com

SAKAKINI, Gillian Cudmore. b 63. St Mellitus Coll 16. **d** 18 **p** 19. C Tadley w Pamber Heath and Silchester *Win* from 18. *The Vicarage St Marys, Bishopswood Road, Tadley RG26 4HQ* E: gilly.sak@gmail.com

SALA, Kuabuleke Meymans. b 68. **d** 08 **p** 09. C Edmonton All SS w St Mich *Lon* 08–16; C Wood Green St Mich w Bounds Green St Gabr etc 16–18; Chapl Mid-Essex Hosp Services NHS Trust from 18. *Mid Essex Hospital NHS Trust, Broomfield Hospital, Chelmsford CM1 7ET* T: (01245) 515244 E: smeymans@hotmail.com

SALEH, Mrs Carey Jane. b 62. Sheff Univ BA 94 RGN 83. Qu Coll Birm 11. **d** 13 **p** 14. C Bromsgrove *Worc* 13–17; V Stourport and Wilden from 17. *The Vicarage, Church Avenue, Stourport-on-Severn DY13 9DD* T: (01299) 822041 M: 07933-744107 E: revcareysaleh@gmail.com

SALES, Canon Patrick David. b 43. K Coll Lon AKC 68 BD 74 Kent Univ MA 00. **d** 69 **p** 70. C Maidstone All SS w St Phil *Cant* 69–71; C Maidstone All SS w St Phil and H Trin 71–72; C Chart next Sutton Valence 72–74; C Birchington w Acol 75–77; V Boughton under Blean w Dunkirk 77–83; V Herne 83–03; P-in-c St Nicholas at Wade w Sarre and Chislet w Hoath 98–03; TV Whitstable 03–06; Hon Min Can Cant Cathl 83–01; Hon Can Cant Cathl 01–06; RD Reculver 86–92; AD 01–06; Dioc Adv in Liturgy 00–06; rtd 06; PtO *Chich* from 14. *The Well House, South Lane, Dallington, Heathfield TN21 9NJ* T: (01435) 830194 M: 07803-257283 E: patricksales@btinternet.com

SALFORD, Archdeacon of. *See* SHARPLES, The Ven David John
SALISBURY, Anne Ruth. b 37. Dalton Ho Bris 63. **d** 87 **p** 94. C Harrow Trin St Mich *Lon* 87–98; C Paddington Em and W Kilburn St Luke w St Simon and St Jude 99–03; rtd 03. *c/o Crockford, Church House, Great Smith Street, London SW1P 3AZ* M: 07986-868667
SALISBURY, Canon Peter Brian Christopher. b 58. UMIST BSc 80 MBCS 85. Sarum & Wells Th Coll BTh 92. **d** 92 **p** 93. C Stanmore *Win* 92–95; V Chilworth w N Baddesley 95–05; V Lymington from 05; AD Lyndhurst from 13; Hon Can Win Cathl from 17. *The Vicarage, Grove Road, Lymington SO41 3RF* T: (01590) 673847 E: vicar@lymingtonchurch.org
SALISBURY, Canon Roger John. b 44. Lon Univ BD 67. Lon Coll of Div 66. **d** 68 **p** 69. C Harold Wood *Chelmsf* 68–73; V Dorking St Paul *Guildf* 73–82; R Rusholme H Trin *Man* 82–90; TR Gt Chesham *Ox* 90–06; RD Amersham 98–04; Hon Can Ch Ch 02–06; C Langham Place All So *Lon* 06–11; rtd 11; Sec Ch Patr Trust 06–15; Sec Peache Trustees 11–19; PtO *B & W* from 12. *6 Church Street, Widcombe, Bath BA2 6AZ* T: (01225) 489076 E: rogerandhilda.salisbury@gmail.com
SALISBURY, Canon Tobias. b 33. Em Coll Cam BA 60. Ripon Hall Ox 60. **d** 62 **p** 63. C Putney St Mary *S'wark* 62–65; C Churchdown St Jo *Glouc* 65–67; V Urchfont w Stert *Sarum* 67–73; R Burton Bradstock w Shipton Gorge and Chilcombe 73–79; P-in-c Long Bredy w Lt Bredy and Kingston Russell 75–79; TR Bride Valley 79–86; V Gt and Lt Bedwyn and Savernake Forest 86–97; Can and Preb Sarum Cathl 92–98; rtd 98; PtO *B & W* from 98. *Anfield, Hayes Lane, Compton Dundon, Somerton TA11 6PB* T: (01458) 274459
SALISBURY, Bishop of. *See* HOLTAM, The Rt Revd Nicholas Roderick
SALISBURY, Dean of. *See* PAPADOPULOS, The Very Revd Nicholas Charles
SALMON, Canon Andrew Ian. b 61. St Jo Coll Nottm BTh 88. **d** 88 **p** 89. C Collyhurst *Man* 88–92; P-in-c Pendleton St Ambrose 92–95; TV Pendleton 95–99; TR 99–04; P-in-c Salford Sacred Trin and St Phil 04–16; V Salford Sacred Trin from 16; AD Salford 06–13; Borough Dean Salford 13–18; Hon Can Man Cathl from 10. *Sacred Trinity Rectory, 52 George Leigh Street, Manchester M4 5DG* T: 0161-834 2041 *or* 839 1180 M: 07990-585037 E: rev.andy@btinternet.com *or* andy@salfordchurch.com
SALMON, Andrew Meredith Bryant. b 30. Jes Coll Cam BA 54 MA 58. Ridley Hall Cam 54. **d** 56 **p** 57. C Enfield Ch Ch Trent Park *Lon* 56–58; Chapl Monkton Combe Sch Bath 58–71; Chapl Milton Abbey Sch Dorset 71–89; TV Bride Valley *Sarum* 89–96; rtd 97; PtO *Sarum* from 97. *Heatherland, Barnhill Road, Wareham BH20 5BD* T: (01929) 554039 E: amsalmonbh20@gmail.com
SALMON, Anthony James Heygate. b 30. CCC Ox BA 53 MA 57. Cuddesdon Coll 54. **d** 56 **p** 57. C S Norwood St Mark *Cant* 56–59; S Africa 59–69; Chapl USPG Coll of the Ascension Selly Oak 69–74; P-in-c Frinsted w Wormshill and Milstead *Cant* 74–78; R Harrietsham 74–85; P-in-c Ulcombe 81–85; V Chobham w Valley End *Guildf* 85–95; rtd 95; PtO *St Alb* from 95. *24 Elmwood, Welwyn Garden City AL8 6LE* T: (01707) 333694
SALMON, Mrs Constance Hazel. b 25. R Holloway Coll Lon BSc 46. Lon Bible Coll 66 Gilmore Course 71. **dss** 80 **d** 87 **p** 96. Sidcup St Andr *Roch* 80–88; NSM 87–88; PtO 88–96; NSM Eynsford w Farningham and Lullingstone 96–05. *43 Old Mill Close, Eynsford, Dartford DA4 0BN* T: (01322) 866034
SALMON, Michael John. b 77. **d** 13. NSM Bishopston and St Andrews *Bris* 13–14. *40 Fenner Square, London SW11 2HQ* M: 07779-107841 E: michaelsalmon@mac.com *or* michael@it-games.co.uk
SALMON, Philip John. b 63. Oak Hill Th Coll 96. **d** 98 **p** 99. C Kington w Huntington, Old Radnor, Kinnerton etc *Heref* 98–02; TV Radipole and Melcombe Regis *Sarum* 02–18; P-in-c Pitsmoor Ch Ch *Sheff* from 18; C Sheff St Cuth from 18; C Ellesmere St Pet from 18. *The Vicarage, 257 Pitsmoor Road, Sheffield S3 9AQ* M: 07799-944436 E: revpip@yahoo.com
SALMON, Richard Harold. b 35. Fitzw Ho Cam BA 57. Clifton Th Coll 57. **d** 59 **p** 60. C Blackheath Park St Mich *S'wark* 59–61; C St Alb St Paul 61–63; OMF 63–65; C Telok Anson St Luke Malaysia 63–65; V Kuanton Pehang Epiphany 65–75; P-in-c March St Wendreda *Ely* 75–76; R 76–85; V Congresbury w Puxton and Hewish St Ann *B & W* 85–00; rtd 00; PtO *Truro* 00–01; *B & W* from 02. *2 Wisteria Avenue, Hutton, Weston-super-Mare BS24 9QF* T: (01934) 813750 M: 07966-038543 E: richardandhelensalmon@gmail.com
SALMON, William John. b 50. Lon Univ BSc 72 DipEd 73. Cranmer Hall Dur 76. **d** 79 **p** 80. C Summerstown *S'wark* 79–81; C Hampreston *Sarum* 81–86; V Sundon *St Alb* 86–90; Dep Chapl HM Young Offender Inst Glen Parva

90–91; Chapl HM Pris Whitemoor 91–95; Chapl HM Pris Blundeston 95–04 and 07–14; Chapl HM Pris Belmarsh 04–07; Chapl HM Pris and YOI Warren Hill from 14; PtO *Nor* from 16. *HM Prison Warren Hill, Grove Road, Hollesley, Woodbridge IP12 3BF* T: (01394) 633400
SALMON, Mrs Yvonne Delysia. b 40. Cant Sch of Min 00. **d** 03 **p** 04. OLM Boughton Monchelsea *Cant* 03–10; PtO from 11. *Elderden Farm Cottage, Maidstone Road, Staplehurst, Tonbridge TN12 0RN* T: (01622) 842598 E: y.salmon@tesco.net
SALOP, Archdeacon of. *See* THOMAS, The Ven Paul Wyndham
SALT, David Thomas Whitehorn. b 32. K Coll Lon AKC 56 BD 57. **d** 57 **p** 58. Chapl Torgil Girls' Sch Aoba New Hebrides 57–59; Warden Catechist Coll Lolowai 59–63; Prin St Andr Coll Guadalcanal Solomon Is 63–66; C Hawley H Trin *Guildf* 66–68; V Shelf *Bradf* 68–73; R Checkendon *Ox* 73–81; RD Henley 78–84; TR Langtree 81–84; V Hungerford and Denford 84–89; Chapl Hungerford Hosp 84–89; P-in-c Harpsden *Ox* 89–95; Gen Sec Melanesian Miss 89–95; rtd 95; PtO *Sarum* 95–05; *Guildf* 06–15; *Win* 06–12; *Portsm* from 16. *1 Victoria Court, 19 Beach Road, Hayling Island PO11 0AB* T: (023) 9246 4764 E: dtwsalt@gmail.com
SALT, Jeremy William. b 56. St Mellitus Coll. **d** 11 **p** 12. NSM Ingatestone w Fryerning *Chelmsf* 11–15; P-in-c Buckden w the Offords *Ely* from 15; Dioc Social Justice Co-ord from 15. *The Vicarage, 16 Church Street, Buckden, St Neots PE19 5TL* T: (01480) 819377 E: jes.salt@btinternet.com
SALT, Neil. b 64. Univ of Wales (Ban) BA 85 New Coll Edin BD 89 Man Metrop Univ BSc 97. Edin Th Coll 86. **d** 89 **p** 90. C Stretford All SS *Man* 89–93; V Smallbridge and Wardle 93–94; PtO *Wakef* 94–01; Hon C Rippondon and Barkisland w W Scammonden 01–06; Chapl Rishworth Sch Rippondon 02–05; V Thornton-le-Fylde *Blackb* 06–14; PtO 14–17; V Grimsargh from 17. *6 Douglas Lane, Grimsargh, Preston PR2 5JF* T: (01772) 796854 E: vicar.grimsargh@gmail.com
SALT, Mrs Susan . b 64. Imp Coll Lon MB, BS 89 Man Univ PhD 10. All SS Cen for Miss & Min 17. **d** 19. C Fellside Team *Blackb* from 19. *6 Douglas Lane, Grimsargh, Preston PR2 5JF* M: 07730-197656 E: sdsalt93@gmail.com
SALTER, Arthur Thomas John. b 34. AKC 60. **d** 61 **p** 62. C Ealing St Pet Mt Park *Lon* 61–65; C Shepherd's Bush St Steph w St Thos 65–66; C Holborn St Alb w Saffron Hill St Pet 66–70; P-in-c Barnsbury St Clem 70–77; P-in-c Islington St Mich 70–77; V Pentonville St Silas w All SS and St Jas 70–00; CF (TAVR) from 75; Gen Sec Angl and E Chs Assn from 76; Chmn from 90; P-in-c St Dunstan in the West *Lon* 79–99; rtd 00. *1 St James's Close, Bishop Street, London N1 8PH* T: (020) 7359 0250 E: salteralexis@aol.com
SALTER, Christopher. *See* SALTER, Nigel Christopher Murray
SALTER, David Whitton. b 69. Bris Univ BEng 90. Trin Coll Bris 06. **d** 08 **p** 09. C Eynsham and Cassington *Ox* 08–11; TV Chipping Norton from 11. *6 The Grange, Kingham, Chipping Norton OX7 6XY* T: (01608) 658852 M: 07768-582285 E: david.w.salter@btinternet.com
SALTER, Janet Elizabeth. b 48. Leeds Univ CertEd 69. SWMTC 92. **d** 95 **p** 98. C Coleshill *Birm* 95–97; Hon C St Dennis *Truro* 97–00; TV Gillingham *Sarum* 00–04; V Stour Vale 04–11; rtd 11; PtO *Truro* from 14. *6 Maple Close, St Columb TR9 6SL* T: (01637) 881552 E: jansalter552@gmail.com
SALTER, John. *See* SALTER, Arthur Thomas John
SALTER, Canon John Frank. b 37. Dur Univ BA 62. Cranmer Hall Dur 62. **d** 64 **p** 65. C Bridlington Priory *York* 64–67; Travelling Sec IVF 67–70; V Stoughton *Guildf* 70–02; RD Guildf 89–94; Hon Can Guildf Cathl 99–02; rtd 03; PtO *Guildf* from 03. *7 Aldershot Road, Guildford GU2 8AE* T: (01483) 511165 E: johnsalter37@gmail.com
SALTER, Nigel Christopher Murray. b 46. Loughb Univ BTech. Ripon Coll Cuddesdon 79. **d** 81 **p** 82. C Glouc St Aldate 81–84; C Solihull *Birm* 84–88; V Highters Heath 88–97; Asst Chapl Greenwich Healthcare NHS Trust 97–01; Asst Chapl Qu Eliz Hosp NHS Trust 01–03; P-in-c Leaton and Albrighton w Battlefield *Lich* 03–06; rtd 06; PtO *Win* from 12. *4 Maple Close, Alton GU34 2AY* T: (01420) 85412
SALTER, Roger John. b 45. Trin Coll Bris 75. **d** 79 **p** 80. C Bedminster St Mich *Bris* 79–82; C Swindon Ch Ch 82–84; V Bedminster Down 84–89; P-in-c Northwood *Portsm* 89–93; P-in-c W Cowes H Trin 89–92; V Cowes H Trin and St Mary 92–94; USA from 94; rtd 10. *1300 Panorama Drive, Vestavia Hill AL 35216-3032, USA* T: (001) (1) 205 7967 E: salter.roger@gmail.com
SALTMARSH, Philip. b 71. Keele Univ MA 03 RN 93. SNWTP 08. **d** 11 **p** 12. NSM Grassendale *Liv* 11–14; C Liv All SS from 14; AD Liv N from 18. *19 Lockerby Road, Liverpool L7 0HG* M: 07715-397390 E: philsaltmarsh@aol.com
SALWAY, Canon Donald Macleay. b 55. St Pet Hall Ox BA 54 MA 59. Oak Hill Th Coll 54. **d** 56 **p** 57. C Holloway St Mary w St Jas *Lon* 56–67; V Cambridge St Phil *Ely* 67–81; V Mile Cross

Nor 81–96; RD Nor N 89–95; Hon Can Nor Cathl 91–96; rtd 96; PtO *B & W* 96–18; C Langport Area 98–00. *29 Capel Court, The Burgage, Prestbury, Cheltenham GL52 3EL* T: (01242) 577261 E: donald.salway@btinternet.com

SAMBROOK, Kenneth Henry. b 42. NOC 04. **d** 05 **p** 06. NSM Wistaston *Ches* 05–15; rtd 15; PtO *Ches* from 15. *6 Westfield Drive, Wistaston, Crewe CW2 8ES* T: (01270) 662455 E: rev.ken@stmaryswistaston.org.uk

SAMMÉ, Raymond Charles. b 50. Anglia Poly Univ MA 03 St Andr Univ MLitt 08 CBiol 80 MRSB 80. Oak Hill Th Coll 85. **d** 87 **p** 88. C Holmer w Huntington *Heref* 87–90; C Derby St Alkmund and St Werburgh 90–93; V Romford Gd Shep *Chelmsf* 93–08; P-in-c Swanley St Paul *Roch* 08–16; rtd 17. *18 Sevenoaks Avenue, Derby DE22 4HU* E: ray.samme@gmail.com

SAMMON, Canon Helen Mary Kirkman. b 57. Newnham Coll Cam MA 79 Bris Univ MB, ChB 82 MRCGP 98 Qu Foundn for Ecum Th Educn MA 10. WEMTC 00. **d** 03 **p** 04. NSM Painswick, Sheepscombe, Cranham, The Edge etc *Glouc* 03–07; P-in-c Tuffley 07–12; Public Preacher 12–16; P-in-c Highnam, Tibberton w Rudford etc from 16; CMD Officer from 15; Hon Can Glouc Cathl from 13. *25 Maidenhall, Highnam, Gloucester GL2 8DJ* E: vicar@highnamchurch.org

SAMPLE, Mrs Fiona Jean. b 55. Dur Univ BA 11. Lindisfarne Regional Tr Partnership 02. **d** 08 **p** 09. Chapl Mowden Hall Sch 06–17; OLM Bolam w Whalton and Hartburn w Meldon *Newc* 08–14; NSM 14–17; C from 17; OLM Nether Witton 08–14; NSM 14–17; C from 17. *South Middleton Farm, Middleton, Morpeth NE61 4EB* T: (01670) 774245 M: 07486-364582 E: f.sample@btinternet.com

SAMPSON, Brian Andrew. b 39. **d** 94 **p** 95. C Glemsford, Hartest w Boxted, Somerton etc *St E* 94–96; C Pentlow, Foxearth, Liston and Borley *Chelmsf* 96–97; P-in-c 97–03; P-in-c N Hinckford 03–04; C 04–09; rtd 09. *4 Friars Court, Edgworth Road, Sudbury CO10 2TG* T: (01787) 371529 E: captainbriance@waitrose.com

SAMPSON, Clive. b 38. St Jo Coll Cam BA 61 MA 64. Ridley Hall Cam 63. **d** 65 **p** 66. C Tunbridge Wells St Jo *Roch* 65–69; Travelling Sec Scripture Union 69–79; V Maidstone St Luke *Cant* 79–94; rtd 98; PtO *Win* from 17. *108 Bure Homage Gardens, Christchurch BH23 4DR* T: (01425) 279029 E: clive.sampson12@gmail.com

SAMPSON, Gemma Sophia Marie. b 75. Huddersfield Univ BA 96 Leic Univ MA 05 Sheff Univ BA 15. Coll of Resurr Mirfield 13. **d** 15 **p** 16. C Hartlepool St Aid and St Columba *Dur* 15–19; P-in-c from 19. *St Luke's Vicarage, 5 Tunstall Avenue, Hartlepool TS26 8NF* M: 07780-675322 E: revdgemma@gmail.com

SAMPSON, Julian Robin Anthony. b 78. St D Coll Lamp BA 00. St Steph Ho Ox 01. **d** 03 **p** 04. C Notting Hill All SS w St Columb *Lon* 03–04; C Staines and Asst Chapl HM Pris Bronzefield 04–07; Chapl HM Pris Birm 07–13; V Handsworth St Mich *Birm* 13–18; P-in-c Birm Bp Latimer w All SS 14–18; V Small Heath from 18. *The Clergy House, 85 Jenkins Street, Birmingham B10 0PQ* T: 0121-772 0621 M: 07801-944520 E: vicarhandsworth@hotmail.com *or* julians@cofebirmingham.com

SAMPSON, Terence Harold Morris. b 41. ACA 64 FCA 75. Bps' Coll Cheshunt 64. **d** 67 **p** 68. C Penrith St Andr *Carl* 67–72; V Carl St Barn 72–80; TR Carl H Trin and St Barn 80–84; Chapl Cumberland Infirmary 83–84; R Workington St Mich *Carl* 84–01; Hon Can Carl Cathl 89–01; RD Solway 90–95; PtO 02–16; *Eur* from 03. *Edificio Balcon de San Miguel, Avenida de Alicante 17/19, 03193 San Miguel de Salinas (Alicante)*, Spain T: (0034) 677 237 496 M: 07775-683275 E: terenceandmargaret@hotmail.co.uk

SAMS, Mrs Jacqueline. b 53. Open Univ BA 82 St Osyth Coll of Educn CertEd 74. NTMTC BA 10. **d** 10 **p** 11. NSM Colchester Ch Ch w St Mary V *Chelmsf* 10–14; PtO 14–16; NSM Berechurch St Marg w St Mich from 16. *17 Chestnut Avenue, Colchester CO2 0AL* T: (01206) 530586 E: revjackiesams@gmail.com

SAMS, Michael Charles. b 34. FCA 62. Ox NSM Course 81. **d** 84 **p** 85. NSM Abingdon *Ox* 84–92 and 99–04; P-in-c Shippon 92–99; PtO from 04. *23 Charney Avenue, Abingdon OX14 2NZ* T: (01235) 529084 E: michael-gwenda@uwclub.net

SAMSON, Canon Hilary Lynn. b 50. SWMTC. **d** 03 **p** 04. NSM St Agnes and Mithian w Mount Hawke *Truro* 03–06; P-in-c St Enoder 06–18; P-in-c Newlyn St Newlyn 06–18; RD Pydar 13–18; Hon Can Truro Cathl 16–18; rtd 18. *The Stable, 12 Newton Road, Troon, Camborne TR14 7SJ* E: hilarysamson@btinternet.com

SAMSON, Mrs Susan Mary. b 50. SWMTC. **d** 09 **p** 10. OLM Sittingbourne w Bobbing *Cant* from 09. *11 Adelaide Drive, Sittingbourne ME10 1YB* T: (01795) 478635 E: suesamson@sky.com

SAMUEL, Brother. *See* DOUBLE, Richard Sydney

SAMUEL, Fiaz. *See* SAMUEL, Luther Fiaz

SAMUEL, Kerry Jay. b 71. Nottm Univ BA 92 Hughes Hall Cam PGCE 93 K Coll Lon PhD 07. NTMTC 05. **d** 07 **p** 08. C Twickenham St Mary *Lon* 07–10; PtO *Glouc* 13–15; Chapl Cheltenham Coll from 13; Chapl All SS Academy Cheltenham from 15. *Chandos Lodge, Thirlestaine Road, Cheltenham GL53 7AA* M: 07774-470403 E: kerrysamuel@hotmail.com

SAMUEL, Luther Fiaz. b 47. Karachi Univ BA 83. St Thos Th Coll Karachi BTh 88. **d** 88 **p** 89. Pakistan 88–96; Oman 96–03; PtO *Lich* 03–04; NSM Walsall St Matt 04–15; Minority Ethnic Angl Concerns Officer 04–05; Asian Missr 05–13; rtd 13; PtO *Lich* 15–17; *Nor* from 17. *3 Charlotte Drive, Costessey, Norwich NR8 5HJ* M: 07736-761754

SAMUELS, Canon Anne Elizabeth. b 51. Birm Univ BA 73 CertEd 74. Trin Coll Bris 85. **d** 87 **p** 94. Par Dn Moreton *Ches* 87–91; Par Dn Halton 91–94; C 94–03; Bp's Adv for Women in Min 94–96; Asst Dir of Ords 96–03; RD Frodsham 99–03; Chapl Halton Gen Hosp NHS Trust 99–00; Chapl N Cheshire Hosps NHS Trust 01–03; V Higher Bebington *Ches* 03–14; Hon Can Ches Cathl 01–14; rtd 14; Chapl Foxhill Retreat and Conf Cen *Ches* from 16. *10 West Heath Court, Gerard Road, West Kirby, Wirral CH48 4ES* T: 0151-625 3492 E: annesamuels47@btinternet.com

SAMUELS, Canon Christopher William John. b 42. AKC 66. **d** 67 **p** 68. C Kirkholt *Man* 67–72; C-in-c Houghton Regis St Thos CD *St Alb* 72–76; R Tarporley *Ches* 76–83; R Ches St Mary 83–05; RD Ches 95–02; Hon Can Ches Cathl 97–05; rtd 05; Chapl to The Queen 01–12; LtO *St As* from 05; PtO *Ches* from 07; *St As* from 16; *Eur* from 09. *Long View, Mannings Lane, Hoole Village, Chester CH2 2PB* M: 07929-420423 E: cwjsamuels@gmail.com

SAMUELS, Canon Raymond John. b 49. Qu Mary Coll Lon BSc 73 Ex Univ PGCE 74. Trin Coll Bris 85. **d** 87 **p** 88. C Moreton *Ches* 87–91; V Halton 91–02; Dioc Dir of Ords 03–14; rtd 14; V Alvanley *Ches* 14–18; Hon Can Ches Cathl 16–18; PtO from 18. *10 West Heath Court, Gerard Road, West Kirby, Wirral CH48 4ES* T: 0151-625 3492 E: raysamuels47@btinternet.com

SAMUELS, Mrs Sheila Tarona. b 70. St Mellitus Coll MA 19. **d** 19. C Godalming *Guildf* from 19. *49 Coopers Rise, Godalming GU7 2NH* M: 07951-215260 E: s.samuels70@hotmail.com

SAMWAYS, Denis Robert. b 37. Leeds Univ BA 62. Coll of Resurr Mirfield 62. **d** 64 **p** 65. C Clun w Chapel Lawn *Heref* 64–69; C Pocklington w Yapham-cum-Meltonby, Owsthorpe etc *York* 69–71; C Millington w Gt Givendale 69–71; R Hinderwell w Roxby 71–76; Hon C 80–91; Hon C Loftus 76–80; V Boosbeck w Moorsholm 91–95; R Kirby Misperton w Normanby, Edston and Salton 95–02; rtd 02. *7 High Street, Gatehouse of Fleet, Castle Douglas DG7 2HR* T: (01557) 814095 E: dennissamways71@sky.com

SAMWAYS, John Feverel. b 44. BA. Trin Coll Bris 81. **d** 83 **p** 84. C Patcham *Chich* 83–86; C Ox St Aldate w St Matt 86–94; R Ox St Matt 95–97; TR Keynsham *B & W* 97–09; rtd 09; PtO *B & W* from 10. *9 Newland Gardens, Frome BA11 1PN* T: (01373) 454047 E: john.samways28@btinternet.com

SANCHEZ RODRIGUEZ, Miguel. b 66. Deusto Univ MA 95. Coll of Resurr Mirfield 12. **d** 14 **p** 15. C Elland *Leeds* 14–17 and from 14; C Barnsley St Mary 17–18; C Gawber 17–18; C Cen Barnsley from 18. *The Vicarage, Church Street, Gawber, Barnsley S75 2RL* M: 07761-501229 E: msanrod@gmail.com

SANDAY, Robert Ward. b 55. Sarum & Wells Th Coll 89. **d** 91 **p** 92. C Swindon Ch Ch *Bris* 91–94; V Lyddington and Wanborough and Bishopstone etc 94–00; Chapl to the Deaf Portsm and Win from 00; V Southampton Lord's Hill and Lord's Wood 10–15; P-in-c Hound from 15; C Bursledon from 15; C Hamble le Rice from 15; Portsm Dioc Disability Adv from 15. *The Vicarage, Grange Road, Netley Abbey, Southampton SO31 5FF* T: (023) 8045 6778 E: robertsanday12@gmail.com

SANDBERG, Canon Peter John. b 37. Lon Univ LLB 59. Lon Coll of Div 67. **d** 69 **p** 70. C Hailsham *Chich* 69–72; C Billericay St Mary *Chelmsf* 72–77; TV Billericay and Lt Burstead 77–83; V Thundersley 83–02; RD Hadleigh 90–00; Hon Can Chelmsf Cathl 00–02; rtd 02; PtO *Chelmsf* from 02. *Hethersett, School Road, Pentlow, Sudbury CO10 7JR* T: (01787) 281006 E: peterandcelia@talktalk.net

SANDELLS-REES, Kathy Louise. *See* JONES, Kathy Louise

SANDER, Thomas William. b 87. Westcott Ho Cam. **d** 11 **p** 12. C Sharnbrook, Felmersham and Knotting w Souldrop *St Alb* 11–14; V Flamstead and Markyate Street from 14. *The Vicarage, 50 Trowley Hill Road, Flamstead, St Albans AL3 8EE* E: thomas.william.sander@gmail.com

SANDER-HEYS, Mrs Jemma Joan. b 79. Ex Univ BA 02 Leeds Univ BA 11 Sheff Univ MA 12. Coll of Resurr Mirfield 09. **d** 12 **p** 13. C R Wootton Bassett *Sarum* 12–15;

TV Gt Yarmouth *Nor* from 15. *1 Osborne Avenue, Great Yarmouth NR30 4EE* T: (01493) 304609 M: 07811-480438 E: jemmajsanders@hotmail.com

SANDERCOCK-PICKLES, Deborah Sharon Agnes. b 62. Coll of Ripon & York St Jo BSc 84 Man Metrop Univ MSc 96 Crewe & Alsager Coll PGCE 87. SNWTP 09. **d** 12 **p** 13. C Chadderton St Matt w St Luke *Man* 12–15; P-in-c Prestwich St Marg 15–18; V from 17; AD Radcliffe and Prestwich 18–19. *St Margaret's Vicarage, 2 St Margaret's Road, Prestwich, Manchester M25 2QB* T: 0161-773 2698 M: 07871-760107 E: deborah.sandercock@hotmail.co.uk

SANDERS, Bryant John. **d** 15 **p** 16. C S Molton w Nymet St George, High Bray etc *Ex* 15–16; C S Molton w Nymet St George, Chittlehamholt etc from 16. *Shears Cottage, Kings Nympton, Umberleigh EX37 9SP* T: (01769) 581420

SANDERS, Diana Faye. b 46. Auckland Univ MA 68 LSE PhD 75 Anglia Ruskin Univ PhD 10. Westcott Ho Cam 02. **d** 04 **p** 05. NSM Cottenham *Ely* 04–08; P-in-c Farley Hill St Jo *St Alb* 08–11; rtd 11; PtO *Ely* 11–16. *48 Tenison Manor, Cottenham, Cambridge CB24 8XL* T: (01954) 205420 E: sandersdianaf@gmail.com

SANDERS, Canon Hilary Clare. b 57. Hull Univ BA 79 UEA CertEd 81. EAMTC 83. **dss** 85 **d** 87 **p** 94. Haverhill w Withersfield, the Wrattings etc *St E* 85–87; Hon Par Dn Melton 87–94; Hon C 94–99; Dioc Dir Educn (Schools) 88–99; P-in-c Earl Soham w Cretingham and Ashfield 99–05; P-in-c Boulge w Burgh, Grundisburgh and Hasketon 05–13; R Carlford from 13; Dioc Adv for Women's Min from 10; RD Woodbridge from 11; Hon Can St E Cathl from 04. *The Rectory, St Michael's Close, Framlingham, Woodbridge IP13 9BJ* T: (01728) 768875 *or* (01473) 735183 E: revclaresanders@tiscali.co.uk

SANDERS, Canon Mark. b 57. Hull Univ BA 79 Cam Univ BA 82. Westcott Ho Cam 80. **d** 83 **p** 84. C Haverhill w Withersfield, the Wrattings etc *St E* 83–87; P-in-c Melton 87–91; R 91–98; Dioc Dir Post-Ord Tr 97–14; Asst Dioc Dir of Ords 98–99; Dioc Dir of Ords 99–14; Dioc Dir of CME 99–01; R Framlingham w Saxtead from 14; RD Loes from 15; Hon Can St E Cathl from 01. *The Rectory, St Michael's Close, Framlingham, Woodbridge IP13 9BJ* T: (01728) 768875 E: revmarksanders@tiscali.co.uk

SANDERS, Michael Barry. b 45. Fitzw Coll Cam BA 67 MA 71 Lon Univ BD 71. St Jo Coll Nottm 68 Lon Coll of Div. **d** 71 **p** 72. C Ashtead *Guildf* 71–74; Chapl St Jo Coll Cam 75–79; V Dorridge *Birm* 79–89; TR Walsall *Lich* 89–97; Preb Lich Cathl 97–01; Chapl The Hague *Eur* 01–07; P-in-c Kemble, Poole Keynes, Somerford Keynes etc *Glouc* 07–12; rtd 12; PtO *Glouc* from 15; Clergy Retirement Officer from 16; PtO *Eur* from 12. *1 Rowena Cade Avenue, Cheltenham GL50 2LA* T: (01242) 515631 E: mbsanders45@gmail.com

SANDERS, Susan Rachel. *See* COLLINGRIDGE, Susan Rachel

SANDERS, Canon Wendy Elizabeth. b 49. Carl Dioc Tr Course 87. **d** 90 **p** 94. NSM Bampton w Mardale *Carl* 90–92; C Walney Is 92–94; C Stanwix 94–98; TV Chippenham St Paul w Hardenhuish etc *Bris* 98–03; TV Kington St Michael 98–03; RD Chippenham 99–03; TR Cockermouth Area *Carl* 03–14; Hon Can Carl Cathl 10–14; rtd 14; RD Derwent *Carl* 11–16. *23 Lowscales Drive, Cockermouth CA13 9DR* T: (01900) 823269 E: revdwes@gmail.com

SANDERS, William John. b 48. Liv Inst of Educn BA 80. Wycliffe Hall Ox 81. **d** 83 **p** 84. C Netherton *Liv* 83–87; P-in-c Wavertree St Bridget 87–97; V Wavertree St Bridget and St Thos 97–14; P-in-c 14–18; rtd 14; PtO *Liv* from 19. *14 Nightingale Road, Liverpool L12 0QF* E: billandalice@virginmedia.com

SANDERSON, Colin James. b 54. Univ of Wales (Cardiff) MA 95 SEN 76 RGN. St Mich Coll Llan 85. **d** 87 **p** 88. C Merthyr Dyfan *Llan* 87–90; C Cadoxton-juxta-Barry 90–91; V Llangeinor 91–99; LtO 04–10; V Congleton St Jas *Ches* from 10; Chapl Mid Cheshire Hosps NHS Foundn Trust 11–12; Lead Chapl from 12. *St James's Vicarage, 116 Holmes Chapel Road, Congleton CW12 4NX* T: (01260) 408203 *or* (01270) 255141 M: 07713-742365 E: cjsanderson2005@hotmail.com

SANDERSON, Daniel. b 40. AKC 66. **d** 67 **p** 68. C Upperby St Jo *Carl* 67–70; V Addingham 72–75; V Ireleth w Askam 75–02; C Dalton-in-Furness and Ireleth-with-Askam 02–05; Hon Can Carl Cathl 95–05; RD Furness 01–04; rtd 05; PtO *Carl* from 13. *52 Parklands Drive, Askam-in-Furness LA16 7JP* T: (01229) 463018

SANDERSON, Canon Gillian. b 47. Cranmer Hall Dur 80. **dss** 82 **d** 87 **p** 94. Allesley *Cov* 82–86; Warwick 86–00; C 87–94; TV 94–00; Hon Can Cov Cathl 94–00; PtO 00–15. *17 Marlborough Drive, Leamington Spa CV31 1XY* T: (01926) 459749 M: 07714-193776 E: gillian7647@gmail.com

SANDERSON, Paul. b 59. Univ of Wales (Abth) BSc 80 Man Univ MEd 92 Ches Coll of HE PGCE 81. **d** 05 **p** 06. OLM

Bury St Jo w St Mark *Man* 05–10; OLM Walmersley Road, Bury 10–19; P-in-c Elton St Steph from 19. *22 Birley Street, Bury BL9 5DT* E: paul270159@gmail.com

SANDERSON, Timothy. b 68. York Univ BSc 89 Glos Univ BA 03 St Jo Coll Dur MATM 09. Cranmer Hall Dur 07. **d** 09 **p** 10. C Jesmond H Trin *Newc* from 09; C Newc St Barn and St Jude 09–17. *36 St Julien Gardens, Newcastle upon Tyne NE2 2QX* T: 0191-281 9452 M: 07592-720879 E: tim@htj.org.uk

SANDES, Denis Lindsay. b 46. CITC BTh 86. **d** 89 **p** 90. C Bandon Union *C, C & R* 89–92; I Kells Gp *C & O* 92–07; Can Leighlin Cathl 03–07; I Omey w Ballynakill, Errislannan and Roundstone *T, K & A* 07–13; Can Tuam Cathl 08–11; Provost Tuam 10–13; rtd 13. *Ballyhasty, Cloughjordan, Co Tipperary, Republic of Ireland* T: (00353) (76) 604 5868 M: 86-647 5056 E: revdlsandes@gmail.com

SANDFORD, Nicholas Robert. b 63. Kent Univ BA 84 Univ of Wales (Cardiff) BD 87. St Mich Coll Llan 84. **d** 87 **p** 88. C Neath w Llantwit *Llan* 87–90; C Cardiff St Jo 90–94; R Cilybebyll 94–97; Chapl HM Pris Swansea 95–97; Chapl HM Pris Parc (Bridgend) 97–04; Chapl HM Pris Usk and Prescoed 04–13; Chapl HM Pris Swansea 13–16; Chapl HM Pris Cardiff from 16; PtO *Llan* from 14. *HM Prison, Knox Road, Cardiff CF40 0UG* T: (029) 2092 3100 E: nick.r.sandford@justice.gov.uk

SANDFORD, Paul Richard. b 47. Em Coll Cam BA 69 MA 73. Wycliffe Hall Ox 72. **d** 75 **p** 76. C Upper Holloway St Pet *Lon* 75–77; C Finchley St Paul Long Lane 77–81; Ind Chapl *Newc* 81–88; TV Cramlington 81–88; TV Dronfield *Derby* 88–90; TV Dronfield w Holmesfield 90–02; P-in-c Sinfin 02–10; V 10–14; RD Derby S 02–10; rtd 14; PtO *Derby* from 14. *4 Dawlish Court, Alvaston, Derby DE24 0QZ* E: prsandford@ntlworld.com

SANDHAM, Daniel Paul. b 82. St Chad's Coll Dur BA 05. St Steph Ho Ox BA 09 MA 14. **d** 09 **p** 10. C Hendon St Mary and Ch Ch *Lon* 09–12; V Brownswood Park 12–18; P-in-c Winchmore Hill St Paul 18–19; V from 19. *St Paul's Vicarage, Church Hill, London N21 1JA* T: (020) 8886 3545 E: vicar@spwh.org

SANDHAM, Stephen McCourt. b 41. K Coll Lon BD 65 AKC 65. **d** 66 **p** 67. C Stockton St Pet *Dur* 66–69; C Bishopwearmouth Gd Shep 69–71; C Bishopwearmouth St Mich w St Hilda 71–75; V Darlington St Mark w St Paul 75–82; P-in-c Sunderland St Chad 82–87; R Shincliffe 87–98; P-in-c 98–06; rtd 06; Chapl Sherburn Hosp Dur 98–07; PtO *Dur* from 07. *21 Hill Meadows, High Shincliffe, Durham DH1 2PE* E: stephensandham@yahoo.co.uk

SANDIFORD, Mrs Christine Krogh. b 44. Smith Coll (USA) BA 66 Man Univ PGCE 87. SNWTP 11. **d** 12 **p** 13. OLM Didsbury St Jas and Em *Man* 12–17; PtO from 17. *330 Lapwing Lane, Manchester M20 6UW* T: 0161-434 1343 E: cksandiford@hotmail.com

SANDLE, Lynne Kirsty. b 75. Paisley Univ BA 98. St Mellitus Coll 15. **d** 18 **p** 19. C Chellington *St Alb* from 18. *The Rectory, Bamfords Lane, Turvey, Bedford MK43 8DS* T: (01234) 881654 M: 07967-509314

SANDOM, Miss Carolyn Elizabeth. b 63. Homerton Coll Cam BEd 85. Wycliffe Hall Ox BTh 93. **d** 94. C St Helen Bishopsgate w St Andr Undershaft etc *Lon* 94–96; C Cambridge H Sepulchre *Ely* 96–05; PtO *Chelmsf* 05–06; NSM Mayfair Ch Ch *Lon* 06–11; NSM Tunbridge Wells St Jo *Roch* 11–18. *57 Green Way, Tunbridge Wells TN2 3HJ* T: (01892) 671629

SANDOVER, Cherry Elizabeth. b 57. Essex Univ BA 98 MA 00 PhD 04 PGCE 04. St Mellitus Coll 14. **d** 15 **p** 16. NSM Leigh St Clem *Chelmsf* from 15; NSM Southend from 19. *7B Victoria Drive, Leigh-on-Sea SS9 1SF* T: (01702) 715845 M: 07859-911997 E: revcherrysandover@gmail.com

SANDS, William James. b 55. Nottm Univ LTh 83 Birm Univ MA 99. St Jo Coll Nottm 80. **d** 83 **p** 84. C St Mary-at-Latton *Chelmsf* 83–86; R Mvurwi Zimbabwe 86–87; C-in-c Barkingside St Cedd *Chelmsf* 87–89; C Woodford St Mary w St Phil and St Jas 87–89; P-in-c Elmsett w Aldham *St E* 89–92; P-in-c Kersey w Lindsey 89–92; R Esigodini Zimbabwe 92–96; Sub Dean Harare 97; Chapl Algarve *Eur* 98–00; V Castle Bromwich St Clem *Birm* 00–09; P-in-c Yardley St Edburgha 09–11; V from 11. *49 Vicarage Road, Yardley, Birmingham B33 8PH* E: williamsands123@btinternet.com

SANER-HAIGH, Robert James. b 73. Birm Univ BA 94 MPhil 98. Wycliffe Hall Ox BA 04 MA 08. **d** 05 **p** 06. C Appleby *Carl* 05–07; Bp's Dom Chapl and C Dalston w Cumdivock, Raughton Head and Wreay 07–10; Officer for IME 4-7 07–08; Dir of Ords 08–10; P-in-c Kendal H Trin from 10. *Holy Trinity Vicarage, 2 Lynngarth Drive, Kendal LA9 4JA* T: (01539) 729403 E: vicar@kendalparishchurch.co.uk

SANGSTER, Andrew. b 45. K Coll Lon BD 67 AKC 67 BA 71 MA 84 Lon Inst of Educn MPhil 93 LLB 97 UEA PhD 14 FCollP. St Boniface Warminster. **d** 69 **p** 70. C Aylesford *Roch* 69–72; C Shirley *Win* 73–76; V Woolston 76–79; Prov Youth Chapl Ch in Wales 79–82; Chapl Collegiate Sch New Zealand 82–89; Chapl Eton Coll 89–92; Hd Master St Edm Sch Hindhead 92–96; Hd Thos Day Schs Lon 96–99; V Ormesby St Marg w Scratby, Ormesby St Mich etc *Nor* 99–04; Chapl Bromley Coll 04–10; rtd 10; PtO *Nor* 10–15; Bp's Officer for Rtd Clergy from 15; Hon PV Nor Cathl from 14. *10 Harvey Lane, Norwich NR7 0BQ* T: (01603) 437402 E: asangster666@btinternet.com

SANKEY, Julian. b 52. Qu Coll Ox BA 74 MA 79. St Jo Coll Nottm 84. **d** 86 **p** 87. C New Barnet St Jas *St Alb* 86–89; C Mansfield SS Pet and Paul *S'well* 89–94; Chapl St Luke's Hospice Sheff 94–07. *29 Grindlow Close, Sheffield S14 1PE* T: 0114-264 9988

SANSBURY, Canon Christopher John. b 34. Peterho Cam BA 57 MA. Westcott Ho Cam 58. **d** 59 **p** 60. C Portsea N End St Mark *Portsm* 59–63; C Weeke *Win* 63–71; V N Eling St Mary 71–78; R Long Melford *St E* 78–00; P-in-c Lawshall w Shimplingthorne and Alpheton 98–00; Hon Can St E Cathl 97–00; rtd 00; PtO *St E* 00–18. *2 Deacon's Close, Lavenham, Sudbury CO10 9TT* T: (01787) 248068

SANSOM, John Reginald. b 40. St Jo Coll Nottm 73. **d** 75 **p** 76. C Ipswich St Marg *St E* 75–79; P-in-c Emneth *Ely* 79–85; P-in-c Hartford 85–86; TV Huntingdon 86–91; R Sawtry 91–97; R Sawtry and Glatton 97–99; TV Ely 99–05; rtd 05; PtO *Ely* from 06. *77 St Ovins Green, Ely CB6 3AW* T: (01353) 614913 E: johnjudysansom@ntlworld.com

SANSOM, Canon Michael Charles. b 44. Bris Univ BA 66 St Jo Coll Dur PhD 74. Cranmer Hall Dur 68. **d** 72 **p** 73. C Ecclesall *Sheff* 72–76; LtO *Ely* 76–88; Dir of Studies Ridley Hall Cam 76–88; Vice-Prin 79–88; Dir of Ords *St Alb* 88–10; Can Res St Alb 88–10; rtd 10. *101 Churchfields Drive, Bovey Tracey, Newton Abbot TQ13 9QZ* T: (01626) 836773 E: michaelsansom123@btinternet.com

SANSUM, Canon David Henry. b 31. Bris Univ BA 52 MA 63. St Aid Birkenhead 54. **d** 56 **p** 57. C Henleaze *Bris* 56–59; C Stratton St Margaret 59–60; C Stoke Bishop 60–64; V Stechford *Birm* 64–76; V Ashbourne St Oswald w Mapleton *Derby* 76–98; P-in-c Fenny Bentley, Thorpe and Tissington 77–83; V Ashbourne St Jo 81–98; RD Ashbourne 91–98; Hon Can Derby Cathl 95–98; rtd 98; PtO *Glouc* 98–15; *Bris* 98–15. *Greenleaze, Main Road, Easter Compton, Bristol BS35 5SQ* T: (01454) 632563 E: davidsansum@btinternet.com

SANTANA, Levy. *See* CAMPOS DE SANTANA, Levy Henrique

✠**SANTER, The Rt Revd Mark.** b 36. Qu Coll Cam BA 60 MA 64 Lambeth DD 99. Westcott Ho Cam. **d** 63 **p** 64 **c** 81. Tutor Cuddesdon Coll 63–67; C Cuddesdon *Ox* 63–67; Fell and Dean Clare Coll Cam 67–72; Tutor 68–72; Prin Westcott Ho Cam 73–81; Hon Can Win Cathl 78–81; Area Bp Kensington *Lon* 81–87; Bp Birm 87–02; rtd 02; Hon Asst Bp Worc from 02 and Birm from 03. *81 Clarence Road, Kings Heath, Birmingham B13 9UH* T: 0121-441 2194

SAPWELL, Mrs Lynette Lilian. b 51. Sussex Univ BEd 73 Middx Univ BA 03. NTMTC 00. **d** 03 **p** 04. NSM Rochford *Chelmsf* 03–07; P-in-c Appleton *Ox* 07–16; rtd 16; PtO *Ox* 16–17; *Bris* 17–19. *The Old Post Office, 45 Queens Road, Hannington, Swindon SN6 7RP* T: (01793) 764418 E: lynsapwell@gmail.com

SARALIS, Preb Christopher Herbert. b 34. Univ of Wales BA 54 St Cath Coll Ox BA 56 MA 60. Wycliffe Hall Ox. **d** 57 **p** 58. C Abergavenny St Mary w Llanwenarth Citra *Mon* 57–61; C Bridgwater St Mary w Chilton Trinity *B & W* 61–65; V Berrow 65–72; R Berrow and Breane 72–76; RD Burnham 72–76; V Minehead 76–92; RD Exmoor 80–86; Preb Wells Cathl 84–92; V Bovey Tracey SS Pet, Paul and Thos w Hennock *Ex* 92–99; rtd 99; PtO *B & W* from 99. *17 George Maher Court, Shudrick Lane, Ilminster TA19 0BP* T: (01460) 52416 E: christophersaralis@talktalk.net

SARGANT, John Raymond. b 38. CCC Cam BA 61 MA 70. Westcott Ho Cam 64 Harvard Div Sch 66. **d** 67 **p** 68. C Croydon St Jo *Cant* 67–72; Sec Zambia Angl Coun 72–75; P-in-c Bradford-on-Avon Ch Ch *Sarum* 76–81; V 81–90; TV Marlborough 90–03; Dioc Inter-Faith Adv 90–00; Can and Preb Sarum Cathl 92–01; rtd 03. *48 Summerhill Road, Lyme Regis DT7 3DT* T: (01297) 445922

✠**SARGEANT, The Rt Revd Frank Pilkington.** b 32. St Jo Coll Dur BA 55. Cranmer Hall Dur 57. **d** 58 **p** 59 **c** 84. C Gainsborough All SS *Linc* 58–62; C Gt Grimsby St Jas 62–66; V Hykeham 66–73; Dir In-Service Tr and Adult Educn *Bradf* 73–84; Can Res Bradf Cathl 73–77; Adn Bradf 77–84; Suff Bp Stockport *Ches* 84–94; Bp at Lambeth (Hd of Staff) *Cant* 94–99; rtd 99; Hon Asst Bp Eur 99–07; Hon

Asst Bp Man from 99; PtO *Ches* from 99. *32 Brotherton Drive, Trinity Gardens, Salford M3 6BH* T: 0161-839 7045 E: franksargeant68@outlook.com

SARGENT, Ann. b 65. **d** 98 **p** 99. C Bris St Andr Hartcliffe 98–01; P-in-c Flax Bourton *B & W* 01–09; P-in-c Barrow Gurney 01–09; P-in-c Long Ashton 05–09; R Long Ashton w Barrow Gurney and Flax Bourton 09–19; Dioc Dir of Ords *Glouc* from 19; Warden of Readers from 19. *4 College Green, Gloucester GL1 2LR* T: (01452) 835547

SARGENT, Charles Edward. b 68. K Coll Lon BD 89 Leeds Univ MA 96. Coll of Resurr Mirfield 94. **d** 96 **p** 97. C Notting Dale St Clem w St Mark and St Jas *Lon* 96–00; P-in-c S Kensington St Aug 00–04; Chapl Imp Coll 00–04; Chapl Brunel Univ 04–10; PtO *S'wark* 05–16; NSM The Windmill from 16; PtO *Truro* 11–16. *12 Toronto Drive, Smallfield, Horley RH6 9RB* T: (01342) 842232 E: charles.sargent@priest.com

SARGENT, Canon David Gareth. b 63. Sheff Univ BA 85 St Jo Coll Dur BA 96. Cranmer Hall Dur 93. **d** 96 **p** 97. C Norbury *Ches* 96–01; V Hooton 01–06; TR Penrith w Newton Reigny and Plumpton Wall *Carl* from 06; RD Penrith from 14; Hon Can Carl Cathl from 18. *The Rectory, 3 Lamley Gardens, Penrith CA11 9LR* T: (01768) 863000

SARGENT, Mrs Janet. b 54. **d** 07 **p** 08. OLM Birchencliffe *Wakef* 07–08; OLM Birkby and Birchencliffe 08–14; *Leeds* from 14. *11 Kirkwood Drive, Huddersfield HD3 3WA* T: (01484) 650390

SARGENT, Miss Philippa Mary. b 68. Oriel Coll Ox MA 94. Ripon Coll Cuddesdon 13. **d** 15 **p** 16. C Kempsey and Severn Stoke w Croome d'Abitot *Worc* 15–18; P-in-c Marnhull *Sarum* from 18; V Sturminster Newton, Hinton St Mary and Lydlinch from 18. *The Vicarage, Church Street, Sturminster Newton DT10 1DB* T: (01258) 473905 M: 07963-273221 E: philippa.sargent@me.com

SARMEZEY, George Arpad. b 61. Qu Mary Coll Lon BA 83 Goldsmiths' Coll Lon PGCE 86. Westcott Ho Cam 89. **d** 92 **p** 93. C Eastville St Anne w St Mark and St Thos *Bris* 92–94; C Stratton St Margaret w S Marston etc 94–97; Asst Chapl Northn Gen Hosp NHS Trust 97–00; Sen Chapl from 00. *Northampton General Hospital, Billing Road, Northampton NN1 5BD* T: (01604) 545773 *or* 634700 F: 544608 E: george.sarmezey@ngh.nhs.uk

SARUM, Archdeacon of. *See* JEANS, The Ven Alan Paul

SARVANANTHAN, Sudharshan. b 70. Trin Coll Bris 06. **d** 08 **p** 09. C Heart of Eden *Carl* 08–12; P-in-c Clifton, Dean and Mosser 12–17; C Brigham, Gt Broughton and Broughton Moor 14–17; P-in-c Brigham, Clifton, Dean and Mosser 17–19; Network Youth Ch Ldr 12–19; R Wyberton *Linc* from 19; V Frampton from 19. *The Rectory, Church Lane, Wyberton, Boston PE21 7AF* M: 07785-334804 E: rev.sudharshan@googlemail.com

SASSER, Canon Howell Crawford. b 37. Maryland Univ BA 72 Geo Mason Univ Virginia MA 74 Westmr Coll Ox MTh 97. Washington Dioc Course 75. **d** 77 **p** 78. W Germany 77–80; Somalia 80–83; Cyprus 84–92; Chapl Montreux w Gstaad *Eur* 92–97; Chapl Oporto 97–05; Adn Gib 02–05; Bp's Chapl and Research Asst 05–06; rtd 06. *5225 Wilson Lane, Apt 3119, Mechanicsburg PA 17055, USA* E: howellsasser@aol.com

SATHYARAJ, Canon Rajkumar Reuben. Bangalore Univ BSc Karnatak Univ MA. Trin Th Coll Singapore MDiv. **d** 97. Egypt 01–11; C Seagoe *D & D* 11–18; P-in-c Kilwarlin Upper w Kilwarlin Lower from 18; Hon Can All SS Cathl Cairo from 05. *Kilwarlin Rectory, 9 St John's Road, Hillsborough BT26 6ED* M: 07927-938185 E: revraj@hotmail.com

SATKUNANAYAGAM, Kuhan. b 76. St Jo Coll Dur BSc 01 BA 11 Univ of E Lon MSc 06 PsychD 08. Cranmer Hall Dur 09. **d** 11 **p** 12. C Leatherhead and Mickleham *Guildf* 11–15; C Long Ditton from 15. *The Rectory, 5 Church Meadow, Long Ditton, Surbiton KT6 5EP* T: (020) 8398 1583 M: 07957-293907 E: kuhan@dunelm.org.uk

SATTERLEY, Gerald Albert. b 34. Lon Univ BA 56 Ex Univ Hon BA. Wycliffe Hall Ox 58. **d** 60 **p** 61. C Southborough St Pet *Roch* 60–63; C S Lyncombe *B & W* 63–66; V Sheff St Barn 66–69; R Adwick-le-Street 69–73; V Awre and Blakeney *Glouc* 73–82; P-in-c Newnham 80–82; V Newnham w Awre and Blakeney 82–90; R Instow *Ex* 90–98; V Westleigh 90–98; rtd 98; PtO *Ex* from 98. *31 Gracey Court, Woodland Road, Broadclyst, Exeter EX5 3GA*

SAUL, Norman Stanley. b 30. St Aid Birkenhead 51. **d** 54 **p** 55. C S Shore H Trin *Blackb* 54–57; C Poulton-le-Fylde 57–59; PC Freckleton 59–66; V Blackb St Luke 66–68; V Barton 68–72; V Foxdale *S & M* 72–77; V Maughold 77–90; CF (ACF) 80–86; rtd 90; PtO *Blackb* from 90. *15 Croft Meadow, Bamber Bridge, Preston PR5 8HX* T: (01772) 314475 E: norman.saul@sky.com

SAUM, Rachel Elizabeth. b 78. Edin Univ BSc 00 K Coll Lon MA 11. St Mellitus Coll BA 16. **d** 16 **p** 17. C Newbold Pacey w Moreton Morrell *Cov* from 16. *The Vicarage,*

Charlecote, Warwick CV35 9EW M: 07815-793625 E: revrachelsaum@gmail.com

SAUNDERS, Alan William. b 67. St Mellitus Coll. **d** 13 **p** 14. C Halliwell St Pet *Man* 13–16; V Pennington from 16. *Christ Church Vicarage, Schofield Street, Leigh WN7 4HT* T: (01942) 673619 M: 07767-643444 E: alan@alongside.me.uk

SAUNDERS, Andrew Vivian. b 44. Leeds Univ BA 65. Coll of Resurr Mirfield 66. **d** 68 **p** 69. C Goodmayes St Paul *Chelmsf* 68–71; C Horfield H Trin *Bris* 71–75; C Oldland 75–77; Ind Chapl *B & W* 77–80; P-in-c Buckland Dinham w Elm, Orchardleigh etc 77–78; P-in-c Buckland Dinham 78–80; V Westfield 80–90; R Clutton w Cameley 90–99; C Christchurch *Win* 99–05; rtd 05; PtO *B & W* from 06. *8 Mill House Court, Willow Vale, Frome BA11 1BG* T: (01373) 467683 E: andrewvsaunders@gmail.com

SAUNDERS, Barry. *See* SAUNDERS, John Barry

SAUNDERS, Brian Gerald. b 28. Pemb Coll Cam BA 49 MA 53. Cuddesdon Coll 63. **d** 66 **p** 67. NSM Gt Berkhamsted *St Alb* 66–87; P-in-c Lt Gaddesden 87–92; rtd 92; PtO *Ox* 92–94; *St Alb* 92–02; Pet from 95; *Linc* from 01; Hon C Newton Longville w Stoke Hammond and Whaddon *Ox* 94–01. *7 Applecroft, Northchurch, Berkhamsted HP4 3RX* T: (01442) 874955

SAUNDERS, Canon Bruce Alexander. b 47. St Cath Coll Cam BA 68 MA 72. Cuddesdon Coll 68. **d** 71 **p** 72. C Westbury-on-Trym H Trin *Bris* 71–74; Hon C Clifton St Paul 74–78; Asst Chapl Bris Univ 74–78; TV Fareham H Trin *Portsm* 78–84; TR Mortlake w E Sheen *S'wark* 84–97; RD Richmond and Barnes 89–94; Can Missr for Ch in Soc 97–03; Can Res S'wark Cathl 03–14; Sub Dean 12–14; C-in-c Bermondsey St Hugh CD *S'wark* 03–14; rtd 14; PtO *Bris* from 15. *10 Reedley Road, Bristol BS9 3ST* T: 0117-373 2123

SAUNDERS, David Anthony. b 48. Trin Coll Bris 76. **d** 78 **p** 79. C Bath Walcot *B & W* 78–80; Asst Dir RE 80–83; Youth Chapl 80–83; C Long Ashton 83–84; V Bath St Bart 84–90; OCM 84–90; V Cullompton *Ex* 90–97; R Kentisbeare w Blackborough 90–97; Dir Shiloh Min USA from 97; rtd 13. *605 Tuscan Valley Drive, Oxford MS 38655, USA* E: dasaunders@mac.com

SAUNDERS, Gareth John McKeith. b 71. St Andr Univ BD 93 Edin Univ MTh 99. TISEC 99. **d** 99 **p** 00. C Inverness St Andr *Mor* 99–03; C Edin St Salvador and Edin Gd Shep 03–06; LtO *St And* from 07; Hon C St Andrews All SS from 10. *45 Lindsay Berwick Place, Anstruther KY10 3YP* T: (01333) 310140 M: 07732-356123 E: gareth@garethjmsaunders.co.uk

SAUNDERS, Ivor John. b 37. Wolv Poly CQSW 81. **d** 04 **p** 05. OLM Wolverhampton St Jude *Lich* 04–17; PtO from 17. *34 Wrottesley Road, Wolverhampton WV6 8SF* T: (01902) 751162

SAUNDERS, James Benedict John. b 72. St Aid Coll Dur BA 93 St Jo Coll Cam PhD 97 St Jo Coll Dur BA 00. Cranmer Hall Dur 98. **d** 01 **p** 02. C Sole Bay *St E* 01–04; P-in-c Teigh w Whissendine and Market Overton *Pet* 04–09; Asst Chapl HM Pris Ashwell 04–07; Chapl Uppingham Sch from 09. *Pentire, 48 High Street West, Uppingham, Oakham LE15 9QD* T: (01572) 829934 E: jbjs@uppingham.co.uk

SAUNDERS, Mrs Joan Mary (Jo). b 44. Univ Coll Lon BA 66 PGCE 67. EAMTC 00. **d** 03 **p** 04. NSM Gt and Lt Casterton w Pickworth and Tickencote *Pet* 03–05; P-in-c 09–16; P-in-c Castle Bytham w Creeton *Linc* 05–09; Hon C Ketton, Collyweston, Easton-on-the-Hill and Tinwell *Pet* 09–16; rtd 17; PtO *Pet* from 17. *Mellstock, Bourne Road, Essendine, Stamford PE9 4LH* T: (01780) 480479 E: revjosaunders@live.co.uk

SAUNDERS, John Barry. b 40. Chich Th Coll. **d** 83 **p** 84. C St Breoke Truro 83–84; C St Breoke and Egloshayle 84–87; V Treverbyn 87–96; RD St Austell 91–96; V Perranzabuloe 96–03; rtd 03; PtO *Truro* from 04. *48 Cormorant Drive, St Austell PL25 3BA* T: (01726) 71994

SAUNDERS, Canon John Michael. b 40. Brasted Th Coll 66 Clifton Th Coll 68. **d** 70 **p** 71. C Homerton St Luke *Lon* 70–74; SAMS Brazil 74–91; P-in-c Horsmonden *Roch* 91–97; Area Sec (SE England) SAMS 91–97; V Gillingham St Mark *Roch* 97–08; rtd 08; Hon C Newton Longville, Mursley, Swanbourne etc *Ox* 08–15; rtd 15; PtO *Ox* from 15; *Cant* from 19. *The Rectory, Roman Road, Aldington, Ashford TN25 7EF* M: 07732-682472 E: canonjohnsaunders@aol.com

SAUNDERS, Mrs Margaret Rose. b 49. Newnham Coll Cam BA 71 St Jo Coll York PGCE 72. St Alb Minl Tr Scheme 85. **d** 88 **p** 94. Hon Par Dn Gt Berkhamsted *St Alb* 88–90; Hon Chapl Asst Gt Ormond Street Hosp for Sick Children Lon 88–90; Asst Chapl Aylesbury Vale HA 90–92; Chapl Milton Keynes Gen NHS Trust 92–98; Chapl Milton Keynes Community NHS Trust 92–98; C Newport Pagnell w Lathbury and Moulsoe *Ox* 98–01; TV Grantham *Linc* 01–02; P-in-c Grantham, Manthorpe 02–04; Chapl United Lincs Hosps NHS Trust

01–14; rtd 14; Gen Preacher *Linc* 05–16; PtO *St Alb* from 16. *7 Applecroft, Northchurch, Berkhamsted HP4 3RX* T: (01442) 874955 E: margar3t.saunders@gmail.com

SAUNDERS, Mark Richard. *See* VASEY-SAUNDERS, Mark Richard

SAUNDERS, Martin Paul. b 54. K Coll Lon BD 76 AKC 76 Univ of Northumbria at Newc DipSW 96. Westcott Ho Cam 77. **d** 78 **p** 79. C Seaton Hirst *Newc* 78–81; Regional Chapl Hong Kong Miss to Seamen 81; C Egglescliffe *Dur* 81–82; Chapl to Arts and Recreation 81–84; C Jarrow *Dur* 82–84; TV 84–88; V Southwick St Columba 88–94; PtO from 94. *55 The Meadows, Burnopfield, Newcastle upon Tyne NE16 6QW* T: (01207) 271242 M: 07710-325197 E: martinsaunders18@gmail.com

SAUNDERS, Martyn Leonard John. b 69. Magd Coll Cam MEng 92. Wycliffe Hall Ox BA 97. **d** 98 **p** 99. C Quinton Road W St Boniface *Birm* 98–02; TV Barnsbury *Lon* 02–10; V Chatham St Phil and St Jas *Roch* from 10. *The Vicarage, 139 Sussex Drive, Walderslade, Chatham ME5 0NR* T: (01634) 861108 E: martyn.saunders@pipnjims.co.uk

SAUNDERS, Michael. b 38. Charing Cross Hosp Medical Sch MB, BS 62 FRCPEd 74 FRCP 78 MSOSc 84. NEOC 82. **d** 84 **p** 85. LtO *York* 84–92; Tutor NEOC 84–93; NSM Stokesley *York* 92–93; C Ripon Cathl 93–95; PtO *York* 93–13; NSM Gt and Lt Ouseburn w Marton cum Grafton etc *Ripon* 95–02; NSM Masham and Healey 02–08; PtO 08–14; *Leeds* from 14. *College Grove, College Lane, Masham, Ripon HG4 4HE* T: (01765) 688306 M: 07711-567160

SAUNDERS, Michael Walter. b 58. Grey Coll Dur BSc 79 CChem MRSC 84. Wycliffe Hall Ox 86. **d** 89 **p** 90. C Deane *Man* 89–93; TV Eccles 93–02; Chapl Eccles Sixth Form Coll 96–02; Dioc Adv on Evang *Man* 98–02; C Yateley and Eversley *Win* 02–06; P-in-c Darby Green 05–06; V Darby Green and Eversley 06–16; V Hungerford and Denford *Ox* from 16. *The Vicarage, Parsonage Lane, Hungerford RG17 0JB* M: 07713-810811 E: mike@mikethevicar.co.uk

SAUNDERS, Moira Ruth Forbes. *See* FORBES, Moira Ruth

SAUNDERS, Richard George. b 54. BNC Ox BA 76 MA 81. St Jo Coll Nottm 82. **d** 85 **p** 86. C Barrow St Mark *Carl* 85–89; C Cranham Park *Chelmsf* 89–97; TV Kinson *Sarum* 97–00; TR Kinson and W Howe 00–12; V Sheet *Portsm* from 12. *Sheet Vicarage, 2 Pulens Lane, Petersfield GU31 4DB* T: (01730) 263673

SAUNDERS, Ronald. b 37. St Pet Coll Birm CertEd 62 Memorial Univ Newfoundland CertEd 80 Columbia Univ MA 82 PhD 87 ACP 67. Sarum Th Coll 69. **d** 68 **p** 70. Lic to Offic Malawi 68–70; C Blantyre 71–72; C Kensington St Mary Abbots w St Geo *Lon* 72–73; C Bournemouth St Fran *Win* 73–75; I Twillingate Canada 75–76; Lic to Offic 77–81; C Gt Marlow *Ox* 81–82; Area Org Leprosy Miss 82–85; V Penycae *St As* 85–87; TV Wrexham 87–89; LtO *Ox* 90–91; Chapl Morden Coll Blackheath 91–97; Master Wyggeston's Hosp Leic 97–03; P-in-c Nerja and Almuñécar *Eur* 05–07. *Barrio San Isidro 92, 18830 Huescar (Granada), Spain* E: ron1937uk@hotmail.co.uk

SAUNDERS (née CORNWALL), Valerie Cecilia. b 40. Bedf Coll Lon BSc 62 Lon Inst of Educn PGCE 63. Scottish Chs Open Coll 96. **d** 03 **p** 04. NSM Dingwall *Mor* from 03; NSM Strathpeffer from 03. *Chessbury, 12 Firthview, Dingwall IV15 9PF* T: (01349) 865445 M: 07747-066993 E: valeriestj@btopenworld.com

SAUNDERS, Ms Wendy Jennifer. b 49. S'wark Ord Course 86. **d** 95 **p** 96. Bp's Adv for Urban Min and Leadership *S'wark* 90–91; C Thamesmead 95–98; P-in-c Eltham St Sav 98–15; rtd 15; PtO *S'wark* from 15; *Nor* from 15. *Thistle Barn, Reepham Road, Felthorpe, Norwich NR10 4DU* M: 07802-603754 E: revwendy@tiscali.co.uk

SAUSBY, John Michael. b 39. AKC. **d** 63 **p** 64. C Crosland Moor *Wakef* 63–65; C Halifax St Jo Bapt 65–67; V Birkby 67–77; V Holmfirth 77–89; TR Upper Holme Valley 89–01; rtd 01; PtO *Wakef* 04–14; *Leeds* 14–16. *15 River Holme View, Brockholes, Huddersfield HD9 7BP* T: (01484) 667228

SAUVEN, Edward Paul. b 82. St Jo Coll Nottm 14. **d** 16 **p** 17. C Tewkesbury w Walton Cardiff and Twyning *Glouc* from 16. *126 Queens Road, Tewkesbury GL20 5ER* M: 07727-241370

SAVAGE, Canon Christopher Marius. b 46. Hull Univ MA 94 FRSA 99. Bps' Coll Cheshunt 66 Qu Coll Birm 68. **d** 70 **p** 71. C Battersea St Luke *S'wark* 70–75; TV Newbury *Ox* 75–80; R Lich St Mary w St Mich 80–85; V Chessington *Guildf* 85–91; Ind Chapl *Win* 91–00; Chapl Basingstoke Coll of Tech 91–00; V Newc Ch Ch w St Ann 00–07; Team Ldr Chapl to People at Work in Cam *Ely* 07–12; rtd 12; PtO *Sarum* from 12. *22 Burcombe Lane, Wilton, Salisbury SP2 0ES* M: 07788-741489 E: chrismsavage@gmail.com

SAVAGE, Helen. b 55. Birm Univ BA 76 Dur Univ BA 82 MA 90 Newc Univ MLitt 83 Dur Univ PhD 05. Cranmer Hall Dur 80. **d** 83 **p** 84. C Newc St Gabr 83–86; Adult Educn Adv

86–94; V Bedlington 94–04; PtO 09–15; V Slaley, Healey and Whittonstall from 15; R Blanchland w Hunstanworth and Edmundbyers etc from 15. *Slaley Vicarage, Hexham NE47 0AA* T: (01434) 673609 E: helensavage1@gmail.com

SAVAGE, Mrs Hilary Linda. b 48. RGN 71 RM 86. WMMTC 89. **d** 92 **p** 94. C Quinton Road W St Boniface *Birm* 92–96; P-in-c Edgbaston SS Mary and Ambrose 96–01; V 01–02; TV Cramlington *Newc* 02–10; R Eckington and Ridgeway *Derby* 10–14; rtd 14; PtO *Ban* from 14. *Ein ty Noddfa, 4 Belle Vue, Ffestiniog, Blaenau Ffestiniog LL41 4NU* T: (01766) 762383 E: hilarysavage@hotmail.com

SAVAGE, Mrs Jennifer Anne. b 52. CertEd 73. NOC 96. **d** 99 **p** 00. C Haworth *Bradf* 99–02; R 02–09; P-in-c Cross Roads cum Lees 07–09; P-in-c Thornton in Lonsdale w Burton in Lonsdale 09–13; Steeton *Leeds* 13–16; V 16–18. *13 Currer Walk, Steeton, Keighley BD20 6TL*

SAVAGE, Lucy Jane. *See* WORMSLEY, Lucy Jane

SAVAGE, Michael Atkinson. b 33. St Pet Hall Ox BA 57 MA 61. Tyndale Hall Bris 57. **d** 59 **p** 60. C Rugby St Matt *Cov* 59–62; C Welling *Roch* 62–66; V Bowling St Steph *Bradf* 66–73; V Ben Rhydding 73–92; RD Otley 87–92; TR Quidenham *Nor* 92–97; R Quidenham Gp 97–99; rtd 99; PtO *Bradf* 00–14; *Leeds* from 14; *Eur* from 17. *42 Hollins Lane, Utley, Keighley BD20 6LT* T: (01535) 606790 E: damsav@talktalk.net

SAVAGE, Paul Andrew. b 78. Univ of Wales (Ban) BA 00 Ches Univ MTh 15. St Jo Coll Nottm 10. **d** 12 **p** 13. C Bawtry w Austerfield and Misson *S'well* 12–15; C Bawtry w Austerfield, Misson, Everton and Mattersey 15; P-in-c Ascension TM *Leic* from 15. *73 Thurnby Lodge, Nursery Road, Leicester LE5 2HQ* T: 0116-241 9526 E: revsavage2013@gmail.com

SAVEGE, Timothy Michael. b 38. **d** 00 **p** 01. OLM Blyth Valley *St E* 00–05; OLM Bury St Edmunds St Mary 05–09; PtO *Chelmsf* from 09. *2 Chequer Square, Bury St Edmunds IP33 1QZ* T: (01284) 728041 E: tim.savege@btinternet.com

SAVIDGE, Graham John. b 47. Univ of Wales (Ban) BSc 69 PhD 78. CITC 89. **d** 92 **p** 94. LtO *D & D* 92–10; NSM Down Cathl 94–97; NSM Lecale Gp 97–10; PtO from 10. *7 Cedar Grove, Ardglass, Downpatrick BT30 7UE* T: (028) 4461 3101

SAVIGEAR, Miss Elfrida Beatrice. b 49. Wye Coll Lon BSc 71 Bath Univ MSc 85 Lambeth STh 94. Ridley Hall Cam 91. **d** 93 **p** 94. C Ross w Brampton Abbotts, Bridstow, Peterstow etc *Heref* 93–97; P-in-c Butlers Marston and the Pillertons w Ettington *Cov* 97–99; P-in-c Alderminster and Halford 97–99; P-in-c Bicknoller w Crowcombe and Sampford Brett *B & W* 99–00; P-in-c Stogumber w Nettlecombe and Monksilver 99–00; R Quantock Towers 00–08; C Darlington H Trin *Dur* 08–11; rtd 11; Hon C Beaminster Area *Sarum* from 11. *7 Trinity Way, Bridport DT6 3XJ* T: (01308) 424031

SAVILL, David. b 27. Em Coll Cam BA 49 MA 52. Ridley Hall Cam 50. **d** 52 **p** 53. Chapl St E Cathl 52–54; C St Martin-in-the-Fields *Lon* 54–57; V Sunbury 57–67; V Heston 67–73; Hon C Mettingham w Ilketshall St John *St E* 73–79; Hon C Mettingham 79–80; Chapl Felixstowe Coll 80–90; rtd 90; PtO *B & W* 90–11; *St E* 11–16. *14 St Anne's Close, Beccles NR34 9SD* T: (01502) 716380 E: david.savill886@btinternet.com

SAVILLE, Andrew. b 66. Worc Coll Ox BA 92 MA 92 Cov Univ PhD 00. Wycliffe Hall Ox. **d** 95 **p** 96. C Tonbridge SS Pet and Paul *Roch* 95–99; NSM Bromley Ch Ch 99–03; Dir Bromley Chr Tr Cen 99–03; C Fordham *Chelmsf* 03–10; V Laleham *Lon* from 10; AD Spelthorne from 14. *The Vicarage, The Broadway, Laleham, Staines TW18 1SB* T: (01784) 455524 E: andy@savilles.org.uk

SAVILLE, Canon Edward Andrew. b 47. Leeds Univ CertEd 70 Open Univ BA 75. Carl Dioc Tr Inst. **d** 90 **p** 91. C Accrington St Jo w Huncoat *Blackb* 90–93; C Standish 93–95; V Brierfield 95–09; P-in-c 09–10; Hon C 10–13; AD Pendle 98–05 and 13–18; Lead Officer Dioc Bd for Soc Resp 09–19; Hon Can Blackb Cathl 11–19; PtO from 19. *6 Blea Close, Burnley BB12 7TP* M: 07912-227144 E: e.saville@btinternet.com

SAVILLE (née McCULLAGH), Mrs Elspeth Jane Alexandra. b 68. Man Univ BSc 90. Wycliffe Hall Ox BTh 95. **d** 95 **p** 96. C Huddersfield H Trin *Wakef* 95–98; NSM Tonbridge SS Pet and Paul *Roch* 98–99; NSM Bromley Ch Ch 99–03; NSM Fordham *Chelmsf* 03–07; PtO *Lon* from 19. *The Vicarage, The Broadway, Laleham, Staines TW18 1SB* T: (01784) 455524

SAVILLE, Mrs Margaret. b 46. SWMTC 93. **d** 94 **p** 95. C Over St Chad *Ches* 94–98; V Crewe All SS and St Paul 98–05; P-in-c Helsby and Dunham-on-the-Hill 05–12; V 12; rtd 12; Hon C Devoran *Truro* 12–15; Hon C Feock 12–15; PtO from 15. *Coombe Lodge, Church Coombe, Redruth TR16 6RT* T: (01872) 863116 E: margaretsaville@rocketmail.com

SAWYER, Andrew William. b 49. AKC 71 St Aug Coll Cant 71. **d** 72 **p** 73. C Farnham *Guildf* 72–75; C Shadwell *Ex* 75–78; R Colkirk w Oxwick, Whissonsett and Horningtoft *Nor* 78–82; R Colkirk w Oxwick w Pattesley, Whissonsett etc 82–90; V

Hungerford and Denford *Ox* 90–15; rtd 15. *22 Lowdale Lane, Sleights, Whitby YO22 5BU* T: (01947) 229123

SAWYER, Derek Claude. b 33. ALCD 58. **d** 58 **p** 59. C Kirby Muxloe *Leic* 58–60; C Braunstone 60–65; R Vacoas St Paul Mauritius 65–68; V Knighton St Mich *Leic* 68–82; Chapl Kifissia *Eur* 82; LtO *Glouc* 85–87; V Glouc St Aldate 87–01; P-in-c Capisterre St Paul and St Jo St Kitts-Nevis 01–08; LtO 09; P-in-c Roseau w Portsmouth Dominica 09–11; LtO St Kitts-Nevis 11–15; Hon C Cayon w Nichola Town from 15. *Rawlins Ground, St Paul's Village, PO Box 4031, Sandy Point, St Kitts 00265, St Kitts and Nevis* T: (001) (869) 466 2773 M: 669 5697 E: derekcsawyer@gmail.com

SAWYER, Frank Denzil. b 71. Toronto Univ BA 93 MDiv 97 Ch Div Sch of the Pacific (USA) DMin 04. **d** 97. C Toronto St Clem Canada 97–99; USA 99–16; P-in-c Corfu *Eur* 14–15; USA 15–16; Chapl Gtr Lisbon *Eur* 16–19. *Address temp unknown* M: (00351) 931 101 805

SAWYER, James Thomas Lawrence . b 66. Middx Poly BA 88. ERMC 12. **d** 15 **p** 16. NSM Baldock w Bygrave *St Alb* 15–17; C 17–18; V Hormead, Wyddial, Anstey, Brent Pelham etc from 18. *The Vicarage, Great Hormead, Buntingford SG9 0NT* M: 07733-368776 E: rev.j.sawyer@btinternet.com

SAX, Ms Katharine Margaret. b 50. Ripon Coll Cuddesdon. **d** 03 **p** 06. NSM Pokesdown All SS and Southbourne St Chris *Win* 04–05; C Swaythling 06–09; Ecum Officer (Wilts Area) *Sarum* 09–11; P-in-c Churchill and Langford *B & W* 11–16; rtd 16; PtO *Win* from 16. *73 Moorcroft Avenue, Burton, Christchurch BH23 7HU* M: 07733-442476 E: kate.kinkiizi@gmail.com

✠**SAXBEE, The Rt Revd John Charles.** b 46. Bris Univ BA 68 St Jo Coll Dur PhD 74. Cranmer Hall Dur 68. **d** 72 **p** 73 **c** 94. C Compton Gifford *Ex* 72–77; P-in-c Weston Mill 77–80; V 80–81; TV Cen Ex 81–87; Jt Dir SWMTC 81–92; Preb Ex Cathl 88–92; Adn Ludlow *Heref* 92–01; Preb Heref Cathl 92–01; P-in-c Wistanstow 92–94; P-in-c Acton Scott 92–94; Suff Bp Ludlow 94–01; Bp Linc 01–11; rtd 11; PtO *St D* from 11. *22 Shelley Road, Priory Park, Haverfordwest SA61 1RX* T: (01437) 768918 E: john.saxbee@btinternet.com

SAXBY, Canon Martin Peter. b 52. St Jo Coll Dur BA 77. Cranmer Hall Dur 74. **d** 78 **p** 79. C Peckham St Mary Magd *S'wark* 78–81; C Ramsey *Ely* 81–84; P-in-c Mattishall w Mattishall Burgh *Nor* 84–89; P-in-c Welborne 84–89; P-in-c Yaxham 84–89; R Mattishall w Mattishall Burgh, Welborne etc 89–90; V Rugby St Matt *Cov* 90–07; V Rugby W 08–13; RD Rugby 06–13; Healthy Churches Development Mentor 13–17; Hon Can Cov Cathl 11–17; rtd 17; PtO *Cov* from 13. *13 Ambleside, Rugby CV21 1JB* F: 07053-480079 M: 07944-670288

SAXBY, Canon Steven Michael Paul. b 70. Fitzw Coll Cam BA 98 MA 02 Heythrop Coll Lon MA 05 Univ Coll Lon MA 08. Aston Tr Scheme 92 Linc Th Coll 94 Westcott Ho Cam 95. **d** 98 **p** 01. C E Ham w Upton Park and Forest Gate *Chelmsf* 98–00; C Barking St Marg w St Patr 00–02; Waltham Forest Deanery Development Worker 02–07; NSM Walthamstow 02–03; V Walthamstow St Pet 03–09; P-in-c Walthamstow St Barn and St Jas Gt 09–14; V from 14; P-in-c Walthamstow St Sav 11–13; RD Waltham Forest 07–12; Exec Officer Lon Chs Soc Action from 13; Hon Can Manila Philippines from 14. *St Barnabas' Vicarage, St Barnabas Road, London E17 8JZ* T: (020) 8520 5323 E: stevensaxby@btinternet.com

SAXON, John. b 61. Ridley Hall Cam 15. **d** 17 **p** 18. NSM Saffron Walden and Villages *Chelmsf* from 17. *The Rectory, Mill Road, Debden, Saffron Walden CB11 3LB* E: debdenwimbishcurate@gmail.com

SAXTON, James. b 54. Lanc Univ BEd 77 Hull Univ MEd 85. Linc Th Coll 84. **d** 86 **p** 87. C Moor Allerton *Ripon* 86–90; C Knaresborough 90–92; TV Seacroft 92–95; V Ireland Wood 95–00; TV Becontree S *Chelmsf* 02–09; C Camberwell St Geo *S'wark* 09–12; Chapl S Lon and Maudsley NHS Foundn Trust 09–12; rtd 12; PtO *S'well* from 18. *11 Stannier Way, Watnall, Nottingham NG16 1GL* E: james_saxton@outlook.com

SAYER, The Ven Penelope Jane. b 59. Newc Univ BA 80 Open Univ BA 93. SEITE 04. **d** 07 **p** 08. NSM Upper St Leonards St Jo *Chich* 07–10; TR Becontree S *Chelmsf* 10–16; NSM Woodham Mortimer w Hazeleigh 16–18; NSM Woodham Walter 16–18; Turnaround Min (Bradwell Area) 16–18; Adn Sherborne *Sarum* from 18. *Aldhelm House, West Stafford, Dorchester DT2 8AB* T: (01202) 659427 M: 07729-372996 E: adsherborne@salisbury.anglican.org

SAYER, Simon Benedict. b 59. Man Univ BA 07. St Steph Ho Ox MTh 11. **d** 10 **p** 11. C Hollinwood and Limeside *Man* 10–13; V Tipton St Jo *Lich* from 13; CMP from 13. *St John's Vicarage, Upper Church Lane, Tipton DY4 9ND* T: 0121-679 7510 M: 07754-100845 E: simonsayer@me.com

SAYER, Vivienne Rosina. b 56. Univ of Wales (Cardiff) BA 78 Trin Coll Carmarthen MA 04 Cardiff Univ BTh 15 PGCE 85. St Mich Coll Llan 13. **d** 15. C Newcastle Emlyn and Llandyfriog etc *St D* 15–19; P-in-c Llansadwrn w Llanwrda and Manordeilo from 19. *The Vicarage, Llanwrda SA19 8HD* T: (01550) 777200 E: revd.viv.sayer@gmail.com

SAYERS, Karen Jane. *See* GARDINER, Karen Jane

SAYERS, Susan. *See* HILL, Susan

SAYLE, Philip David. b 61. Nottm Univ BA 98. St Jo Coll Nottm 92. **d** 94 **p** 95. C Helston and Wendron *Truro* 94–97; R St Stephen in Brannel 97–00; R Kenwyn w St Allen 00–06; V Upton Ascension *Ches* 06–15; P-in-c Diptford, N Huish, Harberton, Harbertonford etc *Ex* 15–18; P-in-c Ermington and Ugborough 15–18; R Diptford w N Huish, Ermington, Halwell etc from 18. *The Rectory, Diptford, Totnes TQ9 7NY* T: (01548) 821199 M: 07703-011531 E: dsayle@me.com

SCAMMAN (née BEWES), Mrs Helen Catherine. b 71. Leeds Univ BA 94 York Univ PGCE 95 Cam Univ BA 01. Ridley Hall Cam 99. **d** 02 **p** 03. C Win Ch Ch 02–06; NSM 06–07; PtO *Ely* 07–10; *Blackb* 10–14; C Lancaster St Thos from 14. *St Thomas's Vicarage, 33 Belle Vue Terrace, Lancaster LA1 4TY* T: (01524) 590410 E: helen@st.tees.org.uk

SCAMMAN, Jonathan Leitch. b 73. St Andr Univ MA 96 Ex Coll Ox MPhil 98 Cam Univ BA 01. Ridley Hall Cam 99. **d** 02 **p** 03. C Win Ch Ch 02–07; C Cambridge St Barn *Ely* 07–10; P-in-c Lancaster St Thos *Blackb* 10–11; V from 11. *St Thomas's Vicarage, 33 Belle Vue Terrace, Lancaster LA1 4TY* T: (01524) 590410 E: scampersons@yahoo.com

SCAMMELL, Canon Frank. b 56. Cam Univ MA. St Jo Coll Nottm BA 83. **d** 82 **p** 83. C Stapenhill w Cauldwell *Derby* 82–86; TV Swanage and Studland *Sarum* 86–92; Min Southgate LEP *St E* 92–03; V Stoughton *Guildf* from 03; AD Guildf 11–17; Hon Can Guildf Cathl from 16. *Stoughton Vicarage, 3 Shepherds Lane, Guildford GU2 9SJ* T: (01483) 560560 E: frankpippa@hotmail.com

SCANLAN, Helen Tracy. b 66. Dioc OLM tr scheme 06. **d** 09 **p** 10. NSM Heaton Reddish *Man* 09–11; C Heatons 11–12; TV from 12; AD Heaton from 18. *The Vicarage, 42 Lea Road, Stockport SK4 4JU* T: 0161-432 1227 E: helen.scanlan@btinternet.com

SCARD, Mrs Linda Joyce. b 52. STETS 11. **d** 14 **p** 15. NSM N Hants Downs *Win* from 14. *Adams Farm, The Street, North Warnborough, Hook RG29 1BL* T: (01256) 704835 M: 07801-089717 E: linda.scard@btinternet.com

SCARGILL, Christopher Morris. b 57. UEA BA 79 York Univ MA 81 Leeds Univ CertEd 81 Nottm Univ BTh 89. Linc Th Coll 86. **d** 89 **p** 90. C Desborough and Brampton Ash w Dingley and Braybrooke *Pet* 89–92; C Buxton w Burbage and King Sterndale *Derby* 92–93; TV 93–98; V Ipstones w Berkhamsytch and Onecote w Bradnop *Lich* 98–09; RD Alstonfield 08–09; Local Min Adv (Stafford) 07–09; Sen Chapl Torrevieja *Eur* 09–14; V St Annes St Thos *Blackb* from 14; PtO *Eur* from 14. *The Vicarage, 2 St Thomas Road, Lytham St Annes FY8 1JL* T: (01253) 725551 E: revdcms@gmail.com

SCARGILL, Mrs Claire Frances. b 49. Birkbeck Coll Lon BSc 83 Heythrop Coll Lon MA 06. St Mellitus Coll 13. **d** 14 **p** 15. OLM Mistley w Manningtree and Bradfield *Chelmsf* from 14. *Mistley Lodge, 32 New Road, Mistley, Manningtree CO11 2AQ* T: (01206) 395417 M: 07714-752100 E: revclairescargill@gmail.com

SCARISBRICK, Canon Helen. b 60. Sheff Univ BA 81 Sheff Poly PGCE 82 Ches Coll of HE BTh 99. NOC 97. **d** 99 **p** 00. C Norbury *Ches* 99–03; P-in-c Cheadle Heath 03–07; C Edgeley and Cheadle Heath 07–09; V Broadheath 09–18; P-in-c Gee Cross from 18; RD Mottram from 18; Hon Can Ches Cathl from 19. *8 Kensington Street, Hyde SK14 5QD* T: 0161-366 7243 E: hscarisbrick@btinternet.com *or* info@holytrinitychurch-gx.org.uk

SCARLATA, Mark. b 72. **d** 13 **p** 14. NSM Cambridge St Mark *Ely* 13–16; Chapl Cam St Edw from 16; Tutor St Mellitus Coll from 16. *10 Roseford Road, Cambridge CB4 2HD* T: (01223) 977345 *or* 655399 E: mwscar@gmail.com

SCARR, Mrs Hazel Anne. b 44. SAOMC. **d** 00 **p** 01. NSM Adderbury w Milton *Ox* 00–04; NSM Chadlington and Spelsbury, Ascott under Wychwood 04–05; NSM Hardington Vale *B & W* 05–07; NSM Hook Norton w Gt Rollright, Swerford etc *Ox* 07–10; PtO 11–19. *Betula House, Barford Road, Bloxham, Banbury OX15 4EZ* T: (01295) 720022 E: revhazel@yahoo.co.uk

SCEATS, Preb David Douglas. b 46. Ch Coll Cam BA 68 MA 72 Bris Univ MA 71. Clifton Th Coll 68. **d** 71 **p** 72. C Cambridge St Paul *Ely* 71–74; Lect Trin Coll Bris 74–83; V Shenstone *Lich* 83–86; Dioc Tr Officer 86–91; P-in-c Colton 86–90; Dir Local Min Development 91–98; Warden of Readers 91–96; C Lich St Chad 94–98; Dioc Board of Min

Team Ldr 96–98; Preb Lich Cathl 96–98; Prin NTMTC 99–07; Preb St Paul's Cathl *Lon* 02–07; P-in-c Selkirk *Edin* 07–11; rtd 11; Hon C Selkirk *Edin* from 11. *11 Shawpark Road, Selkirk TD7 4DS* T: (01750) 779278 E: dsceats@gmail.com *or* d-sceats@sky.com

SCHAEFER, Carl Richard. b 67. Coll of Resurr Mirfield 91. **d** 94 **p** 95. C Ribbleton *Blackb* 94–98; V Blackb St Thos w St Jude 98–08; P-in-c Blackb St Mich w St Jo and H Trin 03–08; V Goldthorpe w Hickleton *Sheff* from 08; P-in-c Bolton-upon-Dearne from 16. *Goldthorpe Presbytery, Lockwood Road, Goldthorpe, Rotherham S63 9JY* T: (01709) 898426 E: frcschaefer@outlook.com *or* carl.schaefer@sheffield.anglican.org

SCHARF, Brian Howard. b 39. Alberta Univ BA 60. Trin Coll Toronto 60 Coll of Resurr Mirfield 61. **d** 63 **p** 65. C Vancouver St Faith Canada 63–65; C Broadstairs *Cant* 65–68. *3236 Robinson Road, North Vancouver BC V7J 3E9, Canada* T: (001) (604) 987 0219 E: brianscharf@shaw.ca

SCHEFFER (née SQUIRES), Mrs Rachel Louise Squires. b 79. Coll of Ripon & York St Jo BA 00. Ripon Coll Cuddesdon MA 07. **d** 07 **p** 08. C Alnwick *Newc* 07–12; C Monkseaton St Pet 13–15; P-in-c Stamfordham w Matfen from 15; Dioc Development Officer for Youth Work from 15. *St Mary's Vicarage, Stamfordham, Newcastle upon Tyne NE18 0QQ* T: (01661) 886853 E: rlsscheffer@gmail.com

SCHEMANOFF, Ms Natasha Anne. b 50. CertEd 71. **d** 96 **p** 97. C Freshford, Limpley Stoke and Hinton Charterhouse *B & W* 96–99; TV Worle 99–00; V Kewstoke w Wick St Lawrence 00–07; Bp's Adv for Racial Justice 00–07; rtd 07; PtO *Truro* 97–16; *Newc* from 17. *30 Green Batt, Alnwick NE66 1TU*

SCHILD, John. b 38. ALCD 64. **d** 64 **p** 65. C Cheltenham Ch Ch *Glouc* 64–67; Area Sec CMS Sheff and S'well 67–73; Area Sec CMS Chelmsf and St Alb 73–76; V Lt Heath *St Alb* 76–88; R Bedford St Pet w St Cuth 88–94; P-in-c King's Walden and Offley w Lilley 94–98; V 98–03; rtd 03; PtO *Truro* from 17. *Trenarren, St Cleer, Liskeard PL14 5DN* T: (01579) 347047 E: john@schild.demon.co.uk

SCHLEGER, Ms Maria Francesca. b 57. LSE BA 78 SS Coll Cam BA 84 MA 89. Westcott Ho Cam 82. **dss** 85 **d** 87 **p** 94. De Beauvoir Town St Pet *Lon* 85–90; Par Dn 87–90; Team Dn Bow H Trin and All Hallows 90–94; Dean of Women's Min (Stepney Area) 90–94; PtO *Birm* 94–98; NSM Stepney St Dunstan and All SS *Lon* 99–03; Chapl Mildmay Miss Hosp 03–12; PtO *Lon* from 12. *75 Lansdowne Drive, London E8 3EP* T: (020) 7683 0051

SCHLOSS, Mrs Sandra Vanessa. b 63. Cant Ch Ch Univ BA 13. **d** 13 **p** 14. NSM Addiscombe St Mildred *S'wark* 13–17; C Camberwell St Luke from 17. *131 Coleman Road, London SE5 7TF* T: (020) 8405 8257 M: 07743-497156 E: sandra.stlukespeckham@gmail.com

SCHLUTER, Nathaniel David. b 71. Pemb Coll Ox BA 93 MA 97 Green Coll Ox DPhil 98. Wycliffe Hall Ox BA. **d** 00 **p** 01. C Gerrards Cross and Fulmer *Ox* 00–05; Prin Johannesburg Bible Coll S Africa from 05; PtO *Ox* from 14. *PO Box 374, Auckland Park, 2006 South Africa*

SCHMIDT, Canon Karen Rosemarie. b 48. Surrey Univ BSc 70 Solicitor 76. STETS 96. **d** 99 **p** 00. NSM Lee-on-the-Solent *Portsm* 99–05; P-in-c Purbrook 05–06; V 06–09; rtd 09; Bp's Dom Chapl *Portsm* 09–12; Hon C Brighstone and Brooke w Mottistone 13–14; Hon C Shorwell w Kingston 13–14; Hon C Chale 13–14; PtO *Glouc* from 15. *31 Truscott Avenue, Swindon SN25 2GR* T: (01793) 753457 M: 07990-518541 E: karenrschmidt@yahoo.co.uk

SCHNYDER, Cécile. b 76. Ausbildungs Schule Bern BA 97 Roehampton Univ MA 10. Westcott Ho Cam BTh 15. **d** 15 **p** 16. C Sutton *S'wark* 15–18; P-in-c Dulwich St Clem w St Pet from 18; Chapl Jas Allen's Girls' Sch Dulwich from 18. *The Vicarage, 140 Friern Road, London SE22 0AY* E: cecile.schnyder@cantab.net

SCHOFIELD, Andrew Thomas. b 47. K Coll Lon BD 70 AKC 71 PGCE 72 Win Univ MA 16. St Aug Coll Cant 70. **d** 81 **p** 82. C Whittlesey *Ely* 81–84; C Ramsey 84–87; P-in-c Ellington, Grafham, Easton and Spaldwick w Barham and Woolley 87–94; R March St Jo 94–05; P-in-c Duxford 05–09; P-in-c Hinxton 05–09; P-in-c Ickleton 05–09; rtd 09; P-in-c Beetham *Carl* 09–12; PtO from 12; *Blackb* from 12. *Holker House, Whittington, Carnforth LA6 2NX* T: (01524) 274391 E: atschofield@outlook.com

SCHOFIELD, Carol Anne. b 62. Coll of Resurr Mirfield BA 19. **d** 19. C Wythenshawe *Man* from 19. *8 Devoke Road, Wythenshawe, Manchester M22 1TY* M: 07875-660379 E: revcarol11@gmail.com

SCHOFIELD, David Leslie. b 40. MISM 89. EMMTC 98. **d** 01 **p** 02. NSM Derby St Mark *Derby* 01–04; PtO *Man* from 05; P-in-c Dukinfield St Luke *Ches* 07–12; rtd 12. *72 Bromley Cross Road, Bromley Cross, Bolton BL7 9LT* T: (01204)

303137   M: 07855-906987   E: fatherschofield@aim.com   *or* fatherschofield@gmail.com

SCHOFIELD, Gary. b 64. Ripon Coll Cuddesdon 97. **d** 99 **p** 00. C Exhall *Cov* 99–02; V Wales *Sheff* from 02; P-in-c Harthill and Thorpe Salvin from 08; P-in-c Todwick 12–13; AD Laughton 11–14. *The Vicarage, Manor Road, Wales, Sheffield S26 5PD*   T: (01909) 771111   E: gary.schofield@sheffield.anglican.org

SCHOFIELD, John Martin. b 47. Selw Coll Cam BA 69 MA 73. St Steph Ho Ox 70. **d** 72 **p** 73. C Palmers Green St Jo *Lon* 72–75; C Friern Barnet St Jas 75–80; V Luton St Aug Limbury *St Alb* 80–89; V Biddenham and Dir CME 89–94; Dir Minl Tr *Guildf* 94–99; Can Res Guildf Cathl 95–99; PtO 03–05; Dir Dioc Min Course 05–09. *81 Pickmere Road, Sheffield S10 1GZ*

SCHOFIELD, Canon Nigel Timothy. b 54. Dur Univ BA 76 Nottm Univ BCombStuds 83 FRCO. Linc Th Coll 80. **d** 83 **p** 84. C Cheshunt *St Alb* 83–86; TV Colyton, Southleigh, Offwell, Widworthy etc *Ex* 86–94; V Seaton 94–03; P-in-c Beer and Branscombe 01–03; V Seaton and Beer 03–06; RD Honiton 99–03; Can Res Chich Cathl from 06. *4 Vicars Close, Chichester PO19 1PT*   T: (01243) 813589   E: precentor@chichestercathedral.org.uk

SCHOFIELD, Ruth Elizabeth. b 65. Imp Coll Lon BEng 87. STETS 06. **d** 09 **p** 10. NSM Botley, Curdridge and Durley *Portsm* 09–12; TV Fareham H Trin 12–17; Asst Chapl Portsm Hosps NHS Trust 11–17; P-in-c Rowde and Bromham *Sarum* 17–18; R from 18. *The Rectory, High Street, Bromham, Chippenham SN15 2HA*   M: 07738-858909   E: revrschofield@gmail.com

SCHOFIELD, Preb Sarah. b 70. Man Univ BA 95 Birm Univ MPhil 99. Qu Coll Birm 95. **d** 97 **p** 98. C Longsight St Luke *Man* 97–02; Tutor (Man Ho) Westcott Ho Cam 00–04; P-in-c Gorton St Phil *Man* 02–06; P-in-c Abbey Hey 04–06; TV Cen Wolverhampton *Lich* 06–18; Rep for Women in Min Wolverhampton Area 15–18; Bp's Adv for Women's Min from 18; Lead Chapl Wolv Univ from 18; Preb Lich Cathl from 16. *27 Adelaide Walk, Wolverhampton WV2 1DX*   M: 07500-780494   E: sarah.schofield@wlv.ac.uk

SCHOFIELD, Simon Whitworth. b 64. Birm Univ BA 88. SNWTP 10. **d** 13 **p** 14. NSM Stretford St Matt *Man* from 13. *20 Langshaw Street, Manchester M16 9LR*   T: 0161-227 8285   M: 07761-636751   E: simon_schodog@yahoo.co.uk

SCHOFIELD, Timothy. *See* SCHOFIELD, Nigel Timothy

SCHOFIELD, Mrs Victoria Louise. b 56. Liv Poly BSc 88 Liv Univ PGCE 91. Wycliffe Hall Ox BTh 05. **d** 02 **p** 03. C Hattersley *Ches* 02–05; P-in-c Runcorn St Mich 05–06; V 06–19; rtd 19. *16 Braemore Road, Wallasey CH44 2BL*   E: vicki_schofield@hotmail.com

SCHOLES, Ms Victoria Prichard. b 68. Man Univ BSc 89. St Jo Coll Nottm 97. **d** 00 **p** 01. C Macclesfield St Jo *Ches* 00–02; NSM 02–03; PtO 03–14. *87B Gawsorth Road, Macclesfield SK11 8UF*   T: (01625) 425049

SCHOLEY, Michael. b 45. **d** 10. NSM Staincross *Wakef* 10–13. *8 Croft Close, Mapplewell, Barnsley S75 6FN*   T: (01226) 386173   E: michael.scholey@virgin.net

SCHOLLAR, Canon Pamela Mary. b 39. Southn Univ DipEd 80. S Dios Minl Tr Scheme 89. **d** 92 **p** 94. NSM Bournemouth St Andr *Win* 92–94; NSM Pokesdown St Jas 94–09; Hon Can Win Cathl 02–09; PtO from 10. *22 Bethia Road, Bournemouth BH8 9BD*   T: (01202) 397925

SCHOLZ, Terence Brinsley. b 44. St Martin's Coll Lanc MA 98. CBDTI 94. **d** 97 **p** 98. NSM St Annes St Thos *Blackb* 97–01; NSM Broughton 01–02; PtO 02–04; NSM Freckleton 04–12; rtd 12; PtO *Blackb* from 12. *14 Further Ends Road, Freckleton, Preston PR4 1RL*   T: (01772) 632966   M: 07989-931909   E: tbscholz@btinternet.com

SCHOOLING, Bruce James. b 47. Rhodes Univ BA 73. St Paul's Coll Grahamstown 76. **d** 76 **p** 77. C Rondebosch St Thos S Africa 76–79; C St Geo Cathl Cape Town 79–83; R Malmesbury 83–86; C Wanstead St Mary *Chelmsf* 87–90; V Leigh-on-Sea St Jas 90–04; PtO from 05; rtd 07. *249 Woodgrange Drive, Southend-on-Sea SS1 2SQ*   T: (01702) 613429   M: 07710-208476   E: b.schooling@btinternet.com

SCHRIMSHAW, Angela Anna Violet. b 51. SRN 73 SCM 76 Hull Univ HVCert 93 BSc 98. NEOC 01. **d** 04 **p** 05. NSM Welton w Melton *York* 04–16; Chapl HM Pris Humber 16–18; PtO from 18. *22 Bricknell Avenue, Hull HU5 4JS*   T: (01482) 446609   E: schrim@schrim.karoo.co.uk

SCHRODER, Edward Amos. b 41. Cant Univ (NZ) BA 64. Cranmer Hall Dur. **d** 67 **p** 68. C St Marylebone All So w SS Pet and Jo *Lon* 67–71; Dean Gordon Coll and C Hamilton Ch Ch USA 71–76; Can Missr and Asst to Bp Florida 76–79; R Orange Park Grace Ch 79–86; R San Antonio Ch Ch 86–00; Chapl Amelia Plantation Chpl 00–06; rtd 06. *15 Hickory Lane, Amelia Island FL 32034, USA*   T: (001) (904) 277 6752   F: 277 8323   E: tschroder100@gmail.com

SCHUIL-BREWER, Miss Sophie Victoria. b 76. Greenwich Univ LLB 98 Cam Univ BTh 18. Westcott Ho Cam 16. **d** 18 **p** 19. C Kensal Rise St Martin *Lon* from 18. *87A Harvist Road, London NW6 6HA*   M: 07771-514691   E: sophie.s-b@hotmail.co.uk

SCHUMAN, Andrew William Edward. b 73. Birm Univ BA 95 MSc 96 Bris Univ PhD 00 FRGS 02. Trin Coll Bris BA 03 MA 04. **d** 04 **p** 05. C Shirehampton *Bris* 04–08; C Bris Ch the Servant Stockwood 08–13; P-in-c Brislington St Chris from 13; Partnership P Bris S from 08. *23 First Avenue, Bristol BS4 4DU*   T: 0117-909 4235   E: andrewschuman@me.com

SCHÜNEMANN, Canon Bernhard George. b 61. K Coll Lon BD 86 AKC 86 LRAM 83. Ripon Coll Cuddesdon 88. **d** 90 **p** 91. C Kirkby *Liv* 90–93; C St Martin-in-the-Fields *Lon* 93–97; Chapl Br Sch of Osteopathy 93–97; P-in-c Littlemore *Ox* 97–06; V S Dulwich St Steph *S'wark* from 06; Dir Ords Woolwich Area from 13; Hon Can Tamale Ghana from 13. *St Stephen's Vicarage, 111 College Road, London SE21 7HN*   T: (020) 8693 3797 *or* 8766 7281   F: 8693 7194   E: schunemann@btinternet.com

SCHUTTE, Ms Margaret Ann. b 50. Natal Univ BA 71. SAOMC. **d** 04 **p** 05. C Overbury w Teddington, Alstone etc *Worc* 04–07; Chapl HM Pris Hewell from 07. *HM Prison Hewell, Hewell Lane, Redditch B97 6QS*   T: (01527) 785000   E: margie.schutte@justice.gov.uk

SCHWIER, Paul David. b 55. **d** 96 **p** 97. OLM Pulham Market, Pulham St Mary and Starston *Nor* 96–99; OLM Dickleburgh and The Pulhams from 99. *Street Farm, Pulham Market, Diss IP21 4SP*   T: (01379) 676240   E: paulschwier@hotmail.co.uk

SCHWIER, Peter Andrew. b 52. **d** 91 **p** 92. NSM Fressingfield, Mendham, Metfield, Weybread etc *St E* 91–13; NSM Sancroft from 13. *Valley Farm, Metfield, Harleston IP20 0JZ*   T: (01379) 586517

SCLATER, Jennifer. b 44. TISEC. **d** 02 **p** 04. Par Dn Elgin w Lossiemouth *Mor* 02–04; NSM from 04. *77 Wards Road, Elgin IV30 1TE*   M: 07950-830017   E: jenny@sclater.com

SCLATER, John Edward. b 46. Nottm Univ BA 68 St Edm Hall Ox CertEd 71. Cuddesdon Coll 69. **d** 71 **p** 72. C Bris St Mary Redcliffe w Temple etc 71–75; Chapl Bede Ho Staplehurst 75–79; Chapl Warw Sch 79; P-in-c Offchurch *Cov* 79–80; Belgium 81–89; Willen Priory 89–91; C Linslade *Ox* 91–94; P-in-c Hedsor and Bourne End 94–02; rtd 02; PtO *B & W* from 03. *3 East Court, South Horrington Village, Wells BA5 3HL*   T: (01749) 671349   M: 07896-893432   E: john.jes007@yahoo.co.uk

SCOBIE, Geoffrey Edward Winsor. b 39. Bris Univ BSc 62 MSc 68 Birm Univ MA 70 Glas Univ PhD 78 FRSA 96 AFBPsS. Tyndale Hall Bris 62. **d** 65 **p** 66. C Summerfield *Birm* 65–66; C Moseley St Anne 66–67; Lect Psychology Glas Univ 67–04; Hon C Glas St Silas 70–83; P-in-c 83–84; Hon R 84–85; TR 85–86; Team Chapl 86–88; Hon Asst Team Chapl 88–99; Assoc P Bishopbriggs 99–08; P-in-c Lenzie 06–09; rtd 14. *3 Norfolk Crescent, Bishopbriggs, Glasgow G64 3BA*   T: 0141-722 2907

SCOFFIELD, Catherine Rosemary. b 61. **d** 16 **p** 17. NSM Barnstaple *Ex* 16–17; NSM Newport and Bishops Tawton from 17. *8 Church Grove, Barnstaple EX32 9DJ*   E: cathy.scoffield@exeter.anglican.org

SCORER, Canon John Robson. b 47. Westcott Ho Cam 73. **d** 75 **p** 76. C Silksworth *Dur* 75–78; C Newton Aycliffe 78–82; V Sherburn 82–83; V Sherburn w Pittington 83–89; P-in-c Croxdale 89–93; Chapl Dur Constabulary 89–11; Chapl Dur Police Tr Cen 93–05; Hon Can Dur Cathl 04–11; rtd 11; PtO *Dur* from 11. *45 Norwich Road, Durham DH1 5QA*

SCOTCHMER, Michael Leslie. b 48. **d** 14 **p** 15. OLM Chingford St Anne *Chelmsf* from 14. *142 Kings Avenue, Woodford Green IG8 0JQ*   T: (020) 8504 7497   M: 07802-483147   E: mls@milesconsulting.co.uk

SCOTFORD, Bethan Lynne. b 44. Univ of Wales (Cardiff) BA 67 PGCE 68. St As Minl Tr Course 95. **d** 99 **p** 00. Fieldworker (Wales) USPG 98–11; C Guilsfield w Pool Quay *St As* 99–02; V Corwen w Llangar, Glyndyfrdwy etc 02–11; rtd 11; PtO *St As* 11–16 and from 17. *7 Fairview Avenue, Guilsfield, Welshpool SY21 9NE*   T: (01938) 555153   M: 07802-656607   E: bscotford@toucansurf.com

SCOTLAND, Nigel Adrian Douglas. b 42. McGill Univ Montreal MA 71 Aber Univ PhD 75 CertEd 75 Bris Univ MLitt 85. Gordon-Conwell Th Sem MDiv 70 Lon Coll of Div ALCD 66 LTh 74. **d** 66 **p** 67. C Harold Wood *Chelmsf* 66–69; USA 69–70; R Lakefield Canada 70–72; LtO *Ab* 72–75; Chapl and Lect St Mary's Coll Cheltenham 75–79; Sen Lect 77–79; Chapl and Sen Lect Coll of SS Paul and Mary Cheltenham 79–84; NSM Cheltenham St Mark *Glouc* 85–92; Ldr Glenfall Fellowship 90–03; Field Chair RS Cheltenham and Glouc Coll of HE 89–01; Field Chair Glos Univ 01–05; Prin Lect 96–08; Research Fell from 08; LtO *Glouc* 90–03; PtO from 03; Tutor Trin Coll Bris from 06; LtO *Bris* from

07; Tutor Bris Univ from 09; PtO *Eur* from 18. *8 The Rowans, Woodmancote, Cheltenham GL52 4RL*   T: (01242) 676969
E: nigel.scotland@btopenworld.com

SCOTLAND, Primus of the Episcopal Church in. *See* STRANGE, The Most Revd Mark Jeremy

SCOTT, Adam. b 47. Ch Ch Ox BA 68 MA 72 City Univ MSc 79 St Andr Univ PhD 10 Barrister 72 FRSA 95 CEng 81 MIET 81 FIEE 94. S'wark Ord Course 73. **d** 75 **p** 76. MSE Blackheath Park St Mich *S'wark* 75–17; Dean for MSE, Woolwich from 90; Prof Fell St Andr Univ *St And* 96–97; Sen Res Fell from 98; CF from 16. *c/o MOD Chaplains (Army)*   T: (01264) 383430
E: adam.scott@btinternet.com

SCOTT, Preb Allan George. b 39. Man Univ BA 61. Coll of Resurr Mirfield 61. **d** 63 **p** 64. C Bradford cum Beswick *Man* 63–66; P-in-c 66–72; Hon C Bramhall *Ches* 72–74; Hon C Tottenham St Jo *Lon* 74–76; Hon C Bush Hill Park St Steph 76–79; R Stoke Newington St Mary 79–02; P-in-c Brownswood Park 95–97; Preb St Paul's Cathl 91–04; rtd 04; PtO *Lon* 14–18. *8 West Hackney House, 15 Northwold Road, London N16 7HJ*   T: (020) 7923 0153 E: allangscott@gmail.com

SCOTT, Barrie. b 63. Birm Univ BA 85 Goldsmiths' Coll Lon PGCE 86. St Steph Ho Ox 93. **d** 95 **p** 96. C Tilehurst St Mich *Ox* 95–98; PtO *Birm* 98–15; V Perry Barr from 15. *The Vicarage, Church Road, Perry Barr, Birmingham B42 2LB*   T: 0121-356 7998 M: 07841-202408 E: vicar@st-johns-perry-barr.org.uk

SCOTT, Basil John Morley. b 34. Qu Coll Cam BA 59 Banaras Hindu Univ MA 65. Ridley Hall Cam 58. **d** 60 **p** 61. C Woking St Pet *Guildf* 60–63; India 63–83; TR Kirby Muxloe *Leic* 83–89; Asian Outreach Worker (Leic Martyrs) 89–95; Derby Asian Chr Min Project 95–00; rtd 00; PtO *Ely* from 00. *14 Scotsdowne Road, Trumpington, Cambridge CB2 9HU*   T: (01223) 476565 E: basil.scott2@ntlworld.com

SCOTT, Charles Geoffrey. b 32. St Jo Coll Cam BA 54 MA 58. Cuddesdon Coll 56. **d** 58 **p** 59. C Brighouse *Wakef* 58–61; C Bathwick w Woolley *B & W* 61–64; V Frome Ch Ch 64–78; R Winchelsea *Chich* 78–93; R Winchelsea and Icklesham 93–95; rtd 95; PtO *Chich* from 95. *Hickstead, Main Street, Iden, Rye TN31 7PT*   T: (01797) 280096

SCOTT, Canon Christopher Michael. b 44. SS Coll Cam BA 66 MA 70. Cuddesdon Coll 66. **d** 68 **p** 69. C New Addington *Cant* 68–73; C Westmr St Steph w St Jo *Lon* 73–78; V Enfield St Mich 78–81; V Effingham w Lt Bookham *Guildf* 81–87; R Esher 87–98; RD Emly 91–96; R Bude Haven and Marhamchurch *Truro* 98–03; Hon Can Truro Cathl 03–08; rtd 08; PtO *Truro* from 15. *Lantyan, Poughill, Bude EX23 9EU*   T: (01288) 350741 E: chriscott98@yahoo.co.uk

SCOTT, Christopher Stuart. b 48. Surrey Univ BA 92 MBPsS 92. Sarum & Wells Th Coll 79. **d** 81 **p** 82. C Enfield Chase St Mary *Lon* 81–82; C Coalbrookdale, Iron-Bridge and Lt Wenlock *Heref* 82–86; P-in-c Breinton 86–89; Chapl Hickey's Almshouses Richmond 89–01; PtO *S'wark* 06–16; Chapl Richmond Charities' Almshouses 08–16; rtd 16; PtO *Win* from 17. *10 King Alfred Terrace, Winchester SO23 7DE*
E: scottcs@blueyonder.co.uk

SCOTT, Claude John. b 37. Qu Mary Coll Lon BSc 60 PhD 64 Lon Inst of Educn PGCE 61 FRSA 94. EAMTC 88. **d** 91 **p** 92. NSM Heigham H Trin *Nor* 91–98; PtO from 98. *26 The Pastures, Blakeney, Holt NR25 7LY*   T: (01263) 740573 E: claudescott@icloud.com

SCOTT, Colin. b 32. Dur Univ BA 54. Coll of Resurr Mirfield 58. **d** 60 **p** 61. C Wallsend St Pet *Newc* 60–64; C Seaton Hirst 64–68; C Longbenton St Bart 68–70; V Benwell St Aid 70–77; V Sleekburn 77–89; P-in-c Cambois 77–88; V Longhoughton w Howick 89–96; rtd 96; PtO *Newc* from 96. *Pele Cottage, Hepple, Morpeth NE65 7LH*   T: (01669) 640258

SCOTT, Daniel Mark. b 82. Trin Coll Cam BA 05 MEd 08. St Mellitus Coll 16. **d** 19. C Stratford St Jo w Ch Ch *Chelmsf* from 19. *29 Rounton Road, London E3 4HA*   M: 07859-053933 E: dmscott46@gmail.com

SCOTT, David. b 40. Rhodes Univ BA 63. St Paul's Coll Grahamstown LTh 65. **d** 65 **p** 66. C Pietermaritzberg St Pet S Africa 66–67; C Durban N St Martin-in-the-Fields 68; R Harding 69; R Newcastle H Trin 70–75; R Bellair 76–78; R Kabega Park All SS 79–87; Chapl Port Elizabeth Univ 88–91; TV Cheltenham St Mark *Glouc* 92–96; R Swanscombe *Roch* 96–10; rtd 10; PtO *Roch* from 11. *103 Hillside Avenue, Gravesend DA12 5QN*   T: (01474) 248735 M: 07949-069019
E: scottrev@uwclub.net

SCOTT, David. *See* SCOTT, Timothy David

SCOTT, Canon David Victor. b 47. St Chad's Coll Dur BA 69 Lambeth DLitt 08. Cuddesdon Coll 69. **d** 71 **p** 72. C St Mary-at-Latton *Chelmsf* 71–73; Chapl Haberdashers' Aske's Sch Elstree 73–80; V Torpenhow *Carl* 80–91; V Allhallows 80–91; R Win St Lawr and St Maurice w St Swithun 91–10; Warden Sch of Spirituality Win 91–10; Hon Can Win Cathl 02–10; rtd 10; Hon Fell Win Univ from 05. *2 Sunnyside,*

Kendal LA9 7DJ   T: (01539) 728650 E: scott.d.v@live.com *or* davidandmiggyscott@hotmail.com

SCOTT, Mrs Erica Jane. b 58. Trin Coll Bris BA 02. **d** 02 **p** 03. C Ilminster and Distr *B & W* 02–05; C Nailsea Ch Ch w Tickenham 05–07; P-in-c Whitchurch *Bris* 07–08; PtO *S & M* 09–12; Chapl K Wm's Coll Is of Man from 12. *King William's College, Castletown, Isle of Man IM9 1TP*   T: (01624) 820400 E: rev.ericaj@gmail.com *or* chaplain@kwc.im

SCOTT, Francis Richard. b 63. St Jo Coll Dur BA 85 Selw Coll Cam PGCE 86. St Jo Coll Nottm MA 02. **d** 00 **p** 01. C Huntington *York* 00–03; TV 03–09; V Swanland from 09. *The Vicarage, St Barnabas Drive, Swanland, North Ferriby HU14 3RL*   T: (01482) 631271   E: fandfscott@aol.com *or* francis@stbchurch.org.uk

SCOTT, Gary James. b 61. Edin Univ BD 87 Heriot-Watt Univ PGCE 98. Edin Th Coll 85. **d** 87 **p** 88. C Edin St Cuth 87–90; R Peebles 90–96; P-in-c Innerleithen 92–96; R Penicuik 96–98; R W Linton 96–98; Sen Chapl ACF 98–08; LtO *Edin* 98–10; Hd Master Tweedbank Sch 06–10; CF 10–18; Chapl Chigwell Sch Essex from 18. *The White House, Radleys Yard, 121A High Road, Chigwell IG7 6QQ*   T: (020) 7998 8308 M: 07710-600953 E: shamrock.racing@btinternet.com

SCOTT, Geoffrey. *See* SCOTT, Charles Geoffrey

SCOTT, Guy Charles. b 61. Coll of Resurr Mirfield. **d** 00 **p** 01. C Abington *Pet* 00–03; P-in-c Mullion *Truro* 03–07; C Cury and Gunwalloe 03–07; R Is of Scilly 07–10; P-in-c Biggleswade *St Alb* 10–13; V from 13; RD from 18. *The Vicarage, Shortmead Street, Biggleswade SG18 0AT*   T: (01767) 312243 E: g.c.scott@btinternet.com

SCOTT, Mrs Inez Margaret Gillette. b 26. St Alb Minl Tr Scheme 76. **dss** 79 **d** 87 **p** 94. Preston w Sutton Poyntz, Littlemoor etc *Sarum* 83–86; Dorchester 86–96; Par Dn 87–88; NSM 88–96; rtd 88; PtO *Sarum* 96–15. *21 Chesil Place, Somerleigh Road, Dorchester DT1 1AF*   T: (01305) 267547 E: pandiscott@googlemail.com

SCOTT, Canon Janice Beasant. b 44. Cam Th Federation MA 08 MCSP 66. EAMTC 89. **d** 92 **p** 94. NSM Fakenham w Alethorpe *Nor* 92–95; C Eaton 95–99; R Dickleburgh and The Pulhams 99–09; RD Redenhall 03–06; PtO 09–13; P-in-c Trowse 13–19; Hon Can Nor Cathl from 08. *21 School Row, Prudhoe NE42 5FE*   M: 07450-480023 E: rockingrector@gmail.com

SCOTT, John. b 54. Heriot-Watt Univ BA 76 Leeds Univ BA 97 Heythrop Coll Lon MA 05. Coll of Resurr Mirfield 95. **d** 97 **p** 98. C Bethnal Green St Matt w St Jas the Gt *Lon* 97–00; Asst Chapl Qu Mary Univ of Lon 97–00; C Heston 00–04; Inter-Faith Adv 00–05; USA 06–11; PtO *Win* 06–08; rtd 11. *Lakeview, Church Street, St Mary Bourne, Andover SP11 6BN*   T: (01264) 738972 M: 07889-977593 E: absalom1662@yahoo.co.uk

SCOTT, John. *See* SCOTT, William John

SCOTT, John Peter. b 47. Open Univ BA 80. Lambeth STh 81 K Coll Lon 69 St Aug Coll Cant 74. **d** 75 **p** 76. C Dartford St Alb *Roch* 75–78; C-in-c Goring-by-Sea *Chich* 78–81; Chapl Wells Hosp 81–86; Chapl Meare Manor Hosp 81–86; CF (TAVR) 82–90; Chapl Pangbourne Coll 86–90; Min Reigate St Phil CD *S'wark* 90–92; P-in-c Reigate St Phil 92–14; Chapl St Bede's Sch Reigate 90–13; rtd 14; PtO *S'wark* from 14. *5 Haine Close, Horley RH6 9SU* E: johnpeterscott@gmail.com

SCOTT, John Vickers. b 48. Open Univ BA 88 MCIOB 81. CBDTI 02. **d** 05 **p** 06. NSM Penwortham St Leon *Blackb* 05–09; P-in-c Chipping and Whitewell 09–15; rtd 15; PtO *Blackb* from 15. *10 Cuerden Rise, Lostock Hall, Preston PR5 5YD*   T: (01772) 335555 M: 07875-895354 E: frjohn.chipping@btinternet.com

SCOTT, Julie Elizabeth. b 68. Ripon Coll Cuddesdon 16. **d** 18 **p** 19. C Wellington and Distr *B & W* from 18. *112 Buckwell, Wellington TA21 8TE*   M: 07935-812736 E: revjuliescott@hotmail.com

SCOTT, Mrs June Christine. b 43. SRN 64 RM 66 RHV 84. **d** 11 **p** 12. OLM Foremark and Repton w Newton Solney *Derby* from 11. *32 Hillcrest Avenue, Burton-on-Trent DE15 0TZ*   T: (01283) 565074 E: jcscott242@gmail.com

SCOTT, Katherine Jane. b 65. Warwick Univ BA 88 Univ of Wales (Trin St Dav) LTh 12 Dur Univ MA 17 PGCE 89. ERMC 14. **d** 17 **p** 18. C Elstow *St Alb* from 17. *The Vicarage, Shortmead Street, Biggleswade SG18 0AT*   T: (01767) 312243 M: 07922-487705 E: k.j.scott@outlook.com

SCOTT (née GOLDIE), Canon Katrina Ruth. b 76. Fitzw Coll Cam BA 97 MPhil 00 MA 01. Westcott Ho Cam 98. **d** 00 **p** 01. C Cov E 00–04; V Willenhall 04–15; Dioc Adv for Women's Min 06–10; Dean Women's Min 10–15; Hon Can Cov Cathl 10–15; R The Guitings, Cutsdean, Farmcote etc *Glouc* from 15; AD N Cotswold from 15; Hon Can Glouc Cathl from 18. *The Rectory, Copse Hill Road, Lower Slaughter, Cheltenham GL54 2HY*   T: (01451) 821777 E: krgscott@hotmail.com

SCOTT, Keith Brounton de Salve. b 55. QUB BD. **d** 83 **p** 84. C Belfast St Matt *Conn* 83–87; I Ardclinis and Tickmacrevan w Layde and Cushendun 87–01; CMS 02–09; P-in-c Rathkeale w Askeaton, Kilcornan and Kilnaughtin *L & K* 09–16; CMS Ireland 16–17; CMS Zambia from 17. *Church Mission Society, Watlington Road, Oxford OX4 6BZ* T: 08456-201799 E: kbs16355@gmail.com

SCOTT, Kenneth James. b 46. Bris Univ BA 68. Trin Coll Bris 71. **d** 73 **p** 74. C Illogan *Truro* 73–76; C Camberley St Paul *Guildf* 76–81; R Bradford Peverell, Stratton, Frampton etc *Sarum* 81–08; RD Dorchester 95–99; rtd 08; PtO *St E* from 09. *2 Fir Close, Wickham Market, Woodbridge IP13 0UB* T: (01728) 747232

SCOTT, Kevin Francis. b 51. Peterho Cam MA Mert Coll Ox DPhil 76 CChem MRSC. Wycliffe Hall Ox BA 83. **d** 83 **p** 84. C Ox St Ebbe w H Trin and St Pet 83–86; P-in-c Prestonpans *Edin* 86–93; R Musselburgh 86–93; R Edin SS Phil and Jas 93–08. *Kirklands, Craigend Road, Stow, Galashiels TD1 2RJ* T: 0131-208 0402 E: drkfs@aol.com

SCOTT, Kevin Willard. b 53. Open Univ BA 96 Glos Univ MA 03. Linc Th Coll 02. **d** 92 **p** 93. C Walton-on-Thames *Guildf* 92–97; R Matson *Glouc* 97–03; RD Glouc City 01–03; V Malden St Jo *S'wark* 03–18; AD Kingston 05–09; Chapl MU 12–16; rtd 18. *43 Henty Road, Worthing BN14 7HE* E: kevinwscott@btinternet.com

SCOTT (*née* CURRELL), Mrs Linda Anne. b 62. K Alfred's Coll Win BEd 84. Trin Coll Bris BA 92. **d** 92 **p** 93. Par Dn Tunbridge Wells St Mark *Roch* 92–94; C 94–97; TV Walthamstow *Chelmsf* 97–02; PtO 02–04; *S'wark* 05–14; *B & W* 14–16; Chapl Yeovil Distr Hosp NHS Foundn Trust from 16. *42 High Street, Yatton, Bristol BS49 4HJ* T: (01934) 838960 M: 07823-324979 E: scottlinda125@gmail.com

SCOTT, Mrs Lissa Melanie. b 58. Birm Univ BA 79 PGCE 80. SAOMC 98. **d** 01 **p** 02. C Risborough *Ox* 01–06; Chapl Bucks Hosps NHS Trust 05–07; TV Monkwearmouth *Dur* 07–11; V Heighington and Darlington St Matt and St Luke from 11. *9 Pinewood Crescent, Heighington Village, Newton Aycliffe DL5 6RR* T: (01325) 312134 E: lissalife@btinternet.com

SCOTT, Canon Malcolm Kenneth Merrett. b 30. ACA 53 FCA 64. Clifton Th Coll 56. **d** 58 **p** 59. C Highbury Ch Ch *Lon* 58–60; CMS 60–61; Uganda 61–74; V Sunnyside w Bourne End *St Alb* 74–90; V Clapham 90–95; rtd 95; PtO *Lich* 96–14. *10 The Ring, Little Haywood, Stafford ST18 0TP* T: (01889) 881464

SCOTT, Canon Paul Malcolm. b 57. Sheff City Poly BA 79 CPFA 85. Ripon Coll Cuddesdon 98. **d** 00 **p** 01. C N Shields *Newc* 00–03; V Shiremoor 03–12; V Alnwick from 12; AD 15–18; Hon Can Newc Cathl from 16. *St Michael's Vicarage, Howling Lane, Alnwick NE66 1DH* T: (01665) 602184 E: paulscott1957@btinternet.com

SCOTT, Canon Pauline Claire Michalak. b 55. St Anne's Coll Ox BA 77 MA 82 Dur Univ PGCE 78. TISEC 98. **d** 01 **p** 02. NSM Papworth *Ely* 01–05; TV Ely 05–09; P-in-c Alresford *Chelmsf* 09–10; P-in-c Gt Bentley and Frating w Thorrington 09–10; V Alresford and Frating w Thorrington 10–17; P-in-c Elmstead 16–17; V Tenpenny Villages 17–18; AD St Osyth 16–18; Hon Can Chelmsf Cathl 17–18; rtd 18. *19A Belle Vue Road, Wivenhoe, Colchester CO7 9LD* M: 07872-968323 E: pauline@pscott.eclipse.co.uk

SCOTT, Peter Lindsay. b 29. Keble Coll Ox BA 54 MA 58. Linc Th Coll 54. **d** 56 **p** 57. C Weston-super-Mare St Sav *B & W* 56–59; C Knowle H Nativity *Bris* 59–61; P-in-c Glas St Pet 61–63; V Heap Bridge *Man* 63–73; V Rochdale St Geo w St Alb 73–86; R Droylsden St Andr 86–94; rtd 94; PtO *Man* from 94; *Ches* from 14. *3 Rothesay Crescent, Sale M33 4NL* T: 0161-972 0139

SCOTT, Prof Peter Manley. b 61. Birm Univ BA 83 MA 84 Bris Univ PhD 91. All SS Cen for Miss y Min 12. **d** 14 **p** 15. NSM Old Trafford St Jo *Man* 14–18; NSM Man Apostles w Miles Platting from 18. *19 Victoria Road, Fallowfield, Manchester M14 6AQ* M: 07932-688503 E: petermanleyscott@outlook.com

SCOTT, Simon James. b 65. Ch Ch Ox BA 87 MA 90. Wycliffe Hall Ox 87. **d** 91 **p** 92. C Cheadle All Hallows *Ches* 91–95; Scripture Union 95–98; C Cambridge H Sepulchre *Ely* 98–05; R Lt Shelford from 05. *The Rectory, 2 Manor Road, Little Shelford, Cambridge CB22 5HF* T: (01223) 841998 M: 07739-984323 E: simonjscott1965@btinternet.com

SCOTT, The Ven Terence. b 56. QUB BSc 77. CITC 77. **d** 80 **p** 81. C Ballymena w Ballyclug *Conn* 80–83; C Antrim All SS 83–85; P-in-c Connor w Antrim St Patr 85–88; I Magherafelt *Arm* from 88; Hon V Choral Arm Cathl 95–06; Can Arm Cathl from 06; Adn Arm from 14. *The Rectory, 1 Churchwell Lane, Magherafelt BT45 6AL* T: (028) 7963 2365 M: 07590-894529 E: terryscott123@btinternet.com

SCOTT, Canon Theresa Anne. b 53. Bris Univ BSc 75 Lon Univ PGCE 76. Ox Min Course 89. **d** 92 **p** 94. NSM Wickham Bishops w Lt Braxted *Chelmsf* 92–93; NSM Drayton St Pet (Abingdon) *Ox* 94–01; NSM Convenor (Berks) 97–01; Bp's Officer for NSM 98–01; Bp's Adv for Women in Ord Min 01–05; P-in-c Hurley and Stubbings 01–02; V Burchetts Green 02–08; AD Maidenhead and Windsor 05–07; TR Bicester w Bucknell, Caversfield and Launton 08–13; Hon Can Ch Ch 05–13; rtd 13; PtO *Ox* from 13. *24 High Street, Thame OX9 2BZ* T: (01844) 218730 E: theresa.scott@driftway.co.uk

SCOTT, Timothy Charles Nairne. b 61. Ex Univ BA 83. Westcott Ho Cam 84. **d** 87 **p** 88. C Romford St Edw *Chelmsf* 87–89; Community Priest 89–94; P-in-c Leytonstone H Trin and St Aug Harrow Green 94–97; V 97–02; Educn and Tr Adv (Bradwell Area) 02–04; R S'wark Ch Ch 04–13; PtO 13–14; TR Yatton Moor *B & W* from 14. *42 High Street, Yatton, Bristol BS49 4HJ* E: timcnscott@gmail.com

SCOTT, Timothy David. b 68. Girton Coll Cam BA 89 Warw Univ PGCE 91. Ridley Hall Cam 13. **d** 15 **p** 16. C Romford Gd Shep *Chelmsf* 15–18; C Northwood Em *Lon* from 18. *4 Church Close, Northwood HA6 1SG* M: 07766-793959 E: dave.scott@ecn.org.uk

SCOTT, Trevor Ian. b 57. Culham Coll Ox CertEd 79. EAMTC 97. **d** 98 **p** 99. NSM Waltham H Cross *Chelmsf* from 98; PtO *Eur* from 16. *Hartland Villas, 208 High Road, Broxbourne EN10 6QF* T: (01992) 420376 or 450321 M: 07748-624051 E: trevor.scott2@ntlworld.com

SCOTT, William John. b 46. TCD BA 70. CITC. **d** 71 **p** 72. C Bangor St Comgall *D & D* 71–74; C Holywood 74–80; Dioc Min of Healing Team from 75; I Carnalea 80–90; N Ireland Wing Chapl ATC from 80; I Seapatrick *D & D* 90–11; Treas Dromore Cathl 02–08; Adn Dromore 05–11; rtd 11. *61 The Rowans, Banbridge BT32 4DQ* T: (028) 4062 5853 M: 07803-147751 E: john@scottsfamily.co.uk

SCOTT, Preb William Sievwright. b 46. Edin Th Coll 67. **d** 70 **p** 71. C Glas St Ninian 70–73; C Bridgwater St Fran *B & W* 73–77; R Shepton Beauchamp w Barrington, Stocklinch etc 77–81; P-in-c Cossington and Woolavington 82–84; Chapl Community of All Hallows Ditchingham 84–91; V Pimlico St Mary Bourne Street *Lon* 91–02; P-in-c Pimlico St Barn 97–01; V 01–02; AD Westmr St Marg 97–04; Preb St Paul's Cathl from 00; Chapl to RVO and Qu Chpl of the Savoy 02–07; Chapl to The Queen 03–07; Sub-Dean HM Chpls R and Dep Clerk of the Closet 07–15; Sub-Almoner and Dom Chapl to The Queen 07–15; rtd 15; Extra Chapl to The Queen from 15; PtO *Lon* from 15. *13 Kylestrome House, Cundy Street, London SW1W 9JT* T: (020) 7730 6920 M: 07941-470399 E: bournebill@btinternet.com

SCOTT-BROMLEY, Ms Deborah Joan. b 58. Open Univ BA 96 Surrey Univ BA 01 K Coll Lon MA 11 AKC 12. STETS 98. **d** 01 **p** 02. C Hale w Badshot Lea *Guildf* 01–05; V Bordon from 05. *St Mark's Vicarage, 58 Forest Road, Bordon GU35 0BP* T: (01420) 477550 E: deborah@stmarkschurchbordon.uk

SCOTT-DEMPSTER, Canon Colin Thomas. b 37. Em Coll Cam BA 65 MA 68. Cuddesdon Coll 64. **d** 66 **p** 67. C Caversham *Ox* 66–69; Chapl Coll of SS Mark and Jo Chelsea 69–73; V Chieveley w Winterbourne and Oare *Ox* 73–02; RD Newbury 77–98; Hon Can Ch Ch 90–02; rtd 02; PtO *St And* from 10. *Whiligh, New Fowlis, Crieff PH7 3NH* T: (01764) 683779 E: colinscottdempster@gmail.com

SCOTT-GARNETT, Linda. b 44. **d** 07 **p** 08. NSM Bermondsey St Hugh CD *S'wark* 07–14; rtd 14; PtO *S'wark* from 14. *6 Bromley College, London Road, Bromley BR1 1PE* T: (020) 3689 0939 M: 07425-135804 E: revlindasg@gmail.com

SCOTT-THOMPSON, Ian Mackenzie. b 57. Ch Ch Ox BA 78. St Jo Coll Nottm BA 82. **d** 83 **p** 84. C Hartley Wintney, Elvetham, Winchfield etc *Win* 83–85; C Bitterne 85–89; V Iford 89–99; P-in-c Holdenhurst 95–99; TR Cove St Jo *Guildf* 99–06; RD Aldershot 03–06; V Wonersh w Blackheath 06–10; P-in-c Marks Tey and Aldham *Chelmsf* from 10. *The Rectory, Church Lane, Marks Tey, Colchester CO6 1LW* T: (01206) 215772 E: ian.scott-thompson@virgin.net

SCRACE, Canon David Peter. b 46. Sarum & Wells Th Coll 79. **d** 81 **p** 82. C Abbots Langley *St Alb* 81–85; TV Chippenham St Paul w Hardenhuish etc *Bris* 85–91; P-in-c Harnham *Sarum* 91–99; V 99–11; RD Salisbury 95–98; Can and Preb Sarum Cathl 10–11; rtd 11; C Budleigh Salterton, E Budleigh w Bicton etc *Ex* 12–14; PtO from 14. *14 Roselands, Sidmouth EX10 8PD* T: (01395) 708239 E: d.scrace@btopenworld.com

✠**SCREECH, The Rt Revd Royden.** b 53. K Coll Lon BD 74 AKC 74. St Aug Coll Cant 75. **d** 76 **p** 77 **c** 00. C Hatcham St Cath *S'wark* 76–80; V Nunhead St Antony 80–87; P-in-c Nunhead St Silas 82–87; RD Camberwell 83–87; V New Addington 87–94; Selection Sec ABM 94–97; Sen Selection Sec Min Division Abps' Coun 97–00; Suff Bp St Germans

Truro 00–11; rtd 12; PtO *Truro* from 15. *61 Edgcumbe Road, St Austell PL25 5DX* E: royscreech@yahoo.com

SCREETON, Kirsty Hayley. *See* DEAKIN, Kirsty Hayley

✠**SCRIVEN, The Rt Revd Henry William.** b 51. Sheff Univ BA 72. St Jo Coll Nottm 73. **d** 75 **p** 76 **c** 95. C Wealdstone H Trin *Lon* 75–79; SAMS Argentina 79–82; USA 82–83; SAMS Spain 84–90; Chapl Madrid w Bilbao *Eur* 90–95; Suff Bp *Eur* 95–02; Dean Brussels 95–97; Dir of Ords 97–02; Asst Bp Pittsburgh USA 02–08; Miss Dir for S America SAMS / CMS 09–17; Hon Asst Bp Ox from 09; Hon Asst Bp Win from 13; PtO *Eur* from 18. *16 East St Helen Street, Abingdon OX14 5EA* T: (01235) 536607 M: 07789-635260 E: henry.scriven@gmail.com

SCRIVEN, Hugh Alexander. b 59. Trin Coll Cam BA 80. Cranmer Hall Dur 81. **d** 84 **p** 85. C Pudsey St Lawr and St Paul *Bradf* 84–87; C Madeley *Heref* 87–91; TV 91–00; V Edgbaston St Germain *Birm* 00–18; P-in-c Accrington St Jo w Huncoat *Blackb* from 18. *36 Bluebell Way, Huncoat, Accrington BB5 6TD* T: (01254) 872911 E: hughscriven@outlook.com

SCRIVENER, Margaret Thelma. b 47. RN. STETS. **d** 12 **p** 13. NSM E Win 12–17; rtd 17; PtO *Win* from 17. *21 Westwood Gardens, Chandlers Ford, Eastleigh SO53 1FN* T: (023) 8026 3471 E: marscriv@gmail.com

SCRIVENER, Robert Allan. b 54. Nottm Univ BEd 78 Hull Univ BTh 98 De Montfort Univ Leic MA 99 Huddersfield Univ BA 03. Linc Th Coll 79. **d** 80 **p** 81. C Sherwood *S'well* 80–83; C Burghclere w Newtown and Ecchinswell w Sydmonton *Win* 83–86; TV Hemel Hempstead *St Alb* 86–93; V Kingston upon Hull St Nic *York* 93–03; V Mansfield Woodhouse *S'well* 03–17; rtd 17. *26 Eastwood Grove, Rugby CV21 4DP* E: allan.scrivener@virginmedia.com

SCROGGIE, Mrs Felicity Marie-Louise. b 62. Pemb Coll Ox BA 86 St Andr Univ MPhil 87. STETS BTh 99. **d** 99 **p** 00. C Brondesbury St Anne w Kilburn H Trin *Lon* 99–02; V Sudbury St Andr 02–13; AD Brent 10–13; TR Kidlington w Hampton Poyle *Ox* from 13. *The Rectory, 19 Mill Street, Kidlington OX5 2EE* T: (01865) 372230 E: felicityscroggie@gmail.com

SCULLY, Kevin John. b 55. NIDA BDA 96. St Steph Ho Ox 91. **d** 93 **p** 94. C Stoke Newington St Mary *Lon* 93–97; C Stepney St Dunstan and All SS 97–00; Dir of Ords and Voc Adv 97–00; P-in-c Bethnal Green St Matt w St Jas the Gt 00–02; R 02–18; Warden Coll of St Barn Lingfield from 18. *The College of St Barnabas, Blackberry Lane, Lingfield RH7 6NJ* T: (01342) 870260

SCURR, David. b 54. Wilson Carlile Coll 98 SAOMC 05. **d** 05 **p** 06. C Thatcham *Ox* 05–08; P-in-c Farndon and Coddington *Ches* 08–12; V from 12. *The Vicarage, Church Lane, Farndon, Chester CH3 6QD* T/F: (01829) 270270

SEABOURNE (née PEARSON), Mrs Joanna Ruth. b 76. St Hilda's Coll Ox BA 97 PGCE 98 St Jo Coll Dur BA 05 MA 09. Cranmer Hall Dur 03. **d** 06 **p** 07. C Leeds St Geo *Ripon* 06–10; TV from 10; P-in-c Woodhouse and Wrangthorn 12–18; Dir Dioc Interns from 18; AD Headingley from 18. *The Rectory, 1 Vicarage View, Leeds LS5 3HF* T: 0113-243 8498 *or* 230 7115 M: 07712-590991 E: joanna.seabourne@stgeorgesleeds.org.uk

SEABRIGHT, Preb Elizabeth Nicola. b 52. SRN 73. WEMTC 01. **d** 04 **p** 05. NSM Ledbury *Heref* 04–17; NSM Hop Churches from 17; PtO *Worc* from 05; Preb Heref Cathl from 16. *The Grove Cottage, Fromes Hill, Ledbury HR8 1HP* T: (01531) 640252 M: 07977-016683 E: revdnick@gmail.com

SEABROOK, Alan Geoffrey. b 43. ALCD 65. **d** 66 **p** 67. C Bethnal Green St Jas Less *Lon* 66–70; C Madeley *Heref* 70–73; V Girlington *Bradf* 74–80; P-in-c Abdon w Clee St Margaret *Heref* 80–83; R Bitterley 80–83; P-in-c Cold Weston 80–83; P-in-c Hopton Cangeford 80–83; P-in-c Stoke St Milburgh w Heath 80–83; R Bitterley w Middleton, Stoke St Milborough etc 83–08; RD Ludlow 01–05; rtd 08; PtO *Heref* from 08; RD Bromyard 12–17. *Penhope House, Ballhurst, Bromyard HR7 4EF* T: (01885) 482184

SEABROOK, Paul. b 60. Univ of Wales (Cardiff) BA 81 Glos Univ BA 08 Nottm Univ PGCE 82. Ridley Hall Cam 01. **d** 03 **p** 04. C Wimborne Minster *Sarum* 03–07; R Taverham *Nor* 07–16; R Taverham w Ringland from 16. *The Rectory, 173 Taverham Road, Taverham, Norwich NR8 6SG* T: (01603) 868217 E: seabrooktribe@talktalk.net

SEABROOK, Mrs Penelope Anne. b 56. Hertf Coll Ox BA 77 K Coll Lon MA 98. SEITE 00. **d** 03 **p** 04. C Southfields St Barn *S'wark* 03–08; NSM 03–07; C Fulham All SS *Lon* 08–19; V from 19. *All Saints' Vicarage, 70 Fulham High Street, London SW6 3LG* T: (020) 7736 3264 M: 07985-108541 E: pennyseabrook@hotmail.com *or* vicar@allsaints-fulham.org.uk

SEABROOK, The Ven Richard Anthony. b 68. Southn Univ BTh 92. Chich Th Coll 92. **d** 92 **p** 93. C Cottingham *York* 92–94; C Hawley H Trin *Guildf* 94–98; V Hockley *Chelmsf*

98–05; R Benalla Australia 05–09; R Mount Barker 09–15; Adn The Murray 09–14; Adn The Murray-Riverland 14–15; Dioc Admin The Murray 10–13; P-in-c Torrevieja *Eur* from 15. *calle Manuel de Falla 240, 03169 Algorfa (Alicante), Spain* T: (0034) 966 840 136 E: frras@blackwater.org.au

SEAFORD, The Very Revd John Nicholas. b 39. Dur Univ BA 67. St Chad's Coll Dur 68. **d** 68 **p** 69. C Bush Hill Park St Mark *Lon* 68–71; C Stanmore *Win* 71–73; V N Baddesley 73–76; V Chilworth w N Baddesley 76–78; V Highcliffe w Hinton Admiral 78–93; RD Christchurch 90–93; Hon Can Win Cathl 93–05; Dean Jersey and R Jersey St Helier 93–05; Angl Adv Channel TV 93–05; Chapl Jersey Airport 98–00; Chapl HM Pris La Moye 03–05; rtd 05; PtO *Sarum* 05; *Win* 05–14. *Claremont, Buffetts Road, Sturminster Newton DT10 1DZ* T: (01258) 471479 E: jolen.claremont@tiscali.co.uk

SEAGO, Aled Niclas. b 88. Lanc Univ BA 09. Oak Hill Th Coll BA 17. **d** 18 **p** 19. C Poynton *Ches* from 18. *18 Ivy Road, Poynton, Stockport SK12 1PE* M: 07952-736369 E: aled.seago@gmail.com *or* curate@poyntonparishchurch.org

SEAGO, Timothy Paul. b 59. Ripon Coll Cuddesdon 06. **d** 08 **p** 09. C Marlborough *Sarum* 08–12; P-in-c Totteridge *St Alb* 12–17; V from 17; AD Barnet from 18. *St Andrew's Vicarage, 78 Greenway, London N20 8EJ* M: 07772-809136 E: revdtim@seago.org.uk

SEAL, Canon Nicholas Peter. b 57. Ex Univ BA. Linc Th Coll 81. **d** 83 **p** 84. C Wareham *Sarum* 83–87; Chapl K Alfred Coll *Win* 87–91; V Stanmore 91–01; P-in-c Win St Matt 01–10; R from 10; RD Win 99–07; Chapl Peter Symonds Coll *Win* from 01; Hon Can Win Cathl from 13. *The Rectory, 44 Cheriton Road, Winchester SO22 5AY* T/F: (01962) 854849 E: peter.seal@ntlworld.com

SEAL (formerly MILLER), Mrs Rosamund Joy. b 56. R Holloway Coll Lon BSc 77 Whitelands Coll Lon PGCE 80. EMMTC 89. **d** 94 **p** 96. NSM Grantham *Linc* 94–96; C Stamford All SS w St Jo 96–00; C Spalding St Mary and St Nic 00–05; P-in-c Moulton 05–13; V Holbeach from 13; RD Elloe E from 09; RD Elloe W 09–13. *The Vicarage, 5 Church Street, Holbeach, Spalding PE12 7LL* T: (01406) 424989 E: rosamund.seal@btinternet.com

SEALY, Stephen. b 52. K Coll Lon BD 86 AKC 86. Linc Th Coll 86. **d** 88 **p** 89. C Botley *Portsm* 88–91; Min Can and Prec Cant Cathl 91–96; V Pembury *Roch* 96–04; V Sidcup St Jo 04–17; P-in-c Footscray w N Cray 16–17; AD Sidcup 08–13; C Wymondham *Nor* from 17. *9 Applegarth, Wymondham NR18 0BZ* E: sealynk@btconnect.com

SEAMAN, Christopher Robert. b 34. St Jo Coll Ox BA 58 MA 74 Solicitor 62. Ox Min Course 92 SAOMC 94. **d** 95 **p** 96. NSM Wallington w Pyrton and Shirburn *Ox* 95–97; NSM Icknield 97–98; PtO 98–99 and from 05; Hon C Shippon 99–04. *5 Curtyn Close, Abingdon OX14 1SE* T: (01235) 520380

SEAMAN, John. *See* SEAMAN, Robert John

SEAMAN, Miss Miranda Kate. b 66. Univ Coll Lon BSc 88 Solicitor 90. EAMTC 02. **d** 05 **p** 06. NSM S Weald *Chelmsf* 05–08; NSM Ingatestone w Fryerning 08–10; NSM Downham w S Hanningfield 10–11; NSM Downham w S Hanningfield and Ramsden Bellhouse from 11. *Copt Hall, 2 High Street, Stock, Ingatestone CM4 9BW* T: (01277) 841921 M: 07909-522763 E: seamanyoung@btinternet.com

SEAMAN (née HEWLINS), Mrs Pauline Elizabeth. b 47. Lon Univ BD 68 AKC. Ox Min Course 93. **d** 96 **p** 97. NSM Radley and Sunningwell *Ox* 96–99; NSM Shippon 99–09; P-in-c 06–09; Chapl SS Helen and Kath Sch Abingdon 96–04; Chapl SW Oxon Primary Care Trust 05–07; PtO *Ox* from 09. *5 Curtyn Close, Abingdon OX14 1SE* T: (01235) 520380

SEAMAN, Robert John. b 44. Glos Univ BA 04 Newland Park Teacher Tr Coll DipEd 69 ACP 84. EAMTC 84. **d** 84 **p** 85. NSM Downham Market w Bexwell *Ely* 84–90; V Southea w Murrow and Parson Drove 90–97; V Guyhirn w Ring's End 90–97; V Newnham w Awre and Blakeney *Glouc* 97–08; AD Forest N 04–08; Hon C Whitwick, Thringstone and Swannington *Leic* 08–11; rtd 11; PtO *Leic* from 11; *Pet* from 11. *6 Hiawatha, Wellingborough NN8 3SH* T: (01933) 382165 E: shipmates2@hotmail.co.uk

SEAMER, Stephen James George. b 50. AKC 73. Ridley Hall Cam 74. **d** 75 **p** 76. C Rustington *Chich* 75–78; C Bulwell St Jo *S'well* 78–79; P-in-c Camber and E Guldeford *Chich* 79–80; TV Rye 80–83; V Knowle *Birm* 83–87; Assoc Chapl Brussels Cathl *Eur* 87–88; P-in-c Tervuren 88–94; Chapl 94–98; P-in-c Liège 90–98; V Tonbridge SS Pet and Paul *Roch* 98–06; Chapl Düsseldorf *Eur* 06–14; rtd 14; PtO *Nor* from 15. *Low Wood, The Street, Erpingham, Norwich NR11 7QB* T: (01263) 768125 E: cromercliftops@gmail.com

SEAR, Benjamin William. b 84. Southn Univ BSc 07. Oak Hill Th Coll BA 15. d 15 p 16. C Patcham *Chich* 15–19; R Maresfield from 19; V Nutley from 19. *Crystals Rest, High Street, Maresfield, Uckfield TN22 2EH* E: benjamin.w.sear@gmail.com *or* vicar.maresfieldandnutley@protonmail.com

SEAR, Mrs Julie Anne Caradoc. b 61. Trin Coll Bris 08. d 10 p 11. C Ashington, Washington and Wiston w Buncton *Chich* 10–13; R Hartfield w Coleman's Hatch from 13. *The Rectory, Church Street, Hartfield TN7 4AG* T: (01892) 770436 M: 07840-021909 E: revjuliesear1@gmail.com

SEAR, Peter Lionel. b 49. Ex Univ BA 72. Linc Th Coll 72. d 74 p 75. C Sheldon *Birm* 74–77; C Caversham *Ox* 77–81; C Caversham St Pet and Mapledurham etc 81–85; TR Thatcham 85–98; V Castle Cary w Ansford *B & W* 98–00; rtd 00; PtO *B & W* from 03. *Plumtree Cottage, 1 Rodmore Road, Evercreech, Shepton Mallet BA4 6JL* T: (01749) 838843 E: peter@knowlecottage.eclipse.co.uk

SEARE, Mrs Janice Mae. b 48. SEN. STETS 99. d 02 p 03. C Holdenhurst and Iford *Win* from 02. *Wood Farm, Holdenhurst Village, Bournemouth BH8 0EE* T: (01202) 302468 F: 391281 E: pete.seare@sky.com

SEARLE, Anthony Miles. b 76. Univ of Wales (Abth) BSc 98 PGCE 99 SS Coll Cam BTh 10. Westcott Ho Cam 08. d 10 p 11. C Bishop's Stortford St Mich *St Alb* 10–13; Asst Chapl Oundle Sch 13–16; P-in-c Corby SS Pet and Andr from 16; P-in-c Gt and Lt Oakley from 16. *The Vicarage, 40 Beanfield Avenue, Corby NN18 0EH* M: 07785-357562 E: asearle76@googlemail.com

SEARLE, David William. b 37. MASI 89 ACIOB 98. d 99 p 00. OLM E Bergholt and Brantham *St E* 99–07; rtd 07; PtO *St E* from 07. *Rowan House, Elm Road, East Bergholt, Colchester CO7 6SG* T: (01206) 298932

SEARLE, Canon Hugh Douglas. b 35. St Cath Coll Cam BA 59 MA 63 Cranfield Inst of Tech MSc 85. Oak Hill Th Coll 59. d 61 p 62. C Islington H Trin Cloudesley Square *Lon* 61–64; Chapl HM Pris Lewes 64–65; Chapl HM Borstal Roch 65–69; Chapl HM Youth Cust Cen Hollesley Bay Colony 70–74; Chapl HM Pris Parkhurst 74–78; P-in-c Barton *Ely* 78–84; V 84–00; P-in-c Coton 78–84; R 84–00; RD Bourn 81–92; Hon Can Ely Cathl 97–00; rtd 00; PtO *Ely* 00–17. *4 Marguerite Drive, Lenzie, Kirkintilloch, Glasgow G66 4HF* E: hugdoug@talktalk.net *or* hughsearle80@gmail.com

✠**SEARLE, The Rt Revd Jacqueline Ann.** b 60. Whitelands Coll Lon BEd 82 Bris Univ MA 01. Trin Coll Bris 90. d 92 p 94 c 18. Par Dn Roxeth *Lon* 92–94; C Ealing St Steph Castle Hill 94–96; Tutor and Dean of Women Trin Coll Bris 96–03; P-in-c Littleover *Derby* 03–04; V 04–12; RD Derby S 10–12; Hon Can Derby Cathl 11–12; Adn Glouc 12–18; Can Res Glouc Cathl 12–18; Suff Bp Crediton *Ex* from 18. *32 The Avenue, Tiverton EX16 4HW* T: (01884) 250002 E: bishop.of.crediton@exeter.anglican.org

SEARLE, John Francis. b 42. Lon Univ MB, BS 66 FRCA 70 FRSocMed 84. SWMTC 92. d 95 p 96. NSM Ex St Leon w H Trin 95–03; Assoc Staff Member SWMTC from 03; Can Res Ex Cathl 15–16; PtO from 15. *Belle Isle Lodge, Belle Isle Drive, Exeter EX2 4RY* T: (01392) 432153 M: 07814-712921 E: j.f.searle@btinternet.com

SEARLE, Mark Robin. b 73. Cen Sch Speech & Drama BA 94. Trin Coll Bris BA 03. d 03 p 04. C Cant St Mary Bredin 03–07; C Ashtead *Guildf* 07–10; P-in-c Upton *Ex* 10–17; R Bath Weston All SS w N Stoke and Langridge *B & W* from 17. *The Rectory, Church Street, Weston, Bath BA1 4BU* E: revmarksearle@gmail.com

SEARLE, Michael Westran. b 47. Leeds Univ LLB 68. Cuddesdon Coll 69. d 71 p 72. C Norton St Mary *Dur* 71–74; C Westbury-on-Trym H Trin *Bris* 74–77; V Bedminster Down 77–84; V Bris Ch the Servant Stockwood 84–88; Dir of Tr *York* 88–00; R Dunnington 00–07; rtd 07; PtO *Truro* from 16. *Lamorna Vean, Lamorna, Penzance TR19 6NY* T: (01736) 810218 E: mike.lamornavean@btinternet.com

SEARLE, Philip Robert. b 67. Westcott Ho Cam. d 95 p 96. C Plymstock *Ex* 95–97; C Plymstock and Hooe 97–98; TV Stoke-upon-Trent *Lich* 98–10; PtO from 10. *164 Vicarage Gardens, Plymouth PL5 1LJ* E: phil.hairetic@hotmail.co.uk

SEARLE-BARNES, Belinda Rosemary. b 51. Lon Univ MA 93 ARCM 72 GRSM 73. Sarum Th Coll 93. d 96 p 97. NSM Pimperne, Stourpaine, Durweston and Bryanston *Sarum* 96–00; Asst Par Development Adv 98–00; Asst Chapl Bryanston Sch 98–00; TV Southampton (City Cen) *Win* 00–04; Chapl Godolphin Sch 04–07; P-in-c Winslow w Gt Horwood and Addington *Ox* 07–08; R 08–14; rtd 14; PtO *Win* from 14; St Alb from 17; NSM Officer Bedford Adnry from 19. *3 Ravensden Grange, Sunderland Hill, Ravensden, Bedford MK44 2SH* T: (01234) 771112 E: belinda@searle-barnes.com *or* ssmobeds@stalbans.anglican.org

SEARS, Jacqueline Isabella. SRN 69. NTMTC 95. d 99 p 00. NSM Hanwell St Mellitus w St Mark *Lon* 99–02; Asst Chapl Essex Rivers Healthcare NHS Trust 03; Chapl 04–06; C Ipswich St Matt *St E* 04–06; C Triangle, St Matt and All SS 06–10; rtd 10; PtO *St E* from 10. *4 Woodward Close, Ipswich IP2 0EA* T: (01473) 214125 E: jackie@jbsears.com

SEATON, Christopher Charles. d 10 p 11. C St Andrews Major w Michaelston-le-Pit *Llan* 10–15; C Cadoxton-juxta-Barry 15–16; C Barry from 16. *13 Hillside Close, Barry CF63 2QP* T: (01446) 747541 E: chris.c.seaton@hotmail.co.uk

SEATON-BURN, Paul Simon. b 70. Ex Univ BA 92. St Jo Coll Nottm MTh 06. d 06 p 07. C Broughton w Loddington and Cransley etc *Pet* 06–09; P-in-c Desborough, Brampton Ash, Dingley and Braybrooke 09–11; P-in-c Chagford, S Tawton, Drewsteignton etc *Ex* 11–13; TR Chagford, Gidleigh, Throwleigh etc from 13. *The Rectory, Chagford, Newton Abbot TQ13 8BW* T: (01647) 432880 E: paulsburn@btinternet.com

SEBBAGE, Lynda Anne. b 54. ERMC 16. d 17 p 18. NSM Stour Valley *St E* from 17. *Clarence House, Clarence Road, Sudbury CO10 1NJ*

SEBER, Derek Morgan. b 43. Man Poly MA 87 Man Metrop Univ MPhil 96. Oak Hill Th Coll 71. d 73 p 74. C Collyhurst *Man* 73–76; C Radcliffe St Thos and St Jo 76–77; Ind Missr 77–89; P-in-c Hulme St Geo 77–83; Hon C Moss Side St Jas w St Clem 83–96; Project Officer Linking Up 89–96; Lic Preacher *Man* 90–96; P-in-c Cheetham St Jo 97; P-in-c Thornton Hough *Ches* 97–05; V 05–08; Ind Chapl 97–05; rtd 08; PtO *Ches* 08–12; *Blackb* from 12. *3 Castle Park, Hornby, Lancaster LA2 8SB* T: (015242) 22011 E: derek.seber@sky.com

SECCOMBE, Marcus John. b 34. Oak Hill Th Coll 60. d 63 p 64. C Woodthorpe *S'well* 63–67; C Doncaster St Mary *Sheff* 67–72; V Owston 72–90; R Rossington 90–99; rtd 99; PtO *Sheff* from 99. *39 Marlborough Road, Doncaster DN2 5DF* T: (01302) 321505 E: marcusseccombe@gmail.com

SEDDON, Mrs Carol Susan. b 44. ARCM 63 GNSM 66 Man Univ DipEd 67. Ripon Coll Cuddesdon 05. d 05 p 06. NSM Alsager St Mary *Ches* 05–08; Asst Chapl HM YOI Stoke Heath 05–08; V Northwich St Luke and H Trin *Ches* 08–17; rtd 17; PtO *Ches* 17–18; P-in-c Northwich H Trin from 18. *The Vicarage, 1 Tall Trees Close, Northwich CW8 4YA* T: (01606) 74632 M: 07973-737038 E: carol_seddon@hotmail.com

SEDDON, Ernest Geoffrey. b 26. Man Univ MA 85 ARIBA 51. St Deiniol's Hawarden 80. d 80 p 81. C Dunham Massey St Marg *Ches* 80–83; P-in-c Warburton 82–87; P-in-c Dunham Massey St Mark 85–86; V 86–92; rtd 92; PtO *Ches* 92–06. *7 Colwyn Place, Llandudno LL30 3AW* T: (01492) 547639 *or* 642107

SEDDON, Philip James. b 45. Jes Coll Cam BA 68 MA 71 Birm Univ MPhil 01. Ridley Hall Cam 67. d 70 p 71. C Tonge w Alkrington *Man* 70–74; CMS Nigeria 74–78; Lect St Jo Coll Nottm 78–79; LtO *Ely* 79–85; Chapl Magd Coll Cam 79–85; Lect Bibl Studies Selly Oak Colls 86–00; LtO *Birm* 87–05; Lect Th Birm Univ 00–05; Dir Min STETS 05–10; rtd 10; PtO *Sarum* from 11. *6 Beech Close, Porton, Salisbury SP4 0NP* T: (01980) 619104 E: philipjseddon@gmail.com

SEDEN, Martin Roy. b 47. Man Univ MSc Salford Univ PhD. EMMTC 79. d 82 p 83. NSM Knighton St Mary Magd *Leic* 82–07; NSM Rutland Deanery *Pet* from 08; SSM Officer Oakham Adnry from 18. *60 Leicester Road, Uppingham, Oakham LE15 9SD* T: (01572) 822244 M: 07806-940407 E: rseden@gmail.com

SEDGEWICK, Clive Malcolm. b 56. Loughb Univ BSc 78 UEA MA 92 PGCE 79. SAOMC 00. d 04 p 05. NSM High Harrogate Ch Ch *Ripon* 04–13; P-in-c Bardsey 13–14; *Leeds* 14–17; TR Axminster, Chardstock, All Saints etc *Ex* from 17. *The Rectory, Church Street, Axminster EX13 5AQ* M: 07903-326053 E: clivesedgewick@yahoo.com

SEDGLEY, Mrs Jean. b 41. Open Univ BA 03 Whitelands Coll Lon CertEd 63. S Dios Minl Tr Scheme 92. d 95 p 96. NSM Haywards Heath St Wilfrid *Chich* 95–01; NSM Cuckfield 01–09; rtd 09; PtO *Chich* from 14. *10 St Nicholas Court, Lindfield, Haywards Heath RH16 2EY* T: (01444) 413974 E: jean@sedgley.org

SEDGLEY, Canon Timothy John. b 42. St Jo Coll Ox BA 63 MA 68. Westcott Ho Cam 64. d 66 p 67. C Nor St Pet Mancroft 66–70; V Costessey 70–79; RD Nor N 75–79; V Walton-on-Thames *Guildf* 79–05; RD Emly 86–91; Hon Can Guildf Cathl 86–05; Dir OLMs and NSMs 93–05; rtd 05; PtO *Glouc* from 06. *6 St Paul's Court, Moreton-in-Marsh, Gloucester GL56 0ET* T: (01608) 652696 E: timsedgley@hotmail.com

SEDGWICK, Jonathan Maurice William. b 63. BNC Ox BA 85 MA 89 Leeds Univ BA 88. Coll of Resurr Mirfield 86. d 89 p 90. C Chich St Paul and St Pet 89–91; Dean of Div and Chapl Magd Coll Ox 91–94; PtO *S'wark* 97–99; Hon C E Dulwich St Jo 99–11; Hon C Walworth St Chris 11–14; P-in-c *S'wark*

St Geo w St Alphege and St Jude 14–18; R from 18. *St George's Rectory, Manciple Street, London SE1 4LW* M: 07585-113773 E: jonathan@stgeorge-themartyr.co.uk

SEDGWICK, Canon Peter Humphrey. b 48. Trin Hall Cam BA 70 Dur Univ PhD 83. Westcott Ho Cam 71. **d** 74 **p** 75. C Stepney St Dunstan and All SS *Lon* 74–77; P-in-c Pittington *Dur* 77–79; Lect Th Birm Univ 79–82; Hon C The Lickey *Birm* 79–82; Th Consultant for NE Ecum Gp *Dur* 82–88; Lect Th Hull Univ 88–94; Abp's Adv on Ind Issues *York* 88–94; Vice-Prin Westcott Ho Cam 94–96; Asst Sec Abps' Coun Bd for Soc Resp 96–04; NSM Pet St Barn 96–98; Prin St Mich Coll Llan 04–14; Can Llan Cathl from 06; PtO from 14. *Church House, Grand Avenue, Cardiff CF5 4HX* T: (029) 2067 9833 E: peter.sedgwick2@btinternet.com

SEEAR, Ms Louise. b 57. St Mary's Coll Dur BA 78. Ripon Coll Cuddesdon 09. **d** 12 **p** 13. NSM N Lambeth *S'wark* 12–15; Asst Chapl King's Coll Hosp NHS Foundn Trust 13–19; NSM Hythe *Cant* from 16; Chapl Lewisham and Greenwich NHS Trust from 19. *The Vicarage, Oak Walk, Hythe CT21 5DN* M: 07813-615150 E: louseear@gmail.com *or* revlouseear@gmail.com

SEED, Richard Edward. b 55. UNISA BTh 86 Westmr Coll Ox MEd. Kalk Bay Bible Inst S Africa. **d** 80 **p** 81. S Africa 80–85 and 87–89; Zimbabwe 85–87; Asst Chapl Kingham Hill Sch Oxon 89–90; C Beckenham Ch Ch *Roch* 90–95; Chapl Düsseldorf *Eur* 96–00; CMS from 00. *CMS, PO Box 1799, Oxford OX4 9BN* T: 08456-201799

SEED, The Ven Richard Murray Crosland. b 49. Leeds Univ MA 91. Edin Th Coll 69. **d** 72 **p** 73. C Skipton Ch Ch *Bradf* 72–75; C Baildon 75–77; Chapl HM Det Cen Kidlington 77–80; TV Kidlington *Ox* 77–80; V Boston Spa *York* 80–99; P-in-c Newton Kyme 84–85; P-in-c Clifford 89–99; P-in-c Thorp Arch w Walton 98–99; Chapl Martin House Hospice for Children Boston Spa 85–99; RD New Ainsty *York* 97–99; Adn York 99–12; R York H Trin Micklegate 00–12; rtd 12; PtO *York* from 14. *Mill Cottage, Main Street, Allerston, Pickering YO18 7PG* T: (01723) 859011

SEED, Susan Mary. b 61. **d** 14 **p** 15. C Lancaster Ch Ch *Blackb* 14–18; R Slyne w Hest and Halton w Aughton from 18. *The Vicarage, 2 Summerfield Drive, Slyne, Lancaster LA2 6AQ* T: (01524) 822128 E: revsusan.seed@btinternet.com

SEELEY, Jutta. *See* BRUECK, Jutta

✠**SEELEY, The Rt Revd Martin Alan.** b 54. Jes Coll Cam BA 76 MA 79. Ripon Coll Cuddesdon 76 Union Th Sem (NY) STM 78. **d** 78 **p** 79 **c** 15. C Bottesford w Ashby *Linc* 78–80; USA 80–90; Selection Sec ABM 90–96; Sec for Continuing Minl Educn 90–96; V Is of Dogs Ch Ch and St Jo w St Luke *Lon* 96–06; Prin Westcott Ho Cam 06–15; Hon Can Ely Cathl 08–15; Bp St E from 15; Hon Asst Bp Ely from 15; PtO *Eur* from 17. *The Bishop's House, 4 Park Road, Ipswich IP1 3ST* T: (01473) 252829 E: bishop.martin@cofesuffolk.org

SEGGAR, Jennifer Mary. b 63. Open Univ PGCE 01. **d** 05 **p** 06. OLM Bildeston w Wattisham and Lindsey, Whatfield etc *St E* 05–09; C Sudbury and Chilton 09–11; P-in-c Bramford 11–19; Spiritual Dir Cursillo 16–19; R Holbrook, Stutton, Freston, Woolverstone etc from 19. *15 Denmark Gardens, Ipswich Road, Holbrook, Ipswich IP9 2BG* E: revjseggar@outlook.com

SEGGIE, Ms Karen Angela. b 75. Roehampton Univ BA 13. Ripon Coll Cuddesdon MTh 15. **d** 15 **p** 16. C Milton next Gravesend Ch Ch *Roch* from 15; C Gravesend St Aid from 15; C Gravesend H Family w Ifield from 15. *28 The Sandpipers, Gravesend DA12 5QB* T: (01474) 362654 E: karenseggie16@gmail.com

SEGRAVE-PRIDE, Mrs Philippa Louise. b 73. Westhill Coll Birm BTh 96. Ripon Coll Cuddesdon 97. **d** 99 **p** 00. C Harborne St Pet *Birm* 99–02; TV Tring *St Alb* 02–04; TV Bp's Hatfield, Lemsford and N Mymms 04–09; P-in-c Harpenden St Jo 09–12; V 12–13; Canada from 13. *1281 Durant Drive, Coquitlam, British Columbia V3B 6K8, Canada* T: (001) (778) 838 3132 E: philippa@segrave.net

SEIVEWRIGHT, Scott Stuart. b 77. PtO *Win* 17–18; *Lich* from 18. *8A Church Street, Audley, Stoke-on-Trent ST7 8DE* M: 07757-806507 E: seivewrightscott@gmail.com

SELBY, Canon Carole Janis. b 50. Chelsea Coll of Physical Educn CertEd 71 Sussex Univ BEd 72 K Coll Lon MA 03. Westcott Ho Cam 93. **d** 95 **p** 96. C Worc St Barn w Ch Ch 95–99; Min Turnford St Clem CD *St Alb* 99–08; TV Cheshunt 08–17; RD 04–12; Hon Can St Alb 13–17; rtd 17. *6 Perrings, Wymondham NR18 0JR* T: (01953) 600635 E: c_selby@talk21.com

SELBY, Michael Ernest. b 59. Preston Poly BEd 80. Ripon Coll Cuddesdon 14. **d** 16 **p** 17. C Ealing St Pet Mt Park *Lon* 16–19; V Ruislip Manor St Paul from 19. *St Paul's Vicarage, Thurlstone Road, Ruislip HA4 0BP* M: 07795-187164 E: revmselby@gmail.com

SELBY, Peter Leslie. b 54. Down Coll Cam BA 75 MA 79 MB, BChir 79 MD 90 FRCP. All SS Cen for Miss & Min 16. **d** 18 **p** 19. NSM Cheadle Hulme St Andr *Ches* from 18. *22 Nevill Road, Bramhall, Stockport SK7 3ET* T: 0161-439 4735 M: 07721-539081 E: peter@theselbys.org *or* peter@standrewscheadlehulme.org.uk

✠**SELBY, The Rt Revd Peter Stephen Maurice.** b 41. St Jo Coll Ox BA 64 MA 67 Episc Th Sch Cam Mass BD 66 K Coll Lon PhD 75 Birm Univ Hon DD 07. Bps' Coll Cheshunt 66. **d** 66 **p** 67 **c** 84. C Queensbury All SS *Lon* 66–69; C Limpsfield and Titsey *S'wark* 69–77; Assoc Dir of Tr 69–73; Vice-Prin *S'wark* Ord Course 70–72; Asst Dioc Missr *S'wark* 73–77; Dioc Missr *Newc* 77–84; Can Res Newc Cathl 77–84; Suff Bp Kingston *S'wark* 84–91; Area Bp 91–92; Wm Leech Prof Fell *Dur* Univ 92–97; Asst Bp Dur and Newc 92–97; Bp Worc 97–07; Hon Prof Univ Coll Worc from 98; Bp HM Pris 01–07; Asst Bp Portsm 08–11; Hon Co-Dir St Paul's Inst 12–14; Hon Asst Bp S'wark from 11; Visiting Prof K Coll Lon from 08. *57 Girton Road, London SE26 5DJ* T: (020) 3538 0220 E: peterselby1941@gmail.com

SELBY, Philip James. b 82. Nottm Univ BSc 04 Derby Univ PGCE 06. Oak Hill Th Coll BA 15. **d** 15 **p** 16. C Buxton Trin Prop Chpl *Derby* 15–19; R Stanton-by-Dale w Dale Abbey and Risley from 19. *The Rectory, Stanhope Street, Stanton-by-Dale, Ilkeston DE7 4QA* M: 07910-321576 E: philselby82@gmail.com

SELBY-BOOTHROYD, Richard George. b 46. SWMTC. **d** 09 **p** 10. NSM St Illogan *Truro* 09–11; NSM Lyneham w Bradenstoke *Sarum* 11–18; P-in-c 15–18; NSM R Wootton Bassett *Sarum* 11–15; NSM Woodhill 11–18; rtd 19. *8 St Josephs Way, Lyneham, Chippenham SN15 4FA* E: rsb@priest.com

SELBY, Suffragan Bishop of. *See* THOMSON, The Rt Revd John Bromilow

SELDON, Francis Peter. b 58. St Jo Coll Nottm 98. **d** 00 **p** 01. C Styvechale *Cov* 00–02; C Cheylesmore 02–04; V 04–11; V Chilvers Coton w Astley from 11; AD Nuneaton 16–19. *Chilvers Coton Vicarage, Coventry Road, Nuneaton CV11 4NJ* T: (024) 7638 3010 *or* 7634 6413

SELF, Canon David Christopher. b 41. Toronto Univ BSc 62 MA 64 K Coll Lon BD 68 AKC 68. **d** 69 **p** 70. C Tupsley *Heref* 69–73; Chapl Dur Univ 73–78; TV Southampton (City Cen) *Win* 78–84; TR Dunstable *St Alb* 84–95; RD 90–91; TR Bris St Paul's 95–06; RD Bris City 98–99; AD City 99–03; Hon Can Bris Cathl 99–06; rtd 06; PtO *Bris* from 07; *Glouc* from 16. *3 Shannon Court, Thornbury, Bristol BS35 2HN* T: (01454) 418006 E: david@dcself.plus.com

SELF, John Andrew. b 47. Trin Coll Bris 74 CMS Tr Coll Crowther Hall 76. **d** 81 **p** 83. CMS Pakistan 77–91; Assoc V Bath Weston All SS w N Stoke *B & W* 91–92; V Sparkhill St Jo *Birm* 92–17; rtd 17; PtO *Birm* 17–19; *Sarum* from 19. *2 Silver Street, Steeple Ashton, Trowbridge BA14 6HB* T: (01380) 871569 E: john.self@me.com

SELFE, John Ronald. b 41. EMMTC 85. **d** 95 **p** 96. OLM Mid Marsh Gp *Linc* from 95. *Bookend, 236 Eastgate, Louth LN11 8DA* T: (01507) 603809

SELLER, Prof Mary Joan. b 40. Qu Mary Coll Lon BSc 61 Lon Univ PhD 64 DSc 82. S'wark Ord Course 89. **d** 91 **p** 94. NSM Hurst Green *S'wark* 91–10; rtd 10; PtO *S'wark* from 10. *11 Home Park, Oxted RH8 0JS* T: (01883) 715675 E: mary.seller@kcl.ac.uk

SELLER, Timothy John. b 46. Qu Mary Coll Lon BSc 67 Lon Univ PhD 71. **d** 08 **p** 09. OLM Ewhurst *Guildf* 08–16; PtO 16–17; rtd 17. *Long Barn, Back Street, Ilmington, Shipston-on-Stour CV36 4LJ* M: 07845-192041 E: tim.seller@outlook.com

SELLERS, Canon Anthony. b 48. Southn Univ BSc 71 PhD 76. Wycliffe Hall Ox 84. **d** 86 **p** 87. C Luton St Mary *St Alb* 86–90; V Luton St Paul 90–16; Hon Can St Alb 12–16; rtd 16; PtO *St Alb* from 16. *Address withheld by request*

SELLERS, George William. b 35. NOC. **d** 89 **p** 90. NSM Rothwell *Ripon* 89–05; rtd 05. *Dolphin Manor Care Home, Stone Brig Lane, Rothwell, Leeds LS26 0UD*

SELLERS, Joseph Matthew Christopher. b 81. Trin Coll Bris 16. **d** 18 **p** 19. C Chorleywood St Andr *St Alb* from 18. *36 Quickley Lane, Chorleywood, Rickmansworth WD3 5AF* E: joe.sellers@st-andrews.org.uk

SELLERS, Mrs Rosalind April. b 48. Liv Univ MA 77. SWMTC 06. **d** 09 **p** 11. NSM Cannington, Otterhampton, Combwich and Stockland *B & W* 09–10; NSM Puriton and Pawlett 10–18; PtO from 18. *1 St Mary's Crescent, North Petherton, Bridgwater TA6 6RA* T: (01278) 661279 M: 07794-666247 E: rosalind.sellers153@gmail.com

SELLERS, Warren John. b 43. Bp Otter Coll Chich TCert 73 W Sussex Inst of HE DipAdEd 88. K Coll Lon 63 Sarum Th Coll 65. **d** 68 **p** 69. C Guildf H Trin w St Mary 68–72; Hon C Chich St Paul and St Pet 72–73; C Epping St Jo *Chelmsf* 73–76;

Hon C Pulborough *Chich* 76–90; Hon C Fleet *Guildf* 90–92; Teacher 73–89; Waltham Abbey St Lawr and H Cross Schs Essex 73–76; Pulborough St Mary, Easeboure & Bp Tuffnell Schs 76–89; Hd Teacher St Pet Jun Sch Farnborough 90–92; TV Upper Kennet *Sarum* 92–95; TR 95–03; rtd 03. *71 Bay Crescent, Swanage BH19 1RD* E: wjandmjs27@btinternet.com

SELLERS, Wendy. b 62. Leeds Univ BA 84 Herts Univ PGCE 00. ERMC 16. **d** 18 **p** 19. NSM Hertford *St Alb* from 18. *59 Attimore Road, Welwyn Garden City AL8 6LG* T: (01707) 372315 M: 07585-553173 E: revwendy55@gmail.com

SELLEY, Paul Edward Henry. b 47. Bris Univ BEd 70 ALCM 67 LTCL 87. Sarum Th Coll 93. **d** 96 **p** 97. C Swindon Dorcan *Bris* 96–00; V Ashton Keynes, Leigh and Minety 00–07; rtd 07; PtO *Sarum* from 07. *5 Miles Gardens, Weymouth DT3 5NH* T: (01305) 814948 E: paul.selley@which.net

SELLGREN, Eric Alfred. b 33. AKC 61. **d** 62 **p** 63. C Ditton St Mich *Liv* 62–66; V Hindley Green 66–72; V Southport St Paul 72–80; Warden Barn Fellowship Winterborne Whitchurch 80–86; V The Iwernes, Sutton Waldron and Fontmell Magna *Sarum* 86–98; rtd 98; PtO *Sarum* from 98. *19 Savoy Court, Shaftesbury SP7 8BN* T: (01747) 853327 E: revsellgren@gmail.com

SELLICK, Canon Peter James. b 67. Wadh Coll Ox BA 89. Edin Th Coll BD 94. **d** 94 **p** 95. C Kippax w Allerton Bywater *Ripon* 94–97; C Stanningley St Thos 97–02; C W Bromwich All SS *Lich* 02–12; Ind Chapl Black Country Urban Ind Miss 02–12; Development Dir Chs and Ind Gp Birm and Solihull from 12; PtO *Lich* from 15; Hon Can Birm Cathl from 16. *41 Wheatley Road, Oldbury B68 9HW* T: 0121-423 4334 *or* 426 0425 M: 07746-299676 E: peters@cofebirmingham.com

✠**SELLIN, The Rt Revd Deborah Mary.** b 64. St Andr Univ MA 86. STETS 04. **d** 07 **p** 08 **c** 19. NSM Guildf St Sav 07–10; V Wonersh w Blackheath 10–19; AD Cranleigh 15–19; Hon Can Guildf Cathl 18–19; Suff Bp Southampton *Win* from 19. *39 Hook Road, Ampfield, Romsey SO51 9DB* M: 07703-194564 E: bishop.debbie@winchester.anglican.org

SELLIN, Jacqueline Mary. b 67. Sarum Coll 14. **d** 17 **p** 18. NSM Southampton (City Cen) *Win* 17–18; NSM Southampton St Mich from 18. *50 Bullar Road, Southampton SO18 1GS*

SELLIX, Mrs Pamela Madge. b 47. Lon Univ BA 68 PGCE 68. SWMTC 00. **d** 04 **p** 05. NSM Saltash *Truro* from 04. *Farthings, Quarry Road, Pensilva, Liskeard PL14 5NT* T: (01579) 363464

SELMAN, Laura Margaret. b 81. **d** 15 **p** 16. C Surbiton St Andr and St Mark *S'wark* 15–17; C Bury St Edmunds All SS w St Jo and St Geo *St E* from 17; C Lark Valley from 17. *2 Fen Way, Bury St Edmunds IP33 3ZA* E: curatelaura@gmail.com

SELMAN, Matthew Robert. b 81. Leic Univ BA 03 SOAS Lon MA 06 St Edm Coll Cam BTh 17. Westcott Ho Cam 17. **d** 17 **p** 18. C Bury St Edmunds All SS w St Jo and St Geo *St E* from 17; C Lark Valley from 17. *2 Fen Way, Bury St Edmunds IP33 3ZA*

SELMAN, Michael Richard. b 47. Sussex Univ BA 68 Bris Univ MA 70. Coll of Resurr Mirfield 71. **d** 73 **p** 74. C Hove All SS *Chich* 73–74; C Horfield H Trin *Bris* 74–78; P-in-c Landkey *Ex* 78–79; C Barnstaple and Goodleigh 78–79; TV Barnstaple, Goodleigh and Landkey 79–82; TR 82–84; P-in-c Sticklepath 83–84; TR Barnstaple 85; RD 83–85; TR Cen Ex 85–00; Chapl Aquitaine *Eur* 00–08; Partnership P E Bris 08–12; rtd 12; PtO *Eur* from 16. *1 Millwey Court, Axminster EX13 5GD* M: 07735-499920 E: revmichael.selman@gmail.com

SELMES, Brian. b 48. Nottm Univ BTh 74 Dur Univ MA 97. Linc Th Coll 70. **d** 74 **p** 75. C Paddock *Liv* 74–77; C Sydenham St Bart *S'wark* 77–80; Chapl Darlington Memorial and Aycliffe Hosps 80–98; Co-ord Chapl S Durham Healthcare NHS Trust 98–02; Sen Chapl Co Durham and Darlington NHS Foundn Trust 02–12; rtd 12; PtO *Dur* 15–18. *19 The Avenue, Richmond DL10 7AZ* T: (01748) 821873 E: bmselmes@tiscali.co.uk

SELVARATNAM, Christian Nathan. b 68. Warwick Univ BSc 90. Cranmer Hall Dur 06. **d** 08 **p** 09. NSM York St Mich-le-Belfrey from 08. *11/12 Minster Yard, York YO1 7HH* T: (01904) 624190 M: 07773-784728 E: christian.selvaratnam@gmail.com

SELVEY, Canon John Brian. b 33. Dur Univ BA 54. Cuddesdon Coll 56. **d** 58 **p** 59. C Lancaster St Mary *Blackb* 58–61; C Blackb Cathl 61–65; Cathl Chapl 64–65; V Foulridge *Blackb* 65–69; V Walton-le-Dale 69–82; V Cleveleys 82–89; Hon Can Bloemfontein Cathl from 88; V Slyne w Hest *Blackb* 89–97; Hon Can Blackb Cathl 93–97; rtd 97; PtO *Carl* 98–19. *Low Quietways, Borrowdale Road, Keswick CA12 5UP* T: (01768) 773538 E: jselvey7@btinternet.com

SELWOOD, Michael. b 40. Oak Hill Th Coll BA 91. **d** 91 **p** 92. Canada 91–95; P-in-c Sherborne, Windrush, the Barringtons etc *Glouc* 95–07; rtd 07; PtO *Glouc* from 16. *17 Croft Holm, Moreton-in-Marsh GL56 0JH* T: (01608) 812384 E: mselwood@btinternet.com

SELWYN, David Gordon. b 38. Clare Coll Cam BA 62 MA 66 DD New Coll Ox MA 66 MEHS. Ripon Hall Ox. **d** 64 **p** 65. C Ecclesall *Sheff* 64–65; Asst Chapl New Coll Ox 65–68; Lect Univ of Wales (Lamp) *St D* 68–98; Reader 98–05; PtO *St D* 68–05. *62A Swiss Valley, Llanelli SA14 8BT* T: (01554) 773983

SEMPER, Jocelyn Rachel. See WALKER, Jocelyn Rachel

SEMPLE, Henry Michael. b 40. K Coll Lon BSc 62 Birkbeck Coll Lon PhD 67 CMath FIMA FCMI FRSA. S Dios Minl Tr Scheme. **d** 87 **p** 88. NSM Steyning *Chich* 87–91; PtO *Guildf* 87–91; *Linc* 92–93; NSM Linc Cathl 93–99; TR Headley All SS *Guildf* 99–02; R 02–10; rtd 10; PtO *Guildf* 10–12; *Chich* from 11. *12 St Michael's Road, Worthing BN11 4SD* T: (01903) 520691 E: michael.semple1@outlook.com

SEMPLE, Sean Alexander John. b 71. Natal Univ BSocSc 93 BTh 03 UNISA BTh 97 Kwazulu-Natal Univ MTh 14. **d** 09 **p** 11. C Hillcrest H Trin S Africa 09–10; Asst P Pinetown St Jo 10–12; Asst P Larnaca Cyprus 13–15; V Weobley w Sarnesfield and Norton Canon *Heref* 15–19; R Letton w Staunton, Byford, Mansel Gamage etc 15–19; R Ross w Walford and Brampton Abbotts from 19. *The Rectory, Church Street, Ross-on-Wye HR9 5HN* T: (01989) 562175 E: sean@rawchurch.org.uk

SEMPLE, Studdert Patrick. b 39. TCD BA 66. CITC 66. **d** 67 **p** 68. C Orangefield *D & D* 67–70; USA 70–71; I Stradbally *C & O* 71–82; Ch of Ireland Adult Educn Officer 82–88; I Donoughmore and Donard w Dunlavin *D & G* 88–96; Bp's C Dublin St Geo and St Thos 96–99; Chapl Mountjoy Pris 96–99; Chapl Mater Hosp 96–99; rtd 99. *49 Richmond Park, Monkstown, Co Dublin, Republic of Ireland* T: (00353) (1) 214 0843 M: 86-375 3207 E: naturesplaythings@gmail.com

SEN, Canon Arani. b 61. R Holloway Coll Lon BA 84 St Martin's Coll Lanc PGCE 86 Open Univ MA 94 Fitzw Coll Cam BA 98 MA 02. Ridley Hall Cam 96. **d** 99 **p** 00. C Mildmay Grove St Jude and St Paul *Lon* 99–02; C-in-c Southall Em CD 02–06; V Southall Em 06–08; V Upper Armley *Ripon* 08–14; *Leeds* from 14; AD Armley *Ripon* 13–14; *Leeds* from 14; Hon Can Bradf Cathl from 17. *22 Hill End Crescent, Leeds LS12 3PW* T: 0113-263 8788 E: revaranisen@gmail.com

SENIOR, Canon Brian Stephen. b 55. Brighton Coll of Educn CertEd 76. Oak Hill Th Coll 91. **d** 93 **p** 94. C Hildenborough *Roch* 93–98; TV Tunbridge Wells St Jas w St Phil 98–04; V Tunbridge Wells St Phil 04–15; RD Tunbridge Wells 07–14; TR S Gillingham from 15; Hon Can Roch Cathl from 16. *The Vicarage, 4 Drewery Drive, Rainham, Gillingham ME8 0NX* T: (01634) 231071 E: rector@stmattswigmore.org.uk *or* revbriansenior@gmail.com

SENIOR, David John. b 47. Oak Hill Th Coll. **d** 82 **p** 83. C Market Harborough *Leic* 82–85; TV Marfleet *York* 85–91; R Desford and Peckleton w Tooley *Leic* 91–96; P-in-c Hall Green Ascension *Birm* 96–99; V 99–12; P-in-c Gospel Lane St Mich 97–03; AD Shirley 10–12; rtd 12; Hon C Londesborough Wold *York* 12–15; Hon C Pocklington Wold 12–15; PtO *Carl* 15–17; *York* from 18. *9 Knott Lane, Easingwold, York YO61 3LX* E: davidsenior3@gmail.com

SENIOR, David Norman. b 59. Cam Univ MA 82. St Mellitus Coll 12. **d** 15 **p** 17. NSM Howell Hill *Guildf* from 15. *65 Higher Drive, Banstead SM7 1PW* M: 07710-313749

SENIOR, Mrs Lisa Elaine. b 65. Leeds Univ BA 09. NOC 06. **d** 09 **p** 10. C Dewsbury *Wakef* 09–14; *Leeds* 14; R Colne *Blackb* from 14. *The Rectory, 30 Grenfell Gardens, Colne BB8 9PL* T: (01282) 869420

SENIOR, Patrick Nicolas Adam. b 63. Univ of Wales (Ban) BA 86. Trin Coll Bris BA 94. **d** 94 **p** 95. C Derringham Bank *York* 94–98; V Brownhill *Wakef* 98–14; R Burnley St Pet and St Steph *Blackb* from 14. *The Rectory, 30 Grenfell Gardens, Colne BB8 9PL* T: (01282) 869420 *or* 413120 E: patricksenior24@gmail.com

✠**SENTAMU, The Most Revd and Rt Hon John Tucker Mugabi.** b 49. Makerere Univ Kampala LLB 71 Selw Coll Cam BA 76 MA MPhil 79 PhD 84. Ridley Hall Cam. **d** 79 **p** 79 **c** 96. Chapl HM Rem Cen Latchmere Ho 79–82; C Ham St Andr *S'wark* 79–82; C Herne Hill St Paul 82–83; P-in-c Tulse Hill H Trin 83–84; V Upper Tulse Hill St Matthias 83–84; V Tulse Hill H Trin and St Matthias 85–96; P-in-c Brixton Hill St Sav 87–89; Hon Can S'wark Cathl 93–96; Area Bp Stepney *Lon* 96–02; Bp Birm 02–05; Abp York from 05. *Bishopthorpe Palace, Bishopthorpe, York YO23 2GE* T: (01904) 707021 F: 772389 E: office@archbishopofyork.org

SENTAMU BAVERSTOCK, Mrs Grace Kathleen Nabanja. b 75. Nottm Univ BA 96 Selw Coll Cam BTh 10. Ridley Hall Cam 06. **d** 10 **p** 11. C Watford St Luke *St Alb* 10–14; V Leagrave from 14. *St Luke's Vicarage, High Street, Luton LU4 9JY* T: (01582) 592361 E: gracesenba@gmail.com

SEPHTON, Mrs Jacqueline Ann Driscoll. b 46. RGN 67. **d** 10 **p** 11. OLM Stoke by Nayland w Leavenheath and

Polstead *St E* 10–13; NSM 13–16; rtd 16. *12 Highlands Road, Hadleigh, Ipswich IP7 5HU* T: (01473) 810072 E: jackie.sephton@tiscali.co.uk

SEPHTON, John. b 43. **d** 01 **p** 02. OLM Newburgh w Westhead *Liv* from 01; Asst Chapl HM Pris Risley 02–09. *37 Brighouse Close, Ormskirk L39 3NA* T: (01695) 576774 E: johnsephton@postmaster.co.uk

SEPPALA, Christopher James. b 59. St Jo Coll Dur BA 82 Ch Ch Coll Cant CertEd 92. Chich Th Coll 83. **d** 85 **p** 86. C Whitstable *Cant* 85–88; C S Ashford Ch Ch 88–91; PtO 01–16. *2 The Briars, Long Reach Close, Whitstable CT5 4QF* T: (01227) 282622 E: xpristopheros@netscapeonline.co.uk

SERBUTT, Rita Eileen. b 33. Man Univ BA 54 Univ of Wales (Cardiff) DipEd 56 FRSA 94. **d** 01 **p** 02. OLM Balham St Mary and St Jo *S'wark* 01–03; rtd 03; PtO *S'wark* from 03. *56 Manville Road, London SW17 8JL* T: (020) 8767 8383 E: eileen.serbutt@btinternet.com

SERGENT, Jean-Luc James. b 78. Paris Univ MSc 02. St Mellitus Coll BA 15. **d** 15 **p** 18. C The Hague *Eur* 15–17; C Kensington St Barn *Lon* from 17. *17 Devonport Road, London W12 8NZ* M: 07528-731953 E: jeanluc.sergent@gmail.com

SERJEANT, Frederick James. b 28. Lon Inst of Educn BEd 73. AKC 53 St Boniface Warminster 53. **d** 54 **p** 55. C Leytonstone St Marg w St Columba *Chelmsf* 54–58; C Parkstone St Pet w Branksea *Sarum* 58–59; V Reigate St Luke S Park *S'wark* 59–65; V Battersea St Pet 65–71; C-in-c Battersea St Paul 67–71; V W Mersea *Chelmsf* 71–73; P-in-c E Mersea 71–73; R W w E Mersea 73–75; rtd 93. *9 Howard Close, Bothenhampton, Bridport DT6 4SR* T: (01308) 424510 E: f.serjeant@gmail.com

SERJEANT, Heather Faith. *See* SMITH, Heather Faith

SERMON, Michael John. b 61. Univ of Cen England in Birm ACIB 85. Qu Coll Birm BA 98 MA 99. **d** 99 **p** 00. C W Heath *Birm* 99–03; V Blackheath from 03; P-in-c Rounds Green from 11. *St Paul's Vicarage, 83 Vicarage Road, Halesowen B62 8HX* T: 0121-559 1000 E: mike@mikesermon.co.uk

SERVANT, Canon Alma Joan. b 51. Nottm Univ BA 76. Westcott Ho Cam 83. **dss** 85 **d** 87 **p** 94. Ordsall *S'well* 85–88; Par Dn 87–88; Par Dn Man Whitworth 88–94; TV 94–96; Chapl Man Poly 88–92; Chapl Man Metrop Univ 92–96; P-in-c Heaton Norris St Thos 96–00; P-in-c Hulme Ascension 00–05; R 05–14; C Man Cathl 14–15; C Man St Ann 14–15; Hon Can Man Cathl 02–15; rtd 15; PtO *Man* from 15. *10 Stoneyfield Close, Manchester M16 8GT*

SESSFORD, Canon Alan. b 34. Bps' Coll Cheshunt 65. **d** 66 **p** 67. C Highcliffe w Hinton Admiral *Win* 66–69; C Minehead *B & W* 70; C Chandler's Ford *Win* 70–73; V Burton and Sopley 73–00; RD Christchurch 93–98; Hon Can Win Cathl 98–00; rtd 00; PtO *Win* from 00; Chapl R Bournemouth and Christchurch Hosps NHS Foundn Trust from 01. *4 Benson Close, Bransgore, Christchurch BH23 8HX* T: (01425) 673412

SETTERFIELD, Canon Nicholas Manley. b 63. Colchester Inst of Educn BA 89. St Steph Ho Ox 89. **d** 92 **p** 93. C Prestbury *Glouc* 92–96; R Letchworth St Alb 96–03; V Northampton St Matt *Pet* from 03; Can Pet Cathl from 17. *St Matthew's Vicarage, 30 East Park Parade, Northampton NN1 4LB* T: (01604) 604412 E: vicar@stmatthews-northampton.org.uk

SETTIMBA, John Henry. b 52. Nairobi Univ BSc 78 Leeds Univ MA 91. Pan Africa Chr Coll BA 78. **d** 78 **p** 80. Kenya 78–81; Uganda 81–85; C Allerton *Bradf* 86–87; C W Ham *Chelmsf* 87–91; C-in-c Forest Gate All SS 91–94; P-in-c 94–96; TV Hackney *Lon* 96–02; rtd 07. *63 Belvedere Court, Upper Richmond Road, London SW15 6HZ* T: (020) 3722 0279 E: henrysettimba@outlook.com

SEVILLE, Thomas Christopher Mann. b 57. Trin Hall Cam MA 80. Coll of Resurr Mirfield 87. **d** 89 **p** 90. C Knowle *Bris* 89–93; CR from 93. *House of the Resurrection, Stocks Bank Road, Mirfield WF14 0BN* T: (01924) 483315 E: tseville@mirfield.org.uk

SEWARD, Jolyon Frantom. b 57. Univ of Wales (Cardiff) BA 81. Chich Th Coll 83. **d** 86 **p** 87. C Llanblethian w Cowbridge and Llandough etc *Llan* 86–88; C Newton Nottage 88–93; Dioc Children's Officer 88–98; V Penyfai w Tondu 93–01; TV Heavitree and St Mary Steps *Ex* from 01. *St Lawrence's Vicarage, 36 Lower Hill Barton Road, Exeter EX1 3EH* T: (01392) 466302 *or* 677152 E: frjolyon@heavitreeteam.org.uk *or* frjolyon@blueyonder.co.uk

SEWARD, Nicholas. b 70. Imp Coll Lon BEng 91 St Jo Coll Dur BA 96 MA 98. Cranmer Hall Dur 94. **d** 98 **p** 99. C Bearsted w Thurnham *Cant* 98–02; Chapl and Hd RS Magd Coll Sch Ox 02–08; Hd Kingham Hill Sch from 08. *Kingham Hill School, Kingham, Chipping Norton OX7 6TH* T: (01608) 658999 E: n.seward@kingham-hill.oxon.sch.uk

SEWELL, Andrew. *See* SEWELL, John Andrew Clarkson

SEWELL, Canon Andrew William. b 61. Nottm Univ BSc 83. St Jo Coll Nottm 93. **d** 93 **p** 94. C Adel *Ripon* 93–96; C Far

---

Headingley St Chad 96–98; Asst Dioc Missr 96–98; P-in-c Otham w Langley *Cant* 98–01; R 01–10; P-in-c Maidstone St Paul from 10; AD Maidstone from 10; Hon Can Cant Cathl from 11. *St Paul's Vicarage, 130 Boxley Road, Maidstone ME14 2AH* T: (01622) 691926 E: andrew@asewell.plus.com

SEWELL, Canon Elizabeth Jill. b 56. Reading Univ BSc 77. Trin Coll Bris BA 97. **d** 97 **p** 98. C Rothley *Leic* 97–01; TV Market Harborough and The Transfiguration etc 01–07; RD Gartree I 06–07; TR Knaresborough *Ripon* 07–13; P-in-c Nidd 11–13; Can Res Ripon Cathl 13–16; rtd 16. *1 The Green, Bewerley, Harrogate HG3 5HU* E: ejsewell13@gmail.com

SEWELL, Jacqueline. b 57. Auckland Univ BMus 80 LTh 85 K Coll Lon MA 00 PhD 15. St Jo Coll Auckland. **d** 84 **p** 85. C Warkworth New Zealand 84–85; P-in-c 85–86; TV Glenfield 87–91; Dioc Youth Facilitator 92–03; Dir Amaze Cen 02–05; Dir Field Educn St Jo Coll Auckland 05–12; Tutor Cuddesdon: Glouc and Heref from 15; Dioc Dir Reader Tr *Heref* from 15. *Diocesan Office, The Palace, Hereford HR4 9BL* T: (01432) 373300 E: jacky.sewell@rcc.ac.uk

SEWELL, John Andrew Clarkson. b 58. Aston Tr Scheme 93 Ripon Coll Cuddesdon 95. **d** 97 **p** 98. C Horsham *Chich* 97–99; C Cleobury Mortimer w Hopton Wafers etc *Heref* 99–01; R 01–03; TV Ludlow, Ludford, Ashford Carbonell etc 03–04; Chapl Shropshire's Community NHS Trust 03–04; Lead Chapl ChAT (Weston-super-Mare Chapl About Town) *B & W* 05–10; Hon C Weston super Mare St Jo 06–07; P-in-c Westbury sub Mendip w Easton 07–09; Retail Chapl Bris City Cen 10–17; Min Can Bris Cathl 15–17; R Redmarley D'Abitot, Bromesberrow, Pauntley etc *Glouc* 17–18. *The Rectory, Redmarley, Gloucester GL19 3HS* E: rectorandy@icloud.com

SEWELL, Canon Richard Michael. b 62. Birm Univ BA 84. SEITE 99. **d** 02 **p** 03. C Putney St Mary *S'wark* 02–05; TV Wimbledon 05–10; TR Barnes 10–18; Dir IME Kingston Area 12–18; Dean St Geo Coll Jerusalem from 18; Hon Can S'wark Cathl from 19. *St George's College, PO Box 1248, Jerusalem 91000, via Israel* T: (00972) (2) 626 4704 M: 07714-265864 E: richardsewell4@virginmedia.com

SEWELL, Miss Sarah Frances. b 61. Wycliffe Hall Ox 87. **d** 91 **p** 94. C Binley *Cov* 91–94; Asst Chapl Derriford Hosp Plymouth 94–96; Chapl Stoke Mandeville Hosp NHS Trust 96–00; Chapl R Marsden NHS Foundn Trust 00–05; Chapl Team Ldr Epsom and St Helier Univ Hosps NHS Trust 05–07; Sen Co-ord Chapl 07–13; Lead Chapl 13–18; C Sutton *S'wark* 14–18; Lead Chapl Ox Univ Hosps NHS Foundn Trust from 18. *Chaplaincy Office, John Radcliffe Hospital, Headley Way, Headington, Oxford OX3 9DU* T: (01865) 857921 M: 07552-262974

SEXTON, Canon Michael Bowers. b 28. SS Coll Cam BA 52 MA 56. Wells Th Coll 52. **d** 54 **p** 55. C Miles Platting St Luke *Man* 54–57; C Bradford cum Beswick 57–58; C-in-c Oldham St Chad Limeside CD 58–62; R Filby w Thrigby w Mautby *Nor* 62–72; P-in-c Runham 67–72; P-in-c Stokesby w Herringby 68–72; R Hethersett w Canteloff 72–85; V Ketteringham 73–84; RD Humbleyard 81–86; Hon Can Nor Cathl 85–93; R Hethersett w Canteloff w Lt and Gt Melton 85–86; V Hunstanton St Mary w Ringstead Parva, Holme etc 86–93; rtd 94; PtO *Nor* from 94. *3 Forge Close, Poringland, Norwich NR14 7SZ* T: (01508) 493885

SEYMOUR, Canon David Raymond Russell. b 56. Keble Coll Ox BA 79 MA 88. St Steph Ho Ox 79. **d** 81 **p** 82. C Tilehurst St Mich *Ox* 81–85; TV Parkstone St Pet w Branksea and St Osmund *Sarum* 85–91; V Bradford-on-Avon Ch Ch 91–01; P-in-c Sturminster Newton and Hinton St Mary 01–02; V Sturminster Newton, Hinton St Mary and Lydlinch 02–18; C Hazelbury Bryan and the Hillside Par 08–18; C Okeford 08–18; P-in-c Marnhull 15–18; RD Blackmore Vale 08–16; Can and Preb Sarum Cathl 13–18; P-in-c Blisland w Temple, St Breward and Helland *Truro* 18–19; P-in-c St Tudy w St Mabyn and Michaelstow 18–19; R Camelside from 19. *The Rectory, Glebe Parc, St Tudy, Bodmin PL30 3AS* T: (01208) 850088 E: drrseymour@hotmail.co.uk

SEYMOUR, John. b 73. Bris Univ BSc 95 MB, ChB 98 Heythrop Coll Lon MA 03 Trin Coll Cam BA 05. Westcott Ho Cam 03. **d** 06 **p** 07. C Poplar *Lon* 06–09; Chapl Twyford C of E High Sch Acton 09–17; Tutor St Aug Coll of Th from 17; PtO *Lon* from 17; Public Preacher *S'wark* from 17. *Trinity House, 4 Chapel Court, London SE1 1HW* T: (020) 7939 9400 E: j.seymour@staugustinescollege.co.uk

SEYMOUR, John Anthony. b 46. SWMTC. **d** 08 **p** 09. NSM Carbis Bay w Lelant *Truro* 08–11; P-in-c 11–13; rtd 13; PtO *Truro* from 16. *5 Station Hill, Lelant, St Ives TR26 3DJ* T: (01736) 449794 E: tonyseymour@talktalk.net

SEYMOUR, Canon John Charles. b 30. Oak Hill Th Coll 51 and 55 Wycliffe Coll Toronto 54. **d** 57 **p** 58. C Islington St Andr w St Thos and St Matthias *Lon* 57–60; C Worthing St Geo *Chich* 60–63; V Thornton *Leic* 63–70; R Kirby

Muxloe 70–81; TR 81–83; RD Sparkenhoe I 83–88; R Market Bosworth w Shenton 83–87; TR Market Bosworth, Cadeby w Sutton Cheney etc 87–93; RD Sparkenhoe W 89–92; Hon Can Leic Cathl 82–93; rtd 93; PtO *Leic* 15–18. *56 Wyggeston Hospital, Hinkley Road, Leicester LE3 0UX* T: 0116-254 8295 E: jams56@btinternet.com

SEYMOUR, Paul Edward. b 62. Humberside Univ BA 92. St Jo Coll Nottm 01. **d** 03 **p** 04. C Ingleby Barwick *York* 03–07; C Hatfield Hyde *St Alb* 07–10; P-in-c Stevenage All SS Pin Green 10–13; V 13–16; TV Bp's Hatfield, Lemsford and N Mymms from 16. *9 Great Braitch Lane, Hatfield AL10 9FD* T: (01707) 21966 M: 07809-839773 E: revpaulseymour@icloud.com *or* revpaulseymour@gmail.com

SEYMOUR-JONES, Michael D'Israeli. b 37. **d** 09. OLM Shiplake w Dunsden and Harpsden *Ox* 09–12; PtO from 13. *6 Heathfield Close, Binfield Heath, Henley-on-Thames RG9 4DS* T: 0118-947 8632 E: m.seymour_jones@btinternet.com

SEYMOUR-WHITELEY, Ms Alison. b 51. City of Lon Poly MA 90 Homerton Coll Cam PGCE 95. CITC 04. **d** 07 **p** 08. LtO *Clogh* 07–11; Chapl HM Pris Morton Hall 11–12; Chapl Notts Healthcare NHS Foundn Trust 12–15; P-in-c Templemore w Thurles and Kilfithmone *C & O* from 15. *The Rectory, The Square, Rathdowney, Co Laois, Republic of Ireland* M: (00353) 85-141 3354 E: alisonsw@hotmail.co.uk

SHACKELL, Daniel William. b 42. **d** 95 **p** 96. Dir Spires Cen S'wark 93–06; OLM Streatham St Leon *S'wark* 95–99; LtO 99–06; rtd 07; PtO *Guildf* 01–09; *Sarum* from 09. *Wynways, 146 West Bay Road, Bridport DT6 4AZ* T: (01308) 426514 M: 07818-808249 E: danshackell@gmail.com

SHACKERLEY, The Very Revd Albert Paul. b 56. K Coll Lon MA 97 Sheff Univ PhD 07. Chich Th Coll 91. **d** 93 **p** 94. C Harlesden All So *Lon* 93–96; P-in-c Chelmsf All SS 96–98; V 98–02; Can Res Sheff Cathl 02–09; Vice Dean 05–09; V Doncaster St Geo 10–14; Hon Can Sheff Cathl 10–14; Dean Brecon *S & B* from 14. *The Cathedral Office, Cathedral Close, Brecon LD3 9DP* T: (01874) 623857　　　　E: paul_shackerley@btinternet.com　　　*or* dean@breconcathedral.org.uk

SHACKLADY, Mrs Thelma. b 38. Liv Univ BA 60. St Alb Minl Tr Scheme 89. **d** 92 **p** 94. NSM Luton St Andr *St Alb* 92–96; NSM Luton All SS w St Pet 96–03; PtO from 03; *Ox* from 06. *45 Lilly Hill, Olney MK46 5EZ* T: (01234) 712997 E: thelma.shacklady@gmail.com

SHACKLETON, Canon Alan. b 31. Sheff Univ BA 53. Wells Th Coll 54. **d** 56 **p** 57. C Ladybarn *Man* 56–58; C Bolton St Pet 58–61; V Middleton Junction 61–70; V Heywood St Luke 70–84; AD Rochdale 82–92; Hon Can Man Cathl 84–97; V Heywood St Luke w All So 85–86; TV Rochdale 86–91; TR 91–97; rtd 97; PtO *Man* 97–17. *28 Taunton Avenue, Rochdale OL11 5LD* T: (01706) 645335

SHAFTO, Robert James. b 38. Univ of Wales (Ban) BTh 06 Heythrop Coll Lon MA 10 FCA 61. OLM course 96. **d** 99 **p** 00. NSM W Dulwich All SS *S'wark* 99–07; rtd 07; PtO *S'wark* from 08. *46 Cedar Close, London SE21 8HX* T: (020) 8761 7395 E: bob.shafto46@gmail.com

SHAKESHAFT, Mrs Petra Jayne. b 60. Anglia Ruskin Univ BA 97 Cam Univ BTh 14. Westcott Ho Cam 12. **d** 14 **p** 15. C Cherry Hinton St Jo *Ely* 14–17; P-in-c Duxford from 17; P-in-c Hinxton from 17; P-in-c Ickleton from 17; P-in-c Pampisford from 17; P-in-c Whittlesford from 17. *The Rectory, 13 St John's Street, Duxford, Cambridge CB22 4RA* T: (01223) 510387 M: 07847-307416 E: petra_paul.shakeshaft@ntlworld.com

SHAKESPEARE, James Douglas Geoffrey. b 71. Fitzw Coll Cam BA 93 MA 97 Man Univ MA 96. Westcott Ho Cam 97. **d** 99 **p** 00. C Cherry Hinton St Jo *Ely* 99–02; Bp's Chapl and Policy Adv *Leic* 02–05; P-in-c Birstall and Wanlip 05–09; V 09–10; NSM Market Harborough and The Transfiguration etc 10–11; TV 11–17; P-in-c Cherry Hinton St Jo *Ely* from 17. *St John's Vicarage, 9 Luard Road, Cambridge CB2 8PJ* E: jshakespeare@btinternet.com

SHAKESPEARE, Steven. b 68. CCC Cam BA 89 PhD 94. Westcott Ho Cam 93. **d** 96 **p** 97. C Cambridge St Jas *Ely* 96–99; V Endcliffe and Chapl Sheff Hallam Univ 99–03; Chapl Liv Hope Univ from 03; PtO *Liv* from 16. *Anglican Chaplaincy, Hope Park, Taggart Avenue, Liverpool L16 9JD* T: 0151-291 3545 E: shakess@hope.ac.uk

SHALLOE, Jacqueline. b 61. St Mellitus Coll 15. **d** 18 **p** 19. NSM Hillingdon St Jo *Lon* from 18. *22 Canfield Drive, Ruislip HA4 6QW* M: 07546-275304

SHAND, Brian Martin. b 53. Univ Coll Lon BA 76 PhD 82. St Steph Ho Ox 85. **d** 87 **p** 88. C Uxbridge St Marg *Lon* 87–88; C Uxbridge 88–90; C Worplesdon *Guildf* 90–94; Relig Affairs Producer BBC Radio Surrey 90–94; V Weston *Guildf* 94–01; V Witley 01–14; rtd 14; PtO *Guildf* from 17. *Tan Cottage, Garden Close, Shamley Green, Guildford GU5 0UW* T: (01483) 894066

SHANKS, Canon Robert Andrew Gulval. b 54. Ball Coll Ox BA 75 G&C Coll Cam BA 79 Leeds Univ PhD 90. Westcott Ho Cam 77. **d** 80 **p** 81. C Potternewton *Ripon* 80–83; C Stanningley St Thos 84–87; Lect Leeds Univ 87–91; Teaching Fell Lanc Univ *Blackb* 91–95; Research Fell in Th Cheltenham and Glouc Coll of HE 95–96; NSM Leeds City *Ripon* 95–96; P-in-c Upper Ryedale and CME Officer Cleveland Adnry *York* 97–04; Can Res Man Cathl 04–14; rtd 14; PtO *York* from 14; *Eur* from 16. *39 Derwent Mews, York YO10 3DN* T: (01904) 500253 E: shanks.york@gmail.com

SHANNON, Alexander David John. b 86. Ch Coll Cam BA 07 MMath 08 PhD 13 Peterho Cam MPhil 16. Westcott Ho Cam 2013. **d** 16 **p** 17. C St Ives *Ely* from 16. *4 Adams Drive, St Ives PE27 6TD* M: 07745-347354 E: adj.shannon@gmail.com

SHANNON, Helen Louise. b 68. NTMTC 07. **d** 10 **p** 12. C Woodside Park St Barn *Lon* from 10. *24 Stable Walk, London N2 9RD* T: (020) 8883 7450 M: 07866-507609 E: helenshannon@stbarnabas.co.uk

SHANNON, Canon Trevor Haslam. b 33. Selw Coll Cam BA 57 MA 61 Lon Univ BD 69. Westcott Ho Cam 57. **d** 59 **p** 60. C Moss Side Ch Ch *Man* 59–62; V Woolfold 62–66; Chapl Forest Sch Snaresbrook 66–80 and 87–88; V Gt Ilford St Marg *Chelmsf* 88–90; TR Gt Ilford St Clem and St Marg 90–96; V 96–99; RD Redbridge 90–95; Hon Can Chelmsf Cathl 93–99; rtd 99; PtO *Nor* from 00. *Honeysuckle Cottage, Clubbs Lane, Wells-next-the-Sea NR23 1DP* T: (01328) 711409 E: tshannon409@btinternet.com

SHARKEY, Philip Michael. b 50. York Univ BA 73 MA 08 CQSW 78. ERMC 06. **d** 08 **p** 09. NSM Shingay Gp *Ely* 08–13; NSM Duxford from 13; NSM Hinxton from 13; NSM Ickleton from 13; Chapl Cam Univ Hosps NHS Foundn Trust from 19. *23 Cherry Drive, Royston SG8 7DL* T: (01763) 221284 M: 07917-619124 E: sharkey_phil@yahoo.co.uk

SHARLAND, Canon Marilyn. b 40. City of Birm Coll CertEd 61. Oak Hill Th Coll 84. **dss** 86 **d** 87 **p** 94. Barkingside St Laur *Chelmsf* 86–88; Hon Par Dn Hucclecote *Glouc* 88–89; C Coney Hill 89–98; P-in-c Tuffley 98–99; V 99–06; Hon Can Glouc Cathl 02–06; rtd 06. *51 Lynmouth Road, Hucclecote, Gloucester GL3 3JD* E: canon.marilyn@blueyonder.co.uk

SHARP, Alexander Mark. b 87. Univ Coll Falmouth BA 08. Oak Hill Th Coll BA 17. **d** 18 **p** 19. C St Illogan *Truro* from 18. *14 Glenfeadon Terrace, Portreath, Redruth TR16 4JX* M: 07717-748353 E: alexsharp353@gmail.com

SHARP, Alfred James Frederick. b 30. Oak Hill Th Coll 62. **d** 64 **p** 65. C Hanley Road St Sav w St Paul *Lon* 64–68; P-in-c Leverton *Linc* 68–84; Chapl Pilgrim Hosp Boston 76–84; P-in-c Benington w Leverton *Linc* 84; V Ch Broughton w Boylestone amd Sutton on the Hill *Derby* 84–89; R Ch Broughton w Barton Blount, Boylestone etc 89–94; rtd 94. *14 Edgefield, Weston, Spalding PE12 6RQ* T: (01406) 370376

SHARP, Mrs Barbara Elaine. b 52. Open Univ BA 84. Ripon Coll Cuddesdon 01. **d** 03 **p** 04. C Timperley *Ches* 03–06; P-in-c Lostock Gralam 06–11; V Sale St Paul from 11. *St Paul's Vicarage, 28 Kilvert Drive, Sale M33 6PN* T: 0161-973 1042 E: revbarb@hotmail.co.uk

SHARP, Brian Phillip. b 48. Cant Sch of Min 85. **d** 88 **p** 89. C S Ashford Ch Ch *Cant* 88–92; C St Laur in Thanet 92–96; V Margate St Jo 96–13; P-in-c Margate All SS 09–13; rtd 13; PtO *Cant* from 14. *32 The Hawthorns, Broadstairs CT10 2NG* T: (01843) 579871 E: brianthevic@yahoo.co.uk

SHARP, Canon David Malcolm. b 33. Hertf Coll Ox BA 56 MA 59. Cuddesdon Coll 56. **d** 58 **p** 59. C Bris St Mary Redcliffe w Temple 58–65; V Henleaze 65–75; V Nor St Pet Mancroft 75–82; R Nor St Pet Mancroft w St Jo Maddermarket 82–98; Hon Can Nor Cathl 86–98; Dioc Eur Contact 91–09; rtd 98; PtO *Nor* from 98. *The Pines, Field Lane, Fakenham NR21 9QX* T: (01328) 864121 E: dmsharp22@btinternet.com

SHARP, Mrs Hazel Patricia. b 39. Qu Eliz Coll Lon BSc 61. SWMTC 05. **d** 06 **p** 07. NSM St Merryn and St Issey w St Petroc Minor *Truro* 06–09; rtd 09; PtO *B & W* 10–11; Chapl Somerset Partnership NHS Foundn Trust 11–14; PtO *B & W* from 14. *22 Bekynton Avenue, Wells BA5 3NF* T: (01749) 674397 M: 07751-258558 E: hh.psharp@btinternet.com

SHARP (née BROWN), Mrs Jane Madeline. b 54. **d** 97 **p** 98. C Aylestone St Andr w St Jas *Leic* 97–00; NSM Knighton St Mary Magd 00–08; NSM Leic St Jas from 08; Chapl Leic Coll of FE from 14. *10 St Mary's Road, Leicester LE2 1XA* T: 0116-270 6002 E: a.sharp53@ntlworld.com

SHARP, Mrs Janice Anne. b 54. Aston Tr Scheme 91 NOC 93. **d** 96 **p** 97. C Skipton H Trin *Bradf* 96–00; V Buttershaw St Paul 00–02; Chapl Hull and E Yorks Hosps NHS Trust 02–17; Hon C Patrington w Hollym, Welwick and Winestead *York* 07–14; Hon C Easington w Skeffling, Keyingham, Ottringham etc from 14. *3 Ringrose Cottages, Northside*

Road, Hollym, Withernsea HU19 2RS T: (01964) 612548 E: jas5000.js@googlemail.com

SHARP, Nicholas Leonard. b 64. Grey Coll Dur BA 85. St Jo Coll Nottm MA 95. **d** 95 **p** 96. C Oakwood St Thos *Lon* 95–99; TV N Farnborough *Guildf* 99–05; Chapl Farnborough Sixth Form Coll 01–05; P-in-c Lt Amwell *St Alb* 05–08; TV Hertford 08–18; V Rye Park St Cuth from 18. *The Vicarage, 8 Ogard Road, Hoddesdon EN11 0NU* E: nicthevic@gmail.com

SHARP, Philip Paul Clayton. b 66. Open Univ BSc 97. Trin Coll Bris 04. **d** 06 **p** 07. C Liskeard and St Keyne *Truro* 06–11; P-in-c St Martin w Looe 11–17; C Duloe, Herodsfoot, Morval and St Pinnock 11–17; R Looe and Morval from 17; RD W Wivelshire 13–18. *The Rectory, St Martin, Looe PL13 1NX* T: (01503) 263070 E: ppsharp@tiscali.co.uk

SHARP, Miss Sarah Elizabeth. b 67. Bp Otter Coll Chich BA 89 Anglia Poly Univ MA 00 K Coll Lon MA 11 Coll of Ripon & York St Jo PGCE 90. Westcott Ho Cam 98. **d** 00 **p** 01. C Ross *Heref* 00–03; R Lower Windrush *Ox* 03–13; V Bodicote from 13; AD Deddington from 19. *2 The Rydes, Bodicote, Banbury OX15 4EJ* T: (01295) 250282 E: ss50sharp@btinternet.com

SHARP, Thomas Matthew. b 91. St Cath Coll Cam BA 12 MA 16 St Jo Coll Dur BA 16. Cranmer Hall Dur 14. **d** 17 **p** 18. C Chapel House *Newc* 17–18; C Newc Cathl from 18. *2 Church House, Hugh Street, Wallsend NE28 6RL* M: 07769-737314 E: fr.tomsharp@gmail.com

SHARP, Trevor Andrew. b 63. Westcott Ho Cam. **d** 14 **p** 15. C St Mary-at-Latton *Chelmsf* 14–17; V Norton *St Alb* from 17. *The Vicarage, 17 Norton Way North, Letchworth Garden City SG6 1BY* M: 07970-284332 E: trevorann@hotmail.co.uk *or* revtrev08@gmail.com

SHARPE, Anthony Mark. b 67. Leeds Univ BA 01. Coll of Resurr Mirfield 99. **d** 01 **p** 02. C Acomb Moor *York* 01–02; C Norton juxta Malton 02–03; C W Buckrose 03–04; Chapl RN 04–05; R Teme Valley S *Worc* 05–09; rtd 09. *Old Rectory, Ceodana, Lannerch-y-Medd LL71 8EW* E: am67sharpe@aol.com

SHARPE, Canon Bruce Warrington. b 41. Ely Th Coll 62 St Steph Ho Ox 64. **d** 65 **p** 66. C Streatham St Pet *S'wark* 65–67; C Castries St Lucia 67–68; Hon C Leic St Matt and St Geo 68–69; Hon C Catford St Laur *S'wark* 69–70; Hon C Deptford St Paul 70–75; Hon C Lamorbey H Redeemer *Roch* 76–83; Hon C Sidcup St Andr 88–99; Locum Chapl Morden Coll Blackheath 98–08; PtO *Roch* 83–88; *Lon* 97–06; *Ex* from 09; *S'wark* 98–10 and from 17; *Roch* 99–01; Hon C Bickley 01–11; Hon Can Windward Is from 01. *Walnut Cottage, Upper Braddons Hill Road, Torquay TQ1 1QE* E: canonbruce1@aol.com

SHARPE, David Francis. b 32. Ex Coll Ox BA 56 MA 59. St Steph Ho Ox 57. **d** 60 **p** 61. C Hunslet St Mary and Stourton *Ripon* 60–63; C Notting Hill St Jo *Lon* 63–68; V Haggerston St Mary w St Chad 68–78; P-in-c Haggerston St Aug w St Steph 73–78; V Haggerston St Chad 78–83; V Mill Hill St Mich 83–98; rtd 98; Chapl St Raphaël *Eur* 98–02; PtO *Lon* 02–13; *S'wark* from 11. *10 Up, The Quadrangle, Morden College, London SE3 0PW* T: (020) 8853 5104 E: davidsharpe32@waitrose.com

SHARPE, Derek Martin Brereton (Pip). b 29. Birkbeck Coll Lon BA 60. NEOC 90. **d** 90 **p** 91. NSM Scarborough St Luke *York* 90–92; Asst Chapl Scarborough Distr Hosp 90–92; P-in-c Sherburn and W and E Heslerton w Yedingham *York* 92–99; Hon C Buckrose Carrs 99; rtd 99; PtO *York* from 00. *Room 6, The Abbey Residential Home, Town Street, Old Malton, Malton YO17 7HB* T: (01663) 692256

SHARPE, Mrs Jennifer Louise. b 74. St Jo Coll Nottm BA 15. **d** 15 **p** 16. C Mansfield St Jo w St Mary *S'well* 15–16; C Warsop 16–19; P-in-c Stockton Christchurch *Dur* from 19. *243 Darlington Lane, Stockton-on-Tees TS19 8AA* E: jenniesharpe2305@gmail.com *or* revdjenniesharpe@gmail.com

SHARPE, Miss Joan Valerie. b 33. EMMTC 73. **dss** 84 **d** 88 **p** 94. Hon Par Dn Warsop *S'well* 88–94; Hon C 94–98; rtd 98; PtO *S'well* 04–18. *1 Forest Court, Eakring Road, Mansfield NG18 3DP* T: (01623) 424051

SHARPE, Canon John Edward. b 50. St Jo Coll Dur BSc 72. Cranmer Hall Dur 73. **d** 76 **p** 77. C Woodford Wells *Chelmsf* 76–79; C Ealing St Mary *Lon* 79–83; Min Walsall St Martin *Lich* 83–87; TV Walsall 87–96; R Glenfield *Leic* 96–15; AD Sparkenhoe E 03–11; Hon Can Leic Cathl 10–15; rtd 15; PtO *Glouc* from 16. *18 Bramble Chase, Bishops Cleeve, Cheltenham GL52 8WN* T: (01242) 677057 E: jesharpe1@btinternet.com

SHARPE, Lance Roland. b 68. Birm Chr Coll MA 10. Birm Bible Inst 91. **d** 16 **p** 17. NSM Morriston *S & B* 16–19; Sen Chapl Abertawe Bro Morgannwg Univ Health Bd 16–19; P-in-c Gwastedyn *S & B* from 19. *20 Nant Rhyd-Hir, Rhayader LD6 5DZ* M: 07938-762570 E: lancersharpe@gmail.com

SHARPE, Mrs Margaret Joy. b 43. Qu Coll Birm. **d** 09 **p** 10. OLM Bilton *Cov* 09–12; NSM 12–18; rtd 18; PtO *Cov* from

18. *60 Cymbeline Way, Bilton, Rugby CV22 6LA* T: (01788) 810794

SHARPE, Mrs Margaret Therèsa. b 48. Man Univ BEd 70. Cranmer Hall Dur 72 WMMTC 90. **d** 91 **p** 94. C W Bromwich H Trin *Lich* 91–96; Asst Chapl Glenfield Hosp NHS Trust Leic 96–99; Chapl 99–00; Chapl Univ Hosps Leic NHS Trust 00–04; Chapl Team Ldr 04–12; rtd 12; PtO *Leic* 13–16; *Glouc* from 16. *18 Bramble Chase, Bishops Cleeve, Cheltenham GL52 8WN* T: (01242) 677057 E: mtsharpe@btinternet.com

SHARPE, Mark. *See* SHARPE, Anthony Mark

SHARPE, Peter Richard. b 55. Salford Univ BSc 76 ACIB 81. STETS 98. **d** 01 **p** 02. C Ex St Jas 01–04; R S Hill w Callington *Truro* 04–12; C St Ive and Pensilva w Quethiock 09–12; P-in-c Linkinhorne and Stoke Climsland 10–12; RD E Wivelshire 11–12; P-in-c St Keverne 12–16; P-in-c St Ruan w St Grade and Landewednack 12–16; R St Keverne, St Ruan w St Grade and Landewednack from 16. *The Vicarage, Lemon Street, St Keverne, Helston TR12 6NG* T: (01326) 280999 E: peter@petersharpe.net

SHARPE, Pip. *See* SHARPE, Derek Martin Brereton

SHARPE, Richard Gordon. b 48. Birm Univ BA 69. St Jo Coll Nottm BA 74. **d** 75 **p** 76. C Hinckley H Trin *Leic* 75–78; C Kingston upon Hull H Trin *York* 78–85; Chapl Marston Green Hosp Birm 85–88; Chapl Chelmsley Hosp Birm 86–88; TV Chelmsley Wood *Birm* 85–88; P-in-c Dosthill 88–93; V 93–97; R Desford and Peckleton w Tooley *Leic* 97–12; rtd 12; PtO *York* from 17. *17 Elmslac Road, Helmsley, York YO62 5AW* T: (01439) 770031 E: sharpeselmslac@hotmail.com

SHARPE, Canon Roger. b 35. TCD BA 60 MA 63. Qu Coll Birm 60. **d** 62 **p** 63. C Stockton H Trin *Dur* 62–64; C Oakdale St Geo *Sarum* 64–68; V Redlynch and Morgan's Vale 68–86; RD Alderbury 82–86; V Warminster St Denys 86–88; R Upton Scudamore 86–88; V Horningsham 86–88; R Warminster St Denys, Upton Scudamore etc 88–95; Can and Preb Sarum Cathl 89–00; RD Heytesbury 89–95; Chmn Dioc Assn for Deaf 91–98; P-in-c Corsley *Sarum* 92–95; TR Cley Hill Warminster 95–00; rtd 00; PtO *Sarum* from 01. *Woodside, Bugmore Lane, East Grinstead SP5 3SA* T: (01722) 712753 E: rsharpe@macline.co.uk

SHARPE, William Wilberforce. b 62. **d** 05 **p** 06. NSM Brixton St Matt w St Jude *S'wark* 05–10; NSM Tulse Hill H Trin and St Matthias from 10; Chapl Guy's and St Thos' NHS Foundn Trust 08–18; Sen Chapl from 18. *1D Lovelace Road, London SE21 8JY* T/F: (020) 8761 8539 M: 07912-205414 E: sharpeww@aol.com *or* william.sharpe@gstt.nhs.uk

SHARPLES, Catherine Ruth. b 70. Nottm Univ BSc 92 Nottm Trent Univ PhD 96. Trin Coll Bris 11. **d** 13 **p** 14. C Stevenage St Pet Broadwater *St Alb* 13–17; V from 17. *St Peter's Vicarage, 1 The Willows, Stevenage SG2 8AN* T: (01438) 217526 M: 07505-459157 E: revkatesharples@gmail.com

SHARPLES, The Ven David John. b 58. Lon Univ BD 81 AKC 81. Coll of Resurr Mirfield. **d** 82 **p** 83. C Prestwich St Mary *Man* 82–87; V Royton St Anne 87–02; AD Tandle 94–02; Dir of Ords from 02; Adn Salford from 09; Hon Can Man Cathl from 06; Can Res Man Cathl from 17. *2 The Walled Gardens, Swinton, Manchester M27 0FR* T: 0161-794 2331 *or* 708 9366 F: 794 2411 M: 07909-231278 E: ddo@bishopscourt.manchester.anglican.org *or* archsalford@manchester.anglican.org

SHARPLES, Gregory Stephen. b 80. **d** 14 **p** 15. C S Widnes *Liv* 14–17; TV from 17. *St Mary's Vicarage, St Mary's Road, Widnes WA8 0DN* M: 07730-512603

SHARPLES, Jean. *See* ROLT, Jean

SHARPLES, Jonathan David. b 65. Lon Bible Coll BA 95. Wycliffe Hall Ox 03. **d** 05 **p** 06. C Ashton-upon-Mersey St Mary Magd *Ches* 05–09; R Astbury and Smallwood 09–14. *Address withheld by request* E: jonsharples@hotmail.com

SHAVE, Canon Norman Rossen. b 60. G&C Coll Cam BA 82 MA 95 Newc Univ MB, BS 85 MRCGP 90. Cranmer Hall Dur 98. **d** 00 **p** 01. C Preston on Tees *Dur* 00–03; C Preston-on-Tees and Longnewton 03–04; V Norton St Mary 04–12; P-in-c Stockton St Chad *and* Stockton St Chad 12–16; V from 16; P-in-c Hartlepool St Luke from 19; Hon Can Dur Cathl from 19. *The Vicarage, 34A Westbourne Road, Hartlepool TS25 5RE* T: (01429) 233609

SHAW, Alan Taylor. b 52. Sarum & Wells Th Coll 88. **d** 90 **p** 91. C Beeston *Ripon* 90–93; C Stanningley St Thos 93–96; TV Seacroft 96–98; V Ryhill *Wakef* 98–02; rtd 03; PtO *Wakef* 04–14; *Leeds* from 14. *65 Hollingthorpe Avenue, Hall Green, Wakefield WF4 3NP* T: (01924) 255210

SHAW, Alan Walter. b 41. TCD BA 63 BAI 63 Chu Coll Cam MSc 66. **d** 94 **p** 95. NSM Drumcliffe w Kilnasoolagh *L & K* 94–97; NSM Kenmare w Sneem, Waterville etc 97–09; Can Limerick Cathl 07–09; rtd 09. *22 Ceann Mara Court, Pairc na*

Gloine, Kenmare, Co Kerry, Republic of Ireland T: (00353) (64) 664 0626 M: 87-678 8700 E: shawa@eircom.net

✠SHAW, The Rt Revd Alexander <u>Martin</u>. b 44. AKC 67. **d** 68 **p** 69 **c** 04. C Glas St Oswald 68–70; C Edin Old St Paul 70–75; Chapl K Coll Cam 75–77; C St Marylebone All SS *Lon* 77–78; R Dunoon *Arg* 78–81; Succ Ex Cathl 81–83; Dioc Miss and Ecum Officer 83–89; TV Cen Ex 83–87; Can Res St E Cathl 89–04; Prec 96–04; Bp Arg 04–09; rtd 09; Hon Asst Bp Ex from 10; Can Res and Prec Ex Cathl 17–18. *11 Russell Terrace, Exeter EX4 4HX* T: (01392) 663511 M: 07801-549615 E: amartinshaw@gmail.com

SHAW, Mrs Alison Barbara. b 55. Open Univ BA 92. SWMTC 98. **d** 01 **p** 02. NSM St Breoke and Egloshayle *Truro* 01–03; C Bodmin w Lanhydrock and Lanivet 03–05; TV 05–10; TV Devonport St Boniface and St Phil *Ex* 10–14; V Devonport St Boniface 14–16; P-in-c Stoke Fleming, Blackawton and Strete 16–17; V Stoke Fleming, Blackawton, Strete and E Allington from 17. *The Rectory, Rectory Lane, Stoke Fleming, Dartmouth TQ6 0QB* T: (01803) 770868 E: alishaw2001@yahoo.co.uk

SHAW, Andrew James. b 54. York Univ MA 97 Cumbria Univ BA 10. LCTP 07. **d** 10 **p** 11. NSM Fleetwood St Dav and Fleetwood St Pet *Blackb* 10–13; NSM Waterside Par 13–15; V from 15; NSM Stalmine w Pilling 13–15; V from 15. *St John's Vicarage, Lancaster Road, Pilling, Preston PR3 6AE* T: (01253) 799895 E: pillingrev@btconnect.com

SHAW, Anne. *See* MORRIS, Anne

SHAW, Ms Anne Lesley. b 50. SRN SCM. Linc Th Coll 77. **dss** 80 **d** 87 **p** 94. Camberwell St Luke *S'wark* 80–85; Chapl Asst R Lon Hosp (Whitechapel) 85–90; Chapl Lewisham Hosp 90–94; Chapl Hither Green Hosp 90–94; Chapl Sydenham Childrens Hosp 90–94; Chapl Lewisham Hosp NHS Trust 94–10; rtd 10; PtO *S'wark* 11–13; *Cant* from 14. *54 Nutcroft Road, London SE15 1AF* T: (020) 7639 4031 E: shawpowell@hotmail.co.uk

SHAW, Anne Patricia Leslie. b 39. MB, BS 63 MRCS 63 LRCP 63. Qu Coll Birm 79. **dss** 81 **d** 87 **p** 94. Pinner *Lon* 81–84; Rickmansworth *St Alb* 84–09; NSM 87–09; rtd 09; PtO *St Alb* from 09. *37 Sandy Lodge Road, Moor Park, Rickmansworth WD3 1LP* T: (01923) 827663 E: anneshaw@doctors.org.uk

SHAW, Anthony Keeble. b 36. K Alfred's Coll Win CertEd 60 Birkbeck Coll Lon CPsychol 98. SWMTC 78. **d** 81 **p** 82. Hd Teacher Wolborough C of E Primary Sch 73–87; NSM E Teignmouth *Ex* 81–83; NSM Highweek and Teigngrace 83–87; Sub Chapl HM Pris Channings Wood 85–87; C Southbourne St Kath *Win* 87–89; Teaching 89–96; NSM Regent's Park St Mark *Lon* 93–96; P-in-c Winthorpe and Langford w Holme *S'well* 96–01; Dioc Chief Insp of Schs 96–01; rtd 01; PtO *Win* from 01. *Manlea Cottage, Centre Lane, Everton, Lymington SO41 0JP* T: (01590) 645451

SHAW, Craig Lee. b 72. Newc Univ LLB 94. Cranmer Hall Dur 12. **d** 14 **p** 15. C Penkridge *Lich* 14–17; PtO *Ches* from 18; P-in-c Essington *Lich* 19; P-in-c Shareshill 19; V Essington, Featherstone and Shareshill from 19. *21 Wolverhampton Road, Essington, Wolverhampton WV11 2BX* T: (011922) 400583 M: 07443-505615

SHAW, David George. b 40. Lon Univ BD 64 MA 03. Tyndale Hall Bris 58. **d** 65 **p** 66. C Kirkdale St Lawr *Liv* 65–68; C Bebington *Ches* 68–70; V Swadlincote *Derby* 70–75; R Eyam 75–04; rtd 04; PtO *Sarum* from 15. *9 North Fields, Sturminster Newton DT10 1FD* T: (01258) 473797 E: berdavshaw@outlook.com

SHAW, Canon David Michael. b 61. Univ Coll Dur BA 83 Bris Univ BA 97. Trin Coll Bris 11. **d** 93 **p** 94. C Wotton-under-Edge w Ozleworth and N Nibley *Glouc* 93–97; P-in-c Jersey St Clem *Win* 97–98; R from 98; Can Mombasa from 11. *The Rectory, La rue du Presbytere, St Clement, Jersey JE2 6RB* T: (01534) 851992

SHAW, David Thomas. b 45. Open Univ BA 78. WMMTC 87. **d** 90 **p** 91. C Sheldon *Birm* 90–93; R Chelmsley Wood 93–02; TR Broughton Astley and Croft w Stoney Stanton *Leic* 02–10; rtd 10; PtO *Cov* from 11. *39 Orchard Way, Stretton on Dunsmore, Rugby CV23 9HP* T: (024) 7654 2036 E: davidshaw139@btinternet.com

SHAW, Mrs Felicity Mary. b 46. UEA BSc 67 MSc 68. NOC 88. **d** 91 **p** 94. Par Dn Benchill *Man* 91–94; C 94–95; TV E Farnworth and Kearsley 95–98; TR 98–03; V Woodhall *Bradf* 03–07; rtd 07; PtO *Man* 08–17. *99 Pennine Road, Horwich, Bolton BL6 7HW* T: (01204) 696851 E: rev.fmshaw@btinternet.com

SHAW, Graham. b 44. Worc Coll Ox BA 65. Cuddesdon Coll. **d** 69 **p** 70. C Esher *Guildf* 69–73; R Winford *B & W* 73–78; Chapl Ex Coll Ox 78–85; R Farnborough *Roch* 88–95; rtd 04. *21 Ulster Court, Albany Park Road, Kingston upon Thames KT2 5SS* E: grahamshaw67@gmail.com

SHAW, Graham Lister. b 81. Fitzw Coll Cam BA 04 MA 08 Ox Brookes Univ MA 11. Wycliffe Hall Ox 05. **d** 07 **p** 08. C Camberley St Paul *Guildf* 07–11; V Ches Ch Ch from 11. *57 Black Diamond Park, Chester CH1 3ET* T: (01244) 325302 E: graham.shaw@christchurchchester.com

SHAW, Canon Grahame David. b 44. Lich Th Coll 65. **d** 68 **p** 69. C Grange St Andr *Ches* 68–73; TV E Runcorn w Halton 73–74; TV Thamesmead *S'wark* 74–79; V Newington St Paul 79–13; S'wark Adnry Ecum Officer 90–13; RD S'wark and Newington 96–02; Hon Can S'wark Cathl 99–13; rtd 13; PtO *Sarum* from 16. *2 St Peter's Close, Pimperne, Blandford Forum DT11 8UZ*

SHAW, Gregory. b 66. Chu Coll Cam MA 90 MEng 89. Ripon Coll Cuddesdon 09. **d** 12 **p** 13. NSM Yardley Hastings, Denton and Grendon etc *Pet* 12–15; NSM Earls Barton 15–17; PtO from 17. *114 Birchfield Road, Northampton NN1 4RH* T: (01604) 459954 E: gregnshaw@hotmail.com

SHAW, Mrs Irene. b 45. Gilmore Course 80 NEOC 82. **dss** 83 **d** 87 **p** 94. Elloughton and Brough w Brantingham *York* 83–86; Westborough *Guildf* 86–88; C 87–88; C Shottermill 88–91; C Lamorbey H Redeemer *Roch* 91–97; V Belvedere All SS 97–02; TV Em TM *Wakef* 02–05; rtd 05; PtO *York* from 07. *26 Brereton Close, Beverley HU17 7QE* T: (01482) 871095

SHAW, Prof Jane Alison. b 63. Ox Univ BA 85 MA 91 Harvard Div Sch MDiv 88 Univ of California Berkeley PhD 94. SAOMC 96. **d** 97 **p** 98. Fell Regent's Park Coll Ox 94–01; Dean 98–01; Hon Cathl Chapl Ch Ch Ox 00–10; Fell, Chapl and Dean of Div New Coll Ox 01–10; NSM Ox St Mary V w St Cross and St Pet 97–01; Hon Can Ch Ch 05–10; Can Th Sarum Cathl 07–10; Dean Grace Cathl San Francisco USA 10–14; Dean Relig Life and Prof RS Stanford Univ 14–18; Prin Harris Manchester Coll Ox from 18. *Harris Manchester College, Mansfield Road, Oxford OX1 3TD* T: (01865) 618082 E: jane.shaw@theology.ox.ac.uk

SHAW, Miss Jane Elizabeth. b 47. New Hall Cam BA 68 MA 72 Brunel Univ MPhil 79. NEOC 98. **d** 01 **p** 02. NSM Moor Allerton *Ripon* 01–05; Presbyter Bp Rockey Chpl Raiwind Pakistan 06–11; NSM Upper Wylye Valley *Sarum* 11–17; PtO from 17. *Manor Farm House, Corton, Warminster BA12 0SZ* T: (01985) 850141 E: shawjane2005@gmail.com

SHAW, Mrs Jane Louise Claridge. b 66. Birm Poly BA 87. WMMTC 00. **d** 03 **p** 04. C Longbridge *Birm* 03–07; V Dosthill from 07; AD Polesworth from 17. *The Vicarage, 1 Church Road, Dosthill, Tamworth B77 1LU* T: (01827) 281349 E: louiseshaw6@yahoo.co.uk

SHAW, Judy Anne. b 57. Lon Metrop Univ BA 05. Linc Sch of Th and Min 12. **d** 17 **p** 18. NSM Nettleham *Linc* from 17. *122 Hermit Street, Lincoln LN5 8EG* T: (01522) 822649 M: 07594-670408 E: judeshaw.shaw3@gmail.com

SHAW, Keith Arthur. b 51. **d** 10 **p** 11. NSM Baswich *Lich* from 10; Chapl S Staffs and Shropshire Healthcare NHS Foundn Trust from 10. *44 Chasewood, Longford Road, Cannock WS11 1RJ* E: keith.shaw@sssft.nhs.uk

SHAW, Kenneth James. b 36. St Jo Coll Nottm 85 Edin Th Coll 88. **d** 87 **p** 89. NSM Troon *Glas* 87–89; C Glas St Mary 89–90; R Lenzie 90–01; Warden of Readers 96–01; rtd 01; Hon C Glas St Mary 02–06; LtO from 08. *19 Mailerbeg Gardens, Moodiesburn, Glasgow G69 0JP* T: (01236) 873987 E: kenneth.shaw24@btinternet.com

SHAW, Louise. *See* SHAW, Jane Louise Claridge

SHAW, Malcolm. b 46. Trin Coll Bris. **d** 01 **p** 02. C Bolsover *Derby* 01–05; R Brimington 05–10; P-in-c Chelford w Lower Withington *Ches* 10–13; rtd 13; PtO *Ches* from 13. *85 Rochester Crescent, Crewe CW1 5YQ* T: (01270) 213317 M: 07713-624005 E: malcolmshaw238@btinternet.com

SHAW, Malcolm Roy. b 47. Lon Univ BA 69 CQSW 76. NEOC 03. **d** 05 **p** 06. NSM Hunmanby w Muston *York* 05–08; NSM Rufforth w Moor Monkton and Hessay 08–13; NSM Long Marston 08–13; NSM Healaugh w Wighill, Bilbrough and Askham Richard 08–13; NSM Tockwith and Bilton w Bickerton 08–13; NSM N Ainsty 13; V 13–17; rtd 17; PtO *York* from 18. *11 Privet Drive, Thorpe Willoughby, Selby YO8 9GD* T: (01757) 212360 E: revroytockwith@btinternet.com

SHAW, Canon Margaret Ann. b 58. Bp Otter Coll Chich BA 80 SS Paul & Mary Coll Cheltenham PGCE 81. EAMTC 00. **d** 03 **p** 04. C Langdon Hills *Chelmsf* 03–06; TV Basildon St Andr w H Cross 06–16; RD Basildon 10–16; TR Harwich Peninsula from 16; Hon Can Chelmsf Cathl from 15. *The Rectory, 51 Highfield Avenue, Harwich CO12 4DR* E: sh.ma@btinternet.com

SHAW, Martin. *See* SHAW, Alexander Martin

SHAW, Michael. *See* SHAW, Ralph Michael

SHAW, Neil Graham. b 61. St Jo Coll Nottm LTh 91. **d** 91 **p** 92. C Leamington Priors St Paul *Cov* 91–95; TV Bestwood *S'well* 95–99; Chapl HM YOI Thorn Cross 99–01; Chapl

HM Pris Hindley 01–07; Chapl HM Pris Liv 07–14; TV Warrington E *Liv* 14–16; TR from 16; AD Warrington from 19. *The Rectory, 33 Station Road South, Padgate, Warrington WA2 0PD* M: 07432-157443 E: rev.ngs1@gmail.com

SHAW, Neil James. b 79. Leeds Univ BA 00 K Coll Lon MA 11 Dur Univ MA 16. Westcott Ho Cam 14 Yale Div Sch 15. **d** 16 **p** 17. C Upper St Leonards St Jo *Chich* 16–17; C Chich St Paul and Westhampnett from 17. *37 Somerstown, Chichester PO19 6AL* M: 07527-447615 E: njshaw1@icloud.com

SHAW, Norman William. b 46. Open Univ BA 94. **d** 13 **p** 14. OLM Glossop *Derby* from 13. *32 Duke Street, Glossop SK13 8DU* T: (01457) 867493

SHAW, Peter William. b 89. Wycliffe Hall Ox 14. **d** 17 **p** 18. C Wollaton *S'well* 17–19; C Aspley from 19; C Bilborough and Strelley from 19. *St John's Vicarage, Graylands Road, Nottingham NG8 4FD* M: 07706-047133 E: peter@stjnotts.org

SHAW, Ralph. b 38. Man Univ MEd 70. Sarum & Wells Th Coll 78. **d** 80 **p** 81. C Consett *Dur* 80–84; P-in-c Tanfield 84–88; V 88–97; R S Shields St Aid and St Steph 97–05; rtd 05. *10 Shipley Court, Gateshead NE8 4EZ* T: 0191-420 5137

SHAW, Ralph Michael. b 45. DipAdEd. Lich Th Coll 68. **d** 70 **p** 71. C Dewsbury All SS *Wakef* 70–75; TV Redcar w Kirkleatham *York* 75–76; Dioc Youth Officer *St Alb* 76–91; Chief Exec Jo Grooms 91–08; Team Ldr Workplace Min *St Alb* 08–10; rtd 10; PtO *St Alb* from 10. *18 Wyton, Welwyn Garden City AL7 2PF* T: (01707) 321813 E: revmshaw@yahoo.co.uk

SHAW, Preb Richard Tom. b 42. AKC 69. St Aug Coll Cant 69. **d** 70 **p** 71. C Dunston St Nic *Dur* 70–73; C Maidstone All SS w St Phil and H Trin *Cant* 73–75; Chapl RN 75–79; V Barrow-on-Humber *Linc* 79–83; V Linc St Faith and St Martin w St Pet 83–91; V Clun w Bettws-y-Crwyn and Newcastle *Heref* 91–11; P-in-c Hopesay 98–02; rtd 11; RD Clun Forest *Heref* 94–05 and 08–11; Preb Heref Cathl 02–11; PtO from 12. *The Granary, Newcastle Court, Newcastle, Craven Arms SY7 8QL* E: richard@rick-shaw.co.uk

SHAW, Canon Robert William. b 46. Lon Univ BD 69. St Aug Coll Cant 69. **d** 70 **p** 71. C Hunslet St Mary and Stourton *Ripon* 70–71; C Hunslet St Mary 71–74; C Hawksworth Wood 74–76; R Stanningley St Thos 76–84; V Potternewton 84–94; V Manston 94–02; P-in-c Beeston Hill H Spirit 02–04; P-in-c Hunslet Moor St Pet and St Cuth 02–04; V Beeston Hill and Hunslet Moor 04–11; Hon Can Ripon Cathl 08–11; rtd 11; PtO *Leeds* from 17. *23 St Chad's Rise, Leeds LS6 3QE* E: bobshaw46@hotmail.co.uk

SHAW, Mrs Rosemary Alice. b 44. CertEd 65 CQSW 78 Heythrop Coll Lon MA 96 MA 04. S'wark Ord Course 87. **d** 89 **p** 94. Par Dn Walworth *S'wark* 89–92; Par Dn E Dulwich St Jo 92–95; NSM 95–96; Eileen Kerr Mental Health Fell Maudsley Hosp 95–96; Chapl King's Healthcare NHS Trust 96–01; Sen Chapl Guy's and St Thos' NHS Foundn Trust 02–07; Chapl from 13; Hon C E Dulwich St Jo *S'wark* 96–12; Hon C Peckham St Sav 12–14; PtO from 14. *19 Scutari Road, London SE22 0NN* T: (020) 8693 6325 M: 07731-693247 E: rosemary.shaw1@ntlworld.com

SHAW, Roy. See SHAW, Malcolm Roy

SHAW, Mrs Sarah. **d** 14 **p** 15. C Edin St Cuth 14–17; R Falkirk from 17. *The Rectory, 33 Carronflats Road, Grangemouth FK3 9DG* T: (01324) 482438 M: 07943-405156 E: sarah.shaw0614@yahoo.co.uk

SHAW, Stewart James. b 64. Wilson Carlile Coll 97 NTMTC BA 07. **d** 07 **p** 08. C Hounslow H Trin w St Paul and St Mary *Lon* 07–09; Chapl RAF from 09. *Chaplaincy Services (RAF), HQ Air Command, RAF High Wycombe HP14 4UE* T: (01494) 496800

SHAW, William John. Edin Coll of Art BSc 96 Bradf Univ MSc 97 Internat Chr Coll BA 10. TISEC 10. **d** 12 **p** 13. Chapl St Mary's Cathl *Edin* 12–15; P-in-c Grangemouth 15–16; R from 16; P-in-c Bo'ness 15–16; R from 16. *The Rectory, 33 Carronflats Road, Grangemouth FK3 9DG* T: (01324) 482438 M: 07749-256547 E: stmarysandstcatharines@virginmedia.com

SHAYLER-WEBB, Peter. b 57. Bath Univ BSc 81 BArch 83. Ripon Coll Cuddesdon 93. **d** 95 **p** 96. C Bedford St Paul *St Alb* 95–99; C Dorking w Ranmore *Guildf* 99–04; R Sherwood Australia from 04. *PO Box 107, Sherwood Qld 4075, Australia* T: (0061) (7) 3278 2498 *or* (7) 3379 3437 F: 3278 2048 E: psw5957@bigpond.net.au

SHEA, Martyn Paul Leathley. b 66. City Univ BSc 89. Wycliffe Hall Ox. **d** 00 **p** 01. C Ches Square St Mich w St Phil *Lon* 00–03; C Stamford St Geo w St Paul *Linc* 03–08; P-in-c Jersey St Mark *Win* 08–10; V from 10. *The Vicarage, St Mark's Road, St Helier, Jersey JE2 4LY* T: (01534) 720595 M: 07976-869467 E: vicar@stmarksjersey.com

SHEARCROFT, Sister Elizabeth Marion. b 57. SRN 76. **d** 94 **p** 95. CA from 84; NSM Margate H Trin *Cant* 94–98; Chapl Thanet Healthcare NHS Trust 94–98; Chapl E Kent Hosps

NHS Trust 99–02; C Kendal H Trin *Carl* 02–05; V Streatham Immanuel and St Andr *S'wark* 05–19; V Taunton All SS *B & W* from 19. *Address temp unknown* E: liz@thekingfishery.co.uk

SHEARD, Andrew Frank. b 60. York Univ BA 81. St Jo Coll Nottm 92. **d** 94 **p** 95. C Uxbridge *Lon* 94–96; TV 96–99; P-in-c 99–01; TR 01–18; R Warblington w Emsworth *Portsm* from 18. *The Rectory, 20 Church Path, Emsworth PO10 7DP* E: andrewf.sheard@btinternet.com

SHEARD, Cindy Heather Shirley. b 67. Open Univ BA 05. Yorks Min Course 14. **d** 16 **p** 17. NSM Birstall *Leeds* 16–17; NSM Heckmondwike (w Norristhorpe) and Liversedge from 17. *5 Ash Grove, Gomersal, Cleckheaton BD19 4SJ* T: (01274) 872615 E: cindy.sheard@hotmail.co.uk

SHEARD, Gillian Freda. See COOKE, Gillian Freda

SHEARD, Canon Michael Rowland. b 42. K Coll Lon BA Man Univ PhD. **d** 95 **p** 95. World Miss Officer Lich 86–09; TV Willenhall H Trin *Lich* 95–09; Preb Lich Cathl 99–09; rtd 09; Hon Can Kuala Lumpur from 10; PtO *Linc* 15–18. *9 Queen Street, Kirton Lindsay, Gainsborough DN21 4NS* T: (01652) 648846 M: 07711-541983 E: m.r.sheard@btinternet.com

SHEARLOCK, The Very Revd David John. b 32. FRSA 91 Birm Univ BA 55. Westcott Ho Cam 56. **d** 57 **p** 58. C Guisborough *York* 57–60; C Christchurch *Win* 60–64; V Kingsclere 64–71; V Romsey 71–82; Dioc Dir of Ords 77–82; Hon Can Win Cathl 78–82; Dean Truro 82–97; R Truro St Mary 82–97; Chapl Cornwall Fire Brigade 91–97; rtd 98; PtO *Sarum* from 98. *3 The Tanyard, Shadrack Street, Beaminster DT8 3BG* T: (01308) 863170 E: davidshearlock@gmail.com

SHEARN, Andrew William. b 43. Ex Univ BA 65. WMMTC 04. **d** 06 **p** 07. NSM Wellesbourne *Cov* 06–09; NSM Studley 10–13; NSM Spernall, Morton Bagot and Oldberrow 10–13; NSM Arden Marches from 13. *58 St Fremund Way, Leamington Spa CV31 1AB* T: (01926) 930552 E: andy_shearn@hotmail.com

SHEATH, Allan Philip. b 48. SWMTC 95. **d** 98 **p** 99. NSM Tiverton St Pet and Chevithorne w Cove *Ex* 98–03; C Honiton, Gittisham, Combe Raleigh, Monkton etc 03–04; TV 04–11; C Tiverton St Andr 12–15; PtO *B & W* from 16. *11 Fairfield, Sampford Peverell, Tiverton EX16 7DE* T: (01884) 820136 E: allan.sheath@gmail.com

SHEDD, Mrs Christine Elizabeth. b 49. City of Birm Coll CertEd 70 St Jo Coll York MA 02. NOC 02. **d** 04 **p** 05. C Thornton St Jas *Bradf* 04–07; TV Oakenshaw, Wyke and Low Moor 07–12; V Low Moor and Oakenshaw 12–13; Warden of Readers 09–13; PtO *Wakef* 14; *Leeds* from 14. *84 New Road, Huddersfield HD5 0HR* T: (01484) 511071 M: 07814-958919 E: c.shedd@btinternet.com

SHEDDEN, Canon Valerie. b 56. Ripon Coll of Educn CertEd 77. Cranmer Hall Dur 81. **dss** 84 **d** 87 **p** 94. Tudhoe Grange *Dur* 84–85; Whitworth w Spennymoor 85–91; Par Dn 87–91; Par Dn E Darlington 91–94; P-in-c Bishop Middleham 94–00; Dioc RE Adv 94–00; V Heworth St Mary 00–10; AD Gateshead 06–10; P-in-c Consett from 10; Hon Can Dur Cathl from 17. *The Vicarage, 10 Aynsley Terrace, Consett DH8 5NF* T: (01207) 500996 E: val.shedden@talk21.com

SHEEHAN, Vincent Thomas Paul. b 77. **d** 16 **p** 17. NSM Enfield St Geo *Lon* from 16. *21 Forty Hill, Enfield EN2 9HT* T: (020) 8362 1213 E: vincentsheehan@talktalk.net

SHEEHY, Jeremy Patrick. b 56. Magd Coll Ox BA 78 MA 81 New Coll Ox DPhil 90. St Steph Ho Ox 78. **d** 81 **p** 82. C Erdington St Barn *Birm* 81–83; C Small Heath St Greg 83–84; Dean Div, Fell and Chapl New Coll Ox 84–90; V Leytonstone St Marg w St Columba *Chelmsf* 90–96; P-in-c Leytonstone St Andr 93–96; Prin St Steph Ho Ox 96–06; TR Swinton and Pendlebury *Man* from 06; AD Eccles 11–13. *St Peter's Rectory, Vicarage Road, Swinton, Manchester M27 0WA* T: 0161-794 1578

SHEEN, David Kenneth. b 70. Cov Univ BSc 95 Univ of Wales (Cardiff) BA 04 MA 08. St Mich Coll Llan 01. **d** 04 **p** 05. C Cowbridge *Llan* 04–07; C Penarth and Llandough 07–10; P-in-c Pwllgwaun and Llanddewi Rhondda 10–14; Warden of Readers 10–14; Chapl Cardiff Univ from 14. *The Anglican Chaplaincy, 61 Park Place, Cardiff CF10 3AT* T: (029) 2023 2550 E: sheend2@cardiff.ac.uk *or* dks101@mac.com

SHEFFIELD, Julia. b 55. MCSP 78 SRP 78. NTMTC BA 05. **d** 05 **p** 06. NSM Yiewsley *Lon* 05–09; Chapl Mid-Essex Hosp Services NHS Trust 09–12; Lead Chapl 12–18; rtd 18; PtO *Chelmsf* from 18. *Latton Vicarage, The Gowers, Harlow CM20 2JP* T: (01279) 423609 E: julishef@hotmail.co.uk

SHEFFIELD, Canon Michael Julian. b 53. Brentwood Coll of Educn CertEd. Sarum & Wells Th Coll 76. **d** 79 **p** 80. C Locks Heath *Portsm* 79–83; C Ryde All SS 83–86; P-in-c Ryde H Trin 86–92; V 92–96; S Ferriby *Linc* 86–92; P-in-c Swanmore St Mich *Portsm* 86–92; V 92–96; V W Leigh 96–04; V Waterlooville 04–17; Hon Can Portsm Cathl 16–17; rtd 17; PtO *Portsm* from 18. *21 David Newberry Drive, Lee-on-the-Solent PO13 8FF* M: 07818-031902 E: mikesheffield@btinternet.com

SHEFFIELD, Sean Andrew. b 70. Trin Coll Bris 15. **d** 17 **p** 18. C Dover Town *Cant* from 17. *St Andrew's Vicarage, 3 Crabble Meadows, Dover CT17 0FL* M: 07710-423432 E: sean.sheffield@outlook.com

SHEFFIELD AND ROTHERHAM, Archdeacon of. *See* CHAMBERLAIN, The Ven Malcolm Leslie

SHEFFIELD, Bishop of. *See* WILCOX, The Rt Revd Peter Jonathan

SHEFFIELD, Dean of. *See* BRADLEY, The Very Revd Peter Edward

SHEGOG, Preb Eric Marshall. b 37. City Univ MA 88. Lich Th Coll 64. **d** 65 **p** 66. C Benhilton *S'wark* 65–68; Asst Youth Adv 68–70; V Abbey Wood 70–76; Chapl Sunderland Town Cen 76–83; C Bishopwearmouth St Mich w St Hilda *Dur* 76–83; Hd Relig Broadcasting IBA 84–90; PtO *Lon* 85–90; *St Alb* 85–89; Hon C Harpenden St Nic 89–97; Dir Communications for C of E 90–97; Dir Communications *Lon* 97–00; Preb St Paul's Cathl 97–00; Acting Dioc Gen Sec 99; rtd 00; PtO *St Alb* from 00. *The Coach House, 7A High Street, Clophill, Bedford MK45 4AB* T: (01525) 864868 E: ericshegog37@gmail.com

SHELDON, Jennifer Christine. b 43. K Coll Lon BA 99. NTMTC 00. **d** 02 **p** 03. NSM Poplar *Lon* from 02. *15 Townshend Road, Chislehurst BR7 6HP* T: (020) 8295 3107 E: jensheldon@aol.com

SHELDRAKE, Mrs Varlie Iris. b 39. SRN 64 SCM 65. **d** 03 **p** 04. OLM E w W Harling, Bridgham w Roudham, Larling etc *Nor* 03–09; rtd 09; PtO *Nor* from 09. *12 Kemp's Barns, Garboldisham Road, East Harling, Norwich NR16 2TS* T: (01953) 717404 E: varlie@eastharling.com

SHELLARD-JAMES, Janet Elizabeth. b 64. Southn Univ BSc 85 Kingston Univ PGCE 92. Sarum Coll BA 17. **d** 17 **p** 18. C Chewton Mendip w Ston Easton, Litton etc *B & W* 17; C Wells St Thos w Horrington from 17. *7 Dodd Avenue, Wells BA5 3JU* T: (01749) 671203 M: 07833-521570

SHELLEY, Catherine Jean. b 65. Down Coll Cam BA 88 LLM 89 MA 93 Man Univ PhD 11 Called to the Bar (Lincoln's Inn) 91 Solicitor 00. Westcott Ho Cam 08. **d** 10 **p** 11. C Kersal Moor *Man* 10–12; C W Didsbury and Withington St Chris 12–13; Chapl Birm Univ 13–15; PtO *S'wark* 16–17; V Mottingham St Edw from 17; PtO *Lon* 16–17; Dep Registrar Ely and Liv 16–17. *St Edward's Vicarage, St Keverne Road, London SE9 4AQ* T: (020) 8857 6278 M: 07711-611201 E: revdrcath@gmail.com

SHELLEY, Derrick Sydney David. b 38. Lon Univ LLB 60 AKC 65. Linc Th Coll 66. **d** 68 **p** 69. C Weybridge *Guildf* 68–72; Chapl Red Bank Schs 71–76; PtO *Blackb* 76–96; rtd 96; PtO *Truro* 96–03; *Lich* 04–09; *Blackb* 11–14. *57 Kenilworth Road, Lytham St Annes FY8 1LB* T: (01253) 780298 E: notatmycage@gmx.com

SHELLEY, Robin Arthur. b 34. CEng MIMechE. St Jo Coll Nottm 85. **d** 87 **p** 88. C Countesthorpe w Foston *Leic* 87–90; V Enderby w Lubbesthorpe and Thurlaston 90–00; rtd 00; PtO *Leic* 00–03; *York* from 02. *10 Old Pond Place, North Ferriby HU14 3JE* T: (01482) 637063 E: robin@shelley10.karoo.co.uk

SHELLEY, Rupert Harry. b 78. Bris Univ BSc 00. Wycliffe Hall Ox BTh 10. **d** 10 **p** 11. C Wimbledon Em Ridgway Prop Chpl *S'wark* 10–14; Ldr Forres Holidays Titus Trust from 14; PtO *Ox* 15–18; Win 15–18. Forres, *12 Lime Tree Mews, 2 Lime Walk, Oxford OX3 7DZ* T: (01865) 766155 M: 07956-914123 E: info@forresholidays.org *or* rupertshelley@hotmail.com

SHELTON, Ian Robert. b 52. BEd 74 Lon Univ MA 79. Ripon Coll Cuddesdon BA 81 MA 90. **d** 82 **p** 83. C Wath-upon-Dearne w Adwick-upon-Dearne *Sheff* 82–86; TV Grantham *Linc* 86–93; P-in-c Waltham 93–97; R 97–11; P-in-c Barnoldby le Beck 93–97; R 97–11; RD Haverstoe 01–11; RD Grimsby and Cleethorpes 10–11; Can and Preb Linc Cathl 05–11; V Rowley Regis *Birm* 11–18; AD Warley 13–17; rtd 18. *2 Mulberry Drive, Golcar, Huddersfield HD7 4FA* E: ianshelton232@hotmail.co.uk

SHELTON, Ms Pauline Mary. b 52. K Coll Lon BA 73. NOC 96. **d** 99 **p** 00. C Baswich *Lich* 99–02; TV Stoke-upon-Trent 02–06; Dioc OLM Course Ldr 06–10; Prin OLM and Reader Tr 10–19; rtd 19. *Dray Cottage, Cheadle Road, Draycott, Stoke-on-Trent ST11 9RQ* T: (01782) 388834 E: pauline.shelton@lichfield.anglican.org

SHEMILT, Lisa. b 69. St Jo Coll Nottm 03. **d** 05 **p** 06. C Walton St Jo *Derby* 05–13; P-in-c Morley w Smalley and Horsley Woodhouse 13–14; V Morley and Smalley 14–16; Dir Studies Initial Reader Tr 13–16; C Heanor from 16; C Langley Mill and Aldercar from 16; C Marlpool from 16. *80 Main Road, Smalley, Ilkeston DE7 6EF* T: (01332) 880380 E: revlisashemilt@hotmail.co.uk

SHENTON, Canon Brian. b 43. Chich Th Coll 73. **d** 75 **p** 76. C Mill Hill Jo Keble Ch *Lon* 75–78; C New Windsor *Ox* 78–81;

TV 81–82; P-in-c Cherbury 82–83; V Calcot 83–89; V Reading St Mary the Virgin 89–13; P-in-c Reading St Matt 96–00; RD Reading 95–13; Hon Can Ch Ch 98–13; rtd 13; PtO *Ox* 13–17; Hon C Nettlebed w Bix, Highmoor, Pishill etc 17–19; Hon C Nuffield 17–19; PtO from 19. *73 Watlington Street, Reading RG1 4RQ* M: 07710-490250 E: canon@waitrose.com

SHEPHARD, Brian Edward. b 34. Magd Coll Cam BA 56 MA 60 Ox Univ CertEd 71. Wycliffe Hall Ox 58. **d** 60 **p** 61. C Wigan St Cath *Liv* 60–62; C Kidderminster St Geo *Worc* 62–65; Lect CA Tr Coll Blackheath 65–70; Lect Hamilton Coll of Educn 70–77; Chapl Buchan Sch Castletown 77–88; Tutor Wilson Carlile Coll of Evang 88–89; C Andreas St Jude *S & M* 89–91; C Jurby 89–91; V Lezayre 91–02; rtd 02; PtO *S & M* from 02. *Keayn Ard, Queens Road, Port St Mary, Isle of Man IM9 5EP* T: (01624) 833315

SHEPHERD, Canon Anthony Michael. b 50. Em Coll Cam BA 72 MA 76. Westcott Ho Cam 72. **d** 74 **p** 75. C Folkestone St Mary and St Eanswythe *Cant* 74–79; Bp's Dom Chapl *Ripon* 79–87; Dioc Communications Officer 79–87; V High Harrogate St Pet 87–14; Leeds 14–15; Hon Can Ripon Cathl from 99; rtd 15; Chapl to The Queen from 09. *3 Heatherdale Mews, Summerbridge, Harrogate HG3 4BQ* T: (01423) 500901 E: ashepherd@talktalk.net

SHEPHERD, Mrs Bridget Clare. b 76. Open Univ BSc 01 K Coll Lon MA 04. Trin Coll Bris BA 08. **d** 08 **p** 09. C S Croydon St *S'wark* 08–14; V Lee Gd Shep w St Pet from 14. *The Vicarage, 47 Handen Road, London SE12 8NR* M: 07833-031258 E: bridget@goodpeter.org.uk

SHEPHERD, Christopher Francis Pleydell. b 44. St Steph Ho Ox 68. **d** 69 **p** 70. C Milber *Ex* 69–72; C Ex St Thos 72–74; TV Ilfracombe, Lee and W Down 74–78; TV Ilfracombe, Lee, W Down, Woolacombe and Bittadon 78–80; P-in-c Tregony w St Cuby and Cornelly *Truro* 80–83; R 83–96; rtd 04. *2 Cherry Meadow, Cheriton Fitzpaine, Crediton EX17 4JX* T: (01363) 866896

SHEPHERD, Mrs Clare Frances. b 75. Cov Univ BA 02. St Mellitus Coll BA 15. **d** 15 **p** 16. C Shottermill *Guildf* 15–18; R Ewhurst w Okewood and Forest Green from 18. *The Rectory, The Street, Ewhurst, Cranleigh GU6 7PX* M: 07825-551412 E: clare.f.shepherd@me.com

SHEPHERD, Jack Eric Bloss. b 88. Edin Univ MA 12. Cranmer Hall Dur 15. **d** 17 **p** 18. C Skelmersdale St Paul *Liv* from 17. *6 Wilcove, Skelmersdale WN8 8NF* M: 07415-122370 E: jshepherd88@outlook.com

SHEPHERD, Miss Jayne Elizabeth. b 57. Reading Univ BA 78. Cranmer Hall Dur 79. **dss** 82 **d** 87 **p** 94. Wombourne *Lich* 82–85; Harlescott 85–90; Par Dn 87–90; Chapl Asst Qu Medical Cen Nottm Univ Hosp NHS Trust 90–97; Asst Chapl Cen Notts Healthcare NHS Trust 90–97; Chapl Pet Hosps NHS Trust 97–02; Chapl St Helens and Knowsley Hosps NHS Trust 02–08; V Knutsford St Cross *Ches* 08–15; P-in-c Alsager St Mary 15–18; rtd 18. *53 News Lane, Rainford, St Helens WA11 7JY* E: j.shepherd57@hotmail.com

SHEPHERD, John Martin. b 68. St Jo Coll Cam BA 90. Oak Hill Th Coll BA 96. **d** 96 **p** 97. C Rusholme H Trin *Man* 96–00; SAMS Brazil 00–03; TV Gt Chesham *Ox* from 03. *14A Manor Way, Chesham HP5 3BG* T: (01494) 771471 E: john@theshepherds.org.uk

SHEPHERD, Canon John Michael. b 42. BNC Ox BA 63 MA 72. Coll of Resurr Mirfield 64. **d** 66 **p** 67. C Clapham H Spirit *S'wark* 66–69; C Kingston All SS 69–72; V Upper Tooting H Trin 73–80; V Wandsworth St Paul 80–90; P-in-c Mitcham SS Pet and Paul 90–92; V 92–97; RD Merton 96–97; V Battersea St Luke 97–07; RD Battersea 01–04; Hon Can S'wark Cathl 01–07; rtd 07; PtO *Portsm* from 08. *36 Lawrence Road, Southsea PO5 1NY* T: (023) 9283 7387 E: johnmshepherd36@gmail.com

SHEPHERD, Mrs Julie Margaret. b 37. **d** 03 **p** 04. OLM Halliwell *Man* 03–08; PtO from 08. *Apple Cottage, 16 Grove Street, Bolton BL1 3PG* T: (01204) 844508 M: 07742-667903   E: julieshepherd15@btinternet.com *or* julieshepherd@hushmail.com

SHEPHERD, Keith Frederick. b 42. EMMTC 86. **d** 89 **p** 90. NSM Stocking Farm *Leic* 89–93; NSM Church Langton w Tur Langton, Thorpe Langton etc 93–99; TV Syston 99–07; rtd 07; PtO *Leic* from 07. *57 Fielding Road, Birstall, Leicester LE4 3AG* T: 0116-267 4172 E: keithshepherd55@btinternet.com

SHEPHERD, Mrs Pauline. b 53. Stockwell Coll of Educn TCert 73. WMMTC 00. **d** 03 **p** 04. C Walsall Pleck and Bescot *Lich* 03–08; P-in-c Yoxall from 09; PtO *Lich* from 10. *5 Newtons College, The Close, Lichfield WS13 7LF* T: (01543) 418451 M: 07814-680304 E: p.shepherd140@btinternet.com

SHEPHERD, Canon Peter William. b 48. Reading Univ BA 71 Lon Univ BD 80 Brighton Poly MPhil 87 Lanc Univ MA 94

Open Univ PhD 04. Chich Th Coll 77. **d** 80 **p** 81. NSM Eastbourne St Sav and St Pet *Chich* 80–82; NSM Clitheroe St Mary *Blackb* 82–14; LtO 14–19; Hd Master Wm Temple Sch Preston 83–88; Hd Master Canon Slade Sch Bolton 89–06; rtd 06; PtO *Man* 89–12; Hon Can Man Cathl from 06; PtO *Blackb* from 19. *Homestead, Eastham Street, Clitheroe BB7 2HY* T/F: (01200) 425053 M: 07934-555891 E: pws.canonslade@btconnect.com

SHEPHERD, Stephen. b 54. All SS Cen for Miss & Min 12. **d** 15 **p** 16. NSM Whitworth w Facit *Man* 15–18; NSM Castleton Moor from 18. *93 Rugby Road, Rochdale OL12 0DZ* T: (01706) 661572 E: stephenshep38@gmail.com

SHEPHERD, Thomas. b 52. Man Univ BA 79 Didsbury Coll Man PGCE 83 SRN 74. NOC 92. **d** 95 **p** 96. C Baguley *Man* 95–99; C Timperley *Ches* 99–03; V Sale St Paul 03–08; V Sandbach 08–19; rtd 19. *Address temp unknown*

SHEPHERDSON, Mrs Maria Thérèse. b 65. STETS. **d** 07 **p** 08. C Warmley, Syston and Bitton *Bris* 07–11; P-in-c Upper Kennet *Sarum* 11–13; R from 13. *The Rectory, 27 High Street, Avebury, Marlborough SN8 1RF* T: (01672) 539643 E: revmariashepherdson@outlook.com

SHEPPARD, Miss Barbara Ann. b 48. Portsm Poly BA 71 Southn Univ PGCE 72 St Paul's Coll Chelt CertEd 82. Trin Coll Bris 14. **d** 16 **p** 17. OLM Swindon All SS w St Barn *Bris* from 16. *8 Southbrook Street, Swindon SN2 1HF* T: (01793) 612682 M: 07785-267721 E: barbarasheppard@btinternet.com

SHEPPARD, David Owain. b 72. Sunderland Univ BA 95 Cam Univ PGCE 99. Westcott Ho Cam 16. **d** 18 **p** 19. C Ware St Mary *St Alb* from 18. *3 The Hawthorns, Ware SG12 0XY* M: 07792-128503 E: revd.d.sheppard@gmail.com

SHEPPARD, Ian Arthur Lough. b 33. Sarum & Wells Th Coll 71. **d** 74 **p** 75. C Bishop's Cleeve *Glouc* 74–77; Chapl RAF 77–81; V Gosberton *Linc* 81–87; V Leven Valley *Carl* 87–90; Deputation and Gen Appeals Org Children's Soc 90–98; rtd 98. *57 Seymour Grove, Eaglescliffe, Stockton-on-Tees TS16 0LE* T: (01642) 791612 E: ials@btopenworld.com

SHEPPARD, Canon Martin. b 37. Hertf Coll Ox BA 61 MA 65. Chich Th Coll 63. **d** 65 **p** 66. C N Hull St Mich *York* 65–68; C Hove St Jo *Chich* 68–71; V Heathfield St Rich 71–77; V New Shoreham and Old Shoreham 77–94; TR Rye 94–03; RD 95–02; Can and Preb Chich Cathl 02–03; rtd 03; PtO *Chich* from 03. *62 St Pancras Road, Lewes BN7 1JG* T: (01273) 474999

SHEPPARD, Roger Malcolm. b 47. Aston Univ MBA 86 Wolv Poly PGCE 88 Solicitor 74. WMMTC 98. **d** 01 **p** 02. NSM Castle Vale w Minworth *Birm* 01–07; NSM Four Oaks 08–13; P-in-c Wylde Green 13–16; P-in-c Bordesley St Benedict from 16; CF(V) 07–16. *193 Dower Road, Sutton Coldfield B75 6SY* T: 0121-308 8850 M: 07775-281777 E: rmsheppard@hotmail.co.uk

SHEPPARD, Preb Susan. b 59. Ex Univ BA 80 MA 99 SS Hild & Bede Coll Dur PGCE 81. SWMTC 95. **d** 06 **p** 07. NSM Stoke Canon, Poltimore w Huxham and Rewe etc *Ex* 98–01; Chapl St Pet High Sch Ex 99–06; Tutor SWMTC from 05; NSM Brampford Speke, Cadbury, Newton St Cyres etc *Ex* from 08; Preb Ex Cathl from 11. *49 Fore Street, Silverton, Exeter EX5 4HZ* T: (01392) 861022 E: sue.sheppard@netherexe.org

SHEPTON, Robert Leonard McIntire. b 35. Jes Coll Cam BA 58 MA 61. Oak Hill Th Coll 59. **d** 61 **p** 62. C Weymouth St Jo *Sarum* 61–63; Boys' Ldr Cam Univ Miss Bermondsey 63–66; Warden Ox-Kilburn Club 66–69; Chapl St D Coll Llandudno 69–77; Chief Instructor Carnoch Outdoor Cen 77–80; Chapl Kingham Hill Sch Oxon 80–92; rtd 92. *Innisfree, Duror, Appin PA38 4DA* T: (01631) 730437 F: 730382 E: bob@innisfree.free-online.co.uk *or* bobshepton1@gmail.com

SHER, Canon Falak. b 65. Coll of Resurr Mirfield. **d** 07 **p** 08. C Radcliffe *Man* 07–10; TV Gorton and Abbey Hey 10–14; P-in-c Chorlton-cum-Hardy St Werburgh 14–17; R from 17; P-in-c Hulme Ascension from 14; C Whalley Range St Edm and Moss Side etc 14–16; Hon Can Man Cathl from 16. *St Werburgh's Rectory, 388 Wilbraham Road, Manchester M21 0UH* T: 0161-881 1642 M: 07930-573624 E: falakfalak@hotmail.com

SHERBORNE, Archdeacon of. *See* SAYER, The Ven Penelope Jane

SHERBORNE, Area Bishop of. *See* GORHAM, The Rt Revd Karen Marisa

SHERBOURNE, Gloria. b 49. STETS 00. **d** 03 **p** 04. NSM Jersey St Brelade *Win* 03–10; Asst Chapl Jersey Gp of Hosps 03–04 and 05–10. *11 Iter Court, Bow, Crediton EX17 6BZ* T: (01363) 881240 E: gsherbourne@gmail.com

SHERDLEY, Mrs Margaret Ann. b 46. Ches Coll of HE BTh 03. NOC 00. **d** 03 **p** 04. NSM Fellside Team *Blackb* 03–14; Chapl Myerscough Coll 06–11; rtd 11; PtO *Blackb* from 15. *Home Barn, Hollowforth Lane, Woodplumpton, Preston PR4 0BD* T: (01772) 691101 M: 07931-592787 E: m.sherdley@sky.com

SHERIDAN, Canon Andrew Robert (Drew). b 61. Edin Univ MA 83 Jordanhill Coll Glas PGCE 86. TISEC 95. **d** 98 **p** 99. C Glas St Mary 98–01; R Greenock 01–16; P-in-c Gourock 06–16; R Lanark from 16; Bp's Dom Chapl from 15; Can St Mary's Cathl from 15. *The Rectory, 1 Cleghorn Road, Lanark ML11 7QT* T: (01555) 663065 E: thecanteringcanon@outlook.com

SHERIDAN, Preb Deborah Jane. b 47. Kent Univ BA 69 ALA 73. WMMTC 90. **d** 93 **p** 94. NSM Lich St Chad 93–03; NSM The Ridwares and Kings Bromley 03–18; NSM Kings Bromley, The Ridwares and Yoxall 18–19; PtO from 19; Voc Educn Officer 06–18; Chapl St Giles Hospice Lich 98–14; Preb Lich Cathl from 16. *45 High Grange, Lichfield WS13 7DU* T: (01543) 264363 *or* 416595 E: d.sheridan@postman.org.uk

SHERIDAN, Stephen Anthony. b 62. RMN 87 Chich Univ BA 11. SEITE 04. **d** 07 **p** 08. NSM Bexhill St Pet *Chich* 07–08; NSM Stone Cross St Luke w N Langney 08–12; NSM Shotton *St As* 12–13; PtO *Ches* 15–17; P-in-c Ches St Oswald and St Thos from 17. *The Vicarage, 33 Abbots Grange, Chester CH2 1AJ* T: (01244) 665984 M: 07770-629875 E: sheridan_steve@yahoo.com

SHERIFF (*née* WORRALL), Canon Suzanne. b 63. Trin Coll Bris BA 86. **d** 87 **p** 94. Par Dn Kingston upon Hull St Nic *York* 87–91; Par Dn Kingston upon Hull St Aid Southcoates 91–94; C 94–96; TV Marfleet 96–00; TR 00–07; V Tadcaster w Newton Kyme 07–14; P-in-c Kirk Fenton w Kirkby Wharfe and Ulleskelfe 10–14; V Tadcaster 14–19; Can and Preb York Minster from 01. *The Vicarage, 78 Station Road, Tadcaster LS24 9JR* T: (01937) 833394 E: sue.sheriff@virgin.net

SHERLOCK, Mrs Barbara Lee Kerney. b 48. Dur Univ PhD 07. Westcott Ho Cam. **d** 05 **p** 06. C Norton St Mary and Stockton St Chad *Dur* 05–07; P-in-c Newport and Widdington *Chelmsf* 07–11; V Barrow *St E* 11–18; rtd 18; PtO *St E* from 18. *Flat 2, 34 Southgate Street, Bury St Edmunds IP33 2AZ* E: barbara_sherlock@btinternet.com

SHERLOCK, Charles Patrick. b 51. New Coll Ox BA 73 MA 76 Open Univ MBA 00. Ripon Coll Cuddesdon 75. **d** 77 **p** 78. C Ashtead *Guildf* 77–81; Ethiopia 81–82; Chapl Belgrade w Zagreb *Eur* 82–84; USPG Ethiopia 84–91; R Dollar *St And* 91–97; Bursar Fistula Hosp Ethiopia 97–00; P-in-c Crieff *St And* 01–04; R 04–07; P-in-c Comrie 01–04; R 04–07; P-in-c Lochearnhead 01–04; R 04–07; PtO 07–13; Assoc Chapl Addis Ababa St Matt Ethiopia 07–13; P-in-c Hilborough w Bodney *Nor* 13–16; P-in-c Oxborough w Foulden and Caldecote 13–16; P-in-c Cockley Cley w Gooderstone 13–17; P-in-c Didlington 13–17; C Mundford w Lynford 16–17; rtd 17; PtO *St And* from 18. *26 Hunter Street, Auchterarder PH3 1PA* T: (01764) 664429 M: 07740-981951 E: cpsherlock@msn.com

SHERLOCK, Helen Georgina. b 69. Southn Univ BEd 93. St Mellitus Coll BA 18. **d** 18. C Alphington, Shillingford St George and Ide *Ex* from 18. *Glenn House, 96 Old Tiverton Road, Exeter EX4 6LD* M: 07919-405212 E: helen@sherlockfamily.co.uk

SHERLOCK, Canon Thomas Alfred. b 40. Aux Course 87. **d** 90 **p** 91. NSM Kilmallock w Kilflynn, Kilfinane, Knockaney etc *L & K* 90–94; C Templemore w Thurles and Kilfithmone *C & O* 95–98; I 98–00; I Castlecomer w Colliery Ch, Mothel and Bilboa 00–11; Preb Ossory Cathl 05–11; rtd 11; Chapl Kingston Coll Mitchelstown from 13. *Castlequarter, Kildorrery, Co Cork, P67 EH74, Republic of Ireland* T: (00353) (22) 40677 M: 86-810 4463 E: hazelsherlock@eircom.net

SHERRATT, David Arthur. b 60. Univ of Wales (Lamp) BA 82 Leeds Univ BA 91. Coll of Resurr Mirfield 92. **d** 92 **p** 93. C St Jo on Bethnal Green *Lon* 92–95; C W Hampstead St Jas 95–98; V Abbey Wood *S'wark* from 98. *St Michael's Vicarage, 1 Conference Road, London SE2 0YH* T: (020) 8311 0377

SHERRED, Peter William. b 47. Kent Univ BA 69. SEITE 96. **d** 99 **p** 00. NSM Dover St Mary *Cant* 99–02; PtO from 02. *Copthorne, Dover Road, Guston, Dover CT15 5EN* T: (01304) 203548 F: 206950

SHERRING, Patrick. b 55. Trent Park Coll of Educn BEd 78 CertEd 77. Ridley Hall Cam 95. **d** 97 **p** 98. C Leyton St Mary w St Edw and St Luke *Chelmsf* 97–01; P-in-c Ingatestone w Buttsbury 01–04; C Fryerning w Margaretting 01–04; V Ingatestone w Fryerning from 04; P-in-c Margaretting w Mountnessing and Buttsbury from 15. *The Rectory, 1 Rectory Close, Fryerning Lane, Ingatestone CM4 0DB* T: (01277) 352562 E: patrick.sherring@ingatestoneparishchurch.org.uk

SHERRING, Toby Bruce. b 76. Ex Univ BA 97 St Luke's Coll Ex PGCE 98. St Steph Ho Ox MTh 04. **d** 02 **p** 03. C W Derby St Jo *Liv* 02–05; Chapl St Hilda's Sch for Girls Perth Australia 06–16; Chapl The Peterborough Sch from 16; PtO *Ely*

from 18. *The Peterborough School, Thorpe Road, Peterborough PE3 6AP* T: (01733) 343357

SHERRINGTON, Penelope. b 51. Kent Univ BA 11. SEITE 08. **d** 11 **p** 12. Chapl Gt Ormond Street Hosp NHS Foundn Trust from 11; NSM Godstone and Blindley Heath *S'wark* 11–14; NSM Bletchingley and Nutfield from 14; PtO *Lon* from 14. *Little Granta, Godstone Road, Bletchingley, Redhill RH1 4PL* T: (01883) 744991   E: martinpenny012000@yahoo.com   *or* penny.sherrington@gosh.nhs.uk

SHERWIN, Canon David Royston. b 56. St Jo Coll Nottm 84. **d** 89 **p** 90. C Conisbrough *Sheff* 89–95; V Wheatley Park and Dioc Adv for Evang 95–01; P-in-c Martley and Wichenford, Knightwick etc *Worc* 01–08; TR Worcs W Rural from 09; RD Martley and Worc W 08–19; Hon Can Worc Cathl from 15. *The Rectory, Martley, Worcester WR6 6QA* T/F: (01886) 888664 E: davidwin56@aol.com

SHERWIN, Mrs Jane. b 41. Sarum Th Coll 93. **d** 96 **p** 97. NSM Brightling, Dallington, Mountfield etc *Chich* 96–02; P-in-c Waldron 02–09; rtd 09; PtO *St E* 10–16; *Chich* from 15. *Treetops at Merlins, Uckfield Road, Ringmer, Lewes BN8 5RU* T: (01273) 812173

SHERWIN, Miss Margaret Miriam. b 32. Ripon Coll Cuddesdon 81. **dss** 83 **d** 87 **p** 94. Holborn St Alb w Saffron Hill St Pet *Lon* 83–88; Par Dn 87–88; Par Dn Highgate St Mich 88–93; rtd 93; Hon C Pucklechurch *Portsm* 93–99; PtO from 99. *16 Lombard Court, Lombard Street, Portsmouth PO1 2HU* T: (023) 9283 8429

SHERWIN, Mrs Philippa Margaret. b 46. Lon Univ BDS 70 LDS 70. **d** 99 **p** 00. OLM Queen Thorne *Sarum* 99–08; rtd 08; PtO *Sarum* 08–15. *Haycroft, Sandford Orcas, Sherborne DT9 4RP* T: (01963) 220380 E: pm.sherwin@btinternet.com

SHERWOOD, David Charles. b 56. LRPS 94. WEMTC 98. **d** 01 **p** 02. C Taunton Lyngford *B & W* 01–05; P-in-c Hemyock w Culm Davy, Clayhidon and Culmstock *Ex* 05–11; P-in-c Ashburton, Bickington, Buckland in the Moor etc 11–17; RD Moreton 12–15; rtd 17. *Address withheld by request*

SHERWOOD, David James. b 45. Univ of Wales (Cardiff) LLM 94 Solicitor 69. St Steph Ho Ox 81. **d** 83 **p** 84. C Westbury-on-Trym H Trin *Bris* 83–85; C Corringham *Chelmsf* 85–87; V Hullbridge 87–94; V Kenton *Lon* 94–06; rtd 06; PtO *Chich* from 06; *Eur* from 98. *130 St Helens Road, Hastings TN34 2EJ* T: (01424) 254510 E: canddsherwood@aol.co.uk

SHERWOOD, Canon Ian Walter Lawrence. b 57. TCD BA 80. **d** 82 **p** 84. C Dublin St Patr Cathl Gp *D & G* 82–83; Chapl Billinge Hosp Wigan 83–86; C Orrell *Liv* 83–86; Chapl Bucharest w Sofia *Eur* 86–89; Chapl Istanbul w Moda from 89; Can Malta Cathl from 97; PtO from 99. *c/o FCO (Istanbul), King Charles Street, London SW1A 2AH* T: (0090) (212) 251 5616 F: 243 5702 E: iansherwo@gmail.com

SHERWOOD, Jane. *See* LEES, Jane

SHERWOOD, Kenneth Henry. b 37. CITC 90. **d** 93 **p** 94. NSM Malahide w Balgriffin *D & G* 93–96 and 01–15; NSM Castleknock and Mulhuddart w Clonsilla 96–97; NSM Leighlin w Grange Sylvae, Shankill etc *C & O* 97–04; NSM Holmpatrick w Balbriggan and Kenure *D & G* 15–18; NSM Swords w Donabate and Kilsallaghan from 18. *49 Mountfield Park, Malahide, Co Dublin, Republic of Ireland* T: (00353) (1) 803 8485 M: 86-258 0002 E: kensherwood07@eircom.net

SHERWOOD, Suffragan Bishop of. *See* PORTER, The Rt Revd Anthony

SHEWAN, Alistair Boyd. b 44. Open Univ BA 83 BSc 95. Edin Th Coll 63. **d** 67 **p** 68. Prec St Andr Cathl Inverness *Mor* 67–69; C Shepherd's Bush St Steph w St Thos *Lon* 70–72; Hon C Edin St Mich and All SS 73–75; PtO 75–81; Hon C Edin Old St Paul 81–86; NSM Edin St Columba 87–91; Asst Dioc Supernumerary from 91; C Edin St Ninian 95–08. *Limegrove, High Street, Gifford, Haddington EH41 4QU* T: (01620) 810402 E: alaistair315@btinternet.com

SHEWRING (*née* SMITH), Mrs Susan Helen. b 51. Univ of Cen England in Birm BEd 87 Warwick Univ PGDE 90. WMMTC 01. **d** 04 **p** 05. NSM Billesley Common *Birm* 04–07; Asst Chapl Univ Hosp Birm NHS Foundn Trust 07–14; rtd 14; PtO *Birm* from 14. *48 St Helens Road, Solihull B91 2DA* T: 0121-448 1846 M: 07914-434058 E: sue_shewring@yahoo.co.uk

SHIELD, Mrs Christine Ann. b 54. Lindisfarne Regional Tr Partnership 13. **d** 15 **p** 16. NSM Warkworth and Acklington *Newc* from 15. *Godric's Hollow, 18 Watershaugh Road, Warkworth, Morpeth NE65 0TX* T: (01665) 711141 E: christineannshield@googlemail.com

SHIELDS, Dennis. b 41. Brighton Coll of Educn CertEd 72 Brighton Poly DipEd 84 Roehampton Inst MA 87 Sheff Univ MA 16. **d** 05 **p** 06. NSM Meltham *Wakef* 05–14; *Leeds* from 14. *11 The Hollow, Meltham, Holmfirth*

HD9 5LA T: (01484) 850074 F: 326222 M: 07974-146120 E: dennis_shields@btinternet.com

SHIELDS, Mrs Jennifer Jill. b 39. Heref Coll of Educn CertEd 74. SAOMC 99. **d** 02 **p** 03. OLM Lenborough *Ox* 02–11; PtO from 11. *8 West Furlong, Padbury, Buckingham MK18 2BP* T: (01280) 814474

SHIELLS, Alex Alan Terry. b 94. Mattersey Hall BA 16 Dur Univ MA 19. St Hild Coll 17. **d** 19. C Worksop Ch Ch and Shireoaks *S'well* from 19. *27 Sunnyside, Worksop S81 7LN* M: 07591-982497 E: alexshiells@gmail.com

SHIELS, Rosalinde Cameron. *See* WALSER, Rosalinde Cameron

SHILL, Kenneth Leslie. b 49. Leic Univ BA 70 Lon Univ BD 73. Ridley Hall Cam 75. **d** 77 **p** 78. C Harborne Heath *Birm* 77–83; V Mansfield St Jo *S'well* 83–93; Bp's Adv on Healing 89–93; Chapl Amsterdam w Heiloo *Eur* 93–95; TR Bath Twerton-on-Avon *B & W* 95–04; V Arnold *S'well* 04–15; TV S Cheltenham *Glouc* from 15. *25 Hatherley Court Road, Cheltenham GL51 3AG* T: (01242) 461784 E: kshill@sky.com

SHILLAKER, Mrs Christine Frances. b 39. Gilmore Ho 74. **dss** 86 **d** 87 **p** 94. Colchester St Leon, St Mary Magd and St Steph *Chelmsf* 86–89; Par Dn 87–89; Par Dn Colchester, New Town and The Hythe 89–94; C 94–96; P-in-c Ramsey w Lt Oakley 96–02; rtd 02; PtO *Chelmsf* from 02. *21 Nelson Road, Colchester CO3 9AP* T: (01206) 570234

SHILLING, Ms Audrey Violet. b 26. Dur Univ BA 69. CA Tr Coll 51 Cranmer Hall Dur 66. **d** 87 **p** 94. CA from 53; NSM Gillingham H Trin *Roch* 87–93; NSM Rainham 94–96; PtO 96–10; *Guildf* 10–18. *Flat 14, Manormead, Tilford Road, Hindhead GU26 6RA* T: (01428) 601514 E: ashilling14@gmail.com

SHILLINGFORD, Brian. b 39. Lich Th Coll 65. **d** 68 **p** 69. C Lewisham St Swithun *S'wark* 68–71; C Egdonside 71–75; TV Croydon St Jo *Cant* 75–81; TV N Creedy *Ex* 81–93; TR 93–05; rtd 05; PtO *Ex* from 05. *Lyndbank, Albert Road, Crediton EX17 2BZ* T: (01363) 877221 E: brianandkayshil@gmail.com

SHILLINGTON, Maureen Lesley. *See* BROWELL, Maureen Lesley

SHILSON-THOMAS, Mrs Annabel Margaret. b 60. Jes Coll Ox BA 82. Westcott Ho Cam 87. **d** 89 **p** 98. Par Dn Sydenham St Bart *S'wark* 89–93; Journalist CAFOD 95–03; Hon C Kingston All SS w St Jo *S'wark* 97–98; PtO *Ely* 00–03; Chapl Anglia Poly Univ 03–04; C Kingston All SS w St Jo *S'wark* 04–05; Spirituality Consultant CAFOD from 05; C Cambridge Gt St Mary w St Mich *Ely* 07–15; Tutor Westcott Ho Cam from 15; PtO *Ely* from 15. *28 Fulbrooke Road, Cambridge CB3 9EE* T: (01223) 729475 E: ams94@cam.ac.uk

SHILSON-THOMAS, Canon Hugh David. b 64. Ex Coll Ox BA 86 MA 98 K Coll Lon MA 99. Westcott Ho Cam 87. **d** 89 **p** 90. C Sydenham All SS *S'wark* 89–92; C Lower Sydenham St Mich 89–92; Ecum Chapl Kingston Univ 93–98; Chapl Rob Coll Cam 98–03; Nat Adv for HE/Chapl Abps' Coun 03–08; Chapl and Dean of Chpl Selw Coll Cam from 08; Chapl Newnham Coll Cam from 08; Chapter Can Ely Cathl from 10. *28 Fulbrooke Road, Cambridge CB3 9EE* T: (01223) 729475 *or* 335846 E: hds21@cam.ac.uk

SHILVOCK, Geoffrey. b 47. Univ of Wales (Lamp) BA 69. Sarum Th Coll 70. **d** 72 **p** 73. C Kidderminster St Mary *Worc* 72–78; P-in-c Gt Malvern Ch Ch 78–85; V Wolverley and Cookley 85–12; RD Kidderminster 95–01; rtd 12; PtO *Worc* from 13. *7 Marsh Grove, Kidderminster DY10 2HS* T: (01562) 228096 E: geoffshilvock@hotmail.com

SHIMWELL, Robert John. b 46. ARCM 65. Trin Coll Bris 75. **d** 78 **p** 79. C Richmond H Trin and Ch Ch *S'wark* 78–79; C Cullompton and Kentisbeare w Blackborough *Ex* 79–81; V S Cave and Ellerker w Broomfleet *York* 81–87; Chapl Lee Abbey 87–88; R Glas St Silas 88–94; V Upton (Overchurch) *Ches* 94–05; RD Wirral N 97–98; Hon Can Ches Cathl 02–05; V Lee St Mildred *S'wark* 05–11; rtd 11; PtO *S'wark* 11–15; *Roch* 12–16; *Ches* from 16. *12 The Oaks, Glossop SK13 6LD* T: (01457) 514601 E: rob.shimwell@btinternet.com

SHIN, Beom Jin (Stephen). b 80. Kyung Hee Univ Korea BA 03 Univ Coll Lon MSc 08. St Steph Ho Ox 08. **d** 11 **p** 12. C Banbury *Ox* 11–15; PtO 16–17; Miss Partner CMS from 16. *Church Mission Society, Watlington Road, Cowley, Oxford OX4 6BZ* E: bjmonani@gmail.com

SHINE, Canon Ann Aisling. RGN SCM. **d** 03 **p** 04. Aux Min Dublin Drumcondra w N Strand *D & G* 03–05; Aux Min Clondalkin w Rathcoole from 05; Can Ch Ch Cathl Dublin from 10. *1 Roselawn Grove, Castleknock, Dublin 15, Republic of Ireland* T: (00353) (1) 820 1797 M: 87-239 7902 E: aislingshine@hotmail.com

SHINHMAR, Joshua Rajbir. b 68. Ridley Hall Cam 16. **d** 18 **p** 19. C Chesterton St Geo *Ely* from 18. *39*

St Kilda Avenue, Cambridge CB4 2PN M: 07730-177765 E: joshuashinhmar@gmail.com

SHINKINS, Pamela Mhairi. b 41. Leeds Univ BSc 62 Open Univ BA 84. TISEC 05. **d** 07 **p** 08. LtO *Mor* from 08. *Homelea, 7 Blair, Poolewe, Achnasheen IV22 2LP* T: (01445) 781346 E: pam.shinkins@btinternet.com

SHINN, William Raymond. b 22. Sarum & Wells Th Coll 71. **d** 73 **p** 74. C Letchworth St Paul *St Alb* 73–75; C Dunstable 76–78; TV 78–80; V Luton St Chris Round Green 80–88; rtd 88; PtO *St Alb* 88–16. *Room 14, Elmside, Elmside Walk, Hitchin SG5 1HB* T: (01462) 641883

SHINTON, Bertram David. b 41. WMMTC 95. **d** 98 **p** 99. NSM Broseley w Benthall, Jackfield, Linley etc *Heref* 98–12; PtO from 10. *Gestiana, Woodlands Road, Broseley TF12 5PU* T: 0121-311 2104 *or* (01952) 883534

SHIPLEY, Christopher John. b 44. Leeds Univ BSc 65 MSc 70 BA 72. Coll of Resurr Mirfield 70. **d** 73 **p** 74. C Preston St Jo *Blackb* 73–77; Chapl Lancs (Preston) Poly 75–77; V Blackb St Mich w St Jo 77–81; P-in-c Blackb H Trin 78–81; V Blackb St Mich w St Jo and H Trin 81–82; V Walthamstow St Pet *Chelmsf* 82–85; Gen Sec Mary Feilding Guild Lon 85–86; Org Waltham Forest Coun for Voluntary Service 86–89; Gen Sec Hull 89–91; Dir Grimsby and Cleethorpes 91; Teacher Upbury Manor High Sch Gillingham 92–94; Hd of Science 94–02; Teacher Whitstable Community Coll 02–03; Hd of Science Cheyne Middle Sch Sheerness 03–09; Team Ldr Science Is of Sheppey Academy 09–10; C Minster-in-Sheppey *Cant* 10–12; C Sheerness H Trin w St Paul 10–12; C Queenborough 10–12; C W Sheppey 12–14; C Eastchurch w Leysdown and Harty 10–12; P-in-c 12–14; R 14–16; PtO from 17. *12 Cumberland Drive, Lower Halstow, Sittingbourne ME9 7JA* T: (01795) 841125 E: chrisshply@gmail.com

SHIPLEY, June Patricia. See ASQUITH, June Patricia

SHIPLEY, Ruth Mary. See HOWLETT-SHIPLEY, Ruth Mary

SHIPLEY, Canon Stephen Edwin Burnham. b 52. Univ Coll Dur BA 74. Westcott Ho Cam 85. **d** 87 **p** 88. C Ipswich St Marg *St E* 87–90; P-in-c Stuntney *Ely* 90–95; Min Can, Prec and Sacr Ely Cathl 90–95; Producer Worship Progr BBC Relig Broadcasting from 95; LtO *Derby* from 96; Hon Can Derby Cathl from 09. *21 Devonshire Road, Buxton SK17 6RZ* T: (01298) 78383 M: 07808-403812 E: sebshipley@gmail.com

SHIPP, Miss Elizabeth Ann. b 81. Leic Univ BA 02 Ox Brookes Univ MA 09. Ripon Coll Cuddesdon BA 06. **d** 07 **p** 08. C Wymondham *Nor* 07–11; Bp's Chapl *Worc* 11–16; Min Can Worc Cathl 12–16; P-in-c Melbourn *Ely* from 16; P-in-c Meldreth from 16. *The Vicarage, Vicarage Close, Melbourn, Royston SG8 6DY* T: (01763) 220626 E: vicar.melbournmeldreth@gmail.com

SHIPP, Linda Mary. b 49. Cranmer Hall Dur 00. **d** 02 **p** 03. Chapl among Deaf People *York* 02–17; C Kirkleatham 02–05; V Whorlton w Carlton and Faceby 05–17; rtd 17; PtO *York* from 18. *23 Marlborough Road, Marton-in-Cleveland, Middlesbrough TS7 8LB* M: 07970-908517

SHIPP, Susan. See HOLLINS, Patricia Susan

SHIPTON, Canon Andrew James. b 60. Leeds Univ BA 82 Univ of Northumbria at Newc MEd 99 Leeds Univ MPhil 06. Cranmer Hall Dur 83. **d** 85 **p** 86. C Fishponds St Jo *Bris* 85–88; C Gosforth All SS *Newc* 88–91; V Long Benton St Mary 91–96; Chapl Northumbria Univ 96–06; TV Ch the King 06–07; TR 07–14; V Gosforth All SS from 14; P-in-c Gosforth St Hugh from 07; Dioc Development Officer for Youth Work from 06; Hon Can Newc Cathl from 07. *All Saints' Vicarage, 33 Brackenfield Road, Newcastle upon Tyne NE3 4DX* T: 0191-284 5540 E: andrewshipton085@aol.com

SHIPTON, Eileen Kay. See OSGOOD, Eileen Kay

SHIPTON, Linda Anne. See GREEN, Linda Anne

SHIRES, Alan William. b 34. Univ Coll BA 60. Oak Hill Th Coll 57. **d** 61 **p** 62. C York St Paul 61–64; C Southgate *Chich* 64–67; V Doncaster St Mary *Sheff* 67–75; PtO *Portsm* 75–96; Student Counsellor Portsm Poly 75–88; Hd Student Services Portsm Poly 88–96; rtd 96; PtO *Lich* 13. *15 Broomfield Road, Admaston, Wellington TF5 0AR* E: aw.shires@btinternet.com

SHIRLEY, Gary Ronald. b 57. Wilson Carlile Coll 96 SWMTC 06. **d** 09 **p** 10. C Devonport St Budeaux *Ex* 09–12; C Yelverton, Meavy, Sheepstor and Walkhampton 12–16; C Yelverton, Meavy, Sheepstor, Walkhampton, Sampford Spiney and Horrabridge 16–19; rtd 19. *47 Hallsfield, Cricklade, Swindon SN6 6LR* E: gary.shirley2@btinternet.com

SHIRLEY, Valerie Joy. b 42. **d** 96 **p** 97. OLM Sydenham H Trin *S'wark* 96–07; OLM Sydenham H Trin and St Aug 07–12; PtO from 12. *9 Faircroft, 5 Westwood Hill, London SE26 6BG* T: (020) 8778 2551 E: valshirley@btinternet.com

SHIRRAS, The Ven Edward Scott. b 37. St Andr Univ BSc 61. Clifton Th Coll 61. **d** 63 **p** 64. C Surbiton Hill Ch Ch *S'wark* 63–66; C Jesmond Clayton Memorial *Newc* 66–68; CPAS

68–75; Hon C Wallington *S'wark* 69–75; V Roxeth Ch Ch *Lon* 75–82; V Roxeth Ch Ch and Harrow St Pet 82–85; AD Harrow 82–85; Adn Northolt 85–92; V Win Ch Ch 92–01; rtd 01; PtO *Ox* 01–02 and 09–17; P-in-c Marcham w Garford 02–09. *4 Culham Close, Abingdon OX14 2AS* T: (01235) 553129 E: epshirras@aol.com

SHIRRAS, Mrs Pamela Susan. b 41. St Andr Univ BSc 62 Brunel Univ PGCE 80. Wycliffe Hall Ox 04. **d** 05 **p** 06. NSM Marcham w Garford *Ox* 05–09; PtO 09; NSM Abingdon 09–11; PtO from 11. *4 Culham Close, Abingdon OX14 2AS* T: (01235) 553129 E: epshirras@aol.com

SHOCK, Rachel Alexandra. b 63. Nottm Trent Univ LLB 94. EMMTC 95. **d** 98 **p** 00. NSM Radford All So w Ch Ch and St Mich *S'well* 98–99; NSM Lenton Abbey 99–02; NSM Wollaton 02–08; Internet Chapl Development Worker 06–10; Workplace Chapl and NSM Nottingham All SS, St Mary and St Pet *S'well* 11–15; PtO from 15; Chapl Costa Brava *Eur* from 18. *Placa Firal 4, 17121 Corçà (Girona), Spain* E: chaplaincostabrava@gmail.com

SHOESMITH (née HALL), Mrs Judith Frances. b 64. SS Coll Cam BA 85 MA 89 MEng 94 BTh 02 CEng 97. Ridley Hall Cam 99. **d** 02 **p** 03. C Drayton in Hales *Lich* 02–05; LtO *Liv* 05–11; TV Walthamstow *Chelmsf* 11–18; TV Wigan All SS *Liv* from 18. *The Vicarage, 141 Whelley, Wigan WN1 3UE* M: 07505-126167 E: fshoesmith@gmail.com

SHOESMITH, Canon Kathia Andree. b 64. Leeds Univ BA 08 RN 98. Coll of Resurr Mirfield 06. **d** 08 **p** 09. C Ripponden and Barkisland w W Scammonden *Wakef* 08–11; V Bradshaw and Holmfield 11–14; *Leeds* from 14; C Southowram and Claremount from 17; AD Halifax from 17; Jt AD Calder Valley from 18; Hon Can Bradf Cathl from 19. *The Vicarage, Pavement Lane, Bradshaw, Halifax HX2 9JJ* T: (01422) 244330 E: reverend.kathia@outlook.com

SHOKRALLA, Adel Salah Makar. b 75. Ain Shams Univ Cairo BSc 96. Alexandria Sch of Th 05 Trin Coll Bris MA 10. **d** 09 **p** 11. C Heavitree and St Mary Steps *Ex* 10–12; CMS Egypt 12–15; V Old Windsor *Ox* from 15. *The Vicarage, Church Road, Old Windsor, Windsor SL4 2PQ* T: (01753) 865778 M: 07729-772276

SHONE, Miss Ursula Ruth. b 34. Stirling Univ BA 75 Open Univ BPhil 88. **dss** 81 **d** 86 **p** 94. Bridge of Allan *St And* 81–85; Lochgelly 85–87; Chapl Cov Cathl 87–90; Ind Chapl 87–90; Par Dn Ainsdale *Liv* 90–94; Dioc Science Adv 90–99; C Ainsdale 94–96; C Childwall St Dav 96–99; rtd 99; NSM Brechin *Bre* 00–12; LtO *Edin* from 12. *5 Abbotsford Court, Kelso TD5 7SQ* T: (01573) 224210 E: u.shone@btinternet.com

SHOOTER, Philippa Margaret. b 49. Hull Univ BA 70 Nottm Univ MA 72 CQSW 72. NOC 04. **d** 06 **p** 07. NSM Fence-in-Pendle and Higham *Blackb* 06–11; Hon C Coppull and Coppull St Jo 11–13; rtd 13; PtO *York* from 13. *23 Nelson Street, Bridlington YO15 3BJ* T: (01262) 424802 E: philippashooter@btinternet.com

SHOOTER, Robert David. b 44. Lon Univ BSc 70 Lanc Univ MA 94 CQSW 72 LRAM 92. NOC 99. **d** 02 **p** 03. NSM Brierfield *Blackb* 02–04; NSM Briercliffe 04–09; PtO 09–13; *York* from 13. *23 Nelson Street, Bridlington YO15 3BJ* T: (01262) 424802 E: robertshooter@btinternet.com

SHOOTER, Ms Susan. b 58. Nottm Univ BA 81 PGCE 82. St Jo Coll Nottm MA 96. **d** 96 **p** 98. C Dartford H Trin *Roch* 96–97; C Crayford 97–00; V Bostall Heath 00–09. *131 Pengelly, Delabole PL33 9AT* T: (01840) 213645 M: 07929-496942 E: shooter160@btinternet.com

SHOREY, Simon Daniel John. b 77. St Mellitus Coll 15. **d** 18 **p** 19. C Wivelsfield *Chich* from 18; C Mid-Sussex Network Ch from 18. *30 Haywards Road, Haywards Heath RH16 4JB* E: simon@thepointchurch.co.uk

SHORT, Bryan Raymond. b 37. Bris Univ BSc 59 CertEd 60. **d** 02 **p** 14. OLM Kirkheaton *Wakef* 02–09; PtO 09–14; *Leeds* from 14. *12 Bankfield Lane, Kirkheaton, Huddersfield HD5 0JG* T: (01484) 425832

SHORT, Ms Clare. b 50. Leic Univ BA 72 St Mary's Coll Twickenham PGCE 73. S Dios Minl Tr Scheme 89. **d** 92 **p** 94. NSM Horsham *Chich* 92–99; PtO *Newc* 04–15. *Hedgelea, South Road, Lowick, Berwick-upon-Tweed TD15 2TX* T: (01289) 389222

SHORT, David Keith. Nottm Univ MSci 01 Chu Coll Cam BTh 13 Warwick Univ PGCE 04. Ridley Hall Cam 10. **d** 13 **p** 14. C Chorleywood Ch Ch *St Alb* 13–16; V Furze Platt *Ox* from 16. *Address withheld by request* T: (01628) 784053 E: vicar@stpetersandstmarks.org.uk

SHORT, Eileen. b 45. Ex Univ BA 66. NOC 93. **d** 96 **p** 97. NSM Castleton Moor *Man* 96–98; NSM Chorlton-cum-Hardy St Clem 98–00; NSM Baguley 00–10; PtO from 10; *Ches* from 16. *2 Netherwood Road, Northenden, Manchester M22 4BQ*

SHORT, Mrs Heather Mary. b 50. LWCMD 71 Cardiff Coll of Educn CertEd 72. WEMTC 98. **d** 01 **p** 02. C Heref S Wye

01–05; P-in-c Bodenham, Felton and Preston Wynne 05–12; P-in-c Marden w Amberley and Wisteston 05–12; P-in-c Sutton St Nicholas w Sutton St Michael 05–12; R Maund Gp 12–17; rtd 17. *24 Boraston Drive, Burford, Tenbury Wells WR15 8AG*

SHORT, Canon John <u>Timothy</u>. b 43. Kelham Th Coll 63. **d** 68 **p** 69. C St Marylebone Ch Ch w St Barn *Lon* 68–70; C Southgate Ch Ch 70–72; P-in-c Mosser and Dioc Youth Officer *Carl* 72–78; R Heyford w Stowe Nine Churches *Pet* 78–87; V Northampton St Jas 87–96; RD Wootton 88–96; TR Kingsthorpe w Northampton St Dav 96–08; Can Pet Cathl 97–08; rtd 08; PtO *Pet* from 09; *Derby* 14–18. *11 Cytringan Close, Kettering NN15 6GW* T: (01536) 310633 E: jtimshort@btinternet.com

SHORT, Kenneth Arthur. b 33. Tyndale Hall Bris 64. **d** 67 **p** 68. C E Twickenham St Steph *Lon* 67–71; C Paddock Wood *Roch* 71–74; SE Area Sec BCMS 74–82; Hon C Sidcup Ch Ch *Roch* 74–82; V Tollington Park St Mark w St Anne *Lon* 82–86; V Holloway St Mark w Em 86–89; R Alfold and Loxwood *Guildf* 89–98; rtd 98; PtO *Roch* 00–13; *Lon* 02–13; *S'wark* from 15. *10 Montague Graham Court, Kidbrooke Gardens, London SE3 0PD* T: (020) 8858 8033 E: jukebox.short@gmail.com

SHORT, Martin Peter. b 54. Peterho Cam BA 77 MA 81. Wycliffe Hall Ox 77. **d** 79 **p** 80. C Shipley St Pet *Bradf* 79–82; C Becontree St Mary *Chelmsf* 82–86; V Bolton St Jas w St Chrys *Bradf* 86–92; Dioc Communications Officer 92–98; C Otley 92–98; Hd Media Tr Communications Dept Abps' Coun 98–05; Hon C and Hon Chapl Bradf Cathl 98–05; Chapl to Bp Dover *Cant* 06–12; Hon Min Can Cant Cathl 06–12; R Stow on the Wold, Condicote and The Swells *Glouc* from 12. *The Rectory, Sheep Street, Stow on the Wold, Cheltenham GL54 1AA* T: (01451) 830607

SHORT, Martin Ronald. b 57. Crewe & Alsager Coll CertEd 78 Leic Univ BEd 85. St Jo Coll Nottm 93. **d** 93 **p** 94. C Frankby w Greasby *Ches* 93–97; TV Horwich and Rivington *Man* 97–02; TV Turton Moorland 02–08; P-in-c Rawtenstall St Mary 08–15; P-in-c Constable Lee 08–15; Borough Dean Rossendale 10–13; AD Rossendale 13–15; R Middleton and Thornham 15–18; V Honley *Leeds* from 18. *The Vicarage, St Mary's Road, Honley, Holmfirth HD9 6AZ* E: martin.short@leeds.anglican.org

SHORT, Canon Michael John. b 38. Univ of Wales (Lamp) BA 59. Sarum Th Coll 59. **d** 61 **p** 62. C Swansea St Nic *S & B* 61–64; C Oystermouth 64–69; V Merthyr Vale w Aberfan *Llan* 69–82; RD Merthyr Tydfil 76–82; R Caerphilly 82–08; RD 83–04; Can Llan Cathl 89–08; Prec 02–08; rtd 08; PtO *Llan* from 10. *238 Abercynon Road, Abercynon, Mountain Ash CF45 4LU* T: (01443) 742650 M: 07831-742515

SHORT, Neil Robert. b 58. Loughb Univ BSc 81 St Jo Coll Dur BA 86. Cranmer Hall Dur 83. **d** 86 **p** 87. C Whitfield *Derby* 86–90; C Bradf St Aug Undercliffe 90–96; V Burscough Bridge *Liv* 96–07; Pioneer Min Toxteth 07–09; V St Jas in the City 09–18; V Blundellsands St Mich from 18. *5 Ramleh Park, Liverpool L23 6YD* E: neil@theshorts.go-plus.net

SHORT, Mrs Patricia Ann (Pip). b 41. K Coll Lon BA 62 AKC 62. **d** 00 **p** 01. NSM Etwall w Egginton *Derby* 00–10; NSM Ashbourne St Jo 10–11; NSM Ashbourne St Oswald w Mapleton 10–11; NSM Clifton 10–11; NSM Norbury w Snelston 10–11; Chapl Asst Derby Teaching Hosps NHS Foundn Trust from 00; PtO *Lich* 05–09 and 14–15; *Derby* from 11; *Lich* from 17. *Ivy Cottage, 19 Monk Street, Tutbury, Burton-on-Trent DE13 9NA* T: (01283) 813640 *or* (01332) 347141 F: (01283) 814373 M: 07711-823082 E: pip.short2011@gmail.com

SHORT, Robert Leslie. b 48. Em Coll Cam BA 70 MA 76. Wycliffe Hall Ox 87. **d** 92 **p** 92. Mexico 92–93; Chapl Repton Sch Derby 93–04; P-in-c Ibiza *Eur* 04–13; rtd 13; PtO *Eur* from 13; *S'well* from 13. *49 Manton Crescent, Beeston, Nottingham NG9 2GD* E: bobthevicar@gmail.com

SHORT, Stephen Timothy. b 71. Cheltenham & Glouc Coll of HE BA 96. Ripon Coll Cuddesdon 05. **d** 07 **p** 08. C Tewkesbury w Walton Cardiff and Twyning *Glouc* 07–11; P-in-c Clowne *Derby* 11–13; C Barlborough and Renishaw 11–13; R Barlborough and Clowne 13–17; V Melbourne, Ticknall, Smisby and Stanton from 17. *The Rectory, Church Square, Melbourne, Derby DE73 8JH* T: (01332) 864741 M: 07801-357612 E: stephen.short71@btinternet.com

SHORT, Timothy. *See* SHORT, John Timothy

SHORT, Vincent Charles. b 57. Oak Hill Th Coll 95. **d** 97 **p** 98. C Chatham St Phil and St Jas *Roch* 97–01; V Istead Rise 01–11; V New Beckenham St Paul 11–16; TV Limpsfield and Tatsfield *S'wark* from 16. *The Rectory, Ricketts Hill Road, Tatsfield, Westerham TN16 2NA* T: (01959) 577289

SHORTER, Mrs Anne Roberta. b 56. Edin Univ BA 77 Cam Univ BTh 09. Westcott Ho Cam 07. **d** 09 **p** 10. C Brackley St Pet w St Jas *Pet* 09–12; P-in-c Stanground *Ely* 13; P-in-c

Farcet 13; V Stanground and Farcet 13–19; rtd 19. *Address temp unknown* E: anne.shorter@btinternet.com

SHORTER, Robert Edward. b 48. Ripon Coll Cuddesdon 89. **d** 91 **p** 92. C Braunton *Ex* 91–94; C Bishopsnympton, Rose Ash, Mariansleigh etc 94–96; TV 96–98; P-in-c E w W Harptree and Hinton Blewett *B & W* 98–03; Dioc Ecum Officer 98–03; rtd 03. *Neduadd Bungalow, Dyffryn Road, Llandrindod Wells LD1 6AN* T: (01597) 829790 E: robertshorter@live.co.uk

SHOTLANDER, Lionel George. b 27. Cant Univ (NZ) BA 49 MA 51. **d** 51 **p** 52. New Zealand 51–58 and 60–74; C Southsea St Pet *Portsm* 58–60; V Curdridge 74–85; R Durley 79–85; V Twyford and Owslebury and Morestead *Win* 85–91; rtd 91; PtO *Win* from 91; *Portsm* from 91. *Cambria, High Street, Shirrell Heath, Southampton SO32 2JN* T: (01329) 832353

SHOTTON, Heather Margaret Elizabeth. b 18 **p** 19. NSM Wrexham *St As* from 18. *10 Brynmally Park, Pentre Broughton, Wrexham LL11 6BP* T: (01978) 721666

SHOULER, Canon the Hon Margaret Fiona. b 55. Nottm Univ BEd 78. St Jo Coll Nottm MTh 03. **d** 01 **p** 02. C Sherwood *S'well* 01–06; P-in-c Selston 06–11; V From 11; AD Newstead from 17; Hon Can S'well Minster from 17. *The Vicarage, 58 Church Lane, Selston, Nottingham NG16 6EW* T: (01773) 813777 E: fionashouler@hotmail.com

SHOULER, Simon Frederic. b 54. Pemb Coll Cam MA 79 FRICS 89. EMMTC 82. **d** 85 **p** 86. NSM Asfordby *Leic* 85–89; LtO from 89. *1 West End, Long Clawson, Melton Mowbray LE14 4PE* T: (01664) 822698 E: oldmanorhouse@shoulers.co.uk

SHOWERS, Cyril Rotimi Sigismond. b 64. Fourah Bay Coll Freetown BA 89. SEITE 09. **d** 12 **p** 13. NSM N Dulwich St Faith *S'wark* 12–17; PtO 17–18; Public Preacher 18–19; NSM Northfleet and Rosherville *Roch* from 19. *St Mark's Vicarage, 123 London Road, Northfleet, Gravesend DA11 9NH* M: 07951-762440 E: cyril_showers@yahoo.com

SHREEVE, The Ven David Herbert. b 34. St Pet Hall Ox BA 57 MA 61. Ridley Hall Cam 57. **d** 59 **p** 60. C Plymouth St Andr *Ex* 59–64; V Bermondsey St Anne *S'wark* 64–71; V Eccleshill *Bradf* 71–84; RD Calverley 78–84; Hon Can Bradf Cathl 83–84; Adn Bradf 84–99; rtd 99; PtO *Bradf* 99–14; *Ripon* 00–14; *Leeds* from 14. *26 Kingsley Drive, Harrogate HG1 4TJ* T: (01423) 886479

SHREEVES, Keir Laurence. b 82. Brunel Univ BA 04. St Mellitus Coll BA 13. **d** 13 **p** 14. C Turnham Green Ch Ch *Lon* 13–16; NSM Brighton St Pet *Chich* from 16. *St Peter's Church, York Place, Brighton BN1 4GU* T: (01273) 698182 E: keir.shreeves@gmail.com *or* keir@stpetersbrighton.org

SHREWSBURY, Preb Michael Buller. b 30. St Jo Coll Dur BA 54. Linc Th Coll 54. **d** 56 **p** 57. C Salford St Phil w St Steph *Man* 56–60; Chapl RN 60–63; Chapl HM Pris Pentonville 64–67; Bermuda 67–70; V Dalston H Trin w St Phil *Lon* 70–86; AD Hackney 79–84; Preb St Paul's Cathl 86–92; R Stepney St Dunstan and All SS 86–92; rtd 92; PtO *Lon* 92–15. *22 Blackcliffe Way, Bearpark, Durham DH7 7TJ* T: 0191-659 9114 E: mike.shrewsbury@btinternet.com

SHREWSBURY, Area Bishop of. *See* BULLOCK, The Rt Revd Sarah Ruth

SHRIMPTON, Mrs Sheila Nan. b 32. Qu Mary Coll Lon BA 54 LSE CertSS 55. St Chris Coll Blackheath 57. **dss** 83 **d** 87 **p** 94. LtO *B & W* 83–90; NSM Barkston and Hough Gp *Linc* 90–97; Asst Local Min Officer 90–97; C Brant Broughton and Beckingham 97–98; P-in-c Churchstanton, Buckland St Mary and Otterford *B & W* 98–02; rtd 02; PtO *B & W* 03–14. *2 King William Mews, Church Street, Curry Rivel, Langport TA10 0HD* T: (01458) 259293

SHRINE, Mrs Susan Elaine Walmsley. b 56. NOC. **d** 02 **p** 03. C Bradshaw and Holmfield *Wakef* 02–04; TV Shelf w Buttershaw St Aid *Bradf* 04–10; P-in-c Queensbury 10–15; V 15–16; P-in-c Bredbury St Barn *Ches* from 16; P-in-c Queensbury *Leeds* from 14. *St Barnabas' Vicarage, Osborne Street, Bredbury, Stockport SK6 2AD* T: 0161-406 6569 E: sue.shrine780@btinternet.com

SHUFFLEBOTHAM, Alastair Vincent. b 32. Nottm Univ CSocSc 57. Lich Th Coll 63. **d** 65 **p** 66. C W Kirby St Bridget *Ches* 65–71; C Stockport St Paul 69–71; V Tranmere St Paul w St Luke 71–78; V Neston 78–97; rtd 97; PtO *St As* 09–16. *Y-Clystyrau, 5 Tan-y-Bryn, Llanbedr Dyffryn Clwyd, Ruthin LL15 1AQ* T: (01824) 704619 E: 2bunches@talktalk.net

SHUKER, Linda Kathleen. b 56. Imp Coll Lon BSc 77 PhD 81. St Jo Coll Nottm 05. **d** 07 **p** 08. C Rothley *Leic* 07–11; R Birling, Addington, Ryarsh and Trottiscliffe *Roch* from 11. *The Vicarage, Birling Road, Ryarsh, West Malling ME19 5LS* T: (01732) 842249 E: dlshuker@aol.com

SHUKMAN, Ann Margaret. b 31. Girton Coll Cam BA 53 MA 58 LMH Ox DPhil 74. WMMTC 80. **dss** 84 **d** 92 **p** 94. Steeple Aston w N Aston and Tackley *Ox* 84–96; NSM 92–96; rtd 96; PtO *Ox* 96–01; Hon C Dumfries *Glas* from 01.

Elshieshields Tower, Lockerbie DG11 1LY T: (01387) 810280
E: revann@stjohnsdumfries.org *or* ann.shukman@gmail.com

SHULER, Patricia Ann Margaret. b 52. Anglia Ruskin Univ
MA 08 Univ of Wales (Ban) BTh 08. Ridley Hall Cam 02.
d 05 **p** 06. C Ipswich St Aug *St E* 05–09; C Woodbridge
St Jo and Bredfield 09–12; P-in-c Martlesham w Brightwell
12–15; rtd 15; Rtd Clergy, Widows and Widowers Officer
Ches from 15; PtO from 16. *27 The Beeches, Upton, Chester
CH2 1PE* T: (01244) 318941 E: tricia.shuler@gmail.com

SHUTT, Anthony John. b 57. Brunel Univ BSc 79. Trin Coll
Bris 87. **d** 89 **p** 90. C Epsom St Martin *Guildf* 89–95; P-in-c
Send from 95. *St Mary's Vicarage, Vicarage Lane, Send, Woking
GU23 7JN* T: (01483) 222193 E: tony@tonyshutt.co.uk

SHUTT, The Ven Nicholas Stephen. b 58. Qu Mary Coll Lon
LLB 80 Univ of Wales (Cardiff) LLM 01 Plymouth Coll of Art
BA 11 Solicitor 83. SWMTC 91. **d** 94 **p** 95. NSM Yelverton,
Meavy, Sheepstor and Walkhampton *Ex* 94–16; P-in-c 08–16;
R Yelverton, Meavy, Sheepstor, Walkhampton, Sampford
Spiney and Horrabridge *Ex* 16–19; Adn Plymouth from 19;
Preb Ex Cathl from 11. *12 Blackbrook Close, Walkhampton,
Yelverton PL20 6JF* T: (01822) 854653 *or* (01752) 858382
E: archdeacon.of.plymouth@exeter.anglican.org *or*
nick.shutt@gmail.com

SHUTTLEWORTH, Caroline Elizabeth. b 59. K Coll Lon
BA 92. St Mellitus Coll BA 16. **d** 16 **p** 17. C Islington
St Mary *Lon* from 16. *20 Ellesmere Road, London
E3 5QX* M: 07986-064025 E: ceshuttleworth@aol.com *or*
caroline.shuttleworth@stmaryislington.org

SHUTTLEWORTH (*née* Gaunt), Rachel. b 81. St Cuth Soc
Dur BA 04. St Mellitus Coll BA 18. **d** 18 **p** 19. C Tanhouse
The Oaks CD *Liv* from 18. *23 Elmridge, Skelmersdale
WN8 6DF* M: 07891-378299 E: gaunt_rachel@yahoo.co.uk

SIBANDA, The Very Revd Melusi Francis. b 72. Univ of
Zimbabwe BSc 96 BA 99 St Martin's Coll Lanc MA 06. Bp
Gaul Th Coll Harare 97. **d** 98 **p** 99. C Bulawayo Cathl
Zimbabwe 98–01; R Bulawayo St Marg 01–03; C Colne
and Villages *Blackb* 03–06; P-in-c Rednal *Birm* 06–12; V
12–16; AD Kings Norton 12–15; R Dunsborough Australia
16–19; Dean St Paul's Cathl Rockhampton from 19. *The
Deanery, 164 Alma Lane, Rockhampton QLD 4700, Australia*
E: melusi.sibanda@gmail.com

SIBANDA, Thabani Isaac. b 84. Cranmer Hall Dur 15. **d** 18
p 19. C Nor Heartsease St Fran from 18; C Thorpe St Matt
from 19. *9 Pine Road, Norwich NR7 9LE* M: 07709-552157
E: thabo.i.sibanda@gmail.com

SIBBALD, Olwyn Eileen. *See* MARLOW, Olwyn Eileen

SIBLEY, Jonathan Paul Eddolls. b 55. Newc Univ BA 77.
Westcott Ho Cam 78 Ripon Coll Cuddesdon 85. **d** 87
p 88. C Waltham Cross *St Alb* 87–90; C Chalfont St Peter
Ox 90–96; P-in-c Sulhamstead Abbots and Bannister w
Ufton Nervet 96–02; P-in-c Sutton St Mary *Linc* 02–11; V
Long Sutton w Lutton etc from 11. *The Vicarage, Market
Place, Long Sutton, Spalding PE12 9JJ* T/F: (01406) 362033
E: jonathan.sibley3@btinternet.com

SIBLEY, Peter Linsey. b 40. Selw Coll Cam BA 61 MA 63. Oak
Hill Th Coll 79. **d** 81 **p** 82. C Crofton *Portsm* 81–84; TV
Cheltenham St Mark *Glouc* 84–93; P-in-c Tewkesbury H Trin
93–96; V 96–05; RD Tewkesbury and Winchcombe 97–02;
rtd 05; PtO *Glouc* from 14. *14 Griffiths Avenue, Cheltenham
GL51 7BH* T: (01242) 514640 E: sibglos@aol.com

SIBSON, Canon Edward John. b 39. Brasted Th Coll 61 St Aid
Birkenhead 63. **d** 65 **p** 66. C Gt Parndon *Chelmsf* 65–69; C
Saffron Walden 69–72; P-in-c Colchester St Leon 72–77;
TV Colchester St Leon, St Mary Magd and St Steph 77–80;
Ind Chapl 72–80; V Layer de la Haye 80–90; R Chipping
Ongar w Shelley 90–98; RD Ongar 94–98; P-in-c High and
Gd Easter w Margaret Roding 98–04; P-in-c Gt Canfield
w High Roding and Aythorpe Roding 98–04; Hon Can
Chelmsf Cathl 01–04; rtd 04; PtO *Chelmsf* from 04. *73
Thaxted Road, Saffron Walden CB11 3AG* T: (01799) 520007
E: ejohnsibson@btinternet.com

SIBSON, Canon Robert Francis. b 46. Leeds Univ CertEd 68.
Sarum & Wells Th Coll 78. **d** 80 **p** 81. C Watford St Mich
St Alb 80–83; TV Digswell and Panshanger 83–90; Chapl
Qu Eliz Hosp Welwyn Garden City 86–88; V Biggleswade
St Alb 90–02; Chapl Bedford and Shires Health and
Care NHS Trust 94–02; RD Biggleswade *St Alb* 96–01; V
Sawbridgeworth 02–12; Hon Can St Alb 98–12; rtd 12; PtO
St Alb from 12; *Ely* from 13; Asst Rtd Clergy Officer from 16.
35 High Street, Offord D'Arcy, St Neots PE19 5RF T: (01480)
812756 M: 07711-705081 E: robert.sibson@btinternet.com

SICHEL, Stephen Mackenzie. b 59. UEA BA 80 Birm Univ
MA 95 K Coll Lon DThMin 16. Ripon Coll Cuddesdon 87.
d 90 **p** 91. C Tettenhall Regis *Lich* 90–95; C Camberwell
St Giles w St Matt *S'wark* 95–01; P-in-c Brixton St Matt
01–02; P-in-c Brixton St Matt w St Jude 02–13; V from 13; AD

Lambeth N 10–12. *The Vicarage, 5 St Matthew's Road, London
SW2 1ND* T/F: (020) 7733 9605 E: sichel@tiscali.co.uk

SIDDALL, Canon Arthur. b 43. Lanc Univ MA 81 Surrey Univ
PGCE 94 MCMI 96. ALCD 67. **d** 67 **p** 68. C Formby H Trin
Liv 67–70; C Childwall All SS 70–72; CMS 72–77; Chapl
Chittagong Ch Ch Bangladesh 74–77; V Clitheroe St Paul
Low Moor *Blackb* 77–82; V Blackb St Gabr 82–90; Dep Gen
Sec Miss to Seamen 90–93; Hon C Leatherhead *Guildf* 93–96;
V Chipping and Whitewell *Blackb* 96–04; Rural Chapl
03–04; Chapl Naples w Sorrento, Capri and Bari *Eur* 04–07;
Chapl Montreux w Anzere, Gstaad and Monthey 07–09;
Adn Italy and Malta 05–09; Switzerland 07–09; rtd 09; PtO
Liv from 16; *Blackb* 16–17; *Eur* from 16. *24 Shaw Crescent,
Liverpool L37 8DA*

SIDDALL, Mark. b 77. Southn Univ BSc 99 PhD 03 Univ
of Bordeaux II MSc 98. St Mellitus Coll MA 18. **d** 18 **p** 19.
C Draycot *Bris* from 18. *11 Aintree Drive, Chippenham
SN14 0FA* M: 07482-316541 E: mr_mark_sid@yahoo.com

SIDDLE, Michael Edward. b 33. Dur Univ BA 54. St Aid
Birkenhead 55. **d** 57 **p** 58. C Fazakerley Em *Liv* 57–59; C
Farnworth 59–62; V Swadlincote *Derby* 62–70; Distr Sec
(Northd and Dur) BFBS 70–72; Yorkshire 72–82; V Bamber
Bridge St Aid *Blackb* 82–87; V Horsforth *Ripon* 87–00; rtd 00;
PtO *Ripon* 00–14; Leeds 14–16. *28 Carr Bridge Drive, Cookridge,
Leeds LS16 7JY* T: 0113-261 0498 M: 07941-209069

SIDEBOTHAM, Canon Stephen Francis. b 35. Qu Coll Cam
BA 58 MA 80. Linc Th Coll 58. **d** 60 **p** 61. C Bitterne Park
Win 60–64; Hong Kong 64–83; Dean 76–83; Adn 78–83;
Chapl Gravesend and N Kent Hosp 83–94; R Gravesend
St Geo *Roch* 83–94; RD Gravesend 91–94; P-in-c Rosherville
91–94; Acorn Chr Foundn 94–19; rtd 97; PtO *Ox* 97–19. *20
The Dovecotes, Allesley Hall Drive, Allesley, Coventry CV5 9RD*
E: sideblot@btinternet.com

SIDEBOTTOM, Andrew John. *See* GRACE, Andrew John

SIDEBOTTOM, Susan Marie. b 60. Yorks Min Course. **d** 09
p 10. NSM Chesterton *Lich* 09–16; NSM Knutton from 16.
18 Leech Avenue, Newcastle ST5 7PN

SIDWELL, Elizabeth Sarah. b 57. Girton Coll Cam BA 79
MA 83 Univ of Wales (Swansea) MSc 94. Ripon Coll
Cuddesdon 08. **d** 10 **p** 11. C Wells St Cuth w Wookey Hole
B & W 10–14; PtO 14–15; R Bredenbury *Heref* from 15. *The
Rectory, Bredenbury, Bromyard HR7 4TF* T: (01885) 482737
E: essidwell@yahoo.ie

SIEBERT, Mrs Rosemary Clare. b 48. Solicitor 03. SEITE 99.
d 08 **p** 09. NSM Folkestone St Mary, St Eanswythe
and St Sav *Cant* 08–15; NSM Marcham w Garford and
Shippon *Ox* from 16. *9 Sweetbriar, North Street, Marcham,
Abingdon OX13 6PD* T: (01865) 392135 M: 07763-330113
E: rsiebert@btinternet.com

SIEJKOWSKI, Piotr Jan. *See* ASHWIN-SIEJKOWSKI, Piotr Jan

SIGRIST, Mrs Catherine Mary. b 55. Westcott Ho Cam.
d 07 **p** 08. C Cheriton St Martin *Cant* 07–10; C Cheriton
All So w Newington 07–10; R Ringwould w Kingsdown
and Ripple etc 10–16; P-in-c Saltash *Truro* from 16; P-in-c
Landrake w St Erney and Botus Fleming from 16. *The
Rectory, St Stephens, Saltash PL12 4AP* T: (01752) 842323
E: rev.cathysigrist@gmail.com

SIGRIST, Richard Martin. b 46. Bernard Gilpin Soc Dur 67
Sarum Th Coll 68. **d** 71 **p** 72. C Yeovil St Mich *B & W*
71–74; Chapl RN 74–84; TV Sidmouth, Woolbrook
and Salcombe Regis *Ex* 84–86; TR 86–91; TR Sidmouth,
Woolbrook, Salcombe Regis, Sidbury etc 91–94; RD Ottery
90–94; USA 94–99; P-in-c Devonport St Bart *Ex* 99–02; V
02–07; V Devonport St Bart and Ford St Mark 08–11; RD
Plymouth Devonport 01–11; rtd 11; PtO *B & W* from 11. *4
Brue Crescent, Burnham-on-Sea TA8 1LR* T: (01278) 780135
E: rmsigrist@hotmail.com

SIGSWORTH, David. b 61. York Univ BA 82 K Coll Lon
MMus 83 Lon Inst of Educn PGCE 84. Trin Coll Bris 12. **d** 14
p 15. C Gt Bookham *Guildf* 14–18; V Lightwater from 18.
The Vicarage, 28 Broadway Road, Lightwater GU18 5SJ

SILCOCK, Donald John. b 30. AKC 59. **d** 60 **p** 61. C Hackney
St Jo *Lon* 60–63; C-in-c Plumstead Wm Temple Ch Abbey
Wood CD *S'wark* 63–68; C Felpham w Middleton *Chich*
68–74; R Ightham *Roch* 74–84; R Cliffe at Hoo w Cooling
84–92; RD Strood 85–91; rtd 92; PtO *Chich* from 92. *Puck's
House, 26 Ancton Way, Bognor Regis PO22 6JN* T: (01243)
582883

SILINS, Jacqueline. *See* JOHNSON, Jacqueline

SILK, Canon Ian Geoffrey. b 60. Pemb Coll Cam BA 81
MA 85. Trin Coll Bris BA 89. **d** 89 **p** 90. C Linc St Giles
89–93; P-in-c Linc St Geo Swallowbeck 93–98; V 98–16; PV
Linc Cathl from 01; Can and Preb Linc Cathl from 07. *5
The Brambles, Littleport, Ely CB6 1XH* M: 07944-688505
E: ian.silk@ntlworld.com

SILK, John Arthur. b 52. Selw Coll Cam BA 73 MA 77 K Coll Lon MTh 80. Westcott Ho Cam 75. **d** 77 **p** 78. C Banstead *Guildf* 77–80; C Dorking w Ranmore 80–84; R Ringwould w Kingsdown *Cant* 84–95; V Thames Ditton *Guildf* 95–14; rtd 14; PtO *B & W* from 15. *Southolme, Church Street, Milborne Port, Sherborne DT9 5DJ* T: (01963) 548472 E: johnsilk@tiscali.co.uk

SILK, Stuart Charles. b 76. SS Mark & Jo Univ Coll Plymouth BA 99. Oak Hill Th Coll BA 10. **d** 10 **p** 11. C Southbourne w W Thorney *Chich* 10–13; C Lindfield from 13. *66 Finches Gardens, Lindfield RH16 2PB* T: (01444) 483547 M: 07866-487535 E: stuartcsilk@gmail.com *or* stuart@linfield.info

SILLER, Canon James Robert William. b 44. Pemb Coll Ox BA 65 MA 70. Westcott Ho Cam 67. **d** 70 **p** 71. C Spring Grove St Mary *Lon* 70–73; C Leeds St Pet *Ripon* 73–77; P-in-c Leeds City 73–77; V Gilling and Kirkby Ravensworth 77–82; P-in-c Middleton Tyas and Melsonby 77–82; R Farnley 82–94; V Potternewton 94–05; Hon Can Ripon Cathl 99–05; rtd 05; PtO *York* 06–11. *1 Sandhill Oval, Leeds LS17 8EB* T: 0113-268 0014

SILLETT, Angela Veronica Isabel. *See* BERNERS-WILSON, Angela Veronica Isabel

SILLEY, Andrew. b 85. Bris Univ BSc 07. Wycliffe Hall Ox BTh 15. **d** 15 **p** 16. C Corby St Jo w Epiphany *Pet* from 15. *13 Honiton Gardens, Corby NN18 8BW* M: 07534-419072 E: andrewsilley@msn.com

SILLEY, Canon Michael John. b 48. Ripon Coll Cuddesdon 82. **d** 84 **p** 85. C Frodingham *Linc* 84–87; V Ingham w Cammeringham w Fillingham 87–96; R Aisthorpe w Scampton w Thorpe le Fallows etc 87–96; RD Lawres 92–96; P-in-c N w S Carlton 93–96; P-in-c Brigg 96–97; V Brigg, Wrawby and Cadney cum Howsham 97–04; RD Yarborough 01–02; Bp's Dom Chapl 05–12; Gen Preacher 05–12; Can and Preb Linc Cathl 09–13; rtd 12; PtO *Linc* from 13. *46 Windsor Way, Broughton, Brigg DN20 0EL* T: (01652) 651055 E: michaelsilley48@outlook.com

SILLIS, Andrew Keith. b 66. Wolv Poly BSc 87. Aston Tr Scheme 91 Westcott Ho Cam 93. **d** 96 **p** 97. C Boyne Hill *Ox* 96–99; C Hayes St Nic CD *Lon* 99–00; C-in-c 00–05; V N Hayes St Nic 05–09; V Cuddington *Guildf* 09–12; Chapl Bonn w Cologne *Eur* 12–15; P-in-c Stourbridge St Thos *Worc* 15–18; V from 18; RD Stourbridge from 17. *The Vicarage, 34 South Road, Stourbridge DY8 3YB* T: (01562) 884155 M: 07951-904122 E: asillis@aol.com

SILLIS, Eric Keith. b 41. NW Ord Course 75. **d** 78 **p** 79. C Blackpool St Steph *Blackb* 78–82; V Huncoat 82–86; V Blackpool St Wilfrid 86–95; V Fleetwood St Dav 95–06; Dioc Chapl MU 99–06; rtd 06; PtO *Blackb* from 06. *23 Fernwood Avenue, Thornton-Cleveleys FY5 5EU* T: (01253) 865449

SILLITOE, William John. b 37. Lich Th Coll 67. **d** 69 **p** 70. C Ettingshall *Lich* 69–71; C March St Jo *Ely* 72–74; P-in-c Kennett 74–77; V Fordham St Pet 74–77; V Castle Bromwich St Clem *Birm* 77–00; rtd 00; PtO *Birm* 00–04; *Lich* 15–18. *St Clement's Croft, 11 Wood Green Road, Wednesbury WS10 9AX* T: 0121-505 5954

SILLS, Canon Peter Michael. b 41. Nottm Univ BA 63 LLM 68 Kent Univ PhD 00 Barrister 76. S'wark Ord Course 78. **d** 81 **p** 82. C W Wimbledon Ch Ch *S'wark* 81–85; P-in-c Barnes H Trin 85–93; Wandsworth Adnry Ecum Officer 90–93; V Purley St Mark 93–00; Can Res Ely Cathl 00–08; rtd 08; PtO *Chich* from 08. *The Coach House, Keymer Road, Hassocks BN6 8JR* T: (01273) 842760 E: peter@peter-sills.co.uk

SILVA, Peter John. b 47. Rhodes Univ BA 73 HDipEd 77 BEd 79. St Paul's Coll Grahamstown 68. **d** 74 **p** 74. C Bloemfontein Cath S Africa 74–75; Chapl Dioc Sch for Girls Grahamstown 75–79; Lect Rhodes Univ 79–81; Dir Academic Support Services Natal Univ 81–85; Regional Manager Performance and Educn 86; Dir Tape Aids for the Blind 87; R Overport Ch Ch 88–89; Chapl Dioc Sch for Girls Grahamstown 89–95; Dir Educn Projects Grahamstown Foundn 95–98; TV Abingdon *Ox* 99–02; Chief Exec Officer Peers Early Educn Partnership 02–11; P-in-c Gt w Lt Tew and Over w Nether Worton *Ox* 11–13; rtd 12; PtO *Ox* from 13. *45 Spring Street, Chipping Norton OX7 5NN* T: (01608) 430234 M: 07980-264472 E: silvapete@gmail.com

SILVERSIDES, Mark. b 51. Lon Univ BD 73. St Jo Coll Nottm 74. **d** 76 **p** 77. C Hornchurch St Andr *Chelmsf* 76–80; P-in-c Becontree St Thos 80–85; TR Becontree W 85–86; CPAS Staff 86–92; New Media Producer from 92. *15 Glenhurst Drive, Whickham, Newcastle upon Tyne NE16 5SH* T: 0191-488 1937 E: msilversides@ambitnewmedia.com

SILVERTHORN, Alan. b 37. St Mich Coll Llan 62. **d** 65 **p** 66. C Machen and Rudry *Mon* 65–71; V New Tredegar 71–83; V Llanfrechfa and Llanddewi Fach w Llandegfeth 83–04; rtd 04; PtO *Llan* 05–17. *14 Davies Street, Ystrad Mynach, Hengoed CF82 8AD* T: (01443) 816649

SILVESTER, Christine. b 51. WMMTC 02. **d** 05 **p** 06. NSM Walsall Wood *Lich* 05–08; NSM Shelfield and High Heath 08–18; Chapl R Wolv NHS Trust 08–14; rtd 18. *Address withheld by request* E: silvesterchristine@hotmail.com

SILVESTER, David. b 59. Qu Mary Coll Lon BSc 80 Nottm Univ BCombStuds 85. Linc Th Coll 82. **d** 85 **p** 86. C Walthamstow St Mary w St Steph *Chelmsf* 85–90; TV Barking St Marg w St Patr 90–96; V Mildmay Grove St Jude and St Paul *Lon* 96–08; AD Islington 03–07; TR Hackney Marsh 08–11; V Studley *Cov* 11–13; P-in-c Spernall, Morton Bagot and Oldberrow 11–13; R Arden Marches 13–17; AD Alcester 14–17; rtd 17; PtO *Cov* from 17. *The Vicarage, 3 Manor Mews, Manor Road, Studley B80 7NA* E: dsilve5737@aol.com

SILVESTER, Canon Stephen David. b 59. Chu Coll Cam BA 80 MA 83 Man Univ PGCE 82. St Jo Coll Nottm 88. **d** 91 **p** 92. C Nottingham St Jude *S'well* 91–96; V Gamston and Bridgford 96–08; AD W Bingham 04–07; P-in-c Nottingham St Nic 08–11; R from 11; P-in-c Sneinton St Chris w St Phil 10–14; AD Nottm S from 16; Hon Can S'well Minster from 13. *37 Lyme Park, West Bridgford, Nottingham NG2 7TR* T: 0115-982 0407

SIMESTER, Paul Stephen. b 57. Oak Hill Th Coll 97. **d** 99 **p** 00. C Branksome Park All SS *Sarum* 99–03; TV Wareham 03–07; PtO from 14. *27 Weyman's Avenue, Bournemouth BH10 7JR* T: (01202) 574995 E: psimester@hotmail.com

SIMISTER, Norman Harold. b 39. Bris Univ BSc 60. **d** 93 **p** 94. OLM Wainford *St E* 93–09; PtO from 10. *Romaine, 1 School Road, Ringsfield, Beccles NR34 8NZ* T: (01502) 715549

SIMMONDS, Paul Andrew Howard. b 50. Nottm Univ BSc 73. Trin Coll Bris 75. **d** 78 **p** 79. C Leic H Trin w St Jo 78–82; SW Regional Co-ord CPAS 83–86; Hd Adult Tr and Resources CPAS 86–95; Hon C Wolston and Church Lawford *Cov* from 89; Dioc Miss Adv 95–03; Research Dir Forward Vision 03–05; Team Ldr Foundations21 BRF from 05; Ind Chapl *Cov* from 08. *31 John Simpson Close, Wolston, Coventry CV8 3HX* T: (024) 7654 3188 E: paul@workcare.org

SIMMONDS, Canon Paul Richard. b 38. AKC 63. **d** 64 **p** 65. C Newington St Mary *S'wark* 64–67; C Cheam 68–73; P-in-c Stockwell Green St Andr 73–87; V 87–03; Hon Can S'wark Cathl 97–03; rtd 03; PtO *Chich* from 15. *Timbers, 37 Ocean Drive, Ferring, Worthing BN12 5QP* T: (01903) 242679 E: paulangela@hotmail.com

SIMMONDS, Robert William. b 52. Nottm Univ BTh 77. Linc Th Coll 72. **d** 80 **p** 81. C Roehampton H Trin *S'wark* 80–83; TV Hemel Hempstead *St Alb* 83–90; V S Woodham Ferrers *Chelmsf* 90–94; rtd 94; PtO *Cant* 03–06; *Blackb* 10–14; *Cant* 14–16. *70 Wynn Road, Whitstable CT5 2JN* T: (01227) 634919 E: bobwsimmonds@tiscali.co.uk

SIMMONS, Andrew John. b 88. Van Mildert Coll Dur MChem 10. Oak Hill Th Coll BA 16. **d** 16 **p** 17. C Houghton *Carl* 16–19; C Toxteth St Philemon w St Gabr and St Cleopas *Liv* from 19. *Address temp unknown* E: andrewjohnsimmons@gmail.com

SIMMONS, Bernard Peter. b 26. CA Tr Coll 48 S'wark Ord Course 86. **d** 88 **p** 88. C Chatham St Wm *Roch* 88–91; rtd 91; P-in-c Underriver and Seal St Lawr *Roch* 91–95; PtO *Pet* 95–11. *5 Sycamore Drive, Desborough, Kettering NN14 2YH* T: (01536) 763302 E: mail@petersimmons.me.uk

SIMMONS, Canon Brian Dudley. b 35. Master Mariner. St Steph Ho Ox 62. **d** 64 **p** 65. C Bournemouth St Pet *Win* 64–67; Miss to Seamen 67–71; Hon C Milton next Gravesend w Denton *Roch* 67–70; Hon C Gravesend St Geo 70–71; V Lamorbey H Trin 71–90; R Hever w Mark Beech 90–93; P-in-c Four Elms 90–93; R Hever, Four Elms and Mark Beech 93–94; V Langton Green 94–01; Hon Can Roch Cathl 91–01; rtd 01; PtO *Roch* from 04. *17 Chancellor House, Mount Ephraim, Tunbridge Wells TN4 8BT* T: (01892) 617262 E: canonsimmons@gmail.com

SIMMONS, Canon Christopher John. b 49. Mert Coll Ox MA 77. NEOC 88. **d** 90 **p** 91. C Kirkleatham *York* 90–93; P-in-c Barlby 93–95; V Barlby and Riccall 95–02; RD Derwent 98–01; R Pocklington and Owsthorpe and Kilnwick Percy etc 02–08; P-in-c Burnby 06–08; P-in-c Londesborough 06–08; P-in-c Nunburnholme and Warter and Huggate 06–08; P-in-c Shiptonthorpe and Hayton 06–08; P-in-c Skirlaugh w Long Riston, Rise and Swine 08–12; C Brandesburton and Leven w Catwick 11–12; RD N Holderness 09–11; Can and Preb York Minster 08–12; rtd 12; Hon C Brandesburton and Leven w Catwick *York* 12–13; PtO *Newc* from 13. *22 Valebrook, Hexham NE46 2BL* E: chris@csimmons.plus.com

SIMMONS, Eric. b 30. Leeds Univ BA 51. Coll of Resurr Mirfield 51. **d** 53 **p** 54. C Chesterton St Luke *Ely* 53–57; Chapl Keele Univ *Lich* 57–61; CR from 63; Warden Hostel of the Resurr Leeds 66–67; Superior CR 74–87; R Foundn of St Kath in Ratcliffe 89–92; Prior St Mich Priory 93–97; rtd 98; PtO *Leeds* from 17. *House of the Resurrection, Stocks Bank*

Road, Mirfield WF14 0BN T: (01924) 494318 F: 490489
E: esimmons@mirfield.org.uk

SIMMONS, Gary David. b 59. Trin Coll Bris BA 86. **d** 87 **p** 88.
C Ecclesfield *Sheff* 87–90; Min Stapenhill Immanuel CD
Derby 90–95; V Stapenhill Immanuel 97–98; R Slaugham
Chich 98–10; P-in-c Staplefield Common 08–10; R Slaugham
and Staplefield Common 10–16; RD Cuckfield 11–16; TR
Glascote and Stonydelph *Lich* from 16. *The Vicarage, 86
Bamford Street, Tamworth B77 2AS*

SIMMONS, John Graham. b 54. Westf Coll Lon BSc 75 Man
Univ PGCE 76. NOC 89. **d** 92 **p** 93. C Thame w Towersey
Ox 92–97; R Heydon, Gt and Lt Chishill, Chrishall etc
Chelmsf 97–05; V Chadderton Ch Ch *Man* from 05;
PtO *Eur* from 16. *The Vicarage, Block Lane, Chadderton,
Oldham OL9 7QB* T: 0161-652 2950 M: 07813-559654
E: chaddertonvicar@gmail.com

SIMMONS, John Harold. b 46. FCCA. Sarum & Wells Th
Coll 86. **d** 89 **p** 90. NSM The Iwernes, Sutton Waldron and
Fontmell Magna *Sarum* 89–01; NSM Iwerne Valley 01–17; RD
Milton and Blandford 13–16; PtO from 17. *Fourways, Frog
Lane, Shroton, Blandford Forum DT11 8QL* T: (01258) 860515
E: john@fourways.plus.com

SIMMONS, Mrs Margaret Irene. b 49. Cov Univ BSc 02
RGN RSCN. **d** 08 **p** 09. NSM Leam Valley *Cov* 08–10;
NSM Hillmorton 10–18; P-in-c 12–18; rtd 18; PtO *Cov*
18–19; Hon C Hillmorton from 19. *The Vicarage, 18
Hoskyn Close, Rugby CV21 4LA* T: (01788) 576279
E: mi.simmons@btinternet.com

SIMMONS, Ms Marion. b 45. NOC 95. **d** 98 **p** 99. NSM
Stoneycroft All SS *Liv* 98–99; C 00–01; TV Fazakerley
Em 01–08; TR 08–14; rtd 14; PtO *Liv* from 16. *1 Rainbow
Drive, Melling, Liverpool L31 1BY* T: 0151-739 4367
E: marionrainbow1@yahoo.co.uk

SIMMONS, Peter. *See* SIMMONS, Bernard Peter

SIMMONS, Peter Maurice. b 51. ERMC 10. **d** 11 **p** 12. C
Kettering Ch the King *Pet* 11–15; V Penn Street *Ox* from 15.
The Vicarage, Penn Street, Amersham HP7 0PX M: 07824-
618875 E: revpeter@live.co.uk

SIMMS, Miss Melanie Laura. b 73. Trin Coll Bris 06. **d** 08
p 09. C Southway *Ex* 08–13; C Rainham *Roch* 13–15;
Chapl Peter Carnley Ang Community Sch Australia from
15. *3 Champagny Way, Secret Harbour WA 6173, Australia*
E: revmelaniesimms@hotmail.co.uk

SIMON, David Sidney. b 49. Univ of Wales (Abth)
BSc(Econ) 70 Hull Univ MA 83 Lanc Univ MA 05.
NEOC 84. **d** 87 **p** 88. NSM Beverley St Mary *York* 87–94;
NSM Beverley Deanery 94–98; Lect Humberside Coll of
HE 87–90; Humberside Poly 90–92; Humberside Univ
York 92–96; Lincs and Humberside Univ 96–98; Admin
Rydal Hall *Carl* 98–01; PtO 01–02; NSM Cartmel Peninsula
02–14; Dioc Officer for NSM 08–14; rtd 14; Lect Halifax
Leeds 14–17; Lect Halifax w Siddal 17–18; PtO from 19. *25
Winterbutlee Grove, Todmorden OL14 7QU* T: (01706) 810336
E: davidsimon25www@btinternet.com

SIMON, Fiona Elizabeth. b 64. Bradf Univ BEng 86. STETS 06.
d 09 **p** 10. C Stoke-next-Guildf *Guildf* 09–13; PtO 13–14;
P-in-c Haw 14–16; V 16–18; Asst Chapl Brussels *Eur* from
18. *Pro-Cathedral of the Holy Trinity, 29 rue Capitaine Crespel,
1050 Brussels, Belgium* T: (0032) (2) 511 7183 M: 07810-
160254 E: fionasimon1964@gmail.com

SIMON, Frederick Fairbanks. b 42. Ripon Coll Cuddesdon 74.
d 77 **p** 78. C Cheddleton *Lich* 77–79; C Woodley St Jo the
Ev *Ox* 79–82; V Spencer's Wood 82–85; P-in-c Steventon
w Milton 85–87; Chapl Grenville Coll Bideford 87–95;
rtd 96; PtO *Ex* 96–04. *26 Castle Street, Calne SN11 0DX*
E: fr.fred@btopenworld.com

SIMON, Haydn Henry England. *See* ENGLAND-SIMON,
Haydn Henry

✠**SIMON, The Rt Revd Oliver.** b 45. Dur Univ BA 67 Sussex
Univ MA 68 Sheff Univ MinnTheol 94 Lon Univ DMin 09.
Cuddesdon Coll 69. **d** 71 **p** 72 **c** 12. C Kidlington *Ox* 71–74;
C Bracknell 74–78; V Frodsham *Ches* 78–88; R Easthampstead
Ox 88–00; Chapl Ripon Coll Cuddesdon 00–05; Chapl
Community of St Mary V Wantage 00–05; Chapl Pemb
Coll Ox 03–04; TV Rugby *Cov* 05–10; OLM Officer and Dir
Studies 06–10; OLM Tutor Qu Foundn Birm 07–10; rtd 10;
Dir Studies Dio Mauritius 10–12; Bp Antsiranana 12–15.
Colcombe Mill Cottage, Colyton EX24 6EU T: (01297) 552870
E: oliversimon@dunelm.org.uk

SIMONS, Miss Christine. b 40. RGN 62 RM 64 RHV 69.
St Jo Coll Nottm 82. dss 84 **d** 87 **p** 94. Claygate *Guildf*
84–87; C Camberley St Paul 87–93; NSM 93–99; C Woking
Ch Ch 99–05; rtd 05; PtO *Guildf* from 05. *25 Kingsway,
Blackwater, Camberley GU17 0JW* T: (01276) 503174
E: chris@spaceagenow.co.uk

SIMONS, Rachel Clare. b 72. ERMC 15. **d** 18 **p** 19. NSM
Bedford St Pet w St Cuth *St Alb* from 18. *1 Soroptimist
House, Green Lane, Clapham, Bedford MK41 6ER*
E: curatestpeterdemerton@gmail.com

SIMONSON, Canon Juergen Werner Dietrich. b 24. Lon
Univ BD 52. ALCD 52. **d** 52 **p** 53. C W Kilburn St Luke
w St Simon and St Jude *Lon* 52–56; Nigeria 57–63; Chapl
CMS Tr Coll Chislehurst 64–65; Vice-Prin 65–67; Prin CMS
Tr Coll Chislehurst 67–69; V Putney St Marg *S'wark* 69–81;
RD Wandsworth 74–81; Hon Can S'wark Cathl 75–90; R
Barnes St Mary 81–90; rtd 90; PtO *Win* 90–15. *33 Barnhill
Court, Barnhill Road, Chipping Sodbury, Bristol BS37 6FG*
E: juergens@tiscali.co.uk

SIMPER, Rachel Dawn. *See* WATTS, Rachel Dawn

SIMPKINS, Canon Lionel Frank. b 46. UEA BSc 68 Lambeth
STh 77. St Jo Coll Nottm LTh 74. **d** 73 **p** 74. C Leic H Apostles
73–77; C Bushbury *Lich* 77–80; V Sudbury w Ballingdon
and Brundon *St E* 80–96; Chapl Sudbury Hosps 80–96; RD
Sudbury *St E* 88–96; V Ipswich St Aug 96–12; Warden of
Readers 03–10; Hon Can St E Cathl 94–12; rtd 12; Widows
Officer *St E* from 12; PtO from 12; *Chelmsf* from 18. *64A
Nowton Road, Bury St Edmunds IP33 2BU* T: (01284) 725108
E: lionelsimpkins@hotmail.com

SIMPKINS, Matthew Jonathan. b 78. Oriel Coll Ox BA 99
MA 08 Essex Univ PGCE 08. Ripon Coll Cuddesdon
MPhil 15. **d** 15 **p** 16. C Wickford and Runwell *Chelmsf* 15–18;
Bp's Chapl 17–18; P-in-c Lexden from 18. *2 Wroxham Close,
Colchester CO3 3RQ* E: revdmatthewsimpkins@gmail.com

SIMPKINS, Susan Carol. b 58. St Steph Ho Ox 03. **d** 05. NSM
Ruislip St Martin *Lon* 05–11; PtO 12–13. *70 Park Avenue,
Ruislip HA4 7UJ* T: (01895) 630170 M: 07742-912664
E: sue.simpkins@btopenworld.com

SIMPSON, Alan Eric. b 52. Ch Ch Ox BA 73 MA 77 Birm Univ
PhD 77 Dur Univ MA 01 CPhys 77 MInstP 77. Cranmer
Hall Dur 96. **d** 98 **p** 99. C Long Benton *Newc* 98–02; P-in-c
Cresswell and Lynemouth 02–06; V 06–17; rtd 17; PtO *Newc*
from 17. *Keeper's Cottage, 8 High Street, Kirk Yetholm, Kelso
TD5 8PH* E: fr.alan@talk21.com

SIMPSON, Alexander. b 31. Oak Hill Th Coll 74. **d** 76
p 77. Hon C Lower Homerton St Paul *Lon* 76–81; Hon C
Homerton St Barn w St Paul 81–85; TV Hackney Marsh
85–87; V Kensington St Helen w H Trin 87–97; rtd 97;
PtO *Derby* 01–07; *Nor* from 08. *2 Ferndale Close, Norwich
NR6 5SD* T: (01603) 443412

SIMPSON, The Very Revd Alison Jane. b 60. St Andr Univ
BSc 83 BD 86 Princeton Univ MTh 87. **d** 99 **p** 99. C Ellon *Ab*
99–02; R Huntly *Mor* 02–09; R Keith 02–09; R Aberchirder
02–09; P-in-c Fochabers 04–09; R Nairn from 09; Can
St Andr Cathl Inverness from 09; Dean Mor from 14. *The
New Rectory, 3 Queen Street, Nairn IV12 4AA* T: (01667)
452458 M: 07548-230745 E: revalison433@btinternet.com
or dean@moray.anglican.org

SIMPSON, Andrew. b 48. Liv Univ BEng 69. Sarum Th Coll 83.
d 86 **p** 87. NSM Canford Magna *Sarum* 86–15; PtO from 15.
17 Sopwith Crescent, Wimborne BH21 1SH T: (01202) 883996
E: andrews.1248@gmail.com

SIMPSON, Andrew Charles. b 65. NEOC 06. **d** 09 **p** 10.
C Hessle *York* 09–12; P-in-c Sigglesthorne w Nunkeeling
and Bewholme from 12; V Skirlaugh, Catwick, Long
Riston, Rise, Swine w Ellerby from 12. *The Vicarage,
Church Lane, Skirlaugh, Hull HU11 5EU* T: (01964) 564634
E: andrew61simpson@hotmail.com

SIMPSON (formerly McGIVERN), Mrs Ann Margaret.
b 49. Newc Poly BSc 79 MPhil 92 Newc Univ PGCE 80.
Lindisfarne Regional Tr Partnership 10. **d** 11. NSM Long
Benton *Newc* 11–15; NSM Balkwell 15–17; Chapl Newcastle
upon Tyne Hosps NHS Foundn Trust 14–17; rtd 17; PtO
Newc from 17. *Keeper's Cottage, 8 High Street, Kirk Yetholm,
Kelso TD5 8PH* M: 07940-211004 E: annpope@hotmail.com

SIMPSON, Catherine Jane. **d** 14 **p** 15. Castledawson
D&R 14–15; C Seapatrick *D&D* 15–19; I Glencraig
from 19. *3 Seahill Road, Holywood BT18 0DA* T: (028)
9042 1691 E: revcatherinesimpson@icloud.com *or*
catherine@holytrinityglencraig.org

SIMPSON, Charles Michael. b 38. St Cath Coll Cam MA 64
Campion Hall Ox MA 65 Heythrop Coll Lon STL 69 K Coll Lon
PhD 71. **d** 68 **p** 69. Lect Th Lon Univ 72–84; Chapl Prince of
Peace Community Greenwich 85–87; Retreat Dir St Beuno's
Clwyd 87–91; P-in-c Selkirk *Edin* 91–94; P-in-c Offchurch *Cov*
94–96; Warden Offa Retreat Ho and Dioc Spirituality Adv
94–00; P-in-c Stoke Canon, Poltimore w Huxham and Rewe
etc *Ex* 00–04; Dioc Adv in Adult Tr 00–04; rtd 04; PtO *Cov*
05–13. *10 Applemede, Silverton, Exeter EX5 4JX* T: (01392)
861757 E: michaelandsharon@simpson4.plus.com

SIMPSON, Christine. b 52. **d** 07 **p** 08. OLM Drayton in
Hales *Lich* 07–14; NSM Cheswardine, Childs Ercall, Hales,

Hinstock etc from 14; RD Hodnet from 17. *18 Mortimer Road, Buntingsdale Park, Market Drayton TF9 2EP* T: (01630) 638794

SIMPSON, David Charles Edward. b 51. NEOC 02. **d** 05 **p** 06. NSM York St Chad 05–09; PtO 09–12; NSM York All SS Pavement w St Crux and St Mich from 12; NSM York St Helen w St Martin from 12; NSM York St Denys from 12; NSM York St Olave w St Giles from 12. *98 Brunswick Street, York YO23 1ED* T: (01904) 635085 E: davidcitycentre@outlook.com

SIMPSON, David John. b 61. Univ Coll Dur BA 85 Univ Coll Lon MA 11. Sarum & Wells Th Coll 89. **d** 91 **p** 92. C Selby Abbey *York* 91–94; C Romsey *Win* 94–97; Chapl Southn Univ 97–05; Chapl RN from 05. *Royal Naval Chaplaincy Service, Mail Point 1-2, Leach Building, Whale Island, Portsmouth PO2 8BY* T: (023) 9262 5055 F: 9262 5134

SIMPSON, Derek John. b 59. Oak Hill Th Coll BA 89. **d** 89 **p** 90. C Alperton *Lon* 89–95; TR Brentford 95–17; AD Hounslow 02–15; R Thirsk *York* from 17. *The Rectory, Cemetery Road, Thirsk YO7 1PR* E: derek.simpson@btinternet.com

SIMPSON, Eleanor Elizabeth Mary. *See* ROBERTSHAW, Eleanor Elizabeth Mary

SIMPSON, Mrs Elizabeth Ann. b 59. Lon Bible Coll BA 80 Trin Coll Bris 84. **dss** 86 **d** 97 **p** 98. Thornbury *Glouc* 86–87; Beckenham Ch Ch *Roch* 87–90; Heydon, Gt and Lt Chishill, Chrishall etc *Chelmsf* 90–93; Shirwell, Loxhore, Kentisbury, Arlington, etc *Ex* 93–97; NSM S Molton w Nymet St George, High Bray etc 97–99; C 99–03; P-in-c W Buckingham *Ox* 03–11; R 11–19; V Adderbury w Milton from 19. *12 Round Close Road, Adderbury, Banbury OX17 3EE*

SIMPSON, Mrs Georgina. b 46. Westmr Coll Ox BTh 93 Birm Univ MA 95 DipEd 98. SAOMC 95. **d** 97 **p** 98. NSM Littlemore *Ox* 97–98; C Ox St Giles and SS Phil and Jas w St Marg 98–09; Hon C 12–18; PtO 09–12 and from 18. *85 Church Road, Sandford-on-Thames, Oxford OX4 4YA* T: (01865) 775160 E: georgie.simpson1@gmail.com

SIMPSON, Jill. b 53. **d** 13 **p** 14. NSM Ferring *Chich* from 13. *Greensward, 64 Lime Tree Avenue, Worthing BN14 0DP* T: (01903) 872746

SIMPSON, Canon John Bernard. b 40. St Paul's Coll Chelt CertEd 62 Ox Univ MTh 95 ACP 66. **d** 93 **p** 93. In URC 63–93; Asst to RD Lothingland *Nor* 93–94; RD 99–10; C Hopton w Corton 93–94; P-in-c 94–99; TR Lowestoft St Marg 99–10; Hon Can Nor Cathl 01–10; rtd 10; P-in-c Publow w Pensford, Compton Dando and Chelwood *B & W* 10–15; PtO *Heref* from 16. *34 Dorchester Way, Belmont, Hereford HR2 7ZP* T: (01432) 269241 M: 07905-013183 E: canonjohn145@btinternet.com

SIMPSON, Canon John Lawrence. b 33. SS Coll Cam BA 55 MA 59 ARCM 60 UWE Hon MMus. Wells Th Coll 63. **d** 65 **p** 66. Chapl Win Cathl 65–66; C Win St Bart 65–69; Chapl Repton Sch Derby 69–71; Hd of RE Helston Sch 71–78; P-in-c Curry Rivel *B & W* 79–80; R Curry Rivel w Fivehead and Swell 80–86; V Tunbridge Wells K Chas *Roch* 86–89; Can Res Bris Cathl 89–99; rtd 99; PtO *B & W* 00–19. *Yardes Cottage, Windmill Hill, Ilminster TA19 9NT* T: (01823) 480593 E: simpson.yardes@btinternet.com

SIMPSON, John Raymond. b 41. Univ of S Aus DipEd 92. Chich Th Coll 65. **d** 67 **p** 68. C Scarborough St Martin *York* 67–71; C Grangetown 71–72; Youth Chapl Bermuda 72–75; C Lewisham St Mary *S'wark* 76; C Albany Australia 76–78; R Carey Park 78–84; Chapl RAAChD 77–84; Chapl RAN 84–90; Chapl RAAF 90–99; Asst P Grace Cathl San Francisco USA 99–00; Chapl RANSR Australia from 00. *44/19 Oakleigh Drive, Erskine Grove, Erskine WA 6210, Australia* T: (0061) (8) 9586 4144 E: simpsonjohnr@googlemail.com

SIMPSON, John Verrent. b 68. Univ of Wales (Cardiff) BScEcon 93. Ripon Coll Cuddesdon 98. **d** 98 **p** 99. C Cardiff St Jo *Llan* 98–00; C Cen Cardiff 00–01; C Upper Chelsea H Trin *Lon* 01–04; P-in-c Lt Missenden *Ox* from 05. *The Vicarage, Little Missenden, Amersham HP7 0RA* T: (01494) 862008 M: 07919-551614 E: vicar@lmchurch.org

SIMPSON, Kevin Gordon. b 54. Univ of Wales BEd 96 MCIPD 94. St Mich Coll Llan. **d** 02 **p** 03. NSM Llantwit Fardre *Llan* 02–16; PtO from 16; St D from 16. *St Ignatius, Caldey Island, Tenby SA70 7UJ* M: 07870-397494 E: kgsimpson4151@gmail.com

SIMPSON, Mrs Madeline Bridget. b 79. Newc Univ BA 01 Regent Coll Vancouver MA 09. St Mellitus Coll 17. **d** 19. C Ulverston St Mary w H Trin *Carl* from 19. *Trinkeld Vicarage, Main Road, Swarthmoor, Ulverston LA12 0RZ* M: 07502-315137 E: simpson.madi@gmail.com

SIMPSON, Miss Margery Patricia. b 36. SRN 57 SCM 59. Oak Hill Th Coll BA 86. **dss** 86 **d** 87 **p** 94. Rodbourne Cheney *Bris* 86–87; Par Dn 87–90; Par Dn Warmley 90–94; C Warmley, Syston and Bitton 94–95; TV Yate New Town 95–96; rtd 97;

PtO *Sarum* 97–04; *Carl* 05–18. *19 Wentworth Park, Stainburn, Workington CA14 1XP* T: (01900) 61523

SIMPSON, Mark Lawrence. b 73. Oak Hill Th Coll BA 03. **d** 03 **p** 04. C Leyland St Andr *Blackb* from 03. *45 Westgate, Leyland PR5 2LX* T: (01772) 622446 E: mark.simpson@wellfieldchurch.org.uk

SIMPSON, Martha Grace. b 83. **d** 14 **p** 15. C Chipping Norton *Ox* from 14. *15 Cross Leys, Chipping Norton OX7 5HG* M: 07828-921518 E: martha.simpson@stmaryscnorton.com

SIMPSON, Matthew John. b 76. Nottm Univ BA 95 Leic Univ MA 01. St Jo Coll Nottm 11. **d** 13 **p** 14. C The Quinton *Birm* 13–16; C Knowle from 16. *49 Newton Road, Knowle, Solihull B93 9HN* M: 07522-586254 E: mattsimpson365@hotmail.com or revmattsimpson@gmail.com

SIMPSON, Michael. *See* SIMPSON, Charles Michael

SIMPSON, Morna Mary Heather. b 79. Cen Lancs Univ BA 00 St Martin's Coll Lanc PGCE 07. Ripon Coll Cuddesdon 15. **d** 17 **p** 18. C Stocking Farm and Beaumont Leys *Leic* 17–19; C Leic H Spirit from 19. *18 Lords Avenue, Leicester LE4 2HX* E: revmorna@icloud.com

SIMPSON, Peter Richard. b 53. Univ Coll Lon BSc(Econ) 74 Qu Mary Coll Lon MSc 75 FRSocMed 09. **d** 97 **p** 11. In RC Ch 97–11; NSM St Andr Cathl Inverness *Mor* 12–18; rtd 18; PtO *York* from 19. *Apartment 32 , Cardinal Court, Bishophill Junior, York YO1 6ES* T: (01904) 638572 M: 07710-123202 E: prs1@waitrose.com

SIMPSON, Philip Alexander. b 54. Keele Univ BA 79 Sunderland Univ MSc 03 CQSW 79. CMS Tr Coll Selly Oak 85. **d** 89 **p** 07. CMS 85–14; Pakistan 85–98; Regional Dir for Eurasia 98–14; PtO *Guildf* 06–07; NSM Woking Ch Ch from 07. *10 Horsell Park Close, Woking GU21 4LZ* T: (01483) 770510 E: phil_simpsoncms@mac.com

SIMPSON, Rachel Victoria. *See* BUNTING, Rachel Victoria

SIMPSON, Raymond James. b 40. Lon Coll of Div ALCD 63 LTh 74. **d** 63 **p** 64. C Longton St Jas *Lich* 64–68; C Upper Tooting H Trin *S'wark* 68–71; BFBS Distr Sec E Anglia 71–77; C-in-c Bowthorpe CD *Nor* 78–84; V Bowthorpe 84–96; Guardian Community of Aid and Hilda 96–11; rtd 11; PtO *Newc* from 96. *7 Wallace Green, Berwick-upon-Tweed TD15 1EB* T: (01289) 306771 E: revd.ray.simpson@btinternet.com

SIMPSON, The Ven Richard Lee. b 66. Keble Coll Ox BA 88 MPhil 91 Westmr Coll Ox PGCE 89. Wycliffe Hall Ox 91. **d** 93 **p** 94. C Newc St Gabr 93–97; P-in-c Jesmond H Trin 97–06; P-in-c Newc St Barn and St Jude 97–06; P-in-c Brancepeth *Dur* 06–18; Dir IME 4-7 Dur and Newc 06–09; Dir IME 4-7 Lindisfarne Coll of Th from 09; Adn Auckland and Can Dur Cathl from 18. *45 Milbank Road, Darlington DL3 9NL* T: (01325) 480444 M: 07867-802671 E: ricksimpson300@btinternet.com or archdeacon.of.auckland@durham.anglican.org

SIMPSON, Canon Robert Charles. b 46. Ridley Hall Cam. **d** 85 **p** 86. C Eastwood *S'well* 85–88; V Yardley St Cypr Hay Mill *Birm* 88–93; P-in-c Newent and Gorsley w Cliffords Mesne *Glouc* 93–95; R 95–05; Dioc Ecum Officer 04–05; P-in-c Glouc St Jas and All SS 05–10; V Glouc St Jas and All SS and Ch Ch 10–12; AD Glouc City 08–11; Hon Can Glouc Cathl 10–12; rtd 12; PtO *Glouc* 12–13; C St Briavels w Hewelsfield and Brockweir from 13. *27 Ryelands Road, Bream, Lydney GL15 6LD* T: (01594) 560202

SIMPSON, Robert David. b 61. Fitzw Coll Cam BA 83 MA 87 Bris Univ MLitt 94. Trin Coll Bris 85. **d** 87 **p** 88. C Beckenham Ch Ch *Roch* 87–90; C Heydon w Gt and Lt Chishill *Chelmsf* 90; C Chrishall 90; C Elmdon w Wendon Lofts and Strethall 90; C Heydon, Gt and Lt Chishill, Chrishall etc 91–93; TV Shirwell, Loxhore, Kentisbury, Arlington, etc *Ex* 93–97; TR S Molton w Nymet St George, High Bray etc 97–03; R Cranborne w Boveridge, Edmondsham etc *Sarum* from 16. *The Rectory, Grugs Lane, Cranborne, Wimborne BH21 5PX* T: (01725) 517232 E: quinetrector3@gmail.com

SIMPSON, Robert John. NUU BA PGCE. **d** 03 **p** 04. NSM Ballymoney w Finvoy and Rasharkin *Conn* 03–08; NSM Ballywillan from 08. *28 Willowfield Park, Coleraine BT52 1RE* T: (028) 7035 8552 M: 07793-059858 E: rev.robertsimpson@gmail.com

SIMPSON, Canon Roger Westgarth. b 51. Lon Univ BSc 72. St Jo Coll Nottm 77. **d** 79 **p** 80. C St Marylebone All So w SS Pet and Jo *Lon* 79–85; R Edin St Paul and St Geo 85–95; R Vancouver H Trin Canada 95–99; V York St Mich-le-Belfrey 99–10; C 10–13; Abp's Evangelist from 10; Hon C York St Barn 14–17; Can and Preb York Minster 10–17; Hon C Chipping Norton *Ox* from 17. *Juxon House, Little Compton, Moreton-in-Marsh GL56 0SE* E: rogerwestgarthsimpson@gmail.com

SIMPSON, Samuel. b 26. TCD BA 55 MA 69 Div Test 56. TCD Div Sch. **d** 56 **p** 57. C Coleraine *Conn* 56–60; I Donagh w

Cloncha and Clonmany *D & R* 60–64; I Ballyscullion 64–81; Can Derry Cathl 78–96; I Errigal w Garvagh 81–96; Adn Derry 89–96; rtd 96. *53 Magheramenagh Drive, Atlantic Road, Portrush BT56 8SP* T: (028) 7082 4292

SIMPSON, Mrs Sarah Jamieson. b 80. Univ Coll Lon BA 03 K Coll Lon PGCE 04. St Mellitus Coll BA 15 MA 17. **d** 17 **p** 18. C Lee Gd Shep w St Pet *S'wark* from 17. *23 Thornwood Road, London SE13 5RG* T: (020) 8355 6112 M: 07801-562018 E: mrssarahsimpson@gmail.com

SIMPSON (née RALPHS), Mrs Sharon Ann. b 55. St Mary's Coll Dur BA 77. Cranmer Hall Dur 81. **dss** 83 **d** 87 **p** 94. Caverswall *Lich* 83–87; Par Dn 87–89; Asst Dioc Officer for Minl Tr *St As* 90–91; NSM Selkirk *Edin* 91–94; C Offchurch *Cov* 94–96; Warden Offa Retreat Ho and Dioc Spirituality Adv 94–00; C Stoke Canon, Poltimore w Huxham and Rewe etc *Ex* 00–04; Dioc Adv in Adult Tr 00–04; rtd 04; PtO *Cov* 05–13. *10 Applemede, Silverton, Exeter EX5 4JX* T: (01392) 861757 E: michaelandsharon@simpson4.plus.com

SIMPSON, Mrs Susan Fiona. b 67. Herts Univ BSc 89. ERMC 09. **d** 11 **p** 12. C Soham and Wicken *Ely* 11–14; V Somersham w Pidley and Oldhurst and Woodhurst from 14. *The Rectory, Rectory Lane, Somersham, Huntingdon PE28 3EL* T: (01487) 840676 M: 07775-828745 E: susan.charlotte@googlemail.com

SIMPSON, Mrs Susie Alexandra. b 58. Hertf Coll Ox BA 81. St Steph Ho Ox BA 98. **d** 99 **p** 00. C High Wycombe *Ox* 99–03; TV 03–08; Chapl HM YOI Roch 09–10; Chapl HM Pris Isis 10–19; Chapl HM Pris E Sutton Park from 19. *HM Prison, East Sutton Park, Sutton Valence, Maidstone ME17 3DF* T: (01622) 785000 E: susie.simpson@justice.gov.uk

SIMPSON, Thomas William Newton. b 89. Ex Univ BA 10. Oak Hill Th Coll BA 17. **d** 17 **p** 18. C Fremington, Instow and Westleigh *Ex* from 17. *The Vicarage, Fremington, Barnstaple EX31 2NX* M: 07940-428313 E: twnsimpson@gmail.com

SIMPSON, Ursula Lucy. b 51. St Anne's Coll Ox MA 73 Leeds Univ MA 05. NOC 02. **d** 05 **p** 06. NSM York St Paul 05–10; P-in-c York St Barn 10–16; rtd 16; PtO *York* 16–19; Hon C Chipping Norton Ox from 17. *Juxon House, Little Compton, Moreton-in-Marsh GL56 0SE* E: u.simpson@btinternet.com *or* ulsimpson@gmail.com

SIMPSON-GRAY, Lennox George (Rickey). b 64. S Bank Univ BA 93 FCMA 96. ERMC 11. **d** 14 **p** 15. NSM Hemel Hempstead *St Alb* 14–19; TV The Claydons and Swan Ox from 19. *The Rectory, Queen Catherine Road, Steeple Claydon, Buckingham MK18 2PY* M: 07783-027603 E: rev-rick@outlook.com

SIMS, Bernard David. b 40. Bath Univ BSc 66. Ox Min Course 91. **d** 94 **p** 95. NSM Beedon and Peasemore w W Ilsley and Farnborough *Ox* 94–98; TV Blakenall Heath *Lich* 98–10; PtO *Lich* from 10. *2 March Way, Walsall WS9 8SG* E: reverenddavid98@gmail.com

SIMS, The Ven Christopher Sidney. b 49. Wycliffe Hall Ox 74. **d** 77 **p** 78. C Walmley *Birm* 77–80; V Yardley St Cypr Hay Mill 80–88; V Stanwix *Carl* 88–96; RD Carl 89–95; Hon Can Carl Cathl 91–95; P-in-c Bassenthwaite, Isel and Setmurthy 96–00; P-in-c Bolton w Ireby and Uldale 96–00; P-in-c Allhallows 96–00; P-in-c Torpenhow 96–00; TR Binsey 00–03; V Shrewsbury H Cross *Lich* 03–09; RD Shrewsbury 08–09; Adn Walsall 09–14; rtd 14; PtO *Carl* from 14. *Stanthwaite, Burgh-by-Sands, Carlisle CA5 6AW* T: (01228) 576629 E: ven.csims@gmail.com

SIMS, James Henry. b 35. St Jo Coll Nottm 87. **d** 89 **p** 91. NSM Bangor Abbey *D & D* 89–93; C Holywood 93; Bp's C Kilbroney 93–01; Min Can Belf Cathl 99–09; P-in-c Clonallon w Warrenpoint *D & D* 01–09; Can Dromore Cathl 03–09; rtd 09. *7 Prior's Lea, Holywood BT18 9QW* T: (028) 9042 4360 E: jim.sims321@tiscali.co.uk

SIMS, Mrs Julia Mary Heaton. b 56. STETS 04. **d** 07 **p** 08. NSM Winscombe and Sandford *B & W* 07–11; Past Co-ord St Monica Trust Sandford Station from 11; PtO *B & W* 11–15; C Banwell 15–17; C Banwell and Congresbury w Hewish, Puxton and W Wick 17–18; PtO from 18. *7 Round Oak Grove, Cheddar BS27 3BW* T: (01934) 740120 M: 07875-340291

SIMS, Keith George. b 29. **d** 95 **p** 96. OLM Forest Hill St Aug *S'wark* 95–04; PtO *Roch* from 04. *196 Long Lane, Bexleyheath DA7 5AQ* T: (020) 8303 0138 E: keithsims7@btinternet.com

SIMS, Canon Vickie Lela. b 56. Iowa State Univ BA 79. Ripon Coll Cuddesdon 00. **d** 02 **p** 03. C Grantham St Wulfram *Linc* 02–05; P-in-c Coulsdon St Andr *S'wark* 05–11; V 11–14; Jt Dir of IME Croydon Area 09–14; Chapl Milan w Lake Como *Eur* from 14; Chapl Genoa 14–18; Adn Italy and Malta *Eur* 16–19; Hon Can from 19. *via Solferino 17, 20121 Milano, Italy* T: (0039) (02) 655 2258 E: allsaintspriest@hotmail.com *or* simstabbat@hotmail.com

SIMS-WILLIAMS, Robert James Alden (Robin). b 79. Trin Hall Cam MEng 02 MA 05 BTh 12. Westcott Ho Cam 10.

d 13 **p** 14. C Paddington St Jo w St Mich *Lon* 13–17; P-in-c Hendon All SS Childs Hill from 17. *All Saints' Vicarage, Church Walk, London NW2 2TJ* T: (020) 8452 8840 M: 07812-167292 E: robin@cantab.net

SINCLAIR, Canon Arthur Alfred. b 46. **d** 87 **p** 89. Hon C St Andr Cathl Inverness *Mor* 87–92; C 93–97; Chapl Asst Inverness Hosp 87–89; Dioc Chapl *Mor* 87–89; NSM Culloden St Mary-in-the-Fields 89–92; P-in-c 93–12; P-in-c Inverness St Jo 93–12; Edin Th Coll 92–93; Chapl Raigmore Hosp NHS Trust Inverness from 93; Can St Andr Cathl Inverness *Mor* 05–12; rtd 12; LtO *Mor* from 12. *Rose Cottage, 8A Southside Place, Inverness IV2 3JF* T: (01463) 716288 E: arthurasinclair@btinternet.com

SINCLAIR, Craig Paul. b 82. Ridley Hall Cam 15. **d** 17 **p** 19. C Wulfric Benefice *B & W* 17–18; C Weston-super-Mare St Paul from 18. *15 Clarence Road North, Weston-super-Mare BS23 4AT*

✠**SINCLAIR, The Rt Revd Gordon Keith.** b 52. Ch Ch Ox MA. Cranmer Hall Dur. **d** 84 **p** 85 **c** 08. C Summerfield *Birm* 84–88; V Aston SS Pet and Paul 88–01; AD Aston 00–01; Hon Can Birm Cathl 00–01; V Cov H Trin 01–07; Suff Bp Birkenhead *Ches* from 07. *Bishop's Lodge, 67 Bidston Road, Prenton CH43 6TR* T: 0151-652 2741 F: 651 2330 E: bpbirkenhead@chester.anglican.org

SINCLAIR, Canon Jane Elizabeth Margaret. b 56. St Hugh's Coll Ox BA 78 MA 80. St Jo Coll Nottm BA 82. **dss** 83 **d** 87 **p** 94. Herne Hill St Paul *S'wark* 83–86; Chapl and Lect St Jo Coll Nottm 86–93; Can Res Sheff Cathl 93–03; Hon Can Sheff Cathl 03–07; V Rotherham 03–07; Adn Stow and Lindsey *Linc* 07–14; Can Steward Westmr Abbey from 14. *2 Little Cloister, London SW1P 3PL* T: (020) 7654 4815 E: jane.sinclair@westminster-abbey.org

SINCLAIR, Canon John Robert. b 58. Oak Hill Th Coll 90. **d** 92 **p** 93. C Ponteland *Newc* 92–96; V Long Benton St Mary 96–01; V Newburn 01–11; AD Newc W 07–11; Hon Can Newc Cathl 08–11; Can Res Newc Cathl 11–19; Dioc Adv in Local Evang 11–19; R Upper Coquetdale from 19; Hon Can Newc Cathl from 19. *The Rectory, Rothbury, Morpeth NE65 7TL* T: (01669) 620482 M: 07706-154383 E: j.sinclair@newcastle.anglican.org *or* rectorjohn@outlook.com

SINCLAIR, Keith. *See* SINCLAIR, Gordon Keith

✠**SINCLAIR, The Rt Revd Maurice Walter.** b 37. Nottm Univ BSc 59 Leic Univ PGCE 60. Tyndale Hall Bris 62 Nashotah Ho Hon DD 01. **d** 64 **p** 65 **c** 90. C Boscombe St Jo *Win* 64–67; SAMS 67–02; Argentina 67–78; Personnel Sec 79–83; Asst Gen Sec 83–84; Prin Crowther Hall CMS Tr Coll Selly Oak 84–90; Bp N Argentina 90–02; Primate of S Cone 95–02; rtd 02; Hon Asst Bp Birm from 02. *55 Selly Wick Drive, Birmingham B29 7JQ* T: 0121-471 2617

SINCLAIR, Peter. b 44. Oak Hill Th Coll. **d** 88 **p** 89. C Darlington H Trin *Dur* 88–91; C-in-c Bishop Auckland Woodhouse Close CD 91–98; P-in-c Consett 98–09; rtd 09; PtO *Dur* from 11. *16 Deanery View, Lanchester, Durham DH7 0NH* E: annandpetersinclair@talktalk.net

SINCLAIR, Peter Monteith. b 52. St Andr Univ BSc 73. NEOC. **d** 01 **p** 02. NSM Darlington St Cuth *Dur* 01–05; Hon Min Can Dur Cathl 05–12; V Woodhorn w Newbiggin *Newc* 12–17; rtd 17; PtO *Newc* 17–18; C Ch the King from 18. *60 Barmoor Drive, Newcastle upon Tyne NE3 5RG* M: 07710-017625 E: peter@aftersunday.org.uk

SINCLAIR, Reginald William. b 53. Wolv Poly BSc 77 CEng MIMechE. Man OLM Scheme 04. **d** 07 **p** 08. OLM Atherton and Hindsford w Howe Bridge *Man* 07–09; TV from 09; Borough Dean Wigan from 13. *Bumbles, 23 Millers Lane, Atherton, Manchester M46 9BW* T: (01942) 892996 M: 07530-162920 E: revreg@btinternet.com

SINDALL, Canon Christine Ann. b 42. ALA 69. EAMTC 84. **d** 87 **p** 94. NSM Sutton *Ely* 87–89; C Cambridge Ascension 89–94; TV 94–96; R Cheveley 96–07; R Ashley w Silverley 96–07; V Kirtling 96–07; V Wood Ditton w Saxon Street 96–07; RD Linton 01–07; Hon Can Ely Cathl 01–07; rtd 07; PtO *Newc* from 07. *9 East Moor, Longhoughton, Alnwick NE66 3JB* T: (01665) 572287 E: csindall@btinternet.com

SINGH, Jonathan James. b 72. Bp Grosseteste Coll BA 96 Drew Univ New Jersey DMin 12. Ripon Coll Cuddesdon 97. **d** 00 **p** 01. C Spalding St Mary and St Nic *Linc* 00–02; C Sanderstead St Mary *S'wark* 02–03; P-in-c 03–05; TV Sanderstead 05–06; V E Crompton *Man* 06–09; R Broughty Ferry *Bre* 09–11; Chapl St Mich Hospice Harrogate 11–13; Bereavement Support Worker from 13; PtO *Ripon* 13–14; NSM Ripon Cathl *Leeds* 14–16; PtO *York* 14–15; *Leeds* from 17; *Man* from 17. *6 Cavendish Mews, Leeds LS17 7AA* T: 0113-226 8754 M: 07745-753343 E: revdrjonathansingh@gmail.com

SINGH, Vivian Soorat. b 30. Trin Coll Cam BA MA 53. Westcott Ho Cam 54. **d** 55 **p** 56. C Yardley Wood *Birm* 55–57; C Birm St Paul 57–59; Asst Master Framlingham Coll 59–72; Chapl 60–72; Chapl Wymondham Coll

72–75; Dep Hd Litcham High Sch 75–88; rtd 88; PtO *Nor* from 88. *Manor Cottage, Wendling Road, Longham, Dereham NR19 2RD* T: (01362) 687382

SINGLETON, David Brinley. b 59. St Steph Ho Ox. **d** 00 **p** 01. C Soham *Ely* 00–01; C Soham and Wicken 02–04; P-in-c Capel St Mary w Lt and Gt Wenham *St E* 04–08; R 08–13; RD Samford 10–13; R Bansfield 13–18; P-in-c Haughley w Wetherden and Stowupland from 18. *The Vicarage, The Folly, Haughley, Stowmarket IP14 3NS* E: brinsingleton@btinternet.com

SINTON, Bernard. b 43. Leic Univ BSc 66. Sarum & Wells Th Coll 87. **d** 90 **p** 91. NSM Horsham *Chich* 90–19; PtO from 19. *Kinsale, 28 Kennedy Road, Horsham RH13 5DA* E: pa.sinton@outlook.com

SINTON, Mrs Patricia Ann. b 41. RGN 62 SCM 64. STETS 95. **d** 98 **p** 99. NSM Horsham *Chich* 98–01; P-in-c Shipley 01–19; rtd 19. *Kinsale, 28 Kennedy Road, Horsham RH13 5DA* E: pa.sinton@outlook.com

SINTON, Vera May. b 43. Somerville Coll Ox BA 65 MA 69 Bris Univ CertEd 66. Trin Coll Bris 79. **dss** 81 **d** 87 **p** 94. Broxbourne w Wormley *St Alb* 81–87; Hon Par Dn 87; Tutor All Nations Chr Coll Ware 81–87; Chapl St Hilda's Coll Ox 87–90; Tutor Wycliffe Hall Ox 87–98; NSM Ox St Clem 99–09; Tutor Ox Cen for Youth Min 01–04; rtd 09; PtO *Ox* from 09; *Leeds* from 10. *Rookhurst, West End, Gayle, Hawes DL8 3RT* T: (01969) 666948 E: vera@vsinton.co.uk

SIRCAR, Deepak Debchandan. b 46. Lon Hosp BDS 72 Leeds Univ BA 06. NOC 03. **d** 06 **p** 07. NSM Doncaster St Geo *Sheff* 06–10; NSM Bath Widcombe *B & W* 10–13; P-in-c Barnby Dun *Sheff* 13–17; rtd 17; PtO *Sheff* from 17. *5 Barnsdale Mews, Campsall, Doncaster DN6 9RH* M: 07768-830393 E: deepaksircar@btinternet.com

SIRR, John Maurice Glover. b 42. TCD BA 63. CITC 65. **d** 65 **p** 66. C Belfast St Mary *Conn* 65–68; C Finaghy 68–69; I Drumcliffe w Lissadell and Munninane *K, E & A* 69–87; Preb Elphin Cathl 81–87; Dean Limerick and Ardfert *L & K* 87–11; I Limerick City 87–11; Chapl Limerick Pris 87–11; rtd 11. *17A Knockhill, Ennis Road, Limerick, V94 CR24, Republic of Ireland* T: (00353) (61) 277372　M: (00353) 87-254 1121 E: maurice42sirr@gmail.com

SISTIG (née STEWART), Mrs Jennifer Jane. b 71. Urban Univ Rome STB 00. St Jos Th Inst Cedara BTh 00. **d** 99 **p** 00. C Kirby-Hilton S Africa 99–00; C Scottsville 00–01; R Woodlands-Montclair-cum-Yellowwood Park 01–05; R Hillcrest 05–08; NSM Fleet *Guildf* from 08; Chapl St Geo Sch Ascot 10–18; Chapl Frimley Health NHS Foundn Trust from 13; PtO *Ox* from 12. *43 Church Road, Bagshot GU19 5EQ* T: (01276) 473348　M: 07546-120844 E: jenniferjanesistig@gmail.com

SITWELL, Mrs Mary Elizabeth. b 49. Brighton Coll of Educn DipEd 71 Sussex Univ BEd 72. **d** 03 **p** 12. Chapl Roedean Sch Brighton 87–05; NSM Bishopstone *Chich* 03–06; rtd 05; NSM Alfriston w Lullington, Litlington and W Dean *Chich* 06–09; PtO 09–12 and from 16; NSM Iford w Kingston and Rodmell 12–13; NSM Iford w Kingston and Rodmell and Southease 13–16. *Chambles, Village Green, Piddinghoe, Newhaven BN9 9AP* T: (01273) 510183 E: isla.sitwell@btinternet.com

SIU, Leslie. b 87. City Univ BSc 09. Wycliffe Hall Ox BA 14. **d** 15 **p** 16. C Westlands St Andr *Lich* 15–18; V Wickham Market w Pettistree *St E* from 18. *The Vicarage, Crown Lane, Wickham Market, Woodbridge IP13 0SA* M: 07732-878076 E: leslie@wickhammarketchurch.org

SIVILL, David Neil. b 69. **d** 14. OLM Atherton and Hindsford w Howe Bridge *Man* from 14. *7 Kennet Way, Leigh WN7 1SN* M: 07535-753594 E: sivilld@manchesterfire.gov.uk

SIVYER, Steven Robert. b 74. RCM BMus 97 Leic Univ MSc 09 PhD 14 Cant Ch Ch Univ PGCE 98. SEITE 12. **d** 15 **p** 16. C Marden *Cant* 15–17; C Boughton Monchelsea 17–18; P-in-c Martham and Repps w Bastwick, Thurne etc *Nor* from 18. *The Rectory, School Road, Marham, Great Yarmouth NR29 4PX* T: (01493) 740823　M: 07725-229841 E: steven@sivyer.org.uk

SIXSMITH, David. b 39. Lon Univ BD 66. **d** 97 **p** 98. NSM Castleacre w Newton, Rougham and Southacre *Nor* 97–99; OLM Narborough w Narford 97–99; OLM Pentney St Mary Magd w W Bilney 97–99; OLM Westacre 97–99; C Hunstanton St Mary w Ringstead Parva etc 99–01; P-in-c Foulsham w Hindolveston and Guestwick 01–06; P-in-c N Elmham w Billingford and Worthing 02–05; rtd 06; PtO *Nor* from 06. *Old Mill Cottage, Broadmeadow Common, Castle Acre, King's Lynn PE32 2BU* T: (01760) 755703 E: david.sixsmith@hotmail.co.uk

SIZER, Stephen Robert. b 53. Sussex Univ BA Ox Univ MTh 94. Trin Coll Bris 80. **d** 83 **p** 84. C St Leonards St Leon *Chich* 83–86; C Guildf St Sav w Stoke-next-Guildford 86–89; R Stoke-next-Guildf 89–97; V Virginia Water

97–17; rtd 17; PtO *Win* 17–18. *39 Bevan Close, Southampton SO19 9PE* M: 07970-789549 E: stephen@peacemakers.ngo

SKELTON, Beresford. b 52. St Chad's Coll Dur BA 74. Chich Th Coll 74. **d** 76 **p** 77. C Byker St Ant *Newc* 76–80; C Newc St Jo 80–82; Chapl Asst Newc Gen Hosp 80–81; Chapl Asst Freeman Hosp Newc 81–82; V Cresswell and Lynemouth *Newc* 82–88; P-in-c Millfield St Mary *Dur* 88–93; V from 93; P-in-c Bishopwearmouth Gd Shep from 04; CMP from 77; Warden from 12. *St Mary Magdalene's Vicarage, Wilson Street, Sunderland SR4 6HJ* T/F: 0191-565 6318

SKELTON (née BOXER), Mrs Caroline Victoria. b 46. Bradf Univ BA 69. Yorks Min Course 09. **d** 11 **p** 12. NSM Baildon *Bradf* 11–14; *Leeds* 14–16; Rtd Clergy and Widows Officer (Bradford) from 16. *2 Highfield Mews, Baildon, Shipley BD17 5PF* T: (01274) 582224 E: caroline.skelton46@gmail.com

SKELTON, Melvyn Nicholas. b 38. St Pet Coll Ox BA 61 MA 65 Selw Coll Cam BA 63 MA 68. Ridley Hall Cam 62. **d** 64 **p** 65. C St Marychurch *Ex* 64–66; C Bury St Edmunds St Mary *St E* 66–69; Hon C 69–78; LtO 78–08; PtO from 09. *Milburn House, The Street, Moulton, Newmarket CB8 8RZ* T: (01638) 750563 E: melvynskelton@gmail.com

SKEPPER, Mrs Suzanne Jayne. b 63. Trin Coll Bris BA 09. **d** 09 **p** 10. C Wotton St Mary *Glouc* 09–13; V Twigworth, Down Hatherley, Norton, The Leigh etc from 13. *The Rectory, Tewkesbury Road, Twigworth, Gloucester GL2 9PQ* M: 07981-429259 E: suzanne.skepper@hotmail.co.uk

SKIDMORE, Iaen Macdonald. b 58. SNWTP 11. **d** 13 **p** 14. C Marown, Foxdale and Baldwin *S & M* 13–16; R Andreas, Ballaugh, Jurby and Sulby from 16. *The Rectory, Churchtown, Ramsey, Isle of Man IM7 2AN* T: (01624) 897873　M: 07624-403945 E: revd.iaenskidmore@gmail.com

SKIDMORE (née CANNINGS), Karen Rachel. b 75. Nottm Univ BA 96. Ridley Hall Cam 04. **d** 06 **p** 07. C Pitsmoor Ch Ch *Sheff* 06–10; P-in-c Herringthorpe 10–15; V from 15. *The Vicarage, 493 Herringthorpe Valley Road, Rotherham S60 4LB* T: (01709) 836052 E: karen.skidmore@yahoo.co.uk *or* karen.skidmore@sheffield.anglican.org

SKIDMORE, Michael Anthony. b 38. **d** 98 **p** 99. NSM Rainworth and Blidworth *S'well* 98–00; P-in-c Basford St Leodegarius 00–05; P-in-c Willoughby-on-the-Wolds w Wysall and Widmerpool 05–07; NSM Carlton-in-the-Willows, Porchester and Woodthorpe 07–09; rtd 09; PtO *S'well* from 09. *11 Graveney Gardens, Arnold, Nottingham NG5 6QW* T: 0115-926 0773 E: mikeskidmore1@sky.com

SKIDMORE, Mrs Sheila Ivy. b 36. **d** 87 **p** 94. Hon Par Dn Leic Resurr 87–91; Par Dn Clarendon Park St Jo w Knighton St Mich 91–94; TV 94–01; rtd 01; PtO *Leic* 01–17. *15 School Lane, Birstall, Leicester LE4 4EA* T: 0116-267 3318 E: skidmore010@btinternet.com

SKIDMORE, Simon Peter. b 88. Univ of Wales (Ban) BD 10. Trin Coll Bris 12. **d** 14 **p** 15. C Wednesbury St Bart *Lich* 14–17; TV Bilston from 18. *The Vicarage, 8 Cumberland Road, Bilston WV14 6LT* M: 07919-800533 E: skiders180@hotmail.co.uk

SKILLEN, John Clifford Tainish. b 50. NUU BA 72 MA 82 TCD BTh 89 QUB DipEd 73. CITC 86. **d** 89 **p** 90. C Bangor Abbey *D & D* 89–92; I Kilwarlin Upper w Kilwarlin Lower 92–96; I Finaghy *Conn* 96–09; Asst Ed The Church of Ireland Gazette 99–15; Bp's Sen Dom Chapl *Conn* from 08. *25 Berkeley Hall Square, Lisburn BT27 5TB* T: (028) 9267 0257　M: 07740-553926 E: revcskillen25@gmail.com

SKILLING, Graham. b 57. **d** 12 **p** 13. NSM Kendal H Trin *Carl* from 12. *7 Danes Road, Staveley, Kendal LA8 9PW* T: (01539) 822695 E: gr36939@yahoo.co.uk

SKILTON, The Ven Christopher John. b 55. Magd Coll Cam BA 76 MA 80. Wycliffe Hall Ox 77. **d** 80 **p** 81. C Ealing St Mary *Lon* 80–84; C New Borough and Leigh *Sarum* 84–88; TV Gt Baddow *Chelmsf* 88–95; TR Sanderstead All SS *S'wark* 95–04; P-in-c Sanderstead St Mary 02–04; RD Croydon S 00–04; Adn Lambeth 04–13; P-in-c Kennington St Mark 08–09; Adn Croydon from 13. *Croydon Episcopal Area Office, 6 St Peter's Road, Croydon CR0 1HD* T: (020) 8256 9630　F: 8256 9631 E: christopher.skilton@southwark.anglican.org

SKILTON, Joseph Laurence. b 41. Univ of Wales TCert 64 Murdoch Univ Aus BA 90 Aus Pacific Coll MA 93. St Mich Coll Llan. **d** 70 **p** 71. C Bicester *Ox* 71–73; C Shrewsbury St Chad *Lich* 73–76; V W Bromwich St Phil 76–80; Australia from 80; rtd 06. *37 Cosmo Crescent, Newstead, Launceston TAS 7250, Australia* E: pax2u2@gmail.com

SKINGLEY, Christopher George. b 49. K Coll Lon MA 98. Oak Hill Th Coll BA 90 Qu Coll Birm. **d** 00 **p** 01. C Enfield St Jas *Lon* 00–03; V Ramsgate St Mark *Cant* 03–15; rtd 15; PtO *Cant* from 16. *18 Royal Native Way, Whitstable CT5 4UE* T: (01227) 272508 E: chris.skingley@btinternet.com

✠**SKINNER, The Rt Revd Brian Antony.** b 39. Reading Univ BSc 60. Tyndale Hall Bris 66. **d** 67 **p** 68 **c** 77. C Woking St Pet

Guildf 67–70; Chile 70–86; Adn Valparaiso 76–77; Suff Bp Valparaiso 77–86; C Chorleywood St Andr *St Alb* 87–96; V Iver *Ox* 96–06; rtd 06; PtO *Ox* from 08. *10 Benton Drive, Chinnor OX39 4DP* T: (01844) 353504 E: b.skinner@dsl.pipex.com

SKINNER, Mrs Elaine Teresa (Terri). b 55. Bath Univ BSc 78. EMMTC 99. **d** 02 **p** 03. NSM Whitwick St Jo the Bapt *Leic* 02–05; NSM Thorpe Acre w Dishley 05–10; P-in-c Leic St Theodore 10–17; rtd 17; PtO *Leic* from 18. *55 Rosslyn Road, Whitwick, Coalville LE67 5PU* T: (01530) 832676 M: 07810-241381 E: terri.skinner@btopenworld.com

SKINNER, Graeme John. b 57. Southn Univ BSc 79. Trin Coll Bris BA 86. **d** 86 **p** 87. C Bebington *Ches* 86–90; V Ashton-upon-Mersey St Mary Magd 90–06; V Upton (Overchurch) 06–18; P-in-c Holme Eden and Wetheral w Warwick *Carl* from 18. *The Rectory, Warwick Bridge, Carlisle CA4 8RF* T: (01228) 561358 E: graemevicarofeden@gmail.com

SKINNER, Mrs Jane Mary. b 59. Leeds Univ BA 81. Cranmer Hall Dur 82. **dss** 84 **d** 87 **p** 94. Chatham St Phil and St Jas *Roch* 84–87; Hon Par Dn Church Coniston *Carl* 87–91; Hon Par Dn Torver 87–91; NSM Dalton-in-Furness 91–97; Chapl HM Pris Haverigg 92–97; Chapl Carl Hosps NHS Trust 97–01; Chapl N Cumbria Acute Hosps NHS Trust 01–02; TV Carl H Trin and St Barn 98–02; Hon C W Swindon and the Lydiards *Bris* 02–09; Chapl Swindon and Marlborough NHS Trust 03–10; NSM Golden Cap Team *Sarum* 09–10; TV 10–18; TR Parkham, Alwington, Buckland Brewer etc *Ex* from 18. *The Rectory, Old Market Drive, Woolsery, Bideford EX39 5QF* E: rectorhartlandcoast@gmail.com

SKINNER, Canon Jean. b 47. Univ of Northumbria at Newc BA 03 RN 68 RM 70. NEOC 93. **d** 96 **p** 97. NSM Ch the King *Newc* 96–03; NSM Newc St Thos Prop Chpl 03–17; NSM City Cen Chapl 03–06; Dioc Child Protection Adv 07–17; NSM Newc Cathl 12–17; Hon Can Newc Cathl 16–17; rtd 17; PtO *Newc* from 17. *32 Easedale Avenue, Melton Park, Newcastle upon Tyne NE3 5TB* T: 0191-236 3474 E: revjeanskinner@yahoo.com *or* jeanskinner1@gmail.com

SKINNER, Preb John Cedric. b 30. Bris Univ BA 55. Tyndale Hall Bris 55. **d** 57 **p** 58. C St Leonard *Ex* 57–62; Univ Sec IVF 62–68; V Guildf St Sav 68–76; R Stoke next Guildf St Jo 74–76; R Guildf St Sav w Stoke-next-Guildford 76–84; R Ex St Leon w H Trin 84–98; Chapl R W of England Sch for the Deaf 84–98; Preb Ex Cathl 92–98; rtd 98; PtO *Ex* from 00. *386 Topsham Road, Exeter EX2 6HE* T: (01392) 876540

SKINNER, John Richard. b 45. NOC 84. **d** 87 **p** 88. C Allerton *Liv* 87–90; C Huyton St Mich 90–97; P-in-c Fairfield 97–03; rtd 04. *15 Dickinson Road, Liverpool L37 4BX* T: (01704) 874899

SKINNER, Maurice Wainwright. b 30. St Jo Coll Ox BA 53 MA 59 FRSC 70. Ox NSM Course. **d** 86 **p** 87. NSM Furze Platt *Ox* 86–94; NSM Hurley and Stubbings 94–00; rtd 00; PtO *Ox* from 00. *133 Beverley Gardens, Maidenhead SL6 6ST* T: (01628) 624875

SKINNER, Michael Thomas. b 39. Open Univ BA 88 BA 90 Heythrop Coll Lon MA 11. S'wark Ord Course 73. **d** 78 **p** 79. NSM Orpington St Andr *Roch* 78–82; P-in-c 99–09; NSM Orpington All SS 82–99; Assoc Bp's Officer for NSMs 90–98; Bp's Officer for NSMs *Roch* 98–09; rtd 09; PtO *Roch* from 09; *Lon* from 11; S'wark 02–05 and from 10; *Truro* from 12. *16 Ambleside Gardens, South Croydon CR2 8SF* T: (020) 8239 1973 E: mikeskinner2@virginmedia.com

SKINNER, Paul Anthony. b 35. Sarum Th Coll. **d** 09 **p** 10. NSM Sixpenny Handley w Gussage St Andrew etc *Sarum* 09–14; PtO from 14. *11 The Parsonage, Sixpenny Handley, Salisbury SP5 5QJ* T: (01785) 552785 E: paulofpaskin@yahoo.com

SKINNER, Raymond Frederick. b 45. St Jo Coll Dur BA 67 Dur Univ MA 93. Cranmer Hall Dur. **d** 70 **p** 71. C High Elswick St Paul *Newc* 70–76; V Newbottle *Dur* 76–87; Ind Chapl 81–87; RD Houghton 84–87; Chapl Oman 87–90; TR Morden S'wark 90–13; rtd 13; Public Preacher S'wark 13–17; PtO from 17. *6 Lawrence Avenue, Bidborough, Tunbridge Wells TN4 0XB* T: (01892) 525913 E: skinhicks@tiscali.co.uk

SKINNER, Stephen John. b 52. Bris Univ St Jo Coll Dur BA Dur Univ MLitt AIA. Cranmer Hall Dur. **d** 83 **p** 84. C Chatham St Phil and St Jas *Roch* 83–87; P-in-c Torver *Carl* 87–90; R 90–91; P-in-c Church Coniston 87–90; V 90–91; V Dalton-in-Furness 91–97; TR Carl H Trin and St Barn 97–02; TR W Swindon and the Lydiards *Bris* 02–09; TR Golden Cap Team *Sarum* 09–18; rtd 18. *Address temp unknown* E: sjmskinners@btinternet.com

SKINNER, Terri. See SKINNER, Elaine Teresa

SKIPPON, Kevin John. b 54. St Steph Ho Ox 78. **d** 81 **p** 82. C Gt Yarmouth *Nor* 81–84; C Kingstanding St Luke *Birm* 84–86; V Smethwick SS Steph and Mich 86–92; Chapl Derbyshire R Infirmary 92–94; Chapl Derbyshire R Infirmary NHS Trust 94–98; Chapl Derby Hosps NHS Foundn Trust 98–04 and 04–08; C Upminster *Chelmsf* 09–14; Chapl

St Andr Healthcare 09–13; Chapl Havering Primary Care Trust 09–13; rtd 14; PtO *Heref* from 16. *Beech Cottage, 25 Banks Head, Bishops Castle SY9 5JL* T: (01588) 630777 E: kevin.skippon@asitis.me.uk

SKIPWORTH, Nicola Rachael. b 72. Southn Inst BA 95. Trin Coll Bris BA 01. **d** 01 **p** 02. C Bassaleg *Mon* 01–05; TV High Wycombe *Ox* 05–13; TV Carew *St D* 13–14; P-in-c Pembroke Dock 14–18; P-in-c Harworth S'well from 18. *The Vicarage, Tickhill Road, Harworth, Doncaster DN11 8PD* M: 07734-233742 E: nickythevicar@gmail.com

SKIRROW, Paul Richard. b 52. Hull Univ BA 82 Ches Coll of HE MTh 00. NOC 97. **d** 00 **p** 01. C St Luke in the City *Liv* 00–03; V Ditton St Mich w St Thos 03–07; Asst Dir CME 03–07; rtd 07; PtO *Ely* 10–15; *Leeds* from 17; *Eur* from 18. *2 The Crosskeys, Church Street, Pateley Bridge, Harrogate HG3 5LB* T: (01832) 293383 E: paulskirrow@googlemail.com

SKUSE, Anne Martha. CITC. **d** 09 **p** 10. NSM Kilmocomogue *C, C & R* 09–15; I Moviddy Union 15–17; Chapl Bandon Gr Sch from 17. *Westlands, Crossmahon, Bandon, Co Cork, Republic of Ireland* T: (00353) (23) 8884 4306 M: (00353) 86-023 9699 E: annemskuse@gmail.com

SLACK, Mrs Moira Elizabeth. b 52. Brunel Univ BTech 74 Leeds Univ BA 06. NOC 03. **d** 06 **p** 07. C Heaton Ch Ch *Man* 06–09; P-in-c Stretford All SS 09–14; C Bolton St Pet w St Phil from 14. *50 Devonshire Road, Bolton BL1 4PQ* T: (01204) 841865 E: moslack@btinternet.com

SLADDEN, Daniel John. b 69. K Coll Cam BA 91 MA 95. Yorks Min Course. **d** 12 **p** 13. NSM Ingleby Barwick *York* 12–16; Min Can Ripon Cathl *Leeds* from 16; PtO *York* from 18. *Ripon Cathedral Office, Liberty Courthouse, Minster Road, Ripon HG4 1QS* T: (01765) 602072 E: dan@sladden.com

SLADDEN, John David. b 49. RN Eng Coll Plymouth BSc 74 St Edm Coll Cam MA 86. Ridley Hall Cam 80. **d** 83 **p** 84. C St Bees *Carl* 83–85; PtO *Lich* 85–87; Miss Co-ord Down to Earth Evangelistic Trust 85–87; V Doncaster St Jas *Sheff* 87–94; PtO *Ely* from 07. *9 Teal Close, Chatteris PE16 6PR* T: (01354) 694097 E: jds25@cantab.net

SLADE, Canon Adrian Barrie. b 47. K Alfred's Coll Win DipEd 68. St Jo Coll Nottm BTh 73 ALCD 72. **d** 73 **p** 74. C Streatham Immanuel w St Anselm S'wark 73–76; C Chipping Barnet *St Alb* 76–78; C Chipping Barnet w Arkley 78–80; V Sundon 80–85; Soc Resp Officer *Glouc* 86–12; Hon Can Glouc Cathl 91–12; rtd 12; PtO *Glouc* from 15. *16 Conway Road, Hucclecote, Gloucester GL3 3PL* T: (01452) 372468 E: glossr@star.co.uk

SLADE, Joanna Elisabeth. See STOBART, Joanna Elisabeth

SLADE, Michael John. b 55. Trin Coll Bris 94. **d** 96 **p** 97. C Blagdon w Compton Martin and Ubley *B & W* 96–99; V Winscombe and Sandford 99–10; RD Locking 05–08; V Chollerton w Birtley and Thockrington *Newc* 10–17; rtd 17; PtO *Newc* from 17. *Meadowfield, Church Lane, Wark, Hexham NE48 3LX* E: emjayslade@gmail.com

SLADE, Roland Gregory. b 88. Southn Univ BSc 09. Ridley Hall Cam 14. **d** 17 **p** 18. C Gt Marlow w Marlow Bottom, Lt Marlow and Bisham *Ox* from 17. *52 Oak Tree Avenue, Marlow SL7 3EJ* M: 07449-330581 E: rolandgslade@gmail.com

SLATER, Andrew Kenneth. b 62. Reading Univ BA 84 PGCE 85 Open Univ MA 99. ERMC 10. **d** 13 **p** 14. NSM Wymondham *Nor* 13–18; NSM Attleborough w Besthorpe from 18. *The Battle, 110 Norwich Road, Attleborough NR17 2JY* T: (01953) 455046 M: 07850-924575 E: joannaandandrewslater@gmail.com

SLATER, Canon Ann. b 46. Somerville Coll Ox BA 67 MA 71. WMMTC 92. **d** 95 **p** 96. C Northampton St Benedict *Pet* 95–99; TV Daventry, Ashby St Ledgers, Braunston etc 99–05; R Heyford w Stowe Nine Churches and Flore etc 05–14; RD Daventry 08–13; Can Pet Cathl 10–14; rtd 14; PtO *Pet* from 15. *34 Millway, Northampton NN5 6ES* T: (01604) 586014 E: annslater34@gmail.com

SLATER, Carol Ann. See COSLETT, Carol Ann

SLATER, Christopher Richard. b 69. Oak Hill Th Coll BA 08. **d** 08. C Rock Ferry *Ches* 08–12; C Tranmere St Cath 08–12; V Rock Ferry from 12. *The Vicarage, St Peter's Road, Birkenhead CH42 1PY* T: 0151-645 1622 M: 07899-807507 E: slater.cr@btinternet.com

SLATER, Ian Stuart. b 47. St Jo Coll Nottm BA 07. **d** 04 **p** 05. NSM Gt Horton *Bradf* 04–11; P-in-c 11–12; C Fairweather Green 12–14; *Leeds* 14; PtO from 17. *Stable Cottage, 5 The Drive, Denholme, Bradford BD13 4DY* T: (01274) 831437 E: revianslater@gmail.com

SLATER, John Ralph. b 38. Kent Univ BA 90. Linc Th Coll 71. **d** 73 **p** 74. C S Hackney St Mich w Haggerston St Paul *Lon* 73–74; C Leytonstone St Marg w St Columba *Chelmsf* 74–77; C Whitstable All SS w St Pet *Cant* 77–80; V Gt Ilford St Alb *Chelmsf* 80–83; V Clipstone S'well 83–87; rtd 87. *4 Rowena Road, Westgate-on-Sea CT8 8NQ* T: (01227) 831593

SLATER, Canon Mark Andrew. b 56. ARCS 79 Imp Coll Lon BSc 79. Ridley Hall Cam 87. **d** 89 **p** 90. C Northampton St Giles *Pet* 89–92; C Stopsley *St Alb* 92–93; C-in-c Bushmead CD 93–99; V St Alb St Luke from 99; RD St Alb from 15; Hon Can St Alb from 18. *St Luke's Vicarage, 46 Cell Barnes Lane, St Albans AL1 5QJ* T: (01727) 865399 F: 865399 E: mark.slater@saint-lukes.co.uk

✠**SLATER, The Rt Revd Paul John.** b 58. CCC Ox MA 83 St Jo Coll Dur BA 83. Cranmer Hall Dur 81. **d** 84 **p** 85 **c** 15. C Keighley St Andr *Bradf* 84–88; P-in-c Cullingworth and Dir Dioc Foundn Course 88–93; Bp's Personal Exec Asst 93–95; Warden of Readers 92–96; R Haworth *Bradf* 95–01; Bp's Officer for Min and Miss 01–15; Adn Craven 05–14; Adn Richmond and Craven *Leeds* 14–15; Suff Bp Kirkstall from 15. *4 Borrowdale Court, 5 Clifton Drive, Menston, Ilkley LS29 6FZ* T: 0113-284 4304 E: paul.slater@leeds.anglican.org *or* bishop.paul@leeds.anglican.org

SLATER, Paul John. *See* CAREY-SLATER, Paul John

SLATER, Robert Adrian. b 48. St Jo Coll Nottm 76. **d** 79 **p** 80. C Bedworth *Cov* 79–82; TV Billericay and Lt Burstead *Chelmsf* 82–88; V Rounds Green *Birm* 88–94; rtd 07. *11 Lewis Road, Birmingham B30 2SU* T: 0121-689 2721 E: robslater@freeuk.com *or* skyblueteddy68@icloud.com

SLATER, Victoria Ruth. b 59. Hertf Coll Ox BA 82 MA 87 Selw Coll Cam BA 89 MA 94 Lon Univ MA 01 Anglia Ruskin Univ DProf 13. Westcott Ho Cam 86. **d** 89 **p** 94. Chapl Asst Man R Infirmary 89–90; Chapl 90–94; Chapl St Mary's Hosp Man 90–94; Chapl Ox Radcliffe Hosp NHS Trust 94–97; Chapl Sir Michael Sobell Ho Palliative Care Unit 97–05; Asst Soc Resp Adv *Ox* 07–05; Chapl Care Co-ord N Lon Hospice 07–08; Research and Development Officer Ox Cen for Ecclesiology and Practical Th 09–13; Chapl Frimley Health NHS Foundn Trust 14–15. *Address withheld by request* E: slaterv2@btinternet.com

SLATER, Preb William Edward. b 51. Aston Tr Scheme 85 Oak Hill Th Coll 87. **d** 89 **p** 90. C Balderstone *Man* 89–94; V Newchapel *Lich* 94–16; RD Stoke N 99–08 and 12–16; Preb Lich Cathl 08–16; rtd 16; PtO *Lich* from 17; *Ches* from 18. *4 Gwyn Avenue, Knypersley, Stoke-on-Trent ST8 7BW* T: (01782) 518350

SLATTER, Barrie John. b 44. Nottm Univ BSc 66 FRICS 97. **d** 00 **p** 01. OLM Hundred River *St E* 00–03; C Alde River 03–06; R 06–14; rtd 14; PtO *St E* from 14. *Moor Farm Barn, Kings Lane, Sotherton, Beccles NR34 8AF* T: (01986) 872100 M: 07802-924738 E: barrie.rectory@btinternet.com

SLATTERY, Maurice Michael. b 43. Southlands Coll Lon TCert 73 Lon Inst of Educn BEd 74. S'wark Ord Course 91. **d** 94 **p** 95. NSM Malden St Jas *S'wark* 94–97; NSM Niton, Whitwell and St Lawrence *Portsm* 97–99; NSM Selsdon St Jo w St Fran *S'wark* 99–03; PtO *Portsm* 03–04 and 07–08 and from 09; P-in-c St Lawrence 04–06; NSM Clayton w Keymer *Chich* 08–09; P-in-c Burpham 13–16; P-in-c Poling 13–16; rtd 16. *1 Woodland Mews, East Hill Road, Ryde PO33 1QU* E: mauricemslattery@hotmail.com

SLAUGHTER, Clive Patrick. b 36. St Paul's Coll Grahamstown. **d** 77 **p** 78. S Africa 77–87; R Thorley w Bishop's Stortford H Trin *St Alb* 87–90; R Thorley 90–01; RD Bishop's Stortford 96–01; rtd 01; PtO *St Alb* 01–03; P-in-c Much Hadham 03–04; P-in-c Braughing w Furneux Pelham and Stocking Pelham 04–05; P-in-c Braughing w Furneux Pelham and Stocking Pelham 04–05; PtO 09–19. *53 High Street, Hunsdon, Ware SG12 8QB* T: (01279) 844955 E: marcia.slaughter@virgin.net

SLAVIC, Jean-Sacha (Sacha). b 68. **d** 12 **p** 13. NSM Foleshill St Laur *Cov* 12–14; NSM Cov Cathl from 15; Chapl Bablake Sch Cov from 14. *1 Crown Green, Coventry CV6 6FA* T: (024) 7627 1200 M: 07714-288352 E: slavic@btinternet.com

SLAYEN, Karen Elizabeth. b 59. **d** 12 **p** 13. OLM Atherton and Hindsford w Howe Bridge *Man* 12–16; NSM Westleigh St Pet 16–18; NSM Westleigh St Paul 16–18; NSM Westleigh St Pet and St Paul from 18; NSM Leigh St Mary from 16. *51 Treen Road, Astley, Tyldesley, Manchester M29 7HD* T: (01942) 891154 M: 07966-643950

SLEDGE, The Ven Richard Kitson. b 30. Peterho Cam BA 52 MA 57. Ridley Hall Cam 52. **d** 54 **p** 55. C Compton Gifford *Ex* 54–57; C Ex St Martin, St Steph, St Laur etc 57–63; V Dronfield *Derby* 63–76; TR 76–78; RD Chesterfield 72–78; Adn Huntingdon *Ely* 78–96; R Hemingford Abbots 78–89; Hon Can Ely Cathl 78–99; rtd 96; Bp's Dom Chapl *Ely* 96–99; Rtd Clergy Officer 98–07; Asst (Huntingdon/Pet Area) 07–16; PtO from 99. *7 Budge Close, Brampton, Huntingdon PE28 4PL* T: (01480) 380284 *or* (01353) 662749 F: (01480) 437789 E: rksledge@supanet.com

SLEDGE, Canon Timothy Charles Kitson. b 64. Coll of Ripon & York St Jo BA 87 York Univ MA 88. Trin Coll Bris. **d** 95 **p** 96. C Huddersfield St Thos *Wakef* 95–98; V Luddenden w Luddenden Foot 98–03; P-in-c Sowerby 02–03; Dioc Miss Enabler *Pet* 03–08; V Romsey *Win* 08–17; AD 13–17; Hon

Can Win Cathl from 14. *Baker Court, 2A Fraser Road, Southsea PO5 1EE* E: timsledge01@gmail.com

SLEE, John Graham. b 51. Brunel Univ BTech 73. Oak Hill Th Coll 85. **d** 87 **p** 88. C St Columb Minor and St Colan *Truro* 87–91; R St Mawgan w St Ervan and St Eval 91–02; RD Pydar 93–95; P-in-c St Just-in-Roseland and St Mawes 02–07; rtd 07; PtO *Ox* 08–13; *Blackb* from 18. *4 Highgrove Road, Lancaster LA1 5FS* E: john@nbepiphany.co.uk

SLEEP, Benjamin Luke. b 78. Ridley Hall Cam 16. **d** 18 **p** 19. C Eastbourne St Jo *Chich* from 18. *12 Upper Dukes Drive, Eastbourne BN20 7XT*

SLEGG, John Edward. b 36. St Pet Coll Ox BA 62 MA 66. Ridley Hall Cam 62. **d** 64 **p** 65. C Perranzabuloe *Truro* 64–66; CF 66–86; V Lyminster and Poling *Chich* 86–05; rtd 06. *4 Bakers Meadow, Billingshurst RH14 9GG*

SLEIGHT, Gordon Frederick. b 47. AKC 69. St Aug Coll Cant 69. **d** 70 **p** 71. C Boston *Linc* 70–74; P-in-c Louth St Mich and Stewton 74; TV Louth 74–81; V Crosby 81–95; P-in-c Nettleham 95–97; V 97–05; RD Lawres 04–05; rtd 05; LtO *Mor* from 05. *17 Kintail Place, Dingwall IV15 9RL* E: gsassynt@gmail.com

SLENNETT, Mrs Jane Alison. b 57. St Mich Coll Llan. **d** 08. NSM Aberavon *Llan* from 08. *42 Carlton Place, Porthcawl CF36 3ET* T: (01656) 784840 E: deacon@parishofaberavon.org

SLINGSBY, Miss Philippa Jane. b 89. Birm Univ BSc 12 St Jo Coll Dur BA 18. Cranmer Hall Dur 15. **d** 18 **p** 19. C Tong and Laisterdyke *Leeds* from 18. *207 Broadstone Way, Bradford BD4 9BT* T: (01274) 4060425 M: 07576-484897 E: philippa.slingsby@leedsanglican.com

SLIPPER, Charles Callan. b 55. Lanc Univ BA 77 PhD 84. S Dios Minl Tr Scheme 91. **d** 93 **p** 94. Focolare Movement from 77; NSM N Acton St Gabr *Lon* 93–96; Nat Ecum Officer Coun for Chr Unity from 17. *Council for Christian Unity, Church House, Great Smith Street, London SW1P 3AZ* T: (01707) 339242 *or* (020) 7898 1479 E: callanslipper@gmail.com *or* callan.slipper@churchofengland.org

SLIPPER, Robert James. b 64. St Jo Coll Cam BA 87 MA 91. Wycliffe Hall Ox BA 92. **d** 92 **p** 93. C Southgate *Chich* 92–95; C Stoughton *Guildf* 95–00; V Terrington St Clement *Ely* from 00. *The Vicarage, 27 Sutton Road, Terrington St Clement, King's Lynn PE34 4PQ* T: (01553) 828430 E: rjslipper@dsl.pipex.com

SLOAN, William. b 49. Lanc Univ CertEd 78 BEd 79 Cumbria Univ MA 11. CBDTI 04. **d** 07 **p** 08. NSM Croston and Bretherton *Blackb* 07–10; NSM Hoole 10–11; PtO 11–13; NSM Hesketh w Becconsall 13–15; rtd 15; PtO *Blackb* from 15. *5 Red House Lane, Eccleston, Chorley PR7 5RH* T: (01257) 453665 M: 07721-923001

SLOANE, The Very Revd Niall James. b 81. TCD BA 03 MA 06 MPhil 05. CITC 03. **d** 05 **p** 06. C Agherton *Conn* 05–07; C Taney *D & G* 07–12; I Killiney H Trin 12–17; Abp's Dom Chapl 08–15; Min Can St Patr Cathl Dublin 08–15; Dean Limerick *L & K* from 17; I Limerick City from 17; Can St Patr Cathl Dublin from 15. *The Deanery, 7 Kilbane, Castletroy, Limerick, Y94 Y4AX, Republic of Ireland*

SLOGGETT, Donald George. b 49. Trin Coll Bris 81. **d** 83 **p** 84. C Horfield H Trin *Bris* 83–86; C Highworth w Sevenhampton and Inglesham etc 86–88; P-in-c Upavon w Rushall *Sarum* 88–90; R Upavon w Rushall and Charlton 90–01; R Stoulton w Drake's Broughton and Pirton etc *Worc* 01–16; rtd 16; PtO *Worc* from 17. *1 Chevalier Close, Pershore WR10 3EE* T: (01386) 244021 E: don.sloggett@gmail.com

SLOW, Leslie John. b 47. Liv Univ BSc 68 MSc 69. NOC 77. **d** 80 **p** 81. NSM Gt Horton *Bradf* 80–07; PtO *York* from 08. *21 Mile End Park, Pocklington, York YO42 2TH* T: (01759) 303888 E: les@theslows.plus.com

SLUMAN, Richard Geoffrey Davies. b 34. St Jo Coll Ox BA 68 MA 68. Sarum Th Coll 68. **d** 70 **p** 71. C Gt Yarmouth *Nor* 70–73; V Churchdown *Glouc* 73–82; P-in-c Blockley w Aston Magna 82–83; V Blockley w Aston Magna and Bourton on the Hill 83–94; rtd 94; PtO *Cov* 94–10. *21 Manor Farm Road, Tredington, Shipston-on-Stour CV36 4NZ* T: (01608) 662317

SLYFIELD, Mrs Margaret Medi. b 61. Linc Sch of Th and Min 11. **d** 14 **p** 15. NSM Buxton w Burbage and King Sterndale *Derby* from 14. *Old Shop, Queen Street, Tideswell, Buxton SK17 8JT* T: (01298) 871478 E: mmslyfield@yahoo.co.uk

SMAIL, Richard Charles. b 57. CCC Ox BA 80 MA 83. Ox Min Course 90. **d** 93 **p** 95. NSM Keble Coll Ox 93–96; Chapl, Fell and Lect BNC Ox 97–02; PtO *Ox* 02–05; P-in-c Rousham from 05. *Top Flat, 256 Abingdon Road, Oxford OX1 4SP* T: (01865) 245553 E: richardsmail@supanet.com

SMAILES, Ian Collingwood. b 46. Brighton Poly BSc 71. NTMTC BA 07. **d** 07 **p** 08. NSM Laleham *Lon* from 07. *Gadebridge House, 211 Thames Side, Staines TW18 1UF* T: (01784) 461195 E: ianandrosalind@gmail.com

SMALE, Ian Keith. b 53. Wycliffe Hall Ox 98. **d** 00 **p** 01. C Overton w Laverstoke and Freefolk *Win* 00–04; P-in-c E Dean w Friston and Jevington *Chich* 04–06; R 06–08; P-in-c Overton w Laverstoke and Freefolk *Win* 08–18; P-in-c N Waltham and Steventon, Ashe and Deane 11–18; rtd 18; PtO *Win* from 18. *33 Mercia Avenue, Charlton, Andover SP10 4EJ*

SMALE, Ian Stuart. b 49. **d** 07. NSM Chich Cathl from 07. *9 Canal Place, Chichester PO19 8DR*   M: 07973-747694   E: ishmael@ishmael.org.uk

SMALE, Irene Euphemia. b 52. Chich Univ BA Win Univ MA Southn Univ PhD 15. **d** 14. NSM Chich St Pancras and St Jo 14–17; Chapl Prebendal Sch Chich from 17. *9 Canal Place, Chichester PO19 8DR*   T: (01273) 421021   M: 07980-617584   E: irene.smale@chichester.anglican.org

SMALING, Christopher James. b 72. Bath Univ BSc 93 K Coll Lon PGCE 95. STETS 11. **d** 14 **p** 15. NSM Aldersbrook *Chelmsf* from 14. *84 St James Road, London E15 1RN*   M: 07977-564035

SMALL, Gary William. b 57. Witwatersrand Univ BSc 81 Stockholm Univ MSc 86 KTH R Inst of Tech Stockholm MSc 94. Qu Foundn (Course) 16. **d** 19. NSM Harlescott *Lich* from 19. *34 Queen Street, Shrewsbury SY1 2JX*   T: (01743) 614803   M: 07891-690010 E: gwmsmall31@gmail.com

SMALL, Gordon Frederick. b 41. St Jo Coll Nottm 77. **d** 79 **p** 80. C Belper *Derby* 79–84; NSM Matlock Bath 90–91; C Ripley 91–93; TV Bucknall and Bagnall *Lich* 93–98; Assoc P Deal St Leon w St Rich and Sholden etc *Cant* 98–06; rtd 06; PtO *Bris* from 07. *10 Elmer Close, Malmesbury SN16 9UE*   T: (01666) 823722 E: gordonsmall@talktalk.net

SMALL, Marcus Jonathan. b 67. Univ of Wales (Ban) BD 94 St Jo Coll Dur MA 13. Ripon Coll Cuddesdon 94. **d** 96 **p** 97. C Moseley St Mary *Birm* 96–99; TV Wenlock *Heref* 99–05; R Eardisley w Bollingham, Willersley, Brilley etc from 05; RD Kington and Weobley 12–14. *Church House, Church Road, Eardisley, Hereford HR3 6NN*   T: (01544) 327440   E: rector@eardisleygroup.org.uk

SMALL, William. *See* SMALL, Gary William

SMALLDON, The Ven Keith. b 48. Open Univ BA 76 Newc Univ MA 94. St Mich Coll Llan. **d** 71 **p** 72. C Cwmbran *Mon* 71–73; C Chepstow 73–75; Dioc Youth Adv *Bradf* 75–79; P-in-c Woolfold *Man* 82–85; Dioc Youth and Community Officer 82–90; P-in-c Thursby *Carl* 90–94; Dir of Clergy Tr 90–94; TR Daventry, Ashby St Ledgers, Braunston etc *Pet* 94–98; Dir Clergy Danetre Hosp 94–98; TR Llantwit Major *Llan* 98–03; Can Res Brecon Cathl *S & B* 03–11; Dioc Dir of Min 03–11; P-in-c Steynton 11–13; rtd 13; PtO *Ox* from 13. *41 Horsham Close, Banbury OX16 1XP*   T: (01295) 269281   E: keithsmalldon@btinternet.com

SMALLEY, The Very Revd Stephen Stewart. b 31. Jes Coll Cam BA 55 MA 58 PhD 79. Eden Th Sem (USA) BD 57 Ridley Hall Cam. **d** 58 **p** 59. C Portman Square St Paul *Lon* 58–60; Chapl Peterho Cam 60–63; Dean 62–63; Lect RS Ibadan Univ Nigeria 63–69; Lect Th Man Univ 70–77; Can Res and Prec Cov Cathl 77–87; Vice-Provost 86–87; Dean Ches 87–01; rtd 01; PtO *Glouc* 02–16. *30 Orchard Park, Elton, Chester CH2 4NQ*   E: stephen.ssmalley@yahoo.com

SMALLMAN, Godfrey John. b 57. St Hild Coll 18. **d** 19. NSM Lodge Moor St Luke *Sheff* from 19. *26 Slayleigh Lane, Sheffield S10 3RH*   T: 0114-230 9690

SMALLMAN, Miss Margaret Anne. b 43. Hull Univ BSc 64 Bris Univ CertEd 65. St Jo Coll Nottm. **dss** 83 **d** 87 **p** 94. Bromsgrove St Jo *Worc* 83–88; Par Dn 87–88; Par Dn Stoke Prior, Wychbold and Upton Warren 88–90; Team Dn Tettenhall Wood *Lich* 91–94; TV 94–99; P-in-c W Bromwich H Trin 99–08; C W Bromwich Gd Shep w St Jo 99–08; RD W Bromwich 04–08; rtd 08; PtO *Lich* 08–09 and from 18; Hon C Wellington All SS w Eyton 09–18. *10 St Agatha's Close, Telford TF1 3QP*   T: (01952) 253643

SMALLS, Peter Harry. b 34. FCCA. **d** 97 **p** 98. OLM Castleacre w Newton, Rougham and Southacre *Nor* 97–99; OLM Narborough w Narford 97–99; OLM Pentney St Mary Magd w W Bilney 97–99; OLM Westacre 97–99; OLM Narborough w Narford and Pentney 99–02; PtO from 03; *St E* from 07. *Windward, Drapers Lane, Ditchingham, Bungay NR35 2JW*   T: (01986) 894667 E: peter.smalls@outlook.com

SMALLWOOD, Simon Laurence. b 58. St Jo Coll Dur BSc 80. Cranmer Hall Dur 89. **d** 92 **p** 93. C Stapenhill w Cauldwell *Derby* 92–96; TV Dagenham *Chelmsf* 96–03; V Becontree St Geo 03–19. *Address temp unknown* E: smallwood164@gmail.com

SMART, Barry Anthony Ignatius. b 57. Lanc Univ BEd 79. St Steph Ho Ox 85. **d** 88 **p** 89. C Wantage *Ox* 88–91; C Abingdon 91–93; TV 93–95; C Princes Risborough w Ilmer 95–97; C Kingstanding St Luke *Birm* 97–00; V Small Heath 00–09; Chapl Compton Hospice 09–13; V Kingstanding

St Luke *Birm* from 13. *The Clergy House, 49 Caversham Road, Birmingham B44 0LW*   T: 0121-354 3281   M: 07952-663872   E: frbarrysmart@yahoo.co.uk

SMART, Mrs Carol. b 45. SSF SRN 67. S Dios Minl Tr Scheme 89. **d** 92 **p** 94. Chapl Isle of Wight Healthcare NHS Trust 92–99; NSM Shorwell w Kingston *Portsm* 99–02; NSM Gatcombe 92–02; NSM Chale 92–02; PtO from 02. *20 Sydney Close, Shide, Newport PO30 1YG*   T: (01983) 526242   E: revcarolsmart@tiscali.co.uk

SMART, Harry Gavin. b 67. St D Coll Lamp BA 90 Sheff Hallam Univ MA 06. Westcott Ho Cam 90. **d** 94 **p** 95. C Thirsk *York* 94–97; C Sheff St Leon Norwood 97–99; Mental Health Chapl Sheff Care Trust 99–06; Lead Mental Health Chapl Lincs Partnership NHS Foundn Trust 07–13. *Address temp unknown*

SMART, Canon Haydn Christopher. b 38. Wells Th Coll 66. **d** 69 **p** 70. C Hillmorton *Cov* 69–72; C Duston *Pet* 72–75; V Woodford Halse 75–79; V Woodford Halse w Eydon 79–82; V Wellingborough All SS 82–92; RD Wellingborough 87–92; V Longthorpe 92–03; Can Pet Cathl 92–03; RD Pet 96–01; rtd 03; P-in-c Madeira *Eur* 03–06; PtO *Pet* from 06; Chapl to Retired Clergy and Clergy Widows' Officer from 08. *4 Silvester Road, Castor, Peterborough PE5 7BA*   T: (01733) 380460 E: havenincastor@btinternet.com

SMART, Mrs Hilary Jean. b 42. SOAS Lon BA 63. EMMTC 85. **d** 88 **p** 94. Par Dn Walsall Pleck and Bescot *Lich* 88–94; TV Sheff Manor 94–02; Bp's Ecum Officer 94–02; rtd 02; Chapl Compton Hospice 02–06; PtO *S'well* from 06. *77 Denton Drive, West Bridgford, Nottingham NG2 7FS*   T: 0115-923 1097

SMART, Lorraine Ann. b 58. Wall Hall Coll Aldenham BEd 79. St Mellitus Coll 14. **d** 15 **p** 16. OLM Loughton St Mich *Chelmsf* from 15. *30 Stonards Hill, Loughton IG10 3EG*   T: (020) 8502 2017 E: lorraine.smart@btopenworld.com

SMART, Neil Robert. b 61. Bris Univ BVSc 84. Ridley Hall Cam 01. **d** 03 **p** 04. C Shirley *Win* 03–07; P-in-c Brockenhurst 07–11; V 11–18; P-in-c Boldre w S Baddesley 09–11; V 11–18; C Southsea St Jude *Portsm* from 18. *St Margaret's Vicarage, 13 Cousins Grove, Southsea PO4 9RP*   E: somesmarts@btopenworld.com

SMART, Russell Martin. b 79. Moorlands Coll BA 06 Anglia Ruskin Univ MA 11. Ridley Hall Cam 09. **d** 11 **p** 12. C Romford Gd Shep *Chelmsf* 11–15; C N Farnborough *Guildf* 15–17; C Farnborough Gd Shep 17–18; V from 18. *The Parsonage, 45 Sand Hill, Farnborough GU14 8ER*   T: (01252) 543789 E: russ@goodshepherdchurch.org.uk

SMEATON, William Brian Alexander. b 37. CITC 69. **d** 71 **p** 72. C Belfast St Luke *Conn* 71–81; I Tullyaughnish w Kilmacrennan and Killygarvan *D & R* 81–02; Bp's Dom Chapl 87–02; Can Raphoe Cathl 88–02; Dioc Radio Officer 90–02; rtd 02. *Bearna Ghaoithe, Drumcavney, Trentagh, Letterkenny, Co Donegal, Republic of Ireland*   M: (00353) 74-913 7917 E: smeaton@indigo.ie

SMEDLEY, Christopher John. b 62. Trent Poly BSc 90. St Jo Coll Nottm MA 98. **d** 98 **p** 99. C Cotmanhay *Derby* 98–02; R Wilne and Draycott w Breaston from 02. *The Rectory, 68 Risley Lane, Breaston, Derby DE72 3AU*   T: (01332) 872242   E: smedley7@btinternet.com

SMEDLEY, Paul Mark. b 59. Bris Univ BA 80 Lanc Univ MA 81. S Dios Minl Tr Scheme 89. **d** 92 **p** 93. NSM Acton St Mary *Lon* 92–08; PtO from 08; *S'wark* from 17. *6 Media House, 32 Coin Street, London SE1 8YG*   M: 07958-438712

SMEETON, (née GRESHAM), Mrs Karen Louise. b 75. Hull Univ LLB 96. Ripon Coll Cuddesdon BA 01. **d** 02 **p** 03. C Leesfield *Man* 02–05; V Hamer 05–11; P-in-c Spotland 11–13; C Oakenrod and Bamford 11–13; V Spotland and Oakenrod from 13; AD Rochdale from 17. *13 Brooklands Court, Rochdale OL11 4EJ* E: therevdksmeeton@gmail.com

SMEETON, Canon Nicholas Guy. b 74. Trin Hall Cam MA 99. Ripon Coll Cuddesdon BA 03. **d** 04 **p** 05. C Ashton Ch Ch *Man* 04–07; P-in-c Oldham St Steph and All Martyrs 07–11; TV Oldham 07–11; V Coldhurst and Oldham St Steph 11–17; Assoc Dir of Ords 15–17; Hon Can Man Cathl from 17; Dir of Ords from 17. *13 Brooklands Court, Rochdale OL11 4EJ* E: frnicksmeeton@gmail.com

SMEJKAL, Yenda Marcel. b 68. Van Mildert Coll Dur BA 97. Coll of Resurr Mirfield 97. **d** 99 **p** 00. C S Shields All SS *Dur* 99–03; TV N Wearside 03–04; P-in-c Sundon *St Alb* from 04; P-in-c Luton St Sav from 12. *St Mary's Vicarage, 1 Selina Close, Luton LU3 3AW*   T: (01582) 583076   E: yenda.smejkal@virgin.net

SMETHAM, Abigail Laura. *See* THOMPSON, Abigail Laura

SMETHURST, David Alan. b 36. Lon Univ BD 60 Man Univ MPhil 84. Tyndale Hall Bris 57. **d** 61 **p** 62. C Burnage St Marg *Man* 61–63; P-in-c Whalley Range St Marg 63–65; R Haughton St Mary 65–74; R Ulverston St Mary w H Trin *Carl* 74–87; Dean Hong Kong 87; Dir Acorn Chr Healing

Trust Resource Cen 88–93; V Epsom St Martin *Guildf* 93–00; RD Epsom 97–00; rtd 01; PtO *Carl* from 01. *16 Helme Lodge, Natland, Kendal LA9 7QA* T: (01539) 729997 E: friarsground@yahoo.com

SMILLIE, Linda Barbara. b 46. Oak Hill Th Coll 85. **d** 87 **p** 94. Par Dn Holloway St Mary w St Jas *Lon* 87–88; Par Dn Holloway St Mary Magd 88–90; Chapl W End Stores 90–91; C Holloway St Mark w Em 90–91; Hon C Islington St Mary 92–94; C-in-c Southall Em CD 95–01; rtd 01; PtO *Ox* 01–04; Hon C Hanger Hill Ascension and W Twyford St Mary *Lon* 04–07; PtO *Chich* 12–17. *20 Wyvern Place, Warnham, Horsham RH12 3QU* T: (01403) 273788

SMITH, Adrian Paul. b 73. Ches Coll of HE BA 94 Linc Univ MA 15. Cranmer Hall Dur 07. **d** 09 **p** 10. C Mablethorpe w Trusthorpe *Linc* 09–12; R Spring Line Gp 12–15; R Owmby Gp 12–15; Dioc Communications Officer from 15; Lic Preacher 15–18; V Linc St Mary Magd w St Paul and St Mich from 18. *Edward King House, The Old Palace, Lincoln LN2 1PU* T: (01522) 504037 E: adrian.smith@lincoln.anglican.org

SMITH, Adrian William Chase. b 62. **d** 18 **p** 18. C Watford St Luke *St Alb* 18–19; P-in-c Woodhouse and Wrangthorn *Leeds* from 19; TV Leeds St Geo from 19. *96 Becketts Park Drive, Leeds LS6 3PL*

SMITH, Aidan John. b 54. Leic Univ BA 76 Man Univ MBA 81 Heythrop Coll Lon MA 17. STETS 04. **d** 07 **p** 08. NSM St Martin Ludgate *Lon* 07–13; NSM Pinner 13–18; NSM Lilliput *Sarum* from 19. *4 Glenair Avenue, Poole BH14 8AD* T: (01202) 718434 E: smithanddenny@hotmail.com

✠**SMITH, The Rt Revd Alan Gregory Clayton.** b 57. Birm Univ BA 78 MA 79 Univ of Wales (Ban) PhD 02. Wycliffe Hall Ox 79. **d** 81 **p** 82 **c** 01. C Pudsey St Lawr *Bradf* 81–82; C Pudsey St Lawr and St Paul 82–84; Chapl Lee Abbey 84–90; TV Walsall *Lich* 90–97; Dioc Missr 90–97; Adn Stoke-upon-Trent 97–01; Area Bp Shrewsbury 01–09; Bp St Alb from 09. *Abbey Gate House, 4 Abbey Mill Lane, St Albans AL3 4HD* T: (01727) 853305 F: 846715 E: bishop@stalbans.anglican.org

SMITH, Alan Leonard. b 51. Madeley Coll of Educn CertEd 72. Trin Coll Bris 93. **d** 95 **p** 96. C Taunton St Mary *B & W* 95–98; V Taunton Lyngford 98–07; RD Taunton 04–06; V Chatham St Steph *Roch* 07–14; RD Roch 11–14; rtd 14. *4 Elm Grove Drive, Dawlish EX7 0EU* T: (01626) 439983 E: revdalansmith@yahoo.co.uk

SMITH, Alan Thomas. b 35. Open Univ BA 78 Sussex Univ DipEd 79. Ridley Hall Cam 82. **d** 84 **p** 85. C Bedworth *Cov* 84–89; R Carlton Colville w Mutford and Rushmere *Nor* 89–97; rtd 97; PtO *Nor* from 01. *17 St Martins Gardens, New Buckenham, Norwich NR16 2AX* T: (01953) 860550 M: 07811-229493

SMITH, John. b 29. AKC 53. **d** 54 **p** 55. C Charlton Kings St Mary *Glouc* 54–56; C-in-c Findon Valley CD *Chich* 56–57; V Viney Hill *Glouc* 57–65; V Churchdown St Jo 65–66; V Bishop's Cannings *Sarum* 66–69; CF 69–88; V Douglas St Thos *S & M* 88–92; rtd 92; PtO *S & M* 92–05. *17 Saddle Mews, Douglas, Isle of Man IM2 1JA* T: (01624) 670093 E: padrealead@gmail.com

SMITH, Andrew. b 84. Southn Univ BSc 06 K Coll Lon MA 12. Wycliffe Hall Ox 06. **d** 09 **p** 10. C Lymington *Win* 09–13; P-in-c Bitterne Park 13–18; V from 18. *Bitterne Park Vicarage, 7 Thorold Road, Southampton SO18 1HZ* E: revandysmith@gmail.com

SMITH, Andrew Clifford. b 67. Ridley Coll Melbourne BMin 00. **d** 01 **p** 01. C Clayton All SS Australia 01–03; C Gainsborough and Morton *Linc* 03–06; TV 06–08; P-in-c Woodhall Spa Gp 08–14; Par Dn Mandelong Australia from 14. *PO Box 148, Kalorama VA 3766, Australia*

SMITH, Andrew David. b 62. All SS Cen for Miss & Min 15. **d** 18 **p** 19. NSM Blackley St Andr *Man* from 18; NSM Blackley St Paul from 18; NSM Blackley St Pet from 18. *5 Heathland Road, Salford M7 3GD* E: smudger1275@gmail.com

SMITH, Andrew Graham. b 81. St Mellitus Coll BA 14. **d** 14 **p** 15. C Basildon St Andr w H Cross *Chelmsf* 14–17; P-in-c Hutton from 17. *The Rectory, 175 Rayleigh Road, Hutton, Brentwood CM13 1LX* M: 07743-870851 E: fatherandysmith@gmail.com

SMITH, Andrew John. b 59. Birm Univ BSc 80 PhD 81. WMMTC 89. **d** 91 **p** 92. C Stourport Worc *Worc* 91–92; C Stourport and Wilden 92–95; TV Redditch, The Ridge 95–05; P-in-c Redditch St Steph 02–05; Ind Chapl 95–05; Chapl Redditch and Bromsgrove Primary Care Trust 01–05; V W Bromwich All SS *Lich* 05–15; RD W Bromwich 08–13; TR March *Ely* from 15; RD from 16. *St Peter's Rectory, 54 High Street, March PE15 9JR* E: andrew.marchurch@gmail.com

SMITH, Andrew John. b 46. Lon Univ BScEng 67 PhD 71 Bath Univ MEd 88 CEng 96 MIET 96. Coll of Resurr Mirfield 74. **d** 76 **p** 77. C Swindon New Town *Bris* 76–78; C Southmead

78–79; PtO 79–91; rtd 11. *15 Dyrham Close, Bristol BS9 4TF* T: 0117-942 8594 E: phillip.bytheway@bt.com

SMITH, Andrew John. b 53. Loughb Univ BTech 74. Lon Bible Coll 95 St Jo Coll Nottm MA 98. **d** 99 **p** 00. C Hailsham *Chich* 99–02; P-in-c Worc St Mich 02–03; TV Almondbury w Farnley Tyas *Wakef* 03–07; V Woolston New Zealand 07–11; C Remuera St Aidan 13–14; Jt P-in-c St Heliers Bay 14–15; Jt V Pahiatua and Eketahuna 15–18; PtO *Chich* from 18. *Tillington Rectory, Tillington, Petworth GU28 9AH* E: ajsinz211@gmail.com

SMITH, Andrew Lewis. b 60. Bris Univ BSc 83 CEng 88 MIET 88. Trin Coll Bris BA 11. **d** 11 **p** 12. C E Dean w Friston and Jevington *Chich* 11–15; R Fetcham *Guildf* from 15. *The Rectory, 10A The Ridgeway, Fetcham, Leatherhead KT22 9AZ* M: 07974-795343 E: revandrewsmith@hotmail.com

SMITH, Andrew Perry Langton. b 56. Sheff City Poly BSc 79 Imp Coll Lon MSc 80. Trin Coll Bris 89. **d** 91 **p** 92. C Littleover *Derby* 91–95; TV Walsall *Lich* 95–09; Ind Chapl Black Country Urban Ind Miss 95–16; Hon C Walsall St Paul and Walsall Pleck and Bescot 05–09; Ecum Dean Telford Chr Coun 10–16; RD Telford 12–16; C Kinnerley w Melverley, Knockin w Maesbrook and Maesbury 18–19; PtO from 19. *St Matthew's Vicarage, St George's Road, Donnington, Telford TF2 7NJ* T: (01952) 604239

SMITH, Mrs Angela. b 64. Portsm Poly BA 86 DipArch 89. Wycliffe Hall Ox 11. **d** 14 **p** 15. C Win Ch Ch 14–17; P-in-c Hartley Wintney, Elvetham, Winchfield etc from 17. *The Vicarage, Church Lane, Hartley Wintney, Hook RG27 8DZ* T: (01252) 842215 M: 07754-877575 E: angierosiesmith@gmail.com *or* angie.smith@stjohnshw.org.uk

SMITH, Angela Elisabeth. b 53. Southn Univ BA 75 Bp Grosseteste Coll PGCE 76. WEMTC 03. **d** 06 **p** 07. NSM Matson *Glouc* 06–09; NSM Glouc St Geo w Whaddon 09–15; NSM N Cheltenham 15–16; rtd 16; PtO *Nor* from 16. *The Rectory, 11 Pinewood Drive, Horning, Norwich NR12 8LZ* T: (01692) 630216 E: angela.draesmith2@btinternet.com

SMITH, Mrs Anita Elisabeth. b 57. Westhill Coll Birm BEd 79. Trin Coll Bris 85. **d** 88 **p** 94. Par Dn Bermondsey St Anne *S'wark* 88–92; Par Dn Brockley Hill St Sav 92–94; C 94–99; Miss Partner CMS Kenya 99–13; V Banbury St Hugh *Ox* from 14. *St Hugh's Vicarage, 4 Longfellow Road, Banbury OX16 9LB* T: (01295) 369021 E: anita.smith.nbi@gmail.com

SMITH, Ann Veronica. b 38. Doncaster Coll of Educn DipEd. Edin Dioc NSM Course 88. **d** 95 **p** 96. NSM S Queensferry *Edin* 95–99; NSM Falkirk 99–10; rtd 10; LtO *Edin* from 10. *16 Mannerston, Linlithgow EH49 7ND* T: (01506) 834361 E: avandmds@btinternet.com

SMITH, Anthony Cyril. b 40. K Coll Lon 65. **d** 69 **p** 70. C Crewkerne *B & W* 69–71; C Crewkerne w Wayford 71–74; TV Hemel Hempstead *St Alb* 74–76; Asst Chapl K Coll Taunton 76–80; Chapl 80–02; rtd 02; PtO *B & W* from 03. *1 Castle Street, Stogursey, Bridgwater TA5 1TG* T: (01278) 733577 E: kayandtony@kayandtony.plus.com *or* kayandtony40@gmail.com

SMITH, Anthony James. b 80. Jes Coll Cam BA 02 MA 06 Sussex Univ MSc 03 DPhil 08 St Jo Coll Dur BA 18. Cranmer Hall Dur 16. **d** 19. C Spennymoor and Whitworth *Dur* from 19. *34 Bluebell Drive, Spennymoor DL16 7YF* M: 07751-143941 E: revdanthonysmith@gmail.com

SMITH, Anthony James. b 57. Sheff Univ BA FCA. Ridley Hall Cam 83. **d** 86 **p** 87. C Woking St Pet *Guildf* 86–90; C Reigate St Mary *S'wark* 90–94; CMS Kenya 94–00; Finance Team Ldr World Vision UK 00–05; NSM Walton Milton Keynes *Ox* 10–12; PtO *Win* from 12; Hd of Resource Development from 13. *The Vicarage, The Plestor, Selborne, Alton GU34 3JQ* T: (01420) 511079 M: 07521-222886 E: anthony.smith@winchester.anglican.org

SMITH, Mrs Antoinette. b 47. NTMTC 94. **d** 98 **p** 99. NSM Chigwell and Chigwell Row *Chelmsf* 98–02; TV 02–10; Chapl Haven Ho Children's Hospice 03–10; V Blackmore and Stondon Massey *Chelmsf* 10–15; RD Ongar 10–13; PtO *Pet* 15–17; R Gt w Lt Harrowden and Orlingbury and Isham etc from 17. *The Rectory, 18 Kings Lane, Little Harrowden, Wellingborough NN9 5BL* T: (01933) 678573 M: 07815-025242 E: reverend.tonismith@gmail.com

SMITH, Austin John Denyer. b 40. Worc Coll Ox BA 62. Cuddesdon Coll 64. **d** 66 **p** 67. C Shepherd's Bush St Steph w St Thos *Lon* 66–69; C W Drayton 69–72; Chapl Sussex Univ *Chich* 72–79; V Caddington *St Alb* 79–06; rtd 06; PtO *St Alb* from 07. *209 Bedford Road, Hitchin SG5 2UE* T: (01462) 437433 E: ajdsmith@waitrose.com

SMITH, Mrs Barbara Ann. b 56. SNWTP 07. **d** 10 **p** 11. NSM Liv St Chris Norris Green from 10. *25 Meadow Lane, Liverpool L12 5EA* T: 0151-226 3534 M: 07957-963546 E: basmith@blueyonder.co.uk

SMITH, Mrs Barbara Mary. b 47. Doncaster Coll of Educn CertEd 68. Cranmer Hall Dur 82. **dss** 85 **d** 87 **p** 94. Beverley St Nic *York* 85–87; Par Dn 87; NSM S'wark H Trin w St Matt 89–90; Ind Chapl Teesside *York* 91–95; Hon C Middlesbrough St Chad 94–95; PtO *St Alb* 96–02; Locum Chapl Anglia Poly Univ *Ely* 96–98; TV Linton 00–04; rtd 04; PtO *Newc* from 04; *Dur* from 10. *14 Glebelands, Corbridge NE45 5DS*

SMITH, Canon Barry. b 41. Univ of Wales (Lamp) BA 62 Fitzw Ho Cam BA 64 MA 68 Man Univ MPhil 91. Ridley Hall Cam. **d** 65 **p** 66. C Rhyl w St Ann *St As* 65–70; Chapl Scargill Ho 70–72; C Flint *St As* 72–74; V Broughton 74–86; Dioc Ecum Officer 82–86; RD Wrexham 82–86; TR 86–95; Can Cursal St As Cathl 86–95; Chan 95; PtO *S'wark* 97–02. *1 Acorn Keep, Rowhills, Farnham GU9 9BL* T: (01252) 322111

SMITH, Barry Roy. b 46. STETS. **d** 00 **p** 04. NSM Blendworth w Chalton w Idsworth *Portsm* 00–05; Asst Chapl Portsm Hosps NHS Trust 03–05; Team Chapl from 05; PtO *Portsm* 05–07 and from 09; NSM Blendworth w Chalton w Idsworth 07–09. *10 Celandine Avenue, Waterlooville PO8 9BE* E: barry.roy.smith@googlemail.com

SMITH, Beverley Anne. b 56. Univ of Wales Coll of Medicine MSc 97 Univ of S Wales MSc 15 RN 78 RM 80 RHV 87 Univ of Wales PGCE 00. St Mich Coll Llan. **d** 05 **p** 06. NSM Whitchurch *Llan* 05–11; NSM Mynyddislwyn *Mon* 11–13; NSM Cyncoed from 15; Chapl Cardiff and Vale Univ Health Bd 08–11. *3 Solva Avenue, Cardiff CF14 0NP* M: 07841-707525 E: beverleyatciw@btinternet.com

SMITH, The Ven Brian. b 44. Westmr Coll Ox MTh 95. Sarum & Wells Th Coll 71. **d** 74 **p** 75. C Pennywell St Thos and Grindon St Oswald CD *Dur* 74–77; Chapl RAF 77–95; P-in-c Keswick St Jo *Carl* 95–96; V 96–05; RD Derwent 98–05; Hon Can Carl Cathl 99–05; Adn of Man *S & M* 05–11; V Douglas St Geo 05–11; rtd 11; PtO *Carl* from 12. *The Coach House, The Street, Westward, Wigton CA7 8AF* T: (01697) 345396 E: brian.smith157@btinternet.com

✠**SMITH, The Rt Revd Brian Arthur.** b 43. Edin Univ MA 66 Fitzw Coll Cam BA 68 MA 72 Jes Coll Cam MLitt 73. Westcott Ho Cam 66. **d** 72 **p** 73 **c** 93. Tutor and Lib Cuddesdon Coll 72–75; Dir of Studies Ripon Coll Cuddesdon 75–78; Sen Tutor 78–79; C Cuddesdon *Ox* 76–79; Dir Tr *Wakef* 79–87; P-in-c Halifax St Jo 79–85; Hon Can Wakef Cathl 81–87; Adn Craven *Bradf* 87–93; Suff Bp Tonbridge *Roch* 93–01; Hon Can Roch Cathl 93–01; Bp Edin 01–11; rtd 11; LtO *Edin* from 11; PtO *Ab* from 12. *Flat E, 2A Dean Path, Edinburgh EH4 3BA* T: 0131-220 6097 E: bishopsmith@btinternet.com

SMITH, Brian Michael. b 42. Kelham Th Coll 69. **d** 69 **p** 70. C Somers Town *Lon* 70–74; C Stamford Hill St Jo 74–75; C Stamford Hill St Bart 75–84; P-in-c Edmonton St Pet w St Martin 84–92; V 92–07; rtd 07. *9 Derwent Gardens, Derwent Avenue, Matlock DE4 3LX* T: (01629) 56559 E: bms.stple@gmail.com

SMITH, Canon Bridget Mary. b 46. Bp Otter Coll CertEd 67. S Dios Minl Tr Scheme 88. **d** 91 **p** 94. C Pet H Spirit Bretton 91–95; P-in-c Silverstone and Abthorpe w Slapton 95–03; R Silverstone and Abthorpe w Slapton etc 03–09; Warden of Past Assts 00–06; Can Pet Cathl 01–09; rtd 09; PtO *S'well* from 10. *2 Merryweather Close, Southwell NG25 0BN* T: (01636) 812215 E: quickvic@lineone.net

SMITH, Mrs Carol. b 55. SEITE 01. **d** 04 **p** 05. C Epping Distr Chelmsf 04–07; Chapl Epping Forest Primary Care Trust 05–07; V Moulsham St Luke *Chelmsf* 07–17; P-in-c Moulsham St Jo 13–17; C Galleywood Common 13–17; C Widford 13–17; Hon Can Chelmsf Cathl 13–17; V Herne *Cant* from 17. *The New Vicarage, Herne Street, Herne Bay CT6 7HE* E: carolrev@gotadsl.co.uk

SMITH, Mrs Catherine Eleanor Louise. b 52. SAOMC 99. **d** 02 **p** 03. NSM Denham *Ox* 02–05; NSM Penn Street 05–15; NSM Beaconsfield 15–17; PtO from 17; Chapl Heatherwood & Wexham Park Hosps NHS Foundn Trust 05–14; Chapl Frimley Health NHS Foundn Trust from 14. *24 Westfield Road, Beaconsfield HP9 1EF* T/F: (01494) 670389 M: 07973-818998 E: catherinesmith52@btinternet.com

SMITH, Mrs Charlene. b 79. Coll of Resurr Mirfield 12. **d** 14 **p** 15. C Meltham *Leeds* 14–18 and from 14. *The Rectory, Cross Hill, Ackworth, Pontefract WF7 7EJ* T: (01977) 599959 E: revd.charlenesmith@gmail.com

SMITH, Charles Henry Neville. b 31. Nottm Univ BA 52 MA 65. Sarum Th Coll 55. **d** 57 **p** 58. C Thirsk w S Kilvington *York* 57–60; C Linthorpe 60–61; V Danby 61–66; Chapl United Camb Hosps 66–76; Chapl Lanc Moor Hosp 76–84; Hon Can Blackb Cathl 81–84; Asst Sec Gen Syn Hosp Chapl Coun 84–88; Hon C Lee St Marg *S'wark* 84–88; Chapl Guy's Hosp Lon 88–96; rtd 96; Hon Chapl S'wark Cathl from 96. *57 Belmont Park, London SE13 5BW* T: (020) 8318 9993 E: revnev@talktalk.net

SMITH, Canon Charles Rycroft. b 46. Sarum & Wells Th Coll 76. **d** 78 **p** 79. C Heref St Martin 78–81; C Southampton Maybush St Pet *Win* 81–83; R The Candover Valley 83–99; RD Alresford 90–99; P-in-c Guernsey St Andr 99–01; R 01–07; Vice-Dean Guernsey 02–07; P-in-c Beaulieu and Exbury and E Boldre 07–14; rtd 14; Hon Can Win Cathl from 14; PtO *Heref* from 15. *Hope Cottage, 25B New Street, Ledbury HR8 2EA* T: (01531) 631104 E: rycs006@gmail.com

SMITH, Christine Lydia. *See* CARTER, Christine Lydia

SMITH, Mrs Christine Mary. b 53. Lanc Univ BA 75. Ox Min Course 13. **d** 15 **p** 16. NSM E Win from 15. *Pilgrim Cottage, Stoke Charity, Winchester SO21 3PF* T: (01962) 760309 M: 07751-303007 E: christine@hymnsam.co.uk

SMITH, The Ven Christopher Blake Walters. b 63. Univ of Wales (Cardiff) BMus 84 BD 88 LLM 95. St Mich Coll Llan 85. **d** 88 **p** 89. C Aberdare *Llan* 88–93; V Tongwynlais 93–00; Dioc Dir Post-Ord Tr 95–05; Dom Chapl Bp Llan and Warden of Ords 01–07; Chapl to Abp Wales 03–07; Adn Morgannwg from 06; P-in-c Cwmbach from 07; Metrop Can from 04. *The Heights, Nant y Groes Drive, Tirfounder Road, Aberdare CF44 0BE* T: (01685) 378455 E: archdeacon.morgannwg@churchinwales.org.uk

SMITH, Canon Christopher Francis. b 46. K Coll Lon BD 68 AKC 68. St Aug Coll Cant 69. **d** 70 **p** 71. C Norwood All SS *Cant* 70–72; Asst Chapl Marlborough Coll 72–76; C Deal St Leon w Sholden *Cant* 77–81; P-in-c Benenden 81–83; V 83–07; P-in-c Sandhurst w Newenden 04–07; Hon Can Cant Cathl 03–07; AD Tenterden 05–07; Chapl Benenden Sch 81–92; Chapl Benenden Hosp 91–07; rtd 07; PtO *Cant* from 07. *34 Richmond Road, Whitstable CT5 3PH* T: (01227) 266569 E: christopherfrancissmith@yahoo.co.uk or cfsmith46@gmail.com

SMITH, Christopher James. b 72. Newc Univ BSc 94. Wycliffe Hall Ox BTh 01. **d** 02 **p** 03. C Cambridge H Trin *Ely* 02–04; Assoc R Manchester Zion Ch USA 04–08; R Chevening *Roch* 09–19; RD Sevenoaks 19; TR Marlborough *Sarum* from 19. *The Rectory, Rawlingswell Lane, St Martins, Marlborough SN8 1AU* E: revcjsmith@gmail.com

SMITH, Christopher John. b 81. Ridley Hall Cam 16. **d** 18 **p** 19. C Colchester St Luke *Chelmsf* from 18. *9 Asquith Drive, Highwoods, Colchester CO4 9FS*

SMITH, Christopher Matthew. b 67. New Coll Ox BA 89 MA 93 Open Univ LLB 07 Cardiff Univ LLM 09 Homerton Coll Cam PGCE 90 Called to the Bar (Gray's Inn) 10. St Steph Ho Ox BA 94. **d** 95 **p** 96. C Wantage *Ox* 95–99; Dom Chapl to Bp Horsham *Chich* 99–01; V Beckenham St Mich w St Aug Roch 01–11; V Holborn St Alb w Saffron Hill St Pet *Lon* from 11; AD S Camden 16–18. *St Alban's Clergy House, 18 Brooke Street, London EC1N 7RD* T: (020) 7405 1831 or (020) 7430 2551

SMITH, Canon Christopher Milne. b 44. Selw Coll Cam BA 66. Cuddesdon Coll 67. **d** 69 **p** 70. C Liv Our Lady and St Nic 69–74; TV Kirkby 74–81; R Walton St Mary 81–91; Can Res Sheff Cathl 91–02; V Doncaster St Geo 02–10; Bp's Adv on the Paranormal 97–10; Hon Can Sheff Cathl 03–10; rtd 10; PtO *Sheff* 10–14; *Newc* from 10; Chapl to The Queen 04–14; PtO *Eur* 10–19. *14 Ravensdowne, Berwick-upon-Tweed TD15 1HX* T: (01289) 330375 E: smithrevem@gmail.com

SMITH, Clifford. b 31. St Aid Birkenhead 59. **d** 61 **p** 62. C Limehouse St Anne *Lon* 61–63; C Ashtead *Guildf* 63–66; R Bromley All Hallows *Lon* 66–76; V Hillsborough and Wadsley Bridge *Sheff* 76–89; V Stainforth 89–96; rtd 96; Hon C Hurst *Ox* 97–12; Hon C Ruscombe and Twyford w Hurst from 12. *33 King Street Lane, Winnersh, Wokingham RG41 5AX* T: 0118-978 9453

SMITH, Clive Leslie. b 50. Leeds Univ BA 72 MA 03 Ch Coll Liv PGCE 73. Coll of Resurr Mirfield 75. **d** 77 **p** 78. C Goldington *St Alb* 77–81; C Cheshunt 81–84; V Watford St Pet 84–89; Chapl Leavesden Hosp Abbots Langley 89–94; Chapl St Alb and Hemel Hempstead NHS Trust 94–00; Chapl W Herts Hosps NHS Trust 00–01; Sen Chapl Doncaster and Bassetlaw Hosps NHS Foundn Trust 01–14; rtd 14; PtO *S'well* 02–17; *Sheff* 14–18; Chapl HM Pris Lindholme from 18. *HM Prison Lindholme, Doncaster DN7 6EE* T: (01302) 524870 E: clive.smith@justice.gov.uk

SMITH, Colin. b 39. Open Univ BA 80 LRSC 65 CChem 88 FRSC 88. NEOC 94. **d** 97 **p** 98. NSM Jesmond H Trin and Newc St Barn and St Jude 97–08; rtd 08; PtO *Newc* from 08. *1 Cayton Grove, Newcastle upon Tyne NE5 1HL* T: 0191-267 9519 E: colinandevelyn@btopenworld.com

SMITH, Colin Richard. b 53. Liv Poly BA 80 Liv Univ MTD 83. Oak Hill Th Coll 84. **d** 86 **p** 87. C Ormskirk *Liv* 86–89; V Wigan St Cath 89–94; C St Helens St Helen 94–99; TV 99–10; P-in-c St Helens St Mark 06–10; TV St Helens Town Cen 10–15; rtd 15; PtO *Liv* from 17. *5 Victoria Avenue, St Helens WA11 7BU*

SMITH, Mrs Corinne Anne. b 52. St Andr Univ MTheol 91. SAOMC 95. **d** 97. **c** Abingdon *Ox* 97–02; Chapl Pemb Coll Ox 02–03; Chapl Ox Radcliffe Hosps NHS Trust 03–07; Chapl Portsm Hosps NHS Trust 07–12; Chapl Sue Ryder Nettlebed Hospice 12–15; PtO *Portsm* 16–17; NSM Shanklin St Sav from 17; NSM Lake from 17; NSM Godshill from 17. *Dovecote, 7 Culver Road, Shanklin PO37 6ER* T: (01983) 861581 M: 07775-628593 E: therevcozza@gmail.com

SMITH, Craig Philip. b 61. Sheff City Poly BA 86. St Jo Coll Nottm 90. **d** 93 **p** 94. C Bramley and Ravenfield w Hooton Roberts etc *Sheff* 93–97; C Rainham w Wennington *Chelmsf* 97–00; TV Gainsborough and Morton *Linc* 00–03; V Catshill and Dodford *Worc* 03–07; New Zealand 07–15; TR Gorton and Abbey Hey *Man* from 16; AD Ardwick from 17. *The Rectory, 42-44 Wellington Street, Manchester M18 8LJ* T: 0161-231 7401 E: craig@gortonchurch.org

SMITH, Daniel Bradley. b 69. Harris Man Coll Ox BTh 05. St Steph Ho Ox 04. **d** 06 **p** 07. C Bexhill St Pet *Chich* 06–11; R W Blatchington from 11. *St Peter's Rectory, 23 Windmill Close, Hove BN3 7LJ* T: (01273) 732459

SMITH, Canon Darren John Anthony. b 62. Nottm Univ BCombStuds 84. Linc Th Coll 84. **d** 86 **p** 87. C Leic Ascension 86–90; C Curdworth w Castle Vale *Birm* 90; C Castle Vale St Cuth 90–91; C Kingstanding St Luke 91–92; P-in-c 92–93; V 93–08; P-in-c Kingstanding St Mark 01–02; Gen Sec ACS from 08; Hon Can Ghana from 18. *Gordon Browning House, 8 Spitfire Road, Birmingham B24 9PB* T: 0121-382 5533 F: 382 6999 E: fr.smith@additionalcurates.co.uk

SMITH, David Earling. b 35. AKC 60. **d** 61 **p** 62. C Knebworth *St Alb* 61–63; C Chipping Barnet 64–66; C S Ormsby w Ketsby, Calceby and Driby *Linc* 66–69; R Claxby w Normanby-le-Wold 69–74; R Nettleton 69–74; R S Kelsey 69–74; R N Owersby w Thornton le Moor 69–74; R Stainton-le-Vale w Kirmond le Mire 69–74; V Ancaster 74–79; Warden and Chapl St Anne Bedehouses Linc 79–89; C Linc Minster Gp 79–89; rtd 89; PtO *Linc* 90–02. *17 Egerton Road, Lincoln LN2 4PJ* T: (01522) 510336

✠**SMITH, The Rt Revd David James.** b 35. AKC 58 FKC 99. **d** 59 **p** 60 **c** 87. C Gosforth All SS *Newc* 59–62; C Newc St Fran 62–64; C Longbenton St Bart 64–68; V Longhirst 68–75; V Monkseaton St Mary 75–82; RD Tynemouth 80–82; Hon Can Newc Cathl 81–87; Adn Lindisfarne 81–87; V Felton 82–83; Suff Bp Maidstone *Cant* 87–92; Bp HM Forces 90–92; Bp Bradf 92–02; rtd 02; Hon Asst Bp York from 02; Hon Asst Bp Eur from 02. *34 Cedar Glade, Dunnington, York YO19 5QZ* T: (01904) 481225 E: david@djmhs.force9.co.uk

SMITH, Canon David John. b 32. Goldsmiths' Coll Lon BA 76 LSE MSc 79. Lon Coll of Div 68. **d** 70 **p** 71. C Clerkenwell St Jas and St Jo w St Pet *Lon* 70–73; P-in-c Penge St Paul *Roch* 74–78; V 78–89; RD Beckenham 86–89; Chapl Bromley and Sheppard's Colls 90–97; PtO *S'wark* 90–97; Dioc Clergy Widows and Retirement Officer *Roch* 90–97; Hon Can Roch Cathl 95–97; rtd 98; PtO *St Alb* from 98; *Lon* from 99; *Ox* 09–19. *13 Park Way, Rickmansworth WD3 7AU* T: (01923) 775963

SMITH, David Robert. b 54. Southn Univ BSc 75 Loughb Univ MSc 86 CEng 84 MRAeS 84. WEMTC 02. **d** 05 **p** 06. C Matson *Glouc* 05–09; P-in-c Glouc St Geo w Whaddon 09–12; V 12–15; AD Glouc City 11–15; TR N Cheltenham 15–16; Hon Can Glouc Cathl 14–16; R Ashmanhaugh, Barton Turf etc *Nor* from 16. *The Rectory, 11 Pinewood Drive, Horning, Norwich NR12 8LZ* T: (01692) 630216 E: draesmith2@btinternet.com

SMITH, David Roy. b 74. Westcott Ho Cam 10. **d** 12 **p** 13. C Thorpe St Andr *Nor* 12–16; P-in-c E w W Harling, Bridgham w Roudham, Larling etc from 16. *The Rectory, Church Road, East Harling, Norwich NR16 2NB* E: revdavidrsmith@gmail.com

SMITH, David Stanley. b 41. Ox NSM Course. **d** 84 **p** 85. NSM Burghfield *Ox* 84–86; NSM Stratfield Mortimer 86–88; NSM Mortimer W End w Padworth 86–88; C St Breoke and Egloshayle *Truro* 88–93; V Penwerris 93–07; rtd 07; PtO *Ox* 09–10. *Emmaus, 1 Webster Close, Reading RG2 8BF* T: 0118-987 2597

SMITH, Mrs Deborah Louise. b 56. WEMTC 02 NOC 03. **d** 05 **p** 06. C Honley *Wakef* 05–07; Chapl HM Pris and YOI New Hall 05–07; NSM Woolston New Zealand 07–11; Chapl Nelson Hosps 11–12; C Remuera St Aidan 13–14; Jt P-in-c St Heliers Bay 14–15; Jt V Pahiatua and Eketahuna 15–18; P-in-c Tillington *Chich* from 18; P-in-c Duncton from 18; P-in-c Upwaltham from 18. *Tillington Rectory, Tillington, Petworth GU28 9AH* E: dlsinz211@gmail.com

SMITH, Mrs Decia Jane. b 47. ALAM 66. WMMTC 92. **d** 95 **p** 96. C Edgbaston St Germain *Birm* 95–99; P-in-c Abbots Leigh w Leigh Woods *Bris* 00–12; rtd 12; PtO *Bris* from 13. *4 Kingsmill, Bristol BS9 1BZ* T: 0117-968 3511 E: revdecia@yahoo.co.uk

SMITH, Declan. *See* SMITH, Godfrey Declan Burfield

SMITH, Denis Richard. b 53. MA 15. St Jo Coll Nottm 83. **d** 85 **p** 86. C Hersham *Guildf* 85–88; C Thatcham *Ox* 88–91; V Shefford *St Alb* 91–02; P-in-c Tilehurst St Cath *Ox* 02–07; V Tilehurst St Cath and Calcot 07–16; rtd 16; PtO *Ox* from 16; *Win* from 17. *32 Basswood Drive, Basingstoke RG24 9SW* E: revdenissmith@hotmail.com

SMITH, Mrs Denise. b 46. Didsbury Coll of Educn CertEd 67. **d** 08 **p** 09. OLM Goodshaw and Crawshawbooth *Man* 08–16; rtd 16; PtO *Man* from 18. *Address temp unknown* M: 07551-361875 E: mrsbucket122@btinternet.com

SMITH, Dennis Austin. b 50. Lanc Univ BA 71 Liv Univ PGCE 72. NW Ord Course 74. **d** 77 **p** 78. NSM Seaforth *Liv* 77–83; NSM Gt Crosby St Faith 77–83; Hon C 83–98; Hon C Gt Crosby St Faith and Waterloo Park St Mary from 98; Asst Chapl Merchant Taylors' Sch Crosby 79–83; Chapl from 83. *16 Fir Road, Liverpool L22 4QL* T: 0151-928 5065

SMITH, Derek Graham. b 52. St Cath Coll Cam BA 74 MA 77. Westcott Ho Cam 74. **d** 76 **p** 77. C Weymouth H Trin *Sarum* 76–79; P-in-c Bradpole 79; TV Bridport 79–84; R Monkton Farleigh, S Wraxall and Winsley 84–98; TR Melksham 98–09; C Atworth w Shaw and Whitley 07–09; C Broughton Gifford, Gt Chalfield and Holt 07–09; RD Bradford 01–08; Chapl Wilts and Swindon Healthcare NHS Trust 00–02; Can and Preb Sarum Cathl 03–09; Chapl Limassol St Barn 09–17; rtd 17; PtO *B & W* from 18. *2 Underleaf Way, Peasedown St John, Bath BA2 8SY* T: (01761) 438976 E: revdgsmith52@gmail.com

SMITH, Donald Edgar. b 56. Oak Hill Th Coll 89. **d** 91 **p** 92. C Holloway St Mark w Em *Lon* 91–92; C Tollington 92–95; TV W Ealing St Jo w St Jas 95–08; R Frinton *Chelmsf* from 08. *The Rectory, 22 Queens Road, Frinton-on-Sea CO13 9BL* T: (01255) 674664 E: donthevic@btinternet.com

SMITH, Miss Dorothea Violet (Thea). b 93. Warwick Univ BA 16. Trin Coll Bris BA 19. **d** 19. C Woking Ch Ch *Guildf* from 19. *4 Orchard Drive, Woking GU21 4BN* M: 07845-232393 E: thea.smith@rocketmail.com

SMITH, Edward George. b 61. Surrey Univ BSc 82 Cov Univ MSc 95. Ox Min Course 06. **d** 09 **p** 10. NSM Aynho and Croughton w Evenley etc *Pet* 09–11; NSM Chenderit 11–14; R Cogenhoe and Gt and Lt Houghton w Brafield from 14; RD Wellingborough from 18. *The Rectory, Church Street, Cogenhoe, Northampton NN7 1LS* T: (01604) 891166 M: 07740-909756 E: eddie.smith@talk21.com

SMITH, Miss Elizabeth Jane. b 50. Birm Univ BA 72. Trin Coll Bris 88. **d** 90 **p** 94. C Lowestoft and Kirkley *Nor* 90–94; TV Rugby *Cov* 94–01; C Shepton Mallet w Doulting *B & W* 01–03; R 03–10; Chapl Mendip Primary Care Trust 01–06; Chapl Somerset Primary Care Trust 06–10; rtd 10; PtO *Sarum* from 11; *B & W* from 15. *19 Alcock Crest, Warminster BA12 8ND* E: lizinwarminster@gmail.com

SMITH, Canon Elizabeth Marion. b 52. ACA 76 FCA 82. Carl Dioc Tr Inst 91. **d** 94 **p** 95. C Appleby *Carl* 94–98; P-in-c Hesket-in-the-Forest and Armathwaite 98–04; P-in-c Skelton and Hutton-in-the-Forest w Ivegill 98–04; R Inglewood Gp 04–12; RD Penrith 06–09; Hon Can Carl Cathl 08–12; rtd 13; PtO *Carl* 13–16; Hon C Harraby 16–19; P-in-c from 19. *Tanglewood, Cumwhinton, Carlisle CA4 8DL* T: (01228) 560310 E: revdesmith@hotmail.com

SMITH, Esther. b 65. Coll of Ripon & York St Jo BA 86 York Univ PGCE 87. Trin Coll Bris BA 13. **d** 13 **p** 14. C Bath Walcot *B & W* 13–17; C Combe Down w Monkton Combe and S Stoke 17–18; R Chilcompton w Downside and Stratton on the Fosse from 18. *The Rectory, The Street, Chilcompton, Radstock BA3 4HN* T: (01761) 233401 E: esthersmith369@gmail.com

SMITH (née DAVIS), Felicity Ann. b 40. Bris Univ MB, ChB 63. Qu Coll Birm 83. **dss** 86 **d** 87 **p** 94. NSM Dioc Bd for Soc Resp *Cov* 86–96; NSM Leamington Spa H Trin from 96. *14 Oakwood Grove, Warwick CV34 5TD* T: (01926) 492452 E: felicity@fandi.me.uk

SMITH, Felix Arran Jerome. b 87. Edin Univ MA 11 Win Univ MA 17. Ripon Coll Cuddesdon MTh 13. **d** 13 **p** 15. C Dundee St Paul *Bre* 13–14; C Coplow *Leic* 14–17; V Lancing St Mich *Chich* from 17. *St Michael's Vicarage, 117 Penhill Road, Lancing BN15 8HD* T: (01903) 753653 M: 07818-407114 E: revfelixsmith@gmail.com

SMITH, Frances Mary. *See* KNIGHT, Frances Mary

SMITH, Francis Malcolm. b 44. Open Univ BA 82 FCMI ACIB 69. EAMTC 90. **d** 93 **p** 94. NSM Prittlewell *Chelmsf* 93–08; PtO 08–16; NSM N Shoebury 16–17; NSM Southchurch H Trin 16–17; PtO from 17. *24 St Augustine's Avenue, Southend-on-Sea SS1 3JH* T: (01702) 586680 F: 291166 E: franksmith44@hotmail.com

SMITH, Gavin Craig. b 71. Ridley Hall Cam 02. **d** 04 **p** 05. C Heatons *Man* 04–07; CF from 07. *c/o MOD Chaplains*

(Army) T: (01264) 383430 F: 381824 M: 07919-354796 E: gavinsmith1971@hotmail.com

SMITH, Geoffrey. b 45. Bernard Gilpin Soc Dur 65 Sarum Th Coll 66. **d** 69 **p** 70. C Hatfield *Sheff* 69–71; C Bolton St Pet *Man* 71–74; V Lt Hulton 74–78; P-in-c Newc St Andr and Soc Resp Adv *Newc* 78–87; Hon Can Newc Cathl 84–87; Dir Cen for Applied Chr Studies 87–91; Team Ldr Home Office Birm Drug Prevention Unit 91–93; Public Preacher *Birm* 87–93; C Brampton and Farlam and Castle Carrock w Cumrew *Carl* 93–96; ACUPA Link Officer 94–96; Can Res Bradf Cathl 96–00; Nat Dir PtO C H 00–02; PtO *Ox* 00–02; Hon C Biddenham *St Alb* 02–07; rtd 07; PtO *Carl* from 07; *Eur* from 07; P-in-c Shotley *Newc* from 18. *St Johns's, Shotley Bridge, Consett DH8 9TL* T: 05602-231702 E: geoffsmith1@btinternet.com

SMITH, Geoffrey Keith. b 37. Lon Coll of Div 57. **d** 60 **p** 61. C Leek St Luke *Lich* 60–63; C Trentham 63–66; V Lilleshall 66–84; P-in-c Sheriffhales w Woodcote 83–84; V Lilleshall and Sheriffhales 84–87; P-in-c Haughton 87–91; R Derrington, Haughton and Ranton 91–03; RD Stafford 95–03; rtd 03; PtO *Lich* from 03; CF (ACF) 73–02. *19 Meadow Drive, Haughton, Stafford ST18 9HU* T: (01785) 259076 E: geoffmar@btinternet.co.uk

SMITH, Geoffrey Raymond. b 49. AKC 71. St Aug Coll Cant 71. **d** 72 **p** 73. C Hendon St Alphage *Lon* 72–75; C Notting Hill St Mich and Ch Ch 75–78; P-in-c Isleworth St Fran 78–83; P-in-c Chipping Ongar *Chelmsf* 83–84; R 84–86; R Shelley 84–86; R Chipping Ongar w Shelley 86–89; RD Ongar 88–89; P-in-c Harlow St Mary Magd 89–90; V 90–98; R Woodford St Mary w St Phil and St Jas 98–08; TR Loughton St Jo 08–09; R 09–15; rtd 15; PtO *Chich* 16–18; R Laughton w Ripe and Chalvington from 18. *The Rectory, Church Lane, Laughton, Lewes BN8 6AH* T: (01323) 811177

SMITH, Georgina Leah. *See* HOLDING, Georgina Leah

SMITH, Gerald. b 36. Sarum Th Coll 61. **d** 63 **p** 64. C Menston w Woodhead *Bradf* 63–66; Chapl RAF 66–70; C Hoylake Ches 70–72; R Inverurie *Ab* 72–74; R Kemnay 72–74; TV Hucknall Torkard *S'well* 74–75; R Falkland Is 75–78; V Luddenden w Luddenden Foot *Wakef* 79–86; V Scopwick Gp *Linc* 86–94; P-in-c Leasingham 94–96; rtd 96; PtO *Ex* from 96. *Ivy Cottage, Woolsery, Bideford EX39 5QS* T/F: (01237) 431298 E: geraldsmithgerould@btinternet.com

SMITH, Mrs Gillian. b 55. EAMTC 02. **d** 05 **p** 06. NSM Burwell w Reach *Ely* 05–09; P-in-c Potton w Sutton and Cockayne Hatley *St Alb* 09–13; R 13–19; rtd 19. *Abel Cottage, New Road, Ashwellthorpe, Norwich NR16 1HF* E: gillsmith.ash@gmail.com

SMITH, Mrs Gillian Angela. b 39. RGN 60 RM 62. All Nations Chr Coll IDC 65. **d** 94 **p** 95. NSM Haydock St Mark *Liv* 94–96; PtO *Ely* 96–02; *Eur* 98–01; Hon C Milton *Win* 02–03; PtO *Ely* 03–11; *Chelmsf* 04–11; *York* from 11. *3 Belvedere Mansions, Lonsdale Road, Scarborough YO11 2QU* T: (01723) 448560 E: gill.rev@outlook.com

SMITH, Gillian Carol. *See* HUBBARD, Gillian Carol

SMITH, Godfrey Declan Burfield. b 42. TCD BA 64 MA 67 PGCE 65. Sarum Th Coll. **d** 69 **p** 70. Zambia 70–75; PtO *D & G* 81–02; S Regional Sec (Ireland) CMS 81–99; Overseas Sec 87–93; Miss Personnel Sec 93–99; I Donoughmore and Donard w Dunlavin *D & G* 02–11; rtd 11. *Moelvra, 1 Marlborough Road, Glenageary, Co Dublin, Republic of Ireland* M: (00353) 87-298 7364 E: declansmith14@gmail.com

SMITH, Graham. b 39. Univ of Wales (Ban) CertEd 60 Lon Univ DipEd 75. **d** 01 **p** 02. OLM Upper Holme Valley *Wakef* 01–05; NSM R Richmond *Ripon* 05–08; rtd 08; PtO *Derby* 08–18. *15 Church Street, Denby Village, Ripley DE5 8PA* T: (01332) 881324 M: 07918-025346 E: graham.smith50@btopenworld.com or gsmith370@btinternet.com or revdgsmith@btinternet.com

SMITH, Graham. *See* SMITH, John Graham

SMITH, The Very Revd Graham Charles Morell. b 47. St Chad's Coll Dur BA 74. Westcott Ho Cam 74. **d** 76 **p** 77. C Tooting All SS *S'wark* 76–80; TV Thamesmead 80–87; TR Kidlington w Hampton Poyle *Ox* 87–97; RD Ox 89–95; TR Leeds City *Ripon* 97–04; Hon Can Ripon Cathl 97–04; Dean Nor 04–13; rtd 13; PtO *Ex* 13–17; P-in-c Ashreigney 17–18; P-in-c Broadwoodkelly 17–18; P-in-c Brushford 17–18; P-in-c Winkleigh 17–18. *Blacksmith's Cottage, Church Street, Ashreigney, Chulmleigh EX18 7LP* T: (01769) 520824 E: gcsmith@uwclub.net

SMITH, Graham David Noel. b 37. Oak Hill Th Coll 72. **d** 73 **p** 74. C Southborough St Pet w Ch Ch and St Matt *Roch* 73–76; C Bedworth *Cov* 76–79; R Treeton *Sheff* 79–84; V Riddlesden *Bradf* 84–96; RD S Craven 91–96; rtd 96; Hon C Ilkley All SS *Bradf* 97–03; PtO 03–14; *Leeds* from 14. *26 Hawthorne Grove, Burley in Wharfdale, Ilkley LS29 7RF* T: (01943) 864754

SMITH, Graham John. b 60. RN Eng Coll Plymouth BScEng 84. Trin Coll Bris BA 90 St Jo Coll Nottm MA 00.

d 90 **p** 91. C Herne *Cant* 90–93; Chapl RN 93–96; C Henfield w Shermanbury and Woodmancote *Chich* 96–98; Chapl Sussex Police 96–98; Chapl Portsm Hosps NHS Trust 98–00; P-in-c Cosham and Chapl Highbury Coll of FE Portsm 00–05; CME Officer *Portsm* 03–05; PtO from 06; *Guildf* from 16. *18 Poynings Place, Portsmouth PO1 2PB* T: (023) 9229 1239 M: 07970-826160 E: gjsmith@first-web.co.uk

SMITH, Graham Russell. b 60. New Coll Ox BA 81 MA 89 Lon Univ BD 89. Qu Coll Birm 02. **d** 04 **p** 05. C Yardley St Edburgha *Birm* 04–08; TV Bushbury *Lich* from 08. *The Good Shepherd Vicarage, 17 Goodyear Avenue, Wolverhampton WV10 9JX* T: (01902) 731713 M: 07746-994186 E: smith-graham32@sky.com

SMITH, Greg Peter. b 60. Warwick Univ BA 86 Qu Coll Birm BA 99. WMMTC 97. **d** 99 **p** 00. C Binley *Cov* 99–04; P-in-c E Green from 04; AD Cov S from 18. *St Andrew's Vicarage, Church Lane, Eastern Green, Coventry CV5 7BX* T: (024) 7642 2856 E: gregsmith31760@aol.com

SMITH, Gregory James. *See* CLIFTON-SMITH, Gregory James

SMITH, Mrs Gwendoline Anne. b 52. K Coll Lon BA 97. SEITE 97. **d** 99 **p** 00. C Erith St Paul *Roch* 99–02; V Hadlow 02–12; RD Paddock Wood 10–12; TV Bideford, Northam, Westward Ho!, Appledore etc *Ex* 12–17; rtd 17; PtO *B & W* from 17. *13 Dillons Road, Creech St Michael, Taunton TA3 5DS* E: gwensmith1252@gmail.com

SMITH, Miss Hannah Joy. b 82. Sheff Univ BA 03 K Coll Lon MA 10. St Mellitus Coll 08. **d** 12 **p** 13. C Leeds City *Ripon* 12–14 and 14–16; P-in-c Leeds Halton St Wilfrid 16–17; V Halton and Osmondthorpe from 17. *St Wilfrid's Vicarage, Selby Road, Leeds LS15 7NP* M: 07766-997287 E: hannahjoysmith@googlemail.com

SMITH, Sister Hazel Ferguson Waide. b 33. Univ Coll Lon BA 55. **dss** 64 **d** 87 **p** 06. CSA 58–77; St Etheldreda's Children's Home Bedf 64–85; Bedford St Paul *St Alb* 85–92; Par Dn 87–92; rtd 92; PtO *St Alb* from 92; *Ox* from 93; Assoc Sister CSA from 03. *Paddock House, 6 Linford Lane, Willen, Milton Keynes MK15 9DL* T: (01908) 397267 M: 07789-654881 E: hazel.s35@talktalk.net

SMITH, Heather Faith. b 60. Stirling Univ BSc 80 Ox Univ BTh 04 Heythrop Coll Lon MA 11. Ripon Coll Cuddesdon 00. **d** 02 **p** 03. C Caversham St Pet and Mapledurham *Ox* 02–06; PtO from 19. *36 Greystones, Bromham, Chippenham SN15 2JT* T: (01380) 850729

SMITH, Henry Robert. b 41. Lanchester Poly Cov BSc 66. Qu Coll Birm 75. **d** 78 **p** 79. Hon C Hillmorton *Cov* 78–81; LtO *S'well* 81–85; Hon C Radcliffe-on-Trent and Shelford etc 85–89; C Sutton in Ashfield St Mary 89–92; P-in-c Forest Town 92–98; P-in-c Babworth w Sutton-cum-Lound 98–02; P-in-c Scofton w Osberton 98–02; P-in-c Babworth w Sutton-cum-Lound and Scofton etc 02–06; rtd 06; PtO *S'well* from 18. *15 Park Lane, Retford DN22 6TX* T: (01777) 949649 E: bobsmith@dircon.co.uk

SMITH, Howard Alan. b 46. St Jo Coll Dur BA 73. Cranmer Hall Dur. **d** 74 **p** 75. C Brighton St Matthias *Chich* 74–77; C Henfield w Shermanbury and Woodmancote 77–80; R Northiam 80–87; Chapl St Ebba's Hosp Epsom 87–94; Chapl Qu Mary's Hosp Carshalton 87–94; Chapl Merton and Sutton Community NHS Trust 94–99; Chapl Epsom and St Helier Univ Hosps NHS Trust 99–08; rtd 08; PtO *S'wark* from 08; Chapl Wandsworth Primary Care Trust 10–13. *72 Park Lane, Wallington SM6 0TL* T: (020) 8643 3300 E: howard_a_smith2003@yahoo.co.uk

SMITH, Howard Gilbert. b 48. Leeds Univ BA 69. St Steph Ho Ox BA 71 MA 75 Ridley Hall Cam 72. **d** 73 **p** 74. C Wallsend St Luke *Newc* 73–76; C Farnworth and Kearsley *Man* 76–77; P-in-c Farnworth All SS 77–78; TV E Farnworth and Kearsley 78–82; V Belfield 82–93; V Leesfield 93–04; V Northallerton w Kirby Sigston *York* 04–13; rtd 13; PtO *York* from 13; *Carl* from 18. *3 Kent Park Avenue, Kendal LA9 5JT* E: howardgsmith@tiscali.co.uk

SMITH, Howard Vincent. b 48. Trin Coll Bris 09. **d** 11 **p** 12. OLM Winterbourne *Bris* 11–16; OLM Coalpit Heath 12–13; OLM Frampton Cotterell and Iron Acton 12–16; OLM Frenchay and Winterbourne Down 12–16; OLM Fromeside from 16. *15 Winchcombe Road, Frampton Cotterell, Bristol BS36 2AG* T: (01454) 773817 M: 07504-435443 E: revd.hvs@gmail.com

SMITH, Ian. b 62. Qu Coll Birm. **d** 14 **p** 15. C Edgbaston St Germain *Birm* 14–18; V Blendon *Roch* from 18. *The Vicarage, 37 Bladindon Drive, Bexley DA5 3BS* T: (020) 8301 5387 M: 07841-615945 E: revd.iansmith@gmail.com

SMITH, Canon Ian. b 62. Hull Univ BA 83 Man Univ MA 09. Oak Hill Th Coll BA 88. **d** 88 **p** 89. C W Hampstead St Luke *Lon* 88–90; C Woking St Pet *Guildf* 90–95; V Leyland St Jo *Blackb* 95–02; C Goole *Sheff* 02–03; P-in-c Sheff St Paul 03–12; R Warmsworth from 12; AD W Doncaster from 15;

Hon Can Sheff Cathl from 12. *Warmsworth Rectory, 187 Warmsworth Road, Doncaster DN4 0TW* T: (01302) 853324 E: ian.smith@sheffield.anglican.org

SMITH, Ian Martin. b 60. ERMC 14. **d** 17 **p** 18. NSM Silsoe, Pulloxhill and Flitton *St Alb* from 17. *67 Manor Road, Toddington, Dunstable LU5 6AJ*

SMITH, Canon Ian Walker. b 29. Leeds Univ BA 52. Coll of Resurr Mirfield 52. **d** 54 **p** 55. C Moulsecoomb *Chich* 54–61; Chapl K Sch Cant 61–62; C Crawley *Chich* 62–79; TV 79–81; R Clenchwarton *Ely* 81–94; RD Lynn Marshland 84–94; Hon Can Ely Cathl 88–94; PtO *Nor* 88–94; rtd 94; PtO *Ely* 94–09. *27 Jubilee Drive, Dersingham, King's Lynn PE31 6YA* T: (01485) 540203 E: iwsadasfra@gmail.com

SMITH, Irene Lillian. b 47. **d** 99 **p** 00. OLM Moston St Chad *Man* 99–16; OLM Moston St Jo 11–14; OLM Newton Heath 11–14; rtd 16; PtO *Man* from 16. *1 Walmersley Road, Manchester M40 3RS* T: 0161-682 5927 M: 07732-301172 E: irenel.smith@ntlworld.com

SMITH, Mrs Irene Mary. b 43. Shenstone Coll of Educn CertEd 64 Lon Univ BD 77. OLM course 96. **d** 99 **p** 00. OLM Uttoxeter Area *Lich* 99–18; PtO from 18. *16 Teanhurst Close, Tean, Stoke-on-Trent ST10 4NN* T: (01538) 722975 E: irene.smith0@btinternet.com

SMITH, Irene Victoria. *See* WATKINS, Irene Victoria

SMITH, Janet. *See* SMITH, Patricia Janet

SMITH, Mrs Janette Elizabeth. b 61. Sarum Coll 13. **d** 16 **p** 17. C Hartley Wintney, Elvetham, Winchfield etc *Win* 16–19; V Crookhorn *Portsm* from 19; C Purbrook from 19; C Portsdown from 19. *87 Perseus Place, Waterlooville PO7 8AW* M: 07928-535696 E: revjanettesmith@gmail.com

SMITH, Janice Lilian. b 51. Open Univ BSc 98. NOC 98. **d** 01 **p** 02. NSM Yeadon St Jo *Bradf* 01–06; P-in-c Bramhope *Ripon* 06–14; *Leeds* 14–18; P-in-c Ireland Wood *Ripon* 09–12; rtd 18. *17 Silverdale Close, Guiseley, Leeds LS20 8BQ* E: revjanice.smith@gmail.com

SMITH, Canon Jeffry Bradford. b 56. Pitzer Coll BA 82. Ripon Coll Cuddesdon 83 Ch Div Sch of the Pacific (USA) MDiv 85. **d** 86 **p** 87. C Visalia USA 86–87; C Frimley *Guildf* 87–91; R E and W Clandon 91–03; Chapl HM Pris Send 94–96; Chapl HM Pris Channings Wood 03–04; Can Res Bermuda 04–07; TV Glendale Gp *Newc* 09–14; rtd 14; PtO *Newc* from 14; R Coldstream *Edin* from 15. *20 Tenter Hill, Wooler NE71 6DG* E: revcanonjsmith@gmail.com

SMITH, Mrs Jennifer Pamela. b 63. Girton Coll Cam BA 85 MA 88. Oak Hill Th Coll BA 91. **d** 91 **p** 94. C Rawdon *Bradf* 91–93; Chapl Bradf Cathl 93–96; P-in-c Kelbrook 96–00; Asst Chapl Airedale NHS Trust 01–07; Chapl Airedale NHS Foundn Trust from 07. *24 Greenacres, Skipton BD23 1BX* T: (01756) 790852 *or* (01535) 294088 E: jenny.smith@leeds.anglican.org

SMITH, Jeremy John Hawthorn. b 52. Birm Univ BSc 73 Lanc Univ MA 97. CBDTI 94. **d** 97 **p** 98. NSM Long Marton w Dufton and w Milburn *Carl* 97–00; NSM Hesket-in-the-Forest and Armathwaite 00–04; NSM Skelton and Hutton-in-the-Forest w Ivegill 00–04; NSM Ainstable 00–04; NSM Inglewood Gp 04–12; PtO 13–19. *Tanglewood, Cumwhinton, Carlisle CA4 8DL* T: (01228) 560310 E: revdesmith@hotmail.com

SMITH, Jesse Lee. b 70. Man Univ BA 93 Nottm Univ MA 96. Linc Th Coll 94 Westcott Ho Cam 95. **d** 96 **p** 97. C Gomersal *Wakef* 96–00; C Penarth All SS *Llan* 00–02; TV Cen Cardiff 02–03; V Hartlepool H Trin *Dur* 03–08; V Caerau w Ely *Llan* from 08. *The Vicarage, Cowbridge Road West, Cardiff CF5 5BQ* T: (029) 2056 32564 E: jesselsmith1970@gmail.com

SMITH, Jessica Clare. b 73. Ex Coll Ox BA 95 Ox Univ PGCE 96. Ridley Hall Cam 16. **d** 18. C Strood St Fran *Roch* from 18. *81 Laburnum Road, Rochester ME2 2LB* M: 07508-958802 E: curate.stfrancisstrood@gmail.com

SMITH, Joanne Sarah. b 79. Salford Univ BSc 01. St Jo Coll Nottm 14. **d** 16 **p** 17. C Horwich and Rivington *Man* from 16. *St Elizabeth's Vicarage, Cedar Avenue, Horwich, Bolton BL6 6HT* T: (01204) 240508 M: 07026-279494 E: revdjosmith@hotmail.com

SMITH, John. *See* SMITH, Stephen John

SMITH, John Alec. b 37. Lon Coll of Div ALCD 62 BD 63. **d** 63 **p** 64. C Cromer *Nor* 63–66; C Barking St Marg *Chelmsf* 66–69; V Attercliffe *Sheff* 69–75; P-in-c Sheff St Barn and St Mary 76–78; V 78–89; Ind Chapl 78–89; RD Ecclesall 80–85; TR Chippenham St Paul w Hardenhuish etc *Bris* 89–00; V Kington St Michael 89–00; rtd 00. *The Willows, Salford Priors, Evesham WR11 8UU* T: (01789) 772072

SMITH, John Bartlett. b 50. St Chad's Coll Dur BA 73 ACIPD. Cuddesdon Coll 73. **d** 76 **p** 77. C Heref St Martin 76–86; NSM Isleworth St Mary *Lon* 86–89; NSM Millom *Carl* 89–92; NSM Balham St Mary and St Jo *S'wark* 92–04; PtO *Ox*

10–14. *91 Willowbourne, Fleet GU51 5BP* M: 07769-990391 E: j29bs@yahoo.com

SMITH, John Denmead. b 44. Keble Coll Ox BA 65 MA 69 St Jo Coll Ox DPhil 71. Coll of Resurr Mirfield 72. **d** 75 **p** 76. NSM Win St Lawr and St Maurice w St Swithun 75–80; Chapl Win Coll 75–04; Sen Chapl 04–06; rtd 06; Lect Uganda Chr Univ Mukono from 06. *56D North Bar Without, Beverley HU17 7AB* T: (01482) 865513 E: jds1000@gmail.com

SMITH, John Ernest. b 52. St Andr Univ MTheol 77. Wycliffe Hall Ox 78. **d** 79 **p** 80. C Bermondsey St Mary w St Olave, St Jo etc *S'wark* 79–87; P-in-c Whyteleafe 87–97; RD Caterham 96–98; P-in-c Merstham and Gatton 98–10; TR Merstham, S Merstham and Gatton 10–12; P-in-c Hoo St Werburgh *Roch* 12–19; rtd 19. *21 Bayfield, Painters Forstal, Faversham ME13 0EF* E: revjohn.e.smith@btinternet.com

SMITH, John Graham. b 32. **d** 78 **p** 79. NSM Hordle *Win* 78–00; rtd 00; PtO *Win* from 00. *3 Marryat Road, New Milton BH25 5LW* T: (01425) 615701 E: rev.smith@ukgateway.net

SMITH, John Lawrence. b 43. Birm Univ BSc 65. Linc Th Coll 67. **d** 70 **p** 71. C Frodingham *Linc* 70–75; TV Gt Grimsby St Mary and St Jas 75–83; V Wolverhampton St Andr *Lich* 83–12; rtd 12; PtO *Ox* from 14. *75 Courtington Lane, Bloxham, Banbury OX15 4HS* T: (01295) 721709

SMITH, Canon John Leslie. b 44. Trin Coll Cam BA 65 MA 71. Ripon Coll Cuddesdon 79. **d** 81 **p** 82. C Ollerton *S'well* 81–84; P-in-c Farndon and Thorpe 84–88; P-in-c Winthorpe and Langford w Holme 88–95; Dioc Chief Insp of Schs 88–95; Dir of Educn *Pet* 95–99; P-in-c Cottingham w E Carlton 97–99; P-in-c Gretton w Rockingham and Cottingham w E Carlton 99; Dir of Educn *Roch* 99–10; Hon Can Roch Cathl 04–10; P-in-c Bredgar w Bicknor and Frinsted w Wormshill etc *Cant* 05–10; rtd 10; PtO *S'well* from 10; *Eur* from 19. *Whiteways, Low Road, Besthorpe, Newark NG23 7HJ* T: (01636) 894277 E: revcanjohn.smith@googlemail.com *or* revcanjohn.smith@me.com

SMITH, John Malcolm. b 36. ACIB 60. NOC 81. **d** 84 **p** 85. NSM Bury St Pet *Man* 84–06; PtO from 06. *46 Ajax Drive, Bury BL9 8EF* T: 0161-766 8378 E: jmalcolmsmith@btinternet.com

SMITH, John Rollin. b 43. **d** 11 **p** 17. OLM Penn and Tylers Green *Ox* 11–12; NSM Gt Marlow w Marlow Bottom, Lt Marlow and Bisham from 16. *The Knoll, Paul's Hill, Penn, High Wycombe HP10 8NZ* T: (01494) 815718 E: jsmithmpg@aol.com

SMITH, John Simon. b 46. Middx Hosp MB, BS 70 FRCGP 91. Ripon Coll Cuddesdon 05. **d** 06 **p** 07. NSM Kettering SS Pet and Paul 06–16; rtd 16; PtO *Pet* from 16. *34 Poplars Farm Road, Barton Seagrave, Kettering NN15 5AG* T: (01536) 513786 E: john@poplarsfarm.org

SMITH, John Sydney. b 36. Lanc Univ MA 97 ALA 59 FLA 68 FISM 82. CBDTI 94. **d** 97 **p** 98. NSM Arthuret, Nicholforest and Kirkandrews on Esk *Carl* 97–02; rtd 02; PtO *Carl* from 01. *The Jays, 3 White House, Walton, Brampton CA8 2DJ* T: (016977) 41114 E: johnandjill.thejays@btinternet.com

SMITH, John Thompson. b 30. Wycliffe Hall Ox 64. **d** 66 **p** 67. C Walsall *Lich* 66–69; V Stoke Prior *Worc* 69–75; Asst Gen Sec Red Triangle Club 75–85; R Tendring and Lt Bentley w Beaumont cum Moze *Chelmsf* 85–89; R Fairstead w Terling and White Notley etc 89–92; Chapl Heath Hosp Tendring 85–92; rtd 92; PtO *B & W* 92–12. *1 Harvey Close, Weston-super-Mare BS22 7DW* T: (01934) 514256

SMITH, John Trevor. b 47. GGSM. Coll of Resurr Mirfield 74. **d** 77 **p** 78. C Loughton St Jo *Chelmsf* 77–80; C Ruislip St Martin *Lon* 80–84; P-in-c Southall Ch Redeemer 84–91; V Kingsbury St Andr 91–13; rtd 13; PtO *Nor* from 13. *1 All Saints Street, King's Lynn PE30 5AD* T: (01553) 775250 E: johntsmith23@btinternet.com

SMITH, John William. b 51. EAMTC 00. **d** 03 **p** 04. NSM Erpingham w Calthorpe, Ingworth, Aldborough etc *Nor* 03–06; P-in-c Roughton and Felbrigg, Metton, Sustead etc 06–15; rtd 15; PtO *Nor* from 15. *18 Pound Lane, Aylsham, Norwich NR11 6DR* T: (01263) 734761 E: ajksmith@btinternet.com

SMITH, Jonathan Paul. b 60. Univ of Wales (Lamp) BA 81. Wycliffe Hall Ox 82. **d** 84 **p** 85. C Baglan *Llan* 84–88; C Gabalfa 88–90; R Llangammarch w Llanganten and Llanlleonfel etc *S & B* 90–01; Dioc Missr 95–01; R Denbigh *St As* 01–15; AD 09–14; TV Wrexham from 15. *Llwyn, 3 Craigmillar Road, Wrexham LL12 7AR* T: (01978) 350797 E: jonathan@plwyfwrecsam.org.uk

SMITH, The Ven Jonathan Peter. b 55. K Coll Lon BD 77 AKC 77 Cam Univ PGCE 78. Westcott Ho Cam 79. **d** 80 **p** 81. C Gosforth All SS *Newc* 80–82; C Waltham Abbey *Chelmsf* 82–85; Chapl City Univ *Lon* 85–88; R Harrold and Carlton w Chellington *St Alb* 88–97; Chapl Beds Police 90–97; V Harpenden St Jo *St Alb* 97–08; RD Wheathampstead

99–04; Adn St Alb from 08. *6 Sopwell Lane, St Albans AL1 1RR* T: (01727) 818121

SMITH, Joseph Paul. b 87. Northn Univ BA 09. Trin Coll Bris 15. d 18 p 19. C Over St Chad *Ches* from 18. *15 Windsor Drive, Winsford CW7 1PJ* M: 07702-425344 E: joe.paul.smith@googlemail.com *or* revjoesmith87@gmail.com

SMITH, Joseph Paul Tobias George. b 73. Ox Univ BTh 95 Ex Univ MA 97. d 08 p 09. OLM Talbot Village *Sarum* 08–11; NSM Branksome St Aldhelm 11–16; PtO from 16; *Win* from 16. *16 Southlea Avenue, Bournemouth BH6 3AB* T: (01202) 424148 M: 07949-794164 E: smithjoe91264316@aol.com

SMITH, Canon Joyce Mary. b 52. Lon Hosp BDS 74 Nottm Univ MMedSc 77 Lon Univ PhD 84 MCCDRCS 89. EAMTC. d 00 p 01. C Harlow St Mary and St Hugh w St Jo the Bapt *Chelmsf* 00–02; C Waltham H Cross 02–03; TV 03–10; NSM from 10; RD Epping Forest 10–13; RD Epping Forest and Ongar 13–18; Chapl St Clare Hospice 10–14; Hon Can Chelmsf Cathl from 15. *2 Takeley Close, Waltham Abbey EN9 1QH* T: (01992) 733655 E: revdjoyces@sky.com

SMITH, Miss Judith. b 74. SS Coll Cam BA 95 MA 98 PGCE 97. Trin Coll Bris BA 09. d 09 p 10. C Beeston *Ripon* 09–13; TV Abbeylands 13–14; *Leeds* 14–17; TR Moor Allerton and Shadwell from 17. *St Stephen's House, Tynwald Drive, Leeds LS17 5DR* E: revjudesmith@gmail.com

SMITH, Sister Judith Lillian. b 56. Cumbria Univ BA 13. All SS Cen for Miss & Min 15. d 17 p 18. NSM Hornby w Claughton and Whittington etc *Blackb* from 17. *St Joseph's House of Prayer, New Vicarage, Church Lane, Tunstall, Carnforth LA6 2RQ.* T: (03330) 119563 E: sisterjudithocmm@gmail.com

SMITH, Julian William. b 64. Liv Univ BSc 85. Trin Coll Bris BA 93. d 93 p 94. C Henfynyw w Aberaeron and Llanddewi Aberarth *St D* 93–97; V Llansantffraed and Llanbadarn Trefeglwys etc 97–05; V Llansantffraed w Llanrhystud and Llanddeiniol from 05. *The Vicarage, 11 Maes Wyre, Llanrhystud SY23 5AH* T: (01974) 202336 E: julian.debs@tiscali.co.uk

SMITH, Julie Lesley. b 64. d 14 p 15. C Saltburn-by-the-Sea *York* 14–17; V Barrowford and Newchurch-in-Pendle *Blackb* from 17. *The Vicarage, Wheatley Lane Road, Barrowford, Nelson BB9 6QS* E: jls446439@gmail.com

SMITH, Mrs Justine Lydia. b 69. d 12 p 13. C Elloughton and Brough w Brantingham *York* 12–16; P-in-c The Marshland *Sheff* from 16. *25 Prospect Close, Swinefleet, Goole DN14 8FB*

SMITH, Mrs Katharine Emma. b 85. Pemb Coll Cam MEng 08. Ridley Hall Cam 11. d 14 p 16. C Battersea St Pet and St Paul *S'wark* 14–19; C Swindon St Aug *Bris* from 19. *8 Figsbury Close, Swindon SN25 1UA* M: 07814-601366 E: kaf@patternchurch.org

SMITH, Mrs Katherine Jane. b 42. Sussex Univ BA 65. d 07 p 08. NSM Battersea St Luke *S'wark* 07; rtd 12; PtO *S'wark* from 12; *Chich* from 19. *74 Alfriston Road, London SW11 6NW* T: (020) 7228 3079 M: 07747-874970 E: katherine.smith42@btopenworld.com

SMITH, Keith. b 46. ACIB. S Dios Minl Tr Scheme 85. d 87 p 88. NSM W Worthing St Jo *Chich* 87–94; NSM Maybridge 94–96; C Durrington 96–01; V Pagham 01–11; rtd 11; PtO *Chich* from 11. *20 Trent Road, Worthing BN12 4EL* T: (01903) 534498 E: keith_smith_99@yahoo.com

SMITH, Kenneth Robert. b 48. K Coll Lon BD 75 AKC 75. St Aug Coll Cant 75. d 76 p 77. C Birtley *Dur* 76–80; V Lamesley 80–90; R Whitburn 90–13; rtd 13. *105 Sidecliffe Road, Sunderland SR6 9JR* T: 0191-549 7704

SMITH, Kevin. b 66. Westmr Coll Ox BA 89. Chich Th Coll 90. d 92 p 93. C Worksop Priory *S'well* 92–96; V New Cantley *Sheff* 96–03; P-in-c Horden *Dur* 03–06; V 06–16; P Admin Shrine of Our Lady of Walsingham from 16. *The Shrine of Our Lady of Walsingham, The College, Knight Street, Walsingham NR22 6EF* T: (01328) 824247 E: ks.horden@btinternet.com *or* pr.adm@olw-shrine.org.uk

SMITH, Laurence Robert. b 91. UEA BA 12. Ridley Hall Cam 12. d 15 p 16. C Bury St Edmunds St Mary *St E* 15–18; V Woodley *Ox* from 18; V Southlake from 18. *St James's Vicarage, 97 Reading Road, Woodley, Reading RG5 3AE* T: 0118-969 3445 M: 07909-331350 E: revlaurencesmith@gmail.com

SMITH, Laurence Sidney. b 37. Sarum & Wells Th Coll 70. d 73 p 74. C Surbiton St Matt *S'wark* 73–76; C Horley 76–81; V W Ewell *Guildf* 81–90; V W Byfleet 90–02; rtd 02; PtO *Glouc* from 03. *Candlemill Cottage, Millbank, George Street, Nailsworth, Stroud GL6 0AG* T: (01453) 836432

SMITH, Lawrence Paul. b 51. Southn Univ BTh 81 Ch Ch Coll Cant CertEd 72. Chich Th Coll 76. d 79 p 80. C Margate St Jo *Cant* 79–84; R Eythorne and Elvington w Waldershare etc 84–97; Par Min Development Adv Kensington Area *Lon* 97–09; NSM Isleworth St Fran 00–09; P-in-c 05–09; TR Northfleet and Rosherville *Roch* 09–18; P-in-c Perry Street 14–18; rtd 18. *36 Thomas Drive, Gravesend DA12 5PZ*

SMITH, Lewis Shand. b 52. Aber Univ MA 74 Edin Univ BD 78 FRSA 00. Edin Th Coll 74. d 77 p 78. C Wishaw *Glas* 77–79; P-in-c 79–80; C Motherwell 77–79; P-in-c 79–80; R Lerwick and Burravoe *Ab* 80–00; Can St Andr Cathl 93–00; R Dumfries *Glas* 00–05; Miss to Seamen 80–00; LtO *Edin* from 08. *Sandview, Bigton, Shetland ZE2 9JA* M: 07785-744610 E: shand.smith@talk21.com

SMITH, Mrs Linda Jean. b 61. Ripon Coll Cuddesdon 97. d 99 p 00. C St Martin w Looe *Truro* 99–03; P-in-c Talland 03–09; C Lanreath, Pelynt and Bradoc 03–09; TV Langtree *Ox* from 09; AD Henley from 16. *The Vicarage, Reading Road, Woodcote, Reading RG8 0QX* T: (01491) 680979 E: woodcotevicarage@btinternet.com

SMITH, Miss Lorna Cassandra. b 43. Open Univ BA 76. Cant Sch of Min 82. dss 86 d 87 p 94. Birchington w Acol and Minnis Bay *Cant* 86–92; Par Dn 87–92; C Addlestone *Guildf* 92–97; V Englefield Green 97–05; rtd 05; PtO *Guildf* 05–18; *Lon* 08–13. *St Mary's Convent and Nursing Home, Burlington Lane, London W4 2QE* T: (020) 8994 4641 E: revlcs@aol.com

SMITH, Lorna Mary. *See* LAVARELLO-SMITH, Lorna Mary

SMITH, Mrs Lorna Rosalind. b 53. Oak Hill NSM Course 89. d 92 p 94. NSM Squirrels Heath *Chelmsf* 92–94; NSM Stanford-le-Hope w Mucking 94–97; P-in-c Fobbing 97–04; P-in-c Tillingham 04–15; rtd 15; PtO *Chelmsf* from 15. *33 Latchingdon Road, Cold Norton CM3 6JG* T: (01621) 828755 E: adrianlorna33@btinternet.com

SMITH, Lydia Jane. b 63. St Mellitus Coll BA 13. d 13 p 14. C Saffron Walden and Villages *Chelmsf* 13–16; TV Thurstable and Winstree from 16. *The Vicarage, 45 Malting Green Road, Layer-de-la-Haye, Colchester CO2 0JJ* E: lydiasmith73@gmail.com

SMITH (née THORNTON), Magdalen Mary. b 69. Warwick Univ BA 90. Qu Coll Birm BD 95. d 96 p 97. C Kirkby *Liv* 96–98; C Birm St Martin w Bordesley St Andr 00–03; NSM Tilston and Shocklach *Ches* 03–08; C Wilmslow 08–17; Asst Dir of Ords 12–14; Dioc Dir of Ords 14–19; Nat Adv for Selection Abps' Coun from 19. *3 Cathedral Close, Guildford GU2 7TL* T: (020) 7898 1593 E: revmagssmith@btinternet.com *or* magdalen.smith@churchofengland.org

SMITH, Margaret Elizabeth. b 46. Bretton Hall Coll CertEd 67. NOC 85. d 88 p 94. Hon Par Dn Battyeford *Wakef* 88–89; Hon C Mirfield 89–91; Chapl HM Pris and YOI New Hall 90–95; Dn-in-c Flockton cum Denby Grange *Wakef* 91–94; P-in-c 94–96; V Scholes 96–01; P-in-c Buckden *Ely* 01–05; P-in-c Offord D'Arcy w Offord Cluny 01–05; R Buckden w the Offords 05–06; rtd 06; PtO *Bradf* 06–14; *Leeds* 14–16. *9 Bobbin Mill Court, Steeton, Keighley BD20 6PU* T: (01535) 654721 E: memagsmith@tesco.net

SMITH, Mrs Marion Elizabeth. b 51. Bris Univ CertEd 73 Middx Univ BA 99. NTMTC. d 98 p 99. NSM Cowley *Lon* 98–00; P-in-c Harlington 00–08; R from 08. *The Rectory, St Peter's Way, Hayes UB3 5AB* T: (020) 8759 9569 M: 07803-617509 E: marionsmith1@tiscali.co.uk

SMITH, Mark Alan. b 85. Peterho Cam BA 06 MA 10. Oak Hill Th Coll 14. d 17 p 18. C Frogmore *St Alb* from 17. *13 Sycamore Drive, Park Street, St Albans AL2 2PJ* M: 07828-065837 E: mark.s@hotfrog.com

SMITH, Mark Andrew. b 59. UNISA BA 86. St Paul's Coll Grahamstown. d 85 p 86. P Port Elizabeth St Mary Magd S Africa 88–89; R Cradock St Pet 89–92; R Alexandra Plurality 93; Chapl St Andr Coll Grahamstown 94–01; Chapl Denstone Coll Uttoxeter 02–07; NSM Alton w Bradley-le-Moors and Oakamoor w Cotton *Lich* 06–07; NSM Denstone w Ellastone and Stanton 06–07; NSM Mayfield 06–07; Chapl K Coll Taunton from 07. *King's College, South Road, Taunton TA1 3LA* T: (01823) 328211 *or* 328137 M: 07969-141242 E: masmith@kings-taunton.co.uk

SMITH, Mark David. *See* LAYNESMITH, Mark David

SMITH, Mark Gordon Robert Davenport. b 56. St Jo Coll Dur BA 77. Ridley Hall Cam 78. d 80 p 81. C Sheff St Jo 80–83; C Brightside w Wincobank 83–86; V Kimberworth Park 86–91; Consultant NE England CPAS 91–98; Nat Co-ord Cert in Evang Studies (CA) 98–04; Chapl for Deaf People *Derby* 04–15; V Rawdon *Leeds* from 15; Min in Deaf Community from 15. *The Vicarage, Layton Avenue, Rawdon, Leeds LS19 6QQ* T: 0113-391 0389 M: 07702-269608 E: mail@revmarksmith.com *or* mark@deafchurch.co.uk

SMITH, Mark Peter. b 61. Reading Univ BA 82 Open Univ BA 93 MA 97 Liv Univ MTh 02 Univ of Wales (Trin St Dav) PhD 12 Keele Univ PGCE 84. NOC 99. d 02 p 03. C Wingerworth *Derby* 02–06; TV Ex St Thos and Em 06–09; P-in-c Kingsteignton and Teigngrace 09–15; V from 15; RD Newton Abbot and Ipplepen 12–16. *The Vicarage, Daws Meadow, Kingsteignton, Newton Abbot TQ12 3UA* T: (01626) 355127 E: marksmith487@btinternet.com

SMITH, Mark Stephen. b 84. Peterho Cam BA 05 PGCE 06 MA 10 MPhil 12 PhD 16. Ridley Hall Cam 08. **d** 12 **p** 13. C Lt Shelford *Ely* 12–15; Chapl Peterho Cam 12–15; Chapl Ch Coll Cam 15–18; Fell and Dean Clare Coll Cam from 19; LtO *Ely* from 15. *Clare College, Trinity Lane, Cambridge CB2 1TL* T: (01223) 333240 E: mss53@cam.ac.uk

SMITH, Mark Winton. b 60. St Jo Coll Dur BA 81 Barrister-at-Law (Middle Temple) 82. SEITE 01. **d** 04 **p** 05. NSM E Wickham *S'wark* from 04. *16 Watersmeet Way, London SE28 8PU* T/F: (020) 8310 5063 E: revdmarksmith@aol.com

SMITH, Martin Stanley. b 53. Univ of Wales (Abth) BScEcon 75. STETS. **d** 99 **p** 00. NSM Woking Ch Ch *Guildf* from 99. *Brackenlea, 11 Heather Close, Horsell, Woking GU21 4JR* T: (01483) 714307 E: martin.wokingsmiffs@googlemail.com

SMITH, Canon Martin William. b 40. K Coll Lon BD 63 AKC 63. **d** 64 **p** 65. C Ashford St Hilda *CD Lon* 64–67; R Labuan Sabah Malaysia 67–69; R Likas Sabah 69–71; V Lakenham St Mark *Nor* 72–85; V N Walsham w Antingham 85–01; P-in-c Neatishead, Barton Turf and Irstead 94–95; RD Tunstead 91–96; RD St Benet 96–99; Hon Can Nor Cathl 93–05; V Wymondham 01–05; rtd 06; PtO *Nor* from 06. *Dragon House, 72 Besthorpe Road, Attleborough NR17 2NQ* T: (01953) 456003 E: smithdragonhouse@btinternet.com

SMITH, Martyn. b 52. CertEd 73. Oak Hill Th Coll BA 81. **d** 81 **p** 82. C Halliwell St Pet *Man* 81–86; V Cambridge St Martin *Ely* 86–89; Vineyard Chr Fellowship 89–15. *6 Rowan Court, Bolton BL1 7SL*

SMITH, Matthew. b 94. Trin Coll Bris 16. **d** 19. C Weston Favell *Pet* from 19. *5 Kestrel Close, Northampton NN3 3JG* E: revdmatthewsmith@gmail.com

SMITH, Melvyn. *See* SMITH, William Melvyn

SMITH, Canon Michael David. b 57. St Steph Ho Ox 81. **d** 83 **p** 84. C Beaconsfield *Ox* 83–87; V Wing w Grove 87–92; R Farnham Royal w Hedgerley 92–01; P-in-c Cookham 01–03; V The Cookhams 03–13; AD Maidenhead and Windsor 11–13; Can Res York Minster from 13. *4 Minster Yard, York YO1 7JD* T: (01904) 557211

SMITH, Michael Ian Antony. b 69. Warwick Univ BSc 91. Oak Hill Th Coll BA 95. **d** 95 **p** 96. C Cheadle *Ches* 95–98; C Hollington St Leon *Chich* 98–01; C Hartford *Ches* 01–04; V from 04. *The Vicarage, 7 The Green, Hartford, Northwich CW8 1QA* T: (01606) 77557 *or* 872255 E: mike@stjohnshartford.org

SMITH, Michael John. b 47. Kelham Th Coll 65. **d** 71 **p** 72. C Cov St Mary 71–75; Chapl RN 75–90; CF 90–95; R Lynch w Iping Marsh and Milland *Chich* 95–03; RD Midhurst 98–03; Community Chapl Bielefeld Station Germany 03–12; rtd 13; PtO *S'well* from 14. *36 Sherwin Road, Stapleford, Nottingham NG9 8PQ* E: revmjsmith@hotmail.com

SMITH, Michael Keith John. b 66. Thames Poly BSc 88. Linc Th Coll BTh 95. **d** 95 **p** 96. C Birch St Agnes w Longsight St Jo w St Cypr *Man* 95–99; TV Pendleton 99–06; P-in-c Lower Kersal 03–06; Bp's Chapl and Policy Adv *Leic* 06–14; R Caversham Thameside and Mapledurham *Ox* from 14. *The Rectory, 20 Church Road, Caversham, Reading RG4 7AD* T: 0118-947 9505 E: mkjsmith@btinternet.com

SMITH, Michael Raymond. b 36. Qu Coll Cam BA 59 MA 63 ARCM 56 ARCO 56. Cuddesdon Coll 64. **d** 65 **p** 66. C Redcar *York* 65–70; V Dormanstown 70–73; Prec Worc Cathl 73–77; TR Worc St Barn w Ch Ch 77–83; RD Worc E 79–83; V Eskdale, Irton, Muncaster and Waberthwaite *Carl* 83–87; Chapl Uppingham Sch 87–93; P-in-c Stoke Lacy, Moreton Jeffries w Much Cowarne etc *Heref* 93–01; Dioc Schs Officer 93–03; rtd 01; PtO *Heref* 04–12; *Mon* from 10. *Upper House, Grosmont, Abergavenny NP7 8EP* T: (01981) 240790 E: michael.smith365@btinternet.com

SMITH, Michael Richard Guy. b 55. Man Univ BA 77. Ripon Coll Cuddesdon 88. **d** 90 **p** 91. C Wallasey St Hilary *Ches* 90–93; C Howden *York* 93–94; TV 94–97; V Gt and Lt Driffield 04–10; RD Harthill 08–10; Chapl Puerto de la Cruz Tenerife *Eur* 10–14; P-in-c Nailsworth w Shortwood, Horsley etc *Glouc* 14–15; V 15–18; AD Stroud 17–18; rtd 18; PtO *Glouc* from 19. *64 Foxwhelp Way, Quedgeley, Gloucester GL2 4BY* M: 07840-260182 E: mike.davica@sky.com

SMITH, Neville. *See* SMITH, Charles Henry Neville

SMITH, Nicholas William. b 87. York Univ BA 10 Peterho Cam BA 16. Ridley Hall Cam 14. **d** 17 **p** 18. C Tulse Hill H Trin and St Matthias *S'wark* from 17. *132 Trinity Rise, London SW2 2QT* M: 07964-560195 E: nickwsmith@hotmail.co.uk

SMITH, Nicola Jane. b 85. Ox Brookes Univ BSc 08. St Mellitus Coll BA 17. **d** 17 **p** 18. C Sholing *Win* from 17; C Bitterne Park from 17. *7 Thorold Road, Southampton SO18 1HZ* T: (023) 8067 9911 E: nicky@ascensionsouthampton.co.uk *or* revnickysmith@gmail.com

SMITH, Preb Olwen. b 44. Birm Univ BA 66. Selly Oak Coll 67. **d** 87 **p** 94. Ind Chapl Black Country Urban Ind Miss *Lich* 84–98; TV Cen Wolverhampton 94–10; Preb Lich Cathl 99–10; rtd 10; PtO *Lich* 10–13; *Ox* from 14. *75 Courtington Lane, Bloxham, Banbury OX15 4HS* T: (01295) 721709 E: smitholwen@btinternet.com

SMITH, Ms Pamela Jane Holden. b 56. Warwick Univ BA 78 Lon Inst of Educn PGCE 82. Qu Coll Birm BA 04. **d** 04 **p** 05. C Coventry Caludon *Cov* 04–08; NSM 04–06; PtO from 08; Web Pastor i-church *Ox* from 08. *34 Styvechale Avenue, Coventry CV5 6DX* T: (024) 7667 2893 E: rev.pam.smith@gmail.com *or* webpastor@i-church.org

SMITH, Canon Patricia Janet. b 45. Oak Hill Th Coll 87. **d** 89 **p** 90. Canada 89–02; V Charminster and Stinsford *Sarum* 02–16; P-in-c Bradford Peverell, Stratton, Frampton etc 09–16; RD Dorchester 09–16; Can and Preb Sarum Cathl 10–16; rtd 16. *Sparrows, New Buildings, Charminster, Dorchester DT2 7SG* M: 07468-580196 E: plumsmith18@gmail.com

SMITH, Patricia Joanna. **d** 12 **p** 13. C Dumbarton *Glas* 12–14; C Johnstone from 14; C Renfrew from 14. *21 Macleod Drive, Helensburgh G84 9QS* T: (01436) 671091 E: patsmithcurate@gmail.com

SMITH, Paul. b 48. STETS 99. **d** 02 **p** 03. NSM Copthorne *Chich* 02–12; rtd 12; PtO *Chich* 12–17. *7 Heather Close, Copthorne, Crawley RH10 3PZ* T: (01342) 714308 E: heatherclose@freenet.co.uk

SMITH, Paul. b 52. **d** 98 **p** 99. OLM Leominster *Heref* from 98. *32 The Meadows, Leominster HR6 8RF* T: (01568) 615862 *or* 612124

SMITH, Paul Aidan. b 59. Birm Univ BA 82. Wycliffe Hall Ox 82. **d** 85 **p** 86. C Selly Park St Steph and St Wulstan *Birm* 85–88; C Kensal Rise St Mark and St Martin *Lon* 88–91; V Water Eaton *Ox* 91–00; TR Hale w Badshot Lea *Guildf* 00–02; TV Stantonbury and Willen *Ox* 02–09; TR from 09. *2 Hooper Gate, Willen, Milton Keynes MK15 9JR* T: (01908) 606689 M: 07930-308644 E: paul_a_smith@bigfoot.com *or* paul.a.smith.mk@btinternet.com

SMITH, Canon Paul Allan. b 66. Ch Coll Cam BA 88 MA 00 PhD 94. WMMTC 98 Ripon Coll Cuddesdon 99. **d** 00 **p** 01. C Moseley St Mary *Birm* 00–03; P-in-c Tilston and Shocklach *Ches* 03–08; Officer for Initial Min Tr 03–08; R Wilmslow 08–17; Can Res Guildf Cathl from 17. *3 Cathedral Close, Guildford GU2 7TL* T: (01483) 547860 E: revpaulsmith@btinternet.com

SMITH, Paul Andrew. b 55. St Chad's Coll Dur BA 76. Chich Th Coll 78. **d** 80 **p** 81. C Habergham Eaves St Matt *Blackb* 80–83; C Ribbleton 83–86; V Rishton 86–05; RD Whalley 95–01; R Cottingham *York* 05–19; AD Cen and N Hull 10–16. *Address temp unknown* E: dreadnoughtfam@aol.com

SMITH, Paul Anthony. b 66. Ripon Coll Cuddesdon. **d** 00 **p** 01. C Prestwood and Gt Hampden *Ox* 00–05; P-in-c W Leigh *Portsm* 05–06; V 06–10; TV Abingdon *Ox* from 10. *St Michael's Vicarage, Faringdon Road, Abingdon OX14 1BG* T: (01235) 534654 E: paul315smith@btinternet.com

SMITH, Preb Paul Gregory. b 39. Ex Univ BA 61. St Steph Ho Ox 61. **d** 63 **p** 64. C Walthamstow St Mich *Chelmsf* 63–66; C Devonport St Mark Ford *Ex* 66–69; C Hemel Hempstead *St Alb* 69–71; TV 71–83; R Bideford *Ex* 83–96; TR Bideford, Northam, Westward Ho!, Appledore etc 96; Chapl Bideford and Torridge Hosps 83–96; P-in-c Ex St Jas 96–98; R 98–03; rtd 03; Preb Ex Cathl from 95. *Valrose, Broad Lane, Appledore, Bideford EX39 1ND* T: (01237) 423513 E: fatherpaulsmith@aol.com *or* pgsmith490@btinternet.com

SMITH, Miss Paula. b 57. Ox Min Course 14. **d** 17 **p** 18. NSM Deddington w Barford, Clifton and Hempton *Ox* from 17. *11 Bishops Close, Barford St Michael, Banbury OX15 0RU* M: 07818-053978 E: paulawoodcote@hotmail.co.uk

SMITH, Mrs Paula Mary. b 57. Sheff Poly BA 79 Qu Coll Birm BA 06. WMMTC 03. **d** 06 **p** 07. C Walsall *Lich* 06–10; P-in-c Donnington Wood from 10; Min Development Adv (Salop) from 10. *St Matthew's Vicarage, St George's Road, Donnington, Telford TF2 7NJ* T: (01952) 604239 E: revdpaula@hotmail.co.uk

SMITH, Mrs Pauline Frances. b 37. Bris Univ BA 58 Lon Univ CertEd 59. Sarum & Wells Th Coll 87. **d** 90 **p** 94. C Cobham *Guildf* 90–96; P-in-c Lower Wylye and Till Valley *Sarum* 96–97; RD Stonehenge 01–03; rtd 03; PtO *Glouc* from 04. *267B London Road, Charlton Kings, Cheltenham GL52 6YG* T: (01242) 222810 E: panda.smith@talktalk.net

SMITH, Peter. b 36. Keele Univ BA 60. Cuddesdon Coll 73. **d** 75 **p** 76. C Shrewsbury St Chad *Lich* 75–80; V Burton St Chad 80–90; P-in-c Berwick w Selmeston and Alciston *Chich* 90–91; R 91–02; rtd 02; PtO *Sarum* from 03. *3 Olivier Place, Hart Close, Wilton, Salisbury SP2 0FW*

SMITH, Peter Alexander. *See* GRAYSMITH, Peter Alexander

SMITH, Peter Denis Frank. b 52. Local Minl Tr Course. **d** 81 **p** 83. OLM Camberwell St Mich w All So w Em S'wark 81–95; OLM Croydon St Jo 95–04; PtO from 10. *57 Alton Road, Croydon CR0 4LZ* T: (020) 8406 3557 E: peter.smith59@live.co.uk

SMITH, Peter Harold. b 53. Cumbria Univ BA 13. LCTP 07. **d** 10 **p** 11. NSM Euxton *Blackb* 10–15; C Chorley St Pet 15–17; V from 17. *St Peter's Vicarage, Harpers Lane, Chorley PR6 0HT* T: (01257) 433308 M: 07412-624931 E: vicarstpeter@gmail.com

SMITH, Peter Henry. b 62. Bris Univ BA 83. SEITE 96. **d** 99 **p** 00. C Romford St Edw *Chelmsf* 99–02; V Aldersbrook 02–10; TR Waltham H Cross from 10. *The Rectory, Highbridge Street, Waltham Abbey EN9 1DG* T: (01992) 701352 E: peterhxsmith@aol.com

SMITH, Peter Howard. b 57. St Jo Coll Dur BSc 78 Selw Coll Cam BA 82 MA 85. Ridley Hall Cam 80. **d** 83 **p** 84. C Welling *Roch* 83–87; C Hubberston w Herbrandston and Hasguard etc *St D* 87–88; C Hubberston 89–91; V Canley *Cov* 91–00; V Burney Lane *Birm* 00–06; P-in-c 06–07; P-in-c Ward End 06–07; P-in-c Bordesley Green 06–07; V Ward End w Bordesley Green 07–17; AD Yardley and Bordesley 05–12; V Penn Fields *Lich* from 17. *St Philip's Vicarage, Church Road, Bradmore, Wolverhampton WV3 7EJ* E: petersmith50@icloud.com

SMITH, Philip David. b 55. Shoreditch Coll Lon BEd 78. Oak Hill Th Coll BA 98. **d** 98 **p** 99. C Cheltenham St Mary, St Matt, St Paul and H Trin *Glouc* 98–03; TV Cheltenham St Mark 03–18; PtO *Ox* from 19. *33 Vicarage Road, Oxford OX1 4RD* E: philipdsmith1304@gmail.com

SMITH, Philip James. b 60. Imp Coll Lon BScEng 82 Fitzw Coll Cam BA 94. Ridley Hall Cam 92. **d** 95 **p** 96. C Aldborough w Boroughbridge and Roecliffe *Ripon* 95–99; V 99–14; *Leeds* 14–15; V E Bedfont *Lon* from 15. *9 Hatton Road, Bedfont, Feltham TW14 9JR* M: 07786-087389 E: revpsmith@gmail.com

SMITH, Philip Lloyd Cyril. b 22. Ch Coll Cam BA 47 MA 49. Wycliffe Hall Ox 47. **d** 49 **p** 50. C St Helens St Helen *Liv* 49–52; V Woking St Jo *Guildf* 52–56; R Burslem St Jo *Lich* 56–83; P-in-c Burslem St Paul 82–83; R Burslem 83–86; rtd 86; PtO *Sheff* 86–01. *Upper Treasurer's House, 42 Bromley College, London Road, Bromley BR1 1PE* T: (020) 8290 1566

SMITH, Philip Raymond. b 56. ERMC 08. **d** 11 **p** 12. NSM Farndon w Thorpe, Hawton and Cotham *S'well* 11–14; NSM E Trent 14–15; NSM Newark w Coddington 15–17; NSM Balderton, Barnby in the Willows and Coddington from 18. *Dart Cottage, 4 Lancaster Road, Coddington, Newark NG24 2TA* T: (01636) 703305 M: 07532-164314 E: dartcottage@btinternet.com

SMITH, Mrs Priscilla Elizabeth. b 48. Open Univ BSc 93 Nottm Univ MA 08. **d** 12 **p** 13. OLM Horncastle Gp *Linc* from 12; OLM Asterby Gp from 12; OLM Hemingby Gp from 12. *Evergreen, Upland Close, Horncastle LN9 5AR* T: (01507) 524611 M: 07798-695950 E: priscilla.smith926@btinternet.com

SMITH, Rachel Ross. *See* ROSS, Rachel Anne

SMITH, Raymond Charles William. b 56. K Coll Lon BD 78 AKC 78. Coll of Resurr Mirfield 79. **d** 80 **p** 81. C Iffley *Ox* 80–83; C Wallingford w Crowmarsh Gifford etc 83–86; V Tilehurst St Mary 86–96; TR Haywards Heath St Wilfrid *Chich* 96–08; V from 08. *The Rectory, St Wilfrid's Way, Haywards Heath RH16 3QH* T: (01444) 413300

SMITH, Raymond George Richard. b 38. Univ of Wales (Ban) BSc 61 MSc 65. WMMTC 91. **d** 94 **p** 95. NSM Edgmond w Kynnersley and Preston Wealdmoors *Lich* 94–97; Chapl Princess R Hosp NHS Trust Telford 95–03; V Llandegfan w Llandysilio *Ban* 03–08; rtd 09; PtO *Ban* 09–14; AD Tindaethwy 11–15; PtO from 15. *41 Cae Mair, Beaumaris LL58 8YN* T: (01248) 810032 E: rayandhazel41@btinternet.com

SMITH, Richard Harwood. b 34. Sarum Th Coll 57. **d** 59 **p** 60. C Kington w Huntington *Heref* 59–62; C Georgetown St Phil Br Guiana 62–64; C Kitty 64–65; V Mackenzie Guyana 65–69; C Broseley w Benthall *Heref* 69–70; Area Sec USPG Heref and Worc 70–76; R Wigmore Abbey *Heref* 76–84; V Eye w Braiseworth and Yaxley *St E* 84–96; P-in-c Bedingfield 84–96; P-in-c Occold 84–96; rtd 96. *30 Townsend Court, Green Lane, Leominster HR6 8TD* T: (01568) 616458

SMITH, Richard Keith. b 44. St Jo Coll Nottm. **d** 84 **p** 85. C Wirksworth w Alderwasley, Carsington etc *Derby* 84–87; R Hulland, Atlow, Bradley and Hognaston 87–96; P-in-c Long Compton, Whichford and Barton-on-the-Heath *Cov* 96–08; P-in-c Wolford w Burmington 97–08; P-in-c Cherington w Stourton 97–08; P-in-c Barcheston 97–08; R S Warks Seven Gp 08–09; RD Shipston 05–09; rtd 09; PtO *Cov* from 09.

12 Moreton Close, Stratford-upon-Avon CV37 7HB T: (01789) 296712 E: rkvjsmith@gmail.com

SMITH, Richard Michael. b 52. Lon Univ BA 74. EAMTC 79. **d** 82 **p** 83. NSM Cambridge Ascension *Ely* 82–84; C Rainham *Roch* 84–88; V Southborough St Thos 88–96; P-in-c Lake *Portsm* 96–99; V 99–06; P-in-c Shanklin St Sav 96–99; V 99–06; V Southsea 06–15; rtd 15; PtO *York* from 16. *159 Prospect Road, Scarborough YO12 7LF*

SMITH, Robert Alfred William. b 53. **d** 08 **p** 09. OLM Withington St Paul *Man* 08–18; rtd 18; PtO *Man* from 18; *Ches* from 15. *4 Brigsteer Walk, Manchester M40 8LW* M: 07896-967043 E: lowchenbob@gmail.com

✠**SMITH, The Rt Revd Robin Jonathan Norman.** b 36. Worc Coll Ox BA 60 MA 64. Ridley Hall Cam 60. **d** 62 **p** 63 **c** 90. C Barking St Marg *Chelmsf* 62–67; Chapl Lee Abbey 67–72; V Chesham St Mary *Ox* 72–80; RD Amersham 79–82; TR Gt Chesham 80–90; Hon Can Ch Ch 88–90; Suff Bp Hertford *St Alb* 90–01; rtd 01; Hon Asst Bp St Alb from 02. *7 Aysgarth Road, Redbourn, St Albans AL3 7PJ* T/F: (01582) 791964 E: bprobin@no7.me.uk

SMITH, Roger. *See* SMITH, Thomas Roger

SMITH, Roger Owen. b 50. Univ of Wales (Abth) BA 72 St Chad's Coll Dur CertEd 73 FRGS. S'wark Ord Course 84. **d** 87 **p** 88. NSM Nunhead St Antony w St Silas S'wark 87–91; NSM Forest Hill St Aug 91–98; NSM Crofton Park St Hilda w St Cypr 91–98; NSM Brockley Hill St Sav 91–98; NSM Camberwell St Giles w St Matt 98–00; PtO *Cant* 01–07; NSM Folkestone Trin from 07. *22 Wear Bay Road, Folkestone CT19 6BN* T: (01303) 259896 E: rohsmith@aol.com

SMITH, Canon Roger Stuart. b 41. Chich Th Coll 65. **d** 66 **p** 67. C Garforth *Ripon* 66–70; C Hilborough Gp Nor 70–73; TV 73–78; V Mendham w Metfield and Withersdale *St E* 78–89; P-in-c Fressingfield w Weybread and Wingfield 86–89; R Fressingfield, Mendham, Metfield, Weybread etc 90–91; RD Hoxne 86–91; R Kelsale-cum-Carlton, Middleton, Theberton etc 91–01; C Yoxmere Conf 01–04; RD Saxmundham *St E* 96–03; Hon Can St E Cathl 97–04; rtd 04; PtO *St E* from 04. *Rookery Nook, Wash Lane, St Margaret South Elmham, Harleston IP20 0PQ* T: (01986) 782465 E: rogerandmolly@mypostoffice.co.uk

SMITH, Roger William. b 48. Imp Coll Lon BSc 70. EAMTC. **d** 00 **p** 01. NSM Rothwell w Orton, Rushton w Glendon and Pipewell *Pet* 00–11; PtO *Eur* from 11. *14 rue du Parc, 34480 Autignac, France* T: (0033) 4 99 57 07 81 E: rogerwilliamsmith@gmail.com

SMITH, Ronald Eric. b 43. EMMTC 93. **d** 93 **p** 94. NSM Wingerworth *Derby* 93–99; NSM Newbold w Dunston 99–01; NSM Loundsley Green 01–05; rtd 05; PtO *Derby* 05–18; *York* from 06. *20 Oak Tree Lane, Haxby, York YO32 2YH* T: (01904) 767691 E: revronsmith@btinternet.com

SMITH, Preb Roy Leonard. b 36. Clifton Th Coll 63. **d** 66 **p** 67. C Clapham St Jas S'wark 66–70; C Kennington St Mark 70–74; C-in-c Southall Em CD *Lon* 74–83; V Stonebridge St Mich 83–06; Preb St Paul's Cathl 96–06; rtd 06; Hon C Kensal Rise St Mark and St Martin *Lon* 06–11; PtO from 11. *4 Biko House, 2 Barry Road, London NW10 8DW* T: (020) 8961 7312 E: prebroy@yahoo.co.uk

SMITH, Ruth. *See* YOUNG, Vivienne Ruth

SMITH, Rycroft. *See* SMITH, Charles Rycroft

SMITH, Mrs Sally Anne. b 63. Ches Univ BA 13 RN 85. St Jo Coll Nottm 07. **d** 09 **p** 10. C Stone St Mich and St Wulfad w Aston St Sav *Lich* 09–12; C Hanley H Ev 12–13; TV from 13; Dioc Officer for Vulnerable Adults from 12. *Hanley Rectory, 35 Harding Road, Stoke-on-Trent ST1 3BQ* T: (01782) 791213 M: 07962-025659 E: revsally6@aol.com

SMITH, Scott Anthony. b 73. K Alfred's Coll Win BA 99. Trin Coll Bris 08. **d** 10 **p** 11. C Clevedon St Andr and Ch Ch *B & W* 10–13; C Beckenham St Jo *Roch* from 13. *30 Ash Road, Croydon CR0 8HU* M: 07810-810313 E: smithscott@hotmail.com

SMITH, Sharon. b 56. Herts Univ BSc 98 PhD 02. ERMC 13. **d** 15 **p** 16. NSM Caddington *St Alb* 15–18; NSM Farley Hill St Jo 15–18; V Orpington Ch Ch *Roch* from 19. *The Vicarage, 165 Charterhouse Road, Orpington BR6 9EP* M: 07821-571283 E: revsharonsmith@outlook.com

SMITH, Mrs Shirley Ann. b 46. Sarum & Wells Th Coll 89. **d** 93 **p** 94. C Totton *Win* 93–96; Chapl Portsm Hosps NHS Trust 96–98; V Lord's Hill *Win* 98–01; TV Beaminster Area *Sarum* 01–05; rtd 05; PtO *Sarum* 05–08; P-in-c Hazelbury Bryan and the Hillside *Sar* 08–11; P-in-c Okeford 08–11; PtO *B & W* 11–12 and 17–19; Chapl Yeovil Distr Hosp NHS Foundn Trust 12–16. *2 Franklyn Place, Kingsbury Episcopi, Martock TA12 6AZ* T: (01935) 508013 E: puddleduckwater@gmail.com

SMITH, Stephen. b 53. CQSW 78. Sarum & Wells Th Coll 87. **d** 89 **p** 90. C Redcar *York* 89–92; C Leeds St Aid *Ripon*

92–96; R Lanteglos by Camelford w Advent *Truro* 96–99; Chapl Hull and E Yorks Hosps NHS Trust 99–01; V Leeds St Marg and All Hallows *Ripon* 08–14; AD Headingley 09–13; P-in-c Mabe *Truro* from 14. *The Vicarage, Church Road, Mabe Burnthouse, Penryn TR10 9HN* T: (01326) 617628 E: revstevesmith53@gmail.com

SMITH, Stephen. b 60. Leeds Univ MA 07. Coll of Resurr Mirfield 02. **d** 04 **p** 05. C Burnley St Cath w St Alb and St Paul *Blackb* 04–07; C St Annes St Anne 07–10; PtO 10–17; V Chadderton St Mark *Man* from 17. *St Mark's Vicarage, Milne Street, Chadderton, Oldham OL9 0HR* M: 07898-301807

SMITH, Stephen John. b 55. Lon Univ BD 80. Trin Coll Bris 77. **d** 81 **p** 82. C Fulham St Matt *Lon* 81–86; C Stoke Gifford *Bris* 86–90; TV 90–01; rtd 01; PtO *Bris* from 01. *47 Saxon Way, Bradley Stoke, Bristol BS32 9AR* T: (01454) 616429 E: stevesmith334@btinternet.com

SMITH, Stephen John. b 46. Kelham Th Coll 65. **d** 69 **p** 70. C Warsop *S'well* 69–73; C Heaton Ch Ch *Man* 73–75; V Bolton St Bede 75–78; R Bilborough w Strelley *S'well* 78–84; R E Leake 84–92; P-in-c Costock 84–92; P-in-c Rempstone 84–92; P-in-c Stanford on Soar 84–92; R E and W Leake, Stanford-on-Soar, Rempstone etc 92–97; RD W Bingham 92–97; V Swaffham *Nor* 97–11; C Gt and Lt Dunham w Gt and Lt Fransham and Sporle 03–11; RD Breckland 02–06; Chapl NW Anglia Healthcare NHS Trust 99–11; rtd 11; PtO *Linc* from 18. *15 Sandpiper Way, King's Lynn PE30 5DN* M: 07837-790712 E: revsjsmith@gmail.com

SMITH, Canon Stephen John Stanyon. b 49. Sussex Univ BA 81 Birm Univ MSocSc 83. Westcott Ho Cam 83. **d** 85 **p** 86. C Four Oaks *Birm* 85–89; Asst P Cheyenne River Reservation USA 89–91; Miss P Rosebud Reservation 91–94; Assoc R Ivoryton and Essex 94–98; Can St Paul's Cathl Buffalo 98–04; Asst P Buffalo St Andr from 04. *3105 Main Street, Buffalo NY 14214, USA* T: (001) (716) 834 9337 F: 836 0558 E: sjsmith6@buffalo.edu

SMITH, Stephen Thomas. b 55. Westcott Ho Cam 95. **d** 97 **p** 98. C Kempston Transfiguration *St Alb* 97–01; C Bromham w Oakley and Stagsden 01–05; TV Elstow from 05. *St Michael's Vicarage, Faldo Road, Bedford MK42 0EH* T: (01234) 266920

SMITH, Stephen Thomas. **d** 16 **p** 17. NSM Goetre w Llanover *Mon* 16–18; NSM Lower Islwyn Min Area from 18. *5 The Rise, Fairview, Blackwood NP12 3PL* T: (01443) 820872 M: 07523-719630 E: stephen.smith11@btinternet.com

SMITH, Steven Barnes. b 60. Cov Poly BA 83 Leeds Univ BA 86 MSc 02 Liv Jo Moores Univ PhD 18. Coll of Resurr Mirfield 84. **d** 87 **p** 88. C Darlington St Mark w St Paul *Dur* 87–89; C Prescot *Liv* 89–91; V Hindley Green 91–96; Asst Chapl Havering Hosps NHS Trust 96–98; Hd Multi-Faith Chapl Chelsea and Westmr Hosp NHS Foundn Trust 98–07; PtO *Lon* 07–13; *Ban* from 12. *Address withheld by request* E: sbsmith01@aol.com

SMITH, Steven Gerald Crosland. b 48. Linc Th Coll 82. **d** 84 **p** 85. Chapl St Jo Sch Tiffield 84–87; C Towcester w Easton Neston *Pet* 84–87; P-in-c Kings Heath 87–89; V 89–93; TV N Creedy *Ex* 93–06; TR 06–13; RD Cadbury 02–13; rtd 13; PtO *Ex* from 13. *5 Melhuish Close, Witheridge, Tiverton EX16 8AZ* E: stevengcsmith@aol.com

SMITH, Susan. b 48. FInstD 87. Ox Min Course 93. **d** 96 **p** 97. C Burnham w Dropmore, Hitcham and Taplow *Ox* 96–00; TV Whitton *Sarum* 00–02; TV W Slough *Ox* 02–08; V Cippenham 08–13; rtd 13; PtO *Ox* from 13; *Portsm* from 16. *Easter Cottage, 36 Britwell Road, Burnham, Slough SL1 8AG* T: (01628) 603046 E: suzone@hotmail.co.uk

SMITH, Miss Susan Ann. b 50. Bris Univ BA 72 St Jo Coll York PGCE 73. Ripon Coll Cuddesdon 97. **d** 99 **p** 00. C Swaffham *Nor* 99–02; R King's Beck 02–12; rtd 12; PtO *Nor* from 13. *9 Eagle Close, Erpingham, Norwich NR11 7AW* T: (01263) 761497

SMITH, Susan Helen. *See* SHEWRING, Susan Helen

SMITH, Susan Jennifer. b 52. MCIPD 90. SAOMC 94. **d** 97 **p** 98. C Ascot Heath *Ox* 97–01; P-in-c Flixton St Mich *Man* 01–10; P-in-c Altcar and Hightown *Liv* 10–14; P-in-c Hightown 14–16; rtd 16; PtO *Liv* from 16. *79 Greenloons Drive, Formby, Liverpool L37 2LX* E: saxoncross@btinternet.com

SMITH, Mrs Susan Penelope Zoë. b 61. Ox Min Course 12. **d** 15 **p** 16. NSM Weston Turville *Ox* 15–17; NSM Broughton from 17; Chapl HM Pris Grendon and HM Pris Spring Hill from 18. *HM Prison Grendon, Grendon Underwood, Aylesbury HP18 0TL* M: 07854-659756 E: suepzsmith@gmail.com

SMITH, Terence. b 38. Brunel Univ BSc 79 Cranfield Inst of Tech MSc 80. Tyndale Hall Bris 67. **d** 69 **p** 70. C Cheylesmore *Cov* 69–71; C Leamington Priors St Paul 71–74; V Halliwell St Paul *Man* 74–75; Lect Uxbridge Coll 80–86; R Medstead w Wield *Win* 86–99; P-in-c Kennington *Ox* 99–03; V 03–08; rtd 08. *15 Grove Road, Seaford BN25 1TP* E: ter.s@btinternet.com

SMITH, Terrence Gordon. b 34. MCSP 58 SRN 60. St Mich Coll Llan 68. **d** 70 **p** 71. C Gelligaer *Llan* 70–73; CF (TA) 72–99; C Aberavon *Llan* 73–75; V Pontlottyn w Fochriw 75–77; V Kenfig Hill 77–84; V Dyffryn 84–99; rtd 99. *1 Gnoll Crescent, Neath SA11 3TF* T: (01639) 633460

SMITH, Thea. *See* SMITH, Dorothea Violet

SMITH, Canon Thomas Roger. b 48. Cant Sch of Min 77. **d** 80 **p** 81. NSM Folkestone St Sav *Cant* 80–82; NSM Lyminge w Paddlesworth, Stanford w Postling etc 82–85; Chapl Cant Sch of Min 82–91; R Biddenden and Smarden *Cant* 86–91; TR Totnes, Bridgetown and Berry Pomeroy etc *Ex* 91–96; P-in-c Haslingden w Grane and Stonefold *Blackb* 96–98; V 98–15; P-in-c Musbury 07–15; AD Accrington 03–13; Hon Can Blackb Cathl 08–15; rtd 15; PtO *Blackb* from 15. *150 Southwood Drive, Accrington BB5 2TU* T: (01254) 237581 E: rsmith9456@aol.com

SMITH, Timothy. b 58. Trin Coll Bris 00. **d** 02 **p** 03. C Warminster Ch Ch *Sarum* 02–06; P-in-c Plymouth St Jude *Ex* from 06. *St Jude's Vicarage, Knighton Road, Plymouth PL4 9BU* T: (01752) 224178 or 263163

SMITH, Timothy Stewart. b 90. Trin Coll Bris 14. **d** 17 **p** 18. C Northampton St Giles *Pet* from 17. *3 The Avalon, 14 The Avenue, Dallington, Northampton NN5 7AN* E: revdtimsmith@gmail.com

SMITH, Toni. *See* SMITH, Antoinette

SMITH (née WOOD), Mrs Valerie Rosemary. b 53. Warwick Univ BA 74. WEMTC 06. **d** 09 **p** 10. NSM Highley w Billingsley, Glazeley etc *Heref* from 09; Par Giving Adv from 17. *20 Yew Tree Grove, Highley, Bridgnorth WV16 6DG* T: (01746) 861966 E: keithandvals@aol.com

SMITH, Mrs Virginia Jane. b 41. Nottm Univ BSc 63. Guildf Dioc Min Course 04. **d** 09 **p** 10. NSM Surrey Weald *Guildf* 09–13; rtd 13; PtO *Guildf* from 13. *Dove Cottage, 14 The Paddock, Westcott, Dorking RH4 3NT* T: (01306) 885349 E: virginia.smith@smartemail.co.uk or rev.virginia.smith@talktalk.net

SMITH, Mrs Wendy Patricia. b 60. **d** 10 **p** 11. OLM Walton and Trimley *St E* 10–13; NSM from 13. *12A Langley Avenue, Felixstowe IP11 2NA* T: (01394) 211755 M: 07708-597808 E: grannysmith57@hotmail.co.uk

SMITH, Canon William Melvyn. b 47. K Coll Lon BD 69 AKC 69 PGCE 70. St Aug Coll Cant 71. **d** 71 **p** 72. C Kingswinford H Trin *Lich* 71–73; Hon C Coseley Ch Ch 73–74; C Wednesbury St Paul Wood Green 75–78; V Coseley St Chad 78–91; TR Wordsley 91–93; RD Himley 83–93; TR Wordsley *Worc* 93–96; RD Himley 93–96; Stewardship and Resources Officer 97–10; Hon Can Worc Cathl 03–10; Asst Chapl Palma de Mallorca *Eur* 10–12; rtd 12; PtO *Worc* from 13; *Lon* 16–18; *Eur* from 17. *14 Beech Tree Close, Kingswinford DY6 7DR* T: (01384) 357062 E: wmelsmith@blueyonder.co.uk

SMITH-CAMERON, Canon Ivor Gill. b 29. Madras Univ BA 50 MA 52. Coll of Resurr Mirfield. **d** 54 **p** 55. C Rumboldswyke *Chich* 54–58; Chapl Imp Coll Lon 58–72; Dioc Missr *S'wark* 72–92; Can Res S'wark Cathl 72–94; C Battersea Park All SS 92–94; Hon C 94–96; Hon C Battersea Fields 96–05; Co-ord All Asian Chr Consultation 92–93; rtd 94; Chapl to The Queen 95–99; PtO *S'wark* from 05. *24 Holmewood Gardens, London SW2 3RS* T: (020) 8678 8977 E: ivorsmithcameron@yahoo.co.uk

SMITHAM, Ann. *See* HOWELLS, Elizabeth Ann

SMITHSON, Philip George Allan. b 55. Bede Coll Dur TCert 76 Open Univ BA 82. **d** 07 **p** 08. OLM Monkwearmouth *Dur* from 07. *2 Sea View Gardens, Sunderland SR6 9PN* E: philipsmithson@talktalk.net

SMITHURST, Jonathan Peter. b 54. FInstLEx 81. EMMTC 91. **d** 94 **p** 95. NSM Bramcote *S'well* 94–03; NSM Attenborough 03–06; AD Beeston 99–06; P-in-c Everton, Mattersey, Clayworth and Gringley 06–11; V 11–14; AD Bassetlaw and Bawtry 09–14; P-in-c Attenborough 14; V from 14; Dioc Assn Officer 14–17. *Vale Cottage, 19 Church Lane, Attenborough, Nottingham NG9 6AS* T: 0115-925 9602 E: office@attenboroughchurch.org.uk

SMYTH, Anthony Irwin. b 40. TCD BA 63 MA 66. Clifton Th Coll 64. **d** 66 **p** 67. C Worthing St Geo *Chich* 66–69; SAMS Chile 70–75; Dir Th Educn Valparaiso 72–75; C Woodley St Jo the Ev *Ox* 75–80; V St Leonards St Ethelburga *Chich* 80–93; R Stopham and Fittleworth 93–05; rtd 05; PtO *Chich* from 05; *Portsm* from 05. *20 Grenehurst Way, Petersfield GU31 4AZ* T: (01730) 260370 E: anthony.smyth@btinternet.com

SMYTH, Elizabeth. *See* LEAVER, Lucinda Elizabeth Jane

SMYTH, Canon Gordon William. b 47. Open Univ BA. St Jo Coll Nottm 81. **d** 83 **p** 84. C St Keverne *Truro* 83–86; V Landrake w St Erney and Botus Fleming 86–95; RD E Wivelshire 94–95; V Highertown and Baldhu 95–14; Hon

Can Truro Cathl 06–14; rtd 14; PtO *Truro* from 14; PV Truro Cathl from 14. *3 Carnon Valley, Carnon Downs, Truro TR3 6LG* T: (01872) 870743 E: gordonsmyth58@gmail.com

SMYTH, Kenneth James. b 44. TCD BA 67 MA 72. **d** 68 **p** 69. C Bangor Abbey *D & D* 68–71; C Holywood 71–74; I Gilnahirk 74–82; I Newtownards w Movilla Abbey 82–88; I Newtownards 89–11; Preb Wicklow St Patr Cathl Dublin 93–11; rtd 11. *3 Mount Royal, Bangor BT20 3BG* T: (028) 9145 8706 E: kennethjsmith@aol.com

SMYTH, Lucinda Elizabeth Jane. *See* LEAVER, Lucinda Elizabeth Jane

SMYTH, Peter Frederick. b 58. SNWTP. **d** 10 **p** 11. C Prescot *Liv* 10–13; TV Kirkby 13–17; V Childwall St Dav from 17. *St David's Vicarage, Rocky Lane, Liverpool L16 1JA* T: 0151-722 4549 M: 07847-456025 E: stdavidsvicar@gmail.com

SMYTH, Robert Andrew Laine (Brother Anselm). b 30. Trin Coll Cam BA 53 MA 59 Lon Univ PGCE 60 DipEd 65. **d** 79 **p** 80. SSF from 53; Min Prov Eur Prov SSF 79–91; LtO *Linc* 84–92; P-in-c Cambridge St Benedict *Ely* 92–93; V 93–00; rtd 00; *Worc* from 08. *Glasshampton Monastery, Shrawley, Worcester WR6 6TQ* T: (01299) 896345

SMYTH, Roderick Lindsay. Ulster Univ MEd QUB BMus PGCE Univ of Wales (Lamp) BTh. **d** 13 **p** 14. C Belfast Malone St Jo *Conn* 14–16; I Nenagh *L & K* from 16. *St Mary's Rectory, Church Road, Nenagh, Co Tipperary, Republic of Ireland* T: (00353) (67) 32598 M: 87-970 6479 E: rsmyth6582@btinternet.com

SMYTH, Trevor Cecil. b 45. Chich Th Coll 66. **d** 69 **p** 70. C Cookridge H Trin *Ripon* 69–73; C Middleton St Mary 73–75; C Felpham w Middleton *Chich* 75–78; P-in-c Wellington Ch *Ch Lich* 78–80; V 80–86; P-in-c W Wittering *Chich* 86; R W Wittering and Birdham w Itchenor 86–94; PtO 00; TV Withycombe Raleigh *Ex* 01–15; Hon C E Blatchington and Bishopstone *Chich* from 15. *St Andrew's House, 14 Marine Drive, Seaford BN25 2RS* T: (01323) 892972

SMYTHE, Mrs Angela Mary. b 53. St Jo Coll Nottm 85. **d** 87 **p** 94. Par Dn Forest Town *S'well* 87–90; Dn-in-c Pleasley Hill 90–94; V 94–03; AD Mansfield 98–03; P-in-c Sneinton St Chris w St Phil 03–08; Chapl Qu Eliz Sch and Samworth Ch Academy 08–13; rtd 13; PtO *S'well* from 13. *Address withheld by request* M: 07443-472401 E: angiesmythe@aol.com *or* angelasmythe1@sky.com

SMYTHE, Peter John Francis. b 32. Lon Univ LLB 56 Barrister-at-Law (Middle Temple) 76. Wells Th Coll 56. **d** 58 **p** 59. C Maidstone All SS *Cant* 58–62; V Barrow St Jo *Carl* 62–65; V Billesdon w Goadby and Rolleston *Leic* 65–71; rtd 97. *The Gables, 16 Geraldine Road, Malvern WR14 3PA* T: (01684) 573266

SNAITH, Bryan Charles. b 33. Univ of Wales BSc 55. St Mich Coll Llan 61. **d** 61 **p** 62. C Bargoed w Brithdir *Llan* 61–62; C Llanishen and Lisvane 62–71; Ind Chapl *Dur* 71–76; Ind Chapl *Worc* 76–81; P-in-c Stone 76–81; C Chaddesley Corbett 77–81; TV Colchester St Leon, St Mary Magd and St Steph *Chelmsf* 81–86; Ind Chapl 81–03; rtd 03; PtO *Chelmsf* from 04. *4 Wren Close, Stanway, Colchester CO3 8ZB* T: (01206) 767793 E: bryansnaith-colchester@msn.com

SNAPE, Paul Anthony Piper. b 44. **d** 98 **p** 99. OLM Tettenhall Wood and Perton *Lich* 98–10; PtO from 10. *24 Windsor Gardens, Castlecroft, Wolverhampton WV3 8LY* T: (01902) 763577 E: p-snape44@tiscali.co.uk *or* rev.ps@outlook.com

SNARE, Peter Brian. b 39. Cape Town Univ BSc 63. SEITE 99. **d** 02 **p** 03. NSM Dymchurch w Burmarsh and Newchurch *Cant* 02–09; NSM New Romney w Old Romney and Midley 07–09; NSM St Mary's Bay w St Mary-in-the-Marsh etc 07–09; PtO from 09. *35 Shepherds Walk, Hythe CT21 6PW* T: (01303) 269242 *or* (020) 7320 1701 E: peter.snare@btinternet.com

SNARES, Ian. b 68. Brunel Univ BEng 91. Ridley Hall Cam 09. **d** 11 **p** 12. C Ilfracombe, Lee, Woolacombe, Bittadon etc *Ex* 11–15; C Ilfracombe SS Phil and Jas w W Down 11–15; V Cowplain *Portsm* from 15; Jt AD Havant from 19. *The Vicarage, Padnell Road, Waterlooville PO8 8DZ* E: iansnares@gmail.com

SNASDELL, Canon Antony John. b 39. St Chad's Coll Dur BA 63. **d** 65 **p** 66. C Boston *Linc* 65–70; Hon C Worksop Priory *S'well* 71–82; P-in-c Gt Massingham *Nor* 82–84; P-in-c Lt Massingham 82–84; P-in-c Harpley 82–84; R Gt and Lt Massingham and Harpley 84–91; R Thorpe St Andr 91–04; Hon Can Nor Cathl 03–04; rtd 04; PtO *Nor* from 05. *1 Speedwell Road, Wymondham NR18 0XQ* T: (01953) 857509

SNEARY, Michael William. b 38. Brentwood Coll of Educn CertEd 71 Open Univ BA 79. Ely Th Coll 61. **d** 64 **p** 65. C Loughton St Jo *Chelmsf* 64–67; Youth Chapl 67–70; Hon C Ingrave 70–71; Teacher Harold Hill Gr Sch Essex 71–74; Ivybridge Sch 74–76; Coombe Dean Sch Plymouth 76–03; rtd 03. *The Lodge, 1 Lower Port View, Saltash PL12 4BY*

SNELL, Mrs Brigitte. b 43. BA 85. EAMTC 86. **d** 89 **p** 94. NSM Cambridge Gt St Mary w St Mich *Ely* 89–91; Par

Dn Cambridge St Jas 91–94; C 94–95; V Sutton 95–03; R Witcham w Mepal 95–03; rtd 03; PtO *Ely* 05–16 and from 19. *45 London Road, Harston, Cambridge CB22 7QQ* T: (01223) 872839 E: brigittesnell@gmail.com

SNELL, Colin. b 53. Trin Coll Bris 94. **d** 96 **p** 97. C Martock w Ash *B & W* 96–00; TV Wilton 00–08; V Galmington 08–18; rtd 18. *Mapperton House, Blind Lane, Bower Hinton, Martock TA12 6LR*

SNELLGROVE, Canon Martin Kenneth. b 54. City Univ BSc 77 CEng 80 MICE 84. Aston Tr Scheme 85 Ridley Hall Cam 87. **d** 89 **p** 90. C Four Oaks *Birm* 89–92; TV Wrexham *St As* 92–01; R Hope 01–13; AD Hawarden 03–10; V Corwen w Llangar w Glyndyfrdwy etc 13–17; I Valle Crucis Miss Area from 18; AD Penllyn and Edeirnion 13–18; AD Valle Crucis from 18; Can Cursal St As Cathl from 13. *The Rectory, Ffordd Ty Cerrig, Corwen LL21 9RP* T: (01490) 413520

SNELLING, Brian. b 40. **d** 69 **p** 70. C Slough *Ox* 69–72; C Hoole *Ches* 72–76; V Millbrook 76–80; V Homerton St Luke *Lon* 80–90; R Marks Tey w Aldham and Lt Tey *Chelmsf* 90–98; V Stebbing w Lindsell 98–04; V Stebbing and Lindsell w Gt and Lt Saling 04–05; rtd 05; PtO *Chelmsf* 06–16. *69 Reymead Close, West Mersea, Colchester CO5 8DN* T: (01206) 383717 E: revbrians@aol.com

SNELLING, Joseph David Griffith. b 90. Clare Coll Cam BA 12 MA 16. St Mellitus Coll 15. **d** 17 **p** 18. C Linc St Swithin from 17. *84 Little Bargate Street, Lincoln LN5 8JL* M: 07585-845793 E: joseph.snelling@mac.com

SNELLING, Stephen Thomas. b 47. City of Lon Poly BA 73. SEITE 08. **d** 10 **p** 11. NSM Seal SS Pet and Paul *Roch* 10–11; NSM Nantwich *Ches* 12–18; PtO from 18. *Silverhurst, 16 Holly Place, Wistaston, Nantwich CW5 6NG* T: (01270) 668858 *or* 665800 M: 07775-833824 E: anantwichpriest@silverhurst.co.uk

SNELSON, William Thomas. b 45. Ex Coll Ox BA 67 Fitzw Coll Cam BA 69 MA 75. Westcott Ho Cam 67. **d** 69 **p** 70. C Godalming *Guildf* 69–72; C Leeds St Pet *Ripon* 72–75; V Chapel Allerton 75–81; V Bardsey 81–93; Dioc Ecum Officer 86–93; W Yorkshire Ecum Officer *Bradf* 93–97; Gen Sec Chs Together in England 97–08; rtd 08; Development Officer Angl Cen Rome 08–15; PtO *Ripon* 09–14; *Leeds* from 14. *6 Abbey Crags Way, Knaresborough HG5 8EF* T: (01423) 862660 M: 07917-663250 E: bill.snelson@btopenworld.com

SNOOK, Mrs Margaret Ann. b 41. S Dios Minl Tr Scheme. **d** 91 **p** 94. NSM Keynsham *B & W* 91–04; Chapl Univ Hosps Bris NHS Foundn Trust from 91; PtO *B & W* from 04. *32 Hurn Lane, Keynsham, Bristol BS31 1RS* T: 0117-986 3439 M: 07802-944528 E: snook926@btinternet.com

SNOW, Frank. b 31. Lon Univ BD 57. **d** 83 **p** 84. Hon C Tweedmouth *Newc* 83–86; Hon C Berwick H Trin 86–89; Hon C Berwick St Mary 86–89; Hon C Berwick H Trin and St Mary 89–90; R Gt Smeaton w Appleton Wiske and Birkby etc *Ripon* 90–97; rtd 97; PtO *Ripon* 97–14; *Leeds* 14–16; *Sheff* from 02. *18D Abbey Lane Dell, Sheffield S8 0BZ* T: 0114-327 5067 E: fersnow@outlook.com

✠**SNOW, The Rt Revd Martyn James.** b 68. Sheff Univ BSc 89. Wycliffe Hall Ox BTh 95. **d** 95 **p** 96 **c** 13. C Brinsworth w Catcliffe and Treeton *Sheff* 95–97; CMS Guinea 98–01; V Pitsmoor Ch Ch *Sheff* 01–10; P-in-c Stocksbridge 07–08; AD Ecclesfield 07–10; Adn Sheff and Rotherham 10–13; Suff Bp Tewkesbury *Glouc* 13–16; Bp Leic from 16. *12 Springfield Road, Leicester LE2 3BD* T: 0116-270 8985 E: bishop.leicester@leccofe.org

SNOW, Peter Richard. b 85. Qu Coll Cam MA 10. Oak Hill Th Coll BA 16. **d** 16 **p** 17. C St Helen Bishopsgate w St Andr Undershaft etc *Lon* from 16; C Harringay St Paul 18–19; P-in-c from 19. *St Paul's Church House, 1 Wightman Road, London N4 1RW* M: 07929-456136 E: snow@cantab.net *or* pete@stpaulsharringay.com

SNOW, Richard John. b 57. Bris Univ BSc 80 K Coll Lon MA 05. **d** 90 **p** 91. C Preston Plucknett *B & W* 90–95; TV Stratton St Margaret w S Marston etc *Bris* 95–02; R Box w Hazlebury and Ditteridge 02–07; TR Kirkby Lonsdale *Carl* from 07. *The Rectory, Vicarage Lane, Kirkby Lonsdale, Carnforth LA6 2BA* T: (01524) 272044 E: rector@therainbowparish.org

SNOWBALL, Miss Deborah Jane. b 67. Middx Poly BEd 90. Ripon Coll Cuddesdon 02. **d** 04 **p** 05. C Sawbridgeworth *St Alb* 04–07; P-in-c Rickmansworth 07–12; V from 12; RD 11–16. *The Vicarage, Bury Lane, Rickmansworth WD3 1ED* T: (01923) 772627 E: vicar@stmarysrickmansworth.org.uk

SNOWBALL, Canon Dorothy Margaret. b 52. Sunderland Univ BA 98. NEOC 98. **d** 01 **p** 02. NSM Heworth St Mary *Dur* 01–07; P-in-c Eighton Banks from 07; AD Gateshead 16–19; Hon Can Dur Cathl from 17. *2 Oval Park View, Felling, Gateshead NE10 9DS* T: 0191-469 5059 E: dorothysnowball@btinternet.com

SNOWDEN (née HALL), The Ven Elizabeth. b 58. Plymouth Poly BSc 79 Birm Univ BA 01 Lon Inst of Educn PGCE 80. Qu Coll Birm 98. **d** 01 **p** 02. C Burntwood *Lich* 01–04; C and Youth Work Co-ord Ogley Hay 04–10; P-in-c Bestwood Em w St Mark *S'well* 10–11; V 11–16; AD Nottm N 13–16; Adn Chelmsf from 16. *The Archdeacon's Lodge, 136 Broomfield Road, Chelmsford CM1 1RN*   T: (01245) 258257   M: 07954-690788 E: revesnowden@yahoo.co.uk *or* a.chelmsford@chelmsford.anglican.org

SNUGGS, Canon David Sidney. b 49. Keble Coll Ox BA 71 PGCE 72 MA 75. S Dios Minl Tr Scheme 89. **d** 92 **p** 93. C Bitterne *Win* 92–96; V Fair Oak 96–14; Hon Can Win Cathl 11–14; rtd 14; PtO *Win* from 14. *13 Cranbourne Park, Hedge End, Southampton SO30 0NX*   M: 07875-733323 E: davidandidane.snuggs@outlook.com

SNYDER, Miss Susanna Jane. b 78. Em Coll Cam BA 00 MA 05 Birm Univ PhD 09. Qu Coll Birm BA 04. **d** 05 **p** 06. C Brownswood Park and Stoke Newington St Mary *Lon* 05–08; PtO *Ox* 08–10 and from 14; USA 10–14; Dir Part-Time Pathway Ripon Coll Cuddesdon from 18. *Ripon College, Cuddesdon, Oxford OX44 9EX*   T: (01865) 877400 E: susannajsnyder@gmail.com

SNYDER GIBSON, Catherine. *See* GIBSON, Catherine Snyder

SOADY, Canon Mark. b 60. Univ of Wales BTh RMN 84. St Mich Coll Llan 96. **d** 96 **p** 97. C Tenby *St D* 96–99; TV 99–03; Min Can St Woolos Cathl *Mon* 03–08; P-in-c Newport All SS 03–12; Chapl Univ of Wales (Newport) 08–12; V Abergavenny St Mary w Llanwenarth Citra from 12; P-in-c Abergavenny H Trin from 12; AD Abergavenny from 14; CF(V) 98–12; Prior Holywell Community from 14; Can St Woolos Cathl *Mon* from 14. *St Mary's Vicarage, Monk Street, Abergavenny NP7 5ND*   T: (01873) 853168   M: 07968-753978 E: vicar@stmarys-priory.org

SOAR, Angela Margaret. *See* PATERSON, Angela Margaret

SOAR, Martin William. b 54. Wye Coll Lon BSc 78. Wycliffe Hall Ox 86. **d** 88 **p** 89. C Henfynyw w Aberaeron and Llanddewi Aberarth *St D* 88–91; C Hubberston 91–93; P-in-c Low Harrogate St Mary *Ripon* 93–95; V 95–06; Chapl Old Swinford Hosp Sch Stourbridge 06–18; C Kinver and Enville *Lich* 10–18; C Alton w Bradley-le-Moors and Denstone etc from 18. *The Vicarage, Church Lane, Mayfield, Ashbourne DE6 2JR* E: msoar@oshsch.com *or* msoar54@gmail.com

SOBCZAK, Mrs Susan Clare. b 49. WEMTC 10. **d** 13 **p** 14. NSM Nailsworth w Shortwood, Horsley etc *Glouc* 13–19; rtd 19. *1 Byways, Horsley, Stroud GL6 0PP*   T: (01453) 833526 E: suesobczak@gmail.com

SOCHON, David Lomas Philipe. b 40. Univ Coll Lon BA 62. **d** 07 **p** 08. OLM Newton Flotman, Swainsthorpe, Tasburgh, etc *Nor* 07–15; RD Depwade 09–13; rtd 15; PtO *St E* from 15; *Nor* from 15. *Greenacre, Stone Street, Spexhall, Halesworth IP19 0RN*   T: (01986)   781151 E: davidsochon@googlemail.com

SODADASI, David Anand Raj. b 63. Osmania Univ Hyderabad BCom 85 MA 99 Union Bibl Sem Pune BD 95 Univ of Wales PhD 12. United Th Coll Bangalore MTh 00. **d** 01 **p** 02. C Jabalpur Cathl India 01–04; Lect Leonard Th Coll 00–04; PtO *Ox* 04–05; NSM Ray Valley 05–10; R Cusop w Blakemere, Bredwardine w Brobury etc *Heref* 10–17; R Icknield Way Villages *Chelmsf* from 17. *The Rectory, 1 Hall Lane, Great Chishill, Royston SG8 8SG* E: anandsodadasi@hotmail.co.uk

SODOR AND MAN, Bishop of. *See* EAGLES, The Rt Revd Peter Andrew

SOER, Patricia Kathleen Mary. b 40. Hull Coll of Educn CertEd 61. **d** 99 **p** 00. OLM Deptford St Jo w H Trin *S'wark* 99–06; OLM Deptford St Jo w H Trin and Ascension 06–10; rtd 10; PtO *S'wark* from 10. *350 Wood Vale, London SE23 3DY*   T: (020) 8699 4616

SOFIELD, Martin. b 60. **d** 02 **p** 03. OLM Clifton *Man* 02–10; NSM Ardrossan *Glas* 10–11; R 11–16; NSM Dalry 10–11; R 11–16; NSM Irvine St Andr LEP 10–11; I 11–16. *44 Gooding Crescent, Stevenston KA20 4AU*   M: 07710-428896 E: martin.sofield@btinternet.com

SOHAIL, Victor. b 67. All SS Cen for Miss & Min 14. **d** 17 **p** 18. C Gt Marsden w Nelson St Phil *Blackb* from 17. *3 Pinewood Drive, Nelson BB9 0WB*

SOKANOVIC (née HARRIS), Mrs Mary Noreen Cecily. b 58. Suffolk Coll BA 97 RGN 79 RN 96. EAMTC 02. **d** 05 **p** 06. NSM Whitton and Thurleston w Akenham *St E* 05–10; Bp's Chapl 10–15; C Ipswich St Mary-le-Tower 10–15; P-in-c Whitton and Thurleston w Akenham from 15; Bp's Adv for Healthcare Chapl 12–16. *Side View, School Road, Coddenham, Ipswich IP6 9PS*   M: 07824-323073 E: marysokanovic@outlook.com

SOKOLOWSKI (née MAHON), Mrs Stephanie Mary. b 56. Liv Univ BSc 80 SRN 80 K Coll Lon BA 00. S'wark Ord Course 91. **d** 94 **p** 95. C Warlingham w Chelsham and Farleigh *S'wark*

94–97; C Godstone and Blindley Heath 97–04; C Shere, Albury and Chilworth *Guildf* from 07. *The Vicarage, Brook Road, Chilworth, Guildford GU4 8ND*   T: (01483) 534293   M: 07731-783924 E: ssokolowski@btinternet.com

SOLMAN, Mrs Fiona Barbara. b 53. SRN 75 RSCN 75 RHV 80. STETS 03. **d** 06 **p** 07. C Cottesmore and Barrow w Ashwell and Burley *Pet* 06–09; C Empingham and Exton w Horn w Whitwell 06–09; C Greetham and Thistleton w Stretton and Clipsham 06–09; R Etwall w Egginton *Derby* 09–18; rtd 18. *The Gables, 21 Castleton Boulevard, Skegness PE25 2TU*   T: (01754) 465698 E: fionasolman@aol.com

SOMASUNDRAM, Ian Mark. b 81. Man Univ MEng 04 Jes Coll Cam PhD 10. Oak Hill Th Coll BA 15. **d** 15 **p** 16. C Hebburn St Jo *Dur* 15–19; P-in-c from 19; C Jarrow Grange 15–19; P-in-c from 19. *23 St John's Avenue, Hebburn NE31 2TZ*   M: 07742-319151 E: ian.m.somasundram@gmail.com

SOMERS-EDGAR, Carl John. b 46. Otago Univ BA 69. St Steph Ho Ox 72. **d** 75 **p** 76. C Northwood H Trin *Lon* 75–79; C St Marylebone All SS 79–82; V Liscard St Mary w St Columba *Ches* 82–85; V Caversham St Pet New Zealand 85–11; rtd 11. *32 Cole Street, Caversham, Dunedin 9012, New Zealand*   T: (0064) (3) 487 9877 E: paratus@xtra.co.nz

SOMERS HESLAM, Peter. *See* HESLAM, Peter Somers

SOMERVILLE, John William Kenneth. b 38. St D Coll Lamp 60. **d** 63 **p** 64. C Rhosllannerchrugog *St As* 63–67; C Llangystennin 67–70; V Gorsedd 70–76; V Gorsedd w Brynford and Ysgeifiog 77–02; RD Holywell 96–02; rtd 02; PtO *St As* from 09. *15 Bryn Marl Road, Mochdre, Colwyn Bay LL28 5DT*

SOPER, Jonathan Alexander James. b 64. Univ Coll Dur BA 85. Wycliffe Hall Ox 94. **d** 96 **p** 97. C Bath Weston All SS w N Stoke and Langridge *B & W* 96–00; C Bryanston Square St Mary w St Marylebone St Mark *Lon* 00–04; LtO *Ex* from 07. *Church Office, 22 Southernhay West, Exeter EX1 1PR*   T: (01392) 434311 E: jon@enc.net.uk

SOPHIANOU, Neofitos Anthony. b 47. Sarum & Wells Th Coll 86. **d** 88 **p** 89. C St Peter-in-Thanet *Cant* 88–91; PtO *St Alb* 97–99; C Stevenage St Nic and Graveley 99–03; PtO 03–04; V Wheatley Park *Sheff* 04–07; V Goole 07–11; R Sprotbrough 11–14; Bp's Urban Adv 05–14; rtd 14; PtO *Sheff* from 14; Ecum Officer Doncaster Adnry from 15. *7 Victoria Avenue, Hatfield, Doncaster DN7 6QG*   T: (01302) 459403   M: 07828-570891

SORENSEN, Ms Anna Katrine Elizabeth. b 58. Man Univ BA 82 MPhil 94 Open Univ PGCE 95. Ripon Coll Cuddesdon 83. **d** 87 **p** 94. Par Dn Ashton H Trin *Man* 87–88; Asst Chapl St Felix Sch Southwold 89–90; Chapl 90–99; Hon Par Dn Reydon *St E* 89–92; Hon Par Dn Blythburgh w Reydon 92–94; Hon C 94–99; C Gislingham and Thorndon 99–03; P-in-c Billingborough Gp *Linc* 03–18; P-in-c N Beltisloe Gp from 18. *The Rectory, 30 High Street, Ropsley, Grantham NG33 4BE*   M: 07793-544238 E: sorensenanna8@gmail.com

SØRENSEN, Michaela Alexandra. b 70. Kent Univ BA 92. ERMC 18. **d** 19. C Watton *Nor* from 19. *44 Jubilee Road, Watton, Thetford IP25 6BJ*   M: 07554-542861 E: michaelasorensen@icloud.com

SOTONWA, Canon Oladapo Oyegbola. b 56. Ibadan Univ Nigeria BEd 79 MEd 81 PhD 86. Immanuel Coll Ibadan 91. **d** 94 **p** 95. C Italupe Em Nigeria 94–95; V Egbeba All SS 95–03; V Simeon Ashiru Mem Ch 03–04; V Odogbonuki St Pet 04–05; Hon Can Ijebu from 05; PtO *S'wark* 06–07; Hon C W Dulwich Em 07–11; Hon C S'wark H Trin w St Matt 11; Chapl HM Pris Nor from 11. *HM Prison Norwich, Knox Road, Norwich NR1 4LU*   T: (01603) 708600   M: 07983-630658 E: oladaposotonwa@yahoo.co.uk *or* oladapo.sotonwa@justice.gov.uk

SOTONWA, Canon Thomas Bamidele Adegboyega. b 78. Ambrose Alli Univ Nigeria BMLS 05 Middx Univ MSc 11. **d** 05 **p** 06. Nigeria 05–13; PtO *Birm* 13–17; V Rednal from 17; Hon Can Ibadan Nigeria from 19. *St Stephen's Vicarage, Edgewood Road, Rednal, Birmingham B45 8SG*   T: 0121-453 3347   M: 07837-421941 E: sotzi2002@gmail.com

SOULSBY, Canon Michael. b 36. Dur Univ BSc 57. Westcott Ho Cam 61. **d** 62 **p** 63. C Selly Oak St Mary *Birm* 62–66; C Kings Norton 66–72; TV 73–76; TR Sutton *Liv* 76–88; RD Prescot 84–88; P-in-c Orton Longueville *Ely* 88–96; RD Yaxley 92–02; TR The Ortons, Alwalton and Chesterton 96–04; Hon Can Ely Cathl 94–04; rtd 04; PtO *Ely* from 05; *Pet* from 14; *Ox* from 17. *8 Leiston Court, Eye, Peterborough PE6 7WL*   T: (01733) 221124 E: m.soulsby@talk21.com

SOULT, Mrs Pamela Elizabeth. b 46. SNWTP. **d** 09 **p** 10. NSM Over Peover w Lower Peover *Ches* 09–11; NSM Goostrey w Swettenham 11–17; rtd 17; PtO *Ches* from 17. *The Tower House, The Courtyard, Swettenham, Congleton CW12 2JZ*   T: (01477) 571844 E: pamelasoult@aol.com

SOUNDY, Mrs Philippa Clare. b 60. BNC Ox BA 81. St Mellitus Coll BA 10. d 10 p 11. CMS 10–13; NSM Amersham on the Hill Ox 10–14; NSM Hawridge w Cholesbury and St Leonard 14–15; PtO St Alb from 15; Ox 15–19. White Lodge, 22 Westbury Road, Warminster BA12 0AW T: (01985) 220573 M: 07791-226162 E: pippasoundy@hotmail.co.uk or pippasoundy@btinternet.com

SOUPPOURIS, Ms Gail Camilla. b 52. Essex Univ BA 75 Anglia Ruskin Univ MA 07. SEITE 02. d 05 p 06. C W Wickham St Fran and St Mary S'wark 05–08; P-in-c Shoreham Beach Chich 08–14; rtd 14; PtO Chich from 16. The Rotyngs, Rottingdean, Brighton BN2 7DX T: (01273) 240420 M: 07950-665051 E: gail.souppouris@gmail.com

SOURBUT, Preb Philip John. b 57. Cam Univ BA MA. Cranmer Hall Dur BA. d 85 p 86. C Springfield All SS Chelmsf 85–88; C Roxeth Ch Ch and Harrow St Pet Lon 88–91; P-in-c Bath St Sav B & W 91–93; R Bath St Sav w Swainswick and Woolley 93–98; V Cullompton and R Kentisbeare w Blackborough Ex 98–01; TR Cullompton, Willand, Uffculme, Kentisbeare etc 01–09; Dioc Voc Development Officer 09–15; Tutor SWMTC 09–15; C Ex St Mark, St Sidwell and St Matt 09–15; Dioc Dir Miss and Min from 15; Jt Prin SWMTC from 17; Preb Ex Cathl from 13. The Old Deanery, The Cloisters, Cathedral Close, Exeter EX1 1HS T: (01392) 294903 E: philip.sourbut@exeter.anglican.org

SOURBUT GROVES, Catherine Ann. b 67. Bath Univ BA 91 MSc 93 PhD 97. STETS MA 07. d 07 p 08. C Saltford w Corston and Newton St Loe B & W 07–11; P-in-c Bath St Barn w Englishcombe 11–16; V from 16. The Vicarage, Mount View, Southdown, Bath BA2 1JX T: (01225) 478952

SOUTER, Ruth Rosemary. b 55. Dur Univ BEd 77. EMMTC 00. d 03 p 04. C Braunstone Park CD Leic 03–07; V Erdington Ch the K Birm from 07. St Margaret's Vicarage, Somerset Road, Erdington, Birmingham B23 6NQ T: 0121-373 9209 E: ruthsouter@yahoo.com

SOUTER, William Ewen Logan. b 66. Em Coll Cam BA 88 Univ Coll Lon PhD 93. Trin Coll Bris BA 94 MA 97. d 97 p 98. C Harborne Heath Birm 97–01; TV Horsham Chich 01–11; PtO Llan from 13. 89 Claude Road, Cardiff CF24 3QD T: (029) 2115 4631 M: 07807-384350 E: willsouter@hotmail.co.uk

SOUTH, Gerald Peter. b 45. d 09 p 10. NSM Limpsfield and Tatsfield S'wark 09–15; PtO from 15; P-in-c Avening w Cherington Glouc from 17. The Rectory, 5 Orchard Field, Avening, Tetbury GL8 8PE T: (01453) 834884 E: gp.south@btopenworld.com

SOUTH, Gillian. See HARWOOD, Gillian

SOUTHAMPTON, Suffragan Bishop of. See SELLIN, The Rt Revd Deborah Mary

SOUTHCOMBE, Matthew Leonard. b 81. Surrey Univ BMus 04 Roehampton Univ MA 08. St Mellitus Coll BA 18. d 18 p 19. C Whitchurch St Aug Bris from 18; C Bedminster from 18. 41 Birchall Road, Bristol BS6 7TT M: 07714-754660 E: matt@stnicholasbristol.org

SOUTHEE, Mrs Sandra Margaret. b 43. EAMTC 97. d 00 p 01. NSM Galleywood Common Chelmsf 00–02; NSM Moulsham St Jo 02–06; Asst Chapl Mid-Essex Hosp Services NHS Trust 01–06; PtO Chelmsf 06–07; NSM Gt Baddow 07–12; rtd 12; PtO Chelmsf from 12. 6 Hampton Road, Chelmsford CM2 8ES T: (01245) 475456 E: sandysouthee@hotmail.co.uk

SOUTHEND, Archdeacon of. See SNOWDEN, The Ven Elizabeth

⚥SOUTHERN, The Rt Revd Humphrey Ivo John. b 60. Ch Ch Ox BA 82 MA 86. Ripon Coll Cuddesdon 83. d 86 p 87 c 07. C Rainham Roch 86–90; C Walton St Mary Liv 90–92; C Walton-on-the-Hill 92; V Hale Guildf 92–96; TR 96–97; TR Hale w Badshot Lea 97–99; Dioc Ecum Officer 92–99; TR Tisbury Sarum 99–01; TR Nadder Valley 01–07; RD Chalke 00–07; Can and Preb Sarum Cathl 06–07; Suff Bp Repton Derby 07–15; Warden of Readers 09–15; Prin Ripon Coll Cuddesdon from 15; Asst Bp Ox from 15. Ripon College, Cuddesdon, Oxford OX44 9EX T: (01865) 877400 E: principal@rcc.ac.uk

SOUTHERN, John Abbott. b 27. Leeds Univ BA 47. Coll of Resurr Mirfield. d 51 p 52. C Leigh St Mary Man 51–55; C Gt Grimsby St Jas Linc 55–58; V Oldham St Jas Man 58–60; V Haigh Liv 60–75; V Pemberton St Jo 75–98; rtd 98; PtO Liv from 00. 145 Moor Road, Orrell, Wigan WN5 8SJ T: (01942) 732132

SOUTHERN, Mrs Lindsay Margaret. b 70. Univ of Wales (Abth) BA 01 Reading Univ PGCE 04 St Jo Coll Dur BA 08. Cranmer Hall Dur 06. d 08 p 09. C Kirklington w Burneston and Wath and Pickhill Ripon 08–12; V Catterick Leeds from 12. The Vicarage, High Green, Catterick, Richmond DL10 7LN T: (01748) 811462 M: 07720-242468

SOUTHERN, Paul Ralph. b 48. Oak Hill Th Coll 85. d 87 p 88. C Chadwell Heath Chelmsf 87–91; P-in-c Tolleshunt

D'Arcy w Tolleshunt Major 91–01; V Tolleshunt D'Arcy and Tolleshunt Major 01–08; rtd 08; PtO Chelmsf from 08; Eur from 19. 12 Guisnes Court, Back Road, Tolleshunt D'Arcy, Maldon CM9 8TW T: (01621) 860380 E: paulsouthern@btinternet.com

SOUTHERON, Kathryn Ruth. See TRIMBY, Kathryn Ruth

SOUTHERTON, Canon Peter Clive. b 38. Univ of Wales (Lamp) BA 59. Qu Coll Birm. d 61 p 62. C Llandrillo-yn-Rhos St As 61–68; Bermuda 68–71; V Esclusham St As 72–82; V Prestatyn 82–04; Hon Can St As Cathl 96–04; rtd 04; PtO St As from 09. 6 Llwyn Mesen, Prestatyn LL19 8NS T: (01745) 853176 E: clivesoutherton@yahoo.co.uk

SOUTHGATE, Mrs Clair Mary. b 67. Trin Coll Bris 09. d 11 p 12. OLM Box w Hazlebury and Ditteridge Bris from 11; OLM Colerne w N Wraxall from 11. 6 Queens Square, Box, Corsham SN13 8EA T: (01225) 743970 M: 07917-117644 E: meddling@tiscali.co.uk

SOUTHGATE, Graham. b 63. GIBiol 85 NE Surrey Coll of Tech PhD 89. Ripon Coll Cuddesdon BTh 93. d 93 p 94. C Tisbury Sarum 93–97; TV Chalke Valley 97–03; R Bratton, Edington and Imber, Erlestoke etc 03–11; TR Nadder Valley from 11; RD Chalke from 19. The Rectory, Shaftesbury Road, Fovant, Salisbury SP3 5JA T: (01722) 714826 E: grahamsouthgate63@hotmail.com

SOUTHGATE, Patricia Elizabeth. b 44. d 03 p 04. OLM Parkstone St Pet and St Osmund w Branksea Sarum from 03. 1 Dune Crest, 105 Banks Road, Poole BH13 7QQ T: (01202) 700124 E: patsouthgate@btinternet.com

SOUTHWARD, Canon James Fisher. b 57. St Martin's Coll Lanc BEd 80. Chich Th Coll 83. d 86 p 87. C Woodford St Barn Chelmsf 86–89; TV Crawley Chich 89–95; V Higham and Merston Roch from 95; RD Strood 02–12; Hon Can Roch Cathl from 09. The Vicarage, Hermitage Road, Higham, Rochester ME3 7NE T/F: (01634) 717360 E: vicar@highamparishchurch.org.uk

SOUTHWARK, Archdeacon of. See STEEN, The Ven Jane Elizabeth

SOUTHWARK, Bishop of. See CHESSUN, The Rt Revd Christopher Thomas James

SOUTHWARK, Dean of. See NUNN, The Very Revd Andrew Peter

SOUTHWELL, Peter John Mackenzie. b 43. New Coll Ox BA 64 MA 68. Wycliffe Hall Ox 66. d 67 p 68. C Crookes St Thos Sheff 67–70; Lect Sheff Univ 67–70; Sen Tutor Wycliffe Hall Ox 70–08; Chapl and Lect Qu Coll Ox 82–10; rtd 10; LtO Ox 10–11; PtO from 19. The Queen's College, Oxford OX1 4AW T: (01865) 279120 E: peter.southwell@queens.ox.ac.uk

SOUTHWELL AND NOTTINGHAM, Bishop of. See WILLIAMS, The Rt Revd Paul Gavin

SOUTHWELL, Dean of. See SULLIVAN, The Very Revd Nicola Ann

SOWDEN, Charles William Bartholomew. b 47. d 97 p 98. OLM Saxonwell Linc 97–06; NSM Metheringham w Blankney and Dunston 06–09; P-in-c Wyberton 09–17; P-in-c Frampton 09–17; rtd 17. Address temp unknown E: charles.sowden1@btinternet.com

SOWDEN, Geoffrey David. b 57. Kingston Poly BA 79. Wycliffe Hall Ox 95. d 97 p 98. C Ware Ch Ch St Alb 97–02; V Highworth w Sevenhampton and Inglesham etc Bris from 02; P-in-c Broad Blunsdon from 05. The Vicarage, 10 Stonefield Drive, Highworth, Swindon SN6 7DA T: (01793) 765554 E: the.sowdens@btinternet.com

SOWDON, Henry Lewis Malcolm. b 37. TCD BA. Bps' Coll Cheshunt. d 64 p 65. C Newport w Longford Lich 64–66; C Caverswall 66–69; Chapl Clayesmore Sch Blandford 69–72; Hon C Hornsey Ch Ch Lon 72–80; Chapl Gordon's Sch Woking 80–86; TV Hodge Hill Birm 86–91; PtO 91–12; rtd 02. 157 Heathfield Road, Birmingham B19 1JD T: 0121-240 3557

SOWERBUTTS, Alan. b 49. Sheff Univ BSc 70 PhD 73 Qu Coll Cam BA 75 MA 79. Westcott Ho Cam 74. d 76 p 77. C Salesbury Blackb 76–80; V Lower Darwen St Jas 80–84; V Musbury 84–93; P-in-c Brindle 93–98; Sec Dioc Adv Cttee for the Care of Chs 93–98; V Read in Whalley 98–14; rtd 14; PtO Man from 14; Blackb from 14. 9 Hapton Way, Rossendale BB4 8QG T: (01706) 219279 M: 07730-535598 E: fralans@yahoo.co.uk

SOWERBUTTS, Philip John. b 67. Ches Coll of HE BEd 89 Edge Hill Coll of HE PGCE 99. Oak Hill Th Coll BA 03. d 03 p 04. C Kirk Ella and Willerby York 03–07; V Castle Church Lich from 07. Castle Church Vicarage, 18 Castle Bank, Stafford ST16 1DJ T: (01785) 607150 M: 07910-606876 E: vicar@castlechurch.org.uk

SOWERBY, Geoffrey Nigel Rake. b 35. St Aid Birkenhead 56. d 60 p 61. C Armley St Bart Ripon 60–63; Min Can Ripon

Cathl 63–65; V Thornthwaite w Thruscross and Darley 65–69; V Leeds All SS 69–73; V Leyburn w Bellerby 73–81; R Edin Old St Paul 81–86; V Hawes and Hardraw *Ripon* 86–92; Dioc Adv in Deliverance Min 91–92; rtd 92; PtO *Dur* 92–13; *Ripon* 92–14; *Leeds* 14. *25 Greendale Court, Bedale DL8 1FB* T: (01677) 425860 M: 07749-229189 E: geoffreynsowerby@btinternet.com

✠SOWERBY, The Rt Revd Mark Crispin Rake. b 63. K Coll Lon BD 85 AKC 85 Lanc Univ MA 94. Coll of Resurr Mirfield 85. d 87 p 88 c 09. C Knaresborough *Ripon* 87–90; C Darwen St Cuth w Tockholes St Steph *Blackb* 90–92; V Accrington St Mary 92–97; Chapl St Chris High Sch Accrington 92–97; Chapl Victoria Hosp Accrington 92–97; Asst Dir of Ords *Blackb* 93–96; Voc Officer and Selection Sec Min Division 97–01; V Harrogate St Wilfrid *Ripon* 01–04; TR 04–09; Asst Dir of Ords 05–09; Area Bp Horsham *Chich* 09–19; Prin Coll of Resurr Mirfield from 19. *College of the Resurrection, Stocks Bank Road, Mirfield WF14 0BW* T: (01924) 490441

SOWTER, Colin Victor. b 35. Ball Coll Ox BA 56 MA 59 DPhil 60. Oak Hill NSM Course 88. d 91 p 92. NSM Cranleigh *Guildf* 91–93; NSM Wonersh 93–98; NSM Wonersh w Blackheath 98–05; rtd 05; PtO *Guildf* from 05. *Hollycroft, Grantley Avenue, Wonersh Park, Guildford GU5 0QN* T: (01483) 892094 F: 892894 E: colin.sowter@btopenworld.com

SOWTON, Mrs Alison. b 62. Qu Coll Birm. d 09 p 10. C Oxhey All SS *St Alb* 09–13; TV Melksham *Sarum* from 13. *The Vicarage, 59 Linnet Lane, Melksham SN12 7FA* T: (01225) 434113 M: 07739-712548 E: alisonsowton@live.com

SPACKMAN (*née* MORRISON), Mrs Ailsa. b 40. Qu Univ Kingston Ontario BA 82. Montreal Dioc Th Coll. d 83 p 85. Canada 83–95; Dn Gaspé 83–85; I Malbay Miss Par 85–92; Chapl Drummondville Penitentiary 92–93; rtd 93; PtO *Ex* from 99. *Cofton Lodge, Cofton Hill, Cockwood, Exeter EX6 8RB* T: (01626) 891584

SPACKMAN, Canon Peter John. b 37. Southn Univ BSc 60. Westcott Ho Cam 65. d 66 p 67. C Boxmoor St Jo *St Alb* 66–69; C Alnwick St Paul *Newc* 69–72; C-in-c Stewart Town Jamaica 72–74; I Sept-Iles Canada 74–77; R Baie Comeau 77–80; R Gaspé 80–92; Adn Gaspé 88–92; R Richmond and Hon Can Quebec Canada 92–94; PtO *Ex* 95–97; Hon C Kenton, Mamhead, Powderham, Cofton and Starcross 97–02; PtO 02–15. *Cofton Lodge, Cofton Hill, Cockwood, Exeter EX6 8RB* T: (01626) 891584

SPAIGHT, Robert George. b 45. Ridley Hall Cam. d 84 p 85. C St Columb Minor and St Colan *Truro* 84–87; C Worksop St Jo S'well 87–89; V Barlings *Linc* 89–13; rtd 13. *The Forge, Cross Roads, Riby, Grimsby DN37 8NH* T: (01469) 569768

SPANKIE, Mrs Susan Jane. b 61. Bp Grosseteste Coll BEd 90. SCRTP 12. d 15. NSM Hanborough and Freeland *Ox* from 15. *9 Oakdale Lane, Witney OX28 1GH* T: (01993) 706469 E: revsue@gst.org.uk

SPANNER, Handley James. b 51. Lanchester Poly Cov BSc 73 BA. Oak Hill Th Coll 82. d 85 p 86. C Cov H Trin 85–89; V Rye Park St Cuth *St Alb* 89–01; V Colney Heath St Mark 01–12; rtd 12; PtO *Chich* from 13. *79 Old Manor Road, Rustington, Littlehampton BN16 3QF* E: jamesspanner@aol.com

SPAREY-TAYLOR, Mrs Rebecca Elizabeth. b 76. Univ of Wales (Cardiff) BSc 99. St Padarn's Inst 12. d 17 p 18. C Wrexham *St As* from 17. *The Vicarage, 37 Acton Gate, Wrexham LL11 2PW* T: (01978) 291621 E: curateofwrexham@outlook.com

SPARGO, Anne Elizabeth. b 51. Newnham Coll Cam MB 76 BChir 77 MA 79. WEMTC 03. d 06 p 07. NSM Frampton on Severn, Arlingham, Saul etc *Glouc* 06–10; P-in-c 10–16; rtd 16; PtO *Heref* from 18. *Quilter, Walwyn Road, Upper Colwall, Malvern WR13 6PX* E: anne.spargo@btinternet.com

SPARHAM, Canon Anthony George. b 41. St Jo Coll Dur BA 69. Cranmer Hall Dur 66. d 71 p 72. C Bourne *Linc* 71–74; TV Tong *Bradf* 74–76; V Windhill 76–81; Dioc Dir of Educn *St E* 82–85; V Goostrey *Ches* 85–99; R Wilmslow 99–08; Jt Dir Lay Tr 85–97; Hon Can *Ches* Cathl 94–08; rtd 08; PtO *Ches* 08–17; *Lich* 08–11 and 14–17; Hon C Whittington and W Felton w Haughton 11–14; Hon C Grantown-on-Spey *Mor* from 16; Hon C Rothiemurchus from 16. *48 Strathspey Drive, Grantown-on-Spey PH26 3EY* T: (01479) 481151 E: t.sparham41@sky.com

SPARKES, Mrs Lynne. b 55. Chelt & Glouc Coll of HE BEd 96. WEMTC 06. d 09 p 10. NSM Barnwood *Glouc* 09–12; C Gt Malvern Ch Ch *Worc* 13–14; TV Malvern Chase from 14. *137 Madresfield Road, Malvern WR14 2HD* E: lynnesparkes@googlemail.com

SPARKS, Ian. b 59. Lanc Univ BSc(Econ) 81. Cranmer Hall Dur 94. d 96 p 97. C Bowdon *Ches* 96–00; V Chelford w Lower Withington 00–06; P-in-c Macclesfield St Jo 06–14; P-in-c Luddenden w Luddenden Foot *Leeds* from 14; C

Ryburn from 14. *The Vicarage, 50 Carr Field Drive, Luddenden, Halifax HX2 6RJ* E: iansparks5@googlemail.com

SPARROW, Miss Elisabeth Joy. b 70. Nottm Univ BEng 94. Qu Coll Birm 11. d 11 p 12. C Bartley Green *Birm* 11–15; P-in-c Bridgwater St Jo *B & W* 15–16; V from 16. *St John's Vicarage, Blake Place, Bridgwater TA6 5BA* T: (01278) 422540 E: lis.sparrow@gmail.com *or* revlisstjohnbridgwater@gmail.com

SPARROW, Michael Kenneth. St Jo Coll Dur BA 74. Coll of Resurr Mirfield 74. d 75 p 76. C N Hinksey *Ox* 75–78; C Portsea St Mary *Portsm* 78–85; V Midsomer Norton w Clandown *B & W* 85–93; Chapl Schiedam Miss to Seafarers *Eur* 93–03; Chapl Mombasa Kenya 04–12; P-in-c N Ockendon *Chelmsf* 14–19; rtd 19. *52 Birch Crescent, South Ockendon RM15 6TZ* T: (01708) 859598 E: mksparrow13@gmail.com

SPEAKE, Emma Louise. b 81. Man Univ BA 12 Sheff Univ MA 16. Yorks Min Course 14. d 16 p 17. C W Kirby St Bridget *Ches* 16–18; V Grange St Andr from 18; Chapl St Chad's Catholic and C of E High Sch from 19. *The Vicarage, 37 Lime Grove, Runcorn WA7 5JZ* T: (01928) 830170 M: 07515-174597 E: rev.em@outlook.com

SPEAKMAN, Anthony Ernest. b 40. d 71 p 72. C Newtown w Llanllwchaiarn w Aberhafesp *St As* 71–72; C Holywell 72–75; C St Marylebone w H Trin *Lon* 75–77; V Camberwell St Phil and St Mark *S'wark* 77–80; LtO *Lon* 94–96; NSM Kensington St Jo 96–05; PtO 10–17. *26 Hughenden House, 33 Jerome Crescent, London NW8 8SH*

SPEAR, Andrew James Michael. b 60. Dur Univ BA 81. Ridley Hall Cam 83. d 86 p 87. C Haughton le Skerne *Dur* 86–90; C Eastbourne H Trin *Chich* 90–95; C Patcham 95–02; V Oldland *Bris* 02–16; P-in-c Longwell Green 13–16; rtd 16; PtO *Chich* 17–18; Hon C E Dean w Friston and Jevington from 18. *36 Summerdown Lane, East Dean, Eastbourne BN20 0LE* E: andrewjmspear@hotmail.com

SPEAR, Miss Jennifer Jane. b 53. Westhill Coll Birm BEd 76. Trin Coll Bris 82. dss 84 d 87 p 95. Reading St Jo *Ox* 84–90; Par Dn 87–90; Hon Par Dn Devonport St Barn *Ex* 90–91; Hon Par Dn Devonport St Mich 90–91; Par Dn Plymstock 91–94; C 94–97; TV Plymstock and Hooe 97–11; rtd 11. *69 Plymstock Road, Plymouth PL9 7PD* T: (01752) 405202

SPEAR, John Cory. b 33. Open Univ BA 87. Ridley Hall Cam 68. d 70 p 71. C Gerrards Cross *Ox* 70–73; TV Washfield, Stoodleigh, Withleigh etc *Ex* 73–79; R Instow 79–90; V Westleigh 79–90; RD Hartland 82–89; V Pilton w Ashford 90–97; TR Barnstaple 97–99; rtd 99; PtO *Ex* from 00. *Abbots Lodge, Abbotsham Court, Abbotsham, Bideford EX39 5BH* T: (01237) 476607

SPEAR, Sylvia Grace. b 36. St Chris Coll Blackheath 60. dss 76 d 87 p 94. S Wimbledon H Trin and St Pet *S'wark* 76–80; Lee Gd Shep w St Pet 80–95; Par Dn 87–94; C 94–95; rtd 95; PtO *Nor* from 95. *19 Grovelands, Ingoldisthorpe, King's Lynn PE31 6PG* T: (01485) 543469

SPEARS, Reginald Robert Derek. b 48. Trin Coll Ox BA 72 MA 75. Cuddesdon Coll 72. d 75 p 76. C Hampton All SS *Lon* 75–79; C Caversham *Ox* 79–81; C Caversham St Pet and Mapledurham etc 81–84; V Reading St Matt 84–94; V Earley St Pet 94–14; rtd 14; PtO *Ox* from 14. *65 Aborn Parade, West End Road, Mortimer Common, Reading RG7 3TQ* T: 0118-933 2722 E: derekspears@compuserve.com *or* dspears.awb@gmail.com

SPECK, Ms Jane Elisabeth. b 72. Univ of Cen England in Birm BA 94 St Jo Coll Dur BA 01 MA 02. Cranmer Hall Dur 98. d 02 p 03. C Stourport and Wilden *Worc* 02–05; C N Lambeth *S'wark* 05–11; Chapl K Coll Lon 05–19; Dir Ords Kingston Area 13–19; NSM St Mary le Strand w St Clem Danes *Lon* 17–19; Chapl York St Jo Univ from 19. *St Wulfstan's Vicarage, 8 Abbotsway, York YO31 9LD* E: janespeck@hotmail.com

SPECK, Preb Peter William. b 42. Univ of Wales (Ban) BSc 64 Birm Univ BA 66 MA 71 Lambeth DM 12. Qu Coll Birm 64. d 67 p 68. C Rhosddu *St As* 67–71; C Wrexham 71–72; Asst Chapl United Sheff Hosps 72–73; Chapl N Gen Hosp Sheff 73–79; Chapl R Free Hosp Lon 79–95; Hon Sen Lect Sch of Med 87–95; Preb St Paul's Cathl *Lon* 92–95; Chapl Southn Univ Hosps NHS Trust 95–02; rtd 02; Public Preacher *Win* from 02; Visiting Fell Southn Univ 02–18; Hon Sen Research Fell and Hon Sen Lect K Coll Lon from 02. *22 The Harrage, Romsey SO51 8AE* T: (01794) 516937

SPECK, Raymond George. b 39. Oak Hill Th Coll 64. d 67 p 68. C Stretford St Bride *Man* 67–70; C Roxeth Ch Ch *Lon* 70–74; V Woodbridge St Jo *St E* 74–85; R Jersey St Ouen w St Geo *Win* 85–98; rtd 98; PtO *Win* from 98. *Rosevale Lodge, rue du Craslin, St Peter, Jersey JE3 7BU* T: (01534) 634987 E: revrayspeck@hotmail.com

SPEDDING, Clare. See FRYER-SPEDDING, Clare Caroline

SPEDDING, William Granville. b 39. Tyndale Hall Bris BD 60. d 62 p 63. C Man Albert Memorial Ch 62–65; Hd RE

Whitecroft Sch Bolton 65–71; Co-ord Humanities Hayward Sch Bolton 71–93; PtO *Man* 65–67 and from 02; NSM New Bury 67–79; NSM Bolton St Paul w Em 79–86; NSM Pennington 86–02. *26 Milverton Close, Lostock, Bolton BL6 4RR* T: (01204) 841248 E: granvillespedding@ntlworld.com

SPEEDY (née BRINDLEY), Mrs Angela Mary. b 44. Oak Hill Th Coll 93 NOC 99. **d** 00 **p** 01. C Handforth *Ches* 00–03; R Whaley Bridge 03–05; rtd 05; Hon C Barthomley *Ches* 07–18; PtO from 18. *19 Church Lane, Sandbach CW11 2LG* T: (01270) 753303 E: darrelspeedy735@gmail.com

SPEEDY, Canon Darrel Craven. b 35. St Chad's Coll Dur BA 57. Wells Th Coll 57. **d** 59 **p** 60. C Frodingham *Linc* 59–63; V Heckington w Howell 63–71; V Barton upon Humber 71–79; R Tain *Mor* 79–85; Dioc Sec 82–85; Can St Andr Cathl Inverness 83–85; Syn Clerk 83–85; R Whaley Bridge *Ches* 85–01; RD Chadkirk 88–95; Hon Can Ches Cathl from 96; rtd 01; P-in-c Barthomley *Ches* 01–19; PtO from 19. *19 Church Lane, Sandbach CW11 2LG* T: (01270) 753303 E: darrelspeedy735@gmail.com

SPEEKS, Mark William Bezerra. b 62. Ex Univ BA 82 Ex Coll Ox MSt 83 Yale Univ MDiv 02. **d** 02 **p** 02. C Los Angeles St Alban USA 02–03; NSM Kilburn St Mary w All So and W Hampstead St Jas *Lon* 04–08; NSM St Botolph Aldgate w H Trin Minories 08–10; CF from 10; NSM Belsize Park *Lon* 10–16; NSM S Hampstead St Sav 10–16; Hon Chapl Ch Ch Ox from 17. *c/o MOD Chaplains (Army)* T: (01264) 383430 F: 381824 M: 07843-518063 E: mspeeks@hotmail.com

SPEERS, Canon Samuel Hall. b 46. TCD BA 70 MA 75. Cuddesdon Coll 70. **d** 73 **p** 74. C Boreham Wood All SS *St Alb* 73–76; Madagascar 76–88; Hon Can Antananarivo from 85; R S Lafford *Linc* 88–02; RD Lafford 96–02; TR Chipping Barnet *St Alb* 02–13; rtd 13; Hon C Chingford SS Pet and Paul *Chelmsf* 13–16. *31 Tennyson Drive, Bourne PE10 9WB* T: (01778) 421657 E: hall.speers@talk21.com

SPELLER, Shaun Lawrence. b 88. Birm Poly BA 88. Ripon Coll Cuddesdon 11. **d** 13 **p** 14. C Harpenden St Nic *St Alb* 13–17; V Henlow and Langford from 17. *The Vicarage, 65 Church Street, Langford, Biggleswade SG18 9QT* T: (01462) 700248 M: 07922-129361

SPENCE, Amanda Jane. b 70. St Aug Coll of Th 17. **d** 19. C Crayford *Roch* from 19. *1A Iron Mill Place, Crayford, Dartford DA1 4RT*

SPENCE, David Royston. b 80. St Jo Coll Cam MA 06 PhD 06. Trin Coll Bris 10. **d** 13 **p** 14. C Shill Valley and Broadshire *Ox* 13–16; C Kirk Ella and Willerby *York* from 16. *14 Kirk Rise, Kirk Ella, Hull HU10 7NG* M: 07754-299275 E: david.r.spence@gmail.com *or* revdspence@gmail.com

SPENCE, James Andrew Deane. b 83. Loughb Univ BSc 06. Oak Hill Th Coll BA 17. **d** 17 **p** 18. C Rusholme H Trin *Man* from 17. *2 The Grange, Manchester M14 5NY* T: 0161-224 1123 M: 07793-739115 E: james@plattchurch.org

SPENCE, Michael James. b 62. Sydney Univ BA 85 LLB 87 St Cath Coll Ox DPhil 96. St Steph Ho Ox. **d** 06 **p** 07. NSM Cowley St Jas *Ox* 06–08; Vice-Chan Sydney Univ Australia from 08. *Vice-Chancellor's Office, Quadrangle A14, University of Sydney, NSW 2006, Australia* T: (0061) (2) 9351 5051 *or* (2) 9389 1603 M: 401-693506 E: vice-chancellor@vcc.usyd.edu.au

SPENCE, Mrs Moira Joan. b 44. SAOMC 96. **d** 01 **p** 02. OLM Risborough *Ox* 01–06; NSM Ewenny w St Brides Major *Llan* 07–18. *Ty Bara, 33 Main Road, Ogmore-by-Sea, Bridgend CF32 0PD*

SPENCELEY, Douglas. b 49. Edin Univ MA 70 SS Mark & Jo Univ Coll Plymouth PGCE 71. ERMC 07. **d** 09 **p** 10. NSM Arthingworth, Harrington w Oxendon and E Farndon *Pet* 09–12; NSM Maidwell w Draughton, Lamport w Faxton 09–12; Bp's V for Ch Schs from 12; NSM Billing 12–17; NSM Northampton Em from 17. *1 Russet Drive, Little Billing, Northampton NN3 9TF* T: (01604) 407977 E: dspenceley@lineone.net

SPENCELEY, Haydon du Garde. b 84. Nottm Univ BA 06 Leeds Univ MA 09. St Jo Coll Nottm 11. **d** 14 **p** 15. C Northampton Em *Pet* 14–17; TR from 17; Asst Dir Ords from 17. *24 The Nurseries, Northampton NN1 5HN* T: (01604) 244391 M: 07985-973773 E: haydon.spenceley@gmail.com

SPENCELEY, Malcolm. b 40. Open Univ BA 92 Dur Inst of Educn CertEd 72. Cranmer Hall Dur 78. **d** 80 **p** 81. C Redcar *York* 80–85; V Middlesbrough Ascension 85–93; V Newby 93–05; rtd 05; PtO *York* from 06. *6 Tameside, Stokesley, Middlesbrough TS9 5PE* T: (01642) 710443

SPENCER, Andrew. b 47. St Matthias Coll Bris BEd 70 Univ of Wales (Ban) BTh 05. **d** 04 **p** 05. Moderator for Reader Tr *Guildf* 01–06; OLM Busbridge and Hambledon from 04; Tutor Local Min Progr from 07.

24 Park Road, Godalming GU7 1SH T: (01483) 416333 E: andy.spencer@bhcgodalming.org

SPENCER, Antony Wade. b 50. Ridley Hall Cam 92. **d** 94 **p** 95. C Bury St Edmunds St Geo *St E* 94–96; PtO 96–97; C Rougham, Beyton w Hessett and Rushbrooke 97–99; TV Mildenhall 99–07; Dir Past Development Harborne Heath *Birm* 07–11; C 11–18; PtO from 18. *74 Croftdown Road, Birmingham B17 8RD* T: 0121-426 6228 M: 07704-324444 E: antonyspencer@stjohnsharborne.org

SPENCER, Miss Christine Patricia. b 66. Man Univ BSc 02. St Steph Ho Ox BTh 16. **d** 15 **p** 16. C Storrington *Chich* 15–18; P-in-c Three Bridges from 18. *St Richard's Vicarage, 1 Crossways, Crawley RH10 1QF* M: 07980-617588 E: christine.spencer66@gmail.com *or* vicarstrichardscrawley@hotmail.com

SPENCER, Christopher Graham. b 61. Magd Coll Cam BA 83 MA 87 Bath Univ MSc 84. St Jo Coll Nottm 93. **d** 93 **p** 94. C Ore St Helen and St Barn *Chich* 93–97; V Deal St Geo *Cant* from 97. *The Vicarage, 8 St George's Road, Deal CT14 6BA* T: (01304) 372587 E: chris.spencer@tiscali.co.uk

SPENCER, Christopher Stuart. b 84. Bournemouth Univ BSc 05. St Jo Coll Nottm 08. **d** 12. C Southbroom *Sarum* 12–14. *22 Grampian Close, Oldland Common, Bristol BS30 8QA* T: 0117-932 8726 M: 07792-098249 E: chris_spencer2000@yahoo.co.uk

SPENCER, David William. b 43. EAMTC 80. **d** 81 **p** 82. NSM Wisbech St Aug *Ely* 81–84; C Whittlesey 84–86; R Upwell Christchurch 86–90; R March St Pet and March St Mary 90–98; TV Stanground and Farcet 98–01; V Farcet 01–04; V Farcet Hampton 04–08; rtd 08; PtO *Ely* 08–10; P-in-c Elton w Stibbington and Water Newton 10–12; PtO from 13. *10 Hemingford Crescent, Peterborough PE2 8LL*

SPENCER, Mrs Gail. b 57. STETS. **d** 03 **p** 04. NSM Wilton w Netherhampton and Fugglestone *Sarum* 03–06; NSM Radcliffe-on-Trent and Shelford *S'well* 06–07; Chapl Qu Medical Cen Nottm Univ Hosp NHS Trust from 07. *2 Gatcombe Close, Radcliffe-on-Trent, Nottingham NG12 2GG* T: 0115-933 6068 E: gailspencer@yahoo.co.uk

SPENCER, George. b 56. Cam Univ BA 77 MA 83 Leeds Metrop Univ DipSW 01. Coll of Resurr Mirfield 80. **d** 83 **p** 84. C Edin Old St Paul 83–85; P-in-c Edin St Ninian 85–92; Chapl Asst St Helens and Knowsley Hosps NHS Trust 92–93; Chapl 93–96; Chapl Calderdale and Huddersfield NHS Foundn Trust from 12; PtO *Wakef* 08–14; *Leeds* from 14. *Chaplaincy, Huddersfield Royal Infirmary, Acre Street, Huddersfield HD3 3EA* T: (01484) 342092 E: george.spencer@cht.nhs.uk

SPENCER, Canon Gilbert Hugh. b 43. Lon Univ BD 67. ALCD 66. **d** 67 **p** 68. C Bexleyheath Ch Ch *Roch* 67–73; C Bexley St Jo 73–76; P-in-c Bromley St Jo 76–78; V 78–81; R Chatham St Mary w St Jo 81–91; V Minster-in-Sheppey *Cant* 91–09; P-in-c Queenborough 99–05; AD Sittingbourne 94–00, 03–04 and 06–09; Hon Can Cant Cathl 99–09; Chapl Sheppey Community Hosp 91–98; Chapl Thames Gateway NHS Trust 98–09; rtd 09; PtO *Cant* from 09; Retirement Officer (Ashford Adnry) from 11. *75 Acorn Close, Kingsnorth, Ashford TN23 3HR* T: (01233) 501774 M: 07961-545934 E: gilbert_spencer@hotmail.com

SPENCER, Graham Lewis. b 48. St Jo Coll Nottm 80. **d** 82 **p** 83. C Leic St Anne 82–85; P-in-c Frisby-on-the-Wreake w Kirby Bellars 85–86; TV Melton Gt Framland 86–93; V Upper Wreake 93–99; V Glen Magna cum Stretton Magna etc 99–05; rtd 05; PtO *Leic* from 05. *18 Chetwynd Drive, Melton Mowbray LE13 0HU* T: (01664) 564266 E: grahamandtrish@talktalk.net

SPENCER, Ian John. b 61. Qu Coll Birm 03. **d** 05 **p** 06. C Gt Malvern St Mary *Worc* 05–08; Warden Dioc Retreat Ho (Holland Ho) Cropthorne from 08. *Holland House, Main Street, Cropthorne, Pershore WR10 3NB* T: (01386) 860330 E: ian.spencer@hollandhouse.org

SPENCER, Joan. b 50. **d** 98 **p** 99. OLM Nor St Mary Magd w St Jas from 98. *94 Mousehold Avenue, Norwich NR3 4RS* T: (01603) 404471 E: revjoan@virginmedia.com

SPENCER, John Edward. b 36. Bris Univ BA 60. Tyndale Hall Bris 60. **d** 61 **p** 62. C St Helens St Mark *Liv* 61–64; Japan 65–70; Area Sec CMS Leic and Pet 70–71; Warden and Chapl Rikkyo Japanese Sch Rudgwick 71–73; Hd Master and Chapl Pennthorpe Sch Rudgwick 74–96; NSM Rudgwick *Chich* 95–96; rtd 96; PtO *Chich* 96–98; *Guildf* 96–98; Hd Master Ardingly Coll Jun Sch Haywards Heath 97–98; Chapl Rowcroft Hospice Torquay 99–01; Hon C Bovey Tracey SS Pet, Paul and Thos w Hennock *Ex* 99–13; PtO *Nor* from 13. *19 Lamsey Lane, Heacham, King's Lynn PE31 7LA* T: (01485) 572029 E: jhnspncr@btinternet.com

SPENCER, Mrs Margot Patricia Winifred. b 48. Coll of St Matthias Bris CertEd 69. STETS 98. **d** 01 **p** 02. NSM Wonersh w Blackheath *Guildf* 01–05; NSM Busbridge and Hambledon from 05. *24 Park Road, Godalming GU7 1SH* T: (01483) 416333 E: margotspencer@btinternet.com

SPENCER, Peter Roy. b 40. CertEd. Sarum & Wells Th Coll 72. **d** 74 **p** 75. C Northampton St Alb *Pet* 74–77; TV Cov E 77–90; V Erdington St Barn *Birm* 90–02; TR Erdington 02–07; Chapl John Taylor Hospice Birm 90–07; rtd 07; PtO *Birm* from 07. *15 Poplar Road, Smethwick B66 4AW* T: 0121-429 4514 E: p.r.spencer@btinternet.com

SPENCER, Richard Dennis. b 50. Imp Coll Lon BSc 71. NTMTC 93. **d** 96 **p** 97. C Leek and Meerbrook *Lich* 96–00; P-in-c Shrewsbury H Trin w St Julian 00–10; V 10–15; TV Saffron Walden and Villages *Chelmsf* from 15. *The Vicarage, Radwinter Road, Ashdon, Saffron Walden CB10 2ET* T: (01799) 584171

SPENCER, Robert. b 48. St Jo Coll Nottm. **d** 93 **p** 94. NSM Ellon *Ab* 93–95 and from 99; NSM Cruden Bay 93–95; NSM Fraserburgh w New Pitsligo 95–99; P-in-c Oldmeldrum from 09. *12 Riverview Place, Ellon AB41 9NW* T: (01358) 723193 E: revbob.spencer@btinternet.com

SPENCER, Canon Stephen Christopher. b 60. Ball Coll Ox BA 82 DPhil 90. Edin Th Coll 88. **d** 90 **p** 91. C Harlesden All So *Lon* 90–93; P-in-c Nyamandhlovu Zimbabwe 93–99; R Bulawayo All SS 96–99; V Caton w Littledale *Blackb* 99–03; Dep Prin CBDTI 99–03; Tutor NOC 03–08; Tutor Yorks Min Course 08–12; Co-ord Yorks Regional Tr Partnership 08–10; P-in-c Brighouse and Clifton *Wakef* 10; V 11–14; Tutor Yorks Min Course 14–17; Vice Prin St Hild Coll from 17; Hon Can Musoma from 13. *St Hild College, Stocks Bank Road, Mirfield WF14 0BW* T: (01924) 481924 E: stephenspencer8@me.com

SPENCER, Stephen Nigel Howard. b 53. Pemb Coll Ox BA 75 MA 03 Jes Coll Cam PGCE 76. Trin Coll Bris 80. **d** 82 **p** 83. C Partington and Carrington *Ches* 82–85; C Brunswick *Man* 85–88; Chapl UEA *Nor* 88–92; rtd 92; PtO *Nor* 92–95; *Ely* from 19. *1 Forty Acre Road, Trumpington, Cambridge CB2 9AL*

SPENCER, Stephen Robert. b 61. NTMTC BA 08. **d** 08 **p** 09. C Langdon Hills *Chelmsf* 08–11; V Eastwood 11–19; V Bromley Common St Aug w St Luke *Roch* from 19. *The Vicarage, Southborough Lane, Bromley BR2 8AT* T: (020) 8467 1351 E: revsteve.spencer@btinternet.com

SPENCER, Canon Susan. b 47. EMMTC 87. **d** 90 **p** 94. Par Dn Cotgrave *S'well* 90–94; C 94–98; P-in-c Rolleston w Fiskerton, Morton and Upton 98–10; Asst Warden of Readers 98–07; AD S'well 07–10; Jt AD S'well and Newark 08–09; Hon Can S'well Minster 08–10; rtd 10; PtO *Linc* from 16. *15 Cherry Avenue, Branston, Lincoln LN4 1UY* T: (01522) 823947 E: suespencer47@googlemail.com

SPENCER, Mrs Susan Lesley. b 55. **d** 00 **p** 01. OLM Middleton and Thornham *Man* from 00. *1 Westbrook Close, Rochdale OL11 2XY* T: (01706) 350668 E: suelspencer@yahoo.co.uk

SPENCER, Sylvia. b 98. Chapl Grampian Univ Hosp NHS Trust 98–03; Chapl NHS Grampian from 04; NSM Ellon *Ab* from 99. *12 Riverview Place, Ellon AB41 9NW* T: (01358) 723193 E: revsylvia.spencer@btinternet.com

SPICER, David John. b 52. Sussex Univ BA 76 Lon Univ MTh 78. Westcott Ho Cam 77. **d** 79 **p** 80. C E Dulwich St Jo *S'wark* 79–82; C Richmond St Mary w St Matthias and St Jo 82–87; V Lewisham St Swithun 87–91; Chapl Community of All Hallows Ditchingham 91–17; rtd 17; PtO *Nor* from 18. *28 Pakefield Road, Lowestoft NR33 0HU* T: (01502) 580129

SPICER, Leigh Edwin. b 56. Birm Univ MA 02. Sarum & Wells Th Coll 78. **d** 81 **p** 82. C Harborne St Pet *Birm* 81–83; C Bloxwich *Lich* 83–87; Chapl RAF 87–11; PtO *S & B* from 12. *Dolyfelin, Llanbister Road, Llandrindod Wells LD1 6SP* T: (01597) 851109

SPICER, Canon Nicolas. b 61. Univ of Wales (Lamp) BA 84. Coll of Resurr Mirfield 84. **d** 86 **p** 87. C Westbury-on-Trym H Trin *Bris* 86–89; C Willesden Green St Andr and St Fran *Lon* 89–93; Chapl Asst Charing Cross Hosp Lon 93–94; Asst Chapl Hammersmith Hosps NHS Trust 94–97; R Ardleigh and The Bromleys *Chelmsf* 97–07; P-in-c Worksop Priory *S'well* 07–11; V from 11; P-in-c Worksop St Paul from 13; Hon Can S'well Minster from 17. *The Vicarage, Cheapside, Worksop S80 2HX* T: (01909) 472180 E: vicar@worksoppriory.co.uk

SPICER, Robert Patrick. b 39. FCA 68. SAOMC 94. **d** 97 **p** 98. NSM Riverside *Ox* 97–01; NSM Beaconsfield 01–07; PtO from 07. *16 Hayse Hill, Windsor SL4 5SZ* T: (01753) 864697 E: spicerrevrob@aol.com

SPIERS, The Ven Peter Hendry. b 61. St Jo Coll Dur BA 82. Ridley Hall Cam 83. **d** 86 **p** 87. C W Derby St Luke *Liv* 86–90; TV Everton St Pet 90–95; V Everton St Geo 95–05; P-in-c Gt Crosby St Luke 05–13; V 13–15; Adn Knowsley and Sefton from 15; Hon Can Liv Cathl from 06. *2A Monfa Road, Bootle L20 6BQ* E: pete@spiersfamily.eclipse.co.uk *or* pete.spiers@liverpool.anglican.org

SPIERS, Philip John. b 55. Reading Univ BSc 76. Ripon Coll Cuddesdon 10. **d** 13 **p** 14. NSM Darby Green and Eversley *Win* 13–17; NSM Minchinhampton w Box and Amberley *Glouc* from 17. *The Rectory, Amberley, Stroud GL5 5JG* T: (01453) 873176 E: spiersjohn@talk21.com

SPIKIN, Simon John Overington. b 48. Nottm Univ BTh 74 K Coll Lon MTh 80 Univ of Wales (Lamp) MA 11. Linc Th Coll 70. **d** 75 **p** 76. C Sawbridgeworth *St Alb* 75–79; C Odiham w S Warnborough and Long Sutton *Win* 79–81; R Dickleburgh w Thelveton w Frenze and Shimpling *Nor* 81–82; P-in-c Dickleburgh w Thelveton, Frenze, Shimpling etc 81–82; R Dickleburgh, Langmere, Shimpling, Thelveton etc 82–96; rtd 96; PtO *Cant* 01–12. *Marley Court, Kingston, Canterbury CT4 6JH* T: (01227) 832405

SPILLER, Canon David Roger. b 44. St Jo Coll Dur BA 70 Fitzw Coll Cam BA 72 MA 76 Nottm Univ DipAdEd 80. Ridley Hall Cam 70. **d** 73 **p** 74. C Bradf Cathl 73–77; C Stratford-on-Avon w Bishopton *Cov* 77–80; Chapl Geo Eliot Hosp Nuneaton 80–90; V Chilvers Coton w Astley *Cov* 80–90; RD Nuneaton 84–90; Prin Aston Tr Scheme 90–97; C Kings Norton *Birm* 98–99; C Shirley 99–00; Dir of Min and Dioc Dir of Ords *Cov* 00–11; Hon Can Cov Cathl 04–11; rtd 11; PtO *Cov* from 12; *Worc* from 12. *Pear Tree Cottage, Wick Road, Little Comberton, Pershore WR10 3EG* T: (01386) 710725 E: rogerspiller@btinternet.com

SPILSBURY, Stephen Ronald Paul. b 39. Nottm Univ BSc 69 MPhil 72 Bris Univ PhD 99. Linc Th Coll 71. **d** 64 **p** 65. In RC Ch 64–71; C Cricklade w Latton *Bris* 72–75; P-in-c Swindon All SS 76–81; V Lawrence Weston 81–95; RD Westbury and Severnside 89–91; rtd 99; PtO *Bris* from 03. *10 Woodside Grove, Bristol BS10 7RF* T: 0117-959 1079 E: paulspilsbury@btinternet.com

SPINDLER, Miss Jane Diana. b 54. Southn Univ BA 75 CertEd 76. Wycliffe Hall Ox 87. **d** 89 **p** 94. C Bishopsworth *Bris* 89–93; C Brislington St Luke 93–94; rtd 95; PtO *Bris* from 95. *143 Highridge Road, Bishopsworth, Bristol BS13 8HT* T: 0117-935 8137

SPINK, Mrs Diana. b 40. Ex Univ BA 63 PGCE 64. SAOMC 97. **d** 00 **p** 01. NSM Hemel Hempstead *St Alb* 00–10; rtd 10; PtO *St Alb* from 10. *39 Garland Close, Hemel Hempstead HP2 5HU* T: (01442) 262133 M: 07808-184321 E: diana2spink@hotmail.com

SPINKS, Prof Bryan Douglas. b 48. St Chad's Coll Dur BA 70 BD 79 K Coll Lon MTh 72 Dur Univ DD 88 Yale Univ Hon MA 98 FRHistS 85. **d** 75 **p** 76. C Witham *Chelmsf* 75–78; C Clacton St Jas 78–79; Chapl Chu Coll Cam 80–97; Affiliated Lect Div Cam Univ 82–97; Prof Liturg Studies Yale Univ and Fell Morse Coll 98–07; Prof Liturg Studies and Past Th Yale Univ from 07; PtO *Ely* from 02. *57 White Birch Drive, Guilford CT 06437, USA* E: bryan.spinks@yale.edu

SPINKS, Christopher George. b 53. Oak Hill Th Coll BA 88. **d** 88 **p** 89. C Hove Bp Hannington Memorial Ch *Chich* 88–92; Travelling Sec UCCF 92–95; Itinerant Min 95–98; Chapl Martlets Hospice Hove 98–11; TV Hove *Chich* 99–10; V Polegate from 11. *Church Office, St John's Church, Church Road, Polegate BN26 5BX* T: (01323) 483259 E: chrisgspinks@hotmail.com

SPINKS, John Frederick. b 40. Westmr Coll Ox MTh 97. Oak Hill Th Coll 79. **d** 82 **p** 83. NSM Roxbourne St Andr *Lon* 82–89; C Northwood H Trin 89–93; P-in-c Greenhill St Jo 93–96; V 96–04; rtd 04; PtO *Lon* from 04; *Ox* from 04; *St Alb* from 04. *Woodpecker Cottage, 232 Northwood Road, Harefield, Uxbridge UB9 6PT* T: (01895) 822477 M: 07711-635199 E: woodpecker232@tiscali.co.uk

SPITTLE, Christopher Bamford. b 74. St Jo Coll Dur BA 95. Ridley Hall Cam 97. **d** 99 **p** 00. C Netherton *Liv* 99–03; TR Sutton 03–11; P-in-c Skelmersdale St Paul from 11. *The Vicarage, Church Road, Skelmersdale WN8 8ND* T: (01695) 722087

SPITTLE, Robin. b 57. St Jo Coll Nottm 84. **d** 86 **p** 87. C Ipswich St Fran *St E* 86–91; Min Shotley St Mary CD 91–92; R Shotley 92–99; P-in-c Copdock w Washbrook and Belstead 93–99; V Kesgrave from 99. *4 Wades Grove, Kesgrave, Ipswich IP5 2EF* T: (01473) 623388 E: robinspittle@btinternet.com

SPIVEY, Colin. b 35. ACII 61. Oak Hill Th Coll 74. **d** 76 **p** 77. C Egham *Guildf* 76–79; C Edgware *Lon* 79–83; R Haworth *Bradf* 83–95; Sub Chapl HM Pris Leeds 94–99; V Thorpe Edge *Bradf* 95–00; rtd 01; PtO *Ripon* 01–14; *Leeds* from 14. *2 Woodhill View, Wetherby LS22 6PP* T: (01937) 581508 E: sawetherby@live.co.uk

SPOKES, David Lawrence. b 57. Nottm Univ BCombStuds 85. Linc Th Coll 82. **d** 85 **p** 86. C Rushall *Lich* 85–89; TV Thornaby on Tees *York* 89–93; R Yardley Hastings, Denton and Grendon etc *Pet* 02–14; Rural Adv Northn Adnry 05–14; P-in-c Howden-le-Wear and Hunwick *Dur* 14–16; P-in-c Willington and Sunnybrow 14–16; V Hunwick and Willington from

16; AD Stanhope from 18. *The Rectory, Willington, Crook DL15 0DE* T: (01388) 747914 E: mail@davidspokes.com *or* vicar@hunwickandwillington.org.uk

SPONG, Bennett Jarod. b 49. Coll of Charleston (USA) BA 74 Thames Poly PGCE 87. **d** 05 **p** 06. OLM Charlton *S'wark* from 05. *10 Mayhill Road, London SE7 7JQ* T: (020) 8853 4457 E: bjspong@hotmail.com

SPONG, Mrs Hilary Vida. b 44. Ex Univ BTh 09 Sarum Coll MA 16. SWMTC 06. **d** 09 **p** 10. NSM St Stythians w Perranarworthal and Gwennap *Truro* 09–12; NSM Feock 11–12; NSM Devoran 11–12; NSM Perranzabuloe and Crantock w Cubert 12–14; rtd 14; PtO *Truro* from 14. *Nansough Manor, Ladock, Truro TR2 4PB* T: (01726) 883315 M: 07855-781134 E: hilaryspong@sent.com

SPONG, Terence John. *See* MESLEY-SPONG, Terence John

SPOOR, Nigel Christopher Oliver. b 51. Univ Coll Dur BA 73 Heythrop Coll Lon MA 16. **d** 18 **p** 19. C Prestwood and Gt Hampden *Ox* from 18. *30 Westwood Drive, Amersham HP6 6RJ* T: (01494) 765108 M: 07724-122981 E: nigel.spoor@talktalk.net *or* nigel@htprestwood.org.uk

SPRATT, Robert Percival. b 31. FCIOB MRSPH ACABE. Carl Dioc Tr Inst 84. **d** 87 **p** 88. NSM Kendal St Thos *Carl* 87–89; Chapl HM Pris Preston 89–96; Dir Miss to Pris from 96; Asst Chapl HM Pris Wymott 97–04; Sessional Chapl HM Pris Lanc 04–06; Asst Chapl HM Pris Haverigg from 06; PtO *Blackb* from 96; *Carl* from 97. *Missions to Prisons, PO Box 37, Kendal LA9 6GF* T/F: (01539) 720475 E: bob@greenstones.org.uk

SPRAY, John William. b 29. Sarum & Wells Th Coll 71. **d** 73 **p** 74. C Clayton *Lich* 73–77; V Hartshill 77–82; P-in-c Aston 82–83; P-in-c Stone St Mich 82–83; P-in-c Stone St Mich w Aston St Sav 83–84; R 84–90; rtd 90; PtO *Lich* 90–16. *2 Belvoir Avenue, Trentham, Stoke-on-Trent ST4 8SY* T: (01782) 644959

SPRAY, Mrs Josephine Ann. b 44. Nottm Coll of Educn TCert 65. SAOMC 95. **d** 98 **p** 99. NSM Watford St Mich *St Alb* 98–02; P-in-c Turvey 02–10; rtd 11; PtO *St Alb* from 11; *Ox* from 11. *121 High Street, Olney MK46 4EF* T: (01234) 713726 E: jo-spray@sky.com

SPRAY, Mrs Karen Patricia. b 55. **d** 06 **p** 07. NSM Littleham w Exmouth *Ex* 06–07; C Honiton, Gittisham, Combe Raleigh, Monkton etc 07–09; P-in-c Clyst St Mary, Clyst St George etc 09–13; C Lympstone and Woodbury w Exton 09–13; C Aylesbeare, Rockbeare, Farringdon etc 09–13; V Aylesbeare, Clyst St George, Clyst St Mary etc 13–17; Hon C E w W Harptree and Hinton Blewett *B & W* from 17. *3 Glanville Drive, Hinton Blewett, Bristol BS39 5GF* T: (01761) 452017 E: unitedparish@revdkaren.org.uk

SPRAY, Richard Alan. b 43. EMMTC 85. **d** 88 **p** 89. NSM Cotgrave *S'well* 88–96; P-in-c Barton in Fabis 96–01; P-in-c Thrumpton 96–01; P-in-c Kingston and Ratcliffe-on-Soar 96–01; P-in-c Blyth 01–02; P-in-c Scrooby 01–02; V Blyth and Scrooby w Ranskill 02–10; AD Bawtry 06–09; rtd 11; PtO *Sheff* from 12; *S'well* from 18. *Thorn Lea, Mattersey Road, Ranskill, Retford DN22 8ND* T: (01777) 816048 M: 07971-637670

SPREADBRIDGE, Alison Margaret. b 50. Open Univ BSc 96. SEITE 04. **d** 07 **p** 08. C Dartford St Edm *Roch* 07–11; P-in-c Gillingham H Trin 11–13; rtd 13. *16 Murhill Lane, Plymouth PL9 7FN* T: 07979-013559

SPREADBRIDGE, Paul Andrew. b 49. Greenwich Univ CertEd 02 Kent Univ BA 05. SEITE 99. **d** 98 **p** 03. In RC Ch 98–01; NSM Chatham St Steph *Roch* 02–04; C Orpington All SS 04–07; V Bexley St Mary 07–11; R Chelsfield 11–13; P-in-c Charlestown *Truro* 13–16; P-in-c Par 13–16; rtd 16; PtO *Truro* 16–17; C Stoke Damerel and Devonport St Aubyn *Ex* 17–18. *16 Murhill Lane, Plymouth PL9 7FN*

SPREADBURY, Canon Joanna Mary Magdalen (Jo). b 65. Magd Coll Ox BA 90 MA 93 K Coll Lon PhD 99. Westcott Ho Cam MA 99. **d** 99 **p** 00. C Watford St Mich *St Alb* 99–03; C Leavesden 03–06; V Abbots Langley 06–15; Can Res Portsm Cathl from 15. *51 High Street, Old Portsmouth PO1 2LU* T: 023-9282 3300 ext 226 E: canonprecentor@portsmouthcathedral.org.uk

SPREDBURY, Mary Jane. b 59. Open Univ BA 99. STETS 03. **d** 06 **p** 07. NSM Acton St Mary *Lon* from 06. *6 St Catherine's Court, Bedford Road, London W4 1UH* T: (02) 8995 8879 M: 07803-759886 E: spredbury@btinternet.com

SPRIGGS, John David Robert. b 36. BNC Ox BA 58 MA 63. S'wark Ord Course 73. **d** 75 **p** 76. LtO *Ox* 75–97; Chapl Pangbourne Coll 95–97; PtO *Linc* 97–18; *Eur* from 18. *Glen House, Great Ponton Road, Boothby Pagnell, Grantham NG33 4DH* T: (01476) 585756

SPRINGATE, Paul Albert Edward. b 48. Oak Hill Th Coll 81. **d** 83 **p** 84. C Pennycross *Ex* 83–87; TV Sileby, Cossington and Seagrave *Leic* 87–96; Chapl and Warden Harnhill Healing Cen 96–13; Bp's Adv on Healing *Glouc* 03–13; rtd 13; PtO *Glouc* from 17. *111 North Home Road, Cirencester GL7 1DU* M: 07748-846164

SPRINGBETT, John Howard. b 47. Pemb Coll Cam BA 70 MA 74. Ridley Hall Cam 70. **d** 72 **p** 73. C Ulverston St Mary w H Trin *Carl* 72–76; V Dewsbury Moor *Wakef* 76–84; V Hoddesdon *St Alb* 84–00; RD Cheshunt 94–00; TR Shelf w Buttershaw St Aid *Bradf* 00–03; V Woodford Bridge *Chelmsf* 03–14; rtd 14. *Walton Farmhouse, 68 Main Street, Walton, Street BA16 9QF* T: (01458) 899641 E: springbett25@hotmail.com

SPRINGER, Richard Kevin. b 76. Middx Univ BA 98 Birkbeck Coll Lon MSc 06 Cam Univ BTh 13. Westcott Ho Cam 11. **d** 13 **p** 14. C De Beauvoir Town St Pet *Lon* 13–16; C St Geo-in-the-East w St Paul 16–18; R from 18. *St George-in-the-East Rectory, 16 Cannon Street Road, London E1 0BH* T: (020) 7481 1345 M: 07730-597513 E: richard.springer@london.anglican.org *or* richard@stgeorgeintheeast.org

✠**SPRINGETT, The Rt Revd Robert Wilfred.** b 62. Nottm Univ BTh 89 Lon Univ MA 92. Linc Th Coll 86. **d** 89 **p** 90 **c** 16. C Colchester St Jas, All SS, St Nic and St Runwald *Chelmsf* 89–92; C Basildon St Martin w Nevendon 92–94; P-in-c Belhus Park and S Ockendon 94–01; RD Thurrock 98–01; R Wanstead St Mary w Ch Ch 01–10; AD Redbridge 08–10; Hon Can Chelmsf Cathl 08–10; Adn Cheltenham *Glouc* 10–16; Suff Bp Tewkesbury from 16. *Bishop's House, 3 Hill Road, Gloucester GL4 6ST* T: (01452) 489456 M: 07962-273544 E: btewkesbury@glosdioc.org.uk

SPRINGETT, Simon Paul. b 56. Warwick Univ LLB 78 Dur Univ MA 10 Plymouth Univ PGCE 07. Wycliffe Hall Ox 78. **d** 81 **p** 82. C Harlow St Mary and St Hugh w St Jo the Bapt *Chelmsf* 81–84; C Gt Clacton 84–86; R Rayne 86–91; Chapl RN 91–14; Chief Exec Officer Aggie Weston's 14–15; Chapl RNR from 14; PtO *Portsm* 14–16; *Ex* from 14. *99 Eggbuckland Road, Plymouth PL3 5JR* T: (01752) 248341 E: simonspringett@yahoo.com

SPRINGFORD, Patrick Francis Alexander. b 45. Wycliffe Hall Ox 71. **d** 74 **p** 75. C Finchley Ch Ch *Lon* 74–79; CF 79–00; Rtd Officer Chapl RAChD 00–12; PtO *Eur* from 12; *Cant* 13–17; *Glouc* from 18. *15 Grouse Gardens, Brockworth, Gloucester GL3 4SE* E: patrick.springford@live.co.uk

SPRINGTHORPE, Canon David Frederick. b 47. Open Univ BA. AKC 72. **d** 73 **p** 74. C Dartford St Alb *Roch* 73–77; C Biggin Hill 77–80; R Ash 80–89; R Ridley 80–89; R Eynsford w Farningham and Lullingstone 89–94; V Barnehurst 94–04; RD Erith 98–04; R Keston 04–12; Hon Can Roch Cathl 02–12; rtd 12; PtO *Roch* from 12; *Cant* from 13. *38 Alvis Avenue, Herne Bay CT6 8AR* T: (01227) 219853 E: david.springthorpe@btopenworld.com

SPROATS, Mrs Beverley Louise. b 73. St Cath Coll Ox BA 94 MA 98 Cam Univ BTh 13. Ridley Hall Cam 11. **d** 13 **p** 14. C Yeadon *Leeds* 13–17; R Jersey St Jo *Win* from 17. *St John's Rectory, La rue des Landes, St John, Jersey JE3 4AF* T: (01534) 861677 M: 07986-937329 E: beverleysproats@gmail.com

SPROSTON, Bernard Melvin. b 37. Cranmer Hall Dur 77. **d** 79 **p** 80. C Westlands St Andr *Lich* 79–82; P-in-c Heage *Derby* 82–87; V Heath 87–02; rtd 02; PtO *Derby* from 02. *2 Upwood Close, Holmehall, Chesterfield S40 4UP* T: (01246) 207401 E: bernel@hotmail.co.uk *or* bernel37@outlook.com

SPRY, Miss Elisabeth Roselie. b 47. Open Univ BA 82. **d** 06 **p** 07. OLM Stratton St Mary w Stratton St Michael etc *Nor* 06–16; OLM Long Stratton and Pilgrim TM 16–17; PtO from 17. *13 Whitehouse Drive, Long Stratton, Norwich NR15 2TD* T: (01508) 530478 E: erspry@yahoo.co.uk

SPURGEON, Michael Paul. b 53. Open Univ BA 02 MIEx. Linc Th Coll 83. **d** 85 **p** 86. C Lillington *Cov* 85–89; C Min Can Ripon Cathl 89–95; R Lower Nidderdale 95–14; *Leeds* from 14. *Lower Nidderdale Rectory, 6 Old Church Green, Kirk Hammerton, York YO26 8DL* T: (01423) 331142

SPURR, Andrew. b 58. St Jo Coll Dur BA 80. Qu Coll Birm 92. **d** 93 **p** 94. C Rainham *Roch* 93–96; C Stansted Mountfitchet *Chelmsf* 96; C Stansted Mountfitchet w Birchanger and Farnham 97; R 97–06; V Evesham w Norton and Lenchwick *Worc* from 06. *Church House, Market Place, Evesham WR11 4RW* T: (01386) 446219 E: vicar@evesham.church

SPURRELL, John Mark. b 34. CCC Ox BA 57 MA 61 FSA 87. Linc Th Coll 58. **d** 60 **p** 61. C Tilbury Docks *Chelmsf* 60–65; C Boston *Linc* 65–76; R Stow in Lindsey 76–85; P-in-c Willingham 76–85; P-in-c Coates 76–85; P-in-c Brightwell w Sotwell *Ox* 85–97; rtd 97; PtO *B & W* from 97. *10 The Liberty, Wells BA5 2SU* T: (01749) 678966 M: 07929-725502 E: mspurrell@gmail.com

SPURWAY, Christine Frances. b 54. Cuddesdon Coll 96. **d** 98 **p** 99. C Coulsdon St Andr *S'wark* 98–02; P-in-c Riddlesdown 02–05; V 05–16; RD Croydon S 04–16; rtd 16; PtO *S'wark* from 16; *Roch* from 17. *6 Highfield Close, Pembury, Tunbridge Wells TN2 4HQ* T: (01892) 824563 E: rev.christine54@btinternet.com

SQUIRE, Geoffrey Frank. b 36. Ex & Truro NSM Scheme. **d** 83 **p** 84. NSM Barnstaple *Ex* 83–98; NSM Swimbridge, W Buckland, Landkey, and E Buckland from 98. *Little Cross, Northleigh Hill, Goodleigh, Barnstaple EX32 7NR* T: (01271) 344935 E: gfsquire@yahoo.co.uk

SQUIRE, Susan Elizabeth. *See* WIGGINS, Susan Elizabeth

SQUIRES, John Wallace Howden. b 45. Sydney Univ BA 67 DipEd 68 MTh 97 PhD 05 Lon Univ BD 75. Moore Th Coll Sydney ThL 74. **d** 76 **p** 76. C Normanhurst Australia 76–78; C Luton St Mary *St Alb* 78–79; Chapl Home of Divine Healing Crowhurst 79–80; C-in-c Putney Australia 80–82; R Longueville 83–97; Dir Inst for Values Univ of NSW 97–02; Dir Aus Human Rights Cen Univ of NSW 03–05. *22 Moorehead Street, Redfern NSW 2016, Australia* T: (0061) (2) 9690 0206 *or* (2) 9385 3637 F: 9385 1778 M: 41-822 6976 E: j.squires@unsw.edu.au

SQUIRES, The Ven Malcolm. b 46. St Chad's Coll Dur BA 72. Cuddesdon Coll 72. **d** 74 **p** 75. C Headingley *Ripon* 74–77; C Stanningley St Thos 77–80; V Bradshaw *Wakef* 80–85; V Ripponden 85–89; V Barkisland w W Scammonden 85–89; V Mirfield 89–96; TR Wrexham *St As* 96–02; Hon Can St As Cathl 00–01; Adn Wrexham 01–10; R Llandegla 02–10; Bp's Chapl 10–11; Can Cursal St As Cathl 10–11; rtd 11; PtO *St As* from 11. *1A Penrhyn Park, Penrhyn Bay, Llandudno LL30 3HW* T: (01492) 544560 M: 07966-200894 E: malcolm@squires1a.plus.com

SQUIRES, Rachel Louise. *See* SCHEFFER, Rachel Louise Squires

SRIKANTHA, Stephen. b 86. K Coll Lon BA 11 MA 12 PhD 16. Westcott Ho Cam 13. **d** 16 **p** 18. C Kennington St Jo w St Jas *S'wark* 16–17; C Redhill St Jo from 17. *6 Artillery Court, 2 Hooley Lane, Redhill RH1 6ET* T: (01737) 511654 M: 07747-351360 E: stephen.srikantha@outlook.com

STABLES, Katharine Ruth. b 45. R Holloway Coll Lon BA 67. WMMTC 90. **d** 93 **p** 94. NSM Knutton *Lich* 93–05; NSM Silverdale and Alsagers Bank 93–96; Soc Resp Officer 96–99; Officer for NSMs 03–05; P-in-c Startforth and Bowes and Rokeby w Brignall *Ripon* 05–09; rtd 10; PtO *Dur* from 10; *Leeds* from 11. *15 Greenbank, Eggleston, Barnard Castle DL12 0BQ* T: (01833) 650006 E: kruth@btopenworld.com

STACE, Michael John. b 44. Open Univ BA 80. SEITE 94. **d** 97 **p** 98. NSM Cant St Dunstan w H Cross 97–01; NSM Cant All SS 01–06; P-in-c 06–14; rtd 14; PtO *Cant* from 15. *124 St Stephen's Road, Canterbury CT2 7JS* T: (01227) 451169 F: 455627 M: 07831-174900 E: michaelstace31@gmail.com

STACEY, Gillian. *See* STILL, Gillian

STACEY, Graham John. b 68. Lon Bible Coll BA 97. Ripon Coll Cuddesdon 05. **d** 08 **p** 09. C Beedon and Peasemore w W Ilsley and Farnborough *Ox* 08–10; C E Downland 10–11; PtO 12–18. *The Vicarage, 58 Cashes Green Road, Stroud GL5 4RA* M: 07753-687389 E: graham@thestaceys.tv

STACEY, Mrs Kate Elizabeth. b 73. Lon Bible Coll BTh 97. Ripon Coll Cuddesdon 05. **d** 08 **p** 09. C E Downland *Ox* 08–11; V Wychwood 11–18; TR Stroud Team *Glouc* from 18. *The Vicarage, 58 Cashes Green Road, Stroud GL5 4RA*

STACEY, Mrs Rosalind Ruth (La). b 54. New Hall Cam MA 81 Bulmershe Coll of HE PGCE 94. Ripon Coll Cuddesdon 09. **d** 11 **p** 12. C Easthampstead *Ox* 11–14; V Eton w Eton Wick, Boveney and Dorney from 14. *The Vicarage, 69A Eton Wick Road, Eton Wick, Windsor SL4 6NE* T: (01753) 852268 E: revlastacey@gmail.com

STACEY (née O'BRIEN), Mrs Shelagh Ann. b 55. RGN 83 Bedf Coll Lon BSc 77. NOC 89. **d** 92 **p** 94. Par Dn S Elmsall *Wakef* 92–94; C 94–95; C Carleton 95–97; P-in-c 97–99; C E Hardwick 95–97; P-in-c 97–99; V Carleton and E Hardwick 99–14; *Leeds* from 14. *The Vicarage, 10 East Close, Pontefract WF8 3NS* T: (01977) 702478

STACEY, The Very Revd Victor George. b 44. NUI BA 69 QUB MTh. CITC 72. **d** 72 **p** 73. C Derriaghy *Conn* 72–76; C Knock *D & D* 76–79; I Ballymacarrett St Martin 79–86; I Dublin Santry w Glasnevin *D & G* 86–94; I Dun Laoghaire 95–12; Bp's Dom Chapl 90–12; Prov and Dioc Registrar 95–12; Preb Maynooth St Patr Cathl Dublin 97–12; Dean St Patr Cathl Dublin 12–16; rtd 16. *27 The Poplars, Monkstown Valley, Monkstown, Co Dublin, A94 Y2W1, Republic of Ireland* T: (00353) (1) 563 7958 M: 87-996 1440 E: victorgstacey@gmail.com

STACY, Christine Rosemary. b 49. UEA BSc 70 Keswick Hall Coll PGCE 71 Univ of Wales (Ban) MSc 75 Northumbria Univ PhD 94. **d** 10 **p** 11. OLM Upper Coquetdale *Newc* 10–18; rtd 18; PtO *Newc* from 18. *Ovenstone, Sharperton, Morpeth NE65 7AT* T: (01669) 640382 E: rosie.stacy65@gmail.com

STAFF, Mrs Jean. b 44. CertEd 64. EMMTC 81. **dss** 84 **d** 87 **p** 94. Old Brumby *Linc* 84–88; C 87–88; C Gainsborough St Geo 88–91; Dn-in-c 91–94; P-in-c 94–96; P-in-c Haxey 96–97; P-in-c Owston 96–97; V Haxey 97–04; V Owston 97–04; rtd 04; PtO *Linc* from 17. *5 South Furlong Croft, Epworth, Doncaster DN9 1GB* T: (01427) 871422

STAFF, Susan. *See* JACKSON, Susan

STAFFORD, Christopher James. b 67. Birm Univ BSc 88 PhD 92. St Jo Coll Nottm MA 98. **d** 99 **p** 00. C Westbrook St Phil *Liv* 99–03; R Newchurch w Croft 03–14; TV Newton 14–16; TR from 16. *All Saints' Vicarage, 243 Crow Lane East, Newton-le-Willows WA12 9UB* T: (01925) 271421 E: chrisj.stafford@virginmedia.com

STAFFORD, David George. b 45. Qu Coll Birm 75. **d** 77 **p** 78. C Chesterfield SS Aug *Derby* 77–80; C Ranmoor *Sheff* 80–83; V Bolton-upon-Dearne 83–11; rtd 11. *4 Rylestone Court, Sheffield S12 4NJ* T: 0114-248 0993

STAFFORD, Matthew Charles. b 73. Wilson Carlile Coll 94 Ripon Coll Cuddesdon 99. **d** 99 **p** 00. C High Wycombe *Ox* 99–02; P-in-c Wrockwardine Wood *Lich* 02–04; R Oakengates and Wrockwardine Wood 04–15; TR Wenlock *Heref* from 15. *The Rectory, 1 New Road, Much Wenlock TF13 6EQ* T: (01952) 727396 M: 07889-376865 E: wenlockrectory@btinternet.com

STAFFORD, Canon Richard William. b 46. Ringsent Tech Inst TCert 69. CITC 96. **d** 99 **p** 00. NSM Annagh w Drumgoon, Ashfield etc *K, E & A* 99–07; P-in-c Drumgoon 07–12; Can Kilmore Cathl 08–12; rtd 12. *12 Cherrymount, Keadue Lane, Cavan, Co Cavan, Republic of Ireland* T: (00353) (49) 437 1173 M: 87-240 4630 E: rwstafford@yahoo.com

STAFFORD, Area Bishop of. *See* ANNAS, The Rt Revd Geoffrey Peter

STAGG, Jeremy Michael. b 47. Leeds Univ BSc 69 Fontainebleau MBA 77 Southn Univ BTh 94. Sarum & Wells Th Coll 90. **d** 92 **p** 93. C Basing *Win* 92–96; P-in-c Barton, Pooley Bridge and Martindale *Carl* 96–99; Hon CMS Rep 96–99; C Burgh-by-Sands and Kirkbampton w Kirkandrews etc *Carl* 99–00; C Barony of Burgh 00–01; P-in-c Distington 01–05; Dioc Past Sec 00–05; TR Cheswardine, Childs Ercall, Hales, Hinstock etc *Lich* 05–10; RD Hodnet 06–11; rtd 10; PtO *Lich* from 11. *27 Fishers Lock, Newport TF10 7ST* T: (01952) 813735

STAGG, Roy Ernest. b 48. **d** 01 **p** 02. OLM Birchington w Acol and Minnis Bay *Cant* 01–04; OLM St Laur in Thanet 04–05. *7 Minster Road, Acol, Birchington CT7 0JB* T: (01843) 841551 M: 07802-406066 E: roystagg@ymail.com

STAGG, Russell James. b 69. SEITE 08. **d** 11 **p** 12. NSM Haggerston St Chad *Lon* 11–12; C Holborn St Alb w Saffron Hill St Pet 12–15; P-in-c Roughey *Chich* 15–17; V Colgate and Roffey from 17. *The Vicarage, 8 Rainbow Field, Faygate, Horsham RH12 0AR* T: (01293) 852870 M: 07834-735002 E: father.russell@me.com

STAINER, David John. b 58. RCM BMus 80. St Mellitus Coll BA 11. **d** 11 **p** 12. NSM Collier Row St Jas and Havering-atte-Bower *Chelmsf* 11–15; NSM Rainham w Wennington from 15. *29 Cormorant Walk, Hornchurch RM12 5HE* T: (01708) 550053 M: 07870-820314 E: davidjstainer@hotmail.co.uk

STAINER, Helene Lindsay. b 59. SWMRC 01. **d** 04 **p** 05. NSM Ivybridge w Harford *Ex* 04–09; P-in-c Milverton w Halse and Fitzhead *B & W* 09–10; R Milverton w Halse, Fitzhead and Ash Priors from 10; RD Tone from 19. *The Vicarage, Parsonage Lane, Milverton, Taunton TA4 1LR* T: (01823) 400305 E: helenestainer@aol.com

STAINER, Canon Richard Bruce. b 62. Anglia Ruskin Univ MA 09. Linc Th Coll 92. **d** 94 **p** 95. C N Walsham w Antingham *Nor* 94–97; R Cogenhoe and Gt and Lt Houghton w Brafield *Pet* 97–14; RD Wootton 01–07; V Higham Ferrers w Chelveston 14–19; R Blisworth, Alderton, Grafton Regis etc from 19; Can Pet Cathl from 12. *The Rectory, 37 High Street, Blisworth, Northampton NN7 3BJ* E: canon.stainer@gmail.com

STAINES, Edward Noel. b 26. Trin Coll Ox BA 48 BSc 49 MA 52 MSc 85. Chich Th Coll 51 57. **d** 57 **p** 58. C Eastbourne St Mary *Chich* 57–61; V Amberley w N Stoke 61–70; V Forest Row 70–75; V Bexhill St Aug 75–79; TR Ovingdean w Rottingdean and Woodingdean 79–85; V Rottingdean 85–86; Chapl Gtr Lisbon *Eur* 88; Chapl Marseille 90; rtd 90; PtO *Worc* 86–09. *4 Little Penny Rope, Pershore WR10 1QN* T: (01386) 554382

STAINSBY, Alan. b 48. NEOC 01. **d** 04 **p** 05. NSM Hart w Elwick Hall *Dur* 04–06; NSM Haswell, Shotton and Thornley 06–18; NSM Haswell and Shotton from 18. *6 Church View, Shotton Colliery, Durham DH6 2YD* T: 0191-526 5200

STALKER, William John. b 49. NOC 89. **d** 91 **p** 92. C Formby H Trin *Liv* 91–94; V Stoneycroft All SS 94–03; Chapl R Liv Univ Hosp NHS Trust 94–03; P-in-c Lowton St Mary *Liv* 03–13; TR Lowton and Golborne 13–14; rtd 14. *Hilltop House, Oubas Hill, Ulverston LA12 7LB* E: flostalker@aol.com

STALLARD, John Charles. b 34. Selw Coll Cam BA 58 MA 62. Ripon Hall Ox 62. **d** 64 **p** 65. C Hall Green Ascension *Birm* 64–66; C Sutton Coldfield H Trin 66–68; C-in-c Brandwood

CD 68–71; Chapl Dame Allan's Schs Newc 71–74; V Warley Woods *Birm* 75–84; TR Droitwich *Worc* 84–87; P-in-c Dodderhill 84–87; TR Droitwich Spa 87–94; V Pensnett 94–00; rtd 00; PtO *St D* 00–07; *St As* from 09. *Craigievar, Abbey Road, Llangollen LL20 8SN* T: (01978) 860654 E: dapharles@gmail.com

STALLARD, The Ven Mary Kathleen Rose. b 67. Selw Coll Cam BA 88 Lon Inst of Educn PGCE 90. Qu Coll Birm 91. **d** 93 **p** 97. C Newport St Matt *Mon* 93–96; P-in-c Ysbyty Cynfyn w Llantrisant and Eglwys Newydd *St D* 96–97; V 97–02; Min Can and Chapl St As Cathl 02–03; Can Res St As Cathl 03–11; Dir of Ords and Co-ord of Minl Formation St As 10–11; Chapl St Jos High Sch Wrexham 11–18; Adn Ban from 18; C Llandudno from 18. *The Rectory, 27 Church Walks, Llandudno LL30 2HL* T: (01492) 876624 M: 07779-418007 E: faithdevwxm@gmail.com *or* archdeacon.bangor@churchinwales.org.uk

STALLEY, Brian Anthony. b 38. Oak Hill Th Coll 60. **d** 63 **p** 64. C Summerstown *S'wark* 63–70; Surrey BFBS Sec 70–73; Manager Action Cen BFBS 73–76; R Branston *Linc* 76–91; rtd 91; PtO *Linc* from 91. *6 Sunningdale Grove, Washingborough, Lincoln LN4 1SP* T: (01522) 794164 F: 794663 M: 07941-508445 E: patchyann104@gmail.com

STAMFORD, Dean of. *Vacant*

STAMP, Andrew Nicholas. b 44. Ex Univ BA 67. Sarum Th Coll 67. **d** 69 **p** 70. C S Beddington St Mich *S'wark* 69–73; Tutor Sarum & Wells Th Coll 73–76; Chapl RN 76–81; C-in-c W Leigh CD *Portsm* 81–82; V W Leigh 82–87; R Botley 87–95; V Curdridge and R Durley 94–95; P-in-c Compton, the Mardens, Stoughton and Racton *Chich* 95–08; P-in-c Stansted 95–08; Tutor Bp Otter Coll Chich 95–98; Dioc Rural Officer *Chich* 00–08; rtd 08; Hon C Arlington, Berwick, Selmeston w Alciston etc *Chich* 11–13; PtO *Portsm* from 15; *Chich* from 17. *36 Up Marden, Chichester PO18 9JR* T: (01243) 535010 E: a.stamp@btinternet.com

STAMP, Canon Ian Jack. b 47. Aston Tr Scheme 82 NOC 83. **d** 86 **p** 87. C Tonge w Alkrington *Man* 86–89; V Heywood St Marg 89–98; P-in-c Heywood St Luke w All So 96–98; TR Heywood 98–01; V Bury St Jo w St Mark 01–10; V Walmersley Road, Bury 10–12; Borough Dean Bury 10–12; Hon Can Man Cathl 11–12; rtd 12; PtO *Man* from 12. *10 Unity Crescent, Heywood OL10 3DW* T: (01706) 367788 M: 07816-425881 E: ianstamp10@btinternet.com

STAMP, Philip Andrew. b 53. Linc Th Coll 86. **d** 88 **p** 89. C Barton w Peel Green *Man* 88–91; R Blackley H Trin 91–19; P-in-c Lightbowne 04–19; rtd 19; PtO *Man* from 19. *29 Mough Lane, Chadderton, Oldham OL9 9PJ*

STAMPS, Canon Dennis Lee. b 55. Biola Univ (USA) BA 78 Trin Evang Div Sch (USA) MDiv 83 MA 87 Dur Univ PhD 95. Westcott Ho Cam 90. **d** 92 **p** 93. C Moseley St Mary *Birm* 92–96; Dir WMMTC 96–01; Dean Qu Coll Birm 01–02; Can Res St Alb 02–12; Minl Development Officer 02–12; Dir Min 11–12; R Harpenden St Nic from 12. *The Rectory, 9 Rothamsted Avenue, Harpenden AL5 2DD* T: (01582) 712202 E: dstampsuk@aol.com

✠**STANCLIFFE, The Rt Revd David Staffurth.** b 42. Trin Coll Ox BA 65 MA 68 Lambeth DD 04. Cuddesdon Coll 65. **d** 67 **p** 68 **c** 93. C Armley St Bart *Ripon* 67–70; Chapl Clifton Coll Bris 70–77; Dir of Ords and Can Res Portsm Cathl 77–82; Provost Portsm 82–93; Bp Sarum 93–10; rtd 10; Hon Asst Bp Eur from 11; Hon Asst Bp Dur from 13. *Butts House, 15 The Butts, Stanhope, Bishop Auckland DL13 2UQ* T: (01388) 526912 E: david.stancliffe@hotmail.com

STAND, Andrew George. b 68. St Jo Coll Dur BA 06. Cranmer Hall Dur 04. **d** 06 **p** 07. C Bromsgrove St Jo *Worc* 06–09; TV Gornal and Sedgley 09–16; TV Worc SE from 16. *The Vicarage, 11 Jasmine Close, Worcester WR5 3LU* T: (01905) 358150 E: andy.stand@sky.com

STANDEN, David Charles. b 68. K Coll Lon BA 91 AKC 91 PGCE 92 Lon Univ PhD 00. Westcott Ho Cam 01. **d** 03 **p** 04. C Prittlewell *Chelmsf* 03–07; P-in-c Stratton and Launcells *Truro* 07–11; P-in-c Bude Haven and Marhamchurch 09–11; R Edin St Mich and All SS 11–13; Chapl K Edw Sch Witley from 13. *King Edward's School, Petworth Road, Wormey, Godalming GU8 5SG* T: (01428) 686700 E: d.c.standen@btinternet.com

STANDEN, Mark Jonathan. b 63. LMH Ox BA 85 Cam Univ BA 94 Barrister 86. Ridley Hall Cam 92. **d** 95 **p** 96. C Sevenoaks St Nic *Roch* 95–99; R Angmering *Chich* from 99; RD Arundel and Bognor from 08; Acting Adn Chich 18–19. *The Rectory, Rectory Lane, Angmering, Littlehampton BN16 4JU* T: (01903) 896417 E: markstanden@stmargaretsangmering.church

STANDEN McDOUGAL, Canon John Anthony Phelps. b 33. AKC 58. **d** 59 **p** 60. C Ipswich St Marg *St E* 59–63; C Bury St Edmunds St Mary 63–65; C Wadhurst *Chich* 65–70; C Tidebrook 65–70; R Tollard Royal w Farnham *Sarum* 70–81; P-in-c Gussage St Michael and Gussage All Saints 71–76; R

76–81; RD Milton and Blandford 81–86; R Tollard Royal w Farnham, Gussage St Michael etc 82–86; Can and Preb Sarum Cathl 86–94; TR Bride Valley 86–94; rtd 94; PtO *Sarum* 94–16. *Silverbridge Cottage, North Chideock, Bridport DT6 6LG* T: (01297) 489408

STANDING, Victor. b 44. Lon Univ BMus 66 Clare Coll Cam PGCE 68 FRCO 67. Ripon Coll Cuddesdon 75. **d** 78 **p** 79. C Wimborne Minster *Sarum* 78–80; TV Wimborne Minster and Holt 80–83; R Ex St Sidwell and St Matt 83–94; Dep PV Ex Cathl 83–01; Chapl R Devon and Ex Hosp 83–94; Chapl W of England Eye Infirmary Ex 83–94; P-in-c Tedburn St Mary, Whitestone, Oldridge etc *Ex* 94–96; P-in-c Dunsford and Doddiscombsleigh 95–96; P-in-c Cheriton Bishop 95–96; TR Tedburn St Mary, Whitestone, Oldridge etc 96–01; RD Kenn 97–01; V New Shoreham and Old Shoreham *Chich* 01–11; rtd 11; P-in-c Shanklin St Blasius *Portsm* 11–15; PtO *Lich* 17–18. *23 Abnalls Croft, Lichfield WS13 7BP* T: (01543) 418890 E: victor@victorstanding.plus.com

STANDRING, Rupert Benjamin Charles. b 68. Pemb Coll Ox BA 90 MA 99 Cam Univ BA 94. Ridley Hall Cam 92. **d** 95 **p** 96. C Bromley Ch Ch *Roch* 95–99; Tutor Cornhill Tr Course 99–04; Hon C W Hampstead St Luke *Lon* 99–04; PtO 04–05; Min Mayfair Ch Ch 05–09; Lic Preacher 09–10; P-in-c Fulham St Pet 10–11; V from 11. *56 Langthorne Street, London SW6 6JY* T: (020) 7385 4950 E: rupert.standring@googlemail.com

STANES, The Ven Ian Thomas. b 39. Sheff Univ BSc 62 Linacre Coll Ox BA 65 MA 69. Wycliffe Hall Ox 63. **d** 65 **p** 66. C Leic H Apostles 65–69; V Broom Leys 69–76; Warden Marrick Priory *Ripon* 76–82; Officer Miss, Min and Evang Willesden Area *Lon* 82–92; CME Officer 82–92; Preb St Paul's Cathl 89–92; Adn Loughborough *Leic* 92–05; rtd 05; PtO *Sarum* from 06. *192 Bath Road, Bradford-on-Avon BA15 1SP* T: (01225) 309036 E: istanes@btinternet.com

STANESBY, Derek Malcolm. b 31. Leeds Univ BA 56 Man Univ MEd 75 PhD 84 SOSc. Coll of Resurr Mirfield 56. **d** 58 **p** 59. C Lakenham St Jo *Nor* 58–61; C Welling *S'wark* 61–63; V Bury St Mark *Man* 63–67; R Ladybarn 67–85; Can and Steward Windsor 85–97; rtd 97; PtO *Leic* 00–15; *Pet* 00–07. *32 Elizabeth Way, Uppingham, Oakham LE15 9PQ* T: (01572) 821298

STANFORD, Timothy Charles. b 61. **d** 11 **p** 12. C Walton Breck *Liv* 11–13; P-in-c Worksop St Jo *S'well* from 13. *St John's Vicarage, 1B Shepherds Avenue, Worksop S81 0JD* E: tcs227@gmail.com

STANGHAN, Eileen. b 40. Whitelands Coll Lon CertEd 75. **d** 98 **p** 99. OLM Reigate St Phil *S'wark* 98–10; rtd 10; PtO *S'wark* from 10. *20 Saxon Way, Reigate RH2 9DH* T: (01737) 240920 *or* (01293) 430043 E: eileenstanghan@ntlworld.com

STANIER, Robert Sebastian. b 75. Magd Coll Ox BA 98 Selw Coll Cam BA 05. Westcott Ho Cam 03. **d** 06 **p** 07. C Perry Hill St Geo w Ch Ch and St Paul *S'wark* 06–09; Chapl Abp Tenison's Sch Kennington 09–13; Hon C N Lambeth and S Lambeth St Anne and All SS *S'wark* 09–13; V Surbiton St Andr and St Mark from 13; AD Kingston from 18. *The Vicarage, St Mark's Hill, Surbiton KT6 4LS* T: (020) 8399 0639 E: robertstanier@btinternet.com

STANIFORD, Canon Doris Gwendoline. b 43. Gilmore Course IDC 79. **dss** 80 **d** 87 **p** 94. Hangleton *Chich* 80–82; Durrington 82–89; Par Dn 87–89; Chich Th Coll 83–89; C Crawley and Chapl Crawley Gen Hosp 89–97; Dioc Voc Adv and Chapl St Cath Hospice Crawley 92–97; Asst Dir of Ords *Chich* 97–12; C Southwick St Mich 97–99; Can and Preb Chich Cathl 08–12; rtd 12; PtO *Chich* from 15. *23 Beechside, Crawley RH10 6TL* E: staniforddoris@gmail.com

STANIFORTH, Julian Martin. b 59. Aston Univ BSc 82 MCIMA 93. SEITE 07. **d** 10 **p** 11. C Herne *Cant* 10–14; V The Six from 14. *The Vicarage, Church Lane, Newington, Sittingbourne ME9 7JU* T: (01795) 227329 M: 07879-626115 E: julian.staniforth@gmail.com

STANLEY, Arthur Patrick. b 32. TCD BA 54 Div Test 55 MA 64. **d** 55 **p** 56. C Waterford H Trin *C & O* 55–57; CF 58–74; Dep Asst Chapl Gen 74–83; USA 84–04; rtd 94; PtO *B & W* 05–12. *9 Westbourne Court, Cooden Drive, Bexhill-on-Sea TN39 3AA* T: (01424) 539307 E: patnpaddy@hotmail.com

STANLEY, Canon John Alexander. b 31. Tyndale Hall Bris. **d** 56 **p** 57. C Preston All SS *Blackb* 56–60; C St Helens St Mark *Liv* 60–63; V Everton St Cuth 63–70; P-in-c Everton St Sav 69–70; V Everton St Sav w St Cuth 70–74; V Huyton St Mich 74–18; Hon Can Liv Cathl 87–18; AD Huyton 89–02; Chapl to The Queen 93–01; rtd 18; PtO *Ches* from 19. *The Vicarage, Bluebell Lane, Liverpool L36 7SA* T: 0151-449 3900 F: 480 6002 M: 07740-621833

STANLEY, Canon Nicola Vere. b 56. Surrey Univ BA 07 MCIPD 83. STETS 99. **d** 02 **p** 03. C Bedford Park *Lon* 02–06; V Twickenham All Hallows 06–14; Asst Dir of Ords Kensington

Area 04–14; Can Res, Prec and Sacr Bris Cathl from 14. *Bristol Cathedral, College Green, Bristol BS1 5TJ* T: 0117-926 4879 E: canon.precentor@bristol-cathedral.co.uk

STANLEY, Patrick. *See* STANLEY, Arthur Patrick

STANLEY, Canon Simon Richard. b 44. Wells Th Coll 66. **d** 69 **p** 70. C Foleshill St Laur *Cov* 69–71; C Hessle *York* 71–75; P-in-c Flamborough 75–80; R Dunnington 80–92; P-in-c York St Barn 92–99; P-in-c York St Chad 99–14; P-in-c York All SS Pavement w St Crux and St Mich 03–09; P-in-c York St Denys 04–09; Relig Progr Producer BBC Radio York 94–03; rtd 09; P-in-c York St Chad 09–14; Can and Preb York Minster 05–14; PtO from 14. *69 Temple Avenue, York YO10 3RS* M: 07946-466364 E: simonstanley@clara.net

STANLEY, Mrs Susan Dorothy Margaret. b 61. Ox Min Course 14. **d** 17 **p** 18. C Potterspury w Furtho and Yardley Gobion etc *Pet* from 17. *Hole in the Wall, Main Street, Upper Stowe, Northampton NN7 4SH* T: (01327) 341307 M: 07745-765575 E: stanley.thehole@btinternet.com

STANLEY-SMITH, James. b 29. Hatf Coll Dur BA 54 DipEd 55. S Dios Minl Tr Scheme 81. **d** 84 **p** 85. C Bournemouth St Jo w St Mich *Win* 84–87; R Hale w S Charford 87–94; rtd 94; PtO *Win* from 94. *10 Rownhams Way, Rownhams, Southampton SO16 8AE* T: (023) 8073 2529 E: jstanley-smith@cwcom.net

STANNARD, Miss Beryl Elizabeth. b 36. SRN 62 SCM 64. Oak Hill Th Coll BA 92. **d** 92 **p** 94. Par Dn Streatham Park St Alb *S'wark* 92–94; C Gerrards Cross and Fulmer *Ox* 96–01; rtd 01; PtO *Ox* from 02. *31 Codmore Crescent, Chesham HP5 3LZ*

STANNARD, Brian. b 46. MICE 71 MIStructE 71. Cranmer Hall Dur 86. **d** 88 **p** 89. C Burnage St Marg *Man* 88–91; V Walmersley 91–03; TV Westhoughton and Wingates 03–04; rtd 04; PtO *Liv* from 16. *63 Portland Street, Southport PR8 5AF* T: (01704) 534632 E: b.stannard@btinternet.com

STANNARD, The Ven Colin Percy. b 24. Selw Coll Cam BA 47 MA 49. Linc Th Coll 47. **d** 49 **p** 50. C St E Cathl 49–52; C-in-c Nunsthorpe CD *Linc* 52–55; CF (TA) 53–67; V Barrow St Jas *Carl* 55–64; V Upperby St Jo 64–70; R Gosforth 70–75; RD Calder 70–75; P-in-c Natland 75–76; V 76–84; RD Kendal 75–84; Hon Can Carl Cathl 75–84; Can Res Carl Cathl 84–93; Adn Carl 84–93; rtd 93; PtO *Carl* 93–14. *Flat 4, Manormead, Tilford Road, Hindhead GU26 6RA*

STANNARD, Neill David. b 74. Brunel Univ BA 99 Univ Coll Lon PGCE 00. Ridley Hall Cam 17. **d** 19. C Worthing St Matt *Chich* from 19. *16 St Michael's Road, Worthing BN11 4SD* M: 07557-337204 E: neill.stannard@gmail.com

STANNARD, Canon Peter Graville. b 59. Univ of Wales (Abth) BSc(Econ) 81. St Steph Ho Ox BA 85 MA 86. **d** 86 **p** 87. C Worksop Priory *S'well* 86–89; Prin St Nic Th Coll Ghana 89–96; Hon Can Koforidua from 93; TR Shelf w Buttershaw St And *Bradf* 96–99; P-in-c Heaton Norris St Thos *Man* 00–02; TV Heatons 02–08; P-in-c S Shields St Hilda w St Thos *Dur* 08–12; P-in-c S Shields St Aid and St Steph 08–12; C Houghton le Spring 12–13; rtd 13; PtO *Dur* 13–15; *S'wark* 16–17; *St Alb* from 17. *10 Johnson Court, Park Side Drive, Houghton Regis, Dunstable LU5 5RQ* M: 07428-519778 E: petergstannard@gmail.com

STANNING (*née* **CROMPTON), Mrs Gillian Kay.** b 65. Univ of Wales (Ban) BA 86 Homerton Coll Cam PGCE 87. SNWTP 07. **d** 10 **p** 11. C Norley, Crowton and Kingsley *Ches* 10–13; V Sandbach Heath w Wheelock 13–17; C Borderlands Miss Area *St As* from 17. *32 Well House Drive, Penymynydd, Chester CH4 0LB* T: (01244) 541420 M: 07840-627725 E: gill.pioneerpriest@gmail.com

STANTON, Ms Angela. b 59. Loughb Univ BSc 80 Ch Coll Liv PGCE 81. Westcott Ho Cam 03. **d** 05 **p** 06. C Atherton and Hindsford w Howe Bridge *Man* 05–08; P-in-c Reddish 08–18; R from 18; Hon Assoc Dioc Dir of Ords from 10; Borough Dean Stockport from 13. *St Elisabeth's Rectory, 28 Bedford Street, Stockport SK5 6DJ* T: 0161-432 3033 E: angiestanton27@yahoo.co.uk

STANTON, The Very Revd David John. b 60. St Andr Univ MTheol 82 Ex Univ MA 00 FSAScot 89 FRSA 98. Ripon Coll Cuddesdon 83. **d** 85 **p** 86. C Beckenham St Geo *Roch* 85–88; Asst Chapl Shrewsbury Sch 88–90; Hon C Shrewsbury All SS w St Mich *Lich* 88–90; P-in-c Abbotskerswell *Ex* 90–94; Chapl Plymouth Univ 92–97; P-in-c Bovey Tracey St Jo, Chudleigh Knighton etc 94–97; V Bovey Tracey St Jo w Heathfield 99–05; Dioc Voc Adv 95–05; Warden of Readers 96–03; Acting Dioc Dir of Ords 03–05; RD Moreton 98–05; Can Prec and Can Past Worc Cathl 05–13; Can and Treas Westmr Abbey from 13; Sub Dean Westmr from 18; Adn Westmr from 18. *1 Little Cloister, London SW1P 3PL* T: (020) 7654 4804 E: david.stanton@westminster-abbey.org

STANTON, Gregory John. b 47. Sarum & Wells Th Coll 84. **d** 86 **p** 87. C Willenhall H Trin *Lich* 86–89; C Plympton St Mary *Ex* 89–91; V Milton Abbot, Dunterton, Lamerton

etc 91–13; rtd 13; P-in-c Bovey Tracey St Jo w Heathfield *Ex* 13–15; V 15–17. *The Granary, Rubbytown Farm, Tavistock PL19 8PA* E: frgregssc@gmail.com

STANTON, Ms Karen Janis. b 55. NOC 00. **d** 03 **p** 04. C Withington St Paul *Man* 03–04; C Urmston 04–07; TV Wythenshawe 07–12; R Kinver and Enville *Lich* 12–19; V Hale and Ashley *Ches* from 19. *1 Harrop Road, Hale, Altrincham WA15 9BU* T: 0161-928 4182 M: 07814-254744 E: kaz@thestantons.me.uk

STANTON, Richard Oliver. b 90. Pemb Coll Cam BA 11 MA 15 MPhil 12. Westcott Ho Cam 12. **d** 15 **p** 16. C Attleborough w Besthorpe *Nor* 15–19; P-in-c Nor St Jo w St Julian from 19. *The Rectory, 8 Kilderkin Way, Norwich NR1 1RD* T: (01603) 626104 E: richard_stanton@btinternet.com

STANTON-HYDE, Mrs Marjorie Elizabeth. b 37. TCert 58. Cranmer Hall Dur 86. **d** 88 **p** 94. Par Dn Elmley Lovett w Hampton Lovett and Elmbridge etc *Worc* 88–91; Par Dn Wilden 88–91; Par Dn Hartlebury 88–91; Dn-in-c 91–94; P-in-c 94–97; R 97–98; rtd 98; Hon C Gt Malvern St Mary *Worc* 99–02; Warden Jes Hosp Cant 02–05; Chapl Worcs Community and Mental Health Trust 05–12; PtO *Worc* from 12. *4 Severn Drive, Malvern WR14 2SZ* T: (01684) 569589 E: marjemoto@gmail.com

STANTON-SARINGER, Maurice Charles. b 49. Bris Univ BSc 71 PGCE 72 Fitzw Coll Cam BA 77 MA 81. Ridley Hall Cam 75. **d** 78 **p** 79. C Gerrards Cross *Ox* 78–80; C Bletchley 80–83; Chapl Stowe Sch 83–91; R Sherington w Chicheley, N Crawley, Astwood etc *Ox* 91–06; RD Newport 95–04; TR Loddon Reach 06–13; rtd 13; PtO *Ox* from 13. *23 Western Avenue, Buckingham MK18 1LJ* E: saringer@btinternet.com

STANWAY, Peter David. b 48. K Coll Lon BD 71. St Aug Coll Cant 72. **d** 73 **p** 74. C Maidstone All SS w St Phil and H Trin *Cant* 73–77; Canada 77–84; C Waterlooville *Portsm* 84–87; R Laughton w Ripe and Chalvington *Chich* 87–90; Chapl Witney Community Hosp 90–91; C Wheatley w Forest Hill and Stanton St John *Ox* 91–92; C Cowley St Jas 93–02; rtd 02; PtO *Ox* from 14. *22 Colleywood, Kennington, Oxford OX1 5NF* T: (01865) 739342 E: peterstroudley060@gmail.com

STAPLE, Miss Patricia Ann. b 54. Birm Univ BA 75. St Steph Ho Ox 00. **d** 02 **p** 05. C Dartmouth and Dittisham *Ex* 02–04; C Colyton, Musbury, Southleigh and Branscombe 04–07; V Athelney *B & W* 07–19; rtd 19. *1 Compton Close, Taunton TA2 7UD* M: 07731-931683 E: triciastaple1@btinternet.com

STAPLEFORD, Robin Duncan. b 62. Aston Tr Scheme 92 St Jo Coll Nottm 94. **d** 96 **p** 97. C Evington *Leic* 96–99; TV Vale of Belvoir 00–08; R Upper Wensum Village Gp *Nor* from 08. *The Rectory, Market Hill, Colkirk, Fakenham NR21 7NU* T: (01328) 853226 E: upperwensumrector@btinternet.com

STAPLES, David. b 35. Jes Coll Ox BA 59 MA 63 BD 75. Linc Th Coll 59. **d** 61 **p** 62. C Kettering St Andr *Pet* 61–64; C Doncaster St Geo *Sheff* 64–66; Dioc Youth Chapl 66–71; V Mexborough 71–83; Chapl Montagu Hosp Mexborough 71–83; RD Wath *Sheff* 77–83; Hon Can Sheff Cathl 80–83; V W Haddon w Winwick *Pet* 83–88; RD Brixworth 83–89; V W Haddon w Winwick and Ravensthorpe 88–00; ACUPA Link Officer 90–00; rtd 00; PtO *Linc* from 00. *1 Sycamore Close, Bourne PE10 9RS* T: (01778) 423121 E: david.staples@talktalk.net

STAPLES, Jeffrey Joseph. b 61. St Jo Coll Nottm 97. **d** 99 **p** 00. C Prenton *Ches* 99–03; P-in-c Wallasey St Nic 03–04; P-in-c New Brighton All SS 03–04; V Wallasey St Nic w All SS from 04. *St Nicholas' Vicarage, 22 Groveland Road, Wallasey CH45 8JY* T: 0151-639 3589 E: jeffstaples4@hotmail.com

STAPLES, John Michael. b 45. STETS 94. **d** 97 **p** 98. C Tisbury *Sarum* 97–02; P-in-c Barford St Martin, Dinton, Baverstock etc 00–01; TV Nadder Valley 01–08; C Fovant, Sutton Mandeville and Teffont Evias etc 06–08; rtd 08; PtO *Sarum* from 08. *Crabstone Cottage, Locarno Road, Swanage BH19 1HY* T: (01929) 421715 E: john_staples@btinternet.com

STAPLES, John Wedgwood. b 42. Hertf Coll Ox BA 64 MA. Wycliffe Hall Ox 64. **d** 66 **p** 67. C Yardley St Edburgha *Birm* 66–69; C Knowle 69–74; R Barcombe *Chich* 74–81; V Old Windsor *Ox* 81–96; P-in-c Pangbourne w Tidmarsh and Sulham 96–99; R 99–07; rtd 07; PtO *Win* from 07. *6 Douglas Road, Bournemouth BH6 3ER* T: (01202) 425859 E: revdjohn.staples@gmail.com

STAPLES, Canon Peter Brian. b 38. Bps' Coll Cheshunt 66. **d** 68 **p** 69. C Birkdale St Jas *Liv* 68–71; C Sevenoaks St Jo *Roch* 71–74; V Treslothan *Truro* 74–80; V Truro St Paul and St Clem 80–02; Hon Can Truro Cathl 98–02; rtd 02; PtO *St E* from 03. *25 Osmund Walk, Bury St Edmunds IP33 3UU* T: (01284) 760620 E: canonpeter@hotmail.com

STAPLETON, The Very Revd Henry Edward Champneys. b 32. FSA 74 Pemb Coll Cam BA 54 MA 58. Ely Th Coll 54. **d** 56 **p** 57. C York St Olave w St Giles 56–59; C Pocklington w Yapham-cum-Meltonby, Owsthorpe etc 59–61; R Seaton Ross w Everingham and Bielby and Harswell 61–67; RD Weighton 66–67; R Skelton by York 67–75; V Wroxham w Hoveton *Nor* 75–81; P-in-c Belaugh 76–81; Can Res and Prec Roch Cathl 81–88; Dean Carl 88–98; rtd 98; PtO *Wakef* 98–14; *Leeds* from 14; *York* from 03. *Rockland House, 20 Marsh Gardens, Honley, Huddersfield HD9 6AF* T: (01484) 666629 E: hec.stapleton@talktalk.net

STAPLETON, Robert Vauvelle. b 47. St Jo Coll Dur BA 70. Cranmer Hall Dur. **d** 71 **p** 72. C Moreton *Ches* 71–73; C Monkwearmouth All SS *Dur* 73–76; C Stranton 76–79; P-in-c Kelloe 79–86; V New Shildon 86–96; R Stoke Albany w Wilbarston and Ashley etc *Pet* 96–04; P-in-c Somborne w Ashley *Win* 04–12; Dioc Rural Officer 04–12; rtd 12; PtO *York* from 12. *14 St Mary's Way, Thirsk YO7 1BS* T: (01845) 522676 E: robertstapleton@hotmail.com

STARES, Mrs Olive Beryl. b 33. Sarum Th Coll 83. **dss** 86 **d** 87 **p** 94. Crofton *Portsm* 86–87; Hon C 87–01; rtd 01; PtO *Portsm* from 05. *62 Mancroft Avenue, Hill Head, Fareham PO14 2DD* T: (01329) 668540 E: berylstares@hotmail.co.uk

STARK, Mrs Beverley Ann. b 52. Bp Otter Coll CertEd 73 EMMTC 92. **d** 92 **p** 94. Par Dn Bulwell St Jo *S'well* 92–94; C 94–97; TV Bestwood 97–03; C Bestwood Em w St Mark 03–04; R Ironstone Villages *Leic* 04–16; RD Framland 06–11; rtd 16; PtO *Linc* from 17. *2 Church Walk, Great Hale, Sleaford NG34 9LL* E: beverley.stark@btinternet.com

STARK, John Jordan. b 40. Hull Univ BA 62. St Chad's Coll Dur. **d** 64 **p** 65. C Buxton *Derby* 64–67; C Wolborough w Newton Abbot *Ex* 67–74; R Belstone 74–79; P-in-c Plymouth St Gabr 79–80; V 80–10; rtd 10. *11 Warwick Orchard Close, Plymouth PL5 3NZ* T: (01752) 787132

STARK, Margaret Alison. b 46. Univ of Wales BA 70 BA 71. St Mich Coll Llan. **d** 90 **p** 97. C Llanishen and Lisvane *Llan* 90–93; C Llanishen 93–94; C Aberavon 94–98; R Llanfabon 98–01; rtd 01; PtO *Llan* from 04. *6 Alexandra House, Beach Road, Penarth CF64 1FN* T: (029) 2070 1303 E: stark545@btinternet.com

STARK TOLLER, Peter Sheridan. b 74. Pemb Coll Ox BA 96 MA Nottm Univ PGCE 97. Wycliffe Hall Ox 11. **d** 13 **p** 14. C Dibden *Win* 13–18; R from 18. *c/o St Andrew's Church, Beaulieu Road, Dibden Purlieu, Southampton SO45 4PT* M: 07758-006578 E: peter@starktoller.co.uk *or* rector@dibdenchurches.org

STARKEY, Michael Stuart. b 63. LMH Ox BA 85 Nottm Univ BTh 92 MA 93. St Jo Coll Nottm 90. **d** 93 **p** 94. C Ealing St Mary *Lon* 93–95; C Brownswood Park 95–97; P-in-c 97–01; V Twickenham Common H Trin 01–09; V Kennington St Mark *S'wark* 09–11; V Llanidloes w Llangurig *Ban* 11–13; Can Ban Cathl 12–13; Tutor Wilson Carlile Coll of Evang from 14; PtO *Man* from 14; Hd of Ch Growth from 19. *1 Princess Court, 38 Circular Road, Manchester M20 3LP* T: 0161-434 6306 M: 07870-281055 E: revstarkey@yahoo.co.uk

STARKEY, Ms Naomi Ernestine. b 65. LMH Ox BA 86. St Seiriol Cen 11. **d** 14 **p** 15. NSM Bro Cyfeiliog and Mawddwy *Ban* 14–15; C Bro Enlli 15–18; C Bro Dwynwen from 18. *The Rectory, Ffordd Caergybi, Llanfairpwllgwyngyll LL61 5SX* T: (01248) 713421 E: naomi.starkey@gmail.com

STARKEY, Susan Anne. b 52. St Jo Coll Nottm. **d** 97 **p** 98. C Watford St Luke *St Alb* 97–02; C Oxhey All SS 02–04; V Findern *Derby* from 04; V Willington from 04. *The Vicarage, 66 Castle Way, Willington, Derby DE65 6BU* T: (01283) 703928 E: susan.starkey@btopenworld.com

STARKIE, Catherine Vivienne. b 54. Qu Foundn (Course) 14. **d** 17 **p** 18. OLM Mid Trent *Lich* from 17. *3 Old School Close, Weston, Stafford ST18 0HF* T: (01889) 271046

STARKINGS, Susan Anne. b 52. Kent Univ BSc 82 Sheff City Poly MSc 90 Punjab Univ PhD 93. SEITE 08. **d** 11 **p** 12. NSM Gt Bredon *Cant* 11–14; C King's Wood 14–19; rtd 19. *The Forge, Godmersham Park, Godmersham, Canterbury CT4 7DT* T: (01227) 730925 E: sue.starkings@btinternet.com

STARLING, Deborah Mary Patricia. b 57. **d** 14 **p** 15. NSM Dawlish, Cofton and Starcross *Ex* 15–16; NSM Melton Mowbray *Leic* 17–18; PtO from 18; Dioc Disability Awareness Adv from 18. *12 Balmoral Road, Melton Mowbray LE13 1JN* T: (01664) 564128 M: 07863-398707 E: debbiestarling@btinternet.com

STARLING, Timothy Gordon James. b 69. Ripon Coll Cuddesdon 16. **d** 18 **p** 19. C StowCaple *Heref* from 18. *The Rectory, King's Caple, Hereford HR1 4TX* M: 07980-204572 E: timgjstarling@gmail.com

STARNS, Helen Edna. *See* PATTEN, Helen Edna

STARR, Michael Richard. b 43. Sarum Th Coll 65. **d** 68 **p** 69. C Plymouth St Pet *Ex* 68–72; C Blackpool St Paul *Blackb* 72–74; V Burnley St Cuth 74–79; C Eastbourne St Mary *Chich* 79–84; P-in-c Eastbourne Ch Ch 84–87; V 87–88;

R Guernsey Ste Marie du Castel *Win* 88–01; V Guernsey St Matt 94–01; Vice-Dean Guernsey 99–01; P-in-c Win St Bart 01–08; rtd 09; PtO *Win* from 09. *62 Beresford Road, Chandler's Ford, Eastleigh SO53 2LY* T: (023) 8036 1505 E: michael_starr@hotmail.co.uk

STARTIN, Frank David. b 60. Qu Foundn (Course) 14. **d** 17 **p** 18. NSM Winshill *Derby* from 17; NSM Hartshorne and Bretby from 17. *91 Scalpcliffe Road, Burton-on-Trent DE15 9AB* T: (01283) 566736 E: frankstartin@gmail.com

STARTIN, Nicola Gail. b 57. K Coll Lon LLB 79. St Steph Ho Ox 88. **d** 90 **p** 96. C Wellingborough All SS *Pet* 90–92; NSM Pyle w Kenfig *Llan* 94–95; Asst Chapl Mid Kent Healthcare NHS Trust 95–97; Chapl HM Pris E Sutton Park 97–00; Chapl HM Pris Haslar 00–02; Chapl Haslar Immigration Removal Cen 02–18. *Address temp unknown*

STATHAM, Brian Edward. b 55. K Coll Lon MA AKC 76. St Steph Ho Ox 77. **d** 78 **p** 79. C Ches H Trin 78–81; C Birkenhead Priory 81–82; TV 82–86; V Newton 86–91; SSF 91–94; TV Horsham *Chich* 95–99; Chapl Horsham Gen Hosp 95–99; TV Ches 99–03; P-in-c Stockport St Matt 03–07; C Edgeley and Cheadle Heath 07–10; V Milton *Lich* from 10; P-in-c Norton in the Moors from 18; RD Leek from 15. *The Vicarage, Baddeley Green Lane, Stoke-on-Trent ST2 7EY* T: (01782) 534062 M: 07724-133215 E: brianstatham1995@btinternet.com

STATHAM, John Francis. b 31. Kelham Th Coll 51. **d** 56 **p** 57. C Ilkeston St Mary *Derby* 56–58; C New Mills 58–59; V 69–81; C Newbold w Dunston 59–62; PC Ridgeway 62–69; RD Glossop 78–81; R Matlock 81–89; R Killamarsh 89–93; rtd 93; PtO *Derby* from 93; *S'well* 93–11. *33 Ackford Drive, The Meadows, Worksop S80 1YG* T: (01909) 476031

STATON, Preb Geoffrey. b 40. Wells Th Coll 64. **d** 66 **p** 67. C Wednesfield St Thos *Lich* 66–69; C Cannock 69–72; V Cheddleton 72–82; RD Leek 77–82; V Harlescott 82–90; TR Penkridge 90–05; rtd 05; C Colton, Colwich and Gt Haywood *Lich* 05–10; C Abbots Bromley, Blithfield, Colton, Colwich etc 11–13; Preb Lich Cathl 87–10; PtO from 13. *5 Hunters Close, Great Haywood, Stafford ST18 0GF* T: (01889) 882081 M: 07971-016494 E: geoffrey.staton@virgin.net

STATTER, Ms Deborah Hilary. b 55. **d** 00 **p** 01. OLM Everton St Pet *Liv* 00–02; OLM Everton St Pet w St Chrys 02–04; C 04–08; P-in-c Netherton 08–14; TR 14–17; TR Netherton and Sefton from 17. *St Oswald's Vicarage, 183 St Oswald's Lane, Bootle L30 5SR* T: 0151-525 1882 M: 07952-105466 E: debbie.statter@btinternet.com

STAUNTON, Mrs Mary Provis. b 52. Leic Univ BSc 74. EMMTC 05. **d** 07 **p** 08. NSM Mickleover All SS *Derby* 07–14; NSM Mickleover St Jo 07–14; NSM Mickleover from 14. *165A Pastures Hill, Littleover, Derby DE23 4AZ* T: (01332) 510264 E: mps52@staunton.force9.co.uk

STAVERT, Miss Rachel Louise. b 66. Coll of Ripon & York St Jo BEd 88. Cranmer Hall Dur 10. **d** 12 **p** 13. C Penrith w Newton Reigny and Plumpton Wall *Carl* 12–16; TV Cartmel Peninsula from 16. *The Vicarage, Boarbank Lane, Allithwaite, Grange-over-Sands LA11 7QR* M: 07813-962740 E: revrachstav@gmail.com

STAVROU, Stephen Francis. b 83. St Jo Coll Cam BA 05 MA 09 Peterho Cam MPhil 09. Westcott Ho Cam 07. **d** 09 **p** 10. C Bedford Park *Lon* 09–13; Succ S'wark Cathl 13–16; Chapl K Coll Lon 13–16; TV Barnes from 16; Dir Ords Kingston Area from 17. *St Michael's Vicarage, 39 Elm Bank Gardens, London SW13 0NX* T: (020) 8878 7589 *or* 8876 5230 E: vicar@stmichaelbarnes.org

STAYNINGS, Margaret Rose. b 42. **d** 13 **p** 14. OLM Bris Lockleaze St Mary Magd w St Fran 13–16; P-in-c 15–16; PtO 16–19. *5 Cotman Walk, Bristol BS7 9UG* T: 0117-935 4540 M: 07542-191959 E: davenmar@hotmail.co.uk

STAYTE, Miss Samantha Mary. b 71. Ex Coll Ox BA 92 MPhil 02 Ex Univ PGCE 95. Westcott Ho Cam 10. **d** 13 **p** 14. C Summertown *Ox* 13–17; P-in-c Combe Martin, Berrynarbor, Lynton, Brendon etc *Ex* 17–18; R Lynton, Brendon, Countisbury etc from 18. *The Rectory, 20 Lee Road, Lynton EX35 6BP* T: (01598) 752289 E: samanthastayte@hotmail.com *or* priest-in-charge@stmarylynton.com

STAZIKER, Catherine. b 61. Hull Univ BA 84 Anglia Ruskin Univ BA 13. Westcott Ho Cam 10. **d** 12 **p** 13. C Millhouses H Trin *Sheff* 12–15; C Abbeydale St Jo 12–15; PtO 15–16 and from 18; TV Digswell and Panshanger *St Alb* 16–18; PtO *Roch* from 18. *125 Machon Bank Road, Sheffield S7 1PH* M: 07968-316812 E: catherinestaziker@btinternet.com

STEACY, William Leslie. b 59. UCD BAgrSc 82 MAgrSc 88 TCD BTh 06. CITC 03. **d** 06 **p** 07. C Dunboyne and Rathmolyon *M & K* 06–10; I Kingscourt w Syddan 10–18; I Athlone w Benown, Kiltoom and Forgney from 18. *The Rectory, Killyon Hill, Bonavalley, Athlone, Co Westmeath,*

N37 XP08, Republic of Ireland T: (00353) (90) 647 9984 E: williamsteacy@eircom.net

STEAD, Canon Andrew Michael. b 63. BA 84 Heythrop Coll Lon MA 12. Coll of Resurr Mirfield 84. **d** 87 **p** 88. C Wellingborough All Hallows *Pet* 87–90; Chapl St Alb Abbey 90–94; Chapl Aldenham Sch Herts 94–04 and 12–13; Ho Master 01–08; Teacher 08–13; PtO *St Alb* 04–12; NSM St Alb Abbey 05–13; Chapl Lich Cathl Sch 13–17; Can Res Lich Cathl 13–17; Can Prec from 17. *24 The Close, Lichfield WS13 7LD* E: rev.amstead@gmail.com *or* andrew.stead@lichfield-cathedral.org

STEAD, Philip John. b 60. Sheff Univ LLB 82 City of Lon Poly ACII 85. Linc Th Coll 95. **d** 95 **p** 96. C Warsop *S'well* 95–99; P-in-c Forest Town from 99; P-in-c Mansfield Oak Tree Lane from 07; P-in-c Mansfield St Lawr from 13. *The Vicarage, Old Mill Lane, Forest Town, Mansfield NG19 0EP* T: (01623) 622177

STEADMAN, Mrs Gloria Ann. b 44. STETS BA 04. **d** 04 **p** 05. NSM Farlington *Portsm* 04–08; NSM W Leigh 08–15; PtO 15–16; *Linc* from 16. *56 Nettleham Road, Lincoln LN2 1RH* T: (01522) 402844 E: gloria@freshvisions.co.uk

STEADMAN, The Ven Mark John. b 74. Southn Univ LLB 95 Ch Coll Cam BA 01 MA 05 Barrister-at-Law (Inner Temple) 96. Westcott Ho Cam 99. **d** 02 **p** 03. C Portsea St Mary *Portsm* 02–05; P-in-c Camberwell St Phil and St Mark *S'wark* 05–12; AD Bermondsey 08–11; Bp's Chapl 11–15; Adn Stow and Lindsey *Linc* from 15. *Edward King House, The Old Palace, Lincoln LN2 1PU* T: (01522) 504050 *or* 504089 M: 07870-266553 E: archdeacon.stow@lincoln.anglican.org

STEADMAN-ALLEN, Miss Barbara. b 53. Birm Univ BMus 77 Spurgeon's Coll Lon MTh 00 Trent Park Coll of Educn CertEd 74 ARCM 83. Cranmer Hall Dur 88. **d** 90 **p** 94. C Chessington *Guildf* 90–94; C Chertsey 94–99; P-in-c Mickleham 99–01; C Leatherhead and Mickleham 01–04; Chapl Box Hill Sch 99–04; TV Surrey Weald *Guildf* from 04. *Holmwood Vicarage, Horsham Road, Holmwood, Dorking RH5 4JX* M: 07711-884941 E: revdbsa@gmail.com

STEAR, Michael Peter Hutchinson. b 47. Goldsmiths' Coll Lon TCert 68. Wycliffe Hall Ox 71. **d** 74 **p** 75. C Streatham Vale H Redeemer *S'wark* 74–77; C-in-c Ramsgate St Mark *Cant* 77–82; V 82–83; Min Jersey St Paul Prop Chpl *Win* 83–94; TR Radipole and Melcombe Regis *Sarum* 94–00; Chapl Weymouth Coll 94–97; rtd 00; PtO *Sarum* from 01. *Flat 3, 5 Widcombe Street, Poundbury, Dorchester DT3 6BH* T: (01305) 520811 E: mphstear@gmail.com

STEBBING, Christopher Henry. b 64. G&C Coll Cam MEng 87 MA 90. Cranmer Hall Dur 98. **d** 00 **p** 01. C Malin Bridge *Sheff* 00–04; V Sheff St Jo 04–12; Dir IME 4-7 08–12; V Lodge Moor St Luke from 12; C Crosspool from 17. *St Luke's House, 18 Blackbrook Road, Sheffield S10 4LP* T: 0114-230 3538 E: chris.stebbing@sheffield.anglican.org

STEBBING, Michael Langdale (Nicolas). b 46. Univ of Zimbabwe BA 68 UNISA MTh 86. Coll of Resurr Mirfield. **d** 74 **p** 75. C Borrowdale Rhodesia 74–75; P-in-c Chikwaka 76–77; S Africa 79–86; CR from 80. *House of the Resurrection, Stocks Bank Road, Mirfield WF14 0BN* T: (01924) 494318 E: nstebbing@mirfield.org.uk

STEDMAN, Preb Michael Sydney. b 34. MRICS 58. Clifton Th Coll 62. **d** 65 **p** 66. C Lindfield *Chich* 65–68; C Gt Baddow *Chelmsf* 68–73; TV Ashby w Thurton, Claxton and Carleton *Nor* 73–75; P-in-c 75–85; TV Rockland St Mary w Hellington 73–75; P-in-c 75–85; TV Framingham Pigot 73–75; P-in-c 75–85; TV Bramerton w Surlingham 73–75; P-in-c 75–85; TV Bergh Apton w Yelverton 73–75; P-in-c 75–85; RD Loddon 78–85; R Church Stretton *Heref* 85–99; RD Condover 88–96; Preb Heref Cathl 94–99; rtd 99; PtO *St E* from 00. *44 The Mowbrays, Framlingham, Woodbridge IP13 9DL* T: (01728) 724479 E: michael.gillstedman@yahoo.co.uk

STEED, Christopher Denis. b 55. Lon Univ BD 92 Bris Univ MSc 03 Ex Univ PGCE 01 EdD 05. Sarum Th Coll 05. **d** 06 **p** 07. C Yatton Moor *B & W* 06–10; P-in-c Combe Martin, Berrynarbor, Lynton, Brendon etc *Ex* 11–15; TR Totton *Win* from 15. *The Rectory, 92 Salisbury Road, Totton, Southampton SO40 3JA* T: (023) 8184 3308 M: 07704-138433 E: chrissteed@uwclub.net

STEED, Mrs Helene. b 70. Uppsala Univ MDiv 95. Past Inst Uppsala 95. **p** 96. C Lican Melby Sweden 96–97; TV Essunga 97–04; Dean's V Cork Cathl *C, C & R* 04–08; I Clones w Killeevan *Clogh* 08–16; Preb Clogh Cathl 11–16; Adn Clogh 14–16; I Dundela St Mark *D & D* from 16. *St Mark's Rectory, 4 Sydenham Avenue, Belfast BT4 2DR* M: (00353) 86-860 3112 E: helenesteed@yahoo.com *or* dundela@down.anglican.org

STEEL, Coralie Mary. b 47. Bedf Coll Lon BA 69 Solicitor 73. St Mich Coll Llan 98. **d** 01 **p** 02. NSM Llangunnor w Cwmffrwd *St D* 01–12; rtd 12; PtO *St D* from 12. *Llwyn Celyn, 24 Picton Terrace, Carmarthen SA31 3BX* T: (01267) 236369

STEEL, Graham Reginald. b 51. Cam Univ MA. Trin Coll Bris 80. **d** 83 **p** 84. C Gt Parndon *Chelmsf* 83–86; C Barking St Marg w St Patr 86–89; P-in-c Westcliff St Cedd 89–96; P-in-c Prittlewell St Pet 92–96; Chapl Southend Health Care NHS Trust 89–92; V Prittlewell St Pet w Westcliff St Cedd *Chelmsf* 96–07; P-in-c S Trin Broads *Nor* 07–08; R 08–16; rtd 16. *5 Tide Way, Bracklesham Bay, Chichester PO20 8FE* E: grahamrsteel@tiscali.co.uk

STEEL, Leslie Frederick. b 34. Webster Univ Geneva MA 88. St Jo Coll Auckland 57 LTh 65. **d** 59 **p** 60. C Roslyn New Zealand 59–62; V Waimea Plains 62–69; CF 70–73; Singapore 72–73; V Dunstan New Zealand 74–81; Adn Otago 77–82; V Anderson's Bay and Chapl Police Force 82–86; Can Dunedin Cathl 82–85; Adn Dunedin 85–86; Hon C Geneva *Eur* 87–90; Chapl Lausanne 90–97; PtO *Pet* 98–99; P-in-c Potterspury, Furtho, Yardley Gobion and Cosgrove 99–02; R Potterspury w Furtho and Yardley Gobion etc 02–04; rtd 04. *14 Kaspar Street, Warkworth 0910, New Zealand* T: (0064) (9) 422 2560 E: ehsteel@xtra.co.nz

STEEL, Norman William. b 53. Sarum & Wells Th Coll 85. **d** 87 **p** 88. C S Woodham Ferrers *Chelmsf* 87–91; R Woolavington w Cossington and Bawdrip *B & W* 91–99; P-in-c Pitminster w Corfe 99–02; Chapl Richard Huish Coll Taunton 99–05; PtO *B & W* 02–05. *28 Wilton Street, Taunton TA1 3JR* T: (01823) 368161

STEEL, Richard John. b 57. Dur Univ BA 79 Cam Univ MA 86 Edin Univ MTh 97. Ridley Hall Cam 81. **d** 84 **p** 85. C Hull St Jo Newland *York* 84–87; Relig Broadcasting Officer *Derby* 88–92; Dioc Communications Officer *Blackb* 92–97; Communication Dir CMS 97–05; NSM Stoke-next-Guildf *Guildf* 00–05; R Kirkheaton *Wakef* 05–14; *Leeds* 14–16; RD Almondbury *Wakef* 06–14; *Leeds* 14–16; Miss Team Ldr Linc from 16. *9 Loweswater Close, Waddington, Lincoln LN5 9PU* M: 07900-216363 E: richardsteel03@icloud.com *or* richard.steel@lincoln.anglican.org

STEEL, Thomas Molyneux. b 39. Man Univ BA 61. Ripon Hall Ox 61. **d** 63 **p** 64. C Newc H Cross 63–66; P-in-c Man St Aid 66–71; R Failsworth St Jo 71–79; P-in-c Farnham Royal *Ox* 79–81; P-in-c Hedgerley 80–81; R Farnham Royal w Hedgerley 81–91; V Prescot *Liv* 91–03; rtd 03; PtO *Lon* from 04. *20 Barnet Way, London NW7 3BH* T: (020) 8906 0271 E: t.steel@virgin.net

STEELE, Edwin Harry. b 80. Mattersey Hall BA 05. Ridley Hall Cam 06. **d** 08 **p** 09. C Ecclesall *Sheff* 08–11; P-in-c Greenhill 11–15; V 15–16; P-in-c Doncaster St Mary and St Paul 16–18; Bp's Interim Min from 18. *30 Millmount Road, Sheffield S8 9EG* E: edwinharrysteele@gmail.com *or* harry.steele@sheffield.anglican.org

STEELE, The Ven Gordon John. b 55. Kent Univ BA 76 Worc Coll Ox BA 82 MA 87. Coll of Resurr Mirfield 82. **d** 84 **p** 85. C Greenhill St Jo *Lon* 84–88; TV Uxbridge 88–94; V Northampton St Alb *Pet* 94–01; V Pet St Jo 01–12; RD Pet 04–10; Adn Oakham from 12; Can Pet Cathl from 04. *Diocesan Office, The Palace, Minster Precincts, Peterborough PE1 1YB* T: (01733) 887017 E: archdeacon.oakham@peterborough-diocese.org.uk

STEELE, Peter Gerald. b 44. Bournemouth Tech Coll BSc 67 Essex Univ MSc 69. Sarum & Wells Th Coll 91. **d** 93 **p** 94. C Beaminster Area *Sarum* 93–97; P-in-c Aldermaston w Wasing and Brimpton *Ox* 97–08; P-in-c Woolhampton w Midgham and Beenham Valance 05–08; R Aldermaston and Woolhampton 08–10; AD Bradfield 07–10; rtd 10; PtO *Sarum* from 14; *Win* from 18. *19 Tolme Way, Picket Piece, Andover SP11 6FF* T: (01264) 393288 E: petesteele@btinternet.com

STEELE, Canon Terence. b 54. Linc Th Coll 85. **d** 87 **p** 88. C New Sleaford *Linc* 87–90; V Cowbit 90–95; P-in-c Burgh le Marsh 95–97; V 97–06; P-in-c Orby 95–97; V 97–06; P-in-c Bratoft w Irby-in-the-Marsh 95–97; R 97–06; P-in-c Welton-le-Marsh w Gunby 95–97; R 97–06; R Burgh Gp from 06; RD Calcewaithe and Candleshoe 05–17; Can and Preb Linc Cathl from 07. *The Vicarage, Glebe Rise, Burgh le Marsh, Skegness PE24 5BL* T: (01754) 810216 E: father.terry@btclick.com

STEELE-PERKINS, Mrs Barbara Anita. b 46. Whitelands Coll Lon CertEd 68 Spurgeon's Coll MTh 98. STETS 99. **d** 01 **p** 02. Tutor Local Min Progr *Guildf* from 95; NSM Wisley w Pyrford 01–04; NSM Haslemere and Grayswood 04–18; rtd 18; PtO *Guildf* from 18. *68 Church Road, Milford, Godalming GU8 5JD* T: (01483) 351467 E: barbarasp46@gmail.com

STEEN, The Ven Jane Elizabeth. b 64. Newnham Coll Cam BA 88 MA 90 PhD 92. Westcott Ho Cam 93. **d** 96 **p** 97. C Chipping Barnet w Arkley *St Alb* 96–99; Chapl and Personal Asst to Bp S'wark 99–05; Hon Chapl S'wark Cathl 00–05; Chan and Can Th and Dir Min Tr 05–13; Adn S'wark from 13. *2 Harmsworth Mews, West Square, London SE11 4SQ* T: (020) 7820 8079 *or* 7939 9409 E: jane.steen@southwark.anglican.org

STEER, Andrew David. b 67. Huddersfield Univ BA 97 PGCE 98 RGN 88 RM 92. Ridley Hall Cam 14. **d** 16 **p** 17. C Almondbury w Farnley Tyas *Leeds* from 16. *50 Longcroft, Huddersfield HD5 8XW* T: (01484) 309973 E: adsteer@icloud.com

STEER, Norman William. b 35. SRN 57. EAMTC 01. **d** 03 **p** 04. NSM Dickleburgh and The Pulhams *Nor* 03–14; PtO from 14. *Brook Cottage, Harleston Road, Starston, Harleston IP20 9NL* T: (01379) 854245 M: 07941-473255 E: steernorman@gmail.com

STEER, Philip Lloyd. b 36. Ex Coll Ox BA 60. Ripon Hall Ox 60. **d** 62 **p** 63. C Ilkeston St Mary *Derby* 62–65; C Eckington 65–67; V Woodville 67–72; P-in-c Stiffkey w Morston and Langham Episcopi *Nor* 72–74; rtd 96. *15 Front Street, Binham, Fakenham NR21 0AN*

STEER, Simon Morrison. b 58. York Univ BA 81. Princeton Th Sem MDiv 87 Westmr Th Sem (USA) PhD 02. **d** 12 **p** 13. Chapl Abingdon Sch from 12; NSM N Abingdon *Ox* 12–18; PtO from 18. *29 Park Road, Abingdon OX14 1DA* T: (01235) 536529 M: 07758-850086 E: simon.steer@abingdon.org.uk

STEERS, Alan James. *See* COOK, Alan James

STEIN, Ms Ann Elizabeth. b 57. Loughb Univ BSc 78 Liv Hope MA 01. NOC 05. **d** 07 **p** 08. C Ormskirk *Liv* 07–11; P-in-c Abram 11–17; P-in-c Bickershaw 11–17; TV Chapelfields from 17. *The Vicarage, 1 Vicarage Gardens, Abram, Wigan WN2 5SA* T: (01942) 865647 E: revannstein@gmail.com

STEINBERG, Eric Reed (Joseph). b 65. Trin Coll Bris BA 94. **d** 94 **p** 95. C Chigwell and Chigwell Row *Chelmsf* 94–99; Dir Y2000 99–00; Dir Jews for Jesus UK 00–05; Dir CMS from 05; PtO *Ox* from 12. *47 New Bridge Street, Witney OX18 1YA* T: (01865) 787400 E: kosherjoe@mac.com

STELL, Peter Donald. b 50. Leeds Univ 74 Southn Univ BA 81 Man Univ 93 MInstM. Sarum & Wells Th Coll 78. **d** 81 **p** 82. C Rothwell w Lofthouse *Ripon* 81–85; TV Brayton *York* 85–87; Chapl Asst Leybourne Grange Hosp W Malling 87–88; Chapl Asst Kent, Sussex and Pembury Hosps Tunbridge Wells 87–88; C Spalding St Jo w Deeping St Nicholas *Linc* 87–93; Chapl S Lincs HA Mental Handicap Unit 88–93; Chapl HM Pris Liv 93–94; Chapl HM Pris Wayland 94–99; Chapl HM Pris Grendon and HM Pris Spring Hill 99–02; Chapl HM Pris Rye Hill 02–05; Chapl HM Pris N Sea Camp 05–13; Chapl Thorpe Hall Hospice 14–15. *8 Van Gogh Drive, Spalding PE11 3HU* T: (01775) 762546

STENTIFORD, Canon Pauline Cecilia Elizabeth. b 48. EAMTC 98. **d** 00 **p** 01. NSM Gt and Lt Bealings w Playford and Culpho *St E* 00–03; P-in-c 03–13; RD Woodbridge 05–11; Hon Can *St E* Cathl 08–13; rtd 14; PtO *St E* from 14. *Sheepstor, Boyton, Woodbridge IP12 3LH* T: (01394) 411469 E: pauline@stentiford.com

STEPHEN, Canon Kenneth George. b 47. Strathclyde Univ BA 69 Edin Univ BD 72. Edin Th Coll 69. **d** 72 **p** 73. C Ayr *Glas* 72–75; R Renfrew 75–80; R Motherwell 80–93; R Wishaw 80–93; R Kilmarnock 93–06; R Dalbeattie 06–14; Syn Clerk 87–12; Can St Mary's Cathl 87–12; Hon Can St Mary's Cathl 12–14; rtd 14; LtO *Glas* from 14. *32 Dalmellington Road, Ayr KA7 3PY* T: (01292) 267065

STEPHENS, Canon Anthony Wayne. b 54. Surrey Univ BSc 80. St Jo Coll Nottm 02. **d** 04 **p** 05. C Preston w Sutton Poyntz, Littlemoor etc *Sarum* 04–08; Pioneer Min Weymouth Town Cen 08–13; P-in-c S Hill w Callington *Truro* 13–16; P-in-c Stoke Climsland 13–16; P-in-c Linkinhorne 13–16; R Callington Cluster from 16; Chapl Duchy Coll from 15; Hon Can Truro Cathl from 18. *The Rectory, Stoke Climsland, Callington PL17 8NZ* T: (01579) 371496 E: revtonystephens@gmail.com

STEPHENS, Canon Harold William Barrow. b 47. Lon Univ BEd 71. S Dios Minl Tr Scheme 80. **d** 82 **p** 83. NSM Heytesbury and Sutton Veny *Sarum* 82–83; NSM Bishopstrow and Boreham 83–91; Dep Hd Master Westwood St Thos Sch Salisbury 91–99; P-in-c Market Lavington and Easterton *Sarum* 99–03; P-in-c W Lavington and the Cheverells 02–03; R The Lavingtons, Cheverells, and Easterton 03–07; TR Dorchester 07–13; P-in-c The Winterbournes and Compton Valence 09–13; Can and Preb Sarum Cathl 09–13; rtd 13; PtO *Sarum* from 13. *40 Ashley Place, Warminster BA12 9QJ* T: (01985) 301137 E: rectoryh@googlemail.com

STEPHENS, Mrs Jean. b 46. St As Minl Tr Course. **d** 89 **p** 97. NSM Gwernaffield and Llanferres *St As* 89–02 and 04–09; NSM Hawarden 02–04; NSM Cilcain, Gwernaffield, Llanferres etc 09–12; rtd 13; PtO *St As* from 14. *Noddfa, Pen y Fron Road, Pantymwyn, Mold CH7 5EF* T: (01352) 740037 E: jean.noddfa@btinternet.com

STEPHENS, Jill. *See* STEPHENS, Rosemary Jill

STEPHENS, Mrs Joanna Louise. b 69. St Jo Coll Nottm BA 08. **d** 08 **p** 09. C Bramcote *S'well* 08–10; C Attenborough 10–12; C Toton 10–12; TV Hucknall Torkard 12–19; V W

Hucknall from 19. *The Vicarage, 63 Ruffs Drive, Hucknall, Nottingham NG15 6JG* T: 0115-963 3640 M: 07890-385133 E: joke.stephens@talktalk.net

STEPHENS, John Michael. b 29. MRICS 52. Lich Th Coll 62. **d** 64 **p** 65. C Birchington w Acol *Cant* 64–70; V Tovil 70–79; V Brabourne w Smeeth 79–94; RD N Lympne 87–94; rtd 94; PtO *York* from 94. *Southacre, Kirby Mills, Kirkbymoorside, York YO62 6NR* T: (01751) 432766

STEPHENS, Martin Nicholas. b 64. Brunel Univ BSc 88 Nottm Univ MTh 01. St Jo Coll Nottm 99. **d** 01 **p** 02. C Newchapel *Lich* 01–04; TV Bucknall 04–16; TR Macclesfield Team *Ches* from 16. *85 Beech Lane, Macclesfield SK10 2DY* T: (01625) 426110 E: teamrector.macc@gmail.com

STEPHENS, Michael. *See* STEPHENS, John Michael

STEPHENS, Paul. b 53. AGSM 73 Newton Park Coll Bath PGCE 74. Trin Coll Bris 91. **d** 93 **p** 94. C S Molton w Nymet St George, High Bray etc *Ex* 93–97; R Norton Fitzwarren *B & W* 97–99; Chapl St Aug Sch Taunton 97–99; Chapl Monkton Combe Sch Bath 99–08; P-in-c Winford w Felton Common Hill *B & W* 08–19; rtd 19. *Sunnymead, Priors Hill, Timsbury, Bath BA2 0DG*

STEPHENS, Mrs Penny Clare. b 60. St Anne's Coll Ox BA 83 Lon Inst of Educn PGCE 85. Oak Hill Th Coll. **d** 99 **p** 00. C Turnham Green Ch Ch *Lon* 99–03; P-in-c Brasted *Roch* 03–10; PtO from 10; Chapl St Joseph's Hospice Hackney 13–17; Chapl Hospice in the Weald from 17. *The Oast House, Forest Farm, Pembury Road, Tonbridge TN11 0ND* T: (01732) 358208 or (01892) 820500 E: pennystephens@btinternet.com

STEPHENS, Canon Peter John. b 42. Oriel Coll Ox BA 64 MA 67. Clifton Th Coll 63. **d** 68 **p** 68. C Lenton *S'well* 68–71; C Brixton Hill St Sav *S'wark* 71–73; P-in-c 73–82; TV Barnham Broom *Nor* 82–89; V Gorleston St Mary 89–94; RD Flegg (Gt Yarmouth) 92–94; P-in-c High Oak 94–97; RD Humbleyard 95–98; C Hingham w Wood Rising w Scoulton 96–97; TR High Oak, Hingham and Scoulton w Wood Rising 97–05; Hon Can Nor Cathl 99–05; rtd 05; PtO *St Alb* 12–16. *15 Church Row, Wootton, Bedford MK43 9HQ* T: (01234) 765403 M: 07768-425349 or 07973-322513 E: peterstephens@aol.com

STEPHENS, Mrs Rebecca Louise. b 76. Birm Univ BSc 97 PGCE 98. Qu Coll Birm 12. **d** 14 **p** 15. C Coleshill *Birm* 14–17; C Maxstoke 14–17; R The Whitacres, Lea Marston, and Shustoke from 17; Bp's Adv for Women's Min from 17; Jt AD Coleshill from 18. *Address withheld by request* T: (01675) 481252 E: revbeckys@gmail.com

STEPHENS, Richard William. b 37. Dur Univ BSc 62. Cranmer Hall Dur 62. **d** 64 **p** 65. C Hensingham *Carl* 64–67; C Norbury *Ches* 67–71; R Elworth and Warmingham 71–79; V Bootle St Matt *Liv* 79–89; P-in-c Litherland St Andr 79–83; P-in-c Failsworth H Trin *Man* 89–93; R 93–02; P-in-c Oldham St Barn 01–02; AD Oldham 99–02; rtd 02; Hon C Dalbeattie *Glas* 02–09; LtO from 09. *Cloverstone, 3 Craignair Street, Dalbeattie DG5 4AX* T: (01556) 610627 E: revrstephens@btinternet.com

STEPHENS, Mrs Rosemary Jill. b 46. SRN 68. WEMTC 96. **d** 08 **p** 13. NSM Goodrich, Marstow, Welsh Bicknor, Llangarron etc *Heref* 08–17; NSM Wye Reaches Gp 08–17; PtO from 17. *Sunnyside Cottage, Coppett Hill, Goodrich, Ross-on-Wye HR9 6JG* T: (01600) 890975 E: jill.stephens1@btinternet.com

STEPHENS, Canon Simon Edward. b 41. Qu Coll Birm PhD 80. Bps' Coll Cheshunt 63. **d** 67 **p** 68. C Cov St Mark 67–71; C Lillington 71–76; C-in-c Canley CD 76–79; V Canley 79–80; Chapl RN 80–97; Asst Chapl Menorca *Eur* 97–98; Chapl 98–99; Chapl Moscow 99–14; Hon Can Malta Cathl 01–14; rtd 14; Chapl Solomon Is 14–15; P-in-c Tangier *Eur* 16–17; PtO from 17. *119 Hoe Court, Citadel Road, Plymouth PL1 2RN* E: apokosar@gmail.com

STEPHENS, Mrs Tessa. b 74. Leeds Univ BA 97. St Jo Coll Nottm MTh 10. **d** 10 **p** 11. C Hipswell *Ripon* 10–14; C Linthorpe *York* 14–18; Chapl Teesside Univ 14–18; V Nunthorpe from 18. *114 Gypsy Lane, Nunthorpe, Middlesbrough TS7 0DR* M: 07944-302344 E: tessa.stephens@btinternet.com

STEPHENSON, David. b 76. Huddersfield Univ BMus 98. Qu Coll Birm 12. **d** 14 **p** 15. C Darwen St Pet *Blackb* 14–18; C Haslingden w Grane and Stonefold 18; V from 18; C Musbury 18; V from 18. *St Mark's Rectory, Walkden Road, Worsley, Manchester M28 2WH* E: frdavidstephenson@gmail.com

STEPHENSON, David John. b 65. Bris Univ BSc(Soc) 87 Dur Univ BA 91. Cranmer Hall Dur 92. **d** 92 **p** 93. C Whickham *Dur* 92–94; C Sunderland Pennywell St Thos 94–97; V Stockton St Jo *Dur* 97–00; V Stockton St Jas 99–06; V W Dulwich All SS *S'wark* 06–18; P-in-c Streatham Hill St Marg 14–16; AD Lambeth S 13–18; V Cotham St Sav w St Mary and Clifton St Paul *Bris* from 18. *12 Belgrave Road, Bristol BS8 2AB*

STEPHENSON, Canon Eric George. b 41. Bede Coll Dur CertEd 63. Qu Coll Birm. **d** 66 **p** 67. C Wakef St Jo 66–69; C Seaham w Seaham Harbour *Dur* 69–73; C Cockerton 73–75; LtO 75–85; V E Boldon 85–08; AD Jarrow 92–01; Hon Can Dur Cathl 93–08; rtd 08; Chapl to The Queen 02–11; PtO *Dur* 14–17. *39 Haversham Park, Sunderland SR5 1HW* T: 0191-549 5278 E: ericgstephenson@googlemail.com

STEPHENSON, Ian Clarke. b 24. Tyndale Hall Bris 52. **d** 56 **p** 57. C Bedworth *Cov* 56–58; C Edgware *Lon* 58–65; R Biddulph Moor *Lich* 65–70; Hon C Biddulph 70–88; Hon C Burslem 85–88; New Zealand from 87; rtd 89. *5 Arthur Terrace, Balclutha 9230, New Zealand* T: (0064) (3) 418 2657 E: clarkeia@es.co.nz

STEPHENSON, James Alexander. b 77. Hatf Coll Dur BSc 00 Ox Univ BTh 15. Ripon Coll Cuddesdon 09. **d** 11 **p** 12. Chapl Canford Sch and C N Poole Ecum Team *Sarum* 11–12; PtO *Ox* 13; Zambia 13–18; Chapl St Paul's Colleg Sch Hamilton New Zealand 15–18; Chapl Blue Coat Sch Reading from 18. *Reading Blue Coat School, Holme Park, Sonning Lane, Sonning, Reading RG4 6SU* M: 07809-125657 E: jxstevo@hotmail.com *or* jas@rbcs.org.uk

STEPHENSON, Mrs Jane Eleanor. b 50. Leeds Univ BA 72 PGCE 73. **d** 05 **p** 06. NSM Bunbury and Tilstone Fearnall *Ches* 05–09; P-in-c Tilston and Shocklach 09–13; R 13–19; Educn and Tr Officer 07–09; Past Worker Tr Officer 06–10; rtd 19; PtO *Ches* from 19. *The Mount, Hobb Hill, Tilston, Malpas SY14 7DU* T: (01829) 250249 E: stephenson256@btinternet.com

STEPHENSON (*née* BRYAN), **Judith Claire.** b 57. Aston Univ BSc 79 PhD 82 Trent Poly PGCE 83. St Jo Coll Nottm BTh 94 LTh 95. **d** 95 **p** 96. C Wolverhampton St Matt *Lich* 95–99; Chapl Hull Univ York 99–08; Chapl W Lon YMCA 08–14; PtO *Lon* 14–18; Chapl HM Pris Wormwood Scrubs from 18. *HM Prison Wormwood Scrubs, Du Cane Road, London W12 0TU* E: stephenson414@btinternet.com

STEPHENSON, Juliet. b 69. St Jo Coll Dur BA 05. Cranmer Hall Dur 03. **d** 05 **p** 06. C Retford *S'well* 05–08; V Newnham w Awre and Blakeney *Glouc* 08–13; V Chapel House *New* 13–18; Dir Good Funerals Co from 18; NSM Toxteth St Marg *Liv* from 19. *42J Central Avenue, Liverpool L24 0TP* T: 0151-486 3990 E: juliet_stephenson@hotmail.com

STEPHENSON, Canon Martin Woodard. b 55. St Cath Coll Cam BA 77 MA 82. Westcott Ho Cam 78. **d** 81 **p** 82. C Eastleigh *Win* 81–85; C Ferryhill *Dur* 85–87; Asst Dir of Ords 87–89; Chapl St Chad's Coll 87–89; TR Clarendon Park St Jo w Knighton St Mich *Leic* 89–98; P-in-c Hall Green St Pet *Birm* 98–99; V from 99; P-in-c Hall Green St Mich from 16; Warden of Readers 08–17; Hon Can Birm Cathl from 14. *St Peter's Vicarage, 33 Paradise Lane, Birmingham B28 0DY* T: 0121-777 1935 E: martin.stephenson@cantab.net

STEPHENSON, Norman Keith. b 62. St Jo Coll Cam MA 88 Strathclyde Univ MBA 91. NEOC 04. **d** 07 **p** 08. NSM Kingston upon Hull H Trin *York* 07–08; NSM Ealing St Pet Mt Park *Lon* 08–13; PtO from 13. *25B Montpelier Road, London W5 2QT* T: (020) 8991 9134 M: 07880-602577 E: n.k.stephenson@btinternet.com

STEPHENSON, Canon Robert. b 36. St Chad's Coll Dur BA 58. **d** 60 **p** 61. C Whickham *Dur* 60–63; C Gateshead St Mary 63–65; PC Low Team 65–67; R Stella 67–74; V Comberton *Ely* 74–04; RD Bourn 94–97; P-in-c Dry Drayton 97–01; Hon Can Ely Cathl 01–04; rtd 04; PtO *Ely* 04–18. *1 Porthmore Close, Highfields, Caldecote, Cambridge CB23 7ZR* T: (01954) 210638 E: robert1pc@yahoo.co.uk

STEPHENSON, Simon George. b 44. St Jo Coll Dur BA 67. Trin Coll Bris 74. **d** 76 **p** 77. C Hildenborough *Roch* 76–82; C Bishopsworth *Bris* 82–85; C-in-c Withywood CD 85–90; TV Wreningham *Nor* 90–97; P-in-c Tasburgh w Tharston, Forncett and Flordon 94–97; rtd 05; Asst Chapl HM Pris Wayland 98–09; PtO *Nor* from 09. *7 Swanton Avenue, Dereham NR19 2HJ* T: (01362) 699537 E: paulineandsimon@talktalk.net

STEPNEY, Area Bishop of. *See* GRENFELL, The Rt Revd Joanne Woolway

STERLING, Anne. *See* HASELHURST, Anne

STERLING, John Haddon. b 40. Pemb Coll Cam BA 62 MA 66. Cuddesdon Coll 63. **d** 65 **p** 66. C Pretoria Cathl S Africa 65–69; Lic to Offic Natal 69–70; Chapl Bris Cathl 71–74; Member Dioc Soc and Ind Team 71–74; Ind Chapl *Linc* 74–87; Ind Chapl *Ripon* 87–92; TV Hanley H Ev *Lich* 92–97; Min in Ind 92–97; P-in-c Hixon w Stowe-by-Chartley 97–02; P-in-c Fradswell, Gayton, Milwich and Weston 97–02; TR Mid Trent 02–06; rtd 06; PtO *Lich* 07–19. *10 Newquay Avenue, Stafford ST17 0EB* T: (01785) 662870 E: dojo.sterling@gmail.com

STERRY, Christopher. b 54. K Coll Lon BD 77 AKC 77. Episc Sem Austin Texas 78 St Jo Coll Nottm 79. **d** 80

p 81. C Huddersfield St Jo *Wakef* 80–84; V Middlestown 84–89; Chapl and Tutor NOC 89–94; Lect Ches Coll of HE 93–94; NSM Padgate *Liv* 92–94; Bp's Dom Chapl *Blackb* 94–97; Chapl Whalley Abbey 94–97; Warden 97–04; V Whalley 97–09; P-in-c Sabden and Pendleton 07–09; C Colne and Villages 09–12; P-in-c Huntley and Longhope, Churcham and Bulley *Glouc* 12–17; C Abenhall w Mitcheldean 12–17; C Westbury-on-Severn w Flaxley, Blaisdon etc 12–17; Warden of Readers 13–15; rtd 17. *3 Woodlands, Newland, Malvern WR13 5AX* M: 07947-753791 E: woodlandschris2017@gmail.com

STERRY, Timothy John. b 34. Oriel Coll Ox BA 58 MA 62. Wycliffe Hall Ox 58. **d** 60 **p** 61. C Cromer *Nor* 60–64; Chapl Oundle Sch 64–72; Teacher Cheam Prep Sch 72–75; Hd Master Temple Grove Sch E Sussex 75–80; Team Ldr Scripture Union Independent Schs 81–99; rtd 00; PtO *Sarum* 02–18. *24 Barn Road, Broadstone BH18 8NJ* T: (01202) 929422 E: tim@sterry.org

STEVEN, Canon David Bowring. b 38. AKC 64. **d** 64 **p** 65. C Grantham St Wulfram *Linc* 64–68; C Kimberley St Cypr S Africa 68–71; R Mafeking 71–75; C Bramley *Ripon* 76–77; V Sutton Valence w E Sutton and Chart Sutton *Cant* 77–82; P-in-c Littlebourne 82–86; Warden of Readers 82–86; V Mansfield Woodhouse *S'well* 86–98; P-in-c Mullion *Truro* 98–03; RD Kerrier 01–03; rtd 03; Hon Can Truro Cathl 03–07; PtO from 03. *5 Guinea Port Parc, Wadebridge PL27 7BY* T: (01208) 815393

STEVEN, Canon James Henry Stevenson. b 62. CCC Cam BA 84 MA 87 St Jo Coll Dur BA 87 K Coll Lon PhD 99. Cranmer Hall Dur 84. **d** 87 **p** 88. C Welling *Roch* 87–91; C Bournemouth St Jo w St Mich *Win* 91–94; TV Bournemouth St Pet w St Swithun, H Trin etc 94–00; Chapl Bournemouth and Poole Coll of FE 94–00; Tutor Trin Coll Bris 00–08; Lect K Coll Lon 08–11; Dir Liturgy and Worship Sarum Coll from 11; Can Th Glouc from 14; PtO *Bris* from 12. *Sarum College, 19 The Close, Salisbury SP1 2EE* T: (01722) 424800 E: jsteven@sarum.ac.uk

STEVEN, Richard John. b 54. Oak Hill Th Coll BA 99. **d** 99 **p** 01. C Bluff Pt Australia 00–03; P-in-c Horsmonden *Roch* 04–09; Chapl HM Pris Blantyre Ho 05–09; Australia 09–11; P-in-c Herstmonceux and Wartling *Chich* from 11. *The Rectory, West End, Herstmonceux, Hailsham BN27 4NY* T: (01323) 833124 E: ra_steven@hotmail.com

STEVENETTE, Canon Simon Melville. b 62. Hull Univ BA 83. Wycliffe Hall Ox 84. **d** 87 **p** 88. C Carterton *Ox* 87–90; C Keynsham *B & W* 90–91; TV 91–98; Chapl Keynsham Hosp Bris 92–98; V Swindon Ch Ch *Bris* from 98; AD Swindon 11–17; Hon Can Bris Cathl from 13. *Christ Church Vicarage, 26 Cricklade Street, Swindon SN1 3HG* T: (01793) 522832 *or* 529166 M: 07902-239936 E: simon.stevenette@gmail.com

STEVENS, Alan Robert. b 55. Warwick Univ BA 77. St Jo Coll Nottm 87. **d** 89 **p** 90. C Ex St Leon w H Trin 89–92; TV Rugby *Cov* 92–97; P-in-c N w S Kilworth and Misterton *Leic* 97–00; PtO from 13. *Address withheld by request* E: hattersbarmyarmy@googlemail.com

STEVENS, Andrew. *See* STEVENS, John David Andrew

STEVENS, Canon Andrew Graham. b 54. BEd MA. Coll of Resurr Mirfield. **d** 83 **p** 84. C Leigh Park *Portsm* 83–87; TV Brighton Resurr *Chich* 87–94; V Plumstead St Nic *S'wark* from 94; Hon Can S'wark Cathl from 14. *St Nicholas's Vicarage, 64 Purrett Road, London SE18 1JP* T: (020) 8854 0461 F: 8265 5065 E: frandrew@dircon.co.uk

STEVENS, Anne Helen. b 61. Warwick Univ BA 82 Fitzw Coll Cam BA 90 MA 94 Heythrop Coll Lon MTh 99. Ridley Hall Cam 88. **d** 91 **p** 94. Par Dn E Greenwich Ch Ch w St Andr and St Mich *S'wark* 91–94; Chapl Trin Coll Cam 94–99; P-in-c Battersea St Mich *S'wark* 99–07; V 07–12; Dir Readers' Tr 99–12; Hon Can S'wark Cathl 05–12; V St Pancras w St Jas and Ch Ch *Lon* from 12; Dean of Women's Ministry Edmonton Area from 15. *St Pancras Vicarage, 6 Sandwich Street, London WC1H 9PL* T: (020) 7388 1461 E: vicar@stpancraschurch.org

STEVENS, Anthony Harold. b 46. CEng 71 MIStructE 71 FIStructE 87 MICE 75 FICE 92. St Mich Coll Llan 94. **d** 95 **p** 96. C Cardiff St Jo *Llan* 95–98; TV Cowbridge 98–01; R Eglwysilan 01–08; R Gelligaer 08–12; AD Caerphilly 04–10; rtd 13; PtO *Llan* from 14; *Mon* from 14. *2 Falcon Grove, Penarth CF64 5FB* T: (029) 2070 7745 E: anthony.stevens@btinternet.com

STEVENS, Brian Henry. b 45. Open Univ BA 80. S Dios Minl Tr Scheme 81. **d** 84 **p** 85. NSM S Malling *Chich* 84–86; C Langney 86–87; TV Wolverton *Ox* 87–88; V Welford w Sibbertoft and Marston Trussell *Pet* 88–91; V Hardingstone and Horton and Piddington 91–11; Chapl Northants Police 06–11; rtd 11. *2C Manor Road, Kingsthorpe, Northampton NN2 6QJ* M: 07710-207201 E: fr.brian@talktalk.net

STEVENS, David John. b 45. Bris Univ BA 67. Clifton Th Coll.
d 70 p 71. C Ex St Leon w H Trin 70–75; P-in-c Lt Burstead
Chelmsf 75–77; TV Billericay and Lt Burstead 77–81; P-in-c
Illogan *Truro* 81–83; R St Illogan 83–96; RD Carnmarth N
96; V Highworth w Sevenhampton and Inglesham etc *Bris*
96–01; P-in-c Constantine *Truro* 01–10; RD Kerrier 03–10;
rtd 10; PtO *Truro* from 10; RD Penwith 14–17. *Bede House,
Primrose Hill, Goldsithney, Penzance TR20 9JR*   T: (01736)
719090 E: djstevens121@btinternet.com

STEVENS, Douglas George. b 47. Lon Univ BA 69. Westcott
Ho Cam 69. d 72 p 73. C Portsea St Geo CD *Portsm* 72–75;
C Portsea N End St Mark 75–79; Chapl NE Lon Poly *Chelmsf*
79–83; C-in-c Orton Goldhay CD *Ely* 83–87; V Elm 87–91; V
Coldham 87–91; V Friday Bridge 87–91; R Woodston 91–98;
P-in-c Fletton 94–98; rtd 98. *28 Francis Gardens, Peterborough
PE1 3XX*   T: (01733) 755430

STEVENS, Miss Gillian. b 51. K Alfred's Coll Win CertEd 72.
EAMTC 98. d 01 p 02. C March St Mary and March St Pet *Ely*
01–03; C Whittlesey, Pondersbridge and Coates 03–05; TV
05–16; rtd 16; PtO *Nor* from 17; *Ely* from 17. *21 Lighthouse
Lane, Hunstanton PE36 6EN* E: gill.stevens8@btinternet.com

STEVENS, James Anthony. b 47. Worc Coll Ox MA 69. Trin Coll
Bris 78. d 80 p 81. C Heref St Pet w St Owen and St Jas 80–84;
C Lowestoft and Kirkley *Nor* 84–85; TV 85–89; V Dorridge
Birm 89–05; AD Shirley 02–05; R Sarratt and Chipperfield
St Alb 05–12; rtd 12; PtO *Roch* from 13. *17 Prospect Park,
Southborough, Tunbridge Wells TN4 0EQ*   T: (01892) 670954
E: revjim@virginmedia.com

STEVENS, Jane. *See* KRAFT, Jane

STEVENS, John David <u>Andrew</u>**.** b 44. Wycliffe Hall Ox. d 68
p 69. C Standish *Blackb* 68–71; C Stonehouse *Glouc* 71–76;
P-in-c Closworth *B & W* 76–77; P-in-c Barwick 76–77;
TV Yeovil 77–80; R Chewton Mendip w Ston Easton,
Litton etc 80–94; R Quantoxhead 94–07; RD Quantock
95–01; rtd 07; PtO *B & W* from 07. *Amberwell, Holywell
Road, Edington, Bridgwater TA7 9LE*   T: (01278) 722327
E: andrewstevens@zetnet.co.uk

STEVENS, Jonathan Mark. b 76. St Mellitus Coll 16. d 19.
NSM Soul Survivor Watford *St Alb* from 19. *18 Rutherford
Way, Bushey Heath, Bushey WD23 1NJ* M: 07798-700685
E: jstevens@soulsurvivorwatford.co.uk

STEVENS, Martin Leonard. b 35. St Jo Coll Dur BA 60 MA 72.
Oak Hill Th Coll 60. d 62 p 63. C Low Elswick *Newc* 62–65;
C S Croydon *Cant* 65–69; Hon C 69–74; S England
Deputation Sec ICM 69–74; V Felling *Dur* 74–86; NSM
Ches Square St Mich w St Phil *Lon* 92–96; rtd 95; Hon C
Cullompton and Kentisbeare w Blackborough *Ex* 96–01; PtO
Cov from 03. *11 Foxes Way, Warwick CV34 6AX*   T: (01926)
490864 E: martin.stevens6@sky.com

STEVENS, Norman William. b 38. St Chad's Coll Dur BA 61.
d 63 p 99. C Wingate Grange *Dur* 63–64; NSM Bulkington w
Shilton and Ansty *Cov* 99–08; PtO from 08. *60 Clinton Lane,
Kenilworth CV8 1AT*   T: (01926) 858090 *or* (024) 7622 7597
E: norstevens@hotmail.com

STEVENS, Canon Olive. b 48. Ex Univ BA 04. SWMTC 01.
d 04 p 05. C Camborne *Truro* 04–13; C Redruth w Lanner
and Treleigh 11–14; TV 14–15; R Camborne and Tuckingmill
15–16; P-in-c Penponds 15–16; R Camborne, Tuckingmill and
Penponds 16–18; RD Carnmarth N 08–16; Hon Can Truro
Cathl 14–18; rtd 18. *Hideaway, The Square, Portreath, Redruth
TR16 4LA*   T: (01209) 842372 E: olivestevens@aol.com

STEVENS, Penelope Ann. *See* PRINCE, Penelope Ann

STEVENS, Philip Terence. b 55. Man Univ BSc 76 Lon Univ
BD 81 St Jo Coll Dur MA 86. Cranmer Hall Dur 81. d 83
p 84. C Withington St Paul *Man* 83–86; C Middleton
86–88; V Saddleworth 88–92; V Sheff St Paul 93–96;
TR Sheff Manor 96–00; PtO 00–06; *Newc* 06–08; *B & W*
09–10; P-in-c Bleadon and Weston-super-Mare St Andr
Bournville 10–13; PtO *York* 13–18; P-in-c Laceby and
Ravendale Gp *Linc* 14; P-in-c Keelby Gp 14; V Wolds
Gateway Group from 14; RD Haverstoe from 14. *The Rectory,
4 Cooper Lane, Laceby, Grimsby DN37 7AX*   T: (01472)
753602 M: 07914-357544 E: philiptstevens@gmail.com *or*
philip.stevens@woldsgateway.org.uk

STEVENS, Richard William. b 36. AKC 59. St Boniface
Warminster 59. d 60 p 61. C Greenhill St Jo *Lon* 60–63;
Chapl RAF 63–79; CF 79–01; rtd 01; PtO *Cant* 02–10. *The
Old Vicarage, Stockbury, Sittingbourne ME9 7UN*   T: (01795)
844891

STEVENS, Robin George. b 43. Leic Univ BA 65. Cuddesdon
Coll 74. d 74 p 75. C Hemel Hempstead *St Alb* 74–77; Chapl
K Coll Sch Wimbledon 77–03; TV Wimbledon *S'wark* 98–08;
rtd 09; PtO *S'wark* 11–13; *Sarum* from 13. *34 Long Street,
Devizes SN10 1NT*

STEVENS, Mrs Sara-Jane. b 72. Southn Univ BEd 97. SEITE 12.
d 15 p 16. C Worthing St Matt *Chich* 15–18; P-in-c Sullington

and Thakeham w Warminghurst from 18. *The Rectory,
The Street, Thakeham, Pulborough RH20 3EP*   T: (01798)
813121 M: 07923-420834 E: revsj@btinternet.com

STEVENS, Mrs Susan Marjorie Earlam. b 52. RGN 74.
WMMTC 97. d 00 p 01. NSM Harborne St Faith and St Laur
Birm 00–02; NSM Publow w Pensford, Compton Dando and
Chelwood *B & W* 03–12; Chapl R United Hosp Bath NHS
Trust 06–12; rtd 12; PtO *B & W* from 15. *Woollard Place,
Woollard, Pensford, Bristol BS39 4HU*   T: (01761) 490898
E: smestevens@hotmail.co.uk

STEVENS, Timothy David. b 80. Leeds Univ BA 01 Sheff
Univ MA 16. Yorks Min Course 13. d 16 p 17. C Wakef
Cathl *Leeds* 16–19; V Darton w Staincross and Mapplewell
from 19. *The Vicarage, 6 Jacobs Hall Court, Darton, Barnsley
S75 5LY* M: 07979-854727 E: tim_stevens@hotmail.com *or*
tim.stevens@leeds.anglican.org

✠**STEVENS, The Rt Revd Timothy John.** b 46. Selw Coll Cam
BA 68 MA 72. Ripon Coll Cuddesdon 75. d 76 p 77 c 95.
C E Ham w Upton Park and Forest Gate *Chelmsf* 76–80;
TR Canvey Is 80–88; Dep Dir Cathl Cen for Research and
Tr 82–84; Bp's Urban Officer 87–91; Hon Can Chelmsf
Cathl 87–91; Adn W Ham 91–95; Suff Bp Dunwich *St E*
95–99; Bp Leic 99–15; rtd 15. *62 Horringer Road, Bury
St Edmunds IP33 2DR*   T: (01284) 768321 M: 07860-692258
E: tjs46@icloud.com

STEVENS, Canon Alastair Rice. b 42. Open Univ BA 78.
Ripon Coll Cuddesdon 78. d 80 p 81. C Bexhill St Pet *Chich*
80–82; C Brighton St Matthias 82–84; C Swindon Ch Ch *Bris*
84–87; Bp's Soc and Ind Adv 87–97; P-in-c Swindon All SS
w St Barn 97–01; V 01–11; P-in-c Swindon St Aug 04–11;
Hon Can Bris Cathl 02–11; rtd 11; PtO *Bris* 12–17. *17 Kelly
Gardens, Swindon SN25 4YH*   T: (01793) 336587 M: 07880-
710172 E: al@stair.me.uk

STEVENSON, Alistair Philip. b 84. Sheff Univ BA 07.
Yorks Min Course 13. d 16 p 17. C Ecclesall *Sheff*
from 16; P-in-c Greystones from 18. *The Vicarage, 1
Cliffe Farm Drive, Sheffield S11 7JW* M: 07769-213581
E: alistair@acstevenson.net *or* alistair.stevenson@allsaintsecclesall.org.uk
or alistair.stevenson@sheffield.anglican.org

STEVENSON, Canon Andrew James. b 63. IEng AMICE MIAT.
SWMTC 94. d 97 p 98. NSM Highertown and Baldhu *Truro*
97–08; NSM Mylor w Flushing from 08; Hon Can Truro Cathl
from 15. *31 Nansavallon Road, Truro TR1 3JU*   T: (01872)
241880 E: theblackstuff@sky.com

STEVENSON, Beaumont. *See* STEVENSON, Frank Beaumont

STEVENSON, Bernard Norman. b 57. Kent Univ BA 78 Fitzw
Coll Cam BA 84 86. Ridley Hall Cam. d 82 p 83. C
Mortlake w E Sheen *S'wark* 82–84; C Kensal Rise St Martin
Lon 84–88; C Headstone St Geo 88–90; V Worfield *Heref*
90–95; R Hutton *B & W* 95–07; RD Locking 04–05. *High
Ridge, 7 Lauderdale, Barnstaple EX32 8DU*   T: (01271) 321972
E: bstevenson@clara.net

STEVENSON, Brian. b 34. NW Ord Course 76. d 79 p 80. C
Padiham *Blackb* 79–82; V Clitheroe St Paul Low Moor 82–89;
V Blackb St Silas 89–01; rtd 01; PtO *Blackb* from 01. *1 Chatburn
Close, Great Harwood, Blackburn BB6 7TL*   T: (01254) 885051

STEVENSON, Brian. *See* STEVENSON, Robert Brian

STEVENSON, Christopher James. b 43. TCD BA 65 MA 73
Em Coll Cam BA 69 MA 73. Westcott Ho Cam 68. d 70
p 71. C Newc H Cross 70–72; C Arm St Mark w Aghavilly
72–73; C Dublin Crumlin *D & G* 73–76; Hon Clerical V Ch
Ch Cathl Dublin 75–76; C-in-c Appley Bridge All SS CD
Blackb 76–82; P-in-c Appley Bridge 82–91; Bp's C Cloonclare
w Killasnett, Lurganboy and Drumlease *K, E & A* 91–12; rtd
12. *7 Merchants Quarter, Cathcart Square, 14 Dublin Road,
Enniskillen BT74 6HJ*   T: (028) 6632 8512 M: 07982-262862

STEVENSON, David Andrew. b 60. Trin Coll Bris BA 92. d 92
p 93. C Nottingham St Sav *S'well* 92–96; P-in-c Darlaston
All SS and Ind Chapl Black Country Urban Ind Miss *Lich*
96–00; C Darlaston St Lawr 99–00; TV Broadwater *Chich*
00–08; P-in-c Eastwood *S'well* from 08; P-in-c Brinsley
w Underwood from 09. *The Rectory, 5A Woodland Way,
Eastwood, Nottingham NG16 3BU*   T: (01773) 710770

STEVENSON, David Eugene. b 66. Luton Univ BA 02.
St Steph Ho Ox 06. d 08 p 09. C Nor St Jo w St Julian
08–11; P-in-c Watford St Jo *St Alb* 11–13; V from
13. *St John's Vicarage, 9 Monmouth Road, Watford
WD1 1QW*   T: (01923)   25775   M: 07980-315534
E: rev.davidstevenson@googlemail.com

STEVENSON, Donald Macdonald. b 48. Lon Univ
BSc(Econ) 70 Leeds Univ MA 72 Univ of Wales (Abth)
PGCE 73 Warwick Univ MEd 78 MBACP 11. Oak Hill Th
Coll BA 88. d 88 p 89. C Gt Malvern St Mary *Worc* 88–92;
Chapl Bedford Sch 92–98; Sen Chapl 96–98; PtO *St Alb*
99–02; rtd 13; PtO *St Alb* from 17. *94 Curlew Crescent, Bedford
MK41 7HZ*   T: (01234) 217013 E: don_xmcds9@gmx.co.uk

STEVENSON, Elizabeth. *See* STEVENSON, Margaret Elizabeth Maud

STEVENSON, Canon Frank Beaumont. b 39. Duke Univ (USA) BA 61 MInstGA. Episc Th Sch Harvard MDiv 64. d 64 p 64. USA 64–66; Zambia 66–68; Lect Th Ox Univ from 68; Bp's Tr Officer *Ox* 69–70; Chapl Keble Coll Ox 71–72; Chapl Oxon Mental Healthcare NHS Trust 75–07; Officer for CME *Ox* from 90; Dioc Adv Past Care from 90; Hon Can Ch Ch from 98. *The School House, Wheatley Road, Stanton St John, Oxford OX33 1ET* T: (01865) 351635 E: beaumont.stevenson@btinternet.com *or* beaumont.stevenson@gmail.com

STEVENSON, Gerald Ernest. b 35. S'wark Ord Course 80. d 83 p 84. NSM Eltham Park St Luke *S'wark* 83–88; Asst Chapl HM Pris Wormwood Scrubs 88–98; PtO *S'wark* 88–99; rtd 99; Hon C Eltham St Barn *S'wark* 99–04. *7 Moira Road, London SE9 1SJ* T: (020) 8850 2748

STEVENSON, Graham. b 82. Ex Coll Ox MBiochem 04 K Coll Lon MA 15. St Mellitus Coll BA 14. d 14 p 15. NSM Stamford Hill St Thos *Lon* 14–16; C 17–18; C Clapton St Jas 16–17; Chapl Fitzw Coll Cam from 18. *Fitzwilliam College, Storey's Way, Cambridge CB3 0DG* T: (01223) 332000 M: 07954-409472 E: stevenson_g@hotmail.com *or* chaplain@fitz.cam.ac.uk

STEVENSON, John. b 39. Glas Univ MA 64 Jordan Hill Coll Glas TCert 65. St Jo Coll Nottm Edin Th Coll. d 87 p 88. NSM Moffat *Glas* 87–92; P-in-c Eastriggs 92–95; P-in-c Gretna 92–95; P-in-c Langholm 92–95; Israel 95–01; P-in-c Thurso and Wick *Mor* 01–06; rtd 06; LtO *Glas* from 07. *Hoppertitty, Beattock, Moffat DG10 9PJ* T: (01683) 300164 M: 07588-342060 E: hoppertitty@msn.com

STEVENSON, John William. b 44. Salford Univ BSc 66 UNISA BTh 89. St Paul's Coll Grahamstown 84. d 87 p 87. C St Mary's Cathl Johannesburg S Africa 87–88; R Bezuidenhout Valley 88–93; V Broom Leys *Leic* 93–11; rtd 11; PtO *Pet* from 12. *5 Roman Way, Daventry NN11 0RW* T: (01327) 700119 E: johnandrene@btinternet.com

STEVENSON, Miss Margaret Elizabeth Maud. b 49. Stranmillis Coll CertEd 70 Ulster Univ BEd 86. CITC 07. d 10 p 11. NSM Drumglass w Moygashel *Arm* from 10. *The Rubrics, 1 Derrycaw Lane, Portadown, Craigavon BT62 1TW* T: (028) 3885 1503 E: elizabethstevenson431@btinternet.com

STEVENSON, Canon Michael Richard Nevin. b 52. Univ Coll Lon MA 77. CITC. d 86 p 87. C Clooney w Strathfoyle *D & R* 86–89; CF 89–12; I Bunclody w Kildavin, Clonegal and Kilrush *C & O* from 12; Can Ferns Cathl from 16. *The Rectory, Ryland Road, Bunclody, Co Wexford, Republic of Ireland* T: (00353) (53) 937 7652 E: bunclody@ferns.anglican.org

STEVENSON, Nikki James Blanton. b 79. d 16 p 17. C Northampton St Mary *Pet* 16–19; C Ingleby Barwick *York* from 19. *3 Bodiam Close, Ingleby Barwick, Stockton-on-Tees TS17 5GQ* M: 07701-024843 E: nikthevic@icloud.com

STEVENSON, Miss Pamela Mary. b 35. CQSW 74. d 97 p 98. OLM Mitcham Ascension *S'wark* 97–05; PtO from 05; Retirement Officer Kingston Area from 08. *7 Robin Hood Close, Mitcham CR4 1JN* T: (020) 8764 8331 M: 07702-928204 E: revpamstevenson@gmail.com

STEVENSON, Robert. b 52. UWIST BSc 73 Cant Ch Ch Univ MA 11 MRTPI 78 MCIM 89. SEITE 03. d 05 p 06. NSM Woodnesborough w Worth and Staple *Cant* 05–12; NSM Eastry and Woodnesborough from 12; Managing Dir Dioc Architects from 11. *The Old Rectory, 5 Cowper Road, Deal CT14 9TW* T: (01304) 366003 E: rev.rob.stevenson@btinternet.com

STEVENSON, Canon Robert Brian. b 40. QUB BA 61 Qu Coll Cam BA 67 MA 71 Pemb Coll Ox BA 69 BD 76 MA 76 Birm Univ PhD 70. Cuddesdon Coll 69. d 70 p 71. C Lewisham St Jo Southend *S'wark* 70–73; C Catford (Southend) and Downham 73–74; Lect and Dir Past Studies Chich Th Coll 74–81; Acting Vice-Prin 80–81; V W Malling w Offham *Roch* 81–10; RD Malling 93–02; Hon Can Roch Cathl 98–10; rtd 10; PtO *Roch* from 10; *Cant* from 18. *Michaelmas Cottage, Stan Lane, West Peckham, Maidstone ME18 5JT* T: (01622) 817693 E: woolystevenson@yahoo.co.uk

STEVENSON, Sheila Reinhardt. *See* SWARBRICK, Sheila Reinhardt

STEVENSON, Canon June Lesley. b 61. Aston Tr Scheme 86 Sarum & Wells Th Coll BTh 91. d 91 p 94. Par Dn Chatham St Steph *Roch* 91–94; C 94–96; PtO *York* 96–97; *Liv* 97–00; V Abram 00–10; V Bickershaw 00–10; P-in-c Winwick 10–15; R from 15; P-in-c Burtonwood 14–15; V from 15; Hon Can Liv Cathl from 06. *The Rectory, Golborne Road, Winwick, Warrington WA2 8SZ* T: (01925) 632760 E: june.steventon123@btinternet.com

STEVENTON, Kenneth. b 59. Cuddesdon Coll 94. d 96 p 97. C Spalding St Mary and St Nic *Linc* 96–99; R Sutterton,

Fosdyke, Algarkirk and Wigtoft 99–05; P-in-c Evenwood *Dur* 05–09; P-in-c Ingleton from 05; P-in-c Staindrop from 05. *St Mary's Vicarage, 7 Beechside, Staindrop, Darlington DL2 3PE* T: (01833) 660237 E: revken@freeuk.co.uk

STEVINSON, Harold John Hardy. b 34. Selw Coll Cam BA 57 MA 61. Qu Coll Birm. d 59 p 60. C Bris St Mary Redcliffe w Temple 59–63; C Caversham *Ox* 63–73; Soc Resp Officer *Dur* 74–82; Sec Dioc Bd for Miss and Unity 82–88; P-in-c Croxdale *Dur* 82–88; P-in-c Leamington Hastings and Birdingbury *Cov* 88–96; rtd 96; PtO *Cov* 96–00; *Glouc* from 96. *8 Greenways, Winchcombe, Cheltenham GL54 5LG* T: (01242) 602195 E: jstevinsons@gmail.com

STEVINSON, Mrs Josephine Mary. b 25. STh 56. Cranmer Hall *Dur* 86. dss 86 d 87 p 94. Croxdale *Dur* 86–87; LtO 87–88; LtO *Cov* 88–96; NSM Leamington Hastings and Birdingbury 94–96; rtd 96; PtO *Glouc* from 96; *Lich* from 18. *8 Greenways, Winchcombe, Cheltenham GL54 5LG* T: (01242) 602195 E: jstevinsons@gmail.com

STEWARD, Mrs Linda Christine. b 46. NE Lon Poly CQSW 82. S'wark Ord Course 84. d 88 p 94. NSM E Ham w Upton Park and Forest Gate *Chelmsf* 88–91; Chapl Newham Healthcare NHS Trust Lon 91–98; NSM Plaistow *Chelmsf* 91–96; NSM Plaistow and N Canning Town 96–98; P-in-c Rawreth w Rettendon 98–06; rtd 06. *2 Belfairs Park Close, Leigh-on-Sea SS9 4TR* T: (01702) 525638 E: lindasteward123@gmail.com

STEWARDSON, Enid Joyce. b 53. d 11 p 12. OLM Heath Hayes *Lich* 11–15; PtO from 15. *Highfield House, 20 Highfield Road, Cannock WS12 2DX* T: (01543) 279817 E: joycestewa@aol.com

STEWART, Alan. *See* STEWART, Hugh Alan

STEWART, Alistair Charles. b 60. St Andr Univ MA 83 Birm Univ PhD 92. Qu Coll Birm 86. d 89 p 90. C Stevenage St Andr and St Geo *St Alb* 89–92; C Castle Vale St Cuth *Birm* 92–93; Lect Codrington Coll Barbados 93–97; C Hanley H Ev *Lich* 97–98; Prof Gen Th Sem NY USA 98–01; V Bridge Par *Sarum* 01–10; C Sherborne w Castleton, Lillington and Longburton 10–12; TV Upton cum Chalvey *Ox* from 13. *St Peter's Vicarage, 52 Montem Lane, Slough SL1 2QJ* T: (01753) 520725

STEWART (née BARBER), Mrs Anne Louise. b 71. QUB BA 93 PGCE 94. CITC 97. d 00 p 01. NSM Belfast Malone St Jo *Conn* 00–09; NSM Finaghy 09–11; I from 11. *St George's Rectory, 6 Royal Lodge Park, Belfast BT8 7YP* T: (028) 9070 1350 *or* 9029 2980 M: 07724-067547

STEWART, Ms Brenda Alice. b 60. ERMC. d 09 p 10. C Abbots Ripton w Wood Walton *Ely* 09–12; C Kings Ripton 09–12; C Houghton w Wyton 09–12; R W Leightonstone 12–18; R Holkham w Egmere w Warham etc *Nor* from 18. *19 Home Piece Road, Wells-next-the-Sea NR23 1PX* E: bas@con-brio.com

STEWART, Brian. b 59. TCD BTh 91. CITC 88. d 91 p 92. C Ballywillan *Conn* 91–94; I Belfast St Geo from 94. *St George's Rectory, 6 Royal Lodge Park, Belfast BT8 7YP* T: (028) 9070 1350 M: 07902-792080 E: bstewart1662@gmail.com

STEWART, Charles. b 55. St Jo Coll Cam BA 77 MA 81 CertEd 79. Wycliffe Hall Ox 85. d 87 p 88. C Bowdon *Ches* 87–90; C Bath Abbey w St Jas *B & W* 90–94; Can Res, Prec and Sacr Win Cathl 94–06; V Walton-on-Thames *Guildf* 06–15; P-in-c Christchurch *Win* 15–19; V from 19. *The Vicarage, 13A Church Street, Christchurch BH23 1BW* T: (01202) 485804 E: vicar@christchurchpriory.org

STEWART, Charles Michael. b 50. Ball Coll Ox MA 82 K Coll Lon BA 05 AKC 05 MA 07 FCA 82. Ripon Coll Cuddesdon 06. d 07 p 08. NSM Leatherhead and Mickleham *Guildf* 07–11; PtO from 13. *Rickstones, Punchbowl Lane, Dorking RH5 4BN* T: (01306) 884153 M: 07936-524152 E: carolandmikestewart@outlook.com

STEWART, Ms Dorothy Elaine. b 51. Man Metrop Univ BA 93 Bradf Univ MA 98. Coll of Resurr Mirfield 08. d 10 p 11. C Potternewton *Ripon* 10–14; *Leeds* 14; V Fairweather Green from 14. *The Vicarage, Ings Way, Bradford BD8 0LU* M: 07826-107049 E: dotelartuna@hotmail.com

STEWART, Hugh Alan. b 67. Lon Inst BA 91 Middx Univ BA 03. NTMTC 00. d 03 p 04. C Gt Stanmore *Lon* 03–06; P-in-c Hertford St Andr *St Alb* 06–08; P-in-c Hertingfordbury 06–08; TV Hertford from 08. *St Andrew's Rectory, 7 Elizabeth Close, Hertford SG14 2DB* T: (01992) 582726 E: h.alanstewart@tiscali.co.uk

STEWART, James. *See* STEWART, Malcolm James

STEWART, Canon James Patrick. b 55. Keele Univ BA 77 Birm Univ MA 78. Ridley Hall Cam 86. d 88 p 89. C Boulton *Derby* 88–91; C Cove St Jo *Guildf* 91–92; TV 92–97; TR Tunbridge Wells St Jas w St Phil *Roch* 97–04; V Tunbridge Wells St Jas from 04; RD Tunbridge Wells 99–07 and 15–18; Hon Can Roch Cathl from 05. *The Vicarage, 12 Shandon Close, Tunbridge Wells TN2 3RE* T: (01892) 530687 *or* 521703 E: jpstewart4@googlemail.com

STEWART, James William. b 71. Selw Coll Cam BA 92 MA 96 Anglia Ruskin Univ MA 12. Westcott Ho Cam 09 Yale Div Sch 10. **d** 11 **p** 12. C Gt Yarmouth *Nor* 11–14; Bp's Chapl 14–16; Hon PV Nor Cathl from 14; R Thorpe St Andr from 16. *The Rectory, 21A South Avenue, Norwich NR7 0EY* T: (01603) 927291 M: 07986-839583 E: jstewart1971@googlemail.com

STEWART, Mrs Janet Margaret. b 41. Roehampton Inst CertEd 62. Cranmer Hall Dur 67. **d** 87 **p** 94. Hon Par Dn Oulton Broad *Nor* 87–94; Chapl Lowestoft Hosp 94–97; PtO *B & W* 97–98; C Quidenham Gp *Nor* 98–01; Chapl Norfolk and Nor Univ Hosps NHS Foundn Trust from 00; Chapl Norfolk Community Health and Care NHS Trust from 04. *30 St Joseph's Road, Sheringham NR26 8JA* T: (01263) 824497 E: janet.stewart10@btinternet.com

STEWART, Jennifer Jane. *See* SISTIG, Jennifer Jane

STEWART, John. b 39. Oak Hill Th Coll 75. **d** 77 **p** 78. C Accrington Ch Ch *Blackb* 77–79; TV Darwen St Pet w Hoddlesden 79–86; R Coppull St Jo 86–04; rtd 04; PtO *Blackb* 05–11. *83 Regents Way, Euxton, Chorley PR7 6PG*

STEWART, Kathryn Susan. b 57. Coll of Ripon & York St Jo BA 79 Glyndŵr Univ BA 17. **d** 18 **p** 19. NSM Mold Miss Area *St As* from 18. *16 Ffordd Trem y Foel, Mold CH7 1NG* T: (01352) 753374 M: 07500-936985 E: kathy12oct@sky.com

STEWART, Keith Malcolm Morris. b 45. **d** 08 **p** 09. OLM Stalybridge *Man* 08–14; PtO from 14; *Ches* from 14. *6 Hillside Close, Weston, Crewe CW2 5FZ* T: (01270) 829044 E: julkeith@btinternet.com

STEWART, Kim Deborah. *See* MATHERS, Kim Deborah

STEWART, Louise. *See* STEWART, Anne Louise

STEWART, Malcolm James. b 44. York Univ MA 66 K Coll Lon MA 68 Lon Inst of Educn PGCE 69 Solicitor 79. NEOC 89. **d** 93 **p** 94. NSM Upper Nidderdale *Ripon* 93–95; C Fountains Gp 95–98; V Catterick 98–03; P-in-c Culmington w Onibury, Bromfield etc *Heref* 03–06; TV Ludlow 06–10; RD 07–10; rtd 10; PtO *Heref* from 11; *Worc* from 17. *3 Leadon Place, Ledbury HR8 2GD* T: (01531) 630237

STEWART, Michael. *See* STEWART, Charles Michael

STEWART, Ms Monica Frances Ethel. b 35. RGN 57 RM 59. **d** 08 **p** 12. NSM Stamford Hill St Thos *Lon* from 08. *2 The Heights, 165 Mountview Road, London N4 4JU* T: (020) 8340 4746 M: 07947-026297 E: monica.f.stewart@googlemail.com

STEWART, Philip John. b 76. Glas Univ MB, ChB 99 MRCGP 03 Westmr Th Sem California MA 16. Ridley Hall Cam 18. **d** 19. NSM Upper Chelsea St Simon *Lon* from 19. *Flat 3, 49 Lennox Gardens, London SW1X 0DF* M: 07967-310796 E: drphilstewart@mac.com

STEWART, The Very Revd Raymond John. b 55. TCD BA 79 MA 82. CITC Div Test 77. **d** 79 **p** 80. C Clooney *D & R* 79–82; I Dunfanaghy 82–87; I Gweedore Union 85–87; Dioc Youth Adv 83–87; Bp's Dom Chapl 85–87; I Castledawson 87–03; I Tamlaght O'Crilly Upper w Lower 03–17; Ed D & R Dioc News 89–93; Dioc Glebes Sec *D & R* 93–17; Stewardship Adv 98–17; Can Derry Cathl 99–17; Dean Derry from 17; I Templemore from 17. *The Deanery, 30 Bishop Street, Londonderry BT48 6PP* M: 07761-585412 E: deanofderry@stcolumbs.net

STEWART, Stephen John. b 62. Oak Hill Th Coll. **d** 99 **p** 00. C Mile Cross *Nor* 99–04; TV Cove St Jo *Guildf* from 04. *Southwood Vicarage, 15 The Copse, Farnborough GU14 0QD* T: (01252) 513422 E: stevestewartc@hotmail.com

STEWART, Susan Catherine. *See* BELL, Susan Catherine

STEWART-DARLING, Fiona Lesley. b 58. Kingston Poly GRSC 79 Lon Univ PhD 82 K Coll Lon MA 99. Trin Coll Bris BA 91. **d** 91 **p** 94. C Cirencester *Glouc* 91–94; Chapl Cheltenham and Glouc Coll of HE 94–97; Chapl Portsm Univ 97–04; Hon Chapl Portsm Cathl 97–04; Bp's Chapl in Docklands *Lon* from 04; PV Westmr Abbey from 13. *143 New Atlas Wharf, 3 Arnhem Place, London E14 3ST* T: (020) 7477 1073 M: 07739-461090 E: fiona.stewart-darling@london.anglican.org

STEWART-SYKES, Teresa Melanie. b 64. Bris Univ BA 85. Qu Coll Birm 87. **d** 89 **p** 16. Par Dn Stevenage St Andr and St Geo *St Alb* 89–92; PtO *Birm* 92–93; Barbados 93–97; C Meir Heath *Lich* 97–98; USA 98–01; NSM Dorchester *Sarum* 12–14; NSM Dorchester and the Winterbournes from 14. *1 Mithras Close, Dorchester DT1 2RF* T: (01305) 319662

STEWART SMITH, Mrs Alison Mary. b 74. St Andr Univ MA 96 St Jo Coll Dur BA 15 Homerton Coll Cam PGCE 97. Cranmer Hall Dur 13. **d** 15 **p** 16. C Swaledale *Leeds* from 15. *Mill House, Swale Hall Lane, Grinton, Richmond DL11 6HL* T: (01748) 884665 E: alisonmstewartsmith@gmail.com

STIBBE, Mrs Hazel Mary. **d** 99 **p** 00. NSM Wolverhampton St Andr *Lich* 99–02; LtO *St As* 03–08; rtd 08; PtO *St As* from 09. *Braemar, Kerry Street, Montgomery SY15 6PG* T: (01686) 668912 E: hazel.stibbe@gmail.com

STICKINGS, James Edmund de Garis. b 76. Magd Coll Ox BA 98 MA 08. Ripon Coll Cuddesdon 08. **d** 12 **p** 13. C Headington Quarry *Ox* 12–16; R Rotherfield Peppard and Kidmore End etc from 16. *The Rectory, Kidmore End, Reading RG4 9AY* T: 0118-972 1459 E: revjstickings@gmail.com

STICKLAND, David Clifford. b 44. Surrey Univ BA 01 CPFA 68 MAAT 77 FCCA 80. STETS 98. **d** 01 **p** 02. NSM Greatham w Empshott and Hawkley w Prior's Dean *Portsm* 01–05; NSM Petersfield and Buriton 05–10; rtd 10; PtO *Portsm* from 11. *14 Captains Row, Portsmouth PO1 2TT* M: 07836-282561 E: david_stickland.t21@btinternet.com

STICKLAND, Geoffrey John Brett. b 42. Open Univ BSc 96. St D Coll Lamp. **d** 66 **p** 67. C Aberavon H Trin *Llan* 66–69; C-in-c Llanrumney Cardiff *Mon* 69–72; C Tetbury w Beverston *Glouc* 72–75; V Hardwicke 75–82; R Hardwicke, Quedgeley and Elmore w Longney 82–98; V Quedgeley 98–11; rtd 11. *19 Tai Cae Mawr, Llanwrtyd Wells LD5 4RJ* T: (01591) 610701 E: geoffstickland@googlemail.com

STICKLEY (*née* **BRAGG**), **Mrs Annette Frances.** b 44. Chich Th Coll 97. **d** 00. NSM Worth *Chich* 00–06; PtO from 06. *14 Elmstead Park Road, West Wittering, Chichester PO20 8NQ* T: (01243) 514619 E: annettestickley@talktalk.net

STIFF, Canon Derrick Malcolm. b 40. Lich Th Coll 69. **d** 72 **p** 73. C Cov St Geo 72–75; R Benhall w Sternfield *St E* 75–79; P-in-c Snape w Friston 75–79; V Cartmel Carl 79–87; R Sudbury and Chilton *St E* 87–94; P-in-c Lavenham 94–95; P-in-c Preston 94–95; R Lavenham w Preston 95–03; Min Can St E Cathl 90–00; Hon Can St E Cathl 00–03; RD Lavenham 95–03; rtd 03; PtO *St E* 03–19; *Sarum* from 03. *8 Keats Close, Saxmundham IP17 1WJ* T: (01728) 652964 E: canonstiff@hotmail.com

STILEMAN, William Mark Charles. b 63. Selw Coll Cam BA 85 MA 89 PGCE 86. Wycliffe Hall Ox. **d** 91 **p** 92. C Ox St Andr 91–95; TV Gt Chesham 95–03; P-in-c Maidenhead St Andr and St Mary 03–04; V from 04; C White Waltham w Shottesbrooke from 19. *St Mary's Vicarage, 14 Juniper Drive, Maidenhead SL6 8RE* T: (01628) 624908 E: will.stileman@stmarysmaidenhead.org

STILL, Colin Charles. b 35. Selw Coll Cam BA 67 MA 71 United Th Sem Dayton STM 69. Cranmer Hall Dur 67. **d** 69 **p** 70. C Drypool St Columba w St Andr and St Pet *York* 69–72; Abp's Dom Chapl 72–75; Recruitment Sec ACCM 76–80; P-in-c Ockham w Hatchford *Guildf* 76–80; R Merstham 80–90; Can Missr and Ecum Officer 80–90; PtO *Chich* from 92; rtd 96. *Flat 9, 16 Lewes Crescent, Brighton BN2 1GB* T: (01273) 686014

STILL (*née* **STACEY**), **Mrs Gillian.** b 53. SWMTC 94. **d** 97 **p** 98. NSM Peter Tavy, Mary Tavy, Lydford and Brent Tor *Ex* 97–06; C Abbotskerswell 06–15; C Totnes w Bridgetown, Berry Pomeroy etc from 15; Chapl Rowcroft Hospice Torquay from 01. *The Vicarage, School Hill, Stoke Gabriel, Totnes TQ9 6QX* M: 07971-412511 E: gillstill@yahoo.co.uk

STILL, Canon Jonathan Trevor Lloyd. b 59. Ex Univ BA 81 Qu Coll Cam BA 84 MA 88. Westcott Ho Cam 82. **d** 85 **p** 86. C Weymouth H Trin *Sarum* 85–88; Chapl for Agric *Heref* 88–93; V N Petherton w Northmoor Green *B & W* 93–00; V The Bourne and Tilford *Guildf* 00–11; RD Farnham 05–10; V Buckland Newton, Cerne Abbas, Godmanstone etc *Sarum* from 11; RD Dorchester from 16; Can and Preb Sarum Cathl from 18. *The Vicarage, 4 Back Lane, Cerne Abbas, Dorchester DT2 7JW* T: (01300) 341251 E: cernevicar@gmail.com

STILL, Michael John. b 63. Reading Univ BSc 84 S Bank Univ PGCE 96. St Mellitus Coll 16. **d** 19. NSM Kenton *Lon* from 19; Chapl Quainton Hall Sch Harrow from 19. *12A Radnor Road, Harrow HA1 1RY* T: (020) 8863 8540 M: 07870-952274 E: mikestill63@gmail.com

STILWELL, Malcolm Thomas. b 54. Coll of Resurr Mirfield 83. **d** 86 **p** 87. C Workington St Mich *Carl* 86–90; P-in-c Flimby 90–93; PtO 93–95; NSM Westfield St Mary 95–11; NSM Workington St Jo from 11; NSM Maryport, Netherton, Flimby and Broughton Moor from 17; NSM Solway Plain from 17. *18 Moorfield Avenue, Workington CA14 4HJ* T: (01900) 66757 E: info@thestilwellstudio.co.uk

STILWELL, Mrs Susan May. b 59. Herts Univ MA 96. ERMC 08. **d** 11 **p** 12. NSM Bp's Hatfield, Lemsford and N Mymms *St Alb* from 11. *Field View, Kimpton Road, Welwyn AL6 9NN* T: (01438) 716338 E: susan.stilwell@clara.co.uk

STILWELL, Timothy James. b 65. Birm Univ BA 87. Wycliffe Hall Ox 96. **d** 98 **p** 99. C Clifton Ch Ch w Em *Bris* 98–02; C Hammersmith St Paul *Lon* 02–05; V Fulham St Dionis from 05; AD Hammersmith and Fulham from 15. *St Dionis' Vicarage, 18 Parson's Green, London SW6 4UH* T: (020) 7731 1376 E: tim@stdionis.org.uk

STIMPSON, Nigel Leslie. b 60. St Martin's Coll Lanc BA 92 Lanc Univ MA 99. Coll of Resurr Mirfield 94. **d** 94 **p** 95. C Heyhouses on Sea *Blackb* 94–96; C Torrisholme 96–99; V

Ravensthorpe and Thornhill Lees w Savile Town *Wakef* 99–05; TR Ribbleton *Blackb* 05–12; R 12–13; Chapl Gtr Lisbon *Eur* 13–14; Asst Chapl Palma de Mallorca 14–19; Chapl Costa del Sol E from 19. *Casa Esperanza, Calle Virgen del Carmen 3, 29640 Fuengirola (Málaga), Spain* T: (0034) 952 472 140 E: nigel.stimpson13@gmail.com *or* vicar.costadelsol@gmail.com

STINSON, Andrew James. b 80. Newc Univ MEng 04 St Jo Coll Dur BA 11. Cranmer Hall Dur 09. **d** 12 **p** 13. C Oxton *Ches* 12–15; R Barrow from 15; Dioc Worship Adv from 15. *The Rectory, Mill Lane, Great Barrow, Chester CH3 7JF* T: (01829) 740263 M: 07847-948976 E: revandystinson@gmail.com

STIRLING, Canon Christina Dorita (Tina). b 48. Lon Univ BEd 73. Wycliffe Hall Ox 87. **d** 89 **p** 94. Par Dn Thame w Towersey *Ox* 89–94; C 94–98; P-in-c Brill, Boarstall, Chilton and Dorton 98; R Bernwode 98–13; AD Aylesbury 05–10; Hon Can Ch Ch 09–13; rtd 13; PtO *Ox* 13–16; *Sarum* from 16. *Sherborne House, Tower Hill, Iwerne Minster, Blandford Forum DT11 8NH* T: (01747) 811451 E: tinadstirling@aol.com

STIRLING TROY, Mrs Margaret Ann. b 63. St Hilda's Coll Ox BA 85 MA Win Univ MA 15. STETS 10. **d** 13 **p** 14. C Farncombe *Guildf* from 13; Chapl HM Pris Send from 17. *10 Dormers Close, Godalming GU7 2QX* T: (01483) 428733 E: mstirling1@hotmail.co.uk

STOBART (formerly SLADE), Joanna Elisabeth. b 70. Leeds Univ BA 91 MA 92 Coll of Ripon & York St Jo PGCE 93. Sarum Coll BA 16. **d** 16 **p** 17. C Yatton Moor *B & W* 16–19; V Ilminster and Whitelackington from 19. *21 Higher Beacon, Ilminster TA19 9AJ* M: 07765-110266 E: joannaslade@aol.com

STOBART, Stuart Malcolm. b 64. Glos Univ BA 07. Yorks Min Course 07. **d** 09 **p** 10. C Clayton *Bradf* 09–12; P-in-c Hellifield 12–14; Leeds 14–15; P-in-c Long Preston w Tosside *Bradf* 12–14; *Leeds* 14–15; V Hellifield and Long Preston from 15; PtO *Eur* from 17. *Kellwell House, Kendal Road, Hellifield, Skipton BD23 4HE* T: (01729) 851511 M: 07545-631387 E: stuart.stobart@yahoo.co.uk

STOBER, Ms Brenda Jacqueline. Liv Univ BSc 79 Leeds Univ BA 08 Cranmer Hall Dur MA 19 Lanc Univ PGCE 80. NOC 04. **d** 07 **p** 08. C Southport Em *Liv* 07–11; C Wavertree H Trin 11–13; V Denton *Newc* 13–18; P-in-c Kirk Langley *Derby* from 18; P-in-c Mackworth All SS from 18; P-in-c Mugginton and Kedleston from 18; RD Duffield 18; RD Longford 18; AD Dove and Derwent from 18. *4 Church Lane, Kirk Langley, Ashbourne DE6 4NG* T: (01332) 824792 E: bjstober@yahoo.com

STOCK, Edward Christopher James. b 85. Heythrop Coll Lon BA 12. Ridley Hall Cam 12. **d** 14 **p** 15. C Eastwood *Chelmsf* 14–17; C Sydenham H Trin and St Aug *S'wark* 17–19; P-in-c Sydenham H Trin and Forest Hill from 19. *20 Gaynesford Road, London SE23 2UQ* M: 07838-156835 E: reveddstock@gmail.com

STOCK, Lionel Crispian. b 58. Nottm Univ BTh 94 ACMA 85 ACIS 94. Linc Th Coll 91. **d** 94 **p** 95. C Preston w Sutton Poyntz, Littlemoor etc *Sarum* 94–97; P-in-c Stalbridge 97–00; Hon C Hillingdon All SS *Lon* 01–04; NSM Kendal H Trin *Carl* 04–10; PtO *Win* 10–12; Min Can Win Cathl 12–13; PtO *Eur* 10–13; P-in-c W Meon and Warnford *Portsm* 13–18; PtO *Eur* from 18. *79 Butts Road, Ottery St Mary EX11 1FP* M: 07814-935715 E: revlstock@hotmail.com

STOCK, Nigel. *See* STOCK, William Nigel

STOCK, Miss Ruth Vaughan. b 51. Birkbeck Coll Lon BA 79 MA 85. Wycliffe Hall Ox 91. **d** 93 **p** 94. Par Dn Toxteth St Philemon w St Gabr and St Cleopas *Liv* 93–94; C 94–97; TV 97–10; TV St Luke in the City 10–13; C 13–16; rtd 16; PtO *Liv* from 17. *88 South Quay, Wapping Quay, Liverpool L3 4BW* E: ruthstock@gmail.com

STOCK, The Very Revd Victor Andrew. b 44. AKC 68 FRSA 95. **d** 69 **p** 70. C Pinner *Lon* 69–73; Chapl Lon Univ 73–79; R Friern Barnet St Jas 79–86; R St Mary le Bow w St Pancras Soper Lane etc 86–02; P-in-c St Mary Aldermary 87–98; Dean Guildf 02–12; rtd 12; PtO *Lon* from 13. *62 Bramwell House, Churchill Gardens, London SW1V 3DS* T: (020) 7828 4921 E: vastock@btinternet.com

✠**STOCK, The Rt Revd William Nigel.** b 50. St Cuth Soc Dur BA 72. Ripon Coll Cuddesdon. **d** 76 **p** 77 **c** 00. C Stockton St Pet *Dur* 76–79; Papua New Guinea 79–84; V Shiremoor *Newc* 85–91; TR N Shields 91–98; RD Tynemouth 92–98; Hon Can Newc Cathl 97–98; Can Res Dur Cathl 98–00; Chapl Grey Coll Dur 99–00; Suff Bp Stockport *Ches* 00–07; Bp St E 07–13; Bp at Lambeth *Cant* 13–17; Hon Asst Bp S'wark 13–17; Hon Asst Bp Lon 14–17; Hon Asst Bp B & W 16–17; Bp Falkland Is 14–17; Bp HM Forces 14–17; rtd 17; PtO *B & W* from 14. *18 Trendale Lane, Bicknoller, Taunton TA4 4EG*

STOCKER, David William George. b 37. Bris Univ BA 58 CertEd. Qu Coll Birm 59. **d** 60 **p** 61. C Sparkhill St Jo *Birm* 60–64; C Keighley *Bradf* 64–66; V Grenoside *Sheff* 66–83; V Sandbach *Ches* 83–01; rtd 01; PtO *Ches* 01–16. *3 Ivy Bank Close, Ingbirchworth, Penistone, Sheffield S36 7GT* T: (01226) 953415 E: davidwgstocker@gmail.com

STOCKER, John Henry. b 48. Cov Univ BSc 71 Sheff Univ BEd 81 ACP 88. St Mich Coll Llan 01. **d** 04 **p** 05. NSM E Radnor *S & B* 04–06; NSM Irfon Valley 06–09; rtd 09; PtO *S & B* from 10. *1 Tai Cae Mawr, Llanwrtyd Wells LD5 4RJ* T: (01592) 610231 M: 07891-086631 E: stocker65@btinternet.com

STOCKER, Rachael Ann. *See* KNAPP, Rachael Ann

STOCKING, Clifford Brian. b 67. Trin Coll Bris 08. **d** 10 **p** 11. C Hadlow *Roch* 10–13; P-in-c March St Wendreda *Ely* 13–15; P-in-c March St Jo 13–15; TV March 15–17; V Margate H Trin *Cant* from 17; Jt AD Thanet from 18. *5 Devonshire Gardens, Margate CT9 3AF* M: 07941-056237 E: clifford2567@gmail.com

STOCKITT, Robin Philip. b 56. Liv Univ BA 77 Crewe & Alsager Coll PGCE 78. Ridley Hall Cam 95. **d** 97 **p** 98. C Billing *Pet* 97–01; P-in-c Freiburg-im-Breisau *Eur* 01–14; Asst Chapl Basle 01–14; I Donagheady *D & R* from 14. *The Rectory, 33 Longland Road, Dunamanagh, Strabane BT82 0PH* T: (028) 7139 8017 M: 07538-243138 E: robin.stockitt@gmail.com

STOCKLEY, Mrs Alexandra Madeleine Reuss. b 43. Cranmer Hall Dur 80 Carl Dioc Tr Inst. **dss** 84 **d** 87 **p** 94. Upperby St Jo *Carl* 84–89; Par Dn 87–89; Dn-in-c Grayrigg, Old Hutton and New Hutton 90–94; P-in-c 94–95; P-in-c Levens 95–03; rtd 03; PtO *Carl* from 03. *Crowberry, Ulpha, Broughton-in-Furness LA20 6DZ* T: (01229) 716875

STOCKPORT, Suffragan Bishop of. *Vacant*

STOCKS, Simon Paul. b 68. Rob Coll Cam BA 89 MA 93 Man Univ PhD 11. Trin Coll Bris BA 03 MPhil 06. **d** 04 **p** 05. C Coulsdon St Jo *S'wark* 04–07; Hon C 07–13; Hon C Purley Ch Ch from 13; Tutor St Aug Coll of Th from 11. *316 Coulsdon Road, Coulsdon CR5 1EB* T: (01737) 553190 E: s.stocks@staugustinescollege.ac.uk

STOCKTON, Canon Ian George. b 49. Selw Coll Cam BA 72 MA 76 Hull Univ PhD 90. St Jo Coll Nottm PGCE 74. **d** 75 **p** 76. C Chell *Lich* 75–78; C Trentham 78–80; R Dalbeattie *Glas* 80–84; P-in-c Scotton w Northorpe *Linc* 84–88; Asst Local Min Officer 84–88; Local Min Officer and LNSM Course Prin 88–97; TR Monkwearmouth *Dur* 97–11; Can Res and Chan Blackb Cathl 11–17; rtd 17. *13 Longdales Road, Lincoln LN2 2JR* E: ian.g.stockton@gmail.com

STODDART, David Easton. b 36. K Coll Dur BSc 60 PhD 66 CEng 66 MIMechE 66 FCMI 72 FIQA 76. WEMTC 92. **d** 95 **p** 96. OLM Stroud H Trin *Glouc* 95–99; OLM Woodchester and Brimscombe 99–00; NSM 00–08; Jt Angl Chapl Severn NHS Trust 99–05; Jt Angl Chapl Glos Primary Care Trust 05–11; rtd 11; PtO *Glouc* from 08. *Woodstock, Hampton Green, Box, Stroud GL6 9AD* T: (01453) 885338 E: stoddart@david-isabel.co.uk

STODDART, Mrs Hazel Elizabeth Jane. b 92. Cranmer Hall Dur 17. **d** 19. C Salford St Phil w St Steph *Man* from 19. *Apartment 6.01, Block A, Adelphi Wharf, Adelphi Street, Salford M3 6DZ*

STOKE-ON-TRENT, Archdeacon of. *See* PARKER, The Ven Matthew John

STOKER, Andrew. b 64. Coll of Ripon & York St Jo BA 86. Coll of Resurr Mirfield 87. **d** 90 **p** 91. C Horton *Newc* 90–92; C Clifford *York* 92–96; P-in-c Cawood 96–98; P-in-c Ryther 96–98; P-in-c Wistow 96–98; R Cawood w Ryther and Wistow 98–04; P-in-c York St Clem w St Mary Bishophill Senior 04–05; R York St Clem w St Mary Bishophill from 05. *13 Nunthorpe Avenue, York YO23 1PF* T: (01904) 624425

STOKER, Canon Howard Charles. b 62. Linc Th Coll BTh 93. **d** 93 **p** 94. C Hessle *York* 93–96; C Richmond w Hudswell *Ripon* 96–99; C Downholme and Marske 96–99; R Holt w High Kelling *Nor* from 99; RD Holt 05–11; Hon Can Nor Cathl from 13. *The Rectory, 11 Church Street, Holt NR25 6BB* T: (01263) 712048 F: 711397 E: holtrectory@tiscali.co.uk

STOKER, Canon Joanna Mary. b 57. Leic Univ BA 79 Nottm Univ BCombStuds 83. Linc Th Coll 80. **dss** 83 **d** 87 **p** 94. Greenford H Cross *Lon* 83–87; Par Dn 87–89; Par Dn Farnham Royal w Hedgerley *Ox* 89–92; Dn-in-c Seer Green and Jordans 92–94; P-in-c 94–97; TV Stantonbury and Willen 97–03; TR Basingstoke *Win* from 03; Hon Can Win Cathl from 08. *The Rectory, Church Street, Basingstoke RG21 7QT* T: (01256) 326654 E: jostoker@dsl.pipex.com

STOKES, Canon Andrew John. b 38. G&C Coll Cam BA 60 MA 64. Ripon Hall Ox 60. **d** 62 **p** 63. C Northampton All SS w St Kath *Pet* 62–65; C Endcliffe *Sheff* 65–68; Ind Missr 65–68; Sen Ind Chapl 69–74; P-in-c Bridport *Sarum* 75–79; TR 79–80; V Holbeach Marsh *Linc* 82–88; Bp's Dom Chapl

88–92; Can Res and Prec Linc Cathl 92–03; rtd 03; PtO *Linc* from 03. *2 Lupin Road, Lincoln LN2 4GD* T: (01522) 537595

STOKES, Colin Arthur (Ted). b 59. Birm Univ BDS 82. WEMTC 00. **d** 03 **p** 04. NSM Bromyard *Heref* 03–08; NSM Bromyard and Stoke Lacy 09–18; PtO from 18. *Solmor Paddocks, Linley Green Road, Whitbourne, Worcester WR6 5RE* T: (01886) 821625

STOKES, Dawn Ann. b 63. **d** 16 **p** 17. C Daventry *Pet* from 16. *28 Osprey Drive, Daventry NN11 0XP* E: dawn.stokes@ymail.com

STOKES, Roger Sidney. b 47. Clare Coll Cam BA 68 MA 72. Sarum & Wells Th Coll 69. **d** 72 **p** 73. C Keighley *Bradf* 72–74; C Bolton St Jas w St Chrys 74–78; V Hightown *Wakef* 78–85; Dep Chapl HM Pris Wakef 85–87; Chapl HM Pris Full Sutton 87–89; PtO *Wakef* 92–95; P-in-c Carlinghow 95–99; P-in-c Bedford St Martin *St Alb* 99–14; rtd 14; PtO *St Alb* from 14. *88 Sovereigns Quay, Bedford MK40 1TF* T: (01234) 261812 E: r.s.stokes.65@cantab.net

STOKES, Canon Simon Colin. b 62. Nene Coll Northn BSc 83. Ridley Hall Cam 89. **d** 92 **p** 93. C New Catton Ch Ch *Nor* 92–96; P-in-c King's Lynn St Jo the Ev *Nor* 96–06; P-in-c Bowthorpe 06–11; Chapl Coll of W Anglia 01–06; R Sprowston w Beeston *Nor* from 11; RD Nor N from 16; Hon Can Nor Cathl from 06. *The Vicarage, 2 Wroxham Road, Norwich NR7 8TZ* T: (01603) 426492 E: simon@simonstokes.co.uk *or* vicar@sprowston.org.uk

STOKES, Simon Jeremy. b 63. St Anne's Coll Ox BA 86 MA 90 Mass Inst of Tech SM 88 Univ of Wales (Cardiff) LLM 97 Solicitor 92. NTMTC BA 08. **d** 08 **p** 09. NSM Clerkenwell H Redeemer *Lon* 08–13; NSM St Marylebone St Cypr 13–17. *4 Stable Court, Charterhouse, 15 Charterhouse Square, London EC1M 6AU* M: 07722-048110

STOKES, Ted. See STOKES, Colin Arthur

STOKES, Terence Harold. b 46. Open Univ BA 89. Sarum & Wells Th Coll 71. **d** 73 **p** 74. C Blakenall Heath *Lich* 73–75; C Walsall Wood 75–78; C Northampton St Alb *Pet* 78–81; TV Swinton St Pet *Man* 81–85; V Daisy Hill 85–92; rtd 09; PtO *Blackb* 09–12; Hon C Chorley St Laur from 12; PtO *Man* 13–14. *17 St John's Court, Chorley Road, Westhoughton, Bolton BL5 3WG* M: 07899-040781 E: revthstokes@aim.com

STOKES-HARRISON, David Neville Hurford. b 41. FCA 65 FCCA 67 FInstM 68. Qu Coll Birm 97. **d** 00 **p** 01. NSM Walsall *Lich* 00–07; NSM Edgmond w Kynnersley and Preston Wealdmoors 07–18; NSM Tibberton w Bolas Magna and Waters Upton 07–18; rtd 18; PtO *Lich* from 18. *The Rectory, Mill Lane, Tibberton, Newport TF10 8NL* T: (01952) 551063 E: stokesharrison@btinternet.com

STOKOE, Wayne Jeffrey. b 56. Coll of Resurr Mirfield 94. **d** 96 **p** 97. C Sheff St Cath Richmond Road 96–99; V Edlington 99–09; P-in-c Doncaster H Trin 09–10; P-in-c New Cantley 09–10; V from 10. *St Hugh's House, Levet Road, Doncaster DN4 6JQ* T: (01302) 371256 E: wjs56@live.co.uk

STOLTZ, Christopher Barry. b 76. St Olaf Coll Minnesota BA 99. Concordia Th Sem Indiana MDiv 03. **d** 06 **p** 07. C Highgate St Mich *Lon* 06–09; Chapl Trin Coll Cam 09–14; Min Can Westmr Abbey from 14; Succ 14–15; Prec from 15. *The Chapter Office, 20 Dean's Yard, London SW1P 3PA* T: (020) 7654 4855 E: christopher.stoltz@westminster-abbey.org

STONE, Adrian Gordon. b 68. Trent Poly BSc 89 Nottm Univ PGCE 92. St Jo Coll Nottm 01. **d** 03 **p** 04. C Bayston Hill *Lich* 03–06; V Stafford St Jo and Tixall w Ingestre 06–17; V Trentham from 17. *The Vicarage, Trentham Park, Stoke-on-Trent ST4 8AE* T: (01782) 691948 M: 07739-043709 E: adrianstone@me.com

STONE, Albert John. b 44. Loughb Univ BTech 67 BSc. Sarum & Wells Th Coll 83. **d** 85 **p** 86. C Plymstock *Ex* 85–88; P-in-c Whitestone 88–92; P-in-c Oldridge 88–92; P-in-c Holcombe Burnell 88–92; R Tedburn St Mary, Whitestone, Oldridge etc 93–94; P-in-c Yarcombe w Membury and Upottery 94; P-in-c Cotleigh 94; V Yarcombe, Membury, Upottery and Cotleigh 95–99; P-in-c Bampton, Morebath, Clayhanger and Petton 99–10; rtd 10; PtO *Ex* from 99. *9 Castle Park, Hemyock, Cullompton EX15 3SA* T: (01823) 681459 E: ajstone@orpheusmail.co.uk

STONE, Christopher. See STONE, John Christopher

STONE, Christopher John. b 49. Lanc Univ MA 89 Keele Univ MA 92. Lambeth STh 84 Linc Th Coll 78. **d** 81 **p** 82. C Bromley St Mark *Roch* 81–84; R Burgh-by-Sands and Kirkbampton w Kirkandrews etc *Carl* 84–89; Chapl N Staffs R Infirmary Stoke-on-Trent 89–93; Co-ord Staff Support Services N Staffs Hosp 93–09; rtd 09. *Coppers Nest, Fore Street, Milton Abbot, Tavistock PL19 0PA* T: (01822) 870721 E: stonecj49@btinternet.com

STONE, Christopher Martyn Luke. b 78. Glam Univ BA 99. St Steph Ho Ox 99. **d** 02 **p** 03. C Merthyr Tydfil Ch Ch *Llan* 02–07; TV Bassaleg *Mon* 07–13; TR from 13. *The Vicarage, 1 Church View, Caerphilly Road, Bassaleg, Newport NP10 8ND* T: (01633) 378354 E: vicchris78@sky.com

STONE, Canon David Adrian. b 56. Oriel Coll Ox BA 78 MA 83 BM, BCh 83. Wycliffe Hall Ox 85. **d** 88 **p** 89. C Holborn St Geo w H Trin and St Bart *Lon* 88–91; C S Kensington St Jude 91–93; V 93–02; AD Chelsea 96–02; TR Newbury *Ox* 02–10; Can Res and Prec Cov Cathl from 10; Sub-Dean from 14. *55 Cotswold Drive, Coventry CV3 6EZ* M: 07973-215927 E: david@dandb.org.uk

STONE, Elizabeth Karen Forbes. See FORBES STONE, Elizabeth Karen

STONE, The Ven Godfrey Owen. b 49. Ex Coll Ox BA 71 MA 75 W Midl Coll of Educn PGCE 72. Wycliffe Hall Ox BA 78. **d** 81 **p** 82. C Rushden w Newton Bromswold *Pet* 81–87; Dir Past Studies Wycliffe Hall Ox 87–92; TR Bucknall and Bagnall *Lich* 92–02; RD Stoke 98–02; Adn Stoke-upon-Trent 02–13; P-in-c Edensor 04–07; rtd 13; PtO *Ox* from 14. *12 William Lucy Way, Oxford OX2 6EQ* E: stonegodfrey03@gmail.com

STONE, Ian Matthew. b 72. Ox Univ BTh 08. Ripon Coll Cuddesdon 03. **d** 05 **p** 06. C Hammersmith St Pet *Lon* 05–08; V Queensbury All SS 08–14; R Gt Stanmore from 14. *14 Chambers Walk, Stanmore HA7 4FN* T: (020) 8954 3876 E: rector@stjohnschurchstanmore.org.uk

STONE, Jeffrey Peter. b 34. Nottm Univ TCert 72 BEd 73. Lich Th Coll 58. **d** 61 **p** 62. C Newark St Mary *S'well* 61–65; C Sutton in Ashfield St Mich 65–69; Robert Smyth Sch Market Harborough 72–89; R Waltham on the Wolds, Stonesby, Saxby etc *Leic* 90–96; rtd 96; PtO *Leic* 99–17. *71 Redland Road, Oakham LE15 6PH* T: (01572) 756842

STONE, John. See STONE, Albert John

STONE, John Anthony. b 46. Univ of Wales (Lamp) MA 05. St Chad's Coll Dur BA 68. **d** 69 **p** 70. C New Addington *Cant* 69–72; C Tewkesbury w Walton Cardiff *Glouc* 72–76; C-in-c Dedworth CD *Ox* 76–82; V Dedworth 82–86; TV Chipping Barnet w Arkley *St Alb* 86–95; R Baldock w Bygrave 95–03; R Ches H Trin 03–11; rtd 11; PtO *St As* from 12; *Ban* from 14. *4 Carpenter Avenue, Llandudno LL30 1YW* E: jastone@dunelm.org.uk

STONE, Canon John Christopher. b 53. Newc Univ BA 74 Birkbeck Coll Lon MA 77 MSTSD 74 LGSM 73 MIPR FRSA. Oak Hill NSM Course 89. **d** 92 **p** 93. NSM Southfleet *Roch* 92–07; Dioc Communications Officer 96–03; Chapl Univ of Greenwich 98–99; Hon Can Roch Cathl 02–18; Bp's Dom Chapl 03–07; Bp's Media Adv 03–07; Bp's Communications Consultant 07–18; R Gravesend St Geo 07–18; rtd 18. *37 The Old Yews, Longfield DA3 7JS*

STONE, Martyn. See STONE, Christopher Martyn Luke

STONE, Matthew. See STONE, Ian Matthew

STONE, Nigel John. b 57. Bedf Coll Lon BSc 82 Lon Bible Coll MA 95. St Jo Coll Nottm 82. **d** 85 **p** 86. C Battersea Park St Sav *S'wark* 85–87; C Battersea St Sav and St Geo w St Andr 87–89; P-in-c Brixton St Paul 89–92; V 92–97; Adult Educn and Tr Officer 97–09; Dioc Olympic Adv 10–12; Par Support P Kingston Area 10–13; Hon Chapl S'wark Cathl 97–13; V Mitcham St Mark from 13. *St Mark's Vicarage, Locks Lane, Mitcham CR4 2JX* T: (020) 8648 2397 *or* 8640 1035 E: nigelstone6@btinternet.com

STONE, Peter Jonathan Michael. b 71. Ripon Coll Cuddesdon 08. **d** 10 **p** 11. C Charminster and Stinsford *Sarum* 10–14; TV Bridport from 14. *The Vicarage, 5 Garden Close, Bridport DT6 3AJ* T: (01308) 426459 M: 07971-425889 E: revpetestone@yahoo.co.uk *or* pete@bridport-team-ministry.org

STONE, Canon Philip William. b 58. Ridley Hall Cam 85. **d** 88 **p** 89. C Hackney Marsh *Lon* 88–97; V Kensal Rise St Mark and St Martin 97–04; TR 04–10; AD Brent 03–10; Dir Scargill Ho from 10; Hon Can Bradf Cathl *Leeds* from 19. *Scargill House, Kettlewell, Skipton BD23 5HU* T: (01756) 761240 E: phil@scargillmovement.org

STONE, Robert David. b 65. St Mellitus Coll 14. **d** 16 **p** 17. NSM Bocking St Pet *Chelmsf* from 16. *20 Oxney Villas, Felsted, Dunmow CM6 3EQ* T: (01371) 821477 E: robertstone1965@gmail.com

STONEHOUSE, Ian Michael. b 66. Westhill Coll Birm BPhil 97. St Mellitus Coll BA 16. **d** 16 **p** 17. C Leatherhead and Mickleham *Guildf* from 16. *52 Woodbridge Avenue, Leatherhead KT22 7QN* M: 07775-681884 E: ian.stonehouse@mac.com

STONES, Preb John Graham. b 49. Southn Univ BSc 72. SWMTC 91. **d** 94 **p** 95. C Okehampton w Inwardleigh, Bratton Clovelly etc *Ex* 94–97; TV Sidmouth, Woolbrook, Salcombe Regis, Sidbury etc 97–04; R Church Stretton *Heref* 04–07; TR Teignmouth, Ideford w Luton, Ashcombe etc *Ex* 07–14; Preb Ex Cathl 13–14; rtd 14; Bp's Chapl *Ex* from 16. *2 West Avenue, Exeter EX4 4SD* T: (01392) 671823 *or* 272362 E: gstones1@icloud.com

STONESTREET, George Malcolm. b 38. AKC 61. **d** 62 **p** 63. C Leeds St Pet *Ripon* 62–64; C Far Headingley St Chad 64–67; V Askrigg w Stallingbusk 67–82; V Bramley 82–85; TR 85–94; V Eskdale, Irton, Muncaster and Waberthwaite *Carl* 94–03; rtd 03; PtO *Carl* from 09. *Northside, Grange, Keswick CA12 5UQ* T: (01768) 777671 E: malcolm@dip.edi.co.uk *or* malcolmstonestreet@gmail.com

STONHAM, Emma Jane. *See* GRAEME, Emma Jane

STONIER, Mrs Mary. b 56. **d** 09 **p** 10. OLM Crowle Gp *Linc* 09–18; NSM Bottesford w Ashby from 18. *28 Windsor Road, Crowle, Scunthorpe DN17 4ES* T: (01724) 710900 E: mary.stonier@tiscali.co.uk

STOPFORD, John Thomas. b 44. AIMLS 67. **d** 16 **p** 17. NSM Whitegate w Lt Budworth *Ches* from 16; Chapl Asst St Luke's Cheshire Hospice from 16. *7 Plover Avenue, Winsford CW7 1LA* T: (01606) 558802 M: 07710-228336 E: jstopford801@btinternet.com

STORDY, Richard Andrew. b 64. St Jo Coll Ox BA 86 Univ of Wales MTh 10 Barrister 86. Cranmer Hall Dur BA 97. **d** 98 **p** 99. C Gt Horton *Bradf* 98–02; V Chapeltown *Sheff* from 02; AD Ecclesfield 10–14. *St John's Vicarage, 23 Housley Park, Chapeltown, Sheffield S35 2UE* T: 0114-257 0966 M: 07812-924926 E: rick@rastordy.plus.com

STORER, Rachael. **d** 16 **p** 17. NSM Gwastedyn *S & B* 16–17; C Ithon Valley from 17. *The Rectory, Crossgates, Llandrindod Wells LD1 6RU* T: (01597) 851204 E: ithonvalleyrectory@googlemail.com

STOREY, Mrs Elizabeth Mary. b 37. Man Univ BA 84. Local Minl Tr Course 81. **dss** 84 **d** 87 **p** 94. Liv All So Springwood 84–91; Par Dn 87–91; C St Helens St Helen 91–94; C Garston 94–97; Asst Chapl Liv Univ 94–98; C Mossley Hill St Matt and St Jas 97–03; Asst Chapl Liv Coll 98–03; rtd 03; PtO *Liv* from 16. *27 Mentmore Road, Mossley Hill, Liverpool L18 4PU* T: 0151-724 2075

STOREY, Gerard Charles Alfred. b 57. Thames Poly BSc 80 Lon Univ PhD 84 GRSC 80. Wycliffe Hall Ox 84. **d** 87 **p** 88. C Broadwater *Chich* 87–92; TV 92–95; Chapl Northbrook Coll of Design and Tech 90–95; Oman 95–99; P-in-c Guernsey H Trin *Win* 99–01; V 01–07; P-in-c Bream *Glouc* 07–12; V 12–14; Tanzania from 14; Public Preacher *Glouc* from 14; PtO *Chich* from 16. *80 Evelyn Avenue, Ruislip HA4 8AS* E: gerardstorey@yahoo.co.uk

STOREY, Canon Michael. b 36. Chich Th Coll 73. **d** 75 **p** 76. C Illingworth *Wakef* 75–78; V Rastrick St Jo 78–87; V Crosland Moor 87–06; Hon Can Wakef Cathl 00–06; rtd 06; PtO *Wakef* 07–14; *Leeds* from 14. *198 Healey Wood Road, Brighouse HD6 3RW* T: (01484) 713663 E: mickthevic@googlemail.com

✠**STOREY, The Most Revd Patricia Louise.** b 60. TCD MA 83. CITC BTh 94. **d** 97 **p** 98 **c** 13. C Ballymena w Ballyclug *Conn* 97–00; C Glenavy w Tunny and Crumlin 00–04; I Londonderry St Aug *D & R* 04–13; Bp M & K from 13. *Bishop's House, Moyglare, Maynooth, Co Kildare, Republic of Ireland* T: (00353) (1) 628 9825 *or* (1) 629 2163 E: patriciastorey56@yahoo.co.uk *or* bishop@meath.anglican.org

STOREY, Timothy. b 60. Trin Coll Bris 92. **d** 94 **p** 95. C Bath Weston St Jo w Kelston *B & W* 94–98; C Shirley *Win* 98–03; R Blandford Forum and Langton Long *Sarum* 03–14; TR Cen Telford *Lich* from 14; RD Telford from 16. *The Rectory, 20 Burlington Close, Dawley, Telford TF4 3TD* T: (01952) 595915 E: revtimstorey@gmail.com

STORK BANKS, Daniel John. b 78. Reading Univ MBA 11 Univ of Wales (Abth) BScEcon 02. Ripon Coll Cuddesdon 13. **d** 15 **p** 16. C Cheswardine, Childs Ercall, Hales, Hinstock etc *Lich* from 15. *The Vicarage, Childs Ercall, Market Drayton TF9 2DA* T: (01952) 840680 M: 07825-951659 E: danstorkbanks@gmail.com

STORY, Victor Leonard. b 45. St Mark & St Jo Coll Lon TCert 66 Brighton Poly BSc 74 LIMA 74. Ripon Coll Cuddesdon 80. **d** 81 **p** 82. C Evesham *Worc* 81–85; P-in-c Ilmington w Stretton on Fosse and Ditchford *Cov* 85–90; P-in-c Ilmington w Stretton-on-Fosse etc 90–96; Chapl Vlissingen (Flushing) Miss to Seamen *Eur* 96–97; Chapl Rotterdam Miss to Seafarers 97–99; Rotterdam 99; R Gt w Lt Milton and Gt Haseley *Ox* 99–15; rtd 15; PtO *Ox* from 15. *66 Rowell Way, Chipping Norton OX7 5BD* E: victor.story@btinternet.com

STOTE, Mrs Judith Ann. b 50. Qu Coll Birm 07. **d** 09 **p** 10. OLM Studley *Cov* 09–12; NSM 12–13; NSM Spernall, Morton Bagot and Oldberrow 12–13; NSM Arden Marches 13–15; rtd 15; PtO *Cov* from 15. *6 Dunstall Close, Redditch B97 5UY* T: (01527) 852515 E: judy@ardenmarches.com

STOTE, Mrs Pamela Anne. b 49. Dudley Coll of Educn TCert 70 Open Univ BA 83. WMMTC 97. **d** 00 **p** 01. NSM Cov St Geo 00–03; NSM Whitley 03–13; P-in-c 05–13; rtd 13; PtO *Cov* 14–15; NSM Allesley Park and Whoberley 15–19.

22 Chetwode Close, Coventry CV5 9NA M: 07905-230924 E: pamstote49@gmail.com

STOTER, David John. b 43. K Coll Lon AKC 66. **d** 67 **p** 68. C Reading St Giles *Ox* 67–71; C Luton Lewsey St Hugh *St Alb* 71–73; Chapl Chelsea and Westmr Hosp Lon 73–79; Convenor of Chapls Notts Distr HA 79–94; Chapl Univ Hosp Nottm 79–94; Chapl Nottm Gen Hosp 79–02; Sen Chapl Qu Medical Cen Nottm Univ Hosp NHS Trust 94–02; Sen Chapl Notts Healthcare NHS Trust 94–02; Manager Chapl and Bereavement Services 94–02; R Gedling *S'well* 02–06; rtd 06; OCM 06–08; PtO *St And* 06–08; Hon C Nettlebed w Bix, Highmoor, Pishill etc *Ox* 08–10; PtO *Ches* from 11; *Heref* from 19. *3 The Hopkilns, Kyrewood, Tenbury Wells WR15 8SG* E: david.stoter@yahoo.co.uk

STOTESBURY, Robert John. **d** 06 **p** 07. NSM Ferns w Kilbride, Toombe, Kilcormack etc *C & O* 06–10; NSM Enniscorthy w Clone, Clonmore, Monart etc 10–16; NSM Ardamine w Kiltennel, Glascarrig etc 16–18; P-in-c Killeshin w Cloydagh and Killabban from 18. *Croneyhorn, Carnew, Arklow, Co Wicklow, Republic of Ireland* T: (00353) (53) 942 6300 M: 87-988 2507 E: rstotesbury@hotmail.com

STOTT, Andrew David. b 61. NOC 03. **d** 05 **p** 06. C Walton Breck *Liv* 05–09; P-in-c W Derby St Luke 09–14; TR 4Saints Team 14–18; AD Huyton 17–18; P-in-c Orrell Hey St Jo and St Jas 18; TR Litherland and Orrell Hey from 19; AD Sefton S from 19. *St Phillip's Vicarage, Orrell Road, Liverpool L21 8NG* M: 07510-222374

STOTT, Christopher John. b 45. Lon Univ BD 68. Tyndale Hall Bris. **d** 69 **p** 70. C Croydon Ch Ch Broad Green *Cant* 69–72; Ethiopia 73–76; Area Sec (SW) BCMS 76–78; Tanzania 78–84; R Harwell w Chilton *Ox* 85–10; RD Wallingford 91–95; rtd 10; Chapl Berks Healthcare NHS Foundn Trust from 10; PtO *Ox* from 10. *1 Dibleys, Blewbury, Didcot OX11 9PT* T: (01235) 850070

STOTT, Mrs Debra Ann. b 60. Univ of Wales (Ban) BA 81 Open Univ BSc 00. All SS Cen for Miss & Min 12. **d** 14 **p** 15. NSM Moreton *Ches* from 14. *20 Broomleigh Close, Wirral CH63 2RH* T: 0151-608 3364 M: 07879-851796 E: debbi.stott@outlook.com

STOTT, Jonathan Robert. b 67. Ripon Coll Cuddesdon 99. **d** 01 **p** 02. C Anfield St Columba *Liv* 01–05; V Dovecot 05–10; Chapl HM Pris Risley 10; P-in-c Dovecot *Liv* 10–13; TR Lowton and Golborne from 15. *St Luke's Vicarage, 246 Slag Lane, Lowton, Warrington WA3 2ED* E: frjonathan@btinternet.com

STOTT, Miss Teresa. b 57. Linc Th Coll 94. **d** 94 **p** 95. C Lee-on-the-Solent *Portsm* 94–97; C Spalding St Jo w Deeping St Nicholas *Linc* 97–98; P-in-c Freiston w Butterwick 98–99; R Freiston w Butterwick and Benington 99–03; R Freiston, Butterwick w Bennington, and Leverton 03–04; C-in-c Cleethorpes St Fran CD 04–09; TV Gt and Lt Coates w Bradley 09–11; Chapl Matthew Humberston Sch 04–11; Chapl St Andr Hospice Grimsby 06–11; Chapl Whiteley Village *Guildf* 11–15; V Skerton St Luke *Blackb* 15–17; rtd 17; PtO *Linc* from 17. *1 Warren Side, North Summercotes, Louth LN11 7NL* E: stott145@btinternet.com

STOW, John Mark. b 51. Selw Coll Cam BA 73 MA 77. Linc Th Coll 76. **d** 78 **p** 79. C Harpenden St Jo *St Alb* 78–82; TV Beaminster Area *Sarum* 82–87; P-in-c Hawkchurch 87–88; P-in-c Marshwood Vale 87–88; TR 88–91; Past Co-ord Millfield Jun Sch 93–98; Manager Somerset Rural Youth Project 99–12; Regional Development Manager Learning SW from 12; PtO *B & W* 09–13; Hon C Somerton w Compton Dundon, the Charltons etc 13. *54 Etsome Terrace, Somerton TA11 6LS* E: stowjm@gmail.com

STOW, Archdeacon of. *See* STEADMAN, The Ven Mark John

STOWE, Mrs Katharine Elizabeth. b 78. Birm Univ BA 01 PGCE 02 Trin Coll Cam BA 06. Westcott Ho Cam 04. **d** 07 **p** 08. C Salter Street and Shirley *Birm* 07–11; Bp's Dom Chapl from 11. *East Wing, Bishop's Croft, Old Church Road, Harborne, Birmingham B17 0BE* T: 0121-427 1163 E: bishopschaplain@cofebirmingham.com

STOWE, Nigel James. b 36. Bris Univ BSc 57. Clifton Th Coll 59. **d** 61 **p** 62. C Ware Ch Ch *St Alb* 61–64; C Reigate St Mary *S'wark* 64–67; V Islington St Jude Mildmay Park *Lon* 67–75; V Penn Street *Ox* 75–01; rtd 01; PtO *Ox* 01–18. *27 Snowdrop Way, Widmer End, High Wycombe HP15 6BL* T: (01494) 717496

STOWE, Canon Rachel Lilian. b 33. Qu Coll Birm 79. **dss** 83 **d** 87 **p** 94. Dean w Yelden, Melchbourne and Shelton *St Alb* 82–87; Pertenhall w Swineshead 82–87; Bp's Officer for NSMs and Asst Dir of Ords 87–93; rtd 93; NSM The Stodden Churches *St Alb* 87–96; Hon Can St Alb 92–96; Convenor Dioc Adv Gp for Chr Healing *Ripon* 98–03; PtO 97–14; *Leeds* from 14; *York* from 98. *Preston Cottage, East Cowton,*

Northallerton DL7 0BD T/F: (01325) 378173 M: 07860-618600 E: rachelstowe2106@outlook.com

STOWELL, Ms Jody. b 75. Spurgeon's Coll BD 09. Ridley Hall Cam 09. **d** 11 **p** 12. C Harrow Weald All SS *Lon* 11–14; V Harrow Weald St Mich from 14. *74 Bishop Ken Road, Harrow HA3 7HR* M: 07940-269148 E: revjody@virginmedia.com

STRACHAN, Donald Philip Michael. b 37. St D Coll Lamp 60. **d** 62 **p** 63. C Aberdeen St Mary *Ab* 62–64; P-in-c Aberdeen St Paul 64–66; Chapl St Andr Cathl 65–68; Itinerant Priest *Mor* 68–73; R Coatbridge *Glas* 73–85; Chapl HM Pris Glas (Barlinnie) 84–87; Dioc Supernumerary *Glas* 85–94; rtd 94; PtO *Arg* 87–06; LtO from 06. *Reul na Mara, Claddach Kirkibost, Isle of North Uist HS6 5EP* T: (01876) 580392

STRACHAN, Robert John. b 90. Ex Coll Ox BA 12. Oak Hill Th Coll BA 17. **d** 18 **p** 19. C Cambridge H Sepulchre *Ely* from 18. *9 Victoria Street, Cambridge CB1 1JP* M: 07900-202168 E: robbiejstrachan@gmail.com

STRAFFORD, Nigel Thomas Bevan. b 53. Univ of Wales (Lamp) BA 80. Sarum & Wells Th Coll 80. **d** 82 **p** 84. C Kidderminster St Mary *Worc* 82; C Kidderminster St Mary and All SS, Trimpley etc 82–83; Hon C Stockton St Mark *Dur* 84–86; Asst P Longwood *Wakef* 86–94; V Athersley 94–97; P-in-c Ferrybridge 97–03; P-in-c Holme and Seaton Ross Gp *York* 03–04; R 04–13; rtd 13; PtO *Dur* from 14. *5 High Street, Stanhope, Bishop Auckland DL13 2UP* T: (01388) 526405

STRAIN, Benjamin Michael. b 90. **d** 16 **p** 17. C Ealing St Paul *Lon* from 16. *23 Littlewood Close, London W13 9XH* T: (020) 8579 9444 M: 07598-389614 E: ben@stpaulsealing.com

STRAIN, Christopher Malcolm. b 56. Solicitor Southn Univ LLB 77. Wycliffe Hall Ox 83. **d** 86 **p** 87. C Werrington *Pet* 86–89; C Broadwater *Chich* 89–94; TV Hampreston *Sarum* 94–00; P-in-c Parkstone St Luke 00–03; V from 03. *The Vicarage, 2 Birchwood Road, Parkstone, Poole BH14 9NP* T: (01202) 741030 E: cmstrain@tiscali.co.uk

STRAIN, John Damian. b 49. Keele Univ BA 72 Birkbeck Coll Lon MSc 83 PhD 89 AFBPsS 89. STETS BTh 00. **d** 00 **p** 01. NSM Hindhead *Guildf* 00–03; NSM Churt and Hindhead 03–09; Work Economy and Business Adv 08–12; P-in-c Compton, the Mardens, Stoughton and Racton *Chich* 09–12; P-in-c Stansted 09–12; R Octagon 12–16; rtd 16; PtO *Guildf* 17–19. *Pinewoods, Church Lane, Grayshott, Hindhead GU26 6LY*

STRANACK, Canon David Arthur Claude. b 43. Chich Th Coll 65. **d** 68 **p** 69. C Forest Gate St Edm *Chelmsf* 68–69; C Colchester St Jas, All SS, St Nic and St Runwald 69–74; V Brentwood St Geo 74–82; V Nayland w Wiston *St E* 82–99; R Hadleigh 99–02; V Hadleigh, Layham and Shelley 02–08; Dean Bocking 99–08; RD Hadleigh 99–07; Hon Can St E Cathl 94–08; rtd 08; PtO *St E* from 08. *12 Sandy Lane, Sudbury CO10 7HG* T: (01787) 881657 E: david.stranack@btinternet.com

STRANACK, Canon Richard Nevill. b 40. Leeds Univ BA 63. Coll of Resurr Mirfield 63. **d** 65 **p** 66. C Bush Hill Park St Mark *Lon* 65–68; C Brighton St Martin *Chich* 68–72; P-in-c Toftrees w Shereford *Nor* 72–74; V 74–81; P-in-c Pensthorpe 72–74; R 74–81; V Hempton and Pudding Norton 72–81; RD Burnham and Walsingham 78–81; V Par *Truro* 81–94; P-in-c St Blazey 87–91; Hon Chapl Miss to Seafarers from 81; V Stratton and Launcells *Truro* 94–06; RD Stratton 02–05; Chapl Cornwall Healthcare NHS Trust 97–02; Chapl N and E Cornwall Primary Care Trust 02–06; rtd 06; P-in-c Duloe, Herodsfoot, Morval and St Pinnock *Truro* 06–08; Hon Can Truro Cathl 98–08. *8 Sunwine Place, Exmouth EX8 2SE* T: (01395) 225638 E: rnstranack@yahoo.co.uk

STRAND, Mrs Christine Ann. b 56. Sussex Univ CertEd 78. Yorks Min Course 13. **d** 15 **p** 16. NSM Bridlington Priory *York* from 15. *Ranamara, Georgian Way, Bridlington YO15 3TB* T: (01262) 679056 E: christine@thestrands.plus.com

STRAND, Matthew David. b 87. Northumbria Univ BSc 08. St Jo Coll Nottm MA 12. **d** 12 **p** 13. C Linthorpe *York* 12–16; V Kirkleatham from 16. *130 Mersey Road, Redcar TS10 4DF* M: 07825-585965 E: matthewstrand@hotmail.com

STRAND, Mrs Sarah Elizabeth. b 90. Ex Univ BA 11 St Jo Coll Dur BA 13 MA 14. Cranmer Hall Dur 11. **d** 14 **p** 15. C Stokesley w Seamer *York* 14–17; C Coatham and Dormanstown 17–18; Tutor Cranmer Hall Dur from 17; PtO *York* from 18. *130 Mersey Road, Redcar TS10 4DF* E: revsarahstrand@outlook.com

STRAND, Tyler Alan. b 51. Augustana Coll (USA) AB 73 Gen Th Sem NY MDiv 78. St Steph Ho Ox 74. **d** 77 **p** 78. C Barrington St Mich USA 77–80; R Whitewater St Luke 80–85; R Frankfurt am Main Ch the K W Germany 85–90; Chapl Helsinki w Moscow *Eur* 90–93; Chapl H Cross Greek Orthodox Sch USA 94–95; V Hoffman Estates H Innocents 96–99; Dean Makati Philippines 00–08; R Healdsburg St Paul USA from 08. *319 North Street Apt 3, Healdsburg CA 95448, USA* T: (001) (707) 433 2107 E: tylerastrand@yahoo.co.uk

STRANG, Martin Guthrie. b 55. Bris Univ BSc 76 Paisley Coll of Tech MSc 83 MIMechE 85. St Jo Coll Nottm 07. **d** 09 **p** 10. C Trowell, Awsworth and Cossall *S'well* 09–12; P-in-c Stafford St Paul Forebridge *Lich* 12–13; P-in-c Castle Town 12–13; V Stafford St Paul and St Thos from 13. *St Thomas's Vicarage, Doxey, Stafford ST16 1EQ* T: (01785) 258796 M: 07908-995450 E: mstrang12@btinternet.com

STRANGE, Canon Alan Michael. b 57. Pemb Coll Ox BA 79 MA 89 Bris Univ MPhil 13. Wycliffe Hall Ox BA 84. **d** 84 **p** 85. C York St Paul 84–87; Asst Chapl Brussels Cathl *Eur* 87–91; Assoc Chapl 91–95; P-in-c Heigham H Trin *Nor* 95–99; R 99–16; RD Nor S 09–16; Hon Can Nor Cathl 10–16; Chapl Amsterdam w Den Helder and Heiloo *Eur* from 16. *Bouwmeester 2, 1188 DT Amstelveen, The Netherlands* M: (0031) (06) 2494 0884 E: alan@christchurch.nl

STRANGE, Malcolm. b 58. Westmr Coll Ox MTh 95 Bris Univ PGCE 02. Sarum & Wells Th Coll 82. **d** 85 **p** 86. C Seaton Hirst *Newc* 85–88; C Ridgeway *Sarum* 88–89; TV 89–91; TV Newbury *Ox* 91–98; TR Bideford, Northam, Westward Ho!, Appledore etc *Ex* 98–01; RD Hartland 99–01; NSM Winterbourne *Bris* 08–16; NSM Frampton Cotterell and Iron Acton 08–16; C Fromeside 16–17; P-in-c from 17. *Orchard House, 70 High Street, Winterbourne, Bristol BS36 1JQ* T: (01454) 775529 M: 07792-275237 E: m.strange@stbcc.org

✠**STRANGE, The Most Revd Mark Jeremy.** b 61. Aber Univ LTh 82. Linc Th Coll 87. **d** 89 **p** 90 **c** 07. C Worc St Barn w Ch Ch 89–92; V Worc St Wulstan 92–98; R Elgin w Lossiemouth *Mor* 98–07; P-in-c Dufftown 04–07; P-in-c Aberlour 04–07; Can St Andr Cathl Inverness 00–07; Syn Clerk 03–07; Bp Mor from 07; Provost St Andr Cathl Inverness from 14; Primus from 17. *Bishop's House, St John's, Arpafeelie, North Kessock, Inverness IV1 3XD* T: (01463) 819900 E: bishop@moray.anglican.org

STRANGE, Canon Peter Robert. b 48. Univ Coll Lon BA 69 Ex Coll Ox BA 71 MA 76. Cuddesdon Coll 71. **d** 72 **p** 73. C Denton *Newc* 72–74; C Newc St Jo 74–79; Chapl for Arts and Recreation 79–90; R Wallsend St Pet 79–86; Can Res Newc Cathl 86–11; Angl Adv Tyne Tees TV 90–10; Asst Dioc Dir of Ords *Newc* 94–98; rtd 11; PtO *Newc* from 11. *4 Woodthorne Road, Jesmond, Newcastle upon Tyne NE2 3PB* T: 0191-284 4468 M: 07712-594950 E: p.strange119@btinternet.com

STRANGE, Preb Robert Lewis. b 45. Sarum & Wells Th Coll 72. **d** 74 **p** 75. C Walthamstow St Barn and St Jas Gt *Chelmsf* 74–77; C Wickford 77–80; P-in-c Treverbyn *Truro* 80–83; V 83–86; Asst Stewardship Adv 82–96; V Newlyn St Pet 86–10; Preb Trehaverock 94–10; rtd 10; Hon Chapl Miss to Seafarers from 86. *The Old School House , Carrallack Lane, St. Just, Penzance TR19 7LZ* T: (01736) 786598 E: strange643@btinternet.com

STRANGE, The Ven William Anthony. b 53. Qu Coll Cam BA 76 MA 80 K Alfred's Coll Win CertEd 77 Ox Univ DPhil 89. Wycliffe Hall Ox 79. **d** 82 **p** 83. Tutor Wycliffe Hall Ox 82–87; C Aberystwyth *St D* 87; TV 87–91; V Llandeilo Fawr and Taliaris 91–96; Hd of Th and RS Trin Coll Carmarthen 96–01; V Carmarthen St Pet *St D* 03–09; AD Carmarthen 00–09; V Pencarreg and Llanycrwys 09–19; Adn Cardigan 09–19; rtd 19. *Mistletoe Cottage, Station Road, Andoversford, Cheltenham GL54 4LA* T: (01242) 820378 E: will.a.strange@gmail.com

STRANRAER-MULL, The Very Revd Gerald Hugh. b 42. AKC 69. St Aug Coll Cant 69. **d** 70 **p** 71. C Hexham *Newc* 70–72; C Corbridge w Halton 72; R Ellon *Ab* 72–08; R Cruden Bay 72–08; Can St Andr Cathl 81–08; Dean Ab 88–08; P-in-c Peterhead 02–04; rtd 08; P-in-c Strathnairn St Paul *Mor* 09–12; Hon C Inverness St Mich from 11; Dioc Dir of Ords from 14. *4 Lochlann Avenue, Culloden, Inverness IV2 7LT* T: (01463) 793943 E: stranraermull@btinternet.com

STRAPPS, Canon Robert David. b 28. St Edm Hall Ox BA 52 MA 56. Wycliffe Hall Ox 52. **d** 54 **p** 55. C Low Leyton *Chelmsf* 54–57; C Ox St Aldate w H Trin 57–60; V Sandal St Helen *Wakef* 60–94; RD Chevet 81–93; Hon Can Wakef Cathl 92–94; rtd 94; PtO *Wakef* 94–98; *Glouc* 94–12; *Worc* 94–12. *Brookside, Hill Road, Kemerton, Tewkesbury GL20 7JN* T: (01386) 725515

STRASZAK, Edmund Norman. b 57. Coll of Resurr Mirfield 88. **d** 90 **p** 91. C Adlington *Blackb* 90–93; C Harrogate St Wilfrid and St Luke *Ripon* 93–95; V Chorley All SS *Blackb* from 95. *All Saints' Vicarage, Moor Road, Chorley PR7 2LR* T: (01257) 265665 E: enstraszak@gmail.com

STRATFORD, Mrs Anne Barbara. Southn Univ CertEd 58 Ox Univ MTh 99. Qu Coll Birm 88. **d** 91 **p** 94. Officer Dioc Bd of Soc Resp (Family Care) *Lich* 85–97; NSM Kinnerley w Melverley and Knockin w Maesbrook 91–95; Chapl

Robert Jones and Agnes Hunt Orthopaedic Hosp 95–97; NSM Maesbury *Lich* 95–96; P-in-c 96–97; Chapl Moreton Hall Sch from 96; P-in-c Ford *Heref* 97–02; V 02–05; P-in-c Alberbury w Cardeston 97–02; V 02–05; rtd 05; PtO *Lich* from 05; *St As* from 05. *Pentre Cleddar, Hengoed, Oswestry SY10 7AB* T: (01691) 650469

STRATFORD, Niall Ralph. CITC. **d** 09. NSM Killiney Ballybrack *D & G* from 09. *8 Hermitage Downs, Grange Road, Rathfarnham, Dublin 16, Republic of Ireland* T: (00353) (1) 493 7535 E: vanstratford@eircom.net

STRATFORD, Terence Stephen. b 45. Chich Th Coll 67. **d** 69 **p** 70. C Old Shoreham *Chich* 69–73; C New Shoreham 69–73; C Uckfield 73–75; C Lt Horsted 73–75; C Isfield 73–75; P-in-c Waldron 76–80; R 80–82; V Blacklands Hastings Ch Ch and St Andr 82–89; P-in-c Ovingdean 89–95; Dioc Ecum Officer 89–95; P-in-c Staplefield Common 95–00; Sussex Ecum Officer 95–01; V Ferring *Chich* 06–08; C New Shoreham and Old Shoreham 08–11; P-in-c Kingston Buci 11–15; Hon C New Shoreham and Shoreham Beach 15–18; RD Hove 14–18; rtd 18. *Tudor Croft, 3 Tudor Close, Seaford BN25 2LU* T: (01273) 453768 E: terry.stratford@yahoo.co.uk

STRATFORD, The Very Revd Timothy Richard. b 61. York Univ BSc 82 Sheff Univ PhD 08. Wycliffe Hall Ox 83. **d** 86 **p** 87. C Mossley Hill St Matt and St Jas *Liv* 86–89; C St Helens St Helen 89–91; Bp's Dom Chapl 91–94; V W Derby Gd Shep 94–03; TR Kirkby 03–12; Adn Leic 12–18; Dean Ches from 18. *The Deanery, 7 Abbey Street, Chester CH1 2JF* T: (01244) 500956 *or* 500971 E: dean@chestercathedral.com

STRATHIE, Duncan John. b 58. Heythrop Coll Lon MA 01. Cranmer Hall Dur BA 97. **d** 97 **p** 98. C Yateley *Win* 97–01; V Kempshott 01–07; Min Tr Officer 07–14; Dioc Convenor of Voc Advisers 03–14; PtO 14–15; Co-ord for Learning and Discipleship *Sarum* 14–15; V Moseley St Mary and St Anne *Birm* from 15. *18 Oxford Road, Moseley, Birmingham B13 9EH* M: 07515-313242 E: duncan@strathie.net

STRATON, Christopher James. b 46. **d** 93 **p** 94. Chapl Miss to Seamen S Africa 93–96; Asst P Gingindlovu All SS 97–99; R 99–00; P-in-c Tyldesley w Shakerley *Man* 00–06; TV Astley, Tyldesley and Mosley Common 06–11; rtd 11; PtO *Liv* from 16. *2 Scarisbrick Court, Scarisbrick New Road, Southport PR8 6QF* E: chris.straton@sky.com

STRATTA, Antony Charles. b 36. ACIS. S'wark Ord Course 82. **d** 85 **p** 86. C Southborough St Pet w Ch Ch and St Matt *Roch* 85–88; R Gt Mongeham w Ripple and Sutton by Dover *Cant* 88–96; rtd 96; PtO *St E* 96–17. *11 Gracey Court, Woodland Road, Broadclyst, Exeter EX5 3GA* T: (01392) 464950 E: antonystratta@btinternet.com

STRATTON, Mrs Anne Margaret. b 58. Nottm Univ BEng 79. EMMTC 03. **d** 06 **p** 07. NSM Bradgate Team *Leic* 06–10; P-in-c Belper *Derby* 10–13; V from 13. *St Peter's Vicarage, 6 Chesterfield Road, Belper DE56 1FD* T: (01773) 821323 *or* 839560 M: 07773-076555 E: rev.annestratton@gmail.com

STRATTON, Henry William. b 39. Bris Univ CertEd 74 BEd 75. Glouc Sch of Min 80. **d** 83 **p** 84. NSM Cainscross w Selsley *Glouc* 83–87; C Odd Rode *Ches* 87–92; V Runcorn H Trin 92–96; V Lostock Gralam 96–05; rtd 05; PtO *Ches* from 05. *63 Hollymere, New Grosvenor Road, Ellesmere Port CH65 2HH* T: 0151-355 3423

STRAUGHAN, Prof Keith. b 60. Imp Coll Lon BSc 81 Lon Univ PhD 87 Imp Coll Lon ARCS 81 CPhys 87 MInstP 87 Trin Coll Cam BA 97 MA 00. Westcott Ho Cam 94. **d** 97 **p** 98. C Abbots Langley *St Alb* 97–00; Fell SS Coll Cam 00–08; Chapl 00–03; Dean 03–05; Sen Tutor 05–08; Dean Univ Cen Milton Keynes 08–17; NSM Milton Keynes *Ox* from 11; PtO *St Alb* from 17. *21 Watercress Way, Broughton, Milton Keynes MK10 7AJ* T: (01908) 200730

STRAW, Mrs Juliet Lesley. b 49. Univ of Wales (Ban) BA 70 Leeds Univ PGCE 71. SAOMC 00. **d** 03 **p** 04. NSM Stratfield Mortimer and Mortimer W End etc *Ox* 03–10; P-in-c Wymering *Portsm* 10–11; V 11–17; P-in-c Cosham 10–11; V 11–17; rtd 17; PtO *Ox* from 19. *Clive Cottage, 68 Windmill Road, Mortimer Common, Reading RG7 3RL* E: juliet.straw@btinternet.com

STRAWBRIDGE, Canon Jennifer Ruth. b 78. Washington & Lee Univ BA 01 Ox Univ MSt 02 DPhil 14. Yale Div Sch MDiv 04. **d** 04 **p** 04. C New Haven Ch Ch and Chapl Bridgeport Hosp USA 04–05; C Arlington St Mary 05–09; Asst Chapl Keble Coll Ox 09–10; Chapl and Fell 10–16; Assoc Prof NT Ox Univ from 16; LtO *Ox* from 10; NSM Headington from 18; Wiccamical Preb Chich Cathl from 18. *Mansfield College, Mansfield Road, Oxford OX1 3TF* M: 07578-296948 E: jennifer.strawbridge@theology.ox.ac.uk

STREATFEILD, Peter Michael Fremlyn. b 53. Newc Univ BSc 77 St Jo Coll Dur BA 03. Cranmer Hall Dur 00. **d** 03 **p** 04. C Solway Plain *Carl* 03–08; TV Binsey 08–18; rtd 18;

PtO *Carl* from 18. *10 The Island, Anthorn, Wigton CA7 5AN* E: peterstreatfeild@btinternet.com

STREET, Anthony James. b 57. Trin Coll Bris 79. **d** 85 **p** 87. SAMS 85–95; C Temuco H Trin Chile 85–87; V Temuco St Matt 87–95; P-in-c Warley *Wakef* 96–99; V 99–14; *Leeds* 14; P-in-c Halifax St Hilda *Wakef* 10–14; *Leeds* 14; R Sawley *Derby* from 14. *The Rectory, 561 Tamworth Road, Long Eaton, Nottingham NG10 3FB* T: 0115-973 4900 E: familiastreet@btinternet.com

STREET, David. b 72. St Jo Coll Nottm. **d** 10 **p** 11. C Bucknall *Lich* 10–13; TV 13–18; TR from 18. *The Rectory, 151 Werrington Road, Stoke-on-Trent ST2 9AQ* T: (01782) 937113 E: revdavestreet@gmail.com

STREET, Peter Jarman. b 29. K Coll Lon BD 59 AKC 59. **d** 59 **p** 60. C Highters Heath *Birm* 59–60; C Shirley 60–62; Lect Cheshire Coll of Educn 62–66; St Pet Coll of Educn Birm 66–70; RE Adv Essex Co Coun 70–92; Hon C Gt Dunmow *Chelmsf* 71–85; Sen Insp RE and Humanities 74–92; R Gt w Lt Yeldham *Chelmsf* 85–92; RD Belchamp 90–92; rtd 92; PtO *Chelmsf* from 92. *18 Jubilee Court, Great Dunmow CM6 1DY* T: (01371) 876871

STREET, Philip. b 47. Lon Univ BPharm 68. NW Ord Course 75. **d** 78 **p** 79. C Heaton St Barn *Bradf* 78–81; C Evington *Leic* 82–84; R Wymondham w Edmondthorpe, Buckminster etc 84–88; V Gosberton Clough and Quadring *Linc* 88–95; Asst Local Min Officer 88–95; V Buttershaw St Paul *Bradf* 95–99; P-in-c Gt and Lt Casterton w Pickworth and Tickencote *Pet* 99–04; R 04–09; P-in-c Empingham and Exton w Horn w Whitwell 02–06; rtd 09; PtO *Pet* from 09; *Cov* from 18. *43 Barton Road, Rugby CV22 7PT* E: p.street08@btinternet.com

STREETER, Brian Thomas. b 68. Reading Univ BSc 89. Ridley Hall Cam 05. **d** 08 **p** 09. C Windermere St Mary and Troutbeck *Carl* 08–12; Par Missr 13–15; P-in-c Egton-cum-Newland and Lowick and Colton *Carl* 15–19; P-in-c Coniston and Torver 18–19; R Coniston and the Crake Valley from 19. *The Vicarage, Penny Bridge, Ulverston LA12 7RQ* T: (01229) 861668 M: 07505-048736 E: streeter787@btinternet.com

STREETER, Christine Mary. See HADDON-REECE, Christine Mary

STRETCH, Richard Mark. b 53. **d** 93 **p** 94. OLM Stowmarket *St E* 93–13; NSM from 13. *91 Kipling Way, Stowmarket IP14 1TS* T: (01449) 676219

STRETTON, Reginald John. b 37. Man Univ BSc 62 Nottm Univ PhD 65 MRPharmS 63 CBiol 70 MRSB 70. EMMTC 88. **d** 91 **p** 92. NSM Loughb Gd Shep *Leic* 91–94; P-in-c Burrough Hill Pars 94–02; rtd 02; PtO *Leic* from 02; *S'well* 02–14; *Derby* 05–14. *19 Paddock Close, Quorn, Loughborough LE12 8BJ* T: (01509) 412935 E: reginaldstretton@btinternet.com

STRETTON, Robert John. b 45. Kelham Th Coll. **d** 69 **p** 70. C Hendon *Dur* 69–73; C Middlesbrough St Thos *York* 73–77; OSB 77–78; V Brandon *Dur* 78–85; SSM from 85; LtO *Dur* 85–91; Tr in Evang Ch in Wales 91–94; PtO *S'wark* 94–01; Lesotho 01–05; PtO *S'wark* from 14. *86B Vassall Road, London SW9 6JA* E: ssmlondon@yahoo.co.uk *or* robssm@icloud.com

STREVENS, Brian Lloyd. b 49. St Jo Coll Dur BA 70. Ripon Hall Ox 70. **d** 73 **p** 74. C Old Trafford St Jo *Man* 73–76; C Bolton St Pet 76–78; Org Sec Southn Coun of Community Service 78–92; PtO *Win* 82–86 and 92–95 and 01–16; Hon C Bitterne Park 86–92; Hon C N Stoneham 95–01. *186 Hill Lane, Southampton SO15 5DB* T: (023) 8033 3301 E: brianstrevens@btinternet.com

STRICKLAND (née CUTTS), Mrs Elizabeth Joan Gabrielle. b 61. St Jo Coll Dur BA 83. Westcott Ho Cam 87. **d** 90 **p** 94. C Cayton w Eastfield *York* 90–92; NSM Biggin Hill *Roch* 93–96; PtO *Ox* 96–00; *Ely* 00–02; P-in-c Holywell w Needingworth 02–07; NSM Hartford and Houghton w Wyton from 15. *Windswept, Holywell, St Ives PE27 4TQ* T: (01480) 495275 *or* 460107 E: epstrickland@ukonline.co.uk *or* epstrickland@yahoo.co.uk

STRIDE, Clifford George. b 58. Win Univ BA 11. STETS 08. **d** 11 **p** 12. NSM Ampfield, Chilworth and N Baddesley *Win* 11–16; TV Upper Wylye Valley *Sarum* from 16. *Ashton Gifford Rectory, Green Lane, Codford, Warminster BA12 0NY* T: (01985) 850941 E: cgstride@btinternet.com

STRIDE, John David. b 46. Ex Univ BSc 68. Oak Hill Th Coll 86. **d** 88 **p** 89. C Ashtead *Guildf* 88–96; V Lodge Moor St Luke *Sheff* 96–11; rtd 11; PtO *Sheff* from 11. *11 Blenheim Mews, Sheffield S11 9PR* T: 0114-235 6220 E: john@jonjax.net

STRIDE, John Michael. b 48. Oak Hill Th Coll BA 77. **d** 80 **p** 81. C Edmonton All SS *Lon* 80–82; C Edmonton All SS w St Mich 82–83; C Wembley St Jo 83–85; P-in-c Hockering *Nor* 85–89; R Hockering, Honingham, E and N Tuddenham 89–91; V Tuckswood 91–93; Chapl HM Pris Leeds 93–94; Chapl HM Pris Littlehey 94–96; V Heeley *Sheff* 96–99; TR Heeley and Gleadless Valley 99–04; AD Attercliffe 02–04;

V Goole 04–06; Chapl Combined Courts 06–11; Hon C Darfield 07–11; V Ludham, Potter Heigham, Hickling and Catfield *Nor* 11–16; rtd 16; PtO *Nor* from 17. *51 Mileham Drive, Aylsham, Norwich NR11 6WD* T: (01263) 479855 E: johnmo.stride@gmail.com

STRIKE, Maurice Arthur. b 44. FRSA 66. Sarum & Wells Th Coll 85. **d** 87 **p** 88. C Chippenham St Andr w Tytherton Lucas *Bris* 87–91; R Corfe Castle, Church Knowle, Kimmeridge etc *Sarum* 91–04; R Guernsey St Philippe de Torteval *Win* 04–13; R Guernsey St Pierre du Bois 04–13; rtd 13; PtO *Nor* from 13; *Win* 13–18. *The Flint House, 49 Mundesley Road, Overstrand, Cromer NR27 0NB* T: (01263) 576805 E: mstrike@hotmail.co.uk

STRINGER, Adrian Nigel. b 60. Univ of Wales (Cardiff) BD 82 Lanc Univ PGCE 83. Sarum & Wells Th Coll 86. **d** 88 **p** 89. C Barrow St Matt *Carl* 88–92; TV Westhoughton *Man* 92–94; I Inver w Mountcharles, Killaghtee and Killybegs *D & R* 94–96; V Tuckingmill *Truro* 96–01; Chapl R Alexandra and Albert Sch Reigate 01–03; I Desertlyn w Ballyeglish *Arm* from 03. *The Rectory, 24 Cookstown Road, Moneymore, Magherafelt BT45 7QF* T: (028) 8674 8200 E: blackdogmaverick@yahoo.co.uk

STRINGER, Harold John. b 36. Peterho Cam BA 58. Ripon Hall Ox 62. **d** 64 **p** 65. C Hackney St Jo *Lon* 64–68; C Roehampton H Trin *S'wark* 68–71; P-in-c Southampton St Mich w H Rood, St Lawr etc *Win* 71–73; TV Southampton (City Cen) 73–82; Ind Chapl 77–82; V Notting Hill St Jo *Lon* 82–87; V Notting Hill St Pet 82–87; V Notting Hill St Jo and St Pet 87–01; AD Kensington 98–01; rtd 02; PtO *Lon* from 03. *56 Mountfield Road, London W5 2NQ* T: (020) 8998 8049 E: mail@haroldstringer.co.uk

STROEBEL, Mrs Stephanie Suzanne. b 47. Middx Univ BA 06. NTMTC 03. **d** 06 **p** 07. NSM Ashingdon w S Fambridge *Chelmsf* 06–08; NSM S Woodham Ferrers 08–10; P-in-c Woodham Mortimer w Hazeleigh 10–15; P-in-c Woodham Walter 10–15; rtd 15; PtO *Chelmsf* 15–17; Hon C Hockley from 17. *27 Orchard Avenue, Hockley SS5 5BA* T: (01702) 200901 M: 07930-105163 E: s.stroebel135@gmail.com or s.stroebel@btinternet.com

STRONG, Christopher Patteson. b 43. Ridley Hall Cam. **d** 83 **p** 84. C Dalton-in-Furness *Carl* 83–87; V Wootton *St Alb* 87–02; RD Elstow 94–02; R Fowlmere, Foxton, Shepreth and Thriplow *Ely* 02–08; rtd 08; PtO *St Alb* from 08. *Kiln Farm, Priory Road, Campton, Shefford SG17 5PG* T: (01462) 819274 E: christopherpstrong@hotmail.com

STRONG, John. *See* STRONG, William John Leonard

STRONG, Canon John David. b 34. Cuddesdon Coll 59. **d** 61 **p** 62. C Gosforth All SS *Newc* 61–65; Chapl Malvern Coll 65–71; R Welford w Weston on Avon *Glouc* 72–79; V Nailsworth 79–01; RD Tetbury 83–00; Hon Can Glouc Cathl 91–01; rtd 01. *Glebe House, The Meads, Leighterton, Tetbury GL8 8UW* T: (01666) 890236 E: canondavid@tiscali.co.uk

STRONG, Matthew John. b 60. Lon Univ BA 81 Cam Univ BA 84 MA 89. Ridley Hall Cam 82. **d** 85 **p** 86. C Houghton *Carl* 85–89; C Hirwaun *Llan* 89–91; V Troedyrhiw w Merthyr Vale 91–95; Tutor Llan Ord Course 91–95; PtO *Birm* from 14. *22 Birch Lane, Oldbury B68 0NZ* T: 0121-421 5978

STRONG, Rowan Gordon William. b 53. Victoria Univ Wellington BA 76 Edin Univ PhD 92 Melbourne Coll of Div ThM 88. St Jo Coll (NZ) LTh 80. **d** 77 **p** 78. C Kapiti New Zealand 77–83; C Palmerston N St Pet 79–81; V Shannon 81–83; Assoc P E Hill Australia 83–89; NSM Edin Old St Paul 89–92; Tutor Edin Univ 91–92; Lect Murdoch Univ Australia from 92; Sen Lect from 02. *150 George Street, East Fremantle WA 6158, Australia* T: (0061) (8) 9339 0643 *or* (8) 9360 6470 F: 9360 6480 M: 439-988896 E: r.strong@murdoch.edu.au

STRONG, Capt William John Leonard. b 44. CA Tr Coll 64 Chich Th Coll 87. **d** 89 **p** 90. CA from 66; C Mayfield *Chich* 89–92; C Seaford w Sutton 92–94; V Crawley Down All SS 94–97; rtd 01. *21 Carroll Close, Poole BH12 1PL* M: 07944-670125

STROUD, Daniel Joseph Shine. **d** 14 **p** 14. C Whitemarsh USA 14–17; TV Mold Miss Area *St As* from 17. *The New Rectory, Rectory Lane, Llanferres, Mold CH7 5SR* T: (01352) 810694 E: djstroud@gmail.com

STROUD, David Alan. b 74. Kent Univ BA 96 Ch Ch Coll Cant PGCE 95. Westcott Ho Cam 02. **d** 04 **p** 05. C Liss *Portsm* 04–08; Asst Chapl Cant Ch Ch Univ from 08. *Canterbury Christ Church University, North Holmes Road, Canterbury CT1 1QU* T: (01227) 922538 E: david.stroud@canterbury.ac.uk

STROUD, Lara Christina Shine. b 83. Appalachian State Univ (USA) BMus 07. Virginia Th Sem MDiv 12. **d** 12 **p** 12. C Omaha All SS USA 12–13; C Rehoboth Beach and Harbeson 13–14; C Whitemarsh 14–17; C Estuary and Mountain Miss

Area *St As* from 17. *The New Rectory, Rectory Lane, Llanferres, Mold CH7 5SR* T: (01352) 810694 E: motherlara@gmail.com

✠STROYAN, The Rt Revd John Ronald Angus. b 55. St Andr Univ MTheol 76 Univ of Wales (Lamp) MA 07 Birm City Univ Hon PhD 15. Qu Coll Birm 81 Bossey Ecum Inst Geneva 82. **d** 83 **p** 84 **c** 05. C Cov E 83–87; V Smethwick St Matt w St Chad *Birm* 87–94; V Bloxham w Milcombe and S Newington *Ox* 94–05; AD Deddington 02–05; Suff Bp Warw *Cov* from 05. *Warwick House, School Hill, Offchurch, Leamington Spa CV33 9AL* E: bishop.warwick@covcofe.org

STRUDWICK, Caroline Mary Easdeale. b 55. Solicitor 84. STETS 12. **d** 15 **p** 16. NSM Upper Itchen *Win* 15–19; PtO from 19. *Corvus Cottage, South Street, Ropley, Alresford SO24 0DY* T: (01962) 773093 E: carolinestrudwick@carolinestrudwick.co.uk

STRUDWICK, Paul. **d** 99 **p** 00. USA 99–04; Canada 04–13; P-in-c Menorca *Eur* from 13. *Apartado de Correos 102, 07720 Es Castell, Menorca, Spain* T: (0034) 617 222 382 E: rev.strudwick@gmail.com

STRUDWICK, Canon Vincent Noel Harold. b 32. Nottm Univ BA 59 DipEd Lambeth DD 09. Kelham Th Coll 52. **d** 59 **p** 60. Tutor Kelham Th Coll 59–63; Sub-Warden 63–70; C Crawley *Chich* 70–73; Adult Educn Adv 73–77; R Fittleworth 73–77; Planning Officer for Educn Milton Keynes 77–80; Dir of Educn *Ox* 81–89; Hon Can Ch Ch from 81; Continuing Minl Educn Adv 85–89; Dir Dioc Inst for Th Educn 89–97; Prin Ox Min Course 89–94; Prin SAOMC 94–96; Fell and Tutor Kellogg Coll Ox 94–00; Hon Fell from 07; C Aylesbury *Ox* 97–98; PtO 98–16. *31 The Square, Brill, Aylesbury HP18 9RP* T: (01844) 237748 E: vincent.strudwick@kellogg.ox.ac.uk

STRUTT, Peter Edward. b 40. SAOMC 94. **d** 97 **p** 98. NSM Penn Street *Ox* 97–02; PtO from 02; St Alb from 10. *59 King's Ride, Penn, High Wycombe HP10 8BP* T: (01494) 812418 E: pestrutt@pennweb.uk

STRUTT, Preb Susan. b 45. Glouc Sch of Min 87. **d** 90 **p** 94. NSM Eye, Croft w Yarpole and Lucton *Heref* 90–94; C Leominster 94–96; Hon Chapl RAF 94–96; P-in-c Bosbury w Wellington Heath etc *Heref* 96–98; TV Ledbury 98–14; Dioc Adv on Women in Min 99–03; Preb Heref Cathl 07–14; rtd 14; PtO *Nor* 16–18; Hon C Gt and Lt Ellingham, Rockland and Shropham etc from 18. *25 Edenside Drive, Attleborough NR17 2EL* E: prebsue@hotmail.com *or* revrichardwebb@googlemail.com

STUART, Sister Ann-Marie Lindsay. b 41. Westmr Coll Lon CertEd 69 Kent Univ BA 80 Univ of Wales (Lamp) MA 03. Franciscan Study Cen 76. **d** 99 **p** 00. NSM Sherborne w Castleton and Lillington *Sarum* 99–01; TV Golden Cap Team 01–05; TR 05–08; rtd 08; Hon C Crosslacon *Carl* 08–11; NSM Brigham, Gt Broughton and Broughton Moor 11–12; Dioc Adv for Spirituality 09–12; PtO *Truro* 13–14; *Sarum* 14–18; C Kilcolman w Kiltallagh, Killorglin, Knockane etc *L & K* from 18. *Seaview House, Gurrane West, Sunhill, Killorglin, Co Kerry, V93 T2C1, Republic of Ireland* T: (00353) (66) 979 0359 E: revamls8@gmail.com

STUART, Brother. *See* BURNS, Stuart Maitland

STUART, Prof Elizabeth Bridget. b 63. Jes Coll Ox BA 84 St Hugh's Coll Ox MA 88 DPhil 88. SCTEI 17. **d** 19. NSM Win St Matt from 19. *5 Wychwood Place, Winchester SO22 6NB* T: (01962) 856501 M: 07711-607234 E: liz@stmatthewstpaul.org

STUART-BLACK, Veronica. *See* CAROLAN, Veronica

STUART-BOURNE, Mrs Rona. b 67. Surrey Univ BSc 89. Ripon Coll Cuddesdon 09. **d** 11 **p** 12. C Freshwater and Yarmouth *Portsm* 11–12; C Portsea St Luke 12–13; C Southsea St Pet 12–13; C Southsea St Luke and St Pet 13–14; C Greatham w Empshott and Hawkley w Prior's Dean 14–16; V Empshott and Hawkley w Priors Dean 16–18; R Merrow *Guildf* from 18. *The Rectory, 232 Epsom Road, Guildford GU4 7AA* E: revrona@gmail.com

STUART-LEE, Nicholas Richard. b 54. Wycliffe Hall Ox. **d** 83 **p** 84. C Costessey *Nor* 83–85; TV Dewsbury *Wakef* 85–90; R Rowlands Castle *Portsm* 90–00; V Nottingham St Jude *S'well* 00–03; TR Thame *Ox* 03–07. *69 Harefields, Oxford OX2 8NR* T: (01865) 511044

STUART-MARTIN, Rosanna. b 60. Bris Univ BA 81. Wycliffe Hall Ox 89. **d** 92 **p** 94. Par Dn Stanford in the Vale w Goosey and Hatford *Ox* 92–94; C 94–96; C Abingdon 96–00; PtO 00–04; P-in-c Uffington, Shellingford, Woolstone and Baulking 04–14; PtO from 15. *7 Limetrees, Chilton, Didcot OX11 0HW* T: (01235) 821861 E: rosanna.martin@btinternet.com

STUART-SMITH, David. b 36. St Pet Coll Ox BA 61 MA 65. Tyndale Hall Bris. **d** 63 **p** 64. C Tooting Graveney St Nic *S'wark* 63–67; C Richmond H Trin 67–70; LtO 70–74; NSM Canonbury St Steph *Lon* 70–74; Travelling Sec IVF 70–74; Bangladesh 74–79; V Clapham Park St Steph *S'wark* 79–95;

RD Streatham 83–87; Chapl Wye Coll Kent 95–99; Chapl Wye Campus Imp Coll *Lon* 99–01; P-in-c Wye w Brook *Cant* 95–01; P-in-c Hastingleigh 00–01; rtd 01; PtO *Cant* 01–07 and from 16; *Lon* 07–15. *100 North Street, Biddenden, Ashford TN27 8AE* T: (01580) 292615 E: speakup5@yahoo.com

STUART-WHITE, Canon William Robert. b 59. Ox Univ BA. Trin Coll Bris BA. **d** 86 **p** 87. C Upper Armley *Ripon* 86–91; P-in-c Austrey *Birm* 91–92; P-in-c Warton 91–92; V Austrey and Warton 92–98; R Camborne *Truro* 98–06; P-in-c Stoke Climsland 06–09; P-in-c Linkinhorne 06–09; P-in-c St Breoke and Egloshayle 09–12; Hon Can Truro Cathl 09–12 and from 18; Adn Cornwall 12–18; P-in-c Falmouth All SS from 18. *5 St Nazaire Close, Falmouth TR11 5FP* T: (01326) 219246 E: wstuartwhite@gmail.com

STUBBINGS, Mrs Paulette Joanne. b 71. Kent Univ BA 92. SEITE 12. **d** 15 **p** 16. C Boughton-under-Blean w Dunkirk etc *Cant* 16–18; TV Whitstable from 18. *35 Douglas Avenue, Whitstable CT5 1RT* E: paulettejstubbings@gmail.com

STUBBS, Ian Kirtley. b 47. Man Univ DipAE 90. Kelham Th Coll 66. **d** 70 **p** 71. C Chandler's Ford *Win* 70–75; C Farnham Royal *Ox* 75–80; Ind Chapl 75–80; Ind Chapl *Man* 81–86; TV Oldham 81–86; TR Langley and Parkfield 86–88; Community Work Officer Dioc Bd of Soc Resp 88–90; Dir Laity Development 90–96; Nat Adv in Adult Learning C of E Bd of Educn 97–02; V Stalybridge *Man* 02–11; P-in-c Glossop *Derby* 11–14; V 14–16; C Hadfield 11–14; C Charlesworth and Dinting Vale 11–14; V Dinting Vale 14–16; rtd 16; PtO *Ches* from 17. *9 Carisbrooke Close, Wistaston, Crewe CW2 8JD* T: (01270) 383391 M: 07712-451710 E: iks1647@gmail.com

STUBBS, Stanley Peter Handley. b 23. Lon Univ BD 52 Lille 3 Univ MèsL 82. Ely Th Coll 53. **d** 55 **p** 56. C Fletton *Ely* 55–58; Hon Min Can Pet Cathl 56–58; C Hounslow Heath St Paul *Lon* 58–63; CF (TA) 59–78; V Northampton St Alb *Pet* 63–76; R Brondesbury Ch Ch and St Laur *Lon* 76–93; rtd 93; PtO *Lon* 93–18. *3 Westbury Lodge Close, Pinner HA5 3FG* T: (020) 8868 8296 E: peter.stubbsuk@gmail.com

STUBBS, Canon Trevor Noel. b 48. AKC 70. St Aug Coll Cant 73. **d** 74 **p** 75. C Heckmondwike *Wakef* 74–77; C Warwick Australia 77–80; V Middleton St Cross *Ripon* 80–89; R Wool and E Stoke *Sarum* 89–95; TR Bridport 95–09; RD Lyme Bay 06–09; rtd 09; Admin Bp Gwynne Th Coll Sudan from 09; LtO *Sarum* from 09; PtO *Bris* from 15; *B & W* from 15; Can and Preb Sarum Cathl from 03. *15 Cleeve Grove, Keynsham, Bristol BS31 2HF* T: 0117-986 9664 E: revtrev.stubbs@gmail.com

STUBENBORD, Jess William. b 48. BA 72. Trin Coll Bris 75. **d** 78 **p** 79. C Cromer *Nor* 78–82; C Gorleston St Mary 82–85; P-in-c Saxthorpe and Corpusty 85–89; P-in-c Blickling 86–89; R Saxthorpe w Corpusty, Blickling, Oulton etc 89–93; P-in-c Mulbarton w Kenningham 93–97; P-in-c Mulbarton w Bracon Ash, Hethel and Flordon 94–97; P-in-c Wreningham 95–97; R Mulbarton w Bracon Ash, Hethel and Flordon 98–13; rtd 13; PtO *Nor* from 13. *Haven Cottage, 13 Cromer Road, Overstrand, Cromer NR27 0NT* T: (01263) 578230 E: jamstubenbord@gmail.com

STUCHFIELD, Nicolas John. b 60. ERMC 15. **d** 17 **p** 18. NSM Saxmundham w Kelsale cum Carlton *St E* from 17. *Address withheld by request* E: nic@stuchfield.com

STUCKES, Stephen. b 62. Trin Coll Bris BA 99. **d** 96 **p** 97. C Dunster, Carhampton and Withycombe w Rodhuish *B & W* 96–00; V Alcombe 00–17; RD Exmoor 09–17; Preb Wells Cathl 12–17; Chapl Berne *Eur* 17–18; C Alfriston w Lullington, Litlington, W Dean and Folkington *Chich* 18; R from 18. *The Rectory, Sloe Lane, Alfriston, Polegate BN26 5UP* E: stephen1962@btinternet.com

STUCKEY, Mrs Ann Marie. b 54. STETS 10. **d** 13 **p** 14. NSM Seaton and Beer *Ex* 13–17; NSM Uplyme w Axmouth from 17. *7 West Acres, Seaton EX12 2HP* T: (01297) 23016 M: 07814-078710

STUDDERT-KENNEDY, Andrew Geoffrey. b 59. Ch Ch Ox BA 80 MA 86. Ripon Coll Cuddesdon BA 88. **d** 89 **p** 90. C Wimbledon *S'wark* 89–94; V Norbury St Oswald 94–02; RD Croydon N 99–02; TR Marlborough *Sarum* 02–18; RD 09–18; Can and Preb Sarum Cathl 12–18; TR Uxbridge *Lon* from 18; Chapl to The Queen from 17. *St Andrew's Vicarage, Nursery Waye, Uxbridge UB8 2BJ* T: (01895) 239055 E: andrewsk1959@btinternet.com

STUDHOLME, Muriel Isabel. b 25. **d** 96. NSM Bromfield w Waverton *Carl* 96–02; NSM Solway Plain 02–09. *Yew Tree Cottage, Dundraw, Wigton CA7 0DP* T: (01697) 342506

STUDMAN, Tom Lucas. b 79. Leic Univ BSc 00 Man Metrop Univ PGCE 01. St Mellitus Coll BA 19. **d** 19. C W Didsbury and Withington St Chris *Man* from 19. *354 Wilbraham Road, Manchester M21 0UX* T: 0161-860 6003 E: tomstudman@hotmail.co.uk

STURCH, Richard Lyman. b 36. Ch Ch Ox BA 58 MA 61 DPhil 70 Open Univ BSc 06. Ely Th Coll. **d** 62 **p** 63. C Hove All SS *Chich* 62–65; C Burgess Hill St Jo 65–66; C Ox St Mich w St Martin and All SS 67–68; Tutor Ripon Hall Ox 67–71; Lect Univ of Nigeria 71–74; Lect Lon Bible Coll 75–80; TV Wolverton *Ox* 80–86; R Islip w Charlton on Otmoor, Oddington, Noke etc 86–01; rtd 01; PtO *Ox* 02–18. *128 Stoke Gifford Retirement Village, Edward Parker Road, Bristol BS16 1YE* E: sturchrichard@gmail.com

STURGEON, Mrs Susan Gerrie. b 53. Man Univ MBA 02. Yorks Min Course 16. **d** 17. NSM Abbeydale and Millhouses *Sheff* from 17. *52 Common Lane, Sheffield S11 7TG* T: 0114-327 7748 E: sgerriesturgeon@gmail.com

STURROCK, Marian Elizabeth. b 46. Westmr Coll Ox BTh 97. St Mich Coll Llan 97. **d** 99 **p** 00. C Swansea St Pet *S & B* 99–03; Chapl Swansea NHS Trust 00–03; R Thundersley *Chelmsf* 03–16; rtd 16; PtO *St D* from 16; *S & B* from 17. *29 Cleviston Park, Llandennech, Llanelli SA14 9UW* T: (01554) 821648 E: mariansturrock@gmail.com

STURT, Mrs Rachel Caroline. b 60. Open Univ BSc 03 RGN 81. STETS 08. **d** 11 **p** 12. NSM Wrecclesham *Guildf* 11–15; NSM Alton *Win* from 17; PtO *Guildf* 15–17. *14 Arthur Road, Farnham GU9 8PB* T: (01252) 710968 E: rachelsturt@btopenworld.com *or* rachel.annachaplain@hotmail.com

STURT, Rock André Daniel. b 56. Liv Univ BSc 79 Lon Inst of Educn CertEd 80. Oak Hill Th Coll BA 88. **d** 88 **p** 89. Chapl St Bede's Sch Cam 88–91; C Cambridge St Martin *Ely* 88–91; P-in-c Alwalton and Chesterton 91–96; TV The Ortons, Alwalton and Chesterton 96–03; R Gravesend St Geo *Roch* 03–06; Chapl HM YOI Roch 13–14; Chapl HM Pris Pentonville 14–18; V Mildmay Grove St Jude and St Paul *Lon* 18–19. *39 Bertram Road, London NW4 3PR* E: sturtrock672@gmail.com

STUTTARD, Ms Anna. b 64. Newc Univ BA 86 Heythrop Coll Lon MA 14 Cam Univ BTh 17. Westcott Ho Cam 15. **d** 17 **p** 18. C Hornsey St Mary w St Geo *Lon* from 17. *11 Falkland Road, London N8 0NU* M: 07941-121748 E: stuttard.tempest@btopenworld.com

STYLER, Jamie Cuming. b 36. Sarum & Wells Th Coll 70. **d** 72 **p** 73. C Whipton *Ex* 72–75; C Paignton St Jo 76–78; V Topsham 78–88; V Plymouth St Simon 88–01; Chapl Plymouth Community Services NHS Trust 94–01; rtd 01; PtO *Ex* from 01. *Drey House, 27 Langham Way, Ivybridge PL21 9BX* T: (01752) 691592 E: maureencumingstyle@yahoo.com

STYLES, Charlie Adam Mark. b 81. St Hild Coll Dur BA 04. Oak Hill Th Coll 06. **d** 09 **p** 10. C Britwell *Ox* 09–11; C Stoke Poges 11–13; P-in-c Lutterworth w Cotesbach and Bitteswell *Leic* 13–16; R from 16. *The Rectory, Coventry Road, Lutterworth LE17 4SH* E: charliestyles@dunelm.org.uk *or* charlie.styles@lutterworthchurch.org

STYLES, Christopher James. b 60. Univ Coll Lon BA 94. Wycliffe Hall Ox 10. **d** 12 **p** 13. C Chich St Pancras and St Jo 12–16; C Polegate from 16. *St Wilfrid's House, 90 Broad Road, Eastbourne BN20 9RA* T: (01323) 370560 M: 07990-433020 E: cjstyles@talk21.com

STYLES, Mary Elise. b 60. Southn Univ BM 85 Univ Coll Lon MSc 97 Anglia Ruskin Univ BA 12. ERMC 09. **d** 12 **p** 13. C Rome *Eur* 12–16; R S Quantock *B & W* from 16. *The Vicarage, Kingston St Mary, Taunton TA2 8HW* E: styles@alice.it *or* revmarye@gmail.com

STYLES, Ross. b 60. **d** 15 **p** 17. C Greystones *D & G* 15–17; C Ch Ch Cathl Dublin from 17. *32 Shandon Drive, Phibsborough, Dublin 7, Republic of Ireland* T: (00353) 87-989 2941 E: stylesross@gmail.com

SUART, Geoffrey Hugh. b 49. Man Univ BSc 70 Nottm Univ PGCE 71. Oak Hill Th Coll. **d** 83 **p** 84. C Ogley Hay *Lich* 83–86; TV Wenlock *Heref* 86–90; TR Kirby Muxloe *Leic* 90–04; RD Sparkenhoe E 99–03; R Snettisham w Ingoldisthorpe and Fring *Nor* 04–14; Chapl Norfolk Hospice 11–14; rtd 14. *285 Station Road, Bagworth, Coalville LE67 1BL* E: geoffsuart.t21@btinternet.com

SUCH, Colin Royston. b 62. UEA LLB 83. Ripon Coll Cuddesdon 94. **d** 97 **p** 98. C Streetly *Lich* 97–00; P-in-c Wednesfield St Greg 00–04; V Rushall from 04; P-in-c Walsall St Pet 08–13. *Rushall Vicarage, 10 Tetley Avenue, Walsall WS4 2HE* T: (01922) 624677 E: suchcol@aol.com

SUCH, Canon Howard Ingram James. b 52. Southn Univ BTh 81 Lon Univ MA 97. Sarum & Wells Th Coll 77. **d** 81 **p** 82. C Cheam *S'wark* 81–84; Prec Cant Cathl 84–91; V Borden 91–03; Hon Min Can Cant Cathl 84–03; AD Sittingbourne 00–03; Can Res and Prec Sheff Cathl 03–07; Warden St Barn Coll Lingfield *S'wark* 07–18; Public Preacher from 18; Hon Can S'wark Cathl from 16; Superior Soc of Retreat Conductors 05–11; PtO *Chich* from 15; *Cant* from

18; Hon Min Can Cant Cathl from 18. *6 Thundersland Road, Herne Bay CT6 6JT*

SUCH, Miss Nicola Jane. b 73. Roehampton Inst BA 95. Trin Coll Bris 12. **d** 14 **p** 15. C Wroughton and Wichelstowe *Bris* 14–18; P-in-c Kempshott *Win* 18–19; V from 19. *St Mark's Vicarage, 171 Kempshott Lane, Basingstoke RG22 5LF*

SUCKLING, Keith Edward. b 47. CChem FRSC Darw Coll Cam PhD 71 Liv Univ BSc 87 DSc 89. Oak Hill NSM Course 91. **d** 94 **p** 95. NSM Digswell and Panshanger *St Alb* 94–14; P-in-c Fraserburgh *Ab* from 14. *6 Crimond Court, Fraserburgh AB43 9QW* T: (01346) 518158 E: keith.suckling@cantab.net

SUDBURY, Archdeacon of. *See* JENKINS, The Ven David Harold

SUDDABY, Susan Eveline. b 43. Bedf Coll of Educn CertEd 64. S'wark Ord Course 93. **d** 96 **p** 97. NSM Rusthall *Roch* 96–00; C Northfleet 00–02; PtO 03–06; P-in-c N Chapel w Ebernoe *Chich* 06–08; rtd 08; PtO *Chich* from 08; *S'wark* from 17. *54 Garden Wood Road, East Grinstead RH19 1JX* T: (01342) 313042

SUDELL, Philip Henry. b 61. Thames Poly BScEng 84 Lon Univ PGCE 85. Wycliffe Hall Ox 89. **d** 92 **p** 93. C Worthing Ch the King *Chich* 92–96; C Muswell Hill St Jas w St Matt *Lon* 96–05; LtO 05–14; P-in-c Chitts Hill St Cuth 14–15; AD W Haringey from 14; Public Preacher 15–19; P-in-c Friern Barnet St Pet le Poer from 19; PtO *Eur* from 18. *163 Colney Hatch Lane, London N10 1HA* T: (020) 8883 7417 E: philip.sudell@gracech.org.uk

SUDRON, David Jeffrey. b 78. Univ Coll Dur BA 99 MA 00. St Steph Ho Ox 01. **d** 03 **p** 04. C Gt Grimsby St Mary and St Jas *Linc* 03–08; Min Can Dur Cathl 08–12; R Wallsend St Pet and St Luke *Newc* 12–19; NSM Crathorne *York* from 19; NSM Rudby in Cleveland w Middleton from 19; NSM Whorlton w Carlton and Faceby from 19. *18 Church Lane, Swainby, Northallerton DL6 3EA* T: (01642) 700321 E: david.sudron@dunelm.org.uk

SUDWORTH, Frank. b 43. Open Univ BA 92. Oak Hill Th Coll. **d** 78 **p** 79. C Deane *Man* 78–81; C Worksop St Jo *S'well* 82–85; V Wollaton Park 85–90; P-in-c Lenton Abbey 85–86; V 86–90; V Upper Armley *Ripon* 90–97; RD Armley 92–95; Dep Chapl HM Pris Liv 97–98; P-in-c Low Moor H Trin *Bradf* 98–03; V Low Moor 03; P-in-c Wyke 03–05; TR Oakenshaw, Wyke and Low Moor 06–07; rtd 07; PtO *Blackb* from 07. *12 Brampton Avenue, Thornton-Cleveleys FY5 2JY* T: (01253) 858377

SUDWORTH, Richard John. b 68. Leeds Univ LLB 90 Spurgeon's Coll MTh 05. Qu Coll Birm 05. **d** 10 **p** 11. C Sparkbrook Ch Ch and Tyseley *Birm* 10–13; P-in-c Sparkbrook Ch Ch 13–18; Tutor Qu Foundn Birm 13–17; Abp's Sec for Inter-Relig Affairs *Cant* from 18. *Lambeth Palace, London SE1 7JU* T: (020) 7898 1247 M: 07891-635664 E: suddy@blueyonder.co.uk

SUDWORTH, Timothy Mark. b 70. St Martin's Coll Lanc BA 93 K Coll Lon MA 00 Anglia Ruskin Univ BA 08. St Paul's Th Cen Lon 06. **d** 08 **p** 09. NSM Egham *Guildf* 08–16; Chapl Strode's Coll 08–16; PtO *Guildf* 15–16; Min Oak Tree Angl Fellowship *Lon* from 16. *100 Creffield Road, London W3 9PX* T: (020) 3624 9184 or 8993 2060 M: 07964-760259 E: timsudworth@btinternet.com *or* tims@oaktree.org.uk

SUEKARRAN, Hannah Louise. Pemb Coll Cam MA 12 St Jo Coll Dur BA 15. Cranmer Hall Dur 13. **d** 16 **p** 17. C Harton *York* from 16. *18 Hollytree Way, Brayton, Selby YO8 9SS* M: 07846-527021 E: hannahsuekarran@gmail.com

SUEKARRAN, Robert Patrick. b 84. Bradf Univ BSc 06 St Jo Coll Dur BA 15 Keele Univ PGCE 08. Cranmer Hall Dur 12. **d** 15 **p** 16. C Strensall *York* 15–19; P-in-c Brayton from 19. *18 Hollytree Way, Brayton, Selby YO8 9SS* M: 07944-592355 E: robert_suekarran@hotmail.com

SUFFERN, Richard William Sefton. b 57. Reading Univ BSc 79. Trin Coll Bris 88. **d** 90 **p** 91. C Radipole and Melcombe Regis *Sarum* 90–94; TV Cheltenham St Mark *Glouc* 94–99; R Whitnash *Cov* from 99. *St Margaret's Rectory, 2 Church Close, Whitnash, Leamington Spa CV31 2HJ* T: (01926) 425070 E: rwss@talktalk.net

SUGDEN, Charles Edward. b 59. Magd Coll Cam PGCE 82 MA 83. Trin Coll Bris 89. **d** 91 **p** 92. C Gidea Park *Chelmsf* 91–94; TV Melksham *Sarum* 94–01; NSM Poole 02–08; V Locks Heath *Portsm* 08–15; P-in-c Frenchay and Winterbourne Down *Bris* 15–16; P-in-c Stapleton 15–16; R Frenchay and Stapleton from 16. *21 Park Road, Stapleton, Bristol BS16 1AZ* T: 0117-958 4714 M: 07729-027969

SUGDEN, Canon Christopher Michael Neville. b 48. St Pet Coll Ox BA 70 MA 74 Westmr Coll Ox PhD 88. St Jo Coll Nottm MPhil 74. **d** 74 **p** 75. C Leeds St Geo *Ripon* 74–77; Assoc P Bangalore St Jo India 77–83; Registrar and Dir Academic Affairs Ox Cen for Miss Studies 83–01; Exec Dir 01–04; Exec Sec Angl Mainstream Internat 04–13; LtO *Ox*

83–13; Sec Ox Cen for Relig and Public Life from 13; PtO *Ox* from 13; Hon Can Jos from 00; Hon Can Sunyani Ghana from 12. *OCRPL, 21 High Street, Eynsham, Oxford OX29 4HE* M: 07808-297043 E: csugden@ocrpl.org

SULLIVAN, Canon Julian Charles. b 49. Lon Univ BSc 74 CertEd 75. Wycliffe Hall Ox 80. **d** 83 **p** 84. C Southall Green St Jo *Lon* 83–87; C Wells St Cuth w Wookey Hole *B & W* 87–90; V Sheff St Barn and St Mary 90–91; V Sheff St Mary w Highfield Trin 91–95; V Sheff St Mary Bramall Lane 95–16; P-in-c Endcliffe 04–07; AD Ecclesall 01–06; Bp's Urban Adv 05–16; Hon Can Sheff Cathl 01–16; rtd 16; PtO *Sheff* from 16. *64 Kingfield Road, Sheffield S11 9AU* T: 0114-258 3087

SULLIVAN, Mrs Linda Mary. b 45. **d** 14 **p** 15. OLM Malmesbury w Westport and Brokenborough *Bris* 14–16; OLM Malmesbury and Upper Avon from 16. *48 Bonners Close, Malmesbury SN16 9UF* T: (01666) 822281

SULLIVAN, Miss Lucy. b 87. Chich Univ BSc 10 Sheff Univ BA 17. Coll of Resurr Mirfield 15. **d** 18 **p** 19. C Rottingdean *Chich* from 18. *3 St Margaret's, High Street, Rottingdean, Brighton BN2 7HS* T: (01273) 933316 M: 07882-244320 E: mthr.lucysullivan@gmail.com *or* mthr.lucy@stmargaret.org.uk

SULLIVAN, The Very Revd Nicola Ann. b 58. SRN 81 RM 84. Wycliffe Hall Ox BTh 95. **d** 95 **p** 96. C Earlham St Anne *Nor* 95–99; Assoc V Bath Abbey w St Jas *B & W* 99–02; Chapl R Nat Hosp for Rheumatic Diseases NHS Trust 99–02; Bp's Chapl and Past Asst *B & W* 02–07; Sub-Dean and Preb Wells Cathl 03–07; Adn Wells and Can Res Wells Cathl 07–16; Dean S'well from 16. *The Residence, Vicars Court, Church Street, Southwell NG25 0HP* T: (01636) 817282 E: dean@southwellminster.org.uk

SULLY, Andrew Charles. b 67. Southn Univ BA 88 Birm Univ MPhil 95. Qu Coll Birm 90. **d** 93 **p** 94. C Maindee Newport *Mon* 93–96; V Llanfihangel w Llanafan and Llanwnnws etc *St D* 96–02; TV St As 03–06; PV St As Cathl 02–06; V Llangollen w Trevor and Llantysilio 06–17; P-in-c Valle Crucis Miss Area 18; AD Llangollen 10–12; V Llandudno *Ban* from 18. *The Rectory, 27 Church Walks, Llandudno LL30 2HL* T: (01978) 860231

SUMMERFIELD, Mrs Nina Mary Joyner. b 59. Leic Univ BSc 80 Wye Coll Lon MSc 82. WEMTC 13. **d** 16 **p** 17. NSM Lydney *Glouc* 16–19; NSM Woolaston w Alvington and Aylburton 16–19; NSM Lydney, Woolaston, Alvington and Aylburton from 19. *2 Hillview, Lydney GL15 5JT* T: (01594) 842997 M: 07747-560351 E: nina.summerfield@hotmail.co.uk

SUMMERS, Canon Alexander William Mark. b 75. Leic Univ BA 98 MA 00 Fitzw Coll Cam BTh 09 Open Univ PGCE 01. Westcott Ho Cam 07. **d** 09 **p** 10. C Chingford SS Pet and Paul *Chelmsf* 09–12; P-in-c Walthamstow St Mich 12–13; V 13–18; AD Waltham Forest 15–16; Public Preacher from 18; V W Ham from 18; CMD Adv Barking Area from 18; Hon Can Chelmsf Cathl from 15. *The Vicarage, 9 Palmerston Road, London E17 6PQ* T: (020) 8509 3895 M: 07434-918410 E: awm.summers@icloud.com *or* asummers@chelmsford.anglican.org

SUMMERS, Graham. b 50. SCRTP 12. **d** 15 **p** 16. C Penn and Tylers Green *Ox* from 15. *43 Kings Ride, Penn, High Wycombe HP10 8BP* T: (01494) 814347 M: 07866-920341 E: gandcsummers@icloud.com

SUMMERS, Jeanne. *See* SUMMERS, Ursula Jeanne

SUMMERS, John Emrys. b 80. G&C Coll Cam LLM 03 Univ Coll Ox MA 07 Barrister-at-Law (Lincoln's Inn) 04. Westcott Ho Cam 13. **d** 16 **p** 17. C Three Valleys *Sarum* 16–19; Chapl Trin Coll Cam from 19. *Trinity College, Cambridge CB2 1TQ* M: 07760-464490 E: johnsummers235@gmail.com

SUMMERS (née PASCOE), Mrs Lorraine Eve. b 51. SAOMC 98. **d** 01 **p** 02. NSM Sandon, Wallington and Rushden w Clothall *St Alb* 01–06; P-in-c Kimpton w Ayot St Lawrence 06–14; Asst Chapl E and N Herts NHS Trust 06–14; rtd 14; PtO *Nor* from 15. *Trafoi, Banham Road, Kenninghall, Norwich NR16 2ED* T: (01953) 888389 E: lorrainesummers51@gmail.com

SUMMERS, Neil Thomas. b 58. Roehampton Inst BA 93 K Coll Lon MA 94 St Mary's Coll Strawberry Hill PGCE 95. SEITE 97. **d** 00 **p** 01. NSM Richmond St Mary w St Matthias and St Jo *S'wark* 00–14; TV from 14. *2 Ravensbourne Road, Twickenham TW1 2DH* T: (020) 8892 8313 M: 07540-974702 E: neil.summers@richmondteamministry.org

SUMMERS, Canon Raymond John. b 41. Univ of Wales TCert 63 Open Univ BA 75. St Mich Coll Llan 77. **d** 77 **p** 78. NSM Mynyddislwyn *Mon* 77–81; NSM Abercarn 81–82; P-in-c 82–89; V 89–91; V Mynyddislwyn 91–95; TR 95–08; RD Bedwellty 93–04; Can St Woolos Cathl 01–08; rtd 08.

12A Maple Gardens, Risca, Newport NP11 6AR T: (01633) 613676

SUMMERS, Canon Stephen Bruce. b 63. St Andr Univ MTheol 95 Chich Univ PhD 08. STETS 98. **d** 00 **p** 01. C Bishop's Waltham *Portsm* 00–02; R Farlington 02–09; Prin Local Min Progr *Guildf* from 09; Hon Can Guildf Cathl from 18. *Church House, 20 Alan Turing Road, Surrey Research Park, Guildford GU2 7YF* T: (01483) 790319 E: steve.summers@cofeguildford.org.uk

SUMMERS, Preb Ursula Jeanne. b 35. Birm Univ BA 56 Liv Univ CertEd 57. Glouc Sch of Min. **dss** 85 **d** 87 **p** 94. Fownhope *Heref* 85–87; Hon C 87; Brockhampton w Fawley 85–87; Hon C 87; C Marden w Amberley and Wisteston 88–94; P-in-c Rural 93–99; RD Heref Rural 93–99; P-in-c Wellington w Pipe-cum-Lyde and Moreton-on-Lugg 96–02; Preb Heref Cathl 96–02; rtd 02; PtO *Heref* from 02. *33 St Botolph's Green, Leominster HR6 8ER* T: (01568) 617456 E: roland.summers@yahoo.co.uk

SUMNER, Angela Diane. b 56. Brighton Poly BSc 78 Sussex Univ PGCE 92 Coll of SS Mark and Jo Plymouth MA 02 Ex Univ BTh 15 MRPharmS. SWMTC 10. **d** 12 **p** 13. NSM Totnes w Bridgetown, Berry Pomeroy etc *Ex* from 12; Asst Chapl S Devon Healthcare NHS Foundn Trust 12–13; Chapl 13–15; Chapl Torbay and S Devon NHS Foundn Trust from 15. *9 Wayside, Brixham TQ5 8PY* T: (01803) 853959 E: angela.sumner@outlook.com

SUMNER, Mrs Judith Elizabeth. b 68. Ox Poly BEd 90. Ripon Coll Cuddesdon 13. **d** 16 **p** 17. OLM Reading St Mary the Virgin *Ox* from 16. *97 Warborough Avenue, Tilehurst, Reading RG31 5LF* T: 0118-377 3286 M: 07866-614836 E: judithsumner29@gmail.com

SUMPTER, Guy. b 60. Leic Univ BA 01 PhD 08. Ripon Coll Cuddesdon 09. **d** 11 **p** 12. C Brentwood St Thos *Chelmsf* 11–14; R Eye *St E* from 14. *The Vicarage, 41 Castle Street, Eye IP23 7AW* T: (01379) 871986 E: fatherguy@btinternet.com

SUMSION, Paul Henry. b 74. UMIST BSc 97. Trin Coll Bris BA 03 MA 06. **d** 04 **p** 05. C Hawkshaw Lane *Man* 04–08; P-in-c 08; C Holcombe 04–08; P-in-c 08; R Holcombe and Hawkshaw from 09; Chapl Bury Coll of FE 05–07; CF (TA) from 11. *St Mary's Vicarage, Bolton Road, Hawkshaw, Bury BL8 4JN* T: (01204) 888060 E: paul@holcombehawkshaw.org

SUNDERLAND, Wendy Jillian. b 47. **d** 99 **p** 00. OLM Bury St Edmunds St Mary *St E* 99–08; rtd 08. *9 Crown Street, Bury St Edmunds IP33 1QU*

SUNDERLAND, Archdeacon of. See COOPER, The Ven Robert Gerard

SUNLEY, Carol. b 49. Leeds Univ BA 12. Yorks Min Course 10. **d** 12. NSM N Ormesby *York* 12–15; NSM Ormesby 15–16; rtd 17; PtO *York* from 18. *21 Norfolk Crescent, Middlesbrough TS3 0LZ* T: (01642) 503468 E: pcsunley@ntlworld.com

SURMAN, Malcolm Colin. b 48. Birm Univ CertEd 72 Southn Univ BTh 88 Worc Univ BA 12. Sarum & Wells Th Coll 76. **d** 78 **p** 79. C Basingstoke *Win* 78–81; P-in-c Alton All SS 81–85; V 85–01; Chapl N Hants Loddon Community NHS Trust 84–01; P-in-c Burton and Sopley *Win* 01–14; rtd 14; PtO *Win* from 14; *Ox* from 15. *31 Van Diemens Close, Chinnor OX39 4QE* T: (01844) 761717 E: mcsurman@me.com

SURREY, Mrs Maureen. b 53. Man OLM Scheme 98. **d** 01 **p** 03. OLM Davyhulme Ch Ch *Man* 01–02; OLM Walkden and Lt Hulton 03–09; OLM Flixton St Jo from 09. *56 Abingdon Road, Urmston, Manchester M41 0GN* T: 0161-748 3961 E: sidandmo@hotmail.com

SURREY, Archdeacon of. See DAVIES, The Ven Richard Paul

SURRIDGE, Jonathan Mark. b 67. Leic Poly BSc 88. Ripon Coll Cuddesdon 10. **d** 12 **p** 13. C Hinckley St Mary *Leic* 12–16; P-in-c Leic St Phil from 16; P-in-c Leic Presentation from 16. *15 Castle Street, Leicester LE1 5WN* T: 0116-318 0680 E: jmsurridge@gmail.com

SURTEES, Timothy John de Leybourne. b 31. G&C Coll Cam BA 54 MA 58. Westcott Ho Cam 54. **d** 56 **p** 57. C Guisborough *York* 56–59; C Grantham St Wulfram *Linc* 59–61; V Cayton w Eastfield *York* 61–72; R Cheam *S'wark* 72–96; rtd 96; PtO *Heref* 96–18. *39 Campbell Road, Hereford HR1 1AD* T: (01432) 371654

SUTCH, The Ven Christopher David. b 47. AKC 69. St Aug Coll Cant 69. **d** 70 **p** 71. C Bris St Andr Hartcliffe 70–75; C Swindon Dorcan 75–78; TV 78–79; P-in-c Alveston 79–83; V 83–89; RD Westbury and Severnside 86–89; CF (TA) 80–03; TR Yate New Town *Bris* 89–99; RD Stapleton 95–99; V Cainscross w Selsley *Glouc* 99–07; AD Stonehouse 04–07; Chapl Costa del Sol E *Eur* 07–13; Adn Gib 08–13; rtd 13; PtO *Eur* from 16. *5 Mostham Place, Brockworth, Gloucester GL3 4BA*

SUTCLIFFE, Crispin Francis Henry. b 48. Keble Coll Ox BA 69. Sarum & Wells Th Coll 73. **d** 74 **p** 75. C Truro St Paul 74–77; C St Jo Cathl Umtata S Africa 77–80; P-in-c Treslothan

Truro 80–85; V 85–91; R Ilchester w Northover, Limington, Yeovilton etc *B & W* 91–11; rtd 11. *57 Wilbert Road, Beverley HU17 0AJ* T: (01482) 864674

SUTCLIFFE, Howard Guest. b 44. Fitzw Coll Cam BA 66 MA 70 Birm Univ MA 75. Westcott Ho Cam 73. **d** 74 **p** 75. C Chorlton-cum-Hardy St Clem *Man* 74–77; Chapl Chetham's Sch of Music 77–80; V Oldham St Paul *Man* 80–94; Co-ord Werneth and Freehold Community Development Project 94–06; PtO 94–09; rtd 09; Hon C Saddleworth *Man* 09–14; PtO from 16. *27 Spurn Lane, Diggle, Oldham OL3 5QP* T: (01457) 879640 E: howardguestsutcliffe@yahoo.co.uk

SUTCLIFFE, Ian. b 31. Surrey Univ BSc 69. Qu Coll Birm 61. **d** 63 **p** 65. C W Wimbledon Ch Ch *S'wark* 63–65; C Battersea St Phil 65–66; C Kingston Hill St Paul 71–73; LtO *Carl* 75–96; rtd 96. *42 Hill Street, Arbroath DD11 1AB*

SUTCLIFFE, John Leslie. b 35. Liv Univ BA 56. Sarum Th Coll 58. **d** 60 **p** 61. C Lytham St Cuth *Blackb* 60–62; C Altham w Clayton le Moors 62–65; C-in-c Penwortham St Leon CD 65–71; Ind Chapl *Liv* 71–74; V Orford St Andr 74–79; V Burnley St Cuth *Blackb* 79–88; Bp's Adv on UPA *Ripon* 88–94; Hon C Leeds Gipton Epiphany 88–94; I Carrickmacross w Magheracloone *Clogh* 94–01; rtd 01; PtO *Blackb* from 02; *Bradf* 13–14; *Leeds* 14–16. *1 Beckside, Barley, Burnley BB12 9JZ* T: (01282) 449687

SUTCLIFFE, Peter John. b 58. BA. Linc Th Coll. **d** 82 **p** 83. C Skipton Ch Ch *Bradf* 82–85; C Tettenhall Regis *Lich* 85–86; TV 86–89; TV Warwick *Cov* 89–93; Relig Producer BBC Radio Cov and Warks 89–93; V Burley in Wharfedale *Bradf* 93–03; RD Otley 97–02; P-in-c Yeadon St Andr 03–06; V Lightcliffe *Wakef* 06–09; V Lesbury w Alnmouth *Newc* 09–11; V Longhoughton w Howick 09–11; rtd 11; PtO *Newc* from 13. *29 Oaky Balks, Alnwick NE66 2QE* T: (01665) 604395 E: peter.sutcliffe@btinternet.com

SUTCLIFFE, Richard John. b 67. ACMA 03. Ripon Coll Cuddesdon 09. **d** 12 **p** 13. NSM Hurstbourne Priors, Longparish etc *Win* from 12. *2 Applegate, St Mary Bourne, Andover SP11 6DT* T: (01264) 738288 M: 07976-672733 E: rev.sutcliffe@btinternet.com

SUTCLIFFE, Stephen Alan. b 71. Ripon Coll Cuddesdon 16. **d** 18 **p** 19. C Gurnard w Cowes St Faith *Portsm* from 18; C Northwood from 18. *2 St Faith's Road, Cowes PO31 7HH* T: (01983) 652506 M: 07800-907300 E: steve.alan.sutcliffe@icloud.com

SUTER (née RENNIE), Mrs Margot Mardelle. b 63. Univ of Wales (Swansea) BSc 84. Ripon Coll Cuddesdon 13. **d** 16 **p** 17. NSM Flackwell Heath *Ox* 16–19; NSM Beaconsfield from 19. *46 Butlers Court Road, Beaconsfield HP9 1SG* T: (01494) 676952 M: 07779-803519 E: margotsuter@hotmail.com

SUTER, Canon Richard Alan. b 48. Rhodes Univ BA 72 St Jo Coll Dur BA 74. Cranmer Hall Dur 72. **d** 75 **p** 76. C Darlington H Trin *Dur* 75–77; C Wrexham *St As* 77–82; R Llansantffraid Glan Conwy and Eglwysbach 82–87; V Broughton 87–92; RD Wrexham 90–97; V Rossett 92–04; V Holt, Rossett and Isycoed 04–09; V Rossett and Isycoed 09–11; Hon Can St As Cathl 11; rtd 11; PtO *St As* from 11. *64 Leaches Lane, Mancot, Deeside CH5 2BL* T: (01244) 534374 E: etsuterra1@gmail.com

SUTHERLAND, Alan. b 55. Sarum & Wells Th Coll. **d** 80 **p** 81. C Hessle *York* 80–83; USA from 83; rtd 10. *18417 Black Bear Trail, Norman OK 73072-9604, USA* E: alansutherland@att.net

SUTHERLAND, Mrs Elaine Anita. b 64. EMMTC 95 Moorlands Bible Coll 86. **d** 10 **p** 11. C Leic H Trin w St Jo from 10. *104 Sports Road, Glenfield, Leicester LE3 8AJ* T: 0116-254 8981 M: 07747-466865 E: esutherland@htl.church

SUTHERLAND, Lesley Ann. b 61. **d** 16 **p** 17. C Cornforth and Ferryhill *Dur* from 16. *4 The Cottages, Rushyford, Ferryhill DL17 0LN* M: 07548-249098 E: lesley.suthrland61@gmail.com

SUTHERLAND, Robert. b 78. Newc Univ BA 00 St Jo Coll Dur MATM 09 SS Hild & Bede Coll Dur PGCE 01 Sheff Univ MA 15. Cranmer Hall Dur 05 Coll of Resurr Mirfield 08. **d** 09 **p** 10. C Morley *Wakef* 09–12; V Mixenden and Illingworth 12–14; *Leeds* from 14. *37 Hops Lane, Halifax HX3 5FB* T: (01422) 353929 E: robb@priest.com

SUTTIE, Miss Jillian. b 53. Ex Univ BA 75 PGCE 76. ERMC 05. **d** 08. NSM Colney Heath St Mark *St Alb* from 08. *51 West Riding, Bricket Wood, St Albans AL2 3QE* T: (01923) 662772 E: jillsuttie@ukgateway.net

SUTTLE, Neville Frank. b 38. Reading Univ BSc 61 Aber Univ PhD 64. **d** 76 **p** 77. NSM Penicuik *Edin* from 76. *44 St James's Gardens, Penicuik EH26 9DU* T/F: (01968) 673819 E: suttle_hints@hotmail.com

SUTTON, Charles Edwin. b 53. Bris Univ CertEd 76 BEd 77 Birkbeck Coll Lon MSc 00 PhD 07. Ripon Coll Cuddesdon 77. **d** 80 **p** 81. C Stanwix *Carl* 80–84; Warden Marrick Priory *Ripon* 84–88; Fell Birkbeck Coll *Lon* 00–10; PtO *Bris* 12–13;

NSM Clifton All SS w St Jo 13–15; V from 15; Bp's Adv for SSM from 14; AD Bris W from 19. *All Saints' Vicarage, 68 Pembroke Road, Clifton, Bristol BS8 3ED* T: 0117-907 8088 *or* 974 1355 M: 07785-912663 E: charleses@me.com

SUTTON, Christopher David. b 69. Kent Univ BSc 90 FIA 93. SEITE 11. **d** 14 **p** 15. NSM Slaugham and Staplefield Common *Chich* 14–17; NSM Ardingly from 17. *Coppers, 19A Denmans Lane, Lindfield, Haywards Heath RH16 2LA* M: 07903-068366 E: christopher.sutton@yahoo.co.uk

SUTTON, David Robert. b 49. Birm Univ BA 69 Ox Univ CertEd 72 Leeds Beckett Univ MA 15. St Steph Ho Ox 70. **d** 72 **p** 73. C Clitheroe St Mary *Blackb* 72–75; C Fleetwood St Pet 75–78; V Calderbrook *Man* 78–88; V Winton 88–08; Chapl Salford Mental Health Services NHS Trust 92–08; Chapl Gtr Man W Mental Health NHS Foundn Trust 08–17; rtd 17; PtO *Ches* from 14; *Man* from 14; *Blackb* from 16. *42 Lulworth Road, Eccles, Manchester M30 8NP* T: 0161-707 3040 E: frlinedancer@talktalk.net

SUTTON, James William. b 41. Oak Hill Th Coll 81. **d** 84 **p** 85. NSM Chorleywood St Andr *St Alb* 84–06; PtO *Eur* 06–18; *St Alb* from 18. *7 Hillside Road, Chorleywood, Rickmansworth WD3 5AP* T: (01923) 282806 E: jsuttonsnr@outlook.com

SUTTON, Jeremy John Ernest. b 60. Ridley Hall Cam 83. **d** 86 **p** 87. C Seacombe *Ches* 86–88; C Northwich St Luke and H Trin 88–90; TV Birkenhead Priory 90–94; V Over St Chad 94–01; V Dunham Massey St Marg and St Mark from 01. *St Margaret's Vicarage, Dunham Road, Altrincham WA14 4AQ* T/F: 0161-928 1609 E: jeremyjsutton@outlook.com

SUTTON, Canon John. b 47. St Jo Coll Dur BA 70. Ridley Hall Cam 70. **d** 72 **p** 73. C Denton St Lawr *Man* 72–77; R 77–82; V High Lane *Ches* 82–88; V Sale St Anne 88–96; V Timperley 96–12; RD Bowdon 03–12; Hon Can Ches Cathl 01–12; rtd 12; PtO *Ches* from 12. *6 Walton Road, Sale M33 4AD* T: 0161-283 8914 E: jfsuttontimp@aol.com

SUTTON, John Stephen. b 33. Em Coll Cam BA 57 MA 61. Wycliffe Hall Ox 57. **d** 59 **p** 60. C Dagenham *Chelmsf* 59–62; C Bishopwearmouth St Gabr *Dur* 62–63; V Over Kellet *Blackb* 63–67; V Darwen St Barn 67–74; V Walthamstow St Jo *Chelmsf* 74–84; V Stebbing w Lindsell 84–98; RD Dunmow 94–98; rtd 98; PtO *Chich* from 98. *20 Firwood Close, Eastbourne BN22 9QL* T: (01323) 504654 E: johnsutton33@hotmail.co.uk

SUTTON, Canon John Wesley. b 48. Rolle Coll CertEd 71. All Nations Chr Coll. **d** 76 **p** 77. Chile 76–77; Peru 79–84; Area Sec SAMS 84–88; Youth Sec 88-91; Personnel Sec and Asst Gen Sec 91–03; Gen Sec 03–09; Dir Strategic Partnerships and Miss Nationwide Chr Trust 09–10; C Hornchurch St Andr *Chelmsf* 10–14; rtd 14; Hon Can Peru from 93. *Apt 1D, Block A Royal Golf, Sev Ballesteros, Mijas Costa, 29649 Málaga, Spain* E: johnsutton2104@gmail.com

SUTTON, Kingsley Edwin. b 70. TCD BTh 94. **d** 97 **p** 98. C Belfast St Matt *Conn* 97–99; C Willowfield *D & D* 99–02; I Newry 02–16; I Kilgariffe Union *C, C & R* from 16. *The Rectory, Gullanes, Clonakilty, Co Cork, Republic of Ireland* T: (00353) (23) 883 3357 E: rev.sutton@gmail.com

SUTTON, Mrs Monica Rosalind. b 48. Sheff Hallam Univ MSc 99 Leeds Univ BA 09. Yorks Min Course. **d** 09 **p** 10. NSM Sheff St Cuth from 09; P-in-c from 16. *124 Dalewood Road, Sheffield S8 0EF* T: 0114-236 4399 E: monica_r_sutton@yahoo.com *or* monica.sutton@sheffield.anglican.org

SUTTON, The Ven Peter Allerton. b 59. Ex Univ BA 85. Linc Th Coll 85. **d** 87 **p** 88. C Fareham H Trin *Portsm* 87–90; C Alverstoke 90–93; Chapl HM Pris Haslar 90–93; V Lee-on-the-Solent 93–12; Warden of Readers 96–00; RD Gosport 06–09; Hon Can Portsm Cathl 09–12; Adn Is of Wight 12–18; P-in-c Empshott and Hawkley w Priors Dean 18; V Greatham, Empshott and Hawkley w Priors Dean from 18; IME Officer from 12. *The Vicarage, Hawkley, Liss GU33 6NF* E: peter.sutton@portsmouth.anglican.org

SUTTON, Philip Frank. b 55. SAOMC 92. **d** 95 **p** 96. NSM Akeman *Ox* 95–00; Chapl Ox Radcliffe Hosps NHS Trust 96–00; Sen Chapl R United Hosp Bath NHS Trust 00–07; Dioc Adv Hosp Chapl *Ox* 04–07; Chapl Team Ldr Ox Radcliffe Hosps NHS Trust 07–12; Chapl Team Ldr Ox Univ Hosps NHS Foundn Trust 12–16; NSM Ox St Matt 16–18; C DAMASCUS from 18. *6 Alexander Close, Abingdon OX14 1XA* T: (01235) 526114 M: 07507-378737 E: revpsutton@btinternet.com

SUTTON, Wesley Alan. b 55. Staffs Univ MA 14 Brentwood Coll of Educn CertEd 77. **d** 16 **p** 17. NSM Grayshott *Guildf* from 16. *Acorn House, High Street, Bordon GU35 0AP* T: (01420) 478121 M: 07734-870291 E: wsutton@acornchristian.org

SWABEY, Brian Frank. b 44. BA. Oak Hill Th Coll 79. **d** 82 **p** 83. C Clapham St Jas *S'wark* 82–84; C Wallington 84–88; Chapl Mt Gould Hosp Plymouth 88–89; V Plymouth St Jude *Ex* 88–92; Chapl RN 92–99; V Penn Fields *Lich* 99–01; rtd 01;

PtO *Ex* 01–09; *Truro* from 15. *30 Treskewes Estate, St Keverne, Helston TR12 6RA* T: (01326) 281168 E: brian@swabey.org

SWABY, Desrene. b 42. SEITE 00. **d** 03 **p** 04. NSM S'wark St Geo w St Alphege and St Jude 03–09; NSM Camberwell St Mich w All So w Em 09–16; PtO from 16. *36 Gabriel House, 10 Odessa Street, London SE16 7HQ* T: (020) 7231 9834 E: desrene.s@hotmail.co.uk

SWAIN, John Edgar. b 44. Lich Th Coll 67. **d** 69 **p** 70. C E Dereham w Hoe *Nor* 69–73; V Haugh *Linc* 73–74; R S Ormsby w Ketsby, Calceby and Driby 73–74; R Harrington w Brinkhill 73–74; R Oxcombe 73–74; R Ruckland w Farforth and Maidenwell 73–74; R Somersby w Bag Enderby 73–74; R Tetford and Salmonby 73–74; R Belchford 73–74; V W Ashby 73–74; C Attleborough *Nor* 74–78; P-in-c Oxford Cen w Eastwood & Princeton Canada 78–84; P-in-c Oldcastle w Colchester N 84–90; P-in-c Kirton w Falkenham *St E* 90–95; Chapl Suffolk Constabulary 90–01; P-in-c Gt and Lt Whelnetham w Bradfield St George 95–01; P-in-c Lawshall w Shimplingthorne and Alpheton 98–01; R Wawa w White River and Hawk Junction Canada 01–09; rtd 09. *70 Mosher Road, RR #2, Iron Bridge ON P0R 1H0, Canada* E: jswain@ontera.net

SWAIN, Canon John Roger. b 29. Fitzw Ho Cam BA 55 MA 59. Bps' Coll Cheshunt 55. **d** 57 **p** 58. C Headingley *Ripon* 57–60; C Moor Allerton 60–65; V Wyther 65–75; V Horsforth 75–86; P-in-c Roundhay St Edm 86–88; V 88–95; RD Allerton 89–94; Hon Can Ripon Cathl 89–95; rtd 95; PtO *Ripon* 05–14; *Leeds* from 14. *3 Harlow Court, Park Avenue, Leeds LS8 2JH* T: 0113-246 1274

SWAIN, Preb Peter John. b 44. Sarum & Wells Th Coll 86. **d** 88 **p** 89. C Beaminster Area *Sarum* 88–92; P-in-c W Newton and Bromfield w Waverton *Carl* 92–98; Member Rural Life and Agric Team 93–96; Ldr 96–98; RD Solway *Carl* 95–98; Hon Can Carl Cathl 96–98; TR Leominster *Heref* 98–05; RD 98–05; Preb Heref Cathl 03–05; rtd 05; PtO *Heref* from 12. *10 Market Hall Street, Kington HR5 3DP* T: (01544) 230999 E: pandpswain@btinternet.com

SWAIN, Mrs Sharon Juanita. b 46. Sussex Univ BA 75 CertEd 76 Heythrop Coll Lon MA 04. Glouc Sch of Min 81. **dss** 84 **d** 87 **p** 94. Upton St Leonards *Glouc* 84–88; C 87–88; Children's Officer *Worc* 88–95; Min Can Worc Cathl 94–95; V Hanley Castle, Hanley Swan and Welland 95–01; R E Bergholt and Brantham *St E* 01–06; RD Samford 01–06; TR Solway Plain *Carl* 06–10; rtd 10; C Carew *St D* 13–14. *Selemat, Jameston, Tenby SA70 8QJ* T: (01834) 871381 E: rev.s.swain@googlemail.com

SWAINE, Judith Ann. b 55. STETS. **d** 09 **p** 10. C Portsea All SS *Portsm* 09–13; PtO *Win* 13–16; Chapl HM Pris Is of Wight from 14. *HM Prison Albany, 55 Parkhurst Road, Newport PO30 5RS* T: (01983) 556573

SWALES, David James. b 58. Warwick Univ BA 79. Cranmer Hall Dur 81. **d** 84 **p** 85. C Eccleshill *Bradf* 84–88; C Prenton *Ches* 88–92; V Oakworth *Bradf* 92–00; V Bolton St Jas w St Chrys 00–09; V Haughley w Wetherden and Stowupland *St E* 09–17; P-in-c Pott Shrigley *Ches* from 17. *The Vicarage, Spuley Lane, Pott Shrigley, Macclesfield SK10 5RS* M: 07806-785714 E: rev.david@btinternet.com

SWALES, Peter. b 52. ACIB 78 Open Univ BA 99. Ridley Hall Cam 85. **d** 87 **p** 88. C Allestree *Derby* 87–91; P-in-c Horsley 91–99; RD Heanor 97–99; V Heckmondwike *Wakef* 99–03; V Chellaston *Derby* 03–10; rtd 10. *18 Kerry Drive, Smalley, Ilkeston DE7 6ER* T: (01332) 881752 E: pasta.swales@gmail.com

SWALLOW, Mrs Alice Gillian. b 51. Birm Univ BA 72 CertEd 73. NEOC 82. **dss** 84 **d** 87 **p** 94. Morpeth *Newc* 84–86; Uttoxeter w Bramshall *Lich* 86–88; Par Dn 87–88; Par Dn Rocester 88; Chapl to the Deaf *Man* 88–90; Par Dn Goodshaw and Crawshawbooth 88–93; C Barkisland w W Scammonden *Wakef* 93–95; V Ripponden 95–97; rtd 97; PtO *Wakef* 02–14; *Leeds* from 14. *22 Scholes Lane, Scholes, Cleckheaton BD19 6NR* T: (01274) 875529 E: jill_swallow@yahoo.co.uk

SWALLOW, John Brian. b 36. Trent Poly 78. **d** 84 **p** 85. C Cleveleys *Blackb* 84–87; V Blackpool St Mich 87–93; P-in-c Burnley St Steph 93–98; V 98–01; RD Burnley 97–00; rtd 01; PtO *Dur* from 01. *6 Chichester Walk, Haughton-le-Skerne, Darlington DL1 2SG* E: swallowj2@hotmail.co.uk

SWAN, Canon Duncan James. b 65. Imp Coll Lon BSc 88 SS Coll Cam BA 91 MA 95 K Coll Lon MA 04 MPhil 18. Ridley Hall Cam 89. **d** 92 **p** 93. C Stevenage St Andr and St Geo *St Alb* 92–95; C Harpenden St Nic 95–99; V Redbourn 99–06; TR Caterham *S'wark* 06–18; AD 11–16; Deaneries Development Adv from 18; Hon C Merton Priory from 18; Hon Can S'wark Cathl from 16. *St John's Vicarage, 135 High Path, London SW19 2JY* M: 07513-337585 E: duncpen@hotmail.com

SWAN, Philip Douglas. b 56. Wye Coll Lon BSc 78 Qu Coll Cam MA 81 CertEd 81. St Jo Coll Nottm 86. **d** 88 **p** 89. C

Birm St Martin w Bordesley St Andr 88–92; C Selly Park St Steph and St Wulstan 92–96; P-in-c The Lickey 96–98; V 98–10; Dir World Miss *Lich* from 10; C Penn 12–14; C Hanley H Ev from 14. *Christ Church Vicarage, 10 Emery Street, Stoke-on-Trent ST6 2JJ*

SWAN, Preb Ronald Frederick. b 35. St Cath Coll Cam BA 59 MA. Coll of Resurr Mirfield. d 61 p 62. C Staveley *Derby* 61–65; Chapl Lon Univ 65–72; C St Martin-in-the-Fields 72–77; V Ealing St Barn 77–88; V Ealing St Steph Castle Hill 81–88; AD Ealing E 84–88; V Harrow St Mary 88–97; AD Harrow 89–94; Preb St Paul's Cathl 91–06; Master R Foundn of St Kath in Ratcliffe 97–06; rtd 06; PtO *Lon* from 10. *8 Moat Lodge, London Road, Harrow HA1 3LU* T: (020) 8864 4625 E: ronaldswan@btinternet.com

SWANBOROUGH, Alan William. b 38. Southn Univ BEd 75. Sarum & Wells Th Coll 77. d 80 p 81. NSM Ventnor H Trin *Portsm* 80–85; NSM Ventnor St Cath 80–85; Chapl Upper Chine Sch Shanklin 85–94; Chapl Ryde Sch w Upper Chine 94–03; NSM Shanklin St Blasius *Portsm* 91–10; P-in-c 93–10; rtd 10; PtO *Portsm* from 10. *6 The Cambria, 32 Broadway, Sandown PO36 9BY* T: (01983) 402686 E: a.swanborough38@btinternet.com

SWANN, Ms Anne Barbara. b 49. St Mich Coll Llan BTh 07 MTh 08. d 08 p 09. Hon C Peterston-super-Ely w St Brides-super-Ely *Llan* 08–10; PtO 10–12; C Glan Ely 12–15; rtd 14; PtO *Llan* from 15. *19 Fairways Crescent, Cardiff CF5 3DZ* T: (029) 2056 2641 M: 07810-798465 E: revdanne@live.co.uk

SWANN, Edgar John. b 42. TCD BA 66 MA 70 BD 77 HDipEd 80. CITC 68. d 68 p 69. C Crumlin *Conn* 68–70; C Howth *D & G* 70–73; I Greystones 73–08; Can Ch Ch Cathl Dublin 90–08; adn Glendalough 93–08; rtd 09. *Noah's Ark, 4 Mount Haven, New Road, Greystones, Co Wicklow, Republic of Ireland* T: (00353) (1) 255 7572 M: 87-255 7032 E: edgarjswann@eircom.net

SWANN, Frederick David. b 38. d 69 p 70. C Lurgan Ch the Redeemer *D & D* 69–77; I Ardmore w Craigavon 77–79; I Comber 79–85; I Drumglass w Moygashel *Arm* 85–06; Can Arm Cathl 96–06; Preb Arm Cathl 98–01; Treas Arm Cathl 01–06; rtd 06; P-in-c Tubbercurry w Killoran *T, K & A* 14–18. *Branchfield, Ballymote, Co Sligo, Republic of Ireland* T: (00353) (71) 919 7097 E: derickswann@eircom.net

SWANN, Paul David James. b 59. Ch Ch Ox BA 81 MA 88. St Jo Coll Nottm 87. d 90 p 91. C Old Hill H Trin *Worc* 90–94; V 94–02; C Worc City and Chapl Worc Tech Coll 02–09; rtd 09; PtO *Worc* from 12. *26 Knotts Avenue, Worcester WR4 0HZ* T: (01905) 619339 E: pdjswann@gmail.com

SWANNACK, David Joseph. b 65. d 11 p 12. C Frodingham and New Brumby *Linc* 11–15; V Messingham 15–16; P-in-c Scotter w E Ferry 15–16; P-in-c Scotton w Northorpe 15–16; R Messingham w E Butterwick, Scotter w E Ferry and Scotton w Northorpe from 16. *The Rectory, Church Lane, Scotter, Gainsborough DN21 3RZ* T: (01724) 647789 E: daveswannack@gmail.com

SWANSEA AND BRECON, Bishop of. *See* DAVIES, The Most Revd John David Edward

SWANTON, Canon John Joseph. b 61. Bradf and Ilkley Coll BA 84 Univ of Wales (Ban) BTh 10 MCIH 89. S Dios Minl Tr Scheme 92. d 95 p 96. NSM Shalford *Guildf* 95–99; NSM Compton w Shackleford and Peper Harow 99–11; TV S Cotswolds *Glouc* 11–14; TR from 14; Hon Can Glouc Cathl from 19. *The Rectory, Ampney Crucis, Cirencester GL7 5RY* T: (01285) 851309 E: john@swanton.plus.com

SWARBRICK, Miss Emma Jayne. b 83. St Martin's Coll Lanc BA(QTS) 05. Trin Coll Bris 16. d 18 p 19. C S Shore H Trin *Blackb* from 18; C S Shore St Pet from 18. *1 Windermere Road, Blackpool FY4 2BX* T: (01253) 348194 E: emmaswarbrick@outlook.com

SWARBRICK (née PITE), Mrs Sheila Reinhardt. b 60. St Jo Coll Dur BA 82 Nottm Univ MA 98. Oak Hill Th Coll BA 88. d 88 p 94. Par Dn Derby St Aug 88–92; C Brampton St Thos 92–95; PtO *St Alb* 95–96; P-in-c The Stodden Churches 96–98; Chapl Papworth Hosp NHS Trust 98–99; TV Braunstone *Leic* 99–02; P-in-c 02–07; PtO *Ex* 07–08; Hon C Cen Ex 08–14; P-in-c from 14; Asst Chapl R Devon and Ex NHS Foundn Trust from 09. *7 Lower Kings Avenue, Exeter EX4 6JT* T: (01392) 438866 E: sheila.pite@cooptel.net *or* s.swarbrick@nhs.net

SWARBRIGG, David Cecil. b 42. TCD BA 64 MA 67. d 65 p 66. C Lisburn Ch Ch *Conn* 65–67; C Thames Ditton *Guildf* 72–76; Chapl Hampton Sch Middx 76–97; rtd 97. *39 Harefield, Hinchley Wood, Esher KT10 9TY* T/F: (020) 8398 3950 E: d.swarbrigg@btinternet.com

SWART-RUSSELL, Phoebe. b 58. Cape Town Univ BA 79 MA 82 DPhil 88. Ox NSM Course 89. d 90 p 94. C Riverside *Ox* 90–95; Hon C Chenies and Lt Chalfont, Latimer and

Flaunden 96–00; PtO from 10. *The Rectory, Latimer, Chesham HP5 1UA* T: (01494) 762281

SWARTZ, Clifford Robert. b 71. Trin Coll Connecticut BA 92 Trin Coll Cam BA 99. Ridley Hall Cam 97. d 00 p 01. C Kirk Ella *York* 00–03; Regional Dir FOCUS USA 03–11; Hon C Tariffville Trin Ch 03–11; P-in-c St Bees *Carl* 11–12; V 12–15; Chapl St Bees Sch 11–15; PtO *Ox* 15–16; Chapl Haberdashers' Monmouth Schs from 16; PtO *Heref* from 17. *Lancaster House, 26 Hereford Road, Monmouth NP25 3HJ* E: clifford.swartz@gmail.com *or* cr.swartz@habsmonmouth.org

SWAYNE, Jeremy Michael Deneys. b 41. Worc Coll Ox BA 63 BM, BCh 67 MRCGP 71 FFHom 91. d 00 p 01. NSM Fosse Trinity *B & W* 00–04; P-in-c 04–05; rtd 05; PtO *B & W* from 05. *Tanzy Cottage, Rimpton, Yeovil BA22 8AQ* T: (01935) 850031 E: jem.swayne@btinternet.com

SWAYZE, Margaret. b 69. d 11 p 12. OLM Diss *Nor* 11–19; rtd 19; PtO *Nor* from 19. *32 Croft Lane, Diss IP22 4NA* T: (01379) 644701 E: maggiecroftlane@live.co.uk

SWEATMAN, John. b 44. Open Univ BA 89. Bernard Gilpin Soc Dur 67 Oak Hill Th Coll 68. d 71 p 72. C Rayleigh *Chelmsf* 71–73; C Seaford w Sutton *Chich* 73–77; Chapl RN 77–82; CF 82–85; V Hellingly and Upper Dicker *Chich* 85–90; Hon C Mayfield 95–96; P-in-c Malborough w S Huish, W Alvington and Churchstow *Ex* 96–02; V Ash w Westmarsh *Cant* 02–11; P-in-c Wingham w Elmstone and Preston w Stourmouth 10–11; AD E Bridge 08–11; rtd 11; PtO *Cant* 12–16; *Sarum* from 16. *78 Keepers Road, Devizes SN10 2FP* T: (01380) 727626 E: johnsrev@btinternet.com

SWEENEY, Andrew James. b 61. Wycliffe Hall Ox 96. d 96 p 97. C Bladon w Woodstock *Ox* 96–99; C Coleraine *Conn* 99–02; V Cogges and S Leigh *Ox* 02–12; V N Leigh 09–12; AD Witney 07–08; I Ballymoney w Finvoy and Rasharkin *Conn* from 12. *The Rectory, 4 Queen Street, Ballymoney BT53 6JA* T: (028) 2766 2149 M: 07720-472556 E: ballymoneyrector@sky.com

SWEENEY, Andrew John. b 59. Ripon Coll Cuddesdon 09. d 11 p 12. C Clapham Ch Ch and St Jo *S'wark* 11–15; P-in-c Hythe *Cant* from 15. *The Vicarage, Oak Walk, Hythe CT21 5DN* T: (01303) 266217 E: vicarofhythe@gmail.com

SWEENEY, Robert Maxwell. b 38. Ch Ch Ox BA 63 MA 66 Birm Univ MA 78. Cuddesdon Coll 63. d 65 p 66. C Prestbury *Glouc* 65–68; C Handsworth St Andr *Birm* 68–70; Asst Chapl Lancing Coll 70–73; V Wotton St Mary *Glouc* 74–79; V Ox St Thos w St Frideswide and Binsey 79–03; Chapl Magd Coll Ox 82–88; rtd 03. *22 Park House, 39 Park Place, Cheltenham GL50 2RF* T: (01242) 254028

SWEENEY, William David. b 89. St Jo Coll Nottm BA 13 LTh 14. d 14 p 15. C Ex St Thos and Em 14–17; C Plympton 17–18; TV from 18. *The Rectory, 31 Wain Park, Plymouth PL7 2HX* T: (01752) 946084 M: 07909-830621 E: fr.willsweeney@aol.co.uk

SWEERTS, Mrs Evelyn Harriet Elisabeth. b 75. Bris Univ BA 96 MA 98 PGCE 99. ERMC 16. d 19. NSM Luxembourg *Eur* from 19. *8 rue de Jardins, Hassel, 5762 Luxembourg* T: (00352) 2667 1135 E: evelyn.sweerts@outlook.com

SWEET, Reginald Charles. b 36. Open Univ BA 74. Ripon Hall Ox 61. d 62 p 63. C Styvechale *Cov* 62–65; Chapl RN 65–69 and 74–93; R Riddlesworth w Gasthorpe and Knettishall *Nor* 69–74; R Brettenham w Rushford 69–74; PtO 93–96; Chapl Miss to Seamen 96–99; rtd 99; Chapl St Cross Hosp 99–12; Master from 12. *The Chaplain's Lodge, The Hospital of St Cross, St Cross Road, Winchester SO23 9SD* T: (01962) 853525 M: 07889-375085 E: master@hospitalofstcross.co.uk

SWEET, Preb Vaughan Carroll. b 46. Aston Univ BSc 69 MSc 70. Linc Th Coll 89. d 91 p 92. C Uttoxeter w Bramshall *Lich* 91–95; P-in-c Hadley 95–98; V 98–07; P-in-c Wellington Ch Ch 03–07; V Hadley and Wellington Ch Ch 07–11; RD Telford 00–11; RD Telford Severn Gorge *Heref* 00–03; Preb Lich Cathl 05–11; rtd 12; PtO *Lich* 12–18; *St As* from 12. *64 Queens Park Flats, Queens Park Close, Mablethorpe LN12 2XA*

SWEETING, David Charles. b 67. Nottm Univ BSc 89. STETS 04. d 08 p 09. C Holbeach *Linc* 08–12; V Glen Gp from 12. *The Vicarage, 19 Spalding Road, Pinchbeck, Spalding PE11 3UD* T: (01775) 725698 M: 07973-841799 E: david@davidsweeting.orangehouse.co.uk

SWEETING, Paul Lee. b 68. Lanc Univ BSc 90 St Martin's Coll Lanc PGCE 92. Cranmer Hall Dur BA 99. d 99 p 00. C Blackb St Gabr 99–03; R Falkland Is 03–06; Chapl Sedbergh Sch from 06; Chapl RAuxAF from 15. *Greenrigg, Loftus Hill, Sedbergh LA10 5SQ* M: 07794-737886 E: sweeting.paul@googlemail.com

SWEETMAN (née BURNIE), Ms Judith. b 57. Leic Univ BA 79. Westcott Ho Cam 05. d 07 p 08. C Coggeshall w Markshall *Chelmsf* 07–10; P-in-c Boxford, Edwardstone, Groton etc

St E 10–18; rtd 18; PtO *Nor* from 18. *15 The Dial, Reepham, Norwich NR10 4LX*

SWENSSON, Sister Gerd Inger. b 51. Lon Univ MPhil 85 Uppsala Univ 70. **dss** 74 **d** 87. In Ch of Sweden 74–75; Notting Hill *Lon* 75–77; CSA from 75; Abbey Ho Malmesbury *Bris* 77–79; R Foundn of St Kath in Ratcliffe 79–81; Notting Hill All SS w St Columb *Lon* 81–84; Kensington St Mary Abbots w St Geo 85–89; C Bedford Park 91–95; Sweden from 95. *Christens Gård, Pl 8, St Slågarp, S-231 95 Trelleborg, Sweden* T/F: (0046) (40) 487059 M: 708-743994 E: tedeum@telia.com

SWIFT, Ainsley Laird. b 56. Liv Univ BEd 80. Ripon Coll Cuddesdon. **d** 94 **p** 95. C Prescot *Liv* 94–98; TV New Windsor *Ox* 98–01; P-in-c 01–15; TR 15–18; V Bray and Braywood from 18; AD Maidenhead and Windsor from 18. *The Vicarage, The Churchyard, Bray, Maidenhead SL6 2UB* T: (01628) 621527

✠**SWIFT, The Rt Revd Andrew Christopher.** b 68. Edin Univ BEng 90 Aber Univ MSc 97. Ripon Coll Cuddesdon BTh 05. **d** 07 **p** 08 **c** 18. C Glouc St Cath 07–10; P-in-c Dunoon *Arg* 10–16; R 16–18; P-in-c Rothesay 10–16; R 16–18; P-in-c Tighnabruaich 10–11; Dean Arg 12–18; Can Cumbrae 13–18; Can St Jo Cathl Oban 13–18; Bp Bre from 18. *Bishop's House, 5 Ballumbie View, Dundee DD4 0NQ* T: (01382) 800458 *or* 459569 E: rev.andrew@familyswift.org.uk *or* bishop@brechin.anglican.org

SWIFT, Andrew Christopher. b 87. K Coll Lon LLB 08. St Steph Ho Ox BTh 12. **d** 12 **p** 13. C Hendon St Mary and Ch Ch *Lon* 12–15; C Smallthorne *Lich* 15–19; P-in-c from 19; P-in-c Burslem St Werburgh from 19. *The Vicarage, Ford Green Road, Stoke-on-Trent ST6 1NX* T: (01782) 827889 M: 07792-809334 E: fr.andrew.c.swift@gmail.com

SWIFT, Christopher James. b 65. Hull Univ BA 86 Man Univ MA 95 Sheff Univ PhD 06. Westcott Ho Cam 89. **d** 91 **p** 92. C Longton *Blackb* 91–94; TV Chipping Barnet w Arkley *St Alb* 94–97; Chapl Wellhouse NHS Trust 97–98; Chapl Dewsbury Health Care NHS Trust 98–01; Hd Chapl Services Leeds Teaching Hosps NHS Trust 01–17; Dir Chapl and Spirituality Methodist Homes for the Aged from 17; PtO *Leeds* from 17; *Sheff* from 17. *MHA, Epworth House, 3 Stuart Street, Derby DE1 2EQ* T: (01332) 221875 M: 07711-485773 E: chris.swift@mha.org.uk

SWIFT, Christopher John. b 54. Linc Coll Ox BA 76 MA Selw Coll Cam BA 80. Westcott Ho Cam 79. **d** 81 **p** 82. C Portsea N End St Mark *Portsm* 81–84; C Alverstoke 84–87; V Whitton SS Phil and Jas *Lon* 87–94; R Shepperton 94–08; R Shepperton and Littleton from 08; AD Spelthorne 98–04. *The Rectory, Church Square, Shepperton TW17 9JY* T/F: (01932) 220511 E: christopher.swift@london.anglican.org *or* chrisswift@tiscali.co.uk

SWIFT, Ian John Edward. b 46. NTMTC 99. **d** 02 **p** 03. NSM Basildon St Martin *Chelmsf* 02–06; C Vange 06–11; Ind Chapl 06–11; Chapl Essex Police 06–11; P-in-c Crosscrake *Carl* 11–16; rtd 16; PtO *Carl* from 17. *4 Wilkinson View, Backbarrow, Ulverston LA12 8RE* M: 07725-037680 E: ijeswift@googlemail.com

SWIFT, Jessica Suzanne. b 75. Univ of New Brunswick BSc 99. Wycliffe Hall Ox 99. **d** 02 **p** 03. C Islington St Mary *Lon* 02–05; C Mildmay Grove St Jude and St Paul 05–09; C Barnsbury 09–19; Dean of Women's Min Stepney Area 14–19; AD Islington 17–19; V S Tottenham St Ann from 19. *St Ann's Vicarage, South Grove, London N15 5QG* M: 07769-338624 E: swift_jessica@hotmail.com

SWIFT, Ms Pamela Joan. b 47. Liv Univ BSc 68. NEOC 85. **d** 88 **p** 94. Par Dn Bermondsey St Jas w Ch Ch *S'wark* 88–91; Par Dn Middleton St Cross *Ripon* 91–92; C Leeds All So and Dioc Stewardship Adv 92–95; TR Bramley 95–99; Miss Adv USPG Blackb, Bradf, Carl and Wakef 99–01; Hon C Kildwick *Bradf* 99–01; R and Community P Glas St Matt 01–05; rtd 05; Hon C Lanercost, Walton, Gilsland and Nether Denton *Carl* 06–10; Chapl N Cumbria Acute Hosps NHS Trust 06–08; PtO *Newc* 11–14; Chapl Northumbria Healthcare NHS Foundn Trust 14–15; P-in-c Glazebury w Hollinfare *Liv* 15. *10 Hesnall Close, Glazebury, Warrington WA3 5PB* M: 07833-938843 E: pam.swift@live.co.uk

SWIFT, Richard Barrie. b 33. Selw Coll Cam BA 58 MA 64. Ripon Hall Ox. **d** 60 **p** 61. C Stepney St Dunstan and All SS *Lon* 60–64; C Sidmouth St Nic *Ex* 64–72; P-in-c W Hyde St Thos *St Alb* 72–77; V Mill End 72–77; V Mill End and Heronsgate w W Hyde 77–82; V Axminster *Ex* 82–83; P-in-c Chardstock 82–83; P-in-c Combe Pyne w Rousdon 82–83; TR Axminster, Chardstock, Combe Pyne and Rousdon 83–94; rtd 94; PtO *Ex* from 94. *28 Gracey Court, Broadclyst, Exeter EX5 3GA* T: (01392) 469436

SWIFT, Sarah Jane. b 65. St Aid Coll Dur BSc 88 Nottm Univ MA 10. St Jo Coll Nottm 05. **d** 06 **p** 07. C Wealdstone H Trin *Lon* 06–10; Chapl Chr Healing Miss from 10. *8 Cambridge*

Court, 210 Shepherd's Bush Road, London W6 7NJ T: (020) 7603 8118 E: sarah@healingmission.org

SWIFT, Stanley. b 47. Open Univ BA 86 ACIS 71. Linc Th Coll 71. **d** 74 **p** 75. C Heaton St Barn *Bradf* 74–77; C Bexhill St Pet *Chich* 77–81; R Crowland *Linc* 81–86; RD Elloe W 82–86; R Upminster *Chelmsf* 86–95; P-in-c N Ockendon 94–95; V Rush Green 95–02; V Gt Burstead 02–11; V Gt Burstead w Ramsden Crays 11–13; rtd 13; PtO *Chelmsf* from 14. *16 Mariners Way, Maldon CM9 6YW* T: (01621) 859955 E: stanswift@hotmail.com

SWINBANK, Jennifer. *See* WOOD, Anne Jennifer

SWINDELL, Anthony Charles. b 50. Selw Coll Cam BA 73 MA 77 Leeds Univ MPhil 77 PhD 07 Lambeth DD 12. Ripon Hall Ox 73. **d** 75 **p** 76. C Hessle *York* 75–78; P-in-c Litlington w W Dean *Chich* 78–80; Adult Educn Adv E Sussex 78–80; TV Heslington *York* 80–81; Chapl York Univ 80–81; R Harlaxton *Linc* 81–91; RD Grantham 85–90; R Jersey St Sav *Win* 91–15; PtO *Nor* 93–96; rtd 15. *Annakisha, 4 Troed y Garth, Y Fan, Llandiloes SY18 6NA* E: anthonyswindell@aol.co.uk

SWINDELL, Brian. b 35. St Jo Coll Nottm 86. **d** 88 **p** 89. C Wombwell *Sheff* 88–91; V Brinsworth w Catcliffe 91–93; TR Brinsworth w Catcliffe and Treeton 93–99; rtd 99; PtO *S'well* from 04. *36 Wasdale Close, West Bridgford, Nottingham NG2 6RG* T: 0115-914 1125

SWINDELL, Richard Carl. b 45. Didsbury Coll Man CertEd 67 Open Univ BA 73 Leeds Univ MEd 86. NOC 79 Qu Coll Birm 77. **d** 82 **p** 83. Hd Teacher Moorside Jun Sch 78–96; NSM Halifax St Aug *Wakef* 82–92; NSM Huddersfield H Trin 92–14; *Leeds* from 14; Family Life and Marriage Officer *Wakef* 96–02; Bp's Adv for Child Protection *Leeds* from 14. *13 Moor Hill Court, Laund Road, Salendine Nook, Huddersfield HD3 3GQ* T: (01484) 640473 M: 07946-761364 E: rswin25004@aol.com

SWINDELLS, Mrs Tracy Jane. b 67. Open Univ BA 01 Warwick Univ MA 09 Man Metrop Univ PGCE 03. LCTP 10. **d** 12 **p** 13. NSM Lostock Hall and Farington Moss *Blackb* 12–14; NSM Leyland St Jas 14–16; V Langho Billington from 16. *1 Higherfield, Langho, Blackburn BB6 8HQ* T: (01254) 247039 E: revtswindells@aol.com

SWINDLEHURST, Christine Frances. *See* SPURWAY, Christine Frances

SWINDON, Suffragan Bishop of. *See* RAYFIELD, The Rt Revd Lee Stephen

SWINERD, Emily Rose Mary. b 86. Ches Univ BTh 08. Trin Coll Bris 17. **d** 19. C Highworth w Sevenhampton and Inglesham etc *Bris* from 19. *14 Brookfield, Highworth, Swindon SN6 7HV* M: 07837-820747 E: emily.swinerd86@gmail.com

SWINHOE, John Robert. b 68. **d** 10 **p** 14. NSM Horton *Newc* 10–18; NSM Blyth St Mary 15–18; C Seaton Hirst from 18; Chapl Northd Fire and Rescue Service from 11. *St Andrew's Vicarage, Hawthorn Road, Ashington NE63 9AU* E: johnswinhoe19@gmail.com

SWINHOE, Terence Leslie. b 49. Man Univ BA 71 PGCE 72 Lon Univ BD 95. NOC. **d** 84 **p** 85. C Harborne St Pet *Birm* 84–87; V Warley *Wakef* 87–96; V Rastrick St Matt 96–06; P-in-c Greetland and W Vale 06–14; *Leeds* 14; rtd 14; PtO *Leeds* from 17. *6 Bent Lea, Huddersfield HD2 1QW* T: (01484) 429767 E: swinfam@aol.com

SWINNEY, Shawn Douglas. b 76. Oak Hills Chr Coll (USA) BA 01 Regent Coll Vancouver MA 04. Ox Min Course 07. **d** 09 **p** 10. NSM Gerrards Cross and Fulmer *Ox* 09–13; C Surbiton Hill Ch Ch *S'wark* 13–18; C Combe Down w Monkton Combe and S Stoke *B & W* from 18. *81 Church Road, Combe Down, Bath BA2 5JJ* M: 07508-078058 E: shawnswinney@hotmail.com

SWINTON, Garry Dunlop. b 59. SS Mark & Jo Univ Coll Plymouth BA 81 CertEd 82. Ripon Coll Cuddesdon 85. **d** 88 **p** 89. C Surbiton St Andr and St Mark *S'wark* 88–92; Succ S'wark Cathl 92–97; P-in-c Wandsworth St Faith 97–01; Chapl YMCA Wimbledon 97–01; Chapl Greycoat Hosp Sch from 01; Chapl Westmr City Sch from 01; PV Westmr Abbey from 06. *4 Greenham Close, London SE1 7RP* T: (020) 7261 9321 M: 07961-422303 E: garry.swinton@gmail.com

SWIRES-HENNESSY, Matthew. b 81. Lon Sch of Th BA 06. Wycliffe Hall Ox MTh 10. **d** 09 **p** 10. C Luton St Fran *St Alb* 09–12; C N Farnborough *Guildf* 12–17; C Farnborough St Pet from 17. *27 Church Road East, Farnborough GU14 6QJ* M: 07803-928006 E: revd.msh@googlemail.com *or* matthew@stpetersfarnborough.org.uk

SWITHINBANK, Mrs Penelope Jane. b 53. St Andr Univ MTheol 74 Hughes Hall Cam PGCE 75. Ridley Hall Cam 00. **d** 02 **p** 03. Dir Connections Falls Ch Virginia USA 02–07; R Johns Island Ch of Our Sav 07–08; Chapl St Mellitus Coll *Lon* from 08; PtO *Bris* 13–18; *B & W* from 18. *Lanston House, 81 Fortescue Street, Norton St Philip, Bath BA2 7PE* M: 07870-497365 E: penelopeswithinbank@mac.com

SWITZERLAND, Archdeacon of. *See* KELHAM, Canon Adèle Mary

SWORD, Bernard James. b 46. **d** 04 **p** 05. NSM Millbrook *Ches* 04–07; P-in-c Bredbury St Barn 07–14; rtd 15; PtO *Ches* 16–18; Hon C Sandbach Heath w Wheelock from 18. *17 Woodlands Park, Wash Lane, Allostock, Knutsford WA16 9LG* T: (01565) 722168 M: 07866-446681 E: revdbsword@gmail.com

SWYER, David Martin. b 64. Univ of Wales (Abth) BA 87 PGCE 89. St Mich Coll Llan 89. **d** 91 **p** 92. C Killay *S & B* 91–93; C Newton St Pet 93–95; R Albourne w Sayers Common and Twineham *Chich* 95–13; Hon C Haywards Heath St Rich 16; Hon C Portslade St Nic and St Andr and Mile Oak 16–17; P-in-c from 17. *18 Amesbury Crescent, Hove BN3 5RD* T: (01273) 425695 E: davidswyer64@gmail.com

SWYER (*née* HARRIS**), Canon Rebecca Jane.** b 67. Univ of Wales (Lamp) BA 88 Univ of Wales (Cardiff) MPhil 93. St Mich Coll Llan 89. **d** 91. C Sketty *S & B* 91–95; PtO *Chich* 95–02; LtO from 02; Lect Th Chich Univ 97–09; Min Development Officer *Chich* from 09; Can and Preb Chich Cathl from 10; Dir Dept Apostolic Life from 15. *18 Amesbury Crescent, Hove BN3 5RD* T: (01273) 425695 E: rebecca.swyer@chichester.anglican.org

SYDNEY, Archbishop of. *See* DAVIES, Glenn Naunton

SYER, Mrs Angela. b 48. ARCM 69 Philippa Fawcett Coll CertEd 71. Qu Coll Birm. **d** 00 **p** 01. C Oakdale *Sarum* 00–04; P-in-c Coxley w Godney, Henton and Wookey *B & W* 04–13; rtd 13; PtO *Sarum* from 13. *The Old Inn, Stalbridge Weston, Sturminster Newton DT10 2LA* T: (01963) 362830 E: angelasyer@hotmail.com

SYKES, Alan Roy. b 53. Sheff Univ BA 75. Dioc OLM Tr Scheme 05. **d** 08 **p** 09. NSM Richmond St Mary w St Matthias and St Jo *S'wark* 08–18; PtO from 18. *251 King's Road, Kingston upon Thames KT2 5JH* T: (020) 8549 3887 E: alan.sykes@richmondteamministry.org

SYKES, Christine Virginia. b 55. **d** 07 **p** 08. NSM Castle Church *Lich* from 07. *18 Delamere Lane, Stafford ST17 9TL* T: (01785) 240529 E: curate@castlechurch.co.uk *or* chris@castlechurch.org.uk

SYKES, Mrs Clare Mary. b 61. Open Univ BA 10. WEMTC 93. **d** 96 **p** 97. C Tupsley w Hampton Bishop *Heref* 96–01; NSM Bromyard and Stanford Bishop, Stoke Lacy, Moreton Jeffries w Much Cowarne etc 01–08; NSM Bromyard and Stoke Lacy 09–12; RD Bromyard 05–12; R Osney *Ox* from 12. *Osney Rectory, 81 West Way, Oxford OX2 9JY* T: (01865) 242345 E: revclare@btinternet.com

SYKES, Cynthia Ann. b 41. **d** 05 **p** 06. OLM Em TM *Wakef* 05–14; Newsome and Armitage Bridge and S Crosland *Leeds* from 14. *The Old Dairy, Parkhead Farm, Birdsedge, Huddersfield HD8 8XW* T: (01484) 603894

SYKES, Mrs Emma Caroline Mary. b 75. Warwick Univ BA 96. St Jo Coll Nottm 06. **d** 08 **p** 09. C Birm St Martin w Bordesley St Andr 08–14; PtO 14–15; NSM Boldmere from 15; Leadership Specialist CPAS from 16; Asst Dioc Dir of Ords *Birm* from 18. *159 Boldmere Road, Sutton Coldfield B73 5UL* T: 0121-354 3130 M: 07859-066510 E: emmarsykes@hotmail.com

SYKES, Gerald Alfred. b 58. Univ of Wales (Abth) BSc 79 PhD 83 Univ of Wales (Cardiff) BD 98. St Mich Coll Llan 95. **d** 98 **p** 99. C Cardigan w Mwnt and Y Ferwig w Llangoedmor *St D* 98–01; P-in-c Brechfa w Abergorlech etc 01–08; P-in-c Alverthorpe *Wakef* 08–14; *Leeds* 14–17; P-in-c Westgate Common *Wakef* 08–14; *Leeds* 14–17; V Highgate *Birm* from 17; Chapl St Alb Academy from 17. *St Alban's Vicarage, 120 Stanhope Street, Birmingham B12 0XB* E: frgerrysykes@gmail.com

SYKES, Graham Timothy Gordon. b 59. ACIB 89. St Jo Coll Nottm BTh 92. **d** 92 **p** 93. C Kington w Huntington, Old Radnor, Kinnerton etc *Heref* 92–95; C Breinton 95–97; TV W Heref 97–98; Dioc Co-ord for Evang 95–01; V Bromyard 01–08; P-in-c Stanford Bishop, Stoke Lacy, Moreton Jeffries w Much Cowarne etc 01–08; P-in-c Bromyard and Stoke Lacy 09–12; Bp's Dom Chapl *Ox* 13–16; Chapl Sobell Ho Hospice from 17. *Sobell House, Churchill Hospital, Old Road, Oxford OX3 7LE* T: (01865) 225860 E: graham.sykes@ouh.nhs.uk

SYKES, Ian. b 44. Leic Univ DipEd. Ripon Coll Cuddesdon 84. **d** 85 **p** 86. In Bapt Min 64–84; C Headington *Ox* 85–88; TV Bourne Valley *Sarum* 88–97; R Peter Tavy, Mary Tavy, Lydford and Brent Tor *Ex* 97–07; Hon C 07–10; PtO *Win* 11–17. *Forge Cottage, East End, Damerham, Fordingbridge SP6 3HQ* T: (01725) 518635 E: iansforgery@btinternet.com

SYKES, James Clement. b 42. Keble Coll Ox BA 64 MA 71. Westcott Ho Cam 65. **d** 67 **p** 68. C Bishop's Stortford St Mich *St Alb* 67–71; Chapl St Jo Sch Leatherhead 71–73; Bermuda 74–79; V Northaw *St Alb* 79–87; Chapl St Marg Sch Bushey 87–98; R Guernsey St Sampson *Win* 99–07; rtd 07; PtO *Win* from 07. *Petit Robinet, Rue de Bouverie, Castel,*

Guernsey GY5 7UA T: (01481) 256381 M: 07781-111459 E: jimandsue@cwgsy.net

SYKES, Miss Jean. b 45. Leeds Univ BA 66 Bris Univ CertEd 67. Ripon Coll Cuddesdon 86. **d** 88 **p** 94. C N Huddersfield *Wakef* 88–91; Team Dn 91–93; TV Kippax w Allerton Bywater *Ripon* 93–13; AD Whitkirk 05–09; rtd 13; PtO *Leeds* from 17. *21 Dearne Hall Road, Barugh Green, Barnsley S75 1LU* T: (01226) 388709

SYKES, Jeremy Gordon. b 63. Hull Univ BA 85. St Alb Minl Tr Scheme 92 Ripon Coll Cuddesdon 97. **d** 99 **p** 00. C Ipswich St Mary-le-Tower *St E* 99–02; P-in-c Briston w Burgh Parva and Melton Constable *Nor* 02–06; P-in-c Briston, Burgh Parva, Hindolveston etc 06–17; R from 17; RD Holt 11–17. *The Vicarage, 1 Grange Close, Briston, Melton Constable NR24 2LY* T: (01263) 860280 E: jeremy@sykes-uk.com *or* briston.vicarage@gmail.com

SYKES, Jeremy Jonathan Nicholas. b 61. Girton Coll Cam BA 83 MA 86. Wycliffe Hall Ox BA 88 MA 91. **d** 89 **p** 90. C Knowle *Birm* 89–92; Asst Chapl Oakham Sch 92–98; Chapl Giggleswick Sch 98–06; Hd Master Gt Walstead Sch 06–10; Chapl Hurstpierpoint Coll from 10. *Hurstpierpoint College, College Lane, Hurstpierpoint, Hassocks BN6 9JS* T: (01273) 836889 E: jeremy.sykes@hppc.co.uk

SYKES, Canon John. b 39. Man Univ BA 62. Ripon Hall Ox 61. **d** 63 **p** 64. C Heywood St Luke *Man* 63–67; C Bolton H Trin 67–71; Chapl Bolton Colls of H&FE 67–71; R Reddish *Man* 71–78; V Saddleworth 78–87; TR Oldham 87–04; Hon Can Man Cathl 91–04; rtd 04; PtO *Man* from 04; Chapl to The Queen 95–09. *53 Ivy Green Drive, Springhead, Oldham OL4 4PR* T: 0161-678 6767 M: 07968-382075 E: sykesjohn76@gmail.com

SYKES, John Harold. b 50. Van Mildert Coll Dur BA 71 K Coll Lon BD 73 AKC 74 MTh 75 Linc Coll Ox MSc 89 ALAM 71 FRSA 92. S'wark Ord Course 75. **d** 09 **p** 09. NSM Ashburnham w Penhurst *Chich* 09–19; PtO *Cant* from 19. *Woodlands, Dorothy Avenue, Cranbrook TN17 3AL* T: (01580) 712793

SYKES, Sandra. b 51. St Mellitus Coll 13. **d** 14 **p** 15. OLM Gt and Lt Leighs and Lt Waltham *Chelmsf* 14–17; NSM from 17; OLM Gt Waltham w Ford End 15–17; NSM from 17; OLM The Chignals w Mashbury 15–17; NSM from 17. *141 Main Road, Great Leighs, Chelmsford CM3 1NP* T: (01245) 362701 E: sandra.sykes59@btinternet.com

SYLVESTER, Jeremy Carl Edmund. b 56. Cape Town Univ BA 78 HDipEd 79. Coll of Resurr Mirfield 84. **d** 87 **p** 88. C St Cypr Cathl Kimberley S Africa 87–89; C Ganyesa 89–92; Chapl Informal Settlements Johannesburg 92–96; P-in-c Stoke Newington St Olave *Lon* 96–98; TV Plymouth Em, St Paul Efford and St Aug *Ex* 98–01; CMS 01–06; V Nether w Upper Poppleton *York* from 06. *The Vicarage, 15 Nether Way, Upper Poppleton, York YO26 6JQ* T: (01904) 789522 E: jeremysylvester@btinternet.com

SYMCOX, Ms Caroline Jane. b 80. Keble Coll Ox BA 01 MSt 02 MLitt 10. Ripon Coll Cuddesdon 09. **d** 11 **p** 12. C Amersham *Ox* 11–14; TV S Cotswolds *Glouc* from 14. *The Vicarage, The Croft, Fairford GL7 4BB* T: (01285) 712467 M: 07811-212370 E: carolinesymcox@googlemail.com

SYMES, Andrew John Barrington. b 66. Magd Coll Cam BA 88 MA 92 Ches Univ MA 13. All Nations Chr Coll 90. **d** 00 **p** 00. C Walmer St Jo S Africa 00–02; Dir Ext Progr Bible Inst E Cape 02–06; P-in-c Kings Heath *Pet* 07–13; C Northampton St Giles 07–13; Exec Sec Angl Mainstream Internat from 13; PtO *Ox* 13–14; C Fyfield w Tubney and Kingston Bagpuize 14–18; PtO from 18. *Red Roof Cottage, Ashfields Lane, East Hanney, Wantage OX12 0HN* T: (01235) 869139 M: 07921-921324 E: asymes@anglican-mainstream.net

SYMES-THOMPSON, Hugh Kynard. b 54. Peterho Cam BA 76 MA 81. Cranmer Hall Dur. **d** 79 **p** 80. C Summerfield *Birm* 79–82; C Harlow New Town w Lt Parndon *Chelmsf* 82–83; Australia 84–89; TV Dagenham *Chelmsf* 89–95; R Cranfield and Hulcote w Salford *St Alb* 95–19; Chapl Cranfield Univ 02–19; rtd 19. *Address temp unknown* E: revhugh.st@gmail.com

SYMINGTON, Patricia Ann. *See* TURNER, Patricia Ann

SYMMONS, Canon Roderic Paul. b 56. Chu Coll Cam BA 77 MA 81 Oak Hill Th Coll BA 83 Fuller Th Sem California DMin 90. **d** 83 **p** 84. C Ox St Aldate w St Matt 83–88; Lic to Offic LA USA 89–90; R Ardingly *Chich* 90–99; RD Cuckfield 95–99; P-in-c Redland *Bris* 99–14; V 14–18; PtO from 18; Tutor Trin Coll Bris 99–10; AD City *Bris* from 14; Hon Can Bris Cathl from 15. *18 Machin Road, Bristol BS10 7HQ*

SYMON, Canon Roger Hugh Crispin. b 34. St Jo Coll Cam BA 59. Coll of Resurr Mirfield 59. **d** 62 **p** 63. C Westmr St Steph w St Jo *Lon* 61–66; P-in-c Hascombe *Guildf* 66–68; Chapl Surrey Univ 66–74; V Paddington Ch Ch *Lon* 74–78; V Paddington St Jas 78–79; USPG 80–87; Abp

Cant's Acting Sec for Angl Communion Affairs 87–94; Can Res Cant Cathl 94–02; rtd 02; PtO *Glouc* from 02. *5 Bath Parade, Cheltenham GL53 7HL* T: (01242) 700645 E: rogersymon@blueyonder.co.uk

SYMONDS, Alan Jeffrey. b 56. Ridley Hall Cam 93. **d** 95 **p** 96. C Bath St Luke *B & W* 95–99; R Abbas and Templecombe w Horsington 99–06; P-in-c Somerton w The Charltons and Kingsdon from 06. *Rosemount, Sutton Road, Somerton TA11 6QP* T: (01458) 272029 E: somerton.vicar@btinternet.com

SYMONDS, James Henry. b 31. Ripon Hall Ox 67. **d** 69 **p** 70. C Southampton (City Cen) *Win* 69–71; CF 71–78 and 79–90; P-in-c Arrington *Ely* 78–79; P-in-c Orwell 78–79; P-in-c Wimpole 78–79; P-in-c Croydon w Clopton 78–79; CF (R of O) 90–96; rtd 96; P-in-c Coughton, Spernall, Morton Bagot and Oldberrow *Cov* 99–02; PtO *Lich* 00–16; *Cov* 02–15; *Worc* from 13. *Thimble Cottage, Kings Coughton, Alcester B49 5QD* T: (01789) 764609 E: jim.marie@btinternet.com

SYMONS, Mrs Susannah Mary. b 59. LMH Ox BA 81 La Sainte Union Coll PGCE 94. STETS 02. **d** 05 **p** 06. C Nadder Valley *Sarum* 05–09; TV Beaminster Area 09–11; R Bradeley, Church Eaton, Derrington and Haughton *Lich* 11–18; R Kingsley and Foxt-w-Whiston and Oakamoor etc from 18. *The Rectory, Holt Lane, Kingsley, Stoke-on-Trent ST10 2BA* E: sue.symons@btinternet.com

SYMS, Richard Arthur. b 43. Ch Coll Cam BA 66 MA 71. Wycliffe Hall Ox 66. **d** 68 **p** 69. C New Eltham All SS *S'wark* 68–72; Chapl to Arts and Recreation *Dur* 72–73; C Hitchin St Mary *St Alb* 73–76; TV Hitchin 77–78; PtO 78–97; P-in-c Datchworth 97–03; rtd 03; PtO *Lon* from 03; *St Alb* from 03. *8 Lytton Fields, Knebworth SG3 6AZ* T: (01438) 811933 M: 07900-241470 E: richard.syms@sky.com

SYNNOTT, Alan Patrick Sutherland. b 59. **d** 85 **p** 86. C Lisburn Ch Ch *Conn* 85–88; CF 88–95; I Galloon w Drummully *Clogh* 95–01; I Monkstown *Conn* 01–04; PtO 04–09; I Skreen w Kilmacshalgan and Dromard *T, K & A* 09–17; Adn Killala 10–17; Can Killala Cathl 10–17; Can Achonry Cathl 10–17; Dioc Dir of Ords 12–17; Can Tuam Cathl 13–17; I Camlough w Mullaglass *Arm* from 17. *The Rectory, 2 Maytown Road, Bessbrook, Newry BT35 7LY* T: (028) 3083 7448 M: (00353) 86-848 4924 E: alanpsynnott@gmail.com

SZEJNMANN, Claus-Christian Werner (Chris). b 65. R Holloway Coll Lon BA 90 K Coll Lon PhD 94 SFHEA 14. St Mellitus Coll 17. **d** 19. C Leic H Trin w St Jo from 19. *Holy Trinity Church, 2 Upper King Street, Leicester LE1 6XE* T: 0116-254 8981 E: cszejnmann@htl.church

T

TABER-HAMILTON, Nigel John. b 53. Univ of Wales (Ban) BA 75. Qu Coll Birm Ch Div Sch of Pacific 77. **d** 78 **p** 81. C W Wimbledon Ch Ch *S'wark* 78–79; C Berkeley St Mark USA 79–81; C Bloomington H Trin 81–90; and 92–94; Interim R Crawfordsville St Jo 90–91; Interim R New Harmony St Steph 91–92; V Seymour All SS 94–00; R St Aug in-the-Woods from 00. *PO Box 11, Freeland WA 98249, USA* T: (001) (360) 331 4887 F: 331 4822 E: rector@whidbey.com

TABOR, John Tranham. b 30. Ball Coll Ox BA 56 MA 58. Ridley Hall Cam 55. **d** 58 **p** 59. C Lindfield *Chich* 58–62; Tutor Ridley Hall Cam 62–63; Chapl 63–68; Warden Scargill Ho 68–75; R Berkhamsted St Mary *St Alb* 75–96; rtd 96; PtO *St Alb* 96–16; Ox 99–00. *1 The Downs, Aldbourne, Marlborough SN8 2RZ* T: (01672) 540640 E: johnttabor@yahoo.co.uk

TAFESSE, Bogale Tiruneh. b 68. **d** 84 **p** 85. PtO *Birm* from 17. *137 Rodney Close, Birmingham B16 8DJ* M: 07534-220148 E: bogye2003@yahoo.com

TAFFINDER, Dawn Anne. b 66. WEMTC 13. **d** 16 **p** 17. NSM Madeley *Heref* from 16. *5 Reynards Meadow, Sutton Hill, Telford TF4 4NQ* T: (01952) 684277 M: 07813-262311 E: dawn.taffinder@blueyonder.co.uk

TAFT, Mrs Janet Anne. b 59. Sheff Univ BA 80 Wolv Univ PGCE 82. Wycliffe Hall Ox 06. **d** 08 **p** 09. NSM Abingdon *Ox* 08–12; Chapl SS Helen and Kath Sch Abingdon 10–13; C Warfield *Ox* 13–16; PtO from 16. *9 The Chestnuts, Abingdon OX14 3YN* T: (01344) 566390 M: 07929-543626

TAGGART, Terence. b 57. Linc Univ BA 13. Linc Sch of Th and Min 09. **d** 13 **p** 14. NSM Fen and Hill Gp *Linc* 13–15; P-in-c Stornoway *Arg* from 15; P-in-c Eoropaidh from 15. *St Peter's House, 10 Springfield Road, Stornoway HS1 2PT* T: (01851) 700841 M: 07768-219984 E: terry_t_2000_uk@yahoo.co.uk

TAGGART, Canon William Joseph. b 54. **d** 85 **p** 86. C Belfast St Mich *Conn* 85–90; I Belfast St Kath from 90; Dioc Registrar from 06; Can Conn Cathl from 12. *St Katharine's Rectory, 24 Lansdowne Road, Belfast BT15 4DB* T: (028) 9077 7647 E: belfast.stkatharine@connor.anglican.org

TAGUE, Russell. b 59. Aston Tr Scheme 90 Linc Th Coll 92. **d** 94 **p** 95. C Astley *Man* 94–97; Chapl HM YOI Swinfen Hall 97–00; Chapl HM Pris Risley 00–05; TV Kirkby *Liv* 05–08; R Arthuret w Kirkandrews-on-Esk and Nicholforest *Carl* 08–17; rtd 17. *159 Hillock Lane, Woolston, Warrington WA1 4PJ* E: taguejosh@yahoo.co.uk

TAILBY, Ms Jane Dorothy. b 56. Culham Coll of Educn BEd 79. WEMTC 01. **d** 04 **p** 05. NSM Frampton Cotterell and Iron Acton *Bris* 04–09; NSM Winterbourne and Frenchay and Winterbourne Down 08–09; TV Nadder Valley *Sarum* 09–16; V Nassington, Apethorpe, Thornhaugh etc *Pet* from 16. *The Vicarage, 34 Station Road, Nassington, Peterborough PE8 6QB* E: jdtailby@aol.com

TAILBY, Peter Alan. b 49. Chich Th Coll 83. **d** 85 **p** 86. C Stocking Farm *Leic* 85–88; C Knighton St Mary Magd 88–90; P-in-c Thurnby Lodge 90–98; P-in-c W Molesey *Guildf*

98–05; V 05–16; rtd 16; PtO *Leic* from 17. *6 Parkside Close, Leicester LE4 1EP* E: ptailby@virginmedia.com

TAIT, Philip Leslie. b 52. Ex Univ BA 73 Hull Univ PGCE 74. NEOC 87. **d** 90 **p** 91. NSM Osbaldwick w Murton *York* 90–92; Chapl and Hd RS Berkhamsted Sch Herts 93–97; P-in-c Woodhorn w Newbiggin *Newc* 98; Chapl HM Pris Wolds 98–00; Chapl R Russell Sch Croydon 00–05; Chapl Hurstpierpoint Coll 05–07; TV Upper Skerne *Dur* 07–13; P-in-c Ashley w Silverley *Ely* 13–18; P-in-c Cheveley 13–18; P-in-c Kirtling 13–18; P-in-c Wood Ditton w Saxon Street 13–18; rtd 19. *51 Farro Drive, York YO30 6QQ* M: 07852-943244 E: philiptait548@btinternet.com

TAIT (née DAVIS), Canon Ruth Elizabeth. b 39. St Andr Univ MA 62 Moray Ho Coll of Educn DipEd 63. Moray Ord Course 89. **dss** 90 **d** 94 **p** 95. Elgin w Lossiemouth *Mor* 90–96; C 94–96; NSM Dufftown *Ab* 96–03; C Forres *Mor* 96–98; NSM Aberlour 98–03; Dioc Dir of Ords 02–08; NSM Elgin w Lossiemouth 04–08; rtd 08; LtO *Mor* from 10; Hon Can St Andr Cathl Inverness from 03. *Benmore, Burnbank, Birnie, Elgin IV30 8RW* T: (01343) 862808 E: ruth.e.tait@btinternet.com

TAIT, Ms Valerie Joan. b 60. Open Univ BA 96 SRN 82 RSCN 82. Trin Coll Bris 99. **d** 01 **p** 02. C W Heref 01–06; P-in-c Ford 06–13; P-in-c Gt Wollaston 08–13; P-in-c Alberbury w Cardeston 06–13; R Ford, Gt Wollaston and Alberbury w Cardeston from 13. *The Vicarage, Ford, Shrewsbury SY5 9LZ* T: (01743) 850254

TAJIMA, Ms Serena . b 82. K Alfred's Coll Win BA 03 Bournemouth Univ MSc 11. Westcott Ho Cam 15. **d** 17 **p** 18. C Reading St Luke w St Bart *Ox* from 17. *19 Carnarvon Road, Reading RG1 5SB* M: 07901-891738 E: serenatajima@icloud.com

TALBOT, Derek Michael. b 55. St Jo Coll Dur BSc 77. St Jo Coll Nottm 84. **d** 87 **p** 88. C Rushden w Newton Bromswold *Pet* 87–90; C Barton Seagrave w Warkton 90–95; V Kettering Ch the King 95–02; V Northwood Em *Lon* 02–16; P-in-c Northolt St Jos 13–14; AD Harrow 02–07; Dir of Ords Willesden Area 10–16; Evang Enabler *Carl* 16–19; Dir Miss Community Development from 19. *1 St Johns Gate, Threlkeld, Keswick CA12 4TZ* M: 07767-763715 E: mike.talbot@lineone.net or mike.talbot@carlislediocese.org.uk

TALBOT (née THOMSON), Mrs Elizabeth Lucy. b 74. Lanc Univ BA 96 Bris Univ BA 00 MA 01. Trin Coll Bris 98. **d** 01 **p** 02. C Bitterne *Win* 01–05; Chapl Dean Close Sch 05–15; C Edin St Paul and St Geo from 16. *St Paul's and St George's Church, 10 Broughton Street, Edinburgh EH1 3RH* T: 0131-556 1335 M: 07777-115923

TALBOT, George Brian. b 37. Qu Coll Birm 78. **d** 80 **p** 81. C Heref St Martin 80–83; R Bishop's Frome w Castle Frome and Fromes Hill 83–90; P-in-c Acton Beauchamp and Evesbatch w Stanford Bishop 83–90; R Burstow *S'wark* 90–02; rtd 02; PtO *Chich* from 16. *14 Locksash Close, West Wittering, Chichester PO20 8QP* T: (01243) 512454

TALBOT, John Herbert Boyle. b 30. TCD BA 51 MA 57. CITC 52. **d** 53 **p** 54. C Dublin St Pet *D & G* 53–57; Chan Vicar St Patrick's Cathl Dub 56–61; C Dublin Zion Ch *D & G* 57–61; Chapl Asst St Thos Hosp Lon 61–64; Min Can and Sacr Cant Cathl 64–67; R Brasted *Roch* 67–84; R Ightham 84–95; P-in-c Shipbourne 87–91; RD Shoreham 89–95; rtd 95; PtO *Roch* from 01. *12 Waterlakes, Edenbridge TN8 5BX* T: (01732) 865729 E: jbtalbot@waitrose.com

TALBOT, Mrs June Phyllis. b 46. Ripon Coll of Educn CertEd 67. NEOC 88. **d** 91 **p** 94. NSM Cleadon *Dur* 91–97; Dioc Voc Adv 94–16; NSM Bishopwearmouth St Gabr 97–16; PtO from 16. *66 Wheatall Drive, Whitburn, Sunderland SR6 7HQ* T: 0191-529 2265 E: talbot886@btinternet.com

TALBOT, Mair Josephine. *See* McFADYEN, Mair Josephine

TALBOT, Michael. *See* TALBOT, Derek Michael

TALBOT, Simon George Guy. b 79. Reading Univ BSc 01. Oak Hill Th Coll BA 07. **d** 07 **p** 08. C Ipswich St Marg *St E* 07–10; C Plymouth Em, St Paul Efford and St Aug *Ex* 10–11; TV 11–15; P-in-c Willand, Uffculme, Kentisbeare etc from 15; RD Tiverton and Cullompton from 17. *The Rectory, Old Village, Willand, Cullompton EX15 2RH* E: simon@thetalbots.org.uk

TALBOT, Susan Gabriel. b 46. Leeds Univ BA 69 Man Poly CertEd 70 Man Univ PhD 00. NOC 91. **d** 94 **p** 95. C Wythenshawe St Martin *Man* 94–98; P-in-c Cheetham St Jo 98–02; I:tO 02–04; C Wilmslow *Ches* 04–05; Dioc Adv Healing 06–08; NSM Bowdon 06–11; PtO from 11. *34 Eaton Road, Bowdon, Altrincham WA14 3EH* T: 0161-233 0630 E: susangabriel@btinternet.com

TALBOT-PONSONBY, Preb Andrew. b 44. Coll of Resurr Mirfield 66. **d** 68 **p** 70. C Radlett *St Alb* 68–70; C Salisbury St Martin *Sarum* 70–73; P-in-c Acton Burnell w Pitchford *Heref* 73–80; P-in-c Frodesley 73–80; P-in-c Cound 73–80; Asst Dioc Youth Officer 73–80; P-in-c Bockleton w Leysters 80–81; V 81–92; P-in-c Kimbolton w Middleton-on-the-Hill 80–81; V Kimbolton w Hamnish and Middleton-on-the-Hill 81–92; P-in-c Wigmore Abbey 92–96; R 97–98; RD Leominster 97–98; Public Preacher 98–14; Warden of Readers 02–12; Preb Heref Cathl from 87; rtd 09; Rtd Clergy Officer *Heref* from 13; PtO from 14. *Well Cottage, 5 Quay Street, Hereford HR1 2NH* T: (01432) 264725 E: andrew@talbot-ponsonby.org

TALBOT-PONSONBY, Preb Gillian. b 50. Sarum & Wells Th Coll 89. **d** 91 **p** 94. C Leominster *Heref* 91–92; NSM Wigmore Abbey 92–98; Public Preacher from 98; Asst Dioc Adv on Women in Min 99–03; Dioc Adv from 03; Preb Heref Cathl from 14. *Well Cottage, 5 Quay Street, Hereford HR1 2NH* T: (01432) 264725 E: jill@talbot-ponsonby.org

TALBOTT, Brian Hugh. b 34. St Pet Hall Ox BA 57 MA 64. Westcott Ho Cam. **d** 59 **p** 60. C Newc H Cross 59–61; C Newc St Jo 61–64; Chapl RNR 63–91; Chapl Barnard Castle Sch 64–71; Chapl Bishop's Stortford Coll 71–96; Hon C Bishop's Stortford St Mich *St Alb* 71–96; rtd 96; PtO *B & W* from 96; Acting Chapl Wells Cathl Sch 97–98. *Four Seasons, Milton Lane, Wookey Hole, Wells BA5 1DG* T: (01749) 679678 E: talbott@talktalk.net

TALBOTT, Scott Malcolm. b 55. SAOMC 00. **d** 03 **p** 04. NSM Watford St Andr *St Alb* 03–10; PtO 10–15; NSM Rickmansworth from 15. *Elmhurst, 40 Berks Hill, Chorleywood, Rickmansworth WD3 5AH* T: (01923) 282370 M: 07802-244877 E: scott.talbott@talk21.com

TALBOTT, Simon John. b 57. Pontifical Univ Maynooth BD 81. **d** 81 **p** 82. In RC Ch 81–87; C Headingley *Ripon* 88–91; V Gt and Lt Ouseburn w Marton cum Grafton 91–97; Chapl Qu Ethelburga's Coll York 91–97; P-in-c Markington w S Stainley and Bishop Thornton *Ripon* 97–01; AD Ripon 97–01; P-in-c Epsom St Martin *Guildf* 01–02; V 02–13; Chapl Univ for the Creative Arts 06–13; P-in-c Gt Shelford *Ely* from 13; P-in-c Stapleford from 16; P-in-c Harston w Hauxton and Newton from 18; RD Granta from 16. *The Vicarage, 12 Church Street, Great Shelford, Cambridge CB22 5EL* T: (01223) 847068 M: 07740-665210 E: simon@thetalbotts.co.uk

TALKS, David. b 57. Trin Hall Cam BA 78 MA 81. Trin Coll Bris BA 06. **d** 06 **p** 07. C Colchester St Jo *Chelmsf* 06–11; P-in-c Lynchmere and Camelsdale *Chich* 11–15; C 15–16; NSM Newton Longville, Mursley, Swanbourne etc *Ox* from 16. *The Rectory, Drayton Road, Newton Longville, Milton Keynes MK17 0BH* T: (01908) 366330 E: david.5parishes@btinternet.com

TALLANT, John. b 45. Edin Th Coll 86. **d** 88 **p** 89. C Cayton w Eastfield *York* 88–90; C N Hull St Mich 90–91; V Scarborough St Sav w All SS 91–93; V Fleetwood St Nic *Blackb* 93–99; P-in-c Sculcoates St Paul w Ch Ch and St Silas *York* 99–03; P-in-c Hull St Mary Sculcoates 99–03; P-in-c Hull St Steph Sculcoates 99–03; R Woldsburn 03–11; P-in-c Dunscroft St Edwin *Sheff* 11–15; rtd 15; PtO *York* 15–18; P-in-c Kingston

upon Hull St Mary from 18. *223 Cottingham Road, Hull HU5 4AU* E: john.tallant@talktalk.net

TALLINN, Dean of. *See* PIIR, Gustav Peeter

TALLON, Jonathan Robert Roe. b 66. Rob Coll Cam BA 88 MA 92 Nottm Univ MPhil 07. St Jo Coll Nottm BTh 94. **d** 97 **p** 98. C Bury St Jo w St Mark *Man* 97–01; P-in-c Cadishead 01–08; V 08–09; Tutor N Bapt Learning Community from 09. *Luther King House, Brighton Grove, Manchester M14 5JP* T: 0161-249 2546 E: jonathan.tallon@northern.org.uk

TALLOWIN (née BOUDIER), Mrs Rosemary. b 57. St Mellitus Coll BA 11. **d** 11 **p** 12. C Colchester St Mich Myland *Chelmsf* 11–14; TV Harwich Peninsula 14–19; P-in-c Fen Drayton w Fenstanton *Ely* from 19. *The Vicarage, 16 Church Street, Fenstanton, Huntingdon PE28 9JL* E: rosie.tallowin@btinternet.com

TAMPLIN, Peter Harry. b 44. Sarum & Wells Th Coll 71. **d** 73 **p** 74. C Digswell *St Alb* 73–76; C Chesterton St Luke *Ely* 76–82; V Chesterton St Geo 82–95; R Durrington *Sarum* 95–07; rtd 07. *1 Gathorne Road, Bristol BS3 1LR* T: 0117-963 9628 E: phtamplin@yahoo.co.uk

TAMS, Adam Michael. b 85. Trin Coll Bris BA 17. **d** 17 **p** 18. C Leamington Priors St Paul *Cov* from 17. *10 Sandown Close, Leamington Spa CV32 7SX* M: 07871-816699 E: atams@mac.com *or* adam@stpl.org.uk

TAMS, Paul William. b 56. Huddersfield Poly CertEd 77. EAMTC 87. **d** 90 **p** 91. NSM Mildenhall *St E* 90–93; NSM Brandon and Santon Downham w Elveden etc 93–17; V Lakenheath, Santon Downham and Elveden from 17. *2 Kitchener Close, Lakenheath, Brandon IP27 9FT* T: (01842) 861819 M: 07503-211323 E: paultams@sky.com

TAN (née MITCHELL), Mrs Sarah Rachel. b 70. Birm Univ BA 00 Fitzw Coll Cam BA 04. Westcott Ho Cam 02. **d** 05 **p** 06. C Reddal Hill St Luke *Worc* 05–08; Chapl HM Pris Wayland 08–13; PtO *Ely* from 08. *Address withheld by request* E: icklesaraht@gmail.com

TANNER, Benjamin Michael. b 84. Loughb Univ BEng 06. Oak Hill Th Coll BA 19. **d** 19. C Endcliffe *Sheff* from 19. *48 Renshaw Road, Sheffield S11 7PD* M: 07912-890512 E: b.m.tanner@me.com

TANNER, Canon Frank Hubert. b 38. St Aid Birkenhead 63. **d** 66 **p** 67. C Ipswich St Marg *St E* 66–69; C Mansfield SS Pet and Paul *S'well* 69–72; V Huthwaite 72–79; Chapl to the Deaf 79–92; Hon Can S'well Minster 90–92; Chapl Northn and Rutland Miss to the Deaf 92–01; rtd 01; PtO *Truro* 03–15. *Caldecote, 1A Garrick Road, Northampton NN1 5ND* T: (01604) 631709 E: franktanner@blue-earth.co.uk

TANNER, Leonard John. **d** 03 **p** 04. C Taney *D & G* 03–07; I Tullow from 07; Dioc Dir Lay Min from 09; Chan V St Patr Cathl Dublin 07–11. *Tullow Rectory, Brighton Road, Carrickmines, Dublin 18, Republic of Ireland* T: (00353) (1) 289 3154 M: 86-302 1376 E: tanner1@eircom.net

✠**TANNER, The Rt Revd Mark Simon Austin.** b 70. Ch Ch Ox BA 92 MA 96 St Jo Coll Dur BA 98 Liv Univ MTh 05. Cranmer Hall Dur 95. **d** 98 **p** 99 **c** 16. C Upton (Overchurch) *Ches* 98–01; V Doncaster St Mary *Sheff* 01–07; V Ripon H Trin 07–11; AD Ripon 09–11; Warden Cranmer Hall Dur 11–16; Vice-Prin St Jo Coll Dur 11–16; Hon Can Dur Cathl 15–16; Suff Bp Berwick *Newc* from 16. *Berwick House, Longhirst Road, Pegswood, Morpeth NE61 6XF* T: (01670) 519000 E: bishopofberwick@newcastle.anglican.org

TANNER, Canon Mark Stuart. b 59. Nottm Univ BA 81. Sarum & Wells Th Coll. **d** 85 **p** 86. C Radcliffe-on-Trent *S'well* 85; C Radcliffe-on-Trent and Shelford etc 85–88; C Bestwood 88–89; TV 89–93; Bp's Research Officer 93–97; P-in-c S'well H Trin 93–98; V 98–13; AD S'well 01–06; Hon Can S'well Minster 07–13; V Hartley Wintney, Elvetham, Winchfield etc *Win* 13–17; RD Odiham 16–17; V Radcliffe-on-Trent and Shelford *S'well* from 17. *The Vicarage, 2 Vicarage Lane, Radcliffe-on-Trent, Nottingham NG12 2FB*

TANNER, Martin Philip. b 54. Univ Coll Lon BSc(Econ) 75. Ridley Hall Cam 79. **d** 82 **p** 83. C Bitterne *Win* 82–85; C Weeke 85–88; V Long Buckby w Watford *Pet* 88–96; P-in-c Desborough 96–97; R Desborough, Brampton Ash, Dingley and Braybrooke 97–08; P-in-c Drayton in Hales *Lich* 08–17; RD Hodnet 14–17; OCM 09–17; rtd 17; PtO *Pet* from 18. *16 Feast Field Close, Wollaston, Wellingborough NN29 7QG* T: (01933) 664246 E: mp.tanner@btinternet.com

TANSEY, Daniel Matthew Robert. b 74. Leeds Metrop Univ BA 97 Cam Univ BTh 17. Ridley Hall Cam 15. **d** 17 **p** 18. C The Ch in the Woottons *Nor* from 17. *34 Castle Rising Road, South Wootton, King's Lynn PE30 3JB* M: 07928-825060 *or* 07866-368272 E: dan@churchinthewoottons.net

TANSILL, Canon Derek Ernest Edward. b 36. Univ of Wales (Lamp) BA 61. Ripon Hall Ox 61. **d** 63 **p** 64. C Chelsea St Luke *Lon* 63–67; C-in-c Saltdean CD *Chich* 67–69; V Saltdean

69–73; V Billingshurst 73–82; R Bexhill St Pet 82–85; RD Battle and Bexhill 84–86; V Horsham 85–86; TR 86–06; RD 77–82 and 85–93; Can and Preb Chich Cathl 81–06; Chapl Chich Cathl from 06. *5 The Chantry, Canon Lane, Chichester PO19 1PZ* T: (01243) 775596 E: derektansill@gmail.com

TANSLEY, Romney. b 41. K Coll Lon BD 64. **d** 65 **p** 66. C Royton St Anne *Man* 65–68; Chapl St Hilda's Coll Br Honduras 68–70; R Stann Creek & Chapl Stann Creek High Sch 70–71; V Westleigh St Pet *Man* 72–77; rtd 06. *Apartment 301, 18 Leftbank, Manchester M3 3AJ* E: romney@tansley.co.uk

TANSWELL, Stuart Keith. b 79. Reading Univ BSc 01. Ripon Coll Cuddesdon BTh 08. **d** 08 **p** 09. C St Blazey *Truro* 08–11; C Luxulyan 08–11; C Tywardreath w Tregaminion 08–11; V N Holmwood *Guildf* 11–18; R Guernsey St Michel du Valle *Win* from 18. *Vale Church Rectory, L'Abbaye, Vale, Guernsey GY3 5SF* T: (01481) 244088 E: stuart@tanswell.net *or* rector@valechurch.org.uk

TAPLIN, Kim. b 58. Lon Bible Coll BA 79 Homerton Coll Cam PGCE 84 Regent's Park Coll Ox MTh 03. S Dios Minl Tr Scheme 94. **d** 94 **p** 95. C Sholing *Win* 94–97; P-in-c Rendcomb *Glouc* 97–00; Chapl Rendcomb Coll Cirencester 97–00; Chapl Clifton Coll Bris 01–13; V Clifton All SS w St Jo *Bris* 14–15; Chapl Malvern St Jas Girls' Sch from 15. *20 Manby Road, Malvern WR14 3BB* E: kimtaplin1@gmail.com

TAPP, Mrs Sarah Alison. b 73. St Mellitus Coll 16. **d** 19. C Woking St Mary *Guildf* from 19. *6 Rapley Lane, Knaphill, Woking GU21 2SN* M: 07889-049019 E: sarah@sarahtapp.co.uk

TAPPER, Canon John A'Court. b 42. FCA 64. Sarum & Wells Th Coll 89. **d** 91 **p** 92. C Ashford *Cant* 91–94; P-in-c Folkestone H Trin w Ch Ch *Cant* 94–96; V 96–06; P-in-c Sandgate St Paul w Folkestone St Geo 01–06; V Folkestone Trin 06–07; AD Elham 00–05; Hon Can Cant Cathl 06–07; rtd 07; PtO *Cant* 07–08 and from 12; Retirement Officer (Maidstone Adnry) 07–08; Hon C Cranbrook 08–12. *Mill Cottage, Mill Lane, Sissinghurst, Cranbrook TN17 2HX* T: (01580) 713836 E: john.tapper@btinternet.com

TARGETT, Kenneth. b 28. Qu Coll Birm 54. **d** 57 **p** 58. C Mansfield Woodhouse *S'well* 57–59; C Skipton Ch Ch *Bradf* 59–62; V Bradf St Jo 62–65; PtO 65–82; Australia 82–87; V Old Leake w Wrangle *Linc* 87–94; rtd 94; PtO *Linc* from 00. *The Sloop, Sea Lane, Old Leake, Boston PE22 9JA* T: (01205) 871991

TARLETON, Canon Peter. b 46. TCD BA 72 MA 80 HDipEd 77. TCD Div Sch Div Test 73. **d** 73 **p** 74. C Cork St Luke w St Ann *C, C & R* 73–75; C Dublin Drumcondra *D & G* 75–77; I Limerick City *L & K* 77–82; I Drumgoon w Dernakesh, Ashfield etc *K, E & A* 82–85; Chapl HM YOI Hindley 85–89; Chapl HM Pris Lindholme 89–99; Hon Can Sheff Cathl 98–99; Chapl HM Pris Leeds 99–06; Chapl Lancs Teaching Hosps NHS Trust 08–11; Co-ord Chapl Southport and Ormskirk Hosp NHS Trust 11; I Killeshin w Cloydagh and Killabban *C & O* 11–18; Can Ossory Cathl 15–18; P-in-c Maryborough w Dysart Enos and Ballyfin from 18; Can Kilkenny Cathl from 18. *The Rectory, Coote Street, Portlaoise, Co Laois, Republic of Ireland* T: (00353) (57) 862 1154 M: 87-769 0050 E: peter.tarleton@hotmail.co.uk

TARLING, Matthew Paul. b 79. Nottm Univ MEng 03. Oak Hill Th Coll BA 09. **d** 09 **p** 10. C Blaydon and Swalwell *Dur* 09–13; V Spennymoor and Whitworth from 13; AD Auckland from 18. *30 Jubilee Close, Spennymoor DL16 6GA* T: (01388) 327603 M: 07714-212374 E: revmatttarling@gmail.com

TARLING, Preb Paul. b 53. Oak Hill Th Coll BA. **d** 85 **p** 86. C Old Hill H Trin *Worc* 85–89; V Walford w Bishopswood *Heref* 89–90; P-in-c Goodrich w Welsh Bicknor and Marstow 89–90; R Walford and St John w Bishopswood, Goodrich etc 90–96; RD Ross and Archenfield 95–96; P-in-c Kington w Huntington, Old Radnor, Kinnerton etc 96–00; R 00–08; RD Kington and Weobley 02–07; Preb Heref Cathl 07–08; rtd 08; PtO *S & B* from 11. *1 Alexandra Road, Llandrindod Wells LD1 5LT* T: (01597) 822615 E: revpt@yahoo.com

TARLTON, Simon John Deverill. b 63. WEMTC 14. **d** 16 **p** 17. NSM Ross w Walford and Brampton Abbotts *Heref* 16–17; C from 17. *Pantry Cottage, Goodrich, Ross-on-Wye HR9 6JE* T: (01600) 890185 M: 07462-893457 E: simon.tarlton@gmail.com

TÄRNEBERG, Helene. *See* STEED, Helene

TARPER, Miss Ann Jennifer. b 47. SRN 71 Nottm Univ BCombStuds 82. Linc Th Coll 79. **dss** 83 **d** 87 **p** 96. Stamford All SS w St Jo *Linc* 82–85; Witham *Chelmsf* 85–90; Par Dn 87–90; Min and Educn Adv to Newmarch Gp Min *Heref* 90–93; PtO 93–95; Dep Chapl HM Pris Dur 95–97; Chapl HM Pris Foston Hall 97–00; PtO *Lich* 97–02; C W End *Win* 02–05; V Slade Green *Roch* 05–16; rtd 16; PtO *Lich* from 17. *5 Ivinson Way, Bramshall, Uttoxeter ST14 5BF* T: (01889) 592728 E: ajtarper@gmail.com

TARRAN, Mrs Susan Ann. b 63. CPFA 92. ERMC 08. **d** 11 **p** 12. NSM Bishop's Stortford *St Alb* 11–12; NSM Hockerill from 12. *47 Church Manor, Bishop's Stortford CM23 5AF* M: 07970-952228 E: su.tarran@ntlworld.com

TARRANT, Canon Ian Denis. b 57. G&C Coll Cam BA MA. St Jo Coll Nottm 81. **d** 84 **p** 85. C Ealing St Mary *Lon* 84–87; CMS Democratic Republic of Congo 88–98; Can Boga from 97; Sen Angl Chapl Nottm Univ *S'well* 98–09; R Woodford St Mary w St Phil and St Jas *Chelmsf* from 09. *The Rectory, 8 Chelmsford Road, London E18 2PL* T: (020) 8504 7981 E: rector@stmaryswoodford.org.uk

TARRANT, John Michael. b 38. St Jo Coll Cam BA 59 MA 63 Ball Coll Ox BA 62 MA 76. Ripon Hall Ox 60. **d** 62 **p** 63. C Chelsea All SS *Lon* 62–65; Chapl and Lect St Pet Coll Saltley 66–70; Belize 70–74; V Forest Row *Chich* 75–87; PtO *Heref* 93–99; NSM Ross 99–00; P-in-c Guilsborough w Hollowell and Cold Ashby *Pet* 00–08; Jt P-in-c Cottesbrooke w Gt Creaton and Thornby 00–08; P-in-c W Haddon w Winwick and Ravensthorpe 03–08; P-in-c Spratton 07–08; rtd 08; PtO *Sarum* from 11; *Win* from 16; *Eur* from 09. *16 Windsor Road, Salisbury SP2 7DX* T: (01722) 340058 E: jandmtarrant1988@gmail.com

TARRIS, Canon Geoffrey John. b 27. Em Coll Cam BA 50 MA 55. Westcott Ho Cam 51. **d** 53 **p** 54. C Abbots Langley *St Alb* 53–55; Prec St E Cathl 55–59; V Bungay H Trin w St Mary 59–72; RD S Elmham 65–72; V Ipswich St Mary le Tower 72–78; V Ipswich St Mary le Tower w St Lawr and St Steph 78–82; Hon Can St E Cathl 74–82; Can Res St E Cathl 82–93; Dioc Dir of Lay Min 82–87; Warden of Readers 82–87; Dioc Dir of Ords 87–93; rtd 93; PtO *Nor* 93–12; *St E* from 93; Hon PV Nor Cathl 94–12. *53 The Close, Norwich NR1 4EG* T: (01603) 622136

TARRIS, Philip Geoffrey. b 54. Univ of Wales (Swansea) BSc 76 Lon Univ MSc 78. ERMC. **d** 10 **p** 11. P-in-c Gt Dunmow and Barnston *Chelmsf* 10–14; P-in-c The Sampfords and Radwinter w Hempstead 14–17; P-in-c Thaxted 15–17; R Thaxted, The Sampfords, Radwinter and Hempstead from 17. *The Vicarage, Watling Lane, Thaxted, Dunmow CM6 2QY* T: (01799) 586570 E: pgtarris@gmail.com

TARRY, Mrs Angela Helen. b 86. Qu Foundn Birm BA 16. **d** 16 **p** 17. C Hinckley St Mary *Leic* 16–19; C Hexagon from 19. *90B Netherley Road, Hinckley LE10 0RF* T: (01455) 230997 E: angelatarry@hotmail.com

TARRY, Canon Gordon Malcolm. b 54. Leeds Univ BSc 75 Lon Bible Coll BA 83. Ridley Hall Cam. **d** 85 **p** 86. C Gt Ilford St Andr *Chelmsf* 85–89; C Rainham 89–92; C Rainham w Wennington 92–93; V Gt Ilford St Jo 93–06; RD Redbridge 01–06; TR Barking St Marg w St Patr 06–11; V Leigh-on-Sea St Aid from 11; Hon Can Chelmsf Cathl from 05. *St Aidan's Vicarage, 78 Moor Park Gardens, Leigh-on-Sea SS9 4PY* T: (01702) 512531 E: gordontarry@yahoo.co.uk

TASH, Elizabeth. *See* ROOKWOOD, Elizabeth

TASH, Stephen Ronald. b 56. Warw Univ BEd 79. WMMTC 88. **d** 91 **p** 92. C Studley *Cov* 91–95; P-in-c Salford Priors 95–09; Dioc Youth Officer 95–00; P-in-c Temple Grafton w Binton 00–09; P-in-c Exhall w Wixford 03–09; V Fulford *York* 09–11; rtd 11; PtO *Cov* from 14; Chapl Univ Hosps Cov and Warks NHS Trust from 17. *16 Eclipse Road, Alcester B49 5EH* T: (01789) 765319 E: stevetash@aol.com

TASSELL, Mrs Stella Venetia. b 39. RGN 60 RNT 63 RMN 66 RHV 72. **d** 01 **p** 02. OLM Woodham *Guildf* 01–09; PtO *Bradf* 10–14; *Leeds* 14–16; *Guildf* from 12. *3 Park Gate Court, Constitution Hill, Woking GU22 7RW* T: (01483) 755481 M: 07790-521567 E: stellatassell@googlemail.com

TATE, Denis Steven. b 53. Lanc Univ MA 76. LCTP 09. **d** 11 **p** 12. NSM Ellel w Shireshead *Blackb* 11–15; TV Bentham, Burton-in-Lonsdale, Chapel-le-Dale etc *Leeds* from 15. *The Vicarage, 21 Manor Close, Burton in Lonsdale, Carnforth LA6 3NE* T: (01524) 61579 E: revden@hotmail.co.uk

TATE, James. b 56. Oak Hill Th Coll 93. **d** 95 **p** 96. C Hammersmith St Simon *Lon* 95–98; C N Hammersmith St Kath 98–99; P-in-c from 99. *St Katherine's Vicarage, Primula Street, London W12 0RF* T: (020) 8746 2213 *or* 8743 3951 E: jim.stkats@gmail.com

TATE, John Robert. b 38. Dur Univ BA 61 MA 71. Cranmer Hall Dur. **d** 70 **p** 71. C Bare *Blackb* 70–73; V Over Darwen St Jas 73–81; V Caton w Littledale 81–98; rtd 98; PtO *Blackb* from 98. *69 Otley Road, Skipton BD23 1HJ* T: (01756) 709235

TATE, Lesley Carole. b 58. St Mellitus Coll 15. **d** 18 **p** 19. NSM N Hammersmith St Kath *Lon* from 18. *The Vicarage, Primula Street, London W12 0RF* T: (020) 8746 2213 E: lestateuk@yahoo.co.uk

TATE, Toby James. b 74. Univ of Wales (Abth) BSc 96 Sheff Univ MEd 00 Warwick Univ PGCE 97. Ripon Coll Cuddesdon 11. **d** 13 **p** 14. C Triangle, St Matt and All SS *St E* 13–16; P-in-c Martlesham w Brightwell from 16. *The*

Rectory, 17 Lark Rise, Martlesham Heath, Ipswich IP5 3SA
E: tobyjtate@gmail.com

TATHAM, Andrew Francis. b 49. Grey Coll Dur BA 71 K Coll Lon PhD 84 AKC 88 FBCartS 96. S'wark Ord Course 89. **d** 92 **p** 93. NSM Headley w Box Hill *Guildf* 92–02; TV Ilminster and Distr *B & W* 02–10; V Isle Valley 10–14; RD Crewkerne and Ilminster 07–12; RD Ilminster 12–14; rtd 14; Hon C Quantock Coast *B & W* from 14. *61 West Street, Watchet TA23 0BH* T: (01984) 633331 E: aftatham@btinternet.com

TATTERSALL, John Hartley. b 52. Ch Coll Cam BA 73 MA 76 FCA 89. SEITE 04. **d** 07 **p** 08. NSM Wykeham *Ox* from 07; PtO *Lon* from 19. *Abingdon House, Park Lane, Swalcliffe, Banbury OX15 5EU* T: (01295) 780283 M: 07711-733978 E: jhtatters@aol.com

TATTERSALL, Jonathan Mark. b 76. Lon Bible Coll BTh 99. St Jo Coll Nottm MA 16. **d** 16 **p** 17. C Dorridge *Birm* 16–19; C Harborne Heath from 19. *2 Milford Copse, Birmingham B17 9TF* M: 07939-139036

TATTON-BROWN, Canon Simon Charles. b 48. Qu Coll Cam BA 70 MA 78 Man Univ CQSW 72. Coll of Resurr Mirfield 78. **d** 79 **p** 80. C Ashton St Mich *Man* 79–82; P-in-c Prestwich St Gabr 82–87; V 87–88; Bp's Dom Chapl 82–88; TR Westhoughton 88–96; TR Westhoughton and Wingates 97–00; V Chippenham St Andr w Tytherton Lucas *Bris* 00–13; RD Chippenham 03–06; Hon Can Bris Cathl 11–13; rtd 14; PtO *B & W* from 14. *259 Bloomfield Road, Bath BA2 2BA* T: (01225) 835404 M: 07891-898472 E: simon@tattonbrown.myzen.co.uk

TATTUM, Ian Stuart. b 58. N Lon Poly BA 79 Fitzw Coll Cam BA 89. Westcott Ho Cam 87. **d** 90 **p** 91. C Beaconsfield *Ox* 90–94; C Bushey *St Alb* 94–96; P-in-c Pirton 96–01; P-in-c St Ippolyts 00–06; P-in-c Gt and Lt Wymondley 01–06; P-in-c Southfields St Barn *S'wark* 06–11; V from 11; P-in-c Earlsfield St Jo from 17; AD Wandsworth from 18. *St Barnabas' Vicarage, 146A Lavenham Road, London SW18 5EP* T: (020) 8480 2290 E: iantattum@gmail.com

TATTUM, Ruth Margaret. *See* LAMPARD, Ruth Margaret

TATTUM, Mrs Josephine Gayle. b 56. St Jo Coll Nottm BATM 12. **d** 12 **p** 13. C Nottingham St Nic *S'well* 12–16; Ind Chapl from 16. *55 St Austell Drive, Nottingham NG11 7BT* T: 0115-846 5760 M: 07504-018386 E: josephinetatum@gmail.com

TAULTY, Mrs Eileen. b 45. **d** 03. OLM Pemberton St Mark Newtown *Liv* 03–07; OLM Marsh Green w Newtown 08–14; OLM Newtown from 14. *38 Alexandra Crescent, Wigan WN5 9JP* T: (01942) 208021

TAUNTON, Archdeacon of. *See* HILL, The Ven Simon James

TAUNTON, Suffragan Bishop of. *See* WORSLEY, The Rt Revd Ruth Elizabeth

TAUSON (née PURVIS), Ms Sandra Anne. b 56. Univ Coll Ches BTh 01. NOC 98. **d** 01 **p** 02. C Blackpool St Jo *Blackb* 01–06; P-in-c Gt Harwood 06–08; Chapl Pennine Acute Hosps NHS Trust 08–17; V Chorley St Pet *Blackb* 11–14; NSM Rochdale *Man* 14–17; PtO *Blackb* 14–17; Chapl Univ Hosp Southn NHS Foundn Trust from 17. *University Hospital Southampton NHS Trust, Tremona Road, Southampton SO16 6YD* T: (023) 8077 7222 M: 07967-136992

TAVERNER, Lorraine Dawn. *See* COLAM, Lorraine Dawn

TAVERNOR (née LLOYD), Mrs Eileen. b 50. FIBMS 74. NOC 88. **d** 91 **p** 94. C Heref St Martin w St Fran 91–95; P-in-c Bucknell w Chapel Lawn, Llanfair Waterdine etc 95–01; V 01–09; rtd 09; PtO *Heref* 09–15. *Froglands, Rosemary Lane, Leintwardine, Craven Arms SY7 0LP* T: (01547) 540365

TAVINOR, The Very Revd Michael Edward. b 53. Univ Coll Dur BA 75 Em Coll Cam CertEd 76 K Coll Lon MMus 77 AKC 77 ARCO 77 Univ of Wales (Lamp) MTh 10. Ripon Coll Cuddesdon BA 81 MA 86. **d** 82 **p** 83. C Ealing St Pet Mt Park *Lon* 82–85; Min Can, Prec and Sacr Ely Cathl 85–90; P-in-c Stuntney 87–90; V Tewkesbury w Walton Cardiff *Glouc* 90–99; P-in-c Twyning 98–99; V Tewkesbury w Walton Cardiff and Twyning 99–02; Hon Can Glouc Cathl 97–02; Dean Heref from 02. *The Deanery, Cathedral Close, Hereford HR1 2NG* T: (01432) 374203 F: 374220 E: dean@herefordcathedral.org

TAWN, Canon Andrew Richard. b 61. Trin Coll Cam BA 83 Ox Univ BA 88 Sheff Univ MA 14. Ripon Coll Cuddesdon 86. **d** 89 **p** 90. C Dovecot *Liv* 89–93; TV Dorchester *Ox* 93–98; Student Supervisor Cuddesdon Coll 93–98; R Addingham Bradf 98–12; Dir Clergy Development *Leeds* from 12; Hon Can Bradf Cathl from 15. *The Vicarage, Morton Lane, East Morton, Keighley BD20 5RS* T: (01274) 567898 E: a.tawn@btinternet.com

TAYLER, Jeremy Charles. b 78. LSE BSc 00 Birkbeck Coll Lon MA 06. Westcott Ho Cam 13. **d** 15 **p** 16. C St John's Wood *Lon* 15–18; R Henley w Remenham *Ox* from 18. *St Mary's Rectory, Hart Street, Henley-on-Thames RG9 2AU* E: jeremyctayler@gmail.com

TAYLER, Mrs Wendy Christian. b 76. **d** 13 **p** 14. C Neath *Llan* 13–16; TV 16–18; C Llansawel, Briton Ferry 16–18; C Caerleon and Llanfrechfa *Mon* from 18. *Ridgeways, Usk Road, Caerleon, Newport NP18 1LN* M: 07808-147619 E: wcsanderson@hotmail.co.uk*or*wendy.stcadocs@gmail.com

TAYLEUR, Mrs Gillian Sarah. b 61. Bedf Coll Lon BSc 82. OLM course 05. **d** 08 **p** 09. NSM Herne Hill *S'wark* from 08. *27 Finsen Road, London SE5 9AX* T: (020) 7737 1991 M: 07546-539737 E: gill@hernehillparish.org

TAYLOR, Alan Clive. b 48. Southn Univ BTh 79 DipEd 73. Sarum Th Coll 69. **d** 74 **p** 75. C Watford St Pet *St Alb* 74–78; C Broxbourne w Wormley 78–83; Chapl to the Deaf 83–91; V Shefford 83–91; R Portishead *B & W* 91–02; TR 02–08; rtd 08; PtO *Bris* from 09; *Sarum* from 15. *Larkhill, The Green, Dauntsey, Chippenham SN15 4HY* T: (01666) 511169 E: padreact@gmail.com

TAYLOR, Canon Alan Leonard. b 43. Chich Th Coll 67. **d** 69 **p** 70. C Walton St Mary *Liv* 69–73; C Toxteth St Marg 73–75; V Stanley 75–83; V Leeds St Aid *Ripon* 84–11; V Leeds Richmond Hill 06–11; TR Leeds All So and St Aid 11–12; Hon Can Ripon Cathl 97–12; AD Allerton 08–12; rtd 13; PtO *Linc* from 16. *Marsh Bank Cottage, Frampton Roads, Frampton, Boston PE20 1AY* T: (01205) 722693 E: alantaylor43@btinternet.com

TAYLOR, Andrew David. b 58. Regent's Park Coll Ox BA 81 MA 86 Toronto Univ MDiv 92 K Coll Lon MTh 95 FRSA 08. Westcott Ho Cam 85. **d** 87 **p** 89. C Leckhampton SS Phil and Jas w Cheltenham St Jas *Glouc* 87–91; P-in-c Swindon w Eaton and Elmstone Hardwicke 92–93; C Highgate St Mich *Lon* 94–97; Chapl R Holloway and Bedf New Coll *Guildf* 97–03; Public Preacher 04; PtO 05–13; C Englefield Green 13; Research Assoc Ox Cen for Christianity and Culture from 12; Chapl Downe Ho Sch Berks 15–17; PtO *Eur* from 18. *25 Great Norwood Street, Cheltenham GL50 2AW* T: (01242) 511955 M: 07952-866581 E: andrew.taylor@regents.ox.ac.uk

TAYLOR, Ann. *See* TAYLOR, Margaret Ann

TAYLOR, Ms Anne Elizabeth. b 68. Ulster Univ BSc 91 MA 99. CITC BTh 94. **d** 94 **p** 95. C Dublin Rathfarnham *D & G* 94–14; Chapl Adelaide and Meath Hosp Dublin 01–03; Abp's Dom Chapl *D & G* 03–14; Children's Min Officer Sunday Sch Soc of Ireland 05–14; V Formby St Pet *Liv* from 14; AD Sefton N from 15. *St Peter's Vicarage, Cricket Path, Formby, Liverpool L37 7DP* T: (01704) 872824 E: revannetaylor@gmail.com

TAYLOR, Arthur Alfred. b 32. Univ Coll Ox MA 56. Ox NSM Course 80. **d** 83 **p** 84. NSM Monks Risborough *Ox* 83–96; NSM Aylesbury Deanery from 96. *9 Place Farm Way, Monks Risborough, Princes Risborough HP27 9JJ* T: (01844) 347197 E: arthyrtaylor16@btinternet.com

TAYLOR, Brian. b 38. Bris Univ BA 60 Liv Univ BA 70 Southn Univ MA 90. Ridley Hall Cam 60. **d** 66 **p** 66. Chapl Victoria Coll Ondo Nigeria 66–72; PtO *Derby* 74–78; Chapl Newbury Coll 76–94; P-in-c Shaw cum Donnington *Ox* 89–90; R 90–08; rtd 08; PtO *Ox* 08–15; *Derby* from 15. *Fairview House Barn, The Moor, Tideswell, Buxton SK17 8LR* M: 07925-126761 E: brian_harker_taylor@yahoo.co.uk

TAYLOR, Brian Lee. b 71. Mattersey Hall BA 97 MA 99. Coll of Resurr Mirfield MA 17. **d** 17 **p** 18. C Chingford SS Pet and Paul *Chelmsf* from 17. *16 Mark Avenue, London E4 7NR* M: 07786-261792 E: fr.lee@parishofchingford.org.uk

TAYLOR, Mrs Bryony Ruthellen. b 77. Leeds Univ BA 99 MA 05 St Jo Coll Dur BA 14. Cranmer Hall Dur 12. **d** 14 **p** 15. C Houghton le Spring *Dur* 14–18; R Barlborough and Clowne *Derby* from 18. *The Rectory, Church Street, Barlborough, Chesterfield S43 4EP* T: (01246) 813569 M: 07960-735352 E: bryony.taylor@gmail.com

TAYLOR, Mrs Caroline Mary. b 85. Nottm Univ BA 07 Kellogg Coll Ox MSc 11 St Jo Coll Dur BATM 18. Cranmer Hall Dur 15. **d** 18 **p** 19. C Hoxton St Jo w Ch Ch *Lon* from 18. *St John's Church, 85 Pitfield Street, London N1 6NP* M: 07538-634352 E: revcarolinetaylor@gmail.com

TAYLOR, Charles Derek. b 36. Trin Hall Cam BA 59 MA 62. Ripon Hall Ox 59. **d** 61 **p** 62. C Nottingham All SS *S'well* 61–64; C Binley *Cov* 64–67; C Stoke 67–70; R Purley *Ox* 70–74; V Milton *B & W* 74–93; RD Locking 86–87 and 90–93; V Wells St Cuth w Wookey Hole 93–98; rtd 98; PtO *Roch* 00–16; *B & W* from 19. *5 Banner Farm Road, Tunbridge Wells TN2 5EA* T: (01892) 526825 E: c.derektaylor5@yahoo.co.uk

TAYLOR, The Very Revd Charles William. b 53. Selw Coll Cam BA 74 MA 78. Cuddesdon Coll 74. **d** 76 **p** 77. C Wolverhampton *Lich* 76–79; Chapl Westmr Abbey 79–84; V Stanmore *Win* 84–90; R N Stoneham 90–95; Can Res and Prec Lich Cathl 95–07; Dean Pet 07–16; PtO *Newc* from 17; *Newc* from 18; Assoc Can Res Sarum Cathl 17–18. *38 Rochester Drive, Felton, Morpeth NE65 9DS* M: 07754-893718 E: charles53taylor@outlook.com

TAYLOR, Christopher Drewett. b 58. Qu Coll Birm 06. **d** 09 **p** 10. C Shepshed and Oaks in Charnwood *Leic* 09–13; Chapl Loughb Univ from 13. *Brockington Building, Loughborough University, Loughborough LE11 3TU* T: (01509) 223742 M: 07946-763257 E: christaylor36beacon@msn.com *or* c.taylor2@lboro.ac.uk

TAYLOR, Christopher Vincent. b 47. Glas Univ MTh 10 PhD 17 R Cen Sch Speech & Drama DipEd 71. Cranmer Hall Dur 94. **d** 96 **p** 97. C Kendal St Geo *Carl* 96–99; TV Wheatley *Ox* 99–03; TV Leeds City *Ripon* 03–06; Chapl Arts and Recreation City of Leeds 03–06; rtd 06; Hon C Beacon *Carl* 08–15; PtO from 15; Dioc Chapl to the Arts from 08. *78 Windermere Road, Kendal LA9 5EZ* T: (01539) 727424 E: christaylor156@btinternet.com

TAYLOR, Colin. d 15 **p** 16. Dromara w Garvaghy *D & D* 15–16; C 16–19; I from 19. *The Rectory, 58 Banbridge Road, Dromara, Dromore BT25 2NE* T: (028) 9753 3919 M: 07852-130463 E: colintayloretc@btinternet.com

TAYLOR, Colin John. b 66. Witwatersrand Univ BCom 87 BTh 94. Wycliffe Hall Ox MTh 97. **d** 97 **p** 98. C Denton Holme *Carl* 97–01; Bp's Dom Chapl 01–06; Dir CME 1-4 00–06; V Felsted and Lt Dunmow *Chelmsf* from 06. *The Vicarage, Bury Chase, Felsted, Dunmow CM6 3DQ* T: (01371) 820242 E: ctaylor585@googlemail.com

TAYLOR, Canon David. b 53. St Jo Coll Dur BA 74 PGCE 75 Liv Univ MTh 04. Sarum & Wells Th Coll 91. **d** 93 **p** 94. C Cheadle Hulme All SS *Ches* 93–97; V Macclesfield St Jo 97–05; RD Macclesfield 03–05; TR Congleton 05–19; RD 08–13; Hon Can Ches Cathl 09–19; rtd 19; PtO *Ches* from 19. *12 Garnett Close, Stapeley, Nantwich CW5 7RF*

TAYLOR, David Christopher Morgan. b 56. Leeds Univ BSc 77 Univ Coll Lon PhD 80 Univ Coll Ches MEd 96 SOSc MRSB. NOC 91. **d** 94 **p** 95. Tutor Liv Univ from 86; NSM Waterloo Ch Ch and St Mary 94–99; P-in-c Altcar 98–00; NSM Altcar and Hightown 03–14; NSM Formby H Trin and Altcar from 14. *20 Liverpool Road, Formby, Liverpool L37 4BW* T: (01704) 873304 F: 0151-794 5337 E: dcmt@liverpool.ac.uk *or* taylordcm@aol.com

TAYLOR, Derek. *See* TAYLOR, Charles Derek

TAYLOR, The Very Revd Derek John. b 31. Univ of Wales (Lamp) BA 52 Fitzw Ho Cam BA 54 MA 58 Ex Univ CertEd 70. St Mich Coll Llan 54. **d** 55 **p** 56. C Newport St Paul *Mon* 55–59; CF (TA) 57–59 and 62–64; CF 59–62; V Bettws *Mon* 62–64; V Exminster *Ex* 64–70; Hd of RE Heathcote Sch Tiverton 70–71; W Germany 71–75; Chapl R Russell Sch Croydon 75–79; Chapl St Andr C of E High Sch Croydon 79–84; P-in-c Croydon St Andr *Cant* 79–81; V 81–84; Chapl Bromsgrove Sch 84–89; Provost St Chris Cathl Bahrain 90–97; Hon Chapl Miss to Seamen 90–97; PtO *Worc* 90–00; P-in-c Bearsden w Milngavie *Glas* 00–03; PtO *Worc* 04–11; *Leeds* from 17. *22 Coxwold View, Wetherby LS22 7PU* T: (01937) 918534 M: 07904-205669 E: dervaltaylor@talktalk.net

TAYLOR, Garry Kenneth. b 53. Edin Univ BMus 75 Southn Univ BTh 81 Ch Ch Coll Cant PGCE 95. Sarum & Wells Th Coll 76. **d** 79 **p** 80. C Southsea H Spirit *Portsm* 79–82; C Croydon St Jo *Cant* 82–84; C Croydon St Jo *S'wark* 85–86; V Choral S'well Minster 86–90; V Portsea St Alb *Portsm* 90–94; NSM Hamble le Rice *Win* 96–97; P-in-c Southampton St Jude 97–04; V Highcliffe w Hinton Admiral 04–09; V Highcliffe 09–15; rtd 15. *Oriel Cottage, 2 Avon View, Castle Street, Salisbury SP1 3SY* T: (01722) 334153 M: 07454-569169 E: garry.k.taylor@btinternet.com

TAYLOR, George James Trueman. b 36. Ripon Hall Ox 66. **d** 69 **p** 70. C Wavertree H Trin *Liv* 69–73; V Newton-le-Willows 73–79; V Stoneycroft All SS 79–83; V Haigh 83–04; Jt P-in-c Aspull and New Springs 02–03; rtd 04. *228 Wigan Road, Aspull, Wigan WN2 1DU* T: (01942) 830430

TAYLOR, Canon Gordon. b 46. AKC 68. St Aug Coll Cant 69. **d** 70 **p** 71. C Rotherham *Sheff* 70–74; P-in-c Brightside St Thos 74–79; P-in-c Brightside St Marg 77–79; V Brightside St Thos and St Marg 79–82; R Kirk Sandall and Edenthorpe 82–91; V Beighton 91–96; V Goole 96–03; AD Snaith and Hatfield 98–03; V Tickhill w Stainton 03–11; Hon Can Sheff Cathl 93–11; rtd 11; PtO *Sheff* from 11. *96 Whitton Close, Doncaster DN4 7RD* T: (01302) 533249 E: gordon.taylor809@btinternet.com

TAYLOR, Canon Graham Smith. b 70. TISEC 98. **d** 01 **p** 02. C Ellon, Cruden Bay and Peterhead *Ab* 01–04; P-in-c 04–06; R Aberdeen St Mary 06–14; Dioc Dir Ords 06–14; Can St Andr Cathl 08–14; R Aberdeen St Clem 09–12; R Perth St Jo *St And* from 14; Can St Ninian's Cathl Perth from 19. *St John's Rectory, 23 Comely Bank, Perth PH2 7HU* T: (01738) 245922 M: 07773-482174 E: revgraham@tiscali.co.uk

TAYLOR, Hugh Nigel James. b 43. MCMI FInstD. NTMTC 04. **d** 06 **p** 07. NSM Loughton St Mary *Chelmsf* 06–14; PtO from

14. 4 Twentyman Close, Woodford Green IG8 0EW T: (020) 8504 8901 M: 07770-365255 E: revhnjt@gmail.com

✠**TAYLOR, The Rt Revd Humphrey Vincent.** b 38. Pemb Coll Cam BA 61 MA 66 Lon Univ MA 70. Coll of Resurr Mirfield 61. **d** 63 **p** 64 **c** 91. C N Hammersmith St Kath *Lon* 63–64; C Notting Hill St Mark 64–66; USPG Malawi 67–71; Chapl Bp Grosseteste Coll Linc 72–74; Sec Chapls in HE Gen Syn Bd of Educn 75–80; Gen Sec USPG 80–91; Sec Miss Progr 80–84; Hon Can Bris Cathl 86–91; LtO *S'wark* 89–91; Suff Bp Selby *York* 91–03; rtd 03; Hon Asst Bp Glouc 03–13; Hon Asst Bp Worc 03–16; PtO *Glouc* from 15. *10 High Street, Honeybourne, Evesham WR11 7PQ* T: (01386) 834846

TAYLOR, Iain William James. b 41. **d** 03 **p** 04. OLM Cant St Pet w St Alphege and St Marg etc 03–11; rtd 11; PtO *Cant* from 12. *30 Deans Mill Court, The Causeway, Canterbury CT1 2BF* T: (01227) 457711 E: revd.iain.taylor@talktalk.net

TAYLOR, Ian. b 53. Saltley Tr Coll Birm CertEd 75. **d** 95 **p** 96. OLM Heywood *Man* 95–10; OLM Sudden and Heywood All So from 10. *818A Edenfield Road, Rochdale OL12 7RB* T: (01706) 355738 E: reviantaylor@gmail.com

TAYLOR, Preb Jacqueline Margaret. b 56. Trin Coll Bris 02. **d** 04 **p** 05. C Bath St Luke *B & W* 04–08; Chapl Univ Hosps Bris NHS Foundn Trust 08–13; P-in-c Kingsbridge and Dodbrooke *Ex* 13–15; R Kingsbridge, Dodbrooke, and W Alvington from 15; RD Woodleigh from 16; Preb Ex Cathl from 19. *Dodbrooke Rectory, Church Street, Kingsbridge TQ7 1NW* T: (01548) 856231 E: jtaylor808@btinternet.com

TAYLOR, James. *See* TAYLOR, Nigel James

TAYLOR, James Charles. b 81. Fitzw Coll Cam BA 03 MA 07. Oak Hill Th Coll BA 11. **d** 12 **p** 13. C W Hampstead St Luke *Lon* 12–17; C Jersey St Helier *Win* 17–19. *8 Fairways, Plat Douet Road, St Clement JE2 6PN* E: james.taylor@cantab.net

TAYLOR, James Richard. b 78. Bath Univ BSc 00. Trin Coll Bris BA 17. **d** 17 **p** 18. C Bridgwater H Trin and Durleigh *B & W* from 17. *16 Bagborough Drive, Bridgwater TA6 6UW* M: 07837-573874 E: jamestaylormail@gmail.com

TAYLOR, Jamie Alexander Franklyn. b 73. Kent Univ BA 95. Westcott Ho Cam. **d** 98 **p** 99. C Walton-on-Thames *Guildf* 98–02; C St Peter-in-Thanet *Cant* 02–08; Chapl E Kent NHS and Soc Care Partnership Trust 03–06; Chapl Kent & Medway NHS and Soc Care Partnership Trust 06–08; V Sonning *Ox* from 08. *The Vicarage, Thames Street, Sonning, Reading RG4 6UR* T: 0118-969 3298 E: revjaft@yahoo.co.uk

TAYLOR, Jane Suzanne. b 54. Ex Univ BA 73. SEITE 96. **d** 99 **p** 00. NSM Knaphill w Brookwood *Guildf* 99–00; C Frimley Green and Mytchett 00–04; PtO *Ex* from 04. *Rocknell Manor Farm, Westleigh, Tiverton EX16 7ES* T: (01884) 829000 E: janetaylor@millhouseretreats.co.uk

TAYLOR (*née* MAYOR), Mrs Janet Hilary. b 55. St Martin's Coll Lanc BA 96 Open Univ PGCE 98. LCTP 10. **d** 11 **p** 12. NSM Chorley St Laur *Blackb* 11–15; NSM Croston, Bretherton and Mawdesley w Bispham from 15. *Orchard House, Old Pope Lane, Whitestake, Preston PR4 4JQ* E: curatejanet@gmail.com

TAYLOR, Miss Jean. b 37. Nottm Univ TCert 58. St Andr Coll Pampisford 62. **dss** 68 **d** 00 **p** 01. CSA 62–79; E Crompton *Man* 79–97; Chadderton St Luke 97–04; OLM 00–04; OLM Chadderton St Matt w St Luke 04–05; Warden Jes Hosp Cant 05–08; PtO *Cant* from 05. *7 Chantry Court, St Radigund's Street, Canterbury CT1 2AD* T: (01227) 761652 E: revjtay7@gmail.com

TAYLOR, Canon Jennifer Anne. b 53. Sussex Univ BEd 75 Surrey Univ BA 01 Win Univ MA 09. STETS 98. **d** 01 **p** 02. Chapl Salisbury Cathl Sch 01–13; NSM Salisbury St Thos and St Edm *Sarum* 01–09; NSM Chalke Valley 09–13; TV from 13; Can and Preb Sarum Cathl from 18. *27 Viking Way, Salisbury SP2 8TA* T/F: (01722) 503081 E: revjennytaylor@gmail.com

TAYLOR, Sister Jennifer Mary. b 41. CA Tr Coll IDC 65. **dss** 77 **d** 87 **p** 07. CA from 65; Chapl Asst HM Pris Holloway 75–79; Ho Mistress Ch Hosp Sch Hertf 78–79; Chapl Asst Rtd Officer Chapl RAChD 80–90; Germany 90–96; rtd 96; PtO *Eur* from 96; *Nor* 06–07 and from 11; Hon C Dereham and Distr 07–11. *4 Eckling Grange, Norwich Road, Dereham NR20 3BB* T: (01362) 692547

TAYLOR, Jeremy Christopher. b 75. Birm Univ BA 97. Oak Hill Th Coll BA 07. **d** 07 **p** 08. C Chell *Lich* 07–10; P-in-c Enderby w Lubbesthorpe and Thurlaston *Leic* 10–18; V from 18. *The Rectory, 16A Desford Road, Leicester LE9 7TE* T: (01455) 888679 M: 07787-514058 E: juneandjerry@btinternet.com

TAYLOR, Joanna Beatrice. *See* NEARY, Joanna Beatrice

TAYLOR, John. b 58. Aston Tr Scheme 94 Ripon Coll Cuddesdon 96. **d** 98 **p** 99. C Southport Em *Liv* 98–03; V Hindley All SS 03–09; R Yanchep Australia from 09. *2 Lagoon Drive, Yanchep WA 6035, Australia* T: (0061) (8) 9561 1357 *or* (8) 9561 1421 F: (8) 9561 1421 E: revj-tay@bigpond.com

TAYLOR, Canon John Andrew. b 53. Linc Th Coll 86. **d** 88 **p** 89. C Stanley *Liv* 88–91; V Wigan St Jas w St Thos 91–04;

AD Wigan W 99–04; Hon Can Liv Cathl 03–04; V Prescot from 04; AD Huyton 06–17; Hon Can Liv Cathl from 07; Chapl to The Queen from 16. *The Vicarage, Vicarage Place, Prescot L34 1LA*   T: 0151-426 6719

TAYLOR, Canon John Michael. b 30. St Aid Birkenhead 56. d 59 p 60. C Chorley St Jas *Blackb* 59–62; C Broughton 62–64; Chapl St Boniface Coll Warminster 64–68; V Altham w Clayton le Moors *Blackb* 68–76; RD Accrington 71–76; Can Res Blackb Cathl 76–96; Tutor CBDTI 88–96; rtd 96; PtO *Blackb* from 96. *8 Fosbrooke House, Clifton Drive, Lytham St Annes FY8 5RQ*

✠**TAYLOR, The Rt Revd John Mitchell.** b 32. Aber Univ MA 54. Edin Th Coll 54. d 56 p 57 c 91. C Aberdeen St Marg *Ab* 56–58; R Glas H Cross 58–64; R Glas St Ninian 64–73; R Dumfries and Chapl Dumfries and Galloway R Infirmary 73–91; Can St Mary's Cathl *Glas* 79–91; Bp Glas 91–98; rtd 98; Hon Asst Bp Glas from 99. *85 Lord Lyell Drive, Kirriemuir DD8 4LF*   T: (01575) 573132

TAYLOR, John Porter. b 48. Ex Univ BA 71 MA 76. Cranmer Hall Dur 93. d 93 p 94. C Ossett cum Gawthorpe *Wakef* 93–96; R Crofton 96–02; Chapl Mid Yorks Hosps NHS Trust 03–06; Chapl Oakham Sch 06–13; rtd 13; PtO *Pet* 13–14; Hon C Empingham, Edith Weston, Lyndon, Manton etc from 14. *24 Main Street, Empingham, Oakham LE15 8PS*   T: (01780) 460735 E: jpt100948@gmail.com

TAYLOR, John Ralph. b 48. St Jo Coll Nottm BTh 74. d 74 p 75. C Clitheroe St Jas *Blackb* 74–77; C Kidsgrove *Lich* 77–79; C Hawkwell *Chelmsf* 79–82; V Linc St Geo Swallowbeck 82–92; rtd 92. *16 Rosedale Close, Cherry Willingham, Lincoln LN3 4RE*

TAYLOR, Canon John Rowland. b 29. St Mich Coll Llan 57. d 58 p 59. C Caerau St Cynfelin *Llan* 58–59; C Aberdare 59–61; Chapl Miss to Seamen 61–88; Dar-es-Salaam Tanzania 61–73; Adn Dar-es-Salaam 65–73; V-Gen 67–73; Hon Can Dar-es-Salaam from 73; V Bangkok Ch Ch Thailand 73–84; Chapl Rotterdam w Schiedam *Eur* 84–88; V Warnham *Chich* 88–98; rtd 98; PtO *Chich* 98–00; P-in-c Streat w Westmeston 00–07. *11 The Cedars, St George's Park, Ditchling Road, Burgess Hill RH15 0GR*   T: (01444) 232232 E: canonjohn@btinternet.com

TAYLOR, Jonathan Paul. b 74. Birm Univ BEng 97 Birm Chr Coll BA 05. Trin Coll Bris 07. d 11 p 12. C Coventry Caludon *Cov* 11–14; V Binley from 14. *St Bartholomew's Vicarage, 68 Brandon Road, Binley, Coventry CV3 2JF* E: jonandsu@gmail.com

TAYLOR, Joseph Robin Christopher. b 34. St Aid Birkenhead 58. d 61 p 62. C Aldershot St Mich *Guildf* 61–64; C Fleet 64–68; R Manaton *Ex* 69–74; R N Bovey 69–74; V Dawlish 74–87; P-in-c Christow, Ashton, Trusham and Bridford 87–88; R 88–95; PtO 95–98; *St E* from 98; rtd 99. *24 Edwin Panks Road, Hadleigh, Ipswich IP7 5JL*   T: (01473) 824262

TAYLOR, Julia Mary. *See* CODY, Julia Mary

TAYLOR, Kane Matthew. b 70. Open Univ BSc 04. Wycliffe Hall Ox 09. d 11 p 12. C Kettering St Andr *Pet* 11–14; P-in-c Weldon w Deene 14–17; R from 17. *The Rectory, 13 School Lane, Weldon, Corby NN17 3JN*   T: (01536) 626361 E: kane.taylor@hotmail.co.uk *or* kane.taylor@virgin.net

TAYLOR, Kelvin John. b 53. Portsm Univ CertEd 94 BA 96. Trin Coll Bris 02. d 04 p 05. C Overton w Laverstoke and Freefolk *Win* 04–08; V Kempshott 08–17; rtd 17; PtO *Win* from 17. *31 Melrose Road, Southampton SO15 7PB*

TAYLOR, Kingsley Graham. b 55. Univ of Wales (Cardiff) BD 93. St Mich Coll Llan 90. d 93 p 94. C Llanelli *St D* 93–97; V Whitland w Cyffig and Henllan Amgoed etc from 97; AD Pembroke from 16. *The Vicarage, North Road, Whitland SA34 0BH*   T: (01994) 240494 E: ktaylor559@aol.com

TAYLOR, Lee Anthony. b 77. Univ of Wales (Lamp) BA 02 Win Univ MA 12. Ripon Coll Cuddesdon 10. d 12 p 13. C Leigh-on-Sea St Marg *Chelmsf* 12–15; C Leigh St Clem 15; C Croydon St Jo *S'wark* 15–18; C Valle Crucis Miss Area *St As* from 18. *The Vicarage, Abbey Road, Llangollen LL20 8SN* E: frleetaylor@hotmail.co.uk

TAYLOR, Lynda Brigid. b 54. Man Univ BA Cam Univ PhD. ERMC. d 10 p 11. NSM Chesterton St Geo *Ely* 10–13; NSM Cambourne LEP 13–16; PtO from 17. *110 School Lane, Lower Cambourne, Cambridge CB23 5DJ* E: lyndabtaylor7@gmail.com

TAYLOR, Lyndon John. b 49. St Mich Coll Llan 92. d 95 p 96. NSM Swansea St Nic *S & B* 95–99; C Llwynderw 99–01; V Waunarllwydd 01–06; V Clydach 08–14; rtd 14; PtO *Mon* from 14; *Llan* 15–18. *85 Pen yr Alltwen, Alltwen, Pontardawe, Swansea SA8 3EA*   T: (01792) 934999

TAYLOR, Lynne. b 51. Sheff Univ BMet 73 Salford Univ PhD 80. Man OLM Scheme 98. d 01 p 02. OLM Turton Moorland *Man* 01–11; rtd 11; PtO *Man* from 11; *Carl* from 12; *Blackb* from 14. *56 Station Road, Turton, Bolton*

BL7 0HA   T: (01204) 852551 *or* 852292   M: 07776-208732 E: innoveras@hotmail.co.uk

TAYLOR, Margaret Ann. b 46. d 98 p 99. OLM Newcastle w Butterton *Lich* 98–17; PtO from 17. *12 Silverton Close, Bradwell, Newcastle ST5 8LU*   T: (01782) 660174 E: revanntaylor@yahoo.co.uk

TAYLOR, Mark Edward. b 54. St Jo Coll Auckland LTh. d 78 p 79. C Claudelands New Zealand 78–80; C Taumarunui 80–81; V Te Aroha 81–86; Chapl RN 86–88; Chapl RN New Zealand 90–94; Can Wellington 94–96; P-in-c Albany Greehithe New Zealand from 96; P-in-c Glen Eden 02–03. *2/2 Whitcombe Road, Bucklands Beach, Manukau 2012, New Zealand*   T: (0064) (27) 495 1767   M: 27-495 1767 E: chalice@xtra.co.nz

TAYLOR, Mark John. b 73. St Andr Univ MTheol 99. Coll of Resurr Mirfield 01. d 03 p 04. C N Meols *Liv* 03–07; TV Sutton 07–18; P-in-c Alfreton *Derby* from 18; P-in-c Riddings and Ironville from 18; C Somercotes from 18. *13 Church Street, Alfreton DE55 7AH*   T: (01773) 833280 E: mjtaylor513@gmail.com

TAYLOR, Canon Martyn Andrew Nicholas. b 66. d 96 p 97. C Stamford St Geo w St Paul *Linc* 96–03; R from 03; P-in-c Stamford Ch Ch 11–15; Can and Preb Linc Cathl from 15. *St George's Rectory, 16 St George's Square, Stamford PE9 2BN*   T: (01780) 757343 *or* 481800 E: rector@stgeorgeschurch.net

TAYLOR, Matthew Anthony. b 87. Van Mildert Coll Dur BSc 08. Wycliffe Hall Ox BTh 16. d 17 p 18. C Sevenoaks St Nic *Roch* from 17. *40 South Park, Sevenoaks TN13 1EJ*   M: 07917-441265 E: matt.taylor1987@gmail.com

TAYLOR, Matthew Timothy. b 62. NTMTC. d 11 p 12. C Rushden St Mary w Newton Bromswold *Pet* 11–17; V Finham *Cov* from 17. *The Vicarage, 136 Green Lane, Coventry CV3 6EA* E: matt_t_taylor@btinternet.com

TAYLOR, Mrs Maureen. b 36. Lon Bible Coll BTh 90 MA 94. d 97 p 98. NSM Borehamwood *St Alb* 97–00; NSM Radlett 00–05; PtO from 06. *57A Loom Lane, Radlett WD7 8NX*   T: (01923) 855197

TAYLOR, Michael. *See* TAYLOR, John Michael

TAYLOR, Michael Allan. b 50. Nottm Univ BTh 80. St Jo Coll Nottm 76. d 80 p 81. C Bowling St Jo *Bradf* 80–82; C Otley 82–85; P-in-c Low Moor St Mark 85–92; P-in-c Bris St Andr w St Bart 92–96; PtO *Llan* from 05. *19 Alexander Place, Abercanaid, Merthyr Tydfil CF48 1SJ*   T: (01443) 691481 E: micktaylor61@gmail.com

TAYLOR, Michael Andrew James. b 40. Univ Coll Ches BTh 96. d 99 p 00. NSM Halliwell *Man* 99–11; TV 03–11; rtd 11; PtO *Man* from 11. *123 Smithills Dean Road, Bolton BL1 6JZ*   T: (01204) 491503 E: majtaylor123@aol.com

TAYLOR, Michael Barry. b 38. Leeds Univ MA 96. Bps' Coll Cheshunt 63. d 65 p 66. C Leeds St Cypr Harehills *Ripon* 65–68; C Stanningley St Thos 68–70; V Hunslet Moor St Pet and St Cuth 70–78; V Starbeck 78–00; rtd 00; PtO *Leic* 00–16; *Glouc* from 16. *13 Capel Court, The Burgage, Prestbury, Cheltenham GL52 3EL*   T: (01242) 517969

TAYLOR, Michael Frank Chatterton. b 30. St Aid Birkenhead 59. d 61 p 62. C Knighton St Jo *Leic* 61–65; V Briningham *Nor* 65–86; R Melton Constable w Swanton Novers 65–86; P-in-c Thornage w Brinton w Hunworth and Stody 85–86; R Lyng w Sparham 86–90; R Elsing w Bylaugh 86–90; R Lyng, Sparham, Elsing and Bylaugh 90–95; RD Sparham 92–95; rtd 95; PtO *Portsm* from 95. *The Rhond, 33 Station Road, St Helens, Ryde PO33 1YF*   T/F: (01983) 873531   M: 07989-274848 E: mfct@uwclub.net

TAYLOR, Michael John. b 50. d 07 p 08. OLM Went Valley *Wakef* 07–11; NSM Pontefract St Giles 11–14; Leeds 14–19; NSM Pontefract from 19. *19 Windsor Rise, Pontefract WF8 4PZ*   T: (01977) 702824   M: 07968-932135 E: michael@darringtonchurch.com

TAYLOR, Canon Michael Joseph. b 49. Gregorian Univ Rome STB 72 PhL 74 Birm Univ MA 81 Nottm Univ PhD 05. English Coll Rome 67. d 72 p 73. In RC Ch 72–83; Hon C Newport Pagnell w Lathbury *Ox* 83–85; Hon C Newport Pagnell w Lathbury and Moulsoe 85–86; TV Langley Marish 86–90; Vice Prin EMMTC *S'well* 90–97; Prin 97–06; R Gedling 06–16; P-in-c Lambley 11–16; Hon Can S'well Minster 00–16; rtd 16; PtO *S'well* from 18. *55 Field Lane, Beeston, Nottingham NG9 5FF*   T: 0115-925 9228

TAYLOR, Michael Noel. b 40. Leeds Univ BSc 62 PGCE 63. EMMTC 95. d 98 p 99. NSM Woodthorpe *S'well* 98–02; NSM Gedling Deanery 02–03; NSM Epperstone, Gonalston, Oxton and Woodborough 03–10; NSM Calverton 03–10; rtd 10; PtO *S'well* from 11. *16 Church Meadow, Calverton, Nottingham NG14 6HG*   T: 0115-847 3718   F: 912 7671   M: 07713-125771 E: michael.taylor21@ntlworld.com

TAYLOR, Michael Stewart. b 58. St Mich Coll Llan BTh 91. **d** 91 **p** 92. C Llangunnor w Cwmffrwd *St D* 91–94; V Llansantffraed and Llanbadarn Trefeglwys etc 94–97; P-in-c Jersey St Andr *Win* 97–99; V 99–16; P-in-c Freshford, Limpley Stoke and Hinton Charterhouse *B & W* from 16. *The Rectory, Crowe Lane, Freshford, Bath BA2 7WB* T: (01225) 723570 E: vicarmike@gmail.com

TAYLOR, Michelle Deborah. b 67. Trin Coll Bris 16. **d** 18 **p** 19. C Trendlewood CD *B & W* from 18. *16 Briar Close, Nailsea, Bristol BS48 1QG* M: 07969-243222

TAYLOR, Mrs Monica. b 39. **d** 06 **p** 07. OLM Wyke *Guildf* 06–09; PtO 09–16; *Cant* from 17. *8 Lime Trees, Staplehurst, Tonbridge TN12 0SS* E: mrsmonicataylor@hotmail.com

TAYLOR, Neil Andrew. b 56. ERMC 13. **d** 15 **p** 16. NSM Chigwell and Chigwell Row *Chelmsf* 15–17; NSM Chipping Ongar w Shelley etc from 17. *The Rectory, 52 Epping Road, Toot Hill, Ongar CM5 9SQ*

TAYLOR, Canon Nicholas Hugh. b 63. Cape Town Univ BA 83 MA 87 Dur Univ PhD 91 Ox Univ MTh 07. **d** 96 **p** 97. Lect and Chapl Univ of Swaziland 95–98; Chapl St Mich Sch Manzini 96–98; Sen Lect Africa Univ Zimbabwe 98–01; Can Th Mutare Cathl from 99; Dioc Dir Th Educn Manicaland 99–01; R Penhalonga 00–01; Assoc Prof Pretoria Univ S Africa 02–04; R Pretoria St Hilda 02–03; R Pretoria N St Mary 03; Hon C Smithfield St Bart Gt *Lon* 04; Research Fell Univ of Zululand S Africa 04–17; Hon Tutor Ripon Coll Cuddesdon 04–05; K Coll Lon 06; PtO *Nor* from 04; *Ox* 05–07; R Clarkston *Glas* from 09; Tutor TISEC 10–14. *St Aidan's Rectory, 8 Golf Road, Clarkston, Glasgow G76 7LZ* T: 0141-638 3080 M: 07944-091132 E: n.h.taylor@ripon.oxon.org *or* rector.staidansclarkston@gmail.com

TAYLOR, Preb Nicholas James. b 46. St Chad's Coll Dur BA 67. **d** 69 **p** 70. C Beamish *Dur* 69–74; C Styvechale *Cov* 74–77; P-in-c Wilmcote w Billesley 77–79; P-in-c Aston Cantlow 77–79; V Aston Cantlow and Wilmcote w Billesley 79–87; V Cov St Fran N Radford 87–97; RD Cov N 93–97; V Wilton *B & W* 97–11; Preb Wells Cathl 08–11; rtd 11; PtO *B & W* from 15. *50 Summerlands Park Avenue, Ilminster TA19 9BT* T: (01460) 929392 M: 07761-437505 E: nickruthtaylor@gmail.com

TAYLOR, Nicholas John. b 48. Leeds Univ BSc 69. St Mich Coll Llan BTh 09. **d** 09 **p** 10. NSM Griffithstown *Mon* 09–13; NSM Panteg and Griffithstown 13–17; rtd 17. *Little Barton, Trelleck, Monmouth NP25 4PE* M: 07860-507258 E: revnjt@btinternet.com

TAYLOR, Nigel James. b 73. Lanc Univ BA 94. Trin Coll Bris BA 11. **d** 11 **p** 12. C Risborough *Ox* 11–15; C Idle *Leeds* 15–18; V from 18. *92 Town Lane, Bradford BD10 8PJ* M: 07749-816265 E: revdjimtaylor@gmail.com

TAYLOR, Nigel Roy. b 63. Keele Univ MA 01 RGN 86 RMN 89. Qu Coll Birm 10. **d** 12 **p** 13. C Walsall St Paul *Lich* 12–15; C Walsall St Luke 12–15; TV Kidderminster Ismere *Worc* 15–18; TR from 18; Ind Chapl from 15. *42 Woodlands Road, Cookley, Kidderminster DY10 3TL* E: revnrt@icloud.com

TAYLOR, Nigel Thomas Wentworth. b 60. Bris Univ BA 82 Ox Univ BA 86. Wycliffe Hall Ox 84. **d** 87 **p** 88. C Ches Square St Mich w St Phil *Lon* 87–91; C Roxeth Ch Ch and Harrow St Pet 91–93; TV Roxeth 93–97; V S Mimms Ch Ch 97–16; AD Cen Barnet 04–09; Dir Tr and Development Edmonton Area from 16. *3 Guildown Avenue, London N12 7DE* T: (020) 8445 8495 M: 07484-230864 E: nigel.taylor@london.anglican.org

TAYLOR, Mrs Noelle Rosemary. b 58. NTMTC 02. **d** 05 **p** 06. C St Mary-at-Latton *Chelmsf* 05–08; TV Gt Parndon 08–14; V 14–15; P-in-c Chipping Ongar w Shelley 15–17; R Chipping Ongar w Shelley etc from 17. *The Rectory, Shakletons, Ongar CM5 9AT* T: (01277) 362173 E: noelletaylor@hotmail.com

TAYLOR, Norman Adrian. b 48. Ho of Sacred Miss 64 St D Coll Lamp 70. **d** 73 **p** 74. C Fleur-de-Lis *Mon* 73–75; C W Drayton *Lon* 75–79; C-in-c Hayes St Edm CD 79–85; V Hayes St Edm 85–87; V Pilton w Ashford *Ex* 87–89; V Sidley *Chich* 89–02; Chapl Hastings and Rother NHS Trust 00–02; V Durrington *Chich* 02–13; rtd 13; PtO *Chich* 13–17. *7 Guernsey Road, Ferring, Worthing BN12 5PN* T: (01903) 245939 E: frnormantaylor@gmail.com

TAYLOR, Mrs Patricia Anne. b 56. TCD BTh 05. CITC 03. **d** 05 **p** 06. C Wicklow w Killiskey *D & G* 05–10; TV Smestow Vale *Lich* 10–13; rtd 13; PtO *Lich* 13–16; *Wakef* 14; *Leeds* from 14. *2 Poplar Avenue, Shafton, Barnsley S72 8PU* E: patricia.taylor@live.com

TAYLOR, Patricia Mary. b 52. Goldsmiths' Coll Lon BEd 80. Wycliffe Hall Ox 06. **d** 09 **p** 10. NSM Upper Holloway *Lon* 09–12 and 12–13; NSM Wandsworth St Mich w St Steph *S'wark* from 13. *1 Beloe Close, London SW15 5RB* M: 07880-656395 E: patricia@stmikes-ststeves.org.uk *or* patricia-taylor@hotmail.co.uk

TAYLOR, Patrick James. b 72. Magd Coll Cam BA 96 MA 99 MEng 96 K Coll Lon MA 11. Ripon Coll Cuddesdon BA 00. **d** 01 **p** 02. C Kenilworth St Nic *Cov* 01–05; TV Solihull *Birm* 05–14; R Stratford-upon-Avon, Luddington etc *Cov* from 14. *The Vicarage, 10 Old Town, Stratford-upon-Avon CV37 6BG* T: (01789) 508155 E: vicar@stratford-upon-avon.org

TAYLOR, Paul. b 63. RGN 85. Sarum & Wells Th Coll 92 Linc Th Coll BTh 95. **d** 95 **p** 96. C Boultham *Linc* 95–98; C Ditton St Mich w St Thos *Liv* 98–00; V Bickerstaffe and Melling 00–06; TV N Meols 06–08; rtd 08; Chapl St Helens and Knowsley Hosps NHS Trust from 13. *139 Sussex Road, Southport PR8 6AF* T: (01704) 500617 E: paulandjotaylor@virginmedia.com

TAYLOR, The Ven Paul Stanley. b 53. Ox Univ BEd 75 MTh 98. Westcott Ho Cam. **d** 84 **p** 85. C Bush Hill Park St Steph *Lon* 84–88; Asst Dir Post Ord Tr Edmonton Episc Area 87–94; Dir Post Ord Tr 94–00 and 02–04; V Southgate St Andr *Lon* 88–97; V Hendon St Mary 97–01; V Hendon St Mary and Ch Ch 01–04; AD W Barnet 00–04; Adn Sherborne *Sarum* 04–18; Can and Preb Sarum Cathl 04–18; rtd 18; PtO *Birm* from 19; *Lich* from 19. *2 Blackwell Lane, Redditch B97 6SS* T: (01527) 591699 M: 07796-691203 E: pstaylor53@gmail.com

TAYLOR, Peter. b 51. St Jo Coll Cam BA 72 MA 76. Ridley Hall Cam 73. **d** 76 **p** 77. C Roch 76–79; PtO *Ely* 79–99 and 05–06; NSM Downham 99–05; P-in-c Coveney 06–17; RD Ely 09–14; Bp's Adv for Self-Supporting Min 10–17; PtO from 17. *Gravel Head Farm, Downham Common, Little Downham, Ely CB6 2TY* T: (01353) 698714 F: 699107 E: peter@taylormonroe.co.uk

TAYLOR, Canon Peter David. b 47. Liv Univ BEd 74 Man Univ MEd 78 Lanc Univ MA 88. NOC 78. **d** 81 **p** 82. C Formby H Trin *Liv* 81–84; V Stoneycroft All SS 84–91; Chapl St Kath Coll 91–96; Dioc RE Field Officer 91–96; Dioc Dir of Educn *Leic* 96–09; Hon Can Leic Cathl 98–09; Dir Operations Ch Academy Services Ltd *Pet* 09–11; PtO *Leic* from 09; rtd 11. *87 Main Street, Humberstone, Leicester LE5 1AE* T: 0116-220 1461 *or* (01733) 566575 E: peter.tay1947@gmail.com

TAYLOR, Peter David. b 38. FCA. NOC 77. **d** 80 **p** 81. C Penwortham St Mary *Blackb* 80–84; V Farington 84–92; V Euxton 92–04; rtd 04; PtO *Blackb* from 04. *33 Aspendale Close, Longton, Preston PR4 5LJ* T: (01772) 614795

TAYLOR, The Ven Peter Flint. b 44. Qu Coll Cam BA 65 MA 69. Lon Coll of Div BD 70. **d** 70 **p** 71. C Highbury New Park St Aug *Lon* 70–73; C Plymouth St Andr w St Paul and St Geo *Ex* 73–77; V Ironville *Derby* 77–83; P-in-c Riddings 82–83; R Rayleigh *Chelmsf* 83–96; Chapl HM YOI Bullwood Hall 85–90; RD Rochford *Chelmsf* 89–96; Adn Harlow 96–09; rtd 09. *5 Springfield Terrace, Springfield Road, South Brent TQ10 9AP* T: (01364) 73427 E: peterftaylor@lineone.net

TAYLOR, Peter John. b 46. Tyndale Hall Bris 70. **d** 73 **p** 74. C Walshaw Ch Ch *Man* 73–75; C Rodbourne Cheney *Bris* 75–78; Asst Chapl HM Pris Pentonville 78–79; Chapl HM Borstal Roch 79–84; Chapl HM Pris Highpoint 84–90; Asst Chapl Gen of Pris 90–01; rtd 01. *The Old Butchery, The Street, Redgrave, Diss IP22 1RY* T: (01379) 890368 E: peterblowingrock@aol.com

TAYLOR, Peter John. b 40. Oak Hill Th Coll 62. **d** 65 **p** 66. C St Paul's Cray St Barn *Roch* 65–69; C Woking St Jo *Guildf* 69–77; R Necton w Holme Hale *Nor* 77–94; R Necton, Holme Hale w N and S Pickenham 95–05; RD Breckland 86–94; Hon Can Nor Cathl 98–03; rtd 05; PtO *Nor* from 05. *5 Starling Close, Aylsham, Norwich NR11 6XG* T: (01263) 731964

TAYLOR, Peter Joseph. b 41. Bps' Coll Cheshunt 66. **d** 68 **p** 69. C Wollaton *S'well* 68–71; C Cockington *Ex* 71–74; V Broadhembury 74–79; V Broadhembury w Payhembury 79–81; V Gt Staughton *Ely* 81–86; V Gt Paxton and R Offord D'Arcy w Offord Cluny 86–01; Chapl HM YOI Gaynes Hall 81–91; rtd 01; PtO *Ely* 01–18; *St Alb* 07–16. *9 Park Way, Offord Cluny, St Neots PE19 5RW* T: (01480) 811662 E: peter.taylor9@talktalk.net

TAYLOR, Mrs Rachel Sara. b 60. Univ Coll Lon BA 81. SEITE 98. **d** 01 **p** 02. C Wimbledon *S'wark* 01–05; V Motspur Park from 05; AD Merton from 19. *The Vicarage, 2 Douglas Avenue, New Malden KT3 6HT* T: (020) 8942 3117 E: holycrossvicarage@btinternet.com

TAYLOR, Ralph Urmson. Tulsa Univ MA 72 Man Coll of Educn DipEd 74 TCert 82. Kelham Th Coll. **d** 56 **p** 57. C Redcar *York* 57–59; C Bridlington Quay H Trin 59–62; C Sewerby w Marton 60–62; Chapl Lich Th Coll 62–65; Chapl Holland Hall Sch 65–93; rtd 93; Sacr Tulsa H Trin USA 93–02. *43 East Cliffe, Lytham St Annes FY8 5DX*

TAYLOR, Raymond. b 34. Lon Coll of Div 62. **d** 65 **p** 66. C Pennington *Man* 65–70; P-in-c Wombridge *Lich* 70–80; R S Normanton *Derby* 80–88; RD Alfreton 86–88; V Youlgreave, Middleton, Stanton-in-Peak etc 88–98; rtd 99; PtO *Derby*

98–18. *4 Jeffries Avenue, Crich, Matlock DE4 5DU* T: (01773) 856845

TAYLOR, Raymond Montgomery. b 43. Oak Hill Th Coll 77. **d** 80 **p** 81. Hon C Cricklewood St Pet *Lon* 80–85; Hon C Golders Green 85–87; V New Southgate St Paul 87–00; AD Cen Barnet 96–00; V Thaxted *Chelmsf* 00–13; rtd 13; PtO *Chelmsf* 13–18. *2 Crescent Close, Dunmow CM6 1DE* T: (01371) 874809 E: vade.mecum@outlook.com

TAYLOR, Richard Godfrey. b 73. Pemb Coll Cam MA 99. Oak Hill Th Coll BA 00. **d** 00 **p** 01. C Brunswick *Man* 00–04; C Aldridge *Lich* 04–09; V Clapham Common St Barn *S'wark* from 09; AD Battersea from 16. *The Vicarage, 8 Lavender Gardens, London SW11 1DL* T: (020) 7223 5953 E: fatboytaylor@gmail.com *or* vicar@shaw.co.uk

TAYLOR, Richard John. b 46. Ripon Coll Cuddesdon 85. **d** 85 **p** 86. C Moseley St Mary *Birm* 85–87; V Kingsbury 87–91; TR Hodge Hill 91–03; P-in-c 03–05; R Weston super Mare St Jo *B & W* 05–16; RD Locking 08–16; rtd 16; PtO *B & W* from 18. *2 Ringwood Grove, Weston-super-Mare BS23 2UA*

TAYLOR, Robert Ian. b 68. St Jo Coll Nottm. **d** 08 **p** 09. C Buttershaw St Paul *Bradf* 08–12; Chapl Bradf Academy from 08. *52 Bowling Park Drive, East Bowling, Bradford BD4 7ES* T: (01274) 788722 E: robtlr@aol.com

TAYLOR, Robin. *See* TAYLOR, Joseph Robin Christopher

TAYLOR, Roger James Benedict. b 42. Glouc Sch of Min 89 WMMTC 95. **d** 96 **p** 97. NSM Cromhall w Tortworth and Tytherington *Glouc* 96–99; P-in-c Wistanstow *Heref* 99–01; Min Can Brecon Cathl *S & B* 01–07; Chapl Brecon War Memorial Hosp 01–07; Chapl St Oswald's Almshouses 08–12; rtd 12. *9 Jubilee Close, Bidford-on-Avon, Alcester B50 4ED* E: rogertaylor.burdon@gmail.com

TAYLOR, Rosemary Edith. *See* JENKINS, Rosemary Edith

TAYLOR, Roy William. b 37. Ch Coll Cam BA 61 MA 64. Clifton Th Coll 61. **d** 63 **p** 64. C Blackb Sav 63–66; C Hensingham *Carl* 66–68; CMS Taiwan 69–79; TV Bushbury *Lich* 79–85; OMF 85–93; Hon C Wolverhampton St Jude *Lich* 93–94; P-in-c Torquay St Jo and Ellacombe *Ex* 94–99; R Instow and V Westleigh 99–03; RD Hartland 01–03; rtd 03. *31 Shore Road, Millisle, Newtownards BT22 2BT* T: (028) 9186 2769 E: roy.31@btinternet.com

TAYLOR, Simon Dominic Kent. b 69. Surrey Univ BSc 90 W Sussex Inst of HE PGCE 91 Sussex Univ MA(Ed) 99. Trin Coll Bris BA 01. **d** 01 **p** 02. C Southgate *Chich* 01–04; TV 04–10; Dioc Officer for Emerging Leadership 04–10; R Busbridge and Hambledon *Guildf* from 10; AD Godalming from 19. *Spinney Copse, Hambledon Road, Godalming GU7 1PJ* T: (01483) 421267 E: simon.taylor@bhcgodalming.org

TAYLOR, Simon John. b 72. Worc Coll Ox BA 94 MPhil 96 MA 99 DPhil 00. St Mich Coll Llan 00 Ven English Coll Rome 01. **d** 02 **p** 03. C Cotham St Sav w St Mary and Clifton St Paul *Bris* 02–06; P-in-c Bris St Mary Redcliffe w Temple etc 06–12; CMD Officer and Can Res Derby Cathl 12–19; AD Derby City 13–19; Hd of Min Development *Bris* from 19. *Bristol Diocesan Board of Finance, Hillside House, Bristol Parkway North, Newbrick Road, Stoke Gifford, Bristol BS34 8YU* T: 0117-906 0100

TAYLOR, Simon Wheldon. b 62. **d** 12 **p** 13. NSM Tunbridge Wells St Phil *Roch* 12–15; NSM Stapleford *Ely* from 15. *The Vicarage, 43 Mingle Lane, Stapleford, Cambridge CB22 5SY* T: (01892) 782043 M: 07970-716163 E: st@cloisters.com

TAYLOR, Stephen Charles. b 53. St Edm Hall Ox BA 75 Ex Univ PGCE 78. WEMTC 05. **d** 08 **p** 09. NSM Highnam, Lassington, Rudford, Tibberton etc *Glouc* 08–13; P-in-c Westbury-on-Severn w Flaxley, Blaisdon etc from 13. *Address withheld by request* T: (01452) 760756 E: stevewillstay@gmail.com

TAYLOR, Stephen Gordon. b 35. Bris Univ BA 60. Ridley Hall Cam 60. **d** 62 **p** 63. C Gt Baddow *Chelmsf* 62–65; C Portsdown *Portsm* 65–69; P-in-c Elvedon *St E* 69–70; R 70–75; P-in-c Eriswell 69–70; R 70–75; P-in-c Icklingham 69–70; R 70–75; Chapl St Felix Sch Southwold 77–77; R Lt Shelford w Newton *Ely* 77–96; rtd 96; PtO *Ely* 96–17. *15 Church Close, Whittlesford, Cambridge CB22 4NY* T: (01223) 830461 E: sgt707@btinternet.com

TAYLOR, Stephen James. b 48. Chich Th Coll 70. **d** 73 **p** 74. C Tottenham St Paul *Lon* 73–76; St Vincent 78–85; Grenada 85–88; C-in-c Hammersmith SS Mich and Geo White City Estate CD *Lon* 88–96; AD Hammersmith 92–96; P-in-c Hammersmith St Luke 94–96; USPG Brazil 96–08; PtO *Lon* from 14. *12 Bletchley Court, Wenlock Street, London N1 7NX* T: (020) 7253 8629 E: stephentaylor2001@hotmail.com

TAYLOR, Stephen Mark. b 65. City Univ BSc 87 Lon Univ PGCE 90. NTMTC 95. **d** 98 **p** 99. Chapl Bp Stopford's Sch Enfield 98–02 and 03–06; NSM Enfield Chase St Mary *Lon* 98–02; PtO *Eur* 02–03; C Hornsey St Mary w St Geo *Lon* 03–06;

P-in-c March St Jo *Ely* 06–08; Hon Asst Dir of Ords 07–08; P-in-c Enfield St Mich *Lon* 08–13; V from 13. *The Vicarage, 2 Gordon Hill, Enfield EN2 0QP* T: (020) 8363 1063 M: 07711-559107 E: stephen.taylor@london.anglican.org

TAYLOR, The Ven Stephen Ronald. b 55. Dur Univ MA 99. Cranmer Hall Dur 80. **d** 83 **p** 84. C Chester le Street *Dur* 83–87; V Newbottle 87–92; V Stranton 92–00; TR Sunderland 00–07; Provost Sunderland Minster 07–11; Hon Can Dur Cathl 06–11; Adn Maidstone *Cant* from 11; Hon Can Rift Valley Tanzania from 00; Hon Fell Sunderland Univ *Dur* from 09. *The Archdeaconry, 4 Redcliffe Lane, Penenden Heath, Maidstone ME14 2AG* T: (01622) 200221 E: stephen.taylor@archdeacmaid.org

TAYLOR, Stewart. b 51. Cranmer Hall Dur 74. **d** 77 **p** 78. C Norwood St Luke *S'wark* 77–81; C Surbiton Hill Ch Ch 81–91; V Cambridge St Phil *Ely* from 91. *St Philip's Vicarage, 252 Mill Road, Cambridge CB1 3NF* T: (01223) 247652 *or* 414775 E: vicar@stphilipschurch.org.uk

TAYLOR, Canon Stuart Bryan. b 40. St Chad's Coll Dur BA 64. **d** 66 **p** 67. C Portsea N End St Mark *Portsm* 66–70; C Epsom St Martin *Guildf* 70–76; Chapl Clifton Coll Bris 76–88; Dir Bloxham Project 88–93; Chapl Giggleswick Sch 93–95; Bp's Officer for Miss and Evang *Bris* 96–01; Bp's Adv for Past Care for Clergy and Families 01–10; Hon Min Can Bris Cathl 02–04; Chapl Bris Cathl Sch 01–09; Hon Can Bris Cathl 04–10; rtd 10; PtO *B & W* from 12. *Bris* from 14. *62 Providence Lane, Long Ashton, Bristol BS41 9DN* T: (01275) 393625 M: 07974-316489 E: sbtbristol@gmail.com

TAYLOR, Susan Ann. b 57. **d** 16 **p** 17. NSM Gillingham St Mary *Roch* 16–17; NSM Gillingham H Trin from 17. *14 Century Road, Gillingham ME8 0BG* T: (01634) 235058 M: 07910-701806 E: susan.taylor3@hotmail.co.uk

TAYLOR, Mrs Susan Mary. b 51. Ex Univ LLB 73 St Anne's Coll Ox BCL 75 Solicitor 78. SEITE 03. **d** 06 **p** 07. NSM Barkingside St Laur *Chelmsf* 06–12; Chapl Evelina Children's Hosp from 12; Chapl Guy's and St Thos' NHS Foundn Trust from 13; PtO *S'wark* 10–13; *Chelmsf* from 12. *Norwood, North End, Buckhurst Hill IG9 5RA* T: (020) 8504 9867 *or* 7188 7188 E: suetaylorathome@aol.com *or* sue.taylor@gstt.nhs.uk

TAYLOR, Mrs Teresa Mary. b 53. SRN 76 SCM 78. WEMTC 98. **d** 02 **p** 03. NSM Kingswood *Bris* 02–12; Chapl Freeways Trust from 07; P-in-c Mangotsfield *Bris* 12–13; V from 13. *19 Hicks Avenue, Emersons Green, Bristol BS16 7HA* E: revtmt@blueyonder.co.uk

TAYLOR, Thomas. b 33. Sarum & Wells Th Coll 77. **d** 80 **p** 81. NSM Heatherlands St Jo *Sarum* 80–82; TV Kinson 82–88; TV Shaston 88–98; Chapl Westmr Memorial Hosp Shaftesbury 88–98; rtd 98; PtO *Sarum* 98–12. *10 Hanover Lane, Gillingham SP8 4TA* T: (01747) 826569

TAYLOR, Thomas. b 42. St Jo Coll Dur BA 64 Leeds Univ MA 02. Linc Th Coll 64. **d** 66 **p** 67. C Clitheroe St Mary *Blackb* 66–69; C Skerton St Luke 69–71; C-in-c Penwortham St Leon CD 71–72; V Penwortham St Leon 72–78; R Poulton-le-Sands 78–81; P-in-c Morecambe St Lawr 78–81; R Poulton-le-Sands w Morecambe St Laur 81–85; Chapl Lord Wandsworth Coll Hook 85–92; V Walton-le-Dale *Blackb* 92–94; P-in-c Samlesbury 92–94; V Walton-le-Dale St Leon w Samlesbury St Leon 95–96; RD Leyland 94–96; Hon C Tarleton 03–11; Hon C Rufford and Tarleton 11–12. *52 Hesketh Lane, Tarleton, Preston PR4 6AQ* T: (01772) 813871 E: rustichouse@bigfoot.com

TAYLOR, Timothy Robert. b 62. W Midl Coll of Educn BEd 87 Cumbria Univ BA 10. LCTP 07. **d** 10 **p** 11. NSM Egremont and Haile *Carl* from 10. *42 Abbey Vale, St Bees CA27 0EF* T: (01946) 822255 E: timothy@trtaylor.co.uk

TAYLOR, Willam Goodacre Campbell. *See* CAMPBELL-TAYLOR, William Goodacre

TAYLOR, Capt William Thomas. b 61. Rob Coll Cam BA 83 BA 90. Ridley Hall Cam 88. **d** 91 **p** 92. C Bromley Ch Ch *Roch* 91–95; C St Helen Bishopsgate w St Andr Undershaft etc *Lon* 95–98; R from 98; R St Pet Cornhill from 01. *The Old Rectory, Merrick Square, London SE1 4JB* T: (020) 7378 8186

TAYLOR-COOK, Andrew. b 62. ERMC. **d** 08 **p** 09. C Wirksworth *Derby* 08–12; Chapl amongst Deaf People *Ox* 12–13; Chapl amongst Deaf People *Pet* 12–15; C Guilsborough and Hollowell and Cold Ashby etc 13–15; P-in-c Codnor *Derby* 15–19; P-in-c Horsley and Denby 15–19; P-in-c Loscoe 15–19; P-in-c Horsley Woodhouse 15–19; V Denby Gp from 19. *The Vicarage, 20 Codnor Denby Lane, Codnor, Ripley DE5 9SN* T: (01773) 740288 M: 07840-848123 E: andrewtc@btinternet.com

TAYLOR-KENYON (née THOMPSON), Louise Margaret. b 61. Clare Coll Cam BA 83 MA 07 Homerton Coll Cam PGCE 84 Leeds Univ MA 07. NOC 04. **d** 07 **p** 08. C Skipton H Trin *Bradf* 07–10; C Skipton Ch Ch w Carleton 07–10; C Embsay w Eastby 10–14; V 14; *Leeds* 14–19; CME Officer

10–19; P-in-c Bamburgh *Newc* from 19; P-in-c Belford and Lucker from 19; AD Bamburgh and Glendale from 19. *20 Radcliffe Park, Bamburgh NE69 7AN* M: 07545-235362 E: revdlouisetk@greennet.org.uk

TEAL, Andrew Robert. b 64. Birm Univ BA 85 PhD 06 Ox Brookes Univ PGCE 05 Pemb Coll Ox MA 08. Ripon Coll Cuddesdon 86. **d** 88 **p** 89. C Wednesbury St Paul Wood Green *Lich* 88–92; TV Sheff Manor 92–97; Asst Post-Ord Tr Officer 93–98; Tutor Ripon Coll Cuddesdon 92–97; V Tickhill w Stainton *Sheff* 97–02; Warden of Readers 98–02; Hd of Th Plater Coll 02–03; Hd of Th and Past Studies 03–05; Chapl Pemb Coll Ox from 05; Fell from 08; Lect Ripon Coll Cuddesdon from 08; Warden SLG from 09; Lect Th Ox Univ from 07. *Pembroke College, Oxford OX1 1DW* T: (01865) 286276 F: 276418 E: andrew.teal@theology.ox.ac.uk

TEALE, Adrian. b 53. Univ of Wales (Abth) BA 74 CertEd 77 MA 80 Univ of Wales (Cardiff) MTh 89. Wycliffe Hall Ox 78. **d** 80 **p** 81. C Betws w Ammanford *St D* 80–84; V Brynaman w Cwmllynfell from 84; RD Dyffryn Aman 95–01. *Y Dalar Deg, 10 Bryn Road, Upper Brynamman, Ammanford SA18 1AU* T: (01269) 822275 E: tinkerteale@googlemail.com

TEAR, Jeremy Charles. b 67. Westmr Coll Ox BA 89 Birm Univ MA 99 MCIPD 94. Aston Tr Scheme 95 Qu Coll Birm 97. **d** 99 **p** 00. C Timperley *Ches* 99–03; V Macclesfield St Paul 03–10; C Caversham Thameside and Mapledurham *Ox* 10–15; TV Warrington W *Liv* 15–17; TR from 17. *St Paul's Vicarage, 6 Poplar Avenue, Penketh, Warrington WA5 2EH* T: (01925) 723492 E: revjtear@btinternet.com

TEARE, Adrian Jeremy. b 79. Van Mildert Coll Dur BA 01 G&C Coll Cam BA 10. Westcott Ho Cam 08. **d** 12. C Tottenham St Paul *Lon* 12–13; C Kilburn St Mary w All So and W Hampstead St Jas 13–14; C Palmers Green St Jo 14–15; PtO 15–18. *34 Greyhound Hill, London NW4 4JP* T: (020) 8203 3172 E: adrian.teare@gmail.com

TEARE, Canon Robert John Hugh. b 39. Bris Univ BSc 62. Coll of Resurr Mirfield 67. **d** 70 **p** 71. C Fareham SS Pet and Paul *Portsm* 70–73; Chapl K Alfred Coll Win 73–78; V Pokesdown St Jas 78–82; R Winnall 82–06; RD Win 89–99; Hon Can Win Cathl 92–06; rtd 06; Chapl CSMV 06–09; PtO *Ox* 09–11; P-in-c Hanney, Denchworth and E Challow 11–12; PtO from 12. *29 Elizabeth Drive, Wantage OX12 9YA* T: (01235) 770966 E: robertteare@googlemail.com

TEARNAN, John Herman Janson. b 37. Bris Univ BSc 59. Kelham Th Coll 62. **d** 66 **p** 67. C Kettering SS Pet and Paul 66–71; LtO 71–85; PtO *St Alb* 82–85; *Pet* 85–94; Chapl HM YOI Wellingborough 89–90; Chapl HM YOI Glen Parva 90–94; Guyana 94–03; rtd 03; PtO *Pet* from 05. *14 Rectory Walk, Barton Seagrave, Kettering NN15 6SP* T: (01536) 510629 E: jaytee1937@btinternet.com

TEARNE, Jonathan Philip. b 84. Goldsmiths' Coll Lon BA 06 Birkbeck Coll Lon MSc 12. Wycliffe Hall Ox BA 18. **d** 19. C Emmaus Par Team *Leic* from 19. *Address withheld by request*

TEASDALE, Angela. b 67. St Hild Coll 16. **d** 18 **p** 19. NSM Wadworth w Loversall and Balby *Sheff* from 18. *Fernwood View, Littleworth Lane, Rossington, Doncaster DN11 0HD* E: teasdaleangela@aol.com

TEASDEL, David Charles. b 77. Coll of Resurr Mirfield 05. **d** 08 **p** 09. C Ouzel Valley *St Alb* 08–11; TV Kingsdown and Barrow Hill *Derby* 11–14; P-in-c Sharlston *Leeds* 14–16; V from 16; P-in-c Altofts 14–16; V from 16. *The Vicarage, 72A Church Road, Normanton WF6 2QG* T: (01928) 893110 M: 07914-045419 E: fatherdavidteasdel@gmail.com

TEBBOTH, Mrs Jennifer Mary. b 61. Univ Coll Lon BSc 82 RGN 87 Ox Brookes Univ PGCE 05. Ox Min Course 12. **d** 15 **p** 16. NSM Chalfont St Giles, Seer Green and Jordans *Ox* from 15. *40 Gaviots Way, Gerrards Cross SL9 7DX* T: (01753) 892940 M: 07708-094532 E: jenny.tebboth@btopenworld.com

TEBBS, Richard Henry. b 52. Southn Univ BTh. Sarum & Wells Th Coll 75. **d** 78 **p** 79. C Cinderhill *S'well* 78–82; C Nor St Pet Mancroft w St Jo Maddermarket 82–85; TV Bridport *Sarum* 85–94; TR Yelverton, Meavy, Sheepstor and Walkhampton *Ex* 94–08; P-in-c Frankley *Birm* 08–13; R 13–17; PtO *Lich* from 18. *Severn Villa, 14 Waterside, Burton-on-Trent DE15 9HE*

TEBBUTT, Canon Christopher Michael. b 55. ACA CTA. St Jo Coll Nottm BA 99. **d** 96 **p** 97. C Catherington and Clanfield *Portsm* 96–00; P-in-c Southbroom *Sarum* 00–07; V 07–09; TR Canford Magna from 09; RD Wimborne 11–16; Can and Preb Sarum Cathl from 12. *The Rectory, Canford Magna, Wimborne BH21 3AF* T: (01202) 882270 M: 07917-190307 E: rev.christebbutt@gmail.com

TEBBUTT, Sandra Eileen. b 56. FBDO 78. STETS 96. **d** 99 **p** 00. NSM Blendworth w Chalton w Idsworth *Portsm* 99–00; Chapl Wilts and Swindon Healthcare NHS Trust 00–05;

Regional Manager Bible Soc from 05; NSM Southbroom *Sarum* 04–09; NSM Canford Magna from 10. *The Rectory, Canford Magna, Wimborne BH21 3AF* T: (01202) 883382 E: sandra.tebbutt@biblesociety.org.uk

TEBBY, Ms Janet Elizabeth. b 52. Open Univ BA 88 Lady Spencer Chu Coll of Educn CertEd 73. ERMC 05. **d** 08 **p** 09. NSM Wootton w Quinton and Preston Deanery *Pet* 08–12; TV Oakham, Ashwell, Braunston, Brooke, Egleton etc 12–17; rtd 17; Hon C Yardley Hastings, Denton and Grendon etc *Pet* from 18. *3 The Drive, Wellingborough NN8 2DB* T: (01933) 384628 E: jtebby@gmail.com

TEDD, Christopher Jonathan Richard. See HOWITZ, Christopher Jonathan Richard

TEGALLY, Narinder Jit Kaur. b 57. RGN 93. SAOMC 99. **d** 02 **p** 03. NSM Welwyn Garden City *St Alb* 02–05; Asst Chapl R Free Hampstead NHS Trust 05–07; Sen Chapl Guy's and St Thos' NHS Foundn Trust 07–12; TV Beaconsfield *Ox* 12–17; Lead Sen Chapl R United Hosps Bath NHS Foundn Trust from 17. *Royal United Hospital, Combe Park, Bath BA1 3NG* T: (01225) 824039 M: 07940-580859 E: narinder.tegally@nhs.net

TEGGARTY, Samuel James Karl. b 53. Dundee Univ BSc 77. CITC 98. **d** 01 **p** 02. NSM Newry *D & D* 01–03; NSM Kilkeel 03–15; P-in-c Aghaderg w Donaghmore and Scarva from 16. *79 Knockchree Avenue, Kilkeel, Newry BT34 4BP* T: (028) 4176 9076 E: karl.teggarty@btinternet.com

TELEMAN, Roxana Tenea. b 63. ERMC 16. **d** 19. NSM Nice w Vence *Eur* from 19. *49 boulevard de L'Océan, Les Demeures de Fontclair, 13009 Marseille, France*

TELEN, Salvador Roberto Sabornido. b 66. **d** 89. C Notting Hill St Jo *Lon* 05–10; Hon C Walthamstow St Sav *Chelmsf* 12–13; P-in-c 13–14; V from 14; Hon C Walthamstow St Barn and St Jas Gt 12–13; PtO *Lon* from 16; *St Alb* from 19. *St Saviour's Vicarage, 210 Markhouse Road, London E17 8EP* T: (020) 8520 2036 M: 07874-888138 E: father.telen@btinternet.com

TELFER, Andrew Julian. b 68. Essex Univ BA 94 Lon Sch of Th MA 18. Wycliffe Hall Ox BTh 97. **d** 97 **p** 98. C Skelmersdale St Paul *Liv* 97–01; C Ashton-in-Makerfield St Thos 01–03; V Whiston from 03. *The Vicarage, 90 Windy Arbor Road, Prescot L35 3SG* T: 0151-426 6329 E: ajtelfer@btinternet.com

TELFER, Canon Frank Somerville. b 30. Trin Hall Cam BA 53 MA 58. Ely Th Coll 53. **d** 55 **p** 56. C Liv Our Lady and St Nic 55–58; Chapl Down Coll Cam 58–62; Bp's Chapl Nor 62–65; Chapl Kent Univ *Cant* 65–73; Can Res Guildf Cathl 73–95; rtd 96; PtO *Nor* from 96. *Holbrook, Glandford, Holt NR25 7JP* T: (01263) 740586 E: fandjtelfer@btinternet.com

TELFORD, Alan. b 46. St Jo Coll Nottm. **d** 83 **p** 84. C Normanton *Derby* 83–86; TV N Wingfield, Pilsley and Tupton 86–90; TV N Wingfield, Clay Cross and Pilsley 90–92; P-in-c Oakwood 92–94; V Leic St Chris 94–05; P-in-c Leic St Theodore 05–09; rtd 09. *2 Springfield Cottage, Newmarket Lane, Clay Cross, Chesterfield S45 9AR* T: (01246) 866988 M: 07854-937449 E: atelford@talktalk.net

TELFORD, John Anthony. b 72. Oak Hill Th Coll BA 96. **d** 13 **p** 14. C Anlaby St Pet *York* from 13; C Anlaby Common St Mark from 13. *St Mark's Vicarage, 1055 Anlaby Road, Hull HU4 7PP* T: (01482) 575232 M: 07956-100383 E: john.telfs@gmail.com *or* telfordj@btinternet.com

TELFORD, Richard Francis. b 46. K Coll Lon 65. **d** 69 **p** 70. C Barkingside H Trin *Chelmsf* 69–72; C Wickford 72–77; P-in-c Romford St Jo 77–80; V 80–82; PtO 93–96; rtd 08. *Juglans, The Street, Wattisfield, Diss IP22 1NS* E: richard_telford@hotmail.com

TEMBEY, David. b 51. **d** 96 **p** 97. NSM Whitehaven *Carl* 96–00; NSM Cultram St Cuth 00–02; NSM Holme Cultram St Mary 00–02; NSM Bromfield w Waverton 00–02; TV Solway Plain 02–15; V Marske in Cleveland *York* from 15; RD Guisborough from 19. *The Vicarage, 6 Windy Hill Lane, Marske-by-the-Sea, Redcar TS11 7BN* T: (01642) 473119 E: tembey6@btinternet.com

TEMPERLEY-BARNES, Mrs Lisa Caroline. Westcott Ho Cam 09. **d** 11 **p** 12. C Newbold de Verdun, Barlestone and Kirkby Mallory *Leic* 11–13; C Bosworth and Sheepy Gp 13–14; R Woodhouse, Woodhouse Eaves and Swithland from 14. *St Paul's Rectory, 11 Paterson Drive, Woodhouse Eaves, Loughborough LE12 8RL* T: (01509) 890972 E: revdlisatemperley@gmail.com

TEMPLE, Mrs Sylvia Mary. b 48. Ex Univ BA 70 Univ of Wales (Abth) PGCE 71. St D Dioc Tr Course 93. **d** 94 **p** 97. NSM Tenby *St D* 94–99; C 99–00; V Martletwy w Lawrenny and Minwear etc 00–05. *Llwyn Onn, Trafalgar Road, Tenby SA70 7DW*

TEMPLEMAN (née WILLIAMS), Mrs Ann Joyce. b 50. St Hugh's Coll Ox BA 72 MA 75 PGCE 73. Cranmer Hall Dur 03. **d** 05 **p** 06. Headmistress Dur High Sch for Girls

98–11; NSM Peterlee *Dur* 05–11; P-in-c Theale and Englefield *Ox* 11–18; R Hoole *Blackb* from 18. *The Rectory, 69 Liverpool Old Road, Much Hoole, Preston PR4 4RB* M: 07877-659156 E: anntempleman@live.co.uk

TEMPLEMAN, Peter Morton. b 49. Ch Ch Ox BA 71 MA 75. Wycliffe Hall Ox MA 75. **d** 76 **p** 77. C Cheltenham St Mary, St Matt, St Paul and H Trin *Glouc* 76–79; Chapl St Jo Coll Cam 79–84; P-in-c Finchley St Paul Long Lane *Lon* 84–85; P-in-c Finchley St Luke 84–85; V Finchley St Paul and St Luke 85–99; V Peterlee *Dur* 99–11; C Theale and Englefield *Ox* 11–18; PtO *Blackb* from 18. *The Rectory, 69 Liverpool Old Road, Much Hoole, Preston PR4 4RB* E: anntempleman@live.co.uk

TEMPLETON, Iain McAllister. b 57. St Andr Coll Drygrange 80. **d** 85 **p** 86. In RC Ch 85–92; NSM Dornoch *Mor* 95; P-in-c Kirriemuir *St And* 95–99; R Eccleston *Blackb* 99–09; V Walsall St Andr *Lich* from 09. *St Andrew's Vicarage, 119 Hollyhedge Lane, Walsall WS2 8PZ* T: (01922) 721658 E: fatheriain@aol.com

TEMPLETON, Susan Prichard Molison. b 83. R Holloway Coll Lon BSc 05 MA 11. Ripon Coll Cuddesdon 15. **d** 18 **p** 19. C Woodley *Ox* from 18. *25 Dunbar Drive, Woodley, Reading RG5 4HA* M: 07834-818751 E: susie.templeton@gmail.com

TEN WOLDE, Christine Caroline. b 57. **d** 99 **p** 00. NSM Llanegryn w Aberdyfi w Tywyn *Ban* 99–12; NSM Tywyn w Llanegryn w Aberdyfi w Pennal 12–13; NSM Bro Ystumanner from 13. *Abergroes, Aberdovey LL35 0RE* T: (01654) 767047 F: 767572 M: 07977-108438 E: curate@stpeterschurch.org.uk

TENGE-HESLOP, Mrs Sabine Ulrike. b 59. Goethe Univ Frankfurt MSc 83. Lindisfarne Regional Tr Partnership 12. **d** 17 **p** 18. NSM Harelaw and Annfield Plain *Dur* from 17. *16 Glebeside, Satley, Bishop Auckland DL13 4HR* T: (01388) 730855 E: s.u.tenge-heslop@durham.ac.uk

TENNANT, Cyril Edwin George. b 37. Keble Coll Ox BA 59 MA 63 Lon Univ BD 61 Ex Univ MA 03 Univ of Wales PhD 11. Clifton Th Coll 59. **d** 62 **p** 63. C Stapleford *S'well* 62–65; C Felixstowe SS Pet and Paul *St E* 65–69; V Gipsy Hill Ch Ch *S'wark* 69–84; V Lee St Mildred 84–90; P-in-c Lundy *Is Ex* 90–92; V Ilfracombe SS Phil and Jas w W Down 90–01; rtd 01; PtO *Ex* 01–06; *Ox* 06–08 and 12–18. *27 Harvest Way, Witney OX28 1BX* T: (01993) 778977 E: cyril.tennant@yahoo.co.uk

TER HAAR, Roger Edward Lound. b 52. Magd Coll Ox BA 73. **d** 06 **p** 07. OLM Bramley and Grafham *Guildf* 06–13; PtO from 17; *St D* from 17. *Testers, Upperton, Petworth GU28 9BE* T: (020) 7797 8100 E: terhaar@crownofficechambers.com

TERRANOVA, Jonathan Rossano (Ross). b 62. Sheff Poly BA 85 Heythrop Coll Lon MA 17. Oak Hill Th Coll BA 88. **d** 88 **p** 89. C Carl St Jo 88–91; C Stoughton *Guildf* 91–94; R Ditton *Roch* from 94; RD Malling 02–07. *The Rectory, 2 The Stream, Ditton, Maidstone ME20 6AG* T: (01732) 842027

TERRELL, Richard Charles Patridge. b 43. Wells Th Coll 69. **d** 71 **p** 72. C Shepton Mallet *B & W* 71–76; P-in-c Drayton 76–77; P-in-c Muchelney 76–77; TV Langport Area 78–82; P-in-c Tatworth 82–89; V 89–96; R W Coker w Hardington Mandeville, E Chinnock etc 96–09; rtd 09; PtO *B & W* from 09. *2 Hamdon View, Norton sub Hamdon, Stoke-sub-Hamdon TA14 6SE* T: (01935) 881330 M: 07736-836004 E: richard.terrell@homecall.co.uk

TERRY, Canon Christopher Laurence. b 51. Heythrop Coll Lon MA 09 FCA 80. St Alb Minl Tr Scheme. **d** 83 **p** 84. Hon C Dunstable *St Alb* 83–89; C Abbots Langley 89–92; TV Chambersbury 92–99; Chapl Abbot's Hill Sch Herts 96–99; R Southwick St Mich *Chich* 99–03; RD Hove 00–03; Finance and Admin Sec Min Division Abps' Coun 04–09; TR Gt Yarmouth *Nor* 09–16; RD 11–16; Hon Can Nor Cathl 13–16; rtd 16; PtO *Nor* from 16. *34 Rightup Lane, Wymondham NR18 9NB* T: (01953) 603522 E: cterry925@btinternet.com

TERRY, Colin Alfred. b 49. Trin Coll Bris 98. **d** 00 **p** 01. C Bexleyheath Ch Ch *Roch* 00–03; V Belvedere All SS 03–10; Chapl Bromley Coll 10–12; P-in-c Lamorbey H Redeemer *Roch* 12–17; AD Sidcup 13–16; rtd 17; PtO *Cant* from 18. *48 Egremont Road, Bearsted, Maidstone ME15 8LX* E: colin.terry.49@btinternet.com

TERRY, Darcy. See CHESTERFIELD-TERRY, John Darcy Francis Malcolm

TERRY, Mrs Hilary June. b 45. SEITE 08. **d** 11 **p** 13. NSM Uckfield *Chich* 11–15; rtd 15; PtO *Roch* from 15. *110 Townsend Road, Snodland ME6 5RL* M: 07947-923513 E: juneterry1@gmail.com

TERRY, Ian Andrew. b 53. St Jo Coll Dur BA 74 St Jo Coll York PGCE 75 St Mary's Coll Twickenham MA 99 Surrey Univ PhD 05. Coll of Resurr Mirfield 78. **d** 80 **p** 81. C Beaconsfield *Ox* 80–83; C N Lynn w St Marg and St Nic *Nor* 83–84; Chapl and Hd RE Eliz Coll Guernsey 84–89; Chapl St Jo Sch Leatherhead 89–92; R Bisley and W End

Guildf 92–02; Asst Chapl HM Pris Coldingley 99–02; Dioc Dir of Educn *Heref* 02–08; Hon TV W Heref 03–08; Chapl St Edm Sch Cant 08–09; TR Bournemouth Town Cen *Win* from 09. *St Peter's Rectory, 18 Wimborne Road, Bournemouth BH2 6NT* T/F: (01202) 554058 E: ianterry@live.co.uk

TERRY, James Richard. b 74. Linc Coll Ox BA 95. Oak Hill Th Coll BA 03. **d** 03 **p** 04. C Harold Wood *Chelmsf* 03–07; NSM Blackb Ch Ch w St Matt 07–13; V Tranmere St Cath *Ches* from 13. *St Catherine's Vicarage, 39 Westbank Road, Birkenhead CH42 7JP* T: 0151-652 7379 E: james_terry1@hotmail.com

TERRY, Jeffrey. See TERRY, Robert Jeffrey

TERRY, John Arthur. b 32. S'wark Ord Course. **d** 66 **p** 67. C Plumstead All SS *S'wark* 66–69; C Peckham St Mary Magd 69–72; V Streatham Vale H Redeemer 72–80; R Sternfield w Benhall and Snape *St E* 80–84; V Stevenage St Mary Shephall *St Alb* 84–86; V Stevenage St Mary Shephall w Aston 86–90; V Cople w Willington 90–97; Chapl Shuttleworth Agric Coll 90–97; rtd 97; PtO *St E* 98–18; *Nor* 98–04; *Ely* 03–16. *2 Kestrel Drive, Brandon IP27 0UA* T: (01842) 812055 E: jterry83@hotmail.com

TERRY, John Darcy Francis Malcolm. See CHESTERFIELD-TERRY, John Darcy Francis Malcolm

TERRY, John Michael. b 56. Ex Univ BSc 78 Southn Univ MSc 88 Anglia Ruskin Univ BA 09 CEng 93 MIMarEST 93. Ridley Hall Cam 06. **d** 09 **p** 10. NSM Fareham St Jo *Portsm* 09–13; NSM Hook w Warsash from 13; Jt P-in-c from 14. *The Vicarage, 113 Church Road, Warsash, Southampton SO31 9GF* T: (01489) 808296 E: mike@terry-home.co.uk

TERRY, June. See TERRY, Hilary June

TERRY, Justyn Charles. b 65. Keble Coll Ox BA 86 St Jo Coll Dur BA 95 K Coll Lon PhD 03. Cranmer Hall Dur 92. **d** 95 **p** 96. C Paddington St Jo w St Mich *Lon* 95–99; V Kensington St Helen w H Trin 99–05; Assoc Prof Trin Episc Sch for Min USA 05–08; Dean and Pres 08–16; Dean Wycliffe Hall Ox from 17. *Wycliffe Hall, 52-54 Banbury Road, Oxford OX2 6PW* T: (01865) 274620 M: 07495-781795 E: justyn.terry@wycliffe.ox.ac.uk

TERRY, Marc David. b 78. Trin Coll Bris 08. **d** 10 **p** 11. C Margate H Trin *Cant* 10–14; C Aylesham w Adisham and Nonington 15–18; TR By Brook *Bris* from 18. *By Brook Rectory, 3 Church Farm, Yatton Keynell, Chippenham SN14 7FD* T: (01249) 782672 E: revmarcterry@gmail.com

TERRY, Neal John. b 66. **d** 17 **p** 18. NSM Long Benton St Mary *Newc* from 17. *4 Sandpiper Place, Newcastle upon Tyne NE12 8PE* T: 0191-266 5285 E: n.j.terry@btinternet.com

TERRY (née LEONARD), Mrs Nicola Susan. b 61. Keele Univ BA 85. Ridley Hall Cam 07. **d** 09 **p** 10. NSM Alverstoke *Portsm* 09–13; NSM Hook w Warsash from 13; Jt P-in-c from 14. *The Vicarage, 113 Church Road, Warsash, Southampton SO31 9GF* T: (01489) 808296 E: revnsterry@gmail.com

TERRY, Robert Jeffrey. b 52. Lon Univ LLB 75 City Univ MA 81 Barrister-at-Law 76 FCIArb 96. SWMTC 17. **d** 19. NSM Boscastle and Tintagel Gp *Truro* from 19; NSM Week St Mary Circle of Par from 19. *St Pirans, Trethevy, Tintagel PL34 0BE* E: stpiran@me.com

TERRY, Stephen John. b 49. K Coll Lon BD 72 AKC 74. **d** 75 **p** 76. C Tokyngton St Mich *Lon* 75–78; C Hampstead St Steph w All Hallows 78–81; V Whetstone St Jo 81–89; TR Aldrington *Chich* 89–07; R 07–17; rtd 17. *36 Church Mead, Hassocks BN6 8BN* E: stephenterry49@gmail.com

TETLEY, Brian. b 38. St Jo Coll Dur BA 82 ACA 62 FCA 72. Cranmer Hall Dur 80. **d** 83 **p** 84. C Chipping Sodbury and Old Sodbury *Glouc* 83–86; Chapl and Succ Roch Cath 86–89; R Gravesend H Family w Ifield 89–93; Tutor Westcott Ho Cam 93–94 and 95–96; Tutor Ridley Hall and Pemb Coll Cam 94–95; C Duxford, Hinxton and Ickleton 97; PtO 98–99; NSM Worc Cathl 00–03; rtd 03; PtO *Worc* 03–08; *Ox* 08–14. *23 Cripley Road, Oxford OX2 0AH* T: (01865) 250209 E: briantetley@btinternet.com

TETLEY, Miss Carol Ruth. b 61. Ches Coll of HE BA 84. NEOC 06. **d** 09 **p** 10. NSM Anlaby St Pet *York* 09–13; NSM Anlaby Common St Mark 11–13; NSM Hessle from 13; Chapl Hull and E Yorks Hosps NHS Trust from 13. *27 Cranberry Way, Hull HU4 7AQ* T: (01482) 351644 E: caroltetley@crt61.karoo.co.uk

TETLEY, The Ven Joy Dawn. b 46. St Mary's Coll Dur BA 68 Leeds Univ CertEd 69 St Hugh's Coll Ox BA 75 MA 80 Dur Univ PhD 88. NW Ord Course 77. **dss** 77 **d** 87 **p** 94. Bentley *Sheff* 77–79; Buttershaw St Aid *Bradf* 79–80; Dur Cathl 80–83; Lect Trin Coll Bris 83–86; Chipping Sodbury and Old Sodbury *Glouc* 83–86; Dn Roch Cathl 87–89; Hon Can 90–93; Assoc Dir of Post Ord Tr 87–88; Dir Post Ord Tr 88–93; Hon Par Dn Gravesend H Family w Ifield 89–93; Prin EAMTC *Ely* 93–99; Adn Worc and Can Res Worc Cathl 99–08; rtd 08; PtO *Ox* 08–11. *23 Cripley Road, Oxford OX2 0AH* T: (01865) 250209 E: briantetley@btinternet.com

TETLEY, Matthew David. b 61. Bucks Coll of Educn BSc 83. Sarum & Wells Th Coll BTh 89. **d** 87 **p** 88. C Kirkby Liv 87–90; C Hindley St Pet 90–93; TV Whorlton Newc 93–96; V Newbiggin Hall 96–01; P-in-c Longhorsley and Hebron 01–06; Chapl HM Pris Acklington 01–06 and 08–15; Chapl HM Pris Frankland 06–08; Chapl HM Pris Dur from 15; PtO Newc from 15. HM Prison Durham, 19B Old Elvet, Durham DH1 3HU T: 0191-332 3400 E: matthew.tetley@justice.gov.uk

TETLOW, John. b 46. St Steph Ho Ox 73. **d** 76 **p** 77. C Stanwell Lon 76–77; C Hanworth All SS 77–80; C Somers Town 80–83; TV Wickford and Runwell Chelmsf 83–90; P-in-c Walthamstow St Mich 90–96. 6A Bushwood, London E11 3AY T: (020) 8989 9076

TETLOW, Richard Jeremy. b 42. Trin Coll Cam MA 66 Goldsmiths' Coll Lon CQSW 74. Qu Coll Birm 81. **d** 83 **p** 84. C Birm St Martin 83–85; C Birm St Martin w Bordesley St Andr 85–88; V Birm St Jo Ladywood 89–01; V Ladywood St Jo and St Pet 01–08; rtd 08; PtO Birm from 08. 26 Sovereign Way, Moseley, Birmingham B13 8AT T: 0121-449 4892

TETT, Richard Colin. b 60. Qu Foundn Birm 14. **d** 16 **p** 17. C Eckington Worc from 16; C Defford w Besford from 16. 5 Crown Court, Crown Lane, Defford, Worcester WR8 9BE T: (01386) 751152 M: 07712-706717 E: captrickt@hotmail.co.uk

TETZLAFF, Mrs Geraldine Vivienne. b 59. St Jo Coll Nottm 10. **d** 12 **p** 13. C Macclesfield Team Ches 12–15; V Chelford and Lower Withington w Marthall 15–19; P-in-c Birkenhead Ch Ch from 19. Christ Church Vicarage, 7 Palm Grove, Prenton CH43 1TE M: 07756-664622 E: gerri.tetzlaff@gmail.com

TETZLAFF, Silke. b 67. Friedrich Schiller Univ 87 K Coll Lon BA 97 AKC 97 Anglia Poly Univ MA 01. Westcott Ho Cam 99. **d** 01 **p** 02. C Leagrave St Alb 01–05; TV Baldock w Bygrave and Weston 05–11; C Sandon, Wallington and Rushden w Clothall 10–11; R Staplehurst Cant from 11. The New Rectory, High Street, Staplehurst, Tonbridge TN12 0BJ T: (01580) 891258 E: silke.tetzlaff@btinternet.com

TEWKESBURY, Suffragan Bishop of. See SPRINGETT, The Rt Revd Robert Wilfred

THACKER, Christine Mary. b 44. Simon Fraser Univ BC BA 90. Vancouver Sch of Th MDiv 93. **d** 92 **p** 93. R Kitimat Ch Ch Canada 93–00; C Boultham Linc 00–09; rtd 10; PtO Nor from 10. 51A South Beach Road, Hunstanton PE36 5BA E: chrism.thacker@gmail.com

THACKER, Ian David. b 59. Univ of Wales (Lamp) MA 13. Oak Hill Th Coll BA 91. **d** 91 **p** 92. C Illogan Truro 91–94; C Eglwysilan Llan 94–96; TV Hornsey Rise Whitehall Park Team Lon 96–97; TV Upper Holloway 97–01; Chapl HM YOI Huntercombe and Finnamore 01–11; Chapl HM Pris Huntercombe from 11. HM Prison Huntercombe, Huntercombe Place, Nuffield, Henley-on-Thames RG9 5SB T: (01491) 632212 M: 07864-095435 E: ian.thacker@justice.gov.uk

THACKER, Jonathan William. b 53. Lon Univ BA 74. Linc Th Coll 76. **d** 79 **p** 80. C Bromyard Heref 79–82; C Penkridge w Stretton Lich 82–87; V Brothertoft Gp Linc 87–96; RD Holland W 92–95; P-in-c Crosby 96–01; V 01–19; RD Manlake 11–14; RD Is of Axholme 11–14; Chapl Scunthorpe and Goole Hosps NHS Trust 99–01; rtd 19. Church Cottage, Front Street, Barnby, Newark NG24 2SA M: 07804-250459 E: pajidog2017@gmail.com

THACKRAY, John Adrian. b 55. Southn Univ BSc 76 ACIB 81. Coll of Resurr Mirfield 81. **d** 84 **p** 85. C Loughton St Jo Chelmsf 84–87; Chapl Bancroft's Sch Woodford Green 87–92; Sen Chapl K Sch Cant 92–01; Chapl Abp's Sch Cant 01–02; Sen Chapl K Sch Roch 02–15; P-in-c Ipswich St Mary at the Elms St E from 15; PtO Chelmsf from 92; Hon Min Can Cant Cathl from 93; Hon PV Roch Cathl 02–15; Bp's Ecum Adv St E from 16. The Vicarage, 68 Blackhorse Lane, Ipswich IP1 2EAF M: 07780-613754

THACKRAY, William Harry. b 44. Leeds Univ CertEd 66. Chich Th Coll 70. **d** 73 **p** 74. C Sheff St Cuth 73–76; C Stocksbridge 76–78; P-in-c Newark St Leon S'well 79–80; TV Newark w Hawton, Cotham and Shelton 80–82; V Choral S'well Minster 82–85; V Bawtry w Austerfield 85; P-in-c Misson 85; V Bawtry w Austerfield and Misson 86–93; RD Bawtry 90–93; P-in-c Balderton 93–03; P-in-c Coddington w Barnby in the Willows 98–03; V Biggleswade St Alb 03–09; RD 07–09; rtd 09; Hon C Lower Swale Ripon 09–14; Leeds 14; PtO York from 14. 8 Newsham Way, Northallerton DL7 8HT T: (01609) 780102 E: williamhthackray@gmail.com

THAKE, Preb Terence. b 44. ALCD 65. **d** 66 **p** 67. C St Faringdon w Lt Coxwell Ox 66–70; C Aldridge Lich 70–73; V Werrington 73–82; Chapl HM Det Cen Werrington Ho 73–82; TR Chell Lich 82–94; Chapl Westcliff Hosp 82–94; RD Stoke N Lich 91–94; V Colwich w Gt Haywood 94–00; P-in-c Colton 95–00; R Colton, Colwich and Gt Haywood 00–04; RD Rugeley 98–06; Preb Lich Cathl 94–10; Dioc Environmental

Adv Derby from 12; rtd 04; PtO Lich 15–16. 18 Middleton Avenue, Codnor, Ripley DE5 9SS E: tthake@tiscali.co.uk or terry.thake@btinternet.com

THATCHER, Ms Catherine Mary. b 72. Em Coll Cam MA 97 City Univ MSc 01 Cam Univ BTh 14 ACCA 98. Westcott Ho Cam 12. **d** 14 **p** 15. C Bradf Cathl Leeds 14–17 and from 14; Clergy Development Officer Bradf Area from 17. 20 Gledhow Drive, Oxenhope, Keighley BD22 9SA E: oxenhopecat@gmail.com

THATCHER, Stephen Bert. b 58. Greenwich Univ PGCE 04. St Jo Coll Nottm LTh 87 ALCD 87. **d** 87 **p** 88. C Bargoed and Deri w Brithdir Llan 87–89; C Llanishen and Lisvane 89–91; V Llanwnda, Goodwick w Manorowen and Llanstinan St D 91–95; P-in-c Coberley, Cowley, Colesbourne and Elkstone Glouc 95–96; Dioc Rural Adv 95–96; R New Radnor and Llanfihangel Nantmelan etc S & B 96–00; Dioc Tourism Officer 96–99; Dioc Chs and Tourism Rep 97–00; CF 00–18; R Seale, Puttenham and Wanborough Guildf from 18. The Rectory, Elstead Road, Seale, Farnham GU10 1JA T: (01252) 783057 M: 07379-526555 E: stephen_thatcher@sky.com

THAXTER, Paul. b 58. **d** 94. Pakistan 94–13; Dir Transcultral Miss CMS from 13; PtO Win from 13. 57 St Edmunds Road, Southampton SO16 4FT E: paul.thaxter@cmsuk.org

THEAKER, David Michael. b 41. **d** 68 **p** 69. C Folkingham w Laughton Linc 68–71; C New Cleethorpes 71–74; P-in-c Gt Grimsby St Andr and St Luke 74–77; P-in-c Thurlby 77–79; PtO Ely from 00. 11 Willow Way, Hauxton, Cambridge CB22 5JB T: (01223) 873132 E: david_theaker@yahoo.co.uk

THEAKSTON, Canon Sally Margaret. b 62. UEA BSc 84 K Coll Lon MA 94. Ripon Coll Cuddesdon BA 89. **d** 89 **p** 94. Par Dn Hackney Lon 89–93; Par Dn Putney St Mary S'wark 93–94; C 94–96; Chapl RN 96–02; TR Gaywood Nor 02–09; TR Dereham and Distr 09–19; P-in-c Shipdham w Bradenham from 14 and 15; Asst Dir of Ords from 16; Hon Can Nor Cathl from 10. 28 Litcham Road, Gressenhall, Dereham NR20 4AR M: 07904-070654 E: stheakston@aol.com or sally.theakston@dioceseofnorwich.org

THELWELL, The Ven John Berry. b 49. Univ of Wales (Ban) BD 72. Qu Coll Birm 73. **d** 73 **p** 74. C Minera St As 73–80; Dioc Youth Chapl 78–86; V Gwernaffield and Llanferres 80–93; Chapl Clwyd Fire Service 88–94; RD Mold St As 91–95; TR Hawarden 93–02; Can Cursal St As Cathl 95–02; Prec 98–02; Adn Montgomery St As 02–12; V Berriew 03–12; rtd 12; PtO St As from 13. O'r Diwedd, 2 Bryn Road, Bryn-y-Baal, Mold CH7 6RY T: (01352) 750962 E: john.thelwell@btinternet.com

THEOBALD, Graham Fitzroy. b 43. ALCD 67. **d** 67 **p** 68. C Crookham Guildf 67–71; C York Town St Mich 71–74; V Wrecclesham 74–83; Chapl Green Lane Hosp 74–81; R Frimley Guildf 83–85; Chapl Frimley Park Hosp 83–85; PtO Ox 90–92; C Easthampstead 92–97; Chapl E Berks NHS Trust 92–03; rtd 03; PtO Ox 03–12; Hon C Ruscombe and Twyford w Hurst from 12. 50 Viking, Bracknell RG12 8UL T: (01344) 428525 M: 07721-408740 E: witsend50gra@gmail.com

THEOBALD, Susan Ann. b 61. La Sainte Union Coll BEd 83. STETS 07. **d** 10 **p** 11. C Southsea St Jude Portsm 10–14; P-in-c Ryde St Jo Oakfield and H Trin from 14. St John's Vicarage, Victoria Crescent, Ryde PO33 1DQ E: theobald.sue.79@gmail.com

THETFORD, Suffragan Bishop of. See WINTON, The Rt Revd Alan Peter

THEWLIS, Andrew James. b 64. Man Univ BSc 86. Cranmer Hall Dur 87. **d** 90 **p** 91. C Walshaw Ch Ch Man 90–95; P-in-c Jersey St Jo Win 95–98; R 98–16; TV Savernake Sarum 16–18. 7 Flathouse, Linthwaite, Huddersfield HD7 5PR T: (01484) 617357 M: 07747-114707 E: thewlisandy@gmail.com

THEWLIS, Canon John Charles. b 49. Van Mildert Coll Dur BA 70 PhD 75. NOC 78. **d** 81 **p** 82. NSM Hull St Mary Sculcoates York 81–83; C Spring Park Cant 83–84; C Spring Park All SS S'wark 85–86; V Eltham Park St Luke 86–01; R Carshalton 01–17; Hon Can S'wark Cathl 14–17; rtd 17; PtO S'wark from 17; Heref from 17. Willow Cottage, The Marsh, Wellington, Hereford HR4 8DU T: 05603-670746 E: jct@thewlis.org.uk

THEWSEY, Robert Sydney. b 65. Sarum Coll MA 18. Ripon Coll Cuddesdon 99. **d** 01 **p** 02. C Chorlton-cum-Hardy St Clem Man 01–04; P-in-c Stretford All SS 04–08; P-in-c Boscastle w Davidstow Truro 08–15; R Boscastle and Tintagel Gp 15–16; RD Stratton 11–16; R Shiplake w Dunsden and Harpsden Ox from 16. The Rectory, Shiplake, Henley-on-Thames RG9 4BS E: robert.thewsey@btinternet.com

THICKE, James Balliston. b 43. Sarum & Wells Th Coll 74. **d** 77 **p** 78. C Wareham Sarum 77–80; TV 80–83; Dioc Youth Adv Dur 83–87; C Portishead B & W 87–90; V Westfield 90–08; RD Midsomer Norton 98–04; Chapl Norton Radstock Coll of FE 00–08; rtd 08; PtO B & W from 09; Chapl ATC from 13. 11

Welton Grove, Midsomer Norton, Radstock BA3 2TS T: (01761) 411905 M: 07971-943654 E: jamesballiston@hotmail.co.uk

THIRLWELL, Miss Margaret. b 36. Bris Univ BA 59 St Aid Coll Dur DipEd 61. **d** 03 **p** 04. OLM Binfield *Ox* 03–09; PtO 09–17 and from 18. *70 Red Rose, Binfield, Bracknell RG42 SLD* T: (01344) 423920 E: margaret.thirlwell@gmail.com

THIRTLE, Ms Lucy Rachel. b 62. Ex Univ BA 85. Cranmer Hall Dur 97. **d** 99 **p** 00. C Basingstoke *Win* 99–04; P-in-c Kingsclere 04–06; P-in-c Ashford Hill w Headley 06; V Kingsclere and Ashford Hill w Headley 06–15; Hon C Ray Valley *Ox* from 15. *3 The Rise, Islip, Kidlington OX5 2TG* T: (01865) 379470 E: revlucy.islip@gmail.com

THISELTON, Prof Anthony Charles. b 37. Lon Univ BD 59 K Coll Lon MTh 64 Sheff Univ PhD 77 Dur Univ DD 93 Lambeth DD 02 FBA 10 FKC 10. Oak Hill Th Coll 58. **d** 60 **p** 61. C Sydenham H Trin *S'wark* 60–63; Tutor Tyndale Hall Bris 63–67; Sen Tutor 67–70; Lect Bibl Studies Sheff Univ 70–79; Sen Lect 79–85; Prof Calvin Coll Grand Rapids USA 82–83; Special Lect Th Nottm Univ 86–88; Prin St Jo Coll Nottm 86–88; Prin St Jo Coll w Cranmer Hall Dur 88–92; Prof Chr Th Nottm Univ from 92; Can Th Leic Cathl from 94; Can Th S'well Minster from 00. *Department of Theology, Nottingham University, University Park, Nottingham NG7 2RD* T: 0115-951 5852 F: 951 5887 E: thiselton@ntlworld.com

THISTLETHWAITE, Canon Nicholas John. b 51. Selw Coll Cam BA 73 MA 77 PhD 80. Ripon Coll Cuddesdon BA 78 MA 83. **d** 79 **p** 80. C Newc St Gabr 79–82; Chapl G&C Coll Cam 82–90; LtO *Ely* 82–90; V Trumpington 90–99; Can Res and Prec Guildf Cathl 99–16; Sub-Dean 06–16; rtd 17; PtO *Ely* from 17; Chapl to The Queen from 14. *16 Douglas Court, Ely CB7 4SE* T: (01353) 663231 E: njt789@gmail.com

THISTLEWOOD, Michael John. b 31. Ch Coll Cam BA 53 MA 57. Linc Th Coll 54. **d** 56 **p** 57. C N Hull St Mich *York* 56–59; C Scarborough St Mary 59–61; V Kingston upon Hull St Jude w St Steph 61–67; V Newland St Aug 67–72; Asst Master Bemrose Sch Derby 72–80; V Derby St Andr w St Osmund 80–82; LtO *Ox* 84–95; rtd 88; PtO *Carl* 88–98; *Derby* 98–05; *Carl* 05–08 and from 09. *44 Blackhall Croft, Blackhall Road, Kendal LA9 4UU* E: mjt06@hotmail.co.uk

THODAY, Margaret Frances. b 38. **d** 03 **p** 04. OLM Roughton and Felbrigg, Metton, Sustead etc *Nor* 03–08; PtO from 08. *Flat 3, 4 Norwich Road, Cromer NR27 0AX* T: (01263) 510945

THODY, Charles Michael Jackson. b 62. Linc Th Coll BTh 94. **d** 94 **p** 95. C Immingham *Linc* 94–97; P-in-c Leasingham and Cranwell 97–01; P-in-c Bishop Norton, Waddingham and Snitterby 01–03; Chapl Doncaster and S Humber Healthcare NHS Trust 01–03; Chapl Notts Healthcare NHS Trust 03–09; Chapl Rotherham, Doncaster and S Humber NHS Foundn Trust 09–11; Sen Chapl N Lincs and Goole NHS Foundn Trust from 12. *Chaplaincy, Scunthorpe General Hospital, Cliff Gardens, Scunthorpe DN15 7BH* T: (01724) 282282 E: c.thody@nhs.net

THOM, Alastair George. b 60. G&C Coll Cam BA 81 MA 84 ACA 86. Ridley Hall Cam 88. **d** 91 **p** 92. C Lindfield *Chich* 91–94; C Finchley St Paul and St Luke *Lon* 94–98; P-in-c W Kilburn St Luke w St Simon and St Jude 98–13; P-in-c Paddington Em Harrow Road 98–13; V W Kilburn St Luke and Harrow Road Em from 13; AD Westmr Paddington 06–11. *The Vicarage, 19 Macroom Road, London W9 3HY* T: (020) 8962 0294 E: alastairthom@yahoo.co.uk

THOM, James. b 31. St Chad's Coll Dur BA 53. **d** 57 **p** 58. C Middlesbrough St Thos *York* 57–60; C Hornsea and Goxhill 60–62; C S Bank 62–63; V Copmanthorpe 63–75; V Coxwold 75–77; V Coxwold and Husthwaite 77–87; RD Easingwold 77–82; Spiritual Dir York Angl Cursillo 86–93; P-in-c Topcliffe 87–93; rtd 93; PtO *York* from 93; *Ripon* 93–14; *Leeds* 14–16. *34 Hell Wath Grove, Ripon HG4 2JT* T: (01765) 605083

THOMAS, Adam Douglas. b 68. All SS Cen for Miss & Min 15. **d** 18 **p** 19. C Lytham St Cuth *Blackb* from 18. *81 Blackpool Road, Lytham St Annes FY8 4EN* M: 07968-434328 E: cathyandadam89@gmail.com

THOMAS, Alan. *See* THOMAS, Thomas Alan

THOMAS, Aled Huw. b 59. Univ of Wales (Abth) BD 81. St Mich Coll Llan 84. **d** 85 **p** 86. C Llandeilo Fawr and Taliaris *St D* 85–86; P-in-c Llangrannog and Llandysiliogogo 86–88;

Chapl RAF 88–92; R Ystradgynlais *S & B* 92–94; CF 94–08; Sen CF 08–10; V St Dogmael's w Moylgrove and Monington w Meline *St D* 10–11; V St Dogmael's and Monington and Nevern etc 11–12; rtd 12. *Y Bwthyn, 8 Church Street, Rhayader LD6 5AY* T: (01597) 810964 E: padrealed@gmail.com

THOMAS, Mrs Alison Margaret. b 55. Birm Univ BSocSc 77. Qu Foundn Birm 13. **d** 16 **p** 17. NSM Stafford St Mary and Marston *Lich* 16–19; C 19; NSM Stafford St Chad 16–19; C 19; C Stafford St Paul and St Thos from 19. *3 Sandringham Close, Stafford ST17 0AB* T: (01785) 259767 M: 07542-887924 E: revdalison@gmail.com

THOMAS, Andrew Herbert Redding. b 41. Lon Coll of Div 66. **d** 69 **p** 70. C Cromer *Nor* 69–72; Holiday Chapl 72–76; R Grimston w Congham *Nor* 76–83; R Roydon All SS 76–83; C-in-c Ewell St Paul Howell Hill CD *Guildf* 83–89; V Howell Hill 89–95; RD Epsom 93–95; TR Beccles St Mich *St E* 95–04; P-in-c Worlingham w Barnby and N Cove 98–01; rtd 04; PtO *St E* 04–16; *Nor* from 04. *9A Corner Street, Cromer NR27 9HW* T: (01263) 515091 E: ahrthomas@waitrose.com

THOMAS, Andrew Nigel. b 75. Ox Brookes Univ BA 13. Westcott Ho Cam 08. **d** 10 **p** 11. C The Cookhams *Ox* 10–13; Chapl RN 13–14; R Dulverton w Brushford, Brompton Regis etc *B & W* from 14. *The Vicarage, High Street, Dulverton TA22 9DW* T: (01398) 323018 E: and73w@me.com *or* dulvertonbenefice@gmail.com

THOMAS, Andrew Robert. b 80. G&C Coll Cam BA 03. Oak Hill Th Coll BA 09. **d** 09 **p** 10. C Angmering *Chich* 09–12; C Cambridge St Matt *Ely* 12–17; P-in-c Doncaster St Mary and St Paul *Sheff* from 17. *The Vicarage, 59 St Mary's Road, Doncaster DN1 2NR* M: 07786-376615 E: andythomas196@yahoo.co.uk

THOMAS, Anina Jane. b 76. Ex Univ BA 97 Edge Hill Coll of HE PGCE 02. St Mellitus Coll 17. **d** 19. C Lache cum Saltney *Ches* from 19. *19 Capeland Close, Saltney, Chester CH4 8PU* M: 07582-199167 E: anina@stmarkssaltney.org.uk

THOMAS, Anne Valerie. *See* NOBLE, Anne Valerie

THOMAS, Barrie. *See* THOMAS, Illtyd Barrie

THOMAS, Canon Barry Wilfred. b 41. Univ of Wales (Cardiff) BD 75. St Mich Coll Llan 72. **d** 75 **p** 76. C Porthmadog *Ban* 75–78; V Llanegryn and Llanfihangel-y-Pennant etc 78–82; TR Llanbeblig w Caernarfon and Betws Garmon etc 82–94; Sec Dioc Coun for Miss and Unity 81–94; Can Ban Cathl 89–94; Chapl Monte Carlo *Eur* 95–00; V Llanfihangel Ystrad and Cilcennin w Trefilan etc *St D* 00–06; rtd 06; PtO *Eur* from 07. *46 Ezel Court, Heol Glan Rheidol, Cardiff CF10 5NS* E: barry.thomas379@btinternet.com

THOMAS, Bernard. *See* THOMAS, Edward Bernard Meredith

THOMAS, Bernard. *See* THOMAS, Elwyn Bernard

THOMAS, Brian. *See* THOMAS, David Brian

THOMAS, The Ven Charles Edward. b 27. Univ of Wales (Lamp) BA 51. Coll of Resurr Mirfield 51. **d** 53 **p** 54. C Ilminster w Whitelackington *B & W* 53–56; Chapl St Mich Coll Tenbury 56–57; C St Alb St Steph 57–58; V Boreham Wood St Mich 58–66; R Monksilver w Brompton Ralph and Nettlecombe *B & W* 66–74; P-in-c Nettlecombe 68–69; R S Petherton w The Seavingtons 74–83; RD Crewkerne 77–83; Adn Wells, Can Res and Preb Wells Cathl 83–93; rtd 93; PtO *St D* 93–17. *Geryfelin, Tregaron SY25 6ND* T: (01974) 298102

THOMAS, Charles Leslie. b 58. Qu Coll Birm 09. **d** 11 **p** 12. C Sevenhampton w Charlton Abbots, Hawling etc *Glouc* 11–15; V Worc St Wulstan 15–18; RD Worc E 16–18; PtO *Lich* 18–19; P-in-c Wolverhampton St Andr 19; V from 19. *The Vicarage, High Street, Albrighton, Wolverhampton WV7 3EQ* T: (01902) 373415 M: 07542-532662 E: revcharlesthomas@gmail.com

THOMAS, Charles Moray Stewart Reid. b 53. BNC Ox BA 74 MA 79. Wycliffe Hall Ox 75. **d** 78 **p** 79. C Bradf Cathl 78–81; C Barnsbury St Andr and H Trin w All SS *Lon* 81–90; TV Barnsbury 90–99; Chapl Lon Goodenough Trust 99–08; V Grayshott *Guildf* 08–18; rtd 18; PtO *Eur* from 16. *Jubilee Cottage, Hospital Road, Shirrell Heath, Southampton SO32 2JR* T: (01329) 833174 E: moray@thethomases.org.uk

THOMAS, Clive Alexander. b 49. Open Univ BA 77 St Luke's Coll Ex CertEd 71. STETS 94. **d** 97 **p** 99. NSM Southwick St Mich *Chich* 97–01; C Bridport *Sarum* 01–04; TV Shaston 04–09; TR Shaftesbury 09–14; rtd 14. *2 Marlborough Park, Ilfracombe EX34 8JB* T: (01271) 600089 E: rev.clivet@gmail.com

THOMAS, David. b 49. **d** 08 **p** 09. NSM Barnes *S'wark* 08–12; PtO 12–14; Asst Chapl Richmond Charities' Almshouses 14–18; rtd 18. *8 Church Estate Almshouses, Richmond TW9 1UX* T: (020) 8948 4188 *or* 8940 7812 M: 07596-018177 E: david.thomas497@googlemail.com

THOMAS, David Brian. b 45. MIEEE. St D Dioc Tr Course 82. **d** 85 **p** 86. NSM Llandysul *St D* 85–87; NSM Lampeter Pont Steffan w Silian 88–92; NSM Lampeter and Ultra-Aeron 92–96; P-in-c Llanfihangel Genau'r-glyn and Llangorwen

96–97; V 97–10; AD Llanbadarn Fawr 00–10; rtd 10; PtO *Lich* from 15. *5 Willowdene, St Martin's Road, Gobowen, Oswestry SY10 7GA* T: (01691) 662629 E: dbrianthomas@yahoo.com

THOMAS, David Edward. b 60. Univ of Wales (Lamp) BA 83. St Mich Coll Llan 85. **d** 86 **p** 87. C Killay *S & B* 86–89; P-in-c Newbridge-on-Wye and Llanfihangel Brynpabuan 89–90; V 90–91; V Brecon St David w Llanspyddid and Llanilltyd 91–09; V Glasbury and Llowes w Clyro and Betws from 09. *The Vicarage, 4 The Birches, Glasbury, Hereford HR3 5NW* T: (01497) 847156 E: thomas3693@btinternet.com

THOMAS, The Very Revd David Glynne. b 41. Dur Univ BSc 63. Westcott Ho Cam 64. **d** 67 **p** 68. C St John's Wood *Lon* 67–70; Min Can St Alb 70–72; Chapl Wadh Coll Ox 72–75; C Ox St Mary V w St Cross and St Pet 72–75; Bp's Dom Chapl 75–78; P-in-c Burnham 78–82; TR Burnham w Dropmore, Hitcham and Taplow 82–83; R Coolangatta Australia 83–86; R Toowoomba 86–87; Can Res Worc Cathl 87–99; Dean Brisbane 99–03; Chapl to Abp Brisbane 03–06; rtd 06. *173 Edgewater Village, 171 David Low Way, Bli Bli QLD 4560, Australia* T: (0061) (7) 5450 8224 E: davidthomas@westnet.com.au

THOMAS, David Godfrey. b 50. St Chad's Coll Dur BA 71 Fitzw Coll Cam BA 74 MA 78. Westcott Ho Cam 72. **d** 75 **p** 76. C Kirkby *Liv* 75–78; TV Cov E 78–88; TR Canvey Is *Chelmsf* 88–92; R Wivenhoe 92–09; R Shenfield 09–16; rtd 16; PtO *Chelmsf* from 18. *6 Inglis Road, Colchester CO3 3HU* T: (01206) 576565 M: 07875-126953 E: davidthomas50@tiscali.co.uk

THOMAS, David Jeffrey. d 15 **p** 16. NSM Llansadwrn w Llanwrda and Manordeilo *St D* from 15. *Llwyncelyn, Manordeilo, Llandeilo SA19 7BP* T: (01550) 777758 E: djt292@btinternet.com

THOMAS, David John. b 34. Univ of Wales (Swansea) St D Coll Lamp. St D Dioc Tr Course 85. **d** 88 **p** 89. NSM Cwmaman *St D* 88–96; Public Preacher 96–11; PtO from 11. *9 New School Road, Garnant, Ammanford SA18 1LL* T: (01269) 823936

THOMAS, David Jonathan. b 80. **d** 19. C Hounslow St Paul and Gd Shep *Lon* from 19. *360 Beavers Lane, Hounslow TW4 6HJ* E: david@hwparish.org.uk

THOMAS, Prof David Richard. b 48. BNC Ox BA 71 MA 74 Fitzw Coll Cam BA 75 MA 80 Lanc Univ PhD 83. Ridley Hall Cam 73 Qu Coll Birm 79. **d** 80 **p** 81. C Anfield St Columba *Liv* 80–83; C Liv Our Lady and St Nic w St Anne 83–85; Chapl CCC Cam 85–90; V Witton *Blackb* 90–93; Bp's Adv on Inter-Faith Relns 90–93; Lect Cen for Study of Islam and Chr-Muslim Relns Selly Oak 93–04; Sen Lect Birm Univ 99–04; Reader 04–07; Prof Christianity and Islam from 07; PtO *Derby* 05–11; LtO 11–16; Hon Can Th Derby Cathl 11–16; PtO *B & W* from 17; Preb Wells Cathl from 18. *Department of Theology and Religion, University of Birmingham, Edgbaston, Birmingham B15 2TT* T: 0121-415 8373 E: d.r.thomas.1@bham.ac.uk

THOMAS, Canon David Thomas. b 44. St Cath Coll Cam BA 66 MA 70. Cranmer Hall Dur. **d** 71 **p** 72. C Chorlton-cum-Hardy St Clem *Man* 71–74; Chapl Salford Tech Coll 74–79; P-in-c Pendleton St Thos *Man* 75–77; V 77–80; TR Gleadless *Sheff* 80–90; RD Attercliffe 86–90; V Benchill *Man* 90–99; TV Wythenshawe 99–00; AD Withington 99–00; P-in-c Stretford St Matt 00–09; Hon Can Man Cathl 09; PtO *Man* from 09; *Carl* 10–15. *40 Longmead Road, Salford M6 7EU* T: 0161-737 5867 E: tom-hil@talk21.com

THOMAS (née THOMSON), Mrs Dorothy Lucille. b 39. Univ of Wales (Lamp). **d** 00 **p** 10. OLM Pontnewydd *Mon* 00–15; rtd 15. *Raldoro, Mount Pleasant Road, Pontnewydd, Cwmbran NP44 1BD* T: (01633) 771353

THOMAS, Edward. *See* THOMAS, Charles Edward

THOMAS, Edward Harald Meredith. b 21. Leeds Univ BA 44 Univ of Qld BEd 68 BD 72. Coll of Resurr Mirfield 47. **d** 49 **p** 50. C St Mary-at-Lambeth *S'wark* 49–54; C Portsea N End St Mark *Portsm* 54–56; V Portsea All SS 56–64; R Woolloongabba Australia 64–72; Perm to Offic Brisbane 72–78; Miss Chapl 78–92; rtd 92. *33 Highfield Street, Durack QLD 4077, Australia* T: (0061) (7) 3372 3517 M: 41-622 7121 E: bernard_thomas@iinet.net.au

THOMAS (née REEVES), Mrs Elizabeth Anne. b 45. Sheff Univ BA 67 PGCE 75. SWMTC 87. **d** 90 **p** 94. Par Dn Stoke Damerel *Ex* 90–93; Dioc Children's Adv *Bradf* 93–01; Par Dn Baildon 93–94; C 94–96; P-in-c Denholme Gate 96–01; P-in-c Tuxford w Weston and Markham Clinton *S'well* 01–08; rtd 08; PtO *S'well* from 18. *The Lyrics, 113 The Oval, Retford DN22 7SD* T: (01777) 700047 E: liz.thomas@sky.com

THOMAS, The Ven Elwyn Bernard. b 45. Univ of Wales (Swansea) BSc 68. St Mich Coll Llan BD 71. **d** 71 **p** 72. C Aberdare St Fagan *Llan* 71–74; C Merthyr Dyfan 74–76; R Dowlais 76–86; V Llangynwyd w Maesteg 86–00; Can

Llan Cathl 98–00; Adn St As 00–11; R Llandyrnog and Llangwyfan 00–11; P-in-c 11–14; rtd 11; PtO St As 15–17; P-in-c Bala 17; TV Penedeyrn Miss Area 18; PtO from 18. *11 Cae Glas, Trefnant, Denbigh LL16 5UB* T: (01745) 731732 E: elwynbernardthomas@btinternet.com

THOMAS, Ernest Keith. b 49. St Mich Coll Llan 73. **d** 76 **p** 77. C Swansea St Gabr *S & B* 76–79; C Killay 79–81; Prec Kimberley Cathl S Africa 81–84; R Kimberley St Aug 84–92; R Kimberley St Alb 89–92; Can Kimberley Cathl 86–92; V Aberdare *Llan* 93–96; Sub-Dean Bloemfontein Cathl S Africa 96–10; R Welkom from 10. *PO Box 231, Welkom, 9460 South Africa* T: (0027) (57) 352 3497 or (57) 352 5664 F: 352 2272 M: 83-709 0976 E: stmatt@global.co.za

THOMAS, Gabrielle Rachael. b 74. Bris Univ BA 95 Ches Univ MTh 13 Nottm Univ PhD 17. St Jo Coll Nottm 11. **d** 15 **p** 16. C Teddington St Mary w St Alb *Lon* 15–17; Research Assoc Dur Univ 17–19; Hon Min Can Dur Cathl 18–19; PtO from 19; Lect Yale Div Sch USA from 19. *Yale Divinity School, 409 Prospect Street, New Haven CT 06511, USA* E: gabrielle.thomas@yale.edu

THOMAS, Mrs Gail Lesley. b 71. Wolv Univ BA 96. Trin Coll Bris 15. **d** 17 **p** 18. C Yate *Bris* from 17. *22 Hampden Close, Yate, Bristol BS37 5UW* T: (01454) 855013 M: 07746-050607 E: gail_l_thomas@hotmail.com or gail@yateparish.org.uk

THOMAS, Gareth David. b 75. Sheff Univ BA 96 Ches Univ PGCE 03. All SS Cen for Miss & Min 10. **d** 13 **p** 14. C Ches St Paul 13–15; C Huntington 13–15; Chapl Ches Univ 14–17; NSM Chester St Pet from 17. *6 Jesmond Road, Chester CH1 4EQ* T: (01244) 374697 E: g-thomas@hotmail.co.uk or g.thomas@chester.ac.uk

THOMAS, Gareth Mark. b 72. Cranmer Hall Dur. **d** 10 **p** 11. C Atherton and Hindsford w Howe Bridge *Man* 10–13; TV Daisy Hill, Westhoughton and Wingates 13–16; TV Blackrod, Daisy Hill, Westhoughton and Wingates 16–17; V Hope St Jas and Pendlebury St Jo from 17. *91 Broomhall Road, Pendlebury, Swinton, Manchester M27 8XR* T: 0161-925 0059 M: 07947-389893 E: garethmthomas@hotmail.com

THOMAS, Geoffrey Brynmor. b 34. K Coll Lon BA 56 AKC 56. Ridley Hall Cam 58. **d** 60 **p** 61. C Harlow New Town w Lt Parndon *Chelmsf* 60–65; V Leyton All SS 65–74; V Haley Hill *Wakef* 74–82; R The Winterbournes and Compton Valence *Sarum* 82–89; TV Cheltenham St Mark *Glouc* 89–92; P-in-c Dowdeswell and Andoversford w the Shiptons etc 92–95; RD Northleach 92–95; rtd 95; PtO *B & W* 96–18. *48 Riverside Walk, Midsomer Norton, Bath BA3 2PD* T: (01761) 414146 E: gbt34@btinternet.com

THOMAS, George. b 46. Leeds Univ BEd 69. Cranmer Hall Dur 75. **d** 78 **p** 79. C Highfield *Liv* 78–83; V Chorley St Jas *Blackb* 83–02; P-in-c Blackb St Gabr 02–08; rtd 08; PtO *Blackb* from 08. *80 Severn Drive, Walton-le-Dale, Preston PR5 4TE* T: (01772) 330152

THOMAS, Glyn. b 36. Lon Univ BPharm 61. St Deiniol's Hawarden 80. **d** 82 **p** 83. C Rhyl w St Ann *St As* 83–85; R Llanycil w Bala and Frongoch and Llangower etc 85–03; RD Penllyn 96–03; rtd 03; PtO *St As* from 09. *Blaen-y-Coed, 7 Lon Helyg, Abergele LL22 7JQ* T: (01745) 827725 E: thombala@aol.com

THOMAS, Gordon Herbert. b 43. Guildf Dioc Min Course 00. **d** 00 **p** 01. OLM Cove St Jo *Guildf* 00–13; rtd 13; PtO *Guildf* from 13. *13 Tay Close, Farnborough GU14 9NB* T: (01252) 512347 E: gh.thomas27@btinternet.com

THOMAS, Greville Stephen. b 64. Qu Coll Birm 94. **d** 96 **p** 97. C Hillingdon All SS *Lon* 96–99; C Acton Green 99–04; P-in-c Northolt St Mary 04–06; R 06–14; V Sudbury St Andr from 14. *St Andrew's Vicarage, 956 Harrow Road, Wembley HA0 2QA* T: (020) 8904 4016 E: greville.thomas@london.anglican.org

THOMAS, Canon Harald Daniel. b 34. FInstTT. **d** 97 **p** 05. Par Dn Pontnewydd *Mon* 97–05; NSM 05–16; NSM Cwmbran from 16; Hon Can St Woolos Cathl from 10. *Raldoro, Mount Pleasant Road, Pontnewydd, Cwmbran NP44 1BD* T: (01633) 771353

THOMAS, Miss Hilary Faith. b 43. Ex Univ BA 65 Southn Univ PGCE 66. Trin Coll Bris 90. **d** 94 **p** 95. C Yeovil w Kingston Pitney *B & W* 94–98; V Brislington St Luke *Bris* 98–07; rtd 07; PtO *B & W* 09–12; NSM Mark w Allerton 12–14; PtO from 15. *Brierley, Lower North Street, Cheddar BS27 3HH* T: (01934) 742207 E: hilarythomas@uwclub.net

THOMAS, Hugh Vivian. b 57. Kingston Poly LLB 80 Barrister-at-Law (Lincoln's Inn) 86. SEITE 02. **d** 05 **p** 06. NSM Knockholt w Halstead *Roch* 05–17; P-in-c St Marg Pattens *Lon* 12–14; NSM St Mich Cornhill w St Pet le Poer etc 14–15; PtO 16–17; NSM Tottenham Ct Marg 17–18; NSM W Hampstead St Cuth from 18. *5 The Meadows, Halstead, Sevenoaks TN14 7HD* T: (01959) 532664 E: hughvthomas@btopenworld.com

THOMAS, Huw. See THOMAS, William Huw

THOMAS, Huw Daniel. b 76. Qu Coll Birm. **d** 13 **p** 14. C Salford Sacred Trin and St Phil *Man* 13–16; P-in-c Flixton St Mich from 16. *348 Church Road, Urmston, Manchester M41 6HR* M: 07708-501527 E: huwcantona@yahoo.co.uk

THOMAS, Canon Huw Glyn. b 42. St D Coll Lamp BA 62 Linacre Coll Ox BA 65 MA 69. Wycliffe Hall Ox 62. **d** 65 **p** 66. C Oystermouth *S & B* 65–68; Asst Chapl Solihull Sch 68–69; Chapl and Hd Div 69–73; Selection Sec ACCM 73–78; C Loughton St Jo *Chelmsf* 73–77; V Bury St Jo *Man* 78–83; V Bury St Jo w St Mark 83–86; Dir of Ords 82–87; Can Res and Treas Liv Cathl 87–95; USPG 95–06; Chapl Addis Ababa Ethiopia 95–97; Provost All SS Cathl Cairo 97-01; Can from 01; Prin Edwardes Coll Peshawar Pakistan 01–06; rtd 06; Hon Sen Fell Liv Hope Univ from 07; PtO *Lon* 07–12; *Blackb* 12–14 and 16–17; P-in-c Overton 14–16. *Flat 3, 36 Knowlys Road, Heysham, Morecambe LA3 2PF* T: (01524) 852292 M: 07981-114255 E: huwapglyn@gmail.com

THOMAS, Ian William. b 53. Bedf Coll of Educn CertEd 74. Ox Min Course 89. **d** 92 **p** 93. NSM Fenny Stratford *Ox* from 92. *5 Laburnum Grove, Bletchley, Milton Keynes MK2 2JW* T: (01908) 644457

THOMAS, Illtyd Barrie. b 54. Nazarene Th Coll Man BA 02 MA 06. Cumbria Chr Learning 17. **d** 18 **p** 18. C Carl H Trin and St Barn from 18. *33 Longlands Road, Carlisle CA3 9AD* T: (01228) 529735 M: 07443-549525 E: barriethomas@outlook.com

THOMAS, Jeffrey. See THOMAS, David Jeffrey

THOMAS, Jeffrey Malcolm. **d** 10 **p** 12. C Morriston *S & B* 10–11; C Swansea St Thos and Kilvey 12–14; P-in-c Porth Newydd *Llan* from 14; P-in-c Dinas w Penygraig from 18; C Tonypandy w Clydach Vale w Williamstown from 18. *4 Kimberley Way, Porth CF39 9HS* T: (01443) 551754 E: jeffreymthomas61@yahoo.com

THOMAS, Canon Jennifer Monica. b 58. Wilson Carlile Coll 79 Sarum & Wells Th Coll 91. **d** 93 **p** 94. Par Dn Wandsworth St Paul *S'wark* 93–94; C 94–97; V Forest Hill 97–02; V Mitcham Ascension from 02; Hon Can S'wark Cathl from 14. *The Vicarage, Sherwood Park Road, Mitcham CR4 1NE* T: (020) 8764 1258 E: ascensionchurch@btinternet.com

THOMAS, Jeremy Paul. b 63. Lanc Univ BSc 87. Trin Coll Bris 04. **d** 06 **p** 07. C Aughton Ch Ch *Liv* 06–10; P-in-c Ashton-in-Makerfield St Thos 10–15; V from 15. *The Vicarage, 18 Warrington Road, Ashton-in-Makerfield, Wigan WN4 9PL* T: (01942) 727275 E: jeremy@holmacre.plus.com

THOMAS, John Thurston. b 28. Univ of Wales (Swansea) BSc 48 DipEd 49 Leeds Univ PhD 58 CChem FRSC 65. Glouc Sch of Min 88. **d** 90 **p** 91. NSM S Cerney w Cerney Wick and Down Ampney *Glouc* 90–96; PtO 96–01; *S & B* from 01. *15 Roman Court, Blackpill, Swansea SA3 5BL* T: (01792) 406671

THOMAS, Julian Mark. b 48. Ex Univ BA 05. SWMTC 00. **d** 03 **p** 04. C Okehampton w Inwardleigh, Bratton Clovelly etc *Ex* 03–07; C Essington *Lich* 07–12; rtd 12; PtO *Lich* 13–16. *9 New Minster House, Bird Street, Lichfield WS13 6PR* T: (01543) 253319 E: mark.thomas108@o2.co.uk

THOMAS, Katie Jane. b 71. **d** 14 **p** 15. C Stoke-next-Guildf *Guildf* 14–15; C Guildf H Trin w St Mary 15–18; P-in-c Malden St Jas *S'wark* 18–19; V from 19. *7 Bodley Road, New Malden KT3 5QD*

THOMAS, Keith. See THOMAS, Ernest Keith

THOMAS, Kimberley Ann. b 59. Cranmer Hall Dur 02. **d** 04 **p** 05. C Chesterton *Lich* 04–07; V Stretton w Claymills 07–16; R Mundaring Australia from 16. *11 Mann Street, Mundaring WA 6073, Australia* T: (0061) (8) 9295 1029 E: mundaringparish@westnet.com.au

THOMAS, Leighton. See THOMAS, Adrian Leighton

THOMAS, Canon Leslie Richard. b 45. Lon Coll of Div 65. **d** 69 **p** 70. C Knotty Ash St Jo *Liv* 69–72; C Sutton 72–74; TV 74–77; V Banks 77–82; V Gt Crosby All SS 82–92; P-in-c Marthall and Chapl David Lewis Cen for Epilepsy *Ches* 92–02; V Bickerton, Bickley, Harthill and Burwardsley 02–10; RD Malpas 04–10; Hon Can Ches Cathl 07–10; rtd 10; PtO *Liv* from 16. *7 Fairhaven Road, Southport PR9 9UJ* T: (01704) 227511 E: sandstone1945@gmail.com

THOMAS, Mark. See THOMAS, Julian Mark

THOMAS, Mark Gareth. b 82. Cam Univ BA 04 MPhil 13. **d** 15 **p** 16. C Battersea Rise St Mark *S'wark* 15–18; C Onslow Square and S Kensington St Aug *Lon* from 18. *Holy Trinity Brompton, Ennismore Gardens Mews, London SW7 1JA* T: 08456-447533 E: mark.thomas@htb.org

THOMAS, Preb Mark Wilson. b 51. Dur Univ BA 72 Hull Univ MA 89. Ripon Coll Cuddesdon 76. **d** 78 **p** 79. C Chapelthorpe *Wakef* 78–81; C Seaford w Sutton *Chich* 81–84; V Gomersal *Wakef* 84–92; TR Almondbury w Farnley Tyas 92–01; RD Almondbury 93–01; Hon Can Wakef Cathl 99–01; P-in-c Shrewsbury St Chad w St Mary *Lich* 01–07;

V Shrewsbury St Chad, St Mary and St Alkmund 07–13; RD Shrewsbury 09–13; Preb Lich Cathl 11–13; rtd 13; PtO *Lich* 14–17; Hon C Witney *Ox* from 17. *Mill Farmhouse, Black Bourton, Bampton OX18 2PE* T: (01993) 840368 E: markthomas51@hotmail.com

THOMAS, Martin Russell. b 66. Edin Univ BMus 88 UEA PhD 13 LRSM 02. Ripon Coll Cuddesdon BTh 05. **d** 03 **p** 04. C Wymondham *Nor* 03–06; P-in-c Fulham St Andr *Lon* 06–07; V 07–11; Can Res St E Cathl 11–12; P-in-c Kennington Park St Agnes *S'wark* 12–13; TR Plaistow and N Canning Town *Chelmsf* 14–15; TR Catford (Southend) and Downham *S'wark* from 15. *The Rectory, 353 Bromley Road, London SE6 2RP* M: 07460-257103 E: fathermartinthomas@gmail.com

THOMAS (formerly **WADE), Mary Ruth.** b 70. Leeds Univ BA 92 Wolv Univ PGCE 94. Qu Coll Birm 10. **d** 12 **p** 13. C Albrighton, Boningale and Donington *Lich* 12–15; V from 15. *The Vicarage, High Street, Albrighton, Wolverhampton WV7 3EQ* T: (01902) 373415 or 373160 M: 07857-039641 E: revmarywade@gmail.com

THOMAS, Michael Longdon Sanby. b 34. Trin Hall Cam BA 55 MA 60. Wells Th Coll 56. **d** 58 **p** 59. C Sandal St Helen *Wakef* 58–60; Chapl Portsm Cathl 60–64; V Shedfield 64–69; V Portchester 69–98; rtd 98. *188 Castle Street, Portchester, Fareham PO16 9QH* T/F: (023) 9242 0416 E: thomasfamily73@cwtv.net or anmithomas@gmail.com

THOMAS, Michael Rosser David. b 74. Kent Univ BA 96. St Steph Ho Ox BTh 02. **d** 02 **p** 03. C Aberavon *Llan* 02–05; Min Can Brecon Cathl *S & B* 05–07; Succ 07–17; P-in-c Brecon St Mary w Llanddew 08–11; P-in-c Brecon St Mary 11–13; Bp's Chapl 14–16; TV Old St Pancras *Lon* from 17. *The Rectory, 191 St Pancras Way, London NW1 9NH* T: (020) 7267 3962 E: fr.michael@posp.co.uk

THOMAS, Moray. See THOMAS, Charles Moray Stewart Reid

THOMAS, Ms Natasha Creighton. b 70. St Hild Coll BA 18. **d** 18 **p** 19. NSM Keighley *Leeds* from 18. *12 Laurel Grove, Bingley BD16 2RY* M: 07887-707221 E: natasha.thomas@leeds.anglican.org

THOMAS, Nigel Bruce. b 63. Univ of Wales BD 91. St Jo Coll Nottm MA 98. **d** 97 **p** 98. C Millom *Carl* 97–02; R Benthom *Bradf* 02–07; P-in-c St Breoke and Egloshayle *Truro* 07–08; TR Carew *St D* 08–12; PtO *Sarum* from 12; Chapl HM Pris The Verne 15–18; Chapl HM YOI Portland 15–18; TV Yatton Moor *B & W* from 18. *The Vicarage, 1 Millier Road, Cleeve, Bristol DT11 7QJ* T: (01258) 459414 M: 07817-356651 E: nigelbthomas1@gmail.com

THOMAS, Nigel Clayton. b 52. Leeds Univ BA 76 Univ of Wales (Cardiff) PGCE 77. ERMC 08. **d** 11 **p** 12. C Madrid *Eur* 11–16; P-in-c Nerja and Almuñécar 16–19; Chapl from 19. *Church House, Paseo Tamango Hill 25, Adosado 7, 29793 Torrox Costa (Málaga), Spain* T: (0034) 951 815 736 M: (0034) 608 695 756 E: cofenerja@gmail.com or nigelthomasnta@gmail.com

THOMAS, Ms Pamela Sybil. b 38. Ripon Coll Cuddesdon 88. **d** 90 **p** 94. Par Dn Preston w Sutton Poyntz, Littlemoor etc *Sarum* 90–94; C 94–96; P-in-c Weymouth St Edm 96–05; P-in-c Abbotsbury, Portesham and Langton Herring 97–08; Chapl Westhaven Hosp Weymouth 96–08; rtd 08; Hon C Cullompton, Willand, Uffculme, Kentisbeare etc *Ex* 08–15; PtO *Sarum* from 16. *Rosewood, 22 North Square, Chickerell, Weymouth DT3 4DX* T: (01305) 750903 E: rev.thomas@btinternet.com or revpsthomas22@gmail.com

THOMAS, Canon Patrick Hungerford Bryan. b 52. St Cath Coll Cam BA 73 MA 77 Leeds Univ BA 78 Univ of Wales PhD 82. Coll of Resurr Mirfield 76. **d** 79 **p** 80. C Aberystwyth *St D* 79–81; C Carmarthen St Pet 81–82; R Llangeitho and Blaenpennal w Betws Leucu etc 82–84; Warden of Ords 83–86; R Brechfa w Abergorlech etc 84–01; V Carmarthen St Dav from 01; Can St D Cathl from 00. *St David's Vicarage, 4 Penllwyn Park, Carmarthen SA31 3BU* T: (01267) 234183 E: canon.patrick@yahoo.co.uk

THOMAS, Paul Richard. b 75. Univ of Wales (Cardiff) BA 96 MA 99 Hon ARAM 11. Ripon Coll Cuddesdon BA 01 MA 06. **d** 02 **p** 03. C Wanstead St Mary w Ch Ch *Chelmsf* 02–06; C St Marylebone w H Trin *Lon* 06–11; V Paddington St Jas from 11; Chapl St Marylebone C of E Sch 08–11; Chapl R Academy of Music *Lon* 08–12; AD Westmr Paddington from 16; Acting Adn Charing Cross 17–19; PtO *Ox* 18–19. *St James's Vicarage, 6 Gloucester Terrace, London W2 3DD* T: (020) 7262 1265 M: 07967-753671 E: vicar@stjamespaddington.org.uk

THOMAS, Canon Paul Robert. b 42. NOC. **d** 82 **p** 83. C Hull St Jo Newland *York* 82–84; P-in-c Rowley 84–87; Soc Resp Officer Hull 84–87; R Rowley w Skidby 87–88; TR Barking St Marg w St Patr *Chelmsf* 88–93; Gen Sec and Admin St Luke's Hosp for Clergy 93–03; Can and Preb Chich Cathl 98–03; P in O 99–12; rtd 03; PtO *Nor* 03–14; P-in-c Erpingham w Calthorpe, Ingworth, Aldborough etc 14–18; PtO 18–19; Hon C Caston, Griston, Merton, Thompson etc from 19. *11 Cecil Road, Dereham NR20 4AN* E: synergyatwork@aol.com

THOMAS, The Ven Paul Wyndham. b 55. Oriel Coll Ox BA 76 BTh 78 MA 80. Wycliffe Hall Ox 77. **d** 79 **p** 80. C Llangynnwyd w Maesteg *Llan* 79–85; TV Langport Area *B & W* 85–90; P-in-c Thorp Arch w Walton *York* 90–93; Clergy Tr Officer 90–04; V Nether w Upper Poppleton 93–04; P-in-c Castle Town *Lich* 04–11; RD Stafford 05–11; Local Par Development Adv Stafford Area 10–11; Adn Salop from 11; P-in-c Forton from 11. *The Vicarage, Tong, Shifnal TF11 8PW* T: (01902) 372622

THOMAS, Peter James. b 53. Lon Univ BSc 75. Trin Coll Bris 77. **d** 80 **p** 81. C Hucclecote *Glouc* 80–84; C Loughborough Em *Leic* 84–85; TV Parr *Liv* 85–92; V Eckington and Defford w Besford *Worc* 92–05; RD Pershore 00–05; P-in-c Norton sub Hamdon, W Chinnock, Chiselborough etc *B & W* 05–17; P-in-c Stoke sub Hamdon 12–17; R Ham Hill Villages 17–19; RD Ivelchester 07–13; rtd 19; PtO *B & W* from 19. *8 Irwell Green, Taunton TA1 2TA* E: pthomas5@aol.com

THOMAS, Peter Rhys. b 37. TCD BA 59 MA 72 MInstPkg MCIPD. **d** 72 **p** 73. C Tuam w Cong, Ballinrobe and Aasleagh *T, K & A* 73–75; I 75–77; C Bingley All SS *Bradf* 77–79; V Shelf 79–81; Producer Relig Broadcasting Viking Radio 81–84; P-in-c Croxton *Linc* 81–82; P-in-c Ulceby 81–82; P-in-c Wootton 81–82; P-in-c Ulceby Gp 82; V 82–84; R E and W Tilbury and Linford *Chelmsf* 84–89; I Celbridge w Straffan and Newcastle-Lyons *D & G* 89–93; I Youghal Union *C, C & R* 93–99; Dioc Communications Officer (Cork) 95–99; Can Cork Cathl 97–99; Preb Cloyne Cathl 97–99; rtd 99; Rep Leprosy Miss Munster from 00. *Abina Cottage, Ballykenneally, Ballymacoda, Co Cork, Republic of Ireland* T/F: (00353) (24) 98082 E: prthomas@iol.ie

THOMAS, Peter Wilson. b 58. K Coll Lon BD 80 AKC 80. Ripon Coll Cuddesdon 80. **d** 82 **p** 83. C Stockton St Pet *Dur* 82–85; TV Solihull *Birm* 85–90; V Rednal 90–05; Chapl MG Rover 95–05; P-in-c Balsall Common 05–10; V from 10. *St Peter's House, Holly Lane, Balsall Common, Coventry CV7 7EA* T/F: (01676) 532721 E: frpeter@uwclub.net

THOMAS, Canon Philip Harold Emlyn. b 41. Cant Univ (NZ) BA 64 MA 77 Dur Univ PhD 82. Melbourne Coll of Div BD 68. **d** 68 **p** 69. C Adelaide H Trin Australia 68–71; LtO Dio Christchurch New Zealand 71–77; Fell and Chapl Univ Coll Dur 77–83; V Heighington *Dur* 84–10; AD Darlington 94–00; Hon Can Dur Cathl 07–10; rtd 10; PtO *Glouc* from 14. *2 Gloucester Street, Cirencester GL7 2DG* E: philip.thomas7@btinternet.com

THOMAS, Philip John. b 52. Liv Poly BSc 74 Leeds Poly 77. Trin Coll Bris 94. **d** 96 **p** 97. C Skelton w Upleatham *York* 96–97; C Acomb St Steph and St Aid 97–01; V Woodthorpe *S'well* 01–15; V Cinderhill 15–17; Chapl MU from 03; rtd 17; PtO *S'well* from 18. *28 Lambley Lane, Gedling, Nottingham NG4 4PA* M: 07897-003409 E: philipthomas323@gmail.com

THOMAS, Ramon Lorenzo. b 44. Victoria Univ Wellington BCA 73 Mass Inst of Tech MSc 80 CA 73. Oak Hill Th Coll 89. **d** 97 **p** 98. NSM Yateley *Win* 97–99; Chairman Judah Trust from 99; PtO *Chich* from 10. *58 Rock Gardens, Bognor Regis PO21 2LF* T: (01243) 825523 E: judahtrust@aol.com

THOMAS, Rhys. *See* THOMAS, Peter Rhys

THOMAS, Richard Nathan. b 76. Ch Ch Coll Cant BA 98. Ridley Hall Cam 11. **d** 13 **p** 14. C Ealing St Paul *Lon* 13–16; V Tunbridge Wells St Phil *Roch* from 16. *St Philip's Vicarage, Birken Road, Tunbridge Wells TN2 3TE* T: (01892) 512071 M: 07786-132897 E: richnthomas@gmail.com

THOMAS, Robert Graham. b 53. G&C Coll Cam BA 75 MA 79 Imp Coll Lon PhD 78 CEng 82 FIMechE 93. SAOMC 04. **d** 06 **p** 07. C Bathampton w Claverton *B & W* 06–10; P-in-c Trowbridge St Jas and Keevil *Sarum* 10–11; R from 11; Chapl Wilts Coun from 11. *The Rectory, Union Street, Trowbridge BA14 8RU* T: (01225) 350647 E: rob.thomas@cantab.net

✠**THOMAS, The Rt Revd Roderick Charles Howell.** b 54. LSE BSc 75. Wycliffe Hall Ox 91. **d** 93 **p** 94 **c** 15. C Plymouth St Andr w St Paul and St Geo *Ex* 93–95; C Plymouth St Andr and Stonehouse 95–99; P-in-c Elburton 99–05; V 05–15; Preb Ex Cathl 12–15; Suff Bp Maidstone *Cant* from 15; Hon Asst Bp Lon, S'wark and Ex from 15; Chelmsf, Sheff, Man, Nor, Ches, Ely, and Roch from 16; Lich, Bris and Birm from 17; Ox from 18. *The Old Vicarage, 29 St John's Meadow, Blindley Heath, Lingfield RH7 6JU* T: (01342) 834140 M: 07906-331110 E: bishop@bishopofmaidstone.org

THOMAS, Mrs Ruth Alison Mary. b 57. York Univ BA 79 Dur Univ PGCE 80 MA 96. NEOC 07. **d** 09 **p** 10. NSM Dur St Giles from 09; NSM Shadforth and Sherburn 09–12. *68 Gilesgate, Durham DH1 1HY* T: 0191-386 0402 M: 07855-236063 E: ruththomas.durham@gmail.com

THOMAS, Mrs Sheila Mary Witton. b 49. STETS 06. **d** 09 **p** 10. NSM Marnhull *Sarum* 09–14; PtO 15–17; NSM W Parley from 17. *11A West Moors Road, Ferndown BH22 9SA* M: 07748-974206 E: sheila2is@yahoo.co.uk

THOMAS, Sonia Patricia. *See* BARRON, Sonia Patricia

THOMAS, Preb Stephen Blayney. b 35. St D Coll Lamp BA 62. Bp Burgess Hall Lamp. **d** 63 **p** 64. C Ledbury *Heref* 63–67; C Bridgnorth w Tasley 67–68; C Clun w Chapel Lawn, Bettws-y-Crwyn and Newcastle 68–73; C Clungunford w Clunbury and Clunton, Bedstone etc 68–73; V Worfield 73–84; RD Bridgnorth 81–83; R Kingsland 84–96; P-in-c Eardisland 84–96; P-in-c Aymestrey and Leinthall Earles w Wigmore etc 84–96; R Kingsland w Eardisland, Aymestrey etc 97–99; Preb Heref Cathl 85–01; rtd 99; PtO *Heref* from 00; *Worc* from 00. *28 Castle Close, Burford, Tenbury Wells WR15 8AY* T: (01584) 819642 E: stephenbthomas@btinternet.com

THOMAS, Canon Stuart Grahame. b 54. Pemb Coll Cam BA 77 MA 81 Ban Univ MPhil 15 ATCL 97. Ridley Hall Cam 85. **d** 87 **p** 88. C Guildf H Trin w St Mary 87–91; V Churt 91–94; V Ewell St Fran 94–14; Dioc Ecum Officer 99–07; RD Epsom 07–14; R Frimley from 14; Hon Can Guildf Cathl from 12. *The Rectory, 3 Parsonage Way, Frimley, Camberley GU16 8HZ* T: (01276) 23291 E: revstuart.thomas@btinternet.com

THOMAS, Miss Susan. b 58. City of Liv Coll of HE BA 80 PGCE 81. SNWTP 10. **d** 13 **p** 14. C Formby H Trin and Altcar *Liv* 13–17; C Chapelfields 17–18. *19 Hampton Road, Formby, Liverpool L37 6EJ* T: (01704) 398990 E: thomass1109@aol.com

THOMAS, Susan Linda. b 60. SEITE 08. **d** 11 **p** 12. NSM Coulsdon St Jo *S'wark* from 11. *40 West Hill, South Croydon CR2 0SA*

THOMAS, Canon Sydney Robert. b 44. Univ of Wales (Swansea) BA 65 MA 83. St D Coll Lamp LTh 67. **d** 67 **p** 68. C Llanelli *St D* 67–77; V Pontyberem 77–01; TR Cwm Gwendraeth 01–08; RD Cydweli 94–05; Can St D Cathl 94–08; Chan St D Cathl 01–03; Treas St D Cathl 03–08; rtd 09; PtO *St D* from 09. *40 Waungoch, Upper Tumble, Llanelli SA14 6BX* T: (01269) 841677 E: sydvic@sydvic.plus.com

THOMAS, Thomas. b 68. Selw Coll Cam BA 90. Wycliffe Hall Ox 91. **d** 93 **p** 94. C Much Woolton *Liv* 93–97; V Carr Mill 97–10; C Springfield *Birm* 10–11; P-in-c 11–15; V from 15. *St Christopher's Vicarage, 172 Woodlands Road, Springfield, Birmingham B11 4ET* T: 0121-702 2745 M: 07980-650801 E: tom172thomas@btinternet.com

THOMAS, Thomas Alan. b 37. K Coll Lon BD 60 AKC 60. St Boniface Warminster 60. **d** 61 **p** 62. C Washington *Dur* 61–65; C Bishopwearmouth St Mary V w St Pet CD 65–70; V Ruishton w Thornfalcon *B & W* 70–82; R Hutton 82–94; V Frome Ch Ch 94–96; Chapl Victoria Hosp Frome 94–96; R Camerton w Dunkerton, Foxcote and Shoscombe *B & W* 96–00; rtd 00; PtO *B & W* from 00. *12 Farrington Way, Farrington Gurney, Bristol BS39 6US* T: (01761) 453434

THOMAS, Timothy Charles Rank. b 75. Trin Coll Bris. **d** 14 **p** 15. C Walkden and Lt Hulton *Man* 14–17; P-in-c Bowling St Jo *Leeds* from 17. *96 Lister Avenue, Bradford BD4 7QS* T: (01274) 681300 E: tim@stjohnsbowling.com

THOMAS, Virginia Jacqueline. b 48. UEA BA 70. Yale Div Sch MDiv 97. **d** 00 **p** 01. NSM Chelsea St Luke and Ch Ch *Lon* 00–04; NSM W Brompton St Mary w St Pet 04–06; P-in-c 05–06; P-in-c W Brompton St Mary w St Peter and St Jude 06–10; V 10–14; rtd 14; V Gt w Lt Tew and Heythrop *Ox* from 14. *The Vicarage, New Road, Great Tew, Chipping Norton OX7 4AG* T: (01608) 683584 E: ginnytea@googlemail.com

THOMAS, Vivian Ivor. b 52. S Bank Univ MSc 95 Regent Coll Vancouver MCS 97 K Coll Lon PhD 02. **d** 08 **p** 09. NSM Hammersmith St Paul *Lon* from 08. *76 Rannoch Road, London W6 9SP* T: (020) 7384 5954 M: 07767-777891 E: vivian.thomas@btinternet.com *or* viv.thomas@formation.org.uk

THOMAS, William Huw. b 65. Yorks Min Course 15. **d** 17 **p** 18. NSM Pitsmoor Ch Ch *Sheff* from 17. *140 Abbeyfield Road, Sheffield S4 7AY* M: 07525-688479 E: huw.thomas@sheffield.anglican.org

THOMAS, The Ven William Jordison. b 27. K Coll Cam BA 50 MA 55. Cuddesdon Coll 51. **d** 53 **p** 54. C Byker St Ant *Newc* 53–56; C Berwick H Trin 56–59; V Alwinton w Holystone and Alnham 59–70; V Alston cum Garrigill w Nenthead and Kirkhaugh 70–80; P-in-c Lambley w Knaresdale 72–80; RD Bamburgh and Glendale 81–83; TR Glendale Gp 80–83; Adn Northd and Can Res Newc Cathl 83–92; rtd 92; PtO *Newc* from 92. *20 Robert Adam Court, Bondgate Without, Alnwick NE66 1PH* T: (01665) 602644

THOMAS, Wilson Hugo. b 40. **d** 01 **p** 05. Barbados 01–05; NSM Frimley *Guildf* 05–07. *3B Ansell Road, Frimley GU16 8BS* T: (01276) 681652 E: wilsonthomas56@googlemail.com

THOMAS ANTHONY, Brother. See DEHOOP, Thomas Anthony
THOMASSON, Keith Duncan. b 69. St Pet Coll Ox BA 91
MA 97 Sarum Coll MA 15 Lon Inst of Educn PGCE 92. Ripon
Coll Cuddesdon BA 01 Bossey Ecum Inst Geneva. d 02 p 03.
C Lancaster St Mary w St John and St Anne *Blackb* 02–04; C
Longridge 04–06; Partnership P E Bris 06–11; Chapl Hants
Colleg Sch 11–14; Hon C Romsey *Win* 11–14; Sen Chapl
Alabaré Chr Care Centres from 14. *Alabaré Christian Care
Centres, 2 Watt Road, Salisbury SP2 7UD* M: 07500-788148
E: k.thomasson@alabare.co.uk
**THOMASSON-ROSINGH, Mrs Anna Clara Abena (Anna-
Claar).** b 74. Ede Chr Coll BEd 97 Utrecht Univ MA 01
Man Univ PhD 09. Leiden Protestant Sem 98 Bossey Ecum
Inst Geneva 01. d 14 p 15. Remonstrant Min 02–14; C
Clarendon *Sarum* 14–18; Dir Studies Sarum Coll 15–18; TV
Chalke Valley *Sarum* from 18. *The Vicarage, Nunton, Salisbury
SP5 4HP* M: 07419-121822
THOMPSON (née SMETHAM), Canon Abigail Laura. b 75.
K Coll Lon BMus 97 Clare Coll Cam BA 05. Westcott Ho
Cam 03. d 06 p 07. C Sheff Manor 06–10; P-in-c Clifton
St Jas 10–15; V 15–18; Dean of Women's Min 15–18; Can
Res and Sub-Dean St Alb from 18. *Deanery Barn, Sumpter
Yard, Holywell Hill, St Albans AL1 1BY* M: 07947-475073
E: rev.abi.thompson@gmail.com
THOMPSON, Adrian David. b 68. Univ of Wales (Abth)
BSc 93 PhD 97 Bris Univ PGCE 98. Wycliffe Hall Ox 93.
d 05 p 06. C Blackb St Gabr 05–08; Chapl Abp Temple
Sch Preston 09–11; TV Cockermouth Area *Carl* from
11; C Gt Broughton from 14. *The Rectory, Lorton Road,
Cockermouth CA13 9DU* T: (01900) 821288 or 829926
E: adrian.cockermouth@gmail.com or adrian@cateam.org.uk
THOMPSON, Canon Andrew David. b 68. Poly of Wales
BSc 90 Nottm Univ MA 03. Wycliffe Hall Ox 98. d 00
p 01. C Oakwood *Derby* 00–04; Asst Chapl UAE 05–06;
Chapl Kuwait 06–10; Chapl Abu Dhabi St Andr UAE from
10; Hon Can Bahrain from 11. *St Andrew's, PO Box 262,
Abu Dhabi, United Arab Emirates* T: (00971) 2446 1361
E: andythompson1968@swissmail.org
THOMPSON, Andrew Robert William. d 13 p 14.
Belfast St Donard *D & D* 13–14; C Donaghcloney
w Waringstown 14–17. *8 Hatchley Close, Sutton
Heath, Woodbridge IP12 3TX* M: 07803-062874
E: andrew7hompson@yahoo.co.uk
THOMPSON, Canon Anthony Edward. b 38. Bris Univ
BA 61. Ridley Hall Cam 61. d 63 p 64. C Peckham St Mary
Magd *S'wark* 63–66; SAMS Paraguay 67–72; C Otley *Bradf*
72–75; TV Woughton *Ox* 75–82; P-in-c Lower Nutfield
S'wark 82–02; V S Nutfield w Outwood 02–03; RD Reigate
91–93; Local Min Adv Croydon Episc Area 93–03; Hon
Can S'wark Cathl 03; rtd 03; PtO *Chich* from 04. *3 The
Curlews, Shoreham-by-Sea BN43 5UQ* T: (01273) 440182
E: tonythompsonsbs@hotmail.com
THOMPSON, Benjamin Joseph Peter. b 79. Trin Coll Cam
BA 00 MA 04. Oak Hill Th Coll MTh 12. d 12 p 13. C Moreton-
in-Marsh w Batsford, Todenham etc *Glouc* 12–16; NSM from
16. *32 Croft Holm, Moreton-in-Marsh GL56 0JH* T: (01608)
238628 M: 07912-675561 E: bjpthompson1@gmail.com
THOMPSON, Brian. b 34. MRICS 65 FRICS 75. St Jo Coll
Nottm 81. d 84 p 85. C Bletchley *Ox* 84–87; V Sneyd Green
Lich 87–99; rtd 99; PtO *Lich* 99–11; *Leic* from 12. *14 Stuart Court,
High Street, Kibworth Beauchamp, Leicester LE8 0LR* T: 0116-
319 7523 E: thompson.brian48@gmail.com
THOMPSON, Carrie Julia Lucy Jadwiga. b 77. Keble Coll
Ox BA 99 MA 04. St Steph Ho Ox MA 06. d 04 p 05. C
Camberwell St Giles w St Matt *S'wark* 04–08; V Forton *Portsm*
from 08; Chapl St Vincent Sixth Form Coll from 08. *The
Vicarage, 10 Spring Garden Lane, Gosport PO12 1HY* T: (023)
9250 3140 E: fortonchurch@gmail.com
THOMPSON, Christopher William. See OGILVIE THOMPSON,
Christopher William
THOMPSON, David. See THOMPSON, John David
THOMPSON, David Arthur. b 37. Clifton Th Coll. d 69
p 70. C Finchley Ch Ch *Lon* 69–72; C Barking St Marg w
St Patr *Chelmsf* 72–75; TV 75–81; V Toxteth Park St Clem
Liv 81–91; TR Parr 91–03; rtd 03; PtO *Sarum* 03–10; *Liv* from
16. *Calm Haven, 21 Arklow Drive, Hale Village, Liverpool
L24 5RN* T: 0151-425 2012
THOMPSON, David John. b 64. Cranmer Hall Dur 92. d 95
p 96. C Poulton-le-Sands w Morecambe St Laur *Blackb*
95–99; V Farington Moss 99–02; V Lea 02–09; Warden
Past Assts 06–09; P-in-c Ringley w Prestolee *Man* 09–10; TV
Farnworth, Kearsley and Stoneclough 10–13; V Walmersley
Road, Bury from 13. *St John's Vicarage, 270 Walmersley Road,
Bury BL9 6NH* T: 0161-797 7652 E: dvjt@outlook.com
THOMPSON, Derrick Lionel. b 65. Trin Coll Bris 13.
d 15 p 16. NSM S Norwood H Innocents *S'wark* 15–18;

P-in-c Thornton Heath St Paul from 18. *19 Oliver Avenue,
London SE25 6TY* T: 020-8768 5387 M: 07342-923138
E: revd.derrick@gmail.com
THOMPSON (née WHEATLEY), Diane. b 59. Goldsmiths'
Coll Lon BMus 80 Anglia Ruskin Univ MA 14 Birm Poly
PGCE 81. Westcott Ho Cam 10. d 12 p 13. C Kings Heath
Birm 12–16; TV Warwick *Cov* from 16. *All Saints' Vicarage,
Vicarage Fields, Warwick CV34 5NJ* T: (01926) 492073
E: revdt.allsaints@gmail.com
THOMPSON, Edward Ronald Charles. b 25. AKC 51. d 52
p 53. C Hinckley St Mary *Leic* 52–54; Asst Master St Geo
Upper Sch Jerusalem 54–55; Chapl St Boniface Coll
Warminster 56–59; R Hawkchurch w Fishpond *Sarum* 59–63;
V Camberwell St Mich w All So w Em *S'wark* 63–67; P-in-c
St Mary le Strand w St Clem Danes *Lon* 67–74; R 74–93; rtd
93; PtO *S'wark* from 95. *3 Woodsyre, Sydenham Hill, London
SE26 6SS* T: (020) 8670 8289 E: woodsyre@btinternet.com
THOMPSON, Ms Eileen Carol. b 46. Lon Univ BA 69.
New Coll Edin MTh 92. d 96 p 97. Par Dn Dhaka St Thos
Bangladesh 96–97; Presbyter Madras H Cross w St Mich
India 97–99; Presbyter in charge Madras St Mary 99–02; V
Pallikunu St Geo and Palla Ch Ch 02–04; Min Livingston
LEP *Edin* 04–13; rtd 13; LtO *Edin* from 13. *4/2 Saxe
Coburg Terrace, Edinburgh EH3 5BU* T: 0131-315 4928
E: eileenthompson@gmail.com
THOMPSON, Canon Elizabeth Gray McManus. d 06 p 07.
NSM Garrison w Slavin and Belleek *Clogh* 06–07; NSM
Rossorry 07–09; NSM Enniskillen 09–11; Bp's C Aghalurcher
w Tattykeeran, Cooneen etc 11–13; NSM Donagh w
Tyholland and Errigal Truagh 13–18; NSM Derryvullen S w
Garvary from 18; Can Clogh Cathl from 19. *En-Rimmon, 6
Tullylammy Road, Irvinestown, Enniskillen BT94 1RN* T: (028)
6862 8258 E: thompson.clogher@btinternet.com
⊕**THOMPSON, The Rt Revd Geoffrey Hewlett.** b 29. Trin
Hall Cam BA 52 MA 56. Cuddesdon Coll 52. d 54 p 55 c 74.
C Northampton St Matt *Pet* 54–59; V Wisbech St Aug *Ely*
59–66; V Folkestone St Sav *Cant* 66–74; Area Bp Willesden
Lon 74–79 and 79–85; Bp Ex 85–99; rtd 99; Hon Asst Bp Carl
from 99. *Low Broomrigg, Warcop, Appleby-in-Westmorland
CA16 6PT* T: (01768) 341281
THOMPSON, Geoffrey Peter. b 58. St Pet Coll Ox BA 80
MA 82. SEITE 99. d 02 p 03. C Cheam *S'wark* 02–06;
C Croydon St Jo 06–11; P-in-c Norbury St Steph and
Thornton Heath 11–15; V from 15. *St Stephen's Vicarage, 9
Warwick Road, Thornton Heath CR7 7NH* T: (020) 8684 3820
E: gtchurch@waitrose.com
THOMPSON, Harold Anthony. b 41. NOC 84. d 87 p 88. C
Leeds Belle Is St Jo and St Barn *Ripon* 87–90; V Leeds St Cypr
Harehills 90–96; V Shadwell 96–06; rtd 06; PtO *Leeds* from
17. *551 Shadwell Lane, Leeds LS17 8AP* T: 0113-266 5913
E: tonythompson1941@gmail.com
THOMPSON, Hewlett. See THOMPSON, Geoffrey Hewlett
THOMPSON, Ian David. b 51. Hull Univ BSc 72. NOC 94.
d 97 p 98. C Blackley St Andr *Man* 97–00; P-in-c 00–06;
R Burnage St Marg 06–16; rtd 16; PtO *Man* from 16. *4
Kinross Avenue, Heywood OL10 3FX* M: 07747-614054
E: iandthompson@virginmedia.com
THOMPSON, Ian George. b 60. SEITE 99. d 02 p 03. NSM
Walworth St Pet *S'wark* 02–05; NSM Dulwich St Clem w
St Pet 05–07; Chapl HM Pris Pentonville 07–11; Chapl
HM YOI Wetherby 11–13; Chapl HM Pris Coldingley
13–16; Chapl HM Pris Wormwood Scrubs 16–18; Chapl
HM Pris Brixton from 18. *HM Prison Brixton, Jebb Avenue,
London SW2 5XF* T: (020) 8588 6052 M: 07985-582257
E: ian.thompson3@justice.gov.uk
THOMPSON, Jane Elspeth Christine. b 58. Sarum
Coll 13. d 16 p 17. NSM Michelmersh and Awbridge and
Braishfield etc *Win* from 16. *36 Five Elms Drive, Romsey
SO51 5RN* T: (01794) 502035 E: jane.thompson@me.com
THOMPSON, Jeremy James Thomas. b 58. Sunderland Univ
BEd 92. Cranmer Hall Dur 94. d 96 p 97. C Bedlington *Newc*
96–00; P-in-c Choppington 00–02; V 02–08; R St John Lee
from 08; V Warden w Newbrough from 08; AD Hexham from
16. *St John Lee Rectory, Acomb, Hexham NE46 4PE* T: (01434)
600268 E: revjjtt@gmail.com
THOMPSON, John David. b 40. Lon Univ BD 65 Ch Ch Ox
DPhil 69. St Steph Ho Ox 65. d 67 p 68. C Solihull *Birm*
67–71; C Biddestone w Slaughterford *Bris* 71–73; Lect Sarum
& Wells Th Coll 71–72; C Yatton Keynell *Bris* 71–73; C Castle
Combe 71–73; V Braughing *St Alb* 74–77; R Digswell 77–82;
TR Digswell and Panshanger 82–98; rtd 00; PtO *Ab* from 15.
11 Russell Street, Boddam, Peterhead AB42 3NG T: (01779)
472680
THOMPSON, Canon John Michael. b 47. Nottm Univ
BTh 77. Linc Th Coll 73. d 77 p 78. C Old Brumby *Linc*
77–80; C Grantham 80–81; TV 81–84; V Holton-le-Clay

84–94; V Holton-le-Clay and Tetney 94–97; R Humshaugh w Simonburn and Wark *Newc* 97–14; Hon Can Newc Cathl 11–14; rtd 14; PtO *Newc* from 14. *2 Woodside Avenue, Corbridge NE45 5EL* E: corbridgemichael@outlook.com

THOMPSON, John Richard. b 62. Birm Univ BA 89. WEMTC 16. **d** 16 **p** 16. C Minchinhampton w Box and Amberley *Glouc* 16–17; C Stroudwater Team from 17; Chapl Glos Hosps NHS Foundn Trust from 13. *Hillgrove, Verney Road, Stonehouse GL10 2QD* T: (01453) 823349 E: cloudend@waitrose.com *or* john.thompson10@nhs.net

THOMPSON, John Turrell. b 57. Sheff Univ BA(Econ) 79 Southn Univ BTh 88. Sarum & Wells Th Coll 83. **d** 86 **p** 87. C Tavistock and Gulworthy *Ex* 86–90; TV Pinhoe and Broadclyst 90–95; P-in-c Northam w Westward Ho! and Appledore 95–96; TV Bideford, Northam, Westward Ho!, Appledore etc 96–00; rtd 00; PtO *Ex* from 00. *Brambles Patch, 39 Westermore Drive, Roundswell, Barnstaple EX31 3XU*

THOMPSON (née LILLIE), Mrs Judith Virginia. b 44. LMH Ox BA 66 Essex Univ MA 73 Univ of E Africa DipEd 67. Gilmore Course IDC 82. **dss** 82 **d** 87 **p** 94. Lawrence Weston *Bris* 82–85; E Bris 85–95; Hon Par Dn 87–95; Chapl HM Rem Cen Pucklechurch 87–91; Chapl Asst Southmead Hosp Bris 91–95; C Knowle St Barn *Bris* 95–02; Bp's Adv for Past Care for Clergy and Families 97–00; Community Th St Mich Coll Llan 00–05; Dir In-House Tr 02–05; Chapl Worcs Acute Hosps NHS Trust 05–09; PtO *Sarum* from 11. *Grove Cottage, Barton Lane, Mere, Warminster BA12 6JA* T: (01747) 860553 E: judithvthompson@aol.com

THOMPSON, Kevin. b 55. Sheff Univ BEd 77 Sheff Hallam Univ MSc 03. Oak Hill Th Coll. **d** 89 **p** 90. C Brinsworth w Catcliffe *Sheff* 89–92; V Kimberworth Park 92–97; V Grenoside 97–98; PtO from 98. *30 Arnold Avenue, Charnock, Sheffield S12 3JB* T: 0114-239 6986 E: kevthompson007@gmail.com

THOMPSON, Louise Margaret. *See* TAYLOR-KENYON, Louise Margaret

THOMPSON, Mark William. b 52. St Jo Coll Nottm 77. **d** 81 **p** 82. C Barnsbury St Andr and H Trin w All SS *Lon* 81–84; C Addiscombe St Mary *S'wark* 84–87; V Thorpe Edge *Bradf* 87–94; Chapl Colchester Hosp Univ NHS Foundn Trust 94–17; rtd 17; PtO *Chelmsf* 18–19. *38 St John's Close, Colchester CO4 0HP* T: (01206) 841648 E: mark.thompson57@virginmedia.com

THOMPSON, Martin Eric. b 52. FCCA. Trin Coll Bris 95. **d** 97 **p** 98. C Heref St Pet w St Owen and St Jas 97–01; P-in-c Huntley and Longhope *Glouc* 01–02; R Huntley and Longhope, Churcham and Bulley 03–05; P-in-c Worfield *Heref* 05–10; V Twigworth, Down Hatherley, Norton, The Leigh etc *Glouc* 10–13; rtd 13; PtO *Heref* 14–19. *1 Church Close, Ross-on-Wye HR9 5HS* T: (01989) 565575 E: revmtthompson123@btinternet.com *or* mandft@hotmail.co.uk

THOMPSON, The Very Revd Matthew. b 68. CCC Cam BA 90 MA 94 MPhil 94. Ridley Hall Cam 91. **d** 94 **p** 95. C Hulme Ascension *Man* 94–97; C Langley and Parkfield 97–98; TV 98–00; P-in-c Man Clayton St Cross w St Paul 00–08; AD Ardwick 03–08; P-in-c Bolton St Pet 08–11; P-in-c Bolton St Phil 08–11; V Bolton St Pet w St Phil 11–17; Borough Dean Bolton 10–17; Hon Can Man Cathl 12–17; Dean Birm from 17. *38 Goodby Road, Birmingham B13 8NJ* T: 0121-262 1840 E: dean@birminghamcathedral.com

THOMPSON, Melvyn Rodney. b 46. K Coll Lon BD 69 MPhil 79 PhD 79 AKC 70. St Aug Coll Cant 69. **d** 70 **p** 71. C Tye Green w Netteswell *Chelmsf* 71–73; C W Brompton St Mary w St Pet *Lon* 73–77; rtd 11. *22 Grasmere Road, Thundersley, Benfleet SS7 3HF* T: (01268) 759268 M: 07963-112512 E: mel@mel-thompson.co.uk

THOMPSON, Mervyn Patrick. b 59. Wilson Carlile Coll 84 Coll of Resurr Mirfield 90. **d** 92 **p** 93. C Sheff St Cath Richmond Road 92–95; V Thurnscoe St Hilda 95–06; P-in-c Thurnscoe St Helen 99–06; R Thurnscoe 06–11; TR S Shields All SS *Dur* from 11. *The Rectory, Tyne Terrace, South Shields NE34 0NF* T: 0191-456 1851 E: mervynthompson@aol.com

THOMPSON, Michael. b 49. NEOC 83. **d** 86 **p** 87. C Ashington *Newc* 86–88; C Ponteland 88–91; TV Newc Epiphany 91–98; P-in-c Choppington 98–99; P-in-c Woldingham *S'wark* 99–02; TV Caterham 02–03; TV Saffron Walden w Wendens Ambo, Littlebury etc *Chelmsf* 03–08; R N Hartismere *St E* 08–14; RD Hartismere 13–14; TV Upper Skerne *Dur* 14–18; rtd 18; PtO *Dur* from 19. *6 Ebberston Court, Spennymoor DL16 6YT* E: fmichael.thompson@btinternet.com

THOMPSON, Michael Bruce. b 53. N Carolina Univ BA 75 Dallas Th Sem ThM 79 Virginia Th Sem 79 Ch Coll Cam PhD 88. **d** 80 **p** 81. Asst Min New Bern N Carolina 80–81; Chair Youth and Evang and Renewal in E Carolina 81–83; Lect Greek Cam Univ 87–88; Lect St Jo Coll Nottm 88–95; Lect NT and Dir of Studies Ridley Hall Cam 95–00; Vice-

Prin from 00. *Ridley Hall, Ridley Hall Road, Cambridge CB3 9HG* T: (01223) 746580 E: mbt2@cam.ac.uk

THOMPSON, Mrs Michelle. b 68. Man Univ BA 89. Ripon Coll Cuddesdon 90. **d** 92 **p** 94. Par Dn Leigh St Mary *Man* 92–94; Asst Chapl HM Pris Full Sutton 95–97; V York St Hilda 97–00; Dir Reader Tr and Local Min Development *Man* 00–03; Chapl HM Pris Styal 04–13; Chapl Wrightington, Wigan and Leigh NHS Foundn Trust 13–17; PtO *Birm* from 18. *38 Goodby Road, Birmingham B13 8NJ* T: 0121-447 9788

THOMPSON, Canon Neil Hamilton. b 48. SS Hild & Bede Coll Dur BEd 72 Leic Univ MA 75. S'wark Ord Course 77 Ven English Coll Rome. **d** 80 **p** 81. C Merton St Mary *S'wark* 80–82; C Dulwich St Barn 82–84; V Shooters Hill Ch Ch 84–87; V S Dulwich St Steph 87–96; Ldr Post Ord Tr Woolwich Area 94–96; R Limpsfield and Titsey 96–08; Can Res and Prec Roch Cathl 08–16; rtd 16. *23 Hathaway Court, Esplanade, Rochester ME1 1QX* T: (01634) 405265 E: neilthompson@houndofheaven.co.uk

THOMPSON, Patrick Arthur. b 36. Dur Univ BA 59. Qu Coll Birm. **d** 61 **p** 62. C W Wickham St Fran *Cant* 61–65; C Portchester *Portsm* 65–68; C Birchington w Acol *Cant* 68–71; V S Norwood St Mark 71–77; P-in-c Norbury St Oswald 77–81; V Norbury St Oswald *S'wark* 81–93; V Sutton New Town St Barn 93–00; rtd 00; LtO *Mor* 00–03 and from 10; Resident P Grantown-on-Spey 04–10. *Rose Cottage, 2 Market Street, Forres IV36 1EF* T: (01309) 675917

THOMPSON, Canon Paul. b 58. Ox Univ BA. Ripon Coll Cuddesdon 80. **d** 83 **p** 84. Chapl Fazakerley Hosp Liv 83–86; C Kirkby *Liv* 83–86; TV Kirkby 86–89; Ind Chapl 86–89; Chapl Kirkby Coll of FE 86–89; CF 89–01; Chapl Epsom Coll 01–19; Hon Can Guildf Cathl 18–19; rtd 19. *The Studio, Dawes Green House, Tapners Road, Leigh, Reigate RH2 8NN* M: 07868-753251

THOMPSON, Canon Paul. b 65. TCD BA 87. CITC 87. **d** 89 **p** 90. C Orangefield w Moneyreagh *D & D* 89–92; I Dromara w Garvaghy 92–97; I Ramoan w Ballycastle and Culfeightrin *Conn* 97–00; Dep Chapl HM Pris Liv 00–01; Chapl HM YOI Portland 01–13; Chapl HM Pris Erlestoke 14–17; I Derryvullen N w Castlearchdale *Clogh* from 17; Preb Clogh Cathl from 19. *The Rectory, 5 Enniskillen Road, Castle Irvine Demesne, Irvinestown, Enniskillen BT94 1BD* T: (028) 6862 1890

THOMPSON, Canon Paul Noble. b 54. Univ of Wales (Cardiff) BMus 77 Univ of Wales (Ban) MPhil 04 Glyndŵr Univ PhD 13. Coll of Resurr Mirfield. **d** 80 **p** 81. C Bargoed and Deri w Brithdir *Llan* 80–83; C Whitchurch 83–84; V Porth w Trealaw 84–90; V Llanharan w Peterston-super-Montem 90–97; Hon C Barry All SS 97–01; Dioc Youth Chapl 90–01; V Lisvane 01–09; Chapl Univ of St Mark and St Jo *Ex* 09–14; C St Woolos Cathl *Mon* from 14; Dioc Dir of Ords from 14; Can St Woolos Cathl from 17. *St Mark's Vicarage, 7 Gold Tops, Newport NP20 4PH* T: (01633) 252046 E: revpaulthompson.pt@gmail.com

THOMPSON, Pauline. *See* WILLCOX, Pauline

THOMPSON, Canon Peter Alrick. b 79. QUB BA 01 TCD MPhil 03 ARIAM 99 FLCM 09. CITC 01. **d** 03 **p** 04. C Clooney w Strathfoyle *D & R* 03–06; I Donaghmore w Upper Donaghmore *Arm* from 06; Hon V Choral Arm Cathl from 06; Succ from 11; Dioc Liturg Officer from 09; St Patr Cathl Dublin from 18. *St Michael's Rectory, 66 Main Street, Castlecaulfield, Dungannon BT70 3NP* T: (028) 8776 1214 M: 07732-856306 E: donaghmore@armagh.anglican.org

THOMPSON, Mrs Rachel Mary. b 65. Roehampton Inst BA 87 Rolle Coll PGCE 88 Nottm Univ MA 08. EMMTC 04. **d** 07 **p** 08. NSM Wilne and Draycott w Breaston *Derby* 07–11; NSM Kirk Hallam 11–14; Missr Erewash Deanery 14–15; PtO *Linc* 15–18; Pet from 18. *159 Cold Overton Road, Oakham LE15 6NU* E: rev.rach@gmail.com

THOMPSON, Raymond Craigmile. b 42. Man Univ BTh. **d** 84 **p** 85. C Clooney *D & R* 84–86; I Urney w Sion Mills 86–92; I Derryvullen N w Castlearchdale *Clogh* 92–05; Chapl to Bp Clogh 02–05; Can Clogh Cathl 03–05; Dean Clogh 05–09; I Clogh w Errigal Portclare 05–09; rtd 09. *En-Rimmon, 6 Tullylammy Road, Irvinestown, Enniskillen BT94 1RN* T: (028) 6862 8258 E: thompson.clogher@btinternet.com

THOMPSON, Robert Craig. b 72. Univ Coll Dur BA 92. Westcott Ho Cam 94. **d** 96 **p** 97. C Wigan All SS *Liv* 96–00; P-in-c Ladybrook *S'well* 00–05; P-in-c Bengeo *St Alb* 05–08; TV Hertford from 08. *The Rectory, Byde Street, Hertford SG14 3BS* T: (01992) 413691 E: revrobert@ntlworld.com

THOMPSON, Robert George. b 71. K Coll Cam BA 93 MA 97. Ripon Coll Cuddesdon MTh 95. **d** 97 **p** 98. C Ruislip St Martin *Lon* 97–01; Chapl Parkside Community NHS Trust Lon 01–09; Chapl R Brompton and Harefield NHS Foundn Trust 09–16; Hon C Holland Park *Lon* 09–15; Hon C Notting Dale St Clem w St Mark and St Jas 15–18; V Kilburn St Mary w All So and W Hampstead St Jas from 18. *St Mary's Vicarage, 134A Abbey Road, London NW6 4SN* T: (020) 7221 3548 E: rgt71@icloud.com

THOMPSON, Roger Quintin. b 63. K Coll Lon BA 85 AKC 85 Nottm Univ PGCE 86 MA 96. Aston Tr Scheme 92 St Jo Coll Nottm 94. **d** 96. C Easton H Trin w St Gabr and St Lawr and St Jude *Bris* 96–00; C Lisburn Ch Ch Cathl *Conn* 00–04; I Kilwaughter w Cairncastle and Craigy Hill 04–15; Partnership Co-ord CMS Ireland from 15. *79 Mill Green, Doagh, Ballyclare BT39 0PH* T: (028) 9334 0518 M: 07734-748919 E: rqtfi@btinternet.com *or* rogerthompson@cmsireland.org

THOMPSON, Ross Keith Arnold. b 53. Sussex Univ BA 75 Bris Univ PhD 82. Coll of Resurr Mirfield 80. **d** 82 **p** 83. C Knowle *Bris* 82–85; TV E Bris 85–94; V Bristol St Aid w St Geo 94–95; V Knowle St Barn and H Cross Inns Court 95–02; Tutor St Mich Coll Llan 02–05; rtd 09. *Grove Cottage, Barton Lane, Mere, Warminster BA12 6JA* T: (01747) 860553 E: rosskathompson@aol.com

THOMPSON, Ruth Jean. *See* GOSTELOW, Ruth Jean

THOMPSON, Mrs Shanthi Hazel Peiris. b 67. Cranmer Hall Dur 07. **d** 09 **p** 10. C Kirkby Lonsdale *Carl* 09–13; P-in-c Staveley, Ings and Kentmere from 13. *The Vicarage, Kentmere Road, Staveley, Kendal LA8 9PA* T: (01539) 821267 M: 07931-446025 E: staveleyvicarage@gmail.com

THOMPSON, Stephen Peter. b 45. Lon Univ BSc 67 Lon Inst of Educn PGCE 71 K Coll Lon BD 77 AKC 77 SOAS Lon BA 82 Poona Univ MPhil 85 PhD 87 FRAS 91. Ripon Coll Cuddesdon. **d** 00. NSM Bedford Park *Lon* 00–01; NSM Isleworth St Fran 01–08; PtO from 08. *12 Minsterley Avenue, Shepperton TW17 8QT* T: (01932) 761956 E: drstephenp.thompson@gmail.com

THOMPSON, Thomas Michael. b 46. **d** 11 **p** 12. NSM Silverton, Butterleigh, Bickleigh and Cadeleigh *Ex* from 11. *Gable Cottage, Bickleigh, Tiverton EX16 8RD* T: (01884) 855309 M: 07866-133640 E: tmdfthompson@uwclub.net

THOMPSON, Timothy Charles. b 51. Lon Univ BSc 73 AKC. Westcott Ho Cam 75. **d** 78 **p** 79. C Ipswich St Mary at Stoke w St Pet etc *St E* 78–81; Ind Chapl *Nor* 81–88; C Lowestoft and Kirkley 81–83; TV 83–88; V Coney Hill *Glouc* 88–94; P-in-c Caister *Nor* 94–00; R 00–16; rtd 16; PtO *Ely* from 16; Hon PV Ely Cathl from 17. *110 Columbine Road, Ely CB6 3WN* T: (01353) 772131 E: tim@timthompson.plus.com

THOMPSON, Canon Timothy William. b 47. Bris Univ CertEd 70 Open Univ BA 78. EMMTC. **d** 88 **p** 89. C Scartho *Linc* 88–91; V Haxey 91–95; P-in-c Surfleet 95–00; Asst Local Min Officer 95–00; RD Elloe W 98–00; P-in-c Linc St Pet-at-Gowts and St Andr 00–09; P-in-c Linc St Botolph 00–09; RD Christianity 02–08; rtd 09; Can and Preb Linc Cathl from 02. *16 Nocton Park Road, Nocton, Lincoln LN4 2BE* T: (01526) 320171 M: 07885-238813 E: timwthompson@btinternet.com

THOMPSON, Canon Tom Malcolm. b 38. Dur Univ BA 60 Man Univ MPhil 93. Bps' Coll Cheshunt 60. **d** 62 **p** 63. C Standish *Blackb* 62–65; C Lancaster St Mary 65–67; V Chorley All SS 67–72; V Barrowford 72–78; RD Pendle 75–78; R Northfield *Birm* 78–82; RD Kings Norton 79–82; V Longton *Blackb* 82–94; RD Leyland 89–94; V Nunthorpe *York* 94–03; Can and Preb York Minster 98–03; RD Stokesley 00–03; rtd 03; PtO *Carl* from 03; *Blackb* from 08. *Wainstones, 6 Greengate Crescent, Levens, Kendal LA8 8QB* T: (015395) 61409 E: tm.levens@btinternet.com

THOMPSON-VEAR, John Arthur. b 76. Sunderland Univ BA 98. St Steph Ho Ox BA 02 MA 06. **d** 03 **p** 04. C Plymouth Crownhill Ascension *Ex* 03–06; Chapl RN 06–08; TV Harrogate St Wilfrid *Ripon* 08–11; CF(V) 10–12. *22 Park House Green, Harrogate HG1 3HW* M: 07377-844888 E: revjatv@gmail.com

THOMPSTONE, Canon John Deaville. b 39. BNC Ox BA 63 MA 67. Ridley Hall Cam 63. **d** 65 **p** 66. C Hoole *Ches* 65–68; C Fulwood *Sheff* 68–71; V Skirbeck H Trin *Linc* 71–77; V Shipley St Pet *Bradf* 77–91; RD Airedale 82–88; V Poynton *Ches* 91–04; Hon Can Ches Cathl 02–04; rtd 04; PtO *Glouc* from 04. *Greyfriars, Broadway Road, Childswickham, Broadway WR12 7HP* T: (01386) 852930 E: johndthompstone@gmail.com

THOMSON, Alexander Keith. b 38. Cranmer Hall Dur BA 63. **d** 64 **p** 65. C Middleton *Man* 64–68; P-in-c Kinloch Rannoch *St And* 68–72; Chapl Rannoch Sch 68–72; Asst Chapl Oundle Sch 72–94; Chapl Laxton Sch 88–94; LtO Pet 73–94; PtO 94–01; rtd 98. *School House Cottage, Alderley Road, Chelford, Macclesfield SK11 9AP* T: (01625) 860996 E: randathomson@outlook.com

THOMSON, Andrew Maitland. b 43. CA(Z) 67. Westcott Ho Cam 78. **d** 80 **p** 81. C Harre Cathl Zimbabwe 80–82;

R Kadoma and P-in-c Chegutu 82–87; R Malborough St Paul Harare 87–92; P-in-c E w N and W Barsham *Nor* 92–95; P-in-c N and S Creake w Waterden 92–94; P-in-c Sculthorpe w Dunton and Doughton 92–94; R N and S Creake w Waterden, Syderstone etc 95–11; rtd 11; C E w W Rudham, Helhoughton etc *Nor* 11–16; PtO from 16. *3 Charles Road, Fakenham NR21 8JX* T: (01328) 862557 E: pandathomson@btinternet.com

THOMSON, Mrs Anja. b 58. STETS. **d** 12 **p** 13. NSM Fishponds St Mary *Bris* 12–17; Chapl HM Pris Ashfield from 17; PtO *Bris* from 17. *HM Prison Ashfield, Shortwood Road, Pucklechurch, Bristol BS16 9QJ* T: 0117-303 8000 M: 07742-968633 E: anjathomson@btinternet.com

THOMSON, Bruce. *See* THOMSON, Sydney Bruce

THOMSON, Miss Caitlin Elizabeth. b 90. Sheff Univ BA 12 MA 14 St Jo Coll Dur BA 17. Cranmer Hall Dur 14. **d** 17 **p** 18. C W Bessacarr *Sheff* 17–19; C Sheff St Mark Broomhill from 19. *26 Elgin Street, Sheffield S10 1UQ* M: 07742-296180 E: caitlin.e.thomson@gmail.com

THOMSON, Canon Celia Stephana Margaret. b 55. LMH Ox MA 83 Birkbeck Coll Lon MA 87 K Coll Lon MA 94. Sarum & Wells Th Coll 89. **d** 91 **p** 94. Par Dn Southfields St Barn *S'wark* 91–94; C 94–95; V W Wimbledon Ch Ch 95–03; Tutor SEITE 95–00; Voc Adv Lambeth Adnry 96–00; Can Res Glouc Cathl from 03. *3 Miller's Green, Gloucester GL1 2BN* T: (01452) 415824 E: cthomson@gloucestercathedral.org.uk

THOMSON, Charles Hector. b 85. UWE BA 07 Reading Univ MSc 08. St Mellitus Coll BA 16. **d** 16 **p** 17. C Upper Chelsea St Simon *Lon* 16–19; C Battersea Rise St Mark *S'wark* from 19. *24 Parma Crescent, London SW11 1LT* M: 07739-825099

THOMSON, Christopher Grant. b 71. Cam Univ BTh 07. Westcott Ho Cam 05. **d** 07 **p** 08. C Bletchingley and Nutfield *S'wark* 07–11; P-in-c Kenley 11–17; P-in-c Purley St Barn 11–17; Asst Dir of Ords Croydon Area 13–17; Chapl Plymouth Univ *Ex* from 17; Public Preacher *Truro* from 17. *Plymouth University, Drake Circus, Plymouth PL4 8AA* T: (01752) 600600 E: revdthomson@btinternet.com

✠**THOMSON, The Rt Revd David.** b 52. Keble Coll Ox MA 78 DPhil 78 Selw Coll Cam BA 80 MA 84 FRSA 06 FSA 08 FRHistS 08. Westcott Ho Cam 78. **d** 81 **p** 82 **c** 08. C Maltby *Sheff* 81–84; TV Banbury *Ox* 84–94; Sec Par and People 84–93; TR Cockermouth w Embleton and Wythop *Carl* 94–02; Adn Carl and Can Res Carl Cathl 02–08; Suff Bp Huntingdon *Ely* 08–18; rtd 18; PtO *Heref* from 19; Hon Asst Bp Heref from 19. *31 Apple Grove, Hereford HR4 0EA* T: (01432) 353008 M: 07771-864550 E: david@skypilots.co.uk

THOMSON, David Francis. b 54. Salford Univ BA 81 CPFA 84. NOC 05. **d** 07 **p** 08. NSM New Bury w Gt Lever *Man* 07–10; P-in-c Ainsworth from 10; C Bury St Mary 13–14; Borough Dean Bury from 17; AD Radcliffe and Prestwich from 19. *The Vicarage, Ainsworth Hall Road, Ainsworth, Bolton BL2 5RY* T: (01204) 398567 M: 07551-437368 E: thomsondf@hotmail.com

THOMSON, Dorothy Lucille. *See* THOMAS, Dorothy Lucille

THOMSON, Canon Elizabeth Jane. b 64. Univ Coll Ox MA 85 DPhil 89 Trin Coll Cam BA 02 Moray Ho Coll of Educn PGCE 90. Westcott Ho Cam 00. **d** 03 **p** 04. C Pilton w Croscombe, N Wootton and Dinder *B & W* 03–07; TV Witney *Ox* 07–14; Can Missr Derby Cathl from 14. *22 Kedleston Road, Derby DE22 1GU* T: (01332) 208995 E: missioner@derbycathedral.org

THOMSON, Elizabeth Lucy. *See* TALBOT, Elizabeth Lucy

THOMSON, Hannah Nadka. b 84. Qu Foundn Birm 16. **d** 18 **p** 19. C Cant St Martin and St Paul from 18. *70 Thanington Road, Canterbury CT1 3XE* E: revhannaht@hotmail.com

THOMSON, James. b 39. St Andr Coll Melrose 58 Episc Sem Austin Texas 88. **d** 62 **p** 63. C Oklahoma City All So USA 89–90; R Oklahoma St Matt 90–95; Assoc R Oklahoma H Trin 95–05; P-in-c Pittenweem *St And* 06–09; P-in-c Elie and Earlsferry 06–09; rtd 09; LtO *St And* 09–11; P-in-c Fraserburgh *Ab* 11–12. *41A South Street, St Andrews KY16 9QR* T: (01334) 479645 E: jim39@talktalk.net

THOMSON, James Maclaren. b 69. Grey Coll Dur BA 91 Univ Coll Lon MA 93. Wycliffe Hall Ox BA 99. **d** 00 **p** 01. C Oulton Broad *Nor* 00–04; V Chatteris *Ely* 04–13; Hon C 13–17; Chapl Qu Eliz Hosp King's Lynn NHS Foundn Trust 13–17; Chapl Kettering Gen Hosp NHS Foundn Trust 17–18; Chapl NW Anglia NHS Foundn Trust from 18. *Chaplaincy Department, Peterborough City Hospital, Bretton Gate, Bretton, Peterborough PE3 9GZ* T: (01733) 673115 E: james.thomson2@nhs.net

✠**THOMSON, The Rt Revd John Bromilow.** b 59. York Univ BA 81 Nottm Univ PhD 01. Wycliffe Hall Ox BA 84 MA 91. **d** 85 **p** 86 **c** 14. C Ecclesall *Sheff* 85–89; Tutor St Paul's Coll Grahamstown S Africa 89–92; Asst P Grahamstown St Bart 90–92; Asst Lect Rhodes Univ 91–92; V Doncaster St Mary *Sheff* 93–01; Dir Min 01–14; Hon Can Sheff

Cathl 01–14; Suff Bp Selby *York* from 14. *Bishop's House, York Road, Barlby, Selby YO8 5JP* T: (01757) 429982 E: bishopofselby@yorkdiocese.org

THOMSON, Julian Harley. b 43. AKC 70. St Aug Coll Cant 70. **d** 71 **p** 72. C Wellingborough All Hallows *Pet* 71–74; Min Can, Prec and Sacr Ely Cathl 74–80; P-in-c Stuntney 76–80; V Arrington 80–91; R Croydon w Clopton 80–91; R Orwell 80–91; R Wimpole 80–91; V Linton 91–96; R Bartlow 91–96; P-in-c Castle Camps 91–96; TR Linton 96–01; RD 99–01; rtd 01; PtO *Nor* from 01. *Lavender Cottage, 7 Abbey Road, Great Massingham, King's Lynn PE32 2HN* T: (01485) 520721 E: thomson5816@btinternet.com

THOMSON, Keith. *See* THOMSON, Alexander Keith

THOMSON, Mark Stephen. b 57. Glas Univ MA 78. Ridley Hall Cam 10. **d** 12 **p** 13. C Market Deeping *Linc* 12–15; C Uffington Gp 15–16; R Quarrington w Old Sleaford from 16. *The Rectory, 6 Spire View, Sleaford NG34 7RN*

THOMSON, Penelope Jane. b 59. ERMC 14. **d** 17 **p** 18. NSM Bp's Hatfield, Lemsford and N Mymms *St Alb* from 17. *74 Pine Grove, Brookmans Park, Hatfield AL9 7BW*

THOMSON, Richard William Byars. b 60. Birm Univ BA 86. Ripon Coll Cuddesdon 86. **d** 88 **p** 89. C Moulsecoomb *Chich* 88–90; P-in-c Kirriemuir *St And* 90–94; P-in-c Piddletrenthide w Plush, Alton Pancras etc *Sarum* 94–02; P-in-c Milborne St Andrew w Dewlish 94–02; Chapl Milton Abbey Sch Dorset 02–12; P-in-c Boxwell, Leighterton, Didmarton, Oldbury etc *Glouc* from 12. *Withymore Vicarage, Old Down Road, Badminton GL9 1EU* T: (01454) 219236 E: revrichardthomson@gmail.com

THOMSON, Robert Douglass. b 37. Lon Univ TCert 61 Newc Univ DAES 70 Dur Univ BEd 75. NEOC 76. **d** 79 **p** 80. NSM Shincliffe *Dur* 79–98; Chapl St Aid Coll Dur 93–99; PtO *Dur* from 99. *11 Hill Meadows, High Shincliffe, Durham DH1 2PE* T: 0191-386 3358 E: rdthomson@btinternet.com

THOMSON, Robin Alexander Stewart. b 43. Ch Coll Cam MA 69 K Coll Lon MTh 72. SEITE 94. **d** 96 **p** 97. NSM Wimbledon Em Ridgway Prop Chpl *S'wark* 96–02 and 10–13; NSM Tooting Graveney St Nic 02–10; rtd 13; PtO *S'wark* from 13. *2 Coppice Road, London SW20 9AS* T: (020) 8540 7748 *or* 8770 9717 F: 8770 9747

THOMSON, Sydney Bruce. b 49. Fuller Th Sem California MA 91 ThM 92 Stirling Univ MLitt 98. Ripon Coll Cuddesdon 05. **d** 07 **p** 08. C Worcs W Rural *Worc* 07–10; TV Leominster *Heref* 10–18; rtd 19. *Address temp unknown* M: 07807-917206 E: beagle67@btinternet.com

THOMSON, Canon Wendy Leigh. b 64. Trin W Univ Vancouver BA 87. Wycliffe Hall Ox BTh 99. **d** 00 **p** 01. C Oulton Broad *Nor* 00–04; C Chatteris *Ely* 04–13; V from 13; Bp's Adv on Women's Min *Chelmsf* from 16; Hon Can Ely Cathl from 16. *The Vicarage, Church Lane, Chatteris PE16 6JA* T: (01354) 692173 E: wendy@chatteris.org

THORBURN, Canon Guy Douglas Anderson. b 50. Trin Coll Ox BA 74 MA 78. Ridley Hall Cam. **d** 83 **p** 84. C Putney St Marg *S'wark* 83–87; R Moresby *Carl* 87–97; V Gt Clacton *Chelmsf* 97–17; C Harwich Peninsula 15–16; AD St Osyth 07–16; AD Harwich 15–16; Hon Can Chelmsf Cathl 15–17; rtd 17; PtO *Chelmsf* 18–19. *51 Pole Barn Lane, Frinton-on-Sea CO13 9NQ* E: revguy.thorburn@virgin.net

THORBURN, Preb Simon Godfrey. b 51. Newc Univ BSc 73 Fitzw Coll Cam BA 77 MA 81 Sheff Univ MMinTheol 97. Westcott Ho Cam 75. **d** 78 **p** 79. C Stafford *Lich* 78–82; C Tettenhall Regis 82–83; TV 83–90; Soc Resp Officer *S'wark* 90–97; V Edgbaston St Geo *Birm* 97–09; AD Edgbaston 03–08; Chapl St Geo Sch Edgbaston 99–08; V Oswestry *Lich* 09–17; R Rhydycroesau 09–17; Preb Lich Cathl 16; rtd 17. *Key Farm, New Road, Far Forest, Kidderminster DY14 9TG* E: simon@thorburns.plus.com

THORIUS, Mrs Lynn Christine. b 51. Leeds Univ BA 11. Yorks Min Course 08. **d** 11 **p** 12. NSM E Richmond *Ripon* 11–14; Bp's Chapl and Policy Adv 14–17; P-in-c Wiske Benefice *Leeds* from 18; Hon Can Ripon Cathl from 19. *The Retreat, Hornby, Northallerton DL6 2JH* T: (01609) 881451 M: 07788-862397 E: lynnthorius12@btinternet.com

THORN (formerly KINGS), Mrs Jean Alison. b 63. RGN 85 Heythrop Coll Lon MTh. Cranmer Hall Dur BA 90. **d** 91 **p** 94. Chapl Bris Poly 91–92; Chapl UWE 92–95; Hon C Bris Lockleaze St Mary Magd w St Fran 91–95; C Fishponds All SS 95–96; Hon C 96–97; V Bris Ch the Servant Stockwood 97–01; Hon C Whitchurch 01–04. *12 Rosamond Avenue, Shipton Gorge, Bridport DT6 4LN* E: jean@jeanandbob.demon.co.uk

THORN, Kevan. b 67. CBDTI 03. **d** 06 **p** 07. NSM Blackpool H Cross *Blackb* 06–10; NSM Kirkham from 10. *16 Bannistre Close, Lytham St Annes FY8 3HS* T: (01253) 713088 E: 08707-621548 E: kevanthorn@btopenworld.com

THORN, Mrs Pamela Mary. b 46. Brentwood Coll of Educn BEd 78. EAMTC 01. **d** 04 **p** 05. NSM Waterbeach

Ely 04–15; PtO from 15. *31 Lode Avenue, Waterbeach, Cambridge CB25 9PX* T: (01223) 864262 M: 07989-491557 E: pamandtrevorthorn@btinternet.com

THORN, Peter. b 50. Man Poly BEd 79. Ridley Hall Cam 82. **d** 84 **p** 85. C Aughton Ch Ch *Liv* 84–87; C Skelmersdale St Paul 87–90; Dioc Children's Officer 87–92; P-in-c Croft w Southworth 90–92; C Streatley *St Alb* 92–95; R Blofield w Hemblington *Nor* 95–96; P-in-c 96–99; Assoc Dioc Dir of Tr 97–99; V Sheff St Bart *Newc* 99–01; P-in-c Shotley St E 01–07; P-in-c Tweedmouth *Newc* 07–09; P-in-c Claydon and Barham *St E* 09–15; C Gt and Lt Blakenham w Baylham and Nettlestead 09–15; rtd 15; P-in-c Flixton St Jo *Man* 15–17; Chapl Bolton NHS Foundn Trust from 16. *St John's Vicarage, Irlam Road, Urmston, Manchester M41 6AP* T: 0161-425 9855 M: 07810-363291 E: peterthorn15@hotmail.co.uk

THORN, Simon Alexander. b 66. Bris Univ BSc 89 PhD 92 FLS 98 FCollP 96. Ox Min Course 06. **d** 09 **p** 10. NSM Abingdon *Ox* 09–12; NSM Hermitage from 12; Chapl Downe Ho Sch Berks 11–14; Chapl Win Coll from 15. *Culver Lodge, St Michael's Road, Winchester SO23 9JE* T: (01962) 856372 M: 07714-194591

THORNALLEY, Graham Paul. b 70. Coll of Resurr Mirfield 05. **d** 07 **p** 08. C Brumby *Linc* 07–09; C Frodingham 09–11; TV Howden *York* 11–17; V Kingston upon Hull St Alb from 17. *St Alban's Vicarage, 62 Hall Road, Hull HU6 8SA* T: (01482) 443566 E: gthornalley@me.com

THORNBURGH, Richard Hugh Perceval. b 52. Sarum & Wells Th Coll. **d** 84 **p** 85. C Broadstone *Sarum* 84–87; TV Beaminster Area 87–95; TV Hanley H Ev *Lich* 96–01; R The Saints *St E* 01–17; C Bungay 14–17; rtd 17. *180 Holmfield Road, Blackpool FY2 9PU* T: (01253) 508850 E: rhpt@pharisaios.co.uk

THORNBY, Mrs Janet. b 40. **d** 06 **p** 07. OLM Cheriton All So w Newington *Cant* 06–10; PtO from 10. *11 Peene Cottages, Peene, Folkestone CT18 8BB* T: (01303) 271267 E: thornbyrobjan@aol.com

THORNE, Mrs Anita Dawn. b 46. Trin Coll Bris 84. **dss** 86 **d** 87 **p** 94. Asst Chapl Bris Poly 86–88; Par Dn Olveston 88–94; P-in-c 94–96; P-in-c Portland All SS w St Pet *Sarum* 96–05; P-in-c Clutton w Cameley *B & W* 05–10; R Clutton w Cameley, Bishop Sutton and Stowey 10–12; rtd 12; PtO *Sarum* from 12; *B & W* 13–18. *2 Armada Way, Dorchester DT1 2TL* T: (01305) 265118 E: thorne391@btinternet.com

THORNE, Mrs Anne. b 55. SWMTC 95. **d** 98 **p** 99. C Crediton and Shobrooke *Ex* 98–01; C Beer and Branscombe 01–03; C Seaton and Beer 03–06; P-in-c Braunton from 06. *The Vicarage, Church Street, Braunton EX33 2EL* T: (01271) 815330 E: vicarthorne@aol.com

THORNE, Mrs Margaret. b 58. Kingston Poly BA 79 Heythrop Coll Lon MA 02 LGSM 78. Ox Min Course 05. **d** 08 **p** 09. C Earley St Pet *Ox* 08–12; V Headington St Mary 12–15; R Chinnor, Sydenham, Aston Rowant and Crowell 15–19; R Coity, Nolton and Brackla w Coychurch *Llan* from 19. *The Rectory, Merthyrmawr Road North, Bridgend CF31 3NH* M: 07512-951780 E: maggie53thorne@gmail.com

THORNE, Valerie Joan. b 60. Chelt & Glouc Coll of HE BA 96. Wycliffe Hall Ox 07. **d** 09 **p** 10. C Wotton-under-Edge w Ozleworth, N Nibley etc *Glouc* 09–10; C Sodbury Vale 10–12; R Brimpsfield w Birdlip, Syde, Daglingworth etc from 12. *The Rectory, Duntisbourne Leer, Cirencester GL7 7AS* T: (01285) 821040 M: 07882-882796 E: rev.val@btinternet.com

THORNETT, Joan. b 38. **d** 07 **p** 09. OLM Stickney Gp *Linc* 07–12; rtd 13; PtO *Linc* 15–18. *Gardeners Cottage, Harrington, Spilsby PE23 4NH* E: fctjw@btinternet.com

THORNEWILL, Canon Mark Lyon. b 25. ALCD 56. **d** 56 **p** 58. C-in-c Bradf Cathl 56–59; C-in-c Otley 59–62; R Lifton *Ex* 62–66; R Kelly w Bradstone 62–66; Dir Past Care Norton Hosps Louisville USA 69–84; Hon Can Louisville Cathl from 70; rtd 96. *116 East Campbell Street, Frankfort KY 40601-3508, USA* T: (001) (502) 696 9274 E: markthornewill@gmail.com

THORNEYCROFT, Preb Pippa Hazel Jeanetta. b 44. Ex Univ BA 65. WMMTC 85. **d** 88 **p** 94. NSM Albrighton *Lich* 88–90; NSM Beckbury, Badger, Kemberton, Ryton, Stockton etc 90–96; P-in-c Shareshill 96–09; P-in-c Essington 07–09; Dioc Adv for Women in Min 93–00; Preb Lich Cathl 99–09; RD Penkridge 01–05; rtd 09; C Tettenhall Wood and Perton *Lich* 10–12; C Hadley and Wellington Ch Ch from 12; Chapl to The Queen 01–14. *Manor Cottage, 21 High Street, Albrighton, Wolverhampton WV7 3JB* T: (01902) 375523 M: 07970-869011 E: pippa@thorneycroft.plus.com

THORNILEY, Canon Richard James Gordon. b 56. Portsm Poly BA 78. St Jo Coll Nottm MTh 95. **d** 97 **p** 98. C Bowbrook S *Worc* 97–01; R Church Lench w Rous Lench and Abbots Morton etc from 01; RD Evesham from 15; Hon Can Worc

Cathl from 17. *The Rectory, Station Road, Harvington, Evesham WR11 8NJ* T: (01386) 870527

THORNLEY, David Howe. b 43. Wycliffe Hall Ox 77. **d** 79 **p** 80. C Burgess Hill St Andr *Chich* 79–83; P-in-c Amberley w N Stoke 83–84; P-in-c Parham and Wiggonholt w Greatham 83–84; V Amberley w N Stoke and Parham, Wiggonholt etc 84–92; P-in-c S w N Bersted 92–99; V 99–08; rtd 08; PtO *Chich* from 14. *Spinaway Cottage, Church Hill, Slindon, Arundel BN18 0RD* M: 07941-834920 E: dhthornley@btinternet.com

THORNLEY, Edward Charles. b 84. Ex Univ BA 05 Anglia Ruskin Univ MA 10. Westcott Ho Cam 08 Yale Div Sch 09. **d** 10 **p** 11. C Dereham and Distr *Nor* 10–13; C St Marylebone w H Trin *Lon* 13–18; Chapl St Marylebone C of E Sch 13–18; Chapl R Academy of Music 13–18; Chapl Fort Worth All SS Episc Sch USA from 18. *All Saints' Episcopal School, 9700 Saints Circle, Fort Worth TX 76108, USA* M: 07709-674615 E: edward.thornley@gmail.com

THORNLEY, Nicholas Andrew. b 56. St Jo Coll Nottm BTh 81. **d** 81 **p** 84. C Frodingham *Linc* 81–84; P-in-c Belton 84–85; V 85–90; V Horncastle w Low Toynton 90–98; V High Toynton 98; R Greetham w Ashby Puerorum 98; RD Horncastle 94–98; TR Gainsborough and Morton 98–11; Can and Preb Linc Cathl 98–11; P-in-c Broughton and Duddon *Carl* 11–17. *Purt ny Shee, Marton Road, Willingham by Stow, Gainsborough DN21 5JU* E: nickthorn1456@gmail.com

THORNS, Mrs Joanne. b 64. Sunderland Univ BSc 86 MRPharmS. Cranmer Hall Dur 97. **d** 99 **p** 00. C Norton St Mary *Dur* 99–04; C Stockton St Chad 02–04; TV Dur N 04–14; Regional Officer NE Chs Acting Together from 14. *19 Lumley Road, Durham DH1 5NP* T: 0191-386 8049 M: 07932-513295 E: regionalofficer@necat.co.uk

THORNTON, Canon Darren Thomas. b 68. Wilson Carlile Coll 90 EAMTC 00. **d** 02 **p** 03. C E Dereham and Scarning *Nor* 02–05; P-in-c Nor St Giles 05–13; V from 13; Chapl UEA from 05; RD Nor E from 14; Hon Can Nor Cathl from 17. *St Giles's Vicarage, 44 Heigham Road, Norwich NR2 3AU* T: (01603) 623724 E: d.thornton@uea.ac.uk

THORNTON, Dominic Oskari. b 83. Kent Univ BA 05 Jes Coll Cam BTh 14. Westcott Ho Cam 12. **d** 15 **p** 16. C Salisbury St Thos and St Edm *Sarum* 15–18. *The Vicarage, Church Lane, Old Basing, Basingstoke RG24 7DJ* M: 07522-862973 E: revdominic@icloud.com

THORNTON, Jackie-Dee. b 80. St Mellitus Coll BA 17. **d** 17 **p** 18. C Gt and Lt Leighs and Lt Waltham *Chelmsf* 17–19; C Gt Waltham w Ford End 17–19; C The Chignals w Mashbury 17–19; NSM Chelmsf Cathl from 19; Chapl Anglia Ruskin Univ from 19. *13 Blackwater Close, Chelmsford CM1 7QJ* T: (01245) 604223 M: 07415-033045 E: jaxdee@hotmail.com

THORNTON, Magdalen Mary. *See* SMITH, Magdalen Mary

THORNTON, Timothy Charles Gordon. b 35. Ch Ch Ox BA 58 MA 61. Linc Th Coll 60. **d** 62 **p** 63. C Kirkholt CD *Man* 62–64; Tutor Linc Th Coll 64–68; Chapl 66–68; Fiji 69–73; Chapl Brasted Place Coll Westerham 73–74; Can Missr *Guildf* 74–79; P-in-c Hascombe 74–79; V Chobham w Valley End 79–84; V Spelsbury and Chadlington Ox 84–87; V Chadlington and Spelsbury, Ascott under Wychwood 87–00; rtd 00; PtO *Carl* from 01. *The Old Cottage, Warcop, Appleby-in-Westmorland CA16 6NX* T: (017683) 41239

⊕**THORNTON, The Rt Revd Timothy Martin.** b 57. Southn Univ BA 78 K Coll Lon MA 97. St Steph Ho Ox 78. **d** 80 **p** 81 **c** 01. C Todmorden *Wakef* 80–82; P-in-c Walsden 82–85; Chapl Univ of Wales (Cardiff) *Llan* 85–86; Sen Chapl 86–87; Bp's Chapl *Wakef* 87–91; Dir of Ords 88–91; Bp's Chapl *Lon* 91–94; Dep P in O 92–01; Prin NTMTC 94–98; V Kensington St Mary Abbots w St Geo *Lon* 98–01; AD Kensington 00–01; Area Bp Sherborne *Sarum* 01–08; Bp Truro 08–17; Bp at Lambeth *Cant* from 17; Bp HM Forces from 17; Hon Asst Bp Lon from 17; Hon Asst Bp Portsm from 17; Hon Asst Bp S'wark from 17. *Lambeth Palace, London SE1 7JU* T: (020) 7898 1200

THOROGOOD, Preb John Martin. b 45. Birm Univ BA 68 PGCE 69. Ox NSM Course 82. **d** 85 **p** 86. NSM Sunningdale *Ox* 85–90; Chapl St Geo Sch Ascot 88–90; TV Camelot Par *B & W* 90–97; V Evercreech w Chesterblade and Milton Clevedon 97–03; RD Cary and Bruton 96–03; R Dulverton and Brushford 03–10; P-in-c Brompton Regis w Upton and Skilgate 08–10; R Dulverton w Brushford, Brompton Regis etc 10–13; RD Exmoor 05–09; Preb Wells Cathl 07–13; rtd 13; PtO *B & W* from 14. *Holden Cottage, 2 West Street, Withycombe, Minehead TA24 6PX* T: (01984) 641745 M: 07966-640771 E: johntvicar@btinternet.com

THOROLD, Alison Susan Joy. *See* HEALY, Alison Susan Joy

THOROLD, Canon Jeremy Stephen. b 59. **d** 04 **p** 05. OLM Gainsborough and Morton *Linc* 04–07; NSM Lanteglos by Camelford w Advent and St Teath *Truro* 07–09; P-in-c

Menheniot and St Ive and Pensilva w Quethiock 09–11; Bp's Dom Chapl 11–16; Minl Development Review Admin 10–14; Bp's Adv for Deliverance Min 14–16; P-in-c Newquay from 16; C St Columb Minor and St Colan from 16; Hon Can Truro Cathl from 16. *Sea Breeze, 28B West Road, Quintrell Downs, Newquay TR8 4LD* M: 07545-961233 E: jem33wheel@aol.com

THOROLD, Canon John Stephen. b 35. Bps' Coll Cheshunt 61. **d** 63 **p** 64. C Cleethorpes *Linc* 63–70; V Cherry Willingham w Greetwell 70–77; P-in-c Firsby w Gt Steeping 77–79; R 79–86; R Aswardby w Sausthorpe 77–86; R Halton Holgate 77–86; R Langton w Sutterby 77–86; V Spilsby w Hundleby 77–86; R Lt Steeping 79–86; R Raithby 79–86; V New Sleaford 86–01; RD Lafford 87–96; Can and Preb Linc Cathl 98–01; rtd 01; PtO *Linc* from 01. *8 Ashwood Close, Horncastle LN9 5HA* T: (01507) 526562

THORP, Mrs Alison Claire. b 63. Kingston Poly BSc 85 Nottm Univ MA 10. EMMTC 06. **d** 09 **p** 10. NSM Bosworth and Sheepy Gp *Leic* 09–13; Chapl Geo Eliot Hosp NHS Trust Nuneaton 12–14; Chapl Burton Hosps NHS Foundn Trust from 14; PtO *Leic* from 13. *Culloden Farm, Gopsall, Atherstone CV9 3QJ* T: (01530) 270350 E: alisonthorp@btconnect.com *or* alison.thorp@burtonft.nhs.uk

THORP, Mrs Helen Mary. b 54. Bris Univ BA 75 MA(Theol) 77 Dur Univ MA 98. Trin Coll Bris 78. **d** 87 **p** 94. NSM Siddal *Wakef* 87–91; NSM Bishopwearmouth St Gabr *Dur* 91–05; NSM Upper Skerne 05–07; NSM Blaydon and Swalwell 07–17; NSM Dinsdale w Sockburn from 17; NSM Hurworth from 17; NSM Middleton St George from 17; Voc Adv 93–05; Tutor Cranmer Hall Dur from 98. *8 Westacres, Middleton St George, Darlington DL2 1LJ* E: h.m.thorp@durham.ac.uk

THORP, Mrs Maureen Sandra. b 47. Man OLM Scheme 92. **d** 95 **p** 96. OLM Heywood *Man* 95–01; P-in-c Shore and Calderbrook 01–06; V Tonge w Alkrington 06–15; Borough Dean Rochdale 10–12; rtd 15; PtO *Man* from 15. *4 Lyn Grove, Heywood OL10 4SS* E: thorpmaureen@aol.com *or* maureensandrathorp@gmail.com

THORP, Norman Arthur. b 29. Tyndale Hall Bris 63. **d** 65 **p** 66. C Southsea St Jude *Portsm* 65–68; C Braintree *Chelmsf* 68–73; P-in-c Tolleshunt D'Arcy w Tolleshunt Major 73–75; V 75–83; R N Buckingham *Ox* 83–95; RD Buckingham 90–95; rtd 95; PtO *Ox* from 97. *27 Baisley Gardens, Napier Street, Bletchley, Milton Keynes MK2 2NE* T: (01908) 370221

THORP, Roderick Cheyne. b 44. Ch Ch Ox BA 65 MA 69. Ridley Hall Cam 66. **d** 69 **p** 70. C Reading Greyfriars *Ox* 69–73; C Kingston upon Hull St Martin *York* 73–76; C Heworth H Trin 76–79; C-in-c N Bletchley CD *Ox* 79–86; TV Washfield, Stoodleigh, Withleigh etc *Ex* 86–96; RD Tiverton 91–96; P-in-c Dolton 96–00; P-in-c Iddesleigh w Dowland 96–00; P-in-c Monkokehampton 96–00; rtd 00; P-in-c Etton w Dalton Holme *York* 00–08; PtO from 09. *4 Stonegate Court, Stonegate, Hunmanby, Filey YO14 0NZ* T: (01723) 892628 E: aranjay@freeuk.com *or* aranjay@phonecoop.coop

THORP, Samuel Stephen. b 92. Lon Sch of Th BA 14. Cranmer Hall Dur 16. **d** 18 **p** 19. C Diss *Nor* from 18. *7 De Lucy Close, Diss IP22 4YL* M: 07506-474538 E: samuel.thorp@disssteamministry.org.uk

THORP, Stephen Linton. b 62. Trin Coll Bris BA 92. **d** 92 **p** 93. C Knutsford St Jo and Toft *Ches* 92–96; TV Newton Tracey, Horwood, Alverdiscott etc *Ex* 96–06; R Necton, Holme Hale w N and S Pickenham *Nor* from 06; RD Breckland from 18. *The Rectory, School Road, Necton, Swaffham PE37 8HT* T: (01760) 722021 E: slthorp@outlook.com

THORP, Susannah Ruth. *See* CURTIS, Susannah Ruth

THORP, Timothy. b 65. St Steph Ho Ox BTh 93. **d** 96 **p** 97. C Jarrow *Dur* 96–99; P-in-c N Hylton St Marg Castletown 99–02; C Felpham and Missr Arundel and Bognor *Chich* 02–07; C Arundel w Tortington and S Stoke 07–08; P-in-c Ernesettle *Ex* 08–11; P-in-c Whitleigh 08–11; C Honicknowle 08–11; P-in-c Plymouth Crownhill Ascension from 11. *The Vicarage, 33 Tavistock Road, Plymouth PL5 3AF* T: (01752) 417618 E: fathertimt@bigfoot.com

THORPE, Preb Christopher David Charles. b 60. Cov Poly BA 83. Ripon Coll Cuddesdon 85. **d** 88 **p** 89. C Norton St Alb 88–92; TV Blakenall Heath *Lich* 92–99; TR Bilston 99–08; V Shifnal and Sheriffhales 08–16; P-in-c Tong 11–16; V Shifnal, Sheriffhales and Tong from 16; Preb Lich Cathl from 07. *The Vicarage, Manor Close, Shifnal TF11 9AJ* T: (01952) 463694 E: chris@christhorpe.org

THORPE, Donald Henry. b 34. St Aid Birkenhead 57. **d** 60 **p** 61. C Mexborough *Sheff* 60–64; C Doncaster St Leon and St Jude 64–67; V Doncaster Intake 67–74; V Millhouses H Trin 74–85; Prec Leic Cathl 85–89; TR Melton Gt Framland 89–93; rtd 93; PtO *Sheff* from 93; *S'well* 93–11. *18 All Hallows Drive, Tickhill, Doncaster DN11 9PP* T: (01302) 743129 E: dsthorpe1@tiscali.co.uk

THORPE (née RICHARDS), Eleanor Poppy. b 93. Ches Univ BA 14. Cranmer Hall Dur 15. **d** 17 **p** 18. C Formby H Trin and Altcar *Liv* from 17. *3 Kenton Close, Formby, Liverpool L37 7EA*

THORPE, Canon Kerry Michael. b 51. Oak Hill Th Coll BD 78. **d** 78 **p** 79. C Upton (Overchurch) *Ches* 78–81; C Chester le Street *Dur* 81–84; V Fatfield 84–93; V Margate H Trin *Cant* 93–98; C 98–09; Dioc Missr 06–11; Min Harvest New Angl Ch 10–11; Dioc Miss and Growth Adv *Cant* 11–16; Hon Can Cant Cathl 08–16; rtd 16; PtO *Cant* from 17. *19 Chapman Fields, Cliffsend, Ramsgate CT12 5LB* T: (01843) 591637 E: kerryandeunice@gmail.com

THORPE, Nathan Andrew. b 93. Univ of Wales (Trin St Dav) BA 14 St Jo Coll Dur BA 17. Cranmer Hall Dur 14. **d** 17 **p** 18. C Formby St Pet *Liv* from 17. *3 Kenton Close, Formby, Liverpool L37 7EA* M: 07505-234115 E: nathanthorpe1@hotmail.co.uk

THORPE, Poppy. *See* THORPE, Eleanor Poppy

✠**THORPE, The Rt Revd Richard Charles.** b 65. Birm Univ BSc 87 Ox Univ BTh 96. Wycliffe Hall Ox 93. **d** 96 **p** 97 **c** 15. C Brompton H Trin w Onslow Square St Paul *Lon* 96–05; P-in-c Shadwell St Paul w Ratcliffe St Jas 05–10; R 10–15; P-in-c Bromley by Bow All Hallows 10–14; Suff Bp Islington from 15; Hon Asst Bp S'wark from 18; P-in-c St Edm the King and St Mary Woolnoth etc *Lon* 17–18; R St Edm and St Mary Woolnoth etc from 18. *26 Canonbury Park South, London N1 2FN* M: 07776-204945 E: bishop.islington@london.anglican.org

THREADGILL, Steven Alan. b 59. Cant Univ (NZ) BA 84 MA 88 Christchurch Teachers' Coll Dip Teaching 88. STETS MA 08. **d** 08 **p** 09. C Lee-on-the-Solent *Portsm* 08–11; C Bundaberg Australia from 11. *8 Hodgetts Court, Bundaberg QLD 4670, Australia* T: (0061) (7) 4151 2621 or (7) 4151 3128 M: 40-769 3897 E: steventhreadgill@yahoo.co.uk

THRELFALL-HOLMES, Miranda. b 73. Ch Coll Cam BA 95 MA 97 Univ Coll Dur PhD 00 St Jo Coll Dur BA 02. Cranmer Hall Dur 00. **d** 03 **p** 04. C Newc St Gabr 03–06; Chapl and Fell Univ Coll Dur 06–12; Interim Prin Ustinov Coll Dur 11–12; V Belmont and Pittington *Dur* 12–17; AD Dur 16–17; TR St Luke in the City *Liv* from 17. *St Bride's Church, Percy Street, Liverpool L8 7LT* M: 07565-521309 E: miranda@threlfall-holmes.net or rector@stlukeinthecity.org.uk

THROUP, Ms Caroline Elizabeth. b 64. St Cath Coll Cam BA 86 MA 90 Man Univ MBA 94 Ches Univ MTh 13. St Jo Coll Nottm 08. **d** 10 **p** 11. C Burnage St Marg *Man* 10–13; R Levenshulme 13–16; Tutor Ridley Hall Cam 16–18; LtO *Ely* 17–18; PtO *Man* 17–18; R Wilmslow *Ches* from 18. *15 Parkway, Wilmslow SK9 1LS* E: caroline.throup@ntlworld.com

THROUP, Marcus. b 78. Nottm Univ PhD 14. **d** 04 **p** 05. Voc Adv and Dioc Dir of Ords *Win* from 16. *The Diocesan Office, Wolvesey Palace, Winchester SO23 9ND* T: (01962) 710984 E: marcus.throup@winchester.anglican.org

THROWER, Clive Alan. b 41. Sheff Univ BSc 62 CEng 90. EMMTC 76. **d** 79 **p** 80. C Derby Cathl 79–86; C Spondon 86–91; Soc Resp Officer 86–91; Faith in the City Link Officer 88–91; Dioc Rural Officer 91; P-in-c Ashford w Sheldon 91; V Ashford w Sheldon and Longstone 92–07; Dioc Rural and Tourism Officer 96–07; RD Bakewell and Eyam 04–07; rtd 07; PtO *Derby* from 07. *Longstone House, 5 Vernon Green, Bakewell DE45 1DT* T: (01629) 814863 E: clive@thrower.org.uk

THROWER, Philip Edward. b 41. Kelham Th Coll 61. **d** 66 **p** 67. C Hayes St Mary *Lon* 66–69; C Yeovil *B & W* 69–71; C Shirley St Jo *Cant* 71–77; P-in-c S Norwood St Mark 77–81; V 81–84; V S Norwood St Mark 85–97; V Malden St Jas 97–07; rtd 07; PtO *S'wark* from 07. *243 Chipstead Way, Banstead SM7 3JN* T: (01737) 218306

THURBURN-HUELIN, David Richard. b 47. St Chad's Coll Dur BA 69 Ex Univ MA 98. Westcott Ho Cam 69. **d** 71 **p** 72. C Poplar *Lon* 71–76; Chapl Liddon Ho Lon 76–80; R Harrold and Carlton w Chellington *St Alb* 81–88; V Goldington 88–95; Dir OLM Truro 95–00; P-in-c Shipston-on-Stour w Honington and Idlicote *Cov* 01–05; R 05–12; rtd 12; PtO *Glouc* from 13. *19 The Firs, Lower Quinton, Stratford-upon-Avon CV37 8TJ* T: (01789) 720967 E: thurburn.huelins@btinternet.com

THURGILL, Sally Elizabeth. b 60. **d** 02 **p** 03. OLM Mattishall and the Tudd Valley *Nor* 02–18; NSM from 18. *3 Dereham Road, Yaxham, Dereham NR19 1RF* T: (01362) 692745 E: sally.thurgill@matvchurch.uk

THURSTON-SMITH, Trevor. b 59. Chich Th Coll 83. **d** 86 **p** 87. C Rawmarsh w Parkgate *Sheff* 86–87; C Horninglow *Lich* 87–91; Chapl for People affected by HIV *Leic* 05–11; P-in-c Broughton Astley and Croft w Stoney Stanton 11–14; V Wigston from 14. *8 Harrogate Way, Wigston LE18 3YB* E: trevor@thursmith.co.uk

THURTELL, Victoria Ann. *See* PASK, Victoria Ann

TIBBO, George Kenneth. b 29. Reading Univ BA 50 MA 54. Coll of Resurr Mirfield 55. **d** 57 **p** 58. C W Hartlepool St Aid *Dur* 57–61; V Darlington St Mark 61–73; V Darlington St Mark w St Paul 73–75; R Crook 75–80; V Stanley 76–80; V Oldham St Chad Limeside *Man* 80–87; V Hipswell *Ripon* 87–95; OCM 90–95; rtd 95; P-in-c Nidd *Ripon* 95–01; PtO 02–04; Hon C Saddleworth *Man* 04–10; Hon C Denshaw 10–14; PtO *Dur* 14–16. *14 Greenside, Greatham, Hartlepool TS25 2HQ* T: (01429) 682854

TIBBOTT (née VINE), Mrs Carolyn Ann. b 63. Anglia Poly Univ BSc 04. NTMTC BA 07. **d** 07 **p** 08. C Gidea Park *Chelmsf* 07–11; V Broomfield from 11. *Broomfield Vicarage, 10 Butlers Close, Chelmsford CM1 7BE* T: (01245) 440318 E: ctibbott@hotmail.com

TIBBS, Simon John. b 71. **d** 08 **p** 09. C Edin Old St Paul 08–11; Lect Coll of Transfiguration Grahamstown S Africa 11–12; PtO *St Alb* 12–13; P-in-c Gt Crosby St Faith and Waterloo Park St Mary *Liv* 13–14; C 14–16; Lect Coll of Transfiguration Grahamstown S Africa from 16. *College of the Transfiguration, PO Box 77, Grahamstown, 6040 South Africa* T: (0027) (46) 622 3332 E: tibbs.simon@gmail.com

TICE, Richard Ian. b 66. Bris Univ BA 88. Wycliffe Hall Ox BTh 94. **d** 94 **p** 95. C Langham Place All So Lon from 94. *12 De Walden Street, London W1G 8RN* T: (020) 7580 8954 or 7580 3522 E: ricospa-grace@allsouls.org

TICKLE, Robert Peter. St Chad's Coll Dur BA 74. St Steph Ho Ox 74. **d** 76 **p** 77. *5 Bramley Court, Orchard Lane, Harrold, Bedford MK43 7BG* T: (01234) 721417

TICKNER, Canon Colin de Fraine. b 37. Chich Th Coll. **d** 66 **p** 67. C Huddersfield SS Pet and Paul *Wakef* 66–68; C Dorking w Ranmore *Guildf* 68–74; V Shottermill 74–91; RD Godalming 89–91; R Ockley, Okewood and Forest Green 91–97; Hon Can Guildf Cathl 96–97; rtd 97; Adv for Past Care *Guildf* 97–12; Chapl St Cath Sch Bramley 97–12; PtO *Guildf* 12–14. *11 Linersh Drive, Bramley, Guildford GU5 0EJ* T: (01483) 898161 E: colin.tickner@sky.com

TICKNER, Canon David Arthur. b 44. AKC 67. **d** 69 **p** 70. C Thornhill Lees *Wakef* 69–71; C Billingham St Aid *Dur* 71–74; TV 74–78; CF 78–98; PtO *Guildf* 96–98; R Heysham *Blackb* 98–13; Hon Can Blackb Cathl 12–13; rtd 13; P-in-c Turners Hill *Chich* from 13. *The Vicarage, Church Road, Turners Hill, Crawley RH10 4PB* T: (01342) 715278 E: david.tickner@gmail.com or stleonardth@gmail.com

TIDESWELL, Mrs Lynne Maureen Ann. b 49. NOC 02. **d** 05 **p** 06. NSM Stoke-upon-Trent *Lich* 05–10; NSM Knutton 10–17; P-in-c 14–17; rtd 17; PtO *Lich* from 17. *74 Grange Road, Cheddleton, Leek ST13 7NP* E: vicarsrest@talktalk.net

TIDEY, Mark James. b 72. Trin Coll Bris 14. **d** 17 **p** 18. NSM Stratton St Margaret w S Marston etc *Bris* from 17. *8 Whitby Grove, Swindon SN2 1NA*

TIDSWELL, David Alan. b 42. CEng 73 FIEE 84 Univ Coll Chich BA 03. St Steph Ho Ox 99. **d** 00 **p** 01. NSM Forest Row *Chich* 00–07; P-in-c Fairwarp 07–10; P-in-c High Hurstwood 07; rtd 17. *Manapouri, Hammerwood Road, Ashurst Wood, East Grinstead RH19 3SA* T: (01342) 822808 E: datidswell@btinternet.com

TIERNAN, Paul Wilson. b 54. Man Univ BA 76. Coll of Resurr Mirfield 77. **d** 79 **p** 80. C Lewisham St Mary *S'wark* 79–83; V Sydenham St Phil from 83. *St Philip's Vicarage, 122 Wells Park Road, London SE26 6AS* T: (020) 8699 4930

TIERNEY, Miss Sarah. b 72. Bp Grosseteste Coll BA(QTS) 94. Trin Coll Bris 17. **d** 19. C Frodingham and New Brumby *Linc* from 19. *The Vicarage, 159 Warwick Road, Scunthorpe DN6 1HH* M: 07765-314456 E: pennine357@gmail.com

TIESEMA-SAMSOM, Mrs Astrid Leonore. b 61. Anglia Ruskin Univ BA 13. ERMC 09. **d** 13 **p** 14. C Harwich Peninsula *Chelmsf* 13–17; V Pill, Portbury and Easton-in-Gordano *B & W* from 17. *The Rectory, 17 Church Road, Easton-in-Gordano, Bristol BS20 0PQ* E: altsamsom@hotmail.com

TIGWELL, Brian Arthur. b 36. S'wark Ord Course 74. **d** 77 **p** 78. C Purley St Mark *S'wark* 77–80; TV Upper Kennet *Sarum* 80–85; V Devizes St Pet 85–99; Wilts Adnry Ecum Officer 88–99; RD Devizes 92–98; rtd 99; PtO *Sarum* from 01; *B & W* 04–18. *15 Sudweeks Court, New Park Street, Devizes SN10 1DX*

TILBY, Canon Angela Clare Wyatt. b 50. Girton Coll Cam BA 72 MA 76. Cranmer Hall Dur 77. **d** 97 **p** 98. Tutor Westcott Ho Cam 97–11; Vice-Prin 01–06; Hon C Cherry Hinton St Jo *Ely* 97–06; V Cambridge St Benedict 07–11; CMD Officer and Can Res Ch Ch *Ox* 11–16; rtd 16; PtO *Portsm* from 16; Hon Can Portsm Cathl from 19. *51 High Street, Portsmouth PO1 2LU* T: (023) 9275 2335 M: 07966-132045 E: angela.tilby@chch.ox.ac.uk

TILDESLEY, Edward William David. b 56. SS Hild & Bede Coll Dur BEd 79. SAOMC 93. **d** 96 **p** 97. Chapl Shiplake Coll Henley 96–99; NSM Emmer Green *Ox* 96–99; Chapl Oakham

Sch 99–00; TV Dorchester *Ox* 00–05; C Aldershot St Mich *Guildf* 05–08; rtd 08; NSM Wyke Regis *Sarum* 10–17; Chapl HM Pris Dorchester from 13; PtO *Sarum* from 17. *Address withheld by request* E: ewdtildesley@outlook.com

TILL, Anthony Richard. b 61. Qu Foundn (Course) 17. **d** 19. NSM Walbrook Epiphany *Derby* from 19. *51 Friary Avenue, Allenton, Derby DE24 9DD* T: (01332) 691354 M: 07801-097859 E: anthonytill@virginmedia.com

TILLBROOK, Richard Ernest. b 50. St Mark & St Jo Coll Lon CertEd 71 ACP 76. NTMTC 96. **d** 99 **p** 00. Hd RE Davenant Foundn Sch Loughton 71–03; NSM High Laver w Magdalen Laver and Lt Laver etc *Chelmsf* 99–03; V Colchester St Barn from 03. *St Barnabas' Vicarage, 13 Abbot's Road, Colchester CO2 8BE* T: (01206) 797481 M: 07818-440530 E: fathercap@hotmail.com

TILLER, Edgar Henry Valentine. b 22. Ex Univ CertEd 69 Open Univ BA 78 ACP 71. Wells Th Coll 57. **d** 59 **p** 60. C Weston-super-Mare St Jo *B & W* 59–62; V Stoke Lane and Leigh upon Mendip 62–67; Asst Master Chaddiford Sch Barnstaple 69–81; PtO *Ex* 67–05; *Llan* 06–12; rtd 91. *42 Llys Pegasus, Ty Glas Road, Llanishen, Cardiff CF14 5ER*

TILLER, The Ven John. b 38. Ch Ch Ox BA 60 MA 64 Bris Univ MLitt 72. Tyndale Hall Bris 60. **d** 62 **p** 63. C Bedford St Cuth *St Alb* 62–65; C Widcombe *B & W* 65–67; Tutor Tyndale Hall Bris 67–71; Chapl 67–71; Lect Trin Coll Bris 71–73; P-in-c Bedford Ch Ch *St Alb* 73–78; Chief Sec ACCM 78–84; Hon Can St Alb 79–84; Can Res Heref Cathl 84–04; Chan 84–02; Dioc Dir of Tr *Heref* 91–00; Adn Heref 02–04; rtd 05; Local Miss and Min Adv (Shrewsbury Area) *Lich* 05–09; Hon C Meole Brace 09; PtO from 10; *Heref* from 17. *2 Pulley Lane, Bayston Hill, Shrewsbury SY3 0JH* T: (01743) 873595 E: canjtiller@btinternet.com

TILLER, Leslie Selwyn. b 54. Peterho Cam BA 75 MA 79 Leeds Univ BA 80. Coll of Resurr Mirfield 78. **d** 81 **p** 82. C W Dulwich All SS and Em *S'wark* 81–85; R Purleigh, Cold Norton and Stow Maries *Chelmsf* 85–93; R Beddington *S'wark* 93–05; R Wensum Benefice *Nor* 05–14; RD Sparham 08–13; P-in-c Flegg Coastal Benefice 14–18; P-in-c Nor St Mary Magd w St Jas from 18. *St Mary Magdalene Vicarage, 10 Crome Road, Norwich NR3 4RQ* E: selwyn@tillett.org.uk

TILLETT, Luke David. b 88. Rob Coll Cam BTh 10. Ridley Hall Cam 07. **d** 10 **p** 11. C Guisborough *York* 10–15; Chapl to Bp Beverley 15; V Acomb Moor from 15; RD City of York from 19. *The Vicarage, 2 Sherringham Drive, York YO24 2SE* T: (01904) 706047   E: vicar@jamesthedeacon.org.uk   *or* lukedavidtillett@gmail.com

TILLETT, Michael John Arthur. b 57. Ridley Hall Cam 96. **d** 98 **p** 99. C Framlingham w Saxtead *St E* 98–01; P-in-c Stoke by Nayland w Leavenheath and Polstead 01–03; R 03–10; RD Hadleigh 07–10; R Ipswich St Helen, H Trin, and St Luke 10–13. *4 Oak Eggar Chase, Pinewood, Ipswich IP8 3TJ* M: 07531-940870 E: revtillett@aol.com

TILLETT, Miss Sarah Louise. b 59. Regent Coll Vancouver MCS 00. Wycliffe Hall Ox 01. **d** 03 **p** 03. C Knowle *Birm* 03–07; P-in-c Bloxham w Milcombe and S Newington *Ox* 07–14; PtO 16–17; Chapl Chantilly *Eur* from 17. *7A Avenue du Bouteiller, 60500 Chantilly, France* E: sarah02tillett@gmail.com

TILLETT, Selwyn. *See* TILLETT, Leslie Selwyn

TILLEY, Canon David Robert. b 38. Kelham Th Coll 58. **d** 63 **p** 64. C Bournemouth St Fran *Win* 63–67; C Moulsecoomb *Chich* 67–70; C Ifield 70–75; TV Warwick *Cov* 76–85; P-in-c Alderminster and Halford 85–96; Dioc Min Tr Adv 85–90; CME Adv 90–04; Assoc Min Willenhall 96–04; Hon Can Cov Cathl 03–04; rtd 04; PtO *Cov* from 04. *17 Coventry Road, Baginton, Coventry CV8 3AD* T/F: (024) 7630 2508 E: david.r.tilley@gmail.com

TILLEY, James Stephen. b 55. St Jo Coll Nottm BTh 84. **d** 84 **p** 85. C Nottingham St Jude *S'well* 84–88; C Chester le Street *Dur* 88–92; Tr and Ed CYFA (CPAS) 92–94; Hd 94–02; PtO *Cov* 92–06; C Nailsea N Trin *B & W* 06–16; Min Trendlewood CD from 17; RD Portishead from 18. *29 Vynes Way, Nailsea, Bristol BS48 2UG* T: (01275) 543332 F: 545803 M: 07971-563229 E: steve.tilley@htnailsea.org.uk

TILLIER, Preb Jane Yvonne. b 59. New Hall Cam BA 81 PhD 85. Ripon Coll Cuddesdon BA 90. **d** 91 **p** 94. Par Dn Sheff St Mark Broomhill 91–94; C 94–95; Chapl Glouc Cathl 95–97; P-in-c Madeley *Lich* 97–03; P-in-c Betley 02–03; PtO 03–04; Chapl and Team Ldr Douglas Macmillan Hospice Blurton 04–08; P-in-c Barlaston *Lich* 08–14; Min Development Adv Stafford Area 10–14; Dioc Adv for Women in Min 11–17; Bp's Adv for Past Care and Wellbeing from 14; Preb Lich Cathl from 11. *10 Plantation Park, University of Keele, Keele, Newcastle ST5 5NA* T: (01782) 639720 E: jane@atherton-tillier.co.uk

TILLOTSON, Simon Christopher. b 67. Lon Univ BA 90 Trin Coll Cam BA 93 MA 96. Ridley Hall Cam 91. **d** 94 **p** 95. C Paddock Wood *Roch* 94–98; C Ormskirk *Liv* 98–00; V Aylesford *Roch* 00–07; TV Whitstable *Cant* from 07. *The Vicarage, Church Street, Whitstable CT5 1PG* T: (01227) 272308 M: 07946-527471 E: tillotsons@gmail.com

TILLYER, Preb Desmond Benjamin. b 40. Ch Coll Cam BA 63 MA 67. Coll of Resurr Mirfield 64. **d** 66 **p** 67. C Hanworth All SS *Lon* 66–70; Chapl Liddon Ho Lon 70–74; V Pimlico St Pet w Westmr Ch Ch *Lon* 74–06; AD Westmr St Marg 85–92; Preb St Paul's Cathl 01–06; rtd 06; PtO *Nor* from 06; *Lon* from 13. *85 Claremont House, 14 Aerodrome Road, London NW9 5NW* T: (020) 8032 5402 E: deslannw9@gmail.com

TILSON, Canon Alan Ernest. b 46. TCD. **d** 70 **p** 71. C Londonderry Ch Ch *D & R* 70–73; I Inver, Mountcharles and Killaghtee 73–79; I Leckpatrick w Dunnalong 79–89; Bermuda 89–05; Hon Can Bermuda Cathl 96–05; I Tullyaughnish w Kilmacrennan and Killygarvan *D & R* 05–10; rtd 10. *Coquina, 28 Castle Way, Glencarse, Perth PH2 7NY* T: (01738) 860914 M: 07470-056227 E: canontilson@gmail.com

TILTMAN, Canon Alan Michael. b 48. Selw Coll Cam BA 70 MA 74. Cuddesdon Coll 71. **d** 73 **p** 74. C Chesterton Gd Shep *Ely* 73–77; C Preston St Jo *Blackb* 77–79; Chapl Lancs (Preston) Poly 77–79; TV Man Whitworth 79–86; Chapl Man Univ (UMIST) 79–86; V Urmston *Man* 86–99; Dir CME 99–03; C Salford Sacred Trin and St Philip 99–02; V Buckley *St As* 04–14; Chan St As Cathl 13–14; rtd 14; PtO *St As* from 14. *The Vicarage, Church Street, Rhosymedre, Wrexham LL14 3EA* T: (01978) 824087 E: a.tiltman@hotmail.com

TILTMAN, Canon Katherine Joan. b 53. St Hugh's Coll Ox MA 74 Man Metrop Univ MSc 02. St Mich Coll Llan 09. **d** 11 **p** 12. C Wrexham *St As* 11–14; C Ruabon and Rhosymedre 14; V 14–16; I Offa Miss Area from 17; Hon Can St As Cathl from 19. *The Vicarage, Church Street, Rhosymedre, Wrexham LL14 3EA* T: (01978) 824087 M: 07753-230644 E: katherinetiltman@gmail.com

TIMBRELL, Keith Stewart. b 48. Edin Th Coll 72. **d** 74 **p** 75. C Chorley St Pet *Blackb* 74–77; C Altham w Clayton le Moors 77–79; Chapl Whittingham Hosp Preston 79–95; Trust Chapl Dorset HealthCare University NHS Foundn Trust 95–08; rtd 08; PtO *Sarum* from 09; *Win* from 10. *9 Whitecross Close, Poole BH17 9HN* T: (01202) 604985 M: 07788-907965 E: clerigo@btinternet.com

TIMMINS, Miss Susan Katherine. b 64. Leic Univ BScEng 85 MICE 91. St Jo Coll Nottm MTh 94. **d** 96 **p** 97. C Iver *Ox* 96–00; P-in-c Pendlebury St Jo *Man* 00–06; V 06–15; Hon Assoc Dioc Dir of Ords 10–15; PtO 15–16; V Appley Bridge and Parbold *Blackb* from 16. *The Vicarage, 5 Tan House Lane, Parbold, Wigan WN8 7HG* T: (01257) 462350 M: 07969-837394 E: susanktimmins@aol.com

TIMMIS (née PITT), Mrs Karen Lesley Finella. b 62. Lon Univ BA 84. Chich Th Coll BTh 94. **d** 94 **p** 95. C Walton-on-the-Hill *Liv* 94–98; P-in-c Warrington St Barn 98–00; V from 00. *The Vicarage, 73 Lovely Lane, Warrington WA5 1TY* T: (01925) 633556

TIMMIS, Vivian Alycia Mary. b 67. Coll of H Cross (USA) BA 89 Birm Univ PhD 98 MA 90 Long Is Univ MSLIS 06. Ripon Coll Cuddesdon 15. **d** 17 **p** 18. C Warwick *Cov* from 17; Chapl Warw Sch from 18. *43 Verdon Place, Barford, Warwick CV35 8BT* T: (01926) 624346 F: 328643 M: 07827-377625   E: asmithhoward@gmail.com   *or* a.timmis@warwickschool.org

TIMS, Brian Anthony. b 43. Solicitor 64. STETS 95. **d** 98 **p** 99. NSM Whitchurch w Tufton and Litchfield *Win* 98–02; NSM Shipton Bellinger 02; PtO 06–13 and from 15; *Ox* from 13. *Fern Bank, Bere Court Road, Pangbourne, Reading RG8 8JT* T: 0118-984 2335 E: brian@timsfamily.com

TINGAY, Kevin Gilbert Xavier. b 43. Sussex Univ BA 79. Chich Th Coll 79. **d** 80 **p** 81. C W Tarring *Chich* 80–83; TV Worth 83–90; R Bradford w Oake, Hillfarrance and Heathfield *B & W* 90–01; RD Tone 96–01; P-in-c Camerton w Dunkerton, Foxcote and Shoscombe 01–10; Bp's Inter Faith Officer 01–10; Bp's Adv for Regional Affairs 01–10; rtd 10; PtO *B & W* from 10. *82B Keyford, Frome BA11 1JJ* T: (01373) 455778 E: kgxt@btinternet.com

TINNISWOOD, Ms Louise. b 71. Staffs Univ BA 96 Cliff Coll MA 11 Huddersfield Univ PGCE 97. St Jo Coll Nottm 10. **d** 12 **p** 13. C Finningley w Auckley *Sheff* 12–15; R Crofton *Leeds* from 15; V Warmfield from 15. *The Vicarage, 2A Ashdene Approach, Crofton, Wakefield WF4 1LZ* M: 07989-862189 E: louise.tinniswood@talktalk.net

TINSLEY, Derek. b 31. ALCM 65 BTh 93 PhD 97. NW Ord Course 73. **d** 76 **p** 77. C Gt Crosby St Faith *Liv* 76–80; V Wigan St Anne 80–85; V Colton w Satterthwaite and Rusland *Carl* 85–93; rtd 93; PtO *Liv* from 93. *Lyndale, 43 Renacres Lane, Ormskirk L39 8SG*

TINSLEY, Preb Derek Michael. b 35. Lon Coll of Div ALCD 66 LTh. **d** 66 **p** 67. C Rainhill *Liv* 66–68; C Chalfont St Peter *Ox* 68–73; P-in-c Maids Moreton w Foxcote 73–74; P-in-c Akeley w Leckhampstead 73–74; P-in-c Lillingstone Dayrell w Lillingstone Lovell 73–74; R N Buckingham 74–82; RD Buckingham 78–82; P-in-c Alstonfield *Lich* 82–84; P-in-c Butterton 82–84; P-in-c Warslow and Elkstones 82–84; P-in-c Wetton 82–84; V Alstonfield, Butterton, Warslow w Elkstone etc 85–95; RD Alstonfield 82–95; Preb Lich Cathl 91–98; V Cheddleton 95–98; Chapl St Edward's Hosp Cheddleton 96–98; rtd 98; PtO *Lich* 98–12; *Derby* 98–17. *30 Gracey Court, Woodland Road, Broadclyst, Exeter EX5 3GA* T: (01392) 466763 E: derekm.tinsley@btinternet.com

TIPLADY, Janet. b 56. Liv Univ BEd 79 St Kath Coll Liv TCert 78. ERMC 10. **d** 12 **p** 13. NSM Warboys w Broughton and Bury w Wistow *Ely* from 12. *22 Locksgate, Somersham, Huntingdon PE28 3HZ* T: (01487) 840193 M: 07713-099346 E: janet.tiplady@gmail.com

TIPP (formerly **NORTHERN**), **Mrs Elaine Joy.** b 54. Leic Univ BSc 75. SEITE 00. **d** 03 **p** 04. C Snodland All SS w Ch Ch *Roch* 03–08. *14 Church Road, Murston, Sittingbourne ME10 3RU* T: (01795) 472574 E: 2xp@talktalk.net

TIPP, James Edward. b 45. Heythrop Coll Lon MA 93. Oak Hill Th Coll 73. **d** 75 **p** 76. C St Mary Cray and St Paul's Cray *Roch* 75–78; C Southborough St Pet w Ch Ch and St Matt 78–82; R Snodland All SS w Ch Ch 82–08; RD Cobham 96–08; Hon Can Roch Cathl 01–08; rtd 08. *14 Church Road, Murston, Sittingbourne ME10 3RU* T: (01795) 472574 E: 2xp@talktalk.net

TIPPING, Canon John Woodman. b 42. AKC 65. **d** 66 **p** 67. C Croydon St Sav *Cant* 66–70; C Plaistow St Mary *Roch* 70–72; V Brockley Hill St Sav *S'wark* 72–83; P-in-c Sittingbourne St Mary *Cant* 83–86; V 86–94; P-in-c Mersham w Hinxhill 94–03; P-in-c Mersham w Hinxhill and Sellindge 03–07; P-in-c Sevington 94–07; P-in-c Brabourne w Smeeth 95–00; AD N Lympne 95–02; Hon Can Cant Cathl 03–07; rtd 07; PtO *St E* from 08. *5 Peace Place, Thorpeness, Leiston IP16 4NA* T: (01728) 454165 E: jwtipping@talk21.com

TIPPLE, Neil. b 58. Loughb Univ BTech 81 Aston Univ MSc 86. WMMTC 01. **d** 04 **p** 05. C Cov E 04–08; V Haywards Heath Ascension *Chich* 08–17. *27 The Warren, Burgess Hill RH15 0DU* M: 07792-198451 E: ginandwhisky@aol.com *or* neiltipple@sky.com

TISDALE, Mark-Aaron Buchanan. b 67. Pittsburgh Univ BA 94. Westcott Ho Cam 00. **d** 02 **p** 03. C Norton *St Alb* 02–05; P-in-c Clifton and Southill 05–11; Chapl St Edm Sch Cant 11–12; C Finchampstead and California *Ox* 12–17; V Glinton, Etton, Maxey, Peakirk and Northborough *Pet* from 17; CF (ACF) 10–18. *The Rectory, 11 Lincoln Road, Glinton, Peterborough PE6 7JR* T: (01733) 252359 E: 9bridgesrector@gmail.com

TITCOMB, Mrs Claire. b 35. SAOMC 95. **d** 98 **p** 99. OLM Witney *Ox* 98–17; Assoc P for Min Development from 01. *30 Beech Road, Witney OX28 6LW* T: (01993) 771234

TITCOMBE, Peter Charles. *See* JONES, Peter Charles

TITFORD, Richard Kimber. b 45. UEA BA 67. Ripon Coll Cuddesdon 78. **d** 80 **p** 80. C Middleton *Man* 80–83; P-in-c Edwardstone w Groton and Lt Waldingfield *St E* 83–90 and 95–02; R 90–94; P-in-c Boxford 00–02; C Assington w Newton Green and Lt Cornard 00–02; R Boxford, Edwardstone, Groton etc 02–03; rtd 03; PtO *St E* from 03; *S'wark* 10–13; *Chelmsf* from 13. *2 Chestnut Mews, Friars Street, Sudbury CO10 2AH* T/F: (01787) 880303 M: 07971-031793 E: richardtitford3@outlook.com

TITLEY, Caroline. *See* TITLEY, Sarah Caroline

TITLEY, Canon David Joseph. b 47. Ex Univ BSc Surrey Univ PhD. Wycliffe Hall Ox. **d** 82 **p** 83. C Stowmarket *St E* 82–85; C Bloxwich *Lich* 85–90; TV 90–95; V Prees and Fauls 95–00; V Clacton St Paul *Chelmsf* 00–13; Hon Can Chelmsf Cathl 12–13; rtd 13; PtO *Chelmsf* from 14. *34 Turner Avenue, Lawford, Manningtree CO11 2LG* T: (01206) 396462 E: titleydj@gmail.com

TITLEY, James Garreth. Bp Grosseteste Coll BA 09. Westcott Ho Cam 16. **d** 19. C Grantham, Manthorpe *Linc* from 19; C Grantham St Wulfram from 19. *12 Lincoln Close, Grantham NG31 8RQ* T: (01476) 576362 E: jtitley@stwulframs.com

TITLEY, Mrs Sarah Caroline. b 58. Newnham Coll Cam MA 83 FCIH 93. SEITE 14 Sarum Coll 15. **d** 17 **p** 18. NSM Wilton w Netherhampton and Fugglestone *Sarum* from 17. *23 The Close, Salisbury SP1 2EH* M: 07808-298137 E: caroline.titley165@btinternet.com

TIZZARD, Canon David John. b 40. LRAM. Sarum Th Coll 65. **d** 68 **p** 69. C Foley Park *Worc* 68–70; Hon C Gravesend St Geo *Roch* 70–73; Miss to Seamen 70–72; PV Truro Cathl 73–75; TV Bemerton *Sarum* 75–79; Dir Soc Resp 79–85; Chapl to the Deaf 79–85; Can and Preb Sarum Cathl 84–85;

R S Hill w Callington *Truro* 85–87; P-in-c Linkinhorne 86–87; Relig Affairs Producer BBC Radio Solent 87–94; V Portswood St Denys *Win* 87–94; P-in-c Distington *Carl* 94–96; Soc Resp Officer 94–96; Hon Can Carl Cathl 94–96; TV Beaminster Area *Sarum* 96–99; rtd 99; PtO *Ex* from 99; *St D* 05–13; P-in-c Cilgerran w Bridell and Llantwyd and Eglwyswrw 13–14. *Chy Trevor, 4 Cambrian Way, Blaenannerch, Cardigan SA43 2BW* T: (01239) 811178

TIZZARD, Peter Francis. b 53. Oak Hill Th Coll 88. **d** 90 **p** 91. C Letchworth St Paul w Willian *St Alb* 90–95; I Drumkeeran w Templecarne and Muckross *Clogh* 95–00; P-in-c Ramsgate Ch Ch *Cant* 00–02; V from 02. *24 St Mildred's Avenue, Ramsgate CT11 0HT* T: (01843) 853732

TOAN, Robert Charles. b 50. Oak Hill Th Coll. **d** 84 **p** 85. C Upton (Overchurch) *Ches* 84–87; V Rock Ferry 87–99; RD Birkenhead 97–99; V Plas Newton 99–06; P-in-c Ches Ch Ch 03–06; V Plas Newton w Ches Ch Ch 07–09; RD Ches 02–08; Cambodia 09–15; rtd 15; PtO *Ches* from 16. *19 Meadows Lane, Saughall, Chester CH1 6AY* T: (01244) 881573 E: bobtoan@gmail.com

TOBIN, Rebecca Louise. b 75. St Martin's Coll Lanc BA 00 Newc Univ MA 12 Sheff Univ BA 14. Coll of Resurr Mirfield 12. **d** 14 **p** 15. C The Boldons *Dur* 14–18; Chapl HM Pris and YOI Stoke Heath 18; Chapl HM YOI Deerbolt from 18; Chapl HM Pris Dur from 18. *HM Prison Durham, 19B Old Elvet, Durham DH1 3HU* T: 0191-332 3400 E: rebecca.tobin@justice.gov.uk

TOBIN, Robert Benjamin. b 70. Harvard Univ AB 93 TCD MPhil 98 Mert Coll Ox DPhil 04 Em Coll Cam BA 07 MA 11 Ox Univ MA 11. Westcott Ho Cam 04. **d** 07 **p** 08. C Beaconsfield *Ox* 07–09; Chapl Harvard Univ USA 09–10; Chapl Oriel Coll Ox 10–17; V Balham St Mary and St Jo *S'wark* from 17; Dir of Ords Kingston Area from 18. *St Mary's Vicarage, 218A Balham High Road, London SW12 9BS* M: 07817-956068 E: vicar@stmarybalham.org.uk *or* rbtobin@cantab.net

TOBIN, Mrs Vanessa Joanne. b 69. Wolv Univ BA 90 Univ of Cen England in Birm PGCE 92. Qu Coll Birm 13. **d** 15 **p** 16. C Wednesfield *Lich* 15–17; C Tettenhall Wood and Perton 17–19; V Pensnett *Worc* from 19. *St Mark's Vicarage, Vicarage Lane, Brierley Hill DY5 4JH* M: 07854-773432 E: revenesstobin@aol.com

TODD, Mrs Abigail Jean. b 85. St Mellitus Coll BA 18. **d** 18 **p** 19. C Woodford Wells *Chelmsf* from 18. *7 Roebuck Lane, Buckhurst Hill IG9 5QR* E: abi@asww.org.uk

TODD, Andrew George. b 67. Worc Coll Ox BA 90 Sheff Univ MA 16 FCA. Coll of Resurr Mirfield 13. **d** 15 **p** 16. C Barbourne *Worc* 15–18; P-in-c from 18. *1 Beech Avenue, Worcester WR3 8PZ* M: 07806-892165 E: revandyt@outlook.com

TODD, Canon Andrew John. b 61. Univ Coll Dur BA 84 K Coll Lon MPhil 98 Cardiff Univ PhD 09. Coll of Resurr Mirfield 85. **d** 87 **p** 88. C Thorpe St Andr *Nor* 87–91; Chapl K Alfred Coll Win 91–94; Sen Asst P E Dereham and Scarning *Nor* 94–97; Dir Studies EAMTC *Ely* 94–01; Vice-Prin 97–01; CME Officer *St E* 01–06; Can Res St E Cathl 01–06; Sub Dean 04–06; Dean Chapl Studies St Mich Coll Llan 06–16; Dir Chapl Studies St Padarn's Inst 16–17; Hon Research Fell Cardiff Univ *Llan* from 07; Progr Dir Sarum Coll from 17; PtO *St E* from 06; *Sarum* from 17. *Sarum College, 19 The Close, Salisbury SP1 2EE* T: (01722) 424836 M: 07785-560558 E: atodd@sarum.ac.uk

TODD, Ms Claire Dianne. b 67. Dur Univ MA 04. Ridley Hall Cam 15. **d** 17 **p** 18. C Marton-in-Cleveland *York* from 17. *31 Grange Wood, Coulby Newham, Middlesbrough TS8 0RT* M: 07940-191383 E: cd.todd@outlook.com

TODD, Clive. b 57. Open Univ BSc 04 Linc Univ MA 11. Linc Th Coll 89. **d** 91 **p** 92. C Consett *Dur* 91–93; C Bensham 93–95; P-in-c S Hetton w Haswell 95–98; R Ebchester 98–04; V Medomsley 98–04; P-in-c S Lawres Gp *Linc* 04–09; RD Lawres 06–07; P-in-c Thanington *Cant* 09–13; Dir of Ords 09–13; R Lower Swale *Leeds* 13–18; P-in-c Brighstone and Brooke w Mottistone *Portsm* 18–19; P-in-c Shorwell w Kingston 18–19; P-in-c Calbourne w Newtown 18–19; P-in-c Shalfleet 18–19; P-in-c Thorley 18–19; P-in-c Freshwater 18–19; P-in-c Yarmouth 18–19; P-in-c Totland Bay 18–19; TR W Wight from 19. *The Rectory, Rectory Lane, Brighstone, Newport PO30 4QH*

TODD, Edward Peter. b 44. Cranmer Hall Dur 86. **d** 88 **p** 89. C Hindley All SS *Liv* 88–91; P-in-c Wigan St Steph 91–96; V 96–98; P-in-c N Meols 98–03; TR 03–05; rtd 05; P-in-c Scarisbrick *Liv* 10–12; PtO from 16. *1B Nixons Lane, Southport PR8 3ES* T: (01704) 570227 E: revtodd6@gmail.com

TODD, Michael Edward. b 62. Brighton Poly BA 84 Surrey Univ PGCE 85. SEITE 96 Ven English Coll Rome 98. **d** 99 **p** 05. C Farnham *Guildf* 99–00; Chapl Surrey Inst Art and Design 99–00; Development Officer Surrey Univ *Guildf*

00–02; Progr Manager and Lect Croydon Coll 02–05; Dep Dir City and Islington Coll 05–07; Hon C Camberwell St Giles w St Matt *S'wark* 04–05; Hon C Newington St Mary from 05; Hd of Sch S Thames Coll 07–10; Chapl Trin Sch Lewisham 11–14; Ch Engagement Manager (Regional) Children's Soc from 15. *The Children's Society, Whitecross Studios, 50 Banner Street, London EC1Y 8ST* T: (020) 7841 4415 M: 07960-517297 E: mike.todd@childrenssociety.org.uk

TODD, Nicholas Stewart. b 61. Open Univ BA 03 MA 08 Cardiff Univ MTh 12. Wycliffe Hall Ox 94. **d** 96 **p** 97. C Gt Wyrley *Lich* 96–99; V Leaton and Albrighton w Battlefield 99–02; R Holbrook, Stutton, Freston, Woolverstone etc *St E* 02–06; CF from 06. *c/o MOD Chaplains (Army)* T: (01264) 383430 F: 381824 E: todds.rus.org

TODD, Canon William Moorhouse. b 26. Lich Th Coll 54. **d** 57 **p** 58. C W Derby St Mary *Liv* 57–61; V Liv St Chris Norris Green 61–97; Hon Can Liv Cathl 92–97; rtd 97; PtO *Liv* from 97. *3 Haymans Grove, West Derby, Liverpool L12 7LD* T: 0151-256 1712 E: williamtodd44@gmail.com

TOLHURST, David. b 72. Cranmer Hall Dur 07. **d** 09 **p** 10. C Middleton St George *Dur* 09–13; C Sadberge 09–13; V Silksworth 13–18; V Sunderland St Matt and St Wilfrid from 18; AD Wearmouth from 17. *St Matthew's Vicarage, Silksworth Road, New Silksworth, Sunderland SR3 2AA* T: 0191-523 9932 E: revtolhurst@btinternet.com *or* vicar@stmatthewsilksworth.org

TOLLEFSEN VAN DER LANS, Alida Thadden Maria (Alja). b 50. Utrecht Univ 89. St Steph Ho Ox 96. **d** 98 **p** 99. C Bramhall *Ches* 98–02; V Knutsford St Cross 02–07; Utrecht Old Catholic Ch *Eur* 07–12; Chapl E Netherlands 12–15; P-in-c Twente from 15; PtO from 18. *Diepenheimseweg 108, 7475 MN Markelo, The Netherlands* T: (0031) (858) 770308 E: alja.tollefsen@xs4all.nl

TOLLER, Peter Sheridan. *See* STARK TOLLER, Peter Sheridan

TÖLLER, Elizabeth Margery. b 53. Leeds Univ BA 75. Ripon Coll Cuddesdon 84. **d** 87 **p** 00. Asst Chapl Leeds Gen Infirmary 87–90; PtO *Nor* 90–91; Chapl Lt Plumstead Hosp 92–93; Chapl Co-ord HM Pris Nor 93–95; Chapl Gt Yarmouth Coll 96–99; PtO *S'wark* 99–00 and 11–18; Hon C Wandsworth St Paul 00–11; Hon Asst Chapl St Chris Hospice Lon 03–10. *Roseneath Cottage, Isle of Iona PA76 6SJ* E: mtoller@gmx.de

TÖLLER, Heinz Dieter. b 52. NEOC 86. **d** 87 **p** 88. C Leeds Gipton Epiphany *Ripon* 87–90; R Coltishall w Gt Hautbois and Horstead *Nor* 90–99; V Wandsworth St Paul *S'wark* 99–18; AD Wandsworth 05–13; rtd 18; Warden Iona Community *Arg* from 18; PtO from 18. *Roseneath Cottage, Isle of Iona PA76 6SJ* T: (01681) 700404 M: 07872-574374 E: htoller@gmail.com

TOLWORTHY, Canon Colin. b 37. Chich Th Coll 64. **d** 67 **p** 68. C Hulme St Phil *Man* 67–70; C Lawton Moor 70–71; C Hangleton *Chich* 72–76; V Eastbourne St Phil 76–87; V Hastings H Trin 87–10; Can and Preb Chich Cathl 03–10; rtd 10; PtO *Lon* from 13. *The Charterhouse, Charterhouse Square, London EC1M 6AN* T: (020) 7250 1019

TOMALIN, Stanley Joseph Edward. b 66. Oak Hill Th Coll BA 93. **d** 96 **p** 97. C Bitterne *Win* 96–00; C Hailsham *Chich* 00; P-in-c Hawkswood CD 01–05; V Hawkswood 05–11; C Hailsham 11–16; RD Dallington 07–14; C Cheadle *Ches* from 16. *1 Warren Avenue, Cheadle SK8 1NB* T: 0161-491 6939 E: stantomalin@gmail.com

TOMBS, Kenneth Roberts. b 42. Open Univ BA 84. S Dios Minl Tr Scheme 92. **d** 95 **p** 96. Dep Hd Twyford C of E High Sch Acton 86–97; Chapl 98–02; rtd 02; NSM Ickenham *Lon* 95–12; PtO from 12. *91 Burns Avenue, Southall UB1 2LT* T: (020) 8574 3738 E: ken.tombs@btinternet.com

TOMKINS, Ian James. b 60. Univ of Wales (Cardiff) LLB 81 Aston Business Sch MBA 90. Ridley Hall Cam. **d** 00 **p** 01. C Bourton-on-the-Water w Clapton *Glouc* 00–04; P-in-c Broxbourne w Wormley *St Alb* 04–07; R 07–10; Adv for Minl Support *Bris* 10–18; Hon C Stoke Gifford 11–14; Hon C Redland 14–18; V Bris St Matt and St Nath from 18. *St Matthew's Church Office, Clare Road, Cotham, Bristol BS6 5TB* T: 0117-944 1598 E: vicar@stmatthews-bristol.org.uk

TOMKINS, James Andrew. b 66. R Holloway & Bedf New Coll Lon BA 88. SAOMC 01. **d** 04 **p** 06. C Lavendon w Cold Brayfield, Clifton Reynes etc *Ox* 04–05; C Risborough 05–08; TV from 08. *The Rectory, Mill Lane, Monks Risborough, Princes Risborough HP27 9JE* T: (01844) 275944 E: jamestomkins@btinternet.com

TOMKINS, Jocelyn Rachel. *See* WALKER, Jocelyn Rachel

TOMKINS, Justin Mark. b 71. Chu Coll Cam BA 93 MA 97 PhD 98. Trin Coll Bris BA 10 MPhil 12. **d** 11 **p** 12. C Longfleet *Sarum* 11–18; C The Hedinghams and Upper Colne *Chelmsf* from 19. *The Rectory, Church Road, Great Yeldham, Halstead CO9 4PT* E: email@justintomkins.org

TOMKINS, Simon Charles Ross. b 83. St Jo Coll Dur BA 06 Cam Univ BA 12. Ridley Hall Cam 10. **d** 13 **p** 14. C Lt Shelford *Ely* 13–16; R Alsagers Bank, Audley and Talke *Lich* from 16. *The Vicarage, 1 Wilbrahams Walk, Audley, Stoke-on-Trent ST7 8HL*

TOMKINSON, Linda Margaret. b 76. QUB BD 97 St Jo Coll Dur MATM 13. Cranmer Hall Dur 10. **d** 12 **p** 13. C Blackpool St Jo *Blackb* 12–16; C Blackpool St Wilfrid 16–19; P-in-c from 19; C Marton 16–19. *St Wilfrid's Vicarage, Langdale Road, Blackpool FY4 4RT* M: 07784-325537 E: revlindat@hotmail.co.uk

TOMKINSON, Raymond David. b 47. Ox Brookes Univ MA 10 SRN 71 MSSCh 72. EAMTC 86. **d** 89 **p** 90. NSM Chesterton St Geo *Ely* 89–91; C Sawston 91–93; C Babraham 91–93; P-in-c Wimbotsham w Stow Bardolph and Stow Bridge etc 93–94; R 94–00; RD Fincham 94–97; Dir Old Alresford Place *Win* 00–06; P-in-c Old Alresford and Bighton 00–06; rtd 06; PtO *Leic* from 07; *Pet* from 07; Chapl Ripon Coll Cuddesdon from 09. *8 Uppingham Road, Oakham LE15 6JD* T: (01572) 756844 E: raymondtomkinson@gmail.com

TOMKINS-RUSSELL, James Anthony. b 67. Oak Hill Th Coll BA 99. **d** 99 **p** 00. C Chadwell *Chelmsf* 99–03; C Patcham *Chich* 03–07; P-in-c N Mundham w Hunston and Merston 07–18; R 18–19; RD Chich 15–19; R Overton w Laverstoke and Freefolk *Win* from 19; P-in-c N Waltham and Steventon, Ashe and Deane from 19. *The Rectory, 54 Lordsfield Gardens, Overton, Basingstoke RG25 3EW* T: (01256) 770207 E: russell.j760@gmail.com

✠**TOMLIN, The Rt Revd Graham Stuart.** b 58. Linc Coll Ox BA 80 MA 83 Ex Univ PhD 96. Wycliffe Hall Ox BA 85. **d** 86 **p** 87 **c** 15. C Ex St Leon w H Trin 86–89; Chapl Jes Coll Ox 89–94; Tutor Wycliffe Hall Ox 89–98; Vice-Prin 98–05; Prin St Paul's Th Cen *Lon* 05–15; Dean St Mellitus Coll 07–15; Area Bp Kensington from 15. *Dial House, Riverside, Twickenham TW1 3DT* T: (020) 7932 1180 M: 07929-048720 E: bishop.kensington@london.anglican.org

TOMLIN, Keith Michael. b 53. Imp Coll Lon BSc 75. Ridley Hall Cam 77. **d** 80 **p** 81. C Heywood St Jas *Man* 80–83; C Rochdale 83–84; TV 84–85; Chapl Rochdale Tech Coll 83–85; R Benington w Leverton *Linc* 85–99; R Leverton 99–01; Chapl HM Pris N Sea Camp 97–01; P-in-c Fotherby *Linc* 01–06; Louthesk Deanery Chapl 06–10; rtd 13; Chapl United Lincs Hosps NHS Trust from 14; PtO *Linc* from 18. *Address withheld by request* E: keithtomlin@live.co.uk

TOMLINE, Stephen Harrald. b 35. Dur Univ BA 57. Cranmer Hall Dur. **d** 61 **p** 62. C Blackley St Pet *Man* 61–66; V Audenshaw St Steph 66–90; V Newhey 90–01; rtd 01; PtO *Carl* 01–16. *3 Humphrey Cottages, Stainton, Kendal LA8 0AD* T: (01539) 560988

TOMLINSON, Anne Lovat. b 56. Edin Univ MA 78 PhD 85 MTh 98. St Jo Coll Nottm 84. **d** 93. Tutor TISEC 93–02; Dir Past Studies 98–00; Dioc Dir of Ords *Edin* 02–05; Prov Local Collaborative Min Officer 02–08; Min Development Officer *Glas* 09–14; Prin Scottish Episc Inst from 14. *Scottish Episcopal Church, General Synod Office, 21 Grosvenor Crescent, Edinburgh EH12 5EE* T: 0131-225 6357 M: 07729-054417 E: principal@scotland.anglican.org

TOMLINSON, Barry William. b 47. Clifton Th Coll 72. **d** 72 **p** 73. C Pennington *Man* 72–76; SAMS 76–80; Chile 77–80; C-in-c Gorleston St Mary CD *Nor* 80; V Gorleston St Mary 80–88; Chapl Jas Paget Hosp Gorleston 81–87; P-in-c Gt w Lt Plumstead *Nor* 88–89; R Gt w Lt Plumstead and Witton 89–93; R Gt and Lt Plumstead w Thorpe End and Witton 93–98; Chapl Lt Plumstead Hosp 88–94; Chapl Norwich Community Health Partnership NHS Trust 94–95; RD Blofield *Nor* 96–98; V Margate H Trin *Cant* 98–99; R Roughton and Felbrigg, Metton, Sustead etc *Nor* 99–02; PtO 02–10; P-in-c Brinton, Briningham, Hunworth, Stody etc 10–16; PtO from 17. *St Clare, 12 Heath Road, Sheringham NR26 8JH* T: (01263) 820266 M: 07796-243436 E: barrywtomlinson@gmail.com

TOMLINSON, Canon David Robert. b 63. Open Univ BA 07 St Jo Coll Dur BA 09 Sarum Coll MA 14. Cranmer Hall Dur 07. **d** 09 **p** 10. C Shildon *Dur* 09–13; P-in-c 13–19; AD Auckland 15–18; Sen Ldr Resourcing Ch Network from 19; Public Preacher from 19; Hon Can Dur Cathl from 17. *The Vicarage, Brookside, Evenwood, Bishop Auckland DL14 9RA* M: 07546-596079 E: smileydavid63@gmail.com *or* david.tomlinson@durham.anglican.org

TOMLINSON, Canon David Robert. b 60. Kent Univ BSc 82 Chelsea Coll Lon PGCE 83 Jes Coll Cam BA 92 MA 96. Ridley Hall Cam 90. **d** 93 **p** 94. C Godalming *Guildf* 93–98; V Grays North *Chelmsf* 98–08; RD Thurrock 03–08; TR Saffron Walden w Wendens Ambo, Littlebury etc 08–11; TR Saffron Walden and Villages from 12; RD Saffron Walden from 09; Hon Can Chelmsf Cathl from 15. *The Rectory, 17*

Borough Lane, Saffron Walden CB11 4AG T: (01799) 500947
E: rector@stmaryssaffronwalden.org

TOMLINSON, David William. b 48. Lon Bible Coll MA 95 Westcott Ho Cam 97. **d** 97 **p** 98. NSM W Holloway St Luke *Lon* 97–00; P-in-c 00–01; V 01–18; rtd 18. *65 Tremadoc Road, London SW4 7NA* E: revdavetomlinson@hotmail.com

TOMLINSON, Eric Joseph. b 45. Lich Th Coll 70 Qu Coll Birm 72. **d** 73 **p** 74. C Cheadle Lich 73–76; C Sedgley All SS 77–79; V Ettingshall 79–94; V Horton, Lonsdon and Rushton Spencer 94–12; rtd 12; PtO *Lich* 12–13. *4 Burgis Close, Cheddleton, Leek ST13 7NR* T: (01538) 361551

TOMLINSON, Helen. b 53. **d** 07 **p** 08. OLM Stretford All SS *Man* 07–12; NSM Blackley St Paul from 12; Chapl Christie NHS Foundn Trust Man 13–18; Chapl Salford Univ *Man* from 18. *118 Crab Lane, Manchester M9 8WD* T: 0161-795 8768 E: helentomlinson116@gmail.com

TOMLINSON, Mrs Jean Mary. b 32. K Coll Lon BEd 75. S Dios Minl Tr Scheme 84. **d** 87 **p** 94. Hon Par Dn Spring Park All SS *S'wark* 87–92; Chapl HM YOI Hatfield 92–98; PtO *S'well* from 92. *6 Cheyne Walk, Bawtry, Doncaster DN10 6RS* T: (01302) 711281

TOMLINSON (née MILLS), The Ven Jennifer Clare. b 61. Trin Hall Cam BA 82 MA 86. Ridley Hall Cam 88. **d** 91 **p** 94. C Busbridge *Guildf* 91–95; C Godalming 95–98; NSM Grays North *Chelmsf* 98–08; Chapl Thurrock Primary Care Trust 99–08; NSM Saffron Walden w Wendens Ambo, Littlebury etc *Chelmsf* 08–11; NSM Saffron Walden and Villages 12–19; NSM N Blackwater 17–18; Bp's Adv on Women's Min 08–19; Par Development Adv (Colchester Area) 11–19; Hon Can Chelmsf Cathl 12–19; Adn Birm from 19. *23 Carisbrooke Road, Birmingham B17 8NN* T: 0121-426 0441 E: jennyt@cofebirmingham.com

TOMLINSON, John Howard. b 54. Newc Univ BSc 76 MICE 83. Chich Th Coll 91. **d** 93 **p** 94. C Blewbury, Hagbourne and Upton *Ox* 93–96; C Cowley St Jas 96–97; TV 97–04; TR Upper Wylye Valley *Sarum* 04–15; RD Heytesbury 07–13; rtd 15; PtO *Cant* from 15. *11 Castle Mews, Folkestone CT20 2BU* T: (01303) 488123 E: johntomlinson73@gmail.com

TOMLINSON, John William Bruce. b 60. Univ of Wales (Abth) BA 82 Man Univ MA 90 Birm Univ PhD 08 Nottm Trent Univ PGCE 11. Hartley Victoria Coll 87 Mar Thoma Th Sem Kottayam 90 Linc Th Coll 91. **d** 92 **p** 93. In Methodist Ch 90–91; C Sawley *Derby* 92–95; P-in-c Man Victoria Park 95–98; Dioc CUF Officer 95–98; Chapl St Anselm Hall Man Univ 96–98; V Shelton and Oxon *Lich* 98–04; Ecum Co-ord for Miss and Chief Exec Officer Lincs Chapl Services *Linc* 04–06; PtO 08–14; V Carrington *S'well* 14–17; Registrar and Course Dir St Jo Coll Nottm from 16; Lic Preacher *S'well* from 17. *St John's College, Chilwell Lane, Bramcote, Nottingham NG9 3DS* T: 0115-968 3209 M: 07983-134597 E: dr.pelican@hotmail.co.uk *or* john.tomlinson@stjohns-nottm.ac.uk

TOMLINSON, Martyn Craig. b 78. Coll of Resurr Mirfield 13. **d** 15 **p** 16. C Barnsley St Mary *Leeds* 15–18; C Cen Barnsley 18; V Royston and Felkirk from 18. *The Vicarage, Church Street, Royston, Barnsley S71 4QZ* M: 07523-260707 E: fr.craig@outlook.com

TOMLINSON, Matthew Robert Edward. b 61. St Chad's Coll Dur BA 83 Univ of Wales (Cardiff) BD 86 St Mich Coll Llan 92. **d** 94 **p** 95. C Abergavenny St Mary w Llanwenarth Citra *Mon* 94–96; PV Llan Cathl and Chapl Llan Cathl Sch 96–00; V Edgbaston St Aug *Birm* from 00. *St Augustine's Vicarage, 44 Vernon Road, Birmingham B16 9SH* T/F: 0121-454 0127 M: 07989-915499 E: matthewtomlinson@me.com

TOMPKINS, April. b 51. Man Univ BEd 75. EMMTC 05. **d** 07 **p** 08. NSM Belper *Derby* from 07. *8 Derwent Grove, Alfreton DE55 7PB* T: (01773) 835122 E: april_tompkins@hotmail.com

TOMPKINS, David John. b 32. Oak Hill Th Coll 55. **d** 58 **p** 59. C Northampton St Giles *Pet* 58–61; C Heatherlands St Jo *Sarum* 61–63; V Selby St Jas and Wistow *York* 63–73; V Retford St Sav *S'well* 73–87; P-in-c Clarborough w Hayton 84–87; V Kidsgrove *Lich* 87–90; V Tockwith and Bilton w Bickerton *York* 90–97; rtd 97; PtO *Pet* 00–03. *49 Wentworth Drive, Oundle, Peterborough PE8 4QF* T: (01832) 275176

TOMPKINS, Michael John Gordon. b 35. Man Univ BSc 58 MPS 59. NOC 82. **d** 85 **p** 86. C Abington *Pet* 85–87; TV Daventry 87–92; P-in-c Braunston 87–92; TV Daventry, Ashby St Ledgers, Braunston etc 92–93; R Paston 93–98; rtd 00; PtO *Ches* from 98. *19 Clarendon Close, Chester CH4 7BL* T: (01244) 659147 E: mjgtompkins@onetel.com

TOMS, Elizabeth Jane. b 66. **d** 13 **p** 14. OLM Crondall and Ewshot *Guildf* 13–18; Chapl Frimley Health NHS Foundn Trust from 15. *48 Danvers Drive, Church*

Crookham, Fleet GU52 0ZD T: (01252) 810624 E: elizabeth.toms@fph-tr.nhs.uk

TOMS, Sheila Patricia. b 33. Cam Univ TCert 54 Univ of Wales (Cardiff) BEd 77. Llan Ord Course 90. **dss** 91 **d** 94 **p** 97. Canton St Luke *Llan* 91–94; NSM Peterston-super-Ely w St Brides-super-Ely 94–00; P-in-c Newport St Paul *Mon* 00–06; PtO 07–13; P-in-c Goetre w Llanover 13–14; PtO from 14. *26 Fairfax View, Raglan, Usk NP15 2DR* T: (01291) 690250 E: sheilaptoms@btinternet.com

TONBRIDGE, Archdeacon of. *See* CONALTY, The Ven Julie Anne

TONBRIDGE, Suffragan Bishop of. *See* BURTON JONES, The Rt Revd Simon David

TONGE, Brian. b 36. St Chad's Coll Dur BA 58. Ely Th Coll 59. **d** 61 **p** 62. C Fleetwood St Pet *Blackb* 61–65; Chapl Ranby Ho Sch Retford 65–69; Hon C Burnley St Andr w St Marg *Blackb* 69–97; rtd 97; PtO *Blackb* from 97. *50 Fountains Avenue, Simonstone, Burnley BB12 7PY* T: (01282) 776518

TONGE, The Very Revd Lister. b 51. K Coll Lon AKC 74 Loyola Univ Chicago MPS 95. St Aug Coll Cant 74. **d** 75 **p** 76. C Liv Our Lady and St Nic w St Anne 75–78; C Johannesburg Cathl S Africa 78–79; CR 79–91; Lic to Offic *Wakef* 83–91; PtO *Man* 89–94; USA 93–95; PtO *Liv* 95–96; Chapl Community of St Jo Bapt from 96; Chapl Ripon Coll Cuddesdon 05–09; Lic to Offic Newark USA from 08; Chapl New Coll Ox 10–11; Dean Mon 12–18; Dean Newport from 18; V Newport St Woolos 12–14; V Newport St Woolos w St Mark from 14. *The Deanery, 105 Stow Hill, Newport NP20 4ED* T: (01633) 259627 E: deanofnewport@churchinwales.org.uk

TONGUE, Canon Paul. b 41. St Chad's Coll Dur BA 63. **d** 64 **p** 65. C Dudley St Edm *Worc* 64–69; C Sedgley All SS *Lich* 69–70; V Amblecote *Worc* 70–07; Chapl Dudley Gp of Hosps NHS Trust 93–07; Hon Can Worc Cathl 93–07; RD Stourbridge 96–01; rtd 07; PtO *Worc* from 09. *99 Woolhope Road, Worcester WR5 2AP* T: (01905) 352052 E: paul_tongue@sky.com

TONKIN, Mrs Jacqueline Anne. b 50. Open Univ BSc 02 DipSW 02. Yorks Min Course. **d** 11 **p** 12. NSM Langtoft w Foxholes, Butterwick, Cottam etc *York* 11–19; NSM Gt and Lt Driffield 12–19; P-in-c Waggoners from 19; RD Harthill from 17. *The Vicarage, 4 Pulham Lane, Wetwang, Driffield YO25 9XT* E: jacki.tonkin1@btinternet.com

TONKINSON, Canon David Boyes. b 47. K Coll Lon BD 71 AKC 71. St Aug Coll Cant 71. **d** 72 **p** 73. C Surbiton St Andr *S'wark* 72–74; C Selsdon St Jo w St Fran *Cant* 75–81; V Croydon St Aug Cant 81–84; V Croydon St Aug *S'wark* 85–89; C Easthampstead and Ind Chapl *Ox* 89–96; Chapl Bracknell Coll 93–96; Soc Resp Adv *Portsm* 96–02; Hon Can Portsm Cathl 96–02; Ind Chapl *Win* 02–08; Hon C Heckfield w Mattingley and Rotherwick 06–07; Hon C Hook and Heckfield w Mattingley and Rotherwick 07–08; Soc Resp Partnership Development Officer *Guildf* 08–11; rtd 11. *17 Squirrel Close, Sandhurst GU47 9DL* E: david.tonkinson@o2.co.uk

TOOBY, Anthony Albert. b 58. Sarum & Wells Th Coll 89. **d** 91 **p** 92. C Warsop *S'well* 91–95; C Ollerton w Boughton 95–98; V Girlington *Bradf* 98–10; P-in-c Mancetter *Cov* 10–17; V Blyth St Cuth *Newc* from 17. *29 Ridley Avenue, Blyth NE24 3BA* E: tonytooby@virginmedia.com

TOOGOOD, Mrs Gillian Mary. b 58. Ridley Hall Cam 08. **d** 10 **p** 11. C Brentford *Lon* 10–13; Lic Preacher Kensington Area from 13. *5 Fulmer Way, London W13 9XQ* T: (020) 8567 1299 M: 07936-793362 E: gill.toogood@tiscali.co.uk

TOOGOOD, John Peter. b 73. Leeds Univ BA 95. Ripon Coll Cuddesdon 98. **d** 00 **p** 01. C Sherborne w Castleton and Lillington *Sarum* 00–03; P-in-c Chieveley w Winterbourne and Oare *Ox* 03–10; R E Downland from 10. *The Vicarage, Church Lane, Chieveley, Newbury RG20 8UT* T: (01635) 247566 E: edownlandrector@gmail.com

TOOGOOD, Ms Melanie Lorraine. b 57. K Coll Lon BD 78 AKC 78. Ripon Coll Cuddesdon 94. **d** 96 **p** 97. C Shepperton *Lon* 96–99; C Greenford H Cross 99–04; P-in-c Tufnell Park St Geo and All SS 04–06; V 06–16; rtd 16; PtO *Lon* from 16. *8 St James' Close, Bishop Street, London N1 8PH* E: meltoogood@me.com

TOOGOOD, Robert Charles. b 45. AKC 70. St Aug Coll Cant 70. **d** 71 **p** 72. C Shepperton *Lon* 71–74; C Kirk Ella *York* 74–76; P-in-c Levisham w Lockton 76–81; P-in-c Ebberston w Allerston 76–81; R Kempsey and Severn Stoke w Croome d'Abitot *Worc* 81–92; V Bramley *Win* 92–10; rtd 10; PtO *Win* 10–19. *14 Huntsmead, Alton GU34 2SE* T: (01420) 87007

TOOGOOD, Robert Frederick. b 43. St Paul's Coll Chelt CertEd 65 Open Univ BA 74. Trin Coll Bris 93. **d** 95 **p** 96. C Southbroom *Sarum* 95–99; TV Langport Area *B & W* 99–04; rtd 04; PtO *Ox* 05–17; *Sarum* from 05. *49 Barrow Close, Marlborough SN8 2BE* T: (01672) 511468

TOOKE, Mrs Sheila. b 44. EAMTC 89. **d** 91 **p** 94. NSM March St Wendreda *Ely* 95–95; P-in-c Upwell Christchurch 95–97; P-in-c Welney 95–97; P-in-c Manea 95–97; R Christchurch and Manea and Welney 97–03; rtd 03; PtO *Ely* from 03. *The Haven, 21 Wisbech Road, March PE15 8ED* T: (01354) 652844 E: stooke@havenmarch.plus.com

TOOKEY, Preb Christopher Tom. b 41. AKC 67. **d** 68 **p** 69. C Stockton St Pet *Dur* 68–71; C Burnham *B & W* 71–77; R Clutton w Cameley 77–81; V Wells St Thos w Horrington 81–06; RD Shepton Mallet 86–95; Chapl Bath and West Community NHS Trust 95–06; Preb Wells Cathl *B & W* 90–11; rtd 06; PtO *B & W* from 06. *47 Drake Road, Wells BA5 3LE* T: (01749) 676006 E: christophertookey@talktalk.net

TOOP, Preb Allan Neil. b 49. St Alb Minl Tr Scheme 79 Linc Th Coll 82. **d** 83 **p** 84. C Kempston Transfiguration *St Alb* 83–87; C Ludlow *Heref* 87–92; P-in-c Stokesay and Sibdon Carwood w Halford 92–01; P-in-c Acton Scott 96–01; RD Condover 96–00; V Minsterley 01–13; R Habberley 01–13; P-in-c Hope w Shelve 07–13; R Minsterley, Habberley and Hope w Shelve 13–15; Preb Heref Cathl 06–15; rtd 15; PtO *Lich* from 16. *The Rectory, 15 Brookside, Bicton, Shrewsbury SY3 8EP* T: (01743) 851375 E: trigger.milward@gmail.com

TOOP, Mrs Mary-Louise. b 55. Glouc Sch of Min 90. **d** 04 **p** 05. Dir of Ords *Heref* 00–15; NSM Minsterley 04–13; NSM Habberley 04–13; NSM Hope w Shelve 04–13; NSM Minsterley, Habberley and Hope w Shelve 13–15; Preb Heref Cathl 12–15; P-in-c Bicton, Montford w Shrawardine and Fitz *Lich* from 15. *The Rectory, 15 Brookside, Bicton, Shrewsbury SY3 8EP* T: (01743) 851375

TOOTH, Nigel David. b 47. RMN 69. Sarum & Wells Th Coll 71. **d** 74 **p** 75. C S Beddington St Mich *S'wark* 74–77; C Whitchurch *Bris* 77–83; TV Bedminster 83–87; Chapl Dorchester Hosps 87–94; Chapl Herrison Hosp Dorchester 87–94; Chapl Dorset County Hosp NHS Foundn Trust 94–11; rtd 11. *5 Pomp Terrace, Martinstown, Dorchester DT2 9JN* T: (01305) 889576 E: nigeltooth@hotmail.co.uk

TOOVEY, Rupert William. b 66. **d** 10 **p** 11. NSM Storrington *Chich* 10–15 and from 18; NSM Steyning 15–18; NSM Ashurst 15–18. *31 Downsview Avenue, Storrington, Pulborough RH20 4PS* T: (01903) 740466 M: 07802-203655

TOPALIAN, Canon Berj. b 51. Sheff Univ BA 72 PhD 77. Sarum Th Coll 95. **d** 97 **p** 98. NSM Clifton Ch Ch w Em *Bris* 97–98; C Bris St Mich and St Paul 98–99; C Cotham St Sav w St Mary and Clifton St Paul 99–01; V Pilning w Compton Greenfield 01–08; Chapl St Monica Home Westbury-on-Trym 08–16; Hon Min Can Bris Cathl 04–11; Hon Can Bris Cathl 11–16; rtd 16; PtO *Bris* from 16. *40 Fenshurst Gardens, Long Ashton, Bristol BS41 9AU*

TOPHAM, Benjamin Mark. b 84. Cliff Coll BA 05. Ridley Hall Cam 13. **d** 14 **p** 15. C Chalfont St Peter *Ox* 14–17; C Gerrards Cross and Fulmer from 17. *54 The Uplands, Gerrards Cross SL9 7JG* M: 07736-953127 E: ben.topham@saintjames.org.uk

TOPLEY (*née* BRANCHE), Caren Teresa. b 59. Avery Hill Coll BEd 81. SEITE 94. **d** 97 **p** 98. NSM Arlesey w Astwick *St Alb* 97–99; NSM Clifton and Southill 99–16; R from 16. *The Rectory, 8 Rectory Close, Clifton, Shefford SG17 5EL* T: (01462) 615499 E: rector@clifton-beds.co.uk

TOPPING, Kenneth Bryan Baldwin. b 27. Bps' Coll Cheshunt 58. **d** 59 **p** 60. C Fleetwood St Pet *Blackb* 59–63; V Ringley *Man* 63–70; V Cleator Moor w Cleator *Carl* 70–91; rtd 92; PtO *Blackb* 92–07. *28 Glebelands, Corbridge NE45 5DS* T: (01434) 634944 E: bryantopping93@gmail.com

TOPPING, Roy William. b 37. S Dios Minl Tr Scheme 91. **d** 92 **p** 93. Bahrain 89–94; Chapl Miss to Seamen Milford Haven 94–99; rtd 99; PtO *Sarum* 00–15; *Chich* from 15. *25 Strand Court, Harsfold Road, Rustington, Littlehampton BN16 2NT* T: (01903) 778939

TORDOFF, Donald William. b 45. Nottm Univ BA 69. Qu Coll Birm 69. **d** 71 **p** 72. C High Harrogate Ch Ch *Ripon* 71–75; C Moor Allerton 75–80; V Bilton 80–92; R Spennithorne w Finghall and Hauxwell 92–01; rtd 01; PtO *Ripon* 02–14; *Leeds* from 10. *13 Dulverton Hall, Esplanade, Scarborough YO11 2AR* E: don@tordoffs.myzen.co.uk

TORDOFF (*née* PARKER), Mrs Margaret Grace. b 40. SRN 65 SCM 67. Cranmer Hall Dur 81. **dss** 83 **d** 87 **p** 94. Bilton *Ripon* 83–87; C 87–92; Chapl Spennithorne Hall 92; NSM Spennithorne w Finghall and Hauxwell 92–00; rtd 00; PtO *M & K* from 00; *Ripon* 00–14; *Leeds* 14–16; *York* from 10. *13 Dulverton Hall, Esplanade, Scarborough YO11 2AR* E: margaret@tordoffs.myzen.co.uk

TORR, Stephen Charles. b 81. Birm Univ BA 05 PhD 12. Ridley Hall Cam 10. **d** 12 **p** 13. C Wilnecote *Lich* 12–13; C Abbots Bromley, Blithfield, Colton, Colwich etc 13–16; P-in-c Norton *Ches* from 16; Tutor St Mellitus Coll

16–19. *The Vicarage, Norton Hill, Windmill Hill, Runcorn WA7 6QE* T: (01928) 716523 E: vicar@stbertschurch.org.uk

TORRANCE, David Alan. b 91. Fitzw Coll Cam BA 12 MA 16 Edin Univ MTh 13. Ridley Hall Cam 14. **d** 17 **p** 18. C Portswood Ch Ch *Win* from 17; C Portswood St Denys from 19. *6 Royston Close, Southampton SO17 1TB* T: (023) 8055 3282 E: torrance@cantab.net

TORRENS, Marianne Rose. *See* ATKINSON, Marianne Rose

TORRENS, Robert Harrington. b 33. Trin Coll Cam BA 56 MA 61. Ridley Hall Cam 56. **d** 58 **p** 59. C Bromley SS Pet and Paul *Roch* 58–60; C Aylesbury *Ox* 60–63; V Eaton Socon *St Alb* 63–73; LtO 73–75; V Pittville All SS *Glouc* 75–84; Chapl Frenchay Hosp Bris 84–94; Chapl Manor Park Hosp Bris 84–94; Chapl St Pet Hospice Bris 94–98; P-in-c Chippenham *Ely* 98–01; P-in-c Snailwell 98–01; PtO 01–18; *St E* from 01. *68 Barons Road, Bury St Edmunds IP33 2LW* T: (01284) 752075 E: torrensatkinson@aol.com

TORRY, Malcolm Norman Alfred. b 55. St Jo Coll Cam BA 76 MA 80 K Coll Lon MTh 79 LSE MSc 96 Lon Univ BD 78 PhD 90 BA 01 BSc 10 Lambeth MPhil 18. Cranmer Hall Dur 79. **d** 80 **p** 81. C S'wark H Trin w St Matt 80–83; C S'wark Ch Ch 83–88; Ind Chapl 83–88; V Hatcham St Cath 88–96; V E Greenwich Ch Ch w St Andr and St Mich 96–97; TR E Greenwich 97–13; TV 13–14; RD Greenwich Thameside 98–01; rtd 14; PtO *S'wark* 15–16; Hon C Nunhead St Antony w St Silas from 16. *286 Ivydale Road, London SE15 3DF* T: (020) 7635 7916 E: malcolm@torry.org.uk

TOSTEVIN, Alan Edwin John. b 41. Trin Coll Bris BA 86. **d** 86 **p** 87. C Hildenborough *Roch* 86–89; TV Ipsley *Worc* 89–06; rtd 06; PtO *Worc* from 06; *Cov* from 16. *3 Canterbury Close, Studley B80 7JF* T: (01527) 852636 E: artostevin@gmail.com

TOTNES, Archdeacon of. *See* DETTMER, The Ven Douglas James

TOTNEY (*née* YATES), Mrs Jennifer Clare. b 83. Dur Univ BA 04 MA 05 Selw Coll Cam BA 08. Westcott Ho Cam 06. **d** 09 **p** 10. C White Horse *Sarum* 09–12; TV Vale of Pewsey from 12; Lic Lay Min Tr Officer from 16. *The Rectory, Church Street, Pewsey SN9 5DL* T: (01672) 562886 E: jennifer.totney@gmail.com

TOTTEN, Andrew James. b 64. QUB BA 87 TCD BTh 90 Univ of Wales (Cardiff) MTh 07. CITC. **d** 90 **p** 91. C Newtownards *D & D* 90–94; CF from 94; QHC from 16. *c/o MOD Chaplains (Army)* T: (01264) 887064 E: andrewjtotten@hotmail.com

TOTTERDELL, Canon Rebecca Helen. b 57. Lon Bible Coll BA 80 MA 99. Oak Hill Th Coll 88. **d** 91 **p** 94. Par Dn Broxbourne w Wormley *St Alb* 91–94; C 94–95; C Stevenage St Nic and Graveley 95–99; P-in-c Benington w Walkern 99–08; Asst Dir of Ords 03–08; Bp's Adv for Women in Min 03–07; Asst Dioc Dir of Ords *Ex* 09–10; Dioc Dir of Ords 10–19; Hon C Bovey Tracey SS Pet, Paul and Thos w Hennock 09–17; Preb Ex Cathl 14–17; Can Res Ex Cathl from 17. *Address temp unknown*

TOTTLE, Nicola Rachael. *See* SKIPWORTH, Nicola Rachael

TOVAR, Gillian Elaine. *See* NICHOLLS, Gillian Elaine

TOVEY, Phillip Noel. b 56. Lon Univ BA 77 Lon Bible Coll BA 83 Nottm Univ MPhil 88 Lambeth STh 95 Ox Brookes Univ PhD 06. St Jo Coll Nottm 85. **d** 87 **p** 88. C Beaconsfield *Ox* 87–90; C Banbury 90–91; TV 91–95; Chapl Ox Brookes Univ 95–98; P-in-c Holton and Waterperry w Albury and Waterstock 95–97; TV Wheatley 97–98; Dioc Tr Officer 98–18; Dir Reader Tr 04–18; NSM Wootton and Dry Sandford 05–10; Lect Ripon Coll Cuddesdon 04–16; Dep Warden Readers 16–19; Warden Readers from 19; Prin Ox Local Min Pathway from 18. *20 Palmer Place, Abingdon OX14 5LZ* T: (01235) 527077 E: phillip.tovey@oxford.anglican.org

TOWERS, Canon David Francis. b 32. G&C Coll Cam BA 56 MA 60. Clifton Th Coll 56. **d** 58 **p** 59. C Gresley *Derby* 58–63; V Brixton St Paul *S'wark* 63–75; V Chatteris *Ely* 75–87; RD March 82–87; Hon Can Ely Cathl 85–87; R Burnley St Pet *Blackb* 87–97; rtd 97; PtO *Bradf* 99–14; *Leeds* from 14. *21 Drovers Walk, Hellifield, Skipton BD23 4DW* T: (01729) 825803 E: dtlongcliffe@gmail.com

TOWERS, Patrick Leo. b 43. AKC 68 Hull Univ CertEd 69. **d** 74 **p** 75. Japan 74–81; TV Bourne Valley *Sarum* 81–83; Dioc Youth Officer 81–83; Chapl Oundle Sch 83–86; I Rathkeale w Askeaton and Kilcornan *L & K* 86–89; I Nenagh 89–00; Can Limerick, Killaloe and Clonfert Cathls 97–00; Provost Tuam *T, K & A* 00–09; Can Tuam Cathl 00–09; I Galway w Kilcummin 00–09; rtd 09. *Doonwood, Mountbellew, Co Galway, H53 Y821, Republic of Ireland* T: (00353) (90) 968 4547 M: 86-814 0649 E: towers.patrick@gmail.com

TOWLER, Canon David George. b 42. Cranmer Hall Dur 73. **d** 76 **p** 77. C Newbarns w Hawcoat *Carl* 76–80; V Huyton St Geo *Liv* 80–98; V Newburgh w Westhead 98–07; AD Ormskirk 01–06; Hon Can Liv Cathl 03–07; rtd 07; PtO *Liv* from 16. *7 Padstow Close, Southport PR9 9RX* E: davidgtowler@gmail.com

TOWLER, John Frederick. b 42. Surrey Univ PhD 05. Bps' Coll Cheshunt 62. **d** 66 **p** 67. C Lowestoft St Marg *Nor* 66–71; R Horstead 71–77; Warden Dioc Conf Ho Horstead 71–77; Prec and Min Can Worc Cathl 77–81; rtd 02; Hon C Fordingbridge and Breamore and Hale etc *Win* 06–12; PtO from 12; *Sarum* from 17. *24 Oak Road, Alderholt, Fordingbridge SP6 3BL* T: (01425) 656595 M: 07940-855952 E: cjtptners@talktalk.net

TOWNEND, John Philip. b 52. Southn Univ BTh 95. Sarum & Wells Th Coll 89. **d** 91 **p** 92. C Sherborne w Castleton and Lillington *Sarum* 91–95; P-in-c Wool and E Stoke 95–98; Sacr and Chapl Westmr Abbey 98–01; P-in-c Brightwalton w Catmore, Leckhampstead etc *Ox* 01–10; P-in-c Beedon and Peasemore w W Ilsley and Farnborough 05–10; R W Downland 10–17; rtd 17. *87 Talmena Avenue, Wadebridge PL27 7RP* E: jptownend@btinternet.com

TOWNEND, The Ven Lee Stuart. b 65. St Jo Coll Dur MA 08. Cranmer Hall Dur 96. **d** 98 **p** 99. C Buxton w Burbage and King Sterndale *Derby* 98–01; V Loose *Cant* 01–08; P-in-c Ilkley All SS *Bradf* 08–12; Ch Growth Officer Chesterfield Adnry *Derby* 12–17; Adn Carl and Can Res Carl Cathl from 17. *The Vicarage, Pooley Bridge, Penrith CA10 2LT* T: 07458-016925 E: leethevicar@gmail.com *or* archdeacon.north@carlislediocese.org.uk

TOWNER, Andrew Paul John. b 76. Bris Univ BSc 98 Surrey Univ Roehampton PGCE 02. Oak Hill Th Coll MTh 07. **d** 07. C St Helen Bishopsgate w St Andr Undershaft etc *Lon* 07–10; C Beckenham Ch Ch *Roch* 10–14; P-in-c Houghton *Carl* from 14. *12 Brunstock Close, Carlisle CA3 0HL* T: (01228) 810076 *or* 515972 M: 07956-569983 E: andrew@hkchurch.org.uk

TOWNER, Colin David. b 39. St Pet Coll Ox BA 61 MA 65 Lon Univ BD 63 ARCM 72 LRAM 73. Tyndale Hall Bris 61. **d** 64 **p** 65. C Southsea St Simon *Portsm* 64–67; C Penge St Jo *Roch* 67–70; V Leic St Chris 70–74; Hon C Southsea St Jude *Portsm* 75–82; PtO 86–90 and 00–01 and from 12; C Southsea St Pet 01–03; P-in-c 03–07; P-in-c Portsea St Luke 05–07; rtd 07; PtO *Ely* 08–12. *10 Ophir Road, Portsmouth PO2 9EN* E: sctowner@btinternet.com

TOWNER, Preb Paul. b 51. Bris Univ BSc 72 BTh 81. Oak Hill Th Coll 78. **d** 81 **p** 82. C Aspley *S'well* 81–84; R Gt Hanwood *Heref* 84–99; RD Pontesbury 93–99; P-in-c Heref St Pet w St Owen and St Jas 99–11; V 11–16; RD Heref City 07–10; RD Heref Rural 07–10; RD Heref 10–16; Preb Heref Cathl 96–16; rtd 16; PtO *Ches* from 17. *14 Bachefield Avenue, Huntington, Chester CH3 6DA* E: preb.paul@btinternet.com

TOWNLEY, The Ven Peter Kenneth. b 55. Sheff Univ BA 78. Ridley Hall Cam 78. **d** 80 **p** 81. C Ashton Ch Ch Man 80–83; C-in-c Holts CD 83–88; R Stretford All SS 88–96; V Ipswich St Mary-le-Tower *St E* 96–08; RD Ipswich 01–08; Hon Can St E Cathl 03–08; Adn Pontefract *Wakef* 08–14; *Leeds* from 14; Hon Can Ripon Cathl from 15; Dioc Chapl MU from 16; Clergy Development Officer Wakefield Area *Leeds* from 19. *The Vicarage, Kirkthorpe Lane, Kirkthorpe, Wakefield WF1 5SZ* T: (01924) 896327 *or* 434459 F: 896327 *or* 364834 E: peter.townley@leeds.anglican.org *or* archdeacon.pontefract@leeds.anglican.org

TOWNLEY, Robert Keith. b 44. TCD MPhil 04. St Jo Coll Auckland LTh 67. **d** 67 **p** 68. C Devonport H Trin New Zealand 67–70; C Lisburn Ch Ch *Conn* 71–74; C Portman Square St Paul *Lon* 75–80; Dean Ross and I Ross Union C, C & R 82–94; Chan Cork Cathl 82–94; Dean Kildare and I Kildare w Kilmeague and Curragh *M & K* 95–06; Chapl Defence Forces 95–06; rtd 06; LtO *Arm* from 06. *Address temp unknown*

TOWNS, Ms Claire Louise. b 69. Portsm Poly BA 90 Univ of Wales (Cardiff) MSc 93 St Jo Coll Nottm MA 01. EMMTC 06. **d** 07 **p** 08. C Beeston *S'well* 07–12; V Swanmore St Barn *Portsm* from 12. *The Vicarage, Church Road, Swanmore, Southampton SO32 2PA* T: (01489) 808968 M: 07766-541152 E: clairetowns@googlemail.com

TOWNS, Paul Robert. b 69. Plymouth Univ BSc 92 Nottm Univ MA 04. Westcott Ho Cam 15. **d** 17 **p** 18. NSM Ab Kettleby and Holwell w Asfordby *Leic* from 17; NSM Old Dalby, Nether Broughton, Saxelbye etc from 17. *Harby Hall, 14 School Lane, Harby, Melton Mowbray LE14 4BZ* T: (01664) 444188 M: 07855-839629 E: prtowns@outlook.com

TOWNSEND, Allan Harvey. b 43. WMMTC 89. **d** 92 **p** 93. NSM Fenton *Lich* 92–96; C Tividale 96–98; P-in-c Saltley and Shaw Hill *Birm* 98–06; P-in-c Washwood Heath 01–06; V Saltley and Washwood Heath 06–09; rtd 09; PtO *Lich* 09–10 and 11–19; C Wolstanton 10; PtO *Derby* 13–18; *Birm* 14–19. *5 The Croft, Stoke-on-Trent ST4 5HT* T: (01782) 416333

TOWNSEND, Anne Jennifer. b 38. Lon Univ MB, BS 60 MRCS 60 LRCP 60. S'wark Ord Course 88. **d** 91 **p** 94. NSM Wandsworth St Paul *S'wark* 91–08; Chapl Asst St Geo Hosp Lon 91–92; Dean MSE *S'wark* 93–99; PtO 08–13; *Roch* from

13. *3 Bromley College, London Road, Bromley BR1 1PE* T: (020) 8460 3869 E: revdrannetow@yahoo.co.uk

TOWNSEND, Christopher Robin. b 47. St Jo Coll Nottm. **d** 74 **p** 75. C Gt Horton *Bradf* 74–77; C Heaton St Barn 77–78; C Wollaton *S'well* 78–80; V Slaithwaite w E Scammonden *Wakef* 80–14; *Leeds* 14–18; P-in-c Marsden 16–18; rtd 18. *9 Vineyard, Leymoor Road, Golcar, Huddersfield HD7 4RN* E: robin.townsend@homecall.co.uk

TOWNSEND, Derek William. b 52. Fitzw Coll Cam BA 74 Man Univ PhD 89. St Jo Coll Nottm 91. **d** 91 **p** 92. C Hazlemere Ox 91–95; TV Banbury 95–98; V Banbury St Paul 98–01; PtO from 11. *24 Lower Lodge Lane, Hazlemere, High Wycombe HP15 7AT* T: (01494) 715964 M: 07855-015519 E: bill.townsend@tiscali.co.uk

TOWNSEND, Mrs Diane Rosalind. b 45. Stockwell Coll of Educn CertEd 66 K Alfred's Coll Win BEd 88. Sarum Th Coll 93. **d** 96 **p** 97. NSM Botley, Durley and Curdridge *Portsm* 96–00; NSM Buriton 00–05; NSM Portsea N End St Mark 05–10; TV 06–10; rtd 10; PtO *Portsm* from 10. *9 Daisy Lane, Locks Heath, Southampton SO31 6RA* T: (01489) 574092 E: dirobdaisy@aol.com

TOWNSEND, Gary. b 65. Trin Coll Bris. **d** 00 **p** 01. C Minster-in-Sheppey *Cant* 00–04; C Tonbridge SS Pet and Paul *Roch* 04–10; V Henham and Elsenham w Ugley *Chelmsf* from 10. *The Vicarage, Carters Lane, Henham, Bishop's Stortford CM22 6AQ* T: (01279) 850281 M: 07719-876452 E: gary.townsend@heuchurch.co.uk

TOWNSEND, Peter. b 37. Open Univ BA 87. Wells Th Coll 67. **d** 69 **p** 70. C Desborough *Pet* 69–72; C Bramley *Ripon* 72–75; C-in-c Newton Hall LEP *Dur* 75–80; P-in-c Newton Hall 80–81; V Hartlepool St Luke 81–03; rtd 03; PtO *Dur* from 03. *348 Stockton Road, Hartlepool TS25 2PW* T: (01429) 291651 E: townsend_peter@yahoo.co.uk

TOWNSEND, Philip Roger. b 51. Sheff Univ BA 78. Trin Coll Bris 78. **d** 80 **p** 81. C Wstrm St Jas *S'wark* 80–85; C Ardsley *Sheff* 85–88; V Crookes St Tim 88–17; AD Hallam 05–12; rtd 17. *71A Palm Street, Sheffield S6 2XF* E: phil@townsend.org.uk

TOWNSEND, Canon Robert William. b 68. Univ of Wales (Ban) BA 90. St Mich Coll Llan BTh 93. **d** 93 **p** 95. C Dolgellau w Llanfachreth and Brithdir etc *Ban* 93–94; Min Can Ban Cathl 94–96; P-in-c Amlwch 96–97; R 97–99; R Llanfair-pwll and Llanddaniel-fab etc 99–03; P-in-c Llanilar w Rhostie and Llangwyryfon etc *St D* 03–06; Dioc Schools Officer 03–06; R Llanberis, Llanrug and Llandinorwig *Ban* 06–11; P-in-c Llandwrog and Llanwnda 11–12; P-in-c Uwch Gwyrfai Beuno Sant 12–13; AD Arfon 12–15; AD Synod Bangor 15–18; Dioc Dir of Educn 10–15; Dioc Communications Officer 12–15; Dioc Dir of Communication 15–18; Bp's Communications Officer from 18; C Bro Eryri from 15; Hon Can Ban Cathl from 12. *12 Llys y Waun, Waunfawr, Caernarfon LL55 4ZA* T: (01286) 650262 M: 07855-492006 E: robert@townsend.cx

TOWNSEND, Robin. *See* TOWNSEND, Christopher Robin

TOWNSEND, Mrs Teresa Lee. b 70. Ox Brookes Univ BA 05. Ox Min Course 16. **d** 18 **p** 19. NSM W Swindon and Lydiard Tregoze *Bris* from 18. *Tryphena, 18 St John Road, Wroughton, Swindon SN4 9ED* T: (01793) 812734 M: 07818-044431 E: rev.teresa.townsend@gmail.com

TOWNSEND, William. *See* TOWNSEND, Derek William

TOWNSHEND (formerly WEAVER), Canon Angela Mary. b 48. WMMTC 92. **d** 95 **p** 96. C Hill *Birm* 95–99; V Hamstead St Paul 99–06; AD Handsworth 05–06; Hon Can Birm Cathl 05–06; Can Res Guildf Cathl 06–11; C-in-c Bath Ch Ch Prop Chpl *B & W* 11–15; PtO *Guildf* 15–17 and from 18; Chapl Birtley Ho Bramley 17–18; Chapl Oak Hall Nursing Home Haslemere from 18. *16 Kings Road, Shalford, Guildford GU4 8JU* M: 07791-551824 E: angelatownshend@btinternet.com

TOWNSHEND, Charles Hume. b 41. St Pet Coll Ox BA 64 MA 69. Westcott Ho Cam 64. **d** 66 **p** 67. C Warlingham w Chelsham and Farleigh *S'wark* 66–75; R Old Cleeve, Leighland and Treborough *B & W* 75–85; R Bishops Lydeard w Bagborough and Cothelstone 85–95; V N Curry 95–06; rtd 06. *Mutterings, Church Road, Colaton Raleigh, Sidmouth EX10 0LW* T: (01395) 567460

TOWNSHEND, Patricia Olwyn. b 53. Univ of Rhodesia BA 74 UNISA BTh MTh 08. Coll of Transfiguration Grahamstown 09. **d** 09 **p** 10. C Pinelands S Africa 09–11; R Factreton 11–17; V Dunchurch *Cov* from 17. *The Vicarage, 11 Critchley Drive, Dunchurch, Rugby CV22 6PJ* T: (01788) 461987 M: 07555-458484 E: revptownshend@gmail.com

TOY, Canon John. b 30. Hatf Coll Dur BA 53 MA 62 Leeds Univ PhD 82 FSA 13. Wells Th Coll 53. **d** 55 **p** 56. C Newington St Paul *S'wark* 55–58; S Sec SCM 58–60; Chapl Ely Th Coll 60–64; Chapl Gothenburg w Halmstad and

Jönköping *Eur* 65–69; Asst Chapl St Jo Coll York 69–72; Sen Lect 72–79; Prin Lect 79–83; Can Res and Chan York Minster 83–99; rtd 99; PtO *Eur* from 99; *S'well* 03–15; *York* from 16. *Dulverton Hall, Esplanade, Scarborough YO11 2AR* T: (01723) 340115 E: johntoy@talktalk.net

TOYNBEE, Claire Louise. *See* ALCOCK, Claire Louise

TOYNE, Mrs Marian Elizabeth Christina. b 63. Rolle Coll BA 84 Swansea Coll of Educn PGCE 85. Linc Sch of Th and Min 11. **d** 14 **p** 15. NSM Frodingham and New Brumby *Linc* 14–16; C 16–19; V Woldmoor Gp from 19. *The Vicarage, Grange Lane, North Kelsey, Market Rasen LN7 6EZ* T: (01724) 859565 E: marian.toyne@live.co.uk

TOZE, Lissa Melanie. *See* SCOTT, Lissa Melanie

TOZE, Stephen James. b 51. Birm Univ BA 79. Qu Coll Birm 76 Westcott Ho Cam 93. **d** 93 **p** 94. C Leominster *Heref* 93–94; R Gt Brickhill w Bow Brickhill and Lt Brickhill *Ox* 94–02; Rural Officer Buckm Adnry 95–02; V Wilshamstead and Houghton Conquest *St Alb* from 02; Ecum Officer Buckm Adnry *Ox* from 13. *The Vicarage, 15 Vicarage Lane, Wilstead, Bedford MK45 3EU* T: (01234) 740423 E: s@steve777.plus.com

TRACEY, Mrs Caroline Patricia. b 56. SNWTP 10. **d** 13 **p** 14. OLM Horwich and Rivington *Man* from 13; OLM Blackrod 13–15; Chapl Wrightington, Wigan and Leigh NHS Foundn Trust from 18. *Wrightington, Wigan and Leigh NHS Foundation Trust, Wigan Lane, Wigan WN1 2NN* T: (01204) 692303 E: caroline@archangelos.co.uk *or* caroline.tracey@wwl.nhs.uk

TRACEY-MacLEOD, Talisker Isobel. b 81. St Andr Univ MA 03. Ripon Coll Cuddesdon BTh 11. **d** 11 **p** 12. C Hove All SS *Chich* 11–15; R Cherbury w Gainfield *Ox* from 15. *The Rectory, Church Lane, Longworth, Abingdon OX13 5DX* T: (01865) 596224 M: 07887-773579 E: rector@alathea.org.uk

TRAFFORD-ROBERTS, Rosamond Jane. b 40. Qu Coll Birm BA. **d** 95 **p** 96. C Ledbury *Heref* 95–00; Lect St Botolph Aldgate w H Trin Minories *Lon* 00–05; Chapl Ho of St Barn-in-Soho 03–05; rtd 05; PtO *Lon* from 05; *Heref* from 18. *9 Ledbury Park, Ledbury HR8 1LF* M: 07736-335959 E: revdros@hotmail.com

TRAILL, Geoffrey Conway. b 58. Ridley Coll Melbourne BA 82 BTh 87. **d** 85 **p** 85. Australia 85–87 and from 88; C Shrub End *Chelmsf* 87–88. *1 Albert Street, Point Lonsdale Vic 3225, Australia* T: (0061) (3) 5258 4624 F: 5258 4623 M: 412-381225 E: gtraill@optusnet.com.au

TRAIN, Paul Michael. b 57. Stellenbosch Univ BChD 82. SEITE 03. **d** 06 **p** 07. NSM Loughton St Jo *Chelmsf* 06–10. *5 Monkchester Close, Loughton IG10 2SN* T: (020) 8508 2937

TRAINOR, Mrs Lynn Joanna. b 65. Bris Univ BSc 87 Ex Univ PGCE 89. SAOMC 99. **d** 02 **p** 03. C Ascot Heath *Ox* 02–06; PtO 15–17; V Langton Green *Roch* from 17. *The Vicarage, The Green, Langton Green, Tunbridge Wells TN3 0JB* T: (01892) 862072 E: lynn@lynnie.co.uk *or* lynn@langtongreenchurch.org.uk

TRANTER, John. b 51. St Jo Coll Nottm 84. **d** 00 **p** 01. C Gt Wyrley *Lich* 00–04; V Altham w Clayton le Moors *Blackb* 04–14; R Chelsfield *Roch* 14–18; P-in-c from 18; AD Orpington 14–18; C Green Street Green and Pratts Bottom from 18. *The Rectory, Skibbs Lane, Orpington BR6 7RH* T: (01689) 825749 E: revjohnt@talktalk.net *or* rector@stmartinchelsfield.org.uk

TRANTER, Stephen. b 61. Lanc Univ BA 81 RGN 87 RMN 89. Trin Coll Bris BA 99. **d** 99 **p** 00. C Blackpool St Thos *Blackb* 99–03; P-in-c Blackb St Jas 03–10; P-in-c Blackb St Steph 04–10; Chapl Univ Hosps of Morecambe Bay NHS Trust 10–12; P-in-c Ellel w Shireshead *Blackb* 11–12; OLM Officer *Man* 12–16; TR W Bolton from 16. *St Matthew's Vicarage, Stanwell Street, Bolton BL1 3RQ* T: (01204) 398552 E: stephentranter@msn.com

TRAPNELL, Mrs Hazel Joan. b 45. Trin Coll Bris. **d** 12 **p** 13. OLM Stoke Bishop *Bris* from 12. *30 Hazelwood Court, Hazelwood Road, Bristol BS9 1PU* T: 0117-968 7190 E: hazeltrapnell@blueyonder.co.uk

TRAPNELL, Canon Stephen Hallam. b 30. G&C Coll Cam BA 53 MA 57 Virginia Th Sem BD 56 MDiv 70 Hon DD 02. Ridley Hall Cam 53. **d** 56 **p** 57. C Upper Tulse Hill St Matthias *S'wark* 56–59; C Reigate St Mary 59–61; V Richmond Ch Ch 61–72; P-in-c Sydenham H Trin 72–80; R Worting *Win* 80–92; Field Officer Decade of Evang 92–96; Can Shyogwe (Rwanda) from 93; rtd 96; PtO *Sarum* from 93; *Win* 96–14. *Yew Tree House, Mill Lane, Shalbourne, Marlborough SN8 3XA* T: (01672) 870460 E: steptrap@btinternet.com

TRASK, Imtiaz Ashley James. b 58. **d** 13 **p** 14. NSM Frant w Eridge *Chich* from 13. *The Rectory, Church Street, Cowden, Edenbridge TN8 7JE* M: 07897-262975 E: ijohnat@hotmail.co.uk

TRASK, Mrs Marion Elizabeth. b 54. Leic Univ BSc 74 Brunel Univ PGCE 76. Moorlands Bible Coll 82 Oak Hill Th Coll 93. **d** 96 **p** 97. C Bermondsey St Mary w

St Olave, St Jo etc *S'wark* 96–00; C Peckham St Mary Magd 00–04; P-in-c Cowden w Hammerwood *Chich* 10–16; P-in-c Cowden from 16; Chapl Qu Victoria Hosp NHS Foundn Trust East Grinstead from 10. *The Rectory, Church Street, Cowden, Edenbridge TN8 7JE* T: (01342) 850221 M: 07931-144260 E: m.traskcwhd@btinternet.com *or* cowdenchurch@hotmail.com

TRASLER, Canon Graham Charles George. b 44. Ch Ch Ox BA 65 MA 69. Cuddesdon Coll 66. **d** 68 **p** 69. C Gateshead St Mary *Dur* 68–71; P-in-c Monkwearmouth St Pet 71–79; R Bentley and Binsted *Win* 79–84; R New Alresford w Ovington and Itchen Stoke 84–01; RD Alresford 99–01; P-in-c Stockbridge and Longstock and Leckford 01–03; R 03–09; Hon Can Win Cath 05–09; rtd 09; PtO *Win* from 09. *3 Langtons Court, Alresford SO24 9UE* T: (01962) 736062 M: 07810-693910 E: costadelanton@gmail.com

TRATHEN, Paul Kevin. b 69. York Univ BA 91 MA 93 Jordanhill Coll Glas PGCE 94 Middx Univ BA 03. NTMTC 00. **d** 03 **p** 04. C Wickford and Runwell *Chelmsf* 03–07; P-in-c Rawreth w Rettendon 07–10; P-in-c Rawreth 10–11; Dioc Adv for Faith in the Public Square 11–12; V Walthamstow St Pet from 12; P-in-c Leytonstone St Andr 16–18; Chapl Forest Sch Snaresbrook from 12. *St Peter's Vicarage, 121 Forest Rise, London E17 3PW* T: (020) 8509 8901 M: 07871-584997 E: stpeterforestvicar-main@yahoo.co.uk *or* paul.trathen@btopenworld.com

TRAVERS, Canon Colin James. b 49. St Pet Coll Ox BA 70 MA 74. Ridley Hall Cam 70. **d** 72 **p** 73. C Hornchurch St Andr *Chelmsf* 72–75; Youth Chapl 75–77; C Aldersbrook 75–77; V Barkingside St Laur 77–82; V Waltham Abbey 82–88; V S Weald 88–95; Co-ord NTMTC and Hon C Gt Warley and Ingrave St Nic 95–98; P-in-c Gt Canfield w High Roding and Aythorpe Roding 98–02; V Theydon Bois 02–09; Hon Can Chelmsf Cathl 01–09; rtd 09; PtO *Ely* from 10. *7 Springhead Lane, Ely CB7 4QY* T: (01353) 659732 E: revtravs@gmail.com

TRAVES, Stephen Charles. b 44. Sheff City Coll of Educn CertEd 66 Open Univ BA 79. NOC 96. **d** 99 **p** 00. NSM Barnsley St Pet and St Jo *Wakef* 99–02; NSM Cudworth 02–07; NSM Lundwood 02–04; PtO 07–14; *Leeds* from 14; *Eur* 08–18. *23 Ecklands Croft, Millhouse Green, Sheffield S36 9AJ* T: 0119-695 6001 E: fr.s.traves2@gmail.com

TRAYNOR, Neil Owen. b 70. Worc Coll Ox BA 91 MA 94 Leeds Univ BA 11 Reading Univ PGCE 94. Coll of Resurr Mirfield 09. **d** 11 **p** 12. C Barnsley St Mary *Wakef* 11–13; Bp's Dom Chapl 13–14; TV Witney *Ox* 14–17; C Holland Park *Lon* from 17; Chapl Guy's and St Thos' NHS Foundn Trust from 18. *25 Sheffield Terrace, London W8 7NQ* M: 07887-778757 E: neil.traynor@yahoo.com

TRAYNOR, Nigel Martin Arthur. b 58. St Jo Coll Nottm 94. **d** 96 **p** 97. C Wellington All SS w Eyton *Lich* 96–00; P-in-c Pype Hayes *Birm* 00–02; TV Erdington 02–16; V Pype Hayes 16–18; AD Aston 12–18; Miss Outreach Co-ord Mercy Air S Africa from 18. *PO Box 1735, White River, 1240 Republic of South Africa* E: nmat1162@gmail.com

TREACY, Richard James. b 74. Aber Univ BD Univ of Wales (Cardiff) MTh 99. **d** 98 **p** 99. C Hillsborough *D & D* 98–02. *14 Downshire Crescent, Hillsborough BT26 6DD* T: (028) 9268 3098 M: 07917-854222 E: richard.treacy@btinternet.com

TREANOR, Timothy Lyons Victor. b 62. St Jo Coll Cam BA 83 MA 87 K Coll Lon MA 95 Cranfield Univ MSc 01. Ripon Coll Cuddesdon BTh 08. **d** 08 **p** 09. C Tavistock and Gulworthy *Ex* 08–10; C Ottery St Mary, Alfington, W Hill, Tipton etc 10–13; TR Wellington and Distr *B & W* from 13. *The Rectory, 72 High Street, Wellington TA21 8RF* T: (01823) 662248 E: tlvtreanor@btinternet.com

TREASURE, Canon Andrew Stephen. b 51. Oriel Coll Ox BA 73 MA 77. St Jo Coll Nottm BA 76. **d** 77 **p** 78. C Beverley Minster *York* 77–81; C Cambridge H Trin *Ely* 81–84; C Cambridge H Trin w St Andr Gt 84–85; V Eccleshill *Bradf* 85–98; P-in-c Bradf St Oswald Chapel Green 98–04; P-in-c Horton 98–04; V Lt Horton 04–14; *Leeds* from 14; C Bowling St Steph *Bradf* 05–14; *Leeds* 14–15; C Bankfoot and Bowling St Steph from 15; Hon Can Bradf Cathl from 04. *St Oswald's Vicarage, Christopher Street, Bradford BD5 9DH* T: (01274) 522717 E: stephen.treasure@leeds.anglican.org

TREASURE, Geoffrey. b 39. Hatf Coll Dur BA 61 Univ of Wales (Cardiff) DipEd 62. Oak Hill NSM Course 90. **d** 93 **p** 94. NSM Forty Hill Jes Ch *Lon* 93–95; Consultant SW England CPAS 95–02; PtO *B & W* 95–04; P-in-c Stoke St Gregory w Burrowbridge and Lyng 04–07; rtd 07; PtO *B & W* from 07. *Gable Cottage, West Lyng, Taunton TA3 5AP* T: (01823) 490458 E: geofftreasure@googlemail.com

TREASURE, James. b 75. Roehampton Inst BSc 99. Ripon Coll Cuddesdon 16. **d** 17 **p** 17. C Kidderminster St Jo and H Innocents *Worc* 17–18; C Dudley from 18. *32*

Chawn Hill, Stourbridge DY9 7JB M: 07747-110847
E: jtreasure@gmail.com

TREBY, David Alan. b 47. FIBMS 72 Bris Poly MSc 90. St Jo Coll Nottm MA 95. **d** 95 **p** 96. C Camborne *Truro* 95–00; V Stoke Gabriel and Collaton *Ex* 00–12; rtd 12; PtO *Sarum* from 12. *28 Ham Meadow, Marnhull, Sturminster Newton DT10 1LR* T: (01258) 820678

TREBY, Stephen Frank. b 46. Man Univ LLB 67 Lambeth STh 01. Cuddesdon Coll 69 Bangalore Th Coll 70. **d** 71 **p** 72. C Ashbourne St Oswald w Mapleton *Derby* 71–74; C Boulton 74–76; Chapl Trowbridge Coll *Sarum* 76–79; TV Melksham 79–87; V Dilton's-Marsh 87–01; Chapl Westbury Hosp 87–91; Chapl Wilts and Swindon Healthcare NHS Trust 92–01; R Spetisbury w Charlton Marshall etc *Sarum* 01–11; rtd 11. *5 Walnut Road, Honiton EX14 2UG* T: (01404) 548715 E: stephentreeby@hotmail.com

TREETOPS, Ms Jacqueline. b 47. NEOC 83. **dss** 86 **d** 87 **p** 94. Low Harrogate St Mary *Ripon* 86–87; C Roundhay St Edm 87–95; C Potternewton 95–97; rtd 97; PtO *Ripon* 01–14; *Leeds* 14–16. *43 Lincombe Bank, Leeds LS8 1QG* T: 0113-237 0474 E: j.treetops@sky.com

TREFUSIS, Charles Rodolph. b 61. Hull Univ BA 83. Wycliffe Hall Ox 85. **d** 90 **p** 91. C Blackheath St Jo *S'wark* 90–94; V Purley Ch 94–18; V Walton H Trin *Ox* from 18. *Walton Rectory, 42 Redwood Drive, Aylesbury HP21 7TN*

TREGALE, Diane Ruth. b 68. Spurgeon's Coll MTh 05. St Jo Coll Nottm 07. **d** 08 **p** 09. C Wilford *S'well* 08–11; C Sherborne w Castleton, Lillington and Longburton *Sarum* from 11; Chapl Gryphon Sch Sherborne from 11. *8 Kings Road, Sherborne DT9 4HU* E: diane@tregale.co.uk *or* diane.tregale@gryphon.dorset.sch.uk

TREGALE, John Ernest. b 69. Ex Univ BSc 90 Sheff Univ MA 01. St Jo Coll Nottm 05. **d** 08 **p** 09. C Wilford *S'well* 08–11; C Sherborne w Castleton, Lillington and Longburton *Sarum* 11–16; TV from 16. *8 Kings Road, Sherborne DT9 4HU* E: jono@tregale.co.uk

TREGENZA, Matthew John. b 69. Univ of Wales (Lamp) BA 92 BA(Theol) 08 SS Coll Cam PGCE 93 Lon Univ MA 01 FRGS 96. Westcott Ho Cam 01. **d** 03 **p** 04. C Marnhull *Sarum* 03–06; TV Mynyddislwyn *Mon* 06–08; P-in-c Blackwood 08–12; R Bishop's Lydeard w Lydeard St Lawrence etc *B & W* 12–19; RD Tone 14–19; R Crediton, Shobrooke and Sandford etc *Ex* from 19. *The Rectory, Church Street, Crediton EX17 2AQ* T: (01363) 894038 E: matthew.tregenza@gmail.com

TREHARNE, David Owen. b 73. Univ of Wales (Cardiff) BMus 94 MPhil 06 Bris Univ MEd 04 Bris Coll PGCE 00. Trin Coll Bris 94. **d** 99 **p** 04. NSM Bassaleg *Mon* 99–00; C Caerphilly *Llan* 04–08; P-in-c Porthkerry and Rhoose 08–12; Dioc Voc Adv 08–12; V Tidenham w Beachley and Lancaut *Glouc* from 12; P-in-c St Briavels w Hewelsfield and Brockweir from 12. *Tidenham Vicarage, Gloucester Road, Tutshill, Chepstow NP16 7DH* T: (01291) 760034 E: dtrevd@aol.com

TRELENBERG, Olaf. b 72. Ridley Hall Cam 06. **d** 08 **p** 09. C Scotforth *Blackb* 08–12; P-in-c Sandiacre *Derby* 12–14; R from 14. *St Giles's Rectory, Church Drive, Sandiacre, Nottingham NG10 5EE* T: 0115-939 7163 M: 07877-357332 E: olaf@talktalk.net

TREMBATH, Martyn Anthony. b 65. Leeds Univ BA 86. Ripon Coll Cuddesdon 88. **d** 90 **p** 91. C Bodmin w Lanhydrock and Lanivet *Truro* 90–91; C St Erth 92–96; C Phillack w Gwithian and Gwinear 94–96; C Hayle 94–96; Asst Chapl R Free Hampstead NHS Trust 96–98; Sen Chapl R Cornwall Hosps Trust 98–10; NSM Godrevy *Truro* 08–10; TR 10–13; Hon Can Truro Cathl 09–13; Chapl Luton and Dunstable Univ Hosp NHS Foundn Trust from 13; Bp's Adv for Hosp Chapl St Alb from 16; PtO *Ox* from 14. *The Chaplaincy, Luton and Dunstable Hospital, Lewsey Road, Luton LU4 0DZ* T: 08451-270127 E: godrevy-tr@hotmail.co.uk

TREMLETT, The Very Revd Andrew. b 64. Pemb Coll Cam BA 86 MA 90 Qu Coll Ox BA 88 MA 95 Ex Univ MPhil 96. Wycliffe Hall Ox 86. **d** 89 **p** 90. C Torquay St Matthias, St Mark and H Trin *Ex* 89–92; Miss to Seamen 92–94; Asst Chapl Rotterdam *Eur* 92–94; Chapl 94–95; TV Fareham H Trin *Portsm* 95–98; Bp's Dom Chapl 98–03; V Goring-by-Sea *Chich* 03–08; Can Res Bris Cathl 08–10; Can Westmr Abbey and R Westmr St Marg 10–16; Adn Westmr 14–16; Dean Dur from 16. *The Deanery, The College, Durham DH1 3EQ* T: 0191-384 7500 E: dean@durhamcathedral.co.uk

TREMTHTHANMOR, Ms Chrys Mymmir Evnath Tristan. b 66. Univ of California BA 88. St Mich Coll Llan BA 05 MPhil 07. **d** 06 **p** 07. C Coity, Nolton and Brackla *Llan* 06–10; TV Daventry, Ashby St Ledgers, Braunston etc *Pet* 10–16; Tr Officer (CMD) from 16; C Abington 16–19. *1 Bouverie Court, The Lakes, Northampton NN4 7YD* T: (01733) 887000 E: vicarwelton@o2.co.uk

TRENDALL, Matthew James. b 72. Oriel Coll Ox BA 93 MA 98. Trin Coll Bris BA 10. **d** 10 **p** 11. C Redland *Bris* 10–13; P-in-c Walton Milton Keynes *Ox* 13–14; R from 14. *The Rectory, Walton Road, Wavendon, Milton Keynes MK17 8LW* T: (01908) 582839 M: 07447-150396 E: trendalls.mk@btinternet.com

TRENDALL, Peter John. b 43. Oak Hill Th Coll 66. **d** 69 **p** 70. C Beckenham Ch Ch *Roch* 69–73; C Bedworth *Cov* 73–76; V Hornsey Rise St Mary *Lon* 76–82; P-in-c Upper Holloway St Steph 80–82; V Hornsey Rise St Mary w St Steph 82–84; TR Walthamstow St Mary w St Steph *Chelmsf* 84–85 and 85–93; P-in-c Chigwell 93–94; TR Chigwell and Chigwell Row 94–08; rtd 08; PtO *St E* from 08. *27 Crick Court, Station Road, Southwold IP18 6DE* T: (01502) 722962 M: 07453-347862 E: peter.trendall@btinternet.com

TRENDER, Lawrence. b 37. Bps' Coll Cheshunt 64. **d** 66 **p** 67. C Petersham *S'wark* 66–71; C Malden St Jo 71–73; R Thornham Magna w Thornham Parva *St E* 73–81; R Thornhams Magna and Parva, Gislingham and Mellis 81–87; P-in-c Mellis 73–81; P-in-c Gislingham 73–81; RD Hartismere 85–87; R Skipsea w Ulrome and Barmston w Fraisthorpe *York* 92–01; rtd 01; PtO *York* from 01. *Stone Cottage, 5 Far Lane, Bewholme, Driffield YO25 8EA* T: (01964) 533020 E: trender@waitrose.com

TRENHOLME (née ROBERTSON), Mrs Jane Lesley. b 54. Man Univ BSc 76 Leeds Univ BA 06. NOC 03. **d** 06 **p** 07. NSM Northowram *Wakef* 06–08; C Tong *Bradf* 08–14; *Leeds* 14; C Laisterdyke *Bradf* 08–10; P-in-c 10–14; *Leeds* 14; PtO 17–18; C Shelf w Buttershaw St Aid from 18; C Wibsey St Paul from 18. *Stretchgate, Rookes Lane, Halifax HX3 8PU* T: (01274) 693392 M: 07771-823281 E: jltrenholme@hotmail.co.uk

TRENHOLME, William Nicholas David. b 85. Grey Coll Dur MSci 08. Oak Hill Th Coll BA 13. **d** 13 **p** 14. C Wollaston w Strixton and Bozeat etc *Pet* 13–16; TV Bentham, Burton-in-Lonsdale, Chapel-le-Dale etc *Leeds* from 16. *St Mary's Vicarage, Main Street, Ingleton, Carnforth LA6 3HF* M: 07712-627243 E: nick.trenholme@gmail.com

TRENIER, Andrew Peter Christopher. b 80. Univ of Wales (Swansea) BScEcon 02 Ox Univ BA 13. Ripon Coll Cuddesdon 09. **d** 12 **p** 13. C Derby Cathl 12–15; R Chingford SS Pet and Paul *Chelmsf* 15–19; Prec and Sacr Win Cathl from 19. *8 The Close, Winchester SO23 9LS* M: 07786-868615 E: andytrenier@gmail.com

TRETHEWEY, The Ven Frederick Martyn. b 49. Lon Univ BA 70 Lambeth STh 79. Oak Hill Th Coll 75. **d** 78 **p** 79. C Tollington Park St Mark w St Anne *Lon* 78–82; C Whitehall Park St Andr Hornsey Lane 82–87; TV Hornsey Rise Whitehall Park Team 87–88; V Brockmoor *Lich* 88–93; V Brockmoor *Worc* 93–01; Chapl Russells Hall Hosp Dudley 88–91; Chapl Dudley Gp of Hosps NHS Trust 92–01; RD Himley *Worc* 96–01; Hon Can Worc Cathl 99–01; Adn Dudley 01–13; rtd 13; P-in-c Brittany *Eur* 13–16; PtO *Leic* from 16; *Glouc* from 17. *Finlock Bungalow, Redesdale Place, Moreton-in-Marsh GL56 0EQ* T: (01608) 654121 E: fred@trethewey.org.uk

TRETHEWEY, Richard John. b 74. Jes Coll Ox MA 02. Wycliffe Hall Ox BA 02. **d** 02 **p** 03. C Biddulph *Lich* 02–06; C Knowle *Birm* 06–16; R Glenfield and Newtown Linford *Leic* from 16. *The Rectory, Main Street, Glenfield, Leicester LE3 8DG* M: 07595-320563 E: richard@trethewey.org.uk

TRETT, Peter John. b 44. **d** 97 **p** 98. OLM High Oak, Hingham and Scoulton w Wood Rising *Nor* 97–14; PtO from 14. *Holly House, 35 Plough Lane, Hardingham, Norwich NR9 4AE* T: (01953) 850369 E: trett@nnbus.co.uk

TREVELYAN, Mrs Rosemary Elizabeth. b 43. Ex Univ CertEd 64 Open Univ BA 91. **d** 11. NSM Washingborough w Heighington and Canwick *Linc* 11–17. *6 Wyebank Place, Tutshill, Chepstow NP16 7EU* E: rtrev911@hotmail.com

TREVITHICK, Janet Anne. b 54. **d** 13. NSM Titchfield *Portsm* from 13. *34 Vicarage Lane, Fareham PO14 2LA* T: (01329) 668957 E: janettrevithick@m8n.com

TREVOR, Canon Charles Frederic. b 27. Sarum Th Coll 54. **d** 56 **p** 57. C Sutton in Ashfield St Mich *S'well* 56–58; C Birstall *Leic* 58–61; V Prestwold w Hoton 61–66; V Thornton in Lonsdale w Burton in Lonsdale *Bradf* 66–74; V Kirkby Malham 74–85; P-in-c Coniston Cold 81–85; Hon Can Bradf Cathl 85–92; V Sutton 85–92; RD S Craven 86–91; rtd 92; PtO *Bradf* 92–14; *Leeds* 14–16. *6 Elbolton Flats, Hebden Road, Skipton BD23 5LH* T: (01756) 752640

TREW, Jeremy Charles. b 66. Univ of Wales (Abth) BSc 89 Leeds Univ MSc 92. St Jo Coll Nottm MA 94. **d** 97 **p** 98. C Roundhay St Edm *Ripon* 97–01; P-in-c Spofforth w Kirk Deighton 01–07; V Seaton and Beer *Ex* from 07; RD Honiton 13–19. *The Vicarage, Colyford Road, Seaton EX12 2DF* T: (01297) 20391 E: jeremytrew@hotmail.com

TREW, Robin Nicholas. b 52. UWIST BSc 74 Open Univ MA 01. St Jo Coll Nottm 87. **d** 89 **p** 90. C Cov H Trin 89–93; V Snitterfield w Bearley 93–02; R Allesley 02–16; AD Cov

N 10–15; rtd 16; PtO *Heref* from 17. *The Hollies, 10 Watling Street South, Church Stretton SY6 7BG*

TREWEEK, Guy Matthew. b 65. LSE BSc(Econ) 87 Peterho Cam BA 07 MA 12. Westcott Ho Cam 05 Yale Div Sch 07. **d** 08 **p** 09. C Hammersmith St Pet *Lon* 08–11; P-in-c St Andr-by-the-Wardrobe w St Ann, Blackfriars 11–15; P-in-c St Jas Garlickhythe w St Mich Queenhithe etc 11–15; PtO from 15; *Glouc* 15–17; Public Preacher from 17; Min Can Glouc Cathl from 17. *Bishopscourt, Pitt Street, Gloucester GL1 2BQ* T: (01452) 524158 E: guy.treweek@gmail.com *or* gtreweek@glosdioc.org.uk

✠**TREWEEK (née MONTGOMERY), The Rt Revd Rachel.** b 63. Reading Univ BA 85. Wycliffe Hall Ox BTh 94. **d** 94 **p** 95 **c** 15. C Tufnell Park St Geo and All SS *Lon* 94–99; V Bethnal Green St Jas Less 99–06; CME Officer 99–06; Adn Northolt 06–11; Adn Hackney 11–15; Bp Glouc from 15. *Bishopscourt, Pitt Street, Gloucester GL1 2BQ* T: (01452) 835512

TREWEEKS, Mrs Angela Elizabeth. b 35. Gilmore Ho IDC 59. **d** 87 **p** 94. Chapl Asst St Nic Hosp Newc 85–87; Chapl 87; Hon C Newc St Geo 87–89; Chapl St Mary's Hosp Stannington 92–95; Hon C Rothbury *Newc* 94–96; rtd 95; PtO *Newc* from 96. *The Nook, Pondicherry, Rothbury, Morpeth NE65 7YS* T: (01669) 620393 E: angelatreweeks@talktalk.net

TRICK, Matthew John Harvey. Univ of Wales (Abth) BSc 02. St Mich Coll Llan BTh 08. **d** 08 **p** 09. C Cowbridge *Llan* 08–10; C Aberavon 10–11; TV 11–14; P-in-c Cambourne *Ely* 14–17; V Ringwood w Ellingham and Harbridge etc *Win* from 17. *The Vicarage, 65 Southampton Road, Ringwood BH24 1HE* T: (01425) 540951 M: 07903-156688 E: matthew.trick@ringwoodbenefice.org.uk

TRICKETT, Canon Judith. b 50. Open Univ BA 00. St Jo Coll Nottm 89. **d** 91 **p** 94. Par Dn Kimberworth *Sheff* 91–93; Dn-in-c Worsbrough Common 93–94; V 94–01; V Herringthorpe 01–10; R Firbeck w Letwell 10–15; V Woodsetts 10–15; Hon Can Sheff Cathl 08–15; rtd 15; Hon C Harthill and Thorpe Salvin *Sheff* 15–16; Hon C Aston cum Aughton w Swallownest and Ulley 16–17; PtO from 17. *9 St Alban's Court, Wickersley, Rotherham S66 1FG* T: (01709) 739666 M: 07974-404831 E: judith.trickett493@btinternet.com

TRICKEY, Christopher Jolyon. b 57. Jes Coll Cam BA 79 MA 83 Barrister-at-Law 80. Trin Coll Bris BA 90. **d** 90 **p** 91. C Chesham Bois *Ox* 90–94; R Busbridge *Guildf* 94–98; P-in-c Hambledon 97–98; R Busbridge and Hambledon 98–09; Chapl Godalming Coll 01–09; R Nailsea H Trin *B & W* 09–17; PtO *Guildf* 17–19; Hon C Oxshott from 19. *The Vicarage, Steels Lane, Oxshott, Leatherhead KT22 0QH* T: (01372) 842071 E: cjtrickey@gmail.com

TRICKEY, Mrs Frances Anne. b 59. Keele Univ BA 81 Lon Inst of Educn PGCE 82 Win Univ BA 11. STETS 08. **d** 11 **p** 12. NSM Wraxall *B & W* 11–17; V Oxshott *Guildf* from 17. *The Vicarage, Steels Lane, Oxshott, Leatherhead KT22 0QH* T: (01372) 842071 E: francestrickey@hotmail.co.uk *or* frances.trickey@standrewsoxshott.org.uk

TRICKEY, The Very Revd Frederick Marc. b 35. Dur Univ BA 62. Cranmer Hall Dur. **d** 64 **p** 65. C Alton St Lawr *Win* 64–68; V Win St Jo cum Winnall 68–77; Angl Adv Channel TV from 77; R Guernsey St Martin *Win* 77–02; P-in-c Sark 02–03; Dean Guernsey 95–03; Hon Can Win Cathl 95–03; rtd 03; PtO *Win* from 03. *L'Esperance, La Route des Camps, St Martin, Guernsey GY4 6AD* T: (01481) 238441 E: fut@ewgsy.net

TRICKEY, Mrs Joanna Charlotte. b 85. Leeds Univ BA 07 Wycliffe Hall Ox BA 10. St Mellitus Coll 14. **d** 17 **p** 19. C Guildf Ch Ch from 17. *2 Ivor Close, Guildford GU1 2ET* M: 07534-908689 E: thejtrickeys@gmail.com *or* jo@christchurchguildford.com

TRICKLEBANK, Steven. b 56. Nottm Univ BTh 88 Keele Univ MA 97. Linc Th Coll 85. **d** 88 **p** 89. C Ditton St Mich *Liv* 88–91; C Wigan All SS 91–93; Chapl Aintree Hosps NHS Trust Liv 93–97; C-in-c St Edm Anchorage Lane CD *Sheff* 97–00; Chapl Doncaster R Infirmary and Montagu Hosp NHS Trust 97–00; V Stocksbridge *Sheff* 00–04; P-in-c Streatham Ch Ch *S'wark* 04–05; P-in-c Streatham Hill St Marg 04–05; V Streatham Ch Ch from 05. *Christ Church Vicarage, 3 Christchurch Road, London SW2 3ET* T: (020) 8674 5723 E: steventricklebank@hotmail.com

TRIFFITT, Jonathan Paul. b 74. St Jo Coll Nottm BA 03. **d** 03 **p** 04. C W Kilburn St Luke w St Simon and St Jude *Lon* 03–06; C Paddington Em Harrow Road 03–06; C Sherborne w Castleton etc and Chapl Gryphon Sch Sherborne 06–10; V Southbroom *Sarum* 10–15; RD Devizes 11–15; R Blandford Forum and Langton Long from 15; RD Milton and Blandford from 16. *The Rectory, 2 Portman Place, Blandford Forum DT11 7DG* T: (01258) 721754 E: jonathantriffitt@icloud.com

TRIGG, Jeremy Michael. b 51. Open Univ BA 88. Ripon Coll Cuddesdon 80. **d** 81 **p** 82. C Roundhay St Edm *Ripon* 81–84; C Harrogate St Wilfrid and St Luke 84–87; TV Pocklington Team *York* 87–90; R Rowley w Skidby 90–97; TV Wolverton *Ox* 97–98; R 98–11; P-in-c Rothwell *Ripon* 11–14; *Leeds* 14–15; TR Rothwell, Lofthouse, Methley etc 15–17; rtd 17. *2 Deep Ghyll Walk, Ripon HG4 1RL* E: jeremy.trigg@gmail.com

TRIGG, Preb Jonathan David. b 49. Ex Coll Ox BA 71 MA 75 Dur Univ PhD 92. Cranmer Hall Dur BA 82. **d** 83 **p** 84. C Enfield St Andr *Lon* 83–87; V Oakwood St Thos 87–96; AD Enfield 92–96; V Highgate St Mich 96–17; P-in-c Highgate All SS 09–14; C 14–17; AD W Haringey 00–06; Dir of Ords Edmonton Area 08–17; Preb St Paul's Cathl 10–17; rtd 17; PtO *B & W* from 17. *2 Park Street, Taunton TA1 4DF* M: 07883-340239 E: jdtrigg@gmail.com

TRIGLE, Alan Neil. b 61. Hertf Coll Ox BA 84 MA 87. St Mellitus Coll BA 15. **d** 15 **p** 17. C Kensal Town St Thos w St Andr and St Phil *Lon* 15–16; C Chiswick St Nic w St Mary from 17. *1 Oldfield Road, London W3 7TD* M: 07711-623834 E: atrigle@icloud.com

TRILL, Barry. b 42. Chich Th Coll 65. **d** 68 **p** 69. C W Hackney St Barn *Lon* 68–73; TV Is of Dogs Ch Ch and St Jo w St Luke 73–78; P-in-c Hastings All So *Chich* 78–79; V 79–99; rtd 99. *17 School Place, Bexhill-on-Sea TN40 2PX* T: (01424) 217765

TRIM, Elizabeth Ann. See VARLEY, Elizabeth Ann

TRIMBLE, Eleanor Louise. b 70. Man Metrop Univ BSc 97. Yorks Min Course. **d** 09 **p** 10. C Old Trafford St Jo *Man* 09–13; P-in-c Man Apostles w Miles Platting from 13. *Church of the Apostles Rectory, Ridgway Street, Manchester M40 7FY* T: 0161-948 4197 M: 07887-601451 E: eleanor.trimble@btinternet.com

TRIMBY (née SOUTHERTON), Kathryn Ruth. b 66. Univ of Wales (Lamp) BA 88. Sarum & Wells Th Coll 90. **d** 92 **p** 97. C Connah's Quay *St As* 92–97; R Halkyn w Caerfallwch w Rhesycae 97–04; I Tubbercurry w Killoran *T, K & A* 04–14; Can Achonry Cathl 11–14; Can Tuam Cathl 13–14; R Llanyblodwel, Llanymynech, Morton and Trefonen *Lich* from 14. *The Rectory, Rectory Lane, Pant, Oswestry SY10 9RA* T: (01691) 831211 E: kathsoutherton@hotmail.com

TRIMMER, Penelope Marynice. See DRAPER, Penelope Marynice

TRINDER, Miss Gillian Joyce. b 68. Birm Univ BA 90 Bp Grosseteste Coll PGCE 91. Westcott Ho Cam 09. **d** 11 **p** 12. C Whitkirk *Ripon* 11–13; C Starbeck 13–14; *Leeds* 14; NSM Bury St Edmunds All SS w St Jo and St Geo *St E* 16–17; NSM Lark Valley 16–17; Chapl Ypres *Eur* 17–19. *Address temp unknown*

TRIST, Richard McLeod. b 55. Univ of NSW BSEd 76. Ridley Coll Melbourne BTh 86. **d** 87 **p** 87. C Camberwell St Jo Australia 87–88; P-in-c Cranbourne 88–91; I 91–92; Sen Assoc Min Kew St Hilary 93–96; C Langham Place All So *Lon* 97–01; V Camberwell St Mark Australia from 01; AD Camberwell 03–05. *1 Canterbury Road, Camberwell Vic 3124, Australia* T: (0061) (3) 9897 1532 *or* (3) 9882 3776 F: 9882 6514 E: richard.trist@bigpond.com *or* stmarksc@bigpond.com

TRISTRAM, Canon Catherine Elizabeth. b 31. Somerville Coll Ox BA 53 MA 57. **dss** 83 **d** 87 **p** 94. Holy Is *Newc* 84–01; Hon C 87–01; Hon Can Newc Cathl 94–01; PtO from 01. *4 Lewins Lane, Holy Island, Berwick-upon-Tweed TD15 2SB* T: (01289) 389306

TRISTRAM, Canon Michael Anthony. b 50. Ch Coll Cam BA 72 MA 76 Solicitor 76. Ripon Coll Cuddesdon 79. **d** 82 **p** 83. C Stanmore *Win* 82–85; R Abbotts Ann and Upper Clatford and Goodworth Clatford 85–92; V Pershore w Pinvin, Wick and Birlingham *Worc* 92–03; Hon Can Worc Cathl 00–03; Can Res Portsm Cathl 03–15; rtd 15; PtO *Portsm* from 15; *Eur* from 18. *39 Oakwood Road, Hayling Island PO11 9AY* T: (023) 9246 3170

TRIVASSE, Keith Malcolm. b 59. Man Univ BA 81 CertEd 82 MPhil 90 Dur Univ MA 98. Qu Coll Birm 84. **d** 86 **p** 87. C Prestwich St Marg *Man* 86–88; C Orford St Marg *Liv* 88–90; TV Sunderland *Dur* 90–91; P-in-c N Hylton St Marg Castletown 91–95; R Bothal and Pegswood w Longhirst *Newc* 95–97; P-in-c Bury Ch King *Man* 01–11; P-in-c Bury St Paul 01–03; C Bury, Roch Valley 11–15; rtd 15; PtO *Man* from 15. *Address withheld by request* T: 0161-258 0649

TRIVASSE, Ms Margaret. b 59. Dur Univ BA 80 MA 97 New Coll Dur PGCE 01 Liv Univ MTh 05. NOC 01. **d** 04 **p** 05. NSM Radcliffe *Man* 04–08; NSM Prestwich St Gabr from 08. *114 Valley Mill Lane, Bury BL9 9BY* T: 0161-258 0649 M: 07796-366220 E: margtriv@yahoo.co.uk

TRODDEN, Canon Michael John. b 54. K Coll Lon BD 77 AKC 77 CertEd. Wycliffe Hall Ox 79. **d** 80 **p** 81. C Woodford St Mary w St Phil and St Jas *Chelmsf* 80–87; V Aldborough

Hatch 87–96; R Ampthill w Millbrook and Steppingley *St Alb* 96–19; Hon Can St Alb 18–19; rtd 19. *Address temp unknown*

TROLLOPE, David Harvey. b 41. BSc 63. Lon Coll of Div 66. **d** 68 **p** 69. C Bermondsey St Jas w Ch Ch *S'wark* 68–71; CMS Namibia 71–72; Uganda 72–77; Kenya 77–82; V Gt Crosby St Luke *Liv* 82–04; rtd 04; PtO *Ches* from 04. *26 Whitehouse Lane, Heswall, Wirral CH60 1UQ* T: 0151-342 2648 E: davidtrollope@btinternet.com

TROMANS, Judith Anne. *See* OLIVER, Judith Anne

TROMANS, Kevin Stanley. b 57. St Martin's Coll Lanc BEd 79 St Jo Coll Dur MA 12. Aston Tr Scheme 90 Coll of Resurr Mirfield 92. **d** 94 **p** 95. C Rawdon *Bradf* 94–96; C Woodhall 96–98; V Liversedge w Hightown *Wakef* 98–02; V Bierley *Bradf* 02–07; Chapl Co Durham and Darlington NHS Foundn Trust 07–12; Sen Chapl from 12; CF(V) 08–18. *University Hospital Durham, North Road, Durham DH1 5TW* T: 0191-333 2183 E: kevintromans@nhs.net

TROMBETTI, Lynda Joan. b 52. **d** 03 **p** 04. OLM Dorking w Ranmore *Guildf* 03–11; NSM 11–12; Chapl Epsom and St Helier Univ Hosps NHS Trust 15–17; PtO *Guildf* 12–15; P-in-c Walton-on-the-Hill 15–17; PtO *Portsm* from 15; Chapl Isle of Wight NHS Trust from 19. *5 Egypt Copse, Cowes PO31 8BA* M: 07968-629364 E: rev.lyndi@gmail.com

TROOD, James William. b 68. Cov Poly BSc 90 St Jo Coll Dur PGCE 91. St Jo Coll Nottm MTh 02. **d** 02 **p** 03. C Anchorsholme *Blackb* 02–06; TV Glascote and Stonydelph *Lich* 06–15; RD Tamworth 09–14; P-in-c Walsall St Matt 15–18; R from 18. *The Rectory, 48 Jesson Road, Walsall WS1 3AX* T: (01922) 626039 M: 07939-587208 E: rector@stmatthewswalsall.co.uk

TROTMAN, Michael Edwin. b 81. Univ of Wales (Cardiff) BSc 02 Kingston Univ PGCE 10. Wycliffe Hall Ox 16. **d** 18 **p** 19. C Fordingbridge and Hyde and Breamore etc *Win* from 18. *The Vicarage, Frogham Hill, Stuckton, Fordingbridge SP6 2HH* M: 07525-662999

TROTT, Daniel Mark. b 84. Hertf Coll Ox BA 08 MA 10 New Coll Ox MSt 10 DPhil 14. Westcott Ho Cam 13. **d** 16 **p** 17. C Upper Norwood St Jo *S'wark* from 16. *3 Enderley House, Sylvan Road, London SE19 2RT* T: (020) 8771 5307

TROTT, Stephen. b 57. Hull Univ BA 79 Fitzw Coll Cam BA 83 MA 87 Univ of Wales (Cardiff) LLM 03 FRSA 86. Westcott Ho Cam 81. **d** 84 **p** 85. C Hessle *York* 84–87; C Kingston upon Hull St Alb 87–88; R Pitsford w Boughton *Pet* from 88; Sec CME 88–93; Chapl Pitsford Sch from 91; RD Brixworth *Pet* from 15; Hon Can Th Richmond Canada from 15; CF (TA) from 16. *The Rectory, Humfrey Lane, Boughton, Northampton NN2 8RQ* T: (01604) 845655 M: 07712-863000 E: revstephentrott@gmail.com

TROTTER, Robin Fenwick. b 56. Qu Foundn (Course) 16. **d** 18 **p** 19. OLM Burton St Modwen *Lich* from 18; OLM Burton St Aid and St Paul from 18. *4 Home Farm, Geary Lane, Bretby, Burton-on-Trent DE15 0QE* T: (01283) 702221 M: 07984-450761 E: robin.trotter@icloud.com

TROUT, Keith. b 49. Trin Coll Bris 90. **d** 92 **p** 93. C Pudsey St Lawr and St Paul *Bradf* 92–97; V Burley *Ripon* 97–14; *Leeds* 14; P-in-c 14–17; rtd 14. *8 South Street, Gargrave, Skipton BD23 3RT*

TROWSDALE, James Andrew. b 61. Yorks Min Course 13. **d** 15 **p** 16. NSM Rudston, Boynton, Carnaby etc *York* 15–19; PtO from 19. *The Rectory, Rudston Road, Burton Agnes, Driffield YO25 4NE* T: (01262) 490148 E: james.trowsdale@hey.nhs.uk *or* revjamestrowsdale@gmail.com

TRUBY, Canon David Charles. b 57. Liv Poly BA 79. Linc Th Coll 79. **d** 82 **p** 83. C Stanley *Liv* 82–85; C Hindley St Pet 85–90; R Brimington *Derby* 90–98; Can Res Derby Cathl 98–03; TR Wirksworth from 03; RD 08–17; Hon Can Derby Cathl from 04. *The Rectory, Coldwell Street, Wirksworth, Matlock DE4 4FB* T: (01629) 822858 E: david.truby@outlook.com

TRUDGETT, Raymond John. b 46. Wilson Carlile Coll 86. **d** 04 **p** 05. Port Chapl and C Aqaba SS Pet and Paul Jordan 04–07; Chapl Medway and Thames Ports *Roch* 07–11; PtO *Cant* 07–11; *Chelmsf* 07–11; rtd 11; PtO *Nor* from 11. *9 Holly Road, Lowestoft NR32 3NH* T: (01502) 583668

TRUMAN, Miss Catherine Jane. b 64. Coll of Ripon & York St Jo BEd 88. St Jo Coll Nottm 01. **d** 03 **p** 04. C Owlerton *Sheff* 03–06; Hd Academic Progr Wilson Carlile Coll of Evang 06–12; Tr Manager 12–19. *14 Park Avenue, Chapeltown, Sheffield S35 1WE*

TRUMAN, Miss Charlotte Jane. b 71. Birm Univ BPhil 96. Westcott Ho Cam 96. **d** 99 **p** 00. C High Harrogate Ch Ch *Ripon* 99–03; P-in-c Oulton w Woodlesford 03–06; Chapl HM YOI Northallerton 06–09; Chapl HM Pris and YOI New Hall 09–18; Chapl Huddersfield Univ *Leeds* from 18. *University of Huddersfield, Queensgate, Huddersfield HD1 3DH* T: (01484) 422288 E: revcjt@hotmail.co.uk

TRUMPER, Roger David. b 52. Ex Univ BSc 74 K Coll Lon MSc 75 Ox Univ BA 80 MA 85. Wycliffe Hall Ox 78. **d** 81 **p** 82. C Tunbridge Wells St Jo *Roch* 81–84; C Slough *Ox* 84–87; TV Shenley and Loughton 87–88; TV Watling Valley 88–93; R Byfleet *Guildf* 93–05; TV Sidmouth, Woolbrook, Salcombe Regis, Sidbury etc *Ex* 05–16; rtd 16. *28 Gilbert Road, Yeovil BA21 5FN* E: nonnobis115@gmail.com

TRUNDLE, Christopher Philip. b 85. Trin Coll Cam BA 07 MA 10 PGCE 08. Coll of Resurr Mirfield 08. **d** 10 **p** 11. C Tottenham St Paul *Lon* 10–12; C Pimlico St Gabr 12–13; P-in-c Clerkenwell H Redeemer 13–14; V from 14; P-in-c Clerkenwell St Mark 13–14; V from 14. *The Clergy House, 24 Exmouth Market, London EC1R 4QE* T: (020) 7837 1861 E: chris.trundle@gmail.com *or* holyredeemerstmark@tiscali.co.uk

TRURO, Bishop of. *See* MOUNSTEPHEN, The Rt Revd Philip Ian

TRURO, Dean of. *See* BUSH, The Very Revd Roger Charles

TRUSCOTT, Stephen Alistair. b 49. **d** 06 **p** 07. OLM Bishopston and St Andrews *Bris* 06–14; OLM Redland from 14. *5 Kent Road, Bristol BS7 9DN* T: 0117-942 4248 E: steve@redland.org.uk

TRUSS, Canon Charles Richard. b 42. Reading Univ BA 63 Linacre Coll Ox BA 66 MA 69 K Coll Lon MPhil 79 Win Univ MA 16. Wycliffe Hall Ox 64. **d** 66 **p** 67. C Leic H Apostles 66–69; C Hampstead St Jo *Lon* 69–72; V Belsize Park 72–79; V Wood Green St Mich 79–82; TR Wood Green St Mich w Bounds Green St Gabr etc 82–85; R Shepperton 85–94; V Waterloo St Jo w St Andr *S'wark* 94–08; RD Lambeth 95–05; Hon Can St Mark Cathl 01–08; Sen Chapl Actors' Ch Union 04–08; rtd 08; PtO *S'wark* from 08; *Guildf* from 10. *12 Camden Cottages, Church Walk, Weybridge KT13 8JT* T: (01932) 702317 E: richard.truss@btinternet.com

TRUSTRAM, Canon David Geoffrey. b 49. Pemb Coll Ox BA 71 MA 76 Qu Coll Cam BA 73 MA 77. Westcott Ho Cam 74. **d** 75 **p** 76. C Surbiton St Mark *S'wark* 75–77; C Surbiton St Andr and St Mark 77–78; C Richmond St Mary w St Matthias and St Jo 78–82; P-in-c Eastry *Cant* 82–88; R Eastry and Northbourne w Tilmanstone etc 88–90; Chapl Eastry Hosp 82–90; V Tenterden St Mildred w Smallhythe *Cant* 90–10; P-in-c Tenterden St Mich 07–10; Hon Can Cant Cathl 96–10; AD Tenterden 99–05; rtd 10; PtO *Cant* from 11. *Hensmead, New Road, Headcorn, Ashford TN27 9SE* T: (01622) 892480 M: 07811-874806 E: trustram@btinternet.com

TSANG, Wing Man. b 52. Lon Univ BSc 74 MPhil 84 MCB 88 MRCPath 88 FRCPath 96. STETS 99. **d** 02 **p** 03. C Merthyr Tydfil Ch Ch *Llan* 02–05; TV Broadwater *Chich* 05–17; rtd 17; PtO *Portsm* from 18. *47 Mulberry Avenue, Fareham PO14 2SN* M: 07961-839018 E: wing2699@hotmail.com

TSUKADA, John Jutaro. **d** 15. NSM Aberdeen St Ninian *Ab* from 15. *25 Ashwood Circle, Bridge of Don, Aberdeen AB22 8XU*

TUAM, Archdeacon of. *See* MACWHIRTER, The Ven Stephen Joseph

TUAM, KILLALA AND ACHONRY, Bishop of. *See* ROOKE, The Rt Revd Patrick William

TUBBS, Preb Brian Ralph. b 44. AKC 66. **d** 67 **p** 68. C Ex St Thos 67–72; TV Sidmouth, Woolbrook and Salcombe Regis 72–77; R Ex St Jas 77–96; RD Christianity 89–95; V Paignton St Jo and Chapl S Devon Healthcare NHS Foundn Trust 96–09; Preb Ex Cathl 95–09; rtd 09; PtO *Eur* from 10. *58 Dorset Avenue, Exeter EX4 1ND* T: (01392) 200506 E: fathertubbs@aol.com

TUCK, Canon Andrew Kenneth. b 42. Kelham Th Coll 63. **d** 68 **p** 69. C Poplar Lon 68–74; TV 74–76; V Walsgrave on Sowe *Cov* 76–90; R Farnham *Guildf* 90–12; Chapl Surrey Hants Borders NHS Trust 90–05; Chapl Surrey and Borders Partnership NHS Foundn Trust 05–12; RD Farnham *Guildf* 00–05; Hon Can Guildf Cathl 09–12; rtd 12; PtO *Guildf* 12–13; Dioc Spiritual Direction Co-ord from 14. *7 Forge Close, Farnham GU9 9PX* T: (01252) 716119 E: andrew.tuck@cofeguildford.org.uk

TUCK, David John. b 36. St Cath Coll Cam BA 61 MA 65. Cuddesdon Coll 61. **d** 63 **p** 64. C Holt and Kelling w Salthouse *Nor* 63–68; Zambia 68–73; V Sprowston *Nor* 73–84; R Beeston St Andr 73–84; RD Nor N 81–84; V Pinner *Lon* 84–01; rtd 01; PtO *Lon* 02–04 and from 18; *St Alb* from 04; Hon C N Harrow St Alb *Lon* 04–17. *119 High Street, Northwood HA6 1ED* T: (01923) 825806 M: 07443-576905 E: dandtuck@btinternet.com

TUCK, Gillian. b 40. SRN 64 SCM 66. Llan Dioc Tr Scheme 93. **d** 97 **p** 98. NSM Pontypridd St Cath w St Matt *Llan* 97–01; P-in-c Pontypridd St Matt w Cilfynydd 01–05; NSM Pontypridd St Matt and Cilfynydd w Llanwynno 05–08; rtd 08; PtO *Llan* from 09. *4 Maes Glas, Coed y Cwm, Pontypridd CF37 3EJ* T: (01443) 791049

TUCK, Rebecca Jane. b 78. Lon Guildhall Univ BSc 99 Univ of E Lon PGCE 00. Ridley Hall Cam 16. **d** 18 **p** 19. C Horsham *Chich* from 18. *18 Queensway, Horsham RH13 5AY* M: 07905-315577 E: rebecca.tuck.rt@gmail.com

TUCK, Canon Ronald James. b 47. S'wark Ord Course 75. **d** 78 **p** 79. C Upper Holloway St Pet w St Jo *Lon* 78–81; P-in-c Scottow and Swanton Abbott w Skeyton *Nor* 81–88; R Bradwell 88–12; Hon Can Nor Cathl 10–12; rtd 12; PtO *Nor* from 12. *5 Gosford Heights, 47 Gosford Road, Beccles NR34 9SP* T: (01502) 717273 E: revtuck@btinternet.com

TUCKER, Canon Anthony Ian. b 50. CA Tr Coll 73 S'wark Ord Course 81. **d** 85 **p** 86. NSM E Ham w Upton Park and Forest Gate *Chelmsf* 85–86; NSM S'well Minster 86–90; C Rolleston w Fiskerton, Morton and Upton 90–93; P-in-c Teversal 93–96; Chapl Sutton Cen 93–96; P-in-c Norwell w Ossington, Cromwell and Caunton 96–04; Dioc Tourism Adv 96–04; V Balderton and Barnby-in-the-Willows 04–15; AD Newark 00–12; Jt AD Newark and S'well 08–12; Hon Can S'well Minster from 08; rtd 15; PtO *Linc* from 16. *4 Swallow Drive, Claypole, Newark NG23 5FG* T: (01636) 626899 E: tonytucker57@gmail.com

TUCKER, Ms Catherine Jane. b 62. Birkbeck Coll Lon BA 97 Jes Coll Cam MPhil 11. Westcott Ho Cam 09. **d** 11 **p** 12. C Forest Hill w Lower Sydenham *S'wark* 11–14; V Croydon H Sav from 14; AD Croydon N from 17. *The Vicarage, 115 St Saviour's Road, Croydon CR0 2XF* T: (020) 3784 3017 M: 07709-618063 E: holysav@hotmail.com

TUCKER, Ian Malcolm. b 46. S Dios Minl Tr Scheme 86. **d** 89 **p** 90. NSM Pill w Easton in Gordano and Portbury *B & W* 89–95; C Frome St Jo and St Mary 95–99; TV Redruth w Lanner and Treleigh *Truro* 99–04; P-in-c Par and Hon Chapl Miss to Seafarers 04–11; rtd 11. *4 Priory Road, Portbury, Bristol BS20 7TH* E: iandm@btinternet.com

TUCKER, Canon Jill. b 47. UMIST BSc 68 MSc 69 PhD 77. Qu Coll Birm 05. **d** 06 **p** 07. NSM Ilmington w Stretton-on-Fosse etc *Cov* 06–09; NSM Shipston-on-Stour w Honington and Idlicote from 09; AD Shipston from 09; Dean of Self-Supporting Min from 11; Hon Can Cov Cathl from 14; PtO *Truro* from 16. *The Old House, Back Lane, Oxhill, Warwick CV35 0QN* T: (01295) 680663 F: 688193 M: 07973-994800 E: revjill.tucker@tiscali.co.uk

TUCKER (née RAMSAY), Kerry. b 59. Heythrop Coll Lon MA 94. Westcott Ho Cam 92. **d** 94 **p** 96. C Westville St Eliz S Africa 95–96; C Charlton St Luke w H Trin *S'wark* 96–99; C Cambridge Gt St Mary w St Mich *Ely* 99–04; V Sunninghill *Ox* 04–08; P-in-c S Ascot 07–08; PtO 08–15; Hon C Byfleet *Guildf* 09–10; Hon C E Horsley and Ockham w Hatchford and Downside 10–14; PtO *S'wark* from 15. *The Homestead, Castle Street, Bletchingley, Redhill RH1 4QA* T: (01883) 742226

TUCKER, Michael. b 33. **d** 84 **p** 85. NSM Sawston *Ely* 84–87; C Ely 87–90; P-in-c Barton Bendish w Beachamwell and Shingham 90–98; P-in-c Wereham 90–98; rtd 98; PtO *Nor* 99–04 and from 13; *Ely* 00–17. *2 Lighthouse Close, Hunstanton PE36 6EL* T: (01485) 298192 E: mandstucker@icloud.com

TUCKER, Canon Michael Owen. b 42. Lon Univ BSc 66 Surrey Univ PhD 69. Glouc Sch of Min 81. **d** 84 **p** 85. NSM Uley w Owlpen and Nympsfield *Glouc* 84–92; P-in-c Amberley 92–09; Dioc NSM Officer 94–09; Hon Can Glouc Cathl 98–09; RD Stonehouse 99–04; rtd 09. *18 Bownham Mead, Rodborough Common, Stroud GL5 5DZ* T: (01453) 873352 E: mike@tuckers.org.uk

TUCKER, Nicholas Harold. b 41. Reading Univ BSc 66. NOC 90. **d** 93 **p** 94. NSM Ilkley All SS *Bradf* 93–98; P-in-c Uley w Owlpen and Nympsfield *Glouc* 98–06; rtd 06; NSM Nailsworth w Shortwood, Horsley etc *Glouc* 07–08; PtO from 16. *The Rowans, 13 Priory Way, Tetbury GL8 8HT* T: (01666) 503188 E: nick@nick-tucker.co.uk

TUCKER, Nicholas John Cuthbert. b 74. Birm Univ BSc 96. Oak Hill Th Coll MTh 04. **d** 04 **p** 05. C Bebington *Ches* 04–07; Research Fell Oak Hill Th Coll 07–15; PtO *St Alb* 08–15; V Edgbaston St Bart *Birm* from 15; AD Edgbaston from 17. *The Vicarage, 1B Arthur Road, Edgbaston, Birmingham B15 2UW* T: 0121-454 5439 M: 07957-566714 E: nick@hellotuckers.com *or* nick@edgbastonoldchurch.org.uk

TUCKER, Richard Parish. b 51. Cam Univ BA 72 MA 76 Lon Univ BD 83. Wycliffe Hall Ox 80. **d** 83 **p** 84. C Wellington w Eyton *Lich* 83–84; C Walsall 84–88; TV Dronfield *Derby* 88–90; TV Dronfield w Holmesfield 90–98; V Sutton Coldfield St Columba *Birm* 98–17; rtd 17; PtO *Birm* from 17. *2 Hopton Cottages, Main Street, Youlgrave, Bakewell DE45 1UW* T: (01629) 636074 E: rev.richardtucker@gmail.com

TUCKER, Stephen Reid. b 51. New Coll Ox BA 72 MA 76. Ripon Coll Cuddesdon. **d** 77 **p** 78. C Hove All SS *Chich* 77–80; Lect Chich Th Coll 80–86; V Portsea St Alb *Portsm*

86–90; Chapl and Dean of Div New Coll Ox 90–95; P-in-c Ovingdean *Chich* 96–01; Bp's Adv on CME 96–01; V Hampstead St Jo *Lon* 01–16; AD N Camden 14–16; rtd 16; PtO *Sarum* from 17. *10 Beechcroft Road, Laverstock, Salisbury SP1 1PF* E: stucker957@btinternet.com

TUCKER, Preb Susan. b 53. Stockwell Coll of Educn CertEd 74. **d** 97 **p** 98. C Taunton St Andr *B & W* 97–01; V Bishops Hull 01–10; RD Taunton 06–10; Chapl St Marg Hospice Taunton 01–07; R Chard St Mary w Combe St Nicholas, Wambrook etc *B & W* 10–17; RD Ilminster 14–17; Preb Wells Cathl 15–17; rtd 17. *The Clock House, Buckerell, Honiton EX14 3QD* E: suetucker99@btinternet.com

TUCKER, Vivian Clive Temple. b 39. Univ of Wales (Swansea) BSc 60 Univ of Wales DipEd 61. St As Minl Tr Course 93. **d** 96 **p** 97. NSM Gresford w Holt *St As* 96–04; NSM Holt, Rossett and Isycoed 04–09; rtd 09; PtO *St As* from 09. *8 Snowdon Drive, Ty Gwyn, Wrexham LL11 2UY* T: (01978) 359226 E: geraldine.tucker26@icloud.com

TUCKETT, Prof Christopher Mark. b 48. Qu Coll Cam MA 71 Lanc Univ PhD 79. Westcott Ho Cam 71. **d** 75 **p** 76. C Lancaster St Mary *Blackb* 75–77; Chapl and Fell Qu Coll Cam 77–79; Lect NT Man Univ 79–89; Sen Lect 89–91; Prof Bibl Studies 91–96; Lect NT Ox Univ 96–00; Prof NT Studies 00–13; rtd 13; PtO *Ox* from 13. *1 Wallingford Road, Cholsey, Wallingford OX10 9LQ* T: (01491) 659091 E: christopher.tuckett@theology.ox.ac.uk

TUCKWELL, Jonathan David. b 77. St Jo Coll Cam MEng 00 MA 02. Oak Hill Th Coll BA 11. **d** 11 **p** 12. C Cambridge St Andr Less *Ely* 11–18; V Enfield Ch Ch Trent Park from 18. *2A Chalk Lane, Cockfosters, Barnet EN4 9JQ* M: 07785-576939 E: jon.tuckwell@christchurchcockfosters.org.uk

TUCKWELL, Richard Graham. b 46. SS Mark & Jo Univ Coll Plymouth TCert 67 Open Univ BA. **d** 07 **p** 08. NSM Tarvin *Ches* 07–09; P-in-c Alvanley 09–12; V 12–14; rtd 14; PtO *Ches* from 14. *Iddesleigh, 5 Walkers Lane, Tarporley CW6 0BX* T: (01829) 732732 M: 07713-485318 E: richard.tuckwell@googlemail.com

TUDGE, Paul Quartus. b 55. Leeds Univ BEd 78. Cranmer Hall Dur 84. **d** 87 **p** 88. C Roundhay St Edm *Ripon* 87–90; C Leeds City 91; V Woodside 91–99; Warden of Readers 96–99; V Ilkley All SS *Bradf* 99–08; RD Otley 02–08; P-in-c Farsley 08–11; V 11–14; *Leeds* from 14; RD Calverley *Bradf* 10–14; AD N Bradford *Leeds* 14–16. *The Vicarage, 9 St John's Avenue, Farsley, Pudsey LS28 5DN* T: 0113-257 0059 E: paul.tudge@leeds.anglican.org

TUDGEY, Stephen John. b 51. Nottm Univ BTh 81 Westmr Coll Ox MTh 00. St Jo Coll Nottm LTh 81. **d** 81 **p** 82. C Grays Thurrock *Chelmsf* 81–83; C Madeley *Heref* 84–87; R Chilcompton w Downside and Stratton on the Fosse *B & W* 87–03; P-in-c Falmouth K Chas *Truro* from 03; Hon Chapl Miss to Seafarers from 04. *The Rectory, 19 Trescobeas Road, Falmouth TR11 2JB* T: (01326) 319141 E: stevetudgey11@gmail.com

TUDOR, Canon David St Clair. b 55. K Coll Lon BD 77 AKC 77 K Coll Lon MTh 89. Ripon Coll Cuddesdon 77. **d** 78 **p** 79. C Plumstead St Nic *S'wark* 78–80; C Redhill St Matt 80–83; C-in-c Reigate St Phil CD 83–87; Asst Sec Gen Syn Bd for Miss and Unity 87–88; PtO *S'wark* 94–97; TV Canvey Is *Chelmsf* 97–00; TR from 00; AD Hadleigh from 08; Hon Can Chelmsf Cathl from 15. *St Nicholas House, 210 Long Road, Canvey Island SS8 0JR* T: (01268) 682586 E: dstudor@tiscali.co.uk

TUDWAY, Stephen William. b 75. Ch Ch Ox MA 97. ERMC 14. **d** 17 **p** 18. NSM Flamstead and Markyate Street *St Alb* from 17. *57 Trowley Hill Road, Flamstead, St Albans AL3 8DL* T: (01582) 842442 M: 07954-441991 E: curatefm@gmail.com

TUFFIN, Mrs Gillian Patricia. b 43. S Dios Minl Tr Scheme 91. **d** 94 **p** 95. C Gidea Park *Chelmsf* 94–98; TV Stoke-upon-Trent *Lich* 98–01; Admin and Prayer Co-ord Shalom Chr Healing Cen from 02; NSM Northolt Park St Barn *Lon* 02–08; PtO from 08. *76 Stowe Crescent, Ruislip HA4 7SS* T: (020) 8864 5394

TUFFNELL, Canon Nigel Owen. b 65. Teesside Poly BSc 90 UEA MSc 01. St Jo Coll Nottm 87. **d** 94 **p** 95. C Guisborough *York* 94–97; P-in-c Northwold *Ely* 97–98; P-in-c Stoke Ferry w Wretton 97–98; P-in-c Whittington 97–98; R Northwold and Wretton w Stoke Ferry etc 98–03; Bp's Adv on Environmental Issues 02–03; TR Kegworth, Hathern, Long Whatton, Diseworth etc *Leic* 03–06; PtO *Nor* 10; Hon C Hopton w Corton 10–12; P-in-c Scole, Brockdish, Billingford, Thorpe Abbots etc 12–14; P-in-c Redenhall, Harleston, Wortwell and Needham 12–14; R Redenhall w Scole from 14; RD Redenhall from 15; Hon Can Nor Cathl from 16. *The Rectory, 10 Swan Lane, Harleston IP20 9AN* T: (01379) 308905 M: 07443-937050 E: rector@7churches.org.uk

TUFNELL, Andrew Stephen Goodwin. b 83. Univ of Wales (Cardiff) BSc 05 PGCE 06. Ridley Hall Cam 12. **d** 15 **p** 16.

C Gamston and Bridgford *S'well* 15–17; V Chilwell from 17. *8 College Road, Beeston, Nottingham NG9 4AS* M: 07779-639507 E: a.tufnell@gmail.com

TUFNELL, Christopher Edward David. b 89. Sheff Univ BA 11. Oak Hill Th Coll BA 17. **d** 17 **p** 18. C Fulwood *Sheff* from 17. *Christ Church Fulwood, Canterbury Avenue, Sheffield S10 3RT* T: 0114-230 1911 E: christufnell@fulwoodchurch.co.uk

TUFNELL, Edward Nicholas Pember. b 45. Chu Coll Cam MA 68. St Jo Coll Nottm BA 73. **d** 73 **p** 74. C Ealing St Mary *Lon* 73–76; BCMS Tanzania 76–88; P-in-c Lt Thurrock St Jo *Chelmsf* 89–91; V Grays North 91–98; Chapl Thurrock Community Hosp Grays 89–98; P-in-c Bourton-on-the-Water w Clapton *Glouc* 98–05; R Bourton-on-the-Water w Clapton etc 05–11; AD Stow 09–10; rtd 11; PtO *St Alb* from 11. *Karibuni, 37 Harrold Priory, Bedford MK41 0SD* T: (01234) 215440 M: 07816-123470

TUFNELL, Michael. b 81. Imp Coll Lon BEng 05. St Mellitus Coll MA 10. **d** 10 **p** 11. C Enfield Ch Ch Trent Park *Lon* 10–14; C Turnham Green Ch Ch 14–18; TV Canford Magna *Sarum* from 18. *359 Sopwith Crescent, Wimborne BH21 1XQ* M: 07977-139544 E: michaeltufnell@gmail.com

TUFT, Preb Patrick Anthony. b 31. Selw Coll Cam BA 56 MA 60. Edin Th Coll 56. **d** 58 **p** 59. C Keighley *Bradf* 58–63; PV Chich Cathl 63–68; Min Can St Paul's Cathl *Lon* 68–74; Hon Min Can St Paul's Cathl 74–91; V Chiswick St Nic w St Mary 74–06; PV Westmr Abbey 74–79; AD Hounslow *Lon* 87–93; P-in-c Chiswick St Paul Grove Park 88–90; Preb St Paul's Cathl 95–06; rtd 07; PtO *Lon* from 07. *68 Worple Road, Isleworth TW7 7HU* T: (020) 8581 3014 M: 07768-892099 E: patrick@tuft.co

TULK, Giles David. b 65. Leeds Univ BA 86. ERMC 06. **d** 09 **p** 10. C Stansted Mountfitchet w Birchanger and Farnham *Chelmsf* 09–11; C Bocking St Mary 11–13; TR Albury, Braughing, Furneux Pelham, Lt Hadham etc *St Alb* 13–16; R Minsterley, Habberley and Hope w Shelve *Heref* from 16; RD Pontesbury from 18. *The New Vicarage, Minsterley, Shrewsbury SY5 0AA* T: (01743) 790672 E: gtulk@waitrose.com *or* stiperstonesrevgiles@gmail.com

TULL, Preb Christopher Stuart. b 36. Hertf Coll Ox BA 60 MA 64. Oak Hill Th Coll 60. **d** 62 **p** 63. C Stoodleigh *Ex* 62–71; C Washfield 62–71; TV Washfield, Stoodleigh, Withleigh etc 71–74; RD Tiverton 74–75; R Bishops Nympton w Rose Ash 75–77; V Mariansleigh 75–77; TR Bishopsnympton, Rose Ash, Mariansleigh etc 77–99; RD S Molton 80–87 and 95–99; Preb Ex Cathl 84–99; rtd 99; PtO *B & W* from 04. *The Old Smithy, Challacombe, Barnstaple EX31 4TU* T: (01598) 763201

TULLETT, Paul Budworth. b 71. Lanc Univ BSc 92 Birm Univ MBA 00 Anglia Ruskin Univ BA 09. Ridley Hall Cam 07. **d** 09 **p** 10. C Taunton St Mary *B & W* 09–13; V Water Orton *Birm* from 13. *The Vicarage, Vicarage Lane, Water Orton, Birmingham B46 1RX* T: 0121-730 2081 M: 07581-544978 E: paulofwaterorton@hotmail.co.uk

TULLETT, Peter Watts. b 46. Qu Coll Birm 92. **d** 94 **p** 95. C Worle *B & W* 94–96; Chapl HM YOI Portland 96–01; PtO *B & W* 02–04 and 07–18; Hon C Uphill 04–06. *2 Ferry Lane, Lympsham, Weston-super-Mare BS24 0BT* T: (01934) 814284 M: 07803-330395 E: peter@valmagnolia.plus.com

TULLOCH, Richard James Anthony. b 52. Wadh Coll Ox BA 74 Selw Coll Cam BA 79. Ridley Hall Cam 76. **d** 79 **p** 80. C Morden *S'wark* 79–83; C Jesmond Clayton Memorial *Newc* 83–94; V New Borough and Leigh *Sarum* 94–11; TR Eden, Gelt and Irthing *Carl* 11–18; RD Brampton 16–18; rtd 18. *12C Grafton Square, London SW4 0DQ* E: rjatulloch@gmail.com

TULLOCH, Canon Yvonne Lorraine. b 63. Sheff Univ MA 07. WEMTC 96. **d** 99 **p** 00. NSM Magor *Mon* 99–00; NSM Kenilworth St Jo *Cov* 00–05; Chapl for Evang Cov Cathl 05–06; Can Res for Miss 06–09; Can for Development Birm Cathl 09–10; PtO 10–13; *Lon* from 13; *S'wark* from 14; Bp's Officer for Clergy Bereavement from 17. *112 Salcott Road, London SW11 6DG* T: 07801-351947 E: yvonne@ataloss.org

TULLY, David John. b 56. St Jo Coll Dur BA 77 Nottm Univ PGCE 78. Ridley Hall Cam 81. **d** 84 **p** 85. C Gosforth St Nic *Newc* 84–86; C Newburn 86–90; TV Whorlton 90–96; V 96–00; R Gateshead Fell *Dur* 00–09; R Chester le Street from 09. *The Rectory, Lindisfarne Avenue, Chester le Street DH3 3PT* T: 0191-388 4027

TULLY, Janet Florence. b 43. **d** 03 **p** 04. OLM Margate St Jo *Cant* 03–08; PtO *Nor* from 09. *4 Westgate Court, Wymondham NR18 0PX* M: 07866-839275

TUNBRIDGE, Genny Louise. b 64. Clare Coll Cam BA 85 St Cross Coll Ox DPhil 93. Qu Coll Birm BD 95. **d** 96 **p** 97. C Boston *Linc* 96–00; Lect 00–01; Prec Chelmsf Cathl 01–06; Can Res Chelmsf Cathl 02–06; V Gosforth All SS *Newc* 06–13; rtd 13; PtO *Birm* from 15. *The Old Rectory, 80 Hodge Hill Common, Birmingham B36 8AG* M: 07891-610868 E: genny.tunbridge@gmail.com

TUNGAY, Michael Ian. b 45. Oak Hill Th Coll 70. **d** 73 **p** 74. C Fulham St Mary N End *Lon* 73–75; C Hammersmith St Simon 76–79; P-in-c 79–84; PtO *S'wark* 09–11. *7 Lily Close, London W14 9YA* T: (020) 8748 3151 E: miketungay@uk2.net

TUNLEY, Timothy Mark. b 61. Ridley Hall Cam 89. **d** 92 **p** 93. C Aldborough w Boroughbridge and Roecliffe *Ripon* 92–95; C Knaresborough 95–98; V Swaledale 98–05; TV Seacroft 05–09; Dioc Adv for NSM 03–08; Chapl Miss to Seafarers from 09. *109 Avalon Gardens, Linlithgow Bridge, Linlithgow EH49 7PL* T: (01506) 842629 M: 07581-625941 E: timothy.tunley@mtsmail.org

TUNNICLIFFE, Canon Martin Wyndham. b 31. Keele Univ BA 56. Qu Coll Birm 59. **d** 60 **p** 61. C Castle Bromwich SS Mary and Marg *Birm* 60–65; V Shard End 65–73; R Over Whitacre w Shustoke 73–78; V Tanworth 78–98; RD Solihull 89–94; Hon Can Birm Cathl 91–98; rtd 98; PtO *Birm* 98–17. *202 Ralph Road, Shirley, Solihull B90 3LE* T/F: 0121-745 6522

TUNNICLIFFE, Mrs Siv. b 33. Stockholm Univ MPhil 58. SAOMC 94. **d** 97 **p** 98. OLM Wingrave w Rowsham, Aston Abbotts and Cublington *Ox* 97–12; OLM Wing w Grove 04–12; OLM Cottesloe 12–10; PtO 10–19; rtd 19. *Baldwy House, Leighton Road, Wingrave, Aylesbury HP22 4PA* T/F: (01296) 681374

TUNSTALL, Mrs Alyson Margaret. b 70. St Mellitus Coll BA 17. **d** 17 **p** 18. C Garston *Liv* from 17. *127 Stamfordham Drive, Liverpool L19 6PY* M: 07795-171269

TUPLIN, Mrs Josette. b 52. Liv Univ BA 73. St Mellitus Coll 18. **d** 19. NSM Woodchurch *Ches* from 19. *5 Beryl Road, Prenton CH43 9RS* T: 0151-677 2266 M: 07592-721399 E: josietuplin@gmail.com

TUPLING, Mrs Catherine Louise. b 74. Westhill Coll Birm BTh 96. Wycliffe Hall Ox 01. **d** 03 **p** 04. C Belper *Derby* 03–07; P-in-c Hathersage w Bamford and Derwent 07–08; P-in-c Hathersage w Bamford and Derwent and Grindleford 08–13; V Dore *Sheff* 13–19; P-in-c Totley 17–19; Dioc Disability Adv and Chapl amongst Deaf People *Ox* from 19. *1 Tithe Barn Court, Manor Way, Kidlington OX5 2BL* E: katie.tupling@oxford.anglican.org

TURAHIRWA, Jean-Bosco. b 40. ERMC 16. **d** 18 **p** 19. NSM Brussels *Eur* from 18. *Pro-Cathedral of the Holy Trinity, 29 rue Capitaine Crespel, 1050 Brussels, Belgium* T: (0032) (2) 511 7183

TURK, James Richard. b 72. WEMTC 14. **d** 17 **p** 18. C Upton St Leonards *Glouc* from 17. *53 Goshawk Road, Quedgeley, Gloucester GL2 4NU* T: (01452) 558990 M: 07758-225113 E: jamesturk@blueyonder.co.uk

TURLEY, Debra. b 67. Oak Hill Th Coll BA 91. LCTP 07. **d** 10 **p** 11. C Utley *Bradf* 10–14; Leeds 14–15; V Taunton Lyngford *B & W* from 15. *62 Eastwick Road, Taunton TA2 7HD* E: debbi.turley@sky.com

✠**TURNBULL, The Rt Revd Anthony <u>Michael</u> Arnold.** b 35. Keble Coll Ox BA 58 MA 62 Greenwich Univ Hon DLitt 94 Dur Univ Hon DD 03. Cranmer Hall Dur. **d** 60 **p** 61 **c** 88. C Middleton *Man* 60–61; C Luton w E Hyde *St Alb* 61–65; Dir of Ords *York* 65–69; Abp's Dom Chapl 65–69; Chapl York Univ 69–76; V Heslington 69–76; Chief Sec CA 76–84; Can Res Roch Cathl 84–88; Adn Roch 84–88; Bp Roch 88–94; Bp Dur 94–03; rtd 03; Hon Asst Bp Cant, Eur and Roch from 03. *3 Gardeners Quay, Upper Strand Street, Sandwich CT13 9DH* T: (01304) 611389 E: amichaelturnbull@yahoo.co.uk

TURNBULL, Brian Robert. b 43. Chich Th Coll 71. **d** 74 **p** 75. C Norbury St Phil *Cant* 74–76; C Folkestone St Sav 76–77; Hon C Tong *Lich* 83–88; C Jarrow *Dur* 88–89; TV 89–94; P-in-c Hartlepool St Oswald 94–96; V 96–04; rtd 04; PtO *Dur* from 05; *Newc* from 05. *50 The Chare, Leazes Square, Newcastle upon Tyne NE1 4DD* T: 0191-221 2312 E: frbrian@onetel.com

TURNBULL, George William <u>Warwick</u>. b 47. Leeds Poly BEd 84 Bradf Univ MSc 06 Open Univ MA 11 Lon Univ TDip 68 CQSW 75. NOC 85. **d** 88. Chapl Asst Leeds Gen Infirmary 88–91; PtO *Ripon* 91–94; NSM Leeds All So and St Aid 15–16; NSM Potternewton w Lt London from 16. *11 North Parade, Leeds LS16 5AY* T: 0113-228 8584 M: 07714-720234 E: warwick.t@ntlworld.com

TURNBULL, James Awty. b 28. Solicitor Bradf Univ HonDLaws 97. Cranmer Hall Dur 89. **d** 89 **p** 90. NSM Bolton Abbey *Bradf* 89–98; PtO 98–14; Leeds from 14. *1 Woodlands Close, Ilkley LS29 9BY*

TURNBULL (née WILKINSON), Mrs Marlene Sandra. b 45. SRN 71. Trin Coll Bris IDC 78. **dss** 78 **d** 93 **p** 94. Wrose *Bradf* 78–82; Chapl St Luke's Hosp Bradf 78–82; Past Tutor Aston Tr Scheme 79–81; W Yorkshire CECS 82–84; Westgate Common *Wakef* 84–86; E Ardsley 86–92; Wakef St Jo 92–94;

NSM 93–94; TV Barrow St Geo w St Luke *Carl* 94–00; TV Darwen St Pet w Hoddlesden *Blackb* 00–02; rtd 03; PtO *Wakef* 10–14; *Bradf* 12–14; *Leeds* 14–16. *9 Victoria Drive, Horsforth, Leeds LS18 4PN* E: wilkingreen2014@gmail.com

TURNBULL, Michael. *See* TURNBULL, Anthony Michael Arnold

TURNBULL, Michael Francis. b 62. Liv Univ BTh 99. NOC 95. **d** 98 **p** 99. C Birkenhead Ch Ch *Ches* 98–02; P-in-c Leasowe 02–08; R Wistaston from 08; Asst Warden of Readers from 04. *The Rectory, 104 Church Lane, Crewe CW2 8ER* T: (01270) 665742 *or* 567119 M: 07595-908644 E: mfturnbull@gmail.com

TURNBULL, Michael Peter. b 56. Chich Univ BA 15. SEITE 09. **d** 12. NSM Sidley *Chich* 12–16; NSM Upper St Leonards St Jo from 16; Asst Chapl E Sussex Healthcare NHS Trust from 17. *17 Knebworth Road, Bexhill-on-Sea TN39 4JH* T: (01424) 221948 M: 07864-628081 E: mpt@michaelturnbull.co.uk

TURNBULL, Peter Frederick. b 64. SS Mark & Jo Univ Coll Plymouth BA 85. Sarum & Wells Th Coll BTh 91. **d** 91 **p** 92. C Upper Norwood All SS *S'wark* 91–95; Chapl HM Pris Dorchester 95–98; C Dorchester *Sarum* 95–98; NSM Melbury 98–99; C Maltby *Sheff* 99–02; TV 02–08; TV Crosslacon *Carl* 08–16; TV Chellington St Alb from 16. *The Rectory, 3 The Moor, Carlton, Bedford MK43 7JR* T: (01234) 720961 E: pfturnbull@gmail.com *or* chellingtonteam@gmail.com

TURNBULL, Richard Duncan. b 60. Reading Univ BA 82 St Jo Coll Dur BA 92 Dur Univ PhD 97 Ox Univ MA 05 MICAS 85 FRHistS. Cranmer Hall Dur 90. **d** 94 **p** 95. C Portswood Ch Ch *Win* 94–98; V Chineham 98–05; Prin Wycliffe Hall Ox 05–12; Dir Cen for Enterprise, Markets and Ethics from 12. *16A Woodstock Road East, Begbroke, Kidlington OX5 1RG* T: (01865) 371358 E: richard.turnbull@theceme.org

TURNBULL, Mrs Sally Elizabeth. b 55. Bp Grosseteste Coll BEd 78. **d** 11 **p** 12. OLM Owmby Gp *Linc* 11–17; R from 17. *Sunnymede, Faldingworth Road, Spridlington, Market Rasen LN8 2DF* T: (01673) 862764 M: 07594-432058 E: supersonicsal55@gmail.com

TURNBULL, Warwick. *See* TURNBULL, George William Warwick

TURNER, Alan James. b 40. Oak Hill Th Coll BA 81. **d** 81 **p** 82. C Bradley *Wakef* 81–84; C Sandal St Helen 84–86; P-in-c Sileby *Leic* 86–87; TR Sileby, Cossington and Seagrave 87–94; R Hollington St Leon *Chich* 94–01; R Frant w Eridge 01–08; rtd 08; PtO *York* from 10. *4 The Limes, Helmsley, York YO62 5DT* T: (01439) 771957 E: alanturner3040@gmail.com

TURNER, Albert Edward. b 41. Glouc Sch of Min 83. **d** 89 **p** 90. C Woodford St Mary w St Phil and St Jas *Chelmsf* 89–91; R Greatworth and Marston St Lawrence etc *Pet* 91–99; R Somersham w Pidley and Oldhurst *Ely* 99–02; rtd 02; PtO *St Alb* from 04; Chapl Asst Bedford Hosp NHS Trust 05–10; Chapl Asst Papworth Hosp NHS Foundn Trust 06–18; PtO *Ely* from 15. *23 Brace Dein, Upper Cambourne, Cambridge CB23 6HT* T: (01954) 269525 M: 07950-097525 E: aet546@hotmail.com

TURNER, Andrew John. b 52. St Jo Coll Nottm. **d** 83 **p** 84. C Framlingham w Saxtead *St E* 83–86; P-in-c Badingham w Bruisyard and Cransford 86–88; P-in-c Dennington 86–88; R Badingham w Bruisyard, Cransford and Dennington 88–91; Chapl RAF 91–12; rtd 12; PtO *Truro* from 16. *2 Spitfire Row, St Eval, Wadebridge PL27 7TF* T: (01841) 540947 E: a.turner682@btinternet.com

TURNER, Ann. *See* TURNER, Patricia Ann

TURNER, Mrs Ann Elizabeth Hamer. b 38. Ex Univ BA 59 PGCE 60. Trin Coll Bris 84. **dss** 86 **d** 87 **p** 94. Bath St Luke *B & W* 86–91; Hon C 87–91; Chapl Dorothy Ho Foundn 89–91; C Bath Twerton-on-Avon *B & W* 91–94; TV 94–96; rtd 98; PtO *Ex* 00–06; Hon C Ottery St Mary, Alfington, W Hill, Tipton etc from 06. *4 Beech Park, West Hill, Ottery St Mary EX11 1UH* T: (01404) 813476 E: jandaturner@btinternet.com

TURNER, Anthony John. b 49. St Mich Coll Llan 89. **d** 91 **p** 92. C Coity w Nolton *Llan* 91–95; R Castlemartin w Warren and Angle etc *St D* 95–04; TV Monkton 04–07; TV Cwmbran *Mon* 07–13; OCM 95–00; rtd 13; PtO *Llan* from 13. *14 Dol Nant Dderwen, Bridgend CF31 5AA* T: (01656) 750713 E: rev.anthony.turner@gmail.com

TURNER, The Ven Antony Hubert Michael. b 30. FCA 63. Tyndale Hall Bris 54. **d** 56 **p** 57. C Nottingham St Ann *S'well* 56–58; C Cheadle *Ches* 58–62; V Macclesfield Ch Ch 62–68; LtO *S'wark* 68–74; Home Sec BCMS 68–74; V Southsea St Jude *Portsm* 74–79; RD Portsm 79–84; Hon Can Portsm Cathl 85–86; Adn Isle of Wight 86–96; rtd 96; PtO *Portsm* from 96. *15 Avenue Road, Hayling Island PO11 0LX* T: (023) 9246 5881 E: ventony@gmail.com

TURNER, Carl Francis. b 60. St Chad's Coll Dur BA 81. St Steph Ho Ox 83. **d** 85 **p** 86. C Leigh-on-Sea St Marg *Chelmsf* 85–88; C Brentwood St Thos 88–90; TV Plaistow 90–95; P-in-c 95–96; TR Plaistow and N Canning Town 96–01; Prec and Can Res Ex Cathl 01–14; R New York St Thos USA from 14. *1 West 53rd Street, New York, NY 10019, USA* T: (001) (212) 757 7013 F: (212) 977 6582 E: rector@saintthomaschurch.org

TURNER, Carlton John. b 79. Univ of W Indies BA 05 Qu Coll Birm MA 09 Glos Univ PhD 15. **d** 05 **p** 06. C Bahamas St Greg Bahamas 05–06; C S Beach All SS & Asst Chapl Main Hosp 06–08; C Nassau Calvery Hill 08–10; TV Bloxwich *Lich* 10–17; Tutor Qu Foundn Birm from 17; PtO *Lich* from 17; *Birm* from 18. *Queen's College, Somerset Road, Edgbaston, Birmingham B15 2QH* T: 0121-454 1527 E: carltonturner07@hotmail.com *or* turnerc@queens.ac.uk

TURNER, Christina Caroline. *See* FFRENCH-HODGES, Christina Caroline

TURNER, Mrs Christine. b 42. EMMTC. **d** 94 **p** 95. Asst Chapl Qu Medical Cen Nottm Univ Hosp NHS Trust 94–97; NSM Hickling w Kinoulton and Broughton Sulney *S'well* 94–97; NSM Cotgrave 97–99; P-in-c Willoughby-on-the-Wolds w Wysall and Widmerpool 99–04; rtd 04; PtO *Ox* from 12. *The Rosarie, Milcombe, Banbury OX15 4RS* T: (01295) 722330 E: revd.christine@care4free.net

TURNER, Christopher Gilbert. b 29. New Coll Ox BA 52 MA 55. Ox Min Course 91. **d** 92 **p** 93. NSM Hook Norton w Gt Rollright, Swerford etc *Ox* from 92. *Rosemullion, High Street, Great Rollright, Chipping Norton OX7 5RQ* T: (01608) 737359 E: rosemullion@cooptel.net

TURNER, Christopher James Shepherd. b 48. Ch Ch Ox BA 70 MA 74. Wycliffe Hall Ox 71. **d** 74 **p** 75. C Rusholme H Trin *Man* 74–78; C Chadderton Ch Ch 78–80; V 80–89; V Selly Park St Steph and St Wulstan *Birm* 89–99; P-in-c Locking *B & W* 99–05; Chapl Weston Hospice 99–05; P-in-c The Quinton *Birm* 05–09; R 09–11; AD Edgbaston 08–10; PtO from 11. *10 Presthope Road, Birmingham B29 4NJ* T: 0121-603 7916 E: cjsturner@gmail.com

TURNER, Christopher Matthew. b 68. Brunel Univ BSc 90. Cranmer Hall Dur 01. **d** 03 **p** 04. C Hykeham *Linc* 03–06; P-in-c Mid Marsh Gp 06–14; R 14–17; P-in-c Saltfleetby 06–14; V 14–17; P-in-c Theddlethorpe 06–14; R 14–17; P-in-c Borough Green *Roch* from 17. *The Vicarage, 24 Maidstone Road, Borough Green, Sevenoaks TN15 8BD* E: reverendchristurner@gmail.com

TURNER, Mrs Claire Elizabeth. b 76. Plymouth Univ BA 99. Qu Coll Birm 08. **d** 11 **p** 12. C Wednesfield *Lich* 11–14; P-in-c Rubery *Birm* 14–15; V from 15. *St Chad's Vicarage, 160A New Road, Rubery, Rednal, Birmingham B45 9JA* T: 0121-238 3168 M: 07748-998227 E: revclaireturner@gmail.com

TURNER, Colin Peter John. b 42. Clifton Th Coll 63. **d** 66 **p** 67. C Kinson *Sarum* 66–68; C York St Paul 68–72; Org Sec (SE Area) CPAS 73–78; TV Radipole and Melcombe Regis *Sarum* 78–87; R Radstock w Writhlington *B & W* 90–07; R Kilmersdon w Babington 90–07; RD Midsomer Norton 04–07; rtd 07; PtO *B & W* 07–13; *Sarum* from 14. *12 Gainsborough Rise, Trowbridge BA14 9HX* E: colinpjt@blueyonder.co.uk

TURNER, Derek John. b 54. Univ of Wales (Ban) BSc 81 PhD 86. St Jo Coll Nottm. **d** 87 **p** 88. C Pelsall *Lich* 87–91; C Stratford-on-Avon w Bishopton *Cov* 91–99; R Leire w Ashby Parva and Dunton Bassett *Leic* 00–06; rtd 06; PtO *Win* 07–16. *The Parsonage, La Rue du Crocquet, St Brelade, Jersey JE3 8BZ* M: 07713-832676 E: frderek@cesmail.net

TURNER, Dylan Lawrence. b 72. Goldsmiths' Coll Lon BMus 96 SS Coll Cam BTh 08. Westcott Ho Cam 06. **d** 08 **p** 09. C Strood St Nic w St Mary *Roch* 08–12; P-in-c Longfield from 12. *The Rectory, 67 Main Road, Longfield DA3 7PQ* T: (01474) 702201 M: 07779-225810 E: dylan.turner@cantab.net

TURNER, Edward. *See* TURNER, Albert Edward

TURNER, Edward Nicholas. b 80. Birm Univ BA 01 Anglia Ruskin Univ MA 08. Westcott Ho Cam 06. **d** 08 **p** 09. C Winchmore Hill St Paul *Lon* 08–11; V Edmonton St Aldhelm 11–14; V Southgate St Andr from 14. *St Andrew's Vicarage, 184 Chase Side, London N14 5HN* T: (020) 8886 7523 M: 07788-782646 E: edd.turner@expertit.net

TURNER, Canon Edward Robert. b 37. Em Coll Cam BA 62 BTh 66 MA 67. Westcott Ho Cam 64. **d** 66 **p** 67. C Salford St Phil w St Steph *Man* 66–69; Chapl Tonbridge Sch 69–81; Adv for In-Service Tr *Roch* 81–89; Dir of Educn 81–96; Can Res Roch Cathl 81–00; Vice-Dean 88–00; Dioc Adv on Community Affairs 96–00; Consultant Rochester 2000 Trust and Bp's Consultant on Public Affairs 00–02; rtd 02; PtO *Nor* from 01. *Glebe House, Church Road, Neatishead, Norwich NR12 8BT* T: (01692) 631295 E: aandeturner@broadlandnet.co.uk

TURNER, Mrs Eileen Margaret. b 45. Goldsmiths' Coll Lon TCert 66 Ches Coll of HE MTh 02. NOC 90. **d** 93 **p** 94.

C Sandal St Cath *Wakef* 93–96; P-in-c Hammerwich *Lich* 96–02; Dir OLM Course 96–02; Dir Ext Studies St Jo Coll Nottm 02–10; rtd 10; PtO *Sheff* 11–18; *S'wark* from 18. *Apartment 25, 4 Gaumont Place, London SW2 4GA* M: 07774-623769 E: eileenmturner@ymail.com

TURNER, Mrs Elaine. b 58. Birm Univ BSc 79 CEng 84 MICE 84 MIStructE 85. **d** 04 **p** 05. OLM Walesby *Linc* 04–18; OLM Walesby Gp from 18. *Rose Cottage, Normanby-le-Wold, Market Rasen LN7 6SS* T: (01673) 828142 E: elaine-turner58@supanex.com

TURNER, Miss Elizabeth Jane. b 67. Leeds Univ BEng 88. Trin Coll Bris 93. **d** 96 **p** 97. C Eccles *Man* 96–00; P-in-c Barrow *Ches* 00–08; Dioc Ecum Officer 00–08; R Thurstaston from 08; Dioc Ecum Officer from 08. *Thurstaston Rectory, 77 Thingwall Road, Wirral CH61 3UB* T: 0151-648 1816 E: rector@thurstaston.org.uk

TURNER, Canon Frederick Glynne. b 30. Univ of Wales (Lamp) BA 52. St Mich Coll Llan 52. **d** 54 **p** 55. C Aberaman *Llan* 54–60; C Oystermouth *S & B* 60–64; V Abercynon *Llan* 64–71; V Ton Pentre 71–73; TR Ystradyfodwg 73–77; R Caerphilly 77–82; V Whitchurch 82–96; Can Llan Cathl 84–96; Prec 95–96; rtd 96; PtO *Llan* from 96. *83 Newborough Avenue, Llanishen, Cardiff CF14 5DA* T: (029) 2075 4443

TURNER, Miss Gaynor. b 44. LNSM course 93. **d** 96 **p** 97. NSM Salford Sacred Trin *Man* 96–99; Asst Chapl among Deaf People from 96; Lic Preacher 99–07; PtO 07–15; NSM Broughton 15–17; PtO from 17. *19 Ellesmere Avenue, Worsley, Manchester M28 0AL* E: gturner157@btinternet.com

TURNER, Gemma Dee. b 78. Coll of Resurr Mirfield BA 16. **d** 16 **p** 17. C Hessle *York* 16–19; V from 19. *167 First Lane, Hessle HU13 9EY* M: 07583-448163 E: darkangel@alias1.karoo.co.uk

TURNER, Geoffrey. b 51. Selw Coll Cam BA 75 MA 78 PGCE 75. NOC 90. **d** 93 **p** 94. C E Crompton *Man* 93–96; C Heywood St Luke w All So 96–98; TV Heywood 98–01; TR 01–08; TR Worsley 08–16; C Swinton H Rood 13–16; rtd 16. *25 Pear Tree Park, Holme, Carnforth LA6 1SD* E: gt1951@btinternet.com

TURNER, Geoffrey Edwin. b 45. Aston Univ BSc 68 Newc Univ MSc 69 PhD 72. Cranmer Hall Dur BA 74. **d** 75 **p** 76. C Wood End *Cov* 75–79; V Huyton Quarry *Liv* 79–86; Press and Communications Officer *Ely* 86–94; P-in-c Gt w Lt Abington 86–94; P-in-c Hildersham 86–94; V Letchworth St Paul w Willian *St Alb* 94–01; P-in-c Willingham *Ely* 01–02; R 02–08; P-in-c Rampton 01–02; R 02–08; rtd 08; PtO *Ripon* 09–14; *Leeds* from 14. *8 Wayside Crescent, Harrogate HG2 8NJ* T: (01423) 885668 E: geoffrey168@btinternet.com

TURNER, Geoffrey James. b 46. St Deiniol's Hawarden 85. **d** 87 **p** 88. C Loughor *S & B* 87–89; C Swansea St Pet 89–90; R New Radnor and Llanfihangel Nantmelan etc 90–96; V Ystalyfera 96–07; RD Cwmtawe 00–06; V Loughor 07–13; rtd 13; PtO *S & B* from 13. *35 Tawe Park, Ystradgynlais, Swansea SA9 1GU* T: (01639) 841760 E: geoffrey.turner2@sky.com

✠**TURNER, The Rt Revd Geoffrey Martin.** b 34. Oak Hill Th Coll 60. **d** 63 **p** 64 **c** 94. C Tonbridge St Steph *Roch* 63–66; C Heatherlands St Jo *Sarum* 66–69; V Derby St Pet 69–73; V Chadderton Ch Ch *Man* 73–79; R Bebington *Ches* 79–93; Hon Can Ches Cathl 89–93; RD Wirral N 89–93; Adn Ches 93–94; Suff Bp Stockport 94–00; rtd 00; PtO *Ches* 00–18; Hon Asst Bp Ches 02–18. *18 Gracey Court, Woodland Road, Broadclyst, Exeter EX5 3GA* T: (01392) 465269 E: geoff@theturners.eu

TURNER, Gerald Garth. b 38. Univ of Wales (Lamp) BA 61 St Edm Hall Ox BA 63 MA 67 Man Univ PhD 11. St Steph Ho Ox 63. **d** 65 **p** 66. C Drayton in Hales *Lich* 65–68; Chapl Prebendal Sch Chich 68–70; PV Chich Cathl 68–70; C Forest Row 70–72; V Hope *Derby* 72–78; Prec Man Cathl 78–86; Can Res Man Cathl 78–86; R Tattenhall and Handley *Ches* 86–04; rtd 04; PtO *S'well* 04–12; *Ches* from 15. *75 London Road, Nantwich CW5 6LN* T: (01270) 749415 E: ggarthturner@hotmail.com

TURNER, Mrs Heather Winifred. b 43. Open Univ BA 08 Win Univ MA 13 SRN 65. Cant Sch of Min 87. **d** 90 **p** 94. Par Dn Orpington All SS *Roch* 90–93; Chapl to the Deaf 93–00; P-in-c Wrotham 95–01; TV E Dereham and Scarning *Nor* 01–02; rtd 02; PtO *Nor* 02–04; C Darsham *St E* 04–06; C Middleton cum Fordley and Theberton w Eastbridge 04–06; C Westleton w Dunwich 04–06; C Yoxford, Peasenhall and Sibton 04–06; C Blyth Valley 06–07; TV 07; PtO 07–12; *Cov* from 08; Chapl Shakespeare Hospice 14–15; PtO *Glouc* from 16. *10 Pembroke Gardens, Wellesbourne, Warwick CV35 9PX* T: (01789) 842442 E: revhwturner@gmail.com

TURNER, Henry John Mansfield. b 24. Magd Coll Cam BA 45 MA 48 BD 12 Man Univ PhD 85. Westcott Ho Cam 48. **d** 50 **p** 51. C Crosby *Linc* 50–52; C Chorlton upon Medlock *Man* 52–55; Inter-Colleg Sec SCM (Man) 52–55; C Leigh St Mary *Man* 55–57; V Rochdale Gd Shep 57–62; India 63–67; V Becontree St Geo *Chelmsf* 67–71; R Weeley 71–79; Chapl

St Deiniol's Lib Hawarden 79–80; Sub-Warden 80–86; PtO *Chelmsf* 86–13; Hon C St Botolph without Bishopgate *Lon* 87–17; PtO from 17. *Merrywood, 25 Fourth Avenue, Frinton-on-Sea CO13 9DU* T: (01255) 677554

TURNER, James Alfred. b 34. MCIPS 76. Ox Min Course 91. **d** 94 **p** 95. NSM Kidlington w Hampton Poyle *Ox* 94–06; PtO 06–07. *11 St Mary's Close, Kidlington, Oxford OX5 2AY* T: (01865) 375562

TURNER, James Henry. b 51. NOC 99. **d** 02 **p** 03. NSM Middleton St Cross *Ripon* 02–13; Beeston *Leeds* 13–15; NSM Leeds Belle Is St Jo and St Barn 15–17; rtd 17; PtO *Leeds* from 17. *38 Acre Crescent, Middleton, Leeds LS10 4DJ* T: 0113-229 6865 E: jamesjpturner@aol.com

TURNER, Jane. *See* TURNER, Elizabeth Jane

TURNER, Jessica Mary. b 60. SS Coll Cam BA 81 PGCE 82. Trin Coll Bris 88. **d** 91 **p** 94. Par Dn Preston Em *Blackb* 91–94; C Bamber Bridge St Aid 94–95; Chapl Preston Acute Hosps NHS Trust 95–98; Chapl Blackpool Victoria Hosp NHS Trust 98–03; Chapl Blackpool, Fylde and Wyre Hosps NHS Trust 03–05; Hon Can Blackb Cathl 02–05; Chapl Ox Radcliffe Hosps NHS Trust 06–12; PtO *Ox* from 12. *33 Mayfield Road, Farmoor, Oxford OX2 9NY* T: (01865) 864435 M: 07966-016399 E: jessicatu196@gmail.com

TURNER, John. *See* TURNER, Henry John Mansfield

TURNER, John William. b 43. Sheff Univ BSc 73. Wycliffe Hall Ox 86. **d** 88 **p** 89. C Clayton *Bradf* 88–91; C Horton 91–92; V Bankfoot 92–01; V Holland-on-Sea *Chelmsf* 01–05; rtd 05. *20 Grantley Drive, Harrogate HG3 2ST* T: (01423) 545994

TURNER, Canon Keith Howard. b 50. Southn Univ BA 71. Wycliffe Hall Ox 72. **d** 75 **p** 76. C Enfield Ch Ch Trent Park *Lon* 75–79; C Chilwell *S'well* 79–83; P-in-c Linby w Papplewick 83–90; R 90–15; Hon Can S'well Minster 02–13; rtd 15; PtO *S'well* from 16. *20 Northfield Avenue, Radcliffe-on-Trent, Nottingham NG12 2HX* T: 0115-933 1737 E: k.h.turner@btinternet.com

TURNER, Keith Stanley. b 51. ACIB 80. NTMTC 96. **d** 99 **p** 00. C S Hornchurch St Jo and St Matt *Chelmsf* 99–12; rtd 12; PtO *Chelmsf* 12–15; Hon C Romford Gd Shep from 15. *16 Wells Gardens, Rainham RM13 7LU* T: (01708) 554274 E: revkeitht@ntlworld.com

TURNER, Mrs Lorraine Elizabeth. b 67. Brunel Univ BSc 90 Open Univ MA 96. Cranmer Hall Dur 01. **d** 03 **p** 04. C Birchwood *Linc* 03–06; TV Louth 06–14; P-in-c Legbourne and Wold Marsh 06–14; V 14–17; Chapl United Lincs Hosps NHS Trust 07–13; RD Louthesk *Linc* 16–17; V Platt *Roch* from 17. *24 Maidstone Road, Borough Green, Sevenoaks TN15 8BD* E: rev.lorraine@btinternet.com

TURNER, Mark. b 60. Aston Tr Scheme 87 Sarum & Wells Th Coll BTh 92. **d** 92 **p** 93. C New Sleaford *Linc* 92–94; C Bottesford and Muston *Leic* 94–98; C Harby, Long Clawson and Hose 94–98; C Barkestone w Plungar, Redmile and Stathern 94–98; P-in-c Thurnby Lodge 98–00; C Aylestone Park CD 00–03; P-in-c Areley Kings *Worc* 03–05; R from 05; C Shrawley, Witley, Astley and Abberley from 15; RD Stourport 06–07 and from 13. *14 Dunley Road, Stourport-on-Severn DY13 0AX* T: (01299) 829557 E: revmturner@tiscali.co.uk

TURNER, Mark Roy James. b 79. All SS Cen for Miss & Min 13. **d** 15 **p** 16. NSM Burton and Shotwick *Ches* 15–16; NSM Eastham from 16; Chapl Birkenhead Sch from 18. *20 The Birches, Neston CH64 3SB* T: 0151-353 8177 M: 07469-893264 E: ddowirral@yahoo.co.uk or fathermarkturner@gmail.com

TURNER, Martin John. b 34. Trin Hall Cam BA 55 MA 59. Cuddesdon Coll 58. **d** 60 **p** 61. C Rugby St Andr *Cov* 60–65; C Cov Cathl 65–68; USA 68–70; V Rushmere *St E* 70–82; V Monkwearmouth St Pet *Dur* 82–90; V Bathford *B & W* 90–99; rtd 99; PtO *B & W* 00–07; *Truro* 97–16; *Newc* from 17. *30 Green Batt, Alnwick NE66 1TU* M: 07929-231167 E: turnerschemanoff@aol.com

TURNER, Michael Andrew. b 34. K Coll Cam BA 59 MA 62. Cuddesdon Coll 59. **d** 61 **p** 62. C Luton St Andr *St Alb* 61–64; V 70–77; C-in-c Northolt St Jos *Lon* 64–70; PtO *St Alb* 77–93; Dep Hd and Chapl Greycoat Hosp Sch 86–93; P-in-c Shilling Okeford *Sarum* 93–99; Chapl Croft Ho Sch Shillingstone 93–99; rtd 99; PtO *Sarum* from 99; V of the Close Sarum Cathl 02–07; Dioc Retirement Officer from 08. *12 Berkshire Road, Harnham, Salisbury SP2 8NY* T: (01722) 504000 E: sarum.turners@ntlworld.com

TURNER, Canon Michael John Royce. b 43. St Jo Coll Dur BA 65. Chich Th Coll 65. **d** 67 **p** 68. C Hodge Hill *Birm* 67–71; C Eling, Testwood and Marchwood *Win* 71–72; TV 72–77; R Kirkwall *Ab* 77–85; R Drumlithie *Bre* from 85; R Drumtochty from 85; R Fasque from 85; R Laurencekirk from 85; Hon Can St Paul's Cathl Dundee from 13. *Beattie Lodge, Laurencekirk AB30 1HJ* T/F: (01561) 377380 E: mjrturner@btinternet.com

TURNER, Canon Nicholas Anthony. b 51. Clare Coll Cam BA 73 MA 77 Keble Coll Ox BA 77 MA 81. Ripon Coll Cuddesdon 76. **d** 78 **p** 79. C Stretford St Matt *Man* 78–80; Tutor St Steph Ho Ox 80–84; V Leeds Richmond Hill *Ripon* 84–91; Offg Chapl RAF and V Ascension Is 91–96; Can Th St Helena Cathl from 94; V Raynes Park St Sav *S'wark* 96–01; P-in-c Broughton, Marton and Thornton *Bradf* 01–02; R from 02; *Leeds* from 14. *The Rectory, 7 Roundell Drive, West Marton, Skipton BD23 3UL* T: (01282) 842332 E: nicholas.turner@leeds.anglican.org

TURNER (*née* **SYMINGTON**)**, Canon Patricia Ann.** b 46. SRN 68 RMN 71 SCM 72. St Steph Ho Ox 82. dss 84 **d** 87. Buttershaw St Aid *Bradf* 84–87; TM Manningham 87–91; Ascension Is 91–96; Par Dn Raynes Park St Sav *S'wark* 96–01; Par Dn Broughton, Marton and Thornton *Bradf* 01–14; *Leeds* from 14; AD Skipton 05–16; Assoc Dioc Dir of Ords *Bradf* 04–07; Dir of Ords 07–14; *Leeds* 14–16; Hon Can Bradf Cathl 09–16. *The Rectory, 7 Roundell Drive, West Marton, Skipton BD23 3UL* T: (01282) 842332 E: canonannturner@gmail.com

TURNER, Peter Carpenter. b 39. Oak Hill Th Coll 63. **d** 66 **p** 67. C Chadwell *Chelmsf* 66–69; C Braintree 69–73; R Fyfield 73–87; P-in-c Moreton 77–83; P-in-c Fyfield and Moreton w Bobbingworth 83–87; C-in-c Bobbingworth 82–83; P-in-c Willingale w Shellow and Berners Roding 84–87; V E Ham St Geo 87–04; rtd 04; PtO *Lon* from 05. *9 Llandovery House, Chipka Street, London E14 3LE* T: (020) 7987 5902

TURNER, The Ven Peter Robin. b 42. St Luke's Coll Ex PGCE 70 Open Univ BA 79 Westmr Coll Ox MTh 96 AKC 65. St Boniface Warminster 65. **d** 66 **p** 67. C Crediton *Ex* 66–69; PtO 69–70; Chapl RAF 70–88; Asst Chapl-in-Chief RAF 88–95; Chapl-in-Chief RAF 95–98; Can and Preb Linc Cathl 95–98; Chapl Dulwich Coll 98–02; Bp's Dom Chapl *S'well* 02–07; Hon Can S'well Minster 02–12; Chapl for Sector Min 07–12; rtd 12; QHC from 92; PtO *S'well* from 17. *12 Chimes Meadow, Southwell NG25 0GB* T: (01636) 812250 M: 07890-633137 E: pr.turner1942@gmail.com

TURNER, Philip James. b 54. **d** 11 **p** 12. NSM Gt Sankey *Liv* 11–14; NSM Warrington W 14–15; Chapl Warrington and Halton Hosps NHS Foundn Trust from 14; NSM Gateacre *Liv* 15–19. *147 Cradley, Widnes WA8 7PN* T: 0151-424 0037 E: philip.turner4@nhs.net

TURNER, Ms Philippa Anne. b 64. Trevelyan Coll Dur BA 86 Yale Univ MDiv 88. **d** 94 **p** 95. Chapl New York Hosp USA 91–95; Assoc P New York Ch of Heavenly Rest 95–08; Chapl R Veterinary Coll *Lon* 08–17; Chapl R Free and Univ Coll Medical Sch 08–17; V Earl's Court Road St Phil from 17; PtO *St Alb* 12–17. *2 Pembroke Road, London W8 6NT* M: 07525-234382 E: pipturn@gmail.com

TURNER, Ricky Ronald. b 84. Middx Univ BA 05 Goldsmiths' Coll Lon PGCE 06. Qu Coll Birm 11. **d** 14 **p** 15. C Oxhey All SS *St Alb* 14–17; TV Dunstable from 17. *St Augustine's Vicarage, 83 Halfmoon Lane, Dunstable LU5 4AE* E: rickyturner@ntlworld.com

TURNER, Canon Roger Dyke. b 39. Trin Coll Bris 79. **d** 81 **p** 82. C Clevedon St Andr and Ch Ch *B & W* 81–85; R Freshford, Limpley Stoke and Hinton Charterhouse 85–88; V Kenilworth St Jo *Cov* 88–04; RD Kenilworth 90–98; Hon Can Cov Cathl 00–04; rtd 04; PtO *Birm* 04–05; *Cov* from 04; P-in-c Barston *Birm* 05–11; PtO 12–18. *15 Caesar Road, Kenilworth CV8 1DL* T: (01926) 734330

TURNER, Mrs Ruth Carpenter. b 62. Anglia Ruskin Univ BA 09 LLCM 83 GLCM 84. Ridley Hall Cam 07. **d** 09 **p** 10. C Brampton St Thos *Derby* 09–13; TV Dronfield w Holmesfield 13–18; C Battersea Fields *S'wark* from 18. *St Saviour's Vicarage, 351A Battersea Park Road, London SW11 4LH* M: 07855-714538 E: ruthturner2632@btinternet.com or ruth.turner@southwark.anglican.org

TURNER, Stewart Gordon. b 54. Ex Univ BA 06. SWMTC 03. **d** 06 **p** 07. NSM Falmouth All SS *Truro* 06–09; C Mawnan 09–13; P-in-c 13–17; C Budock 09–13; P-in-c Constantine from 11. *The Vicarage, Chalbury Heights Brill, Constantine, Falmouth TR11 5UR* T: (01326) 340259 E: rev.stewart.turner@btinternet.com or rev.stewart@stconstantine.plus.com

TURNER (*formerly* **BENBOW**)**, Mrs Susan Catherine.** b 47. Birm Univ BEd 70. St Alb Minl Tr Scheme 82. dss 85 **d** 87 **p** 94. Gt Wyrley *Lich* 85–87; Par Dn 87–88; Par Dn Whitstable *Cant* 88–92; Par Dn Eastry and Northbourne w Tilmanstone etc 92–94; C 94–96; P-in-c Gt Mongeham w Ripple and Sutton by Dover 96–98; rtd 98; PtO *Nor* 99–04; *Sarum* from 08. *9 Whitehill, Puddletown, Dorchester DT2 8SB* T: (01305) 849030 E: bands8turner@uwclub.net

TURNER, Sylvia Jean. b 46. Lon Univ 72 Open Univ BA 77. Westcott Ho Cam 93. **d** 95 **p** 96. C Whitstable *Cant* 95–99; R Wigmore Abbey *Heref* 99–09; P-in-c Pontesbury I and II

09–11; rtd 11; PtO *Heref* from 11. *Wheelwrights, Witton, Ludlow SY8 3DB* T: (01584) 890586 M: 07773-036994 E: sylviaturner812@btinternet.com

TURNER, Vivien Andree Elizabeth. b 53. **d** 13 **p** 17. NSM Banstead *Guildf* 13–18; P-in-c Graffham w Woolavington Chich from 18. *The Rectory, Graffham, Petworth GU28 0NL* E: reverendvivien@gmail.com

TURNER-CALLIS, Mrs Gillian Ruth. b 79. Aber Univ BD 03. Wycliffe Hall Ox MTh 05. **d** 05 **p** 06. C Shepshed and Oaks in Charnwood *Leic* 05–08; TR Kegworth, Hathern, Long Whatton, Diseworth etc 08–15; R W Hallam and Mapperley w Stanley *Derby* from 15; Asst Dir of Ords from 18. *The Rectory, The Village, West Hallam, Ilkeston DE7 6GR* T: 0115-944 5784 M: 07838-881307

TURNER-LOISEL, Mrs Elizabeth Anne. b 57. Lanc Univ BA 79 MA 80 York Univ PGCE 81. EMMTC 96. **d** 99 **p** 00. Chapl Nat Sch Hucknall 99–04; P-in-c Annesley w Newstead *S'well* 04–11; V 11–14; Hon Can S'well Minster 13–14; V Hatfield *Sheff* from 14; AD Snaith and Hatfield from 14. *The Vicarage, 2 Vicarage Close, Hatfield, Doncaster DN7 6HN* T: (01302) 459110 E: revd.liz@gmail.com

TURNHAM, Mrs Dominique Emma. b 90. Homerton Coll Cam BA 11 MA 15. St Steph Ho Ox 13. **d** 15 **p** 16. C Dereham and Distr *Nor* from 15. *15 George Eliot Way, Dereham NR19 1EX* T: (01362) 697388 M: 07788-278460 E: dominiqueturnham@gmail.com

TURNOCK, Geoffrey. b 38. Leeds Univ BSc 61 PhD 64 MSOSc. EMMTC 84. **d** 87 **p** 88. NSM Oadby *Leic* 87–00; NSM Okeford *Sarum* 00–04; PtO 04–18. *10 Billingsmoor Lane, Poundbury, Dorchester DT1 3WT* T: (01305) 757177

TURPIN, Christine Lesley. See DICKSON, Christine Lesley

TURPIN, Canon John Richard. b 41. St D Coll Lamp BA 63 Magd Coll Cam BA 65 MA 70. Cuddesdon Coll 65. **d** 66 **p** 67. C Tadley St Pet *Win* 66–71; V Southampton Thornhill St Chris 71–85; V Ringwood 85–10; Hon Can Win Cathl 99–10; rtd 10; PtO *Win* from 10. *111 Beaufort Road, Bournemouth BH6 5AU* T: (01202) 421321 E: john.turpin4@btinternet.com

TURPIN, Raymond Gerald. b 35. **d** 97 **p** 98. OLM Brockley Hill St Sav *S'wark* 97–05; PtO from 05; Retirement Officer Woolwich Area from 08. *60 Bankhurst Road, London SE6 4XN* T: (020) 8690 6877 or 8311 2000 E: rayturpin@talktalk.net

TURRELL, Peter Charles Morphett. b 47. **d** 01 **p** 02. NSM Carshalton Beeches *S'wark* 01–15; PtO from 15. *62 Stanley Park Road, Carshalton SM5 3HW* T: (020) 8669 0318 E: peterturrell@btinternet.com

TURRELL, Stephen John. b 35. S'wark Ord Course. **d** 83 **p** 84. NSM W Wickham St Jo *Cant* 83–84; NSM Addington *S'wark* 85–92; NSM Blendworth w Chalton w Idsworth *Portsm* 92–97; PtO 97–01; NSM Storrington *Chich* 01–06; rtd 06; PtO *Chich* 13–17; *B & W* from 19. *38 Beaconfield Road, Yeovil BA20 2JN* T: (01935) 479196 E: turrell567@gmail.com

TURTLE, Jessica Ellen. b 79. St Mellitus Coll 15. **d** 17 **p** 18. NSM Bagshot *Guildf* from 17. *1 The Mount, Trumpsgreen Road, Virginia Water GU25 4EJ*

TURTON, Douglas Walter. b 38. Kent Univ BA 77 Surrey Univ MSc 90 Univ of Wales (Ban) PhD 04 Glyndŵr Univ DMin 16 CQSW 70. Oak Hill Th Coll 77. **d** 78 **p** 79. C Cant St Mary Bredin 78–80; P-in-c Thornton Heath St Paul 80–81; V 81–84; V Thornton Heath St Paul *S'wark* 85–91; R Eastling w Ospringe and Stalisfield w Otterden *Cant* 91–00; rtd 00; PtO *Cant* from 13. *16 Weatherall Close, Dunkirk, Faversham ME13 9UL* T: (01227) 752244

TURVILLE, Mrs Janet Elizabeth. b 59. Matlock Coll of Educn BEd 82. Ripon Coll Cuddesdon 11. **d** 12 **p** 13. C Wirksworth *Derby* 12–16; P-in-c Walton-on-Trent w Croxall, Rosliston etc 16–17; P-in-c Stapenhill Immanuel 16–17; C Seale and Lullington w Coton in the Elms 16–17; TV Louth *Linc* from 17. *St Michael's Vicarage, Little Lane, Louth LN11 9DU* M: 07710-550396 E: janetturville@hotmail.co.uk or janet.turville@teamparishoflouth.org.uk

TUSCHLING, Ruth Mary Magdalen. b 65. Freiburg Univ MA 94 CCC Cam PhD 04. Westcott Ho Cam BA 97. **d** 98 **p** 99. C Hampstead St Jo *Lon* 98–01; PtO *Ely* 02–06; OSB 04–08; Warden Offa Retreat Ho and Dioc Spirituality Adv *Cov* 08–12; Dioc Spirituality Adv *Portsm* from 12. *50 Penny Street, Portsmouth PO1 2NL* T: (023) 9281 5044 E: ruth.tuschling@portsmouth.anglican.org

✠**TUSTIN, The Rt Revd David.** b 35. Magd Coll Cam BA 57 MA 61 Lambeth DD 98. Cuddesdon Coll 58. **d** 60 **p** 61 **c** 79. C Stafford St Mary *Lich* 60–63; C St Dunstan in the West *Lon* 63–67; Asst Gen Sec C of E Coun on Foreign Relns 63–67; V Wednesbury St Paul Wood Green *Lich* 67–71; V Tettenhall Regis 71–79; RD Trysull 76–79; Suff Bp Grimsby *Linc* 79–00; Can and Preb Linc Cathl 79–00; rtd 00; Hon

Asst Bp Linc from 01. *The Ashes, Tunnel Road, Wrawby, Brigg DN20 8SF* T/F: (01652) 655584 E: tustindavid@hotmail.com

TUTTON, Jeffrey Richard. b 64. St Aug Coll of Th 14. **d** 17 **p** 18. NSM Ore Ch Ch *Chich* from 17. *Timber House, Main Street, Northiam, Rye TN31 6NB*

TUTTON, Canon John Knight. b 30. Man Univ BSc 51. Ripon Hall Ox 53. **d** 55 **p** 56. C Tonge w Alkrington *Man* 55–57; C Bushbury *Lich* 57–59; R Blackley St Andr *Man* 59–67; R Denton Ch Ch 67–95; Hon Can Man Cathl 90–95; rtd 95; Hon C Exminster and Kenn *Ex* 96–01; PtO from 01. *2 Hescane Park, Cheriton Bishop, Exeter EX6 6JP* T: (01647) 24651 E: johnktutton@hotmail.com

TWEDDLE, David William Joseph. b 28. Dur Univ BSc 50 Open Univ BA 97 ATCL 56. Wycliffe Hall Ox 54. **d** 56 **p** 57. C Darlington H Trin *Dur* 56–60; P-in-c Prestonpans *Edin* 60–63; PV Linc Cathl 63–65; C Pet St Jo 65–71; Hon Min Can Pet Cathl 68–93; V Southwick w Glapthorn 71–83; P-in-c Benefield 80–83; R Benefield and Southwick w Glapthorn 83–93; RD Oundle 84–89; rtd 94; PtO *Ely* 94–07. *6 Barton Square, Ely CB7 4DF* T: (01353) 614393

TWEED, Andrew. b 48. Univ of Wales (Cardiff) BA 69 Trin Coll Carmarthen MA 97. St Deiniol's Hawarden. **d** 81 **p** 84. NSM Llandrindod w Cefnllys *S & B* 81–86; NSM Llandrindod w Cefnllys and Disserth 87–15; NSM Glan Ithon 15–18; PtO from 18. *Gwenallt, Wellington Road, Llandrindod Wells LD1 5NB* T: (01597) 823671 E: andrewtweed1@aol.com

TWEEDIE-SMITH, Ian David. b 60. Newc Univ BA 83. Wycliffe Hall Ox 83. **d** 85 **p** 86. C Hatcham St Jas *S'wark* 85–89; C Bury St Edmunds St Mary *St E* 89–02; TV Woking St Pet *Guildf* 02–12; P-in-c Purton *Bris* 12–14; V from 14. *The Vicarage, 2 Kingsacre, Hyde Lane, Purton, Swindon SN5 4DU* T: (01793) 770077 E: vicarage@stmaryspurton.org.uk

TWEEDY, Andrew Cyril Mark. b 61. Man Univ BA(Econ) 81. SAOMC 98. **d** 01 **p** 02. C Carterton *Ox* 01–03; C Brize Norton and Carterton 03–04; V Bromham w Oakley and Stagsden *St Alb* 04–08; Chapl Barcelona *Eur* 08–14; R Lower Windrush *Ox* 14–19; TR Brize Norton and Carterton from 19. *The Rectory, 6 Burford Road, Carterton OX18 3AA* E: revdrew61@gmail.com

TWIDELL, Canon William James. b 30. St Mich Coll Llan 58. **d** 60 **p** 61. C Tonge w Alkrington *Man* 60–63; C High Wycombe All SS *Ox* 63–65; P-in-c Elkesley w Bothamsall *S'well* 65–66; V Bury St Thos *Man* 66–72; V Daisy Hill 72–84; R Flixton St Mich 84–00; AD Stretford 88–98; Hon Can Man Cathl 97–00; rtd 00; PtO *Man* from 00; *Ches* 00–10. *Flat A5, Trinity Gate, Epsom Road, Guildford GU1 3PJ* T: (01483) 453492

TWIGG (née LATKA), Mrs Allison. b 70. Nene Coll Northn BEd 93. Ripon Coll Cuddesdon 13. **d** 15 **p** 16. C Weston Favell *Pet* 15–18; C Guilsborough and Hollowell and Cold Ashby etc from 18. *The Vicarage, 2 Church Road, Spratton, Northampton NN6 8HR* M: 07759-835011 E: revallisontwigg@gmail.com

TWINE, Mrs Jacqueline Ann. b 64. Middx Univ BA 11. Ripon Coll Cuddesdon 15. **d** 18 **p** 19. C Southsea St Luke and St Pet *Portsm* from 18. *68 Court Lane, Portsmouth PO6 2LR* T: (023) 9279 6318 M: 07922-867552 E: curate.stlukesouthsea@gmail.com

TWINLEY, David Alan. b 66. Ox Univ BTh 00 Heythrop Coll Lon MA 10. St Steph Ho Ox 97. **d** 00 **p** 01. C Saffron Walden w Wendens Ambo, Littlebury etc *Chelmsf* 00–03; V Bury w Houghton and Coldwaltham and Hardham *Chich* 03–16; RD Petworth 10–16; V Arundel w Tortington and S Stoke from 16. *The Vicarage, 26 Maltravers Street, Arundel BN18 9BU* T: (01903) 885209 E: frdavid@twinley.me.uk or vicar@stnicholas-arundel.co.uk

TWISLETON, John Fiennes. b 48. St Jo Coll Ox BA 69 MA 73 DPhil 73. Coll of Resurr Mirfield 73. **d** 76 **p** 77. C New Bentley *Sheff* 76–79; P-in-c Moorends 79–80; V 80–86; USPG 86–90; Prin Alan Knight Tr Cen Guyana 87–90; V Holbrooks *Cov* 90–96; Edmonton Area Missr *Lon* 96–01; Dioc Adv for Miss and Renewal *Chich* 01–09; C Haywards Heath St Rich 01–09; R Horsted Keynes 09–17; rtd 17. *13 Marylands, New England Road, Haywards Heath RH16 3JZ* E: john@twisleton.co.uk

TWISS, Dorothy Elizabeth. Gilmore Ho 68 Linc Th Coll 70. **d** 87 **p** 94. Chapl Asst RAF 78–91; TV Pewsey *Sarum* 91–95; Chapl HM Pris Drake Hall 95–01; Chapl HM Pris Ford 01–03; rtd 03; PtO *Portsm* from 05. *41 Rosecott, Havant Road, Horndean, Waterlooville PO8 0XA* M: 07929-650284 E: dorothy.twiss371@btinternet.com

TWITTY, Miss Rosamond Jane. b 54. Univ of Wales (Ban) BSc 75 CertEd 76. Trin Coll Bris BA 89. **d** 90 **p** 94. Par Dn Lt Thurrock St Jo *Chelmsf* 90–94; C 94–95; C Upper Armley *Ripon* 95–08; TV Langport Area *B & W* 08–14; C 14–17; V Levels

Arc from 17. *The Vicarage, 1 New Street, Long Sutton, Langport TA10 9JW* T: (01458) 241260 E: jane.twitty@btinternet.com

TWOMEY, David James Benedict. b 87. Sheff Univ BSc 08 Northumbria Univ PGCE 09. **d** 14 **p** 15. C Cullercoats St Geo *Newc* 14–18; P-in-c Seaton Hirst from 18. *St John's Vicarage, Newbiggin Road, Ashington NE63 0TQ* E: david.twomey@ymail.com

TYDEMAN, Rosemary. *See* WILLIAMS, Rosemary

TYE, Eric John. b 37. St Alb Minl Tr Scheme 78. **d** 81 **p** 82. NSM Rushden St Mary w Newton Bromswold *Pet* 81–07; PtO from 07. *29 Kingsmead Park, Bedford Road, Rushden NN10 0NF* T: (01933) 353274

TYE, John Raymond. b 31. Lambeth STh 64 Linc Th Coll 66. **d** 68 **p** 69. C Crewe St Mich *Ches* 68–71; C Wednesfield St Thos *Lich* 71–76; P-in-c Petton w Cockshutt 76–79; P-in-c Hordley 79; P-in-c Weston Lullingfield 79; R Petton w Cockshutt and Weston Lullingfield etc 79–81; V Hadley 81–84; R Ightfield w Calverhall 84–89; V Ash 84–89; R Calton, Cauldon, Grindon and Waterfall 89–96; RD Alstonfield 95–96; rtd 96; PtO *Lich* 05–14. *38 Aston Street, Wem, Shrewsbury SY4 5AU* T: (01939) 236218

TYERS, Philip Nicolas. b 56. St Jo Coll Nottm BTh 84. **d** 84 **p** 85. C Rugby St Matt *Cov* 84–88; TV Cov E 88–95; P-in-c Preston St Matt *Blackb* 95–96; TR Preston Risen Lord 96–06; Co-ord Chapl HM Pris Leeds 06–07; Co-ord Chapl HM Pris Wymott 07–16; Chapl HM Pris Liv from 16. *Chaplain's Office, HM Prison, 68 Hornby Road, Liverpool L9 3DF* T: 0151-530 4000 E: ptyers@outlook.com or philip.tyers@justice.gov.uk

TYLDESLEY, Mrs Vera. b 47. Man Coll of Educn BEd 80. **d** 98 **p** 99. OLM Pendlebury St Jo *Man* 98–17; rtd 17; PtO *Man* from 17. *7 Kingsway, Swinton, Manchester M27 4JU* T: 0161-736 3845 E: vera.tyldesley4@ntlworld.com

TYLER, Canon Alan William. b 60. Ridley Hall Cam 84. **d** 86 **p** 87. C Bedwellty *Mon* 86–89; C St Mellons and Michaelston-y-Fedw 89–92; V Abersychan and Garndiffaith 92–97; Chapl Glan Hafren NHS Trust 97–99; Sen Chapl Gwent Healthcare NHS Trust from 99; Can St Woolos Cathl *Mon* from 08. *Chaplaincy Office, The Royal Gwent Hospital, Cardiff Road, Newport NP20 2UB* T: (01633) 234263 or 871457 E: alan.tyler@wales.nhs.uk

TYLER, Alison Ruth. b 51. Keele Univ BA 74 CQSW 78. S'wark Ord Course 93. **d** 95 **p** 96. NSM Hatcham St Cath *S'wark* 95–99; Dep Chapl HM Pris Brixton 99–02; Chapl HM Pris Wormwood Scrubs 02–07; Learning and Development Manager HM Pris Service Chapl 07–15; Hon Min Can S'wark Cathl from 06; PtO from 06; *Cov* 08–15. *Address withheld by request* E: ar.tyler@ntlworld.com

TYLER, Andrew. Univ of Wales (Lamp) BA 79 Warw Univ MA 80 Leeds Univ BA 85 Man Univ BD 86. Coll of Resurr Mirfield 83. **d** 87 **p** 88. C Glen Parva and S Wigston *Leic* 87–90; C Didcot All SS *Ox* 90–92; Asst Chapl Chu Hosp Ox 92–93; NSM Caversham St Andr *Ox* 93–97; Co-ord Tr Portfolio (Berks) 96–97; P-in-c Nor St Giles 97–99; P-in-c Nor St Mary Magd w St Jas 99–00; V 00–08; Hon C Eaton Ch Ch 09–12; Discipleship and Lay Ministry Development Officer *Linc* 09–12; PtO 09–12; C Cawston w Booton and Brandiston etc *Nor* 12–15; PtO from 15; P-in-c Ipswich All Hallows *St E* 17–18; Dir St Marylebone Healing and Counselling Cen from 18. *Address withheld by request* M: 07768-581679 E: xatyler@aol.com

TYLER, Brian Sidney. b 32. MIPI 79. Chich Th Coll 62. **d** 64 **p** 65. C Brighton St Mich *Chich* 64–69; C-in-c Southwick St Pet 69–75; PtO 80; NSM Brighton Resurr 93–94; Chapl St Dunstan's Hosp Brighton 93–95; C Brighton St Matthias *Chich* 95–02; Hon C 02–05; rtd 05; PtO *Chich* from 05. *318 Ditchling Road, Brighton BN1 6JG* T: (01273) 559292

TYLER, Charles Stewart. b 44. **d** 14 **p** 15. OLM Mease Valley *Lich* from 14. *Orchard House, 4 Woodland View, Chilcote, Swadlincote DE12 8DP* T: (01827) 373248 E: stewart.tyler6@btinternet.com

TYLER, Capt Christopher Paul. b 54. Brighton Univ BA 11. **d** 17 **p** 18. C Lavenham w Preston *St E* from 17. *7 Weavers Close, Lavenham, Sudbury CO10 9QN* T: (01787) 829788 E: cpaultyler@hotmail.com

TYLER, David Stuart. b 69. Hull Univ BSc 91 ACA 94. Wycliffe Hall Ox 01. **d** 03 **p** 04. C Ashby-de-la-Zouch St Helen w Coleorton *Leic* 03–05; C Ashby-de-la-Zouch and Breedon on the Hill 05–07; P-in-c Hanborough and Freeland *Ox* 07–11; R from 11; AD Woodstock 12–17 and from 18. *The Rectory, Swan Lane, Long Hanborough, Witney OX29 8BT* T: (01993) 881270 E: revdavidtyler@gmail.com

TYLER (née FOSTER), Mrs Frances Elizabeth. b 55. Linc Th Coll 81. **dss** 84 **d** 87 **p** 94. Hampton All SS *Lon* 84–87; Par Dn Brentford 87–91; NSM Walsgrave on Sowe *Cov* from 91; Dioc Adv for Women's Min 97–05; Chapl S Warks Gen Hosps NHS Trust from 08. *The Vicarage, 4 Farber Road,*

Coventry CV2 2BG T: (024) 7661 5152 E: revftyler@aol.com *or* frances.tyler@swft.nhs.uk

TYLER, Mrs Gaynor. b 46. Univ of Wales (Abth) BA 68. S'wark Ord Course 87. **d** 90 **p** 94. NSM Reigate St Luke S Park *S'wark* 90–97; Deanery NSM Maelienydd *S & B* 97–04; NSM Cwmdauddwr w St Harmon and Llanwrthwl 04–05; NSM Llanwrthwl w St Harmon, Rhayader, Nantmel etc 05–06; PtO from 06. *Dyffryn Farm, Llanwrthwl, Llandrindod Wells LD1 6NU* T: (01597) 811017

TYLER, John Thorne. b 46. Selw Coll Cam BA 68 MA 71. Sarum & Wells Th Coll 70. **d** 72 **p** 73. C Frome St Jo *B & W* 72–74; Chapl Richard Huish Coll Taunton 74–93; Hon C Stoke St Gregory w Burrowbridge and Lyng *B & W* 77–93; P-in-c Shepton Beauchamp w Barrington, Stocklinch etc 93–94; TV Ilminster and Distr 94–98; rtd 99; Hon C Quantock Towers *B & W* 99–01; P-in-c Stogursey w Fiddington 01–06; PtO 06–09; C Chard St Mary w Combe St Nicholas, Wambrook etc 09–10; PtO from 11. *24 Ganges Close, Fivehead, Taunton TA3 6PG* T: (01460) 281574 E: tyleruk@tiscali.co.uk

TYLER, Malcolm. b 56. Kent Univ BSc 77 Cam Univ BA 84. Ridley Hall Cam 82. **d** 85 **p** 86. C Twickenham St Mary *Lon* 85–88; C Acton St Mary 88–91; V Walsgrave on Sowe *Cov* from 91; AD Cov E 07–14; Assoc Dioc Dir of Ords from 15. *The Vicarage, 4 Farber Road, Coventry CV2 2BG* T: (024) 7661 5152 *or* 7661 8845 E: stmaryssowe@aol.com

TYLER, Paul. *See* TYLER, Christopher Paul

TYLER, Canon Paul Graham Edward. b 58. St Jo Coll Dur BA 79 Dur Univ PGCE 93. Cranmer Hall Dur 81. **d** 83 **p** 84. C Stranton *Dur* 83–86; C Collierley w Annfield Plain 86–89; V Esh and Hamsteels 89–92; Chapl HM Pris Frankland 09–16; NSM Cornforth and Ferryhill *Dur* from 16; Hon Can Dur Cathl from 16. *Address withheld by request* E: pgetyler@hotmail.com

TYLER (née WAITE), Mrs Sheila Margaret. b 25. SRN 47. Trin Coll Bris 71. **dss** 79 **d** 87 **p** 94. Easton H Trin w St Gabr and St Lawr *Bris* 79–80; Westbury-on-Trym St Alb 81–85; rtd 85; Hon Par Dn Henleaze *Bris* 87–94; Hon C 94–95; Chapl Stoke Park and Purdown Hosps Stapleton 88–90; PtO *B & W* 95–00; *Bris* 95–08; *Chich* 01–02. *6 Gracey Court, Woodland Road, Broadclyst, Exeter EX5 3GA* T: (01392) 462872

TYLER, Stewart. *See* TYLER, Charles Stewart

TYNDALL, Canon Daniel Frank. b 61. Aston Tr Scheme 90 Sarum & Wells Th Coll BTh 93. **d** 93 **p** 94. C Wolverhampton *Lich* 93–96; C Bris St Mary Redcliffe w Temple etc 96–01; V Earley St Nic *Ox* 01–08; P-in-c Caversham St Pet and Mapledurham 08–10; P-in-c Caversham St Jo 08–10; R Caversham Thameside and Mapledurham 10–13; V Bris St Mary Redcliffe w Temple etc from 13; Hon Can Bris Cathl from 19. *The Vicarage, 10 Redcliffe Parade West, Bristol BS1 6SP* T: 0117-231 0060 E: dftyndall@gmail.com

TYNDALL, Jeremy Hamilton. b 55. Birm Univ MPhil 01. St Jo Coll Nottm BTh 81 LTh 81. **d** 81 **p** 82. C Oakwood St Thos *Lon* 81–84; C Upper Holloway St Pet w St Jo 84–87; TV Halewood *Liv* 87–96; P-in-c Yardley St Edburgha *Birm* 96–99; V 99–01; R Eugene St Thos USA 01–08; Dean Den Convocation 06–08; TR Cove St Jo *Guildf* 08–17; rtd 17; PtO *Newc* from 18. *1 Chevington Green, Hadston, Morpeth NE65 9AX* T: (01670) 946713 M: 07854-595129 E: jeremytyndall@hotmail.com

TYNDALL, Samuel Michael. b 87. York Univ BA 08. Yorks Min Course BA 16. **d** 16 **p** 17. C Linthorpe *York* 16–19; C Marton-in-Cleveland from 19. *26 Emerson Avenue, Middlesbrough TS5 7QH* M: 07914-341750

TYNDALL, Canon Simon James. b 54. LSE BSc(Econ) 77 Lon Univ PGCE 82 Open Univ MA 98. St Jo Coll Nottm 88. **d** 90 **p** 91. C Yeovil w Kingston Pitney *B & W* 90–94; V Rastrick St Jo *Wakef* 94–01; TR Chippenham St Paul w Hardenhuish etc *Bris* 01–13; V Kington St Michael 01–13; AD Chippenham 08–13; Hon Can Bris Cathl 11–13; Chapl Tervuren *Eur* 13–19; rtd 19. *26 Dennenlaan, 3080 Tervuren, Belgium* T: (0032) (2) 767 3435 E: simon@tyndall.plus.com *or* simon.tyndall@stpaulstervuren.be

TYNDALL, Canon Timothy Gardner. b 25. Jes Coll Cam BA 50. Wells Th Coll 50. **d** 51 **p** 52. C Warsop *S'well* 51–55; R Newark St Leon 55–60; V Sherwood 60–75; P-in-c Bishopwearmouth St Mich w St Hilda *Dur* 75–85; RD Wearmouth 75–85; Hon Can Dur Cathl 83–90; Chief Sec ACCM 85–90; rtd 90; PtO *Lon* 90–18; *S'wark* 90–11. *Flat 16, 2B Bollo Lane, London W4 5LE* T: (020) 8994 4516

TYRER, Ms Jayne Linda. b 59. Goldsmiths' Coll Lon BA 81 CertEd 82. Sarum & Wells Th Coll 85. **d** 87 **p** 95. C Rochdale *Man* 87–88; Par Dn Heywood St Luke w All So 88–91; Hon Par Dn Burneside *Carl* 91–07; Hon Par Dn Beacon from 07; Chapl Kendal Hosp 91–94; Chapl Westmorland Hosps NHS Trust 94–98; Chapl Univ Hosps of Morecambe Bay NHS Foundn Trust from 98. *St Oswald's Vicarage, Burneside, Kendal LA9 6QX* T: (01539) 722015 E: jayne.tyrer@mbht.nhs.uk

TYRER, Neil. *See* PURVEY-TYRER, Neil

TYRÉUS, Per Jonas Waldemar (Peter). b 45. Uppsala Univ 66. **p** 71. Sweden 71–00; C Pelton *Dur* 00–03; C Chester le Street 03–11; rtd 11. *27 Castle Riggs, Chester le Street DH2 2DL* E: petertyreus@googlemail.com

TYRRELL, John Patrick Hammond. b 42. Cranmer Hall Dur 62. **d** 65 **p** 66. C Edin St Jo 65–68; Chapl RN 68–72; Chapl St John's Cathl Hong Kong 72–74; 78–82; Area Sec SE Asia SOMA UK 78–82; V Westborough *Guildf* 74–78; C Yateley *Win* 82–83; C-in-c Darby Green CD 83–88; V Darby Green 88–96; V Chineham 96–97; rtd 02; PtO *Linc* from 06. *5 Blacksmith's Court, Metheringham, Lincoln LN4 3YQ* T: (01526) 322147 E: john_tyrrell42@hotmail.com

TYRRELL, Martyn Christopher. b 79. Trin Coll Bris 15. **d** 17 **p** 18. C Shirwell, Loxhore, Kentisbury, Arlington, etc *Ex* from 17. *The Rectory, Shirwell, Barnstaple EX31 4JU* T: (01271) 850844 E: martyntyrrell@hotmail.com

TYRRELL, Stephen Jonathan. b 39. Sheff Univ BA 62. Clifton Th Coll. **d** 65 **p** 66. C Rodbourne Cheney *Bris* 65–68; C Lillington *Cov* 68–72; P-in-c Bishop's Itchington 73–78; V 78–86; V Kingston upon Hull St Nic *York* 86–92; TV Cheltenham St Mary, St Matt, St Paul and H Trin *Glouc* 92–04; rtd 04; PtO *Glouc* from 05. *96A Fosseway Avenue, Moreton-in-Marsh GL56 0EA* T: (01608) 812350

TYSON, Mrs Frances Mary. b 44. Reading Univ BScAgr 68 Wolv Univ PGCE 91. St Jo Coll Nottm 01. **d** 02 **p** 03. NSM Walsall *Lich* 02–07; NSM Portswood Ch Ch *Win* from 07. *26 Reynolds Road, Southampton SO15 5GS*

TYSON, Jacqueline. b 56. **d** 16 **p** 17. NSM Wearmouth Deanery from 16; NSM Sunderland Minster *Dur* from 17. *Address withheld by request* M: 07866-426177 E: revjacquityson@sunderlandminster.org

TYSON, Mrs Nigella Jane. b 44. RGN 66 Kent Univ BA 95. SEITE 96. **d** 97 **p** 98. NSM Aylesham w Adisham, Nonington w Wymynswold and Goodnestone etc *Cant* 97–00; P-in-c Kingsland w Eardisland, Aymestrey etc *Heref* 00–04; R 04–09; rtd 09; PtO *Heref* from 10. *Fairview, Stoke Prior, Leominster HR6 0NE* T: (01568) 760610 E: revnigella@sky.com

U

UDAL, Canon Joanna Elizabeth Margaret. b 64. SS Hild & Bede Coll Dur BSc 86. Ripon Coll Cuddesdon BTh 94. **d** 97 **p** 98. C Whitton St Aug *Lon* 97–00; Asst to Abp Sudan 00–09; Abp's Sec for Angl Communion Affairs *Cant* 09–14; Hon Min Can S'wark Cathl 11–17; PtO from 11; Can Juba S Sudan from 07; PtO *Eur* 18–21. *4 York Square, London E14 7LU* T: (020) 7790 8525

UDDIN, Mohan. b 52. Sussex Univ BA 74 PGCE 75 Lon Bible Coll MA 87 PhD 98 Anglia Poly Univ MA 02 Southn Univ MA 15. Ridley Hall Cam 99. **d** 03 **p** 04. C Hornchurch St Andr *Chelmsf* 03–07; PtO 08–11; *Win* 09–12; TV Newbury *Ox* 10–13; rtd 13; PtO *Win* from 13. *247 Oceana Boulevard,*

Lower Canal Walk, Southampton SO14 3JG M: 07515-386301 E: mohan.uddin@btopenworld.com

UFFINDELL, David Wilfred George. b 37. Qu Coll Birm 72. **d** 75 **p** 76. NSM Harlescott *Lich* 75–07; rtd 07; PtO *Lich* 08–14 and 16. *53 Talbot Court, Salop Street, Bridgnorth WV16 5BR*

UFFINDELL, Harold David. b 61. Down Coll Cam MA 87. Wycliffe Hall Ox BA 86 MA 91 Oak Hill Th Coll 86. **d** 87 **p** 88. C Kingston Hill St Paul *S'wark* 87–91; C Surbiton St Matt 91–98; V Sunningdale *Ox* 98–16; P-in-c Bracknell 15–16; AD 12–15; R Farnham *Guildf* from 16. *The Rectory, Upper Church Lane, Farnham GU9 7PW* T: (01252) 710129 E: daviduffindell@btconnect.com

UGWUNNA, The Ven Sydney Chukwunma. b 45. Nebraska Wesleyan Univ BSc 67 Univ of Nebraska, Linc MSc 70 Wayne State Univ PhD 79. Virginia Th Sem MDiv 96. **d** 96 **p** 97. C Alexandria Resurrection USA 96–97; C Knaresborough *Ripon* 98–02; Dean Trin Th Coll and Adn Umuahia Nigeria 03–06; R Alexandria Meade Memorial Ch USA 06–08; Visiting P Washington Cathl 09–10; R Earleville St Steph 10–11. *189 New Haw Road, Addlestone KT15 2DP*

ULOGWARA, Canon Obinna Chiadikobi. b 68. Univ of Nigeria BA(Ed) 98 Lagos Univ MEd 03. Trin Coll Umuahia 87. **d** 90 **p** 91. V Ahiara H Trin Nigeria 90–05; Chapl Secondary Schs Dio Mbaise 90–93; V Irete St Pet 93–95; Chapl Secondary Schs Dio Owerri 94–99; V Egbeada Em 99; V Sari Iganmu St Phil 00–01; V Igbobi St Steph 01–05; Hon Chapl to Abp Lagos 01–05; C Dublin Whitechurch *D & G* 05–10; Bp's C Dublin St Geo and St Thos 10–17. *96 Lower Drumcondra Road, Dublin 9, Republic of Ireland* M: (00353) 87-247 6339 E: binagwara@yahoo.com

UMPLEBY, Canon Mark Raymond. b 70. Trin Coll Bris BA 99. **d** 99 **p** 00. C Birstall *Wakef* 99–02; TV N Huddersfield 02–06; Dioc Voc Adv 04–06; Chapl David Young Community Academy Leeds 06–13; PtO *Wakef* 14; C Batley St Thos *Leeds* 14–16; C Hanging Heaton 14–16; C Batley from 16; Hon Can Ripon Cathl from 19. *St Thomas's Vicarage, 16 Stockwell Drive, Batley WF17 5PA* E: markumpleby@hotmail.com

UNDERDOWN (née PARE), Margaret Jean. b 49. Univ of Wales (Abth) BSc 70. St Mich Coll Llan 06. **d** 08 **p** 09. Chapl HM Pris Cardiff 03–13; NSM Cathays *Llan* from 13. *22 Caerleon Road, Cardiff CF14 3DR* T: (029) 2033 1988

UNDERDOWN, Steven. b 52. Hull Univ BSc 75 CertEd 76 K Coll Lon PhD 02. **d** 88 **p** 04. CSWG 82–02; Chapl Brighton and Sussex Univ Hosps NHS Trust 03–15; NSM Hove *Chich* 03–09; P-in-c Hove St Patr 09–15; Chapl Burrswood Chr Hosp *Roch* 15–19; PtO from 19. *May Cottage, Burrswood, Groombridge, Tunbridge Wells TN3 9PU* M: 07981-423973 E: steven.underdown@hotmail.com

UNDERHILL, Stanley Robert. b 27. Cant Sch of Min. **d** 82 **p** 83. C New Addington *Cant* 82–84; C Cannock *Lich* 84–86; TV 86–88; R Dymchurch w Burmarsh and Newchurch *Cant* 88–92; rtd 92; Chapl Menorca *Eur* 92–94; PtO *Cant* 94–04; Lon 05–13. *Charterhouse, Charterhouse Square, London EC1M 6AN* T: (020) 7490 5059 M: 07970-954958 E: stanunder@aol.com

UNDERWOOD, Brian. b 35. Dur Univ BA 57 Keble Coll Ox PGCE 76 Dur Univ MA 72. Clifton Th Coll 57. **d** 59 **p** 60. C Blackpool Ch Ch *Blackb* 59–61; C New Malden and Coombe *S'wark* 61–64; Travel Sec Pathfinders 64–68; Chapl Chantilly *Eur* 68–69; Home Sec CCCS 69–71; P-in-c Gatten St Paul *Portsm* 71–72; Chapl Lyon w Grenoble and Aix-les-Bains *Eur* 72–75; Asst Chapl Trent Coll Nottm 76–80; Chapl Qu Eliz Gr Sch Blackb 80–85; R Bentham St Jo *Bradf* 85–92; V St Alb Ch Ch 92–00; rtd 00; PtO *St Alb* 00–14; *Guildf* from 15. *2 Coombe Court, Station Approach, Tadworth KT20 5AL* T: (01737) 479965 E: brian.v255@yahoo.com

UNDERWOOD, Mrs Susannah Lucy. b 72. Westmr Coll Ox BTh 98. ERMC 05. **d** 08 **p** 09. C Stevenage H Trin *St Alb* 08–11; TV Welwyn from 11. *The Rectory, Brook Bridge Lane, Datchworth, Knebworth SG3 6SU* T: (01438) 817183 E: team.vicar@welwyn.org.uk

UNSWORTH, Philip James. b 41. UEA BEd 82 Nottm Coll of Educn CertEd 63 Nottm Univ DipEd 72. EAMTC 94. **d** 97 **p** 98. NSM Hethersett w Canteloff w Lt and Gt Melton *Nor* 97–00; P-in-c Blofield w Hemblington 00–06; rtd 06; PtO *Nor* from 06. *55 Campbell Close, Hunstanton PE36 5PJ* T: (01485) 532436

UNSWORTH, Thomas Foster. b 28. Lon Univ BA 56. Lich Th Coll 60. **d** 62 **p** 63. C Northfield *Birm* 62–64; C The Lickey 64–66; V Forcett *Ripon* 66–68; V Bellerby and Leyburn 68–69; V Leyburn w Bellerby 69–73; Chapl Whittingham Hosp Preston 73–79; V Freckleton *Blackb* 79–83; V S Yardley St Mich *Birm* 83–86; V Sutton w Carlton and Normanton upon Trent etc *S'well* 86–90; Chapl from 90; St Raphaël *Eur* 90–97; PtO *Cant* from 99. *31 Broadlands Avenue, New Romney TN28 8JE* T: (01797) 361922 E: tom.unsworth@outlook.com

UNWIN, Barry. b 70. Sheff Univ BA 91. Oak Hill Th Coll BA 05. **d** 05 **p** 06. C Hebburn St Jo *Dur* 05–09; C Jarrow Grange 05–09; P-in-c New Barnet St Jas *St Alb* 09–13; V 13–16; P-in-c Hanley Castle, Hanley Swan and Welland *Worc* from 16; P-in-c Upton-on-Severn, Ripple, Earls Croome etc from 16. *Rose Bay, Tunnel Hill, Upton-upon-Severn, Worcester WR8 0QL* M: 07757-610345 E: barryunwin@gmail.com

UNWIN, Christopher Michael Fairclough. b 31. Dur Univ BA 57. Linc Th Coll 58. **d** 67 **p** 68. C St Hilda w St Thos *Dur* 67–73; R Tatsfield *S'wark* 73–81; RE Adv to Ch Secondary Schs 73–81; V Newc St Gabr 81–96; RD Newc E 96; rtd 96; PtO *Dur* from 96; *Newc* from 96. *2 The Cottage,*

West Row, Greatham, Hartlepool TS25 2HW T: (01429) 872781 E: jcmfunwin@gmail.com

UPCHURCH, Sarah Louise. b 66. RGN 89 RSCN 95. SEITE BA 15. **d** 12 **p** 13. NSM Ardingly *Chich* 12–16; NSM Haywards Heath Ascension 16–18; C Worth, Pound Hill and Maidenbower from 18. *St Barnabas House, Crawley Lane, Crawley RH10 7EB* T: (01293) 524804 M: 07910-464404 E: vicarstb@worthparish.org

UPHILL, Ms Ann Carol. b 54. Westcott Ho Cam 95. **d** 97 **p** 98. C Strood St Nic w St Mary *Roch* 97–01; R Footscray w N Cray 01–14; rtd 14; PtO *Roch* from 16. *46 St Leonard's Rise, Orpington BR6 9NB* T: (01689) 637515 M: 07802-883121 E: ann.uphill@uwclub.net

UPSON-SMITH (née GOODWIN), Nicola. b 74. Univ of Wales (Lamp) BA 96 Trin Coll Carmarthen PGCE 98. Ripon Coll Cuddesdon 14. **d** 16 **p** 17. C Northampton St Alb *Pet* 16–19; V Chadsmoor *Lich* from 19. *St Aidan's Vicarage, Albert Street, Cannock WS11 5JD* M: 07807-542417 E: nicola.upsonsmith@yahoo.co.uk

UPTON, Anthony Arthur. b 30. Leic Univ MA 97 PhD 03. Wells Th Coll 61. **d** 63 **p** 64. C Milton *Portsm* 63–67; Chapl RN 67–83; V Foleshill St Laur *Cov* 83–91; rtd 91; PtO *Cov* 91–13. *Redlands Bungalow, Banbury Road, Lighthorne CV35 0AH*

UPTON, Caroline Tracey. *See* APPLEGATH, Caroline Tracey

UPTON, Mrs Christina Phoebe. b 61. Man Univ MB, ChB 85 Ches Univ MTh 04 MRCPsych 93. NOC 06. **d** 08 **p** 09. C W Kirby St Bridget *Ches* 08–12; R Ches H Trin from 12. *The Rectory, 50 Norris Road, Chester CH1 5DZ* T: (01244) 372721 E: tina.upton@tesco.net

UPTON, Christopher Martin. b 53. Bp Grosseteste Coll CertEd 74. EAMTC 94. **d** 97 **p** 98. NSM Gorleston St Andr *Nor* 97–05; NSM Bradwell from 05. *27 Curlew Way, Bradwell, Great Yarmouth NR31 8QX* T: (01493) 668184 E: rev.martin.upton@talk21.com

UPTON, Clement Maurice. b 49. Linc Th Coll 88. **d** 90 **p** 91. C Northampton St Alb *Pet* 90–93; V Laxey and Lonan *S & M* 93–96; V Hipswell *Ripon* 96–01; V Wellingborough St Andr *Pet* 01–10; Chapl Northants Police 05–10; rtd 10; PtO *B & W* 12–14; P-in-c Costa Azahar *Eur* 13–14; PtO *Leic* from 15; *Eur* 18–19; Chapl Malta and Gozo from 19. *74 Rodolphe Street, Sliema 1273, Malta GC* E: sheclem26@yahoo.co.uk

UPTON, Canon Julie. b 61. Ripon Coll Cuddesdon 87. **d** 88 **p** 94. C Kirkstall *Ripon* 88–91; Par Dn E Greenwich Ch Ch w St Andr and St Mich *S'wark* 91–94; C 94; PtO 01–03; *St E* 02–03; NSM Manningham *Bradf* 03–04; TV Bramley *Ripon* 04–10; P-in-c Sheff Manor 10–12; TR from 12; Jt AD Attercliffe from 18; Hon Can Sheff Cathl from 14. *St Aidan's Vicarage, 4 Manor Lane, Sheffield S2 1UF* T: 0114-272 4676 E: julie.upton1@gmail.com *or* julie.upton@sheffield.anglican.org

UPTON, Martin. *See* UPTON, Christopher Martin

UPTON, Mrs Susan Dorothy. b 53. Bp Grosseteste Coll CertEd 74 Nottm Univ BEd 75. EAMTC 99. **d** 02 **p** 03. NSM Bradwell *Nor* from 02. *27 Curlew Way, Bradwell, Great Yarmouth NR31 8QX* T: (01493) 668184 E: sue-upton@talk21.com

UPTON-JONES, Peter John. b 38. Selw Coll Cam BA 63 MA 67 Liv Univ CertEd 64. NOC 90. **d** 92 **p** 93. NSM Formby H Trin *Liv* 92–00; P-in-c Lezayre St Olave Ramsey *S & M* 00–03; V 03–08; P-in-c Kirkbride 00–03; R 03–08; rtd 08; PtO *S & M* from 09. *Clock Cottage, Glen Road, Colby, Isle of Man IM9 4NT* T: (01624) 830216 E: peteru_j@hotmail.com

UREN, Malcolm Lawrence. b 37. AKC 63. **d** 64 **p** 65. C Cant St Martin w St Paul 64–67; C Falmouth K Chas *Truro* 67–71; V St Blazey 71–79; P-in-c Tuckingmill 79–83; V 83–89; V Launceston St Steph w St Thos 89–92; V St Stephen by Launceston 92–96; rtd 00; PtO *Truro* from 00. *17 Forth An Tewennow, St Mary's Gardens, Phillack, Hayle TR27 4QE* T: (01736) 756619 E: malcolm.uren1@btinternet.com

URMSON-TAYLOR, Ralph. *See* TAYLOR, Ralph Urmson

✠**URQUHART, The Rt Revd David Andrew.** b 52. Ealing Business Sch BA 77. Wycliffe Hall Ox 82. **d** 84 **p** 85 **c** 00. C Kingston upon Hull St Nic *York* 84–87; TV Drypool 87–92; V Cov H Trin 92–00; Hon Can Cov Cathl 99–00; Suff Bp Birkenhead *Ches* 00–06; Bp Birm from 06. *Bishop's Croft, Old Church Road, Birmingham B17 0BG* T: 0121-427 1163 F: 426 1322 E: bishop@cofebirmingham.com

URQUHART, Canon Edmund Ross. b 39. Univ Coll Ox BA 62 MA 68. St Steph Ho Ox 62. **d** 64 **p** 65. C Milton *Win* 64–69; C Norton *Derby* 69–73; V Bakewell 73–05; RD Bakewell and Eyam 95–04; Hon Can Derby Cathl 02–05; rtd 05; PtO *Derby* from 05; *Lich* 08–13. *1 Hambleton Close, Ashbourne DE6 1NG* T: (01335) 346454 E: edmund991@btinternet.com

URQUHART, Ian Garnham. b 46. Univ Coll Lon LLB 71. Wycliffe Hall Ox 98. **d** 99 **p** 00. C Barnston *Ches* 99–16; rtd 16; PtO *Ches* from 16. *The Corrie, 19 Gayton Parkway, Wirral CH60 3SZ* T: 0151-342 6710 M: 07770-823373 E: ian@papintalo.co.uk

URSELL, Canon Philip Elliott. b 42. Univ of Wales BA 66 Ox Univ MA 82 Nashotah Ho Wisconsin DD 08. St Steph Ho Ox 66. **d** 68 **p** 69. C Newton Nottage *Llan* 68–71; Asst Chapl Univ of Wales (Cardiff) 71–77; Chapl Wales Poly 74–77; LtO *Llan* 77–07; Chapl Em Coll Cam 77–82; Prin Pusey Ho 82–03; Warden Ascot Priory 85–13; LtO *Ox* 82–13; Can Rio Grande from 05; PtO *Llan* from 15. *273 Hayes Apartments, The Hayes, Cardiff CF10 1BZ* T: (029) 2132 8359 E: peu@cantab.net

✠**URWIN, The Rt Revd Lindsay Goodall.** b 56. Heythrop Coll Lon MA 03 Nashotah Ho Wisconsin Hon DD 11. Ripon Coll Cuddesdon 77. **d** 80 **p** 81 **c** 93. C Walworth *S'wark* 80–83; V N Dulwich St Faith 83–88; Dioc Missr *Chich* 88–93; Area Bp Horsham 93–09; Can and Preb Chich Cathl 93–09; P Admin Shrine of Our Lady of Walsingham 09–15; Hon Asst Bp Nor from 09; OGS from 91; Provost Woodard Corp (S Division) 06–15; R Brunswick Ch Ch Australia from 15; Bp for Angl Schs Melbourne from 15. *8 Glenlyon Road, Brunswick, Vic 3056, Australia* T: (0061) 39-380 1064 E: lindsayurwin1@gmail.com

✠**USHER, The Rt Revd Graham Barham.** b 70. Edin Univ BSc 93 CCC Cam BA 95 MA 00. Westcott Ho Cam 93 St Nic Th Coll Ghana 96. **d** 96 **p** 97 **c** 14. C Nunthorpe *York* 96–99; V N Ormesby 99–04; R Hexham *Newc* 04–14; AD 06–11; Suff Bp Dudley *Worc* 14–19; Hon Can Kumasi Ghana 07–14; Bp Nor from 19. *Bishop's House, Norwich NR3 1SB* T: (01603) 629001 E: bishop@dioceseofnorwich.org

USHER, Miss Tracey Louise. b 86. Sunderland Univ BSc 11. Coll of Resurr Mirfield BA 18. **d** 18 **p** 19. C Newc St Gabr from 18. *26 Crompton Road, Newcastle upon Tyne NE6 5QL* T: 0191-906 9259 E: rev.tracey@icloud.com

UTTIN, Suzanne. *See* GRINDROD, Suzanne

UTTLEY, Mrs Valerie Gail. b 43. Man Univ BA 64. NOC 80. **dss** 83 **d** 87 **p** 94. Otley *Bradf* 83–87; Hon Par Dn 87–89; Par Dn Calverley 89–92; Ind Chapl *Ripon* 92–97; C Kirkstall 95–97; V Lofthouse 97–10; rtd 10; PtO *Newc* from 11. *1 Victoria Terrace, Alnwick NE66 1RE*

UZOIGWE, Austin Chuks. b 64. Qu Coll Birm 13. **d** 15 **p** 16. C Mardyke *Chelmsf* 15–19; TV Newton Flotman, Swainsthorpe, Tasburgh, etc *Nor* from 19. *The New Rectory, Church Hill, Tasburgh, Norwich NR15 1NB* M: 07778-135998 E: revaustinuzoigwe@aol.com

V

VACCARO, Canon Alexandra. b 64. Qu Coll Birm 07. **d** 10 **p** 11. NSM Kidderminster St Mary and All SS w Trimpley etc *Worc* 10–15; NSM Kidderminster Ismere 15–19; NSM Kidderminster St Jo and H Innocents from 19; Dean Self-Supporting Min from 18; Hon Can Worc Cathl from 17. *18 Batham Road, Kidderminster DY10 2TN* T: (01562) 515894 E: alex640213@gmail.com

VAIL, David William. b 30. Dur Univ BA 56 Sheff Univ DipEd 71. Oak Hill Th Coll 56. **d** 58 **p** 59. C Toxteth Park St Bede *Liv* 58–61; Kenya 61–77; Chapl Versailles *Eur* 77–82; Gen Sec Rwanda Miss 82–88; V Virginia Water *Guildf* 88–96; rtd 96; PtO *Ox* from 98. *36 Silverthorne Drive, Caversham, Reading RG4 7NS* T: 0118-954 6667

VAIZEY, Martin John. b 43. AKC 64. **d** 65 **p** 66. C Bishopwearmouth Gd Shep *Dur* 65–69; C Darlington H Trin 69–72; V Easington Colliery 72–80; C-in-c Bishopwearmouth St Mary V w St Pet CD 80–85; V Sunderland Springwell w Thorney Close 85–88; R Witton Gilbert 88–96; P-in-c Wingate Grange 96–99; V Wheatley Hill and Wingate w Hutton Henry 99–07; rtd 07; PtO *Dur* from 13. *Elmside, 2 Etherley Lane, Bishop Auckland DL14 7QR* T: (01388) 450093 E: vaizeym@gmail.com

VALE, Thomas Stanley George. b 52. Chich Th Coll 85. **d** 87 **p** 88. C Leic St Phil 87–90; C Knighton St Mary Magd 90–93; P-in-c Leic St Chad 93–97; V 97–01; V Blackfordby and Woodville 01–17; rtd 17; PtO *Llan* from 17. *107 Springfield Gardens, Hirwaun, Aberdare CF44 9LQ*

VALENTINE, Daniel James. b 74. Lon Guildhall Univ LLB 98 Middx Univ LLM 05 Sheff Univ BA 16 Solicitor 04. Yorks Min Course 14. **d** 16 **p** 17. NSM Chorlton-cum-Hardy St Clem *Man* from 16; Chapl Man Airport from 18. *6 Spindle Mews, Manchester M4 6DB* T: 0161-273 8385 M: 07966-224160 E: revdanchorlton@gmail.com *or* d.valentine@stclement-chorlton.org.uk

VALENTINE, Hugh William James. b 56. Bradf Univ BA 83 CQSW. S'wark Ord Course 86. **d** 89 **p** 90. NSM Stoke Newington Common St Mich *Lon* 89–92; NSM Westmr St Jas from 92; Bps' Adv in Child Protection Stepney and Two Cities Areas from 96; Bp's Adv in Child Protection *Ox* 96–05. *The Clerk's House, 127 Kennington Road, London SE11 6SF* T: (020) 7735 3138 M: 07760-176704 E: mail@hughvalentine.net

VALENTINE, Jeremy Wilfred. b 38. NW Ord Course 76. **d** 79 **p** 80. C Cundall *Ripon* 79–82; TV Huntington *York* 82–87; V Sand Hutton 87–08; P-in-c Whitwell w Crambe, Flaxton and Foston 01–08; RD Buckrose and Bulmer and Malton 98–02; rtd 08; PtO *York* from 08. *5 Sand Hutton Court, Sand Hutton, York YO41 1LU* T: (01904) 468443 E: jeremyvalentine38@outlook.com

VALENTINE, John Harvey. b 63. Ch Ch Ox BA 85 MA 85. Ridley Hall Cam BA 92. **d** 93 **p** 94. C Heigham H Trin *Nor* 93–97; C

Ches Square St Mich w St Phil *Lon* 97–00; C Brompton H Trin w Onslow Square St Paul 00–02; P-in-c Holborn St Geo w H Trin and St Bart 02–09; R from 09. *13 Doughty Street, London WC1N 2PL* T: (020) 7404 9606 *or* 7404 4407 F: 7831 0588 M: 07736-066091 E: john.valentine@sgtm.org

VALENTINE, Mrs Katherine Anne. b 58. Newc Poly BA 80 Anglia Ruskin Univ MA 12. ERMC 03. **d** 06 **p** 07. C Haughley w Wetherden and Stowupland *St E* 06–10; P-in-c Pakenham w Norton and Tostock 10–18; C Badwell and Walsham 15–18; R Pakenham w Norton, Tostock etc from 18; Asst Dioc Dir of Ords from 16; RD Ixworth from 17. *The Orwell, Woolpit Road, Norton, Bury St Edmunds IP31 3LU* T: (01359) 235095 E: katherine@kavalentine.plus.com

VALIANT, Mrs Lesley Jean. b 51. Whitelands Coll Lon CertEd 74 Univ Coll Chich BA 99. STETS 99. **d** 01 **p** 02. NSM Bedhampton *Portsm* 01–04; C Southsea St Jude 04–06; Asst to RD Portsm 04–06; TV Pewsey and Swanborough *Sarum* 06–09; TV Modbury, Bigbury, Ringmore, Kingston etc *Ex* 11–13; PtO *Cant* from 14; Chapl MU from 14. *27 Cliffe Avenue, Margate CT9 5DU* T: (01843) 293964 M: 07751-168228 E: ljvaliant@gmail.com

VALLENTE-KERR, Susan Fiona. b 77. St Martin's Coll Lanc BA 98 Ch Ch Coll Cant PGCE 00 Moorlands Coll MA 08. St Mellitus Coll 08. **d** 11 **p** 12. C Frindsbury w Upnor and Chattenden *Roch* from 11; C Strood St Nic w St Mary from 17; C Strood St Fran from 17. *The Vicarage, 3 Central Road, Rochester ME2 3HF* T: (01634) 612984 M: 07875-349029 E: suziqvk@yahoo.co.uk

VALLINS, Canon Christopher. b 43. Hon FRSocMed 06. Lich Th Coll 63. **d** 66 **p** 67. C Cuddington *Guildf* 66–70; C Aldershot St Mich 70–73; V W Ewell 73–81; R Worplesdon and Chapl Merrist Wood Coll of Agric and Horticulture 81–89; RD Guildf 86–89; Chapl Epsom Health Care NHS Trust 89–99; Hd Past Care Epsom and St Helier Univ Hosps NHS Trust 99–07; Bp's Adv on Healing *Guildf* 97–07; Bp's Adv for Hosp Chapl 07–16; Hon Can Guildf Cathl from 01; PtO *S'wark* from 07; *Guildf* from 16. *Little Watermead, Reigate Road, Hookwood, Horley RH6 0HD* T: (01293) 824188 F: 823282 M: 07917-337920 E: chrisvallins@yahoo.com

VAN BEVEREN (née FORBES), Mrs Susan Margaret. b 64. St Hugh's Coll Ox BA 85 MA 89. Trin Th Sch Melbourne 95. **d** 96 **p** 96. Ind Chapl Inter-Ch Trade and Ind Miss Australia 96–99; NSM Amsterdam w Den Helder and Heiloo *Eur* 00–03; Officer for Miss in Work and Economic Life *Ox* 03–07; Dioc Adv 08–13; NSM S Ascot 07–09; NSM Sunninghill and S Ascot 09–13; PtO from 14; Chapl Heatherwood & Wexham Park Hosps NHS Foundn Trust 14–15; Head of Chapl Kingston Hosp NHS Foundn Trust Surrey from 15. *Kingston Hospital NHS Foundation Trust, Kingston Hospital, Galsworthy*

Road, Kingston-upon-Thames KT2 7QB   T: (020) 8546 7711
E: susanvanbeveren@gmail.com or susan.vanbeveren@nhs.net

VAN BLERK, Etienne. b 68. Pretoria Univ BA 91 Stellenbosch Univ BTh 92 Lebanese American Univ BA 96. Ox Min Course 07. **d** 09 **p** 10. C Bicester w Bucknell, Caversfield and Launton Ox 09–11; C Walton H Trin 11–13; Chapl Rossall Sch Fleetwood 13–19; PtO Blackb 19; P-in-c Carbis Bay w Lelant Truro from 19. The Vicarage, Porthrepta Road, Carbis Bay, St Ives TR26 2LD   M: 07795-985942 E: vanblerketienne@gmail.com

VAN CARRAPIETT, Timothy Michael James. b 39. Chich Th Coll 60. **d** 63 **p** 64. C Sugley Newc 63–65; C Newc St Fran 65–69; P-in-c Wrangbrook w N Elmsall CD Wakef 69–74; P-in-c Flushing Truro 74–75; P-in-c Mylor w Flushing 75–76; P-in-c St Day 76–82; R Aldrington Chich 82–87; V Bexhill St Barn 87–01; rtd 01; PtO St E 01–13; Chelmsf from 08. The College of St Barnabas, Blackberry Lane, Lingfield RH7 6NJ

VAN DE KASTEELE, Peter John. b 39. Magd Coll Cam BA 61 MA 65. Clifton Th Coll 61. **d** 63 **p** 64. C Eastbourne H Trin Chich 63–66; C N Pickenham w S Pickenham etc Nor 66–70; R Mursley w Swanbourne and Lt Horwood Ox 70–80; Admin Sec Clinical Th Assn from 83; Gen Dir 88–99; PtO Glouc 83–16; Hon C Westcote w Icomb and Bledington 88–89; rtd 99. 68 Springfield Road, Southwell NG25 0BT

van de WEYER, Robert William Bates. b 50. Lanc Univ BA 76. S'wark Ord Course 78. **d** 81 **p** 82. Warden Lt Gidding Community 77–98; Hon C Gt w Lt Gidding and Steeple Gidding Ely 81–83; P-in-c 83–93; P-in-c Winwick 83–93; P-in-c Hamerton 83–93; P-in-c Upton and Copmanford 83–93; PtO from 93; St Alb from 15. 4 Copse Way, Cambridge CB2 8BJ E: robert@vandeweyer.co.uk

VAN DEN BERG, Jan Jacob. b 56. Sarum & Wells Th Coll 86. **d** 88 **p** 89. C Glouc St Aldate 88–91; C Ollerton w Boughton S'well 91–95; P-in-c Scrooby 95–00; P-in-c Blyth 97–00; C Brampton and Farlam and Castle Carrock w Cumrew Carl 00–02; TV Eden, Gelt and Irthing 02–05; P-in-c Rockcliffe and Blackford from 05. The Vicarage, Rockcliffe, Carlisle CA6 4AA   T: (01228) 674209   F: 672006

VAN DEN BERG-OWENS, Jayne. b 65. **d** 11 **p** 12. C Kirkby Liv 11–14; TV 4Saints Team from 14. St George's Vicarage, St George's Road, Huyton, Liverpool L36 8BE   M: 07828-701890 E: jayne.vdbo@gmail.com

VAN DEN BERGH, Victor Michael Cornelius. b 53. ALBC 92. Ridley Hall Cam 02. **d** 03 **p** 04. C Tamworth Lich from 03. St Francis's Vicarage, Masefield Drive, Tamworth B79 8JB   T: (01827) 65926   M: 07770-900712 E: vic_vdb@btinternet.com

van den HOF, Ariadne Rolanda Magdalena. b 71. Univ of Wales (Cardiff) MTh 96 Leiden Univ MA 05. Old Cath Sem Amersfoort 90 St Mich Coll Llan 98. **d** 99 **p** 00. C Dolgellau w Llanfachreth and Brithdir etc Ban 99–01; Min Can Ban Cathl 01–02; P-in-c Trefdraeth w Aberffraw, Llangadwaladr etc 02–03; R 03–06; R Llanffestiniog w Blaenau Ffestiniog etc 06–11; Rural Life Co-ord 04–11; V Shooters Hill Ch Ch S'wark from 11. Christ Church Vicarage, 1 Craigholm, Shooters Hill, London SE18 3RR   T: (020) 8856 5858 E: armvandenhof@gmail.com

VAN DER HART, William Richard. b 76. Homerton Coll Cam BEd 99. Wycliffe Hall Ox BTh 04. **d** 04 **p** 05. C Bryanston Square St Mary w St Marylebone St Mark Lon 04–08; TV Roxeth 08–11; V W Harrow 11–14; C Onslow Square and S Kensington St Aug from 14. 20 Alderbury Road, London SW13 9BU   M: 07968-132129 E: william.vanderhart@htb.org.uk

VAN DER LELY, Canon Janice Kay. b 55. Sheff Univ BA 76 Dur Univ PhD 79 Webster Univ (USA) MA 05 Ox Brookes Univ MA 10. Ripon Coll Cuddesdon 08. **d** 09 **p** 10. C Cirencester Glouc 09–12; V Thornbury and Oldbury-on-Severn w Shepperdine 12–19; Chan Llan Cathl from 19. 1 St Mary's, The Cathedral Green, Cardiff CF5 2EB   T: (029) 2115 6258   M: 07595-270438 E: janvanderlely@gmail.com or chancellor@llandaffcathedral.org.uk

van der LINDE, Herbert John. b 43. Rhodes Univ BA 66. Coll of Resurr Mirfield. **d** 68 **p** 69. C Kingston St Luke S'wark 68–75; C Chipping Campden w Ebrington Glouc 75–78; V Cheltenham St Pet 78–84; V Bussage 84–13; rtd 13; PtO Bris from 13. Amen Corner, 18 Waylands, Cricklade, Swindon SN6 6BT   T: (01793) 759026 E: frjohn.vanderlinde@gmail.com

VAN DER PUMP, Charles Lyndon. b 25. FRCM. S'wark Ord Course 86. **d** 88 **p** 89. NSM Primrose Hill St Mary w Avenue Road St Paul Lon 88–02; PtO 02–18. 48 Canfield Gardens, London NW6 3EB   T/F: (020) 7624 4517 E: lyndonvdp@waitrose.com

VAN DER TOORN, Canon Stephne. b 53. Natal Univ BA 73 Stellenbosch Univ HDipEd 75. Th Ext Educn Coll. **d** 93

p 95. NSM Pretoria St Mary S Africa 93–01; C Fawley Win 01–07; R E Bergholt and Brantham St E from 07; Hon Can St E Cathl from 13. The Rectory, Rectory Lane, Brantham, Manningtree CO11 1PZ   T: (01206) 392646 E: revsteph3@vodafoneemail.co.uk

van der VALK, Jesse. b 59. Nottm Univ BTh 84 Birm Univ MPhil 88 Avery Hill Coll PGCE 85. St Jo Coll Nottm 81. **d** 88 **p** 89. C Droitwich Spa Worc 88–92; V Hartshead and Hightown Wakef 92–96; R Woolwich St Mary w St Mich S'wark from 96; USPG (Lon Volunteers and Co-workers Team) from 97. The Rectory, 43 Rectory Place, London SE18 5DA   T: (020) 8465 7307 or 8316 4338 E: jvdr09@aol.com

VAN KRIEKEN VANNERLEY, David. See VANNERLEY, David van Krieken

VAN LEEUWEN, Canon Dirk Willem. b 45. Utrecht Univ LLD 71. Th Faculty Brussels 71 S'wark Ord Course 80. **d** 82 **p** 83. Asst Chapl Brussels Cathl Eur 82–84; Chapl Haarlem 84–93; Chapl Antwerp St Boniface 94–06; Assoc Chapl 06–07; Chapl Charleroi 94–00; P-in-c Ypres 97–99; P-in-c Leuven 98–99; Can Brussels Cathl 96–07; Chapl Knokke 01–07; P-in-c Ostend 01–06; P-in-c Bruges 01–03; V Gen to Bp Eur 02–07; Adn NW Eur 05–07; rtd 08. De Gouden Druyfftack, Damplein 21, 4331GC Middelburg, The Netherlands   T: (0031) (615) 494914 E: dlw@skhl.nl

VAN OMMEREN, Ms Gerda Maria Jacoba. b 76. Leiden Univ MA 99. St Mellitus Coll 17. **d** 19. C Goodrington and Collaton St Mary Ex from 19. 40 Steed Close, Paignton TQ4 7SN   M: 07787-127983 E: reverendgerda@outlook.com

VAN ROSSUM, Paul Anthony. b 53. Sheff Univ BScTech 74 Birm Univ PGCE 75 Open Univ MA 92. Trin Coll Bris 09. **d** 12 **p** 13. OLM Almondsbury and Olveston Bris from 12; Bp's Chapl 16–18; rtd 19. 18 Townsend Lane, Almondsbury, Bristol BS32 4EQ   T: (01454) 626160 E: paulvanrossum@gmail.com

VAN STRAATEN, Christopher Jan. b 55. Bris Univ BA 77 Natal Univ HDipEd 78. Oak Hill Th Coll 90. **d** 92 **p** 93. C Woodley Ox 92–96; V Gillingham St Aug Roch 96–07; V Aylesford 07–16; V Sutton Park York 16–18; P-in-c Wawne 16–18; V Sutton Park and Wawne from 18; AD E Hull from 19. 11 Sovereign Way, Kingswood, Hull HU7 3JG   T: (01482) 838486 E: cjvanstraaten@gmail.com

van WENGEN, Rosemary Margaret. See KOBUS van WENGEN, Rosemary Margaret

VAN ZANDBERGEN, Karen. See BURNETT-HALL, Karen

VANE, Benjamin Christopher George. b 81. Bath Univ BSc 03. Oak Hill Th Coll BA 15. **d** 15 **p** 16. C Oakwood St Thos Lon 15–19; C Ox St Ebbe w H Trin and St Pet from 19. 14 Kelburne Road, Oxford OX4 3SJ   M: 07967-602513 E: ben.vane@gmail.com

VANN, The Ven Cherry Elizabeth. b 58. ARCM 78 GRSM 80. Westcott Ho Cam 86. **d** 89 **p** 94. Par Dn Flixton St Mich Man 89–92; Chapl Bolton Inst of F&HE 92–98; Par Dn Bolton St Pet 92–94; C 94–98; TV E Farnworth and Kearsley 98–04; TR 04–08; Chapl among Deaf People 98–04; AD Farnworth 05–08; Adn Rochdale from 08. 57 Melling Road, Oldham OL4 1PN   T: 0161-678 1454   F: 678 1455   M: 07587-132707 E: archrochdale@manchester.anglican.org

VANNERLEY, David van Krieken. b 50. Kent Univ BA 78 MPhil 07 Cant Ch Ch Univ MA 11 Ch Ch Coll Cant CertEd 71. SEITE 00. **d** 05 **p** 06. NSM St Laur in Thanet Cant 05–13; PtO Roch from 13; Cant 13–14; TV Whitstable from 14; Chapl Kent Critical Incident Chapl Service from 10. The Rectory, 69 Swalecliffe Court Drive, Whitstable CT5 2NF   T: (01227) 792826 E: vannerley@aol.com

VANNOZZI, Peter. b 62. Lon Univ BA 83 Heythrop Coll Lon MA 06. Ripon Coll Cuddesdon BA 86 MA 91. **d** 87 **p** 88. C Kenton Lon 87–90; C Fleet Guildf 90–93; V Northwood Hills St Edm Lon 93–97; AD Harrow 95–97; V S Dulwich St Steph S'wark 97–05; RD Dulwich 02–05; Can Res Wakef Cathl 05–07; V Hampton Hill Lon 07–15; V Highgate St Aug 15–19; V Isleworth St Fran from 19. Vicarage of St Francis of Assisi, 865 Great West Road, Isleworth TW7 5PD   T: (020) 8374 6985 E: revpetervannozzi@gmail.com

VANSTONE, Preb Walford David Frederick. b 38. Open Univ BA 81. AKC 69. **d** 70 **p** 71. C Feltham Lon 70–75; TV E Runcorn w Halton Ches 75–80; V Grange St Andr 80–82; V Hampton All SS Lon 82–05; P-in-c Teddington SS Pet and Paul and Fulwell 99–00; AD Hampton 95–03; Preb St Paul's Cathl 99–05; Chapl Richmond Coll 02–05; rtd 05; PtO Lon from 05. 13 Lammas Close, Staines TW18 4XT E: wvanstone@aol.com

VARAH, Canon Paul Hugh. b 46. St Deiniol's Hawarden 83. **d** 85 **p** 86. C Prestatyn St As 85–87; P-in-c Hawarden 87–88; TV 88–89; V Esclusham 89–96; V Connah's Quay 96–13; Can Cursal St As Cathl 08–13; rtd 13; PtO St As from 14. 4 New Road, Dobshill, Deeside CH5 3LU   T: (01244) 540728 E: paulhvarah@gmail.com

VARGESON, Canon Peter Andrew. b 53. Wycliffe Hall Ox 85. **d** 87 **p** 88. C Yateley *Win* 87–92; V Bursledon 92–17; AD Eastleigh 99–06 and 09–16; P-in-c Hound 07–15; C 15–17; rtd 17; PtO *Win* from 17; Hon Can Tororo Uganda from 99. *4 Knoll Gardens, St Ives, Ringwood BH24 2LW* T: (01425) 839343 E: peter.vargeson@gmail.com

VARLEY (*née* TRIM), Elizabeth Ann. b 52. Homerton Coll Cam BEd 75 Van Mildert Coll Dur PhD 85 St Jo Coll Dur BA 96. NEOC 94. **d** 96 **p** 97. C Sedgefield *Dur* 96–99; Dir Post-Ord Tr Stepney Area *Lon* 99–02; V Hipswell *Ripon* 02–07; Hon Can Ripon Cathl 05–07; R Bacton w Wyverstone, Cotton and Old Newton etc *St E* 07–15; C Bro Arwystli *Ban* 15–16; PtO *Portsm* from 17. *Society of the Sisters of Bethany, 7 Nelson Road, Southsea PO5 2AR* T: 07922-012703 E: lizpssb@gmail.com

VARLEY, Robert. b 36. St Jo Coll Cam BA 57 MA 64 Man Poly PGCE 92. NW Ord Course 71. **d** 74 **p** 75. C Wallasey St Hilary *Ches* 74–77; V Rock Ferry 77–81; PtO *Man* 82–83; Hon C E Farnworth and Kearsley 83–86; Hon C Walkden Moor 86–87; C 87–89; V Lt Hulton 89–90; PtO from 97. *66 Normanby Road, Worsley, Manchester M28 7TS* T: 0161-790 8420 M: 07801-064602 E: revrobvarley@hotmail.com

VARNEY, Peter David. b 38. Univ Coll Dur BA 61 MA 64. Qu Coll Birm 61. **d** 64 **p** 65. C Newington St Paul *S'wark* 64–66; C Camberwell St Mich w All So w Em 66–67; Perm to Offic Kuching Malaysia 67–68; Hon C Croxley Green All SS *St Alb* 69; Asst Sec Gen Syn Bd for Miss and Unity 69–72; PtO *Roch* 69–72 and 74–84; Asst Chapl CSJB 72–73; Asst Sec Chrs Abroad 74–79; Dir Bloxham Project 84–85; PtO *Cant* 84–85; *S'wark* 85–86; P-in-c Thornage w Brinton w Hunworth and Stody *Nor* 87–88; P-in-c Briningham 87–88; C Melton Constable w Swanton Novers 87–88; PtO from 88; Chapl Yare and Norvic Clinics and St Andr Hosp *Nor* 90–95; rtd 03. *280 The Pavilion, St Stephens Road, Norwich NR1 3SN* T: (01603) 760838 E: varney@waitrose.com

VARNEY, Stephen Clive. b 59. Qu Mary Coll Lon BSc 80 Sussex Univ MSc 82 Southn Univ BTh 88. Sarum & Wells Th Coll 83. **d** 86 **p** 87. C Riverhead w Dunton Green *Roch* 86–91; V Bostall Heath 91–99; V Bromley St Mark 99–19; rtd 19. *56 High Street, Overton, Basingstoke RG25 3HG* M: 07961-117578

VARNON, Nicholas Charles Harbord. b 45. St Luke's Coll Ex CertEd 71 Open Univ BA 83 BPhil 91 MA 94 Univ of Wales MPhil 00. St Mich Coll Llan 91. **d** 93 **p** 94. C Pontypridd St Cath w St Matt *Llan* 93–97; P-in-c Sutton St Nicholas w Sutton St Michael *Heref* 97–04; P-in-c Withington w Westhide 97–04; P-in-c Weybourne Gp *Nor* 04–06; R N Elmham, Billingford, Bintree, Guist etc 06–16; CF (ACF) 00–16; rtd 16; PtO *Nor* from 16. *Willow Lodge, Springwell Road, Whissonsett, Dereham NR20 5TU* E: nicholas.varnon@btinternet.com

VARQUEZ, Leo Bacleon. b 61. St Andr Th Sem Manila 82. **d** 86 **p** 86. P St Andr Philippines 86–91; P St Isidore 92–94; SSF 95–99; NSM Edin St Jo 98–99; NSM Mill End and Heronsgate w W Hyde *St Alb* 99–00; Asst Chapl HM Pris Featherstone 00–02; C Hednesford *Lich* 00–04; C Kingstanding St Luke *Birm* 04–06; Asst Chapl Univ Coll Lon Hosps NHS Foundn Trust 06–08; Chapl Univ Hosp of N Staffs NHS Trust from 08. *University Hospital of North Staffs, Newcastle Road, Stoke-on-Trent ST4 6QG* T: (01782) 676400 E: leo.varquez@uhns.nhs.uk

VARTY, John Eric. b 44. Tyndale Hall Bris 68. **d** 71 **p** 72. C Barrow St Mark *Carl* 71–74; C Cheadle *Ches* 74–82; V Cheadle All Hallows 82–89; V Alsager Ch Ch 89–06; rtd 06; Chapl to Bp Stockport *Ches* 07–14; C Acton and Worleston, Church Minshull etc 12–14; PtO from 14. *14 Gowy Close, Alsager, Stoke-on-Trent ST7 2HX* T: (01270) 877360 E: john.varty@homecall.co.uk

VASBY-BURNIE, Timothy Roy. b 79. Trin Coll Cam MA 00. Wycliffe Hall Ox BTh 07. **d** 07 **p** 08. C Stone Ch Ch and Oulton *Lich* 07–10; V Wednesbury St Bart 10–16; V Shrewsbury St Geo w Greenfields from 16. *The Vicarage, St George's Street, Shrewsbury SY3 8QA* E: tim@vasbyburnie.net

VASEY, Mrs Janet Mary. b 41. Margaret McMillan Coll of Educn CertEd 62. Local MinI Tr Course 11. **d** 11. NSM Gt Grimsby St Mary and St Jas *Linc* from 11. *34 Western Outway, Grimsby DN34 5EX* T: (01472) 753145 E: jan.vasey@btinternet.com

VASEY-SAUNDERS, Canon Leah Beverley. b 77. Huddersfield Univ BMus 98 St Jo Coll Dur BA 03. Cranmer Hall Dur 00. **d** 03 **p** 04. C Whorlton *Newc* 03–04; Hon C Newc St Geo 05–08; TV Cannock *Lich* 08–09; TV Cannock and Huntington 09–10; V Heath Hayes 10–11; C Hednesford 08–11; PtO *S'well* 12–13; P-in-c Harworth 13–16; Can Prec Wakef Cathl *Leeds* from 16. *4 Cathedral Close, Margaret Street, Wakefield WF1 2DP* T: (01924) 373923 E: leah@vasey-saunders.co.uk *or* leah.vasey-saunders@wakefield.cathedral.org.uk

VASEY-SAUNDERS, Mark Richard. b 74. Coll of Ripon & York St Jo BA 95 St Jo Coll Dur BA 00. Cranmer Hall

Dur 98. **d** 01 **p** 02. C Ponteland *Newc* 01–04; Chapl Newc Univ 04–08; PtO *Lich* 10–11; TV Retford Area *S'well* 11–16; Tutor St Hild Coll from 17; PV Wakef Cathl *Leeds* from 17. *4 Cathedral Close, Margaret Street, Wakefield WF1 2DP* E: mark@vasey-saunders.co.uk

VAUGHAN, Canon Andrew Christopher James. b 61. Univ of Wales (Lamp) BA 82. Linc Th Coll 82. **d** 84 **p** 85. C Caerleon *Mon* 84–86; C Magor w Redwick and Undy 86–88; Ind Chapl 84–94; Linc Ind Miss 94–17; P-in-c Swinderby from 17; Can and Preb Linc Cathl from 05. *46 Post Mill Close, North Hykeham, Lincoln LN6 9HL* T: (01522) 687242 M: 07702-468549 E: andrewvaughan@ntlworld.com

VAUGHAN, Andrew Kenneth. b 64. MCIOB 01. Ridley Hall Cam 04. **d** 07 **p** 08. C Chislehurst Ch Ch *Roch* 07–11; V Istead Rise from 11. *The Vicarage, Upper Avenue, Istead Rise, Gravesend DA13 9DA* T: (01474) 832403 M: 07977-154809 E: andrewvaughan@akv64s.com

VAUGHAN, Brian John. b 38. Lich Th Coll 65. **d** 68 **p** 69. C Fisherton Anger *Sarum* 68–70; C Wareham w Arne 70–73; Asst P Mt Lawley Australia 73; R Dalwallinu 73–76; R Morawa 75–78; Field Officer Bible Soc of W Australia 78–81; Assoc P Mt Lawley 82–86; R Pinjarra 86–96; R Manjimup 96–00; rtd 00. *Milborne, 6 Steeple Retreat, Busselton WA 6280, Australia* T: (0061) (8) 9751 1225 M: (0061) 42-407 4414 E: sherton38@gmail.com

VAUGHAN, Carole Ann. b 47. Leeds Univ CertEd 68. STETS 95. **d** 98 **p** 99. NSM Oakley w Wootton St Lawrence *Win* 98–18; rtd 18; PtO *Sheff* from 19. *365 Fox Hill Road, Sheffield S6 1BG* E: carole@cjvaughan.co.uk

VAUGHAN, Miss Catherine Margaret. b 64. Bp Grosseteste Coll BEd 88 Moorlands Coll BA 05. STETS MA 12. **d** 12 **p** 13. C Bath Twerton-on-Avon *B & W* 12–15; V Owlsmoor Ox from 15. *The Vicarage, 107 Owlsmoor Road, Owlsmoor, Sandhurst GU47 0SS* M: 07879-498474

VAUGHAN, Charles Jeremy Marshall. b 52. Man Univ BSc 75. St Jo Coll Nottm 83. **d** 85 **p** 86. C Epsom Common Ch Ch *Guildf* 85–88; C Woking Ch Ch 88–93; R Worting *Win* 93–07; R Winklebury and Worting 07–10; R Oakley w Wootton St Lawrence 10–18; rtd 18; PtO *Sheff* from 19. *365 Fox Hill Road, Sheffield S6 1BG* E: jeremy@cjvaughan.co.uk

VAUGHAN, Craig Aaron. **d** 12 **p** 13. NSM Newton Nottage *Llan* 12–17; TV Llantwit Major 17–18; TV Glamorgan Heritage Coast from 18. *The Vicarage, Trepit Road, Wick, Cowbridge CF71 7QL* T: (01656) 890468 E: fathercraig.70@btinternet.com

VAUGHAN, Edward Michael. b 59. Univ of NSW BA 80 Sydney Univ DipEd 81. Moore Th Coll Sydney BTh 87. **d** 89 **p** 89. C Jannali Australia 89–91; C Rozelle 92–94; R Darling Street 95–05; I Crinken *D & G* 05–10; Australia from 10. *PO Box 465, Kings Cross NSW 1340, Australia* T: (0061) (2) 9360 6844 E: edwardv@ughan.net

VAUGHAN, Idris Samuel. b 46. Sarum Th Coll 70. **d** 72 **p** 73. C Workington St Jo *Carl* 72–76; C Foley Park *Worc* 76–79; V Hayton St Mary *Carl* 79–85; Chapl Asst Univ Hosp Nottm 85–90; Chapl Asst Nottm Gen Hosp 85–90; Chapl Stafford Distr Gen Hosp 90–94; Chapl Chase Hosp Cannock 90–94; Chapl Mid Staffs Gen Hosps NHS Trust 94–06; rtd 06; P-in-c Lanzarote *Eur* 06–10. *43 Silmore Crescent, Stafford ST17 4JL*

VAUGHAN, Jeremy. *See* VAUGHAN, Charles Jeremy Marshall

VAUGHAN, Jonathan Michael. b 84. Bris Univ BSc 06. Wycliffe Hall Ox BTh 11. **d** 13 **p** 14. NSM Ox St Andr 13–17; V Wolvey, Copston Magna and Withybrook *Cov* from 17. *The Vicarage, School Lane, Wolvey, Hinckley LE10 3LH* T: (01455) 220385 E: revjonathanvaughan@gmail.com

VAUGHAN, Patrick Handley. b 38. TCD BA 60 BD 65 Selw Coll Cam BA 62 MA 66 Nottm Univ PhD 88. Ridley Hall Cam 61. **d** 63 **p** 64. Min Can Bradf Cathl 63–66; Uganda 67–73; P-in-c Slingsby *York* 74–77; Tutor NW Ord Course 74–77; P-in-c Hovingham *York* 74–77; Prin EMMTC *S'well* 77–90; Hon Can Leic Cathl 87–90; Assoc Lect Open Univ from 94. *113 Upperthorpe Road, Sheffield S6 3EA* T: 0114-272 2675 E: patrickvaughan38@yahoo.co.uk

✠**VAUGHAN, The Rt Revd Peter St George.** b 30. Selw Coll Cam BA 55 MA 59 BNC Ox MA 63. Ridley Hall Cam. **d** 57 **p** 58 **c** 89. C Birm St Martin 57–63; Chapl Ox Pastorate 63–67; Asst Chapl BNC Ox 63–67; V Galle Face Ch Ch Ceylon 67–72; Prec H Trin Cathl Auckland New Zealand 72–75; Prin Crowther Hall CMS Tr Coll Selly Oak 75–83; Adn Westmorland and Furness *Carl* 83–89; Hon Can Carl Cathl 83–89; Area Bp Ramsbury *Sarum* 89–98; Can and Preb Sarum Cathl 89–98; rtd 98; Hon Asst Bp Bradf 98–01; Hon Can Bradf Cathl 98–01; PtO *Glouc* 01–06; Hon Asst Bp Glouc 06–11; Hon Asst Bp Bris from 02. *Willowbrook, Downington, Lechlade GL7 3DL* T: (01367) 252216

VAUGHAN, Preb Roger Maxwell. b 39. AKC 62. **d** 63 **p** 64. C W Bromwich All SS *Lich* 63–65; C Wolverhampton 65–70;

V Tunstall Ch Ch 70–79; V Abbots Bromley 79–86; P-in-c Blithfield 85–86; V Abbots Bromley w Blithfield 86–93; V Stafford St Jo and Tixall w Ingestre 93–04; Preb Lich Cathl 99–04; rtd 04; PtO *Lich* from 04. *51 Crestwood Drive, Stone ST15 0LW* T: (01785) 812192

VAUGHAN, Trevor. b 41. Cen Lancs Univ BA 91. Linc Th Coll 66. **d** 69 **p** 70. C Wyken *Cov* 69–72; C Stratford-on-Avon w Bishopton 72–73; P-in-c Monks Kirby w Withybrook and Copston Magna 73–75; P-in-c Wolvey, Burton Hastings and Stretton Baskerville 73–77; P-in-c Withybrook w Copston Magna 73–77; V Heyhouses *Blackb* 77–80; CF (TA) from 79; V Chorley St Geo *Blackb* 80–83; R Bolton by Bowland w Grindleton *Bradf* 83–89; V Settle 89–91; R Broughton, Marton and Thornton 91–00; V Morecambe St Barn *Blackb* 00–03; P-in-c Sabden and Pendleton 03–06; rtd 06; PtO *Leeds* from 17. *Throstle Nest Cottage, Old Road, Thornton in Craven, Skipton BD23 3TB* T: (01282) 842383 E: trevor.vaughan3@outlook.com

VAUGHAN-WILSON, Canon Jane Elizabeth. b 61. Magd Coll Ox MA 87. Cranmer Hall Dur. **d** 89 **p** 94. Par Dn Ormesby *York* 89–93; Dn-in-c Middlesbrough St Agnes 93–94; P-in-c 94–95; TV Basingstoke *Win* 95–03; PtO *Truro* from 03; Dioc Dir of Ords from 14; Hon Can Truro Cathl from 16. *4 Tolver Road, Penzance TR18 2AG* T: (01736) 351825 E: jvaughanwi@hotmail.co.uk

VELLACOTT, Peter Graham. b 38. EAMTC 90. **d** 93 **p** 94. NSM Framlingham w Saxtead *St E* 93–95; NSM Brandeston w Kettleburgh 95–99; NSM Easton 95–99; P-in-c Brandeston w Kettleburgh and Easton 99–07; rtd 07; PtO *St E* 07–16. *Stretham House, The Street, Earl Soham, Woodbridge IP13 7SF* T: (01728) 685423

VENABLES, Deborah. b 70. **d** 12 **p** 13. NSM Presteigne w Discoed, Kinsham, Lingen and Knill *Heref* from 12. *17 Caenbrook Meadow, Presteigne LD8 2NE* T: (01544) 267663 E: revdebbiev@aol.com

VENABLES, Canon Margaret Joy. b 37. Bp Otter Coll CertEd 57. S Dios Minl Tr Scheme 86. **d** 89 **p** 94. NSM Wilton *B & W* 89–91; C Taunton St Andr 91–97; P-in-c Haynes *St Alb* 97–03; P-in-c Clophill 00–03; R Campton, Clophill and Haynes 03–06; RD Shefford 01–06; Hon Can St Alb 05–06; rtd 06; P-in-c Barnack w Ufford and Bainton *Pet* 06–10; PtO from 10. *The Cottage, Millstone Lane, Barnack, Stamford PE9 3ET* T: (01780) 749127 E: margsv@waitrose.com or margaretvenables@gmail.com

VENABLES, Philip Richard Meredith. b 58. Magd Coll Ox BA 79 CertEd 80. Wycliffe Hall Ox 85. **d** 88 **p** 89. C Gillingham St Mark *Roch* 88–93; V Penge St Jo 93–07; R Bebington *Ches* 07–12; V Whittle-le-Woods *Blackb* from 12. *The Vicarage, Preston Road, Whittle-le-Woods, Chorley PR6 7PS* T: (01257) 241291 E: philip.venables@ntlworld.com

VENESS, David Roger. b 48. Brunel Univ BTech 70. St Jo Coll Nottm 73. **d** 75 **p** 76. C Selly Hill St Steph *Birm* 75–80; V Colney Heath St Mark *St Alb* 80–98; RD Hatfield 88–93; rtd 13; PtO *St Alb* from 15. *125 Westfields, St Albans AL3 4JR* M: 07930-430033 E: 100drv@gmail.com

VENETUCCI, Lisa. *See* REDFERN, Lisa

VENN, Richard Frank. b 49. Leeds Univ BSc 72 Strathclyde Univ PhD 77 CChem FRSC 97. Ridley Hall Cam 04. **d** 05 **p** 06. C Margate H Trin *Cant* 05–08; P-in-c Len Valley 08–16; AD N Downs 15–16; rtd 16; PtO *Bris* from 17; *Eur* from 18. *27 Abbey Row, Malmesbury SN16 0AG* T: (01666) 238315 M: 07970-288669 E: richardfvenn@gmail.com

VENNELLS, Ms Paula Anne. b 59. Bradf Univ BA 81 FRSA 88. SAOMC 02. **d** 05 **p** 06. NSM Bromham w Oakley and Stagsden *St Alb* from 05. *Rushey Ford House, West End Road, Kempston, Bedford MK43 8RU* T: (01234) 851594 M: 07786-174638 E: paula.vennells@gmail.com

✠**VENNER, The Rt Revd Stephen Squires.** b 44. Birm Univ BA 65 Linacre Coll Ox BA 67 MA 71 Lon Univ PGCE 72 Birm Univ Hon DD 09 Cant Ch Ch Univ DUniv 10. St Steph Ho Ox 65. **d** 68 **p** 69 **c** 94. C Streatham St Pet *S'wark* 68–71; C Streatham Hill St Marg 71–72; C Balham Hill Ascension 72–74; V Clapham St Pet 74–76; Bp's Chapl to Overseas Students 74–76; P-in-c Studley *Sarum* 76; V 76–82; V Weymouth H Trin 82–94; RD Weymouth 88–93; Can and Preb Sarum Cathl 89–94; Suff Bp Middleton *Man* 94–99; Suff Bp Dover *Cant* from 99; Area Bp Falkland 15–14; Bp HM Forces 09–14; Hon Asst Bp Eur from 11; Hon Asst Bp St Alb from 13. *81 King Harry Lane, St Albans AL3 4AS* T: (01727) 831704 M: 07980-743628 E: stephen@venner.org.uk

VENNING, Miss Alice Helen. b 83. St Mellitus Coll 12. **d** 15 **p** 16. C Blenheim *Ox* 15–17; C Woodstock and Bladon from 17. *73 Heath Lane, Bladon, Woodstock OX20 1RZ* M: 07966-977157 E: alice.venning@gmail.com

VENNING, Nigel Christopher. b 50. K Coll Lon BD 75 AKC 75. St Aug Coll Cant 75. **d** 76 **p** 77. C Minehead *B & W* 76–80;

C Fawley *Win* 80–83; P-in-c Whitestaunton and Combe St Nicholas w Wambrook *B & W* 83–89; R Staplegrove 89–01; P-in-c Norton Fitzwarren 00–01; R Staplegrove w Norton Fitzwarren 01–03; R Blackdown 03–05; RD Taunton 96–01; rtd 05; PtO *B & W* from 05. *Crispin House, 5 Mendip Edge, Weston-super-Mare BS24 9JF* T: (01934) 814112 E: nigelvenning@hotmail.com

VERE NICOLL, Charles Fiennes. b 55. Solicitor 79. SAOMC 96. **d** 99 **p** 00. NSM Basildon w Aldworth and Ashampstead *Ox* 99–08; P-in-c St Barthélemy French W Indies 02–16; PtO *Ox* 08–10; *Lon* from 09. *61 Eaton Terrace, London SW1W 8TR* M: 07768-238128 E: cvn@cvnsbh.com

VEREKER, Jennifer Lesley. b 45. Totley Hall Coll CertEd 66. WMMTC 96. **d** 99 **p** 00. NSM Rugby *Cov* 99–03; TV Gt and Lt Coates w Bradley *Linc* 03–08; rtd 08; PtO *St E* from 08. *5 Chancellery Mews, Bury St Edmunds IP33 3AB* T: (01284) 701918 E: j.vereker@btinternet.com

VEREY, Christopher Douglas. b 46. St Chad's Coll Dur BA 68 MA 70. Ripon Coll Cuddesdon 02. **d** 04 **p** 05. NSM Yate New Town *Bris* 04–09; PtO *Glouc* from 16. *2 The Green, Heathend, Wotton-under-Edge GL12 8AR* E: chrisverey@tiscali.co.uk

VERNON, Bryan Graham. b 50. Qu Coll Cam BA 72 MA 76. Qu Coll Birm 73. **d** 75 **p** 76. C Newc St Gabr 75–79; Chapl Newc Univ 79–91; Lect Health Care Ethics from 91; Chmn Newc Mental Health Trust 91–94; PtO from 94. *34 Queens Road, Jesmond, Newcastle upon Tyne NE2 2PQ* T: 0191-281 3861 E: b.g.vernon@ncl.ac.uk

VERNON, John Christie. b 40. Imp Coll Lon BScEng 62. Linc Th Coll 63. **d** 65 **p** 66. C Barnard Castle *Dur* 65–69; CF 69–90; Asst Chapl Gen 90–92; Chapl Ellesmere Coll 92–99; PtO *Lich* 99–01; NSM Ellesmere Deanery 01–05 and 06–08; P-in-c Petton w Cockshutt, Welshampton and Lyneal etc 05–06; RD Ellesmere 02–08; PtO from 08. *The Drift House, Lake House Mews, Grange Road, Ellesmere SY12 9DE* T: (01691) 623765 M: 07778-312226 E: revjcv@gmail.com

VERNON, Canon Matthew James. b 71. Collingwood Coll Dur BSc 93 Fitzw Coll Cam BA 96 MA 98. Westcott Ho Cam 94. **d** 97 **p** 98. C Guildf H Trin w St Mary 97–01; Chapl St Jo Cathl and P-in-c Pokfulam Em Hong Kong 01–09; Can Res St E Cathl from 09; Sub Dean from 12. *2 Abbey Precincts, Bury St Edmunds IP33 1RS* T: (01284) 748720 or 701472 E: canon.pastor@stedscathedral.co.uk

VERNON, Rachele Evie. b 16. NSM Croydon Ch Ch *S'wark* from 16. *49 Dron House, Adelina Grove, London E1 3AA*

VERRALL-KELLY, Laura Joanne. b 91. Trin Coll Bris 16. **d** 19. C Knowle St Martin *Bris* from 19. *18 Hill Street, Totterdown, Bristol BS3 4TP* E: laurajverrall91@gmail.com

VERWEY, Mrs Eileen Susan Vivien. b 41. Open Univ BA 78 BA 93 Goldsmiths' Coll Lon PGCE 82. WEMTC 03. **d** 05 **p** 06. NSM Burghill *Heref* from 05; NSM Stretton Sugwas from 05; NSM Pipe-cum-Lyde and Moreton-on-Lugg from 05. *Mill Croft House, Staunton-on-Wye, Hereford HR4 7LW* T: (01981) 500626

VESEY, Nicholas Ivo. b 54. Bris Univ BSc 73. Cranmer Hall Dur 95. **d** 97 **p** 98. C Tunbridge Wells St Mark *Roch* 97–01; V New Catton St Luke w St Aug *Nor* 01–14; Chapl Aspen Chpl Colorado USA from 14. *77 Meadowood Drive, Aspen CO 81611, USA* T: (001) (970) 925 7184 E: nicholas@vesey.net

VESSEY, Canon Andrew John. b 45. Bp Otter Coll CertEd 67. Sarum & Wells Th Coll 84. **d** 86 **p** 87. C Framlingham w Saxtead *St E* 86–89; V Catshill and Dodford *Worc* 89–94; P-in-c Areley Kings 94–95; R 95–02; RD Stourport 00–02; TV Kidderminster St Jo and H Innocents 02–05; TR Cen Swansea *S & B* 05–10; Hon Can Brecon Cathl 10; rtd 10; PtO *Nor* from 10; *St E* from 10. *3 The Laurels, Fressingfield, Eye IP21 5NZ* T: (01379) 588389 E: andrew.vessey@btinternet.com

VESSEY, Peter Allan Beaumont. b 36. ALCD 65. **d** 64 **p** 65. C Rayleigh *Chelmsf* 64–67; C Cambridge H Trin *Ely* 67–71; V Kingston upon Hull St Aid Southcoates *York* 71–80; V Swanwick and Pentrich *Derby* 80–94; PtO from 94; rtd 96; PtO *Portsm* from 15. *5 Aman Court, Granville Road, Totland Bay PO39 0BG* M: 07983-759048 or 07990-509455 E: pnuvessey@hotmail.co.uk

VESTERGAARD, David Andrew. b 64. Reading Univ BSc 86. Wycliffe Hall Ox 97. **d** 99 **p** 00. C Chadderton Ch Ch *Man* 99–02; V Wednesfield Heath *Lich* 02–13; AD Wolverhampton 07–11; RD 11–13; Preb Lich Cathl 12–13; R Bebington *Ches* from 13. *The Rectory, Church Road, Bebington, Wirral CH63 3EX* E: david@vestergaard.co.uk

VEVERS, Canon Geoffrey Martin. b 51. Oak Hill Th Coll. **d** 82 **p** 83. C Wealdstone H Trin *Lon* 82–84; C Harrow Trin St Mich 84–88; V Wandsworth St Steph *S'wark* 88–96; V Battersea Fields 96–15; RD Battersea 04–10; Hon Can S'wark Cathl from 06; rtd 16; Hon C Furzedown *S'wark* from 16. *The*

Vicarage, 63 Chillerton Road, London SW17 9BE T: (020) 3417 6811 M: 07903-357092 E: g.vevers@pobroadband.co.uk

VIBERT (*née* GREEN), Imogen Elizabeth. b 73. Birm Univ BA 96 Cam Univ BTh 02. Westcott Ho Cam 99. **d** 02 **p** 03. C Poplar *Lon* 02–06; Hon C Upper Clapton St Matt 06–12; Hon C Stamford Hill St Thos 06–12; Chapl St Sav and St Olave's Sch Newington from 12; Chapl S'wark Cathl from 13. *St Saviour's and St Olave's School, New Kent Road, London SE1 4AN* T: (020) 7407 1843 M: 07799-101075 E: imogen.vibert@gmail.com

VIBERT, Simon David Newman. b 63. Glas Univ MTh 94. Oak Hill Th Coll BA 89. **d** 89 **p** 90. C Houghton *Carl* 89–92; C-in-c Buxton Trin Prop Chpl *Derby* 92–99; V Wimbledon Park St Luke *S'wark* 99–07; Vice Prin Wycliffe Hall Ox 07–12; Acting Prin 12–13; Dir Sch of Preaching 08–17; V Virginia Water *Guildf* from 17. *Christchurch Vicarage, Callow Hill, Virginia Water GU25 4LD* T: (01344) 430230 E: simon.vibert@cc-vw.org

VICCAJEE, Rutton Behram. b 55. SCRTP 15. **d** 18 **p** 19. C Tongham *Guildf* from 18. *Salix House, 2 Willow Fields, Ash Green, Aldershot GU12 6HF* T: (01252) 910212 M: 07770-750248

VICENCIO PRIOR, Mrs Carla Alexandra Torres Lopes. b 70. Bath Univ BSc 93 SSEES Lon MA 97 Ches Univ MTh 15. St Jo Coll Nottm 12. **d** 15 **p** 16. C Kirk Hallam *Derby* 15–18; C Derby Cathl 18–19; TV Wirksworth from 19. *58 Yokecliffe Drive, Wirksworth, Matlock DE4 4EX* M: 07767-087530 E: revcarla@talktalk.net

VICKERMAN, Canon John. b 42. Chich Th Coll 69. **d** 72 **p** 73. C Horbury *Wakef* 72–76; C Elland 76–78; V Glass Houghton 78–89; V Bruntcliffe 89–96; V King Cross 96–11; RD Halifax 00–06; Hon Can Wakef Cathl 02–11; rtd 11; PtO *Worc* from 15. *6 St Barnabas, Newland, Malvern WR13 5AX* T: (01684) 563741 E: john.vickerman42@gmail.com

VICKERS, Dennis William George. b 30. RIBA 72 York Univ MA 91 IHBC 99. Glouc Th Course. **d** 86 **p** 87. NSM Stokesay *Heref* 86–88; NSM Bucknell w Chapel Lawn, Llanfair Waterdine etc 88–92; NSM Wigmore Abbey 93–01; PtO from 01. *The Willows, Norbury, Bishops Castle SY9 5DX* E: dennisvickers02@btinternet.com

VICKERS, Donald. b 48. Edge Hill Coll of HE DASE 80 Univ of Wales (Ban) MEd 87. NOC 97. **d** 00 **p** 01. NSM Leigh St Mary *Man* 00–05; NSM Westleigh St Pet 05–12; Asst Chapl HM Pris Man 00–12; rtd 12; PtO *Man* 12–17. *21 Broom Way, Westhoughton, Bolton BL5 3TZ* T: (01942) 815193 M: 07768-492581 E: frdonvickers@gmail.com

VICKERS, Mrs Janice Audrey Maureen. b 56. **d** 96 **p** 97. OLM Woking Ch Ch *Guildf* 96–06; OLM Ottershaw 06–18; NSM Goldsworth Park from 18. *7 Langdale Close, Woking GU21 4RS* T: (01483) 720873 E: janvickers1520@gmail.com

VICKERS, Mrs Mary Janet. b 57. Westmr Coll Ox MTh 97. St Jo Coll Nottm BTh 85. **dss** 85 **d** 87 **p** 99. Worc City St Paul and Old St Martin etc 85–89; Par Dn 87–89; World Miss Officer Worc 89–92; USPG 92–00; LtO *Eur* 95–99; PtO from 99; PtO Adnry of the Army from 97; NSM Cheswardine, Childs Ercall, Hales, Hinstock etc *Lich* 99–01; NSM Wrecclesham *Guildf* 01–02; NSM Pimperne, Stourpaine, Durweston and Bryanston *Sarum* 03–05; NSM Hipswell *Ripon* 05–06; NSM W Andover *Win* 07–09; NSM Portway and Danebury 09–10; Ind Chapl *Linc* 10–17. *2 Meadow Drive, Healing, Grimsby DN41 7RU* T: (01472) 280148 M: 07730-972403 E: vickers983@btinternet.com

VICKERS, Michael. b 60. Cranmer Hall Dur BA 98. **d** 98 **p** 99. C Monkwearmouth *Dur* 98–00; C Kowloon St Andr Hong Kong 00–07; V Cranham Park *Chelmsf* from 07. *St Luke's Vicarage, 201 Front Lane, Upminster RM14 1LD* T: (01708) 222562 F: 223253 E: revmichaelvickers@gmail.com

✠**VICKERS, The Rt Revd Michael Edwin.** b 29. Worc Coll Ox BA 56 MA 56. Cranmer Hall Dur. **d** 59 **p** 60 **c** 88. C Bexleyheath Ch Ch *Roch* 59–62; Chapl Lee Abbey 62–67; V Hull St Jo Newland *York* 67–81; AD Cen and N Hull 72–81; Can and Preb York Minster 81–88; Adn E Riding 81–88; Area Bp Colchester *Chelmsf* 88–94; rtd 94; Hon Asst Bp Blackb 94–13. *137 Canalside, Redhill RH1 2FH* T: (01737) 642984 E: micjan38@btinternet.com

VICKERS, Peter. b 56. St Jo Coll Nottm LTh 85. **d** 85 **p** 86. C Worc St Barn w Ch Ch 85–88; TV Kidderminster St Mary and All SS w Trimpley etc 88–92; Ind Chapl 88–92; CF 92–11; RD Grimsby and Cleethorpes *Linc* 11–13; RD Haverstoe 11–13; Ind Chapl 13–17. *2 Meadow Drive, Healing, Grimsby DN41 7RU* T: (01472) 280148 E: revd.p.vickers@hotmail.co.uk

VICKERS, Peter George. b 41. Local Minl Tr Course 90. **d** 93 **p** 94. OLM Cobham *Guildf* 93–04; OLM Cobham and Stoke D'Abernon 04–11; rtd 11; PtO *Guildf* from 11. *24 Station*

Road, Stoke D'Abernon, Cobham KT11 3BN T: (01932) 862497 E: revpgv@googlemail.com

VICKERS, Randolph. b 36. Newc Univ MA 93 FCIM FInstD. St Alb Minl Tr Scheme 77. **d** 80 **p** 82. NSM Hitchin *St Alb* 80–87; NSM Luton Lewsey St Hugh 87–89; NSM Shotley *Newc* 89–01; rtd 01; PtO *Newc* from 01; *Dur* from 14. *4 The Paddock, Stocksfield NE43 7PH* T/F: (01661) 842364 E: rvickers@christian-healing.com

VICKERS, Timothy Hugh. b 81. Jes Coll Cam BA 03 MA 06 Birkbeck Coll Lon MA 10. Ox Min Course 14. **d** 16 **p** 17. C Redbourn *St Alb* from 16. *11 Blackhorse Lane, Redbourn, St Albans AL3 7EP* T: (01582) 622530 E: tim@stmarysredbourn.org *or* timvickers@hotmail.co.uk

VICKERY, Jonathan Laurie. b 58. Bretton Hall Coll BEd 80. Wycliffe Hall Ox 81. **d** 84 **p** 85. C Gorseinon *S & B* 84–86; P-in-c Whitton and Pilleth and Cascob etc 86–87; R 87–91; V Crickhowell w Cwmdu and Tretower 91–02; P-in-c Downend *Bris* 02–07; V from 07. *Christ Church Vicarage, Shrubbery Road, Bristol BS16 5TB* T: 0117-908 9868 E: vicar@christchurchdownend.com

VICKERY, Robin Francis. b 48. K Coll Lon BD 73 AKC 73. **d** 74 **p** 75. C Clapham St Jo *S'wark* 74–77; C Clapham Ch Ch and St Jo 75–77; C Reigate St Luke S Park 77–79; Hon C Clapham H Spirit 80–87 and 02–10; Hon C Clapham Team 87–01; Hon C N Lambeth 10–18; PtO from 18. *13 Chelsham Road, London SW4 6NR* T: (020) 7622 4792 M: 07748-781376 E: rf.vickery@gmail.com

VIDAL-HALL, Roderic Mark. b 37. Sheff Univ BSc 60. Lich Th Coll 62. **d** 64 **p** 65. C Ilkeston St Mary *Derby* 64–67; C Nether and Over Seale 67–70; V Chellaston 70–84; C Marchington w Marchington Woodlands *Lich* 84–97; C Kingstone w Gratwich 85–97; TV Uttoxeter Area 97–01; rtd 01. *Le Perhou, 22630 Saint-Juvat, France* T: (0033) 2 96 88 16 34 E: mark@vidalhall.co.uk

VIGARS, Anthony Roy. b 54. St Jo Coll Dur BA 75. Trin Coll Bris 77. **d** 78 **p** 79. C Barking St Marg w St Patr *Chelmsf* 78–81; C Littleover *Derby* 81–84; C-in-c Stapenhill Immanuel CD 84–90; V Meltham *Wakef* 90–97; V Reading St Jo *Ox* 97–06; rtd 07; PtO *Ox* 07–08; *Ex* from 09. *15 Edgcumbe Drive, Tavistock PL19 0ET* T: (01822) 610539 E: vigars@lineone.net

VIGEON, Canon Owen George. b 28. Peterho Cam BA 52 MA 57. Ely Th Coll 52. **d** 54 **p** 55. C Barrow St Luke *Carl* 54–58; Chapl St Jo Coll York 58–61; V Burnley St Steph *Blackb* 61–69; V Bilsborrow and Asst Dir RE 69–73; V St Annes St Thos 74–85; RD Fylde 80–85; R Halton w Aughton 85–93; Hon Can Blackb Cathl 92–93; rtd 93; PtO *Worc* 93–04; *Cov* from 04. *10 Hall Lane, Coventry CV2 2AW* T: (024) 7661 1712 E: owenvig@virginmedia.com

VIGERS, Neil Simon. b 62. K Coll Lon BD 84 MTh 87. Linc Th Coll 88. **d** 90 **p** 91. C Chelsea St Luke and Ch Ch *Lon* 90–93; C Staines St Mary and St Pet 93–96; P-in-c Hook *Win* 96–02; R 02–07; PtO *Guildf* from 14; *S'wark* from 18. *St Andrew's House, 16 Tavistock Crescent, London W11 1AP* T: (020) 7313 3900 F: 7313 3999

VIGOR, Ms Margaret Ann. b 45. Ripon Coll Cuddesdon 85. **d** 87 **p** 96. Chapl Asst All SS Convent Ox 87–89; Par Dn Basildon St Martin w Nevendon *Chelmsf* 89–91; Chapl Billingham St Cuth *Dur* 96–11; rtd 11; PtO *Dur* from 11. *15 Mitchell Street, Hartlepool TS26 9EZ* T: (01429) 867458

VILASECA-BRUCH, John. b 89. Cam Univ BA 16. Westcott Ho Cam 14. **d** 16 **p** 17. C Berwick H Trin and St Mary *Newc* 16–19; V Tynemouth Cullercoats St Paul from 19. *53 Grosvenor Drive, Whitley Bay NE26 2JR* M: 07860-828852 E: vilaseca26@yahoo.es

VILES, Joan Mary. b 47. **d** 13 **p** 14. NSM Thornes *Wakef* 13–14; Leeds 14–17; PtO from 17. *4 Thornes Moor Close, Wakefield WF2 8QA* T: (01924) 383564 E: revjoanviles@sky.com

VILLAGE, Andrew. b 54. Collingwood Coll Dur BSc 75 Edin Univ PhD 80 Bris Univ PhD 03. Trin Coll Bris BA 92. **d** 92 **p** 93. C Northampton St Giles *Pet* 92–95; R Middleton Cheney w Chacombe 95–04; Dir Cen for Min Studies Univ of Wales (Ban) *Ban* 04–07; Lect York St Jo Univ from 07; PtO *York* from 08. *York St John University, Lord Mayor's Walk, York YO31 7EX* T: (01904) 876723 M: 07749-484425 E: a.village@yorksj.ac.uk

VILLER, Canon Allan George Frederick. b 38. EAMTC 78. **d** 81 **p** 82. NSM Ely 81–85; V Emneth 85–92; V Littleport 92–03; RD Ely 98–03; rtd 03; Hon Can Ely Cathl 01–06; Hon C Barton Bendish w Beachamwell etc 03–06; PtO *Ely* from 06; *Nor* from 07. *41 Westfields, Narborough, King's Lynn PE32 1SX* T/F: (01760) 337633 E: allan@viller.net

VINCENT, Preb Alfred James. b 30. Bris Univ BA 54 Lon Univ BD 56. Tyndale Hall Bris 50. **d** 54 **p** 55. C Shrewsbury St Julian *Lich* 54–56; C Camborne *Truro* 56–59; V Kenwyn 59–68; LtO *St Alb* 68; Lect Qu Coll Birm 68–70; LtO *Birm* 68–70; V Bordesley St Oswald 70–76; V S Shields St Hilda w

St Thos *Dur* 76–84; Hon Chapl Miss to Seafarers from 79; V Bude Haven *Truro* 84–89; R Bude Haven and Marhamchurch 89–92; RD Stratton 88–92; Preb St Endellion 90–95; rtd 92; P-in-c Chacewater *Truro* 92–95; PtO 95–17. *5 Raymond Road, Redruth TR15 2HD* T: (01209) 219263

VINCENT, David Cyril. b 37. Selw Coll Cam BA 60 MA 64. Coll of Resurr Mirfield 60. **d** 62 **p** 63. C Cheetwood St Alb *Man* 62–65; C Lawton Moor 65–67; V Wandsworth Common St Mary *S'wark* 67–84; RD Tooting 75–80; R Stoke D'Abernon *Guildf* 84–02; rtd 02; PtO *B & W* 04–16. *23 Wingfield Court, Lenthay Road, Sherborne DT9 6EG*   T: (01935) 817516 E: dajovincent@btinternet.com

VINCENT, Jacqueline Margaret. *See* RODWELL, Jacqueline Margaret

VINCENT, James. *See* VINCENT, Alfred James

VINCENT, John Leonard. b 61. Univ of Wales (Lamp) BA 83 Southn Univ BTh 87 Cardiff Univ MTh 14. Chich Th Coll 84. **d** 87 **p** 88. C Hampton All SS *Lon* 87–90; C Shepperton 90–95; V Whitton SS Phil and Jas 95–03; CF from 03. *c/o MOD Chaplains (Army)*   T: (01264) 383430   F: 381824 E: padrejohn@live.co.uk

VINCENT, Michael Francis. b 48. CertEd 70 Open Univ BA 83. Sarum & Wells Th Coll 85. **d** 87 **p** 88. C Nuneaton St Mary *Cov* 87–90; C Stockingford 90–91; P-in-c 91–99; V 99–14; rtd 14; PtO *Leic* 15–18. *11 Elmcroft Road, North Kilworth, Lutterworth LE17 6HX*   T: (01858) 881194 E: mick.vincent@gmail.com

VINCENT, Roy David. b 37. Chich Th Coll 81. **d** 83 **p** 84. C Atherton *Man* 83–86; V E Crompton 86–95; P-in-c Burwash *Chich* 95–00; R 00–04; rtd 04; PtO *Carl* 05–11; *Mor* from 12. *24 Stewart Street, Portgordon, Buckie AB56 5QT*   T: (01542) 834705

VINCER, Ms Louise Claire. b 69. Roehampton Inst BA 90 Edin Univ MTh 93. Westcott Ho Cam 97. **d** 00 **p** 01. C Waltham H Cross *Chelmsf* 00–04; C Perry Hill St Geo w Ch Ch and St Paul *S'wark* 04–06; C Bermondsey St Anne and St Aug 06–11; C Bermondsey St Jas w Ch Ch and St Crispin 06–11; Community P N Lincs *Linc* 11–13; Developing Discipleship Progr Co-ord 14–17; C Humberston from 17. *The Rectory, 49 Park Drive, Grimsby DN32 0EG*   T: (01472) 351815

VINE, Carolyn Ann. *See* TIBBOTT, Carolyn Ann

VINE, James David. b 67. Brighton Univ BSc 95. St Steph Ho Ox. **d** 00 **p** 01. C Eastbourne St Mary *Chich* 00–03; V Stone Cross St Luke w N Langney from 03. *The Vicarage, 8 Culver Close, Eastbourne BN23 8EA*   T: (01323) 764473 E: jamesdavidvine@gmail.com

VINE, Michael Charles. b 51. Worc Coll Ox BA 73 MA 80. Cuddesdon Coll 73. **d** 76 **p** 77. C Wallsend St Luke *Newc* 76–79; C Denton 79–81; V Sugley 81–91; V Shiremoor 91–02; R Wallsend St Pet and St Luke 02–11; rtd 11; PtO *Newc* from 11. *26 Percy Street, North Shields NE30 4HA*   T: 0191-257 4711 E: vinemichael@freeuk.co.uk

VINE, Canon Neville Peter. b 54. K Coll Lon BD 80 AKC 80. Linc Th Coll 80. **d** 81 **p** 82. C Peterlee *Dur* 81–86; Chapl Peterlee Coll 84–86; V Auckland St Pet *Dur* 86–89; PtO 89–91; R Easington 91–99; R Easington, Easington Colliery and S Hetton 99–03; AD Easington 98–03; V Auckland St Andr and St Anne 03–14; V Bishop Auckland 14–16; AD Auckland 03–15; Hon Can Dur Cathl 03–16; rtd 16; PtO *Dur* from 17. *4 Conway Grove, Bishop Auckland DL14 6AF*   T: (01388) 604397 E: neville.vine@btinternet.com

VINER, Canon Leonard Edwin. b 20. Univ Coll Dur BA 43. St Aug Coll Cant 38. **d** 43 **p** 44. C W Molesey *Guildf* 43–45; Miss Likoma Nyasaland 46–52; Warden St Andr Th Coll Likoma 52–56 and 58–60; C Roxbourne St Andr *Lon* 56–58; Chapl St Mich Teacher Tr Coll Malindi Malawi 60–64; Warden St Andr Th Coll Mponda's 64–67; P-in-c Malindi 67–69; R Zomba 69–71; Hon Can S Malawi from 71; R Honing w Crostwight *Nor* 71–75; P-in-c E Ruston 71–73; V 73–75; P-in-c Witton w Ridlington 71–73; V 73–75; C Corby Epiphany w St Jo *Pet* 75–79; V Brigstock w Stanion 79–86; rtd 86; Asst Chapl Lisbon *Eur* 86–87; Chapl Tangier 87–89; PtO *Pet* from 90. *Old Vicarage Residential and Nursing Home, Weekley, Kettering NN16 9UP*

VINEY, Peter. b 43. Ox NSM Course. **d** 76 **p** 77. NSM High Wycombe *Ox* from 76. *76 Westmead, Princes Risborough HP27 9HS*   T: (01844) 275461

VIRDEN, Richard. b 40. K Coll Lon BSc 61 Univ Coll Lon MSc 62 PhD 66. **d** 04 **p** 05. OLM N Tyne and Redesdale *Newc* 04–10; PtO from 10. *Ingram Cottage, West Woodburn, Hexham NE48 2SB*   T: (01434) 270334

VIVASH, Peter Henry. b 57. Hockerill Coll of Educn CertEd 78 CQSW 85. Cranmer Hall Dur 90. **d** 92 **p** 93. C Malpas *Mon* 92–95; R Bettws 95–01; P-in-c Upper Derwent *Carl* 01–16; Dioc Rep CMS 01–16; Warden of Readers *Carl* 05–16; V Acomb St Steph and St Aid *York* from 16. *The Vicarage, 32 Carr Lane, York YO26 5HX* E: peter.vivash@dsl.pipex.com

VIVIAN, Adrian John. b 42. K Coll Lon BD 65 AKC 66. St Denys Warminster 62. **d** 66 **p** 67. C Bromley St Andr *Roch* 66–69; C Egg Buckland *Ex* 69–73; PtO 73–84; P-in-c Newton Ferrers w Revelstoke 84–87. *9 Munro Avenue, Yealmpton, Plymouth PL8 2NQ*

VIVIAN, Simon John. b 70. Edin Univ BMus 96. Ripon Coll Cuddesdon 14. **d** 16 **p** 17. C Gt Berkhamsted, Gt and Lt Gaddesden etc *St Alb* from 16. *All Saints' House, Shrublands Road, Berkhamsted HP4 3HY*   T: (01442) 864199 E: curate@greatberkhamsted.org.uk

VIVIAN, Thomas Keith. b 27. St Jo Coll Cam BA 48 MA 52. St Deiniol's Hawarden 76. **d** 80 **p** 81. Hd Master Lucton Sch Leominster 62–85; LtO *Heref* 80–85; P-in-c Chew Stoke w Nempnett Thrubwell *B & W* 85–88; R 88–97; P-in-c Norton Malreward 85–88; R 88–97; RD Chew Magna 92–97; rtd 97; PtO *Sarum* from 97; *B & W* 97–11. *Timberley, Sidmouth Road, Lyme Regis DT7 3ES*   T: (01297) 443547

VIVIAN, Victor Ivan. b 38. Nottm Poly LLB 87. EMMTC 91. **d** 94 **p** 95. NSM Bestwood *S'well* 94–99; Korea 99–03; rtd 03; PtO *S'well* from 03. *12 Deepdale Road, Wollaton, Nottingham NG8 2FU*   T: 0115-928 3954 E: vicvivian@icloud.com

VOCKINS, Preb Michael David. b 44. Univ of Wales (Abth) BSc 69. Glouc Sch of Min 85. **d** 88 **p** 89. NSM Cradley w Mathon and Storridge *Heref* 88–14; PtO 14–18; RD Ledbury 02–13; PtO *Worc* 88–18; Chapl Heref Sixth Form Coll 05–09; Bp's Adv for SSM *Heref* 06–15; Preb Heref Cathl 09–15; PtO *B & W* from 18. *The Chantry, Charlton Musgrove, Wincanton BA9 8HG*   T: (01963) 34837 E: mdvockins@btinternet.com

VOLLAND, Michael John. b 74. Northumbria Univ BA 96 K Coll Lon MA 04 Dur Univ DThM 13. Ridley Hall Cam 04. **d** 06 **p** 07. Pioneer Min Glouc City 06–09; C Glouc Cathl 07–09; Dir Missr Cranmer Hall Dur 09–15; P Missr E Dur Miss Project 14–15; AD Easington *Dur* 14–15; PtO *Ely* from 15; Tutor Ridley Hall Cam 15–17; Prin from 17; CF (ACF) from 13. *Ridley Hall, Ridley Hall Road, Cambridge CB3 9HG*   T: (01223) 746585 E: mjv22@cam.ac.uk

VOLOSSEVICH, Alexander. b 55. St Mellitus Coll 15. **d** 18 **p** 19. NSM Ealing St Mary *Lon* from 18. *26 Beech Gardens, London W5 4AJ*   M: 07743-602256 E: avolos@yahoo.com

VOLTZENLOGEL, Timothy John. b 60. St Jo Coll Dur BA 81. Wycliffe Hall Ox BTh 00. **d** 00 **p** 01. C Eastbourne All SS *Chich* 00–04; V Church Langley *Chelmsf* 04–11; V Bexhill St Steph *Chich* 11–17; V Linc St Geo Swallowbeck from 17. *St George's Vicarage, Eastbrook Road, Lincoln LN6 7EP*   T: (01522) 689033

VON FRAUNHOFER, Nicola Anne. b 63. Bris Univ MB, ChB 88 Lon Univ MSc 05 MRCPsych 88. SEITE 14. **d** 14 **p** 16. NSM Wandsworth St Paul *S'wark* from 14. *St Paul's Community Centre, 23 Inner Park Road, London SW19 6ED*   T: (020) 8785 2341 E: nickyvonfr@yahoo.co.uk

VON MALAISÉ, Nicolas Axel Christoph. b 62. Univ Coll Ox BA 84 MA. Ripon Coll Cuddesdon BA 87. **d** 87 **p** 88. C Oxhey St Matt *St Alb* 87–90; C Northfield *Birm* 90–92; Asst Chapl Win Coll 92–05; V Bordesley St Benedict *Birm* 06–10; PtO *Win* 06–10. *27 Kensington Place, London W8 7PR* E: utunumsint7@aol.com

VOOGHT, Canon Michael George Peter. b 38. St Pet Hall Ox BA 61 MA 65. Chich Th Coll 61. **d** 63 **p** 64. C E Dulwich St Jo *S'wark* 63–66; C Prestbury *Glouc* 66–72; R Minchinhampton 72–85; RD Stonehouse 79–85; V Thornbury 85–02; Hon Can Glouc Cathl 86–02; rtd 02; PtO *Glouc* from 03; *Bris* 05–18. *62 High Street, Thornbury, Bristol BS35 2AN*   T: (01454) 414915

VOST, Mrs Jane. b 62. **d** 04 **p** 08. OLM Radcliffe *Man* 04–10; OLM Radcliffe St Andr 10–13; PtO from 13; Chapl Wrightington, Wigan and Leigh NHS Foundn Trust 12–16; Chapl Man Univ NHS Foundn Trust 16–19. *Address withheld by request*   M: 07986-668144 E: jane.vost@hotmail.co.uk

VOTH HARMAN, Karin. b 65. Virginia Univ BA 87 Sussex Univ MA 93 DPhil 99. Westcott Ho Cam 09. **d** 11 **p** 12. NSM King's Cliffe, Bulwick and Blatherwycke etc *Pet* 11–16; NSM Ketton, Collyweston, Easton-on-the-Hill etc 13–16; P-in-c Cherry Hinton St Andr *Ely* from 16. *The Vicarage, 2 Fulbourn Old Drift, Cambridge CB1 9NE*   T: (01223) 242954   M: 07971-936253 E: karinvothharman@gmail.com

VOUSDEN, Canon Alan Thomas. b 48. K Coll Lon BSc 69. Qu Coll Birm. **d** 72 **p** 73. C Orpington All SS *Roch* 72–76; C Belvedere All SS 76–80; R Cuxton and Halling 80–86; V Bromley St Mark 86–98; Chapl Bromley Hosp 86–94; Chapl Bromley Hosps NHS Trust 94–98; V Rainham *Roch* 98–10; RD Gillingham 00–10; Bp's Dom Chapl 10–13; Hon Can Roch Cathl 99–13; rtd 13; PtO *Roch* from 13. *3 Fartherwell Avenue, West Malling ME19 6NG* E: alanvousden@btinternet.com

VOWLES, Ms Patricia. b 50. S'wark Ord Course 84. **d** 87 **p** 94. USPG 70–91; NSM Nunhead St Antony w St Silas *S'wark* 87–91; Par Dn Newington St Mary 91–94; Par Dn Camberwell St Mich w All So w Em 91–94; V 94–06; Chapl Cautley Ho Chr Cen 06–10; C Croydon St Jo *S'wark* from 11.

Church House, Barrow Road, Croydon CR0 4EZ T: (020) 8688 7006 M: 07709-253496 E: patricia.vowles@yahoo.com

VOWLES, Canon Peter John Henry. b 25. Magd Coll Ox BA 50 MA 55. Westcott Ho Cam 50. **d** 52 **p** 53. C Kings Heath *Birm* 52–56; C Huddersfield St Pet *Wakef* 56–57; V Perry Beeches *Birm* 57–64 and 64–72; R Cottingham *York* 72–83; R Man St Ann 83–91; Hon Can Man Cathl 83–91; rtd 91; PtO *Man* 91–17. *10 Redshaw Close, Manchester M14 6JB* T: 0161-257 2065

VROLIJK, The Ven Paul Dick. b 64. Delft Univ of Tech MSc 88. Trin Coll Bris BA 03 PhD 08. **d** 04 **p** 05. NSM Stoke Gifford *Bris* 04–08; Chapl Aquitaine *Eur* 09–15; Sen Chapl and Chan Brussels Cathl from 15; Adn NW Eur from 16. *Rue Capitaine Crespel 29 , B-1050 Brussels, Belgium* T: (0032) (2) 511 7183 M: (0032) 47-685 0744 E: paul.vrolijk@gmail.com *or* paul.vrolijk@europe.anglican.org

VROOM, Richard Adriaan. **d** 88 **p** 88. Utrecht Old Catholic Ch *Eur* 88–07; V Llanegryn w Aberdyfi w Tywyn *Ban* 07–12;

V Tywyn w Llanegryn w Aberdyfi w Pennal 12–13; V Bro Ystumanner 13–17; rtd 17. *Karvel, 15 38, 8231 AX, Lelystad, The Netherlands* E: ravroom@mac.com

VYE, Mrs Georgina Ann. b 57. SWMTC 06. **d** 09 **p** 10. C Littleham w Exmouth and Lympstone and Woodbury w Exton *Ex* 09–10; C Ex St Thos and Em 10–14; C Chard St Mary w Combe St Nicholas, Wambrook etc *B & W* from 14. *57 Caraway Close, Chard TA20 1HP* T: (01460) 66159 M: 07950-989916 E: g.vye@btinternet.com

VYSE, James Michael Owen. b 72. Leeds Univ BA 95. St Steph Ho Ox 16. **d** 18 **p** 19. C Worksop Priory *S'well* from 18. *6 Conrad Close, Worksop S80 2EN* M: 07951-859911 E: curate@worksoppriory.co.uk

VYVYAN, Michael David. b 78. Loughb Univ BSc 02 De Montfort Univ PGCE 03. Westcott Ho Cam 12. **d** 15 **p** 16. C Camberwell St Phil and St Mark *S'wark* 15–19; P-in-c Brockley Hill St Sav from 19. *31 Siddons Road, London SE23 2JH* E: fathervyvyan@gmail.com

W

WAAKO, Samuel. b 80. Makerere Univ Kampala BA 05. St Mellitus Coll 15. **d** 18 **p** 19. C Woking St Pet *Guildf* from 18. *The Rectory, 28 High Street, Old Woking, Woking GU22 9ER* M: 07923-331108 E: samyol2000@yahoo.com

WADDELL, James William Boece. b 74. Trin Coll Bris 06. **d** 08 **p** 09. C Slaugham *Chich* 08–11; C Slaugham and Staplefield Common 11–12; USA 12–13; V Leyton St Cath and St Paul *Chelmsf* 13–18; C Chanctonbury *Chich* from 18. *Fryern House, Fryern Park, Fryern Road, Storrington, Pulborough RH20 4FF* T: (01903) 740182 M: 07813-872871 E: jim@thecornerstone.org.uk *or* jim.waddell@chanctonbury.org.uk

WADDELL, Peter Matthew. b 75. Keble Coll Ox BA 96 Fitzw Coll Cam MPhil 98 PhD 02. Westcott Ho Cam 98. **d** 02 **p** 03. C Oxton *Ches* 02–04; Chapl SS Coll Cam 05–10; Past Dean 10–12; Dean of Chpl Win Univ 12–16; P-in-c Abbots Langley *St Alb* from 16. *26 Greenways, Abbots Langley WD5 0EU* E: vicar@abbotslangley.org.uk

WADDINGTON, Gary Richard. b 69. St Chad's Coll Dur BSc 91 Heythrop Coll Lon MA 05. St Steph Ho Ox BTh 96. **d** 96 **p** 97. C Southsea H Spirit *Portsm* 96–00; V Paulsgrove 00–10; TR Harrogate St Wilfrid *Ripon* 10–14; Leeds from 14. *St Wilfrid's Vicarage, 51B Kent Road, Harrogate HG1 2EU* M: 07920-464818 E: teamrector@stwilfrid.org

WADE, Canon Andrew John. b 50. Trin Coll Bris. **d** 86 **p** 87. C St Keverne *Truro* 86–89; TV Probus, Ladock and Grampound w Creed and St Erme 89–92; V Constantine 92–00; P-in-c Ludgvan 00–01; P-in-c Marazion 00–01; P-in-c St Hilary w Perranuthnoe 00–01; R Ludgvan, Marazion, St Hilary and Perranuthnoe 01–08; RD Penwith 03–08; TR Probus, Ladock and Grampound w Creed and St Erme 08–17; Hon Can Truro Cathl 08–17; Rural Link Officer from 12; rtd 17. *34 Gloucester Avenue, Carlyon Bay, St Austell PL25 3PT* T: (01726) 882746 E: andrewsanctuary@aol.com

WADE, Christopher John. b 54. Trent Poly BSc 81 MRICS 82 ACIArb 88. Aston Tr Scheme 88 Trin Coll Bris. **d** 92 **p** 93. C Barnsley St Geo *Wakef* 92–95; C Whittle-le-Woods *Blackb* 95–99; P-in-c Bulwell St Jo *S'well* 99–03; Dir Heavenfire Min from 03. *3 Brierdene Court, Whitley Bay NE26 3HP* T: 084516-65277 E: chris@heavenfire.org

WADE, Canon David Peter. b 65. St Jo Coll Nottm LTh 92. **d** 92 **p** 93. C Victoria Docks Ascension *Chelmsf* 92–95; P-in-c Victoria Docks St Luke 95–97; V 97–19; P-in-c Canning Town 18–19; AD Newham 07–15; Hd of Development Growing Chr Communities from 19; NSM W Ham from 19; Hon Can Chelmsf Cathl from 18. *The Vicarage, 16A Ruscoe Road, London E16 1JB* T: (020) 7476 2076 E: davenicky@hotmail.com

WADE, Geoffrey Adrian. b 61. Ripon Coll Cuddesdon. **d** 01 **p** 02. C Worc City St Paul and Old St Martin etc 01–02; C Wordsley 02–04; TV Ilminster and Distr *B & W* 04–10; V Winsmoor from 10; RD Crewkerne from 18. *The Rectory, Shepton Beauchamp, Ilminster TA19 0LP* T: (01460) 240228 E: gw@winsmoor.plus.com

WADE, Mark John. b 84. St Mary's Coll Twickenham BA 06 St Jo Coll Dur BA 17. Cranmer Hall Dur 14. **d** 17 **p** 18. C Goose Green *Liv* from 17. *6 Netherwood Grove, Wigan WN3 6NF* M: 07827-811530 E: mark-wade@live.com

WADE, Mary Ruth. *See* THOMAS, Mary Ruth

WADEY, Rachel Susan. *See* ALLEN, Rachel Susan

WADGE, Alan. b 46. Grey Coll Dur BA 68 MA 72. St Chad's Coll Dur. **d** 70 **p** 71. C Cockerton *Dur* 70–74; C Whitworth w Spennymoor 74–75; P-in-c Shipton Moyne w Westonbirt and Lasborough *Glouc* 75–80; Chapl Westonbirt Sch 75–80; V Dean Forest H Trin *Glouc* 80–83; Chapl Gresham's Sch Holt 83–91; R Ridgeway *Ox* 91–11; RD Wantage 95–01; rtd 11; PtO *Sarum* from 12. *8 Underhill, Mere, Warminster BA12 6LU* E: alanwadge@hotmail.com

WADMAN, Vera Margaret. b 51. EAMTC 97. **d** 00 **p** 01. NSM Burnham *Chelmsf* 00–02; NSM Creeksea w Althorne, Latchingdon and N Fambridge 02–09; NSM Creeksea from 09; P-in-c from 10. *Fernlea Cottage, 8 Fernlea Road, Burnham-on-Crouch CM0 8EJ* T: (01621) 783963 E: vera.wadman@allsaintscreeksea.org.uk

WADSWORTH (née REID), Mrs Alison Margaret. b 36. Bris Univ CertEd 57. **d** 97 **p** 98. OLM Cley Hill Warminster *Sarum* 97–06; PtO from 06. *2 Saxon's Acre, Warminster BA12 8HT* T: (01985) 212510 E: awap@blueyonder.co.uk

WADSWORTH, Andrew James. b 56. St Jo Coll Dur BA 79 Cam Univ CertEd 80 Lambeth STh 95 FRSA 99. Sarum & Wells Th Coll 84 Chich Th Coll 86. **d** 87 **p** 88. NSM Forest Road and E Grinstead St Swithun *Chich* 87–89; C Shrewsbury St Chad w St Mary *Lich* 89–91; TV Honiton, Gittisham, Combe Raleigh, Monkton etc *Ex* 91–97; V Bulkington w Shilton and Ansty *Cov* 97–06; P-in-c Bognor *Chich* 06–07; V 07–18; rtd 18. *3 Shaftesbury Place, Rustington, Littlehampton BN16 2GA* E: andrewwadsworth@btinternet.com

WADSWORTH, Andrew John. b 67. Reading Univ BSc 88 MRICS 90. Wycliffe Hall Ox 99. **d** 01 **p** 02. C Plymouth St Andr and Stonehouse *Ex* 01–05; C Enfield Ch Ch Trent Park *Lon* 05–13; C Grange Park St Pet 13–18; R Trull w Angersleigh *B & W* from 18. *The New Rectory, Wild Oak Lane, Trull, Taunton TA3 7JT* T: (01823) 368084 E: wadsworth.andy@outlook.com

WADSWORTH, Jean. b 44. St Jo Coll Dur BA 71. Cranmer Hall Dur 85. **d** 87 **p** 94. Par Dn Thamesmead *S'wark* 87–92; Par Dn Rotherhithe H Trin 92–94; C 94–98; V New Eltham All SS 98–08; RD Eltham and Mottingham 01–05; rtd 08. *2 Peak Coach House, Cotmaton Road, Sidmouth EX10 8SY*

WADSWORTH, Canon Peter Richard. b 52. Qu Coll Ox BA 73 MA 77. Cuddesdon Coll 74 English Coll Rome 76. **d** 77 **p** 78. C High Wycombe *Ox* 77–81; C Farnham Royal w Hedgerley 81–84; Dioc Ecum Officer *Portsm* 84–90; V E Meon 84–96; V Langrish 84–96; V Elson 96–04; RD Gosport 96–02; V St Alb St Sav 04–17; Hon Can St Alb 16–17; rtd 17; PtO *York* from 17. *45 Normandy Avenue, Beverley HU17 8PF* T: (01482) 865662 E: peter.wadsworth52@gmail.com

WAGGETT, Geoffrey James. b 49. Sarum & Wells Th Coll 83. **d** 85 **p** 86. C Newton Nottage *Llan* 85–88; TV Glyncorrwg w Afan Vale and Cymmer Afan 88–89; R 89–99; V Glyncorrwg and Upper Afan Valley 99–00; TR Ebbw Vale *Mon* 00–13; TV Upper Ebbw Valleys 13–16; P-in-c Upper Ebbw Valleys *Mon* 16–17; PtO *Llan* from 17. *43 Rushfield Gardens, Bridgend CF31 1DF* T: (01656) 658635 E: geoffandjennifer@hotmail.co.uk

WAGSTAFF (née JONES), Ms Alison. b 40. K Coll Dur BA 63 Man Univ CertEd 64. TISEC 95. **d** 98 **p** 99. C Edin St Cuth 98–00; Assoc P Edin St Columba from 00; Chapl St Columba's Hospice 01–05. *27 Cambridge Gardens, Edinburgh EH6 5DH* T: 0131-554 6702 M: 07766-383117 E: alisonwagstaff7@gmail.com

WAGSTAFF, Canon Andrew Robert. b 56. K Coll Lon BD 79 AKC 79. Coll of Resurr Mirfield 81. **d** 83 **p** 84. C Newark w Hawton, Cotham and Shelton *S'well* 83–86; C Dublin St Bart w Leeson Park *D & G* 86–89; V Nottingham St Geo w St Jo *S'well* 89–95; V Worksop Priory 95–06; Chapl Antwerp St Boniface *Eur* from 06; Hon Can from 12. *Grétrystraat 39, 2018 Antwerp, Belgium* T: (0032) (3) 239 3339 E: chaplain@boniface.be

WAGSTAFF, The Ven Christopher John Harold. b 36. St D Coll Lamp BA 62. **d** 63 **p** 64. C Queensbury All SS *Lon* 63–68; V Tokyngton St Mich 68–73; V Coleford w Staunton *Glouc* 73–83; RD Forest S 76–82; Adn Glouc 83–00; Hon Can Glouc Cathl 83–00; Hon Can St Andr Cathl Njombe (Tanzania) from 93; rtd 00; PtO *Glouc* from 00. *Karibuni, Collafield, Littledean, Cinderford GL14 3LG* T: (01594) 825282 E: mc.wagstaff@btinternet.com

WAGSTAFF, Miss Joan. b 33. Gilmore Ho. **dss** 75 **d** 87 **p** 94. Ellesmere Port *Ches* 86–87; Par Dn 87–93; rtd 93; PtO *Ches* from 93. *41 Heywood Road, Great Sutton, South Wirral CH66 3PS* T: 0151-348 0884

WAGSTAFF, Ms Julie. b 48. Univ of Wales (Swansea) BA 93. St Mich Coll Llan 10. **d** 13 **p** 15. NSM Waunarllwydd *S & B* 13–18; rtd 18; PtO *S & B* from 18. *14 Bethania Road, Clydach, Swansea SA6 5DE* T: (01792) 845426 E: juliewagstaff1948@gmail.com

WAGSTAFF, Michael. b 59. R Holloway Coll Lon BA 81. Coll of Resurr Mirfield 88. **d** 89 **p** 90. C Worksop Priory *S'well* 89–92; C Ab Kettleby Gp *Leic* 92–94; TV Leic Resurr 94–00; Dioc Soc Resp Officer *Sheff* 00–08; Chapl RN from 08. *Royal Naval Chaplaincy Service, Mail Point 1-2, Leach Building, Whale Island, Portsmouth PO2 8BY* T: (023) 9262 5055 F: 9262 5134

WAGSTAFF, Robert William. b 36. Edin Th Coll 61. **d** 63 **p** 64. C Harringay St Paul *Lon* 63–64; C Mill Hill Jo Keble Ch 64–69; NSM N Lambeth *S'wark* 70–80; NSM Wilden *Worc* 80–92; NSM Stourport and Wilden 92–97; NSM Hartlebury 80–97; NSM Ombersley w Doverdale 80–97; C Shrawley, Witley, Astley and Abberley 98–02; rtd 02; PtO *Worc* from 02. *The Red House, Quarry Bank, Hartlebury, Kidderminster DY11 7TE* T: (01299) 250883

WAGSTAFFE, Eric Herbert. b 25. St Aid Birkenhead 55. **d** 57 **p** 58. C Harpurhey Ch Ch *Man* 57–60; R 60–69; V Pendlebury St Jo 69–84; V Hoghton *Blackb* 84–91; rtd 91; PtO *Blackb* 91–02; *Man* 95–17. *3 Chelwood Close, Bolton BL1 7LN* T: (01204) 596048

WAIN, Phillip. b 54. Aston Tr Scheme 89 Linc Th Coll 93. **d** 93 **p** 94. C Witton *Ches* 93–97; R Lea Gp *Linc* 97–14 and from 14; RD Corringham from 13. *Oaktree House, Padmoor Lane, Upton, Gainsborough DN21 5NH* T: (01427) 639933 E: phillip.wain@btinternet.com

WAINAINA, Canon Francis Samson Kamoko. b 51. St Jo Coll Dur MA 89. Oak Hill Th Coll BA 84. **d** 84 **p** 85. Kenya 84–88; C Upton (Overchurch) *Ches* 88–92; V Ellesmere St Pet *Sheff* 92–95; C York St Mich-le-Belfrey 95–01; V Starbeck *Ripon* 01–14; *Leeds* 14–16; Hon Can Ripon Cathl 12–16; rtd 16; PtO *S'well* from 16. *40 Elder Street, Sutton-in-Ashfield NG17 3FE* E: francis.wainaina51@gmail.com

✠**WAINE, The Rt Revd John.** b 30. Man Univ BA 51. Ridley Hall Cam 53. **d** 55 **p** 56 **c** 75. C W Derby St Mary *Liv* 55–58; C Sutton 58–60; V Ditton St Mich 60–64; V Southport H Trin 64–69; V Kirkby 69–71; TR 71–75; Suff Bp Stafford *Lich* 75–78; Preb Lich Cathl 75–78; Bp St E 78–86; Bp Chelmsf 86–96; Clerk of the Closet 89–96; rtd 96; PtO *St E* from 96; Hon Asst Bp St E from 08. *Broadmere, Ipswich Road, Grundisburgh, Woodbridge IP13 6TJ* T: (01473) 738296 E: john@jwaine.co.uk

WAINE, The Very Revd Stephen John. b 59. Westcott Ho Cam 81. **d** 84 **p** 85. C Wolverhampton *Lich* 84–88; Min Can and Succ St Paul's Cathl *Lon* 88–93; V Romford St Edw *Chelmsf* 93–10; P-in-c Romford St Jo 02–10; Adn Dorset *Sarum* 10–15; Can and Preb Sarum Cathl 10–15; Dean Chich from 15. *The Deanery, Canon Lane, Chichester PO19 1PX* T: 812484 *or* (01243) 812494 E: dean@chichestercathedral.org.uk

WAINMAN, Mrs Caroline Sarah Elizabeth. b 65. Aston Univ BSc 88 Mansf Coll Ox PGCE 90. ERMC 14. **d** 17 **p** 18. C Hemel Hempstead *St Alb* from 17. *7 Mountfield Road, Hemel Hempstead HP2 5DR* M: 07889-788664

WAINWRIGHT, John Pounsberry. b 42. St Steph Ho Ox 64. **d** 66 **p** 67. C Palmers Green St Jo *Lon* 66–70; C Primrose Hill St Mary w Avenue Road St Paul 70–71; P-in-c St John's Wood

All SS 71–73; V Hendon All SS Childs Hill 73–17; PtO from 16; rtd 17. *55 Silkstream Road, Edgware HA8 0DD*

WAINWRIGHT, Kevin Frank. b 46. Linc Th Coll 73. **d** 75 **p** 76. C Stand *Man* 75–78; C Radcliffe St Thos and St Jo 78–80; V Kearsley Moor 80–13; rtd 13; PtO *Man* from 13. *216 Oldham Road, Middleton, Manchester M24 2JZ* M: 07939-311124 E: kfw.kiwi@yahoo.co.uk

WAINWRIGHT, Mrs Kirsty Anne. b 73. ERMC 16. **d** 19. C St Alb St Steph from 19. *12 Tavistock Avenue, St Albans AL1 2NH* T: (01727) 857613

WAINWRIGHT, Malcolm Hugh. b 47. Man Univ BA 68 Nottm Univ MA 89. St Jo Coll Nottm MA 98. **d** 98 **p** 99. NSM Cotgrave and Owthorpe *S'well* 98–02; P-in-c Plumtree and Tollerton 02–09; Hon C Burton Fleming w Fordon, Grindale etc *York* 09–11; P-in-c Skelton w Shipton and Newton on Ouse from 11; C Alne from 17; C Brafferton w Pilmoor, Myton-on-Swale etc from 17; C Coxwold and Husthwaite from 17; C Crayke w Brandsby and Yearsley from 17; C Easingwold w Raskelf from 17; C Strensall from 17; C Forest of Galtres from 17. *The Rectory, Church Lane, Skelton, York YO30 1XT* T: (01904) 471351 E: malcolm@mhwainwright.eclipse.co.uk

WAINWRIGHT, Mrs Margaret Gillian. b 45. Qu Mary Coll Lon BA 68. EAMTC 00. **d** 03 **p** 04. NSM Combs and Lt Finborough *St E* 03–05; NSM The Creetings and Earl Stonham w Stonham Parva 05–11; rtd 11. *The Cottage, Elmswell Road, Wetherden, Stowmarket IP14 3LN* T: (01359) 242653 E: margwain@btopenworld.com

WAINWRIGHT, Martin John. b 69. Loughb Univ BEng 92. Trin Coll Bris BA 98. **d** 98 **p** 99. C Chislehurst Ch Ch *Roch* 98–02; V Camberley St Mary *Guildf* 02–10; V Howell Hill from 10; CF(V) from 16. *St Paul's Vicarage, 17 Northey Avenue, Sutton SM2 7HS* T: (020) 8224 9927 E: martinw@saintpauls.co.uk *or* martinjwainwright@gmail.com

WAINWRIGHT, Pauline Barbara. See FLORANCE, Pauline Barbara

WAINWRIGHT, Peter Anthony. b 45. K Coll Lon BD 73 MRICS 67. Ridley Hall Cam 73. **d** 75 **p** 76. C Ashtead *Guildf* 76–79; V Woking St Paul 79–84; PtO *Ox* 87–92 and 03–05; P-in-c Harston w Hauxton and Newton *Ely* 05–10; rtd 10; PtO *Ox* from 10. *19 Rosebery Avenue, High Wycombe HP13 7AL* T: (01494) 267913 M: 07814-835528 E: rev@peterwainwright.plus.com

WAINWRIGHT, Robert James David. b 86. St Jo Coll Dur BA 07 Ch Ch Ox MSt 08 DPhil 11. Wycliffe Hall Ox BA 14 MA 18. **d** 15 **p** 16. C Burford w Fulbrook, Taynton, Asthall etc *Ox* 15–17; NSM from 18; Chapl and Fell Oriel Coll Ox from 18. *Oriel College, Oriel Square, Oxford OX1 4EW* M: 07799-262056 E: robert.wainwright@chch.oxon.org

WAINWRIGHT, Robert Neil. b 52. NEOC 99. **d** 02 **p** 03. NSM Barlby and Riccall *York* 02–05; NSM Selby Abbey 05–12; TV Tenby *St D* from 12; Dioc Lay Development Officer from 14. *The Vicarage, Penally, Tenby SA70 7PN* T: (01834) 849459 M: 07768-390060 E: robbwain@gmail.com

WAITE, Daniel Alfred Norman. b 42. **d** 04 **p** 05. OLM Gorleston St Andr *Nor* 04–12; PtO from 12. *15 Laburnum Close, Bradwell, Great Yarmouth NR31 8JB* T: (01493) 664591

WAITE, Julian Henry. b 47. Open Univ BA 98. Brasted Th Coll 68 Ridley Hall Cam 70. **d** 72 **p** 73. C Wollaton *S'well* 72–76; C Herne Bay Ch Ch *Cant* 76–79; P-in-c Mersham *Cant* 79–87; Chapl Wm Harvey Hosp Ashford 79–87; V Marden *Cant* 87–93; Chapl HM Pris Blantyre Ho 90–93; Chapl HM Pris Swaleside 01–12; rtd 12; PtO *Cant* from 12. *31 Shearwater, Maidstone ME16 0DW* T: (01622) 664957

WAITE, Kathryn Joy. b 69. Univ Coll Lon BSc 92 MB, BS 95 MRCP 98 FRCR 03. ERMC 14. **d** 17 **p** 18. C Chesterton St Andr *Ely* from 17. *3 Natal Road, Cambridge CB1 3NS* T: (01223) 211286 M: 07826-835410 E: kathrynw@freenetname.co.uk

WAITE, Sheila Margaret. See TYLER, Sheila Margaret

WAIZENEKER, Canon Ann Elizabeth. b 56. Southn Univ BSc 78. SEITE 05. **d** 08 **p** 09. C Chich St Paul and Westhampnett 08–12; P-in-c New Shoreham 12–14; V New Shoreham and Shoreham Beach from 14; P-in-c Old Shoreham 12–15; R Old Shoreham and Kingston Buci 15–19; Dean of Women's Min from 17; Can and Preb Chich Cathl from 15. *The Vicarage, Church Street, Shoreham-by-Sea BN43 5DQ* T: (01273) 965303 E: annwaizeneker@gmail.com

WAKE, Colin Walter. b 50. Oriel Coll Ox BA 72 MA. Cuddesdon Coll 74. **d** 75 **p** 76. C Sandhurst *Ox* 75–78; C Faversham *Cant* 79–80; TV High Wycombe *Ox* 80–89; R Weston Favell *Pet* 89–06; Chapl St Jo Hosp Weston Favell 89–06; rtd 06. *35 Greenhill, Royal Wootton Bassett, Swindon SN4 8EH*

WAKEFIELD, Allan. b 31. Qu Coll Birm 72. **d** 74 **p** 75. C Kingsthorpe w Northampton St Dav *Pet* 74–77; TV Clifton *S'well* 77–81; V Bilborough St Jo 81–85; R Bere Ferrers *Ex*

85–91; R Mevagissey and St Ewe *Truro* 91–96; rtd 96; PtO *Truro* 96–98; Hon C Malborough w S Huish, W Alvington and Churchstow *Ex* 98–02; PtO 01–11. *4 Eden Cottages, Exeter Road, Ivybridge PL21 0BL* T: (01752) 698724

WAKEFIELD, Anne Frances. b 58. St Aid Coll Dur BSc 79 Sheff Univ PGCE 80. NTMTC 94. **d** 97 **p** 98. NSM Danbury *Chelmsf* 97–98; NSM Sherburn w Pittington *Dur* 98–01; Asst Chapl HM Pris Dur 01–03; Chapl HM YOI Northallerton 03–05; Chapl HM Pris Low Newton 05–08; P-in-c Stamford Bridge Gp *York* 09–12; R 12–18; RD S Wold 12–17; P-in-c York St Hilda from 18. *St Hilda's Vicarage, 155 Tang Hall Lane, York YO10 3SD* E: fran.wakefield@btopenworld.com

WAKEFIELD, David Kenneth. b 64. Ridley Hall Cam 02. **d** 04 **p** 05. C Bures w Assington and Lt Cornard *St E* 04–07; P-in-c Burlingham St Edmund w Lingwood, Strumpshaw etc *Nor* 07–09; R from 09. *The Rectory, Barn Close, Lingwood, Norwich NR13 4TS* T: (01603) 713880 E: revd.wake@btinternet.com

WAKEFIELD, Frances. *See* WAKEFIELD, Anne Frances

WAKEFIELD, Gavin Tracy. b 57. Van Mildert Coll Dur BSc 78 Sheff Univ CertEd 80 Kent Univ PhD 98. St Jo Coll Nottm 83. **d** 86 **p** 87. C Anston *Sheff* 86–89; C Aston cum Aughton and Ulley 89–91; TV Billericay and Lt Burstead *Chelmsf* 91–98; Dir Miss and Past Studies Cranmer Hall Dur 98–08; Dir Tr, Miss and Min *York* from 09; NSM Stamford Bridge Gp 13–18. *St Hilda's Vicarage, 155 Tang Hall Lane, York YO10 3SD* T: (01904) 699504 E: gavin.wakefield@yorkdiocese.org

WAKEFIELD, Mark Jeremy. b 55. York Univ BA 77. NTMTC BA 07. **d** 07 **p** 08. NSM Primrose Hill St Mary w Avenue Road St Paul *Lon* from 07. *15 Evangelist Road, London NW5 1UA* T: (020) 7267 8202 M: 07899-668493 E: mark.wakefield@blueyonder.co.uk

WAKEFIELD, Peter. b 48. St Jo Coll Nottm BTh 72 ALCD 72. **d** 72 **p** 73. C Hinckley H Trin *Leic* 72–75; C Kirby Muxloe 75–78; V Barlestone 78–85; TV Padgate *Liv* 85–88; V Quinton w Marston Sicca *Glouc* 91–97; rtd 97. *295 Leach Green Lane, Rednal, Birmingham B45 8EB* T: 0121-453 6979

WAKEFIELD, Dean of. *See* COWLING, The Very Revd Simon Charles

WAKEFIELD, Suffragan Bishop of. *See* ROBINSON, The Rt Revd Anthony William

WAKEHAM, Ellen Liesel. *See* EAMES, Ellen Liesel

WAKEHAM-DAWSON, Andrew Whistler. b 65. Wye Coll Lon BSc 87 Open Univ PhD 94. STETS 98. **d** 01 **p** 02. NSM Paddington St Sav *Lon* 01–04; Chapl RAF from 04. *Chaplaincy Services (RAF), HQ Air Command, RAF High Wycombe HP14 4UE* T: (01494) 496800 E: andrew.wakeham-dawson519@mod.gov.uk

WAKELIN, Alan Frank. b 32. Univ of Wales (Lamp) BA 58. Coll of Resurr Mirfield 58. **d** 60 **p** 61. C Northampton St Matt *Pet* 60–63; C Pet All SS 63–65; C Spalding St Mary and St Nic *Linc* 65–68; R Skirbeck St Nic 68–97; rtd 97. *Address temp unknown*

WAKELIN, Canon Brian Roy. b 53. Westf Coll Lon BSc 74. STETS 96. **d** 99 **p** 00. NSM Win Ch Ch from 99; Hon Can Win Cathl from 17. *11 Elm Court, Elm Road, Winchester SO22 5BA* T: (01962) 868679 E: brian.wakelin@ccwinch.org.uk

WAKELING, Canon Bruce. b 50. Lon Univ BA 74. Westcott Ho Cam 74. **d** 77 **p** 78. C Weymouth H Trin *Sarum* 77–82; TV Oakdale 82–89; R Clopton w Otley, Swilland and Ashbocking *St E* 89–98; V Rushmere 98–16; Hon Can St E Cathl 14–16; rtd 16. *1 Queech Place, Barham, Ipswich IP6 0GD*

WAKELING, Miss Faith Georgina. b 65. Anglia Ruskin Univ BA 10. Westcott Ho Cam 08. **d** 10 **p** 11. C Loughton St Jo *Chelmsf* 10–14; C Plaistow and N Canning Town 14–17; PtO from 17; NSM Greenwich St Alfege *S'wark* from 18. *Address withheld by request* M: 07837-968967 E: faithwakeling@gmail.com

WAKELING, Hugh Michael. b 42. Cape Town Univ BSc 63. Wycliffe Hall Ox 71. **d** 74 **p** 75. C Kennington St Mark *S'wark* 74–78; C Surbiton Hill Ch Ch 78–80; NSM Richmond H Trin and Ch Ch 80–84; NSM California *Ox* 85–89 and 00–07; NSM Arborfield w Barkham 89–00; PtO 07–17; *Heref* from 18. *Sunnybank, Dunns Copse, Ledbury HR8 2HR*

WAKELING, Mrs Joan. b 44. Hockerill Coll Cam CertEd 65. S'wark Ord Course 76. **dss** 79 **d** 90 **p** 94. Subiton Hill Ch Ch *S'wark* 79–80; Richmond H Trin and Ch Ch 80–84; California *Ox* 84–89; Arborfield w Barkham 89–00; NSM 90–00; Chapl Luckley-Oakfield Sch Wokingham 90–05; NSM Finchampstead *Ox* 00–05; P-in-c Raglan w Llandenny and Bryngwyn *Mon* 05–14; rtd 14; PtO *Heref* from 14. *28 Pound Meadow, Ledbury HR8 2EU* T: (01531) 633188 E: revdjwakeling@gmail.com

WAKELING, Rayner Alan. b 58. Portsm Poly BSc 79 Bris Univ PGCE 80. St Steph Ho Ox. **d** 01 **p** 02. C Willesden Green St Andr and St Fran *Lon* 01–05; V Greenhill St Jo 05–11; V

Pentonville St Silas w All SS and St Jas from 11. *St Silas House, 45 Cloudesley Road, London N1 0EL* T: (020) 7837 4228 E: raynerwakeling@hotmail.com

WAKELY, Marcus. b 40. Solicitor 62 FRSA 88. EMMTC 84. **d** 87 **p** 88. NSM Carrington *S'well* 87–91; C Worksop Priory 91–95; V Sheff St Matt 95–01; rtd 01. *16 Park House Gates, Nottingham NG3 5LX* T: 0115-960 9038 E: marcopaulo.w@outlook.com

WAKEMAN, Canon Hilary Margaret. b 38. EAMTC. **dss** 85 **d** 87 **p** 94. Heigham St Thos *Nor* 85–90; C 87–90; C Nor St Mary Magd w St Jas 90–91; Dn-in-c Norwich-over-the-Water Colegate St Geo 90–91; Team Dn Norwich Over-the-Water 91–94; TV 94–96; Hon Can Nor Cathl 94–96; I Kilmoe Union *C, C & R* 96–01; Dir of Ords 99–01; rtd 01; PtO *Nor* from 17. *15 Sherwyn House, 61 St George's Street, Norwich NR3 1BL* M: 07548-313030 E: hilary.wakeman@gmail.com

WALDEN, Alan Howard. b 64. Bris Univ BSc 86 Lon Business Sch MBA 93. Trin Coll Bris BA 09. **d** 09 **p** 10. C Frimley *Guildf* 09–12; TV Madeley *Heref* from 12. *St Michael's Vicarage, Church Street, Madeley, Telford TF7 5BN* T: (01952) 586645 M: 07957-773043 E: ahwalden@gmail.com *or* alan.walden@tf7.org.uk

WALDEN, Mrs Jane. b 55. Cartrefle Coll of Educn CertEd 76 Chelt & Glouc Coll of HE BA 01. WEMTC 02. **d** 05 **p** 06. NSM Minchinhampton *Glouc* 05–09; NSM Minchinhampton w Box and Amberley 09–12; V Brockworth 12–19; rtd 19. *13 Sheppard Way, Minchinhampton, Stroud GL6 9BZ* E: janewalden7255@gmail.com

WALDEN, John Edward Frank. b 38. FInstSMM. Oak Hill Th Coll 67. **d** 69 **p** 70. C Rainham *Chelmsf* 69–73; P-in-c Bris H Cross Inns Court 73–78; Conf and Publicity Sec SAMS 78–81; Hon C Southborough St Pet w Ch Ch and St Matt *Roch* 78–81; Exec Sec Spanish and Portuguese Ch Aid Soc 80–81; Hon C Tonbridge St Steph *Roch* 81–84; R Earsham w Alburgh and Denton *Nor* 84–89; PtO from 01. *2 Wentworth Drive, Harrogate HG2 7LA* E: revjefw@gmail.com

WALDSAX, Mrs Heather. b 58. Bris Univ BA 79 PGCE 80. STETS 06. **d** 08 **p** 09. NSM Canford Magna *Sarum* 08–17; NSM Wimborne Minster and the N Villages from 17. *60 Floral Farm, Canford Magna, Wimborne BH21 3AU* T: (01202) 889269 E: heather@waldsax.net

WALE (née BROWN), Wendy Anne. b 71. Homerton Coll Cam BEd 93. Trin Coll Bris BA 11. **d** 11 **p** 12. C Summerfield *Birm* 11–14; C Edgbaston St Germain 11–14; Chapl Wadh Coll Ox 14–18; C Beverley Minster *York* from 18. *28 Newton Drive, Beverley HU17 8NX* M: 07825-288779 E: wendy@beverleyminster.org.uk

WALES, David Neville. b 55. Rhodes Univ BA 78 Open Univ BSc 01. Coll of Resurr Mirfield 80. **d** 82 **p** 83. Zimbabwe 82–88; C Linslade *Ox* 89–91; P-in-c Weston Turville 91–07; R from 07; Voc Adv from 99. *The Rectory, Church Walk, Weston Turville, Aylesbury HP22 5SH* T: (01296) 613212 M: 07534-001044 E: d.wales512@btinternet.com

WALES, Mrs Janet Mary. b 56. Rhodes Univ MA 80 CTABRSM 98. Ox Min Course 11. **d** 14 **p** 15. NSM Ellesborough, The Kimbles and Stoke Mandeville *Ox* 14–17; PtO from 17. *The Rectory, Church Walk, Weston Turville, Aylesbury HP22 5SH* T: (01296) 612936 E: janetmwales@gmail.com

WALES, Archbishop of. *See* DAVIES, The Most Revd John David Edward

WALFORD, Mrs Angela. b 44. Whitelands Coll Lon CertEd 76. S Dios Minl Tr Scheme 85. **d** 92 **p** 94. NSM Boyatt Wood *Win* 92–99; Asst Chapl Epsom and St Helier Univ Hosps NHS Trust 99–07; PtO *S'wark* 07–13. *58 Wolseley Road, Mitcham Junction, Mitcham CR4 4JQ* T: (020) 8646 2841 E: wols1@tiscali.co.uk

WALFORD, David. b 45. S'wark Ord Course 75. **d** 78 **p** 79. NSM Hackbridge and N Beddington *S'wark* 78–83; C Fawley *Win* 83–87; C-in-c Boyatt Wood CD 87–90; V Boyatt Wood 90–97; rtd 97; PtO *S'wark* 98–02; Assoc P S Beddington and Roundshaw 00–07; Hon Chapl Epsom and St Helier NHS Trust 00–03; Asst Chapl Epsom and St Helier Univ Hosps NHS Trust 03–10; PtO *S'wark* 10–13. *58 Wolseley Road, Mitcham Junction, Mitcham CR4 4JQ* T: (020) 8646 2841

WALFORD, James Nicholas. b 80. Bris Univ BSc 02. Wycliffe Hall Ox 11. **d** 14 **p** 15. C Clifton Ch Ch w Em *Bris* from 14; C Redland from 18. *89 Kings Drive, Bishopston, Bristol BS7 8JQ* M: 07852-674317 E: jimw@emmanuelbristol.org.uk

WALFORD, Marc-Ashton. b 88. Aber Univ BSc 11. Wycliffe Hall Ox BTh 16. **d** 16 **p** 17. C Llanstadwel and Burton and Rosemarket *St D* 16–18; C Glamorgan Heritage Coast *Llan* from 18. *The Vicarage, St Brides Major, Bridgend CF32 0SD* T: (01656) 880328 M: 07535-015332 E: marc2k1@yahoo.com

WALFORD, Mrs Marion Gladys. b 54. NTMTC BA 08. **d** 08 **p** 09. C Canvey Is *Chelmsf* 08–12; TV from 12. *37*

Ruskoi Road, Canvey Island SS8 9QN T: (01268) 698991
E: revmarion@googlemail.com

WALFORD, Robin Peter. b 46. Qu Coll Birm 75. **d** 78 **p** 79.
C Radcliffe-on-Trent *S'well* 78–81; TV Newark w Hawton,
Cotham and Shelton 81–84; P-in-c Forest Town 84–92;
Co-ord Chapl Leeds Community and Mental Health
Services 92–97; PtO *Ripon* 97–14; *Leeds* from 14. *15
Oaklands Drive, Adel, Leeds LS16 8NZ* T: 0113-281 7251
E: robin.walford@btinternet.com

WALKER, Alan Robert Glaister. b 52. K Coll Cam BA 76
MA 79 New Coll Ox MA 84 Poly Cen Lon LLB 91 Heythrop
Coll Lon MTh 93 Univ of Wales LLM 96. St Steph Ho Ox 82.
d 84 **p** 85. C St John's Wood *Lon* 84–86; Chapl Poly Cen
Lon 87–92; Chapl Univ of Westmr 92–94; Chapl Univ Ch
Ch the K 87–94; V Hampstead Garden Suburb from 94. *The
Vicarage, 1 Central Square, London NW11 7AH* T/F: (020)
8455 7206 M: 07956-491037 E: fatherwalker@aol.com

WALKER, Mrs Alison Mary. b 91. St Pet Coll Ox MChem 13.
Trin Coll Bris MA 17. **d** 18 **p** 19. C Wenlock *Heref* from 18. *3
Grenville Drive, Much Wenlock TF13 6HB* M: 07817-610973

WALKER, Canon Allen Ross. b 46. Portsm Univ BA 94 MA 98.
Chich Th Coll 86. **d** 88. C Cosham *Portsm* 88–91; Chapl
Portsm Mental Health Community 91–97; Dn Portsm
Deanery 91–97; Community Chapl Burnham and Slough
Deanery *Ox* 97–12; AD Burnham and Slough 05–12; Hon
Can Ch Ch 08–12; rtd 12. *2 Juniper Gardens, Gillingham
SP8 4RF* E: mrarwalker@aol.com

WALKER, Mrs Amanda Frances. b 62. Cen Sch Speech &
Drama BSc 85 Univ Coll Lon MSc 94 Qu Coll Birm BA 09.
WMMTC 06. **d** 09 **p** 10. C Stafford *Lich* 09–12; V Streetly
from 12. *All Saints' Vicarage, 2 Foley Church Close, Sutton
Coldfield B74 3JX* T: 0121-353 5875 M: 07811-326204
E: revdmandywalker@btinternet.com

WALKER, Andrew David. b 84. BSc 06. Trin Coll Bris BA 10.
d 11 **p** 12. C S Dales *Derby* 11–15; R Eckington and Ridgeway
from 15. *The Rectory, 17 Church Street, Eckington, Sheffield
S21 4BG* T: (01246) 432196 E: adwalker2@googlemail.com

WALKER, Andrew James. b 70. Liv Hope Univ BA 10.
SNWTP 15. **d** 17 **p** 18. C Cotes Heath and Standon and
Swynnerton etc *Lich* 17–19; C Caverswall and Weston
Coyney w Dilhorne from 19. *The Vicarage, Church
Street, Eccleshall, Stafford ST21 6BY* M: 07933-293528
E: ajw0212@gmail.com

WALKER, Andrew Stephen. b 58. St Chad's Coll Dur BA 80
Heythrop Coll Lon MA 99. St Steph Ho Ox 83. **d** 85 **p** 86.
C Fareham SS Pet and Paul *Portsm* 85–87; C St John's Wood
Lon 87–93; V Streatham St Pet *S'wark* 93–98; PtO *Bris* 98–00;
S'wark 98–09; R St Edm the King and St Mary Woolnoth etc
Lon 00–10; P-in-c Lewes St Mich and St Thos at Cliffe w All
SS *Chich* 09–14; NSM Brighton St Mich and St Paul 14–15;
C St Marylebone w H Trin *Lon* 15–17; V Pimlico St Mary
Bourne Street from 17; PtO *Eur* from 16. *The Presbytery,
30 Bourne Street, London SW1W 8JJ* M: 07931-745853
E: andrew.walker@operamail.com

WALKER, Ms Angela Jean. b 55. St Jo Coll Nottm 03.
d 05 **p** 06. C Kempshott *Win* 05–09; P-in-c Cobham w
Luddesdowne and Dode *Roch* from 10. *The Vicarage, Battle
Street, Cobham, Gravesend DA12 3DB* T: (01474) 814332
E: ahiangel@aol.com

WALKER, Canon Anthony Charles St John. b 55. Trin Coll
Ox MA 80. Wycliffe Hall Ox 78. **d** 81 **p** 82. C Bradf Cathl
81–84; C Nottingham St Ann w Em *S'well* 84–88; V Retford
St Sav 88–01; TR Retford 02–11; TR Retford Area 11–17; AD
Retford 00–09; Hon Can S'well Minster 04–11; V Morton
and Riddlesden *Leeds* from 17. *The Vicarage, St Mary's Road,
Riddlesden, Keighley BD20 5PA* E: tony@tonywalker.f9.co.uk

WALKER, Arthur Daniel. b 60. Nene Coll Northn BA 86
St Martin's Coll Lanc PGCE 90 Leeds Univ BA 10. Yorks
Min Course 07. **d** 10 **p** 11. C Northallerton w Kirby
Sigston *York* 10–14; V Birkenshaw w Hunsworth *Leeds*
14–19; P-in-c Easington w Liverton *York* from 19. *2
Grinkle Lane, Easington, Saltburn-by-the-Sea TS13 4NT*
E: revdannywalker@outlook.com

WALKER (*née* JEYES), Mrs Caroline Helen. b 58. Wye Coll
Lon BSc 81 Anglia Ruskin Univ MA 11. ERMC 08. **d** 10 **p** 11.
NSM Desborough, Brampton Ash, Dingley and Braybrooke
Pet 10–13; Chapl Kettering Gen Hosp NHS Foundn Trust
10–13; R Hardington Vale *B & W* from 13. *The Rectory,
Vicarage Lane, Norton St Philip, Bath BA2 7LY* T: (01373)
834258 E: carolinehwalker@btinternet.com

WALKER, Catherine Jane. b 76. Birm City Univ MA 08. Qu
Foundn Birm 15. **d** 17 **p** 18. C Boldmere *Birm* from 17. *19
Southam Drive, Sutton Coldfield B73 5PD* M: 07803-718776
or 07484-111614 E: revvcath@gmail.com

WALKER, Ms Cherie Pauline. b 57. LCTP BA 15. **d** 15 **p** 16.
C Broughton *Blackb* 15–19; C Ingol 18–19; P-in-c from

19. *St Margaret's Vicarage, 1A St Margaret's Close, Ingol,
Preston PR2 3ZU* T: (01772) 727208 M: 07840-328846
E: revrie52@outlook.com

WALKER, Christopher James Anthony. b 43. Sarum &
Wells Th Coll 85. **d** 87 **p** 88. Hon C Durrington *Sarum*
87–89; CF 87–98; MOD Civil Service Chapl 98–15; rtd
15; PtO *Sarum* from 99; *Win* from 99. *Horseshoe Meadow
Farm, Cholderton, Salisbury SP4 0ED* T: (01980) 629234
E: horseshoewalkers@gmail.com

WALKER, Christopher Simon John. b 87. **d** 19. NSM Padiham
w Hapton and Padiham Green *Blackb* from 19. *14 Bendwood
Close, Padiham, Burnley BB12 8RT* E: kit@padihamparish.org

WALKER, Mrs Claire Victoria. b 79. Van Mildert Coll Dur
BA 03. Westcott Ho Cam 15. **d** 17 **p** 18. C Market Rasen
Linc from 17. *Turnstone, Willingham Road, Market Rasen
LN8 3RE* M: 07495-190310

WALKER, Daniel. *See* WALKER, Arthur Daniel

WALKER, Canon David. b 48. Linc Th Coll 71. **d** 74 **p** 75.
C Arnold *S'well* 74–77; C Crosby *Linc* 77–79; V Scrooby
S'well 79–86; V Sutton in Ashfield St Mary 86–94; P-in-c
Sutton in Ashfield St Mich 89–94; TR Birkenhead Priory
Ches 94–05; RD Birkenhead 99–05; R Bromborough
05–13; Hon Can Ches Cathl 03–13; rtd 13; PtO *Newc*
from 14. *12 Mead Court, Newcastle upon Tyne NE12 9RF*
E: dave.walker48@outlook.com

WALKER, Canon David Andrew. b 52. St Andr Univ
MTheol 75 MA Hull Univ MPhil 00. Linc Th Coll 79. **d** 81
p 82. C Hessle *York* 81–84; C N Hull St Mich 84–86; V from
86; AD Cen and N Hull 99–10; RD Hull 00–10; Can and Preb
York Minster from 01. *St Michael's Vicarage, 214 Orchard Park
Road, Hull HU6 9BX* T: (01482) 803375

WALKER, David Andrew. b 76. Van Mildert Coll Dur BSc 97.
Oak Hill Th Coll MTh 07. **d** 07 **p** 08. C Cheadle All Hallows
Ches 07–11; V Finchley Ch Ch *Lon* from 11. *Christ Church
Vicarage, 616 High Road, London N12 0AA* T: (020) 8445
2532 M: 07980-360408 E: davasarahwava@yahoo.co.uk

WALKER, David Ian. b 41. Bernard Gilpin Soc Dur 64 Bps'
Coll Cheshunt 65. **d** 68 **p** 69. C Todmorden *Wakef* 68–72;
V Rastrick St Jo 72–77; V Crosland Moor 77–86; R Kirton in
Lindsey w Manton *Linc* 86–99; R Grayingham 86–99; OCM
88–99; V Clee *Linc* 96–06; rtd 07; PtO *Linc* from 07; Asst Chapl
N Lincs and Goole Hosps NHS Trust 08–11. *48 Pretymen
Crescent, New Waltham, Grimsby DN36 4PB* T: (01472)
826958 M: 07592-548852 E: davidian8@virginmedia.com

WALKER, David John. b 69. Yorks Min Course. **d** 16 **p** 17.
NSM Dronfield w Holmesfield *Derby* from 16. *Foxlyn,
Owlthorpe Lane, Mosborough, Sheffield S20 5BA* M: 07802-
374763 E: walkerd2@btconnect.com

✠**WALKER, The Rt Revd David Stuart.** b 57. K Coll Cam
MA 81 Warwick Univ PhD 15. Qu Coll Birm. **d** 83 **p** 84
c 00. C Handsworth *Sheff* 83–86; TV Maltby 86–91; Ind
Chapl 86–91; V Bramley and Ravenfield 91–95; R Bramley
and Ravenfield w Hooton Roberts etc 95–00; Hon Can Sheff
Cathl 00; Suff Bp Dudley *Worc* 00–13; Bp Man from 13.
Bishopscourt, Bury New Road, Salford M7 4LE T: 0161-792
2096 E: bishop.david@manchester.anglican.org

WALKER, Derek Fred. b 46. Trin Coll Bris 71. **d** 74 **p** 75. C
St Paul's Cray St Barn *Roch* 74–78; C Rushden w Newton
Bromswold *Pet* 78–80; R Kirkby Thore w Temple Sowerby and
Newbiggin *Carl* 80–83; V Coppull *Blackb* 83–87; V New Ferry
Ches 87–96; R Akeman *Ox* 96–11; rtd 11; PtO *Nor* from 13.
34 Valley Rise, Dersingham, King's Lynn PE31 6PT T: (01485)
541124 E: derek.dersingham@yahoo.co.uk

✠**WALKER, The Rt Revd Edward William Murray (Dominic).**
b 48. AKC 73 Heythrop Coll Lon MA 97 Brighton Univ
Hon DLitt 98 Univ of Wales LLM 05. **d** 72 **p** 72 **c** 97. CGA
67–83; C Wandsworth St Faith *S'wark* 72–73; Bp's Dom
Chapl 73–76; R Newington St Mary 76–85; RD S'wark and
Newington 80–85; OGS from 83; Superior 90–96; V Brighton
St Pet w Chpl Royal and St Jo *Chich* 85–86; P-in-c Brighton
St Nic 85–86; TR Brighton St Pet and St Nic w Chpl Royal
86–97; RD Brighton 85–97; Can and Preb Chich Cathl
85–97; Area Bp Reading *Ox* 97–03; Bp Mon 03–13; rtd 13;
Hon Asst Bp S & B from 13; Hon Asst Bp Llan from 17. *2
St Vincent's Drive, Monmouth NP25 5DS* T: (01600) 772151
E: dwalker.ogs@btinternet.com

WALKER, Mrs Elizabeth. b 42. CQSW 85. NEOC 91. **d** 94 **p** 00.
NSM Stockton St Chad *Dur* 94–08; rtd 08; PtO *Dur* from 08.
29 Bramble Road, Stockton-on-Tees TS19 0NQ T: (01642)
615332

WALKER, Canon Elizabeth Margaret Rea. b 49. Ch Ch Coll
Cant CertEd 70. S'wark Ord Course 89. **d** 92 **p** 94. NSM
Ash and Ridley *Roch* 92–97; Chapl St Geo Sch Gravesend
92–97; P-in-c Burham and Wouldham *Roch* 97–05; P-in-c
Platt 05–12; V 12–15; Assoc Dir of Ords 97–15; Hon Can
Roch Cathl 09–15; rtd 15; PtO *Roch* from 16; *Cant* from

18. *26 Howard Drive, Maidstone ME16 0QD* T: (01622) 759609 M: 07434-156563 E: revliz.walker@btinternet.com

WALKER, Gavin Russell. b 43. FCA 78. Coll of Resurr Mirfield 76. **d** 78 **p** 79. C Wakef St Jo 78–81; C Northallerton w Kirby Sigston *York* 81–83; V Whorlton w Carlton and Faceby 83–85; P-in-c Brotherton *Wakef* 85–89; V Earl's Heaton 89–97; TV Dewsbury 97–99; TV Egremont and Haile *Carl* 99–04; rtd 04; PtO *Carl* from 05. *37 Fell View Park, Gosforth, Seascale CA20 1HY* T: (019467) 25386 M: 07986-505886 E: gavinstaffa@sky.com

WALKER, Gerald Roger. b 41. K Coll Lon BD 67 AKC 67. **d** 68 **p** 69. C High Elswick St Phil *Newc* 68–70; C Goring-by-Sea *Chich* 70–75; R Selsey 75–81; V Hove St Andr Old Ch 81–91; V Copthorne 91–95; rtd 95; NSM Streat w Westmeston *Chich* 95–99; PtO *S'wark* 00–15; *Guildf* 00–15; *Chich* 12–17. *1 Ramsay Hall, 9-13 Byron Road, Worthing BN11 3HN* T: (01903) 217493 E: clergyoncall@btinternet.com

WALKER, Canon Harvey William. b 26. Edin Univ MA 52. St Steph Ho Ox 58. **d** 60 **p** 61. C Newc St Matt w St Mary 60–64; V 64–94; Hon Can Newc Cathl 80–94; rtd 95; PtO *Newc* from 95. *16 Eastbourne House, The Links, Whitley Bay NE26 1PG*

WALKER, Ian Richard Stevenson. b 51. Univ of Wales (Lamp) BA 73. Qu Coll Birm. **d** 76 **p** 77. C Stainton-in-Cleveland *York* 76–79; C Fulford 79–81; C Kidderminster St Mary *Worc* 81–82; TV Kidderminster St Mary and All SS, Trimpley etc 82–86; R Keyingham w Ottringham, Halsham and Sunk Is *York* 86–98; RD S Holderness 94–98; R Scartho *Linc* 98–08; P-in-c Epworth Gp 08–12; R 12–17; rtd 17; PtO *York* from 17. *The Vicarage, Main Road, Thorngumbald, Hull HU12 9NA* E: irsw@btinternet.com

WALKER, Mrs Jane Louise. b 63. STETS 03. **d** 06 **p** 07. NSM Alton All SS *Win* 06–09; Chapl Phyllis Tuckwell Hospice Farnham from 10; NSM Rowledge and Frensham *Guildf* 11–16; V Frensham from 16; AD Farnham from 17. *The Vicarage, The Street, Frensham, Farnham GU10 3DT* T: (01252) 792137 E: revjanewalker@gmail.com

WALKER (formerly **WARHAM), Mrs Jean.** b 55. **d** 00 **p** 01. OLM Newcastle w Butterton *Lich* from 00. *166 High Street, Alsagers Bank, Stoke-on-Trent ST7 8BA* T: (01782) 721505 E: mrspopasmurf@hotmail.com

WALKER, Mrs Jillian Francesca. b 41. **d** 99 **p** 00. OLM Blackbourne *St E* 99–11; PtO from 11. *2 The Causeway, Walsham-le-Willows, Bury St Edmunds IP31 3AB* E: digger.walker@mac.com

WALKER (née **SEMPER), Canon Jocelyn Rachel.** b 64. Univ of Wales (Ban) BA 85 Wan Univ PGCE 86. NOC 98. **d** 01 **p** 02. C Chadderton St Matt *Man* 01–04; Chapl Asst Salford R Hosps NHS Trust 04–07; P-in-c Maidstone St Martin *Cant* 07–14; Voc Officer from 14; Dioc Dir of Ords from 13; Hon Can Cant Cathl from 14. *St Mary's Vicarage, Taswell Street, Dover CT16 1SE* E: jwalker@diocant.org

WALKER, Canon John. b 51. Aber Univ MA 74 Edin Univ BD 78. Edin Th Coll 75. **d** 78 **p** 79. C Broughty Ferry *Bre* 78–81; P-in-c Dundee St Jo 81–85; Ind Chapl 83–88; R Dundee St Luke 85–95; R Alford *Ab* 95–02; R Inverurie from 95; R Auchindoir from 95; P-in-c Kemnay from 95; R Whiterashes from 11; Syn Clerk from 08; Can St Andr Cathl from 01. *The Rectory, St Mary's Place, Inverurie AB51 3NW* T: (01467) 620470 E: jwcan@btinternet.com

WALKER, John Anthony Patrick. b 58. Kent Univ PhD 12. Trin Coll Bris BA 86. **d** 86 **p** 87. C Canford Magna *Sarum* 86–90; TV Glyncorrwg w Afan Vale and Cymmer Afan *Llan* 90–96; Hd of RE Wentworth High Sch Eccles 97–99; Community Chapl and C Gorton St Phil *Man* 00–03; P-in-c Oldham St Paul 03–04; PtO 04–07; Cant 07–12; Hon C Maidstone St Martin 12–14; TR Dover Town from 15; AD Dover 16–17; Jt AD 17–18. *St Mary's Vicarage, Taswell Street, Dover CT16 1SE* M: 07980-692813 E: johnwalker_uk@btinternet.com

WALKER, John David. b 44. St Jo Coll Dur BA 76. Cranmer Hall Dur 77. **d** 77 **p** 78. C Heworth H Trin *York* 77–81; P-in-c Allerthorpe and Barmby on the Moor w Fangfoss 81–83; TV Pocklington Team 84–89; P-in-c Hovingham 89; TV Street 89–92; R Dunnington 92–99; V Thorne *Sheff* 99–03; rtd 03; PtO *York* from 03. *9 Bishop Blunt Close, Hessle HU13 9NJ* T: (01482) 642110

WALKER, John Frank. b 53. Leeds Univ BEd 76 Ripon Coll of Educn CertEd 75. NW Ord Course 78. **d** 81 **p** 82. NSM Whitkirk *Ripon* 81–82; C 82–85; V Sutton Courtenay w Appleford *Ox* 85–90; Dioc Children's Adv *S'wark* 90–94; V Walworth St Jo from 94; Youth and Children's Officer Woolwich Episc Area 95–99. *St John's Vicarage, 18 Larcom Street, London SE17 1NQ* T: (020) 7703 4375

WALKER, John Howard. b 47. Brasted Th Coll 67 Clifton Th Coll 69. **d** 72 **p** 73. C Upton (Overchurch) *Ches* 72–76; Asst

Chapl Liv Univ 76–79; V Everton St Chrys 79–82; C Parr Mt 83–86; SAMS 86–94; Area Sec (NE and E Midl) SAMS 86–89; Paraguay 89–94; V Calverley *Bradf* 95–12; rtd 12; Hon C Leeds St Geo *Ripon* 12–14 and from 14. *103 Harehills Avenue, Leeds LS8 4HU* T: 0113-249 6239 M: 07903-836806

WALKER, Canon John Percival. b 45. CITC 68. **d** 71 **p** 72. C Belfast St Clem *D & D* 71–74; C Magheraculmoney *Clogh* 74–78; C Lisburn St Paul *Conn* 78–81; I Belfast St Ninian 81–88; I Belfast St Mary w H Redeemer 88–12; Preb Conn Cathl 98–12; Treas Conn Cathl 04–12; rtd 12. *4 Sprucefield Court, Lisburn BT27 5UL* M: 07835-866914 E: walkerjohnpercival@googlemail.com

WALKER, John Richard. *See* WALKER, Richard John

WALKER, Judith Anne. *See* WALKER-HUTCHINSON, Judith Anne

WALKER, Julie Lorraine. b 68. Liv Univ BTh 05 Ches Univ MTh 09. St Jo Coll Nottm 10. **d** 12 **p** 13. C Wybunbury and Audlem w Doddington *Ches* 12–15; V Haslington w Crewe Green 15–18; V Eccleshall *Lich* from 18; RD from 18. *The Vicarage, Church Street, Eccleshall, Stafford ST21 6BY* T: (01785) 850351 M: 07581-540435 E: juleswalker68@gmail.com or vicar.eccleshall@gmail.com

WALKER, Keith. b 48. Linc Th Coll 82. **d** 84 **p** 85. C Whickham *Dur* 84–87; C Trimdon Station 87; P-in-c 87–89; V 89–90; R Penshaw 90–98; P-in-c Shiney Row 92–95; P-in-c Herrington 93–95; rtd 98; Hon C Jersey St Brelade *Win* 01–03; PtO *Dur* from 03. *16 Westfields, School Aycliffe, Newton Aycliffe DL5 6PX* T: (01325) 495715 M: 07906-542095 E: revdkwalker@hotmail.com

WALKER, Canon Lesley Ann. b 53. Westmr Coll Ox MTh 00. S Dios Minl Tr Scheme 85. **d** 88 **p** 94. Par Dn Oakdale *Sarum* 88–92; Team Dn Bridgnorth, Tasley, Astley Abbotts, etc *Heref* 92–94; TV 94–03; Vice-Prin OLM Tr Scheme *Cant* 03–04; PtO 06–07; R Meneage *Truro* 07–17; RD Kerrier 10–17; Hon Can Truro Cathl from 15 and from 15. Lis *Escop, Feock, Truro TR3 6QQ* T: (01872) 862657 E: chaplain@truro.anglican.org

WALKER, Mrs Linda Joan. b 47. **d** 04 **p** 05. OLM Blurton *Lich* 04–11; OLM Blurton and Dresden 11–17; PtO from 18. *6 Thackeray Drive, Blurton, Stoke-on-Trent ST3 2HE* T: (01782) 324895 E: linda.walker910@ntlworld.com

WALKER, Mrs Margaret Joy. b 44. Westhill Coll Birm TCert 66 Newc Univ MA 93. CA Tr Coll 80. dss 86 **d** 87 **p** 94. Scargill Ho 86–87; Hon Par Dn Monkwearmouth St Andr *Dur* 87; Hon Par Dn Chester le Street 87–93; Hon Chapl Wells Cathl *B & W* 93–01; PtO *Cant* 02–05; NSM Stone Street Gp 05–11; AD W Bridge 09–11; PtO 11–13; *Leeds* from 13. *109 Hurrs Road, Skipton BD23 2JF* T: (01756) 229056 E: margiwalker@uwclub.net

WALKER, Mark Alexander (Marcus). b 81. Oriel Coll Ox BA 02 MA 08 MSt 04. Ripon Coll Cuddesdon MA 10. **d** 11 **p** 12. C Winchmore Hill St Paul *Lon* 11–14; Assoc Dir Angl Cen Rome 14–18; R Smithfield Gt St Bart *Lon* from 18. *15 Wilmington Square, London WC1X 0ER* M: 07919-201244 E: marcus.walker@greatstbarts.com

WALKER, Lt Col Mark George. b 68. Univ of New England BProfStud 00 Canberra Univ MDefStud 00 Chas Sturt Univ NSW BTheol 07. **d** 06 **p** 07. C Albany St Jo Australia 06–08; PtO Perth 09; C Balga w Mirrabooka 09–11; NSM Frampton on Severn, Arlingham, Saul etc *Glouc* 11; P-in-c Lesmurdie Australia 12–13; PtO Perth 14; Chapl Ocean Reef Primary Sch from 14. *33 Semaphore Avenue, Burns Beach WA 6028, Australia* T: (0061) (4) 1415 4885 M: 07580-756141 E: markwalker68@me.com

WALKER, Martin John. b 52. Linc Coll Ox BA 73 PGCE 74 St Jo Coll Dur BA 78. Cranmer Hall Dur. **d** 79 **p** 80. C Harlow New Town w Lt Parndon *Chelmsf* 79–81; C Dorchester *Ox* 81–83; Chapl Bath Coll of HE 83–89; TV Southampton (City Cen) *Win* 89–91; Adv in RE and Resources *Sarum* 91–92; Hon C Northolt St Mary *Lon* 92–00; Chapl Bancroft's Sch Woodford Green 92–99; Chapl St Helen's Sch Northwood 99–18; Chapl Wellingborough Sch 00–18; R Wiveliscombe and the Hills *B & W* from 18. *The Rectory, South Street, Wiveliscombe, Taunton TA4 2LZ* E: revmjwalker@yahoo.com

WALKER, Martin John. b 66. Greenwich Univ CertEd 98 Brighton Univ MBA 00. St Mellitus Coll 15. **d** 18 **p** 19. C Crawley *Chich* from 18. *23 Smoke Lane, Reigate RH2 7HJ* T: (01293) 279028 M: 07768-774099 E: martin.john.walker@icloud.com

WALKER, Michael John. b 39. St D Coll Lamp BA 61. St Aid Birkenhead 61. **d** 63 **p** 64. C Clifton *York* 63–66; C Marfleet 66–69; V Salterhebble St Jude *Wakef* 69–83; V Llangollen w Trevor and Llantysilio *St As* 83–93; RD Llangollen 87–93; V Kerry and Llanmerewig and Dolfor 93–01; RD Cedewain 97–01; rtd 01; PtO *Ban* 01–17; *Heref* from 12. *41 Oldfields Close, Leominster HR6 8TL* T: (01568) 617472 E: margaretwalker299@gmail.com

WALKER, Michael Maynard. b 82. Imp Coll Lon MEng 05. Trin Coll Bris 16. **d** 18 **p** 19. C Westcliff St Mich *Chelmsf* from 18. *144 Alexandra Road, Southend-on-Sea SS1 1HB* M: 07989-498412 E: michaelwalker.mw@gmail.com *or* mike@stmichaelswestcliff.org

WALKER, Canon Nigel Maynard. b 39. ALCD 66. **d** 67 **p** 68. C Southsea St Jude *Portsm* 67–70; C Addington S Africa 70–73; R 73–76; C Abingdon w Shippon *Ox* 76–80; V Upton (Overchurch) *Ches* 80–94; Chapl Brussels and Chan Brussels Cathl *Eur* 94–04; P-in-c Leuven 02–04; rtd 05; PtO *Cant* 05–10; *Eur* from 05; *Portsm* from 10; *Win* from 10; *Chich* from 12; *Guildf* from 13. *12 The Sands, Whitehill, Bordon GU35 9QW* T: (01420) 477323 E: nigelmwalker@gmail.com

WALKER, Paul Colin. b 77. Thames Valley Univ BMus 01 Roehampton Inst PGCE 02. Trin Coll Bris 16. **d** 18 **p** 19. C Gt Faringdon w Lt Coxwell *Ox* from 18. *17 Gloucester Street, Faringdon SN7 7JA* M: 07825-372527 E: revpaulwalker@icloud.com

WALKER, Paul Gary. b 59. Lon Univ BD. St Jo Coll Nottm 82. **d** 84 **p** 85. C Bowling St Steph *Bradf* 84–87; C Tong 87–90; P-in-c Oakenshaw cum Woodlands 90–97; V Wrose 97–13; P-in-c Bolton St Jas w St Chrys 10–13; RD Calverley 01–09; R Wortley and Farnley *Leeds* 16–18; V Drighlington and Gildersome from 18. *The New Vicarage, 2A Church Street, Gildersome, Morley, Leeds LS12 4RU* M: 07907-802135 E: paulwalker71@blueyonder.co.uk *or* paulwalker71@me.com

WALKER, Paul Laurence. b 63. St Chad's Coll Dur BA 84. Chich Th Coll BTh 90. **d** 88 **p** 89. C Shildon w Eldon *Dur* 88–91; C Barnard Castle w Whorlton 91–93; C Silksworth 93–96; C-in-c Moorside St Wilfrid CD 96–99; V Norton St Mary 99–04; Chapl Manager Tees and NE Yorks NHS Trust 04–06; Chapl Manager Tees, Esk and Wear Valleys NHS Foundn Trust from 06; PtO *Dur* from 04. *Tees, Esk and Wear Valleys NHS Foundation Trust, Flatts Lane Centre, Flatts Lane, Middlesbrough TS6 0SZ* T: (01642) 451665 E: paul.walker8@nhs.net

WALKER, Mrs Pepita. b 35. **d** 07 **p** 08. OLM Kemble, Poole Keynes, Somerford Keynes etc *Glouc* 07–11; NSM 11–14; rtd 14; PtO *Glouc* from 14. *Woodstock, Frampton Mansell, Stroud GL6 8JE* T: (01285) 760211 E: pepita@pepitawalker.co.uk

WALKER, Percival. See WALKER, John Percival

WALKER, Peter Anthony. b 57. Pemb Coll Cam BA 79 MA 83 St Jo Coll Dur BA 86. Cranmer Hall Dur 84. **d** 87 **p** 88. C Chesham Bois *Ox* 87–90; Chapl Bradf Cathl 90–93; TV W Swindon and the Lydiards *Bris* 93–99; V Keresley and Coundon *Cov* 99–10; P-in-c Bidford-on-Avon 10–12; V 12–15; P-in-c Exhall w Wixford 10–15; P-in-c Salford Priors 10–15; P-in-c Temple Grafton w Binton 10–15; R Heart of England from 15. *The Vicarage, 5 Howard Close, Bidford-on-Avon, Alcester B50 4EL* T: (01789) 772217 E: peter@heartparishes.org.uk

WALKER, Canon Peter Anthony Ashley. b 46. Chich Th Coll 67. **d** 70 **p** 71. C Stamford Hill St Thos *Lon* 70–74; C Bethnal Green St Matt 74–77; V Hackney Wick St Mary of Eton w St Aug 77–84; Warden Rydal Hall *Carl* 84–95; P-in-c Rydal 84–95; P-in-c Porthleven w Sithney *Truro* 95–01; RD Kerrier 96–01; Can Res Truro Cathl 01–11; P-in-c Feock 01–10; Chapl Is of Scilly 10–12; rtd 12; PtO *Truro* from 13. *Ryancot, Wansford Meadows, Gorran Haven, St Austell PL26 6HU* T: (01726) 843621 E: petelynne@btinternet.com *or* peter.walker2@btinternet.com

WALKER, Peter Ronald. b 50. Southn Univ BA 72 K Alfred's Coll Win PGCE 73. WMMTC 02. **d** 05 **p** 06. NSM Hadley and Wellington Ch Ch *Lich* 05–10; Chapl Shrewsbury and Telford NHS Trust 09–10; TV Rhos-Cystennin *St As* 10–16; Asst P Aberconwy Miss Area 17–19; PtO *Ban* from 14. *The Rectory, Glyn y Marl Road, Llandudno Junction LL31 9NS* T: (01492) 583579

WALKER, Peter Sidney Caleb. b 50. St Mich Th Coll Crafers 76. **d** 80 **p** 81. C Devonport Australia 80–81; P-in-c Fingal Valley 81–84; R E Devonport and Spreyton 84–88; R Swallow *Linc* 88–94; R Selworthy, Timberscombe, Wootton Courtenay etc *B & W* 94–01; Chapl Costa del Sol W *Eur* 01–04; R Coxheath, E Farleigh, Hunton, Linton etc *Roch* 05–12; P-in-c Offwell, Northleigh, Farway, Cotleigh etc *Ex* 12–17; rtd 17; P-in-c Ashburnham w Penhurst *Chich* from 17. *Agmerhurst Granary, Kitchenham Road, Ashburnham, Battle TN33 9NA* E: p.walker977@btinternet.com

WALKER, Canon Peter Stanley. b 56. SRN RMN Nottm Univ BCombStuds. Linc Th Coll 80. **d** 83 **p** 84. C Woodford St Barn *Chelmsf* 83–86; C Brentwood St Thos 86–88; V Colchester St Barn 88–94; P-in-c Colchester St Jas, All SS, St Nic and St Runwald 94–96; R Colchester St Jas and St Paul w All SS etc 96–17; Hon Can Chelmsf Cathl 09–17; rtd 17; PtO *Chelmsf* from 17. *55 Sweet Briar Road, Stanway,*

Colchester CO3 0HH T: (01206) 545192 M: 07867-972231 E: frpeterwalker@gmail.com

WALKER, Philip Kingsley. b 47. Ox Univ BA 70. St Mich Coll Llan. **d** 90 **p** 91. C Maindee Newport *Mon* 90–92; C Llanmartin 92–94; V Bishton 94–98; R Panteg 98–03; R Panteg w Llanfihangel Pontymoile 03–07; rtd 07. *Glan Aber, Lon Isallt, Trearddur Bay, Holyhead LL65 2UP*

WALKER, Richard David. b 45. Hull Univ BSc 68. S Dios Minl Tr Scheme 92. **d** 95 **p** 96. NSM Horfield St Greg *Bris* 95–98; NSM Lawrence Weston and Avonmouth 98–00; Chapl HM Pris Leic 00–01; Chapl HM Pris Usk and Prescoed 01–03; Hon C Cromhall, Tortworth, Tytherington, Falfield etc *Glouc* 04–07. *Ford House, Bronllys Road, Talgarth, Brecon LD3 0HH* T: (01874) 712292 E: richard-walker@live.co.uk

WALKER, Richard John. b 67. Humberside Coll of Educn BSc 88 Leeds Univ MSc(Eng) 97 St Jo Coll Dur BA 04 St Jo Coll Nottm MA 14. Cranmer Hall Dur 02. **d** 04 **p** 05. C Scarborough St Mary w Ch Ch and H Apostles *York* 04–08; V Elloughton and Brough w Brantingham 08–13; V Beverley St Nic 13–17; Asst Dioc Dir of Ords 13–15; 15–17; V Scarborough St Mary w Ch Ch and H Apostles from 17. *The Vicarage, 1 North Cliff Gardens, Scarborough YO12 6PR* T: (01723) 371354 E: revrichardjwalker@gmail.com

WALKER, Richard Mark. b 63. York Univ BSc 84. St Jo Coll Nottm MA 00. **d** 00 **p** 01. C Ben Rhydding *Bradf* 00–04; P-in-c Yeadon St Jo 04–08; V Yeadon 08–14; *Leeds* from 14. *St John's Vicarage, Barcroft Grove, Yeadon, Leeds LS19 7XZ* T: 0113-250 2272 E: richard.walker@leeds.anglican.org

WALKER, Rie. See WALKER, Cherie Pauline

WALKER, Rodney Graham. b 59. St Hild Coll 14. **d** 17 **p** 18. NSM Pontefract St Giles *Leeds* 17–19; NSM Pontefract from 19. *11A Ashgap Lane, Normanton WF6 2DT* M: 07746-980727 E: rod@carletoncourt.co.uk

WALKER, Roger. See WALKER, Gerald Roger

WALKER, Mrs Ruth. b 51. MAAT 95. **d** 03 **p** 04. OLM Camberley St Mary *Guildf* from 03. *73 Verran Road, Camberley GU15 2ND* T: (01276) 503551 E: tandr.walker@ntlworld.com

WALKER (née APPLETON), Mrs Ruth Elizabeth. b 58. St Jo Coll Dur BA 79 Hughes Hall Cam PGCE 80. St Jo Coll Nottm 86. **d** 88 **p** 94. Par Dn Princes Risborough w Ilmer *Ox* 88–90; C and Congr Chapl Bradf Cathl 90–93; C The Lydiards *Bris* 93–94; NSM W Swindon and the Lydiards 94–96; C Swindon St Jo and St Andr 96–98; PtO 98–99; C Keresley and Coundon *Cov* 99–10; AD Cov N 04–10; C Bidford-on-Avon 10–15; C Exhall w Wixford 10–15; C Salford Priors 10–15; C Temple Grafton w Binton 10–15; C Heart of England 15–16; Project Dir Calling Young Disciples *Worc* from 16. *The Vicarage, 5 Howard Close, Bidford-on-Avon, Alcester B50 4EL* T: (01789) 772217 E: ruth@heartparishes.org.uk

WALKER, Sharon Anne. b 60. Derby Univ BA 99. St Jo Coll Nottm. **d** 02 **p** 03. C Greetham and Thistleton w Stretton and Clipsham *Pet* 02–05; C Cottesmore and Barrow w Ashwell and Burley 02–05; P-in-c Pet St Mary Boongate 05–10; R Street w Walton and Compton Dundon *B & W* 10–19; P-in-c Compton Dundon 13–19; C W Cheltenham *Glouc* from 19. *111 Brooklyn Road, Cheltenham GL51 8DX* E: sharonannewalker@hotmail.com

WALKER, Mrs Sheila. b 45. Ex Univ MA 66 PGCE 66. SWMTC 12. **d** 14 **p** 15. NSM Whimple, Talaton, Clyst St Lawr and Clyst Hydon *Ex* 14–17; NSM Bradninch 14–17; NSM Rotherfield Peppard and Kidmore End etc *Ox* from 17. *2 Priory Copse, Peppard Common, Henley-on-Thames RG9 5LH* T: 0118-972 4861 E: swalk2@btinternet.com

WALKER, Stephen Michael Maynard. b 62. St Jo Coll Dur BA 84. Trin Coll Bris 86. **d** 88 **p** 89. C Eastwood *S'well* 88–92; CF 92–02; C Marple All SS *Ches* 02–06; P-in-c Tewkesbury H Trin *Glouc* 06–10; V from 10. *Holy Trinity Vicarage, 49 Barton Street, Tewkesbury GL20 5PU* T: (01684) 293233 E: vicar@trinitytewkesbury.org.uk

WALKER, Stephen Patrick. b 62. York Univ BSc 83 PGCE 84. St Jo Coll Nottm 87. **d** 90 **p** 91. C Hull St Jo Newland *York* 90–94; Min Grove Green LEP *Cant* 94–98; Children's Min Adv 96–98; TV Drypool *York* 98–99; TR 99–04; TR Binsey *Carl* 04–11; RD Derwent 10–11; P-in-c Theydon Bois and Theydon Garnon *Chelmsf* 11; V 11–16; R W Buckrose *York* from 16. *The Rectory, 2 Sudnicton Croft, Westow, York YO60 7NB* T: (01653) 619715 E: rectorwestbuckrose@icloud.com

WALKER, Susan Ann. b 57. All SS Cen for Miss & Min 16. **d** 18 **p** 19. NSM Prestwich St Marg *Man* from 18. *Bishopscourt, Bury New Road, Salford M7 4LE* E: sue256@gmail.com

WALKER, Mrs Susan Joy. b 52. Univ of Wales (Lamp) BA 73 Hull Univ MA 91. Qu Coll Birm 75. **dss** 83 **d** 87 **p** 94. Kidderminster St Mary and All SS, Trimpley etc *Worc* 83–86; Keyingham w Ottringham, Halsham and Sunk Is *York* 86–87; Hon Par Dn 87–94; Hon C 94–98; Chapl Hull Coll of FE 89–98;

Chapl N Lindsey Coll *Linc* 98–12; V Burstwick, Burton Pidsea etc *York* from 12; RD S Holderness from 19. *The Vicarage, Main Road, Thorngumbald, Hull HU12 9NA* T: (01964) 601381 E: susanwalkerfe@hotmail.co.uk

WALKER, Terry Edward. b 55. St Mellitus Coll 15. **d** 17 **p** 18. C W w E Mersea, Peldon, Gt and Lt Wigborough *Chelmsf* from 17. *26 Garden Farm, West Mersea, Colchester CO5 8ES* T: (01206) 383640 E: terryinmersea@live.co.uk

WALKER, Trevor John. b 51. Southn Univ BTh 80. Sarum & Wells Th Coll 75. **d** 78 **p** 79. C Standish *Blackb* 78–81; P-in-c N Somercotes *Linc* 81–82; P-in-c S Somercotes 81–82; V Somercotes 82–85; R Binbrook Gp 85–17; rtd 17. *1 Neville Turner Way, Waltham, Grimsby DN37 0YJ* E: priest1@compuserve.com

WALKER, Yaroslav Sky. b 92. St Pet Coll Ox BA 15. St Steph Ho Ox 17. **d** 19. C Ruislip St Martin *Lon* from 19. *5 Wyteleaf Close, Ruislip HA4 7SP* M: 07719-167101 E: fr.yswalker@gmail.com

WALKER-HILL, Richard John. b 51. WMMTC 06. **d** 09 **p** 10. C Oakengates and Wrockwardine Wood *Lich* 09–13; V Gravelly Hill *Birm* from 13; P-in-c Stockland Green from 13; AD Aston 18–19; Jt AD Aston and Sutton Coldfield from 19. *All Saints' Vicarage, Broomfield Road, Birmingham B23 7QA* T: 0121-373 0730 E: r.walkerhill@sky.com

WALKER-HUTCHINSON, Mrs Judith Anne. b 58. St Jo Coll Dur BA 07 CPFA 88. Cranmer Hall Dur 05. **d** 07 **p** 08. C Penhill *Ripon* 07–10; R Haddington *Edin* 10–11; rtd 11; PtO *Dur* from 11. *Westrill, Cotherstone, Barnard Castle DL12 9PF* T: (01833) 650396 M: 07977-507038 E: revjudith@outlook.com

WALKEY, Malcolm Gregory Taylor. b 44. Lon Univ. Kelham Th Coll 63. **d** 68 **p** 69. C Oadby *Leic* 68–72; TV Corby SS Pet and Andr w Gt and Lt Oakley 72–79; R Ashton w Hartwell 79–86; TR Halesworth w Linstead, Chediston, Holton etc *St E* 86–91; P-in-c Laxfield 93–01; rtd 01; PtO *St E* 02–18. *4 Church View, Holton, Halesworth IP19 8PB* T: (01986) 872594 E: walkeys4446@gmail.com

WALL, Miss Elizabeth Anne. b 51. Birm Univ BDS 73 St Andr Univ MLitt 17. WMMTC 97. **d** 00 **p** 01. NSM Lich St Chad 00–14; NSM Alrewas from 14; NSM Wychnor from 14. *15 Gaia Lane, Lichfield WS13 7LW* T: (01543) 254891 M: 07711-557770 E: ayton265@gmail.com

WALL, John Caswallen. b 60. York Univ BA 83 MA 85. St Steph Ho Ox BA 89. **d** 89 **p** 90. C Ifield *Chich* 89–94; C Brighton St Pet and St Nic w Chpl Royal 94–97; C Brighton St Pet w Chpl Royal 97–98; TV Newbury *Ox* 98–05; P-in-c Moulsecoomb *Chich* 05–16; P-in-c Uckfield from 16. *The Rectory, 1 Sand Ridge, Ridgewood, Uckfield TN22 5ET* T: (01825) 371688 E: jocaswall@hotmail.com

WALL, Canon Márcia Zélia. b 59. NOC 04. **d** 07 **p** 08. C Oakenrod and Bamford *Man* 07–10; V Rhodes and Parkfield 10–16; Borough Dean Rochdale 12–16; Bp's Adv for Women's Min 13–16; AD Heywood and Middleton 15–16; Can Res Man Cathl from 16. *Manchester Cathedral, Victoria Street, Manchester M3 1SX* M: 07823-332110 E: revdmarciawall@hotmail.co.uk

WALL, Matthew William. b 74. Westcott Ho Cam 12. **d** 14 **p** 15. C Stoke Newington St Mary *Lon* 14–17; TV Poplar from 17. *St Nicholas' Vicarage, 2N Dee Street, London E14 0PT* T: (020) 7515 8405 M: 07764-823266 E: rev.matt.wall@gmail.com

WALL, Nicholas John. b 46. Brasted Th Coll 69 Trin Coll Bris 71. **d** 73 **p** 74. C Morden *S'wark* 73–78; R Dunkeswell and Dunkeswell Abbey *Ex* 78–83; V Sheldon 78–83; P-in-c Upottery, Luppitt and Monkton 81–83; V Dunkeswell, Sheldon and Luppitt 83–03; V Dunkeswell, Luppitt, Sheldon and Upottery 03–11; rtd 11; CF(V) from 87. *The Glasshouse Flat, Old Sheldon Grange, Dunkeswell, Honiton EX14 4SE* M: 07811-105090

WALL, Richard David. b 78. Ch Ch Ox BA 99. St Steph Ho Ox 00. **d** 02 **p** 03. C Bocking St Mary *Chelmsf* 02–05; C Philadelphia St Clem USA 05–15; R Washington St Paul from 15. *St Paul's Parish, 2430 K Street NW, Washington DC 20037, USA* T: (001) (202) 337 2020 E: frrichardwall@yahoo.com *or* wall@stpauls-kst.com

WALL, Timothy. b 87. Van Mildert Coll Dur MMath 09 St Jo Coll Dur BA 14. Cranmer Hall Dur 12. **d** 15 **p** 16. C Peterlee *Dur* 15–18; P-in-c Hetton-Lyons w Eppleton from 18. *The Rectory, Houghton Road, Hetton-le-Hole, Houghton le Spring DH5 9PH* M: 07805-744253 E: revtwall@gmail.com

WALLACE, Preb Alastair Robert. b 52. St Cath Coll Cam BA 71 MA 75 Lon Univ BD 75. Trin Coll Bris 72. **d** 75 **p** 76. C Ex St Leon w H Trin 75–79; Chapl Ridley Hall Cam 79–86; R Bath St Mich w St Paul *B & W* 83–96; RD Bath 90–96; Sub-Dean Wells Cathl 96–99; TR Ilminster and Distr 99–10; V Ilminster and Whitelackington 10–12; Hon Asst Dioc Missr 96–12; Preb Wells Cathl 96–12;

rtd 12; PtO *B & W* from 15. *Houses Barton, Thurloxton, Taunton TA2 8RH* T: (01823) 412712 M: 07746-961191 E: alastair.wallace@btinternet.com

WALLACE, Mrs Brenda Claire. b 52. Linc Th Coll 73 S'wark Ord Course 78. **dss** 80 **d** 87 **p** 94. Sutton at Hone *Roch* 80–83; Borstal 83–89; Hon Par Dn 87–89; HM Pris Cookham Wood 83–89; Asst Chapl 87–89; NSM Stansted Mountfitchet *Chelmsf* 89–96; NSM Stansted Mountfitchet w Birchanger and Farnham 97; C Hutton 97–13; P-in-c Rettendon and Hullbridge 13–17; rtd 17; Hon C Rawreth *Chelmsf* from 17; Hon C Rettendon and Hullbridge from 17. *The Forge Nurseries, Church Road, Rawreth, Wickford SS11 8SH* E: brenda.wallace93@outlook.com

WALLACE, David Alexander Rippon. b 39. CEng MIET. Ox Min Course 94. **d** 96 **p** 97. NSM Haddenham w Cuddington, Kingsey etc *Ox* 96–97; NSM Worminghall w Ickford, Oakley and Shabbington 97–02; NSM Aylesbury Deanery 02–12; rtd 12; PtO *Ox* from 12. *11 Station Road, Haddenham, Aylesbury HP17 8AN* T/F: (01844) 290670 E: revd@wallaces.org

WALLACE, Mrs Edwina Margaret. b 49. EMMTC 00. **d** 03 **p** 04. C Broughton Astley and Croft w Stoney Stanton *Leic* 03–07; C Sutton Coldfield St Chad *Birm* 07–11; P-in-c V 11–14; rtd 14; PtO *Birm* from 14; *Leic* from 14. *The Hawthorns, Acresford Road, Donisthorpe, Swadlincote DE12 7PT* T: (01530) 274002 M: 07766-714261 E: edwinawallace41@gmail.com

WALLACE, Godfrey Everingham. See EVERINGHAM, Georgina Wendy

WALLACE, Ian Malcolm. b 57. Southn Univ LLB 78 Solicitor 79. STETS 06. **d** 09 **p** 10. C Wisley w Pyrford *Guildf* 09–13; P-in-c Yate New Town *Bris* 13–14; TR Yate from 14. *The Rectory, 97 Canterbury Close, Yate, Bristol BS37 5TU* T: (01454) 311483 M: 07799-076697 E: rector@yateparish.org.uk

WALLACE, James Marchant. **d** 11 **p** 12. C Waterford w Killea, Drumcannon and Dunhill *C & O* 11–17. *Address temp unknown* M: (00353) 87-272 1789 E: wallace1.jim@gmail.com

WALLACE, Julie Michele. See BARRELL, Julie Michele

WALLACE, Mark David. b 76. Worc Coll Ox BA 98 MA 01. Oak Hill Th Coll 05. **d** 08 **p** 09. C Trull w Angersleigh *B & W* 08–12; P-in-c Colchester St Pet and St Botolph *Chelmsf* from 12. *St Peter's Vicarage, Balkerne Close, Colchester CO1 1NZ* T: (01206) 572641 M: 07772-615378 E: towncentrevicar@gmail.com

WALLACE, Mark George. b 72. Qu Coll Cam BA 94. Oak Hill Th Coll BA 08. **d** 08 **p** 09. C Guildf Ch Ch w St Martha-on-the-Hill 08–12; V Lightwater 12–17; AD Surrey Heath 16–17; V Woking St Mary from 17. *St Mary's Vicarage, West Hill Road, Woking GU22 7UJ* E: vicar@stmaryofbethany.org.uk

⊕**WALLACE, The Rt Revd Martin William.** b 48. K Coll Lon BD 70 AKC 70. St Aug Coll Cant 70. **d** 71 **p** 72 **c** 03. C Attercliffe *Sheff* 71–74; C New Malden and Coombe *S'wark* 74–77; V Forest Gate St Mark *Chelmsf* 77–93; RD Newham 82–91; P-in-c Forest Gate Em w Upton Cross 85–89; Hon Can Chelmsf Cathl 89–03; P-in-c Forest Gate All SS 91–93; Dioc ACUPA Link Officer 91–97; P-in-c Bradwell on Sea 93–97; P-in-c St Lawrence 93–97; Ind Chapl Maldon and Dengie Deanery 93–97; Adn Colchester 97–03; Bp's Adv for Hosp Chapl 97–03; Suff Bp Selby *York* 03–13; rtd 13; Hon Asst Bp York from 13. *28 Alexandra Court, Bridlington YO15 2LB* T: (01262) 670265 E: mdw28@btinternet.com

WALLACE, Matt. b 75. Liv Univ BA 96. Trin Coll Bris BA 11. **d** 11 **p** 12. C Chase Terrace *Lich* 11–15; TV Burntwood, Chase Terrace etc from 15. *3 Chapel Street, Chase Terrace WS7 1NL* M: 07855-960179 E: matt.wallace@o2.co.uk

WALLACE (*née* ALEXANDER), Mrs Nancy Joan.** b 42. Roehampton Inst TCert 64 Ox Brookes Univ BA 97 PQCSW 97. SAOMC 95. **d** 98 **p** 99. NSM Worminghall w Ickford, Oakley and Shabbington *Ox* 98–02; NSM Aylesbury Deanery 02–12; rtd 12; PtO *Ox* from 12. *11 Station Road, Haddenham, Aylesbury HP17 8AN* T/F: (01844) 290670 E: revn@wallaces.org

WALLACE, Nicholas Robert. b 56. Trin Coll Bris 93. **d** 95 **p** 96. C Fishponds St Jo *Bris* 95–98; P-in-c Barton Hill St Luke w Ch Ch 98–99; P-in-c Barton Hill St Luke w Ch Ch and Moorfields 99–00; R Binstead *Portsm* 00–10; V Havenstreet St Pet 00–10; P Adelaide St Mary Australia 10–13; V Sorrento w Rye from 13. *The Vicarage, 3473 Point Nepean Road, Sorrento Vic 3943, Australia* E: nrwallace@hotmail.com

WALLACE, Robert. b 52. Sussex Univ BSc 73. Linc Th Coll 73. **d** 76 **p** 77. C Plaistow St Mary *Roch* 76–79; C Dartford H Trin 79–83; V Borstal 83–89; Chapl The Foord Almshouses 83–89; Chapl HM Pris Cookham Wood 83–89; P-in-c Farnham *Chelmsf* 89–96; V Stansted Mountfitchet 89–96; R Stansted Mountfitchet w Birchanger and Farnham 97; R Hutton 97–15; rtd 15; PtO *Roch* from 16. *30 Bromley College, London*

Road, Bromley BR1 1PE T: (020) 8001 1055 M: 07950-613932 E: fatherbobwallace@hotmail.com

WALLACE, Susan Marilyn. b 67. Ch Ch Coll Cant BA(Ed) 90 Leeds Univ MA 06 Sheff Univ MA 15. NOC 03. d 06 p 07. NSM Acomb St Steph and St Aid *York* 06–10; NSM York St Mich-le-Belfrey 10; TV Leeds City *Ripon* 10–13; Can Res, Prec and Sacr Win Cathl 14–18; Liturg Dir and Creative Worship Consultant Transcendence Trust from 19; PtO *Win* from 19; *Sarum* from 19. *111 London Road, Salisbury SP1 3HA* M: 07962-071621 E: sue@transcendence.org.uk

WALLACE-JONES, Sally. b 66. Man Univ BA 87 PhD 91 Lucy Cavendish Coll Cam BTh 17. Ridley Hall Cam 15. d 17 p 18. C High Oak, Hingham and Scoulton w Wood Rising *Nor* from 17. *17 Bell Meadow, Hingham, Norwich NR9 4HT* T: (01953) 853165 E: revsamwj@gmail.com

WALLBANK, Alison Patricia. b 59. d 09 p 10. OLM Whitworth w Facit *Man* 09–14; NSM Norden w Ashworth and Bamford 13–14; NSM Eggleston *Dur* from 14; NSM Middleton-in-Teesdale w Forest and Frith from 14; NSM Lower Teesdale *Leeds* from 14. *1 Greta Place, Wesley Terrace, Middleton-in-Teesdale, Barnard Castle DL12 0SW* M: 07800-955791 E: alisonwallbank59@gmail.com

WALLER, Allen Ranson. b 82. James Madison Univ USA BA 05. Wycliffe Hall Ox BTh 16. d 16 p 17. C Oxton *Ches* 16–19; R Raleigh St Tim USA from 19. *116 East Wind Lane, Cary NC 27518, USA*

WALLER, Annalu. b 63. Cape Town Univ BSc 83 MSc 88 Dundee Univ PhD 92. TISEC 01. d 04 p 05. Hon C Dundee St Marg *Bre* 04–13; Hon C Dundee St Martin 10–13; Hon Chapl Dundee Univ from 07. *9 Invergowrie Drive, Dundee DD2 1RD* T: (01382) 644570 *or* 388223 E: awaller@dundee.ac.uk

WALLER, Canon David James. b 58. Whitelands Coll Lon BA 85 K Coll Lon MA 95. Ripon Coll Cuddesdon 85. d 88 p 89. C Tettenhall Regis *Lich* 88–91; Chapl Greenwich Univ *S'wark* 92–97; P-in-c Yiewsley *Lon* 97–01; TR Plymstock and Hooe *Ex* 01–12; Chapl Palma de Mallorca *Eur* from 12; Hon Can from 19. *Calle Nuñez de Balboa 6, 07014 Son Armadans, Palma de Mallorca, Spain* T: (0034) 971 737 279 *or* 600 400 600 E: davidwaller2000@btinternet.com *or* chaplain@anglican-mallorca.org

WALLER, Canon Derek James Keith. b 54. Em Coll Cam BA 75 PGCE 76. Trin Coll Bris 88. d 91 p 92. C Church Stretton *Heref* 91–95; R Appleby Gp *Leic* 95–04; P-in-c Rushden St Pet *Pet* 04–07; V 08–14; RD Higham 11–14; Can Pet Cathl 13–14; CMS S Sudan from 14. *Church Mission Society, Watlington Road, Cowley, Oxford OX4 6BZ*

WALLER, Mrs Elizabeth Alison. b 49. Open Univ BA 89 Univ of Cen England in Birm MA 99 Wolfs Coll Cam PGCE 91. EAMTC 02. d 05 p 06. NSM Oundle w Ashton and Benefield w Glapthorn *Pet* 05–08; NSM Aldwincle, Clopton, Pilton, Stoke Doyle etc from 08. *Priory Cottage, 40 Church Street, Stilton, Peterborough PE7 3RF* T: (01733) 242412 E: eawaller@btinternet.com

WALLER, Gordon Robert. b 50. Jes Coll Cam BA 72 MA 75. d 03 p 05. OLM Tooting St SS *S'wark* from 03. *131 Ribblesdale Road, London SW16 6SP* T: (020) 8769 6733 E: gordon.waller2012@yahoo.co.uk

WALLER, John. b 60. Man Univ BA 84 Liv Univ MA 07. St Jo Coll Nottm 85. d 87 p 88. C Chorlton-cum-Hardy St Clem *Man* 87–90; R Openshaw 90–95; Chapl Ancoats Hosp Man 93–95; TV Watling Valley *Ox* 95–96; TR 96–03; R Brickhills and Stoke Hammond from 03; AD Mursley 06–11. *The Rectory, 10 Pound Hill, Great Brickhill, Milton Keynes MK17 9AS* T: (01525) 261062 E: rector@brickhillschurches.org.uk

WALLER, Maxine Dawn. b 62. St Hild Coll 17. d 19. NSM Bridlington Priory *York* from 19. *15 Queen Street, Bridlington YO15 2SF* M: 07737-816894 E: maxinewaller@hotmail.co.uk

WALLER, Philip Thomas. b 56. Ex Coll Ox BA 78 MA 88 St Jo Coll Dur BA 87. Cranmer Hall Dur 85. d 88 p 89. C Enfield St Andr *Lon* 88–91; C Belper Derby 91–95; P-in-c Oakwood 95–05; P-in-c Long Eaton St Jo 05–10; V 10–15; Asst Dir of Ords 09–15; TV Welwyn *St Alb* from 15; Asst Dir of Ords from 15. *The Vicarage, 4 Bury Lane, Codicote, Hitchin SG4 8XT* T: (01438) 504318 E: vicar@stgiles-church.org.uk

WALLER, William John. b 38. Bps' Coll Cheshunt 66. d 68 p 69. C Luton Lewsey St Hugh *St Alb* 68–73; C Oxhey All SS 73–75; C Henllys w Bettws *Mon* 75–77. *Bell House with Brodawel, Church Road, Llandegfedd Village, Newport NP18 1HX*

WALLEY, Mark Nathan. b 83. Ox Brookes Univ BA 06. Oak Hill Th Coll 17. d 19. C Linthorpe *York* from 19. *45 Lothian Road, Middlesbrough TS4 2HS* M: 07752-050746 E: markwalley@gmail.com

WALLEY, Canon Peter Francis. b 60. Bris Univ BSc 82 CEng 89 MICE 89. Trin Coll Bris 96. d 98 p 99. C Ex St Jas 98–01; Asst Chapl Brussels *Eur* 01–05; Bp's Dom Chapl *Lich* 05–12; P-in-c Mickleover All SS *Derby* 12–14; P-in-c Mickleover St Jo 12–14; V Mickleover from 14; RD Derby S 15–16; Hon Can Derby Cathl from 17. *All Saints' Vicarage, Etwall Road, Mickleover, Derby DE3 0DL* T: (01332) 513793 E: peterwalley@btinternet.com

WALLINGTON, Martin John. b 59. SAOMC 95. d 98 p 99. NSM Chorleywood St Andr *St Alb* 98–03; P-in-c Wooburn *Ox* 03–08; V from 08. *Wooburn Vicarage, Windsor Hill, Wooburn Green, High Wycombe HP10 0EH* T: (01628) 521209

WALLINGTON, Paul. b 62. Birm Univ BCom 83 ACA 86. Trin Coll Bris BA 94. d 94 p 95. C Chorley St Laur *Blackb* 94–97; C Darwen St Pet w Hoddlesden 97–98; TV 98–00; rtd 00; PtO *Man* from 13; Chapl Canon Slade Sch Bolton 08–16; Chapl St Swithun's Sch Win from 16. *St Swithun's School, Alresford Road, Winchester SO21 1HA* T: (01962) 835700 E: thewallingtons@hotmail.com *or* wallingtonp@stswithuns.com

WALLIS, Anna Louise. b 73. Leic Univ BSc 95 PhD 99 Selw Coll Cam BA 05 MA 09. Westcott Ho Cam 03. d 06 p 07. C Huddersfield St Pet *Wakef* 06–09; Chapl Sheff Teaching Hosps NHS Foundn Trust 09–11; PtO *Sheff* 11–12; NSM Huddersfield St Pet *Leeds* 12–17. *Address withheld by request* E: anna.wallis121@gmail.com

WALLIS, Benjamin John. b 55. Wimbledon Sch of Art BA 79. Chich Th Coll 92. d 94 p 95. C Battersea Ch Ch and St Steph *S'wark* 94–98; C Wood Green St Mich w Bounds Green St Gabr etc *Lon* 98–03; V Barkingside St Geo *Chelmsf* from 03. *St George's Vicarage, Woodford Avenue, Ilford IG2 6XQ* T: (020) 8550 4149 E: pam@herdom.com

WALLIS, David Peter. b 72. Ripon Coll Cuddesdon BTh 03. d 03 p 04. C Eastbourne St Mary *Chich* 03–07; P-in-c Ditchling, Streat and Westmeston 07–08; R from 08. *St Margaret's Vicarage, 2 Charlton Gardens, Lewes Road, Ditchling, Hassocks BN6 8WA* T: (01273) 843165 E: revdavidwallis@yahoo.co.uk

WALLIS, Ian George. b 57. Sheff Univ BA 79 PhD 92 St Edm Ho Cam MLitt 87. Ridley Hall Cam 88. d 90 p 91. C Armthorpe *Sheff* 90–92; Chapl and Fell SS Coll Cam 92–95; Hon C Chesterton Gd Shep *Ely* 93–95; R Houghton le Spring *Dur* 95–07; AD Houghton 04–07; Tutor Aston Tr Scheme 93–97; Prin NOC 07–08; V Sheff St Mark Broomhill 09–14; rtd 14; PtO *Sheff* from 14; *Leeds* from 17. *1 Sike Close, Holmfirth HD9 1JD* M: 07717-417760 E: ian.wallis@sero.co.uk

WALLIS, John Anthony. b 36. St Pet Coll Ox BA 60 MA 65. Clifton Th Coll 60. d 62 p 63. C Blackpool St Mark *Blackb* 62–65; C Leeds St Geo *Ripon* 65–69; Korea 69–74; Nat Sec (Scotland) OMF 75–78; Home Dir OMF 78–89; Hon C Sevenoaks St Nic *Roch* 78–89; Chapl The Hague *Eur* 89–95; V Northwood Em *Lon* 95–01; rtd 01; PtO *Nor* from 03; *Ely* from 13. *Church Cottage, 61 Gayton Road, Grimston, King's Lynn PE32 1BG* T: (01485) 600336 E: johna.wallis@btinternet.com

WALLIS, Raymond Christopher. b 38. Moor Park Coll Farnham 62 Sarum Th Coll 63. d 66 p 67. C Allerton *Bradf* 66–68; C Langley Marish *Ox* 68–69; C Caister *Nor* 69–73; P-in-c E w W Bradenham 73–80; R Upwell St Pet and Outwell *Ely* 80–84; V Bishopstone *Chich* 84–97; rtd 97; PtO *Chich* from 97. *Lanthorn, Park Lane, Bexhill-on-Sea TN39 4DS* E: wallis.raymond@yahoo.co.uk

WALLIS, Richard David. b 69. Herts Univ BA 96. SWMTC 15. d 18 p 19. C Chacewater w St Day and Carharrack *Truro* from 18; C Devoran from 18; C Feock from 18; C St Stythians w Perranarworthal and Gwennap from 18. *13 Kingston Way, Mabe Burnthouse, Penryn TR10 9FD* M: 07484-616499 E: rwallis1969@gmail.com

WALLMAN-GIRDLESTONE, Jane Elizabeth. b 61. Homerton Coll Cam BEd 83. St Steph Ho Ox 89 Sarum & Wells Th Coll BTh 92. d 93 p 94. C Woodbridge St Mary *St E* 93–96; V Ipswich St Thos 96–00; Dir Past Studies and Adv for Women's Min St Mich Coll Llandaff 00–02; Lect TISEC 03–07; Lect Qu Foundn Birm 04–05; LtO *Mor* from 06. *St Columba House, The Clattach, Alturlie Point, Allanfearn, Inverness IV2 7HZ* T: (01463) 230708 M: 07776-181824 E: janewallman@hotmail.co.uk *or* janewallmangirdlestone@gmail.com

WALLS, Michael Peter. b 38. Cape Town Univ BA 57. Wells Th Coll 59. d 61 p 62. C Morecambe St Barn *Blackb* 61–64; C Birm St Paul 64–66; Ind Chapl 64–74; V Temple Balsall 66–74; Chapl Wroxall Abbey Sch 72–74; V Kings Heath *Birm* 74–76; Hon C Bordesley St Benedict 76–78; Sen Chapl Oakham Sch 78–83; P-in-c Leic St Sav 83–85; P-in-c Knossington and Cold Overton 85–87; P-in-c Owston and Withcote 85–87; V Tilton w Lowesby 85–87; P-in-c 87; V Whatborough Gp 87–90; Bp's

Adv on Relns w People of Other Faiths 89–93; Hon Can Leic Cathl 89–95; V Leic St Mary 90–93; rtd 93; PtO *Ban* 02–17. *4 Partridge Way, Oakham LE15 6BX* E: brompton01@gmail.com

WALMSLEY, Canon Derek. b 57. Oak Hill Th Coll 89. **d** 91 **p** 92. C Bletchley *Ox* 91–95; C Utley *Bradf* 95–00; V 00–15; P-in-c Keighley St Andr 14–15; Hon Can Bradf Cathl 13–15; Dir of Ords *Leeds* from 15; Can Res Wakef Cathl from 15. *14 Belgravia Road, Wakefield WF1 3JP* T: (01924) 314284 *or* 371802 M: 07743-338690 E: dwalmsley9@aol.com *or* derek.walmsley@leeds.anglican.org

WALPOLE, Neil Derek. b 63. St Hild Coll 17. **d** 18 **p** 19. C Dewsbury *Leeds* from 18. *St John's Vicarage, 68 Staincliffe Road, Dewsbury WF13 4ED* T: (01924) 451247 M: 07419-334234

WALROND-SKINNER, Susan Mary. *See* PARFITT, Susan Mary

WALSALL, Archdeacon of. *Vacant*

WALSER (née SHIELS), Mrs Rosalinde Cameron. b 47. Edin Univ MA 68 Moray Ho Coll of Educn PGCE 69. NOC 92. **d** 95 **p** 97. NSM Scarborough St Mary w Ch Ch and H Apostles *York* 95–97; Chapl St Cath Hospice Scarborough 95–97; Chapl Scarborough Coll 95–97; P-in-c E Ayton *York* 97–06; rtd 06; PtO *York* from 07. *29 Sea Cliff Road, Scarborough YO11 2XU* T: (01723) 372382

WALSH, Mrs Alexandra Mary (Gussie). b 50. Wycliffe Hall Ox 06. **d** 08 **p** 09. C Penrith w Newton Reigny and Plumpton Wall *Carl* 08–12; C Buckingham *Ox* 12–18; rtd 18; PtO *Guildf* from 19. *Farm View, Upper House Lane, Shamley Green, Guildford GU5 0SX* E: gussiewalsh@hotmail.com

WALSH, Carys Ruth. b 62. Ex Univ BA 83 MPhil 89 Heythrop Coll Lon MA 00 PhD 11 Win Univ MA 15. STETS 10. **d** 13 **p** 14. Selection Sec Min Division Abps' Coun 07–14; C Chelsea St Luke and Ch Ch *Lon* 13–16; Tutor St Mellitus Coll 15–18; PtO *Chelmsf* from 16; *Pet* 16–17; C Kettering SS Pet and Paul from 17; C Tr Officer from 18. *Bouverie Court, 6 The Lakes, Bedford Road, Northampton NN4 7YD* T: (01604) 887054 M: 07707-556761 E: carys.walsh@peterborough-diocese.org.uk

WALSH, David Christopher. b 59. Warwick Univ BA 81. St Jo Coll Nottm BA 83 Ripon Coll Cuddesdon 00. **d** 02 **p** 03. C Greenwich St Alfege *S'wark* 02–06; C Kensington St Mary Abbots w Ch Ch and St Phil *Lon* 06–16; AD Kensington 11–16; R Kettering SS Pet and Paul from 16. *The Rectory, Church Walk, Kettering NN16 0DJ* T: (01536) 513385 M: 07957-656643 E: rector@peterandpaul.org.uk

✠**WALSH, The Rt Revd Geoffrey David Jeremy.** b 29. Pemb Coll Cam BA 53 MA 58. Linc Th Coll 53. **d** 55 **p** 56 **c** 86. C Southgate Ch Ch *Lon* 55–58; SCM Sec Cam 58–61; C Cambridge Gt St Mary w St Mich *Ely* 58–61; V Moorfields *Bris* 61–66; R Marlborough *Sarum* 66–76; Can and Preb Sarum Cathl 73–76; Adn Ipswich *St E* 76–86; R Elmsett w Aldham 76–80; Suff Bp Tewkesbury *Glouc* 86–95; rtd 95; PtO *St E* from 95; Hon Asst Bp St E from 08. *6 Warren Lane, Martlesham Heath, Ipswich IP5 3SH* T: (01473) 620797 E: jandcwalsh61@gmail.com

WALSH, Geoffrey Malcolm. b 46. Sarum & Wells Th Coll 82. **d** 84 **p** 85. C Wellington and Distr *B & W* 84–87; TV Axminster, Chardstock, Combe Pyne and Rousdon *Ex* 87–90; Chapl RN 90–94; R Huntspill *B & W* 94–11; rtd 11; PtO *Sarum* 12–17; C Axminster, Chardstock, All Saints etc *Ex* 14–18. *Thimbles, 70 Flax Meadow Lane, Axminster EX13 5FJ* T: (01297) 598361 E: geoffreywalsh@talktalk.net

WALSH, Gussie. *See* WALSH, Alexandra Mary

WALSH, Canon Neil-Allan. b 72. Cant Ch Ch Univ BA 03 Cape Town Univ DipEd 97. Westcott Ho Cam 06. **d** 08 **p** 09. C Lt Ilford St Mich *Chelmsf* 08–11; P-in-c Leytonstone St Marg w St Columba from 11; P-in-c Leytonstone H Trin and St Aug Harrow Green from 14; Black and Minority Ethnic Adv to Bp Barking from 14; Hon Can Cape Town from 16. *St Margaret's Vicarage, 15 Woodhouse Road, London E11 3NG* T: (020) 8519 0813 M: 07903-652874 E: neilallanwalsh@yahoo.com

WALSH, Nicholas Sean. b 83. Moorlands Coll BA 07 K Coll Lon MA 13. St Mellitus Coll 11. **d** 13 **p** 14. C Luton Lewsey St Hugh *St Alb* 13–17; TV Catford (Southend) and Downham *S'wark* from 17. *233 Bellingham Road, London SE6 1EH* M: 07774-516204 E: nswalsh@gmail.com

WALSH, Peter. b 64. Liv Univ BA 86 Nottm Univ BTh 90. Linc Th Coll 87. **d** 90 **p** 91. C Cantley *Sheff* 90–93; C Poulton-le-Fylde *Blackb* 93–95; V Blackpool St Steph 95–03; TR Ches 03–05; V Ches St Oswald and St Thos 05–11; Min Can Ches Cathl 04–05; V W Kirby St Andr 11–19; Minl Development Review Officer 11–14; rtd 19. *6 Coronation Road, Kirkham, Preston PR4 2HE* E: revpeterwalsh@btconnect.com

WALSH, Sarah Elaine. b 60. LLCM(TD) 90 CTABRSM 95. NEOC 04. **d** 07 **p** 10. NSM Waggoners *York* 07–08; NSM Crookes St Tim *Sheff* 09–11; NSM Walkley 11–12; Chapl HM Pris Nottm 12–13; Chapl HM Pris Stocken 12–13; Chapl

HM Pris Lindholme 13–19; Chapl HM Pris Moorland 13–19; NSM Doncaster St Geo *Sheff* 18–19; R Dickleburgh and The Pulhams *Nor* from 19. *The Rectory, Station Road, Pulham Market, Diss IP21 4TE* E: sarahwalsh967@btinternet.com

WALSHAW, Mrs Caroline Elaine. b 59. St Jo Coll Dur BA 81 Goldsmiths' Coll Lon PGCE 82. SEITE 13. **d** 15 **p** 16. NSM Pembury *Roch* from 15. *40 Ridgeway, Pembury, Tunbridge Wells TN2 4ES* T: (01892) 278675 M: 07810-633389 E: canrwalshaw@outlook.com

WALSHE, Marie Sylvia. b 54. RGN RCNT. **d** 99 **p** 00. NSM Kilkeel *D & D* 99–00; NSM Down H Trin w Hollymount 00–08; NSM Rathmullan w Tyrella 00–08; NSM Newcastle 08–13; NSM Gilnahirk from 13. *8 Castle View, Dundrum, Newcastle BT33 0SA* T: (028) 4377 1757 E: walshemarie@hotmail.com

WALT, Canon Trevor William. b 52. RMN 74 RNT 79. Ox NSM Course 83. **d** 86 **p** 87. NSM Crowthorne *Ox* 86–89; Chapl Asst Broadmoor Hosp Crowthorne 86–89; Chapl 89–10; Hon Can Ch Ch *Ox* 00–07; Bp's Adv for Healing and Deliverance Min *Chelmsf* 11–17; Chapl St Helena Hospice Colchester 13–17; rtd 17; PtO *Chelmsf* from 10. *Address withheld by request*

WALTER, Donald Alex. b 34. Ripon Hall Ox 57. **d** 60 **p** 61. C Ealing St Steph Castle Hill *Lon* 60–63; Jamaica 63–80; V Twickenham Common H Trin *Lon* 81–00; rtd 00; PtO *Lon* from 03. *Ebenezer, 23 Hawley Close, Hampton TW12 3XX* T: (020) 8941 5193 E: alexwalter@maperche.co.uk

WALTER, Giles Robert. b 54. Cam Univ MA 76. Cranmer Hall Dur 78. **d** 82 **p** 83. C Finchley Ch Ch *Lon* 82–86; C Cambridge H Sepulchre w All SS *Ely* 86–92; C Cambridge H Sepulchre 92–93; P-in-c Tunbridge Wells St Jo *Roch* 93–95; V 95–19; rtd 19. *36 Belvoir Road, Cambridge CB4 1JJ*

WALTER, Ian Edward. b 47. Edin Univ MA 69 Keble Coll Ox BA 71 MA 78. Cuddesdon Coll 71. **d** 73 **p** 74. C Greenock *Glas* 73–76; C Glas St Mary and Chapl Angl Students Glas 76–79; R Paisley St Barn 79–84; P-in-c Bolton St Phil *Man* 84–86; V 86–91; Dioc Ecum Officer 88–94; V Elton All SS 91–98; V Stalybridge 98–01; R Hawick *Edin* 01–08; rtd 08; Hon C Oban St Jo *Arg* from 08. *Balaclava, 56 Dalriach Road, Oban PA34 5JE* T: (01631) 564855 E: ian_walter@btinternet.com

WALTER, Noël. b 41. St D Coll Lamp. **d** 66 **p** 67. C Mitcham Ascension *S'wark* 66–71; C Caterham 71–74; OCM 71–74; V Welling *S'wark* 74–82; C Warlingham w Chelsham and Farleigh 82–88; Chapl Warlingham Park Hosp Croydon 82–88; Chapl R Earlswood Hosp Redhill 88–90; Chapl Redhill Gen Hosp 88–91; Chapl E Surrey Hosp Redhill 88–96; Sen Chapl Gt Ormond Street Hosp for Children NHS Trust 96–06; rtd 06; PtO *Ex* 98–07; C Chagford, S Tawton, Drewsteignton etc 07–12; PtO from 13. *Whiddon View, 13 Bretteville Close, Chagford, Newton Abbot TQ13 8DW* T: (01647) 432610 E: panda.walter@icloud.com

WALTER, Robin. b 37. Univ Coll Dur BA 63 MA 90 Linacre Coll Ox BA 65 MA 69. St Steph Ho Ox 63 Pontigny Seminary 65. **d** 66 **p** 68. C Peckham St Jo *S'wark* 66–69; Chapl Lon Univ 69–70; C Dur St Marg 70–74; R Burnmoor 74–79; Asst Master Barnard Castle Sch 79–97; NSM Barnard Castle Deanery 80–82 and 88–97; Hon C Whorlton *Dur* 82–83; Hon C Barnard Castle w Whorlton 83–88; P-in-c Redmarshall 97–01; R 01–03; P-in-c Bishopton w Gt Stainton 97–01; V 01–03; rtd 03; PtO *York* from 03; *Worc* from 04. *The Laurels, Worcester Road, Great Witley, Worcester WR6 6HR* T: (01299) 890190 E: rfw@myric.net

WALTERS, Christopher Rowland. b 47. Open Univ BA 78 Univ of Wales PGCE 94 MEd 95 Texas Wesleyan Univ PhD 02. **d** 02 **p** 10. Hd Master Mayflower Chr Sch Pontypool 90–05; OLM Abergavenny H Trin *Mon* 02–12; P-in-c Govilon w Llanfoist w Llanelen from 12; PtO *S & B* from 14. *The Rectory, Merthyr Road, Govilon, Abergavenny NP7 9PT* T: (01873) 831048 M: 07967-945320 E: church@chriswalters.co.uk

WALTERS, Daniel Geoffrey Thomas. b 81. K Coll Cam BA 02 MA 06. Coll of Resurr Mirfield BA 15. **d** 16 **p** 17. C High Crompton and Thornham *Man* 16–19; C Ox St Giles and SS Phil and Jas w St Marg from 19. *19A St Margaret's Road, Oxford OX2 6RX* M: 07469-738948 E: dgtwalters@outlook.com

WALTERS, David Allan. b 48. Southn Univ MA 87 Bath Univ MEd 95. **d** 09 **p** 10. OLM Wylye and Till Valley *Sarum* 09–12; NSM Lower Wylye and Till Valley 12–14; NSM Salisbury Plain 14–18; rtd 18; PtO *Sarum* from 18. *Hillside, Chapel Lane, Shrewton, Salisbury SP3 4BX* T: (01980) 620038 E: david.a.walters@hotmail.com

WALTERS, David Trevor. b 37. Ex Coll Ox BA 58 MA 62. St Steph Ho Ox 62. **d** 64 **p** 65. C Cardiff St Mary *Llan* 64–69; C Brecon w Battle *S & B* 69–73; Min Can Brecon Cathl 69–73; V Llanddew and Talachddu 73–78; V Cefncoed and Capel Nantddu 78–80; V Cefn Coed and Capel Nantddu w Vaynor etc 80–87; V Talgarth and Llanelieu 87–04; rtd 04. *16 Dan-y-Bryn, Glasbury, Hereford HR3 5NH* T: (01497) 842966

WALTERS, Mrs Felicity Ann. b 56. WEMTC. d 01 p 02. C Glouc St Geo w Whaddon 01–05; C Matson 05–06; P-in-c Huntley and Longhope, Churcham and Bulley 06–11; P-in-c Hadfield *Derby* 11–14; V from 14; V Charlesworth and Gamesley from 14. *St Andrew's Vicarage, 122 Hadfield Road, Hadfield, Glossop SK13 2DR* T: (01457) 852431 E: walters@revfelicity.plus.com

WALTERS, Ian Robert. b 51. ACA 74 FCA 81. d 85 p 86. OLM Ingoldsby *Linc* 85–92; NSM Grantham St Anne New Somerby and Spitalgate 92–94; NSM Ingoldsby 94–06; NSM Ropsley 94–06; NSM Old Somerby 94–06; NSM Sapperton w Braceby 94–06; P-in-c Gosberton, Gosberton Clough and Quadring 06–15; V from 15. *The Vicarage, 6 Wargate Way, Gosberton, Spalding PE11 4NH* T/F: (01775) 840694 M: 07831-645683 E: vicar@gosberton.org

WALTERS, Ivan. *See* WALTERS, William Ivan

WALTERS, Canon James Arthur. b 78. Selw Coll Cam BA 00 PhD 07. Westcott Ho Cam 03. d 07 p 08. C Hampstead St Jo *Lon* 07–10; Chapl LSE from 10; NSM Bloomsbury St Geo w Woburn Square Ch Ch from 11; Can and Preb Chich Cathl from 16. *London School of Economics, Houghton Street, London WC2A 2AE* T: (020) 7955 7965 E: j.walters2@lse.ac.uk

WALTERS, Canon John Philip Hewitt. b 50. Bp Burgess Hall Lamp 69 Coll of Resurr Mirfield 72. d 73 p 74. C Llangiwg *S & B* 73–76; Min Can Brecon Cathl 76–79; C Brecon w Battle 76–79; V Merthyr Cynog and Dyffryn Honddu etc 79–83; V Llandeilo Tal-y-bont 83–15; Hon Can Brecon Cathl 12–15; PtO *St D* 14–15; rtd 15; PtO *S & B* from 15. *12 Coles Close, Swansea SA1 2GD* T: (01792) 455026 E: jphwalters12@gmail.com

WALTERS, Canon Michael William. b 39. Dur Univ BSc 61. Clifton Th Coll 61. d 63 p 64. C Aldershot H Trin *Guildf* 63–66; C Upper Armley *Ripon* 66–69; NE Area Sec CPAS 69–75; V Hyde St Geo *Ches* 75–82; V Knutsford St Jo and Toft 82–97; P-in-c Congleton St Pet 97–98; TR Congleton 98–05; rtd 05; Hon Can Ches Cathl 94–13; Hon C Davenham 05–13; PtO from 13. *27 Alvanley Rise, Northwich CW9 8AY* T: (01606) 333126 E: michael@alvanleyrise.co.uk

WALTERS, Nicholas Humphrey. b 45. K Coll Lon BD 67 AKC 67. d 68 p 69. C Weston *Guildf* 68–71; Chapl and Lect NE Surrey Coll of Tech Ewell 71–77; Hon C Ewell *Guildf* 71–77; Warden Moor Park Coll Farnham 77–80; Tutor Surrey Univ *Guildf* from 80; Dir of Studies Guildf Inst from 82; Public Preacher *Guildf* 84–15. *9 Valley View, Godalming GU7 1RD* T: (01483) 415106 or 562142

WALTERS, Nicholas Rhys. b 88. St Steph Ho Ox 14. d 17 p 18. C Primrose Hill St Mary w Avenue Road St Paul *Lon* from 17. *2 St John's Hall, St John's Wood High Street, London NW8 7NE* M: 07704-715367 E: nickrwalters@gmail.com

WALTERS, Mrs Sheila Ann Beatrice. b 37. Bris Univ DipEd 58. EMMTC 85. d 89 p 94. NSM Ashby-de-la-Zouch St Helen w Coleorton *Leic* 89–98; PtO 99–02; NSM Packington w Normanton-le-Heath 02–05; rtd 05; PtO *Sheff* from 06. *8 Kensington Park, Sheffield S10 4NJ* T: 0114-229 5497

WALTERS, William Ivan. b 49. CBDTI 04. d 07 p 08. NSM Lea *Blackb* 07–14; rtd 14; PtO *Blackb* from 14. *9 Thornpark Drive, Lea, Preston PR2 1RE* T: (01772) 732573 E: ivanwalters@btinternet.com

WALTNER, Moise (Mike). b 75. ERMC 13. d 15 p 16. C Vienna *Eur* from 15. *Address temp unknown* E: rmwccv@gmail.com

WALTON, Mrs Alison Claire. b 59. Homerton Coll Cam BEd 82. Lon Bible Coll Oak Hill Th Coll BA 90 MPhil 92. d 92 p 98. C Bedford Ch Ch *St Alb* 92–94; PtO 94–95; *S'well* 95–98; NSM Lenton Abbey 98–99; Assoc Lect St Jo Coll Nottm 97–99; C Thorley *St Alb* 00–03; V Croxley Green St Oswald 03–07; Dir Ch Study and Practice Ridley Hall Cam 07–16; Public Preacher *Ely* 07–16; V Isleworth All SS *Lon* from 16. *Butterfield House, 63 Church Street, Isleworth TW7 6BE* T: (020) 8560 7511 E: ali.walton@cantab.net or ali.walton@allsaints-isleworth.org

WALTON, Ann Beverley. b 56. Huddersfield Poly BSc 78 Sheff Poly MPhil 84 Coll of Ripon & York St Jo MA 97. NOC 00. d 03 p 04. C Ecclesfield *Sheff* 03–06; R Adwick-le-Street w Skelbrooke from 06; P-in-c Owston from 14. *The Rectory, Village Street, Adwick-le-Street, Doncaster DN6 7AD* T: (01302) 723224 E: ann.walton@sheffield.anglican.org

WALTON, Mrs Camilla Iris. b 56. STETS 97. d 00 p 01. C Lyndhurst and Emery Down and Minstead *Win* 00–04; V Boldre w S Baddesley 04–08; TV Beaconsfield *Ox* 08–12; AD Amersham 12–17; rtd 18; PtO *Bris* from 19. *1A Fore Street, Ashton Keynes, Swindon SN6 6NP* E: camillawalton@gmail.com

WALTON, Mrs Catherine. b 66. Lindisfarne Regional Tr Partnership. d 15 p 16. NSM Norton St Mary *Dur* from 15; NSM Norton St Mich from 15. *23 Wadham Grove, Darlington DL1 2GJ* T: (01325)

260274 M: 07581-043061 E: revd.catherine@gmail.com or archdeacons.secretary@durham.anglican.org

WALTON, Deborah Ruth. b 68. Wolv Poly LLB 90 Barrister-at-Law 91 Solicitor 97. St Mellitus Coll BA 17. d 17 p 18. C Kinver and Enville *Lich* from 17. *The Vicarage, The Close, Enville, Stourbridge DY7 5HX* T: (01384) 878880 M: 07954-338902 E: deborah.r.walton@me.com

WALTON, Frank. b 39. d 04 p 05. OLM Woodhorn w Newbiggin *Newc* 04–09; PtO from 09. *6 New Queen Street, Newbiggin-by-the-Sea NE64 6AZ* T: (01670) 817568

WALTON, The Ven Geoffrey Elmer. b 34. Dur Univ BA 59. Qu Coll Birm. d 61 p 62. C Warsop *S'well* 61–65; Dioc Youth Chapl 65–69; V Norwell 65–69; Recruitment Sec ACCM 69–75; V Weymouth H Trin *Sarum* 75–82; RD Weymouth 79–82; Can and Preb Sarum Cathl 81–00; Adn Dorset 82–00; P-in-c Witchampton and Hinton Parva, Long Crichel etc 82–93; P-in-c Vale of Allen 93–96; V Witchampton, Stanbridge and Long Crichel etc 96–00; rtd 00; PtO *Sarum* from 01. *Priory Cottage, 6 Hibberds Field, Cranborne, Wimborne BH21 5QL* T: (01725) 517167 E: geoffreywalton34@gmail.com

WALTON, John Victor. b 45. Lon Univ BSc 67. Linc Th Coll 79. d 81 p 82. C Stevenage St Mary Shephall *St Alb* 81–85; TV Bourne Valley *Sarum* 85–95; P-in-c Puddletown and Tolpuddle 95–02; R Puddletown, Tolpuddle and Milborne w Dewlish 02–04; rtd 04; PtO *Sarum* from 12. *Serenity, Wootton Grove, Sherborne DT9 4DL* T: (01935) 814435 E: revjvw@hotmail.com

WALTON, Canon Kevin Anthony. b 64. St Chad's Coll Dur BA 87 Dur Univ PhD 99. Trin Coll Bris BA 91. d 92 p 93. C Stranton *Dur* 92–95; C Hartlepool H Trin 95–96; V Sunderland St Mary and St Pet 96–08; AD Wearmouth 05–08; Can and Chan St Alb from 08. *2 Sumpter Yard, St Albans AL1 1BY* T: (01727) 890242 E: canon@stalbanscathedral.org

WALTON, Luke. b 64. Leeds Univ LLB 87. Cranmer Hall Dur BA 94. d 97 p 98. C Didsbury St Jas and Em *Man* 97–02; C Clifton Ch Ch w Em *Bris* 02–06; Arts Development Officer Bible Soc from 06; PtO *Bris* from 06. *Bible Society, Stonehill Green, Westlea, Swindon SN5 7DG* T: (01793) 418100 F: 418118 M: 07799-414199

WALTON, Michael Roy. b 74. St Cuth Soc Dur BA 95. Oak Hill Th Coll BA 09. d 09 p 10. C W Kilburn St Luke w St Simon and St Jude *Lon* 09–12; R Chadwell *Chelmsf* from 12. *The Rectory, 10 Rigby Gardens, Grays RM16 4JJ* T: (01375) 842176 M: 07949-637377 E: mikewalton.online@gmail.com

WALTON, Reginald Arthur. b 40. St Jo Coll Nottm 80. d 81 p 82. C Woodthorpe *S'well* 81–84; P-in-c Nottingham St Andr 84–85; V 85–91; R Moreton *Ches* 91–01; P-in-c Whatton w Aslockton, Hawksworth, Scarrington etc *S'well* 01–05; V 05–07; rtd 07; PtO *S'well* from 17. *19 The Maltsters, Newark NG24 4RU* T: (01636) 659869 E: regwalton40@gmail.com

WALTON, Richard James. b 55. UMIST BSc 77 Sheff Univ MEd 84 Leeds Univ PhD 98 MA 10 CPhys MInstP SFHEA 13. NOC 07. d 09 p 10. NSM Warmsworth *Sheff* 09–11; P-in-c Burghwallis and Campsall from 11; Bp's Adv for SSM from 14; Asst Dioc Dir of Ords from 14; AD Adwick from 19. *The Rectory, Village Street, Adwick-le-Street, Doncaster DN6 7AD* T: (01302) 723224 M: 07931-526333 E: r.j.walton94@gmail.com

WALTON, Stephen James. b 71. Mert Coll Ox BA 92 MA 97. Oak Hill Th Coll BA 01. d 02 p 03. C Thurnby w Stoughton *Leic* 02–07; R Marbury w Tushingham and Whitewell *Ches* 07–15; Chapl Düsseldorf *Eur* from 15. *Mulvany House, Rotterdamer Strasse 135, 40474 Düsseldorf, Germany* E: walton_stephen@hotmail.com

WALTON, Prof Stephen John. b 55. Birm Univ BSc 76 Fitzw Coll Cam BA 79 MA 82 Sheff Univ PhD 97. Ridley Hall Cam 77. d 83 p 84. C Bebington *Ches* 83–86; Voc and Min Adv CPAS 86–92; LtO *St Alb* 86–94; Public Preacher 00–04; Bp's Dom Chapl 94–95; Lect St Jo Coll Nottm 95–99; Lect Greek and NT Lon Sch of Th 99–03; Sen Lect Greek and NT 03–11; Prof NT 11–13; Hon Research Fell Tyndale Ho Cam 13–15; Affiliated Lect Div Cam Univ 13–17; Prof NT and Research Fell St Mary's Univ Twickenham *Lon* 13–17; Public Preacher *Ely* 12–16; Lic Preacher *Lon* from 16; Assoc Research Fell Trin Coll Bris from 18. *Butterfield House, 63 Church Street, Isleworth TW7 6BE* T: (020) 8560 7511 M: 07897-630462 E: steve.walton@cantab.net or s.walton@trinitycollegebristol.ac.uk

WALTON, Teresa Margaret. b 52. d 12 p 13. NSM Washington *Dur* 12–17; PtO *Newc* from 17. *18 Wingate Grange, Houghton le Spring DH4 6GQ* E: twalton2207@gmail.com

WALTON, William Frederick. b 59. IEng 98 CEnv 05. Qu Foundn (Course) 16. d 18 p 19. NSM Cov H Trin from

18. *1 Rookery Lane, Coventry CV6 4GL* T: (024) 7668 0137 M: 07771-555764 E: bill.walton@hotmail.co.uk

WANDREY, Bryce Philip. b 77. St Olaf Coll Minnesota BA 99. Concordia Th Sem Indiana MDiv 03 St Steph Ho Ox 07. **d** 08 **p** 09. C Highgate St Mich *Lon* 08–17; C Highgate All SS 09–14; P-in-c 14–17; Chapl Porter Gaud Sch USA from 17. *5 Fields Place, Charleston SC 92403, USA* E: brycepwandrey@gmail.com

WANDSWORTH, Archdeacon of. *See* KIDDLE, The Ven John

WANJIE, Lukas Macharia. b 50. Fitzw Coll Cam BA 79 MA 83 Birkbeck Coll Lon MSc 98. St Paul's Coll Limuru 72 Ridley Hall Cam 76. **d** 75 **p** 76. C Uthiru St Pet Kenya 75–76; C Mill End and Heronsgate w W Hyde *St Alb* 79; V Westlands St Mark Nairobi Kenya 80–84; Prin Trin Bible Coll Nairobi 85–91; C St Alb St Steph 91–94; PtO 94–95; Race Relations Adv Croydon *S'wark* 95–01; V Bermondsey St Kath w St Bart 01–12; rtd 13. *7 Bute Walk, Derby DE21 6BN* E: wanjiel@yahoo.co.uk

WANSTALL, Noelle Margaret. *See* HALL, Noelle Margaret

WARBRICK, Canon Quentin David. b 66. Jes Coll Ox BA 88. Cranmer Hall Dur 89. **d** 92 **p** 93. C Birm St Martin w Bordesley St Andr 92–96; C Handsworth St Jas 96–00; V Packwood w Hockley Heath 00–10; AD Shirley 05–10; P-in-c Kings Heath 10–14; V from 14; AD Moseley from 17; Hon Can Birm Cathl from 14. *The Vicarage, 4 Vicarage Road, Kings Heath, Birmingham B14 7RA* T: 0121-444 0260 *or* 444 0760 E: info@davidwarbrick.co.uk

WARBURTON, Andrew James. b 44. Oak Hill Th Coll 64. **d** 69 **p** 70. C New Milverton *Cov* 69–72; C Fulham St Matt *Lon* 72–76; C Chesham St Mary *Ox* 76–80; TV Gt Chesham 80–94; Chapl Paris St Mich *Eur* 94–97; Asst Chapl Amsterdam w Heiloo 97–99; rtd 99; PtO *Carl* from 11. *Burnbrae, Riccarton, Newcastleton TD9 0SN* T: (01387) 376293 M: 07962-622740 E: borderwarburton@gmail.com

WARD, Alan William. b 56. Trin Coll Bris 80. **d** 81 **p** 82. C New Ferry *Ches* 81–86; Dioc Youth Officer 86–91; C Charlesworth and Dinting Vale *Derby* 91–96; V Mickleover All SS 96–11; C Mickleover St Jo 06–11; R Wallasey St Hilary *Ches* from 11; RD Wallasey from 18. *St Hilary's Rectory, Church Hill, Wallasey CH45 3NH* T: 0151-638 4771 E: rector@sthilarywallasey-org.uk

WARD, Mrs Alice Belinda. b 58. Dur Univ BSc 79 MA 01 MBACP 04. Cranmer Hall Dur 15. **d** 17 **p** 18. NSM Jesmond H Trin *Newc* 17–18; NSM Newc St Luke from 18. *1 Hawthorn Villas, Wallsend NE28 7NT* E: aliceward1@mac.com

WARD, Alistair William McKenzie. b 62. Ridley Hall Cam 16. **d** 18 **p** 19. C Linc St Pet in Eastgate from 18. *15 Queensway, Lincoln LN2 4AJ* T: (01522) 520512 M: 07999-426560 E: alistairward@virginmedia.com

WARD (née WEIGHTMAN), Mrs Andrea Frances. b 66. Sheff Univ BA 87. Ridley Hall Cam 00. **d** 03 **p** 04. C Handforth *Ches* 03–07; V Blendon *Roch* 07–17; P-in-c Chatham St Paul w All SS from 17. *The Vicarage, 2A Waghorn Street, Chatham ME4 5LT* T: (01634) 845419 M: 07983-851105 E: andreaward72@gmail.com

WARD, Andrew John. b 65. Cliff Th Coll 85 Trin Coll Bris BA 99. **d** 99 **p** 00. C Belper *Derby* 99–03; TV Walbrook Epiphany 03–11; TR from 11; RD Derby S 12–15. *St Augustine's Rectory, 155 Almond Street, Derby DE23 6LY* T: (01332) 766603 *or* 760846 E: rector.walbrooke@gmail.com

WARD, Canon Anthony Peter. b 46. Bris Univ BSc 67 Ox Univ DipEd 68. St Jo Coll Nottm. **d** 82 **p** 83. C Hellesdon *Nor* 82–85; P-in-c Nor St Aug w St Mary 85–91; P-in-c Norwich-over-the-Water Colegate St Geo 85–90; Norfolk Churches' Radio Officer 85–95; TV Norwich Over-the-Water 91–95; V Gorleston St Andr 95–11; RD Gt Yarmouth 98–02; Hon Can Nor Cathl 03–11; rtd 11. *20 The Butts, Belper DE56 1HX* T: (01773) 821639 E: revtw@btinternet.com *or* revtw@live.com

WARD, Arthur John. b 32. Lon Univ BD 57. St Aid Birkenhead 57. **d** 57 **p** 58. C Ecclesfield *Sheff* 57–60; C Fulwood 60–63; Tutor St Aid Birkenhead 63–66; R Denton St Lawr *Man* 66–74; CMS 74–82; TV Wolverhampton *Lich* 82–90; V Edgbaston SS Mary and Ambrose *Birm* 90–96; rtd 96; PtO *Heref* from 97. *Bramble Cottage, 6 Lower Forge, Eardington, Bridgnorth WV16 5LQ* T: (01746) 764758 E: revjohnward@aol.com

WARD, Miss Beverley Jayne. b 61. Bolton Inst of Educn CertEd 97. St Steph Ho Ox 00. **d** 02 **p** 07. C Standish *Blackb* 02–07; C Thornton-le-Fylde 07–09; P-in-c Eccleston 09–12; V Cleveleys from 12. *The Vicarage, Rough Lea Road, Thornton-Cleveleys FY5 1DP* T: (01253) 852153 M: 07811-907274 E: rev.jayneward@gmail.com

WARD, Brett Ernest. b 62. Univ of Wales MTh 06. ACT 86. **d** 89 **p** 89. C E Maitland Australia 89; Asst P 89–91; Asst P Singleton 91–92; P-in-c Weston 92–97; C Forton *Portsm*

97–99; P-in-c 99–05; V 05–07; P-in-c Eltham H Trin *S'wark* 07–10; V from 10; AD Eltham and Mottingham from 13; Asst Dir of Ords Woolwich Area from 16. *Holy Trinity Vicarage, 59 Southend Crescent, London SE9 2SD* T: (020) 8850 1246 *or* 8859 6274 E: fr.brett@ht-e.org.uk

WARD, Canon Calvin. b 34. Univ of Wales BA 57 DipEd 60 Fitzw Ho Cam BA 63 MA 67. Westcott Ho Cam 61. **d** 64 **p** 65. C Handsworth St Mich *Birm* 64–66; C Shaw Hill 66–69; V Windhill *Bradf* 69–76; V Esholt 76–81; V Oakworth 81–91; V Allerton 91–99; Hon Can Bradf Cathl 94–99; rtd 99; PtO *Bradf* 99–14; *Leeds* from 14. *47 Wheatlands Drive, Bradford BD9 5JN* E: candmward@blueyonder.co.uk *or* calvin.ward28@gmail.com

WARD, Daran. b 65. Brunel Univ BSc 88. St Jo Coll Nottm 07. **d** 09 **p** 10. C Hartley Wintney, Elvetham, Winchfield etc *Win* 09–13; V Bramley *Sheff* 13–19; P-in-c Thrybergh 13–19; V Alsager Ch Ch Ches from 19. *43 Church Road, Alsager, Stoke-on-Trent ST7 2HS* E: daran.ward@gmail.com

WARD, David. b 40. St Jo Coll Nottm 83. **d** 85 **p** 86. C Aspley *S'well* 85–89; V 89–04; rtd 04; PtO *S'well* from 04. *150 Robins Wood Road, Nottingham NG8 3LD* T: 0115-929 3231 M: 07971-092089 E: david.jeans.ward@gmail.com

WARD, David Graham. b 51. CBDTI 03. **d** 06 **p** 07. OLM Higher Walton *Blackb* 06–07; NSM 07–10; P-in-c Brindle 10–11; R from 11. *Coppice Farm, Goose Foot Lane, Samlesbury, Preston PR5 0RQ* T: (01254) 852995 F: 851101

WARD, Edward. *See* WARD, William Edward

WARD, Mrs Elisabeth. b 63. Trevelyan Coll Dur BA 85 St Mellitus Coll MA 18 Bath Spa Univ PGCE 99. Linc Sch of Th and Min 11. **d** 14 **p** 15. C Stamford St Geo w St Paul *Linc* 14–18; V Skirbeck H Trin from 18. *Holy Trinity Vicarage, 64 Spilsby Road, Boston PE21 9NS* T: (01205) 355172 M: 07768-814698 E: rev.lisward@holytrinity.org.uk

WARD, Elizabeth Joyce. *See* HOLMES, Elizabeth Joyce

WARD, Frances Elizabeth Fearn. b 59. St Andr Univ MTheol 83 Man Univ PhD 00 Bradf Univ MA 06 RGN 87. Westcott Ho Cam 87. **d** 89 **p** 94. Par Dn Westhoughton *Man* 89–93; Tutor Practical Th N Coll Man 93–98; Hon C Bury St Pet *Man* 93–98; C Unsworth 98–99; V Bury St Pet 99–05; C Leverhulme 05–06; Bp's Adv on Women in Min 02–04; Hon Can Man Cathl 04–06; Can Res Bradf Cathl 06–10; Dean St E 10–18; LtO *Carl* from 18. *St Michael's Rectory, Dora Crescent, Workington CA14 2EZ* M: 07791-165774 E: fefward@gmail.com

WARD, Frank Wyatt. b 30. Oak Hill NSM Course 84. **d** 92 **p** 94. NSM Paddington St Pet *Lon* 92–09; NSM Paddington St Mary Magd and St Pet 09–15; rtd 15; PtO *Lon* from 15. *82 Hill Rise, Greenford UB6 8PE* T: (020) 8575 5515

WARD, Garry William. b 67. Anglia Ruskin Univ MA 11 RGN 90 RM 92. Qu Coll Birm 01. **d** 03 **p** 04. C Wednesfield *Lich* 03–06; TV Wordsley *Worc* 06–11; V Claverley w Tuckhill *Heref* from 11. *The Vicarage, Lodge Park, Claverley, Wolverhampton WV5 7DP* T: (01746) 710304 E: garry@penfold.email

WARD, Helen Frances. b 48. EAMTC 02. **d** 04 **p** 05. NSM Gorleston St Andr *Nor* 04–11; rtd 11. *20 The Butts, Belper DE56 1HX* T: (01773) 821639 E: revhw@btinternet.com

WARD, Ian Stanley. b 62. K Coll Lon BD 83. Cranmer Hall Dur 84. **d** 86 **p** 87. C Moreton *Ches* 86–89; Chapl RAF 89–18; C Skirbeck H Trin *Linc* from 18. *Holy Trinity Vicarage, 64 Spilsby Road, Boston PE21 9NS* T: (01205) 355172

WARD, Canon Janice Ann. b 65. Univ of Wales (Lamp) BA 86. ERMC 05. **d** 08 **p** 09. C Haverhill w Withersfield *St E* 08–12; P-in-c Marown, Foxdale and Baldwin *S & M* 12–13; V from 13; Can St German's Cathl from 16. *Marown Vicarage, Main Road, Crosby, Isle of Man IM4 4BH* T: (01624) 851378 M: 07624-406084 E: revjaniceward@manx.net

WARD, Jason David. b 71. Glas Univ BSc 93 PhD 98. Oak Hill Th Coll BA 06. **d** 06 **p** 07. C Cheadle Hulme St Andr *Ches* 06–09; C Harold Wood *Chelmsf* 09–13; V Chaddesden St Mary *Derby* from 13. *The Vicarage, 133 Chaddesden Lane, Chaddesden, Derby DE21 6LL* T: (01332) 280924 M: 07866-361054 E: jasethebass@gmail.com *or* jason@chaddesdenchurch.org.uk

WARD, Jayne. *See* WARD, Beverley Jayne

WARD, John. *See* WARD, Arthur John

WARD, Canon John Frederick. b 55. St Mich Coll Llan 81. **d** 84 **p** 85. C Pembroke Dock *St D* 84–86; PV Llan Cathl 86–89; R St Brides Minor w Bettws 89–97; V Shard End *Birm* 97–04; V Twigworth, Down Hatherley, Norton, The Leigh etc *Glouc* 04–10; C Wotton-under-Edge w Ozleworth, N Nibley etc 10–12; C Charfield and Kingswood 10–11; C Charfield and Kingswood w Wickwar etc 11–12; V Quedgeley from 12; Hon Can Glouc Cathl from 18. *The New Rectory, School Lane, Quedgeley, Gloucester GL2 4PN* T: (01452) 720411 M: 07967-636094 E: jfmw23@gmail.com

WARD, Prof John Stephen Keith. b 38. Univ of Wales (Cardiff) BA 62 Linacre Coll Ox BLitt 68 DD 98 Trin Hall Cam MA 72 DD 99 FBA 01. Westcott Ho Cam 72. **d** 72 **p** 73. Lect Philosophy of Relig Lon Univ 71–75; Hon C Hampstead St Jo 72–75; Dean Trin Hall Cam 75–82; Prof Moral and Soc Th K Coll Lon 82–85; Prof Hist and Philosophy of Relig 85–91; Regius Prof Div Ox Univ 91–03; Can Res Ch Ch Ox 91–03; rtd 03; PtO Ox 03–15 and 17–19; Professorial Research Fell Heythrop Coll Lon 10–18. *39 Coopers Lane, Abingdon OX14 5GU* T: (01235) 539799 E: keith.ward@chch.ox.ac.uk

WARD, Keith Raymond. b 37. Dur Univ BSc 60. Chich Th Coll 63. **d** 65 **p** 66. C Wallsend St Luke *Newc* 65–68; C Wooler 68–74; V Dinnington 74–81; V Bedlington 81–93; V Stannington 93–99; rtd 99; PtO *Newc* from 00. *2 Ethel's Close, Gloster Meadows, Amble, Morpeth NE65 0GD* T: (01665) 714357 E: raymond987@btinternet.com

WARD, Kevin. b 47. Edin Univ MA 69 Trin Coll Cam PhD 76. **d** 78 **p** 79. CMS 75–92; Uganda 76–90; Qu Coll Birm 91; PtO *Birm* 91; C Halifax *Wakef* 91–92; P-in-c Charlestown 92–95; NSM Headingley *Ripon* 95–14; Lect Leeds Univ from 95. *8 North Grange Mews, Leeds LS6 2EW* T: 0113-278 7801 E: trskw@leeds.ac.uk

WARD, Lionel Owen. b 37. Univ of Wales (Cardiff) BA 58 Univ of Wales (Swansea) DipEd 59 MA 65 Lon Univ PhD 70. St Mich Coll Llan 83. **d** 85 **p** 86. NSM Swansea St Mary w H Trin *S & B* 85–89; P-in-c Swansea St Matt w Greenhill 89–00; TV Cen Swansea 00–01; Dioc Dir of Educn 97–01; RD Swansea 98–01; rtd 02; PtO *S'wark* 10–11. *17 Gresham Court, 11 Pampisford Road, Purley CR8 2UU* E: lionelward@hotmail.co.uk

WARD, Mark. b 62. Imp Coll Lon BScEng 84. Wycliffe Hall Ox BTh 93. **d** 93 **p** 94. C Parkham, Alwington, Buckland Brewer etc *Ex* 93–96; C S Molton w Nymet St George, High Bray etc 96–97; TV 97–05; TV Ottery St Mary, Alfington, W Hill, Tipton etc from 05; RD Ottery from 17. *The Vicarage, Newton Poppleford, Sidmouth EX10 0HB* T: (01395) 568390 E: revmarkward@btinternet.com

WARD, Matthew Alan James. b 69. Nottm Poly BSc 91 Dur Univ DThM 16. Ridley Hall Cam 94. **d** 97 **p** 98. C Birchwood *Linc* 97–00; Chapl Cov Univ 00–05; Chapl Leeds Univ 05–18; Chapl Leeds Beckett Univ 05–18. *6 Barony, Millgate, Cupar KY15 5ER*

WARD, Michael Reginald. b 31. BNC Ox BA 54 MA 58. Tyndale Hall Bris 54. **d** 56 **p** 57. C Ealing St Mary *Lon* 56–59; C Morden *S'wark* 59–61; Area Sec (Midl and E Anglia) CCCS 61–66; V Chelsea St Jo *Lon* 66–73; P-in-c Chelsea St Andr 72–73; V Chelsea St Jo w St Andr 73–76; P-in-c Hawkesbury *Glouc* 76–80; P-in-c Alderley w Hillesley 79–80; P-in-c Bibury w Winson and Barnsley 80–85; V Barkby and Queniborough *Leic* 85–90; R Gunthorpe w Bale w Field Dalling, Saxlingham etc *Nor* 90–98; rtd 98; PtO *Heref* 98–08; *Glouc* 00–08. *4 Framland Drive, Melton Mowbray LE13 1HY* T: (01664) 500039

WARD (née MASSEY), Michelle Elaine (Shellie). Plymouth Univ BA 00. Trin Coll Bris BA 04. **d** 04 **p** 05. C Barrowby and Gt Gonerby *Linc* 04–09; P-in-c Saxonwell 09–12; P-in-c Claypole 11–12; P-in-c Broadway w Wickhamford *Worc* from 12. *The Vicarage, Church Street, Broadway WR12 7AE* T: 07780-002565 E: michelleward36@aol.com

WARD, Nigel Andrew. b 50. Peterho Cam BA 72 MA 76. Oak Hill NSM Course 89. **d** 92 **p** 93. NSM Frogmore *St Alb* from 92. *15 Park Street, St Albans AL2 2PE* T: (01727) 872667

WARD, Peter Macdonald. b 41. **d** 09 **p** 10. NSM Harrow Weald All SS *Lon* from 09. *129 Sylvia Avenue, Pinner HA5 4QL* T: (020) 8428 7887 M: 07733-001777 E: wardhatchend@hotmail.com

WARD, Peter Nicholas. b 59. Ban Ord Course 03. **d** 08 **p** 09. NSM Llanwnnog and Caersws w Carno *Ban* 08–11; NSM Bro Ddyfi Uchaf 11–14; NSM Bro Cyfeiliog and Mawddwy from 14. *Coed Cae, Clatter, Caersws SY17 5NW* T: (01686) 688034 E: peteandsand@btopenworld.com

WARD, Robert. b 60. Em Coll Cam BA 81 MA 85. Chich Th Coll. **d** 86 **p** 87. C Horfield H Trin *Bris* 86–90; C Stantonbury and Willen *Ox* 90; TV 90–96; V Knowle St Martin *Bris* 96–07; R Cradley w Mathon and Storridge *Heref* from 07; RD Ledbury from 13. *The Rectory, Cradley, Malvern WR13 5LQ* T: (01886) 880438 E: robert.ward776@gmail.com

WARD, Robert Arthur Philip. b 53. Lon Univ BD 82 Open Univ BA 88. Qu Coll Birm 77. **d** 79 **p** 80. C Balsall Heath St Paul *Birm* 79–82; Chapl RAF 82–98; TR Blakenall Heath *Lich* 98–01; PtO 05–07; V Ravensthorpe and Thornhill Lees w Savile Town *Wakef* 07–13; P-in-c St Marychurch *Ex* from 13. *The Vicarage, Hampton Avenue, Torquay TQ1 3LA* T: (01803) 269258 E: father.robert@hotmail.co.uk

WARD, Robert Charles Irwin. b 48. Leic Univ LLB 70 Madras Bible Sem DD 01 Called to the Bar (Inner Temple) 72.

Cranmer Hall Dur 78. **d** 80 **p** 81. C Byker St Mich w St Lawr *Newc* 80–85; PtO 86–07; NSM Newc St Luke from 07; Dir Clarence Trust and NE Area Revival Min from 86; Asst Chapl HM Pris Frankland 91–95; rtd 13. *1 Hawthorn Villas, The Green, Wallsend NE28 7NT* T/F: 0191-234 3969 M: 07768-528181 E: rwarduk@mac.com

WARD, Canon Robin. b 66. Magd Coll Ox BA 87 MA 91 K Coll Lon PhD 03. St Steph Ho Ox 88. **d** 91 **p** 92. C Romford St Andr *Chelmsf* 91–94; C Willesden Green St Andr and St Fran *Lon* 94–96; V Sevenoaks St Jo *Roch* 96–06; Chapl Invicta Community Care NHS Trust 97–06; Hon Can Roch Cathl 04–06; Prin St Steph Ho Ox from 06. *St Stephen's House, 16 Marston Street, Oxford OX4 1JX* T: (01865) 613500 E: robin.ward@ssho.ox.ac.uk

WARD, Mrs Rosemary Clare. b 57. Westf Coll Lon BA 79 Liv Univ MA 80 MPhil 82. Trin Coll Bris BA 94. **d** 94 **p** 95. C Bris St Andr Hartcliffe 94–98; C Downend 98–02; P-in-c Broad Blunsdon 02–05; C Highworth w Sevenhampton and Inglesham etc 02–05; Dioc Lay Tr Adv 02–05; Leadership Development Adv CPAS 05–11; R Sawtry and Glatton *Ely* 12–16; rtd 16; PtO *Win* from 17. *24 Farnleys Mead, Lymington SO41 3TJ* T: (01590) 679651 E: wardrosie@btinternet.com

WARD, Mrs Sandra Elizabeth. b 53. Lady Spencer Chu Coll of Educn TCert 75 Anglia Ruskin Univ MA 07. LCTP 08. **d** 13 **p** 14. NSM Orton and Tebay w Ravenstonedale etc *Carl* 13–16; NSM Shap w Swindale and Bampton w Mardale 13–16; NSM High Westmorland 16–18; P-in-c Lorton and Loweswater w Buttermere from 18. *The Vicarage, Loweswater, Cockermouth CA13 0RU* T: (01900) 85237 M: 07946-633334 E: revd.sandra@btinternet.com *or* vicarlolobu@hotmail.com

WARD, Mrs Sheena Mary. b 55. Newc Univ BA 76 PGCE 77. **d** 00 **p** 01. OLM Cramlington *Newc* 00–18; rtd 18; PtO *Newc* from 18. *17 Yarmouth Drive, Cramlington NE23 1TL* T: (01670) 732211 E: reverendsheena@gmail.com

WARD, Canon Simon William James. b 71. Dur Univ BA 94 Westmr Coll Ox PGCE 96. Ripon Coll Cuddesdon 98. **d** 00 **p** 01. C Aldershot St Mich *Guildf* 00–03; TV Sole Bay St E 03–09; Bp's Chapl *Nor* 09–14; P-in-c Earlham 14–17; TR Gt Yarmouth from 17; Hon Can Nor Cathl from 17. *The Rectory, Town Wall Road, Great Yarmouth NR30 1DJ* E: revdsimon@msn.com

WARD, Mrs Susan Elizabeth. b 50. NOC 92. **d** 95 **p** 96. NSM Heyside *Man* 95–09; NSM Newhey 09–16; NSM Belfield from 09; NSM Milnrow 09–16; NSM Milnrow and New Hey from 16; Chapl Pennine Acute Hosps NHS Trust 04–16; PtO *Leeds* from 17. *12 Airedale Quay, Rodley, Leeds LS13 1NZ* T: 0113-229 3839 M: 07595-593605 E: sue.ward1950@live.co.uk

WARD, Timothy James. b 67. CCC Ox BA 90 MA 95 Edin Univ PhD 99. Oak Hill Th Coll BA 95. **d** 99 **p** 00. C Crowborough *Chich* 99–04; TV Hinckley H Trin *Leic* 04–10; R 10–13; Assoc Dir Cornhill Tr Course 13–16; PtO *Roch* 14–16; Tutor Oak Hill Coll from 16. *Oak Hill College, Chase Side, London N14 4PS* T: (020) 8449 0467

WARD, Timothy John Conisbee. b 62. New Coll Ox BA 85 MA 02 PGCE 86. Wycliffe Hall Ox BA 91. **d** 92 **p** 93. C Dorking St Paul *Guildf* 92–96; C Herne Hill *S'wark* 96–02; V Walberton w Binsted *Chich* from 02. *St Mary's Vicarage, The Street, Walberton, Arundel BN18 0PQ* T: (01243) 551488 E: tjcward@uwclub.net

WARD, Timothy William. b 49. Open Univ BA 74 Birm Univ BPhil(Ed) 93. St Deiniol's Hawarden 78. **d** 79 **p** 80. NSM Handsworth St Mary *Birm* 79–95; PtO 95–05; NSM Gt Barr *Lich* 95–19; PtO from 19. *3 Dale Close, Birmingham B43 6AS* T: 0121-358 1880 *or* 358 2807 E: curate.greatbarr@btinternet.com

WARD, Tracy. b 63. RGN RSCN 89. All SS Cen for Miss & Min 13. **d** 16 **p** 17. C Sale St Anne *Ches* 16–18; V Mellor from 18. *The Vicarage, 51 Church Road, Mellor, Stockport SK6 5LX* M: 07875-059113 E: revdtracyward@icloud.com

WARD, Preb William Edward. b 48. FSAScot 71. AKC 71. **d** 72 **p** 73. C Heref St Martin 72–77; C Blakenall Heath *Lich* 77–78; TV 78–82; V Astley, Clive, Grinshill and Hadnall 82–91; R Edgmond w Kynnersley and Preston Wealdmoors 91–17; P-in-c Tibberton w Bolas Magna and Waters Upton 02–17; Chapl Harper Adams Univ Coll 91–17; Preb Lich Cathl 09–17; CF (TA) 83–05; CF (ACF) 05–10; rtd 17. *31 Fair Oak, Newport TF10 7LR* E: e.ward17@btinternet.com

WARDALE, Robert Christopher. b 46. Newc Univ BA 69 MA 93. Coll of Resurr Mirfield 77. **d** 79 **p** 80. C Cockerton *Dur* 79–84; P-in-c Hedworth 84–87; V 87–92; V Darlington H Trin 92–06; rtd 06; PtO *Newc* from 06; *Dur* from 12. *24 Beechcroft, Kenton Road, Newcastle upon Tyne NE3 4NB* T: 0191-285 5284 E: wardalerc@aol.com

WARDELL, Gareth Kevin. b 59. York Univ BA 81 MA 01. Ridley Hall Cam 03. **d** 05 **p** 06. C Selby Abbey *York*

05–08; C Kensington St Mary Abbots w Ch Ch and St Phil *Lon* 08–13; V Hampton All SS from 13. *All Saints' Vicarage, 40 The Avenue, Hampton TW12 3RS* T: (020) 8487 3823 E: wardellgareth@hotmail.com *or* vicar@allsaintshampton.co.uk

WARDEN, Richard James. b 57. Kent Univ BA 79 K Coll Lon MTh 86. Wycliffe Hall Ox 81. **d** 83 **p** 84. C Fulham St Mary N End *Lon* 83–85; CF 85–89; Chapl Wycombe Abbey Sch 89–01; Sen Chapl and Hd RS Wellington Coll Berks 01–04; P-in-c Finchampstead *Ox* 04–10; Chapl Mill Hill Sch Lon from 10. *Mill Hill School, The Ridgeway, London NW7 1QS* T: (020) 8959 1176 E: rjw@millhill.org.uk

WARDLE, John Argyle. b 47. St Jo Coll Dur BA 71 ARCM 67 CertEd 73. **d** 73 **p** 74. C Mansfield SS Pet and Paul *S'well* 73–77; Chapl St Felix Sch Southwold 77–87; TV Haverhill w Withersfield, the Wrattings etc *St E* 87–90; V Choral S'well Minster 90–99; Bp's Adv on Healing 94–99; R Bridlington Priory *York* 99–08; RD Bridlington 03–08; rtd 08; PtO *York* 12–17. *27 First Avenue, Bridlington YO15 2JW* T: (01262) 400127 E: jawardle27@btinternet.com

WARDMAN, Canon Carol Joy. b 56. Lon Univ BA 79 Man Univ MPhil 02. NOC 91. **d** 94 **p** 95. NSM Hebden Bridge *Wakef* 94–97; NSM Sowerby 97–10; Dioc Adv for Older People's Issues 08–11; NSM Halifax 10–11; Bps' Adv for Ch and Soc Ch in Wales from 11; PtO *St As* from 12; Metrop Can Llan Cathl from 15. *39 Cathedral Road, Cardiff CF11 9XF* T: (029) 2034 8260 E: carol.wardman@gmail.com *or* carolwardman@churchinwales.org.uk

WARE, Canon John Lawrence. b 37. Nottm Univ BA 59. Ridley Hall Cam 59. **d** 62 **p** 63. C Attercliffe *Sheff* 62–66; C Ranmoor 66–68; R Liddington and Soc and Ind Chapl Bris 68–74; Bp's Soc and Ind Adv and C-in-c Bris St Thos 74–79; V Kingswood 79–88; RD Bitton 85–87; P-in-c Broad Blunsdon 88–94; P-in-c Blunsdon St Andrew 88–94; R The Blunsdons 94–01; RD Cricklade 88–94; Hon Can Bris Cathl 76–01; rtd 01; PtO *Bris* from 01; Chapl HM Pris Bris 03–07. *26 Dongola Road, Bishopston, Bristol BS7 9HP* T: 0117-924 1304 E: jlwdongola@gmail.com

WARE, Ms Judith Marian. b 52. St Hugh's Coll Ox BA 74 MA 78 PGCE 75. CBDTI 00. **d** 02 **p** 03. NSM Windermere St Mary and Troutbeck *Carl* 02–05; C Thornes and Lupset *Wakef* 05–10; Chapl Wakef Cathl Sch 05–06; R Crumpsall *Man* 10–17; rtd 17; PtO *Man* from 17. *22 Kingsway Close, Oldham OL8 1BE* T: 0161-971 6326 E: jmware30@gmail.com

WARE, Stephen John. b 55. Univ of Wales (Lamp) BA 76. Ripon Coll Cuddesdon 77. **d** 79 **p** 80. C Lighthorne *Cov* 79–82; Chapl RAF 82–00; Command Chapl RAF 00–05; Selection Sec Min Division 05; V Bloxham w Milcombe and S Newington *Ox* 05–06; Warden of Readers *Glouc* 06–12; Asst Dioc Dir of Ords 06–14. *25 Beauchamp Meadow, Lydney GL15 5NS* T: (01594) 842299

WAREHAM, Mrs Caroline. b 32. Lightfoot Ho Dur 55. **dss** 80 **d** 87 **p** 94. Stanwell *Lon* 80–88; Par Dn 87–88; C Epsom St Barn *Guildf* 88–95; C Aldershot St Mich 95–98; rtd 98; PtO *Sarum* 00–18. *17 Homefield, Mere, Warminster BA12 6LT* T: (01747) 861716

WARHAM, Jean. *See* WALKER, Jean

WARHURST (*née* HART), Mrs Jane Elizabeth. b 56. Sheff Univ BA 77. NOC 98. **d** 01 **p** 02. C Edge Hill St Cypr w St Mary *Liv* 01–06; V Toxteth St Bede w St Clem 06–14; V Irlam *Man* from 14; Dioc Ecum Officer 14–16. *The Vicarage, Vicarage Road, Irlam, Manchester M44 6WA*

WARHURST, Richard. b 76. Univ Coll Chich BA 99. St Steph Ho Ox 00. **d** 02 **p** 03. C New Shoreham *Chich* 02–06; C Old Shoreham 02–06; R Chailey 06–10; Chapl Dorothy House Hospice Winsley 10–15; PtO *B & W* 11–15; R St Bartholomew *Sarum* from 15. *The Rectory, Semley, Shaftesbury SP7 9AU* T: (01747) 830174

WARING, Graham George Albert. b 37. ACII 62. Portsm Dioc Tr Course 86. **d** 87 **p** 02. Chapl Qu Alexandra Hosp Portsm 87–92; NSM Portsea All SS *Portsm* 92–94; NSM Widley w Wymering 94–95; NSM Wisbech St Aug *Ely* 95–98; Chapl King's Lynn and Wisbech Hosps NHS Trust 96–00; NSM Leverington *Ely* 98–00; NSM Southea w Murrow and Parson Drove 98–00; PtO *York* 00–02; NSM Scarborough St Sav w All SS 02–09; PtO from 09. *28 Newby Farm Road, Newby, Scarborough YO12 6UN* T: (01723) 353545 E: grachel.waring@gmail.com

WARING, Jeffery Edwin. b 53. Trin Coll Bris 80. **d** 83 **p** 84. C Harpurhey Ch Ch *Man* 83–86; TV Eccles 86–92; P-in-c Hamworthy *Sarum* 92–04; P-in-c Red Post 04–13; rtd 13; Hon C Iwerne Valley *Sarum* from 14. *Glen View, Church Lane, Sutton Waldron, Blandford Forum DT11 8PB* E: jeffwaring@btinternet.com

WARING, Mrs Margaret Ruth. b 44. Keele Univ CertEd 65. SWMTC 86. **d** 90 **p** 94. Par Dn Tavistock and Gulworthy *Ex*

90–94; C 94–96; TV Axminster, Chardstock, All Saints etc 96–04; rtd 04; PtO *Ex* from 04. *13 Latches Walk, Axminster EX13 5DQ* T: (01297) 639112

✠**WARKE, The Rt Revd Robert Alexander.** b 30. TCD BA 52 BD 60. **d** 53 **p** 54 **c** 88. C Newtownards *D & D* 53–56; C Dublin St Cath w St Victor *D & G* 56–58; C Dublin Rathfarnham 58–64; Min Can St Patr Cathl Dublin 59–64; I Dunlavin w Ballymore Eustace and Hollywood *D & G* 64–67; I Dublin Drumcondra w N Strand 67–71; I Dublin St Barn 67–71; I Dublin Zion Ch 71–88; Adn Dublin 80–88; Bp C, C & R 88–98; rtd 98. *6 Kerdiff Park, Monread Road, Naas, Co Kildare, Republic of Ireland* T: (00353) (45) 898144 E: rawarke@eircom.net

WARLAND, Peter William. b 35. K Coll Lon 56. **d** 60 **p** 61. C Pemberton St Jo *Liv* 60–64; C Warrington St Elphin 64–66; V Farnworth All SS *Man* 66–71; Chapl RN 71–92; QHC 88–92; Chapl Greenbank and Freedom Fields Hosps Ex 92–00; Chapl St Luke's Hospice Plymouth 94–00; rtd 00; PtO *Ex* from 00. *5 Evans Court, 6 Craigie Drive, Plymouth PL1 3TP* T: (01752) 663274

WARMAN, Miss Marion Alice. b 20. Newnham Coll Cam BA 43 MA 50. S'wark Ord Course 76. **dss** 79 **d** 87 **p** 94. Spring Grove St Mary *Lon* 79–87; Hon Par Dn 87–94; Hon C from 94; Chapl Asst W Middx Univ Hosp Isleworth 80–93; Chapl Volunteer Hounslow and Spelthorne NHS Trust 93–04; PtO *Lon* from 93. *43 Thornbury Road, Isleworth TW7 4LE* T: (020) 8560 5905

WARMAN, Philip Noel. b 64. Roehampton Inst BSc 85 PGCE 86. Ridley Hall Cam 99. **d** 01 **p** 02. C Burney Lane *Birm* 01–06; C Luton St Mary *St Alb* 06–09; V Brightside w Wincobank *Sheff* from 09. *The Vicarage, 24 Beacon Road, Sheffield S9 1AD* T: 0114-281 9360 E: phil.warman@sheffield.anglican.org

WARMINGTON, Thomas Zane. b 82. Ridley Hall Cam 16. **d** 18 **p** 19. C Epping Distr *Chelmsf* from 18. *2 Lower Swaines, Epping CM16 5ER* E: tomwarmit@gmail.com

WARNE, Miss Susan Annette. b 39. Man Univ BSc 61 Nottm Univ DipEd 62. **d** 00 **p** 01. OLM Yoxmere *St E* 00–09; PtO from 09. *Wynkyns, 22 Oakwood Park, Yoxford, Saxmundham IP17 3JU* T: (01728) 668410

WARNER, Alan Winston. b 51. Lon Univ BSc 73. Coll of Resurr Mirfield 73. **d** 76 **p** 77. C Willenhall St Anne *Lich* 76–78; C Baswich 78–81; V Wednesfield St Greg 81–87; Chapl Frimley Park Hosp 87–94; Chapl Frimley Park Hosp NHS Trust 94–04; Team Ldr Shrewsbury and Telford NHS Trust 04–10; Bp's Adv on Hosp Chapl *Lich* 06–10; rtd 10; PtO *Nor* from 11. *9 Beachmans Court, Wilson Road, Lowestoft NR33 0HZ* T: (01502) 218864 E: alan.warner@talktalk.net

WARNER, Canon Andrew Compton. b 35. Fitzw Ho Cam BA 58 MA 62. Westcott Ho Cam 59. **d** 60 **p** 61. C Addlestone *Guildf* 60–64; C-in-c Ash Vale CD 64–71; V Hinchley Wood 71–80; R Gt Bookham 80–00; RD Leatherhead 88–93; Hon Can Guildf Cathl 99–00; rtd 00; PtO *Win* from 00. *5 Pearman Drive, Andover SP10 2SB* T: (01264) 391325 E: dandawarner@yahoo.co.uk

WARNER, Clifford Chorley. b 38. Hull Univ MA 88. EMMTC 76. **d** 79 **p** 80. NSM Swanwick and Pentrich *Derby* 79–88; NSM Allestree 88–98; PtO 98–18. *3 Meadow Reach, Station Approach, Duffield, Belper DE56 4HT* T: (01332) 843389 E: cliffgwen@gmail.com

WARNER, David. b 40. AKC 63. **d** 64 **p** 65. C Castleford All SS *Wakef* 64–68; Warden Hollowford Tr and Conf Cen Sheff 68–72; R Wombwell *Sheff* 72–83; V Wortley w Thurgoland 83–95; RD Tankersley 88–93; V Worsbrough St Mary 95–00; P-in-c Bildeston w Wattisham *St E* 00–02; P-in-c Whatfield w Semer, Nedging and Naughton 00–02; R Bildeston w Wattisham and Lindsey, Whatfield etc 02–05; rtd 05; PtO *St E* from 05. *10 Magdalen Street, Eye IP23 7AJ* T: (01379) 870459 M: 07050-111478

WARNER, David. b 80. Leic Univ BA 02 Sheff Univ BA 13. Coll of Resurr Mirfield 10. **d** 13 **p** 14. C Abbots Langley *St Alb* 13–16; V Mossley *Man* from 16. *St John's Vicarage, Carrhill Road, Mossley, Ashton-under-Lyne OL5 0SA* T: (01457) 237667 E: frdavidwarner@gmail.com *or* vicarofmossley@gmail.com

WARNER, David Leonard John. b 24. Kelham Th Coll 47. **d** 51 **p** 52. C Mill Hill St Mich *Lon* 51–54; C Pimlico St Sav 54–56; R Rustenburg S Africa 56–64; R Hillcrest St Wilfrid 64–68; V Bournemouth H Epiphany *Win* 68–78; V Whitchurch w Tufton and Litchfield 78–89; RD Whitchurch 79–89; rtd 89; PtO *Win* 89–15; Hon Chapl Win Cathl from 97. *17 Lions Hall, St Swithun Street, Winchester SO23 9HW* T: (01962) 867343

WARNER, Dennis Vernon. b 46. Lon Univ BA 68 K Coll Lon BD 71. **d** 72 **p** 73. C W Bromwich All SS *Lich* 72–75; C Uttoxeter w Bramshall 75–79; NSM Stretton w Claymills 79–16; NSM Burton St Chad 16; PtO from 17. *90 Beech*

Lane, Stretton, Burton-on-Trent DE13 0DU T: (01283) 548058
E: densue@uku.co.uk

WARNER, Canon George Francis. b 36. Trin Coll Ox BA 60 MA 64 Qu Coll Cam BA 63. Westcott Ho Cam 61. **d** 63 **p** 64. C Birm St Geo 63–66; C Maidstone All SS w St Phil and H Trin *Cant* 66–69; Chapl Wellington Coll Berks 69–78; TR Coventry Caludon *Cov* 78–95; Hon Can Cov Cathl 85–02; RD Cov E 89–95; P-in-c Leamington Priors All SS 95–02; P-in-c Leamington Spa H Trin and Old Milverton 95–02; rtd 02; PtO *Cov* from 02. *Coll Leys Edge, Fant Hill, Upper Brailes, Banbury OX15 5AY* T: (01608) 685550 E: sandgwarner@btinternet.com

WARNER, John Philip. b 59. Keble Coll Ox BA 80 MA 84. St Steph Ho Ox 81. **d** 83 **p** 84. C Brighton Resurr *Chich* 83–87; C Paddington St Mary *Lon* 87–90; V Teddington St Mark and Hampton Wick 90–00; P-in-c Belgrade *Eur* 00–03; P-in-c St Magnus the Martyr w St Marg New Fish Street *Lon* 03–10; R from 10; P-in-c St Mary Abchurch 04–13; P-in-c St Clem Eastcheap w St Martin Orgar 08–11. *St Magnus the Martyr, Lower Thames Street, London EC3R 6DN* T: (020) 7626 4481 E: rector@stmagnusmartyr.org.uk

WARNER, Mrs Marjorie Anne. b 53. York Univ BA 74 York St Jo Univ MA 04. NEOC 06. **d** 09 **p** 10. NSM Masham and Healey *Leeds* 09–16; PtO from 17. *26 Larkhill Crescent, Ripon HG4 2HN* T: (01765) 606961 E: marjorieawarner@gmail.com

✠**WARNER, The Rt Revd Martin Clive.** b 58. St Chad's Coll Dur BA 80 MA 85 PhD 03. St Steph Ho Ox 82. **d** 84 **p** 85 **c** 10. C Plymouth St Pet *Ex* 84–88; TV Leic Resurr 88–93; Admin Shrine of Our Lady of Walsingham 93–02; P-in-c Hempton and Pudding Norton *Nor* 98–00; Hon Can Nor Cathl 00–02; C St Andr Holborn *Lon* 02–03; Can Res St Paul's Cathl 03–10; Suff Bp Whitby *York* 10–12; Bp Chich from 12; Master of Guardians Shrine of Our Lady of Walsingham 06–16. *The Palace, Chichester PO19 1PY* T: (01243) 782161 F: 531332 E: bishop@chichester.anglican.org

WARNER, Canon Mary. b 52. Univ of Wales (Swansea) BSc 73 Aber Univ PhD 77. NEOC 90. **d** 93 **p** 94. C Bensham *Dur* 93–96; Asst Chapl Newcastle upon Tyne Hosps NHS Trust 96–98; Chapl Hartlepool and E Durham NHS Trust 98–99; Chapl N Tees and Hartlepool NHS Trust 99–04; Chapl City Hosps Sunderland NHS Foundn Trust 04–15; Hon Can Dur Cathl 10–15; rtd 15; PtO *Dur* from 15; *Newc* from 16. *47 Wydon Park, Hexham NE46 2DA* T: (01434) 607931

WARNER, Canon Michael John William. b 41. Ex Univ MPhil 06. Sarum Th Coll 68. **d** 71 **p** 72. C Plympton St Mary *Ex* 71–75; V St Goran w Caerhays *Truro* 75–78; V Bishops Tawton *Ex* 78–79; V Newport *Truro* 79–83; V St Stythians w Perranarworthal and Gwennap 83–93; Sec Dioc Adv Cttee 93–01; P-in-c Budock 93–97; P-in-c Tregony w St Cuby and Cornelly 97–03; C Probus, Ladock and Grampound w Creed and St Erme 02–03; Hon Can Truro Cathl 98–03; rtd 03; PtO *Truro* from 03. *98 Porthpean Road, St Austell PL25 4PN* T: (01726) 64130 E: m.j.w.w@btinternet.com

WARNER, Nigel Bruce. b 51. St Jo Coll Cam BA 72 MA 76 ALCM 67. Wycliffe Hall Ox 75. **d** 77 **p** 78. C Luton St Mary *St Alb* 77–80; Prec Dur Cathl 80–84; R St John Lee *Newc* 84–91; V Lamesley *Dur* 91–98; V Bishopwearmouth St Nic 98–11; AD Wearmouth 99–05; V Heworth St Mary 11–16; rtd 16; PtO *Dur* from 17; *Newc* from 17. *47 Wydon Park, Hexham NE46 2DA* T: (01434) 607931 E: nigelwarmer275@btinternet.com

WARNER, Philip. *See* WARNER, John Philip

WARNER, Canon Robert William. b 32. TCD BA 54 MA 65 BD 65. TCD Div Sch Div Test 56. **d** 56 **p** 57. C Wythenshawe St Martin CD *Man* 56–60; R Hulme St Steph w St Mark 60–66; R Droylsden St Mary 66–76; R Stand 76–97; AD Radcliffe and Prestwich 85–96; Hon Can Man Cathl 87–97; rtd 97; PtO *Man* from 99. *28 Cow Lees, Westhoughton, Bolton BL5 3EG* T: (01942) 818821

WARNER, Mrs Stephanie Patricia. b 49. Lon Inst BA 96. SEITE 05. **d** 07 **p** 08. NSM Mottingham St Andr w St Alban *S'wark* 07–11. *20 Millbrook Gardens, Chadwell Heath, Romford RM6 6RP* T: (020) 8503 8379 M: 07365-181414 E: renwars@btinternet.com

WARNER, Terence. b 36. **d** 92 **p** 93. NSM Leek and Meerbrook *Lich* 92–98; NSM Odd Rode *Ches* 98–03; PtO *Lich* 03–15; NSM Brown Edge 15; rtd 15; PtO *Lich* 15–18. *36 Haig Road, Leek ST13 6BZ* T: (01538) 371988

WARNES, Brian Leslie Stephen. b 40. Natal Univ BSocSc 76. Kelham Th Coll 59. **d** 67 **p** 68. C Tonge Moor *Man* 67–71; S Africa 71–87; V Blean *Cant* 87–94; V Te Awamutu St Jo New Zealand 94–98; Chapl to Bp Christchurch 98–04; rtd 05. *57 Killarney Avenue, Torbay, North Shore City 0630, New Zealand* E: stephen.warnes@gmail.com

WARNES, David John. b 50. Jes Coll Cam BA 72 MA 76 PGCE 73. EAMTC 01. **d** 04 **p** 05. Chapl Ipswich Sch and NSM Ipswich St Mary-le-Tower *St E* 04–10; NSM Edin St Martin from 10. *7E Devon Place, Edinburgh EH12 5HJ* T: 0131-337 3574 M: 07732-654603 E: warnesdavid@googlemail.com

WARR, Timothy Gerald. b 59. Trin Coll Bris BA 86. **d** 88 **p** 89. C Yateley *Win* 88–91; C Chapel Allerton *Ripon* 91–93; V Wortley-de-Leeds 93–01; TR Borehamwood *St Alb* 01–05; TR Elstree and Borehamwood from 05. *The Rectory, 94 Shenley Road, Borehamwood WD6 1EB* T: (020) 8207 6603 *or* 8905 1365 F: 8207 6603 E: tim.warr@btinternet.com

WARRELL (*née* Lester), Stephanie Helen. b 94. Ches Univ BA 16. St Mellitus Coll MA 18. **d** 18 **p** 19. C Upton (Overchurch) *Ches* from 18. *43 Grafton Drive, Wirral CH49 0TX* M: 07503-128253 E: stephanie_helen_@hotmail.co.uk

WARREN, The Very Revd Alan Christopher. b 32. CCC Cam BA 56 MA 60. Ridley Hall Cam 56. **d** 57 **p** 58. C Cliftonville *Cant* 57–59; C Plymouth St Andr *Ex* 59–62; Chapl Kelly Coll Tavistock 62–64; V Leic H Apostles 64–72; Hon Can Cov Cathl 72–78; Dioc Missr 72–78; Provost Leic 78–92; rtd 92; PtO *Nor* from 92. *9 Queen's Drive, Hunstanton PE36 6EY* T: (01485) 534533

WARREN, Bunny. *See* WARREN, Gordon Lenham

WARREN, Mrs Gillian. b 53. Sheff Univ BA 74 PGCE 75. WMMTC 89. **d** 92 **p** 94. Par Dn Tettenhall Regis *Lich* 92–94; C 94–95; TV Bilston 95–00; R Lich St Chad 00–02; V Wednesbury St Paul Wood Green 02–10; V Albrighton, Boningale and Donington 10–14; rtd 14; PtO *Lich* from 18. *12 Walsall Road, Aldridge, Walsall WS9 0JL*

WARREN, Gordon Lenham (Bunny). b 45. Wycliffe Hall Ox 91. **d** 93 **p** 94. C Sunbury *Lon* 93–96; C Laleham 96–98; R Limehouse 98–13; rtd 13; Hon Chapl RN 08–16; PtO *Cant* from 14. *Hideaway Cottage, Avenue Road, Ramsgate CT11 8ES* T: (01843) 597299 E: gordonlwarren@aol.com

WARREN, James Randolph. b 54. St Paul's Coll Chelt CertEd 75 Bris Univ BEd 76 Birm Univ MEd 84. Ridley Hall Cam 90. **d** 92 **p** 93. C Boldmere *Birm* 92–95; V Torpoint *Truro* 95–01; Hon Chapl RN 98–01; V Shottery St Andr *Cov* 01–18; P-in-c Winnersh *Ox* from 18. *6 St Catherine's Close, Sindlesham, Wokingham RG41 5BZ* E: ssmarycath@gmx.co.uk

WARREN, Malcolm Clive. b 46. St D Coll Lamp. **d** 74 **p** 75. C Newport St Andr *Mon* 74–78; C Risca 78–79; V St Hilary Greenway 79–84; TV Grantham *Linc* 84–90; Ind Chapl *Linc* 87–90 and Worc 90–05; P-in-c Dudley St Aug Holly Hall *Worc* 95–96; PtO 96–97; TV Kidderminster St Mary and All SS w Trimpley etc 97–05; Ind Chapl *Bris* 05–10; TV Pontypool *Mon* 10–16; rtd 16; PtO *Mon* from 16. *31 Overdene, Pontllanfraith, Blackwood NP12 2JS* T: (01495) 741879 M: 07971-222739 E: malcolm.warren296@btinternet.com

WARREN, Martin John. b 59. Ch Coll Cam BA 81 MA 85. St Jo Coll Nottm LTh 85. **d** 86 **p** 87. C Littleover *Derby* 86–90; C Hermitage and Hampstead Norreys, Cold Ash etc *Ox* 90–91; TV 91–97; TV Hermitage 97–02; P-in-c Shebbear, Buckland Filleigh, Sheepwash etc *Ex* 02–15; TR from 15. *The Rectory, Shebbear, Beaworthy EX21 5RU* T: (01409) 281424 E: martinwarren535@btinternet.com

WARREN, Michael Philip. b 62. Oak Hill Th Coll BA 91 MA 04. **d** 94 **p** 95. C Tunbridge Wells St Jo *Roch* 94–98; Assoc Min Heydon, Gt and Lt Chishill, Chrishall etc *Chelmsf* 98–04; V Tunbridge Wells St Pet *Roch* from 04. *St Peter's Vicarage, Bayhall Road, Tunbridge Wells TN2 4TP* T: (01892) 530384 E: vicar@stpeterstw.com

WARREN, Canon Paul Kenneth. b 41. Selw Coll Cam BA 63 MA 67. Cuddesdon Coll 64. **d** 67 **p** 68. C Lancaster St Mary *Blackb* 67–70; Chapl Lanc Univ 70–78; V Langho Billington 78–83; Bp's Dom Chapl and Chapl Whalley Abbey 83–88; R Standish 88–01; P-in-c Silverdale 01–19; Hon Can Blackb Cathl 91–19; RD Chorley 92–98; AD Tunstall 08–14; PtO from 19. *The Vicarage, St John's Grove, Silverdale, Carnforth LA5 0RH* T: (01524) 701268 E: paulkwarren@btinternet.com

WARREN, Peter. b 40. Hull Univ MA 90 FCA 64. Oak Hill Th Coll 77. **d** 79 **p** 80. C Newcastle w Butterton *Lich* 79–82; TV Sutton St Jas and Wawne *York* 82–87; V Ledsham w Fairburn 87–95; R Ainderby Steeple w Yafforth and Kirby Wiske etc *Ripon* 95–03; rtd 03; PtO *York* from 04; *Sheff* from 08. *5 Bridge Farm, Pollington, Goole DN14 0BF* T: (01405) 862925 E: peter@rabbit22.plus.com

WARREN, Peter John. b 55. Worc Coll of Educn CertEd 76. Trin Coll Bris BA 86. **d** 86 **p** 87. C W Streatham St Jas *S'wark* 86–91; P-in-c Edin Clermiston Em 91–98; P-in-c Blackpool Ch Ch w All SS *Blackb* 98–03; V 03–09; Co-Pastor Internat Chr Fellowship Phnom Penh 09–13; Pastor from 13. *ICF, PO Box 98, Phnom Penh, Cambodia* T: (00855) 7788 6846 E: revpwarren@googlemail.com

WARREN, Robert. b 54. TCD BA 78 MA 81. CITC 76. **d** 78 **p** 79. C Limerick City *L & K* 78–81; Dioc Youth Adv

(Limerick) 79–86; I Adare w Kilpeacon and Croom 81–88; Bp's Dom Chapl 81–95; Dioc Registrar (Limerick etc) 81–12; Dioc Registrar (Killaloe etc) 86–12; I Tralee w Kilmoyley, Ballymacelligott etc 88–12; Can Limerick, Killaloe and Clonfert Cathls 95–96; Chan 97–12; Asst Dioc Sec L & K 90–12; Adn Limerick, Ardfert and Aghadoe *L & K* 10–12; I Taney *D & G* from 12; Preb Taney St Patr Cathl Dublin 04–12; Preb Tipperkevin from 12. *Taney Rectory, 6 Stoney Road, Dundrum, Dublin 14, Republic of Ireland* T: (00353) (1) 298 4497 M: 87-252 1133 E: taney@dublin.anglican.org

WARREN, Canon Robert Peter Resker. b 39. Jes Coll Cam BA 63 MA. ALCD 65. d 65 p 66. C Rusholme H Trin *Man* 65–68; C Bushbury *Lich* 68–71; V Crookes St Thos *Sheff* 71–90; TR 90–93; RD Hallam 78–83; Hon Can Sheff Cathl 82–93; Can Th Sheff Cathl 93–04; Nat Officer for Evang 93–04; Springboard Missr 98–04; rtd 04; PtO *Ripon* 03–10; *Newc* from 10. *2 The Fairway, High Hauxley, Morpeth NE65 0JW* T: (01665) 714697 E: robertwarren27@yahoo.com

WARREN, William Frederick. b 55. Sarum & Wells Th Coll 83. d 86 p 87. C E Greenwich Ch Ch w St Andr and St Mich *S'wark* 86–91; C Richmond St Mary w St Matthias and St Jo 91–95; TV 96–97; V Putney St Marg 97–08; V S Croydon St Pet and St Aug 08–18; AD Croydon Cen 17–18; Chapl Morden Coll Blackheath from 18. *Morden College, 19 St Germans Place, London SE3 0JW* T: (020) 8463 8324 M: 07920-506421 E: chaplain@mordencollege.org.uk

WARREN, William John. b 86. Warwick Univ BA 08. Wycliffe Hall Ox BTh 13. d 13 p 14. C Heigham H Trin *Nor* 13–17; C Nor St Andr 17–18; Public Preacher from 18. *68 Clarendon Road, Norwich NR2 2PW* T: (01603) 396757 M: 07843-731598

WARRICK, Mark. b 54. Aston Univ BSc 76 Nottm Univ BCombStuds 83. Linc Th Coll 80. d 83 p 84. C Grantham *Linc* 83–87; C Cirencester *Glouc* 87–91; V Over *Ely* 91–97; V Deeping St James *Linc* 97–09; P-in-c Stamford All SS w St Jo 09–13; V 13–19; RD Aveland and Ness w Stamford 06–09 and 10–14; RD Stamford 14–19; Dean Stamford 17; rtd 19. *2 The Old Builders Yard, Newboults Lane, Stamford PE9 1FA*

WARRILLOW, Brian Ellis. b 39. Linc Th Coll 81. d 83 p 84. C Tunstall *Lich* 83–85; C Shrewsbury H Cross 86–87; P-in-c Tilstock 88; P-in-c Whixall 88; V Tilstock and Whixall 89–92; TV Hanley H Ev 92–94; rtd 94; PtO *Lich* 01–02; P-in-c Menton *Eur* 02–05; Hon C Wolstanton *Lich* 07–10; PtO from 14; *Eur* from 00. *12 Sutton Avenue, Silverdale, Newcastle ST5 6TB* T: (01782) 700925 E: brian.warrillow@gmail.com

WARRILOW, Mrs Christine. b 42. Lanc Univ BA 86. NOC 86. d 89 p 94. C Netherton *Liv* 89–92; C Cantril Farm 92–94; V 94–96; V Hindley Green 96–02; rtd 02; PtO *Liv* 03–08; Hon C Stanley and Stoneycroft St Paul from 08; PtO *Blackb* 16–17. *10 Beacon View Drive, Upholland, Skelmersdale WN8 0HL*

WARRINGTON, Archdeacon of. *Vacant*
WARRINGTON, Suffragan Bishop of. *See* MASON, The Rt Revd Beverley Anne

WARWICK, Gordon Melvin. b 31. NOC 79. d 80 p 81. NSM Darrington *Wakef* 80–87; TV Almondbury w Farnley Tyas 87–95; rtd 95; PtO *Newc* 95–09; Hon C Dumfries *Glas* from 11. *4 Glencaple Avenue, Dumfries DG1 4SJ* T: (01387) 731357 E: gordonwarwick1931@btinternet.com

WARWICK, Hugh Johnston. b 39. ARCM 63. SAOMC 97. d 00 p 01. NSM Rotherfield Peppard *Ox* 00–02; NSM Rotherfield Peppard and Kidmore End etc 02–08; rtd 08; PtO *Ox* from 08; *Pet* from 08. *Witan House, 38 Wheeler's Rise, Croughton, Brackley NN13 5ND* T: (01869) 819577 or 819596 E: hugh@pukekos.co.uk

WARWICK, Canon John Michael. b 37. Fitzw Ho Cam BA 58 MA 62. Ely Th Coll 58. d 60 p 61. C Towcester w Easton Neston *Pet* 60–63; C Leighton Buzzard *St Alb* 63–64; C Boston *Linc* 64–66; P-in-c Sutterton 66–72; V 72–74; V Sutton St Mary 74–84; V Bourne 84–02; Can and Preb Linc Cathl 89–02; RD Aveland and Ness w Stamford 93–00; Chapl Bourne Hosps Lincs 84–93; Chapl NW Anglia Healthcare NHS Trust 93–98; rtd 02; PtO *Ox* 03–17. *24 Hurst Park Road, Twyford, Reading RG10 0EY* T: 0118-932 0649

WARWICK, The Ven Neil Michael. b 64. Nottm Univ BA 86. Ridley Hall Cam 03. d 05 p 06. C Towcester w Caldecote and Easton Neston etc *Pet* 05–09; V Earley St Nic *Ox* 09–19; Adn Bris from 19. *Bristol Diocesan Board of Finance, Hillside House, Bristol Parkway North, Newbrick Road, Stoke Gifford, Bristol BS34 8YU* T: 0117-906 0100 E: neil.warwick@bristoldiocese.org

WARWICK, Archdeacon of. *See* DUGMORE, Barry John
WARWICK, Suffragan Bishop of. *See* STROYAN, The Rt Revd John Ronald Angus

WASEY, Kim Alexandra Clare. b 77. Man Univ BA 99 Birm Univ MPhil 03. Qu Coll Birm 00. d 02 p 03. C Rochdale *Man* 02–04; Chapl Man Univ 04–06; Chapl Man Metrop Univ 04–06; Chapl Salford Univ 06–09; Hon C Man Victoria Park from 09; Chapl Salford Univ from 12. *St Chrysostom's Rectory, 38 Park Range, Manchester M14 5HQ* T: 0161-224 6971 M: 07944-155772 E: kim.wasey@gmail.com *or* k.wasey@salford.ac.uk

WASHBROOK, Mrs Mary. d 12 p 13. OLM Peak Forest and Dove Holes *Derby* 12–18; OLM Fairfield, Peak Forest and Dove Holes from 18. *22 Alexander Road, Dove Holes, Buxton SK17 8BN* T: (01298) 815187 E: maryatdove@gmail.com

WASHFORD, Mrs Rhonwen Richarde Foster. b 50. RGN 99. ERMC 05. d 08 p 09. NSM Stalham, E Ruston, Brunstead, Sutton and Ingham *Nor* 08–11; NSM Thorpe St Andr 11–15; rtd 15; PtO *Nor* from 15. *60B The Close, Norwich NR1 4EH* T: (01603) 302800 E: rhonwenwashford@hotmail.com

WASSALL, Canon Keith Leonard. b 45. Bede Coll Dur TCert 67. Chich Th Coll 68. d 71 p 72. C Upper Gornal *Lich* 71–74; C Codsall 74–75; TV Hanley All SS 75–79; Asst P Pembroke Bermuda 79–81; V Rickerscote *Lich* 81–92; P-in-c Coven 92–99; Asst Chapl HM Pris Featherstone 92–99; Can Res Bermuda 99–04; C Houghton le Spring *Dur* 04–06; C Eppleton and Hetton le Hole 04–06; C Lyons 04–06; C Millfield St Mark and Pallion St Luke 06–09; rtd 09; PtO *Dur* from 10. *28 Monteigne Drive, Bowburn, Durham DH6 5QB* T: 0191-377 8709 E: klwassall@tiscali.co.uk

WASTELL, Canon Eric Morse. b 33. St Mich Coll Llan. d 62 p 63. C Oystermouth *S & B* 62–65; C St Jo Cathl Antigua 65–66; R St Mary 66–73; R St Paul 73–74; Dioc Registrar 69–74; Hon Can Antigua 71–74; V Swansea St Gabr *S & B* 74–98; RD Clyne 88–96; Can Brecon Cathl 90–98; rtd 98. *Stella Maris Care Home, Eaton Crescent, Swansea SA1 4QR* T: (01792) 473453

WASTIE, Canon David Vernon. b 37. Open Univ BA 84. Chich Th Coll 79. d 81 p 82. C Bitterne Park *Win* 81–83; TV Chambersbury *St Alb* 83–87; V Jersey St Luke *Win* 87–94; P-in-c Jersey St Jas 87–93; V 93–94; V Jersey St Luke w St Jas 94–95; V Southbourne St Kath 95–99; Hon Can Bukavu Congo from 94; rtd 02; PtO *Derby* 05–08; *Win* 09–13; C Bournemouth St Fran 13–14; PtO *Sheff* from 16. *28 Cuthbert Cooper Place, Sheffield S9 4JS* T: 0114-242 1612 E: canonwastie@hotmail.com

WATCHORN, Canon Brian. b 39. Em Coll Cam BA 61 MA 65 Ex Coll Ox BA 62. Ripon Hall Ox 61. d 63 p 64. C Bolton St Pet *Man* 63–66; Chapl G&C Coll Cam 66–74; V Chesterton St Geo *Ely* 75–82; Fell Dean and Chapl Pemb Coll Cam 82–96; Hon Can Ely Cathl 94–04; Chapter Can 00–10. *34 Petersfield Mansions, Petersfield, Cambridge CB1 1BB* T: (01223) 322378 E: bw214@pem.cam.ac.uk

WATERFIELD, Janet Lyn. b 50. Birm Univ BA 06. WMMTC 99. d 02 p 03. C Bilston *Lich* 02–07; TV 07–12; P-in-c Lich Ch Ch 12–15; P-in-c Longdon 12–15; V Lichfield and Longdon from 15; RD Lich from 18. *Christ Church Vicarage, 95 Christ Church Lane, Lichfield WS13 8AL* T: (01543) 410751 M: 07905-539111 E: janwaterfield@blueyonder.co.uk

WATERFORD, Dean of. *See* JANSSON, The Very Revd Maria Patricia

WATERMAN, Canon Albert Thomas. b 33. Roch Th Coll 61. d 64 p 65. C Dartford St Alb *Roch* 64–67; V Ilkeston St Jo *Derby* 67–75; V Mackworth St Fran 75–79; V Dartford St Alb *Roch* 79–98; RD Dartford 84–97; Hon Can Roch Cathl 96–98; rtd 98. *19 Beachfield Road, Bembridge PO35 5TN* T: (01983) 874286

WATERMAN, Mrs Jacqueline Mahalah. b 45. ALCM 71. Cant Sch of Min 82. dss 85 d 87 p 94. Wavertree H Trin *Liv* 85–90; Par Dn 87–90; Par Dn Anfield St Columba 90–94; C 94; P-in-c Walton St Jo 97–99; V 99–01; C Baildon *Bradf* 01–05; rtd 05; PtO *Bradf* 05–14; *Leeds* from 14. *5 Lansdowne Close, Baildon, Shipley BD17 7LA* T: (01274) 468556

WATERS (née MUNRO-SMITH), Alison Jean. b 73. Regent's Park Coll Ox MA 94. Wycliffe Hall Ox 02. d 04 p 05. C Lostwithiel, St Winnow w St Nectan's Chpl etc *Truro* 04–08; C Shepperton and Littleton *Lon* 08–12; C Sonning *Ox* 12–16; R Cannington, Otterhampton, Combwich and Stockland *B & W* from 16. *The Rectory, 27 Brook Street, Cannington, Bridgwater TA5 2HP* T: (01278) 652636 E: alwaters@hotmail.co.uk

WATERS, Brenda Mary. *See* COUZENS, Brenda Mary

WATERS, Mrs Carolyn Anne. b 52. St Jo Coll Nottm BA 02. d 00 p 01. NSM Frodsham *Ches* 00–02; C Penhill *Bris* 02–06; P-in-c Stopham and Fittleworth *Chich* 06–09; rtd 09; PtO *Newc* from 10. *5 Leybourne Avenue, Newcastle upon Tyne NE12 7AP* M: 07789-430317 E: carolyn.anne.waters@googlemail.com

WATERS, Geoffrey John. b 64. UMIST BSc 85 Trin Coll Bris BA 99 Qu Coll Birm MA 08 St Hild Coll Dur PGCE 86.

WMMTC 06. **d** 08 **p** 09. NSM Northampton St Giles *Pet* 08–13; P-in-c Shirehampton *Bris* 13–15; C Oldland 15–19; PtO from 19; Chapl Partis Coll Bath from 19. *Address temp unknown* E: geoffreyjwaters@btinternet.com

WATERS, John Michael. b 30. Qu Coll Cam BA 53 MA 58. Ridley Hall Cam 53. **d** 55 **p** 56. C Southport Ch Ch *Liv* 55–57; C Farnworth 57–62; V Blackb H Trin 63–70; Sec Birm Coun Chr Chs 70–77; Chapl Birm Cathl 70–74; Dioc Ecum Officer 74–77; V Hednesford *Lich* 77–93; RD Rugeley 78–88; rtd 93; P-in-c Etton w Dalton Holme *York* 93–99; PtO from 00. *Blacksmith's Cottage, Middlewood Lane, Fylingthorpe, Whitby YO22 4UB* T: (01947) 880422

WATERS, John Sangster. b 48. CQSW 75. St Mich Coll Llan 67. **d** 13 **p** 13. NSM Caerwent w Dinham and Llanvair Discoed etc *Mon* 13–14; NSM Wentwood from 14. *Cae Golwg, Mynyddbach, Shirenewton, Chepstow NP16 6RT* T: (01291) 641449 M: 07836-585250 E: john@transientwaters.com

WATERS, Kenneth Robert. b 51. ERMC 08. **d** 10 **p** 11. NSM Grimshoe *Ely* 10–19; R Wissey Valley from 19. *6 The Avenue, Brookville, Thetford IP26 4RF* T: (01366) 727220 E: ken.waters@btinternet.com

WATERS, Mark. b 51. Southn Univ BTh 85. Sarum & Wells Th Coll 79. **d** 82 **p** 83. C Clifton All SS w St Jo *Bris* 82–85; P-in-c Brislington St Anne 85–91; Dioc Soc Resp Officer *Sheff* 91–94; Community Org Citizen Organisation Foundn 94–00; NSM Rotherham *Sheff* 94–97; Hon C Gt Crosby St Faith and Waterloo Park St Mary *Liv* 97–00; NSM 05–09; TV Kirkby 00–04; Progr Manager Participation for Change Ch Action on Poverty 04–05; PtO *Man* 06–13; NSM Toxteth Park Ch Ch and St Mich w St Andr *Liv* 09–14; NSM St Luke in the City 12–14; TV 14–19; rtd 19. *30 Victoria Road West, Crosby, Liverpool L23 8UQ* E: marko.waters@gmail.com

WATERS, Stephen. b 49. Chich Th Coll 83. **d** 85 **p** 86. C Baildon *Bradf* 85–87; C Altrincham St Geo *Ches* 87–89; TV Ellesmere Port 89–91; P-in-c Crewe St Jo 91–93; V Mossley 93–98; TV Congleton 98–99; P-in-c Alvanley 99–02; V Penhill *Bris* 02–05; rtd 05; PtO *Newc* from 10. *5 Leybourne Avenue, Newcastle upon Tyne NE12 7AP* M: 07796-694139 E: stephen@soulfriend.org.uk

WATERS, William Paul. b 52. Aston Tr Scheme 84 Chich Th Coll 86. **d** 88 **p** 89. C Tottenham St Paul *Lon* 88–91; C Stroud Green H Trin 91–95; TV Wickford and Runwell *Chelmsf* 95–98; Chapl Runwell Hosp Wickford 95–98; Chapl Qu Medical Cen Nottm Univ Hosp NHS Trust 98–10; C Ilkeston H Trin *Derby* 10–12; rtd 12; P-in-c Ilkeston St Jo *Derby* 15–16; C Kirk Hallam 15–16; C Spondon from 17. *22 Teesdale Court, Beeston, Nottingham NG9 5PJ* T: 0115-917 3429 E: paulwat04@gmail.com

WATERSON, Graham Peter. b 50. **d** 07 **p** 08. OLM Astley Bridge *Man* 07–10; NSM Thame *Ox* from 10. *The Rectory, 46 High Street, Tetsworth, Thames OX9 7AS* T: (01844) 281462 M: 07747-757657

WATERSTREET, Canon John Donald. b 34. Trin Hall Cam BA 58 MA 62. Lich Th Coll 58. **d** 60 **p** 61. C Blackheath *Birm* 60–64; C Aston SS Pet and Paul 64–67; R Sheldon 67–77; RD Coleshill 75–77; V Selly Oak St Mary 77–89; RD Edgbaston 84–89; Hon Can Birm Cathl 86–00; R The Whitacres and Shustoke 89–97; C Acocks Green 97–00; rtd 00; PtO *Birm* 00–12 and 15–18. *67 Rivendell Court, 1071 Stratford Road, Hall Green, Birmingham B28 8AT* E: jwaterstreet81@gmail.com

WATERSTREET, Mark Andrew. b 61. Qu Foundn (Course) 15. **d** 18 **p** 19. NSM Dosthill *Birm* from 18. *4 Cross Heath Cottages, Station Road, Nether Whitacre, Coleshill, Birmingham B46 2AG* T: (01675) 466403 M: 07976-800481 E: m.waterstreet@btopenworld.com

WATES, John Norman. b 43. BNC Ox MA 65 Solicitor 72 FRSA 00 Hon FRAM 09. **d** 02 **p** 03. OLM Chipstead *S'wark* 02–13; PtO from 13. *Elmore, High Road, Chipstead, Coulsdon CR5 3SB* T: (01737) 557550 F: 552918 E: john.wates@btinternet.com

WATHERSTON, Peter David. b 42. Lon Univ BSc 69 FCA 76. Ridley Hall Cam 75. **d** 77 **p** 78. C Barnsbury St Andr *Lon* 77–81; Chapl Mayflower Family Cen Canning Town *Chelmsf* 81–96; PtO 96–16; Dir First Fruit Charity from 97; PtO *Dur* from 14. *Manor Stables, 2A Staindrop Road, West Auckland, Bishop Auckland DL14 9JX* T: (01388) 606357 M: 07913-694678 E: pwatherston@aol.com

WATKIN, David Glynne. b 52. Univ of Wales (Lamp) BA 74 PhD 78 Wolv Univ PGCE 87 MTS FRGS. **d** 02 **p** 03. OLM Wolverhampton St Matt *Lich* 02–09; OLM Bilston 09–12; Bp's Officer for OLM 07–11; V Heath Hayes from 12. *St John's Vicarage, 226 Hednesford Road, Heath Hayes, Cannock WS12 3DZ* T: (01543) 274104 M: 07810-412377 E: revglynne@hotmail.co.uk

WATKIN, David William. b 42. FCA 70. Qu Coll Birm 84. **d** 86 **p** 87. C Tunstall *Lich* 86–89; Camberwell Deanery Missr

---

S'wark 89–95; V Trent Vale *Lich* 95–01; V Milton 01–10; rtd 10; PtO *Lich* from 10. *33 Station Grove, Stoke-on-Trent ST2 7EA* T: (01782) 253237 E: davidwwatkin@hotmail.com

WATKIN, Paul Stephen George. b 75. Anglia Ruskin Univ BA 08. Westcott Ho Cam 06. **d** 08 **p** 09. C Harwich Peninsula *Chelmsf* 08–11; P-in-c Rivenhall 11–14; TV Witham and Villages from 14. *The Rectory, Western Lane, Silver End, Witham CM8 3SA* T: (01376) 583930 E: psgw100@aol.com

WATKIN, Prof Thomas Glyn. b 52. Pemb Coll Ox BA 74 MA 77 BCL 75 Barrister-at-Law (Middle Temple) 76. Llan Dioc Tr Scheme 89. **d** 92 **p** 94. NSM Roath St Martin *Llan* from 92. *49 Cyncoed Road, Penylan, Cardiff CF23 5SB* T: (029) 2049 5662

WATKINS, Adrian Raymond. b 57. St Andr Univ MA 80 Ox Univ MTh 15. Lon Bible Coll 82 Ripon Coll Cuddesdon 12. **d** 07 **p** 08. Regional Manager (Asia) CMS 00–12; Lic to Offic Amritsar India from 07; PtO *St E* 08–12; C Newmarket All SS 12–15; R N Hartismere from 15. *The Rectory, Oakley, Diss IP21 4BW* T: (01379) 741949 M: 07958-617665 E: adrianrwatkins@gmail.com *or* rectornorthhartismere@gmail.com

WATKINS, Mrs Andrea. b 71. ERMC. **d** 08 **p** 09. C Heyford w Stowe Nine Churches and Flore etc *Pet* 08–11; R Blisworth, Alderton, Grafton Regis etc 11–19; R Brington w Whilton and Norton etc from 19; Tr Co-ord for Lic Ev from 11. *The Rectory, Main Street, Great Brington, Northampton NN7 4JB* E: andrealwatkins@hotmail.co.uk

WATKINS, Anthony John. b 42. St D Coll Lamp BA 64. St Steph Ho Ox 64. **d** 66 **p** 67. C E Dulwich St Jo *S'wark* 66–71; C Tewkesbury w Walton Cardiff *Glouc* 71–75; Prec and Chapl Choral Ches Cathl 75–81; R Brixworth w Holcot *Pet* 81–12; rtd 12. *20 Bromley College, London Road, Bromley BR1 1PE* T: (020) 8290 4700

WATKINS, Betty Anne. See MOCKFORD, Betty Anne

WATKINS, Charles Mark. b 57. Bradf Univ BTech 79. Westcott Ho Cam 06. **d** 08 **p** 09. C Almondbury w Farnley Tyas *Wakef* 08–11; TV Castleford 11–14; *Leeds* 14–18; C Smawthorpe *Wakef* 11–12; Pontefract All SS *Leeds* 18–19; C Pontefract St Giles 18–19; C Pontefract from 19. *Grenton, South Baileygate, Pontefract WF8 2JL* M: 07751-930968 E: wattycm@me.com

WATKINS, Christopher. b 43. Sarum & Wells Th Coll 88. **d** 90 **p** 91. C Abergavenny St Mary w Llanwenarth Citra *Mon* 90–94; TV Cwmbran 94–96; TV Wordsley *Worc* 00–09; rtd 09; PtO *Mon* 09–15; P-in-c Newport All SS from 15. *287 Malpas Road, Newport NP20 6WA* T: (01633) 556583 E: chriswat1943@gmail.com

WATKINS (née ROBERTS), Mrs Gwyneth. b 35. Univ of Wales (Swansea) BA MEd. St Mich Coll Llan 90. **d** 91 **p** 97. C Llanbadarn Fawr w Capel Bangor and Goginan *St D* 91–94; P-in-c Maenordeifi and Capel Colman w Llanfihangel etc 94–97; R 97–98; rtd 98; PtO *Win* 09–15. *17 Carlinford, 26 Boscombe Cliff Road, Bournemouth BH5 1JW* T: (02102) 391076 E: gwynethwatkins1@hotmail.com

WATKINS (née SMITH), Mrs Irene Victoria. b 45. SRN 66 SCM 69. **d** 03 **p** 04. OLM Lawton Moor *Man* 03–11; rtd 11; PtO *Man* from 11. *288 Wythenshawe Road, Manchester M23 9DA* T: 0161-998 4100 M: 07889-116856

WATKINS, John Graham. b 48. N Lon Poly CQSW 74. WEMTC 04. **d** 07 **p** 08. NSM Ledbury *Heref* 07–17; NSM Hop Churches 17–18; PtO from 19. *18 Pound Close, Tarrington, Hereford HR1 4AZ* T: (01432) 890595 E: john.watkins_48@yahoo.co.uk

WATKINS, Jonathan. b 58. Padgate Coll of Educn BEd 79. Trin Coll Bris 90. **d** 92 **p** 93. C Wallington *S'wark* 92–97; C Hartley Wintney, Elvetham, Winchfield etc *Win* 97–99; Chapl Win Univ 99–08; P-in-c Stockbridge and Longstock and Leckford *Win* 10–12; R Test Valley 12–17; P-in-c Knutton *Lich* 18; V from 18. *St Mary's Vicarage, Church Lane, Knutton, Newcastle ST5 6DU* T: (01782) 618367

WATKINS, Mark. See WATKINS, Charles Mark

WATKINS, Michael Morris. b 32. MRCS 60 LRCP 60. St Jo Coll Nottm 74. **d** 81 **p** 81. C Hornchurch St Andr *Chelmsf* 81–84; P-in-c Snitterfield w Bearley *Cov* 84–90; V 90–92; rtd 93; PtO *Cov* from 93. *Glaslyn, Riverside, Tiddington Road, Stratford-upon-Avon CV37 7BD* T: (01789) 298085 E: michaelwatkins@talktalk.net

WATKINS, Canon Peter. b 51. Oak Hill Th Coll BA. **d** 82 **p** 83. C Whitnash *Cov* 82–86; V Wolston and Church Lawford 86–99; RD Rugby 94–99; V Finham 99–10; Hon Can Cov Cathl 04–10; rtd 10; PtO *Cov* from 11; AD Rugby 13–17; PtO *S'well* from 16. *4 Medway Drive, Bingham, Nottingham NG13 8YD* T: (01949) 729525 M: 07772-001812 E: watkins51@icloud.com

WATKINS, Peter Gordon. b 34. St Pet Coll Ox BA 57 MA 61. Wycliffe Hall Ox 58. **d** 59 **p** 60. C Wolverhampton St Geo

Lich 59–60; C Burton St Chad 60–61; C Westmr St Jas *Lon* 61–63; USA 63–65; V Ealing Common St Matt *Lon* 67–15; rtd 15. *Charterhouse Sutton's Hospital, The Charterhouse, Charterhouse Square, London EC1M 6AN*

WATKINS, Robert Henry. b 30. New Coll Ox BA 54 MA 60. Westcott Ho Cam 59. **d** 60 **p** 61. C Newc H Cross 60–63; C Morpeth 63–67; V Delaval 67–80; V Lanercost w Kirkcambeck and Walton *Carl* 80–90; rtd 90; PtO *Carl* from 90. *Lowpark, Loweswater, Cockermouth CA13 0RU* T: (01900) 85242 E: bob@lowpark242.plus.com

WATKINS, Susan Jane. *See* HEIGHT, Susan Jane

WATKINSON, Adam John McNicol. b 68. Keble Coll Ox BA 89 MA 93 St Martin's Coll Lanc PGCE 90. NOC 01. **d** 03 **p** 04. NSM Croston and Bretherton *Blackb* 03–05; Chapl Ormskirk Sch 02–03; Chapl Liv Coll 03–06; Chapl Repton Sch Derby 06–16; PtO *Lich* 14–16; Chapl Charterhouse Sch Godalming from 16; PtO *Carl* from 15; *Guildf* from 16. *Charterhouse School, Brooke Hall, Charterhouse, Godalming GU7 2DX* T: (01483) 291500 *or* 291603 E: ajmw@charterhouse.org.uk

WATKINSON, Mrs Denise. b 59. St Jo Coll Nottm 13. **d** 15 **p** 16. NSM Hyson Green and Forest Fields *S'well* from 15. *51 Oxclose Lane, Arnold, Nottingham NG5 6FW* M: 07806-385621 E: denise.watkinson1@sky.com

WATKINSON, George Albion. b 87. Wycliffe Hall Ox 14. **d** 17 **p** 18. C Win Ch Ch from 17. *8 Juniper Close, Winchester SO22 4LU*

WATKINSON, Simon Thomas. b 89. Hatf Coll Dur BA 12 K Coll Lon MA 13 AKC 14. St Mellitus Coll MA 18. **d** 18 **p** 19. C Salford St Phil w St Steph *Man* from 18. *68 The Royal, Wilton Place, Salford M3 6FT* M: 07882-940280 E: simon.w@stphilips.org.uk

WATMORE, Mrs Georgina Jane Ann. b 63. Univ Coll Ox BA 85 MA 92 Ox Brookes Univ BA 10. SNWTP 10. **d** 12 **p** 13. C Hale and Ashley *Ches* 12–15; R Tarporley from 15. *The Rectory, High Street, Tarporley CW6 0AG* T: (01829) 732491 M: 07926-654707 E: revgeorgina@me.com

WATSON, Adam Stewart. b 75. Southn Univ BA 99. St Jo Coll Nottm 08. **d** 10 **p** 11. C Alton *Win* 10–14; V Welton and Dunholme w Scothern *Linc* from 14. *The Vicarage, Holmes Lane, Dunholme, Lincoln LN2 3QT* E: watson_adam3@sky.com

WATSON, Alan. b 41. AKC 64. St Boniface Warminster. **d** 65 **p** 66. C Hendon St Ignatius *Dur* 65–68; C Sheff St Cecilia Parson Cross 68–70; C Harton Colliery *Dur* 70–72; TV 72–74; R Gorton Our Lady and St Thos *Man* 74–82; TR Swinton St Pet 82–87; TR Swinton and Pendlebury 87–89; R Rawmarsh w Parkgate *Sheff* 89–94; P-in-c Dunscroft St Edwin 96–99; V 99–09; rtd 10; PtO *Sheff* 10–15; Hon C Sheff St Matt from 15; CMP from 98. *28 Shrewsbury Hospital, Norfolk Road, Sheffield S2 2SU* T: 0114-270 0212 M: 07884-230859 E: alan.watson61945@gmail.com

WATSON, Canon Alan. b 34. Lon Univ LLB 58. Linc Th Coll 58. **d** 60 **p** 61. C Spring Park *Cant* 60–63; C Sheerness H Trin w St Paul 63–68; R Allington 68–73; P-in-c Maidstone St Pet 73; R Allington and Maidstone St Pet 73–99; Hon Can Cant Cathl 85–99; RD Sutton 86–92; rtd 99; PtO *B & W* from 00; *Sarum* from 00. *68 Southgate Drive, Wincanton BA9 9ET* T: (01963) 34368 E: arw68@mypostoffice.co.uk

WATSON, Albert Victor. b 44. Ridley Hall Cam 85. **d** 87 **p** 88. C Hornchurch St Andr *Chelmsf* 87–94; P-in-c Tye Green w Netteswell 94–95; R 95–12; RD Harlow 99–04; rtd 12; Hon C Fyfield, Moreton w Bobbingworth etc *Chelmsf* 12–15; PtO from 15. *107 The Hoo, Harlow CM17 0HS* T: (01279) 453224 E: revalbie1944@gmail.com

WATSON, Alice Lydia Joy. b 87. G&C Coll Cam MA 08 K Coll Lon MSc 11. Ripon Coll Cuddesdon BA 18 MA 19. **d** 19. C Kettering SS Pet and Paul from 19. *2 Moorhouse Way, Kettering NN15 7LX* E: revalicewatson@gmail.com

⊕**WATSON, The Rt Revd Andrew John.** b 61. CCC Cam BA 82 MA 90. Ridley Hall Cam 84. **d** 87 **p** 88 **c** 08. C Ipsley *Worc* 87–91; C Notting Hill St Jo and St Pet *Lon* 91–96; V E Twickenham St Steph 96–08; AD Hampton 03–08; Suff Bp Aston *Birm* 08–14; Bp Guildf from 14. *Willow Grange, Woking Road, Guildford GU4 7QS* T: (01483) 590500 E: bishop.andrew@cofeguildford.org.uk

WATSON, Anne-Marie Louise. *See* RENSHAW, Anne-Marie Louise

WATSON, Beverly Anne. b 64. K Coll Cam BA 86 MA 90 Surrey Univ MA 08 ALCM 83. STETS 05. **d** 08 **p** 09. C Spring Grove St Mary *Lon* 08; C Aston and Nechells *Birm* 08–12; TV Salter Street and Shirley 12–15; V Guildf All SS from 15. *Willow Grange, Woking Road, Guildford GU4 7QS,* or *The Vicarage, 18 Vicarage Gate, Guildford GU2 7QJ* T: (01483) 841970 *or* 563173 M: 07547-416721 E: beverlyannewatson@btinternet.com

WATSON, Bruce Maclaren. b 68. Wolv Poly BA 90 Birm Univ PGCE 91. St Mellitus Coll 18. **d** 19. C Ashford Town

Cant from 19. *21 Grange Road, Deal CT14 9TS* T: (01304) 374139 M: 07790-538284 E: bruised@btinternet.com

WATSON, Cathryn Dawn. b 67. Man Poly BSc 88. Trin Coll Bris 15. **d** 17 **p** 18. C Tipton St Matt *Lich* 17–18; C Tipton St Matt w St Martin and St Paul from 19. *54 Oxford Way, Tipton DY4 8AL* T: 0121-439 6615 M: 07986-407000 E: curate@stmattstipton.com

WATSON, David. **d** 12 **p** 18. NSM Honicknowle *Ex* 12–14; NSM Ernesettle, Whitleigh and Honicknowle from 14. *23 Norfolk Road, Plymouth PL3 6BS* T: (01752) 670207 E: david@compton-vit.co.uk

WATSON, David. *See* WATSON, Leonard Alexander David

WATSON, Miss Dawn Louise. b 79. Greenwich Univ BA(QTS) 01. Ripon Coll Cuddesdon 14. **d** 16 **p** 17. C Margate St Jo *Cant* 16–18; P-in-c from 18; C Margate All SS 16–18; P-in-c from 18. *24 St Peter's Road, Margate CT9 1TH* M: 07805-699519 E: dawnlouise_watson@hotmail.co.uk

WATSON, The Very Revd Derek Richard. b 38. Selw Coll Cam BA 61 MA 65. Cuddesdon Coll 62. **d** 64 **p** 65. C New Eltham All SS *S'wark* 64–66; Chapl Ch Coll Cam 66–70; Bp's Dom Chapl *S'wark* 70–73; V Surbiton St Mark 73–77; V Surbiton St Andr and St Mark 77–78; Can Res and Treas S'wark Cathl 78–82; Dioc Dir of Ords 78–82; P-in-c Chelsea St Luke *Lon* 82–85; R 85–87; P-in-c Chelsea Ch Ch 86–87; R Chelsea St Luke and Ch Ch 87–96; AD Chelsea 94–96; Dean Sarum 96–02; rtd 02; PtO *Lon* from 17. *83 Winchester Street, London SW1V 4NU* T: (020) 7828 7377 E: dandswatson@googlemail.com

WATSON, Derek Stanley. b 54. NEOC 92. **d** 95 **p** 96. C W Acklam *York* 95–98; C-in-c Ingleby Barwick CD 98–00; V Ingleby Barwick 00–06; V Middlesbrough St Martin w St Cuth 06–11; rtd 12; PtO *Dur* 14–17. *3 The Brother House, Greatham, Hartlepool TS25 2HS* T: (01429) 872848 E: d.watson909@btinternet.com

WATSON, Geoffrey. b 48. Liv Univ BEd 71. Linc Th Coll 81. **d** 83 **p** 84. C Hartlepool St Luke *Dur* 83–87; P-in-c Shadforth 87–94; Soc Resp Officer 87–94; Dioc Rural Development Adv 90–94; V Staveley, Ings and Kentmere *Carl* 94–13; rtd 13. *15 Hawkins Way, Helston TR13 8FQ* T: (01326) 619984 E: geof_watson@talktalk.net

WATSON, Graeme Campbell Hubert. b 35. Ch Ch Ox BA 58 BA 59 MA 61. Coll of Resurr Mirfield 59. **d** 61 **p** 62. C Edin St Mary 61–63; C Carrington *S'well* 63–67; Tutor St Cyprian's Coll Ngala Tanzania 67–69; Vice-Prin St Mark's Th Coll Dar es Salaam 69–73; P-in-c Dar es Salaam St Alb 74–77; P-in-c Kingston St Mary w Broomfield *B & W* 77–80; V 80–81; R Kingston St Mary w Broomfield etc 81–95; P-in-c Feock *Truro* 95–00; Tutor SWMTC 95–00; rtd 00; PtO *Truro* 00–02; *Lon* from 02. *75 Winston Road, London N16 9LN* T: (020) 7249 8701 E: gchwatson@blueyonder.co.uk

WATSON, Henry Stanley. b 36. **d** 72 **p** 74. NSM Bethnal Green St Jas Less *Lon* 72–83 and 89–93; NSM Old Ford St Paul w St Steph and St Mark 83–88; NSM Scarborough St Mary w Ch Ch and H Apostles *York* 93–97; P-in-c Seamer 97–03; rtd 03; Hon C Fauls *Lich* 03–08; PtO *Heref* from 09. *14 Oakfield Park, Much Wenlock TF13 6HJ* T: (01952) 728794

WATSON, The Ven Ian Leslie Stewart. b 50. Wycliffe Hall Ox 79. **d** 81 **p** 82. C Plymouth St Andr w St Paul and St Geo *Ex* 81–85; TV Ipsley *Worc* 85–90; V Woodley St Jo the Ev *Ox* 90–92; TR Woodley 92–95; Chapl Amsterdam w Den Helder and Heiloo *Eur* 95–01; Chief Exec ICS 01–07; Can Gib Cathl *Eur* 02–07; Adn Cov 07–12; rtd 12; PtO *Linc* from 16. *The Cottages, 43 Station Road, Hibaldstow, Brigg DN20 9DY* T: (01652) 651040 M: 07714-214790 E: i.watson440@btinternet.com

WATSON, James Valentine John Giles. b 65. Newc Univ BA 87 Ox Univ BA 91 MA 97 Buckingham Univ PGCE 15. Ripon Coll Cuddesdon 89. **d** 92 **p** 93. C Newc St Geo 92–95; TV Daventry, Ashby St Ledgers, Braunston etc *Pet* 95–00; V Woodplumpton *Blackb* 00–03; TR Wheatley *Ox* 03–10; Chapl Old Buckenham Hall Sch 10–15; Chapl Maidwell Hall Sch from 15; C Maidwell w Draughton, Lamport w Faxton *Pet* from 15; C Arthingworth, Harrington w Oxendon and E Farndon from 15. *The Rectory, 35 Main Street, Great Oxenden, Market Harborough LE16 8NE* T: (01858) 469808 M: 07881-577149 E: jvjgwatson1@gmail.com

WATSON, The Ven Jeffrey John Seagrief. b 39. Em Coll Cam BA 61 MA 65. Clifton Th Coll 62. **d** 65 **p** 66. C Beckenham Ch Ch *Roch* 65–69; C Southsea St Jude *Portsm* 69–71; V Win Ch Ch 71–81; V Bitterne 81–93; RD Southampton 83–93; Hon Can Win Cathl 91–93; Adn Ely 93–04; Hon Can Ely Cathl 93–04; rtd 04; PtO *Win* from 04. *7 Ferry Road, Hythe, Southampton SO45 5GB* T: (023) 8084 1189 E: jjswatson@gmail.com

WATSON, Mrs Joanna Margaret. b 57. All SS Cen for Miss & Min. **d** 14 **p** 15. NSM Norden w Ashworth and Bamford

Man 14–16; NSM Chadderton St Matt w St Luke 16–17; NSM Whitworth w Facit from 17. *21 Westfield Close, Rochdale OL11 5XB*   T: (01706) 524657 E: jo.mwatson@tiscali.co.uk

WATSON, John Calum. b 69. Spurgeon's Coll BD 96 K Coll Lon MA 14. Trin Coll Bris MA 03. **d** 03 **p** 04. C Richmond H Trin and Ch Ch *S'wark* 03–06; TV Deptford St Jo w H Trin and Ascension 06–08; V Tupsley w Hampton Bishop *Heref* 08–14; V Dulwich St Barn *S'wark* from 14; Dir Ords Woolwich Area from 17. *38 Calton Avenue, London SE21 7DG* E: john@allyu.org.uk

WATSON, Jonathan Ramsay George. b 38. Oriel Coll Ox BA 61 MA 65 DipEd 62. Ridley Hall Cam 88. **d** 90 **p** 91. C Locks Heath *Portsm* 90–94; V Erith St Paul *Roch* 94–01; rtd 01; PtO *Chich* from 01. *14 Park Crescent, Midhurst GU29 9ED*   T: (01730) 816145 E: jrgwatson@netscapeonline.co.uk

WATSON, Ms Joyce. b 46. Ilkley Coll TCert 68. TISEC 06. **d** 09 **p** 10. NSM Iona *Arg* 10–16; rtd 16; PtO *Arg* from 16. *Beannachd, Isle of Iona PA76 6SP*   T: (01681) 700525 E: joyce@iona76.plus.com

WATSON, Mrs Julie Ann. b 61. UWE BA 95 SS Coll Cam BTh 12. Westcott Ho Cam 09. **d** 11 **p** 12. C Malvern Link w Cowleigh *Worc* 11–14; TR Worc St Barn w Ch Ch from 14. *St Barnabas' Rectory, Church Road, Worcester WR3 8NX*   T: (01905) 23785 E: revjulieann@btinternet.com

WATSON, Julie Sandra. b 59. Liv Poly BSc 81 Teesside Poly PhD 86. NEOC 99. **d** 02 **p** 03. NSM Redcar *York* 02–12; NSM Selby Abbey from 12; Dean Self-Supporting Min from 09. *8 Sherwood Drive, Thorpe Willoughby, Selby YO8 9TN* E: j.s.watson@tees.ac.uk *or* julie.watson@yorkdiocese.org *or* julie301watson@btinternet.com

WATSON, Canon Leonard Alexander David. b 37. Man Univ BSc 59. Coll of Resurr Mirfield 62. **d** 64 **p** 65. C Rawmarsh w Parkgate *Sheff* 64–68; C Empangeni S Africa 69–74; TV E Runcorn w Halton *Ches* 74–79; TV Sanderstead All SS *S'wark* 79–86; TR Selsdon St Jo w St Fran 86–98; RD Croydon Addington 90–95; P-in-c Horne and Outwood 98–02; Hon Can S'wark Cathl 02–03; rtd 02; PtO *Win* 03–13. *49 Hilley Field Lane, Fetcham, Leatherhead KT22 9UP* E: dadiwatson@hotmail.com

WATSON, Mrs Linda Marie. b 58. St Mich Coll Llan 14. **d** 15 **p** 16. C New Radnor and Llanfihangel Nantmelan etc *S & B* 15–16; C Colwyn from 17. *The Rectory, Llanelwedd, Builth Wells LD2 3TY*   T: (01982) 553533 E: revlindawatson@gmail.com

WATSON, Mark Edward. b 68. Birm Univ BEng 91. St Jo Coll Nottm 07. **d** 09 **p** 10. C Higher Bebington *Ches* 09–13; P-in-c Frizinghall St Marg *Bradf* 13–14; *Leeds* from 14; P-in-c Windhill *Bradf* 13–14; *Leeds* from 14. *7 Red Beck Vale, Shipley BD18 3BN*   T: (01274) 986447   M: 07838-441568 E: lordsmyshepherd@yahoo.co.uk

WATSON, Nicholas Edgar. b 67. St Cath Coll Cam BA 88 MA 92. Wycliffe Hall Ox BA 91. **d** 92 **p** 93. C Benfieldside *Dur* 92–95; C-in-c Stockton Green Vale H Trin CD 95; P-in-c Stockton H Trin 96–00; Chapl Ian Ramsey Sch Stockton 95–00; P-in-c Hardwall *Derby* 00–09; Warden of Readers 00–09; TR Wednesfield *Lich* from 09; RD Wulfrun from 14. *The Rectory, 9 Vicarage Road, Wednesfield, Wolverhampton WV11 1SB*   T: (01902) 731462 E: newatson@btopenworld.com

WATSON, Prof Paul Frederick. b 44. MRCVS 69 RVC(Lon) BSc 66 BVetMed 69 Sydney Univ PhD 73 Lon Univ DSc 95. Oak Hill NSM Course 86. **d** 88 **p** 89. NSM Muswell Hill St Jas w St Matt *Lon* 88–96; NSM Edmonton St Aldhelm 96–01; PtO 01–09; *St Alb* from 01. *50 New Road, Ware SG12 7BY*   T: (01920) 466941 E: pwatson@rvc.ac.uk

WATSON, Paul William. b 55. Huddersfield Poly BA. St Jo Coll Nottm. **d** 86 **p** 87. C Meltham Mills *Wakef* 86–89; C Meltham 89–90; TV Borehamwood *St Alb* 90–96; V Oswaldtwistle Immanuel and All SS *Blackb* 96–08; rtd 08. *214 Union Road, Oswaldtwistle, Accrington BB5 3EG*   T: (01254) 381441

WATSON, Philip. b 60. RGN 83. Qu Coll Birm 86. **d** 89 **p** 90. C Ordsall *S'well* 89–93; TV Benwell *Newc* 93–99; V Stocking Farm *Leic* 99–10; R Barwell w Potters Marston and Stapleton from 10. *The Rectory, 14 Church Lane, Barwell, Leicester LE9 8DG*   T: (01455) 446993 E: frpwatson@virginmedia.com

WATSON, Richard Francis. b 40. Yorks Min Course 08. **d** 09 **p** 10. NSM Ilkley All SS *Bradf* 09–14; *Leeds* from 14. *23 St Helen's Way, Ilkley LS29 8NP*   T: (01943) 430108

WATSON, Canon Richard Frederick. b 66. Avery Hill Coll BA 87. Trin Coll Bris 91. **d** 93 **p** 94. C Kempston Transfiguration *St Alb* 93–97; TV Dunstable 97–03; R E Barnet 03–11; RD Barnet 05–11; Can Res and Sub-Dean St Alb 11–17; V St Alb St Saw from 17. *St Saviour's Vicarage, 25 Sandpit Lane, St Albans AL1 4DF* E: rf.watson@btopenworld.com *or* vicar.stsaviours@gmail.com

WATSON, Robert Bewley. b 34. Bris Univ BA 59. Clifton Th Coll 56. **d** 61 **p** 62. C Bebington *Ches* 61–65; C Woking St Jo *Guildf* 65–68; V Knaphill 68–98; rtd 98; PtO *Guildf* from 98. *Endrise, 1 Wychelm Road, Lightwater GU18 5RT*   T: (01276) 453822

WATSON, Roger Brian. b 45. Cranmer Hall Dur 67. **d** 70 **p** 71. C Sandylands *Blackb* 70–74; C Wallingford *Ox* 74–77; C Winchmore Hill St Paul *Lon* 77–83; rtd 10. *20 Ferndene Road, London SE24 0AQ*

WATSON, Mrs Sarah Louise. b 73. SS Hild & Bede Coll Dur BA 95 Sheff Univ MA 17 PGCE 96. St Hild Coll 15. **d** 17 **p** 18. C Walbrook Epiphany *Derby* from 17. *Address withheld by request*   M: 07966-548868 E: sarahwatson311@gmail.com *or* curate.walbrook@gmail.com

WATSON, The Ven Sheila Anne. b 53. St Andr Univ MA 75 MPhil 80 Kent Univ Hon DD 13. Edin Th Coll 79. **dss** 79 **d** 87 **p** 94. Bridge of Allan *St And* 79–80; Alloa 79–80; Monkseaton St Mary *Newc* 80–84; Adult Educn Officer *Lon* 84–87; Hon C Chelsea St Luke and Ch Ch 87–96; Selection Sec ABM 92–93; Sen Selection Sec 93–96; Adv on CME *Sarum* 97–02; Dir of Min 98–02; Can and Preb Sarum Cathl 00–02; Adn Buckingham *Ox* 02–07; Adn Cant and Can Res Cant Cathl 07–16; PtO *Lon* from 16; Preacher Lincoln's Inn from 17; Chapter Can St Paul's Cathl *Lon* from 17. *83 Winchester Street, London SW1V 4NU*   T: (020) 7828 7377 E: vensheilawatson@gmail.com

WATSON, Stephanie Abigail. See MOYES, Stephanie Abigail

WATSON, Mrs Susan Judith. b 50. Birm Univ BA 72. Qu Coll Birm 09. **d** 12 **p** 13. C Cen Wolverhampton *Lich* 12–16; TV Smestow Vale 17–18; PtO 18–19; C Smestow Vale from 19. *6 Newbridge Avenue, Wolverhampton WV6 0LW*   T: (01902) 680689   M: 07932-175846 E: suewatson@telecomplus.org.uk *or* suewatson6@gmail.com

WATSON, Timothy Daniel. b 71. ERMC. **d** 11 **p** 12. C Liv Cathl 11–15; CME Officer *Chich* 15–18; Chemin Neuf Community P Hove 15–18; R Hackett H Cross Australia from 18. *Address temp unknown*   M: 07427-685651

WATSON, Canon Timothy Patrick. b 38. ALCD 66. **d** 66 **p** 67. C Northwood Em *Lon* 66–70; TV High Wycombe *Ox* 70–76; Gen Sec ICS 76–82; R Bath Weston All SS w N Stoke *B & W* 82–93; R Bath Weston All SS w N Stoke and Langridge 93–94; TR Cheltenham St Mary, St Matt, St Paul and H Trin *Glouc* 94–03; rtd 03; PtO *Glouc* from 04; Can Kitgum from 05. *The Gateways, Farm Lane, Leckhampton, Cheltenham GL53 0NN*   T: (01242) 514298 E: tigertimwatson@yahoo.co.uk

WATSON, William. b 36. Ripon Hall Ox 64. **d** 66 **p** 67. C Leamington Priors H Trin *Cov* 66–69; V Salford Priors 69–74; V Malin Bridge *Sheff* 74–79; Chapl Shrewsbury R Hosps 79–89; Chapl R Hallamshire Hosp Sheff 89–92; Chapl Cen Sheff Univ Hosps NHS Trust 92–93; P-in-c Alveley and Quatt *Heref* 93–96; Chapl N Gen Hosp NHS Trust Sheff 96–01; Chapl Weston Park Hosp Sheff 96–99; Chapl Cen Sheff Univ Hosps NHS Trust 99–01; rtd 96; PtO *Sheff* 01–07; *Liv* from 16. *7 Sandiway Court, Preston Road, Southport PR9 9EG*   T: (01704) 541017 E: billandolwyn@outlook.com

WATSON, William Lysander Rowan. b 26. TCD BA 47 MA 50 Clare Coll Cam MA 52 St Pet Hall Ox MA 57. **d** 49 **p** 50. C Chapelizod and Kilmainham *D & G* 49–51; Tutor Ridley Hall Cam 51–55; Chapl 55–57; Chapl St Pet Coll Ox 57–93; Fell and Tutor 59–93; Sen Tutor 77–81; Vice Master 83–85; Lect Th Ox Univ 60–93; rtd 93. *Llandaff Barn, 11 Thames Street, Eynsham, Witney OX29 4HF*   T: (01865) 464198 E: lysander.watson@ntlworld.com

WATSON LEE, Christopher James. Leic Univ BA 04 Anglia Ruskin Univ PGCE 05. Oak Hill Th Coll BA 16. **d** 17 **p** 18. NSM Loose *Cant* 17–18; C from 19. *Address withheld by request* E: chris.watsonlee@allsaintsloose.org.uk

WATSON WILLIAMS, Richard Hamilton Patrick. b 31. SS Coll Cam BA 57 MA 62. St Aug Coll Cant. **d** 59 **p** 60. C Dorking St Paul *Guildf* 59–63; C Portsea St Mary *Portsm* 63–66; V Culgaith *Carl* 66–71; V Kirkland 66–71; V Wigton 72–79; Warden Dioc Conf Ho Crawshawbooth *Man* 79–82; P-in-c Crawshawbooth 79–82; Master Lady Kath Leveson Hosp 82–98; P-in-c Temple Balsall *Birm* 82–84; V 84–98; rtd 98; PtO *Glouc* from 98. *16 Barton Mews, Barton Road, Tewkesbury GL20 5RP*   T: (01684) 290509

WATT, John Cameron. b 67. Keele Univ BA 89. Linc Sch of Th and Min 12. **d** 15 **p** 16. C Linc St Nic w St Jo Newport 15–19; C S Lafford from 19; C Billingborough Gp from 19. *24 Roselea Avenue, Welton, Lincoln LN2 3RT*   T: (01673) 860028   M: 078887-802784 E: cameron.watt@aol.com

WATTERS, Mrs Kay. b 44. SAOMC 98. **d** 01 **p** 02. OLM Prestwood and Gt Hampden *Ox* 01–07; Chapl to Bp Buckingham 04–07; rtd 07; PtO *Ox* from 07; Cyprus and the Gulf 07–15; PtO *Sarum* from 15. *17 Pasture Way, Bridport DT6 4DW* E: kay_watters@hotmail.com

WATTLEY, Jeffery Richard. b 57. Univ of Wales (Abth) BSc(Econ) 79. Trin Coll Bris BA 92. **d** 92 **p** 93. C Reading Greyfriars *Ox* 92–96; V Wonersh *Guildf* 96–98; V Wonersh w Blackheath 98–06; V Egham 06–17; RD Runnymede 13–16; V Jersey Gouray St Martin *Win* from 17. *The Vicarage, Le Mont Gabard, St Martin, Jersey JE3 6UA* T: (01534) 853255

WATTS, Mrs Aline Patricia. b 57. St Jo Coll Nottm 02. **d** 04 **p** 05. C Lache cum Saltney *Ches* 04–08; P-in-c Leasowe 08–17; rtd 17; PtO *Ches* from 17. *9 Ash Close, Weston Rhyn, Oswestry SY10 7TW* E: enyakwatts@gmail.com

WATTS (née DUCKWORTH), Mrs Angela Denise. b 58. RN 95 RM 98. Ripon Coll Cuddesdon 05. **d** 07 **p** 08. C Malvern H Trin and St Jas *Worc* 07–10; PtO *Roch* 10–11; S'wark 11–12; *Portsm* from 11; *Win* 12; Chapl St Mich Hospice Basingstoke 12–13; Chapl Hants Hosps NHS Foundn Trust 13–15; Lead Chapl 15–17; rtd 17; PtO *Win* from 17; *Sarum* from 18. *6 Church Farm Close, North Waltham, Basingstoke RG25 2BN* T: (01256) 397626 E: angelawatts.tssf@gmail.com

WATTS, Anthony John. b 30. AKC 59. **d** 60 **p** 61. C Whitburn *Dur* 60–63; C Croxdale 63–65; V Warrington St Pet *Liv* 65–70; V Peel *Man* 70–78; P-in-c Bury St Mark 78–81; V Davyhulme Ch Ch 81–99; Chapl Trafford Gen Hosp 89–94; Chapl Trafford Healthcare NHS Trust 94–98; rtd 99; PtO *Ches* from 00; *Man* 00–17. *11 Brackenfield Way, Winsford CW7 2UX* T: (01606) 590803

WATTS, Clive Roger. b 69. RGN 92. Ripon Coll Cuddesdon 14. **d** 16 **p** 17. C Wigston *Leic* 16–19; P-in-c Barrow upon Soar w Walton le Wolds from 19; P-in-c Wymeswold and Prestwold w Hoton from 19. *Holy Trinity Rectory, 27 Cotes Road, Barrow upon Soar, Loughborough LE12 8JP* M: 07905-230857 E: fr.clive.watts@gmail.com

WATTS, Daniel John. b 70. Wycliffe Hall Ox 04. **d** 06 **p** 07. C Paddock Wood *Roch* 06–09; C Harrogate St Mark *Ripon* 09–14; Leeds from 14. *2 Rossett Beck, Harrogate HG2 9NT* M: 07977-126438 E: daniel.watts11@btinternet.com *or* daniel.watts11@icloud.com

WATTS, David Henry. b 27. Ex Coll Ox BA 50 MA 55. Wells Th Coll 51. **d** 53 **p** 54. C Haslemere *Guildf* 53–55; C Chelmsf Cathl 55–58; Succ Chelmsf Cathl 55–58; V Chessington *Guildf* 58–62; Educn Officer Essex Educn Cttee 62–70; HMI of Schs 70–87; Hon C Wetherby *Ripon* 79–87; P-in-c Healaugh w Wighill, Bilbrough and Askham Richard *York* 87–89; Chapl HM Pris Askham Grange 87–96; rtd 89; PtO *York* 98–10. *Address temp unknown*

WATTS, Gordon Sidney Stewart. b 40. CITC 63. **d** 66 **p** 67. C Belfast St Steph *Conn* 66–69; CF 69–74; V Boldre w S Baddesley *Win* 94–96; P-in-c Warmfield *Wakef* 96–02; Sub Chapl HM Pris Wakef 97–02; Chapl Huggens Coll Northfleet 02–07; rtd 07; PtO *Ches* from 07. *8 Bramwell Avenue, Prenton CH43 0RH* T: 0151-200 0861 M: 07967-134101 E: gss.watts@ntlworld.com

WATTS, Graham Hadley Lundie. b 74. Man Metrop Univ BA 95. Ridley Hall Cam 98. **d** 02 **p** 03. C Camberley St Paul *Guildf* 02–06; C Northwood Em *Lon* 06–14; TV Gt Marlow w Marlow Bottom, Lt Marlow and Bisham *Ox* from 14. *165 Marlow Bottom, Marlow SL7 3PL* T: (01628) 473548 E: graham.watts@4u-team.org

WATTS, John Michael. b 45. **d** 04 **p** 10. OLM Ashtead *Guildf* 04–15; PtO from 15; Asst Chapl Guy's and St Thos' NHS Foundn Trust from 04; PtO *S'wark* from 05. *31 Broadhurst, Ashtead KT21 1QB* T: (01372) 275134 E: john.watts@gstt.nhs.uk

WATTS, John Robert. b 39. Leeds Univ BSc 60 MSc 63 DipEd 63. Oak Hill Th Coll 88. **d** 90 **p** 91. C Partington and Carrington *Ches* 90–93; P-in-c Tintwistle 93–98; V Hollingworth w Tintwistle 98–04; RD Mottram 99–03; rtd 04; PtO *Ches* from 04. *16 Norley Drive, Vicars Cross, Chester CH3 5PG* T: (01244) 350439 E: revrobwatts@hotmail.co.uk

WATTS, Jonathan Peter (Jonah). b 52. Lon Univ BA 74. Ripon Coll Cuddesdon BTh 11. **d** 08 **p** 09. C Crayford *Roch* 08–11; V Twyford and Owslebury and Morestead etc *Win* 11–17; rtd 17; PtO *Win* from 17. *6 Church Farm Close, North Waltham, Basingstoke RG25 2BN* T: (01256) 397626 E: jonah.watts1@icloud.com

WATTS, Mrs Mary Kathleen. b 31. Lon Univ BA 86. Gilmore Ho 73. **dss** 77 **d** 87 **p** 94. Lower Streatham St Andr *S'wark* 77–88; C 87–88; C Streatham Immanuel w St Anselm 87–88; C Streatham Immanuel and St Andr 90–91; rtd 91; PtO *S'wark* 91–94 and 05–06; Hon C Norbury St Oswald 94–05; PtO *Roch* 10–16; Church from 16. *25 Ramsay Hall, 9-13 Byron Road, Worthing BN11 3HN*

WATTS, Matthew David. b 79. Clare Coll Cam BA 01 MA 04 MSci 01 St Jo Coll Dur BA 05. Cranmer Hall Dur 03. **d** 06 **p** 07.

C Comberton and Toft w Caldecote and Childerley *Ely* 06–09; V Burnside-Harewood New Zealand 09–19; V Buller from 19. *13A Lyndhurst Street, Westport 7825, New Zealand* T: (0064) (22) 639 6093 E: mattdwatts@hotmail.com

WATTS, Paul George. b 43. Nottm Univ BA 67. Wells Th Coll 67. **d** 69 **p** 70. C Sherwood *S'well* 69–74; Chapl Trent (Nottm) Poly 74–80; V Nottingham All SS 80–84; Public Preacher 84–06; rtd 06. *14 Chestnut Grove, Nottingham NG3 5AD* T: 0115-960 9964 M: 07952-369066 E: wattses@yahoo.co.uk

WATTS, Sir Philip Beverley. b 45. Leeds Univ BSc 66 MSc 69 Ox Brookes Univ BA 11 FInstP 80 FEI 90 FGS 98 FRGS 98. Ox Min Course 09. **d** 11 **p** 12. NSM Binfield *Ox* 11–13; P-in-c Waltham St Lawrence 13–16; PtO from 16. *Sunnyridge, Hill Farm Lane, Binfield, Bracknell RG42 5NR* T: (01344) 305965 E: philbwatts@gmail.com

WATTS (née SIMPER), Rachel Dawn. b 67. K Coll Lon BD 89. Westcott Ho Cam 90. **d** 92 **p** 94. Par Dn Clitheroe St Mary *Blackb* 92–94; C 94–95; C Nor St Pet Mancroft w St Jo Maddermarket 95–97; V Slyne w Hest *Blackb* 97–04; V Briercliffe 04–11; Women's Min Adv 00–11; Hon Can Blackb Cathl 10–11; R Uppingham w Ayston and Belton w Wardley *Pet* from 11; Asst Dir Ords from 14. *The Rectory, 45 Lime Tree Avenue, Uppingham, Oakham LE15 9SS* T: (01572) 829956 E: rwatts789@btinternet.com *or* rectorofuppingham@gmail.com

WATTS, Ms Rebecca Harriet. b 61. St Cath Coll Cam BA 83 MA. Wycliffe Hall Ox 87. **d** 90 **p** 94. C Goldsworth Park *Guildf* 90–94; Chapl Wadh Coll Ox 94–97; C Ox St Mary V w St Cross and St Pet 94–97; Chapl Somerville Coll Ox 97–98; PtO *Newc* 98–99 and from 02. *7 Westfield Avenue, Newcastle upon Tyne NE3 4YH* T: 0191-285 9840 E: rebecca.h.watts@blueyonder.co.uk

WATTS, Robert. *See* WATTS, John Robert

WATTS, Roger Mansfield. b 41. Univ of Wales (Cardiff) BSc 63 CEng 76 MIET 76. Chich Th Coll 89. **d** 91 **p** 92. C Chippenham St Andr w Tytherton Lucas *Bris* 91–93; C Henfield w Shermanbury and Woodmancote *Chich* 93–96; R Jedburgh *Edin* 96–99; R Wingerworth *Derby* 99–06; rtd 06; PtO *Llan* 14–16; *St As* 16; Hon C Aled Miss Area from 16. *The Rectory, 1 Rhodfa Sant Elian, Colwyn Bay LL29 8PY* T: (01492) 209147 E: revrwatts@gmail.com

WATTS, Ms Samantha Alison Lundie. b 70. Birm Univ BA 92 Cam Univ BA 01. Ridley Hall Cam 99. **d** 02 **p** 03. C Camberley St Paul *Guildf* 02–06; NSM Northwood Em *Lon* 06–14; TV Gt Marlow w Marlow Bottom, Lt Marlow and Bisham *Ox* from 14; Chapl St Geo Sch Ascot from 18. *165 Marlow Bottom, Marlow SL7 3PL* T: (01628) 473548 E: sami.watts@4u-team.org

WATTS, Scott Antony. b 67. Anglia Ruskin Univ MA 18 FRSA 12. EAMTC 00. **d** 03 **p** 04. NSM Brampton *Ely* 03–07; Chapl St Jo Hospice Moggerhanger 07–09; Lead Chapl Hinchingbrooke Health Care NHS Trust 09–17; TV Vale and Cotswold Edge *Glouc* from 17. *The New Vicarage, Stratford Road, Honeybourne, Evesham WR11 7PP* T: (01386) 834946 E: revscottwatts@hotmail.com

WATTS, Thomas Annesley. b 79. K Coll Cam BA 01 MA 05. Oak Hill Th Coll MTh 08. **d** 08 **p** 09. C Wharton *Ches* 08–12; C Gt Chesham *Ox* 12–18; Min Hampstead St Jo Downshire Hill Prop Chpl *Lon* from 18. *St John's Church, Downshire Hill, London NW3 1NU* T: (020) 7099 9360 M: 07764-679210 E: tom@tomandsue.net

WATTS, Mrs Valerie Anne. b 44. UEA BEd 79. EAMTC 90. **d** 93 **p** 94. NSM N Walsham and Edingthorpe *Nor* 93–14; PtO from 15. *15 Millfield Road, North Walsham NR28 0EB* T: (01692) 405119 E: rev.valwatts@outlook.com

WATTS, William Henry Norbury. b 51. CertEd. St Jo Coll Nottm 87. **d** 89 **p** 90. C S Molton w Nymet St George, High Bray etc *Ex* 89–93; TV Swanage and Studland *Sarum* 93–10; P-in-c Basildon w Aldworth and Ashampstead *Ox* 10–14; V from 14; P-in-c Sulhamstead Abbots and Bannister w Ufton Nervet 14–17; AD Bradfield 11–17. *The Vicarage, Pangbourne Road, Upper Basildon, Reading RG8 8LS* T: (01491) 671714 E: revwillwatts@btinternet.com

WAUDBY, Miss Christine. b 45. TCert 66. Trin Coll Bris. **d** 90 **p** 94. C Weston-super-Mare Ch Ch *B & W* 90–94; C Blackheath *Birm* 94–99; PtO 99–03; NSM Ipsley *Worc* 03–10; rtd 10; PtO *Heref* from 11. *2 Coppice Close, Withington, Hereford HR1 3PP*

WAUGH, Nigel John William. b 56. TCD BA 78 MA 81. CITC 76. **d** 79 **p** 80. C Ballymena w Ballyclug *Conn* 79–82; C Ballyholme *D & D* 82–84; I Bunclody w Kildavin *C & O* 84–85; I Bunclody w Kildavin, Clonegal and Kilrush 86–91 and 91–98; Preb Ferns Cathl 88-91; Treas 91–96; Radio Officer (Cashel) 90-91; (Ferns) 92–98; Dioc Info Officer (Ferns) *C & O* 91–98; Prec Ferns Cathl 96–98; I Delgany

D & G from 98. *The Rectory, 8 Elsinore, Delgany, Greystones, Co Wicklow, Republic of Ireland* T: (00353) (1) 287 4515 M: 86-102 8888 E: nigelwaugh@gmail.com

WAY, Miss Alison Janet. b 61. York Univ BSc 83 FIBMS 86. St Mich Coll Llan 02. **d** 04 **p** 05. C Basingstoke *Win* 04–08; P-in-c Woodhill *Sarum* 08–10; R 10–14; NSM R Wootton Bassett and Lyneham w Bradenstoke 11–14; P-in-c S Nutfield w Outwood *S'wark* 14–15; V S Nutfield from 15; Officer for Lay Miss and Min Croydon Area from 14. *The Vicarage, 136 Mid Street, South Nutfield, Redhill RH1 5RP* T: (01737) 822211 E: revalisonway@gmail.com

WAY, Andrew Lindsay. b 43. Linc Th Coll 76. **d** 78 **p** 79. C Shenfield *Chelmsf* 78–82; C Waltham *Linc* 82–84; V New Waltham 84–89; R Duxford *Ely* 89–94; V Hinxton 89–94; V Ickleton 89–94; P-in-c Doddington w Benwick 94–97; P-in-c Wimblington 94–97; R Doddington w Benwick and Wimblington 97–98; R Eythorne and Elvington w Waldershare etc *Cant* 98–09; AD Dover 00–03; rtd 09; PtO *Cant* from 09. *17 Chequer Lane, Ash, Canterbury CT3 2AX* E: albeway@clara.net

WAY, Mrs Barbara Elizabeth. b 47. Open Univ BA 82 Hull Univ PGCE 86. Linc Th Coll IDC 78. **dss** 78 **d** 87 **p** 94. Shenfield *Chelmsf* 78–82; Adult Educn Adv *Linc* 82–85; Dioc Lay Min Adv 85; New Waltham 82–89; Min 87–89; Tetney 86–89; Min 87–89; NSM Duxford, Ickleton and Hinxton *Ely* 89–94; Dir Past Studies EAMTC 91–94; Min Pampisford 92–94; P-in-c Coates 94–95; TV Whittlesey, Pondersbridge and Coates 95–98; Local Min Adv *Cant* 98–02; Dioc Dir of Reader Selection and Tr 00–02; Dioc Adv in Women's Min 02–04; P-in-c Whitfield w Guston 02–10; Chapl E Kent Hosps NHS Trust 06–08; rtd 10; PtO *Cant* 10–13; C Westgate St Sav 13–16; PtO from 16. *17 Chequer Lane, Ash, Canterbury CT3 2AX* E: belway@clara.co.uk

WAY, Colin George. b 31. St Cath Coll Cam BA 55 MA 59 Lon Inst of Educn PGCE 58. EAMTC. **d** 84 **p** 85. NSM Hempnall *Nor* 84–87; C Gaywood, Bawsey and Mintlyn 87–90; R Acle w Fishley and N Burlingham 90–96; RD Blofield 95–96; rtd 96; PtO *Nor* 96–97 and from 02; P-in-c Pulham Market, Pulham St Mary and Starston 97–99; Hon C Eaton 99–02. *347 Unthank Road, Norwich NR4 7QG* T: (01603) 458363 E: colin.way@ntlworld.com

WAY, Matthew Paul. b 87. Univ of Wales (Newport) BA 09. St Mellitus Coll BA 18. **d** 18 **p** 19. C Hope Ch Islington *Lon* from 18. *28 Witherington Road, London N5 1PP* M: 07715-578198 E: mattway222@gmail.com *or* matt@hopechurchislington.org

WEAKLEY, Susan Margaret. b 52. SEITE 05. **d** 08 **p** 09. NSM Merstham and Gatton *S'wark* 08–10; NSM Merstham, S Merstham and Gatton 10–13; NSM Reigate St Mark 13–16; P-in-c Charlwood from 16; P-in-c Sidlow Bridge from 16. *81 Parkhurst Road, Horley RH6 8EX* T: (01293) 773954 M: 07887-888372

WEARING, Miss Julie Ann. b 65. Cov Poly BSc 89 St Jo Coll Dur BA 12. Cranmer Hall Dur 10. **d** 12 **p** 13. C Upton cum Chalvey *Ox* 12–15; V Linc St Faith and St Martin w St Pet from 15. *The Vicarage, 16SC Carholme Road, Lincoln LN1 1RU* T: (01522) 415858 M: 07710-592553 E: revjulie.stfaiths@gmail.com

WEARING, Malcolm Jamieson. b 72. Salford Univ BEng 94 PhD 00. All SS Cen for Miss & Min 11. **d** 14 **p** 15. OLM Farnworth, Kearsley and Stonecleugh *Man* from 14. *16 Butterfield Road, Bolton BL5 1DU* T: (01204) 658334 E: malcolm@stjohnsfarnworth.co.uk

WEARMOUTH, Alan Wilfred. b 54. Bris Univ BEd 76. Glouc Sch of Min 85. **d** 88 **p** 89. NSM Coleford w Staunton *Glouc* 88–06; C Coleford, Staunton, Newland, Redbrook etc 06–19; rtd 19. *Windhover, 2 Broadwell Bridge, Broadwell, Coleford GL16 7GA* T: (01594) 832660 M: 07811-118736 E: alanw22uk@yahoo.co.uk

WEARN, Simon Joseph. b 76. Pemb Coll Cam BA 00 MEng 00. Oak Hill Th Coll BA 09. **d** 09 **p** 10. C Gt Faringdon w Lt Coxwell *Ox* 09–13; R Hinckley H Trin *Leic* from 13. *Holy Trinity Vicarage, 1 Cleveland Road, Hinckley LE10 0AJ* M: 07980-910104 E: sjwearn@gmail.com

WEATHERHOGG, Susanne. *See* JUKES, Susanne

WEATHERILL, Martha Grace. b 77. Brunel Univ BSc 00 K Coll Lon MSc 01 MPhil 06. St Steph Ho Ox 15. **d** 17 **p** 18. C Chich St Paul and Westhampnett from 17. *19 Whistler Avenue, Chichester PO19 6DL* M: 07472-909011 E: jmweatherill@icloud.com

WEATHERSTONE, Timothy Andrew Patrick. b 59. Bedf Coll Lon BSc 81 UEA MSc 82 Anglia Ruskin Univ BA 12 Tilburg Univ PhD 16. ERMC 05. **d** 08 **p** 09. C Bowthorpe *Nor* 08–11; C Shipdham w Bradenham 11–12; TV Barnham Broom and Upper Yare 11–15; R from 15. *The Rectory, The Street, Reymerston, Norwich NR9 4AG* T: (01362) 858748 *or*

858021 M: 07967-190976 E: timweatherstone@mac.com *or* bb.office@weatherstone.net

WEAVER, Alan William. b 63. Linc Th Coll 95. **d** 95 **p** 96. C Seaford w Sutton *Chich* 95–98; C Langney 98–01; P-in-c The Haven CD 02–05; P-in-c Jarvis Brook 05–07; V from 07. *St Michael's Vicarage, Crowborough Hill, Crowborough TN6 2HJ* T: (01892) 661565 E: angyalanweaver@waitrose.com

WEAVER, Angela Mary. *See* TOWNSHEND, Angela Mary

WEAVER, Brian John. b 34. Oak Hill Th Coll 82. **d** 84 **p** 85. C Nailsea H Trin *B & W* 84–88; R Nettlebed w Bix and Highmore *Ox* 88–98; rtd 98; Hon C Warfield *Ox* 99–05; PtO *Lich* from 06. *11A Leslie Road, Sutton Coldfield B74 3BS* T: 0121-580 8086 E: bri_jac@talktalk.net

WEAVER, David Sidney George. b 46. Univ of Wales (Cardiff) BA 67 MA 71 Goldsmiths' Coll Lon MA 01 Lon Univ CertEd 76. SEITE 07. **d** 09 **p** 10. NSM Hove All SS *Chich* 09–12; P-in-c Haywards Heath St Rich 12–16; V 16; rtd 16; PtO *Chich* 16–17; P-in-c Eastbourne St Mich from 17. *123 Ringwood Road, Eastbourne BN22 8TG* M: 07811-145656 E: frdavidweaver@gmail.com

WEAVER, Mrs Diane Beverley. b 57. LCTP 06. **d** 09 **p** 10. C Steeton *Bradf* 09–13; V Barnoldswick w Bracewell *Leeds* 13–18; rtd 18. *5 Oakwood Close, Thornton-Cleveleys FY5 4EL* E: revdianeweaver@btinternet.com

WEAVER, Duncan Charles. b 60. St Jo Coll Nottm BA 99 Cardiff Univ MA 09 St Andr Univ MLitt 14. St Jo Coll Nottm 92. **d** 94 **p** 95. C Watford *St Alb* 94–98; TV Bourne Valley *Sarum* 98–01; CF 01–17; Chapl Bloxham Sch from 17. *Bloxham School, Banbury Road, Bloxham, Banbury OX15 4PE* T: (01295) 720222 E: dcweaver60@hotmail.com

WEAVER, Elaine. b 54. St Mellitus Coll 15. **d** 18 **p** 19. NSM Roxeth *Lon* from 18. *37 Yeading Avenue, Harrow HA2 9RL* T: (020) 8868 1081 M: 07964-748891 E: elaine_weaver37@hotmail.com

WEAVER, Fiona Margaret. b 61. Westcott Ho Cam 99. **d** 00 **p** 01. C Islington St Jas w St Pet *Lon* 00–03; Asst Chapl Univ of N Lon 00–02; Asst Chapl Lon Metrop Univ 01–03; Chapl 03–05; Lead Chapl 05–11; Family and Youth Work Adv 12–13; P-in-c Purley St Swithun *S'wark* 13–18; P-in-c Purley St Mark 13–18; V Purley St Mark and St Swithun from 18. *The Vicarage, 2 Church Road, Purley CR8 3QQ* T: (020) 8668 0063 E: revfionaweaver@gmail.com

WEAVER, Mrs Joyce Margaret. b 43. **d** 00 **p** 01. OLM Warrington St Ann *Liv* 00–13; rtd 13; PtO *Liv* from 16. *71 Orford Avenue, Warrington WA2 8PQ* T: (01925) 634993 E: joycearniew@aol.com

WEAVER, Martyn Graham. b 71. Salford Univ BEng 93 St Jo Coll Dur BA 12. Cranmer Hall Dur 10. **d** 12 **p** 13. C Selby Abbey *York* 12–16; V Bingley All SS *Leeds* from 16; PtO *York* from 18. *26 Falcon Road, Bingley BD16 4DW* E: martyn.weaver@tesco.net

WEAVER, Canon Michael Howard. b 39. Southn Univ MPhil 95 DipArch. Chich Th Coll 63. **d** 66 **p** 67. C Kidderminster St Jo *Worc* 66–69; Cathl Chapl and Dioc Architect Br Honduras 69–71; TV Droitwich *Worc* 71–76; V Arundel w Tortington and S Stoke *Chich* 76–96; P-in-c Clymping 84–87; RD Arundel and Bognor 88–93; Sub-Chapl HM Pris Ford 77–96; V Lymington *Win* 96–04; Chapl Southn Community Services NHS Trust 96–01; Chapl Southn City Primary Care Trust 01–04; rtd 04; Hon Can Enugu from 94; PtO *Win* 04–14; *Portsm* from 04; AD W Wight 10–12; PtO *Chich* from 14. *Tau Cottage, Crossbush, Arundel BN18 9PJ* T: (01903) 885087 E: junovicarage@hotmail.com

WEAVER, Canon William. b 40. Man Univ BA 63 BD 65. **d** 74 **p** 75. Lect Th Leeds Univ 67–91; Hon C Clifford *York* 82–86; Chapl K Edw Sch Birm 91–94; Provost Woodard Schs (Midl Division) 94–03; Hon Can Derby Cathl from 96; PtO 96–18; *Blackb* from 18. *1 Douglas Avenue, Stalmine, Poulton-le-Fylde FY6 0NB* T: (01253) 700849 E: william.antheaweaver@btinternet.com

WEBB, Alwyn Charles. b 62. Oak Hill Th Coll BA 95 K Coll Lon PGCE 96 MA 13. St Mellitus Coll 11. **d** 13 **p** 14. C Richmond H Trin and Ch Ch *S'wark* 13–18. *23 Grena Road, Richmond TW9 1XU* T: (020) 8404 1112 E: alwynwebb87@hotmail.com

WEBB, Amy Lavinia. b 75. STETS 12. **d** 15 **p** 16. C Botley *Portsm* 15–17; C Curdridge 15–17; C Durley 15–17; C Locks Heath 17–19; V Wymering from 19; V Cosham from 19. *Wymering Vicarage, Medina Road, Portsmouth PO6 3NH* E: rev.amywebb@yahoo.co.uk

WEBB, Arthur <u>Robert</u>. b 33. Lanc Univ MA 82 FRSA LCP 67. Wells Th Coll 69. **d** 70 **p** 70. C W Drayton *Lon* 70–72; Hd Master St Jas Cathl Sch Bury St Edmunds 72–86; Min Can St E Cathl 72–87; Succ St E Cathl 81–87; P-in-c Seend and Bulkington *Sarum* 87–88; V 88–91; R Heytesbury and Sutton

Veny 91–96; rtd 96; PtO *B & W* from 96; *Sarum* from 98; *Bris* 00–04; P-in-c Las Palmas *Eur* 04–08; PtO from 09. *27 Marlborough Buildings, Bath BA1 2LY* T: (01225) 484042

WEBB, Mrs Barbara Mary. b 39. Bedf Coll Lon BA 60 Cam Univ DipEd 61. Wycliffe Hall Ox 00. **d** 02 **p** 03. NSM Cumnor *Ox* 02–05; NSM Stanford in the Vale w Goosey and Hatford 05–09; P-in-c Shippon 09–10; rtd 10; PtO *Ox* 10–14; *Ches* from 14. *72A Station Road, Marple, Stockport SK6 6NY* T: 0161-221 2414 E: derry_barbara@msn.com

WEBB, Mrs Brenda Lynn. b 45. Stockwell Coll of Educn CertEd 66. EAMTC 97. **d** 00 **p** 01. NSM Saxmundham w Kelsale cum Carlton *St E* 00–10; Teacher Beacon Hill Sch 00–10; rtd 10; PtO *St E* from 12. *48 Pightle Close, Elmswell, Bury St Edmunds IP30 9EL* T: (01359) 242925 E: brenda.l.webb@gmail.com

WEBB, Catharine Rosemary Wheatley. b 39. **d** 05 **p** 06. OLM Redhill St Matt *S'wark* 05–09; PtO from 09. *6 Hurstleigh Drive, Redhill RH1 2AA* T/F: (01737) 769763 M: 07709-700602 E: webbcrw8@ntlworld.com

WEBB, Christopher Scott. b 70. Univ of Wales (Abth) BSc. Trin Coll Bris BA 96. **d** 96 **p** 97. C Dafen *St D* 96–98; C Cowbridge *Llan* 98–01; Officer for Renewal, Par Development and Local Ecum 01–04; V Llanfair Caereinion, Llanllugan and Manafon *St As* 04–07; President of Renovaré USA 07–12; V Lampeter *St D* 12–14; Dioc Spirituality Adv and Dep Warden Launde Abbey *Leic* from 14. *Launde Abbey, Launde Road, Launde, Leicester LE7 9XB* T: (01572) 717254 E: cw@launde.org.uk

WEBB, Dominic Mark. b 68. Oriel Coll Ox BA 91. Wycliffe Hall Ox BA 93. **d** 96 **p** 97. C Cradley *Worc* 96–99; C Leyton Ch Ch *Chelmsf* 99–02; P-in-c St Helier *S'wark* 02–06; Hon C Stratford St Paul and St Jas *Chelmsf* 07–15; PtO from 15. *32A Lister Road, London E11 3DS* T: (020) 8558 6354 E: webbdom@googlemail.com

WEBB, Mrs Eileen Marion. b 46. Bingley Coll of Educn CertEd. **d** 08 **p** 09. OLM Cheriton St Martin *Cant* 08–11; OLM Cheriton All So w Newington 08–11; OLM Cheriton w Newington 11–16; rtd 16; PtO *Cant* from 16. *4 Westfield Lane, Etchinghill, Folkestone CT18 8BZ* T: (01303) 864272 F: 864272 M: 07867-546929 E: bryleen@aol.com

WEBB, Mrs Gillian Anne. b 49. Whitelands Coll Lon CertEd 71 Heythrop Coll Lon MA 04. St Alb Minl Tr Scheme 83. **dss** 86 **d** 87 **p** 94. Kempston Transfiguration *St Alb* 86–96; NSM 87–96; NSM Kempston All SS 96–08; P-in-c Marston Morteyne w Lidlington 08–16; rtd 16; PtO *St Alb* from 16. *2 Hillson Close, Marston Moretaine, Bedford MK43 0QN* T: (01234) 767256

WEBB, Mrs Glenda Marjorie. St Jo Coll Nottm BA 13 Sheff Univ MA 16. Yorks Min Course 13. **d** 15 **p** 16. NSM Brayton *York* 15–19; NSM Askham Bryan from 19; NSM Copmanthorpe from 19; NSM Bolton Percy from 19; Asst Chapl York Teaching Hosp NHS Foundn Trust from 19. *Rockside, Springfield, Boston Spa, Wetherby LS23 6EB* M: 07871-241933 E: glendamwebb@gmail.com

WEBB (*née* EDWARDS), **Mrs Helen Glynne.** b 57. SRN 79 RMN 81 Birkbeck Coll Lon MSc 94. Wycliffe Hall Ox 88. **d** 90 **p** 94. Par Dn Clapham St Jas *S'wark* 90–94; Chapl Asst Southmead Health Services NHS Trust 94–97; PtO *Bris* 97–19. *13 The Green, Olveston, Bristol BS35 4DN* T/F: (01454) 615827 E: helenw13@gmail.com

WEBB, Ian. b 77. UWE BA 00. Trin Coll Bris 12. **d** 14 **p** 15. C Dronfield w Holmesfield *Derby* 14–18; P-in-c Clipstone *S'well* from 18; P-in-c Edwinstowe from 18; P-in-c Perlethorpe from 18. *The Vicarage, West Lane, Edwinstowe, Mansfield NG21 9QT* M: 07795-030241 E: ian@webbhome.co.uk

WEBB, Mrs Janice Beryl. b 49. Dioc OLM tr scheme 05. **d** 08 **p** 09. NSM Stour Vale *Sarum* 08–11; NSM Barbourne *Worc* 11–17; rtd 17; PtO *Worc* from 17; *Heref* from 18. *Seaview, Upper House, Wolferlow, Bromyard HR7 4QA* T: (01886) 853096 E: jan.dorset@gmail.com

WEBB, Jennifer Rose. b 48. Leeds Univ BA 70 Bedf Coll Lon CQSW 72. **d** 96 **p** 97. OLM Ham St Rich *S'wark* 96–05; NSM March St Mary *Ely* 05–14; P-in-c 14–15; NSM March St Pet 05–14; P-in-c 14–15; NSM March St Wendr 15; rtd 18; PtO *Ely* from 18. *3 Wherry Close, March PE15 9BX* T: (01354) 650855 E: revdjennywebb@btinternet.com

WEBB, John. *See* WEBB, William John

WEBB, John Christopher Richard. b 38. ACA 63 FCA 74. Wycliffe Hall Ox 64. **d** 67 **p** 68. C Hendon St Paul Mill Hill *Lon* 67–71; CF 71–93; R Bentworth and Shalden and Lasham *Win* 93–03; RD Alton 98–02; rtd 03; PtO *B & W* from 04. *Lower Farm Cottage, Church Street, Podimore, Yeovil BA22 8JE* T: (01935) 841465 E: john-cr.webb465@tiscali.co.uk

WEBB, Jonathan Paul. b 62. Bapt Th Coll Johannesburg BTh 98. **d** 02 **p** 03. NSM Linden S Africa 02–04; Asst P Bryanston 04–06; TV Bury St Edmunds All SS w St Jo and

St Geo *St E* 07–10; V E Molesey *Guildf* 10–15; V Brighouse and Clifton *Leeds* from 15. *47 Bracken Road, Brighouse HD6 2HX* E: revpaulwebb@gmail.com

WEBB, Kenneth Gordon. b 47. Lon Univ MB, BS 71. Trin Coll Bris BA 92. **d** 93 **p** 94. C Cheltenham St Mark *Glouc* 93–97; Banchang Ch Ch Thailand 97–02; P-in-c Duns *Edin* 02–17. *9/32 Western Harbour View, Edinburgh EH6 6PG* T: 0131-629 2102 M: 07990-866918 E: kenwebb275@icloud.com

WEBB, Mrs Linda. b 61. Qu Foundn (Course) 15. **d** 17 **p** 18. NSM Hulland, Atlow, Kniveton, Bradley and Hognaston *Derby* from 17. *Brambledene, Stanton Lees, Matlock DE4 2LQ* T: (01629) 312206 E: linwebb@btinternet.com

WEBB (*née* NAGEL), **Mrs Lucy Mary.** b 86. Bris Univ BA 07 PGCE 08 Anglia Ruskin Univ MA 15. Ridley Hall Cam 13. **d** 15 **p** 16. C Redland *Bris* 15–18; C Guildf St Sav from 18. *27 Agraria Road, Guildford GU2 4LF* T: (01483) 445152 M: 07813-405361 E: lucynagel@hotmail.com *or* lucy.webb@st-saviours.org.uk

WEBB, Lyndon James Stuart. b 89. G&C Coll Cam BA 11 MPhil 12. Ripon Coll Cuddesdon BA 18. **d** 19. C Broadstone *Sarum* from 19. *1A Mission Road, Broadstone BH18 8JJ* M: 07805-582432 E: revlyndonwebb@gmail.com

WEBB, Michael David. b 59. K Coll Lon BD 82 PGCE 83. Ripon Coll Cuddesdon 88. **d** 90 **p** 91. C Broughton Astley *Leic* 90–93; C Hugglescote w Donington, Ellistown and Snibston 93–94; TV 94–98; R Castleford All SS and Whitwood *Wakef* 98–01; P-in-c Glass Houghton 98–01; TR Castleford 02; rtd 02; PtO *S'well* 06–16; *York* 13–18; *Leic* from 17. *31 Bramley Road, Birstall, Leicester LE4 4FH* T: 0116-212 8466 M: 07813-144645 E: michael@michaelshouse.co.uk

WEBB, Canon Michael John. b 49. Linc Coll Ox BA 70 MA 74. Linc Th Coll 70. **d** 72 **p** 73. C Tring *St Alb* 72–75; C Chipping Barnet 75–78; C Chipping Barnet w Arkley 78–82; TV Cullercoats St Geo *Newc* 82–89; V Newc H Cross 89–97; Chapl MU 96–02; V Newc St Gabr 97–06; AD Newc E 97–04; V Alnwick 06–11; Hon Can Newc Cathl 02–11; rtd 11; PtO *Carl* from 12. *Underne, 24 Wordsworth Street, Keswick CA12 4BZ* T: (01768) 771180 E: michaeljwebb1@btinternet.com

WEBB, Miss Miriam May. b 50. **d** 19. NSM Lark Valley *St E* from 19; NSM Bury St Edmunds All SS w St Jo and St Geo from 19. *Address withheld by request* T: (01284) 704593 E: webbmiriamm@gmail.com

WEBB, Norma Fay. b 39. K Coll Dur BDS 62. **d** 04 **p** 05. OLM Thornhill and Whitley Lower *Wakef* 04–09; PtO 09–14; *Leeds* from 14. *24 High Street, Thornhill, Dewsbury WF12 0PS* T: (01924) 463574 E: normafwebb@btinternet.com

WEBB, Patrick James. b 84. Moorlands Th Coll BA 11 Greenwich Univ PGCE 08. Wycliffe Hall Ox BA 19. **d** 19. C Bleadon and Bournville *B & W* from 19. *6 Burrington Avenue, Weston-super-Mare BS24 9LP* M: 07581-719116 E: p.j.webb1984@gmail.com

WEBB, Paul. *See* WEBB, Jonathan Paul

WEBB, Peter Henry. b 55. Nottm Univ BA 77. St Steph Ho Ox 77. **d** 79 **p** 80. C Lancing w Coombes *Chich* 79–82; C The Hydneye 82–84; C-in-c 84–86; Chapl Sunderland Distr Gen Hosp 86–94; Chapl City Hosps Sunderland NHS Foundn Trust from 94. *The Chaplain's Office, Sunderland Royal General Hospital, Kayll Road, Sunderland SR4 7TP* T: 0191-565 6256 *or* 569 9180

WEBB, Richard. b 38. Oak Hill NSM Course 91. **d** 94 **p** 95. NSM Hanwell St Mary w St Chris *Lon* 94–04; rtd 04; PtO *Cant* from 05. *1 Haffenden Meadow, Charing, Ashford TN27 0JR* T: (01233) 714663 E: revrichardwebb@googlemail.com

WEBB, Canon Richard Frederick. b 42. Cant Sch of Min. **d** 84 **p** 85. C Ipswich St Clem w H Trin *St E* 84–87; R Rougham and Beyton w Hessett 87–91; R Rougham, Beyton w Hessett and Rushbrooke 91–92; P-in-c Woodbridge St Jo 92–98; P-in-c Saxmundham 98–04; P-in-c Kelsale-cum-Carlton, Middleton, Theberton etc 02–04; R Saxmundham w Kelsale cum Carlton 04–10; RD Saxmundham 03–05; Hon Can St E Cathl 06–10; rtd 10; PtO *St E* from 10. *48 Pightle Close, Elmswell, Bury St Edmunds IP30 9EL* T: (01359) 242925 E: richard.webb380@btinternet.com

WEBB, Robert. *See* WEBB, Arthur Robert

WEBB, Rosemary. b 59. **d** 10 **p** 11. NSM Ascot Heath *Ox* 10–13; P-in-c Clewer St Andr 13–15; R from 15; C New Windsor 13–14. *St Andrew's Rectory, 16 Parsonage Lane, Windsor SL4 5EN* T: (01753) 852334 E: rosiewebb@btinternet.com

WEBB, Rosemary. *See* WEBB, Catharine Rosemary Wheatley

WEBB, Timothy Robert. b 57. Univ of Wales (Abth) BA 79 Univ of Wales (Ban) BTh 03 CQSW 89. **d** 03 **p** 04. C Machynlleth w Llanwrin and Penegoes *Ban* 03–06; C Deanery of Llyn and Eifionydd 07–14; R Bro Cymer from 14. *The Rectory, Pencefn Road, Dolgellau LL40 2YW* M: 07748-962193 E: timbrocymer@outlook.com

WEBB, William John. b 43. Cuddesdon Coll 68. **d** 71 **p** 72. C Weston Favell *Pet* 71–73; C Newport w Longford *Lich* 74–77; C Baswich 77–79; P-in-c Stonnall and Wall 79–83; V Prees and Fauls 83–95; V St Martin's 95–06; rtd 06; PtO *Heref* from 06; *Lich* from 09. *72 Market Street, Kingswinford DY6 9LH* T: (01384) 295856

WEBBER, John Arthur. b 45. Keble Coll Ox BA 67 MA 71 Gen Th Sem NY STM 85. Cuddesdon Coll 70. **d** 71 **p** 72. C Penarth All SS *Llan* 71–74; USPG Bangladesh 75–84; 85–91; USA 84–85; Asst P Stepney St Dunstan and All SS *Lon* 91–97; Bp's Adv Relns w People of Other Faiths 91–04; P-in-c Bethnal Green St Barn 97–00; Dir of Ords 00–04; TR Llantwit Major *Llan* 04–10; rtd 10; PtO *Llan* from 10. *2 Arundel Place, Cardiff CF11 8DP* T: (029) 2019 6400 M: 07745-874839 E: johnwebber342@btinternet.com

WEBBER, Lionel Frank. b 35. Kelham Th Coll St Mich Coll *Llan.* **d** 60 **p** 61. C Bolton Sav *Man* 60–63; C Aberavon *Llan* 63–65; R Salford Stowell Memorial *Man* 65–69; V Aberavon H Trin *Llan* 69–74; TV Stantonbury *Ox* 74–76; TR Basildon St Martin w H Cross and Laindon *Chelmsf* 76–79; P-in-c Nevendon 77–79; RD Basildon 79–89; R Basildon St Martin w Nevendon 79–95; R Basildon St Martin 95–01; Hon Can Chelmsf Cathl 84–01; Chapl to The Queen 94–01; rtd 01; PtO *Chelmsf* from 07. *12 Ramblers Way, Burnham-on-Crouch CM0 8LR* T: (01621) 785152

WEBBER, Lorna Violet. b 40. **d** 06 **p** 07. OLM Woodbridge St Jo and Bredfield *St E* 06–10; rtd 10; PtO *St E* from 10. *Deo Gratias, 43 Through Duncans, Woodbridge IP12 4EA* T: (01394) 384634 E: lorna@stjohnswoodbridge.org.uk

WEBBER, Canon Michael Champneys Wilfred. b 48. Man Univ BA 71 MA(Theol) 78. Cuddesdon Coll 73. **d** 75 **p** 76. C Caterham *S'wark* 75–79; P-in-c Kidbrooke St Jas 79–84; TV 84–85; V Earls Barton *Pet* 87–09; RD Wellingborough 00–06; P-in-c Daventry, Ashby St Ledgers, Braunston etc 09–16; TR Daventry 16–19; RD 18; Can Pet Cathl 04–19; rtd 19; PtO *Pet* from 19. *12 Rowlandson Close, Northampton NN3 3PB* T: (01604) 403499 E: michaelc.webber@btinternet.com

WEBBER, Raymond John. b 40. Linc Th Coll 84. **d** 85 **p** 86. C Helston *Truro* 85; C Helston and Wendron 85–90; TV 90–93; R Kenton, Mamhead, Powderham, Cofton and Starcross *Ex* 93–03; rtd 03; PtO *Truro* from 03. *1 Seton Gardens, Camborne TR14 7JS* T: (01209) 711360

WEBBER, Thomas George Edward. b 63. LSE BSc 84. Trin Coll Bris. **d** 98 **p** 99. C Churchdown *Glouc* 98–02; TV Stoke Gifford *Bris* 02–12; V Weston super Mare Ch Ch and Em *B & W* from 12. *The Cedar, Montpelier, Weston-super-Mare BS23 2RQ* T: (01934) 709343 E: tomandchriswebber@tiscali.co.uk

WEBBER, Toby Roderic. b 75. St Jo Coll Dur BA 96. Wycliffe Hall Ox BA 01. **d** 02 **p** 03. C Chorley St Laur *Blackb* 02–06; P-in-c Bamber Bridge St Aid 06–12; P-in-c Walton-le-Dale St Leon w Samlesbury St Leon 11–12; Bp's Dom Chapl 12–15; V Altham w Clayton le Moors from 15. *The Vicarage, Church Street, Clayton le Moors, Accrington BB5 5HT*

WEBBLEY, Ms Rachel Catharine. b 75. Hatf Coll Dur BA 98. Qu Coll Birm BA 03. **d** 04 **p** 05. C Bicester w Bucknell, Caversfield and Launton *Ox* 04–07; TV Whitstable *Cant* 07–18; TR from 18. *28A West Cliff, Whitstable CT5 1DN* T: (01227) 273329

WEBSTER, Dennis Eric. b 39. Fitzw Ho Cam BA 60 MA 64 Linacre Coll Ox MA 70 Lon Univ CertEd 61. Wycliffe Hall Ox 62. **d** 65 **p** 66. C Herne Bay Ch Ch *Cant* 65–68; C Tulse Hill H Trin *S'wark* 68–69; Missr Kenya 70–75; Chapl Pierrepont Sch Frensham 75–91; R Chiddingfold *Guildf* 91–02; rtd 02; PtO *Guildf* from 02. *Sylvan Cottage, 24 Longdown Road, Lower Bourne, Farnham GU10 3JL* T: (01252) 713919 E: denwb@talktalk.net

WEBSTER, Derek Herbert. b 34. FRSA 82 Hull Univ BA 55 Lon Univ BD 55 Leic Univ MEd 68 PhD 73. Lambeth STh 67 Linc Th Coll 76. **d** 76 **p** 77. Lect Hull Univ from 72; Reader from 97; NSM Cleethorpes *Linc* from 76. *60 Queen's Parade, Cleethorpes DN35 0DG* T: (01472) 693786 E: dwebster@edrev.demon.co.uk *or* revwebster@btinternet.com

WEBSTER, Canon Diane Margaret. b 43. Oak Hill NSM Course 91. **d** 94 **p** 95. NSM Welwyn Garden City *St Alb* 94–99; P-in-c Burley Ville *Win* 99–10; RD Christchurch 03–10; Hon Can Win Cathl 08–10; rtd 10; PtO *Win* from 10. *Burwood, The Rise, Brockenhurst SO42 7SJ* T: (01590) 624927 E: diane.mwebster@tiscali.co.uk

⌖**WEBSTER, The Rt Revd Glyn Hamilton.** b 51. SRN 73. Cranmer Hall Dur 74. **d** 77 **p** 78 **c** 13. C Huntington *York* 77–81; V York St Luke 81–92; Chapl York Distr Hosp 81–92; Sen Chapl York Health Services NHS Trust 92–99; Can and Preb York Minster 94–99; Can Res York Minster 99–13; RD City of York 97–04; Assoc Dioc Dir of Ords 05–10; Suff Bp Beverley (PEV) from 13; Hon Asst Bp Liv from 13; Hon Asst Bp Ches from 13; Hon Asst Bp Sheff 13–14; Asst Bp Sheff from 14; Hon Asst Bp Dur from 14; Hon Asst Bp Man from 14; Hon Asst Bp Leeds from 14. *Holy Trinity Rectory, Micklegate, York YO1 6LE* T: (01904) 628155 M: 07983-341323 E: office@seeofbeverley.org.uk *or* bishopofbeverley@yorkdiocese.org

WEBSTER, James. *See* WEBSTER, Robin James Cook

WEBSTER, The Ven Martin Duncan. b 52. Nottm Univ BSc 74. Linc Th Coll 75. **d** 78 **p** 79. C Thundersley *Chelmsf* 78–81; C Canvey Is 81–82; TV 82–86; V Nazeing 86–99; RD Harlow 88–99; TR Waltham H Cross 99–09; Hon Can Chelmsf Cathl 00–09; Adn Harlow 09–17; rtd 17; PtO *Sarum* from 17. *22 Ashlands, Ford, Salisbury SP4 6DY* E: martinwebster52@me.com

WEBSTER, Mrs Patricia Eileen. b 34. St Gabr Coll Lon TCert 54. Gilmore Ho 56. **d** 87 **p** 94. Par Dn Belmont *Dur* 87–93; rtd 93; PtO *Dur* 04–15. *25 Eldon Grove, Hartlepool TS26 9LY* T: (01429) 425915

WEBSTER, Robin James Cook. b 62. Plymouth Poly BSc 86 Cranfield Inst of Tech MSc 87 Cranfield Univ PhD 06. St Jo Coll Nottm MTh 13. **d** 13 **p** 14. C Broxbourne w Wormley *St Alb* 13–16; V Langleybury St Paul from 16; Dioc Officer for IME (2) from 16. *The Vicarage, Langleybury Lane, Kings Langley WD4 8QQ* T: (01923) 270634 M: 07875-080949 E: stpaulslangleybury@gmail.com

WEBSTER, Rosamond Mary. *See* LATHAM, Rosamond Mary

WEBSTER, Sarah Vernoy. b 38. Univ of Georgia BSc 61. S'wark Ord Course 87. **d** 90 **p** 94. NSM Primrose Hill St Mary w Avenue Road St Paul *Lon* 90–01; Hon C Ann Arbor St Andr USA from 02. *4179 Eastgate Drive, Ann Arbor MI 48103, USA* T: (001) (734) 424 2750 E: revsallyweb@comcast.net

WEBSTER, Canon Stephen Jeremy. b 71. Leic Univ BA 92 PGCE 93. Wycliffe Hall Ox 05. **d** 07 **p** 08. C Oundle w Ashton and Benefield w Glapthorn *Pet* 07–14; R from 14; RD Oundle from 13; Can Pet Cathl from 19. *2 Herons Wood Close, Oundle, Peterborough PE8 4HW* T: (01832) 275631 E: stephen.webster@yahoo.co.uk

WEDGBURY, John William. b 53. RMCS BSc 78. St Jo Coll Nottm 84. **d** 87 **p** 88. C Folkestone St Jo *Cant* 87–91; V Mangotsfield *Bris* 91–92; NSM Manselton *S & B* 00–02; P-in-c Caereithin 02–05; NSM Swansea St Thos and Kilvey 05–12; PtO 12–15. *4 Ffynone Drive, Swansea SA1 6DD* T: (01792) 464194

WEDGE, Christopher Graham. b 67. LSE BSc(Econ) 89 Huddersfield Univ PGCE 94. NOC 00. **d** 06 **p** 07. C Castleford *Wakef* 06–09; Dep Chapl Manager United Lincs Hosps NHS Trust 09–11; C Boston *Linc* 11–12; TV 12–14; P-in-c Prestwich St Mary *Man* 14–18; R 18–19; AD Bury 15–16; PtO from 19. *Address temp unknown* E: chrisshef@hotmail.com

WEDGEWORTH, Canon Michael John. b 40. Nottm Univ BSc 62. Wesley Ho Cam MA 66. **d** 93 **p** 94. In Methodist Ch 66–93; NSM Feniscowles *Blackb* 93–96; Sec DBF 95–05; Hon P Blackb Cathl from 95; LtO 96–05; PtO from 05; Hon Can Blackb Cathl 03–10. *Abbott House, 74 King Street, Whalley, Clitheroe BB7 9SN* T: (01254) 825694 E: mike.wedgeworth@blackburn.anglican.org.uk *or* michael_wedgeworth@hotmail.com

WEEDEN, Canon Simon Andrew. b 55. York Univ BA 79. Wycliffe Hall Ox 88. **d** 90 **p** 91. C Gt Chesham *Ox* 90–94; P-in-c Haversham w Lt Linford, Tyringham w Filgrave 94–97; R Lamp 97–99; P-in-c Bramshott and Liphook *Portsm* 99–00; R 00–10; RD Petersfield 04–09; TR Whitton *Sarum* 10–19; Can and Preb Sarum Cathl 16–19; rtd 19. *5 Newbolt Close, Newport Pagnell MK16 8ND* E: simon@weeden.plus.com

WEEKES, David John. b 34. Magd Coll Cam BA 59 MA 68 Lon Univ PGCE 68 Aber Univ MTh 79 St Andr Univ PhD 17 FSAScot. Clifton Th Coll 62. **d** 64 **p** 65. C Cheadle *Ches* 64–68; Chapl Ntare Sch Mbarara Uganda 69–73; PtO *St And* 73–74; Chapl and Hd of RE Fettes Coll Edin 74–94; Warden and Chapl Lee Abbey Internat Students' Club Kensington 94–01; rtd 01; PtO *Lon* 94–03. *Loaning Hill House, Kilmany, Cupar KY15 4PT* T: (01382) 330183 M: 07855-761970 E: dw62@st-andrews.ac.uk

WEEKES, Robin Alasdair Rutley. b 73. Peterho Cam MA 94. Wycliffe Hall Ox BA 98 MA 98. **d** 99 **p** 00. C Wimbledon Em Ridgway Prop Chpl *S'wark* 99–03; Crosslinks India 03–10; Tutor Cornhill Tr Course 10–13; Min Wimbledon Em Ridgway Prop Chpl *S'wark* from 13. *Emmanuel Parsonage, 8 Sheep Walk Mews, London SW19 4QL* T: (020) 8946 4613 M: 07811-384350 E: robin.weekes@emmanuelwimbledon.org.uk

WEEKS, Ms Jane Anne. b 61. UEA BA 00. Aston Tr Scheme 95 EAMTC 97. **d** 00 **p** 01. C Hadleigh *St E* 00–02; C Hadleigh, Layham and Shelley 02–03; Chapl HM Pris Bullwood Hall 03–06; Chapl HM Pris Cookham Wood 06–08; PtO *Cant*

09–10; R Hever, Four Elms and Mark Beech *Roch* 10–16; P-in-c Elham w Denton and Wootton and Acrise *Cant* from 16; P-in-c Lyminge w Paddlesworth, Stanford w Postling etc from 18; AD Elham from 19. *The Vicarage, Vicarage Lane, Elham, Canterbury CT4 6TT* T: (01303) 840219 E: revweeks@hotmail.com

WEEKS, Mrs Rachel Elizabeth (Kim). b 51. STETS 09. **d** 14. NSM Portsea N End St Mark *Portsm* from 14. *7 Kingfisher Court, Portsmouth PO3 5XE* T: (023) 9269 8969 M: 07878-299231 E: kimeweeks@gmail.com

WEEKS, Timothy Robert. b 47. SAOMC 03. **d** 08 **p** 09. NSM Royston *St Alb* 08–12; LtO 12–17; Chapl Princess Alexandra Hosp NHS Trust from 08; PtO *Chelmsf* 09–16; *St Alb* from 17. *6 Chantry Road, Bishop's Stortford CM23 2SF* T: (01279) 831404 *or* (01763) 243265 M: 07974-866016

WEETMAN, Mrs Dorothy. b 41. **d** 03 **p** 04. OLM Prudhoe *Newc* 03–09; rtd 09; PtO *Newc* from 09. *Station Gate East, Eltringham Road, Prudhoe NE42 6LA* T: (01661) 834538

WEETMAN, Canon John Charles. b 66. Qu Coll Ox BA 87 MA 92. Trin Coll Bris BA 91. **d** 91 **p** 92. C Hull St Jo Newland *York* 91–95; V Boosbeck w Moorsholm 95–02; V Redcar 02–11; RD Guisborough 99–11; V Selby Abbey from 11; Can and Preb York Minster from 05. *The Abbey Vicarage, 32A Leeds Road, Selby YO8 4HX* T: (01757) 705130 E: weetman217@btinternet.com

WEIGHTMAN, Andrea Frances. *See* WARD, Andrea Frances
WEIGHTMAN, David Courtenay. b 47. FRICS 88. **d** 04 **p** 05. OLM Oxted and Tandridge *S'wark* 04–14; OLM Oxted 14–17; PtO from 17. *13 Silkham Road, Oxted RH8 0NP* T: (01883) 715420 F: 717336 M: 07739-456947 E: davidcweightman@gmail.com

WEIL, Thomas James. b 53. K Coll Lon BSc 74 PhD 79 AKC 74. S Tr Scheme 95. **d** 97 **p** 99. NSM Stoughton *Guildf* 97–03; PtO *Lon* 03–13; *Guildf* 04–15; NSM Worplesdon from 15. *Address withheld by request.*

WEIR, David Alexander. b 69. City Univ BSc 91 Fitzw Coll Cam BA 94 MA 99 Chich Univ BA 08. Westcott Ho Cam 92. **d** 95 **p** 97. C Locks Heath *Portsm* 95–96; C W Leigh 96–00; C Leigh Park and Warren Park 00–01; PtO 03–05; NSM Portsea St Mary 05–08; PtO *Truro* 08–09; P-in-c Exford, Exmoor, Hawkridge and Withypool *B & W* 09–12; P-in-c Exton and Winsford and Cutcombe w Luxborough 11–12; R Exmoor from 12; Warden of Readers Taunton Adnry 14–17. *The Rectory, Exford, Minehead TA24 7LX* T: (01643) 831330 E: david.weir122@btinternet.com

WEIR, Graham Francis. b 52. GSM LASI. NOC 88. **d** 91 **p** 92. NSM High Crompton *Man* 91–92; NSM Heyside 92–94; Asst Chapl Bolton Hosps NHS Trust 94–96; Chapl Bolton NHS Foundn Trust 96–12; Dep Hd of Chapl 04–12; PtO *Man* 13–18; Chapl OHP 13–17; rtd 17; PtO *York* from 17. *10 Field Close, Whitby YO21 3LR* E: gweir52@hotmail.co.uk

WEIR, John Michael Vavasour. b 48. K Coll Lon BD 72 AKC 72 MA 00. **d** 73 **p** 74. C Hatfield Hyde *St Alb* 73–76; C Watford St Mich 76–79; Asst Chapl Oslo St Edm *Eur* 80–81; V Bethnal Green St Pet w St Thos *Lon* 81–04; Chapl Qu Eliz Hosp for Children Lon 81–98; Chapl Team Ldr Toc H 01–10; Sen Chapl Dubai and Sharjah w N Emirates 04–10; rtd 10; PtO *Lon* from 13. *38 Belgrave Street, London E1 0NQ* T: (020) 7791 7957 E: jmvweir@gmail.com

WEIR, John William Moon. b 36. St Luke's Coll Ex CertEd 69 Ex Univ BEd 76. SWMTC 82. **d** 85 **p** 86. NSM Meavy, Sheepstor and Walkhampton *Ex* 85–87; NSM Yelverton, Meavy, Sheepstor and Walkhampton 87–05; Hd Master Princetown Primary Sch 86–94; Sub-Chapl HM Pris Dartmoor 86–94; PtO *Ex* from 05. *Goblin's Green, Dousland, Yelverton PL20 6ND* T: (01822) 852671

WEIR, Nicholas James. b 77. Pemb Coll Cam BA 98 MA 02 Green Coll Ox BM, BCh 01 MRCPsych 05. Oak Hill Th Coll MTh 11. **d** 11 **p** 12. C Eastrop *Win* 11–15; V Frogmore *St Alb* from 15. *The Vicarage, 39 Frogmore, St Albans AL2 2JU* T: (01727) 872172

WEIR, Ms Rachel Sian Shapland. b 66. Newnham Coll Cam BA 88 MA 91 Called to the Bar 91. Ripon Coll Cuddesdon MTh 07. **d** 07 **p** 08. Asst Nat Adv for Inter Faith Relns Abps' Coun 07–08; NSM Wolvercote *Ox* 07–08; NSM Headington Quarry 09–11; Chapl Highgate Sch Lon 14–18; Min Can St Paul's Cathl *Lon* from 18. *7B Amen Court, London EC4M 7BU* M: 07815-729565 E: rachelssweir@yahoo.co.uk

WEIR, William Daniel Niall. b 57. UEA BA 79. Ripon Coll Cuddesdon 80. **d** 83 **p** 84. C Chelsea St Luke *Lon* 83–87; PV Westmr Abbey 85–89; C Poplar *Lon* 87–88; TV 88–93; P-in-c Forest Gate Em w Upton Cross *Chelmsf* 93–97; V 97–99; Asst Chapl Southn Univ Hosps NHS Trust 99–00; Trust Chapl 00–03; R W Hackney *Lon* from 03. *The Rectory, 306 Amhurst Road, London N16 7UE* T: (020) 7254 3235 E: niall.weir@mac.com

WEISSERHORN, Julian Timothy David Moritz. *See* GADSBY, Julian Timothy David Moritz

WEITZMANN, Benjamin Edward Albert. b 80. Surrey Univ BSc 03. St Steph Ho Ox BTh 15. **d** 15 **p** 16. C Boxmoor St Jo *St Alb* 15–18; TV Portsea N End St Mark *Portsm* from 18; P-in-c Portsea St Sav from 18; C Portsea Ascension from 18. *The Vicarage, 98 Kirby Road, Portsmouth PO2 0PW* M: 07887-484080 E: benjamin@weitzmann.co.uk

WELBOURN, David Anthony. b 41. K Coll Lon BD 63 AKC 63. St Boniface Warminster 63. **d** 64 **p** 65. C Stockton St Chad *Dur* 64–67; C S Westoe 69–74; Ind Chapl 69–80; Ind Chapl *Nor* 80–90; Ind and Commerce Officer *Guildf* 90–06; rtd 06; PtO *Guildf* 06–17. *3 Windgates, Guildford GU4 7DJ* T/F: (01483) 825541 E: welbourn@ntlworld.com

✠**WELBY, The Most Revd and Rt Hon Justin Portal.** b 56. Trin Coll Cam BA 78 MA 90 St Jo Coll Dur BA 91 Hon FCT. Cranmer Hall Dur 89. **d** 92 **p** 93 **c** 11. C Chilvers Coton w Astley *Cov* 92–95; R Southam 95–02; V Ufton 96–02; Can Res Cov Cathl 02–07; Co-Dir Internat Min 02–05; Sub-Dean 05–07; P-in-c Cov H Trin 07; Dean Liv 07–11; Bp Dur 11–13; Abp Cant from 13. *Lambeth Palace, London SE1 7JU* T: (020) 7898 1200 E: contact@lambethpalace.org.uk

WELBY, Peter Edlin Brown. b 34. Open Univ BA 75. Cranmer Hall Dur 75. **d** 77 **p** 78. C Auckland St Andr and St Anne *Dur* 77–79; C S Westoe 79–81; V Tudhoe 81–93; R Croxdale and Tudhoe 93–99; rtd 99; PtO *Dur* from 04. *Blyth House, 9 Rhodes Terrace, Nevilles Cross, Durham DH1 4JW* T: 0191-384 8295

WELCH, Amanda Jane. b 58. **d** 04 **p** 05. OLM Worplesdon *Guildf* 04–17; rtd 17; PtO *Heref* from 18. *Oak Barn, Brinsop Court Park, Brinsop, Hereford HR4 7AX* E: revmandywelch@gmail.com

WELCH, Gordon Joseph. b 47. Man Univ BSc 68 MSc 69 PhD 72. NOC 84. **d** 87 **p** 88. NSM Upton Ascension *Ches* 87–98; LtO 99–00; NSM Backford and Capenhurst 00–02; NSM Ellesmere Port from 02; RD Wirral S 06–11. *6 St James's Avenue, Upton, Chester CH2 1NA* T: (01244) 382196 M: 07890-993948 E: gordonwelch@btinternet.com

WELCH, John Harry. b 52. Oak Hill Th Coll 85. **d** 87 **p** 88. C Parr *Liv* 87–90; V W Derby St Luke 90–00; V Eccleston Park 00–07; P-in-c St Helens St Matt Thatto Heath 06–07; TR Eccleston Team 07–17; Chapl Willowbrook Hospice 01–12; rtd 17. *10 Bobbin Mill, Spark Bridge, Ulverston LA12 8BS*

WELCH, Paul Baxter. b 47. Lanc Univ BEd 74 MA 75. St Alb Minl Tr Scheme 80. **d** 83 **p** 84. NSM Heath and Reach *St Alb* 83–84; Bp's Sch Adv *Win* 84–89; P-in-c Clungunford w Clunbury and Clunton, Bedstone etc *Heref* 89–93; V Wellingborough All SS *Pet* 93–01; R Pulborough *Chich* 01–16; RD Storrington 04–11; TV Crawley 16–17; V W Green from 17. *Priesthouse, 128 Ifield Road, Crawley RH11 7BW* T: (01293) 544046 M: 07759-695110 E: paulbwelch@live.co.uk

WELCH, Rebecca Anne. *See* JONES, Rebecca Anne

WELCH, Mrs Sally Ann. b 62. Pemb Coll Ox MA 88. SAOMC 96. **d** 99 **p** 00. NSM Abingdon *Ox* 99–01; P-in-c Kintbury w Avington 01–05; R Cherbury w Gainfield 05–09; C Ox St Giles and SS Phil and Jas w St Marg 09–15; V Charlbury w Shorthampton from 15; AD Chipping Norton from 15. *The Vicarage, Church Lane, Charlbury, Chipping Norton OX7 3PX* M: 07974-439630 E: vicar@stmaryscharlbury.com

WELCH, The Ven Stephan John. b 50. Hull Univ BA 74 Lon Univ MTh 98. Qu Coll Birm 74. **d** 77 **p** 78. C Waltham Cross *St Alb* 77–80; P-in-c Reculver *Cant* 80–86; P-in-c Herne Bay St Bart 82–86; V Reculver and Herne Bay St Bart 86–92; V Hurley and Stubbings *Ox* 92–00; P-in-c Hammersmith St Pet *Lon* 00–06; AD Hammersmith and Fulham 01–06; Adn Middx from 06. *98 Dukes Avenue, London W4 2AF* T: (020) 8742 8308 E: archdeacon.middlesex@london.anglican.org

WELDON, Nicholas Patrick. b 77. UWE BSc 99. Oak Hill Th Coll BA 07. **d** 07 **p** 08. C Moreton-in-Marsh w Batsford, Todenham etc *Glouc* 07–11; P-in-c N Tawton, Bondleigh, Sampford Courtenay etc *Ex* 11–13; TV Chagford, Gidleigh, Throwleigh etc from 13; RD Okehampton from 16. *The Rectory, Essington Close, North Tawton EX20 2EX* T: (01837) 880183 M: 07970-984190 E: npweldon@gmail.com

WELDON, Robert Price. b 57. Cant Ch Ch Univ BA 12. SEITE 06. **d** 09 **p** 10. NSM Caterham *S'wark* 09–13; C G7 Benefice *Cant* 13–16; V Folkestone Trin from 16. *The Trinity Benefice Vicarage, 21 Manor Road, Folkestone CT20 2SA* T: (01303) 253831 M: 07929-866879 E: revbob62@gmail.com

WELDON, William Ernest. b 41. TCD BA 62 MA 66. **d** 64 **p** 65. C Belfast Trin Coll Miss *Conn* 64–67; C Carnmoney 67–71; Chapl RN 71–96; QHC 93–96; Hon C Holbeton *Ex* 96–01; PtO from 01. *3 Garden Close, Holbeton, Plymouth PL8 1NQ* T: (01752) 830139 E: billanddinahweldon@btopenworld.com

WELFORD, Gillian Margaret. b 51. Westf Coll Lon BA 65. **d** 04 **p** 05. OLM Chiddingfold *Guildf* 04–14; PtO from 14. *15 Woodberry Close, Chiddingfold, Godalming GU8 4SF* T: (01428) 683620 E: gill@welford.myzen.co.uk

WELHAM, Clive Richard. b 54. **d** 80 **p** 81. C Bellingham St Dunstan *S'wark* 80–84; Chapl Goldsmiths' Coll Lon 84–95; V Plumstead Ascension 95–10; P-in-c Plumstead St Mark and St Marg 07–10; V Plumstead Common from 10; AD Plumstead from 14. *The Vicarage, 42 Jago Close, London SE18 2TY* T: (020) 8854 3395

WELLBELOVE, Miss Sophie Rebecca. b 86. Chich Univ BA 08. St Mellitus Coll BA 18. **d** 18 **p** 19. C Camberley St Paul *Guildf* from 18. *3 Upper Gordon Road, Camberley GU15 2HJ* M: 07709-690632 E: sophiewellbelove@gmail.com

WELLER (née SPENCE), The Ven Susan Karen. b 65. Leeds Univ BSc 86 Liv Univ PhD 89. Wycliffe Hall Ox BA 95. **d** 96 **p** 97. C Caverswall and Weston Coyney w Dilhorne *Lich* 96–00; C Wilnecote 00–05; Dioc Adv for Women in Min 00–04; Brazil 05–11; PtO *Lich* 11–14; Adn Walsall 15–19; Adn Lich from 19. *Unit 1 Three Spires House, Station Road, Lichfield WS13 6HX*

WELLINGTON, James Frederick. b 51. Leic Univ LLB 72 Fitzw Coll Cam BA 76 MA 11 Nottm Univ MPhil 91 Lambeth PhD 14. Ridley Hall Cam 74. **d** 77 **p** 78. C Mill Hill Jo Keble Ch *Lon* 77–80; C Wood Green St Mich w Bounds Green St Gabr etc 80–83; V Stocking Farm *Leic* 83–90; V Gt Glen, Stretton Magna and Wistow etc 90–98; Warden of Readers 91–97; RD Gartree II 96–98; TR Syston 98–07; RD Goscote 00–06; Hon Can Leic Cathl 94–07; R Keyworth and Stanton-on-the-Wolds and Bunny etc *S'well* 07–16; AD E Bingham 08–15; rtd 16; PtO *S'well* from 16. *Michaelmas House, 28 Dunholme Avenue, Newark NG24 4AR* T: (01636) 674490 E: jhcwelli@btinternet.com

WELLMAN, Mrs Karen Ann. b 62. BNC Ox BA 84. Ox Min Course 09. **d** 12 **p** 13. C Basingstoke *Win* 12–15; P-in-c Teddington St Mark *Lon* 15–17; V from 17. *The Vicarage, St Marks Road, Teddington TW11 9DE* E: revkarenwellman@btinternet.com

WELLS, Adrian Mosedale. b 61. SWMTC 96. **d** 99 **p** 00. NSM Kingskerswell w Coffinswell *Ex* 99–02; C Wolborough and Ogwell 02–13; TV Burrington, Chawleigh, Cheldon, Chulmleigh etc from 13; RD S Molton from 13. *The Vicarage, The Square, Witheridge, Tiverton EX16 8AE* T: (01884) 861383 E: vicaradrian@btinternet.com

WELLS, Andrew Peter. b 54. Birm Poly BEd 83 Birm Univ BPhil 86 Open Univ MA 92. Qu Foundn Birm 12. **d** 15 **p** 16. NSM The Quinton *Birm* from 15. *89 Upper Meadow Road, Quinton, Birmingham B32 1NR* T: 0121-689 0376 M: 07977-579894 E: apwells1954@hotmail.com

WELLS, Andrew Stuart. b 48. St Jo Coll Dur BA 71 Man Metrop Univ PGCE 04. Cranmer Hall Dur. **d** 74 **p** 75. C Walmsley *Man* 74–77; C Failsworth H Family 77–79; R Openshaw 79–90; V Hindsford 90–98. *1 Henry Street, Haslington, Crewe CW1 5PS* T: (01270) 585303 E: andrewwells@hotmail.com

WELLS, Antony Ernest. b 36. Oak Hill Th Coll 58. **d** 61 **p** 62. C Bethnal Green St Jas Less *Lon* 61–64; SAMS Paraguay 64–69; V Kirkdale St Athanasius *Liv* 69–73; SAMS Argentina 73–75; V Warfield *Ox* 75–81; V Fairfield *Liv* 81–83; C Rainhill 83–85; TV Cheltenham St Mark *Glouc* 85–89; P-in-c Forest of Dean Ch Ch w English Bicknor 89–95; rtd 97; C Pinhoe and Broadclyst *Ex* 02–04. *4 Case Gardens, Seaton EX12 2AP* T: (01297) 20482 E: gentonwells@btinternet.com

WELLS, Daniel Michael. b 74. Trin Coll Cam MA 95 Cam Inst of Educn PGCE 97. Wycliffe Hall Ox BTh 05. **d** 06 **p** 07. C Plymouth St Andr and Stonehouse *Ex* 06–09; C W Hampstead St Luke *Lon* 09–12; C Langham Place All So 12–18; V Richmond H Trin and Ch Ch *S'wark* from 18. *The Vicarage, Sheen Park, Richmond TW9 1UP* E: dan@wellsweb.org.uk or dan.wells@htrichmond.org.uk

WELLS, David. b 63. Imp Coll Lon BSc 85 ARCS 85. EAMTC 97. **d** 00 **p** 01. C Sprowston w Beeston *Nor* 00–03; P-in-c Drayton w Felthorpe 03–05; R Drayton 05–18; R Caister from 18. *The Rectory, Rectory Close, Caister-on-Sea, Great Yarmouth NR30 5EG* E: david.wells@btinternet.com

WELLS, Mrs Gillian Lesley. b 50. Anglia Ruskin Univ BA 14. Nor Ord Course 07. **d** 10 **p** 11. OLM Reepham, Hackford w Whitwell, Kerdiston etc *Nor* 10–15; C Dereham and Distr 15; TV from 15. *The Rectory, Church Close, Shipdham, Thetford IP25 7LX* T: (01362) 822404 M: 07597-306414 E: gilliewells1@btinternet.com

WELLS, Jeremy Stephen. b 47. Nottm Univ BA 69 UWE MSc 97. Chich Th Coll 72. **d** 73 **p** 74. C S Yardley St Mich *Birm* 73–76; C St Marychurch *Ex* 76–78; P-in-c Bridgwater H Trin *B & W* 78–82; P-in-c Brent Knoll 82–84; P-in-c E Brent w Lympsham 82–84; R Brent Knoll, E Brent and Lympsham

84–99; PtO *Chich* 99–07; rtd 07. *15A Victoria Close, Burgess Hill RH15 9QS* T: (01444) 244275

✠**WELLS, The Rt Revd Joanne Caladine Bailey.** b 65. CCC Cam BA 87 MA 90 Univ of Minnesota MA 90 St Jo Coll Dur BA 92 PhD 97. Cranmer Hall Dur. **d** 95 **p** 96 **c** 16. Chapl Clare Coll Cam 95–98; Dean 98–01; Tutor Ridley Hall Cam 01–05; PtO *Ely* 95–05; *Nor* 99–04; Dir Angl Episc Ho of Studies Duke Div Sch N Carolina USA 05–12; Abp's Chapl *Cant* 13–16; Can Th Liv Cathl 15–16; Suff Bp Dorking *Guildf* from 16. *Church House, 20 Alan Turing Road, Surrey Research Park, Guildford GU2 7YF* T: (01483) 570829 E: bishop.jo@cofeguildford.org.uk

WELLS, John Charles. b 44. St Jo Coll Nottm 00. **d** 19. NSM Scarborough St Mary w Ch Ch and H Apostles *York* from 19. *38 Newby Farm Crescent, Scarborough YO12 6UW* T: (01723) 352777 M: 07812-707628 E: john@sllew.go-plus.net

WELLS, Judith Margaret. b 48. Whitelands Coll Lon CertEd 71. Trin Coll Bris 09. **d** 11 **p** 12. OLM Purton *Bris* from 11. *The Live and Let Live, 7 Upper Pavenhill, Purton, Swindon SN5 4DQ* T: (01793) 770627 M: 07760-400257

WELLS, Kirsty Julia. b 73. Coll of SS Mark and Jo Plymouth BEd 95. Sarum Coll BA 16. **d** 16 **p** 17. C Sturminster Newton, Hinton St Mary and Lydlinch *Sarum* from 16. *12 Rookery Close, Gillingham SP8 4LH* T: (01747) 823562 M: 07525-250608 E: revkirsty@hotmail.com

WELLS, Canon Leslie John. b 61. Univ of Wales (Ban) BTh 06. **d** 04 **p** 05. OLM St Helier *S'wark* 04–08; C Morden 08–10; TV 10–17; AD Merton 16–17; TR Horley from 17; Hon Can S'wark Cathl from 17. *4 Russells Crescent, Horley RH6 7DN* T: (01293) 782218 M: 07804-231492 E: leswells80@hotmail.com or parishoffice@stbartshorley.org

WELLS, Canon Lydia Margaret Debert. b 50. Dur Univ BA 72 Sheff Univ MPhil 92 Leeds Univ MA 00. NOC 97. **d** 00 **p** 01. C Adwick-le-Street w Skelbrooke *Sheff* 00–03; V Doncaster Intake 03–09; V Sheff St Pet and St Oswald 09–14; AD Ecclesall 12–14; Hon Can Sheff Cathl 12–14; rtd 14; PtO *Sheff* from 14. *Apartment 1, 17 Bluecoat Rise, Sheffield S11 9DW* T: 0114-258 3097 M: 07803-710573 E: lydmwells@gmail.com

WELLS, Michael John. b 46. Univ Coll Ox BA 68 MA 73 Solicitor 74. S Dios Minl Tr Scheme 92. **d** 95 **p** 96. NSM Brighton St Pet w Chpl Royal *Chich* 95–98; Sen C 99–04; NSM Brighton St Bart 98–99; rtd 04; PtO *Chich* 04–10; P-in-c Brighton Annunciation 10–16; PtO from 16. *35 Park Crescent, Brighton BN2 3HB* T: (01273) 600735

WELLS, Nicholas Anthony. b 60. Cranmer Hall Dur 88. **d** 91 **p** 92. C Accrington St Jo w Huncoat *Blackb* 91–94; C Douglas St Geo and St Barn *S & M* 94–95; C Douglas All SS and St Thos 95–97; V Onchan 97–03; V Netherton *Liv* 03–07; AD Bootle 05–07; P-in-c Maghull 07–09; TR Maghull and Melling 09–16; AD Ormskirk 10–16; V Lytham St Cuth *Blackb* from 16; Hon Can Liv Cathl 05–16. *St Cuthbert's Vicarage, Church Road, Lytham, Lytham St Annes FY8 5PX* E: nick.the-vic@blueyonder.co.uk

WELLS, Canon Peter Robert. b 59. Wilson Carlile Coll 78 Sarum & Wells Th Coll 87. **d** 89 **p** 90. CA from 81; C Mortlake w E Sheen *S'wark* 89–93; Dir St Marylebone Healing and Counselling Cen 93–97; TV N Lambeth *S'wark* 97–00; Chapl Trin Hospice Lon 97–03; Chapl Brighton and Sussex Univ Hosps NHS Trust 03–19; Can and Preb Chich Cathl 10–19; rtd 19. *10 Lewes Mews, Arundel Place, Brighton BN2 1GR*

WELLS, Philip Anthony. b 83. UEA BA 04 Leeds Univ BA 07 MA 08. Coll of Resurr Mirfield 05. **d** 08 **p** 09. C Holt w High Kelling *Nor* 08–11; Bp's Dom Chapl *Wakef* 11–13; V Lamorbey H Trin *Roch* 13–19; AD Sidcup 16–19; V Wantage Ox from 19. *The Vicarage, The Cloisters, Wantage OX12 8AQ*

WELLS, The Ven Roderick John. b 36. Dur Univ BA 63 Hull Univ MA 85. Cuddesdon Coll 63. **d** 65 **p** 66. C Lambeth St Mary the Less *S'wark* 65–66; C Kennington Cross St Anselm 66–68; P-in-c 68–71; R Skegness *Linc* 71–77; P-in-c Winthorpe 77; R Skegness and Winthorpe 77–78; TR Gt and Lt Coates w Bradley 78–89; RD Grimsby and Cleethorpes 83–89; Can and Preb Linc Cathl 86–01; Adn Stow 89–01; V Hackthorn w Cold Hanworth 89–93; P-in-c N w S Carlton 89–93; rtd 01; PtO *Linc* 01–17; *Pet* from 01; *Leic* from 10. *5 Wheatfield Way, Barleythorpe, Oakham LE15 7UD* T: (01572) 492778 E: venrjw@gmail.com

WELLS, Ruth Mary. b 80. Ox Brookes Univ BA 03. Ripon Coll Cuddesdon MA 17. **d** 17 **p** 18. C W Moors *Sarum* from 17. *57 Moorlands Road, West Moors, Ferndown BH22 0JN* M: 07715-670319 E: ruthwells@rocketmail.com

WELLS, Mrs Sally Ursula. b 40. St Mark's Coll Canberra BTh 93 Ripon Coll Cuddesdon 96. **d** 97 **p** 98. Asst Chapl Vienna *Eur* 97–02; PtO 02–06; rtd 06; PtO *Sarum* from 11. *10 Park Street, Salisbury SP1 3AU* T: (01722) 322954 E: wellsfrance@gmail.com

WELLS, Canon Samuel Martin Bailey. b 65. Mert Coll Ox BA 87 MA 95 Edin Univ BD 91 Dur Univ PhD 96. Edin Th Coll 88. **d** 91 **p** 92. C Wallsend St Luke *Newc* 91–95; C Cherry Hinton St Andr *Ely* 95–97; C Teversham 95–97; P-in-c Earlham St Eliz *Nor* 97–03; RD Nor S 99–03; P-in-c Cambridge St Mark *Ely* 03–05; Can Th and Wiccamical Preb Chich Cathl from 04; Dean Duke Chpl Duke Univ N Carolina USA 05–12; V St Martin-in-the-Fields *Lon* from 12; Hon Can Th Guildf Cathl from 18. *6 St Martin's Place, London WC2N 4JJ* T: (020) 7766 1107 E: sam.wells@smitf.org

WELLS, Terry Roy John. b 45. EAMTC 89. **d** 92 **p** 93. C Martlesham w Brightwell *St E* 92–95; R Higham, Holton St Mary, Raydon and Stratford 95–00; TV Walton and Trimley 00–07; rtd 07; PtO *Chelmsf* 07–16; *St E* from 07. *Apartment 2, 1 The Maltings, The Quayside Maltings, High Street, Mistley, Manningtree CO11 1AL* T: (01206) 392957 E: terry.wells987@gmail.com

WELLS, Archdeacon of. *See* GELL, The Ven Anne Elizabeth

WELLS, Dean of. *See* DAVIES, The Very Revd John Harverd

WELSBY, George Andrew. b 61. St Martin's Coll Lanc BA 82 Leeds Univ BA 98 De Montfort Univ BA 09. Coll of Resurr Mirfield 96. **d** 98 **p** 99. C W Derby St Jo *Liv* 98–02; V Nuneaton St Mary *Cov* 02–07; PtO *Lich* 08–10; V Willenhall St Giles 10–18; P-in-c Willenhall St Anne 10–14; V 14–18; V Haydock St Jas *Liv* from 18; CMP from 06. *The Vicarage, 169 Church Road, Haydock, St Helens WA11 0NJ* T: (01942) 727956 E: andrew.welsby@hotmail.co.uk

WELSH, Jennifer Ann. b 48. Univ Coll Lon BA. **d** 81 **p** 98. NSM Newport St Matt *Mon* 81–85; NSM Risca 85–04; NSM Maindee Newport 04–09; PtO *Worc* from 12. *470 Caerleon Road, Newport NP19 7LW* T: (01633) 258287 E: mtrjen@btinternet.com

WELSH, Mrs Jennifer Lee. b 59. Calgary Univ BSc 81. Cam Episc Div Sch (USA) MDiv 87. **d** 87 **p** 88. C Calgary H Nativity Canada 87–89; Asst Chapl HM Pris Linc 89–94; Asst Chapl HM Pris Win 95–02; Chapl to Lutheran Students 03–08; PtO *Win* 95–02; *Lon* 03–08; Chapl Univ Coll 08–13; C St Pancras w St Jas and Ch Ch 08–13; C Kensington St Mary Abbots 13–17; V W Brompton St Mary w St Peter and St Jude from 17; AD Chelsea from 19. *St Mary's Vicarage, 24 Fawcett Street, London SW10 9EZ* E: vicar@stmarytheboltons.org.uk

WELSH, Philip Peter. b 48. Keble Coll Ox BA 69 MA 73 Selw Coll Cam BA 72 MA 76. Westcott Ho Cam 71. **d** 73 **p** 74. C W Dulwich All SS and Em *S'wark* 73–76; C Surbiton St Andr and St Mark 76–79; Lect St Steph Coll Delhi India 79–81; V Malden St Jo *S'wark* 81–87; Min Officer *Linc* 87–94; TR Basingstoke *Win* 94–02; V Westmr St Steph w St Jo *Lon* 02–13; rtd 13; PtO *Lon* from 13. *St Mary's Vicarage, 24 Fawcett Street, London SW10 9EZ* E: philipwelsh66@gmail.com

WELSH, Robert Leslie. b 32. Sheff Univ BA 54. St Jo Coll Dur. **d** 58 **p** 59. C S Westoe *Dur* 58–62; C Darlington St Cuth 62–66; CF (TA) 64–67; V E Rainton *Dur* 66–85; R W Rainton 66–85; R Wolsingham and Thornley 85–97; rtd 97; PtO *Dur* 97–17. *12 Lea Green, Wolsingham, Bishop Auckland DL13 3DU* T: (01388) 528529 E: r.l.welsh@btinternet.com

WELSMAN, Derek Brian. b 65. Trin Coll Bris. **d** 99 **p** 00. C Ash *Guildf* 99–02; V Easebourne *Chich* 02–10; P-in-c Lurgashall, Lodsworth and Selham 08–10; V Easebourne, Lodsworth and Selham from 10; P-in-c Lynchmere and Camelsdale 15–16; RD Midhurst from 10. *Northgate, Dodsley Grove, Easebourne, Midhurst GU29 9BE* T: (01730) 812655 *or* 813341 E: derekwelsman@btinternet.com

WELTERS, Mrs Elizabeth Ann. b 49. Bris Univ BSc 70 Reading Univ PGCE 71. SAOMC 94. **d** 97 **p** 98. NSM Aylesbury *Ox* 97–03; NSM Schorne 03–10; rtd 10; PtO *Ox* from 11. *19 Scampton Close, Bicester OX26 4FF* T: (01869) 249481 E: lizwelters@yahoo.co.uk

WEMYSS, Canon Gary. b 52. Cranmer Hall Dur 79. **d** 80 **p** 81. C Blackb St Jas 80–83; C Padiham 83–86; V Stalmine 86–90; P-in-c Egton-cum-Newland and Lowick *Carl* 90–03; V Egton-cum-Newland and Lowick and Colton 03–03; RD Furness 04–10; Hon Can Carl Cathl 08–14; rtd 14; PtO *Carl* from 14. *5 Highfield Road, Sedbergh LA10 5DH* T: (015396) 22021 E: gwemyss@clara.co.uk *or* gary@eandgwemyss.co.uk

WENHAM, David. b 45. Pemb Coll Cam BA 67 MA Man Univ PhD 70. Ridley Hall Cam 81. **d** 84 **p** 85. Tutor Wycliffe Hall Ox 84–07; Dean 02–05; Vice-Prin 05–06; NSM Shelswell *Ox* 96–02; NSM Cumnor 03–07 and 13–17; Tutor Trin Coll Bris 07–12; Vice Prin 08–12; PtO *Ox* from 17. *66 Pinnocks Way, Oxford OX2 9DQ* T: (01865) 682984 E: todavidwenham@gmail.com

WENHAM, Michael Timothy. b 49. Pemb Coll Cam MA 75. Wycliffe Hall Ox. **d** 86 **p** 87. C Norbury *Ches* 86–89; V Stanford in the Vale w Goosey and Hatford *Ox* 89–09; rtd 09; PtO *Ox* 09–19. *19 Churchward Close, Grove, Wantage*

OX12 0QZ T: (01235) 760094 M: 07719-715640 E: michaeltwenham@gmail.com

WENHAM, Peter William. b 47. Pemb Coll Cam MA 73 MD 85 FRCS 76. St Jo Coll Nottm 98. **d** 01 **p** 02. NSM Wollaton Park *S'well* 01–06; NSM Nottingham W Deanery 06–07; P-in-c Edwalton *S'well* 07–12; rtd 12; PtO *S'well* from 13. *31 Sutton Passeys Crescent, Nottingham NG8 1BX* T: 0115-970 2481

✠**WENT, The Rt Revd John Stewart.** b 44. CCC Cam BA 66 MA 70. Oak Hill Th Coll 67. **d** 69 **p** 70 **c** 96. C Northwood Em *Lon* 69–75; V Margate H Trin *Cant* 75–83; Vice-Prin Wycliffe Hall Ox 83–89; Adn Surrey *Guildf* 89–96; Chmn Dioc Coun for Unity and Miss 90–96; Suff Bp Tewkesbury *Glouc* 96–13; Hon Can Glouc Cathl 96–13; rtd 13; Hon C Chenies and Lt Chalfont, Latimer and Flaunden *Ox* 13–18; Hon Asst Bp Ox from 13. *31 Pandorea House, 35 Lismore Boulevard, London NW9 4DL*

WENZEL, Andreas. b 81. St Steph Ho Ox MTh 14. **d** 14 **p** 15. C Horbury w Horbury Bridge *Leeds* 14–17 and from 14. *The Shrine of Our Lady of Walsingham, The College, Knight Street, Walsingham NR22 6EF* T: (01328) 824204 E: frandreas.wenzel@gmail.com *or* shrine.pr@olw-shrine.org.uk

WERNER, Canon Donald Kilgour. b 39. Univ of Wales BA 61 Linacre Coll Ox BA 64 MA 67. Wycliffe Hall Ox 61. **d** 64 **p** 65. C Wrexham *St As* 64–69; Chapl Brasted Place Coll Westerham 69–73; Chapl Bris Univ 73–76; Hon C Clifton St Paul 73–76; Chapl Keele Univ *Lich* 77–79; P-in-c Keele 77–79; C York St Mich-le-Belfrey 79–83; Dir of Evang 79–83; R Holborn St Geo w H Trin and St Bart *Lon* 83–02; Hon Can Bujumbura from 99; Prof and Dean Th Univ Burundi from 03; Lic Preacher *Lon* 02–04; Vice-Chan Bujumbura Chr Univ 14–17; PtO *York* from 17. *25 Dulverton Hall, Esplanade, Scarborough YO11 2AR* M: 07927-295371 E: donaldinburundi@hotmail.com

WERRELL, Ralph Sidney. b 29. Hull Univ PhD 02. Tyndale Hall Bris 54. **d** 56 **p** 57. C Penn Fields *Lich* 56–60; C Champion Hill St Sav *S'wark* 60–61; R Danby Wiske w Yafforth *Ripon* 61–65; P-in-c Hutton Bonville *York* 61–65; R Combs *St E* 65–75; V Bootle Ch Ch *Liv* 75–80; R Scole, Brockdish, Billingford, Thorpe Abbots etc *Nor* 80–83; R Southam w Stockton *Cov* 83–89; R Southam 89–94; rtd 95; PtO *Birm* 95–12; *Cov* from 95; *Lich* 01–16. *Sameach, 2A Queens Road, Kenilworth CV8 1JQ* T/F: (01926) 858677 E: rswerrell@hotmail.com

WERRETT, Olivia Margaret. b 50. Brighton Univ BA 08 Eastbourne Tr Coll FETC 82. **d** 03. NSM Bexhill St Pet *Chich* from 03. *127 Pebsham Lane, Bexhill-on-Sea TN40 2RP* T: (01424) 214144 M: 07772-383084 E: owerrett@btinternet.com

WESSON, Preb John Graham. b 38. St Pet Coll Ox BA 62 MA 68. Clifton Th Coll 63. **d** 65 **p** 66. C Southport Ch Ch w St Andr *Liv* 65–68; C Ox St Ebbe w St Pet 68–71; Chapl Poly Cen Lon 71–76; C-in-c Edin St Thos 76–82; Dir Past Studies Trin Coll Bris 82–86; R Birm St Martin w Bordesley St Andr 86–96; RD Birm City 88–95; Hon Can Birm Cathl 91–96; Dir Local Min Development 91–96; Team Ldr Min Division 99–03; Team Ldr Bd of Min 99–03; C Lich St Mich w St Mary and Wall 96–03; Preb Lich Cathl 99–03; rtd 03. *11 Gordon Drive, Abingdon OX14 3SW* T: (01235) 526088 E: john.gwesson1@gmail.com

WEST, Alan David. b 61. Southn Univ BTh 92 Thames Valley Univ MA 97. Aston Tr Scheme 87 Sarum & Wells Th Coll 89. **d** 92 **p** 93. C S'wark St Geo the Martyr w St Jude 92–94; C S'wark St Geo w St Alphege and St Jude 95–96; V Boscoppa *Truro* 96–02; Chapl Mt Edgcumbe Hospice 02–05; Chapl R Cornwall Hosps Trust 05–10; Public Preacher *Truro* 10–12; Hon C St Blazey 12–14; Hon C Lanlivery 12–14; Hon C Luxulyan 12–14. *c/o Crockford, Church House, Great Smith Street, London SW1P 3AZ*

WEST, Andrew Victor. b 59. Wycliffe Hall Ox 87. **d** 90 **p** 91. C Leyland St Andr *Blackb* 90–94; C Blackpool St Jo 94–96; TV Bedworth *Cov* 96–98; Chapl Cheltenham and Glouc Coll of HE 98–01; Chapl Glos Univ 01–03; Chapl St Martin's Coll *Carl* 03–07; Chapl Cumbria Univ 07–10; C Carl St Jo 03–10; R Gateshead Fell *Dur* 10–17; P-in-c Gateshead St Geo 14–16; Chapl HM Pris Frankland from 17. *HM Prison Frankland, Brasside, Durham DH1 5YD* T: 0191-376 5000

WEST, Bryan Edward. b 39. Avery Hill Coll CertEd 69 BEd 80 Kent Univ MA 86. Cant Sch of Min 85. **d** 88 **p** 89. NSM Gravesend H Family w Ifield *Roch* 88–92; C Gravesend St Geo 92–95; NSM Hatcham Park All SS *S'wark* 95–98; NSM Stambridge and Ashingdon w S Fambridge *Chelmsf* 98–01; NSM Canvey Is 01–06; Chapl Southend Health Care NHS Trust 99–06; PtO *Chelmsf* 06–13; *Truro* from 16. *4 Barton Court, Central Treviscoe, St Austell PL26 7PD* T: (01726) 823102 E: roadbuilder2013@gmail.com

WEST, Miss Caroline Elisabeth. b 61. RGN 84. Wycliffe Hall Ox 93. **d** 95. NSM Eastrop *Win* from 95. *19 Beaulieu Court, Riverdene, Basingstoke RG21 4DQ* T: (01256) 350389 *or* 464249 E: caroline.west@stmarys-basingstoke.org.uk

WEST, Mrs Christine Cecily. TCD BA 60 MA 63 HDipEd 61. CITC 91. **d** 94 **p** 95. NSM Bray *D & G* 94–96; NSM Kilternan 96–99; LtO from 99. *55 Beech Park Road, Foxrock, Dublin 18, Republic of Ireland* T: (00353) (1) 289 6374 E: johncecily@eircom.net

WEST, David Marshall. b 48. St Jo Coll Dur BA 70. **d** 73 **p** 74. C Wylde Green *Birm* 73–76; C Wokingham St Paul *Ox* 76–79; V Hurst 79–88; V Maidenhead St Luke 88–95; C Whitley Ch Ch 95–99; P-in-c Reading Ch Ch 99–05; V 05–12; rtd 13; PtO *Ox* from 18. *The Old Tannery, Church Lane, Ledbury HR8 1DW* T: (01531) 636580 E: oldtannery@hotmail.co.uk

WEST, Derek Elvin. b 47. Hull Univ BA 69. Westcott Ho Cam 71. **d** 73 **p** 74. C Walthamstow St Pet *Chelmsf* 73–77; C Chingford SS Pet and Paul 77–80; TV W Slough *Ox* 80–88; Slough Community Chapl 88–95; TV Upton cum Chalvey 95–12; rtd 12; PtO *Lon* from 12. *35 Wallasey Crescent, Ickenham, Uxbridge UB10 8SA* M: 07957-158069 E: derekewest@gmail.com

WEST, Mrs Elizabeth Maxine. b 47. Liv Univ BA 69 Lon Inst of Educn PGCE 70 K Coll Lon BA 95 AKC. NTMTC. **d** 99 **p** 00. NSM Hornsey H Innocents *Lon* 99–00; NSM Highgate St Mich 00–03; C 03–11; rtd 12; PtO *Lon* from 13. *West Villa, Inderwick Road, London N8 9JU* T: (020) 8348 3042 E: maxineanddennis@hotmail.com

WEST, Canon Eric Robert Glenn. b 55. QUB BA 79 Man Univ DipEd 80. CITC BTh 92. **d** 92 **p** 93. C Enniskillen *Clogh* 92–95; I Lisbellaw 95–00; CF 00–03; I Annagh w Drumgoon, Ashfield etc *K, E & A* 03–06; I Derryvullen N w Castlearchdale *Clogh* 06–15; I Carnteel and Crilly *Arm* from 15; Can St Patr Cathl Dublin from 11. *St James's Rectory, 22 Carnteel Road, Aughnacloy BT69 6DU* M: 07969-332530 E: glenn.west55@hotmail.com

WEST, Mrs Heather June. b 55. Dur Univ BA 18. SWMTC 12. **d** 15 **p** 16. NSM Three Rivers *Truro* 15–17; C 17–19; P-in-c from 19; C Moorland Gp from 19. *52 Trelinnoe Gardens, South Petherwin, Launceston PL15 7TH* T: (01566) 770649 M: 07734-810664 E: pronter@btinternet.com

WEST, Canon Jeffrey James. b 50. Worc Coll Ox BA 72 BPhil 74 MA 76 FSA 11 FRSA 01. Ripon Coll Cuddesdon 05. **d** 07 **p** 08. NSM Banbury *Ox* from 07; AD Deddington 12–17; Hon Can Ch Ch from 17. *St Mary's Centre, Horse Fair, Banbury OX16 0AA* T: (01608) 811136 M: 07766-198484 E: jeff@banburystmary.org.uk

WEST, Jennifer. **d** 16 **p** 17. NSM Holton-le-Clay, Tetney and N Cotes *Linc* from 16. *11 Belmont, Holton-le-Clay, Grimsby DN36 5HQ* T: (01472) 453029 E: revjennywest@outlook.com

WEST (formerly WINDIATE), Mrs Mary Elizabeth. b 49. Linc Th Coll 94. **d** 94 **p** 95. C Loughton St Jo *Chelmsf* 94–98; P-in-c Ashingdon w S Fambridge 98–01; P-in-c Stambridge 98–01; TV Canvey Is 01–07; P-in-c Greenstead w Colchester St Anne 07–08; TR 08–13; rtd 13; PtO *Truro* from 14. *4 Barton Court, Central Treviscoe, St Austell PL26 7PD* T: (01726) 823102 E: m.west653@btinternet.com

WEST, Maxine. *See* WEST, Elizabeth Maxine

WEST, Canon Michael Brian. b 39. Sheff Univ BSc 60. Linc Th Coll 64. **d** 66 **p** 67. C Bp's Hatfield *St Alb* 66–69; Ind Chapl 69–81; Sen Ind Chapl 71–81; Hon Can St Alb 78–81; Sen Ind Chapl and Hon Can Sheff Cathl 81–01; Dir Open Forum for Economic Regeneration 02–04; rtd 04; PtO *Sheff* from 02. *23 Walton Road, Sheffield S11 8RE* T: 0114-266 2188 E: mike.west23@tiscali.co.uk

WEST, The Ven Michael Frederick. b 50. Trin Coll Ox BA 72 MA 76 UEA PhD 96. Westcott Ho Cam 72. **d** 74 **p** 75. C Wolverhampton *Lich* 74–78; C Hanley H Ev 78–79; TV 79–82; Dioc Youth Officer *St E* 83–88; V Ipswich St Thos 88–95; Prin OLM Scheme 96–03; Hon Can St E Cathl 96–03; Can Res and Chan Linc Cathl 03–08; Dioc Dir Formation in Discipleship and Min 03–06; TR Wrexham *St As* 08–13; AD 08–13; Chan St As Cathl 11–13; Res Can Ban Cathl 13–14; Tr Adn from 14; CMD Officer from 13. *The Vicarage, Newgate Street, Y Felinheli LL56 4SQ* T: (01248) 671159 E: ministryarchdeacon@gmail.com

WEST, Canon Paul John Francis. b 66. Newc Univ Aus BA 87 DipEd 93. Westcott Ho Cam 04. **d** 06 **p** 07. C Albury Australia 06–08; C Dee Why 08–09; C King Street 09–10; P-in-c Wisbech SS Pet and Paul *Ely* 10–16; Chapl Wisbech Gr Sch 10–15; Chapl Newcastle Gr Sch Australia 16–17; Can Res Newcastle Cathl from 16; R Maitland from 17. *St Mary's Rectory, 68 Church Street, Maitland NSW 2320, Australia* E: fatherpjfwest@gmail.com

WEST, Paul Leslie. b 57. OLM course 96. **d** 99 **p** 00. OLM Kinnerley w Melverley and Knockin w Maesbrook *Lich* 99–16; OLM Kinnerley w Melverley, Knockin w Maesbrook and Maesbury from 16. *2 Braddan, Farm Hall, Kinnerley, Oswestry SY10 8EG* T: (01691) 682600

WEST, Penelope Ann. b 52. Chelt & Glouc Coll of HE MA 98 Univ of Wales (Lamp) MPhil 08 FIBMS 72. **d** 00 **p** 01. NSM Hartpury w Corse and Staunton *Glouc* 00–09; NSM Ashleworth, Corse, Hartpury, Hasfield etc 09–12; PtO from 13. *Catsbury Cottage, Corsend Road, Hartpury GL19 3BP* T: (01425) 700314 E: revpennywest@gmail.com

WEST, Peter Harcourt. b 29. **d** 59 **p** 60. C Histon *Ely* 59–60; C Hampreston *Sarum* 60–61; C Braintree *Chelmsf* 61–63; PtO from 72; rtd 94. *12A The Piccards, Chestnut Avenue, Guildford GU2 4DW* T: (01483) 389487

WEST, Philip William. b 48. Magd Coll Ox BA 70 MA 78. St Jo Coll Nottm BA 72. **d** 75 **p** 76. C Rushden w Newton Bromswold *Pet* 75–79; C Pitsmoor w Ellesmere *Sheff* 79–83; V Attercliffe 83–89; Ind Chapl 85–90; P-in-c Darnall 86–89; V Stannington 89–13; P-in-c Sheff St Bart 02–07; AD Hallam 96–02; Hon Can Sheff Cathl 01–13; rtd 13; PtO *Sheff* from 13; Hon C S Holderness Coast *York* from 16; Hon C Easington w Skeffling, Keyingham, Ottringham etc from 16; Hon C Hedon, Paull, Sproatley and Preston from 16. *The Rectory, Ottringham Road, Keyingham, Hull HU12 9RX* T: (01964) 622228 E: philipwest65@gmail.com

WEST, Richard Barry. b 47. Mather Coll of Educn TCert 72. **d** 16 **p** 17. NSM Whaley Bridge *Ches* 16–19; PtO from 19. *Beech House, Kettleshulme, High Peak SK23 7EJ* T: (01663) 734497 M: 07751-834832 E: rickangelawest@yahoo.co.uk

WEST, Roderic. *See* WEST, Thomas Roderic

WEST, Ruth. BSc BTh. **d** 09 **p** 10. C Waterford w Killea, Drumcannon and Dunhill *C & O* 09–12; I Inver w Mountcharles, Killaghtee and Killybegs *D & R* 12–17; I Killesher *K, E & A* from 17. *Killesher Rectory, 10 Mill Road, Tully, Florencecourt, Enniskillen BT92 1FN* M: (00353) 87-625 9077 E: ruthjwest@hotmail.com

WEST, Stephen Peter. b 52. Liv Univ CertEd 74. Oak Hill Th Coll 87. **d** 89 **p** 90. C Gateacre *Liv* 89–92; V Liv All So Springwood 92–02; TV Teignmouth, Ideford w Luton, Ashcombe etc *Ex* 02–18; rtd 18. *98 Mulberry Close, Paignton TQ3 3GD* E: spwest33@gmail.com

WEST, Mrs Suzanne Elizabeth. b 46. STETS 04. **d** 07 **p** 08. NSM Portsea St Geo *Portsm* 07–11; Asst to RD Gosport from 11; PtO from 18. *64 Melville Road, Gosport PO12 4QX* T: (023) 9278 8782 E: melville64@ntlworld.com *or* sue.melville64@ntlworld.com

WEST, The Ven Thomas Roderic. b 55. BTh 90. TCD Div Sch. **d** 86 **p** 87. C Dromore Cathl *D & D* 86–89; I Carrowdore w Millisle 89–95; I Moira 95–12; I Seapatrick from 12; Can Dromore Cathl from 05; Chan Dromore Cathl 08–12; Adn Dromore from 11. *The Rectory, 63 Lurgan Road, Banbridge BT32 4LY* T: (028) 4062 2612 *or* 4062 2744 E: rodric@btinternet.com *or* roderic@bchurch.co.uk

WEST, Canon Timothy Ralph. b 53. Bath Univ BSc 75. Ridley Hall Cam 82. **d** 85 **p** 86. C Mildenhall *St E* 85–88; TV Melbury *Sarum* 88–92; TR 92–98; TR Preston w Sutton Poyntz, Littlemoor etc 98–15; TR Weymouth Ridgeway from 15; RD Weymouth and Portland 12–17; Can and Preb Sarum Cathl from 17. *The Rectory, Sutton Road, Preston, Weymouth DT3 6BX* T: (01305) 833142 E: weymouth.ridgeway.rector@gmail.com

WEST CUMBERLAND, Archdeacon of. *See* PRATT, The Ven Richard David

WEST HAM, Archdeacon of. *See* COCKETT, The Ven Elwin Wesley

WEST-LINDELL, Stein Erik. b 54. BA. Linc Th Coll 82. **d** 84 **p** 85. C Allington and Maidstone St Pet *Cant* 84–87; R Orlestone w Snave and Ruckinge w Warehorne 87–93; R Byfield w Boddington and Aston le Walls *Pet* 93–99; V Nor Lakenham St Alb and St Mark 99–17; V Nor Lakenham St Mark from 17. *2 Conesford Drive, Norwich NR1 2BB* T: (01603) 621843

✠**WESTALL, The Rt Revd Michael Robert.** b 39. Qu Coll Cam BA 62 MA 66. Cuddesdon Coll 63 Harvard Div Sch 65. **d** 66 **p** 67 **c** 01. C Heref St Martin 66–70; Lect Bp's Coll Calcutta India 70–76; Vice Prin 76–79; Prin 79–83; Prin St Mark's Th Coll Dar-es-Salaam Tanzania 84–92; R Alfrick, Lulsley, Suckley, Leigh and Bransford *Worc* 93–00; Bp SW Tanganyika 01–06; rtd 06; P-in-c Torquay St Luke *Ex* 07–12; Hon Asst Bp Ex 07–12; Hon Asst Bp Heref from 12. *Oak House, Kingstone, Hereford HR2 9ET* T: (01981) 250259 E: michaelwestall39@gmail.com

WESTBROOK, Canon Colin David. b 36. Oriel Coll Ox BA 59. St Steph Ho Ox MA 63. **d** 62 **p** 63. C Roath St Martin *Llan* 61–66; C Roath 66–74; V Llantarnam *Mon* 74–79; V Newport St Jo Bapt 79–07; Hon Can St Woolos Cathl 88–91; Can St Woolos Cathl from 91; Warden of Ords 91–99. *St John's*

Vicarage, 62 Oakfield Road, Newport NP20 4LP T: (01633) 265581 E: colinwestbrook@talktalk.net

WESTBROOK (*née* REED), **Mrs Ethel Patricia Ivy.** b 42. Bris Univ CertEd 63. Cant Sch of Min 82. **dss** 84 **d** 87 **p** 94. Fawkham and Hartley *Roch* 84–85; Asst Dir of Educn 84–86; Cliffe at Hoo w Cooling 85–86; Corby SS Pet and Andr w Gt and Lt Oakley 86–90; Par Dn 87–90; Par Dn *Roch* 90–94; C Rainham 94–99; V Joydens Wood St Barn 99–05; Dioc Chapl MU 01–05; rtd 05; Hon C Banstead *Guildf* 05–11; PtO *Roch* from 05; *Cant* from 12. *5 Victoria Mews, Station Road, Westgate-on-Sea CT8 8RQ* T: (01843) 836022 E: patriciawipe@yahoo.co.uk

WESTERMANN-CHILDS, Miss Emma Jane. b 71. Univ of Wales (Ban) BA 93 Ox Univ MTh 99. Ripon Coll Cuddesdon 96. **d** 98 **p** 99. C Launceston *Truro* 98–01; P-in-c St Stephen in Brannel from 01. *The Rectory, 70 Rectory Road, St Stephen, St Austell PL26 7RL* T: (01726) 822236

WESTERN, Canon Robert Geoffrey. b 37. Man Univ BSc 60. Qu Coll Birm. **d** 62 **p** 63. C Sedbergh *Bradf* 62–65; PV Linc Cathl 65–73; Hd Master Linc Cathl Sch 74–96; Can and Preb Linc Cathl 74–96; rtd 97; PtO *Carl* from 05. *2 Guldrey House, Guldrey Lane, Sedbergh LA10 5DS* T: (015396) 21426 E: robthel1@aol.com

WESTHAVER, George Derrick. b 68. St Mary's Univ Halifax NS BA 92. Wycliffe Coll Toronto MDiv 98. **d** 97 **p** 98. C Teversham and Cherry Hinton St Andr *Ely* 97–00; TV The Ramseys and Upwood 00–03; Chapl Linc Coll Ox 03–06; C Ox St Mich w St Martin and All SS 03–06; R Halifax St Geo Canada 07–13; Prin Pusey Ho from 13; Fell St Cross Coll Ox from 13. *Pusey House, St Giles, Oxford OX1 3LZ* T: (01865) 278415 E: gwesthaver@gmail.com

WESTLAKE, Michael Paul. b 34. Ex Coll Ox BA 56 MA 64. Wells Th Coll 59. **d** 61 **p** 62. C Southmead *Bris* 61–67; V Eastville St Thos 67–74; V Eastville St Thos w St Anne 74–83; P-in-c Easton St Mark 79–83; V Marshfield w Cold Ashton and Tormarton etc 83–01; rtd 01; PtO *Birm* 03–14. *65 Duxford Road, Great Barr, Birmingham B42 2JD* T: 0121-358 7030

WESTLAND, Richard Theodore. b 27. **d** 87 **p** 88. OLM Freiston w Butterwick *Linc* 87–97; rtd 97; PtO *Linc* from 97. *76 Brand End Road, Butterwick, Boston PE22 0JD* T: (01205) 760572

WESTMACOTT, Rosemary Margaret. *See* FRANKLIN, Rosemary Margaret

WESTMINSTER, Archdeacon of. *See* STANTON, The Ven David John

WESTMINSTER, Dean of. *See* HOYLE, The Very Revd David Michael

WESTMORLAND AND FURNESS, Archdeacon of. *See* ROSS, The Ven Vernon

WESTON, Canon David Wilfrid Valentine. b 37. Lanc Univ PhD 93. **d** 68 **p** 69. OSB 60–84; LtO *Ox* 67–84; Prior Nashdom Abbey 71–74; Abbot 74–84; C Chorley St Pet *Blackb* 84–85; V Pilling 85–89; Bp's Dom Chapl *Carl* 89–94; Can Res Carl Cathl 94–05; Lib 95–05; Vice-Dean 00; rtd 05; PtO *Carl* from 06. *The Pond House, Ratten Row, Dalston, Carlisle CA5 7AY* T: (01228) 710673 E: helweston@gmail.com

WESTON, Evelyn Sarah. b 68. **d** 17 **p** 18. NSM Heswall *Ches* from 17. *3 The Pipers, Heswall, Wirral CH60 9LL* T: 0151-342 4472 E: lyn.weston@chester.anglican.org *or* lyn_weston@yahoo.co.uk *or* lyn.weston@heswallparish.co.uk

WESTON, Gary James. b 72. Westmr Coll Ox BTh 95. Wycliffe Hall Ox 02. **d** 04 **p** 05. C Barrow St Paul *Carl* 04–08; C S Barrow 08–09; P-in-c Hinckley H Trin *Leic* 09–10; V Hinckley St Jo from 10; AD Sparkenhoe W from 15. *21 Windrush Drive, Hinckley LE10 0NY* T: (01455) 233552 E: gary@stjohnshinckley.org

WESTON, Mrs Judith. b 36. Open Univ BA 75 MSR 56. St Jo Coll Nottm 84. **dss** 85 **d** 87 **p** 94. Huddersfield H Trin *Wakef* 85–87; Par Dn 87–91; Par Dn Wakef St Andr and St Mary 91–94; C 94–95; Chapl Huddersfield NHS Trust 95–98; rtd 96; PtO *Wakef* 98–14; *Leeds* 14–16. *Overcroft, 8A Newland Road, Huddersfield HD5 0QT* T: (01484) 453591

WESTON, Mrs Katherine. b 48. Ripon Coll Cuddesdon 18. **d** 19. NSM Basildon w Aldworth and Ashampstead *Ox* from 19. *Willow Tree Cottage, Ashampstead, Reading RG8 8RA* T: (01635) 201356 M: 07765-255569 E: westonkaty@hotmail.com

WESTON, Neil. b 51. Jes Coll Ox BA 73 MA 78. Ridley Hall Cam 74. **d** 76 **p** 77. C Ealing St Mary *Lon* 76–80; P-in-c Pertenhall w Swineshead *St Alb* 80–89; P-in-c Dean w Yelden, Melchbourne and Shelton 80–89; R The Stodden Churches 89–91; R Newhaven *Chich* 91–98; P-in-c Radcliffe-on-Trent and Shelford etc *S'well* 98–04; R 04–05; V Radcliffe-on-Trent and Shelford 06–09; R Kington w Huntington, Old Radnor, Kinnerton etc *Heref* 09–14; rtd 14; PtO *Ox* from 14. *15 Longmead, Abingdon OX14 1JQ* T: (01235) 204147

WESTON, Paul David Astley. b 57. Trin Hall Cam BA 80 MA 83 Westmr Coll Ox MPhil 92 K Coll Lon PhD 02. Wycliffe Hall Ox 83. **d** 85 **p** 86. C New Malden and Coombe *S'wark* 85–89; Lect Oak Hill Th Coll 89–97; Vice-Prin 97–00; Gen Sec UCCF 00–01; Assoc Lect Ridley Hall Cam 02–03; Tutor from 03; PtO *Ely* 01–06. *Ridley Hall, Ridley Hall Road, Cambridge CB3 9HG* T: (01223) 746580 F: 746581 E: pdaw2@cam.ac.uk

WESTON, Phillip Richard. b 76. Bath Univ BSc 99 York Univ MSc 02 Lon Sch of Th PhD 18. Wycliffe Hall Ox BA 09. **d** 10 **p** 11. C Aughton Ch Ch *Liv* 10–14; P-in-c Gidea Park *Chelmsf* 14–16; V 16–18; V Ashton Hayes *Ches* from 18; Tutor St Mellitus NW from 18. *14 Dums Lane, Ashton, Chester CH3 8BU* T: (01829) 752272 M: 07939-129631 E: vicar@ashtonhayes.church

WESTON, Stephen John Astley. b 55. Aston Univ BSc 77. Ridley Hall Cam 78. **d** 81 **p** 82. C Gt Chesham *Ox* 81–85; C Southport Ch Ch *Liv* 85–87; P-in-c Gayhurst w Ravenstone, Stoke Goldington etc *Ox* 87–91; R 91–96; RD Newport 92–95; V Chipping Norton 96–01; TR 01–13; AD 02–07; Hon Can Ch Ch 06–13; P-in-c Ottery St Mary, Alfington, W Hill, Tipton etc *Ex* 13–16; TR from 17. *The Vicar's House, The College, Ottery St Mary EX11 1DQ* T: (01404) 812979

WESTON, Timothy Bernard Charles. b 48. **d** 03 **p** 04. OLM Watton w Carbrooke and Ovington *Nor* 03–07; OLM Ashill, Carbrooke, Ovington and Saham Toney 07–14; PtO from 14. *Sunset Barn, Morton Lane, Weston Longville, Norwich NR9 5JL* T: (01603) 879115 E: reverendweston@gmail.com

WESTON, Ms Virginia Anne. b 58. UEA BSc 79. Wycliffe Hall Ox 84. **d** 87 **p** 02. Par Dn New Malden and Coombe *S'wark* 87–89; LtO *Lon* 89–01; Chapl to People at Work in Cam *Ely* 02–06; Chapl Cam Univ Hosps NHS Foundn Trust from 18. *22 Ravensworth Gardens, Cambridge CB1 2XL* E: virginiaweston@yahoo.co.uk

WESTWOOD, Canon John Richard. b 55. Clare Coll Cam BA 77 MA 81 Lambeth MA 98. Ripon Coll Cuddesdon 77. **d** 79 **p** 80. C Oakham w Hambleton and Egleton *Pet* 79–81; C Oakham, Hambleton, Egleton, Braunston and Brooke 81–83; V Gt w Lt Harrowden and Orlingbury 83–90; V Wellingborough St Andr 90–99; RD Wellingborough 92–97; R Irthlingborough 99–10; P-in-c Rothwell w Orton, Rushton w Glendon and Pipewell 10–18; R Rothwell w Orton and Rushton w Glendon etc from 18; C Broughton w Loddington and Cransley etc 10–18; Warden of Readers 95–05; Can Pet Cathl from 97. *The Vicarage, High Street, Rothwell, Kettering NN16 6BQ* T: (01536) 710268 E: revdjohn.westwood@gmail.com

WESTWOOD, Peter. b 38. Open Univ BA 76. AKC 65. **d** 65 **p** 66. C Acomb St Steph and St Aid *York* 65–68; Chapl HM Youth Cust Cen Onley 69–73; Chapl HM Pris Leic 73–77; Maidstone 77–81; Dur 81–87; Brixton 87–93; Wormwood Scrubs 93–98; PtO *S'wark* from 98; rtd 99. *St Stephen's Church, College Road, London SE21 7HN* T: (020) 8693 0082 E: westwood773@btinternet.com

WESTWOOD, Richard Andrew. b 64. Nottm Univ BSc 85 PGCE 86. St Jo Coll Nottm 02. **d** 04 **p** 05. C Gt Wyrley *Lich* 04–15; TV Burntwood, Chase Terrace etc from 15. *The Vicarage, 158A High Street, Chasetown, Burntwood WS7 3XG* T: (01543) 682336 E: westwood.richard@btinternet.com

WESTWOOD, Timothy. b 61. Wolv Poly MBA 91. WMMTC 95. **d** 98 **p** 99. NSM Sedgley St Mary *Worc* from 98. *85 High Park Crescent, Dudley DY3 1QY* T: (01902) 831078 E: twestwood@mac.com

WETHERALL, Canon Nicholas Guy. b 52. Lon Univ BMus 73 Ox Univ CertEd 75. Chich Th Coll 82. **d** 84 **p** 85. C Cleobury Mortimer w Hopton Wafers *Heref* 84–87; TV Leominster 87–92; V Cuckfield *Chich* 92–14; RD Hurst 92–03; Can and Preb Chich Cathl 08–14; rtd 14. *3 Brookward Terrace, Heamoor, Penzance TR18 3QZ* T: (01736) 368887 E: nick.4epnewlyn@gmail.com

WETHERELL, Ms Eileen Joyce. b 44. Westf Coll Lon BSc 66. S Dios Minl Tr Scheme 89. **d** 92 **p** 94. Par Dn Southampton Maybush St Pet *Win* 92–94; C 94–96; TV Totton 96–04; V Hythe 04–12; Dioc Adv for Women's Min 02–12; rtd 12; PtO *Win* from 12. *3 Creighton Road, Southampton SO15 4JF* T: (023) 8184 8598 E: ewetherell@tiscali.co.uk

WETHERELL, Philippa Clare. *See* LEA, Philippa Clare

WEYMONT, Martin Eric. b 48. St Jo Coll Dur BA 69 MA 74 Fitzw Coll Cam PGCE 73 Lon Inst of Educn PhD 89 Open Univ BSc 96. Westcott Ho Cam 71. **d** 73 **p** 74. C Blackheath *Birm* 73–76; Hon C Willesden St Matt *Lon* 76–77; Hon C Belmont 77–79; P-in-c W Twyford 79–85; NSM Cricklewood St Mich 85–88; Chapl St Pet Colleg Sch Wolv 88–91; Hon C Wolverhampton *Lich* 88–91; NSM Bickershaw *Liv* 91–97; P-in-c Mells w Buckland Dinham, Elm, Whatley etc *B & W*

97–15; rtd 15; PtO *Sarum* from 16; *B & W* from 16. *33 Ludlow Close, Warminster BA12 8BJ*

WHAITE, Richard Patrick. b 80. Univ Coll Lon BSc 01 Man Univ MPhil 04 K Coll Lon MA 10 Ox Univ BA 14. Ripon Coll Cuddesdon 11. **d** 14 **p** 15. C Fulham All SS *Lon* 14–17; Assoc Tutor St Mellitus Coll 15–17; Chapl and Fell Dur Univ 17–19; Chapl Cranmer Hall Dur 18–19; R Ches St Mary from 19. *St Mary's Parish Hall, Overleigh Road, Chester CH4 7HL* T: (01244) 671202 M: 07857-776247 E: office@stmaryschester@btconnect.com

WHALE, David. b 81. Univ of Wales (Ban) BSc 02 Glos Univ PGCE 06. Wycliffe Hall Ox BTh 15. **d** 15 **p** 16. C Glouc St Cath 15–18; P-in-c Chenies and Lt Chalfont, Latimer and Flaunden from 18. *The Rectory, Chenies, Rickmansworth WD3 6ER* E: revdwhale@gmail.com

WHALE, Noel Raymond. b 41. Ox Univ 67. **d** 70 **p** 71. C Amersham *Ox* 70–73; C Geelong Australia 73–76; P-in-c Altona 76–79; I 79–85; I Ivanhoe 86–97; Prec and Min Can St Paul's Cathl 97–01; I Bundoora St Pet 01–11. *Unit 1, 33-35 Ligar Street, Sunbury VIC 3429, Australia* T: (0061) (3) 9740 3315 M: 41-219 6127 E: jonahnoel@hotmail.com

WHALE, Peter Richard. b 49. Auckland Univ MA 72 BSc 73 Down Coll Cam BA 74 MA 79 Otago Univ BD 78 Ex Univ PhD 90. St Jo Coll Auckland 75. **d** 77 **p** 78. C Takapuna New Zealand 77–80; Chapl K Coll Auckland 81–85; TV Saltash *Truro* 85–90; Jt Dir SW Minl Tr Course 86–90; Preb St Endellion *Truro* 89–90; Prin WMMTC 90–92; rtd 04. *6 Bluebell Walk, Coventry CV4 9XR* T: (024) 7646 4894

WHALEY, Stephen John. b 57. York Univ BA 79. Cranmer Hall Dur BA 85. **d** 86 **p** 87. C Selby Abbey *York* 86–90; V Derringham Bank from 90; AD W Hull 98–00. *110 Calvert Road, Hull HU5 5DH* T: (01482) 352175

WHALLEY, Miss Alice Elizabeth. b 87. Univ Coll Lon BSc 09. St Steph Ho Ox BA 13. **d** 14 **p** 15. C Moulsecoomb *Chich* 14–17; C E Grinstead St Swithun 17–18; V Brownswood Park *Lon* from 18. *St John's Vicarage, 2A Gloucester Drive, London N4 2LW* M: 07745-809669 E: alice.whalley@me.com

WHALLEY, Anthony Allen. b 41. Linc Th Coll 77. **d** 79 **p** 80. C Upton cum Chalvey *Ox* 79–83; R Newton Longville w Stoke Hammond and Whaddon 83–96; R Winslow w Gt Horwood and Addington 99–06; rtd 06; PtO *Worc* from 07. *2 Charlock Road, Malvern WR14 3SR* T: (01684) 562897 E: tony.rosemary@btinternet.com

WHALLEY, Mrs Constance Mary. b 55. CBDTI 99. **d** 02 **p** 03. NSM Garstang St Helen and St Michaels-on-Wyre *Blackb* 02–16; rtd 16; PtO *Blackb* from 17. *4 Leicester Avenue, Garstang, Preston PR3 1FH* T: (01995) 238206 E: cwwhalley56@gmail.com

WHALLEY, Edward Ryder Watson. b 31. G&C Coll Cam BA 54 MA 59. Westcott Ho Cam 55. **d** 57 **p** 58. C Ashton-on-Ribble St Andr *Blackb* 57–60; Chapl Magd Coll Cam 60–63; C Arnold *S'well* 63–67; rtd 96; PtO *Lon* from 03. *6 Cranleigh, 137-139 Ladbroke Road, London W11 3PX* T: (020) 7727 1985

WHALLEY, Eleanor Jean. b 72. **d** 14 **p** 15. C St Neots *Ely* 14–16; P-in-c Soham and Wicken 16–18; R Soham from 18. *The Vicarage, 27 The Oaks, Soham, Ely CB7 5FF* E: eleanorjw@gmail.com

WHALLEY, George Peter. b 40. **d** 86 **p** 86. NSM Ellon *Ab* from 86; NSM Cruden Bay from 86. *128 Braehead Drive, Cruden Bay, Peterhead AB42 0NW* T: (01779) 812511 E: peter_whalley@btinternet.com

WHALLEY, Jonathan Peter Lambert. b 60. Wm Booth Memorial Coll 87. St Jo Coll Nottm BA 97. **d** 97 **p** 98. C Hattersley *Ches* 97–01; V The Marshland *Sheff* 01–09; P-in-c Wolsingham and Thornley *Dur* from 09; P-in-c Satley, Stanley and Tow Law from 09; CF(V) from 02. *The Rectory, 14 Rectory Lane, Wolsingham, Bishop Auckland DL13 3AJ* T: (01388) 527340

WHALLEY, Peter. *See* WHALLEY, George Peter

✠WHALON, The Rt Revd Pierre Welté. b 52. Boston Univ BMus 74 Duquesne Univ MMus 81. Virginia Th Sem MDiv 85. **d** 85 **p** 85 **c** 01. R N Versailles All So USA 85–91; R Philadelphia St Paul 91–93; R Fort Pierce St Andr 93–01; Bp in Charge Convocation of American Chs in Eur from 01; Hon Asst Bp Eur from 02. *23 avenue George V, 75008 Paris, France* T: (0033) 1 53 23 84 04 *or* 1 47 20 02 23 F: 1 47 20 02 23 E: bppwhalon@aol.com *or* cathedral@american.cathedral.net

WHARTON, Canon Gillian Vera. b 66. TCD BTh 93 MPhil 99 HDipEd 02. CITC 90. **d** 93 **p** 94. C Glenageary *D & G* 93–96; Hon PV Ch Ch Cathl Dublin from 96; Dioc Youth Officer 96–00; C Lucan w Leixlip 96–00; Chapl Rathdown Sch 00–04; I Dublin Booterstown *D & G* from 04; I Dublin Mt Merrion from 04; Can St Patr Cathl Dublin from 17. *The Rectory, Cross Avenue, Booterstown, Blackrock, Co Dublin, A94*

W7R6, Republic of Ireland T: (00353) (1) 288 7118 *or* (1) 283 5873 M: 87-230 0767 E: booterstown@dublin.anglican.org *or* gillwharton@gmail.com

✠WHARTON, The Rt Revd John Martin. b 44. Van Mildert Coll Dur BA 69 Linacre Coll Ox BTh 71 MA 76. Ripon Hall Ox 69. **d** 72 **p** 73 **c** 92. C Birm St Pet 72–75; C Croydon St Jo *Cant* 76–77; Dir Past Studies Ripon Coll Cuddesdon 77–83; C Cuddesdon *Ox* 79–83; Sec to Bd of Min and Tr *Bradf* 83–92; Dir Post-Ord Tr 84–92; Hon Can Bradf Cathl 84–92; Can Res Bradf Cathl 92; Bp's Officer for Min and Tr 92; Area Bp Kingston *S'wark* 92–97; Bp Newc 97–14; rtd 14; PtO *Dur* from 15; Hon Asst Bp Lon from 15; Hon Asst Bp Eur from 16; Hon Asst Bp S'wark from 16. *20 Thamespoint, Fairways, Teddington TW11 9PP* T: (020) 8977 8347

WHARTON, Canon Kate Elizabeth. b 78. Leeds Metrop Univ BSc 00. Wycliffe Hall Ox BTh 05. **d** 05 **p** 06. C W Derby St Luke *Liv* 05–09; P-in-c Everton St Geo 09–15; V 15–17; AD Liv N 13–17; V Roby from 17; Hon Can Liv Cathl from 13. *St Bartholomew's Vicarage, 11 Church Road, Roby, Liverpool L36 9TL* T: 0151-489 1698 E: vicar@stbartholomewsroby.org.uk

WHARTON, Canon Richard Malcolm. b 69. Univ of Cen England in Birm BA 91 PGCE 92. Ripon Coll Cuddesdon BTh 98. **d** 98 **p** 99. C Weoley Castle *Birm* 98–01; C Hall Green Ascension 01–04; P-in-c Hall Green St Mich 03–08; Chapl Univ Hosp Birm NHS Foundn Trust from 08; Hon Can Birm Cathl from 16. *18 Pineapple Grove, Birmingham B30 2TJ* T: 0121-627 1627 ext 52599 *or* 443 1371 E: richard.wharton@ubh.nhs.uk

WHARTON, Susan Jane. b 58. Leeds Univ BSc 79 Coll of Ripon & York St Jo MA 00. NOC 96. **d** 99 **p** 00. C Bingley All SS *Bradf* 99–03; P-in-c Weston w Denton 03–08; P-in-c Leathley w Farnley, Fewston and Blubberhouses 03–08; C Washburn and Mid-Wharfe 08–09; P-in-c 09–12; P-in-c Bethersden w High Halden and Woodchurch *Cant* from 12. *The Vicarage, Bull Lane, Bethersden, Ashford TN26 3HA* T: (01233) 820266 E: sue@whartons.org.uk

WHARTON, Thomas Geoffrey. b 72. Glas Univ BA 93. Westcott Ho Cam 03. **d** 05 **p** 06. C Linton in Craven and Burnsall w Rylstone *Bradf* 05–09; TV Knight's Enham and Smannell w Enham Alamein *Win* 09–13; P-in-c W End 13–18; V Romsey from 18. *The Vicarage, Church Lane, Romsey SO51 8EP* E: rev.thomaswharton@gmail.com

WHATELEY, Stuart David. b 44. Ripon Hall Ox 71. **d** 73 **p** 74. C Chilvers Coton w Astley *Cov* 73–76; Chapl Miss to Seafarers from 76; PtO *Sheff* 10–17. *10 Merryman Garth, Hedon, Hull HU12 8NJ* T: (01405) 764730 M: 07551-777717 E: whateleysd@gmail.com

WHATELEY, Thomas Roderick (Rod). b 52. St Jo Coll Nottm 94. **d** 96 **p** 97. C Willesborough *Cant* 96–99; P-in-c Cliftonville 99–03; R Orlestone w Snave and Ruckinge w Warehorne etc 03–13; R Saxon Shoreline 13–19; rtd 19; PtO *Eur* from 16. *Address temp unknown*

WHATLEY, Roger James. b 49. Chich Th Coll 94. **d** 96 **p** 04. NSM Newport St Thos and Newport St Jo *Portsm* 96–11; Chapl Is of Wight Fire and Rescue Service from 11. *Beechcroft, 46 Trafalgar Road, Newport PO30 1QG* T: (01983) 825938 E: whatleys138@uwclub.net

WHATMOUGH, Michael Anthony. b 50. ARCO 71 Ex Univ BA 72. Edin Th Coll BD 81. **d** 81 **p** 82. C Edin St Hilda and Edin St Fillan 81–84; C Salisbury St Thos and St Edm *Sarum* 84–86; R 86–93; RD Salisbury 90–93; V Bris St Mary Redcliffe w Temple etc 93–04; PtO *Lich* 08–10; C Cannock and Huntington 10–12; C Hatherton 10–12; P-in-c Headingley *Ripon* 12–14; TR Leeds from 14. *Headingley Vicarage, 16 Shire Oak Road, Leeds LS6 2DE* T: 0113-274 3238 M: 07711-335050 E: tony@whatmough.org.uk

WHATSON, Mark Edwin Chadwick. b 57. Southn Univ BSc 79 CEng 83 MIMechE 83. NOC 86. **d** 88 **p** 91. NSM Church Hulme *Ches* 88–91; NSM Goostrey 91–95; NSM Hardwicke, Quedgeley and Elmore w Longney *Glouc* 95–98; C Thornbury 98–01; Ind Chapl 99–01; R Freshwater *Portsm* 01–17; R Yarmouth 01–17; rtd 17; PtO *Portsm* from 18. *26 Albert Road, Sandown PO36 8AW* T: (01983) 406236

WHATTON, Joanna Nicola. *See* PAYNE, Joanna Nicola

WHEALE, Alan Leon. b 43. Hull Univ MA 92 AKC 69. St Aug Coll Cant 69. **d** 70 **p** 71. C Tamworth *Lich* 70–73; C Cheddleton 73–75; V Garretts Green *Birm* 75–78; V Perry Beeches 78–83; V Winshill *Derby* 83–84; Deputation Appeals Org (E Midl) CECS 84–86; C Arnold *S'well* 86–88; V Daybrook 88–96; R Clifton Campville w Edingale and Harlaston *Lich* 96–06; P-in-c Thorpe Constantine 96–06; P-in-c Elford 97–06; rtd 06; PtO *Lich* 06–08; Hon C Tamworth 08–12; PtO 12–14; Hon C Rolleston 14–15; Hon C Anslow 14–15; Hon C Hanbury, Newborough, Rangemore and Tutbury

14–15; PtO *Derby* from 15. *1 Redbrick Gardens, Swadlincote DE11 0WJ* T: (01283) 221022 E: alan-wheale@supanet.com

WHEALE, Sarah Ruth. *See* BULLOCK, Sarah Ruth

WHEATLEY, Diane. *See* THOMPSON, Diane

WHEATLEY (née GRAHAM), Mrs Fiona Karen. b 57. Hull Univ BA 84 De Montfort Univ PGCE 94. SAOMC 03. **d** 06 **p** 07. C Stevenage St Hugh and St Jo *St Alb* 06–10; TV Bp's Hatfield, Lemsford and N Mymms 10–14; R Clothall, Rushden, Sandon, Wallington and Weston from 14. *The Vicarage, Payne End, Sandon, Buntingford SG9 0QU* T: (01763) 284189 E: fkwheatley@gmail.com

WHEATLEY, Jane. *See* WHEATLEY, Sarah Jane

WHEATLEY, The Ven Paul Charles. b 38. St Jo Coll Dur BA 61. Linc Th Coll 61. **d** 63 **p** 64. C Bishopston *Bris* 63–68; Youth Chapl 68–73; V Swindon St Paul 73–77; TR Swindon Dorcan 77–79; R Ross *Heref* 79–81; P-in-c Brampton Abbotts 79–81; RD Ross and Archenfield 79–91; TR Ross w Brampton Abbotts, Bridstow and Peterstow 81–91; Preb Heref Cathl 87–91; Adn Sherborne *Sarum* 91–03; P-in-c W Stafford w Frome Billet 91–03; rtd 03; PtO *Heref* from 04. *The Farthings, Bridstow, Ross-on-Wye HR9 6QF* T: (01989) 566965 E: paulwheatley@buckcastle.plus.com

✠**WHEATLEY, The Rt Revd Peter William.** b 47. Qu Coll Ox BA 69 MA 73 Pemb Coll Cam BA 71 MA 75. Ripon Hall Ox 72. **d** 73 **p** 74 **c** 99. C Fulham All SS *Lon* 73–78; V St Pancras H Cross w St Jude and St Pet 78–82; P-in-c Hampstead All So 82–90; P-in-c Kilburn St Mary 82–90; P-in-c Kilburn St Mary w All So 90–95; V W Hampstead St Jas 82–95; Dir Post-Ord Tr 85–95; AD N Camden 88–93; Adn Hampstead 95–99; Area Bp Edmonton 99–14; rtd 15; Hon Asst Bp S'wark from 13; Hon Asst Bp Lon from 15; P-in-c St Leonards Ch Ch and St Mary etc *Chich* from 19. *47 Sedlescombe Road South, St Leonards-on-Sea TN38 0TB* T: (01424) 424814

WHEATLEY, Miss Sarah Jane. b 45. St Gabr Coll Lon Dip Teaching 67. St Alb Minl Tr Scheme 77. **d** 96 **p** 97. NSM Meppershall w Campton and Stondon *St Alb* 96–99; P-in-c Shillington 99–03; V Gravenhurst, Shillington and Stondon 03–12; rtd 12; PtO *St Alb* from 12. *16 Queen Street, Stotfold, Hitchin SG5 4NX* T: (01462) 731170 E: jane.wheatley5@btinternet.com

WHEATLEY PRICE, Canon John. b 31. Em Coll Cam BA 54 MA 58. Ridley Hall Cam 54. **d** 56 **p** 57. C Drypool St Andr and St Pet *York* 56–59; CMS 59–76; Uganda 60–74; Adn Soroti 72–74; Hon Can Soroti 78–97; Adn N Maseno Kenya 74–76; V Clevedon St Andr *B & W* 76–82; V Clevedon St Andr and Ch Ch 82–87; Chapl Amsterdam w Heiloo *Eur* 87–92; P-in-c Cromford *Derby* 92–95; P-in-c Matlock Bath 92–95; V Matlock Bath and Cromford 95–96; rtd 96; PtO *Sarum* 96–01; *Birm* 01–18. *2 Beausale Drive, Knowle, Solihull B93 0NS* T: (01564) 730067 E: john@wheatleyprice.co.uk

WHEATON, Canon Christopher. b 49. St Jo Coll Nottm BTh 80. **d** 80 **p** 81. C Hatcham St Jas *S'wark* 80–83; C Warlingham w Chelsham and Farleigh 83–87; V Carshalton Beeches 87–13; Hon Can S'wark Cathl 07–13; rtd 13; PtO *S'well* from 14. *70 Gordon Road, West Bridgford, Nottingham NG2 5LS* T: 0115-982 7192 E: christopherwheaton@btinternet.com

WHEATON, Patrick Edward. b 78. Ex Coll Ox BA 00. Trin Coll Bris BA 08. **d** 09 **p** 10. C Shill Valley and Broadshire *Ox* 09–13; C Cheltenham St Mary w St Matt and St Luke *Glouc* from 13; PtO *Eur* from 16. *38 College Road, Cheltenham GL53 7HX* M: 07974-986608

WHEELER, Preb Alexander Quintin Henry (Alastair). b 51. Lon Univ BA 73 MBACP 07. St Jo Coll Nottm 74. **d** 77 **p** 78. C Kenilworth St Jo *Cov* 77–80; C Madeley *Heref* 80–83; P-in-c Draycott-le-Moors *Lich* 83–84; P-in-c Forsbrook 83–84; R Draycott-le-Moors w Forsbrook 84–91; V Nailsea Ch Ch *B & W* 91–96; R Nailsea Ch Ch w Tickenham 96–10; RD Portishead 95–01; V Wells St Cuth w Wookey Hole 10–16; RD Shepton Mallet 11–16; Preb Wells Cathl 03–16; rtd 16; PtO *B & W* from 16; *Sarum* from 16. *32 Windy Ridge, Beaminster DT8 3SR* T: (01308) 862093 E: aqhw02@gmail.com

WHEELER, Andrew Charles. b 48. CCC Cam BA 69 MA 72 Makerere Univ Kampala MA 72 Leeds Univ PGCE 72. Trin Coll Bris BA 88. **d** 88 **p** 88. CMS from 76; C Whitton *Sarum* 88–89; C All SS Cathl Cairo Egypt 89–92; Co-ord for Th Educn Sudan 92–00; C All SS Cathl Nairobi Kenya 92–00; Abp's Sec for Angl Communion Affairs *Cant* 00–01; C Guildf St Sav 02–16; rtd 16; Dioc World Miss Adv *Guildf* 06–19; Hon C Guildf H Trin w St Mary 18–19; PtO from 19. *16 Little Street, Guildford GU2 9QG* E: andy.wheeler2@gmail.com

WHEELER (née MILLAR), Mrs Christine. b 55. City of Lon Poly BSc 76 DipCOT 81. S Dios Minl Tr Scheme 84. **d** 87 **p** 94. NSM Kingston Buci *Chich* 87–89; Par Dn Merstham and Gatton *S'wark* 89–94; C 94–96; R Rockland St Mary w Hellington, Bramerton etc *Nor* 96–04; PtO from 04. *Mayland,*

Low Road, Strumpshaw, Norwich NR13 4HU T: (01603) 713583 E: emailcw@sky.com

WHEELER, David Ian. b 49. Southn Univ BSc 70 PhD 78. NOC 87. **d** 90 **p** 91. C Blackpool St Jo *Blackb* 90–94; R Old Trafford St Jo *Man* 94–05; P-in-c Irlam 05–08; V 08–13; rtd 13; PtO *Win* from 15; *Sarum* from 16. *22 Glamis Avenue, Northbourne, Bournemouth BH10 6DP* T: (01202) 577820

WHEELER, David James. b 49. Leeds Univ MA 95 CQSW 74. S Dios Minl Tr Scheme 87. **d** 90 **p** 91. C Hythe *Cant* 90–92; C Knaresborough *Ripon* 92–97; Asst Soc Resp Officer 94–97; P-in-c Gt and Lt Ouseburn w Marton cum Grafton etc 97–01; V 01–05; Jt AD Ripon 01–05; V Cobbold Road St Sav w St Mary *Lon* 05–12; rtd 12; PtO *St E* 13–18; Hon C Lower Wharfedale *Leeds* from 18. *The Vicarage, Old Pool Bank, Pool in Wharfedale, Otley LS21 1EJ* E: david.wheeler@phonecoop.coop

WHEELER, Mrs Helen Mary. b 38. Qu Coll Birm 04. **d** 06 **p** 07. NSM Smethwick Resurr *Birm* 06–12; rtd 12; PtO *Birm* from 12. *99 Brookfield Road, Birmingham B18 7JA* T: 0121-554 4721 M: 07804-450099 E: revhwheeler@hotmail.co.uk

WHEELER, James Albert. b 49. Sarum & Wells Th Coll 74. **d** 76 **p** 77. C Orpington All SS *Roch* 76–79; C Roch 79–81; C Bexley St Jo 81–84; V Penge Lane H Trin 84–93; P-in-c Tunbridge Wells St Luke 93–99; V 99–09; P-in-c Southborough St Thos 09–15; rtd 15; PtO *Chich* from 16. *19 Plover Close, Eastbourne BN23 7SB* T: (01323) 767533 E: j.wheeler@mybroadbandmail.com

WHEELER, Julian Aldous. b 48. Nottm Univ BTh 74. Kelham Th Coll 70. **d** 75 **p** 76. C Bideford *Ex* 75–79; LtO 79–86; Hon C Parkham, Alwington, Buckland Brewer etc 86–03. *Manorfield, Mount Raleigh Avenue, Bideford EX39 3NR* T: (01237) 477271

WHEELER, Preb Madeleine. b 42. Gilmore Course 76. dss 78 **d** 87 **p** 94. Ruislip Manor St Paul *Lon* 78–92; Par Dn 87–91; Team Dn 91–92; Chapl for Women's Min (Willesden Episc Area) 86–95; P-in-c N Greenford All Hallows *Lon* 94–00; Preb St Paul's Cathl 95–00; rtd 00; PtO *St Alb* from 00; *Lon* from 02. *178A Harefield Road, Uxbridge UB8 1PP* T: (01895) 257274 E: mm.wheeler@tiscali.co.uk *or* mwheeler7442@gmail.com

WHEELER, Nicholas Charles. b 50. Leic Univ BA 72. SEITE 00. **d** 03 **p** 04. NSM Blackheath St Jo *S'wark* 03–08; PtO 08–11; NSM Eltham H Trin 11–16; NSM Chipping Barnet *St Alb* from 16. *St Peter's House, Barnet Road, Barnet EN5 3JF* E: teamvicar.aurkley@gmail.com

WHEELER, Nicholas Gordon Timothy. b 59. BCombStuds 84. Linc Th Coll. **d** 84 **p** 85. C Hendon St Alphage *Lon* 84–87; C Wood Green St Mich w Bounds Green St Gabr etc 87–89; TV 89–93; R Cranford 93–02; V Ruislip St Mary 02–16; R Hayes St Mary from 16. *The Rectory, 170 Church Road, Hayes UB3 2LR* T: (020) 8845 3485 M: 07769-339529 E: frnicholaswheeler@virginmedia.com

WHEELER, Canon Nicholas Paul. b 60. Ox Univ BA 86 MA 91. Wycliffe Hall Ox 83. **d** 87 **p** 88. C Wood Green St Mich w Bounds Green St Gabr etc *Lon* 87–91; Chapl to Bp Edmonton 91–96; P-in-c Somers Town 96–03; P-in-c Old St Pancras w Bedford New Town St Matt 96–03; P-in-c Camden Town St Mich w All SS and St Thos 96–03; P-in-c Camden Square St Paul 96–03; TR Old St Pancras 03–08; Brazil 08–15; R Upper Chelsea H Trin and St Sav *Lon* from 15. *97A Cadogan Lane, London SW1X 9DU* T: (020) 7730 7270 E: nicholaspaulwheeler@gmail.com

WHEELER, Paul Kenneth. b 81. Coll of Resurr Mirfield 17. **d** 19. C Nantwich *Ches* from 19. *12 Hallams Drive, Nantwich CW5 7RN* E: paulwheeler508@gmail.com

WHEELER, Canon Richard Roy. b 44. K Coll Lon BD 72. St Aug Coll Cant. **d** 74 **p** 74. C Brixton St Matt *S'wark* 74–79; Dir St Matt Meeting Place Brixton 78–79; Sec BCC Community Work Resource Unit 79–82; TV Southampton (City Cen) *Win* 83–88; TR 88–98; Hon Can Win Cathl 94–98; Soc Resp Adv *St Alb* 98–09; Can Res St Alb 01–09; rtd 09; PtO *S'wark* from 16. *143 Well Hall Road, London SE9 6TS* T: (020) 8856 5271 E: canonrwheeler@btinternet.com

WHEELER, Richenda Mary Celia. b 71. St Mary's Coll Strawberry Hill BA 93. Ripon Coll Cuddesdon BTh 98. **d** 99 **p** 00. C Dalston H Trin w St Phil and Haggerston All SS *Lon* 99–02; Asst Chapl R Free Hampstead NHS Trust 02–05; Chapl Lon Metrop Univ 05–10; Chapl Derby Univ 10–14; Chapl Derby Cathl 10–14; PtO *S'wark* 15; V Dalston H Trin w St Phil and Haggerston All SS *Lon* 15–17; PtO 17–19; Chapl Hartpury Coll from 18. *Hartpury College, Hartpury House, Hartpury, Gloucester GL19 3BE* T: (01452) 702100 M: 07971-659534 E: richenda@leigh.me

WHEELER, Mrs Sally Ann Violet. b 59. Westmr Coll Ox BEd 81. SAOMC 94. **d** 97 **p** 98. NSM Chippenham St Paul w Hardenhuish etc *Bris* 97–01; C Gtr Corsham and Lacock 01–04; TV 04–12; P-in-c Marshfield w Cold Ashton and Tormarton etc 12–17; V from 17; AD Chippenham from 15. *The Vicarage,*

Church Lane, Marshfield, Chippenham SN14 8NT T: (01225) 892180 E: marshfield.benefice@gmail.com

WHEELER-KILEY, Mrs Susan Elizabeth. b 47. d 06 p 07. NSM S Norwood St Mark *S'wark* 06–17; NSM S Norwood H Innocents 15–17; PtO from 17. *35 St Luke's Close, London SE25 4SX* T: (020) 8656 9923 M: 07890-780572 E: fs.kiley@btinternet.com

WHEELHOUSE, Paul Andrew. b 72. Bradf Univ BEd 95 Ox Brookes Univ MA 11 St Jo Coll Dur BATM 12. Cranmer Hall Dur 10. d 12 p 13. C Burley in Wharfedale *Bradf* 12–16; Ilkley St Marg *Leeds* 16–18; V Bierley from 18. *Bierley Vicarage, Bierley Lane, Bradford BD4 6AA* M: 07832-892854 E: pawheelhouse@gmail.com

WHEELWRIGHT, Michael Harvey. b 39. Bps' Coll Cheshunt 64. d 67 p 68. C Glen Parva and S Wigston *Leic* 67–70; C Evington 70–74; V Leic St Eliz Nether Hall 74–79; Chapl Prudhoe Hosp Northd 79–99; PtO *Dur* from 79; *Newc* from 99; rtd 04. *6 Nunnykirk Close, Ovingham, Prudhoe NE42 6BP* T: (01661) 835749

WHELAN, Miss Patricia Jean. b 33. ACA 55 FCA 82. Dalton Ho Bris 58. dss 64 d 87 p 94. Stapleford *S'well* 62–69; Aylesbury *Ox* 69–75; Bushbury *Lich* 75–77; Patchway *Bris* 77–81; Trin Coll Bris 81–82; W Swindon LEP 82–86; High Wycombe *Ox* 86–87; Par Dn 87–91; Par Dn Ox St Ebbe w H Trin and St Pet 91–93; rtd 93. *81 Cogges Hill Road, Witney OX28 3XU* T: (01993) 779099 E: patwhelan81@btinternet.com

WHELAN, Peter Warwick Armstrong. b 34. Southn Univ BTh 80 Open Univ BA 80. Sarum Th Coll 69. d 71 p 72. C Salisbury St Mark *Sarum* 71–73; C Solihull *Birm* 73–77; TR Shirley 77–86; Chapl Whittington Hosp NHS Trust 86–99; Chapl Camden and Islington Community Health NHS Trust 86–99; rtd 99; PtO *Ex* from 98. *5 Greenacres, Asheldon Road, Torquay TQ1 2QS* T: (01803) 212483 E: warwickw@talktalk.net

WHELAN, Raymond Keith. b 40. Cant Sch of Min 85. d 88 p 91. C Eastbourne St Andr *Chich* 88–93; C-in-c Parklands St Wilfrid CD 93–95; TV Chich 95–00; V Chich St Wilfrid 00–01; rtd 04; PtO *Chich* from 04. *9 Ruislip Gardens, Aldwick, Bognor Regis PO21 4LB* T: (01243) 264865 E: wdiosc@aol.com

WHERRY, Anthony Michael. b 44. Nottm Univ BA 65. WMMTC 88. d 91 p 92. NSM Worc City St Paul and Old St Martin etc 91–95; NSM Worc E Deanery 95–02; NSM Worc SE 02–17. *2 Thomas Stock Gardens, Abbeymead, Gloucester GL4 5GH* T: (01905) 358532 E: tonywherry@btinternet.com

WHETTER, Linda Carol. b 56. d 16 p 17. NSM Probus, Ladock and Grampound w Creed and St Erme *Truro* from 16. *Pencoose Barn, Tregony, Truro TR2 5TR* M: 07866-455952 E: lindaw23@outlook.com

WHETTINGSTEEL, Raymond Edward. b 44. S Dios Minl Tr Scheme 79. d 82 p 83. NSM Sholing *Win* 82–84; C Southampton Maybush St Pet 84–89; R Hatherden w Tangley, Weyhill and Penton Mewsey 89–99; rtd 99; PtO *Win* from 11. *20 Clover Way, Hedge End, Southampton SO30 4RP* T: (01489) 787033 E: ray_whettingsteel@hotmail.com

WHETTON, Nicholas John. b 56. Open Univ BA 94. St Jo Coll Nottm 83. d 86 p 87. C Hatfield *Sheff* 86–90; V Cornholme *Wakef* 90–96; P-in-c Livesey *Blackb* 96–99; V 99–03; P-in-c Ewood 96–97; Chapl HM Pris Hull from 03. *The Chaplain's Office, HM Prison, Hedon Road, Hull HU9 5LS* T: (01482) 282200 E: nicholas.whetton@justice.gov.uk

WHIFFIN, Mrs Vanessa Janet. b 68. Birm Univ BMus 89 ABSM 87. STETS 10. d 14 p 15. C Marshfield w Cold Ashton and Tormarton etc *Bris* 14–17; TV Witney *Ox* from 17. *Address withheld by request* E: ness@witneyparish.org

WHINNEY, Nigel Patrick Maurice. b 43. Open Univ BA 91. SWMTC 95. d 97 p 98. NSM Ilminster and Distr *B & W* 97–08; Bp's Officer for Ord NSM (Taunton Adnry) 99–06; RD Crewkerne and Ilminster 01–07; rtd 08; PtO *B & W* 08–12; Perm to Offic Nelson New Zealand from 12. *376B Hardy Street, Nelson 7010, New Zealand* T: (0064) (354) 67765

WHINTON, William Francis Ivan. b 35. NOC 77. d 80 p 81. NSM Stockport St Mary *Ches* 80–82; NSM Disley 82–87; V Birtles 87–00; Dioc Officer for Disabled 89–00; rtd 00; Chapl for Deaf People *Ches* 00–04; PtO from 05; *Lich* 09–15. *Allmeadows Cottage, Wincle, Macclesfield SK11 0QJ* T: (01260) 227278

WHIPP, Antony Douglas. b 46. Leeds Univ BSc 68 Lanc Univ PhD 04. Ripon Coll Cuddesdon 84. d 86 p 87. C Dalston *Carl* 86–89; V Holme Cultram St Mary 89–96; V Holme Cultram St Cuth 89–96; V Kells 96–00; V Hartlepool St Aid *Dur* 00–05; R Ebchester 05–13; V Medomsley 05–13; rtd 13; PtO *Dur* 14–17. *34 Egglestone Drive, Consett DH8 7UB* T: (01207) 588407 E: tony.whipp@durham.anglican.org *or* tony.whipp@outlook.com

WHIPP, Canon Margaret Jane. b 55. LMH Ox BA 76 Sheff Univ MB, ChB 79 MRCP 82 FRCR 86 Hull Univ MA 99 Glas Univ PhD 08. NOC 87. d 90 p 94. NSM Wickersley *Sheff* 90–98; Tutor Cranmer Hall Dur 98–99; Dir Practical Th NEOC 00–04; Ecum Chapl Ox Brookes Univ 04–08; Lect Past Studies Ox Min Course 06–08; Dean of Studies Ripon Coll Cuddesdon 08–12; Chapl Ox Univ Hosps NHS Foundn Trust 13–19; Lead Chapl 16–18; rtd 19; PtO *Ox* from 19; Hon Can Ch Ch from 16. *2 All Saints Road, Oxford OX3 7AU* T: (01865) 765409 M: 07775-617129 E: margaretwhipp@btinternet.com

WHITAKER, Anthony. b 50. SS Mark & Jo Coll Chelsea CertEd 72 Middx Univ BA 02. NTMTC 99. d 02 p 03. C Blackmore and Stondon Massey *Chelmsf* 02–06; P-in-c St Keverne *Truro* 06–11; C Churt and Hindhead *Guildf* 11–15; rtd 15; Hon C Stow on the Wold, Condicote and The Swells *Glouc* from 16. *The Vicarage, 27 Mosedale, Moreton-in-Marsh GL56 0HP* T: (01608) 652415 M: 07905-013017 E: tony_whitaker@btinternet.com

WHITAKER, Benjamin. See WHITAKER, Michael Benjamin

WHITAKER, Irene Anne. b 57. d 01 p 02. OLM Parr *Liv* 01–06; TV Bootle 06–18; TR 18–19; R from 19. *The Vicarage, Elm Road, Seaforth, Liverpool L21 1BH* T: 0151-920 2205 M: 07771-581886

WHITAKER, Margaret Scott. b 45. Dioc OLM tr scheme 00 EAMTC 04. d 03 p 04. OLM Eaton *Nor* 03–05; C Sprowston w Beeston 05–07; C New Catton Ch Ch 07–11; R Horsford, Felthorpe and Hevingham 11–15; rtd 15; PtO *Nor* from 15. *West End Lodge, Norwich Road, Ludham, Great Yarmouth NR29 5PB* T: (01692) 678302 M: 07717-317900 E: mwhitaker1@btinternet.com

WHITAKER, Michael Benjamin. b 60. Nottm Univ BA 83. Sarum & Wells Th Coll 85. d 87 p 88. C Gt Grimsby St Mary and St Jas *Linc* 87–91; C Abingdon *Ox* 91–95; Chapl to the Deaf *Sarum* 95–00; PtO *Win* 97–00; Asst Chapl amongst Deaf People *Ox* from 00; Chapl HM Pris Grendon and HM Pris Spring Hill from 07. *HM Prison Grendon, Grendon Underwood, Aylesbury HP18 0TL* T: (01865) 736100 E: whitakerben5@gmail.com

WHITAKER, Neil Robert. b 71. All SS Cen for Miss & Min 16. d 18 p 19. NSM Langley *Man* from 18. *43 Melverley Road, Manchester M9 0PD* E: revneilster@outlook.com

WHITBY, Raymond Thomas. b 57. d 14 p 15. NSM Wigan All SS *Liv* 15–17. *52 Coroners Lane, Widnes WA8 9JB* T: 0151-423 6375 E: ramonw57@sky.com

WHITBY, Suffragan Bishop of. See FERGUSON, The Rt Revd Paul John

WHITCROFT, Graham Frederick. b 42. Oak Hill Th Coll 64. d 66 p 67. C Cromer *Nor* 66–69; C Attercliffe *Sheff* 69–72; V Kimberworth Park 72–85; V Lepton *Wakef* 85–07; RD Kirkburton 98–05; rtd 07; PtO *Wakef* 14; *Leeds* from 14. *18 Far Croft, Lepton, Huddersfield HD8 0LS* T: (01484) 609868 E: gswhitcroft@yahoo.com

WHITE, Preb Alan. b 43. Ex Univ BA 65. Chich Th Coll 65. d 68 p 69. C Upper Clapton St Matt *Lon* 68–72; C Southgate Ch Ch 72–76; P-in-c Friern Barnet St Pet le Poer 76–79; V 79–85; TR Ex St Thos and Em 85–99; Preb Ex Cathl 03–08; rtd 08; RD Newton Abbot and Ipplepen *Ex* 16–18. *Flat 3, 7 Courtenay Road, Newton Abbot TQ12 1HP* T: (01626) 332451 E: revalanwhite@tiscali.com

⊕**WHITE, The Rt Revd Alison Mary.** b 56. St Aid Coll Dur BA 78 Leeds Univ MA 94. Cranmer Hall Dur 83. dss 86 d 87 p 94. c 15. NSM Chester le Street *Dur* 86–89; Dioc Adv in Local Miss 89–93; Hon Par Dn Birtley 89–93; Dir Past Studies Cranmer Hall Dur 93–98; Dir of Ords *Dur* 98–00; Springboard Missr 00–04; Adult Educn Officer *Pet* 05–10; Can Pet Cathl 09–10; Hon Can Th Sheff Cathl 10–15; P-in-c Riding Mill *Newc* 11–15; Adv for Spirituality and Spiritual Direction 11–15; Suff Bp Hull *York* from 15. *Hullen House, Woodfield Lane, Hessle HU13 0ES* T: (01482) 649019 F: 647449 E: alisonmarywhite@btinternet.com *or* bishophull@yorkdiocese.org

WHITE, Canon Andrew Paul Bartholomew. b 64. MIOT 85 ABIST 85. Ridley Hall Cam 86. d 90 p 91. C Battersea Rise St Mark *S'wark* 90–93; P-in-c Balham Hill Ascension 93–97; V 97–98; Dir Internat Min and Can Res Cov Cathl 98–05; Chapl Iraq from 05; President Foundn for Relief and Reconciliation in the Middle E from 05. *The Croft, 66 Shepherds Way, Liphook GU30 7HH* T: (01428) 723939 *or* (00964) (7901) 265723 E: apbw2@cam.ac.uk

WHITE, Anne Margaret. b 55. Nottm Univ BEd 78. STETS 07. d 10 p 11. NSM Guernsey St Andr *Win* 10–13; P-in-c Aldbrough, Mappleton w Goxhill and Withernwick *York* from 13; RD N Holderness from 16. *The Vicarage, Carlton Drive, Aldbrough, Hull HU11 4SF* T: (01964) 527230 M: 07911-712274 E: white.anne19@gmail.com

WHITE, Camilla Elizabeth Zoë. b 56. Somerville Coll Ox BA 78 MA 83 Heythrop Coll Lon MA 06. Ripon Coll Cuddesdon 05. d 07 p 08. NSM Bramley and Grafham *Guildf* 07–17; PtO 17–19; NSM Bramley and Grafham from 19. *Bramley Mill, Mill Lane, Bramley, Guildford GU5 0HW* T: (01483) 892645 E: camillawhite@waitrose.com

WHITE, Colin Davidson. b 44. St And Dioc Tr Course 86. d 88 p 89. NSM Glenrothes *St And* 88–89; P-in-c 89–90; P-in-c Leven 90–92; R 92–95; V Grimethorpe *Wakef* 95–01; P-in-c Kellington w Whitley 01–02; TV Knottingley and Kellington w Whitley 02–10; rtd 10. *42 Glendale Avenue North, Belfast BT8 6LB* T: (028) 9029 6037 M: 07973-795560 E: col_the_rev@hotmail.co.uk

WHITE, Crispin Michael. b 42. Southn Univ MA 98 PhD 06 FRSA 94. Bps' Coll Cheshunt 62. d 65 p 66. C S Harrow St Paul *Lon* 65–67; C Mill Hill St Mich 67–68; I Labrador St Clem Canada 68–71; Toc H Padre (W Region) 71–75; (E Midl Region) 75–82; Ind Chapl *Portsm* 82–98; P-in-c Hatfield Broad Oak and Bush End *Chelmsf* 98–04; Ind Chapl 98–07; Harlow 98-04; Lon Thames Gateway 04–07; rtd 07; PtO *Chich* 12–17. *6 Downlands, Firsdown Close, Worthing BN13 3BQ* T/F: (01903) 830785 M: 07962-057436 E: postmaster@crispinwhite.plus.com *or* postmaster@erispiwhite.plus.com

WHITE, David. b 75. All Hallows Coll Dublin BA 09 Irish Sch of Ecum MPhil 10. St Jo Coll Nottm 10 CITC MTh 13. d 12 p 13. C Clonsast w Rathangan, Thomastown etc *M & K* 12–13; C Bandon Union *C, C & R* 13–16; I Carlow w Urglin and Staplestown *C & O* from 16. *The Rectory, Green Road, Carlow, Republic of Ireland* T: (00353) (59) 913 2565 E: whitedk@eircom.net

WHITE, Canon David Christopher. b 51. Lon Univ LLB 73. St Jo Coll Nottm 86. d 88 p 89. C Bulwell St Mary *S'well* 88–92; V Nottingham All SS 92–98; TR Clarendon Park St Jo w Knighton St Mich *Leic* 98–05; R Emmaus Par Team 05–07; P-in-c Fosse Team 07–12; TR 12–16; Bp's NSM Officer 02–08; Hon Can Leic Cathl 08–16; rtd 16; PtO *Leic* from 16; *S'well* from 17. *Lindum, 11 Gainsborough Road, Winthorpe, Newark NG24 2NN* E: davidwhite264@virginmedia.com

WHITE, David Martin. b 50. St Jo Coll Dur BA 72. Cranmer Hall Dur DipTh 73. d 74 p 75. C Ripley *Derby* 74–78; C Normanton 78–80; C-in-c Sinfin 78–80; P-in-c 80; V 80–88; P-in-c Belper 88–91; V 91–97; RD Duffield 96–97; rtd 11. *Water's Edge, 18 Clipper View, Birmingham B16 9DJ* T: 0121-454 2758 E: dmartinwhite@gmail.com

WHITE, Canon David Paul. b 58. Oak Hill Th Coll. d 84 p 85. C Toxteth Park St Clem *Liv* 84–87; C Woodford Wells *Chelmsf* 87–89; C Woodside Park St Barn *Lon* 89–90; TV Canford Magna *Sarum* 90–93; V York St Mich-le-Belfrey 93–99; V St Austell *Truro* 99–10; Dioc Dir Miss 05–10; Hon Can Truro Cathl 05–10; V Chorleywood St Andr *St Alb* 10–16; Public Preacher *Truro* from 16. *74 Boxwell Park, Bodmin PL31 2BE* E: dprm58@hotmail.com

WHITE, David Peter. b 55. Anglia Ruskin Univ MA 07 AMICE 78. ERMC 09. d 12 p 13. NSM Felixstowe St Jo *St E* 12–16; NSM Bacton w Wyverstone, Cotton and Old Newton etc 16–18; PtO from 19. *154 Colneis Road, Felixstowe IP11 9LQ* M: 07982-003144 E: david.pwhite@icloud.com

WHITE, Derek. b 35. d 84 p 85. C St Marylebone St Cypr *Lon* 84–96; Bp's Chapl for the Homeless 87–01; P-in-c St Mary le Strand w St Clem Danes 96–01; rtd 01; PtO *S'wark* from 04. *80 Coleraine Road, London SE3 7PE* T: (020) 8858 3622 E: david.godsquad@sky.com

WHITE, Douglas Richard Leon. b 49. Linc Th Coll 81. d 83 p 84. C Warsop *S'well* 83–88; V Kirkby in Ashfield St Thos 88–93; Asst Chapl Qu Medical Cen Nottm Univ Hosp NHS Trust 93–98; Chapl Cen Notts Healthcare NHS Trust 98–01; Chapl Mansfield Distr Primary Care Trust 01–02; Chapl Geo Eliot Hosp NHS Trust Nuneaton 02–06; Chapl Mary Ann Evans Hospice 02–06; Chapl Compton Hospice 06–08; Chapl Marie Curie Hospice Solihull 08–11; Chapl Primrose Hospice Bromsgrove from 08; PtO *Birm* 11–14; *Cov* from 06. *1 Glebe Avenue, Bedworth CV12 0DP* T: (024) 7636 0417 E: rickwhite29@btinternet.com

WHITE, Duncan Ernest. b 45. d 07 p 08. OLM Tilehurst St Geo and Tilehurst St Mary *Ox* 07–11; PtO from 11. *41 Cambrian Way, Calcot, Reading RG31 7DD* T: 0118-380 0367 E: rev.duncan.white@gmail.com

WHITE, Mrs Elaine. b 63. Leeds Univ BA 85 Ches Univ PGCE 89. All SS Cen for Miss & Min 16. d 19. C Liscard Resurr *Ches* from 19; C Seacombe w Poulton from 19. *22 Elleray Park Road, Wallasey CH45 0LH* M: 07856-709714

✠**WHITE, The Rt Revd Francis.** b 49. Univ of Wales (Cardiff) BSc(Econ) 70. St Jo Coll Nottm. d 80 p 81 c 02. C Dur St Nic 80–84; C Chester le Street 84–87; Chapl Dur and Chester le Street Hosps 87–89; V Birtley *Dur* 89–97; RD Chester-

le-Street 93–97; Adn Sunderland and Hon Can Dur Cathl 97–02; Suff Bp Brixworth *Pet* 02–10; Can Pet Cathl 02–10; Asst Bp Newc 10–16; rtd 16; Hon Asst Bp York from 17; P-in-c Kingston upon Hull H Trin from 19. *Hullen House, Woodfield Lane, Hessle HU13 0ES* T: (01482) 649019 E: white6.francis1949@gmail.com

WHITE, Geoffrey Brian. b 54. Jes Coll Ox BA 76 MA 80 BD 16. St Steph Ho Ox 76. d 79 p 80. C Huddersfield St Pet *Wakef* 79–82; C Flixton St Mich *Man* 82–84; TV Westhoughton 84–91; V Stevenage St Mary Shephall w Aston *St Alb* 91–06; RD Stevenage 01–06; R Norton *Sheff* from 06; C Norton Lees St Paul from 17; C Greenhill from 17; C Woodseats St Chad from 17. *Norton Rectory, Norton Church Road, Norton, Sheffield S8 8JQ* T: 0114-274 5066 E: geoffreywhite_333@hotmail.com *or* geoffrey.white@sheffield.anglican.org

WHITE, Canon Geoffrey Gordon. b 28. Selw Coll Cam BA 50 MA 54. Cuddesdon Coll 51. d 53 p 54. C Bradford-on-Avon H Trin *Sarum* 53–56; C Kennington St Jo *S'wark* 56–61; V Leeds St Wilfrid *Ripon* 61–63; Chapl K Coll Hosp Lon 63–66; V Aldwick *Chich* 66–76; V Brighton Gd Shep Preston 76–93; Can and Preb Chich Cathl 90–93; rtd 93; Hon C Stepney St Dunstan and All SS *Lon* 94–10; PtO 13–19; *Leic* from 15; *Pet* from 17. *7 Lime Tree Place, Great Bowden, Market Harborough LE16 7JE* T: (01858) 465186

WHITE, George Trevor. b 93. Heythrop Coll Lon BA 15. St Mellitus Coll 15. d 18 p 19. C Lenton Abbey *S'well* from 18. *18 Boyce Gardens, Nottingham NG3 3FB* M: 07807-645583 E: georgetrevorwhite@icloud.com

WHITE, Gillian Margaret. b 57. Qu Eliz Coll Lon BSc 79 Sheff Univ MEd 96 PhD 02 Nottm Univ MA 07. EMMTC 05. d 07 p 08. NSM Derby St Paul 07–13; PtO 14–15; NSM Tideswell from 15. *The Vicarage, 6 Pursglove Drive, Tideswell, Buxton SK17 8PA* T: (01298) 871317 M: 07973-866848 E: g.m.white@tesco.net *or* gillianwhite1@me.com *or* gillianwhite470@gmail.com

WHITE, Graham John. b 76. Lon Bible Coll BTh 99 K Coll Lon MA 08. Ripon Coll Cuddesdon 13. d 15. C Tring *St Alb* 15–16. *14 Leach Road, Aylesbury HP21 8LG* M: 07963-584458

WHITE, Miss Hazel Susan. b 65. Nottm Univ BA 88 Birm Univ MPhil 11. Qu Coll Birm 05. d 07 p 08. C Woodfield *Leic* 07–12; C Moseley St Mary and St Anne *Birm* from 12. *15 Park Hill, Birmingham B13 8DU* T: 0121-449 1071 *or* 449 2243 E: hazelwhite1@btinternet.com

WHITE, Ian Jeffrey. b 57. Leeds Univ BSc 80 PhD 86 BA 05 CChem 83 MRSC 83. Coll of Resurr Mirfield 03. d 05 p 06. C Stanningley St Thos *Ripon* 05–09; P-in-c Adel 09–14; Leeds 14–19; P-in-c Ireland Wood *Ripon* 12–14; *Leeds* 14–16; Dioc Environment Officer *Ripon* 06–14; *Leeds* 14–19; rtd 19. *17 Haven Gardens, Leeds LS16 6SN* T: 0113-267 2923 E: ian.white.uk@outlook.com

WHITE, Ian Terence. b 56. CertEd. Ripon Coll Cuddesdon 83. d 86 p 87. C Maidstone St Martin *Cant* 86–89; C Earley St Pet Ox 89–91; TV Schorne 91–96; V St Osyth *Chelmsf* 96–00; R The Suttons w Tydd *Linc* 00–04; rtd 04; PtO *Nor* from 06; *St E* from 10. *9 Haling Way, Thetford IP24 1EY* T: (01842) 820180 E: revianwhite@aol.com

WHITE, James Robert. b 88. St Steph Ho Ox 14. d 18 p 19. NSM Ruislip St Martin *Lon* from 18. *20 Lymington Drive, Ruislip HA4 7EZ* M: 07716-086302 E: whitejr@hotmail.co.uk

WHITE, Miss Janice. b 49. Trin Coll Bris IDC 76. d 91 p 94. C Claygate *Guildf* 91–98; Assoc Min Stanford-le-Hope w Mucking *Chelmsf* 98–12; rtd 12; PtO *St E* from 12. *27 Canterbury Gardens, Hadleigh IP7 5BS* T: (01473) 808835 E: wheeze4god@talktalk.net

WHITE, Jo. *See* WHITE, Julia Mary

WHITE, Canon John Austin. b 42. Hull Univ BA 64. Coll of Resurr Mirfield 64. d 66 p 67. C Leeds St Aid *Ripon* 66–69; Asst Chapl Leeds Univ 69–73; Chapl NOC 73–82; Can and Prec Windsor 82–12; rtd 12. *24 Camm Avenue, Windsor SL4 4NW* E: johnaustinwhite@hotmail.com

WHITE, John Christopher. b 62. Keble Coll Ox BA 84 Ex Univ MA 98 PhD 10. Wycliffe Hall Ox BA 88. d 89 p 90. C Southway *Ex* 89–93; TV Plymouth Em, St Paul Efford and St Aug 93–99; Hon C Abbotskerswell 99–05; PtO *Birm* 05–10; TV Kings Norton 10–14; P-in-c Kingsbury from 14; P-in-c Baxterley w Hurley and Wood End and Merevale etc from 14. *The Vicarage, Church Lane, Kingsbury, Tamworth B78 2LR* T: (01827) 874252 E: jwhite.harborne@live.co.uk

WHITE, John David. b 77. Univ of Missouri BA 05. Trin Coll Bris 16. d 18 p 19. C Stoke Bishop *Bris* from 18. *9 Dorset Road, Westbury-on-Trym, Bristol BS9 4BJ* M: 07540-960254 E: johndwhite77@gmail.com

WHITE, John Emlyn. *See* HARRIS-WHITE, John Emlyn

WHITE, Canon John Francis. b 47. Qu Coll Cam BA 69 MA 73. Cuddesdon Coll 72. **d** 72 **p** 73. Sacr Wakef Cathl 72–73; Prec 73–76; V Thurlstone *Wakef* 76–82; P-in-c Hoyland Swaine 81–82; V Chapelthorpe 82–06; RD Chevet 96–05; V Lindley 06–10; Hon Can Wakef Cathl 00–10; rtd 10. *16 Thorne End Road, Staincross, Barnsley S75 6NR* T: (01226) 217440 E: john.white110@virginmedia.com

WHITE, John Malcolm. b 54. Aston Univ BSc 77. Trin Coll Bris BA 87. **d** 87 **p** 88. C Harborne Heath *Birm* 87–91; C S Harrow St Paul *Lon* 91–93; TV Roxeth 93–96; V Derby St Alkmund and St Werburgh 96–13; PtO *Sheff* 13–18. *284 Springvale Road, Sheffield S10 1LJ* T: 0114-263 1447 E: whitejm@globalnet.co.uk *or* johnemw@gmail.com

WHITE, John William. b 37. CEng 71 MIMechE 71. SAOMC 98. **d** 01 **p** 02. NSM Sandhurst *Ox* 01–10; PtO from 10. *21 Broom Acres, Sandhurst GU47 8PN* T: (01344) 774349

WHITE (née REDMAN), Mrs Julia Elizabeth Hithersay. b 43. St Alb Minl Tr Scheme 87 SAOMC 99. **d** 99 **p** 00. NSM Harpenden St Jo *St Alb* 99–13; PtO from 13. *The Folly, 71 Station Road, Harpenden AL5 4RL* T: (01582) 763869

WHITE, Julia Mary (Jo). b 52. Harris Coll CertEd 73 Man Univ BEd 85 MEd 87 PhD 92. NOC 00. **d** 03 **p** 04. C Ashbourne St Oswald w Mapleton *Derby* 03–07; R Wingerworth 07–13; R Thornton Dale w Allerston, Ebberston etc *York* 13–18; rtd 18; PtO *York* from 18. *31 Low Moorgate, Rillington, Malton YO17 8JW* T: (01944) 758875 E: jo@handjwhite.uk

WHITE, Justin Michael. b 70. Keble Coll Ox MEng 93 Warwick Univ MA 94 Trin Coll Cam BA 00. Westcott Ho Cam 98. **d** 01 **p** 02. C Chippenham St Andr w Tytherton Lucas *Bris* 01–04; Chapl SS Helen and Kath Sch Abingdon 04–06; Jun Chapl Win Coll 06–14; Can Res San Francisco USA 14–15; Chapl Dulwich Coll 15–18; Hon C Dulwich St Barn *S'wark* 15–18; Chapl Win Coll from 18; PV Westmr Abbey from 16. *Winchester College, College Street, Winchester SO23 9NA* E: justin_white@mac.com

WHITE, Keith Robert. b 48. Open Univ BA 88. St Jo Coll Nottm 82. **d** 84 **p** 85. C Erith St Paul *Roch* 84–88; Chapl Salisbury Coll of Tech *Sarum* 88; PtO *Roch* 11–13; V Crockenhill All So from 13. *The Vicarage, Eynsford Road, Crockenhill, Swanley BR8 8JS* T: (01322) 662157 E: keith.acts101@gmail.com

WHITE, Kenneth Charles. b 26. Tyndale Hall Bris 48. **d** 54 **p** 56. Chapl Lotome Sch Karamoja Uganda 54–55; Lic to Offic Mombasa Kenya 55–57; C Morden *S'wark* 57–60; V Ramsey St Mary's w Ponds Bridge *Ely* 60–66; V Leyton Ch Ch *Chelmsf* 66–81; V Totland Bay *Portsm* 81–91; rtd 91; PtO *Llan* 91–07; *Lon* from 08. *286A Torbay Road, Harrow HA2 9QW* T: (020) 8868 2431

WHITE, Malcolm Robert. b 46. Man Univ BSc 68. Cranmer Hall Dur 74. **d** 77 **p** 78. C Linthorpe *York* 77–81; C Sutton St Jas and Wawne 81–83; V Upper Holloway St Pet w St Jo *Lon* 83–95; TV Burnham w Dropmore, Hitcham and Taplow *Ox* 95–00; CMS Jordan 00–07; rtd 07; PtO *Ox* from 08. *Cherry Cottage, 1 Wymers Wood Road, Burnham, Slough SL1 8JQ* T: (01628) 669085 E: whitesmv@gmail.com

WHITE, Matthew Peter. b 87. Lon Sch of Th BA 14 St Jo Coll Dur MA 18. Cranmer Hall Dur 16. **d** 18 **p** 19. C W Byfleet *Guildf* from 18. *St John's Church, Camphill Road, West Byfleet KT14 6EH* T: (01932) 988773 E: matt@stjohnswestbyfleet.org.uk

WHITE, Michael Godfrey. b 46. SAOMC 98. **d** 02 **p** 03. OLM Shelswell *Ox* 02–07; NSM Fawley *Win* 07–13; rtd 13; PtO *Win* 13–15; *Ox* from 15. *32 Fortescue Drive, Chesterton, Bicester OX26 1UT* T: (01869) 572559 E: revmikewhite@yahoo.co.uk

WHITE, Mrs Natalie Jane. b 65. Ridley Hall Cam 13. **d** 15 **p** 16. C Corby St Columba *Pet* 15–18; TV Daventry from 18. *The Rectory, 71 High Street, Braunston, Daventry NN11 7HS* M: 07806-664495 E: revnatwhite@gmail.com

WHITE, Nicholas John. b 71. Southn Univ BA 93 Open Univ PGCE 95. Ripon Coll Cuddesdon 15. **d** 18 **p** 19. C St Helens Town Cen *Liv* from 18. *14 Alpine Close, St Helens WA10 4EY* M: 07562-560695

WHITE, Paul John. b 68. Middx Univ LLB 90 Bris Univ LLM 92 Dur Univ MA 19 Solicitor 91. St Mellitus Coll BA 08. **d** 08 **p** 09. C Woodchurch *Cant* 08–12; V Hadlow *Roch* from 13. *The Vicarage, Maidstone Road, Hadlow, Tonbridge TN11 0DJ* T: (01732) 850238 M: 07970-072757 E: pauljohnwhite@gmail.com

WHITE, Philip Craston. b 59. York Univ BA 81 Nottm Univ PGCE 84. Trin Coll Bris. **d** 99 **p** 00. C Countesthorpe w Foston *Leic* 99–03; C-in-c Hamilton CD 03–09; C Leic H Trin w St Jo 09–12; V Broughton *Ox* from 12. *24 King Edward Avenue, Aylesbury HP21 7JD* T: (01296) 484555 M: 07725-339236 E: phil@broughtonchurch.org

WHITE, Philip William. b 53. Bede Coll Dur CertEd 75 Coll of Ripon & York St Jo MA 01. St Jo Coll Nottm 89. **d** 91 **p** 92. C Clifton *York* 91–95; TV Heworth H Trin 95–01; P-in-c Scarborough St Jas w H Trin 01–15; Tr Officer E Riding 01–13; P-in-c Cayton w Eastfield 13–15; P-in-c Thurgarton w Hoveringham and Bleasby etc *S'well* 15–17; P-in-c Rolleston w Fiskerton, Morton and Upton 15–17; V W Trent from 17. *The Vicarage, Southwell Road, Thurgarton, Nottingham NG14 7GP* M: 07720-010066 E: phil_07@btinternet.com

WHITE, Ms Philippa Jane. b 77. Bris Univ BSc 99 MSc 03. Trin Coll Bris 17. **d** 19. C Cotham St Sav w St Mary and Clifton St Paul *Bris* from 19. *9 Dorset Road, Westbury-on-Trym, Bristol BS9 4BJ* M: 07540-959522 E: pippakendall@hotmail.com

WHITE, Mrs Philippa Judith. b 86. CCC Cam BA 08 MA 12. Ripon Coll Cuddesdon BA 13. **d** 14 **p** 15. C Linc St Jo 14–18; C Linc Cathl 14–15; PV 15–18; Succ Ch Ch Ox from 18. *Christ Church, St Aldates, Oxford OX1 1DP* M: 07474-958658 E: revdpjwhite@gmail.com

WHITE, Canon Phillip George. b 33. Univ of Wales (Lamp) BA 54. St Mich Coll Llan 54. **d** 56 **p** 57. C Tongwynlais *Llan* 56–58; C Mountain Ash 58–60; C Aberavon 60–62; Area Sec (Middx) CMS 62–64; V Treherbert *Llan* 64–75; P-in-c Treorchy 75–76; V Treherbert w Treorchy 76–77; V Pyle w Kenfig 77–99; RD Margam 86–99; Can Llan Cathl 91–99; rtd 99; PtO *Llan* from 99. *8 Heol Fair, Porthcawl CF36 5LA* T: (01656) 786297

WHITE, Canon Priscilla Audrey. b 62. St Hugh's Coll Ox BA 84 MA 88 Birm Univ MA 12. Wycliffe Hall Ox 87. **d** 89 **p** 94. Par Dn Southway *Ex* 89–93; NSM Plymouth Em, St Paul Efford and St Aug 93–99; P-in-c Abbotskerswell 99–05; P-in-c Harborne St Faith and St Laur *Birm* 05–10; V from 10; AD Edgbaston 10–17; Hon Can Birm Cathl from 15. *The Vicarage, Church Lane, Kingsbury, Tamworth B78 2LR* T: (01827) 874252 *or* 0121-427 2410 E: priscillawhite.harborne@btinternet.com

WHITE, Richard. *See* WHITE, Douglas Richard Leon

WHITE, Richard Alfred. b 49. CQSW. St Jo Coll Nottm. **d** 90 **p** 91. C Leic St Phil 90–95; C Old Dalby and Nether Broughton 95–98; R Ibstock w Heather 98–10; rtd 10; PtO *Leic* 10–16 and from 21. *3 Marston Way, Heather, Coalfield LE67 2RR* T: (01530) 260676 E: richard49white@googlemail.com

WHITE, Richard Michael. b 84. Ox Brookes Univ BA 07 PGCE 08. St Mellitus Coll BA 16. **d** 16 **p** 17. C Cogges and S Leigh *Ox* 16–19; TR Bath Twerton-on-Avon *B & W* from 19. *The Rectory, Watery Lane, Bath BA2 1RL* M: 07716-688681 E: richardwhite115@hotmail.com

WHITE, Canon Richard Stanley. b 70. Trin Coll Bris BA 02. **d** 03 **p** 04. C Haydock St Mark *Liv* 03–06; Pioneer Min Dream Network 06–09; Can for Miss and Evang 09–18; Dir Making and Nurturing Disciples *York* from 18. *47 Hempland Avenue, York YO31 1DD* M: 07989-312758

WHITE, Canon Robert Charles. b 61. Mansf Coll Ox BA 83. St Steph Ho Ox 83. **d** 85 **p** 86. C Fratton *Portsm* 85–88; C Portsea N End St Mark 88–92; V Warren Park 92–00; P-in-c Leigh Park 94–96; V 96–00; RD Havant 98–00; V Portsea St Mary from 00; P-in-c Portsea All SS from 19; AD Portsm from 11; Hon Can Portsm Cathl from 97. *St Mary's Vicarage, Fratton Road, Portsmouth PO1 5PA* T: (023) 9282 2687 *or* 9282 2990 F: 9235 9320 E: revrcwhite@gmail.com

WHITE, Robin Edward Bantry. b 47. TCD BA 70 BD 79. CITC 72. **d** 72 **p** 73. C Dublin Zion Ch *D & G* 72–76; Min Can St Patr Cathl Dublin 76–79; C Taney Ch Ch *D & G* 76–79; I Abbeystrewry Union *C, C & R* 79–89; I Douglas Union w Frankfield 89–02; I Moviddy Union 02–14; Can Cork Cathl 89–14; Can Ross Cathl 89–93; Adn Cork, Cloyne and Ross 93–14; Preb Castleknock St Patr Cathl Dublin 09–14; rtd 14. *Ardcairn, 26 Marble Court, Paulstown, Co Kilkenny, R95 KT22, Republic of Ireland* T: (00353) (59) 972 6089 M: 87-286 2178 E: rebw@eircom.net *or* robinbantrywhite@gmail.com

WHITE, Roderick Harry. b 55. Trin Coll Bris BA 86. **d** 86 **p** 87. C Northampton St Giles *Pet* 86–89; C Godley cum Newton Green *Ches* 89–93; P-in-c 93–99; R Northiam *Chich* from 99. *The Rectory, 24 High Meadow, Northiam, Rye TN31 6GA* T: (01797) 253118 E: rod@rodwhite.freeuk.com

WHITE, Roger David. b 37. Univ of Wales (Cardiff) BTh 91. St Mich Coll Llan. **d** 66 **p** 67. C Mountain Ash *Llan* 66–71; C Port Talbot St Theodore 71–74; V Caerhun w Llangelynin w Llanbedr-y-Cennin *Ban* 74–85; R Llanbedrog w Llannor w Llanfihangel etc 85–88; V Llangeinor *Llan* 88–90; V Spittal w Trefgarn and Ambleston w St Dogwells *St D* 90–98; V Abergwili w Llanfihangel-uwch-Gwili etc 98–00; rtd 00. *Tir Na Nog, 18 Bryn Cir, Llanerchymedd LL71 8EG* T: (01248) 470159

WHITE, Roger Ian Scott. b 41. Leeds Univ BA 62 Culham Coll Ox PGCE 70. Coll of Resurr Mirfield 62. **d** 64 **p** 65. C Wotton-under-Edge *Glouc* 64–69; NSM Rugby St Andr *Cov*

71–80; W Germany 80–82; P-in-c Brinklow *Cov* 82–86; R 86–90; P-in-c Harborough Magna 82–86; R 86–90; P-in-c Monks Kirby w Pailton and Stretton-under-Fosse 82–86; V 86–90; Germany 90–92; V Lydgate w Friezland *Man* 92–01; Chapl Hamburg *Eur* 01–11; rtd 11; PtO *Eur* from 16. *Spannwisch 7, 22159 Hamburg, Germany* T: (0049) (40) 664316 E: roger.white@gmx.de

WHITE, Ronald Henry. b 36. Bris Univ BSc 58. SWMTC 82. **d** 85 **p** 86. C Ivybridge *Ex* 85–87; C Ivybridge w Harford 87–88; V Blackawton and Stoke Fleming 88–95; V Stoke Fleming, Blackawton and Strete 95–00; RD Woodleigh 95–99; rtd 00; PtO *Ex* from 02. *10 Hollingarth Way, Hemyock, Cullompton EX15 3XB* T: (01823) 681020 E: revron@btinternet.com

WHITE, Sandy Dulcie. b 44. **d** 98 **p** 99. OLM W Streatham St Jas *S'wark* 98–05; PtO *Wakef* 05–07; NSM Cornholme and Walsden 07–14; PtO *Leeds* from 14. *774 Rochdale Road, Todmorden OL14 7UA* T: (01706) 812007 E: revsandyd@gmail.com

WHITE, Sheelagh Mary. *See* ASTON, Sheelagh Mary

WHITE, Simon Inigo Dexter. b 58. York Univ BA 80 Nottm Univ PGCE 81. St Jo Coll Nottm 87. **d** 90 **p** 91. C Chadkirk *Ches* 90–94; C Stockport St Geo 94; TV Stockport SW 94–99; Chapl Stockport Gr Sch 94–99; P-in-c W Hallam and Mapperley *Derby* 99–02; P-in-c Stanley 99–02; R W Hallam and Mapperley w Stanley 02–13; V Tideswell from 13. *The Vicarage, 6 Pursglove Drive, Tideswell, Buxton SK17 8PA* T: 0115-932 4695 *or* (01298) 871317 E: s.i.d.white@tesco.net *or* simon.white44@btinternet.com

WHITE, Simon James Hithersay. b 65. St Jo Coll Nottm 01. **d** 03 **p** 04. C Alnwick *Newc* 03–06; P-in-c Felton and Longframlington w Brinkburn 06–13; Dioc Youth Officer 06–13; R Morpeth from 13. *The Rectory, Cottingwood Lane, Morpeth NE61 1ED* T: (01670) 517716 M: 07749-866402 E: rev.simonjhwhite@gmail.com

WHITE, Simon John. b 60. Southn Univ BSc 82. ERMC 13. **d** 16. NSM Hadleigh, Layham and Shelley *St E* from 16. *20 The Street, Assington, Sudbury CO10 5LJ* T: (01787) 211228 M: 07572-418555 E: simon@sjwhite.co.uk

WHITE, Stephen Ross. b 58. Hull Univ BA 81 QUB PhD 94. Ripon Coll Cuddesdon BA 84. **d** 85 **p** 86. C Redcar *York* 85–88; P-in-c Gweedore, Carrickfin and Templecrone *D & R* 88–92; Bp's Dom Chapl 91–92; Dean Raphoe 92–02; I Raphoe w Raymochy and Clonleigh 93–01; Dean Killaloe and Clonfert *L & K* 02–12; Chan St Patr Cathl Dublin 11–12; P-in-c Dunsfold and Hascombe *Guildf* 12–19. *The Rectory, Church Green, Dunsfold, Godalming GU8 4LT* T: (01483) 200048 E: stephenwhite14@btinternet.com

WHITE, Mrs Susan Margaret. b 48. Univ of E Lon BA 84 Brunel Univ MBA 94 Anglia Poly Univ MA 04. EAMTC 01. **d** 04 **p** 05. C Harwich Peninsula *Chelmsf* 04–08; P-in-c Alkham w Capel le Ferne and Hougham *Cant* 08–12; P-in-c Eythorne and Elvington w Waldershare etc 12; P-in-c Whitfield w Guston 12; R Bewsborough 13–18; AD Dover 11–16; rtd 18. *29 Mount Road, Canterbury CT1 1YD* E: revsuewhite@gmail.com

WHITE, (*née* BUTLER), Mrs Valerie Joyce. b 58. EAMTC 99. **d** 02 **p** 03. NSM Southminster *Chelmsf* 02–06; Hon Chapl Miss to Seafarers Tilbury 05–06; C Bury St Edmunds All SS w St Jo and St Geo *St E* 06–08; TV Walton and Trimley 08–16; P-in-c Bacton w Wyverstone, Cotton and Old Newton etc 16–18; rtd 19; PtO *St E* from 19. *154 Colneis Road, Felixstowe IP11 9LQ* M: 07859-464932 E: valthevic@talktalk.net

WHITE, Canon Vernon Philip. b 53. Clare Coll Cam BA 75 MA 79 Oriel Coll Ox MLitt 80. Wycliffe Hall Ox. **d** 77 **p** 78. Tutor Wycliffe Hall Ox 77–83; Chapl and Lect Ex Univ 83–87; R Wotton and Holmbury St Mary *Guildf* 87–93; Dir of Ords 87–93; Can Res and Chan Linc Cathl 93–01; Prin STETS 01–11; Can Th Win Cathl 06–11; Can Th Westmr Abbey 11–18; Sub-Dean 15–18; Visiting Prof K Coll Lon 11–18. *Address temp unknown*

WHITE, William Frederick. b 30. St Jo Coll Nottm. **d** 02. NSM Hillingdon St Jo *Lon* 02–06; NSM Cowley 06–08; Asst Chapl Hillingdon Hosp NHS Trust 02–08; PtO *Lon* 08–18. *31A Copperfield Avenue, Hillingdon, Uxbridge UB8 3NU* T: (01895) 236746 M: 07754-234233 E: billwhite2001@hotmail.com

WHITE-DUNDAS, Maithre Cecilia. b 60. Nottm Univ PhD. CITI. **d** 17. Ballyholme *D & D* from 17. *59 Sharman Road, Belfast BT9 5FX* M: 07921-567094 E: whitedum@tcd.ie

WHITEHALL, Adrian Leslie. b 53. Leeds Univ MB, ChB 76 Sheff Univ MMedSc 93 MRCGP 80. Ridley Hall Cam 04. **d** 06 **p** 07. C Todwick *Sheff* 06–09; Tanzania 10–11; PtO *Derby* from 12; CMS Tanzania 13–15; PtO *Eur* from 19. *Meadow House, Ashbourne Road, Belper DE56 2DA* T: (01773) 826410 M: 07866-454148 E: adrian.whitehall@gmail.com

WHITEHEAD, Alexander. *See* WHITEHEAD, Matthew Alexander

WHITEHEAD, Andrew Paul. b 77. Lanc Univ BA 01 Cam Univ BTh 12. Westcott Ho Cam 10. **d** 12 **p** 13. C Clitheroe St Mary *Blackb* 12–15; C Cawston w Booton and Brandiston etc *Nor* 15–17; TV Aylsham and Distr from 17; Dioc Chapl MU from 19. *The Rectory, Ames Court, Cawston, Norwich NR10 4QD* T: (01603) 872236 M: 07801-290649 E: a.p.whitehead@me.com

WHITEHEAD, Anwyl David. b 67. St Hild Coll 16. **d** 18. NSM Chapeltown *Sheff* from 18. *68 The Rookery, Deepcar, Sheffield S36 2NA*

WHITEHEAD, Christopher Martin Field. b 36. ALCD 62. **d** 62 **p** 63. C Higher Openshaw *Man* 62–63; C Halliwell St Pet 64–66; V Owlerton *Sheff* 66–75; V Hunmanby w Muston *York* 75–95; RD Scarborough 91–94; R Lockington and Lund and Scarborough w Leconfield 95–01; rtd 01; PtO *York* 01–15. *59 Cornelian Drive, Scarborough YO11 3AL* T: (01723) 377837 E: candjwhitehead59@gmail.com

WHITEHEAD, David. b 62. Newc Univ BSc 83 MSc 85 PhD 89. St Jo Coll Nottm BA 09. **d** 07 **p** 08. C Ambleside w Brathay *Carl* 07–10; TV Kirkby Lonsdale 10–14; P-in-c Whitehaven 14–15; Dioc Healing Adv 13–15; rtd 15; PtO *Carl* from 16. *Brandle Howe, Helm Road, Bowness-on-Windermere, Windermere LA23 3AA* T: (015394) 44393 E: davidcwhitehead@btopenworld.com

WHITEHEAD, David. *See* WHITEHEAD, Anwyl David

WHITEHEAD, Gordon James. b 42. Culham Coll of Educn DipEd 64. Clifton Th Coll 66. **d** 73 **p** 74. C Romford Gd Shep *Chelmsf* 73; SAMS Santiago Chile 74–87; C Coleraine *Conn* 87–94; I Errigle Keerogue w Ballygawley and Killeshil *Arm* 94–02; I Bright w Ballee and Killough *D & D* 02–07; rtd 07. *75 Kensington Manor, Dollingstown, Craigavon BT66 7HR* T: (028) 3831 7989 E: whitehead105@btinternet.com

WHITEHEAD, Ian Richard. b 63. St Jo Coll Nottm BA 95. **d** 95 **p** 96. C Hillmorton *Cov* 95–97; C Whitnash 97–99; R Rolleston *Lich* 99–18; V Anslow 99–18; C Hanbury, Newborough, Rangemore and Tutbury 14–18; R Anslow, Rolleston and Tutbury 18–19; P-in-c Crich and S Wingfield *Derby* from 19. *New Vicarage, Coasthill, Crich, Matlock DE4 5JS* T: (01773) 425077 E: cswvicar@gmail.com

WHITEHEAD, Mrs Jennifer Jane. b 45. St Jo Coll York CertEd 67. **d** 98 **p** 99. OLM Winterton Gp *Linc* from 98. *11 Queen Street, Winterton, Scunthorpe DN15 9TR* T: (01724) 734027 E: jennifer.whitehead@btinternet.com

WHITEHEAD, Mrs Joanne Louise. b 71. Hull Univ BA 92 PGCE 93 Nottm Univ MA 08. EMMTC 05. **d** 08 **p** 09. C Oakwood *Derby* 08–13; P-in-c Newhall 13–16; Lead Chapl Derbyshire Constabulary and Fire and Rescue Services 16–17; Dioc Enablement Officer 18–19; PtO *Derby* from 18. *4 Bromyard Drive, Chellaston, Derby DE73 6PF* T: (01332) 388650 M: 07816-281023

WHITEHEAD, John Stanley. b 38. Jes Coll Cam BA 63 MA 62 MPhil. Westcott Ho Cam 63. **d** 64 **p** 65. C Batley All SS *Wakef* 64–67; C Mitcham St Mark *S'wark* 67–70; C Frindsbury w Upnor *Roch* 70–72; TV Strood 72–75; R Halstead 75–82; V Betley *Lich* 82–85; V Betley and Keele 85–01; Asst Chapl Keele Univ 82–01; PtO *Ches* 02–09 and from 11; C Acton and Worleston, Church Minshull etc 10; PtO *Lich* from 09. *Paddock House, Longhill Lane, Hankelow, Crewe CW3 0JG* T: (01270) 812607

WHITEHEAD, Canon Matthew Alexander. b 44. Leeds Univ BA 65 Birm Univ MA 75 St Chad's Coll Dur DipEd 66 Newc Univ MPhil 03. Qu Coll Birm. **d** 69 **p** 70. C Bingley All SS *Bradf* 69–72; C Keele and Asst Chapl Keele Univ *Lich* 72–74; Bp's Dom Chapl *Dur* 74–80; V Escomb and Witton Park 74–80; V Birtley 80–89; RD Chester-le-Street 84–89; V Stockton St Pet 89–00; V The Trimdons 00–03; Dioc Warden of Readers 94–03; Hon Can Dur Cathl 96–03; P-in-c Stow Gp *Linc* 03–09; rtd 09; Dioc Warden of Readers *Linc* 03–11; Can and Preb Linc Cathl 04–18; V Linc St Mary Magd w St Paul and St Mich 14–18. *77 Yarborough Crescent, Lincoln LN1 3NE* M: 07518-746643 E: alex.whitehead@lincoln.anglican.org

WHITEHEAD, Canon Nicholas James. b 53. Univ of Wales (Ban) BTh 07 ACIB. Ridley Hall Cam 86. **d** 88 **p** 89. C Bourne *Guildf* 88–92; V Hersham 92–10; RD Emly 06–10; P-in-c Shere, Albury and Chilworth 10–14; R 14–18; RD Cranleigh 13–15; Hon Can Guildf Cathl 12–18; rtd 18; PtO *Portsm* from 19. *Rowan House, Dean Lane, Bishops Waltham, Southampton SO32 1FX* M: 07946-389583

WHITEHEAD, Paul Conrad. b 60. St Jo Coll Nottm LTh 92. **d** 92 **p** 93. C Mansfield Woodhouse *S'well* 92–96; C Carlton-in-the-Willows 96–02; C Colwick 96–02; CF (TA) from 96; NSM Trowell, Awsworth and Cossall *S'well* from 04. *84 Hillside Road, Beeston, Nottingham NG9 3AT* T: 0115-919 7030 M: 07973-727221

WHITEHEAD, Canon Robin Lawson. b 53. Bris Univ BA 76 Lon Univ MA 96. St Steph Ho Ox 77. **d** 80 **p** 81. C Cheshunt *St Alb* 80–83; C E Grinstead St Swithun *Chich* 83–85; V Friern Barnet St Pet le Poer *Lon* 85–92; R Friern Barnet St Jas 92–95; C Wood Green St Mich w Bounds Green St Gabr etc 96–97; TR Leic Resurr 97–04; V Boston *Linc* 04–05; TR 05–13; RD Holland E 09–10; RD Holland W 09–10; RD Holland 10–13; Can and Preb Linc Cathl 09–13; rtd 13; PtO *Cant* 13–16; R Winchelsea and Icklesham *Chich* 13–17; PtO *Glas* from 17. *8 Galla Crescent, Dalbeattie DG5 4JY* T: (01556) 611829 E: robinwhitehead6@btinternet.com

WHITEHOUSE, Alan Edward. b 35. CEng 66. Glouc Sch of Min 89. **d** 92 **p** 93. NSM Evesham *Worc* 92–96; NSM Evesham w Norton and Lenchwick 96–02; rtd 02; PtO *Worc* from 03. *The Coppice, 56 Elm Road, Evesham WR11 3DW* T: (01386) 442427 M: 07789-081595 E: alan.coppice@tiscali.co.uk

WHITEHOUSE, David Garner. b 70. Sheff Univ BEng 91. EAMTC 03. **d** 05 **p** 06. C Cheadle *Ches* 05–10; P-in-c Southport SS Simon and Jude w All So *Liv* 10–19; V Leyland St Andr *Blackb* from 19. *St Andrew's Vicarage, 1 Crocus Field, Leyland PR25 3DY* E: davidgwhitehouse@googlemail.com

WHITEHOUSE, Nigel Andrew. b 57. St Mary's RC Sem Birm 75 Westcott Ho Cam 91. **d** 80 **p** 81. In RC Ch 81–87; C Whittlesey and Pondersbridge *Ely* 92–94; P-in-c Newton 94–98; R 98–03; P-in-c Gorefield 94–98; V 98–03; P-in-c Tydd St Giles 94–98; R 98–03; TR Whittlesey, Pondersbridge and Coates from 03; Hon Asst Dir of Ords 09–12; RD March 09–15. *The Rectory, 9A St Mary's Street, Whittlesey, Peterborough PE7 1BG* T: (01733) 203676 E: nigel.whitehouse@hotmail.com

WHITEHOUSE, Mrs Sarah Alice. b 61. St Andr Univ MA 83. St Aug Coll of Th 16. **d** 19. NSM Tooting All SS *S'wark* from 19. *21 Nottingham Road, London SW17 7EA* M: 07831-613358 E: sarah.whitehouse@6kbw.com

WHITEHOUSE, Canon Susan Clara. b 48. R Holloway Coll Lon BA 70. Westcott Ho Cam 87. **d** 89 **p** 94. Par Dn Farnley *Ripon* 89–93; Dioc Development Rep 92–03; C Bedale and Thornton Watlass w Thornton Steward 93–96; V Aysgarth and Bolton cum Redmire 96–06; R Penhill 06–13; Hon Can Ripon Cathl 02–13; AD Wensley 03–05; rtd 13; LtO *Edin* from 14. *157 The Murrays, Edinburgh EH17 8UN* E: revsuewhitehouse@btinternet.com

WHITELEY, Capt Paul Nigel. b 64. **d** 18 **p** 19. C Spalding St Paul *Linc* from 18. *St John's House, 6 Wedgewood Drive, Spalding PE11 3FJ* T: (01775) 711491 M: 07952-224304 E: paulwhiteley@btinternet.com

WHITELEY, Raewynne Jean. b 66. Melbourne Univ BA 89 MA 92 ACT BTh 95 BMin 95 Princeton Th Sem PhD 03. **d** 96 **p** 93. C Hunters Hill Australia 96–98; C Princeton Trin Ch USA 98–01; C Trin Cathl Trenton 01–02; V Swedesboro 02–06; R New York St Jas 07–17; Can Th Long Is 09–17; Dioc Discipleship and Voc Missr *S'wark* from 18; Hon C Sanderstead St Mary from 18. *Trinity House, 4 Chapel Court, Borough High Street, London SE1 1UH* M: 07426-903725 E: raewynne.whiteley@southwark.anglican.org

WHITELEY, Canon Robert Louis. b 28. Leeds Univ BA 48. Coll of Resurr Mirfield 50. **d** 52 **p** 53. C Hollinwood *Man* 52–55; Br Honduras 56–61; V Illingworth *Wakef* 61–68; V Westgate Common 68–75; Can Res Wakef Cathl 75–80; Hon Can Wakef Cathl 80–93; V Almondbury 80–82; TR Almondbury w Farnley Tyas 82–92; RD Almondbury 81–93; rtd 93; PtO *Wakef* 93–14; *Leeds* 14–16; *Ox* 98–10; *Guildf* 10–13; *Ox* from 13. *34 Elizabeth Court, Victoria Road, Wargrave, Reading RG10 8BP* E: r.whitley505@btinternet.com

WHITELOCK, Mrs Susan Karen. b 62. STETS 98. **d** 01 **p** 06. NSM Portsea N End St Mark *Portsm* 01–06; NSM Portsea St Mary from 06. *404 Copnor Road, Portsmouth PO3 5EW* M: 07903-414029 E: sue.whitelock@ntlworld.com

WHITEMAN, Christopher Henry Raymond. b 51. Portsm Poly BA 73 Worc Coll of Educn PGCE 74 Open Univ BSc 97. St Jo Coll Nottm MA 99. **d** 90 **p** 91. C Rockland St Mary w Hellington, Bramerton etc *Nor* 90–93; P-in-c Gillingham w Geldeston, Stockton, Ellingham etc 93–94; R 94–04; R Culworth w Sulgrave and Thorpe Mandeville etc *Pet* 04–11; rtd 11. *28 Penterry Park, Chepstow NP16 5AZ* E: chrwhiteman@aol.com

WHITEMAN, The Ven Rodney David Carter. b 40. Ely Th Coll 61. **d** 64 **p** 65. C Kings Heath *Birm* 64–70; V Rednal 70–79; V Erdington St Barn 79–89; RD Aston 81–86 and 88–89; Hon Can Birm Cathl 85–89; Adn Bodmin *Truro* 89–00; Adn Cornwall 00–05; P-in-c Cardynham and Helland 89–94; Hon Can Truro Cathl 89–95; rtd 06; PtO *Truro* from 16. *22 Treverbyn Gardens, Sandy Hill, St Austell PL25 3AW* T: (01726) 879043 E: rodneywhiteman@talktalk.net

WHITFIELD, Joy Verity. *See* CHAPMAN, Joy Verity

WHITFIELD, Leslie Turnbull. b 43. Cardiff Univ LLM 10 CEng 72 MIET 72 MCMI 74. St Jo Coll Nottm MA 00.

d 00 **p** 01. C Bottesford w Ashby *Linc* 00–03; P-in-c Mablethorpe w Trusthorpe 03–07; Ind Chapl 07–08; rtd 08; PtO *Linc* from 17. *3 Burland Court, Washingborough, Lincoln LN4 1HL* T: (01522) 791195 M: 07913-247783 E: rev.les@tiscali.co.uk

WHITFIELD, Miss Vivien Elizabeth. b 46. Westhill Coll Birm CertEd 68. Open Th Coll BA 01 Lon Sch of Th MA 04. **d** 17 **p** 18. NSM Colchester St Jo *Chelmsf* from 17. *21 Broad Oaks Park, Colchester CO4 0JX* M: 07752-888273 (text only) E: vivien.whitfield@talk21.com

WHITFIELD, William. b 47. Open Univ BA 80 Univ of Wales (Cardiff) LLM 95 FRSH 81. STETS 01. **d** 04 **p** 05. NSM Marchwood *Win* 04–08; NSM Millbrook 08–11; PtO from 11; *Portsm* from 13. *35 The Rowans, Marchwood, Southampton SO40 4YW* T: (023) 8086 0399 E: william.whitfield@btinternet.com

WHITFORD, Judith. *See* POLLINGER, Judith

WHITFORD (née FAULKNER), Mrs Margaret Evelyn. b 54. Goldsmiths' Coll Lon BEd 77. EAMTC 98. **d** 01 **p** 02. C Grays Thurrock *Chelmsf* 01–05; C Bradwell on Sea 05–08; C Bradwell on Sea and St Lawrence 08–11; C Brandon and Santon Downham w Elveden etc *St E* 11–15; rtd 15. *19 High Street, West Mersea, Colchester CO5 8QA* E: mandlz@btinternet.com

WHITFORD, William Laurence. b 56. Open Univ BA 92. NOC 92. **d** 95 **p** 96. C Hindley All SS *Liv* 95–99; P-in-c E and W Tilbury and Linford *Chelmsf* 99–04; R 04–05; P-in-c Bradwell on Sea 05–08; R Bradwell on Sea and St Lawrence 08–11; R Brandon and Santon Downham w Elveden etc *St E* 11–15; rtd 15. *19 High Street, West Mersea, Colchester CO5 8QA* E: mandlz@btinternet.com

WHITING, Alison Ruth. b 73. STETS. **d** 14 **p** 15. NSM Dorchester and the Winterbournes *Sarum* 14–16. *10 Royal Mews, Princes Street, Dorchester DT1 1RL* T: (01305) 751716 E: ally_whiting@hotmail.com

WHITING, Joseph Alfred. b 41. Oak Hill Th Coll 82. **d** 85 **p** 86. Hon C Sidcup St Andr *Roch* 85–88; C Southborough St Pet w Ch Ch and St Matt 88–92; C Aldridge *Lich* 92–97; TV Rye *Chich* 97–02; rtd 02; PtO *Roch* 02–14. *238 Ralph Perring Court, Stone Park Avenue, Beckenham BR3 3LX* T: (020) 3583 3431 E: whitings71@tiscali.co.uk or whitings71@talktalk.net

WHITLEY, Brian. b 58. Dundee Univ BA 97 Portsm Univ MA(Ed) 00 RMN 84 RGN 84. STETS 04. **d** 07 **p** 08. C Easthampstead *Ox* 07–10; P-in-c Woodplumpton *Blackb* 10–15; PtO 15–17; P-in-c Cockfield *Dur* from 17; P-in-c Lynesack from 17; P-in-c Evenwood from 17. *The Rectory, 107 Front Street, Cockfield, Bishop Auckland DL13 5AA* T: (01388) 718584 M: 07825-487536 E: bwhitley2@btinternet.com

WHITLEY, Eric Keir. b 45. Salford Univ BSc 68. Trin Coll Bris 77. **d** 79 **p** 80. C Nottingham St Ann w Em *S'well* 79–83; V Donisthorpe and Moira w Stretton-en-le-Field *Leic* 83–91; V Thorpe Acre w Dishley 91–00; V Loughb Gd Shep 00–15; rtd 15; PtO *Leic* from 15. *4 Lamport Close, Loughborough LE11 2TT* T: (01509) 324821

WHITLEY, Ian Peter. b 61. Ox Min Course 16. **d** 17 **p** 18. C Banstead *Guildf* from 17. *14 Glenfield Road, Banstead SM7 2DG* M: 07961-382293 E: kittyandwitty@aol.com

WHITLEY, John William. b 46. TCD BA 68. Cranmer Hall Dur BA 71. **d** 71 **p** 72. C Belfast St Mary Magd *Conn* 71–73; C Toxteth St Philemon w St Gabr *Liv* 73–78; P-in-c Toxteth St Cleopas 78–88; TV Toxteth St Philemon w St Gabr and St Cleopas 89–95; P-in-c Litherland St Paul Hatton Hill 95–02; V 02–16; rtd 16; PtO *Dur* from 17. *3 Bishop's Close, Durham DH1 2BU* T: 0191-386 0328 E: anthea.whitley@virgin.net

WHITLEY (née ALLISON), Rosemary Jean. b 45. LTCL 67. Trin Coll Bris 75 St Jo Coll Nottm 94. **d** 95 **p** 99. NSM Loughb Gd Shep *Leic* 95–98 and 00–15; NSM Thorpe Acre w Dishley 98–00; rtd 15; PtO *Leic* from 15. *4 Lamport Close, Loughborough LE11 2TT*

WHITLOCK, Canon James Frederick. b 44. Ch Coll Cam BA 75 MA 78. Westcott Ho Cam 73. **d** 76 **p** 77. C Newquay *Truro* 76–79; P-in-c St Mawgan w St Ervan and St Eval 79–81; R 81; Bp's Dom Chapl 82–85; Dioc Dir of Ords 82–85; V Leagrave *St Alb* 85–89; TR Probus, Ladock and Grampound w Creed and St Erme *Truro* 89–95; V Penzance St Mary w St Paul 95–00; P-in-c Penzance St Jo 97–00; Hon Can Truro Cathl 98–00; rtd 00. *10 Barlandhu, Newlyn, Penzance TR18 5QT* T: (01736) 330474

WHITMARSH, Mrs Pauline. b 45. **d** 04 **p** 05. OLM Bramshaw and Landford w Plaitford *Sarum* 04–06; OLM Forest and Avon 06–14; rtd 14; PtO *Sarum* from 14. *Address temp unknown* E: paulinewhitmarsh@gmail.com

WHITMORE, Preb Benjamin Nicholas. b 66. Imp Coll Lon BEng 88. Cranmer Hall Dur 89. **d** 92 **p** 93. C Gt Wyrley *Lich* 92–95; C Hednesford 95–00; V Walsall Pleck and Bescot 00–07; Hon C Walsall and Walsall St Paul 05–07; V Penn from 07; Preb Lich Cathl from 13. *St Bartholomew's Vicarage,*

68 Church Hill, Penn, Wolverhampton WV4 5JD T: (01902) 332351 M: 07742-020246 E: benjowhitmore@gmail.com

WHITMORE, Edward James. b 36. Lon Univ BD 66. Tyndale Hall Bris. **d** 68 **p** 69. Tanzania 68–76; LtO *Blackb* 77–09. *74 Greencroft, Penwortham, Preston PR1 9LB* T: (01772) 746522

WHITMORE, Stephen Andrew. b 53. Sheff Univ BSc 74. St Jo Coll Nottm 89. **d** 91 **p** 92. C Newbury *Ox* 91–95; TV High Wycombe 95–16; rtd 16; PtO *Ox* from 16. *128 Templewood, Walters Ash, High Wycombe HP14 4UF* E: banjovicar@hotmail.com

WHITNEY, Charles Edward. b 46. Goldsmiths' Coll Lon BA 71 TCert 72 ACP 75 Glos Univ MA 18. WEMTC 01. **d** 04 **p** 05. NSM Tewkesbury w Walton Cardiff and Twyning *Glouc* 04–17; NSM Deerhurst and Apperley w Forthampton etc 10–17; rtd 17; PtO *Glouc* from 17. *Sarn Hill Lodge, Bushley Green, Bushley, Tewkesbury GL20 6AD* T: (01684) 296764 E: whitneyok@sky.com

WHITNEY, John Charles. b 59. St Jo Coll Dur BATM 11. Cranmer Hall Dur 09. **d** 11 **p** 12. C Kirkheaton *Wakef* 11–14; Leeds 14–15; V Alvaston *Derby* from 15. *The Vicarage, 8 Church Street, Alvaston, Derby DE24 0PR* T: (01332) 571143 E: rev_john@whitney.org.uk *or* rev_john@alvaston.church

WHITTAKER, Canon Angela. b 68. Birm Univ BA 89 St Martin's Coll Lanc PGCE 91. NEOC 98. **d** 00 **p** 01. C Houghton le Spring *Dur* 00–04; TV Kirkby Lonsdale *Carl* 04–09; P-in-c Natland from 09; P-in-c Old Hutton and New Hutton from 09; RD Kendal 12–18; Hon Can Carl Cathl from 14. *The Vicarage, Natland, Kendal LA9 7QQ* T: (01539) 560355 E: a-awhittaker@tiscali.co.uk

WHITTAKER, Brian Lawrence. b 39. Univ of Wales MTh 06. Clifton Th Coll 63. **d** 66 **p** 67. C Whitton and Thurleston w Akenham *St E* 66–69; C Normanton *Wakef* 69–74; P-in-c Castle Hall, Stalybridge and Dukinfield Ch Ch *Ches* 74–77; V Stalybridge H Trin and Ch Ch 77–83; TR Bucknall and Bagnall *Lich* 83–91; R Draycott-le-Moors w Forsbrook 91–05; rtd 05; PtO *Lich* from 05. *6 Rubens Way, Stoke-on-Trent ST3 7GQ* T: (01782) 397765 E: brianlwhittaker@gmail.com

WHITTAKER, Derek. b 30. Liv Univ BEng 51 PhD 58 CEng 65. **d** 93 **p** 95. Zambia 93–96; NSM Broom Leys *Leic* 97–00; rtd 00; PtO *Leic* 00–16; *Leeds* from 17. *4 Spa Court, Park Street, Ripon HG4 2BX* E: derek.whittaker777@gmail.com

WHITTAKER, Mrs Diane Claire. b 57. Newc Poly BA 79 Thames Poly BSc 87 Univ of Wales (Abth) MA 92. ERMC 06. **d** 08. C Welwyn *St Alb* 08–12; P-in-c Potterspury w Furtho and Yardley Gobion etc *Pet* 12–15; R from 15. *The Vicarage, 11 Church Lane, Potterspury, Towcester NN12 7PU* T: (01908) 542043 E: diane.whittaker7@btinternet.com

WHITTAKER, Edward Geoffrey. b 59. Birm Univ BSc 82 Avery Hill Coll PGCE 85 Dur Univ MA 95. Westcott Ho Cam 97. **d** 99 **p** 00. C Neston *Ches* 99–02; V Rocester and Croxden w Hollington *Lich* 02–10; P-in-c Uttoxeter Area 07–11; TR 11–15; P-in-c Upper Tean 13–14; RD Uttoxeter 04–11; P-in-c Shrawley, Witley, Astley and Abberley *Worc* from 15; P-in-c Teme Valley N from 15. *The Rectory, 1 Chiltern Close, Great Witley WR6 6HL* T: (01299) 890100 M: 07791-484774 E: ted@clovermail.net

WHITTAKER, Garry. b 59. St Jo Coll Nottm 89. **d** 91 **p** 92. C Denton Ch Ch *Man* 91–95; P-in-c Waterhead 95–05; TR Bacup and Stacksteads 05–15; TV Fellside Team *Blackb* from 15. *The Vicarage, Church Lane, Goosnargh, Preston PR3 0RL* T: (01995) 643245 E: braincapers59@aol.com

WHITTAKER, Helena Jane. b 69. Leic Univ BA 91 Open Univ MA 00. Qu Coll Birm 09. **d** 12 **p** 13. NSM Braunstone Park *Leic* 12–15; NSM Hinckley St Mary 15–18; Hon Chapl Leic Gr Sch 15–18; Chapl Ark Burlington Danes Academy London from 18. *Ark Burlington Danes Academy, Wood Lane, London W12 0HR* T: (020) 8735 4950 M: 07787-383282 E: hjwhittaker@tiscali.co.uk *or* helena.whittaker@burlingtondanes.org

WHITTAKER, Mrs Jennifer Margaret. b 43. Glas Univ MA 64. SAOMC 00. **d** 03 **p** 04. NSM Martley and Wichenford, Knightwick etc *Worc* 03–08; NSM Worcs W Rural 09–13; PtO from 13. *The Key Barn, Half Key, Malvern WR14 1UP* T: (01886) 833897 E: jen.whittaker@tiscali.co.uk

WHITTAKER, Jeremy Paul. b 59. Ox Univ MA. Ripon Coll Cuddesdon 82. **d** 84 **p** 85. C Crowthorne *Ox* 84–87; C Westborough *Guildf* 87–88; TV 88–91; Chapl Pierrepont Sch Frensham 91–95; PtO *Guildf* from 95. *6 Springhaven Close, Guildford GU1 2JP*

WHITTAKER, John. b 69. Leic Univ BA 90 ACA 93. Ripon Coll Cuddesdon BTh 00. **d** 00 **p** 01. C Melton Mowbray *Leic* 00–03; P-in-c Barrow upon Soar w Walton le Wolds 03–11; P-in-c Wymeswold and Prestwold w Hoton 05–11; V Hinckley St Mary 11–18; TR Putney St Mary *S'wark* from 18. *17 Monserrat Road, London SW15 2LD* E: johnwhittaker2010@gmail.com *or* john.whittaker@parishofputney.co.uk

68 Church Hill, Penn, Wolverhampton WV4 5JD T: (01902)

WHITTAKER, Karl Paul. b 55. ATL. CITC BTh 95. **d** 95 **p** 96. C Killowen *D & R* 95–99; I Annaghmore *Arm* 99–04; P-in-c Sunbury St Mary Australia 04–05; I Errigal w Garvagh *D & R* 05–19; I Leckpatrick w Dunnalong from 19. *Address temp unknown* E: revpaul07@btinternet.com

WHITTAKER, Canon Peter Harold. b 39. AKC 62. **d** 63 **p** 64. C Walton St Mary *Liv* 63–67; C Ross *Heref* 67–70; R Bridgnorth St Mary 70–78; P-in-c Oldbury 70–78; TR Bridgnorth, Tasley, Astley Abbotts and Oldbury 78–81; RD Bridgnorth 78–81; Preb Heref Cathl 80–81; V Leighton Buzzard w Eggington, Hockliffe etc *St Alb* 81–92; RD Dunstable 84–85; R Barton-le-Cley w Higham Gobion and Hexton 92–04; Hon Can St Alb 92–04; rtd 04; PtO *Lich* 06–17. *11 Llewellyn Place, Shrewsbury SY3 8QY* T: (01743) 361736

WHITTAKER, Robert Andrew. b 49. Open Univ BA 75 Nottm Univ MA 83 DipEd. Linc Th Coll 85. **d** 87 **p** 88. C Mansfield Woodhouse *S'well* 87–90; V Norwell w Ossington, Cromwell and Caunton 90–95; Chapl Ranby Ho Sch Retford 95–03; rtd 06; PtO *S'well* from 14. *23 Birchcroft Road, Retford DN22 7ZD* T: (01777) 470153

WHITTAM, Canon Kenneth Michael. b 26. Ball Coll Ox BA 50 MA 54. Cuddesdon Coll 50. **d** 52 **p** 53. C Adlington *Blackb* 52–55; C St Annes St Thos 55–58; R Halton w Aughton 58–62; R Colne St Bart 62–66; Chapl Highgate Sch Lon 66–75; V Shotwick *Ches* 75–89; Can Res Ches Cathl and Dioc Missr 75–85; Hon Can Ches Cathl 85–90; Clergy Study Officer 85–91; rtd 91; PtO *Ches* 91–10. *22 Warwick Close, Little Neston, Neston CH64 0SR* T: 0151-336 8541

WHITTICK, Emma Louise. b 81. Univ of Wales (Abth) MSc 05 PhD 10 New Coll Ox PGCE 03. St Jo Coll Nottm 09. **d** 15 **p** 16. C Dafen and Felinfoel *St D* 15–17; C Bro Lliedi from 17; Chapl Univ of Wales (Trin St Dav) from 18. *The Chaplaincy, Forest Road, Lampeter SA48 8AN* T: (01570) 424781 E: revdremmawhittick@gmail.com

WHITTING, Dominic Peter. b 85. Cant Ch Ch Univ BA 07. Ripon Coll Cuddesdon 07. **d** 10 **p** 11. C St Breoke and Egloshayle Truro 10–14; V Crowan and Treslothan 14–18; Chapl R Cornwall Hosps Trust from 18. *79 Egloshayle Road, Wadebridge PL27 6AF* T: (01208) 812726 E: domwhitting@hotmail.com

WHITTINGHAM, Janet Irene. *See* HULSE, Janet Irene

WHITTINGHAM, Peter. b 58. Sheff Univ BA 79 PGCE. St Jo Coll Nottm 88. **d** 90 **p** 91. C Northowram *Wakef* 90–93; C Airedale w Fryston 93–96; V Wrenthorpe 96–06; P-in-c Alverthorpe 02–06; V Attercliffe and Darnall *Sheff* 06–11; Chapl Shrewsbury Hosp from 11. *The Chaplain's House, Shrewsbury Hospital, Norfolk Road, Sheffield S2 2SU* T: 0114-275 9997 E: peter.whittingham@sheffield.anglican.org

WHITTINGHAM, Ronald Norman. b 43. Linc Coll Ox BA 65 MA 68. Coll of Resurr Mirfield 65. **d** 67 **p** 68. C Horninglow *Lich* 67–69; C Drayton in Hales 69–70; C Uttoxeter w Bramshall 71–75; P-in-c Burton St Paul 75–80; V Shareshill 80–83; V Silverdale and Knutton Heath 83–89; P-in-c Alsagers Bank 83–89; V Silverdale and Alsagers Bank 89–92; V Honley *Wakef* 92–99; TV Hugglescote w Donington, Ellistown and Snibston *Leic* 99–02; TV Leic Presentation 02–07; C Leic St Chad 02–07; rtd 07; PtO *Lich* from 08. *848 High Lane, Stoke-on-Trent ST6 6HG* T: (01782) 860460 E: ronwhittingham@ntlworld.com

WHITTINGHAM, David John. b 45. Qu Coll Ox BA 67 MA 71. Coll of Resurr Mirfield 69. **d** 71 **p** 72. Chapl St Woolos Cathl *Mon* 71–72; Chapl Qu Coll and C Ox St Mary V w St Cross and St Pet 72–76; V Stockton *Dur* 77–98; Hon Can Dur Cathl 93–98; Can Res and Dioc Dir of Educn 98–03; Nat Sch Development Officer Abps' Coun 03–08; rtd 08. *79 Alderney Street, London SW1V 4HF* M: 07702-036344 E: dj.whittingham@btinternet.com

WHITTINGTON, Peter Graham. b 68. Ox Poly BA 90 Ches Univ MA 14. Trin Coll Bris BA 95. **d** 95 **p** 96. C Gateacre *Liv* 95–99; V Huyton St Geo 99–05; V Orrell 05–16; Dir Studies from 16. *6 Winchester Close, Orrell, Wigan WN5 8PA* T: (01942) 221017 *or* 0151-709 9722 E: peter.whittington@liverpool.anglican.org

WHITTINGTON, Richard Hugh. b 47. Sarum & Wells Th Coll. **d** 93 **p** 94. C Enfield St Jas *Lon* 93–96; P-in-c Ightham *Roch* 96–97; R 97–01; Chapl R Hosp Chelsea 01–13; PtO *Lon* from 13; *Ox* from 14. *60 Walker Drive, Faringdon SN7 7FZ* T: (01367) 243738 M: 07979-360025 E: rhw47@btinternet.com

WHITTINGTON, Mrs Sharon Ann. b 56. Leeds Univ BA 79 PGCE 80. NEOC. **d** 00 **p** 01. NSM The Street Par *York* 00–03; P-in-c York St Thos w St Maurice 03–05; NSM York St Olave w St Giles 03–09; NSM York St Helen w St Martin 04–09; PtO from 09; Chapl St Leon Hospice York from 11. *30 Marygate, York YO30 7BH* T: (01904) 627401 E: sa.whittington@btinternet.com

WHITTLE, Adam Charles. b 87. Liv Univ BA 09 MA 10. Trin Coll Bris 15. **d** 18 **p** 19. C Pennington *Man* from 18. *43 The Pines, Woodside, Hazelwood Road, Bristol BS9 1QD* M: 07919-382278 E: adamwhittle17@hotmail.com

WHITTLE, Ian Christopher. b 60. Univ Coll Dur BA 81 Fitzw Coll Cam BA 88 MA 91. Ridley Hall Cam 85. **d** 88 **p** 89. C S Petherton w The Seavingtons *B & W* 88–91; Asst Chapl The Hague *Eur* 91–97; P-in-c Gayton Gp of Par *Nor* 97–99; R Gayton, Gayton Thorpe, E Walton, E Winch etc 99–10; RD Lynn 02–08; R Stiffkey and Bale from 10. *The Rectory, Langham, Holt NR25 7BX* T: (01328) 830246

WHITTLE, Canon Naomi Clare. b 54. Colchester Inst of Educn BA 75 Lon Univ PGCE 76 Middx Univ MA(Theol) 99 LGSM 77. SEITE 95. **d** 98 **p** 99. C Catford (Southend) and Downham *S'wark* 98–02; P-in-c Shooters Hill Ch Ch 02; V 02–10; Chapl Oxleas NHS Foundn Trust 06–10; V Stockwell St Andr and St Mich *S'wark* 10–16; rtd 16; PtO *S'wark* 16–17; Public Preacher from 17; Dioc Retirement Officer from 19; Hon Can S'wark Cathl from 15. *163 Abbotsbury Road, Morden SM4 5JS* T: (020) 8640 5639 E: n.whittle954@btinternet.com

WHITTLE, Robin Jeffrey. b 51. Bris Univ BA 72 Leic Univ CQSW 75. Sarum & Wells Th Coll 85. **d** 87 **p** 88. C Henbury *Bris* 87–91; V Capel *Guildf* 91–96; Chapl among Deaf People 96–09; PtO *S'wark* 97–99; *Roch* 97–99; P-in-c Walkon-the-Hill *Guildf* 99–04; V Tattenham Corner 04–09; V Findon w Clapham and Patching *Chich* 09–13; rtd 13; PtO *Chich* from 14. *3 Hillside Road, Storrington, Pulborough RH20 3LZ* T: (01903) 740542 E: bobwhittle@btinternet.com

WHITTLE, Mrs Sheila Margaret. b 36. Glouc Th Course 83 NY Th Sem MA 88 Vancouver Sch of Th. **d** 90 **p** 90. R Bulkley Valley Canada 90–93; C Dunbar St Phil 93; P-in-c Maple Ridge St Jo the Divine 93–95; Lethbridge St Mary the Virgin 95–97; NSM Portsea N End St Mark *Portsm* 97–98; P-in-c Lezant w Lawhitton and S Petherwin w Trewen *Truro* 98–02; rtd 02; PtO *Glouc* from 03. *71 Graylag Crescent, Walton Cardiff, Tewkesbury GL20 7RR* T: (01684) 299981 E: sheilawhittle5@gmail.com

WHITTLESEA, Grahame Stanley Jack Hammond. b 37. Kent Univ LLM 95. **d** 05 **p** 06. OLM Blean *Cant* 05–09; rtd 09; PtO *Cant* from 09; Retirement Officer (Cant Adnry) from 10. *4 Eastbridge Hospital, High Street, Canterbury CT1 2BD* T: (01227)   472536   M: 07866-037774 E: gandawhittlesea@tiscali.co.uk

WHITTOCK (née MARBUS), Alida Janny. b 52. RGN 78. STETS 00. **d** 03 **p** 07. NSM Weymouth H Trin *Sarum* 03–09; NSM Abbotsbury, Portesham and Langton Herring 09–14; PtO from 14. *79 Clearmount Road, Weymouth DT4 9LE* T: (01305) 788045 E: adamarbus@aol.com

WHITTOCK, Preb Michael Graham. b 47. Hull Univ BA 69 Fitzw Coll Cam BA 71 MA 76. Westcott Ho Cam 69 Union Th Sem Virginia 71. **d** 72 **p** 73. C Kirkby *Liv* 72–76; C Prescot 76–79; R Methley w Mickletown *Ripon* 79–92; RD Whitkirk 88–92; V Morley St Pet w Churwell *Wakef* 92–01; R Gt Hanwood *Heref* 01–13; R Longden and Annscroft w Pulverbatch 01–13; R Gt Hanwood and Longden and Annscroft etc 13–14; RD Pontesbury 08–13; Preb Heref Cathl 10–14; rtd 14; PtO *Heref* from 15. *The Vicarage, Church Stoke, Montgomery SY15 6AF* T: (01588) 620693 E: mgwhittock@gmail.com

WHITTON, Alysoun. b 55. St Steph Ho Ox 09. **d** 10 **p** 11. NSM Hampstead Em W End *Lon* 10–14; PtO *Cant* 15–16; NSM W Hampstead St Cuth *Lon* 16–18; PtO *Cant* from 18. *5 St Christopher's Green, Broadstairs CT10 2SS* T: (01843) 579936 M: 07985-020203 E: alysoun.whitton@gmail.com

WHITWELL, Canon John Peter. b 36. Open Univ BA 07. Qu Coll Birm 62. **d** 65 **p** 66. C Stepney St Dunstan and All SS *Lon* 65–68; C Chingford SS Pet and Paul *Chelmsf* 68–71; V Walthamstow St Sav 71–78; P-in-c Lt Ilford St Mich 78–88; R 88–98; RD Newham 91–97; Hon Can Chelmsf Cathl 96–98; rtd 98; PtO *Ox* from 99. *152 Bath Road, Banbury OX16 0TT* T: (01295) 266243 E: jandawhitwell@aol.com

WHITWORTH, Benjamin Charles Battams. b 49. CCC Ox BA 71 MA 85. Linc Th Coll 83. **d** 85 **p** 86. C Swanborough *Sarum* 85–88; C Sherborne w Castleton and Lillington 88–91; V Milborne Port w Goathill *B & W* 91–98; rtd 98; PtO *B & W* from 00. *13 The Avenue, Taunton TA1 1EA* T: (01823) 272442 E: whitworth@talktalk.net

WHITWORTH, Canon Duncan. b 47. K Coll Lon BD 69 AKC 69. St Aug Coll Cant 69. **d** 70 **p** 71. C Tonge Moor *Man* 70–73; C Upper Norwood St Jo *Cant* 73–78; Asst Chapl Madrid *Eur* 78–82; Chapl Ankara 82–83; V Douglas St Matt *S & M* 84–12; RD Douglas 91–12; Can St German's Cathl 96–12; rtd 12. *24 Ballafurt Close, Port Erin, Isle of Man IM9 6HS* T: (01624) 837350 E: duncando@manx.net

WHITWORTH, Canon Patrick John. b 51. Ch Ch Ox BA 72 MA 76 St Jo Coll Dur MA 78. **d** 76 **p** 77. C York St Mich-le-

Belfrey 76–79; C Brompton H Trin w Onslow Square St Paul *Lon* 79–84; V Gipsy Hill Ch Ch *S'wark* 84–95; R Bath Weston All SS w N Stoke and Langridge *B & W* 95–16; RD Bath 03–10; Preb Wells Cathl 12–16; rtd 16; PtO *Ox* from 17; Hon Can Bauchi from 95. *Elcot Lodge, Elcot, Newbury RG20 8NJ* E: pwhitworth@metronet.co.uk

WHITWORTH, Vincent Craig. b 80. Nottm Univ BA 01. St Jo Coll Nottm MTh 06. **d** 07 **p** 08. C Parr *Liv* 07–11; C Halliwell St Pet *Man* 11–19; AD Bolton 15–19; P-in-c Bolton St Bede from 19; TV Deane from 19; AD from 19. *St Paul's Vicarage, Vicarage Lane, Halliwell, Bolton BL1 8BP* T: (01204) 849079 M: 07759-920922

WHORTON, Mrs Ailsa Claire. b 67. All SS Cen for Miss & Min 16. **d** 18 **p** 19. C Newton *Ches* from 18. *4 Yew Tree Close, Wirral CH49 5PA* T: 0151-678 4733 M: 07971-569812 E: ailsacwhorton@gmail.com

WHYBORN, Robert. b 42. NOC 87. **d** 90 **p** 91. NSM Milnrow *Man* 90–97; NSM Greenfield 97–03; NSM Saddleworth 03–05; rtd 05; PtO *Man* from 05. *6 Burnell Court, Heywood OL10 2NW* T: (01706) 369397 E: revrob8@aol.com

WHYBROW, Paul Andrew. b 59. St Paul's Coll Chelt BEd 80 Oak Hill Th Coll BA 90. Wycliffe Hall Ox 95. **d** 97 **p** 98. C Magor *Mon* 97–00; V Poughill *Truro* 00–18; rtd 18. *12 The Old Station, Horrabridge, Yelverton PL20 7RQ* E: pa.whybrow59@icloud.com

WHYSALL, Canon Joan. b 42. Lady Mabel Coll CertEd 64 Nottm Univ MA 01. EMMTC 98. **d** 01 **p** 02. NSM Trowell, Awsworth and Cossall *S'well* 01–06; P-in-c Cinderhill 06–14; Hon Can S'well Minster 10–12; rtd 14; PtO *S'well* from 15. *55 Trowell Park Drive, Trowell, Nottingham NG9 3RA* T: 0115-939 6903 E: joan.whysall@btinternet.com

WHYTE, Henry Lewis. b 38. ALCD 70 LTh 74. **d** 70 **p** 71. C Crawley *Chich* 70–74; V Bermondsey St Jas w Ch Ch *S'wark* 74–82; V Kingston Hill St Paul 82–94; V Blackheath Park St Mich 94–02; rtd 02; PtO *S'wark* from 03. *6 Horn Park Lane, London SE12 8UU* T: (020) 8318 9837 E: henrywhyte@hotmail.com

WHYTE, Canon Robert Euan. b 44. St Pet Coll Ox BA 67. Cuddesdon Coll 67. **d** 69 **p** 70. C Blackheath Ascension *S'wark* 69–73; BCC 73–87; NSM Lewisham St Swithun *S'wark* 73–76; NSM Heston *Lon* 76–77; C Rusthall *Roch* 77–88; V 88–08; RD Tunbridge Wells 91–96; Hon Can Roch Cathl 00–08; rtd 08. *9 Thornhill Avenue, Belper DE56 1SH* T: (01773) 880531 E: whyterobert@hotmail.com

WHYTE, William Hadden. b 75. Wadh Coll Ox BA 97 MA 03 MSt 98 DPhil 02. SAOMC 03. **d** 06 **p** 07. NSM Kidlington w Hampton Poyle *Ox* 06–17; NSM Wolvercote and Wytham from 17. *St John's College, Oxford OX1 3JP* T: (01865) 277338 F: 277300 E: william.whyte@sjc.ox.ac.uk

WIBBERLEY, Anthony Norman. b 36. K Coll Lon BSc 58 AKC 58. Sarum & Wells Th Coll 76. **d** 79 **p** 80. Hon C Tavistock and Gulworthy *Ex* 79–86; R Hoby cum Rotherby w Brooksby, Ragdale & Thru'ton *Leic* 86–90; V Ingol *Blackb* 90–96; PtO *Ely* 97–05; rtd 00. *13 Missleton Court, Cherry Hinton Road, Cambridge CB1 8BL* E: anwibbs@hotmail.co.uk

WICK, Canon Patricia Anne. b 54. Lon Bible Coll BA 80 Redcliffe Coll Glouc MA 12. Oak Hill Th Coll 84. **dss** 86 **d** 87 **p** 94. Halliwell St Luke *Man* 86–87; Par Dn 87–91; Par Dn Drypool *York* 91–94; C 94–95; TV 95–97; CMS Sudan 98–14; PtO *York* 15; C Sutton St Mich from 15; Canon Maridi from 09. *14 Cherry Tree Close, Bilton, Hull HU11 4EZ* M: 07527-523098 E: patricia@rcs-communication.com

WICKENS, Andrew Peter. b 63. St Jo Coll Dur BA 85 Magd Coll Cam MEd 97 PGCE 95 ARCM 84 FRSA 14. Westcott Ho Cam 98. **d** 00 **p** 01. C Louth *Linc* 00–03; TV 03–07; Lect Boston 07–10; PV Linc Cathl 01–13; R Newton Heath *Man* from 11; P-in-c Moston St Chad and Moston St Jo 11–13; Min Can Man Cathl from 18. *All Saints' Rectory, 2 Culcheth Lane, Manchester M40 1LR* T: 0161-219 1807 E: andrew.wickens08@btinternet.com

WICKENS, Andrew St Lawrence John. b 63. Mert Coll Ox BA 85 Birm Univ MPhil 94 Dur Univ PGCE 86. Qu Coll Birm 89. **d** 92 **p** 93. C Birchfield *Birm* 92–96; PtO 96–97 and 00–01; Zambia 97–00; P-in-c St Mich Cathl Kitwe 99–00; Lect St Paul's United Th Coll Limuru Kenya 01–05; P-in-c Dudley St Jas *Worc* 05–09; TV Dudley 09–17; Educn Chapl 05–17; Hon Can Worc Cathl 15–17; TR Stoke-upon-Trent and Fenton *Lich* from 17. *172 Smithpool Road, Stoke-on-Trent ST4 4PP* T: (01782) 413915 E: astljwickens@gmail.com

WICKENS, Laurence Paul. b 52. Selw Coll Cam BA 74 MA 78 Leeds Univ PhD 90 CEng 80 MIET 80 MIMechE 81 EurIng 90. EAMTC 02. **d** 06 **p** 07. NSM Cambridge St Barn *Ely* 06–08; NSM Meole Brace *Lich* 08–17; PtO *Cov* from 13. *31 Paddocks Close, Wolston, Coventry CV8 3GW* T: (024) 7651 0305 M: 07811-551583 E: laurence.wickens@gmail.com

WICKENS, Canon Moira. b 56. S Dios Minl Tr Scheme 91. **d** 94 **p** 08. NSM Ifield *Chich* 94–96; C Saltdean 96–03; C Ovingdean and Schs Liaison Officer 03–06; C Kingston Buci 06–08; P-in-c 08–10; Dioc Voc Adv 06–10; R New Fishbourne from 10; P-in-c Appledram from 10; Can and Preb Chich Cathl from 12. *The Rectory, 31 Caspian Close, Fishbourne, Chichester PO18 8AY* T: (01273) 783364

WICKENS, Mrs Sandra Ruth. b 68. St Mellitus Coll BA 19. **d** 19. C Rotherfield w Mark Cross *Chich* from 19. *15 Court Meadow, Rotherfield, Crowborough TN6 3LQ* M: 07743-459685 E: sandiwickens@gmail.com

WICKERT, Keith Frederick. b 59. Birkbeck Coll Lon BSc 84. STETS 09. **d** 12 **p** 13. NSM Fareham H Trin *Portsm* 12–16; NSM Bishop's Waltham from 16; NSM Upham from 16. *14 Denewulf Close, Bishops Waltham, Southampton SO32 1GZ* T: (01489) 809403 M: 07717-312426 E: wickertkeith@gmail.com

WICKETT, Prof Reginald Ernest Yeatman. b 43. Toronto Univ BA 65 MEd 71 EdD 78 Em Coll Saskatoon Hon DCnL 96. Trin Coll Toronto 65. **d** 00 **p** 01. NSM Saskatoon All SS Canada 00–02; NSM St Jo Cathl from 02; PtO *Ely* 12–15. *14-102 Willow Street, Saskatoon SK S7J 0C2, Canada* M: 07984-909693 E: reg.wickett@usask.ca *or* rw461@cam.ac.uk

WICKHAM, Mrs Jennifer Ruth. b 68. Univ of W Ontario BA 91. Cranmer Hall Dur BA 98. **d** 98 **p** 99. C Ponteland *Newc* 98–00; Assoc P Ottawa St Geo Canada 01–18; V Cov St Geo from 18. *101 Moseley Avenue, Coventry CV6 1HR* E: ajwickham@yahoo.com *or* vicarstgs@gmail.com

✠**WICKHAM, The Rt Revd Robert James.** b 72. Grey Coll Dur BA 94 K Coll Lon MA 12. Ridley Hall Cam 95. **d** 98 **p** 99 **c** 15. C Willesden St Mary *Lon* 98–01; C Somers Town 01–03; TV Old St Pancras 03–07; R St John-at-Hackney 07–15; AD Hackney 14–15; Area Bp Edmonton from 15. *27 Thurlow Road, London NW3 5PP* T: (020) 3837 5250 E: bishop.edmonton@london.anglican.org

WICKHAM, Timothy James. b 86. Oak Hill Th Coll 12. **d** 15 **p** 16. C Balderstone *Man* 15–18; C Rusholme H Trin from 18. *32 Gilbrook Way, Rochdale OL16 4RT* M: 07595-919627 E: tjwickham1986@googlemail.com

WICKINGS, Luke Iden. b 59. Sheff Poly BA 81 K Coll Lon PGCE 07. Oak Hill Th Coll BA 90. **d** 90 **p** 91. C Fulham St Mary N End *Lon* 90–92; C Bletchley *Ox* 94–00; V W Norwood St Luke *S'wark* 00–07; Hon C New Malden and Coombe 13–15; C Tolworth, Hook and Surbiton 15–16; TV from 16. *The Vicarage, 278 Hook Road, Chessington KT9 1PF* M: 07983-398984 E: lukewickings@gmail.com

WICKREMASINGHE, Ms Deepthi Frances. b 62. Birkbeck Coll Lon BA 98 Lon Metrop Univ MA 05. St Aug Coll of Th 16. **d** 19. NSM Walworth St Chris *S'wark* from 19. *Basement Flat, 87 Camberwell Grove, London SE5 8JE* T: (020) 7708 1972

WICKREMASINGHE, Rosemary Ethel. b 32. Reading Univ ATD 52 K Coll Lon BD 85 AKC 85. SAOMC 93. **d** 96 **p** 97. NSM Godrevy *Truro* 96–05; rtd 05; PtO *Truro* from 05. *10 Glebe Row, Phillack, Hayle TR27 5AJ* T: (01736) 757850

WICKS, Christopher Blair. b 59. Oak Hill Th Coll BA 88. **d** 88 **p** 89. C Edmonton All SS w St Mich *Lon* 88–92; C Southborough St Pet w Ch Ch and St Matt etc *Roch* 92–96; TV 96–19; V High Brooms from 19. *72 Powder Mill Lane, Southborough, Tunbridge Wells TN4 9EJ* T: (01892) 529098 E: chris@stmattschurch.org.uk

WICKSTEAD, Canon Gavin John. b 46. St Chad's Coll Dur BA 67. Linc Th Coll 82. **d** 84 **p** 85. C Louth *Linc* 84–87; P-in-c E Markham and Askham *S'well* 87–89; P-in-c Headon w Upton 87–89; P-in-c Grove 87–89; R E Markham w Askham, Headon w Upton and Grove 90–92; P-in-c Skegness and Winthorpe *Linc* 92–97; R 97–01; V Holbeach 01–11; RD Elloe F. 05–07; Can and Preb Linc Cathl from 05; rtd 11; PtO *Ely* from 16. *1 Aspen Drive, Sleaford NG34 7GN* T: (01529) 410231 E: wickstead@btinternet.com

WIDDECOMBE, Roger James. b 70. Wycliffe Hall Ox 01. **d** 03 **p** 04. C Downend *Bris* 03–06; C Cheltenham St Mary, St Matt, St Paul and H Trin *Glouc* 06–07; TV Cheltenham H Trin and St Paul from 07. *85 Brunswick Street, Cheltenham GL50 4HA* T/F: (01242) 519520 E: roger@widde.com

WIDDESS, Jonathan Mark. b 73. Univ of Wales (Abth) BScEcon 95. Wycliffe Hall Ox 07 08. **d** 09 **p** 10. C Gabalfa *Llan* 09–13; P-in-c Bargoed and Deri w Brithdir 13–17; V Cumnor *Ox* from 17. *The Vicarage, Abingdon Road, Cumnor, Oxford OX2 9QN* T: (01865) 863702 M: 07595-996534 E: revjonathan@icloud.com *or* revjonathan@cumnor.org *or* vicar@cumnor.org

WIDDESS, Mrs Margaret Jennifer. b 48. Bedf Coll Lon BA 70 Clare Hall Cam PGCE 75 Lambeth MA 03. EAMTC 94. **d** 97 **p** 98. NSM Cambridge St Botolph *Ely* 97–16; rtd 16; PtO *Ely* from 17. *69 Gwydir Street, Cambridge CB1 2LG* T: (01223) 313908 E: mjwiddess@btinternet.com

WIDDOWS, David Charles Roland. b 52. Hertf Coll Ox BA 75 MA 79. St Jo Coll Nottm BA 77. **d** 79 **p** 80. C Blackley St Andr *Man* 79–83; P-in-c Rochdale Deeplish St Luke 83–84; V 84–92; TR Stoke Gifford *Bris* 92–06; Chapl Lee Abbey 06–10; P-in-c Wiveliscombe and the Hills *B & W* 10–11; R 11–17; rtd 17. *1 Butterleigh Drive, Tiverton EX16 4PN* M: 07890-758751

WIDDOWS, Edward John. b 45. Lon Coll of Div 66. **d** 70 **p** 71. C Formby St Pet *Liv* 70–72; C Uckfield, Isfield and Lt Horsted *Chich* 72–73; C Babbacombe *Ex* 73–76; V Sithney *Truro* 76–78; RD Kerrier 77–78; V Bude Haven 78–84; P-in-c Laneast w St Clether and Tresmere 84–85; P-in-c N Hill w Altarnon, Bolventor and Lewannick 84–85; P-in-c Boyton w N Tamerton 84–85; P-in-c N Petherwin 84–85; R Collingham w S Scarle and Besthorpe and Girton *S'well* 85–92; R Guernsey St Michel du Valle *Win* 92–99; R Compton and Otterbourne 99–02; rtd 02; PtO *Win* from 02; *Leic* 08–12. *Glebe Cottage, 4 Spring Back Way, Uppingham, Oakham LE15 9TT* T: (01572) 821980 E: ewiddows01@btinternet.com

WIDDOWS, Heather Susan. b 45. Open Univ BA 76. Moray Ord Course 91. **d** 96 **p** 97. NSM Kishorn *Mor* from 96; NSM Poolewe from 96. *2 Fasaich, Strath, Gairloch IV21 2DB* T: (01445) 712176 E: heather_widdows@yahoo.co.uk

WIDDOWSON, Robert William. b 47. Linc Th Coll 83. **d** 85 **p** 86. C Syston *Leic* 85–88; R Husbands Bosworth w Mowsley and Knaptoft etc 88–93; R Asfordby 93–98; P-in-c Ab Kettleby Gp 93–98; P-in-c Old Dalby and Nether Broughton 95–98; P-in-c Charlton Musgrove, Cucklington and Stoke Trister *B & W* 98–03; P-in-c Ashwick w Oakhill and Binegar 03–12; Adv in Rural Affairs 98–12; rtd 12; PtO *B & W* from 15. *23 The Leaze, Radstock BA3 3YH* T: (01761) 439814 E: robvalwidd@gmail.com

WIECK, Malcolm Rayment. b 44. Solicitor 70. **d** 08 **p** 09. OLM Bratton, Edington and Imber, Erlestoke etc *Sarum* 08–12; NSM 12–14; PtO from 14. *Sandy Lane Cottage, 12 Westbury Road, Edington, Westbury BA13 4QD* T: (01380) 830256 M: 07623-483986 E: malcolm.wieck@btinternet.com

WIEGMAN, Mrs Jacqueline Anne Cecilia. b 52. ERMC 10. **d** 13 **p** 14. NSM Longthorpe *Pet* 13–16; NSM Pet H Spirit Bretton 13–16; Sen Chapl HM Pris Peterborough from 13. *HM Prison Peterborough, Saville Road, Peterborough PE3 7PD* T: (01733) 217500 E: jackie.wiegman@sodexojusticeservices.com

WIFFEN, Ronald. b 38. Glos Univ BA 99. SEITE 99. **d** 01 **p** 02. NSM Canvey Is *Chelmsf* 01–04; P-in-c Bowers Gifford w N Benfleet 04–06; NSM SW Gower *S & B* 06–08; P-in-c Southport St Luke *Liv* 08–09; rtd 09; PtO *Chelmsf* 09–11; P-in-c Mundford w Lynford *Nor* 11–15; P-in-c Ickburgh w Langford 11–15; P-in-c Cranwich 11–15; P-in-c W Tofts and Buckenham Parva 11–15; PtO *Chelmsf* from 15. *Southwycke, 197 Southchurch Boulevard, Southend-on-Sea SS2 4UU* T: (01702) 585608 E: revdronaldwiffen@gmail.com

WIFFIN, Susan Elizabeth. *See* MACDONALD, Susan Elizabeth

WIGGEN, Richard Martin. b 42. Open Univ BA 78 Hull Univ MA 86. Qu Coll Birm 64. **d** 67 **p** 68. C Penistone w Midhope *Wakef* 67–70; C Leeds St Pet *Ripon* 70–73; Asst Youth Chapl *Glouc* 73–76; Youth Officer *Liv* 76–80; V Kirkstall *Ripon* 80–90; V Meanwood 90–07; rtd 07; PtO *Leeds* from 17. *19 Shadwell Lane, Leeds LS17 6DP* T: 0113-266 5241 E: wiggen@btopenworld.com

WIGGINS, Karl Patrick. b 38. MRICS 64 FRICS 87. Trin Coll Bris BD 72. **d** 72 **p** 73. C Hildenborough *Roch* 72–76; Hon C Reading St Barn *Ox* 76–78; Hon C Chieveley w Winterbourne and Oare 78–83; Hon C Earley St Nic 80–83; Hon C Reading St Jo 83–88; Hon C Beech Hill, Grazeley and Spencers Wood 88–98; rtd 98; PtO *Ox* 99; *Sarum* from 05; *B & W* 16–19. *Willow Cottage, 37 New Road, Bradford-on-Avon BA15 1AP* T: (01225) 867007 E: kk-wiggins@msn.com

WIGGINS, Robert Carl Wesley. b 51. All SS Cen for Miss & Min 12. **d** 14 **p** 15. NSM Beeston *S'well* from 14. *31 Woodbridge Avenue, Nottingham NG11 8GP* T: 0115-914 2513 M: 07906-664263 E: rob.wiggins@ntlworld.com

WIGGINS (née SQUIRE), Susan Elizabeth. b 53. St Mellitus Coll 13. **d** 14 **p** 15. OLM Holland-on-Sea *Chelmsf* from 14. *18 Southcliff Hall, 55-57 Marine Parade East, Clacton-on-Sea CO15 6AD* T: (01255) 427724 M: 07974-100069

WIGGLESWORTH, Canon Mark. b 60. Clare Coll Cam BA 82 MA 96 St Jo Coll Dur MA 14. Cranmer Hall Dur 89. **d** 92 **p** 93. C Brinsworth w Catcliffe *Sheff* 92–93; C Brinsworth w Catcliffe and Treeton 93–95; C Goole 95–96; V Askern 96–11; AD Adwick 05–11; Dir Miss and Pioneer Min 11–14; Miss Development Adv Doncaster Adnry from 14; Hon Can Sheff Cathl from 14. *177 Harlington Road, Mexborough S64 0QR* T: (01709) 322952 M: 07818-416424 E: mark.dpmm@gmail.com

WIGGS, Robert James. b 50. Pemb Coll Cam BA 72 MA CertEd. Qu Coll Birm 78. **d** 80 **p** 81. C Stratford St Jo and Ch Ch w Forest Gate St Jas *Chelmsf* 80–83; C E Ham w Upton

Park and Forest Gate 83–86; TV 86–91; TR Grays Thurrock 91–99; PtO 99–16; NSM Maldon St Mary w Mundon from 16. *113 Moulsham Street, Chelmsford CM2 0JN* T: (01245) 359138 E: robwiggs@virginmedia.com

WIGHT, The Ven Dennis Marley. b 53. Southn Univ BTh 87. Sarum & Wells Th Coll 82. **d** 85 **p** 86. C Gillingham *Sarum* 85–87; Appeals Org CECS from 87; PtO *Birm* 89–90; V Coseley Ch Ch *Lich* 90–93; V Coseley Ch Ch *Worc* 93–94; R Stoke Prior, Wychbold and Upton Warren 94–02; RD Droitwich 96–99; V Dale and St Brides w Marloes *St D* 02–10; AD Roose 05–10; Dioc Warden Ords 09–11 and 12–14 and 15; Bp's Chapl 10–14; Dir of Min 10–18; Hon Can St D Cathl 09–18; Adn St D 13–18; P-in-c Wiston w Walton E and Clarbeston 15–18; C Llawhaden w Bletherston and Uzmaston 15–18; rtd 18; PtO *St D* from 18. *6 Llys Holcwm, Ferryside SA17 5SY*

WIGHTMAN, William David. b 39. Birm Univ BA 61. Wells Th Coll 61. **d** 63 **p** 64. C Rotherham *Sheff* 63–67; C Castle Church *Lich* 67–70; V Buttershaw St Aid *Bradf* 70–76; V Cullingworth 76–83; R Peterhead *Ab* 83–91; R Strichen, Old Deer and Longside 90–91; Provost St Andr Cathl 91–02; R Aberdeen St Andr 91–02; P-in-c Aberdeen St Ninian 91–02; Hon Can Ch Ch Cathl Connecticut from 91; rtd 02; PtO *York* from 04. *6 Wold Road, Pocklington, York YO42 2QG* T: (01759) 301369 E: wightmandavid@sky.com

WIGLEY, Brian Arthur. b 31. Qu Coll Birm. **d** 82 **p** 83. C Houghton le Spring *Dur* 82–85; C Louth *Linc* 85–86; TV 86–89; Chapl City Hosp NHS Trust Birm 89–95; rtd 95; PtO *Ex* 95–09; *Leic* 13–16. *11 Stuart Court, High Street, Kibworth Beauchamp, Leicester LE8 0LR* T: 0116-279 3682 E: p-bwigley@tiscali.co.uk

WIGLEY, Canon Harry Maxwell (Max). b 38. Oak Hill Th Coll 61. **d** 64 **p** 65. C Upton (Overchurch) *Ches* 64–67; C Gateacre *Liv* 67–69; C Chadderton Ch Ch *Man* 67; V Gt Horton *Bradf* 69–88; Hon Can Bradf Cathl 85–03; V Pudsey St Lawr and St Paul 88–96; V Yeadon St Jo 96–03; rtd 03; Hon Dioc Ev *Bradf* 04–10; PtO 10–14; *Leeds* 14–18; *Ox* from 18. *1 Bluebell Close, Buckingham MK18 1FP* T: (01280) 309796 E: maxwigley@sky.com

WIGLEY, Canon Jennifer. b 53. Bris Univ BA 74 Birm Univ MA 75 Ox Univ CertEd 76. Qu Coll Birm 86. **d** 87 **p** 97. C Llangollen w Trevor and Llantysilio *St As* 87–89; C Swansea St Jas *S & B* 89–94; NSM Aberystwyth *St D* 95–98; Tutor St Mich Coll Llan 98–00; C Sketty *S & B* 98–00; Chapl Univ of Wales (Swansea) 00–02; Dep Dir S Wales Ord Course 02–18; TV Cen Cardiff *Llan* 03–06; R Radyr 06–18; AD Llan 10–15; Can Llan Cathl 11–18; rtd 18. *12 Llwyn-y-Grant Road, Penylan, Cardiff CF23 9ET* E: jennifer.wigley@btinternet.com

WIGLEY, Trudie Anne. Somerville Coll Ox BA 91 MA 12 ACIB 94. Ripon Coll Cuddesdon 09. **d** 11 **p** 12. C Swindon Ch Ch *Bris* 11–14; P-in-c Swindon Dorcan 14–19; R from 19. *11 Merlin Way, Swindon SN3 5AN* T: (01793) 326128 M: 07505-652781 E: rev.trudie@wigley.org.uk

WIGMORE, John Anthony Kingsland. b 62. Oak Hill Th Coll 05. **d** 07 **p** 08. C Braintree *Chelmsf* 07–11; R Winklebury and Worting *Win* from 11. *The Rectory, Glebe Lane, Worting, Basingstoke RG23 8QA* T: (01256) 327305 E: rector@winkleburyandworting.org.uk

WIGNALL, Daniel Robert Phillip. b 65. Ox Poly BEd 88. St Jo Coll Nottm MA 98. **d** 98 **p** 99. C Fletchamstead *Cov* 98–01; C Abingdon *Ox* 01–07; V Shottermill *Guildf* 07–18; Local Miss Adv from 18. *311 Woodland Walk, Aldershot GU12 4FY*

WIGNALL, Mrs Deborah. b 66. Ox Brookes Univ BSc 87 PGCE 04. St Mellitus Coll BA 17. **d** 17 **p** 18. C Aldershot H Trin *Guildf* from 17. *311 Woodland Walk, Aldershot GU12 4FY* M: 07906-686645

WIGNALL, Canon Paul Graham. b 49. Lanc Univ BA 72 Qu Coll Cam BA 74 MA 78. Westcott Ho Cam 72. **d** 74 **p** 75. C Chesterton Gd Shep *Ely* 74–76; Min Can Dur Cathl 76–79; Tutor Ripon Coll Cuddesdon 80–84; P-in-c Aston Rowant w Crowell *Ox* 81–83; C Shepherd's Bush St Steph w St Thos *Lon* 84–85; P-in-c St Just-in-Roseland and St Mawes *Truro* 99–01; C St Agnes and Mithian w Mount Hawke 01–06; Dir Tr and Development 01–05; Dir Min and Miss Resources 05–06; Hon Can Truro Cathl 05–06; rtd 06; IME Adv *Cov* 08–12; Hon C Aston Cantlow and Wilmcote w Billesley 08–11; Hon C Baginton w Bubbenhall and Ryton-on-Dunsmore 11–12; P-in-c Clun w Bettws-y-Crwyn and Newcastle *Heref* 12–14; P-in-c Clungunford w Clunbury and Clunton, Bedstone etc 12–14; P-in-c Hopesay 12–14; V Clun Valley 14; C Edstaston, Fauls, Prees, Tilstock and Whixall *Lich* 14–18; Chapl Málaga *Eur* 18–19; Chapl Las Palmas from 19. *Holy Trinity, Rafael Ramirez 13, 35005 Las Palmas, Spain* T: (0034) 928 267 202 E: paul@box-tree.me.uk

WIGRAM, Andrew Oswald. b 39. Lon Univ BD 64. Bps' Coll Cheshunt 61. **d** 64 **p** 65. C Marton-in-Cleveland

York 64–69; Kenya 69–82; Warden Trin Coll Nairobi 77–82; V Westcliff St Mich *Chelmsf* 82–95; RD Southend 89–94; R Cropwell Bishop w Colston Bassett, Granby etc *S'well* 95–05; rtd 05; PtO *Dur* from 05. *38 Pierremont Crescent, Darlington DL3 9PB* T: (01325) 371473 E: andrew.wigram@ntlworld.com

WIGRAM, Miss Ruth Margaret. b 41. CertEd 63. Cranmer Hall Dur 83. **dss** 84 **d** 87 **p** 94. Shipley St Paul and Frizinghall *Bradf* 84–90; Par Dn 87–90; Asst Dioc Dir of Ords 90–96; C Skipton H Trin 90–96; V Easby w Skeeby and Brompton on Swale etc *Ripon* 96–06; rtd 07; PtO *York* from 07; *Leeds* from 17. *Maythorn, 30 Ainderby Road, Northallerton DL7 8HD* T: (01609) 761852 E: ruthwigram@hotmail.co.uk

WIKELEY, Canon John Roger Ian. b 41. AKC 64. **d** 65 **p** 66. C Southport H Trin *Liv* 65–69; C Padgate 69–71; TV 71–73; R 73–74; TR 74–85; TR W Derby St Mary 85–98; V 98–06; P-in-c W Derby St Jas 04–06; AD W Derby 89–06; Hon Can Liv Cathl 94–06; rtd 06; PtO *Eur* from 07. *72 Carisbrooke Drive, Southport PR9 7JD* T: (01704) 225412 E: rogel4152@yahoo.co.uk *or* jriw4152@gmail.com

WIKNER, Richard Hugh. b 46. MSI. St Alb Minl Tr Scheme 79. **d** 94 **p** 95. NSM Lt Heath *St Alb* from 94. *Koinonia, 5 The Avenue, Potters Bar EN6 1EG* T: (01707) 650437 E: hughwikner@lineone.net

✠**WILBOURNE, The Rt Revd David Jeffrey.** b 55. Jes Coll Cam BA 78 MA 82. Westcott Ho Cam 79. **d** 81 **p** 82 **c** 09. C Stainton-in-Cleveland *York* 81–85; Chapl Asst Hemlington Hosp 81–85; R Monk Fryston and S Milford *York* 85–91; Abp's Dom Chapl 91–97; Dir of Ords 91–97; V Helmsley 97–09; P-in-c Upper Ryedale 09; Can and Preb York Minster 08–09; Asst Bp Llan 09–17; Dir of Min 10–15; Hon Asst Bp York from 17. *8 Bielby Close, Scarborough YO12 6UU* T: (01723) 362850 E: davidwilbourne1983@btinternet.com

WILBRAHAM, Canon David. b 59. Oak Hill Th Coll BA 88. **d** 88 **p** 89. C Ince Ch Ch *Liv* 88–91; Min St Helens St Helen 91–93; PtO *Guildf* 96–99; NSM Hindhead 99–00; V 00–03; V Churt and Hindhead 03–07; Chapl Thames Valley Police *Ox* 07–17; Nat Police Chapl from 18; Hon Can Ch Ch *Ox* from 11. *28 Tyndalls, Hindhead GU26 6AP* T: (01428) 609665 M: 07973-367786 E: david.wilbraham@thamesvalley.pnn.police.uk *or* davidwilbraham@lineone.net

WILBY, Canon Wendy Ann. b 49. St Hugh's Coll Ox BA 71 MA 93 Leeds Univ MA 01 ARCM 69 LRAM 72. NEOC. **d** 90 **p** 94. Par Dn Barwick in Elmet *Ripon* 90–93; C High Harrogate St Pet 93–94; P-in-c Birstwith 94–01; AD Harrogate 00–01; Chapl St Aid Sch Harrogate 94–01; V Halifax *Wakef* 01–07; RD 06–07; Can Res Bris Cathl 07–13; Dean of Women's Min 11–13; rtd 13; Hon Min Can Ripon Cathl 13; PtO *Leeds* from 14. *Skelton Windmill, Ripon Road, Boroughbridge, York YO51 9DP* M: 07720-141548 E: wilbywindmill@gmail.com

WILCOCK, Mrs Linda Jane. b 46. Nottm Univ TDip 67. **d** 09 **p** 10. OLM Melbury *Sarum* 09–12; TV from 12. *4 Beech Tree Close, Cattistock, Dorchester DT2 0JN* T: (01300) 321112 M: 07788-618412 E: linda.wilcock@virgin.net

WILCOCK, Michael Jarvis. b 32. Dur Univ BA 54. Tyndale Hall Bris 60. **d** 62 **p** 63. C Southport Ch Ch *Liv* 62–65; C St Marylebone All So w SS Pet and Jo *Lon* 65–69; V Maidstone St Faith *Cant* 69–77; Dir Past Studies Trin Coll Bris 77–82; V Dur St Nic 82–98; rtd 98; PtO *Chich* from 98. *1 Tudor Court, 51 Carlisle Road, Eastbourne BN21 4JR* T: (01323) 417170

WILCOCK, Paul Trevor. b 59. Bris Univ BA Leeds Univ MA 93 Huddersfield Univ PhD 15 FHEA 08. Trin Coll Bris 83. **d** 87 **p** 88. C Kirkheaton *Wakef* 87–90; Chapl Huddersfield Poly 90–92; Chapl Huddersfield Univ 92–93; Dir Student Services 93–16; rtd 17; Chapl W Yorkshire Police from 02; NSM Huddersfield H Trin *Wakef* 92–09; NSM Bradley 09–14; PtO *York* from 13; *Leeds* from 14. *25 Mendip Avenue, Huddersfield HD3 3QG* T: (01484) 325232 E: paulwilcock@aol.com

WILCOCK, Terence Granville. b 50. Open Univ BA 82. EAMTC 99. **d** 02 **p** 03. NSM Oundle w Ashton and Benefield w Glapthorn *Pet* 02–04; NSM Crosscrake *Carl* 04–11; P-in-c 06–11; NSM Old Hutton and New Hutton 06–09; Asst Chapl Gtr Athens *Eur* 11–14; V Patterdale *Carl* 14–18; rtd 18; PtO *Carl* from 18. *17 Graythwaite Court, Fernhill Road, Grange-over-Sands LA11 7BN* T: (015395) 34004 E: terryatash@aol.com

WILCOCKSON, Michael Leslie. b 59. Ball Coll Ox BA 81 MA 84 Pemb Coll Cam PGCE 82. **d** 18 **p** 19. NSM Eton w Eton Wick, Boveney and Dorney *Ox* 18–19; Asst Chapl Eton Coll 18–19; C Linton *Ely* from 19. *Queen's House, 16 High Street, Linton, Cambridge CB21 4HS* T: (01223) 891005 M: 07929-451302 E: m.wilcockson@hotmail.com

WILCOCKSON, The Ven Stephen Anthony. b 51. Nottm Univ BA 73 Ox Univ BA 75 MA 81. Wycliffe Hall Ox 73. **d** 76 **p** 77. C Pudsey St Lawr *Bradf* 76–78; C Wandsworth All SS *S'wark* 78–81; V Rock Ferry *Ches* 81–86; V Lache cum Saltney 86–95; V Howell Hill w Burgh Heath *Guildf*

95–09; RD Epsom 00–07; Par Development Officer *Ches* 09–12; Adn Doncaster *Sheff* from 12. *75 Orion Way, Balby, Doncaster DN4 8AE* T: (01709) 309110 M: 07799-874572 E: steve.wilcockson@sheffield.anglican.org

WILCOX, Allan Frank Carey. b 47. Birm Univ CertEd 70 BA 77 Univ of Wales (Ban) MA 09. St Padarn's Inst 16. **d** 17 **p** 18. NSM Bro Eryri *Ban* from 17. *Tyn y Ffynnon, Nant Peris, Caernarfon LL55 4UH* T: (01286) 872281 M: 07972-242118 E: afcwilcox@gmail.com

WILCOX, Anthony Gordon. b 41. ALCD 67. **d** 67 **p** 68. C Cheltenham Ch Ch *Glouc* 67–72; C Beccles St Mich *St E* 72–74; TV 74–81; V Ipswich All SS 81–06; rtd 06; PtO *St E* from 08. *58 Sproughton Court Mews, Sproughton, Ipswich IP8 3AJ* T: (01473) 461561 E: tony.wilcox@caringhandsry.rog

WILCOX, Brian Howard. b 46. Westcott Ho Cam 71. **d** 73 **p** 74. C Kettering SS Pet and Paul 73–78; V Eye 78–82; R Clipston w Naseby and Haselbech w Kelmarsh 82–90; V Hornsea w Atwick *York* 90–97; RD N Holderness 95–97; R Uckfield, Isfield and Lt Horsted *Chich* 97–11; rtd 11; PtO *Nor* from 12. *7 Bramble Way, Wymondham NR18 0UN* T: (01953) 605053 E: brian@wilcoxbh.plus.com

WILCOX, Canon Colin John. b 43. St Mich Coll Llan 84. **d** 86 **p** 87. C Newport St Andr *Mon* 86–88; C Llanmartin 88–90; TV 90–92; V Griffithstown 92–08; Hon Can St Woolos Cathl 07–08; rtd 08; PtO *Mon* from 08; *Llan* from 09. T: (029) 2025 4294 *or* (01600) 740680 E: colin.wilcox63@gmail.com

✠**WILCOX, The Rt Revd David Peter.** b 30. St Jo Coll Ox BA 52 MA 56. Linc Th Coll 52. **d** 54 **p** 55 **c** 86. C St Helier *S'wark* 54–56; C Ox St Mary V 56–59; Tutor Linc Th Coll 59–60; Chapl 60–61; Sub-Warden 61–63; India 64–70; R Gt w Lt Gransden *Ely* 70–72; Can Res Derby Cathl 72–77; Warden EMMTC 73–77; Prin Ripon Coll Cuddesdon 77–85; V Cuddesdon *Ox* 77–85; Suff Bp Dorking *Guildf* 86–95; rtd 95; Hon Asst Bp Chich from 95. *4 The Court, Hoo Gardens, Willingdon, Eastbourne BN20 9AX* T: (01323) 506108 E: davidandpam.wilcox@tiscali.co.uk

WILCOX, David Thomas Richard. b 42. Down Coll Cam BA 63 Regent's Park Coll Ox BA 66. **d** 95 **p** 96. C Bris St Mary Redcliffe w Temple etc 95–97; TV Yate New Town 97–02; Hon C 02–06; rtd 02; PtO *B & W* from 06. *26 Lethbridge Road, Wells BA5 2FN* T: (01749) 673689 E: davidtwilcox@hotmail.co.uk

WILCOX, Graham James. b 43. Qu Coll Ox BA 64 MA 75 Lon Univ BD 97 MTh 02. Ridley Hall Cam 64. **d** 66 **p** 67. C Edgbaston St Aug *Birm* 66–69; C Sheldon 69–72; Asst Chapl Wrekin Coll Telford 72–74; C Asterby w Goulceby *Linc* 74–77; R 77–81; R Benniworth w Market Stainton and Ranby 77–81; R Donington on Bain 77–81; R Stenigot 77–81; R Gayton le Wold w Biscathorpe 77–81; V Scamblesby w Cawkwell 77–81; R Asterby Gp 81–88; V Sutton le Marsh 88–90; R Sutton, Huttoft and Anderby 90–98; R Fyfield, Moreton w Bobbingworth etc *Chelmsf* 98–07; rtd 07; PtO *Cov* from 07. *7 Swallow Close, Stratford-upon-Avon CV37 6TT* T: (01789) 551759 E: g.wilcox4@ntlworld.com

WILCOX, Haydon Howard. b 56. Sarum & Wells Th Coll. **d** 82 **p** 83. C Fishponds St Jo *Bris* 82–85; TV Hucknall Torkard *S'well* 85–91; R Bilsthorpe 91–99; R Eakring 91–99; P-in-c Maplebeck 91–99; P-in-c Winkburn 91–99; P-in-c Aldershot St Mich *Guildf* 99–03; V 03; PtO 03–09; Chapl CSP from 07. *46 Barn Meadow Close, Church Crookham, Aldershot GU52 0YB* T/F: (01252) 621639 E: haydonwilcox@mac.com

WILCOX, Heather Yvonne. b 72. ERMC 05. **d** 08 **p** 09. C Pakefield *Nor* 08–11; R Stratton St Mary w Stratton St Michael etc 11–16; P-in-c Bunwell, Carleton Rode, Tibenham, Gt Moulton etc 14–16; TR Long Stratton and Pilgrim TM from 16; RD Depwade from 16. *The Rectory, 8 Flowerpot Lane, Long Stratton, Norwich NR15 2TS* M: 07932-416233 E: rev.heather@btconnect.com

✠**WILCOX, The Rt Revd Peter Jonathan.** b 61. St Jo Coll Dur BA 84 MA 91 St Jo Coll Ox DPhil 93. Ridley Hall Cam 86. **d** 87 **p** 88 **c** 17. C Preston on Tees *Dur* 87–90; NSM Ox St Giles and SS Phil and Jas w St Marg 90–93; TV Gateshead *Dur* 93–98; Dir Urban Miss Cen Cranmer Hall 93–98; P-in-c Walsall St Paul *Lich* 98–06; Hon C Walsall and Walsall Pleck and Bescot 05–06; Can Res Lich Cathl 06–12; Dean Liv 12–17; Bp Sheff from 17. *Bishopscroft, Snaithing Lane, Sheffield S10 3LG* T: 0114-230 2170 E: bishop@sheffield.anglican.org

WILCOX, Stephen Charles Frederick. b 75. Qu Coll Ox BA 97 ACA 00. Oak Hill Th Coll 04. **d** 07 **p** 08. C Kirk Ella and Willerby *York* 07–11; V Anlaby St Pet from 11; V Anlaby Common St Mark from 11. *The Vicarage, Church Street, Anlaby, Hull HU10 7DG* T: (01482) 653024 E: scfwilcoxw@yahoo.co.uk

WILD, Canon Alan James. b 46. **d** 97 **p** 98. OLM Walworth St Pet *S'wark* 97–07; NSM 07–16; PtO from 16; Hon Can S'wark Cathl from 15. *67 Liverpool Grove, London

SE17 2HP T: (020) 7708 1216 M: 07903-371769 E: therevajwild@googlemail.com

WILD, Hilda Jean. b 48. Linc Th Coll 95. **d** 95 **p** 96. C Newark *S'well* 95–99; V Earlsdon *Cov* 99–13; rtd 13; PtO *Man* from 13. *8 Littondale Close, Royton, Oldham OL2 6PN* T: 0161-652 3790 M: 07580-837760 E: hilda@hwild.plus.com *or* hildajw@virginmedia.com

WILD, Laura Ruth. b 78. St Hild Coll 17. **d** 19. C Nunthorpe *York* from 19. *15 Ripon Road, Nunthorpe, Middlesbrough TS7 0HX* E: lauraruth.wild@gmail.com

WILD, Roger Bedingham Barratt. b 40. Hull Univ MA 93. ALCD 64. **d** 65 **p** 65. C Shipley St Pet *Bradf* 65–68; C Pudsey St Lawr 68–71; P-in-c Rawthorpe *Wakef* 71–73; V 73–78; V Ripon H Trin 78–93; RD Ripon 86–93; OCM 80–91; R Barwick in Elmet *Ripon* 93–01; Asst Chapl Trin Th Coll Singapore 02–05; rtd 05; PtO *York* from 06. *Saddlers Cottage, 15 Chapel Street, Thirsk YO7 1LU* T: (01845) 524985 E: rbbwild@hotmail.com

WILDING, Canon Anita Pamela. b 38. Blackpool and Fylde Coll of Further Tech TCert 61. CMS Tr Coll Chislehurst 65. **dss** 89 **d** 92 **p** 93. Chapl Kabare Girls' High Sch Kenya 92–04; Chapl St Andr Primary Boarding Sch Kabare 92–04; rtd 04; PtO *Blackb* from 04. *5 The Fairways, 35 The Esplanade, Knott End-on-Sea, Poulton-le-Fylde FY6 0AD* T: (01253) 810642 E: pamwilding@gofast.co.uk *or* pamwilding@btinternet.com

WILDING, David. b 43. K Coll Lon BD 67 AKC 67. **d** 68 **p** 69. C Thornhill *Wakef* 68–70; C Halifax St Jo Bapt 70–72; V Scholes 72–79; V Lightcliffe 79–97; rtd 97; PtO *Wakef* 97–14; *Leeds* from 14. *10 Stratton Park, Rastrick, Brighouse HD6 3SN* T: (01484) 387651 E: revd.d.wilding@blueyonder.co.uk

WILDING, Michael Paul. b 57. Chich Th Coll 82. **d** 85 **p** 86. C Treboeth *S & B* 85–87; C Llangiwg 87–88; V Defynnog w Rhydybriw and Llandeilo'r-fan 88–00; V Blaenwysg from 00; AD Brecon 14–15. *Brynorsaf, Sennybridge, Brecon LD3 8RR* T: (01874) 638927 E: frpwilding@btinternet.com

WILDING, Pamela. *See* WILDING, Anita Pamela

WILDS, Canon Anthony Ronald. b 43. Hatf Coll Dur BA 64. Bps' Coll Cheshunt 64. **d** 66 **p** 67. C Newport Pagnell *Ox* 66–72; P-in-c Chipili Zambia 72–75; V Chandler's Ford Win 75–85; V Andover w Foxcott 85–97; RD Andover 89–94; Hon Can Win Cathl 91–97; TR Solihull *Birm* 97–01; Hon Can Birm Cathl 00–01; Adn Plymouth *Ex* 01–10; rtd 10; Hon C Marnhull *Sarum* from 15; PtO *B & W* from 19. *The Rectory, New Street, Marnhull, Sturminster Newton DT10 1PY* T: (01258) 268971 E: tonywilds@gmail.com

WILES, Roger Kenneth. b 58. Witwatersrand Univ BA 80. St Paul's Coll Grahamstown 81. **d** 83 **p** 84. C Johannesburg St Gabr S Africa 83–84; C Belgravia St Jo 84–85; Chapl Jeppe Boys' High Sch 85–86; Chapl Witwatersrand Univ 86–93; R Edenvale Em 94–99; P-in-c Edin Clermiston Em 99–05; V Poulton Lancelyn H Trin *Ches* from 05. *6 Chorley Way, Wirral CH63 9LS* T: 0151-334 6780 *or* 334 9815

WILFORD (*formerly* GIBSON), Laura Mary. b 50. NOC 85. **d** 88 **p** 94. Par Dn Foley Park *Worc* 88–90; Par Dn Kidderminster St Jo and H Innocents 90–94; TV 94–96; P-in-c Mamble w Bayton, Rock w Heightington etc 96–99; TV Cartmel Peninsula *Carl* 99–01; Jt Dir of Ords 00–01; P-in-c Worminghall w Ickford, Oakley and Shabbington *Ox* 01–06; rtd 06; PtO *Leeds* from 17. *5 Cookson Way, Brough with St Giles, Catterick Garrison DL9 4XG* T: (01748) 830017 E: laura.wilford@gmail.com

WILKES, Elizabeth Ann. *See* FRANKLIN, Elizabeth Ann

WILKES, Jonathan Peter. b 66. Leic Poly BA 88 K Coll Lon MA 00. Ripon Coll Cuddesdon BTh 96. **d** 96 **p** 97. C Hackney *Lon* 96–00; P-in-c Paddington St Pet 00–06; P-in-c Paddington St Mary Magd 04–06; P-in-c Kingston All SS w St Jo *S'wark* 06–07; TR 07–12; TR Kingston from 12. *All Saints' Vicarage, 15 Woodbines Avenue, Kingston upon Thames KT1 2AZ* T: (020) 3132 8717 *or* 8546 5964

WILKES, Robert Anthony. b 48. Trin Coll Ox BA 70 MA 73. Wycliffe Hall Ox 71. **d** 74 **p** 75. C Netherton *Liv* 74–77; V 77–81; Bp's Dom Chapl 81–85; CMS 85–98; Pakistan 85–86; Regional Sec Middle E and Pakistan 87–90; PtO *S'wark* 87–90; *Ox* 90–98; P-in-c Mossley Hill St Matt and St Jas *Liv* 98–05; TR Mossley Hill 05–06; Hon Can Liv Cathl 03–06; Dean Birm 06–09; P-in-c Ox St Mich w St Martin and All SS 09–13; V 13–17; rtd 17; PtO *Ox* from 17. *4 Dashwood Mews, Kirtlington, Oxford OX5 3JX* E: revwilkes@btinternet.com

WILKIE, Mrs Donna Louise. b 81. Plymouth Univ BA 02 Leeds Univ MSc 04. Trin Coll Bris 12. **d** 15 **p** 16. C Clevedon St Andr and Ch Ch *B & W* 15–18; C Clevedon Ch 18; C Bris St Matt and St Nath from 18. *Address temp unknown* M: 07789-771110 E: donnawilkie81@gmail.com

WILKIE, Mrs Erica Anne. Open Univ BSc 02. Ripon Coll Cuddesdon 16. **d** 19. NSM Alverstoke *Portsm* from

19. *Address withheld by request* T: (023) 9258 0939
E: reveriwilkie@hotmail.com

WILKIN, Paul John. b 56. Linc Th Coll 88. **d** 90 **p** 91. C Leavesden *St Alb* 90–93; C Jersey St Brelade *Win* 93–97; V Squirrels Heath *Chelmsf* 97–07; R Stansted Mountfitchet w Birchanger and Farnham from 07. *The Rectory, 5 St John's Road, Stansted CM24 8JP* T: (01279) 812203
E: paulwilkin@iname.com

WILKIN, Rose Josephine. *See* HUDSON-WILKIN, Rose Josephine

WILKINS, Mrs Anne Louise. b 65. St Jo Coll Nottm BTh 90. Wycliffe Hall Ox 94. **d** 95 **p** 96. C Wembley St Jo *Lon* 95–98; NSM S Gillingham *Roch* 98–07; Jt P-in-c Locking *B & W* 07–09; Jt P-in-c Hutton and Locking 09–13; P-in-c from 15. *The Vicarage, The Green, Locking, Weston-super-Mare BS24 8DA* T: (01934) 823556 E: revdannelee@yahoo.co.uk

WILKINS, Graham Paul. b 82. York Univ MChem 05 Cam Univ BTh 12. Ridley Hall Cam 09. **d** 12 **p** 13. C N w S Wootton *Nor* 12–16; R Cringleford and Colney from 16. *The Vicarage, 7A Newmarket Road, Cringleford, Norwich NR4 6UE* E: revd.wilkins@gmail.com

WILKINS, Mrs Julia. Brighton Univ BA 96 UWE PGCE 04. St Hild Coll 16. **d** 19. C Leeds St Geo from 19. *Kirkstall Vicarage, Vicarage View, Leeds LS5 3HF* E: julia.wilkins@leeds.anglican.org

WILKINS, Michael Richard. b 71. W Sussex Inst of HE BA 92. Trin Coll Bris 07. **d** 09 **p** 10. C Bath Walcot *B & W* 09–13; V Huddersfield H Trin *Wakef* 13–14; *Leeds* from 14. *2 Norfolk Close, Huddersfield HD1 5NJ* T: (01484) 513213 E: mike@ladytrinityhuddersfield.com

WILKINS, Ralph Herbert. b 29. Lon Univ BD 61. St Aug Coll Cant 72. **d** 73 **p** 74. C Epsom Common Ch Ch *Guildf* 73–76; C Haslemere 77–79; P-in-c Market Lavington and Easterton *Sarum* 79–82; V 82–90; P-in-c Puddletown and Tolpuddle 90–94; P-in-c Milborne St Andrew w Dewlish 92–94; P-in-c Piddletrenthide w Plush, Alton Pancras etc 92–94; rtd 94; PtO *Ab* 94–01; *Heref* 02–15. *The Mill, Marton, Welshpool SY21 8JY* T: (01938) 580566 E: rhwilkins@hotmail.co.uk

WILKINS, Miss Susan Stafford. b 47. Dur Univ BA. Sarum Th Coll. **dss** 82 **d** 87 **p** 94. Redlynch and Morgan's Vale *Sarum* 82–88; Hon Par Dn 87–88; Hon Par Dn Bemerton 88–90; Par Dn Hilperton w Whaddon and Staverton etc 90–94; TV Worle *B & W* 94–99; P-in-c Hallwood *Ches* 99–04; V Hallwood Ecum Par 04–11; RD Frodsham 06–11; rtd 11; PtO *Ches* from 11. *84 Wallerscote Road, Weaverham, Northwich CW8 3LY* T: (01606) 246039 E: suewilkins1@sky.com

WILKINS, The Ven Adrian Mark. b 68. TCD BA 90 MA 94 BTh 94 NUI MA 00 HDipEd 91. CITC 91. **d** 94 **p** 95. C Douglas Union w Frankfield *C, C & R* 94–97; I Dunboyne Union *M & K* 97–02; Chapl NUI 97–02; Min Can St Patr Cathl Dublin 97–02; I Rathmolyon w Castlerickard, Rathcore and Agher *M & K* 01–02; I Douglas Union w Frankfield *C, C & R* from 02; Adn Cork, Cloyne and Ross from 14. *The Rectory, Carrigaline Road, Douglas, Cork, Republic of Ireland* T: (00353) (21) 489 1539 *or* (21) 436 9578 M: 86-166 4805 E: archdeacon@cork.anglican.org

WILKINSON, Canon Alan Bassindale. b 31. St Cath Coll Cam BA 54 MA 58 PhD 59 DD 97. Coll of Resurr Mirfield 57. **d** 59 **p** 60. C Kilburn St Aug *Lon* 59–61; Chapl St Cath Coll Cam 61–67; V Barrow Gurney *B & W* 67–70; Asst Chapl and Lect St Matthias's Coll Bris 67–70; Prin Chich Th Coll 70–74; Can and Preb Chich Cathl 70–74; Warden Verulam Ho 74–75; Dir of Aux Min Tr *St Alb* 74–75; Sen Lect Crewe and Alsager Coll of HE 75–78; Hon C Alsager St Mary *Ches* 76–78; Dioc Dir of Tr *Ripon* 78–84; P-in-c Thornthwaite w Thruscross and Darley 84–88; Hon Can Ripon Cathl 84–88; Tutor Open Univ 88–96; PtO *Portsm* from 88; Hon P Portsm Cathl 88–14; Hon Dioc Th 93–01; Hon Chapl Portsm Cathl 94–01; rtd 96; Visiting Lect Portsm Univ 98–05; Fell Geo Bell Inst Chich Univ from 96. *8 Byron Court, Stockbridge Road, Chichester PO19 8ES* T: (01243) 839578

WILKINSON (née PHILPOTT), Canon Barbara May. b 48. Leeds Univ BA 69 CertEd 70 MA 90. NOC 90. **d** 93 **p** 94. NSM Carleton and Lotherdale *Bradf* 93–96; C Steeton 96–00; Asst Chapl Airedale NHS Trust 96–01; Hd Chapl Services 01–07; Hon Can Bradf Cathl 04–13; RD S Craven 04–07; rtd 13; PtO *York* 13–18. *Carlton House, Market Place, Easingwold, York YO61 3AN* T: (01347) 823620 E: bnkwilkinson@gmail.com

WILKINSON, Benjamin Michael. b 84. Warwick Univ BSc 05. Wycliffe Hall Ox BA 17. **d** 18 **p** 19. C Deane *Man* from 18; C Lostock St Thos and St Jo from 18. *9 Lowside Avenue, Bolton BL1 5XQ* M: 07737-240729 E: bmwpost@gmail.com

WILKINSON, Carol Ann. b 54. Lon Univ BD 88 Man Univ PhD 95. CBDTI 04. **d** 06 **p** 07. NSM Poulton Carleton and Singleton *Blackb* 06–09; LtO from 09. *52 Lowick Drive, Poulton-le-Fylde FY6 8HB* T: (01253) 350700 M: 07894-830305

WILKINSON, Mrs Christine Margaret. b 52. Man Univ BA 74 Neville's Cross Coll of Educn Dur PGCE 75 Birm Univ MEd 78. **d** 04 **p** 05. OLM Eythorne and Elvington w Waldershare etc *Cant* 04–11; C Littlebourne and Ickham w Wickhambreaux etc 11–16; rtd 16. *36 Coach Road, Acrise, Folkestone CT18 8LT*

WILKINSON, Dagmar Ludmila Veronica. b 80. Ostrava Univ MA 06 MA 09. Ripon Coll Cuddesdon 15. **d** 17 **p** 18. C Aston cum Aughton w Swallownest and Ulley *Sheff* 17–19; C Gleadless from 19; C Hackenthorpe from 19; C Woodhouse St Jas from 19; Asst Chapl Sheff Univ from 19. *27 Skipton Road, Swallownest, Sheffield S26 4NQ* T: 0114-327 5697 M: 07745-306954 E: dagmarv@yahoo.com

WILKINSON, Edward. b 55. Cranmer Hall Dur 86. **d** 88 **p** 89. C Bishopwearmouth St Nic *Dur* 88–92; P-in-c Newbottle 92–96; V from 96; AD Houghton 08–14. *The Vicarage, Front Street, Newbottle, Houghton le Spring DH4 4EP* T: 0191-584 3244 E: wilkinson.edward.rev@gmail.com

WILKINSON, Canon Elizabeth Mary. b 65. St Edm Hall Ox MA 91. NEOC 02. **d** 05 **p** 06. C Harlow Green and Lamesley *Dur* 05–09; P-in-c Burnmoor 09–16; AD Houghton 14–16; V Bishopwearmouth St Gabr from 16; Hon Can Dur Cathl from 19. *St Gabriel's Vicarage, 1 St Gabriel's Avenue, Sunderland SR4 7TF* T: 0191-477 3990

WILKINSON, Miss Gemma Louise. b 88. Lanc Univ BA 06. Ripon Coll Cuddesdon 88. **d** 18 **p** 19. C Finchampstead and California *Ox* from 18. *43 McCarthy Way, Finchampstead, Wokingham RG40 4UA* M: 07809-376352 E: reverendgemmaw@outlook.com

WILKINSON, Geoffrey. *See* WILKINSON, Roy Geoffrey

WILKINSON, Canon Guy Alexander. b 48. Magd Coll Cam BA 69. Ripon Coll Cuddesdon 85. **d** 87 **p** 88. C Coventry Caludon *Cov* 87–90; P-in-c Ockham w Hatchford *Guildf* 90–91; R 91–94; Bp's Dom Chapl 90–94; V Small Heath *Birm* 94–99; Adn Bradf 99–04; Abp's Sec for Inter Faith Relns 05–11; Nat Adv for Inter Faith Relns 05–11; V Fulham St Andr *Lon* 12–15; AD Hammersmith and Fulham 12–15; rtd 15; PtO *Sarum* from 16; *Heref* 16–19; NSM Eardisley w Bollingham, Willersley, Brilley etc from 19. *Church House, Almeley, Hereford HR3 6LD* T: (01722) 680057 M: 07515-327757 E: guy@gwilkinson.org.uk

WILKINSON, Miss Helen Mary. b 53. Homerton Coll Cam BEd 76. Trin Coll Bris 02. **d** 04 **p** 05. C Newbury *Ox* 04–08; C Northwood Em *Lon* 08–19; rtd 19. *22 Ullswater Drive, Tilehurst, Reading RG31 6RS* M: 07790-262631

WILKINSON, James Daniel. b 73. Westmr Coll Ox BTh 95 Reading Univ MA 07 MBACP 04. St Steph Ho Ox 97. **d** 99 **p** 00. C Wantage *Ox* 99–02; P-in-c S Hinksey 02–13; V 13–18; Sec to Bp Ebbsfleet *Cant* 02–04; Chapl to Bp Fulham *Lon* from 18; C St Dunstan in the West from 18. *184A Fleet Street, London EC4A 2HD* E: frjwilkinson@gmail.com

WILKINSON, John Andrew. b 59. Pemb Coll Ox BA 83 MA 87 St Jo Coll Dur BA 86. Cranmer Hall Dur 84. **d** 87 **p** 88. C Broadheath *Ches* 87–91; TV Worthing Ch the King *Chich* 91–97; Chapl Chantilly *Eur* 97–06; Asst Chapl Fontainebleau 06–11; Chapl 11–15; Assoc Chapl Brussels Cathl from 15; Can Malta Cathl from 10. *Pro-Cathedral of the Holy Trinity, 29 rue Capitaine Crespel, 1050 Brussels, Belgium* T: (0032) (2) 289 0928 *or* 511 7183 E: john.wilkinson@holytrinity.be

WILKINSON, John Lawrence. b 43. Ch Coll Cam BA 65 MA 69 Birm Univ MLitt 91. Qu Coll Birm 67 Gen Th Sem (NY) STB 69. **d** 69 **p** 70. C Braunstone *Leic* 69–71; C Hodge Hill *Birm* 71–74; P-in-c Aston St Jas 75–84; Tutor Qu Coll Birm 85–95; Hon C Birm St Geo 86–95; V Kings Heath 95–08; Hon Can Birm Cathl 99–08; rtd 09; PtO *Birm* from 09; *Lich* from 15. *203 Barclay Road, Smethwick B67 5LA* T: 0121-434 3526 E: jrwilkinson@dsl.pipex.com

WILKINSON, Jonathan Charles. b 61. Leeds Univ BA 83. Wycliffe Hall Ox 85. **d** 87 **p** 88. C Plymouth St Andr w St Paul and St Geo *Ex* 87–90; C Oulton Broad *Nor* 90–93; V Hallwood *Ches* 93–99; TR Gateshead *Dur* 99–17; C Chester le Street from 17. *St Gabriel's Vicarage, 1 St Gabriel's Avenue, Sunderland SR4 7TF* T: 0191-477 3990 E: jonwilko@virginmedia.com

WILKINSON, Mrs Joyce Aileen. b 29. BSc(Econ) MA. **d** 99 **p** 00. NSM Bredon w Bredon's Norton *Worc* 99–04; rtd 04; PtO *Worc* 04–14. *Foxgloves, Back Lane, Bredon, Tewkesbury GL20 7LH* T: (01684) 773389

WILKINSON, Mrs Judith Felicity. b 64. St Mellitus Coll 16. **d** 19. NSM Southend St Sav Westcliff *Chelmsf* from 19. *188 Westcliff Park Drive, Westcliff-on-Sea SS0 9LR* T: (01702) 343528 E: judith.wilkinson@rocketmail.com

WILKINSON, Canon Keith Howard. b 48. Hull Univ BA 70 FRSA 94 MCT 99. Westcott Ho Cam 74. **d** 76 **p** 77. C Pet St Jude 76–79; Chapl Eton Coll 79–84; PtO *Pet* 82–94; Chapl Malvern Coll 84–89; Hd Master Berkhamsted Sch Herts 89–96; LtO *St Alb* 89–96; Hd Master K Sch Cant 96–07; Hon

Can Cant Cathl 96–07; Sen Chapl Eton Coll 08–18; rtd 18. *Trinity Cottage, 24 Link Terrace, Malvern WR14 2JE*

WILKINSON, Margaret Anne. b 46. Lon Univ MB, BS 70 MSc 74 MRCPsych 77. SAOMC 95. **d** 98 **p** 99. NSM Heston *Lon* 98–06; Chapl HM YOI Feltham 01–06; NSM Penge Lane H Trin *Roch* from 07. *27 River Grove Park, Beckenham BR3 1HX* T: (020) 8650 2312

WILKINSON, Marlene Sandra. *See* TURNBULL, Marlene Sandra

WILKINSON, Matthew John George. b 81. St Cuth Soc Dur BSc 02. St Mich Coll Llan BA 06. **d** 06 **p** 07. C Wrexham *St As* 06–11; PtO 11–12; C Minera w Coedpoeth and Bwlchgwyn 12–14; V Chirk 14–16; TV Offa Miss Area from 17. *The Vicarage, Trevor Road, Chirk, Wrexham LL14 5HD* T: (01691) 778519 E: vicarofchirk@hotmail.com

WILKINSON, Paul. b 51. Sarum & Wells Th Coll 75. **d** 78 **p** 79. C Allerton *Bradf* 78–80; C Baildon 80–83; V Hengoed w Gobowen *Lich* 83–90; V Potterne w Worton and Marston *Sarum* 90–03; Chapl Roundway Hosp Devizes 92–03; P-in-c Leckhampton St Pet *Glouc* 03–09; P-in-c Cheltenham Em w St Steph 08–09; TR S Cheltenham 10–15; rtd 15; PtO *Glouc* from 16. *41 Wheatway, Abbeydale, Gloucester GL4 5ET*

WILKINSON, Paul. b 69. **d** 11 **p** 12. OLM Fountain of Life *Nor* 11–19; Sen Min from 19. *10 Church Street, Ashill, Thetford IP25 7AW* T: (01760) 441443 E: paulwilkinson500@gmail.com

WILKINSON, Paul Martin. b 56. Brunel Univ BSc. Wycliffe Hall Ox 83. **d** 86 **p** 87. C Hinckley H Trin *Leic* 86–90; V Newbold on Avon *Cov* from 90. *The Vicarage, Main Street, Newbold, Rugby CV21 1HH* T: (01788) 543055 F: 542458 E: paulwilkinson54@btinternet.com

WILKINSON, Peter David Lloyd. b 67. Trin Coll Ox BA 89 MA 93. Ridley Hall Cam BA 94. **d** 95 **p** 96. C Brampton St Thos *Derby* 95–98; C Tunbridge Wells St Jo *Roch* 98–02; C Ox St Ebbe w H Trin and St Pet from 02. *10 Lincoln Road, Oxford OX1 4TB* T: (01865) 728885 E: peter.wilkinson@stebbes.org

WILKINSON, Robert. *See* WILKINSON, Walter Edward Robert

WILKINSON, Robert Ian. b 43. MIMunE 73 MICE 84 CEng 73. Oak Hill NSM Course. **d** 88 **p** 89. NSM Hawkwell *Chelmsf* 88–89; NSM Thundersley 89–91; C New Thundersley 91–94; V Berechurch St Marg w St Mich 94–06; rtd 06; PtO *Bradf* 07–14; *Leeds* from 14. *140 Keighley Road, Skipton BD23 2QT* T: (01756) 799748

WILKINSON, Robert John. b 66. Birkbeck Coll Lon BA 98 Fitzw Coll Cam BA 00 ACIB 90. Westcott Ho Cam 98. **d** 01 **p** 02. C Southgate Ch Ch *Lon* 01–04; TV Wood Green St Mich w Bounds Green St Gabr etc 04–11; V Tottenham St Paul 11–18; C Friern Barnet All SS from 18. *4 Highlands, Oakleigh Road North, London N20 9HA* E: robert.wilkinson@london.anglican.org

WILKINSON, Robert Matthew. b 21. TCD BA 46. TCD Div Sch 47. **d** 47 **p** 48. C Limerick St Lawr w H Trin and St Jo *L & K* 47–49; C Arm St Mark 49–51; I Mullavilly 51–55; I Derryloran 55–73; Can Arm Cathl 67–73; I Ballymore 73–87; Treas Arm Cathl 73–75; Chan Arm Cathl 75–83; Prec Arm Cathl 83–87; rtd 87. *60 Coleraine Road, Portrush BT56 8HN* T: (028) 7082 2758

WILKINSON, Robert Samuel. b 52. Wycliffe Hall Ox 92. **d** 94 **p** 95. C Boughton Monchelsea *Cant* 94–96; C Parkwood CD 95–96; C Plymouth St Andr and Stonehouse *Ex* 96–01; P-in-c Whimple, Talaton and Clyst St Lawr 01–11; TV Cullompton, Willand, Uffculme, Kentisbeare etc 11–14; rtd 14. *60 Heavitree Road, Exeter EX1 2LQ*

WILKINSON, Roy Geoffrey. b 42. Open Univ BSc 93 Linc Univ MSc 99. Sarum Th Coll 67. **d** 70 **p** 71. C Belsize Park *Lon* 70–73; C Heston 73–75; C Hythe *Cant* 75–79; V Croydon Woodside *S'wark* 79–86; Asst Mental Health Chapl Skegness and Winthorpe *Linc* 96–97; Asst Chapl Linc Distr Healthcare NHS Trust 96–97; Chapl Lincs Partnership NHS Trust 97–05; rtd 05. *287 Monks Road, Lincoln LN2 5JZ* T: (01522) 522671 M: 07745-755614 E: geoffreyandsarah@ntlworld.com

WILKINSON, Sharon Theresa. b 58. **d** 12 **p** 13. C Scotforth *Blackb* 12–16; V W Ardsley *Leeds* from 16. *The Vicarage, 1168 Dewsbury Road, Dewsbury WF12 7JL* E: fantine2001@aol.com

WILKINSON, Canon Simon Evelyn. b 49. Nottm Univ BA 74. Cuddesdon Coll 74. **d** 76 **p** 77. C Cheam *S'wark* 76–78; P-in-c Warlingham w Chelsham and Farleigh 78–83; Hd RS Radley Coll 83–89; R Bishop's Waltham and Upham *Portsm* 89–97; TR Shaston *Sarum* 97–03; P-in-c Amesbury 03–12; V 12–14; RD Stonehenge 03–10; Can and Preb Sarum Cathl 05–14; rtd 14; PtO *Sarum* from 16. *5 Berkshire Road, Salisbury SP2 8NY*

WILKINSON, Stephen. b 69. Brighton Poly BEng 91. Ridley Hall Cam 08. **d** 10 **p** 11. C Gtr Corsham and Lacock *Bris* 10–14; P-in-c Brinkworth w Dauntsey 14–16; P-in-c Gt

Somerford, Lt Somerford, Seagry, Corston etc 14–16; P-in-c Garsdon, Lea and Cleverton and Charlton 14–16; R Woodbridge from 16. *The Rectory, Frog Lane, Great Somerford, Chippenham SN15 5JA* T: (01249) 723733 E: rector@woodbridgegroup.co.uk

WILKINSON, Stephen Graham. b 64. Leeds Univ BA 08. NOC 05. **d** 08 **p** 09. Chapl to Police and NSM Pennington *Man* 08–11; TV Cramlington *Newc* 11–16; P-in-c Humshaugh w Simonburn and Wark from 16; AD Bellingham from 16. *The Vicarage, Humshaugh, Hexham NE46 4AA* T: (01434) 681304 E: revd.steve.wilkinson@googlemail.com

WILKINSON, Mrs Susan Ann. b 62. SEITE 10. **d** 14. NSM Lewes St Anne and St Mich and St Thos etc *Chich* 14–17; NSM Willingdon from 17. *150 Macquarie Quay, Eastbourne BN23 5AW* T: (01323) 318510 M: 07713-097661 E: sueann_27@hotmail.com

WILKINSON, Walter Edward Robert. b 38. St Andr Univ MA 60. Lon Coll of Div BD 63 ALCD 63. **d** 63 **p** 64. C High Wycombe *Ox* 63–70; PV, Succ and Sacr Roch Cathl 70–73; P-in-c Asby w Ormside *Carl* 73–80; R Cherry Burton *York* 80–95; RD Beverley 88–94; P-in-c Grasmere *Carl* 95–03; rtd 03; PtO *Carl* from 03. *4 Heversham Gardens, Heversham, Milnthorpe LA7 7RA* T: (015395) 64044 E: bob@carliol.clara.co.uk

WILKS, Eric Percival. b 32. Wells Th Coll 67. **d** 68 **p** 69. C Fladbury w Throckmorton, Wyre Piddle and Moor *Worc* 68–70; PtO from 70. *4 Catherine Cottages, Droitwich Road, Hartlebury, Kidderminster DY10 4EL* T: (01299) 251580

WILL, Nicholas James. b 53. Birm Univ LLB 75. Qu Coll Birm 93. **d** 95 **p** 96. C Bridgnorth, Tasley, Astley Abbotts, etc *Heref* 95–00; R Raveningham Gp *Nor* 00–18; rtd 18. *59 Tonning Street, Lowestoft NR32 2AN*

WILLANS, Jonathan Michael Arthur. b 60. QUB BD. CITC 83. **d** 85 **p** 86. C Larne and Inver *Conn* 85–88; R Hawick *Edin* 88–91; P-in-c Brockham Green *S'wark* 91–16; P-in-c Leigh 91–16; V Brockham Green and Leigh from 17. *The Vicarage, Clayhill Road, Leigh, Reigate RH2 8PD* T/F: (01306) 611224 E: jmawilliams@gmail.com

WILLANS, William Richard Gore. b 48. Qu Coll Ox BA 70 MA 74 Ox Univ PGCE 71. CITC 77. **d** 79 **p** 80. C Bonne Bay Canada 79–80; P-in-c Bonne Bay N 80–82; R 82–87; R Thunder Bay St Thos 87–98; I Craigs w Dunaghy and Killagan *Conn* 98–18; rtd 18. *97 Hillmount Road, Cullybackey, Ballymena BT42 1NZ* T: (028) 2588 0428 M: 07880-992425 E: willans@btinternet.com

WILLARD, John Fordham. b 38. K Coll Lon BD 62 AKC 62. **d** 63 **p** 64. C Balham Hill Ascension *S'wark* 63–67; C Leigh Park *Portsm* 67–73; C-in-c Leigh Park St Clare CD 73–75; R Bishop's Waltham 75–87; P-in-c Upham 78–79; R 79–87; V Dalston H Trin w St Phil *Lon* 87–97; P-in-c Haggerston All SS 90–97; P-in-c Fairford *Glouc* 97–98; V Fairford and Kempsford w Whelford 98–04; rtd 04; PtO *Glouc* from 05. *15 Highwood Avenue, Cheltenham GL53 0JJ* T: (01242) 530051 E: john.willard2@btinternet.com

WILLCOCK, Canon Richard William. b 39. Hertf Coll Ox BA 62 MA 66. Ripon Hall Ox 62. **d** 64 **p** 65. C Ashton St Mich *Man* 64–68; Bp's Dom Chapl 68–72; V Charlestown 72–75; Chapl Casterton Sch Lancs 75–80; V Bamford *Man* 80–92; R Framlingham w Saxtead *St E* 92–04; RD Loes 95–97; Warden of Readers 98–03; Hon Can St E Cathl 00–04; rtd 04; PtO *Carl* from 05. *High Green Cottage, Sandford, Appleby-in-Westmorland CA16 6NR* T: (017683) 51021

WILLCOX, Canon Frederick John. b 29. Kelham Th Coll 49. **d** 54 **p** 55. C Tranmere St Paul *Ches* 54–56; LtO *S'well* 57–61; Miss P St Patr Miss Bloemfontein S Africa 62–65; Dir 65–70; P-in-c Derby St Andr w St Osmund 70–74; V 74–80; V Netherton St Andr *Worc* 80–94; Hon Can Worc Cathl 91–94; rtd 94; PtO *Worc* 94–10. *22 Capel Court, The Burgage, Prestbury, Cheltenham GL52 3EL* T: (01242) 256373

WILLCOX (née THOMPSON), Mrs Pauline. b 44. EMMTC 81. **dss** 84 **d** 87 **p** 94. Derby St Aug 84–88; Par Dn 87–88; Par Dn Boulton 88–90; Par Dn Allestree 91–94; C 94–97; Sub-Chapl HM Pris Sudbury 92–94; P-in-c Hartington, Biggin and Earl Sterndale *Derby* 97–01; rtd 01; PtO *Derby* 01–06; Chapl HM Pris Jersey 06–09; PtO *Win* from 10. *9 Clos du Roncherez, Le Pont du Val, St Brelade, Jersey JE3 8FG* T: (01534) 745160 E: willcoxpauline@gmail.com

WILLCOX, Richard John Michael. b 39. Birm Univ BSc 62 PhD 67. Qu Coll Birm 78. **d** 80 **p** 81. C Boldmere *Birm* 80–83; V Edgbaston SS Mary and Ambrose 83–89; V Evercreech w Chesterblade and Milton Clevedon *B & W* 89–97; Dioc Development Rep 90–01; V Bridgwater H Trin 97–01; PtO *Heref* 05–13; *Bris* 14–19. *58 Forrester Green, Colerne, Chippenham SN14 8EA* E: rswillcox@waitrose.com

WILLESDEN, Area Bishop of. *See* BROADBENT, The Rt Revd Peter Alan

WILLETT, Frank Edwin. b 45. Kelham Th Coll 64. **d** 68 **p** 69. C Oswestry H Trin *Lich* 68–71; C Bilston St Leon 71–74; USPG Zambia 75–80; V Curbar and Stoney Middleton *Derby* 80–88; Area Sec USPG Derby and Leic 88–91; V Chesterfield SS Aug *Derby* 91–98; Chapl Walton Hosp 91–98; Ind Chapl *Derby* 98–03; P-in-c Brampton St Mark 03–09; Hon P-in-c Loundsley Green 03–09; rtd 10; Hon C Boldre w S Baddesley *Win* 09–13; PtO from 13. *57 Fawn Gardens, New Milton BH25 5GJ* E: frankfranceswillett@yahoo.com

WILLETT, Canon Geoffrey Thomas. b 38. Dur Univ BA 59 MA 82. Cranmer Hall Dur. **d** 62 **p** 63. C Widnes St Paul *Liv* 62–65; C Harborne Heath *Birm* 65–68; V Wakef St Andr and St Mary 68–75; V Hinckley H Trin *Leic* 75–89; TR 89; RD Sparkenhoe II 84–87; RD Sparkenhoe W 87–89; P-in-c Markfield 89–90; R 90–99; P-in-c Thornton, Bagworth and Stanton 96–99; R Markfield, Thornton, Bagworth and Stanton etc 99–04; RD Sparkenhoe E 91–99; Hon Can Leic Cathl 87–04; rtd 04; PtO *Derby* from 04; *Leic* from 04; *Lich* from 10. *22 Clifton Way, Burton-on-Trent DE15 9DW* T: (01283) 548868 E: carolynwillett79@googlemail.com

WILLETT, Canon John Ivon. b 40. Ch Ch Ox BA 63 MA 65. Chich Th Coll 61. **d** 63 **p** 64. C Leic St Andr 63–66; C Bordesley St Alb *Birm* 66–72; Min Can, Prec and Sacr Pet Cathl 72–82; R Uppingham w Ayston and Wardley w Belton 82–99; Can Pet Cathl 97–99; V Cantley *Sheff* 99–12; AD Doncaster 04–10; rtd 12; PtO *Sheff* from 12; *S'well* from 18. *16 Rosemary Close, Doncaster DN4 6BP* T: (01302) 370808

WILLETTS, Ms Mary Elizabeth Willetts. b 33. St Hild Coll Dur BA 54 Hughes Hall Cam CertEd 55. Cranmer Hall Dur 02. **d** 02 **p** 03. NSM Stockton-on-the-Forest w Holtby and Warthill *York* 02–12; NSM Rural E York 12–13; rtd 13; PtO *York* from 13. *Walnut Cottage, Warthill, York YO19 5XL* T: (01904) 489874

WILLETTS, Mrs Susan. b 60. EMMTC 05. **d** 08 **p** 09. C Burton All SS w Ch Ch *Lich* 08–11; TV Uttoxeter Area 11–16; V Loughb Gd Shep *Leic* from 16. *21 Parklands Drive, Loughborough LE11 2SZ*

WILLEY, Canon David Geoffrey. b 53. Imp Coll Lon BSc 74. Oak Hill Th Coll BA 86. **d** 86 **p** 87. C Cromer *Nor* 86–90; R High Halstow w All Hallows and Hoo St Mary *Roch* 90–94; R Gravesend St Geo 94–02; TR N Farnborough *Guildf* 02–17; V Farnborough St Pet 17–18; RD Aldershot 06–11; Hon Can Guildf Cathl 13–18; rtd 18; PtO *Chelmsf* from 18. *22 New Captains Road, West Mersea, Colchester CO5 8QP* E: david@willeyfamily.plus.com

WILLEY, Canon Graham John. b 38. Moray Ord Course 91. **d** 93 **p** 94. NSM W Coast Jt Congregations *Mor* 93–99; NSM Stirling *St And* 99–03; rtd 03; Hon C Killin *St And* 04–13; Hon C Stirling from 13. *9 Victoria Terrace, Menstrie FK11 7EE* T: (01259) 761932 E: graham.john.willey@btinternet.com

WILLIAMS, Alan Ronald Norman. b 60. RMN 85. Linc Th Coll 95. **d** 95 **p** 96. C Malvern Link w Cowleigh *Worc* 95–99; TV 03–08; V Risca *Mon* 99–03; P-in-c Amblecote *Worc* 08–17; V from 17. *The Vicarage, 4 The Holloway, Amblecote, Stourbridge DY8 4DL* T: (01384) 394057 E: fr.alan.williams@gmail.com

WILLIAMS, Canon Aled Wyn. b 47. Univ of Wales (Abth) BA 69. St Mich Coll Llan 69. **d** 71 **p** 72. C Llanelli *St D* 71–73; P-in-c Capel Colman w Llanfihangel Penbedw etc 73–74; V 74–81; V Llanddewi Brefi w Llanbadarn Odwyn 81–84; V Llanddewi Brefi w Llanbadarn Odwyn, Cellan etc 84–01; V Lampeter and Llanddewibrefi Gp 01–06; TR Bro Teifi Sarn Helen 06–11; AD Lampeter and Ultra-Aeron 96–11; Can St D Cathl 97–11; rtd 11; PtO *St D* 11–16. *Cwmawel, Llanllwni, Pencader SA39 9DR* E: pedrbrefi@btopenworld.com

WILLIAMS, Alexandra Christine. b 66. Victoria Univ Man BSc 87. Ripon Coll Cuddesdon 15. **d** 17 **p** 18. C Edgehill Churches *Cov* from 17. *6 King John's Road, Kineton, Warwick CV35 0HS* T: (01789) 292777 M: 07718-646863 E: alexcwilliams66@gmail.com

WILLIAMS, Miss Alison Lindsay. b 47. Univ of Wales (Abth) BA 69 PGCE 70. Wycliffe Hall Ox 00. **d** 00 **p** 01. C Stratton St Margaret w S Marston etc *Bris* 00–04; TV Chalke Valley *Sarum* 04–12; rtd 12; PtO *Bris* 13–19. *5 Cherry Orchard, Highworth, Swindon SN6 7AU* T: (01793) 979110 E: alisonlwilliams@talktalk.net

WILLIAMS, Andrew. b 68. **d** 19. NSM Woodbridge St Jo and Bredfield *St E* from 19. *Address temp unknown*

WILLIAMS, Andrew Barrington. b 62. Ripon Coll Cuddesdon 96. **d** 98 **p** 99. C Oswaldtwistle Immanuel and All SS *Blackb* 98–01; C Whittle-le-Woods 01–02; P-in-c Hillock *Man* 02–08; P-in-c Unsworth 07–08; P-in-c Radcliffe St Andr 08–14; V Brinnington w Portwood *Ches* 14–18; TV Macclesfield Team from 18. *2 The Mallards, Chester Road, Macclesfield SK11 8PT* T: (01625) 432919 M: 07565-483455 E: revandywilliams@me.com *or* teamvicar.macc@gmail.com

WILLIAMS, Andrew David. b 67. Univ of Wales (Lamp) BA 91. Linc Th Coll 93. **d** 93 **p** 94. C Perry Street *Roch* 93–96; C Ealing St Pet Mt Park *Lon* 96–00; R Finchley St Mary 00–08; Warden of Readers Edmonton Area 05–08; R Applecross Australia 08–14; C Tottenham H Trin *Lon* from 14. *1 Eagle Heights, Waterside Way, London N17 9FU* E: perth08@googlemail.com

WILLIAMS, Andrew Gibson. b 31. Edin Univ MA 57. Edin Th Coll 56. **d** 59 **p** 60. C Todmorden *Wakef* 59–61; C Clitheroe St Mary *Blackb* 61–63; V Burnley St Jas 63–65; CF (TA) 64–65; CF 65–71; R Winterslow *Sarum* 71–84; P-in-c Condover *Heref* 84–88; P-in-c Acton Burnell w Pitchford 84–88; P-in-c Frodesley 84–88; R Condover w Frodesley, Acton Burnell etc 88–90; R Whimple, Talaton and Clyst St Lawr *Ex* 90–94; rtd 94; PtO *Ex* 94–08. *Flat 7, Manormead, Tilford Road, Hindhead GU26 6RA* T: (01428) 601507

WILLIAMS, Andrew John. b 64. Univ Coll Lon BSc 85 Keele Univ PGCE 87 Lon Univ MSc 91. STETS 08. **d** 11 **p** 12. NSM Twickenham All Hallows *Lon* 11–14; NSM Kingston *S'wark* 14–18; NSM Richmond St Mary w St Matthias and St Jo from 18. *51 Moor Mead Road, Twickenham TW1 1JS* M: 07824-310311 E: andrew.williams.london@gmail.com

WILLIAMS, Ann Joyce. See TEMPLEMAN, Ann Joyce

WILLIAMS, Anthea Elizabeth. b 50. Trevelyan Coll Dur BA 71 Kent Univ MA 97 Middx Univ MSc 00 Univ of E Lon PhD 10. Linc Th Coll 72. **dss** 79 **d** 87 **p** 94. St Marylebone Ch Ch *Lon* 79–84; Maidstone St Martin *Cant* 84–91; Par Dn 87–91; Dn-in-c Rolvenden 91–94; P-in-c 94–04; P-in-c Sandhurst w Newenden 01–04; Chapl E Kent NHS and Soc Care Partnership Trust 91–04; Hon Chapl Kent Police *Cant* from 95; PtO from 04; *Chich* from 15. *2 Great Wigsell Cottages, Hastings Road, Bodiam, Robertsbridge TN32 5PU* T: (01580) 754948 E: chaplain2sk@btinternet.com

WILLIAMS, Anthony Clive. b 61. Ex Univ BA 83 Coll of SS Mark and Jo Plymouth MEd 04. SWMTC 09. **d** 11 **p** 12. NSM Elburton *Ex* 11–16; TV Plymouth Em, St Paul Efford and St Aug from 16. *22 Cranmere Road, Plymouth PL3 5JY* T: 03301-139088 E: tony.williams@emmanuelplymouth.co.uk

WILLIAMS, Capt Anthony James. b 57. **d** 08 **p** 09. NSM Bream *Glouc* 08–13; P-in-c Forest of Dean Ch Ch w English Bicknor 13–14; V from 14; Chapl HM Pris Glouc 12–13; Chapl HM Pris Eastwood Park from 13. *HM Prison Eastwood Park, Falfield, Wotton-under-Edge GL12 8DB* T: (01454) 382100 E: revtonyw@hotmail.com *or* anthony.williams@justice.gov.uk

WILLIAMS, The Very Revd Arfon. b 58. Univ of Wales (Abth) BD 83 Univ of Wales (Ban) MA 84. Wycliffe Hall Ox 83. **d** 84 **p** 85. C Carmarthen St Dav *St D* 84–86; TV Aberystwyth 86–88; V Glanogwen *Ban* 88–94; C Ewhurst and Dir Oast Ho Retreat Cen *Chich* 95–98; Asst to RD Rye 95–98; Co-ord for Adult Educn (E Sussex Area) *Chich* 97–98; I Jordanstown *Conn* 98–02; Adn Meirionnydd *Ban* 02–04; R Dolgellau w Llanfachreth and Brithdir etc 02–04; Dean Elphin and Ardagh *K, E & A* from 04; I Sligo w Knocknarea and Rosses Pt from 04. *The Deanery, Strandhill Road, Sligo, Republic of Ireland* T: (00353) (71) 915 7993 E: arvonwilliams@eircom.net

WILLIAMS, Brian. b 48. WMMTC. **d** 83 **p** 84. NSM Lich St Chad 83–03; Asst Chapl Sandwell Health Care NHS Trust 98; Angl Chapl 98–99; Chapl Burton Hosps NHS Trust 99–03; Chapl R Bournemouth and Christchurch Hosps NHS Foundn Trust 03–14; rtd 14; PtO *Lich* from 16. *82 Walsall Road, Lichfield WS13 8AF*

WILLIAMS, Brian Frederick. b 55. Philippa Fawcett Coll CertEd 77 BEd 78. SEITE 98. **d** 01 **p** 02. NSM Folkestone St Mary and St Eanswythe *Cant* 01–10; NSM Folkestone St Mary, St Eanswythe and St Sav 09–11; PtO 11–12; C Alkham w Capel le Ferne and Hougham from 12. *The Vicarage, 20 Alexandra Road, Capel-le-Ferne, Folkestone CT18 7LD* T: (01303) 244119 E: capelvicarage@gmail.com

WILLIAMS, Canon Brian Luke. b 54. AKC 75. St Steph Ho Ox 76. **d** 77 **p** 78. C Kettering St Mary *Pet* 77–80; C Walsall St Gabr Fulbrook *Lich* 80–83; P-in-c Sneyd 83–85; V from 85; RD Stoke N 94–99; Preb Lich Cathl from 13; Can Ho Ghana from 14. *Sneyd Vicarage, Hamil Road, Stoke-on-Trent ST6 1AP* T/F: (01782) 825841

WILLIAMS, Ms Carol Jean Picknell. b 45. FCIPD 89. Ox NSM Course 86. **d** 89 **p** 94. NSM High Wycombe *Ox* 89–97; P-in-c Penn 97–01; rtd 01; PtO *Heref* 02–16; *Chich* from 16. *3 Gillham Wood Road, Bexhill-on-Sea TN39 3BN*

WILLIAMS, Carole. See GARNER, Carole

WILLIAMS, Mrs Catherine Anne. b 65. Selw Coll Cam BA 87 MA 91. SEITE 98. **d** 00 **p** 01. C Chatham St Steph *Roch* 00–02; C Bishop's Cleeve *Glouc* 03–06; Dioc Voc Officer 06–10; Asst Dioc Dir of Ords 08–10; Selection Sec Min Division 10–18; Nat Adv for Voc 11–15; Public Preacher *Glouc* from 11.

Abbey House, Church Street, Tewkesbury GL20 5SR M: 07966-709577 E: revdcawilliams@gmail.com

WILLIAMS, Ms Catherine Lois. b 51. Swansea Coll of Educn CertEd 74 Univ of Wales (Swansea) BEd 80. St Mich Coll Llan. **d** 00 **p** 01. C Gorseinon *S & B* 00–02; C Cen Swansea 03; TV 03–11; rtd 11; PtO *S & B* from 12; *Llan* from 13; *St D* from 14. *41 Ffordd y Glowyr, Godrergraig, Swansea SA9 2BQ* T: (01639) 844814

WILLIAMS (*née* BRERETON), Mrs Catherine Louise. b 69. St Aid Coll Dur BSc 90 Cranfield Univ MSc 92 Fitzw Coll Cam BTh 00. Ridley Hall Cam 97. **d** 00 **p** 01. C S Bank *York* 00–03; V Middlesbrough St Chad 03–09; TV Woughton *Ox* 09–14; Miss and Evang Officer *Glouc* from 14. *Church House, College Green, Gloucester GL1 2LY* T: (01452) 410022

WILLIAMS, Canon Cecil Peter. b 41. TCD BA 63 MA 67 Lon Univ BD 67 PhD 86 Bris Univ MLitt 77. Clifton Th Coll 64. **d** 67 **p** 68. C Maghull *Liv* 67–70; LtO *Bris* 70–91; Tutor Clifton Th Coll 70–72; Tutor Trin Coll Bris 72–91; Lib 73–81; Course Ldr 81–85; Vice-Prin 85–91; V Ecclesall *Sheff* 91–06; Hon Can Sheff Cathl 01–06; rtd 06; V Jersey Gouray St Martin *Win* 06–12; PtO *Ox* from 13. *Shalom, 23 Sandmartin Close, Buckingham MK18 1SD* T: (01280) 308394 M: 07801-353786 E: peter.williams@shalom23.co.uk

WILLIAMS, Mrs Christine Mary. b 51. City Univ BSc 72 Middx Univ BA 05. NTMTC 02. **d** 05 **p** 06. NSM Pitsea w Nevendon *Chelmsf* 05–08; TV Grays Thurrock 08–19; rtd 19. *2 Foxleigh, Billericay CM12 9NS* T: (01277) 654370 E: christine.mwilliams@btopenworld.com

WILLIAMS, Christopher David. b 62. Spurgeon's Coll BD 99. St Jo Coll Nottm MA 06. **d** 06 **p** 07. C Haslemere and Grayswood *Guildf* 06–08; C Godalming 08–09; R Liss *Portsm* from 09. *The Rectory, 111 Station Road, Liss GU33 7AQ.* M: 07803-135739 E: revchris007@gmail.com

WILLIAMS, Preb Clive Gregory. b 45. Trin Coll Bris 83. **d** 85 **p** 86. C Bedhampton *Portsm* 85–88; V Highley w Billingsley, Glazeley etc *Heref* 88–12; P-in-c Stottesdon w Farlow, Cleeton St Mary etc 08–10; RD Bridgnorth 96–05; Preb Heref Cathl 99–12; rtd 12; PtO *Portsm* from 13. *120 Hazleton Way, Waterlooville PO8 9DW* T: (023) 9257 1745 E: cliveandsue2012@btinternet.com

WILLIAMS, Canon Colin Henry. b 52. Pemb Coll Ox BA 73 MA 78. St Steph Ho Ox BA 80. **d** 81 **p** 82. C Liv St Paul Stoneycroft 81–84; TV Walton St Mary 84–89; Chapl Walton Hosp *Liv* 86–89; Bp's Dom Chapl *Blackb* 89–94; Chapl Whalley Abbey 89–94; V Poulton-le-Fylde *Blackb* 94–99; adn Lancaster 99–05; Gen Sec Conf of Eur Chs 05–10; Can Gib Cathl *Eur* 07–10; TR Ludlow *Heref* 10–15; Preb Heref Cathl 14–15; Adn Germany and N Eur 15–19; Adn E Adnry 15–19; rtd 19; PtO *Blackb* from 19; *Eur* from 19. *Flat 1, 3 Ash Drive, Poulton-le-Fylde FY6 8DZ* E: colinw834@gmail.com

WILLIAMS, David. b 43. ACA 65 FCA. K Coll Lon AKC 69 BD 69. **d** 70 **p** 71. C Walkden Moor *Man* 70–72; C Deane 72–75; V Horwich St Cath 75–81; Hon C Chorley All SS *Blackb* 84–86; P-in-c Weeton 86–87; V Singleton w Weeton 87–97; C Lancaster St Mary w St John and St Anne 98–00; Chapl HM Pris Lanc Castle 98–00; rtd 00; PtO *Man* 02–08 and 10–18. *153 Crompton Way, Bolton BL2 2SQ* T: (01204) 373353 E: goodfornow2@sky.com

WILLIAMS, David. b 49. BTh. **d** 88 **p** 89. C Lurgan etc w Ballymachugh, Kildrumferton etc *K, E & A* 88–91; I Kinsale Union *C, C & R* 91–14; Miss to Seafarers 91–14; Can Cork and Cloyne Cathls *C, C & R* 95–97; Treas Cork Cathl 97–14; Preb Tymothan St Patr Cathl Dublin 97–14; rtd 14. *Kilbeg Upper, Clonbur, Co Galway, Republic of Ireland* E: dhw@gofree.indigo.ie or dhwkilbeg@gmail.com

WILLIAMS, David Frank. b 48. S Dios Minl Tr Scheme 91. **d** 94 **p** 95. NSM Romsey *Win* from 94. *24 Feltham Close, Romsey SO51 8PB* T: (01794) 524050 E: revdfw@talk21.com

WILLIAMS, David Gareth. b 58. Lon Univ BD 81. Ripon Coll Cuddesdon 82. **d** 84 **p** 85. C Chandler's Ford *Win* 84–88; C Alton St Lawr 88–90; R Crawley and Littleton and Sparsholt w Lainston 90–97; P-in-c Andover 97–09; TR Risborough *Ox* from 09; AD Aylesbury from 17. *The Rectory, Church Lane, Princes Risborough HP27 9AW* T: (01844) 344784 E: rector@stmarysrisborough.org.uk

WILLIAMS, Canon David Gordon. b 43. Selw Coll Cam BA 65 MA 69. Oak Hill Th Coll 66. **d** 68 **p** 69. C Maidstone St Luke *Cant* 68–71; C Rugby St Matt *Cov* 71–73; P-in-c Budbrooke 73–74; V 74–81; V Lenton *S'well* 81–87; TR Cheltenham St Mark *Glouc* 87–03; Hon Can Glouc Cathl 96–03; R Toodyay w Goomalling Australia 03–08; rtd 08; Miss Development P Avon Deanery 08–09; PtO *Derby* 09–11; *Worc* 12–17. *2 Butchers Row, High Street, Broadway WR12 7DP* T: (01386) 853849 M: 07766-837571 E: canondwilliams@westnet.com.au

⊕**WILLIAMS, The Rt Revd David Grant.** b 61. Bris Univ BSocSc 83. Wycliffe Hall Ox 86. **d** 89 **p** 90 **c** 14. C Ecclesall *Sheff* 89–92; V Dore 92–02; RD Ecclesall 97–02; V Win Ch Ch 02–14; Hon Can Win Cathl 12–14; Suff Bp Basingstoke from 14. *Bishop's Lodge, Colden Lane, Old Alresford, Alresford SO24 9DY* M: 07889-547095 E: bishop.david@winchester.anglican.org

WILLIAMS, David Henry. b 33. Trin Coll Cam BA 56 MA 60 PhD 77. St D Coll Lamp 67. **d** 69 **p** 70. C Monmouth *Mon* 69–70; Chapl St Woolos Cathl 70–71; P-in-c Six Bells 71–76; Libya 76–79; P-in-c Crumlin *Mon* 79–80; R Llanddewi Skirrid w Llanvetherine etc 80–83; PtO 83–87; Guest Master Caldey Abbey 83–87; V Buttington and Pool Quay *St As* 87–95; Chapl Warsaw *Eur* 95–97; rtd 97; PtO *St D* from 14. *Flat W16, The College of St Barnabas, Blackberry Lane, Lingfield RH7 6NJ* T: (01342) 870260 E: dhw.1933@gmail.com

WILLIAMS, David Ivan Ross. b 47. Imp Coll Lon BSc 70 Leic Univ MSc 72 ARCS 70 FBIS. STETS 00. **d** 03 **p** 04. NSM Havant *Portsm* 03–10; PtO *Ex* from 10. *11 Manor Gardens, Exbourne, Okehampton EX20 3RW* T: (01837) 851710 M: 07866-772025 E: david@dirw.demon.co.uk or davidivanross@gmail.com

WILLIAMS, Canon David John. b 38. AKC 62. **d** 63 **p** 64. C Benchill *Man* 63–66; C Heywood St Jas 66–69; V Leesfield 69–73; Chapl TS Arethusa 73–74; TV Southend St Jo w St Mark, All SS w St Fran etc *Chelmsf* 74–80; V Horndon on the Hill 80–93; RD Thurrock 83–92; P-in-c Rochford 93–02; RD 96–02; P-in-c Sutton w Shopland 98–02; Hon Can Chelmsf Cathl 99–02; rtd 02; PtO *Ripon* 02–14; *Leeds* from 14. *29 Stonebeck Avenue, Harrogate HG1 2BN* T: (01423) 522828

WILLIAMS, David John. b 52. NOC 92. **d** 95 **p** 96. C Gt Crosby St Luke *Liv* 95–99; V W Derby St Jas 99–04; Chapl R Liverpool Children's NHS Trust 99–08; Chapl Alder Hey Children's NHS Foundn Trust from 08. *Alder Hey Children's Hospital, Eaton Road, Liverpool L12 2AP* T: 0151-228 4811 E: revdw1999@hotmail.com or david.j.williams@alderhey.nhs.uk

WILLIAMS, David John. b 43. Wadh Coll Ox BA 64. St Jo Coll Nottm 73. **d** 75 **p** 76. C Newcastle w Butterton *Lich* 75–79; P-in-c Oulton 79–89; P-in-c Stone Ch Ch 84–89; V Stone Ch Ch and Oulton 89–96; P-in-c Ashley 96–04; P-in-c Mucklestone 96–04; R Ashley and Mucklestone 04–07; rtd 07; PtO *Heref* from 08. *23 Gravel Hill, Ludlow SY8 1QR* T: (01584) 875884 E: williamsjandm@btinternet.com

WILLIAMS, David John. b 30. Open Univ BA 79. St D Coll Lamp 64. **d** 66 **p** 67. C Mold *St As* 66–69; C Llanrhos 69–71; R Llangynhafal and Llanbedr Dyffryn Clwyd 71–86; P-in-c Llanychan 77–85; P-in-c Llanbedr DC w Llangynhafal, Llanychan etc 86; RD Dyffryn Clwyd 86–95; R Ruthin w Llanrhydd 86–95; rtd 95; PtO *St As* from 09. *16 The Park, Ruthin LL15 1PW* T: (01824) 705746

WILLIAMS, David Michael. b 50. Ex Univ BA 71 Lon Univ MA 77 FSA 81 FRSA 82. SEITE 05. **d** 08 **p** 09. NSM Redhill St Jo *S'wark* 08–10; NSM Redhill St Matt 10–11; P-in-c Gt Coxwell w Buscot, Coleshill etc *Ox* 11–14; V from 14; AD Vale of White Horse 15–18. *The Vicarage, Great Coxwell, Faringdon SN7 7NG* T: (01367) 240665 E: davidwilliams24@btinternet.com

WILLIAMS, David Michael Rochfort. b 40. St Mich Coll Llan 62. **d** 65 **p** 66. C Pembroke Dock *St D* 65–68; Chapl Miss to Seamen and Ind Chapl 68–71; P-in-c Walwyn's Castle w Robeston W 68–70; R 70–71; Ind Chapl *Mon* 71–74; Hon Chapl St Woolos Cathl 71–74; V Blaenavon w Capel Newydd 74–77; Ind Chapl *St As* 77–88; V Whitford 81–87; V Ruabon 87–92; TR Cen Telford *Lich* 92–00; R Burton and Rosemarket *St D* 00–02; Chapl Miss to Seafarers Milford Haven 00–02; Southampton 02–05; rtd 05; PtO *Ox* from 05. *13 Sturt Road, Charlbury, Chipping Norton OX7 3SX* T: (01608) 811284 E: michael@michaelcara1965.plus.com

WILLIAMS, David Norman. b 54. Lanc Univ BSc 76 Leeds Univ BA 83. Coll of Resurr Mirfield 81. **d** 84 **p** 85. C Ireland Wood *Ripon* 84–87; C Beeston 87–91; V Cross Roads cum Lees *Bradf* 91–99; V Skipton Ch Ch 99–07; P-in-c Carleton and Lothersdale 03–07; V Skipton Ch Ch w Carleton 07–14; *Leeds* 14–15; rtd 15. *Shorley Croft, 8 Penrith Road, Keswick CA12 4HF* E: dngc@hotmail.co.uk

WILLIAMS, David Paul. *See* HOWELL, David Paul

WILLIAMS, Canon David Roger. b 49. Open Univ BA. St D Coll Lamp. **d** 73 **p** 74. C Llansamlet *S & B* 73–76; C Oystermouth 76–79; V Aberedw w Llandeilo Graban and Llanbadarn etc 79–81; V Brynmawr 81–89; V Newport St Julian *Mon* 89–09; R Penarth and Llandough *Llan* 09–15; Hon Can St Woolos Cathl *Mon* 09–15; rtd 15; PtO *Mon* from 15; *Llan* from 16. *36 Priory Gardens, Usk NP15 1BB* E: fr.rogerwilliams@uwclub.net

WILLIAMS, Denise Laraine. b 50. Liv Univ TCert 71. NOC 00. **d** 03 **p** 04. C Padgate *Liv* 03–08; P-in-c Cinnamon Brow 08–13; TR Warrington E 13–15; rtd 15; PtO *Ches* from 15; PV Ches Cathl from 16. *30 Rowcliffe Avenue, Chester CH4 7PW* M: 07889-861869   E: denisewilliams50@btinternet.com   or priest.vicar@chestercathedral.com

WILLIAMS, Derek Ivor. b 37. ACA 61 FCA 71. **d** 05 **p** 06. OLM Chollerton w Birtley and Thockrington *Newc* 05–07; PtO from 07. *Buteland House, Bellingham, Hexham NE48 2EX* T: (01434) 220389

WILLIAMS, Derek Lawrence. b 45. Tyndale Hall Bris 65. **d** 69 **p** 70. C Cant St Mary Bredin 69–71; Gen Sec Inter-Coll Chr Fellowship 71–75; LtO *St Alb* 78–84; LtO *Bris* 85–92; PtO *Pet* 92–02; Par and Miss Co-ord Northampton St Giles 93–97; Dioc Millennium Officer 98–00; Dioc Communications Officer 00–02; Dioc Communications Officer *Eur* 02–05; Bp's Admin and Press Officer *Pet* 05–10; Hon C Brington w Whilton and Norton etc 02–08; LtO from 08; rtd 11; Dioc Media Adv *Pet* from 11; PtO from 12. *7 Montrose Close, Market Harborough LE16 9LJ* T: (01858) 432709 M: 07770-981172 E: derek.williams@peterborough-diocese.org.uk

WILLIAMS, Diana Mary. b 36. Bris Univ CertEd 56 Leeds Univ BSc 57. Oak Hill Th Coll 86. **d** 87 **p** 94. C S Mymms K Chas *St Alb* 87–95; V 95–98; R Sandon, Wallington and Rushden w Clothall 98–04; RD Buntingford 01–06; rtd 04; PtO *Ely* 05–13; *Sheff* from 14. *27 Newfield Crescent, Sheffield S17 3DE* E: di.williams@btinternet.com

WILLIAMS, Diane Patricia. *See* BLAKEY WILLIAMS, Diane Patricia

WILLIAMS, Canon Diane Ruth. b 52. Hull Univ BA 80 Nottm Univ MA 94. Linc Th Coll 92. **d** 94 **p** 95. C Stokesley *York* 94–98; TV Louth *Linc* 98–06; Chapl Linc and Louth NHS Trust 98–01; Chapl United Lincs Hosps NHS Trust 01–06; P-in-c Needham Market w Badley *St E* from 06; RD Bosmere from 09; RD Stowmarket from 17; Hon Can St E Cathl from 17. *10 Meadow View, Needham Market, Ipswich IP6 8RH* T: (01449) 720316 E: diane.rev@btinternet.com

WILLIAMS, Doiran George. b 26. Barrister-at-Law (Gray's Inn) 52. WMMTC 91. **d** 93 **p** 94. NSM Edvin Loach w Tedstone Delamere etc *Heref* 93–98; PtO from 98. *Howberry, Whitbourne, Worcester WR6 5RZ* T: (01886) 821189

WILLIAMS, Donna. b 67. UNISA BA 97 Witwatersrand Univ HDipEd 89. St Mellitus Coll 15. **d** 18 **p** 19. C Hounslow H Trin *Lon* from 18. *19 Royal Road, Teddington TW11 0SD* T: (020) 8577 9048 M: 07762-900979 E: donna@hthounslow.org.uk

WILLIAMS, Canon Dylan John. b 72. Univ of Wales (Ban) BTh 97. Ripon Coll Cuddesdon 97. **d** 99 **p** 00. C Holyhead *Ban* 99–01; C Dolgellau w Llanfachreth and Brithdir etc 01–02; P-in-c Amlwch 02–03; R 03–10; P-in-c Porthmadog and Ynyscynhaearn and Dolbenmaen 10–11; P-in-c Bro Eifionydd 11–12; TR 12; V Bro'r Holl Saint 12–16; V Bro Eifionydd from 16; AD Llyn and Eifionydd 10–15; AD Synod Gogledd Meirionnydd 15–18; AD Synod Meirionnydd from 18; Asst Dir of Ords 11–15; Can Ban Cathl from 12. *The Rectory, Y Maes, Criccieth LL52 0AG* T: (01766) 523743 E: canondylan@gmail.com

WILLIAMS (née WITHERS), Eleanor Jane. b 61. Univ of Wales Coll of Medicine MB, BCh 85 Anglia Ruskin Univ MA 07 MRCGP 89. ERMC 04. **d** 07 **p** 08. NSM Milton *Ely* 07–11; V Burwell w Reach from 11. *The Vicarage, 22 Isaacson Road, Burwell, Cambridge CB25 0AF* T: (01638) 741262 E: vicar@stmarysburwell.org.uk

WILLIAMS, Canon Emlyn Cadwaladr. b 64. St Jo Coll Nottm 02. **d** 04 **p** 05. C Glanogwen w St Ann's w Llanllechid *Ban* 04–07; R Llanfihangel Ysgeifiog w Llangristiolus etc 07–12; R Seintiau Braint a Chefni 12–15; AD Malltraeth 13–15; AD Synod Ynys Mon from 15. *The Rectory, Holyhead Road, Gaerwen LL60 6HP* T: (01248) 421275

WILLIAMS (née CALDERWOOD), Emma Louise. b 74. Derby Univ BSc 96 Univ of Wales (Cardiff) MTh 07. St Mich Coll Llan BTh 05. **d** 06 **p** 07. C Stanley w Stoneycroft St Paul *Liv* 06–11; V Stanley and Stoneycroft St Paul from 11; AD W Derby from 17. *28 Brookland Road West, Liverpool L13 3BQ* T: 0151-228 2426 E: revdem1411@btinternet.com

WILLIAMS, Frederick Errol. b 41. MBIM 80. Sarum & Wells Th Coll 86. **d** 88 **p** 89. C Milton *Win* 88–91; P-in-c Chilbolton cum Wherwell 91–94; R 94–06; RD Andover 99–06; rtd 06; TV S Cotswolds *Glouc* 10–14; PtO *Sarum* from 15. *1A Central Street, Ludgershall, Andover SP11 9RA* T: (01264) 791487 E: mail@errolsue69.plus.com

WILLIAMS, Gareth Wynn. *See* RAYNER-WILLIAMS, Gareth Wynn

WILLIAMS, Gavin John. b 61. Down Coll Cam BA 84 Wycliffe Hall Ox BA 88 Barrister-at-Law 85. **d** 89 **p** 90.

C Muswell Hill St Jas w St Matt *Lon* 89–92; Asst Chapl Shrewsbury Sch 92–95; Chapl 95–02; Chapl Westmr Sch from 02; PV Westmr Abbey from 05. *Westminster School, Little Dean's Yard, London SW1P 3PF* T: (020) 7963 1128 E: gavin.williams@westminster.org.uk

WILLIAMS, George Ola. b 55. Bradf Univ PhD 90 Waterloo Lutheran Univ MA 83. St Jo Coll Nottm MTh 95. **d** 96 **p** 97. C Enfield St Jas *Lon* 96–00; V Allerton *Bradf* 00–14; *Leeds* from 14. *The Vicarage, Ley Top Lane, Allerton, Bradford BD15 7LT* T: (01274) 541948   E: george.williams@leeds.anglican.org   or george.ola13@gmail.com

WILLIAMS, Canon Giles Peter. b 54. Lon Univ BA 77 MA 78. Trin Coll Bris 80. **d** 82 **p** 83. C Reading Greyfriars *Ox* 82–85; Rwanda Miss 85–90; Mid-Africa Min (CMS) 90–94; Can Kigali Cathl Rwanda from 90; V Woking St Jo *Guildf* 95–10; RD Woking 08–10; Chapl Cannes *Eur* from 10. *Résidence Kent, 4 avenue Général Ferrié, 06400 Cannes, France* T: (0033) 4 93 94 54 61 F: 4 93 94 04 43 E: mail@holytrinitycannes.org

WILLIAMS, Gillian Jean Richeldis. b 47. St Mich Coll Llan. **d** 99 **p** 02. C Llanishen *Llan* 99–05; P-in-c Rhondda Fach Uchaf 05; rtd 06; P-in-c Llanishen w Trellech Grange and Llanfihangel etc *Mon* 13–14; P-in-c Rockfield and Dingestow Gp 17–18. *Faith House, 82 Kings Fee, Monmouth NP25 5BQ* T: (01600) 716696 E: retired.rev@hotmail.com

WILLIAMS, Graham Parry. b 46. Bp Burgess Hall Lamp 67. **d** 70 **p** 71. C Ebbw Vale *Mon* 70–73; V Trevethin 73–74; V Nantyglo 74–76; Chapl RN 76–85; R Northlew w Ashbury *Ex* 85–87; R Bratton Clovelly w Germansweek 85–87; TV Pontypool *Mon* 88–90; C Skegness and Winthorpe *Linc* 90–91; V Sutton Bridge 91–94; P-in-c Witham Gp 94–97; P-in-c Ruskington 97–01; R 01–03; RD Lafford 02–03; P-in-c Ringstone in Aveland Gp 03–10; rtd 10; PtO *Linc* from 17. *7 Wilkie Drive, Folkingham, Sleaford NG34 0UE* T: (01529) 497632 E: frgraham@hotmail.com

WILLIAMS, Harri Alan McClelland. b 85. Ball Coll Ox BA 07 MA 13 Univ of Wales PhD 18. St Mich Coll Llan BA 10. **d** 10 **p** 11. C Haverfordwest *St D* 10–13; V Milford Haven 13–18; P-in-c Walsingham, Houghton and Barsham *Nor* from 18. *The Vicarage, Church Street, Walsingham NR22 6BL* T: (01328) 821316 E: harri1985@gmail.com

WILLIAMS, Haydn Clifford. b 32. Univ of Wales (Abth) BA 54 DipEd 55. EMMTC 89. **d** 95 **p** 99. NSM Anstey *Leic* 95–01; NSM Broom Leys 01–03; rtd 03; PtO *Leic* from 03. *9 Stamford Drive, Coalville LE67 4TA* T: (01530) 837889

WILLIAMS, Helena Maria Alija. *See* CERMAKOVA, Helena Maria Alija

WILLIAMS, Hilary Susan. *See* PETTMAN, Hilary Susan

WILLIAMS, Howell Mark. b 56. Univ of Wales (Cardiff) BD 87. St Mich Coll Llan 84. **d** 87 **p** 88. C Swansea St Thos and Kilvey *S & B* 87–89; TV Aberystwyth *St D* 89–93; V Hirwaun *Llan* 93–99; V Swansea St Pet *S & B* 99–12; AD Penderi 05–12; V Swansea St Jas from 12; AD Swansea 13–15. *The Vicarage, 1 Ffynone Drive, Swansea SA1 6DB* T: (01792) 470532 E: stjamesuplands1@googlemail.com

WILLIAMS, Canon Hugh Martin. b 45. AKC 73. St Aug Coll Cant 73. **d** 74 **p** 75. C Heston *Lon* 74–78; Chapl City Univ 78–84; PV Westmr Abbey 82–84; V Newquay *Truro* 84–93; V Christchurch *Win* 93–10; Hon Can Win Cathl 04–10; Preacher Charterhouse and Dep Master 10–14; V Cricket St Thomas *B & W* from 14. *14 Church Street, Crewkerne TA18 7HU* T: (01460) 394814 M: 07904-186414 E: hugh.m.williams@ukgateway.net

WILLIAMS, Ian Withers. b 43. Linc Th Coll 68. **d** 69 **p** 70. C Burney Lane *Birm* 69–72; C Cleobury Mortimer w Hopton Wafers *Heref* 72–75; V Knowbury 75–79; P-in-c Coreley w Doddington 75–79; V Lich Ch Ch 79–06; rtd 06; PtO *Heref* from 07; *Worc* from 07. *23 The Oaklands, Tenbury Wells WR15 8FB* T: (01584) 810528 M: 07711-260521 E: ian@theoaklands.com

WILLIAMS, James Llanfair Warren. b 48. St Mich Coll Llan 92. **d** 92 **p** 93. C Pembroke Dock *St D* 92–93; C Pembroke Dock w Cosheston w Nash and Upton 93–95; V Cwmaman 95–98; Chapl Costa Blanca *Eur* 98–00; V Meifod w Llangynyw w Pont Robert w Pont Dolanog *St As* 01–13; rtd 13; Hon C Yatton Moor *B & W* 13–18; PtO from 18. *White Gates, Skinners Lane, Churchill, Winscombe BS25 5PW* E: jlww2@outlook.com

WILLIAMS, James Nicholas Owen. b 39. CEng. S'wark Ord Course. **d** 82 **p** 83. C Petersfield w Sheet *Portsm* 82–86; TV Droitwich Spa *Worc* 86–88; R Church Lench w Rous Lench and Abbots Morton 88–94; V Milton *B & W* 94–04; RD Locking 99–04; rtd 04; Dioc Ecum Officer *B & W* 04–08; Hon C Pill, Portbury and Easton-in-Gordano 04–09; PtO from 09; *Bris* from 04. *151 Charlton Mead Drive, Brentry,*

Bristol BS10 6LP T: 0117-950 4152 M: 07808-772908 E: jnowil64@gmail.com

WILLIAMS, Mrs Jane Lorette. b 66. Univ of Wales (Swansea) BSc 03 Dur Univ BA 16. **d** 16 **p** 17. C Wareham *Sarum* 16–19; R Bride Valley from 19. *The Rectory, Church Street, Burton Bradstock, Bridport DT6 4QS* T: (01308) 898799 E: bvrector@outlook.com

WILLIAMS, Janet Patricia. b 61. Univ Coll Ox BA 83 MSt 85 K Alfred's Coll Win PhD 98. WEMTC 06. **d** 09 **p** 10. NSM Cirencester *Glouc* 09–12; Tutor WEMTC 12–18; Dir Reader Tr 12–18; Hon Can Glouc Cathl 14–18; Vice Prin St Hild Coll from 18. *St Hild College, Stocks Bank Road, Mirfield WF14 0BW* M: 07989-707257 E: janet.williams@sthild.org

WILLIAMS, Janet Patricia. *See* FFRENCH, Janet Patricia

WILLIAMS, Jeffrey. b 52. Univ of Wales (Ban) BTh 06. Llan Ord Course 99. **d** 03 **p** 04. NSM Cardiff St Mary and St Steph w St Dyfrig etc *Llan* 03–07; Chapl Malta and Gozo *Eur* 07–13; P-in-c Chard Gd Shep Furnham *B & W* 13; V from 13. *The Vicarage, Furnham Road, Chard TA20 1AE* T: (01460) 419527 M: 07928-171187 E: fr.jeff@hotmail.com

WILLIAMS, Jeffrey. *See* WILLIAMS, Robert Jeffrey Hopkin

WILLIAMS, Jennifer Ruth. b 72. St Hugh's Coll Ox BA 88 PGCE 89 Man Univ MA 00 PhD 11. Wycliffe Hall Ox 98 NOC 00. **d** 00 **p** 01. C Heatons *Man* 00–04; Hon C Burnage St Marg 04–05; Tutor Wycliffe Hall Ox 05–19; NSM Wootton Ox 11–19; R Ox St Matt from 19. *St Matthew's Vicarage, 65 Marlborough Road, Oxford OX1 4LW* M: 07784-304985

WILLIAMS, John. *See* WILLIAMS, David John

WILLIAMS, John Anthony. b 53. G&C Coll Cam BA 75 MA 79 St Jo Coll Dur BA 83 PhD 86. Cranmer Hall Dur 81. **d** 86 **p** 87. C Beverley Minster *York* 86–89; C Cloughton 89–90; P-in-c 90–93; Clergy Tr Officer E Riding 89–93; P-in-c Emley *Wakef* 93–98; Dioc Minl Tr Officer 93–02; Wakef Min Scheme Officer 97–06; Co-ord for Local Min *Wakef* 02–06; Dean Wakef Min Scheme 06–08; Hon Can Wakef Cathl 08; Sen Lect York St Jo Univ 08–17; rtd 17; PtO *York* 17–18. *75 Quarrydale Road, Sutton-in-Ashfield NG17 4DR* T: (01623) 550830 E: j.a.williams23@btinternet.com

WILLIAMS, John Barrie. b 38. Univ of Wales (Cardiff) MSc 77 DipEd 80 PhD 91. St Mich Coll Llan 89. **d** 87 **p** 88. NSM Newcastle *Llan* 87–89; C Port Talbot St Theodore 89; PtO from 89. *Shorncliffe, 11 Priory Oak, Bridgend CF31 2HY* T: (01656) 660369

WILLIAMS, John Beattie. b 42. Univ of Wales BA 66. Cuddesdon Coll 67. **d** 69 **p** 69. C St Helier *S'wark* 69–70; C Yeovil H Trin *B & W* 70–76; Chapl to the Deaf *Sarum* 76–78; P-in-c Ebbesbourne Wake w Fifield Bavant and Alvediston 76–78; Chapl to the Deaf *B & W* 78–83; TV Fareham H Trin *Portsm* 83–94; R W Wittering and Birdham w Itchenor *Chich* 94–11; rtd 11; PtO *Chich* from 12. *28 Harrow Drive, West Wittering, Chichester PO20 8EJ* T: (01243) 670843 E: witteringjb@outlook.com

WILLIAMS, John David Anthony. b 55. Open Univ BA 98. St Steph Ho Ox 85. **d** 87 **p** 88. C Paignton St Jo *Ex* 87–90; C Heavitree w Ex St Paul 90–91; TV 91–01; P-in-c Exminster and Kenn 01–15; R Exminster, Kenn, Kenton w Mamhead, and Powderham from 15. *The Rectory, Milbury Lane, Exminster, Exeter EX6 8AD* T: (01392) 824283 E: john_williams55@btinternet.com

WILLIAMS, John Francis Meyler. b 34. St Jo Coll Cam BA 56 MA 60. Sarum & Wells Th Coll 79. **d** 81 **p** 82. C Hadleigh w Layham and Shelley *St E* 81–84; P-in-c Campsey Ashe and Marlesford 84–87; R Campsea Ashe w Marlesford, Parham and Hacheston 87–95; P-in-c Kedington 95–97; rtd 97; Chapl St Kath Convent Parmoor 97–98; PtO *Ox* 01–05. *2 Capel Court, The Burgage, Prestbury, Cheltenham GL52 3EL* T: (01242) 577764 E: denbygreen@gmail.com

WILLIAMS, John Frederick Arthur. b 26. Lon Univ BSc 50 Southn Univ PhD 53. Ridley Hall Cam 63. **d** 65 **p** 66. C Cambridge H Sepulchre w All SS *Ely* 65–66; P-in-c Cambridge St Mark 66–67; V Portswood Ch Ch *Win* 67–90; Assoc V 90–93; C Win Ch Ch 93–96; rtd 96; PtO *Win* 96–16. *120 Bellemoor Road, Southampton SO15 7QY* T: (023) 8077 1482

WILLIAMS, John Gilbert. b 36. St Aid Birkenhead 64. **d** 67 **p** 68. C Bollington St Jo *Ches* 67; C Oxton 69–72; P-in-c Acton Beauchamp and Evesbatch w Stanford Bishop *Heref* 72–76; P-in-c Castle Frome 72–76; P-in-c Bishop's Frome 72–76; R Kingsland 76–83; P-in-c Eardisland 77–83; P-in-c Aymestrey and Leinthall Earles w Wigmore etc 82–83; R Cradley w Mathon and Storridge 83–94; R Norton St Philip w Hemington, Hardington etc *B & W* 94–01; rtd 01; PtO *St D* from 02; *S & B* from 14. *Bronydd, 69 St Davids Park, Llanfaes, Brecon LD3 8EQ* T: (01874) 938196 E: cynwyl@tiscali.co.uk

WILLIAMS, Canon John Heard. b 35. Bris Univ BA 58. Clifton Th Coll 59. **d** 59 **p** 60. C Tunbridge Wells Ch Ch *Roch* 59–65;

V Forest Gate St Sav *Chelmsf* 65–75; P-in-c W Ham St Matt 72–75; TR Forest Gate St Sav w W Ham St Matt 75–12; Hon Can Chelmsf Cathl 82–05; rtd 12. *15 Sheldrake Drive, Bristol BS16 1UD* T: 0117-279 6038 E: jheardwilliams@yahoo.co.uk

WILLIAMS, Canon John Keith. b 63. Ridley Hall Cam 95. **d** 97 **p** 98. C Potters Bar *St Alb* 97–99; C Bishop's Stortford St Mich 99–01; P-in-c Bishop's Stortford 01–08; TR Cheshunt 08–17; TR Hemel Hempstead from 17; Hon Can St Alb from 15. *The Rectory, High Street, Hemel Hempstead HP1 3AE* T: (01442) 265272 E: teamrector@hotmail.com

WILLIAMS, Prof John Mark Gruffydd. b 52. St Pet Coll Ox BA 73 MSc 76 MA 77 DPhil 79 Ox Univ DSc FBPsS 84. EAMTC 86. **d** 89 **p** 90. NSM Girton *Ely* 91–03; PtO *Ban* 91–03; NSM Wheatley *Ox* 03–09; PtO 09–11; Hon Can Ch Ch 11–19. *Hollyfield Cottage, 17 Bell Lane, Wheatley, Oxford OX33 1XY* T: (01865) 422037 E: mark.williams@psychiatry.oxford.ac.uk

WILLIAMS, Canon John Peter Philip. b 49. Open Univ BA 84. Chich Th Coll 71. **d** 72 **p** 73. C Abergele *St As* 72–77; R Henllan and Llanefydd 77–82; R Henllan and Llanefydd and Bylchau 82–11; rtd 11; PtO *St As* from 11. *72 Crud y Castell, Denbigh LL16 4PQ* T: (01745) 817319 E: jppwilliams@tiscali.co.uk

WILLIAMS, Canon John Richard. b 48. Rhodes Univ BA 68 K Coll Lon BD 72 AKC 72. **d** 73 **p** 74. C E London St Alb S Africa 73–74; C King William's Town 74–76; C Addington *Cant* 77–80; C Minster-in-Sheppey 80–86; R Temple Ewell w Lydden 86–90; V Hound *Win* 90–94; V Highcliffe w Hinton Admiral 94–03; RD Christchurch 98–03; Chapl Montreux w Gstaad *Eur* 03–06; Switzerland 04–06; rtd 08; PtO *Sarum* from 14. *The Old Bakery, Gussage All Saints, Wimborne BH21 5ET* T: (01258) 841464 E: jmwilliams@mbzonline.net

WILLIAMS, Canon John Roger. b 37. Westmr Coll Ox MTh 97. Lich Th Coll 60. **d** 63 **p** 64. C Wem *Lich* 63–66; C Wolverhampton St Pet 66–69; R Pudleston w Hatf *Heref* 69–74; P-in-c Stoke Prior w Humber 69–74; P-in-c Docklow 69–74; V Fenton *Lich* 74–81; R Shipston-on-Stour w Honington and Idlicote *Cov* 81–92; RD Shipston 83–90; Hon Can Cov Cathl 90–00; R Lighthorne 92–00; V Chesterton 92–00; V Newbold Pacey w Moreton Morrell 92–00; P-in-c Denstone w Ellastone and Stanton *Lich* 00–05; Master St Jo Hosp Lich 05–11; rtd 11; PtO *Lich* from 11. *3 Curborough Road, Lichfield WS13 7NG* T: (01543) 419339

WILLIAMS, John Roger. b 31. Bris Univ BA 55 Lon Univ BD 57. Tyndale Hall Bris 57. **d** 57 **p** 58. C Islington H Trin Cloudesley Square *Lon* 57–60; Travelling Sec IVF 60–64; V Selly Hill St Steph *Birm* 64–74; P-in-c Chilwell *S'well* 74–75; V 75–90; Dioc Tourism Officer 90–95; P-in-c Perlethorpe 90–95; P-in-c Norton Cuckney 90–95; rtd 95; PtO *Derby* 95–11; *S'well* from 11. *21 Chestnut Avenue, Nottingham NG3 6FU* T: 0115-962 2897 E: jrefw.chestnut@btinternet.com

WILLIAMS, John Strettle. b 44. DipEd 73 BA 84. NOC 77. **d** 80 **p** 81. Chapl Cen Liv Coll of FE 80–85; Chapl City Coll Liv 85–09; NSM Liv St Paul Stoneycroft 80–83; NSM Liv Our Lady and St Nic 83–09; Chapl RNR 84–90; CF (TA) from 95; rtd 09. *3 Orchard Dene, Craven Road, Rainhill, Prescot L35 0LT* T: 0151-426 9598 M: 07736-629453

WILLIAMS, Jonathan Anthony. b 65. Wycliffe Hall Ox BTh 95. **d** 98 **p** 99. C Denton Ch Ch *Man* 98–02; R Burnage St Marg 02–05; Hon C Ox St Matt 09–11; P-in-c Wootton 11–18; V 18–19; Hon C Ox St Matt from 19. *St Matthew's Vicarage, 65 Marlborough Road, Oxford OX1 4LW*

WILLIAMS, Jonathan Lane. b 59. Dorset Inst of HE 85. STETS 96. **d** 99 **p** 00. NSM Moordown *Win* 99–16; NSM Winton, Moordown and Charminster from 16; Chapl Hants Hosps NHS Foundn Trust from 07. *28 Queen Mary Avenue, Moordown, Bournemouth BH9 1TS* T/F: (01202) 531630 M: 07977-444186 E: jonathan.williams7@ntlworld.com

WILLIAMS, The Ven Jonathan Simon. b 60. Univ of Wales (Cardiff) BSc 81. Coll of Resurr Mirfield 83. **d** 86 **p** 87. C Gelligaer *Llan* 86–89; C Cwmbran *Mon* 89–90; TV 90–97; V Marshfield and Peterstone Wentloog etc 97–00; TR Bassaleg 00–12; AD 99–12; Adn Newport from 12; Can St Woolos Cathl from 07; Prec from 14. *The Archdeaconry, 93 Stow Hill, Newport NP20 4EA* T: (01633) 215206 E: venjsw@gmail.com

WILLIAMS, Mrs Josephine. b 42. NOC 05. **d** 07 **p** 08. NSM Bootle Ch Ch *Liv* 07–16; PtO from 16. *1 Clayfield Close, Bootle L20 3QN* T: 0151-933 7729 F: 525 1995 E: josiewilliams1@aol.com

WILLIAMS, Ms Josephine Mary. b 47. Reading Univ BEd 78 Hatf Poly MEd 87. SAOMC 96. **d** 99 **p** 00. NSM Terriers Ox 99–02; Chapl HM YOI Aylesbury 02–09; rtd 09; PtO Ox 09–13; *Birm* from 13. *85 Newton Road, Knowle, Solihull B93 9HN* T: (01564) 898607 E: jo.williams58@gmail.com

WILLIAMS, Miss Josephine Sharne Emma. b 76. **d** 13 **p** 14. C Cen Wolverhampton *Lich* 13–16; V Reading St Mark and

All SS *Ox* from 16. *Hamelsham, Downshire Square, Reading RT1 6NJ* M: 07977-142450 E: revdjowilliams@gmail.com

WILLIAMS, Joyce. *See* WILLIAMS, Kathleen Joyce

WILLIAMS, Julian Thomas. b 65. Clare Coll Cam BA 87. Wycliffe Hall Ox BA 90. **d** 91 **p** 92. Min Can St D Cathl 91–94; C St D Cathl 91–94; V Cil-y-Cwm and Ystrad-ffin w Rhandir-mwyn etc 94–00; R Nursling and Rownhams *Win* 00–19. *Address temp unknown*

WILLIAMS, Karl André. b 61. All SS Cen for Miss & Min 10. **d** 16 **p** 17. C Gt Meols *Ches* 16–19; V Dukinfield St Mark from 19. *St Mark's Vicarage, 2 Church Square, Dukinfield SK16 4PX* T: 0161-330 2783 M: 07463-876753

WILLIAMS, Mrs Kathleen Joyce. b 47. Dur Univ TCert 71. St Jo Coll Nottm 03. **d** 05 **p** 06. C Exning St Martin w Landwade *St E* 05–08; V 08–12; rtd 12; Hon C Bath St Sav w Swainswick and Woolley *B & W* 12–18. *Coastlands, Oxwich, Swansea SA3 1LS* E: joyfulwilliams2004@yahoo.co.uk

WILLIAMS, Keith. b 37. St Jo Coll Nottm 83. **d** 85 **p** 86. C Holbeck *Ripon* 85–88; R Swanstead 88–95; V Batley All SS *Wakef* 95–01; P-in-c Purlwell 95–00; rtd 01; PtO *Ripon* 01–14; *Leeds* from 14. *17 Kirkfield Drive, Colton, Leeds LS15 9DR* T: 0113-260 5852 M: 07709-027328

WILLIAMS, Keith Douglas. b 41. EMMTC 86. **d** 89 **p** 90. NSM Netherfield *S'well* 89–07; NSM Colwick 89–07; NSM Gedling 95–07; Chapl Notts Healthcare NHS Trust 93–03; rtd 07; PtO *S'well* from 07. *36 Bramble Court, Carnarvon Grove, Gedling, Nottingham NG4 3HX* T: 0115-961 4850 E: keiwil@ntlworld.com

WILLIAMS, Keith Graham. b 38. Reading Univ MSc 70 MRICS 62. Cranmer Hall Dur. **d** 77 **p** 78. C Almondbury *Wakef* 77–81; C Chapelthorpe 81–82; V Ryhill 82–88; V E Ardsley 88–99; RD Wakef 96–99; rtd 03; PtO *Chich* from 03. *The Granary, 52-54 Belle Hill, Bexhill-on-Sea TN40 2AP* T: (01424) 734093

WILLIAMS, Kelvin George John. b 36. ALCD 62. **d** 62 **p** 63. C Bath Abbey w St Jas *B & W* 62–65; CF (TA) 64–65 and 70–79; Chapl R Nat Hosp for Rheumatic Diseases Bath 64–65; CF 65–68; C Clevedon St Andr *B & W* 68–70; V Ston Easton w Farrington Gurney 70–74; P-in-c Bradford 74–75; R Bradford w Oake, Hillfarrance and Heathfield 75–76; NSM Puriton and Pawlett 89–91; V 92–02; NSM Bridgwater Deanery 91–92; rtd 02; PtO *B & W* 03–04 and from 07; P-in-c Weston Zoyland w Chedzoy 04–07. *Highlands, Knowleyards Road, Middlezoy, Bridgwater TA7 0NY* T: (01823) 698413 E: reverendwilliams@btinternet.com

WILLIAMS, Lea John. b 84. Wolv Univ BA 06 Aber Univ BA 10. Ripon Coll Cuddesdon MTh 16. **d** 16 **p** 17. C Gt Dunmow and Barnston *Chelmsf* from 16. *17 Standrums, Great Dunmow CM6 1TY* T: (01371) 705066 E: lea@stmarysgreatdunmow.org.uk

WILLIAMS, Lee Lawrence. b 75. St Steph Ho Ox 98. **d** 01 **p** 02. C Cowbridge *Llan* 01–04. *34 Queens Drive, Llantwit Fadre, Pontypridd CF83 2NT*

WILLIAMS, Mrs Linda Leonie Paula. b 56. UEA BA 79. SEITE 04. **d** 07 **p** 08. NSM Kenley *S'wark* 07–10; C Harpenden St Nic *St Alb* 10–19; P-in-c Kimpton w Ayot St Lawrence from 19. *The Vicarage, 11 High Street, Kimpton, Hitchin SG4 8RA*

WILLIAMS, Lloyd. b 43. Oak Hill Th Coll 71. **d** 74 **p** 75. C Laisterdyke *Bradf* 74–77; C Hoole *Ches* 77–80; V Rawthorpe *Wakef* 80–84; HM Pris Leeds 84–85; Chapl HM Pris Cardiff 85–88; Chapl HM Pris Aldington 88–95; R Aldington w Bonnington and Bilsington *Cant* 88–95; RD N Lympne 94–95; P-in-c Tuen Mun Hong Kong 95–99; V Clayton *Bradf* 99–03; rtd 03; PtO *York* 04–07; *Wakef* 07–14; *Blackb* from 14. *18 Fosbrooke House, 8 Clifton Drive, Lytham St Annes FY8 5RQ* T: (01253) 667011 M: 07866-604345 E: revlloydwilliams@aol.com

WILLIAMS, Lois. *See* WILLIAMS, Catherine Lois

WILLIAMS, Canon Louise Margaret. b 66. Lanc Univ BA 87. St Jo Coll Nottm 88. **d** 91 **p** 94. Par Dn W Ham *Chelmsf* 91–94; C Harold Hill St Geo 94–95; PtO 95–96; C Southend St Sav Westcliff 95–10; Chapl Asst Southend Health Care NHS Trust 97–10; R S Shoebury *Chelmsf* from 10; Hon Can Chelmsf Cathl from 17. *The Rectory, 42 Church Road, Shoeburyness, Southend-on-Sea SS3 9EU* T: (01702) 292778 E: revlwilliams@aol.com

WILLIAMS, Marion. b 56. St Mellitus Coll 13. **d** 14 **p** 15. NSM Romford St Andr *Chelmsf* 14–15; NSM Cranham 15–18; P-in-c 17–19; R from 19; Chapl St Clare Hospice 15–17. *1 Boyd Close, Upminster RM14 3BG* T: (01708) 228308 *or* (01279) 773700 E: marionbubbs@aol.com

WILLIAMS, Canon Mark. b 73. Pemb Coll Cam BA 94 MA 98 Ox Univ BA 98 MA 02. Ripon Coll Cuddesdon 95 Ven English Coll Rome 97. **d** 98 **p** 99. C Caerphilly *Llan* 98–00; V Walworth St Chris *S'wark* 00–10; Warden Pemb Coll Miss Walworth 00–10; V Kennington St Jo w St Jas from 10; Dioc

Voc Adv from 02; Hon Can Asante Mampong Ghana from 15. *The Vicarage, 92 Vassall Road, London SW9 6JA* T: (020) 7735 9340 E: fr_mark@yahoo.com

WILLIAMS, Mark. b 64. St Mich Coll Llan BTh 94. **d** 97 **p** 98. C Mountain Ash *Llan* 97; C Mountain Ash and Miskin 97–99; C Neath w Llantwit 99–01; C Neath 01–02; V Skewen 02–12; V Port Talbot St Theodore from 12. *St Theodore's Vicarage, Talbot Road, Port Talbot SA13 1LB* T: (01639) 883935

WILLIAMS, Mark. *See* WILLIAMS, Howell Mark

WILLIAMS, Mark Andrew. b 71. STETS 11. **d** 14 **p** 15. C Portchester *Portsm* 14–17; P-in-c Gatten St Paul from 17; P-in-c Sandown Ch Ch from 17. *St Paul's Vicarage, 2 St Paul's Crescent, Shanklin PO37 7AW* M: 07873-406558 E: williams_mark1@sky.com *or* revwilliams71@gmail.com

WILLIAMS, Mark John. b 66. St Martin's Coll Lanc BA 88 PGCE 92 Heythrop Coll Lon MA 07 Man Univ MPhil 17. Cranmer Hall Dur 98. **d** 00 **p** 01. C Hockerill *St Alb* 00–03; TV Chipping Barnet 03–09; V Burnley St Matt w H Trin *Blackb* 09–17; TR Worsley *Man* from 17. *St Mark's Rectory, Walkden Road, Worsley, Manchester M28 2WH* T: 0161-799 6082 E: rector.mark.john.williams@gmail.com

WILLIAMS, Mark Robert. b 62. Spurgeon's Coll Lon BA 83 Univ Coll of Swansea PGCE 84. Ripon Coll Cuddesdon 99. **d** 01 **p** 02. C Wellington and Distr *B & W* 01–05; V Belmont *S'wark* 05–19; Ecum Adv Croydon Area 13–19; V Deeping St James *Linc* from 19. *The Vicarage, 16 Church Street, Deeping St James, Peterborough PE6 8HD* E: revblots@outlook.com

WILLIAMS, The Ven Martin Infeld. b 37. SS Coll Cam BA 62 MA 92. Chich Th Coll 62. **d** 64 **p** 65. C Greenford H Cross *Lon* 64–70; Tutor Chich Th Coll 70–75; Vice-Prin 75–77; V Roath St German *Llan* 77–92; Adn Margam 92–01; Adn Morgannwg 02–04; Treas Llan Cathl 92–04; V Penydarren 92–04; rtd 04. *82 Walker Road, Splott, Cardiff CF24 2EN* T: (029) 2221 9392

WILLIAMS, Martin Jonathan. b 63. Birm Univ BA 84. Trin Coll Bris 96. **d** 98 **p** 99. C Bisley and W End *Guildf* 98–01; C Gerrards Cross and Fulmer *Ox* 01–09; R 09–18; Jt AD Amersham from 17. *Evenley House, Sly Corner, Lee Common, Great Missenden HP16 9LD* M: 07974-010703

WILLIAMS, Mary Edith. b 50. Darlington Tr Coll BEd 73. Cranmer Hall Dur 00. **d** 02 **p** 03. C Filey *York* 02–06; V 06–12; rtd 12; PtO *Ripon* 13–14; *Leeds* from 14. *The Mill House, Parkgate Lane, Brompton on Swale, Richmond DL10 7HA* T: (01748) 811241 E: wilbaric@hotmail.co.uk

WILLIAMS, The Ven Meurig Llwyd. b 61. Univ of Wales (Abth) BA 83 PGCE 84 Univ of Wales (Cardiff) BD 90. Westcott Ho Cam 90. **d** 92 **p** 93. C Holyhead w Rhoscolyn w Llanfair-yn-Neubwll *Ban* 92–95; P-in-c Denio w Abererch 95–96; V 96–99; V Cardiff Dewi Sant *Llan* 99–05; Adn Ban 05–11; TR Bangor 06–11; TV 11; Bp's Commissary and Chapl *Eur* from 11; Adn France from 16; Can Malta Cathl from 11. *47 rue Capitaine Crespel, 1050 Brussels, Belgium* T: (0032) (2) 213 7480 *or* (47) 285 0629 E: meurig.williams@churchofengland.org

WILLIAMS, Michael. *See* WILLIAMS, David Michael Rochfort

WILLIAMS, Canon Michael Dermot Andrew. b 57. Ex Univ BA 86 Lon Univ MA 02. Ripon Coll Cuddesdon 90. **d** 92 **p** 93. NSM Christow, Ashton, Trusham and Bridford *Ex* 92–97; NSM Marston w Elsfield *Ox* 97–99; Chief Exec Radcliffe Infirmary NHS Trust 97–99; V Shipton-under-Wychwood w Milton, Fifield etc *Ox* 99–02; RD Chipping Norton 01–02; Exec Dir Thames Valley HA 02–05; NSM Kennington *Ox* 04–05; Chief Exec Taunton and Somerset NHS Foundn Trust from 05; Hon C Topsham *Ex* 07–14; Hon C Wear 09–14; Hon C Topsham and Wear 14–17; Can Res Ex Cathl from 17; Treas from 18. *9 Cathedral Close, Exeter EX1 1EZ* T: (01392) 421832 E: williamsmda@btinternet.com

WILLIAMS, Canon Michael Joseph. b 42. St Jo Coll Dur BA 68. Bernard Gilpin Soc Dur 63 Cranmer Hall Dur 64. **d** 70 **p** 71. C Toxteth Park St Philemon *Liv* 70–75; TV Toxteth St Philemon w St Gabr 75–78; Dir Past Studies St Jo Coll Dur 78–88; Prin NOC 89–99; Hon Can Liv Cathl 92–99; P-in-c Bolton St Pet *Man* 99–04; V 04–07; P-in-c Bolton St Phil 04–07; Hon Can Man Cathl 00–07; AD Bolton 02–05; rtd 07; PtO *Man* from 08. *51 Cotswold Drive, Horwich, Bolton BL6 7DE* T: (01204) 667162 E: m.j.williams42@hotmail.co.uk

WILLIAMS, Michael Robert John. b 41. Cranmer Hall Dur 67. **d** 70 **p** 71. C Middleton *Man* 70–73; C-in-c Blackley White Moss St Mark CD 73–79; R Blackley St Mark White Moss 79–86; R Gorton Em 86–96; R Gorton Em w St Jas 96–06; rtd 06; PtO *Man* from 06. *26 Hawthorn Avenue, Bury BL8 1DU* T: 0161-761 4712

WILLIAMS, Nia Catrin. b 69. Univ of Wales (Cardiff) BTh 96. St As Minl Tr Course 97. **d** 98 **p** 99. C Llanrhos *St As* 98–02; C Colwyn Bay 02–06; P-in-c Towyn and St George 06–08; V Glanogwen and Llanllechid w St Ann's and Pentir *Ban* 08–12; AD Ogwen 10–12; Can Missr Ban Cathl 12–15; CMD

Officer 12–15; Dir of Ords 12–14; Dir of Voc *St As* 15–16; CF from 16. *c/o MOD Chaplains (Army)* T: (01264) 383430 E: niacatrin13@gmail.com

WILLIAMS, Nicholas Jolyon. b 68. Univ of Wales (Swansea) BA 89. Wycliffe Hall Ox BTh 96. **d** 96 **p** 97. C Ditton *Roch* 96–99; C N Farnborough *Guildf* 99–05; P-in-c Tongham 05–11; V Guildf Ch Ch from 11; AD Guildf from 17. *Christ Church Vicarage, 25 Waterden Road, Guildford GU1 2AZ* T: (01483) 568870 E: nick@christchurchguildford.com

WILLIAMS, Nicholas Lindsey. b 62. Birkbeck Coll Lon BA 02 MA 18 Kent Univ BA 09. SEITE 06. **d** 09 **p** 10. NSM Dartford H Trin *Roch* 09–11; P-in-c Darenth 11–14; P-in-c Horton Kirby and Sutton-at-Hone 13–14; V Darent Valley 14–16; V E Malling, Wateringbury and Teston 16–19; V E Malling and Teston from 19; P-in-c Larkfield from 19. *The Vicarage, 2 The Grange, East Malling, West Malling ME19 6AH* T: (01732) 843282 E: father.nick@btinternet.com

WILLIAMS, Nick. *See* WILLIAMS, James Nicholas Owen

WILLIAMS, The Very Revd Nigel Howard. b 63. St Mich Coll Llan 93. **d** 95 **p** 96. C Denbigh and Nantglyn *St As* 95–97; P-in-c Llanrwst and Llanddoget and Capel Garmon 97–98; R 98–04; V Colwyn Bay 04–08; V Colwyn Bay w Brynymaen 08–11; AD Rhos 04–09; Dean and Lib St As Cathl from 11; TR St Asaph 11–14. *The Deanery, Upper Denbigh Road, St Asaph LL17 0RL* T: (01745) 583597 E: nigelwilliams@churchinwales.org.uk

WILLIAMS, Nigel Mark. b 89. Trin Coll Bris 17. **d** 19. C Keynsham *B & W* from 19. *37 Mayfields, Keynsham, Bristol BS31 1BW* E: nigelwilliams@keynshamparish.org.uk

WILLIAMS, Olivia Hazel. b 55. Dun Laoghaire Inst CertEd 98 TCD BTh 01. CITC 98. **d** 01 **p** 02. C Greystones *D & G* 01–05; Abp's Dom Chapl 03–05; I Carlow w Urglin and Staplestown *C & O* 05–16; rtd 16. *Tig an tSagairt, Slaney Rise, Ballymurphy Road, Tullow, Co Carlow, R93 FR90, Republic of Ireland* T: (00353) (59) 915 2780 M: 86-837 0794 E: williams.olivia2@gmail.com

WILLIAMS, Owen Leslie. b 80. Sussex Univ BSc 01 MSc Cam Univ BTh 13. Ridley Hall Cam 10. **d** 13 **p** 14. C Uppingham w Ayston and Belton w Wardley *Pet* 13–16; C Oakham, Ashwell, Braunston, Brooke, Egleton etc 16–17. *64A Nowton Road, Bury St Edmunds IP33 2BU* E: rev.o.l.williams@gmail.com

WILLIAMS, Canon Paul Andrew. b 62. Oak Hill Th Coll BA 91. **d** 91 **p** 92. C Ware Ch Ch *St Alb* 91–94; C Harold Wood *Chelmsf* 94–99; C Langham Place All So *Lon* 99–06; V Fulwood *Sheff* from 06; Hon Can Sheff Cathl from 11. *The Vicarage, 2 Chorley Drive, Sheffield S10 3RR* T: 0114-230 1911 E: paulwilliams@fulwoodchurch.co.uk

✠**WILLIAMS, The Rt Revd Paul Gavin.** b 68. Grey Coll Dur BA 89. Wycliffe Hall Ox 90. **d** 92 **p** 93 **c** 09. C Muswell Hill St Jas w St Matt *Lon* 92–96; C Clifton Ch Ch w Em *Bris* 96–99; R Gerrards Cross and Fulmer *Ox* 99–09; Hon Can Ch Ch 07–09; Area Bp Kensington *Lon* 09–15; Bp S'well and Nottm from 15. *Bishop's Manor, Bishop's Drive, Southwell NG25 0JR* T: (01636) 812112 E: bishop@southwell.anglican.org

WILLIAMS, Canon Paul Rhys. b 58. St Andr Univ MTheol 82. Westcott Ho Cam 83. **d** 86 **p** 87. Asst Chapl Selw Coll Cam 86–87; C Chatham St Steph *Roch* 87–90; V Gillingham St Aug 90–95; Bp's Dom Chapl 95–03; Hon Can Roch Cathl 01–03; V Tewkesbury w Walton Cardiff and Twyning *Glouc* from 03; AD Tewkesbury and Winchcombe 09–16; Hon Can Glouc Cathl from 06. *Abbey House, Church Street, Tewkesbury GL20 5SR* T: (01684) 293333 *or* 850959 F: 273113 E: vicar@tewkesburyabbey.org.uk

WILLIAMS, Mrs Pauline Mary. b 52. Univ of Wales (Cardiff) BD 96 Trin Coll Carmarthen PGCE 97. St Mich Coll Llan 00. **d** 02 **p** 03. C Coity w Nolton *Llan* 02–06; P-in-c Abercynon 06–11; V Baglan 11–13; Dioc Children's Officer 06–13; P-in-c Costa Almeria and Costa Calida *Eur* 13–16; PtO *Llan* from 16. *3 Ewenny Road, Wick, Cowbridge CF71 7QA* T: (01656) 890066 E: williamspm89@hotmail.com

WILLIAMS, Peter. *See* WILLIAMS, Cecil Peter

WILLIAMS, Peter Charles. b 50. SWMTC 98. **d** 01 **p** 02. OLM Landrake w St Erney and Botus Fleming *Truro* 01–15; rtd 15; PtO *B & W* from 15. *8 Parsons Close, Nether Stowey, Bridgwater TA5 1JS* E: peter.freda@btinternet.com

WILLIAMS, Canon Peter John. b 55. Southn Univ BTh 80. Chich Th Coll 76. **d** 80 **p** 81. C Chepstow *Mon* 80–84; C Morriston *S & B* 84–85; V Glantawe 85–88; R Reynoldston w Penrice and Llangennith 88–05; R Llangennith w Llanmadoc and Cheriton 05–14; Dioc Soc Resp Officer 88–14; Hon Can Brecon Cathl 04–11; Can Res Brecon Cathl 11–14; rtd 15; PtO *S & B* from 15. *10 Woodcote Green, Grovesend, Swansea SA4 8DR* T: (01792) 386391 E: canon.peter.williams@dreamorchid.co.uk

WILLIAMS, Philip Allan. b 48. Bris Univ BSc 69 CertEd 74. Trin Coll Bris 86. **d** 88 **p** 89. C Heref St Pet w St Owen and St Jas 88–93; R Peterchurch w Vowchurch, Turnastone and Dorstone 93–96; P-in-c Holmer w Huntington 96–01; V 01–13; rtd 13; PtO *Ches* from 14. *128 Rugby Drive, Macclesfield SK10 2JF* T: (01625) 432037 E: philtherev@gmail.com

WILLIAMS, The Ven Philip Andrew. b 64. Sheff Univ BA 86. Cranmer Hall Dur 88. **d** 90 **p** 91. C Hillsborough and Wadsley Bridge *Sheff* 90–94; C Lenton Abbey S'well 94–96; P-in-c 96–02; C Wollaton Park 94–96; V Porchester 02–17; AD Gedling 05–17; Assoc Adn Transition Min 17–19; Adn Nottingham *S'well* from 19; Hon Can S'well Minster from 11. *The Vicarage, 2 Cocker Beck, Lambley, Nottingham NG4 4QP* T: 0115-931 3874 E: archd-nottm@southwell.anglican.org

WILLIAMS, Philip James. b 52. St Chad's Coll Dur BA 73. Coll of Resurr Mirfield 74. **d** 76 **p** 77. C Stoke upon Trent *Lich* 76–80; TV 80; Chapl N Staffs Poly 80–84; TV Stoke-upon-Trent 80–84; R Shrewsbury St Giles w Sutton and Atcham 84–14; rtd 14. *6 Latchford Lane, Shrewsbury SY1 4YG* E: flyingvic@btinternet.com

WILLIAMS, Philip Robert. b 78. St Mellitus Coll. **d** 13 **p** 14. C Onslow Square and S Kensington St Aug *Lon* 13–14; C Spitalfields Ch Ch w All SS 14–16; R Shadwell St Paul w Ratcliffe St Jas from 16. *St Paul's Shadwell Rectory, 298 The Highway, London E1W 3DH* M: 07815-146350

WILLIAMS, Mrs Rachel Mary. b 65. All SS Cen for Miss & Min 12. **d** 15 **p** 16. NSM Bolsover *Derby* from 15. *Manor Farm, 25 Dawgates Lane, Sutton-in-Ashfield NG17 3DA* T: (01623) 513048 M: 07975-631066 E: revrwilliams25@gmail.com

WILLIAMS, Canon Richard Elwyn. b 57. Hull Univ BA 79. Coll of Resurr Mirfield 79. **d** 81 **p** 82. C Altrincham St Geo *Ches* 81–84; C Stockport St Thos 84–85; C Stockport St Thos w St Pet 86; R Withington St Crispin *Man* 86–95; V Alveston *Cov* from 95; RD Fosse 99–07; Hon Can Cov Cathl from 06. *The Vicarage, Wellesbourne Road, Alveston, Stratford-upon-Avon CV37 7QB* T: (01789) 292777 E: rickthevic@googlemail.com

WILLIAMS, Canon Richard Henry Lowe. b 31. Liv Univ BA 52. K Coll (NS) BD 64 Ridley Hall Cam 54. **d** 56 **p** 57. C Drypool St Andr and St Pet *York* 56–59; Canada 59–64; V Kirkdale St Athanasius *Liv* 64–68; R Much Woolton 68–79; R Croft w Southworth 79–89; Dioc Communications Officer 79–97; Hon Can Liv Cathl 88–97; R Wavertree St Mary 89–97; rtd 97; PtO *Liv* from 97. *16 Childwall Crescent, Liverpool L16 7PQ* T: 0151-722 7962

WILLIAMS, Richard Lawrence. b 62. Warw Univ BSc 83 ACA 87. Wycliffe Hall Ox 95. **d** 97 **p** 98. C Wallington S'wark 97–00; V Addiscombe St Mary Magd w St Martin 00–09; P-in-c Cranbrook *Cant* 09–13; V 13–15; AD Weald 12–13; Finance Dir Roch DBF from 17; PtO *Cant* from 18. *Old Tannery Cottage, 3A Smallhythe Road, Tenterden TN30 7LH* T: (01634) 560009 M: 07947-010382

WILLIAMS, Robert Jeffrey Hopkin. b 62. Univ of Wales (Abth) BA 84 ALAM. Chich Th Coll BTh 90. **d** 90 **p** 91. C Eastbourne St Mary *Chich* 90–94; R Upper St Leonards St Jo 94–02; V Twickenham St Mary *Lon* from 02. *37 Arragon Road, Twickenham TW1 3NG* T: (020) 8892 2318

WILLIAMS, The Ven Robert John. b 51. Cartrefle Coll of Educn CertEd 72 Univ of Wales (Ban) BEd 73 MA 92. St Mich Coll Llan BD 76. **d** 76 **p** 77. C Swansea St Mary and H Trin *S & B* 76–78; Chapl Univ of Wales (Swansea) 78–88; Children's Adv 81–88; Asst Dir of Educn 81–88; Bp's Chapl for Th Educn 83–88; R Reynoldston w Penrice and Llangennith 84–88; R Denbigh and Nantglyn *St As* 88–94; V Sketty *S & B* 94–99; Dir of Ords 94–99; P-in-c Port Eynon w Rhosili and Llanddewi and Knelston 99–03; Can Brecon Cathl 95–00; Adn Gower 00–16; rtd 16; PtO *S & B* from 16; *Llan* from 18. *11 Raleigh Close, Sketty, Swansea SA2 8LE* T: (01792) 555501

WILLIAMS, Roger. *See* WILLIAMS, David Roger

WILLIAMS, Roger. *See* WILLIAMS, John Roger

WILLIAMS, Roger Anthony. b 54. Univ of Wales (Lamp) BA 76. Bp Burgess Hall Lamp 72 Qu Coll Birm 76. **d** 78 **p** 79. C Llanelli St D 78–82; V Monkton 82–86; Chapl to the Deaf *B & W* 86–90; Chapl amongst Deaf People *Ox* 90–16; rtd 16; PtO *Ox* from 16. *Denchworth House, Denchworth, Wantage OX12 0DX* T: (01235) 868248 E: roger@rawapt.org.uk

WILLIAMS, Roger Stewart. b 54. Qu Coll Cam BA 75 MA 79. Wycliffe Hall Ox BA 78 MA 82. **d** 79 **p** 80. C Hamstead St Paul *Birm* 79–82; C Barking St Marg w St Patr *Chelmsf* 82–85; V Mildmay Grove St Jude and St Paul *Lon* 85–95; P-in-c Charles w Plymouth St Matthias *Ex* 95–09; Chapl Plymouth Univ 95–09; TR Bloxwich *Lich* from 09. *Bloxwich Rectory, 3 Elmore Row, Walsall WS3 2HR* T: (01922) 476598 E: williams.roger@gmail.com

WILLIAMS, Ronald Ernest Nathan. b 66. Univ of Sierra Leone BSc 95. St Jo Coll Nottm MTh 05. **d** 05 **p** 06. C Cowplain

Portsm 05–09; V Rusthall *Roch* from 09. *The Vicarage, Bretland Road, Rusthall, Tunbridge Wells TN4 8PB* T: (01892) 521357 M: 07796-655225 E: ronnierenw@hotmail.com

WILLIAMS, Ronald Hywel. b 35. St D Coll Lamp BA 62. **d** 63 **p** 64. C Machynlleth and Llanwrin *Ban* 63–66; C Llanaber w Caerdeon 66–69; C Hawarden *St As* 69–73; R Llansantffraid Glan Conwy and Eglwysbach 73–77; V Rhosllannerchrugog 77–88; R Cilcain and Nannerch and Rhydymwyn 88–92; V Llanbadarn Fawr w Capel Bangor and Goginan *St D* 92–95; V Llanbadarn Fawr 95–00; RD 94–00; rtd 00; PtO *St D* from 05. *15 Maes y Garn, Bow Street SY24 5DS* T: (01970) 820247

WILLIAMS (née TYDEMAN), Mrs Rosemary (Rose). b 47. Roehampton Inst TCert 69. SAOMC 97. **d** 00 **p** 01. NSM Walton H Trin *Ox* 00–03; NSM E and W Horndon w Lt Warley and Childerditch *Chelmsf* 03–12; rtd 12; PtO *Ox* from 12. *17 Wellington Avenue, Princes Risborough HP27 9HY* T: (01844) 274225 E: rosewilliamsgp@yahoo.co.uk

WILLIAMS, Canon Rowan Clare. b 67. K Coll Cam BA 90 MA 93 Jes Coll Cam BA 05 Clare Coll Cam PhD 14. Westcott Ho Cam 02. **d** 05 **p** 06. C Leic Resurr 05–08; Chapl Univ Hosps Leic NHS Trust 08–10; Chapl York Univ 10–18; Can Res and Prec *Pet* from 18. *Norman Hall, 15A Minster Precincts, Peterborough PE1 1XX* T: (01733) 355310 M: 07919-861912 E: rcw514@york.ac.uk *or* canon.precentor@peterborough-cathedral.org.uk

WILLIAMS, Rowan Douglas. *See* WILLIAMS OF OYSTERMOUTH, Rowan Douglas

WILLIAMS, Mrs Sandra Elizabeth. b 60. STETS 06. **d** 09 **p** 10. C Wrockwardine Deanery *Lich* 09–13; C Appleshaw, Kimpton, Thruxton, Fyfield etc *Win* 13–17; P-in-c 17–19; C W Purbeck *Sarum* from 19. *The Vicarage, West Street, Bere Regis, Wareham BH20 7HQ* E: sandra.williams3@btinternet.com

WILLIAMS (née CROSLAND), Mrs Sarah Rosita. b 50. St Mary's Coll Chelt CertEd 71 BEd 72. EAMTC 01. **d** 03 **p** 04. C Warmley, Syston and Bitton *Bris* 03–06; Asst Chapl Tervuren *Eur* 06–09; P-in-c Lydd *Cant* 10–13; R Brookland, Fairfield, Brenzett w Snargate etc 13–16; rtd 16; PtO *Cant* from 17. *Porfa Las, 15 Wheler Court, Faversham ME13 7NR* M: 07778-450357 E: revsarahwilliams@porfalas.plus.com

WILLIAMS, Canon Shamus Frank Charles. b 57. St Cath Coll Cam BA 79 MA 83. Ripon Coll Cuddesdon 81. **d** 84 **p** 85. C Swanage and Studland *Sarum* 84–87; C St Alb St Pet 87–90; TV Saffron Walden w Wendens Ambo and Littlebury *Chelmsf* 90–95; R Shingay Gp *Ely* from 95; RD Shingay 97–13; Hon Can Ely Cathl from 05. *18 High Street, Guilden Morden, Royston SG8 0JP* T: (01763) 853067 E: shamuswilliams@waitrose.com

WILLIAMS, Mrs Sheena Jane. b 72. Aber Univ LLB 95 Win Univ MA 11. STETS 07. **d** 10 **p** 11. C Swaythling *Win* 10–14; C Chandler's Ford 14–17; P-in-c N Stoneham and Bassett from 17. *The Rectory, 62 Glen Eyre Road, Southampton SO16 3NL* T: (023) 8076 8123 M: 07787-155321 E: rev@williamspost.me.uk

WILLIAMS, Stephen Clark. b 47. Univ of Wales (Cardiff) BSc(Econ) 69 Warw Univ MSc 70. Wycliffe Hall Ox 91. **d** 93 **p** 94. C High Wycombe *Ox* 93–96; C Walton H Trin 96–97; TV 97–03; Acting TR 01–03; P-in-c E and W Horndon w Lt Warley and Childerditch *Chelmsf* 03–12; Ind Chapl 05–12; rtd 12; PtO *Ox* from 12. *17 Wellington Avenue, Princes Risborough HP27 9HY* T: (01844) 274225 E: stevecwilliams@btinternet.com

WILLIAMS, Stephen Grant. b 51. K Coll Lon BD 73 AKC 73. **d** 75 **p** 76. C Paddington Ch Ch *Lon* 75–78; C Paddington St Jas 78–80; Chapl LSE 80–91; Chapl (Sen) Lon Univs 91–15; rtd 15. *4 Stanton Prior, 71 Darley Road, Eastbourne BN20 7UH* E: stephenwilliams6@gmail.com

WILLIAMS, Stephen James. b 52. Lon Univ BSc 73. Ridley Hall Cam 73. **d** 78 **p** 79. C Waltham Abbey *Chelmsf* 78–82; C Bedford St Paul *St Alb* 82–86; P-in-c Chalgrave 86–88; V Harlington from 86; Chapl Luton Sixth Form Coll 08–09; Chapl Luton and Dunstable Univ Hosp NHS Foundn Trust 04–11. *The Vicarage, Church Road, Harlington, Dunstable LU5 6LE* T: (01525) 872413 M: 07530-783196 E: sjw@harlingtonchurch.org.uk *or* sjw@lutonsfc.ac.uk

WILLIAMS, Stephen Lionel. b 48. St Kath Coll Liv CertEd 73 Open Univ BA 77. NOC 93. **d** 96 **p** 97. NSM Hough Green St Basil and All SS *Liv* 96–99; C Padgate 99–02; V Walton St Jo 02–13; rtd 13; PtO *Liv* from 16. *32 Kendal Park, Liverpool L12 9LS* M: 07913-603024 E: frstephen320@hotmail.com

WILLIAMS, Canon Stephen Stuart. b 60. Magd Coll Ox BA 82 Dur Univ BA 88. Cranmer Hall Dur 86. **d** 89 **p** 90. C W Derby Gd Shep *Liv* 89–93; Relig Affairs Producer BBC Radio Merseyside 92–00; TV Liv Our Lady and St Nic w St Anne 93–01; P-in-c Prestwich St Gabr *Man* 01–19; V from 19; C Prestwich St Mary from 10; C Prestwich St Marg from 10; Bp's Dom Chapl 01–05; Interfaith Adv from 05; Hon Can Man Cathl from 10. *St Gabriel's Vicarage, 8 Bishops Road, Prestwich,*

Manchester M25 0HT T: 0161-773 8839 M: 07757-411377 E: saintgabriel@talktalk.net

WILLIAMS, Susan. b 50. Swansea Coll of Educn CertEd 72. Ban Ord Course 94. **d** 97 **p** 98. NSM Criccieth w Treflys *Ban* 97–00; P-in-c 00–01; P-in-c Criccieth and Treflys w Llanystumdwy etc 01–02; R 02–10; rtd 11; PtO *Ban* from 11. *Taleifion, High Street, Criccieth LL52 0RN* T: (01766) 523222 *or* (01248) 354999 F: 523183

WILLIAMS, Ms Susan Jean. b 54. Ches Coll of HE MTh 00 Lanc Univ MA 02 PhD 09. NOC 95. **d** 98 **p** 99. C Prescot *Liv* 98–01; PtO *Blackb* 01–02; C Scotforth 02–05; P-in-c Chipping and Whitewell 05–09; Warden of Readers and Past Assts 09–13; Hon C Balderstone, Mellor and Samlesbury 11–13; V 13–16; Hon C Salesbury and Langho Billington 11–13; Vice-Prin LCTP 05–13; rtd 16; Hon C E Lonsdale *Blackb* from 16. *The New Vicarage, Church Lane, Tunstall, Carnforth LA6 2RQ* E: williams.ammasue@gmail.com

WILLIAMS, Mrs Susan Merrilyn Marsh. b 62. Univ of Wales (Ban) BTh 05. Ban Ord Course 00. **d** 03 **p** 04. C Botwnnog w Bryncroes w Llangwnnadl w Penllech *Ban* 03–08; P-in-c Nefyn w Tudweiliog w Llandudwen w Edern 08–11; V 11–12; TV Sidmouth, Woolbrook, Salcombe Regis, Sidbury etc *Ex* 12–18; R Chipstead *S'wark* from 18. *The Rectory, Starrock Lane, Chipstead, Coulsdon CR5 3QD* T: (01737) 552160

WILLIAMS, Terence. b 36. Univ of Wales (Abth) BSc 57 Univ of Wales (Cardiff) MA 67 Aston Univ PhD 71. Glouc Sch of Min 78. **d** 81 **p** 81. NSM Deerhurst, Apperley w Forthampton and Chaceley *Glouc* 81–87; NSM Tarrington w Stoke Edith, Aylton, Pixley etc *Heref* 87–88; P-in-c Upper and Lower Slaughter w Eyford and Naunton *Glouc* 88–91; P-in-c Redmarley D'Abitot, Bromesberrow w Pauntley etc 91–95; R 95–99; RD Forest N 95–99; rtd 99; PtO *Glouc* 99–02; P-in-c Hasfield w Tirley and Ashleworth 02–05. *4 University Farm, Moreton-in-Marsh GL56 0DN*

WILLIAMS, Terence James. b 76. St Jo Coll Nottm BA 05. Cranmer Hall Dur 02. **d** 05 **p** 06. C Bolsover *Derby* 05–09; P-in-c Codnor 09–13; P-in-c Horsley and Denby and C Morley w Smalley and Horsley Woodhouse 11–13; P-in-c Loscoe 12–13; RD Heanor 11–13; PtO 13–16; Dioc President Children's Soc from 14; C Burton All SS w Ch Ch *Lich* 15–16; C Branston 15–16; C Burton All SS w Ch Ch from 15. *Address withheld by request* E: wterry774@aol.com

WILLIAMS, Timothy John. b 64. Ch Ch Coll Cant BA 86. St Mich Coll Llan BD 89. **d** 89 **p** 90. C Killay *S & B* 89–91; C Llwynderw 91–94; Chapl Swansea NHS Trust 91–93; V Knighton and Norton *S & B* 94–00; Chapl Knighton Hosp 94–00; P-in-c Whitton and Pilleth and Cascob etc *S & B* 99–00; V Killay 00–15; Dioc Communications Officer 10–15; TR Kidderminster St Jo and H Innocents *Worc* from 15; RD Kidderminster from 19. *St John's Vicarage, 33 Lea Bank Avenue, Kidderminster DY11 6PA* T: (01562) 631856 M: 07901-502675 E: teamrector.kwtm@gmail.com

WILLIAMS, Timothy John. b 54. BEd 83. Trin Coll Carmarthen. **d** 89 **p** 90. NSM Llansamlet *S & B* 89–97; P-in-c Bryngwyn and Newchurch and Llanbedr etc 97–01; V Aberedw w Llandeilo Graban and Llanbadarn etc 01–10; V Brecon St David w Llanspyddid and Llanilltyd 10–15; P-in-c Penderyn Mellte from 15; P-in-c Cefn Coed w Vaynor from 15. *The Rectory, 6 Lamb Road, Penderyn, Aberdare CF44 9JU* T: (01685) 811864 E: timothy.williams462@btinternet.com

WILLIAMS, Mrs Tracey Lyn. b 62. Bris Univ BSc 83 MSc 85 PhD 88. Ripon Coll Cuddesdon 08. **d** 11 **p** 12. NSM Sunninghill and S Ascot *Ox* 11–18; PtO from 18. *14 Devon Chase, Warfield, Bracknell RG42 3JN* M: 07856-745434 E: revdtraceywilliams@gmail.com

WILLIAMS, Tracy Grant. b 61. Sheff Univ BMus 84. ERMC 17. **d** 19. C Nor Heartsease St Fran from 19; C Thorpe St Matt from 19. *59 Douro Place, Norwich NR2 4BQ* M: 07834-845623 E: thetracyisland@gmail.com

✠**WILLIAMS, The Rt Revd Trevor Russell.** b 48. TCD BA 71. St Jo Coll Nottm BA 73. **d** 74 **p** 75 **c** 08. C Maidenhead St Andr and St Mary *Ox* 74–77; Asst Chapl QUB 77–81; Relig Broadcasting Producer BBC 81–88; I Newcastle *D & D* 88–93; Ldr Corrymeela Community 93–03; I Belfast H Trin and St Silas *Conn* 03–08; Preb Rathmichael St Patr Cathl Dublin 02–08; Bp L & K 08–14; rtd 14. *50 Murlough View, Dundrum, Newcastle BT33 0WE* T: (028) 4375 1838 E: bishoptrevor.williams@gmail.com

WILLIAMS, Canon Trevor Stanley Morlais. b 38. Jes Coll Ox BA 63 Univ of E Africa MA 67. Westcott Ho Cam BA 67. **d** 67 **p** 68. C Clifton St Paul *Bris* 67–70; Asst Chapl Bris Univ 67–70; Chapl and Fell Trin Coll Ox 70–05; Hon Can Ch Ch *Ox* 95–05; rtd 05. *c/o Dr Catherine Williams, 17 Balmoral Place, Edinburgh EH3 5JA* M: 07740-585562 E: trevor.williams@trinity.ox.ac.uk

WILLIAMS, Victoria Louise. *See* MORGAN, Victoria Louise

WILLIAMS, Mrs Virginia Grace. b 66. Man Univ BN 88 Brunel Univ MSc 01 RGN 88. ERMC 17. **d** 19. C Sancroft *St E* from 19. *4 Samuel Vince Road, Fressingfield, Eye IP21 5SP* M: 07572-872512 E: gini@godsearth.co.uk

WILLIAMS, Walter Haydn. b 31. Univ of Wales (Lamp) BA 53 Selw Coll Cam BA 55 MA 60. St Mich Coll Llan 55. **d** 56 **p** 57. C Denbigh *St As* 56–58; V Choral St As Cathl 58–61; C St As 58–61; R Llanfyllin 61–68; V Northop 68–73; V Mold 73–86; RD 79–86; Can St As Cathl 77–82; Prec 81–82; Preb and Chan 82–86; R Overton and Erbistock and Penley *St As* 86–94; Chmn Ch of Wales Liturg Cttee 86–94; rtd 94; PtO *St As* 09–14. *2 Park Lane, Craig y Don, Llandudno LL30 1PQ* T: (01492) 877294

WILLIAMS, Warren. *See* WILLIAMS, James Llanfair Warren

WILLIAMS, Miss Wendy Irene. b 35. Univ of Wales (Ban) BA 57 MA 73 Man Univ BD 60. **d** 17 **p** 17. NSM Burscough Bridge *Liv* from 17; PtO *Blackb* from 17. *17 Middleccot Close, Orrell, Wigan WN5 8SQ* T: (01695) 623269 E: hughesedith@aol.com

WILLIAMS, William Garmon. b 42. Univ of Wales (Abth) BA 64. Linc Univ Sch of Th & Min Studies 04. **d** 09 **p** 10. OLM Spring Line Gp *Linc* from 09; Chapl Linc Distr Health Services and Hosps NHS Trust from 10. *16 The Green, Ingham, Lincoln LN1 2XT* T/F: (01522) 730365 M: 07811-347579 E: jennywilliams.bees@virgin.net

WILLIAMS-HUNTER, Ian Roy. b 44. Trin Coll Bris 71. **d** 73 **p** 74. C Redhill H Trin *S'wark* 73–75; C Deane *Man* 76–80; R Hartshorne *Derby* 80–02; P-in-c Bretby w Newton Solney 01–02; R Hartshorne and Bretby 02–11; rtd 11; PtO *Derby* 11–18. *85 Hall Street, Church Gresley, Swadlincote DE11 9QT* T: (01283) 217866 *or* 224602

✠**WILLIAMS OF OYSTERMOUTH, The Rt Revd and Rt Hon Lord (Rowan Douglas).** b 50. Ch Coll Cam BA 71 MA 75 Wadh Coll Ox DPhil 75 DD 89 Erlangen Hon DrTheol 99 FBA 90 Hon FGCM 00. Coll of Resurr Mirfield 75. **d** 77 **p** 78 **c** 92. Tutor Westcott Ho Cam 77–80; Hon C Chesterton St Geo *Ely* 80–83; Lect Div Cam Univ 80–86; Dean Clare Coll Cam 84–86; Can Th Leic Cathl 81–92; Lady Marg Prof Div Ox Univ 86–92; Can Res Ch Ch Ox 86–92; Bp Mon 92–02; Abp Wales 99–02; Abp Cant 02–12; Master Magd Coll Cam from 13; Hon Asst Bp Ely from 13; Hon Can Ely Cathl from 14. *Magdalene College, Cambridge CB3 0AG* T: (01223) 332100

WILLIAMSON, Andrew John. b 39. MRPharmS 62. St Alb Minl Tr Scheme 82. **d** 85 **p** 86. NSM Oxhey All SS *St Alb* 85–88; NSM Bricket Wood 88–97; NSM Campbeltown *Arg* 97–08; LtO 08–13; PtO *Win* from 13. *6 Julius Close, Chandlers Ford SO53 2AB* M: 07970-708191 E: andrew.ajgsw@gmail.com

WILLIAMSON, David Barry. b 56. St Jo Coll Nottm 80. **d** 83 **p** 84. C N Mymms *St Alb* 83–86; C Burley *Ripon* 86–92; Project Worker CECS 92–96; Youth and Children's Adv *B & W* 96–04; Dir Time For God 04–11; P-in-c Shepton Mallet w Doulting *B & W* 11–14; PtO *Leeds* from 15; Chapl St Leon Hospice York from 15. *12 Spencers Way, Harrogate HG1 3DN*

WILLIAMSON, Desmond Carl. b 63. QUB BSc 84 Westmr Coll Ox MTh 03. Trin Coll Bris 03. **d** 05 **p** 06. C Portishead *B & W* 05–10; V Tattenham Corner *Guildf* from 10; AD Epsom from 15. *St Mark's Vicarage, St Mark's Road, Epsom KT18 5RD* T: (01737) 353011

WILLIAMSON, Gary. b 50. Surrey Univ BA 72 MA 92 MITI 01 MCIL 07. **d** 14 **p** 15. OLM Pirbright *Guildf* 14–18; PtO from 18. *Round Meadow, Aldershot Road, Pirbright, Woking GU24 0DQ* T: (01483) 236909 M: 07780-872897 E: revdgarywilliamson@yahoo.co.uk

WILLIAMSON, Mrs Jennifer Irene. b 44. Glas Univ MA 66 Sunderland Poly Dip Teaching 79. NEOC 89. **d** 92 **p** 94. NSM Easby w Brompton on Swale and Bolton on Swale *Ripon* 92–95; P-in-c Gilling and Kirkby Ravensworth 95–05; rtd 05; PtO *Leeds* from 17. *65 Whitefields Drive, Richmond DL10 7DL* T: (01748) 824365

WILLIAMSON, Kathleen Lindsay. b 50. Leeds Univ Medical Sch MB, ChB 74 Liv Univ BSc 87. NOC 00. **d** 03 **p** 04. NSM Stretton and Appleton Thorn *Ches* 03–06; NSM Frodsham 06–13; PtO from 13. *37 Waterside Drive, Frodsham WA6 7NF* M: 07899-664068 E: kath@kathwilliamson.org.uk

WILLIAMSON, Mrs Mary Christine. b 46. Bulmershe Coll of HE BEd 79. SWMTC 05. **d** 09 **p** 10. NSM Launceston *Truro* 09–16; rtd 16; NSM Abingdon *Ox* 16–19. *2 Musson Close, Abingdon OX14 5RE* T: (01235) 538862

WILLIAMSON, Canon Michael John. b 39. ALCD 63. **d** 64 **p** 65. C Pennington *Man* 64–67; C Higher Openshaw 67–69; P-in-c Man St Jerome w Ardwick St Silas 69–72; C-in-c Holts CD 72–77; R Droylsden St Mary 77–04; Hon Can Man Cathl 97–04; rtd 04; PtO *Man* from 04. *49 Ennerdale Road, Astley, Tyldesley, Manchester M29 7AR* T: (01942) 870274

WILLIAMSON, Olwen Joan. b 43. **d** 03 **p** 04. OLM Mortlake w E Sheen *S'wark* 03–13; PtO from 13. *25 Christchurch Road, London SW14 7AB* T/F: (020) 8876 7183 E: olwenontour@hotmail.com

WILLIAMSON, Paul Stewart. b 48. K Coll Lon BD 71 AKC 71. **d** 72 **p** 73. C Deptford St Paul *S'wark* 72–75; Hon C Kennington St Jo 76–77; C Hoxton H Trin w St Mary *Lon* 78–83; C St Marylebone All SS 83–84; C Willesden St Mary 84–85; PtO 86–89; C Hanworth St Geo 89–92; P-in-c 92–19; rtd 19. *The Rectory, 7 Blakewood Close, Feltham TW13 7NL* T: (020) 8844 0457 E: 1stewart1@live.co.uk

WILLIAMSON, Philip Howard. b 59. Yorks Min Course. **d** 16 **p** 17. NSM Saddleworth *Man* from 16. *Thorn, Moorside Road, Slaithwaite, Huddersfield HD7 5UU* M: 07736-416126

WILLIAMSON, Ralph James. b 62. LSE BSc(Econ) 84. Ripon Coll Cuddesdon BA 89 MA 97 MTh 05. **d** 90 **p** 91. C Southgate St Andr *Lon* 90–93; TV Ross w Brampton Abbotts, Bridstow, Peterstow etc *Heref* 93–97; Chapl Ch Ch Ox 97–15; V Pimlico St Pet w Westmr Ch Ch *Lon* from 15. *1 St Peter's House, 119 Eaton Square, London SW1W 9AL* T: (020) 7235 4242 E: vicar@stpetereatonsquare.co.uk

WILLIAMSON, Robert Harvey (Robin). b 45. **d** 02 **p** 03. OLM Maidstone St Luke *Cant* 02–15; rtd 15; PtO *Cant* from 15. *Holly Bank, Bower Mount Road, Maidstone ME16 8AU* T: (01622) 682959 E: robin.helen@tesco.net

WILLIAMSON, Robert John. b 55. K Coll Lon BA 77. Coll of Resurr Mirfield 78. **d** 79 **p** 80. C Kirkby *Liv* 79–82; C Warrington St Elphin 82–84; P-in-c Burneside *Carl* 84–90; V Walney Is 90–00; V Darlington St Cuth *Dur* 00–16; V The Thorntons and The Otteringtons *York* from 16; Chapl N Yorks Police 16–18. *4 Endican Lane, Thornton-le-Moor, Northallerton DL7 9FB* T: (01609) 773758 E: revrobertwilliamson@gmail.com

✠**WILLIAMSON, The Rt Revd Robert Kerr (Roy).** b 32. Kingston Univ DEd 98. Oak Hill Th Coll 61. **d** 63 **p** 64 **c** 84. C Crowborough *Chich* 63–66; V Hyson Green *S'well* 66–72; V Nottingham St Ann w Em 72–76; V Bramcote 76–79; Adn Nottingham 78–84; Bp Bradf 84–91; Bp S'wark 91–98; rtd 98; Hon Asst Bp S'well and Nottm from 98. *30 Sidney Road, Beeston, Nottingham NG9 1AN* T/F: 0115-925 4901

WILLIAMSON, Robin. *See* WILLIAMSON, Robert Harvey

WILLIAMSON, Roger Brian. b 38. Imp Coll Lon BSc 59 MIET 61. St Steph Ho Ox 01. **d** 02 **p** 03. NSM Harting w Elsted and Treyford cum Didling *Chich* 02–05; P-in-c Stedham w Iping 05–15; rtd 15; PtO *Chich* from 16. *Hawthorn Cottage, North Lane, South Harting, Petersfield GU31 5PY* M: 07767-266031 E: rogerwilliamson1@btinternet.com

WILLIAMSON, Canon Thomas George. b 33. AKC 57. **d** 58 **p** 59. C Winshill *Derby* 58–61; C Hykeham *Linc* 61–64; V Brauncewell w Dunsby 64–78; R S w N Leasingham 64–78; RD Lafford 78–87; V Cranwell 78–80; R Leasingham 78–80; V Billinghay 80–87; V Gosberton 87–97; V Gosberton, Gosberton Clough and Quadring 97–98; Can and Preb Linc Cathl 94–98; rtd 98; PtO *Linc* 98–01. *10 Newton Way, Woolsthorpe, Grantham NG33 5NR* T: (01476) 861749 E: thomaswilliamson99@btinternet.com

WILLIE, Canon Andrew Robert. b 43. Bris Univ BA 65 Fitzw Coll Cam BA 73 MA 77. Ridley Hall Cam 71. **d** 74 **p** 75. Chapl St Woolos Cathl *Mon* 74–79; Chapl St Woolos Hosp Newport 75–79; V Newbridge *Mon* 79–85; V Mathern and Mounton w St Pierre 85–98; Post-Ord Tr Officer 85–98; V Newport St Mark 98–13; Warden of Readers 91–13; Can St Woolos Cathl *Mon* 02–13; rtd 13; PtO *Mon* from 14. *6 Cordell Close, Llanfoist, Abergavenny NP7 9FE* T: (01873) 852063 E: andrew.robert.willie@gmail.com

WILLIS, Andrew Lyn. b 48. Univ of Wales (Lamp) BA 73. **d** 74 **p** 75. C Swansea St Mary w H Trin and St Mark *S & B* 74–81; V Glasbury and Llowes 81–83; Chapl RAF 83–03; Chapl Moray Hosps from 04; LtO *Mor* from 09. *Deanshaugh Croft, Mulben, Keith AB55 6YJ* T: (01542) 860240 E: andylwillis@hotmail.co.uk

WILLIS, Anthony Charles Sabine. b 53. Ex Coll Ox MA 82. ERMC 05. **d** 07 **p** 08. NSM Hatfield Hyde *St Alb* 07–10; PtO *Newc* 08–10. *Leazes House, Alston CA9 3NH* T: (01434) 382682 E: acswillis@gmail.com

WILLIS, Anthony David. b 40. Sarum & Wells Th Coll 87. **d** 89 **p** 90. C Ivybridge w Harford *Ex* 89–92; C Catherington and Clanfield *Portsm* 92–94; R Ellesborough, The Kimbles and Stoke Mandeville *Ox* 94–08; rtd 09; C Aylesbury *Ox* 19–12; PtO from 12. *12 Fairford Leys Way, Aylesbury HP19 7FQ* T: (01296) 431934 E: revwillis@btinternet.com

WILLIS, Canon Anthony John. b 38. Univ of Wales (Lamp) BA 62. Qu Coll Birm. **d** 64 **p** 65. C Kidderminster St Jo *Worc* 64–68; C Dunstable *St Alb* 68–72; V Rubery *Birm* 72–80; R Salwarpe and Hindlip w Martin Hussingtree *Worc* 80–92; Chapl to Agric and Rural Life 85–03; Hon Can *Worc*

Cathl 99–03; rtd 03; PtO *Worc* 04–08. *1 Snowberry Avenue, Home Meadow, Worcester WR4 0JA* T: (01905) 723509 E: johnjosewillis@aol.com

WILLIS, David Anthony. b 81. Ripon Coll Cuddesdon BA 10. **d** 10 **p** 11. C Ifield *Chich* 10–13; V Midhurst from 13; R Woolbeding from 13. *The Vicarage, June Lane, Midhurst GU29 9EW* E: revdavewillis@live.co.uk

WILLIS, Geoffrey Stephen Murrell. b 58. Sussex Univ BA 80. Wycliffe Hall Ox 83. **d** 86 **p** 87. C Ashtead *Guildf* 86–89; Chapl Lee Abbey 89–94; R Dunsfold *Guildf* 94–01; R Dunsfold and Hascombe 01–06; PtO from 06. *The Barn, Stephens Orchard, Headley Road, Grayshott, Hindhead GU26 6DL* T: (01428) 609382 E: willisgeoffrey@mac.com

WILLIS, Guy Robin Fraser. b 86. Jes Coll Cam BA 08 MA 11. St Steph Ho Ox 12. **d** 15 **p** 16. C Holborn St Alb w Saffron Hill St Pet *Lon* 15–18; C Old St Pancras from 18; C St Andr Holborn from 18. *33 Crowndale Road, London NW1 1TN* T: (020) 7388 3797 E: grfwillis@gmail.com

WILLIS, Hugh. b 39. Bris Univ BDS 63 MGDSRCSEng 82 FRSH 87. **d** 98 **p** 99. OLM Charminster and Stinsford *Sarum* 98–08; PtO from 09. *Glebe Farmhouse, West Hill, Charminster, Dorchester DT2 9RD* T/F: (01305) 262940 E: tournai@aol.com

WILLIS, Mrs Jane Elizabeth. b 59. Wycliffe Hall Ox 06. **d** 08 **p** 09. C Shrewsbury H Cross *Lich* 08–11; TV S Molton w Nymet St George, High Bray etc *Ex* 11–14; P-in-c Hurstpierpoint *Chich* 14–16; R from 16. *The Rectory, 21 Cuckfield Road, Hurstpierpoint, Hassocks BN6 9RP* T: (01273) 832203

WILLIS, Mrs Jennifer Anne. b 41. Bp Otter Coll TCert 62. **d** 11 **p** 12. OLM Wingerworth *Derby* from 11. *9 Pond Lane, Wingerworth, Chesterfield S42 6TW* T: (01246) 554430 E: jenn.willis@uwclub.net

WILLIS, John. *See* WILLIS, Anthony John

WILLIS, Joyce Muriel. b 42. Open Univ BA 86 CQSW 73. EAMTC 86. **d** 89 **p** 94. NSM Hadleigh *St E* 89–02; NSM Hadleigh, Layham and Shelley 02–07; rtd 07; PtO *St E* from 07. *26 Ramsey Road, Hadleigh, Ipswich IP7 6AN* T: (01473) 823165 E: willisjm@lineone.net

WILLIS, Maureen. **d** 15 **p** 16. C Branksome St Clem *Sarum* from 15. *72 Halstock Crescent, Poole BH17 9BA*

WILLIS, Mrs Patricia. b 50. RGN 85 Brunel Univ BSc 95 Ox Brookes Univ PGDE 98. SAOMC 96. **d** 99 **p** 00. C Warmley, Syston and Bitton *Bris* 99–03; V Hanham 03–10; rtd 10; PtO Ox from 10. *30 Tallis Lane, Reading RG30 3EB* M: 07731-331154 E: revpatwillis@yahoo.com

WILLIS, Peter Ambrose Duncan. b 34. Kelham Th Coll 55 Lich Th Coll 58. **d** 59 **p** 64. C Sevenoaks St Jo *Roch* 59–63; Trinidad and Tobago 63–68; P-in-c Diptford *Ex* 68–69; R 69–85; P-in-c N Huish 68–69; R 69–85; R Diptford, N Huish, Harberton and Harbertonford 85–96; rtd 99. *Sun Cottage, Church Street, Modbury, Ivybridge PL21 0QR* T: (01548) 830541

WILLIS, The Very Revd Robert Andrew. b 47. Warw Univ BA 68. Cuddesdon Coll 70. **d** 72 **p** 73. C Shrewsbury St Chad *Lich* 72–75; V Choral Sarum Cathl 75–78; TR Tisbury 78–87; RD Chalke 82–87; V Sherborne w Castleton and Lillington 87–92; Can and Preb Sarum Cathl 88–92; RD Sherborne 91–92; Chapl Cranborne Chase Sch 78–92; Dean Heref 92–01; P-in-c Heref St Jo 92–01; Dean Cant from 01. *The Deanery, The Precincts, Canterbury CT1 2EP* T: (01227) 865264 *or* 762862 E: dean@canterbury-cathedral.org

WILLMONT, Anthony Vernon. b 35. Lich Th Coll 62. **d** 63 **p** 64. C Yardley St Edburgha *Birm* 63–65; C Smethwick H Trin w St Alb 65–68; V Ropley w W Tisted *Win* 68–77; V Ipswich St Aug *St E* 77–84; R King's Worthy *Win* 84–90; R Headbourne Worthy 84–90; R Lapworth *Birm* 90–99; P-in-c Baddesley Clinton 90–99; P-in-c Thornton in Lonsdale w Burton in Lonsdale *Bradf* 99–02; rtd 02; PtO *Bradf* 02–14; *Leeds* from 14. *9 Lowcroft, Butts Lane, Bentham, Lancaster LA2 2FD* T: (01524) 261655

WILLMOT, Julie. b 66. St Mellitus Coll BA 16. **d** 16 **p** 17. NSM Maldon All SS w St Pet *Chelmsf* 16–19; P-in-c Purleigh from 19; NSM Woodham Mortimer w Hazeleigh 16–19; P-in-c from 19; NSM Woodham Walter 16–19; P-in-c from 19. *8 Mayflower Drive, Maldon CM9 6XX* M: 07413-416226 E: revjuliewillmot@gmail.com

WILLMOTT, Robert Owen Noel. b 41. Lich Th Coll 65. **d** 68 **p** 69. C Perry Hill St Geo *S'wark* 68–71; C Denham *Ox* 71–76; P-in-c Tingewick w Water Stratford 76–77; P-in-c Radclive 76–77; R Tingewick w Water Stratford, Radclive etc 77–89; R Wingrave w Rowsham, Aston Abbotts and Cublington 89–06; P-in-c Wing w Grove 04–06; rtd 06; PtO *Ox* from 10. *34 Portfield Way, Buckingham MK18 1BB* T: (01280) 813057

✠**WILLMOTT, The Rt Revd Trevor.** b 50. St Pet Coll Ox BA 71 MA 74. Westcott Ho Cam. **d** 74 **p** 75 c 02. C Norton *St Alb* 74–77; Asst Chapl Oslo w Bergen, Trondheim and Stavanger

Eur 78–79; Chapl Naples w Sorrento, Capri and Bari 79–83; R Ecton *Pet* 83–89; Warden Ecton Ho 83–89; Dioc Dir of Ords and Dir Post-Ord Tr *Pet* 86–97; Can Res, Prec and Sacr *Pet* Cathl 89–97; Adn Dur and Can Res Dur Cathl 97–02; Suff Bp Basingstoke *Win* 02–09; Suff Bp Dover *Cant* 10–19; Hon Asst Bp Ox from 18; rtd 19. *Rose Cottage, 3 Compton Street, Butleigh, Glastonbury BA6 8SE*

WILLOUGHBY, Diane Joyce. b 56. Ex Univ BTh 12. SWMTC 07. **d** 10 **p** 11. C St Agnes and Mount Hawke w Mithian *Truro* from 10; C St Clement 12–15; V from 15; C Perranzabuloe and Crantock w Cubert from 17. *The Vicarage, Mount Hawke, Truro TR4 8DE* M: 07776-152759 E: illogan@hotmail.co.uk

WILLOUGHBY, Francis Edward John. b 38. St Jo Coll Nottm. **d** 83 **p** 84. C Tonbridge SS Pet and Paul *Roch* 83–87; V Sutton at Hone 87–02; P-in-c Horton Kirby 00–02; rtd 03; PtO *Chich* from 03. *23 Mountjoy, Battle TN33 0EQ* T: (01424) 777270

WILLOWS, Michael John. b 35. Sarum & Wells Th Coll 70. **d** 72 **p** 73. C Pershore w Wick *Worc* 72–75; Ind Chapl 75–88; P-in-c Astley 75–81; P-in-c Hallow 81–85; V 85–88; V Wollaston 88–05; rtd 05; PtO *Worc* from 05; *Lich* 12–17. *39 Hyperion Road, Stourton, Stourbridge DY7 6SD* T: (01384) 379794 E: rev.willows@gmail.com

WILLOX, Peter. b 63. Sunderland Poly BSc 85. Cranmer Hall Dur 86. **d** 89 **p** 90. C Bradley *Wakef* 89–92; C Utley *Bradf* 92–95; TV Bingley All SS 95–02; Chapl St Martin's Coll and C Ambleside w Brathay *Carl* 02–07; P-in-c Ben Rhydding *Bradf* 07–12; V 12–14; *Leeds* from 14. *St John's Vicarage, 28 Wheatley Avenue, Ben Rhydding, Ilkley LS29 8PT* T: (01943) 607363 *or* 601430 E: peterwillox@yahoo.co.uk

WILLS, Canon Andrea Jennifer. CITC. **d** 09 **p** 10. NSM Killala w Dunfeeny, Crossmolina, Kilmoremoy etc *T, K & A* 09–13; P-in-c Straid from 13; Can Tuam Cathl from 13; Can Killala Cathl from 16. *Robin Hill, Foxford, Co Mayo, Republic of Ireland* T: (00353) (94) 925 6403 M: 86-261 7572 E: andreajwills@gmail.com

WILLS, David. b 58. Oak Hill Th Coll 92. **d** 94 **p** 95. C Chadwell *Chelmsf* 94–99; P-in-c Darlaston St Lawr *Lich* 99–09; R 09–10; C Darlaston All SS 99–10; TR Bilston from 10. *The Vicarage, Dover Street, Bilston WV14 6AW* T: (01902) 491560

WILLS, Preb David Stuart Ralph. b 36. Chich Th Coll 64. **d** 66 **p** 67. C Bodmin *Truro* 66–70; V Bude Haven 70–78; TV Banbury *Ox* 78–83; Accredited Cllr from 81; V Launceston St Steph w St Thos *Truro* 83–88; P-in-c Kenwyn St Geo 88–93; V Truro St Geo and St Jo 93–96; Preb St Endellion 95–01; rtd 96; Chapl Cornwall Partnership NHS Foundn Trust 99–06; PtO *Truro* from 16. *21 Park Kres, St Agnes TR5 0AL* T: (01872) 555822 M: 07773-402109 E: 8392dsrw@gmail.com

WILLS, Edward Richard. b 64. STETS 07. **d** 10 **p** 11. NSM Wedmore w Theale and Blackford *B & W* 10–13; Chapl RN from 13. *Royal Naval Chaplaincy Service, Mail Point 1.2, Leach Building, Whale Island, Portsmouth PO2 8BY* T: (023) 9262 5055 F: 9262 5134 M: 07971-511564 E: eddie@beonna.co.uk

WILLS, Canon Ian Leslie. b 49. Wycliffe Hall Ox 77. **d** 80 **p** 81. C Henbury *Bris* 80; C Gtr Corsham 80–83; C Whitchurch 83–86; Chapl HM Rem Cen Pucklechurch 86–96; P-in-c Pucklechurch and Abson w Dyrham *Bris* 86–87; V Pucklechurch and Abson 87–99; V Soundwell 99–15; Hon Can Bris Cathl 06–15; rtd 15; PtO *Bris* from 16. *39 The Laurels, Mangotsfield, Bristol BS16 9BT* T: 0117-239 0877 E: ianwills@icloud.com

WILLSON, Andrew William. b 64. Oriel Coll Ox BA 85 Nottm Univ BTh 90 MA 98. Linc Th Coll 87. **d** 90 **p** 91. C Northampton St Mary *Pet* 90–93; C Cov E 93–96; PtO 96–01; Chapl Solihull Sixth Form Coll 98–01; Assoc Chapl Imp Coll Lon 01–03; Co-ord Chapl Imp Coll Lon from 03; Assoc Chapl R Coll of Art 01–03; Co-ord Chapl from 03; Chapl (Sen) Lon Univs from 15. *1 Porchester Gardens, London W2 3LA* T: (020) 7229 6359 E: a.willson@imperial.ac.uk

WILLSON, Mrs Patricia Rosemary. b 45. Trin Coll Bris 12. **d** 13 **p** 14. OLM Horfield St Greg *Bris* 13–16; PtO *Linc* from 16. *100 Pinchbeck Road, Spalding PE11 1QL* T: (01775) 422815 M: 07976-986694 E: pat.willson@yahoo.co.uk

WILLSON, Stephen Geoffrey. b 63. St Jo Coll Nottm BTh 90. **d** 90 **p** 91. C Newport St Andr *Mon* 90–92; C Risca 92–94; TV Cyncoed 94–96; Dioc Youth Chapl 94–99; Lay Past Asst 96–98; TV Cyncoed *Mon* 98–01; TR 01–11; R Welshpool, Castle Caereinion and Pool Quay *St As* 11–14; R Welshpool and Castle Caereinion 14–17; I Pool Miss Area from 18; AD Pool from 15. *The Vicarage, Church Street, Welshpool SY21 7DP* T: (01938) 553164 E: revswillson@btinternet.com

WILMAN, Arthur Garth. b 37. EAMTC 84. **d** 87 **p** 88. NSM Swavesey *Ely* 87–90; NSM Fen Drayton w Conington 87–90; NSM Hardwick 90–98; NSM Toft w Caldecote and Childerley

90–98; PtO from 98. *37 Prentice Close, Longstanton, Cambridge CB24 3DY* T: (01954) 781400

WILMAN, Mrs Dorothy Ann Jane. b 38. Reading Univ BSc 60. Westcott Ho Cam 89. **d** 90 **p** 94. NSM Toft w Caldecote and Childerley *Ely* 90–93; Dean's Asst Trin Hall Cam 92–98; Asst Chapl Cam St Edw *Ely* 93–98; P-in-c Hemingford Abbots 98–02; P-in-c Houghton w Wyton 98–02; rtd 02; PtO *Ely* from 02. *37 Prentice Close, Longstanton, Cambridge CB24 3DY* T: (01954) 781400 E: dorothywilman@btinternet.com

WILMAN, Leslie Alan. b 37. Selw Coll Cam BA 61 MA 65. Ridley Hall Cam 61. **d** 63 **p** 64. C Skipton H Trin *Bradf* 63–67; C Guiseley 67–69; V Morton St Luke 69–79; R Swanton Morley w Worthing *Nor* 79–82; P-in-c E Bilney w Beetley 79–82; P-in-c Hoe 80–82; R Swanton Morley w Beetley w E Bilney and Hoe 82–89 and 89–00; RD Brisley and Elmham 87–93; rtd 00; PtO *Nor* from 00. *7 Wallers Lane, Foulsham, Dereham NR20 5TN* T: (01328) 684109 E: lesliewilman@btinternet.com

WILMER, John Watts. b 26. Lich Th Coll 56. **d** 58 **p** 59. C Wolverhampton Ch Ch *Lich* 58–60; C Fenton 60–63; V Dresden 63–76; TV Sutton St Jas and Wawne *York* 76–80; R Bishop Wilton w Full Sutton 80; P-in-c Kirby Underdale w Bugthorpe 80; R Bishop Wilton w Full Sutton, Kirby Underdale etc 80–87; V York St Hilda 87–91; rtd 92; PtO *York* from 92. *27 Hunter's Way, York YO24 1JL* T: (01904) 709591

WILMOT, David Mark Baty. b 60. Liv Univ BA 82. Sarum & Wells Th Coll 84. **d** 87 **p** 88. C Penrith w Newton Reigny and Plumpton Wall *Carl* 87–91; C St Alb St Pet 91–93; Chapl City Coll St Alb 92–93; V Milton *Lich* 93–01; RD Leek 96–01; RD Windermere from 16. *St Mary's Vicarage, Ambleside Road, Windermere LA23 1BA* T: (01539) 443032 E: vicar@stmaryswindermere.co.uk

WILMOT, Canon Jonathan Anthony de Burgh. b 48. St Jo Coll Nottm BTh 74. **d** 74 **p** 75. C Cambridge St Martin *Ely* 74–77; Chapl Chantilly *Eur* 77–82; Asst Chapl Paris St Mich 80–82; Chapl Versailles 82–87; V Blackheath St Jo *S'wark* 88–95; V Reading Greyfriars *Ox* 95–14; Hon Can Ch Ch 08–14; rtd 14. *7 Birkett Way, Chalfont St Giles HP8 4BH* E: jon.wilmot@gmail.com

WILMOT, Stuart Leslie. b 42. Oak Hill Th Coll 64. **d** 68 **p** 69. C Spitalfields Ch Ch w All SS *Lon* 68–71; C Islington St Mary 71–74; P-in-c Brixton St Paul *S'wark* 75–81; R Mursley w Swanbourne and Lt Horwood *Ox* 81–91; P-in-c Bermondsey St Jas w Ch Ch and St Crispin 99–02; P-in-c Bermondsey St Anne 91–93; P-in-c Bermondsey St Anne and St Aug 93–96; V 96–02; RD Bermondsey 96–00; rtd 02. *Amberlea, College, East Chinnock, Yeovil BA22 9DY*

WILSHERE, Daile Marie. b 70. STETS 06. **d** 09 **p** 10. C Preston w Sutton Poyntz, Littlemoor etc *Sarum* 09–13; TV Savernake 13–15; R Saltford w Corston and Newton St Loe *B & W* from 15. *12 Beech Road, Saltford, Bristol BS31 3BE* T: (01225) 872275 M: 07810-551447 E: dailewilshere@live.co.uk

WILSHIRE, Rosanne Elizabeth. b 74. Herts Univ BSc 97. Westcott Ho Cam 14. **d** 16 **p** 17. C Heath Town *Lich* from 16. *2A Victoria Road, Wednesfield, Wolverhampton WV11 1RZ* T: (01902) 737793 M: 07910-686171 E: revrosht@gmail.com

✠**WILSON, The Rt Revd Alan Thomas Lawrence.** b 55. St Jo Coll Cam BA 77 MA 81 Ball Coll Ox DPhil 89. Wycliffe Hall Ox 77. **d** 79 **p** 80 **c** 03. C Eynsham *Ox* 79–81; C 81–82; C Caversham St Pet and Mapledurham etc 82–89; V Caversham St Jo 89–92; R Sandhurst 92–03; RD Sonning 98–03; Hon Can Ch Ch 02–03; Area Bp Buckingham from 03. *Sheridan, Grimms Hill, Great Missenden HP16 9BG* T: (01494) 862173 F: 890508 M: 07525-655756 E: bishopbucks@oxford.anglican.org

WILSON, Andrew. *See* WILSON, James Andrew Christopher

WILSON, Canon Andrew Alan. b 47. Nottm Univ BA 68. St Steph Ho Ox 68. **d** 71 **p** 72. C Streatham St Paul *S'wark* 71–75; TV Catford (Southend) and Downham 75–80; V Malden St Jas 80–89; Chapl Croydon Community Mental Health Unit 89–94; Chapl Bethlem and Maudsley NHS Trust Lon 94–99; Chapl S Lon and Maudsley NHS Foundn Trust 99–11; Mental Health Chapl (Croydon) 00–11; Hon Can S'wark Cathl 05–11; rtd 11; PtO *S'wark* from 11. *7 Roman Rise, London SE19 1JG* T: (020) 8761 0969 E: arwiljohn@btinternet.com

WILSON, Andrew Marcus William. b 69. Ex Coll Ox BA 91 CCC Cam BA 93 K Coll Lon MA 99. Westcott Ho Cam 91. **d** 94 **p** 95. C Forest Gate Em w Upton Cross *Chelmsf* 94–99; TV Poplar *Lon* 99–09; R S Hackney St Jo w Ch Ch from 09. *The Rectory, 9 Church Crescent, London E9 7DH* T: (020) 8985 5145 E: andrewmwwilson@tiscali.co.uk

WILSON, Andrew Martin. b 60. Bris Univ BSc 82 Univ Coll Chich BA 04. Trin Coll Bris 97. **d** 99 **p** 00. C Broadwater *Chich* 99–07; V Portsdown *Portsm* from 07; C Crookhorn from 13; C Purbrook 13–19; P-in-c from 19; Jt AD Havant 14–19. *St John's Vicarage, 9 Marrels Wood Gardens, Purbrook, Waterlooville PO7 5RS* E: vicar@christchurchportsdown.org

WILSON, Antony Charles. b 69. Em Coll Cam MA 92 PGCE 92. Wycliffe Hall Ox 01. **d** 03 **p** 04. C Bath Walcot *B & W* 03–08; V Ipswich St Jo *St E* 08–12; CF 12–16; P-in-c Dedham *Chelmsf* 16–17; C Ardleigh and The Bromleys 16–17; V Dedham and Ardleigh from 17. *The Vicarage, High Street, Dedham, Colchester CO7 6DE* T: (01206) 323919 E: office@dedham-parishchurch.org.uk

WILSON, Arthur Neville. *See* RUSDELL-WILSON, Arthur Neville

WILSON, Ashley Peter. b 58. Edin Univ BSc 81 BVM&S 83 St Jo Coll Dur BA 99 PhD 08. Cranmer Hall Dur 97. **d** 00 **p** 01. C Nunthorpe *York* 00–03; P-in-c Rounton w Welbury 03–08; Chapl St Chad's Coll *Dur* 08–17; Vice Prin from 16; PtO from 17. *St Chad's College, 18 North Bailey, Durham DH1 3RH* T: 0191-334 3362 or 334 3358 E: ashley.wilson@durham.ac.uk

WILSON, Mrs Barbara Anne. b 38. Brighton Poly BEd 79. **d** 04. NSM Southwick *Chich* 04–11; NSM Kingston Buci 11–15; NSM Old Shoreham and Kingston Buci from 15. *10 Phoenix Crescent, Southwick, Brighton BN42 4HR* T: (01273) 269771 M: 07814-655121

WILSON, Mrs Barbara Joyce. b 51. CBDTI 98. **d** 01 **p** 02. OLM Leyland St Jo *Blackb* 01–07; NSM from 07. *43 Hall Lane, Leyland PR25 3YD* T: (01772) 435340 E: barbara.j.wilson@btinternet.com

WILSON, The Ven Barry Frank. b 58. Man Metrop Univ BA 89 MPhil 94 MTh 99 Keele Univ PGCE 90. NOC 94. **d** 97 **p** 98. C Stone St Mich w Aston St Sav *Lich* 97–99; Chapl Abbots Bromley Sch 00–04; V Madeley and Betley *Lich* 04–13; R Nantwich *Ches* 13–17; Can Res Ches Cathl 17–18; Adn Montgomery *St As* from 18. *The Rectory, Four Crosses, Llanymynech SY22 6RW* T: (01691) 839667 E: archdeacon.montgomery@cinw.org.uk

WILSON, Barry Richard. b 46. WMMTC 88. **d** 91 **p** 92. NSM Leek and Meerbrook *Lich* 91–93; C Styvechale *Cov* 93–98; V Chesterton *Lich* 98–12; rtd 12; PtO *Lich* from 13. *9 Westwood Park Avenue, Leek ST13 8LR* T: (01538) 384090

WILSON, Bernard Martin. b 40. St Jo Coll Cam BA 63 MA 68 Lon Univ CertEd 67. Ripon Hall Ox 72. **d** 73 **p** 74. C Bilton *Cov* 73–77; Dioc Development Officer *Birm* 78–83; Soc Resp Officer *Derby* 83–90; V Darley Abbey 83–90; Chapl Derbyshire R Infirmary 88–90; Educn Unit Dir Traidcraft Exchange 91; V Mickleover St Jo *Derby* 92–98; Adv to Bd of Miss and Soc Resp *Leic* 98–03; rtd 03; PtO *Leic* 03–06, *Lich* from 06; *Heref* from 14. *2 Dargate Close, Shrewsbury SY3 9QE* T: (01743) 236300

WILSON, Mrs Caroline Susan. b 62. St Cath Coll Cam BA 83 MA 87 ALCM 79. Ox Min Course 06. **d** 09 **p** 10. NSM Caversham St Andr *Ox* 09–11; PtO 11–12; *St Alb* 12–14; NSM St Alb St Sav 14–15; NSM Whittlesford *Ely* 15–18; NSM Pampisford 15–18; V Rushmere *St E* 18–19. *27 Norfolk Road, Buntingford SG9 9AN* T: (01763) 274804 E: revd.carolinew@gmail.com

WILSON, Mrs Catherine Ann. b 61. Southn Univ BA 83 Leic Univ PGCE 84. SEITE 11. **d** 14 **p** 15. C Biddenden and Smarden Cant 14–18; V Bromham w Oakley and Stagsden *St Alb* from 18. *The Vicarage, 47 Stagsden Road, Bromham, Bedford MK43 8PY* T: (01234) 825665 M: 07511-625107 E: vicar@bromhambenefice.org

WILSON, Cecil Henry. b 40. CITC 67. **d** 69 **p** 70. C Lurgan St Jo *D & D* 69–72; Min Can Dromore Cathl 72–75; Youth Sec CMS Ireland 75–80; N Regional Sec 80–87; Gen Sec 87–07; Can Belf Cathl 00–07; rtd 07. *42A Magheraknock Road, Ballynahinch BT24 8TJ* T: (028) 9756 4300 E: cecilwilson@gmail.com

WILSON, Christella Helen. b 62. Leeds Univ MA 11. Yorks Min Course 08. **d** 11 **p** 12. C Pannal w Beckwithshaw *Ripon* 11–14; *Leeds* 14; V Hampsthwaite and Killinghall and Birstwith 14–19. *Address temp unknown* E: revchrissywilson@yahoo.com

WILSON (née BRAVERY), The Very Revd Christine Louise. b 58. STETS 94. **d** 97 **p** 98. C Henfield w Shermanbury and Woodmancote *Chich* 97–02; TV Hove 02–08; P-in-c Goring-by-Sea 08–16; Adn Chesterfield *Derby* 10–16; Dean Linc from 16. *The Deanery, 11 Minster Yard, Lincoln LN2 1PJ* T: (01522) 561630 E: dean@lincolncathedral.com

WILSON, Christopher Harry. b 59. Man Univ MusB 80 Ox Univ MTh 01. Wycliffe Hall Ox 88. **d** 91 **p** 92. C S Lafford *Linc* 91–95; P-in-c Billingborough 95–96; P-in-c Sempringham w Pointon and Birthorpe 95–96; P-in-c

Horbling 95–96; P-in-c Billingborough Gp 95–96; V 96–03; P-in-c Leamington Priors All SS *Cov* 03–15; V from 15; P-in-c Leamington Spa H Trin 03–15; V from 15. *Clive House, Kenilworth Road, Leamington Spa CV32 5TL* T: (01926) 424016 E: holy.trinity@btopenworld.com

WILSON, Mrs Claire Frances. b 43. Hull Univ BA 65. SWMTC 85. **d** 87 **p** 94. Par Dn Belsize Park *Lon* 87–94; C 94–97; C Chingford SS Pet and Paul *Chelmsf* 97–09; rtd 09; PtO *Lon* from 10. *Ground Floor Flat, 26 Frognal Lane, London NW3 7DT* T: (020) 7794 3801 E: revclairewilson@btinternet.com

WILSON, Colin Edward. b 63. Ripon Coll Cuddesdon BTh 94. **d** 94 **p** 95. C High Wycombe *Ox* 94–98; P-in-c Broadwell, Evenlode, Oddington and Adlestrop *Glouc* 98–00; P-in-c Westcote w Icomb and Bledington 98–00; R Broadwell, Evenlode, Oddington, Adlestrop etc 00–03; PtO *Eur* 03–05; P-in-c Finchingfield and Cornish Hall End etc *Chelmsf* 05–19; R Gawsworth w North Rode *Ches* from 19. *The Rectory, Church Lane, Gawsworth, Macclesfield SK11 9RJ*

WILSON, Preb David Gordon. b 40. Man Univ BSc 61 Clare Coll Cam BA 63 MA 68. Ridley Hall Cam 63. **d** 65 **p** 66. C Clapham Common St Barn *S'wark* 65–69; C Onslow Square St Paul *Lon* 69–73; V Leic H Apostles 73–84; V Spring Grove St Mary *Lon* 84–05; P-in-c Isleworth St Fran 00–05; Chapl Brunel Univ 90–02; AD Hounslow 97–02; Preb St Paul's Cathl 02–05; rtd 05; PtO *Portsm* from 05. *8 Clover Close, Locks Heath, Southampton SO31 6SQ* T/F: (01489) 571426 E: david.gwilson20@ntlworld.com

WILSON, David Mark. b 53. Lon Univ BSc 75. Wycliffe Hall Ox BA 77 MA 82. **d** 78 **p** 79. C Romford Gd Shep *Chelmsf* 78–81; C Cheadle Hulme St Andr *Ches* 81–85; V Huntington and Chapl Bp's Blue Coat C of E High Sch 85–95; V Birkenhead Ch Ch *Ches* 95–04; V Over St Jo 04–10; P-in-c W Coker w Hardington Mandeville, E Chinnock etc *B & W* 10–13; R Coker Ridge 13–15; rtd 15; PtO *Sarum* from 15. *6 Helston Close, Portesham, Weymouth DT3 4EY* E: Revdavidwilson@gmail.com

WILSON, Delyth Anne. b 15 **p** 16. NSM Cynwyl Gaeo w Llansawel and Talley etc *St D* from 15; P-in-c from 18. *Y Felin, Abergorlech, Carmarthen SA32 7SN* T: (01558) 685764 E: delythawilson@gmail.com

WILSON, Derick. b 33. Oak Hill Th Coll 69. **d** 71 **p** 72. C Lurgan Ch the Redeemer *D & D* 71–74; C Willowfield 74–75; I 83–88; I Knocknamuckley 75–83; I Tullylish 88–98; rtd 98. *Hollycroft, 6 Thornhill Crescent, Tandragee, Craigavon BT62 2NZ* T: (028) 3884 9900

WILSON, Mrs Dorothy Jean. b 35. St Mary's Coll Dur BA 57 DipEd 58 Newc Poly LLB 78. NEOC 86. **d** 88 **p** 96. NSM Dur St Giles 88–03; PtO *Newc* 88–96; Chapl Northumbria Univ 94–96; Chapl N Dur Healthcare NHS Trust 97–02; NSM Pittington, Shadforth and Sherburn *Dur* 03–05; rtd 05; PtO *Dur* from 05. *86 Gilesgate, Durham DH1 1HY* T: 0191-386 5016 E: dorothy9.wilson@gmail.com

WILSON, Edith Yvonne. b 43. St Martin's Coll Lanc MA 98. CBDTI 97. **d** 97 **p** 98. NSM Skerton St Chad *Blackb* 97–05; PtO from 05. *28 Roedean Avenue, Morecambe LA4 6SB* T: (01524) 417097

WILSON, Miss Elizabeth Ann. b 76. Leic Univ BA 98 Southn Univ MA 01. St Jo Coll Nottm MTh 14. **d** 14 **p** 15. C Evington *Leic* 14–17; TV Oadby 17–19; V Leic St Anne, St Paul w St Aug from 19; Chapl Leic Gr Sch from 17. *Address temp unknown* M: 07510-797399 E: lizwilson738@gmail.com

WILSON, Canon Erik. b 51. Lanc Univ BA 72. Trin Coll Bris 83. **d** 85 **p** 86. C Linthorpe *York* 85–89; V Hull St Martin w Transfiguration 89–98; AD W Hull 96–98; V Linthorpe 98–18; RD Middlesbrough 05–11; Can and Preb York Minster 05–18; rtd 18; PtO *York* from 18. *10 Dominican Walk, Eastgate, Beverley HU17 0HF* T: (01482) 867639 E: erik.wilson@btinternet.com

WILSON, Frances Mary. b 61. Leeds Univ BA 98 MPhil 06. Westcott Ho Cam. **d** 00 **p** 01. C Rothwell *Ripon* 00–04; V Catterick 04–11; Initial Reader Tr Officer 04–11; P-in-c Balkwell *Newc* 11–18; AD Tynemouth 15–18; Bp's Dir of Ords *Lich* from 18. *715 Uttoxeter Road, Stoke-on-Trent ST3 7AE* E: franceswilson59@gmail.com

WILSON, Geoffrey. b 42. **d** 97 **p** 98. OLM Gunton St Pet *Nor* 97–08; NSM Lowestoft St Marg 08–12; PtO *Nor* from 13. *7 Monet Square, Gunton, Lowestoft NR32 4LZ* T: (01502) 564064 E: g.wilson570@btinternet.com

WILSON, Geoffrey. *See* WILSON, Samuel Geoffrey

WILSON, Geoffrey Samuel Alan. b 46. TCD BA 69 QUB DipEd 70 TCD MA 72. CITC BTh 93. **d** 96 **p** 97. C Glendermott *D & R* 96–99; I Camus-juxta-Mourne 99–12; rtd 12. *42 Ferndale Park, Portstewart BT55 7JB* T: (028) 7083 3542 *or* 3834 2969 M: 07803-554386 E: revgeoffwilson@comail.com

WILSON, George Thomas. b 47. CBDTI 97. **d** 00 **p** 01. NSM Barrow St Paul *Carl* 00–06; P-in-c Bootle, Corney, Whicham and Whitbeck 06–10; NSM Cartmel Peninsula 10–19; rtd 19. *10 Fairfield, Flookburgh, Grange-over-Sands LA11 7NB* T: (01539) 559215 E: george860@btinternet.com

WILSON, Graham Whitelaw. b 46. Leeds Univ CertEd 77 Birm Univ MPhil 00 Derby Univ DMin 03. EMMTC. **d** 95 **p** 96. NSM Burbage w Aston Flamville *Leic* 95–97; C 97–01; C Fenn Lanes Gp 01–04; PtO from 04. *10 The Courtyard, Higham Lane, Stoke Golding, Nuneaton CV13 6EX* T: (01455) 213598 E: gwwilson@btinternet.com

WILSON, Mrs Heather Clarissa. b 49. Hull Univ BA 71 Leic Univ PGCE 72 Anglia Poly Univ MA 05. EAMTC 01. **d** 03 **p** 04. NSM Duston *Pet* 03–15; TV 06–15; rtd 15; PtO *Pet* from 15. *12 Ardens Grove, Rotherthorpe, Northampton NN7 3JJ* T: (01604) 830714 M: 07702-033727 E: revdheather@gmail.com

WILSON, Canon Ian Andrew. b 57. Nottm Univ BTh 89. Linc Th Coll 86. **d** 89 **p** 90. C Whitton and Thurleston w Akenham *St E* 89–93; P-in-c Elmsett w Aldham 93–02; R Elmsett w Aldham, Hintlesham, Chattisham etc 02; Chapl Woodbridge Sch 03–16; P-in-c Nacton and Levington w Bucklesham etc *St E* from 16; P-in-c Waldringfield w Hemley and Newbourne from 16; Hon Can St E Cathl from 12. *The Rectory, Nacton, Ipswich IP10 0HY* T: (01473) 659875 E: reviwilson@yahoo.co.uk *or* revcanian@yahoo.com

WILSON, Mrs Irene Margaret. b 49. Leeds Univ BA 83 ALCM 69. Yorks Min Course 09. **d** 11 **p** 12. NSM Kingston upon Hull H Trin *York* from 11. *10 Westgate, North Cave, Brough HU15 2NJ* T: (01430) 470719 M: 07711-996519 E: irene@hullminster.org

WILSON, Canon James. b 65. St Steph Ho Ox. **d** 01 **p** 02. C Whitchurch *Bris* 01–03; C Horfield St Greg 03–05; P-in-c from 05; Hon Can Bris Cathl from 13. *St Gregory's Vicarage, Filton Road, Horfield, Bristol BS7 0PD* T: 0117-969 2839 E: revjameswilson@aol.com

WILSON, Canon James Andrew Christopher. b 48. Ex & Truro Min Scheme. **d** 82 **p** 83. NSM Plymouth Crownhill Ascension *Ex* 82–83; NSM Yelverton 83–85; C Plymstock 85–87; R Lifton 87–92; R Kelly w Bradstone 87–92; V Broadwoodwidger 87–92; R Calstock *Truro* 92–13; RD E Wivelshire 00–11; P-in-c St Dominic, Landulph and St Mellion w Pillaton 12–13; rtd 14; Hon Can Truro Cathl from 04; PtO from 14. *22 Riverside Mills, Launceston PL15 8GX* T: (01566) 774998 E: andrew.wilson1111@btinternet.com

WILSON, James Kenneth. b 47. **d** 88 **p** 89. C Holyhead w Rhoscolyn w Llanfair-yn-Neubwll *Ban* 88–91; Chapl RAF 91–97; Mental Health Chapl Lincs Partnership NHS Foundn Trust 07–12; rtd 12; P-in-c Llaneugrad w Llanallgo and Penrhosllugwy etc *Ban* 15; PtO 16–18. *29 Minffordd Estate, Benllech, Tyn-y-Gongl LL74 8QG* T: (01248) 852079 E: ken@kw22.co.uk *or* padre.ken.wilson@gmail.com

WILSON, James Lewis. b 39. TCD BA 62 HDipEd 63 MA 65 BD 71. TCD Div Sch Div Test 74. **d** 74 **p** 75. C Enniskillen *Clogh* 74–76; C Belfast St Matt *Conn* 76–79; I Killeshandra w Killegar *K, E & A* 79–81; I Derrylane 79–81; I Loughgilly w Clare *Arm* 81–10; rtd 10. *2 Tramway Drive, Bushmills BT57 8YS* T: (028) 2073 1353

WILSON, James Robert. b 36. CITC. **d** 66 **p** 67. C Ballywillan *Conn* 67–73; I Drummaul 73–79; I Drummaul w Duneane and Ballyscullion 79–01; Preb Conn Cathl 96; Treas Conn Cathl 96–98; Chan Conn Cathl 98–01; rtd 01. *90 Killycowan Road, Glarryford, Ballymena BT44 9HJ* T: (028) 2568 5737

WILSON, Canon Jane Jennifer. b 43. Ch Ch Coll Cant TCert 65 Open Univ BA 84. Wycliffe Hall Ox 89. **d** 91 **p** 94. Par Dn Northwood Em *Lon* 91–94; C 94–98; TV Blythburgh w Reydon *St E* 98; TV Sole Bay 98–02; TR 02–07; RD Halesworth 01–07; Hon Can St E Cathl 05–07; P-in-c Offwell, Northleigh, Farway, Cotleigh etc *Ex* 07–11; rtd 11; Bp's Adv for Women in Min *Ex* 11–15; PtO from 15. *Hawthorns, 17 Ashleigh Park, Bampton, Tiverton EX16 9LF* T: (01398) 332135 E: janeoffwell@aol.com

WILSON, Mrs Janet Mary. b 44. Bedf Coll of Educn TCert 66 SRN 74. **d** 03 **p** 04. OLM S Croydon Em *S'wark* 03–10; PtO from 11. *Elmwood, 2 Weybourne Place, Sanderstead CR2 0RZ* T: (020) 8657 2195 E: revjanwilson@blueyonder.co.uk

WILSON, Jeffery. b 59. **d** 06 **p** 07. OLM Kirton in Lindsey w Manton *Linc* from 06; OLM Grayingham from 06. *34 Richdale Avenue, Kirton Lindsey, Gainsborough DN21 4BL* T: (01652) 648687

WILSON, John Anthony. b 34. Linc Th Coll. **d** 83 **p** 84. C Nunthorpe *York* 83–85; V Whorlton w Carlton and Faceby 85–94; V E Coatham 94–99; rtd 99; PtO *York* 00–08; *Ripon* 00–03; P-in-c Lower Swale 03–08; PtO *Glouc* 08–19; *York* 10–15. *29 Letch Hill Drive, Bourton-on-*

the-Water, Cheltenham GL54 2DQ T: (01451) 820571 E: johnjeanwilson58@gmail.com

WILSON, John Frederick. b 33. Qu Coll Birm 58. d 61 p 62. C Jarrow St Paul Dur 61–65; C Monkwearmouth All SS 65–68; Br Honduras 68–71; V Scunthorpe Resurr Linc 71–90; Chapl Divine Healing Miss Crowhurst 90–91; V Terrington St Clement Ely 91–99; rtd 99; PtO Ely from 99. 7 Oakleigh Crescent, Godmanchester, Huntingdon PE29 2JJ T: (01480) 392791 E: alex.wilson2@ntlworld.com

WILSON, Canon John Hamilton. b 29. St Chad's Coll Dur BA 53. Sarum Th Coll 53. d 55 p 56. C W End Win 55–59; C Fishponds St Mary Bris 59–64; V Bedminster St Fran 64–73; RD Bedminster 68–73; R Horfield H Trin 73–96; Hon Can Bris Cathl 77–96; rtd 96; PtO Bris from 96. 2 West Croft, Bristol BS9 4PQ T/F: 0117-962 9204 E: johnhollow72@hotmail.com

WILSON, John Lake. b 34. Linc Th Coll 74. d 76 p 77. C N Lynn w St Marg and St Nic Nor 76–80; V Narborough w Narford 80–85; R Pentney St Mary Magd w W Bilney 80–85; V Lakenham St Mark 85–93; P-in-c Trowse 92–93; V Lakenham St Mark w Trowse 93–98; Chapl Whitlingham Hosp 93–98; rtd 98; PtO Nor from 98; Eur from 00. Slinmoor, Warham Road, Wells-next-the-Sea NR23 1NE T: (01328) 711035 E: wslinmoor@aol.com

WILSON, Canon Judith Anne. b 48. Keele Univ BA 71 Leic Univ PGCE 72. S Dios Minl Tr Scheme 92. d 95 p 96. NSM Slaugham Chich 95–96; Sub Chapl HM Pris Wandsworth 95–96; Chapl HM Pris and YOI Hollesley Bay 96–01; Chapl HM Pris Nor 01–09; Chapl Gt Hosp Nor 09–15; P-in-c Nor St Helen 09–14; V 14–15; Bp's Adv for Women's Min 04–10; Hon Asst Dioc Dir of Ords 09–15; Hon Can Nor Cathl 07–15; rtd 15; PtO Nor from 15. 13 Hunters Close, Blofield, Norwich NR13 4LS T: (01603) 211509 E: revjudithwilson@gmail.com

WILSON, Julian. b 63. Plymouth Univ BSc 92. Ox Min Course 15. d 17 p 18. C Cirencester Glouc from 17. The Parish Centre, Gosditch Street, Cirencester GL7 2AG T: (01285) 659317

WILSON, Julian John. b 64. Collingwood Coll Dur BSc 85 Liv Univ BTh. NOC 01. d 04 p 05. C Uttoxeter Area Lich 04–07; Chapl Denstone Coll Uttoxeter 07–09; R Baschurch and Weston Lullingfield w Hordley Lich 09–15; World Development Officer (Salop) 11–15; RD Ellesmere 13–15; P-in-c Corfu Eur from 15. Holy Trinity Corfu, 21 L.Mavili Street, Corfu 49100 E: julesjwilson@gmail.com

WILSON, Karen Amanda Francesca. b 67. St Mellitus Coll 15. d 18 p 19. C Okeford Sarum from 18. The Stables, Mill Farm, Shillingstone Lane, Okeford Fitzpaine, Blandford Forum DT11 0RB E: revdkarenwilson@outlook.com

WILSON, Mrs Kathleen. b 47. Bucks Coll of Educn BSc 90 Ox Brookes Univ MBA 93 RGN 69. d 03 p 04. OLM Iver Ox 03–10; P-in-c Colbury Win 10–13; Chapl Oakhaven Hospice Trust 12–17; rtd 17; PtO Win from 18. 16 Waverley Road, Fordingbridge SP6 1EX T: (01425) 540669 M: 07770-944054 E: kate.wilson501@gmail.com

WILSON, Ms Lauretta Joy. b 64. Bath Univ BSc 87 CertEd 87. SAOMC 02. d 05 p 06. C Boxmoor St Jo St Alb 05–08; TV Langelei 08–15; TR Kegworth, Hathern, Long Whatton, Diseworth etc Leic from 15. The Rectory, 24 Nottingham Road, Kegworth, Derby DE74 2FH M: 07840-753202 E: ljwilson33@btinternet.com

WILSON, Louis. See WILSON, Philip Louis

WILSON, Mark Anthony John. b 56. TCD BA 80. CITC 75. d 80 p 81. C Dublin Rathfarnham D & G 80–84; Bp's C Dublin Finglas 83–84; I Celbridge w Straffan and Newcastle-Lyons 85–88; CF 88–93; I Dundalk w Heynestown Arm 93–03; Chapl Adelaide and Meath Hosp Dublin 04–16; Chapl Algarve Eur 16–17; P-in-c Walbury Beacon Ox from 17. The Vicarage, 3 Elizabeth Gardens, Kintbury, Hungerford RG17 9TB E: markajwilson1@gmail.com

WILSON, Mark Ashley John. b 87. Cranmer Hall Dur 12. d 15 p 16. C Kidsgrove Lich 15–18; P-in-c W Bromwich St Jas w St Paul from 18. 90 Hall Green Road, West Bromwich B71 3LB T: 0121-532 2865 E: vicar@stjameswithstpauls.co.uk

WILSON, Martin. See WILSON, Bernard Martin

WILSON, Canon Mavis Kirby. b 42. Ex Univ BA 64 Cam Univ CertEd 71. S Dios Minl Tr Scheme 82. dss 84 d 87 p 94. Chessington Guildf 84–85; Epsom St Martin 85–86; Epsom Common Ch Ch 86–87; C 87–96; Dioc Adv in Miss, Evang, and Par Development 90–02; R Frimley 02–13; Hon Can Guildf Cathl 94–13; rtd 13. 48 Byrefield Road, Guildford GU2 9UB T: (01483) 808097 E: maviswilson2@gmail.com

WILSON, Mervyn Raynold Alwyn. b 33. Qu Coll Cam BA 57 MA 61. Ripon Hall Ox 57. d 59 p 60. C Rubery Birm 59–62; C Kings Norton 62–63; V Hamstead St Bernard 63–69; R Bermondsey St Mary w St Olave, St Jo etc S'wark

69–78; R Bulwick, Blatherwycke w Harringworth and Laxton Pet 78–03; rtd 03; PtO B & W from 04. The Red Post House, Fivehead, Taunton TA3 6PX T: (01460) 281558 E: margaretwilson426@gmail.com

WILSON, The Very Revd Mervyn Robert. b 22. Bris Univ BA 51 Lon Univ BD 58. Tyndale Hall Bris 52. d 52 p 53. C Ballymacarrett St Patr D & D 52–56; C Donaghcloney 56–59; C Newtownards 59–61; I Ballyphilip w Ardquin 61–70; I Newry St Patr 70–92; Preb Dromore Cathl 83–85; Can Belf Cathl 85–89; Dean Dromore D & D 90–92; rtd 92. 31 Manor Drive, Lisburn BT28 1JH T: (028) 9266 6361

WILSON, Canon Michael. b 44. Liv Univ BA 66 Fitzw Coll Cam BA 68 MA 73 De Montfort Univ MBA 94. Westcott Ho Cam. d 69 p 70. C Worksop Priory S'well 69–71; C Gt Malvern St Mary Worc 71–75; V Leic St Anne 75–85; TR Leic Ascension 85–88; Hon Can Leic Cathl 85–88; Can Res and Treas Leic Cathl 88–09; rtd 09; PtO Pet from 09; Leic from 10. 8 Wensum Close, Oakham LE15 6FU T: (01572) 720853 E: mwilson@keme.co.uk

WILSON, Neil. b 61. Newc Univ BA 83. Ripon Coll Cuddesdon 85. d 88 p 89. C Wallsend St Luke Newc 88–91; C Monkseaton St Pet 91–93; V Earsdon and Backworth 93–04; P-in-c Newc St Jo 04–11; V Haltwhistle and Greenhead 11–18; Chapl Northumbria Healthcare NHS Foundn Trust from 15. 25 Albany Mews, Montague Avenue, Newcastle upon Tyne NE3 4JW E: neilwilson50@btinternet.com

WILSON, Paul David. b 64. Cranmer Hall Dur 96. d 98 p 99. C Bramley and Ravenfield w Hooton Roberts etc Sheff 98–01; V Hatfield 01–13; AD Snaith and Hatfield 11–13; Hon Can Sheff Cathl 12–13; R Warrington St Elphin Liv 13–19; AD Warrington 17–19; R Epworth Gp Linc from 19. The Vicarage, Church Street, Haxey, Doncaster DN9 2HY E: revpdwilson@aol.com

WILSON, Peter Sheppard. b 39. TCD BA 61. CITC Div Test 62. d 62 p 63. C Killowen D & R 62–68; C Portadown St Columba Arm 68–70; I Convoy w Monellan and Donaghmore D & R 70–78; V Castletown S & M 78–83; R Kilmacolm and Bridge of Weir Glas 83–85; I Camus-juxta-Bann D & R 85–92; Bp's Dom Chapl 90–92; I Maguiresbridge w Derrybrusk Clogh 92–05; Chapl to Bp Clogh 98–00; Can Clogh Cathl 03–05; rtd 05. 25 Grogey Road, Fivemiletown BT75 0SQ T: (028) 8952 1883

WILSON, Peter Stuart. b 45. Yorks Min Course 08. d 09 p 10. NSM Cross Roads cum Lees Bradf 09–14; Leeds 14–15; NSM Haworth 09–14; Leeds 14–15; rtd 15; PtO Leeds from 17. 3 Epworth Place, Oakworth, Keighley BD22 7ST M: 07870-134272 E: revdpeterwilson@gmail.com

WILSON, Philip Louis. b 68. Bris Univ LLB 91. Oak Hill Th Coll BA 09. d 09 p 10. NSM Broadwell, Evenlode, Oddington, Adlestrop etc Glouc 09–12; R Denton w S Heighton and Tarring Neville Chich from 12. The Rectory, 6 Heighton Road, Newhaven BN9 0RB T: (01273) 514319 E: landjwilson@btinternet.com

WILSON, Rachel Claire. b 68. d 12 p 13. C Dartford St Edm Roch 12–16; P-in-c Southborough St Thos from 16. St Thomas's Vicarage, 30 Pennington Road, Tunbridge Wells TN4 0SL T: (01892) 525869 E: reverendrachelwilson@gmail.com

WILSON, Mrs Rachel Elizabeth. b 56. Keswick Hall Coll BEd 79. NOC 00. d 03 p 04. NSM Slaidburn and Long Preston w Tosside Bradf 03–10; NSM Lower Wharfedale Leeds 10–16; Min in Deaf Community 09–16; NSM Pocklington Wold York 16–17; NSM Londesborough Wold 16–17; rtd 17; PtO Leeds from 17. 39 Carlton Street, Haworth, Keighley BD21 8JY

WILSON, Richard Graham. b 67. Bris Univ BSc 91 DipSW 93. Trin Coll Bris BA 01. d 01 p 02. C Wandsworth St Mich S'wark 01–05; TR Bath Twerton-on-Avon B & W 05–18; RD Bath 15–18; V Reigate St Mary S'wark from 18. 76 Church Street, Reigate RH2 0SP T: (01225) 421438 M: 07792-693062 E: richard@stmichaelstwerton.com

WILSON, Canon Robert Malcolm (Robin). b 35. St Andr Univ MA 59. ALCD 62. d 62 p 63. C Wallington S'wark 62–66; C Dur St Nic 66–70; V Colchester St Pet Chelmsf 70–01; RD Colchester 93–98; Hon Can Chelmsf Cathl 94–01; rtd 01; PtO St E from 01; Chelmsf 01–10. Hawthorns, Melton Road, Melton, Woodbridge IP12 1NH T: (01394) 383514

WILSON, Robert Stoker. b 39. Dur Univ BSc 62. Oak Hill Th Coll 62. d 64 p 65. C High Elswick St Paul Newc 64–68; C Kirkheaton 68–70; Youth Chapl Liv 70–73; P-in-c S Shields St Steph Dur 73–78; R 78–83; Youth Chapl 73–77; P-in-c S Shields St Aid 81–83; V Greenside 83–94; P-in-c Fatfield 94–98; P-in-c Coniscliffe 98–04; Dioc Adv for IT 98–04; rtd 04; PtO Dur from 13. 9 Augusta Close, Darlington DL1 3HT T: (01325) 350324 M: 07808-

911928 E: stoker.wilson@durham.anglican.org *or* stoker@stokerwilson.me.uk

WILSON, Ross Robert. b 70. Bath Univ BSc 94. Trin Coll Bris MA 12. **d** 12 **p** 13. C Willowfield *D & D* 12–15; I Orangefield w Moneyreagh from 15. *The Rectory, 397A Castlereagh Road, Belfast BT5 6AB* T: (028) 9070 4493 M: 07564-232344 E: ross.wilson@sent.com *or* ross@stjohnsorangefield.org

WILSON, Mrs Sally Jayne. b 57. Ripon Coll of Educn BA 79 PGCE 80 Teesside Univ MA(Ed) 99. **d** 19. NSM Danby w Castleton and Commondale *York* from 19. *17 Dale End, Danby, Whitby YO21 2JF* T: (01287) 660190 E: danbychurch@gmail.com

WILSON, The Very Revd Samuel Geoffrey. b 62. CITC BTh 04. **d** 04 **p** 05. C Swanlinbar w Tomregan, Kinawley, Drumlane etc *K, E & A* 04–07; I Kildallon and Swanlinbar 07–09; I Lurgan Ch the Redeemer *D & D* 09–16; Dean Dromore from 16; I Dromore Cathl from 16. *The Deanery, 28 Church Street, Dromore BT25 1AA* T: (028) 9269 3968 M: 07803-554386 E: revgeoffwilson@gmail.com

WILSON, Simon Anthony. b 67. Portsm Poly BA 88. Cranmer Hall Dur 96. **d** 99 **p** 00. NSM Barnham Broom *Nor* 99–00; NSM Barnham Broom and Upper Yare 00–02; NSM Hellesdon 02–03; Public Preacher from 03; Chapl Norfolk Constabulary (Cen Area) 05–13; Chapl Norfolk Fire Service 05–13; Co-ord Dioc Forum for Soc and Community Concerns 06–13; Co Ecum Officer 10–13. *The Vicarage, Church Lane, Heacham, King's Lynn PE31 7HJ* T: (01485) 570697 E: simon.wilson@dioceseofnorwich.org *or* revsimonwilson@btinternet.com

WILSON, Stephen Charles. b 51. Newc Univ BA 73 Cam Univ BA 78 MA 82. Westcott Ho Cam. **d** 79 **p** 80. C Fulham All SS *Lon* 79–82; C W Hampstead St Jas 82–85; P-in-c Alexandra Park St Sav 85–93; V Preston next Faversham, Goodnestone and Graveney *Cant* 93–14; V Preston-next-Faversham 14–15; Hon Min Can Cant Cathl 98–15; Asst Dir of Ords 07–10; rtd 15; PtO *S'wark* from 16. *42 Mount Ash Road, London SE26 6LY* T: (020) 8699 8386 E: revdscwilson@gmail.com

WILSON, Stephen Graham. b 70. Ridley Hall Cam 09. **d** 11 **p** 12. C Overton w Laverstoke and Freefolk *Win* 11–15; CF from 15. *c/o MOD Chaplains (Army)* T: (01264) 383430 F: 381824 M: 07968-272116 E: revstephenwilson@btinternet.com

WILSON, Canon Stephen John. b 45. Bradf Univ BTech 69. Trin Coll Bris 90. **d** 92 **p** 93. C Marple All SS *Ches* 92–96; P-in-c Moulton 96–01; Chapl Mid Cheshire Hosps Trust 96–99; V Hyde St Geo *Ches* 01–10; RD Mottram 03–08; Hon Can Ches Cathl 06–10; rtd 10; PtO *Ches* from 11. *18 Green Park, Weaverham, Northwich CW8 3EH* T: (01606) 851294 E: stephen.wilson888@btinternet.com

WILSON, Stoker. *See* WILSON, Robert Stoker

WILSON, Stuart Arnold. b 47. SWMTC 94. **d** 97 **p** 98. NSM Okehampton w Inwardleigh, Bratton Clovelly etc *Ex* 97–02; TV 02–09; rtd 10. *Red Spider Cottage, Bratton Clovelly, Okehampton EX20 4JD* T: (01837) 871248 E: s.wilson45@btinternet.com

WILSON, Susan Annette. b 60. Bath Univ BPharm 81 PhD 86 MRPharmS 82. Westcott Ho Cam 98. **d** 00 **p** 01. C Newc St Geo 00–03; Chapl Dame Allan's Schs Newc 02–03; TV Willington *Newc* 03–07; V Newc St Gabr 07–13; rtd 13; PtO *Newc* from 13. *2 Amberdale Avenue, Newcastle upon Tyne NE6 4UF* E: wilsonsrh@btinternet.com

WILSON, Miss Susan Elizabeth. b 52. Lady Spencer Chu Coll of Educn BEd 75. WEMTC 96. **d** 99 **p** 00. NSM Saltford w Corston and Newton St Loe *B & W* 99–06; P-in-c Heversham and Milnthorpe *Carl* 06–16; rtd 16. *Penholme House, Church Road, Grange-over-Sands LA11 6BP* E: revsuewilson@tiscali.co.uk

WILSON, Mrs Sylvia. b 57. Teesside Univ BA 96 Newc Univ MA 99. **d** 08 **p** 09. OLM Preston-on-Tees and Longnewton *Dur* 08–14; P-in-c Egglescliffe from 14. *7 Daltry Close, Yarm TS15 9XQ* T: (01642) 892254 M: 07886-852154 E: sylviawilson.stjohns@gmail.com

WILSON, Thomas D. b 58. Univ of W Ontario BA 80 MDiv 99 Drew Univ New Jersey DMin 10. **d** 01 **p** 01. R Blyth and Brussels Canada 01–07; Hon C Nice w Vence *Eur* 07–08; Lic to Offic Huron Canada 08–11; P-in-c Cambridge St Luke 11–12; R Paisley H Trin and St Barn *Glas* 12–17; R Glas Gd Shep 16–17; Chapl St Raphaël *Eur* from 17. *Le Périgord, 2me étage, appartement droit, 91 rue Alphonse Daudet, 83600 Fréjus, France* T: (0033) 7 83 77 63 63 E: tomdwilson@gmail.com

WILSON, Thomas Kazimir. b 78. Ox Univ BA 01. Wycliffe Hall Ox BA 07. **d** 07 **p** 08. C Toxteth St Philemon w St Gabr and St Cleopas *Liv* 07–12; V Glouc St Jas and All SS and Ch Ch 12–15; Dir St Phil Cen *Leic* from 15. *St Philip's Centre, 2A Stoughton Drive North, Leicester*

LE5 5UB T: 0116-273 3459 E: revtomwilson@gmail.com *or* director@stphilipscentre.co.uk

WILSON, Canon Thomas Roderick. b 26. St Pet Hall Ox BA 50 MA 55. Sarum Th Coll 50. **d** 52 **p** 53. C Poulton-le-Sands *Blackb* 52–56; C Altham w Clayton le Moors 56–58; V Habergham Eaves H Trin 58–78; RD Burnley 70–78; Hon Can Blackb Cathl 75–89; V Bare 78–81; P-in-c Accrington St Jas 81–82; P-in-c Accrington St Paul 81–82; V Accrington St Jas w St Paul 82–89; rtd 89; PtO *Blackb* 89–11. *34 Fosbrooke House, 8 Clifton Drive, Lytham St Annes FY8 5RQ*

WILSON, Timothy Charles. b 62. Oak Hill Th Coll BA 90. **d** 90 **p** 91. C Highley *Heref* 90–94; C Margate H Trin *Cant* 94–98; P-in-c Margate St Phil 98–02; V 02–03; V Gt Chart 03–16; TV Ashford Town 16–18; AD Ashford 11–18; Hon Can Cant Cathl 11–18; P-in-c Wilden w Colmworth and Ravensden *St Alb* from 19; P-in-c Bolnhurst w Keysoe from 19. *The Vicarage, 47 Stagsden Road, Bromham, Bedford MK43 8PY* M: 07808-865716 E: revtimwilson@wcrchurches.org

WILSON, Timothy John. b 58. St Pet Coll Ox MA 80. Trin Coll Bris 81. **d** 83 **p** 84. C Gt Horton *Bradf* 83–86; C Handforth *Ches* 86–90; V Halifax All SS *Wakef* 90–07; TR S Crawley *Chich* from 07. *The Rectory, Forester Road, Crawley RH10 6EH* T: (01293) 523463 E: wilsons@domini.org

WILSON, William Adam. b 53. Sheff Univ BA 74 St Jo Coll Dur BA 84. Cranmer Hall Dur 82. **d** 85 **p** 86. C S Croydon Em *S'wark* 85–89; C Wandsworth All SS 89–93; Chapl Fontainebleau *Eur* 93–00; V S Lambeth St Steph *S'wark* from 00. *The Vicarage, St Stephen's Terrace, London SW8 1DH* T: (020) 7564 1930 *or* 7735 8461 F: 7735 7171 E: vicar@ststephenssouthlambeth.org.uk

WILSON, William Gerard. b 42. St Chad's Coll Dur BA 65. **d** 67 **p** 68. C Hollinwood *Man* 67–71; V Oldham St Jas 71–79; R Birch w Fallowfield 79–93; V Paddington St Jas *Lon* 93–10; AD Westmr Paddington 97–06; rtd 10; PtO *Lon* from 10; *Chich* from 15. *20 Portland Street, Brighton BN1 1RN* M: 07976-363480 E: synaxis52@hotmail.com

WILSON, Yvonne. *See* WILSON, Edith Yvonne

WILSON-BARKER, Mrs Carol Amanda. b 64. Ex Univ BA 08. SWMTC 00. **d** 03 **p** 05. C Godrevy *Truro* 03–07; TV Hale w Badshot Lea *Guildf* 07–12; P-in-c Mere w W Knoyle and Maiden Bradley *Sarum* from 12. *The Vicarage, Angel Lane, Mere, Warminster BA12 6DH* T: (01747) 861859 E: carolw953@aol.com

WILTON, Mrs Carlyn Zena. b 54. R Holloway Coll Lon BA 75 Southn Univ PGCE 76. SWMTC 99. **d** 02 **p** 03. NSM Carbis Bay w Lelant *Truro* from 02. *Venton Elwyn, 61 Queensway, Hayle TR27 4NL* T: (01736) 752863 E: ventonelwyn@aol.com

WILTON, Canon Christopher. b 52. Lon Univ LLB 75 Solicitor 79. NEOC 97. **d** 00 **p** 01. NSM Sherburn in Elmet w Saxton *York* from 03; P-in-c 03–09; V from 09; P-in-c Aberford w Micklefield from 12; RD Selby from 06; Hon Can Ho Ghana from 14; Can and Preb York Minster from 16. *The Vicarage, 2 Sir John's Lane, Sherburn in Elmet, Leeds LS25 6BJ* T: (01977) 682122 *or* 732222 M: 07968-268622 E: frwilton@aol.com

WILTON, Canon Gary Ian. b 60. Bath Univ BSc 83 Trin Coll Bris MA 93 Nottm Univ EdD 05. Wycliffe Hall Ox 85. **d** 88 **p** 89. C Clevedon St Andr and Ch Ch *B & W* 88–92; Lect UWE Bris 92–93; TV Bath Twerton-on-Avon *B & W* 93–97; Dir Studies and Lect Wilson Carlile Coll of Evang 98–04; Assoc Prin 04–05; Sen Lect York St Jo Univ 05–08; Hd Postgraduate Progr 06–08; C of E Rep Eur Union 08–13; Abp Cant's Rep 11–13; Can Brussels Cathl *Eur* 08–13; V Ecclesall *Sheff* 13–19; PtO *Eur* 18–19; Chapl Dinard from 19. *Eglise Anglicaine de Dinard (St Bartholomew), rue Faber, 35800 Dinard, France* T: (0033) 2 99 46 77 00

WILTON (née ADAMS), Mrs Gillian Linda. b 57. SRN 79 SCM 81. Trin Coll Bris 82. **dss** 85 **d** 87 **p** 94. Easton H Trin w St Gabr and St Lawr and St Jude *Bris* 85–91; Par Dn 87–91; Regional Adv (SW) CMJ 91–97; PtO *B & W* 92–93; NSM Bath Twerton-on-Avon 93–97; Chapl Sheff Children's Hosp NHS Trust 98–06; Chapl Team Ldr Sheff Children's NHS Foundn Trust 06–10; PtO *Eur* 08–10; Asst Chapl Tervuren 10–13; P-in-c Leuven 10–11; PtO *Sheff* 13–14; Chapl St Luke's Hospice Sheff from 14; Chapl Sheff Teaching Hosps NHS Foundn Trust from 14. *Ecclesall Vicarage, Ringinglow Road, Sheffield S11 7PQ* T: 0114-236 0084 E: gillian.wilton@hotmail.co.uk

WILTON, Glenn Warner Paul. b 33. Miami Univ Ohio BSc 55 Catholic Univ of America 69 Univ of Washington Seattle MSW 76. Pontifical Beda Coll Rome 66 Ch Div Sch of the Pacific (USA) 77. **d** 65 **p** 66. In RC Ch 65–72; NSM Seattle USA 77–81; Chapl Pastures Hosp Derby 82–88; Chapl St Martin's Hosp Cant 89–93; Chapl St Aug Hosp Cant 89–93; Chapl E Kent NHS and Soc Care Partnership Trust 93–03; rtd 03; PtO *Cant* from 03. *10 Lichfield Avenue, Canterbury CT1 3YA* T: (01227) 454230

WILTS, Archdeacon of. *See* GROOM, The Ven Susan Anne

WILTSHIRE, Mrs Jennifer Mary. b 42. Trin Coll Bris 09. d 11 p 12. OLM Soundwell *Bris* from 11; PtO *Portsm* from 17. *19 Yew Tree Drive, Bristol BS15 4UA* T: 0117-957 0435 E: jenny.wiltshire410@btinternet.com

WILTSHIRE, Robert Michael. b 50. WMMTC. d 89 p 90. NSM Droitwich Spa *Worc* 89–93; Asst Chapl HM Pris Wormwood Scrubs 93–94; Chapl HM Pris Standford Hill 94–97; Chapl HM Pris Whitemoor 97–99; Asst Chapl Gen of Pris 99–06; Chapl HM Pris Shrewsbury 06–13; C Edstaston, Fauls, Prees, Tilstock and Whixall *Lich* 13–14; rtd 14; Hon C Hodnet *Lich* 15–16; C Wrockwardine Deanery 16–17; RD Wrockwardine 16–17; PtO from 17. *Whitehayes, Whitchurch Road, Prees SY13 3JZ* E: rm_wiltshire@btinternet.com

WIMSETT, Paul. b 58. Univ of Wales (Abth) BSc(Econ) 79 Hull Univ MA 86. St Jo Coll Nottm 82. d 85 p 86. C Nuneaton St Nic *Cov* 85–89; C Loughborough Em *Leic* 89–92; TV Totnes, Bridgetown and Berry Pomeroy etc *Ex* 92–99; V Chudleigh w Chudleigh Knighton and Trusham from 99; RD Moreton 05–11. *The Vicarage, Parade, Chudleigh, Newton Abbot TQ13 0JF* T: (01626) 853241 E: chudleigh.cofe@gmail.com

WINBOLT-LEWIS, Martin John. b 46. Fitzw Coll Cam BA 69 MA 72. St Jo Coll Nottm. d 75 p 76. C Highbury Ch Ch *Lon* 75–78; C Nottingham St Nic *S'well* 79–82; R Carlton Colville *Nor* 82–83; R Carlton Colville w Mutford and Rushmere 83–88; V Burley *Ripon* 88–96; Asst Chapl Pinderfields and Pontefract Hosps NHS Trust 96–99; Chapl 99–00; Lead Chapl 00–02; Lead Chapl Mid Yorks Hosps NHS Trust 02–05; Hd Chapl Services 05–10; rtd 11; PtO *Leeds* from 11. *Owl Pen, 2 Old Manor Farm, Church Hill, Bramhope, Leeds LS16 9BA* T: 0113-284 2274 E: winboltlewis@btinternet.com

WINCHESTER, Paul. b 44. St Pet Coll Ox BA 66 MA 70 Weymouth Coll of Educn PGCE 73. Ridley Hall Cam 67. d 69 p 70. C Wednesfield Heath *Lich* 69–72; PtO *Sarum* 73–84; R Tushingham and Whitewell *Ches* 84–02; PtO *Ox* from 02. *12 The Pines, Faringdon SN7 8AU* T: (01367) 240725 E: p.winchester123@btinternet.com

WINCHESTER, Paul Marc. b 53. Univ of Wales (Lamp) BA 80. St Mich Coll Llan 82. d 84 p 85. C Bedwellty *Mon* 84–86; C Chepstow 86–89; V Cwmcarn 89–93; V Fleur-de-Lis 93–98; R Bedwas and Rudry 98–05; P-in-c Llantilio Pertholey w Bettws Chpl etc 05–10; V Brynmawr *S & B* 10–17; rtd 17; PtO *Mon* from 18. *12 Briardene, Llanfoist, Abergavenny NP7 9LJ* T: (01873) 598557 E: marcw1953@sky.com

WINCHESTER, Archdeacon of. *See* BRAND, The Ven Richard Harold Guthrie

WINCHESTER, Bishop of. *See* DAKIN, The Rt Revd Timothy John

WINCHESTER, Dean of. *See* OGLE, The Very Revd Catherine

WINDEBANK, Clive Leonard. b 41. New Coll Ox BA 62 MA 85. Ox NSM Course 75. d 78 p 79. Asst Chapl Ahmadi Kuwait 78–83; NSM Brompton H Trin w Onslow Square St Paul *Lon* 83–84; NSM Basildon w Aldworth and Ashampstead *Ox* 85–88; NSM Streatley w Moulsford 88–00; NSM Wallingford 00–03; Chapl Abu Dhabi St Andr UAE 03–09; PtO *Ox* from 13. *The Coombe House, The Coombe, Streatley, Reading RG8 9QL* T: (01491) 872174

WINDER, Cynthia Frances. *See* CLEMOW, Cynthia Frances

WINDIATE, Mary Elizabeth. *See* WEST, Mary Elizabeth

WINDLE, Mrs Catharine Elizabeth. b 72. Hatf Coll Dur BA 95 Homerton Coll Cam PGCE 96. St Jo Coll Nottm MTh 02. d 03 p 04. C Hucknall Torkard *S'well* 03–05; Hon C Hullavington, Norton and Stanton St Quintin *Bris* 05–06; P-in-c Bath Widcombe *B & W* 06–08; Hon C Malmesbury w Westport and Brokenborough *Bris* 09–13; Chapl SS Helen and Kath Sch Abingdon 13–17; PtO *Ox* 15–18; Chapl Sherborne Sch for Girls from 18. *Sherborne School for Girls, Bradford Road, Sherborne DT9 3QN* T: (01935) 812245 E: royandkatie@gmail.com

WINDLE, Christopher Rodney. b 45. Univ of Wales (Lamp) BA 66. Qu Coll Birm. d 70 p 71. C Lache cum Saltney *Ches* 70–73; C Stockton Heath 73–76; P-in-c Bredbury St Barn 76–83; V 83–07; rtd 07; PtO *Ches* from 07. *6 Norbury Avenue, Marple, Stockport SK6 6NB* T: 0161-427 0375 E: kit.windle@gmail.com

WINDLEY, Caroline Judith. b 62. Trent Poly BA 84 Nottm Univ MA 97 CQSW 84. St Jo Coll Nottm MA 96. d 97 p 98. C Kidderminster St Geo *Worc* 97–01; P-in-c Quarry Bank 01–07; TV Brierley Hill 07–08; RD Kingswinford 04–08; Area Dir of Ord and Adv in Voc Development *Ox* 08–15; Dioc Dir of Ords from 15. *1 Cavalry Path, Aylesbury HP19 9RP* T: (01296) 432921 *or* (01865) 208283 E: caroline.windley@oxford.anglican.org

WINDRIDGE, Michael Harry. b 47. Sarum & Wells Th Coll 91. d 93 p 94. C Hempnall *Nor* 93–96; NSM Twickenham

St Mary *Lon* 96–97; PtO *Nor* from 98. *Fritton Cottage, The Common, Fritton, Norwich NR15 2QS* T: (01508) 498577

WINDROSS, Anthony Michael. b 50. CCC Cam BA 72 MA 75 Birm Univ PGCE 73. S Dios Minl Tr Scheme 90. d 93 p 94. NSM Eastbourne St Mary *Chich* 93–97; C E Grinstead St Swithun 97–99; V Sheringham *Nor* 99–08; V Hythe *Cant* 08–14; R Week St Mary Circle of Par *Truro* 14–18; RD Stratton 16–18; P-in-c Pevensey *Chich* from 18. *15 Peppercombe Road, Eastbourne BN20 8JH* M: 07484-786035   E: amwindross@btinternet.com   *or* anthonywindross@btinternet.com

WINDSLOW, Kathryn Alison. b 62. Southn Univ BTh 83 K Coll Lon MPhil 01. Linc Th Coll 84. dss 86 d 87 p 94. Littlehampton and Wick *Chich* 86–89; Par Dn 87–89; Dn-in-c Scotton w Northorpe *Linc* 89–94; P-in-c 94–97; Asst Local Min Officer 89–97; Local Min Officer and Prin OLM Course 97–02; R Graffoe Gp 02–14; Can and Preb Linc Cathl 09–14; Bp's Adv in Women's Min 08–14; R Storrington *Chich* from 14; RD from 16. *The Rectory, Rectory Road, Storrington, Pulborough RH20 4EF* T: (01903) 742888 E: kathryn.windslow@btinternet.com

WINDSOR, Joy Kathleen. b 66. Ox Min Course 15. d 17 p 18. NSM Alton *Win* from 17. *15 Walnut Close, Alton GU34 2BA* T: (01420) 83746

WINDSOR, The Ven Julie Fiona. b 59. Ridley Hall Cam 98. d 00 p 01. C Chertsey *Guildf* 00–04; TV Papworth *Ely* 04–08; TR 08–14; Hon Can Ely Cathl 12–14; Adn Horsham *Chich* from 14. *20 Langley Lane, Ifield, Crawley RH11 0NA* E: archhorsham@chichester.anglican.org

WINDSOR, Mark James. b 75. Bath Univ BSc 98. Wycliffe Hall Ox BTh 08. d 08 p 09. C Felsted and Lt Dunmow *Chelmsf* 08–12; Par Missr Harwich Peninsula 12–13; TV Vale of Pewsey *Sarum* from 13. *The Vicarage, Wilcot, Pewsey SN9 5NS* T: (01672) 564265 M: 07544-718191 E: markwindsor923@btinternet.com

WINDSOR, Dean of. *See* CONNER, The Rt Revd David John

WINFIELD, Canon Flora Jane Louise. b 64. Univ of Wales (Lamp) BA 85 Virginia Th Sem DD 10 FRSA 98. Ripon Coll Cuddesdon 87. d 89 p 94. Par Dn Stantonbury and Willen *Ox* 89–92; Co Ecum Officer *Glouc* 92–94; Chapl Mansf Coll Ox 94–97; Local Unity Sec Coun for Chr Unity 97–02; CF (TA) from 97; Can Res Win Cathl 02–05; Asst Sec Gen World Conf of Relig for Peace 05–06; Special Adv from 06; Sec Internat Affairs CTBI 06–09; Abp's Sec for Angl Relns *Cant* 07–14; P-in-c St Mary at Hill w St Andr Hubbard etc *Lon* 08–14; Angl Communion Rep UN Institutions Geneva 14–17; PtO *Lon* from 15; Abp's Special Rep to the Commonwealth from 17. *Lambeth Palace, London SE1 7JU* T: (020) 7898 1697 E: flora.winfield@lambethpalace.org.uk

WINFIELD, Miss June Mary. b 29. Gilmore Ho 57. dss 66 d 87 p 94. Is of Dogs Ch Ch and St Jo w St Luke *Lon* 66–68; Bracknell *Ox* 68–74; Dean of Women's Min 74–80; St Marylebone w H Trin *Lon* 80–82; Ind Chapl 82–89; rtd 89; NSM Ealing St Steph Castle Hill *Lon* 89–97; Asst Dioc Dir Ords Willesden Area 94–97; PtO *Lon* 97–02. *25 Trinity Road, Marlow SL7 3AN* T: (01628) 484317 E: winfieldjune@live.co.uk

WINFIELD, Russell James. b 79. Sheff Hallam Univ BA 00 Down Coll Cam BTh 12. St Mellitus Coll MA 14. d 14 p 15. C Brentford *Lon* 14–17; Internat Development Manager St Mellitus Coll from 17; Public Preacher from 17. *St Mellitus College, 24 Collingham Road, London SW5 0LX* T: (020) 7052 0573   M: 07805-160853   E: russjw@outlook.com   *or* russell.winfield@stmellitus.ac.uk

WINFREY, Rebecca Anne. b 66. Newnham Coll Cam BA 88 MB, BCh 90 Anglia Ruskin Univ MA 14. ERMC 10. d 13 p 14. C Barnack w Ufford and Bainton *Pet* 13–14; C The Ortons *Ely* 14–16; C Castor w Upton and Stibbington etc *Pet* 16–17. *Manor Farm House, Manor Farm Lane, Castor, Peterborough PE5 7BW*

WING, Mrs Julie. b 62. Teesside Univ BSc 99. NEOC 02. d 05 p 06. C Sunderland St Chad *Dur* 05–09; TV Gt Aycliffe 09–14; R Usworth from 14. *Usworth Rectory, 14 Prestwick Close, Washington NE37 2LP* M: 07812-589653

WING, Miss Myra Susan. b 45. Cranmer Hall Dur 92. d 94 p 95. C Appledore w Brookland, Fairfield, Brenzett etc *Cant* 94–98; Hon C Wittersham w Stone and Ebony 95–98; V Grayshott *Guildf* 98–08; rtd 08; PtO *Cant* from 09. *142 Minster Road, Westgate-on-Sea CT8 8DQ* T: (01843) 836430 E: susanwing14@gmail.com

WINGATE, Canon Andrew David Carlile. b 44. Worc Coll Ox BA 66 MA 71 MPhil 68 Birm Univ PhD 95. Linc Th Coll 70. d 72 p 73. C Halesowen *Worc* 72–75; Lect Tamilnadu Th Sem India 76–82; Prin WMMTC 82–90; Prin United Coll of Ascension India 90–00; Hon Can Birm Cathl 97–00; Dir Min and Tr *Leic* 00–03; Dir Interfaith Relns and Co-ord Lay Tr 03–10; rtd 10; Can Th Leic Cathl from 00; Chapl to

The Queen 07–14; PtO *Chich* from 16; *Leic* from 17; Assoc Dioc Interfaith Adv *Chich* from 18. *25 Prince Charles Road, Lewes BN7 2HY* T: (01273) 479012   M: 07808-586259 E: andrewwingate5@gmail.com

WINGFIELD, Christopher Laurence. b 57. Westmr Coll Ox BTh 99. Ripon Coll Cuddesdon 93. **d** 95 **p** 96. C Hadleigh *St E* 95–99; P-in-c Melton 99–00; R 00–01; R Sproughton w Burstall, Copdock w Washbrook etc 01–09; RD Samford 06–09; P-in-c Bromsgrove St Jo *Worc* 09–12; TR Bromsgrove 12–14; R Harton *York* from 14; RD S Ryedale from 18. *The Vicarage, Sand Hutton, York YO41 1LB* T: (01904) 468418 E: chris.wingfield@btinternet.com

WINGFIELD DIGBY, Canon Andrew Richard. b 50. Keble Coll Ox BA 72. Wycliffe Hall Ox 74. **d** 77 **p** 78. C Cockfosters Ch Ch CD *Lon* 77–80; C Hadley Wood St Paul Prop Chpl 80–84; Dir Chrs in Sport 84–02; V Ox St Andr 02–16; Six Preacher Cant Cathl 97–07; Hon Can Ch Ch *Ox* 13–16; rtd 16; PtO *Ox* from 17. *The Valley, Asthall Leigh, Witney OX29 9PX* T: (01993) 878243   M: 07768-611232 E: revandrew.wd@btinternet.com

WINKETT, Miss Lucy Clare. b 68. Selw Coll Cam BA 90 MA 94 ARCM 92. Qu Coll Birm BD 94. **d** 95 **p** 96. C Lt Ilford St Mich *Chelmsf* 95–97; Min Can and Chapl St Paul's Cathl *Lon* 97–03; Can Res and Prec 03–10; R Westmr St Jas from 10. *St James's Rectory, 197 Piccadilly, London W1 9LL* T: (020) 7734 4511 *or* 7292 4860 E: rector@sjp.org.uk

WINN, Alan John. b 42. FRSA 73. **d** 01 **p** 02. OLM Ringwould w Kingsdown *Cant* 01–04; OLM Ringwould w Kingsdown and Ripple etc 05–12; rtd 12; PtO *Cant* from 12. *Chilterns, Back Street, Ringwould, Deal CT14 8HL* T: (01304) 361030 E: revjohnwinn@aol.com

WINN, Paul William James. b 44. Liv Univ BSc 66. EMMTC 86. **d** 89 **p** 90. NSM Spalding St Paul *Linc* 89–98; PtO 98–00; P-in-c Cowbit 00–01; V 01–07; rtd 07; PtO *Linc* from 17. *6 Hawthorn Chase, Moulton, Spalding PE12 6GA* T: (01406) 373662 E: paulwinn80@hotmail.com

WINN, Peter Anthony. b 60. Worc Coll Ox BA 82 MA 86. Wycliffe Hall Ox 83. **d** 86 **p** 87. C W Derby Gd Shep *Liv* 86–89; V Seaforth 89–02; P-in-c Anfield St Marg 02–09; V from 09. *St Margaret's Vicarage, Rocky Lane, Liverpool L6 4BA* T: 0151-263 3118

WINN, Canon Simon Reynolds. b 66. Bris Univ BA 88. Trin Coll Bris 96. **d** 98 **p** 99. C Portswood Ch Ch *Win* 98–02; V Northolt St Jos *Lon* 02–10; Dir of Ords Willesden Area 07–10; V Hataitai-Kilbirnie New Zealand 10–15; Dir Ords Wellington from 12; Can Wellington from 15. *Wellington Cathedral of St Paul, PO BOX 12044, Wellington 6144, New Zealand* T: (0064) (21) 207 4867 *or* (4) 472 0286 E: simonwinn66@yahoo.co.uk *or* canon@wellingtoncathedral.org.nz

WINNARD, Jack. b 30. Oak Hill Th Coll 79. **d** 81 **p** 82. C Skelmersdale St Paul *Liv* 81–84; C Goose Green 84–85; V Wigan St Barn Marsh Green 85–98; rtd 99; PtO *Liv* from 00. *Maranatha, 11 Beech Walk, Winstanley, Wigan WN3 6DH* T: (01942) 222339

WINNINGTON-INGRAM, David Robert. b 59. Hertf Coll Ox BA 82 MA 85 K Coll Cam BA 89. Westcott Ho Cam 87. **d** 90 **p** 91. C Bishop's Cleeve *Glouc* 90–94; TV Colyton, Southleigh, Offwell, Widworthy etc *Ex* 94–00; V S Brent and Rattery 00–17; rtd 17. *4 Wesley Place, Harberton, Totnes TQ9 7SW*

WINSBURY, Leigh Darren. b 67. St Jo Coll Nottm 13. **d** 15 **p** 16. C Bideford, Northam, Westward Ho!, Appledore etc *Ex* 15–17; C Bideford, Landcross, Littleham etc 17–19; TV Okehampton, Inwardleigh, Belstone, Sourton etc from 19. *The Rectory, Hatherleigh, Okehampton EX20 3JY* E: lwinsbury@googlemail.com

WINSLADE, Richard Clive. b 69. Aston Tr Scheme 91 Linc Th Coll BTh 93. **d** 96 **p** 97. C Waltham Cross *St Alb* 96–99; C Leavesden 99–03; R Maulden 03–13; V Gravenhurst, Shillington and Stondon from 13. *All Saints' Vicarage, Vicarage Close, Shillington, Hitchin SG5 3LS* T: (01462) 713797 E: richardrev@btinternet.com

WINSPER, Arthur William (Brother Benedict). b 46. Ox Brookes Univ BA 10. Glas NSM Course 89. **d** 91 **p** 92. SSF from 70; Min Eur Prov from 17; NSM Barrowfield *Glas* 91–96; P-in-c St Aug Miss Penhalonga Zimbabwe 96–98; PtO *Worc* 98–08; Sheff 09–12; *Chelmsf* 13–16; *Leeds* from 17; *Eur* from 14. *25 Karnac Road, Leeds LS8 5BL* T: 0113-226 0647   E: ministerssf@franciscans.org.uk *or* benedictssf@franciscans.org.uk

⍭**WINSTANLEY, The Rt Revd Alan Leslie.** b 49. Nottm Univ BTh 72. St Jo Coll Nottm 68 ALCD 72. **d** 72 **p** 73 **c** 88. C Livesey *Blackb* 72–75; C Gt Sankey *Liv* 75–77; P-in-c Penketh 75–77; V 78–81; SAMS 81–93; Bp Bolivia and Peru 88–93; V Eastham *Ches* 94–03; Hon Asst Bp Ches 94–03; V

Whittle le Woods *Blackb* 03–12; Hon Asst Bp *Blackb* 03–12; TV Shirwell, Loxhore, Kentisbury, Arlington, etc *Ex* 12–14; Hon Asst Bp Ex 12–14; rtd 14; Hon Asst Bp Ches from 15. *11 Thorneycroft Way, Crewe CW1 4FZ* M: 07774-314534 E: alanlwinstanley@gmail.com

WINSTANLEY, John Graham. b 47. K Coll Lon 67. **d** 71 **p** 72. C Wandsworth St Paul *S'wark* 71–74; Chapl Salford Univ *Man* 75–79; R Kersal Moor 79–87. *14 Lyndhurst Avenue, Prestwich, Manchester M25 0GF* T: 0161-740 2715   F: 720 6916 E: john@blots.co.uk

WINSTONE, Canon Peter John. b 30. Jes Coll Ox BA 52 MA 56. Ridley Hall Cam 53. **d** 55 **p** 56. C Bitterne *Win* 55–58; C Keighley *Bradf* 58–60; PC Fairweather Green 60–67; V Clapham 67–84; R Leathley w Farnley, Fewston and Blubberhouses 84–95; Hon Can Bradf Cathl 89–95; rtd 95; PtO *Worc* 95–14. *24 Rose Court, St Cyriacs, Chichester PO19 1AW*

WINTER, Andrew Christopher. b 73. Dur Univ BSc 95 PGCE 96. **d** 03 **p** 04. C Mosman St Clem Australia 03–05; NSM Hinckley H Trin *Leic* 06–10; Chapl Ipswich Sch 10–15; Chapl Reed's School 15. *Reed's School, Sandy Lane, Cobham KT11 2ES* T: (01932) 869044

WINTER, Anthony Cathcart. b 28. FCA. Ridley Hall Cam 54. **d** 56 **p** 57. C Childwall St Dav *Liv* 56–58; C Hackney St Jo *Lon* 58–63; V Newmarket All SS *St E* 63–73; LtO 74–81; PtO *Lon* 78–81 and 97–99; Hon C St Andr-by-the-Wardrobe w St Ann, Blackfriars 81–86; Hon C Smithfield St Bart St 86–95; Chapl S'wark Cathl from 99; PtO *Lon* from 08; S'wark from 99. *25 Bowater House, Golden Lane Estate, London EC1Y 0RJ* T: (020) 7490 5765   F: 7490 1064 E: a.c.winter@btinternet.com

⍭**WINTER, The Rt Revd Dagmar.** b 63. Heidelberg Univ DrTheol 96. Herborn Th Sem 93. **d** 96 **p** 97 **c** 19. C Bromley St Mark *Roch* 96–99; C Hexham *Newc* 99–06; P-in-c Kirkwhelpington, Kirkharle, Kirkheaton and Cambo 06–15; Dioc Officer for Rural Affairs 06–15; AD Morpeth 11–13; R Hexham 15–19; Bp's Adv for Women in Min 12–19; Hon Can Newc Cathl 11–19; Suff Bp Huntingdon *Ely* from 19. *14 Lynn Road, Ely CB6 1DA* T: (01353) 662137 E: bishop.huntingdon@elydiocese.org

WINTER, Canon David Brian. b 29. K Coll Lon BA 53 CertEd 54. Oak Hill NSM Course. **d** 87 **p** 88. NSM Finchley St Paul and St Luke *Lon* 87–89; Hd Relig Broadcasting BBC 87–89; Bp's Officer for Evang *Ox* 89–95; P-in-c Ducklington 89–95; Hon Can Ch Ch 95; rtd 95; Hon C Hermitage *Ox* 95–00; Hon C Dorchester 02–05; PtO 00–02 and 06–18. *51 Nideggen Close, Thatcham RG19 4HS* T: (01635) 873639 E: david_winter1@btinternet.com

WINTER, Mrs Jane Marion. b 62. Avery Hill Coll BEd 84 York St Jo Coll MA 09. Ripon Coll Cuddesdon 12. **d** 14 **p** 15. C Orpington St Andr *Roch* 14–15; C Cray Valley from 15; Dioc Facilitator for Formation, Learning and Discipleship from 18. *39 Chelsfield Road, Orpington BR5 4DS* T: (01689) 872282   M: 07734-962140 E: revjanewinter@gmail.com *or* jane.winter@rochester.anglican.org

WINTER, Mrs Mary Elizabeth. b 56. Man Univ BEd 78 Leeds Univ AdDipEd 85. Yorks Min Course 08. **d** 11 **p** 12. C Skipton Ch Ch w Carleton *Bradf* 11–14; Leeds 14–15; C Skipton H Trin *Bradf* 11–14; Leeds 14–15; P-in-c Greengates 15–16; P-in-c Thorpe Edge 15–16; V Greengates and Thorpe Edge from 16. *The Vicarage, Northwood Crescent, Bradford BD10 9HX* T: (01274) 614898   M: 07813-687680 E: mary.winter@hotmail.com

WINTER, Nichola Jane. b 58. Trevelyan Coll Dur BA 79. **d** 02 **p** 03. OLM Aldeburgh w Hazlewood *St E* 02–13; NSM 13–17; NSM Alde Sandlings from 17; Chapl Suffolk Coastal Primary Care Trust from 06. *Threeways, Donkey Lane, Friston, Saxmundham IP17 1PL* T: (01728) 688979 E: njwinter@clara.co.uk

WINTER, Rebecca Anne. *See* BEVAN, Rebecca Anne

WINTER, Stephen Christopher. b 55. Southn Univ BA 76. Trin Coll Bris 85. **d** 88 **p** 89. C Birm St Luke 88–92; TV Kings Norton 92–98; Ind Chapl *Worc* 98–04; Asst Dir Development (Discipleship) 04–11; C Finstall 04–11; rtd 11; PtO *Worc* 11–18; R Elmley Lovett w Hampton Lovett and Elmbridge w Rushock and Hartlebury and Ombersley w Doverdale from 18. *2 Canal Cottages, Hanbury Wharf, Hanbury Road, Droitwich WR9 7DU* E: mail@stephenwinter.net

WINTERBOTTOM, Canon Ian Edmund. b 42. St Andr Univ MA 66. Linc Th Coll 66. **d** 68 **p** 69. C Blackb St Steph 68–71; C Wingerworth *Derby* 71–73; P-in-c Brimington 73–77; R 77–89; RD Bolsover and Staveley 86–93; R Pleasley 89–94; P-in-c Shirebrook 92–94; TR E Scarsdale 94–00; Hon Can Derby Cathl 95–08; Prin Ind Chapl 00–08; rtd 08; PtO *Ely* from 17. *54 Wilkin Walk, Cottenham, Cambridge CB24 8TS* E: ianwinterbottom@aol.com

WINTERBURN, Derek Neil. b 60. Bris Univ BSc 82 Ox Univ BA 85. Wycliffe Hall Ox 83. **d** 86 **p** 87. C Mildmay Grove St Jude and St Paul *Lon* 86–89; C Hackney Marsh 89–91; TV 91–96; V Hampton St Mary 96–16; V Hampton Hill from 16; AD Hampton 08–14. *The Vicarage, 46 St James's Road, Hampton Hill, Hampton TW12 1DQ* E: vicar@winterburn.me.uk

WINTGENS, Peter Brendon. b 47. Surrey Univ BSc 70 Cant Ch Ch Univ BA 12. SEITE 06. **d** 09 **p** 10. NSM Battersea St Mary *S'wark* 09–16; rtd 16; PtO *St E* from 17. *Priory Gate, 11 Seckford Street, Woodbridge IP12 4LY* T: (01394) 382097 E: wintgens@btinternet.com

WINTLE, Anthony Robert. b 44. K Coll Lon 64. St Mich Coll Llan. **d** 68 **p** 69. C Llandaff N *Llan* 68–70; C Baglan 70–75; V Treharris 75–85; V Treharris w Bedlinog 86–90; R St Fagans and Michaelston-super-Ely 90–13; rtd 13; PtO *St D* 13–16; Hon C W Preseli Gp 17. *Porth y Castell, Market Street, Newport SA42 0PH* T: (01239) 820414 E: anthonywintle@btinternet.com

WINTLE, Graham. b 52. Bris Univ BSc 73. Oak Hill Th Coll BA 86. **d** 86 **p** 87. C Southgate *Chich* 86–89; C New Malden and Coombe *S'wark* 89–92; V Surbiton Hill Ch Ch 92–06; R Willoughby Australia from 06. *211 Mowbray Road, Willoughby NSW 2068, Australia* T: (0061) (2) 9411 2172 E: graham.wintle@gmail.com

WINTLE, Canon Ruth Elizabeth. b 31. Westf Coll Lon BA 53 St Hugh's Coll Ox BA 67 MA 74. St Mich Ho Ox 63. **dss** 72 **d** 87 **p** 94. Tutor St Jo Coll Dur 72–74; Selection Sec ACCM 74–83; St Jo in Bedwardine *Worc* 83–87; Par Dn 87–94; Dir of Ords 84–92; Hon Can Worc Cathl 87–97; rtd 95; Bp's Adv on Women's Min *Worc* 95–97; PtO from 98. *6 Coronation Avenue, Rushwick, Worcester WR2 5TF* T: (01905) 427109 E: ruth.wintle@btinternet.com

WINTLE, Thomas Gerrard. b 82. Stirling Univ BA 09 Nottm Univ MA 11. St Steph Ho Ox BTh 15. **d** 15 **p** 16. C Nuneaton St Mary *Cov* 15–18; V from 18. *The Vicarage, 99 Bottrill Street, Nuneaton CV11 5JB* T: (024) 7638 2936 M: 07812-377004 E: t.g.b.wintle@gmail.com

✠**WINTON, The Rt Revd Alan Peter.** b 58. Sheff Univ BA 83 PhD 87. Linc Th Coll 91. **d** 91 **p** 92 **c** 09. C Southgate Ch Ch *Lon* 91–95; P-in-c St Paul's Walden and Dioc CME Officer *St Alb* 95–99; R Welwyn w Ayot St Peter 99–05; TR Welwyn 05–09; Hon Can St Alb 07–09; Suff Bp Thetford *Nor* from 09. *Herfast House, 5 Vicar Street, Wymondham NR18 0PL* T: (01953) 528010 E: bishop.thetford@dioceseofnorwich.org

WIPPELL, David Stanley. b 46. Univ of Qld BSc 67 Selw Coll Cam BA 77 MA. Westcott Ho Cam 76. **d** 78 **p** 79. C Wolvercote w Summertown *Ox* 78–80; Asst Chapl St Edw Sch Ox 78–00; Chapl 00–06; Housemaster 85–97; Chapl St Hugh's Coll Ox 80–85; NSM Ray Valley Ox 06–15; PtO from 15; *Eur* from 99. *Rivermead, 1A Mill Road, Islip, Kidlington OX5 2SZ* T: (01865) 849497 M: 07970-024316 E: davidwippell@gmail.com

WISE, Canon Pamela Margaret. b 51. CertEd 73 BA 79. Ripon Coll Cuddesdon 89. **d** 91 **p** 94. Par Dn Tokyngton St Mich *Lon* 91–94; C N Greenford All Hallows 94; C Bedford All SS *St Alb* 94–97; TV Hitchin 97–03; V Oxhey All SS from 03; Hon Can St Alb from 09; PtO *Lon* from 16. *All Saints' Vicarage, Gosforth Lane, Watford WD19 7AX* T: (020) 8421 5949 E: pamela.wise@gmail.com *or* revpamwise@hotmail.co.uk

WISE, Richard Edmund. b 67. Clare Coll Cam BA 88 MusB 89 LRAM 91. Cranmer Hall Dur 01. **d** 03 **p** 04. C Stanmore *Win* 03–07; P-in-c Bishopstoke 07–09; R from 09. *The Rectory, 10 Stoke Park Road, Eastleigh SO50 6DA* T: (023) 8061 2192 E: rwise@talktalk.net

WISE, Mrs Susan Jacqueline. b 57. Anglia Poly Univ BEd 92. St Mellitus Coll 14. **d** 15 **p** 16. NSM Wickford and Runwell *Chelmsf* from 15. *6 Tamarisk, Benfleet SS7 5PW* T: (01268) 754629 M: 07941-506156 E: sue.wise@sky.com

WISEMAN, Canon David John. b 51. Lon Univ BD 80 Derby Univ MA 99. Cranmer Hall Dur 77. **d** 80 **p** 81. C Bilston *Lich* 80–84; P-in-c W Bromwich St Phil 84–86; V 86–89; P-in-c Cheetham St Mark *Man* 89–94; Dioc Community Relns Officer 89–96; C Ashton H Trin 94–99; TR Ashton 00–03; Chapl Tameside Coll 94–03; Soc Resp Adv *Pet* 03–07; P-in-c Northampton Ch Ch 07–16; AD Gtr Northn 07–16; Can Pet Cathl 09–16; rtd 16; PtO *Heref* from 17. *Myndtown, Clun Road, Craven Arms SY7 9QS* T: (01588) 674738 E: davidwiseman50@gmail.com

WISEMAN, John. b 56. Sarum & Wells Th Coll 80. **d** 83 **p** 84. C Swinton St Pet *Man* 83–87; C Swinton and Pendlebury 87–88; TV Atherton 88–93; V Bedford Leigh 93–02; V Lt Lever from 02. *The Vicarage, Market Street, Little Lever, Bolton BL3 1HH* T: (01204) 700936

WISEMAN, Sister Julie. b 53. ERMC 05. **d** 08 **p** 09. NSM Roughton and Felbrigg, Metton, Sustead etc *Nor* 08–10;

Public Preacher from 10. *32B Beeston Common, Sheringham NR26 8ES* T: (01263) 825623 E: juliessl@btinternet.com

WISHART, Michael Leslie. b 45. St Mich Coll Llan 70. **d** 73 **p** 74. C Llangyfelach *S & B* 73–76; Chapl RN 76–80 and 85–96; V Beguildy and Heyope *S & B* 80–84; V Gowerton 84–85; Chapl RNR 80–85; R Dowlais *Llan* 97–04; R Bishops Lydeard w Bagborough and Cothelstone *B & W* 04–11; P-in-c Lydeard St Lawrence and Combe Florey 10–11; rtd 11; PtO *Llan* from 11. *Hollands Cottage, Higher End, St Athan, Barry CF62 4LW* T: (01446) 751600 E: michael.wishart@btopenworld.com

WISKEN, Canon Brian Leonard. b 34. Dur Univ BA 58. Linc Th Coll 58. **d** 60 **p** 61. C Lobley Hill *Dur* 60–63; C Ipswich All Hallows *St E* 63–65; P-in-c Scunthorpe All SS *Linc* 65–69; V 69–71; Dioc Stewardship Adv 70–75; R Panton w Wragby 71–75; V Langton by Wragby 71–75; R Cleethorpes 75–77; TR 77–89; V Linc St Nic w St Jo Newport 89–99; Can and Preb Linc Cathl 88–00; rtd 99; PtO *Nor* from 99; St E 99–17. *49 Gainsborough Drive, Lowestoft NR32 4NJ* T: (01502) 512378

WISKEN, Robert Daniel. b 30. ACT. **d** 60 **p** 60. C N Rockhampton St Barn Australia 60; V N Rockhampton St Matt 61–63; V Winton *Man* 63–65; R Luddington w Hemington and Thurning *Pet* 65–69; P-in-c Clopton *St E* 66–69; V Ipswich All SS 69–73; V Sompting *Chich* 74–78; Org Sec (SW England) CECS 78–80; R Edmundbyers w Muggleswick *Dur* 80–83; R Wexham *Ox* 83–86; Australia from 86; rtd 95. *11-64 Riverwalk Avenue, Robina QLD 4226, Australia* E: randjwisken@bigpond.com

WITCHELL, David William. b 47. St Jo Coll Nottm BTh 75. **d** 75 **p** 76. C Northampton St Mary *Pet* 75–78; C Oakham w Hambleton and Egleton 78–81; C Oakham, Hambleton, Egleton, Braunston and Brooke 81–82; V Weedon Bec w Everdon 82–90; V Wellingborough St Barn 90–00; RD Wellingborough 98–00; P-in-c Paignton St Paul Preston *Ex* 00–02; V Paignton Ch Ch and Preston St Paul 03–16; RD Torbay 03–09; rtd 16; PtO *Ex* from 11. *1 Kintyre Close, Torquay, Paignton TQ2 7BQ* T: (01803) 316636

WITCHELL, Derek William Frederick. b 49. SAOMC 00. **d** 03 **p** 04. C Bloxham w Milcombe and S Newington *Ox* 03–06; P-in-c Wing w Grove 06–12; P-in-c Wingrave w Rowsham, Aston Abbotts and Cublington 06–12; P-in-c Cheddington w Mentmore 08–12; TV Cottesloe 12–13; rtd 13; PtO *Ox* from 13. *11 Hunt Road, Thame OX9 3LG* T: (01844) 215798 M: 07847-167507

WITCOMBE, The Very Revd John Julian. b 59. Cam Univ MA 84 Nottm Univ MPhil 91. St Jo Coll Nottm BA 83. **d** 84 **p** 85. C Birtley *Dur* 84–87; C Chilwell *S'well* 87–91; V Lodge Moor St Luke *Sheff* 91–95; TR Uxbridge *Lon* 95–98; Dean St Jo Coll Nottm 98–05; Officer for Min *Glouc* 05–10; Hon Can Glouc Cathl 09–10; Can Res Glouc Cathl 10–13; Dir Discipleship and Min 10–13; Dean Cov from 13. *8 Priory Row, Coventry CV1 5EX* T: (024) 7652 1391

WITCOMBE, Michael David. b 53. Univ of Wales (Lamp) BA 76. Qu Coll Birm 76. **d** 78 **p** 79. C Neath w Llantwit *Llan* 78–80; C Whitchurch 80–83; V Newcastle 83–02; P-in-c Ewenny 84–86; V Llanishen 02–19. *Address temp unknown* E: fatherm@btinternet.com

WITCOMBE, Ricarda Jane. b 64. St Jo Coll Cam BA 86 MA 90. St Jo Coll Nottm MA(TS) 99. **d** 01 **p** 02. C Wilford *S'well* 01–05; P-in-c Glouc St Paul 05–09; V Glouc St Paul and St Steph 09–13; PtO 13–14; Chapl Team Ldr Geo Eliot Hosp NHS Trust Nuneaton from 14. *The Chaplaincy, George Eliot Hospital, College Street, Nuneaton CV10 7DJ* T: (024) 7686 5281 E: ricarda.witcombe@geh.nhs.uk

WITCOMBE, Simon Christopher. b 61. Dundee Univ MA 83 PGCE 84 St Jo Coll Dur BA 90. Cranmer Hall Dur 88. **d** 91 **p** 92. C Earlham St Anne *Nor* 91–95; Assoc P Skegness and Winthorpe *Linc* 95–98; Gen Preacher 95–98; R Woodhall Spa Gp 98–07; V Codsall *Lich* 07–17; P-in-c Bilbrook and Coven 13–14; RD Penkridge 11–16; Sen Chapl Glos Univ *Glouc* from 17. *9 Loweswater Road, Cheltenham GL51 3AZ* M: 07715-041525 E: simonwitcombe50@gmail.com *or* switcombe@glos.ac.uk

WITHERIDGE, John Stephen. b 53. Kent Univ BA 76 Ch Coll Cam BA 78 MA 82 FRHistS. Ridley Hall Cam 78. **d** 79 **p** 80. C Luton St Mary *St Alb* 79–82; Asst Chapl Marlborough Coll 82–84; Abp's Chapl *Cant* 84–87; Conduct Eton Coll 87–96; Headmaster Charterhouse Sch Godalming 96–13; PtO *Guildf* 96–09; rtd 13; PtO *Ox* from 14; Hon Chapl Ch Ch from 14; Chapl to The Queen from 17. *Minster Cottage, Church Street, Charlbury, Chipping Norton OX7 3PR* T: (01608) 810383 E: john.witheridge@outlook.com

WITHERS, Mrs Christine Mary. b 37. ALA 60. Gilmore Ho. **dss** 81 **d** 87 **p** 94. Chorleywood Ch Ch *St Alb* 81–86; Darley *Derby* 86–92; C 87–92; Chapl HM Pris Drake Hall 92–95;

P-in-c Standon and Cotes Heath *Lich* 96–98; PtO *Heref* from 98. *2 Ash Meadow, Westbury, Shrewsbury SY5 9QJ* T: (01743) 885038

WITHERS, Eleanor Jane. *See* WILLIAMS, Eleanor Jane

WITHERS, Geoffrey Edward. b 68. QUB BSc 90 TCD BTh 93. CITC 90. **d** 93 **p** 94. C Ballymena w Ballyclug *Conn* 93–97; I Monkstown 97–01; Chapl RAF from 01. *Chaplaincy Services (RAF), HQ Air Command, RAF High Wycombe HP14 4UE* T: (01494) 496800 E: geoff.withers944@mod.gov.uk

WITHERS, Miss Gillian. b 58. Stranmillis Coll BEd 80. St Jo Coll Nottm 94. **d** 97 **p** 98. NSM Mossley *Conn* 97–03; C Bangor St Comgall *D & D* 03–05; V Knock 05–08; I Grey Abbey w Kircubbin from 08. *4 Rectory Wood, Portaferry, Newtownards BT22 1LJ* T: (028) 4272 9307 E: vicarofdibley@hotmail.com

WITHERS, John Geoffrey. b 39. St Jo Coll Dur BA 61 Birm Univ CertEd 63 CQSW 72. SWMTC 84. **d** 87 **p** 88. NSM Drewsteignton *Ex* 87–01; P-in-c 99–01; P-in-c Hittisleigh and Spreyton 99–01; C 01–07; Sub Chapl HM Pris *Ex* 96–07; PtO *Ex* from 07. *Lane's End, Broadwoodwidger, Lifton PL16 0JH* T: (01566) 780544

WITHEY, Michael John. b 45. Open Univ BA 80 Ox Univ MTh 98 SRN 66. Oak Hill Th Coll 71. **d** 74 **p** 75. C St Alb St Paul 74–76; C Luton St Mary 77; C Luton St Fran 77–80; V Woodside w E Hyde 80–87; CF (TA) 83–87; Dioc Stewardship Adv *Ox* 87–89; Chapl HM YOI Onley 89–91; V Hengoed w Gobowen *Lich* 91–95; Chapl Robert Jones and Agnes Hunt Orthopaedic Hosp 91–95; P-in-c Chasetown *Lich* 95–00; V 00–02; V Stroud H Trin *Glouc* 02–13; Chapl Cotswold and Vale Primary Care Trust 02–06; Chapl Glos Primary Care Trust 06–11; Chapl Glos Partnership Trust 02–11; rtd 13. *24 Cwrt Deri, Cwmann, Lampeter SA48 8EJ* E: meic.clydogau@media-maker.com

WITHINGTON, Canon Brian James. b 54. Leic Univ MSc 01 CQSW 76. EAMTC 94. **d** 97 **p** 98. NSM Pet St Jo 97–04; P-in-c Broughton w Loddington and Cransley etc 04–10; C 10–17; RD Kettering 07–17; R Aldwincle, Clopton, Pilton, Stoke Doyle etc from 17; Bp's Adv for Pioneer Min 10–13; Asst Dir Ords from 14; Can Pet Cathl from 13. *The Rectory, 60 Main Street, Aldwincle, Kettering NN14 3EP* T: (01832) 720613 E: rectornv7@uwclub.net

WITHINGTON, George Kenneth. b 37. Birm Univ BA 59. Wells Th Coll 59. **d** 61 **p** 62. C Hartcliffe St Andr CD *Bris* 61–65; V Swindon St Jo 65–73; V Cricklade w Latton 73–97; RD Cricklade 94–97; rtd 97; PtO *Heref* from 97; *Worc* 97–16. *19 Oak Drive, Colwall, Malvern WR13 6RA* T: (01684) 540590 E: kandjw@btinternet.com

WITHINGTON, Canon Keith. b 32. Univ of Wales (Lamp) BA 55. Qu Coll Birm 55. **d** 57 **p** 58. C Bournville *Birm* 57–61; V 61–00; RD Moseley 81–91; Hon Can Birm Cathl 83–00; rtd 00; PtO *Birm* from 00; *Worc* from 00. *44 Dugard Way, Droitwich WR9 8UX* T: (01905) 795847 E: keithkw1000@aol.com

WITHINGTON, Paul Martin. b 60. Kent Univ BSc 86. Trin Coll Bris 01. **d** 03 **p** 04. C Elworth and Warmingham *Ches* 03–06; TV Congleton 06–18; V Weaverham from 18. *St Mary's Vicarage, Church Street, Weaverham, Northwich CW8 3NJ* T: (01606) 851880 E: revpaul9@outlook.com

WITHNELL, Roderick David. b 55. EMMTC 86 Ridley Hall Cam 89. **d** 90 **p** 91. C Shenfield *Chelmsf* 90–94; C Woodleigh and Loddiswell *Ex* 94–95; TV Modbury, Bigbury, Ringmore w Kingston etc 95–00; Canada 00–01; TR Burrington, Chawleigh, Cheldon, Chulmleigh etc *Ex* 01–15; TR Teignmouth, Ideford w Luton, Ashcombe etc from 15. *The Rectory, 30 Dawlish Road, Teignmouth TQ14 8TG* E: roderickwithnell@btinternet.com

WITT, Canon Bryan Douglas. b 52. St Mich Coll Llan BD 84. **d** 84 **p** 85. C Betws w Ammanford *St D* 84–87; V Llanllwni 87–91; V Llangennech and Hendy 91–04; V St Clears w Llangynin and Llanddowror etc 04–15; AD St Clears 13–14; P-in-c Llanarthne and Llanddarog from 15; Hon Can St D Cathl 11–13; Can Cursal from 13. *The New Vicarage, Llanddarog, Carmarthen SA32 8PA* T: (01267) 275504 E: canonwitt@gmail.com

WITT, Caroline Elizabeth. *See* SACKLEY, Caroline Elizabeth

WITTER, Mrs Tania Judy Ingram. b 37. Girton Coll Cam BA 58 MA 63. Oak Hill Th Coll 94. **d** 95 **p** 96. NSM Highbury Ch Ch w St Jo and St Sav *Lon* 95–03 and from 14; PtO 03–13; *Eur* from 03. *26 Viewpoint Apartments, 30–32 Highbury Grove, London N5 2DL* T: (020) 7226 6908 E: tania.witter@btinternet.com

WITTS, Donald Roger. b 47. Cranmer Hall Dur 86. **d** 88 **p** 89. C Leyland St Ambrose *Blackb* 88–90; C Staines St Mary and St Pet *Lon* 90–93; Ind Missr *Man* 93–95; Dioc Communications Officer *Cant* 95–00; P-in-c Blean 95–01; V Birchington w Acol and Minnis Bay 01–17; rtd 17; Asst

Chapl Costa Blanca *Eur* from 18. *Calle Amsterdam 67, Bello Horizonte 2, 03530 La Nucia (Alicante), Spain* T: (0034) 966 896 426 or 611 242 476 M: 07749-201947 or (0034) 612 242 496 E: don.witts@btopenworld.com

WITTS, Preb Graham Robert. b 53. Newc Univ BEd Bris Univ MA 01. Linc Th Coll 79. **d** 82 **p** 83. C Horncastle w Low Toynton *Linc* 82–85; TV Gt Grimsby St Mary and St Jas 85–89; TR Yelverton, Meavy, Sheepstor and Walkhampton *Ex* 89–93; C Glastonbury w Meare *B & W* 93–03; RD Glastonbury 00–03; V Burnham from 03; Warden of Readers Wells Adnry from 10; Preb Wells Cathl from 18. *The Vicarage, Rectory Road, Burnham-on-Sea TA8 2BZ* T: (01278) 782991 E: thewittsonweb@hotmail.com

WIXON, Jack. b 44. Lich Th Coll 68. **d** 71 **p** 72. C Adlington *Blackb* 71–74; C St Annes St Thos 74–76; V Chorley St Jas 76–82; V Preston Em 82–94; V Ribby w Wrea 94–04; V Ribby cum Wrea and Weeton 04–08; rtd 08; Hon C Lytham St Jo *Blackb* 08–14; PtO *Leic* 15–18; Hon C Market Harborough and The Transfiguration etc 18–21; PtO *Pet* from 17. *14 Ryelands Close, Market Harborough LE16 7XE* T: (01858) 439974 E: j.wixon@btinternet.com

WOADDEN, Christopher Martyn. b 56. St Jo Coll Nottm LTh. **d** 87 **p** 88. C Mickleover All SS *Derby* 87–90; C Wirksworth w Alderwasley, Carsington etc 90–92; C Wirksworth 92; TV Gt and Lt Coates w Bradley *Linc* 92–98; V Holton-le-Clay and Tetney 98–07; V Holton-le-Clay, Tetney and N Cotes from 07. *The Vicarage, Church Walk, Holton-le-Clay, Grimsby DN36 5AN* T: (01472) 824082

WOAN, Susan Ann. b 52. Univ of Wales (Abth) BSc 72 Lon Univ PGCE 73 Ch Ch Coll Cant MA 91 Rob Coll Cam BA 95 Ex Univ PhD 08. Ridley Hall Cam 93. **d** 96 **p** 97. C Histon *Ely* 96–97; C Radipole and Melcombe Regis *Sarum* 97–00; Chapl Bournemouth and Poole Coll of FE *Win* 00–04; Hon C Bournemouth St Jo w St Mich 00–04; Vice-Prin Dioc Min Course *Nor* 04–06; Prin Dioc Min Course 07–13; Vice-Prin ERMC 07–10; rtd 13; PtO *Cant* from 14. *12 St Mildred's Avenue, Birchington CT7 9LD* T: (01843) 843336 M: 07710-869135 E: sue.woan1@gmail.com

WODEHOUSE, Carol Lylie. *See* KIMBERLEY, Countess of

WODEMAN, Cyril Peter Guy. b 28. Qu Coll Cam BA 50 MA 55 ARCO 54 LRAM 58 ARCM 58. Cranmer Hall Dur 72. **d** 73 **p** 74. C Penwortham St Mary *Blackb* 73–77; V Burnley St Steph 77–85; V Hornby w Claughton 85–93; rtd 93; PtO *Blackb* from 93; *Carl* from 93. *5 Harling Bank, Kirkby Lonsdale, Carnforth LA6 2DJ* T: (015242) 72474

WOFFENDEN (née HANCOCK), Mrs Dorothy Myfanwy. b 41. NOC 01. **d** 03 **p** 04. NSM Brinnington w Portwood *Ches* 03–05; C Waverton w Aldford and Bruera 05–09; PtO from 09. *8 Churchill Crescent, Marple, Stockport SK6 6HJ* T: 0161-427 6839 E: dwoffenden@talktalk.net

WOGAN, Adam Charles. b 87. Hull Univ BA 12. St Steph Ho Ox BTh 15. **d** 15 **p** 16. C Scarborough St Martin *York* 15–18; C Scarborough St Sav w All SS 15–18; V E Grinstead St Mary *Chich* from 18. *St Mary's Vicarage, Windmill Lane, East Grinstead RH19 2DS* M: 07768-195363 E: adamwogan@hotmail.co.uk

WOLFE, Canon Michael Matheson. b 29. Pemb Coll Ox BA 49 MA 53. Cuddesdon Coll 51. **d** 53 **p** 54. C Moorfields *Bris* 53–57; P-in-c Fochabers *Mor* 57–58; Sub-Warden and Chapl Aberlour Orphanage 58–59; V Southport St Paul *Liv* 59–65; V Upholland 65–73; TR 73–82; RD Ormskirk 78–82; RD Ormskirk and Hon Can Liv Cathl 78–82; Can Res Liv Cathl 82–96; Merseyside Ecum Officer 82–89; AD Toxteth and Wavertree 89–96; rtd 96; PtO *Liv* from 97; Hon Chapl Liv Cathl from 97; Hon Sen Fell Liv Hope Univ from 10. *23 Hunters Lane, Liverpool L15 8HL* T: 0151-733 1541 M: 07712-258027 E: mwolfe@hotmail.co.uk

WOLFENDEN, Peter Graham. b 40. St Pet Coll Ox BA 63 MA 66. Linc Th Coll 62. **d** 64 **p** 65. C Adlington *Blackb* 64–66; Asst Master Barton Peveril Gr Sch 66–69; Chapl Bp Wordsworth's Sch Salisbury 69–72; Hon C Bishopstoke *Win* 66–72; Hon C Ponteland *Newc* 72–02; Hd Master Richard Coates Middle Sch Ponteland 78–01; Chapl Malta and Gozo *Eur* 02–07; Chapl Málaga 07–10; P-in-c Ovingdean *Chich* 10–18. *St James Cottage, 17 Western Road, Shoreham-by-Sea BN43 5WD* E: pgwolfenden@gmail.com

WOLSTENCROFT, The Ven Alan. b 37. Cuddesdon Coll. **d** 69 **p** 70. C Halliwell St Thos *Man* 69–71; C Stand 71–73; V Wythenshawe St Martin 73–80; AD Withington 78–91; Chapl Wythenshawe Hosp Man 80–89; V Baguley *Man* 80–91; V Bolton St Pet 91–98; Hon Can Man Cathl 86–98; Can Res Man Cathl 98–04; Adn Man 98–04; rtd 04; PtO *Man* from 04; Rtd Clergy and Widows Officer from 04; PtO *Eur* from 07. *The Bakehouse, 1 Latham Row, Horwich, Bolton BL6 6QZ* T: (01204) 469985 M: 07714-705535 E: wolstencroftalan@gmail.com

WOLTON, Andrew John. b 54. Cranfield Univ MDA 00. St Jo Coll Nottm BA 08. **d** 08 **p** 09. C Bures w Assington and Lt Cornard *St E* 08–11; R Saxmundham w Kelsale cum Carlton from 11. *The Rectory, Manor Gardens, Saxmundham IP17 1ET* T: (01728) 602687 M: 07769-946364 E: andywolton@btinternet.com

WOLVERHAMPTON, Area Bishop of. *See* GREGORY, The Rt Revd Clive Malcolm

WOLVERSON, Marc Ali Morad. b 68. Univ of Kansas BA 91. Ripon Coll Cuddesdon 93. **d** 96 **p** 97. C Nantwich *Ches* 96–99; C Baton Rouge St Luke USA 99–00; C Bramhall *Ches* 00–04; V High Lane 04–09; P-in-c Douglas All SS *S & M* 09–13; AD Douglas 12; P-in-c Leyland St Jas *Blackb* from 13; AD Leyland from 16. *St James's Vicarage, 201 Slater Lane, Leyland PR26 7SH* T: (01772) 421034

WOMACK, Michael John. b 62. Anglia Ruskin Univ MA 07. Westcott Ho Cam 08. **d** 10 **p** 11. C Framlingham w Saxtead *St E* 10–13; R Athelington, Denham, Horham, Hoxne etc from 13. *St Andrew's House, Vicarage Road, Wingfield, Diss IP21 5RB* T: (01379) 388889 E: hoxnebenefice@gmail.com

WOMERSLEY, Sally Ann. b 61. Westcott Ho Cam 06. **d** 08 **p** 09. C Charing w Charing Heath and Lt Chart *Cant* 08–11; Chapl Cant Ch Ch Univ 11–14; TV N Hinckford *Chelmsf* 14–19; V Milton next Gravesend Ch Ch *Roch* from 19. *Christ Church Vicarage, 48 Old Road East, Gravesend DA12 1NR* T: (01474) 362654 E: sallywomersley@yahoo.co.uk

WONG (née RUNDLE), Hilary. b 65. St Hugh's Coll Ox BA 88 Cheltenham & Glouc Coll of HE PGCE 90. Trin Coll Bris 01. **d** 03 **p** 04. C Chipping Sodbury and Old Sodbury *Glouc* 03–07; P-in-c St Helier *S'wark* 07–11; V 11–17; R Wyoming Australia from 18. *72 Bourbon Street, Wyoming NSW 2250, Australia* E: hilary193wong@hotmail.co.uk

WOO, Arthur Cheumin. b 66. Qu Univ Kingston Ontario BSc 89 MEng 91. St Jo Coll Nottm MTh 08. **d** 08 **p** 09. C Highworth w Sevenhampton and Inglesham etc *Bris* 08–12; V Cheylesmore *Cov* from 12. *Christ Church Vicarage, 11 Frankpledge Road, Coventry CV3 5GT* T: (024) 7650 2770 E: arthur@2woos.co.uk

WOOD, Alastair Paul. b 59. Ox Min Course 06. **d** 09 **p** 10. C Headington Quarry *Ox* 09–13; V Hadley and Wellington Ch Ch *Lich* 13–18; V Studley *Sarum* from 18. *St John's Vicarage, 340 Frome Road, Trowbridge BA14 0ED* M: 07948-989153 E: narniacurate09@btinternet.com

WOOD, Mrs Alison Jaye (Alice). b 57. La Sainte Union Coll BEd 79. STETS 09. **d** 12 **p** 13. NSM Farlington *Portsm* 12–16; C Blackmoor and Whitehill from 16; C Greatham 16–18. *The Brackens, Drift Road, Whitehill, Borden GU35 9EA* T: (01420) 472656 M: 07808-276964 E: woodcrew@tiscali.co.uk

WOOD, Mrs Ann Rene. b 49. St Deiniol's Hawarden 87. **d** 90 **p** 94. Par Dn Bamber Bridge St Aid *Blackb* 90–93; C W Burnley All SS 93–95; V Marton Moss 95–00; Hon Can Blackb Cathl 98–00; R Whiston *Sheff* 00–07; V Kimberworth 07–11; AD Rotherham 04–08; P-in-c Kimberworth Park 10–11; C Rawmarsh w Parkgate 10–11; C Greasbrough 10–11; rtd 11; PtO *Blackb* 11–14; AD Kirkham 14–15; P-in-c Lytham St Jo from 15. *St John's Vicarage, East Beach, Lytham St Annes FY8 5EX* E: ann.wood6@btopenworld.com

WOOD (née BLACKBURN), Mrs Anne Dorothy. b 54. Keele Univ BA 76 Bradf Univ MSc 90. NOC 95. **d** 98 **p** 99. NSM Batley St Thos *Wakef* 98–00; C Morley St Paul 01–02; C Bruntcliffe 01–02; C Morley 02–03; TV 03–07; TV Oakenshaw, Wyke and Low Moor *Bradf* 07–10; Chapl Wakefield Hospice 09–13; Tutor Leeds Dioc Sch Min from 13; PtO *Leeds* from 17. *24 Heaton Avenue, Earlsheaton, Dewsbury WF12 8AQ* T: (01924) 455343 M: 07929-452439 E: anne.d.wood@talk21.com

WOOD (formerly SWINBANK), Mrs Anne Jennifer. b 52. SS Paul & Mary Coll Cheltenham BA 90. St Steph Ho Ox 08. **d** 09. NSM N Cheltenham *Glouc* from 09. *5 Priory Mews, Sidney Street, Cheltenham GL52 6DJ* T: (01242) 700128 E: jennifer.swinbank@northchelt.org.uk

WOOD, Preb Anthony James. b 38. Kelham Th Coll 58. **d** 63 **p** 64. C Shrewsbury St Alkmund *Lich* 63; C Harlescott 63–66; C Porthill 66–70; P-in-c Priorslee 70–76; Chapl Telford Town Cen 73–76; V Barton-under-Needwood *Lich* 76–97; V Barton under Needwood w Dunstall 97–09; V Barton under Needwood w Dunstall and Tatenhill 09–10; RD Tutbury 02–10; Preb Lich Cathl 08–09; rtd 10; PtO *Lich* 11–14 and from 15; *Leic* from 14. *2 Shipley Close, Branston, Burton-on-Trent DE14 3HB* T: (01283) 516772 E: tonywood@preb.co.uk

WOOD, Audrey Elizabeth. *See* COUPER, Audrey Elizabeth

WOOD, Barbara Ann. b 49. St Mich Coll Llan 00. **d** 02 **p** 03. C Glan Ely *Llan* 02–05; P-in-c Llanharan w Peterston-super-Montem from 05. *The Vicarage, Brynna Road, Brynna, Pontyclun CF72 9QE* T: (01443) 226307 E: babswood01@hotmail.com

WOOD, Beresford Donald Richard. b 32. Leeds Univ BA 58. Cant Sch of Min 91. **d** 94 **p** 95. Chapl St Mary's Sch Westbrook 94–02; NSM Folkestone St Mary and St Eanswythe *Cant* 94–02; PtO 02–15. *St Katherine's Cottage, Pound Lane, Elham, Canterbury CT4 6TS* T: (01303) 840817

WOOD, Canon Beryl Jean. b 54. Linc Th Coll 85. **d** 87 **p** 94. C Gaywood, Bawsey and Mintlyn *Nor* 87–92; Asst Chapl Univ Hosp Nottm 93–95; R Shipdham w Bradenham *Nor* 95–06; RD Dereham in Mitford 00–04; Dep Warden Launde Abbey *Leic* 06–09; TR Gaywood *Nor* 10–15; Hon Can Nor Cathl 05–06 and 13–15; rtd 15; PtO *Nor* from 16. *51 Peckover Way, South Wootton, King's Lynn PE30 3UE* T: (01553) 676710 E: beryljwood@yahoo.com

WOOD, Mrs Brenda. b 46. Eliz Gaskell Coll Man TCert 67 Leeds Metrop Univ BEd 94 Leeds Univ MA 04. NOC 00. **d** 03 **p** 04. NSM Kirkstall *Ripon* 03–11; rtd 11. *18 Wentworth Crescent, Leeds LS17 7TW* T: 0113-226 7991 E: bwood@ntlworld.com

WOOD, Brian Richard. b 49. Sheff Univ BA 70 MCMI 78 RIBA 85 MRICS 00 FCIOB 00. Ox Min Course 04. **d** 07 **p** 08. NSM Blenheim *Ox* 07–12; NSM Akeman 12–19; rtd 19; PtO *Ox* 19. *Address temp unknown* E: revbrianwood@gmail.com

WOOD, Mrs Bryony Ann. b 59. St Jo Coll Nottm BA 10. **d** 10 **p** 11. C Derby St Pet and Ch Ch w H Trin 10–11; C Ashbourne St Oswald w Mapleton 11–12; C Hadfield 12–14; V Whatton w Aslockton, Hawksworth, Scarrington etc *S'well* 14–17; TV Market Harborough and The Transfiguration etc *Leic* from 17. *The Rectory, Dingley Road, Great Bowden, Market Harborough LE16 7ET* T: (01858) 469109 M: 07967-113028 E: bryony.wood@yahoo.com

WOOD, Sister Catherine Rosemary. b 54. Melbourne Coll of Div 82 St Jo Coll Auckland 83. **d** 83 **p** 84. C Howick New Zealand 83–87; C Auckland St Paul 88; P-in-c Mangere E 89–90; Co-ord Environmental Educn 90–95; N Fieldworker Chr World Service 96–01; Hon C Glen Eden 90–97; NSM Auckland Cathl 98–01; PtO *S'wark* 01–02; P-in-c Tatsfield 02–08; C Limpsfield and Titsey 02–03; Min Limpsfield Chart St Andr CD 03–08; PtO 08–11; Chapl HM Pris Latchmere Ho 09–11; Chapl HM Pris Wormwood Scrubs 12–14; PtO *Lon* 13–17; *S'wark* 13–17; *Ox* from 17. *St Michael's Convent, Vicarage Way, Gerrards Cross SL9 8AT* T: 07960-088873 E: silentmiaow@yahoo.co.uk

WOOD, Christine Denise. b 48. EMMTC. **d** 05 **p** 06. NSM Clifton *S'well* 05–07; Asst Chapl Notts Healthcare NHS Trust 07–10; Lead Chapl St Andr Healthcare 10–13; NSM Morton and Stonebroom w Shirland *Derby* from 09. *The Old Post Office, 8 Main Road, Higham, Alfreton DE55 6EF* T: (01773) 833152 E: cdjoakwood8@btinternet.com

WOOD, Christopher David. b 60. Worc Coll Ox BA 83 Leeds Univ MA 06. Coll of Resurr Mirfield 04. **d** 06 **p** 07. C King's Lynn St Marg w St Nic *Nor* 06–09; R Hunstanton St Mary w Ringstead Parva etc 09–14; R Nor St Jo w St Julian 14–19; Chapl Norfolk Constabulary 16–19; V Waddington *Blackb* from 19. *The Vicarage, Slaidburn Road, Waddington, Clitheroe BB7 3JQ* E: christopherd1760@hotmail.co.uk *or* rector.timberhill@gmail.com

WOOD, Christopher William. b 44. Rhodes Univ BA 66 UNISA BTh 82. St Bede's Coll Umtata 79. **d** 80 **p** 82. S Africa 80–87; C Houghton Regis *St Alb* 87–00; C Milton *Portsm* 00–03; PtO *Lich* from 04. *27 Penton Walk, Stoke-on-Trent ST3 3DG* T: (01782) 311779 E: candbwood@hotmail.com

WOOD, Clive Marcus. b 52. Bradf Univ BSc 75. SEITE BA 14. **d** 14 **p** 15. NSM Belvedere All SS *Roch* 14–18; LtO 18–19; TV Bexley from 19. *15 Denver Road, Dartford DA1 3LA* T: (01322) 270942 M: 07982-392809 E: clivemwood@yahoo.co.uk

WOOD, Canon Colin Arthur. b 41. S'wark Ord Course 86. **d** 89 **p** 90. C Tadworth *S'wark* 89–93; TV Morden 93–06; Hon Can S'wark Cathl 05–06; rtd 06; PtO *Chich* from 17. *44 Leonora Drive, Bognor Regis PO21 3NH* T: (01243) 264192 E: colinwood685@btinternet.com

WOOD, David Christopher. b 52. Oak Hill Th Coll 89. **d** 91 **p** 92. C Kendal St Thos *Carl* 91–95; P-in-c Asby, Bolton and Crosby Ravensworth 95–05; P-in-c Barton, Pooley Bridge and Martindale 05–13; V Barton, Pooley Bridge, Martindale etc 13–18; rtd 18. *10 Graham Street, Penrith CA11 9LG* E: revdavidcwood@hotmail.com

WOOD, David John. b 48. Newc Univ BSc 70 PGCE 71 Open Univ MA 91. **d** 01 **p** 02. OLM Bedlington *Newc* 01–07; OLM Shotley 07–15; NSM 15–17; rtd 17; PtO *Newc* from 17. *12 Wilding Place, Longhorsley, Morpeth NE65 8LB* E: davwd50@hotmail.com

WOOD, David Michael. b 39. Chich Th Coll. **d** 82 **p** 83. C Epping St Jo *Chelmsf* 82–85; C Totton *Win* 85–88; V Southway *Ex* 88–97; P-in-c Black Torrington, Bradford w Cookbury etc 97–01; R 01–04; rtd 04; PtO *Portsm* from

04. *47 Queens Crescent, Stubbington, Fareham PO14 2QG* E: davidwood@virginmedia.com

WOOD, Dennis William. b 28. Qu Mary Coll Lon BSc 53 Glas Univ PhD 57. NEOC 82. d 85 p 85. NSM Stanhope *Dur* 85–86; NSM Stanhope w Frosterley 86–94; NSM Eastgate w Rookhope 86–94; NSM Melrose *Edin* from 94. *Gordonlee, Ormiston Terrace, Melrose TD6 9SP* T: (01896) 823835 E: d.wood835@btinternet.com

WOOD, Donald. b 40. d 95 p 96. NSM Caldicot *Mon* 95–99; P-in-c Llangwm Uchaf and Llangwm Isaf w Gwernesney etc 99–06; LtO from 06. *13 Deepweir, Caldicot NP26 5JG* T: (01291) 425214

WOOD, Elaine Mary. *See* RICHARDSON, Elaine Mary

WOOD, Elizabeth Lucy. b 35. WMMTC 89. d 92 p 94. NSM Wellingborough St Mark *Pet* 92–95; P-in-c Stanwick w Hargrave 95–00; PtO 00–13; Chapl to Retired Clergy and Clergy Widows' Officer 08–12. *18 Stuart Court, High Street, Kibworth Beauchamp, Leicester LE8 0LR* T: 0116-429 8978 E: elizwood@tiscali.co.uk

WOOD, Geoffrey James. b 47. NOC 88. d 91 p 92. C Stainton-in-Cleveland *York* 91–94; V Middlesbrough St Oswald 94–99; V Eskdaleside w Ugglebarnby and Sneaton 99–06; rtd 06; PtO *York* from 06. *22 Hedley Street, Guisborough TS14 6EG* T: (01287) 619286 E: frgeoff@btinternet.com

WOOD, George Albert. b 22. St Paul's Coll Grahamstown. d 54 p 55. C Hillcrest S Africa 54–57; C W Suburbs Pretoria 57–60; C Cheam S'wark 60–63; R Eshowe S Africa 63–69; Can Zululand 68–73; Dean Eshowe 70–73; R Port Elizabeth Ch the K 74–77; Area Sec United Soc Chich from 78; TV Littlehampton and Wick *Chich* 86–88; rtd 88; PtO *Chich* from 88. *The College of St Barnabas, Blackberry Lane, Lingfield RH7 6NJ* T: (01903) 787746

WOOD, Heather Dawn. *See* ATKINSON, Heather Dawn

WOOD, Miss Helen Ruth. b 54. Bedf Coll Lon BA 75. Glouc Sch of Min 87. d 91 p 94. NSM Up Hatherley *Glouc* 91–94; NSM Cheltenham Em w St Steph 94–09; NSM S Cheltenham from 10; Asst Chapl Cheltenham Ladies' Coll from 91. *9 Southfield Manor Park, Sandy Lane, Charlton Kings, Cheltenham GL53 9DJ* T: (01242) 242793 E: woodh@cheltladiescollege.org

WOOD, Henry. b 70. SNWTP. d 13 p 14. NSM St Helens Town Cen *Liv* from 13. *12 Clipsley Crescent, Haydock, St Helens WA11 0UH* T: (01744) 454671 E: a1harry.wood@gmail.com

WOOD, Mrs Jane Lesley. b 60. Trent Poly BA 82. WEMTC 15. d 18 p 19. NSM Dursley, Uley, Owlpen etc *Glouc* from 18. *11 Spouthouse Lane, Cam, Dursley GL11 5JP* T: (01453) 544350 M: 07443-606582 E: jane_l_wood@yahoo.co.uk

WOOD, Mrs Jennifer Sarah. b 40. Sarum Dioc Tr Coll CertEd 60. Oak Hill Th Coll 92. d 94 p 95. C St Illogan *Truro* 94–98; R Heanton Punchardon w Marwood *Ex* 98–10; C Ilfracombe SS Phil and Jas w W Down 09–10; rtd 10; PtO *Ex* from 11. *32 Stallards, Braunton EX33 1BP* T: (01271) 812730 E: revjswood@hotmail.co.uk

WOOD, Mrs Joanne. b 81. Derby Univ BA 03. Qu Foundn (Course) 14. d 17 p 18. NSM Peel Parishes *Lich* 17–19; NSM Brereton and Rugeley w Armitage from 19. *14 Peakes Road, Rugeley WS15 2LY* M: 07399-539139 E: revjowood@hotmail.com

WOOD, John. b 37. LNSM course 75. d 77 p 79. NSM Haddington *Edin* from 77. *7 Herdmanflatt, Haddington EH41 3LN* T: (01620) 822838

WOOD, John Anthony Scriven. b 48. Leeds Univ BSc 70. St Jo Coll Nottm 76. d 79 p 80. C Colwich *Lich* 79–82; C W Bridgford S'well 82–90; V Gamston and Bridgford 90–95; Chapl Kings Mill Cen NHS Trust 95–01; Chapl Sherwood Forest Hosps NHS Foundn Trust 01–13; rtd 13; NSM Morton and Stonebroom w Shirland *Derby* 08–18; PtO from 18. *The Old Post Office, 8 Main Road, Higham, Alfreton DE55 6EF* T: (01773) 833152 E: john.wood1948@btinternet.com

WOOD, Preb John Maurice. b 58. Qu Coll Cam BA 80 MA 83. Wycliffe Hall Ox BA 87. d 87 p 88. C Northwood Em *Lon* 87–91; C Muswell Hill St Jas w St Matt 91–94; P-in-c S Tottenham St Ann 94–01; V 01–18; AD E Haringey 16–17; Preb St Paul's Cathl 17–18. *c/o Hope in Tottenham, The Trampery, 639 High Road, London N17 8AA* M: 07771-867359 E: johnmauricewood@btconnect.com

WOOD, Canon Samuel. b 47. Lancaster Poly Cov BSc 69 Sheff Univ DipEd. Westcott Ho Cam 72. d 81 p 82. NSM Haverhill St E 81–82; NSM Haverhill w Withersfield, the Wrattings etc 82–83; C Whitton and Thurleston w Akenham 83–86; P-in-c Walsham le Willows 86–88; P-in-c Finningham w Westhorpe 86–88; R Walsham le Willows and Finningham w Westhorpe 88–94; Min Can St E Cathl 89–94; TR Whitstable *Cant* 94–02; Chapl E Kent Community NHS Trust 94–02; Hon Min Can Cant Cathl

96–02; TR Swanage and Studland *Sarum* 02–16; RD Purbeck 07–15; Can and Preb Sarum Cathl 12–16; rtd 16; PtO *Sarum* from 16; Dioc Retirement Officer from 16. *16 Dunnabridge Street, Poundbury, Dorchester DT1 3TQ* T: (01305) 268749 E: john.s.wood@btinternet.com

WOOD, Kathleen. b 46. EMMTC 04. d 06 p 07. NSM Newhall *Derby* 06–09; NSM Etwall w Egginton 09–10; P-in-c Stapenhill Immanuel 10–14; rtd 14; PtO *Derby* 14–16 and from 17; Hon C Newhall 16–17; PtO *Lich* from 14. *28 Eastfield Road, Midway, Swadlincote DE11 0DG* T: (01283) 212490 M: 07401-292180 E: rkw28@btinternet.com

WOOD, Canon Keith Ernest. b 33. Qu Coll Ox BA 55 BCL 56 MA 70. Wycliffe Hall Ox 56. d 58 p 59. C Barking St Marg *Chelmsf* 58–61; Min Basildon St Andr ED 61–70; V Brampton Bierlow *Sheff* 70–82; R Grasmere *Carl* 82–94; RD Windermere 89–94; Hon Can Carl Cathl 91–94 and 98–01; Bp's Dom Chapl 94–01; rtd 01; PtO *Carl* from 01. *The Old Tower, Brackenburgh, Calthwaite CA11 9PW* T: (01768) 894273

WOOD (née DROBIG), Mrs Marion. b 76. Hannover Univ MA 01 Pemb Coll Ox DPhil 05. ERMC 04. d 06 p 07. C Newmarket All SS *St E* 06–09; R Shaw cum Donnington *Ox* from 09. *The Rectory, Well Meadow, Shaw, Newbury RG14 2DS* T: (01635) 600532 M: 07979-534948 E: mariondrobig@hotmail.com

WOOD, Mark Robert. b 68. Trin Coll Ox BA 89 ALCM 83 ARCO 89. STETS 02. d 05 p 06. C Mere w W Knoyle and Maiden Bradley *Sarum* 05–08; P-in-c Wilton w Netherhampton and Fugglestone 08–13; R from 13; RD Chalke 15–19. *The Rectory, 27A West Street, Wilton, Salisbury SP2 0DL* T: (01722) 742571 M: 07770-305990 E: rectorwilton@gmail.com

WOOD, Martin. *See* WOOD, Nicholas Martin

WOOD, Martin Robert. b 65. Birm Univ BSc 86. Trin Coll Bris 98. d 00 p 01. C Wells St Cuth w Wookey Hole *B & W* 00–03; C Shepton Mallet w Doulting 03–07; P-in-c Tedburn St Mary, Whitestone, Oldridge etc *Ex* 07–10; V Tedburn St Mary, Cheriton Bishop, Whitestone etc from 10; RD Kenn 11–19. *The Rectory, Church Lane, Cheriton Bishop, Exeter EX6 6HY* T: (01647) 24119 E: revwood163@gmail.com

WOOD, Canon Michael Frank. b 55. Nottm Univ BCombStuds. Linc Th Coll. d 84 p 85. C Marton *Blackb* 84–88; TV Ribbleton 88–93; V Blackpool St Mary 93–00; P-in-c S Shore St Pet 98–00; RD Blackpool 96–00; TR Brighouse and Clifton *Wakef* 00–08; RD Brighouse and Elland 06–08; TR Castleford 08–14; *Leeds* 14–16; P-in-c Smawthorpe *Wakef* 11–12; Armley w New Wortley *Leeds* from 16; Hon Can Bradf Cathl from 19. *31 Hill End Crescent, Leeds LS12 3PW* M: 07974-274001 E: frmw@hotmail.co.uk

WOOD, Mrs Michaela. b 67. d 01 p 02. NSM Sunbury *Lon* 01–04; NSM Whitton St Aug 04–06; NSM Aylesbury *Ox* 06–13; NSM Salfords *S'wark* 13–19; NSM Weston *Guildf* from 19. *The Vicarage, 1 Chestnut Avenue, Esher KT10 8JL* E: michaelawood@aol.com

WOOD, Canon Nicholas Martin. b 51. Univ of Wales (Lamp) MTh 09. AKC 74. d 75 p 76. C E Ham w Upton Park and Forest Gate *Chelmsf* 75–78; C Leyton St Luke 78–81; V Rush Green 81–91; RD Brighouse and Elland 96–05; Hon Can Wakef 91–05; RD Brighouse and Elland 96–05; Hon Can Wakef Cathl 00–05; Par Development Adv (Bradwell Area) *Chelmsf* 05–12; Miss and Min Adv (Bradwell Area) 12–19; Chapl to Bp Bradwell 11–12; Hon C Basildon St Martin 11–19; Hon Can Chelmsf Cathl 08–19; rtd 19; PtO *Chelmsf* from 19. *126 The Willows, Colchester CO2 8PZ* T: (01206) 562343 E: frmartinwood@gmail.com

WOOD, Canon Rachel Astrid. b 71. Birm Univ BA 92 MA 99. Qu Coll Birm BD 98. d 99 p 00. C Attercliffe, Darnall and Tinsley *Sheff* 99–01; C Roundhay St Edm *Ripon* 01–04; Local Min Development Officer *Newc* 12–17; V Monkseaton St Mary from 17; Hon Can Newc Cathl from 18. *St Mary's Vicarage, 77 Holywell Avenue, Whitley Bay NE26 3AG* T: 0191-252 9319 M: 07591-280905 E: rachel.astrid.wood@gmail.com

WOOD, Raymond John Lee. b 28. ACII 55 ACIArb. Linc Th Coll 66. d 68 p 69. C Beaconsfield *Ox* 68–72; CF 70–72; V Wath-upon-Dearne w Adwick-upon-Dearne *Sheff* 72–77; R St Tudy w Michaelstow *Truro* 77–86; P-in-c St Mabyn 82–86; R St Tudy w St Mabyn and Michaelstow 86–95; Chapl Bodmin Fire Brigade 91–14; rtd 95; PtO *Truro* 96–14; *Chich* from 14. *11 Gannon Road, Worthing BN11 2DT* T: (01903) 232303 E: rjlwood@btinternet.com

WOOD, Richard. *See* WOOD, Beresford Donald Richard

WOOD, Richard James. b 71. Oak Hill Th Coll BA 07. d 08 p 09. C Dagenham *Chelmsf* 08–09; C Aberporth w Blaenporth w Betws Ifan *St D* 12–14; P-in-c Aberporth w Blaenporth w Betws Ifan *St D* 12–14; PtO *Ban* from 12; NSM Tranmere St Cath *Ches* 16–19; PtO from

19. *c/o St Catherine's Vicarage, 39 Westbank Road, Birkenhead CH42 7JP*

WOOD, Richard Stanton. b 79. Univ of Wales (Abth) BSc 02 Univ of Wales (Cardiff) BA 08. d 08 p 09. C Henfynyw w Aberaeron and Llanddewi Aberarth etc *St D* 08–11; TV Llanelli 11–13; V Bro Madryn *Ban* from 13. *3 Llys Madryn, Morfa Nefyn, Pwllheli LL53 6EX* T: (01758) 720707 M: 07855-817740 E: richard@bromadryn.church

WOOD, Roger Graham. b 49. K Coll Lon BD. Chich Th Coll 74. d 76 p 77. C Skipton H Trin *Bradf* 76–79; Dioc Youth Chapl 79–87; V Queensbury 87–96; P-in-c Langcliffe w Stainforth and Horton 96–01; V 01–13; RD Bowland 08–14; R Bolton by Bowland w Grindleton 13–14; R Bolton by Bowland w Grindleton *Blackb* 14–19; rtd 19. *Address temp unknown* E: rgwood49@gmail.com

WOOD, Roger William. b 43. Leeds Univ BA 65 MA 67 Fitzw Coll Cam BA 69 MA 75. Westcott Ho Cam 67. d 70 p 71. C Bishop's Stortford St Mich *St Alb* 70–74; C Sundon w Streatley 75–79; V Streatley 80–09; rtd 09; PtO *St Alb* from 09. *8 Ramsey Road, Barton-le-Clay, Bedford MK45 4PE* T: (01582) 883277

WOOD, Ronald Ernest. b 49. Sarum & Wells Th Coll 79. d 81 p 82. C Weston-super-Mare Cen Par *B & W* 81–84; C Forest of Dean Ch Ch w English Bicknor *Glouc* 84–88; R Sixpenny Handley w Gussage St Andrew etc *Sarum* 88–05; P-in-c Seale, Puttenham and Wanborough *Guildf* 05–10; rtd 10; Hon C Camelot Par *B & W* 10–18; PtO from 18. *5 The Paddock, Galhampton, Yeovil BA22 7AR* T: (01963) 441192

WOOD, Sarah. *See* WOOD, Jennifer Sarah

WOOD, Shane Grant Lindsay. b 60. Southn Univ BTh 91. St Steph Ho Ox 95. d 97 p 98. C Parkstone St Pet w Branksea and St Osmund *Sarum* 97–00; V Teddington SS Pet and Paul and Fulwell *Lon* 00–06; TR Aylesbury *Ox* 06–13; V Salfords *S'wark* 13–19; Bp's Adv for Min Development 13–19; V Weston *Guildf* from 19. *The Vicarage, 1 Chestnut Avenue, Esher KT10 8JL* E: shaneglwood@aol.com

WOOD, Stella Margaret. b 70. Trin Coll Ox BA 91 MA DPhil 95. STETS 95. d 97 p 98. NSM Mere w W Knoyle and Maiden Bradley *Sarum* 97–08; Chapl Sherborne Sch for Girls 00–08; Teacher 08–14; Lic to RD Sarum 08–11; Co-ord for Learning and Discipleship *Sarum* 11–14; Chapl Godolphin Sch from 14; NSM Wilton w Netherhampton and Fugglestone *Sarum* from 14. *The Rectory, 27A West Street, Wilton, Salisbury SP2 0DL* T: (01722) 742571 E: woods@godolphin.wilts.sch.uk *or* stella.wood70@gmail.com

WOOD, Steven Paul. b 54. Fitzw Coll Cam MA 75. ERMC. d 07 p 08. NSM Hitchin *St Alb* 07–10; P-in-c Streatley 10–15; V 15–19; P-in-c Burnham Gp of Par *Nor* from 19. *The Rectory, The Pound, Burnham Market, King's Lynn PE31 8UL* M: 07704-922984

WOOD, Susan Joyce. b 52. Sheff City Coll of Educn CertEd 74. d 09 p 10. OLM Ramsbottom and Edenfield *Man* 09–14 and from 16. *243 Whittingham Drive, Ramsbottom, Bury BL0 9NY* T: (01706) 825464 E: woodsuej@btinternet.com

WOOD, Susan Pauline. b 47. Maria Grey Coll Lon TCert 68. STETS 07. d 10 p 11. NSM Staines *Lon* 10–17; rtd 17; PtO *Lon* from 19. *60 St Nicholas Drive, Shepperton TW17 9LD* T: (01932) 228712

WOOD, Valerie Rosemary. *See* SMITH, Valerie Rosemary

WOOD-ROBINSON, David Michael. b 28. Glas Univ BSc 50 Lon Univ BD 54. d 57 p 57. C Erith St Jo *Roch* 57–58; CMS Japan 58–71; R Holton and Waterperry *Ox* 71–88; RD Aston and Cuddesdon 88–92; R Holton and Waterperry w Albury and Waterstock 88–94; Chapl Ox Brookes Univ 90–94; rtd 94; PtO *Heref* from 15. *16 Pound Meadow, Ledbury HR8 2EU* T: (01531) 632347

WOOD-ROE (née BRYANT), Mrs Sarah Elizabeth. b 82. Grey Coll Dur BA 05 Wolfs Coll Cam MPhil 07. Westcott Ho Cam 06. d 08 p 09. C Branksome St Aldhelm *Sarum* 08–11; Chapl St Jo Sch Leatherhead 11–15; C Clarendon *Sarum* 15–17; C Salisbury St Fran and Stratford sub Castle from 17. *9 Swaynes Close, Salisbury SP1 3AE*

WOODALL, Ms Bridget Ann. b 65. CQSW 92. St Jo Coll Nottm 11. d 13 p 14. C Brierley Hill *Worc* 13–17; TV Kidderminster Ismere from 17. *St Barnabas' Vicarage, 50 Nursery Grove, Kidderminster DY11 5BG* T: (01562) 743545 E: revbridget.woodall@gmail.com

WOODALL, David Paul. b 59. Ches Coll of HE BTh 03. NOC 00. d 03 p 04. C Darwen St Pet w Hoddlesden *Blackb* 03–06; TV Bacup and Stacksteads *Man* 06–12; P-in-c Norden w Ashworth 12–13; C Oakenrod and Bamford 12–13; V Norden w Ashworth and Bamford 13–15; Warden Foxhill Retreat and Conf Cen *Ches* 15–16; PtO *Man* 16–17; V E Crompton from 17. *1 Owen Fold, Lees, Oldham OL4 3DT* M: 07940-721097 E: dpwoodall3@gmail.com

WOODALL, Ms Rosemary Helen. b 80. Newc Univ BSc 01. Ripon Coll Cuddesdon BA 09. d 10 p 11. C Glouc City and Hempsted 10–13; P-in-c Bisley, Chalford, France Lynch, and Oakridge 13–15; V Bisley, Chalford, France Lynch, and Oakridge etc 15–17; Bp's Chapl and Policy Adv *Leic* from 17. *9 Springfield Road, Leicester LE2 3BB* T: 0116-270 8985 M: 07816-420788 E: rosiewoodall@hotmail.co.uk

WOODCOCK, Anne Caroline. *See* McMULLEN, Anne Caroline

WOODCOCK, Edward Marsden. b 47. Hull Univ MSc 01 Leeds Univ BA 03. Coll of Resurr Mirfield 01. d 03 p 04. C Wrenthorpe *Wakef* 03–06; C Alverthorpe 03–06; P-in-c Brotherton *Leeds* 06–15; V 15–17; P-in-c Ferrybridge 06–17; rtd 17. *11 Aldbury Close, Barnsley S71 2BW* E: edward@thewoodcocks.plus.com

WOODCOCK, Michael David. b 67. Avery Hill Coll BEd 91. Wycliffe Hall Ox BTh 96. d 96 p 97. C Orpington Ch Ch *Roch* 96–99; R Knockholt w Halstead 99–06; P-in-c Crosthwaite Kendal *Carl* from 06; P-in-c Cartmel Fell from 06; P-in-c Winster from 06; P-in-c Witherslack from 06. *The Vicarage, Crosthwaite, Kendal LA8 8HX* T: (015395) 68276 E: mich@elwoodcock.com

WOODCOCK, Mrs Michelle Lisa. b 74. Dartington Coll of Art BA 96 Cant Ch Ch Univ PGCE 98. LCTP 08. d 10 p 11. NSM Crosthwaite, Cartmel Fell, Winster and Witherslack *Carl* 10–15; TV Cartmel Peninsula 15–17. *The Vicarage, Crosthwaite, Kendal LA8 8HX* T: (015395) 68276 E: michellewoodcock74@hotmail.com

WOODE, Mrs Elizabeth. b 43. d 06 p 07. NSM Middlewich w Byley *Ches* from 06. *6 The Grange, Hartford, Northwich CW8 1QH* T: (01606) 75030 E: tonylizwoode@hotmail.com

WOODERSON, Mrs Marguerite Ann. b 44. RGN SCM. Qu Coll Birm 86. d 89 p 94. Par Dn Stoneydelph St Martin CD *Lich* 89–90; Par Dn Glascote and Stonydelph 90–91; Par Dn Chasetown 91–94; C 94; C-in-c Chase Terrace St Jo Distr Ch 92–94; Chapl Naas Gen Hosp 94–98; I Celbridge w Straffan and Newcastle-Lyons *D & G* 98–06. *Lazena, Rosses Point, Co Sligo, Republic of Ireland* T: (00353) (71) 911 7852 E: annwooderson@gmail.com

WOODERSON, Michael George. b 39. Southn Univ BA 61. Lon Coll of Div BD 69. d 69 p 70. C Morden *S'wark* 69–73; C Aldridge *Lich* 73–81; V Chasetown and P-in-c Hammerwich 91–94; RD Lich 86–94; Preb Lich Cathl 89–94; I Naas w Kill and Rathmore *M & K* 94–06; rtd 06. *Lazena, Rosses Point, Co Sligo, Republic of Ireland* T: (00353) (71) 911 7852 M: 86-336 8503 E: michaelwooderson@icloud.com

WOODFIELD, Benjamin Robert. b 81. St Jo Coll Nottm. d 14 p 15. C Astley Bridge *Man* 14–18; LtO from 18. *24 Mackenzie Street, Bolton BL1 6QW* M: 07800-746918 E: revbenwoodfield@gmail.com

WOODGATE, Elizabeth Mary. *See* McCLEAVE, Elizabeth Mary

WOODGER, John McRae. b 36. Univ of Wales MTh 08. Tyndale Hall Bris 60. d 63 p 64. C Heref St Pet w St Owen 63–66; C Macclesfield St Mich *Ches* 66–69; V Llangarron w Llangrove *Heref* 69–74; P-in-c Garway 70–74; R Church Stretton 74–84; Preb Heref Cathl 82–84; V Watford *St Alb* 84–01; rtd 01; PtO *Heref* 01–16; *Chich* from 17. *22 Clock Tower Court, Park Avenue, Bexhill-on-Sea TN39 3HP* T: (01424) 552953 E: woodger@talktalk.net

WOODGER, John Page. b 30. Master Mariner 56. St Aid Birkenhead 56. d 59 p 60. C Kimberworth *Sheff* 59–62; Chapl HM Borstal Pollington 62–70; C Goole *Sheff* 62–63; V Balne 63–70; C Halesowen *Worc* 70–74; V Cookley 74–81; TV Droitwich 81–85; TV Bedminster *Bris* 85–93; rtd 93; PtO *Bris* 93–97; *Worc* from 98. *1 Barbel Crescent, Worcester WR5 3QU* T: (01905) 769065 E: john.woodger@cmail.co.uk

WOODGER, Richard William. b 50. Sarum & Wells Th Coll 76. d 79 p 80. C Chessington *Guildf* 79–82; C Frimley and Frimley Green 82–85; V N Holmwood 85–90; TR Headley All SS 90–98; TR Penrith w Newton Reigny and Plumpton Wall *Carl* 98–05; P-in-c Northleach w Hampnett and Farmington etc *Glouc* 05–13; C Sherborne, Windrush, the Barringtons etc 08–13; AD Northleach 09–10; rtd 13; PtO *Lon* from 14. *6 Sylvia Avenue, Pinner HA5 4QE* E: dickwoodger@yahoo.co.uk

WOODHALL, Neil Baxter. b 53. Yorks Min Course 13. d 15 p 16. C Selby Abbey *York* from 15. *6 Priory Park Grove, Monk Fryston, Leeds LS25 5EU* T: (01977) 682091 E: nbwoodhall@btinternet.com

WOODHALL, Peter. b 32. Edin Th Coll 57. d 60 p 61. C Carl St Barn 60–63; Hon Chapl Estoril *Eur* 63–65; Chapl RN 66–82; TR Is of Scilly *Truro* 82–90; V Mithian w Mount Hawke 90–95; rtd 97. *17 Emu Close, Heath and Reach, Leighton Buzzard LU7 0AT*

WOODHAM, Richard Medley Swift. b 43. Master Mariner 70. S'wark Ord Course 71. d 73 p 74. C Gravesend St Aid *Roch* 73–75; C Chessington *Guildf* 75–78; Warden Dioc Conf

Ho Horstead *Nor* 78–87; R Horstead 78–87; Youth Chapl 78–88; V Nor St Mary Magd w St Jas 87–91; TR Norwich Over-the-Water 91–98; P-in-c Lakenham St Jo 98–99; V Nor Lakenham St Jo and All SS and Tuckswood 99–06; RD Nor E 02–06; rtd 06; PtO *Nor* from 06. *40 Anchor Street, Coltishall, Norwich NR12 7AQ* T: (01603) 736411 E: richardmwoodham@gmail.com

WOODHAMS, Raymond John. b 40. Garnett Coll Lon CertEd 68 IEng 68. STETS 98 Coll of Resurr Mirfield 01. **d** 01 **p** 02. NSM E Blatchington *Chich* 01–07; NSM Eastbourne St Sav and St Pet 07–10; PtO from 10. *23 Penlands Vale, Steyning BN44 3PL* T: (01903) 367163 E: raymondj.woodhams@googlemail.com

WOODHAMS, Roy Owen. b 57. ARCM 76 GRSM 78 Lon Inst of Educn TCert 79. Ripon Coll Cuddesdon 91. **d** 93 **p** 94. C Deal St Leon and St Rich and Sholden *Cant* 93–97; P-in-c Cherbury *Ox* 97–02; P-in-c Gainfield 99–02; R Cherbury w Gainfield 02–04; AD Vale of White Horse 01–04; V Fleet *Guildf* 04–13; R Cranleigh from 13; AD from 19. *The Rectory, 15 High Street, Cranleigh GU6 8AS* T: (01483) 800655 E: roy.woodhams@gmail.com

WOODHEAD, Miss Helen Mary. b 35. Bedf Coll Lon BA 57. Westcott Ho Cam 86. **d** 87 **p** 94. Par Dn Daventry *Pet* 87–90; Asst Dioc Dir of Ords *Guildf* 90–00; C Godalming 90–95; C Worplesdon 95–00; rtd 00; PtO *Lich* 00–13 and 18–19. *48 Monks Close, Lichfield WS13 6QR*

WOODHEAD, Canon Michael. b 51. St Jo Coll Nottm 88. **d** 90 **p** 91. C Stannington *Sheff* 90–93; V Deepcar 93–01; TV Crookes St Thos 01–05; TR from 05; Hon Can Sheff Cathl from 11. *St Thomas Church, Nairn Street, Sheffield S10 1UL* T: 0114-267 1090 E: mick.woodhead@sheffield.anglican.org

WOODHOUSE, Canon Alison Ruth. b 43. Bedf Coll of Educn CertEd 64. Dalton Ho Bris 68. **dss** 79 **d** 87 **p** 94. Bayston Hill *Lich* 79–81; W Derby St Luke *Liv* 81–86; Burscough Bridge 86–95; Par Dn 87–94; C 94–95; V Formby St Luke 95–07; AD Sefton 00–05; Hon Can Liv Cathl 02–07; rtd 07; Chapl to The Queen 06–13. *16 Fountains Way, Liverpool L37 4HE* T: (01704) 877423

WOODHOUSE, The Ven Andrew Henry. b 23. Qu Coll Ox BA 48 MA 49. Linc Th Coll 48. **d** 50 **p** 51. C Poplar All SS w St Frideswide *Lon* 50–56; V W Drayton 56–70; RD Hillingdon 67–70; Adn Ludlow *Heref* 70–82; R Wistanstow 70–82; P-in-c Acton Scott 70–73; Can Res Heref Cathl 82–91; Treas Heref Cathl 82–85; Adn Heref 82–91; rtd 91; PtO *Guildf* 91–15. *Orchard Cottage, Bracken Close, Woking GU22 7HD* T: (01483) 760671

WOODHOUSE, The Ven Charles <u>David</u> Stewart. b 34. Kelham Th Coll 55. **d** 59 **p** 60. C Leeds Halton St Wilfrid *Ripon* 59–63; Youth Chapl *Liv* 63–66; Bermuda 66–69; Asst Gen Sec CEMS 69–70; Gen Sec 70–76; Bp's Dom Chapl *Ex* 76–81; R Ideford, Luton and Ashcombe 76–81; V Hindley St Pet *Liv* 81–92; Hon Can Liv Cathl 83–01; rtd 01; PtO *Liv* from 03. *9 Rob Lane, Newton-le-Willows WA12 0DR*

WOODHOUSE, David Edwin. b 45. Lon Univ BSc 68. Cuddesdon Coll 68. **d** 71 **p** 72. C E Dulwich St Jo *S'wark* 71–74; LtO 74–77; PtO *Bris* 77–79; LtO 79–98; PtO *Sarum* from 04; rtd 10; PtO *Bris* from 10. *34 Cambria Place, Swindon SN1 5DN* E: kingsburyhallcd@aol.com

WOODHOUSE, David Maurice. b 40. Lon Univ BA 62. Clifton Th Coll 63. **d** 65 **p** 66. C Wellington w Eyton *Lich* 65–68; C Meole Brace 68–71; V Colwich 71–82; P-in-c Gt Haywood 78–82; R Clitheroe St Jas *Blackb* 82–88; Ellel Grange Chr Healing Cen 88–91; V The Lye and Stambermill *Worc* 91–99; Chapl Acorn Chr Foundn 99–02; Dioc Healing Adv *Guildf* 00–02; rtd 02; PtO *Blackb* from 04. *1 Lilac Avenue, Penwortham, Preston PR1 9PB* T: (01772) 742088

WOODHOUSE, Canon Keith Ian. b 33. K Coll Lon 54. **d** 58 **p** 59. C Stockton St Chad CD *Dur* 58–61; C Man St Aid 61–64; V Peterlee *Dur* 64–99; AD Easington 72–98; Hon Can Dur Cathl 79–99; rtd 99; Dioc Pensions and Widows Officer *Dur* from 00; PtO from 04. *85 Baulkham Hills, Penshaw, Houghton le Spring DH4 7RZ* T/F: 0191-584 3977 E: keithianwoodhouse@excite.com *or* keith.woodhouse@durham.anglican.org

WOODHOUSE, Canon Patrick Henry Forbes. b 47. Ch Ch Ox BA 69 MA 81. St Jo Coll Nottm 69 Lon Coll of Div ALCD 71 LTh 71. **d** 72 **p** 73. C Birm St Martin 72–74; C Whitchurch *Bris* 75–76; C Harpenden St Nic *St Alb* 76–80; Tanzania 80–81; Soc Resp Officer *Carl* 81–85; P-in-c Dean 81–85; Dir Soc Resp *Win* 85–90; V Chippenham St Andr w Tytherton Lucas *Bris* 90–00; Can Res and Prec Wells Cathl *B & W* 00–12; rtd 12; PtO *B & W* 14–19. *Woodside, Rimpton, Yeovil BA22 8AF* T: (01935) 850915 M: 07812-395912 E: pwoodhouse09@gmail.com

WOODHOUSE, Canon Thomas Mark Bews. b 66. Chelt & Glouc Coll of HE BA 98 Glos Univ MA 05 FRSA 05. Aston

Tr Scheme 90 Westcott Ho Cam 92. **d** 95 **p** 96. C Cainscross w Selsley *Glouc* 95–98; V Hardwicke and Elmore w Longney 98–05; P-in-c Wootton Bassett *Sarum* 05–10; V R Wootton Bassett 10–14; P-in-c Lyneham w Bradenstoke 11–14; NSM Woodhill 11–14; RD Calne 06–14; TR Dorchester and the Winterbournes from 14; Can and Preb Sarum Cathl from 09. *The Rectory, 17A Edward Road, Dorchester DT1 2HL* T: (01305) 267944 E: tmbwoodhouse@gmail.com

WOODING, Alison. b 67. Yorks Min Course 05. **d** 10 **p** 11. C Ranmoor *Sheff* 10–15; P-in-c Kimberworth and Kimberworth Park 15–17; C Rawmarsh w Parkgate 15–17; C Greasbrough 15–17; Asst Dean CA from 17. *Wilson Carlile Centre, 50 Cavendish Street, Sheffield S3 7RZ* T: 0114-278 7020 M: 07891-064370 E: revalisonwooding@gmail.com

WOODING JONES, The Ven Andrew David. b 61. Hull Univ MBA 01. Oak Hill Th Coll BA 91. **d** 91 **p** 92. C Welling *Roch* 91–95; TV Crookes St Thos *Sheff* 95–00; Resident Dir Ashburnham Trust 00–12; NSM Ashburnham w Penhurst *Chich* 01–12; Dir World Prayer Cen Birm 12–14; PtO *Roch* 14–18; *Chich* 15–18; Adn Roch from 18. *Lytlewood, Riding Lane, Hildenborough, Tonbridge TN11 9LR* T: (01634) 560023 M: 07843-358553 E: archdeacon.rochester@rochester.anglican.org

WOODLEY, David James. b 38. K Coll Lon BD 61 AKC 61 Open Univ BA 98. **d** 62 **p** 63. C Lancing St Jas *Chich* 62–64; C St Alb St Pet 64–67; Malaysia 67–70; LtO *Linc* 71–72; V Westoning w Tingrith *St Alb* 72–77; Asst Chapl HM Pris Wormwood Scrubs 77–78; Chapl HM Pris Cardiff 78–84; Chapl HM Rem Cen Risley 84–92; Chapl HM Pris Styal 92–98; rtd 98; PtO *Ches* 98–06; *B & W* 08–19. *18 Longcroft Road, Yeovil BA21 4RR* T: (01935) 474072

WOODLEY, Canon John Francis Chapman. b 33. Univ of Wales (Lamp) BA 58. Edin Th Coll 58. **d** 60 **p** 61. C Edin All SS 60–65; Chapl St Andr Cathl *Ab* 65–67; Prec 67–71; R Glas St Oswald 71–77; P-in-c Cumbernauld 77–93; Can St Mary's Cathl 82–99; CSG from 82; R Dalbeattie *Glas* 93–99; rtd 99; Hon Can St Mary's Cathl *Glas* from 99; Dioc Supernumerary 99–03; LtO from 03. *McMillan House, 33 Buchanan Drive, Rutherglen, Glasgow G73 3PF* T: 0141-647 3118 E: jonfwoodley@icloud.com

WOODLEY, Simon Andrew. b 66. Liv Univ BA 88 Univ of Cen England in Birm 96. Ridley Hall Cam BTh 00. **d** 00 **p** 01. C Birm St Martin w Bordesley St Andr 00–04; TR Bemerton *Sarum* 04–18; V Alderholt from 18. *The Vicarage, Daggons Road, Alderholt, Fordingbridge SP6 3DN* E: revwoodley@yahoo.co.uk

WOODMAN, Andrew Christopher. b 83. Ridley Hall Cam 15. **d** 17 **p** 18. C The Mitre Benefice *Nor* from 17. *St Mary's Vicarage, Douglas Haig Road, Norwich NR5 8LD* M: 07834-189519 E: andy.woodman@stn.org.uk

WOODMAN, Oliver Nigel. b 47. FCIPD. Sarum Th Coll 67. **d** 70 **p** 82. C Stepney St Dunstan and All SS *Lon* 70–71; NSM Ovingdean w Rottingdean and Woodingdean *Chich* 81–87; NSM Eastbourne St Sav and St Pet 88–93; Asst to RD Eastbourne 93–98; NSM Eastbourne St Sav and St Pet 98–01; PtO *Win* 02–10; Hon Chapl Win and Eastleigh Healthcare NHS Trust 09–10; PtO *Lich* 10–16. *25A Wissage Lane, Lichfield WS13 6DF* T: (01543) 256655 E: ojwoodman56@googlemail.com

WOODMAN, The Ven Peter Wilfred. b 36. Univ of Wales (Lamp) BA 58. Wycliffe Hall Ox 58. **d** 60 **p** 61. C New Tredegar *Mon* 60–61; C Newport St Paul 61–64; C Llanfrechfa All SS 64–66; Abp of Wales's Messenger 66–67; V Llantilio Pertholey w Bettws Chpl etc *Mon* 67–74; V Bassaleg 74–90; Can St Woolos Cathl 84–01; V Caerwent w Dinham and Llanfair Discoed etc 90–96; Adn Mon 93–01; R Mamhilad and Llanfihangel Pontymoile 96–01; rtd 01. *Glaslyn, 40 Longhouse Barn, Penperlleni, Pontypool NP4 0BD* T: (01873) 881322 E: petglen@gmail.com

WOODMANSEY, Michael Balfour. b 55. Leic Univ BSc. Ridley Hall Cam. **d** 83 **p** 84. C St Paul's Cray St Barn *Roch* 83–89; C S Shoebury *Chelmsf* 89–93; R Stifford 93–01; TR Heworth H Trin *York* 01–07; R Heworth H Trin and St Wulstan from 07. *Heworth Rectory, Melrosegate, York YO31 0RP* T/F: (01904) 422958 E: vicar@holytrinitystwulstan.org.uk

WOODMORE, Mrs Dilys Mary. b 44. SAOMC 98. **d** 01 **p** 02. NSM Dedworth *Ox* 01–04; NSM Burchetts Green 04–14; rtd 14; PtO *Ox* from 14. *59 Terrington Hill, Marlow SL7 2RE* T: (01628) 486274

WOODROW, Mark Jason. b 72. MInstLM 10. Ripon Coll Cuddesdon 11. **d** 13 **p** 14. C Lavenham w Preston *St E* 13–16; P-in-c Stoke by Nayland w Leavenheath and Polstead from 16; P-in-c Nayland w Wiston from 16; RD Hadleigh from 18. *St James's Vicarage, Bear Street, Nayland, Colchester CO6 4LA* T: (01206) 262150 M: 07890-871271 E: revdmarkwoodrow@gmail.com

WOODRUFF, Mrs Celia Mary. b 52. d 14 p 15. NSM Vale and Cotswold Edge *Glouc* 14–17; P-in-c Burpham *Chich* from 17; P-in-c Poling from 17. *The Vicarage, Burpham, Arundel BN18 9RJ* E: ronaldandcelia@btinternet.com

WOODS, The Very Revd Alan Geoffrey. b 42. ACCA 65 FCCA 80. Sarum Th Coll 67. d 70 p 71. C Bedminster St Fran *Bris* 70–73; Youth Chapl 73–76; Warden Legge Ho Res Youth Cen 73–76; P-in-c Neston *Bris* 76–79; TV Gtr Corsham 79–81; CF (TA) 80–94; P-in-c Charminster *Sarum* 81–83; V Charminster and Stinsford 83–90; RD Dorchester 85–90; Chapl Dorchester Hosps 86–87; V Calne and Blackland *Sarum* 90–96; RD Calne 90–96; Chapl St Mary's Sch Calne 90–96; Can and Preb Sarum Cathl 92–96; Sen Chapl Malta and Gozo *Eur* 96–03; Chan Malta Cathl 96–03; Dean Gib 03–08; V Gen to Bp Eur 03–05; Adn Gib 05–08; P-in-c Málaga 06–07; rtd 08; PtO *Sarum* from 08; *Eur* from 08; Dioc Retirement Officer *Sarum* 10–16. *6 Maumbury Square, Weymouth Avenue, Dorchester DT1 1TY* T: (01305) 264877 E: abwoods@tiscali.co.uk

WOODS, Andrea Ruth. b 68. ERMC 17. d 19. C Mattishall and the Tudd Valley *Nor* from 19. *The New Rectory, Rectory Road, Hockering, Dereham NR20 3HP* T: (01603) 928279 M: 07870-786212 E: andrea.woods@matvchurch.uk

WOODS, Christopher Guy Alistair. b 35. Dur Univ BA 60. Clifton Th Coll 60. d 62 p 63. C Rainham *Chelmsf* 62–65; C Edin St Thos 65–69; Sec Spanish and Portuguese Ch Aid Soc 69–79; C Willesborough w Hinxhill *Cant* 74–80; P-in-c Murston w Bapchild and Tonge 80–87; R 87–90; R Gt Horkesley *Chelmsf* 90–98; RD Dedham and Tey 91–98; rtd 98; P-in-c Tenerife Sur *Eur* 99–00; PtO *Chelmsf* from 00. *Bluebonnet, Mill Lane, Bradfield, Manningtree CO11 2UT* T: (01255) 870411

WOODS, Christopher Morrison. b 77. St Andr Univ MA 00 TCD BTh 04. CITC 01. d 04 p 05. C Dundela St Mark *D & D* 04–07; Chapl Ch Coll Cam 07–10; Sec C of E Liturg Commn and Nat Worship Development Officer Abps' Coun 11–13; Tutor Westcott Ho Cam 12–13; PV St Jo Coll Cam 12–13; P-in-c Hoxton St Anne w St Columba *Lon* 13–15; V 15–19; Educator in Adult Learning and Development Stepney Area 13–19; V Ox St Barn and St Paul w St Thos from 19. *St Barnabas' Vicarage, St Barnabas Street, Oxford OX2 6BG* T: (01865) 964041 E: revdchris@icloud.com

WOODS, David Arthur. b 28. Bris Univ BA 52. Tyndale Hall Bris 48. d 53 p 54. C Camborne *Truro* 53–56; C Bromley Ch Ch *Roch* 56–58; V Tewkesbury H Trin *Glouc* 58–66; V Stapleford *S'well* 66–70; Hon Chapl Miss to Seamen 70–93; V Fowey *Truro* 70–93; RD St Austell 80–88; rtd 93. *Linden, 7 Richmond Road, Pelynt, Looe PL13 2NH* T: (01503) 220374

WOODS, David Benjamin. b 42. Linc Th Coll 88. d 90 p 91. C Louth *Linc* 90–93; P-in-c Ingoldmells w Addlethorpe 93–97; R 97–01; P-in-c Sutton Bridge 01–08; rtd 08; Hon C Digby Gp *Linc* from 08. *10 Mayflower Drive, Heckington, Sleaford NG34 9UX* M: 07840-544384 E: woods_david4@sky.com

WOODS, Edward Christopher John. b 44. NUI BA 67. CITC 66. d 67 p 68. C Drumglass *Arm* 67–70; C Belfast St Mark *Conn* 70–73; I Kilcolman *L & K* 73–78; I Portarlington w Cloneyhurke and Lea *M & K* 78–84; Chan Kildare Cathl 81–84; I Killiney Ballybrack *D & G* 85–92; I Dublin Rathfarnham 93–14; Dir of Ords (Dub) 98–14; Internship Co-ord CITC 10–14; rtd 14; PtO *Liv* from 16. *St Peter's Vicarage, Cricket Path, Formby, Liverpool L37 7DP* T: (01704) 872824 E: tedwoods1607@gmail.com

WOODS, Canon Eric John. b 51. Magd Coll Ox BA 72 MA 77 Trin Coll Cam BA 77 MA 83 FRSA 94. Westcott Ho Cam 75. d 78 p 79. C Bris St Mary Redcliffe w Temple etc 78–81; Hon C Clifton St Paul 81–83; Asst Chapl Bris Univ 81–83; V Wroughton 83–93; RD 88–93; V Sherborne w Castleton, Lillington and Longburton *Sarum* 93–16; TR from 16; Chapl Sherborne Sch for Girls 93–99; RD Sherborne *Sarum* 96–04; Can and Preb Sarum Cathl from 98; Chapl Dorset Community NHS Trust 93–00; Chapl SW Dorset Primary Care Trust from 01; Chapl St Antony's Leweston Sch Sherborne 03–17. *The Vicarage, Abbey Close, Sherborne DT9 3LQ* T: (01935) 812452 F: 812206 E: vicar@sherborneabbey.com

WOODS, Frederick James. b 45. Southn Univ BA 66 MPhil 74 Fitzw Coll Cam BA 76 MA 79. Ridley Hall Cam 74. d 77 p 78. C Stratford-on-Avon w Bishopton *Cov* 77–81; V Warminster Ch Ch *Sarum* 81–96; RD Heytesbury 95–96; TR Woodley *Ox* 96–01; V Colchester St Pet and St Botolph *Chelmsf* 01–11; rtd 11; PtO *St E* from 16. *36 Church Road, Otley, Ipswich IP6 9NP* T: (01473) 890786 E: fredjwoods@hotmail.com

WOODS, Geoffrey Edward. b 49. Lon Univ BD 70 K Coll Lon MA 94. Tyndale Hall Bris 67. d 72 p 74. C Gipsy Hill Ch Ch *S'wark* 73–76; C Uphill *B & W* 76–79; R Swainswick w Langridge and Woolley 79–84; PtO *Bris* 84–96; NSM Colerne w N Wraxall 96–12; NSM By Brook 06–11; NSM Box w Hazlebury and Ditteridge 11–12; rtd 14; PtO *Bris* 12–19. *22 Watergates, Colerne, Chippenham SN14 8DR* T: (01225) 743675

WOODS, Michael. b 57. Ripon Coll Cuddesdon 99. d 01 p 02. C Bamber Bridge St Aid *Blackb* 01–06; P-in-c Rishton 06–11; V 11–15; AD Whalley 11–15; R Croston, Bretherton and Mawdesley w Bispham from 15. *The Rectory, 22 Out Lane, Croston, Leyland PR26 9HJ* T: (01772) 600548 E: revmwoods@gmail.com

WOODS, Canon Norman Harman. b 35. K Coll Lon BD 62 AKC 62. d 63 p 64. C Poplar All SS w St Frideswide *Lon* 63–68; C-in-c W Leigh CD *Portsm* 68–76; V Hythe *Cant* 76–01; RD Elham 83–89; Hon Can Cant Cathl 90–01; rtd 01; PtO *Cant* from 01. *36 Abbey Gardens, Canterbury CT2 7EU* T: (01227) 470957 E: normanwoods@talktalk.net

WOODS, Richard Thomas Evelyn Brownrigg. b 51. St Steph Ho Ox 83. d 85 p 86. C Southgate Ch Ch *Lon* 85–88; C Northampton All SS w St Kath *Pet* 88–89; V Maybridge *Chich* 89–99; V E Dean 99–05; R Singleton 99–05; V W Dean 99–05; R E Dean, Singleton, and W Dean 05–13; rtd 13; PtO *Cant* from 15. *12 Whittington Terrace, Cox Hill, Shepherdswell, Dover CT15 7NH* T: (01304) 268013 M: 07717-473774 E: rwoods@onetel.com

WOODS, Roger Andrew. b 60. Southn Univ BSc 81. Oak Hill Th Coll BA 01. d 98 p 99. C Audley *Lich* 98–02; TV Leek and Meerbrook 02–15; V Kings Heath *Pet* from 15; Dioc Urban Support Officer from 15. *The Vicarage, The Bartons Close, Northampton NN5 7HQ* T: (01604) 599902 E: rogerwoodsinbox@gmail.com

WOODS, Stephanie Ruth. b 64. Westhill Coll Birm BEd 92 TCD MTh 12. d 11 p 12. C Drung w Castleterra, Larah and Lavey etc *K, E & A* 12–15; I Lisbellaw *Clogh* from 15. *The Rectory, Drummeer Road, Faughard, Lisbellaw, Enniskillen BT94 5ES* T: (028) 6638 5894 M: 07759-949932 or (00353) 86-160 1318 E: alldonkeysneedshelter@yahoo.ie

WOODS, Timothy James. b 52. Poly Cen Lon BA 78 MSc 79 Ex Univ MA 96 ACIB 75. Qu Coll Birm 81. d 83 p 84. C Brierley Hill *Lich* 83–86; C Stoneydelph St Martin CD 86–88; World Development Officer 86–88; Chr Aid Area Sec (SE Lon) 88–91; V Estover *Ex* 91–97; TR Brixham w Churston Ferrers and Kingswear 97–00; Dir Bd of Ch and Soc *Sarum* 00–05; RD Salisbury 04–07; Advocacy and Middle E Desk Officer USPG 05–08; Regional Co-ord Wales and W of England 10; In Methodist Ch 08–09; LtO *Ex* 10–12; Miss Enabler Devonport St Aubyn and Plymouth Waterfront 13–17; rtd 17; PtO *Ex* from 18; *B & W* from 18. *72 Parkhouse Road, Minehead TA24 8AF* T: (01643) 818665 E: timber.woods@yahoo.co.uk

WOODSFORD, Canon Andrew Norman. b 43. Nottm Univ BA 65. Ridley Hall Cam 65. d 67 p 68. C Radcliffe-on-Trent *S'well* 67–70; P-in-c Ladybrook 70–73; P-in-c Barton in Fabis 73–81; P-in-c Thrumpton 73–81; R Gamston w Eaton and W Drayton 81–88; Chapl Bramcote Sch Notts 81–93; Warden of Readers *S'well* 88; Hon Can S'well Minster 93–08; RD Retford 93–00; rtd 08; PtO *S'well* from 08. *Address temp unknown* E: woodsford@msn.com

WOODSFORD, Martyn Paul. b 64. Oak Hill Th Coll 01 Adelaide Coll of Div BMin 15. d 03 p 04. C Southover *Chich* 03–07; P-in-c S Malling 07–09; P-in-c Adelaide St Luke Australia 09–14; P-in-c Adelaide St Oswald 14–18; TR Halewood and Hunts Cross *Liv* from 18. *The Rectory, 3 Rectory Drive, Liverpool L26 6LJ* E: revwoody@me.com

WOODWARD, Andrew John. b 59. ACIB 85. SEITE 96. d 99 p 00. NSM Weybridge *Guildf* 99–03; NSM St Botolph Aldgate w H Trin Minories *Lon* 03–07; PtO *Guildf* 03–07; P-in-c Kemp Town St Mary *Chich* 07–19; V from 19; RD Brighton from 15. *10 Chesham Street, Brighton BN2 1NA* T: (01273) 698601 M: 07434-605749 E: ruraldeanbrighton@gmail.com

WOODWARD, Anthony John. b 50. Salford Univ BSc 78. St Jo Coll Nottm 79. d 81 p 82. C Deane *Man* 81–84; CF 84–87; R Norris Bank *Man* 87–90; V Lostock St Thos and St Jo 92–96; PtO 96–01; C Halliwell 01–02; TV 02–04; P-in-c Chard and Distr *B & W* 04–06; V Chard St Mary 06–09; P-in-c Combe St Nicholas w Wambrook and Whitestaunton 08–09; rtd 09; PtO *Man* from 14; C W Monkton w Kingston St Mary, Broomfield etc *B & W* 15–17. *58 Woodstock Drive, Bolton BL1 6BB* M: 07827-917209 E: tonyjohn1950@gmail.com

WOODWARD, Clive Ian. b 49. City of Lon Poly BSc 84 Win Univ MA 16. STETS 01. d 04 p 05. NSM Willingdon *Chich* 04–06 and 12–19; Chapl E Sussex Hosps NHS Trust 06–12; rtd 19. *61 Rowan Avenue, Eastbourne BN22 0RX* T: (01323) 509891 E: revd.clive@hotmail.com

WOODWARD, Canon Ian. b 44. OLM course 96. d 97 p 98. OLM Queen Thorne *Sarum* 97–99; Adv to Bd of Ch and Soc 97–00; NSM Wilton w Netherhampton and Fugglestone *Sarum* 00–02; R Bere Regis and Affpuddle w Turnerspuddle 02–14; Can and Preb Sarum Cathl 07–14;

rtd 14; V of the Close Sarum Cathl from 14. *68A The Close, Salisbury SP1 2EN* T: (01722) 555192 M: 07973-318866 E: revianw@btinternet.com *or* voc@salcath.org

WOODWARD, Prof James Welford. b 61. K Coll Lon BD 82 AKC 82 Lambeth STh 85 Birm Univ MPhil 91 Open Univ PhD 99 FRSA 07. Westcott Ho Cam 83. **d** 85 **p** 86. C Consett *Dur* 85–87; Bp's Dom Chapl *Ox* 87–90; Chapl Qu Eliz Hosp Birm 90–96; Distr Chapl Co-ord S Birm HA 90–96; Chapl Manager Univ Hosp Birm NHS Trust 92–96; P-in-c Middleton *Birm* 96–98; P-in-c Wishaw 96–98; Bp's Adv on Health and Soc Care 96–09; V Temple Balsall 98–09; Master Foundn and Hosp of Lady Katherine Leveson 98–09; Dir Leveson Cen for the Study of Ageing, Spirituality and Soc Policy 00–09; Can Windsor 09–15; Prin Sarum Coll from 15; Visiting Prof Th Win Univ from 17; Can and Preb Sarum Cathl from 15. *Sarum College, 19 The Close, Salisbury SP1 2EE* T: (01722) 424801 E: jww@sarum.ac.uk

WOODWARD, Canon John Clive. b 35. Univ of Wales (Lamp) BA 56. St Jo Coll Dur 56. **d** 58 **p** 59. C Risca *Mon* 58–63; C Chepstow 63–66; V Ynysddu 66–74; V Newport Ch Ch 74–84; Can St Woolos Cathl 82–00; TR Cyncoed 84–00; rtd 00. *17 Carisbrooke Way, Cyncoed, Cardiff CF23 9HS* T: (029) 2048 4448

WOODWARD, Mrs Margaret Ruth. b 59. EMMTC 04. **d** 08 **p** 09. NSM Flintham *S'well* 08–14; NSM Car Colston w Screveton 08–14; NSM Hickling w Kinoulton and Broughton Sulney from 14. *The Rectory, 41 Main Street, Kinoulton, Nottingham NG12 3EN* T: (01949) 81183

WOODWARD, Mark Christian. b 73. Univ of Wales (Lamp) BA 95 Trin Coll Carmarthen PGCE 97. Trin Coll Bris MA 02. **d** 02 **p** 03. C Egham *Guildf* 02–06; R Stoke-next-Guildf from 06; Chapl Guildf Coll of FE and HE from 06. *8 Brockway Close, Guildford GU1 2LW* T: (01483) 559886 M: 07949-630031 E: mark@stjohnstoke.com

WOODWARD, Matthew Thomas. b 75. Brunel Univ BA 97 K Coll Lon MA 99 Anglia Poly Univ MA 05. Westcott Ho Cam 99. **d** 01 **p** 02. C Hampstead St Jo *Lon* 01–05; P-in-c Pimlico St Sav 05–10; R San Mateo Transfiguration USA from 10. *3900 Alameda de las Pulgas, San Mateo CA 94403-4110, USA* T: (001) (650) 341 8206 E: matthewwoodward@mac.com

WOODWARD, Merriel Frances. b 55. Brighton Univ BA 08 RGN 81. Ripon Coll Cuddesdon 10. **d** 11 **p** 12. NSM Langney *Chich* 11–17; NSM Willingdon from 17. *61 Rowan Avenue, Eastbourne BN22 0RX* T: (01323) 509891 E: revd.merriel@hotmail.co.uk

WOODWARD (née HIGGINS), Natasha Caroline. b 76. Clare Coll Cam BA 98 MA 02. Westcott Ho Cam 03. **d** 06 **p** 07. C Crayford *Roch* 06–07; C Orpington All SS 08–10; C Chingford SS Pet and Paul *Chelmsf* 10–13; V Kingsbury H Innocents *Lon* from 13; Lic Lay Min Tr Officer Willesden Area from 15; Dean of Women's Min Willesden Area from 19. *Kingsbury Vicarage, 54 Roe Green, London NW9 0PJ* T: (020) 8204 7531 E: natasha.c.woodward@gmail.com

WOODWARD, Canon Peter Cavell. b 36. St Cath Coll Cam BA 58 MA 62. Bps' Coll Cheshunt 58. **d** 60 **p** 61. C Chingford St Anne *Chelmsf* 60–63; Madagascar 63–75; V Weedon Bec *Pet* 75–76; P-in-c Everdon w Farthingstone 75–76; V Weedon Bec w Everdon 76–81; RD Daventry 79–81; Can Pet Cathl 81–02; V Brackley St Pet w St Jas 81–02; Chapl Brackley Cottage Hosp 81–02; RD Brackley *Pet* 82–88; rtd 02; PtO *Pet* from 02; Chapl to Retired Clergy and Clergy Widows' Officer from 08. *7 Glastonbury Road, Northampton NN4 8BB* T: (01604) 660679 E: peterandmary@oddbod.org.uk

WOODWARD, Roger David. b 38. WMMTC 87. **d** 90 **p** 91. C Castle Bromwich SS Mary and Marg *Birm* 90–93; C Kingstanding St Luke 93–04; C Kingstanding St Mark 93–04; rtd 04; Hon C Kingstanding St Mark *Birm* 04–07; PtO *Worc* from 10. *10 Baldwin Road, Bewdley DY12 2BP* T: (01827) 918037

WOODWARD-RUSSELL, Andrew Gregory. b 80. UEA BSc 02 St Edm Coll Cam BTh 05. Westcott Ho Cam 14. **d** 16 **p** 18. C E Greenwich *S'wark* 16–19; Chapl Methodist Homes for the Aged from 19. *Herondale and Kingfisher House Care Home, 175 Yardley Green Road, Bordesley Green, Birmingham B9 5PU* M: 07952-856044 E: andrew.russell@gmx.com

WOODWELL, Sister Anita Marie. b 42. Nottm Univ BA 74 CertEd 80. St Deiniol's Hawarden 85. **dss** 86 **d** 87 **p** 05. Mottram in Longdendale w Woodhead *Ches* 86–89; Par Dn 87–89; Team Dn Birkenhead Priory 89; PtO *Ban* from 01; *St D* from 04; P-in-c Llanfrechfa and Llanddewi Fach w Llandegfeth *Mon* 05–09; Dioc Adv on Spirituality 09–13; PtO from 13. *1 White Houses, Pentwyn, Abersychan, Pontypool NP4 7SY* T: (01495) 753195 E: awoodwell@yahoo.com

WOOFF, Ms Erica Mielle. b 67. City Univ BSc 90 Lon Inst of Educn MA 95 Heythrop Coll Lon MA 05. SEITE 02. **d** 05

p 06. C Sydenham St Bart *S'wark* 05–08; P-in-c Charlton 08–09; R 09–16; P-in-c Stockwell St Andr and St Mich 16–19; V from 19. *St Michael's Vicarage, 78 Stockwell Park Road, London SW9 0DA* T: (020) 7274 6480

WOOKEY, Canon Frances Anne. b 52. ACII 73. WEMTC 94. **d** 97 **p** 98. C Glouc St Jas and All SS 97–01; V Hanley Castle, Hanley Swan and Welland *Worc* 01–15; P-in-c Upton-on-Severn, Ripple, Earls Croome etc 11–15; RD Upton 05–11; Hon Can Worc Cathl 07–15; rtd 15; PtO *Glouc* from 15; *Worc* from 15. *51 Marlstone Road, Norman Hill, Dursley GL11 5SA* T: (01453) 519099 E: fawookey@gmail.com

WOOKEY, Stephen Mark. b 54. Em Coll Cam BA 76 MA 80. Wycliffe Hall Ox 77. **d** 80 **p** 81. C Enfield Ch Ch Trent Park *Lon* 80–84; Asst Chapl Paris St Mich *Eur* 84–87; C Langham Place All So *Lon* 87–96; R Moreton-in-Marsh w Batsford, Todenham etc *Glouc* from 96; RD Stow 99–04. *The Rectory, Bourton Road, Moreton-in-Marsh GL56 0BG* T: (01608) 652680 E: stevewookey@mac.com

WOOLCOCK, Christine Ann. *See* FROUDE, Christine Ann

WOOLCOCK, John. b 47. Open Univ BA 82 BA 86. Wm Temple Coll Rugby 69 Sarum & Wells Th Coll 70. **d** 72 **p** 73. C Kells *Carl* 72–76; C Barrow St Matt 76–78; R Distington 78–86; V Staveley w Kentmere 86–93; Soc Resp Officer 89–93; Hon Can Carl Cathl 91–93; TR Egremont and Haile 93–08; P-in-c Seascale and Drigg 08–13; RD Calder 07–12; rtd 13; PtO *Carl* from 13. *6 Highfields, Whitehaven CA28 6TS* T: (01946) 590685 E: john.woolcock@btinternet.com

WOOLCOCK, Mrs Olwen Sylvia. b 57. Birm Univ BA 78. WEMTC 02. **d** 05 **p** 06. C Claines St Jo *Worc* 05–08; TR Hugglescote w Donington, Ellistown and Snibston *Leic* from 08. *The Rectory, 12 Grange Road, Hugglescote, Coalville LE67 2BQ* T: (01530) 839368 E: olwen@woolcock.org

WOOLDRIDGE, Nicholas Lee. b 83. Aus Catholic Univ BEd 07. Wycliffe Hall Ox BTh 17. **d** 17 **p** 18. C Battersea Rise St Mark *S'wark* from 17. *22 Rochelle Close, London SW11 2RX* M: 07534-040554 E: nicklwooldridge@hotmail.com

WOOLF, Canon Elizabeth Louise. b 73. Qu Coll Cam BA 95 MA 99. Wycliffe Hall Ox BA 05. **d** 06 **p** 07. C Holborn St Geo w H Trin and St Bart *Lon* 06–08; C Hammersmith St Paul 08–09; C Leamington Priors St Paul *Cov* 09–17; TR Leeds St Geo from 17; Hon Can Bradf Cathl from 19. *208 Kirkstall Lane, Leeds LS5 2AB* E: lizzy.woolf@stgeorgesleeds.org.uk

WOOLFORD, Thomas Alan. b 85. Oak Hill Th Coll 13. **d** 17 **p** 18. C Bispham *Blackb* from 17. *422 Ashfield Road, Thornton-Cleveleys FY5 3PJ*

WOOLHOUSE, Kenneth. b 38. BNC Ox BA 61 MA 65. Cuddesdon Coll 61. **d** 64 **p** 65. C Old Brumby *Linc* 64–67; Pastor Michaelshoven Soc Work Village W Germany 67–68; Chapl Cov Cathl 68–75; C-in-c Hammersmith SS Mich and Geo White City Estate CD *Lon* 75–81; Dir Past Studies Chich Th Coll 81–86; P-in-c Birdham w W Itchenor *Chich* 81–86; Chapl W Sussex Inst of HE 86–95; TV N Lambeth *S'wark* 95–01; rtd 01; PtO *S'wark* from 01. *15 Tavistock Tower, Russell Place, London SE16 7PQ* T: (020) 7237 8147

WOOLLARD, Miss Bridget Marianne. b 56. K Coll Cam BA 77 MA 80 Sheff Univ PGCE 78 St Jo Coll Dur BA 81 Birm Univ MPhil 87. Cranmer Hall Dur 79. **dss** 82 **d** 87 **p** 94. Battersea St Pet and St Paul *S'wark* 82–84; Chapl Southn Univ *Win* 84–89; Tutor Past Th and Dir Past Studies Qu Coll Birm 89–92; LtO *Birm* 89–92; Telford Chr Coun Officer for Ind and Commerce *Lich* 92–97; PtO *Heref* 92–97; Lect in Past Th Trin Coll Melbourne Australia 97–98; Chapl Addenbrooke's NHS Trust 98–02; PtO *Lich* 98–08. *37 Hatters Court, Bedworth CV12 9AU*

WOOLLARD, David John. b 39. Leic Univ BSc 62. Trin Coll Bris 86. **d** 88 **p** 89. C Clifton *York* 88–91; C York St Luke 91–94; V Selby St Jas 94–07; V Wistow 94–96; rtd 07; PtO *York* from 07. *6 Town Street, Settrington, Malton YO17 8NR* T: (01944) 768665 E: dwoollard@yahoo.co.uk

WOOLLASTON, Brian. b 53. CertEd 76. St Paul's Coll Grahamstown 81. **d** 83 **p** 84. C Kington w Huntington, Old Radnor, Kinnerton etc *Heref* 88–89; C Tupsley 89–91; V Newbridge-on-Wye and Llanfihangel Brynpabuan etc *S & B* 91–98; CF 98–03; V Whiteshill and Randwick *Glouc* 03–14; TV Stroud Team 14–19; rtd 19. *Address temp unknown*

WOOLLCOMBE (née DEARMER), Mrs Juliet. b 38. St Mary's Coll Dur BA 60 Hughes Hall Cam DipEd 61. Gilmore Course 74. **dss** 77 **d** 87 **p** 94. St Marylebone Ch Ch *Lon* 77–80; Dean of Women's Min (Lon Area) 87–89; Dn-in-c Upton Snodsbury and Broughton Hackett etc *Worc* 89–94; NSM Pershore w Pinvin, Wick and Birlingham 94–98; rtd 98; PtO *Worc* 98–10; Cant from 11. *3 Sturry Court Mews, Sturry Hill, Sturry, Canterbury CT2 0ND* T: (01227) 710346 E: juliet.woollcombe1238@btinternet.com

WOOLLEY, Justine Clare. *See* RICHARDS, Justine Clare

WOOLMER, Preb John Shirley Thursby. b 44. Wadh Coll Ox BA 63 MA 69. St Jo Coll Nottm 70. **d** 71 **p** 72. Asst Chapl Win Coll 72–75; C Ox St Aldate w H Trin 75–82; R Shepton Mallet w Doulting *B & W* 82–02; Chapl Bath and West Community NHS Trust 97–01; Preb Wells Cathl *B & W* 00–02; NSM Leic H Trin w St Jo 02–07; Par Evang 02–07; Springboard Missr 02–04; rtd 07; PtO *Leic* from 15. *Fig Tree Cottage, Roecliffe Road, Cropston, Leicester LE7 7HQ* T: 0116-235 5237 E: jstwoolmer@googlemail.com *or* jstwoolmerf@gmail.com

WOOLMER, Kelvin Frederick. b 55. EAMTC 98. **d** 01 **p** 02. NSM Squirrels Heath *Chelmsf* 01–05; NSM Harold Hill St Paul 05–06; P-in-c Stratford New Town St Paul 06–12; Ind Chapl 06–12; TV Waltham H Cross 12–17; Chapl Lon City Airport 12–17; R Bedford St Pet w St Cuth *St Alb* from 17; PtO *Eur* from 18. *The Rectory, 36 De Parys Avenue, Bedford MK40 2TP* E: kelvin.fwoolmer@gmail.com

WOOLVEN, Mrs Catherine Merris. b 60. Trin Coll Bris 07. **d** 09 **p** 10. Chapl Lee Abbey 09–10; C Kilmington, Stockland, Dalwood, Yarcombe etc *Ex* 10–14; P-in-c Uplyme w Axmouth 14–15; R 15–19; PtO *Sarum* from 19. *The Forge, Church Street, Bowerchalke, Salisbury SP5 5BE* M: 07754-582395

WOOLVEN, Ronald. b 36. Oak Hill Th Coll 60. **d** 63 **p** 64. C Romford Gd Shep *Chelmsf* 63–68; C Widford 68–73; P-in-c Barling w Lt Wakering 73–84; V 84–05; rtd 05; PtO *Chelmsf* from 05. *119 Ness Road, Shoeburyness, Southend-on-Sea SS3 9ES* T: (01702) 294436 E: ronaldwoolven38@gmail.com

WOOLWAY, Joanne. *See* GRENFELL, Joanne Woolway

WOOLWICH, Area Bishop of. *See* DORGU, The Rt Revd Woyin Karowei

WOON, Canon Edward Charles. b 43. SWMTC 94. **d** 96 **p** 97. OLM Tuckingmill *Truro* 96–02; P-in-c 02–11; TV Redruth w Lanner and Treleigh 04–13; Hon Can Truro Cathl 09–13; rtd 13; PtO *Truro* from 16. *31 Trevelthan Road, Redruth TR16 4DX* T: (01209) 212191 M: 07974-431863 E: eddie.woon@btopenworld.com

WOOSTER, Patrick Charles Francis. b 38. Qu Coll Birm 63. **d** 65 **p** 66. C Chippenham St Andr w Tytherton Lucas *Bris* 65–70; C Cockington *Ex* 70–72; V Stone w Woodford *Glouc* 72–73; P-in-c Hill 72–73; V Stone w Woodford and Hill 73–99; rtd 99; PtO *Worc* from 99. *20 Hylton Road, Hampton, Evesham WR11 2QB* T: (01386) 45907

WOOSTER, Mrs Ruth Mary. b 45. SAOMC 95. **d** 98 **p** 99. OLM High Wycombe *Ox* 98–16; PtO from 16. *2 Beechwood View, Wycombe Road, Saunderton, High Wycombe HP14 4HR* T: (01494) 566117 E: ruth.mikewooster@gmail.com

WOOTTON, Philip Charles. b 63. Hatf Coll Dur BA 85 Dur Inst of Educn PGCE 86. Cranmer Hall Dur 98. **d** 00 **p** 01. C Meopham w Nurstead *Roch* 00–04; TV S Chatham H Trin 04–12; TR Tettenhall Wood and Perton *Lich* from 12. *Tettenhall Wood Rectory, 7 Broxwood Park, Wolverhampton WV6 8LZ* T: (01902) 751116 E: philwootton@supanet.com *or* philwootton@sky.com

WORCESTER, Archdeacon of. *See* JONES, The Ven Robert George

WORCESTER, Bishop of. *See* INGE, The Rt Revd John Geoffrey

WORCESTER, Dean of. *See* ATKINSON, The Very Revd Peter Gordon

WORDSWORTH, Paul. b 42. Birm Univ BA 64. Wells Th Coll 64. **d** 66 **p** 67. C Anlaby St Pet *York* 66–71; C Marfleet 71–72; TV 72–77; V Sowerby 77–90; P-in-c Sessay 77–90; V York St Thos w St Maurice 90–01; Local Community Miss Project Ldr 90–96; Abp's Miss Adv *York* 96–00; Miss Strategy Development Officer 01–07; Abp's Officer for Miss and Evang 01–07; rtd 07; PtO *York* from 07. *10 Burniston Grove, York YO10 3RP* T: (01904) 426891 M: 07711-371046 E: pandomw04@gmail.com

WORGAN, Maurice William. b 40. Ely Th Coll 62 Sarum Th Coll 64. **d** 65 **p** 66. C Cranbrook *Cant* 65–69; C Maidstone St Martin 69–72; R Lyminge w Paddlesworth 72–73; P-in-c Stanford w Postling and Radegund 72–73; R Lyminge w Paddlesworth, Stanford w Postling etc 73–88; V Cant St Dunstan w H Cross 88–09; rtd 09; PtO *Cant* from 09. *Old Trees, 13 Weatherall Close, Dunkirk, Faversham ME13 9UL* T: (01227) 363339 E: maurice@maurice-worgan.co.uk

WORKMAN, Aileen Joan. b 55. Linc Sch of Th and Min 11. **d** 15 **p** 16. NSM Spalding St Paul *Linc* 15–17; NSM Spalding St Mary and St Nic 15–17; C from 17. *18 Maple Grove, Spalding PE11 2LE* T: (01775) 768944 M: 07980-436097 E: aileenworkman@hotmail.co.uk

WORKMAN, John Lewis. b 26. St Deiniol's Hawarden 82. **d** 83 **p** 84. C Brecon St Mary and Battle w Llanddew *S & B* 83–86; Min Can Brecon Cathl 83–86; P-in-c Swansea St Luke 86–87; V 87–95; rtd 95. *12 Grove House, Clyne Close, Mayals, Swansea SA3 5HL* T: (01792) 405674

WORLEDGE, Paul Robert. b 70. Hertf Coll Ox BA 91 Lon Inst of Educn PGCE 92. Oak Hill Th Coll BA 00. **d** 00 **p** 01. C Boscombe St Jo *Win* 00–04; V Ramsgate St Luke *Cant* from 04; P-in-c Westgate St Sav 13–16; AD Thanet 09–15. *St Luke's Vicarage, St Luke's Avenue, Ramsgate CT11 7JX* T: (01843) 592562 E: worledge@bigfoot.com

WORLEY, William. b 37. Cranmer Hall Dur 69. **d** 72 **p** 73. C Consett *Dur* 72–76; V Seaton Carew 76–03; CF (TA) from 77; rtd 03; PtO *Dur* from 03. *5 Peakston Close, Hartlepool TS26 0PN* T: (01429) 293494

WORMALD, Roy Henry. b 42. Chich Th Coll 64. **d** 67 **p** 68. C Walthamstow St Mich *Chelmsf* 67–69; C Cov St Thos 69–72; C Cov St Jo 69–72; C Wood Green St Mich *Lon* 72–77; P-in-c Hanwell St Mellitus 77–80; V Hanwell St Mellitus w St Mark 80–95; C Hillingdon St Jo 95–99; R Kirkley St Pet and St Jo *Nor* 99–09; rtd 09; PtO *Nor* from 09; *St E* from 11. *12 Coppleston Close, Worlingham, Beccles NR34 7SF* T: (01502) 713331

WORMSLEY (née SAVAGE), Lucy Jane. b 90. Nottm Univ BA 11. St Jo Sch of Miss Nottm BA 16. **d** 16 **p** 17. C Ossett and Gawthorpe *Leeds* 16–19; V Wyke from 19. *The Vicarage, 6 Vicarage Close, Wyke, Bradford BD12 8QW* E: revdlucy16@hotmail.com

WORN, Nigel John. b 56. Sarum & Wells Th Coll. **d** 84 **p** 85. C Walworth St Jo *S'wark* 84–88; Succ S'wark Cathl 88–92; V Mitcham Ascension 92–01; RD Merton 97; V Kew from 01. *The Vicarage, 278 Kew Road, Kew, Richmond TW9 3EE* T: (020) 8940 4616 E: nigel.worn@gmail.com

WORRALL, Suzanne. *See* SHERIFF, Suzanne

WORSDALE, Barry. b 46. **d** 10 **p** 11. NSM Elloughton and Brough w Brantingham *York* 10–13; P-in-c N Cave w Cliffe from 13; P-in-c Hotham from 13; Chapl HM Pris Wolds from 11. *The Vicarage, Church Lane, North Cave, Brough HU15 2GJ* T: (01430) 470716 E: bworsdale@hotmail.co.uk

WORSFOLD, Canon Caroline Jayne. b 61. St Steph Ho Ox. **d** 88 **p** 94. Chapl Asst Leic R Infirmary 88–90; C Sunderland Pennywell St Thos *Dur* 90–91; Sunderland HA Chapl 90–94; Chapl Priority Healthcare Wearside NHS Trust 94–06; Chapl Northumberland, Tyne and Wear NHS Foundn Trust from 06; Hon Can Dur Cathl from 15. *The Barton Centre, Cherry Knowle Hospital, Ryhope, Sunderland SR2 0NB* T: 0191-522 7347 *or* 565 6256 ext 43370 E: caroline.worsfold@stw.nhs.uk

WORSFOLD, Mrs Natalie Kim. b 70. St Mellitus Coll BA 18. **d** 18 **p** 19. C High Wycombe Ox from 18. *6 Coopers Rise, High Wycombe HP13 7FF* T: (01494) 471315 M: 07867-537604 E: natinthecloud@mail.com

WORSFOLD, The Ven Richard Vernon. b 64. Ex Univ LLB 86. Cranmer Hall Dur BA 94. **d** 95 **p** 96. C Countesthorpe w Foston *Leic* 95–99; TV Bradgate Team 99–01; TR 01–09; V Leic Martyrs 09–18; AD City of Leic 14–18; Adn Leic from 18. *46 Southernhay Road, Leicester LE2 3TJ* M: 07948-385097 E: rworsfold@virginmedia.com

WORSLEY, Christine Anne. b 52. Hull Univ BA 73 Bris Univ CertEd 74 Birm Univ MPhil 94. WMMTC 82. **dss** 84 **d** 87 **p** 94. Smethwick St Mary *Birm* 84–87; Par Dn Smethwick H Trin w St Alb 87–89; Par Dn Coventry Caludon *Cov* 89–91; Chapl Myton Hamlet Hospice 91–95; Tutor WMMTC 95–04; Minl and Adult Learning Officer *Ely* 05–13; Hon Can Ely Cathl 12–13; Kingdom People Development Officer *Worc* 13–15; NSM Bredon w Bredon's Norton 15–17; NSM Defford w Besford 15–17; NSM Eckington 15–17; NSM Elmley Castle w Bricklehampton and Combertons 15–17; NSM Overbury w Teddington, Alstone etc 15–17; rtd 17. *11 Oberon Way, Cottingley, Bingley BD16 1WH*

WORSLEY, Howard John. b 61. Man Univ BA 83 Leeds Univ PGCE 85 Birm Univ PhD 00. St Jo Coll Nottm MTh 93. **d** 93 **p** 94. C Huthwaite *S'well* 93–96; V Radford St Pet 96–01; Dir Studies St Jo Coll Nottm 02–04; Dir of Educn *S'well* 04–10; Dir of Educn *Lon* 10–11; Chapl Lon S Bank Univ *S'wark* 11–12; Sen Lect Cant Ch Ch Univ 12–15; Vice-Prin Trin Coll Bris from 13; Dir *S'wark* 12–13; *B & W* 15–17; NSM Banwell and Congresbury w Hewish, Puxton and W Wick from 17. *72 Bath Road, Wells BA5 3LJ* M: 07528-565600 E: h.worsley@trinitycollegebristol.ac.uk *or* hjworsley4@gmail.com

WORSLEY, Richard John. b 52. Qu Coll Cam BA 74 MA 78 Univ of Wales CertEd 76 Birm Univ MPhil 91 Warwick Univ MA 96. Qu Coll Birm 77. **d** 80 **p** 81. C Styvechale *Cov* 80–84; V Smethwick H Trin w St Alb *Birm* 84–89; TV Coventry Caludon *Cov* 89–96; Hon C Binley 96–05; PtO *Ely* 05–08; Hon C Soham and Wicken 08–13; P-in-c Overbury w Teddington, Alstone etc *Worc* 13–17; P-in-c Elmley Castle w Bricklehampton and Combertons 13–17; rtd 17. *11 Oberon Way, Cottingley, Bingley BD16 1WH* M: 07854-543218

✠**WORSLEY, The Rt Revd Ruth Elizabeth.** b 62. **d** 96 **p** 97. C Basford w Hyson Green *S'well* 96–98; C Hyson Green and Forest Fields 98–01; P-in-c 01–08; AD Nottm N 06–08; P-in-c Sneinton St Chris w St Phil 08–10; Dean of Women's Min 07–10; Hon Can S'well Minster 07–10; Par Development Officer Woolwich Area *S'wark* 10–13; Adn Wilts *Sarum* 13–15; Chapl to The Queen 09–15; Suff Bp Taunton *B & W* from 15. *The Palace, Wells BA5 2PD* T: 01749 672341 M: 07917-693285 E: bishop.taunton@bathwells.anglican.org

WORSLEY, Thomas Robert. b 54. Sunderland Univ CertEd 00. Lindisfarne Regional Tr Partnership 10. **d** 12 **p** 13. NSM Felling *Dur* from 12; P-in-c from 16. *28 Rectory Road East, Gateshead NE10 9DN* M: 07757-949836 E: tom.worsley@blueyonder.co.uk *or* trw@christchurchfelling.org

WORSSAM, Brother Nicholas Alan. b 65. Selw Coll Cam BA 87 MA 91. Qu Coll Birm MA 04. **d** 06 **p** 07. SSF from 99; PtO *Worc* from 15. *Glasshampton Monastery, Shrawley, Worcester WR6 6TQ* T: (01299) 896345 F: 896083 E: nicholasalanssf@btconnect.com

WORSSAM, Richard Mark. b 61. St Jo Coll Dur BA 83 Selw Coll Cam BA 92 Heythrop Coll Lon MA 06 K Coll Lon MSc 09. Ridley Hall Cam 90. **d** 93 **p** 94. C Green Street Green and Pratts Bottom *Roch* 93–97; R Fawkham and Hartley 97–08; V Otford 08–19; V Pembury from 19. *The Vicarage, Hastings Road, Pembury, Tunbridge Wells TN2 4PD* E: richard.worssam@tiscali.co.uk

WORT, Gavin. b 78. K Alfred's Coll Win BTh 99 St Jo Coll Dur MA 10. Westcott Ho Cam 00. **d** 02 **p** 03. C Eastleigh *Win* 02–06; Chapl Northumbria Univ *Newc* 06–11; V Newc H Cross 11–18; Co-ord Chapl Dur Univ from 18; Chapl Collingwood Coll Dur from 18; Chapl Grey Coll Dur from 18; Chapl Trev Coll Dur from 18; Chapl Van Mildert Coll Dur from 18. *Student Wellbeing and Community Engagement Office, Durham University, Stockton Road, Durham DH1 3LE* T: 0191-334 4519 E: gavin.wort@durham.ac.uk

WORTHEN, Canon Jeremy Frederick. b 65. Rob Coll Cam BA 86 MPhil 88 Toronto Univ PhD 92. Ripon Coll Cuddesdon 92. **d** 94 **p** 95. C Bromley SS Pet and Paul *Roch* 94–97; Tutor SEITE 97–05; Prin 05–13; Sec Ecum Relns and Th Coun for Chr Unity from 14; Wiccamical Preb Chich Cathl from 09; Hon Can Cant Cathl from 11. *Council for Christian Unity, Church House, Great Smith Street, London SW1P 3AZ* T: (020) 7898 1488 E: jeremy.worthen@churchofengland.org

WORTLEY, Canon Lyn Sharon. b 59. Open Univ BA 94 Coll of Ripon & York St Jo MA 98. NOC 95. **d** 98 **p** 99. C Greasbrough *Sheff* 98–01; P-in-c Bramley and Ravenfield w Hooton Roberts etc 01–04; V Bramley 04–12; P-in-c Greasbrough from 12; C Rawmarsh w Parkgate 12–17; P-in-c from 17; C Kimberworth and Kimberworth Park from 12; AD Rotherham 14–16; Hon Can Sheff Cathl from 15. *81 Church Street, Greasbrough, Rotherham S61 4DY* T: (01709) 279192 E: lyn.wortley@gmail.com *or* lyn.wortley@sheffield.anglican.org

WORTON, David Reginald Paschal. b 56. St Steph Ho Ox 88. **d** 90 **p** 90. SSF 77–11; NSM Anfield St Columba *Liv* 90–92; Asst P Harare Cathl Zimbabwe 92–93; Asst P St Aug Miss Penhalonga 93–94; LtO *Newc* 94–08; Guardian Almnouth Friary 01–08; Asst P Shrine of Our Lady of Walsingham 08–11; TV Old St Pancras *Lon* from 12. *St Mary's House, Eversholt Street, London NW1 1BN* T: (020) 7387 7301 E: fr.paschal@posp.co.uk

WOSTENHOLM, David Kenneth. b 56. Edin Univ BSc 77 MB, ChB 80 Southn Univ BTh 88. Chich Th Coll 82. **d** 85 **p** 86. C Leytonstone St Marg w St Columba *Chelmsf* 85–90; V Brighton Annunciation *Chich* 90–01; TR Hove 01–07; RD 03–05; P-in-c Glas St Matt from 07. *104 Erradale Street, Glasgow G22 6PT* T: 0141-336 7480 *or* 347 1726 M: 07908-537085 E: stmatthews@btclick.com *or* david.wostenholm@hotmail.co.uk

WOTTON, David Ashley. b 44. Chich Th Coll 71. **d** 74 **p** 75. C Allington and Maidstone St Pet *Cant* 74–77; C Ham St Andr *S'wark* 78–79; Chapl HM Rem Cen Latchmere Ho 78–79; C Tattenham Corner and Burgh Heath *Guildf* 85–88; P-in-c E Molesey St Mary 88–93; R Headley w Box Hill 93–06; OCM 93–06; rtd 06; PtO *Chich* 12–17. *Lion House, 6 Copper Beeches, St Leonards-on-Sea TN37 7RR* T: (01424) 756122 E: dwottonatlion@tiscali.co.uk

WRAGG, Christopher William. b 60. SEITE 97. **d** 00 **p** 01. C Gt Warley Ch Ch *Chelmsf* 00–01; C Warley Ch Ch and Gt Warley St Mary 01–04; TV Buckhurst Hill 04–08; V Squirrels Heath from 08. *30 Wakerfield Close, Hornchurch RM11 2TH* T: (01708) 446571 M: 07714-507147 E: vicarchris@btinternet.com

WRAGG, Peter Robert. b 46. Lon Univ BSc 68. Sarum & Wells Th Coll 71. **d** 74 **p** 75. C Feltham *Lon* 74–79; TV Hackney 79–85; P-in-c Isleworth St Mary 85–94; V Feltham 94–12;

rtd 12; PtO *Chich* from 13. *3 Woodland Avenue, Eastbourne BN22 0HD* T: (01323) 507338 E: peter.wragg@tesco.net

WRATTEN, Martyn Stephen. b 34. AKC 58 St Boniface Warminster 58. **d** 59 **p** 60. C Wandsworth Common St Mary *S'wark* 59–62; C Putney St Mary 62–65; C Pembury *Roch* 65–70; R Stone 70–76; Chapl Joyce Green Hosp Dartford 70–73; Stone Ho Hosp Kent 73–76; Hillcrest Hosp and Netherne Hosp Coulsdon 76–87; Hon C Netherne St Luke CD *S'wark* 76–87; V Gt Doddington *Pet* 87–88; V Gt Doddington and Wilby 88–95; Hon C N Petherton w Northmoor Green *B & W* 95–96; rtd 95; PtO *B & W* from 96. *1 Baymead Close, North Petherton, Bridgwater TA6 6QZ* T: (01278) 662873 E: martyn.wratten@btinternet.com

WRATTEN, Sonya Helen Joan. b 77. Liv Jo Moores Univ BA 00. St Mich Coll Llan 07. **d** 10 **p** 11. C Leic St Phil 10–14; P-in-c Bedford All SS *St Alb* 14–17; Chapl Univ Hosps Leic NHS Trust from 17. *University Hospitals of Leicester NHS Trust, Groby Road, Leicester LE3 9QP* T: 03003-031573 M: 07948-714922 E: sonya.reverend@gmail.com

WRAY, Christopher. b 48. Hull Univ BA 70. Cuddesdon Coll 70. **d** 73 **p** 74. C Brighouse *Wakef* 73–76; C Almondbury 76–78; C Tong *Bradf* 78–80; V Ingleton w Chapel le Dale 80–86; R Brompton Regis w Upton and Skilgate *B & W* 86–91; V Yoxford and Peasenhall w Sibton *St E* 91–94; PtO *Carl* 94–97; R Brough w Stainmore, Musgrave and Warcop 97–02; R Walkingham Hill *Ripon* 02–07; V Ripponden and Barkisland w W Scammonden *Wakef* 07–13; rtd 13. *3 Stonelea, Barkisland, Halifax HX4 0HD* T: (01422) 825208

WRAY, Christopher Brownlow. b 46. Open Univ BA 91. Oak Hill Th Coll 86. **d** 88 **p** 89. C Quidenham *Nor* 88–91; TV Chippenham St Paul w Hardenhuish etc *Bris* 91–97; P-in-c Chipping Sodbury and Old Sodbury *Glouc* 97–09; P-in-c Horton and Lt Sodbury 04–09; rtd 09; Hon C Hardington Vale *B & W* 11–12; PtO *Sarum* from 10. *52 Linden Park, Shaftesbury SP7 8RN* T: (01747) 851961 E: wrays1@directsave.net

WRAY, Martin John. b 51. St Steph Ho Ox 86. **d** 88 **p** 89. C E Boldon *Dur* 88–90; C Seaham w Seaham Harbour 90–92; P-in-c Chopwell 92–95; V 95–97; C Shildon 98–00; C Croxdale and Tudhoe 00–04; P-in-c 04–06; C Spennymoor, Whitworth and Merrington 04–06; V Horsley Hill St Lawr 06–11; rtd 11. *68 Bainbridge Avenue, South Shields NE34 9QY* E: m.wray@sky.com

WRAY, Michael. b 49. Univ of Wales (Cardiff) BSc(Econ) 77 Keele Univ PGCE 78 RGN 87. Ripon Coll Cuddesdon 80. **d** 82 **p** 83. C Blackpool St Steph *Blackb* 82–83; C Torrisholme 83–84; NSM Headington Quarry *Ox* 93–95; C Kennington *Cant* 95–99; CF (TA) 95–99; P-in-c Isham w Pytchley *Pet* 99–04; Chapl Rockingham Forest NHS Trust 99–01; Chapl Northants Healthcare NHS Trust 01–04; R Potterspury w Furtho and Yardley Gobion etc *Pet* 04–11; rtd 11. *19 Cosgrove Road, Old Stratford, Milton Keynes MK19 6AG* T: (01908) 566824 E: revwray@btinternet.com

WRAY-WEAR, Lucinda Jane. b 61. S Bank Univ MSc 03. Qu Foundn (Course) 15. **d** 18 **p** 19. NSM Uttoxeter Area *Lich* from 18. *5 Beech Close, Uttoxeter ST14 7PY* T: (01889) 565052 E: revlucindabww@gmail.com

WRAYFORD, Geoffrey John. b 38. Ex Coll Ox BA 61 MA 65. Linc Th Coll 61. **d** 63 **p** 64. C Cirencester *Glouc* 63–69; V 70–74; Chapl Chelmsf Cathl 69–74; V Canvey Is 74–76; TR 76–80; P-in-c Woodlands *B & W* 80–88; V 89–92; P-in-c Frome St Jo 80–88; P-in-c Frome Ch Ch 80–85; P-in-c Frome St Mary 85–88; V Frome St Jo and St Mary 89–92; V Minehead 92–03; Chapl Taunton and Somerset NHS Trust 92–03; rtd 03; PtO *B & W* 07–15. *Little Garth, Longmeadow Road, Lympstone, Exmouth EX8 5LF* T: (01395) 267838 E: geoffjanw@googlemail.com

WREN, Ann. *See* WREN, Kathleen Ann

WREN, Christopher John. b 54. Dur Univ BEd 76 MA 85. St Steph Ho Ox 77. **d** 79 **p** 80. C Stockton St Pet *Dur* 79–82; C Newton Aycliffe 82–85; V Gateshead St Chad Bensham 85–91; TR Bensham 91–98; V Marton *Blackb* 98–16; rtd 16; LtO *Glas* from 17. *40 Park, Thornhill DG3 5JP* T: (01848) 332543 M: 07900-006795 E: parkhouse4012@gmail.com

WREN, Douglas Peter. b 59. Lanc Univ BA 82. Trin Coll Bris BA 88. **d** 88 **p** 89. C Nantwich *Ches* 88–91; C Chatham St Phil and St Jas *Roch* 91–94; R Kingsdown 94–02; R Speldhurst w Groombridge and Ashurst from 02; RD Tunbridge Wells from 18. *The Rectory, Southfields, Speldhurst, Tunbridge Wells TN3 0PD* T: (01892) 862821 E: douglas.wren12@gmail.com

WREN, Mrs Kathleen Ann. b 50. St Steph Ho Ox 83. **dss** 85 **d** 87. Gateshead St Cuth w St Paul *Dur* 85–86; Gateshead St Chad Bensham 86–91; Par Dn 87–91; Adv for Women's Min 90–98; Par Dn Bensham 91–94; C 94–98; Hon Can Dur Cathl 93–98; C Marton *Blackb* 98–16; rtd 16; LtO *Glas* from 17. *40 Park, Thornhill DG3 5JP* T: (01848) 332543 M: 07900-512062

WREN, Comdr Richard. b 35. S Dios Minl Tr Scheme 88. **d** 90 **p** 91. NSM Tisbury *Sarum* 90–01; TV 95–01; TV Nadder Valley *Sarum* 01–05; rtd 05; PtO *Sarum* from 06. *Gaston House, Tisbury, Salisbury SP3 6LG* T: (01747) 870674 E: twowrens@cuffslane.plus.com

WRIGHT, Alan William. b 44. Hull Univ BA 66 Bris Univ PGCE 67 AMusTCL 71. **d** 95 **p** 96. OLM Barton upon Humber *Linc* from 95. *1 Birchdale, Barton-upon-Humber DN18 5ED* T: (01652) 632364 E: wrightherewrightnow@hotmail.com

WRIGHT, Canon Andrew David Gibson. b 58. St Andr Univ MTheol 81. Ridley Hall Cam. **d** 83 **p** 84. C W Derby Gd Shep *Liv* 83–86; C Carl H Trin and St Barn 86–88; V Wigan St Jas w St Thos *Liv* 88–91; Chapl St Edw Sch Ox 91–97 and 06–07; Ho Master 97–07; Miss Chapl R Nat Miss to Deep Sea Fishermen 07–13; Sec Gen Miss to Seafarers from 13; Asst Chapl St Mich Paternoster Royal *Lon* from 14; PtO *Ox* from 15; Hon Can *Eur* from 16. *11 Davenant Road, Oxford OX2 8BT* T: (020) 7246 2934 M: 07876-824414 E: andrew.wright@missiontoseafarers.org

WRIGHT, Anne. *See* WRIGHT, Jacqueline Anne

WRIGHT, Anthony. *See* WRIGHT, Derek Anthony

WRIGHT, Canon Anthony John. b 47. Ex Univ MA 98 ACA 70 FCA 77. Ripon Coll Cuddesdon 86. **d** 88 **p** 89. C Kidderminster St Mary and All SS w Trimpley etc *Worc* 88–91; P-in-c Offenham and Bretforton 91–96; R Backwell w Chelvey and Brockley *B & W* 96–02; RD Portishead 01–02; P-in-c Tetbury w Beverston *Glouc* 02–03; R 03–06; R Tetbury, Beverston, Long Newnton etc 07–13; Hon Can Glouc Cathl 11–13; rtd 13; PtO *Worc* from 13; *Glouc* from 16. *Fair House, 1 Bromwich Road, Worcester WR2 4AD* T: (01905) 339661 E: fairfieldwright@gmail.com

WRIGHT, Canon Anthony Robert. b 49. Lanchester Poly Cov BA 70. St Steph Ho Ox 70. **d** 73 **p** 74. C Amersham on the Hill *Ox* 73–76; C Reading St Giles 76–78; P-in-c Prestwood 78–84; P-in-c Wantage 84–87; V 87–92; RD 84–92; P-in-c W w E Hanney 88–91; V Portsea St Mary *Portsm* 92–98; Hon Can Portsm Cathl 96–98; R Westmr St Marg and Chapl to Speaker of Ho of Commons 98–10; Can Westmr Abbey 98–10; Sub Dean Westmr 05–10; Adn Westmr 09–10; rtd 10; PtO *Ox* from 11. *23 Quarry High Street, Headington, Oxford OX3 8JU* T: (01865) 750656 E: priestpainter@googlemail.com

WRIGHT, Canon Barry Owen. b 38. S'wark Ord Course 66. **d** 69 **p** 70. C Plumstead Ascension *S'wark* 69–74; Hon C Welling 74–89; Hon Can S'wark Cathl 79–89; Sen Chapl W Midl Police *Birm* 89–93; Sen Chapl Metrop Police *Lon* 93–09; V Mill Hill St Mich 02–10; rtd 10; PtO *Roch* from 10; *S'wark* from 18. *54 Elmbourne Drive, Belvedere DA17 6JF* T: (01322) 463564 E: bwrg8@aol.com

WRIGHT, Catherine Jane. b 62. Bris Univ BA 84 MA 92 PhD 00 Selw Coll Cam BA 96. Ridley Hall Cam 94. **d** 97 **p** 98. C Highworth w Sevenhampton and Inglesham etc *Bris* 97–00; PtO *Ex* 00–01; NSM Stoke St Gregory w Burrowbridge and Lyng *B & W* 01–05; Dioc Voc Adv 02–10; Dir of Voc 10–14; Assoc Dir of Ords 02–14; Dean of Women Clergy and Preb Wells Cathl 05–14; Dir IME 4-7 10–14; Tutor Ridley Hall Cam from 14; PtO *B & W* 15–19. *Ridley Hall, Ridley Hall Road, Cambridge CB3 9HG* T: (01223) 746580 E: cjw28@cam.ac.uk

WRIGHT, Charles Kenneth. b 38. CEng MICE 73 MBIM 91. Sarum & Wells Th Coll 91. **d** 93 **p** 94. C Bridgwater St Mary, Chilton Trinity and Durleigh *B & W* 93–96; Chapl Workington *Carl* 96–03; C Camerton, Seaton and W Seaton 96–03; Chapl W Cumbria Health Care NHS Trust 96–01; Chapl N Cumbria Acute Hosps NHS Trust 01–03; rtd 03; PtO *Carl* from 03. *Naemair, 72 Ruskin Close, High Harrington, Workington CA14 4LS* T: (01946) 833536 E: kenwright@talktalk.net

WRIGHT, Canon Clifford Nelson. b 35. K Coll Lon BD 59 AKC 59. **d** 60 **p** 61. C Stevenage *St Alb* 60–67; V Camberwell St Luke *S'wark* 67–81; RD Camberwell 75–80; Hon Can S'wark Cathl 79–80; TR Basingstoke *Win* 81–93; RD Basingstoke 83–89; Hon Can Win Cathl 89–00; R Win St Matt 93–00; rtd 00; PtO *Win* from 01. *1 Valley Dene, Dibden Purlieu, Southampton SO45 4NG* T: (023) 8084 5898 E: cliffwright@waitrose.com

WRIGHT, Preb David William. b 63. Liv Univ LLB 85 Fitzw Coll Cam BA 92 Cam Univ MA 96 Univ of Wales (Cardiff) LLM 99 Barrister 86. Westcott Ho Cam 90. **d** 93 **p** 94. C Chorlton-cum-Hardy St Clem *Man* 93–97; P-in-c Donnington Wood *Lich* 97–99; V 99–09; TR Cen Wolverhampton from 09; Adn Wolverhampton from 11; Preb Lich Cathl from 15. *The Rectory, 42 Park Road East, Wolverhampton WV1 4QA* T: (01902) 423388 M: 07977-543735 E: david.wright@lichfield.anglican.org

WRIGHT, Derek Anthony. b 35. ACP 66 Lon Univ CertEd 57. Cranmer Hall Dur 80. **d** 81 **p** 82. C Auckland St Andr and

St Anne *Dur* 81–83; V Cornforth 83–87; P-in-c Thornley 87–88; R Gt and Lt Glemham, Blaxhall etc *St E* 88–90; V Evenwood *Dur* 90–93; P-in-c Satley and Tow Law 93–95; V 95–99; rtd 99; PtO *Dur* 00–16. *39 Hilltop Road, Bearpark, Durham DH7 7TA* E: tonywright39@btinternet.com

WRIGHT, Edward Maurice Alexanderson. b 54. Wycliffe Hall Ox. **d** 88 **p** 91. C Maidstone St Luke *Cant* 88–93; R Cliffe at Hoo w Cooling *Roch* 93–15; R Wrotham from 15. *The Rectory, Borough Green Road, Wrotham, Sevenoaks TN15 7RA* T: (01732) 882211

WRIGHT, Edward Michael. b 37. St Cath Soc Ox BA 61 MA 65. Cuddesdon Coll. **d** 64 **p** 65. C Willesden St Andr *Lon* 64–68; Bahamas 68–71; V Lewisham St Steph and St Mark *S'wark* 72–80; V Ox St Barn and St Paul 80–07; rtd 07; PtO *Ox* 08–17. *F16, Marine Gate, Marine Drive, Brighton BN2 5TQ* M: 07973-952664 E: michael19371901@gmail.com

WRIGHT, Frank Albert. b 51. Portsm Univ MA 02. Sarum & Wells Th Coll 80. **d** 83 **p** 84. C Buckingham *Ox* 83–86; C Newport Pagnell w Lathbury and Moulsoe 86–89; TV W Slough 89–95; TR 95–99; TR Fareham H Trin *Portsm* 99–09; Dioc Interfaith Adv 01–06; R Westbourne *Chich* 09–16; rtd 16; PtO *B & W* from 17. *55 London Road, Milborne Port, Sherborne DT9 5DW*

WRIGHT, Frederic Ian. b 64. City Univ BSc 85. Wycliffe Hall Ox BTh 94. **d** 94 **p** 95. C Carl St Jo 94–98; C Bassenthwaite, Isel and Setmurthy 98–00; C Binsey 00–02; TV 02–07. *Aden House, The Square, Allonby, Maryport CA15 6QA* T: (01900) 881095

WRIGHT, Graham John Aston. b 57. Moorlands Th Coll 77 Wycliffe Hall Ox 05. **d** 06 **p** 07. NSM Marston w Elsfield *Ox* 06–08; Asst Chapl St Edw Sch Ox 06–08; Chapl Queenswood Sch Herts 09–12; Chapl Qu Mary's Sch Baldersby Park from 13. *Queen Mary's School, Baldersby Park, Topcliffe, Thirsk YO7 3BZ* T: (01845) 575000 E: chaplain@queenmarys.org

WRIGHT, Gwynne Ann. b 49. Marymount Coll California BA 71 Keller Graduate Sch of Management Illinois MA 98. Seabury-Western Th Sem MDiv 04. **d** 04 **p** 04. C Arlington Heights USA 04–06; P-in-c W Dundee 06–08; P-in-c Dekalb 08–10; R Northfield St Jas 10–14; PtO *York* from 14. *43 Rawcliffe Croft, York YO30 5US* T: (01904) 635095 M: 07710-496594 E: gwynne.wright@me.com

WRIGHT, Mrs Heather Margaret. b 47. EAMTC 93. **d** 96 **p** 97. NSM Heigham St Thos *Nor* 96–99; Hon Asst Dioc Chapl among deaf and deaf-blind people from 99; NSM Sprowston w Beeston 03–16; PtO from 16. *133 Moore Avenue, Norwich NR6 7LQ* T: (01603) 301329 E: and minicom as telephone E: heatherwright404@btinternet.com

WRIGHT, Mrs Hilary. b 44. **d** 08. OLM Parkstone St Pet and St Osmund w Branksea *Sarum* 08–12; NSM 12–15; PtO from 15. *18 Springfield Crescent, Poole BH14 0LL* T: (01202) 747369 E: hilary@stpetersparkstone.org.uk or whilary18@gmail.com

WRIGHT, Canon Howard John Douglas. b 64. BA 85. Trin Coll Bris BA 94. **d** 96 **p** 97. C Ipswich St Matt *St E* 96–00; V Four Marks *Win* from 00; RD Alton 09–17; Hon Can Win Cathl from 16. *The Vicarage, 22 Lymington Bottom, Four Marks, Alton GU34 5AA* T: (01420) 563344 E: howardwright.cogs@gmail.com

WRIGHT, Canon Hugh Edward. b 57. BNC Ox BA 79 MA 87 Ex Univ CertEd 81. Sarum & Wells Th Coll 85. **d** 87 **p** 88. C Hobs Moat *Birm* 87–90; C W Drayton *Lon* 90–92; V Oakfield St Jo *Portsm* 92–13; RD E Wight 00–05; V Ventnor H Trin from 13; V Ventnor St Cath from 13; R Bonchurch from 13; Hon Can Portsm Cathl from 17. *The Vicarage, Maples Drive, Ventnor PO38 1NR* T: (01983) 853729 E: hugh.wright1957@btinternet.com

WRIGHT, Ian. b 65. Coll of Resurr Mirfield 97. **d** 99 **p** 00. C S Lafford *Linc* 99–01; C Hawley H Trin *Guildf* 01–03; Chapl Bonn w Cologne *Eur* 03–06; P-in-c Armley w New Wortley *Ripon* 06–14; *Leeds* 14–15; P-in-c Leeds Richmond Hill *Ripon* 12–14 and 14–15; V Eyres Monsell *Leic* 15–17. *c/o St Martin's House, 7 Peacock Lane, Leicester LE1 5PZ*

WRIGHT, Ian. *See* WRIGHT, Frederic Ian

WRIGHT, Miss Jacqueline Anne. b 39. Dalton Ho Bris 67. **dss** 76 **d** 87 **p** 94. BCMS Uganda 71–77; N Area Sec BCMS 78–88; Pudsey St Lawr and St Paul *Bradf* 82–88; Hon Par Dn 87–88; Par Dn Kingston upon Hull H Trin *York* 88–93; Hd of Min amongst Women CPAS 93–02; CPAS Consultant (W Midl) 96–02; Regional Consultant (Midl) 99–02; PtO *Cov* 93–04; *Birm* 96–02; *Worc* 96–02; *Leic* 99–02; rtd 02; PtO *York* from 04. *Oxenby, Whitby Road, Pickering YO18 7HL* T: (01751) 472689 E: jacqw@talktalk.net

WRIGHT, Mrs Jean. b 41. Man Univ BA 63 CertEd 64. Carl Dioc Tr Inst 88. **d** 91 **p** 94. NSM Kirkby Stephen w Mallerstang etc *Carl* 91–13; PtO from 13. *Mains View, Crosby Garrett, Kirkby Stephen CA17 4PR* T: (017683) 71457 E: j.wright347@btinternet.com

WRIGHT, Jenny Anne. b 82. Stellenbosch Univ Bth 04 MTh 07 DTh 11. Scottish Episc Inst 14. **d** 15 **p** 16. C Edin St Paul and St Geo 15–18; C Edin Ch Ch from 18. *41 Jeffrey Street, Edinburgh EH1 1DH* T: 0131-538 7096 M: 07591-255056

WRIGHT, John. *See* WRIGHT, Anthony John

WRIGHT, Canon John Harold. b 36. Dur Univ BA 58 Ch Ch Coll Cant MA 96 ATCL. Ely Th Coll 58. **d** 61 **p** 62. C Boston *Linc* 61–64; C Willesborough w Hinxhill *Cant* 64–68; V Westwell 68–75; R Eastwell w Boughton Aluph 68–75; V Rolvenden 75–84; R Cheriton St Martin 84–01; Hon Can Cant Cathl 97–01; rtd 01; PtO *Cant* from 01. *1 Cliff Road, Hythe CT21 5XA* T: (01303) 265303

WRIGHT, Jonathan James Gerald. b 67. Oak Hill Th Coll. **d** 10 **p** 11. C Horncastle Gp *Linc* 10–14; R Hedon, Paull, Sproatley and Preston *York* 14–17; R Bingham *S'well* from 17. *The Rectory, East Street, Bingham, Nottingham NG13 8DR*

WRIGHT, Jonathon Stuart. b 84. Girton Coll Cam BA 06 MA 12 MPhil 07. St Steph Ho Ox 12. **d** 15 **p** 16. C Whitchurch *Llan* 15–18; P-in-c Swansea St Pet *S & B* from 18. *235 Cockett Road, Cockett, Swansea SA2 0FH* T: (01792) 578700 E: priest@cockettparish.org.uk

WRIGHT, Judith Mary. b 44. Ex Univ MSc 98 BA 10 SRN 10 SCM 10. SWMTC 04. **d** 07 **p** 08. NSM Silverton, Butterleigh, Bickleigh and Cadeleigh *Ex* 07–11; C Bradninch and Clyst Hydon 11–16; C Broadhembury, Payhembury and Plymtree 11–16; rtd 16. *4 Hele Square, Hele, Exeter EX5 4PN* T: (01392) 882019 E: d.j.wright@btinternet.com

WRIGHT, Kenneth. *See* WRIGHT, Charles Kenneth

WRIGHT, Kevin John. b 54. Southn Univ BSc 75 PGCE 76. Ox Min Course 06. **d** 10 **p** 11. C Radley and Sunningwell *Ox* 10–13; C Kennington 10–13; R Woolavington w Cossington and Bawdrip *B & W* 13–19; P-in-c Brent Knoll, E Brent and Lympsham from 19. *3 Ash Trees, East Brent, Highbridge TA9 4DQ* M: 07764-170463 E: revdkjwright@btinternet.com

WRIGHT, Mrs Kim Beatrice Elizabeth. b 66. STETS 07. **d** 10 **p** 11. NSM Walton-on-Thames *Guildf* 10–12; NSM Oxshott 12–14. *Address withheld by request* M: 07941-947866 E: kbewright@live.co.uk

WRIGHT, Lawrence Charles. b 57. Hull Univ MA 94. EMMTC 93. **d** 96 **p** 96. C Heathridge and Joondalup Australia 96–98; C Penzance St Jo *Truro* 98–02; TV Penzance St Mary w St Paul and St Jo 02–04; Chapl Yarlswood Immigration and Detention Cen 04–06; Chapl W Lon YMCA 06–07; SSF 07–09; R Birm St Geo 09–16; P-in-c Lozells St Paul and St Silas 14–16; TR Kings Norton from 16. *The Rectory, 273 Pershore Road South, Birmingham B30 3EX* E: stgeorge100@live.co.uk *or* parishoffice@kingsnorton.org.uk

WRIGHT, Mrs Louisa Mary (Lisa). b 33. S'wark Ord Course. **d** 87 **p** 94. NSM Streatham Hill St Marg *S'wark* 87–95; Hon C Streatham St Leon 95–02; rtd 02; PtO *S'wark* from 02. *19 Hillside Road, London SW2 3HL* T: (020) 8671 8037 E: lisaw@phonecoop.coop

WRIGHT, Mrs Marion Jane. b 47. Whitelands Coll Lon CertEd 69. Cranmer Hall Dur 73. **d** 00 **p** 02. NSM Scalby *York* 00–15; NSM Cloughton and Burniston 14–15; NSM Ravenscar and Staintondale 14–15; PtO from 15. *3 East Park Road, Scalby, Scarborough YO13 0PZ* T: (01723) 350208 E: marianne.forsyth@hotmail.co.uk

WRIGHT, Martin. b 48. Avery Hill Coll BEd 81 K Alfred's Coll Win CertEd 69 LRAM 76. SAOMC 95. **d** 98 **p** 99. NSM St Alb St Mary Marshalswick 98–01; C Gt Berkhamsted 02–05; V Reigate St Mark *S'wark* 05–13; rtd 13; PtO *Guildf* from 13. *18 Brocks Drive, Fairlands, Guildford GU3 3NE* M: 07774-923550

WRIGHT, Canon Martin Neave. b 37. AKC 61. St Boniface Warminster. **d** 62 **p** 63. C Corby St Columba *Pet* 62–65; Ind Chapl 65–71; Nigeria 71–75; P-in-c Honiley *Cov* 75–84; P-in-c Wroxall 75–84; Ind Chapl 75–84; Soc Resp Officer 84–96; Hon Can Cov Cathl 95–96; Bp's Chapl and Past Asst *B & W* 96–02; Preb Wells Cathl 96–02; Sub-Dean Wells Cathl 00–02; rtd 02; PtO *Cov* 02–19. *2 Honiwell Close, Harbury, Leamington Spa CV33 9LY* T: (01926) 613699

WRIGHT, Canon Michael. b 30. St Chad's Coll Dur BA 55 De Montfort Univ MPhil 04. **d** 56 **p** 57. C New Cleethorpes *Linc* 56–59; C Skegness 59–62; V Louth St Mich 62–73; R Stewton 62–73; R Warmsworth *Sheff* 73–86; Warden Dioc Readers' Assn 81–86; Hon Can Sheff Cathl 82–95; V Wath-upon-Dearne w Adwick-upon-Dearne 86–94; V Wath-upon-Dearne 94–95; RD Wath 92–95; rtd 95; PtO *Linc* from 95. *17 Ashfield Road, Sleaford NG34 7DZ* T: (01529) 415698 E: seacroft2@btinternet.com

WRIGHT, Michael. *See* WRIGHT, Edward Michael

WRIGHT, Michael Christopher. b 44. Leeds Univ BA 65 CertEd 67 MSc 75 Sheff Univ PhD 02 FRSA 95. Wells Th Coll 65. **d** 67 **p** 68. C Dormanstown *York* 67–69; PtO *Linc*

69–88; *Sheff* 71–95; Hd Master Eastmoor High Sch Wakef 84–87; Hd Master Carleton High Sch Pontefract 87–95; C-in-c St Edm Anchorage Lane CD *Sheff* 95–96; Chapl Doncaster R Infirmary and Montagu Hosp NHS Trust 95–01; Research Fell Sheff Univ 01–03; Sen Research Fell Lanc Univ *Blackb* from 03; Hon C Gt Snaith *Sheff* 01–07; PtO *Wakef* 01–14; *Leeds* 14–16; *Eur* from 06; *Sheff* from 07. *Orchard End, Finkle Street, Hensall, Goole DN14 0QY* T: (01977) 661900 *or* (01524) 593152 E: mc.wright@btinternet.com

WRIGHT, Michael George. b 52. WEMTC 01. **d** 04 **p** 05. NSM Woodchester and Brimscombe *Glouc* 04–15. *The Trumpet, West End, Minchinhampton, Stroud GL6 9JA* T: (01453) 883027 M: 07974-303527

WRIGHT, Michael John. b 38. Dur Univ MA 91. Chich Th Coll 59. **d** 62 **p** 63. C Yate *Glouc* 62–65; C Kirby Moorside w Gillamoor *York* 65–68; V 68–72; V Bransdale cum Farndale 68–72; V Kirkbymoorside w Gillamoor, Farndale etc 72–73; Dioc Communications Officer 72–74; V Ormesby 74–80; P-in-c Middlesbrough St Cuth 81–88; PtO 88–99; NSM W Acklam 91–97; Chapl Butterwick Hospice Stockton-on-Tees 97–99; Chapl S Dur Hospice Bp Auckland 97–99; rtd 03. *25 Thornfield Road, Middlesbrough TS5 5DD* T: (01642) 816247 E: michaelwright80@virginmedia.com

WRIGHT, Canon Nicholas Mark. b 59. Loughb Univ BSc 80. Qu Coll Birm 82. **d** 85 **p** 86. C Coney Hill *Glouc* 85–89; C Rotherham *Sheff* 89–91; TV Worc SE 91–98; R Inkberrow w Cookhill and Kington w Dormston 98–15; Hon Can Worc Cathl 11–15; rtd 15; NSM Bengeworth *Worc* 15–18; NSM Bengeworth and Hampton etc from 18. *6 St David's Drive, Evesham WR11 2AU* T: (01386) 443310 E: revnmwright@btinternet.com

✠**WRIGHT, The Rt Revd Prof Nicholas Thomas.** b 48. Ex Coll Ox BA 71 MA 75 DPhil 81 DD 00. Wycliffe Hall Ox BA 73. **d** 75 **p** 76 **c** 03. Fell Mert Coll Ox 75–78; Chapl 76–78; Chapl and Fell Down Coll Cam 78–81; Asst Prof NT Studies McGill Univ Montreal 81–86; Chapl and Fell Worc Coll Ox and Univ Lect Th 86–93; Dean Lich 93–99; Can Th Cov Cathl 92–99; Lector Theologiae and Can Westmr Abbey 00–03; Bp Dur 03–10; Chair NT and Early Christianity St Andr Univ St And from 10. *St Mary's College, South Street, St Andrews KY16 9JU* E: ntw2@st-andrews.ac.uk

WRIGHT, Nigel Christopher James. b 67. Leeds Univ BA 07 MA 13 FCCA 99. NOC 04. **d** 07 **p** 08. NSM Utley *Bradf* 07–10; NSM Oxenhope 10–13; P-in-c 13–14; *Leeds* 14–16; V Roundhay St Edm from 16. *5A North Park Avenue, Leeds LS8 1DN* M: 07970-751670 E: nigel.wright@parishes.leeds.anglican.org *or* revnigelwright@gmail.com

WRIGHT, Miss Pamela Jean. b 38. ALA 63. NTMTC 02. **d** 03 **p** 04. NSM Harrow Trin St Mich *Lon* 03–05; NSM Harrow Weald St Mich 05–12; PtO from 12. *14 Broadlawns Court, Harrow HA3 7HN* T: (020) 8954 9821 E: pamela.jwright@btinternet.com

WRIGHT, Patricia. b 46. SRN 68. S'wark Ord Course 80. **dss** 85 **d** 89. Asst Chapl R Lon Hosp (Mile End) 83–85; Bethnal Green St Matt w St Jas the Gt *Lon* 85–88; Hon C St Botolph Aldgate w H Trin Minories 89–05; Cathl Dn and Dioc HIV/ AIDS Co-ord Swaziland 00–04; Hon C St Geo-in-the-East St Mary *Lon* 06–14; PtO *Cant* from 15. *62 College Road, Deal CT14 6BS* T: (01304) 239031 E: patw@patthedeacon.com

WRIGHT, The Ven Paul. b 54. K Coll Lon BD 78 AKC 78 Heythrop Coll Lon MTh 90 Univ of Wales (Lamp) DMin 09. Ripon Coll Cuddesdon 78. **d** 79 **p** 80. C Beckenham St Geo *Roch* 79–83; Chapl C'h Sch Richmond 83–85; C Richmond St Mary w St Matthias and St Jo *S'wark* 83–85; V Gillingham St Aug *Roch* 85–90; R Crayford 90–99; RD Erith 93–97; V Sidcup St Jo 99–03; Adn Bromley and Bexley from 03; Bp's Adv for Inter-Faith Concerns 11–15; P-in-c Bromley Common St Luke 12–15; P-in-c Slade Green from 16; Hon Can Roch Cathl from 98. *The Archdeaconry, The Glebe, Chislehurst BR7 5PX* T/F: (020) 8467 8743 M: 07985-902601 E: archdeacon.bromley@rochester.anglican.org

WRIGHT, Canon Paul Stephen. b 66. Cen Lancs Univ BA 88 Liv Univ MA 96 Univ of Wales (Cardiff) MTh 11. Westcott Ho Cam 90. **d** 93 **p** 94. C Upholland *Liv* 93–96; CF 96–08; Sen CF 08–14; Chapl Guards Chpl Lon 08–10; Chapl R Memorial Chpl Sandhurst 12–14; Dom Chapl to The Queen from 14 and from 15; Can Chpls R from 15; G S Beckwith Gilbert Fell Princeton Univ USA from 16. *The Chapel Royal, St James's Palace, London SW1A 1BL* T: (020) 7024 5576 E: paul.wright@royal.uk

WRIGHT, Canon Peter. b 35. K Coll Lon AKC 61 Hull Univ MA 86. St Boniface Warminster 61. **d** 62 **p** 63. C Goole *Sheff* 62–67; V Norton Woodseats St Chad 67–80; R Aston cum Aughton 80–84; P-in-c Ulley 80–84; Chapl Rotherham Priority Health Services NHS Trust 80–84; R Aston cum

Aughton and Ulley *Sheff* 84–93; TR Aston cum Aughton w Swallownest, Todwick etc 93–00; RD Laughton 85–93; Chapter Clerk and Hon Can Sheff Cathl 92–00; rtd 00; PtO *Sheff* from 01; Chapl to Rtd Clergy and Clergy Widows Officer from 09. *40 Chancet Wood Drive, Sheffield S8 7TR* T/F: 0114-274 7218 E: allsaints.pw@talk21.com

WRIGHT, Peter Geoffrey. b 60. Ex Univ BSc 81 FCIM 09. Ox Min Course 09. **d** 12 **p** 13. NSM Bicester w Bucknell, Caversfield and Launton Ox 12–18; TV from 18. *10 Hamilton Close, Bicester OX26 2HX* T: (01869) 572272 M: 07966-531921 E: revpeterwright@gmail.com

WRIGHT, Peter Reginald. b 34. St Chad's Coll Dur BA 60. Linc Th Coll 60. **d** 62 **p** 63. C Lt Ilford St Mich *Chelmsf* 62–65; C Billingham St Aid *Dur* 65–68; TV 68–71; TR 71–76; Chapl Portsm Poly 76–87; Sec Chapls in HE Gen Syn Bd of Educn 88–95; rtd 95; PtO *Portsm* 95–10. *6 Garden Lane, Southsea PO5 3DP* T: (023) 9273 6651

WRIGHT, Philip John. b 69. Anglia Ruskin Univ MA 11. St Mellitus Coll BA 14. **d** 14 **p** 15. Chapl Barking Havering and Redbridge Hosps NHS Trust from 08; NSM Cranham Park *Chelmsf* 14–17; PtO from 17. *57 Heron Way, Upminster RM14 1EW* M: 07976-378042 E: philwright69@gmail.com

WRIGHT, Robert. *See* WRIGHT, Anthony Robert

WRIGHT, Robert James. b 74. St Chad's Coll Dur BA 96 K Coll Lon MA 98. St Steph Ho Ox 00. **d** 02 **p** 04. C Ilfracombe, Lee, Woolacombe, Bittadon etc *Ex* 02–05; PtO *S'wark* 11–14; P-in-c Mitcham St Olave 14–18; TV N Cheltenham *Glouc* from 18. *8 Boulton Road, Cheltenham GL50 4RZ* M: 07909-043811 E: robwri99@gmail.com

WRIGHT, Robert John. b 47. St Jo Coll Dur BA 70. SEITE 00. **d** 03 **p** 04. NSM Notting Hill St Jo *Lon* 03–06; NSM Notting Hill St Pet 03–06; NSM N Hammersmith St Kath 06–08; NSM Cheddington w Mentmore *Ox* 08–12; TV Cottesloe 12–13; PtO from 14. *17 Clarence Court, Forest Close, Wendover, Aylesbury HP22 6AB* M: 07988-978419 E: robert@robert-wright.com

WRIGHT (née PRECIOUS), Sally Joanne. b 75. Hatf Coll Dur BA 97 Anglia Poly Univ MA 03. Westcott Ho Cam 00. **d** 02 **p** 03. C Chich St Paul and Westhampnett 02–05; PtO *S'wark* 05–06; Hon C Peckham St Jo w St Andr 06–09; Chapl Guildhall Sch of Music and Drama *Lon* 06–09; Hon C Witney *Ox* from 09. *The Rectory, 13 Station Lane, Witney OX28 4BB* T: (01993) 704441 E: sally-wright@btconnect.com

WRIGHT, Samuel. *See* WRIGHT, William Samuel

WRIGHT, Sarah Jane. b 64. Nottm Trent Univ BA 99. Ripon Coll Cuddesdon 99. **d** 01 **p** 02. C Clarendon Park St Jo w Knighton St Mich *Leic* 01–03; C Leic Martyrs 04–05; PtO 17–18; Chapl Univ Hosps Leic NHS Trust from 18. *3 Wren Close, Melton Mowbray LE13 0QE* T: (01664) 850664 M: 07908-757027 E: dragonfire.phoenixrising@outlook.com

WRIGHT, Simon Andrew. b 63. Clare Coll Cam BA 84 MA 88 Lon Univ MB, BS 87. SNWTP 10. **d** 12 **p** 13. OLM Davyhulme St Mary *Man* 12–19; C from 19. *12 Davyhulme Road, Urmston, Manchester M41 7DS* T: 0161-746 8758 M: 07759-814499 E: revdocwright@hotmail.com

WRIGHT, Canon Simon Christopher. b 44. AKC 67. **d** 68 **p** 69. C Bitterne Park *Win* 68–72; C Kirkby *Liv* 72–74; V Wigan St Anne 74–79; Abp's Dom Chapl and Dioc Dir of Ords *York* 79–84; V W Acklam 84–00; RD Middlesbrough 87–98; Can and Preb York Minster 94–00; V Dartmouth and Dittisham *Ex* 00–10; rtd 10; PtO *York* from 10. *48 Langton Road, Norton, Malton YO17 9AD* T: (01653) 698106 E: scwright44@btinternet.com

WRIGHT, Stephen Irwin. b 58. Ex Coll Ox BA 80 MA 84 Selw Coll Cam BA 85 MA 90 Lanc Univ MA 92 St Jo Coll Dur PhD 97. Ridley Hall Cam 83. **d** 86 **p** 87. C Newbarns w Hawcoat *Carl* 86–90; C Burton and Holme 90–94; NSM Esh *Dur* 94–97; NSM Hamsteels 94–97; C Consett 97–98; Dir Coll of Preachers 98–06; Tutor Spurgeon's Coll from 06; PtO *S'wark* from 99. *Spurgeon's College, 189 South Norwood Hill, London SE25 6DJ* T: (020) 8653 0850 *or* 8768 0878 ext 233 F: 8711 0959 E: s.wright@spurgeons.ac.uk

WRIGHT, Canon Stephen Mark. b 60. Keele Univ BA 83. Trin Coll Bris BA 89. **d** 89 **p** 90. C Thorne *Sheff* 89–92; CMS 92–05; Dioc Missr Asaba Nigeria 93–98; Hon Can Asaba from 98; Chapl Ahmadi St Paul Kuwait 99–03; Chapl Dubai and Sharjah w N Emirates 03–14; P-in-c Quidenham Gp *Nor* from 15. *The Rectory, Church Hill, Banham, Norwich NR16 2HN* T: (01953) 887183 M: 07952-813786 E: canonstevewright@gmail.com

WRIGHT, Stewart. *See* WRIGHT, William Charles Stewart

WRIGHT, Stuart Kendle. b 73. **d** 08 **p** 09. C Tollington *Lon* 08–14; P-in-c Hounslow H Trin w St Paul and St Mary 14–15; P-in-c Hounslow H Trin 15–19; V from 19. *14 Lampton Park Road, Hounslow TW3 4HS* T: (020) 8577 9048 M: 07867-888999

WRIGHT, Thomas. *See* WRIGHT, Nicholas Thomas

WRIGHT, The Very Revd Timothy. b 63. NUU BSc 85 Univ of Wales (Cardiff) MTh 06. Cranmer Hall Dur 86. **d** 89 **p** 90. C Bramcote *S'well* 89–93; I Glenavy w Tunny and Crumlin *Conn* 93–98; Chapl RAF 98–18; Dep Chapl-in-Chief 13–18; Dean Kildare *M & K* from 18; I Kildare w Kilmeague and Curragh from 18; I Newbridge w Carnalway and Kilcullen from 18; QHC from 15; PtO *Eur* from 16. *The Deanery, Morristown Road, Newbridge, Co Kildare, Republic of Ireland* T: (00353) (45) 431352 E: dean@kildare.anglican.org

WRIGHT, Timothy John. b 41. K Coll Lon BD 63 AKC 63. **d** 64 **p** 65. C Highfield *Ox* 64–68; Asst Chapl Worksop Coll Notts 68–71; Chapl Malvern Coll 71–77; Ho Master 77–86; Hd Master Jo Lyon Sch Harrow 86–01; rtd 01; PtO *Worc* from 09. *Beech House, Colwall Green, Malvern WR13 6DX* T: (01684) 541102 E: tm41wright@gmail.com

WRIGHT, Timothy Stanley. b 63. Derby Coll of Educn BEd 86. Cranmer Hall Dur 89. **d** 92 **p** 93. C Eccleshill *Bradf* 92–96; TV Southend *Chelmsf* 96–00; V Boulton *Derby* 00–13; Chapl HM YOI Glen Parva 13–15; PtO *Derby* 13–18; Chapl HM Pris Stocken from 15. *HM Prison Stocken, Stocken Hall Road, Stretton, Oakham LE15 7RD* T: (01780) 795100 E: timwright2005@talktalk.net *or* timothy.wright@justice.gov.uk

WRIGHT, Toby Christopher. b 75. New Coll Ox BA 98 MA 01 Leeds Univ MA 01. Coll of Resurr Mirfield 99. **d** 01 **p** 02. C Petersfield *Portsm* 01–04; P-in-c Peckham St Jo w St Andr *S'wark* 04–06; V Witney w Gartan *D & R* 08–16; Can Raphoe Cathl 10–16; rtd 16. *43 Mallory Park, Eglinton, Londonderry BT47 3XJ* T: (028) 7181 1222 E: stewartwright@live.ie

Ox from 09; AD from 13. *The Rectory, 13 Station Lane, Witney OX28 4BB* T: (01993) 704441 E: rector@witneyparish.org.uk

WRIGHT, Mrs Vyvienne Mary. b 35. S Dios Minl Tr Scheme 80. **dss** 83 **d** 87 **p** 94. Martock w Ash *B & W* 83–00; Hon C 87–00; PtO from 00. *36 Church Close, Martock TA12 6DS* T: (01935) 823292 M: 07931-686362

WRIGHT, William Charles Stewart. b 53. Ulster Poly BSc 81. CITC BTh 95. **d** 95 **p** 96. C Ballyholme *D & D* 95–98; I Conwal Union w Gartan *D & R* 98–16; Can Raphoe Cathl 10–16; rtd 16. *43 Mallory Park, Eglinton, Londonderry BT47 3XJ* T: (028) 7181 1222 E: stewartwright@live.ie

WRIGHT, The Very Revd William Samuel. b 59. TCD BTh 89 MA 90. **d** 87 **p** 88. C Belfast St Aid *Conn* 87–91; Sec Dioc Bd of Miss 90–91; I Cleenish w Mullaghdun *Clogh* 91–99; I Lisburn Ch Ch Cathl *Conn* from 99; Can and Preb Conn Cathl 01–16; Prec 12–16; Dean Conn from 16. *Cathedral Rectory, 11D Magheralave, Lisburn BT28 3BE* T: (028) 9209 0260 E: sam.wright@lisburncathedral.org

WRIGLEY, George Garnett. b 50. St Cath Coll Cam BA 71 Loughb Coll of Educn PGCE 72. NTMTC 02. **d** 04 **p** 05. NSM Hounslow H Trin w St Paul and St Mary *Lon* 04–08; P-in-c Langdale *Carl* 08–10; TV Loughrigg from 10. *The Vicarage, Chapel Stile, Ambleside LA22 9JG* T: (015394) 37267 E: georgewrig@hotmail.com

WROE, The Ven Mark. b 69. Surrey Univ BA 92 Anglia Poly Univ MA 00. Ridley Hall Cam 94. **d** 96 **p** 97. C Chilvers Coton w Astley *Cov* 96–00; P-in-c Heworth St Alb *Dur* 00–03; V Windy Nook St Alb 03–07; V Jesmond H Trin *Newc* 07–19; P-in-c Newc St Barn and St Jude 07–17; AD Newc Cen 17–19; Adn Northd and Can Res Newc Cathl from 19. *80 Moorside North, Newcastle upon Tyne NE4 9DU* T: 0191-273 8245 E: northumberland@newcastle.anglican.org

WUTSCHER, Christoph Johannes. b 79. Ban Univ MA 12. Westcott Ho Cam 10. **d** 13 **p** 14. C Wanstead St Mary w Ch Ch *Chelmsf* 13–16; R Stirling *St And* from 16. *The Rectory, 4 Bracken Lane, Stirling FK9 5AB* T: (01786) 359821 M: 07583-270533 E: christoph.wutscher@hotmail.com

WUYTS, Fabian René Marc. b 73. ISFSC BA 96. Tyndale Th Sem Amsterdam MA 99 Evang Th Faculty Leuven MTh 08. **d** 14 **p** 15. C Whitstable *Cant* 14–18; V Taunton St Jas *B & W* from 18. *69 Richmond Road, Taunton TA1 1EN* M: 07547-195760 E: fabian.wuyts@gmail.com

WYARD, Peter Joseph. b 54. Pemb Coll Cam MA 76 Sussex Univ MSc 80 Brunel Univ MSc 88 Anglia Ruskin Univ MA 07. EAMTC 99. **d** 02 **p** 03. C Framlingham w Saxtead *St E* 02–05; P-in-c Riverside *Ox* 05–08; V Colnbrook and Datchet 08–18; PtO from 18; Miss Partner CMS from 18. *Church Mission Society, Watlington Road, Oxford OX4 6BZ* T: (01865) 787400 E: peter.wyard@btinternet.com

WYATT, Colin. b 27. Ex Coll Ox BA 54 MA 55 Lon Univ BD 62. Tyndale Hall Bris 60. **d** 63 **p** 64. C Radipole *Sarum* 63–66; C Southborough St Pet *Roch* 66–67; V Tetsworth *Ox* 67–72; Lect Bible Tr Inst Glas 72–74; R Hurworth *Dur* 74–79; P-in-c Dinsdale w Sockburn 74–76; R 76–79; R Sadberge 79–84; R Bacton w Wyverstone and Cotton *St E* 84–92; rtd 92; PtO *Ripon* 92–14; *Leeds* 14–16. *St Francis' Vicarage, 146 Tedder Road, South Croydon CR2 8AH* T: (020) 8657 7864

WYATT, David John. b 89. Heythrop Coll Lon BA 11. Ripon Coll Cuddesdon 17. **d** 19. C Canon Pyon w King's Pyon, Birley and Wellington *Heref* from 19. *Sunnybrook, Wellington, Hereford HR4 8AZ* E: revdavid.wyatt@outlook.com

WYATT, Canon David Stanley Chadwick. b 36. Fitzw Ho Cam BA 59 MA 71. Ely Th Coll 59. **d** 61 **p** 62. C Rochdale *Man* 61–63; Bp's Dom Chapl 63–68; R Salford St Paul w Ch Ch from 68; P-in-c Salford Ordsall St Clem 91–96; P-in-c Lower Broughton Ascension from 05; AD Salford 97; Hon Can Man Cathl from 82. *St Paul's Church House, Broadwalk, Salford M6 5FX* T: 0161-736 8868 E: salfordwyatts@yahoo.co.uk

WYATT, Peter Charles. b 62. Bris Univ BSc 85 CEng MIEE 92. St Jo Coll Nottm 05. **d** 07 **p** 08. C Becontree St Thos *Chelmsf* 07–11; Min Selsdon St Fran CD *S'wark* from 11. *St Francis' Vicarage, 146 Tedder Road, Croydon CR2 8AH* T: (020) 8657 7864 E: peter.michelle@gmail.com

WYATT, Peter John. b 38. Kelham Th Coll 58. **d** 64 **p** 65. C N Stoneham *Win* 64–68; C Brixham *Ex* 68–69; Dominica 69–75; Zambia 76–78; P-in-c Ettington *Cov* 78–79; V Butlers Marston and the Pillertons w Ettington 79–86; V Codnor and Loscoe *Derby* 86–91; Chapl for Deaf People 91–03; rtd 03; PtO *Heref* from 04; *St As* from 09. *16 Cae Melyn, Tregynon, Newtown SY16 3EF* T: (01686) 650368 E: pandpwyatt@btinternet.com

WYATT, Royston Dennis. b 36. FRICS 67. Sarum & Wells Th Coll 74. **d** 77 **p** 78. NSM Canford Magna *Sarum* 77–82; V Abbotsbury, Portesham and Langton Herring 82–88; Dioc Missr *Linc* 88–95; R Welford w Weston *Glouc* 95–05; RD Campden 96–01; rtd 05; PtO *B & W* 06–14. *78 Lower Meadow, Ilminster TA19 9DP* T: (01460) 53996 E: revrdw@gmail.com

WYATT (née OWEN), Canon Susan Elizabeth. b 53. Bris Univ BSc 75 Bath Univ PGCE 78. EAMTC 97. **d** 00 **p** 01. Asst Dioc Adv in Miss and Evang *Ely* 00–16; C Sovr 00–06; C Long Stanton w St Mich 02–06; V Cherry Hinton St Jo 06–16; Hon Can Ely Cathl 10–16; rtd 16; PtO *Ely* from 16; RD Bourn from 18. *5 Cottons Field, Dry Drayton, Cambridge CB23 8DG* M: 07713-241261 E: sue.e.wyatt@btinternet.com

WYATT, Trevor. b 60. Keele Univ BSc 81. SEITE 97. **d** 00 **p** 01. NSM Wilmington *Roch* 00–14; V Bexleyheath Ch Ch from 14. *The Vicarage, 57 Townley Road, Bexleyheath DA6 7HY* T: (020) 8301 5086 M: 07860-306746 E: revtrevorwyatt@btinternet.com

WYBER, Richard John. b 47. G&C Coll Cam BA 69 MA 72 FCA 73. SEITE 03. **d** 06 **p** 07. NSM Wanstead St Mary w Ch Ch *Chelmsf* from 06. *7 Mornington Close, Woodford Green IG8 0TT* T: (020) 8504 2447

WYBREW, Canon Hugh Malcolm. b 34. Qu Coll Ox BA 58 MA. Linc Th Coll 59. **d** 60 **p** 61. C E Dulwich St Jo *S'wark* 60–64; Tutor St Steph Ho Ox 65–71; Chapl Bucharest *Eur* 71–73; V Pinner *Lon* 73–83; Sec Fellowship of SS Alb and Sergius 84–86; Dean Jerusalem 86–89; Hon Can Gib Cathl *Eur* 89–04; V Ox St Mary Magd 89–04; Hon Can Ch Ch 01–04; rtd 04. *96 Warwick Street, Oxford OX4 1SY* T: (01865) 241355 E: hugh.wybrew@queens.ox.ac.uk

WYER, Mrs Janet Beatrice. b 58. UEA BA 00. ERMC 04. **d** 07 **p** 08. C Loddon, Sisland, Chedgrave, Hardley and Langley *Nor* 07–10; C Nor St Pet Mancroft w St Jo Maddermarket 10–15; R Kessingland, Gisleham and Rushmere 15–19; rtd 19. *135 Hulver Hill, Woodland Holiday Park, Cromer Road, Trimingham, Norwich NR11 8QJ* M: 07990-576118 E: revdjanetwyer@outlook.com

WYER, Keith George. b 45. St Paul's Coll Chelt CertEd 66 K Coll Lon BD 71 AKC 71. St Aug Coll Cant 71. **d** 72 **p** 73. C Moseley St Mary *Birm* 72–76; Chapl RNR 73–92; C Walsall *Lich* 76–77; Min Walsall St Martin 77–79; Chapl Colston's Sch Bris 79–86; Chapl Kelly Coll Tavistock 86–92; R Combe Martin and Berrynarbor *Ex* 92–95; TR Combe Martin, Berrynarbor, Lynton, Brendon etc 96–10; RD Shirwell 95–01; rtd 10. *Highlands, 6 Holland Park Avenue, Combe Martin, Ilfracombe EX34 0HL*

WYKES, Elaine Karen. b 74. Qu Foundn Birm 13. **d** 16 **p** 17. NSM Anstey and Thurcaston w Cropston *Leic* 16–19; Chapl HM Pris Drake Hall from 19. *HM Prison and Young Offender Institution, Drake Hall, Eccleshall, Stafford* T: (01785) 774100 M: 07572-007100 E: elaine.wykes@justice.gov.uk

WYKES, Canon Peter. b 44. Lon Univ MB, BS 68. Ban & St As Minl Tr Course 97. **d** 00 **p** 01. NSM Trefnant w Tremeirchion *St As* 00–01; NSM Cefn w Trefnant w Tremeirchion 01–14; Hon Can St As Cathl 12–14; rtd 14; PtO *St As* from 14. *2 Llys y Tywysog, Tremeirchion, St Asaph LL17 0UL* T: (01745) 710363 E: peterwykes@gmail.com

WYLAM, John. b 43. AKC 66 FE TCert 75. **d** 67 **p** 68. C Derby St Bart 67–70; SSF 70–72; C Seaton Hirst *Newc* 74–77; V Byker St Silas 77–83; V Alwinton w Holystone and Alnham 83–98; V Chollerton w Birtley and Thockrington

98–09; rtd 09; PtO *Newc* from 09. *Nether House, Garleigh Road, Rothbury, Morpeth NE65 7RG* T: (01669) 622805 E: johnwylam@btopenworld.com

WYLD, Kevin Andrew. b 58. St Cath Coll Ox BA 79 MA 85 Univ Coll Dur MSc 83 Edin Univ BD 85. Edin Th Coll 82. **d** 85 **p** 86. C Winlaton *Dur* 85–87; C Houghton le Spring 87–90; V Medomsley 90–95; V High Spen and Rowlands Gill 95–00; R Winter Park St Rich USA 00–04. *15 Hullock Road, Newton Aycliffe DL5 4LT* T: (01325) 312286 E: kevinwyld@gmail.com

WYLD, Richard Michael. b 81. Surrey Univ BMus 04 St Jo Coll Dur BA 09 MA 10 PhD 14. Cranmer Hall Dur 06. **d** 13 **p** 14. C Sherborne w Castleton, Lillington and Longburton *Sarum* 13–17; Bp's Dom Chapl *Portsm* from 17. *Bishopsgrove, 26 Osborn Road, Fareham PO16 7DQ* T: (01329) 280247 M: 07971-876699 E: rickwyld4@hotmail.com

WYLD, Ruth Elizabeth. *See* CHAPMAN, Ruth Elizabeth

WYLES, Mrs Kate Elizabeth. b 66. Bournemouth Univ BA 89 Win Univ BA 11. STETS 07. **d** 11 **p** 12. C Godalming *Guildf* 11–13; C Stoke-next-Guildf 13–15; V Goldsworth Park from 15. *St Andrew's Vicarage, 8 Cardingham, Woking GU21 3LN* T: (01483) 764523 E: jkwyles@hotmail.co.uk

WYLIE, Alan. b 47. Is of Man Tr Inst 88. **d** 92 **p** 93. NSM Douglas St Geo *S & M* 92–97; NSM Challoch *Glas* 97–00; P-in-c Motherwell 00–16; P-in-c Wishaw 00–16; rtd 16. *8 Millard Avenue, Carfin, Motherwell ML1 4GA* T: (01698) 230869 E: alan.rev@hotmail.com

WYLIE, Clive George. b 64. QUB BSc 86 TCD BTh 90 MA 93. CITC 87. **d** 90 **p** 91. C Drumglass w Moygashel *Arm* 90–93; I Tynan, Aghavilly and Middletown 93–98; Hon V Choral Arm Cathl 93–98; Team P Glas E End 98–03; TR 03–08; Miss 21 Co-ord 98–03; PtO *Nor* 09–12; R N and S Creake w Waterden, Syderstone etc from 12. *The Rectory, 18 Front Street, South Creake, Fakenham NR21 9PE* T: (01328) 823293 M: 07970-875052 E: rector@creakesbenefice.org

WYLIE, David Victor. b 61. ACA 86 LSE BSc(Econ) 82 Leeds Univ BA 91. Coll of Resurr Mirfield 89. **d** 92 **p** 93. C Kilburn St Aug w St Jo *Lon* 92–95; C Heston 95–98; Chapl RN 98–17; P-in-c Leigh-on-Sea St Marg *Chelmsf* from 17. *The Vicarage, 1465 London Road, Leigh-on-Sea SS9 2SB* E: fr.alan.williams@gmail.com

WYLIE, Mrs Emma Clare Anna. b 75. Kent Univ BA 96 MA 01. St Mellitus Coll 13. **d** 16 **p** 17. C Langdon Hills *Chelmsf* 16–19; P-in-c Boreham from 19. *The Vicarage, Church Road, Boreham, Chelmsford CM3 3EG* M: 07982-723539 E: revemswylie@gmail.com

WYNBURNE, Canon John Paterson Barry. b 48. St Jo Coll Dur BA 70. Wycliffe Coll Toronto MDiv 72 Ridley Hall Cam 72. **d** 73 **p** 74. C Gt Stanmore *Lon* 73–76; Chapl Bucharest w Sofia *Eur* 76–77; C Dorking w Ranmore *Guildf* 77–80; V Send 80–88; V York Town St Mich 88–93; V Camberley St Mich Yorktown 93–95; TR Beaconsfield *Ox* 95–09; AD Amersham 04–09; V Long Crendon w Chearsley and Nether Winchendon 09–15; Hon Can Ch Ch 11–15; rtd 15; PtO *Ox* from 15. *66 Windmill Street, Brill, Aylesbury HP18 9TG* T: (01844) 238387 E: revwynburne@btinternet.com

WYNFORD-HARRIS, Robert William. b 61. Anglia Ruskin Univ BA 10 MA 14 LGSM 90. Ridley Hall Cam 06. **d** 08 **p** 09. C Sawbridgeworth *St Alb* 08–11; C Thorley 11–14; P-in-c St Helens *Portsm* 14–17; P-in-c Sea View 14–17; rtd 17; PtO *Ox* from 17. *Whiteoaks, Bucklebury Alley, Cold Ash, Thatcham RG18 9NN* M: 07722-068018 E: wynhar@hotmail.com

WYNN, Edward Laurence. b 65. Leeds Metrop Univ BSc 96 Leeds Univ MA 02 RGN 88. NOC 98. **d** 01 **p** 02. C Emley *Wakef* 01–04; C Flockton cum Denby Grange 01–04; Chapl RAF 04–12; Chapl Wolv Univ *Lich* 12–15; Chapl Birm Women's NHS Foundn Trust 12–15; Chapl RAuxAF 12–15; Chapl RAF from 15. *Chaplaincy Services (RAF), HQ Air Command, RAF High Wycombe HP14 4UE* T: (01494) 496800

WYNN (née ARMSTRONG), Rosemary. b 40. **d** 06. OLM Sturminster Newton, Hinton St Mary and Lydlinch *Sarum* 06–14; PtO 14–17. *2 Mounters Close, Marnhull, Sturminster Newton DT10 1NT* T: (01258) 820806

WYNNE, Preb Alan John. b 46. St Luke's Coll Ex CertEd 71. St Steph Ho Ox BA 71 MA 75. **d** 71 **p** 72. C Watford St Pet *St Alb* 71–74; Chapl Liddon Ho Lon 74–75; Chapl Abp Tenison's Sch Kennington 75–86; Hon C St Marylebone Annunciation Bryanston Street *Lon* 81–86; V Hoxton St Anne w St Columba 86–94; TR Poplar 94–14; Preb St Paul's Cathl 01–14; AD Tower Hamlets 01–06; rtd 14. *194 Long Lane, London SE1 4PZ* E: alanjwynne@tiscali.co.uk

WYNNE (née GORTON), Mrs Angela Deborah. b 60. Leeds Univ BSc 82 CSci 04. CBDTI 04. **d** 07 **p** 08. NSM Penwortham St Mary *Blackb* 07–11; NSM Charnock Richard 11–16; NSM Eccleston 13–16; TV Blackrod, Daisy Hill,

Westhoughton and Wingates *Man* from 16. *St Katherine's Vicarage, Blackhorse Street, Blackrod, Bolton BL6 5EN* E: adwynne@yahoo.co.uk

WYNNE, The Very Revd Frederick John Gordon. b 44. Chu Coll Cam B66 MA 70. CITC 81. **d** 84 **p** 85. C Dublin St Patr Cathl Gp *D & G* 84–86; C Romsey *Win* 86–89; R Broughton, Bossington, Houghton and Mottisfont 89–97; I Dunleckney w Nurney, Lorum and Kiltennel *C & O* 97–08; I Leighlin w Grange Sylvae, Shankill etc 08–10; Chan Ossory Cathl 00–10; Chan Leighlin Cathl 00–04; Dean Leighlin 04–10; rtd 10; PtO *Win* from 13. *12 Avenue Road, Lymington SO41 9GJ* T: (01590) 672082

WYNNE, Ian Charles. b 53. Bris Univ MB, ChB 76 FRCGP 06. SNWTP 09. **d** 11 **p** 12. NSM Haydock St Jas *Liv* from 11. *123 Ashton Road, Newton-le-Willows WA12 0AH* M: 07885-823786 E: ian_cw@hotmail.com

WYNNE, Jago Robert Owen. b 76. Magd Coll Cam BA 98 MA 01. Wycliffe Hall Ox 08. **d** 10 **p** 11. C Onslow Square and S Kensington St Aug *Lon* 10–12; C Clapham H Trin *S'wark* 12–15; V from 15; P-in-c Clapham Park All SS from 16. *25 The Chase, London SW4 0NP* M: 07976-033602 E: jago.wynne@holytrinityclapham.org

WYNNE, Teresa Anne Jane. b 58. Anglia Poly Univ BEd 94 Middx Univ BA 07. NTMTC 04. **d** 07 **p** 08. C Takeley w Lt Canfield *Chelmsf* 07–10; P-in-c Lexden 10–17; TV Cheshunt *St Alb* from 17. *The Vicarage, 5 Longlands Close, Cheshunt, Waltham Cross EN8 8LW* T: (01992) 640338 E: vicarccwc@gmail.com

WYNNE-GREEN, Roy Rowland. b 36. Chich Th Coll 67. **d** 70 **p** 71. C Fleetwood St Pet *Blackb* 70–73; C Cen Torquay *Ex* 73–75; Chapl SW Hosp Lon 75–85; Asst Chapl St Thos Hosp 75–85; Chapl R Surrey Co Hosp Guildf 85–94; Chapl R Surrey Co Hosp NHS Trust 94–01; Chapl Heathlands Mental Health Trust Surrey 94–98; Chapl Surrey Hants Borders NHS Trust 98–01; rtd 01; PtO *Guildf* 02–17. *St Benedict's House, 6 Lawn Road, Guildford GU2 5DE* T: (01483) 574582

WYNNE-JONES, Nicholas Winder. b 45. Jes Coll Ox BA 67 MA 72 Selw Coll Cam 71. Oak Hill Th Coll 69. **d** 72 **p** 73. C St Marylebone All So w SS Pet and Jo *Lon* 72–75; Chapl Stowe Sch 75–83; V Gt Clacton *Chelmsf* 83–95; V Beckenham Ch Ch *Roch* 95–13; RD Beckenham 00–05; rtd 13; Hon C Theale and Englefield *Ox* 13–18; V Englefield from 18. *St Mark's House, Englefield, Reading RG7 5EP* T: 0118-930 3595 E: nwwj@stmarksenglefield.org.uk

Y

YABBACOME, David Wallace. b 55. Bp Otter Coll BEd. Linc Th Coll. **d** 83 **p** 84. C Egham Hythe *Guildf* 83–86; C Cen Telford *Lich* 86–87; TV 87–92; R Cheadle w Freehay 92–00; V Linc St Nic w St Jo Newport 00–13; V E Trent *S'well* 13–15; rtd 15; PtO *Ely* from 16. *67 Primrose Avenue, Downham Market PE38 9GF* T: (01366) 386920 M: 07779-557541 E: revyabb@gmail.com

YABSLEY, Mrs Janet. b 42. St Alb Minl Tr Scheme 81. **dss** 86 **d** 87 **p** 94. Luton St Andr *St Alb* 84–87; NSM Luton St Aug Limbury 87–00; NSM Luton All SS w St Pet 00–06; PtO from 06. *11 Dale Road, Dunstable LU5 4PY* T: (01582) 661480

YACOMENI, Peter Frederick. b 34. Worc Coll Ox BA 58 MA 61. Wycliffe Hall Ox 58. **d** 60 **p** 61. C New Malden and Coombe *S'wark* 60–64; C Bethnal Green St Jas Less *Lon* 64–68; V Barton Hill St Luke w Ch Ch *Bris* 68–75; V Bishopsworth 75–86; RD Bedminster 84–86; P-in-c Wick w Doynton 86–87; V Wick w Doynton and Dyrham 87–98; RD Bitton 95–98; rtd 98; Chapl Wilts and Swindon Healthcare NHS Trust 08–10; Chapl Gt Western Hosps NHS Foundn Trust 08–10; PtO *Bris* 98–19. *15 Orwell Close, Malmesbury SN16 9UB* T: (01666) 826628 E: peter.yacomeni@gmail.com

YACOMENI, Thomas Peter Bruce. b 71. Ex Univ BEng 94. Trin Coll Bris BA 09. **d** 09 **p** 10. C Weston-super-Mare St Paul *B & W* 09–13; Pioneer Min from 13; RD Locking from 18. *78 Bransby Way, Weston-super-Mare BS24 7BW* T: (01934) 517954 M: 07786-806640 E: tom.yacomeni@googlemail.com

YANDELL, Caroline Jane. b 63. St Hugh's Coll Ox BA 85 MA 92 Bris Univ MB, ChB 97 LSHTM MSc 05 Bris Univ PhD 07 Wolfs Coll Cam BTh 08 St Jo Coll Cam MPhil 09 MRCGP 01. Ridley Hall Cam 06. **d** 09 **p** 10. C Henleaze *Bris* 09–13; P-in-c Bassingbourn *Ely* 13–15; V from 15; P-in-c Whaddon 13–15; V from 15. *The Vicarage, 21 North End, Bassingbourn, Royston SG8 5NZ* T: (01763) 244836 E: caroline.yandell@cantab.net

YAP, Thomas Fook Piau. b 75. Leeds Univ BA 98 MA 99. St Jo Coll Nottm MTh 02. **d** 03 **p** 04. C Starbeck *Ripon* 03–07; Chapl Essex Univ *Chelmsf* 07–12; Chapl S Lon and Maudsley NHS Foundn Trust 12–15; PtO *Lon* from 12; *S'wark* from 15. *5 Howerd Court, 20 Love Lane, London SE18 6GR* E: revthomas@hotmail.co.uk

YARRIEN (née FRYER), Cora Lynette. b 74. Man Univ BSc 95 Warwick Univ MSc 97 BA 01. Cranmer Hall Dur 12. **d** 14 **p** 15. C Epperstone, Gonalston, Oxton and Woodborough *S'well* 14–16; C Daybrook 16–18; C Retford Area from 18. *The Vicarage, 3 Maple Drive, Elkesley, Retford DN22 8AX* M: 07885-635374 E: cora.yarrien@icloud.com

YATES, Andrew Martin. b 55. St Chad's Coll Dur BA 77. Linc Th Coll 78. **d** 80 **p** 81. C Brightside St Thos and St Marg *Sheff* 80–83; TV Haverhill w Withersfield, the Wrattings etc *St E* 84–90; Ind Chapl 84–90; R Aylesham w Adisham *Cant* 90–96; P-in-c Dudley St Aug Holly Hall *Worc* 96–03;

Chapl Merry Hill Shopping Cen 96–03; Dioc Soc Resp Officer *Truro* from 03; P-in-c Tresillian and Lamorran w Merther 03–12; P-in-c St Michael Penkevil 03–12; P-in-c Paul from 12; C Newlyn St Pet from 12; C Penzance St Mary w St Paul and St Jo from 12. *Hanover House, 6A Kings Road, Penzance TR18 4LG* T: (01736) 367863 E: andrew.yates@truro.anglican.org

YATES, Christopher David. Open Univ CSocSc 05. Ox Min Course 08. **d** 10 **p** 11. C Williamstown w Medowie and Mallabula Australia 10–12; R Raymond Terrace 12–16; Chapl NSW Police 11–16; V Eastbourne St Sav and St Pet *Chich* 16–17. *St Saviour's Vicarage, Spencer Road, Eastbourne BN21 4PA* T: (01323) 722317 M: 07597-825107 E: chrsyates@yahoo.co.uk

YATES, Mrs Esther Christine. b 46. Moray Ho Coll of Educn DipEd 67 Cartrefle Coll of Educn BEd 80. St As Minl Tr Course 02. **d** 05 **p** 06. NSM Newtown w Llanllwchaiarn w Aberhafesp *St As* 05–07; NSM Llanllwchaiarn and Newtown w Aberhafesp 07–10; NSM Berriew 10–17; NSM Pool Miss Area from 18. *Gwawr-y-Grug, 7 Mill Fields, Milford, Newtown SY16 3JP* T: (01686) 625559 E: esther.yates@talktalk.net

YATES, Francis Edmund. b 49. Ox Univ BEd 72 Sheff Univ MEd 88. Linc Th Coll 95. **d** 95 **p** 96. C Chesterfield St Mary and All SS *Derby* 95–98; P-in-c Newlyn St Newlyn *Truro* 98–03; Dioc Adv for Schs and RE 98–03; P-in-c Tideswell *Derby* 03–11; V 11–12; C Wormhill, Peak Forest w Peak Dale and Dove Holes 07–11; rtd 12; PtO *Linc* from 16. *Tanners, Alford Road, Bilsby, Alford LN13 9PY* T: (01507) 464890 E: frank298@btinternet.com

YATES, Herbert. See YATES, William Herbert

YATES, Jennifer Clare. See TOTNEY, Jennifer Clare

YATES, Miss Joanna Mary. b 49. St Anne's Coll Ox BA 71 MA 74 K Coll Lon PGCE 72. S'wark Ord Course 89. **d** 91 **p** 94. Promotions and Publications Officer Nat Soc 85–95; Chapl Ch Ho Westmr 91–95; C Regent's Park St Mark *Lon* 91–95; C Finchley St Mary 95–01; TV Leeds City *Ripon* 01–09; rtd 09; PtO *Lon* from 10. *8 Frith Court, London NW7 1JP* T: (020) 8349 1076 M: 07961-654430 E: revjoannayates325@btinternet.com

YATES, Lindsay Anne. b 69. Selw Coll Cam BA 91 MA 95 Univ of Wales (Lamp) MTh 10 Barrister 92. Ripon Coll Cuddesdon BTh 99. **d** 99 **p** 00. C Bampton w Clanfield *Ox* 99–02; Chapl Pemb Coll Cam 02–06; Chapl Westcott Ho Cam 07–14; NSM Winchmore Hill St Paul *Lon* 14–17; Tutor St Mellitus Coll 14–17; P-in-c Octagon *Chich* 17–18; R from 18. *The Vicarage, Compton, Chichester PO18 9HD* T: (023) 9263 1252 E: vicar@theoctagonparish.org.uk

YATES, Margaret Helen. b 51. **d** 10 **p** 11. NSM Walbury Beacon *Ox* 10–14; NSM Newbury St Nic and Speen 15–18; PtO from 18. *5 Halfway Cottages, Bath Road, Newbury RG20 8NG* T: (01488) 658092

YATES, Michael Anthony. b 48. Oak Hill Th Coll. d 82 p 83. C Hebburn St Jo *Dur* 82–85; C Sheldon *Birm* 85–87; V Lea Hall 87–92; TV Old Brampton and Loundsley Green *Derby* 92–98; V Loundsley Green 98–01; V Riddings and Ironville 01–07; P-in-c Seale and Lullington w Coton in the Elms 07–11; R 11–17; C Walton-on-Trent w Croxall, Rosliston etc 13–17; rtd 17; PtO *York* from 18. *10 Park Avenue, Beverley HU17 7AT* E: mermaid23@hotmail.co.uk

YATES, Michael **Peter**. b 47. Leeds Univ BA 69 MA 70 MPhil 85 Potchefstroom Univ PhD 03. Coll of Resurr Mirfield 69. d 71 p 72. C Crewe St Andr *Ches* 71–76; V Wheelock 76–79; Chapl Rainhill Hosp Liv 79–89; Chapl Barnsley Distr Gen Hosp 89–94; Chapl Barnsley Distr Gen Hosp NHS Trust 94–11; Chapl Barnsley Hosp NHS Foundn Trust 05–11; rtd 11; PtO *Leeds* from 17. *40 Rainton Grove, Barnsley S75 2QZ* E: mpyates@hotmail.com

YATES, Paul David. b 47. Sussex Univ BA 73 DPhil 80. Sarum & Wells Th Coll 88. d 91 p 92. NSM Lewes All SS, St Anne, St Mich and St Thos *Chich* 91–00; NSM Lewes St Mich and St Thos at Cliffe w All SS 00–10; NSM Lewes St Anne and St Mich and St Thos etc from 10. *17 St Swithun's Terrace, Lewes BN7 1UJ* T: (01273) 473463

YATES, Peter Francis. b 47. Sheff Univ BA 69. Kelham Th Coll 69 NW Ord Course 73. d 74 p 75. C Mexborough *Sheff* 74–78; C Sevenoaks St Jo *Roch* 78–81; CSWG from 81; LtO *Chich* from 85. *The Monastery, Crawley Down, Crawley RH10 4LH* T: (01342) 712074 E: father.peter@cswg.org.uk

YATES, Raymond Paul. b 55. Oak Hill Th Coll BA 88. d 88 p 89. C Bootle St Mary w St Paul *Liv* 88–91; C Drypool *York* 91–92; TV 92–97; C Orpington All SS *Roch* 97–00; R Beeford w Frodingham and Foston *York* 00–06; RD N Holderness 02–06; Chapl HM Pris Hull 01–02; P-in-c Quinton Road W St Boniface *Birm* 06–09; V 09–20. *The Vicarage, Quinton Road West, Birmingham B32 2QD* T: 0121-427 8551 *or* 426 3166 E: ray@stboniface.co.uk

YATES, Ricky. *See* YATES, Warwick John

YATES, Canon Roger Alan. b 47. Trin Coll Cam BA 68 MA 72 MB, BChir 71 Bris Univ PhD 75 MRCP 77 FFPM 93. NOC 84. d 87 p 88. NSM Wilmslow *Ches* from 87; Bp's Officer for NSM 93–17; Hon Can Ches Cathl from 99; RD Knutsford 06–13. *3 Racecourse Park, Wilmslow SK9 5LU* T: (01625) 520246 E: raycandoc@yahoo.co.uk

YATES, Mrs Siân. b 57. Univ of Wales (Ban) Westmr Coll Ox MTh 91. Linc Th Coll 78. d 80 p 94. C Risca *Mon* 80–83; Chapl Ch Hosp Horsham 83–85; Team Dn Haverhill w Withersfield, the Wrattings etc *St E* 85–90; Dioc Youth Chapl *Cant* 90–93; Assoc Min Cant St Martin and St Paul 93–96; Educn Chapl *Worc* 96–03; P-in-c Dudley St Jas 96–03; P-in-c Dudley St Barn 01–02; P-in-c Tregony w St Cuby and Cornelly *Truro* 03–12; Dioc Adv in RE 03–10; TR Penzance St Mary w St Paul and St Jo from 12; C Newlyn St Pet from 12; C Paul from 12. *Hanover House, 6A Kings Road, Penzance TR18 4LG* T: (01736) 367863 E: yates252@btinternet.com *or* teamleader@penleecluster.org.uk

YATES, Stephen Richard. b 79. Univ of Wales (Ban) BSc 01. Trin Coll Bris 14. d 16. C Torquay St Matthias, St Mark and H Trin *Ex* from 16. *3 Redgate Close, Torquay TQ1 3UG* M: 07840-785426

YATES, Timothy John Sturgis. b 56. Bradf Univ BTech 83 Univ Coll Lon PhD 86. ERMC 05. d 07 p 08. NSM Gt Chesham *Ox* from 07. *16 Chapmans Crescent, Chesham HP5 2QU* T: (01494) 772914 M: 07802-155072 E: tim.yates3@btinternet.com

YATES, Warwick John (**Ricky**). b 52. Univ of Wales (Lamp) BA 78. Wycliffe Hall Ox 87. d 89 p 90. C Hoddesdon *St Alb* 89–93; R Finmere w Mixbury, Cottisford, Hardwick etc *Ox* 93–95; R Shelswell 95–08; P-in-c Prague *Eur* 08–17; rtd 17; PtO *Eur* from 17. *Stará Oleška 44, 405 02 Huntířov, Czech Republic* M: (00420) 73-577 8426 E: ry@rickyyates.com

YATES, William **Herbert**. b 35. Man Univ BA 59. Chich Th Coll 60. d 61 p 62. C Blackpool St Steph *Blackb* 61–65; C Wednesbury St Jo *Lich* 65–69; V Porthill 69–78; R Norton in the Moors 78–84; R Church Aston 84–00; rtd 00; PtO *Lich* from 01. *2 Red Lees, Telford TF1 5DE* T: (01952) 619218

YATES, Mrs Yvonne Louise. b 52. NEOC 01. d 04 p 05. NSM Kirkbymoorside w Gillamoor, Farndale etc *York* 04–07; Chapl Oakhill Secure Tr Cen 07–08; Co-ord Chapl HM Pris Kirklevington Grange 08–11; TV Combe Martin, Berrynarbor, Lynton, Brendon etc *Ex* 11–14; Chapl HM Pris Styal from 14. *HM Prison, Styal Road, Styal, Wilmslow SK9 4HR* T: (01625) 553000 E: yvonne.yates@justice.gov.uk

YAU, Timothy Sang. b 71. Ridley Hall Cam 06. d 08 p 09. C Farcet Hampton *Ely* 08–12; C Cringleford and Colney *Nor* from 17. *5 Poppy Close, Cringleford, Norwich NR4 7JZ* M: 07964-078330

YEADON, Ms Victoria Jane. b 69. Univ Coll Lon BSc 91 MSc 92 Anglia Ruskin Univ BA 09. Ridley Hall Cam 07. d 09 p 10. C Deptford St Nic and St Luke *S'wark* 09–12; TV Thameshead from 12. *5 Finchdale Road, London SE2 9PG* T: (020) 8312 2566 E: janeyeadon@gmail.com

YEAGER, Robert **Timothy**. b 50. Univ of Iowa BA 72 JD 77. d 10 p 11. USA 10–14; TV E Greenwich *S'wark* from 14. *89 Westcombe Park Road, London SE3 7RZ* T: (020) 8090 2036 M: 07804-614245 E: rtyeager@gmail.com

YEARWOOD, Jean Cornilia. b 43. Heythrop Coll Lon MA 05 RGN 74 RM 76. d 07 p 08. NSM Croydon Woodside *S'wark* 07–14; rtd 14; PtO *S'wark* from 14. *59 Bradley Road, London SE19 3NT* T: (020) 8771 7743 M: 07913-005545 E: j.yearwood@btopenworld.com

YELDHAM, Anthony Paul Richard. *See* KYRIAKIDES-YELDHAM, Anthony Paul Richard

YELDHAM, Denise Linda. b 51. Leeds Univ BSc 72 MB, ChB 75 Univ of Wales (Lamp) MA 08 MRCPsych 80. Westcott Ho Cam 06. d 08 p 09. C Plymstock and Hooe *Ex* 08–11; C Westmr St Steph w St Jo *Lon* 11–14; P-in-c Margate All SS *Cant* 14–17; P-in-c Margate St Jo 14–17; Chapl Eden Hall Marie Curie Hospice from 18; NSM Kilburn St Mary w All So and W Hampstead St Jas *Lon* from 19. *14 Neville House, 19 Page Street, London SW1P 4JX* T: (020) 7932 0235 M: 07814-193632

YELLAND, Jeffrey Charles. b 46. CEng MIStructE 72. STETS 98. d 01 p 02. NSM Effingham w Lt Bookham *Guildf* 01–04; NSM Dorking St Paul 04–16; PtO from 16. *9 Mulberry Heights, Harrowlands Park, Dorking RH4 2RA* M: 07877-040770 E: jeff@stpaulsdorking.org.uk

YENDALL, John **Edward** Thomas. b 52. St Jo Coll Dur BA 88. Cranmer Hall Dur 84. d 88 p 89. C Bangor *Ban* 88–90; C Botwnnog 90–91; R Trefdraeth w Aberffraw etc 91–01; RD Malltraeth 97–01; V Llanwddyn and Llanfihangel-yng-Nghwynfa etc *St As* 01–07; V Llanrhaeadr ym Mochnant etc 07–11; P-in-c Llansantffraid Glyn Ceirog and Llanarmon etc 11–17; I Boyle and Elphin w Aghanagh, Kilbryan etc *K, E & A* from 17. *Tus Nua, Forest View, Boyle, Co Roscommon, Republic of Ireland* T: (00353) (71) 966 2639 E: edward.yendall2@btinternet.com

✠YEOMAN, The Rt Revd David. b 44. St Mich Coll Llan 66. d 70 p 71 c 04. C Cardiff St Jo Llan 70–72; C Caerphilly 72–76; V Ystrad Rhondda w Ynyscynon 76–81; V Mountain Ash 81–96; R Coity w Nolton 96–04; Can Llan Cathl 00–09; Asst Bp Llan 04–09; Adn Morgannwg 04–06; rtd 09; PtO Llan from 09. *4 Llety Gwyn, Bridgend CF31 1RG* T: (01656) 649919 M: 07971-926631

YEOMAN, Miss Ruth Jane. b 60. Sheff Univ BSc 82 MSc 85 Dur Univ PGCE 83. Ripon Coll Cuddesdon BA 90 MA 94. d 91 p 94. C Coleshill *Birm* 91–95; C Hodge Hill 95–01; Bp's Adv for Children's Work 95–01; L'Arche Lambeth Community 01–03; PtO *S'wark* 03; *Birm* 03; V Menston w Woodhead *Bradf* 03–14; *Leeds* 14–17; C Baildon from 17. *93 Hoyle Court Road, Baildon, Shipley BD17 6EL* M: 07752-912646 E: ruthjyeoman@hotmail.com

YERBURGH, Canon David Savile. b 34. Magd Coll Cam BA 57 MA 61. Wells Th Coll 57. d 59 p 60. C Cirencester *Glouc* 59–63; C Bitterne Park *Win* 63–67; V Churchdown St Jo *Glouc* 67–74; RD Glouc N 73–74; V Charlton Kings St Mary 74–85; R Minchinhampton 85–95; Hon Can Glouc Cathl 86–95; rtd 95; PtO *Sarum* from 95. *2 Mill Race Close, Mill Road, Salisbury SP2 7RX* T: (01722) 320064 E: d.yerburgh@btinternet.com

YERBURY, Gregory Howard. b 67. Trin Coll Bris BA 93. St Jo Coll Nottm 94. d 96 p 97. C Crofton *Portsm* 96–00; P-in-c Bolton St Jo *Man* 00–06; P-in-c Bolton Breightmet St Jas 05–06; TR Leverhulme 06–11; TR Penkridge *Lich* from 11; RD from 16. *The Rectory, New Road, Penkridge, Stafford ST19 5DN* T: (01785) 714344 E: rector@stmichaelspenkridge.co.uk

YETMAN, Miss Sarah Elizabeth. b 85. St Mary's Coll Dur BA 09 Cam Univ BTh 13. Ridley Hall Cam 10. d 13 p 14. C Yateley *Win* 13–17; P-in-c Bournemouth St Jo w St Mich 17–18; V from 18. *13 Durley Chine Road South, Bournemouth BH2 5JT* T: (01202) 241507 *or* 556645 E: sarah.yetman@gmail.com *or* revd.s.yetman@btinternet.com

YILDIRIM, Engin. d 07 p 08. C Istanbul *Eur* 07–17; TV Wood Green St Mich w Bounds Green St Gabr etc *Lon* from 17. *27 Collings Close, London N22 8RL* M: 07908-335400 E: engnyldrm@icloud.com

YONG, Sok Han. b 61. Ox Brookes Univ MA 14. Malaysia Th Sem BTheol 86. d 10 p 11. NSM Ox St Aldate 10–11; NSM Abingdon 11–14; NSM St Andr Hong Kong from 14. *138 Nathan Road, Kowloon, Hong Kong* T: (00852) 2367 1478 E: info@standrews.org.hk

YONGE, James Mohun (Brother Amos). b 47. Keele Univ BA 71. WMMTC 91. **d** 94 **p** 95. SSF from 76; PtO *Worc* 09–17. *Glasshampton Monastery, Shrawley, Worcester WR6 6TQ* T: (01299) 896345 F: 896083 E: amosssf@franciscans.org.uk

YORK, Mrs Elizabeth Joy. b 70. Nottm Univ BA 94 Nottm Trent Univ PGCE 97 Ches Univ MTh 17. St Jo Coll Nottm 13. **d** 15 **p** 16. C Barrow upon Soar w Walton le Wolds *Leic* 15–17; C Wymeswold and Prestwold w Hoton 15–17; C Loughb Gd Shep 17–19; Chapl Loughborough Schs Foundn from 19. *Address withheld by request*

YORK, Canon Humphrey Bowmar. b 28. St Chad's Coll Dur BA 54 Univ of Wales (Lamp) MA 04. **d** 55 **p** 56. C Beamish *Dur* 55–57; C Tettenhall Regis *Lich* 57–62; P-in-c Lansallos w Pelynt *Truro* 62–63; R Lanreath 62–67; V Pelynt 63–67; P-in-c Lanlivery 67–74; P-in-c Luxulyan 67–74; P-in-c Lanlivery w Luxulyan 74–83; RD Bodmin 76–82; R Antony w Sheviock 83–93; Hon Can Truro Cathl 90–93; rtd 93; PtO *Truro* 93–12; *Sarum* 93–17. *8 Huntingdon Street, Bradford-on-Avon BA15 1RF* E: canonhumphrey@tinyworld.co.uk

YORK, Mrs Paula. b 67. **d** 12 **p** 13. C Earls Barton *Pet* 12–15; R Yardley Hastings, Denton and Grendon etc from 15. *14 The Leys, Denton, Northampton NN7 1DH* E: revpaulayork@gmail.com

YORK, Archbishop of. See SENTAMU, The Most Revd and Rt Hon John Tucker Mugabi

YORK, Archdeacon of. *Vacant*

YORK, Dean of. See FROST, The Rt Revd Jonathan Hugh

YORKE, John Andrew. b 47. Cranmer Hall Dur 70. **d** 73 **p** 74. C Spitalfields Ch Ch w All SS *Lon* 73–78; R Tuktoyaktuk Canada 78–88; R Fort McPherson 89–92; V Totland Bay *Portsm* 92–12; V Thorley 95–12; rtd 12; PtO *Portsm* from 12; *Sarum* from 15. *7 Broadmead, Trowbridge BA14 9BX* T: (01225) 680529 E: andyyorke.iow@tiscali.co.uk

YORKSTONE, Peter. b 48. Loughb Univ BTech 72. Oak Hill Th Coll 79. **d** 81 **p** 82. C Blackpool St Thos *Blackb* 81–85; V Copp 85–00; P-in-c Giggleswick and Rathmell w Wigglesworth *Bradf* 00–07; V Kettlewell w Conistone, Hubberholme etc 07–14; rtd 14; PtO *Leic* from 16. *45 Hawthorne Avenue, Hathern, Loughborough LE12 5LP* E: peter@yorkstone.me.uk

YOUATT, Jennifer Alison. See MONTGOMERY, Jennifer Alison

YOUDE, Paul Crosland. b 47. Birm Univ LLB 68. WEMTC 93. **d** 96 **p** 97. NSM Cheltenham St Luke and St Jo *Glouc* 96–99; C Cirencester 99–03; P-in-c Lydney 03–09; P-in-c Woolaston w Alvington and Aylburton 07–09; rtd 09; Hon C Kemble, Poole Keynes, Somerford Keynes etc *Glouc* 09–13; PtO from 16. *107 Painswick Road, Cheltenham GL50 2EX* T: (01242) 463174 E: paul.youde@yahoo.co.uk

YOUELL, Mrs Deborah Mary. b 57. STETS 01. **d** 04 **p** 14. NSM Cowplain *Portsm* 04–08; NSM Crookhorn from 08. *42 The Yews, Horndean, Waterlooville PO8 0BH* T: (023) 9279 9946 *or* 9225 6814 M: 07513-314441 E: debbie@cogs.org.uk

YOUINGS, The Ven Adrian. b 65. Ex Univ BSc 86 Bath Univ PhD 90. Wycliffe Hall Ox 93. **d** 96 **p** 97. C Dorking St Paul *Guildf* 96–99; C S Croydon Em *S'wark* 99–03; R Trull w Angersleigh *B & W* 03–17; RD Taunton 15–17; Adn Bath and Preb Wells Cathl from 17. *56 Claverton Road, Saltford, Bristol BS31 3AG* T: (01225) 873609 M: 07902-804569 E: adbath@bathwells.anglican.org

YOUNG, Andrew Charles. b 54. FIBMS 83. NOC 98. **d** 01 **p** 02. C Heywood *Man* 01–05; TV Eccles 05–16; AD 13–16; CMS Nepal from 16. *22 Southgate, Scarborough YO12 4NB* E: andrew.young66@ntlworld.com

YOUNG, Arthur. b 65. Belf Bible Coll BTh 92. CITC 99. **d** 01 **p** 02. C Donaghadee *D & D* 01–04; I Tullylish 04–13; I Kill *D & G* 13–16; I Lisburn St Paul *Conn* from 16. *St Paul's Rectory, 3 Ballinderry Road, Lisburn BT28 1UD*

YOUNG, Mrs Carole Jane. b 58. Qu Foundn (Course) 16. **d** 18 **p** 19. NSM Kingsbury *Birm* from 18; NSM Baxterley w Hurley and Wood End and Merevale etc from 18. *84 Sycamore Road, Kingsbury, Tamworth B78 2JL* T: (01827) 874194 M: 07960-368524 E: rev.cj.young@gmail.com

YOUNG, Daniel George Harding. b 52. New Coll Ox BA 73 MA 83 Westmr Coll Ox PGCE 74. Cranmer Hall Dur 77. **d** 80 **p** 81. C Bushbury *Lich* 80–83; Chapl Dean Close Sch 83–99; Titus Trust 99–10; PtO *Win* 01–10; C Knutsford St Jo and Toft *Ches* from 10. *35 Beggarmans Lane, Knutsford WA16 9BA* T: (01565) 632128 226116 M: 07974-945651 E: youngdan52@talktalk.net

YOUNG, David Charles. b 54. Open Univ BA 95 PGCE 97 CQSW 82. SEITE 03. **d** 06 **p** 07. NSM Haywards Heath St Wilfrid *Chich* from 06. *4 Ashurst Place, Heath Road, Haywards Heath RH16 3EJ* T: (01444) 416074 M: 07921-144480

YOUNG, David John. b 43. Nottm Univ BA 64 MPhil 89 Lambeth STh 87. Coll of Resurr Mirfield 64. **d** 66 **p** 67.

C Warsop *S'well* 66–68; C Harworth 68–71; P-in-c Hackenthorpe Ch Ch *Derby* 71–72; TV Frecheville and Hackenthorpe 73–75; V Chaddesden St Phil 75–83; R Narborough and Huncote *Leic* 83–89; RD Guthlaxton I 87–90; Chapl Leic Univ 90–95; V Eyres Monsell 95–98; PtO 98–99; rtd 03. *57 Castle Fields, Leicester LE4 1AN* T: 0116-236 5634 E: johnyoung58@virginmedia.com

YOUNG, David Lun Ming. b 81. Leeds Univ BA 02 St Jo Coll Dur BA 09 MA 12. Cranmer Hall Dur 07. **d** 10 **p** 11. C Upper Armley *Ripon* 10–14; TV Moor Allerton and Shadwell 14; *Leeds* from 14; Asst Dir of Ords from 15. *The Vicarage, 2 Church Farm Garth, Leeds LS17 8HD* M: 07736-678558 E: revdaveyoung@gmail.com

YOUNG, Derek John. b 42. St D Coll Lamp. **d** 73 **p** 74. C Griffithstown *Mon* 73–76; C Ebbw Vale 76–77; V Penmaen 77–81; V Penmaen and Crumlin 81–87; Chapl Oakdale Hosp Gwent 83–87; V New Tredegar *Mon* 87–99; V Llanfihangel Crucorney w Oldcastle etc 99–11; P-in-c from 12. *The Vicarage, Llanfihangel Crucorney, Abergavenny NP7 8DH* T: (01873) 890349

YOUNG, Mrs Diana Joan. b 56. St Hilda's Coll Ox BA 78 MA 82. Ripon Coll Cuddesdon 11. **d** 13 **p** 14. C Hampstead St Jo *Lon* 13–17; V Woburn Sands *St Alb* from 17. *30 Church Road, Woburn Sands, Milton Keynes MK17 8TA* E: revdianay@gmail.com

YOUNG, Emma. b 89. Trin Coll Ox BA 10 Aber Univ MTh 12. Ripon Coll Cuddesdon MTh 14. **d** 14 **p** 15. C Luton St Aug Limbury *St Alb* 14–17; V Darent Valley *Roch* from 17. *Darenth Vicarage, Green Street Green Road, Lane End, Dartford DA2 7JR* T: (01322) 227153 M: 07593-652689 E: revd.emma.young@hotmail.co.uk

YOUNG, George William. b 31. Lon Coll of Div ALCD 55. **d** 56 **p** 57. C Everton Em *Liv* 56–58; C Halliwell St Pet *Man* 58–61; V Newburn *Newc* 61–67; P-in-c Tyler's Green *Ox* 67–69; V 69–80; LtO 80–84; Area Sec (W England) SAMS 80–84; Hon C Purley Ch Ch *S'wark* 84–87; V Beckenham St Jo *Roch* 87–92; rtd 92; PtO *S'wark* 92–18. *9 Shortacres, High Street, Nutfield, Redhill RH1 4HJ* T: (01737) 822363 E: theyoungs88@yahoo.com

YOUNG, Graham Mark. b 83. UWE BSc 06 St Jo Coll Dur BA 17 Bath Univ QTS 07. Cranmer Hall Dur 16. **d** 17 **p** 18. C Sunderland St Mary and St Pet *Dur* from 17. *The Good Shepherd Clergy House, Forest Road, Sunderland SR4 0DX* E: revdgrahamyoung@outlook.com

YOUNG, Hyacinth Loretta. NTMTC 95. **d** 98 **p** 99. NSM Harlesden All So *Lon* 98–00; TV Wembley Park 00–12; V Tokyngton St Mich 12–19; rtd 19. *8 Nettleden Avenue, Wembley HA9 6DP* T: (020) 8900 1585 E: hyacinth513@hotmail.com

YOUNG, Iain Clavering. b 56. Newc Poly BA 79. Coll of Resurr Mirfield 80. **d** 83 **p** 84. C Wallsend St Luke *Newc* 83–86; C Horton 86–87; V 87–92; V Friern Barnet St Pet le Poer *Lon* 92–95; C Holborn St Alb w Saffron Hill St Pet 96–97; P-in-c Hoxton H Trin w St Mary 97–02; V 02–09; Chapl Moorfields Eye Hosp NHS Foundn Trust 97–03; P-in-c Lavender Hill Ascension etc *S'wark* 09–12; V from 12. *The Clergy House, Pountney Road, London SW11 5TU* T: (020) 7228 5340 E: iain.young@ifightpoverty.com

YOUNG, James Andrew. b 80. St Jo Coll Nottm. **d** 14 **p** 15. C Horsham *Chich* 14–18; C Crawley from 18. *60A Malthouse Road, Crawley RH10 6BG* M: 07903-813077 E: jimmy@christianjimmy.com *or* jimmy@stjohnscrawley.com

YOUNG, Jeremy Michael. b 54. Ch Coll Cam BA 76 MA 80 Lon Univ MTh 94. Coll of Resurr Mirfield 78. **d** 80 **p** 81. C Whitworth w Spennymoor *Dur* 80–83; C Boxmoor St Jo *St Alb* 83–86; V Croxley Green St Oswald 86–94; Dir Past Studies CITC 94–99; LtO *D & G* 99–03; PtO *B & W* from 06. *Westerley House, Tellisford, Bath BA2 7RL* T: (01373) 830920 E: jeremy_young@mac.com

YOUNG, John. See YOUNG, David John

YOUNG, Canon John David. b 37. Lon Univ BD 65 Sussex Univ MA 77. Clifton Th Coll 62. **d** 65 **p** 66. C Plymouth St Jude *Ex* 65–68; Hd of RE Northgate Sch Ipswich 68–71; Chapl and Sen Lect Bp Otter Coll Chich 71–81; Chapl and Sen Lect W Sussex Inst of HE 77–81; Chapl and Sen Lect York St Jo Coll 81–87; C York St Paul 87–88; Dioc Ev 88–02; Can and Preb York Minster 92–03; Miss Strategy Development Officer 00–02; rtd 02; LtO *York* 02–10; PtO from 10. *72 Middlethorpe Grove, York YO24 1JY* T: (01904) 704195 E: john.young@yorkcourses.co.uk

YOUNG, John Kenneth. Edin Th Coll 62. **d** 64 **p** 65. C Gosforth All SS *Newc* 64–67; C Newc St Gabr 67–69; R Bowers Gifford *Chelmsf* 69–72; R Bowers Gifford w N Benfleet 72–75; P-in-c Kirkwhelpington *Newc* 75–79; P-in-c Kirkharle 77–79; P-in-c Kirkheaton 75–79; P-in-c Cambo 77–79; V Kirkwhelpington, Kirkharle, Kirkheaton and Cambo 79–82; V Gosforth St Nic

82–92; V Healey and Slaley 92–97; rtd 97; PtO *Newc* from 97. *1 Raynes Close, Morpeth NE61 2XX* T: (01670) 515191

YOUNG, Canon Jonathan Priestland. b 44. AKC 68 Whitelands Coll Lon CertEd 74 Roehampton Univ Hon BEd 17. St Boniface Warminster 68. **d** 69 **p** 70. C Clapham H Trin *S'wark* 69–73; C Mitcham St Mark 73–74; V Godmanchester *Ely* 74–82; P-in-c Cambridge St Giles w St Pet 82; P-in-c Chesterton St Luke 82; TR Cambridge Ascension 82–01; Chapl St Jo Coll Sch Cam 88–93; P-in-c Ellington *Ely* 01–02; P-in-c Grafham 01–02; P-in-c Easton 01–02; P-in-c Spaldwick w Barham and Woolley 01–02; R E Leightonstone 02–14; P-in-c Alconbury cum Weston 04–11; P-in-c Buckworth 04–11; P-in-c Hamerton 09–11; P-in-c Winwick 09–11; P-in-c Gt w Lt Gidding and Steeple Gidding 09–11; RD Leightonstone 02–04; Hon Can Ely Cathl 01–14; rtd 14; PtO *Ely* from 14. *Charis House, 15 Causeway, Godmanchester, Huntingdon PE29 2HA* T: (01480) 453350 E: jonathan.young@ely.anglican.org

YOUNG, Joshua Mark. b 87. Nottm Univ BA 10. Ripon Coll Cuddesdon MTh 13. **d** 13 **p** 14. C Welwyn Garden City *St Alb* 13–17; P-in-c Southfleet *Roch* from 18. *Darenth Vicarage, Green Street Green Road, Lane End, Dartford DA2 7JR* M: 07957-978184 E: revdjoshyoung@hotmail.co.uk

YOUNG, Karen Georgina. b 58. Ox Poly BA 87 Dur Univ MA 14. Cranmer Hall Dur. **d** 13 **p** 14. C Chich St Paul and Westhampnett 13–16; V Heckmondwike (w Norristhorpe) and Liversedge *Leeds* from 16. *St James's Vicarage, 25 Church Street, Heckmondwike WF16 0AX* T: (01924) 405881 M: 07836-254320 E: karenyoung58@gmail.com

YOUNG, Karen Heather. b 66. Nottm Univ BA 01. Westcott Ho Cam 02. **d** 05 **p** 07. C Airedale w Fryston *Wakef* 05–06; Hon C Ravenshead *S'well* 07–08; Mental Health Chapl Notts Healthcare NHS Trust 08–09; NSM Shill Valley and Broadshire *Ox* 14–18; NSM Budleigh Salterton, E Budleigh w Bicton etc *Ex* from 18. *Maranatha, Boucher Way, Budleigh Salterton EX9 6HQ* E: thereverendkarenyoung@gmail.com

YOUNG, Kathleen Margaret. See BROWN, Kathleen Margaret
YOUNG, Kenneth. See YOUNG, John Kenneth
YOUNG, Leonard Thomas. b 55. Ches Coll of HE BTh 04 Leeds Univ MA 06. Coll of Resurr Mirfield 04. **d** 06 **p** 07. C Failsworth H Family *Man* 06–09; P-in-c Man Clayton St Cross w St Paul 09–15; R 15–16; P-in-c Derby St Bart 16–17; P-in-c Derby St Luke 16–17; V Derby St Bart and St Luke from 17. *The Vicarage, 49 Addison Road, Derby DE24 8FH*

YOUNG, Mandy Elizabeth. b 58. Leeds Univ BA 91 PhD 94. SEITE 11. **d** 14 **p** 15. C Snodland All SS w Ch Ch *Roch* 14–19; C Dartford St Alb from 19; C Dartford St Edm from 19. *12 Keyes Road, Dartford DA1 5EQ* M: 07551-993619 E: mandyyoung612@outlook.com

YOUNG, Margaret Dorothy. See COOLING, Margaret Dorothy
YOUNG, Mrs Margaret Elizabeth. b 66. Open Univ BSc 00. All SS Cen for Miss & Min 07. **d** 10 **p** 11. C Wythenshawe *Man* 10–13; TV 13–15; V Easingwold w Raskelf *York* from 15; C Alne from 17; C Brafferton w Pilmoor, Myton-on-Swale etc from 17; C Coxwold and Husthwaite from 17; C Crayke w Brandsby and Yearsley from 17; C Skelton w Shipton and Newton on Ouse from 17; C Strensall from 17; C Forest of Galtres from 17. *The Vicarage, Church Hill, Easingwold, York YO61 3JT* T: (01347) 821394 E: margareteyoung@btopenworld.com

YOUNG, Mark Gilbert Campbell. b 60. Mert Coll Ox BA 88. Wycliffe Hall Ox 86. **d** 91 **p** 92. C Holborn St Geo w H Trin and St Bart *Lon* 91–95; C St Pancras w St Jas and Ch Ch 95–99; V W Hampstead Trin 99–06; P-in-c W Hampstead St Cuth 01–06; Hon C Smithfield St Bart Gt 09–15; Hon C St Bart Less 12–15; C St Andr Holborn from 15. *22A Huddleston Road, London N7 0AG* T: (020) 7583 7394 E: marky@standrewholborn.org.uk

YOUNG, Martin John. b 72. Univ Coll Lon BSc 93. Oak Hill Th Coll BA 01. **d** 01 **p** 02. C Heigham H Trin *Nor* 01–05; P-in-c Nor St Andr 05–16; V from 16; Chapl Nor Univ of the Arts from 16. *24 Carnoustie, Norwich NR4 6AY* T: (01603) 498821 E: martin@standrewsnorwich.org

YOUNG, Mrs Maureen. b 47. SEITE 02. **d** 04 **p** 12. NSM Roughey *Chich* 04–11; NSM Rusper w Colgate 11–13; NSM Bishop's Lydeard w Lydeard St Lawrence etc *B & W* from 13. *The Rectory, Lydeard St Lawrence, Taunton TA4 3SF* T: (01984) 667472 E: reverendmaureenyoung@gmail.com

YOUNG, Maurice. See YOUNG, William Maurice
YOUNG, Michael. b 47. STETS 08. **d** 11 **p** 12. NSM Wareham *Sarum* from 11. *5 Tuckers Mill Close, Wareham BH20 5BS* T: (01929) 552582 E: myng220@btopenworld.com

YOUNG, Philip Anderson. b 53. St Jo Coll Dur BA 75 Fitzw Coll Cam BA 78 MA 89. Ridley Hall Cam 75. **d** 78 **p** 79. C Surbiton St Andr and St Mark *S'wark* 78–80; NSM

Aylsham *Nor* 04–05; C Bressingham w N and S Lopham and Fersfield 05–07; C Roydon St Remigius 05–07; V Heigham St Thos 07–12; Dioc Environmental Officer 12–14; PtO from 14; *St E* from 16. *Cambridge House, South Hill, Felixstowe IP11 2AA* T: (01394) 809069 M: 07527-574982 E: philipyoung@btinternet.com

YOUNG, Phillip Andrew. b 82. Melbourne Univ BCom 04 Down Coll Cam BTh 19. Ridley Hall Cam 17. **d** 19. C Wootton *St Alb* from 19. *14 Folkes Road, Wootton, Bedford MK43 9BX* M: 07981-976179 E: payoung1982@gmail.com

YOUNG, Rachel Elizabeth. b 61. Man Univ MusB 82 Leeds Univ MA 09 Lon Inst of Educn PGCE 84. NOC 06. **d** 09 **p** 10. NSM Beverley Minster *York* 09–15; R Walkington, Bishop Burton, Rowley etc 15–17; Succ S'wark Cathl from 17. *Southwark Cathedral Office, Montague Chambers, Montague Close, London SE1 9DA* E: rachel.e.young@tesco.net

YOUNG, Richard Christian. b 65. Southn Univ LLB 87 Solicitor 91. St Jo Coll Nottm 02. **d** 04 **p** 05. C Alperton *Lon* 04–07; V Yiewsley from 07; AD Hillingdon from 18. *St Matthew's Vicarage, 93 High Street, Yiewsley, West Drayton UB7 7QH* T: (01895) 442093 M: 07886-782473 E: richard.youngsofyiewsley@gmail.com *or* vicar@stmatthewsyiewsley.org.uk

YOUNG, Richard Michael. b 63. **d** 96 **p** 97. NSM Brunswick *Man* 96–16; Lic Preacher 16–18; R Birch w Fallowfield from 18. *2 Birch Grove, Rusholme, Manchester M14 5JY* T: 0161-225 0884 M: 07778-817784 E: richardyoung09@gmail.com

YOUNG, Robert William. b 47. MRTPI 73. Cranmer Hall Dur 10. **d** 11 **p** 12. NSM Owlerton *Sheff* 11–12; P-in-c Wadsley 12–14; PtO 14–15; NSM Owlerton 15–17; NSM Tadley w Pamber Heath and Silchester *Win* from 17. *St Mary's House, 10 Romans Field, Silchester, Reading RG7 2QH* T: 0118-970 2353 E: robwyoung101@gmail.com

YOUNG, Ruth. See YOUNG, Vivienne Ruth
YOUNG, Simon Robert. b 72. Trevelyan Coll Dur BSc 94 Fitzw Coll Cam BA 98. Westcott Ho Cam BA 98 CTM 99. **d** 99 **p** 15. C Plaistow St Mary *Roch* 99–00; C Kingsnorth and Shadoxhurst *Cant* 14–15; C Faversham 15–17; C The Brents and Davington 15–17; C Faversham 17–19; C Milton Regis w Murston, Bapchild and Tonge from 19; Chapl Bapchild and Tonge C of E Primary Sch from 19. *The Vicarage, School Lane, Bapchild, Sittingbourne ME9 9NL* E: simonryoung@aol.com

YOUNG, Mrs Sophie Alexandra. b 81. St Aid Coll Dur BA 03 Univ of W of England MA 12. Ridley Hall Cam 17. **d** 19. C Cambridge St Paul *Ely* from 19. *Bridge End Cottage, Sawston Road, Stapleford, Cambridge CB22 5DY* M: 07759-558011 E: sophie_young10@yahoo.co.uk

YOUNG, Stephen Edward. b 52. K Coll Lon BD 73 AKC 73 Open Univ PhD 04 Ch Ch Coll Cant CertEd 74. **d** 75 **p** 76. C Walton St Mary *Liv* 75–79; C Pimlico St Gabr *Lon* 83–85; Chapl Whitelands Coll of HE *S'wark* 85–88; Asst Chapl St Paul's Sch Barnes 88–91; Chapl 91–02; Chapl Dulwich Coll 02–11; Hon C Pimlico St Mary Bourne Street *Lon* 94–11; C Wilton Place St Paul 11–13; P-in-c Deal St Andr *Cant* 13–17; rtd 17; PtO *Cant* from 18; P in O 91–11; Dep P in O from 11. *28 St George's Road, Deal CT14 6BA* M: 07828-033399 E: stephenedwardyoung52@gmail.com

YOUNG, Steven Peter. b 81. Lon Inst BA 02 Leeds Univ BA 07 MA 08. Coll of Resurr Mirfield 05. **d** 08 **p** 09. C W Hendon St Jo *Lon* 08–11; P-in-c Mill Hill St Mich 11–17; V from 17; C Mill Hill Jo Keble Ch 11–15; Chapl N Lon Hospice from 16. *St Michael's Vicarage, 9 Flower Lane, London NW7 2JA* T: (020) 8343 8841 *or* 8959 1857 M: 07590-636912 E: steven_young81@hotmail.com *or* priest@smmh.org.uk

YOUNG, Stuart Kincaid. b 59. **d** 95 **p** 96. C Letchworth St Paul w Willian *St Alb* 95–00; V Pucklechurch and Abson *Bris* from 00. *The Vicarage, Westerleigh Road, Pucklechurch, Bristol BS16 9RD* T: 0117-937 2260 E: skypilot1@go-plus.net

YOUNG (née SMITH), Mrs Vivienne Ruth. b 57. St Jo Coll Dur BA 79. NOC 95. **d** 00 **p** 01. C Heckmondwike *Wakef* 00–03; TV Dewsbury 03–06; Community Miss Adv Livability from 06; PtO *Dur* from 15. *107 Lake Avenue, South Shields NE34 7AY* M: 07443-547906 E: ruth61157@gmail.com

YOUNG, William Maurice. b 32. St Jo Coll Nottm 80. **d** 81 **p** 82. C Harlescott *Lich* 81–84; V Hadley 84–94; rtd 94; PtO *Heref* from 94. *Old Chapel School, Newport Street, Clun, Craven Arms SY7 8JZ* T: (01588) 640846

YOUNGER, Gillian Margaret. b 55. SNWTP 16. **d** 17 **p** 18. NSM Daresbury *Ches* from 17. *56 Norleane Crescent, Runcorn WA7 5ER* E: curate@daresburycofe.com

YOUNGS, Denise. b 48. WMMTC. **d** 09 **p** 10. NSM Lich St Mich w St Mary and Wall from 09; PtO *Ely* from 19. *25 Rowan Close, Haddenham, Ely CB6 3QF*

YOUNGS-DUNNETT, Elizabeth Nigella. b 43. **d** 05 **p** 06. OLM Alde River *St E* 05–13; NSM 13; rtd 13; PtO *St E* from 14. *The*

Cottage, Ship Corner, Blaxhall, Woodbridge IP12 2DY T: (01728) 688660 E: nigellaatblaxhall@btinternet.com

YOUNGSON, David Thoms. b 38. Cuddesdon Coll 71. **d** 73 **p** 74. C Norton St Mary *Dur* 73–76; C Hartlepool St Paul 76–79; P-in-c Stockton St Jo CD 79–84; V Stockton St Jo 84–86; V Owton Manor 86–90; rtd 90; PtO *Dur* from 90. *35 Buxton Gardens, Billingham TS22 5AJ* E: david.youngson@ntlworld.com

YULE, John David. b 49. G&C Coll Cam BA 70 MA 74 PhD 76. Westcott Ho Cam 79. **d** 81 **p** 82. C Cherry Hinton St Andr *Ely* 81–84; C Almondbury w Farnley Tyas *Wakef* 84–87; V Swavesey *Ely* 87–95; V Fen Drayton w Conington 87–95; R Fen Drayton w Conington and Lolworth etc 95–15; rtd 15; PtO *Ely* from 16. *46 Fen Road, Cambridge CB4 1TX* T: (01223) 561070 E: john.yule@gmail.com

Z

ZAIR, Canon Richard George. b 52. Newc Univ BSc 74. Trin Coll Bris 75 Cranmer Hall Dur 79. **d** 80 **p** 81. C Bishopsworth *Bris* 80–83; C New Malden and Coombe *S'wark* 83–91; Dir of Evang CPAS 91–99; Regional Dir 99–09; P-in-c Marcham w Garford *Ox* 09–14; P-in-c Shippon 11–14; AD Abingdon 13–16; V Marcham w Garford and Shippon from 14; Hon Can Ch Ch from 16. *41 North Street, Marcham, Abingdon OX13 6NQ* T: (01865) 391319 M: 07411-234710 E: r_zair@yahoo.co.uk

ZAMMIT, Mark Timothy Paul. b 60. Ox Brookes Univ MA 07. Aston Tr Scheme 90 Sarum & Wells Th Coll 94. **d** 94 **p** 95. C Bitterne Park *Win* 94–98; TV Shaston *Sarum* 98–03; TR 03–08; RD Blackmore Vale 01–08; Chapl Port Regis Sch 99–08; P-in-c Durrington *Sarum* 08–11; C Avon Valley 08–11; TR Avon River 11–15; RD Stonehenge 10–15; TR Almondbury w Farnley Tyas *Leeds* from 15; AD Almondbury from 16; Jt AD Kirkburton from 18. *The Rectory, 2 Westgate, Almondbury, Huddersfield HD5 8XE* T: (01484) 302914 M: 07733-077957 E: zammitparish@yahoo.co.uk

ZAPHIRIOU, Paul Victor. b 49. Hamilton Coll (NY) BA 73 INSEAD MBA 74. Wycliffe Hall Ox 00. **d** 02 **p** 03. C Holborn St Geo w H Trin and St Bart *Lon* 02–06; V Hope Ch Islington from 06; Bp's Adv for Corporate Soc Resp from 05. *108 Liverpool Road, London N1 0RE* T: (020) 7226 0854 M: 07899-796409 E: paul@hoptchurchislington.org

ZAREK, Jennifer Hilary. b 51. Newnham Coll Cam BA 72 MA 76 Southn Univ MSc 73 PhD 78 Ox Univ BTh 98 Garnett Coll Lon CertEd 83. St Steph Ho Ox 95. **d** 97 **p** 98. C Caterham *S'wark* 97–00; V Hutton Cranswick w Skerne, Watton and Beswick *York* 00–05; rtd 05; PtO *York* from 06. *Horsedale House, Silver Street, Huggate, York YO42 1YB* T: (01377) 288525 E: jzarek@btinternet.com

ZASS-OGILVIE, Ian David. b 38. ARICS 72 FRICS 80 AKC 65. K Coll Lon 62 St Boniface Warminster 65. **d** 66 **p** 67. C Washington *Dur* 66–70; Bp's Soc and Ind Adv for N Dur 70–73; Hon C Newc St Jo 73–75; V Tynemouth St Jo 75–78; Hon C St Marylebone St Mary *Lon* 78–81; V Bromley St Jo *Roch* 81–84; R Keith *Mor* 84–88; R Huntly 84–88; R Aberchirder 84–88; R Edin St Pet 88–00; Dir Churches' Regional Commn in the NE Newc and *Dur* 00–05; PtO *Ab* from 05; *Dur* from 05; Research Fell and Tutor St Chad's Coll from 06. *12 St Giles Close, Gilesgate, Durham DH1 1XH* T: 0191-383 0887 E: ianzassogilvie@tiscali.co.uk

ZIHNI, Andrew Stephen. b 77. Mert Coll Ox BA 99 MA 06. St Steph Ho Ox BA 01. **d** 02 **p** 03. C Goldthorpe w Hickleton *Sheff* 02–06; Min Can Windsor 06–14; Chapl St Geo Sch Windsor 06–14; Asst Dioc Dir of Ords *S'wark* from 14; Asst Dir of Voc from 18; PV Westmr Abbey from 18. *Trinity House, 4 Chapel Court, London SE1 1HW* T: (020) 7939 9400 F: 7939 9468 E: andrew.zihni@southwark.anglican.org

ZIMMERMAN, Douglas Lee. b 69. Rhodes Coll Memphis BA 91. Virginia Th Sem MDiv 98. **d** 98. USA 98–14; TR Aylesbury *Ox* from 14. *St Mary's Vicarage, Parsons Fee, Aylesbury HP20 2QZ*

ZIPFEL, Marilyn Ellen. b 48. Open Univ BA 94 MA 98 Goldsmiths' Coll Lon TCert 70 LTCL 97. Dioc OLM tr scheme 01. **d** 03 **p** 04. OLM Oulton Broad *Nor* 03–18; Chapl Jas Paget Healthcare NHS Trust 11–15; PtO *Nor* from 18. *Rozel, Station Road, Lowestoft NR32 4QF* M: 07818-093133 E: marilynzipfel@outlook.com

ZIPPERLEN, John Marcus. b 71. **d** 13 **p** 14. C Haverfordwest St D 13–16; P-in-c Llangwm w Freystrop and Johnston from 16. *The Rectory, The Kilns, Llangwm, Haverfordwest SA62 4NG* T: (01437) 899548 E: marcus@zipperlen.com

ZUCCA, Peter Rennie. b 43. **d** 96 **p** 97. NSM Spotland *Man* 96–99; NSM Bamford 99–05; NSM Rochdale St Geo w St Alb 99–05; NSM Oakenrod and Bamford 05–13; rtd 13. *19 Judith Street, Rochdale OL12 7HS* T: (01706) 675830 *or* 346003 E: peterrucca@hotmail.com

ZUCKERT, Calum Bruno. b 91. SS Hild & Bede Coll Dur BA 12 K Coll Cam BA 16 MMus 17. St Mellitus Coll 18. **d** 19. NSM Winchmore Hill St Paul *Lon* from 19. *St Paul's Lodge, 58 Church Hill, London N21 1JA* T: (020) 3659 4543 M: 07986-301650 E: curate@spwh.org

ZWALF, Canon Willem Anthony Louis (Wim). b 46. AKC 68. **d** 71 **p** 72. C Fulham St Etheldreda w St Clem *Lon* 71–74; Chapl City Univ 74–78; R Coalbrookdale, Iron-Bridge and Lt Wenlock *Heref* 78–90; V Wisbech SS Pet and Paul *Ely* 90–08; P-in-c Wisbech St Aug 03–04; C 04–08; RD Wisbech Lynn Marshland 02–08; Hon Can Ely Cathl 07–08; rtd 09; PtO *Pet* 12–18. *1 The Dell, Oakham LE15 6JG* T: (01572) 770082 E: wimzwalf@aol.com

ZYCH, Berkeley James. b 83. SS Coll Cam BA 05 MSci 05 MA 08 PhD 09 Fitzw Coll Cam BA 12. Westcott Ho Cam 10. **d** 13 **p** 14. C Grimshoe *Ely* 13–16; Prec and Min Can St Alb 16–19; V Harpenden St Jo from 19. *The Vicarage, 5 St John's Road, Harpenden AL5 1DJ* T: (01582) 469343 E: b.j.zych.01@cantab.net *or* vicar@stjohnsharpenden.org.uk

DEACONESSES

COOPER, Janet Pamela. b 46. Glos Coll of Educn TCert 67 Ox Poly CETD 79. Trin Coll Bris. **dss** 83. Patchway *Bris* 83–88; PtO *Glouc* 90–96. *Ephraim Cottage, Kington Mead Farm, Kington Road, Thornbury, Bristol BS35 1PQ* T: (01454) 415280 E: jan.ephraim@talktalk.net

GOUGH, Janet Ainley. b 46. SRN 67 RSCN 68 SCM 70. Dalton Ho Bris 70. **dss** 76. Leic H Apostles 73–80; Kansas City All SS USA 80–81; PtO *Leic* 81–96; from 05. *1 Clarefield Road, Leicester LE3 6FB* E: jangough@hotmail.com

HINDE, Miss Mavis Mary. b 29. Lightfoot Ho Dur. **dss** 65. Hitchin St Mary *St Alb* 65–68; Ensbury *Sarum* 69–70; Portsea St Alb *Portsm* 70–76; Houghton Regis *St Alb* 77–85; Eaton Socon 85–94; rtd 94; PtO *Ely* 94–15. *8 Burnt Close, Eynesbury, St Neots PE19 2LZ* T: (01480) 218219 E: mmavishinde@gmail.com

HORNBY-NORTHCOTE, Mrs Vivien Sheena. b 42. Birkbeck Coll Lon BA 91 Warwick Univ MA 96. Gilmore Course 74. **dss** 79. Mitcham St Olave *S'wark* 79–81; St Dunstan in the West *Lon* 82–86; St Marg Lothbury and St Steph Coleman Street etc 86; rtd 98. *37 Carlton Mews, Wells BA5 1SG*

PIERSON, Mrs Valerie Susan. b 44. TCert 65. Trin Coll Bris 76. **dss** 79. Fulham St Matt *Lon* from 79. *48 Peterborough Road, London SW6 3EB* T: (020) 7731 6544 F: 7731 1858 E: sue@lancepierson.org

SCHMIEGELOW, Patricia Kate Lunn. b 37. St Mich Ho Ox IDC 65. **dss** 86. The Hague *Eur* 86–89; PtO *Glouc* from 90; Gen Sec ICS 92–97; rtd 97. *61 Coln St Aldwyns, Cirencester GL7 5AJ* T/F: (01285) 750218

DIOCESAN, AREA, SUFFRAGAN AND ASSISTANT BISHOPS AND PROVINCIAL EPISCOPAL VISITORS IN ENGLAND, WALES, SCOTLAND AND IRELAND

BATH AND WELLS
Bishop of Bath and Wells — P HANCOCK
Honorary Assistant Bishops — B C CASTLE
B ROGERSON
G H CASSIDY
J F PERRY
J M GOODALL
M A HILL
P E BARBER
R D M MARTIN
R F SAINSBURY
W M D PERSSON
Suffragan Bishop of Taunton — R E WORSLEY

BIRMINGHAM
Bishop of Birmingham — D A URQUHART
Honorary Assistant Bishops — I K MOTTAHEDEH
J M GOODALL
M SANTER
M W SINCLAIR
R C H THOMAS
Suffragan Bishop of Aston — A E HOLLINGHURST

BLACKBURN
Bishop of Blackburn — J T HENDERSON
Honorary Assistant Bishops — C G ASHTON
LORD HOPE OF THORNES
J W GODDARD
Suffragan Bishop of Burnley — P J NORTH
Suffragan Bishop of Lancaster — J L C DUFF

BRISTOL
Bishop of Bristol — V F FAULL
Honorary Assistant Bishops — G H CASSIDY
J M GOODALL
P J FIRTH
P ST G VAUGHAN
R C H THOMAS
Suffragan Bishop of Swindon — L S RAYFIELD

CANTERBURY
Archbishop of Canterbury, Primate of All England and Metropolitan — J P WELBY
Honorary Assistant Bishops — A M A TURNBULL
J R A LLEWELLIN
Suffragan Bishop of Dover — R J HUDSON-WILKIN
Suffragan Bishop of Ebbsfleet (Provincial Episcopal Visitor) — J M GOODALL
Suffragan Bishop of Maidstone — R C H THOMAS
Suffragan Bishop of Richborough (Provincial Episcopal Visitor) — N BANKS

CARLISLE
Bishop of Carlisle — J W S NEWCOME
Honorary Assistant Bishops — A A K GRAHAM
G H THOMPSON
G L HACKER
I M GRIGGS
J H RICHARDSON
N S MCCULLOCH
P S RAMSDEN
R C A HENDERSON
R M HARDY
Suffragan Bishop of Penrith — E G INESON

CHELMSFORD
Bishop of Chelmsford — S G COTTRELL
Honorary Assistant Bishops — M T S MWAMBA
R C H THOMAS
Area Bishop of Barking — P HILL
Area Bishop of Bradwell — J PERUMBALATH
Area Bishop of Colchester — R A B MORRIS

CHESTER
Bishop of Chester — *Vacant*
Honorary Assistant Bishops — A L WINSTANLEY
C F BAZLEY
G G DOW
G H WEBSTER
J D HAYDEN
R C H THOMAS
Suffragan Bishop of Birkenhead — G K SINCLAIR
Suffragan Bishop of Stockport — *Vacant*

CHICHESTER
Bishop of Chichester — M C WARNER
Honorary Assistant Bishops — A D CHESTERS
C H MORGAN
D P WILCOX
K L BARHAM
L A GREEN
M E ADIE
M E MARSHALL
M L LANGRISH
N S READE
Area Bishop of Horsham — *Vacant*
Area Bishop of Lewes — R C JACKSON

COVENTRY
Bishop of Coventry — C J COCKSWORTH
Honorary Assistant Bishops — D R J EVANS
J M GOODALL
Suffragan Bishop of Warwick — J R A STROYAN

DERBY
Bishop of Derby — E J H LANE
Honorary Assistant Bishops — J NICHOLLS
T W ELLIS
Suffragan Bishop of Repton — J E MCFARLANE

DURHAM
Bishop of Durham — P R BUTLER
Honorary Assistant Bishops — D S STANCLIFFE
G H WEBSTER
J L PRITCHARD
Suffragan Bishop of Jarrow — S E CLARK

ELY
Bishop of Ely — S D CONWAY
Honorary Assistant Bishops — G P KNOWLES
M A SEELEY
N BANKS
P S DAWES
R C H THOMAS
R D WILLIAMS OF OYSTERMOUTH
S BARRINGTON-WARD
Suffragan Bishop of Huntingdon — D WINTER

EXETER
Bishop of Exeter — R R ATWELL
Honorary Assistant Bishops — A M SHAW
G W E C ASHBY
J M GOODALL
M J RYLANDS
R C H THOMAS
R S HAWKINS
Suffragan Bishop of Crediton — J A SEARLE
Suffragan Bishop of Plymouth — N H P MCKINNEL

GLOUCESTER

Bishop of Gloucester	R TREWEEK
Honorary Assistant Bishops	A M PRIDDIS
	C J HILL
	D W M JENNINGS
	J R G NEALE
	P B HARRIS
	P J FIRTH
	R J S EVENS
Suffragan Bishop of Tewkesbury	R W SPRINGETT

GUILDFORD

Bishop of Guildford	A J WATSON
Honorary Assistant Bishops	C W HERBERT
	M A BAUGHEN
	N BANKS
Suffragan Bishop of Dorking	J C B WELLS

HEREFORD

Bishop of Hereford	R M C FRITH
Honorary Assistant Bishops	D THOMSON
	M G BOURKE
	M R WESTALL
	R M E PATERSON
Suffragan Bishop of Ludlow	A J MAGOWAN

LEEDS

Bishop of Leeds	N BAINES
Honorary Assistant Bishops	C O BUCHANAN
	C P EDMONDSON
	D J L HAWKINS
	D M HOPE OF THORNES
	G C HANDFORD
	G H WEBSTER
	J L PRITCHARD
	J R FLACK
	T F BUTLER
Suffragan Bishop of Bradford	T M HOWARTH
Suffragan Bishop of Huddersfield	J R GIBBS
Suffragan Bishop of Kirkstall	P J SLATER
Suffragan Bishop of Ripon	H M HARTLEY
Suffragan Bishop of Wakefield	A W ROBINSON

LEICESTER

Bishop of Leicester	M J SNOW
Honorary Assistant Bishops	P J FOX
	C J BOYLE
	R J FREEMAN
Suffragan Bishop of Loughborough	G E FRANCIS-DEHQANI

LICHFIELD

Bishop of Lichfield	M G IPGRAVE
Honorary Assistant Bishops	D E BENTLEY
	I K MOTTAHEDEH
	J M GOODALL
	R C H THOMAS
Area Bishop of Shrewsbury	S R BULLOCK
Area Bishop of Stafford	G P ANNAS
Area Bishop of Wolverhampton	C M GREGORY

LINCOLN

Bishop of Lincoln	C LOWSON
Honorary Assistant Bishops	A R GILLION
	D D J ROSSDALE
	D TUSTIN
	N BANKS
	N PEYTON
	T W ELLIS
Suffragan Bishop of Grantham	N A CHAMBERLAIN
Suffragan Bishop of Grimsby	D E COURT

LIVERPOOL

Bishop of Liverpool	P BAYES
Honorary Assistant Bishops	C G ASHTON
	G H WEBSTER
	J W GODDARD
	S R LOWE
Suffragan Bishop of Warrington	B A MASON

LONDON

Bishop of London	DAME SARAH MULLALLY
Honorary Assistant Bishops	A D POGGO
	E HOLLAND
	J A IDOWU-FEARON
	J A K MILLAR
	J M WHARTON
	M J COLCLOUGH
	P W WHEATLEY
	R C H THOMAS
	R D HARRIES OF PENTREGARTH
	R S LADDS
	S G PLATTEN
	T M THORNTON
	W P K MAKHULU
Area Bishop of Edmonton	R J WICKHAM
Area Bishop of Kensington	G S TOMLIN
Area Bishop of Stepney	J W GRENFELL
Area Bishop of Willesden	P A BROADBENT
Suffragan Bishop of Fulham	J M R BAKER
Suffragan Bishop of Islington	R C THORPE

MANCHESTER

Bishop of Manchester	D S WALKER
Honorary Assistant Bishops	F P SARGEANT
	G G DOW
	G H WEBSTER
	J NICHOLLS
	J W GODDARD
	R C H THOMAS
	R W N HOARE
Suffragan Bishop of Bolton	M D ASHCROFT
Suffragan Bishop of Hulme	*Vacant*
Suffragan Bishop of Middleton	M DAVIES

NEWCASTLE

Bishop of Newcastle	C E HARDMAN
Honorary Assistant Bishops	J H RICHARDSON
	J R PACKER
	S G PLATTEN
Suffragan Bishop of Berwick	M S A TANNER

NORWICH

Bishop of Norwich	G B USHER
Honorary Assistant Bishops	A C FOOTTIT
	D K GILLETT
	D LEAKE
	L G URWIN
	M J MENIN
	N BANKS
	P J FOX
	R C H THOMAS
	R GARRARD
Suffragan Bishop of Lynn	C J MEYRICK
Suffragan Bishop of Thetford	A P WINTON

OXFORD

Bishop of Oxford	S J L CROFT
Honorary Assistant Bishops	D W M JENNINGS
	H I J SOUTHERN
	H W SCRIVEN
	J M GOODALL
	J N JOHNSON
	J S WENT
	K A ARNOLD
	R C H THOMAS
	T WILLMOTT
	W J D DOWN
Area Bishop of Buckingham	A T L WILSON
Area Bishop of Dorchester	C W FLETCHER
Area Bishop of Reading	O J GRAHAM

PETERBOROUGH

Bishop of Peterborough	D S ALLISTER
Honorary Assistant Bishop	E F CONDRY
Suffragan Bishop of Brixworth	J E HOLBROOK

PORTSMOUTH
Bishop of Portsmouth	C R J FOSTER
Honorary Assistant Bishops	I J BRACKLEY
	J W HIND
	K M GORHAM
	T J BAVIN
	T M THORNTON

ROCHESTER
Bishop of Rochester	J H LANGSTAFF
Honorary Assistant Bishops	A M A TURNBULL
	G A CRAY
	K S E OKEKE
	L A GREEN
	M J NAZIR-ALI
	R C H THOMAS
Suffragan Bishop of Tonbridge	S D BURTON-JONES

SALISBURY
Bishop of Salisbury	N R HOLTAM
Honorary Assistant Bishops	D M HALLATT
	J D G KIRKHAM
Area Bishop of Ramsbury	A P RUMSEY
Area Bishop of Sherborne	K M GORHAM

SHEFFIELD
Bishop of Sheffield	P J WILCOX
Honorary Assistant Bishops	D C HAWTIN
	G H WEBSTER
	R C H THOMAS
	R F BLACKBURN
	T W ELLIS
Suffragan Bishop of Doncaster	*Vacant*

SODOR AND MAN
Bishop of Sodor and Man	P A EAGLES
Assistant Bishop of Sodor and Man	P J FERGUSON

SOUTHWARK
Bishop of Southwark	C T J CHESSUN
Honorary Assistant Bishops	A D POGGO
	D J ATKINSON
	G R KINGS
	J A IDOWU-FEARON
	J M WHARTON
	M D DOE
	P S M SELBY
	P S OMUKU
	P W WHEATLEY
	R C H THOMAS
	R C THORPE
	R D HARRIES OF PENTREGARTH
	S G PLATTEN
	T M THORNTON
Area Bishop of Croydon	J D CLARK
Area Bishop of Kingston-upon-Thames	R I CHEETHAM
Area Bishop of Woolwich	W K DORGU

SOUTHWELL AND NOTTINGHAM
Bishop of Southwell and Nottingham	P G WILLIAMS
Honorary Assistant Bishops	J T FINNEY
	M W JARRETT
	R J MILNER
Suffragan Bishop of Sherwood	A PORTER

ST ALBANS
Bishop of St Albans	A G C SMITH
Honorary Assistant Bishops	N BANKS
	R J N SMITH
	S S VENNER
Suffragan Bishop of Bedford	R W B ATKINSON
Suffragan Bishop of Hertford	N M R BEASLEY

ST EDMUNDSBURY AND IPSWICH
Bishop of St Edmundsbury and Ipswich	M A SEELEY
Honorary Assistant Bishops	G D J WALSH
	G H REID
	G P KNOWLES
	J A K MILLAR
	J WAINE
	N BANKS
Suffragan Bishop of Dunwich	M R HARRISON

TRURO
Bishop of Truro	P I MOUNSTEPHEN
Honorary Assistant Bishop	J M GOODALL
Suffragan Bishop of St Germans	*Vacant*

WINCHESTER
Bishop of Winchester	T J DAKIN
Honorary Assistant Bishops	C W HERBERT
	H W SCRIVEN
	J DENNIS
	T J BAVIN
Suffragan Bishop of Basingstoke	D G WILLIAMS
Suffragan Bishop of Southampton	D M SELLIN

WORCESTER
Bishop of Worcester	J G INGE
Honorary Assistant Bishops	A M PRIDDIS
	C J MAYFIELD
	J M GOODALL
	M SANTER
	M W HOOPER
	R M E PATERSON
Suffragan Bishop of Dudley	*Vacant*

YORK
Archbishop of York, Primate of England and Metropolitan	J T M SENTAMU
Honorary Assistant Bishops	D C JAMES
	D J SMITH
	D J WILBOURNE
	F WHITE
	G A CRAY
	G BATES
	J H FROST
	J S JONES
	M W WALLACE
	N BAINES
Suffragan Bishop of Beverley (Provincial Episcopal Visitor)	G H WEBSTER
Suffragan Bishop of Hull	A M WHITE
Suffragan Bishop of Selby	J B THOMSON
Suffragan Bishop of Whitby	P J FERGUSON

GIBRALTAR IN EUROPE
Bishop of Gibraltar in Europe	R N INNES
Honorary Assistant Bishops	A M A TURNBULL
	D J SMITH
	D S STANCLIFFE
	E HOLLAND
	F L SOARES
	F-R MULLER
	J M WHARTON
	J R FLACK
	M J COLCLOUGH
	M L LANGRISH
	N S READE
	P B HARRIS
	P W WHALON
	R GARRARD
	LORD CHARTRES
	S S VENNER
Suffragan Bishop in Europe	D HAMID

CHURCH IN WALES

BANGOR	
Bishop of Bangor	A T G JOHN
LLANDAFF	
Assistant Bishop	E W M WALKER
Bishop of Llandaff	J OSBORNE
MONMOUTH	
Bishop of Monmouth	C E VANN

ST ASAPH	
Bishop of St Asaph	G K CAMERON
ST DAVIDS	
Bishop of St Davids	J S PENBERTHY
SWANSEA AND BRECON	
Bishop of Swansea and Brecon	J D E DAVIES
Honorary Assistant Bishops	E W M WALKER
	J K OLIVER

SCOTTISH EPISCOPAL CHURCH

ABERDEEN AND ORKNEY	
Bishop of Aberdeen and Orkney	A C DYER
ARGYLL AND THE ISLES	
Bishop of Argyll and The Isles	K PEARSON
BRECHIN	
Bishop of Brechin	A C SWIFT
EDINBURGH	
Bishop of Edinburgh	J A ARMES

GLASGOW AND GALLOWAY	
Bishop of Glasgow and Galloway	*Vacant*
Honorary Assistant Bishop	J M TAYLOR
MORAY, ROSS AND CAITHNESS	
Bishop of Moray, Ross and Caithness	M J STRANGE
ST ANDREWS, DUNKELD AND DUNBLANE	
Bishop of St Andrews, Dunkeld and Dunblane	I J PATON

CHURCH OF IRELAND

ARMAGH	
Archbishop of Armagh and Primate of All Ireland and Metropolitan	R L CLARKE
CASHEL AND OSSORY	
Bishop of Cashel and Ossory	M A J BURROWS
CLOGHER	
Bishop of Clogher	F J MCDOWELL
CONNOR	
Bishop of Connor	A F ABERNETHY
CORK, CLOYNE AND ROSS	
Bishop of Cork, Cloyne and Ross	W P COLTON
DERRY AND RAPHOE	
Bishop of Derry and Raphoe	*Vacant*
DOWN AND DROMORE	
Bishop of Down and Dromore	*Vacant*

DUBLIN AND GLENDALOUGH	
Archbishop of Dublin, Bishop of Glendalough, Primate of Ireland and Metropolitan	M G ST A JACKSON
KILMORE, ELPHIN AND ARDAGH	
Bishop of Kilmore, Elphin and Ardagh	S F GLENFIELD
LIMERICK AND KILLALOE	
Bishop of Limerick and Killaloe	K A KEARON
MEATH AND KILDARE	
Bishop of Meath and Kildare	P L STOREY
TUAM, KILLALA AND ACHONRY	
Bishop of Tuam, Killala and Achonry	P W ROOKE

BISHOPS IN THE HOUSE OF LORDS

The Archbishops of Canterbury and York, and the Bishops of London, Durham and Winchester always have seats in the House of Lords. Twenty-one of the remaining Diocesan Bishops also sit in the Upper House. In general those places are filled on the basis of seniority in office as a Diocesan Bishop, any vacant place being filled by the Diocesan Bishop who has been longest in office without sitting in the House of Lords. However, for a transitional period of ten years from 2015, if there is a female Diocesan Bishop in office when a vacancy arises, she (or the most senior female Diocesan Bishop, if more than one are in office) will take up the place. Translation of a Bishop from one diocesan See to another does not affect his or her right to sit in the House of Lords.

The Bishop of Sodor and Man and the Bishop of Gibraltar in Europe are not eligible to sit in the House of Lords, but the former has a seat in the Upper House of the Tynwald, Isle of Man.

ARCHBISHOPS

	Enthroned	Introduced in the House of Lords
CANTERBURY	2013	2012
YORK	2005	2005

BISHOPS SITTING IN THE HOUSE OF LORDS
(as at 1 December 2019)

	Became Diocesan Bishop	Introduced in the House of Lords
LONDON	2018	2018
DURHAM	2009	2014
WINCHESTER	2011	2012
BIRMINGHAM	2006	2010
WORCESTER	2007	2012
COVENTRY	2008	2012
OXFORD	2009	2013
CARLISLE	2009	2013
ST ALBANS	2009	2013
PETERBOROUGH	2010	2014
PORTSMOUTH	2010	2014
CHELMSFORD	2010	2014
ROCHESTER	2010	2014
ELY	2010	2014
SOUTHWARK	2011	2014
LEEDS	2011	2014
SALISBURY	2011	2014
GLOUCESTER	2015	2015
NEWCASTLE	2015	2015
LINCOLN	2011	2017
CHICHESTER	2012	2018
BRISTOL	2018	2018
DERBY	2019	2019

BISHOPS AWAITING SEATS IN THE HOUSE OF LORDS
(in order of seniority)

	Became Diocesan Bishop
BLACKBURN	2013
MANCHESTER	2013
BATH AND WELLS	2014
EXETER	2014
LIVERPOOL	2014
GUILDFORD	2014
ST EDMUNDSBURY & IPSWICH	2015
SOUTHWELL & NOTTINGHAM	2015
LEICESTER	2016
LICHFIELD	2016
SHEFFIELD	2017
TRURO	2018
NORWICH	2019
CHESTER	*vacant*
HEREFORD	*vacant*

HISTORICAL SUCCESSION OF ARCHBISHOPS AND BISHOPS

In a number of dioceses, especially for the mediaeval period, the dating of some episcopal appointments is not known for certain. For ease of reference, the date of consecration is given when known, or, in the case of more modern appointments, the date of confirmation of election. More information on the dates of individual bishops can be found in the Royal Historical Society's *Handbook of British Chronology*.

ENGLAND

PROVINCE OF CANTERBURY

Canterbury

Description of arms. Azure, an archiepiscopal cross in pale or surmounted by a pall proper charged with four crosses patée fitchée sable.

597	Augustine
604	Laurentius
619	Mellitus
624	Justus
627	Honorius
655	Deusdedit
668	Theodorus
693	Berhtwald
731	Tatwine
735	Nothelm
740	Cuthbert
761	Bregowine
765	Jaenberht
793	Æthelheard
805	Wulfred
832	Feologild
833	Ceolnoth
870	Æthelred
890	Plegmund
914	Æthelhelm
923	Wulfhelm
942	Oda
959	Ælfsige
959	Byrhthelm
960	Dunstan
c.988	Athelgar
990	Sigeric Serio
995	Ælfric
1005	Ælfheah
1013	Lyfing [Ælfstan]
1020	Æthelnoth
1038	Eadsige
1051	Robert of Jumièges
1052	Stigand
1070	Lanfranc
1093	Anselm
1114	Ralph d'Escures
1123	William de Corbeil
1139	Theobald of Bec
1162	Thomas Becket
1174	Richard [of Dover]
1184	Baldwin
1193	Hubert Walter
1207	Stephen Langton

1229	Richard le Grant
1234	Edmund Rich
1245	Boniface of Savoy
1273	Robert Kilwardby
1279	John Pecham
1294	Robert Winchelsey
1313	Walter Reynolds
1328	Simon Mepham
1333	John Stratford
1349	Thomas Bradwardine
1349	Simon Islip
1366	Simon Langham
1368	William Whittlesey
1375	Simon Sudbury
1381	William Courtenay
1396	Thomas Arundel[1]
1398	Roger Walden
1414	Henry Chichele
1443	John Stafford
1452	John Kempe
1454	Thomas Bourgchier
1486	John Morton
1501	Henry Deane
1503	William Warham
1533	Thomas Cranmer
1556	Reginald Pole
1559	Matthew Parker
1576	Edmund Grindal
1583	John Whitgift
1604	Richard Bancroft
1611	George Abbot
1633	William Laud
1660	William Juxon
1663	Gilbert Sheldon
1678	William Sancroft
1691	John Tillotson
1695	Thomas Tenison
1716	William Wake
1737	John Potter
1747	Thomas Herring
1757	Matthew Hutton
1758	Thomas Secker
1768	Frederick Cornwallis
1783	John Moore
1805	Charles Manners Sutton
1828	William Howley
1848	John Bird Sumner
1862	Charles Thomas Longley
1868	Archibald Campbell Tait
1883	Edward White Benson
1896	Frederick Temple
1903	Randall Thomas Davidson
1928	Cosmo Gordon Lang
1942	William Temple
1945	Geoffrey Francis Fisher
1961	Arthur Michael Ramsey
1974	Frederick Donald Coggan
1980	Robert Alexander Kennedy Runcie
1991	George Leonard Carey
2002	Rowan Douglas Williams
2013	Justin Portal Welby

London

Description of arms. Gules, two swords in saltire argent hilts and pommels or.

	Theanus
	Eluanus
	Cadar
	Obinus
	Conanus
	Palladius
	Stephanus
	Iltutus
	Theodwinus
	Theodredus
	Hilarius
314	Restitutus
	Guitelinus
	Fastidius
	Vodinus
	Theonus
c.604	Mellitus
664	Cedd[2]
666	Wini
675	Eorcenwald
693	Waldhere
716	Ingwald
745	Ecgwulf
772	Wigheah
782	Eadbeorht
789	Eadgar
793	Coenwalh
796	Eadbald
798	Heathoberht
803	Osmund
c.811	Æthelnoth
824	Ceolberht
862	Deorwulf
898	Swithwulf
898	Heahstan
900	Wulfsige
c.926	Æthelweard
926	Leofstan
926	Theodred
—	Wulfstan I
953	Brihthelm
959	Dunstan
964	Ælfstan
996	Wulfstan II
1004	Ælfhun
1014	Ælfwig

1035	Ælfweard
1044	Robert of Jumièges
1051	William
1075	Hugh of Orival
1086	Maurice
1108	Richard de Belmeis
1128	Gilbert [the Universal]
1141	Robert de Sigillo
1152	Richard de Belmeis II
1163	Gilbert Foliot
1189	Richard Fitz Neal
1199	William of Ste-Mere-Eglise
1221	Eustace de Fauconberg
1229	Roger Niger
1244	Fulk Basset
1260	Henry Wingham
1263	Henry of Sandwich
1274	John Chishull
1280	Richard Gravesend
1306	Ralph Baldock
1313	Gilbert Segrave
1317	Richard Newport
1319	Stephen Gravesend
1338	Richard Bintworth
1340	Ralph Stratford
1355	Michael Northburgh
1362	Simon Sudbury
1375	William Courtenay
1382	Robert Braybrooke
1404	Roger Walden
1406	Nicholas Bubwith
1407	Richard Clifford
1421	John Kempe
1426	William Gray
1431	Robert Fitz-Hugh
1436	Robert Gilbert
1450	Thomas Kempe
1489	Richard Hill
1496	Thomas Savage
1502	William Warham
1504	William Barons [Barnes]
1506	Richard Fitz-James
1522	Cuthbert Tunstall [Tonstall]
1530	John Stokesley
1540	Edmund Bonner
1550	Nicholas Ridley
1553	Edmund Bonner (restored)
1559	Edmund Grindal
1570	Edwin Sandys
1577	John Aylmer
1595	Richard Fletcher
1597	Richard Bancroft
1604	Richard Vaughan
1607	Thomas Ravis
1610	George Abbot
1611	John King
1621	George Monteigne [Mountain]
1628	William Laud
1633	William Juxon
1660	Gilbert Sheldon
1663	Humfrey Henchman
1676	Henry Compton
1714	John Robinson
1723	Edmund Gibson
1748	Thomas Sherlock
1761	Thomas Hayter
1762	Richard Osbaldeston
1764	Richard Terrick
1778	Robert Lowth
1787	Beilby Porteus
1809	John Randolph
1813	William Howley
1828	Charles James Blomfield
1856	Archibald Campbell Tait
1869	John Jackson
1885	Frederick Temple
1897	Mandell Creighton
1901	Arthur Foley Winnington-Ingram
1939	Geoffrey Francis Fisher
1945	John William Charles Wand

1956	Henry Colville Montgomery Campbell
1961	Robert Wright Stopford
1973	Gerald Alexander Ellison
1981	Graham Douglas Leonard
1991	David Michael Hope
1995	Richard John Carew Chartres
2018	Sarah Elisabeth Mullally

Westminster[1]

1540	Thomas Thirlby

Winchester

Description of arms. Gules, two keys endorsed and conjoined at the bows in bend, the upper or, the lower argent, between which a sword in bend sinister of the third, hilt and pommel gold.

BISHOPS OF THE WEST SAXONS

634	Birinus
650	Ægilberht

BISHOPS OF WINCHESTER

660	Wine
670	Leutherius
676	Haedde
705	Daniel
744	Hunfrith
756	Cyneheard
778	Æthelheard
778	Ecbald
785	Dudd
c.785	Cyneberht
803	Eahlmund
814	Wigthegn
825	Herefrith[2]
838	Eadmund
c.838	Eadhun
839	Helmstan
852	Swithhun
867	Ealhferth
877	Tunberht
879	Denewulf
909	Frithestan
931	Byrnstan
934	Ælfheah I
951	Ælfsige I
960	Brihthelm
963	Æthelwold I
984	Ælfheah II
1006	Cenwulf
1006	Æthelwold II
c.1014	Ælfsige II
1032	Ælfwine
1043	Stigand
	Ælfsige III?
1070	Walkelin
1107	William Giffard
1129	Henry of Blois
1174	Richard of Ilchester (Toclyve)
1189	Godfrey de Lucy
1205	Peter des Roches
1244	Will. de Raleigh
1260	Aymer de Valance [of Lusignan]

1262	John Gervaise
1268	Nicholas of Ely
1282	John of Pontoise
1305	Henry Merewell [or Woodlock]
1316	John Sandale
1320	Rigaud of Assier
1323	John Stratford
1333	Adam Orleton
1346	William Edendon [Edington]
1367	William of Wykeham
1404	Henry Beaufort
1447	William of Waynflete
1487	Peter Courtenay
1493	Thomas Langton
1501	Richard Fox
1529	Thomas Wolsey
1531	Stephen Gardiner (deposed)
1551	John Ponet [Poynet]
1553	Stephen Gardiner (restored)
1556	John White (deposed)
1561	Robert Horne
1580	John Watson
1584	Thomas Cowper [Cooper]
1595	William Wickham [Wykeham]
1596	William Day
1597	Thomas Bilson
1616	James Montague
1619	Lancelot Andrewes
1628	Richard Neile
1632	Walter Curll
1660	Brian Duppa
1662	George Morley
1684	Peter Mews
1707	Jonathan Trelawney
1721	Charles Trimnell
1723	Richard Willis
1734	Benjamin Hoadly
1761	John Thomas
1781	Brownlow North
1820	George Pretyman Tomline
1827	Charles Richard Sumner
1869	Samuel Wilberforce
1873	Edward Harold Browne
1891	Anthony Wilson Thorold
1895	Randall Thomas Davidson
1903	Herbert Edward Ryle
1911	Edward Stuart Talbot
1923	Frank Theodore Woods
1932	Cyril Forster Garbett
1942	Mervyn George Haigh
1952	Alwyn Terrell Petre Williams
1961	Sherard Falkner Allison
1975	John Vernon Taylor
1985	Colin Clement Walter James
1995	Michael Charles Scott-Joynt
2011	Timothy John Dakin

Bath and Wells

Description of arms. Azure, a saltire per saltire quarterly counterchanged or and argent.

BISHOPS OF WELLS

909	Athelm
925	Wulfhelm I
928	Ælfheah
938	Wulfhelm II
956	Byrhthelm

---

[1] Indicates a diocese no longer extant, or united with another diocese.
[2] Never signed without Wigthegn.

974	Cyneweard
979	Sigegar
997	Ælfwine
999	Lyfing
1013	Æthelwine (ejected)
1013	Beorhtwine (deposed)
	Æthelwine (restored)
	Beorhtwine (restored)
1024	Brihtwig [also Merehwit]
1033	Duduc
1061	Gisa
1088	John of Tours [de Villula]

BISHOPS OF BATH

1090	John of Tours [de Villula]
1123	Godfrey
1136	Robert
1174	Reg. Fitz Jocelin
1192	Savaric FitzGeldewin

BATH AND GLASTONBURY

1206	Jocelin of Wells

BATH AND WELLS

1244	Roger of Salisbury
1248	William Bitton I
1265	Walter Giffard
1267	William Bitton II
1275	Robert Burnell
1293	William of March
1302	Walter Hasleshaw
1309	John Droxford
1329	Ralph of Shrewsbury
1364	John Barnet
1367	John Harewell
1386	Walter Skirlaw
1388	Ralph Erghum
1401	Henry Bowet
1407	Nicholas Bubwith
1425	John Stafford
1443	Thomas Beckington
1466	Robert Stillington
1492	Richard Fox
1495	Oliver King
1504	Adriano de Castello [di Corneto]
1518	Thomas Wolsey
1523	John Clerk
1541	William Knight
1548	William Barlow
1554	Gilbert Bourne
1560	Gilbert Berkeley
1584	Thomas Godwin
1593	John Still
1608	James Montague
1616	Arthur Lake
1626	William Laud
1628	Leonard Mawe
1629	Walter Curll
1632	William Piers
1670	Robert Creighton
1673	Peter Mews
1685	Thomas Ken (deposed)
1691	Richard Kidder
1704	George Hooper
1727	John Wynne
1743	Edward Willes
1774	Charles Moss
1802	Richard Beadon
1824	George Henry Law
1845	Richard Bagot
1854	Robert John Eden, Lord Auckland
1869	Arthur Charles Hervey
1894	George Wyndham Kennion
1921	St John Basil Wynne Wilson
1937	Francis Underhill
1943	John William Charles Wand
1946	Harold William Bradfield
1960	Edward Barry Henderson
1975	John Monier Bickersteth
1987	George Leonard Carey
1991	James Lawton Thompson
2002	Peter Bryan Price
2014	Peter Hancock

Birmingham

Description of arms. Per pale indented or and gules, five roundels, two, two, and one, and in chief two crosses patée all counterchanged.

1905	Charles Gore
1911	Henry Russell Wakefield
1924	Ernest William Barnes
1953	John Leonard Wilson
1969	Laurence Ambrose Brown
1978	Hugh William Montefiore
1987	Mark Santer
2002	John Mugabi Sentamu
2006	David Andrew Urquhart

Bristol

Description of arms. Sable, three ducal coronets in pale or.

1542	Paul Bush
1554	John Holyman
1562	Richard Cheyney
1581	John Bullingham (held Gloucester and Bristol 1586–9)
1589	Richard Fletcher
	[See vacant for ten years]
1603	John Thornborough
1617	Nicholas Felton
1619	Rowland Searchfield
1623	Robert Wright
1633	George Coke
1637	Robert Skinner
1642	Thomas Westfield
1644	Thomas Howell
1661	Gilbert Ironside
1672	Guy Carleton
1679	William Gulston
1684	John Lake
1685	Jonathan Trelawney
1689	Gilbert Ironside
1691	John Hall
1710	John Robinson
1714	George Smalridge
1719	Hugh Boulter
1724	William Bradshaw
1733	Charles Cecil
1735	Thomas Secker
1737	Thomas Gooch
1738	Joseph Butler
1750	John Conybeare
1756	John Hume
1758	Philip Yonge
1761	Thomas Newton
1782	Lewis Bagot
1783	Christopher Wilson
1792	Spencer Madan
1794	Henry Reginald Courtenay
1797	Ffolliott Herbert Walker Cornewall

1803	George Pelham
1807	John Luxmoore
1808	William Lort Mansel
1820	John Kaye
1827	Robert Gray
1834	Joseph Allen
[1836	to 1897 united with Gloucester]
1897	George Forrest Browne
1914	George Nickson
1933	Clifford Salisbury Woodward
1946	Frederick Arthur Cockin
1959	Oliver Stratford Tomkins
1976	Ernest John Tinsley
1985	Barry Rogerson
2003	Michael Arthur Hill
2018	Vivenne Frances Faull

Chelmsford

Description of arms. Or, on a saltire gules a pastoral staff of the first and a sword argent, hilt and pommel gold.

1914	John Edwin Watts-Ditchfield
1923	Frederic Sumpter Guy Warman
1929	Henry Albert Wilson
1951	Sherard Falkner Allison
1962	John Gerhard Tiarks
1971	Albert John Trillo
1986	John Waine
1996	John Freeman Perry
2003	John Warren Gladwin
2010	Stephen Geoffrey Cottrell

Chichester

Description of arms. Azure, our blessed Lord in judgement seated in His throne, His dexter hand upraised or, His sinister hand holding an open book proper, and issuant from His mouth a two-edged sword point to the sinister gules.

BISHOPS OF SELSEY

681	Wilfrid
716	Eadberht
731	Eolla
733	Sigga [Sigeferth]
765	Aaluberht
c.765	Oswald [Osa]
780	Gislhere
786	Tota
c.789	Wihthun
c.811	Æthelwulf
824	Cynered
845	Guthheard
900	Wighelm
909	Beornheah

931	Wulfhun
943	Ælfred
955	Daniel
956	Brihthelm
963	Eadhelm
980	Æthelgar
990	Ordbriht
1009	Ælfmaer
1032	Æthelric I
1039	Grimketel
1047	Heca
1058	Æthelric II
1070	Stigand

BISHOPS OF CHICHESTER

1075	Stigand
1088	Godfrey
1091	Ralph Luffa
1125	Seffrid I [d'Escures Pelochin]
1147	Hilary
1174	John Greenford
1180	Seffrid II
1204	Simon FitzRobert
1215	Richard Poore
1218	Ranulf of Wareham
1224	Ralph Nevill
1245	Richard Wich
1254	John Climping
1262	Stephen Bersted [or Pagham]
1288	Gilbert de St Leofard
1305	John Langton
1337	Robert Stratford
1362	William Lenn
1369	William Reade
1386	Thomas Rushock
1390	Richard Mitford
1396	Robert Waldby
1397	Robert Reade
1417	Stephen Patrington
1418	Henry de la Ware
1421	John Kempe
1421	Thomas Polton
1426	John Rickingale
1431	Simon Sydenham
1438	Richard Praty
1446	Adam de Moleyns
1450	Reginald Pecock
1459	John Arundel
1478	Edward Story
1504	Richard Fitz-James
1508	Robert Sherburne
1536	Richard Sampson
1543	George Day (deposed)
1552	John Scory
1553	George Day (restored)
1557	John Christopherson
1559	William Barlow
1570	Richard Curtis
1586	Thomas Bickley
1596	Anthony Watson
1605	Lancelot Andrewes
1609	Samuel Harsnett
1619	George Carleton
1628	Richard Montague
1638	Brian Duppa
1642	Henry King
1670	Peter Gunning
1675	Ralph Brideoake
1679	Guy Carleton
1685	John Lake
1689	Simon Patrick
1691	Robert Grove
1696	John Williams
1709	Thomas Manningham
1722	Thomas Bowers
1724	Edward Waddington
1731	Francis Hare
1740	Matthias Mawson
1754	William Ashburnham
1798	John Buckner
1824	Robert James Carr
1831	Edward Maltby

1836	William Otter
1840	Philip Nicholas Shuttleworth
1842	Ashurst Turner Gilbert
1870	Richard Durnford
1896	Ernest Roland Wilberforce
1908	Charles John Ridgeway
1919	Winfrid Oldfield Burrows
1929	George Kennedy Allen Bell
1958	Roger Plumpton Wilson
1974	Eric Waldram Kemp
2001	John William Hind
2012	Martin Clive Warner

Coventry

Description of arms. Gules, within a bordure argent charged with eight torteaux, a cross potent quadrate of the second.

1918	Huyshe Wolcott Yeatman-Biggs
1922	Charles Lisle Carr
1931	Mervyn George Haigh
1943	Neville Vincent Gorton
1956	Cuthbert Killick Norman Bardsley
1976	John Gibbs
1985	Simon Barrington-Ward
1998	Colin James Bennetts
2008	Christopher John Cocksworth

Derby

Description of arms. Purpure, a cross of St Chad argent beneath three fountains in chief.

1927	Edmund Courtenay Pearce
1936	Alfred Edward John Rawlinson
1959	Geoffrey Francis Allen
1969	Cyril William Johnston Bowles
1988	Peter Spencer Dawes
1995	Jonathan Sansbury Bailey
2005	Alastair Llewellyn John Redfern
2019	Elizabeth Jane Holden Lane

Dorchester[1]

634	Birinus
650	Agilbert
c.660	Ætla
c.888	Ahlheard

Ely

Description of arms. Gules, three ducal coronets or.

1109	Hervey
1133	Nigel
1174	Geoffrey Ridel
1189	William Longchamp
1198	Eustace
1220	John of Fountains
1225	Geoffrey de Burgo
1229	Hugh of Northwold
1255	William of Kilkenny
1258	Hugh of Balsham
1286	John of Kirkby
1290	William of Louth
1299	Ralph Walpole
1303	Robert Orford
1310	John Ketton
1316	John Hotham
1337	Simon Montacute
1345	Thomas de Lisle
1362	Simon Langham
1367	John Barnet
1374	Thomas Arundel
1388	John Fordham
1426	Philip Morgan
1438	Lewis of Luxembourg
1444	Thomas Bourgchier
1454	William Grey
1479	John Morton
1486	John Alcock
1501	Richard Redman
1506	James Stanley
1515	Nicholas West
1534	Thomas Goodrich
1555	Thomas Thirlby
1559	Richard Cox
1600	Martin Heton
1609	Lancelot Andrewes
1619	Nicolas Felton
1628	John Buckeridge
1631	Francis White
1638	Matthew Wren
1667	Benjamin Laney
1675	Peter Gunning
1684	Francis Turner
1691	Simon Patrick
1707	John Moore
1714	William Fleetwood
1723	Thomas Greene
1738	Robert Butts
1748	Thomas Gooch
1754	Matthias Mawson
1771	Edmund Keene
1781	James Yorke
1808	Thomas Dampier
1812	Bowyer Edward Sparke
1836	Joseph Allen
1845	Thomas Turton
1864	Edward Harold Browne
1873	James Russell Woodford
1886	Alwyne Frederick Compton
1905	Frederick Henry Chase
1924	Leonard Jauncey White-Thomson
1934	Bernard Oliver Francis Heywood
1941	Harold Edward Wynn
1957	Noel Baring Hudson
1964	Edward James Keymer Roberts

[1] Originally a West Saxon, after Ahlheard's time a Mercian, bishopric. See transferred to Lincoln 1077.

1977	Peter Knight Walker	1496	Richard Redman	1947	Cecil Douglas Horsley
1990	Stephen Whitefield Sykes	1502	John Arundel	1953	Frederick William Thomas
2000	Anthony John Russell	1505	Hugh Oldham		Craske
2010	Stephen David Conway	1519	John Veysey (resigned)	1960	Stanley Albert Hallam Eley
		1551	Miles Coverdale	1970	John Richard Satterthwaite[2]

Exeter

Description of arms. Gules, a sword erect in pale argent hilt or surmounted by two keys addorsed in saltire gold.

BISHOPS OF CORNWALL

870	Kenstec
893	Asser
931	Conan
950	Æthelge[ard]
c.955	Daniel
963	Wulfsige Comoere
990	Ealdred
1009	Æthelsige
1018	Buruhwold
1027	Lyfing, Bishop of Crediton, Cornwall and Worcester
1046	Leofric, Bishop of Crediton and Cornwall [See transferred to Exeter 1050]

BISHOPS OF CREDITON

909	Eadwulf
934	Æthelgar
953	Ælfwold I
973	Sideman
979	Ælfric
987	Ælfwold II
1008	Ælfwold III
1015	Eadnoth
1027	Lyfing
1046	Leofric[1]

BISHOPS OF EXETER

1050	Leofric
1072	Osbern Fitz-Osbern
1107	Will. Warelwast
1138	Robert Warelwast
1155	Robert II of Chichester
1161	Bartholomew
1186	John the Chanter
1194	Henry Marshall
1214	Simon of Apulia
1224	William Brewer
1245	Richard Blund
1258	Walter Bronescombe
1280	Peter Quinel [Wyvill]
1292	Thomas Bitton
1308	Walter Stapeldon
1327	James Berkeley
1328	John Grandisson
1370	Thomas Brantingham
1395	Edmund Stafford
1419	John Catterick
1420	Edmund Lacy
1458	George Nevill
1465	John Booth
1478	Peter Courtenay
1487	Richard Fox
1493	Oliver King

1553	John Veysey (restored)
1555	James Turberville
1560	William Alley [or Allei]
1571	William Bradbridge
1579	John Woolton
1595	Gervase Babington
1598	William Cotton
1621	Valentine Carey
1627	Joseph Hall
1642	Ralph Brownrigg
1660	John Gauden
1662	Seth Ward
1667	Anthony Sparrow
1676	Thomas Lamplugh
1689	Jonathan Trelawney
1708	Offspring Blackall
1717	Lancelot Blackburn
1724	Stephen Weston
1742	Nicholas Claget
1747	George Lavington
1762	Frederick Keppel
1778	John Ross
1792	William Buller
1797	Henry Reginald Courtenay
1803	John Fisher
1807	George Pelham
1820	William Carey
1830	Christopher Bethell
1831	Henry Phillpotts
1869	Frederick Temple
1885	Edward Henry Bickersteth
1901	Herbert Edward Ryle
1903	Archibald Robertson
1916	Rupert Ernest William Gascoyne Cecil
1936	Charles Edward Curzon
1949	Robert Cecil Mortimer
1973	Eric Arthur John Mercer
1985	Geoffrey Hewlett Thompson
1999	Michael Laurence Langrish
2014	Robert Ronald Atwell

Gibraltar in Europe

Description of arms. Argent, in base rising out of the waves of the sea a rock proper, thereon a lion guardant or supporting a passion cross erect gules, on a chief engrailed of the last a crosier in bend dexter and a key in bend sinister or surmounted by a Maltese cross argent fimbriated gold.

BISHOPS OF GIBRALTAR

1842	George Tomlinson
1863	Walter John Trower
1868	Charles Amyand Harris
1874	Charles Waldegrave Sandford
1904	William Edward Collins
1911	Henry Joseph Corbett Knight
1921	John Harold Greig
1927	Frederick Cyril Nugent Hicks
1933	Harold Jocelyn Buxton

BISHOPS OF GIBRALTAR IN EUROPE

1980	John Richard Satterthwaite
1993	John William Hind
2001	Douglas Geoffrey Rowell
2014	Robert Neil Innes

Gloucester

Description of arms. zure, two keys addorsed in saltire the wards upwards or.

1541	John Wakeman *alias* Wiche
1551	John Hooper
1554	James Brooks
1562	Richard Cheyney[3]
1581	John Bullingham[4]
1598	Godfrey Goldsborough
1605	Thomas Ravis
1607	Henry Parry
1611	Giles Thompson
1612	Miles Smith
1625	Godfrey Goodman
1661	William Nicolson
1672	John Pritchett
1681	Robert Frampton
1691	Edward Fowler
1715	Richard Willis
1721	Joseph Wilcocks
1731	Elias Sydall
1735	Martin Benson
1752	James Johnson
1760	William Warburton
1779	James Yorke
1781	Samuel Hallifax
1789	Richard Beadon
1802	George Isaac Huntingford
1815	Henry Ryder
1824	Christopher Bethell
1830	James Henry Monk
[1836	to 1897, united with Bristol]

BISHOPS OF GLOUCESTER AND BRISTOL

1836	James Henry Monk
1856	Charles Baring
1861	William Thomson
1863	Charles John Ellicott[5]

BISHOPS OF GLOUCESTER

1897	Charles John Ellicott
1905	Edgar Charles Sumner Gibson
1923	Arthur Cayley Headlam
1946	Clifford Salisbury Woodward
1954	Wilfred Marcus Askwith
1962	Basil Tudor Guy
1975	John Yates
1992	Peter John Ball
1993	David Edward Bentley
2004	Michael Francis Perham
2015	Rachel Treweek

---

[1] Removed See from Crediton.
[4] Held Gloucester and Bristol 1581-9.

[2] Bishop of Fulham and Gibraltar from 1970 to 1980.
[5] Gloucester only from 1897.

[3] Also Bishop of Bristol.

Guildford

Description of arms. Gules, two keys conjoined wards outwards in bend, the uppermost or, the other argent, interposed between them in bend sinister a sword of the third, hilt and pommel gold, all within a bordure azure charged with ten wool-packs argent.

1927	John Harold Greig
1934	John Victor Macmillan
1949	Henry Colville Montgomery Campbell
1956	Ivor Stanley Watkins
1961	George Edmund Reindorp
1973	David Alan Brown
1983	Michael Edgar Adie
1994	John Warren Gladwin
2004	Christopher John Hill
2014	Andrew John Watson

Hereford

Description of arms. Gules, three leopards' faces jessant-de-lis reversed or.

676	Putta
688	Tyrhtel
710	Torhthere
c.731	Wahistod
736	Cuthberht
741	Podda
c.758	Acca
c.770	Headda
777	Aldberht
786	Esne
c.788	Ceolmund
c.798	Utel
801	Wulfheard
824	Beonna
c.832	Eadwulf
c.839	Cuthwulf
866	Mucel
c.866	Deorlaf
888	Cynemund
890	EadBar
c.931	Tidhelm
940	Wulfhelm
c.940	Ælfric
971	Æthelwulf
1016	Æthelstan
1056	Leofgar
1056	Ealdred, Bishop of Hereford and Worcester
1060	Walter
1079	Robert Losinga
1096	Gerard

1107	Reinhelm
1115	Geoffrey de Clive
1121	Richard de Capella
1131	Robert de Bethune
1148	Gilbert Foliot
1163	Robert of Melun
1174	Robert Foliot
1186	William de Vere
1200	Giles de Braose
1216	Hugh of Mapenore
1219	Hugh Foliot
1234	Ralph Maidstone
1240	Peter d'Aigueblanche
1269	John Breton
1275	Thomas Cantilupe
1283	Richard Swinfield
1317	Adam Orleton
1327	Thomas Chariton
1344	John Trilleck
1361	Lewis Charleton
1370	William Courtenay
1375	John Gilbert
1389	John Trefnant
1404	Robert Mascall
1417	Edmund Lacy
1420	Thomas Polton
1422	Thomas Spofford
1449	Richard Beauchamp
1451	Reginald Boulers
1453	John Stanbury
1474	Thomas Milling
1492	Edmund Audley
1502	Adriano de Castello [di Corneto]
1504	Richard Mayeu
1516	Charles Booth
1535	Edward Fox
1539	John Skip
1553	John Harley
1554	Robert Parfew or Wharton
1559	John Scory
1586	Herbert Westfaling
1603	Robert Bennett
1617	Francis Godwin
1634	Augustine Lindsell
1635	Matthew Wren
1635	Theophilus Field
1636	George Coke
1661	Nicolas Monk
1662	Herbert Croft
1691	Gilbert Ironside
1701	Humphrey Humphries
1713	Philip Bisse
1721	Benjamin Hoadly
1724	Henry Egerton
1746	James Beauclerk
1787	John Harley
1788	John Butler
1803	Ffolliott Herbert Walker Cornewall
1808	John Luxmoore
1815	George Isaac Huntingford
1832	Edward Grey
1837	Thomas Musgrave
1848	Renn Dickson Hampden
1868	James Atlay
1895	John Percival
1918	Herbert Hensley Henson
1920	Martin Linton Smith
1931	Charles Lisle Carr
1941	Richard Godfrey Parsons
1949	Tom Longworth
1961	Mark Allin Hodson
1974	John Richard Gordon Eastaugh
1990	John Keith Oliver
2004	Anthony Martin Priddis
2014	Richard Michael Cokayne Frith

Leicester

see also under Lincoln

Description of arms. Gules, a pierced cinquefoil ermine, in chief a lion passant guardant grasping in the dexter forepaw a cross crosslet fitchée or.

NEW FOUNDATION

1927	Cyril Charles Bowman Bardsley
1940	Guy Vernon Smith
1953	Ronald Ralph Williams
1979	Cecil Richard Rutt
1991	Thomas Frederick Butler
1999	Timothy John Stevens
2016	Martyn James Snow

Lichfield

Description of arms. Per pale gules and argent, a cross potent quadrate in the centre per pale argent and or between four crosses patée those to the dexter argent and those to the sinister gold.

BISHOPS OF MERCIA

656	Diuma[1]
658	Ceollach
659	Trumhere
662	Jaruman

BISHOPS OF LICHFIELD

669	Chad[2]
672	Winfrith
676	Seaxwulf
691	Headda[3]
731	Aldwine
737	Hwita
757	Hemele
765	Cuthfrith
769	Berhthun
779	Hygeberht[4]
801	Aldwulf
816	Herewine
818	Æthelwald
830	Hunberht
836	Cyneferth
845	Tunberht
869	Eadberht
883	Wulfred
900	Wigmund or Wilferth
915	Ælfwine
941	Wulfgar
949	Cynesige
964	Wynsige

---

[1] Archbishop of the Mercians, the Lindisfari, and the Middle Angles.   [2] Bishop of the Mercians and the Lindisfari.
[3] Bishop of Lichfield and Leicester.   [4] Archbishop of Lichfield after 787.

975   Ælfheah
1004   Godwine
1020   Leofgar
1026   Brihtmaer
1039   Wulfsige
1053   Leofwine
1072   Peter

BISHOPS OF LICHFIELD, CHESTER AND COVENTRY[1]

1075   Peter
1086   Robert de Limesey
1121   Robert Peche
1129   Roger de Clinton
1149   Walter Durdent
1161   Richard Peche
1183   Gerard La Pucelle
1188   Hugh Nonant
1198   Geoffrey Muschamp
1215   William Cornhill
1224   Alex. Stavensby
1240   Hugh Pattishall
1246   Roger Weseham
1258   Roger Longespee
1296   Walter Langton
1322   Roger Northburgh
1360   Robert Stretton
1386   Walter Skirlaw
1386   Richard le Scrope
1398   John Burghill
1415   John Catterick
1420   William Heyworth
1447   William Booth
1452   Nicholas Close
1453   Reginald Boulers
1459   John Hales
1493   William Smith
1496   John Arundel
1503   Geoffrey Blyth
1534   Rowland Lee
1541   [Chester formed as a
         bishopric]
1543   Richard Sampson
1554   Ralph Baynes
1560   Thomas Bentham
1580   William Overton
1609   George Abbot
1610   Richard Neile
1614   John Overall
1619   Thomas Morton
1632   Robert Wright
1644   Accepted Frewen
1661   John Hackett
1671   Thomas Wood
1692   William Lloyd
1699   John Hough
1717   Edward Chandler
1731   Richard Smalbroke
1750   Fred. Cornwallis
1768   John Egerton
1771   Brownlow North
1775   Richard Hurd
1781   James Cornwallis [4th Earl
         Cornwallis]
1824   Henry Ryder
1836   [Coventry transferred to
         Worcester diocese]
1836   Samuel Butler
1840   James Bowstead
1843   John Lonsdale
1868   George Augustus Selwyn
1878   William Dalrymple Maclagan
1891   Augustus Legge
1913   John Augustine Kempthorne
1937   Edward Sydney Woods
1953   Arthur Stretton Reeve
1975   Kenneth John Fraser Skelton

1984   Keith Norman Sutton
2003   Jonathan Michael Gledhill
2016   Michael Geoffrey Ipgrave

Lincoln

Description of arms. Gules, two lions passant guardant or, on a chief azure, the Virgin ducally crowned sitting on a throne issuant from the chief, on her dexter arm the infant Jesus, and in her sinister hand a sceptre all gold.

BISHOPS OF LINDSEY

634   Birinus
650   Agilbert
660   Aetlai
678   Eadhaed
680   Æthelwine
693   (?)Edgar
731   (?)Cyneberht
733   Alwig
750   Aldwulf
767   Ceolwulf
796   Eadwulf
839   Beorhtred
869   Burgheard
933   Ælfred
953   Leofwine
996   Sigefrith

BISHOPS OF LEICESTER

664   Wilfrid, translated from York
679   Cuthwine
691   Headda[2] (founder of Lichfield
         Cathedral 705–37)
727   Aldwine
737   Torhthelm
764   Eadberht
785   Unwona
803   Wernberht
816   Raethhun
840   Ealdred
844   Ceolred
874   [See of Leicester removed to
         Dorchester]

BISHOPS OF DORCHESTER

(after   it became a Mercian See)
c.888   Ahlheard
900   Wigmund or Wilferth
909   Cenwulf
925   Wynsige
c.951   Osketel
953   Leofwine
975   Ælfnoth
979   Æscwig
1002   Ælfheln
1006   Eadnoth I
1016   Æthelric
1034   Eadnoth II
1049   Ulf
1053   Wulfwig
1067   Remigius

BISHOPS OF LINCOLN

1072   Remigius
1094   Robert Bloett
1123   Alexander
1148   Robert de Chesney
1183   Walter de Coutances
1186   Hugh of Avalon
1203   William of Blois
1209   Hugh of Wells
1235   Robert Grosseteste
1254   Henry Lexington [Sutton]
1258   Richard Gravesend
1280   Oliver Sutton [Lexington]
1300   John Dalderby
1320   Henry Burghersh
1342   Thomas Bek
1347   John Gynewell
1363   John Bokyngham
         [Buckingham]
1398   Henry Beaufort
1405   Philip Repingdon
1420   Richard Fleming
1431   William Gray
1436   William Alnwick
1450   Marmaduke Lumley
1452   John Chedworth
1472   Thomas Rotherham [Scott]
1480   John Russell
1495   William Smith
1514   Thomas Wolsey
1514   William Atwater
1521   John Longland
1547   Henry Holbeach [Rands]
1552   John Taylor
1554   John White
1557   Thomas Watson
1560   Nicholas Bullingham
1571   Thomas Cooper
1584   William Wickham
1595   William Chaderton
1608   William Barlow
1614   Richard Neile
1617   George Monteigne [Mountain]
1621   John Williams
1642   Thomas Winniffe
1660   Robt. Sanderson
1663   Benjamin Laney
1667   William Fuller
1675   Thomas Barlow
1692   Thomas Tenison
1695   James Gardiner
1705   William Wake
1716   Edmund Gibson
1723   Richard Reynolds
1744   John Thomas
1761   John Green
1779   Thomas Thurlow
1787   George Pretyman [Pretyman
         Tomline after June 1803]
1820   George Pelham
1827   John Kaye
1853   John Jackson
1869   Christopher Wordsworth
1885   Edward King
1910   Edward Lee Hicks
1920   William Shuckburgh Swayne
1933   Frederick Cyril Nugent Hicks
1942   Henry Aylmer Skelton
1946   Leslie Owen
1947   Maurice Henry Harland
1956   Kenneth Riches
1975   Simon Wilton Phipps
1987   Robert Maynard Hardy
2001   John Charles Saxbee
2011   Christopher Lowson

---

[1] 1102 Robert de Limesey, Bishop of Lichfield, moved the See to Coventry. Succeeding bishops are usually termed *of Coventry* until 1228. Then *Coventry and Lichfield* was the habitual title until the Reformation. *Chester* was used by some 12th-century bishops, and popularly afterwards. After the Reformation *Lichfield and Coventry* was used until 1846.
[2] Bishop of Leicester and Lichfield.

Norwich

Description of arms. Azure, three labelled mitres or.

BISHOPS OF DUNWICH

631	Felix
648	Thomas
c.653	Berhtgils [Boniface]
c.670	Bisi
c.673	Æcce
693	Alric (?)
716	Eardred
731	Aldbeorht I
747	Æscwulf
747	Eardwulf
775	Cuthwine
775	Aldbeorht II
781	Ecglaf
781	Heardred
793	Ælfhun
798	Tidferth
824	Waermund[1]
825	Wilred
836	Husa
870	Æthelwold

BISHOPS OF ELMHAM

673	Beaduwine
706	Nothberht
c.731	Heathulac
736	Æthelfrith
758	Eanfrith
c.781	Æthelwulf
c.785	Alhheard
814	Sibba
824	Hunferth
824	Hunbeorht
836	Cunda[2]
c.933	Ælfred[3]
c.945	Æthelweald
956	Eadwulf
970	Ælfric I
974	Theodred I
982	Theodred II
997	Æthelstan
1001	Ælfgar
1021	Ælfwine
1038	Ælfric II
1039	Ælfric III
1043	Stigand[4]
1043	Grimketel[5]
1044	Stigand (restored)
1047	Æthelmaer

BISHOPS OF THETFORD

1070	Herfast
1086	William de Beaufai
1091	Herbert Losinga

BISHOPS OF NORWICH

1091	Herbert Losinga
1121	Everard of Montgomery
1146	William de Turbe
1175	John of Oxford
1200	John de Gray
1222	Pandulf Masca

1226	Thomas Blundeville
1239	William Raleigh
1245	Walter Suffield or Calthorp
1258	Simon Walton
1266	Roger Skerning
1278	William Middleton
1289	Ralph Walpole
1299	John Salmon
1325	[Robert de Baldock]
1325	William Ayermine
1337	Anthony Bek
1344	William of Norwich [Bateman]
1356	Thomas Percy
1370	Henry Spencer [Dispenser]
1407	Alexander Tottington
1413	Richard Courtenay
1416	John Wakeryng
1426	William Ainwick
1436	Thomas Brown
1446	Walter Lyhert [le Hart]
1472	James Goldwell
1499	Thomas Jane
1501	Richard Nykke
1536	William Reppes [Rugge]
1550	Thomas Thirlby
1554	John Hopton
1560	John Parkhurst
1575	Edmund Freke
1585	Edmund Scambler
1595	William Redman
1603	John Jegon
1618	John Overall
1619	Samuel Harsnett
1629	Francis White
1632	Richard Corbet
1635	Matthew Wren
1638	Richard Montagu
1641	Joseph Hall
1661	Edward Reynolds
1676	Antony Sparrow
1685	William Lloyd
1691	John Moore
1708	Charles Trimnell
1721	Thomas Green
1723	John Leng
1727	William Baker
1733	Robert Butts
1738	Thomas Gooch
1748	Samuel Lisle
1749	Thomas Hayter
1761	Philip Yonge
1783	Lewis Bagot
1790	George Horne
1792	Charles Manners Sutton
1805	Henry Bathurst
1837	Edward Stanley
1849	Samuel Hinds
1857	John Thomas Pelham
1893	John Sheepshanks
1910	Bertram Pollock
1942	Percy Mark Herbert
1959	William Launcelot Scott Fleming
1971	Maurice Arthur Ponsonby Wood
1985	Peter John Nott
1999	Graham Richard James
2019	Graham Barham Usher

Oxford

Description of arms. Sable, a fess argent, in chief three demi-ladies couped at the waist heads affrontée proper crowned or arrayed and veiled of the second, in base an ox of the last, horned and hoofed gold, passing a ford barry wavy of six azure and argent.

1542	Robert King[6]
1558	[Thomas Goldwell]
1567	Hugh Curen [Curwen]
1589	John Underhill
1604	John Bridges
1619	John Howson
1628	Richard Corbet
1632	John Bancroft
1641	Robert Skinner
1663	William Paul
1665	Walter Blandford
1671	Nathaniel Crewe [Lord Crewe]
1674	Henry Compton
1676	John Fell
1686	Samuel Parker
1688	Timothy Hall
1690	John Hough
1699	William Talbot
1715	John Potter
1737	Thomas Secker
1758	John Hume
1766	Robert Lowth
1777	John Butler
1788	Edward Smallwell
1799	John Randolph
1807	Charles Moss
1812	William Jackson
1816	Edward Legge
1827	Charles Lloyd
1829	Richard Bagot
1845	Samuel Wilberforce
1870	John Fielder Mackarness
1889	William Stubbs
1901	Francis Paget
1911	Charles Gore
1919	Hubert Murray Burge
1925	Thomas Banks Strong
1937	Kenneth Escott Kirk
1955	Harry James Carpenter
1971	Kenneth John Woollcombe
1978	Patrick Campbell Rodger
1987	Richard Douglas Harries
2007	John Lawrence Pritchard
2016	Steven John Lindsey Croft

---

[1] Bishop of Dunwich or Elmham. [2] Bishop of Elmham or Dunwich. [3] Bishop of Elmham or Lindsey.
[4] Deposed before consecration. [5] Bishop of Selsey and Elmham.
[6] Bishop Rheon. *in partibus*. Of Oseney 1542-5. See transferred to Oxford 1545.

Peterborough

Description of arms. Gules, two keys in saltire the wards upwards between four cross crosslets fitchée or.

1541	John Chamber
1557	David Pole
1561	Edmund Scambler
1585	Richard Howland
1601	Thomas Dove
1630	William Piers
1633	Augustine Lindsell
1634	Francis Dee
1639	John Towers
1660	Benjamin Laney
1663	Joseph Henshaw
1679	William Lloyd
1685	Thomas White
1691	Richard Cumberland
1718	White Kennett
1729	Robert Clavering
1747	John Thomas
1757	Richard Terrick
1764	Robert Lambe
1769	John Hinchliffe
1794	Spencer Madan
1813	John Parsons
1819	Herbert Marsh
1839	George Davys
1864	Francis Jeune
1868	William Connor Magee
1891	Mandell Creighton
1897	Edward Carr Glyn
1916	Frank Theodore Woods
1924	Cyril Charles Bowman Bardsley
1927	Claude Martin Blagden
1949	Spencer Stottisbury Gwatkin Leeson
1956	Robert Wright Stopford
1961	Cyril Eastaugh
1972	Douglas Russell Feaver
1984	William John Westwood
1996	Ian Patrick Martyn Cundy
2010	Donald Spargo Allister

Portsmouth

Description of arms. Per fess or and gules, in chief upon waves of the sea proper a lymphad sable, and in base two keys conjoined wards outwards in bend, the uppermost or, the other argent, interposed between them in bend sinister a sword also argent, hilt and pommel gold.

1927	Ernest Neville Lovett
1936	Frank Partridge
1942	William Louis Anderson
1949	William Launcelot Scott Fleming

1960	John Henry Lawrence Phillips
1975	Archibald Ronald McDonald Gordon
1985	Timothy John Bavin
1995	Kenneth William Stevenson
2010	Christopher Richard James Foster

Rochester

Description of arms. Argent, on a saltire gules an escallop or.

604	Justus
624	Romanus
633	Paulinus
644	Ithamar
664	Damianus
669	Putta
676	Cwichelm
678	Gebmund
716	Tobias
727	Aldwulf
741	Dunn
747	Eardwulf
772	Diora
785	Waermund I
805	Beornmod
844	Tatnoth
868	Badenoth
868	Waermund II
868	Cuthwulf
880	Swithwulf
900	Ceolmund
c.926	Cyneferth
c.934	Burhric
949	Beorhtsige
955	[Daniel?] Rochester or Selsey
964	Ælfstan
995	Godwine I
1046	Godwine II
1058	Siward
1076	Arnost
1077	Gundulf
1108	Ralph d'Escures
1115	Ernulf
1125	John
1137	John II
1142	Ascelin
1148	Walter
1182	Waleran
1185	Gilbert Glanvill
1215	Benedict of Sausetun [Sawston]
1227	Henry Sandford
1238	Richard Wendene
1251	Lawrence of St Martin
1274	Walter Merton
1278	John Bradfield
1283	Thomas Ingoldsthorpe
1292	Thomas of Wouldham
1319	Hamo Hethe
1353	John Sheppey
1362	William of Whittlesey
1364	Thomas Trilleck
1373	Thomas Brinton
1389	William Bottlesham [Bottisham]
1400	John Bottlesham
1404	Richard Young
1419	John Kempe
1422	John Langdon
1435	Thomas Brouns
1437	William Wells

1444	John Low
1468	Thomas Rotherham [otherwise Scott]
1472	John Alcock
1476	John Russell
1480	Edmund Audley
1493	Thomas Savage
1497	Richard Fitz-James
1504	John Fisher
1535	John Hilsey [Hildesleigh]
1540	Nicolas Heath
1544	Henry Holbeach
1547	Nicholas Ridley
1550	John Ponet [Poynet]
1551	John Scory
1554	Maurice Griffith
1560	Edmund Gheast [Guest]
1572	Edmund Freke
1576	John Piers
1578	John Young
1605	William Barlow
1608	Richard Neile
1611	John Buckeridge
1628	Walter Curil
1630	John Bowle
1638	John Warner
1666	John Dolben
1683	Francis Turner
1684	Thomas Sprat
1713	Francis Atterbury
1723	Samuel Bradford
1731	Joseph Wilcocks
1756	Zachary Pearce
1774	John Thomas
1793	Samuel Horsley
1802	Thomas Dampier
1809	Walker King
1827	Hugh Percy
1827	George Murray
1860	Joseph Cotton Wigram
1867	Thomas Legh Claughton
1877	Anthony Wilson Thorold
1891	Randall Thomas Davidson
1895	Edward Stuart Talbot
1905	John Reginald Harmer
1930	Martin Linton Smith
1940	Christopher Maude Chavasse
1961	Richard David Say
1988	Anthony Michael Arnold Turnbull
1994	Michael James Nazir-Ali
2010	James Henry Langstaff

St Albans

Description of arms. Azure, a saltire or, overall a sword erect in pale proper, hilt and pommel gold, in chief a celestial crown of the same.

1877	Thomas Legh Claughton
1890	John Wogan Festing
1903	Edgar Jacob
1920	Michael Bolton Furse
1944	Philip Henry Loyd
1950	Edward Michael Gresford Jones
1970	Robert Alexander Kennedy Runcie
1980	John Bernard Taylor
1995	Christopher William Herbert
2009	Alan Gregory Clayton Smith

St Edmundsbury and Ipswich

Description of arms. Per pale gules and azure, between three ducal coronets a demi-lion passant guardant conjoined to the demi-hulk of an ancient ship or.

1914	Henry Bernard Hodgson
1921	Albert Augustus David
1923	Walter Godfrey Whittingham
1940	Richard Brook
1954	Arthur Harold Morris
1966	Leslie Wilfrid Brown
1978	John Waine
1986	John Dennis
1997	John Hubert Richard Lewis
2007	William Nigel Stock
2015	Martin Alan Seeley

Salisbury

Description of arms. Azure, our Lady crowned, holding in her dexter arm the infant Jesus, and in her sinister arm a sceptre all or, round both the heads circles of glory gold.

BISHOPS OF SHERBORNE

705	Ealdhelm
709	Forthhere
736	Hereweald
774	Æthelmod
793	Denefrith
801	Wigberht
825	Ealhstan
868	Heahmund
877	Æthelheah
889	Wulfsige I
900	Asser
c.909	Æthelweard
c.909	Waerstan
925	Æthelbald
925	Sigehelm
934	Ælfred
943	Wulfsige II
958	Ælfwold I
979	Æthelsige I
992	Wulfsige III
1002	Æthelric
1012	Æthelsige II
1017	Brihtwine I
1017	Ælfmaer
1023	Brihtwine II
1045	Ælfwold II
1058	Hereman, Bishop of Ramsbury

BISHOPS OF RAMSBURY

909	Æthelstan
927	Oda
949	Ælfric I
951	Osulf
970	Ælfstan
981	Wulfgar
986	Sigeric
993	Ælfric II
1005	Brihtwold
1045	Hereman[1]

BISHOPS OF SALISBURY

1078	Osmund Osmer
1107	Roger
1142	Jocelin de Bohun
1189	Hubert Walter
1194	Herbert Poore
1217	Richard Poore
1229	Robert Bingham
1247	William of York
1257	Giles of Bridport
1263	Walter de la Wyle
1274	Robert Wickhampton
1284	Walter Scammel
1287	Henry Brandeston
1289	William de la Corner
1292	Nicholas Longespee
1297	Simon of Ghent
1315	Roger de Mortival
1330	Robert Wyville
1375	Ralph Erghum
1388	John Waltham
1395	Richard Mitford
1407	Nicholas Bubwith
1407	Robert Hallum
1417	John Chaundler
1427	Robert Nevill
1438	William Aiscough
1450	Richard Beauchamp
1482	Lionel Woodville
1485	Thomas Langton
1494	John Blythe
1500	Henry Deane
1502	Edmund Audley
1525	Lorenzo Campeggio
1535	Nicholas Shaxton
1539	John Salcot [Capon]
1560	John Jewell
1571	Edmund Gheast [Guest]
1577	John Piers
1591	John Coldwell
1598	Henry Cotton
1615	Robert Abbot
1618	Martin Fotherby
1620	Robert Townson [Toulson]
1621	John Davenant
1641	Brian Duppa
1660	Humfrey Henchman
1663	John Earle
1665	Alexander Hyde
1667	Seth Ward
1689	Gilbert Burnet
1715	William Talbot
1721	Richard Wilis
1723	Benjamin Hoadly
1734	Thomas Sherlock
1748	John Gilbert
1757	John Thomas
1761	Robert Hay Drummond
1761	John Thomas
1766	John Hume
1782	Shute Barrington
1791	John Douglas
1807	John Fisher
1825	Thomas Burgess
1837	Edward Denison
1854	Walter Kerr Hamilton
1869	George Moberly
1885	John Wordsworth

1911	Frederic Edward Ridgeway
1921	St Clair George Alfred Donaldson
1936	Ernest Neville Lovett
1946	Geoffrey Charles Lester Lunt
1949	William Louis Anderson
1963	Joseph Edward Fison
1973	George Edmund Reindorp
1982	John Austin Baker
1993	David Staffurth Stancliffe
2011	Nicholas Roderick Holtam

Southwark

Description of arms. Argent, eleven fusils in cross conjoined, seven in pale fesswise, four in fess palewise, in the dexter chief a mitre all gules.

1905	Edward Stuart Talbot
1911	Hubert Murray Burge
1919	Cyril Forster Garbett
1932	Richard Godfrey Parsons
1942	Bertram Fitzgerald Simpson
1959	Arthur Mervyn Stockwood
1980	Ronald Oliver Bowlby
1991	Robert Kerr Williamson
1998	Thomas Frederick Butler
2011	Christopher Thomas James Chessun

Truro

Description of arms. Argent, on a saltire gules a sword and key or and in base a fleur-de-lis sable all within a bordure of the last charged with fifteen besants.

1877	Edward White Benson
1883	George Howard Wilkinson
1891	John Gott
1906	Charles William Stubbs
1912	Winfrid Oldfield Burrows
1919	Frederic Sumpter Guy Warman
1923	Walter Howard Frere
1935	Joseph Wellington Hunkin
1951	Edmund Robert Morgan
1960	John Maurice Key
1973	Graham Douglas Leonard
1981	Peter Mumford
1990	Michael Thomas Ball
1997	William Ind
2008	Timothy Martin Thornton
2018	Philip Ian Mounstephen

[1] Ramsbury was added to Sherbourne in 1058 when Hereman became Bishop of Sherbourne. The See was moved to Salisbury in 1078.

Worcester

Description of arms. Argent, ten torteaux, four, three, two, and one.

680	Bosel
691	Oftfor
693	Ecgwine
718	Wilfrid I
745	Milred
775	Waermund
777	Tilhere
781	Heathured
798	Deneberht
822	Heahberht
845	Alhhun
873	Waerferth
915	Æthelhun
922	Wilferth II
929	Cenwald
957	Dunstan
961	Oswald
992	Ealdwulf
1002	Wulfstan I
1016	Leofsige
1027	Lyfing
1033	Brihtheah
1040	Æltric Puttoc, Bishop of York and Worcester
1041	Lyfing (restored)
1046	Ealdred Bishop of Hereford and Worcester 1056–60
1062	Wulfstan II
1096	Samson
1115	Theulf
1125	Simon

1151	John of Pagham
1158	Aldred
1164	Roger of Gloucester
1180	Baldwin
1186	William of Northolt
1191	Robert Fitz Ralph
1193	Henry de Sully
1196	John of Coutances
1200	Mauger
1214	Walter de Gray
1216	Silvester of Evesham
1218	William of Blois
1237	Walter Cantilupe
1266	Nicolas of Ely
1268	Godfrey Giffard
1302	William Gainsborough
1308	Walter Reynolds
1313	Walter Maidstone
1317	Thomas Cobham
1327	Adam Orleton
1334	Simon Montacute
1337	Thomas Hempnall
1339	Wulstan Bransford
1350	John Thoresby
1353	Reginald Brian
1362	John Barnet
1364	William of Whittlesey
1369	William Lenn
1375	Henry Wakefield
1396	Robert Tideman of Winchcomb
1401	Richard Clifford
1407	Thomas Peverel
1419	Philip Morgan
1426	Thomas Polton
1435	Thomas Bourgchier
1444	John Carpenter
1476	John Alcock
1487	Robert Morton
1497	Giovanni de' Gigli
1499	Silvestro de' Gigli
1521	Julius de Medici Guilio de Medici (administrator)
1523	Geronimo Ghinucci
1535	Hugh Latimer
1539	John Bell
1544	Nicholas Heath (deposed)

1552	John Hooper
1554	Nicholas Heath (restored)
1555	Richard Pates
1559	Edwin Sandys
1571	Nicholas Bullingham
1577	John Whitgift
1584	Edmund Freke
1593	Richard Fletcher
1596	Thomas Bilson
1597	Gervase Babington
1610	Henry Parry
1617	John Thornborough
1641	John Prideaux
1660	George Morley
1662	John Gauden
1662	John Earle
1663	Robert Skinner
1671	Walter Blandford
1675	James Fleetwood
1683	William Thomas
1689	Edward Stillingfleet
1699	William Lloyd
1717	John Hough
1743	Isaac Maddox
1759	James Johnson
1774	Brownlow North
1781	Richard Hurd
1808	Ffolliott Herbert Walker Cornewall
1831	Robert James Carr
1841	Henry Pepys
1861	Henry Philpott
1891	John James Stewart Perowne
1902	Charles Gore
1905	Huyshe Wolcott Yeatman-Biggs
1919	Ernest Harold Pearce
1931	Arthur William Thomson Perowne
1941	William Wilson Cash
1956	Lewis Mervyn Charles-Edwards
1971	Robert Wylmer Woods
1982	Philip Harold Ernest Goodrich
1997	Peter Stephen Maurice Selby
2007	John Geoffrey Inge

PROVINCE OF YORK

York

Description of arms. Gules, two keys in saltire argent, in chief a regal crown proper.

BISHOPS

314	Eborius
625	Paulinus [Vacancy 633–64]
664	Cedda
664	Wilfrid I
678	Bosa (retired)
686	Bosa (restored)
691	Wilfrith (restored)
706	John of Beverley
718	Wilfrid II

ARCHBISHOPS

734	Egberht
767	Æthelberht
780	Eanbald I
796	Eanbald II
808	Wulfsige
837	Wigmund
854	Wulfhere
900	Æthelbald
c.928	Hrothweard
931	Wulfstan I
956	Osketel
971	Oswald
971	Edwald
992	Ealdwulf[1]
1003	Wulfstan II
1023	Ælfric Puttoc
1041	Æthelric
1051	Cynesige
1061	Ealdred
1070	Thomas I of Bayeux
1100	Gerard
1109	Thomas II
1119	Thurstan
1143	William Fitzherbert
1147	Henry Murdac
1153	William Fitzherbert (restored)
1154	Roger of Pont l'Eveque

1191	Geoffrey Plantagenet
1215	Walter de Gray
1256	Sewal de Bovill
1258	Godfrey Ludham [Kineton]
1266	Walter Giffard
1279	William Wickwane
1286	John Romanus [le Romeyn]
1298	Henry Newark
1300	Thomas Corbridge
1306	William Greenfield
1317	William Melton
1342	William de la Zouche
1352	John Thoresby
1374	Alexander Neville
1388	Thomas Arundel
1396	Robert Waldby
1398	Richard le Scrope
1407	Henry Bowet
1426	John Kempe
1452	William Booth
1464	George Nevill
1476	Lawrence Booth
1480	Thomas Rotherham [Scott]
1501	Thomas Savage
1508	Christopher Bainbridge
1514	Thomas Wolsey
1531	Edward Lee
1545	Robert Holgate

[1] Ealdwulf and Wulfstan II held the Sees of York and Worcester together, Ælfric Puttoc held both 1040-41 and Ealdred 1060-61.

1555 Nicholas Heath
1561 Thomas Young
1570 Edmund Grindal
1577 Edwin Sandys
1589 John Piers
1595 Matthew Hutton
1606 Tobias Matthew
1628 George Monteigne [Mountain]
1629 Samuel Harsnett
1632 Richard Neile
1641 John Williams
1660 Accepted Frewen
1664 Richard Sterne
1683 John Dolben
1688 Thomas Lamplugh
1691 John Sharp
1714 William Dawes
1724 Lancelot Blackburn
1743 Thomas Herring
1747 Matthew Hutton
1757 John Gilben
1761 Roben Hay Drummond
1777 William Markham
1808 Edward Venables Vernon
      Harcourt
1847 Thomas Musgrave
1860 Charles Thomas Longley
1863 William Thomson
1891 William Connor Magee
1891 William Dalrymple Maclagan
1909 Cosmo Gordon Lang
1929 William Temple
1942 Cyril Forster Garbett
1956 Arthur Michael Ramsey
1961 Frederick Donald Coggan
1975 Stuart Yarworth Blanch
1983 John Stapylton Habgood
1995 David Michael Hope
2005 John Tucker Mugabi Sentamu

Durham

Description of arms. Azure, a cross or between four lions rampant argent.

BISHOPS OF LINDISFARNE[1]

635 Aidan
651 Finan

661 Colman
664 Tuda [Complications
      involving Wilfrid and
      Chad]
681 Eata
685 Cuthberht [Vacancy during
      which Wilfrid administered
      the See]
688 Eadberht
698 Eadfenh
731 Æthelweald
740 Cynewulf
781 Higbald
803 Ecgberht
821 Heathwred
830 Ecgred
845 Eanberht
854 Eardwulf

BISHOPS OF HEXHAM

664 Wilfrith
678 Eata
681 Tunberht
684 Cuthbert
685 Eata (restored)
687 John of Beverley
709 Acca
734 Frithoberht
767 Ahimund
781 Tilberht
789 Æthelberht
797 Heardred
800 Eanberht
813 Tidferth

BISHOPS OF CHESTER-LE-STREET[2]

899 Eardwulf
899 Cutheard
915 Tilred
925 Wigred
944 Uhtred
944 Seaxhelm
944 Ealdred
968 Ælfsige
990 Aldhun

BISHOPS OF DURHAM

990 Aldhun d. 1018 [See vacant
      1018–1020]
1020 Edmund
*c.*1040 Eadred
1041 Æthelric
1056 Æthelwine
1071 Walcher
1081 William of Saint Calais
1099 Ralph [Ranulf] Flambard
1133 Geoffrey Rufus
1143 William of Sainte-Barbe
1153 Hugh of le Puiset
1197 Philip of Poitiers

1217 Richard Marsh
1228 Richard Poore
1241 Nicholas Farnham
1249 Walter Kirkham
1261 Robert Stichill
1274 Robert of Holy Island
1284 Anthony Bek
1311 Richard Kellaw
1318 Lewis de Beaumont
1333 Richard of Bury
1345 Thomas Hatfield
1382 John Fordham
1388 Walter Skirlaw
1406 Thomas Langley
1438 Robert Nevill
1457 Lawrence Booth
1476 William Dudley
1485 John Shirwood
1494 Richard Fox
1502 William Senhouse [Sever]
1507 Christopher Bainbridge
1509 Thomas Ruthall
1523 Thomas Wolsey
1530 Cuthbert Tunstall
1561 James Pilkington
1577 Richard Barnes
1589 Matthew Hutton
1595 Tobias Matthew
1606 William James
1617 Richard Neile
1628 George Monteigne [Mountain]
1628 John Howson
1632 Thomas Morton
1660 John Cosin
1674 Nathaniel Crew [Lord Crew]
1721 William Talbot
1730 Edward Chandler
1750 Joseph Butler
1752 Richard Trevor
1771 John Egerton
1787 Thomas Thurlow
1791 Shute Barrington
1826 William Van Mildert
1836 Edward Maltby
1856 Charles Thomas Longley
1860 Henry Montagu Villiers
1861 Charles Baring
1879 Joseph Barber Lightfoot
1890 Brooke Foss Westcott
1901 Handley Carr Glyn Moule
1920 Herbert Hensley Henson
1939 Alwyn Terrell Petre Williams
1952 Arthur Michael Ramsey
1956 Maurice Henry Harland
1966 Ian Thomas Ramsey
1973 John Stapylton Habgood
1984 David Edward Jenkins
1994 Anthony Michael Arnold
      Turnbull
2003 Nicholas Thomas Wright
2011 Justin Portal Welby
2014 Paul Roger Butler

---

[1] See transferred to Chester-le-Street 883.   [2] See transferred to Durham 995.

Blackburn

Description of arms. Per fess gules and or, in chief two keys in saltire wards downwards argent, in base a rose of the first barbed and seeded proper.

1926	Percy Mark Herbert
1942	Wilfred Marcus Askwith
1954	Walter Hubert Baddeley
1960	Charles Robert Claxton
1972	Robert Arnold Schürhoff Martineau
1982	David Stewart Cross
1989	Alan David Chesters
2004	Nicholas Stewart Reade
2013	Julian Tudor Henderson

Bradford

Description of arms. Azure, two keys in saltire or, in chief a woolpack proper corded gold.

1920	Arthur William Thomson Perowne
1931	Alfred Walter Frank Blunt
1956	Frederick Donald Coggan
1961	Clement George St Michael Parker
1972	Ross Sydney Hook
1981	Geoffrey John Paul
1984	Robert Kerr Williamson
1992	David James Smith
2002	David Charles James
2011	Nicholas Baines
2014	Dissolved upon the creation of the new Diocese of Leeds (q.v.)

Carlisle

Description of arms. Argent, on a cross sable a labelled mitre or.

1133	Æthelwulf
1203	Bernard
1219	Hugh of Beaulieu
1224	Walter Mauclerc
1247	Silvester Everdon
1255	Thomas Vipont
1258	Robert de Chause
1280	Ralph Ireton
1292	John of Halton
1325	John Ross
1332	John Kirkby
1353	Gilbert Welton
1363	Thomas Appleby
1396	Robert Reade
1397	Thomas Merks
1400	William Strickland
1420	Roger Whelpdale
1424	William Barrow
1430	Marmaduke Lumley
1450	Nicholas Close
1452	William Percy
1462	John Kingscote
1464	Richard le Scrope
1468	Edward Story
1478	Richard Bell
1496	William Senhouse [Sever]
1504	Roger Layburne
1508	John Penny
1521	John Kite
1537	Robert Aldrich
1556	Owen Oglethorpe
1561	John Best
1570	Richard Barnes
1577	John May
1598	Henry Robinson
1616	Robert Snowden
1621	Richard Milbourne
1624	Richard Senhouse
1626	Francis White
1629	Barnabas Potter
1642	James Ussher
1660	Richard Sterne
1664	Edward Rainbowe
1684	Thomas Smith
1702	William Nicolson
1718	Samuel Bradford
1723	John Waugh
1735	George Fleming
1747	Richard Osbaldeston
1762	Charles Lyttleton
1769	Edmund Law
1787	John Douglas
1791	Edward Venables Vernon [Harcourt]
1808	Samuel Goodenough
1827	Hugh Percy
1856	Henry Montagu Villiers
1860	Samuel Waldegrave
1869	Harvey Goodwin
1892	John Wareing Bardsley
1905	John William Diggle
1920	Henry Herbert Williams
1946	Thomas Bloomer
1966	Sydney Cyril Bulley
1972	Henry David Halsey
1989	Ian Harland
2000	Geoffrey Graham Dow
2009	James William Scobie Newcome

Chester

Description of arms. Gules, three labelled mitres or.

1541	John Bird
1554	George Cotes
1556	Cuthbert Scott
1561	William Downham
1579	William Chaderton
1595	Hugh Bellott
1597	Richard Vaughan
1604	George Lloyd
1616	Thomas Morton
1619	John Bridgeman
1660	Brian Walton
1662	Henry Ferne
1662	George Hall
1668	John Wilkins
1673	John Pearson
1686	Thomas Cartwright
1689	Nicolas Stratford
1708	William Dawes
1714	Francis Gastrell
1726	Samuel Peploe
1752	Edmund Keene
1771	William Markham
1777	Beilby Porteus
1788	William Cleaver
1800	Henry William Majendie
1810	Bowyer Edward Sparke
1812	George Henry Law
1824	Charles James Blomfield
1828	John Bird Sumner
1848	John Graham
1865	William Jacobson
1884	William Stubbs
1889	Francis John Jayne
1919	Henry Luke Paget
1932	Geoffrey Francis Fisher
1939	Douglas Henry Crick
1955	Gerald Alexander Ellison
1974	Hubert Victor Whitsey
1982	Michael Alfred Baughen
1996	Peter Robert Forster

Leeds

Description of arms. Azure a cross formy throughout the limbs in pale taking the form of a Greek rho or, in the first quarter a rose argent barbed and seeded proper.

2014	Nicholas Baines

Liverpool

Description of arms. Argent, an eagle with wings expanded sable, holding in its dexter claw an ancient inkhorn proper, around its head a nimbus or, a chief paly azure and gules, the dexter charged with an open book or, inscribed with the words 'Thy Word is Truth', the sinister charged with a lymphad gold.

1880   John Charles Ryle
1900   Francis James Chavasse
1923   Albert Augustus David
1944   Clifford Arthur Martin
1966   Stuart Yarworth Blanch
1975   David Stuart Sheppard
1998   James Stuart Jones
2014   Paul Bayes

Manchester

Description of arms. Or, on a pale engrailed gules three mitres of the first, on a canton of the second three bendlets enhanced gold.

1848   James Prince Lee
1870   James Fraser
1886   James Moorhouse
1903   Edmund Arbuthnott Knox
1921   William Temple
1929   Frederic Sumpter Guy Warman
1947   William Derrick Lindsay Greer
1970   Patrick Campbell Rodger
1979   Stanley Eric Francis Booth-
        Clibborn
1993   Christopher John Mayfield
2002   Nigel Simeon McCulloch
2013   David Stuart Walker

Newcastle

Description of arms. Gules, a cross between four lions rampant or, on a chief gold three triple-towered castles of the first.

1882   Ernest Roland Wilberforce
1896   Edgar Jacob
1903   Arthur Thomas Lloyd
1907   Norman Dumenil John
        Straton
1915   Herbert Louis Wild
1927   Harold Ernest Bilbrough
1941   Noel Baring Hudson
1957   Hugh Edward Ashdown
1973   Ronald Oliver Bowlby
1981   Andrew Alexander Kenny
        Graham
1997   John Martin Wharton
2015   Christine Elizabeth Hardman

Ripon and Leeds (Ripon until 1999)

Description of arms. Argent, on a saltire gules two keys wards upwards or, on a chief of the second a Holy Lamb proper.

*c.*678   Eadheath
        NEW FOUNDATION
1836   Charles Thomas Longley
1857   Robert Bickersteth
1884   William Boyd Carpenter
1912   Thomas Wortley Drury
1920   Thomas Banks Strong
1926   Edward Arthur Burroughs
1935   Geoffrey Charles Lester Lunt
1946   George Armitage Chase
1959   John Richard Humpidge
        Moorman
1975   Stuart Hetley Price
1977   David Nigel de Lorentz Young
2000   John Richard Packer
2014   Dissolved upon the creation
        of the new Diocese of Leeds
        (q.v.)

Sheffield

Description of arms. Azure, a crosier in pale ensigned by a fleur-de-lis vert, between in fess a key surmounted by a sword in saltire to the dexter, and to the sinister eight arrows interlaced and banded saltirewise, all or.

1914   Leonard Hedley Burrows
1939   Leslie Stannard Hunter
1962   Francis John Taylor
1971   William Gordon Fallows
1980   David Ramsay Lunn
1997   John Nicholls
2009   Steven John Lindsey Croft
2017   Peter Jonathan Wilcox

Sodor and Man[1]

Description of arms. Argent, upon a pedestal between two coronetted pillars the Virgin Mary with arms extended, in her dexter hand a church proper and in base upon an escutcheon, surmounted by a mitre, the arms of Man – viz. gules, three legs in armour conjoined at the thigh and flexed at the knee.

447   Germanus
        Conindrius
        Romulus
        Machutus
        Conanus
        Contentus
        Baldus
        Malchus
        Torkinus
        Brendanus
        [Before 1080 Roolwer]
        William
        Hamond
1113   Wimund
1151   John
1160   Gamaliel
        Ragnald
        Christian of Argyle
        Michael
1203   Nicholas de Meaux
        Nicholas II
1217   Reginald
1226   John
1229   Simon of Argyle
1252   Richard
1275   Mark of Galloway
1305   Alan
1321   Gilbert Maclelan
1329   Bernard de Linton

---

[1] Included in the province of York by Act of Parliament 1542. Prior to Richard Oldham there is some uncertainty as to several names and dates. From 1425 to 1553 there was an English and Scottish succession. It is not easy to say which claimant was Bishop either *de jure* or *de facto.*

1334	Thomas	1892	Norman Dumenil John Straton	1928	Henry Mosley
1348	William Russell	1907	Thomas Wortley Drury	1941	Frank Russell Barry
1387	John Donegan	1912	James Denton Thompson	1964	Gordon David Savage
1387	Michael	1925	Charles Leonard Thornton-Duesbery	1970	John Denis Wakeling
1392	John Sproten			1985	Michael Humphrey Dickens Whinney
1402	Conrad	1928	William Stanton Jones	1988	Patrick Burnet Harris
1402	Theodore Bloc	1943	John Ralph Strickland Taylor	1999	George Henry Cassidy
1429	Richard Messing Andrew	1954	Benjamin Pollard	2009	Paul Roger Butler
1435	John Seyre	1966	George Eric Gordon	2015	Paul Gavin Williams
1455	Thomas Burton	1974	Vernon Sampson Nicholls		
1458	Thomas Kirklam	1983	Arthur Henry Attwell		
1472	Angus	1989	Noël Debroy Jones		
1478	Richard Oldham	2003	Graeme Paul Knowles		
1487	Hugh Blackleach	2008	Robert Mar Erskine Paterson		
1513	Hugh Hesketh	2017	Peter Andrew Eagles		

Wakefield

1523	John Howden
1546	Henry Man
1556	Thomas Stanley
1570	John Salisbury
1576	John Meyrick

Southwell and Nottingham (Southwell until 2005)

1600	George Lloyd
1605	John Philips
1634	William Forster
1635	Richard Parr
1661	Samuel Rutter
1663	Isaac Barrow
1671	Henry Bridgman
1683	John Lake
1685	Baptist Levinz

Description of arms. Or, a fleur-de-lis azure, on a chief of the last three celestial crowns gold.

1698	Thomas Wilson
1755	Mark Hildesley
1773	Richard Richmond
1780	George Mason
1784	Claudius Crigan
1814	George Murray
1828	William Ward
1838	James Bowstead

Description of arms. Sable, three fountains proper, on a chief or a pale azure, charged with a representation of the Virgin Mary seated bearing the Infant Christ or between a stag lodged proper and two staves raguly crossed vert.

1888	William Walsham How
1897	George Rodney Eden
1928	James Buchanan Seaton
1938	Campbell Richard Hone
1946	Henry McGowan
1949	Roger Plumpton Wilson
1958	John Alexander Ramsbotham
1968	Eric Treacy

1840	Henry Pepys
1841	Thomas Vowler Short
1847	Walter Augustus Shirley
1847	Robert John Eden
1854	Horatio Powys
1877	Rowley Hill
1887	John Wareing Bardsley

1884	George Ridding
1904	Edwyn Hoskyns
1926	Bernard Oliver Francis Heywood

1977	Colin Clement Walter James
1985	David Michael Hope
1992	Nigel Simeon McCulloch
2003	Stephen George Platten
2014	Dissolved upon the creation of the new Diocese of Leeds (q.v.)

BISHOPS SUFFRAGAN IN ENGLAND

Alnwick (Newcastle)

never filled

Aston (Birmingham)

1954	Clement George St Michael Parker
1962	David Brownfield Porter
1972	Mark Green
1982	Michael Humphrey Dickens Whinney
1985	Colin Ogilvie Buchanan
1989–92	*no appointment*
1992	John Michael Austin
2005–2008	*no appointment*
2008	Andrew John Watson
2015	Anne Elizabeth Hollinghurst

Aylesbury (Oxford)

never filled

Barking (Chelmsford)

[in St Albans diocese to 1914]
1901	Thomas Stevens
1919	James Theodore Inskip
1948	Hugh Rowlands Gough
1959	William Frank Percival Chadwick
1975	Albert James Adams
1983	James William Roxburgh

1991	Roger Frederick Sainsbury
2002	David John Leader Hawkins
2014	Peter Hill

Barrow-in-Furness (Carlisle)

1889	Henry Ware
1909	Campbell West-Watson
1926	Henry Sidney Pelham
1944	*in abeyance*

Basingstoke (Winchester)

1973	Colin Clement Walter James
1977	Michael Richard John Manktelow
1994	Douglas Geoffrey Rowell
2002	Trevor Willmott
2010	Peter Hancock
2014	David Grant Williams

Bedford (St Albans)

1537	John Hodgkins[1]
1560–1879	*in abeyance*
1879	William Walsham How[2]
1888	Robert Claudius Billing[3]
1898–1935	*in abeyance*
1935	James Lumsden Barkway
1939	Aylmer Skelton
1948	Claude Thomas Thellusson Wood
1953	Angus Campbell MacInnes

1957	Basil Tudor Guy
1963	Albert John Trillo
1968	John Tyrrell Holmes Hare
1977	Andrew Alexander Kenny Graham
1981	David John Farmbrough
1994	John Henry Richardson
2003	Richard Neil Inwood
2012	Richard William Bryant Atkinson

Berwick (Newcastle)

[in Durham diocese to 2016]
1536	Thomas Sparke
1572–2016	*in abeyance*
2016	Mark Simon Austin Tanner

Beverley (York)

1889	Robert Jarratt Crosthwaite
1923–94	*in abeyance*
1994	John Scott Gaisford
2000	Martyn William Jarrett
2013	Glyn Hamilton Webster

Birkenhead (Chester)

1965	Eric Arthur John Mercer
1974	Ronald Brown
1993	Michael Laurence Langrish
2000	David Andrew Urquhart
2007	Gordon Keith Sinclair

---

[1] Appointed for the diocese of London.   [2] Appointed for the diocese of London.
[3] Appointed for the diocese of London, and retained title after resigning his suffragan duties in 1895.

Bishopwearmouth (Durham)

never filled

Bolton (Manchester)

1984	David George Galliford
1991	David Bonser
1999	David Keith Gillett
2008	Christopher Paul Edmondson
2016	Mark David Ashcroft

Boston (Lincoln)

never filled

Bradford (Leeds)

2014	Toby Matthew Howarth

Bradwell (Chelmsford)

1968	William Neville Welch
1973	John Gibbs
1976	Charles Derek Bond
1993	Laurence Alexander Green
2011	John Michael Wraw
2018	John Perumbalath

Bridgewater (Bath and Wells)

never filled

Bristol (Worcester)

1538	Henry Holbeach [Rands]
1542	*became diocesan see*

Brixworth (Peterborough)

1989	Paul Everard Barber
2002	Francis White
2011	John Edward Holbrook

Buckingham (Oxford)

1914	Edward Domett Shaw
1921	Philip Herbert Eliot
1944	Robert Milton Hay
1960	Gordon David Savage
1964	George Christopher Cutts Pepys
1974	Simon Hedley Burrows
1994	Colin James Bennetts
1998	Michael Arthur Hill
2003	Alan Thomas Lawrence Wilson

Burnley (Blackburn)

[in Manchester diocese to 1926]

1901	Edwyn Hoskyns
1905	Alfred Pearson
1909	Henry Henn
1931	Edgar Priestley Swain
1950	Charles Keith Kipling Prosser
1955	George Edward Holderness
1970	Richard Charles Challinor Watson
1988	Ronald James Milner
1994	Martyn William Jarrett
2000	John William Goddard
2015	Philip John North

Cambridge (Ely)

never filled

Chelsea (London)

never filled

Cirencester (Gloucester)

never filled

Colchester (Chelmsford)

[in London diocese to 1845
in Rochester diocese to 1877
in St Albans diocese 1877–1914]

1536	William More
1541–91	*in abeyance*
1592	John Sterne
1608–1882	*in abeyance*
1882	Alfred Blomfield
1894	Henry Frank Johnson
1909	Robert Henry Whitcombe
1922	Thomas Alfred Chapman
1933	Charles Henry Ridsdale
1946	Frederick Dudley Vaughan Narborough
1966	Roderic Norman Coote
1988	Michael Edwin Vickers
1995	Edward Holland
2001	Christopher Heudebourck Morgan
2014	Roger Anthony Brett Morris

Coventry (Worcester)

see also under Lichfield

1891	Henry Bond Bowlby
1894	Edmund Arbuthnott Knox
1903–18	*no appointment*
1918	*became diocesan see*

Crediton (Exeter)

1897	Robert Edward Trefusis
1930	William Frederick Surtees
1954	Wilfred Arthur Edmund Westall
1974	Philip John Pasterfield
1984	Peter Everard Coleman
1996	Richard Stephen Hawkins
2004	Robert John Scott Evans
2012	Nicholas Howard Paul McKinnel
2015	Sarah Elisabeth Mullally
2018	Jacqueline Ann Searle

Croydon (Southwark)

(in Canterbury diocese to 1985)

1904	Henry Horace Pereira
1924–30	*no appointment*
1930	Edward Sydney Woods
1937	William Louis Anderson
1942	Maurice Henry Harland
1947	Cuthbert Killick Norman Bardsley
1957	John Taylor Hughes
1977	Geoffrey Stuart Snell
1985	Wilfred Denniston Wood
2003	Nicholas Baines
2012	Jonathan Dunnett Clark

Derby (Southwell)

1889	Edward Ash Were
1909	Charles Thomas Abraham
1927	*became diocesan see*

Doncaster (Sheffield)

1972	Stuart Hetley Price
1976	David Stewart Cross
1982	William Michael Dermot Persson
1993	Michael Frederick Gear
2000	Cyril Guy Ashton
2012	Peter Burrows

Dorchester (Oxford)

see also under Dorchester (*diocesan see*) *and* Lincoln

1939	Gerald Burton Allen
1952	Kenneth Riches
1957	David Goodwin Loveday
1972	Peter Knight Walker

1979	Conrad John Eustace Meyer
1988	Anthony John Russell
2000	Colin William Fletcher

Dorking (Guildford)

[in Winchester diocese to 1927]

1905	Cecil Henry Boutflower
1909–68	*in abeyance*
1968	Kenneth Dawson Evans
1986	David Peter Wilcox
1996	Ian James Brackley
2016	Joanne Caladine Bailey Wells

Dover (Canterbury)

1537	Richard Yngworth
1545	Richard Thornden
1557–69	*no appointment*
1569	Richard Rogers
1597–1870	*in abeyance*
1870	Edward Parry
1890	George Rodney Eden
1898	William Walsh
1916	Harold Ernest Bilbrough
1927	John Victor Macmillan
1935	Alfred Careywollaston Rose
1957	Lewis Evan Meredith
1964	Anthony Paul Tremlett
1980	Richard Henry McPhail Third
1992	John Richard Allan Llewellin
1999	Stephen Squires Venner
2010	Trevor Willmott
2019	Rose Josephine Hudson-Wilkin

Dudley (Worcester)

1974	Michael Ashley Mann
1977	Anthony Charles Dumper
1993	Rupert William Noel Hoare
2000	David Stuart Walker
2014	Graham Barham Usher

Dunwich (St Edmundsbury and Ipswich)

see also under Norwich

1934	Maxwell Homfray Maxwell-Gumbleton
1945	Clement Mallory Ricketts
1955	Thomas Herbert Cashmore
1967	David Rokeby Maddock
1977	William Johnston
1980	Eric Nash Devenport
1992	Jonathan Sansbury Bailey
1995	Timothy John Stevens
1999	Clive Young
2016	Michael Robert Harrison

Ebbsfleet (Canterbury)

1994	John Richards
1998	Michael Alan Houghton
2000	Andrew Burnham
2011	Jonathan Mark Richard Baker
2013	Jonathan Michael Goodall

Edmonton (London)

1970	Alan Francis Bright Rogers
1975	William John Westwood
1985	Brian John Masters
1999	Peter William Wheatley
2015	Robert James Wickham

Europe (Europe)

1980	Ambrose Walter Marcus Weekes
1986	Edward Holland
1995	Henry William Scriven
2002	David Hamid

Fulham (London)[1]

1926	Basil Staunton Batty
1947	William Marshall Selwyn
1949	George Ernest Ingle
1955	Robert Wright Stopford
1957	Roderic Norman Coote
1966	Alan Francis Bright Rogers
1970	John Richard Satterthwaite[2]
1980–1982	*no appointment*
1982	Brian John Masters
1985	Charles John Klyberg
1996	John Charles Broadhurst
2013	Jonathan Mark Richard Baker

Grantham (Lincoln)

1905	Welbore MacCarthy
1920	John Edward Hine
1930	Ernest Morell Blackie
1935	Arthur Ivan Greaves
1937	Algernon Augustus Markham
1949	Anthony Otter
1965	Ross Sydney Hook
1972	Dennis Gascoyne Hawker
1987	William Ind
1997	Alastair Lewellyn John Redfern
2006	Timothy William Ellis
2015	Nicholas Alan Chamberlain

Grimsby (Lincoln)

1935	Ernest Morell Blackie
1937	Anhur Ivan Greaves
1958	Kenneth Healey
1966	Gerald Fitzmaurice Colin
1979	David Tustin
2000	David Douglas James Rossdale
2014	David Eric Court

Guildford (Winchester)

1874	John Sutton Utterton
1888	George Henry Sumner
1909	John Hugh Granville Randolph
1927	*became diocesan see*

Halifax (Leeds)

never filled

Hertford (St Albans)

1968	Albert John Trillo
1971	Hubert Victor Whitsey
1974	Peter Mumford
1982	Kenneth Harold Pillar
1990	Robin Jonathan Norman Smith
2001	Christopher Richard James Foster
2010	Paul Bayes
2015	Noel Michael Roy Beasley

Hexham (Newcastle)

never filled

Horsham (Chichester)

1968	Simon Wilton Phipps
1975	Ivor Colin Docker
1991	John William Hind
1993	Lindsay Goodall Urwin
2009	Mark Crispin Rake Sowerby

Huddersfield (Leeds)

2014	Jonathan Robert Gibbs

Hull (York)

1538	Robert Sylvester (Pursglove)
1579–1891	*in abeyance*
1891	Richard Frederick Lefevre Blunt
1910	John Augustus Kempthome
1913	Francis Gurdon
1929–31	*no appointment*
1931	Bemard Oliver Francis Heywood
1934	Henry Townsend Vodden
1957	George Fredenck Townley
1965	Hubert Laurence Higgs
1977	Geoffrey John Paul
1981	Donald George Snelgrove
1994	James Stuart Jones
1998	Richard Michael Cockayne Frith
2015	Alison Mary White

Hulme (Manchester)

1924	John Charles Hill
1930	Thomas Sherwood Jones
1945	Hugh Leycester Homby
1953	Kenneth Venner Ramsey
1975	David George Galliford
1984	Colin John Fraser Scott
1999	Stephen Richard Lowe

Huntingdon (Ely)

1966	Robert Arnold Schürhoff Martineau
1972	Eric St Quintin Wall
1980	William Gordon Roe
1997	John Robert Flack
2003	John Geoffrey Inge
2008	David Thomson
2019	Dagmar Winter

Ipswich (Norwich)

1536	Thomas Manning[3]
?–1899	*in abeyance*[4]
1899	George Carnac Fisher
1906	Henry Luke Paget
1909	*no appointment*
1914	*became diocesan see with St Edmundsbury*

Isle of Wight (Portsmouth)

never filled

Islington (London)

1898	Charles Henry Turner
1923–2015	*in abeyance*
2015	Richard Charles Thorpe

Jarrow (Durham)

1906	George Nickson
1914	John Nathaniel Quirk
1924	Samuel Kirshbaum Knight
1932	James Geoffrey Gordon
1939	Leslie Owen
1944	David Colin Dunlop
1950	John Alexander Ramsbotham
1958	Mervyn Armstrong
1965	Alexander Kenneth Hamilton
1980	Michael Thomas Ball
1990	Alan Smithson
2002	John Lawrence Pritchard
2007	Mark Watts Bryant
2019	Sarah Elizabeth Clark

Kendal (Carlisle)

never filled

Kensington (London)

1901	Frederic Edward Ridgeway
1911	John Primatt Maud
1932	Bertram Fitzgerald Simpson
1942	Henry Colville Montgomery Campbell
1949	Cyril Eastaugh
1962	Edward James Keymer Roberts
1964	Ronald Cedric Osbourne Goodchild
1981	Mark Santer
1987	John George Hughes
1994–96	*no appointment*
1996	Michael John Colclough
2009	Paul Gavin Williams
2015	Graham Stuart Tomlin

Kingston-upon-Thames (Southwark)

1905	Cecil Hook
1915	Samuel Mumford Taylor
1922	Percy Mark Herbert
1927	Frederick Ochterlony Taylor Hawkes
1952	William Percy Gilpin
1970	Hugh William Montefiore
1978	Keith Norman Sutton
1984	Peter Stephen Maurice Selby
1992	John Martin Wharton
1997	Peter Bryan Price
2002	Richard Ian Cheetham

Kirkstall (Leeds)

formerly Richmond
2015	Paul John Slater

Knaresborough (Ripon)

1905	Lucius Frederick Moses Bottomley Smith
1934	Paul Fulcrand Dalacour de Labilliere
1938	John Norman Bateman-Champain
1948	Henry Handley Vully de Candole
1965	John Howard Cruse
1972	Ralph Emmerson
1979	John Dennis
1986	Malcolm James Menin
1997	Frank Valentine Weston
2004	James Harold Bell
2014	*renamed Ripon*

Lancaster (Blackburn)

1936	Benjamin Pollard
1955	Anthony Leigh Egerton Hoskyns-Abrahall
1975	Dennis Fountain Page
1985	Ian Harland
1990	John Nicholls
1998	Geoffrey Stephen Pedley
2006	Geoffrey Seagrave Pearson
2018	Jillian Louise Calland Duff

Leicester (Peterborough)

see also under Lichfield *and* Lincoln
1888	Francis Henry Thickness
1903	Lewis Clayton
1913	Norman MacLeod Lang
1927	*became diocesan see*

Leominster (Hereford)

never filled

---

[1] From 1926 to 1980 exercised the Bishop of London's extra-diocesan jurisdiction over chaplaincies in Northern and Central Europe. Since 1996 has assisted the Diocesan Bishop in all matters not delegated to the Areas, and in pastoral care of parishes operating under the London Plan.

[2] Bishop of Fulham and Gibraltar.   [3] Manning does not appear to have acted as a suffragan bishop in the diocese of Norwich.

[4] The date of Manning's death is not known.

Lewes (Chichester)

1909	Leonard Hedley Burrows
1914	Herbert Edward Jones
1920	Henry Kemble Southwell
1926	Thomas William Cook
1929	William Champion Streatfield
1929	Hugh Maudsley Hordern
1946	Geoffrey Hodgson Warde
1959	James Herbert Lloyd Morrell
1977	Peter John Ball
1992	Ian Patrick Martyn Cundy
1997	Wallace Parke Benn
2014	Richard Charles Jackson

Loughborough (Leicester)

2017	Gulnar Eleanor Francis-Dehqani

Ludlow (Hereford)

1981	Stanley Mark Wood
1987	Ian Macdonald Griggs
1994	John Charles Saxbee
2002	Michael Wrenford Hooper
2009	Alistair James Magowan

Lynn (Norwich)

1963	William Somers Llewellyn
1972	William Aubrey Aitken
1986	David Edward Bentley
1994	David John Conner
1999	Anthony Charles Foottit
2004	James Henry Langstaff
2011	Cyril Jonathan Meyrick

Maidstone (Canterbury)

1944	Leslie Owen
1946–56	*no appointment*
1956	Stanley Woodley Betts
1966–69	*no appointment*
1969	Geoffrey Lewis Tiarks
1976	Richard Henry McPhail Third
1980	Robert Maynard Hardy
1987	David James Smith
1992	Gavin Hunter Reid
2001	Graham Alan Cray
2009–2015	*no appointment*
2015	Roderick Charles Howell Thomas

Malmesbury (Bristol)

1927	Ronald Erskine Ramsay
1946	Ivor Stanley Watkins
1956	Edward James Keymer Roberts
1962	Clifford Leofric Purdy Bishop
1973	Frederick Stephen Temple
1983	Peter James Firth
1994	*renamed* Swindon

Marlborough

1537	Thomas Morley (Bickley)[1]
c.1561–1888	*in abeyance*
1888	Alfred Earle[2]
1919	*in abeyance*

Middleton (Manchester)

1927	Richard Godfrey Parsons
1932	Cecil Wilfred Wilson
1938	Arthur Fawssett Alston
1943	Edward Worsfold Mowll
1952	Frank Woods
1958	Robert Nelson
1959	Edward Ralph Wickham
1982	Donald Alexander Tytler
1994	Stephen Squires Venner

1999	Michael Augustine Owen Lewis
2008	Mark Davies

Molton (Exeter)

never filled

Northampton (Peterborough)

never filled

Nottingham (Lincoln)

[in York diocese to 1837]	
1567	Richard Barnes
1570–1870	*in abeyance*
1870	Henry Mackenzie
1877	Edward Trollope
1893	*in abeyance*

Oswestry (Lichfield)

never filled

Penrith (Carlisle)

see also under Richmond

1537	John Bird[3]
1539–1888	*in abeyance*
1888	John James Pulleine[4]
1939	Grandage Edwards Powell
1944	Herbert Victor Turner
1959	Sydney Cyril Bulley
1967	Reginald Foskett
1970	William Edward Augustus Pugh
1979	George Lanyon Hacker
1994	Richard Garrard
2002	James William Scobie Newcome
2011	Robert John Freeman
2019	Emma Gwynneth Ineson

Plymouth (Exeter)

1923	John Howard Bertram Masterman
1934	Francis Whitfield Daukes
1950	Norman Harry Clarke
1962	Wilfred Guy Sanderson
1972	Richard Fox Cartwright
1982	Kenneth Albert Newing
1988	Richard Stephen Hawkins
1996	John Henry Garton
2005	John Frank Ford
2015	Nicholas Howard Paul McKinnel

Pontefract (Wakefield)

1931	Campbell Richard Hone
1939	Tom Longworth
1949	Arthur Harold Morris
1954	George William Clarkson
1961	Eric Treacy
1968	William Gordon Fallows
1971	Thomas Richard Hare
1993	John Thornley Finney
1998	David Charles James
2002	Anthony William Robinson
2014	*renamed* Wakefield

Ramsbury (Salisbury)

see also under Salisbury

1974	John Robert Geoffrey Neale
1989	Peter St George Vaughan
1999	Peter Fearnley Hullah
2006	Stephen David Conway
2012	Edward Francis Condry
2019	Andrew Paul Rumsey

Reading (Oxford)

1889	James Leslie Randall
1909–42	*in abeyance*
1942	Arthur Groom Parham
1954	Eric Henry Knell
1972	Eric Wild
1982	Ronald Graham Gregory Foley
1989	John Frank Ewan Bone
1997	Edward William Murray Walker
2004	Stephen Geoffrey Cottrell
2011	Andrew John Proud
2019	Olivia Josephine Graham

Repton (Derby)

1965	William Warren Hunt
1977	Stephen Edmund Verney
1986	Francis Henry Arthur Richmond
1999	David Christopher Hawtin
2007	Humphrey Ivo John Southern
2016	Janet Elizabeth McFarlane

Richborough (Canterbury)

1995	Edwin Ronald Barnes
2002	Keith Newton
2011	Norman Banks

Richmond (Leeds)

1889	John James Pulleine[5]
1913	Francis Charles Kilner
1921–2015	*in abeyance*
2015	Paul John Slater
2018	*renamed* Kirkstall

Ripon (Leeds)

formerly Knaresborough

2004	James Harold Bell
2018	Helen-Ann Macleod Hartley

Rochdale (Manchester)

never filled

St Germans (Truro)

1905	John Rundle Cornish
1918–74	*in abeyance*
1974	Cecil Richard Rutt
1979	Reginald Lindsay Fisher
1985	John Richard Allan Llewellin
1993	Graham Richard James
2000	Royden Screech
2013	Christopher David Goldsmith

Selby (York)

1939	Henry St John Stirling Woollcombe
1941	Carey Frederick Knyvett
1962	Douglas Noel Sargent
1972	Morris Henry St John Maddocks
1983	Clifford Conder Barker
1991	Humphrey Vincent Taylor
2003	Martin William Wallace
2014	John Bromilow Thomson

Shaftesbury (Salisbury)

[in Bristol diocese 1542–1836]	
1539	John Bradley
?	*in abeyance*[6]

Sheffield (York)

1901	John Nathaniel Quirk
1914	*became diocesan see*

---

[1] Appointed for the diocese of London.   [2] Appointed for the diocese of London, but retained the title while Dean of Exeter 1900–18.
[3] Appointed for the diocese of Lichfield.   [4] Appointed for the diocese of Ripon.
[5] His suffragan title was changed from Penrith to Richmond by Royal Warrant.   [6] The date of Bradley's death is not known.

Sherborne (Salisbury)

1925	Robert Crowther Abbott
1928	Gerald Burton Allen
1936	Harold Nickinson Rodgers
1947	John Maurice Key
1960	Victor Joseph Pike
1976	John Dudley Galtrey Kirkham
2001	Timothy Martin Thornton
2009	Graham Ralph Kings
2016	Karen Marisa Gorham

Sherwood (Southwell)

1965	Kenneth George Thompson
1975	Harold Richard Darby
1989	Alan Wyndham Morgan
2006	Anthony Porter

Shrewsbury (Lichfield)

1537	Lewis Thomas[1]
1561–1888	*in abeyance*
1888	Sir Lovelace Tomlinson Stamer
1905–40	*in abeyance*
1940	Eric Knightley Chetwode Hamilton
1944	Robert Leighton Hodson
1959	William Alonzo Parker
1970	Francis William Cocks
1980	Leslie Lloyd Rees
1987	John Dudley Davies
1994	David Marrison Hallatt
2001	Alan Gregory Clayton Smith
2009	Mark James Rylands
2019	Sarah Ruth Bullock

Southampton (Winchester)

1895	William Awdry
1896	George Carnac Fisher
1898	The Hon Arthur Temple Lyttelton
1903	James Macarthur
1921	Cecil Henry Boutflower
1933	Arthur Baillie Lumsdaine Karney
1943	Edmund Robert Morgan
1951	Kenneth Edward Norman Lamplugh
1972	John Kingsmill Cavell
1984	Edward David Cartwright
1989	John Freeman Perry
1996	Jonathan Michael Gledhill
2004	Paul Roger Butler
2010	Jonathan Hugh Frost
2019	Deborah Mary Sellin

Southwark (Rochester)

1891	Huyshe Wolcott Yeatman-Biggs
1905	*became diocesan see*

Stafford (Lichfield)

1909	Edward Ash Were
1915	Lionel Payne Crawfurd
1934	Douglas Henry Crick
1938	Leprière Durell Hammond
1958	Richard George Clitherow
1975	John Waine
1979	John Stevens Waller
1987	Michael Charles Scott-Joynt
1996	Christopher John Hill
2005	Alfred Gordon Mursell
2010	Geoffrey Peter Annas

Stepney (London)

1895	George Forrest Browne
1897	Arthur Foley Winnington-Ingram

1901	Cosmo Gordon Lang
1909	Henry Luke Paget
1919	Henry Mosley
1928	Charles Edward Curzon
1936	Robert Hamilton Moberly
1952	Joost de Blank
1957	Francis Evered Lunt
1968	Ernest Urban Trevor Huddleston
1978	James Lawton Thompson
1992	Richard John Carew Chartres
1996	John Mugabi Sentamu
2003	Stephen John Oliver
2011	Adrian Newman
2019	Joanne Woolway Grenfell

Stockport (Chester)

1949	Frank Jackson Okell
1951	David Henry Saunders Saunders-Davies
1965	Rupert Gordon Strutt
1984	Frank Pilkington Sargeant
1994	Geoffrey Martin Turner
2000	William Nigel Stock
2008	Robert Ronald Atwell
2015	Elizabeth Jane Holden Lane

Swindon (Bristol)

formerly Malmesbury

1994	Michael David Doe
2005	Lee Stephen Rayfield

Taunton (Bath and Wells)

1538	William Finch
1559–1911	*in abeyance*
1911	Charles Fane de Salis
1931	George Arthur Hollis
1945	Harry Thomas
1955	Mark Allin Hodson
1962	Francis Horner West
1977	Peter John Nott
1986	Nigel Simeon McCulloch
1992	John Hubert Richard Lewis
1997	William Allen Stewart
1998	Andrew John Radford
2006	Peter David Maurice
2015	Ruth Elizabeth Worsley

Tewkesbury (Gloucester)

1938	Augustine John Hodson
1955	Edward Barry Henderson
1960	Forbes Trevor Horan
1973	Thomas Carlyle Joseph Robert Hamish Deakin
1986	Geoffrey David Jeremy Walsh
1996	John Stewart Went
2013	Martyn James Snow
2016	Robert Wilfred Springett

Thetford (Norwich)

see also under Norwich

1536	John Salisbury
1570–1894	*in abeyance*
1894	Arthur Thomas Lloyd
1903	John Philips Alcott Bowers
1926–45	*no appointment*
1945	John Walker Woodhouse
1953	Martin Patrick Grainge Leonard
1963	Eric William Bradley Cordingly
1977	Hugh Charles Blackburne
1981	Timothy Dudley-Smith
1992	Hugo Ferdinand de Waal
2001	David John Atkinson
2009	Alan Peter Winton

Tonbridge (Rochester)

1959	Russell Berridge White
1968	Henry David Halsey
1973	Philip Harold Ernest Goodrich
1982	David Henry Bartleet
1993	Brian Arthur Smith
2002	Brian Colin Castle
2018	Simon David Burton-Jones

Wakefield (Leeds)

formerly Pontefract

2014	Anthony William Robinson

Warrington (Liverpool)

1918	Martin Linton Smith
1920	Edwin Hone Kempson
1927	Herbert Gresford Jones
1946	Charles Robert Claxton
1960	Laurence Ambrose Brown
1970	John Monier Bickersteth
1976	Michael Henshall
1996	John Richard Packer
2000	David Wilfred Michael Jennings
2009	Richard Finn Blackburn
2018	Beverly Anne Mason

Warwick (Coventry)

1980	Keith Appleby Arnold
1990	Clive Handford
1996	Anthony Martin Priddis
2005	John Ronald Angus Stroyan

Whalley (Blackburn)

[in Manchester diocese to 1926]

1909	Atherton Gwillym Rawstorne
1936	*in abeyance*

Whitby (York)

1923	Harry St John Stirling Woollcombe
1939	Harold Evelyn Hubbard
1947	Walter Hubert Baddeley
1954	Philip William Wheeldon
1961	George D'Oyly Snow
1972	John Yates
1976	Clifford Conder Barker
1983	Gordon Bates
1999	Robert Sidney Ladds
2010	Martin Clive Warner
2014	Paul John Ferguson

Wigan (Liverpool)

never filled

Willesden (London)

1911	William Willcox Perrin
1929	Guy Vernon Smith
1940	Henry Colville Montgomery Campbell
1942	Edward Michael Gresford Jones
1950	Gerald Alexander Ellison
1955	George Ernest Ingle
1964	Graham Douglas Leonard
1974	Geoffrey Hewlett Thompson
1985	Thomas Frederick Butler
1992	Geoffrey Graham Dow
2001	Peter Alan Broadbent

Wolverhampton (Lichfield)

1979	Barry Rogerson
1985	Christopher John Mayfield
1994	Michael Gay Bourke
2007	Clive Malcolm Gregory

---

[1] Not appointed for Lichfield, but probably for Llandaff.

Woolwich (Southwark)

1905	John Cox Leeke
1918	William Woodcock Hough
1932	Arthur Llewellyn Preston
1936	Leslie Hamilton Lang

WALES

Archbishops of Wales

1920	Alfred George Edwards (St Asaph 1889–1934)
1934	Charles Alfred Howell Green (Bangor 1928–44)
1944	David Lewis Prosser (St Davids 1927–50)
1949	John Morgan (Llandaff 1939–57)
1957	Alfred Edwin Morris (Monmouth 1945–67)
1968	William Glyn Hughes Simon (Llandaff 1957–71)
1971	Gwilym Owen Williams (Bangor 1957–82)
1983	Derrick Greenslade Childs (Monmouth 1972–87)
1987	George Noakes (St Davids 1982–91)
1991	Alwyn Rice Jones (St Asaph 1982–99)
1999	Rowan Douglas Williams (Monmouth 1992–2002)
2003	Barry Cennydd Morgan (Llandaff 1999–2017)
2017	John David Edward Davies (Swansea and Brecon 2008–)

Bangor[1]

Description of arms. Gules, a bend or guttée de poix between two mullets pierced argent.

c.550	Deiniol [Daniel]
c.775	Elfod [Elbodugen]
1092	Herve
	[Vacancy 1109–20]
1120	David the Scot
1140	Maurice (Meurig)
	[Vacancy 1161–77]
1177	Guy Rufus [Gwion Goch]
	[Vacancy c.1190–95]
1195	Alan [Alban]
1197	Robert of Shrewsbury
	[Vacancy 1212–15]
1215	Cadwgan
1237	Richard
1267	Anian [or Einion]
1307	Gruflydd ab Iowerth
1309	Anian [Einion] Sais
1328	Matthew de Englefield
1357	Thomas de Ringstead
1366	Gervase de Castro
1371	Hywel ap Gronwy
1372	John Gilbert
1376	John Swaffham

1947	Robert William Stannard
1959	John Arthur Thomas Robinson
1969	David Stuart Sheppard
1975	Michael Eric Marshall
1984	Albert Peter Hall

1400	Richard Young
	[Vacancy c.1404–8]
1408	Benedict Nicolls
1418	William Barrow
1425	John Cliderow
1436	Thomas Cheriton
1448	John Stanbury
1453	James Blakedon
1465	Richard Edenham
1495	Henry Dean
1500	Thomas Pigot
1505	Thomas Penny
1509	Thomas Skevington
1534	John Salcot [or Capon]
1539	John Bird
1542	Arthur Bulkeley
1555	William Glynn
1559	Rowland Meyrick
1566	Nicholas Robinson
1586	Hugh Bellot
1596	Richard Vaughan
1598	Henry Rowlands
1616	Lewis Bayly
1632	David Dolben
1634	Edmund Griffith
1637	William Roberts
1666	Robert Morgan
1673	Humphrey Lloyd
1689	Humphrey Humphreys
1702	John Evans
1716	Benjamin Hoadley
1721	Richard Reynolds
1723	William Baker
1728	Thomas Sherlock
1734	Charles Cecil
1738	Thomas Herring
1743	Matthew Hutton
1748	Zachary Pearce
1756	John Egerton
1769	John Ewer
1775	John Moore
1783	John Warren
1800	William Cleaver
1807	John Randolph
1809	Henry William Majendie
1830	Christopher Bethell
1859	James Colquhoun Campbell
1890	Daniel Lewis Lloyd
1899	Watkin Herbert Williams
1925	Daniel Davies
1928	Charles Alfred Howell Green (Archbishop of Wales 1934)
1944	David Edwardes Davies
1949	John Charles Jones
1957	Gwilym Owen Williams (Archbishop of Wales 1971)
1982	John Cledan Mears
1993	Barry Cennydd Morgan
1999	Francis James Saunders Davies
2004	Phillip Anthony Crockett
2008	Andrew Thomas Griffith John

1996	Colin Ogilvie Buchanan
2005	Christopher Thomas James Chessun
2012	Michael Geoffrey Ipgrave
2017	Woyin Karowei Dorgu

Llandaff[2]

Description of arms. Sable, two pastoral staves endorsed in saltire, the dexter or, the sinister argent. On a chief azure three labelled mitres or.

c.550	Teiliau
c.872	Cyfeiliag
c.880	Libiau
c.940	Marchlwys
982	Gwyzan
c.995	Bledri
1027	Joseph
1056	Herewald
1107	Urban
	[Vacancy of six years]
1140	Uchtryd
1148	Nicolas ap Gwrgant
	[Vacancy of two years]
1186	William Saltmarsh
1193	Henry of Abergavenny
1219	William of Goldcliff
1230	Elias of Radnor
1245	William de Burgh
1254	John de Ware
1257	William of Radnor
1266	Willam de Breuse [or Brus]
1297	John of Monmouth
1323	John of Eaglescliffe
1344	John Paschal
1361	Roger Cradock
1383	Thomas Rushook
1386	William Bottesham
1389	Edmund Bromfield
1393	Tideman de Winchcomb
1395	Andrew Barret
1396	John Burghill
1398	Thomas Peverel
1408	John de la Zouch [Fulford]
1425	John Wells
1441	Nicholas Ashby
1458	John Hunden
1476	John Smith
1478	John Marshall
1496	John Ingleby
1500	Miles Salley
1517	George de Athequa
1537	Robert Holdgate [or Holgate]
1545	Anthony Kitchin
1567	Hugh Jones
1575	William Blethin
1591	Gervase Babington
1595	William Morgan
1601	Francis Godwin
1618	George Carleton
1619	Theophilus Field
1627	William Murray
1640	Morgan Owen

---

[1] Very few of the names of the Celtic bishops have been preserved.

[2] The traditional list of bishops of the Celtic Church has little historical foundation. But the names of the following, prior to Urban, may be regarded as fairly trustworthy, though the dates are very uncertain.

1660	Hugh Lloyd
1667	Francis Davies
1675	William Lloyd
1679	William Beaw
1706	John Tyler
1725	Robert Clavering
1729	John Harris
1739	Matthias Mawson
1740	John Gilbert
1749	Edward Cressett
1755	Richard Newcome
1761	John Ewer
1769	Jonathan Shipley
1769	Shute Barrington
1782	Richard Watson
1816	Herbert Marsh
1819	William Van Mildert
1826	Charles Richard Sumner
1828	Edward Copleston
1849	Alfred Ollivant
1883	Richard Lewis
1905	Joshua Pritchard Hughes
1931	Timothy Rees
1939	John Morgan (Archbishop of Wales 1949)
1957	William Glyn Hughes Simon (Archbishop of Wales 1968)
1971	Eryl Stephen Thomas
1975	John Richard Worthington Poole-Hughes
1985	Roy Thomas Davies
1999	Barry Cennydd Morgan (Archbishop of Wales 2003)
2017	June Osborne

Monmouth

Description of arms. Per pale azure and sable, two crosiers in satire or between in chief a besant charged with a lion passant guardant gules, in fess two fleurs-de-lis and in base a fleur-de-lis all of the third.

1921	Charles Alfred Howell Green
1928	Gilbert Cunningham Joyce
1940	Alfred Edwin Monahan
1945	Alfred Edwin Morris (Archbishop of Wales 1957)
1968	Eryl Stephen Thomas
1972	Derrick Greenslade Childs (Archbishop of Wales 1983)
1986	Royston Clifford Wright
1992	Rowan Douglas Williams (Archbishop of Wales 1999)
2003	Edward William Murray Walker
2013	Richard Edward Pain
2019	Cherry Elizabeth Vann

St Asaph[1]

Description of arms. Sable, two keys endorsed in saltire the wards upwards argent.

*c.*560	Kentigern
*c.*573	Asaph
1143	Gilbert
1152	Geoffrey of Monmouth
1154	Richard
1160	Godfrey
1175	Adam
1183	John I
1186	Reiner
1225	Abraham
1235	Hugh
1242	Hywel Ab Ednyfed
1249	Anian I [or Einion]
1267	John II
1268	Anian II
1293	Llywelyn de Bromfield
1315	Dafydd ap Bleddyn
1346	John Trevor I
1357	Llywelyn ap Madoc ab Ellis
1377	William de Spridlington
1382	Lawrence Child
1390	Alexander Bache
1395	John Trevor II
1411	Robert de Lancaster
1433	John Lowe
1444	Reginald Pecock
1451	Thomas Bird *alias* Knight
1471	Richard Redman
1496	Michael Deacon
1500	Dafydd ab Iorwerth
1504	Dafydd ab Owain
1513	Edmund Birkhead
1518	Henry Standish
1536	Robert Warton [or Parfew]
1555	Thomas Goldwell
1560	Richard Davies
1561	Thomas Davies
1573	William Hughes
1601	William Morgan
1604	Richard Parry
1624	John Hanmer
1629	John Owen
1660	George Griffith
1667	Henry Glemham
1670	Isaac Barrow
1680	William Lloyd
1692	Edward Jones
1703	George Hooper
1704	William Beveridge
1708	Will. Fleetwood
1715	John Wynne
1727	Francis Hare
1732	Thomas Tanner
1736	Isaac Maddox
1744	Samuel Lisle
1748	Robert Hay Drummond
1761	Richard Newcome
1769	Jonathan Shipley
1789	Samuel Hallifax
1790	Lewis Bagot
1802	Samuel Horsley
1806	William Cleaver
1815	John Luxmore
1830	William Carey
1846	Thomas Vowler Short

1870	Joshua Hughes
1889	Alfred George Edwards (Archbishop of Wales 1920)
1934	William Thomas Havard
1950	David Daniel Bartlett
1971	Harold John Charles
1982	Alwyn Rice Jones (Archbishop of Wales 1991)
1999	John Stewart Davies
2009	Gregory Kenneth Cameron

St Davids[2]

Description of arms. Sable, on a cross or five cinquefoils of the first.

*c.*601	David
*c.*606	Cynog
831	Sadyrnfyw
	Meurig
*c.*840	Novis
	?Idwal
*c.*906	Asser
	Llunwerth
944	Eneuris
*c.*961	Rhydderch
*c.*999	Morgeneu
1023	Morgeneu
1023	Erwyn
1039	Tramerin
1061	Joseph
1061	Bleddud
1072	Sulien
1078	Abraham
1080	Sulien
1085	Wilfrid
1115	Bernard
1148	David Fitz-Gerald
1176	Peter de Leia
1203	Geoffrey de Henlaw
1215	Gervase [Iorwerth]
1231	Anselm le Gras
1248	Thomas le Waleys
1256	Richard de Carew
1280	Thomas Bek
1296	David Martin
1328	Henry Gower
1347	John Thoresby
1350	Reginald Brian
1352	Thomas Fastolf
1362	Adam Houghton
1389	John Gilbert
1397	Guy de Mohne
1408	Henry Chichele
1414	John Catterick
1415	Stephen Patrington
1418	Benedict Nichols
1434	Thomas Rodburn [Rudborne]
1442	William Lindwood
1447	John Langton
1447	John de la Bere
1460	Robert Tully
1482	Richard Martin
1483	Thomas Langton
1485	Hugh Pavy
1496	John Morgan [Young]
1505	Robert Sherborn
1509	Edward Vaughan
1523	Richard Rawlins
1536	William Barlow

[1] Prior to the Norman period there is considerable uncertainty as to names and dates.
[2] The following names occur in early records though the dates given cannot always be reconciled.

1548	Robert Ferrar
1554	Henry Morgan
1560	Thomas Young
1561	Richard Davies
1582	Marmaduke Middleton
1594	Anthony Rudd
1615	Richard Milbourne
1621	William Laud
1627	Theophilus Field
1636	Roger Mainwaring
1660	William Lucy
1678	William Thomas
1683	Laurence Womock
1686	John Lloyd
1687	Thomas Watson
	[*Vacancy* 1699–1705]
1705	George Bull
1710	Philip Bisse
1713	Adam Ottley
1724	Richard Smallbrooke
1731	Elias Sydall
1732	Nicholas Claggett
1743	Edward Willes
1744	Richard Trevor
1753	Anthony Ellis
1761	Samuel Squire
1766	Robert Lowth
1766	Charles Moss
1774	James Yorke
1779	John Warren
1783	Edward Smallwell
1788	Samuel Horsley
1794	William Stewart
1801	George Murray

1803	Thomas Burgess
1825	John Banks Jenkinson
1840	Connop Thirlwall
1874	William Basil Tickell Jones
1897	John Owen
1927	David Lewis Prosser
	(Archbishop of Wales 1944)
1950	William Thomas Havard
1956	John Richards Richards
1971	Eric Matthias Roberts
1982	George Noakes (Archbishop of Wales 1987)
1991	John Ivor Rees
1996	David Huw Jones
2002	Carl Norman Cooper
2008	John Wyn Evans
2016	Joanna Susan Penberthy

Swansea and Brecon

Description of arms. Per fess azure and or, in chief surmounting a catherine wheel issuant an eagle rising regardant of the second and in base a fleur-de-lis of the first.

1923	Edward Latham Bevan
1934	John Morgan
1939	Edward William Williamson
1953	William Glyn Hughes Simon
1958	John James Absalom Thomas
1976	Benjamin Noel Young Vaughan
1988	Dewi Morris Bridges
1999	Anthony Edward Pierce
2008	John David Edward Davies (Archbishop of Wales 2017)

Provincial Assistant Bishop

1996–2008 David Thomas

SCOTLAND

Sources: Bp Dowden's *The Bishops of Scotland* (Glasgow 1912), for all the sees up to the Reformation, and for Aberdeen and Moray to the present time.

For bishops after the Reformation (and for a few of the earliest ones before Queen Margaret) – Grub, *Ecclesiastical History of Scotland* (Edinburgh 1861, 4 Vols.) and Bp Keith and Bp Russel, *Scottish Bishops* (2nd ed. Edinburgh 1824).

Scottish episcopal elections became subject immediately to Roman confirmation in 1192. The subordination of the Scottish Church to York became less direct in 1165, and its independence was recognized in a bill of Celestine III in 1192. St Andrews was raised to metropolitan rank on 17 August 1472 and the Archbishop became primate of all Scotland with the same legative rights as the Archbishop of Canterbury on 27 March 1487.

The dates in the margin are those of the consecration or translation to the particular see of the bishops named; or in the case of bishops elect, who are not known to have been consecrated, they are those of the election; or in the case of titular bishops, of the date of their appointment.

The date of the death has been given where there was a long interregnum, or where there is dislocation (as at the Reformation and at the Revolution), or for some special reason to make the history intelligible.

The extra information in the list of College Bishops is given for the reason just stated.

St Andrews

St Andrews, Dunkeld and Dunblane

Description of arms. Quarterly, 1st azure, a saltire argent (for the See of St Andrews); 2nd per fess sable and vert, an open book proper in base, fore-edges and binding or, a dove argent, her wings displayed in chief perching thereon and holding in her beak a spray of olive of the second (for the See of Dunkeld); 3rd chevronny or and gules, a saltire engrailed azure, charged at the fess point with a crescent inverted argent (for the See of Dunblane); 4th azure, a saltire argent supported in front of and by St Andrew enhaloed or and vested pupure with mantle vert, and in base a crescent inverted of the second (for the See of St Andrews).

906	Cellach I
915(?)	Fothad I
955	Malisius I
963	Maelbridge
970	Cellach II
996(?)	Malasius II
(?)	Malmore
1025	Alwyn
1028	Maelduin
1055	Tuthald or Tuadal
1059	Fothad II
1077	Gregory (elect)
to	Catharas (elect)
1107	Edmarus (elect)
	Godricus (elect)
1109	Turgot
1120	Eadmer (elect)
1127	Robert
1159	Waldeve (elect)
1160	Ernald
1165	Richard
1178	Hugh
1180	John the Scot
1198	Roger de Beaumon
1202	William Malveisin
1238	Geoffrey (elect)
1240	David de Bernham
1253	Robert de Stuteville (elect)
1254	Abel de Golin
1255	Gamelin
1273	William Wischard

1280	William Fraser
1298	William de Lamberton
1328	James Bennet
1342	William de Laundels
1385	Stephen de Pay (elect)
1386(?)	Walter Trayl
1388	Alexander de Neville
1398	Thomas de Arundel
1401	Thomas Stewart (elect)
1402	Walter de Danielston (elect)
1403(?)	Gilbert Greenlaw
1403	Henry Wardlaw
1408	John Trevor
1440	James Kennedy

ARCHBISHOPS

1465	Patrick Graham
1478	William Scheves
1497	James Stewart (elect)
1504	Alexander Stewart (elect)
1513	John Hepburn (elect)
1513	Innocenzo Cibo (elect)
1514	Andrew Forman
1522	James Betoun
1538	David Betoun [coadjutor]
1547	John Hamilton
1551	Gavin Hamilton [coadjutor] died 1571
1572	John Douglas (titular)
1576	Patrick Adamson (titular) died 1592
1611	George Gladstanes
1615	John Spottiswoode, died 1639
1661	James Sharp
1679	Alexander Burnet
1684	Arthur Rose, died 1704

BISHOPS OF FIFE

[1704–26	See vacant]
1726	James Rose
1733	Robert Keith
1743	Robert White
1761	Henry Edgar

BISHOPS OF ST ANDREWS

1842	Patrick Torry
1853	Charles Wordsworth
1893	George Howard Wilkinson
1908	Charles Edward Plumb
1931	Edward Thomas Scott Reid
1938	James Lumsden Barkway
1949	Arnold Brian Burrowes
1955	John William Alexander Howe
1969	Michael Geoffrey Hare Duke
1995	Michael Harry George Henley
2005	David Robert Chillingworth
2018	Ian James Paton

†Dunkeld

849(?)	Tuathal
865(?)	Flaithbertach

1114	Cormac
1147	Gregory
1170	Richard I
1178	Walter de Bidun (elect)
1183(?)	John I, the Scot
1203	Richard II, de Prebenda
1212(?)	John II, de Leycester
1214(?)	Hugh de Sigillo
1229	Matthew Scot (elect)
1229	Gilbert
1236(?)	Geoffrey de Liberatione
1252	Richard III, of Inverkeithing
1273(?)	Robert de Stuteville
1283(?)	Hugh de Strivelin [Stirling] (elect)
1283	William
1288	Matthew de Crambeth
1309	John de Leek (elect)
1312	William Sinclair
1337	Malcolm de Innerpeffray (elect)
1344	Richard de Pilmor
1347	Robert de Den (elect)
1347(?)	Duncan de Strathearn
1355	John Luce
1370	John de Carrick (elect)
1371(?)	Michael de Monymusk
1377(?)	Andrew Umfray (elect)
1379	John de Peblys [? of Peebles]
1379	Robert de Derling
1390(?)	Nicholas Duffield
1391	Robert Sinclair
1398(?)	Robert de Cardeny
1430	William Gunwardby
1437	Donald MacNaughton (elect)
1438	James Kennedy
1440(?)	Thomas Livingston
1440	Alexander de Lawedre [Lauder] (elect)
1442	James de Brois [Brewhous]
1447	William Turnbull (elect)
1448	John Ralston
1452(?)	Thomas Lauder
1476	James Livingston
1483	Alexander Inglis (elect)
1484	George Brown
1515	Andrew Stewart (elect)
1516	Gavin Dougias
1524	Robert Cockburn
1526(?)	George Crichton
1546	John Hamilton
1552	Robert Crichton
1572	James Paton (titular)
1585	Peter Rollock (titular)
1607	James Nicolson (titular)
1611(?)	Alexander Lindsay (deposed 1638)
1662	George Haliburton
1665	Henry Guthrie
1677	William Lindsay
1679	Andrew Bruce
1686	John Hamilton
1717	Thomas Rattray
1743	John Alexander

† Indicates a diocese no longer extant, or united with another diocese.

1776(?) Charles Rose
1792 Jonathan Watson
1808 Patrick Torry
1842 Held with St Andrews

†Dunblane

1162 Laurence
c.1180 Symon
1196 W[illelmus]
1198 Jonathan
1215 Abraham
1225 Ralph (elect)
1227 Osbert
1233 Clement
1259 Robert de Prebenda
1284 William I
1296 Alpin
1301 Nicholas
1307 Nicholas de Balmyle
1318(?) Roger de Balnebrich (elect)
1322 Maurice
c.1347 William II
c.1361 Walter de Coventre
c.1372 Andrew
c.1380 Dougal
1403(?) Finlay or Dermoch
1419 William Stephen
1430 Michael Ochiltree
1447(?) Robert Lauder
1468 John Hepburn
1487 James Chisolm
1527 William Chisolm I
1561 William Chisolm II [coadjutor]
1575 Andrew Graham (titular)
1611 George Graham
1616 Adam Bellenden
1636 James Wedderburn
1661 Robert Leighton
1673 James Ramsay
1684 Robert Douglas
[1716–31 See vacant]
1731 John Gillan
1735 Robert White
1744 Thomas Ogilvie (elect)
1774 Charles Rose, died 1791
1776 Held with Dunkeld

Edinburgh

Description of arms. Azure, a saltire and, in chief, a labelled mitre argent.

1634 William Forbes
1634 David Lindsay
1662 George Wishart
1672 Alexander Young
1679 John Paterson
1687 Alexander Rose
1720 John Fullarton
1727 Arthur Millar
1727 Andrew Lumsden
1733 David Freebairn
[1739–76 See vacant]
1776 William Falconer
1787 William Abernethy Drummond
1806 Daniel Sandford
1830 James Walker
1841 Charles Hughes Terrot
1872 Henry Cotterill
1886 John Dowden

1910 George Henry Somerset Walpole
1929 Harry Seymour Reid
1939 Ernest Denny Logie Danson
1947 Kenneth Charles Harman Warner
1961 Kenneth Moir Carey
1975 Alastair Iain Macdonald Haggart
1986 Richard Frederick Holloway
2001 Brian Arthur Smith
2012 John Andrew Armes

Aberdeen

Aberdeen and Orkney

Description of arms. Azure, parted per pale: dexter, a chevron round embattled on its upper edge between a fleur-de-lis argent ensigned of an open crown or in dexter chief, and in base a bishop proper, attired of the second, mitred and holding in his sinister hand a pastoral staff of the third, his dexter hand raised in benediction over three children gules issuant from a cauldron of the third; sinister, an open boat or, an anchor argent pendant from its prow, issuant therefrom a saint proper, attired of the third, enhaloed and holding in his sinister hand a pastoral staff of the second; over all and issuant from the chief a sunburst or, the central ray projected along the palar line to the base.

BISHOPS AT MURTHLAC

(?) Beyn [Beanus]
(?) Donort
(?) Cormac

BISHOPS AT ABERDEEN

1132 Nechtan
c.1150 Edward
c.1172 Matthew
c.1201 John
c.1208 Adam de Kalder
1228 Matthew Scot (elect)
1230 Gilbert de Strivelyn
1240 Radulf de Lamley
1247 Peter de Ramsey
1258 Richard de Pottun
1272 Hugh de Bennum
1282 Henry le Chene
1329 Walter Herok (elect)
1329 Alexander I, de Kyninmund
1344 William de Deyn
1351 John de Rate
1356 Alexander II, de Kyninmund
1380 Adam de Tynyngham
1391 Gilbert de Grenlaw
1422 Henry de Lychton [Leighton]
c.1441 Ingram de Lindsay
1458 Thomas Spens
1480 Robert Blackadder (elect)
1488 William Elphinstone
1515 Robert Forman (elect)
1516 Alexander Gordon
1519 Gavin Dunbar
1529 George Learmonth [coadjutor]
1533 William Stewart

1547 William Gordon
1577 David Cunningham (elect)
1611 Peter Blackburn
1616 Alexander Forbes
1618 Patrick Forbes of Corse
1635 Adam Bellenden [Bannatyne]
1662 David Mitchell
1663 Alexander Burnet
1664 Patrick Scougal
1682 George Halyburton
[1715–21 See vacant]
1721 Archibald Campbell
1724 James Gadderar
1733 William Dunbar
1746 Andrew Gerard
1768 Robert Kilgour
1786 John Skinner
1816 William Skinner
1857 Thomas George Spink Suther
1883 Arthur Gascoigne Douglas
1906 Rowland Ellis
1912 Anthony Mitchell
1917 Frederic Llewellyn Deane
1943 Herbert William Hall
1956 Edward Frederick Easson
1973 Ian Forbes Begg
1978 Frederick Charles Darwent
1992 Andrew Bruce Cameron
2007 Robert Arthur Gillies
2018 Anne Catherine Dyer

†Orkney

1035 Henry
1050 Turolf
1072 John I
1072 Adalbert
1073 Radulf
1102 William I, 'the Old'
1108 Roger
1114 Radulf Novell
1168(?) William II
1188(?) Bjarni
1224 Jofreyrr
1248 Henry I
1270 Peter
1286 Dolgfinn
1310 William III
c.1369 William IV
c.1384 Robert Sinclair
1384(?) John
1394 Henry II
1396(?) John Pak
1407 Alexander Vaus (elect)
1415 William Stephenson
1420 Thomas Tulloch
1461 William Tulloch
1477 Andrew Painter
1500 Edward Stewart
1524 John Benston [coadjutor]
1526(?) Robert Maxwell
1541 Robert Reid
1559 Adam Bothwell
1611 James Law
1615 George Graham
1639 Robert Barron (elect)
1661 Thomas Sydserf
1664 Andrew Honeyman
1677 Murdo Mackenzie
1688 Andrew Bruce, See afterwards administered with Caithness
1857 Held with Aberdeen

Brechin

Description of arms. Or, three piles in point purpure.

1153(?)	Samson
1178	Turpin
1202	Radulf
1215	Hugh
1218	Gregory
1246	Albin
1269(?)	William de Crachin (elect)
1275	William Comyn
1296	Nicholas
1298	John de Kyninmund
1328	Adam de Moravia
1350	Philip Wilde
1351	Patrick de Locrys [Leuchars]
1383	Stephen de Cellario
1411	Walter Forrester
1426	John de Crannach
1455	George Schoriswood
1464	Patrick Graham
1465	John Balfour
1489	William Meldrum
1523	John Hepburn
1557	Donald Campbell (elect)
1565(?)	John Sinclair (elect)
1566	Alexander Campbell (titular)
1610	Andrew Lamb
1619	David Lindsay
1634	Thomas Sydserf
1635	Walter Whitford
1662	David Strachan
1672	Robert Laurie
1678	George Haliburton
1682	Robert Douglas
1684	Alexander Cairncross
1684	James Drummond
1695–1709	Held with Edinburgh
1709	John Falconar
1724	Robert Norrie
1726	John Ochterlonie
1742	James Rait
1778	George Innes
1787	William Abernethy Drummond
1788	John Strachan
1810	George Gleig
1840	David Moir
1847	Alexander Penrose Forbes
1876	Hugh Willoughby Jermyn
1904	Walter John Forbes Robberds
1935	Kenneth Donald Mackenzie
1944	Eric Graham
1959	John Chappell Sprott
1975	Lawrence Edward Luscombe
1990	Robert Taylor Halliday
1997	Neville Chamberlain
2005	John Ambrose Cyril Mantle
2011	Nigel Peyton
2018	Andrew Christopher Swift

Moray

Moray, Ross and Caithness

Description of arms. Party per fess and in chief per pale: 1 or, two lions combatant gules, pulling at a cushion of the last issuant from a crescent azure, on a chief wavy of the third three mullets argent (for the See of Moray); 2 argent, a bishop standing in the sinister vested purpure, mitred and holding in his sinister hand a crosier or and pointing with the dexter hand to a saint affontée, his hands clasped on this breast proper, habited gules, above his head a halo of the third (for the See of Ross); 3 azure, issuant from an antique boat or, a demi-bishop proper vested argent, his mitre and pastoral staff in hand sinister of the second, accompanied by two demi-angels, one in the dexter and the other in the sinister chief holding open books proper, their wings addorsed, also of the second (for the See of Caithness).

1114	Gregory
1153(?)	William
1164	Felix
1172	Simon de Tonei
1187	Richard de Lincoln
1203	Brice de Douglas
1224(?)	Andrew de Moravia
1244(?)	Simon
1251	Radulf de Leycester (elect)
1253	Archibald
1299	David de Moravia
1326	John de Pilmor
1363	Alexander Bur
1397	William de Spyny
1407	John de Innes
1415	Henry Leighton
1422	Columba de Dunbar
1437	John de Winchester
1460(?)	James Stewart
1463	David Stewart
1477	William de Tulloch
1487	Andrew Stewart
1501(?)	Andrew Forman
1516(?)	James Hepburn
1525	Robert Shaw
1532(?)	Alexander Stewart
1538(?)	Patrick Hepburn
1574	George Douglas
1611	Alexander Douglas
1623	John Guthrie
1662	Murdo Mackenzie
1677	James Aitken
1680	Colin Falconer
1687	Alexander Rose
1688	William Hay
1707	Held with Edinburgh
1725	Held with Aberdeen
1727	William Dunbar
1737	George Hay (elect)
1742	William Falconar
1777	Arthur Petrie
1787	Andrew Macfarlane
1798	Alexander Jolly
1838	Held with Ross
1851	Robert Eden
1886	James Butler Knill Kelly
1904	Arthur John Maclean
1943	Piers Holt Wilson

1953	Duncan Macinnes
1970	George Minshull Sessford
1994	Gregor Macgregor
1999	John Michael Crook
2007	Mark Jeremy Strange

†Ross

1131(?)	Macbeth
1150(?)	Simon
1161	Gregory
1195	Reginald
1213	Andrew de Moravia (elect)
1215(?)	Robert I
1250	Robert II
1272	Matthew
1275(?)	Robert II de Fyvin
1295(?)	Adam de Derlingtun (elect)
1297(?)	Thomas de Dundee
1325	Roger
1351	Alexander Stewart
1372	Alexander de Kylwos
1398(?)	Alexander de Waghorn
1418	Thomas Lyell (elect)
	Griffin Yonge (elect)
1420	John Bulloch
1441(?)	Andrew de Munro (elect)
1441(?)	Thomas Tulloch
1464(?)	Henry Cockburn
1478	John Wodman
1481	William Elphinstone (elect)
1483	Thomas Hay
1492	John Guthrie
1498	John Frisel [Fraser]
c.1507	Robert Cockburn
1525	James Hay
c.1539	Robert Cairncross
1552	David Painter
1561(?)	Henry Sinclair
1566	John Lesley
1575	Alexander Hepburn
1611	David Lindsay
1613	Patrick Lindsay
1633	John Maxwell
1662	John Paterson
1679	Alexander Young
1684	James Ramsay
1696	See vacant or held with Caithness until 1727
1727	Held with Moray
1742	Held with Caithness
1762	Robert Forbes
1777	Held with Moray
1819	David Low
1851	Held with Moray

†Caithness

c.1146	Andrew
c.1187	John
1214	Adam
1223(?)	Gilbert de Moravia
1250(?)	William
1263	Walter de Baltrodin
1273(?)	Nicholas (elect)
1275	Archibald Herok
1278	Richard (elect)
1279(?)	Hervey de Dundee (elect)
1282	Alan de St Edmund
1295	John or James (elect)
1296	Adam de Derlingtun
1297	Andrew
1306	Fercard Belegaumbe
1328(?)	David
1341	Alan de Moravia
1343	Thomas de Fingask
1370	Malcolm de Dumbrek
1381	Alexander Man
1414	Alexander Vaus
1425	John de Crannach
1428	Robert Strabrok
1446	John Innes
1448	William Mudy
1478(?)	Prospero Camogli de Medici
1484(?)	John Sinclair (elect)

1502	Andrew Stewart I
1517(?)	Andrew Stewart II
1542	Robert Stewart (elect)
1600	George Gledstanes (elect)
1611	Alexander Forbes
1616	John Abernethy
1662	Patrick Forbes
1680	Andrew Wood
[1695	See vacant]
1731	Robert Keith
1741	Wm. Falconas
1762	Held with Ross
[1742	See Vacant]
1777	Held with Moray

Glasgow

Glasgow and Galloway

Description of arms. Party per pale: dexter, vert, a fess wavy argent charged with a bar wavy azure between a representation of St Mungo issuant from the fess proper, habited or, his dexter hand raised in benediction and in his sinister hand a Celtic cross of the same in chief, in nombril point a salmon proper and in base an annulet of the fourth; sinister, argent a representation of St Ninian standing full-faced proper, clothed in a pontifical robe purpure, on his head a mitre and in his dexter hand a crosier or.

550(?)	Kentigern or Mungo (no record of his successors)
1114(?)	(Michael)
1118(?)	John
1147	Herbert
1164	Ingram
1175	Jocelin
1199	Hugh de Roxburgh (elect)
1200	William Malveisin
1202	Florence (elect)
1208	Walter de St Albans
1233	William de Bondington
1259	Nicholas de Moffat (elect)
1259	John de Cheam
1268	Nicholas de Moffat (elect)
1271	William Wischard (elect)
1273	Robert Wischard
1317	Stephen de Donydouer (elect)
1318	John de Eglescliffe
1323	John de Lindsay
1337	John Wischard
1339	William Rae
1367	Walter Wardlaw
1388	Matthew de Glendonwyn
1391	John Framisden (titular)
1408	William Lauder
1427	John Cameron
1447	James de Brois [Brewhouse]
1448	William Turnbull
1456	Andrew de Durrisdeer
1475	John Laing
1483	George Carmichael (elect)

ARCHBISHOPS

1483	Robert Blackadder (Archbishop 9 Jan 1492)
1509	James Betoun I
1525	Gavin Dunbar
1551	Alexander Gordon
1552	James Betoun II (restored 1587)
1571	John Porterfield (titular)
1573	James Boyd (titular)
1581	Robert Montgomery (titular)
1585	William Erskine (titular)
1610	John Spottiswoode
1615	James Law
1633	Patrick Lindsay
1661	Andrew Fairfoul
1664	Alexander Burnet (restored 1674)
1671	Robert Leighton, died 1684 (resigned 1674)
1679	Arthur Rose
1684	Alexander Cairncross, died 1701
1687	John Paterson,[1] died 1708
[1708	Vacant]

BISHOPS

1731	Alexander Duncan, died 1733
[1733	Vacant]
1787	Held with Edinburgh
1805	William Abernethy Drummond
1809–37	Held with Edinburgh
1837	Michael Russell
1848	Walter John Trower
1859	William Scott Wilson
1888	William Thomas Harrison
1904	Archibald Ean Campbell
1921	Edward Thomas Scott Reid
1931	John Russell Darbyshire
1938	John Charles Halland How
1952	Francis Hamilton Moncreiff
1974	Frederick Goldie
1981	Derek Alec Rawcliffe
1991	John Mitchell Taylor
1998	Idris Jones
2010	Gregor Duthrie Duncan

†Galloway or Candida Casa or Whithorn[2]

	Ninian, died 432(?)
(?)	Octa
681	Trumwine
731	Penthelm, died 735(?)
735	Frithowald, died 764
763	Pehtwine, died 776
777	Ethelbert
791	Beadwulf
1140	Gilla-Aldan
1154	Christian
1189	John
1214	Walter
1235	Odo Ydonc (elect)
1235	Gilbert
1255	Henry
1294	Thomas de Kircudbright [de Daltoun]
1327	Simon de Wedale
1355	Michael Malconhalgh
1359(?)	Thomas Macdowell (elect)
1359	Thomas
1364	Adam de Lanark
(?)	David Douglas, died 1373
(?)	James Carron (resigned 1373)
1378	Ingram de Kethnis (elect)
1379	Oswald
1380	Thomas de Rossy
(?)	Francis Ramsay, died 1402

1406	Elisaeus Adougan
1414(?)	Gilbert Cavan (elect)
1415	Thomas de Butil
1422	Alexander Vaus
1451	Thomas Spens
1457(?)	Thomas Vaus (elect)
1459	Ninian Spot
1482(?)	George Vaus
1508(?)	James Betoun (elect)
1509(?)	David Arnot
1526	Henry Wemyss
1541(?)	Andrew Dury
1559(?)	Alexander Gordon
1610	Gavin Hamilton
1612(?)	William Couper
1619	Andrew Lamb
1635	Thomas Sydserf
1661	James Hamilton
1675	John Paterson
1679	Arthur Rose
1680	James Aitken
1688	John Gordon, died 1726
1697	Held with Edinburgh
1837	Held with Glasgow

Argyll or Lismore

Argyll and The Isles

Description of arms. Azure, two crosiers in saltire and in chief a mitre or.

1193	Harald
1240	William
1253	Alan
1268	Laurence de Erganis
1300	Andrew
1342	Angusde Ergadia (elect)
1344	Martinde Ergaill
1387	John Dugaldi
1397(?)	Bean Johannis
1420(?)	Finlay de Albany
1428	George Lauder
1476	Robert Colquhoun
1504	David Hamilton
1532	Robert Montgomery
1539(?)	William Cunningham (elect)
1553(?)	James Hamilton (elect)
1580	Neil Campbell (titular)
1611	John Campbell (titular)
1613	Andrew Boyd
1637	James Fairlie
1662	David Fletcher
1665	John Young (elect)
1666	William Scroggie
1675	Arthur Rose
1679	Colin Falconer
1680	Hector Maclean
1688	Alexander Monro (elect)
	Held with Ross
1847	Alexander Ewing
1874	George Mackarness
1883	James Robert Alexander Chinnery-Haldane
1907	Kenneth Mackenzie
1942	Thomas Hannay
1963	Richard Knyvet Wimbush
1977	George Kennedy Buchanan Henderson

---

[1] After the deposition of John Paterson at the Revolution the See ceased to be Archiepiscopal.

[2] The traditional founder of the See is St Ninian, but nothing authentic is known of the bishops prior to the accession of Gilla-Aldan between 1133 and 1140.

1993 Douglas MacLean Cameron	1680 Archibald Graham [or McIlvernock]	1782 Robert Kilgour (Aberdeen 1768–86)
2004 Alexander Martin Shaw	Held with Orkney and Caithness	1788 John Skinner (Aberdeen 1786–1816)
2011 Kevin Pearson	1819 Held with Argyll	1816 George Gleig (Brechin 1810–40)

†The Isles

	1837 James Walker (Edinburgh 1880–41)

900 Patrick	
1080 Roolwer	
1080 William	
1095 Hamundr	
1138 Wimund	
1152 John I	
1152(?) Ragnald	
1154 Gamaliel	
1170 Christian	
1194 Michael	
1210 Nicholas I	
1219 Nicholas II of Meaux	
1226(?) Reginald	
1226 Simon	
1249 Laurence (elect)	
1253 Richard	
1275 Gilbert (elect)	
1275 Mark	
1305 Alan	
1324 Gilbert Maclelan	
1328 Bernard de Linton	
1331 Thomas de Rossy	
1349 William Russell	
1374 John Donkan	
1387 Michael	
1392 John Sproten (Man) (titular)	
1402(?) Conrad (Man) (titular)	
1402(?) Theodore Bloc (Man) (titular)	
1410 Richard Messing (Man)	
1422 Michael Anchire	
1425(?) John Burgherlinus (Man)	
1428 Angus I	
1441(?) John Hectoris [McCachane] Macgilleon	
1472 Angus II	
1487 John Campbell	
1511 George Hepburn	
1514 John Campbell (elect)	
1530(?) Ferchar MacEachan (elect)	
1550(?) Roderick Maclean	
1553(?) Alexander Gordon	
1567 John Carswell (titular)	
1573 John Campbell	
1605 Andrew Knox	
1619 Thomas Knox	
1628 John Leslie	
1634 Neil Campbell	
1662 Robert Wallace	
1677 Andrew Wood	

College

Bishops, Consecrated without Sees

1705 John Sage, died 1711	
1705 John Fullarton (Edinburgh 1720), died 1727	
1709 Henry Christie, died 1718	
1709 John Falconar (Fife 1720), died 1723	
1711 Archibald Campbell (Aberdeen 1721), died 1744	
1712 James Gadderar (Aberdeen 1725, Moray 1725), died 1733	
1718 Arthur Millar (Edinburgh 1727), died 1727	
1718 William Irvine, died 1725	
1722 Andrew Cant, died 1730	
1722 David Freebairn (Edinburgh 1733)	
1726 John Ochterlonie (Brechin 1731), died 1742	
1726 James Ross (Fife 1731), died 1733	
1727 John Gillan (Dunblane 1731), died 1735	
1727 David Ranken, died 1728	

Bishops who have held the Office of Primus

1704 Alexander Rose (Edinburgh 1704–20)	
1720 John Fullarton (Edinburgh 1720–27)	
1727 Arthur Millar (Edinburgh 1727)	
1727 Andrew Lumsden (Edinburgh 1727–33)	
1731 David Freebairn (Edinburgh 1733–39)	
1738 Thomas Rattray (Dunkeld 1727–43)	
1743 Robert Keith (Caithness 1731–41)	
1757 Robert White (Dunblane 1735–43, St Andrews 1743–61)	
1762 William Falconar (Orkney and Caithness 1741–62)	

1841 William Skinner (Aberdeen 1816–57)	
1857 Charles Hughes Terrot (Edinburgh 1841–72)	
1862 Robert Eden (Moray, Ross, and Caithness 1851–86)	
1886 Hugh Willoughby Jermyn (Brechin 1875–1903)	
1901 James Butler Knill Kelly (Moray, Ross, and Caithness 1886–1904)	
1904 George Howard Wilkinson (St Andrews, Dunkeld, and Dunblane 1893–1907)	
1908 Walter John Forbes Robberds (Brechin 1904–34)	
1935 Arthur John Maclean (Moray, Ross, and Caithness 1904–43)	
1943 Ernest Denny Logie Danson (Edinburgh 1939–46)	
1946 John Charles Halland How (Glasgow and Galloway 1938–52)	
1952 Thomas Hannay (Argyll and The Isles 1942–62)	
1962 Francis Hamilton Moncreiff (Glasgow and Galloway 1952–74)	
1974 Richard Knyvet Wimbush (Argyll and The Isles 1963–77)	
1977 Alastair Iain Macdonald Haggart (Edinburgh 1975–85)	
1985 Lawrence Edward Luscombe (Brechin 1975–90)	
1990 George Kennedy Buchanan Henderson (Argyll and The Isles 1977–92)	
1992 Richard Frederick Holloway (Edinburgh 1986–2000)	
2000 Andrew Bruce Cameron (Aberdeen 1992–2006)	
2006 Idris Jones (Glasgow and Galloway 1998–2009)	
2009 David Robert Chillingworth (St Andrews, Dunkeld, and Dunblane 2005–17)	
2017 Mark Jeremy Strange (Moray, Ross and Caithness 2007–)	

IRELAND

PROVINCE OF ARMAGH

†Achonry

BISHOPS

c.558 Cathfuidh	
1152 Mael Ruanaid ua Ruadain	
1159 Gille na Naehm O Ruadain [Gelasius]	
1208 Clemens O Sniadaig	
1220 Connmach O Torpaig [Carus]	
1226 Gilla Isu O Cleirig [Gelasius]	
1237 Tomas O Ruadhan	
1238 Oengus O Clumain [Elias]	
1251 Tomas O Maicin	

1266 Tomas O Miadachain [Dionysus]	
1286 Benedict O Bracain	
1312 David of Kilheny	
1348 David II	
1348 Nicol Alias Muircheartach O hEadhra	
1374 William Andrew	
1385 Simon	
c.1390 Tomas mac Muirgheasa MacDonn-chadha	
1401 Brian mac Seaain O hEadhra	
1410 Maghnus O h Eadhra	
1424 Donatus	

1424 Richard Belmer	
1436 Tadhg O Dalaigh	
1442 James Blakedon	
1449 Cornelius O Mochain	
1463 Brian O hEasdhra [Benedictus]	
1470 Nicholas Forden	
1475 Robert Wellys	
1484 Thomas fitzRichard	
1484 Tomas O Conghalain	
1489 John Bustamente	
1492 Thomas Ford	
1508 Eugenius O Flannagain	
1522 Cormac O Snighe	
1547 Thomas O Fihilly	

† Indicates a diocese no longer extant, or united with another diocese.

1562   Eugene O'Harte
1613   Miler Magrath (with Cashel)
       United to Killala 1622

†Annadown

BISHOPS

1189   Conn ua Mellaig [Concors]
1202   Murchad ua Flaithbertaig
1242   Tomas O Mellaig
1251   Conchobar [Concors]
1283   John de Ufford
1308   Gilbert O Tigernaig
1323   Jacobus O Cethernaig
1326   Robert Petit
1328   Albertus
1329   Tomas O Mellaig
1359   Dionysius
1393   Johannes
1394   Henry Trillow
1402   John Bryt
1408   John Wynn
1421   John Boner [Camere]
1425   Seean Mac Braddaigh
1428   Seamus O Lonnghargain
1431   Donatus O Madagain
1446   Thomas Salscot
1450   Redmund Bermingham
1458   Thomas Barrett
1496   Francis Brunand
1540   John Moore
       United to Tuam c.1555

†Ardagh

454   Mel
c.670   Erard
874   Faelghus
       Cele 1048
1152   Mac Raith ua Morain
1172   Gilla Crist O hEothaig
       [Christianus]
       O'Tirlenain 1187
       ua hEislinnen
       Annud O Muiredaig 1216
1217   Robert
1224   M.
1228   Loseph mac Teichthechain
1229   Mac Raith Mac Serraig
1232   Gilla Isu mac in Scelaige O
       Tormaid [Gelasius]
1232   Iocelinus
1238   Brendan Mac Teichthechain
1256   Milo of Dunstable
1290   Matha O'h-Eothaig [Mattheus]
1323   Robert Wirsop (did not get
       possession)
1324   Mac Eoaighseoan
1347   Eoghan O Ferghail
       [Audovenus]
1368   William Mac Carmaic
1373   Cairbre O'Ferghail [Charles]
1373   John Aubrey
1392   Henry Nony (did not get
       possession)
1396   Comedinus Mac Bradaigh
       [Gilbert]
1400   Adam Leyns
1419   Conchobar O'Ferghail
       [Cornelius]
1425   Risdeard O'Ferghail
[1444   O'Murtry, not consecrated
       resigned]
1445   Cormac Mac Shamhradhain
1462   Seaan O'Ferghail
1467   Donatus O'Ferghail
1482   William O'Ferghail
1517   Ruaidri O'Maoileoin
1517   Rory O'Mallone [Roger O
       Melleine]
1541   Richard O'Ferrall
1553   Patrick MacMahon
[1572   John Garvey, not consecrated]
1583   Lysach O'Ferrall

1604   Robert Draper
1613   Thomas Moigne
1679   William Bedell
1633   John Richardson
1661   Robert Maxwell
1673   Francis Marsh
1682   William Sheridan
1692   Ulysses Burgh
1604–33, 1661–92 and 1692–1751 Held
       by the Bishops of Kilmore
1751–1839 Held by the Archbishops of
       Tuam
United to Kilmore 1839

Armagh

Description of arms. Azure, an
archiepiscopal staff in pale argent
ensigned with a cross pattée or,
surmounted by a pall argent fimbriated
and fringed or, charged with four
crosses pattées-fitchées sable.

BISHOPS

444   Patrick
       Benignus 467
       Jarlath 481
       Cormac 497
       Dubthach 513
       Ailill I 526
       Ailill II 536
       David O'Faranan 551
       Carlaen 588
       MacLaisre 623
–640   Thomian MacRonan
       Segeni 688
       Suibhne 730
–732   Congusa
       Affinth 794
–811   Nundha
–818   Artri
835   Forannan
       Mael Patraic I 862
       Fethgna 875
       Cathasach MacRobartach 883
       Mochta 893
900   Maelaithghin
       Cellach
       Mael Ciarain 915
       Joseph 936
       Mael Patraic II 936
       Cathasach MacDolgen 966
       Maelmiure 994
       Airindach 1000
       Maeltuile 1032
1032   Hugh O'Ferris
       Mael Patraic III 1096
1099   Caincomrac O'Boyle

ARCHBISHOPS

1105   Cellach mac Aeda meic Mael
       Isu [Celsus]
1132   Mael maedoc Ua Morgair
       [Malachais]
1137   Gilla Meic Liac mac Diarmata
       meic Ruaidri [Gelasius]
1174   Conchobar O Conchaille
       [Concors]
1175   Gille in Coimhedh O Caran
       [Gilbertus]
1180   Tomaltach O Conchobair
       [Thomas]

1184   Mael Isu Ua Cerbaill
       [Malachias]
1202   Echdonn mac Gilla Uidir
       [Eugenius]
1217   Lucas Neterville
1227   Donatus O Fidabra
1240   Albert Suebeer of Cologne
1247   Reginald
1258   Abraham O'Conallain
1261   Mael Patraic O Scannail
1270   Nicol Mac Mael Isu
1303   Michael MacLochlainn (not
       confirmed)
1304   Dionysius (not confirmed)
1306   John Taaffe
1307   Walter Jorz
1311   Roland Jorz
1324   Stephen Segrave
1334   David Mag Oireachtaigh
1347   Richard FitzRalph
1362   Milo Sweetman
1383   John Colton
1404   Nicholas Fleming
1418   John Swayne
1439   John Prene
1444   John Mey
1457   John Bole [Bull]
1471   John Foxhals or Foxholes
1475   Edmund Connesburgh
1480   Ottaviano Spinelli [de Palatio]
1513   John Kite
1521   George Cromer
1543   George Dowdall
1552   Hugh Goodacre
1553   George Dowdall (again)
[1560   Donat MacTeague, not
       recognized by the Crown,
       1562]
1563   Adam Loftus
1568   Thomas Lancaster
1584   John Long
1589   John Garvey
1595   Henry Ussher
1613   Christopher Hampton
1625   James Ussher
       [Interregnum 1656–61]
1661   John Bramhall
1663   James Margetson
1679   Michael Boyle
1703   Narcissus Marsh
1714   Thomas Lindsay
1724   Hugh Boulter
1742   John Hoadly
1747   George Stone
1765   Richard Robinson [afterwards
       Baron Rokeby]
1795   William Newcome
1800   William Stuart
1822   John George Beresford
       United to Clogher 1850–86
1862   Marcus Gervais Beresford
1886   Robert Bentknox
1893   Robert Samuel Gregg
1896   William Alexander
1911   John Baptist Crozier
1920   Charles Frederick D'Arcy
1938   John Godfrey FitzMaurice Day
1939   John Allen Fitzgerald Gregg
1959   James McCann
1969   George Otto Simms
1980   John Ward Armstrong
1986   Robert Henry Alexander
       Eames
2007   Alan Edwin Thomas Harper
2012   Richard Lionel Clarke

Clogher

Description of arms. Azure, a bishop seated in full pontificals proper, in the act of benediction, and holding his pastoral staff in the left hand.

c.493	MacCarthinn or Ferdachrioch Ailill 869
1135	Cinaeth O Baigill
1135	Gilla Crist O Morgair [Christianus] (moved his see to Louth)

BISHOPS OF LOUTH

1135	Gilla Crist O Morgair [Christianus]
1138	Aed O Ceallaide [Edanus]
1178	Mael Isu O Cerbaill [Malachias]
1187	Gilla Crist O Mucaran [Christinus]
1194	Mael Isu Ua Mael Chiarain
1197	Gilla Tigernaig Mac Gilla Ronain [Thomas]

BISHOPS OF CLOGHER

1218	Donatus O Fidabra
1228	Nehemias
1245	David O Bracain
1268	Michael Mac an tSair
1287	Matthew Mac Cathasaigh I
–1310	Henricus
1316	Gelasius O Banain
1320	Nicholas Mac Cathasaigh
1356	Brian Mac Cathmaoil [Bernard]
1362	Matthew Mac Cathasaigh II
—	Aodh O hEothaigh [alias O Neill]
1373	John O Corcrain [Wurzburg]
1390	Art Mac Cathmhail
1433	Piaras Mag Uidhir [Petrus]
1450	Rossa mac Tomais Oig Mag Uidhir [Rogerius]
1475	Florence Woolley
[1484	Niall mac Seamuis Mac Mathghamna]
1484	John Edmund de Courci
1494	Seamus Mac Pilip Mac Mathghamna
1500	Andreas
1502	Nehemias O Cluainin
1504	Giolla Padraig O Conalaigh [Patrick]
1505	Eoghan Mac Cathmhail [Eugenius]
1517	Padraig O Cuilin
1535	Aodh O Cearbhalain [Odo]
1517	Patrick O'Cullen
1535	Hugh O'Carolan
1570	Miler Magrath
1605	George Montgomery
1621	James Spottiswood
1645	Henry Jones
1661	John Leslie
1671	Robert Leslie
1672	Roger Boyle
1691	Richard Tennison
1697	St George Ashe
1717	John Stearne
1745	Robert Clayton
1758	John Garnett
1782	John Hotham

1796	William Foster
1797	John Porter
1819	John George Beresford
1820	Percy Jocelyn
1822	Robert Ponsonby Tottenham Luftus
	United to Armagh 1850–86
1886	Charles Maurice Stack
1903	Charles Frederick D'Arcy
1908	Maurice Day
1923	James MacManaway
1944	Richard Tyner
1958	Alan Alexander Buchanan
1970	Richard Patrick Crosland Hanson
1973	Robert William Heavener
1980	Gordon McMullan
1986	Brian Desmond Anthony Hannon
2002	Michael Geoffrey St Aubyn Jackson
2011	Francis John McDowell

Connor

Description of arms. Azure, a lamb passant supporting with the dexter foreleg a staff proper flying therefrom a pennant argent charged with a saltire gules between three cross crosslets or; on a chief of the last two crosiers in saltire of the first.

506	Oengus MacNessa 514 Lughadh 543
640	Dimma Dubh [the Black] Duchonna the Pious 725 Cunnen or Cuinden 1038 Flann O'Sculu 1117
1124	Mael Maedoc Ua Morgair [Malachias]
–1152	MaelPatraic O'Banain
1172	Nehemias
1178	Reginaldus
1226	Eustacius
1242	Adam
1245	Isaac de Newcastle-on-Tyne
1258	William de Portroyal
1261	William de Hay [or la Haye]
1263	Robert de Flanders
1275	Peter de Dunach
1293	Johannes
1320	Richard
1321	James de Couplith
1323	John de Eglecliff
1323	Robert Wirsop
1324	Jacabus O Cethernaig
1353	William Mercier
1374	Paulus
1389	Johannes
[1420	Seaan O Luachrain, not consecrated]
1423	Eoghan O'Domhnaill
1429	Domhnall O'Meraich
1431	John Fossade [Festade]
1459	Patricius
1459	Simon Elvington
	United to Down 1441
1945	Charles King Irwin
1956	Robert Cyril Hamilton Glover Elliott
1969	Arthur Hamilton Butler
1981	William John McCappin
1987	Samuel Greenfield Poyntz

1995	James Edward Moore
2002	Alan Edwin Thomas Harper
2007	Alan Francis Abernethy

Derry

Derry and Raphoe

Description of arms. Party per pale: dexter gules, two swords in saltire proper, the hilts in base or, and on a chief azure a harp or stringed argent (for the See of Derry); sinister ermine, a chief per pale azure and or, the first charged with a sun in splendour of the last, the second with a cross pattée gules (for the See of Raphoe).

	Caencomhrac 927
–937	Finachta MacKellach
–949	Mael Finnen

BISHOPS OF MAGHERA

(Where the See was in the twelfth and the thirteenth centuries)

1107	Mael Coluim O Brolchain
—	Mael Brigte O Brolchain
1152	O Gormgaile Muiredach O Cobthaig [Mauricius]
1173	Amhlaim O Muirethaig
1185	Fogartach O Cerballain [Florentius]
c.1230	Gilla in Coimhded O Cerballain [Germanus]
c.1280	Fogartach O Cerballain II [Florentius]

BISHOPS OF DERRY

(Where the See was resettled)

1295	Enri Mac Airechtaig [O'Reghly] [of Ardagh]
1297	Gofraid MacLochlainn [Godfrey]
1316	Aed O Neill [Odo]
1319	Michael Mac Lochlainn [Maurice]
1349	Simon
1391	Johannes
1391	John Dongan
1394	Seoan O Mochain
1398	Aodh [Hugo]
1401	Seoan O Flannabhra
1415	Domhnall Mac Cathmhail
1419	Domhnall O Mearaich
1429	Eoghan O Domhnaill [Eugenius]
1433	John Oguguin
[1456	John Bole, appointment not completed, translated to Armagh]
1458	Bartholomew O Flannagain
c.1464	Johannes
1467	Nicholas Weston
1485	Domhnall O Fallamhain
1501	Seamus mac Pilip Mac Mathghamna [MacMahon]
1520	Ruaidhri O Domhnaill
1520	Rory O'Donnell
1554	Eugene O'Doherty
1568	F. [doubtful authority]
1569	Redmond O'Gallagher
[1603	Denis Campbell, not consecrated]

1605	George Montgomery
1610	Brutus Babington
[1611	Christopher Hampton, consecrated]
1613	John Tanner
1617	George Downham
1634	John Bramhall
1661	George Wild
1666	Robert Mossom
1680	Michael Ward
1681	Ezekiel Hopkins
1691	William King
1703	Charles Hickman
1714	John Hartstonge
1717	St George Ashe
1718	William Nicolson
1727	Henry Downes
1735	Thomas Rundle
1743	Carew Reynell
1745	George Stone
1747	William Barnard
1768	Frederick Augustus Hervey [afterwards Earl of Bristol]
1803	William Knox
1831	Richard Ponsonby Raphoe united to Derry from 1834
1853	William Higgin
1867	William Alexander
1896	George Alexander Chadwick (resigned)
1916	Joseph Irvine Peacocke
1945	Robert M'Neil Boyd
1958	Charles John Tyndall
1970	Cuthbert Irvine Peacocke
1975	Robert Henry Alexander Eames
1980	James Mehaffey
2002	Kenneth Raymond Good

Down

Down and Dromore

Description of arms. Quarterly, 1 and 4 azure, two keys endorsed in saltire the wards in chief or, surmounted in the fess point by a lamb passant proper (for the See of Down); 2 and 3 Argent, two keys endorsed in saltire the wards in chief gules, surmounted by an open book in fess proper between two crosses pattées-fitchées in pale sable (for the See of Dromore).

	Fergus 584
	Suibhne 825
	Graithene 956
	Finghin 964
	Flaithbertach 1043
	MaelKevin 1086
—	Mael Muire 1117
	Oengus Ua Gormain 1123
—	[Anonymous]
c.1124	Mael Maedoc O Morgair [Malachias]
1152	Mael Isu mac in Chleirig Chuirr [Malachias]
1175	Gilla Domangairt Mac Cormaic
c.1176	Echmilid [Malachias]
c.1202	Radulfus
1224	Thomas
1251	Randulphus

1258	Reginaldus
1265	Thomas Lydel
1277	Nicholas le Blund
1305	Thomas Ketel
1314	Thomas Bright
1328	John of Baliconingham
1329	Ralph of Kilmessan
1353	Richard Calf I
1365	Robert of Aketon
1367	William White
1369	Richard Calf [II]
1386	John Ross
1394	John Dongan
1413	John Cely [or Sely]
1445	Ralph Alderle

BISHOPS OF DOWN AND CONNOR

1441	John Fossard
1447	Thomas Pollard
1451	Richard Wolsey
1456	Thomas Knight
1469	Tadhg O Muirgheasa [Thaddaeus]
1489	Tiberio Ugolino
1520	Robert Blyth
1542	Eugene Magennis
1565	James MacCawell
1569	John Merriman
1572	Hugh Allen
1593	Edward Edgeworth
1596	John Charden
1602	Roben Humpston
1607	John Todd (resigned)
1612	James Dundas
1613	Robert Echlin
1635	Henry Leslie
1661	Jeremy Taylor
1667	Roger Boyle
1672	Thomas Hacket
1694	Samuel Foley
1695	Edward Walkington
1699	Edward Smyth
1721	Francis Hutchinson
1739	Carew Reynell
1743	John Ryder
1752	John Whitcombe
1752	Robert Downes
1753	Arthur Smyth
1765	James Traill
1784	William Dickson
1804	Nathaniel Alexander
1823	Richard Mant

BISHOPS OF DOWN, CONNOR AND DROMORE

1849	Robert Bent Knox
1886	William Reeves
1892	Thomas James Welland
1907	John Baptist Crozier
1911	Charles Frederick D'Arcy
1919	Charles Thornton Primrose Grierson
1934	John Frederick McNeice
1942	Charles King Irwin

BISHOPS OF DOWN AND DROMORE

1945	William Shaw Kerr
1955	Frederick Julian Mitchell
1970	George Alderson Quin
1980	Robert Henry Alexander Eames
1986	Gordon McMullan
1997	Harold Creeth Miller

†Dromore

	Mael Brighde 974
	Riagan 1101
1197	Ua Ruanada
1227	Geraldus
1245	Andreas
1284	Tigernach I
1290	Gervasius
—	Tigernach II

1309	Florentius Mac Donnocain
1351	Anonymous
1366	Milo
1369	Christophorus Cornelius 1382
1382	John O'Lannoy
1398	Thomas Orwell
1400	John Waltham
1402	Roger Appleby
1408	Richard Payl
1410	Marcus
1411	John Chourles
1414	Seaan O Ruanadha
1419	Nicholas Wartre
1429	Thomas Rackelf
1431	William
1431	David Chirbury
1450	Thomas Scrope [Bradley]
1450	Thomas Radcliff
1456	Donatus O h-Anluain [Ohendua]
1457	Richard Messing
1463	William Egremond
—	Aonghus [Aeneas] 1476
1476	Robert Kirke
1480	Yvo Guillen
1483	George Braua
1511	Tadhg O Raghallaigh [Thaddeus]
1536	Quintin O Quigley [Cogley]
1539	Roger McHugh
1540	Arthur Magennis
1607	John Todd
[1613	John Tanner, not consecrated]
1613	Theophilus Buckworth
1661	Robert Leslie
1661	Jeremy Taylor (administered the diocese)
1667	George Rust
1671	Essex Digby
1683	Capel Wiseman
1695	Tobias Pullein
1713	John Stearne
1717	Ralph Lambert
1727	Charles Cobbe
1732	Henry Maule
1744	Thomas Fletcher
1745	Jemmett Browne
1745	George Marlay
1763	John Oswald
1763	Edward Young
1765	Henry Maxwell
1766	William Newcome
1775	James Hawkins
1780	William de la Poer Beresford
1782	Thomas Percy
1811	George Hall
1812	John Leslie
1819	James Saurin
	United to Down since 1842

†Elphin

	Domnall mac Flannacain Ua Dubhthaig 1136
	Muiredach O Dubhthaig 1150
1152	Mael Isu O Connachtain Flannacan O Dubhthaig 1168
c.1177	Tomaltach mac Aeda Ua Conchobhair [Thomas]
c.1180	Florint Ua Riacain Ui Maelrvanaid
1206	Ardgar O Conchobhair
1226	Dionysius O Mordha
c.1230	Alanus
1231	Donnchad mac Fingein O Conchobhair [Dionysius Donatus]
1245	Eoin O Mugroin
1247	Tomaltach macToirrdelbaig O Conchobhair [Thomas]
1260	Mael Sechlainn O Conchobhair [Milo]
1262	Tomas mac Fergail mac Diarmata
1266	Muiris O Conchobhair

[1285　Amiaim O Tommaltaig, not consecrated]
1285　Gilla Isu mac in Liathana O Conchobhair
1297　Maelsechlainn mac Briain [Malachias]
1303　Donnchad O Flannacain, [Donatus]
1307　Cathal O Conchobair
1310　Mael Sechlainn Mac Aedha
1313　Lurint O Lachtnain [Laurence]
1326　Sean O Finnachta
1355　Carolus
1357　Gregory O Mochain
1372　Thomas Barrett
1383　Seoan O Mochain
1407　Seaan O Grada
1405　Gerald Caneton
1412　Thomas Colby
1418　Robert Fosten
1421　Edmund Barrett
1427　Johannes
1429　Laurence O Beolain
1429　William O hEidighean
1448　Conchobhar O Maolalaidh
1458　Nicholas O Flanagan
1487　Hugo Arward
1492　Rlocard mac Briain O gCuanach
1499　George Brana
1501　Cornelius O Flannagain
1508　Christopher Fisher
1525　John Maxey
1539　William Maginn 1541(?)
1539　Gabriel de Sancto Serio
1541　Conach or Con O'Negall or O'Shyagall
1552　Roland Burke [de Burgo]
1582　Thomas Chester
1583　John Lynch
1611　Edward King
1639　Henry Tilson
1661　John Parker
1667　John Hodson
1691　Simon Digby
1720　Henry Downes
1724　Theophilus Bolton
1730　Robert Howard
1740　Edward Synge
1762　William Gore
1772　Jemmett Browne
1775　Charles Dodgson
1795　John Law
1810　Power le Poer Trench
1819　John Leslie 1854
　　　United to Kilmore and Ardagh on the death of Bishop Beresford in 1841, when Bishop Leslie became Bishop of the united dioceses.

†Killala

Muiredach
Kellach
O Maolfogmair I 1137
O Maolfogmair II 1151
Imar O Ruaidhin 1176
1179　O Maolfogmair III
1199　Domnall Ua Becdha
1207　Cormac O'Tarpy
　　　O'Kelly 1214
1226　Aengus O Maolfogmair [Elias]
　　　Gille Cellaig O Ruaidhin
1253　Seoan O Laidlg
1281　Donnchad O Flaithbertaig [Donatus]
1307　John Tankard
　　　Sean O Flaithim 1343
1344　James Bermingham
1347　William O DusucBhda
1351　Robert Elyot
1381　Thomas Lodowys

1383　Conchobar O Coineoil [Cornelius]
1390　Thomas Horwell [Orwell]
1400　Thomas Barrett
1403　Muircheartach Cleirach mac Donnchadha O DusucBhda Connor O'Connell 1423
1427　Fergal Mac Martain
1431　Thaddeus Mac Creagh
1432　Brian O Coneoil
1447　Robert Barrett
1452　Ruaidhri Bairead [Barrett]
1453　Thomas
1459　Richard Viel
　　　Miler O'Connell
1461　Donatus O Conchobhair
1470　Tomas Bairead [Barrett]
1487　John de Tuderto [Seaan O Caissin]
1500　Thomas Clerke
1508　Malachias O Clumhain
1513　Risdeard Bairead
1545　Redmond O'Gallagher
1570　Donat O'Gallagher
1580　John O'Casey
1592　Owen O'Conor
1613　Miler Magrath
　　　Achonry united to Killala 1622
1623　Archibald Hamilton
1630　Archibald Adair (deposed, but subsequently restored)
164?　John Maxwell
1661　Henry Hall
1664　Thomas Bayly
1671　Thomas Otway
1680　John Smith
1681　William Smyth
1682　Richard Tennison
1691　William Lloyd
1717　Henry Downes
1720　Charles Cobbe
1727　Robert Howard
1730　Robert Clayton
173?　Mordecai Cary
175?　Richard Robinson [afterwards Baron Rokeby]
1759　Samuel Hutchinson
1781　William Cecil Pery
1784　William Preston
1787　John Law
1795　John Porter
1798　Joseph Stock
1810　James Verschoyle
　　　United to Tuam since 1834

Kilmore

Kilmore, Elphin and Ardagh

Description of arms. Argent, on a cross azure a pastoral staff enfiling a mitre, all or (for the See of Kilmore). Sable, two pastoral staves in saltire or, in base a lamb couchant, argent (for the See of Elphin). Or, a cross gules between four trefoils slipped vert, on a chief sable, a key erect of the first (for the See of Ardagh).

—　Aed Ua Finn 1136
—　Muirchenach Ua Maelmoeherge 1149
1152　Tuathal Ua Connachtaig [Thadeus]

1202　Mi Ua Dobailen
—　Flann O Connachtaig [Florentius] 1231
1237　Congalach Mac Idneoil
1251　Simon O Ruairc
1286　Mauricius
—　Matha Mac Duibne 1314
1320　Padraig O Cridecain
—　Conchobhar Mac Conshnamha [Ford] 1355
1356　Richard O Raghilligh
1373　Johannes
1388　Thomas Rushook
1392　Sean O Raghilligh I [John]
1398　Nicol Mac Bradaigh
1401　Sean O'Raghilligh II
1407　John Stokes
1409　David O'Fairchellaigh
1422　Domhnall O Gabhann
1445　Aindrias Mac Bradaigh
1455　Fear Sithe Mag Dhuibhne
1465　Sean O Raghilligh II
1476　Cormac Mag Shamhradhain
1480　Tomas MacBradaigh
1512　Diarmaid O Raghilligh
1530　Edmund Nugent
1540　Sean Mac Bradaigh
1585　John Garvey
1604　Robert Draper
1613　Thomas Moigne
1629　William Bedell
1643　Robert Maxwell
1673　Francis Marsh
1682　William Sheridan
1693　William Smyth
1699　Edward Wetenhall
1715　Timothy Godwin
1727　Josiah Hort
1742　Joseph Story
1757　John Cradock
1772　Denison Cumberland
1775　George Lewis Jones
1790　William Foster
1796　Charles Broderick
1802　George de la Poer Beresford
　　　Ardagh united to Kilmore 1839
　　　Elphin united to Kilmore 1841
1841　John Leslie
1854　Marcus Gervais Beresford
1862　Hamilton Verschoyle
1870　Charles Leslie
1870　Thomas Carson
1874　John Richard Darley
1884　Samuel Shone
1897　Alfred George Elliott
1915　William Richard Moore
1930　Arthur William Barton
1939　Albert Edward Hughes
1950　Frederick Julian Mitchell
1956　Charles John Tyndall
1959　Edward Francis Butler Moore
1981　William Gilbert Wilson
1993　Michael Hugh Gunton Mayes
2001　Kenneth Harbert Clarke
2013　Samuel Ferran Glenfield

†Mayo

Gerald 732
Muiredach [or Murray]
Mcinracht 732
Aidan 773
1172　Gilla Isu Ua Mailin
　　　Cele O Dubhthaig 1210
1210　?Patricius
1428　William Prendergast
1430　Nicholas 'Wogmay'
1439　Odo O h-Uiginn
1432　Martin Campania
1457　Simon de Duren
1493　John Bel
1541　Eugenius Macan Brehon
　　　United to Tuam 1559

†Raphoe

Sean O Gairedain
Donell O Garvan
Felemy O Syda
Oengus O'Lappin 959
1150 Muiredhach O'Cofley
1156 Gille in Coimhded Ua Carain [Gilbertus]
— Anonymous
1204 Mael Isu Ua Doirig
— Anonymous
1253 Mael Padraig O Scannail [Patricius]
1263 John de Alneto
1265 Cairpre O Scuapa
1275 Fergal O Firghil [Florentius]
1306 Enri Mac-in-Chrossain [Henricus]
1319 Tomas Mac Carmaic Ui Domhnaill
1363 Padraig Mac Maonghail
1367 Conchobar Mac Carmaic Ui Domhnaill [Cornelius]
1397 Seoan MacMenmain
1400 Eoin MacCarmaic [Johannes]
-1413 Anthony
-1414 Robert Rubire
1416 John McCormic
1420 Lochlainn O Gallchobhair I [Laurentius]
1440 Cornelius Mac Giolla Brighde
1443 Lochlainn O Gallchobhair II [Laurentius]
1479 John de Rogeriis
1482 Meanma Mac Carmail [Menclaus Mac Carmacain]
1514 Conn O Cathain [Cornelius]
1534 Eamonn O Gallchobhair
1547 Arthur o'Gallagher
1563 Donnell Magonigle [or McCongail]
[1603 Denis Campbell, not consecrated]
1605 George Montgomery
1611 Andrew Knox
1633 John Leslie
1661 Robert Leslie
1671 Ezekiel Hopkins
1682 William Smyth
1693 Alexander Cairncross
1701 Robert Huntington
1702 John Pooley
1713 Thomas Lindsay
1714 Edward Synge
1716 Nicholas Forster
1744 William Barnard
1747 Philip Twysden
1753 Robert Downes
1763 John Oswald
1780 James Hawkins
1807 John George Beresford
1819 William Magee
1822 William Bissett
    United to Derry since 1834

Tuam

Tuam, Killala and Achonry

Description of arms. Azure beneath a triple architectural canopy three figures, in the centre the Blessed Virgin Mary holding in her arms the Holy Child, between, on the dexter the figure of a bishop (St Jarlath) in pontificalibus and in the act of benediction, and, on the sinister St John supporting with his left arm a lamb argent, each in proper vestments or, the hands, feet, and faces proper.

BISHOPS

Murrough O'Nioc 1032
Hugh O'Hessian 1085
Cathusach Ua Conaill 1117
O Clerig 1137
Muiredach Ua Dubhthaig 1150

ARCHBISHOPS

1152 Aed Ua h-Oisin [Edanus]
1167 Cadhla Ua Dubhthaig [Catholicus]
1202 Felix Ua Ruanada
1236 Mael Muire O Lachtain [Marianus]
1250 Flann Mac Flainn [Florentius]
[1256 James O'Laghtnan, not confirmed or consecrated]
1257 Walter de Salerno
1258 Tomaltach O Conchobair [Thomas]
1286 Stephen de Fulbourn
1289 William de Bermingham
1312 Mael Sechlainn Mac Aeda
1348 Tomas MacCerbhaill [MacCarwill]
1364 Eoin O Grada
1372 Gregory O Mochain I
1384 Gregory O Mochain II
1387 William O Cormacain
1393 Muirchertach mac Pilb O Cellaigh
1410 John Babingle
1411 Cornelius
1430 John Bermingham [Winfield]
1438 Tomas mac Muirchearthaigh O Cellaigh
1441 John de Burgo
1452 Donatus O Muiredaigh
1485 William Seoighe [Joyce]
1503 Philip Pinson
1506 Muiris O Fithcheallaigh
1514 Tomas O Maolalaidh
1537 Christopher Bodkin
1573 William O'Mullally [or Lealy] Annadown united to Tuam c.1555
    Mayo united to Tuam 1559
1595 Nehemiah Donnellan
1609 William O'Donnell [or Daniel]
1629 Randolph or Ralph Barlow
1638 Richard Boyle
1645 John Maxwell
1661 Samuel Pullen
1667 John Parker
1679 John Vesey
1716 Edward Synge
1742 Josiah Hort
1752 John Ryder
1775 Jemmett Browne
1782 Joseph Dean Bourke [afterwards Earl of Mayo]
1794 William Beresford [afterwards Baron Decies]
1819 Power le Poer Trench Killala united to Tuam from 1834

BISHOPS

1839 Thomas Plunket [afterwards Baron Plunket]
1867 Charles Brodrick Bernard
1890 James O'Sullivan
1913 Benjamin John Plunket
1920 Arthur Edwin Ross
1923 John Ort
1928 John Mason Harden
1932 William Hardy Holmes
1939 John Winthrop Crozier
1958 Arthur Hamilton Butler
1970 John Coote Duggan
1986 John Robert Winder Neill
1998 Richard Crosbie Aitken Henderson
2011 Patrick William Rooke

†Ardfert

BISHOPS

Anmchad O h-Anmchada 1117
1152 Mael Brenain Ua Ronain
Gilla Mac Aiblen O'Anmehadha 1166
Domnall O Connairche 1193
1200 David Ua Duibdithrib
Anonymous 1217
1218 John
1218 Gilbertus
1237 Brendan
1253 Christianus
1257 Philippus
1265 Johannes
1286 Nicolaus

PROVINCE OF DUBLIN

1288 Nicol O Samradain
1336 Ailin O hEichthighirn
1331 Edmund of Caermaerthen
1348 John de Valle
1372 Cornelius O Tigernach
1380 William Bull
1411 Nicholas FitzMaurice
1404 Nicholas Ball
1405 Tomas O Ceallaigh
1409 John Attilburgh [Artilburch]
1450 Maurice Stack
1452 Maurice O Conchobhair
1461 John Stack
1461 John Pigge
1473 Philip Stack
1495 John FitzGerald [See vacant in 1534]
1536 James FitzMaurice
1588 Nicholas Kenan
1600 John Crosbie
1622 John Steere
1628 William Steere
1641 Thomas Fulwar United to Limerick 1661

†Ardmore

1153 Eugenius
    Incorporated with Lismore 1192

Cashel

Cashel, Waterford, Lismore, Ossory, Ferns and Leighlin

Description of arms. Gules, two keys addorsed in saltire the wards in chief, or.

BISHOPS

Cormac MacCuillenan 908
Donnell O'Heney 1096 *or* 1098

ARCHBISHOPS

*c.*1111	Mael Ios Ua h-Ainmire
	Mael Iosa Ua Fogludha [Mauricius] 1131
	Domnall Ua Conaing 1137
	Gilla Naomh O'Marty 1149
−1152	Donat O'Lonergan I
−*c.*1160	M.
1172	Domnall O h-Ualla-chain [Donatus]
1186	Muirghes O h-Enna [Matheus]
*c.*1208	Donnchad Ua Longargain I [Donatus]
1216	Donnchad Ua Longargain II [Donatus]
1224	Mairin O Briain [Marianus]
1238	David mac Ceallaig [O'Kelly]
1254	David Mac Cearbaill [Mac Carwill]
1290	Stiamna O Bracain
1303	Maurice Mac Cearbaill
1317	William FitzJohn
1327	Seoan Mac Cerbaill
1329	Walter le Rede
1332	Eoin O Grada
1346	Radulphus O Cellaigh [Kelly]
1362	George Roche [de Rupe]
1365	Tomas Mac Cearbhaill
1374	Philip of Torrington
1382	Michael
1384	Peter Hackett
1406	Richard O Hedian
1442	John Cantwell I
1452	John Cantwell II
1484	David Creagh
1504	Maurice FitzGerald
1525	Edmund Butler
1553	Roland Baron or FitzGerald
1567	James MacCawell
	Emly united to Cashel 1569
1571	Miler Magrath (Bishop of Cashel and Waterford from 1582)
1623	Malcolm Hamilton
1630	Archibald Hamilton
1661	Thomas Fulwar
1667	Thomas Price
	[See vacant 1685–91]
1691	Narcissus Marsh
1694	William Palliser
[1727	William Nicolson, not enthroned]
1727	Timothy Goodwin
1730	Theophilus Bolton
1744	Arthur Price
1752	John Whitcombe
1754	Michael Cox
1779	Charles Agar
1801	Charles Brodrick

1822	Richard Laurence
	Waterford and Lismore united to Cashel from 1833; on the death of Abp Laurence in 1838 the province was united to Dublin and the see ceased to be an Archbishopric

BISHOPS

1839	Stephen Creagh Sandes
1843	Robert Daly
1872	Maurice FitzGerald Day
1900	Henry Stewart O'Hara
1919	Robert Miller
1931	John Frederick McNeice
1935	Thomas Arnold Harvey
1958	William Cecil De Pauley
1968	John Ward Armstrong
	Ossory united to Cashel 1977
1980	Noel Vincent Willoughby
1997	John Robert Winder Neill
2003	Peter Francis Barrett
2006	Michael Andrew James Burrows

†Clonfert

	Moena, or Moynean, or Moeinend 572
	Cummin the Tall 662
	Ceannfaeladh 807
	Laithbheartach 822
	Ruthnel or Ruthme 826
	Cormac MacEdain 922
	Ciaran O'Gabbla 953
	Cathal 963
	Eochu 1031
	O'Corcoran 1095
	Muiredach Ua h-Enlainge 1117
	Gille Patraic Ua Ailcinned 1149
*c.*1152	Petrus Ua Mordha
1172	Mail Isu mac in Baird
1179	Celechair Ua h-Armedaig
	Muirchertach Ua'Maeluidir 1187
	Domnall Ua Finn 1195
	Muirchertach Ua Carmacain 1204
1205	Mael Brigte Ua hErurain
1224	Cormac O Luimlin [Carus]
1248	Thomas
1259	Tomas mac Domnaill Moire O Cellaig
1266	Johannes de Alatre
1296	Robert
*c.*1302	John
1308	Gregorius O Brocaig
1320	Robert Le Petit
1322	Seoan O Leaain
1347	Tomas mac Gilbert O Cellaigh I
1378	Muircheartach mac Pilib O Cellaigh [Maurice]
1393	William O Cormacain
1398	David Corre
1398	Enri O Conmaigh
1405	Tomasi O Cellaigh II
1410	Cobhthach O Madagain
1438	Seaan O hEidin
1441	John White
1447	Conchobhar O Maolalaidh
1448	Cornelius O Cuinnlis
1463	Matthaeus Mag Raith
1508	David de Burgo
1509	Dionysius O'Mordha
1534	Roland de Burgo
1536	Richard Nangle
1580	Hugh
1582	Stephen Kirwan
1602	Roland Lynch
1627	Robert Dawson
1644	William Baily

1665	Edward Wolley
1691	William FitzGerald
1722	Theophilus Bolton
1724	Arthur Price
1730	Edward Synye
1732	Mordecai Cary
1716	John Whitcombe
1752	Arthur Smyth
1753	William Carmichael
1758	William Gote
1762	John Oswald
1763	Denison Cumberland
1772	Walter Cope
1782	John Law
1787	Richard Marlay
1795	Charles Broderick
1796	Hugh Hamilton
1798	Matthew Young
1801	George de la l'oer Beresford
1802	Nathaniel Alexander
1804	Christopher Butson
	United to Killaloe since 1834

†Clonmacnoise

−663	Baitan O'Cormac
−839	Joseph [of Rossmore]
	Maclodhar 890
	Cairbre Crom 904
	Loingsech 919
−940	Donough I
−953	Donough II
−966	Cormae O Cillin
	Maenach 971
	Conaing O'Cosgraigh 998
	Male Poil 1001
	Flaithbertach 1038
	Celechar 1067
	O'Mallaen 1093
	Christian Aherne 1104
?1111	Domnall mac Flannacain Ua Dubthaig
1152	Muirchertach Ua Maeluidir
	Cathal Ua Maeileoin 1207
*c.*1207	Muirchertach Ua Muiricen
1214	Aed O Maeileoin I
1227	Aed O Maeileoin II [Elias]
1236	Thomas Fitzpatrick
1252	Tomas O Cuinn
1280	Anonymous
1282	Gilbert (not consecrated)
1290	William O Dubhthaig
1298	William O Finnein
1303	Domnall O Braein
1324	Lughaid O Dalaigh
1337	Henricus
1349	Simon
1369	Richard [Braybroke]
1371	Hugo
1388	Philippus O Maoil
1389	Milo Corr
1397	O'Gallagher
1397	Philip Nangle
1423	David Prendergast
1426	Cormac Mac Cochlain [Cornelius]
1444	Sean O Dalaigh
1449	Thomas
1458	Robertus
1458	William
1459	John
1487	Walter Blake
1509	Tomas O Maolalaidh
1516	Quintin O h-Uiginn
1539	Richard O'Hogan
1539	Florence Kirwan
1556	Peter Wall [Wale]
	United to Meath 1569

†Cloyne

Reachtaidh 887
1148	Gilla na Naem O Muirchertaig [Nehemias]
	Ua Dubcroin 1159
	Ua Flannacain 1167
1177	Matthaeus Ua Mongaig
1201	Laurence Ua Suilleabain
1205	C.
1281	Luke
c.1224	Florence
1226	Daniel
1237	David mac Cellaig [O'Kelly]
1240	Ailinn O Suilleabain
1247	Daniel
1265	Reginaldus
1275	Alan O Longain
1284	Nicholas of Effingham
1323	Maurice O Solchain
1333	John Brid
1351	John Whitekot
1363	John Swaffham
1376	Richard Wye
1394	Gerard Caneton
1413	Adam Payn
	United to Cork 1418–1638
1638	George Synge
1661–78	Held by the Bishops of Cork
1679	Patrick Sheridan
1683	Edward Jones
1693	William Palliser
1694	Tobias Pullein
1695	St George Ashe
1697	John Pooley
1702	Charles Crow
1726	Henry Maule
1732	Edward Synge
1734	George Berkeley
1753	James Stopford
1759	Robert Johnson
1767	Frederick Augustus Hervery
1768	Charles Agar
1780	George Chinnery
1781	Richard Woodward
1794	William Bennett
1820	Charles Mongan Warhurton
1826	John Brinkley
	United to Cork on the death of Bp Brinkley in 1835

Cork

Cork, Cloyne and Ross

Description of arms. Argent, on a plain cross, the ends pattée, gules, a pastoral staff, surmounted on a mitre, or (for the See of Cork). Azure, a mitre proper labelled or, between three crosses pattées-fitchées argent (for the See of Cloyne). No arms are borne for the See of Ross.

Donnell 876
Soer Bhreatach 892
DusucBhdhurn O'Stefam 959
Cathmogh 969
Mugron O'Mutan 1057
1138	Gregory
?	Ua Menngorain 1147
1148	Gilla Aedha Ua Maigin
1174	[Gregorius] O h-Aedha [O Hea]
c.1182	Reginaldus I

1187	Aicher
1192	Murchad Ua h-Aedha
	Anonymous 1214
1215	Mairin Ua Briain [Marianus]
1225	Gilbertus
1248	Laurentius
1265	William of Jerpoint
1267	Reginaldus
1277	Robert Mac Donnchada
1302	Seoan Mac Cearbaill [Mac Carwill]
1321	Philip of Slane
1327	Walter le Rede
1330	John of Ballyconingham
1347	John Roche
1359	Gerald de Barri
1396	Roger Ellesmere
1406	Richard Kynmoure
1409	Patrick Fox
1409	Milo fitzJohn
1425	John Paston
1418	Adam Payn
1429	Jordan Purcell
1463	Gerald FitzGerald
1472	William Roche (Coadjutor)
1490	Tadhg Mac Carthaigh
1499	John FitzEdmund FitzGerald
1499	Patrick Cant
1523	John Benet
1536	Dominic Tyrre [Tirrey]
1562	Roger Skiddy
1570	Richard Dyxon
1572	Matthew Sheyn
	Ross united to Cork 1583
1583	William Lyon
1618	John Boyle
1620	Richard Boyle
1638	William Chappell
1661	Michael Boyle
1663	Edward Synge
1679	Edward Wetenhall
1699	Dive Downes
1710	Peter Browne
1735	Robert Clayton
1745	Jemmett Browne
1772	Isaac Mann
1789	Euseby Cleaver
1789	William Foster
1790	William Bennet
1794	Thomas Stopford
1805	John George Beresford
1807	Thomas St Laurence
1831	Samuel Kyle
	Cloyne united to Cork from 1835
1848	James Wilson
1857	William FitzGerald
1862	John Gregg
1878	Robert Samuel Gregg
1894	William Edward Meade
1912	Charles Benjamin Dowse
1933	William Edward Flewett
1938	Robert Thomas Hearn
1952	George Otto Sims
1957	Richard Gordon Perdue
1978	Samuel Greenfield Poyntz
1988	Robert Alexander Warke
1999	William Paul Colton

Dublin

Dublin and Glendalough

Description of arms. Azure, an episcopal staff argent, ensigned with a cross pattée or, surmounted by a pallium of the second edged and fringed or, charged with five crosses formée fitchée, sable.

BISHOPS

	Sinhail 790
c.1028	Dunan [Donatus]
1074	Gilla Patraic
1085	Donngus
1096	Samuel Ua'h-Aingliu

ARCHBISHOPS

1121	Grene [Gregorius]
1162	Lorcan Ua'Tuathail [Laurentius]
1182	John Cumin
1213	Henry de Loundres
	Glendalough united to Dublin
1230	Luke
125?	Fulk de Sandford
1279	John de Derlington
1286	John de Sandford
1295	Thomas de Chadworth
1296	William de Hotham
1299	Richard de Ferings
[1307	Richard de Havering, not consecrated]
1311	John de Leche
1317	Alexander de Bicknor
1349	John de St Paul
1363	Thomas Minot
1376	Robert de Wikeford
1391	Robert Waldeby
1396	Richard Northalis
1397	Thomas Cranley
1418	Richard Talbot
1451	Michael Tregury
1472	John Walton
1484	Walter Fitzsimons
1512	William Rokeby
1521	Hugh Inge
1529	John Alan
1535	George Browne
1555	Hugh Curwin
1567	Adam Loftus
1605	Thomas Jones
1619	Lancelot Bulkeley
1661	James Margetson
1663	Michael Boyle
1679	John Parker
1682	Francis Marsh
1694	Narcissus Marsh
1703	William King
1730	John Hoadly
1743	Charles Cobbe
1765	William Carmichael
1766	Arthur Smyth
1772	John Cradock
1779	Robert Fowler
1801	Charles Agar [Earl of Normanton]
1809	Euseby Cleaver
1820	John George Beresford
1822	William Magee
1831	Richard Whately
	Kildare united to Dublin 1846

1864	Richard Chenevix Trench (resigned)
1885	William Conyngham [Lord Plunket]
1897	Joseph Ferguson Peacocke
1915	John Henry Bernard
1919	Charles Frederick D'Arcy
1920	John Allen Fitzgerald Gregg
1939	Arthur William Barton
1956	George Otto Simms
1969	Alan Alexander Buchanan
1977	Henry Robert McAdoo
1985	Donald Arthur Richard Caird
1996	Walton Newcome Francis Empey
2002	John Robert Winder Neill
2011	Michael Geoffrey St Aubyn Jackson

†Emly

	Raidghil 881
	Ua Ruaich 953
	Faelan 980
	MaelFinan 1030
	Diarmait Ua Flainnchua 1114
1152	Gilla in Choimhded Ua h-Ardmhail Mael Isu Ua Laigenain 1163
1172	Ua Meic Stia
1177	Charles O'Buacalla
1177	Isaac O'Hamery
1192	Ragnall Ua Flainnchua
1205	M.
1209	William
1212	Henry
1227	John Collingham
1238	Daniel
1238	Christianus
1251	Gilbert O'Doverty
1266	Florence or Laurence O'hAirt
1272	Matthew MacGormain
1275	David O Cossaig
1286	William de Clifford
1306	Thomas Cantock [Quantock]
1309	William Roughead
1335	Richard le Walleys
1353	John Esmond
1363	David Penlyn [Foynlyn]
1363	William
1405	Nicholas Ball
1421	John Rishberry
1422	Robert Windell
1428	Thomas de Burgo
1428	Robert Portland
1445	Cornelius O Cuinnlis
1444	Robert
1448	Cornelius O Maolalaidh
1449	William O Hetigan
1476	Pilib O Cathail
1494	Donatus Mac Briain
1498	Cinneidigh Mac Briain
1507	Tomas O hUrthaille
1543	Angus O'Hernan
1551	Raymond de Burgo
	United to Cashel 1569
	Transferred to Limerick 1976

†Ferns

−598	Edan [or Maedoc or Hugh]
	Maeldogair 676
	Coman 678
	Diratus 693
	Cillenius 715
	Cairbre O'Kearney 1095
	Ceallach Ua Colmain 1117
	Mael Eoin Ua Dunacain 1125
	Ua Cattain 1135
1178	Loseph Ua h-Aeda
1186	Ailbe Ua Maelmuaid [Albinus]
1224	John of St John
1254	Geoffrey of St John
1258	Hugh of Lamport
1283	Richard of Northampton

1304	Simon of Evesham
1305	Robert Walrand
1312	Adam of Northampton
1347	Hugh de Saltu [of Leixlip]
1347	Geoffrey Grandfeld
1349	John Esmond
1350	William Charnells
1363	Thomas Dene
1400	Patrick Barret
1418	Robert Whittey
1453	Tadhg O Beirn
1457	John Purcell I
1479	Laurence Nevill
1505	Edmund Comerford
1510	Nicholas Comyn
1519	John Purcell II
1539	Alexander Devereux
1566	John Devereux
1582	Hugh Allen
	Leighlin united to Ferns 1597
1600	Robert Grave
1601	Nicholas Statford
1605	Thomas Ram
1635	George Andrews
1661	Robert Price
1667	Richard Boyle
1683	Narcissus Marsh
1691	Bartholomew Vigors
1722	Josiah Hort
1727	John Hoadly
1730	Arthur Price
1734	Edward Synge
1740	George Stone
1743	William Cottrell
1744	Robert Downes
1752	John Garnet
1758	William Carmichael
1758	Thomas Salmon
1759	Richard Robinson
1761	Charles Jackson
1765	Edward Young
1772	Joseph Deane Bourke
1782	Walter Cope
1787	William Preston
1789	Euseby Cleaver
1809	Percy Jocelyn
1820	Robert Ponsonby Tottenham Loftus
1822	Thomas Elrington
	United to Ossory 1835

†Glendalough

	Dairchell 678
	Eterscel 814
	Dungal 904
	Cormac 927
	Nuadha 920 [or Neva]
	Gilda Na Naomh c.1080
	Cormac O'Mail 1101
	Aed Ua Modain 1126
1140	Anonymous
1152	Gilla na Naem
1157	Cinaed O Ronain [Celestinus]
1176	Maelcallann Ua Cleirchen [Malchus]
1186	Macrobius
1192	William Piro
1214	Robert de Bedford
	United to Dublin
	After the union with Dublin some rival bishops appear.
c.1216	Bricheus
1468	John
1475	Michael
1481	Denis White John 1494
1494	Ivo Ruffi
1495	John
1500	Francis Fitzjohn of Corduba

†Iniscattery (Scattery Island)

861	Aidan
959	Cinaeda O'Chommind
973	Scandlam O'Lenz
	O'Bruil 1069
	O'Bruil II 1081
	Dermot O Lennain 1119
	Aed Ua Bechain I 1188
	Cearbhal Ua'h-Enna [Carolus] 1193
1360	Tomas Mac Mathghamhna
1392	John Donkan
1414	Richard Belmer
	Dionysius 1447
1447	John Grene
	Incorporated with Limerick

†Kells

	Mael Finnen 968
c.1152	Tuathal Ua Connachtarg
1185	Anonymous
1202	M. Ua Dobailen
	Incorporated with Meath

†Kildare

	Conlaedh 520
	Hugh [or Hed] the Black 639
	Maeldoborcon 709
	Eutigern 762
	Lomthiull 787
	Snedbran 787
	Tuatchar 834
	Orthanach 840
	Aedgene Britt 864
	Macnghal 870
	Lachtnan 875
	Suibhne 881
	Scannal 885
	Lergus 888
	Mael Findan 950
	Annchadh 981
	Murrough McFlan 986
1030	MaelMartain
	MaelBrighde 1042
	Finn 1085
	MaelBrighde O Brolchan 1097
	Hugh [Heremon] 1100
	Ferdomnach 1101
	Cormac O Cathassaig 1146
	Ua Duibhin 1148
1152	Finn mac Mael Muire Mac Cianain
	Fin mac Gussain Ua Gormain
1161	Malachias Ua Brain
1177	Nehemias
1206	Cornelius Mac Fealain
1223	Ralph of Bristol
1233	John of Taunton
1258	Simon of Kilkenny
1280	Nicholas Cusack
1300	Walter Calf [de Veel]
1333	Richard Houlot
1352	Thomas Giffard
1366	Robert of Aketon [Acton]
1404	John Madock
1431	William fitzEdward
1449	Geoffrey Hereford
1456	John Bole [Bull]
1464	Richard Lang
1474	David Cone
1475	James Wall
	William Barret
1480	Edward Lane
1526	Thomas Dillon
1529	Walter Wellesley
1540	William Miagh
1550	Thomas Lancaster
1555	Thomas Leverous
1560	Alexander Craik
1564	Robert Daly
1583	Daniel Neylan

1604	William Pilsworth
1636	Robert Ussher
1644	William Golborne
1661	Thomas Price
1667	Ambrose Jones
1679	Anthony Dopping
1682	William Moreton
1705	Welbore Ellis
1731	Charles Cobbe
1743	George Stone
1745	Thomas Fletcher
1761	Richard Robinson
1765	Charles Jackson
1790	George Lewis Jones
1804	Charles Lindsay
	United to Dublin after the death of Bp Lindsay in 1846
1976	Separated from Dublin and united to Meath

†Kilfenora

1172	Anonymous
1205	F.
1224	Johannes
1254	Christianus
	Anonymous 1264
1266	Mauricius
1273	Florentius O Tigernaig
1281	Congalach [O Lochlainn]
1291	G.
1299	Simon O Cuirrin
1303	Maurice O Briain
1323	Risdeard O Lochlainn
c.1355	Dionysius
1372	Henricus
	Cornelius
1390	Patricius
1421	Feidhlimidh mac Mathghamhna O Lochlainn [Florentius]
1433	Fearghal
1434	Dionysius O Connmhaigh
1447	John Greni
1476	[? Denis] O Tombaigh
1491	Muircheartach mac Murchadha O Briain [Mauricius]
1514	Maurice O'Kelly
1541	John O'Neylan
–1585	Daniel, bishop-elect
1606	Bernard Adams [with Limerick q.v.]
1617	John Steere
1622	William Murray
[1628	Richard Betts, not consecrated]
1630	James Heygate
1638	Robert Sibthorp
1661–1741	Held by the Archbishops of Tuam
1742–52	Held by the Bishop of Clonfert
	United to Killaloe 1752

†Killaloe

BISHOPS

	O'Gerruidher 1054
	Domnall Ua hEnna 1098
	Mael Muire O Dunain 1117
	Domnall Ua Conaing 1131
	Domnall Ua Longargain 1137
	Tadg Ua Longargain 1161
	Donnchad mac Diarmata Ua Briain 1164
1179	Constantin mac Toirrdelbaig Ua Briain
1194	Diarmait Ua Conaing
1201	Conchobhar Ua h-Enna [Cornelius]
1217	Robert Travers
1221	Domnall Ua h-Enna [Donatus]
1231	Domnall O Cenneitig [Donatus]

1253	Isoc O Cormacain [Isaac]
1268	Mathgamain O h-Ocain [O Hogan]
1281	Maurice O h-Ocain
1299	David Mac Mathghamna [Mac Mahon]
1317	Tomas O Cormacain I
1323	Brian O Cosgraig
1326	David Mac Briain [David of Emly]
?1326	Natus O Heime
1343	Tomas O h-Ogain
1355	Tomas O Cormacain II
1389	Mathghamain Mag Raith
1400	Donatus Mag Raith
1409	Robert Mulfield
1418	Eugenius O Faolain
1423	Thadeus Mag Raith I
1429	Seamus O Lonnghargain
1443	Donnchadh mac Toirdhealbhaigh O Briain
1460	Thadeus Mag Raith II
1463	Matthaeus O Griobhtha
1483	Toirdhealbhach mac Mathghamhna O Briain [Theodoricus]
1523	Thadeus
1526	Seamus O Cuirrin
1546	Cornelius O Dea
1554	Turlough [or Terence] O'Brien II
1570	Maurice [or Murtagh] O'Brien-Arra
1613	John Rider
1633	Lewis Jones
1647	Edward Parry
1661	Edward Worth
1669	Daniel Wytter
1675	John Roan
1693	Henry Ryder
1696	Thomas Lindsay
1713	Thomas Vesey
1714	Nicholas Forster
1716	Charles Carr
1740	Joseph Story
1742	John Ryder
1743	Jemmet Browne
1745	Richard Chenevix
1746	Nicholas Synge
	Kilfenora united to Killaloe 1752
1771	Robert Fowler
1779	George Chinnery
1780	Thomas Barnard
1794	William Knox
1803	Charles Dalrymple Lindsay
1804	Nathaniel Alexander
1804	Robert Ponsonby Tottenham Loftus
1820	Richard Mant
1823	Alexander Arbuthnot
1828	Richard Ponsonby
1831	Edmund Knox [with Clonfert]
	Clonfert united to Killaloe 1834
	Kilmacduagh united to Killaloe 1834
1834	Christopher Butson
1836	Stephen Crengh Sandes
1839	Ludlow Tonson [afterwards Baron Riversdale]
1862	William FitzGerald
1884	William Bennet Chester
1893	Frederick Richards Wynne
1897	Mervyn Archdall
1912	Charles Benjamin Dowse
1913	Thomas Sterling Berry (resigned)
1924	Henry Edmund Patton
1943	Robert M'Neil Boyd
1945	Hedley Webster
1953	Richard Gordon Perdue
1957	Henry Arthur Stanistreet
1972	Edwin Owen
1976	United to Limerick

†Kilmacduagh

?	Ua Cleirig 1137
	Imar Ua Ruaidin 1176
	Rugnad O'Rowan 1178
1179	Mac Gilla Cellaig Ua Ruaidin
1206	Ua Cellaig
	Mael Muire O Connmaig 1224
1227	Aed [Odo]
	Conchobhar O Muiredaig 1247
1248	Gilla Cellaig O Ruaidin [Gilbertus]
1249	David yFredrakern
1254	Mauricius O Leaain
1284	David O Setachain
1290	Luirint O Lachtnain [Laurentius]
1307	Lucas
1326	Johannes
1360	Nicol O Leaain
1394	Gregory O Leaain
1405	Enri O Connmhaigh
1409	Dionysius
1409	Eugene O Faolain
1418	Diarmaid O Donnchadha
1419	Nicol O Duibhghiolla
1419	Seaan O Connmhaigh
1441	Dionysius O Donnchadha
1479	Cornelius O Mullony
1503	Matthaeus O Briain
1533	Christopher Bodkin
1573	Stephen O'Kirwan
[1584	Thomas Burke, not consecrated]
1587	Roland Lynch
1627–1836	Held in commendam by the Bishops of Clonfert
	United to Killaloe since 1834

†Leighlin

–633	Laserian or Molaise
–865	Mainchin
–940	Conella McDonegan Daniel 969
	Cleitic O'Muinic 1050
c.1096	Ferdomnac
	Mael Eoin Ua Dunacain 1125
	Sluaigedach Ua Cathain 1145
1152	Dungal O Caellaide
1192	Johannes
1197	Johannes
1202	Herlewin
1217	Richard [Fleming]
1228	William le Chauniver
1252	Thomas
1275	Nicholas Chever
1309	Maurice de Blanchville
1321	Meiler le Poer
1344	Radulphus O Ceallaigh
1349	Thomas of Brakenberg
1360	Johannes
1362	William (not consecrated)
1363	John Young
1371	Philip FitzPeter
1385	John Griffin
1398	Thomas Peverell
1400	Richard Bocomb
1419	John Mulgan
1432	Thomas Fleming
—	Diarmaid 1464
1464	Milo Roche
1490	Nicholas Magwyr
1513	Thomas Halsey
1524	Mauricius O Deoradhain
1527	Matthew Sanders
1550	Robert Travers
1555	Thomas O'Fihelly
1567	Donnell or Daniel Cavanagh
1589	Richard Meredith
	United to Ferns since 1597 on the death of Bp Meredith

Limerick

Limerick, Ardfert, Aghadoe, Killaloe, Kilfenora, Clonfert, Kilmacduagh and Emly

Description of arms. Azure two keys addorsed in saltire the wards upwards; in the dexter chief a crosier paleways, in the sinister a mitre, all or.

–1106	Gilli alias Gilla Espaic
1140	Patricius
1150	Erolb [? = Harold]
1152	Torgesius
1179	Brictius
1203	Donnchad Ua'Briain [Donatus]
1207	Geoffrey
–1215	Edmund
1223	Hubert de Burgo
1252	Robert de Emly or Neil
1273	Gerald [or Miles] de Mareshall
1302	Robert de Dundonald
1312	Eustace de Aqua or de l'Eau
1336	Maurice de Rochfort
1354	Stephen Lawless
1360	Stephen Wall [de Valle]
1369	Peter Curragh
1399	Bernardus O Conchobhair
1400	Conchobhar O Deadhaidh
1426	John Mothel (resigned)
	Iniscattery incorporated with Limerick
1456	Thomas Leger
1458	William Russel, *alias* Creagh
1463	Thomas Arthur
[1486	Richard Stakpoll, not consecrated]
1486	John Dunowe
1489	John O'Phelan [Folan]
1524	Sean O Cuinn
1551	William Casey
1557	Hugh de Lacey or Lees (deposed)
1571	William Casey
1594	John Thornburgh
1604	Bernard Adams
1626	Francis Gough
1634	George Webb
1643	Robert Sibthorp
	Ardfert united to Limerick 1661
1661	Edward Synge
1664	William Fuller
1667	Francis Marsh
1673	John Vesey
1679	Simon Digby
1692	Nathaniel Wilson
1695	Thomas Smyth
1725	William Burscough
1755	James Leslie
1771	James Averill
1772	William Gore
1784	William Cecil Pery
1794	Thomas Barnard
1806	Charles Morgan Warburton
1820	Thomas Elrington
1823	John Jebb
1834	Edmund Knox
1849	William Higgin
1854	Henry Griffin
1866	Charles Graves
1899	Thomas Bunbury
1907	Raymond D'Audemra Orpen
1921	Harry Vere White

1934	Charles King Irwin
1942	Evelyn Charles Hodges
1961	Robert Wyse Jackson
1970	Donald Arthur Richard Caird
	Killaloe united to Limerick 1976
	Emly transferred to Limerick 1976
1976	Edwin Owen
1981	Walton Newcome Francis Empey
1985	Edward Flewett Darling
2000	Michael Hugh Gunton Mayes
2008	Trevor Russell Williams
2015	Kenneth Arthur Kearon

†Lismore

	Ronan 764
	Cormac MacCuillenan 918
–999	Cinneda O'Chonmind
	Niall mac Meic Aedacain 1113
	Ua Daightig 1119
1121	Mael Isu Ua h-Ainmere
	Mael Muire Ua Loingsig 1150
1151	Gilla Crist Ua Connairche [Christianus]
1179	Felix
	Ardmore incorporated with Lismore 1192
1203	Malachias, O'Heda or O'Danus
1216	Thomas
1219	Robert of Bedford
1228	Griffin Christopher
1248	Ailinn O Suilleabain
1253	Thomas
1270	John Roche
1280	Richard Corre
1309	William Fleming
1310	R.
1322	John Leynagh
1356	Roger Cradock, provision annulled
1358	Thomas le Reve
	United to Waterford 1363

Meath

Meath and Kildare

Description of arms. Sable three mitres argent, two, and one.

BISHOPS OF THE SEE OF CLONARD

	Senach 588
–640	Colman 654
	DusucBhduin O'Phelan 718
	Tole 738
–778	Fulartach 779
	Clothcu 796
	Clemens 826
	Cormac MacSuibhne
	Cumsuth 858
	Suarlech 870
	Ruman MacCathasaid 922
	Colman MacAilild 926
	Tuathal O'Dubhamaigh 1028

BISHOPS OF MEATH

1096	Mael Muire Ua Dunain
1128	Eochaid O Cellaig
1151	Etru Ua Miadacain [Eleuzerius]

1177	Echtigern mac Mael Chiarain [Eugenius]
1192	Simon Rochfort (The See was transferred from Clonard to Newtown near Trim, 1202)
	Kells incorporated with Meath
1224	Donan De [Deodatus] (not consecrated)
1227	Ralph Petit
1231	Richard de la Corner
1253	Geoffrey Cusack
1255	Hugo de Taghmon
1283	Walter de Fulburn
1287	Thomas St Leger
1322	Seoan Mac Cerbaill [John MacCarwill]
1327	William de Paul
1350	William St Leger
1353	Nicholas [Allen]
1369	Stephen de Valle [Wall]
1380	William Andrew
1385	Alexander Petit [or de Balscot]
1401	Robert Montayne
1412	Edward Dantesey
[1430	Thomas Scurlog, apparently not consecrated]
1430	William Hadsor
1435	William Silk
1450	Edmund Ouldhall
1460	William Shirwood
1483	John Payne
1507	William Rokeby
1512	Hugh Inge
1523	Richard Wilson
1529	Edward Staples
1554	William Walsh
1563	Hugh Brady
	Clonmacnoise united to Meath 1569
1584	Thomas Jones
1605	Roger Dod
1612	George Montgomery
1621	James Usher
1625	Anthony Martin [Interregnum 1650–61]
1661	Henry Leslie
1661	Henry Jones
1682	Anthony Dopping
1697	Richard Tennison
1705	William Moreton
1716	John Evans
1724	Henry Downes
1727	Ralph Lambert
1732	Welbore Ellis
1734	Arthur Price
1744	Henry Maule
1758	William Carmichael
1765	Richard Pococke
1765	Arthur Smyth
1766	Henry Maxwell
1798	Thomas Lewis O'Beirne
1823	Nathaniel Alexander
1840	Charles Dickinson
1842	Edward Stopford
1850	Thomas Stewart Townsend
1852	James Henderson Singer
1866	Samuel Butcher
1876	William Conyngham [Lord Plunket]
1885	Charles Parsons Reichel
1894	Joseph Ferguson Peacocke
1897	James Bennett Keene
1919	Benjamin John Plunket
1926	Thomas Gibson George Collins
1927	John Orr
1938	William Hardy Holmes
1945	James McCann
1959	Robert Bonsall Pike
	Kildare united to Meath 1976
1976	Donald Arthur Richard Caird
1985	Walton Newcome Francis Empey
1996	Richard Lionel Clarke
2013	Patricia Louise Storey

†Ossory

Dermot 973
1152 Domnall Ua Fogartaig
1180 Felix Ua Duib Slaine
1202 Hugo de Rous [Hugo Rufus]
1220 Peter Mauveisin
1231 William of Kilkenny
1233 Walter de Brackley
1245 Geoffrey de Turville
1251 Hugh de Mapilton
1260 Geoffrey St Leger
1287 Roger of Wexford
1289 Michael d'Exeter
1303 William FitzJohn
1317 Richard Ledred
1361 John de Tatenhale
1366 William
—   John of Oxford
1371 Alexander Petit [de Balscot]
1387 Richard Northalis
1396 Thomas Peverell
1399 John Waltham
1400 John Griffin
1400 John
1401 Roger Appleby
1402 John Waltham
1407 Thomas Snell
1417 Patrick Foxe
1421 Dionysius O Deadhaidh
1427 Thomas Barry
1460 David Hacket
1479 Seaan O hEidigheain
1487 Oliver Cantwell
1528 Milo Baron [or FitzGerald]
1553 John Bale
1554 John Tonory
1567 Christopher Gaffney
1577 Nicholas Walsh
1586 John Horsfall
1610 Richard Deane
1613 Jonas Wheeler
1641 Griffith Williams
1672 John Parry
1678 Benjamin Parry
1678 Michael Ward
1680 Thomas Otway
1693 John Hartstonge
1714 Thomas Vesey
1731 Edward Tennison
1736 Charles Este
1741 Anthony Dopping
1743 Michael Cox
1754 Edward Maurice
1755 Richard Pococke
1765 Charles Dodgson
1775 William Newcome
1779 John Hotham
1782 William Heresford
1795 Thomas Lewis O'Beirne
1799 Hugh Hamilton
1806 John Kearney
1813 Robert Fowler
     Ferns united to Ossory 1835
1842 James Thomas O'Brien
1874 Robert Samuel Gregg

1878 William Pakenham Walsh
1897 John Baptist Crozier
1907 Charles Frederick D'Arcy
1911 John Henry Bernard
1915 John Allen Fitzgerald Gregg
1920 John Godfrey FitzMaurice Day
1938 Ford Tichbourne
1940 John Percy Phair
1962 Henry Robert McAdoo
     United to Cashel 1977

†Ross

Nechtan MacNechtain 1160
Isaac O'Cowen 1161
O'Carroll 1168
1177 Benedictus
1192 Mauricius
1198 Daniel
1224 Fineen O Clothna [Florentius]
c.1250 Malachy
1254 Mauricius
1269 Walter O Mithigein
1275 Peter O h-Uallachain [?
     Patrick]
1291 Laurentius
1310 Matthaeus O Finn
1331 Laurentius O h-Uallachain
1336 Dionysius
1379 Bernard O Conchobhair
1399 Peter Curragh
1400 Thadeus O Ceallaigh
1401 Mac Raith O hEidirsgeoil
     [Macrobius]
1402 Stephen Brown
1403 Matthew
1418 Walter Formay
1424 John Bloxworth
1426 Conchobhar Mac Fhaolchadha
     [Cornelius]
     Maurice Brown 1431
1431 Walter of Leicester
1434 Richard Clerk
1448 Domhnall O Donnobhain
     John 1460
1460 Robert Colynson
-1464 Thomas
1464 John Hornse alias Skipton
1473 Aodh O hEidirsgeoil [Odo]
1482 Tadhg Mac Carthaigh
1494 John Edmund Courci
1517 Seaan O Muirthile
1519 Tadgh O Raghallaigh
     [Thaddeus]
1523 Bonaventura
1526 Diarmaid Mac Carthaigh
1544 Dermot McDonnell
1551 John
1554 Maurice O'Fihelly
1559 Maurice O'Hea
1561 Thomas O'Herlihy
1582 William Lyon [with Cork and
     Cloyne after 1581]
     United to Cork 1583

†Waterford

1096 Mael lus Ua h-Ainmere
1152 Toistius
1175 Augustinus Ua Selbaig
     Anonymous 1199
1200 Robert I
1204 David the Welshman
1210 Robert II [Breathnach]
1223 William Wace
1227 Walter
1232 Stephen
1250 Henry
1252 Philip
1255 Walter de Southwell
1274 Stephen de Fulbourn
1286 Walter de Fulbourn
1308 Matthew
1323 Nicholas Welifed
1338 Richard Francis
1349 Robert Elyot
1350 Roger Cradock
     Lismore united to Waterford
     1363
1363 Thomas le Reve
1394 Robert Read
1396 Thomas Sparklord
1397 John Deping
1400 Thomas Snell
1407 Roger of Appleby (see under
     Ossory)
1409 John Geese
1414 Thomas Colby
1421 John Geese
1426 Richard Cantwell
1446 Robert Poer
1473 Richard Martin
1475 John Bulcomb
1480 Nicol O hAonghusa
1483 Thomas Purcell
1519 Nicholas Comyn
1551 Patrick Walsh
1579 Marmaduke Middleton
1582 Miler Magrath (Bishop of
     Cashel and Waterford)
1589 Thomas Wetherhead [or
     Walley]
1592 Miler Magrath
1608 John Lancaster
1619 Michael Boyle
1636 John Atherton
1641 Archibald Adair
1661 George Baker
1666 Hugh Gore
1691 Nathaniel Foy
1708 Thomas Mills
1740 Charles Este
1746 Richard Chenevix
1779 William Newcome
1795 Richard Marlay
1802 Power le Poer Trench
1810 Joseph Stock
1813 Richard Bourke
     United to Cashel under
     Church Temporalities Act
     1833

CATHEDRALS

CHURCH OF ENGLAND

(BATH AND) WELLS (St Andrew) Dean J H DAVIES
Can Res N L JEPSON-BIDDLE, R M PAUL
BIRMINGHAM (St Phillip) Dean M THOMPSON
Can Res J E M HOUGHTON
BLACKBURN (St Mary) Dean P HOWELL-JONES
Can Res A D HINDLEY, A S HORSFALL, P J NORTH, R F PAILING
BRADFORD (St Peter) Dean J J LEPINE Can Res J B QUASH,
K N MEDHURST, M R COUTTS, P D MAYBURY
BRISTOL (Holy Trinity) Dean *vacant*
Can Res J M GAINSBOROUGH, M A H RODEN, N V STANLEY
Min Can S R EVANS, T M DAY
CANTERBURY (Christ) Dean R A WILLIS
Can Res E L PENNINGTON, J A IDOWU-FEARON, T J N NAISH
Min Can B D FENTON, M J KRAMER
CARLISLE (Holy Trinity) Dean M C BOYLING
Can Res J E KEARTON, M A MANLEY, P J CLEMENT
CHELMSFORD (St Mary, St Peter and St Cedd)
Dean N J HENSHALL Can Res A M KENNEDY, I J NAY,
I R MOODY
CHESTER (Christ and Blessed Virgin Mary)
Dean T R STRATFORD Can Res J N J C DUSSEK,
M R GILBERTSON, R J BROOKE
CHICHESTER (Holy Trinity) Dean S J WAINE
Can Res D D INMAN, N T SCHOFIELD, S A D FERNS
COVENTRY (St Michael) Dean J J WITCOMBE
Can Res C A LAMB, D A STONE, J B QUASH, K C FLEMING
DERBY (All Saints) Dean *vacant* Can Res E J THOMSON,
R J ANDREWS
DURHAM (Christ and Blessed Virgin Mary)
Dean A TREMLETT Can Res C ALLEN, M H J HAMPEL,
M J EVERITT, S A OLIVER, S R JELLEY
ELY (Holy Trinity) Dean M P J BONNEY Can Res C A BARBER,
H D SHILSON-THOMAS, J H MARTIN, J R GARRARD,
V L JOHNSON
EXETER (St Peter) Dean J D F GREENER
Can Res C J I PALMER, J E A MUSTARD, M D A WILLIAMS,
S GILLINGHAM, T P JONES
GLOUCESTER (St Peter and Holy Trinity) Dean S D LAKE
Can Res A J BRADDOCK, C S M THOMSON,
H J DAWSON, J H S STEVEN, N M ARTHY, R J A MITCHELL
Min Can G M TREWEEK
GUILDFORD (Holy Spirit) Dean D L GWILLIAMS
Can Res P A SMITH
HEREFORD (Blessed Virgin Mary and St Ethelbert)
Dean M E TAVINOR Can Res A PIPER, C PULLIN
LEICESTER (St Martin) Dean D R M MONTEITH
Can Res A C THISELTON, A D C WINGATE, A G MURSELL,
A M ADAMS, F D JENNINGS, J D MALTBY, K S F ROOMS,
P D RATTIGAN
LICHFIELD (Blessed Virgin Mary and St Chad)
Dean A J DORBER Can Res A M STEAD, P S HAWKINS
Min Can J E EVANS, R J LLOYD, T R PLANT
LINCOLN (Blessed Virgin Mary) Dean C L WILSON
Can Res J A PATRICK, P OVEREND, S MCDOUGALL
Min Can I G SILK, P G GREEN
LIVERPOOL (Christ) Dean S H JONES
Can Res J C POLKINGHORNE, M C DAVIES, M L KAVANAGH,
M S NORTHCOTT, N D BARNES
LONDON (St Paul) Dean D J ISON Can Res J D BREWSTER,
J H MILNE, M A POULSON, P D HILLAS, R J MORTON,
R L COUPLAND, S A WATSON Min Can R S S WEIR
MANCHESTER (St Mary, St Denys and St George)
Dean R M GOVENDER Can Res D A HOLGATE, D J SHARPLES,
M Z WALL Min Can A P WICKENS
NEWCASTLE (St Nicholas) Dean G V MILLER
Can Res C MACLAREN, P D DOBSON
NORWICH (Holy Trinity) Dean J B HEDGES
Can Res A S G PLATTEN, A W BRYANT, K N JAMES, P M DOLL
Min Can P J G BARNES-CLAY

OXFORD (Christ Church) Dean M W PERCY
Can Res E J NEWEY, G D BAYLISS, G J WARD, N J BIGGAR
Min Can P C NICHOLSON
PETERBOROUGH (St Peter, St Paul and St Andrew)
Dean C C DALLISTON Can Res I C BLACK, R C WILLIAMS,
S R D BROWN, T M ALBAN JONES
PORTSMOUTH (St Thomas of Canterbury)
Dean A W N S CANE Can Res A C RUSTELL,
J M M SPREADBURY, N R RALPH
RIPON (St Peter and St Wilfred) Dean J R DOBSON
Can Res A B NEWBY, B J PYKE, M A GISBOURNE
Min Can D J SLADDEN
ROCHESTER (Christ and Blessed Virgin Mary)
Dean P J HESKETH Can Res C D DENCH, M J RUSHTON,
S C BREWER Min Can B A A LAWAL, D V GOWER, P J PLUMLEY
ST ALBANS (St Alban) Dean J P H JOHN
Can Res A L THOMPSON, D C FITZGERALD CLARK,
J J B LLOYD, K A WALTON, T M BULL, T M LOMAX
Min Can K QUAK-WINSLOW
ST EDMUNDSBURY (St James) Dean J P HAWES
Can Res M J VERNON, P C BANKS, S A GAZE
SALISBURY (Blessed Virgin Mary) Dean N C PAPADOPULOS
Can Res A MACHAM, E C PROBERT, R A BURRIDGE, R J TITLEY
SHEFFIELD (St Peter and St Paul) Dean P E BRADLEY
Can Res K FARROW Min Can I MAHER, M W P REEDER
SODOR AND MAN (St German) Dean N P GODFREY
Can Res J A T HEATON, J A WARD, J P COLDWELL
Min Can I C FAULDS
SOUTHWARK (St Saviour and St Mary Overie)
Dean A P NUNN Can Res A C WINTER, A K FORD, G M MYERS,
I E VIBERT, J P COLWILL, L K ROBERTS, M G RAWSON,
R E YOUNG, S FAN
SOUTHWELL (Blessed Virgin Mary) Dean N A SULLIVAN
Can Res A C THISELTON, A G MILBANK, E C KIRK, R J FRITH
TRURO (St Mary) Dean R C BUSH Can Res A G BASHFORTH,
L M BARLEY, M D CHAPMAN, S M GRIFFITHS
Min Can G W SMYTH
WAKEFIELD (All Saints) Dean S C COWLING
Can Res D WALMSLEY, L B VASEY-SAUNDERS,
M R VASEY-SAUNDERS
WINCHESTER (Holy Trinity, St Peter, St Paul and St
Swithun) Dean C OGLE Can Res F I L ORR-EWING,
M P C COLLINSON, R G A RIEM Min Can A P C TRENIER,
N P FENNEMORE
WORCESTER (Christ and Blessed Virgin Mary)
Dean P G ATKINSON Can Res G A BYRNE, M W BRIERLEY,
S M EDWARDS Min Can M R DORSETT
YORK (St Peter) Dean J H FROST
Can Res C P COLLINGWOOD, M A MCLEAN, M D SMITH,
O M T O'DONOVAN Min Can C M CUMMING

Collegiate Churches

WESTMINSTER ABBEY
ST GEORGE'S CHAPEL, WINDSOR
See Royal Peculiars, p. 1063.

Diocese in Europe

GIBRALTAR (Holy Trinity) Dean *vacant*
MALTA Valletta (St Paul) Pro-Cathedral
Chan S H M GODFREY
BRUSSELS (Holy Trinity) Pro-Cathedral Chan P D VROLIJK

CHURCH IN WALES

ST ASAPH (St Asaph)   **Dean** N H WILLIAMS
BANGOR (St Dieniol)   Dean K L JONES
ST DAVIDS (St David and St Andrew)
   Dean S C ROWLAND JONES

LLANDAFF (St Peter and St Paul)   Dean G H CAPON
MONMOUTH Newport (St Woolos)   Dean L TONGE
(SWANSEA AND) BRECON (St John the Evangelist)
   Dean A P SHACKERLEY

SCOTTISH EPISCOPAL CHURCH

For the members of the chapter the *Scottish Episcopal Church Directory* should be consulted.

Aberdeen and Orkney
ABERDEEN (St Andrew)   Provost I M POOBALAN

Argyll and The Isles
OBAN (St John)   Provost M R CAMPBELL
CUMBRAE (Holy Spirit) Cathedral of The Isles
   Provost K PEARSON*Bishop of Argyll and The Isles*

Brechin
DUNDEE (St Paul)   Provost J R AULD

Edinburgh
EDINBURGH (St Mary)   Provost J A CONWAY

Glasgow and Galloway
GLASGOW (St Mary)   Provost K HOLDSWORTH

Moray, Ross and Caithness
INVERNESS (St Andrew)   Provost M J STRANGE *Bishop of*
   Moray, Ross and Caithness

St Andrews, Dunkeld and Dunblane
PERTH (St Ninian)   Provost H B FARQUHARSON

CHURCH OF IRELAND

Most cathedrals are parish churches, and the dean is usually, but not always, the incumbent. For the members of the chapter the *Church of Ireland Directory* should be consulted. The name of the dean is given, together with those of other clergy holding full-time appointments.

NATIONAL CATHEDRAL OF ST PATRICK, Dublin   Dean W W MORTON **Dean's V** C W MULLEN

CATHEDRAL OF ST ANNE, Belfast   Dean *vacant*
(St Anne's is a cathedral of the dioceses of Down and Dromore and of Connor)

Province of Armagh

Armagh
ARMAGH (St Patrick)   G J O DUNSTAN

Clogher
CLOGHER (St Macartan)   K R J HALL
ENNISKILLEN (St Macartin)   K R J HALL

Derry and Raphoe
DERRY (St Columb)   R J STEWART
RAPHOE (St Eunan)   K A L BARRETT

Down and Dromore
DOWN (Holy and Undivided Trinity)   T H HULL
DROMORE (Christ the Redeemer)   S G WILSON

Connor
LISBURN (Christ)   *(Dean of Connor)*   W S WRIGHT

Kilmore, Elphin and Ardagh
KILMORE (St Fethlimidh)   N N CROSSEY
SLIGO (St Mary and St John the Baptist)   A WILLIAMS

Tuam, Killala and Achonry
TUAM (St Mary)   L E A PEILOW
KILLALA (St Patrick)   A J GRIMASON

Province of Dublin

Dublin and Glendalough
DUBLIN (Holy Trinity) Christ Church   D P M DUNNE

Meath and Kildare
TRIM (St Patrick)   P D BOGLE *Dean of Clonmacnoise*
KILDARE (St Brigid)   P D BOGLE

Cashel and Ossory
CASHEL (St John the Baptist)   G G FIELD
WATERFORD (Blessed Trinity) Christ Church   M P JANSSON
LISMORE (St Carthage)   P R DRAPER
KILKENNY (St Canice)   D MACDONNELL *Dean of Ossory*
LEIGHLIN (St Laserian)   T W GORDON
FERNS (St Edan)   P G MOONEY

Cork, Cloyne and Ross
CORK (St Fin Barre)   N K DUNNE
CLOYNE (St Colman)   S D GREEN
ROSS (St Fachtna)   C L PETERS

Limerick and Killaloe
LIMERICK (St Mary)   N J SLOANE
KILLALOE (St Flannan)   *vacant*

ROYAL PECULIARS, CLERGY OF THE QUEEN'S HOUSEHOLD, ETC

Royal Peculiars

Description of arms. Azure the reputed arms of Edward the Confessor, viz. a cross patonce between five martlets or, on a chief of the same, between two double roses of Lancaster and York, barbed and seeded proper, a pale charged with the Royal arms (*viz.* Quarterly of France and England).

Collegiate Church of St Peter in Westminster (Westminster Abbey)
Dean D M HOYLE
Can A J BALL, J D T HAWKEY, J E M SINCLAIR, D J STANTON
Min Can M R BIRCH, J E PETERSEN, C B STOLTZ
PV S E ARCHER, P A BAGOTT, A R BODDY, S R BUCKLEY, N J BUNKER, P A E CHESTER, C M CHIVERS, B D FENTON, R C GODSALL, J M GOODALL, A G GYLE, J IDOWU-FEARON, L J JØRGENSEN, A P R KYRIAKIDES-YELDHAM, G P KNOWLES, M D MACEY, P MCGEARY, A D P MOUGHTIN-MUMBY, J L OSBORNE, F L STEWART-DARLING, V A STOCK, G D SWINTON, J M WHITE, G J WILLIAMS, A S ZIHNI

Description of arms. The arms of the Order of the Garter, viz. Argent, a St George's Cross gules. The shield is encircled by the blue Garter with its motto.

Queen's Free Chapel of St George Windsor Castle (St George's Chapel)
Dean THE RT REVD D J CONNER
Can H E FINLAY, M G POLL, M POWELL
Min Can J COORE, B H RUSSELL

The Queen's Household

Royal Almonry
High Almoner THE RT REVD J G INGE (Bishop of Worcester)
Sub-Almoner P S WRIGHT

The College of Chaplains
Clerk of the Closet THE RT REVD J W S NEWCOME (Bishop of Carlisle)
Deputy Clerk of the Closet P S WRIGHT

Chaplains to The Queen

E ADEKUNLE	J D T HAWKEY	G P RAVALDE
H W BEARN	G I KOVOOR	V J H REES
M E BIDE	E J LEWIS	J B V RIVIERE
G A BYRNE	K S MCCORMACK	R B RUDDOCK
R A CHARKHAM	T E MASON	A M SHEPHERD
A CLITHEROW	D NICHOLSON	A G STUDDERT-KENNEDY
I A DAVENPORT	W A NOBLETT	J A TAYLOR
S E FIELD	H PALMER	N J THISTLETHWAITE
D C GLOVER	G P POND	J S WITHERIDGE
J M HASELOCK	R M PRYCE	

Extra Chaplains to The Queen

J P ROBSON	W S SCOTT

Chapels Royal
Dean of the Chapels Royal THE BISHOP OF LONDON
Sub-Dean of the Chapels Royal P S WRIGHT
Priests in Ordinary R D E BOLTON, W A WHITCOMBE
Deputy Priests in Ordinary S D BROOKES, C L FRANSELLA, R J HALL, A G HOWE, M D OAKLEY, J L OSBORNE, S E YOUNG
Domestic Chaplain, Buckingham Palace P S WRIGHT
Domestic Chaplain, Windsor Castle THE DEAN OF WINDSOR
Domestic Chaplain, Sandringham J B V RIVIERE
Chaplain, Royal Chapel, Windsor Great Park M G POLL
Chaplain, Hampton Court Palace A G HOWE
Chaplain, HM Tower of London R J HALL

The Queen's Chapel of the Savoy

Chaplain T M B WOODHOUSE

Royal Foundation of St Katharine in Ratcliffe

Master R M H PREECE

DIOCESAN OFFICES

CHURCH OF ENGLAND

BATH AND WELLS	Diocesan Office, The Old Deanery, Wells BA5 2UG T: (01749) 670777 F: 674240 E: general@bathwells.anglican.org W: www.bathwells.anglican.org
BIRMINGHAM	Diocesan Office, 1 Colmore Row, Birmingham B3 2BJ T: 0121-426 0400 W: www.cofebirmingham.com
BLACKBURN	Clayton House, Walker Industrial Estate, Walker Road, Guide, Blackburn BB1 2QE T: (01254) 503070 F: 667309 E: diocese@blackburn.anglican.org W: www.blackburn.anglican.org
BRISTOL	Unit 1500, Hillside House, Bristol Parkway North, Newbrick Road, Stoke Gifford, Bristol BS34 8YU T: 0117-906 0100 W: www.bristol.anglican.org
CANTERBURY	Diocesan House, Lady Wootton's Green, Canterbury CT1 1NQ T: (01227) 459401 E: reception@diocant.org W: www.canterburydiocese.org
CARLISLE	Church House, 19-24 Friargate, Penrith CA11 7XR T: (01768) 807777 F: 868918 E: enquiries@carlislediocese.org.uk W: www.carlislediocese.org.uk
CHELMSFORD	Diocesan Office, 53 New Street, Chelmsford CM1 1AT T: (01245) 294400 F: 294477 E: reception@chelmsford.anglican.org W: www.chelmsford.anglican.org
CHESTER	Church House, 5500 Daresbury Park, Daresbury, Warrington WA4 4GE T: (01928) 718834 E: churchhouse@chester.anglican.org W: www.chester.anglican.org
CHICHESTER	Diocesan Church House, 211 New Church Road, Hove BN3 4ED T: (01273) 421021 F: 421041 E: enquiry@chichester.anglican.org W: www.chichester.anglican.org
COVENTRY	Cathedral and Diocesan Offices, 1 Hill Top, Coventry CV1 5AB T: (024) 7652 1200 F: 7652 1330 E: ruth.marlow@covcofe.org W: www.dioceseofcoventry.org
DERBY	Derby Church House, 1 Full Street, Derby DE1 3DR T: (01332) 388650 E: enquiries@derby.anglican.org W: www.derby.anglican.org
DURHAM	Cuthbert House, Stonebridge, Durham DH1 3RY T: (01388) 604515 E: diocesan.office@durham.anglican.org W: www.durham.anglican.org
ELY	Diocesan Office, Bishop Woodford House, Barton Road, Ely CB7 4DX T: (01353) 652701 E: office@elydiocese.org W: www.ely.anglican.org
EUROPE	Diocesan Office, 14 Tufton Street, London SW1P 3QZ T: (020) 7898 1155 F: 7898 1166 E: bron.panter@churchofengland.org W: www.europe.anglican.org
EXETER	The Old Deanery, The Cloisters, Exeter EX1 1HS T: (01392) 272686 F: 499594 E: admin@exeter.anglican.org W: www.exeter.anglican.org
GLOUCESTER	Church House, College Green, Gloucester GL1 2LY T: (01452) 410022 E: church.house@glosdioc.org.uk W: www.gloucester.anglican.org
GUILDFORD	Church House, 20 Alan Turing Road, Surrey Research Park, Guildford GU2 7YF T: (01483) 790300 F: 790333 E: guildford.info@cofeguildford.org.uk W: www.guildford.anglican.org
HEREFORD	Diocesan Office, The Palace, Hereford HR4 9BL T: (01432) 373300 F: 352952 E: diooffice@hereford.anglican.org W: www.hereford.anglican.org
LEEDS	Church House, 17-19 York Place, Leeds LS1 2EX T: 0113-200 0540 E: enquiries@leeds.anglican.org W: www.leeds.anglican.org
LEICESTER	St Martin's House, 7 Peacock Lane Leicester LE1 5PZ T: 0116-261 5200 E: leicesterreception@stmartinshouse.com W: www.leicester.anglican.org
LICHFIELD	St Mary's House, The Close, Lichfield WS13 7LD T: (01543) 306030 F: 306039 E: info@lichfield.anglican.org W: www.lichfield.anglican.org

LINCOLN	Diocesan Office, Edward King House, Minster Yard, Lincoln LN2 1PU T: (01522) 504050 E: reception@lincoln.anglican.org W: www.lincoln.anglican.org
LIVERPOOL	St James's House, 20 St James Road, Liverpool L1 7BY T: 0151-709 9722 F: 709 2885 E: enquiries@liverpool.anglican.org W: www.liverpool.anglican.org
LONDON	Diocesan House, 36 Causton Street, London SW1P 4AU T: (020) 7932 1100 F: 7932 1110 E: reception@london.anglican.org W: www.london.anglican.org
MANCHESTER	Diocesan Office, Church House, 90 Deansgate, Manchester M3 2GH T: 0161-828 1400 F: 828 1480 E: manchesterdbf@manchester.anglican.org W: www.manchester.anglican.org
NEWCASTLE	Church House, St John's Terrace, North Shields NE29 6HS T: 0191-270 4100 F: 270 4101 E: info@newcastle.anglican.org W: www.newcastle.anglican.org
NORWICH	Diocesan House, 109 Dereham Road, Easton, Norwich NR9 5ES T: (01603) 880853 E: diocesan.house@dioceseofnorwich.org W: www.norwich.anglican.org
OXFORD	Church House Oxford, Langford Locks, Kidlington OX5 1GF T: (01865) 208200 E: reception@oxford.anglican.org W: www.oxford.anglican.org
PETERBOROUGH	Diocesan Office, The Palace, Minster Precincts, Peterborough PE1 1YB T: (01733) 887000 E: office@peterborough-diocese.org.uk W: www.peterborough-diocese.org.uk
PORTSMOUTH	First Floor, Peninsular House, Wharf Road, Portsmouth PO2 8HB T: (023) 9289 9650 E: admin@portsmouth.anglican.org W: www.portsmouth.anglican.org
ROCHESTER	St Nicholas Church, Boley Hill, Rochester ME1 1SL T: (01634) 560000 E: enquiries@rochester.anglican.org W: www.rochester.anglican.org
ST ALBANS	Holywell Lodge, 41 Holywell Hill, St Albans AL1 1HE T: (01727) 854532 F: 844469 E: mail@stalbans.anglican.org W: www.stalbans.anglican.org
ST EDMUNDSBURY AND IPSWICH	St Nicholas Centre, 4 Cutler Street, Ipswich IP1 1UQ T: (01473) 298500 F: 298501 E: dbf@cofesuffolk.org W: www.stedmundsbury.anglican.org
SALISBURY	Church House, Crane Street, Salisbury SP1 2QB T: (01722) 411922 F: 411990 E: enquiries@salisbury.anglican.org W: www.salisbury.anglican.org
SHEFFIELD	Diocesan Church House, 95-99 Effingham Street, Rotherham S65 1BL T: (01709) 309100 F: 512550 E: reception@sheffield.anglican.org W: www.sheffield.anglican.org
SODOR AND MAN	Thie yn Aspick, 4 The Falls, Tromode Road, Cronkbourne, Isle of Man IM4 4PZ T: (01624) 622108 E: secretary@sodorandman.im W: www.sodorman.anglican.org
SOUTHWARK	Trinity House, 4 Chapel Court, Borough High Street, London SE1 1HW T: (020) 7939 9400 F: 7939 9468 E: trinity@southwark.anglican.org W: www.southwark.anglican.org
SOUTHWELL AND NOTTINGHAM	Jubilee House, 8 Westgate, Southwell NG25 0JH T: (01636) 814331 E: mail@southwell.anglican.org W: www.southwell.anglican.org
TRURO	Church House, Woodlands Court, Truro Business Park, Threemilestone, Truro TR4 9NH T: (01872) 274351 E: info@truro.anglican.org W: www.truro.anglican.org
WINCHESTER	The Diocesan Office, Old Alresford Place, Old Alresford, Alresford SO24 9DH T: (01962) 737300 F: 737358 E: reception@winchester.anglican.org W: www. winchester.anglican.org
WORCESTER	The Old Palace, Deansway, Worcester WR1 2JE T: (01905) 20537 F: 612302 E: generalinfo@cofe-worcester.org.uk W: www.cofe-worcester.org.uk
YORK	The Diocese of York, Amy Johnson Way, York YO30 4XT T: (01904) 699500 E: office@yorkdiocese.org W: www.dioceseofyork.org.uk

CHURCH IN WALES

ST ASAPH	Diocesan Office, High Street, St Asaph LL17 0RD T: (01745) 582245 W: http://stasaph.churchinwales.org.uk
BANGOR	Diocesan Office, Cathedral Close, Bangor LL57 1RL T: (01248) 354999 F: 353882 E: bangor@churchinwales.org.uk W: http://bangor.churchinwales.org.uk
ST DAVIDS	Diocesan Office, Abergwili, Carmarthen SA31 2JG T: (01267) 236145 E: diocese.stdavids@churchinwales.org.uk W: http://stdavids.churchinwales.org.uk
LLANDAFF	Diocesan Office, The Court, Coychurch, Bridgend CF35 5EH T: (01656) 868868 F: 868869 E: rowenasmall@churchinwales.org.uk W: http://llandaff.churchinwales.org.uk
MONMOUTH	Diocesan Office, 64 Caerau Road, Newport NP20 4HJ T: (01633) 267490 F: 265586 W: http://monmouth.churchinwales.org.uk
SWANSEA AND BRECON	Diocesan Centre, Cathedral Close, Brecon LD3 9DP T: (01874) 623716 F: 623716 E: diocese.swanbrec@churchinwales.org.uk W: http://swanseaandbrecon.churchinwales.org.uk

SCOTTISH EPISCOPAL CHURCH

ABERDEEN AND ORKNEY	Diocesan Office, St Clement's Church House, Mastrick Drive, Aberdeen AB16 6UF T: (01224) 662247 E: office@aberdeen.anglican.org W: http://aberdeen.anglican.org
ARGYLL AND THE ISLES	St Moluag's Diocesan Centre, Croft Avenue, Oban PA34 5JJ T: (01631) 570870 E: office@argyll.anglican.org W: www.argyll.anglican.org
BRECHIN	Brechin Diocesan Office, 38 Langlands Street, Dundee DD4 6SZ T: (01382) 459569 E: office@brechin.anglican.org W: http://brechin.anglican.org
EDINBURGH	Diocesan Office, 21A Grosvenor Crescent, Edinburgh EH12 5EL T: 0131-538 7033 E: office@edinburgh.anglican.org W: www.edinburgh.anglican.org
GLASGOW AND GALLOWAY	Diocesan Centre, 5 St Vincent Place, Glasgow G1 2DH T: 0141-221 5720 or 221 6911 E: office@glasgow.anglican.org W: www.glasgow.anglican.org
MORAY, ROSS AND CAITHNESS	Diocesan Office, 9-11 Kenneth Street, Inverness IV3 5NR T: (01463) 237503 E: office@moray.anglican.org W: www.morayepiscopalchurch.scot
ST ANDREWS, DUNKELD AND DUNBLANE	Perth Diocesan Centre, 28A Balhousie Street, Perth PH1 5HJ T: (01738) 443173 E: office@standrews.anglican.org W: www.standrews.anglican.org

CHURCH OF IRELAND

PROVINCE OF ARMAGH

ARMAGH	Church House, 46 Abbey Street, Armagh BT61 7DZ T: (028) 3752 2858 F: 3751 0596 E: office@armagh.anglican.org W: http://armagh.anglican.org
CLOGHER	Diocesan Office, St Macartin's Cathedral Hall, Hall's Lane, Enniskillen BT74 7DR T/F: (028) 6634 7879 E: secretary@clogher.anglican.org W: www.clogher.anglican.org
CONNOR	Diocesan Office, Church of Ireland House, 61-67 Donegall Street, Belfast BT1 2QH T: (028) 9082 8830 F: 9032 1635 E: office@diocoff-belfast.org W: www.connor.anglican.org
DERRY AND RAPHOE	Diocesan Office, 24 London Street, Londonderry BT48 6RQ T: (028) 7126 2440 E: gavin@derryandraphoe.org W: http://derryandraphoe.org
DOWN AND DROMORE	Diocesan Office, Church of Ireland House, 61-67 Donegall Street, Belfast BT1 2QH T: (028) 9082 8850 F: 9032 1902 E: dco@downdromorediocese.org W: www.downanddromore.org
KILMORE	Kilmore Diocesan Office, The Rectory, Cootehill, Co Cavan, Republic of Ireland T: (00353) (49) 555 9954 F: 555 9957 E: office@kilmore.anglican.org W: http://www.dkea.ie
ELPHIN AND ARDAGH	69 Teemore Road, Garvary, Derrylin, Enniskillen BT92 9QB T: (00353) (89) 459 3219 E: diocesea@eirom.net W: http://www.dkea.ie/

| TUAM, KILLALA AND ACHONRY | Stonehall House, Ballisodare, Co Sligo, Republic of Ireland
T: (00353) (71) 916 7280   E: heathersherlock7@gmail.com
W: www.tuam.anglican.org |

PROVINCE OF DUBLIN

CASHEL AND OSSORY	Diocesan Office, The Palace Coach House, Church Lane, Kilkenny, Republic of Ireland T: (00353) (56) 776 1910 F: 775 1813 E: office@cashel.anglican.org W: www.cashel.anglican.org
CORK, CLOYNE AND ROSS	Diocesan Office, St Nicholas' House, 14 Cove Street, Cork, T12 RP40, Republic of Ireland T: (00353) (21) 500 5080 F: 432 0960 E: secretary@corkchurchofireland.com W: www.cork.anglican.org
DUBLIN AND GLENDALOUGH	Diocesan Office, Church of Ireland House, Church Avenue, Rathmines, Dublin 6, Republic of Ireland T: (00353) (1) 496 6981 F: 497 2865 E: admin@dublin.anglican.org W: www.dublin.anglican.org
LIMERICK AND KILLALOE	St John's Rectory, Ashe Street, Tralee, Co Kerry, Republic of Ireland T: (00353) (66) 712 3182 E: secretary@limerick.anglican.org W: www.limerick.anglican.org
MEATH AND KILDARE	Meath and Kildare Diocesan Centre, Moyglare, Maynooth, Co Kildare, Republic of Ireland T: (00353) (1) 629 2163 E: secretary@meath.anglican.org W: www.meathandkildare.org

ARCHDEACONRIES, DEANERIES AND RURAL/AREA DEANS OF THE CHURCH OF ENGLAND AND THE CHURCH IN WALES

CHURCH OF ENGLAND

BATH AND WELLS

ARCHDEACONRY OF WELLS

1. AXBRIDGE   R W NEILL
2. BRUTON AND CARY   E A DUDLEY
3. FROME   G A OWEN
4. GLASTONBURY JURISDICTION   D J L MACGEOCH
5. IVELCHESTER   B S FAULKNER
6. YEOVIL   J DUDLEY-SMITH
7. SHEPTON MALLET   S DENYER

ARCHDEACONRY OF BATH

8. BATH   M D H FRANKUM
9. CHEW MAGNA   S A M'CAW
10. LOCKING   T P B YACOMENI
11. MIDSOMER NORTON   M G STREET
12. PORTISHEAD   J S TILLEY

ARCHDEACONRY OF TAUNTON

13. SEDGEMOOR   J HASLAM
14. CREWKERNE   G A WADE
15. EXMOOR   C S RALPH
16. ILMINSTER   J ABBOTT
17. QUANTOCK   B R G FLENLEY
18. TAUNTON   R S HARRIS
19. TONE   H L STAINER

BIRMINGHAM

ARCHDEACONRY OF BIRMINGHAM

1. EDGBASTON   N J C TUCKER
2. HANDSWORTH AND CENTRAL   I HARPER, P CALVGRT (JT)
3. KINGS NORTON   R S FIELDSON
4. MOSELEY   Q D WARBRICK
5. SHIRLEY   T D HILL-BROWN
6. WARLEY   D BUCKLEY

ARCHDEACONRY OF ASTON

7. ASTON AND SUTTON COLDFIELD   A RICHARDSON
8. COLESHILL   A D BARRETT, R L STEPHENS (JT)
9. POLESWORTH   J L C SHAW
10. SOLIHULL   T N CROWE
11. YARDLEY AND BORDESLEY   A T BULLOCK

BLACKBURN

ARCHDEACONRY OF BLACKBURN

1. ACCRINGTON   I P ENTICOTT
2. BLACKBURN AND DARWEN   F E GREEN
3. BURNLEY   P N A SENIOR
4. CHORLEY   D A ARNOLD
5. LEYLAND   M A M WOLVERSON
6. PENDLE   G S JAMIESON
7. WHALLEY   R J CARMYLLIE

ARCHDEACONRY OF LANCASTER

8. BLACKPOOL   P A LILLICRAP
9. GARSTANG   A W WILKINSON
10. KIRKHAM   A D LYON
11. LANCASTER AND MORECAMBE   C J RIGNEY
12. POULTON   M P KEIGHLEY
13. PRESTON   A MCHAFFIE
14. TUNSTALL   N E GOODRICH

BRISTOL

ARCHDEACONRY OF BRISTOL

1. BRISTOL SOUTH   N J HAY
2. BRISTOL WEST   C E SUTTON
3. CITY DEANERY   R P SYMMONS

ARCHDEACONRY OF MALMESBURY

4. CHIPPENHAM   S A V WHEELER
5. KINGSWOOD AND SOUTH GLOUCESTERSHIRE   J C E ANDREW
6. NORTH WILTSHIRE   A J LOVE
7. SWINDON   C D DEVERELL

CANTERBURY

ARCHDEACONRY OF CANTERBURY

1. EAST BRIDGE   S C THOMAS
2. WEST BRIDGE   R HOLY
3. CANTERBURY   K MADDY
4. RECULVER   A W EVERETT
5. THANET   C B STOCKING, A R BRADDY (JT)

ARCHDEACONRY OF ASHFORD

6. ASHFORD   J C N MACKENZIE, C A B MANSLEY (JT)
7. DOVER   A J BAWTREE
8. ELHAM   J A WEEKS
9. SANDWICH   S W COOPER
10. ROMNEY AND TENTERDEN   A BIENFAIT

ARCHDEACONRY OF MAIDSTONE

11. WEALD   A E J POLLINGTON
12. MAIDSTONE   A W SEWELL
13. NORTH DOWNS   J CORBYN
14. OSPRINGE   S H LILLICRAP
15. SITTINGBOURNE   M J RESCH

CARLISLE

ARCHDEACONRY OF CARLISLE

1. APPLEBY   S J FYFE
2. BRAMPTON   E A JOHNSEN
3. CARLISLE   N D BEER
4. PENRITH   D G SARGENT

ARCHDEACONRY OF WEST CUMBERLAND

5. CALDER   A J BANKS
6. DERWENT   C H HOPE
7. SOLWAY   T D HERBERT

ARCHDEACONRY OF WESTMORLAND AND FURNESS

8. BARROW   *vacant*
9. FURNESS   R J CROSSLEY
10. KENDAL   A E PETTIFOR
11. WINDERMERE   D M B WILMOT

CHELMSFORD

ARCHDEACONRY OF BARKING (BISHOP OF BARKING)

1. BARKING AND DAGENHAM   M J COURT
2. HAVERING   M A POWER

ARCHDEACONRY OF HARLOW (BISHOP OF BARKING)

3. EPPING FOREST AND ONGAR   L P BATSON
4. HARLOW   M J HARRIS

ARCHDEACONRY OF WEST HAM (BISHOP OF BARKING)

5. NEWHAM   *vacant*
6. REDBRIDGE   M J HAWKES
7. WALTHAM FOREST   D R BRITTON

ARCHDEACONRY OF CHELMSFORD (BISHOP OF BRADWELL)

8. BRENTWOOD   P S HAMILTON
9. CHELMSFORD NORTH   T W BALL
10. CHELMSFORD SOUTH   T W BALL
11. MALDON AND DENGIE   P E C BEGLEY

ARCHDEACONRY OF SOUTHEND (BISHOP OF BRADWELL)

12. BASILDON   J S RICHARDS
13. HADLEIGH   D S C TUDOR
14. ROCHFORD   N E ROWAN
15. SOUTHEND-ON-SEA   J COLLIS
16. THURROCK   D BARLOW

ARCHDEACONRY OF STANSTED (BISHOP OF COLCHESTER)

17. BRAINTREE   C M DAVEY
18. DUNMOW AND STANSTED   C M HAWKES
19. HINCKFORD   J D LOWE
20. SAFFRON WALDEN   D R TOMLINSON

ARCHDEACONRY OF COLCHESTER (BISHOP OF COLCHESTER)

21. COLCHESTER   P R NORRINGTON
22. HARWICH   S A HERON
23. ST OSYTH   L BOND
24. WITHAM   *vacant*

CHESTER

ARCHDEACONRY OF CHESTER

1. BIRKENHEAD   R E IVESON
2. CHESTER   H E A JOHNSTON
3. FRODSHAM   D W GUEST
4. GREAT BUDWORTH   A G BROWN
5. MALPAS   I A DAVENPORT
6. MIDDLEWICH   S M DREW
7. WALLASEY   A W WARD
8. WIRRAL NORTH   P M FROGGATT
9. WIRRAL SOUTH   E A GLOVER

ARCHDEACONRY OF MACCLESFIELD

10. BOWDON   G C JAQUISS
11. CONGLETON   S J CLAPHAM
12. KNUTSFORD   I BLAY
13. MACCLESFIELD   J E HARRIES
14. MOTTRAM   H SCARISBRICK
15. NANTWICH   H F CHANTRY
16. CHADKIRK   L S CURRIE
17. CHEADLE   R S MUNRO
18. STOCKPORT   D T BREWSTER

CHICHESTER

ARCHDEACONRY OF CHICHESTER

1. ARUNDEL AND BOGNOR   M J STANDEN
2. CHICHESTER   D JARRATT
3. WESTBOURNE   M J LANE
4. WORTHING   H M BUQUÉ

ARCHDEACONRY OF HORSHAM

5. CUCKFIELD   M J MAINE
6. EAST GRINSTEAD   A F MARTIN
7. HORSHAM   D M BEAL
8. HURST   P S J DOICK
9. MIDHURST   D B WELSMAN
10. PETWORTH   P M GILBERT
11. STORRINGTON   K A WINDSLOW

ARCHDEACONRY OF HASTINGS

12. BATTLE AND BEXHILL   J J FRAIS
13. DALLINGTON   M A LLOYD
14. EASTBOURNE   D J GILLARD
15. HASTINGS   R M M CREIGHTON
16. ROTHERFIELD   S E FRANCIS
17. RYE   C P IRVINE
18. UCKFIELD   P MACBAIN

ARCHDEACONRY OF BRIGHTON AND LEWES

19. BRIGHTON   A J WOODWARD
20. HOVE   D T HENDERSON
21. LEWES AND SEAFORD   J A EGAR

COVENTRY

ARCHDEACONRY OF COVENTRY

1. COVENTRY EAST   E K FORBES STONE
2. COVENTRY NORTH   E B JACKSON
3. COVENTRY SOUTH   G P SMITH
4. KENILWORTH   S BAILEY
5. NUNEATON   D E POULTNEY
6. RUGBY   T D COCKELL

ARCHDEACONRY OF WARWICK

7. ALCESTER   *vacant*
8. FOSSE   *vacant*
9. SHIPSTON   J TUCKER
10. SOUTHAM   M C GREEN
11. WARWICK AND LEAMINGTON   S PARKER

DERBY

ARCHDEACONRY OF CHESTERFIELD

1. CARSINGTON   *vacant*
2. HARDWICK   G MANLEY
3. DERBYSHIRE, NORTH EAST   K E HAMBLIN
4. PEAK   C G PEARSON

ARCHDEACONRY OF DERBY

5. DERBY CITY   *vacant*
6. DOVE AND DERWENT   B J STOBER
7. MERCIA   *vacant*
8. DERBYSHIRE, SOUTH EAST   K PADLEY

DURHAM

ARCHDEACONRY OF DURHAM

1. DURHAM   H MURRAY
2. EASINGTON   F J GRIEVE
3. HARTLEPOOL   J BURBURY
4. LANCHESTER   S CLARK

ARCHDEACONRY OF AUCKLAND

5. AUCKLAND   M P TARLING
6. BARNARD CASTLE   A J HARDING
7. DARLINGTON   M R EAST
8. STANHOPE   D L SPOKES
9. STOCKTON   P S D NEVILLE

ARCHDEACONRY OF SUNDERLAND

10. CHESTER LE STREET AND HOUGHTON   D C GLOVER
11. GATESHEAD   Y GREENER
12. GATESHEAD WEST   T I BRAZIER
13. JARROW   V J CUTHBERT
14. WEARMOUTH   D TOLHURST

ELY

ARCHDEACONRY OF CAMBRIDGE

1. BOURN   S E WYATT
2. CAMBRIDGE NORTH   D J MAHER
3. CAMBRIDGE SOUTH   R M MACKLEY
4. FORDHAM AND QUY   S J GILES
5. GRANTA   S J TALBOTT
6. NORTH STOWE   N J BLANDFORD-BAKER
7. SHINGAY   F A COUCH

ARCHDEACONRIES, DEANERIES AND RURAL/AREA DEANS

ARCHDEACONRY OF HUNTINGDON AND WISBECH

8. ELY   J H ROBSON
9. FINCHAM AND FELTWELL   W S D BURKE
10. HUNTINGDON   I P BRENNAN
11. MARCH   A J SMITH
12. ST IVES   F J KILNER
13. ST NEOTS   G FELLOWS
14. WISBECH LYNN MARSHLAND   R A HINES
15. YAXLEY   S C GOWER

EXETER

ARCHDEACONRY OF EXETER

1. AYLESBEARE   R SELLERS
2. CADBURY   D C FRANCIS
3. CHRISTIANITY   D J NIXON
4. HONITON   C E EDMONDS
5. KENN   D J AYLING
6. OTTERY   M WARD
7. TIVERTON AND CULLOMPTON   S G G TALBOT

ARCHDEACONRY OF TOTNES

8. MORETON   A C RYLANDS
9. NEWTON ABBOT AND IPPLEPEN   E P PARKES
10. OKEHAMPTON   N P WELDON
11. TORBAY   R J CARLTON
12. TOTNES   D A PARSONS
13. WOODLEIGH   J M TAYLOR

ARCHDEACONRY OF BARNSTAPLE

14. BARNSTAPLE   A DODWELL
15. HARTLAND   D J ARNOLD
16. HOLSWORTHY   R A FREEMAN
17. SHIRWELL   R E AUSTIN
18. SOUTH MOLTON   A M WELLS
19. TORRINGTON   S METZ

ARCHDEACONRY OF PLYMOUTH

20. IVYBRIDGE   A C LEGGE
21. PLYMOUTH CITY   D B M GILL
22. TAVISTOCK   N C LAW

GLOUCESTER

ARCHDEACONRY OF GLOUCESTER

1. FOREST SOUTH   C W MACLAY
2. GLOUCESTER CITY   M GARLAND
3. SEVERN VALE   S I V MASON
4. STROUD   S J MURRAY
5. WOTTON   D J RUSSELL

ARCHDEACONRY OF CHELTENHAM

6. CHELTENHAM   G B GRADY
7. CIRENCESTER   V J HUGHES
8. NORTH COTSWOLD   K R SCOTT
9. TEWKESBURY AND WINCHCOMBE   M ALLEN

GUILDFORD

ARCHDEACONRY OF SURREY

1. ALDERSHOT   M W HAYTON
2. CRANLEIGH   R O WOODHAMS
3. FARNHAM   J L WALKER
4. GODALMING   S D K TAYLOR
5. GUILDFORD   N J WILLIAMS
6. SURREY HEATH   J HILLMAN

ARCHDEACONRY OF DORKING

7. DORKING   R K F BUSHYAGER
8. EMLY   A C COWIE
9. EPSOM   D C WILLIAMSON
10. LEATHERHEAD   A D JENKINS
11. RUNNYMEDE   S C FACCINI
12. WOKING   vacant

HEREFORD

ARCHDEACONRY OF HEREFORD

1. ABBEYDORE   N G LOWTON
2. BROMYARD   C R EVANS
3. HEREFORD   N S PATTERSON
4. KINGTON AND WEOBLEY   S HOLLINGHURST
5. LEDBURY   R WARD
6. LEOMINSTER   M J KNEEN
7. ROSS AND ARCHENFIELD   M JOHNSON

ARCHDEACONRY OF LUDLOW

8. BRIDGNORTH   M H DABORN
9. CLUN FOREST   S A C FOUNTAIN
10. CONDOVER   G D GARRETT
11. LUDLOW   W A BUCK
12. PONTESBURY   G D TULK
13. TELFORD SEVERN GORGE   I S NAYLOR

LEEDS

ARCHDEACONRY OF BRADFORD

1. AIRE AND WORTH   S R BENHAM
2. INNER BRADFORD   J E BAVINGTON
3. OUTER BRADFORD   V POLLARD
4. SOUTH CRAVEN AND WHARFEDALE   P C GRAY

ARCHDEACONRY OF HALIFAX

5. ALMONDBURY   M T P ZAMMIT
6. BIRSTALL   S A CASH
7. BRIGHOUSE AND ELLAND   M E RUSSELL
8. CALDER VALLEY   M E RUSSELL, K A SHOESMITH (JT)
9. DEWSBURY   S A CASH
10. HALIFAX   K A SHOESMITH
11. HUDDERSFIELD   R N FIRTH
12. KIRKBURTON   M T P ZAMMIT, R N FIRTH (JT)

ARCHDEACONRY OF LEEDS

13. ALLERTON   K A FITZSIMONS
14. ARMLEY   A SEN
15. HEADINGLEY   J R SEABOURNE
16. WHITKIRK   M PEAT

ARCHDEACONRY OF PONTEFRACT

17. BARNSLEY   S P RACE
18. PONTEFRACT   M GALLAGHER
19. WAKEFIELD   D I GERRARD

ARCHDEACONRY OF RICHMOND AND CRAVEN

20. BOWLAND AND EWECROSS   S C DAWSON
21. HARROGATE   J SMITH
22. RICHMOND   Y S CALLAGHAN
23. RIPON   D C HALL
24. SKIPTON   R HARRIS
25. WENSLEY   P S YEADON

LEICESTER

ARCHDEACONRY OF LEICESTER

1. CITY OF LEICESTER   vacant
2. FRAMLAND (Melton)   P G HOOPER
3. GARTREE   A S W BOOKER
4. GOSCOTE   R M GLADSTONE
5. LAUNDE   A S W BOOKER

ARCHDEACONRY OF LOUGHBOROUGH

6. AKELEY EAST (Loughborough)   W M DALRYMPLE
7. GUTHLAXTON   S J CONSTABLE
8. NORTH WEST LEICESTERSHIRE   V M ELPHICK
9. SPARKENHOE EAST   T L RINGLAND
10. SPARKENHOE WEST   M S POSKITT

LICHFIELD

ARCHDEACONRY OF LICHFIELD

1. LICHFIELD   J L WATERFIELD
2. PENKRIDGE   G H YERBURY
3. RUGELEY   S C DAVIS
4. TAMWORTH   D A DYSON

ARCHDEACONRY OF STOKE-UPON-TRENT

5. ALSTONFIELD   M J EVANS
6. CHEADLE   M S FOLLIN
7. ECCLESHALL   J L WALKER
8. LEEK   B E STATHAM
9. NEWCASTLE   T B BLOOR
10. STAFFORD   *vacant*
11. STOKE-ON-TRENT   S A MORRIS
12. STONE   I R CARDINAL
13. TUTBURY   M R FREEMAN
14. UTTOXETER   B S P LEATHERS

ARCHDEACONRY OF SALOP

15. EDGMOND AND SHIFNAL   K HODSON
16. ELLESMERE   L J COX
17. HODNET   C SIMPSON
18. OSWESTRY   P T DARLINGTON
19. SHREWSBURY   P J CANSDALE
20. TELFORD   T STOREY
21. WEM AND WHITCHURCH   A J B CLAYTON
22. WROCKWARDINE   D A ACKROYD

ARCHDEACONRY OF WALSALL

23. TRYSULL   J M CODY
24. WALSALL   C A ST A RAMSAY
25. WEDNESBURY   M M ENNIS
26. WEST BROMWICH   R A FARRELL
27. WOLVERHAMPTON   D W WRIGHT
28. WULFRUN   N E WATSON

LINCOLN

ARCHDEACONRY OF STOW AND LINDSEY

1. ISLE OF AXHOLME   C KAY
2. CORRINGHAM   P WAIN
3. GRIMSBY AND CLEETHORPES   A P DODD
4. HAVERSTOE   P T STEVENS
5. LAWRES   R H CROSSLAND
6. MANLAKE   C A B MARTIN
7. WEST WOLD   *vacant*
8. YARBOROUGH   D P ROWETT

ARCHDEACONRY OF LINCOLN

9. BOLINGBROKE   P F COATES
10. CALCEWAITHE AND CANDLESHOE   R M LATHAM
11. CHRISTIANITY   H W F JONES
12. GRAFFOE   A R BARBER
13. HORNCASTLE   M N HOLDEN
14. LAFFORD   P A JOHNSON
15. LOUTHESK   N J W BROWN

ARCHDEACONRY OF BOSTON

16. STAMFORD   *vacant*
17. BELTISLOE   C J ATKINSON
18. ELLOE EAST   R J SEAL
19. ELLOE WEST   M J HOWARD
20. GRANTHAM   *vacant*
21. HOLLAND   A J HIGGINSON
22. LOVEDEN   A I TUCKER

LIVERPOOL

ARCHDEACONRY OF LIVERPOOL

1. LIVERPOOL NORTH   *vacant*
2. LIVERPOOL SOUTH   N C MILFORD
3. TOXTETH AND WAVERTREE   E JONES
4. WALTON   *vacant*
5. WEST DERBY   E L WILLIAMS

ARCHDEACONRY OF KNOWSLEY AND SEFTON

6. SEFTON SOUTH   A D STOTT
7. HUYTON   M K ROGERS
8. SEFTON NORTH   A E TAYLOR
9. NORTH MEOLS   S MCGANITY

ARCHDEACONRY OF ST HELENS AND WARRINGTON

10. ST HELENS   *vacant*
11. WARRINGTON   N G SHAW
12. WIDNES   R HARVEY
13. WINWICK   S B GREY

ARCHDEACONRY OF WIGAN AND WEST LANCASHIRE

14. ORMSKIRK   W D PETTY
15. WIGAN   P G ANDERSON

LONDON

ARCHDEACONRY OF LONDON

1. THE CITY   K HEDDERLY

ARCHDEACONRY OF CHARING CROSS

2. WESTMINSTER PADDINGTON   P R THOMAS
3. WESTMINSTER ST MARGARET   P A E CHESTER
4. WESTMINSTER ST MARYLEBONE   L A MOSES

ARCHDEACONRY OF HACKNEY
(STEPNEY AREA)

5. HACKNEY   R BROWN
6. ISLINGTON   *vacant*
7. TOWER HAMLETS   A RIDER

ARCHDEACONRY OF MIDDLESEX
(KENSINGTON AREA)

8. CHELSEA   J L WELSH
9. HAMMERSMITH AND FULHAM   T J STILWELL
10. HAMPTON   T M GARRETT
11. HOUNSLOW   R S FRANK
12. KENSINGTON   M R O'DONOGHUE
13. SPELTHORNE   A SAVILLE

ARCHDEACONRY OF HAMPSTEAD
(EDMONTON AREA)

14. CENTRAL BARNET   G A D PLATTEN
15. WEST BARNET   G A D PLATTEN
16. NORTH CAMDEN (Hampstead)   J G F KESTER
17. SOUTH CAMDEN (Holborn and
    St Pancras)   J G F KESTER
18. ENFIELD   S J OWEN
19. EAST HARINGEY   I G BOOTH
20. WEST HARINGEY   P H SUDELL

ARCHDEACONRY OF NORTHOLT
(WILLESDEN AREA)

21. BRENT   A J TEATHER
22. EALING   S M NEWBOLD
23. HARROW   I P DOWSETT
24. HILLINGDON   R C YOUNG

MANCHESTER

ARCHDEACONRY OF MANCHESTER

1. ARDWICK   C P SMITH
2. HEATON   H T SCANLAN
3. HULME   A W HARDY
4. NORTH MANCHESTER   E M ROBERTS
5. STRETFORD   C S FORD
6. WITHINGTON   R MANN

ARCHDEACONRY OF BOLTON

7. BOLTON   C A BRACEGIRDLE
8. BURY   S D J COOK
9. DEANE   V C WHITWORTH
10. RADCLIFFE AND PRESTWICH   D F THOMSON
11. ROSSENDALE   R BEVAN
12. WALMSLEY   J J HARTLEY

ARCHDEACONRY OF ROCHDALE

13. ASHTON-UNDER-LYNE   P R DIXON
14. HEYWOOD AND MIDDLETON   F C GUITE
15. OLDHAM EAST   L E M WOODALL
16. OLDHAM WEST   N J ANDREWES
17. ROCHDALE   K L SMEETON

ARCHDEACONRY OF SALFORD

18. ECCLES   K HOPWOOD OWEN
19. LEIGH   M B COX
20. SALFORD   D J A BURTON

ARCHDEACONRIES, DEANERIES AND RURAL/AREA DEANS

NEWCASTLE

ARCHDEACONRY OF NORTHUMBERLAND

1. BEDLINGTON   P G J HUGHES
2. NEWCASTLE CENTRAL   E J NATTRASS
3. NEWCASTLE EAST   R W LAWRANCE
4. NEWCASTLE WEST   C L BROWN
5. TYNEMOUTH   T J E MAYFIELD

ARCHDEACONRY OF LINDISFARNE

6. ALNWICK   A J HARDY
7. BAMBURGH AND GLENDALE   L M TAYLOR-KENYON
8. BELLINGHAM   S G WILKINSON
9. CORBRIDGE   *vacant*
10. HEXHAM   J J T THOMPSON
11. MORPETH   J C PARK
12. NORHAM   G R J KELSEY

NORWICH

ARCHDEACONRY OF NORWICH

1. NORWICH EAST   D T THORNTON
2. NORWICH NORTH   S C STOKES
3. NORWICH SOUTH   P H RICHMOND

ARCHDEACONRY OF NORFOLK

4. BLOFIELD   M GREENLAND, P-J B LEECH (JT)
5. DEPWADE   H Y WILCOX
6. GREAT YARMOUTH   J M KINCHIN-SMITH
7. HUMBLEYARD   C B REED
8. LODDON   D C OWEN
9. LOTHINGLAND   D ROGERS, M J ASQUITH (JT)
10. REDENHALL   N O TUFFNELL
11. THETFORD AND ROCKLAND   M C JACKSON
12. ST BENET AT WAXHAM AND TUNSTEAD   C H DOBSON

ARCHDEACONRY OF LYNN

13. BRECKLAND   S L THORP
14. BURNHAM AND WALSINGHAM   A B ELKINS
15. HEACHAM AND RISING   P R COOK
16. DEREHAM IN MITFORD   M A MCCAGHREY
17. HOLT   J G SYKES
18. INGWORTH AND SPARHAM   K A F RENGERT
19. LYNN   J A NASH
20. REPPS   C J HEYCOCKS

OXFORD

ARCHDEACONRY OF OXFORD

1. COWLEY   G B T BAYLISS
2. OXFORD   A G BUCKLEY

ARCHDEACONRY OF BERKSHIRE (BISHOP OF READING)

3. BRACKNELL   G S COLE
4. BRADFIELD   H C W PARBURY
5. MAIDENHEAD AND WINDSOR   A L SWIFT
6. NEWBURY   M D BENNET
7. READING   G FANCOURT
8. SONNING   R J LAMEY

ARCHDEACONRY OF BUCKINGHAM

9. AMERSHAM   T J L HARPER, M J WILLIAMS (JT)
10. AYLESBURY   D G WILLIAMS
11. BUCKINGHAM   R M ROBERTS
12. BURNHAM AND SLOUGH   R J COSH
13. CLAYDON   D J MEAKIN
14. MILTON KEYNES   T NORWOOD
15. MURSLEY   *vacant*
16. NEWPORT   G E ECCLESTONE
17. WENDOVER   D J O KEARLEY-HEYWOOD
18. WYCOMBE   D T BULL

ARCHDEACONRY OF DORCHESTER

19. ABINGDON   H G KENDRICK
20. ASTON AND CUDDESDON   S N CRONK
21. BICESTER AND ISLIP   J G MILLER
22. CHIPPING NORTON   S A WELCH
23. DEDDINGTON   S E SHARP
24. HENLEY   L J SMITH

25. VALE OF WHITE HORSE   J P ST JOHN NICOLLE
26. WALLINGFORD   D RICE
27. WANTAGE   J P ST JOHN NICOLLE
28. WITNEY   T C WRIGHT
29. WOODSTOCK   D S TYLER

PETERBOROUGH

ARCHDEACONRY OF NORTHAMPTON

1. BRACKLEY   *vacant*
2. BRIXWORTH   S TROTT
3. DAVENTRY   M Y GARBUTT
4. GREATER NORTHAMPTON   B J HOLLINS
5. TOWCESTER   P D MCLEOD
6. WELLINGBOROUGH   E G SMITH

ARCHDEACONRY OF OAKHAM

7. CORBY   I A PULLINGER
8. HIGHAM   C A YOUNGMAN
9. KETTERING   H M JEFFERY
10. OUNDLE   S J WEBSTER
11. PETERBOROUGH   I C BLACK
12. RUTLAND   J E BAXTER

PORTSMOUTH

ARCHDEACONRY OF THE MEON

1. BISHOP'S WALTHAM   D T ISAAC
2. FAREHAM   I MEREDITH
3. GOSPORT   K I MITCHELL
4. PETERSFIELD   J BALL

ARCHDEACONRY OF PORTSDOWN

5. HAVANT   K B GREEN, I SNARES (JT)
6. PORTSMOUTH   R C WHITE

ARCHDEACONRY OF ISLE OF WIGHT

7. ISLE OF WIGHT   A COLLINSON

ROCHESTER

ARCHDEACONRY OF ROCHESTER

1. COBHAM   A E DAVIE
2. DARTFORD   R J MORTIMER
3. GILLINGHAM   *vacant*
4. GRAVESEND   N I BOURNE
5. ROCHESTER   H M BURN
6. STROOD   S L COPESTAKE

ARCHDEACONRY OF TONBRIDGE

7. MALLING   W W NORTH
8. PADDOCK WOOD   A J AXON
9. SEVENOAKS   *vacant*
10. SHOREHAM   T R HATWELL
11. TONBRIDGE   M S A BARKER
12. TUNBRIDGE WELLS   D P WREN

ARCHDEACONRY OF BROMLEY AND BEXLEY

13. BECKENHAM   R M HINTON
14. BROMLEY   A KEELER
15. ERITH   A J D FOOT
16. ORPINGTON   W J MUSSON
17. SIDCUP   M J JEMMETT

ST ALBANS

ARCHDEACONRY OF ST ALBANS

1. BERKHAMSTED   J A GORDON
2. HEMEL HEMPSTEAD   E M HOOD
3. HITCHIN   J F MAINWARING
4. RICKMANSWORTH   D M HALL
5. ST ALBANS   M A SLATER
6. WATFORD   *vacant*
7. WHEATHAMPSTEAD   R M BANHAM

ARCHDEACONRY OF BEDFORD

8. AMPTHILL AND SHEFFORD   L KLIMAS
9. BEDFORD   R C HIBBERT
10. BIGGLESWADE   G C SCOTT
11. DUNSTABLE   N Y LENTHALL
12. LUTON   D W KESTERTON
13. SHARNBROOK   S J LILEY

ARCHDEACONRY OF HERTFORD

14. BARNET   T P SEAGO
15. BISHOP'S STORTFORD   M K BROWN
16. BUNTINGFORD   *vacant*
17. CHESHUNT   C E C HUDSON
18. WELWYN HATFIELD   J E FENNELL
19. HERTFORD AND WARE   J M H LOVERIDGE
20. STEVENAGE   C E BUNCE

ST EDMUNDSBURY AND IPSWICH

ARCHDEACONRY OF IPSWICH

1. IPSWICH   N S ATKINS

ARCHDEACONRY OF SUDBURY

2. BOSMERE   D R WILLIAMS
3. CLARE   S MITCHELL
4. HADLEIGH   M J WOODROW
5. IXWORTH   K A VALENTINE
6. LAVENHAM   C M S ROBINSON
7. MILDENHALL   M E OSBORNE
8. STOWMARKET   D R WILLIAMS
9. SUDBURY   S R MORLEY
10. THINGOE   M N HAWORTH

ARCHDEACONRY OF SUFFOLK

11. COLNEYS   A S DOTCHIN
12. HARTISMERE   S A LOXTON
13. HOXNE   S A LOXTON
14. LOES   M SANDERS
15. SAMFORD   L OOSTERHOF
16. SAXMUNDHAM   S E HART
17. WAVENEY AND BLYTH   S J PITCHER
18. WOODBRIDGE   H C SANDERS

SALISBURY

ARCHDEACONRY OF SHERBORNE

1. DORCHESTER   J T L STILL
2. LYME BAY   D F B BALDWIN
3. SHERBORNE   A J D GILBERT
4. WEYMOUTH AND PORTLAND   N J CLARKE
5. BLACKMORE VALE   L M S COOK

ARCHDEACONRY OF DORSET

6. MILTON AND BLANDFORD   J P TRIFFITT
7. POOLE AND NORTH BOURNEMOUTH   L J HOLT
8. PURBECK   S F EVERETT
9. WIMBORNE   A J W ROWLAND

ARCHDEACONRY OF SARUM

10. ALDERBURY   D G BACON
11. CHALKE   G SOUTHGATE
12. HEYTESBURY   P A REID
13. SALISBURY   K J INGLIS
14. STONEHENGE   E J RANCE

ARCHDEACONRY OF WILTS

15. BRADFORD   A E EVANS
16. CALNE   J D CURTIS
17. DEVIZES   P RICHARDSON
18. MARLBOROUGH   R R POWELL
19. PEWSEY   G E R OSBORNE

SHEFFIELD

ARCHDEACONRY OF SHEFFIELD AND ROTHERHAM

1. ATTERCLIFFE   J UPTON, P A KNOWLES (JT)
2. ECCLESALL   T K HOLE
3. ECCLESFIELD   A T ISAACSON
4. HALLAM   M I RHODES

5. LAUGHTON   F M ECCLESTON
6. ROTHERHAM   *vacant*

ARCHDEACONRY OF DONCASTER

7. ADWICK-LE-STREET   R J WALTON
8. DONCASTER   R A HEARD, A HOWARD (JT)
9. DONCASTER, WEST   I SMITH
10. SNAITH AND HATFIELD   E A TURNER-LOISEL
11. TANKERSLEY   D J HOPKIN
12. WATH   A R BREWERTON

SODOR AND MAN

ARCHDEACONRY OF SODOR AND MAN

Deaneries, deanery synods and the office of rural dean were abolished with effect from 1 January 2013 by the Mission and Pastoral Mesure (Isle of Man) 2012 s. 46, and deaneries were replaced by groupings of parishes known as "mission partnerships".

SOUTHWARK

ARCHDEACONRY OF LEWISHAM AND GREENWICH
(BISHOP OF WOOLWICH)

1. CHARLTON   *vacant*
2. DEPTFORD   P J FARLEY-MOORE
3. ELTHAM AND MOTTINGHAM   B E WARD
4. EAST LEWISHAM   S P HALL
5. WEST LEWISHAM   M BROOKS
6. PLUMSTEAD   C R WELHAM

ARCHDEACONRY OF SOUTHWARK
(BISHOP OF WOOLWICH)

7. BERMONDSEY   G J JENKINS
8. CAMBERWELL   *vacant*
9. DULWICH   S J HEIGHT
10. SOUTHWARK AND
     NEWINGTON   A D P MOUGHTIN-MUMBY

ARCHDEACONRY OF LAMBETH
(BISHOP OF KINGSTON)

11. LAMBETH NORTH   C A CLARKE
12. LAMBETH SOUTH   J E CROUCHER
13. MERTON   R S TAYLOR

ARCHDEACONRY OF WANDSWORTH
(BISHOP OF KINGSTON)

14. BATTERSEA   R G TAYLOR
15. KINGSTON   R S STANIER
16. RICHMOND AND BARNES   P W HART
17. TOOTING   S E M CLARKE
18. WANDSWORTH   I S TATTUM

ARCHDEACONRY OF CROYDON

19. CROYDON ADDINGTON   J J E ROWLEY
20. CROYDON CENTRAL   S J D FOSTER
21. CROYDON NORTH   C J TUCKER
22. CROYDON SOUTH   P C ROBERTS

ARCHDEACONRY OF REIGATE
(BISHOP OF CROYDON)

23. SUTTON   A M A GBEBIKAN
24. REIGATE   A C COLPUS
25. TANDRIDGE   K J PERCIVAL

SOUTHWELL AND NOTTINGHAM

ARCHDEACONRY OF NEWARK

1. BASSETLAW AND BAWTRY   D R GOUGH
2. MANSFIELD   *vacant*
3. NEWARK AND SOUTHWELL   M ADAMS
4. NEWSTEAD   M F SHOULER

ARCHDEACONRY OF NOTTINGHAM

5. EAST BINGHAM   S D HIPPISLEY-COX
6. WEST BINGHAM   *vacant*
7. GEDLING   A R GILES
8. NOTTINGHAM NORTH   P A HUXTABLE
9. NOTTINGHAM SOUTH   C D BOURNE

TRURO

ARCHDEACONRY OF CORNWALL

1. ST AUSTELL   H M FLINT
2. CARNMARTH NORTH   C J B BUSH
3. CARNMARTH SOUTH   G K BENNETT
4. KERRIER   D G MILLER
5. PENWITH   J E RISBRIDGER
6. POWDER   L M BARLEY
7. PYDAR   C C MCQUILLEN-WRIGHT

ARCHDEACONRY OF BODMIN

8. STRATTON   D K BARNES
9. TRIGG MAJOR   P M KNIGHT
10. TRIGG MINOR AND BODMIN   P R HOLLEY
11. EAST WIVELSHIRE   C M PAINTER
12. WEST WIVELSHIRE   S J MORGAN

WINCHESTER

ARCHDEACONRY OF WINCHESTER

1. ALRESFORD   D M CHATTELL
2. ALTON   B J PRITCHARD
3. ANDOVER   T A LEWIS
4. BASINGSTOKE   R J S C HARLOW
5. ODIHAM   M E DE QUIDT
6. WHITCHURCH   C L MARSHALL
7. WINCHESTER   K P KOUSSEFF

ARCHDEACONRY OF BOURNEMOUTH

8. BOURNEMOUTH   J C NIGHTINGALE
9. CHRISTCHURCH   G J PHILBRICK
10. EASTLEIGH   *vacant*
11. LYNDHURST   P B C SALISBURY
12. ROMSEY   J M PITKIN
13. SOUTHAMPTON   *vacant*

THE CHANNEL ISLANDS

14. GUERNSEY   T R BARKER
15. JERSEY   M R KEIRLE

WORCESTER

ARCHDEACONRY OF WORCESTER

1. EVESHAM   R J G THORNILEY

2. MALVERN   *vacant*
3. MARTLEY AND WORCESTER WEST   A M POTTER
4. PERSHORE   S A DANGERFIELD
5. UPTON   C A MOSS
6. WORCESTER EAST   D M COOKSEY

ARCHDEACONRY OF DUDLEY

7. BROMSGROVE   P LAWLOR
8. DROITWICH   V W BEYNON
9. DUDLEY   D MELVILLE
10. KINGSWINFORD   D J HOSKIN
11. KIDDERMINSTER   T J WILLIAMS
12. STOURBRIDGE   A K SILLIS
13. STOURPORT   E G WHITTAKER

YORK

ARCHDEACONRY OF YORK
(BISHOP OF SELBY)

1. NEW AINSTY   G R MUMFORD
2. DERWENT   N W R BIRD
3. EASINGWOLD   E C HASSALL
4. SELBY   C WILTON
5. SOUTH WOLD   C R PINCHBECK
6. SOUTHERN RYEDALE   C L WINGFIELD
7. CITY OF YORK   L D TILLET

ARCHDEACONRY OF EAST RIDING
(BISHOP OF HULL)

8. BEVERLEY   R F PARKINSON
9. BRIDLINGTON   M R POLLARD
10. HARTHILL   J A TONKIN
11. NORTH HOLDERNESS   A M WHITE
12. SOUTH HOLDERNESS   S J WALKER
13. HOWDEN   M J PROCTOR
14. HULL   J C COWAN
15. SCARBOROUGH   M J LEIGH

ARCHDEACONRY OF CLEVELAND
(BISHOP OF WHITBY)

16. GUISBOROUGH   D TEMBEY
17. MIDDLESBROUGH   D P BLACK
18. MOWBRAY   F R MAYER-JONES
19. NORTHERN RYEDALE   T J ROBINSON
20. STOKESLEY   W J FORD
21. WHITBY   M G T GOBBETT

CHURCH IN WALES

ST ASAPH

ARCHDEACONRY OF ST ASAPH

1. ST ASAPH   *vacant*
2. DENBIGH   *vacant*
3. DYFFRYN CLWYD   *vacant*
4. HOLYWELL   *vacant*
5. LLANRWST AND RHOS   N W CARTER

ARCHDEACONRY OF MONTGOMERY

6. CEDEWAIN   N W MORRIS
7. MATHRAFAL   *vacant*
8. PENEDEYRN   *vacant*
9. POOL   S G WILLSON
10. VALLE CRUCIS   M K SNELLGROVE

ARCHDEACONRY OF WREXHAM

11. ALYN   P R-M DE G GOWER
12. DEE VALLEY   S M HUYTON
13. HAWARDEN   M J BATCHELOR
14. MOLD   *vacant*
15. WREXHAM   *vacant*

BANGOR

ARCHDEACONRY OF ANGLESEY

1. SYNOD YNYS MON   E C WILLIAMS

ARCHDEACONRY OF BANGOR

2. SYNOD BANGOR   J L JONES

ARCHDEACONRY OF MEIRIONNYDD

3. SYNOD MEIRIONYDD   D J WILLIAMS

ST DAVIDS

ARCHDEACONRY OF ST DAVIDS

1. DAUGLEDDAU   *vacant*
2. DEWISLAND AND FISHGUARD   C C BROWN
3. PEMBROKE   K G TAYLOR
4. ROOSE   A M CHADWICK

ARCHDEACONRY OF CARDIGAN

5. CEMAIS AND SUB-AERON   J S BENNETT
6. EMLYN   D J L ROBERTS
7. GLYN AERON   C L BOLTON
8. LAMPETER AND ULTRA-AERON   P W DAVIES
9. LLANBADARN FAWR   *vacant*

ARCHDEACONRY OF CARMARTHEN

10. CARMARTHEN   *vacant*
11. CYDWELI   *vacant*
12. DYFFRYN AMAN   *vacant*
13. LLANDEILO   S E JONES
14. LLANDOVERY   *vacant*
15. ST CLEARS   *vacant*
16. BRO LLIEDI   D H E MOSFORD

LLANDAFF

ARCHDEACONRY OF LLANDAFF

1. CARDIFF   S LISK
2. LLANDAFF   S M JOHN
3. PENARTH AND BARRY   A P JAMES

ARCHDEACONRY OF MARGAM

4. BRIDGEND   I M HODGES
5. MARGAM   E JENKYNS
6. NEATH   C W COLES
7. VALE OF GLAMORGAN   M J DAVIES

ARCHDEACONRY OF MORGANNWG

8. CYNON VALLEY   M K JONES
9. MERTHYR TYDFIL AND CAERPHILLY   S P KIRK
10. PONTYPRIDD   M D GABLE
11. RHONDDA   R E MOVERLEY

MONMOUTH

ARCHDEACONRY OF MONMOUTH

1. ABERGAVENNY   M SOADY
2. MONMOUTH   *vacant*
3. NETHERWENT   J D HARRIS
4. RAGLAN-USK   T G CLEMENT

ARCHDEACONRY OF NEWPORT

5. BASSALEG   J R CONNELL
6. NEWPORT   J S J GROVES

ARCHDEACONRY OF THE GWENT VALLEYS

7. BEDWELLTY   M OWEN
8. PONTYPOOL   P A GOLLEDGE

SWANSEA AND BRECON

ARCHDEACONRY OF BRECON

1. GREATER BRECON   S E GRIFFITH
2. RADNOR AND BUILTH   M T BEATON

ARCHDEACONRY OF GOWER

3. AFON TAWE (SWANSEA)   H M LERVY
4. GREATER GOWER   P BROOKS

ENGLISH BENEFICES AND CHURCHES

An index of benefices, conventional districts, local ecumenical projects, and proprietary chapels (shown in bold type), together with entries for churches and other licensed places of worship listed on the Parish Index of the Central Board of Finance. Where the church name is the same as that of the benefice (or as that of the place whose name forms the beginning of the benefice name), the church entry is omitted. Church dedications are indicated in brackets.

The benefice entry gives the full legal name, followed by the diocese, its deanery number (p. 909), the patron(s), and the name(s) and appointment(s) of clergy serving there. The following are the main abbreviations used; for others see the full list of abbreviations.

C	Curate	OLM	Ordained Local Minister
C-in-c	Curate-in-charge	P	Patron(s)
Dn-in-c	Deacon-in-charge	P-in-c	Priest-in-charge
Dss	Deaconess	Par Dn	Parish Deacon
Hon C	Honorary Curate	R	Rector
Hon Par Dn	Honorary Parish Deacon	TM	Team Minister
I	Incumbent (includes Rector or Vicar)	TR	Team Rector
Min	Minister	TV	Team Vicar
NSM	Non-stipendiary Minister	V	Vicar

Listed below are the elements in place names which are not normally treated as substantive in the index:

CENTRAL	HIGHER	MUCH	OVER
EAST	LITTLE	NETHER	SOUTH
GREAT	LOW	NEW	THE
GREATER	LOWER	NORTH	UPPER
HIGH	MIDDLE	OLD	WEST

Thus WEST WIMBLEDON (Christ Church) appears as **WIMBLEDON, WEST (Christ Church)** and CENTRAL TELFORD as **TELFORD, CENTRAL**. The only exception occurs where the second element of the place name is a common noun, thus NEW LANE remains as **NEW LANE**, and WEST TOWN as **WEST TOWN**.

4SAINTS TEAM (Huyton Deanery), comprising Huyton, Knowsley, Stockbridge Village, and West Derby *Liv 7* **P** *Patr Bd* **TV** J VAN DEN BERG-OWENS, N H LEA-WILSON **NSM** R E PRYCE

A453 churches of South Nottinghamshire, The, comprising Barton-in-Fabis, Gotham, Kingston-on-Soar, Ratcliffe-on-Soar, and Thrumpton *S'well 6* **P** *D&C, Bp and Ms M Seymour (1 turn), Ld Chan (1 turn)* **R** R I COLEMAN

AB KETTLEBY (St James) and Holwell w Asfordby *Leic 2* **P** *DBP, MMCET and V Rothley (jt)* **P-in-c** P G HOOPER **NSM** P R TOWNS

ABBAS AND TEMPLECOMBE (Blessed Virgin Mary), Henstridge and Horsington *B & W 2* **P** *Bp and Ch Trust Fund Trust* **R** K ROGERS

ABBERLEY (St Mary) *see* Shrawley, Witley, Astley and Abberley *Worc*

ABBERLEY (St Michael) *as above*

ABBERTON (St Andrew) *see* Fingringhoe w E Donyland and Abberton etc *Chelmsf*

ABBERTON (St Edburga), The Flyfords, Naunton Beauchamp and Bishampton w Throckmorton *Worc 4* **P** *Bp and Croome Estate Trustees (1 turn), and Ld Chan (1 turn)* **P-in-c** G R NOYES **C** E L GOLDBY, S A DANGERFIELD

ABBESS RODING (St Edmund King and Martyr) *see* S Rodings *Chelmsf*

ABBEY CHAPEL (St Mary) *see* Annesley w Newstead and Kirkby Woodhouse *S'well*

ABBEY Group of Parishes, The, comprising East Halton, Habrough, Killingholme, Thornton Curtis, Ulceby, and Wootton *Linc 4* **P** *Ld Chan (1 turn), Bp and DBP (1 turn), Bp, DBP, Earl of Yarborough, J E Spilman Esq, and Trustees (1 turn)* **V** *vacant*

ABBEY HULTON (St John) *see* Bucknall *Lich*

ABBEY WOOD (St Michael and All Angels) *S'wark 6* **P** *Bp* **V** D A SHERRATT

ABBEY WOOD (William Temple) *see* Thamesmead *S'wark*

ABBEYDALE *see* Sheff St Pet and St Oswald *Sheff*

ABBEYDALE (St John the Evangelist) and Millhouses *Sheff 2* **P** *Bp and Trustees (jt)* **V** P A INGRAM **NSM** A M LAUENER, S G STURGEON

ABBEYDORE (St Mary) *see* Ewyas Harold w Dulas, Kenderchurch etc *Heref*

ABBEYLANDS Team Ministry, comprising Hawksworth Wood w Moor Grange, Horsforth, and Kirkstall *Leeds 15* **P** *Patr Bd* **TR** N C SINCLAIR **TV** S M KAYE **C** R J FORD

ABBEYSTEAD (Christ Church) *see* Dolphinholme w Quernmore and Over Wyresdale *Blackb*

ABBOTS BICKINGTON (St James) *see* Bradworthy, Sutcombe etc *Ex*

ABBOTS BROMLEY (St Nicholas), Blithfield, Colton, Colwich and Great Haywood *Lich 3* **P** *Bp and D&C (jt)* **R** S C DAVIS **C** S C DEALL **NSM** A V NOBLE, L J FARRINGTON, M A DAVYS **OLM** P A MERRIOTT

ABBOTS LANGLEY (St Lawrence) *St Alb 6* **P** *Bp* **P-in-c** P M WADDELL **C** V J KERSWILL

ABBOTS LEIGH (Holy Trinity) w Leigh Woods *Bris 2* **P** *Bp* **V** S H E JONES

ABBOTS MORTON (St Peter) *see* Church Lench w Rous Lench and Abbots Morton etc *Worc*

ABBOTS RIPTON (St Andrew) *see* N Leightonstone *Ely*

ABBOTSBURY (St Mary) *see* Newton Abbot *Ex*

ABBOTSBURY (St Nicholas), Portesham and Langton Herring *Sarum 4* **P** *The Hon C A Townshend and Bp (alt)* **P-in-c** J C BRADING **NSM** M PREUSS-HIGHAM

ABBOTSHAM (St Helen) *Ex 15* **P** *PCC* **C** R M ELKS

ABBOTSKERSWELL (The Blessed Virgin Mary) *see* Kingskerswell, Abbotskerswell and Coffinswell *Ex*

ABBOTSLEY (St Margaret) *see* Gt Gransden and Abbotsley and Lt Gransden etc *Ely*

ABBOTSWOOD (St Nicholas Family Centre) *see* Yate *Bris*

ABBOTTS ANN (St Mary) and Upper Clatford and Goodworth Clatford *Win 3* **P** *Exors T P de Paravicini Esq and Bp (jt)* **P-in-c** K M DYKES **NSM** N J JUDD

ABDON (St Margaret) *see* Corvedale Benefice *Heref*

ABENHALL (St Michael) w Mitcheldean *Glouc 3* **P** *DBP* **R** D A GILL

ABERFORD (St Ricarius) w Micklefield *York 4* **P** *Abp and Oriel Coll Ox (jt)* **P-in-c** C WILTON

ABINGDON, NORTH (Christ Church) *Ox 19* **P** *Bp* **V** K O DUNNETT **C** K M COOKE, V J WATTS **NSM** P G COOKE

ABINGDON-ON-THAMES (St Helen) and St Michael and All Angels) (St Nicolas) *Ox 19* **P** *Patr Bd* **TR** E C MILLER **TV** P A SMITH **NSM** J E BROWN

ABINGER (St James) and Coldharbour and Wotton and Holmbury St Mary *Guildf 7* **P** *Bp, Ch Patr Trust, and J P M H Evelyn Esq (jt)* **R** A N BERRY

ABINGTON (St Peter and St Paul) *Pet 4* **P** *Bp* **R** B J KIM

ABINGTON PIGOTTS (St Michael and All Angels) *see* Shingay Gp *Ely*

ABINGTON, GREAT (St Mary the Virgin) *see* Granta Vale Gp *Ely*

ABINGTON, LITTLE (St Mary) *as above*

ABRAM (St John) *see* Chapelfields *Liv*

ABRIDGE (Holy Trinity) *see* Vale of Roding *Chelmsf*

ABSON (St James the Great) *see* Pucklechurch and Abson *Bris*

ABTHORPE (St John the Baptist) *see* Silverstone and Abthorpe w Slapton etc *Pet*

ACASTER MALBIS (Holy Trinity) *York 1* **P** *R A G Raimes Esq* **V** C I COATES **NSM** P J MACNAUGHTON

ACASTER SELBY (St John) *see* Appleton Roebuck w Acaster Selby *York*

ACCRINGTON (Christ Church) *Blackb 1* **P** *Bp and V S Shore H Trin (jt)* **P-in-c** I P ENTICOTT **C** P MCNALLY

ACCRINGTON (St Andrew) (St Mary Magdalene) (St Peter) and Church Kirk *Blackb 1* **P** *Bp and DBP (jt)* **R** *vacant*

ACCRINGTON (St James) (St Paul) *Blackb 1* **P** *Bp and DBP (jt)* **V** I P ENTICOTT

ACCRINGTON (St John) w Huncoat St Augustine *Blackb 1* **P** *Bp and V Accrington St Jas w St Paul (jt)* **P-in-c** H A SCRIVEN

ACKLAM (St John the Baptist) *see* W Buckrose *York*

ACKLAM, WEST (St Mary) *York 17* **P** *Trustees* **V** N R RAO

ACKLETON (Mission Room) *see* Worfield *Heref*

ACKLINGTON (St John the Divine) *see* Warkworth and Acklington *Newc*

ACKWORTH (All Saints) (St Cuthbert) *Leeds 18* **P** *Duchy of Lanc* **P-in-c** C SMITH **NSM** P A FOX

ACLE (St Edmund) and Bure to Yare *Nor 4* **P** *Bp, Ch Soc Trust, Personal Reps K M Mills Esq, and DBP (jt)* **R** M GREENLAND

ACOCKS GREEN (St Mary) *Birm 11* **P** *Trustees* **V** A T BULLOCK

ACOL (St Mildred) *see* Birchington w Acol and Minnis Bay *Cant*

ACOMB (Holy Redeemer) *York 7* **P** *The Crown* **V** M A HAND

ACOMB (St Stephen and St Aidan) *York 7* **P** *Trustees* **V** P H VIVASH

ACOMB MOOR (James the Deacon) *York 7* **P** *Abp* **V** L D TILLETT

ACRISE (St Martin) *see* Elham w Denton and Wootton and Acrise *Cant*

ACTON (All Saints) w Great Waldingfield *St E 9* **P** *Bp* **P-in-c** C M HALLETT **NSM** F E M MARSDEN

ACTON (St Gabriel) *see* N Acton St Gabr *Lon*

ACTON (St Martin) *see* W Acton St Martin *Lon*

ACTON (St Mary) *Lon 22* **P** *Bp* **R** N G JONES **C** D M AYRES **NSM** M J SPREDBURY

ACTON (St Mary) and Worleston, Church Minshull and Wettenhall *Ches 15* **P** *Bp, V Over St Chad, and R C Roundell Esq (jt)* **V** S A LAWSON

ACTON BEAUCHAMP (St Giles) *see* Frome Valley *Heref*

ACTON BURNELL (St Mary) *see* Condover w Frodesley, Acton Burnell etc *Heref*

ACTON GREEN (St Peter) *Lon 22* **P** *Bp* **V** K J MORRIS

ACTON ROUND (St Mary) *see* Bridgnorth and Morville Par *Heref*

ACTON SCOTT (St Margaret) *Heref 10* **P** *DBP* **NSM** M G WILLIAMS

ACTON TRUSSELL (St James) *see* Penkridge *Lich*

ACTON TURVILLE (St Mary) *see* Boxwell, Leighterton, Didmarton, Oldbury etc *Glouc*

ACTON, EAST (St Dunstan w St Thomas) *Lon 22* **P** *Bp* **V** J M WESTALL

ACTON, EAST (St Dunstan w St Thomas) *see* E Acton St Dunstan w St Thos *Lon*

ACTON, NORTH (St Gabriel) *Lon 22* **P** *Bp* **V** T J N L'ESTRANGE

ACTON, SOUTH (All Saints) *see* Acton St Mary *Lon*

ACTON, WEST (St Martin) *Lon 22* **P** *Bp* **V** J E PALMER **NSM** B D FRANKLIN, B E F PEARSON

ADBASTON (St Michael and All Angels), High Offley, Knightley, Norbury, Woodseaves, Gnosall and Moreton *Lich 7* **P** *Bp* **R** K M HAMMOND

ADDERBURY (St Mary) w Milton *Ox 23* **P** *New Coll Ox* **V** E A SIMPSON

ADDERLEY (St Peter), Ash, Calverhall, Ightfield and Moreton Say *Lich 17* **P** *C C Corbet Esq, Sir Algernon Heber-Percy KCVO, T C Heywood-Lonsdale Esq, and R Whitchurch (jt)* **R** R A CLARKSON

ADDINGHAM (St Michael) *see* Cross Fell Gp *Carl*

ADDINGHAM (St Peter) *Leeds 4* **P** *J R Thompson-Ashby Esq* **R** J PERRETT **Hon C** P A SUMMERS

ADDINGTON (St Margaret) *see* Birling, Addington, Ryarsh and Trottiscliffe *Roch*

ADDINGTON (St Mary) *S'wark 19* **P** *Abp* **V** D J FORMAN **C** J M NJUE **NSM** B C GENTILELLA

ADDINGTON (St Mary) *see* Winslow w Gt Horwood and Addington *Ox*

ADDINGTON, GREAT (All Saints) *see* Irthlingborough, Gt Addington, Lt Addington etc *Pet*

ADDINGTON, LITTLE (St Mary the Virgin) *as above*

ADDINGTON, NEW (St Edward) *S'wark 19* **P** *Bp* **P-in-c** P C DHANARAJ

ADDISCOMBE (St Mary Magdalene) *S'wark 20* **P** *Trustees* **V** A S JOHNSON

ADDISCOMBE (St Mildred) *S'wark 20* **P** *Bp* **V** R C HAGON

ADDLESTONE (St Augustine) (St Paul) *Guildf 11* **P** *Bp* **V** B H BEECROFT **C** C M BEECROFT

ADDLETHORPE (St Nicholas) *see* Skegness Gp *Linc*

ADEL (St John the Baptist) *Leeds 15* **P** *Brig R G Lewthwaite, D R Lewthwaite Esq, and J V Lewthwaite Esq (jt)* **R** A J BATTYE

ADEYFIELD (St Barnabas) *see* Hemel Hempstead *St Alb*

ADFORTON (St Andrew) *see* Wigmore Abbey *Heref*

ADISHAM (Holy Innocents) *see* Barham Downs w Adisham *Cant*

ADLESTROP (St Mary Magdalene) *see* Broadwell, Evenlode, Oddington, Adlestrop etc *Glouc*

ADLINGFLEET (All Saints) *see* The Marshland *Sheff*

ADLINGTON (St John's Mission Church) *see* Prestbury *Ches*

ADLINGTON (St Paul) *Blackb 4* **P** *Bp* **V** D A ARNOLD **C** E W C CARR

ADSTOCK (St Cecilia) *see* Lenborough *Ox*

ADSTONE (All Saints) *see* Lambfold *Pet*

ADSWOOD (St Gabriel's Mission Church) *see* Stockport St Geo *Ches*

ADVENT (St Adwena) *see* Camel-Allen *Truro*

ADWELL (St Mary) *see* Thame *Ox*

ADWICK-LE-STREET (St Laurence) w Skelbrooke *Sheff 7* **P** *Mrs P N Fullerton and Bp (alt)* **R** A B WALTON **NSM** J M GARDNER

ADWICK-UPON-DEARNE (St John the Baptist) *see* Barnburgh w Melton on the Hill etc *Sheff*

AFFPUDDLE (St Laurence) *see* W Purbeck *Sarum*

AIGBURTH (St Anne) *Liv 2* **P** *Trustees* **V** I R GREENWOOD **C** M W DAVIS

AIKTON (St Andrew) *see* Barony of Burgh *Carl*

AINDERBY STEEPLE (St Helen) *see* Lower Swale *Leeds*

AINSDALE (St John) *Liv 9* **P** *R Walton, Bp, and Adn (jt)* **V** *vacant*

AINSTABLE (St Michael and All Angels) *see* Inglewood Gp *Carl*

AINSTY, NORTH *see* Marston Moor *York*

AINSTY, RURAL, comprising Bilton, Healaugh, Moor Monkton, and Wighill *York 1* **P** *Abp (3 turns), D&C (1 turn)* **C** L J BRENCHER, R D BATTERSBY

AINSWORTH (Christ Church) *Man 10* **P** *Bp* **P-in-c** D F THOMSON **OLM** D J JOHNSTONE, E V LARKIN

AINTREE (St Giles) w St Peter *Liv 8* **P** *Bp* **V** *vacant*

AIREDALE (Holy Cross) w Fryston *Leeds 18* **P** *Bp* **V** T A IBBOTSON **NSM** A L BROWNRIDGE

AIRMYN (St David), Hook and Rawcliffe *Sheff 10* **P** *Bp and Ch Soc Trust (jt)* **V** P J BALL

AISHOLT (All Saints), Enmore, Goathurst, Nether Stowey, Over Stowey and Spaxton w Charlynch *B & W 17* **P** *Bp, D&C Windsor, MMCET, and Ch Trust Fund Trust (jt)* **R** E O KING

AISLABY (St Margaret) *see* Lower Esk *York*

AISTHORPE (St Peter) *see* Spring Line Gp *Linc*

AKELEY (St James) *see* N Buckingham *Ox*

AKEMAN, comprising Bletchingdon, Chesterton, Hampton Gay, Kirtlington, Middleton Stoney, Wendlebury, Weston-on-the-Green *Ox 21* **P** *New Coll and Ch Ch (1 turn), Qu Coll, St Jo Coll, and Period and Country Houses Ltd (1 turn)* **R** J G MILLER

ALBERBURY (St Michael and All Angels) *see* Ford, Gt Wollaston and Alberbury w Cardeston *Heref*

ALBOURNE (St Bartholomew) w Sayers Common and Twineham *Chich 8* **P** *Bp (2 turns), Ex Coll Ox (1 turn)* **R** *vacant*

ALBRIGHTON (St John the Baptist) *see* Leaton and Albrighton w Battlefield *Lich*

ALBRIGHTON (St Mary Magdalene), Boningale and Donington *Lich 15* **P** *Haberdashers' Co and MMCET (jt)* **V** M R THOMAS **C** A J LAWRENCE

ALBURGH (All Saints) *see* Ditchingham, Hedenham, Broome, Earsham etc *Nor*

ALBURY (St Helen) w Tiddington, Holton, Waterperry, Waterstock and Wheatley *Ox 20* **P** *Bp and DBP (jt)* **V** N A R HAWKES **C** D C BENDOR-SAMUEL

ALBURY (St Mary), Little Hadham and Much Hadham *St Alb 15* **P** *Bp Lon* **R** S D BATE

ALBURY (St Peter and St Paul) *see* Shere, Albury and Chilworth *Guildf*

ALBY (St Ethelbert) *see* Erpingham w Calthorpe, Ingworth, Aldborough etc *Nor*
ALCESTER MINSTER (St Nicholas) *Cov 7*   **P** *Bp and Marquess of Hertford (jt)*   **R** A M GUTHRIE   **NSM** S M HENWOOD
ALCISTON (not known) *see* Arlington, Berwick, Selmeston w Alciston etc *Chich*
ALCOMBE (St Michael the Archangel) *B & W 15*   **P** *Bp*
   V K J CROSS
ALCONBURY (St Peter and St Paul) *see* N Leightonstone *Ely*
ALDBOROUGH (St Andrew) w Boroughbridge and Roecliffe *Leeds 23*   **P** *D&C York and Bp (alt)*
   V K J GARDINER
ALDBOROUGH (St Mary) *see* Erpingham w Calthorpe, Ingworth, Aldborough etc *Nor*
ALDBOROUGH HATCH (St Peter) *Chelmsf 6*   **P** *The Crown*
   P-in-c K P B LOVESEY
ALDBOURNE (St Michael) *see* Whitton *Sarum*
ALDBROUGH (St Bartholomew) and Mappleton w Goxhill and Withernwick *York 11*   **P** *Ld Chan, Abp, and Adn E Riding (by turn)*   **P-in-c** A M WHITE
   NSM M M DESBOROUGH
ALDBROUGH (St Paul) *see* Forcett and Aldbrough and Melsonby *Leeds*
ALDBURY (St John the Baptist) *see* Tring *St Alb*
ALDE RIVER Benefice, The, comprising Benhall, Blaxhall, Farnham St Mary w Stafford St Andrew, Great Glemham, Little Glemham, Snape, and Sternfield *St E 16*   **P** *Earl of Guilford, Major P W Hope-Cobbold, DBP, CPAS, Miss S F R Heycock-Hollond, and Exors Mrs A C V Wentworth (jt)*
   R R CORNISH
ALDE SANDLINGS, comprising Aldeburgh w Hazelwood, Aldringham w Thorpe, Friston, and Knodishall w Buxlow *St E 16*   **P** *Mrs A C V Wentworth, Ch Patr Trust, and Ch Soc Trust (jt)*   **R** P M LOWTHER   **C** J D MARSTON
   NSM J S MABEY, N J WINTER, S E HART
ALDE, UPPER, comprising Badingham, Bruisyard, Cransford, Dennington, Rendham, and Sweffling *St E 14*   **P** R C Rous *Esq, DBP, and CPAS (jt)*   **P-in-c** M E PERCIVAL
ALDEBURGH (St Peter and St Paul) *see* Alde Sandlings *St E*
ALDEBY (St Mary) *see* Raveningham Gp *Nor*
ALDENHAM (St John the Baptist), Radlett and Shenley *St Alb 5*   **P** *Patr Bd*   **TR** J IQBAL   **TV** D M MCCARTHY,
   R A FLETCHER
ALDERBROOK (St Richard) *see* Crowborough *Chich*
ALDERBURY (St Mary the Virgin) *see* Clarendon *Sarum*
ALDERCAR (St John) *see* Langley Mill and Aldercar *Derby*
ALDERFORD (St John the Baptist) *see* Reepham and Wensum Valley *Nor*
ALDERHOLT (St James) *Sarum 9*   **P** *DBP*   **V** S A WOODLEY
ALDERLEY (St Kenelm) *see* Tyndale *Glouc*
ALDERLEY (St Mary) w Birtles *Ches 12*   **P** *Trustees and Bp (alt)*   **R** A J HALE
ALDERLEY EDGE (St Philip) *Ches 12*   **P** *Trustees*   **V** R PYE
   NSM L C A ALEXANDER
ALDERMASTON (St Mary the Virgin) and Woolhampton *Ox 4*   **P** *Bp, Keble Coll Ox, CPAS, Lady Dugdale, Worc Coll Ox, and DBP (jt)*   **R** J E MANLEY
ALDERMINSTER (St Mary and Holy Cross) *see* Stourdene Gp *Cov*
ALDERNEY (St Anne) *Win 14*   **P** *The Crown*   **V** J K B FOWLER
   C A L FOWLER
ALDERSBROOK (St Gabriel) *Chelmsf 6*   **P** *DBP*
   V M J HAWKES   **NSM** C J SMALING, M A KENNY, P E WALLSON
ALDERSHOT (Holy Trinity) *Guildf 1*   **P** *CPAS*
   V G P H NEWTON   **C** D WIGNALL, J MAW
   NSM C J B KELLAGHER
ALDERSHOT (St Augustine) *Guildf 1*   **P** *Bp*   **V** K M HODGES
ALDERSHOT (St Michael the Archangel) (Ascension) *Guildf 1*   **P** *Bp*   **V** A A B PEREIRA
ALDERSLEY (Christ the King) *see* Tettenhall Regis *Lich*
ALDERTON (St Andrew) *see* Wilford Peninsula *St E*
ALDERTON (St Giles) *see* Gauzebrook *Bris*
ALDERTON (St Margaret of Antioch) *see* Winchcombe *Glouc*
ALDERTON (St Margaret) *see* Blisworth, Alderton, Grafton Regis etc *Pet*
ALDERWASLEY (All Saints) *see* Wirksworth *Derby*
ALDFIELD (St Lawrence) *see* Fountains Gp *Leeds*
ALDFORD (St John the Baptist) *see* Waverton w Aldford and Bruera *Ches*
ALDHAM (St Margaret and St Catherine) *see* Marks Tey and Aldham *Chelmsf*
ALDHAM (St Mary) *see* Elmsett w Aldham, Hintlesham, Chattisham etc *St E*
ALDINGBOURNE (St Mary the Virgin), Barnham and Eastergate *Chich 1*   **P** *Bp and D&C (jt)*   **NSM** A R BRANT,
   G REEVES, S M HIGGINS

ALDINGHAM (St Cuthbert) and Dendron and Rampside and Urswick *Carl 9*   **P** *The Crown (1 turn), V Dalton-in-Furness and Resident Landowners of Urswick (1 turn)*
   P-in-c L A LUNN
ALDINGTON (St Martin) *see* Saxon Shoreline *Cant*
ALDRIDGE (St Mary the Virgin) (St Thomas) *Lich 24*
   P *MMCET*   **R** P S DOEL   **C** J A MIDDLETON
   OLM J E BAKEWELL, S E QUIBELL
ALDRINGHAM (St Andrew) *see* Alde Sandlings *St E*
ALDRINGTON (St Leonard) *Chich 20*   **P** *Bp*   **V** vacant
ALDSWORTH (St Bartholomew) *see* Sherborne, Windrush, the Barringtons etc *Glouc*
ALDWARK (St Stephen) *see* Alne *York*
ALDWICK (St Richard) *Chich 1*   **P** *Bp*   **V** vacant
ALDWINCLE (St Peter), Clopton, Pilton, Stoke Doyle, Thorpe Achurch, Titchmarsh and Wadenhoe *Pet 10*
   P *G C Capron Esq, Wadenhoe Trust, Soc Merchant Venturers Bris, and DBP (jt)*   **R** B J WITHINGTON   **NSM** E A WALLER,
   H B BRANDON
ALDWORTH (St Mary the Virgin) *see* Basildon w Aldworth and Ashampstead *Ox*
ALEXANDRA PARK (St Andrew) *Lon 20*   **P** *Bp*   **V** A F PYBUS
ALFINGTON (St James and St Anne) *see* Ottery St Mary, Alfington, W Hill, Tipton etc *Ex*
ALFOLD (St Nicholas) and Loxwood *Guildf 2*   **P** *Bp and CPAS (jt)*   **P-in-c** G D CUSHING
ALFORD (All Saints) *see* Six Pilgrims *B & W*
ALFORD Group, The (St Wilfrid), including Beesby w Maltby, Bilsby, Farlesthorpe, Hannah cum Hagnaby w Markby, Saleby, Ulceby w Fordington, Well, and Willoughby w Sloothby w Claxby *Linc 10*   **P** *Bp, Ball Coll Ox, Baroness Willoughby de Eresby, Mrs A M Johnson, and DBP (jt)*
   R R M LATHAM   **C** S V ANGUS   **NSM** J M MORTON
ALFRED JEWEL, comprising Durston, North Newton, North Petherton, Northmoor Green, and Thurloxton *B & W 13*
   P *D&C Windsor (4 turns), Bp (2 turns), Sir Benjamin Slade Bt (1 turn)*   **R** J HASLAM   **C** S J TANCOCK   **NSM** J W SUTTON,
   M H HASLAM
ALFRETON (St Martin) *Derby 2*   **P** *Bp*   **P-in-c** M J TAYLOR
   C I N L BLACK   **NSM** J O K PENFOLD
ALFRICK (St Mary Magdalene) *see* Worcs W Rural *Worc*
ALFRISTON (St Andrew) w Lullington, Litlington, West Dean and Folkington *Chich 21*   **P** *Ld Chan (3 turns), Duke of Devonshire, R A Brown Esq, and Mrs S J Harcourt-Smith (1 turn each)*   **R** S STUCKES
ALGARKIRK (St Peter and St Paul) *see* Kirton in Holland w Algarkirk and Fosdyke *Linc*
ALHAM VALE, comprising Batcombe, Evercreech w Chesterblade, Lamyatt, Milton Clevedon, and Upton Noble *B & W 2*   **P** *DBP*   **Hon C** M D ELLIS
ALHAMPTON (Mission Church) *see* Fosse Trinity *B & W*
ALKBOROUGH (St John the Baptist) *Linc 6*   **P** *Bp*
   V A F PLEDGER
ALKERTON (St Michael and All Angels) *see* Ironstone *Ox*
ALKHAM (St Anthony) w Capel le Ferne and Hougham *Cant 7*   **P** *Abp*   **C** B F WILLIAMS
ALKMONTON (St John) *see* S Dales *Derby*
ALL CANNINGS (All Saints) *see* Cannings and Redhorn *Sarum*
ALL SOULS, NORTH WARWICKSHIRE, comprising Austrey, Newton Regis, Seckington, Shuttington, and Warton *Birm 9*
   P *Ld Chan (1 turn), V Polesworth, Birm Dioc Trustees and Mrs E V G Inge-Innes Lillington (1 turn)*   **R** vacant
ALL STRETTON (St Michael and All Angels) *see* Church Stretton *Heref*
ALLENDALE (St Cuthbert) w Whitfield *Newc 10*   **P** *Viscount Allendale and J C Blackett-Ord Esq (alt)*   **R** J W RUSSELL
ALLENS CROSS (St Bartholomew) *Birm 3*   **P** *Bp*
   P-in-c A DE C LADD   **C** N M LADD
ALLENSMORE (St Andrew) *see* Cagebrook *Heref*
ALLENTON (St Edmund) *see* Pride Park, Wilmorton, Allenton and Shelton Lock *Derby*
ALLER (St Andrew), High Ham w Low Ham and Huish Episcopi cum Langport *B & W 5*   **P** *Adn Wells and Worc Coll Ox (jt)*   **R** J PITMAN   **C** J L BELL-WINFROW
ALLERSTON (St John) *see* Thornton Dale w Allerston, Ebberston etc *York*
ALLERTHORPE (St Botolph) *see* Barmby Moor Gp *York*
ALLERTON (All Hallows) *see* Mossley Hill *Liv*
ALLERTON (not known) *see* Isle of Wedmore *B & W*
ALLERTON (St Peter) (St Francis of Assisi) *Leeds 3*   **P** *Bp*
   V G O WILLIAMS
ALLERTON BYWATER (St Mary the Less), Kippax and Swillington *Leeds 16*   **P** *Bp*   **TR** R E HAYES   **TV** D M FLYNN
ALLESLEY (All Saints) *Cov 2*   **P** *D R D Hamilton Esq*
   R M A BAKER

ALLESLEY PARK (St Christopher) and Whoberley *Cov 3*
P *Bp* V A MARCH C J C LANGLANDS
ALLESTREE (St Edmund King and Martyr) and Darley
Abbey St Matthew *Derby 5* P *Bp and DBP (jt)*
V P BARHAM
ALLESTREE (St Nicholas) *Derby 5* P *Bp* V R C MATHEW
C D M KNIGHT
ALLHALLOWS (All Saints) *see Binsey Carl*
ALLINGTON (St Nicholas) and Maidstone St Peter *Cant 12*
P *Abp* **P-in-c** C P LAVENDER C B J F KNOTT
ALLINGTON (St Swithin) *see Bridport Sarum*
ALLINGTON, EAST (St Andrew) *see Stoke Fleming,*
Blackawton, Strete and E Allington Ex
ALLINGTON, WEST (Holy Trinity) *see Saxonwell Linc*
ALLITHWAITE (St Mary) *see Cartmel Peninsula Carl*
ALLONBY (Christ Church), Cross Canonby and Dearham
Carl 7 P *TR Solway Plain, D&C, and Bp (jt)* V M E DAY
ALMELEY (St Mary) *see Eardisley w Bollingham, Willersley,*
Brilley etc Heref
ALMER (St Mary) *see Red Post Sarum*
ALMONDBURY (St Michael and St Helen) (St Mary) (All
Hallows) w Farnley Tyas *Leeds 5* P *DBP*
TR M T P ZAMMIT **C** A D STEER **NSM** J L MALAY, M FOSSEY
ALMONDSBURY (St Mary the Virgin) and Olveston *Bris 2*
P *Bp and D&C (jt)* V P W ROWE C D S MOSS
OLM A LLOYD, D H BONE, P A VAN ROSSUM
ALNE (St Mary) *York 3* P *CPAS and MMCET (alt)*
P-in-c D M COYNE C E C HASSALL, M E YOUNG,
M H WAINWRIGHT, M HARRISON, S WHITING
NSM C C CRANFIELD, C C GITTENS, C J TOASE, S P POPE,
T M GANT
ALNE, GREAT (St Mary Magdalene) *see Alcester Minster Cov*
ALNHAM (St Michael and All Angels) *see Upper Coquetdale*
Newc
ALNMOUTH (St John the Baptist) *see Lesbury w Alnmouth*
Newc
ALNWICK (St Michael and St Paul) *Newc 6* P *Duke of*
Northumberland V P M SCOTT C G K B RUNDELL
ALPERTON (St James) *Lon 21* P *CPAS* V A I TAYLOR
C A S JACOB, S G TAYLOR
ALPHAMSTONE (not known) *see N Hinckford Chelmsf*
ALPHETON (St Peter and St Paul) *see Chadbrook St E*
ALPHINGTON (St Michael and All Angels), Shillingford
St George and Ide *Ex 3* P *DBP, D&C, and Mrs J M*
Michelmore (jt) R M J PARTRIDGE C H G SHERLOCK
ALRESFORD (St Andrew) *see Tenpenny Villages Chelmsf*
ALRESFORD, NEW (St John the Baptist) *see Arle Valley Win*
ALRESFORD, OLD (St Mary) *as above*
ALREWAS (All Saints) *Lich 1* P *Bp* V J W ALLAN
NSM E A WALL
ALSAGER (Christ Church) *Ches 11* P *Bp* V D WARD
NSM H S KEMBALL
ALSAGER (St Mary Magdalene) (St Patrick's Mission
Church) *Ches 11* P *Bp* **P-in-c** M S GOODRICH
ALSAGERS BANK (St John), Audley and Talke *Lich 9* P *Patr*
Bd R S C R TOMKINS
ALSOP-EN-LE-DALE (St Michael and All Angels) *see Fenny*
Bentley, Thorpe, Tissington, Parwich etc Derby
ALSTON MOOR (St Augustine), including Garrigill,
Kirkhaugh, Knaresdale, Lambley, and Nenthead *Newc 10*
P *Bp* R M C V NASH-WILLIAMS
ALSTONE (St Margaret) *see Overbury w Teddington, Alstone*
etc Worc
ALSTONFIELD (St Peter), Ilam and Wetton *Lich 5* P *DBP,*
Bp, and Sir Andrew Walker-Okeover Bt (jt) **Hon C** L R PRICE
ALTARNON (St Nonna) *see Moorland Gp Truro*
ALTCAR (St Michael and All Angels) *see Formby H Trin and*
Altcar Liv
ALTHAM (St James) w Clayton le Moors *Blackb 1* P *DBP*
and Trustees (alt) V T R WEBBER
ALTHORNE (St Andrew) and North Fambridge *Chelmsf 11*
P *Ld Chan* V S E MANLEY
ALTHORPE (St Oswald) *see Belton Gp Linc*
ALTOFTS (St Mary Magdalene) *Leeds 19* P *SMF*
V D C TEASDEL
ALTON (St Peter) w Bradley-le-Moors and Denstone w
Ellastone and Stanton and Mayfield *Lich 14* P *Earl of*
Shrewsbury and Waterford, DBP, Personal Reps Col Sir Walter
Bromley-Davenport, Bp, and Ch Soc Trust (jt)
V B S P LEATHERS C E J JONES, M W SOAR
ALTON BARNES (St Mary the Virgin) *see Vale of Pewsey*
Sarum
ALTON PANCRAS (St Pancras) *see Piddle Valley, Hilton and*
Ansty, Cheselbourne etc Sarum

ALTON Resurrection (All Saints) (St Lawrence) *Win 2* P *Bp*
and D&C (jt) V A M MICKLEFIELD C G C RANDALL
NSM J K WINDSOR, L D POWER, R C STURT
ALTRINCHAM (St George) *Ches 10* P *Bp* V E J BETTS
NSM D R LAW
ALVANLEY (St John the Evangelist) *Ches 3* P *Bp* V *vacant*
ALVASTON (St Michael and All Angels) *Derby 5* P *PCC*
V J C WHITNEY **NSM** I P MUNRO
ALVECHURCH (St Lawrence) *Worc 7* P *Bp* R R D BUBBERS
ALVEDISTON (St Mary) *see Chalke Valley Sarum*
ALVELEY (St Mary the Virgin) and Quatt *Heref 8*
P *J W H Thompson Esq and Lady Labouchere (jt)*
R N S DUNLOP **NSM** R M SIMS
ALVERDISCOTT (All Saints) *see Newton Tracey, Horwood,*
Alverdiscott etc Ex
ALVERSTOKE (St Faith) (St Francis) (St Mary) *Portsm 3*
P *Bp* R A P NORRIS C H O'SULLIVAN **NSM** E A WILKIE
ALVERTHORPE (St Paul) *Leeds 19* P *Bp* **P-in-c** G COGGINS
ALVESCOT (St Peter) *see Shill Valley and Broadshire Ox*
ALVESTON (St Helen) and Littleton-on-Severn w Elberton
Bris 2 P *Bp and D&C (jt)* **P-in-c** D S MOSS
Hon C S J ORAM
ALVESTON (St James) *Cov 8* P *R Hampton Lucy w Charlecote*
and Loxley V R E WILLIAMS
ALVINGHAM (St Adelwold) *see Mid Marsh Gp Linc*
ALVINGTON (St Andrew) *see Lydney, Woolaston, Alvington*
and Aylburton Glouc
ALVINGTON, WEST (All Saints) *see Kingsbridge, Dodbrooke,*
and W Alvington Ex
ALWALTON (St Andrew) and Chesterton *Ely 15* P *Bp and*
Sir Philip Naylor-Leyland Bt (jt) V M J INGHAM
ALWINGTON (St Andrew) *see Parkham, Alwington,*
Buckland Brewer etc Ex
ALWINTON (St Michael and All Angels) *see Upper*
Coquetdale Newc
ALWOODLEY (St Barnabas) *see Moor Allerton and Shadwell*
Leeds
AMBERGATE (St Anne) and Heage *Derby 6* P *V Duffield and*
Exors M A T Johnson Esq **P-in-c** V M HART
AMBERLEY (Holy Trinity) *see Minchinhampton w Box and*
Amberley Glouc
AMBERLEY (no dedication) *see Maund Gp Heref*
AMBERLEY (St Michael) w North Stoke and Parham,
Wiggonholt and Greatham *Chich 11* P *Bp and Parham*
Estate Trustees (jt) **P-in-c** G M BURGESS
AMBLE (St Cuthbert) *Newc 6* P *Bp* **P-in-c** J A J MCDERMOTT
AMBLECOTE (Holy Trinity) *Worc 12* P *Bp*
V A R N WILLIAMS
AMBLESIDE (St Mary) *see Loughrigg Carl*
AMBROSDEN (St Mary the Virgin) *see Ray Valley Ox*
AMCOTTS (St Mark) *see Belton Gp Linc*
AMERSHAM (St Mary the Virgin) *Ox 9* P *Capt F Tyrwhitt*
Drake R T J L HARPER **NSM** S M GILL
OLM T J W BARNARD
AMERSHAM ON THE HILL (St Michael and All Angels) *Ox 9*
P *Bp* V D G OADES **NSM** P R BINNS
AMESBURY (St Mary and St Melor) *Sarum 14* P *D&C*
Windsor **P-in-c** D A'COURT C H G BREAREY
AMINGTON (St Editha) *Birm 9* P *Bp* V B C GREEN
AMOTHERBY (St Helen) *see The Street Par York*
AMPFIELD (St Mark), Chilworth and N Baddesley *Win 12*
P *Mrs P M A T Chamberlayne-MacDonald* V V L ASHDOWN
NSM V J LAWRENCE
AMPLEFORTH (St Hilda) w Oswaldkirk, Gilling East and
Stonegrave *York 19* P *Abp and Trin Coll Cam (jt) and The*
Crown (by turn) V C E REID
AMPNEY (St Mary) *see S Cotswolds Glouc*
AMPNEY (St Peter) *as above*
AMPNEY CRUCIS (Holy Rood) *as above*
AMPORT (St Mary) *see Portway and Danebury Win*
AMPTHILL (St Andrew) w Millbrook and Steppingley
St Alb 8 P *Ld Chan* V *vacant*
AMPTON (St Peter) *see Blackbourne St E*
AMWELL, GREAT (St John the Baptist) w St Margaret's and
Stanstead Abbots *St Alb 19* P *Bp, Peache Trustees, and*
Haileybury Coll (jt) V E A DONALDSON
AMWELL, LITTLE (Holy Trinity) *see Hertford St Alb*
ANCASTER (St Martin) *see E Loveden Linc*
ANCHORSHOLME (All Saints) *Blackb 8* P *Bp, V Bispham,*
and Ch Soc Trust (jt) V *vacant*
ANCROFT (St Anne) *see Lowick and Kyloe w Ancroft Newc*
ANDERBY (St Andrew) *see Sutton, Huttoft and Anderby Linc*
ANDOVER (St Mary) *Win 3* P *St Mary's Coll Win*
V C J BRADISH C S J ROBERTSON, S O SCOTT
ANDOVER (St Thomas) *see Pastrow Win*

ANDOVER, WEST (St Michael and All Angels) *see* Portway and Danebury *Win*

ANDREAS (St Andrew) (St Jude), Ballaugh, Jurby and Sulby *S & M* P *The Crown* R I M SKIDMORE
C W J MACKAY

ANERLEY (Christ Church) (St Paul) *Roch 13* P *Patr Bd*
TR M D FITTER

ANFIELD (St Columba) *Liv 4* P *Bp* NSM K L MILLER

ANFIELD (St Margaret) *Liv 1* P *Bp* V P A WINN
NSM J E WINN

ANGELL TOWN (St John the Evangelist) *S'wark 11* P *Bp*
V M R MALLETT NSM J N N ANAND, P J MILLIGAN

ANGERSLEIGH (St Michael) *see* Trull w Angersleigh *B & W*

ANGLESEY Group, The, comprising Bottisham, Lode w Longmeadow, Swaffham Bulbeck, and Swaffham Prior *Ely 4*
P *Trin Coll Cam, D&C, and Bp (jt)* V S J GILES

ANGMERING (St Margaret) *Chich 1* P C C F *Somerset Esq and Ch Patr Trust (jt)* R M J STANDEN NSM P S GILES

ANLABY (St Peter) *York 14* P *Trustees* V S C F WILCOX
C J A TELFORD

ANLABY COMMON (St Mark) Hull *York 14* P *Abp*
V S C F WILCOX C J A TELFORD

ANMER (St Mary) *see* Dersingham, Anmer, Ingoldisthorpe etc *Nor*

ANNESLEY (Our Lady and All Saints) w Newstead and Kirkby Woodhouse *S'well 4* P *Bp and Exors Major R P Chaworth-Musters (jt)* P-in-c H ROBINSON
NSM S D COTTERILL

ANNSCROFT (Christ Church) *see* Gt Hanwood and Longden and Annscroft etc *Heref*

ANSFORD (St Andrew) *see* Castle Cary and Ansford *B & W*

ANSLEY (St Lawrence) and Arley *Cov 5* P *Ch Patr Trust, N W H Sylvester Esq, and A C D'O Ransom Esq (jt)* R vacant

ANSLOW (Holy Trinity), Rolleston and Tutbury *Lich 13*
P *Duchy of Lancaster and MMCET (alt)* R vacant

ANSTEY (St George) *see* Hormead, Wyddial, Anstey, Brent Pelham etc *St Alb*

ANSTEY (St Mary) and Thurcaston w Cropston *Leic 9* P *Bp and Em Coll Cam (jt)* R D S MCDONOUGH

ANSTEY, EAST (St Michael) *see* Bishopsnympton, Charles, E Anstey, High Bray etc *Ex*

ANSTEY, WEST (St Petrock) *as above*

ANSTON (St James) *Sheff 5* P *Bp* V J M HIDDEN
NSM B A CUSHING

ANSTY (St James) *see* Nadder Valley *Sarum*

ANSTY (St James) and Shilton *Cov 2* P *Ld Chan*
P-in-c A D COLEMAN

ANTINGHAM (St Mary) *see* Poppyland *Nor*

ANTONY (St James the Great) *see* St Germans w Antony and Sheviock *Truro*

ANTROBUS (St Mark) *Ches 4* P V *Gt Budworth*
P-in-c A G BROWN

ANWICK (St Edith) *see* N Lafford Gp *Linc*

APEDALE Group, The, comprising Cardington, Eaton under Heywood, Hope Bowdler, and Rushbury *Heref 10* P *DBP, Mrs R Bell, Bp Birm, and S Pennington Esq (by turn)*
R N T CLEATON NSM S JELLEYMAN OLM V CLEMENTS

APETHORPE (St Leonard) *see* Nassington, Apethorpe, Thornhaugh etc *Pet*

APLEY (St Andrew) *see* Bardney *Linc*

APPERLEY (Holy Trinity) *see* Deerhurst and Apperley w Forthampton etc *Glouc*

APPLEBY (St Bartholomew) *see* Winterton Gp *Linc*

APPLEBY (St Lawrence) *see* Heart of Eden *Carl*

APPLEBY MAGNA (St Michael and All Angels) *see* Woodfield *Leic*

APPLEDORE (St Mary), Northam, and Westward Ho! *Ex 15*
P *Patr Bd* TR D J ARNOLD TV R M ELKS NSM S E JUNIPER

APPLEDORE (St Peter and St Paul) *see* Tenterden, Rother and Oxney *Cant*

APPLEDRAM (St Mary the Virgin) *Chich 2* P *D&C*
P-in-c M WICKENS

APPLEFORD (St Peter and St Paul) *see* DAMASCUS *Ox*

APPLESHAW (St Peter) Kimpton, Thruxton, Fyfield and Shipton Bellinger *Win 3* P *Bp (1 turn), and Bp, D&C, and R H Routh Esq (1 turn)* R vacant

APPLETHWAITE (St Mary) *see* Windermere St Mary and Troutbeck *Carl*

APPLETON (All Saints) *see* The Street Par *York*

APPLETON (St Laurence) *Ox 19* P *Magd Coll Ox*
R K W CAMPBELL

APPLETON (St Mary Magdalene) *see* Stockton Heath *Ches*

APPLETON ROEBUCK (All Saints) w Acaster Selby *York 1*
P *Abp* V C I COATES NSM P J MACNAUGHTON

APPLETON THORN (St Cross) *see* Stretton and Appleton Thorn *Ches*

APPLETON WISKE (St Mary) *see* Wiske Benefice *Leeds*

APPLETON-LE-MOORS (Christ Church) *see* Lastingham w Appleton-le-Moors, Rosedale etc *York*

APPLETREEWICK (St John the Baptist) *see* Burnsall w Rylstone *Leeds*

APPLEY BRIDGE (All Saints) and Parbold *Blackb 4* P *Bp*
V S K TIMMINS NSM M PLANT

APSLEY END (St Mary) *see* Langelei *St Alb*

ARBORFIELD (St Bartholomew) w Barkham *Ox 8* P *DBP*
R E P BICKERSTETH C J P BIDGOOD, M G HUDDLESTON

ARBORY (St Columba) and Castletown *S & M* P *The Crown and Bp (alt)* V I C COWELL NSM C L BARRY

ARBOURTHORNE (St Paul) and Norfolk Park *Sheff 1* P *Bp and V Sheffield (jt)* V vacant

ARDELEY (St Lawrence), Benington, Cottered w Throcking and Walkern *St Alb 16* P *K Coll Cam, D&C St Paul's, and Bp (jt)* R vacant

ARDEN MARCHES, comprising Spernall, Morton Bagot and Oldberrow, and Studley w Mappleborough Green *Cov 7*
P *Ld Chan, Mrs J M Pinney, and Bp (by turn)* R C E MIER
C D J CORLETT NSM A W SHEARN

ARDEN VALLEY, comprising Bearley, Snitterfield, and Wolverton w Norton Lindsey and Langley *Cov 7* P *Bp and V Wootton Wawen (jt)* R R D MUTTER

ARDINGLY (St Peter) *Chich 5* P *MMCET* R J H CRUTCHLEY
NSM C D SUTTON

ARDINGTON (Holy Trinity) *see* Wantage Downs *Ox*

ARDLEIGH (St Mary the Virgin) *see* Dedham and Ardleigh *Chelmsf*

ARDLEY (St Mary) *see* Cherwell Valley *Ox*

ARDSLEY (Christ Church) *Sheff 12* P R *Darfield*
V F M KOUBLE

ARDSLEY, EAST (St Gabriel) (St Michael) *Leeds 14*
P E C S J G *Brudenell Esq* V vacant

ARDSLEY, WEST (St Mary) *Leeds 14* P E C S J G *Brudenell Esq*
V S T WILKINSON

ARELEY KINGS (St Bartholomew) *Worc 13* P R *Martley*
R M TURNER NSM J M CALAM

ARICONIUM: Aston Ingham, Hope Mansel, Linton, The Lea, Upton Bishop and Weston-under-Penyard *Heref 7*
P *Bp (3 turns), St Jo Coll Ox (2 turns), Exors Preb H L Whatley (1 turn)* R D P HOWELL

ARKENDALE (St Bartholomew) *see* Walkingham Hill *Leeds*

ARKENGARTHDALE (St Mary) *see* Swaledale *Leeds*

ARKESDEN (St Mary the Virgin) *see* Clavering w Langley, Arkesden etc *Chelmsf*

ARKHOLME (St John the Baptist) *see* Hornby w Claughton and Whittington etc *Blackb*

ARKLEY (St Peter) *see* Chipping Barnet *St Alb*

ARKSEY (All Saints) *see* New Bentley w Arksey *Sheff*

ARLE VALLEY Benefice, The, comprising Bighton, New Alresford, Old Alresford, and Ovington w Itchen Stoke *Win 1* P *Bp* P-in-c J M MYLES C N S ANDERSON

ARLECDON (St Michael) *see* Crosslacon *Carl*

ARLESEY (St Andrew) (St Peter) w Astwick *St Alb 8* P *DBP*
V G M BOULT

ARLEY (St Michael) *see* Ansley and Arley *Cov*

ARLEY (St Wilfred) *as above*

ARLEY, UPPER (St Peter) *see* Kidderminster Ismere *Worc*

ARLINGHAM (St Mary the Virgin) *see* Stroudwater Team *Glouc*

ARLINGTON (St James) *see* Shirwell, Loxhore, Kentisbury, Arlington, etc *Ex*

ARLINGTON (St Pancras), Berwick, Selmeston w Alciston and Wilmington *Chich 21* P *Bp Lon, D&C, J Fitzherbert Esq, and Mrs R Fitzherbert (jt)* R P M BLEE
Hon C F J FOX-WILSON

ARMATHWAITE (Christ and St Mary) *see* Inglewood Gp *Carl*

ARMINGHALL (St Mary) *see* Stoke H Cross w Dunston, Arminghall etc *Nor*

ARMITAGE (St John the Baptist) *see* Brereton and Rugeley w Armitage *Lich*

ARMITAGE BRIDGE (St Paul) *see* Newsome and Armitage Bridge and S Crosland *Leeds*

ARMLEY (St Bartholomew) w New Wortley *Leeds 14* P *Bp, DBP, and Hyndman Trustees (jt)* P-in-c M F WOOD

ARMLEY HEIGHTS (Church of the Ascension) *see* Upper Armley *Leeds*

ARMLEY, UPPER (Christ Church) *Leeds 14* P *Ch Patr Trust*
V A SEN C D J ROSS

ARMTHORPE (St Leonard and St Mary) *Sheff 8* P *Bp*
R J M FODEN NSM S J MAUGHAN

ARNCLIFFE (St Oswald) *see* Upper Wharfedale and Littondale *Leeds*

ARNE (St Nicholas) *see* Wareham *Sarum*

ARNESBY (St Peter) *see* Hexagon *Leic*

ARNOLD (Emmanuel) *see* Bestwood Em and St Mark w Rise Park *S'well*

ARNOLD (St Mary) *S'well 7* **P** *Bp* **V** M CAUNT

ARNSIDE (St James) *Carl 10* **P** *Bp* **P-in-c** A B NORMAN **NSM** A MILLER

ARRETON (St George) *Portsm 7* **P** *Bp* **V** J F O'SHAUGHNESSY

ARRINGTON (St Nicholas) *see* Orwell Gp *Ely*

ARROW (Holy Trinity) *see* Alcester Minster *Cov*

ARROWVALE *see* Pembridge w Moor Court, Shobdon, Staunton etc *Heref*

ARTHINGWORTH (St Andrew) and Harrington w Oxendon and East Farndon *Pet 2* **P** *St Jo Coll Ox (2 turns), Nugee Foundn (2 turns), and Bp (1 turn)* **C** J V J G WATSON

ARTHURET (St Michael and All Angels) w Kirkandrews-on-Esk and Nicholforest *Carl 2* **P** *Sir James Graham Bt (2 turns), Bp (1 turn)* **P-in-c** B A MURPHY

ARUNDEL (St Nicholas) w Tortington and South Stoke *Chich 1* **P** *Bp (2 turns), Duke of Norfolk (1 turn)* **V** D A TWINLEY **C** D A CHMIELEWSKI, S R MERRIMAN

ASBY (St Peter) *see* Heart of Eden *Carl*

ASCENSION Team Ministry, The, comprising Humberstone and Thurnby Lodge *Leic 1* **P** *Patr Bd* **P-in-c** P A SAVAGE

ASCOT HEATH (All Saints) *Ox 3* **P** *Bp* **R** D D HANNAH

ASCOT, SOUTH (All Souls) *see* Sunninghill and S Ascot *Ox*

ASCOTT UNDER WYCHWOOD (Holy Trinity) *see* Chase *Ox*

ASFORDBY (All Saints) *see* Ab Kettleby and Holwell w Asfordby *Leic*

ASGARBY (St Andrew) *see* Heckington and Helpringham Gp *Linc*

ASH (Christ Church) *see* Adderley, Ash, Calverhall, Ightfield etc *Lich*

ASH (Holy Trinity) *see* Martock w Kingsbury Episcopi and Ash *B & W*

ASH (St Nicholas) *see* Canonry *Cant*

ASH (St Peter and St Paul) *Roch 1* **P** J R A B Scott Esq **R** H M REEVES **NSM** E M ROBERTSON

ASH (St Peter) *Guildf 1* **P** *Win Coll* **R** K R M BRISTOW **NSM** C L MONK

ASH (Thomas Chapel) *see* Sampford Peverell, Uplowman, Holcombe Rogus etc *Ex*

ASH PRIORS (Holy Trinity) *see* Milverton w Halse, Fitzhead and Ash Priors *B & W*

ASH VALE (St Mary) *Guildf 1* **P** *Bp* **V** N J LAMBERT

ASHAMPSTEAD (St Clement) *see* Basildon w Aldworth and Ashampstead *Ox*

ASHBOCKING (All Saints) *see* Carlford *St E*

ASHBOURNE (St John the Baptist) *Derby 1* **P** *Wright Trustees* **P-in-c** D C J BALLARD **C** A J MARSHALL, C E MCDONALD

ASHBOURNE (St Oswald) w Mapleton *Derby 1* **P** *Bp* **P-in-c** D C J BALLARD **C** A J MARSHALL, C E MCDONALD

ASHBRITTLE (St John the Baptist) *see* Wellington and Distr *B & W*

ASHBURNHAM (St Peter) w Penhurst *Chich 12* **P** *Ashburnham Chr Trust* **P-in-c** P S C WALKER

ASHBURTON (St Andrew), Bickington, Buckland in the Moor, Holne, Huccaby, Leusdon, Princetown, Postbridge, and Widecombe-in-the-Moor *Ex 8* **P** *Duchy of Cornwall (1 turn), Patr Bd (1 turn)* **P-in-c** M J RYLANDS **TV** G E C FENTON

ASHBURY (St Mary the Virgin) *see* Shrivenham and Ashbury *Ox*

ASHBY (St Mary) *see* Somerleyton, Ashby, Fritton, Herringfleet etc *Nor*

ASHBY (St Mary) *see* Thurton w Ashby St Mary, Bergh Apton etc *Nor*

ASHBY (St Paul) *see* Bottesford w Ashby *Linc*

ASHBY CUM FENBY (St Peter) *see* Waltham Gp *Linc*

ASHBY DE LA LAUNDE (St Hybald) *see* Digby Gp *Linc*

ASHBY FOLVILLE (St Mary) *see* S Croxton Gp *Leic*

ASHBY MAGNA (St Mary) *see* Avon-Swift *Leic*

ASHBY PARVA (St Peter) *see* Upper Soar *Leic*

ASHBY PUERORUM (St Andrew) *see* Horncastle Gp *Linc*

ASHBY ST LEDGERS (St Mary) *see* Daventry *Pet*

ASHBY, WEST (All Saints) *see* Hemingby Gp *Linc*

ASHBY-BY-PARTNEY (St Helen) *see* Bolingbroke Deanery *Linc*

ASHBY-DE-LA-ZOUCH (Holy Trinity) (St Helen) and Breedon on the Hill *Leic 8* **P** *Patr Bd* **TR** M E GREGORY **TV** T L PHILLIPS **C** S D BETTS

ASHCHURCH (St Nicholas) and Kemerton *Glouc 9* **P** *DBP and K Storey Esq (jt)* **P-in-c** S GRINDROD

ASHCOMBE (St Nectan) *see* Teignmouth, Ideford w Luton, Ashcombe etc *Ex*

ASHCOTT (All Saints) *see* Polden Wheel *B & W*

ASHDON (All Saints) *see* Saffron Walden and Villages *Chelmsf*

ASHE (Holy Trinity and St Andrew) *see* N Waltham and Steventon, Ashe and Deane *Win*

ASHEN (St Augustine) *see* Two Rivers *Chelmsf*

ASHENDON (St Mary) *see* Bernwode *Ox*

ASHFIELD CUM THORPE (St Mary) *see* Mid Loes *St E*

ASHFIELD, GREAT (All Saints) *see* Pakenham w Norton, Tostock etc *St E*

ASHFORD (St Hilda) *Lon 13* **P** *Bp* **V** J A D S FERNANDES

ASHFORD (St Matthew) *Lon 13* **P** *Ld Chan* **P-in-c** S J KING **C** A D GARNER

ASHFORD (St Peter) *see* Pilton w Ashford *Ex*

ASHFORD BOWDLER (St Andrew) *see* The Ashfords *Heref*

ASHFORD CARBONELL (St Mary) *as above*

ASHFORD HILL (St Paul) *see* Kingsclere and Ashford Hill w Headley *Win*

ASHFORD IN THE WATER (Holy Trinity) *see* Bakewell, Ashford w Sheldon and Rowsley *Derby*

ASHFORD TOWN (Christ Church) (St Francis) (St Mary the Virgin), including Great Chart, Kennington, Kingsnorth, Sevington, Shadoxhurst, Stubbs Cross, and Willesborough *Cant 6* **P** *Patr Bd* **TR** J C N MACKENZIE **TV** C A B MANSLEY, E L LANCHANTIN-PIGGOTT, R W BELLAMY **C** A R J BROWN, B M WATSON **NSM** C M ALDIS, D C STAMPER

ASHFORD, SOUTH (Christ Church) *see* Ashford Town *Cant*

ASHFORDS, The, including Ashford Bowdler, Ashford Carbonel, Caynham, Knowbury, Ludford, and Richards Castle *Heref 11* **P** *Bp* **R** L A MONEY

ASHILL (Blessed Virgin Mary) *see* Isle Valley *B & W*

ASHILL (St Nicholas), Carbrooke, Ovington and Saham Toney *Nor 13* **P** *Bp, New Coll Ox, Cam Univ, and SMF (jt)* **V** J E ATKINS

ASHILL (St Stephen) *see* Willand, Uffculme, Kentisbeare etc *Ex*

ASHINGDON (St Andrew) w South Fambridge, Canewdon and Paglesham *Chelmsf 14* **P** *D&C Westmr, Hyndman Trustees, and CCC Cam (jt)* **P-in-c** E A GUEST **NSM** G N EDWARDS

ASHINGTON (Holy Sepulchre) *Newc 11* **P** *Bp* **P-in-c** C J GROOCOCK

ASHINGTON (St Vincent) *see* Chilton Cantelo, Ashington, Mudford, Rimpton etc *B & W*

ASHLEWORTH (St Bartholomew), Corse, Hartpury, Hasfield, Maisemore, Staunton and Tirley *Glouc 3* **P** *Bp and W G F Meath-Baker Esq (1 turn), Ld Chan (1 turn), Bp (1 turn), and Bp and DBP (1 turn)* **R** J LONGUET-HIGGINS **C** S P GODSELL

ASHLEY (St Elizabeth) *see* Hale and Ashley *Ches*

ASHLEY (St James) *see* Braydon Brook *Bris*

ASHLEY (St John the Baptist) and Mucklestone and Broughton and Croxton *Lich 7* **P** *Bp, SMF, Mrs F F Friend, and T A J Hall Esq (jt)* **OLM** S A HUMPHRIES

ASHLEY (St Mary the Virgin) *see* Stoke Albany w Wilbarston and Ashley etc *Pet*

ASHLEY (St Mary) w Silverley *Ely 4* **P** *Bp and DBP (alt)* **R** *vacant*

ASHLEY (St Peter and St Paul) *see* Somborne w Ashley *Win*

ASHLEY (St Peter) *see* Milton *Win*

ASHLEY GREEN (St John the Evangelist) *see* Gt Chesham *Ox*

ASHMANHAUGH (St Swithin), Barton Turf, Beeston St Laurence, Horning, Irstead and Neatishead *Nor 12* **P** *Bp and Sir Ronald Preston Bt (jt)* **R** D R SMITH

ASHMANSWORTH (St James) *see* NW Hants *Win*

ASHMORE (St Nicholas) *see* Iwerne Valley *Sarum*

ASHMORE PARK (St Alban) *see* Wednesfield *Lich*

ASHOVER (All Saints) and Brackenfield w Wessington *Derby 2* **P** *Exors Revd J J C Nodder, Duke of Devonshire, V Crich and S Wingfield, and DBF (jt)* **R** R G LAWRENCE

ASHOW (Assumption of Our Lady) *see* Stoneleigh w Ashow *Cov*

ASHPERTON (St Bartholomew) *see* Hop Churches *Heref*

ASHPRINGTON (St David) *see* Totnes w Bridgetown, Berry Pomeroy etc *Ex*

ASHREIGNEY (St James) *Ex 19* **P** *DBP* **P-in-c** H S E BLAINE

ASHTEAD (St George) (St Giles) *Guildf 10* **P** *Bp* **R** J R JONES **C** N HILDING OHLSSON

ASHTON (Annunciation) *see* W Kerrier *Truro*

ASHTON (St John the Baptist) *see* Christow, Ashton, Bridford, Dunchideock etc *Ex*

ASHTON (St Michael and All Angels) *see* Salcey *Pet*

ASHTON GATE (St Francis) *see* Bedminster *Bris*

ASHTON HAYES (St John the Evangelist) *Ches 2* **P** *Keble Coll Ox* **V** P R WESTON

ASHTON KEYNES (Holy Cross) *see* Upper Thames *Bris*

ASHTON UNDER HILL (St Barbara) *see* Overbury w Teddington, Alstone etc *Worc*

ASHTON, WEST (St John)   *see* Trowbridge St Thos and W Ashton *Sarum*
ASHTON-IN-MAKERFIELD (Holy Trinity) *Liv 15*   **P** *Bp*   **R** *vacant*
ASHTON-IN-MAKERFIELD (St Thomas) *Liv 15*   **P** *R* Ashton-in-Makerfield H Trin   **V** J P THOMAS   **C** F G COWLING, S J M GREEN   **NSM** I SCHAFER
ASHTON-ON-RIBBLE (St Andrew) *Blackb 13*   **P** *Trustees*   **V** J D G NASH   **C** J W S LEE
ASHTON-ON-RIBBLE (St Michael and All Angels) w Preston St Mark *Blackb 13*   **P** *Trustees*   **V** A EVANS
ASHTON-UNDER-LYNE (Christ Church) *Man 13*   **P** *Bp*   **V** D JACKS   **C** B E BRADY   **OLM** A A HILLS
ASHTON-UNDER-LYNE Good Shepherd (Holy Trinity) (St James) (St Michael and All Angels) (St Gabriel) (St Peter) *Man 13*   **P** *Patr Bd*   **TR** R FARNWORTH   **TV** R D BATTERSHELL
ASHTON-UPON-MERSEY (St Martin) *Ches 10*   **P** *SMF*   **P-in-c** S CONLON
ASHTON-UPON-MERSEY (St Mary Magdalene) *Ches 10*   **P** *Trustees*   **V** S B RANKIN   **C** J BEAUMONT
ASHURST (St James) *Chich 11*   **P** *Bp*   **R** M D G HEATHER   **C** S P MILLS
ASHURST (St Martin of Tours)   *see* Speldhurst w Groombridge and Ashurst *Roch*
ASHURST WOOD (St Dunstan)   *see* Forest Row *Chich*
ASHWATER (St Peter ad Vincula), Halwill, Beaworthy, Clawton and Tetcott w Luffincott *Ex 16*   **P** *Ld Chan (1 turn), Ms C A Friswell, Lt Col Sir John Molesworth St Aubyn Bt, and Bp (jt) (2 turns)*   **R** *vacant*
ASHWELL (St Mary the Virgin) w Hinxworth and Newnham *St Alb 16*   **P** *Bp, N J A Farr Esq, and T D Smyth Esq (jt) (1 turn), Bp (3 turns)*   **R** R A EVENS
ASHWELL (St Mary)   *see* Oakham, Ashwell, Braunston, Brooke, Egleton etc *Pet*
ASHWELLTHORPE (All Saints)   *see* Upper Tas Valley *Nor*
ASHWICK (St James)   *see* Beacon Trinity *B & W*
ASHWICKEN (All Saints) w Leziate, Bawsey and Mintlyn, Congham, E Walton, Gayton, Gayton Thorpe, Gt Massingham, Grimston, Harpley, Lt Massingham and Roydon *Nor 19*   **P** *Patr Bd*   **TR** J M HOLMES   **TV** J M POLLARD
ASHWORTH (St James)   *see* Norden w Ashworth and Bamford *Man*
ASKAM (Church Centre)   *see* Dalton-in-Furness and Ireleth-with-Askam *Carl*
ASKAM (St Peter) *as above*
ASKERN (St Peter) *Sheff 7*   **P** *Bp*   **V** D J FRANKLIN
ASKHAM (St Nicholas)   *see* Retford Area *S'well*
ASKHAM (St Peter)   *see* N Westmorland *Carl*
ASKHAM BRYAN (St Nicholas) *York 1*   **P** *Abp*   **V** G R MUMFORD   **NSM** G M WEBB
ASKHAM RICHARD (St Mary)   *see* Marston Moor *York*
ASKRIGG (St Oswald)   *see* Upper Wensleydale *Leeds*
ASLACKBY (St James)   *see* Billingborough Gp *Linc*
ASLACTON (St Michael)   *see* Long Stratton and Pilgrim TM *Nor*
ASLOCKTON (St Thomas)   *see* Whatton w Aslockton, Hawksworth, Scarrington etc *S'well*
ASPALL (St Mary of Grace)   *see* Debenham and Helmingham *St E*
ASPATRIA (St Kentigern) w Hayton and Gilcrux *Carl 7*   **P** *Bp*   **P-in-c** T D HERBERT   **C** R O GOODFELLOW   **Hon C** D R KING   **NSM** C J KENNEDY
ASPENDEN (St Mary), Buntingford and Westmill *St Alb 16*   **P** *CPAS, MCET, and K Coll Lon (jt)*   **R** I R HILL
ASPLEY (St Margaret) *S'well 8*   **P** *Trustees*   **V** R T K ATKINSON   **C** J W J MORING, P W SHAW, M J BRADLEY
ASPLEY GUISE (St Botolph) w Husborne Crawley and Ridgmont *St Alb 8*   **P** *Ld Chan (1 turn), Trustees Bedf Estates (1 turn), and Bp (2 turns)*   **R** G BRADSHAW
ASPULL (St Elizabeth)   *see* Wigan All SS *Liv*
ASSINGTON (St Edmund)   *see* Bures w Assington and Lt Cornard *St E*
ASTBURY (St Mary) and Smallwood *Ches 11*   **P** *Sir Richard Baker Wilbraham Bt*   **R** *vacant*
ASTERBY Group, The, comprising Benniworth, Biscathorpe, Burgh-on-Bain, Donington-on-Bain, Gayton le Wold, Goulceby, Ranby, Scamblesby, and Stenigot *Linc 13*   **P** *Bp, DBP, C N A F Heneage Esq, and F Smith Esq (jt)*   **OLM** P E SMITH
ASTHALL (St Nicholas)   *see* Burford w Fulbrook, Taynton, Asthall etc *Ox*
ASTLEY (St Mary the Virgin)   *see* Chilvers Coton w Astley *Cov*
ASTLEY (St Mary), Clive, Grinshill and Hadnall *Lich 21*   **P** *D R B Thompson Esq*   **P-in-c** P H CAWTHORNE

ASTLEY (St Peter)   *see* Shrawley, Witley, Astley and Abberley *Worc*
ASTLEY (St Stephen), Tyldesley and Mosley Common *Man 19*   **P** *DBP and V Leigh*   **TR** M B COX   **OLM** A J DAND
ASTLEY ABBOTTS (St Calixtus)   *see* Bridgnorth and Morville Par *Heref*
ASTLEY BRIDGE (St Paul) *Man 12*   **P** *The Crown*   **V** J J HARTLEY
ASTON (St Giles)   *see* Wigmore Abbey *Heref*
ASTON (St James) (St Peter and St Paul) and Nechells *Birm 7*   **P** *Patr Bd*   **V** P J NOTT   **NSM** G S KAYLA
ASTON (St Mary)   *see* Woore and Norton in Hales *Lich*
ASTON (St Peter)   *see* Aston by Sutton, Lt Leigh and Lower Whitley *Ches*
ASTON (St Saviour)   *see* Stone St Mich and St Wulfad w Aston St Sav *Lich*
ASTON ABBOTS (St James the Great)   *see* Cottesloe *Ox*
ASTON BOTTERELL (St Michael and All Angels)   *see* Ditton Priors w Neenton, Burwarton etc *Heref*
ASTON BY SUTTON (St Peter), Little Leigh and Lower Whitley *Ches 4*   **P** *Bp, V Gt Budworth, Lord Daresbury, and B H Talbot Esq (jt)*   **V** C M Y JONES
ASTON CANTLOW (St John the Baptist) and Wilmcote w Billesley *Cov 7*   **P** *SMF*   **P-in-c** D P BENSKIN   **C** J B HOLDEN
ASTON CLINTON (St Michael and All Angels) w Buckland and Drayton Beauchamp *Ox 17*   **P** *Bp, A R Pegg Esq, and Jes Coll Ox (jt)*   **R** S A BOTTOMER   **OLM** A J ROBERTS
ASTON CUM AUGHTON (All Saints) w Swallownest and Ulley *Sheff 5*   **P** *Bp*   **TR** *vacant*
ASTON EYRE (not known)   *see* Bridgnorth and Morville Par *Heref*
ASTON FLAMVILLE (St Peter)   *see* Burbage w Aston Flamville *Leic*
ASTON INGHAM (St John the Baptist)   *see* Ariconium *Heref*
ASTON ON TRENT (All Saints), Elvaston, Weston on Trent and Shardlow, Barrow upon Trent with Twyford and Swarkestone *Derby 7*   **P** *Bp, Earl of Harrington, and Repton Sch (jt)*   **R** A LUKE   **C** E G BACKHOUSE   **NSM** J L PLACKETT-FERGUSON, P HYGATE
ASTON ROWANT (St Peter and St Paul)   *see* Chinnor, Sydenham, Aston Rowant and Crowell *Ox*
ASTON SANDFORD (St Michael and All Angels)   *see* Wychert Vale *Ox*
ASTON SOMERVILLE (St Mary)   *see* Winchcombe *Glouc*
ASTON TIRROLD (St Michael)   *see* The Churn *Ox*
ASTON UPTHORPE (All Saints) *as above*
ASTON, LITTLE (St Peter) *Lich 1*   **P** *Patr Bd*   **V** P S DANIEL
ASTON, NORTH (St Mary the Virgin)   *see* Steeple Aston w N Aston and Tackley *Ox*
ASTON-LE-WALLS (St Leonard), Byfield, Boddington, Eydon and Woodford Halse *Pet 1*   **P** *Bp, CCC Ox, and Em Coll Cam (2 turns), Ld Chan (1 turn)*   **R** S CROSS   **NSM** G D MOORE
ASTON-SUB-EDGE (St Andrew)   *see* Vale and Cotswold Edge *Glouc*
ASTWELL Group of Parishes, The, comprising Helmdon w Stuchbury and Radstone, Lois Weedon, Syresham, Wappenham, and Whitfield *Pet 1*   **P** *Bp, Worc Coll Ox, Ox Univ, Mert Coll Ox, DBP, and Jes Coll Ox (jt)*   **R** *vacant*
ASTWICK (St Guthlac)   *see* Arlesey w Astwick *St Alb*
ASTWOOD BANK (St Matthias and St George)   *see* Redditch Ch the K *Worc*
ASUM GROUP   *see* Bengeworth and Hampton etc *Worc*
ASWARBY (St Denys)   *see* S Lafford *Linc*
ASWARDBY (St Helen)   *see* Bolingbroke Deanery *Linc*
ATCHAM (St Eata)   *see* Shrewsbury St Giles w Sutton and Atcham *Lich*
ATHELINGTON (St Peter), Denham, Horham, Hoxne, Redlingfield, Syleham and Wingfield *St E 13*   **P** *Bp, DBP, Lt Comdr G C Marshall, and H F Soden Esq (jt)*   **R** M J WOMACK   **NSM** E M GOODISON, V J MCCRACKEN
ATHELNEY Benefice, The, comprising Burrowbridge, Lyng, North Curry, and Stoke St Gregory *B & W 13*   **P** *D&C*   **V** *vacant*
ATHERINGTON (St Mary)   *see* Newton Tracey, Horwood, Alverdiscott etc *Ex*
ATHERSLEY (St Helen) and Carlton *Leeds 17*   **P** *DBP and Bp (jt)*   **V** P D NEEDHAM
ATHERSTONE (St Mary) *Cov 5*   **P** *Ch Patr Trust*   **V** M J BRANDSMA
ATHERTON (St John the Baptist) (St George) (St Philip) and Hindsford w Howe Bridge *Man 19*   **P** *DBP*   **TV** R W SINCLAIR   **OLM** D N SIVILL
ATLOW (St Philip and St James)   *see* Hulland, Atlow, Kniveton, Bradley and Hognaston *Derby*

ATTENBOROUGH (St Mary the Virgin) *S'well 9* **P** *CPAS*
V J P SMITHURST

ATTERCLIFFE (St Alban) and Darnall *Sheff 1* **P** *Bp, Dean Sheff, and Sheff Ch Burgesses Trust (jt)* **V** *vacant*

ATTLEBOROUGH (Assumption of the Blessed Virgin Mary) w Besthorpe *Nor 11* **P** *CR and Mrs N Bayntun (jt)*
R M C JACKSON **NSM** A K SLATER

ATTLEBOROUGH (Holy Trinity) *Cov 5* **P** *V Nuneaton*
V A J EVANS **C** A J POULTNEY

ATTLEBRIDGE (St Andrew) *see* Reepham and Wensum Valley *Nor*

ATWICK (St Lawrence) *see* Hornsea, Atwick and Skipsea *York*

ATWORTH (St Michael and All Angels) w Shaw and Whitley *Sarum 15* **P** *D&C Bris and R Melksham (alt)*
V J A PALMER **C** A E EVANS **NSM** R E GILLINGS

AUBOURN (St Peter) *see* Withamside *Linc*

AUCKLAND (St Andrew) *see* Bishop Auckland *Dur*

AUCKLAND (St Anne) *as above*

AUCKLAND (St Helen) *Dur 5* **P** *Bp* **V** R I MCTEER

AUCKLEY (St Saviour) *see* Finningley w Auckley *Sheff*

AUDENSHAW (St Hilda) *Man 13* **P** *Bp* **V** J H KERSHAW

AUDENSHAW (St Stephen) *Man 13* **P** *Bp* **V** P R DIXON
C M HOWARTH

AUDLEM (St James) *see* Wybunbury and Audlem w Doddington *Ches*

AUDLEY (St James the Great) *see* Alsagers Bank, Audley and Talke *Lich*

AUGHTON (All Saints) *see* Bubwith w Skipwith *York*

AUGHTON (Christ Church) *Liv 14* **P** *R Aughton St Mich*
V S H O'DONOGHUE

AUGHTON (St Michael) and Bickerstaffe *Liv 14* **P** *Bp and Earl of Derby (jt)* **R** A A HOUSLEY

AUGHTON (St Saviour) *see* Slyne w Hest and Halton w Aughton *Blackb*

AULT HUCKNALL (St John the Baptist) and Scarcliffe *Derby 2* **P** *Bp and Duke of Devonshire (alt)*
V J H HENDERSON SMITH

AUNSBY (St Thomas of Canterbury) *see* S Lafford *Linc*

AUST (not known) *see* Almondsbury and Olveston *Bris*

AUSTERFIELD (St Helen) *see* Bawtry w Austerfield, Misson, Everton and Mattersey *S'well*

AUSTREY (St Nicholas) *see* All So N Warks *Birm*

AUSTWICK (Epiphany) *see* Clapham-with-Keasden and Austwick *Leeds*

AVEBURY (St James) *see* Upper Kennet *Sarum*

AVELEY (St Michael) *see* Mardyke *Chelmsf*

AVENING (Holy Cross) w Cherington *Glouc 7* **P** *E A Tarlton Esq (1 turn), D&C (2 turns)* **P-in-c** G P SOUTH

AVERHAM (St Michael and All Angels) w Kelham *S'well 3*
P *DBP* **C** G A L HADLEY

AVETON GIFFORD (St Andrew) *see* Modbury, Bigbury, Ringmore etc *Ex*

AVINGTON (St Mary) *see* Itchen Valley *Win*

AVON DASSETT w Farnborough and Fenny Compton *Cov 8*
P *G V L Holbech Esq and Mrs A D Seyfried (jt), CCC Ox, and Bp (alt)* **P-in-c** N M CHATTERTON

AVON RIVER Team, comprising Bulford, Durrington, Enford, Figheldean, Fittleton, Milston w Brigmerston, and Netheravon *Sarum 14* **P** *Patr Bd* **TR** P A BROMILEY
TV G A HUNT

AVON VALLEY PARTNERSHIP *see* Fordingbridge and Hyde and Breamore etc *Win*

AVONMOUTH (St Andrew) *see* Lawrence Weston and Avonmouth *Bris*

AVON-SWIFT Benefice, The, comprising Ashby Magna, Catthorpe, Gilmorton, Kimcote, Misterton, North Kilworth, Peatling Parva, Shawel, South Kilworth, Stanford, and Swinford *Leic 7* **P** *Patr Bd (5 turns), Ld Chan (1 turn)*
TV E L DAVIES **NSM** R A HAY

AVONWICK (St James' Chapel) *see* Diptford w N Huish, Ermington, Halwell etc *Ex*

AWBRIDGE (All Saints) *see* Michelmersh and Awbridge and Braishfield etc *Win*

AWLISCOMBE (St Michael and All Angels) *see* Honiton, Gittisham, Combe Raleigh, Monkton etc *Ex*

AWRE (St Andrew) *see* Newnham w Awre and Blakeney *Glouc*

AWSWORTH (St Peter) *see* Trowell, Awsworth and Cossall *S'well*

AXBRIDGE (St John the Baptist) w Shipham and Rowberrow *B & W 1* **P** *Bp and D&C (alt)*
R T D HAWKINGS

AXFORD (St Michael) *see* Whitton *Sarum*

AXMINSTER (St Mary), Chardstock, All Saints, Combpyne w Rousdon and Membury *Ex 4* **P** *Bp* **TR** C M SEDGEWICK

AXMOUTH (St Michael) *see* Uplyme w Axmouth *Ex*

AYCLIFFE (Church Centre) *see* Dover Town *Cant*

AYCLIFFE, GREAT (St Andrew) (St Clare) *Dur 5* **P** *Patr Bd*
TR A ANDERSON **TV** J ANDERSON **C** D J HUDSON

AYLBURTON (St Mary) *see* Lydney, Woolaston, Alvington and Aylburton *Glouc*

AYLBURTON COMMON (Mission Church) *as above*

AYLESBEARE (Blessed Virgin Mary), Clyst St George, Clyst St Mary, Farringdon, Woodbury w Exton, and Woodbury Salterton *Ex 1* **P** *Bp, D&C, Lord Wraxall, and Mrs S Radcliffe (jt)* **C** N J MASON

AYLESBURY (Holy Trinity) *see* Walton H Trin *Ox*

AYLESBURY (St Mary the Virgin) *Ox 10* **P** *Bp and Patr Bd (jt)*
TR D L ZIMMERMAN **TV** G E LANE **C** P J WHEELER

AYLESBY (St Lawrence) *see* Wolds Gateway Group *Linc*

AYLESFORD (St Peter and St Paul) *Roch 7* **P** *D&C*
V R M PEET

AYLESHAM (St Peter) *Cant 1* **P** *Abp* **V** *vacant*

AYLESTONE (St Andrew) w St James *Leic 1* **P** *Bp*
R R M BASS

AYLMERTON (St John the Baptist), Runton, Beeston Regis, Gresham *Nor 20* **P** *Bp and Guild of All So (2 turns), Duchy of Lanc (1 turn)* **NSM** R M ADAMSON

AYLSHAM (St Michael and All Angels) and District Team Ministry, The, including Badersfield, Blickling, Brampton, Burgh-next-Aylsham, Buxton w Oxnead, Cawston, Haveringland, Heydon, Itteringham w Mannington, Little Barningham, Marsham, Oulton w Imingland, and Wickmere w Wolterton *Nor 18*
P *Patr Bd* **TV** A P WHITEHEAD, D E HAGAN-PALMER
C J O BRANFORD

AYLTON (not known) *see* Cider Churches *Heref*

AYMESTREY (St John the Baptist and St Alkmund) *see* Kingsland w Eardisland, Aymestrey etc *Heref*

AYNHO (St Michael) and Croughton w Evenley and Farthinghoe and Hinton-in-the-Hedges w Steane *Pet 1*
P *Bp (2 turns), Mrs E A J Cartwright-Hignett (1 turn), Magd Coll Ox (1 turn), and Ld Chan (1 turn)* **R** S T COOPER

AYOT ST LAWRENCE (St Lawrence) *see* Kimpton w Ayot St Lawrence *St Alb*

AYOT ST PETER (St Peter) *see* Welwyn *St Alb*

AYSGARTH (St Andrew) *see* Penhill *Leeds*

AYTHORPE RODING (St Mary) *see* Gt Canfield w High Roding and Aythorpe Roding *Chelmsf*

AYTON, EAST (St John the Baptist) *see* Seamer, E Ayton and Cayton *York*

AYTON, GREAT (All Saints) (Christ Church) w Easby and Newton under Roseberry *York 20* **P** *Abp* **V** P H PEVERELL
NSM J C DEAN

BABBACOMBE (All Saints) *Ex 11* **P** *V St Marychurch*
V P E JONES

BABCARY (Holy Cross) *see* Six Pilgrims *B & W*

BABRAHAM (St Peter) *Ely 5* **P** *H R T Adeane Esq*
V A C PARTRIDGE

BABWORTH (All Saints) *see* Retford Area *S'well*

BACKFORD (St Oswald) and Capenhurst *Ches 9* **P** *Bp*
P-in-c S M MANSFIELD

BACKWELL (St Andrew) w Chelvey and Brockley *B & W 12*
P *DBP* **R** C E GARNER

BACKWORTH (St John) *see* Earsdon and Backworth *Newc*

BACONSTHORPE (St Mary) *see* Matlaske *Nor*

BACTON (St Andrew), Happisburgh, Hempstead w Eccles and Lessingham, Ridlington, Sea Palling w Waxham, Walcott, and Witton *Nor 12* **P** *Bp, Earl of Kimberley, K Coll Cam, and Sir Edward Evans-Lombe (jt)* **R** C H DOBSON

BACTON (St Faith) *see* Ewyas Harold w Dulas, Kenderchurch etc *Heref*

BACTON (St Mary the Virgin) w Wyverstone, Cotton and Old Newton, and Wickham Skeith *St E 8* **P** *Patr Bd (2 turns), Ld Chan (1 turn)* **R** *vacant*

BACUP Christ Church and Stacksteads *Man 11* **P** *Patr Bd*
TR D BRAE **TV** D ALLEN **NSM** L M ALLEN
OLM D R J COOK

BADBY (St Mary) w Newnham and Charwelton w Fawsley and Preston Capes *Pet 3* **P** *Bp* **R** *vacant*

BADDESLEY CLINTON (St Michael) *Birm 5* **P** *T W Ferrers-Walker Esq* **R** P H GERARD

BADDESLEY ENSOR (St Nicholas) w Grendon *Birm 9* **P** *Bp, V Polesworth, and PCC (jt)* **V** *vacant*

BADDESLEY, NORTH (All Saints' Mission Church) *see* Ampfield, Chilworth and N Baddesley *Win*

BADDESLEY, NORTH (St John the Baptist) *as above*

BADDESLEY, SOUTH (St Mary the Virgin) *see* Boldre w S Baddesley *Win*

BADDILEY (St Michael) and Wrenbury w Burleydam *Ches 15* **P** *V Acton and Bp (alt)* **P-in-c** A J FULFORD
NSM D WOODS

BADDOW, GREAT (Meadgate Church Centre) (St Mary the Virgin) (St Paul) *Chelmsf 10* **P** *Patr Bd* **TR** D P RITCHIE **TV** P J W SHELDRAKE, T W BALL **Hon C** R C MATTHEWS **NSM** S FINCH

BADDOW, LITTLE (St Mary the Virgin) *Chelmsf 10* **P** *Bp* **P-in-c** J D JONES

BADGER (St Giles) *see* Beckbury, Badger, Kemberton, Ryton, Stockton etc *Lich*

BADGEWORTH (Holy Trinity), Shurdington and Witcombe w Bentham *Glouc 3* **P** *Bp and F D Hicks Beach Esq (jt)* **R** S P COOKE

BADGWORTH (St Congar) *see* Crook Peak *B & W*

BADINGHAM (St John the Baptist) *see* Upper Alde *St E*

BADLESMERE (St Leonard) *see* Shepherds Lees *Cant*

BADMINTON (St Michael and All Angels) *see* Boxwell, Leighterton, Didmarton, Oldbury etc *Glouc*

BADMINTON, LITTLE (St Michael and All Angels) *as above*

BADSEY (St James) *see* E Vale and Avon Villages *Worc*

BADSHOT LEA (St George) and Hale *Guildf 3* **P** *Bp* **R** L J CRAWLEY **C** H T MOORE **NSM** A J CRAWLEY

BADSWORTH (St Mary the Virgin) *Leeds 18* **P** *DBP* **R** *vacant*

BADWELL (St Mary) and Walsham, including Finningham, Langham, Walsham-le-Willows, Wattisfield, and Westhorpe *St E 5* **P** *Bp, MMCET, DBP, R M Martineau Esq, and Ch Union (jt)* **V** J MERRY

BAG ENDERBY (St Margaret) *see* S Ormsby Gp *Linc*

BAGBOROUGH (St Pancras) *see* Bishop's Lydeard w Lydeard St Lawrence etc *B & W*

BAGBY (St Mary) *see* Thirkleby w Kilburn and Bagby *York*

BAGENDON (St Margaret) *see* Churn Valley *Glouc*

BAGINTON (St John the Baptist) w Bubbenhall and Ryton-on-Dunsmore *Cov 6* **P** *D&C (2 turns), Bp (1 turn), Lord Leigh and Bp (1 turn)* **V** D R WINTLE

BAGNALL (St Chad) w Endon *Lich 8* **P** *R Leek and Meerbrook and A D Owen Esq (jt)* **V** A J BETTS

BAGSHOT (Good Shepherd) *see* Savernake *Sarum*

BAGSHOT (St Anne) *Guildf 6* **P** *Ld Chan* **V** A SISTIG **NSM** J E TURTLE

BAGULEY (St John the Divine) Brooklands *Man 6* **P** *Bp and A W Hargreaves Esq (jt)* **V** R J SHERRATT

BAILDON (St John the Evangelist) (St Hugh Mission Church) (St James) *Leeds 1* **P** J P Baxter Esq **V** S R BENHAM **C** R J YEOMAN

BAIN VALLEY Group, The, comprising Coningsby, Kirkby on Bain, Roughton, and Tattershall *Linc 13* **P** *Baroness Willoughby de Eresby, T J Spurrier Esq, and DBP (1 turn), Ld Chan (1 turn)* **R** S A ALLISON **NSM** R E DONE **OLM** M DONE

BAINTON (St Andrew) *see* Woldsburn *York*

BAINTON (St Mary) *see* Barnack w Ufford, Bainton, Helpston and Wittering *Pet*

BAKEWELL (All Saints), Ashford in the Water w Sheldon and Rowsley *Derby 4* **P** *Bp, D&C, and Duke of Rutland (jt)* **V** A P KAUNHOVEN **C** S BEECHAM **NSM** B J JACKSON

BALBY (St John the Evangelist) *see* Wadworth w Loversall and Balby *Sheff*

BALCOMBE (St Mary) *Chich 5* **P** *W Gibson Esq* **R** K D RICHARDS

BALDERSBY (St James) *see* Topcliffe, Baldersby w Dishforth, Dalton etc *York*

BALDERSTONE (St Leonard), Mellor and Samlesbury *Blackb 7* **P** *V Blackb St Mary and St Paul* **V** *vacant*

BALDERTON (St Giles), Barnby in the Willows and Coddington *S'well 3* **P** *Ld Chan and Bp (alt)* **V** E L HOLLIDAY **NSM** P R SMITH

BALDOCK (St Mary the Virgin) w Bygrave *St Alb 16* **P** *Bp and Marquess of Salisbury (jt)* **R** A P HOLFORD

BALDWIN (St Luke) *see* Marown, Foxdale and Baldwin *S & M*

BALE (All Saints) *see* Stiffkey and Bale *Nor*

BALHAM (St Mary and St John the Divine) *S'wark 17* **P** *Bp and Keble Coll Ox (jt)* **V** R B TOBIN **C** B Y C EXCELL

BALHAM HILL (Ascension) *S'wark 17* **P** *Bp* **V** M T GIBBS **C** T D COLLINS

BALKWELL (St Peter) *Newc 5* **P** *Bp* **C** L J CLEMINSON

BALLAM (St Matthew) *see* Ribby cum Wrea and Weeton *Blackb*

BALLAUGH (St Mary Old Church) *see* Andreas, Ballaugh, Jurby and Sulby *S & M*

BALLAUGH (St Mary) *as above*

BALLINGER (St Mary Mission Hall) *see* Gt Missenden w Ballinger and Lt Hampden *Ox*

BALSALL COMMON (St Peter) *Birm 10* **P** *Bp* **V** P W THOMAS

BALSALL HEATH (St Barnabas) *see* Sparkbrook St Agatha w Balsall Heath St Barn *Birm*

BALSALL HEATH (St Paul) and Edgbaston *Birm 4* **P** *Bp and Sir Euan Anstruther-Gough-Calthorpe Bt (jt)* **V** P R LECKEY

BALSCOTE (St Mary Magdalene) *see* Ironstone *Ox*

BALSHAM (Holy Trinity) *see* Granta Vale Gp *Ely*

BALTERLEY (All Saints' Memorial Church) *see* Barthomley *Ches*

BALTONSBOROUGH (St Dunstan) w Butleigh, West Bradley and West Pennard *B & W 4* **P** *Bp* **P-in-c** C J HOPKINS

BAMBER BRIDGE (St Aidan) *Blackb 5* **P** *Bp* **NSM** N J PROCTER

BAMBER BRIDGE (St Saviour) *Blackb 5* **P** *V Blackb* **V** G HALSALL

BAMBURGH (St Aidan) *Newc 7* **P** *Exors Lady Armstrong* **P-in-c** L M TAYLOR-KENYON

BAMFORD (St John the Baptist) *see* Hathersage w Bamford and Derwent and Grindleford *Derby*

BAMFORD (St Michael) *see* Norden w Ashworth and Bamford *Man*

BAMFURLONG (Good Shepherd) *see* Chapelfields *Liv*

BAMPTON (Holy Trinity) (St James) (St Mary) w Clanfield *Ox 28* **P** *Bp, DBP, St Jo Coll Ox, D&C Ex, and B Babington-Smith Esq (jt)* **V** J M COLLIER **NSM** T KUIN LAWTON

BAMPTON (St Michael and All Angels), Morebath, Clayhanger, Petton and Huntsham *Ex 7* **P** *Bp, DBP, and D&C (jt)* **V** K D N CHANDRA

BAMPTON (St Patrick) *see* High Westmorland *Carl*

BAMPTON ASTON (St James) *see* Bampton w Clanfield *Ox*

BAMPTON LEW (Holy Trinity) *as above*

BAMPTON PROPER (St Mary) *as above*

BANBURY (St Francis) *Ox 23* **P** *Bp* **V** C T GAYNOR

BANBURY (St Hugh) *Ox 23* **P** *Bp* **V** A E SMITH **NSM** C G SMITH

BANBURY (St Leonard) *Ox 23* **P** *Bp* **V** E S BURCHELL

BANBURY (St Mary) *Ox 23* **P** *Bp* **NSM** H L ADEY HUISH, J J WEST, S M BOURNE

BANBURY (St Paul) *Ox 23* **P** *Bp* **V** D R H MCGOWAN **C** J H EGGERTSEN

BANHAM (St Mary) *see* Quidenham Gp *Nor*

BANKFOOT (St Matthew) and Bowling St Stephen *Leeds 2* **P** *Bp and CPAS (jt)* **V** J W HINTON **C** A S TREASURE, H E RAITT

BANNINGHAM (St Botolph) *see* King's Beck *Nor*

BANSFIELD, comprising Cowlinge, Denston, Lidgate, Ousden, Stansfield, Stradishall, and Wickhambrook *St E 3* **P** *DBP, Mrs G S M Slater, and Ld Chan (by turn)* **R** *vacant*

BANSTEAD (All Saints) *Guildf 9* **P** *Bp* **V** M PALLIS **C** I P WHITLEY

BANWELL (St Andrew) and Congresbury w Hewish, Puxton and West Wick *B & W 10* **P** *MMCET and D&C Bris (jt)* **V** M J THOMSON **NSM** H J WORSLEY

BAPCHILD (St Lawrence) *see* Milton Regis w Murston, Bapchild and Tonge *Cant*

BAR HILL (not known) *Ely 6* **P** *Bp* **V** *vacant*

BARBON (St Bartholomew) *see* Kirkby Lonsdale *Carl*

BARBOURNE (St Stephen) *Worc 6* **P** *Bp* **P-in-c** A G TODD **NSM** G D MORPHY

BARBY (St Mary) *see* Daventry *Pet*

BARCHESTON (St Martin) *see* S Warks Seven Gp *Cov*

BARCOMBE (St Francis) (St Mary the Virgin) *Chich 21* **P** *Ld Chan* **R** J W HOLLINGSWORTH

BARDFIELD SALING (St Peter and St Paul) *see* Stebbing and Lindsell w Gt and Lt Saling *Chelmsf*

BARDFIELD, GREAT (St Mary the Virgin) and LITTLE (St Katherine) *Chelmsf 18* **P** *Ch Union Trust* **P-in-c** R W F BEAKEN

BARDNEY (St Lawrence) *Linc 13* **P** *DBP (1 turn), Bp (2 turns), and St Jo Coll Cam (1 turn)* **R** D W BARTLETT **NSM** H E JEFFERY

BARDON HILL (St Peter) *see* Coalville w Bardon Hill and Ravenstone *Leic*

BARDSEA (Holy Trinity) *see* Pennington and Lindal w Marton and Bardsea *Carl*

BARDSEY (All Hallows) *Leeds 13* **P** *G L Fox Esq* **V** A J HANNAFIN

BARDSLEY (Holy Trinity) *Man 16* **P** *Wm Hulme Trustees* **V** A D GRANT **OLM** E M LOWE

BARDWELL (St Peter and St Paul) *see* Blackbourne *St E*

BARE (St Christopher) *Blackb 11* **P** *Bp* **V** D L HEAP

BARFORD (St Botolph) *see* Barnham Broom and Upper Yare *Nor*

BARFORD (St John) *see* Deddington w Barford, Clifton and Hempton *Ox*

BARFORD (St Martin) *see* Nadder Valley *Sarum*

BARFORD (St Michael) *see* Deddington w Barford, Clifton and Hempton *Ox*

BARFORD (St Peter) w Wasperton and Sherbourne *Cov 8*
P *Major J M Mills, R Hampton Lucy, and Lady Jeryl*
Smith-Ryland (jt)   R *vacant*
BARFORD, GREAT (All Saints)   *see Riversmeet St Alb*
BARFREYSTONE (St Nicholas)   *see Bewsborough Cant*
BARHAM (St Giles)   *see S Leightonstone Ely*
BARHAM (St John the Baptist)   *see Barham Downs w*
Adisham Cant
BARHAM (St Mary)   *see Claydon St E*
BARHAM DOWNS w Adisham *Cant 1*   P *Abp*   R S C THOMAS
BARHOLME (St Martin)   *see Uffington Gp Linc*
BARKBY (St Mary)   *see Fosse Team Leic*
BARKESTONE (St Peter and St Paul)   *see Vale of Belvoir Leic*
BARKHAM (St James)   *see Arborfield w Barkham Ox*
BARKING (Christ Church)   *see Thames View Chelmsf*
BARKING (St Erkenwald) *Chelmsf 1*   P *Bp*   P-in-c Y LEE
BARKING (St Margaret) *Chelmsf 1*   P *Patr Bd*
TR M T S MWAMBA   NSM E JOHN
BARKING (St Mary)   *see S Bosmere St E*
BARKING (St Patrick) *Chelmsf 1*   P *Bp*   V C D BOLSTER
BARKINGSIDE (Holy Trinity) *Chelmsf 6*   P *V Gt Ilford*
P-in-c S W BATTEN   C K A APPIAH   NSM R E POTTEN
BARKINGSIDE (St Cedd) *Chelmsf 6*   P *Bp*
P-in-c P G HARCOURT
BARKINGSIDE (St Francis of Assisi) *Chelmsf 6*   P *Bp*
P-in-c S W BATTEN   NSM M L BRADLEY
BARKINGSIDE (St George) *Chelmsf 6*   P *Bp*   V B J WALLIS
BARKINGSIDE (St Laurence) *Chelmsf 6*   P *Bp*
P-in-c C M BURROWS   OLM I P ELLIOTT
BARKSTON (St Nicholas)   *see S Cliff Villages Gp Linc*
BARKSTON ASH (Holy Trinity)   *see Sherburn in Elmet w*
Saxton York
BARKWAY (St Mary Magdalene), Barley, Reed and
Buckland *St Alb 16*   P *The Crown and DBP (alt)*   R R C PYKE
BARKWITH Group, The, comprising East Barkwith, Hainton,
Sixhills, East Torrington, and South Willingham *Linc 7*
P *D&C, C N A F Heneage Esq, K Coll Lon, and DBP (by turn)*
R *vacant*
BARKWITH, EAST (St Mary)   *see Barkwith Gp Linc*
BARLASTON (St John the Baptist) *Lich 12*   P *Countess of*
Sutherland   V S W JONES
BARLAVINGTON (St Mary), Burton w Coates and Sutton w
Bignor *Chich 10*   P *Lord Egremont and Miss J B Courtauld (jt)*
P-in-c J F H GREEN
BARLBOROUGH (St James) and Clowne *Derby 3*   P *Ld Chan*
and Mrs A Hayward (alt)   R B R TAYLOR
BARLBY (All Saints)   *see Riccall, Barlby and Hemingbrough*
York
BARLESTONE (St Giles)   *see Newbold de Verdun, Barlestone*
and Kirkby Mallory Leic
BARLEY (St Margaret of Antioch)   *see Barkway, Barley, Reed*
and Buckland St Alb
BARLEY HILL   *see Thame Ox*
BARLING MAGNA (All Saints)   *see Roach Par Chelmsf*
BARLINGS (St Edward) *Linc 5*   P *DBP*   V D P GREEN
BARLOW MOOR (Emmanuel)   *see Didsbury St Jas and Em*
Man
BARLOW, GREAT (St Lawrence)   *see Old Brampton and Great*
Barlow Derby
BARMBY MOOR Group, The (St Catherine), including
Allerthorpe, Fangfoss, Thornton and Melbourne, and
Yapham-cum-Meltonby *York 5*   P *Abp (1 turn), Abp and*
Trustees Duke of Norfolk's Settlement Everingham Fund
(2 turns)   V J F HARDY   NSM K G TOWNLEY
BARMING (St Margaret of Antioch) w West Barming
Roch 7   P *Ld Chan*   R W W NORTH
BARMING HEATH (St Andrew) *Cant 12*   P *Abp*
P-in-c C P LAVENDER   C B J F KNOTT
BARMSTON (All Saints)   *see Bridlington Em and Barmston w*
Fraisthorpe York
BARNACK (St John the Baptist) w Ufford, Bainton,
Helpston and Wittering *Pet 11*   P *Bp, St Jo Coll Cam,*
Burghley Ho Preservation Trust Ltd, and Sir Philip Naylor-
Leyland Bt (jt)   V D C MAYLOR
BARNACRE (All Saints)   *see Scorton and Barnacre and Calder*
Vale Blackb
BARNARD CASTLE (St Mary) w Whorlton *Dur 6*   P *Trin Coll*
Cam   V A J HARDING   C S J CLIFF
BARNARDISTON (All Saints)   *see Stourhead St E*
BARNBURGH (St Peter) w Melton on the Hill and
Adwick-upon-Dearne *Sheff 12*   P *Ld Chan (2 turns), Bp*
(1 turn)   P-in-c K HERROD
BARNBY (St John the Baptist)   *see Worlingham w Barnby and*
N Cove St E
BARNBY DUN (St Peter and St Paul) *Sheff 8*   P *Bp*   V *vacant*

BARNBY IN THE WILLOWS (All Saints)   *see Balderton, Barnby*
in the Willows and Coddington S'well
BARNEHURST (St Martin) *Roch 15*   P *Bp*   V G J BOWEN
NSM P DAVIES
BARNES Team Ministry, The (St Mary) (Holy Trinity)
(St Michael and All Angels) *S'wark 16*   P *Patr Bd*
TR J B B HUTCHINGS   TV D M R COOKE, S F STAVROU
NSM M N CALDERBANK
BARNET (Christ Church)   *see S Mimms Ch Ch Lon*
BARNET (St John the Baptist)   *see Chipping Barnet St Alb*
BARNET (St Stephen) *as above*
BARNET VALE (St Mark) *as above*
BARNET, EAST (St Mary the Virgin) *St Alb 14*   P *The Crown*
R A S CORIO
BARNET, NEW (St James) *St Alb 14*   P *Ch Patr Trust*
V L J HEWITT
BARNETBY LE WOLD (St Barnabas)   *see Brocklesby Park,*
Croxton and North Wolds Linc
BARNEY (St Mary), Hindringham, Thursford, Great
Snoring, Little Snoring and Kettlestone and Pensthorpe
Nor 14   P *D&C (1 turn), DBP and Lord Hastings (1 turn), St Jo*
Coll Cam (1 turn)   R J MUGGLETON
BARNHAM (St Gregory)   *see Blackbourne St E*
BARNHAM (St Mary)   *see Aldingbourne, Barnham and*
Eastergate Chich
BARNHAM BROOM (St Peter and St Paul) and Upper Yare
Nor 16   P *Bp, Mrs A C Briggs, the Revd J B Boston, Ch Soc*
Trust, H Edwards Esq, MMCET, and the Earl of Kimberley (jt)
R T A P WEATHERSTONE   C L PITTMAN   Hon C A J HAWES
BARNINGHAM (St Andrew)   *see Stanton St E*
BARNINGHAM (St Michael and All Angels)   *see Holmedale*
Leeds
BARNINGHAM WINTER (St Mary the Virgin)   *see Matlaske*
Nor
BARNINGHAM, LITTLE (St Andrew)   *see Aylsham and Distr*
Nor
BARNOLDBY LE BECK (St Helen)   *see Waltham Gp Linc*
BARNOLDSWICK (Holy Trinity) (St Mary le Gill) w
Bracewell *Leeds 24*   P *Bp*   V S S MCMAIN   C J M CLARKSON
C M FLETCHER
BARNSBURY (St Andrew) *Lon 6*   P *Patr Bd*   TV D E FELL
C M FLETCHER
BARNSLEY (St Edward the Confessor)   *see Cen Barnsley Leeds*
BARNSLEY (St Mary) *as above*
BARNSLEY (St Mary)   *see S Cotswolds Glouc*
BARNSLEY (St Paul) Old Town   *see Cen Barnsley Leeds*
BARNSLEY (St Peter and St John the Baptist) *Leeds 17*   P *Bp*
V *vacant*
BARNSLEY, CENTRAL (St Edward the Confessor)
(St George) (St Mary) (St Thomas) *Leeds 17*   P *Bp and V*
Darton w Staincross and Mapplewell (jt)   R S P RACE
C J L HEWITT, M SANCHEZ RODRIGUEZ, P J MARIES
NSM M J BURNS, S A OAKLEY
BARNSLEY, WEST, comprising Cawthorne, Dodworth,
Hoylandswaine, and Silkstone *Leeds 17*   P *A J Fraser Esq and*
Bp (jt)   V M L BROWELL   C K I FREEMAN, M S DOERING
BARNSTAPLE (Holy Trinity) and Goodleigh *Ex 14*   P *Bp and*
DBP (jt)   V B J LILLIE   NSM S A PATERSON
BARNSTAPLE (St Peter and St Mary Magdalene) *Ex 14*
P *Bp*   V D M FLETCHER
BARNSTON (Christ Church) *Ches 8*   P *Bp*   V P M FROGGATT
C C C MURPHY
BARNSTON (St Andrew)   *see Gt Dunmow and Barnston*
Chelmsf
BARNSTONE (St Mary Mission Room)   *see Wiverton in the*
Vale S'well
BARNT GREEN (St Andrew)   *see Cofton Hackett w Barnt*
Green Birm
BARNTON (Christ Church) *Ches 4*   P *Bp*   P-in-c D L MOCK
C P J PRITCHARD
BARNWELL (All Saints) (St Andrew), Hemington,
Luddington in the Brook, Lutton, Polebrook and
Thurning *Pet 10*   P *Bp, MMCET, Em Coll Cam, DBP, and Sir*
Philip Naylor-Leyland Bt (jt)   R C H BRAZIER
BARNWOOD (St Lawrence) *Glouc 2*   P *D&C*
V R E CROFTON   NSM A D HAYMAN
BARONY OF BURGH, The (St Michael) *Carl 3*   P *Patr Bd*
P-in-c T A BODDAM-WHETHAM
BARR, GREAT (St Margaret) *Lich 24*   P *M D S Farnham*
V M C RUTTER
BARRINGTON (All Saints)   *see Orwell Gp Ely*
BARRINGTON (Blessed Virgin Mary)   *see Winsmoor B & W*
BARRINGTON, GREAT (St Mary)   *see Sherborne, Windrush,*
the Barringtons etc Glouc
BARRINGTON, LITTLE (St Peter) *as above*

BARROW (All Saints) *St E 10*   **P** *Ld Chan (1 turn), Mrs E C Gordon-Lennox, the Russell-Cooke Trust Co and Bp (1 turn), and St Jo Coll Cam (1 turn)*   **V** *vacant*

BARROW (Holy Trinity) and Goxhill *Linc 8*   **P** *Ld Chan*   **V** J C GIRTCHEN   **C** A E BROWN

BARROW (St Bartholomew) *Ches 2*   **P** *D Okell Esq*   **R** A J STINSON

BARROW (St Giles) *see* Broseley w Benthall, Jackfield, Linley etc *Heref*

BARROW GURNEY (The Blessed Virgin Mary and St Edward King and Martyr) *see* Long Ashton w Barrow Gurney and Flax Bourton *B & W*

BARROW HILL (St Andrew) *see* Staveley and Barrow Hill *Derby*

BARROW IN FURNESS (St Paul) *Carl 8*   **P** *Simeon's Trustees*   **NSM** E A BATES

BARROW UPON SOAR (Holy Trinity) w Walton le Wolds *Leic 6*   **P** *St Jo Coll Cam and DBP (jt)*   **P-in-c** C R WATTS

BARROW, NORTH (St Nicholas) *see* Six Pilgrims *B & W*

BARROW, NORTH Team Ministry, The (St Francis) St Matthew St James the Great *Carl 8*   **P** *Patr Bd*   **TR** J W KNILL-JONES

BARROW, SOUTH (St Peter) *see* Six Pilgrims *B & W*

BARROW, SOUTH Team Ministry, The (St Aidan) (St George) *Carl 8*   **P** *Bp*   **C** R P HAM

BARROWBY (All Saints) and Great Gonerby *Linc 20*   **P** *R Grantham, and Duke of Devonshire (by turn)*   **R** *vacant*

BARROWDEN (St Peter) and Wakerley w South Luffenham and Morcott w Duddington and Tixover *Pet 12*   **P** *Burghley Ho Preservation Trust Ltd, P W Rowley Esq, and Bp (3 turns), Ball Coll Ox (1 turn)*   **P-in-c** C J ARMSTRONG

BARROWFORD (St Thomas) and Newchurch-in-Pendle *Blackb 6*   **P** *Ld Chan and trustees (alt)*   **V** J L SMITH

BARROW-IN-FURNESS (St Aidan) *see* S Barrow *Carl*

BARROW-IN-FURNESS (St George) *as above*

BARROW-IN-FURNESS (St James the Great) *see* N Barrow *Carl*

BARROW-IN-FURNESS (St John the Evangelist) *Carl 8*   **P** *DBP*   **P-in-c** A G BATCHELOR

BARROW-IN-FURNESS (St Mark) *Carl 8*   **P** *Bp*   **P-in-c** A FORD

BARROW-IN-FURNESS (St Mary the Virgin) *see* Walney Is *Carl*

BARROW-ON-HUMBER (Holy Trinity) *see* Barrow and Goxhill *Linc*

BARROW-ON-TRENT (St Wilfrid) *see* Aston on Trent, Elvaston, Weston on Trent etc *Derby*

BARSHAM (Holy Trinity) *see* Bungay *St E*

BARSHAM, EAST (All Saints) *see* Walsingham, Houghton and Barsham *Nor*

BARSHAM, NORTH (All Saints) *as above*

BARSHAM, WEST (The Assumption of the Blessed Virgin Mary) *as above*

BARSTON (St Swithin) *Birm 10*   **P** *MMCET*   **P-in-c** S C L DIMES

BARTESTREE CROSS Group of Parishes, comprising Dormington, Lugwardine w Bartestree, Weston Beggard, and Withington *Heref 3*   **P** *D&C (3 turns), Bp (1 turn), Personal Reps A T Foley (1 turn)*   **R** *vacant*

BARTHOMLEY (St Bertoline) *Ches 11*   **P** *Lord O'Neill*   **R** *vacant*

BARTLEY GREEN (St Michael and All Angels) *Birm 1*   **P** *Bp*   **V** R I ATKINSON

BARTLOW (St Mary) *see* Linton *Ely*

BARTON (St Cuthbert w St Mary) *see* E Dere Street *Leeds*

BARTON (St Lawrence) *see* Fellside Team *Blackb*

BARTON (St Mark's Chapel) w Peel Green and Winton *Man 18*   **P** *Bp, TR Eccles, and TR Worsley (jt)*   **V** I A HALL

BARTON (St Martin) *see* Torquay St Martin Barton *Ex*

BARTON (St Michael), Pooley Bridge, Martindale and Watermillock *Carl 4*   **P** *Bp and Earl of Lonsdale (jt)*   **V** *vacant*

BARTON (St Paul) *Portsm 7*   **P** *R Whippingham*   **V** *vacant*

BARTON (St Peter) *see* Lordsbridge *Ely*

BARTON BENDISH (St Andrew) *see* Wissey Valley *Ely*

BARTON HARTSHORN (St James) *see* The Claydons and Swan *Ox*

BARTON HILL (St Luke w Ch Ch) and Moorfields St Matthew *Bris 3*   **P** *Bp, CPAS, and V Bris St Phil and St Jacob n Em (jt)*   **P-in-c** N J COLEMAN   **OLM** W D GARDINER

BARTON IN FABIS (St George) *see* A453 churches of S Notts *S'well*

BARTON MILLS (St Mary) *see* Mildenhall *St E*

BARTON SEAGRAVE (St Botolph) w Warkton *Pet 9*   **P** *Ch Soc Trust (2 turns), Duke of Buccleuch (1 turn)*   **R** M W LUCAS   **C** A J CLARK

BARTON ST DAVID (St David) *see* Wheathill Priory Gp *B & W*

BARTON STACEY (All Saints) *see* Lower Dever *Win*

BARTON TURF (St Michael) *see* Ashmanhaugh, Barton Turf etc *Nor*

BARTON UNDER NEEDWOOD (St James) w Dunstall and Tatenhill *Lich 13*   **P** *Bp and Sir Rupert Hardy Bt (jt)*   **V** A R RIDLEY

BARTON UPON HUMBER (St Mary) *Linc 8*   **P** *Bp*   **V** D P ROWETT   **NSM** R M JAGGS-FOWLER   **OLM** A W WRIGHT

BARTON, GREAT (Holy Innocents) and Thurston *St E 10*   **P** *Bp and Sir Michael Bunbury Bt (jt)*   **V** M A CROSSMAN

BARTON-LE-CLEY (St Nicholas) w Higham Gobion and Hexton *St Alb 8*   **P** *The Crown (3 turns), Mrs F A A Cooper (1 turn)*   **R** A P JOHNSON

BARTON-LE-STREET (St Michael) *see* The Street Par *York*

BARTON-ON-THE-HEATH (St Lawrence) *see* S Warks Seven Gp *Cov*

BARWELL (St Mary) w Potters Marston and Stapleton *Leic 10*   **P** R J W Titley Esq   **R** P WATSON

BARWICK (St Mary Magdalene) *see* Yeovil H Trin w Barwick *B & W*

BARWICK IN ELMET (All Saints) *see* Elmete Trin *Leeds*

BASCHURCH (All Saints) and Weston Lullingfield w Hordley *Lich 16*   **P** *Ch Patr Trust and Bp (jt)*   **R** L J COX   **NSM** D M COATSWORTH

BASEGREEN (St Peter) *see* Gleadless *Sheff*

BASFORD (St Leodegarius) (St Aidan) *S'well 8*   **P** *Bp*   **V** R SHAW

BASFORD (St Mark) *Lich 9*   **P** *Bp*   **P-in-c** T B BLOOR   **C** P M GRIFFIN

BASHLEY (St John) *see* Milton *Win*

BASILDON (St Andrew) (Holy Cross) *Chelmsf 12*   **P** *Bp*   **V** J S RICHARDS   **C** S M PEARCE

BASILDON (St Martin of Tours) *Chelmsf 12*   **P** *Bp*   **P-in-c** T J G BRAMPTON

BASILDON (St Stephen) w Aldworth and Ashampstead *Ox 4*   **P** *St Jo Coll Cam, Simeon's Trustees, and DBF (by turn)*   **V** W H N WATTS   **NSM** K WESTON

BASING, OLD (St Mary) and Lychpit *Win 4*   **P** *Magd Coll Ox*   **V** H S LEPPARD

BASINGSTOKE (All Saints) (St Michael) *Win 4*   **P** *Patr Bd*   **TR** J M STOKER   **TV** A BENNETT   **NSM** P PALMER

BASINGSTOKE (St Gabriel) *see* Popley w Limes Park and Rooksdown *Win*

BASINGSTOKE Brighton Hill (Christ the King) *see* Basingstoke *Win*

BASINGSTOKE Popley (Bethlehem Chapel) *as above*

BASINGSTOKE South Ham (St Peter) *as above*

BASLOW (St Anne) and Eyam *Derby 4*   **P** *Duke of Devonshire and Earl Temple (jt)*   **R** M V GILBERT

BASSENTHWAITE (St Bega) *see* Binsey *Carl*

BASSENTHWAITE (St John) *as above*

BASSETT (St Michael and All Angels) *see* N Stoneham and Bassett *Win*

BASSINGBOURN (St Peter and St Paul) *Ely 7*   **P** *D&C Westmr*   **V** C J YANDELL

BASSINGHAM (St Michael and All Angels) *see* Withamside *Linc*

BASSINGTHORPE (St Thomas à Becket) *see* N Beltisloe Gp *Linc*

BASTON (St John the Baptist) *see* Ness Gp *Linc*

BASWICH or Berkswich (Holy Trinity) *Lich 10*   **P** *Bp*   **V** G W ADAMSON   **NSM** D CLARK, K A SHAW

BATCOMBE (Blessed Virgin Mary) *see* Alham Vale *B & W*

BATCOMBE (St Mary) *see* Three Valleys *Sarum*

BATH (Christ Church) Proprietary Chapel *B & W 10*   **P-in-c** L E J CHUMBLEY

BATH (St Barnabas) w Englishcombe *B & W 8*   **P** *Bp*   **V** C A SOURBUT GROVES   **C** A S PITT

BATH (St Bartholomew) *B & W 8*   **P** *Simeon's Trustees*   **V** I R LEWIS   **NSM** J R G HOVIL, T C LING

BATH (St Luke) *B & W 8*   **P** *Simeon's Trustees*   **V** M D H FRANKUM   **NSM** L A WORTELHOCK

BATH (St Mary Magdalene) Holloway, Extra-parochial Chapelry *B & W 10*   **Chapl** D J PROTHERO

BATH (St Michael w St Paul) *B & W 8*   **P** *CPAS*   **R** J DRIVER   **C** C S A DEAKIN

BATH (St Saviour) w Swainswick and Woolley *B & W 8*   **P** *Ch Patr Trust and Or Coll Ox (jt)*   **R** M J NORMAN   **Hon C** D J PARR

BATH (St Stephen) *see* Charlcombe w Bath St Steph *B & W*

BATH ABBEY (St Peter and St Paul) w St James *B & W 8*
P *Simeon's Trustees*   R G S BRIDGEWATER   C J M HOFFMANN,
K U MADDEN, S P GIRLING   **NSM** E M LEE-BARBER
BATH Bathwick (St John the Baptist) (Blessed Virgin Mary)
B & W 8   **P** *Bp*   **R** P R H EDWARDS
BATH Odd Down (St Philip and St James) w Combe Hay
B & W 8   **P** *Simeon's Trustees*   **V** P S FERGUSON
NSM M JOYCE
BATH Twerton-on-Avon (Ascension) (St Michael) *B & W 8*
P *Patr Bd*   **TR** R M WHITE   **TV** R J PIMM   **C** J J MENNIE
BATH Walcot (St Andrew) (St Swithin) *B & W 8*   **P** *Simeon's*
Trustees   **R** T GLEGHORN   **C** F A YOUINGS
BATH Weston (All Saints) w North Stoke and Langridge
B & W 8   **P** *Ld Chan*   **R** M R SEARLE
BATH Weston (St John the Evangelist) (Emmanuel) w
Kelston *B & W 8*   **P** *Ld Chan*   **R** vacant
BATH Widcombe (St Matthew) (St Thomas à Becket)
B & W 8   **P** *Simeon's Trustees*   **V** T S BUCKLEY
C J A BUCKLER
BATHAMPTON (St Nicholas) w Claverton *B & W 8*   **P** *D&C*
Bris and the Revd C W D Skrine (jt)   **R** J P FRITH
BATHEALTON (St Bartholomew) *see* Wellington and Distr
B & W
BATHEASTON (St John the Baptist) (St Catherine) *B & W 8*
P *Ch Ch Ox*   **V** vacant
BATHFORD (St Swithun) *B & W 8*   **P** *D&C Bris*
P-in-c S E BUDDLE
BATHWICK (Blessed Virgin Mary) *see* Bath Bathwick *B & W*
BATHWICK (St John the Baptist) *as above*
BATLEY (All Saints) (St Thomas) *Leeds 9*   **P** *Bp, R E Brudenell*
Esq, and R Dewsbury (jt)   **V** M NAYLOR   **C** M R UMPLEBY
BATLEY CARR (Holy Trinity) *see* Dewsbury *Leeds*
BATSFORD (St Mary) *see* Moreton-in-Marsh w Batsford,
Todenham etc *Glouc*
BATTERSEA (Christ Church and St Stephen) *S'wark 14*
P *Bp and V Battersea St Mary (alt)*   **V** G N OWEN
BATTERSEA (St George) *see* Battersea Fields *S'wark*
BATTERSEA (St Luke) *S'wark 14*   **P** *Bp*
P-in-c L M M FERNANDEZ-VICENTE
BATTERSEA (St Mary) *S'wark 14*   **P** *Earl Spencer*   **V** S BUTLER
C A J KENNEDY
BATTERSEA (St Michael) Wandsworth Common *S'wark 14*
P *V Battersea St Mary*   **V** vacant
BATTERSEA (St Peter) (St Paul) *S'wark 14*   **P** *V Battersea*
St Mary   **P-in-c** R P MALONE
BATTERSEA FIELDS (St Saviour) (All Saints) (St George)
S'wark 14   **P** *Bp, CPAS, and Ch Patr Trust (jt)*
P-in-c L W CARR   **C** E BLATCHLEY, R C TURNER, S A A ANAND,
V J ELSTON
BATTERSEA PARK (All Saints) *see* Battersea Fields *S'wark*
BATTERSEA PARK (St Saviour) *as above*
BATTERSEA RISE (St Mark) *S'wark 14*   **P** *V Battersea St Mary*
V P J S PERKIN   **C** C H THOMSON, N L WOOLDRIDGE
BATTISFORD (St Mary) *see* S Bosmere *St E*
BATTLE (Church of the Ascension) (St Mary the Virgin)
Chich 12   **P** *The Crown*   **V** vacant
BATTLE HILL (Good Shepherd) *see* Willington *Newc*
BATTLESDEN (St Peter and All Saints) *see* Woburn w
Eversholt, Milton Bryan, Battlesden etc *St Alb*
BATTYEFORD (Christ the King) *Leeds 9*   **P** *V Mirfield*
V M A MCLEAN
BAUGHURST (St Stephen) and Ramsdell and Wolverton w
Ewhurst and Hannington *Win 4*   **P** *Ld Chan, Duke of*
Wellington, and Bp (by turn)   **R** vacant
BAULKING (St Nicholas) *see* Uffington, Shellingford,
Woolstone and Baulking *Ox*
BAUMBER (St Swithin) *see* Hemingby Gp *Linc*
BAUNTON (St Mary Magdalene) *see* Churn Valley *Glouc*
BAVERSTOCK (St Editha) *see* Nadder Valley *Sarum*
BAWBURGH (St Mary and St Walstan) *see* Easton, Colton,
Marlingford and Bawburgh *Nor*
BAWDESWELL (All Saints) *see* Heart of Norfolk *Nor*
BAWDRIP (St Michael and All Angels) *see* Woolavington w
Cossington and Bawdrip *B & W*
BAWDSEY (St Mary) *see* Wilford Peninsula *St E*
BAWTRY (St Nicholas) w Austerfield, Misson, Everton and
Mattersey *S'well 1*   **P** *Bp and Ld Chan (alt)*
V J E T STRICKLAND   **C** R J HANCOCK
BAXENDEN (St John) *Blackb 1*   **P** *Bp*   **V** T A DONAGHEY
BAXTERLEY (not known) w Hurley and Wood End and
Merevale w Bentley *Birm 9*   **P** *Ld Chan (1 turn), Bp and Sir*
William Dugdale Bt (1 turn)   **P-in-c** J C WHITE
NSM C J YOUNG
BAYDON (St Nicholas) *see* Whitton *Sarum*
BAYFORD (Mission Room) *see* Charlton Musgrove,
Cucklington and Stoke Trister *B & W*

BAYFORD (St Mary) *see* Lt Berkhamsted and Bayford,
Essendon etc *St Alb*
BAYLHAM (St Peter) *see* Bramford w Lt Blakenham, Baylham
and Nettlestead *St E*
BAYSTON HILL (Christ Church) *Lich 19*   **P** *V Shrewsbury H*
Trin w St Julian   **V** P J HUBBARD   **C** R T FARNHAM,
U F PENCAVEL
BAYSWATER (St Matthew) *Lon 2*   **P** *Exors Dame Jewell*
Magnus-Allcroft   **V** W P H COLERIDGE   **NSM** M J LEE
BAYTON (St Bartholomew) *see* Mamble w Bayton, Rock w
Heightington etc *Worc*
BEACHAMPTON (Assumption of the Blessed Virgin Mary) *see*
Buckingham *Ox*
BEACHAMWELL (St Mary) *see* Wissey Valley *Ely*
BEACON Parishes *see* Painswick, Sheepscombe, Cranham,
The Edge etc *Glouc*
BEACON Team Ministry, The, comprising Burneside,
Grayrigg, Kendal St George, Longsleddale, Selside, and
Skelsmergh *Carl 10*   **P** *Patr Bd*   **TR** N L DAVIES
C P A ROGERS   **OLM** J F RADLEY   **Hon Par Dn** J L TYRER
BEACON TRINITY, comprising Ashwick, Binegar, and Oakhill
B & W 7   **P** *Bp*   **P-in-c** R A PRIESTLEY   **C** M L PRIESTLEY,
R J MILES
BEACON, The, comprising Burton Agnes, Harpham, and
Lowthorpe *York 10*   **P** *Ld Chan (2 turns), Sir Charles Legard*
Bt (1 turn)   **P-in-c** J H ANDERSON
BEACONSFIELD (St Mary and All Saints) (St Michael and
All Angels) *Ox 9*   **P** *Patr Bd*   **TR** J P BROOKS
TV M R JOHNSON, S ROBERTS   **NSM** M M SUTER
BEADLAM (St Hilda) *see* Kirkdale w Harome, Nunnington
and Pockley *York*
BEADNELL (St Ebba) *Newc 7*   **P** *Newc Dioc Soc*
P-in-c A S MACPHERSON
BEAFORD (All Saints) *see* Newton Tracey, Horwood,
Alverdiscott etc *Ex*
BEALINGS, GREAT (St Mary) and LITTLE (All Saints) w
Playford and Culpho *St E 18*   **P** *Lord Cranworth (1 turn), Bp*
(3 turns)   **R** vacant
BEAMINSTER AREA (St Mary of the Annunciation),
including Broadwindsor w Burstock, Drimpton, Hooke,
Melplash and Mapperton, Mosterton, Netherbury, Salway
Ash, Seaborough, South Perrott and Chedington, Stoke
Abbott, and Toller Porcorum *Sarum 2*   **P** *Patr Bd*
TR D F B BALDWIN   **TV** J B NEARY   **C** F J BEALE
Hon C E B SAVIGEAR
BEAMISH (St Andrew) *see* Stanley and S Moor *Dur*
BEANE VALLEY Benefice, The, comprising Aston, Bramfield,
Stapleford, Waterford and Watton at Stone *St Alb 19*
P *Grocers' Co (1 turn), R M A Smith Esq (3 turns), Bp (1 turn)*
R J GRAY   **NSM** A LYNAS
BEARLEY (St Mary the Virgin) *see* Arden Valley *Cov*
BEARPARK (St Edmund) *see* Dur N *Dur*
BEARSTED (Holy Cross) *see* N Downs *Cant*
BEARWOOD (St Catherine) *see* Winnersh *Ox*
BEARWOOD (St Mary the Virgin) *Birm 6*   **P** *V Smethwick*
V A H PERRY
BEAUCHAMP RODING (St Botolph) *see* S Rodings *Chelmsf*
BEAUDESERT (St Nicholas) and Henley-in-Arden w
Ullenhall *Cov 7*   **P** *MMCET, Bp, and High Bailiff of*
Henley-in-Arden (jt)   **R** J F GANJAVI
BEAULIEU (Blessed Virgin and Holy Child) and Exbury and
East Boldre *Win 11*   **P** *Bp and Lord Montagu of Beaulieu (jt)*
V J C WHITE
BEAUMONT CUM MOZE (St Leonard and St Mary) *see* Gt
Oakley, Wix, Wrabness etc *Chelmsf*
BEAUMONT LEYS (Christ the King) *see* Stocking Farm and
Beaumont Leys *Leic*
BEAUWORTH (St James) *see* Upper Itchen *Win*
BEAUXFIELD (St Peter) *see* Bewsborough *Cant*
BEAWORTHY (St Alban) *see* Ashwater, Halwill, Beaworthy,
Clawton etc *Ex*
BEBINGTON (St Andrew) *Ches 8*   **P** *M C Saunders-Griffiths*
Esq   **R** D A VESTERGAARD   **C** A A METCALFE, A M RODGERS
BEBINGTON, HIGHER (Christ Church) *Ches 8*   **P** *Bp*
V M G LOACH   **NSM** E S BLACKMORE
BECCLES (St Michael the Archangel) (St Luke's Church
Centre) *St E 17*   **P** *Simeon's Trustees*   **R** H ENDERSON
C B J EDWARDS   **NSM** C E KIDDY, P M CUDMORE
BECK ROW (St John) *see* Mildenhall *St E*
BECKBURY (St Milburga), Badger, Kemberton, Ryton,
Stockton and Sutton Maddock *Lich 15*   **P** *Lord Hamilton*
of Dalzell, Or Coll Ox, and MMCET (2 turns), Ld Chan (1 turn)
R K HODSON
BECKENHAM (Christ Church) *Roch 13*   **P** *Ch Trust Fund*
Trust   **V** R M HINTON   **C** L N BACON
BECKENHAM (Holy Trinity) *see* Penge Lane H Trin *Roch*

BECKENHAM (St George) (St Barnabas) *Roch 13* **P** *Bp and Keble Coll Ox (jt)* **R** J A BLUNDEN **C** E R PRITCHETT, T J HIDE **NSM** J W FOULGER

BECKENHAM (St James) (St Michael and All Angels) and St Augustine *Roch 13* **P** *Bp and SMF (jt)* **V** L C CARBERRY **C** G E LUNN

BECKENHAM (St John the Baptist) Eden Park *Roch 13* **P** *Ch Trust Fund Trust, Bp and Adn Bromley (jt)* **V** D E JONES **C** S A SMITH

BECKENHAM, NEW (St Paul) *Roch 13* **P** *Bp* **V** S P M COUPER

BECKERMET (St Bridget Old Church) *see Seatallan Carl*

BECKERMET (St Bridget) *as above*

BECKERMET (St John) *as above*

BECKFORD (St John the Baptist) *see Overbury w Teddington, Alstone etc Worc*

BECKHAM, WEST (St Helen and All Saints) *see Weybourne Gp Nor*

BECKINGHAM (All Saints) *see Brant Broughton and Beckingham Linc*

BECKINGHAM (All Saints), Walkeringham, Misterton, West Stockwith, Clayworth and Gringley-on-the-Hill *S'well 1* **P** *D&C York (3 turns), Ld Chanc (1 turn), Bp (1 turn)* **V** J D HENSON

BECKINGTON (St George) w Standerwick, Berkley, Rodden, Lullington and Orchardleigh *B & W 3* **P** *Bp (3 turns), Ch Soc Trust (1 turn), and Exors A Duckworth Esq* **R** *vacant*

BECKLEY (All Saints) *see Brede w Udimore and Beckley and Peasmarsh Chich*

BECKLEY (Assumption of the Blessed Virgin Mary), Forest Hill, Horton-cum-Studley and Stanton St John *Ox 20* **P** *Linc Coll Ox and New Coll Ox (jt)* **NSM** J C H M LEE

BECKTON (St Mark) *Chelmsf 5* **P** *Bp* **P-in-c** P M NGUGI

BECKWITHSHAW (St Michael and All Angels) *see Pannal w Beckwithshaw Leeds*

BECONTREE (St Cedd) *Chelmsf 1* **P** *Bp* **NSM** R A DOWLEY

BECONTREE (St Elisabeth) *Chelmsf 1* **P** *Bp* **V** S J HANNA

BECONTREE (St George) *Chelmsf 1* **P** *Bp* **V** *vacant*

BECONTREE (St Mary) *Chelmsf 1* **P** CPAS **V** K R MILLER

BECONTREE (St Thomas) *Chelmsf 1* **P** *Bp* **P-in-c** G H E STOCK

BECONTREE SOUTH (St Alban) (St John the Divine) (St Martin) *Chelmsf 1* **P** *Patr Bd* **TR** F BAILEY **OLM** R P C DESCOMBES

BEDALE (St Gregory) and Leeming and Thornton Watlass *Leeds 25* **P** *Bp, Sir Henry Beresford-Peirse Bt, R Kirklington w Burneston and Wath and Pickhill, and D S Dodsworth Esq (jt)* **R** S A MOOR

BEDDINGHAM (St Andrew) *see Glynde, W Firle and Beddingham Chich*

BEDDINGTON (St Mary) *S'wark 23* **P** *D&C* **R** A R FENBY

BEDDINGTON, SOUTH (St Michael and All Angels) and Roundshaw *S'wark 23* **P** *Bp* **V** A M A GBEBIKAN **C** P T FITZPATRICK

BEDFIELD (St Nicholas) *see Four Rivers St E*

BEDFONT, EAST (St Mary the Virgin) *Lon 11* **P** *Ld Chan* **V** P J SMITH

BEDFORD (All Saints) *St Alb 9* **P** *Bp* **P-in-c** P S DAVIES

BEDFORD (Christ Church) *St Alb 9* **P** *Bp* **V** R C HIBBERT **C** J G BELL

BEDFORD (St Andrew) *St Alb 9* **P** *Ld Chan* **V** J S REVELEY **C** D R GOLDTHORPE

BEDFORD (St John the Baptist) (St Leonard) *St Alb 9* **P** MMCET **R** V E BRYSON

BEDFORD (St Mark) *St Alb 9* **P** *Bp* **V** C ROYDEN

BEDFORD (St Martin) *St Alb 9* **P** *Bp* **V** A PIMENTA

BEDFORD (St Michael and All Angels) *see Elstow St Alb*

BEDFORD (St Paul) *St Alb 9* **P** *Bp* **V** K I GOSS

BEDFORD (St Peter de Merton) w St Cuthbert *St Alb 9* **P** *Ld Chan* **R** K F WOOLMER **NSM** R C SIMONS

BEDFORD LEIGH St Thomas (All Saints' Mission) *Man 19* **P** *V Leigh St Mary* **V** *vacant*

BEDFORD PARK (St Michael and All Angels) *Lon 11* **P** *Bp* **V** K J MORRIS **C** F PESCE, T G I COUPER **NSM** G MORGAN

BEDGROVE (Holy Spirit) *Ox 10* **P** DBP **V** M G KUHRT

BEDHAMPTON (St Nicholas's Mission Church) (St Thomas) *Portsm 5* **P** *Bp* **R** M D CROSS

BEDINGFIELD (St Mary) *see Eye St E*

BEDINGHAM (St Andrew) *see Hempnall Nor*

BEDLINGTON (St Cuthbert), Cambois and Sleekburn *Newc 1* **P** *D&C Dur and D&C (alt)* **V** I J HENNEBRY

BEDMINSTER (St Aldhelm) (St Paul) *Bris 1* **P** *Bp* **P-in-c** N J HAY **C** A J CARTER, A J DOARKS, J C KEAN, L E DOE, M L SOUTHCOMBE

BEDMINSTER (St Michael and All Angels) *Bris 1* **P** *Bp* **P-in-c** A J DOARKS

BEDMINSTER DOWN (St Oswald) *see Bishopsworth and Bedminster Down Bris*

BEDMOND (Ascension) *see Abbots Langley St Alb*

BEDNALL (All Saints) *see Penkridge Lich*

BEDSTONE (St Mary) *see Middle Marches Heref*

BEDWORTH (All Saints) *Cov 5* **P** *Patr Bd* **TR** D E POULTNEY

BEDWYN, GREAT (St Mary) *see Savernake Sarum*

BEDWYN, LITTLE (St Michael) *as above*

BEECH (St Peter) *see Alton Win*

BEECH HILL (St Mary the Virgin) *see Loddon Reach Ox*

BEECH, HIGH (Holy Innocents) *see Waltham H Cross Chelmsf*

BEECHDALE ESTATE (St Chad) *see Blakenall Heath Lich*

BEECHINGSTOKE (St Stephen) *see Vale of Pewsey Sarum*

BEEDING (St Peter) and Bramber w Botolphs *Chich 11* **P** *Bp* **R** E J GRAEME **C** S H TUPPER

BEEDING, LOWER (Holy Trinity) (St John the Evangelist) *Chich 7* **P** *Bp* **V** *vacant*

BEEDON (St Nicholas) *see E Downland Ox*

BEEFORD (St Leonard) w Frodingham and Foston *York 11* **P** *Abp and Ch Soc Trust (jt)* **R** J E GRAINGER-SMITH **NSM** M M DESBOROUGH, S E HEBDEN

BEELEY (St Anne) and Edensor *Derby 4* **P** *Duke of Devonshire* **V** D PERKINS

BEELSBY (St Andrew) *see Wolds Gateway Group Linc*

BEENHAM VALENCE (St Mary) *see Aldermaston and Woolhampton Ox*

BEER (St Michael) *see Seaton and Beer Ex*

BEER HACKETT (St Michael) *see Three Valleys Sarum*

BEERCROCOMBE (St James) *see Beercrocombe w Curry Mallet, Hatch Beauchamp etc B & W*

BEERCROCOMBE (St James) w Curry Mallet, Hatch Beauchamp, Orchard Portman, Staple Fitzpaine, Stoke St Mary w Thurlbear and West Hatch *B & W 16* **P** *Bp, Ch Trust Fund Trust, and D&C (4 turns), Duchy of Cornwall (1 turn)* **Hon C** S R JONES **NSM** C R AGER

BEESANDS (St Andrew) *see Stokenham, Slapton, Charleton w Buckland etc Ex*

BEESBY (St Andrew) *see Alford Gp Linc*

BEESTON (St John the Baptist) *S'well 9* **P** *Duke of Devonshire* **V** W R PLIMMER **C** T F BYRNE **NSM** K D BUCHAN, R C W WIGGINS

BEESTON (St Lawrence) *see Ashmanhaugh, Barton Turf etc Nor*

BEESTON (St Mary the Virgin) *Leeds 14* **P** *Patr Bd* **P-in-c** L C PEARSON **NSM** O OGUNYINKA

BEESTON NEXT MILEHAM (St Mary the Virgin) *see Launditch and the Upper Nar Nor*

BEESTON REGIS (All Saints) *see Aylmerton, Runton, Beeston Regis and Gresham Nor*

BEETHAM (St Michael and All Angels) *Carl 10* **P** *Bp* **P-in-c** A B NORMAN

BEETLEY (St Mary) *see Dereham and Distr Nor*

BEGBROKE (St Michael) *see Yarnton w Begbroke and Shipton-on-Cherwell Ox*

BEIGHTON (All Saints) *see Acle and Bure to Yare Nor*

BEIGHTON (St Mary the Virgin) *Sheff 1* **P** *Bp* **P-in-c** M H E HEALEY

BEKESBOURNE (St Peter) *see Bridge Cant*

BELAUGH (St Peter) *see Wroxham w Hoveton, Belaugh and Tunstead etc Nor*

BELBROUGHTON (Holy Trinity) w Fairfield and Clent *Worc 12* **P** *Ld Chan and St Jo Coll Ox (alt)* **C** S J OLIVER **Hon C** R J C NEWTON

BELCHALWELL (St Aldheim) *see Hazelbury Bryan and the Hillside Par Sarum*

BELCHAMP (St Paul and St Andrew) *see N Hinckford Chelmsf*

BELCHAMP OTTEN (St Ethelbert and All Saints) *as above*

BELCHAMP WALTER (St Mary the Virgin) *as above*

BELCHFORD (St Peter and St Paul) *see Hemingby Gp Linc*

BELFIELD (St Ann) *Man 17* **P** *Bp* **P-in-c** G BARNETT **NSM** S E WARD

BELFORD (St Mary) and Lucker *Newc 7* **P** *V Bamburgh and Beadnell and Bp (alt)* **P-in-c** L M TAYLOR-KENYON

BELGRAVE (All Saints) *see Leic Resurr Leic*

BELGRAVE (St Peter) *as above*

BELHUS PARK (All Saints) *see Mardyke Chelmsf*

BELLE ABBEY (St Cairbre) *see Arbory and Castletown S & M*

BELLE GREEN (Mission) *see Wigan All SS Liv*

BELLE ISLE (St John and St Barnabas) and Hunslet *Leeds 14* **P** *Bp and R Leeds City* **V** A C N BUCKLEY

BELLEAU (St John the Baptist) *see Legbourne and Wold Marsh Linc*

BELLERBY (St John) *see Leyburn w Bellerby Leeds*

BELLINGDON (St John the Evangelist) *see Gt Chesham Ox*

BELLINGHAM (St Cuthbert) *see* N Tyne and Redesdale *Newc*
BELLINGHAM (St Dunstan) *S'wark 4* **P** *Bp* **P-in-c** T B SINGH **NSM** D L RILEY
BELMONT (St Anselm) *Lon 23* **P** *Bp* **V** C M A ROBINSON
BELMONT (St John) *S'wark 23* **P** *R Cheam* **V** vacant
BELMONT (St Mary Magdalene) and Pittington *Dur 1* **P** *The Crown and D&C (alt)* **P-in-c** H MURRAY **C** E J HOLLIS
BELMONT (St Peter) *see* Turton Moorland *Man*
BELPER (Christ Church) w Turnditch *Derby 6* **P** *Bp* **V** J M PAGE **NSM** B G JOHNSON
BELPER (St Peter) *Derby 6* **P** *V Duffield* **V** A M STRATTON **C** J M LYON **NSM** A TOMPKINS
BELSIZE PARK (St Peter) *Lon 16* **P** *D&C Westmr* **P-in-c** P S NICHOLSON
BELSTEAD (St Mary the Virgin) *see* Sproughton w Burstall, Copdock w Washbrook etc *St E*
BELSTONE (St Mary) *see* Okehampton, Inwardleigh, Belstone, Sourton etc *Ex*
BELTINGHAM (St Cuthbert) *see* Haydon Bridge and Beltingham w Henshaw *Newc*
BELTISLOE, NORTH Group, comprising Bassingthorpe w Westby, Bitchfield, Boothby Pagnell, Burton le Coggles, Ingoldsby, Lenton, Old Somerby, Ropsley, and Sapperton w Braceby *Linc 17* **P** *Ch Coll Cam, Sir Lyonel Tollemache Bt, D&C, Bp, DBP, Sir Richard Welby Bt, and Baroness Willoughby de Eresby (jt)* **P-in-c** A K E SORENSEN **OLM** M KING
BELTON (All Saints) and Burgh Castle *Nor 6* **P** *Bp and Ld Chan (alt)* **R** R J BUNN **OLM** V E T RIDPATH
BELTON (St John the Baptist) *see* Kegworth, Hathern, Long Whatton, Diseworth etc *Leic*
BELTON (St Peter and St Paul) *see* S Cliff Villages Gp *Linc*
BELTON (St Peter) *see* Uppingham w Ayston and Belton w Wardley *Pet*
BELTON Group, The (All Saints), including Althorpe and Keadby, and Amcotts *Linc 1* **P** *Bp and The Crown (alt)* **V** C KAY
BELVEDERE (All Saints) *Roch 15* **P** *DBP* **P-in-c** S F ARCHER
BELVEDERE (St Augustine) *Roch 15* **P** *Bp* **V** C W JONES
BEMBRIDGE (Holy Trinity) (St Luke's Mission Church) *Portsm 7* **P** *V Brading* **P-in-c** A E BLOOR
BEMERTON (St Andrew) (St John the Evangelist) (St Michael and All Angels) *Sarum 13* **P** *The Crown (2 turns) and Bp (1 turn)* **TR** vacant
BEMPTON (St Michael) w Flamborough, Reighton w Speeton *York 9* **P** *Patr Bd* **P-in-c** S J PENN
BEN RHYDDING (St John the Evangelist) *Leeds 4* **P** *V Ilkey* **V** P WILLOX **NSM** J H COPSEY
BENCHILL (St Luke the Physician) *see* Wythenshawe *Man*
BENEFIELD (St Mary the Virgin) *see* Oundle w Ashton and Benefield w Glapthorn *Pet*
BENENDEN (St George and St Margaret) and Sandhurst *Cant 12* **P** *Abp* **V** D J COMMANDER
BENFIELDSIDE (St Cuthbert) *Dur 4* **P** *Bp* **V** M JACKSON
BENFLEET, SOUTH (St Mary the Virgin) *Chelmsf 13* **P** *D&C Westmr* **V** L S DRAKE
BENGEO (Holy Trinity) *see* Hertford *St Alb*
BENGEO (St Leonard) *as above*
BENGEWORTH (St Peter) and Hampton w Sedgeberrow and Hinton-on-the-Green *Worc 1* **P** *Patr Bd* **R** M J G BINNEY **NSM** N M WRIGHT
BENHALL (St Mary) *see* Alde River *St E*
BENHILTON (All Saints) *S'wark 23* **P** *Bp* **V** D E CHISLETT
BENINGTON (St Peter) *see* Ardeley, Benington, Cottered w Throcking etc *St Alb*
BENNETTS END (St Benedict) *see* Langelei *St Alb*
BENNIWORTH (St Julian) *see* Asterby Gp *Linc*
BENSHAM AND TEAMS (St Chad) *Dur 11* **P** *Bp* **V** M M GILLEY **C** A I G CRAWFORD, Y GREENER
BENSON (St Helen) w Ewelme *Ox 20* **P** *Merton Coll Ox, Ch Ch Ox, and Brigadier J N B Mogg (1 turn), The Crown (1 turn)* **R** P E GILDAY **S** M COUSINS
BENTHAM (St John the Baptist), Burton-in-Lonsdale, Chapel-le-Dale, Ingleton and Thornton-in-Lonsdale *Leeds 20* **P** *Bp* **TR** A RUSSELL **TV** D S TATE, W N D TRENHOLME
BENTILEE (St Stephen) *see* Bucknall *Lich*
BENTLEY (Emmanuel) and Willenhall Holy Trinity *Lich 28* **P** *Patr Bd* **TR** J D DEAKIN **TV** H L DUCKETT, S L HOUGH
BENTLEY (St Mary) *see* Sproughton w Burstall, Copdock w Washbrook etc *St E*
BENTLEY (St Mary), Binsted and Froyle *Win 2* **P** *D&C, Adn Surrey, and Guild of All So (jt)* **R** Y DUBREUIL **NSM** C W OGILVIE THOMPSON
BENTLEY (St Peter) *Sheff 7* **P** *Bp* **V** D N BERRY
BENTLEY COMMON (St Paul), Kelvedon Hatch and Navestock *Chelmsf 8* **P** *Bp* **NSM** J W BIDDULPH

BENTLEY HEATH (St James) *see* Dorridge *Birm*
BENTLEY, GREAT (St Mary the Virgin) *see* St Osyth and Great Bentley *Chelmsf*
BENTLEY, LITTLE (St Mary) *see* Lawford, Lt Bentley and The Bromleys *Chelmsf*
BENTLEY, LOWER (St Mary) *see* Tardebigge *Worc*
BENTLEY, NEW (St Philip and St James) w Arksey *Sheff 7* **P** *Bp and DBP (jt)* **V** S P DICKINSON
BENTWORTH (St Mary), Lasham, Medstead and Shalden *Win 2* **P** *J L Jervoise Esq and Ld Chan (alt)* **P-in-c** E B PRUEN
BENWELL (St James) (St John) (Venerable Bede) and Scotswood Team, The *Newc 4* **P** *Bp* **TR** A D KIRKWOOD **TV** D J COAD **C** C D MINCHIN
BEOLEY (St Leonard) *see* Redditch H Trin *Worc*
BEOLEY Church Hill (St Andrew's Church Centre) *as above*
BEPTON (St Mary) *see* Cocking w W Lavington, Bepton and Heyshott *Chich*
BERDEN (St Nicholas) *see* Clavering w Langley, Arkesden etc *Chelmsf*
BERE ALSTON (Holy Trinity) *see* Bere Ferrers *Ex*
BERE FERRERS (St Andrew) *Ex 22* **P** *DBP* **R** N C LAW **C** D OAKLEY
BERE REGIS (St John the Baptist) *see* W Purbeck *Sarum*
BERECHURCH (St Margaret w St Michael) *Chelmsf 21* **P** *Bp* **NSM** J SAMS
BERGH APTON (St Peter and St Paul) *see* Thurton w Ashby St Mary, Bergh Apton etc *Nor*
BERGHOLT, EAST (St Mary the Virgin) and Brantham *St E 15* **P** *Em Coll Cam* **R** S VAN DER TOORN **NSM** R J NEEDLE
BERGHOLT, WEST (St Mary the Virgin) and Great Horkesley *Chelmsf 21* **P** *Bp and Ball Coll Ox (alt)* **P-in-c** A J ELMES **C** H R COOPER, R G GIBBS, S L HAYWARD **NSM** A L MASON, P W MANN
BERINSFIELD (St Mary and St Berin) *see* Dorchester *Ox*
BERKELEY (St Mary the Virgin) w Wick, Breadstone, Newport, Stone, Woodford and Hill *Glouc 5* **P** *Bp, Berkeley Will Trustees, and Mrs J D Jenner-Fust (jt)* **V** J M MCHALE
BERKHAMSTED, GREAT (All Saints) (St Peter), Great Gaddesden, Little Gaddesden, Nettleden and Potten End *St Alb 1* **P** *Patr Bd* **TR** T W PILKINGTON **TV** J B RUSSELL **C** S J VIVIAN **NSM** L GEOGHEGAN
BERKHAMSTED, LITTLE (St Andrew) and Bayford, Essendon and Ponsbourne *St Alb 19* **P** *Marquess of Salisbury (2 turns), CPAS (1 turn), and Bp (1 turn)* **R** vacant
BERKHAMSYTCH (St Mary and St John) *see* Butterton, Ipstones-w-Berkhamsytch etc *Lich*
BERKLEY (Blessed Virgin Mary) *see* Beckington w Standerwick, Berkley, Rodden etc *B & W*
BERKSWELL (St John the Baptist) *Cov 4* **P** *Trustees Col C J H Wheatley* **R** M Q BRATTON **C** E A HOLLAND
BERMONDSEY (St Hugh) Charterhouse Mission Conventional District *S'wark 10* **C** D W D ADAMSON **Min** M G RAWSON
BERMONDSEY (St James w Christ Church) (St Anne) *S'wark 7* **P** *Bp, R Bermondsey St Mary, and F W Smith Esq (3 turns), The Crown (1 turn)* **V** G J JENKINS **C** J L C MERCER **NSM** S O LEWIS
BERMONDSEY (St Katharine) w St Bartholomew *S'wark 7* **P** *Bp and R Rotherhithe St Mary w All SS (jt)* **P-in-c** M R NICHOLLS **NSM** E J F GBONDA
BERMONDSEY (St Mary Magdalen w St Olave, St John and St Luke) *S'wark 7* **P** *Ch Patr Soc (2 turns), Ld Chan (1 turn), and Bp (1 turn)* **R** C D MOORE
BERNWODE, comprising Ashendon, Boarstall, Brill, Chilton, Dorton, Ludgershall, and Wotton Underwood *Ox 10* **P** *Bp, CPAS, Earl Temple of Stowe, and Sir Henry Aubrey-Fletcher Bt (jt)* **R** P E SLUSAR **C** J EDMANS
BERRICK SALOME (St Helen) *see* Chalgrove w Berrick Salome *Ox*
BERRINGTON (All Saints) *see* Wenlock *Heref*
BERROW (Blessed Virgin Mary) and Breane *B & W 1* **P** *Adn Wells* **P-in-c** J M PHILPOTT **C** J M A BARR
BERROW (St Faith) w Pendock, Eldersfield, Hollybush and Birtsmorton *Worc 5* **P** *Bp, D&C, and Exors Sir Berwick Lechmere Bt (jt)* **R** J M JAMES **NSM** A E L ELSTON
BERRY POMEROY (St Mary) *see* Totnes w Bridgetown, Berry Pomeroy etc *Ex*
BERRY, GREAT (St John) *see* Langdon Hills *Chelmsf*
BERRYNARBOR (St Peter) *see* Ilfracombe SS Phil and Jas, Combe Martin and Berrynarbor *Ex*
BERSTED, NORTH (Holy Cross) *Chich 1* **P** *Abp* **V** J C KING
BERSTED, SOUTH (St Mary Magdalene) w NORTH *Chich 1* **P** *Abp* **V** T M CROOK

BERWICK (Holy Trinity) (St Mary) *Newc 12* **P** *Bp (2 turns), D&C Dur (1 turn)* **V** D F HANDLEY

BERWICK (St John) *see Chalke Valley Sarum*

BERWICK (St Michael and All Angels) *see Arlington, Berwick, Selmeston w Alciston etc Chich*

BERWICK ST JAMES (St James) *see Wylye and Till Valley Sarum*

BESFORD (St Peter's Chapelry) *see Defford w Besford Worc*

BESSACARR, WEST (St Francis of Assisi) *Sheff 8* **P** *Bp* **V** R A HEARD

BESSELSLEIGH (St Lawrence) *Ox 19* **P** *Ox Ch Trust* **R** K W CAMPBELL

BESSINGBY (St Magnus) *see Bridlington Ch Ch w Bessingby and Ulrome York*

BESSINGBY (St Mark) *as above*

BESSINGHAM (St Mary) *see Roughton and Felbrigg, Metton, Sustead etc Nor*

BESTHORPE (All Saints) *see Attleborough w Besthorpe Nor*

BESTHORPE (Holy Trinity) *see E Trent S'well*

BESTWOOD (Emmanuel) (St Mark) w Rise Park *S'well 8* **P** *Bp and Ch Patr Trust (jt)* **V** N J BATES **C** C LITTLE

BESTWOOD (St Matthew on the Hill) (St Philip) *S'well 8* **P** *Bp and Ch Patr Trust (jt)* **V** E A MORRIS

BESTWOOD PARK (no dedication) *S'well 8* **P** *Bp and Ch Patr Trust (jt)* **V** *vacant*

BESWICK (St Margaret) *see Hutton Cranswick w Skerne, Watton and Beswick York*

BETCHWORTH (St Michael and All Angels) and Buckland *S'wark 24* **P** *D&C Windsor and All So Coll Ox (jt)* **R** A MOORE

BETHERSDEN (St Margaret) w High Halden and Woodchurch *Cant 10* **P** *Abp* **P-in-c** S J WHARTON

BETHESDA (Shared Church) *see Hallwood Ecum Par Ches*

BETHNAL GREEN (St Barnabas) *Lon 7* **P** *D&C Cant* **V** B C RALPH **NSM** S M LEE

BETHNAL GREEN (St James the Less) *Lon 7* **P** *CPAS* **V** C D NEWMAN-DAY

BETHNAL GREEN (St John) *see St Jo on Bethnal Green Lon*

BETHNAL GREEN (St Matthew w St James the Great) *Lon 7* **P** *Bp* **R** E M CLARK **NSM** J E BLACKBURN

BETHNAL GREEN (St Peter) (St Thomas) *Lon 7* **P** *City Corp* **V** H M A ATKINSON **C** T G MAY

BETLEY (St Margaret) *Lich 9* **P** *DBP* **V** P T CHANTRY **C** J J BESWICK PALLISTER **NSM** G A BAILEY

BETTISCOMBE (St Stephen) *see Golden Cap Team Sarum*

BETTON STRANGE (St Margaret) *see Wenlock Heref*

BETTWS-Y-CRWYN (St Mary) *see Clun Valley Heref*

BEVENDEAN (Holy Nativity) *see Moulsecoomb Chich*

BEVERLEY (St Mary) *York 8* **P** *Abp* **V** R A LUMLEY **NSM** A R DOOLAN

BEVERLEY (St Nicholas) *York 8* **P** *Abp* **V** M R PEATMAN **NSM** E A ALMOND

BEVERLEY MINSTER (St John and St Martin) *York 8* **P** *Simeon's Trustees* **V** J W BAKER **C** T P KELLY, W A WALE

BEVERSTON (St Mary the Virgin) *see Tetbury, Beverston, Long Newnton etc Glouc*

BEWBUSH (St Mary Magdalene) *see Gossops Green and Bewbush Chich*

BEWCASTLE (St Cuthbert), Stapleton and Kirklinton w Hethersgill *Carl 2* **P** *Bp, D&C, and DBP (jt)* **P-in-c** R P C BROWN

BEWDLEY (St Anne) *see Ribbesford w Bewdley and Dowles and Wribbenhall Worc*

BEWERLEY GRANGE (Chapel) *see Upper Nidderdale Leeds*

BEWHOLME (St John the Baptist) *see Sigglesthorne w Nunkeeling and Bewholme York*

BEWICK, OLD (Holy Trinity) *see Chatton w Chillingham, Eglingham and S Charlton and Ingram Newc*

BEWSBOROUGH, comprising Barfreystone, Coldred, Eythorne, Sibertswold, and Whitfield *Cant 7* **P** *Abp, D&C, St Jo Coll Ox, and Earl of Guilford (jt)* **R** *vacant*

BEXHILL (All Saints) *see Sidley Chich*

BEXHILL (St Augustine) *Chich 12* **P** *Bp* **V** R COATES

BEXHILL (St Barnabas) *Chich 12* **P** *Bp* **P-in-c** M J BAILEY **C** A G J BIRKS **Hon C** S D HUGGINS

BEXHILL (St Mark) *Chich 12* **P** *Bp* **R** J J FRAIS

BEXHILL (St Peter) (St Michael) (Good Shepherd) (St Andrew) *Chich 12* **P** *Bp* **TR** D S REYNISH **TV** S R EARL **NSM** O M WERRETT

BEXHILL (St Stephen) *Chich 12* **P** *Bp* **P-in-c** K J ROBINSON

BEXLEY Team Ministry (St John the Evangelist) (St Mary) *Roch 17* **P** *The Crown and Patr Bd (alt)* **TR** R E L HARDING **TV** C M WOOD, E R BARLOW **NSM** S E TWYNAM

BEXLEYHEATH (Christ Church) *Roch 15* **P** *Bp* **V** T WYATT

BEXLEYHEATH (St Peter) *Roch 15* **P** *Bp* **V** J R CHARLES

BEXWELL (St Mary) *see Denver and Ryston w Roxham etc Ely*

BEYTON (All Saints) *see Rougham, Beyton w Hessett and Rushbrooke St E*

BIBURY (St Mary) *see S Cotswolds Glouc*

BICESTER (St Edburg) w Bucknell, Caversfield and Launton *Ox 21* **P** *Patr Bd* **TR** V BREED **TV** I R BISCOE, P G WRIGHT **C** A C BECKERLEG, E J BISCOE **NSM** C HILL, P G HILL

BICKENHILL (St Peter) *see Hampton-in-Arden w Bickenhill Birm*

BICKER (St Swithin) *see Haven Gp Linc*

BICKERSHAW (St James and St Elizabeth) *see Chapelfields Liv*

BICKERSTAFFE (Holy Trinity) *see Aughton St Mich and Bickerstaffe Liv*

BICKERTON (Holy Trinity) *see Malpas and Threapwood and Bickerton Ches*

BICKINGTON (St Andrew) *see Fremington, Instow and Westleigh Ex*

BICKINGTON (St Mary the Virgin) *see Ashburton, Bickington, Buckland in the Moor etc Ex*

BICKINGTON, HIGH (St Mary) *see Newton Tracey, Horwood, Alverdiscott etc Ex*

BICKLEIGH (St Mary) *see Silverton, Butterleigh, Bickleigh and Cadeleigh Ex*

BICKLEIGH Roborough (St Mary the Virgin) and Shaugh Prior *Ex 21* **P** *Patr Bd* **P-in-c** S P RUNDELL **C** C J ROUTLEDGE **NSM** M J FAIRALL

BICKLEY (St George) *Roch 14* **P** *SMF* **V** R J NORMAN

BICKLEY (St Wenefrede) *Ches 5* **P** *Marquess of Cholmondeley* **P-in-c** J DIGGLE

BICKNACRE (St Andrew) *see Woodham Ferrers and Bicknacre Chelmsf*

BICKNOLLER (St George) *see Quantock Towers B & W*

BICKNOR (St James) *see Tunstall and Bredgar Cant*

BICTON (Holy Trinity), Montford w Shrawardine and Fitz *Lich 19* **P** *Earl of Powis, N E E Stephens Esq, and J G O Wingfield Esq (jt)* **P-in-c** M TOOP **C** H M LINS, P G ALLAN

BICTON (St Mary) *see Budleigh Salterton, E Budleigh w Bicton etc Ex*

BIDBOROUGH (St Lawrence) and Southborough St Peter *Roch 12* **P** *CPAS Patr Trust* **R** S A HILLS

BIDDENDEN (All Saints) and Smarden *Cant 10* **P** *Abp* **P-in-c** A BIENFAIT

BIDDENHAM (St James) *St Alb 9* **P** *Bp* **V** E J LOMAX

BIDDESTONE (St Nicholas) *see By Brook Bris*

BIDDISHAM (St John the Baptist) *see Crook Peak B & W*

BIDDLESDEN (St Margaret) *see W Buckingham Ox*

BIDDULPH (St Lawrence) *Lich 8* **P** *MMCET* **V** S J DYSON

BIDDULPH MOOR (Christ Church) and Knypersley *Lich 8* **P** *Ch Patr Trust and MMCET (jt)* **R** D A FRASER

BIDEFORD (St Mary), Landcross, Littleham, Monkleigh, and Weare Gifford *Ex 15* **P** *Patr Bd* **TR** C P ROSE-CASEMORE **TV** M COCKFIELD **NSM** A GLOVER

BIDFORD-ON-AVON (St Laurence) *see Heart of England Cov*

BIDSTON (St Oswald) *Ches 1* **P** *Bp* **V** R E IVESON

BIELBY (St Giles) *see Holme and Seaton Ross Gp York*

BIERLEY (St John the Evangelist) *Leeds 3* **P** *Bp* **V** P A WHEELHOUSE

BIERLEY, EAST (St Luke) *see Birkenshaw w Hunsworth Leeds*

BIERTON (St James the Great) and Hulcott *Ox 10* **P** *Bp and D&C Linc (jt)* **V** *vacant*

BIGBURY (St Lawrence) *see Modbury, Bigbury, Ringmore etc Ex*

BIGBY (All Saints) *see Brocklesby Park, Croxton and North Wolds Linc*

BIGGIN (St Thomas) *see Taddington, Chelmorton and Monyash etc Derby*

BIGGIN HILL (St Mark) *Roch 16* **P** *Bp* **V** A M NEWMAN **C** R L ARCHER

BIGGLESWADE (St Andrew) *St Alb 10* **P** *Bp* **V** G C SCOTT

BIGHTON (All Saints) *see Arle Valley Win*

BIGNOR (Holy Cross) *see Barlavington, Burton w Coates, Sutton and Bignor Chich*

BIGRIGG (St John) *see Egremont and Haile Carl*

BILBOROUGH (St John) (St Martin) and Strelley *S'well 8* **P** *SMF and Bp (jt)* **P-in-c** R T K ATKINSON **C** P W SHAW

BILBROOK (Holy Cross) *see Tettenhall Regis Lich*

BILBROUGH (St James) *see Marston Moor York*

BILDESTON (St Mary Magdalene) w Wattisham and Lindsey, Whatfield w Semer, Nedging and Naughton *St E 4* **P** *Abp, Bp, CPAS, Jes Coll Cam, and Reformation Ch Trust (jt)* **R** *vacant*

BILHAM, comprising Brodsworth, Frickley, Hooton Pagnell, and Marr *Sheff 12* **P** *Bp, Major W Warde-Aldam,*

W G A Warde-Norbury Esq, and Mrs S Grant-Dalton (jt)
P-in-c K HERROD
BILLERICAY (Christ Church) (Emmanuel) (St John the Divine) (St Mary Magdalen) and Little Bursted
Chelmsf 12 **P** *Bp* **TR** P A CARR **NSM** M J FOWLER
BILLESDON (St John the Baptist) *see* Coplow *Leic*
BILLESLEY COMMON (Holy Cross) *Birm 4* **P** *Bp*
V D M COLLINS
BILLING, GREAT (St Andrew) w LITTLE (All Saints) *Pet 4*
P *BNC Ox and Bp (alt)* **R** R J BURBIDGE **Hon C** D LUNN
BILLINGBOROUGH Group, The (St Andrew), including
Aslackby, Dowsby, Horbling, and Sempringham w Pointon
Linc 14 **P** *The Crown (2 turns), Bp and St Jo Coll Dur (1 turn)*
P-in-c N A KNOX **C** J C WATT **OLM** J G SPREADBURY
BILLINGE (St Aidan) *Liv 15* **P** *R Wigan* **V** *vacant*
BILLINGFORD (St Leonard) *see* Redenhall w Scole *Nor*
BILLINGFORD (St Peter) *see* Heart of Norfolk *Nor*
BILLINGHAM (St Aidan) (St Cuthbert) (St Luke) (St Mary Magdalene) (St Peter) *Dur 9* **P** *Patr Bd* **TV** R B RADLEY
NSM P J JOHNSON
BILLINGHAY (St Michael) *see* Carr Dyke Gp *Linc*
BILLINGSHURST (St Mary) *Chich 7* **P** *Bp* **V** D M BEAL
BILLINGSLEY (St Mary) *see* Highley w Billingsley, Glazeley
etc *Heref*
BILLINGTON (St Michael and All Angels) *see* Ouzel Valley
St Alb
BILLOCKBY (All Saints) *see* S Trin Broads *Nor*
BILLY MILL (St Aidan) *Newc 5* **P** *Bp* **V** P S BAGSHAW
BILNEY, EAST (St Mary) *see* Dereham and Distr *Nor*
BILSBORROW (St Hilda) *see* Fellside Team *Blackb*
BILSBY (Holy Trinity) *see* Alford Gp *Linc*
BILSDALE MIDCABLE (St John) *see* Upper Ryedale *York*
BILSDALE PRIORY (St Hilda) *see* Ingleby Greenhow, Bilsdale
Priory etc *York*
BILSINGTON (St Peter and St Paul) *see* Saxon Shoreline *Cant*
BILSON (Mission Church) *see* Cinderford w Littledean *Glouc*
BILSTHORPE (St Margaret) *S'well 3* **P** *DBP*
P-in-c Z BURTON **C** A K ALLS **NSM** M A GROVES
BILSTON (St Leonard) (St Chad) (St Mary the Virgin)
Lich 27 **P** *Patr Bd* **TR** D WILLS **TV** S P SKIDMORE
BILTON (St John the Evangelist) and St Luke *Leeds 21* **P** *Bp*
TR S P DOWSON **TV** A PATRICK **C** R K DONEGAN-CROSS
BILTON (St Mark) *Cov 6* **P** N M Assheton Esq
R T D COCKELL **C** J E SMITH
BILTON IN HOLDERNESS (St Peter) *York 12* **P** *Abp*
V *vacant*
BILTON, NEW (St Matthew and St Oswald) *see* Rugby W *Cov*
BILTON-IN-AINSTY (St Helen) *see* Rural Ainsty *York*
BINBROOK Group, The (St Mary), including Kelstern,
Ludford Magna, Swinhope, Thorganby, and Wold Newton
Linc 4 **P** *Ld Chan, DBP and G F Sleight Esq (alt)*
R P J MCEUNE
BINCOMBE (Holy Trinity) *see* Weymouth Ridgeway *Sarum*
BINEGAR (Holy Trinity) *see* Beacon Trinity *B & W*
BINFIELD (All Saints) (St Mark) *Ox 3* **P** *Ld Chan*
R L A J TAYLOR
BINGFIELD (St Mary) *see* St Oswald in Lee w Bingfield *Newc*
BINGHAM (St Mary and All Saints) *S'well 5* **P** *The Crown*
R J J G WRIGHT
BINGLEY (All Saints) *Leeds 1* **P** *Bp* **V** M G WEAVER
C P MAYO-SMITH, R H DOWSON
BINGLEY (Holy Trinity) *Leeds 1* **P** *Bp* **V** A J CLARKE
BINHAM (St Mary) *see* Stiffkey and Bale *Nor*
BINLEY (St Bartholomew) *Cov 1* **P** *Bp* **V** J P TAYLOR
BINSEY (St Margaret) *see* Osney *Ox*
BINSEY Team Ministry, comprising Allhallows,
Bassenthwaite, Bolton All Saints, Ireby, Isel, Plumbland,
Setmurthy, Torpenhow, Uldale, and Wythop *Carl 6* **P** *Patr*
Bd **TR** S J BANKS **TV** P W GILROY
NSM C C FRYER-SPEDDING
BINSTEAD (Holy Cross) *Portsm 7* **P** *Bp* **R** V M BROWN
BINSTED (Holy Cross) *see* Bentley, Binsted and Froyle *Win*
BINSTED (St Mary) *see* Walberton w Binsted *Chich*
BINTON (St Peter) *see* Heart of England *Cov*
BINTREE (St Swithin) *see* Heart of Norfolk *Nor*
BIRCH (St James) w Fallowfield *Man 3* **P** *Bp* **R** R M YOUNG
NSM J WALKER
BIRCH (St Mary) *see* Langley *Man*
BIRCHAM NEWTON (All Saints) *see* Docking, The Birchams,
Fring etc *Nor*
BIRCHAM, GREAT (St Mary the Virgin) *as above*
BIRCHANGER (St Mary the Virgin) *see* Stansted Mountfitchet
w Birchanger and Farnham *Chelmsf*
BIRCHENCLIFFE (St Philip the Apostle) *see* Birkby and
Birchencliffe *Leeds*
BIRCHES HEAD (St Matthew) *see* Hanley H Ev *Lich*

BIRCHFIELD (Holy Trinity) *Birm 2* **P** *Bp* **V** E I PITTS
BIRCHILLS, THE (St Andrew) *see* Walsall St Andr *Lich*
BIRCHIN COPPICE (St Peter) *see* Kidderminster St Jo and H
Innocents *Worc*
BIRCHINGTON (All Saints) w Acol and Minnis Bay *Cant 5*
P *Abp* **V** *vacant*
**BIRCH-IN-RUSHOLME (St Agnes) w Longsight St John w
St Cyprian** *Man 1* **P** *The Crown and Bp (alt)*
P-in-c E O ADOYO
BIRCHMOOR (St John) *see* Polesworth *Birm*
BIRCHOVER (St Michael) *see* Youlgreave, Middleton,
Stanton-in-Peak etc *Derby*
BIRCHWOOD (Mission Church) *see* Blackdown *B & W*
BIRCHWOOD (St Luke) *Linc 11* **P** *Bp* **V** L M HARRIS
BIRCHWOOD (Transfiguration) *see* Warrington E *Liv*
BIRCLE (St John the Baptist) *Man 8* **P** *R Middleton St Leon*
V *vacant*
BIRDBROOK (St Augustine) *see* Two Rivers *Chelmsf*
BIRDHAM (St James) *see* W Wittering and Birdham w
Itchenor *Chich*
BIRDINGBURY (St Leonards) *see* Draycote Gp *Cov*
BIRDLIP (St Mary in Hamlet) *see* Brimpsfield w Birdlip, Syde,
Daglingworth etc *Glouc*
BIRDSALL (St Mary) *see* W Buckrose *York*
BIRKBY (St Cuthbert) Huddersfield and Birchencliffe
Leeds 11 **P** *V Lindley and Bp (jt)* **V** J P HUSTWICK
OLM J SARGENT
**BIRKBY (St John the Evangelist) Huddersfield and
Woodhouse** *Leeds 11* **P** *Bp and DBP (jt)* **V** *vacant*
BIRKBY (St Peter) *see* Wiske Benefice *Leeds*
BIRKDALE (St James) *Liv 9* **P** *Trustees* **V** I G MAINEY
BIRKDALE (St John) *Liv 9* **P** *Trustees* **P-in-c** J P LEFFLER
BIRKDALE (St Peter) *Liv 9* **P** *Trustees* **P-in-c** I G MAINEY
BIRKENHEAD (Christ Church) *Ches 1* **P** *Bp*
P-in-c G V TETZLAFF **NSM** A W GOODE
BIRKENHEAD (St James) w St Bede *Ches 1* **P** *Trustees*
V K P ADDENBROOKE
BIRKENHEAD PRIORY (Christ the King) *Ches 1* **P** *Patr Bd*
R P N BENTLEY
BIRKENSHAW (St Paul) w Hunsworth *Leeds 6* **P** *V Birstall*
P-in-c K NICHOLL **NSM** C WALKER **OLM** R DAVIDSON
BIRKIN (St Mary) *see* Haddlesey w Hambleton and Birkin
York
BIRLEY (St Peter) *see* Canon Pyon w King's Pyon, Birley and
Wellington *Heref*
BIRLING (All Saints), Addington, Ryarsh and Trottiscliffe
Roch 7 **P** R L K SHUKER
BIRLING, LOWER (Christ Church) *see* Snodland All SS w Ch
Ch *Roch*
BIRLINGHAM (St James the Great) *see* Pershore w Pinvin,
Wick and Birlingham *Worc*
BIRMINGHAM (Bishop Latimer w All Saints) *Birm 2*
P *St Martin's Trustees* **R** *vacant*
BIRMINGHAM (St George w St Michael) *see* Edgbaston
St Geo *Birm*
BIRMINGHAM (St George) *Birm 2* **P** *St Martin's Trustees*
P-in-c A J COZENS
BIRMINGHAM (St John the Evangelist) *see* Ladywood St Jo
and St Pet *Birm*
BIRMINGHAM (St Luke) *Birm 2* **P** *Trustees*
P-in-c T D L HUGHES **C** A E HERBERT, N J DRAKE
**BIRMINGHAM (St Martin-in-the-Bull-Ring) w Bordesley
St Andrew** *Birm 2* **P** *St Martin's Trustees* **R** J R ALLCOCK
NSM E BLAIR-CHAPPELL
BIRMINGHAM (St Paul) *Birm 2* **P** *St Martin's Trustees*
P-in-c A A GORHAM **NSM** C M M CHITHAM-MOSLEY
BIRSTALL (St James the Great) and Wanlip *Leic 4* **P** *Bp and
C A Palmer-Tomkinson Esq (jt)* **V** V J JUPP
BIRSTALL (St Peter) *Leeds 6* **P** *Bp* **V** P J KNIGHT
BIRSTWITH (St James) *see* Hampsthwaite and Killinghall and
Birstwith *Leeds*
BIRTLES (St Catherine) *see* Alderley w Birtles *Ches*
BIRTLEY (St Giles) *see* Chollerton w Birtley and
Thockrington *Newc*
BIRTLEY (St John the Evangelist) *Dur 10* **P** *R Chester le Street*
V E G LLOYD **Hon C** B M C BROGGIO
BIRTSMORTON (St Peter and St Paul) *see* Berrow w Pendock,
Eldersfield, Hollybush etc *Worc*
BISBROOKE (St John the Baptist) *see* Lyddington, Bisbrooke,
Caldecott, Glaston etc *Pet*
BISCATHORPE (St Helen) *see* Asterby Gp *Linc*
BISCOT (Holy Trinity) *St Alb 12* **P** *Bp* **V** T B SINGH
BISHAM (All Saints) *see* Gt Marlow w Marlow Bottom,
Lt Marlow and Bisham *Ox*
BISHAMPTON (St James) *see* Abberton, The Flyfords,
Naunton Beauchamp etc *Worc*

BISHOP AUCKLAND (St Andrew) (St Anne) *Dur 5*   **P** *The Crown and Bp (alt)*   **V** M P KEDDILTY   **C** E K G HARROP   **NSM** F COOPER

BISHOP AUCKLAND Woodhouse Close Area of Ecumenical Experiment (Conventional District) *Dur 9*   **C-in-c** S S GILL

BISHOP BURTON (All Saints)   *see* Walkington, Bishop Burton, Rowley etc *York*

BISHOP CAUNDLE (not known)   *see* Three Valleys *Sarum*

BISHOP MIDDLEHAM (St Michael)   *see* Upper Skerne *Dur*

BISHOP NORTON (St Peter), Waddingham and Snitterby *Linc 8*   **P** *Bp and The Crown (alt)*   **P-in-c** K E COLWELL

BISHOP SUTTON (Holy Trinity)   *see* Clutton w Cameley, Bishop Sutton and Stowey *B & W*

BISHOP THORNTON (St John the Evangelist), Burnt Yates, Markington, Ripley and South Stainley *Leeds 23*   **P** *Sir Thomas Ingilby Bt*   **R** P R HARFORD   **NSM** L M C BOON

BISHOP WILTON (St Edith)   *see* Garrowby Hill *York*

BISHOPHILL JUNIOR (St Mary)   *see* York St Clem w St Mary Bishophill *York*

BISHOPHILL SENIOR (St Clement w St Mary)   *as above*

BISHOP'S CANNINGS (St Mary the Virgin)   *see* Cannings and Redhorn *Sarum*

BISHOP'S CASTLE (St John the Baptist) w Mainstone, Lydbury North and Edgton *Heref 9*   **P** *Earl of Powis (3 turns), Ld Chan (1 turn), and Mrs R E Bell (1 turn)*   **P-in-c** S A C FOUNTAIN

BISHOP'S CLEEVE (St Michael and All Angels) and Woolstone w Gotherington and Oxenton *Glouc 9*   **P** *Patr Bd*   **TR** M ALLEN   **TV** R F REAKES

BISHOP'S FROME (St Mary the Virgin)   *see* Frome Valley *Heref*

BISHOP'S HATFIELD (St Etheldreda) (St Luke) (St John) (St Michael and All Angels), Lemsford and North Mymms *St Alb 18*   **P** *Patr Bd*   **TR** D V COLLINS   **TV** P E SEYMOUR   **NSM** P J THOMSON, S M STILWELL

BISHOP'S HULL (St John the Evangelist)   *see* Taunton St Mary and St Jo *B & W*

BISHOPS HULL (St Peter and St Paul) *B & W 18*   **P** *Adn Taunton*   **V** P J HUGHES

BISHOP'S ITCHINGTON (St Michael) *Cov 10*   **P** *Bp*   **P-in-c** M C GREEN

BISHOP'S LAVINGTON (All Saints)   *see* The Lavingtons, Cheverells, and Easterton *Sarum*

BISHOP'S LYDEARD (Blessed Virgin Mary) w Lydeard St Lawrence, Bagborough, Combe Florey and Cothelstone *B & W 19*   **P** *Bp, D&C, W H J Hancock Esq, and Mrs P M G Mitford (jt)*   **NSM** M YOUNG

BISHOP'S STORTFORD (Holy Trinity) *St Alb 15*   **P** *Bp*   **V** M K BROWN   **C** S L FORREST

BISHOP'S STORTFORD (St Michael) *St Alb 15*   **P** *Bp*   **V** D G WILLIAMS

BISHOP'S SUTTON (St Nicholas) and Ropley and West Tisted *Win 1*   **P** *Peache Trustees*   **P-in-c** C WELHAM

BISHOP'S TACHBROOK (St Chad) *Cov 11*   **P** *Bp*   **P-in-c** E SCRIVENS

BISHOPS TAWTON (St John the Baptist)   *see* Newport and Bishops Tawton *Ex*

BISHOP'S WALTHAM (St Peter) *Portsm 1*   **P** *Bp*   **R** J C HUNT   **NSM** J BELOE, K F WICKERT

BISHOPS WOOD (St John the Evangelist) *Lich 2*   **P** *V Brewood*   **V** P MOON

BISHOP'S WOOD (St Mary)   *see* Elmley Lovett w Hampton Lovett and Elmbridge w Rushock and Hartlebury and Ombersley w Doverdale *Worc*

BISHOPSBOURNE (St Mary)   *see* Barham Downs w Adisham *Cant*

BISHOPSNYMPTON (St Mary the Virgin), Charles, East Anstey, High Bray, Knowstone, Mariansleigh, Molland, North Molton w Twitchen, Rose Ash, and West Anstey *Ex 18*   **P** *Patr Bd*   **TR** D P BAKER   **TV** A G FORMAN   **NSM** P A LAWSON

BISHOPSTEIGNTON (St John the Baptist)   *see* Teignmouth, Ideford w Luton, Ashcombe etc *Ex*

BISHOPSTOKE (St Mary) (St Paul) *Win 10*   **P** *Bp*   **R** R E WISE   **C** K M MEPHAM

BISHOPSTON (Church of the Good Shepherd)   *see* Bishopston and St Andrews *Bris*

BISHOPSTON (St Michael and All Angels)   *as above*

BISHOPSTON (St Michael and All Angels) (Church of the Good Shepherd) and St Andrews *Bris 3*   **P** *Patr Bd*   **P-in-c** J C W STEVENSON   **TV** W P MASSEY   **NSM** B J PULLAN

BISHOPSTONE (St Lawrence)   *see* Magnis Gp *Heref*

BISHOPSTONE (St Mary the Virgin)   *see* Lyddington and Wanborough and Bishopstone etc *Bris*

BISHOPSTONE (St Andrew)   *see* E Blatchington and Bishopstone *Chich*

BISHOPSTONE (St John the Baptist)   *see* Chalke Valley *Sarum*

BISHOPSTROW (St Aldhelm)   *see* River Were *Sarum*

BISHOPSWOOD (All Saints)   *see* Wye Reaches Gp *Heref*

BISHOPSWORTH (St Peter) and Bedminster Down *Bris 1*   **P** *Bp*   **TR** T R J GODDEN

BISHOPTHORPE (St Andrew) *York 1*   **P** *Abp*   **V** C I COATES   **NSM** P J MACNAUGHTON

BISHOPTON (St Peter)   *see* Stockton Country Par *Dur*

BISHOPWEARMOUTH (Good Shepherd) *Dur 14*   **P** *Bp*   **P-in-c** B SKELTON

BISHOPWEARMOUTH (St Gabriel) *Dur 14*   **P** *V Sunderland*   **V** E M WILKINSON   **C** P HEIDARI

BISHOPWEARMOUTH (St Luke Pallion)   *see* Millfield St Mark and Pallion St Luke *Dur*

BISHOPWEARMOUTH (St Mary)   *see* Millfield St Mary *Dur*

BISHOPWEARMOUTH (St Nicholas) (Christ Church) *Dur 14*   **P** *Bp*   **V** *vacant*

BISLEY (All Saints), Chalford, France Lynch, and Oakridge and Bussage w Eastcombe *Glouc 4*   **P** *Ld Chan (1 turn), Bp and Adn (1 turn)*   **V** S J MURRAY

BISLEY (St John the Baptist) and West End (Holy Trinity) *Guildf 6*   **P** *Bp*   **R** A J ARMITT

BISPHAM (All Hallows) *Blackb 8*   **P** *Ch Soc Trust*   **R** S J COX   **C** J R H CRAWFORD, T A WOOLFORD

BISTERNE (St Paul)   *see* Ringwood w Ellingham and Harbridge etc *Win*

BITCHFIELD (St Mary Magdalene)   *see* N Beltisloe Gp *Linc*

BITTADON (St Peter)   *see* Ilfracombe, Lee, Woolacombe, Bittadon etc *Ex*

BITTERING PARVA (St Peter and St Paul)   *see* Launditch and the Upper Nar *Nor*

BITTERLEY (St Mary)   *see* Bromfield *Heref*

BITTERNE (Holy Saviour) *Win 13*   **P** *Bp*   **V** A P S PALMER   **NSM** J L PARFITT

BITTERNE PARK (All Hallows) (Ascension) *Win 13*   **P** *Bp*   **V** A SMITH   **C** N J SMITH, W J FAIRBAIRN

BITTESWELL (St Mary)   *see* Lutterworth w Cotesbach and Bitteswell *Leic*

BITTON (St Mary)   *see* Warmley, Syston and Bitton *Bris*

BIX (St James)   *see* Nettlebed w Bix, Highmoor, Pishill etc *Ox*

BIXLEY (St Wandregesilus)   *see* Poringland *Nor*

BLABY (All Saints) *Leic 7*   **P** *Bp*   **P-in-c** J C MICKLETHWAITE

BLACK BOURTON (St Mary the Virgin)   *see* Shill Valley and Broadshire *Ox*

BLACK COMBE, Drigg, Eskdale, Irton, Muncaster and Waberthwaite *Carl 5*   **P** *Bp, Adn W Cumberland, Mrs I Frost-Pennington, the Hon J N Lowther, P Stanley Esq, and DBP (jt)*   **R** G M HART   **C** A M OVERTON-BENGE

BLACK MOUNTAINS Group, The, comprising Craswall, Clodock, Llanveynoe, Longtown, Michaelchurch Escley, Newton, and St Margaret's *Heref 1*   **P** *DBP (2 turns), MMCET (1 turn)*   **V** N G LOWTON

BLACK NOTLEY (St Peter and St Paul), Great Notley and Rayne *Chelmsf 17*   **P** *St Jo Coll Cam and DBP (jt)*   **V** E J BENDREY   **NSM** I R BENDREY, P J HOWLETT, R H KUKIEWICZ

BLACK TORRINGTON (St Mary), Bradford w Cookbury, Thornbury and Highampton *Ex 16*   **P** *DBP*   **R** *vacant*

BLACKAWTON (St Michael)   *see* Stoke Fleming, Blackawton, Strete and E Allington *Ex*

BLACKBIRD LEYS (Holy Family) *Ox 1*   **P** *Bp*   **V** H R CARTER

BLACKBOURNE, comprising Bardwell, Barnham, Euston, Fakenham Magna, Honington, Ingham, Ixworth, and Troston *St E 5*   **P** *Patr Bd*   **TR** K BURTON   **NSM** A J REDMAN, L J NORBURN

BLACKBROOK (St Paul)   *see* Parr *Liv*

BLACKBURN (Christ Church w St Matthew) *Blackb 2*   **P** *Bp*   **V** A RAYNES   **C** M DIN

BLACKBURN (Holy Trinity Worship Centre)   *see* N and E Blackb *Blackb*

BLACKBURN (St Aidan) (St Luke) St Mark and St Philip *Blackb 2*   **P** *Bp and V Blackb (jt)*   **V** C E BROOKS   **NSM** B D PACK

BLACKBURN (St Barnabas) *Blackb 2*   **P** *Bp*   **V** J P MILTON-THOMPSON

BLACKBURN (St Gabriel) *Blackb 2*   **P** *Bp*   **V** S P CORBETT

BLACKBURN (St Jude)   *see* N and E Blackb *Blackb*

BLACKBURN (St Luke)   *see* Blackb St Aid, St Luke, St Mark and St Phil *Blackb*

BLACKBURN (St Michael and All Angels)   *see* N and E Blackb *Blackb*

BLACKBURN (St Silas) *Blackb 2*   **P** *Trustees*   **P-in-c** S M ASTON

BLACKBURN (St Stephen) (St James) *Blackb 2*   **P** *Bp, DBP, and Exors the Ven C W D Carroll (jt)*   **NSM** J C MACHOLC

BLACKBURN The Redeemer (St Bartholomew) (The Saviour) *Blackb 2* **P** *Bp and CPAS (jt)* **V** R A H MARSHALL **C** C D ANDERTON

BLACKBURN, NORTH and EAST (St Jude) (St Michael and All Angels) (Holy Trinity Worship Centre) *Blackb 2* **P** *V Blackb, J Whittaker Esq, and Mrs V Edge (jt)* **P-in-c** N J HEALE

BLACKDOWN (Holy Trinity) *see* Beaminster Area *Sarum*

BLACKDOWN Benefice, The, comprising Buckland St Mary, Churchstanton, Corfe, Otterford, and Pitminster *B & W 16* **P** *DBP (4 turns), Pitminster PCC and Corfe PCC (1 turn)* **R** J A FALLON **Hon C** N P GRIFFIN

BLACKFEN (Good Shepherd) *see* Lamorbey H Redeemer *Roch*

BLACKFORD (Holy Trinity) *see* Isle of Wedmore *B & W*

BLACKFORD (St John the Baptist) *see* Rockcliffe and Blackford *Carl*

BLACKFORD (St Michael) *see* Camelot Par *B & W*

BLACKFORDBY (St Margaret) and Woodville *Leic 8* **P** *Bp* **V** M FISH

BLACKHALL (St Andrew), Castle Eden and Monkhesleden *Dur 2* **P** *Bp* **P-in-c** K G MCNEIL **Hon C** R C DAVIES

BLACKHAM (All Saints) *see* Withyham St Mich *Chich*

BLACKHEATH (All Saints) *S'wark 4* **P** *V Lewisham St Mary* **V** N W S CRANFIELD **C** T W CHATTERTON

BLACKHEATH (Ascension) *see* Deptford St Jo w H Trin and Ascension *S'wark*

BLACKHEATH (St John the Evangelist) *S'wark 1* **P** *CPAS* **V** E F A L SCRASE-FIELD **C** C W A HANNING

BLACKHEATH (St Martin) *see* Wonersh w Blackheath *Guildf*

BLACKHEATH (St Paul) *Birm 6* **P** *Bp* **V** M J SERMON **C** A ANEES

BLACKHEATH PARK (St Michael and All Angels) *S'wark 1* **P** *Bp* **V** A R CHRISTIE **C** T T AJAYI

BLACKLAND (St Peter) *see* Marden Vale *Sarum*

BLACKLANDS Hastings (Christchurch and St Andrew) *Chich 15* **P** *Ch Patr Trust* **P-in-c** C M HILL

BLACKLEY (Holy Trinity) *Man 4* **P** *Bp* **R** *vacant*

BLACKLEY (St Andrew) *Man 4* **P** *Bp* **P-in-c** E M ROBERTS **NSM** A D SMITH, C NIGHTINGALE

BLACKLEY (St Paul) *Man 4* **P** *Bp* **P-in-c** E M ROBERTS **NSM** A D SMITH, H TOMLINSON

BLACKLEY (St Peter) *Man 4* **P** *D&C* **P-in-c** E M ROBERTS **NSM** A D SMITH

BLACKMOOR (St Matthew) and Whitehill *Portsm 4* **P** *Bp* **V** D J CLARKE **C** A J WOOD

BLACKMORE (St Laurence) and Stondon Massey *Chelmsf 3* **P** *Bp* **V** S E BRAZIER-GIBBS

BLACKPOOL (Christ Church w All Saints) (St Andrew) *Blackb 8* **P** *Bp and Trustees (jt)* **V** *vacant*

BLACKPOOL (Holy Cross) South Shore *Blackb 8* **P** *Bp* **V** *vacant*

BLACKPOOL (Holy Trinity) *see* S Shore H Trin *Blackb*

BLACKPOOL (St Christopher) *see* Hawes Side and Marton Moss *Blackb*

BLACKPOOL (St John) *Blackb 8* **P** *Trustees* **V** S I HASKETT

BLACKPOOL (St Mark) *see* Layton and Staining *Blackb*

BLACKPOOL (St Mary) South Shore *Blackb 8* **P** *Bp* **V** *vacant*

BLACKPOOL (St Michael and All Angels) *see* Layton and Staining *Blackb*

BLACKPOOL (St Nicholas) *see* Hawes Side and Marton Moss *Blackb*

BLACKPOOL (St Paul's Worship Centre) *Blackb 8* **P** *Trustees* **P-in-c** D A PREST

BLACKPOOL (St Peter) *see* S Shore St Pet *Blackb*

BLACKPOOL (St Stephen on the Cliffs) *Blackb 8* **P** *Bp, R Bispham All Hallows, and Ch Wardens (jt)* **V** A G SAGE

BLACKPOOL (St Thomas) *Blackb 8* **P** *CPAS* **V** D O'BRIEN

BLACKPOOL (St Wilfrid) Mereside *Blackb 8* **P** *Bp* **P-in-c** L M TOMKINSON

BLACKROD (St Katharine), Daisy Hill, Westhoughton and Wingates *Man 9* **P** *Patr Bd* **TR** C H PHARAOH **TV** A D WYNNE **C** K H DEAKIN

BLACKTOFT (Holy Trinity) *see* Howden *York*

BLACKWATER, NORTH, comprising Salcott Virley, Tollesbury, Tolleshunt d'Arcy, and Tolleshunt Major *Chelmsf 24* **P** *Patr Bd* **V** *vacant*

BLACKWELL (All Saints) and Salutation *Dur 7* **P** *Bp* **NSM** S C JAY

BLACKWELL (St Catherine) *see* The Lickey *Birm*

BLACKWELL (St Werburgh) w Tibshelf *Derby 2* **P** *Bp and MMCET (jt)* **V** G MANLEY **NSM** S L MASON **OLM** D HESKETH

BLADON (St Martin) *see* Woodstock and Bladon *Ox*

BLAGDON (St Andrew) w Compton Martin and Ubley *B & W 9* **P** *Bp and Sir John Wills Bt (jt)* **R** S W LEWIS **C** A J HOLMES

BLAGREAVES (St Andrew) *Derby 5* **P** *Bp, Churchwardens, and CPAS (jt)* **P-in-c** A C M DRING

BLAISDON (St Michael and All Angels) *see* Westbury-on-Severn w Flaxley, Blaisdon etc *Glouc*

BLAKEDOWN (St James the Great) *see* Churchill-in-Halfshire w Blakedown and Broome *Worc*

BLAKEMERE (St Leonard) *see* Cusop w Blakemere, Bredwardine w Brobury etc *Heref*

BLAKENALL HEATH (Christ Church) *Lich 24* **P** *Patr Bd* **TR** *vacant*

BLAKENEY (All Saints) *see* Newnham w Awre and Blakeney *Glouc*

BLAKENEY (St Nicholas w St Mary and St Thomas) w Cley, Wiveton, Glandford and Letheringsett *Nor 17* **P** *Bp and Keble Coll Ox (jt)* **R** R H LAWRY

BLAKENHAM, GREAT (St Mary) *see* Claydon *St E*

BLAKENHAM, LITTLE (St Mary) *see* Bramford w Lt Blakenham, Baylham and Nettlestead *St E*

BLAKESLEY (St Mary) *see* Lambfold *Pet*

BLANCHLAND (St Mary's Abbey) w Hunstanworth and Edmundbyers and Muggleswick *Newc 9* **P** *D E Scott-Harden Esq, Lord Crewe's Trustees and D&C (alt)* **R** H SAVAGE

BLANDFORD FORUM (St Peter and St Paul) and Langton Long *Sarum 6* **P** *Bp* **R** J P TRIFFITT **C** N M J ROBERTSON

BLANDFORD ST MARY (St Mary) *see* Spetisbury w Charlton Marshall etc *Sarum*

BLANKNEY (St Oswald) *see* Metheringham w Blankney and Dunston *Linc*

BLASTON (St Giles) *see* Six Saints circa Holt *Leic*

BLATCHINGTON, EAST (St John the Evangelist) (St Peter) and Bishopstone *Chich 21* **P** *Bp and Bp Lon (alt)* **R** A M C FOLKES **Hon C** T C SMYTH

BLATCHINGTON, WEST (St Peter) *Chich 20* **P** *Bp* **R** D B SMITH

BLAXHALL (St Peter) *see* Alde River *St E*

BLAYDON (St Cuthbert) and Swalwell *Dur 12* **P** *Bp* **NSM** L O GARDNER

BLEADON (St Peter and St Paul) and Bournville *B & W 10* **P** *Bp and Guild of All So (jt)* **R** T J ERRIDGE **C** P J WEBB

BLEAN (St Cosmus and St Damian) *Cant 3* **P** *Master of Eastbridge Hosp* **P-in-c** S C E LAIRD

BLEASBY (St Mary) *see* W Trent *S'well*

BLEASDALE (St Eadmor) *see* Fellside Team *Blackb*

BLEATARN (Chapel of Ease) *see* Heart of Eden *Carl*

BLECHINGLEY *see* Bletchingley and Nutfield *S'wark*

BLEDINGTON (St Leonard) *see* Broadwell, Evenlode, Oddington, Adlestrop etc *Glouc*

BLEDLOW (Holy Trinity) *see* Risborough *Ox*

BLEDLOW RIDGE (St Paul) *see* W Wycombe w Bledlow Ridge, Bradenham and Radnage *Ox*

BLENDON (St James the Great) *Roch 17* **P** *The Crown* **V** I SMITH **NSM** P A PERCIVAL

BLENDWORTH (Holy Trinity) w Chalton w Idsworth *Portsm 5* **P** *Bp* **P-in-c** V L MORGAN

BLETCHINGDON (St Giles) *see* Akeman *Ox*

BLETCHINGLEY (St Mary) and Nutfield *S'wark 25* **P** *Em Coll Cam and Jes Coll Ox (jt)* **R** P K PAMPHILON-GREEN **NSM** P J SHERRINGTON

BLETCHLEY (St Mary) St John's District Church *Ox 14* **P** *DBP* **R** D R MCDOUGALL **C** B M THORPE, M BEER, P C PAVLOU **NSM** H M AKIBO-BETTS

BLETSOE (St Mary) *see* Riseley w Bletsoe *St Alb*

BLEWBURY (St Michael and All Angels) *see* The Churn *Ox*

BLICKLING (St Andrew) *see* Aylsham and Distr *Nor*

BLIDWORTH (St Mary of the Purification) w Rainworth *S'well 2* **P** *DBP and Ld Chan (alt)* **V** *vacant*

BLIDWORTH, NEW (St Andrew) *see* Blidworth w Rainworth *S'well*

BLINDLEY HEATH (St John the Evangelist) *see* Godstone and Blindley Heath *S'wark*

BLISLAND (St Protus and St Hyacinth) *see* Camelside *Truro*

BLISWORTH (St John the Baptist), Alderton, Grafton Regis, Milton Malsor and Stoke Bruerne w Shutlanger *Pet 5* **P** *Bp, MMCET and Hyndman Trustees (2 turns), Ld Chan (1 turn)* **R** R B STAINER

BLITHFIELD (St Leonard) *see* Abbots Bromley, Blithfield, Colton, Colwich etc *Lich*

BLO' NORTON (St Andrew) *see* Guiltcross *Nor*

BLOCKLEY (St Peter and St Paul) *see* Vale and Cotswold Edge *Glouc*

BLOFIELD (St Andrew and St Peter) *Nor 4* **P** *G&C Coll Cam and Ch Soc Trust (jt)* **R** K M BILLSON

BLOOMSBURY (St George) w Woburn Square (Christ Church) *Lon 17* P *Ld Chan* R D T PEEBLES C J HOGAN NSM J A WALTERS

BLORE RAY (St Bartholomew) *see* Calton, Cauldon, Grindon, Waterfall etc *Lich*

BLOXHAM (Our Lady of Bloxham) w Milcombe and South Newington *Ox 23* P *Ex Coll Ox and Eton Coll (jt)* V D R GINGRICH

BLOXHOLME (St Mary) *see* Digby Gp *Linc*

BLOXWICH (All Saints) (Holy Ascension) *Lich 24* P *Patr Bd* TR R S WILLIAMS TV C E DAVIES OLM P A NESBITT

BLOXWORTH (St Andrew) *see* Red Post *Sarum*

BLUBBERHOUSES (St Andrew) *see* Washburn and Mid-Wharfe *Leeds*

BLUE BELL HILL (St Alban) *see* S Chatham H Trin *Roch*

BLUNDELLSANDS (St Michael) *Liv 8* P *Trustees* V N R SHORT

BLUNDELLSANDS (St Nicholas) *Liv 8* P *Trustees* OLM K R THORNBOROUGH

BLUNDESTON (St Mary) *see* Somerleyton, Ashby, Fritton, Herringfleet etc *Nor*

BLUNHAM (St Edmund King and Martyr and St James) *see* Riversmeet *St Alb*

BLUNSDON (St Andrew) *see* N Swindon St Andr *Bris*

BLUNTISHAM (St Mary) cum Earith w Colne and Holywell cum Needingworth *Ely 12* P *Ch Ch Ox and Bp (jt)* V S M ANTHONY

BLURTON (St Alban) *see* Blurton and Dresden *Lich*

BLURTON (St Bartholomew) (St Alban) and Dresden *Lich 11* P *Bp* V *vacant*

BLYBOROUGH (St Alkmund) *see* Trentcliffe Gp *Linc*

BLYFORD (All Saints) *see* Blyth Valley *St E*

BLYMHILL (St Mary) *see* Watershed *Lich*

BLYTH (St Cuthbert) *Newc 1* P *Bp* V A A TOOBY

BLYTH (St Mary and St Martin) and Scrooby w Ranskill *S'well 1* P *Bp and Trin Coll Cam (jt)* P-in-c J L MCKENNA

BLYTH (St Mary) *Newc 1* P *Bp* V *vacant*

BLYTH VALLEY Team Ministry, The, comprising Blyford, Bramfield, Chediston, Halesworth, Holton, Linstead Parva, Spexhall, Thorington, Walpole, Wenhaston, and Wissett *St E 17* P *Patr Bd* TR E L RENNARD NSM A K R ALDER, C J HELD, L M BERRY

BLYTHBURGH (Holy Trinity) *see* Sole Bay *St E*

BLYTON (St Martin) *see* Trentcliffe Gp *Linc*

BOARHUNT (St Nicholas) *see* Southwick w Boarhunt *Portsm*

BOARSTALL (St James) *see* Bernwode *Ox*

BOBBING (St Bartholomew) *see* Sittingbourne w Bobbing *Cant*

BOBBINGTON (Holy Cross) *see* Smestow Vale *Lich*

BOBBINGWORTH (St Germain) *see* Fyfield, Moreton w Bobbingworth etc *Chelmsf*

BOCKING (St Mary) and Panfield *Chelmsf 17* P *Abp Cant and Bp (jt)* P-in-c R A M REID

BOCKING (St Peter) *Chelmsf 17* P *Abp Cant* P-in-c T BARNES NSM R D STONE

BOCONNOC (not known) *see* Lostwithiel Parishes *Truro*

BODDINGTON (St John the Baptist) *see* Aston-le-Walls, Byfield, Boddington, Eydon etc *Pet*

BODDINGTON (St Mary Magdalene) *see* Twigworth, Down Hatherley, Norton, The Leigh etc *Glouc*

BODENHAM (St Michael and All Angels) *see* Maund Gp *Heref*

BODHAM (All Saints) *see* Weybourne Gp *Nor*

BODIAM (St Giles) *Chich 17* P *All So Coll Ox* P-in-c C P IRVINE

BODICOTE (St John the Baptist) *Ox 23* P *New Coll Ox* V S E SHARP

BODINNICK (St John) *see* Trelawny *Truro*

BODLE STREET GREEN (St John the Evangelist) *see* Warbleton, Bodle Street Green and Dallington *Chich*

BODMIN (St Petroc) Team Benefice, The, including Cardynham, Lanhydrock, and Lanivet *Truro 10* P *Patr Bd* TR P R HOLLEY C C R JONES NSM C F CLEMOW, E J MUNDAY

BODNEY (St Mary) *see* Hilborough w Bodney *Nor*

BOGNOR (St Wilfrid) *Chich 1* P *Abp* V *vacant*

BOLAM (St Andrew) *see* Heighington and Darlington St Matt and St Luke *Dur*

BOLAM (St Andrew) w Whalton and Hartburn w Meldon *Newc 11* P *Ld Chan (2 turns), J I K Walker Esq (1 turn), and D&C Dur (1 turn)* P-in-c J P MASON C F J SAMPLE

BOLAS MAGNA (St John the Baptist) *see* Tibberton w Bolas Magna and Waters Upton *Lich*

BOLDMERE (St Michael) *Birm 7* P *Birm Dioc Trustees* V R G BIRCHALL C C J WALKER NSM E C M SYKES

BOLDONS, The (St George) (St Nicholas) *Dur 13* P *Bp (2 turns), The Crown (1 turn)* Hon C D M DUKE

BOLDRE (St John the Baptist) w South Baddesley *Win 11* P *Bp and Lord Teynham (jt)* V S F E NEWHAM NSM R D C ELLIOTT

BOLDRE, EAST (St Paul) *see* Beaulieu and Exbury and E Boldre *Win*

BOLE (St Martin) *see* Retford Area *S'well*

BOLINGBROKE Deanery (St Peter and St Paul) *Linc 9* P *Patr Bd* TR P F COATES TV F A JEFFRIES, T M I M MCLAUGHLIN OLM J COATES

BOLINGBROKE, NEW (St Peter) *see* Sibsey w Frithville *Linc*

BOLLINGHAM (St Silas) *see* Eardisley w Bollingham, Willersley, Brilley etc *Heref*

BOLLINGTON (Holy Trinity) *see* Rostherne w Bollington *Ches*

BOLLINGTON (St Oswald) (Holy Trinity) *Ches 13* P *V Prestbury* V V W HYDON

BOLNEY (St Mary Magdalene) *Chich 5* P *K Coll Lon* NSM M MILLS

BOLNHURST (St Dunstan) w Keysoe *St Alb 13* P *Bp* P-in-c T C WILSON

BOLSOVER (St Mary and St Laurence) *Derby 2* P *Bp* V R C GOULDTHORPE NSM R M WILLIAMS

BOLSTERSTONE (St Mary) *see* Cornerstone *Sheff*

BOLTBY (Holy Trinity) *see* Felixkirk w Boltby *York*

BOLTON (All Saints) *see* Binsey *Carl*

BOLTON (All Saints) *see* N Westmorland *Carl*

BOLTON (Christ Church) *see* Heaton Ch Ch w Halliwell St Marg *Man*

BOLTON (Emmanuel) *see* W Bolton *Man*

BOLTON (St Chad) *see* Leverhulme *Man*

BOLTON (St James w St Chrysostom) *Leeds 3* P *Bp* V S D LEES Hon C P B STOODLEY

BOLTON (St Matthew w St Barnabas) *see* W Bolton *Man*

BOLTON (St Thomas the Apostle) *as above*

BOLTON ABBEY (St Mary and St Cuthbert) *Leeds 24* P *Duke of Devonshire* R N J MERCER

BOLTON Breightmet (St James) *see* Leverhulme *Man*

BOLTON BY BOWLAND (St Peter and St Paul) w Grindleton *Blackb 7* P *Bp and V Hurst Green and Mitton* R *vacant*

BOLTON Chapel (unknown) *see* Whittingham and Edlingham w Bolton Chapel *Newc*

BOLTON LE MOORS (St Bede) *Man 9* P *Bp* P-in-c V C WHITWORTH

BOLTON ON SWALE (St Mary) *see* Easby w Skeeby and Brompton on Swale etc *Leeds*

BOLTON PERCY (All Saints) *York 1* P *Abp* R G R MUMFORD NSM G M WEBB

BOLTON Top o' th' Moss (St John the Evangelist) *see* Leverhulme *Man*

BOLTON, WEST (Emmanuel) (St Luke) (St Matthew w St Barnabas) (St Paul) (St Thomas the Apostle) *Man 7* P *Patr Bd* TR S TRANTER TV D R PETCH, F ADMAN C J O'NEILL

BOLTON-LE-MOORS (St Peter) (St Philip) *Man 7* P *Bp* V C A BRACEGIRDLE C I M G HEPBURN, M E SLACK NSM B S GASKELL, K G C NEWPORT

BOLTON-LE-SANDS (Holy Trinity) *Blackb 14* P *Bp* V N E GOODRICH

BOLTONS, THE *see* W Brompton St Mary w St Peter and St Jude *Lon*

BOLTON-UPON-DEARNE (St Andrew the Apostle) *Sheff 12* P *SMF* P-in-c C R SCHAEFER

BOLVENTOR (Holy Trinity) *see* Moorland Gp *Truro*

BOMERE HEATH (Mission Room) *see* Leaton and Albrighton w Battlefield *Lich*

BONBY (St Andrew) *Linc 8* P *DBP* V G O MITCHELL

BONCHURCH (St Boniface) (St Boniface Old Church) *Portsm 7* P *Ch Patr Trust* R H E WRIGHT

BONDLEIGH (St James the Apostle) *see* Chagford, Gidleigh, Throwleigh etc *Ex*

BONINGALE (St Chad) *see* Albrighton, Boningale and Donington *Lich*

BONNINGTON (St Rumwold) *see* Saxon Shoreline *Cant*

BONSALL (St James the Apostle) *see* Wirksworth *Derby*

BOOKER (Christ the Servant King) *see* High Wycombe *Ox*

BOOKHAM, GREAT (St Nicolas) *Guildf 10* P *Bp* R A D JENKINS C J K HEINE OLM B J MCDONALD

BOOKHAM, LITTLE (All Saints) *see* Effingham w Lt Bookham *Guildf*

BOOSBECK (St Aidan) and Lingdale *York 16* P *Abp* V E M-B HAYNES

BOOTHBY GRAFFOE (St Andrew) *see* Graffoe Gp *Linc*

BOOTHBY PAGNELL (St Andrew) *see* N Beltisloe Gp *Linc*

BOOTHSTOWN (St Andrew's Church Institute) *see* Worsley *Man*

BOOTLE (Christ Church) *Liv 6* P *Bp* V *vacant*

BOOTLE (St Matthew w St Mary) (St Leonard) *Liv 6*   **P** *Patr Bd*   **R** I A WHITAKER   **C** P R A BRIDSON

BOOTLE (St Michael)   *see* Black Combe, Drigg, Eskdale etc *Carl*

BORASTON (not known)   *see* Tenbury *Heref*

BORDEN (St Peter and St Paul) *Cant 15*   **P** *SMF*
P-in-c R D LANE

BORDER Group of Parishes   *see* Llanyblodwel, Llanymynech, Morton and Trefonen *Lich*

BORDESLEY (St Alban the Martyr and St Patrick)   *see* Highgate *Birm*

BORDESLEY (St Benedict) *Birm 11*   **P** *Keble Coll Ox*
P-in-c R M SHEPPARD

BORDESLEY GREEN (St Paul)   *see* Ward End w Bordesley Green *Birm*

BORDON (St Mark) *Guildf 3*   **P** *Bp*   **V** D J SCOTT-BROMLEY

BOREHAM (St Andrew) *Chelmsf 9*   **P** *Bp*   **P-in-c** E C A WYLIE
C D C PIERCE, J S PEARSON

BOREHAM (St John the Evangelist)   *see* River Were *Sarum*

BOREHAMWOOD (All Saints)   *see* Elstree and Borehamwood *St Alb*

BOREHAMWOOD (Holy Cross) *as above*

BOREHAMWOOD (St Michael and All Angels) *as above*

BORLEY (not known)   *see* N Hinckford *Chelmsf*

BOROUGH GREEN (Good Shepherd) *Roch 10*   **P** *Bp*
P-in-c C M TURNER

BOROUGHBRIDGE (St James)   *see* Aldborough w Boroughbridge and Roecliffe *Leeds*

BORROWASH (St Stephen's Chapel)   *see* Ockbrook *Derby*

BORROWDALE (St Andrew)   *see* Keswick St Jo w Borrowdale *Carl*

BORSTAL (St Matthew) *Roch 5*   **P** *V Rochester St Marg*
P-in-c S C BREWER

BORWICK (St Mary)   *see* Warton St Oswald w Yealand Conyers *Blackb*

BOSBURY (Holy Trinity)   *see* Hop Churches *Heref*

BOSCASTLE and Tintagel Group, The, comprising Forrabury, Lewsnewth Otterham, St Juliot, Tintagel, and Trevalga *Truro 8*   **P** *DBP and D&C Windsor (jt)*
P-in-c H J ASTON   **NSM** R J TERRY

BOSCOMBE (St Andrew) *Win 8*   **P** *Bp*   **P-in-c** N J HOULTON

BOSCOMBE (St Andrew)   *see* Bourne Valley *Sarum*

BOSCOMBE (St Clement)   *see* Bournemouth St Clem *Win*

BOSCOMBE (St John the Evangelist) *Win 8*   **P** *Peache Trustees*   **V** R P KHAKHRIA

BOSCOPPA (St Luke) *Truro 1*   **P** *The Crown*
P-in-c J S J WILLIAMS

BOSHAM (Holy Trinity) *Chich 3*   **P** *Bp*   **V** M J LANE

BOSLEY (St Mary the Virgin)   *see* Sutton, Wincle, Wildboarclough and Bosley *Ches*

BOSMERE, NORTH, comprising Coddenham, Creeting St Mary, Creeting St Peter, Crowfield, Earl Stonham w Stonham Parva, Gosbeck, Hemingstone, and Stonham Aspal and Mickfield *St E 2*   **P** *Bp, Pemb Coll Cam, and DBP (jt)*   **R** P J PAYNE   **NSM** H NORRIS

BOSMERE, SOUTH, comprising Barking w Darmsden, Battisford, Flowton, Great Bricett, Offton, Ringshall, Somersham, and Willisham *St E 2*   **P** *Bp, MMCET, Dr I de la Bere, and Ch Patr Trust (jt)*   **R** D D HARRISON

BOSSALL (St Botolph)   *see* Harton *York*

BOSSINGTON (St James)   *see* Mid Test *Win*

BOSTALL HEATH (St Andrew) *Roch 15*   **P** *DBP*
V S SHAHZAD

BOSTON (St Botolph) (St Christopher) (St Thomas) *Linc 21*   **P** *Bp*   **TR** A C BUXTON   **TV** J E ROBERTSON
C S E ROSE

BOSTON SPA (St Mary)   *see* Bramham *York*

BOSWORTH (St Peter) and Sheepy Group, including Orton-on-the-Hill, Ratcliffe Culey, Sibson, and Twycross *Leic 10*   **P** *Patr Bd (2 turns), Ld Chan (1 turn)*
P-in-c M S POSKITT   **TV** J G HARGREAVES   **NSM** A E HALL

BOTCHERBY (St Andrew)   *see* Carl St Aid and Ch Ch *Carl*

BOTESDALE (St Botolph)   *see* Redgrave cum Botesdale w Rickinghall *St E*

BOTHAL (St Andrew) and Pegswood w Longhirst *Newc 11*
P *Bp*   **R** J C PARK

BOTHAMSALL (Our Lady and St Peter)   *see* Retford Area *S'well*

BOTHENHAMPTON (Holy Trinity)   *see* Bridport *Sarum*

BOTLEY (All Saints) *Portsm 1*   **P** *Bp*   **R** G R MENSINGH

BOTLEY (St Peter and St Paul)   *see* Osney *Ox*

BOTLEYS AND LYNE (Holy Trinity)   *see* Chertsey, Lyne and Longcross *Guildf*

BOTTESFORD (St Mary the Virgin)   *see* Vale of Belvoir *Leic*

BOTTESFORD (St Peter) w Ashby *Linc 6*   **P** *Patr Bd*
TR K R DYKE   **C** S C DEAN   **NSM** M STONIER

BOTTISHAM (Holy Trinity)   *see* Anglesey Gp *Ely*

BOTUS FLEMING (St Mary)   *see* Landrake w St Erney and Botus Fleming *Truro*

BOUGHTON (All Saints)   *see* Wissey Valley *Ely*

BOUGHTON (St John the Baptist)   *see* Pitsford w Boughton *Pet*

BOUGHTON (St Matthew)   *see* Ollerton w Boughton *S'well*

BOUGHTON ALUPH (All Saints)   *see* Wye *Cant*

BOUGHTON ALUPH (St Christopher) *as above*

BOUGHTON MALHERBE (St Nicholas)   *see* Len Valley *Cant*

BOUGHTON MONCHELSEA (St Augustine) (St Peter) *Cant 13*   **P** *Abp*   **V** P J F GOODEY

BOUGHTON-UNDER-BLEAN (St Barnabas) (St Peter and St Paul) w Dunkirk, Goodnestone w Graveney, and Hernhill *Cant 14*   **P** *Abp*   **V** J BURROWS

BOULGE (St Michael)   *see* Carlford *St E*

BOULTHAM (Holy Cross) (St Helen) *Linc 11*   **P** *DBP*
R D J OSBOURNE

BOULTON (St Mary the Virgin) *Derby 5*   **P** *Bp*
C P DESBOROUGH

BOURN (St Helena and St Mary)   *see* Papworth *Ely*

BOURNE (St Peter and St Paul) *Linc 17*   **P** *DBP*
V C J ATKINSON   **OLM** P W R LISTER

BOURNE END (St John)   *see* Sunnyside w Bourne End *St Alb*

BOURNE END (St Mark)   *see* Hedsor and Bourne End *Ox*

BOURNE VALLEY, comprising Allington w Boscombe, Cholderton, Idmiston w Porton and Gomeldon, Newton Tony, Winterbourne Earls and Dauntsey, and Winterbourne Gunner *Sarum 10*   **P** *Oriel Coll Ox and Bp (jt)*
P-in-c P A OSTLI-EAST   **C** P OSLER   **NSM** D M COATES

BOURNE, LOWER (St Martin)   *see* The Bourne and Tilford *Guildf*

BOURNE, The (St Thomas) and Tilford *Guildf 3*   **P** *Bp and Adn Surrey (alt)*   **V** J O MORRIS   **C** S L CLARKE
Hon C N FAIRLAMB   **NSM** E J COLLINS, E M LANE

BOURNEMOUTH (Holy Epiphany) *Win 8*   **P** *Bp*
P-in-c D S THOMPSON

BOURNEMOUTH (St Alban)   *see* Winton, Moordown and Charminster *Win*

BOURNEMOUTH (St Ambrose) *Win 8*   **P** *Bp*
P-in-c A F PEARCE

BOURNEMOUTH (St Andrew) Bennett Road *Win 8*
P *Trustees*   **V** G M ROBERTS   **Hon C** J W DAVIES

BOURNEMOUTH (St Barnabas) Queen's Park   *see* Holdenhurst and Iford *Win*

BOURNEMOUTH (St Christopher)   *see* Southbourne St Chris *Win*

BOURNEMOUTH (St Clement) (St Swithun) *Win 8*   **P** *DBP*
P-in-c T J MATTHEWS   **C** S R NICHOLLS

BOURNEMOUTH (St Francis) *Win 8*   **P** *CR*
P-in-c J C NIGHTINGALE

BOURNEMOUTH (St John the Baptist)   *see* Winton, Moordown and Charminster *Win*

BOURNEMOUTH (St John) (St Michael and All Angels) *Win 8*   **P** *Bp and S R Willcox Esq (jt)*   **V** S E YETMAN

BOURNEMOUTH (St Luke)   *see* Winton, Moordown and Charminster *Win*

BOURNEMOUTH Town Centre (St Augustin) (St Peter) (St Stephen) w St Swithun and Holy Trinity *Win 8*   **P** *Patr Bd*   **TR** I A TERRY   **C** M A CLAYTON

BOURNVILLE (St Andrew)   *see* Bleadon and Bournville *B & W*

BOURNVILLE (St Francis) *Birm 4*   **P** *Bp*   **V** P G BABINGTON
C G ROGERS

BOURTON (Holy Trinity)   *see* Wenlock *Heref*

BOURTON (St George)   *see* Upper Stour *Sarum*

BOURTON (St James)   *see* Shrivenham and Ashbury *Ox*

BOURTON (St Peter)   *see* Draycote Gp *Cov*

BOURTON ON THE HILL (St Lawrence)   *see* Vale and Cotswold Edge *Glouc*

BOURTON, GREAT (All Saints)   *see* Shires' Edge *Ox*

BOURTON-ON-THE-WATER (St Lawrence) w Clapton and The Rissingtons *Glouc 8*   **P** *Wadh Coll Ox, DBP, and C T R Wingfield Esq, and Ld Chan (by turn)*   **R** R N KING

BOVEY TRACEY (St John the Evangelist) w Heathfield *Ex 8*   **P** *Guild of All So*   **P-in-c** N J DEBNEY

BOVEY TRACEY (St Peter and St Paul and St Thomas of Canterbury) w Hennock *Ex 8*   **P** *The Crown (2 turns), MMCET (1 turn)*   **V** W G HAMILTON

BOVEY, NORTH (St John the Baptist)   *see* Moretonhampstead, Manaton, N Bovey and Lustleigh *Ex*

BOVINGDON (St Lawrence) *St Alb 4*   **P** *Ch Soc Trust*
V C E BURCH   **NSM** S P WOODMORE

BOW (All Hallows)   *see* Bromley by Bow All Hallows *Lon*

BOW (St Bartholomew) w Broad Nymet *Ex 2*   **P** *DBP*
R *vacant*

BOW (St Mary) and Holy Trinity w Bromley St Leonard
Lon 7 **P** *Bp and Grocers' Co (jt)* **NSM** W A O'REILLY
BOW BRICKHILL (All Saints) *see* Brickhills and Stoke
Hammond *Ox*
BOW COMMON (St Paul) *Lon 7* **P** *Bp* **V** B G HEGARTY
**BOWBROOK NORTH: Feckenham and Hanbury and Stock
and Bradley** *Worc 8* **P** *Bp and D&C (jt)* **P-in-c** A D MORRIS
NSM V W BEYNON
**BOWBROOK SOUTH: Crowle w Bredicot and Hadzor w
Oddingley and Tibberton and Himbleton and
Huddington** *Worc 8* **P** *Bp, D&C, R J G Berkeley Esq, and
J F Bennett Esq (jt)* **P-in-c** A D MORRIS **NSM** V W BEYNON
BOWBURN (Christ the King) and Tudhoe Grange
St Andrew Dur 5 **P** *Bp* **V** J LIVESLEY
BOWDEN HILL (St Anne) *see* Gtr Corsham and Lacock *Bris*
BOWDEN, GREAT (St Peter and St Paul) *see* Market
Harborough and The Transfiguration etc *Leic*
BOWDEN, LITTLE (St Hugh) *as above*
BOWDEN, LITTLE (St Nicholas) *as above*
BOWDON (St Luke) (St Mary the Virgin) *Ches 10* **P** *Bp*
V I M RUMSEY **C** J A PIPER
BOWERCHALKE (Holy Trinity) *see* Chalke Valley *Sarum*
**BOWERS GIFFORD (St John) (St Margaret) w North
Benfleet** *Chelmsf 12* **P** *Em Coll Cam and J R F Bryers Esq
(alt)* **P-in-c** D A O IBIAYO
BOWES (St Giles) *see* Lower Teesdale *Leeds*
BOWES PARK (St Michael-at-Bowes) *see* Wood Green St Mich
w Bounds Green St Gabr etc *Lon*
BOWLAND and The Flyfords *see* Abberton, The Flyfords,
Naunton Beauchamp etc *Worc*
BOWLEE (St Thomas) *see* Langley *Man*
BOWLING (St John) *Leeds 2* **P** *V Bradford*
P-in-c T C R THOMAS **NSM** C BARNES
BOWLING (St Stephen) *see* Bankfoot and Bowling St Steph
Leeds
**BOWNESS-ON-SOLWAY (St Michael), Kirkbride and
Newton Arlosh** *Carl 3* **P** *Earl of Lonsdale (2 turns), V Holme
Cultram (1 turn)* **R** *vacant*
BOWTHORPE (St Michael) *Nor 3* **P** *Bp and CPAS (jt)*
V *vacant*
BOX (St Barnabas) *see* Minchinhampton w Box and
Amberley *Glouc*
BOX (St Thomas à Becket) w Hazlebury and Ditteridge
Bris 4 **P** *Bp* **P-in-c** J M ANDERSON-MACKENZIE
OLM C M SOUTHGATE
BOX HILL (St Andrew) *see* Headley and Box Hill w Walton
on the Hill *Guildf*
BOX RIVER *see* Boxford, Edwardstone, Groton etc *St E*
BOXFORD (St Andrew) *see* E Downland *Ox*
**BOXFORD (St Mary), Edwardstone, Groton, Little
Waldingfield and Newton** *St E 9* **P** *DBP and The Hon
Thomas Lindsay (1 turn), Ld Chan (2 turns), Peterho Cam
(1 turn)* **R** R T PARKER-MCGEE
BOXGROVE (St Mary and St Blaise) *Chich 2* **P** *Duke of
Richmond and Gordon* **P-in-c** I M FORRESTER
BOXLEY (St Mary the Virgin and All Saints) *see* N Downs
Cant
BOXMOOR (St John the Evangelist) *St Alb 2* **P** *Bp*
V M D MACEY **NSM** R C GOATLY
BOXTED (Holy Trinity) *see* Glemsford, Hartest w Boxted,
Somerton etc *St E*
BOXTED (St Peter) *see* Langham w Boxted *Chelmsf*
**BOXWELL (St Mary the Virgin), Leighterton, Didmarton,
Oldbury-on-the-Hill, Sopworth, Badminton w Little
Badminton, Acton Turville, Hawkesbury, Westonbirt
and Lasborough** *Glouc 5* **P** *Duke of Beaufort, J A Huntley
Esq, and Westonbirt Sch (jt)* **P-in-c** R W B THOMSON
BOXWORTH (St Peter) *see* Papworth *Ely*
BOYATT WOOD (St Peter) *Win 10* **P** *Bp* **V** I S MCFARLANE
**BOYLESTONE (St John the Baptist), Church Broughton,
Dalbury, Longford, Long Lane, Radbourne, Sutton on
the Hill and Trusley** *Derby 6* **P** *Patr Bd* **P-in-c** J M LEGH
BOYNE HILL (All Saints) *Ox 5* **P** *Bp* **V** J M HARRIS
BOYNTON (St Andrew) *see* Rudston, Boynton, Carnaby etc
York
BOYTHORPE (St Francis) *see* Chesterfield SS Aug *Derby*
**BOYTON (Holy Name), North Tamerton, Werrington,
St Giles-in-the-Heath and Virginstow** *Truro 9* **P** *Duchy of
Cornwall, MMCET, Ld Chan, and R Williams Esq (by turn)*
R *vacant*
BOYTON (St Andrew) *see* Wilford Peninsula *St E*
BOYTON (St Mary the Virgin) *see* Upper Wylye Valley *Sarum*
BOZEAT (St Mary) *see* Wollaston w Strixton and Bozeat etc
Pet
BRABOURNE (St Mary the Blessed Virgin) *see* Stour Downs
Cant

BRACEBOROUGH (St Margaret) *see* Uffington Gp *Linc*
BRACEBRIDGE (All Saints) *Linc 11* **P** *Mrs B M Ellison-
Lendrum* **V** A J JACKSON-PARR
BRACEBRIDGE HEATH (St John the Evangelist) *Linc 11*
P *Bp* **V** J A BELL
BRACEBY (St Margaret) *see* N Beltisloe Gp *Linc*
BRACEWELL (St Michael) *see* Barnoldswick w Bracewell *Leeds*
BRACKENFIELD (Holy Trinity) *see* Ashover and Brackenfield
w Wessington *Derby*
BRACKLEY (St Peter w St James) *Pet 1* **P** *Bp*
V R W DUNCAN
BRACKNELL (Holy Trinity) *Ox 3* **P** *Bp* **P-in-c** J D BARLOW
C M M CHALMERS
BRACON ASH (St Nicholas) *see* Mulbarton w Bracon Ash,
Hethel and Flordon *Nor*
BRADBOURNE (All Saints) *see* Wirksworth *Derby*
BRADDAN (St Brendan) *S & M* **P** *Bp* **V** D M H RICHARDS
BRADDEN (St Michael) *see* Towcester w Caldecote and
Easton Neston etc *Pet*
**BRADELEY (St Mary and All Saints), Church Eaton,
Derrington and Haughton** *Lich 10* **P** *Bp and Mrs M N
Nutt (jt)* **R** *vacant*
BRADENHAM (St Botolph) *see* W Wycombe w Bledlow
Ridge, Bradenham and Radnage *Ox*
BRADENHAM, WEST (St Andrew) *see* Dereham and Distr *Nor*
BRADENSTOKE (St Mary) *see* Lyneham and Woodhill *Sarum*
BRADFIELD (St Giles) *see* Trunch Group *Nor*
BRADFIELD (St Lawrence) *see* Mistley w Manningtree and
Bradfield *Chelmsf*
BRADFIELD (St Nicholas) *Sheff 3* **P** *V Ecclesfield*
R A T ISAACSON
BRADFIELD and Stanford Dingley *Ox 4* **P** *Ch Soc Trust*
NSM L E BLISS
BRADFIELD COMBUST (All Saints) *see* St Edm Way *St E*
**BRADFIELD ST CLARE (St Clare), Bradfield St George w
Little Whelnetham, Cockfield, Felsham and Gedding**
St E 6 **P** *St Jo Coll Cam (1 turn), Bp and Lt Col J G Aldous
(1 turn)* **R** S J POTTER
BRADFIELD ST GEORGE (St George) *see* Bradfield St Clare,
Bradfield St George etc *St E*
BRADFORD (All Saints) *see* Black Torrington, Bradford w
Cookbury etc *Ex*
BRADFORD (St Augustine) (St Clement) *Leeds 2* **P** *Bp and
V Bradf* **V** R A FAIRHURST
BRADFORD (St Martin) *see* Girlington, Heaton and
Manningham *Leeds*
BRADFORD (St Oswald) *see* Lt Horton *Leeds*
BRADFORD (St Saviour) *see* Fairweather Green *Leeds*
BRADFORD (St Stephen) *see* Bankfoot and Bowling St Steph
Leeds
BRADFORD (St Wilfrid) (St Columba w St Andrew) *Leeds 2*
P *Bp* **C** J E BAVINGTON
BRADFORD ABBAS (St Mary the Virgin) *see* Three Valleys
Sarum
**BRADFORD ON AVON (Holy Trinity), Westwood and
Wingfield** *Sarum 15* **P** *Bp, D&C Sarum, D&C Bris, and CPAS
(jt)* **R** J M ABECASSIS **NSM** A M GREEN
**BRADFORD ON AVON, NORTH (Christ Church) and
Villages**, including Monkton Farleigh, South Wraxall,
and Winsley *Sarum 15* **P** *D&C Bris (2 turns), Bp (1 turn),
V Bradf H Trin (1 turn)* **R** A B KEATING **C** T G MANN
NSM A K CHARNLEY
BRADFORD ON TONE (St Giles) *see* Wellington and Distr
B & W
BRADFORD PEVERELL (Church of the Assumption) *see*
Charminster, Stinsford and the Chalk Stream villages *Sarum*
BRADFORD, WEST (St Catherine) *see* Waddington *Blackb*
BRADING (St Mary the Virgin) *see* Seaview, St Helens,
Brading and Yaverland *Portsm*
BRADLEY (All Saints) *see* Farleigh, Candover and Wield *Win*
BRADLEY (All Saints) *see* Hulland, Atlow, Kniveton, Bradley
and Hognaston *Derby*
BRADLEY (St George) *see* Gt and Lt Coates w Bradley *Linc*
BRADLEY (St John the Baptist) *see* Bowbrook N *Worc*
BRADLEY (St Martin) *Lich 27* **P** *Baldwin Pugh Trustees*
V *vacant*
BRADLEY (St Mary) *see* Cononley w Bradley *Leeds*
BRADLEY (St Thomas) *Leeds 11* **P** *Bp* **P-in-c** I D JAMIESON
BRADLEY STOKE (Christ the King) (Holy Trinity) *Bris 5*
P *Bp and Bris Ch Trustees (jt)* **V** P F HINCKLEY
BRADLEY, GREAT (St Mary the Virgin) *see* Stourhead *St E*
BRADLEY, LITTLE (All Saints) *as above*
**BRADLEY, NORTH (St Nicholas), Southwick, Heywood and
Steeple Ashton** *Sarum 15* **P** *Win Coll and Magd Coll Cam
(jt)* **V** O J LEARMONT

BRADLEY, WEST (not known)   see Baltonsborough w Butleigh, W Bradley etc *B & W*

BRADLEY-LE-MOORS (St Leonard)   see Alton w Bradley-le-Moors and Denstone etc *Lich*

BRADMORE (Mission Room)   see Keyworth and Stanton-on-the-Wolds and Bunny etc *S'well*

BRADNINCH (St Disen) *Ex 7*   P *D&C Windsor*   P-in-c O H J MEARS

BRADNOP (Mission Church)   see Butterton, Ipstones-w-Berkhamsytch etc *Lich*

BRADOC (Blessed Virgin Mary)   see Lostwithiel Parishes *Truro*

BRADPOLE (Holy Trinity)   see Bridport *Sarum*

BRADSHAW (St John the Evangelist) and Holmfield *Leeds 10*   P *Bp*   V K A SHOESMITH   C J A CLARKE   NSM S M HEPTINSTALL

BRADSHAW (St Maxentius)   see Turton Moorland *Man*

BRADWELL (Holy Trinity)   see Cressing w Stisted and Bradwell etc *Chelmsf*

BRADWELL (St Barnabas)   see Hope, Castleton and Bradwell *Derby*

BRADWELL (St Barnabas) and Porthill *Lich 9*   P *Bp*   V C S B ROUTLEDGE   C K E PETHERICK

BRADWELL (St Lawrence and Methodist United)   see Stantonbury and Willen *Ox*

BRADWELL (St Nicholas) *Nor 6*   P *Bp*   NSM C M UPTON, S D UPTON

BRADWELL ON SEA (St Thomas) (St Peter-on-the-Wall) and St Lawrence *Chelmsf 11*   P *Bp*   P-in-c S K POSS

BRADWELL, NEW (St James)   see Stantonbury and Willen *Ox*

BRADWORTHY (St John the Baptist), Sutcombe, Putford, Abbots Bickington, Bulkworthy, and Milton Damerel *Ex 16*   P *The Crown (1 turn), Bp and Exors Mrs F M Palmer (1 turn)*   R R A FREEMAN

BRAFFERTON (St Peter) w Pilmoor, Myton-on-Swale and Thormanby *York 3*   P *Abp and Prof Sir Anthony Milnes Coates Bt (jt)*   P-in-c D M COYNE   C E C HASSALL, M E YOUNG, M H WAINWRIGHT, M HARRISON, S WHITING   NSM C C CRANFIELD, C C GITTENS, C J TOASE, S P POPE, T M GANT

BRAFIELD ON THE GREEN (St Laurence)   see Cogenhoe and Gt and Lt Houghton w Brafield *Pet*

BRAILES (St George) *Cov 9*   P *D&C*   V G HEIGHTON   NSM J W ROLFE

BRAILSFORD (All Saints) w Shirley, Osmaston w Edlaston and Yeaveley *Derby 1*   P *Bp, Earl Ferrers, and Sir Peter Walker-Okeover Bt (by turn)*   R P M TAYLOR   NSM F M GRANT

BRAINTREE (St Michael) *Chelmsf 17*   P *Ch Trust Fund Trust*   P-in-c N C ADAMS

BRAINTREE (St Paul) *Chelmsf 17*   P *Ch Trust Fund Trust*   C C M FAIRWEATHER

BRAISHFIELD (All Saints)   see Michelmersh and Awbridge and Braishfield etc *Win*

BRAITHWAITE (St Herbert)   see Upper Derwent *Carl*

BRAITHWELL (St James)   see Ravenfield, Hooton Roberts and Braithwell *Sheff*

BRAMBER (St Nicholas)   see Beeding and Bramber w Botolphs *Chich*

BRAMBLETON (not known)   see The Bourne and Tilford *Guildf*

BRAMCOTE (St Michael and All Angels) *S'well 9*   P *CPAS*   V P F REYNOLDS

BRAMDEAN (St Simon and St Jude)   see Upper Itchen *Win*

BRAMDEAN COMMON (Church in the Wood)   as above

BRAMERTON (St Peter)   see Rockland St Mary w Hellington, Bramerton etc *Nor*

BRAMFIELD (St Andrew)   see Beane Valley *St Alb*

BRAMFIELD (St Andrew)   see Blyth Valley *St E*

BRAMFORD (St Mary the Virgin) w Little Blakenham, Baylham and Nettlestead *St E 2*   P *MMCET, Bp and D&C Cant (jt)*   V vacant

BRAMHALL (St Michael and All Angels) (Hall Chapel) *Ches 17*   P *Trustees*   V C L PIPER

BRAMHAM (All Saints) *York 1*   P *Ch Ch Ox, G F Lane Fox Esq, and Lady Elizabeth Hastings Estate Charity (jt)*   P-in-c N J MORGAN, NSM P M ANSLOW

BRAMHOPE (St Giles) *Leeds 15*   P *Trustees*   V T P LUSTY

BRAMLEY (Holy Trinity) and Grafham *Guildf 2*   P *Ld Chan*   NSM C E Z WHITE

BRAMLEY (St Francis) *Sheff 6*   P *Bp and Sir Philip Naylor-Leyland Bt (jt)*   Hon C N BOWLER

BRAMLEY (St James)   see Sherfield-on-Loddon and Stratfield Saye etc *Win*

BRAMLEY (St Peter) *Leeds 14*   P *V Leeds City*   R P A CRABB

BRAMPFORD SPEKE (St Peter), Cadbury, Newton St Cyres, Poltimore, Rewe, Stoke Canon, Thorverton and Upton

Pyne *Ex 2*   P *Bp, Earl of Iddlesleigh, DBP, D&C (1 turn), Ld Chan (1 turn)*   R K L CROSS   NSM J A DALLEN, S SHEPPARD

BRAMPTON (St Mark) *Derby 3*   P *Bp*   P-in-c K E HAMBLIN   C J D LOMAS   NSM H J MOORE

BRAMPTON (St Martin)   see Eden, Gelt and Irthing *Carl*

BRAMPTON (St Mary Magdalene)   see E Leightonstone *Ely*

BRAMPTON (St Peter)   see Aylsham and Distr *Nor*

BRAMPTON (St Thomas the Martyr) *Derby 3*   P *Bp*   R M J BARNES   C D M OWENS, M R BROOMHEAD   NSM H J MOORE

BRAMPTON ASH (St Mary)   see Desborough, Brampton Ash, Dingley and Braybrooke *Pet*

BRAMPTON BIERLOW (Christ Church) *Sheff 12*   P *V Wath-upon-Dearne*   V vacant

BRAMPTON BRYAN (St Barnabas)   see Wigmore Abbey *Heref*

BRAMPTON, OLD (St Peter and St Paul) (Cutthorpe Institute) and Great Barlow *Derby 3*   P *Bp and TR Staveley and Barrow Hill (jt)*   R P J GREEN   C D P MOUNCER

BRAMSHALL (St Laurence)   see Uttoxeter Area *Lich*

BRAMSHAW (St Peter)   see Forest and Avon *Sarum*

BRAMSHILL (Mission Church)   see Darby Green and Eversley *Win*

BRAMSHOTT (St Mary the Virgin) and Liphook *Portsm 4*   P *Qu Coll Ox*   P-in-c V W INGLIS-JONES

BRANCASTER (St Mary the Virgin)   see Hunstanton St Mary w Ringstead Parva etc *Nor*

BRANCEPETH (St Brandon) *Dur 1*   P *Bp*   P-in-c A L BROOKER   NSM A C HOBBS

BRANDESBURTON (St Mary) and Leven *York 11*   P *St Jo Coll Cam and Simeon's Trustees (jt)*   V J E GRAINGER-SMITH   NSM M M DESBOROUGH

BRANDESTON (All Saints)   see Orebeck *St E*

BRANDLESHOLME (St Francis House Chapel)   see Kirklees Valley *Man*

BRANDON (Chapel)   see S Cliff Villages Gp *Linc*

BRANDON (St John the Evangelist) and Ushaw Moor *Dur 1*   P *R Brancepeth*   P-in-c C R PETERS

BRANDON (St Peter) *St E 7*   P M A F *Carter Esq*   V S D COBURN   NSM D A COBURN, K PALMER

BRANDON PARVA (All Saints)   see Barnham Broom and Upper Yare *Nor*

BRANDSBY (All Saints)   see Crayke w Brandsby and Yearsley *York*

BRANDWOOD (St Bede) *Birm 4*   P *Bp*   V A M DELMEGE

BRANKSEA ISLAND (St Mary)   see Parkstone St Pet and St Osmund w Branksea *Sarum*

BRANKSOME (St Aldhelm) (St Francis) *Sarum 7*   P *Bp*   V P J MARTIN   NSM S J FLATT

BRANKSOME (St Clement) (St Barnabas) *Sarum 7*   P *MMCET*   V J G V FOSTER   C L J BOWERMAN, M WILLIS

BRANKSOME PARK (All Saints) *Sarum 7*   P *MMCET*   V C R BOYLE

BRANSCOMBE (St Winifred)   see Colyton, Musbury, Southleigh and Branscombe *Ex*

BRANSDALE (St Nicholas)   see Kirkbymoorside w Gillamoor, Farndale etc *York*

BRANSFORD (St John the Baptist)   see Worcs W Rural *Worc*

BRANSGORE (St Mary the Virgin) and Hinton Admiral *Win 9*   P *Sir George Meyrick Bt and Exors P W Jesson (jt)*   P-in-c B C SARGENT

BRANSHOLME (St John the Evangelist) *York 14*   P *Abp*   V vacant

BRANSTON (All Saints) w Nocton and Potterhanworth *Linc 12*   P *Stowe Sch (2 turns), Ld Chan (1 turn), and Nocton Ltd (1 turn)*   R L D BRABIN-SMITH   NSM A J BORMAN

BRANSTON (St Saviour) and Burton All Saints w Christ Church *Lich 13*   P *CPAS, Ch Soc Trust, and Simeon's Trustees (jt)*   V D L COLLIER

BRANSTON BY BELVOIR (St Guthlac)   see High Framland Par *Leic*

BRANT BROUGHTON (St Helen) and Beckingham *Linc 22*   P *Bp and Sir Richard Sutton Bt (alt)*   R C A GOLDSMITH

BRANT ROAD (Church Centre)   see Bracebridge *Linc*

BRANTHAM (St Michael and All Angels)   see E Bergholt and Brantham *St E*

BRANTINGHAM (All Saints)   see Elloughton and Brough w Brantingham *York*

BRANXTON (St Paul) *Newc 12*   P *Abp*   P-in-c G R J KELSEY   NSM J B CARR

BRASSINGTON (St James)   see Wirksworth *Derby*

BRASTED (St Martin) *Roch 9*   P *Abp*   R L A GREEN

BRATHAY (Holy Trinity)   see Loughrigg *Carl*

BRATOFT (St Peter and St Paul)   see Burgh Gp *Linc*

BRATTLEBY (St Cuthbert)   see Spring Line Gp *Linc*

BRATTON (St James the Great) (Oratory), Edington and Imber, Erlestoke and Coulston *Sarum 17* **P** *Bp and V Westbury (jt)* **R** A J M SINCLAIR

BRATTON CLOVELLY (St Mary the Virgin) *see* Okehampton, Inwardleigh, Belstone, Sourton etc *Ex*

BRATTON FLEMING (St Peter) *see* Shirwell, Loxhore, Kentisbury, Arlington, etc *Ex*

BRATTON ST MAUR (St Nicholas) *see* Camelot Par *B & W*

BRAUGHING (St Mary the Virgin), Furneux Pelham and Stocking Pelham *St Alb 15* **P** *Bp and the Hon R P Hamilton (jt)* **R** J A GAWTHROPE

BRAUNSTON (All Saints) *see* Daventry *Pet*

BRAUNSTON (All Saints) *see* Oakham, Ashwell, Braunston, Brooke, Egleton etc *Pet*

BRAUNSTONE PARK (St Peter) *Leic 1* **P** *Bp* **V** K R MAGEE **NSM** N J ROOMS

BRAUNSTONE TOWN (St Crispin) w Thorpe Astley *Leic 9* **P** *Bp* **P-in-c** D J HOVER

BRAUNTON (St Brannock) *Ex 14* **P** *Bp* **P-in-c** A THORNE **Hon C** L A BUTTLE

BRAXTED, GREAT (All Saints) *see* Thurstable and Winstree *Chelmsf*

BRAXTED, LITTLE (St Nicholas) *see* Wickham Bishops w Lt Braxted *Chelmsf*

BRAY (St Michael) and Braywood *Ox 5* **P** *Bp* **V** A L SWIFT

BRAY, HIGH (All Saints) *see* Bishopsnympton, Charles, E Anstey, High Bray etc *Ex*

BRAYBROOKE (All Saints) *see* Desborough, Brampton Ash, Dingley and Braybrooke *Pet*

BRAYDESTON (St Michael) *see* Yare Valley *Nor*

BRAYDON BROOK, comprising Ashley, Charlton, Crudwell, Hankerton, Minety, and Oaksey *Bris 6* **P** *Duchy of Lancaster (1 turn), Bp and Ch Soc Trust (3 turns)* **R** T NIXON **OLM** S J WYMAN

BRAYTON (St Wilfrid) *York 4* **P** *Abp* **R** P D WATSON **C** R P SUEKARRAN

BREADSALL (All Saints) *Derby 5* **P** *Miss A I M Harpur-Crewe* **P-in-c** K J PLANT

BREAGE (St Breaca) *see* W Kerrier *Truro*

BREAM (St James) *Glouc 1* **P** *Bp* **V** C W MACLAY

BREAMORE (St Mary) *see* Fordingbridge and Hyde and Breamore etc *Win*

BREAN (St Bridget) *see* Berrow and Breane *B & W*

BREARTON (St John the Baptist) *see* Knaresborough, Goldsborough, Nidd and Brearton *Leeds*

BREASTON (St Michael) *see* Wilne and Draycott w Breaston *Derby*

BRECKLES (St Margaret) *see* Caston, Griston, Merton, Thompson etc *Nor*

BREDBURY (St Barnabas) *Ches 16* **P** *V Bredbury St Mark* **P-in-c** S E W SHRINE

BREDBURY (St Mark) *Ches 16* **P** *Bp* **P-in-c** A D BULL

BREDE (St George) *see* Brede w Udimore and Beckley and Peasmarsh *Chich*

BREDE (St George) w Udimore and Beckley and Peasmarsh *Chich 17* **P** *Bp, SS Coll Cam, Univ Coll Ox, and Dr P M J Crook (jt)* **Hon C** J D JELLEY

BREDENBURY (St Andrew) *Heref 2* **P** *DBP, V Bromyard, and J H Barneby Esq (jt)* **R** E S SIDWELL

BREDFIELD (St Andrew) *see* Woodbridge St Jo and Bredfield *St E*

BREDGAR (St John the Baptist) *see* Tunstall and Bredgar *Cant*

BREDHURST (St Peter) *see* S Gillingham *Roch*

BREDICOT (St James the Less) *see* Bowbrook S *Worc*

BREDON (St Giles) w Bredon's Norton *Worc 4* **P** *Bp* **R** *vacant*

BREDON'S NORTON (not known) *see* Bredon w Bredon's Norton *Worc*

BREDWARDINE (St Andrew) *see* Cusop w Blakemere, Bredwardine w Brobury etc *Heref*

BREDY, LITTLE (St Michael and All Angels) *see* Bride Valley *Sarum*

BREEDON ON THE HILL (St Mary and St Hardulph) *see* Ashby-de-la-Zouch and Breedon on the Hill *Leic*

BREIGHTMET (St James) *see* Leverhulme *Man*

BREIGHTMET Top o' th' Moss (St John the Evangelist) *as above*

BREINTON (St Michael) *see* W Heref *Heref*

BREMHILL (St Martin) *see* Marden Vale *Sarum*

BRENCHLEY (All Saints) *Roch 8* **P** *D&C Cant* **V** R C PAGET

BRENDON (St Brendon) *see* Lynton, Brendon, Countisbury etc *Ex*

BRENT ELEIGH (St Mary) *see* Monks Eleigh w Chelsworth and Brent Eleigh etc *St E*

BRENT KNOLL (St Michael) and East Brent and Lympsham *B & W 1* **P** *Adn Wells (1 turn), Bp (2 turns)* **P-in-c** K J WRIGHT

BRENT PELHAM (St Mary the Virgin) *see* Hormead, Wyddial, Anstey, Brent Pelham etc *St Alb*

BRENT TOR (Christ Church) *see* Tavistock, Gulworthy and Brent Tor *Ex*

BRENT TOR (St Michael) *as above*

BRENT, EAST (The Blessed Virgin Mary) *see* Brent Knoll, E Brent and Lympsham *B & W*

BRENT, SOUTH (St Petroc) *see* Buckfastleigh, Dean Prior, Littlehempston etc *Ex*

BRENTFORD (St Paul w St Lawrence and St George) (St Faith) *Lon 11* **P** *Bp* **P-in-c** S H GUINNESS **C** O D PENNANT

BRENTWOOD (St George the Martyr) *Chelmsf 8* **P** *DBP* **V** *vacant*

BRENTWOOD (St Thomas) *Chelmsf 8* **P** *DBP* **P-in-c** M R NORTH

BRENZETT (St Eanswith) *see* Brookland, Fairfield, Brenzett w Snargate etc *Cant*

BRERETON (St Michael) and Rugeley w Armitage *Lich 3* **P** *Patr Bd* **TR** D M A EVANS **TV** G L HOLDING, P O HART **NSM** J WOOD **OLM** B D TABERNOR

BRERETON (St Oswald) *Ches 11* **P** *DBP* **C** A C FISHER

BRESSINGHAM (St John the Baptist) *see* Diss *Nor*

BRETBY (St Wystan) *see* Hartshorne and Bretby *Derby*

BRETFORTON (St Leonard) *see* E Vale and Avon Villages *Worc*

BRETHERTON (St John the Baptist) *see* Croston, Bretherton and Mawdesley w Bispham *Blackb*

BRETTENHAM (St Andrew) *see* E w W Harling, Bridgham w Roudham, Larling etc *Nor*

BRETTENHAM (St Mary) *see* Rattlesden w Thorpe Morieux, Brettenham etc *St E*

BRETTON (Holy Spirit) *see* Pet H Spirit Bretton *Pet*

BREWHAM, SOUTH (St John the Baptist) *see* Bruton, Brewham, Pitcombe and Shepton Montague *B & W*

BREWOOD (St Mary and St Chad) *Lich 2* **P** *Bp* **V** P MOON

BRICETT, GREAT (St Mary and St Lawrence) *see* S Bosmere *St E*

BRICKENDON (Holy Cross and St Alban) *see* Lt Berkhamsted and Bayford, Essendon etc *St Alb*

BRICKET WOOD (St Luke) *St Alb 5* **P** *CPAS* **V** K A HODGINS

BRICKHILL, GREAT (St Mary the Virgin) *see* Brickhills and Stoke Hammond *Ox*

BRICKHILL, LITTLE (St Mary Magdalene) *as above*

BRICKHILL, NORTH (St Mark) *see* Bedf St Mark *St Alb*

BRICKHILLS and Stoke Hammond, The *Ox 15* **P** *Bp, Major Sir Philip Pauncefort-Duncombe Bt, St Edw Sch Ox, and Cam Univ (jt)* **R** J WALLER

BRICKLEHAMPTON (St Michael) *see* Elmley Castle w Bricklehampton and Combertons *Worc*

BRIDE (St Bridget), Lezayre and North Ramsey *S & M* **P** *The Crown* **R** B G EVANS-SMITH

BRIDE VALLEY, comprising Burton Bradstock and Chilcombe, Little Bredy, Litton Cheney, Long Bredy, Puncknowle, Shipton Gorge, and Swyre *Sarum 2* **P** *Sir Robert Williams Bt and G A L-F Pitt-Rivers Esq (jt)* **R** J L WILLIAMS **NSM** S LINFORD

BRIDEKIRK (St Bridget) *see* Cockermouth Area *Carl*

BRIDESTOWE (St Bridget) *see* Okehampton, Inwardleigh, Belstone, Sourton etc *Ex*

BRIDFORD (St Thomas à Becket) *see* Christow, Ashton, Bridford, Dunchideock etc *Ex*

BRIDGE (St Peter) *Cant 1* **P** *Abp and St Jo Coll Ox (jt)* **P-in-c** T E LAST

BRIDGE Parishes, The, comprising Kingston Lacy, Shapwick, and Sturminster Marshall *Sarum 6* **P** *Eton Coll and Nat Trust (alt)* **P-in-c** C M COUZENS

BRIDGE SOLLARS (St Andrew) *see* Magnis Gp *Heref*

BRIDGE, The *see* Meon Bridge *Portsm*

BRIDGEMARY (St Matthew) *Portsm 3* **P** *Bp* **V** K I MITCHELL

BRIDGERULE (St Bridget) *see* Holsworthy, Hollacombe, Pyworthy etc *Ex*

BRIDGFORD, EAST (St Peter) and Kneeton *S'well 5* **P** *Magd Coll Ox (2 turns), C G Neale Esq (1 turn)* **P-in-c** R M COLBY

BRIDGFORD, WEST (St Giles) *S'well 6* **P** *Waddington Trustees* **R** L J PROUDLOVE **C** T J E CHAMBERS

BRIDGHAM (St Mary) *see* E w W Harling, Bridgham w Roudham, Larling etc *Nor*

BRIDGNORTH (St Mary Magdalene) (St Leonard) (St James) and Morville Parishes Team Ministry, including Acton Round, Astley Abbotts, Aston Eyre, Monkhopton w Upton Cressett, Morville, Oldbury, Quatford, and Tasley *Heref 8* **P** *Ld Chan (1 turn), DBP (3 turns)* **TR** S H CAWDELL **TV** S H L CAWDELL **C** C I MUNDAY **Hon C** H J PATTERSON **NSM** M A BROOKS

BRIDGWATER (Holy Trinity) and Durleigh St Hugh
B & W 13   **P** *Bp (2 turns) and Ld Chan (1 turn)*
V W H H LANE   **C** J R TAYLOR

BRIDGWATER (St Francis of Assisi) *B & W 13*   **P** *Bp*
V *vacant*

BRIDGWATER (St John the Baptist) *B & W 13*   **P** *Bp*
V E J SPARROW

BRIDGWATER (St Mary) and Chilton Trinity *B & W 13*   **P** *Ld Chan*   **V** P A OLLIVE   **C** S J ISON-STIERER

BRIDLINGTON (Christ Church) w Bessingby and Ulrome
York 9   **P** *Abp, R Bridlington Priory, and R J Wright Esq (jt)*
V M J CAREY

BRIDLINGTON (Emmanuel) and Barmston w Fraisthorpe
York 9   **P** *Trustees and The Hon S E Cunliffe-Lister (jt)*
V R W HARE   **NSM** B F BANCROFT

BRIDLINGTON (Holy Trinity) and Sewerby w Marton *York 9*
P *Abp*   **V** D J MATHER

BRIDLINGTON (St Mary's Priory Church) *York 9*   **P** *Simeon's Trustees*   **R** M R POLLARD   **NSM** C A STRAND, J E FOWLER,
M D WALLER

BRIDPORT (St Mary) *Sarum 2*   **P** *Patr Bd (2 turns) and Ld Chan (1 turn)*   **TR** D J SMITH   **TV** P J M STONE
NSM L D JOHNSON

BRIDSTOW (St Bridget)   *see* StowCaple *Heref*

BRIERCLIFFE (St James) *Blackb 3*   **P** *Hulme Trustees*
V P J PAYTON

BRIERFIELD (St Luke) *Blackb 6*   **P** *Bp*   **V** S A ADESANYA
NSM S J LARGE

BRIERLEY HILL (St Michael) (St Paul) *Worc 10*   **P** *Ld Chan (2 turns), Patr Bd (1 turn)*   **TR** D J HOSKIN   **NSM** B I PRITCHETT

BRIGG (St John the Evangelist), Wrawby and Cadney cum Howsham *Linc 8*   **P** *Bp*   **V** G O MITCHELL

BRIGHAM (St Bridget), Clifton, Dean and Mosser *Carl 6*
P *Patr Bd*   **R** *vacant*

BRIGHOUSE (St Chad)   *see* Lightcliffe and Hove Edge *Leeds*

BRIGHOUSE (St Martin) and Clifton *Leeds 7*   **P** *Bp*
V J P WEBB

BRIGHSTONE (St Mary the Virgin)   *see* W Wight *Portsm*

BRIGHTLING (St Thomas of Canterbury), Mountfield and Netherfield *Chich 13*   **P** *Bp, Adn Lewes and Hastings,
H C Grissell Esq, Mrs A Egerton, and Mrs L A Fraser (jt)*
P-in-c A-M CROSSE

BRIGHTLINGSEA (All Saints) (St James) *Chelmsf 23*   **P** *Ld Chan*   **V** C E BECKETT

BRIGHTON (Annunciation) *Chich 19*   **P** *Wagner Trustees*
P-in-c A J R MURLEY

BRIGHTON (Chapel Royal) *Chich 19*   **P** *Bp*   **V** D J BIGGS

BRIGHTON (Good Shepherd) Preston *Chich 19*   **P** *Bp*
V F P A MASCARENHAS

BRIGHTON (St Bartholomew) *Chich 19*   **P** *Wagner Trustees*
V *vacant*

BRIGHTON (St Cuthman)   *see* Whitehawk *Chich*

BRIGHTON (St George w St Anne and St Mark) *Chich 19*
P *Bp and V Brighton (jt)*   **V** A H MANSON-BRAILSFORD

BRIGHTON (St John)   *see* Preston St Jo w Brighton St Aug and
St Sav *Chich*

BRIGHTON (St Luke) Queen's Park *Chich 19*   **P** *Bp*
C J NEWSON

BRIGHTON (St Martin) w St Wilfrid and St Alban *Chich 19*
P SMF   **V** T G BUXTON

BRIGHTON (St Mary the Virgin)   *see* Kemp Town St Mary
Chich

BRIGHTON (St Matthias) *Chich 19*   **P** *V Preston*
P-in-c T J HOLBIRD

BRIGHTON (St Michael and All Angels) (St Paul) *Chich 19*
P SMF   **V** R J NORBURY   **C** R J BUTCHER-TUSET
NSM K L HUMPHRYS

BRIGHTON (St Nicholas of Myra) *Chich 19*   **P** *Bp*
V D KEECH   **C** J A J C REID

BRIGHTON (St Peter) *Chich 19*   **P** *Bp and V Brompton H Trin (jt)*   **V** R M COATES   **C** A J MARSHALL, H L F GARRATT,
J P GUMBEL, T J HOLBIRD   **NSM** K L SHREEVES

BRIGHTON, NEW (St James) (Emmanuel) *Ches 7*   **P** *Bp*
V H D ATKINSON

BRIGHTSIDE (St Thomas and St Margaret) w Wincobank
Sheff 3   **P** *The Crown and Sheff Ch Burgesses (alt)*
V P N WARMAN

BRIGHTWALTON (All Saints)   *see* W Downland *Ox*

BRIGHTWELL (St Agatha)   *see* Wallingford *Ox*

BRIGHTWELL (St John the Baptist)   *see* Martlesham w
Brightwell *St E*

BRIGHTWELL BALDWIN (St Bartholomew)   *see* Benson w
Ewelme *Ox*

BRIGNALL (St Mary)   *see* Lower Teesdale *Leeds*

BRIGSLEY (St Helen)   *see* Waltham Gp *Linc*

BRIGSTOCK (St Andrew) w Stanion and Lowick and Sudborough *Pet 7*   **P** *Bp (2 turns), L G Stopford Sackville Esq (1 turn)*   **R** H J LOWE

BRILL (All Saints)   *see* Bernwode *Ox*

BRILLEY (St Mary)   *see* Eardisley w Bollingham, Willersley,
Brilley etc *Heref*

BRIMFIELD (St Michael)   *see* Leominster *Heref*

BRIMINGTON (St Michael) *Derby 3*   **P** *V Chesterfield*
R D B COOKE

**BRIMPSFIELD (St Michael) w Birdlip, Syde, Daglingworth,
The Duntisbournes, Winstone, Miserden and Edgeworth** *Glouc 7*   **P** *Ld Chan (1 turn), Bp, DBP,
Major M N T H Wills and CCC Ox (1 turn)*   **R** V J THORNE

BRIMPTON (St Peter)   *see* Aldermaston and Woolhampton
Ox

BRIMSCOMBE (Holy Trinity)   *see* Rodborough, Woodchester
and Brimscombe *Glouc*

BRINDLE (St James) *Blackb 4*   **P** *Trustees*   **R** D G WARD

BRINGHURST (St Nicholas)   *see* Six Saints circa Holt *Leic*

BRINGTON (All Saints)   *see* W Leightonstone *Ely*

**BRINGTON (St Mary w St John) w Whilton and Norton
and Church Brampton w Chapel Brampton and Harlestone and East Haddon and Holdenby** *Pet 2*   **P** *Patr Bd (5 turns), The Crown (1 turn)*   **R** A L WATKINS
C K R EVANS

BRININGHAM (St Maurice)   *see* Brinton, Briningham,
Hunworth, Stody etc *Nor*

BRINKBURN (St Peter and St Paul)   *see* Longframlington w
Brinkburn *Newc*

BRINKHILL (St Philip)   *see* S Ormsby Gp *Linc*

BRINKLEY (St Mary)   *see* Raddesley Gp *Ely*

BRINKLOW (St John the Baptist)   *see* Revel Gp *Cov*

BRINKWORTH (St Michael and All Angels)   *see* Woodbridge
Bris

BRINNINGTON (St Luke)   *see* Stockport and Brinnington
Ches

BRINSCALL (St Luke)   *see* Heapey and Withnell *Blackb*

BRINSLEY (St James the Great) w Underwood *S'well 4*
P *Bp*   **P-in-c** D A STEVENSON

BRINSOP (St George)   *see* Magnis Gp *Heref*

BRINSWORTH (St Andrew)   *see* Rivers Team *Sheff*

**BRINTON (St Andrew), Briningham, Hunworth, Stody,
Swanton Novers and Thornage** *Nor 17*   **P** J S Howlett Esq,
Lord Hastings, and DBP (by turn)   **R** J K ELLIOTT DE RIVEROL

BRISLEY (St Bartholomew)   *see* Upper Wensum Village Gp
Nor

BRISLINGTON (St Anne) *Bris 1*   **P** *Bp*   **P-in-c** I L GARRETT

BRISLINGTON (St Christopher) *Bris 1*   **P** *Simeon's Trustees*
P-in-c A W E SCHUMAN

BRISLINGTON (St Cuthbert) *Bris 1*   **P** *Bp*
P-in-c I L GARRETT

BRISLINGTON (St Luke) *Bris 1*   **P** *Bp*   **V** D M DEWES

BRISTOL (Christ Church w Emmanuel)   *see* Clifton Ch Ch w
Em *Bris*

BRISTOL (Christ Church) w St Ewen, All SS and St George
Bris 3   **P** J E Heal Esq   **P-in-c** J G PEDLAR

BRISTOL (Christ the Servant) Stockwood *Bris 1*   **P** *Bp*
V D G OWEN

BRISTOL (St Aidan) w St George *Bris 3*   **P** *Bp and SMF*
P-in-c R J LING   **C** M HOTCHKISS   **NSM** M M CRITCHLOW
OLM N G CALLEN, T M DENLEY

BRISTOL (St Andrew w St Bartholomew)   *see* Bishopston and
St Andrews *Bris*

BRISTOL (St Andrew) Hartcliffe *Bris 1*   **P** *Bp*
P-in-c D A J MADDOX

BRISTOL (St Anne w St Mark and St Thomas)   *see* Eastville
St Anne w St Mark and St Thos *Bris*

BRISTOL (St Mary the Virgin) Redcliffe w Temple and Bedminster St John the Baptist *Bris 1*   **P** *Bp*
V D F TYNDALL   **C** A K Y PALAIRET, K M CAMPION-SPALL
NSM A D EVERITT

BRISTOL (St Matthew and St Nathanael) (St Katharine)
Bris 3   **P** *Bp and CPAS (jt)*   **V** I J TOMKINS   **C** D L WILKIE
OLM A J HULL, R N PENDLEBURY

BRISTOL (St Michael) Two Mile Hill   *see* Two Mile Hill
St Mich *Bris*

BRISTOL (St Philip and St Jacob w Emmanuel) *Bris 3*
P *Trustees*   **V** T J SILK

**BRISTOL (St Stephen) w St James and St John the Baptist
w St Michael and St George** *Bris 3*   **P** *Ld Chan (1 turn), Bp,
Bris Ch Trustees, and D&C (2 turns)*   **P-in-c** L BARNES
NSM R G CROFT   **OLM** F M HOUGHTON,
J D A BROOKE-TAYLOR

BRISTOL Lockleaze (St Mary Magdalene w St Francis)
Bris 3   **P** *Bp*   **V** *vacant*

BRISTOL St Paul's (St Agnes) *Bris 3* **P** *Bp and Bris Ch Trustees (1 turn), Ld Chan (1 turn)* **R** *vacant*

BRISTOL, EAST (St Aidan) *see Bristol St Aid w St Geo Bris*

BRISTOL, EAST (St Ambrose) (St Leonard) *Bris 3* **P** *Bp*
P-in-c N J COLEMAN

BRISTON (All Saints), Burgh Parva, Hindolveston and Melton Constable *Nor 17* **P** *Bp, Lord Hastings, and D&C (jt)* **R** J G SYKES

BRITFORD (St Peter) *see Chalke Valley Sarum*

BRITWELL (St George) *Ox 12* **P** *Eton Coll* **V** N MCCATHIE
C J A GRIFFITHS

BRITWELL SALOME (St Nicholas) *see Icknield Ox*

BRIXHAM (St Mary) (All Saints) w Churston Ferrers and Kingswear *Ex 11* **P** *The Crown* **TV** J C N GAY

BRIXTON (St Mary) *see Yealmpton and Brixton Ex*

BRIXTON (St Matthew) (St Jude) *S'wark 11* **P** *Abp and Ch Soc Trust (jt)* **V** S M SICHEL **NSM** A HOLE

BRIXTON (St Paul) (St Saviour) *S'wark 11* **P** *Ch Soc Trust*
V S J WHITTINGTON

BRIXTON DEVERILL (St Michael) *see Cley Hill Villages Sarum*

BRIXTON ROAD (Christ Church) *S'wark 11* **P** *CPAS*
V T J JEFFREYS

BRIXTON, NORTH (Christ Church) *see Brixton Road Ch Ch S'wark*

BRIXWORTH (All Saints) w Holcot *Pet 2* **P** *Bp*
R C A M THOMAS

BRIZE NORTON (St Britius) and Carterton *Ox 28* **P** *Patr Bd*
TR A C M TWEEDY **NSM** I B HOWARD

BROAD BLUNSDON (St Leonard) *Bris 7* **P** *Bp*
P-in-c G D SOWDEN

BROAD CAMPDEN (St Michael and All Angels) *see Vale and Cotswold Edge Glouc*

BROAD HINTON (St Peter ad Vincula) *see Upper Kennet Sarum*

BROAD OAK (St George) *see Heathfield Chich*

BROAD TOWN (Christ Church) *see Lyneham and Woodhill Sarum*

BROADBOTTOM (St Mary Magdalene) *see Mottram in Longdendale Ches*

BROADBRIDGE HEATH (St John) *see Horsham Chich*

BROADCHALKE (All Saints) *see Chalke Valley Sarum*

BROADCLYST (St John the Baptist), Clyst Honiton, Pinhoe, Rockbeare and Sowton *Ex 1* **P** *Patr Bd* **TR** E M SLATER
TV B C LANE **NSM** A M HOUGH

BROADFIELD (Christ the Lord) *see S Crawley Chich*

BROADHEATH (Christ Church) *see Worc St Clem and Lower Broadheath Worc*

BROADHEATH (St Alban) *Ches 10* **P** *Bp* **V** D GILL
NSM L REDFERN

BROADHEMBURY (St Andrew the Apostle and Martyr), Dunkeswell, Luppitt, Plymtree, Sheldon, and Upottery
Ex 4 **P** *Bp, D&C, MMCET, Oriel Coll Ox, and M Corfield Esq (jt)* **R** G J S HAYHOE

BROADHEMPSTON (St Peter and St Paul) *see Ipplepen w Torbryan, Denbury, Broadhempston and Woodland Ex*

BROADMAYNE (St Martin) *see Watercombe Sarum*

BROADOAK (St Paul) *see Eggardon and Colmers Sarum*

BROADSIDE, comprising Ranworth, South Walsham, Upton and Fishley, and Woodbastwick *Nor 4* **P** *Bp, Qu Coll Cam, and J Cator Esq (jt)* **R** N J H GARRARD **OLM** E H GARRARD

BROADSTAIRS (Holy Trinity) *Cant 5* **P** *V St Peter-in-Thanet*
R B D FENTON

BROADSTAIRS (St Andrew) *see Reading Street Cant*

BROADSTONE (not known) *see Corvedale Benefice Heref*

BROADSTONE (St John the Baptist) *Sarum 7* **P** *Bp*
V H M BAILEY **C** L J S WEBB

BROADWAS (St Mary Magdalene) *see Worcs W Rural Worc*

BROADWATER (Queen Street Church Centre) *see Broadwater Chich*

BROADWATER (St Mary) (St Stephen) (Queen Street Church Centre) *Chich 4* **P** *Patr Bd* **TR** G J DALY
TV G R NEAL

BROADWATER DOWN *see Tunbridge Wells St Mark Roch*

BROADWATERS (St Oswald) *see Kidderminster Ismere Worc*

BROADWAY (St Aldhem and St Eadburga) *see Isle Valley B & W*

BROADWAY (St Eadburgha) (St Michael and All Angels) w Wickhamford *Worc 1* **P** *Peache Trustees and Ch Ch Ox (jt)*
P-in-c M E WARD **NSM** J M WILLIAMSON

BROADWELL (Good Shepherd) *see Coleford, Staunton, Newland, Redbrook etc Glouc*

BROADWELL (St Paul), Evenlode, Oddington, Adlestrop and Westcote w Icomb and Bledington *Glouc 8* **P** *Bp, Ch Soc Trust, Lord Leigh and DBP (1 turn), and Ch Ch Ox and D&C Worc (1 turn)* **R** R J RENDALL **C** H MAPIMHIDZE
NSM S BLAKE

BROADWELL (St Peter and St Paul) *see Shill Valley and Broadshire Ox*

BROADWEY (St Nicholas) *see Weymouth Ridgeway Sarum*

BROADWINDSOR (St John the Baptist) *see Beaminster Area Sarum*

BROADWOODKELLY (All Saints) *Ex 19* **P** *DBP*
P-in-c H S E BLAINE

BROADWOODWIDGER (St Nicholas) *see Lifton, Broadwoodwidger, Stowford etc Ex*

BROCKDISH (St Peter and St Paul) *see Redenhall w Scole Nor*

BROCKENHURST (St Nicholas) (St Saviour) *Win 11*
P E J F MORANT Esq **V** S F E NEWHAM

BROCKHALL (St Peter and St Paul) *see Heyford w Stowe Nine Churches and Flore etc Pet*

BROCKHAM GREEN (Christ Church) and Leigh *S'wark 24*
P *The Hon R P Hamilton and J N Charrington Esq (jt)*
V J M A WILLANS

BROCKHAMPTON (All Saints) *see Fownhope w Mordiford, Brockhampton etc Heref*

BROCKHAMPTON (Chapel) *see Bromyard and Stoke Lacy Heref*

BROCKHOLES (St George) *see Honley Leeds*

BROCKLESBY PARK (All Saints), Croxton and North Wolds
Linc 8 **P** *Earl of Yarborough (3 turns), Ld Chan (1 turn), Bp, D&C and DBP (1 turn)* **R** L GABEL

BROCKLEY (St Andrew) *see Horringer St E*

BROCKLEY (St Peter) *S'wark 2* **P** *Bp* **P-in-c** B M JONES

BROCKLEY HILL (St Saviour) *S'wark 5* **P** *V Forest Hill Ch Ch*
P-in-c M D VYVYAN

BROCKMOOR (St John) *see Brierley Hill Worc*

BROCKWORTH (St George) *Glouc 3* **P** *DBP* **V** *vacant*

BROCTON (All Saints) *see Baswich Lich*

BRODSWORTH (St Michael and All Angels) *see Bilham Sheff*

BROKENBOROUGH (St John the Baptist) *see Malmesbury and Upper Avon Bris*

BROKERS WOOD (All Saints) *see White Horse Sarum*

BROMBOROUGH (St Barnabas) *Ches 9* **P** *D&C*
R J S GILLIES

BROME (St Mary) *see N Hartismere St E*

BROMESWELL (St Edmund) *see Wilford Peninsula St E*

BROMFIELD (St Mary the Virgin), including Bitterley w Middleton, Bromfield, Clee St Margaret and Cold Weston, Onibury, Stanton Lacy, and Stoke St Milborough w The Heath and Hopton Cangeford *Heref 11* **P** *Bp, Earl of Plymouth, Mrs O T M Rogers-Coltman, Exors Miss M F Rouse-Boughton, DBP and Walcot Trustees (by turn)*
R J T PARKER

BROMFIELD (St Mungo) *see Solway Plain Carl*

BROMFORD FIRS (not known) *see Hodge Hill Birm*

BROMHAM (St Nicholas) *see Rowde and Bromham Sarum*

BROMHAM (St Owen) w Oakley and Stagsden *St Alb 13*
P *Bp* **V** C A WILSON **NSM** P A VENNELLS

BROMLEY (Christ Church) *Roch 14* **P** *CPAS*
V I J BROOMFIELD **C** D M LLOYD **Hon C** V G WILKINS

BROMLEY (St Andrew) *Roch 14* **P** *Bp* **V** J E BOWEN
NSM E J DAVIS

BROMLEY (St John the Evangelist) *Roch 14* **P** *Bp*
V A D MCCLELLAN **C** D R WHIFFIN

BROMLEY (St Mark) *Roch 14* **P** *V Bromley SS Pet & Paul*
C B L LEWIS

BROMLEY (St Mary) *see Plaistow St Mary Roch*

BROMLEY (St Peter and St Paul) *Roch 14* **P** *Bp*
V J M HARRATT **NSM** S L SUTHERLAND

BROMLEY BY BOW (All Hallows) *Lon 7* **P** *Bp and Grocers' Co (jt)* **R** C I ROGERS **NSM** R M ROGERS

BROMLEY COMMON (Holy Trinity) *Roch 14* **P** *The Crown*
V R BRISTOW

BROMLEY COMMON (St Augustine) (St Luke) *Roch 14*
P *Bp* **V** S R SPENCER

BROMLEY CROSS (St Andrew's Mission Church) *see Turton Moorland Man*

BROMLEY, GREAT (St George) *see Lawford, Lt Bentley and The Bromleys Chelmsf*

BROMLEY, LITTLE (St Mary the Virgin) *as above*

BROMPTON (Holy Trinity) *see Onslow Square and S Kensington St Aug Lon*

BROMPTON (St Thomas) w Deighton *York 18* **P** *D&C Dur*
V J M E COOPER

BROMPTON ON SWALE (St Paul) *see Easby w Skeeby and Brompton on Swale etc Leeds*

BROMPTON RALPH (The Blessed Virgin Mary) *see Wiveliscombe and the Hills B & W*

BROMPTON REGIS (Blessed Virgin Mary) *see Dulverton w Brushford, Brompton Regis etc B & W*

BROMPTON, NEW (St Luke) *Roch 3*   P *Bp*
P-in-c G F JENKINS
BROMPTON, WEST (St Jude) (St Mary) St Peter *Lon 8*   P *Bp and Sir Laurence Magnus Bt (jt)*   V J L WELSH
BROMPTON-BY-SAWDON (All Saints)   *see* Upper Derwent *York*
BROMSBERROW (St Mary the Virgin)   *see* Redmarley D'Abitot, Bromesberrow, Pauntley etc *Glouc*
BROMSGROVE (All Saints) (St John the Baptist), including Catshill, Charford, Finstall, and Marlbrook *Worc 7*   P *Patr Bd* TR D S FORD   TV B A ROBERTSON, R A KHAN
NSM J A HATTON
BROMWICH, WEST (All Saints) (St Mary Magdalene) *Lich 26*   P *Bp*   V J E M DICKER   C L J MITCHELL, N P ELY
BROMWICH, WEST (Good Shepherd w St John) *Lich 26*   P *Bp*   V *vacant*
BROMWICH, WEST (Holy Trinity) *Lich 26*   P *Peache Trustees*   V J N ROBBIE
BROMWICH, WEST (St Andrew) (Christ Church) *Lich 26*   P *Bp and V W Bromwich All SS (jt)*   C N P ELY
BROMWICH, WEST (St Francis of Assisi) *Lich 26*   P *Bp*   V R A FARRELL
BROMWICH, WEST (St James) (St Paul) *Lich 26*   P *Bp and V Tipton St Martin and St Paul*   P-in-c M A J WILSON
BROMWICH, WEST (St Peter) *Lich 26*   P *Bp*   V *vacant*
BROMWICH, WEST (St Philip) *Lich 26*   P *Bp*   V *vacant*
BROMYARD (St Peter) and Stoke Lacy *Heref 2*   P *Bp (4 turns), Exors P H G Morgan Esq (1 turn)*   V C R EVANS
C K P N ROBERTSHAW
BRONDESBURY (Christ Church) (St Laurence) *Lon 21*   P *Ld Chan*   R S M FRANCE
BRONDESBURY St Anne w Kilburn (Holy Trinity) *Lon 21*   P *Bp and Ch Patr Soc (alt)*   V C E CARGILL
BROOKE (St Mary the Virgin)   *see* W Wight *Portsm*
BROOKE (St Peter)   *see* Oakham, Ashwell, Braunston, Brooke, Egleton etc *Pet*
BROOKE (St Peter), Kirstead, Mundham w Seething and Thwaite *Nor 5*   P *G&C Coll Cam, Gt Hosp and Countess Ferrers, and Ld Chan (by turn)*   P-in-c L M CHAPMAN
BROOKFIELD (St Anne), Highgate Rise *Lon 17*   P *Bp*   V A J B MELDRUM   NSM S P WALSH
BROOKFIELD (St Margaret) *York 20*   P *Abp*   V V G HATTON
BROOKFIELD (St Mary) *Lon 17*   P *Bp*   V D D R MASON
BROOKHOUSE (St Paul)   *see* Caton w Littledale *Blackb*
BROOKLAND (St Augustine), Fairfield, Brenzett w Snargate and Lydd *Cant 12*   P *Abp*   P-in-c C G MACLEAN
NSM J DARLING, S J BODY
BROOKSBY (St Michael and All Angels)   *see* Upper Wreake *Leic*
BROOKSIDE (Pastoral Centre)   *see* Cen Telford *Lich*
BROOKWOOD (St Saviour)   *see* Knaphill w Brookwood *Guildf*
BROOM (St Matthew)   *see* Heart of England *Cov*
BROOM LEYS (St David) *Leic 8*   P *Bp*   V *vacant*
BROOME (St Michael)   *see* Ditchingham, Hedenham, Broome, Earsham etc *Nor*
BROOME (St Peter)   *see* Churchill-in-Halfshire w Blakedown and Broome *Worc*
BROOMFIELD (St Margaret)   *see* N Downs *Cant*
BROOMFIELD (St Mary and All Saints)   *see* S Quantock *B & W*
BROOMFIELD (St Mary w St Leonard) *Chelmsf 9*   P *Bp*   V C A TIBBOTT   C D C PIERCE, J A HARDY
NSM D M GARFIELD, R A HARVEY
BROOMFLEET (St Mary)   *see* S Cave and Ellerker w Broomfleet
BROOMHILL (St Mark)   *see* Sheff St Mark Broomhill *Sheff*
BROSELEY (All Saints) w Benthall, Jackfield, Linley, Willey and Barrow *Heref 13*   P *Patr Bd*   R C W PENN
BROTHERTOFT Group, The (St Gilbert of Sempringham), including Holland Fen, Kirton Holme, Langrick, and Thornton Le Fen *Linc 21*   P *Bp (2 turns), V Algarkirk (1 turn)*   V *vacant*
BROTHERTON (St Edward the Confessor) *Leeds 18*   P *D&C York*   P-in-c S L BROWN   NSM S HULME
BROTTON PARVA (St Margaret) *York 16*   P *Abp*   R J P RHODES
BROUGH (All Saints)   *see* Elloughton and Brough w Brantingham *York*
BROUGH (St Michael)   *see* Upper Eden *Carl*
BROUGHAM (St Wilfrid Chapel)   *see* N Westmorland *Carl*
BROUGHTON (All Saints)   *see* Warboys w Broughton and Bury w Wistow *Ely*
BROUGHTON (All Saints), Marton and Thornton *Leeds 24*   P *Ch Ch Ox and Exors Dame Harriet Nelson (jt)*   R N A TURNER   C P A TURNER   NSM A J LADDS
BROUGHTON (Ascension)   *see* Lower Broughton Ascension *Man*

BROUGHTON (no church) *Ox 10*   P *Ch Patr Trust*   V P C WHITE   C J E TALBOT   NSM S P Z SMITH
BROUGHTON (St Andrew) w Cransley and Mawsley *Pet 9*   P *Bp*   R N HOBBS
BROUGHTON (St James) (St Clement and St Matthias) St John the Evangelist *Man 20*   P *Patr Bd*   P-in-c C E THRELFALL
BROUGHTON (St John the Baptist) *Blackb 13*   P *Trustees*   V S BALDWIN   OLM P F TAYLOR
BROUGHTON (St Mary Magdalene) (Holy Innocents) and Duddon *Carl 9*   P *V Millom, Lt Col D A S Pennefather, and Ch Patr Trust (by turn)*   V *vacant*
BROUGHTON (St Mary the Virgin)   *see* Wykeham *Ox*
BROUGHTON (St Mary) *Lich 21*   P *D R B Thompson Esq*   V A J B CLAYTON
BROUGHTON (St Mary) *Linc 8*   P *MMCET*   P-in-c D J EAMES
BROUGHTON (St Mary)   *see* Mid Trent *Win*
BROUGHTON (St Peter)   *see* Ashley and Mucklestone and Broughton and Croxton *Lich*
BROUGHTON ASTLEY (St Mary) and Croft w Stoney Stanton *Leic 7*   P *Bp and A I Steele Esq (jt)*   R S J CONSTABLE
C J S BENNER   NSM L M JACKSON
BROUGHTON GIFFORD (St Mary the Virgin), Great Chalfield and Holt St Katharine *Sarum 15*   P *D&C Bris (3 turns), Ld Chan (2 turns), and R C Floyd Esq (1 turn)*   R A E EVANS   NSM R MECREDY
BROUGHTON HACKETT (St Leonard)   *see* Peopleton and White Ladies Aston w Churchill etc *Worc*
BROUGHTON IN FURNESS (St Mary Magdalene)   *see* Broughton and Duddon *Carl*
BROUGHTON MILLS (Holy Innocents)   *as above*
BROUGHTON MOOR (St Columba)   *see* Maryport, Netherton, Flimby and Broughton Moor *Carl*
BROUGHTON POGGS (St Peter)   *see* Shill Valley and Broadshire *Ox*
BROUGHTON, GREAT (Christ Church)   *see* Cockermouth Area *Carl*
BROUGHTON, LOWER (Ascension) *Man 20*   P *Trustees*   P-in-c D S C WYATT
BROUGHTON, NETHER (St Mary the Virgin)   *see* Old Dalby, Nether Broughton, Saxelbye etc *Leic*
BROUGHTON, UPPER (St Luke)   *see* Hickling w Kinoulton and Broughton Sulney *S'well*
BROWN CANDOVER (St Peter)   *see* Farleigh, Candover and Wield *Win*
BROWN CLEE   *see* Ditton Priors w Neenton, Burwarton etc *Heref*
BROWN EDGE (St Anne) *Lich 8*   P *Bp*   P-in-c A J BETTS
BROWNHILL (St Saviour) *Leeds 6*   P *V Batley*   V L A MATTACKS   C M A GREEN
BROWNSOVER (Christ Church)   *see* Clifton w Newton and Brownsover *Cov*
BROWNSWOOD PARK (St John the Evangelist) *Lon 5*   P *City Corp*   V A E WHALLEY
BROXBOURNE (St Augustine) w Wormley *St Alb 17*   P *Bp and Peache Trustees (jt)*   R C E C HUDSON
C G L FENSOME
BROXTED (St Mary the Virgin) w Chickney and Tilty and Great and Little Easton *Chelmsf 18*   P *Bp (2 turns), DBP (1 turn), and MMCET (1 turn)*   P-in-c T E GOODBODY
C S E HURLEY   NSM C M HAWKES, J E PARKER
BROXTOWE (St Martha) *S'well 8*   P *Bp*   V *vacant*
BRUERA (St Mary)   *see* Waverton w Aldford and Bruera *Ches*
BRUISYARD (St Peter)   *see* Upper Alde *St E*
BRUMBY (St Hugh) (All Saints) *Linc 6*   P *Bp*   TR C A B MARTIN   C P J DICKINSON   NSM J A CLARK
BRUNDALL (St Lawrence)   *see* Yare Valley *Nor*
BRUNDISH (St Lawrence)   *see* Four Rivers *St E*
BRUNSTEAD (St Peter)   *see* Stalham, E Ruston, Brunstead, Sutton and Ingham *Nor*
BRUNSWICK (Christ Church) *Man 3*   P *Ch Soc Trust*   R S J T GATENBY   C J H DAVIS
BRUNSWICK (St Cuthbert)   *see* Ch the King *Newc*
BRUNTCLIFFE (St Andrew)   *see* Morley *Leeds*
BRUNTINGTHORPE (St Mary)   *see* Hexagon *Leic*
BRUNTON PARK (St Aidan)   *see* Ch the King *Newc*
BRUSHFORD (St Mary the Virgin) *Ex 19*   P *D&C*   P-in-c H S E BLAINE
BRUSHFORD (St Nicholas)   *see* Dulverton w Brushford, Brompton Regis etc *B & W*
BRUTON (St Mary the Virgin), Brewham, Pitcombe and Shepton Montague *B & W 2*   P *Bp*   R J M BAILEY
Hon C M D ELLIS

BRYANSTON SQUARE (St Mary) w St Marylebone
(St Mark) *Lon 4* **P** *The Crown* **R** J P T PETERS
C M R COOMBS **NSM** B J KISSELL
BRYANSTON STREET (Annunciation) *see* St Marylebone
Annunciation Bryanston Street *Lon*
BRYHER (All Saints) *see* Is of Scilly *Truro*
BRYMPTON (St Andrew) *B & W 6* **P** C E B Clive-Ponsonby-
Fane Esq **R** *vacant*
BRYN St Peter *Liv 15* **P** *Bp* **V** *vacant*
BUBBENHALL (St Giles) *see* Baginton w Bubbenhall and
Ryton-on-Dunsmore *Cov*
BUBWITH (All Saints) w Skipwith *York 2* **P** *Abp and D&C,*
and Ld Chan (alt) **P-in-c** R M KIRKMAN
BUCKDEN (St Mary) w the Offords *Ely 13* **P** *Bp and Ld*
Chan (alt) **P-in-c** J W SALT
BUCKENHAM, NEW (St Martin) *see* Quidenham Gp *Nor*
BUCKENHAM, OLD (All Saints) *as above*
BUCKERELL (St Mary and St Giles) *see* Honiton, Gittisham,
Combe Raleigh, Monkton etc *Ex*
BUCKFAST SANCTUARY (not known) *see* Buckfastleigh,
Dean Prior, Littlehempston etc *Ex*
BUCKFASTLEIGH (Holy Trinity) (St Luke), Dean Prior,
Littlehempston, Rattery, South Brent and Staverton w
Landscove *Ex 12* **P** *Patr Bd* **TR** T H F BENSON
TV G M RADFORD **C** F WIMSETT, L E MCADAM
BUCKHORN WESTON (St John the Baptist) *see* Stour Vale
Sarum
BUCKHURST HILL (St Elisabeth) (St John the Baptist)
(St Stephen) *Chelmsf 3* **P** *Patr Bd* **TR** I D FARLEY
NSM T L PAYNE
BUCKINGHAM (St Peter and St Paul) *Ox 11* **P** *Bp, Adn*
Buckm, Mrs S A J Doulton, G&C Coll Cam, New Coll Ox, and
Exors R J Dalziel Smith Esq (jt) **R** W O C PEARSON-GEE
C D C RODGERS **NSM** J F KING
BUCKINGHAM, NORTH, comprising Akeley, Leckhampstead,
Lillingstone Dayrell, Lillingstone Lovell, and Maids Moreton
Ox 11 **P** *Ch Soc Trust, Mrs J M Williams, and D J Robarts Esq*
(by turn) **R** J A TALING
BUCKINGHAM, WEST, comprising Biddlesden, Shalstone,
Tingewick, Turweston, Water Stratford, and Westbury *Ox 11*
P *Bp, D&C Westmr, G&C Coll Cam, New Coll Ox (1 turn),*
(1 turn), New Coll Ox (1 turn), and DBP (1 turn) **R** *vacant*
BUCKLAND (All Saints) *see* Aston Clinton w Buckland and
Drayton Beauchamp *Ox*
BUCKLAND (St Mary the Virgin) *see* Betchworth and
Buckland *S'wark*
BUCKLAND (St Mary the Virgin) *see* Cherbury w Gainfield
Ox
BUCKLAND (St Michael) *see* Winchcombe *Glouc*
BUCKLAND BREWER (St Mary and St Benedict) *see* Parkham,
Alwington, Buckland Brewer etc *Ex*
BUCKLAND DINHAM (St Michael and All Angels) *see* Mells w
Buckland Dinham, Elm, Whatley etc *B & W*
BUCKLAND FILLEIGH (St Mary and Holy Trinity) *see*
Shebbear, Buckland Filleigh, Sheepwash etc *Ex*
BUCKLAND IN THE MOOR (St Peter) *see* Ashburton,
Bickington, Buckland in the Moor etc *Ex*
BUCKLAND MONACHORUM (St Andrew) *Ex 22* **P** *Bp*
C A FARMER
BUCKLAND NEWTON (Holy Rood), Cerne Abbas,
Godmanstone and Minterne Magna *Sarum 1* **P** *Adn*
Sherborne, Lord Digby, D H C Batten Esq, H E Gallia Esq, and
Col J L Yeatman (jt) **V** J T L STILL
BUCKLAND RIPERS (St Nicholas) *see* Weymouth Ridgeway
Sarum
BUCKLAND ST MARY (Blessed Virgin Mary) *see* Blackdown
B & W
BUCKLAND TOUT SAINTS (St Peter) *see* Stokenham,
Slapton, Charleton w Buckland etc *Ex*
BUCKLAND VALLEY (St Nicholas) *see* Dover Town *Cant*
BUCKLAND, EAST (St Michael) *see* Swimbridge, W Buckland,
Landkey, and E Buckland *Ex*
BUCKLAND, WEST (Blessed Virgin Mary) *see* Wellington and
Distr *B & W*
BUCKLAND, WEST (St Peter) *see* Swimbridge, W Buckland,
Landkey, and E Buckland *Ex*
BUCKLAND-IN-DOVER (St Andrew) *see* Dover Town *Cant*
BUCKLEBURY (St Mary) w Marlston *Ox 4* **P** *C J Pratt Esq*
P-in-c J T D M GADSBY **NSM** L E BLISS
BUCKLEBURY, UPPER (All Saints) *see* Bucklebury w Marlston
Ox
BUCKLERS HARD (St Mary) *see* Beaulieu and Exbury and E
Boldre *Win*
BUCKLESHAM (St Mary) *see* Nacton and Levington w
Bucklesham etc *St E*
BUCKMINSTER (St John the Baptist) *see* S Framland *Leic*

BUCKNALL (St Margaret) *see* Woodhall Spa Gp *Linc*
BUCKNALL Team Ministry, The (St Mary the Virgin),
including Abbey Hulton and Bentilee *Lich 11* **P** *Patr Bd*
TR D STREET **TV** D EDGE **C** M G R MYCOCK
OLM J MARSHALL, M C BRIDGEWATER
BUCKNELL (St Mary) *see* Middle Marches *Heref*
BUCKNELL (St Peter) *see* Bicester w Bucknell, Caversfield
and Launton *Ox*
BUCKROSE CARRS, comprising Rillington, Scampston w
Wintringham, Sherburn, Thorpe Bassett, and West
Heslerton *York 6* **P** *The Crown, H J N Cholmley Esq, Sir Philip*
Naylor-Leyland Bt, and D&C (by turn) **R** J T KINSELLA
BUCKROSE, WEST, comprising Acklam, Birdsall, Burythorpe,
Langton, Leavening, North Grimston, Settrington, and
Westow *York 6* **P** *Ld Chan (1 turn), Lord Middleton and Abp*
(3 turns) **R** S P WALKER **NSM** P M HALL
BUCKS MILLS (St Anne) *see* Parkham, Alwington, Buckland
Brewer etc *Ex*
BUCKSHAW VILLAGE CHURCH (Conventional District)
Blackb 5 **Min** J J GWYN-THOMAS
BUCKWORTH (All Saints) *see* N Leightonstone *Ely*
BUDBROOKE (St Michael) *Cov 11* **P** *MMCET* **V** D A BROWN
BUDE HAVEN (St Michael and All Angels) *see* N Kernow
Truro
BUDLEIGH SALTERTON (St Peter), East Budleigh w Bicton,
and Otterton *Ex 1* **P** *Lord Clinton* **V** M JACQUES
NSM K H YOUNG
BUDLEIGH, EAST (All Saints) *see* Budleigh Salterton, E
Budleigh w Bicton etc *Ex*
BUDOCK (St Budock) *Truro 3* **P** *Bp* **V** G K BENNETT
C B R MORGAN LUNDIE
BUDWORTH, GREAT (St Mary and All Saints) *Ches 4* **P** *Ch*
Ch Ox **V** A G BROWN **NSM** C K B WESTWELL, J S MCKAY
BUDWORTH, LITTLE (St Peter) *see* Whitegate w Lt Budworth
Ches
BUGBROOKE (St Michael and All Angels), Harpole,
Kislingbury and Rothersthorpe *Pet 3* **P** *Bp, Exors E W*
Harrison, DBP, and Sir Philip Naylor-Leyland Bt (jt)
R S R J FRENCH
BUGLAWTON (St John the Evangelist) *see* Congleton *Ches*
BUGTHORPE (St Andrew) *see* Garrowby Hill *York*
BUILDWAS (Holy Trinity) *see* Wrockwardine Deanery *Lich*
BULCOTE (Holy Trinity) *see* Burton Joyce, Bulcote and Stoke
Bardolph etc *S'well*
BULFORD (St Leonard) *see* Avon River *Sarum*
BULKINGTON (Christ Church) *see* Wellsprings *Sarum*
BULKINGTON (St James) *Cov 5* **P** *Ld Chan* **V** C C HIGGINS
BULKWORTHY (St Michael) *see* Bradworthy, Sutcombe etc *Ex*
BULLEY (St Michael and All Angels) *see* Huntley and
Longhope, Churcham and Bulley *Glouc*
BULLINGHOPE, UPPER (St Peter) *see* Heref S Wye *Heref*
BULLINGTON (St Michael and All Angels) *see* Lower Dever
Win
BULMER (St Andrew) *see* N Hinckford *Chelmsf*
BULMER (St Martin) *see* Howardian Gp *York*
BULPHAN (St Mary the Virgin) *see* Orsett and Bulphan and
Horndon on the Hill *Chelmsf*
BULWELL (St John the Divine) *S'well 8* **P** *Bp* **V** D GRAY
BULWELL (St Mary the Virgin and All Souls) *S'well 8* **P** *Bp*
R A J FISHER
BULWICK (St Nicholas) *see* King's Cliffe, Bulwick and
Blatherwycke, Collyweston etc *Pet*
BUNBURY (St Boniface) and Tilstone Fearnall *Ches 5*
P *Haberdashers' Co* **V** T D M HAYWARD
BUNCTON (All Saints) *see* Chanctonbury *Chich*
BUNGAY (Holy Trinity) *St E 17* **P** *DBP, Mrs B I T Suckling,*
and CPAS (jt) **V** I B BYRNE
BUNGAY (Holy Trinity) *see* Bungay *St E*
BUNNY (St Mary the Virgin) *see* Keyworth and Stanton-on-
the-Wolds and Bunny etc *S'well*
BUNTINGFORD (St Peter) *see* Aspenden, Buntingford and
Westmill *St Alb*
BUNWELL (St Michael and All Angels) *see* Long Stratton and
Pilgrim TM *Nor*
BURBAGE (All Saints) *see* Savernake *Sarum*
BURBAGE (Christ Church) *see* Buxton w Burbage and King
Sterndale *Derby*
BURBAGE (St Catherine) w Aston Flamville *Leic 10* **P** *Ball*
Coll Ox **R** A D HALL
BURCHETTS GREEN, comprising Hurley, Littlewick, and
Stubbings *Ox 5* **P** *DBP and Bp (jt)* **V** K B NICHOLLS
NSM T M MOLYNEUX
BURES (St Mary the Virgin) w Assington and Lt Cornard
St E 9 **P** *DBP and Bp (jt)* **V** S R MORLEY
NSM M J CANTACUZENE, P J BOX

BURFORD (St John the Baptist) w Fulbrook, Taynton, Asthall, Swinbrook and Widford *Ox 28* **P** *Bp and Capt D Mackinnon (jt)* **V** T D PUTT **C** O J STRANGE **NSM** R J D WAINWRIGHT **OLM** C REAVLEY
BURFORD (St Mary) *see Tenbury Heref*
BURGATE (St Mary) *see N Hartismere St E*
BURGESS HILL (St Andrew) *Chich 8* **P** *Bp* **V** A R ANGEL **C** I T PAIN
BURGESS HILL (St Edward) *Chich 8* **P** *Bp Chich, Bp Horsham, and R Clayton w Keymer (jt)* **V** *vacant*
BURGESS HILL (St John the Evangelist) *Chich 8* **P** *Bp Chich, Bp Horsham, and R Clayton w Keymer (jt)* **V** K M O'BRIEN **NSM** S S MACCARTHY
BURGH (St Botolph) *see Carlford St E*
BURGH (St Margaret and St Mary) *see S Trin Broads Nor*
BURGH (St Peter) *see Raveningham Gp Nor*
BURGH CASTLE (St Peter and St Paul) *see Belton and Burgh Castle Nor*
BURGH Group, The, comprising Bratoft, Burgh le Marsh, Gunby, Irby-in-the-Marsh, Orby, Welton le Marsh *Linc 10* **P** *Bp (2 turns), H J Montgomery-Massingberd Esq (1 turn), SMF (1 turn)* **R** T STEELE
BURGH HEATH (St Mary the Virgin) *see Nork w Burgh Heath Guildf*
BURGH LE MARSH (St Peter and St Paul) *see Burgh Gp Linc*
BURGH PARVA (St Mary) *see Briston, Burgh Parva, Hindolveston etc Nor*
BURGH-BY-SANDS (St Michael) *see Barony of Burgh Carl*
BURGHCLERE (Ascension) (All Saints) w Newtown and Ecchinswell w Sydmonton *Win 6* **P** *Earl of Carnarvon* **R** D G BARTHOLOMEW
BURGHFIELD (St Mary the Virgin) *Ox 4* **P** *Earl of Shrewsbury* **R** G V LAUTENBACH **NSM** L D COLAM
BURGHILL (St Mary the Virgin) *Heref 3* **P** *DBP* **P-in-c** P J BROWN **NSM** E S V VERWEY
BURGH-NEXT-AYLSHAM (St Mary) *see Aylsham and Distr Nor*
BURGH-ON-BAIN (St Helen) *see Asterby Gp Linc*
BURGHWALLIS (St Helen) and Campsall *Sheff 7* **P** *Bp (2 turns), Mrs E H I Ellison-Anne (1 turn)* **P-in-c** R J WALTON **NSM** C HERBERT
BURHAM (Methodist Church) and Wouldham *Roch 5* **P** *Bp and Ld Chan (alt)* **R** M J HAYES
BURITON (St Mary the Virgin) *Portsm 4* **P** *Bp* **R** W P M HUGHES **C** S A CULLEN **NSM** J M BEE
BURLESCOMBE (St Mary) *see Sampford Peverell, Uplowman, Holcombe Rogus etc Ex*
BURLEY (St Matthias) *Leeds 15* **P** *G M Bedford Esq, J C Yeadon Esq, E Beety Esq, Mrs M E Dunham, and Mrs L M Rawse (jt)* **P-in-c** J A M BARNETT **C** N W LATTIMER
BURLEY IN WHARFEDALE (St Mary the Virgin) *Leeds 4* **P** *Bp* **V** A J KIRK
BURLEY VILLE (St John the Baptist) *Win 9* **P** *V Ringwood* **P-in-c** E A M GAMMON
BURLEYDAM (St Mary and St Michael) *see Baddiley and Wrenbury w Burleydam Ches*
BURLINGHAM (St Andrew) *see Blofield Nor*
BURLINGHAM (St Edmund King and Martyr) w Lingwood, Strumpshaw w Hassingham and Buckenham *Nor 4* **P** *Ch Soc Trust, MMCET, and Bp (jt)* **R** D K WAKEFIELD
BURLTON (St Anne) *see Loppington w Newtown Lich*
BURMANTOFTS (St Agnes) and Harehills, Leeds *Leeds 13* **P** *Ch Trust Fund Trust and Bp (jt)* **V** A S KASIBANTE
BURMARSH (All Saints) *see Romney Marsh Cant*
BURMINGTON (St Nicholas and St Barnabas) *see S Warks Seven Gp Cov*
BURNAGE (St Margaret) *Man 2* **P** *Bp* **R** M R M CALLADINE
BURNAGE (St Nicholas) *Man 6* **P** *Trustees* **R** R MANN **C** A M K BENNISON, M R HEWERDINE **NSM** A J SIMPSON
BURNBY (St Giles) *see Londesborough Wold York*
BURNESIDE (St Oswald) *see Beacon Carl*
BURNESTON (St Lambert) *see Kirklington w Burneston and Wath and Pickhill Leeds*
BURNETT (St Michael) *see Keynsham B & W*
BURNEY LANE (Christ Church) *see Ward End w Bordesley Green Birm*
BURNHAM (St Andrew) *B & W 1* **P** *D&C* **V** G R WITTS **NSM** M H I HAYWARD, S A ELDERGILL
BURNHAM (St Mary the Virgin) *Chelmsf 11* **P** *N D Beckett Esq and Walsingham Coll Trust (jt)* **V** *vacant*
BURNHAM (St Peter) *Ox 12* **P** *Eton Coll* **V** *vacant*
BURNHAM DEEPDALE (St Mary) *see Hunstanton St Mary w Ringstead Parva etc Nor*
BURNHAM NORTON (St Margaret) *see Burnham Gp of Par Nor*
BURNHAM OVERY (St Clement) *as above*

BURNHAM THORPE (All Saints) *as above*
BURNHAM ULPH (All Saints) *as above*
BURNHAM WESTGATE (St Mary), Burnham Norton, Burnham Overy, Burnham Thorpe, and Burnham Sutton w Ulph (The Burnham Group of Parishes) *Nor 14* **P** *Ch Coll Cam (1 turn), Ld Chan (2 turns), and DBP (1 turn)* **P-in-c** S P WOOD
BURNHAM-ON-CROUCH (St Mary the Virgin) *see Burnham Chelmsf*
BURNHAM-ON-SEA (St Andrew) *as above*
BURNLEY (St Andrew) w St Margaret and Burnley St James *Blackb 3* **P** *The Crown and R Burnley St Pet (alt)* **V** P R HAPGOOD-STRICKLAND **C** P J BENFIELD
BURNLEY (St Catherine) (St Alban) and St Paul *Blackb 3* **P** *R Burnley* **V** R T D PARKER
BURNLEY (St Cuthbert) *Blackb 3* **P** *R Burnley* **V** S A ADESANYA **NSM** S J LARGE
BURNLEY (St Mark) *Blackb 3* **P** *Bp* **P-in-c** P J NORTH **C** P J BENFIELD
BURNLEY (St Matthew the Apostle) Habergham Eaves w Holy Trinity *Blackb 3* **P** *R Burnley* **V** A D J FROST **C** K F M GREGORY-WITHAM
BURNLEY (St Peter) (St Stephen) *Blackb 3* **P** *Bp and DBP (jt)* **R** P N A SENIOR
BURNLEY, WEST (All Saints) *Blackb 3* **P** *Bp and R Burnley (jt)* **V** C W HILL
BURNMOOR (St Barnabas) *Dur 10* **P** *Lord Lambton* **R** *vacant*
BURNOPFIELD (St James) *see Tanfield w Burnopfield and Dipton Dur*
BURNSALL (St Wilfrid) w Rylstone *Leeds 24* **P** *Exors Earl of Craven and CPAS (jt)* **P-in-c** D MACHA
BURNT OAK (St Alphage) *see Hendon St Alphage Lon*
BURNT YATES (St Andrew) *see Bishop Thornton, Burnt Yates, Markington etc Leeds*
BURNTWOOD (Christ Church), Chase Terrace, Chasetown and Hammerwich *Lich 1* **P** *Patr Bd* **TV** M WALLACE, R A WESTWOOD **NSM** S R D MORGAN
BURPHAM (Holy Spirit) (St Luke) Guildford *Guildf 5* **P** *Bp* **V** J A LEVASIER **C** D MCCARLEY, J M LEVASIER
BURPHAM (St Mary the Virgin) *Chich 1* **P** *D&C* **P-in-c** C M WOODRUFF
BURRADON (Good Shepherd) *see Weetslade Newc*
BURRILL (Mission Church) *see Bedale and Leeming and Thornton Watlass Leeds*
BURRINGTON (Holy Trinity) *see Wrington w Butcombe and Burrington B & W*
BURRINGTON (Holy Trinity), Chawleigh, Cheldon, Chulmleigh, Meshaw, Romansleigh, Thelbridge, Wembworthy w Eggesford, Witheridge w Creacombe, East Worlington and West Worlington *Ex 18* **P** *Patr Bd* **TR** A N ROCKEY **TV** A M WELLS **C** J M MAY **NSM** J C JOBBINS
BURRINGTON (St George) *see Wigmore Abbey Heref*
BURROUGH GREEN (St Augustine of Canterbury) *see Raddesley Gp Ely*
BURROUGH HILL Parishes, The: Burrough on the Hill, Great Dalby, Little Dalby, Pickwell and Somerby *Leic 2* **P** *Bp, DBP, and Mrs M Burdett Fisher (jt)* **P-in-c** N STOTHERS
BURROUGH ON THE HILL (St Mary the Virgin) *see Burrough Hill Pars Leic*
BURROWBRIDGE (St Michael) *see Athelney B & W*
BURRSVILLE (St Mark) *see Gt Clacton Chelmsf*
BURSCOUGH BRIDGE (St John) (St Andrew) (St Cyprian) *Liv 14* **P** *V Ormskirk* **P-in-c** D P BANBURY **C** E J IRETON **NSM** W I WILLIAMS
BURSDON MOOR (St Martin) *see Parkham, Alwington, Buckland Brewer etc Ex*
BURSEA (Chapel) *see Holme and Seaton Ross Gp York*
BURSLEDON (St Leonard) *Win 10* **P** *Bp* **P-in-c** J PAWSON **C** J E KELLS, R W SANDAY
BURSLEDON Pilands Wood (St Paul) *see Bursledon Win*
BURSLEM (St John the Baptist) (St Paul) *Lich 11* **P** *Bp and MMCET (jt)* **V** *vacant*
BURSLEM (St Werburgh) *Lich 11* **P** *Bp* **P-in-c** A C SWIFT
BURSTALL (St Mary the Virgin) *see Sproughton w Burstall, Copdock w Washbrook etc St E*
BURSTEAD, GREAT (St Mary Magdalene) w Ramsden Crays *Chelmsf 12* **P** *Bp* **P-in-c** M A HALL
BURSTEAD, LITTLE (St Mary) *see Billericay and Lt Burstead Chelmsf*
BURSTOCK (St Andrew) *see Beaminster Area Sarum*
BURSTON (St Mary) *see Winfarthing w Shelfanger w Burston w Gissing etc Nor*
BURSTON (St Rufin) *see Mid Trent Lich*
BURSTOW (St Bartholomew) *see The Windmill S'wark*

BURSTWICK (All Saints), Burton Pidsea, Humbleton w Elsternwick, Halsham, and Thorngumbald *York 12*
P *Abp (2 turns), Ld Chan (1 turn), D&C (1 turn)*
V S J WALKER   **Hon C** P W WEST
BURTLE (St Philip and St James) *see* Polden Wheel *B & W*
BURTON (St Aidan) (St Paul) *Lich 13*   P *Bp and Lord Burton (jt)*   V W S MONKHOUSE   **OLM** R F TROTTER
BURTON (St James) and Holme *Carl 10*   P *Simeon's Trustees*
V G J BURROWS
BURTON (St Luke) and Sopley *Win 9*   P *Bp and D&C Cant (alt)*   **P-in-c** N J LACEY
BURTON (St Nicholas) and Shotwick *Ches 9*   P *D&C (1 turn) and St Jo Hosp Lich (2 turns)*   V C M HELM
BURTON (St Richard) *see* Barlavington, Burton w Coates, Sutton and Bignor *Chich*
BURTON AGNES (St Martin) *see* The Beacon *York*
BURTON BRADSTOCK (St Mary) *see* Bride Valley *Sarum*
BURTON BY LINCOLN (St Vincent) *see* Spring Line Gp *Linc*
BURTON COGGLES (St Thomas à Becket) *see* N Beltisloe Gp *Linc*
BURTON DASSETT (All Saints) *Cov 8*   P *Bp*
P-in-c N M CHATTERTON
BURTON FLEMING (St Cuthbert) *see* Rudston, Boynton, Carnaby etc *York*
BURTON GREEN (Chapel of Ease) *see* Kenilworth St Nic *Cov*
BURTON HASTINGS (St Botolph) *Cov 5*   P *Bp*
V C C HIGGINS
BURTON JOYCE (St Helen), Bulcote and Stoke Bardolph w Lowdham, Caythorpe and Gunthorpe *S'well 7*   P *MMCET and Bp (jt)*   **C** S N JONES
BURTON LATIMER (St Mary the Virgin) *Pet 9*   P *Bp*
R J SAFFORD   **C** T M HOUSTON
BURTON LAZARS (St James) *see* Melton Mowbray *Leic*
BURTON OVERY (St Andrew) *see* Oadby Gt Glen *Leic*
BURTON PEDWARDINE (St Andrew and the Blessed Virgin Mary and St Nicholas) *see* Heckington and Helpringham Gp *Linc*
BURTON PIDSEA (St Peter) *see* Burstwick, Burton Pidsea etc *York*
BURTON UPON STATHER (St Andrew) *see* Flixborough w Burton upon Stather *Linc*
BURTON w COATES (St Agatha) *see* Barlavington, Burton w Coates, Sutton and Bignor *Chich*
BURTON-IN-LONSDALE (All Saints) *see* Bentham, Burton-in-Lonsdale, Chapel-le-Dale etc *Leeds*
BURTON-ON-TRENT (All Saints) *see* Branston and Burton All SS w Ch Ch *Lich*
BURTON-ON-TRENT (St Aidan) *see* Burton St Aid and St Paul *Lich*
BURTON-ON-TRENT (St Chad) *Lich 13*   P *Bp*
P-in-c G J CROSSLEY   **C** B L CARE
BURTON-ON-TRENT (St Modwen) *see* Burton St Modwen *Lich*
BURTON-ON-TRENT (St Paul) *see* Burton St Aid and St Paul *Lich*
BURTON-UPON-TRENT (St Modwen) *Lich 13*   P *Bp*
V W S MONKHOUSE   **OLM** R F TROTTER
BURTONWOOD (St Michael) *Liv 13*   P *R Warrington*
V J L STEVENTON   **Hon C** A LITTON   **NSM** V M HANCOCK
BURWARDSLEY (St John) *see* Tattenhall w Burwardsley and Handley *Ches*
BURWASH (St Bartholomew), Burwash Weald and Etchingham *Chich 13*   P *Bp and BNC Ox (jt)*   R S A EPPS
NSM G R LEWIS
BURWASH WEALD (St Philip) *see* Burwash, Burwash Weald and Etchingham *Chich*
BURWELL (St Andrew) (St Mary) w Reach *Ely 4*   P *DBP*
V E J WILLIAMS   **NSM** P SPALDING
BURY (All Saints) *see* Kirklees Valley *Man*
BURY (Christ Church) *see* Walmersley Road, Bury *Man*
BURY (Christ the King) *see* Bury, Roch Valley *Man*
BURY (Holy Cross) *see* Warboys w Broughton and Bury w Wistow *Ely*
BURY (St John the Evangelist) w Houghton and Coldwaltham and Hardham *Chich 10*   P *Pemb Coll Ox, D&C, and Col Sir Brian Barttelot Bt (jt)*   V P A MALLINSON
BURY (St John w St Mark) *see* Walmersley Road, Bury *Man*
BURY (St Mary the Virgin) *Man 8*   P *Earl of Derby*
R J R HEATON   **C** R E JONES   **OLM** S R BEATTIE
BURY (St Peter) *see* Bury, Roch Valley *Man*
BURY ST EDMUNDS (All Saints) (St John the Evangelist) (St George) *St E 10*   P *Patr Bd*   **TR** M N HAWORTH
C L M SELMAN, M R SELMAN   **Hon C** T L JONES
NSM J C MANN, M M WEBB, V E GAGEN
BURY ST EDMUNDS (Cathedral of St James) District *St E 10*
C S J GEILESKEY

BURY ST EDMUNDS (Christ Church) Moreton Hall *St E 10*
P *Bp, V Bury St Edm St Jas, and V Bury St Edm St Mary (jt)*
V J L ALDERTON-FORD   **NSM** D CARPENTER
BURY ST EDMUNDS (St Mary) (St Peter's District Church)
St E 10   P *Hyndman Trustees*   V S J HARVEY
C N E ALEXANDER
BURY St Paul *Man 8*   P *Trustees*   V J R HEATON   **C** R E JONES
OLM S R BEATTIE
BURY, NEW (St Catherine) (St George) (St James) w Great Lever *Man 7*   P *Bp*   **TR** M A COWLING   **TV** J I MOORES
OLM N A COWELL
BURY, NORTH *see* Bury St Edmunds All SS w St Jo and St Geo *St E*
BURY, ROCH VALLEY (Christ the King) (St Peter) *Man 8*
P *Patr Bd*   **NSM** J L LYSSEJKO
BURYTHORPE (All Saints) *see* W Buckrose *York*
BUSBRIDGE (St John the Baptist) and Hambledon *Guildf 4*
P *Patr Bd*   R S D K TAYLOR   **C** S P WILLETTS   **NSM** C A SOH,
M P W SPENCER   **OLM** A SPENCER, D W JENKINS
BUSCOT (St Mary) *see* Gt Coxwell w Buscot, Coleshill etc *Ox*
BUSH END (St John the Evangelist) *see* Hatfield Broad Oak and Bush End *Chelmsf*
BUSH HILL PARK (St Mark) *Lon 18*   P *Bp*   **NSM** J M FOOT
BUSH HILL PARK (St Stephen) *Lon 18*   P *V Edmonton All SS*
NSM J M FOOT
BUSHBURY (St Mary) *Lich 28*   P *Patr Bd*   **TR** I R M POOLE
TV G R SMITH   **C** R P CLAY
BUSHEY (Holy Trinity) (St James) (St Paul) *St Alb 6*   P *Bp*
R J G EDWARDS   **C** A G BURGESS
BUSHEY HEATH (St Peter) *St Alb 6*   P *Bp*   V A J BURTON
BUSHLEY (St Peter) *see* Longdon, Castlemorton, Bushley, Queenhill etc *Worc*
BUSHMEAD (Christ Church) *St Alb 12*   P *Bp*
V T P MADELEY
BUSSAGE (St Michael and All Angels) *see* Bisley, Chalford, France Lynch, and Oakridge etc *Glouc*
BUTCOMBE (St Michael and All Angels) *see* Wrington w Butcombe and Burrington *B & W*
BUTLEIGH (St Leonard) *see* Baltonsborough w Butleigh, W Bradley etc *B & W*
BUTLERS MARSTON (St Peter and St Paul) *see* Stourdene Gp *Cov*
BUTLEY (St John the Baptist) *see* Wilford Peninsula *St E*
BUTTERCRAMBE (St John the Evangelist) *see* Harton *York*
BUTTERLEIGH (St Matthew) *see* Silverton, Butterleigh, Bickleigh and Cadeleigh *Ex*
BUTTERMERE (St James the Great) *see* Savernake *Sarum*
BUTTERMERE (St James) *see* Lorton and Loweswater w Buttermere *Carl*
BUTTERSHAW (St Aidan) *see* Shelf w Buttershaw St Aid *Leeds*
BUTTERTON (St Bartholomew), Ipstones-w-Berkhamsytch and Onecote-w-Bradnop *Lich 5*   P *Bp, R Leek and Meerbrook, and V Alton etc (jt)*   V M J EVANS
BUTTERTON (St Thomas) *see* Newcastle w Butterton *Lich*
BUTTERWICK (St Andrew) *see* Freiston, Butterwick w Bennington, and Leverton *Linc*
BUTTERWICK (St Nicholas) *see* Langtoft w Foxholes, Butterwick, Cottam etc *York*
BUTTERWICK, EAST (St Andrew) *see* Messingham w E Butterwick, Scotter w E Ferry and Scotton w Northorpe *Linc*
BUTTERWICK, WEST (St Mary the Virgin) *see* Epworth Gp *Linc*
BUTTSBURY (St Mary) *see* Margaretting w Mountnessing and Buttsbury *Chelmsf*
BUXHALL (St Mary) *see* Combs and Finborough *St E*
BUXTED (St Margaret the Queen) (St Mary) and Hadlow Down *Chich 18*   P *Abp, Bp, and Wagner Trustees (jt)*
R *vacant*
BUXTON (St Andrew) *see* Aylsham and Distr *Nor*
BUXTON (St Anne) (St John the Baptist) (St Mary the Virgin) w Burbage and King Sterndale *Derby 4*   P *Patr Bd*
TR E A ENGLAND   **TV** K COCKING   **NSM** J M OVERTON,
M M SLYFIELD
BUXTON (Trinity Chapel) Proprietary Chapel *Derby 4*
C-in-c R MARSDEN
BUXWORTH (St James) *see* Hayfield and Chinley w Buxworth *Derby*
BY BROOK, comprising Biddestone, Castle Combe, Grittleton and Leigh Delamere, Littleton Drew, Nettleton, Slaughterford, West Kington, and Yatton Keynell *Bris 4*
P *Patr Bd*   **TR** M D TERRY   **NSM** M V GUBBINS
OLM G E PARKIN
BYERS GREEN (St Peter) *Dur 5*   P *Bp*   **P-in-c** C A FRISWELL
BYFIELD (Holy Cross) *see* Aston-le-Walls, Byfield, Boddington, Eydon etc *Pet*

BYFLEET (St Mary) *Guildf 12*   **P** *Ld Chan*   **R** J H MCCABE **Hon C** P M S ROSS-MCCABE
BYFLEET, WEST (St John) *Guildf 12*   **P** *Bp*
  V C P HOLLINGSHURST   **C** M P WHITE
BYFORD (St John the Baptist) *see* Letton w Staunton, Byford, Mansel Gamage etc *Heref*
BYGRAVE (St Margaret of Antioch) *see* Baldock w Bygrave *St Alb*
BYKER (St Anthony) *Newc 3*   **P** *Bp*   **V** S E HERBERT   **C** R S CARO
BYKER (St Martin) Newcastle upon Tyne *Newc 3*   **P** *Bp*
  V S E HERBERT   **C** R S CARO   **NSM** H M LUNN
BYKER (St Michael w St Lawrence) *Newc 3*   **P** *Bp*
  V P J A MEDLEY
BYKER (St Silas) *Newc 3*   **P** *Bp*   **V** H B GILL   **NSM** A F TAYLOR
BYKER St Mark and Walkergate (St Oswald) *Newc 3*   **P** *Bp and Ch Trust Fund Trust (jt)*   **V** K MOULDER
BYLAND, OLD (All Saints) *see* Upper Ryedale *York*
BYLAUGH (St Mary) *see* Reepham and Wensum Valley *Nor*
BYLEY CUM LEES (St John the Evangelist) *see* Middlewich w Byley *Ches*
BYRNESS (St Francis) *see* N Tyne and Redesdale *Newc*
BYTHAM, LITTLE (St Medardus) *see* Castle Bytham w Creeton *Linc*
BYTHORN (St Lawrence) *see* W Leightonstone *Ely*
BYTON (St Mary) *see* Pembridge w Moor Court, Shobdon, Staunton etc *Heref*
BYWELL (St Peter) and Mickley *Newc 9*   **P** *Bp and Adn Lindisfarne (jt)*   **P-in-c** P M MORAN
BYWORTH (St Francis) *see* Farnham *Guildf*
CABLE STREET (St Mary) *see* St Geo-in-the-East St Mary *Lon*
CABOURNE (St Nicholas) *see* Caistor *Linc*
CADBURY (St Michael and All Angels) *see* Brampford Speke, Cadbury, Newton St Cyres etc *Ex*
CADBURY, NORTH (St Michael the Archangel) *see* Camelot Par *B & W*
CADBURY, SOUTH (St Thomas à Becket) *as above*
CADDINGTON (All Saints) *St Alb 12*   **P** *D&C St Paul's*
  V R P O'NEILL   **NSM** L MOSS
CADEBY (All Saints) *see* Bosworth and Sheepy Gp *Leic*
CADELEIGH (St Bartholomew) *see* Silverton, Butterleigh, Bickleigh and Cadeleigh *Ex*
CADGWITH (St Mary) *see* St Keverne, St Ruan w St Grade and Landewednack *Truro*
CADISHEAD (St Mary the Virgin) *Man 18*   **P** *Bp*   **V** A E KAY
CADMORE END (St Mary le Moor) *see* S Chilterns *Ox*
CADNEY (All Saints) *see* Brigg, Wrawby and Cadney cum Howsham *Linc*
CADOGAN SQUARE (St Simon Zelotes) *see* Upper Chelsea St Simon *Lon*
CAERHAYS (St Michael) *see* St Goran w Caerhays *Truro*
CAGE GREEN (St Philip) *see* Tonbridge SS Pet and Paul *Roch*
CAGEBROOK Parishes, comprising Allensmore, Clehonger, Eaton Bishop, Kingstone, and Thruxton *Heref 1*
  P *Bp (2 turns), The Crown (1 turn)*   **R** H J MORGAN
  NSM E A HITCHINER
CAINSCROSS (St Matthew) *see* Stroud Team *Glouc*
CAISTER NEXT YARMOUTH (Holy Trinity) (St Edmund) *Nor 6*   **P** *SMF*   **R** D WELLS
CAISTOR (St Peter and St Paul), including Cabourn, Clixby, Cuxwold, Grasby, Rothwell, Searby w Owmby, and Swallow *Linc 7*   **P** *Bp and D&C (3 turns), Earl of Yarborough and J R Thorold Esq (1 turn)*   **V** I ROBINSON   **Hon C** S W ANDREW   **NSM** C J WYLIE, J MCMANN
CAISTOR ST EDMUNDS (St Edmund) *see* Stoke H Cross w Dunston, Arminghall etc *Nor*
CALBOURNE (All Saints) *see* W Wight *Portsm*
CALCOT (St Birinus) *see* Tilehurst St Cath and Calcot *Ox*
CALDBECK (St Mungo) (Fellside), Castle Sowerby and Sebergham *Carl 3*   **P** *Bp and D&C (alt)*   **P-in-c** E REID
CALDECOTE (All Saints), Northill and Old Warden *St Alb 10*   **P** *Grocers' Co (2 turns), R O Shuttleworth Remembrance Trust (1 turn)*   **V** F COLEMAN
CALDECOTE (St Michael and All Saints) *see* Lordsbridge *Ely*
CALDECOTT (St John the Evangelist) *see* Lyddington, Bisbrooke, Caldecott, Glaston etc *Pet*
CALDER VALE (Mission) *see* Scorton and Barnacre and Calder Vale *Blackb*
CALDER VALE (St John the Evangelist) *as above*
CALDERBROOK (St James the Great) *see* Littleborough *Man*
CALDWELL (Chapel) *see* Forcett and Aldbrough and Melsonby *Leeds*
CALDWELL (St Giles) *see* Stapenhill w Cauldwell *Derby*
CALDY (Church of the Resurrection and All Saints) *see* W Kirby St Bridget *Ches*
CALEDONIAN ROAD (All Saints Hall) *see* Barnsbury *Lon*

CALIFORNIA (St Mary and St John) *see* Finchampstead and California *Ox*
CALLINGTON (St Mary) *see* Callington Cluster *Truro*
CALLINGTON Cluster, The, including Linkinhorne, South Hill, and Stoke Climsland *Truro 11*   **P** *Duchy of Cornwall (1 turn), Bp, DBP, PCC South Hill, and PCC Callington (1 turn)*
  R A W STEPHENS   **NSM** A I KING
CALLOW END (St James) *see* Powick and Guarlford and Madresfield w Newland *Worc*
CALMORE (St Anne) *see* Totton *Win*
CALNE (Holy Trinity) *see* Marden Vale *Sarum*
CALNE (St Mary the Virgin) *as above*
CALOW (St Peter) and Sutton cum Duckmanton *Derby 3*   **P** *Bp and V Chesterfield (jt)*   **R** K H BALL
CALSHOT (St George) *see* Fawley *Win*
CALSTOCK (St Andrew) *see* Tamar Valley *Truro*
CALSTONE WELLINGTON (St Mary the Virgin) *see* Oldbury *Sarum*
CALTHORPE (Our Lady w St Margaret) *see* Erpingham w Calthorpe, Ingworth, Aldborough etc *Nor*
CALTHWAITE (All Saints) *see* Inglewood Gp *Carl*
CALTON (St Mary the Virgin), Cauldon, Grindon, Waterfall and Blore Ray w Okeover *Lich 5*   **P** *Bp and Sir Peter Walker-Okeover Bt (jt)*   **R** A BEAHAN
CALUDON (Holy Cross) Coventry *Cov 1*   **P** *Ld Chan and Bp (alt)*   **OLM** E A HARRIS
CALVELEY CHURCH (not known) *see* Bunbury and Tilstone Fearnall *Ches*
CALVERHALL or CORRA (Holy Trinity) *see* Adderley, Ash, Calverhall, Ightfield etc *Lich*
CALVERLEIGH (St Mary the Virgin) *see* Washfield, Stoodleigh, Withleigh etc *Ex*
CALVERLEY (St Wilfrid) *Leeds 14*   **P** *Bp*   **V** P R ARNOLD   **NSM** S E MCWHINNEY
CALVERTON (All Saints) *see* Stony Stratford w Calverton *Ox*
CALVERTON (St Wilfrid) *S'well 7*   **P** *Bp*   **V** S J HUSTWAYTE
CAM (St George) w Stinchcombe *Glouc 5*   **P** *Bp*
  V F J CROCKER   **NSM** A N L HILL, S C A ACLAND
CAM VALE, comprising Corton Denham, Queen Camel, Sparkford, Sutton Montis, West Camel, and Weston Bampfylde *B & W 2*   **P** *Bp and DBP (2 turns), CPAS, MMCET and Revd G Bennett (1 turn)*   **NSM** R A HOSKINS
CAM, LOWER (St Bartholomew) w Coaley *Glouc 5*   **P** *Bp*
  V S K GREATOREX
CAMBER (St Thomas) *see* Rye *Chich*
CAMBERLEY (St Martin) Old Dean *Guildf 6*   **P** *Bp*
  V C E RICHARDSON   **OLM** K M MURRAY
CAMBERLEY (St Mary) *Guildf 6*   **P** *Bp*   **V** A J KNOWLES
  OLM R WALKER
CAMBERLEY (St Michael) Yorktown *Guildf 6*   **P** *Bp*
  V B NICOLE   **NSM** A MITCHELL
CAMBERLEY (St Paul) *Guildf 6*   **P** *Bp*   **V** T J DARWENT
  C D NATNAEL, S R WELLBELOVE   **OLM** C V ISHERWOOD
CAMBERLEY HEATHERSIDE (Community Centre) *Guildf 6*
  P *Bp*   **P-in-c** L J W BAIN
CAMBERWELL (Christ Church) *S'wark 8*   **P** *MMCET*
  V H R BALFOUR
CAMBERWELL (St George) *S'wark 8*   **P** *Bp and Trin Coll Cam (jt)*   **P-in-c** S DAWSON
CAMBERWELL (St Giles) (St Matthew) *S'wark 8*   **P** *Bp*
  V N P GEORGE
CAMBERWELL (St Luke) *S'wark 8*   **P** *Bp*   **P-in-c** I J MOBSBY
  C S V SCHLOSS   **NSM** C DURUEKE
CAMBERWELL (St Michael and All Angels w All Souls w Emmanuel) *S'wark 10*   **P** *DBP*   **P-in-c** J G A ROBERTS
CAMBERWELL (St Philip) and St Mark *S'wark 7*   **P** *The Crown*   **V** *vacant*
CAMBO (Holy Trinity) *see* Kirkwhelpington, Kirkharle, Kirkheaton and Cambo *Newc*
CAMBOIS (St Andrew's Mission Church) *see* Bedlington, Cambois and Sleekburn *Newc*
CAMBORNE (St Martin and St Meriadoc), Tuckingmill and Penponds *Truro 2*   **P** *The Crown and Patr Bd (alt)*
  P-in-c R E BROWNING   **NSM** N J POTTER
CAMBOURNE (no dedication) *Ely 1*   **P** *Bp*   **V** *vacant*
CAMBRIDGE (Christ Church) *see* Cambridge St Andr Less *Ely*
CAMBRIDGE (Good Shepherd) *see* Chesterton Gd Shep *Ely*
CAMBRIDGE (Holy Cross) *Ely 2*   **P** *Bp*   **V** R T WILLIAMS
CAMBRIDGE (Holy Sepulchre) (St Andrew the Great) *Ely 2*
  P *PCC*   **V** A D M PAINE   **C** R J STRACHAN, T G HUTCHINGS
CAMBRIDGE (Holy Trinity) *Ely 3*   **P** *D&C and Peache Trustees (jt)*   **V** R A CHARKHAM   **C** O W Y BENYON, S J BROWNING
CAMBRIDGE (St Andrew the Great) *see* Cambridge H Sepulchre *Ely*

CAMBRIDGE (St Andrew the Less) (Christ Church) *Ely 2*
P *Ch Trust Fund Trust* V s n MIDGLEY C D A TODD,
R A H EVANS NSM P D MYERS
CAMBRIDGE (St Augustine of Canterbury) *see* Cambridge
Ascension *Ely*
CAMBRIDGE (St Barnabas) *Ely 3* P *V Cam St Paul*
V A F MACLAURIN C D J DRIVER, J F C NEAL
CAMBRIDGE (St Benedict) *Ely 3* P *CCC Cam*
V A R MATTHEWS C Z M GUILIANO
CAMBRIDGE (St Botolph) *Ely 3* P *Qu Coll Cam*
P-in-c s g ANDERSON
CAMBRIDGE (St Clement) *Ely 2* P *Jes Coll Cam*
P-in-c N I MOIR NSM A J ROSS
CAMBRIDGE (St Edward King and Martyr) Proprietary
Chapel *Ely 3* C-in-c M SCARLATA, M GREBE
CAMBRIDGE (St Giles) *see* Cambridge Ascension *Ely*
CAMBRIDGE (St James) *Ely 3* P *Bp* P-in-c s ROTHWELL
C A E STRAUSS NSM D P FORD, S J PLANT
CAMBRIDGE (St Luke the Evangelist) *see* Cambridge
Ascension *Ely*
CAMBRIDGE (St Mark) *Ely 3* P *DBP*
P-in-c R C ROSBOROUGH
CAMBRIDGE (St Martin) (St Thomas) *Ely 3* P *V Cam
St Paul* P-in-c J ROTH
CAMBRIDGE (St Mary the Great), w St Michael *Ely 2* P *Trin
Coll Cam* V A M DAFFERN C A C DAY, D S MCLACHLAN,
H M ORR
CAMBRIDGE (St Mary the Less) *Ely 3* P *Peterho Cam*
V R M MACKLEY NSM M A BISHOP
CAMBRIDGE (St Matthew) *Ely 2* P *V Cam St Andr the Less*
V F L PRICE
CAMBRIDGE (St Paul) *Ely 3* P *Ch Trust Fund Trust*
V M S BECKETT C J G CANESSA, S A YOUNG NSM C J ROSE
CAMBRIDGE (St Philip) (St Stephen) *Ely 3* P *Ch Trust Fund
Trust* V s TAYLOR Hon C C R IEVINS
NSM T O BUCHANAN
CAMBRIDGE (St Thomas) *see* Cambridge St Martin *Ely*
CAMBRIDGE Ascension (St Giles) (St Luke the Evangelist)
(St Augustine of Canterbury) (All Souls Chapel) *Ely 2*
P *Bp* TR P A KING TV J C BUNKER Hon C T AMBROSE
CAMDEN SQUARE (St Paul) *see* Old St Pancras *Lon*
CAMDEN TOWN (St Michael) *see* Old St Pancras *Lon*
CAMEL (All Saints) *see* Cam Vale *B & W*
CAMEL-ALLEN Benefice, The, comprising Advent,
Lanteglos-by-Camelford, and St Teath *Truro 10* P *Duchy of
Cornwall and Bp (by turn)* R A J COOPER
CAMELFORD (St Julitta) *see* Camel-Allen *Truro*
CAMELFORD (St Thomas of Canterbury) *as above*
CAMELOT Parishes, The, comprising Blackford, Bratton
St Maur, Compton Pauncefoot, Holton, Maperton, North
Cadbury, North Cheriton, South Cadbury, and Yarlington
B & W 2 P *Patr Bd* R T G RAE SMITH C A C CREEDON
NSM A L PARRIS
CAMELSDALE (St Paul) *see* Fernhurst, Lynchmere and
Camelsdale *Chich*
CAMELSIDE Benefice, The, comprising Blisland, Helland,
St Berward, St Mabyn, and St Tudy w Michaelstow *Truro 10*
P *Duchy of Cornwall (1 turn), D&C, Ch Ch Ox, SMF, MMCET,
and Viscount Falmouth (1 turn)* R D R R SEYMOUR
NSM S E WILLIAMS
CAMERTON (St Peter) *see* Timsbury w Priston, Camerton
and Dunkerton *B & W*
CAMERTON (St Peter), Seaton and West Seaton *Carl 7*
P *D&C and Ch Trust Fund Trust (jt)* V I GRAINGER
NSM I FEARON
CAMMERINGHAM (St Michael) *see* Spring Line Gp *Linc*
CAMP HILL (St Mary and St John) *Cov 5* P *Bp* V *vacant*
CAMPDEN HILL (St George) *see* Holland Park *Lon*
CAMPSALL (St Mary Magdalene) *see* Burghwallis and
Campsall *Sheff*
CAMPSEA ASHE (St John the Baptist) *see* Orebeck *St E*
CAMPTON (All Saints), Clophill and Haynes *St Alb 8* P *Bp
and Ball Coll Ox (alt)* R *vacant*
CANALSIDE Benefice, The, comprising Hilperton w
Whaddon, Semington, and Staverton w Hilperton Marsh
Sarum 15 P *Viscount Long, Magd Coll Cam, and R Trowbridge
St Jas and Keevil (by turn)* R J N REES NSM J E ALBONE
CANDLESBY (St Benedict) *see* Bolingbroke Deanery *Linc*
CANEWDON (St Nicholas) *see* Ashingdon w S Fambridge,
Canewdon and Paglesham *Chelmsf*
CANFIELD, GREAT (St Mary) w High Roding and Aythorpe
Roding *Chelmsf 18* P *A Sainthill Esq, Ch Soc Trust, and Bp
(by turn)* R *vacant*
CANFIELD, LITTLE (All Saints) *see* Takeley w Lt Canfield
Chelmsf

CANFORD CLIFFS (Transfiguration) and Sandbanks
Sarum 7 P *Bp* V A D O'BRIEN C T J PELHAM
CANFORD HEATH (St Paul) *Sarum 7* P *Bp* V M D WILLIAMS
CANFORD MAGNA (no dedication) (Bearwood) (The
Lantern) *Sarum 9* P *Patr Bd* TR C M TEBBUTT
TV G BOLAND, M TUFNELL C P J NESBITT
NSM S E TEBBUTT
CANLEY (St Stephen) *Cov 3* P *Bp* P-in-c D G HAMMOND
CANNING TOWN (St Matthias) *Chelmsf 5* P *Bp*
P-in-c B A ATKINS
CANNINGS AND REDHORN, The, comprising All Cannings,
Bishop's Cannings and Etchilhampton, Chirton and Patney,
Marden, Urchfont w Stert, and Wilsford *Sarum 17* P *Patr Bd*
TR L R CURTIS C J K PORTER
CANNINGTON (Blessed Virgin Mary), Otterhampton,
Combwich and Stockland *B & W 17* P *Bp* R A J WATERS
CANNOCK (St Luke) and Huntington *Lich 3* P *Bp and D&C
(jt)* C A E MANN OLM G M JOYNSON
CANON FROME (St James) *see* Hop Churches *Heref*
CANON PYON (St Lawrence) w King's Pyon, Birley and
Wellington *Heref 6* P *Bp, Ch Union, and D&C (jt)*
V J A DAVIES C D J WYATT
CANONBURY (St Stephen) *Lon 6* P *V Islington St Mary*
V J N BEAUCHAMP
CANONRY Benefice, The, comprising Ash w Westmarsh,
Chillenden w Knowlton, Elmstone w Preston and
Stourmouth, Goodnestone, Nonington, and Wingham
Cant 1 P *Abp, D&C, and Lord Fitzwalter (jt)*
V D I MOULDEN
CANTERBURY (All Saints) *Cant 3* P *Abp* C P GREIG
CANTERBURY (St Dunstan w Holy Cross) (St Mildred)
(St Peter w St Alphege) *Cant 3* P *Abp, Ld Chan, and D&C
(by turn)* R J S RICHARDS NSM K C GOODMAN
CANTERBURY (St Martin) (St Paul) *Cant 3* P *Abp*
R M R GRIFFIN C H N THOMSON
CANTERBURY (St Mary Bredin) *Cant 3* P *Simeon's Trustees*
V B J D L T DE BERRY C S L CARTER
CANTERBURY (St Stephen) *see* Hackington *Cant*
CANTLEY (St Margaret) *see* Acle and Bure to Yare *Nor*
CANTLEY (St Wilfrid) *Sheff 8* P *Guild of All So* V A HOWARD
CANTLEY, NEW (St Hugh of Lincoln) (Holy Trinity) *Sheff 8*
P *Guild of All So and SMF (jt)* V W J STOKOE
CANVEY ISLAND (St Anne) (St Katherine's Worship
Centre) (St Nicholas) *Chelmsf 13* P *Bp and Patr Bd (jt)*
TR D S C TUDOR TV M G WALFORD OLM L A MCGLYNN,
T F BROWN
CANWICK (All Saints) *see* Washingborough w Heighington
and Canwick *Linc*
CAPEL (St John the Baptist) *see* Surrey Weald *Guildf*
CAPEL (St Thomas à Becket) United Benefice, including
Tudeley and Five Oak Green *Roch 8* P *Bp* V J G A IVE
C P F IVE
CAPEL LE FERNE (St Radigund) *see* Alkham w Capel le Ferne
and Hougham *Cant*
CAPEL ST MARY (St Mary) w Little Wenham and Great
Wenham *St E 15* P *Bp and SMF (jt)* R *vacant*
CAPENHURST (Holy Trinity) *see* Backford and Capenhurst
Ches
CAPESTHORNE (Holy Trinity) *see* Marton, Siddington w
Capesthorne etc *Ches*
CAR COLSTON (St Mary) w Screveton *S'well 5* P *H S Blagg
Esq* P-in-c R M COLBY
CARBIS BAY (St Anta and All Saints) w Lelant (St Uny)
Truro 5 P *Bp* P-in-c E VAN BLERK NSM C Z WILTON
CARBROOKE (St Peter and St Paul) *see* Watton *Nor*
CARDESTON (St Michael) *see* Ford, Gt Wollaston and
Alberbury w Cardeston *Heref*
CARDINGTON (St James) *see* Apedale Gp *Heref*
CARDINGTON (St Mary) *see* Elstow *St Alb*
CARDYNHAM (St Meubred) *see* Bodmin *Truro*
CAREBY (St Stephen) *see* Castle Bytham w Creeton *Linc*
CARHAM (St Cuthbert) *see* Cornhill w Carham *Newc*
CARHAMPTON (St John the Baptist) *see* Dunster,
Carhampton, Withycombe w Rodhuish etc *B & W*
CARHARRACK (St Piran's Mission Church) *see* Chacewater w
St Day and Carharrack *Truro*
CARISBROOKE (St Mary the Virgin) *Portsm 7* P *Qu Coll Ox*
V M C BAGG
CARISBROOKE (St Nicholas in the Castle) *Portsm 7*
P *Qu Coll Ox* V M C BAGG
CARLBY (St Stephen) *see* Ryhall w Essendine and Carlby *Pet*
CARLETON (St Chad) *see* Poulton Carleton and Singleton
Blackb
CARLETON (St Mary the Virgin) *see* Skipton Ch Ch w
Carleton *Leeds*

CARLETON (St Michael) and E Hardwick *Leeds 18*
P *V Pontefract and Cawood Trustees (jt)* **V** S A STACEY
NSM K REYNOLDS

CARLETON (St Peter) *see* Rockland St Mary w Hellington, Bramerton etc *Nor*

CARLETON IN CRAVEN *see* Skipton Ch Ch w Carleton *Leeds*

CARLETON RODE (All Saints) *see* Long Stratton and Pilgrim TM *Nor*

CARLETON, EAST (St Mary) *see* Swardeston w E Carleton, Intwood, Keswick etc *Nor*

CARLFORD, comprising Ashbocking, Boulge, Burgh, Clopton, Grundisburgh, Hasketon, Otley, and Swilland *St E 18* **P** *Ld Chan (1 turn), Bp and DBP (2 turns)* **R** H C SANDERS **NSM** M C S CRESSWELL

CARLIN HOW (St Helen) *see* Loftus and Carlin How w Skinningrove *York*

CARLINGHOW (St John the Evangelist) *see* Staincliffe and Carlinghow *Leeds*

CARLISLE (Holy Trinity) (St Barnabas) *Carl 3* **P** *Patr Bd*
P-in-c M A MARTINSON **C** I B THOMAS **NSM** I JOHNSTON

CARLISLE (St Aidan) and Christ Church *Carl 3* **P** *Bp*
P-in-c K TEASDALE

CARLISLE (St Cuthbert) *Carl 3* **P** *D&C* **V** K TEASDALE

CARLISLE (St Elisabeth) Harraby *see* Harraby *Carl*

CARLISLE (St Herbert) w St Stephen *Carl 3* **P** *Bp*
V A JONES

CARLISLE (St James) *see* Denton Holme *Carl*

CARLISLE (St John the Evangelist) *Carl 3* **P** *CPAS*
V S DONALD

CARLISLE (St Luke) Morton *Carl 3* **P** *Bp*
P-in-c M A MARTINSON

CARLISLE (St Michael) *see* Stanwix *Carl*

CARLISLE Belah (St Mark) *as above*

CARLTON (St Aidan) *see* Helmsley *York*

CARLTON (St Andrew) *see* Nailstone and Carlton w Shackerstone *Leic*

CARLTON (St Botolph) *see* Whorlton w Carlton and Faceby *York*

CARLTON (St John the Baptist) *S'well 7* **P** *Bp*
P-in-c A H DIGMAN **C** D E MOYO

CARLTON (St John the Evangelist) *see* Athersley and Carlton *Leeds*

CARLTON (St Mary) *see* Chellington *St Alb*

CARLTON (St Peter) *see* Raddesley Gp *Ely*

CARLTON (St Peter) *see* Saxmundham w Kelsale cum Carlton *St E*

CARLTON BY SNAITH (St Mary) and Drax *York 4* **P** *Abp and Ch Trust Fund Trust (jt)* **P-in-c** A V BURR **C** R J ALLRIGHT

CARLTON COLVILLE (St Peter) and Mutford *Nor 9*
P *Simeon's Trustees and G&C Coll Cam (jt)* **V** *vacant*

CARLTON CURLIEU (St Mary the Virgin) *see* Oadby Gt Glen *Leic*

CARLTON FOREHOE (St Mary) *see* Barnham Broom and Upper Yare *Nor*

CARLTON HUSTHWAITE (St Mary) *see* Coxwold and Husthwaite *York*

CARLTON MINIOTT (St Lawrence) *see* Thirsk *York*

CARLTON SCROOP (St Nicholas) *see* S Cliff Villages Gp *Linc*

CARLTON, EAST (St Peter) *see* Gretton w Rockingham and Cottingham w E Carlton *Pet*

CARLTON, GREAT (St John the Baptist) *see* Mid Marsh Gp *Linc*

CARLTON, NORTH (St Luke) *see* Spring Line Gp *Linc*

CARLTON, SOUTH (St John the Baptist) *as above*

CARLTON-IN-LINDRICK (St John the Evangelist) and Langold w Oldcotes *S'well 1* **P** *Bp and Ld Chan (alt)*
R M ORR

CARLTON-IN-THE-WILLOWS (St Paul) *S'well 7* **P** *MMCET*
NSM W S MURPHY

CARLTON-LE-MOORLAND (St Mary) *see* Withamside *Linc*

CARLTON-ON-TRENT (St Mary) *see* Norwell w Ossington, Cromwell etc *S'well*

CARNABY (St John the Baptist) *see* Rudston, Boynton, Carnaby etc *York*

CARNFORTH (Christ Church) *Blackb 14* **P** *Bp* **V** S L JONES

CARNFORTH (Holy Trinity) *see* Bolton-le-Sands *Blackb*

CARR CLOUGH (St Andrew) *see* Kersal Moor *Man*

CARR DYKE GROUP, The, comprising Billinghay, Martin, North Kyme, South Kyme, Timberland, and Walcott *Linc 14*
P *Sir Philip Naylor-Leyland Bt and Ld Chan (alt)* **V** S R HOLT **OLM** D E WESTON

CARR MILL (St David) *Liv 10* **P** *V St Helens St Mark and Bp (jt)* **V** S L DAVIES

CARRINGTON (St John the Evangelist) *S'well 9* **P** *Bp*
V J S PACEY

CARRINGTON (St Paul) *see* Sibsey w Frithville *Linc*

CARSHALTON (All Saints) *S'wark 23* **P** *Bp*
P-in-c D S FISHER

CARSHALTON BEECHES (Good Shepherd) *S'wark 23* **P** *Bp*
V K J LEWIS **C** H GORDON

CARSINGTON (St Margaret) *see* Wirksworth *Derby*

CARTERTON (St John the Evangelist) *see* Brize Norton and Carterton *Ox*

CARTMEL FELL (St Anthony) *Carl 10* **P** *Bp*
P-in-c M D WOODCOCK

CARTMEL PENINSULA Team Ministry, The (St Mary and St Michael), including Allithwaite, Field Broughton, Finsthwaite, Flookburgh, Grange-over-Sands, Haverthwaite, Lindale, and Staveley-in-Cartmel *Carl 11* **P** *Patr Bd*
P-in-c J H BRUCE **TV** N E DEVENISH, R L STAVERT

CASSINGTON (St Peter) *see* Eynsham and Cassington *Ox*

CASTERTON (Holy Trinity) *see* Kirkby Lonsdale *Carl*

CASTERTON, GREAT (St Peter and St Paul) and LITTLE (All Saints) w Pickworth and Tickencote *Pet 12* **P** *Burghley Ho Preservation Trust Ltd (2 turns), Lord Chesham (1 turn), and Bp (1 turn)* **P-in-c** J J S MCGARRIGLE

CASTLE ACRE (St James) *see* Nar Valley *Nor*

CASTLE ASHBY (St Mary Magdalene) *see* Yardley Hastings, Denton and Grendon etc *Pet*

CASTLE BOLTON (St Oswald) *see* Penhill *Leeds*

CASTLE BROMWICH (St Clement) *Birm 8* **P** *Bp*
V S C CARTER **C** A B THOMAS

CASTLE BROMWICH (St Mary and St Margaret) *Birm 8*
P *Earl of Bradf* **R** M J HOPKINS

CASTLE BYTHAM (St James) w Creeton *Linc 17* **P** *D&C, Bp, Ld Chan, and DBP (by turn)* **R** *vacant*

CASTLE CAMPS (All Saints) *see* Linton *Ely*

CASTLE CARROCK (St Peter) *see* Eden, Gelt and Irthing *Carl*

CASTLE CARY (All Saints) and Ansford *B & W 2* **P** *Bp*
P-in-c E A DUDLEY

CASTLE CHURCH (St Mary) *Lich 10* **P** *Bp*
V P J SOWERBUTTS **NSM** C V SYKES

CASTLE COMBE (St Andrew) *see* By Brook *Bris*

CASTLE DONINGTON (St Edward the King and Martyr) and Lockington cum Hemington *Leic 6* **P** *Lady Gretton and C H C Coaker Esq (jt)* **V** A J RACE **NSM** M J BENNETT

CASTLE EATON (St Mary the Virgin) *see* S Cotswolds *Glouc*

CASTLE FROME (St Michael) *see* Frome Valley *Heref*

CASTLE HEDINGHAM (St Nicholas) *see* The Hedinghams and Upper Colne *Chelmsf*

CASTLE HILL (St Philip) *see* Chapelfields *Liv*

CASTLE NORTHWICH (Holy Trinity) *see* Northwich H Trin *Ches*

CASTLE RISING (St Lawrence) *Nor 15* **P** *G Howard Esq*
R J B V RIVIERE

CASTLE SOWERBY (St Kentigern) *see* Caldbeck, Castle Sowerby and Sebergham *Carl*

CASTLE VALE (St Cuthbert of Lindisfarne) w Minworth *Birm 7* **P** *Bp* **V** J B A COPE

CASTLE VIEW ESTATE (St Francis) *see* Langley Marish *Ox*

CASTLECROFT (The Good Shepherd) *see* Tettenhall Wood and Perton *Lich*

CASTLEFIELDS (All Saints and St Michael) *see* Shrewsbury All SS w St Mich *Lich*

CASTLEFORD Team Parish (All Saints) (St Michael and All Angels), including Glasshoughton, Hightown, and Whitwood *Leeds 18* **P** *Duchy of Lanc and Bp (alt)*
TR J C MILNES **TV** G K RUSZCZYNSKI

CASTLEMORTON (St Gregory) *see* Longdon, Castlemorton, Bushley, Queenhill etc *Worc*

CASTLESIDE (St John the Evangelist) *Dur 4* **P** *Bp*
P-in-c M JACKSON

CASTLETHORPE (St Simon and St Jude) *see* Hanslope w Castlethorpe *Ox*

CASTLETON (St Edmund) *see* Hope, Castleton and Bradwell *Derby*

CASTLETON (St Mary Magdalene) *see* Sherborne w Castleton, Lillington and Longburton *Sarum*

CASTLETON (St Michael and St George) *see* Danby w Castleton and Commondale *York*

CASTLETON MOOR (St Martin) *Man 14* **P** *Bp* **V** F C GUITE **NSM** S SHEPHERD

CASTON (St Cross), Griston, Merton, Thompson, Stow Bedon, Breckles and Great Hockham *Nor 13* **P** *Bp and DBP (jt)* **Hon C** A C BELL, P R THOMAS

CASTOR (St Kyneburgha) w Upton and Stibbington and Water Newton, Marholm and Sutton *Pet 11* **P** *Mrs V S V Gunnery, Sir Philip Naylor-Leyland Bt, and Keble Coll Ox (jt)* **R** D RIDGEWAY

CATCLIFFE (St Mary) *see* Rivers Team *Sheff*

CATCOTT (St Peter) *see* Polden Wheel *B & W*

CATERHAM (St Mary the Virgin) (St Laurence) (St Paul) (St John the Evangelist) *S'wark 25* **P** *Bp*
P-in-c T A MAPSTONE **TV** C L DOWLAND-PILLINGER,
H J BURNETT, J GARTON, P A KURK **NSM** A-M GARTON,
F M LONG, S J ELLISON
CATESBY (St Mary) *see Daventry Pet*
CATFIELD (All Saints) *see Ludham, Potter Heigham, Hickling and Catfield Nor*
CATFORD (St Andrew) *S'wark 4* **P** *Bp* **V** L T F MCKENNA
CATFORD (St John) Southend and Downham *S'wark 4*
P *Bp* **TR** M R THOMAS **TV** N S WALSH, S D LECK
C C T A ROGERS
CATFORD (St Laurence) *S'wark 4* **P** *Bp* **V** C F PICKSTONE
CATHERINGTON (All Saints) and Clanfield *Portsm 5* **P** *Bp*
NSM A M GOTHARD
CATHERSTON LEWESTON (St Mary) *see Golden Cap Team Sarum*
CATON (St Paul) w Littledale *Blackb 14* **P** *V Lanc*
V P R BOULTER
CATSFIELD (St Laurence) and Crowhurst *Chich 12* **P** *Bp and J P Papillon (alt)* **R** M A BRYDON
CATSHILL (Christ Church) *see Bromsgrove Worc*
CATTERICK (St Anne) *Leeds 22* **P** *Bp* **V** L M SOUTHERN
CATTHORPE (St Thomas) *see Avon-Swift Leic*
CATTISTOCK (St Peter and St Paul) *see Melbury Sarum*
CATTON (All Saints) *see Stamford Bridge Gp York*
CATTON (St Nicholas and the Blessed Virgin Mary) *see Walton-on-Trent w Croxall, Rosliston etc Derby*
CATTON, NEW (Christ Church) *Nor 2* **P** *Bp*
P-in-c L M BAKER
CATTON, NEW (St Luke) w St Augustine *Nor 2* **P** *Bp, D&C, and CPAS (jt)* **P-in-c** S E QUANTRILL
CATTON, OLD (St Margaret) *Nor 2* **P** *D&C* **V** A D PARSONS
CATWICK (St Michael) *see Skirlaugh, Catwick, Long Riston, Rise, Swine w Ellerby York*
CATWORTH, GREAT (St Leonard) *see W Leightonstone Ely*
CAULDON (St Mary and St Laurence) *see Calton, Cauldon, Grindon, Waterfall etc Lich*
CAUNDLE MARSH (St Peter and St Paul) *see Three Valleys Sarum*
CAUNTON (St Andrew) *see Norwell w Ossington, Cromwell etc S'well*
CAUSEWAY HEAD (St Paul) *see Solway Plain Carl*
CAUTLEY (St Mark) *see Sedbergh, Cautley and Garsdale Carl*
CAVENDISH (St Mary) *see Stour Valley St E*
CAVENHAM (St Andrew) *see Mildenhall St E*
CAVERSFIELD (St Laurence) *see Bicester w Bucknell, Caversfield and Launton Ox*
CAVERSHAM (Park Church) *see Emmer Green w Caversham Park Ox*
CAVERSHAM (St Andrew) *Ox 7* **P** *Bp* **V** N D JONES
CAVERSHAM (St John the Baptist) *see Caversham Thameside and Mapledurham Ox*
CAVERSHAM (St Peter) *as above*
CAVERSHAM HEIGHTS (St Andrew) *see Caversham St Andr Ox*
CAVERSHAM THAMESIDE (St Peter) (St John the Baptist) and Mapledurham *Ox 7* **P** *Ch Ch Ox, Eton Coll, and Bp (jt)*
R M K J SMITH C J R RYDER, P J CUTHBERT
NSM A J STORCH, R A ROSS
CAVERSWALL (St Peter) and Weston Coyney w Dilhorne *Lich 6* **P** *D&C* **C** A J WALKER, L P LUCKING
CAWOOD (All Saints) w Ryther and Wistow *York 4* **P** *Abp and Ld Chan (alt)* **P-in-c** T N DYER
CAWSAND (St Andrew's Mission Church) *see Maker w Rame, Millbrook, St John and Torpoint Truro*
CAWSTON (St Agnes) *see Aylsham and Distr Nor*
CAWTHORNE (All Saints) *see W Barnsley Leeds*
CAXTON (St Andrew) *see Papworth Ely*
CAYNHAM (St Mary) *see The Ashfords Heref*
CAYTHORPE (St Aidan) *see Burton Joyce, Bulcote and Stoke Bardolph etc S'well*
CAYTHORPE (St Vincent) *see S Cliff Villages Gp Linc*
CAYTON (St John the Baptist) *see Seamer, E Ayton and Cayton York*
CENTRAL *see under substantive place name*
CERNE ABBAS (St Mary) *see Buckland Newton, Cerne Abbas, Godmanstone etc Sarum*
CERNEY WICK (Holy Trinity) *see S Cerney w Cerney Wick, Siddington and Preston Glouc*
CERNEY, NORTH (All Saints) *see Churn Valley Glouc*
CERNEY, SOUTH (All Hallows) w Cerney Wick, Siddington and Preston *Glouc 7* **P** *Bp and Mrs P Chester-Master (1 turn), Ld Chan (1 turn)* **V** J M MCKENZIE
CHACELEY (St John the Baptist) *see Deerhurst and Apperley w Forthampton etc Glouc*

CHACEWATER (St Paul) w St Day and Carharrack *Truro 2*
P *D&C and R Kenwyn w St Allen (jt)* **P-in-c** S A BONE
C K E JONES, R D WALLIS **NSM** J ROWE, S J C FLETCHER
CHACOMBE (St Peter and St Paul) *see Chenderit Pet*
CHADBROOK, comprising Alpheton, Shimplingthorne, and Long Melford *St E 9* **P** *Bp and DBP (jt)* **R** M C O LAWSON
CHADDERTON (Christ Church) (St Saviour) *Man 16* **P** *Ch Soc Trust* **V** J G SIMMONS **NSM** R D BREWIS
CHADDERTON (St Mark) and Middleton Junction *Man 16*
P *The Crown and Bp (alt)* **V** S SMITH
CHADDERTON (St Matthew) St Luke *Man 16* **P** *Bp and The Crown (alt)* **V** D R PENNY
CHADDERTON Emmanuel (St George) *Man 16* **P** *Trustees*
V E D H LEAF
CHADDESDEN (St Mary) *Derby 5* **P** *MMCET* **V** J D WARD
CHADDESDEN (St Philip) w Derby St Mark *Derby 5* **P** *Bp*
Hon C M R FUTERS
CHADDESLEY CORBETT (St Cassian) *see Kidderminster E Worc*
CHADDLEWORTH (St Andrew) *see W Downland Ox*
CHADLINGTON (St Nicholas) *see Chase Ox*
CHADSMOOR (St Aidan) (St Chad) *Lich 3* **P** *Bp and D&C (jt)* **V** N UPSON-SMITH
CHADWELL (Emmanuel) (St Mary) *Chelmsf 16* **P** *Ch Soc Trust* **R** M R WALTON
CHADWELL HEATH (St Chad) *Chelmsf 1* **P** *Vs Dagenham and Ilford (alt)* **V** M J COURT **C** C F NDUKU
NSM C J HARDING
CHAFFCOMBE (St Michael and All Angels), Cricket Malherbie w Knowle St Giles, Tatworth, Thorncombe and Winsham *B & W 16* **P** *Bp and C G S Eyre Esq (jt)*
V P I C BUTCHER **NSM** J ABBOTT
CHAGFORD (St Michael), Gidleigh, Throwleigh, Drewsteignton, South Tawton, Spreyton, Hittisleigh, North Tawton, Bondleigh, Honeychurch and Sampford Courtenay *Ex 10* **P** *Patr Bd* **TR** P S SEATON-BURN
TV N P WELDON **NSM** H M EVERY, R I BULLWORTHY
CHAILEY (St Peter) *Chich 18* **P** *J P B Tillard Esq* **R** *vacant*
CHALBURY (All Saints) *see Wimborne Minster and the N Villages Sarum*
CHALDON (St Peter and St Paul) *see Caterham S'wark*
CHALDON HERRING (St Nicholas) *see The Lulworths, Winfrith Newburgh and Chaldon Sarum*
CHALE (St Andrew) *Portsm 7* **P** *Keble Coll Ox* **R** N J PORTER
CHALFIELD, GREAT (All Saints) *see Broughton Gifford, Gt Chalfield and Holt Sarum*
CHALFONT ST GILES (St Giles), Seer Green and Jordans *Ox 9* **P** *Bp* **R** J D BROWN **C** M MESSERVY,
P E HENDERSON **NSM** J M TEBBOTH, M T BLEAKLEY
CHALFONT ST PETER (St Peter) *Ox 9* **P** *St Jo Coll Ox*
R J P GOODMAN **OLM** W GRAHAM
CHALFONT, LITTLE (St George) *see Chenies and Lt Chalfont, Latimer and Flaunden Ox*
CHALFORD (Christ Church) *see Bisley, Chalford, France Lynch, and Oakridge etc Glouc*
CHALGRAVE (All Saints) *see Toddington and Chalgrave St Alb*
CHALGROVE (St Mary) w Berrick Salome *Ox 20* **P** *Ch Ch Ox* **V** M J LAKEY
CHALK (St Mary) *Roch 4* **P** *R Milton* **V** N I BOURNE
CHALKE VALLEY (Team Ministry), comprising Berwick St John, Bishopstone and Stratford Tony, Bowerchalke, Britford, Broadchalke, Charlton-All-Saints, Coombe Bissett w Homington, Ebbesbourne Wake w Fifield Bavant and Alvediston, and Odstock w Nunton and Bodenham *Sarum 11* **P** *Bp, DBP, and K Coll Cam (by turn)*
TR C BLUNDELL **TV** A C A THOMASSON-ROSINGH,
J A TAYLOR **NSM** R N S LEAKE
CHALLACOMBE (Holy Trinity) *see Shirwell, Loxhore, Kentisbury, Arlington, etc Ex*
CHALLOCK (St Cosmas and St Damian) *see King's Wood Cant*
CHALLOW, EAST (St Nicolas) *see Vale Ox*
CHALLOW, WEST (St Laurence) *see Ridgeway Ox*
CHALTON (St Michael and All Angels) *see Blendworth w Chalton w Idsworth Portsm*
CHALVEY (St Peter) *see Upton cum Chalvey Ox*
CHALVINGTON (St Bartholomew) *see Laughton w Ripe and Chalvington Chich*
CHANCTONBURY, comprising Ashington, Washington and Wiston w Buncton *Chich 11* **P** *Bp and R H Goring Esq (alt)*
R J A DI CASTIGLIONE **C** J W B WADDELL
CHANDLER'S FORD (St Boniface) (St Martin in the Wood) *Win 10* **P** *Bp* **V** I N BIRD **C** G P ROBERTS
CHANTRY (Holy Trinity) *see Mells w Buckland Dinham, Elm, Whatley etc B & W*

CHAPEL ALLERTON (St Matthew) Leeds 13   P V Leeds St Pet
V D M ROBINSON   NSM S RUSHOLME
CHAPEL CHORLTON (St Laurence), Maer and Whitmore
Lich 7   P Bp and G Cavenagh-Mainwaring Esq (jt)
R N A CLEMAS
CHAPEL GREEN (St Oswald)   see Lt Horton Leeds
CHAPEL HOUSE (Holy Nativity) Newc 4   P Bp   V vacant
CHAPEL LAWN (St Mary)   see Middle Marches Heref
CHAPEL PLAISTER (not known)   see Box w Hazlebury and
Ditteridge Bris
CHAPEL ST LEONARDS (St Leonard) and Hogsthorpe and
Mumby and Cumberworth Linc 10   P Bp, Ball Coll Ox,
and Baroness Willoughby de Eresby (jt)   V vacant
CHAPEL-EN-LE-FRITH (St Thomas Becket) Derby 4   P PCC
P-in-c C G PEARSON
CHAPELFIELDS TEAM, The, comprising Abram, Bickershaw,
Hindley, Hindley Green, and Platt Bridge Liv 15   P Patr Bd
TR D M BROOKE   TV A E STEIN   NSM S D CLARKE
CHAPEL-LE-DALE (St Leonard)   see Bentham, Burton-in-
Lonsdale, Chapel-le-Dale etc Leeds
CHAPELTHORPE (St James) Leeds 19   P V Sandal
V K A N GREAVES   C K J A GOLDSMITH
CHAPELTOWN (St John the Baptist) Sheff 3   P Bp
V R A STORDY   NSM A D WHITEHEAD
CHAPMANSLADE (St Philip and St James)   see Cley Hill
Villages Sarum
CHAPPEL (St Barnabas)   see Gt and Lt Tey w Wakes Colne
and Chappel Chelmsf
CHARD (Blessed Virgin Mary) w Combe St Nicholas,
Wambrook and Whitestaunton B & W 16   P Bp and
T V D Eames Esq (jt)   R A E KEMBER   C G A VYE,
K M HAWKSLEY
CHARD (Good Shepherd) Furnham B & W 14   P Bp
V J WILLIAMS
CHARDSTOCK (All Saints)   see Axminster, Chardstock, All
Saints etc Ex
CHARDSTOCK (St Andrew) as above
CHARFIELD (St John) and Kingswood w Wickwar,
Rangeworthy and Hillesley Glouc 5   P Bp, DBP, R W Neeld
Esq, and Earl of Ducie (jt)   R D J RUSSELL
Hon C R H WILLIAMS
CHARFORD (St Andrew)   see Bromsgrove Worc
CHARING (St Peter and St Paul)   see G7 Benefice Cant
CHARING HEATH (Holy Trinity) as above
CHARLBURY (St Mary the Virgin) w Shorthampton
Ox 22   P St Jo Coll Ox   V S A WELCH   NSM J W FIELDEN,
P M BIRD
CHARLCOMBE (Blessed Virgin Mary) w Bath (St Stephen)
B & W 8   P DBP and Simeon's Trustees (jt)   R P A HAWTHORN
NSM D J POW
CHARLECOTE (St Leonard)   see Hampton Lucy w Charlecote
and Loxley Cov
CHARLES (St John the Baptist)   see Bishopsnympton, Charles,
E Anstey, High Bray etc Ex
CHARLES w Plymouth St Matthias Ex 21   P Ch Patr Trust
P-in-c O H D RYDER   C R C M FOWLER, R V CROSSLEY
CHARLESTOWN (St George)   see Salford All SS Man
CHARLESTOWN (St Paul) Truro 1   P The Crown
P-in-c D J P ISIORHO
CHARLESTOWN (St Thomas the Apostle)   see Southowram
and Claremount Leeds
CHARLESWORTH (St John the Evangelist) and Gamesley
Derby 4   P The Crown   V F A WALTERS
CHARLETON (St Mary)   see Stokenham, Slapton, Charleton
w Buckland etc Ex
CHARLTON (Holy Trinity)   see Wantage Ox
CHARLTON (St John the Baptist)   see Braydon Brook Bris
CHARLTON (St John the Baptist)   see St Bartholomew Sarum
CHARLTON (St John)   see Fladbury, Hill and Moor, Wyre
Piddle etc Worc
CHARLTON (St Luke w Holy Trinity) (St Richard)
(St Thomas) S'wark 1   P Bp and Viscount Gough (jt)
P-in-c E A NEWMAN   NSM J P LEE   OLM B J SPONG
CHARLTON (St Peter and St Paul)   see Dover Town Cant
CHARLTON (St Peter)   see Vale of Pewsey Sarum
CHARLTON (St Thomas the Apostle)   see Pastrow Win
CHARLTON ABBOTS (St Martin)   see Sevenhampton w
Charlton Abbots, Hawling etc Glouc
CHARLTON ADAM (St Peter and St Paul)   see Somerton w
The Charltons and Kingsdon B & W
CHARLTON HORETHORNE (St Peter and St Paul)   see
Milborne Port w Goathill etc B & W
CHARLTON KINGS (Holy Apostles) Glouc 6   P R Cheltenham
V A S COLLISHAW
CHARLTON KINGS (St Mary) Glouc 6   P Bp   V G P BOWKETT
C A M BEERE

CHARLTON MACKRELL (St Mary the Virgin)   see Somerton w
The Charltons and Kingsdon B & W
CHARLTON MARSHALL (St Mary the Virgin)   see Spetisbury w
Charlton Marshall etc Sarum
CHARLTON MUSGROVE (St John) (St Stephen),
Cucklington and Stoke Trister B & W 2   P Bp
R R C ASHLEY
CHARLTON ON OTMOOR (St Mary)   see Ray Valley Ox
CHARLTON, SOUTH (St James)   see Chatton w Chillingham,
Eglingham and S Charlton and Ingram Newc
CHARLTON-ALL-SAINTS (All Saints)   see Chalke Valley Sarum
CHARLWOOD (St Nicholas) S'wark 24   P DBP
P-in-c S M WEAKLEY
CHARMINSTER (St Mary the Virgin), Stinsford and the
Chalk Stream villages Sarum 1   P Bp, the Hon C
Townshend, and Win Coll (jt)   R M S PHILLIPS
NSM P A C KENNEDY
CHARMOUTH (St Andrew)   see Golden Cap Team Sarum
CHARNEY BASSETT (St Peter)   see Cherbury w Gainfield Ox
CHARNOCK RICHARD (Christ Church)   see Eccleston and
Charnock Richard Blackb
CHARSFIELD W DEBACH (St Peter)   see Mid Loes St E
CHART SUTTON (St Michael)   see Headcorn and The Suttons
Cant
CHART, GREAT (St Mary)   see Ashford Town Cant
CHART, LITTLE (St Mary)   see G7 Benefice Cant
CHARTERHOUSE-ON-MENDIP (St Hugh)   see Blagdon w
Compton Martin and Ubley B & W
CHARTHAM (St Mary) and Upper Hardres w Stelling
Cant 2   P Abp and Trustees Lord Tomlin (jt)   V P A BROWN
CHARWELTON (Holy Trinity)   see Badby w Newnham and
Charwelton w Fawsley etc Pet
CHASE, comprising Ascott-under-Wychwood, Chadlington,
Enstone, and Spelsbury Ox 22   P Bp and D&C Ch Ch (jt)
R M E J ABREY   NSM I C CHEYNE
CHASE, comprising Chettle, Farnham, Gussage All Saints,
Gussage St Michael, Tarrant Gunville, Tarrant Hinton,
Tarrant Keynston w Tarrant Crawford, Tarrant Monkton w
Tarrant Launceston, and Tollard Royal Sarum 6   P Bp, Adn
Dorset, Ch Soc Trust, Pemb Coll Cam, Univ Coll Ox, T
Sweet-Escott Esq (4 turns), Ld Chan (1 turn)   R M J FOSTER
CHASETOWN (St Anne)   see Burntwood, Chase Terrace etc
Lich
CHASETOWN (St John) as above
CHASTLETON (St Mary the Virgin)   see Chipping Norton Ox
CHATBURN (Christ Church)   see Clitheroe St Mary and
St Paul, Chatburn and Downham Blackb
CHATHAM (St David)   see S Chatham H Trin Roch
CHATHAM (St Mary and St John) Roch 5   P D&C
P-in-c C J A MORGAN
CHATHAM (St Paul w All Saints) Roch 5   P Bp
P-in-c A F WARD   NSM J M WARRINGTON
CHATHAM (St Philip and St James) Roch 5   P Ch Soc Trust
V M L J SAUNDERS   C A BARKER   NSM S C SPENCER
CHATHAM (St Stephen) Roch 5   P Bp   V B J LINNEY
CHATHAM, SOUTH Holy Trinity (St William) (St Alban)
(St David) Roch 5   P Bp   TR E CRANMER
TV D A KICHENSIDE   NSM P A ROBINSON
CHATTERIS (St Peter and St Paul) Ely 11   P G&C Coll Cam
V W L THOMSON
CHATTISHAM (All Saints and St Margaret)   see Elmsett w
Aldham, Hintlesham, Chattisham etc St E
CHATTON (Holy Cross) w Chillingham, Eglingham and
South Charlton and Ingram Newc 7   P Bp and Duke of
Northumberland (1 turn), Ld Chan (1 turn)   V vacant
CHAVEY DOWN (St Martin)   see Winkfield and Cranbourne Ox
CHAWLEIGH (St James)   see Burrington, Chawleigh,
Cheldon, Chulmleigh etc Ex
CHAWTON (St Nicholas)   see Northanger Win
CHEADLE (All Hallows) (St Philip's Mission Church)
Ches 17   P R Cheadle   V P J CUMMING
CHEADLE (St Cuthbert) (St Mary) Ches 17   P Ch Soc Trust
R R S MUNRO   C I L CHIDLOW, J E M NEWMAN,
S J E TOMALIN   NSM P M DOOLEY
CHEADLE (St Giles) w Freehay Lich 6   P DBP   R N J F GREY
CHEADLE HULME (All Saints) Ches 17   P Bp   V J A BACON
CHEADLE HULME (St Andrew) Ches 17   P R Cheadle
V C J P HOBBS   C A J BARNSHAW   NSM P L SELBY
CHEAM (St Dunstan) (St Alban the Martyr) (St Oswald)
S'wark 23   P Patr Bd   NSM F A NORRIS
CHEARSLEY (St Nicholas)   see Long Crendon w Chearsley
and Nether Winchendon Ox
CHEBSEY (All Saints), Creswell, Ellenhall, Ranton and
Seighford Lich 7   P D&C, Qu Eliz Grant Trustees, Trustees
Earl of Lich, and J Eld Esq (jt)   P-in-c D HEMING
CHECKENDON (St Peter and St Paul)   see Langtree Ox

CHECKLEY (Mission Room) *see* Fownhope w Mordiford, Brockhampton etc *Heref*

CHECKLEY (St Mary and All Saints) *see* Uttoxeter Area *Lich*

CHEDBURGH (All Saints) *see* Chevington w Hargrave, Chedburgh w Depden etc *St E*

CHEDDAR (St Andrew), Draycott and Rodney Stoke *B & W 1* **P** *Bp and D&C (jt)* **R** S S BURNS

CHEDDINGTON (St Giles) *see* Cottesloe *Ox*

CHEDDLETON (St Edward the Confessor), Horton, Longsdon and Rushton Spencer *Lich 8* **P** *Bp and R Leek and Meerbrook (jt)* **V** A S G PIKE

CHEDDON FITZPAINE (The Blessed Virgin Mary) *see* S Quantock *B & W*

CHEDGRAVE (All Saints) *see* Loddon, Sisland, Chedgrave, Hardley and Langley *Nor*

CHEDISTON (St Mary) *see* Blyth Valley *St E*

CHEDWORTH (St Andrew), Yanworth and Stowell, Coln Rogers and Coln St Denys *Glouc 8* **P** *Ld Chan (2 turns), Qu Coll Ox (1 turn)* **V** S J GOUNDREY-SMITH

CHEDZOY (The Blessed Virgin Mary) *see* Weston Zoyland w Chedzoy *B & W*

CHEETHAM (St Mark) and Lower Crumpsall *Man 4* **P** *Patr Bd* **V** S L FLETCHER

CHELBOROUGH, EAST (St James) *see* Melbury *Sarum*

CHELBOROUGH, WEST (St Andrew) *as above*

CHELDON (St Mary) *see* Burrington, Chawleigh, Cheldon, Chulmleigh etc *Ex*

CHELFORD (St John the Evangelist) and Lower Withington w Marthall *Ches 12* **P** *DBP* **NSM** F H A ROBINSON

CHELL (St Michael) *Lich 11* **P** *Ch Patr Trust and V Newchapel St Jas (jt)* **V** C J COUPE **NSM** P A LUCKING

CHELL HEATH (Saviour) *see* Chell *Lich*

CHELLASTON (St Peter) *Derby 5* **P** *Bp* **V** J FACEY

CHELLINGTON Team Benefice, The, comprising Carlton w Chellington, Harrold, Odell, Podington w Farndish, Stevington, Turvey, and Wymington *St Alb 13* **P** *Patr Bd* **TR** J E CURTIS **TV** P F TURNBULL **C** L K SANDLE

CHELLS (St Hugh and St John) *see* Stevenage St Hugh and St Jo *St Alb*

CHELMARSH (St Peter) *see* Highley w Billingsley, Glazeley etc *Heref*

CHELMONDISTON (St Andrew) *see* Shoreline *St E*

CHELMORTON AND FLAGG (St John the Baptist) *see* Taddington, Chelmorton and Monyash etc *Derby*

CHELMSFORD (Ascension) (All Saints) (St Michael's Church Centre) *Chelmsf 9* **P** *Bp* **V** T W PAGE

CHELMSFORD (St Andrew) *Chelmsf 9* **P** *Bp* **V** P H GREENLAND

CHELMSLEY WOOD (St Andrew) *Birm 8* **P** *Bp* **R** M E HARMON **NSM** H HORAN

CHELSEA (All Saints) (Old Church) *Lon 8* **P** *R Chelsea St Luke and Earl Cadogan (jt)* **V** D P E REINDORP

CHELSEA (St John w St Andrew) (St John) *Lon 8* **P** *CPAS and Lon Coll of Div (jt)* **V** P R DAWSON **C** E J G LEES-MILLAIS **NSM** A MASON

CHELSEA (St Luke) (Christ Church) *Lon 8* **P** *Earl Cadogan* **R** B LEATHARD **C** J L RUSSELL

CHELSEA, UPPER (Holy Trinity) (St Saviour) *Lon 8* **P** *Earl Cadogan* **R** N P WHEELER **C** G W V BOLTON-DEBBAGE **Hon C** N NASSAR **NSM** P A GISMONDI

CHELSEA, UPPER (St Simon Zelotes) *Lon 8* **P** *Hyndman's Trustees* **V** M R J NEVILLE **NSM** P J STEWART

CHELSFIELD (St Martin of Tours) *Roch 16* **P** *All So Coll Ox* **P-in-c** J TRANTER

CHELSHAM (St Christopher) *see* Warlingham w Chelsham and Farleigh *S'wark*

CHELSHAM (St Leonard) *as above*

CHELSTON (St Peter) *see* Cockington *Ex*

CHELSWORTH (All Saints) *see* Monks Eleigh w Chelsworth and Brent Eleigh etc *St E*

CHELTENHAM (All Saints) *see* N Cheltenham *Glouc*

CHELTENHAM (Christ Church) *Glouc 6* **P** *Simeon's Trustees* **V** vacant

CHELTENHAM (Emmanuel) *see* S Cheltenham *Glouc*

CHELTENHAM (Holy Trinity) (St Paul) *Glouc 6* **P** *Patr Bd* **TR** A K E BLYTH **TV** R J WIDDECOMBE, T R GREW **NSM** G L DICKINSON

CHELTENHAM (St Luke) (St Mary) (St Matthew) *Glouc 6* **P** *Simeon's Trustees* **R** R M COOMBS **C** P E WHEATON **NSM** C L DYSON, S E KNIGHT

CHELTENHAM (St Michael) *Glouc 6* **P** *Bp* **P-in-c** A S COLLISHAW **C** J H WHITE

CHELTENHAM (St Stephen) *see* S Cheltenham *Glouc*

CHELTENHAM, NORTH, comprising Pittville, Elmstone Hardwicke, Prestbury, and Swindon *Glouc 6* **P** *Patr Bd*

TR N R BROMFIELD **TV** G S DAVIS, R J WRIGHT **NSM** A J WOOD, M J FRENCH

CHELTENHAM, SOUTH (Emmanuel) (St Stephen), including Leckhampton *Glouc 6* **P** *Patr Bd* **TR** N D DAVIES **TV** G B GRADY, K L SHILL **Hon C** P F QUINNELL **NSM** E E MITCHELL, H R WOOD

CHELTENHAM, WEST (St Mark) (St Barnabas) (St Aidan) (Emmanuel) *Glouc 6* **P** *MMCET* **R** R J PATERSON **C** R HURLEY, S A WALKER, T A COOK **NSM** A P HOLDERNESS

CHELVESTON (St John the Baptist) *see* Higham Ferrers w Chelveston *Pet*

CHELVEY (St Bridget) *see* Backwell w Chelvey and Brockley *B & W*

CHELWOOD (St Leonard) *see* Publow w Pensford, Compton Dando and Chelwood *B & W*

CHELWOOD GATE (not known) *see* Danehill *Chich*

CHENDERIT, comprising Chacombe, Greatworth, Marston St Lawrence, Middleton Cheney, Thenford, and Warkworth *Pet 1* **P** *Bp and BNC Ox (2 turns), Ld Chan (1 turn)* **R** N W M LEGGETT **Hon C** C J M OLEY

CHENIES (St Michael) and Little Chalfont, Latimer and Flaunden *Ox 9* **P** *Bedford Estates Trustees and Lord Chesham (jt)* **P-in-c** D WHALE **NSM** R F BOUGHTON

CHEQUERFIELD (St Mary) *see* Pontefract *Leeds*

CHERBURY w Gainfield, including Buckland, Charney Bassett, Hinton Waldrist, Littleworth, Longworth, Lyford, and Pusey *Ox 25* **P** *Bp, DBP, Jes Coll, Oriel Coll, and Worc Coll Ox (jt)* **R** T I TRACEY-MACLEOD

CHERHILL (St James the Great) *see* Oldbury *Sarum*

CHERINGTON (St John the Baptist) *see* S Warks Seven Gp *Cov*

CHERINGTON (St Nicholas) *see* Avening w Cherington *Glouc*

CHERITON (St Martin) w Newington Benefice, The *Cant 8* **P** *Abp* **P-in-c** J A ROBERTSON

CHERITON (St Michael and All Angels) *see* Upper Itchen *Win*

CHERITON BISHOP (St Mary) *see* Tedburn St Mary, Cheriton Bishop, Whitestone etc *Ex*

CHERITON FITZPAINE (St Matthew) *see* N Creedy *Ex*

CHERITON STREET (All Souls) *see* Cheriton w Newington *Cant*

CHERITON, NORTH (St John the Baptist) *see* Camelot Par *B & W*

CHERRY BURTON (St Michael) *York 8* **P** *E D F Burton* **R** R F PARKINSON

CHERRY HINTON (St Andrew) *Ely 3* **P** *Peterho Cam* **P-in-c** K VOTH HARMAN **C** R M BARRY **NSM** P V IEVINS

CHERRY HINTON (St John the Evangelist) *Ely 3* **P** *Bp* **P-in-c** J D G SHAKESPEARE **C** C E CAMPBELL **Hon C** P S HESLAM

CHERRY WILLINGHAM (St Peter and St Paul) *see* S Lawres Gp *Linc*

CHERTSEY (St Peter w All Saints), Lyne and Longcross *Guildf 11* **P** *Bp and Haberdashers' Co (jt)* **V** T J HILLIER **C** L W GAMLEN

CHERWELL VALLEY, comprising Ardley w Fewcott, Fritwell, Lower Heyford, Somerton, Souldern, and Upper Heyford *Ox 21* **P** *Patr Bd* **TV** G D G PRICE

CHESELBORNE (St Martin) *see* Piddle Valley, Hilton and Ansty, Cheselbourne etc *Sarum*

CHESHAM BOIS (St Leonard) *Ox 9* **P** *Peache Trustees* **R** L S CLOW **NSM** C CLARE

CHESHAM, GREAT (Christ Church) (Emmanuel) (St Mary the Virgin) *Ox 9* **P** *Patr Bd* **TV** J M SHEPHERD **C** C J GERCKE, J J BAILEY **NSM** T J S YATES

CHESHUNT (St Mary the Virgin) *St Alb 17* **P** *Patr Bd* **TV** E E HANSHAW, H A BRYAN, T A J WYNNE

CHESSINGTON (St Mary the Virgin) *Guildf 9* **P** *Mert Coll Ox* **V** S EDWARDS **NSM** H A JOHNSON

CHESTER (Christ Church) *Ches 2* **P** *Bp and Simeon's Trustees (jt)* **V** G L SHAW **NSM** G JONES, R J KEMP

CHESTER (Holy Trinity without the Walls) *Ches 2* **P** *Bp* **R** C P UPTON **C** C P BURKETT, L M ANNISON

CHESTER (St John the Baptist) *Ches 2* **P** *Duke of Westminster* **V** D N CHESTERS

CHESTER (St Mary-without-the-Walls) *Ches 2* **P** *Duke of Westmr* **R** R P WHAITE **NSM** L C RHODES

CHESTER (St Peter) *Ches 2* **P** *Bp* **P-in-c** J R PHILLIPS **NSM** G D THOMAS, M J LEYDEN

CHESTER GREEN (St Paul) *see* Derby St Paul *Derby*

CHESTER LE STREET (St Mary and St Cuthbert) *Dur 10* **P** *St Jo Coll Dur* **R** D J TULLY **C** J C WILKINSON, M HARRISON

CHESTER SQUARE (St Michael) (St Philip) *Lon 3* **P** *CPAS* **V** C C MARNHAM **C** G A AXELSON

CHESTER St Oswald (St Thomas of Canterbury) *Ches 2*
  P *D&C* **P-in-c** S A SHERIDAN
CHESTER St Paul (St Luke) *Ches 2* **P** *R Ches* **V** C J S BLUNT
CHESTERFIELD (Holy Trinity) (Christ Church) *Derby 3*
  P *CPAS* **R** D J HORSFALL **C** K E HAMBLIN, M R BROOMHEAD
**CHESTERFIELD (St Augustine of Hippo and St Augustine
  of Canterbury)** *Derby 3* **P** *Bp* **C** K E HAMBLIN,
  L H A PEARSON, S BEECHAM **NSM** H J MOORE
CHESTERFIELD (St Mary and All Saints) *Derby 3* **P** *Bp*
  V P F COLEMAN **C** J C MILWAIN, K E HAMBLIN,
  M R BROOMHEAD **NSM** H J MOORE
CHESTERFORD, GREAT (All Saints) *see* Saffron Walden and
  Villages *Chelmsf*
CHESTERFORD, LITTLE (St Mary the Virgin) *as above*
CHESTERTON (Good Shepherd) *Ely 2* **P** *Bp* **V** D J MAHER
  C C A LOWE, M A OSBORNE **NSM** J A GRETTON-DANN
CHESTERTON (Holy Trinity) (St Chad) *Lich 9* **P** *The Crown*
  V S R BOXALL
CHESTERTON (St Andrew) *Ely 2* **P** *Trin Coll Cam*
  V N I MOIR **C** K J WAITE **NSM** A J COLES,
  D H PEYTON JONES
CHESTERTON (St George) *Ely 2* **P** *Bp* **V** R H ADAMS
  C A ATKINS, J A RIGLIN, J R SHINHMAR
CHESTERTON (St Giles) *Cov 8* **P** *Lady Willoughby de Broke*
  V *vacant*
CHESTERTON (St Lawrence) *see* Cirencester *Glouc*
CHESTERTON (St Michael) *see* Alwalton and Chesterton *Ely*
CHESTERTON, GREAT (St Mary) *see* Akeman *Ox*
**CHESWARDINE (St Swithun), Childs Ercall, Hales,
  Hinstock, Sambrook and Stoke on Tern** *Lich 17* **P** *Patr Bd*
  TR R M RICHARDS **C** D J STORK BANKS **NSM** C SIMPSON
CHET VALLEY, The *see* Loddon, Sisland, Chedgrave, Hardley
  and Langley *Nor*
CHETNOLE (St Peter) *see* Three Valleys *Sarum*
CHETTISHAM (St Michael and All Angels) *see* Ely *Ely*
CHETTLE (St Mary) *see* Chase *Sarum*
CHETTON (St Giles) *see* Ditton Priors w Neenton, Burwarton
  etc *Heref*
CHETWODE (St Mary and St Nicholas) *see* The Claydons
  and Swan *Ox*
CHETWYND (St Michael and All Angels) *see* Newport w
  Longford, and Chetwynd *Lich*
CHEVELEY (St Mary) *Ely 4* **P** *DBP and Mrs D A Bowlby (alt)*
  R *vacant*
CHEVENING (St Botolph) *Roch 9* **P** *Abp* **R** *vacant*
CHEVERELL, GREAT (St Peter) *see* The Lavingtons,
  Cheverells, and Easterton *Sarum*
CHEVERELL, LITTLE (St Peter) *as above*
**CHEVINGTON (All Saints) w Hargrave, Chedburgh w
  Depden, Rede and Hawkedon** *St E 3* **P** *Guild of All So
  (1 turn), Ld Chan (2 turns), Bp and DBP (1 turn)* **R** S G HILL
CHEVINGTON (St John the Divine) *Newc 6* **P** *Bp*
  P-in-c S J REILLY
CHEVITHORNE (St Thomas) *see* Tiverton St Pet and
  Chevithorne w Cove *Ex*
**CHEW MAGNA (St Andrew) w Dundry, Norton Malreward
  and Stanton Drew** *B & W 9* **P** *Bp and Adn (jt)*
  R C R M ROBERTS **NSM** S E LOVERN
CHEW STOKE (St Andrew) w Nempnett Thrubwell *B & W 9*
  P *Bp and SMF (jt)* **P-in-c** C R M ROBERTS
  Hon C S A MUNDAY
CHEWTON (Mission Church) *see* Keynsham *B & W*
**CHEWTON MENDIP (St Mary Magdalene) w Ston Easton,
  Litton and Emborough** *B & W 7* **P** *Earl Waldegrave
  (2 turns), Bp (1 turn)* **P-in-c** T C OSMOND
  C J E SHELLARD-JAMES **NSM** H J LATTY
CHEYLESMORE (Christ Church) *Cov 3* **P** *Ch Trust Fund Trust*
  V A C WOO
CHICHELEY (St Laurence) *see* Sherington w Chicheley, N
  Crawley, Astwood etc *Ox*
CHICHESTER (St Pancras and St John) *Chich 2* **P** *Simeon's
  Trustees (2 turns), St Jo Chpl Trustees (1 turn)* **R** M J T PAYNE
  C M D MILMINE, P M COLLINS **NSM** J A NICKOLS
**CHICHESTER (St Paul) (Immanuel) and Westhampnett
  St Peter** *Chich 2* **P** *Bp and D&C (jt)* **R** S P HOLLAND
  C M G WEATHERILL, N J SHAW **NSM** B M COUZENS, R HAWES
CHICHESTER (St Wilfrid) *Chich 2* **P** *Bp* **P-in-c** S P HOLLAND
CHICKERELL (St Mary) w Fleet *Sarum 4* **P** *Bp*
  R J C BRADING
CHICKLADE (All Saints) *see* Nadder Valley *Sarum*
CHIDDINGFOLD (St Mary) *Guildf 4* **P** *Ld Chan*
  R R E GREENE
CHIDDINGLY (not known) w East Hoathly *Chich 18* **P** *Bp*
  R P A HODGINS

CHIDDINGSTONE (St Mary) w Chiddingstone Causeway
  Roch 11 **P** *Abp and Bp (jt)* **P-in-c** T E HOLME
  C W D MACDOUGALL
CHIDDINGSTONE CAUSEWAY (St Luke) *see* Chiddingstone
  w Chiddingstone Causeway *Roch*
CHIDEOCK (St Giles) *see* Golden Cap Team *Sarum*
CHIDHAM (St Mary) *Chich 3* **P** *Bp* **V** *vacant*
CHIEVELEY (St Mary the Virgin) *see* E Downland *Ox*
CHIGNAL SMEALEY (St Nicholas) *see* The Chignals w
  Mashbury *Chelmsf*
CHIGNALS w Mashbury, The *Chelmsf 9* **P** *CPAS (2 turns), Bp
  (1 turn)* **C** D C PIERCE **NSM** S SYKES
CHIGWELL (St Mary) *see* Vale of Roding *Chelmsf*
CHIGWELL (St Winifred) *as above*
CHIGWELL ROW (All Saints) *as above*
CHILBOLTON (St Mary) *see* The Downs *Win*
CHILCOMB (St Andrew) *see* E Win *Win*
CHILCOMBE (not known) *see* Bride Valley *Sarum*
**CHILCOMPTON (St John the Baptist) w Downside and
  Stratton on the Fosse** *B & W 11* **P** *Bp, MMCET, and V
  Midsomer Norton (jt)* **R** E SMITH
CHILCOTE (St Matthew's Chapel) *see* Mease Valley *Lich*
CHILDE OKEFORD (St Nicholas) *see* Okeford *Sarum*
CHILDERDITCH (All Saints and St Faith) *see* E and W
  Horndon w Lt Warley and Childerditch *Chelmsf*
CHILDREY (St Mary the Virgin) *see* Ridgeway *Ox*
CHILDS ERCALL (St Michael and All Angels) *see*
  Cheswardine, Childs Ercall, Hales, Hinstock etc *Lich*
CHILDS HILL (All Saints) *see* Hendon All SS Childs Hill *Lon*
CHILDSWYCKHAM (St Mary the Virgin) *see* Winchcombe
  Glouc
CHILDWALL (All Saints) *Liv 2* **P** *Bp* **V** A J COLMER
  OLM S J GILLIES
CHILDWALL (St David) *Liv 5* **P** *Bp* **V** P F SMYTH
CHILDWALL VALLEY (St Mark) *see* Gateacre *Liv*
CHILDWICK (St Mary) *see* St Alb St Mich *St Alb*
CHILFROME (Holy Trinity) *see* Melbury *Sarum*
CHILHAM (St Mary) *see* King's Wood *Cant*
CHILLENDEN (All Saints) *see* Canonry *Cant*
CHILLESFORD (St Peter) *see* Wilford Peninsula *St E*
CHILLINGHAM (St Peter) *see* Chatton w Chillingham,
  Eglingham and S Charlton and Ingram *Newc*
CHILLINGTON (St James) *see* Winsmoor *B & W*
CHILMARK (St Margaret of Antioch) *see* Nadder Valley *Sarum*
**CHILTERNS, SOUTH, comprising Cadmore End, Ibstone,
  Lane End, and Stokenchurch** *Ox 18* **P** *Patr Bd*
  TR C M ACKFORD
CHILTHORNE DOMER (Blessed Virgin Mary) *see* Tintinhull w
  Chilthorne Domer, Yeovil Marsh etc *B & W*
CHILTINGTON, EAST (not known) *see* Plumpton w E
  Chiltington cum Novington *Chich*
CHILTINGTON, WEST (St Mary) *Chich 11* **P** *Bp* **R** *vacant*
CHILTON (All Saints) *see* Harwell w Chilton *Ox*
CHILTON (St Aidan) *Dur 1* **P** *Bp* **V** *vacant*
CHILTON (St Mary) *see* Bernwode *Ox*
**CHILTON CANTELO (St James) w Ashington, Mudford,
  Rimpton and Marston Magna** *B & W 6* **P** *DBP and D&C,
  D&C Bris, and Bp Lon (by turn)* **R** B STANTON
CHILTON FOLIAT (St Mary) *see* Whitton *Sarum*
CHILTON MOOR (St Andrew) *Dur 10* **P** *Bp*
  P-in-c D NEWTON
CHILTON POLDEN (St Edward) *see* Polden Wheel *B & W*
CHILTON TRINITY (Holy Trinity) *see* Bridgwater St Mary and
  Chilton Trinity *B & W*
CHILVERS COTON (All Saints) w Astley *Cov 5* **P** *Viscount
  Daventry* **V** F P SELDON **NSM** D WATERTON, J L FRYER
  OLM R ALLEN
CHILWELL (Christ Church) *S'well 9* **P** *CPAS*
  V A S G TUFNELL **C** L P B O'BOYLE, M S FORSYTH
CHILWORTH (St Denys) *see* Ampfield, Chilworth and N
  Baddesley *Win*
CHILWORTH (St Thomas) *see* Shere, Albury and Chilworth
  Guildf
CHINEHAM (Christ Church) *Win 4* **P** *Bp* **V** J G CLARK
CHINESE CONGREGATION *see* St Martin-in-the-Fields *Lon*
CHINGFORD (All Saints) (St Peter and St Paul) *Chelmsf 7*
  P *Bp* **C** B L TAYLOR, J M HUTCHINSON **NSM** A SUBARAN,
  H MUSKER, K R WARD **OLM** M P CLAYDON
CHINGFORD (St Anne) *Chelmsf 7* **P** *Bp* **V** J R BULLOCK
  OLM M L SCOTCHMER
CHINGFORD (St Edmund) *Chelmsf 7* **P** *Bp*
  V L A GOLDSMITH **C** J B GILDER
CHINLEY (St Mary) *see* Hayfield and Chinley w Buxworth
  Derby
CHINNOCK, EAST (Blessed Virgin Mary) *see* Coker Ridge
  B & W

CHINNOCK, MIDDLE (St Margaret)   *see* Ham Hill Villages *B & W*

CHINNOCK, WEST (Blessed Virgin Mary) *as above*

CHINNOR (St Andrew), Sydenham, Aston Rowant and Crowell *Ox 20*   **P** *Bp, DBP, and Peache Trustees (jt)*   **C** J A BARR

CHIPPENHAM (St Andrew) w Tytherton Lucas *Bris 4*   **P** *Ch Ch Ox*   **V** R C H KEY

CHIPPENHAM (St Margaret)   *see* Three Rivers Gp *Ely*

CHIPPENHAM (St Paul) w Hardenhuish and Langley Burrell *Bris 4*   **P** *Patr Bd*   **P-in-c** S D DUNN   **C** S P S WILLIAMS, T M HUNTON   **OLM** D J KILMISTER

CHIPPENHAM (St Peter) *Bris 4*   **P** *Bp*   **P-in-c** A M GUBBINS

CHIPPERFIELD (St Paul)   *see* Sarratt and Chipperfield *St Alb*

CHIPPING (St Bartholomew) *Blackb 7*   **P** *Bp*   **V** F JENKINS

CHIPPING BARNET (St John the Baptist) (St Mark) (St Stephen) *St Alb 14*   **P** *The Crown (2 turns) and Bp (1 turn)*   **TR** S C FERRIS   **TV** T D CHAPMAN   **NSM** N C WHEELER

CHIPPING CAMPDEN (St James)   *see* Vale and Cotswold Edge *Glouc*

CHIPPING NORTON (St Mary the Virgin) *Ox 22*   **P** *Patr Bd*   **TR** J E KENNEDY   **TV** D W SALTER   **C** J P JONES, M G SIMPSON, T L ARTIS   **Hon C** R W SIMPSON, U L SIMPSON   **OLM** J E MARSHALL

CHIPPING ONGAR (St Martin) w Shelley, Greensted juxta Ongar and Stanford Rivers *Chelmsf 3*   **P** *Duchy of Lancaster (1 turn), Keble Coll Ox, Guild of All So, and Bp Lon (2 turns)*   **R** N R TAYLOR   **C** J QUINTON   **NSM** N A TAYLOR

CHIPPING SODBURY (St John the Baptist)   *see* Sodbury Vale *Glouc*

CHIPPING WARDEN (St Peter and St Paul)   *see* Culworth w Sulgrave and Thorpe Mandeville etc *Pet*

CHIPSTABLE (All Saints)   *see* Wiveliscombe and the Hills *B & W*

CHIPSTEAD (Good Shepherd)   *see* Chevening *Roch*

CHIPSTEAD (St Margaret of Antioch) *S'wark 24*   **P** *Abp*   **R** S M M WILLIAMS   **NSM** A J ELSON

CHIRBURY (St Michael), Marton, Middleton and Trelystan w Leighton *Heref 12*   **P** *Bp (3 turns), N E E Stephens Esq (1 turn)*   **V** *vacant*

CHIRTON (St John the Baptist)   *see* Cannings and Redhorn *Sarum*

CHISELBOROUGH (St Peter and St Paul)   *see* Ham Hill Villages *B & W*

CHISHILL, GREAT (St Swithun)   *see* Icknield Way Villages *Chelmsf*

CHISHILL, LITTLE (St Nicholas) *as above*

CHISLEDON (Holy Cross)   *see* Ridgeway *Sarum*

CHISLEHURST (Annunciation) *Roch 14*   **P** *Keble Coll*   **V** P A FARTHING

CHISLEHURST (Christ Church) *Roch 14*   **P** *CPAS*   **V** D G S JOHNSTON

CHISLEHURST (St Nicholas) *Roch 14*   **P** *Bp*   **R** A A MUSTOE   **C** T R BONIFACE   **NSM** J B HURN

CHISLET (St Mary the Virgin)   *see* Wantsum Gp *Cant*

CHISWICK (St Michael and All Angels)   *see* Bedford Park *Lon*

CHISWICK (St Michael) *Lon 11*   **P** *V St Martin-in-the-Fields*   **V** M A OBORNE

CHISWICK (St Nicholas w St Mary Magdalene) *Lon 11*   **P** *D&C St Paul's*   **V** S F BRANDES   **C** A N TRIGLE   **NSM** E MCGREGOR

CHISWICK (St Paul) Grove Park *Lon 11*   **P** *V Chiswick*   **V** M C RILEY

CHITHURST (St Mary)   *see* Rogate w Terwick and Trotton w Chithurst *Chich*

CHITTERNE (All Saints and St Mary)   *see* Salisbury Plain *Sarum*

CHITTLEHAMHOLT (St John)   *see* S Molton w Nymet St George, Chittlehamholt etc *Ex*

CHITTLEHAMPTON (St Hieritha) *as above*

CHITTS HILL (St Cuthbert) *Lon 19*   **P** *CPAS*   **P-in-c** M JONES PARRY

CHIVELSTONE (St Sylvester)   *see* Stokenham, Slapton, Charleton w Buckland etc *Ex*

CHOBHAM (St Lawrence) w Valley End *Guildf 6*   **P** *Bp and Brig R W Acworth (alt)*   **V** C D BESSANT

CHOLDERTON (St Nicholas)   *see* Bourne Valley *Sarum*

CHOLESBURY (St Lawrence)   *see* Hawridge w Cholesbury and St Leonard *Ox*

CHOLLERTON (St Giles) w Birtley and Thockrington *Newc 8*   **P** *Mrs P I Enderby (2 turns), Newc Dioc Soc (1 turn)*   **P-in-c** S A LUNN   **NSM** C F BULL

CHOLSEY (St Mary) and Moulsford *Ox 26*   **P** *Ld Chan and Bp (alt)*   **V** A M PETIT   **OLM** V M L GIBBONS

CHOPPARDS (Mission Room)   *see* Upper Holme Valley *Leeds*

CHOPPINGTON (St Paul the Apostle) *Newc 1*   **P** *D&C*   **V** T MOAT

CHOPWELL (St John the Evangelist) *Dur 12*   **P** *Bp*   **P-in-c** P R MURRAY

CHORLEY (All Saints) *Blackb 4*   **P** *Bp*   **V** E N STRASZAK

CHORLEY (St George) *Blackb 4*   **P** *R Chorley*   **V** M G PRINT

CHORLEY (St James) *Blackb 4*   **P** *R Chorley*   **V** D K PHILLIPS

CHORLEY (St Laurence) *Blackb 4*   **P** *Bp*   **R** N G KELLEY   **Hon C** T H STOKES   **NSM** M T BALDWIN

CHORLEY (St Peter) *Blackb 4*   **P** *R Chorley*   **V** P H SMITH

CHORLEY (St Philip)   *see* Alderley Edge *Ches*

CHORLEYWOOD (Christ Church) *St Alb 4*   **P** *CPAS*   **V** D M HALL   **C** J A N HARRISON   **NSM** T W RUSSOFF

CHORLEYWOOD (St Andrew) *St Alb 4*   **P** *Bp*   **V** T E HORLOCK   **C** J M C SELLERS

CHORLTON-CUM-HARDY (St Clement) (St Barnabas) *Man 3*   **P** *D&C*   **R** K FLOOD   **NSM** D J VALENTINE   **OLM** J KING, L M WINDLE

CHORLTON-CUM-HARDY (St Werburgh) *Man 3*   **P** *Bp*   **R** F SHER   **NSM** P J HIBBERT

CHRISHALL (Holy Trinity)   *see* Icknield Way Villages *Chelmsf*

CHRIST THE KING in the Diocese of Newcastle, comprising Brunswick, Brunton Park, Dinnington, and North Gosforth *Newc 2*   **P** *Patr Bd*   **TV** M A EDWARDS   **C** P M SINCLAIR   **NSM** R E HEWETT

CHRISTCHURCH (Christ Church) and Manea and Welney *Ely 11*   **P** *Bp and R T Townley Esq (jt)*   **P-in-c** I BRADY   **NSM** L BRADY

CHRISTCHURCH (Holy Trinity) *Win 9*   **P** *Bp*   **V** C STEWART   **C** J E EVANS, R B PARTRIDGE   **NSM** A M NEWTON

CHRISTCHURCH Stourvale (St George)   *see* Christchurch *Win*

CHRISTIAN MALFORD (All Saints)   *see* Draycot *Bris*

CHRISTLETON (St James) *Ches 2*   **P** *Bp*   **R** S J COLLIER

CHRISTON (Blessed Virgin Mary)   *see* Crook Peak *B & W*

CHRISTOW (St James), Ashton, Bridford, Dunchideock, Dunsford and Doddiscombsleigh *Ex 5*   **P** *Bp, MMCET, SMF, Mrs J M Michelmore, Viscount Exmouth, and F C Fulford Esq (jt)*   **P-in-c** R FRAMPTON

CHUDLEIGH (St Mary and St Martin) w Chudleigh Knighton and Trusham *Ex 8*   **P** *Patr Bd*   **V** P WIMSETT   **NSM** M J FLETCHER

CHUDLEIGH KNIGHTON (St Paul)   *see* Chudleigh w Chudleigh Knighton and Trusham *Ex*

CHULMLEIGH (St Mary Magdalene)   *see* Burrington, Chawleigh, Cheldon, Chulmleigh etc *Ex*

CHURCH ASTON (St Andrew) *Lich 15*   **P** *R Edgmond*   **P-in-c** Z N HEMING

CHURCH BRAMPTON (St Botolph)   *see* Brington w Whilton and Norton etc *Pet*

CHURCH BROUGHTON (St Michael)   *see* Boylestone, Church Broughton, Dalbury, etc *Derby*

CHURCH EATON (St Editha)   *see* Bradeley, Church Eaton, Derrington and Haughton *Lich*

CHURCH HONEYBOURNE (St Ecgwyn)   *see* Vale and Cotswold Edge *Glouc*

CHURCH HULME (St Luke) *Ches 11*   **P** *V Sandbach*   **V** *vacant*

CHURCH IN THE WOOTTONS, The *Nor 19*   **P** *Ld Chan and G Howard Esq (alt)*   **R** J A NASH   **C** D M R TANSEY   **OLM** L ASHBY

CHURCH KNOWLE (St Peter)   *see* St Aldhelm *Sarum*

CHURCH LANGLEY (Church and Community Centre) *Chelmsf 4*   **P** *V Harlow*   **V** A L KOSLA

CHURCH LANGTON (St Peter)   *see* The Langtons and Shangton *Leic*

CHURCH LAWFORD (St Peter)   *see* Wolston and Church Lawford *Cov*

CHURCH LAWTON (All Saints) *Ches 11*   **P** *J Lawton Esq*   **P-in-c** S J CLAPHAM

CHURCH LENCH (All Saints) w Rous Lench and Abbots Morton and Harvington *Worc 1*   **P** *Bp and D&C (jt)*   **R** R J G THORNILEY   **NSM** C P SHEEHAN

CHURCH MINSHULL (St Bartholomew)   *see* Acton and Worleston, Church Minshull etc *Ches*

CHURCH OAKLEY (St Leonard)   *see* Oakley w Wootton St Lawrence *Win*

CHURCH ON THE HEATH (Northampton)   *see* Kings Heath *Pet*

CHURCH PREEN (St John the Baptist)   *see* Wenlock *Heref*

CHURCH STRETTON (St Laurence) *Heref 10*   **P** *Ch Patr Trust*   **R** S G JOHNSON   **Hon C** V R MORRIS   **NSM** M L MAGOWAN

CHURCHAM (St Andrew)   *see* Huntley and Longhope, Churcham and Bulley *Glouc*

CHURCHDOWN (St Andrew) (St Bartholomew) *Glouc 3*   **P** *D&C*   **V** J G PERKIN

CHURCHDOWN (St John the Evangelist) and Innsworth *Glouc 3*   **P** *Bp*   **V** J D HYDE

CHURCHILL (All Saints)   *see* Chipping Norton *Ox*

CHURCHILL (St John the Baptist) and Langford *B & W* 10
  P *D&C Bris*   **P-in-c** T E JESSIMAN

CHURCHILL-IN-HALFSHIRE (St James) w Blakedown and
  Broome *Worc* 12   **P** *Exors Viscount Cobham and N A Bourne
  Esq (alt)*   **P-in-c** S J OLIVER

CHURCHOVER (Holy Trinity)   *see* Revel Gp *Cov*

CHURCHSTANTON (St Peter and St Paul)   *see* Blackdown
  B & W

CHURCHSTOKE (St Nicholas) w Hyssington and Sarn
  Heref 9   **P** *The Crown (1 turn), Earl of Powis (2 turns)*
  P-in-c S A C FOUNTAIN   **C** C J WHITTOCK

CHURCHSTOW (St Mary)   *see* Thurlestone, S Milton,
  Churchstow etc *Ex*

CHURCHTOWN (St Helen)   *see* Garstang St Helen and
  St Michaels-on-Wyre *Blackb*

CHURN VALLEY Benefice, The, comprising Bagendon,
  Baunton, Coberley, Colesbourne, Cowley, Elkstone, North
  Cerney, Rendcomb, and Stratton *Glouc* 7   **P** *Jes Coll Ox,
  Univ Coll Ox, Mrs P Chester-Master, Sir H Elwes, Mrs S Pearce,
  Major M Wills (2 turns), Ld Chan (1 turn)*   **R** D A MINNS
  NSM A CHAMPION, C R POOLEY

CHURN, THE (Aston Tirrold w Aston Upthorpe, Blewbury,
  Hagbourne, North Moreton, South Moreton, and
  Upton) *Ox* 26   **P** *Bp and Magd Coll Ox (1 turn), Adn Berks
  and Hertf Coll Ox (1 turn)*   **R** J P ST JOHN NICOLLE
  Hon C J P H CLARKE   **OLM** L G N BUTLER

CHURNSIDE   *see* S Cerney w Cerney Wick, Siddington and
  Preston *Glouc*

CHURSTON FERRERS (St Mary the Virgin)   *see* Brixham w
  Churston Ferrers and Kingswear *Ex*

CHURT (St John the Evangelist) and Hindhead *Guildf* 3
  P *Adn Surrey*   **V** R T BODLE   **C** C E CHALLIS, D J HOLBIRD
  OLM R J MANLEY-COOPER

CHURWELL (All Saints)   *see* Morley *Leeds*

CHUTE (St Nicholas)   *see* Savernake *Sarum*

CIDER CHURCHES Benefice, The, comprising Aylton, Little
  Marcle, Much Marcle w Yatton, Pixley, Putley, and
  Wellington Heath *Heref* 5   **P** *Bp (3 turns), D&C (1 turn), J F S
  Hervey-Bathhurst Esq (1 turn), C E Money-Kyrle Esq (1 turn)*
  NSM J A RHODES

CINDERFORD (St John the Evangelist) (St Stephen) w
  Littledean *Glouc* 1   **P** *The Crown and Ch Patr Trust (alt)*
  V M J BARNSLEY   **NSM** A C BERESFORD

CINNAMON BROW (Resurrection)   *see* Warrington E *Liv*

CIPPENHAM (St Andrew) *Ox* 12   **P** *Eton Coll*
  V J M MINKKINEN

CIRENCESTER (St John the Baptist) *Glouc* 7   **P** *Bp*
  V G E MORRIS   **C** J WILSON   **Hon C** M J BETTIS
  NSM K R RICHARDSON

CLACTON, GREAT (St John the Baptist) *Chelmsf* 23   **P** *Ch
  Patr Trust*   **V** T M MULRYNE

CLACTON, LITTLE (St James)   *see* Weeley and Lt Clacton
  Chelmsf

CLACTON-ON-SEA (St Christopher) (St James) *Chelmsf* 23
  P *Bp*   **V** J F HUTCHERSON

CLACTON-ON-SEA (St Paul) *Chelmsf* 23   **P** *Ch Patr Trust*
  V D J LOWER

CLAINES (St George w St Mary Magdalene)   *see* Worc St Geo
  w St Mary Magd *Worc*

CLAINES (St John the Baptist) *Worc* 6   **P** *Bp*
  P-in-c J C MUSSON   **NSM** D P DAVIES, P HONNIBALL,
  S E POLLARD

CLANDON, EAST (St Thomas of Canterbury) and WEST
  (St Peter and St Paul) *Guildf* 5   **P** *Earl of Onslow and Bp
  (alt)*   **R** B C R PERKINS

CLANFIELD (St James)   *see* Catherington and Clanfield
  Portsm

CLANFIELD (St Stephen)   *see* Bampton w Clanfield *Ox*

CLANNABOROUGH (St Petrock)   *see* N Creedy *Ex*

CLAPHAM (Christ Church) (St John the Evangelist)
  S'wark 11   **P** *Bp*   **V** P J ROSE-CASEMORE   **C** R S FAULKNER

CLAPHAM (Holy Spirit) *S'wark* 11   **P** *Bp*
  V R A BURGE-THOMAS

CLAPHAM (Holy Trinity) *S'wark* 11   **P** *DBP*   **V** J R O WYNNE
  C J E J MULVANEY, M I JOHN, T G JONES   **NSM** C A CLARKE

CLAPHAM (St James) *S'wark* 12   **P** *CPAS*   **V** N K GUNASEKERA
  Hon C J MARSHALL

CLAPHAM (St Mary the Virgin)   *see* Findon w Clapham and
  Patching *Chich*

CLAPHAM (St Paul) *S'wark* 11   **P** *Bp*   **V** J T BOARDMAN

CLAPHAM (St Peter) *S'wark* 11   **P** *Bp*   **V** vacant

CLAPHAM (St Thomas of Canterbury) *St Alb* 13   **P** *MMCET*
  V S J LILEY

CLAPHAM COMMON (St Barnabas) *S'wark* 14   **P** *Ch Trust
  Fund Trust*   **V** R G TAYLOR   **NSM** A F P COCKING

CLAPHAM PARK (All Saints) *S'wark* 12   **P** *CPAS*
  P-in-c J R O WYNNE

CLAPHAM PARK (St Stephen)   *see* Telford Park *S'wark*

CLAPHAM-WITH-KEASDEN (St James) and Austwick
  Leeds 20   **P** *Bp*   **P-in-c** J DAVIES

CLAPTON (St James) *Lon* 5   **P** *Bp*   **V** R BROWN
  NSM J A ALTY

CLAPTON (St James)   *see* Bourton-on-the-Water w Clapton
  etc *Glouc*

CLAPTON, UPPER (St Matthew) *Lon* 5   **P** *D&C Cant*
  P-in-c W G CAMPBELL-TAYLOR   **C** A O BADEJO

CLARBOROUGH (St John the Baptist)   *see* Retford Area *S'well*

CLARE (St Peter and St Paul)   *see* Stour Valley *St E*

CLAREMOUNT (St Thomas the Apostle)   *see* Southowram
  and Claremount *Leeds*

CLARENCE GATE GARDENS (St Cyprian)   *see* St Marylebone
  St Cypr *Lon*

CLARENDON (Team Ministry), comprising Alderbury, Farley
  w Pitton, West Dean w East Grimstead, West Grimstead,
  Whiteparish, and Winterslow *Sarum* 10   **P** *Patr Bd*
  TR S P CHAMBERS   **TV** S E HUTTON   **NSM** D PERRY,
  F J DUNLOP

CLARENDON PARK (St John the Baptist)   *see* Emmaus Par
  Team *Leic*

CLARKSFIELD (St Barnabas) and Waterhead *Man* 15   **P** *The
  Crown*   **V** P M S MONK   **C** D OWEN   **NSM** J HYDE

CLATFORD, UPPER (All Saints)   *see* Abbotts Ann and Upper
  Clatford and Goodworth Clatford *Win*

CLATWORTHY (St Mary Magdalene)   *see* Wiveliscombe and
  the Hills *B & W*

CLAUGHTON VILLAGE (St Bede)   *see* Birkenhead St Jas w
  St Bede *Ches*

CLAVERDON (St Michael and All Angels) w Preston Bagot
  Cov 7   **P** *Bp*   **P-in-c** A B LARKIN   **NSM** P A HANSON

CLAVERHAM (St Barnabas)   *see* Yatton Moor *B & W*

CLAVERING (St Mary and St Clement) w Langley,
  Arkesden, Wicken Bonhunt, Manuden and Berden
  Chelmsf 21   **P** *Ch Hosp and Keble Coll Ox (jt)*   **V** M A DAVIS

CLAVERLEY (All Saints) w Tuckhill *Heref* 8   **P** *Bp and E M A
  Thompson Esq (jt)*   **V** G W WARD

CLAVERTON (Blessed Virgin Mary)   *see* Bathampton w
  Claverton *B & W*

CLAWTON (St Leonard)   *see* Ashwater, Halwill, Beaworthy,
  Clawton etc *Ex*

CLAXBY (St Mary)   *see* Walesby Gp *Linc*

CLAXTON (St Andrew)   *see* Rockland St Mary w Hellington,
  Bramerton etc *Nor*

CLAY CROSS (St Bartholomew)   *see* N Wingfield, Clay Cross
  and Pilsley *Derby*

CLAY HILL (St John the Baptist) (St Luke) *Lon* 18
  P *V Enfield St Andr and Bp (jt)*   **V** P J H GODDEN

CLAYBROOKE (St Peter)   *see* Upper Soar *Leic*

CLAYDON (no church), including Barham, Great Blakenham,
  and Henley *St E* 2   **P** *Bp, DBP, MMCET and Mrs M Rusinow
  (jt)*   **R** C N MELVILLE   **NSM** C B AUSTIN

CLAYDON (St James the Great)   *see* Shires' Edge *Ox*

CLAYDONS, The, (St Mary) (All Saints) and Swan *Ox* 13
  P *Patr Bd*   **TR** D A HISCOCK   **TV** L G SIMPSON-GRAY
  NSM A MANN

CLAYGATE (Holy Trinity) *Guildf* 8   **P** *Ch Patr Trust*
  V P J BATEMAN   **C** R E RUGG, S P SADLER, T HILL
  NSM M R HARLE

CLAYHANGER (Holy Trinity Worship Centre)   *see* Ogley Hay
  Lich

CLAYHANGER (St Peter)   *see* Bampton, Morebath,
  Clayhanger, Petton etc *Ex*

CLAYHIDON (St Andrew)   *see* Hemyock w Culm Davy,
  Clayhidon and Culmstock *Ex*

CLAYPOLE (St Peter) *Linc* 22   **P** *DBP (2 turns), J R Thorold Esq
  (1 turn)*   **R** vacant

CLAYTON (St Cross w St Paul)   *see* Man Clayton St Cross w
  St Paul *Man*

CLAYTON (St James the Great) *Lich* 9   **P** *Bp*   **V** J B BABB
  C S S GREENSMITH   **NSM** G SHILKOFF

CLAYTON (St John the Baptist) *Leeds* 3   **P** *V Bradf*
  V V POLLARD

CLAYTON (St John the Baptist) w Keymer *Chich* 8   **P** *BNC
  Ox*   **R** A BAXTER   **NSM** T E CAMERON

CLAYTON BROOK (Community Church)   *see* Whittle-le-
  Woods *Blackb*

CLAYTON LE MOORS (All Saints)   *see* Altham w Clayton le
  Moors *Blackb*

CLAYTON LE MOORS (St James) *as above*

CLAYTON WEST w HIGH HOYLAND (All Saints)   *see* High
  Hoyland, Scissett and Clayton W *Leeds*

CLAYWORTH (St Peter)   *see* Beckingham, Walkeringham, Misterton, etc *S'well*
CLEADON (All Saints) *Dur 13*   **P** *R Whitburn*
P-in-c V J CUTHBERT
CLEADON PARK (St Mark and St Cuthbert) *Dur 13*   **P** *Bp*
P-in-c K L BOARDMAN
CLEARWELL (St Peter)   *see* Coleford, Staunton, Newland, Redbrook etc *Glouc*
CLEASBY (St Peter)   *see* E Dere Street *Leeds*
CLEATOR (St Leonard)   *see* Crosslacon *Carl*
CLECKHEATON (St John the Evangelist)   *see* Cleckheaton *Leeds*
CLECKHEATON (St Luke)   *as above*
CLECKHEATON (St Luke) (St John the Evangelist) (Whitechapel) *Leeds 6*   **P** *Bp and V Birstall (jt)*
V B H G JAMES   **NSM** J C PARKES, R M CLARKE
CLECKHEATON (Whitechapel)   *see* Cleckheaton *Leeds*
CLEDFORD (Mission Room)   *see* Middlewich w Byley *Ches*
CLEE HILL (St Peter)   *see* Tenbury *Heref*
CLEE HILL (St Peter's Mission Room)   *see* Wigmore Abbey *Heref*
CLEE ST MARGARET (St Margaret)   *see* Bromfield *Heref*
CLEE, NEW (St John the Evangelist) (St Stephen) *Linc 3*
P *Bp*   **P-in-c** K S JONES   **NSM** A P TAPPIN
CLEE, OLD (Holy Trinity and St Mary the Virgin) *Linc 3*
P *Bp*   **V** N D NAWROCKYI
CLEETHORPE (Christ Church)   *see* Clee *Linc*
CLEETHORPES (St Aidan) *Linc 3*   **P** *Bp*   **V** N D NAWROCKYI
CLEETHORPES (St Francis) Conventional District *Linc 3*
Min N D NAWROCKYI
CLEETHORPES (St Peter) *Linc 3*   **P** *Bp*   **R** P HUNTER
NSM D H WEBSTER
CLEETON (St Mary)   *see* Stottesdon w Farlow, Cleeton St Mary etc *Heref*
CLEEVE (Holy Trinity)   *see* Yatton Moor *B & W*
CLEEVE PRIOR (St Andrew)   *see* E Vale and Avon Villages *Worc*
CLEEVE, OLD (St Andrew), Leighland and Treborough
B & W 15   **P** *Selw Coll Cam (2 turns), Personal Reps G R Wolseley Esq (1 turn)*   **R** *vacant*
CLEHONGER (All Saints)   *see* Cagebrook *Heref*
CLENCHWARTON (St Margaret) and West Lynn *Ely 14*
P *DBP*   **R** *vacant*
CLENT (St Leonard)   *see* Belbroughton w Fairfield and Clent *Worc*
CLEOBURY MORTIMER (St Mary the Virgin) w Hopton Wafers, Neen Sollars and Milson, Neen Savage w Kinlet and Doddington *Heref 11*   **P** *Patr Bd (2 turns), Ld Chan (1 turn)*   **R** W A BUCK   **NSM** M S QUAYLE
CLEOBURY NORTH (St Peter and St Paul)   *see* Ditton Priors w Neenton, Burwarton etc *Heref*
CLERKENWELL (Our Most Holy Redeemer) *Lon 6*
P *Trustees*   **V** C P TRUNDLE   **C** A D BARTLETT
NSM A S MCGREGOR
CLERKENWELL (St James and St John) (St Peter) *Lon 6*
P *Ch Patr Trust and PCC (jt)*   **P-in-c** P J NICHOLAS
C A J BAUGHEN, M B JACKSON
CLERKENWELL (St Mark) *Lon 6*   **P** *City Corp*   **V** C P TRUNDLE
C A D BARTLETT, J G HOBSON
CLEVEDON (Christchurch) *B & W 12*   **P** *Simeon's Trustees*
V C J JENNINGS
CLEVEDON (St Andrew) (St Peter) *B & W 12*   **P** *Ld Chan*
V T R CRANSHAW
CLEVEDON (St John the Evangelist) *B & W 12*   **P** *SMF*
P-in-c T P JORDAN
CLEVEDON, EAST (All Saints) w Clapton in Gordano, Walton Clevedon, Walton in Gordano and Weston in Gordano *B & W 12*   **P** *Bp and SMF (jt)*   **R** N A HECTOR
C B M LITTLE   **Hon C** A I COOK, C E SACKLEY
CLEVELEYS (St Andrew) *Blackb 12*   **P** *Trustees*   **V** B J WARD
CLEWER (St Andrew) *Ox 5*   **P** *Eton Coll*   **R** R WEBB
CLEWER (St Stephen and St Agnes)   *see* New Windsor *Ox*
CLEY (St Margaret)   *see* Blakeney w Cley, Wiveton, Glandford etc *Nor*
CLEY HILL Villages, The, comprising Corsley and Chadmanslade, and the Deverills and Horningsham
Sarum 12   **P** *Bp and DBP (jt)*   **R** P A REID   **C** G C MAYNARD
CLIBURN (St Cuthbert)   *see* N Westmorland *Carl*
CLIDDESDEN (St Leonard)   *see* Farleigh, Candover and Wield *Win*
CLIFF VILLAGES Group, The SOUTH, comprising Barkston, Belton, Carlton Scroop w Normanton, Caythorpe, Fulbeck, Honington, Hough-on-the-Hill, Hougham, Marston, and Syston *Linc 22*   **P** *Sir Anthony Thorold Bt (1 turn), J R Thorold Esq (1 turn), Lord Brownlow (1 turn), Sir Lyonel Tollemache Bt*

(1 turn), J F Fane Esq, Exors S J Packe-Drury-Lowe Esq, and Bp
(1 turn)   **R** S J HADLEY   **C** L E M HALL
CLIFFE (St Andrew)   *see* Riccall, Barlby and Hemingbrough *York*
CLIFFE AT HOO (St Helen) w Cooling *Roch 6*   **P** *D&C*
P-in-c A D HOBBS   **NSM** J E WRIGHT
CLIFFE, SOUTH (St John)   *see* N Cave w Cliffe *York*
CLIFFORD (St Luke) *York 1*   **P** *G Lane-Fox Esq*
P-in-c K F A GABBADON
CLIFFORD (St Mary the Virgin)   *see* Cusop w Blakemere, Bredwardine w Brobury etc *Heref*
CLIFFORD CHAMBERS (St Helen)   *see* Stratford-upon-Avon, Luddington etc *Cov*
CLIFFORDS MESNE (St Peter)   *see* Newent and Gorsley w Cliffords Mesne *Glouc*
CLIFFSEND (St Mary the Virgin)   *see* St Laur in Thanet *Cant*
CLIFTON (All Saints w St John) *Bris 2*   **P** *Bp*   **V** C E SUTTON
C W E BRAY
CLIFTON (All Saints) and Southill *St Alb 8*   **P** *Bp and C E S Whitbread Esq (jt)*   **R** C T TOPLEY
CLIFTON (Christ Church w Emmanuel) *Bris 2*   **P** *Simeon's Trustees*   **V** P J LANGHAM   **C** J N WALFORD, N E SHEPHERD
NSM E C BEBB, R M LILLINGTON   **OLM** J LEE
CLIFTON (Holy Trinity) *Derby 1*   **P** *Mrs M F Stanton, T W Clowes Esq, and V Ashbourne (by turn)*
P-in-c D C J BALLARD   **C** A J MARSHALL, C E MCDONALD
CLIFTON (Holy Trinity) (St Francis) (St Mary the Virgin)
S'well 6   **P** *DBP*   **C** R H DAVEY
CLIFTON (Holy Trinity, St Andrew the Less and St Peter)
Bris 3   **P** *Simeon's Trustees*   **P-in-c** L BARNES
NSM R G CROFT   **OLM** F M HOUGHTON,
J D A BROOKE-TAYLOR
CLIFTON (Mission Church)   *see* Conisbrough *Sheff*
CLIFTON (St Anne) (St Thomas) *Man 18*   **P** *Bp*
NSM A P GORDON
CLIFTON (St Cuthbert)   *see* N Westmorland *Carl*
CLIFTON (St George)   *see* E Trent *S'well*
CLIFTON (St James) *Sheff 6*   **P** *Bp*   **V** *vacant*
CLIFTON (St John the Evangelist)   *see* Brighouse and Clifton *Leeds*
CLIFTON (St John the Evangelist)   *see* Lund *Blackb*
CLIFTON (St Luke)   *see* Brigham, Clifton, Dean and Mosser *Carl*
CLIFTON (St Paul)   *see* Cotham St Sav w St Mary and Clifton St Paul *Bris*
CLIFTON (St Philip and St James) *York 7*   **P** *Trustees*
V A J GREADY   **C** P R MILLARD
CLIFTON CAMPVILLE (St Andrew)   *see* Mease Valley *Lich*
CLIFTON HAMPDEN (St Michael and All Angels)   *see* Dorchester *Ox*
CLIFTON REYNES (St Mary the Virgin)   *see* Lavendon w Cold Brayfield, Clifton Reynes etc *Ox*
CLIFTON UPON DUNSMORE (St Mary) w Newton and Brownsover *Cov 6*   **P** *Bp and H A F W Boughton-Leigh Esq (jt)*   **V** *vacant*
CLIFTON-ON-TEME (St Kenelm)   *see* Worcs W Rural *Worc*
CLIFTONVILLE (St Paul) *Cant 5*   **P** *Ch Patr Trust*
V P L S ELLISDON   **NSM** N H B RATCLIFFE
CLIPPESBY (St Peter)   *see* Martham and Repps w Bastwick, Thurne etc *Nor*
CLIPSHAM (St Mary)   *see* Cottesmore and Burley, Clipsham, Exton etc *Pet*
CLIPSTON (All Saints), Haselbech, Kelmarsh, Marston Trussell, Naseby, Sibbertoft and Welford *Pet 2*   **P** *Bp, Kelmarsh Trust, Ch Coll Cam, and DBP (4 turns), Bp (1 turn)*
R M J HAYES
CLIPSTONE (All Saints) *S'well 2*   **P** *Bp*   **P-in-c** I WEBB
CLITHEROE (St James) *Blackb 7*   **P** *Trustees*
R M W L PICKETT   **C** I SARGINSON
CLITHEROE (St Mary Magdalene) (St Paul), Chatburn and Downham *Blackb 7*   **P** *Bp and Lord Clitheroe (jt)*
V A W FROUD   **NSM** C A HALE-HEIGHWAY
CLIVE (All Saints)   *see* Astley, Clive, Grinshill and Hadnall *Lich*
CLOFORD (St Mary)   *see* Nunney and Witham Friary, Marston Bigot etc *B & W*
CLOPHILL (St Mary the Virgin)   *see* Campton, Clophill and Haynes *St Alb*
CLOPTON (St Mary)   *see* Carlford *St E*
CLOPTON (St Peter)   *see* Aldwincle, Clopton, Pilton, Stoke Doyle etc *Pet*
CLOSWORTH (All Saints)   *see* Coker Ridge *B & W*
CLOTHALL (St Mary the Virgin), Rushden, Sandon, Wallington and Weston *St Alb 16*   **P** *Duchy of Lanc (1 turn), Bp, Marquess of Salisbury, and J A Cherry (4 turns)*
R F K WHEATLEY

CLOUGHTON (St Mary) and Burniston *York 15* **P** *Abp*
V M J LEIGH

CLOVELLY (All Saints) *see* Parkham, Alwington, Buckland
Brewer etc *Ex*

CLOVELLY (St Peter) *as above*

CLOWNE (St John the Baptist) *see* Barlborough and Clowne
Derby

CLOWS TOP (Mission Room) *see* Mamble w Bayton, Rock w
Heightington etc *Worc*

CLUBMOOR (St Andrew) *Liv 5* **P** *Bp* **V** J E M GREEN
C T J GRIFFITHS   **OLM** S J JAMIESON

CLUMBER PARK (St Mary the Virgin) *see* Worksop Priory
S'well

CLUN (St George) *see* Clun Valley *Heref*

CLUN VALLEY Benefice, The, comprising Bettwys-y-Crwyn,
Clun, Clunbury w Clunton, Hopesay, and Newcastle *Heref 9*
P *Earl of Powis (5 turns), Earl of Powis and Mrs R E Bell*
(1 turn) **V** S C MONDON

CLUNBURY (St Swithin) *see* Clun Valley *Heref*

CLUNGUNFORD (St Cuthbert) *see* Middle Marches *Heref*

CLUNTON (St Mary) *see* Clun Valley *Heref*

**CLUTTON (St Augustine of Hippo) w Cameley, Bishop
Sutton and Stowey** *B & W 9* **P** *Bp, DBP, and Exors J P*
Hippisley Esq (jt) **R** M CREGAN

CLYFFE PYPARD (St Peter) *see* Lyneham and Woodhill *Sarum*

CLYMPING (St Mary the Virgin) and Yapton w Ford *Chich 1*
P *Bp (2 turns), Ld Chan (1 turn)* **R** R H HAYES

CLYST HEATH *see* Ex H Trin *Ex*

CLYST HONITON (St Michael and All Angels) *see* Broadclyst,
Clyst Honiton, Pinhoe, Rockbeare etc *Ex*

CLYST HYDON (St Andrew) *see* Whimple, Talaton, Clyst
St Lawr and Clyst Hydon *Ex*

CLYST ST GEORGE (St George) *see* Aylesbeare, Clyst
St George, Clyst St Mary etc *Ex*

CLYST ST LAWRENCE (St Lawrence) *see* Whimple, Talaton,
Clyst St Lawr and Clyst Hydon *Ex*

CLYST ST MARY (St Mary) *see* Aylesbeare, Clyst St George,
Clyst St Mary etc *Ex*

**COALBROOKDALE (Holy Trinity), Iron-Bridge and Little
Wenlock** *Heref 13* **P** *Bp, Lord Forester, V Madeley, and*
V Much Wenlock (jt) **P-in-c** I S NAYLOR **C** S A MANN
NSM J M EDWARDS, P M JORDAN

COALEY (St Bartholomew) *see* Lower Cam w Coaley *Glouc*

COALPIT HEATH (St Saviour) *Bris 5* **P** *Bp* **V** C P LUNT

COALVILLE (Christ Church) w Bardon Hill and Ravenstone
Leic 8 **P** *Simeon's Trustees and R Hugglescote (2 turns), Ld*
Chan (1 turn) **V** G PINNINGTON

COASTAL Group, The *see* Bacton, Happisburgh, Hempstead
w Eccles etc *Nor*

COATES (Holy Trinity) *see* Whittlesey, Pondersbridge and
Coates *Ely*

COATES (St Edith) *see* Stow Gp *Linc*

COATES (St Matthew) *see* Kemble, Poole Keynes, Somerford
Keynes etc *Glouc*

**COATES, GREAT (St Nicholas) and LITTLE (Bishop Edward
King Church) (St Michael) w Bradley** *Linc 3* **P** *Patr Bd*
TR D M MCCORMICK **TV** A I MCCORMICK

COATES, NORTH (St Nicholas) *see* Holton-le-Clay, Tetney
and N Cotes *Linc*

COATHAM (Christ Church) and Dormanstown *York 16*
P *Trustees* **V** R M HAUGHTY

COBBOLD ROAD (St Saviour) w St Mary *Lon 9* **P** *Bp*
V C J B LEE

COBERLEY (St Giles) *see* Churn Valley *Glouc*

COBHAM (St Andrew) (St John the Divine) *Guildf 10* **P** *D*
C H Combe Esq **V** M P BRANSCOMBE **OLM** M BABATUNDE

**COBHAM (St Mary Magdalene) w Luddesdowne and
Dode** *Roch 1* **P** *Earl of Darnley and CPAS (alt)*
P-in-c A J WALKER

COBHAM Sole Street (St Mary's Church Room) *see* Cobham
w Luddesdowne and Dode *Roch*

COBRIDGE (Christ Church) *see* Hanley H Ev *Lich*

COCKAYNE HATLEY (St John the Baptist) *see* Potton w
Sutton and Cockayne Hatley *St Alb*

**COCKERHAM (St Michael) w Winmarleigh St Luke and
Glasson Christ Church** *Blackb 11* **P** *Bp (2 turns), Trustees*
(1 turn) **V** G LEWIS

COCKERINGTON, SOUTH (St Leonard) *see* Mid Marsh Gp
Linc

**COCKERMOUTH AREA Team, The (All Saints) (Christ
Church),** including Bridekirk and Great Broughton *Carl 6*
P *Patr Bd* **TR** G J BUTLAND **TV** A D THOMPSON

COCKERNHOE (St Hugh) *see* Luton St Fran *St Alb*

COCKERTON (St Mary) *Dur 7* **P** *Bp* **V** D J BAGE
C C P ABERNETHY

COCKFIELD (St Mary) *Dur 6* **P** *Bp* **P-in-c** B WHITLEY

COCKFIELD (St Peter) *see* Bradfield St Clare, Bradfield
St George etc *St E*

COCKFOSTERS (Christ Church) Trent Park *see* Enfield Ch Ch
Trent Park *Lon*

**COCKING (not known) w West Lavington, Bepton and
Heyshott** *Chich 9* **P** *Ld Chan and Bp (alt)*
R L M ROBERTSON

COCKINGTON (St George and St Mary) (St Matthew)
Ex 11 **P** *Bp* **P-in-c** D GEORGE **NSM** P D EVANS

COCKLEY CLEY (All Saints) w Gooderstone *Nor 13* **P** *Bp*
R *vacant*

COCKSHUTT (St Simon and St Jude) *see* Petton w
Cockshutt, Welshampton and Lyneal etc *Lich*

COCKYARD (Church Hall) *see* Chapel-en-le-Frith *Derby*

CODDENHAM (St Mary) *see* N Bosmere *St E*

CODDINGTON (All Saints) *see* Balderton, Barnby in the
Willows and Coddington *S'well*

CODDINGTON (All Saints) *see* Colwall w Upper Colwall and
Coddington *Heref*

CODDINGTON (St Mary) *see* Farndon and Coddington *Ches*

CODFORD (St Mary) *see* Upper Wylye Valley *Sarum*

CODFORD (St Peter) *as above*

CODICOTE (St Giles) *see* Welwyn *St Alb*

CODNOR (St James) *see* Denby Gp *Derby*

CODSALL (St Nicholas) *Lich 2* **P** *Bp and Lady Wrottesley (jt)*
V M M MATTOCKS

CODSALL WOOD (St Peter) *see* Codsall *Lich*

COFFINSWELL (St Bartholomew) *see* Kingskerswell,
Abbotskerswell and Coffinswell *Ex*

COFTON (St Mary) *see* Dawlish w Holcombe, Cofton and
Starcross *Ex*

COFTON HACKETT (St Michael) w Barnt Green *Birm 3*
P *Bp* **V** R S FIELDSON

**COGENHOE (St Peter) and Great Houghton and Little
Houghton w Brafield on the Green** *Pet 6* **P** *C G V*
Davidge Esq, Mrs A C Usher, Magd Coll Ox, and DBP (jt)
R E G SMITH **NSM** I P M COBLEY

COGGES (St Mary) and South Leigh *Ox 28* **P** *Bp and Ch*
Patr Trust (jt) **V** S T KIRBY **C** A S MCCULLOCH, M I G DIXON
NSM N K PIKE

COGGESHALL (St Peter ad Vincula) w Markshall *Chelmsf 17*
P *Bp (2 turns), SMF (1 turn)* **P-in-c** C M DAVEY **C** S L BATTS,
T L HARVEY **NSM** K M KING, R J BURDEN

COGGESHALL, LITTLE (St Nicholas) *see* Coggeshall w
Markshall *Chelmsf*

COKER RIDGE, The, comprising Closworth, East Chinnock,
East Coker, Hardington Mandeville, Pendomer, Sutton
Bingham, and West Coker *B & W 6* **P** *D&C Ex, MMCET, Ox*
Chs Trust, and DBP (jt) **R** C G SIMPSON **Hon C** C L O'NEILL

COKER, EAST (St Michael and All Angels) *see* Coker Ridge
B & W

COKER, WEST (St Martin of Tours) *as above*

COLATON RALEIGH (St John the Baptist) *see* Ottery St Mary,
Alfington, W Hill, Tipton etc *Ex*

COLBURN (St Cuthbert) *see* Hipswell *Leeds*

COLBURY (Christ Church) *Win 11* **P** *Bp* **P-in-c** G K MAYER

COLBY (St Giles) *see* King's Beck *Nor*

COLCHESTER (Christ Church w St Mary at the Walls)
Chelmsf 21 **P** *Bp* **R** P R NORRINGTON
Hon C P C M PRESTNEY

COLCHESTER (St Anne) *see* Greenstead w Colchester
St Anne *Chelmsf*

COLCHESTER (St Barnabas) Old Heath *Chelmsf 21* **P** *Bp*
V R E TILLBROOK

**COLCHESTER (St James) and St Paul w All Saints,
St Nicholas and St Runwald** *Chelmsf 21* **P** *Bp*
R J T MCCLUSKEY

COLCHESTER (St John the Evangelist) *Chelmsf 21* **P** *Adn*
Colchester **P-in-c** A J SACHS **C** T M SOLOSY
NSM V E WHITFIELD

COLCHESTER (St Luke) *Chelmsf 21* **P** *Adn Colchester*
P-in-c H R COOPER **C** A J ELMES, C J SMITH, R G GIBBS,
S L HAYWARD **NSM** A L MASON, P W MANN

COLCHESTER (St Michael) Myland *Chelmsf 21* **P** *Ball Coll*
Ox **P-in-c** R G GIBBS **C** A J ELMES, H GREENLAND,
H R COOPER, S L HAYWARD **NSM** P W MANN

COLCHESTER (St Peter) (St Botolph) *Chelmsf 21* **P** *Bp and*
Simeon's Trustees (jt) **P-in-c** M D WALLACE **C** A R F B GAGE

COLCHESTER (St Stephen) *see* Colchester, New Town and
The Hythe *Chelmsf*

**COLCHESTER, New Town and The Hythe (St Stephen,
St Mary Magdalen and St Leonard)** *Chelmsf 21*
R L G BADGER-WATTS

COLD ASH (St Mark) *see* Hermitage *Ox*

COLD ASHBY (St Denys) *see* Guilsborough and Hollowell
and Cold Ashby etc *Pet*

COLD ASHTON (Holy Trinity)   *see* Marshfield w Cold Ashton and Tormarton etc *Bris*
COLD ASTON (St Andrew)   *see* Northleach w Hampnett and Farmington etc *Glouc*
COLD BRAYFIELD (St Mary)   *see* Lavendon w Cold Brayfield, Clifton Reynes etc *Ox*
COLD HIGHAM (St Luke)   *see* Pattishall w Cold Higham and Gayton w Tiffield *Pet*
COLD KIRBY (St Michael)   *see* Upper Ryedale *York*
COLD NORTON (St Stephen) w Stow Maries *Chelmsf 11*   **P** *Bp and Charterhouse (jt)*   **V** S E MANLEY
COLD OVERTON (St John the Baptist)   *see* Whatborough Gp *Leic*
COLD SALPERTON (All Saints)   *see* Sevenhampton w Charlton Abbots, Hawling etc *Glouc*
COLDEAN (St Mary Magdalene)   *see* Moulsecoomb *Chich*
COLDEN COMMON (Holy Trinity)   *see* S Downs Gateway Churches *Win*
COLDHARBOUR (Christ Church)   *see* Abinger and Coldharbour and Wotton and Holmbury St Mary *Guildf*
COLDHARBOUR (St Alban Mission Church)   *see* Mottingham St Andr w St Alban *S'wark*
COLDHURST (Holy Trinity) and Oldham St Stephen and All Martyrs *Man 16*   **P** *Patr Bd*   **V** D S J AUSTIN
COLDRED (St Pancras)   *see* Bewsborough *Cant*
COLDRIDGE (St Matthew)   *see* N Creedy *Ex*
COLDWALTHAM (St Giles)   *see* Bury w Houghton and Coldwaltham and Hardham *Chich*
COLEBROOKE (St Andrew) *Ex 2*   **P** *D&C*   **V** *vacant*
COLEBY (All Saints)   *see* Graffoe Gp *Linc*
COLEFORD (Holy Trinity) w Holcombe *B & W 11*   **P** *Bp and V Kilmersdon (jt)*   **NSM** C R D CRIDLAND
COLEFORD (St John the Evangelist), Staunton, Newland, Redbrook and Clearwell *Glouc 1*   **P** *Bp*   **V** S BICK
COLEGATE (St George)   *see* Nor Colegate and Tombland *Nor*
COLEHILL (St Michael and All Angels) *Sarum 9*   **P** *Governors of Wimborne Minster*   **V** S M PATTLE   **OLM** L L MCGREGOR
COLEMAN'S HATCH (Holy Trinity)   *see* Hartfield w Coleman's Hatch *Chich*
COLEORTON (St Mary the Virgin)   *see* Ashby-de-la-Zouch and Breedon on the Hill *Leic*
COLERNE (St John the Baptist) w North Wraxall *Bris 4*   **P** *New Coll and Oriel Coll Ox (alt)*
   C J M ANDERSON-MACKENZIE   **OLM** C M SOUTHGATE, G E PARKIN
COLESBOURNE (St James)   *see* Churn Valley *Glouc*
COLESHILL (All Saints)   *see* Amersham *Ox*
COLESHILL (All Saints)   *see* Gt Coxwell w Buscot, Coleshill etc *Ox*
COLESHILL (St Peter and St Paul) *Birm 8*   **P** J K Wingfield Digby Esq   **V** R N PARKER
COLEY (St John the Baptist) *Leeds 7*   **P** *V Halifax*
   P-in-c J T ALLISON
COLGATE (St Saviour) and Roffey *Chich 7*   **P** *Bp and P H Calvert Esq (alt)*   **V** R J STAGG   **NSM** D J HOWLAND
COLINDALE (St Matthias) *Lon 15*   **P** *Bp*
   P-in-c M R DUCKETT   **NSM** S J ATKINSON
COLKIRK (St Mary)   *see* Upper Wensum Village Gp *Nor*
COLLATON (St Mary the Virgin)   *see* Goodrington and Collaton St Mary *Ex*
COLLIER ROW (Ascension)   *see* Romford Ascension Collier Row *Chelmsf*
COLLIER ROW (Good Shepherd)   *see* Romford Gd Shep *Chelmsf*
COLLIER ROW (St James) and Havering-atte-Bower *Chelmsf 2*   **P** *CPAS and Bp (jt)*   **V** D E ANDERTON
   C A C MOSS
COLLIER STREET (St Margaret)   *see* Yalding w Collier Street *Roch*
COLLIERLEY (St Thomas)   *see* Harelaw and Annfield Plain *Dur*
COLLIERS END (St Mary)   *see* High Cross *St Alb*
COLLIERS WOOD (Christ Church)   *see* Merton Priory *S'wark*
COLLINGBOURNE DUCIS (St Andrew)   *see* Savernake *Sarum*
COLLINGBOURNE KINGSTON (St Mary)   *as above*
COLLINGHAM (All Saints)   *see* E Trent *S'well*
COLLINGHAM (St John the Baptist)   *as above*
COLLINGHAM (St Oswald) w Harewood *Leeds 21*   **P** *Earl of Harewood and G H H Wheler Esq (jt)*   **P-in-c** S EARLE
COLLINGTON (St Mary)   *see* Bredenbury *Heref*
COLLINGTREE (St Columba)   *see* Salcey *Pet*
COLLYHURST (The Saviour) *Man 4*   **P** *Bp and Trustees (jt)*
   P-in-c N R ELLIOTT   **OLM** M B ROGERS, S PAGE
COLLYWESTON (St Andrew)   *see* King's Cliffe, Bulwick and Blatherwycke, Collyweston etc *Pet*

COLMWORTH (St Denys)   *see* Wilden w Colmworth and Ravensden *St Alb*
COLN RIVER GROUP, The   *see* Sevenhampton w Charlton Abbots, Hawling etc *Glouc*
COLN ROGERS (St Andrew)   *see* Chedworth, Yanworth and Stowell, Coln Rogers etc *Glouc*
COLN ST ALDWYN (St John the Baptist)   *see* S Cotswolds *Glouc*
COLN ST DENYS (St James the Great)   *see* Chedworth, Yanworth and Stowell, Coln Rogers etc *Glouc*
COLNBROOK (St Thomas) and Datchet *Ox 12*   **P** *Bp and D&C Windsor (jt)*   **V** J D F M CHESTERFIELD-TERRY
   C R J COSH
COLNE (Christ Church)   *see* Foulridge, Laneshawbridge and Trawden *Blackb*
COLNE (Holy Trinity) (St Bartholomew) *Blackb 6*   **P** *Bp and DBP*   **R** L E SENIOR
COLNE (St Helen)   *see* Bluntisham cum Earith w Colne and Holywell *Ely*
COLNE ENGAINE (St Andrew)   *see* Halstead Area *Chelmsf*
COLNEY (St Andrew)   *see* Cringleford and Colney *Nor*
COLNEY (St Peter)   *see* London Colney *St Alb*
COLNEY HEATH (St Mark) *St Alb 5*   **P** *Trustees*   **V** G P TRACEY
   NSM J SUTTIE
COLSTERWORTH Group, The (St John the Baptist), including Great Ponton, Little Ponton, North and South Stoke w Easton, and Skillington *Linc 17*   **P** *Bp (2 turns), N E McCorquodale Esq and J R Thorold Esq (1 turn)*
   P-in-c N T GRIFFITHS
COLSTON BASSETT (St John the Divine)   *see* Wiverton in the Vale *S'well*
COLTISHALL (St John the Baptist) w Great Hautbois, Frettenham, Hainford, Horstead and Stratton Strawless *Nor 18*   **P** *D&C, Bp, K Coll Cam, and Ch Soc Trust (jt)*
   R C J ENGELSEN   **OLM** K A DIGNUM
COLTON (Holy Trinity)   *see* Coniston and the Crake Valley *Carl*
COLTON (St Andrew)   *see* Easton, Colton, Marlingford and Bawburgh *Nor*
COLTON (St Mary the Virgin)   *see* Abbots Bromley, Blithfield, Colton, Colwich etc *Lich*
COLTON (St Paul)   *see* Bolton Percy *York*
COLWALL (St Crispin's Chapel) (St James the Great) w Upper Colwall (Good Shepherd) and Coddington *Heref 5*   **P** *Bp*   **R** M J HORTON
COLWICH (St Michael and All Angels)   *see* Abbots Bromley, Blithfield, Colton, Colwich etc *Lich*
COLWICK (St John the Baptist) *S'well 7*   **P** *DBP*
   P-in-c A H DIGMAN   **C** D E MOYO
COLYFORD (St Michael)   *see* Colyton, Musbury, Southleigh and Branscombe *Ex*
COLYTON (St Andrew), Musbury, Southleigh and Branscombe *Ex 4*   **P** *D&C*   **R** S E MARTIN   **C** C J LEES, S GEORGE
COMBE (St Swithin)   *see* Walbury Beacon *Ox*
COMBE DOWN (Holy Trinity) (St Andrew) w Monkton Combe and South Stoke *B & W 8*   **P** *R Bath, Ox Chs Trust, and Comdr H R Salmer (jt)*   **C** S D SWINNEY
COMBE FLOREY (St Peter and St Paul)   *see* Bishop's Lydeard w Lydeard St Lawrence etc *B & W*
COMBE HAY (not known)   *see* Bath Odd Down w Combe Hay *B & W*
COMBE LONGA (St Laurence)   *see* Stonesfield w Combe Longa *Ox*
COMBE MARTIN (St Peter ad Vincula)   *see* Ilfracombe SS Phil and Jas, Combe Martin and Berrynarbor *Ex*
COMBE PYNE (St Mary the Virgin)   *see* Axminster, Chardstock, All Saints etc *Ex*
COMBE RALEIGH (St Nicholas)   *see* Honiton, Gittisham, Combe Raleigh, Monkton etc *Ex*
COMBE ST NICHOLAS (St Nicholas)   *see* Chard St Mary w Combe St Nicholas, Wambrook etc *B & W*
COMBEINTEIGNHEAD (All Saints)   *see* Shaldon, Stokeinteignhead, Combeinteignhead etc *Ex*
COMBERFORD (St Mary and St George)   *see* Wigginton *Lich*
COMBERTON (St Mary)   *see* Lordsbridge *Ely*
COMBERTON, GREAT (St Michael)   *see* Elmley Castle w Bricklehampton and Combertons *Worc*
COMBERTON, LITTLE (St Peter)   *as above*
COMBROOK (St Mary and St Margaret)   *see* Edgehill Churches *Cov*
COMBS (St Mary) and Finborough, including Buxhall, Harleston, Onehouse, and Shelland *St E 8*   **P** *Bp (2 turns), Pemb Coll Ox (1 turn)*   **R** C CHILDS   **Hon C** P M HIGHAM
COMBWICH (St Peter)   *see* Cannington, Otterhampton, Combwich and Stockland *B & W*

COMER GARDENS (St David) *see* Worc St Clem and Lower Broadheath *Worc*

COMMONDALE (St Peter) *see* Danby w Castleton and Commondale *York*

COMPTON (All Saints), Hursley, and Otterbourne *Win 7* **P** *Bp, Mrs P M A T Chamberlayne-Macdonald, and Lord Lifford (jt)* **R** W A PRESCOTT

COMPTON (St Mary and St Nicholas) *see* Hermitage *Ox*

COMPTON (St Mary) *see* Farnham *Guildf*

COMPTON (St Mary) *see* Octagon *Chich*

COMPTON (St Nicholas) w Shackleford and Peper Harow *Guildf 4* **P** *Bp and Major J R More-Molyneux (jt)* **R** *vacant*

COMPTON ABBAS (St Mary the Virgin) *see* Shaftesbury *Sarum*

COMPTON ABDALE (St Oswald) *see* Northleach w Hampnett and Farmington etc *Glouc*

COMPTON BASSETT (St Swithin) *see* Oldbury *Sarum*

COMPTON BEAUCHAMP (St Swithun) *see* Shrivenham and Ashbury *Ox*

COMPTON BISHOP (St Andrew) *see* Crook Peak *B & W*

COMPTON CHAMBERLAYNE (St Michael) *see* Nadder Valley *Sarum*

COMPTON DANDO (Blessed Virgin Mary) *see* Publow w Pensford, Compton Dando and Chelwood *B & W*

COMPTON DUNDON (St Andrew) *see* Street w Walton and Compton Dundon *B & W*

COMPTON GREENFIELD (All Saints) *see* Pilning w Compton Greenfield *Bris*

COMPTON MARTIN (St Michael) *see* Blagdon w Compton Martin and Ubley *B & W*

COMPTON PAUNCEFOOT (Blessed Virgin Mary) *see* Camelot Par *B & W*

COMPTON VALENCE (St Thomas à Beckett) *see* Dorchester and the Winterbournes *Sarum*

COMPTON, LITTLE (St Denys) *see* Chipping Norton *Ox*

COMPTON, NETHER (St Nicholas) *see* Queen Thorne *Sarum*

COMPTON, OVER (St Michael) *as above*

CONDICOTE (St Nicholas) *see* Stow on the Wold, Condicote and The Swells *Glouc*

CONDOVER (St Andrew and St Mary) w Frodesley, Acton Burnell and Pitchford *Heref 10* **P** *Bp, Revd E W Serjeantson, and Mrs C R Colthurst (jt)* **R** G D GARRETT

CONEY HILL (St Oswald) *Glouc 2* **P** *The Crown* **V** J P FARAGHER **C** S T NEWTON

CONEY WESTON (St Mary) *see* Stanton *St E*

CONEYSTHORPE (Chapel) *see* The Street Par *York*

CONGERSTONE (St Mary the Virgin) *see* Bosworth and Sheepy Gp *Leic*

CONGHAM (St Andrew) *see* Ashwicken w Leziate, Bawsey etc *Nor*

CONGLETON (St James) *Ches 11* **P** *Bp* **V** C J SANDERSON

CONGLETON (St John the Evangelist) (St Peter) (St Stephen) *Ches 11* **P** *Patr Bd* **R** *vacant*

CONGRESBURY (St Andrew) *see* Banwell and Congresbury w Hewish, Puxton and W Wick *B & W*

CONINGSBY (St Michael) *see* Bain Valley Gp *Linc*

CONISBROUGH (St Peter) *Sheff 9* **P** *Bp* **P-in-c** M MUGGE

CONISCLIFFE (St Edwin) *Dur 7* **P** *Bp* **NSM** D V ROBINSON

CONISHOLME (St Peter) *see* Marshchapel, Somercotes and Grainthorpe w Conisholme *Linc*

CONISTON (St Andrew) and the Crake Valley *Carl 9* **P** *Bp, MMCET, Peache Trustees, Trustees, patron landowners of Colton, and A C I Naylor Esq (jt)* **R** B T STREETER

CONISTON COLD (St Peter) *see* Gargrave w Coniston Cold *Leeds*

CONISTONE (St Mary) *see* Upper Wharfedale and Littondale *Leeds*

CONONLEY (St John the Evangelist) w Bradley *Leeds 4* **P** *Bp* **P-in-c** J S BACON

CONSETT (Christ Church) *Dur 4* **P** *Bp* **P-in-c** V SHEDDEN

CONSTABLE LEE (St Paul) *see* Rawtenstall and Constable Lee *Man*

CONSTANTINE (St Constantine) *Truro 4* **P** *D&C* **P-in-c** S G TURNER

COOKBURY (St John the Baptist and the Seven Maccabees) *see* Black Torrington, Bradford w Cookbury etc *Ex*

COOKHAMS, The (Holy Trinity) (St John the Baptist) *Ox 5* **P** *Mrs E U Rogers* **V** N PLANT **C** H CHAMBERLAIN, J F AINSLIE **NSM** D JOYNES

COOKHILL (St Paul) *see* Inkberrow w Cookhill and Kington w Dormston *Worc*

COOKLEY (St Michael and All Angels) *see* Heveningham *St E*

COOKLEY (St Peter) *see* Kidderminster Ismere *Worc*

COOKRIDGE (Holy Trinity) *Leeds 15* **P** *R Adel* **V** P W ATKINSON

COOMBE (Christ Church) *see* New Malden and Coombe *S'wark*

COOMBE BISSETT (St Michael and All Angels) *see* Chalke Valley *Sarum*

COOMBES (not known) *see* Lancing w Coombes *Chich*

COOPERSALE (St Alban) *see* Epping Distr *Chelmsf*

COPDOCK (St Peter) *see* Sproughton w Burstall, Copdock w Washbrook etc *St E*

COPFORD (St Michael and All Angels) *see* Thurstable and Winstree *Chelmsf*

COPGROVE (St Michael) *see* Walkingham Hill *Leeds*

COPLE (All Saints), Moggerhanger and Willington *St Alb 10* **P** *Bp (2 turns), Ch Ch Ox (1 turn)* **V** F R GIBSON

COPLOW Benefice, The, comprising Billesdon cum Goadby and Rolleston, Hungarton, and Skeffington *Leic 5* **P** *Bp* **V** A S W BOOKER **C** R L HOMER

COPMANTHORPE (St Giles) *York 1* **P** *R York St Clement w St Mary Bishophill* **V** G R MUMFORD **NSM** G M WEBB

COPNOR (St Alban) *see* Portsea St Alb *Portsm*

COPNOR (St Cuthbert) *see* Portsea St Cuth *Portsm*

COPP (St Anne) w Inskip *Blackb 9* **P** *V Garstang St Helen and St Michaels-on-Wyre* **P-in-c** S J COX **C** P G HUNTER

COPPENHALL (All Saints and St Paul) *see* Crewe All SS and St Paul w St Pet *Ches*

COPPENHALL (St Laurence) *see* Penkridge *Lich*

COPPENHALL (St Michael) *Ches 15* **P** *Bp* **R** J X LEAL

COPPULL (not known) *see* Coppull *Blackb*

COPPULL (St John the Divine) *Blackb 4* **P** *R Standish* **R** M HORNBY

COPSTON MAGNA (St John) *see* Wolvey, Copston Magna and Withybrook *Cov*

COPT OAK (St Peter) *see* Markfield, Thornton, Bagworth and Stanton etc *Leic*

COPTHORNE (St John the Evangelist) *Chich 6* **P** *Bp* **V** W J MAURITZ **NSM** A J WHEELER

COPYTHORNE (St Mary) *Win 11* **P** *Bp Liv* **P-in-c** J R REEVE

COQUETDALE, UPPER, comprising Alnham, Alwinton, Hepple, Holystone, Rothbury, and Thropton *Newc 6* **P** *Duchy of Lanc (2 turns), Ld Chan (1 turn), and Duke of Northumberland (1 turn)* **R** J R SINCLAIR **NSM** A M PETERS-WOTHERSPOON, S D JOYNER

CORBRIDGE (St Andrew) w Halton and Newton Hall *Newc 9* **P** *D&C Carl* **V** D J KENNEDY **C** L F CAUDWELL

CORBY (St Columba and the Northern Saints) *Pet 7* **P** *Bp* **V** I A PULLINGER

CORBY (St John the Baptist) (Epiphany) *Pet 7* **P** *E Brudenell Esq* **R** P W FROST **C** A SILLEY

CORBY (St Peter and St Andrew) (Kingswood Church) *Pet 7* **P** *Bp* **P-in-c** A M SEARLE

CORBY GLEN (St John the Evangelist) *Linc 17* **P** *Ld Chan (2 turns), Margaret Lady Benton Jones (1 turn)* **P-in-c** S L BUCKMAN **C** A W F DONALDSON

CORELEY (St Peter) *see* Tenbury *Heref*

CORFE (St Nicholas) *see* Blackdown *B & W*

CORFE CASTLE (St Edward the Martyr) *see* St Aldhelm *Sarum*

CORFE MULLEN (St Hubert) *Sarum 9* **P** *Bp* **R** J E BURGESS **Hon C** A R BURGESS

CORHAMPTON (not known) *see* Meon Bridge *Portsm*

CORLEY (not known) *see* Fillongley and Corley *Cov*

CORNARD, GREAT (St Andrew) *St E 9* **P** *Bp* **V** C J RAMSEY **NSM** J M RIDLEY

CORNARD, LITTLE (All Saints) *see* Bures w Assington and Lt Cornard *St E*

CORNELLY (St Cornelius) *see* Tregony w St Cuby and Cornelly *Truro*

CORNERSTONE Benefice, The, comprising Bolsterstone, Deepcar, and Stocksbridge *Sheff 3* **P** *Bp (2 turns), R B Rimington Wilson Esq (1 turn)* **V** H R ISAACSON **Hon C** S T PENDLEBURY **NSM** K J CROOKES

CORNERSTONE TEAM, The, comprising Houghton on the Hill and Thurnby *Leic 3* **P** *Patr Bd* **TR** R A MILES **TV** S E RANSLEY **C** T C DEVAS **NSM** H M BENCE

CORNEY (St John the Baptist) *see* Black Combe, Drigg, Eskdale etc *Carl*

CORNFORTH (Holy Trinity) and Ferryhill *Dur 1* **P** *D&C (2 turns), Bp (1 turn)* **V** G NORMAN **C** L A SUTHERLAND **NSM** P G E TYLER

CORNHILL (St Helen) w Carham *Newc 12* **P** *Abp (2 turns), E M Straker-Smith Esq (1 turn)* **P-in-c** G R J KELSEY **NSM** J B CARR

CORNHOLME (St Michael and All Angels) *see* Todmorden w Cornholme and Walsden *Leeds*

CORNISH HALL END (St John the Evangelist) *see* Finchingfield and Cornish Hall End etc *Chelmsf*

CORNWELL (St Peter) *see* Chipping Norton *Ox*

CORNWOOD (St Michael and All Angels) *Ex 20* **P** *Bp*
V *vacant*
CORNWORTHY (St Peter) *see* Totnes w Bridgetown, Berry
Pomeroy etc *Ex*
CORONATION SQUARE (St Aidan) *see* W Cheltenham *Glouc*
CORRINGHAM (St John the Evangelist) (St Mary the
Virgin) and Fobbing *Chelmsf 16* **P** *Bp and SMF (jt)*
R D ROLLINS **C** J M NODDINGS **OLM** W S MOTT
CORRINGHAM (St Lawrence) *see* Lea Gp *Linc*
CORSCOMBE (St Mary the Virgin) *see* Melbury *Sarum*
CORSE (St Margaret) *see* Ashleworth, Corse, Hartpury,
Hasfield etc *Glouc*
CORSENSIDE (All Saints) *see* N Tyne and Redesdale *Newc*
CORSENSIDE (St Cuthbert) *as above*
CORSHAM, GREATER (St Bartholomew) and Lacock *Bris 4*
P *Patr Bd* **P-in-c** A R JOHNSON **TV** A J BEAUMONT
CORSLEY (St Margaret of Antioch) *see* Cley Hill Villages
Sarum
CORSLEY (St Mary the Virgin) *as above*
CORSTON (All Saints) *see* Malmesbury and Upper Avon *Bris*
CORSTON (All Saints) *see* Saltford w Corston and Newton
St Loe *B & W*
CORTON (St Bartholomew) *see* Abbotsbury, Portesham and
Langton Herring *Sarum*
CORTON (St Bartholomew) *see* Hopton w Corton *Nor*
CORTON DENHAM (St Andrew) *see* Cam Vale *B & W*
CORVEDALE Benefice, The, comprising Culmington,
Diddlebury, Holdgate, Munslow, and Tugford *Heref 11*
P *Bp (3 turns), D&C (1 turn), Bp Lich (1 turn), Mrs O T M*
Togers-Coltman (1 turn) **R** J S BEESLEY
CORYTON (St Andrew) *see* Milton Abbot, Dunterton,
Lamerton etc *Ex*
COSBY (St Michael and All Angels) and Whetstone *Leic 7*
P *Bp* **V** C D ALLEN
COSELEY (Christ Church) (St Cuthbert) *Worc 10* **P** *Bp*
P-in-c E J STANFORD
COSELEY (St Chad) *Worc 10* **P** *Bp* **V** *vacant*
COSGROVE (St Peter and St Paul) *see* Potterspury w Furtho
and Yardley Gobion etc *Pet*
COSHAM (St Philip) *Portsm 6* **P** *Bp* **V** A L WEBB
COSSALL (St Catherine) *see* Trowell, Awsworth and Cossall
S'well
COSSINGTON (All Saints) *see* Sileby, Cossington and
Seagrave *Leic*
COSSINGTON (Blessed Virgin Mary) *see* Woolavington w
Cossington and Bawdrip *B & W*
COSTESSEY (St Edmund) *Nor 3* **P** *Gt Hosp Nor*
P-in-c E C LAND **C** I H DYBLE
COSTESSEY, NEW (St Helen) *see* Costessey *Nor*
COSTOCK (St Giles) *see* E and W Leake, Stanford-on-Soar,
Rempstone etc *S'well*
COSTON (St Andrew) *see* S Framland *Leic*
COTEBROOKE (St John and Holy Cross) *see* Tarporley *Ches*
COTEHELE HOUSE (Chapel) *see* Tamar Valley *Truro*
COTEHILL (St John the Evangelist) *see* Scotby and Cotehill w
Cumwhinton *Carl*
COTES HEATH (St James) and Standon and Swynnerton
and Tittensor (jt) *Lich 12* **P** *Bp, V Eccleshall, and Simeon's*
Trustees (jt) **R** S G MCKENZIE
COTESBACH (St Mary) *see* Lutterworth w Cotesbach and
Bitteswell *Leic*
COTGRAVE (All Saints) *S'well 5* **P** *DBP* **R** P D S MASSEY
COTHAM (St Saviour w St Mary) and Clifton St Paul *Bris 3*
P *Bp* **V** D J STEPHENSON **C** P J WHITE **NSM** V H ROYSTON
COTHELSTONE (St Thomas of Canterbury) *see* Bishop's
Lydeard w Lydeard St Lawrence etc *B & W*
COTHERIDGE (St Leonard) *see* Worcs W Rural *Worc*
COTHERSTONE (St Cuthbert) *see* Lower Teesdale *Leeds*
COTLEIGH (St Michael and All Angels) *see* Offwell,
Northleigh, Farway, Cotleigh etc *Ex*
COTMANHAY (Christ Church) *Derby 8* **P** *Bp* **V** P J DAVEY
COTON (St Peter) *see* Lordsbridge *Ely*
COTON-IN-THE-ELMS (St Mary) *see* Seale and Lullington w
Coton in the Elms *Derby*
COTSWOLDS, SOUTH Team Ministry, comprising Ampney
Crucis, Ampney St Peter w St Mary, Barnsley, Bibury and
Winston, Castle Easton, Coln St Aldwyn, Down Ampney,
Driffield, Eastleach, Fairford, Kempsford w Whelford,
Lechlade, Meysey Hampton w Marston Meysey, Poulton,
and Southrop *Glouc 7* **P** *Patr Bd* **TR** J J SWANTON
TV A V CINNAMOND, C J SYMCOX **NSM** D HYDE, H CAINE,
T M HASTIE-SMITH
COTTENHAM (All Saints) w Rampton *Ely 6* **P** *Bp*
R L DAVIES
COTTERED (St John the Baptist) *see* Ardeley, Benington,
Cottered w Throcking etc *St Alb*

COTTERIDGE (St Agnes) *Birm 3* **P** *R Kings Norton*
P-in-c M J CLARIDGE **NSM** R R COLLINS
COTTERSTOCK (St Andrew) *see* Warmington, Tansor and
Cotterstock etc *Pet*
COTTESBROOKE (All Saints) *see* Guilsborough and Hollowell
and Cold Ashby etc *Pet*
COTTESLOE, comprising Aston Abbots, Cheddington w
Mentmore, Cublington, Soulbury, Stewkley, Wing w Grove,
and Wingrave *Ox 15* **P** *Patr Bd* **TR** P D DERBYSHIRE
TV H C BARNES **Hon C** P LYMBERY
COTTESMORE (St Nicholas) and Burley, Clipsham, Exton,
Greetham, Stretton and Thistleton *Pet 12* **P** *Bp, DBP, E R*
Hanbury Esq, and Sir David Davenport-Handley (jt)
V A ORAM
COTTIMORE (St John) *see* Walton-on-Thames *Guildf*
COTTINGHAM (St Mary Magdalene) *see* Gretton w
Rockingham and Cottingham w E Carlton *Pet*
COTTINGHAM (St Mary) *York 14* **P** *Abp* **R** *vacant*
COTTINGLEY (St Michael and All Angels) *Leeds 1* **P** *Bp*
V M G HENDRY
COTTINGWITH, EAST (St Mary) *see* Derwent Ings *York*
COTTISFORD (St Mary the Virgin) *see* Shelswell *Ox*
COTTON (St Andrew) *see* Bacton w Wyverstone, Cotton
and Old Newton etc *St E*
COTTON (St John the Baptist) *see* Kingsley and Foxt-w-
Whiston and Oakamoor etc *Lich*
COTTON MILL (St Julian) *see* St Alb St Steph *St Alb*
COTTONSTONES (St Mary) *see* Ryburn *Leeds*
COUGHTON (St Peter) *see* Alcester Minster *Cov*
COULSDON (St Andrew) *S'wark 22* **P** *Bp* **V** E R FOSS
COULSDON (St John) *S'wark 22* **P** *Abp* **R** P C ROBERTS
NSM S L THOMAS
COULSTON, EAST (St Thomas of Canterbury) *see* Bratton,
Edington and Imber, Erlestoke etc *Sarum*
COUND (St Peter) *see* Wenlock *Heref*
COUNDON (St George) *see* Cov St Geo *Cov*
COUNDON (St James) and Eldon *Dur 5* **P** *Bp and The Crown*
(alt) **P-in-c** G NICHOLSON
COUNTESS WEAR (St Luke) *see* Topsham and Wear *Ex*
COUNTESTHORPE (St Andrew) *see* Four Saints *Leic*
COUNTISBURY (St John the Evangelist) *see* Lynton, Brendon,
Countisbury etc *Ex*
COURTEENHALL (St Peter and St Paul) *see* Salcey *Pet*
COVE (St John the Baptist) (St Christopher) *Guildf 1* **P** *Bp*
P-in-c G M H FOSTER **TV** S J STEWART
COVEHITHE (St Andrew) *see* Wrentham, Covehithe w
Benacre etc *St E*
COVEN (St Paul) *Lich 2* **P** *Bp* **V** S P IREDALE
COVENEY (St Peter ad Vincula) *Ely 8* **P** *Bp* **R** *vacant*
COVENHAM (Annunciation of the Blessed Virgin Mary)
see Fotherby, N Thoresby and Grainsby w Waithe *Linc*
COVENT GARDEN (St Paul) *Lon 3* **P** *Bp* **R** S J GRIGG
NSM S E LENTON
COVENTRY (Holy Trinity) *Cov 2* **P** *Ld Chan*
V G E ANDERSON **NSM** W F WALTON
COVENTRY (St Alban) *Cov 1* **P** *Bp* **R** Z L PIMENTEL
C B PIMENTEL
COVENTRY (St Francis of Assisi) North Radford *Cov 2* **P** *Bp*
P-in-c E B JACKSON
COVENTRY (St George) *Cov 2* **P** *Bp* **V** J R WICKHAM
C C Y POWELL
COVENTRY (St John the Baptist) *Cov 2* **P** *Trustees*
R D L BRACEY
COVENTRY (St Mark) Swanswell (Conventional District)
Cov 1 **C-in-c** T R EAGLES **Min** P J ATKINSON
COVENTRY (St Mary Magdalen) *Cov 3* **P** *Bp* **V** D D ENGH
COVENTRY (St Michael) Stoke *see* Stoke St Mich, Coventry
Cov
COVENTRY (St Nicholas) *see* Radford *Cov*
COVENTRY (St Peter) *Cov 1* **P** *Bp* **R** B A BOYDE
COVENTRY ALL SAINTS (St Anne and All Saints)
(St Margaret) *Cov 1* **P** *Bp* **R** C D HOGGER
COVENTRY Holbrooks (St Luke) *see* Holbrooks *Cov*
COVERACK (St Peter) *see* St Keverne, St Ruan w St Grade and
Landewednack *Truro*
COVERDALE (St Botolph) *see* Middleham w Coverdale and
E Witton etc *Leeds*
COVINGHAM (St Paul) *see* Swindon Dorcan *Bris*
COVINGTON (All Saints) *see* S Leightonstone *Ely*
COWARNE, LITTLE (not known) *see* Bredenbury *Heref*
COWARNE, MUCH (St Mary the Virgin) *see* Frome Valley
Heref
COWBIT (St Mary) *Linc 19* **P** *Ld Chan and DBP (alt)*
V *vacant*
COWCLIFFE (St Hilda) *see* Fixby and Cowcliffe *Leeds*

COWDEN (St Mary Magdalene) *Chich 6*   **P** *Ch Soc Trust* **P-in-c** M E TRASK

COWES (Holy Trinity) (St Mary the Virgin) *Portsm 7* **P** *Trustees and V Carisbrooke St Mary (jt)*   **V** A N POPPE

COWES, EAST (St James) *see* Whippingham w E Cowes *Portsm*

COWESBY (St Michael) *York 18*   **P** *Abp*   **P-in-c** D E GAMBLE **NSM** W A DEWING

COWFOLD (St Peter) *Chich 5*   **P** *Bp Lon*   **NSM** M MILLS

COWGATE (St Peter) *Newc 4*   **P** *Bp*   **V** A M PATERSON **C** W H M NION   **NSM** I H FLINTOFT

COWGILL (St John the Evangelist) *see* Dent w Cowgill *Carl*

COWICK (Holy Trinity) *see* Gt Snaith *Sheff*

COWLAM (St Mary) *see* Waggoners *York*

COWLEIGH (St Peter) *see* Malvern Link w Cowleigh *Worc*

COWLEY (St James) (St Francis) *Ox 1*   **P** *Patr Bd* **TR** G B T BAYLISS   **C** G L BEESLEY   **NSM** R W CHAND

COWLEY (St John) (St Alban) (St Bartholomew) (St Mary and St John) *Ox 1*   **P** *St Steph Ho Ox*   **V** P S J RITCHIE **NSM** S M ALKIRE

COWLEY (St Laurence) *Lon 24*   **P** *Bp*   **R** S M HARDWICKE **NSM** A CLARRIDGE

COWLEY (St Mary) *see* Churn Valley *Glouc*

COWLEY CHAPEL (St Antony) *see* Brampford Speke, Cadbury, Newton St Cyres etc *Ex*

COWLING (Holy Trinity) *see* Sutton w Cowling and Lothersdale *Leeds*

COWLINGE (St Margaret) *see* Bansfield *St E*

COWPEN (St Benedict) *Newc 1*   **P** *Bp*   **R** *vacant*

COWPLAIN (St Wilfrid) *Portsm 5*   **P** *Bp*   **V** I SNARES **C** J L MINTER

COWTON, EAST (All Saints) *see* Wiske Benefice *Leeds*

COX GREEN (Good Shepherd) *Ox 5*   **P** *Bp*   **V** J R HICKS

COXFORD Group, The *see* E w W Rudham, Helhoughton etc *Nor*

COXHEATH (Holy Trinity), East Farleigh, Hunton, Linton and West Farleigh *Roch 7*   **P** *Ld Chan (1 turn), Abp, Lord Cornwallis, and D&C (1 turn)*   **R** P S CALLWAY **C** L C FAULKNER   **NSM** E A DOYLE

COXHOE (St Mary) *see* Kelloe and Coxhoe *Dur*

COXLEY (Christ Church) w Godney, Henton and Wookey *B & W 7*   **P** *Bp*   **V** P I CLARKE   **C** G E MARTIN-SCOTT

COXWELL, GREAT (St Giles) w Buscot, Coleshill and Eaton Hastings *Ox 25*   **P** *Bp and Lord Faringdon (jt)* **V** D M WILLIAMS

COXWELL, LITTLE (St Mary) *see* Gt Faringdon w Lt Coxwell *Ox*

COXWOLD (St Michael) and Husthwaite *York 3*   **P** *Abp* **V** E C HASSALL   **C** D M COYNE, M E YOUNG, M H WAINWRIGHT, M HARRISON, S WHITING **NSM** C C CRANFIELD, C C GITTENS, C J TOASE, S P POPE, T M GANT

CRABBS CROSS (St Peter) *see* Redditch Ch the K *Worc*

CRADLEY (St James) w Mathon and Storridge *Heref 5*   **P** *Bp and D&C Westmr (jt)*   **R** R WARD

CRADLEY (St Peter) *see* Halas *Worc*

CRADLEY HEATH (St Luke) *see* Dudley Wood and Cradley Heath *Worc*

CRAGG VALE (St John the Baptist in the Wilderness) *see* Erringden *Leeds*

CRAKEHALL (St Gregory) *see* Lower Wensleydale *Leeds*

CRAMBE (St Michael) *see* Harton *York*

CRAMLINGTON (St Nicholas) *Newc 1*   **P** *Bp* **TR** W S H DOCHERTY   **TV** D M GRAY   **C** E R A HUDSON

CRAMPMOOR (St Swithun) *see* Romsey *Win*

CRANBORNE (St Mary and St Bartholomew) w Boveridge, Edmondsham, Wimborne St Giles and Woodlands *Sarum 9*   **P** *Viscount Cranborne, Earl of Shaftesbury, and Mrs J E Smith (jt)*   **R** R D SIMPSON

CRANBOURNE (St Peter) *see* Winkfield and Cranbourne *Ox*

CRANBROOK (St Dunstan) *Cant 11*   **P** *Abp* **V** A E J POLLINGTON

CRANFIELD (St Peter and St Paul) and Hulcote w Salford *St Alb 9*   **P** *MMCET*   **R** *vacant*

CRANFORD (Holy Angels) (St Dunstan) *Lon 11*   **P** *R J G Berkeley Esq and W Cardale Esq (jt)*   **R** M J GILL

CRANFORD (St John the Baptist) w Grafton Underwood and Twywell *Pet 9*   **P** *Boughton Estates, DBP, and Sir John Robinson Bt (by turn)*   **R** *vacant*

CRANHAM (All Saints) *Chelmsf 2*   **P** *St Jo Coll Ox*   **R** *vacant*

CRANHAM (St James the Great) *see* Painswick, Sheepscombe, Cranham, The Edge etc *Glouc*

CRANHAM PARK (St Luke) *Chelmsf 2*   **P** *Bp*   **V** M VICKERS **C** C E COZIER   **NSM** J A HEININK, K R PERKINS

CRANHAM PARK Moor Lane (not known) *see* Cranham Park *Chelmsf*

CRANLEIGH (St Nicolas) *Guildf 2*   **P** *Bp*   **R** R O WOODHAMS **C** I MASLIN

CRANMORE, WEST (St Bartholomew) *see* Shepton Mallet w Doulting *B & W*

CRANOE (St Michael) *see* Welham, Glooston and Cranoe and Stonton Wyville *Leic*

CRANSFORD (St Peter) *see* Upper Alde *St E*

CRANSLEY (St Andrew) *see* Broughton w Cransley and Mawsley *Pet*

CRANTOCK (St Carantoc) *see* Perranzabuloe and Crantock w Cubert *Truro*

CRANWELL (St Andrew) *see* N Lafford Gp *Linc*

CRANWICH (St Mary) *Nor 13*   **P** *CPAS*   **R** *vacant*

CRANWORTH (St Mary the Virgin) *see* Barnham Broom and Upper Yare *Nor*

CRASSWALL (St Mary) *see* Black Mountains Gp *Heref*

CRASTER (Mission Church) *see* Embleton w Rennington and Rock *Newc*

CRATFIELD (St Mary) *see* Four Rivers *St E*

CRATHORNE (All Saints) *York 20*   **P** *Lord Crathorne* **P-in-c** W J FORD   **Hon C** A J HUTCHINSON **NSM** D J SUDRON, R OPALA

CRAWCROOK (Church of the Holy Spirit) *see* Greenside *Dur*

CRAWLEY (St John the Baptist) *Chich 6*   **P** *Bp*   **V** S BURSTON **C** J A YOUNG, M J WALKER

CRAWLEY (St Mary) *see* The Downs *Win*

CRAWLEY DOWN (All Saints) *Chich 6*   **P** *R Worth* **V** C E KEYTE   **NSM** E J LOGAN, S J BALE

CRAWLEY, NORTH (St Firmin) *see* Sherington w Chicheley, N Crawley, Astwood etc *Ox*

CRAWLEY, SOUTH (St Mary) *Chich 6*   **P** *Patr Bd* **TR** T J WILSON   **TV** H W SCHNAAR, R J EDWARDS **NSM** G D M RICHARDS, J A E ALDERTON

CRAY (St Barnabas) *see* St Paul's Cray St Barn *Roch*

CRAY VALLEY (St Mary and St Paulinus) (St Andrew) *Roch 16*   **P** *Bp*   **V** J J E DANIELS-WHITE   **C** J M WINTER

CRAY, NORTH (St James) *see* Bexley *Roch*

CRAYFORD (St Paulinus) *Roch 15*   **P** *Bp*   **R** P F PRENTICE **C** AJ SPENCE

CRAYKE (St Cuthbert) w Brandsby and Yearsley *York 3* **P** *The Crown and Abp (alt)*   **R** E C HASSALL   **C** D M COYNE, M E YOUNG, M H WAINWRIGHT, M HARRISON, S WHITING **NSM** C C CRANFIELD, C C GITTENS, C J TOASE, S P POPE, T M GANT

CRAZIES HILL (Mission Room) *see* Wargrave w Knowl Hill *Ox*

CREAKE, NORTH (St Mary) and SOUTH (St Mary) w Waterden, Syderstone w Barmer and Sculthorpe *Nor 14* **P** *Bp, Earl Spencer, Earl of Leicester, Guild of All So, J Labouchere Esq, Mrs M E Russell, and DBP (jt)*   **R** C G WYLIE

CREATON, GREAT (St Michael and All Angels) *see* Guilsborough and Hollowell and Cold Ashby etc *Pet*

CREDITON (Holy Cross) (St Lawrence) Shobrooke and Sandford w Upton Hellions *Ex 2*   **J** *12 Govs of Crediton Ch* **R** M J TREGENZA   **C** H DREVER, P L FILLERY

CREECH ST MICHAEL (St Michael) and Ruishton w Thornfalcon *B & W 18*   **P** *Bp, MMCET, and Dr W R C Batten (jt)*   **V** R S HARRIS

CREED (St Crida) *see* Probus, Ladock and Grampound w Creed and St Erme *Truro*

CREEDY, NORTH: Cheriton Fitzpaine, Woolfardisworthy, Kennerley, Washford Pyne, Puddington, Poughill, Stockleigh English, Morchard Bishop, Stockleigh Pomeroy, Down St Mary, Clannaborough, Lapford, Nymet Rowland, and Coldridge *Ex 2*   **P** *Ld Chan (1 turn), Patr Bd (5 turns)*   **P-in-c** K J CROSS

CREEKMOOR (Christ Church) *Sarum 7*   **P** *Bp* **V** J E AUDIBERT   **NSM** J R A AUDIBERT

CREEKSEA (All Saints) *Chelmsf 11*   **P** *Bp* **P-in-c** V M WADMAN

CREETING (St Mary) *see* N Bosmere *St E*

CREETING (St Peter) *as above*

CREETON (St Peter) *see* Castle Bytham w Creeton *Linc*

CREGNEISH (St Peter) *see* Rushen *S & M*

CRESSAGE (Christ Church) *see* Wenlock *Heref*

CRESSBROOK (St John the Evangelist) *see* Tideswell *Derby*

CRESSING (All Saints) w Stisted and Bradwell-juxt-Coggeshall and Pattiswick *Chelmsf 17*   **P** *Bp, Exors Mrs D E G Keen, and Abp (by turn)*   **P-in-c** C M DAVEY **C** S L BATTS, T L HARVEY   **NSM** K M KING, R J BURDEN

CRESSINGHAM, GREAT (St Michael) and LITTLE (St Andrew), w Threxton *Nor 13*   **P** *Bp and Sec of State for Defence*   **C** G FOSTER

CRESSWELL (St Bartholomew) and Lynemouth *Newc 11* **P** *Bp*   **P-in-c** A W MUNNS

CRESWELL (St Mary Magdalene) *see* Elmton w Creswell and Whitwell w Steetley *Derby*

CRETINGHAM (St Peter) *see* Mid Loes *St E*

CREWE (All Saints and St Paul) (St Peter) *Ches 15* **P** *Bp*
C C G CLEGHORN

CREWE (St Andrew w St John the Baptist) *Ches 15* **P** *Bp*
C C G CLEGHORN

CREWE (St Barnabas) *Ches 15* **P** *Bp* **V** R D POWELL

CREWE GREEN (St Michael and All Angels) *see* Haslington w
Crewe Green *Ches*

CREWKERNE (St Bartholomew) *see* Wulfric Benefice *B & W*

CRICH (St Mary) and South Wingfield *Derby 2* **P** *Ch Trust
Fund Trust and Duke of Devonshire (jt)*
P-in-c I R WHITEHEAD

**CRICK (St Margaret) and Yelvertoft w Clay Coton and
Lilbourne** *Pet 2* **P** *MMCET and St Jo Coll Ox (jt)*
R D M LAKE

CRICKET MALHERBIE (St Mary Magdalene) *see* Chaffcombe,
Cricket Malherbie etc *B & W*

CRICKET ST THOMAS (St Thomas) *B & W 16* **P** *Bp*
V H M WILLIAMS

CRICKLADE (St Sampson) *see* Upper Thames *Bris*

CRICKLEWOOD (St Gabriel) and St Michael *Lon 21* **P** *Bp*
V *vacant*

CRIFTINS (St Matthew) w Dudleston and Welsh Frankton
Lich 16 **P** *Bp and V Ellesmere (jt)* **V** S C AIREY

CRIMPLESHAM (St Mary) *see* Denver and Ryston w Roxham
etc *Ely*

CRINGLEFORD (St Peter) and Colney *Nor 7* **P** *Exors E H
Barclay Esq and Gt Hosp Nor (alt)* **R** G P WILKINS **C** T S YAU

CROCKENHILL (All Souls) *Roch 2* **P** *Bp* **V** K R WHITE

CROCKHAM HILL (Holy Trinity) *Roch 11* **P** *J St A Warde Esq*
V S J DIGGORY

CROFT (All Saints) *see* The Wainfleet Gp *Linc*

CROFT (Christ Church) *see* Newchurch w Croft *Liv*

CROFT (St Michael and All Angels) *see* Broughton Astley and
Croft w Stoney Stanton *Leic*

CROFT (St Peter) *see* E Dere Street *Leeds*

CROFTON (All Saints) *Leeds 19* **P** *Duchy of Lanc*
R L TINNISWOOD **NSM** H WALKER **OLM** A JORDAN

CROFTON (Holy Rood) (St Edmund) *Portsm 2* **P** *Bp*
V R A ENGLAND **C** D J GREENFIELD, J C GREENFIELD
NSM C R PRESTIDGE

CROFTON (St Paul) *Roch 16* **P** *V Orpington*
V B A ABAYOMI-COLE **C** M H LAVENDER

CROFTON PARK (St Hilda w St Cyprian) *S'wark 5*
P *V Lewisham St Mary* **V** S G BATES

CROMER (St Peter and St Paul) *Nor 20* **P** *CPAS*
V J R PORTER **OLM** J M HODGKINSON

CROMFORD (St Mary) *see* Matlock Bath and Cromford
Derby

**CROMHALL (St Andrew), Tortworth, Tytherington,
Falfield and Rockhampton** *Glouc 5* **P** *Bp, R Thornbury and
Oldbury etc, Adn, and J Leigh Esq (1 turn), Earl of Ducie, Oriel
Coll Ox, and MMCET (1 turn)*
Hon C S P PHILLIPSON-MASTERS

CROMPTON FOLD (St Saviour) *see* E Crompton *Man*

CROMPTON, EAST (St James) *Man 15* **P** *Bp*
V D P WOODALL **OLM** W H MOSTON

CROMPTON, HIGH (St Mary) and Thornham *Man 15* **P** *Bp*
OLM D MORRIS

CROMWELL (St Giles) *see* Norwell w Ossington, Cromwell
etc *S'well*

CRONDALL (All Saints) and Ewshot *Guildf 3* **P** *Bp*
V T C L HELLINGS **NSM** S M R CUMMING-LATTEY

CROOK (St Catherine) *Carl 10* **P** *CPAS* **P-in-c** G W BRIGGS

CROOK (St Catherine) *Dur 8* **P** *R Brancepeth* **V** V T FENTON
NSM L LINDSAY

**CROOK PEAK, comprising Badgworth, Biddisham, Christon,
Compton Bishop, Loxton, and Weare** *B & W 1* **P** *R M Dodd
Esq (1 turn), Ld Chan (2 turns), Bp Lon (1 turn)* **R** J A JEFFERY

CROOKES (St Thomas) *Sheff 4* **P** *Patr Bd* **TR** M WOODHEAD
C T J FINNEMORE **NSM** C A STRINE

CROOKES (St Timothy) *Sheff 4* **P** *Sheff Ch Burgesses*
P-in-c M E LAMBERT

CROOKHAM (Christ Church) *Guildf 1* **P** *V Crondall and
Ewshot* **V** S A FRANKLIN

CROOKHORN (Good Shepherd) *Portsm 5* **P** *Simeon's
Trustees* **V** J E SMITH **C** A M WILSON **NSM** M YOUELL

CROPREDY (St Mary the Virgin) *see* Shires' Edge *Ox*

CROPTHORNE (St Michael) *see* Fladbury, Hill and Moor,
Wyre Piddle etc *Worc*

CROPTON (St Gregory) *see* Lastingham w Appleton-le-
Moors, Rosedale etc *York*

CROPWELL BISHOP (St Giles) *see* Wiverton in the Vale *S'well*

CROSBY (St George) (St Michael) *Linc 6* **P** *Sir Reginald
Sheffield Bt* **V** *vacant*

CROSBY GARRETT (St Andrew) *see* Upper Eden *Carl*

CROSBY RAVENSWORTH (St Lawrence) *see* N Westmorland
Carl

CROSBY, GREAT (All Saints) *see* Thornton and Crosby *Liv*

**CROSBY, GREAT (St Faith) and Waterloo Park St Mary the
Virgin** *Liv 6* **P** *St Chad's Coll Dur and Trustees (jt)*
P-in-c J W REED **Hon C** D A SMITH

CROSBY, GREAT (St Luke) *Liv 8* **P** *Bp* **V** A J BRUCE
C L J N PARRY **NSM** D A LOWRIE

CROSBY-ON-EDEN (St John the Evangelist) *see* Eden, Gelt
and Irthing *Carl*

CROSCOMBE (Blessed Virgin Mary) *see* Pilton w Croscombe,
N Wootton and Dinder *B & W*

CROSLAND MOOR (St Barnabas) and Linthwaite *Leeds 11*
P *Bp and R Almondbury (jt)* **P-in-c** P M WITTS
NSM S V BROOKS

CROSLAND, SOUTH (Holy Trinity) *see* Newsome and
Armitage Bridge and S Crosland *Leeds*

CROSS CANONBY (St John the Evangelist) *see* Allonby,
Cross Canonby and Dearham *Carl*

CROSS FELL GROUP, The, comprising Addingham, Culgaith,
Edenhall, Kirkland, Langwathby, Melmerby, Ousby, and
Skirwith *Carl 4* **P** *D&C (2 turns) and DBP (1 turn)* **V** A S PYE
C K M BUTTERFIELD, M R HOUSTON

CROSS GREEN (St Hilda) *Leeds 14* **P** *Bp and Keble Coll Ox (jt)*
P-in-c D J PERCIVAL

CROSS GREEN (St Saviour) *see* Leeds Richmond Hill *Leeds*

CROSS HEATH (St Michael and All Angels) *Lich 9* **P** *Bp*
V S C MADDISON

CROSS IN HAND (St Bartholomew) *see* Waldron *Chich*

CROSS ROADS CUM LEES (St James) *see* Haworth and Cross
Roads cum Lees *Leeds*

CROSS TOWN (St Cross) *see* Knutsford St Cross *Ches*

CROSSCRAKE (St Thomas) *Carl 10* **P** *V Heversham and
Milnthorpe* **V** *vacant*

CROSSENS (St John) *see* N Meols *Liv*

CROSSFLATTS (St Aidan) *see* Bingley All SS *Leeds*

CROSSLACON TEAM MINISTRY, comprising Arlecdon, Cleator,
Cleator Moor, and Frizington *Carl 5* **P** *Patr Bd*
P-in-c N G PENNINGTON

CROSSPOOL (St Columba) *Sheff 4* **P** *Bp*
P-in-c I N C LOTHIAN **C** C H STEBBING

CROSTHWAITE (St Kentigern) Keswick *Carl 6* **P** *Bp*
P-in-c A G MURPHIE

CROSTHWAITE (St Mary) Kendal *Carl 10* **P** *DBP*
P-in-c M D WOODCOCK

**CROSTON (St Michael and All Angels), Bretherton and
Mawdesley w Bispham** *Blackb 4* **P** *M G Rawstorne Esq and
Patr Bd (jt)* **R** M WOODS **NSM** J H TAYLOR

CROSTWICK (St Peter) *see* Horsham St Faith, Spixworth and
Crostwick *Nor*

CROSTWIGHT (All Saints) *see* Smallburgh w Dilham w
Honing and Crostwight *Nor*

CROUCH END HILL (Christ Church) *see* Hornsey Ch Ch *Lon*

CROUGHTON (All Saints) *see* Aynho and Croughton w
Evenley etc *Pet*

CROWAN (St Crewenna) and Treslothan *Truro 2*
P *D L C Roberts Esq and Mrs W A Pendarves (jt)*
P-in-c R E BROWNING

CROWBOROUGH (All Saints) *Chich 16* **P** *Ld Chan*
V S P REES **C** B R THORNDIKE, M S ASHWORTH, T J HIORNS
NSM J A HOBBS, R P DILLINGHAM

CROWBOROUGH (St John the Evangelist) *Chich 16*
P *Guild of All So* **V** P R REDPARTH

CROWCOMBE (Holy Ghost) *see* Quantock Towers *B & W*

CROWELL (Nativity of the Blessed Virgin Mary) *see* Chinnor,
Sydenham, Aston Rowant and Crowell *Ox*

CROWFIELD (All Saints) *see* N Bosmere *St E*

CROWHURST (St George) *see* Catsfield and Crowhurst *Chich*

CROWHURST (St George) *see* Oxted *S'wark*

**CROWLAND (St Mary and St Bartholomew and
St Guthlac)** *Linc 19* **P** *Earl of Normanton*
P-in-c C H BROWN **NSM** J A M BILLSON

CROWLE (St John the Baptist) *see* Bowbrook S *Worc*

CROWLE GROUP, The (St Oswald), including Garthorpe and
Luddington *Linc 1* **P** *Bp (2 turns), The Crown (1 turn)*
V G M LINES

CROWMARSH GIFFORD (St Mary Magdalene) *see*
Wallingford *Ox*

CROWN EAST AND RUSHWICK (St Thomas) *see* Worc Dines
Green St Mich and Crown E, Rushwick *Worc*

CROWNHILL (Ascension) *see* Plymouth Crownhill Ascension
Ex

CROWTHORNE (St John the Baptist) *Ox 8* **P** *Bp*
V L M CORNWELL

CROWTON (Christ Church) *see* Norley, Crowton and
Kingsley *Ches*

CROXALL-CUM-OAKLEY (St John the Baptist)   *see* Seale and Lullington w Coton in the Elms *Derby*
CROXBY (All Saints)   *see* Walesby Gp *Linc*
CROXDALE (St Bartholomew) and Tudhoe *Dur 5*   **P** *D&C*   **P-in-c** B A HILTON   **NSM** D T ACKERLEY
CROXDEN (St Giles)   *see* Rocester and Croxden w Hollington *Lich*
CROXLEY GREEN (All Saints) *St Alb 4*   **P** V Rickmansworth   **V** M R MUGAN
CROXLEY GREEN (St Oswald) *St Alb 4*   **P** *Bp*   **V** R J RILEY-BRALEY
CROXTETH (St Paul) *Liv 5*   **P** R W Derby and Bp *(jt)*   **V** *vacant*
CROXTETH PARK (St Cuthbert) *Liv 5*   **P** *Bp*   **P-in-c** L LEATHERBARROW
CROXTON (All Saints)   *see* Thetford *Nor*
CROXTON (St James)   *see* Papworth *Ely*
CROXTON (St John the Baptist)   *see* S Croxton Gp *Leic*
CROXTON (St John the Evangelist)   *see* Brocklesby Park, Croxton and North Wolds *Linc*
CROXTON (St Paul)   *see* Ashley and Mucklestone and Broughton and Croxton *Lich*
CROXTON Group, The SOUTH (St John the Baptist), including Ashby Folville, Beeby, Gaddesby, Thorpe Satchville, and Twyford *Leic 2*   **P** DBP, Ch Soc Trust, and MMCET *(jt)*   **P-in-c** N STOTHERS
CROXTON KERRIAL (St Botolph and St John the Baptist)   *see* High Framland Par *Leic*
CROYDE (St Mary Magdalene)   *see* Georgeham *Ex*
CROYDON (All Saints)   *see* Orwell Gp *Ely*
CROYDON (Christ Church) Broad Green *S'wark 20*   **P** Simeon's Trustees   **V** L P P JESUDASON   **NSM** R E VERNON
CROYDON (Emmanuel)   *see* S Croydon Em *S'wark*
CROYDON (Holy Saviour) *S'wark 21*   **P** *Bp*   **V** C J TUCKER
CROYDON (St Andrew) *S'wark 20*   **P** *Trustees*   **P-in-c** A S BISHOP   **NSM** C MBANUDE
CROYDON (St Augustine)   *see* S Croydon St Pet and St Aug *S'wark*
CROYDON (St John the Baptist) *S'wark 20*   **P** *Abp*   **P-in-c** A S BISHOP   **C** F A BAYES, J A MOORE, P VOWLES   **NSM** G S A I GERMAIN-POWELL
CROYDON (St Luke)   *see* Croydon Woodside *S'wark*
CROYDON (St Mary Magdalene)   *see* Addiscombe St Mary Magd w St Martin *S'wark*
CROYDON (St Matthew) *S'wark 20*   **P** V Croydon   **V** S J D FOSTER   **C** D O WEITHERS
CROYDON (St Michael and All Angels w St James) *S'wark 20*   **P** *Trustees*   **V** T D PIKE   **C** P R J KENNEDY
CROYDON (St Peter)   *see* S Croydon St Pet and St Aug *S'wark*
CROYDON MINSTER   *see* Croydon St Jo *S'wark*
CROYDON Woodside (St Luke) *S'wark 21*   **P** *Bp*   **V** S J DENNIS   **C** C DAWSON
CROYDON, SOUTH (Emmanuel) *S'wark 20*   **P** Ch Trust Fund Trust   **C** B M O JONES
CROYDON, SOUTH (St Peter) (St Augustine) *S'wark 20*   **P** V Croydon and Bp *(jt)*   **V** G J W DUMBRECK   **NSM** A ONYEKWELU, L M FOX
CRUDGINGTON (St Mary Mission Church)   *see* Wrockwardine Deanery *Lich*
CRUDWELL (All Saints)   *see* Braydon Brook *Bris*
CRUMPSALL (St Matthew w St Mary) *Man 4*   **P** *Bp*   **R** *vacant*
CRUMPSALL, LOWER (St Thomas)   *see* Cheetham and Lower Crumpsall *Man*
CRUNDALE (St Mary the Blessed Virgin)   *see* King's Wood *Cant*
CRUWYS MORCHARD (Holy Cross)   *see* Washfield, Stoodleigh, Withleigh etc *Ex*
CRUX EASTON (St Michael and All Angels)   *see* NW Hants *Win*
CUBBINGTON (St Mary) *Cov 11*   **P** *Bp*   **V** G R COLES
CUBERT (St Cubert)   *see* Perranzabuloe and Crantock w Cubert *Truro*
CUBLEY (St Andrew)   *see* S Dales *Derby*
CUBLINGTON (St Nicholas)   *see* Cottesloe *Ox*
CUCKFIELD (Holy Trinity) *Chich 5*   **P** *Bp*   **V** M J MAINE
CUCKLINGTON (St Lawrence)   *see* Charlton Musgrove, Cucklington and Stoke Trister *B & W*
CUDDESDON (All Saints)   *see* Garsington, Cuddesdon and Horspath *Ox*
CUDDINGTON (St Mary) *Guildf 9*   **P** *Bp*   **P-in-c** T L RICKETTS
CUDDINGTON (St Nicholas)   *see* Wychert Vale *Ox*
CUDHAM (St Peter and St Paul) and Downe *Roch 16*   **P** Ch Soc Trust and Bp *(jt)*   **V** W J MUSSON
CUDWORTH (St John) *Leeds 17*   **P** *Bp*   **V** D NICHOLSON
CUDWORTH (St Michael)   *see* Winsmoor *B & W*

CUFFLEY (St Andrew)   *see* Northaw and Cuffley *St Alb*
CULBONE (St Beuno)   *see* Oare w Culbone *B & W*
CULFORD (St Mary)   *see* Lark Valley *St E*
CULGAITH (All Saints)   *see* Cross Fell Gp *Carl*
CULHAM (St Paul)   *see* Dorchester *Ox*
CULLERCOATS (St George) *Newc 5*   **P** Duke of Northumberland   **V** A J HUGHES
CULLERCOATS (St Paul)   *see* Tynemouth Cullercoats St Paul *Newc*
CULLINGWORTH (St John the Evangelist)   *see* Harden and Wilsden, Cullingworth and Denholme *Leeds*
CULLOMPTON (St Andrew) (Langford Chapel) *Ex 7*   **P** *CPAS*   **R** E Q HOBBS   **C** O H J MEARS
CULM DAVY (St Mary's Chapel)   *see* Hemyock w Culm Davy, Clayhidon and Culmstock *Ex*
CULMINGTON (All Saints)   *see* Corvedale Benefice *Heref*
CULMSTOCK (All Saints)   *see* Hemyock w Culm Davy, Clayhidon and Culmstock *Ex*
CULPHO (St Botolph)   *see* Gt and Lt Bealings w Playford and Culpho *St E*
CULWORTH (St Mary the Virgin) w Sulgrave and Thorpe Mandeville and Chipping Warden w Edgcote and Moreton Pinkney *Pet 1*   **P** T M Sergison-Brooke Esq, DBP, D L P Humfrey Esq, Ch Patr Trust, and Oriel Coll Ox *(jt)*   **R** B D S FAIRBANK
CUMBERWORTH (St Nicholas), Denby, Denby Dale and Shepley *Leeds 12*   **P** V Kirkburton, V Penistone, and Bp *(jt)*   **R** J R JONES   **C** S L HUNTER
CUMDIVOCK (St John)   *see* Dalston w Cumdivock, Raughton Head and Wreay *Carl*
CUMMERSDALE (St James)   *see* Denton Holme *Carl*
CUMNOR (St Michael) *Ox 19*   **P** St Pet Coll Ox   **V** J M WIDDESS   **C** C L SCHNEIDER   **NSM** H A AZER
CUMREW (St Mary the Virgin)   *see* Eden, Gelt and Irthing *Carl*
CUMWHINTON (St John's Hall)   *see* Scotby and Cotehill w Cumwhinton *Carl*
CUMWHITTON (St Mary the Virgin)   *see* Eden, Gelt and Irthing *Carl*
CUNDALL (St Mary and All Saints)   *see* Kirby-on-the-Moor, Cundall w Norton-le-Clay etc *Leeds*
CURBAR (All Saints)   *see* Longstone, Curbar and Stony Middleton *Derby*
CURBRIDGE (St John the Baptist)   *see* Witney *Ox*
CURDRIDGE (St Peter) *Portsm 1*   **P** D&C Win   **V** G R MENSINGH
CURDWORTH (St Nicholas and St Peter ad Vincula) (St George), Middleton and Wishaw *Birm 7*   **P** *Bp*   **R** *vacant*
CURRY MALLET (All Saints)   *see* Beercrocombe w Curry Mallet, Hatch Beauchamp etc *B & W*
CURRY RIVEL (St Andrew) w Fivehead and Swell *B & W 5*   **P** D&C Bris *(1 turn)*, P G H Speke Esq *(2 turns)*   **R** S R PATTERSON
CURRY, NORTH (St Peter and St Paul)   *see* Athelney *B & W*
CURY (St Corentine)   *see* Mullion and Cury w Gunwalloe *Truro*
CUSOP (St Mary) w Blakemere, Bredwardine w Brobury, Clifford, Dorstone, Hardwicke, Moccas and Preston-on-Wye *Heref 1*   **P** Bp, D&C, CPAS, MMCET, P M I S Trumper Esq, S Penoyre Esq, and F Chester-Master Esq *(jt)*   **P-in-c** L J MORRISS   **NSM** C J LISVANE
CUTCOMBE (St John the Evangelist)   *see* Exmoor *B & W*
CUTSDEAN (St James)   *see* The Guitings, Cutsdean, Farmcote etc *Glouc*
CUXHAM (Holy Rood)   *see* Benson w Ewelme *Ox*
CUXTON (St Michael and All Angels) and Halling *Roch 6*   **P** Bp and D&C *(jt)*   **R** R I KNIGHT
CUXWOLD (St Nicholas)   *see* Caistor *Linc*
DACRE (Holy Trinity) w Hartwith and Darley w Thornthwaite *Leeds 23*   **P** Bp, D&C Ripon, V Masham and Healey, and Mrs K A Dunbar *(jt)*   **V** A J FERNELEY
DACRE (St Andrew) *Carl 4*   **P** *Trustees*   **V** *vacant*
DADLINGTON (St James)   *see* Fenn Lanes Gp *Leic*
DAGENHAM (St Cedd)   *see* Becontree St Cedd *Chelmsf*
DAGENHAM (St Martin)   *see* Becontree St Martin *Chelmsf*
DAGENHAM (St Peter and St Paul) *Chelmsf 1*   **P** Ch Soc Trust   **V** J K EDWARDS
DAGLINGWORTH (Holy Rood)   *see* Brimpsfield w Birdlip, Syde, Daglingworth etc *Glouc*
DAISY HILL (St James)   *see* Blackrod, Daisy Hill, Westhoughton and Wingates *Man*
DALBURY (All Saints)   *see* Boylestone, Church Broughton, Dalbury, etc *Derby*
DALBY (St James)   *see* W Coast *S & M*

DALBY (St Lawrence and Blessed Edward King) *see* Bolingbroke Deanery *Linc*
DALBY (St Peter) *see* Howardian Gp *York*
DALBY, GREAT (St Swithun) *see* Burrough Hill Pars *Leic*
DALBY, LITTLE (St James) *as above*
DALBY, OLD (St John the Baptist), Nether Broughton, Saxelbye w Shoby, Grimston and Wartnaby *Leic 2* **P** *Bp, MMCET, V Rothley, and Personal Reps K J M Madocks-Wright Esq (jt)* **P-in-c** J H MACKAY **C** P G HOOPER **NSM** P R TOWNS
DALE ABBEY (All Saints) *see* Stanton-by-Dale w Dale Abbey and Risley *Derby*
DALE HEAD (St James) *see* Slaidburn w Tosside *Leeds*
DALHAM (St Mary), Gazeley, Higham, Kentford and Moulton *St E 7* **P** *Bp (2 turns), Ch Coll Cam (1 turn), C E L Philipps Esq (1 turn), and D W Barclay Esq (1 turn)* **P-in-c** C R I S RYCRAFT
DALLAM (St Mark) *Liv 11* **P** *R Warrington and Bp (jt)* **V** *vacant*
DALLINGHOO (St Mary) *see* Mid Loes *St E*
DALLINGTON (St Giles) *see* Warbleton, Bodle Street Green and Dallington *Chich*
DALLINGTON (St Mary the Virgin) and St James *Pet 4* **P** *Bp and Earl Spencer (jt)* **V** S A FAULKNER
DALSTON (Holy Trinity) w St Philip and Haggerston All Saints *Lon 5* **P** *Bp, Ch Ox (alt)* **V** L J FAWCETT
DALSTON (St Mark w St Bartholomew) *Lon 5* **P** *Ch Patr Trust* **V** J ZVIMBA
DALSTON (St Michael) w Cumdivock, Raughton Head and Wreay *Carl 3* **P** *Bp, DBP, and D&C (jt)* **V** *vacant*
DALTON (Holy Trinity) *Sheff 6* **P** *Bp* **P-in-c** S Y LEE
DALTON (St James) *see* Holmedale *Leeds*
DALTON (St John the Evangelist) *see* Topcliffe, Baldersby w Dishforth, Dalton etc *York*
DALTON (St Michael and All Angels) *Liv 14* **P** *Bp* **P-in-c** P A LOCK
DALTON HOLME (St Mary) *see* Etton w Dalton Holme *York*
DALTON LE DALE (St Andrew) and New Seaham *Dur 2* **P** *Bp and D&C (alt)* **V** P T HARRISON
DALTON, NORTH (All Saints) *see* Woldsburn *York*
DALTON, SOUTH *see* Dalton le Dale and New Seaham *Dur*
DALTON-IN-FURNESS (St Mary) and Ireleth-with-Askam *Carl 9* **P** *Bp* **P-in-c** R J CROSSLEY **C** A E LYNCH
DALWOOD (St Peter) *see* Kilmington, Stockland, Dalwood, Yarcombe etc *Ex*
DAMASCUS, comprising Appleford, Drayton, Milton, Steventon, and Sutton Courtenay *Ox 19* **P** *Bp, Ch Ch Ox, D&C Westmr, and D&C Windsor (jt)* **R** H G KENDRICK **C** P F SUTTON **NSM** K HYDE, M A HEYWOOD, R BRUCE
DAMERHAM (St George) *see* W Downland *Sarum*
DANBURY (St John the Baptist) *Chelmsf 10* **P** *Lord Fitzwalter* **P-in-c** J D JONES
DANBY (St Hilda) w Castleton and Commondale *York 21* **P** *Viscountess Downe* **NSM** S J WILSON
DANBY WISKE (not known) *see* Wiske Benefice *Leeds*
DANE BANK (St George) *see* Denton Ch Ch *Man*
DANEHILL (All Saints) *Chich 18* **P** *Ch Soc Trust* **V** P MACBAIN
DANESMOOR (St Barnabas) *see* N Wingfield, Clay Cross and Pilsley *Derby*
DARBY END (St Peter) and Netherton *Worc 9* **P** *Bp* **V** *vacant*
DARBY GREEN (St Barnabas) and Eversley *Win 5* **P** *Bp* **P-in-c** L W CAMPBELL **NSM** R F HARTLAND
DARENT VALLEY (St Margaret) *Roch 2* **P** *Bp and D&C (jt)* **V** E J YOUNG
DARESBURY (All Saints) *Ches 4* **P** D G Greenhall Esq **V** D R FELIX **NSM** G M YOUNGER
DARFIELD (All Saints) *Sheff 12* **P** *MMCET* **R** D HILDRED
DARLASTON (All Saints) (St Lawrence) and Moxley *Lich 25* **P** *Patr Bd (2 turns), The Crown (1 turn)* **TV** G DAVID **OLM** A J DUCKWORTH
DARLEY (Christ Church) *see* Dacre w Hartwith and Darley w Thornthwaite *Leeds*
DARLEY (St Helen), South Darley and Winster *Derby 1* **P** *Bp* **R** S D MONK
DARLEY ABBEY (St Matthew) *see* Allestree St Edm and Darley Abbey *Derby*
DARLEY, SOUTH (St Mary the Virgin) *see* Darley, S Darley and Winster *Derby*
DARLINGSCOTT (St George) *see* Tredington and Darlingscott *Cov*
DARLINGTON (All Saints) *see* Blackwell All SS and Salutation *Dur*
DARLINGTON (Holy Trinity) *Dur 7* **P** *Adn Dur* **P-in-c** M P FIRTH

DARLINGTON (St Cuthbert) *Dur 7* **P** *Lord Barnard* **P-in-c** M P FIRTH
DARLINGTON (St Herbert) *Dur 7* **P** *The Crown* **V** *vacant*
DARLINGTON (St James) *Dur 7* **P** *The Crown* **P-in-c** K I CRAWFORD
DARLINGTON (St John) *Dur 7* **P** *The Crown* **P-in-c** A ROACHE
DARLINGTON (St Mark) w St Paul *Dur 7* **P** *Bp and St Jo Coll Dur* **V** P A BAKER
DARLINGTON (St Matthew) *see* Heighington and Darlington St Matt and St Luke *Dur*
DARLINGTON St Hilda and (St Columba) *Dur 7* **P** *Bp* **P-in-c** A ROACHE
DARNALL (Church of Christ) *see* Attercliffe and Darnall *Sheff*
DARRINGTON (St Luke and All Saints) *see* Went Valley *Leeds*
DARSHAM (All Saints) *see* Yoxmere *St E*
DARTFORD (Christ Church) *Roch 2* **P** *V Dartford H Trin* **V** R J MORTIMER **C** L J FATUROTI
DARTFORD (Holy Trinity) *Roch 2* **P** *Bp* **V** M J HENWOOD
DARTFORD (St Alban) *Roch 2* **P** *V Dartford H Trin* **P-in-c** M P HAM **C** M E YOUNG
DARTFORD (St Edmund the King and Martyr) *Roch 2* **P** *Bp* **P-in-c** M P HAM **C** M E YOUNG
DARTINGTON (St Mary) *see* Totnes w Bridgetown, Berry Pomeroy etc *Ex*
DARTMOUTH (St Petrox) (St Saviour) and Dittisham *Ex 12* **P** *Sir John Seale Bt, DBP, and Bp (jt)* **V** W P G HAZLEWOOD **C** A P LANGLEY, R L BOYLE
DARTON (All Saints) w Staincross and Mapplewell *Leeds 17* **P** *Bp* **V** T D STEVENS
DARWEN (St Barnabas) *Blackb 2* **P** *Bp* **V** D J BACON
DARWEN (St Cuthbert) w Tockholes St Stephen *Blackb 2* **P** *Bp* **P-in-c** N E DAVIS
DARWEN (St Peter) *Blackb 2* **P** *Bp and V Blackburn (jt)* **V** F E GREEN
DARWEN, LOWER (St James) *Blackb 2* **P** *V Blackb* **V** T J HOROBIN **C** A A J COLE
DARWEN, OVER (St James) and Hoddlesden *Blackb 2* **P** *Bp and V Blackb (jt)* **P-in-c** T J HOROBIN, **C** A A J COLE
DATCHET (St Mary the Virgin) *see* Colnbrook and Datchet *Ox*
DATCHWORTH (All Saints) *see* Welwyn *St Alb*
DAUBHILL (St George the Martyr) *see* W Bolton *Man*
DAUNTSEY (St James Great) *see* Woodbridge *Bris*
DAVENHAM (St Wilfrid) *Ches 6* **P** *Bp* **R** R G IVESON **NSM** V G GERAERTS
DAVENTRY (Holy Cross) *Pet 3* **P** *Patr Bd* **TV** M Y GARBUTT, N E FRY, N J WHITE **C** D A STOKES
DAVIDSTOW (St David) *see* Moorland Gp *Truro*
DAVINGTON (St Mary Magdalene) *see* Faversham *Cant*
DAVYHULME (Christ Church) and Urmston *Man 5* **P** *Bp* **OLM** C A BAILEY
DAVYHULME (St Mary) *Man 5* **P** *Bp* **V** C S FORD **C** J M BEAUMONT, S A WRIGHT **OLM** D J BLAIR
DAWLEY (Holy Trinity) *see* Cen Telford *Lich*
DAWLEY (St Jerome) *see* W Hayes *Lon*
DAWLISH (St Gregory) w Holcombe, Cofton and Starcross *Ex 5* **P** *D&C Ex, D&C Sarum, and Earl of Devon (jt)* **R** D J AYLING **C** T P COLLINS **NSM** C V CURD
DAWLISH WARREN (Church Hall) *see* Dawlish w Holcombe, Cofton and Starcross *Ex*
DAYBROOK (St Paul) *S'well 7* **P** *Bp* **V** S A BAYLIS
DAYLESFORD (St Peter) *see* Chipping Norton *Ox*
DE BEAUVOIR TOWN (St Peter) *Lon 5* **P** *Bp* **V** J F PORTER-PRYCE
DEAL (St Andrew) *Cant 9* **P** *Abp* **R** *vacant*
DEAL (St George the Martyr) *Cant 9* **P** *Abp* **V** C G SPENCER **C** S PORTER
DEAL (St Leonard) (St Richard) and Sholden w Great Mongeham *Cant 9* **P** *Abp* **NSM** P T KAVANAGH
DEAN (All Hallows) *see* The Stodden Churches *St Alb*
DEAN (St Oswald) *see* Brigham, Clifton, Dean and Mosser *Carl*
DEAN COURT (St Andrew) *see* Cumnor *Ox*
DEAN FOREST (Christ Church) *see* Forest of Dean Ch Ch w English Bicknor *Glouc*
DEAN FOREST (St Paul) *see* Parkend and Viney Hill *Glouc*
DEAN PRIOR (St George the Martyr) *see* Buckfastleigh, Dean Prior, Littlehempston etc *Ex*
DEANE (All Saints) *see* N Waltham and Steventon, Ashe and Deane *Win*
DEANE (St Mary the Virgin) *Man 9* **P** *Patr Bd* **TR** T P CLARK **TV** V C WHITWORTH **C** B M WILKINSON
DEANE VALE Benefice, The, comprising Heathfield w Cotford St Luke, Hillfarrance, and Oake *B & W 19* **P** *Bp and PCCs Heathfield, Hillfarrance, and Oake (jt)* **R** *vacant*

DEANSHANGER (Holy Trinity) *see* Passenham *Pet*

DEARHAM (St Mungo) *see* Allonby, Cross Canonby and Dearham *Carl*

DEARNLEY (St Andrew), Wardle and Smallbridge *Man 17*
P *Bp* **C** A E GILBERT

DEBDEN (St Mary the Virgin) *see* Saffron Walden and Villages *Chelmsf*

DEBENHAM (St Mary Magdalene) and Helmingham *St E 14*
P *Ld Chan, Lord Henniker, MMCET, Bp, and Lord Tollemache (by turn)* **R** S R BATES

DEDDINGTON (St Peter and St Paul) Barford, Clifton and Hempton *Ox 23* **P** *D&C Windsor and Bp (jt)*
V A L GOLDTHORP **NSM** P SMITH

DEDHAM (St Mary the Virgin) and Ardleigh *Chelmsf 22*
P *Duchy of Lanc, Lectureship Trustees, and Ld Chan (by turn)*
V A C WILSON

DEDWORTH (All Saints) *Ox 5* **P** *Bp* **V** N C RICHARDS

DEEPCAR (St John the Evangelist) *see* Cornerstone *Sheff*

DEEPING ST JAMES (St James) *Linc 19* **P** *Burghley Ho Preservation Trust Ltd* **V** M R WILLIAMS
NSM S M C MARSHALL

DEEPING ST NICHOLAS (St Nicholas) *see* Spalding St Jo w Deeping St Nicholas *Linc*

DEEPING, WEST (St Andrew) *see* Uffington Gp *Linc*

DEEPLISH (St Luke) and Newbold *Man 17* **P** *Bp*
V S P WATKINSON **NSM** R K GRAY

DEERHURST (St Mary) and Apperley w Forthampton, Chaceley, Tredington, Stoke Orchard and Hardwicke *Glouc 9* **P** *Bp, V Longdon, and J S Yorke Esq (jt)*
P-in-c I FERWERDA **C** K MUNDY

DEFFORD (St James) w Besford *Worc 4* **P** *D&C Westmr*
C R C TETT

DEIGHTON (All Saints) *see* Brompton w Deighton *York*

DELABOLE (St John the Evangelist) *see* Camel-Allen *Truro*

DELAMERE (St Peter) *Ches 6* **P** *The Crown* **R** *vacant*

DELAVAL (Our Lady) *Newc 1* **P** *Lord Hastings*
V D E BOWLER **C** K CHARMAN

DEMBLEBY (St Lucia) *see* S Lafford *Linc*

DENABY MAIN (All Saints) *Sheff 7* **P** *Bp* **V** R C DAVIES

DENBURY (St Mary the Virgin) *see* Ipplepen w Torbryan, Denbury, Broadhempston and Woodland *Ex*

DENBY (St John the Evangelist) *see* Cumberworth, Denby, Denby Dale etc *Leeds*

DENBY DALE (Holy Trinity) *as above*

DENBY Group, The (St Mary the Virgin), comprising Codnor, Denby, Horsley, Horsley Woodhouse, and Loscoe *Derby 8* **P** *The Crown (1 turn), Bp (1 turn), Mrs L B Palmer and Bp (1 turn)* **V** A TAYLOR-COOK **OLM** C C HOLDEN, M D JONES

DENCHWORTH (St James) *see* Vale *Ox*

DENDRON (St Matthew) *see* Aldingham, Dendron, Rampside and Urswick *Carl*

DENESIDE (All Saints) *see* Seaham and Dawdon *Dur*

DENFORD (Holy Trinity) *see* Thrapston, Denford and Islip *Pet*

DENGIE (St James) w Asheldham *Chelmsf 11* **P** *Bp*
P-in-c S K POSS

DENHAM (St John the Baptist) *see* Athelington, Denham, Horham, Hoxne etc *St E*

DENHAM (St Mark) (St Mary the Virgin) *Ox 9* **P** *L J Way Esq* **R** C W LINDNER **Hon C** I M JENNINGS
NSM N R MADUKA

DENHAM (St Mary) *see* Barrow *St E*

DENHAM, NEW (St Francis) *see* Denham *Ox*

DENMEAD (All Saints) *Portsm 5* **P** *Ld Chan*
V E J RACKLYEFT **NSM** A C L JOHNSON

DENNINGTON (St Mary) *see* Upper Alde *St E*

DENSHAW (Christ Church) *see* Saddleworth *Man*

DENSTON (St Nicholas) *see* Bansfield *St E*

DENSTONE (All Saints) *see* Alton w Bradley-le-Moors and Denstone etc *Lich*

DENT (St Andrew) w Cowgill *Carl 10* **P** *Bp and Sidesmen of Dent (alt)* **V** *vacant*

DENTON (Christ Church) (St George) *Man 13* **P** *Bp*
P-in-c M HOWARTH **C** P R DIXON **OLM** C MASTERS

DENTON (Holy Spirit) *Newc 4* **P** *Bp* **V** *vacant*

DENTON (St Andrew) *see* Harlaxton Gp *Linc*

DENTON (St Helen) *see* Washburn and Mid-Wharfe *Leeds*

DENTON (St Lawrence) *Man 13* **P** *Earl of Wilton*
P-in-c K J MAMBU **C** M HOWARTH, P R DIXON
OLM S P CANT

DENTON (St Leonard) w South Heighton and Tarring Neville *Chich 21* **P** *MMCET and Bp (alt)* **R** P L WILSON
C J H LOWRIES

DENTON (St Margaret) *see* Yardley Hastings, Denton and Grendon etc *Pet*

DENTON (St Mary Magdalene) *see* Elham w Denton and Wootton and Acrise *Cant*

DENTON (St Mary) *see* Ditchingham, Hedenham, Broome, Earsham etc *Nor*

DENTON HOLME (St James) *Carl 3* **P** *Trustees*
P-in-c S C BICKERSTETH

DENTON, NETHER (St Cuthbert) *see* Lanercost, Walton, Gilsland and Nether Denton *Carl*

DENVER (St Mary) and Ryston w Roxham and Bexwell and Crimplesham *Ely 9* **P** *Bp and G&C Coll Cam (jt)*
R J M T M GRUNDY

DEOPHAM (St Andrew) *see* High Oak, Hingham and Scoulton w Wood Rising *Nor*

DEPDEN (St Mary the Virgin) *see* Chevington w Hargrave, Chedburgh w Depden etc *St E*

DEPTFORD (St John) (Holy Trinity) (Ascension) *S'wark 2*
P *Patr Bd* **TR** P J FARLEY-MOORE **TV** A Y BENNETT
C L MASEKO

DEPTFORD (St Nicholas) (St Luke) *S'wark 2* **P** *MMCET, Peache Trustees, and CPAS (jt)*
V L A J CODRINGTON-MARSHALL

DEPTFORD (St Paul) *S'wark 2* **P** *Bp* **R** P D BUTLER

DEPTFORD Brockley (St Peter) *see* Brockley St Pet *S'wark*

DERBY (St Alkmund) (St Werburgh) *Derby 5* **P** *Simeon's Trustees* **C** A J D BOND, I D MOUNTFORD, J M NEWMAN, P D MANN, S R CURTIS

DERBY (St Andrew w St Osmund) *see* Pride Park, Wilmorton, Allenton and Shelton Lock *Derby*

DERBY (St Anne) *Derby 5* **P** *Bp* **V** *vacant*

DERBY (St Augustine) *see* Walbrook Epiphany *Derby*

DERBY (St Barnabas) *Derby 5* **P** *Bp* **V** D G HONOUR

DERBY (St Bartholomew) (St Luke) *Derby 5* **P** *Bp*
V L T YOUNG

DERBY (St John the Evangelist) *Derby 5* **P** *Bp* **C** E J JONES

DERBY (St Mark) *see* Chaddesden St Phil w Derby St Mark *Derby*

DERBY (St Paul) *Derby 5* **P** *Bp* **V** *vacant*

DERBY (St Peter and Christ Church w Holy Trinity) *Derby 5*
P *CPAS* **V** P D MORRIS **C** A K MATTHEWS

DERBY (St Thomas) *see* Walbrook Epiphany *Derby*

DERBY, WEST (Good Shepherd) *Liv 5* **P** *Bp and R W Derby (jt)* **OLM** S TRAPNELL

DERBY, WEST (St James) (St Mary) *Liv 5* **P** *Bp and Adn Liv (jt)* **V** S W BOYD

DERBY, WEST (St John) *Liv 5* **P** *Trustees* **V** S J P FISHER

DERBY, WEST (St Luke) *see* 4Saints Team *Liv*

DERBYSHIRE HILL (St Philip) *see* Parr *Liv*

DERE STREET, EAST, comprising Barton, Cleasby w Stapleton, Croft, Eryholme, Manfield, and Middleton Tyas w Moulton *Leeds 22* **P** *The Crown (1 turn), Bp, R Forcett and Aldbrough and Melsonby, V Gilling and Kirkby Ravensworth, and D&C Ripon (1 turn)* **R** *vacant*

DEREHAM (St Nicholas) and District *Nor 16* **P** *Ld Chan (2 turns), Patr Bd (1 turn)* **TV** G L WELLS, J R ROSIE
C D E TURNHAM **NSM** K G PILGRIM **OLM** J L NURSEY

DEREHAM, WEST (St Andrew) *see* Wissey Valley *Ely*

DERRINGHAM BANK (Ascension) (St Thomas) *York 14*
P *Abp* **V** S J WHALEY

DERRINGTON (St Matthew) *see* Bradeley, Church Eaton, Derrington and Haughton *Lich*

DERRY HILL (Christ Church) *see* Marden Vale *Sarum*

DERSINGHAM (St Nicholas), Anmer, Ingoldisthorpe and Shernborne *Nor 15* **P** *HM The Queen and Bp (alt)*
R M A CAPRON **C** D J COSSEY

DERWENT INGS, comprising Elvington, Sutton-on-Derwent, Thorganby, and Wheldrake *York 2* **P** *Abp, Lt Col J Darlington, and Lady Caroline Dunnington-Jefferson (jt)*
R I B KITCHEN

DERWENT, UPPER, comprising Borrowdale, Newlands, and Thornthwaite *Carl 6* **P** *V Keswick St Jo (1 turn), V Crosthwaite (2 turns)* **P-in-c** J A ASHURST

DERWENT, UPPER, comprising Brompton-by-Sawdon, Hutton Buscell, Snainton, and Wykeham *York 19*
P *Viscountess Downe (1 turn), Sir Philip Naylor-Leyland Bt (1 turn), Abp (2 turns)* **NSM** P WOOD

DESBOROUGH (St Giles), Brampton Ash, Dingley and Braybrooke *Pet 9* **P** *Bp, Earl Spencer, and DBP (by turn)*
R H M JEFFERY **C** S V COWAN **NSM** N M CLARKE

DESFORD (St Martin) and Kirby Muxloe *Leic 9* **P** *Bp and Ld Chan (alt)* **R** T L RINGLAND **NSM** R C MARSH

DETHICK (St John the Baptist) *see* Matlock, Dethick, Lea and Holloway *Derby*

DETLING (St Martin) *see* N Downs *Cant*

DEVER, LOWER, comprising Barton Stacey, Bullington, and South Wonston *Win 7* **P** *Bp and D&C (jt)* **R** M D BAILEY

DEVER, UPPER, comprising East Stratton, Micheldever, Stoke Charity w Hunton, Wonston, and Woodmancote w Popham *Win 7* **P** *Lord Northbrook (3 turns), Bp (2 turns)* **P-in-c** J A RENNIE
DEVIZES (St John) (St Mary) *Sarum 17* **P** *Ld Chan* **R** P RICHARDSON **C** B O RUNDELL-EVANS **NSM** J M CLARK
DEVIZES (St Peter) *Sarum 17* **P** *Bp* **V** *vacant*
DEVONPORT (St Bartholomew) and Ford St Mark *Ex 21* **P** *Bp and Trustees (jt)* **V** R T SILK
DEVONPORT (St Boniface) *Ex 21* **P** *Bp* **P-in-c** M C DOYLE
DEVONPORT (St Budeaux) *Ex 21* **P** *CPAS* **V** S J BEACH **C** A J PRICE
DEVONPORT (St Michael) (St Barnabas) (St Aubyn) *Ex 21* **P** *Bp* **V** T J BUCKLEY
DEVONPORT (St Thomas) *see* Plymouth St Pet and H Apostles *Ex*
DEVORAN (St John the Evangelist and St Petroc) *Truro 6* **P** *Bp* **P-in-c** S A BONE **C** K E JONES, R D WALLIS **NSM** J ROWE, S J C FLETCHER
DEWCHURCH, LITTLE (St David) *see* S Wye Rural Par *Heref*
DEWCHURCH, MUCH (St David) *see* Wormelow Hundred *Heref*
DEWLISH (All Saints) *see* Puddletown, Tolpuddle and Milborne w Dewlish *Sarum*
DEWSALL (St Michael) *see* Wormelow Hundred *Heref*
DEWSBURY (All Saints) (St Mark) (St Matthew and St John the Baptist) *Leeds 9* **P** *Bp, Adn Pontefract, RD Dewsbury, and Lay Chmn Dewsbury Deanery Syn (jt)* **TR** S A CASH **C** N D WALPOLE **NSM** A B POLLARD, H THURLOW
DEWSBURY MOOR (St John the Evangelist) *see* Dewsbury *Leeds*
DHOON (Christ Church) *see* Maughold and S Ramsey *S & M*
DIBDEN (All Saints) *Win 11* **P** *MMCET* **R** P S STARK TOLLER
DIBDEN PURLIEU (St Andrew) *see* Dibden *Win*
DICKER, UPPER (Holy Trinity) *see* Hellingly and Upper Dicker *Chich*
DICKLEBURGH (All Saints) and The Pulhams *Nor 10* **P** *Ld Chan (1 turn), Patr Bd (2 turns), The Crown (1 turn)* **R** S E WALSH **OLM** D J ADLAM, P D SCHWIER
DIDBROOK (St George) *see* Winchcombe *Glouc*
DIDCOT (All Saints) *Ox 26* **P** *BNC Ox* **P-in-c** A M LORD **C** B M BODEKER, H R BOORMAN
DIDCOT (St Peter) *Ox 26* **P** *Bp* **P-in-c** H C REYNOLDS **OLM** F M CHILDS
DIDCOT Ladygrove *see* Didcot All SS *Ox*
DIDDINGTON (St Laurence) *see* The Paxtons w Diddington and Southoe *Ely*
DIDLINGTON (St Michael) *Nor 13* **P** *CPAS* **V** *vacant*
DIDMARTON (St Lawrence) *see* Boxwell, Leighterton, Didmarton, Oldbury etc *Glouc*
DIDSBURY (St James) (Emmanuel) *Man 6* **P** *Patr Bd* **TR** N J BUNDOCK **TV** L K BATTYE **C** T A MARSHALL **NSM** J A WHITTELL
DIDSBURY, WEST (Christ Church) and Withington St Christopher *Man 6* **P** *Trustees and The Crown (alt)* **R** A PILKINGTON **C** T L STUDMAN
DIGBY GROUP, The (St Thomas of Canterbury), including Ashby-de-la-Launde, Bloxholme, Dorrington, Kirkby Green, Rowston, and Scopwick *Linc 14* **P** *Mrs H E Gillatt, Ld Chan, and DBP (by turn)* **P-in-c** M P D KENNARD **Hon C** D B WOODS
DIGMOOR (Christ the Servant) *see* Upholland *Liv*
DIGSWELL (Christ the King) (St John the Evangelist) *St Alb 18* **P** *SMF* **R** R P MARSHALL **NSM** S A EVANS
DILHAM (St Nicholas) *see* Smallburgh w Dilham w Honing and Crostwight *Nor*
DILHORNE (All Saints) *see* Caverswall and Weston Coyney w Dilhorne *Lich*
DILTON MARSH (Holy Trinity) *see* White Horse *Sarum*
DILTON or LEIGH (Holy Saviour) *as above*
DILWYN AND STRETFORD (St Mary the Virgin) *see* Leominster *Heref*
DINDER (St Michael and All Angels) *see* Pilton w Croscombe, N Wootton and Dinder *B & W*
DINEDOR (St Andrew) *see* S Wye Rural Par *Heref*
DINES GREEN (St Michael) *see* Worc Dines Green St Mich and Crown E, Rushwick *Worc*
DINGLE (St Gabriel) (St Cleopas) *Liv 3* **P** *Simeon's Trustees* **V** S GASSON
DINGLEY (All Saints) *see* Desborough, Brampton Ash, Dingley and Braybrooke *Pet*
DINNINGTON (St Leonard) *Sheff 5* **P** S B V Weston Esq **R** H A JOWETT
DINNINGTON (St Matthew) *see* Ch the King *Newc*
DINNINGTON (St Nicholas) *see* Merriott w Hinton, Dinnington and Lopen *B & W*

DINSDALE (St John the Baptist) w Sockburn *Dur 7* **P** *D&C and Sherburn Hosp (alt)* **P-in-c** A THORP **NSM** H M THORP
DINTING VALE (Holy Trinity) *Derby 4* **P** *Bp* **P-in-c** N P GURNEY
DINTON (St Mary) *see* Nadder Valley *Sarum*
DINTON (St Peter and St Paul) *see* Wychert Vale *Ox*
DIPTFORD (St Mary the Virgin) w North Huish, Ermington, Halwell, Harberton, Harbertonford, Moreleigh and Ugborough *Ex 12* **P** *The Crown (1 turn), Bp, D&C and Grocers' Co (3 turns)* **R** P D SAYLE
DISCOED (St Michael) *see* Presteigne w Discoed, Kinsham, Lingen and Knill *Heref*
DISEWORTH (St Michael and All Angels) *see* Kegworth, Hathern, Long Whatton, Diseworth etc *Leic*
DISHLEY (All Saints) *see* Thorpe Acre w Dishley *Leic*
DISLEY (St Mary the Virgin) *Ches 16* **P** *Lord Newton* **V** A S CORNES
DISS (St Mary) *see* Diss *Nor*
DISS Team Ministry, The (St Mary), including Bressingham, Fersfield, North Lopham, Roydon, and South Lopham *Nor 10* **P** *Patr Bd* **TR** A C BILLETT **TV** J J CRUSE **C** S S THORP
DISTINGTON (Holy Spirit) *see* Harrington and Distington *Carl*
DITCHEAT (St Mary Magdalene) *see* Fosse Trinity *B & W*
DITCHINGHAM (St Mary), Hedenham, Broome, Earsham, Alburgh and Denton *Nor 10* **P** *Abp, Bp, Countess Ferrers, J M Meade Esq, and St Jo Coll Cam (jt)* **R** C HUTTON **OLM** R A KIRKPATRICK, S L CRAMP
DITCHLING (St Margaret), Streat and Westmeston *Chich 8* **P** *Bp* **R** D P WALLIS
DITTERIDGE (St Christopher) *see* Box w Hazlebury and Ditteridge *Bris*
DITTISHAM (St George) *see* Dartmouth and Dittisham *Ex*
DITTON (St Basil and All Saints) *see* Hough Green St Basil and All SS *Liv*
DITTON (St Michael) (St Thomas) *Liv 12* **P** *Bp* **V** L RILEY-DAWKIN **OLM** L MOSS
DITTON (St Peter ad Vincula) *Roch 7* **P** *Ch Trust Fund Trust* **R** J R TERRANOVA
DITTON PRIORS (St John the Baptist) w Neenton, Burwarton, Cleobury North, Aston Botterell, Wheathill and Loughton and Chetton *Heref 8* **P** *Bp, Princess Josephine zu Loewenstein, and Exors Viscount Boyne (jt)* **R** T M MASON
DIXTON NEWTON (St Peter) *see* Wye Reaches Gp *Heref*
DOBCROSS (Holy Trinity) *see* Saddleworth *Man*
DOCCOMBE (Chapel) *see* Moretonhampstead, Manaton, N Bovey and Lustleigh *Ex*
DOCK (Mission Church) *see* Immingham *Linc*
DOCKENFIELD (Church of the Good Shepherd) *see* Frensham *Guildf*
DOCKING (St Mary), The Birchams, Fring, Stanhoe and Sedgeford *Nor 15* **P** *Bp, D&C, and Mrs A J Ralli (3 turns), HM The Queen (1 turn)* **R** P R COOK **NSM** R J M COLLIER
DOCKLOW (St Bartholomew) *see* Leominster *Heref*
DODBROOKE (St Thomas à Beckett) *see* Kingsbridge, Dodbrooke, and W Alvington *Ex*
DODDERHILL (St Augustine) *see* Droitwich Spa *Worc*
DODDINGHURST (All Saints) *Chelmsf 8* **P** *Bp* **P-in-c** A V COLEMAN **NSM** J W BIDDULPH
DODDINGTON (St John the Baptist) *see* Cleobury Mortimer w Hopton Wafers etc *Heref*
DODDINGTON (St John the Baptist) *see* Kingsdown and Creekside *Cant*
DODDINGTON (St John) *see* Wybunbury and Audlem w Doddington *Ches*
DODDINGTON (St Mary and St Michael), Ilderton, Kirknewton and Wooler *Newc 7* **P** *Bp and Duke of Northumberland (1 turn), Ld Chan (1 turn)* **V** S COOKE **NSM** E J DOBSON
DODDINGTON (St Mary) w Benwick and Wimblington *Ely 11* **P** *Bp, St Jo Coll Dur, and R Raynar Esq (jt)* **R** I BRADY
DODDINGTON (St Peter) *see* Skellingthorpe w Doddington *Linc*
DODDINGTON, GREAT (St Nicholas) and Wilby and Ecton *Pet 6* **P** *Ld Chan, Exors Lt Col H C M Stockdale, and The Crown (by turn)* **R** J R BUCK
DODDISCOMBSLEIGH (St Michael) *see* Christow, Ashton, Bridford, Dunchideock etc *Ex*
DODFORD (Holy Trinity and St Mary) *Worc 7* **P** *Bp* **V** D S FORD
DODFORD (St Mary the Virgin) *see* Weedon Bec w Everdon and Dodford *Pet*
DODLESTON (St Mary) *Ches 2* **P** *D&C* **R** E H CLARKE
DODWORTH (St John the Baptist) *see* W Barnsley *Leeds*

DOGMERSFIELD (All Saints) *see* Hartley Wintney, Elvetham, Winchfield etc *Win*

DOGSTHORPE (Christ the Carpenter) *see* Pet Ch Carpenter *Pet*

DOLPHINHOLME (St Mark) w Quernmore and Over Wyresdale *Blackb 11* **P** *Bp and V Lanc (jt)* **V** C J RIGNEY

DOLTON (St Edmund King and Martyr), Dowland, Iddesleigh, and Monkokehampton *Ex 19* **P** *Bp and Ch Soc Trust (jt)* **R** S Y OLDHAM **NSM** A CONNELL, D J URSELL

DONCASTER (Holy Trinity) *see* New Cantley *Sheff*

DONCASTER (St George) *Sheff 8* **P** *Bp* **V** D L STEVENS **C** D J PARKINSON **NSM** S F BEDFORD

DONCASTER (St Hugh of Lincoln) *see* New Cantley *Sheff*

DONCASTER (St James) *Sheff 8* **P** *Hyndman's Trustees* **P-in-c** C J MCCARTHY **NSM** M G PARNELL

DONCASTER (St Jude) *see* Edlington and Hexthorpe *Sheff*

DONCASTER (St Leonard and St Jude) *Sheff 7* **P** *The Crown* **C** D P D'SILVA

DONCASTER (St Mary) (St Paul) *Sheff 8* **P** *Hyndman's Trustees and Bp (jt)* **P-in-c** A R THOMAS **C** A J PRIESTLEY

DONHEAD ST ANDREW (St Andrew) *see* St Bartholomew *Sarum*

DONHEAD ST MARY (St Mary the Virgin) *as above*

DONINGTON (St Cuthbert) *see* Albrighton, Boningale and Donington *Lich*

DONINGTON (St Mary and the Holy Rood) *see* Haven Gp *Linc*

DONINGTON-ON-BAIN (St Andrew) *see* Asterby Gp *Linc*

DONISTHORPE (St John) *see* Woodfield *Leic*

DONNINGTON (St George) *Chich 2* **P** *Bp* **V** J P COOPER

DONNINGTON (St Mary) *see* Redmarley D'Abitot, Bromesberrow, Pauntley etc *Glouc*

DONNINGTON WOOD (St Matthew) *Lich 20* **P** *Bp* **P-in-c** P M SMITH

DONYATT (Blessed Virgin Mary) *see* Isle Valley *B & W*

DONYLAND, EAST (St Lawrence) *see* Fingringhoe w E Donyland and Abberton etc *Chelmsf*

DORCHESTER (St George) (St Mary the Virgin) (St Peter, Holy Trinity and All Saints) and the Winterbournes *Sarum 1* **P** *Ld Chan (1 turn), Patr Bd (4 turns)* **TR** T M B WOODHOUSE **TV** C L MCCLELLAND **NSM** J LACY-SMITH, J M CULLIFORD, J SADDINGTON, T M STEWART-SYKES

DORCHESTER (St Peter and St Paul) *Ox 20* **P** *Patr Bd* **TR** S E BOOYS **TV** C N KING **C** J C ROBERTS **NSM** J P MORTON

DORDON (St Leonard) *Birm 9* **P** *V Polesworth* **V** *vacant*

DORE (Christ Church) *Sheff 2* **P** *Sir Philip Naylor-Leyland Bt* **V** *vacant*

DORKING (St Martin) w Ranmore *Guildf 7* **P** *Bp* **V** D J TIGHE

DORKING (St Paul) *Guildf 7* **P** *Ch Patr Trust* **V** R K F BUSHYAGER **C** A X CACOURIS, P NEVINS **OLM** J A FIRTH

DORMANSLAND (St John) *see* Lingfield and Dormansland *S'wark*

DORMANSTOWN (All Saints) *see* Coatham and Dormanstown *York*

DORMINGTON (St Peter) *see* Bartestree Cross *Heref*

DORMSTON (St Nicholas) *see* Inkberrow w Cookhill and Kington w Dormston *Worc*

DORNEY (St James the Less) *see* Eton w Eton Wick, Boveney and Dorney *Ox*

DORRIDGE (St Philip) *Birm 5* **P** *Bp* **V** T D HILL-BROWN **Hon C** R J HILL-BROWN

DORRINGTON (St Edward) w Leebotwood, Longnor, Stapleton, Smethcote and Woolstaston *Heref 10* **P** *DBP and J J C Coldwell Esq (jt)* **R** L M DALTON

DORRINGTON (St James) *see* Digby Gp *Linc*

DORSINGTON (St Peter) *see* Vale and Cotswold Edge *Glouc*

DORSTONE (St Faith) *see* Cusop w Blakemere, Bredwardine w Brobury etc *Heref*

DORTON (St John the Baptist) *see* Bernwode *Ox*

DOSTHILL (St Paul) *Birm 9* **P** *Bp* **V** J L C SHAW **NSM** M A WATERSTREET

DOTTERY (St Saviour) *see* Eggardon and Colmers *Sarum*

DOUGLAS (St George) (All Saints) *S & M* **P** *Bp* **V** A BROWN **C** A M DI CHIARA **NSM** A R BROWN **OLM** S A FERRIS

DOUGLAS (St Matthew the Apostle) *S & M* **P** *Bp* **V** T H DAVIS

DOUGLAS (St Ninian) *S & M* **P** *CPAS* **V** J P COLDWELL **NSM** J E GUILFORD

DOUGLAS (St-Thomas the Apostle *S & M* **P** *Bp* **V** *vacant*

DOUGLAS-IN-PARBOLD (Christ Church) *see* Appley Bridge and Parbold *Blackb*

DOULTING (St Aldhelm) *see* Shepton Mallet w Doulting *B & W*

DOVE HOLES (St Paul) *see* Fairfield, Peak Forest and Dove Holes *Derby*

DOVECOT (Holy Spirit) *Liv 5* **P** *Bp* **V** *vacant*

DOVER (St Martin) *see* Dover Town *Cant*

DOVER TOWN (St Mary the Virgin) *Cant 7* **P** *Patr Bd* **TR** J A P WALKER **TV** M J CARTER **C** J P DE SOUZA JÚNIOR, S A SHEFFIELD

DOVERCOURT (All Saints) *see* Harwich Peninsula *Chelmsf*

DOVERDALE (St Mary) *see* Elmley Lovett w Hampton Lovett and Elmbridge w Rushock and Hartlebury and Ombersley w Doverdale *Worc*

DOVERIDGE (St Cuthbert) *see* S Dales *Derby*

DOWDESWELL (St Michael) *see* Sevenhampton w Charlton Abbots, Hawling etc *Glouc*

DOWLAND (St Peter) *see* Dolton, Dowland, Iddesleigh etc *Ex*

DOWLES Button Oak (St Andrew) *see* Ribbesford w Bewdley and Dowles and Wribbenhall *Worc*

DOWLISHWAKE (St Andrew) *see* Winsmoor *B & W*

DOWN AMPNEY (All Saints) *see* S Cotswolds *Glouc*

DOWN HATHERLEY (St Mary and Corpus Christi) *see* Twigworth, Down Hatherley, Norton, The Leigh etc *Glouc*

DOWN ST MARY (St Mary the Virgin) *see* N Creedy *Ex*

DOWN, East (St John the Baptist) *see* Shirwell, Loxhore, Kentisbury, Arlington, etc *Ex*

DOWNDERRY (St Nicholas) *see* St Germans w Antony and Sheviock *Truro*

DOWNE (St Mary Magdalene) *see* Cudham and Downe *Roch*

DOWNEND (Christ Church) (Church Centre) *Bris 5* **P** *Peache Trustees* **V** J L VICKERY **C** A P L WATSON, P J PETERSON **Hon C** C J DOBSON

DOWNHAM (St Barnabas) *see* Catford (Southend) and Downham *S'wark*

DOWNHAM (St Leonard) *see* Clitheroe St Mary and St Paul, Chatburn and Downham *Blackb*

DOWNHAM (St Leonard) *see* Ely *Ely*

DOWNHAM (St Luke) *see* Catford (Southend) and Downham *S'wark*

DOWNHAM (St Margaret) w S Hanningfield and Ramsden Bellhouse *Chelmsf 10* **P** *Bp and Reformation Ch Trust (jt)* **NSM** J ANDREWS, M K SEAMAN, S S EDMUNDSON

DOWNHAM MARKET (St Edmund) and Stradsett *Ely 9* **P** *Bp* **R** J W MATHER **NSM** A D DAVIES

DOWNHAM, NORTH (St Mark) *see* Catford (Southend) and Downham *S'wark*

DOWNHEAD (All Saints) *see* Leigh upon Mendip w Stoke St Michael *B & W*

DOWNHOLME (St Michael and All Angels) *see* Richmond w Hudswell and Downholme and Marske *Leeds*

DOWNLEY (St James the Great) *see* High Wycombe *Ox*

DOWNS BARN and NEAT HILL (Community Church) *see* Stantonbury and Willen *Ox*

DOWNS Benefice, The, comprising Chilbolton, Crawley, Littleton, Sparsholt w Lainston, and Wherwell *Win 3* **P** *Ld Chan (1 turn), Bp and Marquess Camden (1 turn)* **R** J J MACHIN

DOWNSIDE (St Michael's Chapel) *see* Ockham w Hatchford and Downside *Guildf*

DOWNSWAY (All Souls Worship Centre) *see* Southwick *Chich*

DOWNTON (St Giles) *see* Wigmore Abbey *Heref*

DOWNTON (St Laurence) *see* Forest and Avon *Sarum*

DOWSBY (St Andrew) *see* Billingborough Gp *Linc*

DOXEY (St Thomas and St Andrew) *see* Stafford St Paul and St Thos *Lich*

DOYNTON (Holy Trinity) *see* Wick w Doynton and Dyrham *Bris*

DRAKES BROUGHTON (St Barnabas) *see* Stoulton w Drake's Broughton and Pirton etc *Worc*

DRAUGHTON (St Augustine) *see* Skipton H Trin *Leeds*

DRAUGHTON (St Catherine) *see* Maidwell w Draughton, Lamport w Faxton *Pet*

DRAX (St Peter and St Paul) *see* Carlton and Drax *York*

DRAYCOT, comprising Christian Malford, Kington Langley and Draycot Cerne, Seagry, Sutton Benger, and Tytherton Kellaways *Bris 6* **P** *Bp, M Neeld Esq, D&C Sarum, and MMCET (jt)* **R** A J LOVE **C** M SIDDALL

DRAYCOTE Group, The, comprising Birdingbury, Bourton, Frankton, and Stretton-on-Dunsmore *Cov 6* **P** *Bp (2 turns), Simeon's Trustees (1 turn), and Mrs J H Shaw-Fox (1 turn)* **R** *vacant*

DRAYCOTT (St Mary) *see* Wilne and Draycott w Breaston *Derby*

DRAYCOTT (St Peter) *see* Cheddar, Draycott and Rodney Stoke *B & W*

DRAYCOTT IN THE CLAY (St Augustine) *see* Hanbury, Newborough and Rangemoor *Lich*

DRAYCOTT-LE-MOORS (St Margaret) w Forsbrook *Lich 6*
P *Bp*   **R** J P H ROBERTS   **C** S T CROSSLEY
DRAYTON (St Catherine)   *see Levels Arc B & W*
DRAYTON (St Margaret) *Nor 2*   **P** *Bp*   **P-in-c** M R PALMER
DRAYTON (St Peter)   *see DAMASCUS Ox*
DRAYTON (St Peter) Banbury   *see Ironstone Ox*
DRAYTON BASSETT (St Peter)   *see Peel Parishes Lich*
DRAYTON IN HALES (St Mary) *Lich 17*   **P** C C Corbet Esq
V C S MCBRIDE   **NSM** N I MACFARLANE
DRAYTON PARSLOW (Holy Trinity)   *see Newton Longville,
Mursley, Swanbourne etc Ox*
DRAYTON ST LEONARD (St Leonard and St Catherine)   *see
Dorchester Ox*
DRAYTON, EAST (St Peter)   *see Retford Area S'well*
DRAYTON, LITTLE (Christ Church) *Lich 17*   **P** V Drayton in
Hales   **P-in-c** J A MORRIS
DRAYTON, WEST (St Martin) *Lon 24*   **P** *Bp*   **V** R J BARRIE
DRAYTON, WEST (St Paul)   *see Retford Area S'well*
DRAYTON-BEAUCHAMP (St Mary the Virgin)   *see Aston
Clinton w Buckland and Drayton Beauchamp Ox*
DRESDEN (Resurrection)   *see Blurton and Dresden Lich*
DREWSTEIGNTON (Holy Trinity)   *see Chagford, Gidleigh,
Throwleigh etc Ex*
DRIFFIELD (St Mary)   *see S Cotswolds Glouc*
DRIFFIELD, GREAT (All Saints) and LITTLE (St Peter) *York 10*
P *Abp*   **V** S P GRANT
DRIGG (St Peter)   *see Black Combe, Drigg, Eskdale etc Carl*
DRIGHLINGTON (St Paul) and Gildersome *Leeds 14*   **P** *Bp*
and V Batley (jt)   **V** P G WALKER   **NSM** B DUXBURY
DRIMPTON (St Mary)   *see Beaminster Area Sarum*
DRINGHOUSES (St Edward the Confessor) *York 7*   **P** *Abp*
V R C CAREW   **C** R B GIBBONS
DRINKSTONE (All Saints)   *see Woolpit w Drinkstone St E*
**DROITWICH SPA (St Andrew w St Mary de Witton)
(St Nicholas) (St Peter) (St Richard)** *Worc 8*   **P** *Bp*
P-in-c L J HANDY
DRONFIELD (St John the Baptist) w Holmesfield   *Derby 3*
P Ld Chan   **TR** P E BOLD   **TV** P D MELLARS   **C** J T BIRD
NSM C G BAKER, D J WALKER, I A PRICE
DROPMORE (St Anne)   *see Taplow and Dropmore Ox*
DROXFORD (St Mary and All Saints)   *see Meon Bridge Portsm*
DROYLSDEN (St Andrew) (St Martin) *Man 13*   **P** *Bp*
R J H FARNWORTH   **C** E C ROWLES
DROYLSDEN (St Mary) (St John) *Man 13*   **P** *Bp*
R A M BAILIE   **OLM** N ALEXANDER, S BALL
DRY DODDINGTON (St James)   *see Claypole Linc*
DRY DRAYTON (St Peter and St Paul)   *see Lordsbridge Ely*
DRY SANDFORD (St Helen) *Ox 19*   **P** Ox Churches Trust
V vacant
DRYBROOK (Holy Trinity), Lydbrook and Ruardean *Glouc 1*
P The Crown and Bp (alt)   **R** D C EDWARDS
DRYPOOL (St Columba) (St John) *York 14*   **P** Patr Bd
TR D L GRIFFITH-JONES   **TV** M J WESTBY
DUCKLINGTON (St Bartholomew) *Ox 28*   **P** DBP
R P N BODDAM-WHETHAM
DUCKMANTON (St Peter and St Paul)   *see Calow and Sutton
cum Duckmanton Derby*
DUDDENHOE END (The Hamlet Church)   *see Icknield Way
Villages Chelmsf*
DUDDESTON (St Matthew)   *see Aston and Nechells Birm*
DUDDINGTON (St Mary)   *see Barrowden and Wakerley w S
Luffenham etc Pet*
DUDDON (St Peter)   *see Tarvin Ches*
DUDLESTON (St Mary)   *see Criftins w Dudleston and Welsh
Frankton Lich*
DUDLEY (St Andrew)   *see Darby End and Netherton Worc*
**DUDLEY (St Augustine) (St Barnabas) (St Francis)
(St James) (St Thomas and St Luke)** *Worc 9*   **P** Patr Bd
TR H A BURTON   **TV** R L AKERS   **C** J TREASURE, S R BARDELL
DUDLEY (St John) Kate's Hill *Worc 9*   **P** *Bp*   **V** vacant
DUDLEY (St Paul)   *see Weetslade Newc*
DUDLEY WOOD (St John) and Cradley Heath *Worc 9*   **P** The
Crown and V Darby End and Netherton (alt)   **V** A M BAKER
C C O ENWEREM
DUFFIELD (St Alkmund) and Little Eaton *Derby 6*   **P** Patr Bd
V J T HUGHES   **C** D E BARNSLEY
DUFTON (St Cuthbert)   *see Heart of Eden Carl*
DUKINFIELD (St John) (St Alban Mission Church) *Ches 14*
P R Stockport St Mary   **V** T J HAYES   **C** C W VINEY
DUKINFIELD (St Luke) *Ches 14*   **P** *Bp*   **V** vacant
DUKINFIELD (St Mark) *Ches 14*   **P** *Bp*   **V** K A WILLIAMS
NSM J M DUNLOP
DULLINGHAM (St Mary)   *see Raddesley Gp Ely*
DULOE (St Cuby) and Herodsfoot *Truro 12*   **P** Ch Soc Trust
and Ball Coll Ox (jt)   **P-in-c** M JONES

**DULVERTON (All Saints) w Brushford, Brompton Regis,
Upton and Skilgate** *B & W 15*   **P** *Bp, D&C, Em Coll Cam,
and Keble Coll Ox (jt)*   **R** A N THOMAS   **NSM** P A KINGDOM,
R M V COLLETT
DULWICH (St Barnabas) *S'wark 9*   **P** *Bp*   **V** J C WATSON
C E A BARNETT   **NSM** E A LANDER, T BUCKLER
DULWICH (St Clement) St Peter *S'wark 9*   **P** *Bp*
P-in-c C SCHNYDER
DULWICH, EAST (St John the Evangelist) *S'wark 9*   **P** Ripon
Coll Cuddesdon   **V** G O'NEILL   **C** R J G BAUDON
OLM A CLARKE
DULWICH, NORTH (St Faith) *S'wark 9*   **P** *Bp*   **V** S J HEIGHT
DULWICH, SOUTH (St Stephen) *S'wark 9*   **P** Dulwich Coll
V B G SCHÜNEMANN   **C** T L REED
DULWICH, WEST (All Saints) *S'wark 12*   **P** *Bp*
V A N EVERETT   **C** G C DAVIES   **Hon C** C WILES
DULWICH, WEST (Emmanuel) *S'wark 12*   **P** *Bp*
V K G A ANSAH
DUMBLETON (St Peter)   *see Winchcombe Glouc*
DUMMER (All Saints)   *see Farleigh, Candover and Wield Win*
DUNCHIDEOCK (St Michael and All Angels)   *see Christow,
Ashton, Bridford, Dunchideock etc Ex*
DUNCHURCH (St Peter) *Cov 6*   **P** *Bp*   **V** P O TOWNSHEND
DUNCTON (Holy Trinity) *Chich 10*   **P** Lord Egremont
P-in-c D L SMITH
DUNDRY (St Michael)   *see Chew Magna w Dundry, Norton
Malreward etc B & W*
DUNHAM MASSEY (St Margaret) (St Mark) (All Saints)
Ches 10   **P** J G Turnbull Esq   **V** J J E SUTTON
NSM A G RUSTED
DUNHAM, GREAT (St Andrew)   *see Launditch and the Upper
Nar Nor*
DUNHAM, LITTLE (St Margaret) *as above*
DUNHAM-ON-THE-HILL (St Luke)   *see Helsby and
Dunham-on-the-Hill Ches*
DUNHOLME (St Chad)   *see Welton and Dunholme w
Scothern Linc*
DUNKERTON (All Saints)   *see Timsbury w Priston, Camerton
and Dunkerton B & W*
DUNKESWELL ABBEY (Holy Trinity)   *see Broadhembury,
Dunkeswell, Luppitt, Plymtree, Sheldon, and Upottery Ex*
DUNKESWELL AND DUNKESWELL ABBEY (St Nicholas) *as
above*
DUNMOW, GREAT (St Mary the Virgin) and Barnston
Chelmsf 18   **P** Ld Chan (2 turns), CPAS (1 turn)
C L J WILLIAMS
DUNMOW, LITTLE (St Mary the Virgin)   *see Felsted and Lt
Dunmow Chelmsf*
DUNNINGTON (not known)   *see Heart of England Cov*
DUNNINGTON (St Nicholas)   *see Beeford w Frodingham and
Foston York*
DUNNINGTON (St Nicholas)   *see Rural E York York*
DUNS TEW (St Mary Magdalene)   *see Westcote Barton w
Steeple Barton, Duns Tew etc Ox*
DUNSBY (All Saints)   *see Ringstone in Aveland Gp Linc*
DUNSCROFT (St Edwin) *Sheff 10*   **P** *Bp*   **V** vacant
DUNSDEN (All Saints)   *see Shiplake w Dunsden and
Harpsden Ox*
DUNSFOLD (St Mary and All Saints) and Hascombe
Guildf 2   **P** *Bp* and SMF (jt)   **R** vacant
DUNSFORD (St Mary)   *see Christow, Ashton, Bridford,
Dunchideock etc Ex*
DUNSFORTH (St Mary)   *see Aldborough w Boroughbridge
and Roecliffe Leeds*
DUNSMORE (Chapel of the Resurrection)   *see Ellesborough,
The Kimbles and Stoke Mandeville Ox*
DUNSOP BRIDGE (St George)   *see Slaidburn w Tosside Leeds*
**DUNSTABLE (St Augustine of Canterbury) (St Fremund
the Martyr) (St Peter)** *St Alb 11*   **P** *Bp*   **TR** R S PHILLIPS
TV R R TURNER, T A DAVIS
DUNSTALL (St Mary)   *see Barton under Needwood w
Dunstall and Tatenhill Lich*
**DUNSTER (St George), Carhampton, Withycombe w
Rodhuish, Timberscombe and Wootton Courtenay**
B & W 15   **P** *Bp*   **R** C S RALPH   **Hon C** M J JACKSON
DUNSTON (Church House)   *see Newbold w Dunston Derby*
DUNSTON (St Leonard)   *see Penkridge Lich*
DUNSTON (St Nicholas) w (Christ Church) *Dur 12*   **P** *Bp*
V D ATKINSON
DUNSTON (St Peter)   *see Metheringham w Blankney and
Dunston Linc*
DUNSTON (St Remigius)   *see Stoke H Cross w Dunston,
Arminghall etc Nor*
DUNSWELL (St Faith's Mission Church)   *see Hull St Jo
Newland York*

DUNTERTON (All Saints)   *see* Milton Abbot, Dunterton, Lamerton etc *Ex*

DUNTISBOURNE ABBOTS (St Peter)   *see* Brimpsfield w Birdlip, Syde, Daglingworth etc *Glouc*

DUNTISBOURNE ROUS (St Michael and All Angels) *as above*

DUNTON (St Martin)   *see* Schorne *Ox*

DUNTON (St Mary Magdalene) w Wrestlingworth and Eyeworth *St Alb* 10   **P** *Ld Chan and DBP (alt)*   **R** *vacant*

DUNTON BASSETT (All Saints)   *see* Upper Soar *Leic*

DUNWICH (St James)   *see* Yoxmere *St E*

DURHAM (All Saints)   *see* Dur N *Dur*

DURHAM (St Giles) *Dur* 1   **P** *D&C*   **P-in-c** T E GLOVER
NSM R A M THOMAS, R S BRIGGS

DURHAM (St Margaret of Antioch) and Neville's Cross St John *Dur* 1   **P** *D&C*   **R** B T HUISH   **NSM** J HIRST, N C CHATER

DURHAM (St Nicholas) *Dur* 1   **P** *CPAS*   **V** A ARORA
C C S ELWOOD   **NSM** M C M SHERLOCK

DURHAM (St Oswald King and Martyr) and Shincliffe
Dur 1   **P** *D&C*   **P-in-c** P Z KASHOURIS

DURHAM NORTH (St Cuthbert) *Dur* 1   **P** *Patr Bd*
TR C A DICK   **TV** F M COLLIN

DURLEIGH (St Hugh)   *see* Bridgwater H Trin and Durleigh *B & W*

DURLEY (Holy Cross) *Portsm* 1   **P** *Ld Chan*   **R** G R MENSINGH

DURNFORD (St Andrew)   *see* Woodford Valley w Archers Gate *Sarum*

DURRINGTON (All Saints)   *see* Avon River *Sarum*

DURRINGTON (St Symphorian) *Chich* 4   **P** *Bp*
V B M EADON   **C** I H EDGAR

DURSLEY (St James the Great), Uley, Owlpen and Nympsfield (The Ewelme Benefice) *Glouc* 5   **P** *Ld Chan and Bp (alt)*   **R** M G COZENS   **NSM** I N GARDNER, J L WOOD

DURSTON (St John the Baptist)   *see* Alfred Jewel *B & W*

DURWESTON (St Nicholas)   *see* Pimperne, Stourpaine, Durweston and Bryanston *Sarum*

DUSTON (St Francis) (St Luke) and Upton *Pet* 4   **P** *Bp*
TR A J MARRIOTT   **TV** R J KELLOW   **C** L J HOLLAND

DUXFORD (St Peter) w St John *Ely* 5   **P** *Bp*
P-in-c P J SHAKESHAFT   **NSM** P M SHARKEY

DYMCHURCH (St Peter and St Paul)   *see* Romney Marsh *Cant*

DYMOCK (St Mary the Virgin)   *see* Redmarley D'Abitot, Bromesberrow, Pauntley etc *Glouc*

DYRHAM (St Peter)   *see* Wick w Doynton and Dyrham *Bris*

EAGLE (All Saints)   *see* Swinderby *Linc*

EAKRING (St Andrew) *S'well* 3   **P** *DBP*   **P-in-c** Z BURTON
C A K ALLS   **NSM** M A GROVES

EALING (All Saints) *Lon* 22   **P** *Bp*   **V** R E MARSZALEK

EALING (Ascension)   *see* Hanger Hill Ascension and W Twyford St Mary *Lon*

EALING (Christ the Saviour) *Lon* 22   **P** *Bp*   **V** R A COLLINS

EALING (St Barnabas) *Lon* 22   **P** *Bp*   **V** J D C DODD
NSM J V SCOTT

EALING (St Mary) *Lon* 22   **P** *Bp*   **V** S D PAYNTER
NSM A VOLOSSEVICH, W M CHOW

EALING (St Paul) *Lon* 22   **P** *Bp*   **V** M P MELLUISH
C B M STRAIN, C FOX, S P PLUMB   **NSM** C S BURRELL

EALING (St Peter) Mount Park *Lon* 22   **P** *Bp*   **V** D E NENO
C A A DOBRZYNSKI   **NSM** J O A CHOUFAR

EALING (St Stephen) Castle Hill *Lon* 22   **P** *D&C St Paul's*
V S M NEWBOLD   **C** S SANYA   **Hon C** C S NEWBOLD

EALING COMMON (St Matthew) *Lon* 22   **P** *Bp*
V M C C BARTER

EARBY (All Saints) w Kelbrook *Leeds* 24   **P** *Bp*   **V** H FIELDEN

EARDISLAND (St Mary the Virgin)   *see* Kingsland w Eardisland, Aymestrey etc *Heref*

EARDISLEY (St Mary Magdalene) w Bollingham, Willersley, Brilley, Michaelchurch, Whitney, Winforton, Almeley and Kinnersley *Heref* 4   **P** *Patr Bd*   **R** M J SMALL
NSM G A WILKINSON, R O MULLIS

EARL SHILTON (St Simon and St Jude) w Elmesthorpe
Leic 10   **P** *Bp*   **P-in-c** M R CASTLE

EARL SOHAM (St Mary)   *see* Mid Loes *St E*

EARL STERNDALE (St Michael and All Angels)   *see* Taddington, Chelmorton and Monyash etc *Derby*

EARL STONHAM (St Mary)   *see* N Bosmere *St E*

EARLESTOWN (St John the Baptist)   *see* Newton *Liv*

EARLEY (St Bartholomew)   *see* Reading St Luke w St Bart *Ox*

EARLEY (St Nicolas) *Ox* 7   **P** *DBP*   **NSM** E M NEWMAN

EARLEY (St Peter) *Ox* 7   **P** *DBP*   **V** P P HOBDAY
C H E HOBDAY, P H PRICE

EARLEY (Trinity Church) *Ox* 7   **P** *DBP*   **V** J SALMON

EARLHAM (St Anne) (St Elizabeth) (St Mary) *Nor* 3   **P** *Bp and Trustees (jt)*   **R** D M ROWLANDSON   **C** I H DYBLE
NSM T J WATTS   **OLM** D DORAN-SMITH

EARLS BARTON (All Saints) *Pet* 6   **P** *DBP*   **V** J R INGRAM

EARLS COLNE (St Andrew)   *see* Halstead Area *Chelmsf*

EARL'S COURT (St Cuthbert) (St Matthias) *Lon* 8
P *Trustees*   **P-in-c** P A BAGOTT

EARL'S COURT ROAD (St Philip) *Lon* 12   **P** *Bp*
V P A TURNER   **NSM** L A PERRY, M F A AYO

EARLS CROOME (St Nicholas)   *see* Upton-on-Severn, Ripple, Earls Croome etc *Worc*

EARL'S HEATON   *see* Dewsbury *Leeds*

EARLSDON (St Barbara) *Cov* 3   **P** *Bp*   **V** T D RAISTRICK

EARLSFIELD (St Andrew) *S'wark* 18   **P** *Bp*   **V** J BROWN
NSM J P B SERTIN

EARLSFIELD (St John the Divine) *S'wark* 18   **P** *Bp*
P-in-c I S TATTUM

EARNLEY (not known) and East Wittering *Chich* 2   **P** *Bp (2 turns), Bp Lon (1 turn)*   **R** S J DAVIES

EARNSHAW BRIDGE (St John)   *see* Leyland St Jo *Blackb*

EARSDON (St Alban) and Backworth *Newc* 5   **P** *Bp*
V T J E MAYFIELD

EARSHAM (All Saints)   *see* Ditchingham, Hedenham, Broome, Earsham etc *Nor*

EARSWICK, NEW (St Andrew)   *see* Huntington *York*

EARTHAM (St Margaret)   *see* Slindon, Eartham and Madehurst *Chich*

EASBY (St Agatha) w Skeeby and Brompton on Swale and Bolton on Swale *Leeds* 22   **P** *Bp*   **V** Y S CALLAGHAN

EASEBOURNE (St Mary), Lodsworth and Selham *Chich* 9
P *Bp*   **V** D B WELSMAN   **NSM** A M HALLIWELL

EASINGTON (All Saints) w Liverton *York* 16   **P** *Ld Chan*
P-in-c A D WALKER

EASINGTON (All Saints) w Skeffling, Keyingham, Ottringham, Patrington, Welwick and Winestead *York* 12
P *Abp and CPAS (1 turn), Ld Chan (1 turn)*   **Hon C** J A SHARP, P W WEST

EASINGTON (St Hugh)   *see* Banbury St Hugh *Ox*

EASINGTON (St Mary) and Easington Colliery *Dur* 2   **P** *Bp*
C L M MOSS

EASINGTON (St Peter)   *see* Benson w Ewelme *Ox*

EASINGTON COLLIERY (The Ascension)   *see* Easington and Easington Colliery *Dur*

EASINGWOLD (St John the Baptist and All Saints) w Raskelf *York* 3   **P** *Abp*   **V** M E YOUNG   **C** D M COYNE, E C HASSALL, M H WAINWRIGHT, M HARRISON, S WHITING
NSM C C CRANFIELD, C C GITTENS, C J TOASE, S P POPE, T M GANT

EAST   *see also under substantive place name*

EAST DEAN (All Saints), Singleton, and West Dean *Chich* 3
P *Bp (2 turns), D&C (1 turn)*   **R** *vacant*

EAST DEAN (St Simon and St Jude) w Friston and Jevington *Chich* 14   **P** *Duke of Devonshire (1 turn), D&C (2 turns)*   **R** D A BAKER   **Hon C** A J M SPEAR

EAST DEAN (St Winifred)   *see* Lockerley and E Dean w E and W Tytherley *Win*

EAST DOWNLAND, comprising Beedon, Boxford, Chieveley w Winterbourne and Oare, Farnborough, Peasemore, Stockcross, and West Ilsley *Ox* 6   **P** *Bp and Adn (jt)*
R J P TOOGOOD   **C** W MCDOWELL   **NSM** D J DALES

EAST HAM (St George and St Ethelbert) *Chelmsf* 5   **P** *Bp*
V D T HAOKIP

EAST HAM (St Paul) *Chelmsf* 5   **P** *Ch Patr Trust*
V M L PLAYLE   **C** O E CHIKE

EAST HAM Holy Trinity (St Mary Magdalene) (St Bartholomew) (St Alban) (St Edmund King and Martyr) *Chelmsf* 5   **P** *Patr Bd*   **TR** S J LUCAS
TV Q B D PEPPIATT   **C** M G FILIPE LOPES   **NSM** A R EASTER, F ASHFORD-OKAI   **OLM** J R KING

EAST LANE (St Mary)   *see* W Horsley *Guildf*

EAST MARSHLAND, comprising Terrington St John, Tilney All Saints, Tilney St Lawrence, Wiggenhall St Germans w St Mary the Virgin, and Wiggenhall St Mary Magdalene *Ely* 14   **P** *Bp and MMCET (1 turn), Pemb Coll Cam (2 turns, The Crown (1 turn), and Ld Chan (1 turn)*   **V** M N DALE

EAST TRENT Group of Parishes, The, comprising Collingham, Harby w Swinethorpe, Holme, Langford, North and South Clifton, South Scarle w Besthorpe, Girton and Spalford, Thorney w Wigsley, and Winthorpe *S'well* 3   **P** *Bp, Ld Chan, D&C Pet, and Keble Coll Ox (by turn)*
V A J CARTWRIGHT

EAST VALE AND AVON VILLAGES, comprising Badsey w Aldington, Bretforton, Cleeve Prior, North and Middle Littleton, Offenham, and South Littleton *Worc* 1   **P** *Patr Bd*
V P J MORTON   **C** T HUPFIELD

EAST WINCH (All Saints)   *see* Middlewinch *Nor*

EASTBOURNE (All Saints) *Chich 14* **P** *Trustees*
V W R LOVATT **C** J P HAINES
EASTBOURNE (All Souls) *Chich 14* **P** *Ch Soc Trust*
V M D REDHOUSE **C** S N C CARTER
EASTBOURNE (Christ Church) (St Philip) *Chich 14* **P** *Bp and V Eastbourne (jt)* **V** D G CHARLES
EASTBOURNE (Holy Trinity) *Chich 14* **P** *V Eastbourne*
V P J COEKIN **C** J B P BROOK
EASTBOURNE (St Andrew) *Chich 14* **P** *Bp* **V** D J KING
C J S L UNDERHILL
EASTBOURNE (St Elisabeth) *Chich 14* **P** *Bp* **V** D J GILLARD
EASTBOURNE (St John) Meads *Chich 14* **P** *Trustees*
V G M G CARPENTER **C** B L SLEEP **NSM** J A PREECE
EASTBOURNE (St Mary) *Chich 14* **P** *Bp* **V** T O MENDEL
EASTBOURNE (St Michael and All Angels) Ocklynge
Chich 14 **P** *V Eastbourne* **P-in-c** D S G WEAVER
EASTBOURNE (St Saviour and St Peter) *Chich 14* **P** *Keble Coll Ox* **V** M J S MCAULAY **C** T P V CROWLEY
EASTBURY (St James the Great) *see* Lambourn Valley *Ox*
EASTCHURCH (All Saints) w Leysdown and Harty *Cant 15*
P *Abp and Keble Coll Ox (jt)* **P-in-c** T FOREMAN
EASTCOMBE (St Augustine) *see* Bisley, Chalford, France Lynch, and Oakridge etc *Glouc*
EASTCOTE (St Lawrence) *Lon 24* **P** *Bp* **V** C B RANKINE
NSM J M BEVIS-KNOWLES
EASTER, HIGH (St Mary the Virgin) and Good Easter w Margaret Roding *Chelmsf 18* **P** *Bp Lon, Mrs H Shepherd, and D&C St Paul's (by turn)* **R** *vacant*
EASTERGATE (St George) *see* Aldingbourne, Barnham and Eastergate *Chich*
EASTERN GREEN (St Andrew) *Cov 3* **P** *R Allesley*
P-in-c G P SMITH **C** P D RICHARDSON
EASTERTON (St Barnabas) *see* The Lavingtons, Cheverells, and Easterton *Sarum*
EASTFIELD (Holy Nativity) *York 15* **P** *Abp* **V** S TAYLOR
C J C PARKER
EASTGATE (All Saints) *see* Upper Weardale *Dur*
EASTHAM (St Mary the Blessed Virgin) (St Peter's Chapel) (Chapel of the Holy Spirit) *Ches 9* **P** *D&C* **V** E A GLOVER
NSM M R J TURNER
EASTHAM (St Peter and St Paul) *see* Teme Valley S *Worc*
EASTHAMPSTEAD (St Michael and St Mary Magdalene)
Ox 3 **P** *Ch Ch Ox* **R** G S COLE **C** E L DAVIS
EASTHOPE (St Peter) *see* Wenlock *Heref*
EASTHORPE (St Mary the Virgin) *see* Thurstable and Winstree *Chelmsf*
EASTINGTON (St Michael and All Angels) *see* Stroudwater Team *Glouc*
EASTLEACH (St Andrew) *see* S Cotswolds *Glouc*
EASTLEIGH (All Saints) *Win 10* **P** *Bp* **V** I P FLETCHER
EASTLEIGH Nightingale Avenue (St Francis) *see* Eastleigh *Win*
EASTLING (St Mary) *see* High Downs *Cant*
EASTMOORS (St Mary Magdalene) *see* Helmsley *York*
EASTNEY (St Margaret) *see* Southsea *Portsm*
EASTNOR (St John the Baptist) *see* Ledbury w Eastnor *Heref*
EASTOFT (St Bartholomew) *see* The Marshland *Sheff*
EASTOKE (St Andrew) *see* Hayling Is St Andr *Portsm*
EASTON (All Hallows) *Bris 3* **P** *Guild of All So*
V J C MUTEMWAKWENDA
EASTON (All Saints) *see* Orebeck *St E*
EASTON (Holy Trinity w St Gabriel and St Lawrence and St Jude) *Bris 3* **P** *Trustees* **P-in-c** D J P MOORE
EASTON (St Mary) *see* Itchen Valley *Win*
EASTON (St Paul) *see* Westbury sub Mendip w Easton *B & W*
EASTON (St Peter) *see* S Leightonstone *Ely*
EASTON (St Peter), Colton, Marlingford and Bawburgh
Nor 14 **P** *Bp, D&C, Adn, and Sir Edward Evans-Lombe (jt)*
V L A MONTGOMERY **NSM** P J GOODMAN
EASTON GREY (not known) *see* Gauzebrook *Bris*
EASTON IN GORDANO (St George) *see* Pill, Portbury and Easton-in-Gordano *B & W*
EASTON MAUDIT (St Peter and St Paul) *see* Wollaston w Strixton and Bozeat etc *Pet*
EASTON NESTON (St Mary) *see* Towcester w Caldecote and Easton Neston etc *Pet*
EASTON ON THE HILL (All Saints) *see* King's Cliffe, Bulwick and Blatherwycke, Collyweston etc *Pet*
EASTON ROYAL (Holy Trinity) *see* Vale of Pewsey *Sarum*
EASTON, GREAT (St Andrew) *see* Six Saints circa Holt *Leic*
EASTON, GREAT (St John and St Giles) *see* Broxted w Chickney and Tilty etc *Chelmsf*
EASTON, LITTLE (St Mary the Virgin) *as above*
EASTRINGTON (St Michael) *see* Howden *York*
EASTROP (St Mary) *Win 4* **P** *CPAS* **R** C L HAWKINS
C R G PHILLIPS **NSM** C E WEST

EASTRY (St Mary Blessed Virgin) and Woodnesborough
Cant 9 **P** *Abp and Lord Northbourne (jt)* **R** D G RIDLEY
C E A MARSH **NSM** L A HARDY, R STEVENSON
EASTTHORPE (St Paul) *see* Mirfield *Leeds*
EASTVILLE (St Anne w St Mark and St Thomas) *Bris 3* **P** *Bp*
V *vacant*
EASTWELL (St Michael) *see* Ironstone Villages *Leic*
EASTWICK (St Botolph) *see* High Wych and Gilston w Eastwick *St Alb*
EASTWOOD (St David) *Chelmsf 13* **P** *Bp* **V** P D JOYCE
EASTWOOD (St Laurence and All Saints) *Chelmsf 13* **P** *Ld Chan* **V** *vacant*
EASTWOOD (St Mary) *S'well 4* **P** *J N Plumptre Esq*
P-in-c D A STEVENSON
EATON (All Saints) *see* Retford Area *S'well*
EATON (Christ Church) *Nor 3* **P** *D&C* **V** P H RICHMOND
NSM S TOMLINSON
EATON (Christ Church) *see* Marton, Siddington w Capesthorne etc *Ches*
EATON (St Andrew) *Nor 3* **P** *D&C* **V** P R RODD
EATON (St Denys) *see* Ironstone Villages *Leic*
EATON (St Thomas) *see* Tarporley *Ches*
EATON BISHOP (St Michael and All Angels) *see* Cagebrook *Heref*
EATON BRAY (St Mary the Virgin) w Edlesborough
St Alb 11 **P** *DBP* **V** J E COUSANS **NSM** S R BURGE
EATON HASTINGS (St Michael and All Angels) *see* Gt Coxwell w Buscot, Coleshill etc *Ox*
EATON SOCON (St Mary) *St Alb 10* **P** *E W Harper Esq*
V T S ROBB **C** K E FRANKS
EATON, LITTLE (St Paul) *see* Duffield and Lt Eaton *Derby*
EATON-UNDER-HEYWOOD (St Edith) *see* Apedale Gp *Heref*
EBBERSTON (St Mary) *see* Thornton Dale w Allerston, Ebberston etc *York*
EBBESBOURNE WAKE (St John the Baptist) *see* Chalke Valley *Sarum*
EBCHESTER (St Ebba) *Dur 4* **P** *Bp* **NSM** I W WAUGH
EBERNOE (Holy Trinity) *see* N Chapel w Ebernoe *Chich*
EBONY (St Mary the Virgin) *see* Tenterden, Rother and Oxney *Cant*
EBRINGTON (St Eadburgha) *see* Vale and Cotswold Edge *Glouc*
ECCHINSWELL (St Lawrence) *see* Burghclere w Newtown and Ecchinswell w Sydmonton *Win*
ECCLES (St Mary the Virgin) *see* Quidenham Gp *Nor*
ECCLES (St Mary the Virgin) (St Andrew) *Man 18* **P** *Patr Bd and Ld Chan (alt)* **TR** A R GARNER **OLM** J J LEWIS
ECCLESALL (St Gabriel) *see* Greystones *Sheff*
ECCLESALL BIERLOW (All Saints) *Sheff 2* **P** *Dean*
C A P STEVENSON, D C CHRISTIAN, E G KEITH
ECCLESFIELD (St Mary the Virgin) *Sheff 3* **P** *DBF*
V T C GILL
ECCLESHALL (Holy Trinity) *Lich 7* **P** *Bp* **V** J L WALKER
ECCLESHILL (St Luke) *Leeds 3* **P** *V Bradf* **V** J P HARTLEY
ECCLESTON (Christ Church) *see* Eccleston Team *Liv*
ECCLESTON (St Luke) *as above*
ECCLESTON (St Mary the Virgin) and Charnock Richard Christ Church *Blackb 4* **P** *DBP* **R** A J BROWN
ECCLESTON (St Mary the Virgin) and Pulford *Ches 2*
P *Duke of Westmr* **R** R D CLARKE
ECCLESTON (St Thomas) *see* St Helens Town Cen *Liv*
ECCLESTON PARK (St James) *see* Eccleston Team *Liv*
ECCLESTON Team, The (Christ Church) (St Luke) (St James), including Ravenshead and Thatto Heath *Liv 10*
P *Patr Bd* **TR** H T COFFEY **TV** D C MONEME, S J DORAGH
NSM A G FATH
ECCLESTON, GREAT *see* Copp w Inskip *Blackb*
ECKINGTON (Holy Trinity) *Worc 4* **P** *D&C Westmr*
V A C DAVIES **C** R C TETT
ECKINGTON (St Peter and St Paul) and Ridgeway *Derby 3*
P *The Crown and Patr Bd (alt)* **R** A D WALKER
ECKINGTON, UPPER (St Luke) *see* Eckington and Ridgeway *Derby*
ECTON (St Mary Magdalene) *see* Gt Doddington and Wilby and Ecton *Pet*
EDALE (Holy and Undivided Trinity) *Derby 4* **P** *Rep Landowners* **P-in-c** S H COCKSEDGE
EDBURTON (St Andrew) *see* Poynings w Edburton, Newtimber and Pyecombe *Chich*
EDEN PARK (St John the Baptist) *see* Beckenham St Jo *Roch*
EDEN, Gelt and Irthing Team Ministry, The, comprising Brampton, Castle Carrock, Crosby-on-Eden, Cumrew, Cumwhitton, Farlam, Hayton, Irthington, Scaleby, and Talkin *Carl 2* **P** *Patr Bd* **TR** S A ROBERTSON
TV E A JOHNSEN

EDEN, UPPER, comprising Brough w Stainmore, and Kirkby Stephen w Mallerstang and Crosby Garrett w Soulby *Carl 1*   **P** *Bp, Lord Hothfield, and the Hon J N Lowther (jt)*   **R** S M A HELD

EDENBRIDGE (St Peter and St Paul) *Roch 11*   **P** *Bp*   **V** S A J MITCHELL

EDENFIELD (not known) *see* Ramsbottom and Edenfield *Man*

EDENHALL (St Cuthbert) *see* Cross Fell Gp *Carl*

EDENHAM (St Michael) w Witham on the Hill and Swinstead *Linc 17*   **P** *Baroness Willoughby de Eresby, Ld Chan, and Bp (by turn)*   **V** E J R MARTIN   **NSM** I K WILLIAMS

EDENSOR (St Paul) *see* Longton Hall *Lich*

EDENSOR (St Peter) *see* Beeley and Edensor *Derby*

EDGBASTON (St Augustine) *Birm 1*   **P** *Bp*   **V** M R E TOMLINSON

EDGBASTON (St Bartholomew) *Birm 1*   **P** *Sir Euan Anstruther-Gough-Calthorpe Bt*   **V** N J C TUCKER   **C** C H BUTLER

EDGBASTON (St George w St Michael) (St Michael's Hall) *Birm 1*   **P** *Sir Euan Anstruther-Gough-Calthorpe Bt*   **V** J M FRANCIS

EDGBASTON (St Germain) *Birm 1*   **P** *Trustees*   **V** S C HAYES

EDGBASTON (St Mary and St Ambrose) *see* Balsall Heath and Edgbaston SS Mary and Ambrose *Birm*

EDGCOTE (St James) *see* Culworth w Sulgrave and Thorpe Mandeville etc *Pet*

EDGCOTT (St Michael) *see* The Claydons and Swan *Ox*

EDGE HILL (St Dunstan) *see* St Luke in the City *Liv*

EDGE HILL (St Mary) *see* Liv All SS *Liv*

EDGE, THE (St John the Baptist) *see* Painswick, Sheepscombe, Cranham, The Edge etc *Glouc*

EDGEFIELD (St Peter and St Paul) *see* Matlaske *Nor*

EDGEHILL CHURCHES, comprising Combroke, Kineton, Radway, Ratley, Shotteswell, and Warmington *Cov 8*   **P** *Bp and Lord Willoughby de Broke (jt)*   **R** B J JACKSON   **C** A C WILLIAMS, R J COOKE   **Hon C** B I D L T HARTLESS

EDGELEY (St Mark) (St Matthew) and Cheadle Heath *Ches 18*   **P** *Bp*   **V** D T BREWSTER   **NSM** J M JOHNSON

EDGESIDE (St Anne) *Man 11*   **P** *CPAS*   **V** R BEVAN

EDGEWORTH (St Mary) *see* Brimpsfield w Birdlip, Syde, Daglingworth etc *Glouc*

EDGMOND (St Peter) w Kynnersley and Preston Wealdmoors *Lich 15*   **P** *Bp, Adn Salop, Chan Lich, MMCET, and Preston Trust Homes Trustees (jt)*   **R** H M MORBY

EDGTON (St Michael the Archangel) *see* Bishop's Castle w Mainstone, Lydbury N etc *Heref*

EDGWARE (St Alphage) *see* Hendon St Alphage *Lon*

EDGWARE (St Andrew) (St Margaret) (St Peter) *Lon 15*   **P** *MMCET*   **TR** F ADU-BOACHIE   **TV** S BAILY   **C** S W J REA   **NSM** K CHRISTODOULOU

EDINGALE (Holy Trinity) *see* Mease Valley *Lich*

EDINGLEY (St Giles) w Halam *S'well 3*   **P** *Bp*   **V** *vacant*

EDINGTHORPE (All Saints) *see* N Walsham, Edingthorpe, Worstead and Westwick *Nor*

EDINGTON (St George) *see* Polden Wheel *B & W*

EDINGTON (St Mary, St Katharine and All Saints) *see* Bratton, Edington and Imber, Erlestoke etc *Sarum*

EDITH WESTON (St Mary) *see* Empingham, Edith Weston, Lyndon, Manton etc *Pet*

EDLASTON (St James) *see* Brailsford w Shirley, Osmaston w Edlaston etc *Derby*

EDLINGHAM (St John the Baptist w Bolton Chapel) *see* Whittingham and Edlingham w Bolton Chapel *Newc*

EDLINGTON (St Helen) *see* Hemingby Gp *Linc*

EDLINGTON (St John the Baptist) and Hexthorpe *Sheff 9*   **P** *Bp*   **V** S H J EDMONDS

EDMONDSHAM (St Nicholas) *see* Cranborne w Boveridge, Edmondsham etc *Sarum*

EDMONTON (All Saints) (St Michael) *Lon 18*   **P** *D&C St Paul's*   **V** S J OWEN   **NSM** A C PHILLIPS

EDMONTON (St Aldhelm) *Lon 18*   **P** *V Edmonton All SS*   **NSM** H J GRAHAM

EDMONTON (St Alphege) *Lon 18*   **P** *Bp*   **P-in-c** S G BROWN

EDMONTON (St Mary w St John) (St Mary's Centre) *Lon 18*   **P** *D&C St Paul's*   **V** N H ASBRIDGE

EDMONTON (St Peter w St Martin) *Lon 18*   **P** *Bp*   **V** T J KELSEY

EDMUNDBYERS (St Edmund) *see* Blanchland w Hunstanworth and Edmundbyers etc *Newc*

EDSTASTON (St Mary the Virgin), Fauls, Prees, Tilstock and Whixall *Lich 21*   **P** *R Wem, R Whitchurch, and Bp (jt)*   **C** E ATACK, E QUIREY, J M HUNT

EDSTONE (St Michael) *see* Kirkbymoorside w Gillamoor, Farndale etc *York*

EDVIN LOACH (St Mary) w Tedstone Delamere, Tedstone Wafer, Upper Sapey, Wolferlow and Whitbourne *Heref 2*

P *Bp, BNC Ox, Sir Francis Winnington Bt, and D P Barneby Esq (jt)*   **NSM** D B HYETT

EDWALTON (Holy Rood) *S'well 6*   **P** *Exors Major R P Chaworth-Musters*   **P-in-c** M A FRASER

EDWARDSTONE (St Mary the Virgin) *see* Boxford, Edwardstone, Groton etc *St E*

EDWINSTOWE (St Mary) *S'well 2*   **P** *Earl Manvers' Trustees*   **P-in-c** I WEBB

EDWYN RALPH (St Michael) *see* Bredenbury *Heref*

EFFINGHAM (St Lawrence) w Little Bookham *Guildf 10*   **P** *Keble Coll Ox*   **V** A S MACVEAN

EFFORD (St Paul) *see* Plymouth Em, St Paul Efford and St Aug *Ex*

EGDEAN (St Bartholomew) *Chich 10*   **P** *Bp*   **R** P M GILBERT

EGERTON (St James) *see* G7 Benefice *Cant*

EGGARDON and Colmers, comprising Askerswell, Loders, Powerstock, and Symondsbury *Sarum 2*   **P** *Bp, D&C, and Lady Laskey (3 turns), Ld Chan (1 turn)*   **R** C K GRASSKE

EGGBUCKLAND (St Edward) w Estover *Ex 21*   **P** *Ld Chan and Bp (alt)*   **V** C J ROUTLEDGE   **C** K A MURPHY, S P RUNDELL

EGGESFORD (All Saints) *see* Burrington, Chawleigh, Cheldon, Chulmleigh etc *Ex*

EGGINGTON (St Michael) *see* Ouzel Valley *St Alb*

EGGINTON (St Wilfrid) *see* Etwall w Egginton *Derby*

EGGLESCLIFFE (St John the Baptist) *Dur 9*   **P** *Bp*   **P-in-c** S WILSON

EGGLESTON (Holy Trinity) *Dur 6*   **P** *The Crown*   **P-in-c** J BARKER   **NSM** A P WALLBANK

EGHAM (St John the Baptist) *Guildf 11*   **P** *Ch Soc Trust*   **V** E T PRIOR   **C** S B L FRASER   **NSM** M J CALLAGHAN, M T PRIOR

EGHAM HYTHE (St Paul) *Guildf 11*   **P** *Bp*   **V** R C HOAD   **OLM** J FRANCK

EGLETON (St Edmund) *see* Oakham, Ashwell, Braunston, Brooke, Egleton etc *Pet*

EGLINGHAM (St Maurice) *see* Chatton w Chillingham, Eglingham and S Charlton and Ingram *Newc*

EGLOSHAYLE (St Petroc) *see* St Breoke and Egloshayle *Truro*

EGLOSKERRY (St Petrock and St Keri), North Petherwin, Tremaine, Tresmere and Trewen *Truro 9*   **P** *Duchy of Cornwall and Bp (alt)*   **V** G PENGELLY

EGMANTON (Our Lady of Egmanton) *S'well 3*   **P** *SMF*   **P-in-c** Z BURTON   **C** A K ALLS   **NSM** M A GROVES

EGREMONT (St Mary and St Michael) and Haile *Carl 5*   **P** *Patr Bd*   **NSM** T R TAYLOR

EGTON (St Hilda) *see* Middle Esk Moor *York*

EGTON-CUM-NEWLAND (St Mary the Virgin) *see* Coniston and the Crake Valley *Carl*

EIGHT ASH GREEN (All Saints) *see* Fordham *Chelmsf*

EIGHTON BANKS (St Thomas) *Dur 11*   **P** *Bp*   **P-in-c** D M SNOWBALL   **NSM** N CLEE

ELBERTON (St John) *see* Alveston and Littleton-on-Severn w Elberton *Bris*

ELBURTON (St Matthew) *Ex 21*   **P** *CPAS*   **V** J C W CROUCHER   **C** T J BRASSIL

ELDENE (not known) *see* Swindon Dorcan *Bris*

ELDERSFIELD (St John the Baptist) *see* Berrow w Pendock, Eldersfield, Hollybush etc *Worc*

ELDON (St Mark) *see* Coundon and Eldon *Dur*

ELDWICK (St Lawrence) *see* Bingley All SS *Leeds*

ELFORD (St Peter) *see* Mease Valley *Lich*

ELHAM (St Mary the Virgin) w Denton and Wootton and Acrise *Cant 8*   **P** *Abp and Mert Coll Ox (jt)*   **P-in-c** J A WEEKS

ELING (St Mary) *see* Totton *Win*

ELING, NORTH (St Mary) *see* Copythorne *Win*

ELKESLEY (St Giles) *see* Retford Area *S'well*

ELKINGTON, SOUTH (All Saints) *see* Louth *Linc*

ELKSTONE (St John the Baptist) *see* Longnor, Quarnford, Sheen etc *Lich*

ELKSTONE (St John the Evangelist) *see* Churn Valley *Glouc*

ELLAND (All Saints) (St Mary the Virgin) *Leeds 7*   **P** *V Halifax*   **R** D BURROWS   **C** R A CHAPMAN   **OLM** P E CHADWICK

ELLASTONE (St Peter) *see* Alton w Bradley-le-Moors and Denstone etc *Lich*

ELLEL (St John the Evangelist) *Blackb 11*   **P** *V Cockerham w Winmarleigh and Glasson*   **V** C A ABBOTT

ELLENBROOK (St Mary's Chapel) *see* Worsley *Man*

ELLENHALL (St Mary) *see* Chebsey, Creswell, Ellenhall, Ranton etc *Lich*

ELLERBURN (St Hilda) *see* Thornton Dale w Allerston, Ebberston etc *York*

ELLERBY (St James) *see* Skirlaugh, Catwick, Long Riston, Rise, Swine w Ellerby *York*

ELLERKER (not known) see S Cave and Ellerker w Broomfleet York

ELLESBOROUGH (St Peter and St Paul), The Kimbles and Stoke Mandeville Ox 17 P Chequers Trustees, The Hon I Hope-Morley, and D&C Linc (by turn) R vacant

ELLESMERE (St Mary) Lich 16 P Bp V vacant

ELLESMERE (St Peter) Sheff 3 P Bp C P J SALMON

ELLESMERE PORT, comprising Stoak and Whitby Ches 9 P Bp R G B MCGUINNESS C G S FOSTER NSM G J WELCH

ELLINGHAM (St Mary and All Saints) see Ringwood w Ellingham and Harbridge etc Win

ELLINGHAM (St Mary) see Gillingham w Geldeston, Stockton, Ellingham etc Nor

ELLINGHAM (St Maurice) Newc 7 P D&C Dur P-in-c A S MACPHERSON

ELLINGHAM, GREAT (St James), LITTLE (St Peter), Rockland All Saints, Rockland St Peter and Shrapham w Snetterton Nor 11 P Bp, Major E H C Garnier, and CCC Cam (jt) P-in-c C M MASON Hon C S STRUTT

ELLINGTON (All Saints) see E Leightonstone Ely

ELLISFIELD (St Martin) see Farleigh, Candover and Wield Win

ELLISTOWN (St Christopher) see Hugglescote w Donington, Ellistown and Snibston Leic

ELLOE FEN Group, The, comprising Gedney Hill, Sutton St Edmund, Sutton St James, and Whaplode Drove Linc 18 P Bp, Feoffees, and V Long Sutton w Lutton etc (jt) V M G ONGYERTH

ELLOE STONE Parishes, The, comprising Moulton, Holbeach Fen, and Whaplode Linc 18 P Bp and DBP (1 turn), Ld Chan (1 turn) V G W ATHA OLM B A HUTCHINSON

ELLOE, MID see Mid Elloe Gp Linc

ELLOUGHTON (St Mary) and Brough w Brantingham York 13 P Abp and D&C Dur (jt) V M A FRYER

ELM (All Saints) see Fen Orchards Ely

ELM (St Mary Magdalene) see Mells w Buckland Dinham, Elm, Whatley etc B & W

ELM PARK (St Nicholas) Hornchurch Chelmsf 2 P Bp V A J KEIGHLEY NSM D M PERRY, T C KEIGHLEY

ELMBRIDGE (St Mary) see Elmley Lovett w Hampton Lovett and Elmbridge w Rushock and Hartlebury and Ombersley w Doverdale Worc

ELMDON (St Nicholas) see Icknield Way Villages Chelmsf

ELMDON (St Nicholas) (St Stephen's Church Centre) (Valley Church Centre) Birm 10 P Ch Trust Fund Trust R T N CROWE

ELMERS END (St James) see Beckenham St Jas w St Mich and St Aug Roch

ELMESTHORPE (St Mary) see Earl Shilton w Elmesthorpe Leic

ELMETE TRINITY, comprising Barwick, Scholes, and Thorner Leeds 16 P Duchy of Lanc and Earl of Mexborough (alt) R A J NICHOLSON C R D BAILEY NSM A B HAIGH

ELMHAM, NORTH (St Mary) see Heart of Norfolk Nor

ELMHURST (Mission Room) see Lich St Chad Lich

ELMLEY see Lepton, Emley and Flockton w Denby Grange Leeds

ELMLEY CASTLE (St Mary) w Bricklehampton and the Combertons Worc 4 P Bp R D T LEWIS

ELMLEY LOVETT (St Michael) w Hampton Lovett and Elmbridge w Rushock and Hartlebury and Ombersley w Doverdale Worc 8 P Patr Bd R S C WINTER

ELMORE (St John the Baptist) see Hardwicke and Elmore w Longney Glouc

ELMSALL, NORTH (St Margaret) see Badsworth Leeds

ELMSALL, SOUTH (St Mary the Virgin) Leeds 18 P Bp V M GALLAGHER

ELMSETT (St Peter) w Aldham, Hintlesham, Chattisham and Kersey St E 4 P Bp, MMCET, and St Chad's Coll Dur (jt) P-in-c S J CROMPTON-BATTERSBY

ELMSTEAD (St Anne and St Laurence) see Tenpenny Villages Chelmsf

ELMSTONE (not known) see Canonry Cant

ELMSTONE HARDWICKE (St Mary Magdalene) see N Cheltenham Glouc

ELMSWELL (St John the Divine) St E 6 P MMCET R P W GOODRIDGE C I E OKEKE

ELMTON (St Peter) w Creswell and Whitwell w Steetley Derby 3 P Bp R vacant

ELSDON (St Cuthbert) see N Tyne and Redesdale Newc

ELSECAR (Holy Trinity) see Worsbrough w Elsecar Sheff

ELSENHAM (St Mary the Virgin) see Henham and Elsenham w Ugley Chelmsf

ELSFIELD (St Thomas of Canterbury) see Marston w Elsfield Ox

ELSHAM (All Saints) see Brocklesby Park, Croxton and North Wolds Linc

ELSING (St Mary) see Reepham and Wensum Valley Nor

ELSON (St Thomas) Portsm 3 P DBP V K I MITCHELL NSM M A HAY

ELSTEAD (St James) Guildf 4 P Adn Surrey NSM D J ORME

ELSTED (St Paul) see Harting w Elsted and Treyford cum Didling Chich

ELSTERNWICK (St Laurence) see Burstwick, Burton Pidsea etc York

ELSTON (All Saints) w Elston Chapelry S'well 3 P J C S Darwin Esq P-in-c E I MURRAY

ELSTOW (St Mary and St Helena) St Alb 9 P Patr Bd P-in-c P J MESSAM TV S T SMITH C K J SCOTT

ELSTREE (St Nicholas) and Borehamwood St Alb 14 P Patr Bd (3 turns), Ld Chan (1 turn) TR T G WARR TV L R COLLINS

ELSWICK (St Stephen) (St Paul) Newc 4 P Ch Soc Trust and Trustees (jt) V G R CURRY

ELSWICK, HIGH (St Philip) see Newc St Phil and St Aug and St Matt w St Mary Newc

ELSWORTH (Holy Trinity) see Papworth Ely

ELTHAM (Holy Trinity) S'wark 3 P Bp V B E WARD

ELTHAM (St Barnabas) S'wark 3 P Bp V S COOK

ELTHAM (St John the Baptist) S'wark 3 P DBP P-in-c J F BRYSON

ELTHAM (St Saviour) S'wark 3 P Bp V vacant

ELTHAM PARK (St Luke) S'wark 3 P Bp V E J OGLESBY

ELTHAM, NEW (All Saints) S'wark 3 P Bp V A S ROSE

ELTISLEY (St Pandionia and St John the Baptist) see Papworth Ely

ELTON (All Saints) Ely 15 P Sir William Proby Bt C M W PYBUS

ELTON (All Saints) see Kirklees Valley Man

ELTON (St John) Dur 9 P St Chad Coll Dur P-in-c W E BRAVINER C P MURRAY

ELTON (St Mary the Virgin) see Wigmore Abbey Heref

ELTON (St Stephen) Man 8 P V Elton All SS P-in-c P SANDERSON

ELTON-ON-THE-HILL (St Michael) see Wiverton in the Vale S'well

ELVASTON (St Bartholomew) see Aston on Trent, Elvaston, Weston on Trent etc Derby

ELVEDEN (St Andrew and St Patrick) see Lakenheath, Santon Downham and Elveden St E

ELVINGTON (Holy Trinity) see Derwent Ings York

ELWICK HALL (St Peter) see Hart w Elwick Hall Dur

ELWORTH (St Peter) Ches 11 P V Sandbach V D J PAGE

ELY (Holy Trinity w St Mary), including Chettisham, Downham, Little Thetford, Prickwillow, Stretham, and Stuntney Ely 8 P Patr Bd TR C M HILL TV N J ANDREWS C M P PHILLIPS NSM J R HICKISH

ELY (St Peter) Proprietary Chapel Ely 8 P-in-c P D ANDREWS

EMBERTON (All Saints) see Lamp Ox

EMBLETON (Holy Trinity) w Rennington and Rock Newc 6 P Mert Coll Ox P-in-c A J HARDY NSM I P CHADWICK

EMBLETON (St Cuthbert) see Binsey Carl

EMBROOK (Community of St Nicholas) see Wokingham St Paul Ox

EMBSAY (St Mary the Virgin) w Eastby Leeds 24 P R Skipton H Trin NSM T CALOW

EMERY DOWN (Christ Church) see Lyndhurst and Emery Down and Minstead Win

EMLEY (St Michael the Archangel) see Lepton, Emley and Flockton w Denby Grange Leeds

EMMAUS Parish Team, The Leic 1 P Bp P-in-c J LINDSEY C C S BEAUMONT, J P TEARNE NSM I BENNETT

EMMER GREEN (St Barnabas) w Caversham Park Ox 7 P Bp and Ch Ch Ox (jt) R D E CHANDLER

EMNETH (St Edmund) see Fen Orchards Ely

EMPINGHAM (St Peter), Edith Weston, Lyndon, Manton, North Luffenham, Pilton, Preston, Ridlington, Whitwell and Wing Pet 12 P Bp, Baroness Willoughby de Eresby, Sir John Conant Bt, Em Coll Cam, and DBP (jt) R P J MADGWICK Hon C J P TAYLOR NSM J L DUFFY

EMPSHOTT (Holy Rood) see Greatham, Empshott and Hawkley w Priors Dean Portsm

EMSCOTE (All Saints) see Warwick Cov

EMSWORTH (St James) see Warblington w Emsworth Portsm

ENBORNE (St Michael and All Angels) see Walbury Beacon Ox

ENDCLIFFE (St Augustine) Sheff 2 P Ch Burgesses P-in-c C L DAWSON C B M TANNER NSM L M N HALL

ENDERBY (St John the Baptist) w Lubbesthorpe and Thurlaston Leic 7 P Bp and F B Drummond Esq V J C TAYLOR C R I BALMER

ENDON (St Luke) see Bagnall w Endon Lich

ENFIELD (Christ Church) Trent Park *Lon 18* **P** *Ch Trust Fund Trust* **V** J D TUCKWELL **C** J M FEATHERSTONE, J R KNOWLES

ENFIELD (St Andrew) *Lon 18* **P** *Trin Coll Cam* **V** S M GRIFFITHS

ENFIELD (St George) *Lon 18* **P** *Bp* **V** A T OH **NSM** V T P SHEEHAN

ENFIELD (St James) (St Barnabas) *Lon 18* **P** *V Enfield* **V** I M GALLAGHER **NSM** H R GEORGE, K C ONWUKA

ENFIELD (St John the Baptist) *see Clay Hill St Jo and St Luke Lon*

ENFIELD (St Luke) *as above*

ENFIELD (St Mark) *see Bush Hill Park St Mark Lon*

ENFIELD (St Matthew) *see Ponders End St Matt Lon*

ENFIELD (St Michael and All Angels) *Lon 18* **P** *V Enfield* **V** S M TAYLOR

ENFIELD (St Peter and St Paul) *Lon 18* **P** *Bp* **P-in-c** S GALLAGHER

ENFIELD (St Stephen) *see Bush Hill Park St Steph Lon*

ENFIELD CHASE (St Mary Magdalene) *Lon 18* **P** *Bp* **V** G J GILES

ENFORD (All Saints) *see Avon River Sarum*

ENGLEFIELD (St Mark) *Ox 4* **P** *Englefield Estate Trust* **V** N W WYNNE-JONES

ENGLEFIELD GREEN (St Jude) *Guildf 11* **P** *Bp* **V** J M ALLFORD

ENGLISH BICKNOR (St Mary) *see Forest of Dean Ch Ch w English Bicknor Glouc*

ENGLISHCOMBE (St Peter) *see Bath St Barn w Englishcombe B & W*

ENHAM ALAMEIN (St George) *see Pastrow Win*

ENMORE (St Michael) *see Aisholt, Enmore, Goathurst, Nether Stowey etc B & W*

ENMORE GREEN (St John the Evangelist) *see Shaftesbury Sarum*

ENNERDALE (St Mary) *see Lamplugh w Ennerdale Carl*

ENSBURY PARK (St Thomas) *Sarum 7* **P** *Bp* **V** S A EVANS

ENSTONE (St Kenelm) *see Chase Ox*

ENVILLE (St Mary the Virgin) *see Kinver and Enville Lich*

EPPERSTONE (Holy Cross), Gonalston, Oxton and Woodborough *S'well 7* **P** *Bp, Ld Chan, and C P L Francklin Esq (by turn)* **R** A R GILES **NSM** L M RAYNOR

EPPING District (All Saints) (St John the Baptist) *Chelmsf 3* **P** *Patr Bd* **TR** L P BATSON **TV** O C MAXFIELD-COOTE **C** T Z WARMINGTON

EPSOM (St Barnabas) *Guildf 9* **P** *Bp* **P-in-c** M D A ROPER

EPSOM (St Martin) (St Stephen on the Downs) *Guildf 9* **P** *Bp* **V** N A PARISH **C** D J CANDLIN

EPSOM COMMON (Christ Church) *Guildf 9* **P** *Bp* **V** R A DONOVAN **C** D F FOX-BRANCH **NSM** S A CURTIS

EPWELL (St Anne) *see Wykeham Ox*

EPWORTH Group, The (St Andrew), including West Butterwick and Wroot *Linc 1* **P** *The Crown (2 turns), Ld Chan (1 turn)* **R** P D WILSON

ERCALL, HIGH (St Michael and All Angels) *see Wrockwardine Deanery Lich*

ERDINGTON (St Barnabas) *Birm 7* **P** *Bp and Aston Patr Trust (jt)* **C** S C BRIDGE

ERDINGTON (St Chad) *Birm 7* **P** *Bp and Aston Patr Trust (jt)* **V** *vacant*

ERDINGTON Christ the King *Birm 7* **P** *Bp* **V** R R SOUTER

ERIDGE GREEN (Holy Trinity) *see Frant w Eridge Chich*

ERISWELL (St Laurence and St Peter) *see Mildenhall St E*

ERITH (Christ Church) *Roch 15* **P** *Bp* **V** M E CAMERON

ERITH (St John the Baptist) *Roch 15* **P** *Bp* **V** R M RADCLIFFE

ERITH (St Paul) Northumberland Heath *Roch 15* **P** *CPAS* **V** C BEAZLEY-LONG

ERLESTOKE (Holy Saviour) *see Bratton, Edington and Imber, Erlestoke etc Sarum*

ERMINGTON (St Peter and St Paul) *see Diptford w N Huish, Ermington, Halwell etc Ex*

ERNESETTLE (St Aidan), Whitleigh and Honicknowle *Ex 21* **P** *Ld Chan and Bp (alt)* **V** D R BAILEY **NSM** D WATSON

ERPINGHAM (St Mary) w Calthorpe, Ingworth, Aldborough, Thurgarton and Alby w Thwaite *Nor 18* **P** *Bp, Lord Walpole, Gt Hosp Nor, Mrs S M Lilly, and DBP (by turn)* **P-in-c** E C ROBINSON

ERRINGDEN, comprising Cragg Vale and Mytholmroyd *Leeds 8* **P** *Bp and V Halifax (jt)* **V** C B REARDON **C** D J MILES **NSM** M D BULL, M S H MACDONALD

ERWARTON (St Mary the Virgin) *see Shoreline St E*

ERYHOLME (St Mary) *see E Dere Street Leeds*

ESCOMB (no dedication) *Dur 5* **P** *Bp* **P-in-c** B E MECHANIC

ESCOT (St Philip and St James) *see Ottery St Mary, Alfington, W Hill, Tipton etc Ex*

ESCRICK (St Helen) and Stillingfleet w Naburn *York 2* **P** *Abp, D&C, and C D Forbes Adam Esq (jt)* **R** R M KIRKMAN

ESH (St Michael and All Angels) and Hamsteels *Dur 1* **P** *The Crown* **V** M J PEERS **NSM** T HOLDEN

ESHER (Christ Church) (St George) *Guildf 8* **P** *Wadh Coll Ox* **R** *vacant*

ESHOLT (St Paul) *see Guiseley w Esholt Leeds*

ESK MOOR, MIDDLE, comprising Egton, Glaisdale, Goathland, and Grosmont *York 21* **P** *Abp* **V** P A JACKSON **NSM** P J HIGSON

ESK, LOWER, comprising Aislaby, Eskdaleside, and Sneaton *York 21* **P** *Abp* **V** *vacant*

ESKDALE (St Bega's Mission) *see Black Combe, Drigg, Eskdale etc Carl*

ESKDALE (St Catherine) *as above*

ESSENDINE (St Mary the Virgin) *see Ryhall w Essendine and Carlby Pet*

ESSENDON (St Mary the Virgin) *see Lt Berkhamsted and Bayford, Essendon etc St Alb*

ESSINGTON (St John the Evangelist), Featherstone and Shareshill *Lich 2* **P** *Simeon's Trustees, Bp, and R Bushbury (jt)* **V** C L SHAW

ESTON (Christ Church) w Normanby *York 17* **P** *Abp* **TR** J G BLAKELEY

ESTOVER (Christ Church) *see Eggbuckland w Estover Ex*

ETAL (St Mary the Virgin) *see Ford and Etal Newc*

ETCHILHAMPTON (St Andrew) *see Cannings and Redhorn Sarum*

ETCHING HILL (The Holy Spirit) *see Brereton and Rugeley w Armitage Lich*

ETCHINGHAM (The Assumption and St Nicholas) *see Burwash, Burwash Weald and Etchingham Chich*

ETHERLEY (St Cuthbert) *Dur 5* **P** *Bp* **P-in-c** B E MECHANIC

ETON (St John the Evangelist) w Eton Wick, Boveney and Dorney *Ox 12* **P** *Eton Coll and Mrs J M Palmer (jt)* **V** R R STACEY

ETON WICK (St John the Baptist) *see Eton w Eton Wick, Boveney and Dorney Ox*

ETTINGSHALL (Holy Trinity) *Lich 27* **P** *Bp* **V** D P A FEENEY **NSM** A P M EDWARDS

ETTINGTON (Holy Trinity and St Thomas of Canterbury) *see Stourdene Gp Cov*

ETTON (St Stephen) *see Glinton, Etton, Maxey, Peakirk and Northborough Pet*

ETTON (St Mary) w Dalton Holme *York 8* **P** *Lord Hotham* **P-in-c** R F PARKINSON

ETWALL (St Helen) w Egginton *Derby 6* **P** *Bp, Sir Henry Every Bt, Major J W Chandos-Pole, and DBP (by turn)* **R** *vacant*

EUSTON (St Genevieve) *see Blackbourne St E*

EUXTON (not known) *Blackb 4* **P** *Bp* **V** *vacant*

EVE HILL (St James the Great) *see Dudley Worc*

EVEDON (St Mary) *see N Lafford Gp Linc*

EVENLEY (St George) *see Aynho and Croughton w Evenley etc Pet*

EVENLODE (St Edward King and Martyr) *see Broadwell, Evenlode, Oddington, Adlestrop etc Glouc*

EVENWOOD (St Paul) *Dur 6* **P** *Bp* **P-in-c** B WHITLEY

EVERDON (St Mary) *see Weedon Bec w Everdon and Dodford Pet*

EVERINGHAM (St Everilda) *see Holme and Seaton Ross Gp York*

EVERSDEN, GREAT (St Mary) *see Lordsbridge Ely*

EVERSDEN, LITTLE (St Helen) *as above*

EVERSHOLT (St John the Evangelist) *see Woburn w Eversholt, Milton Bryan, Battlesden etc St Alb*

EVERSHOT (St Osmund) *see Melbury Sarum*

EVERSLEY (St Mary) *see Darby Green and Eversley Win*

EVERTON (Holy Trinity) *see Bawtry w Austerfield, Misson, Everton and Mattersey S'well*

EVERTON (St George) *Liv 1* **P** *Bp* **V** A R MAYNARD

EVERTON (St Mary) *see Gamlingay and Everton Ely*

EVERTON (St Mary) *see Milford Win*

EVERTON (St Peter) (St John Chrysostom) (Emmanuel) *Liv 1* **P** *Patr Bd* **R** H CORBETT

EVESBATCH (St Andrew) *see Frome Valley Heref*

EVESHAM (All Saints w St Lawrence) w Norton and Lenchwick *Worc 1* **P** *Bp and D&C (jt)* **V** A SPURR

EVINGTON (St Denys) *Leic 1* **P** *Bp* **V** A J LEES-SMITH **C** N ROSTOCK

EVINGTON, NORTH (St Stephen) *Leic 1* **P** *Bp* **P-in-c** I ST C RICHARDS

EWELL (St Francis of Assisi) Ruxley Lane *Guildf 9* **P** *Bp* **V** *vacant*

EWELL (St Mary the Virgin) *Guildf 9* **P** *Bp* **V** R J E DEWHURST

EWELL, WEST (All Saints) *Guildf 9* **P** *Bp* **V** S M COOKE
NSM V RAKIN
EWELME *see* Dursley, Uley, Owlpen etc *Glouc*
EWELME (St Mary the Virgin) *see* Benson w Ewelme *Ox*
EWERBY (St Andrew) *see* Kirkby Laythorpe *Linc*
EWHURST (St James the Great) *Chich 17* **P** K Coll Cam
P-in-c C P IRVINE
EWHURST (St Peter and St Paul) w Okewood and Forest
Green *Guildf 2* **P** Ld Chan (1 turn), Bp and J P M H Evelyn
Esq (1 turn) **R** C F SHEPHERD **NSM** J MARSH
OLM J MARSH
EWOOD (St Bartholomew) *see* Blackb Redeemer *Blackb*
EWSHOT (St Mary the Virgin) *see* Crondall and Ewshot
Guildf
EWYAS HAROLD (St Michael and All Angels) w Dulas,
Kenderchurch, Abbeydore, Bacton, Kentchurch,
Llangua, Rowlestone, Llancillo, Walterstone, Kilpeck,
St Devereux and Wormbridge *Heref 1* **P** Bp, E Harley Esq,
Mrs B Sexton, J Lucas-Scudamore Esq, Mrs M Barneby, G Clive
Esq, and D&C (2 turns), Ld Chan (1 turn)
P-in-c M R GODSON
EXBOURNE (St Mary the Virgin) *see* Okehampton,
Inwardleigh, Belstone, Sourton etc *Ex*
EXBURY (St Katherine) *see* Beaulieu and Exbury and E Boldre
Win
EXE, WEST (St Paul) *see* Tiverton St Geo and St Paul *Ex*
EXETER (St David) (St Michael and All Angels) *Ex 3* **P** D&C
V N GUTHRIE **Hon C** P A LEE
EXETER (St James) *Ex 3* **P** D&C **R** H H D PRYSE
EXETER (St Leonard w Holy Trinity) *Ex 3* **P** CPAS
R S N AUSTEN **C** C J KEANE
EXETER (St Mark) *Ex 3* **P** Bp **R** T HOCKLEY-STILL
EXETER (St Mary Steps) *see* Heavitree and St Mary Steps *Ex*
EXETER (St Matthew) (St Sidwell) *Ex 3* **P** D&C
P-in-c E R J HODGES
EXETER (St Thomas the Apostle) (Emmanuel) (St Andrew)
(St Philip) *Ex 3* **P** Bp **TR** D J NIXON **TV** C E KEAY
EXETER Holy Trinity *Ex 3* **P** Bp and Ch Soc Trust (jt)
V J P A ELVIN **C** P L BROKENSHIRE
EXETER, CENTRAL (St Martin) (St Mary Arches) (St Olave)
(St Pancras) (St Petrock) (St Stephen) *Ex 3* **P** Patr Bd
P-in-c S R SWARBRICK
EXFORD (St Mary Magdalene) *see* Exmoor *B & W*
EXHALL (St Giles) *see* Heart of England *Cov*
EXHALL (St Giles) *Cov 5* **P** Bp **V** G A PHILLIP
EXMINSTER (St Martin), Kenn, Kenton w Mamhead, and
Powderham *Ex 5* **P** 12 Govs of Crediton Ch, D&C Sarum,
SMF, Mrs M P L Bate, and Earl of Devon (jt)
R J D A WILLIAMS **Hon C** P DAWKES
EXMOOR (St Luke) *B & W 15* **P** Ld Chan (1 turn), Bp, Em
Coll Cam, Peterho Cam, G A Warren Esq, and D M Warren Esq
(2 turns) **R** D A WEIR **NSM** N M BUTT
EXMOUTH (All Saints) *see* Withycombe Raleigh *Ex*
EXMOUTH (Holy Trinity) *see* Littleham-cum-Exmouth w
Lympstone *Ex*
EXMOUTH (St John in the Wilderness) *see* Withycombe
Raleigh *Ex*
EXMOUTH (St John the Evangelist) *as above*
EXNING (St Agnes) *see* Newmarket St Mary w Exning
St Agnes *St E*
EXNING (St Martin) (St Philip) w Landwade *St E 7* **P** D&C
Cant **P-in-c** J C HARDY
EXTON (St Andrew) *see* Aylesbeare, Clyst St George, Clyst
St Mary etc *Ex*
EXTON (St Peter and St Paul) *see* Cottesmore and Burley,
Clipsham, Exton etc *Pet*
EXTON (St Peter and St Paul) *see* Meon Bridge *Portsm*
EXTON (St Peter) *see* Exmoor *B & W*
EXWICK (St Andrew) *Ex 3* **P** Lord Wraxall **P-in-c** J P BIRD
EYAM (St Lawrence) *see* Baslow and Eyam *Derby*
EYDON (St Nicholas) *see* Aston-le-Walls, Byfield,
Boddington, Eydon etc *Pet*
EYE (St Matthew), Newborough and Thorney *Pet 11* **P** Bp
and The Crown (alt) **V** C HURST
EYE (St Peter and St Paul) *St E 12* **P** Bp, SMF, and Lt Comdr
G C Marshall (jt) **R** G SUMPTER
EYEWORTH (All Saints) *see* Dunton w Wrestlingworth and
Eyeworth *St Alb*
EYKE (All Saints) *see* Wilford Peninsula *St E*
EYNESBURY (St Mary) *Ely 13* **P** Bp **R** vacant
EYNSFORD (St Martin) w Farningham and Lullingstone
Roch 10 **P** D&C **NSM** M D MCGARVEY
EYNSHAM (St Leonard) and Cassington *Ox 29* **P** Wycliffe
Hall Ox and Ch Ch Ox (alt) **V** D P FRASER
NSM A C ATHERSTONE **OLM** R ASTON
EYPE (St Peter) *see* Eggardon and Colmers *Sarum*

EYRES MONSELL (St Hugh) *Leic 1* **P** Bp **V** vacant
EYTHORNE (St Peter and St Paul) *see* Bewsborough *Cant*
EYTON (All Saints) *see* Leominster *Heref*
EYTON (St Catherine) *see* Wellington All SS w Eyton *Lich*
FACCOMBE (St Barnabas) *see* Hurstbourne Tarrant,
Faccombe, Vernham Dean etc *Win*
FACEBY (St Mary Magdalene) *see* Whorlton w Carlton and
Faceby *York*
FACIT (St John the Evangelist) *see* Whitworth w Facit *Man*
FAILAND (St Bartholomew) *see* Wraxall *B & W*
FAILSWORTH (Holy Family) *Man 16* **P** The Crown and Bp
(alt) **R** P HUTCHINS
FAILSWORTH (St John) (St John the Evangelist) *Man 16*
P Bp **R** vacant
FAIR OAK (St Thomas) *Win 10* **P** Bp **V** A H MEPHAM
C K M MEPHAM **NSM** R G NICHOLLS
FAIRBURN (St James) *see* Ledsham w Fairburn *York*
FAIRFIELD (St Mark) *see* Belbroughton w Fairfield and Clent
Worc
FAIRFIELD (St Peter), Peak Forest and Dove Holes *Derby 4*
P Patr Bd **V** C F EDWARDS **OLM** M WASHBROOK
FAIRFIELD (St Thomas à Becket) *see* Brookland, Fairfield,
Brenzett w Snargate etc *Cant*
FAIRFORD (St Mary the Virgin) *see* S Cotswolds *Glouc*
FAIRHAVEN (St Paul) *Blackb 10* **P** J C Hilton Esq **V** P A BYE
FAIRLIGHT (St Andrew) (St Peter) and Pett *Chich 17* **P** Patr
Bd **R** R D BARRON **Hon C** H E PATTEN
FAIRSEAT (Holy Innocents) *see* Stansted w Fairseat and Vigo
Roch
FAIRSTEAD (St Mary) *see* Witham and Villages *Chelmsf*
FAIRWARP (Christ Church) *Chich 18* **P** Bp
P-in-c J P CAPERON
FAIRWEATHER GREEN (St Saviour) *Leeds 3* **P** Bp
V D E STEWART
FAKENHAM (St Peter and St Paul) w Alethorpe *Nor 14*
P Trin Coll Cam **R** F R A MASON
FAKENHAM MAGNA (St Peter) *see* Blackbourne *St E*
FALCONWOOD (Bishop Ridley Church) *Roch 15* **P** Bp
V M TARIQ
FALDINGWORTH (All Saints) *see* Middle Rasen Gp *Linc*
FALFIELD (St George) *see* Cromhall, Tortworth,
Tytherington, Falfield etc *Glouc*
FALKENHAM (St Ethelbert) *see* Nacton and Levington w
Bucklesham etc *St E*
FALLOWFIELD (Holy Innocents) *see* Birch w Fallowfield *Man*
FALLOWFIELD (St Crispin) *see* Withington St Crispin *Man*
FALMER (St Laurence) *see* Stanmer w Falmer *Chich*
FALMOUTH (All Saints) *Truro 3* **P** Bp
P-in-c W R STUART-WHITE **C** C J HASSELL
NSM S Y GARDNER
FALMOUTH (King Charles the Martyr) *Truro 3* **P** Bp
P-in-c S J TUDGEY
FALSTONE (St Peter) *see* N Tyne and Redesdale *Newc*
FAMBRIDGE, NORTH (Holy Trinity) *see* Althorne and
N Fambridge *Chelmsf*
FAMBRIDGE, SOUTH (All Saints) *see* Ashingdon w S
Fambridge, Canewdon and Paglesham *Chelmsf*
FANGFOSS (St Martin) *see* Barmby Moor Gp *York*
FAR FOREST (Holy Trinity) *see* Mamble w Bayton, Rock w
Heightington etc *Worc*
FARCET (St Mary) *see* Stanground and Farcet *Ely*
FAREHAM (Holy Trinity) (St Columba) *Portsm 2* **P** Bp
TR S E DAVENPORT **C** G K BAKKER, W M JACOBS
FAREHAM (St John the Evangelist) *Portsm 2* **P** CPAS
V B G DEANS
FAREHAM (St Peter and St Paul) *Portsm 2* **P** Bp
P-in-c R JACKSON
FAREWELL (St Bartholomew) *Lich 1* **P** MMCET
P-in-c L M MCKEON
FARFORTH (St Peter) *see* S Ormsby Gp *Linc*
FARINGDON, GREAT (All Saints) w Little Coxwell *Ox 25*
P Simeon's Trustees **V** J S BELLAMY **C** P C WALKER
FARINGDON, LITTLE (St Margaret of England) *see* Shill
Valley and Broadshire *Ox*
FARLAM (St Thomas à Becket) *see* Eden, Gelt and Irthing
Carl
FARLEIGH (St Andrew), Candover and Wield, including
Bradley, and Northington w Swarraton *Win 1* **P** Ld Chan
(1 turn), Bp, D&C, Earl of Portsmouth, and Lord Ashburton
(1 turn) **R** D M CHATTELL **C** S P E MOURANT
FARLEIGH (St Mary) *see* Warlingham w Chelsham and
Farleigh *S'wark*
FARLEIGH HUNGERFORD (St Leonard) *see* Hardington Vale
B & W
FARLEIGH WALLOP (St Andrew) *see* Farleigh, Candover and
Wield *Win*

FARLEIGH, EAST (not known) *see* Coxheath, E Farleigh, Hunton, Linton etc *Roch*

FARLEIGH, WEST (All Saints) *as above*

FARLESTHORPE (St Andrew) *see* Alford Gp *Linc*

FARLEY (All Saints) *see* Clarendon *Sarum*

FARLEY CHAMBERLAYNE (St John) *see* Michelmersh and Awbridge and Braishfield etc *Win*

FARLEY GREEN (St Michael) *see* Shere, Albury and Chilworth *Guildf*

FARLEY HILL (St John the Baptist) *St Alb 12* **P** *Bp*
V R P O'NEILL

FARLEY HILL (St John the Evangelist) *see* Loddon Reach *Ox*

FARLINGTON (St Andrew) (Church of the Resurrection) *Portsm 6* **P** *Mrs S J Wynter-Bee and Nugee Foundn (jt)*
R P D GULLY **C** P L GOOD

FARLINGTON (St Leonard) *see* Forest of Galtres *York*

FARLOW (St Giles) *see* Stottesdon w Farlow, Cleeton St Mary etc *Heref*

FARMBOROUGH (All Saints) and Marksbury and Stanton Prior *B & W 9* **P** *MMCET (3 turns), Duchy of Cornwall (1 turn), and DBF (1 turn)* **R** J P KNOTT

FARMCOTE (St Faith) *see* The Guitings, Cutsdean, Farmcote etc *Glouc*

FARMINGTON (St Peter) *see* Northleach w Hampnett and Farmington etc *Glouc*

FARMOOR (St Mary) *see* Cumnor *Ox*

FARNBOROUGH (All Saints) *see* E Downland *Ox*

FARNBOROUGH (Good Shepherd) *Guildf 1* **P** *CPAS Patr Trust* **V** R M SMART

FARNBOROUGH (St Botolph) *see* Avon Dassett w Farnborough and Fenny Compton *Cov*

FARNBOROUGH (St Giles) (St Nicholas) *Roch 16* **P** *Em Coll Cam* **R** M J HUGHES **C** S K BROADIE

FARNBOROUGH (St Peter) *Guildf 1* **P** *CPAS Patr Trust*
V E A ETHERINGTON **C** M SWIRES-HENNESSY, S J NORBRON **NSM** R N COBBOLD

FARNBOROUGH, SOUTH (St Mark) *Guildf 1* **P** *Bp*
V I C HEDGES

FARNCOMBE (St John the Evangelist) *Guildf 4* **P** *Bp*
R J RATTUE **C** M A STIRLING TROY

FARNDALE (St Mary) *see* Kirkbymoorside w Gillamoor, Farndale etc *York*

FARNDON (St Chad) and Coddington *Ches 5* **P** *Duke of Westmr and D&C (jt)* **V** D SCURR

FARNDON (St Peter) w Thorpe, Hawton and Cotham *S'well 3* **P** *Ld Chan* **P-in-c** E I MURRAY

FARNDON, EAST (St John the Baptist) *see* Arthingworth, Harrington w Oxendon and E Farndon *Pet*

FARNHAM (St Andrew) (St Francis) (St Mary) *Guildf 3*
P *Bp* **R** H D UFFINDELL **C** J W MARROW

FARNHAM (St Laurence) *see* Chase *Sarum*

FARNHAM (St Mary the Virgin) *see* Stansted Mountfitchet w Birchanger and Farnham *Chelmsf*

FARNHAM (St Mary) *see* Alde River *St E*

FARNHAM (St Oswald) *see* Walkingham Hill *Leeds*

FARNHAM COMMON (St John the Evangelist) *see* Farnham Royal w Hedgerley *Ox*

FARNHAM ROYAL (St Mary the Virgin) w Hedgerley *Ox 12*
P *Bp and Eton Coll (jt)* **R** *vacant*

FARNHAM ROYAL SOUTH (St Michael) *see* Manor Park and Whitby Road *Ox*

FARNINGHAM (St Peter and St Paul) *see* Eynsford w Farningham and Lullingstone *Roch*

FARNLEY (All Saints) *see* Washburn and Mid-Wharfe *Leeds*

FARNLEY TYAS (St Lucias) *see* Almondbury w Farnley Tyas *Leeds*

FARNLEY, NEW (St James) *see* Wortley and Farnley *Leeds*

FARNSFIELD (St Michael) *S'well 3* **P** *Bp* **P-in-c** C G PEARSE

FARNWORTH (All Saints) (St John), Kearsley and Stoneclough *Man 7* **P** *Ld Chan and Patr Bd (alt)*
TV K E LAFFERTY **OLM** M J WEARING

FARNWORTH (Cronton Mission) *see* E Widnes *Liv*

FARNWORTH (St George) *see* New Bury w Gt Lever *Man*

FARNWORTH (St Luke) *see* E Widnes *Liv*

FARRINGDON (All Saints) *see* Northanger *Win*

FARRINGDON (St Petrock and St Barnabas) *see* Aylesbeare, Clyst St George, Clyst St Mary etc *Ex*

FARRINGTON GURNEY (St John the Baptist) *see* Paulton w Farrington Gurney and High Littleton *B & W*

FARSLEY (St John the Evangelist) *Leeds 14* **P** *V Calverley*
V P Q TUDGE **NSM** L M STEVENSON TATE

FARTHINGHOE (St Michael and All Angels) *see* Aynho and Croughton w Evenley etc *Pet*

FARTHINGSTONE (St Mary the Virgin) *see* Lambfold *Pet*

FARWAY (St Michael and All Angels) *see* Offwell, Northleigh, Farway, Cotleigh etc *Ex*

FATFIELD (St George) *Dur 10* **P** *Lord Lambton*
V N J BARR-HAMILTON

FAULKBOURNE (St Germanus) *see* Witham and Villages *Chelmsf*

FAULS (Holy Emmanuel) *see* Edstaston, Fauls, Prees, Tilstock and Whixall *Lich*

FAVELL, WEST (Emmanuel) *see* Northampton Em *Pet*

FAVERSHAM (St Mary of Charity), including Ospringe, Preston-next-Faversham, and The Brents and Davington *Cant 14* **P** *D&C, St Jo Coll Cam, and Abp (jt)*
V S D ROWLANDS **C** D C CORCORAN

FAWDON (St Mary the Virgin) *Newc 2* **P** *Bp*
P-in-c C A MACPHERSON **OLM** M A ATKINSON

FAWKHAM (St Mary) and Hartley *Roch 1* **P** *Bp and D&C (jt)*
R *vacant*

FAWLEY (All Saints) *Win 11* **P** *Bp* **P-in-c** C J BASTON
Hon C A E FAULKNER

FAWLEY (St Mary the Virgin) *see* Hambleden Valley *Ox*

FAWLEY (St Mary) *see* W Downland *Ox*

FAWSLEY (St Mary the Virgin) *see* Badby w Newham and Charwelton w Fawsley etc *Pet*

FAZAKERLEY (Emmanuel) (St Paul) *Liv 4* **P** *Patr Bd*
TR A J BROWN **TV** M A HINDLEY

FAZAKERLEY (St Nathanael) *see* Walton-on-the-Hill *Liv*

FAZELEY (St Paul) *see* Peel Parishes *Lich*

FAZELEY Mile Oak (St Barnabas) *as above*

FEATHERSTONE (All Saints) (St Thomas) *Leeds 18* **P** *Ch Ch Ox and Bp (jt)* **V** I GROSU **NSM** P J CLAPHAM

FECKENHAM (St John the Baptist) *see* Bowbrook N *Worc*

FEERING (All Saints) *see* Kelvedon and Feering *Chelmsf*

FELBRIDGE (St John) *S'wark 25* **P** *DBP* **V** M S FRANCIS

FELBRIGG (St Margaret) *see* Roughton and Felbrigg, Metton, Sustead etc *Nor*

FELIXKIRK (St Felix) w Boltby *York 18* **P** *Abp*
P-in-c D E GAMBLE **NSM** W A DEWING

FELIXSTOWE (Christ Church) *St E 11* **P** *Ch Patr Trust*
V M A MAK

FELIXSTOWE (St John the Baptist) (St Edmund) *St E 11*
P *Bp* **P-in-c** A S DOTCHIN **NSM** P H BRINKLEY

FELIXSTOWE (St Peter and St Paul) (St Andrew) (St Nicholas) *St E 11* **P** *Ch Trust Fund Trust* **V** C A HOOD

FELKIRK (St Peter) *see* Royston and Felkirk *Leeds*

FELLING (Christ Church) *Dur 11* **P** *CPAS*
NSM T R WORSLEY

FELLISCLIFFE (Mission Church) *see* Hampsthwaite and Killinghall and Birstwith *Leeds*

FELLSIDE TEAM, The, comprising Barton, Bilsborrow, Bleasdale, Goosnargh, and Whitechapel *Blackb 9* **P** *Patr Bd*
TR S P C COOPER **TV** G WHITTAKER **C** S SALT

FELMERSHAM (St Mary) *see* Sharnbrook, Felmersham and Knotting w Souldrop *St Alb*

FELMINGHAM (St Andrew) *see* King's Beck *Nor*

FELPHAM (St Mary the Virgin) *Chich 1* **P** *D&C*
R J W A CHALLIS

FELSHAM (St Peter) *see* Bradfield St Clare, Bradfield St George etc *St E*

FELSTED (Holy Cross) and Little Dunmow *Chelmsf 18*
P *CPAS* **V** C J TAYLOR

FELTHAM (St Dunstan) *Lon 11* **P** *Bp* **V** A M E DOLLERY

FELTHORPE (St Margaret) *see* Horsford, Felthorpe and Hevingham *Nor*

FELTON (St Katharine and the Noble Army of Martyrs) *see* Winford w Felton Common Hill *B & W*

FELTON (St Michael and All Angels) *Newc 6* **P** *Bp*
P-in-c T J HARVEY **NSM** C M A HEPPER

FELTON (St Michael the Archangel) *see* Maund Gp *Heref*

FELTON, WEST (St Michael) *see* Whittington and W Felton w Haughton *Lich*

FELTWELL (St Mary) *see* Grimshoe *Ely*

FEN AND HILL Group, The, comprising Hameringham, Mareham le Fen, Mareham on the Hill, and Scrivelsby *Linc 13* **P** *Bp, DBP, G J R Wiggins-Davies Esq, and Lt Col J L M Dymoke (jt)* **R** A J ROBERTS **OLM** K A BUSH

FEN DITTON (St Mary the Virgin) *Ely 2* **P** *Bp*
P-in-c A J FORD

FEN DRAYTON (St Mary the Virgin) w Fenstanton *Ely 10*
P *Ch Coll Cam and Bp (jt)* **P-in-c** R TALLOWIN

FEN ORCHARDS, The, comprising Elm, Emneth, and Friday Bridge w Coldham *Ely 14* **P** *Bp* **V** D L MASON

FENCE-IN-PENDLE (St Anne) and Higham *Blackb 6* **P** *Bp and Ld Chan (alt)* **V** L HINCHCLIFFE

FENCOTE (St Andrew) *see* Lower Swale *Leeds*

FENHAM (Holy Cross) *see* Newc H Cross *Newc*

FENHAM (St James and St Basil) *Newc 4* **P** *Bp*
V J MCGOWAN **NSM** B O OMOBUDE

FENISCLIFFE (St Francis) *Blackb 2* **P** *Bp* **P-in-c** D J ROSCOE

FENISCOWLES (Immanuel) *Blackb 2* **P** *V Blackb*
P-in-c D J ROSCOE
FENITON (St Andrew) *see* Ottery St Mary, Alfington, W Hill, Tipton etc *Ex*
FENN LANES Group, The, comprising Fenny Drayton, Higham-on-the-Hill, Stoke Golding, and Witherley *Leic 10*
P *Bp, D&C, and Lord O'Neill (jt)* **R** L J BLAY
FENNY BENTLEY (St Edmund King and Martyr), Thorpe, Tissington, Parwich and Alsop-en-le-Dale *Derby 1* **P** *Bp, D A G Shields Esq, and Sir Richard FitzHerbert Bt (jt)*
P-in-c C E MCDONALD **NSM** A P GRIGGS
FENNY COMPTON (St Peter and St Clare) *see* Avon Dassett w Farnborough and Fenny Compton *Cov*
FENNY DRAYTON (St Michael and All Angels) *see* Fenn Lanes Gp *Leic*
FENNY STRATFORD (St Martin) *Ox 14* **P** *Bp*
V V J A BULLOCK **NSM** I W THOMAS
FENSTANTON (St Peter and St Paul) *see* Fen Drayton w Fenstanton *Ely*
FENTON (Christ Church) *see* Stoke-upon-Trent and Fenton *Lich*
FEOCK (St Feock) *Truro 6* **P** *Bp* **P-in-c** S A BONE
C K E JONES, R D WALLIS **NSM** J ROWE, S J C FLETCHER
FERNDOWN (St Mary) *see* Hampreston *Sarum*
FERNHAM (St John the Evangelist) *see* Shrivenham and Ashbury *Ox*
FERNHURST (St Margaret), Lynchmere and Camelsdale *Chich 9* **P** *The Crown and Bp (alt)* **V** N P HAIGH
FERNILEE (Holy Trinity) *see* Whaley Bridge *Ches*
FERRIBY, NORTH (All Saints) *York 14* **P** *CPAS*
V M C BRAILSFORD
FERRIBY, SOUTH (St Nicholas) *Linc 8* **P** *Bp* **R** D P ROWETT
NSM R M JAGGS-FOWLER
FERRING (St Andrew) *Chich 4* **P** *D&C* **V** G S INGRAM
NSM J SIMPSON
FERRYBRIDGE (St Andrew) *Leeds 18* **P** *D&C York*
P-in-c S L BROWN **NSM** S HULME
FERRYHILL (St Luke) *see* Cornforth and Ferryhill *Dur*
FERSFIELD (St Andrew) *see* Diss *Nor*
FETCHAM (St Mary) *Guildf 10* **P** *Bp* **R** A L SMITH
FEWSTON (St Michael and St Lawrence) *see* Washburn and Mid-Wharfe *Leeds*
FIDDINGTON (St Martin) *see* Quantock Coast *B & W*
FIELD BROUGHTON (St Peter) *see* Cartmel Peninsula *Carl*
FIELD DALLING (St Andrew) *see* Stiffkey and Bale *Nor*
FIFEHEAD MAGDALEN (St Mary Magdalene) *see* Stour Vale *Sarum*
FIFEHEAD NEVILLE (All Saints) *see* Hazelbury Bryan and the Hillside Par *Sarum*
FIFIELD (St John the Baptist) *see* Wychwood *Ox*
FIFIELD BAVANT (St Martin) *see* Chalke Valley *Sarum*
FIGHELDEAN (St Michael and All Angels) *see* Avon River *Sarum*
FILBY (All Saints) *see* S Trin Broads *Nor*
FILEY (St John) (St Oswald) *York 15* **P** *PCC*
V N L CHAPMAN
FILKINS (St Peter) *see* Shill Valley and Broadshire *Ox*
FILLEIGH (St Paul) *see* S Molton w Nymet St George, Chittlehamholt etc *Ex*
FILLINGHAM (St Andrew) *see* Spring Line Gp *Linc*
FILTON (St Gregory) *see* Horfield St Greg *Bris*
FILTON (St Peter) *Bris 5* **P** *Bp* **R** E L A GREGORY
FILWOOD PARK (St Barnabas) *Bris 1* **P** *Bp and Bris Ch Trustees (jt)* **P-in-c** C L GARDINER **C** S SHEPPARD
FIMBER (St Mary) *see* Waggoners *York*
FINBOROUGH, GREAT (St Andrew) *see* Combs and Finborough *St E*
FINBOROUGH, LITTLE (St Mary) *as above*
FINCHAM (St Martin) *see* W Norfolk Priory Gp *Ely*
FINCHAMPSTEAD (St James) and California *Ox 8* **P** *DBP*
R J F RAMSBOTTOM **C** A ELLIOTT, G L WILKINSON, J W MCALLEN **NSM** J R EDWARDS
FINCHINGFIELD (St John the Baptist) and Cornish Hall End and Wethersfield w Shalford *Chelmsf 17* **P** *CPAS and Bp (alt)* **V** *vacant*
FINCHLEY (Christ Church) *Lon 14* **P** *Ch Patr Trust*
V D A WALKER
FINCHLEY (Holy Trinity) *Lon 16* **P** *Bp* **P-in-c** M MIRT
FINCHLEY (St Barnabas) *see* Woodside Park St Barn *Lon*
FINCHLEY (St Mary) *Lon 14* **P** *Bp* **R** P A DAVISON
C R D MAGRATH
FINCHLEY (St Paul) (St Luke) *Lon 14* **P** *Simeon Trustees and Ch Patr Trust (jt)* **V** N R PYE **NSM** M A CRISPIN
FINCHLEY, EAST (All Saints) *Lon 14* **P** *Bp* **V** *vacant*
FINDERN (All Saints) *Derby 7* **P** *Bp* **V** S A STARKEY

FINDON (St John the Baptist) w Clapham and Patching *Chich 4* **P** *Abp, Bp, and C C F Somerset Esq (jt)*
P-in-c H M BUQUÉ **NSM** C J COX
FINDON VALLEY (All Saints) *Chich 4* **P** *Bp* **P-in-c** B A MILES
FINEDON (St Mary the Virgin) *Pet 8* **P** *Bp* **V** R K R COLES
NSM J E BURNS
FINGEST (St Bartholomew) *see* Hambleden Valley *Ox*
FINGHALL (St Andrew) *see* Lower Wensleydale *Leeds*
FINGRINGHOE (St Andrew) w East Donyland and Abberton w Langenhoe *Chelmsf 24* **P** *Bp (3 turns), Ld Chan (1 turn)* **R** *vacant*
FINHAM (St Martin in the Fields) *Cov 3* **P** *Bp*
V M T TAYLOR **C** A L RHODES
FINMERE (St Michael) *see* Shelswell *Ox*
FINNINGHAM (St Bartholomew) *see* Badwell and Walsham *St E*
FINNINGLEY (Holy Trinity and St Oswald) w Auckley *Sheff 9*
P *Bp* **R** N M REDEYOFF
FINSBURY (St Clement) (St Barnabas) (St Matthew) *Lon 6*
P *D&C St Paul's* **V** D E ALLEN
FINSBURY PARK (St Thomas) *Lon 6* **P** *Abp* **V** S R COLES
FINSTALL (St Godwald) *see* Bromsgrove *Worc*
FINSTHWAITE (St Peter) *see* Cartmel Peninsula *Carl*
FINSTOCK (Holy Trinity) *see* Forest Edge *Ox*
FIR VALE (St Cuthbert) *see* Sheff St Cuth *Sheff*
FIRBANK (St John the Evangelist), Howgill and Killington *Carl 10* **P** *Ld Chan and V Sedbergh (jt)*
P-in-c A B MCMULLON
FIRBECK (St Martin) w Letwell *Sheff 5* **P** *Bp* **R** *vacant*
FIRLE, WEST (St Peter) *see* Glynde, W Firle and Beddingham *Chich*
FIRSBY (St Andrew) *see* Bolingbroke Deanery *Linc*
FIRSWOOD (St Hilda) and Gorse Hill *Man 5* **P** *The Crown*
R T R MALKIN
FISHBOURNE, NEW (St Peter and St Mary) *Chich 2* **P** *Ld Chan* **R** M WICKENS
FISHBURN (St Catherine) *see* Upper Skerne *Dur*
FISHERMEAD (Trinity Church) *see* Woughton *Ox*
FISHERTON ANGER (St Paul) *Sarum 13* **P** *Ch Patr Trust*
R C J RYALLS **NSM** A ETHERIDGE
FISHLAKE (St Cuthbert) w Sykehouse and Kirk Bramwith w Fenwick and Moss *Sheff 10* **P** *Duchy of Lanc (1 turn), D&C Dur (2 turns), and Bp (1 turn)* **R** *vacant*
FISHLEY (St Mary) *see* Broadside *Nor*
FISHPOND (St John the Baptist) *see* Golden Cap Team *Sarum*
FISHPONDS (All Saints) (St Mary) *Bris 3* **P** *Bp*
V E A KESTEVEN
FISHPONDS (St John) *Bris 3* **P** *Bp* **P-in-c** R J LING
C M HOTCHKISS **NSM** M M CRITCHLOW **NSM** N G CALLEN
FISHTOFT (St Guthlac) *Linc 21* **P** *DBP* **R** M A R COOPER
FISKERTON (St Clement) *see* S Lawres Gp *Linc*
FITTLETON (All Saints) *see* Avon River *Sarum*
FITTLEWORTH (St Mary the Virgin) *see* Stopham and Fittleworth *Chich*
FITTON HILL (St Cuthbert) *see* Bardsley *Man*
FITZ (St Peter and St Paul) *see* Bicton, Montford w Shrawardine and Fitz *Lich*
FITZHEAD (St James) *see* Milverton w Halse, Fitzhead and Ash Priors *B & W*
FIVE ALIVE *see* Fladbury, Hill and Moor, Wyre Piddle etc *Worc*
FIVE ASHES (Church of the Good Shepherd) *see* Mayfield *Chich*
FIVE OAK GREEN (St Luke) *see* Capel United Ben *Roch*
FIVEHEAD (St Martin) *see* Curry Rivel w Fivehead and Swell *B & W*
FIXBY (St Francis) and Cowcliffe, Huddersfield *Leeds 11*
P *DBP* **P-in-c** I D JAMIESON
FLACKWELL HEATH (Christ Church) *Ox 18* **P** *DBP*
V C D BULL **C** I J KNIGHT **OLM** M H COURTNEY
FLADBURY (St John the Baptist), Hill and Moor, Wyre Piddle, Cropthorne and Charlton *Worc 4* **P** *Bp and D&C (jt)* **P-in-c** S A DANGERFIELD **C** E L GOLDBY, G R NOYES
FLAMBOROUGH (St Oswald) *see* Bempton w Flamborough, Reighton w Speeton *York*
FLAMSTEAD (St Leonard) and Markyate Street *St Alb 7*
P *Bp and Univ Coll Ox (jt)* **V** T W SANDER
NSM S W TUDWAY
FLAUNDEN (St Mary Magdalene) *see* Chenies and Lt Chalfont, Latimer and Flaunden *Ox*
FLAX BOURTON (St Michael and All Angels) *see* Long Ashton w Barrow Gurney and Flax Bourton *B & W*
FLAXLEY (St Mary the Virgin) *see* Westbury-on-Severn w Flaxley, Blaisdon etc *Glouc*
FLAXTON (St Lawrence) *see* Harton *York*

FLECKNEY (St Nicholas)   *see* Wistow *Leic*
FLECKNOE (St Mark)   *see* Leam Valley *Cov*
FLEET (All Saints) (St Philip and St James) *Guildf 1*   P *Bp*
V M W HAYTON   C C A DUNK   NSM J J SISTIG
FLEET (Holy Trinity)   *see* Chickerell w Fleet *Sarum*
FLEET (St Mary Magdalene)   *see* Mid Elloe Gp *Linc*
FLEETWOOD (St Nicholas) *Blackb 12*   P *Bp and SMF (jt)*
V C A LEITCH
FLEETWOOD (St Peter) (St David's Church Centre)
Blackb 12   P *SMF*   V J M HALL   C C L DINGWALL-JONES
FLEGG COASTAL Benefice, The: Hemsby, Winterton, East
and West Somerton and Horsey *Nor 6*   P *Bp, D&C, SMF,
and Major R A Ferrier (jt)*   P-in-c J S BLOOMFIELD
FLEGG GROUP (Martham)   *see* Martham and Repps w
Bastwick, Thurne etc *Nor*
FLEGG GROUP (Ormesby)   *see* Ormesby St Marg w Scratby,
Ormesby St Mich etc *Nor*
FLEGG GROUP (South Trinity Broads)   *see* S Trin Broads *Nor*
FLEGGBURGH *as above*
FLEMPTON (St Catherine of Alexandria)   *see* Lark Valley *St E*
FLETCHAMSTEAD (St James) *Cov 3*   P *Bp*   V S R BURCH
FLETCHING (St Mary and St Andrew) *Chich 18*   P *Abp*
V B C MURPHY
FLETTON (St Margaret) *Ely 15*   P *Sir Philip Naylor-Leyland Bt*
P-in-c W P L GAMMON
FLIMBY (St Nicholas)   *see* Maryport, Netherton, Flimby and
Broughton Moor *Carl*
FLIMWELL (St Augustine of Canterbury)   *see* Ticehurst and
Flimwell *Chich*
FLINTHAM (St Augustine of Canterbury) *S'well 5*   P *R H T
Hildyard Esq*   P-in-c R M COLBY
FLITCHAM (St Mary the Virgin)   *see* Sandringham w W
Newton and Appleton etc *Nor*
FLITTON (St John the Baptist)   *see* Silsoe, Pulloxhill and
Flitton *St Alb*
FLITWICK (St Andrew) (St Peter and St Paul) *St Alb 8*
P *DBP*   V L F DAVIS   C A J MAFFEI
FLIXBOROUGH (All Saints) w Burton upon Stather *Linc 6*
P *Sir Reginald Sheffield Bt*   P-in-c A F PLEDGER
FLIXTON (St John) *Man 5*   P *Bp*   OLM M SURREY, R W GREEN
FLIXTON (St Mary)   *see* The Saints *St E*
FLIXTON (St Michael) *Man 5*   P *Bp*   P-in-c H D THOMAS
NSM A H CLEPHANE, O B MORETT   OLM F A JENKINSON
FLOCKTON (St James the Great)   *see* Lepton, Emley and
Flockton w Denby Grange *Leeds*
FLOOKBURGH (St John the Baptist)   *see* Cartmel Peninsula
Carl
FLORDON (St Michael)   *see* Mulbarton w Bracon Ash, Hethel
and Flordon *Nor*
FLORE (All Saints)   *see* Heyford w Stowe Nine Churches and
Flore etc *Pet*
FLOWTON (St Mary)   *see* S Bosmere *St E*
FLUSHING (St Peter)   *see* Mylor w Flushing *Truro*
FLYFORD FLAVELL (St Peter)   *see* Abberton, The Flyfords,
Naunton Beauchamp etc *Worc*
FOBBING (St Michael)   *see* Corringham and Fobbing
Chelmsf
FOLESHILL (St Laurence) *Cov 2*   P *Ld Chan*   V G I IRVINE
NSM J A IRVINE
FOLESHILL (St Paul) *Cov 2*   P *Ld Chan*   V A HOGGER-GADSBY
FOLEY PARK (Holy Innocents)   *see* Kidderminster St Jo and H
Innocents *Worc*
FOLKE (St Lawrence)   *see* Three Valleys *Sarum*
FOLKESTONE (St Augustine) (St Mary and St Eanswythe)
St Saviour *Cant 8*   P *Abp*   V *vacant*
FOLKESTONE (St John the Baptist) *Cant 8*   P *CPAS*
V S J BRADFORD   C J L PURLE
FOLKESTONE (St Peter) *Cant 8*   P *Trustees*
P-in-c M V HALDON-JONES
FOLKESTONE Trinity Benefice, The (Holy Trinity w Christ
Church) (St George) (St Paul) *Cant 8*   P *Abp and Ld Chan
(alt)*   V R P WELDON   NSM K M MCNEICE, R O SMITH
FOLKESWORTH (St Helen)   *see* Stilton w Denton and
Caldecote etc *Ely*
FOLKINGHAM (St Andrew)   *see* S Lafford *Linc*
FOLKINGTON (St Peter ad Vincula)   *see* Alfriston w
Lullington, Litlington, W Dean and Folkington *Chich*
FOLKTON (St John)   *see* Hertford York
FOLLIFOOT (St Joseph and St James)   *see* Spofforth w Kirk
Deighton *Leeds*
FONTHILL BISHOP (All Saints)   *see* Nadder Valley *Sarum*
FONTHILL GIFFORD (Holy Trinity) *as above*
FONTMELL MAGNA (St Andrew)   *see* Iwerne Valley *Sarum*
FOOLOW (St Hugh)   *see* Baslow and Eyam *Derby*
FOORD (St John the Baptist)   *see* Folkestone St Jo *Cant*
FOOTSCRAY (All Saints)   *see* Sidcup St Jo w Footscray *Roch*

FORCETT (St Cuthbert) and Aldbrough and Melsonby
Leeds 22   P *DBP and Univ Coll Ox (alt)*
R C A CAMPLING-DENTON
FORD (St Andrew)   *see* Clymping and Yapton w Ford *Chich*
FORD (St John of Jerusalem)   *see* Leominster *Heref*
FORD (St Mark)   *see* Devonport St Bart and Ford St Mark *Ex*
FORD (St Michael and All Angels) and Etal *Newc 12*   P *Lord
Joicey*   R *vacant*
FORD (St Michael), Gt Wollaston and Alberbury w
Cardeston *Heref 12*   P *Bp (3 turns), Sir Michael Leighton Bt
(1 turn)*   R V J TAIT   OLM M E NEAL
FORD END (St John the Evangelist)   *see* Gt Waltham w Ford
End *Chelmsf*
FORDCOMBE (St Peter)   *see* Penshurst and Fordcombe *Roch*
FORDHAM (All Saints) *Chelmsf 21*   P *Reformation Ch Trust,
Ball Coll Ox (alt)*   C F C BLIGHT
FORDHAM (St Peter and St Mary Magdalene)   *see* Three
Rivers Gp *Ely*
FORDHOUSES (St James)   *see* Bushbury *Lich*
FORDINGBRIDGE (St Mary) and Hyde and Breamore and
Hale with Woodgreen *Win 9*   P *K Coll Cam, Keble Coll Ox,
Sir Edward Hulse Bt, and Mrs C R d'O Hickman (jt)*
R G J PHILBRICK   C M E TROTMAN   NSM N L DAVIES
FORDON (St James)   *see* Rudston, Boynton, Carnaby etc *York*
FOREMARK (St Saviour) and Repton w Newton Solney
Derby 7   P *Bp and DBP (jt)*   V M J FLOWERDEW
OLM J C SCOTT
FOREST (St Stephen)   *see* Rainow w Saltersford and Forest
Ches
FOREST AND AVON, comprising Bramshaw, Downton,
Landford, Morgan's Vale, Plaitford, and Redlynch *Sarum 10*
P *Patr Bd*   TR F H GIMSON   TV D G BACON
Hon C C W ROGERS   NSM V BATCHELOR
FOREST EDGE   *see* Huntley and Longhope, Churcham and
Bulley *Glouc*
FOREST EDGE, comprising Finstock w Fawler, Leafield w
Wychwood, Ramsden, and Wilcote *Ox 22*   P *Bp,
V Charlbury, and Sir Mark Norman Bt (jt)*   V P J MANSELL
FOREST GATE (All Saints) *Chelmsf 5*   P *Bp*   P-in-c J S FRASER
C M G P BENNETT
FOREST GATE (Emmanuel w St Peter) Upton Cross
Chelmsf 5   P *Bp*   V C CHIKE   C K N AKWASI-YEBOAH,
P D ODOEMENA
FOREST GATE (St Edmund)   *see* E Ham H Trin *Chelmsf*
FOREST GATE (St James)   *see* Stratford St Jo w Ch Ch *Chelmsf*
FOREST GATE (St Mark) *Chelmsf 5*   P *Ch Patr Trust*
V B W KING
FOREST GATE (St Saviour) (St James) *Chelmsf 5*   P *CPAS*
V C A HENRY
FOREST GREEN (Holy Trinity)   *see* Ewhurst w Okewood and
Forest Green *Guildf*
FOREST HILL (Christ Church) (St George) w Lower
Sydenham St Michael and All Angels *S'wark 5*   P *Patr Bd*
P-in-c P LANE   TV I E C CHUKUKA
FOREST HILL (St Nicholas)   *see* Beckley, Forest Hill,
Horton-cum-Studley and Stanton St John *Ox*
FOREST OF DEAN (Christ Church) w English Bicknor
Glouc 1   P *The Crown (3 turns), SMF (1 turn)*
V A J WILLIAMS
FOREST OF DEAN (Holy Trinity)   *see* Drybrook, Lydbrook and
Ruardean *Glouc*
FOREST OF GALTRES (Farlington, Marton w Moxby, Sheriff
Hutton, and Sutton-on-the-Forest) *York 3*   P *Abp (2
turns), Ld Chan (1 turn)*   P-in-c S WHITING   C D M COYNE,
E C HASSALL, M E YOUNG, M H WAINWRIGHT, M HARRISON
NSM C C CRANFIELD, C C GITTENS, C J TOASE, S P POPE,
T M GANT
FOREST ROW (Holy Trinity) *Chich 6*   P V E Grinstead
V A F MARTIN
FOREST TOWN (St Alban) *S'well 2*   P *Bp*   P-in-c P J STEAD
FOREST-IN-TEESDALE (St Mary the Virgin)   *see* Middleton-in-
Teesdale w Forest and Frith *Dur*
FORESTSIDE (Christ Church)   *see* Octagon *Chich*
FORMBY (Holy Trinity) and Altcar *Liv 8*   P *Bp and Trustees
(jt)*   V M R STANFORD   C E P THORPE   NSM D C M TAYLOR
FORMBY (St Luke) *Liv 8*   P *Bp*   V H T NICOL
FORMBY (St Peter) *Liv 8*   P *R Walton*   V A E TAYLOR
C N A THORPE
FORNCETT (St Mary)   *see* Upper Tas Valley *Nor*
FORNCETT (St Peter) *as above*
FORNCETT END (St Edmund) *as above*
FORNHAM ALL SAINTS (All Saints)   *see* Lark Valley *St E*
FORNHAM ST MARTIN (St Martin) *as above*
FORRABURY (St Symphorian)   *see* Boscastle and Tintagel Gp
Truro

FORSBROOK (St Peter) *see* Draycott-le-Moors w Forsbrook *Lich*

FORTHAMPTON (St Mary) *see* Deerhurst and Apperley w Forthampton etc *Glouc*

FORTON (All Saints) *Lich 15* **P** *Bp* **P-in-c** P W THOMAS

FORTON (St James) *see* Shireshead *Blackb*

FORTON (St John the Evangelist) *Portsm 3* **P** *DBP*
V C J L J THOMPSON

FORTY HILL (Jesus Church) *Lon 18* **P** *V Enfield*
V I H CROFTS

FOSDYKE (All Saints) *see* Kirton in Holland w Algarkirk and Fosdyke *Linc*

FOSSE Team, The, comprising Barkby, East Goscote, Queniborough, Rearsby, Syston, Thrussington w Ratcliffe on the Wreake, and Thurmaston *Leic 4* **P** *Patr Bd*
TR L T FRANCIS-DEHQANI **TV** M C A'HERNE-SMITH, T R DAY
NSM J M HILL

FOSSE TRINITY, comprising Ditcheat, East Pennard, and Pylle *B & W 7* **P** *Bp and Canon D S Salter (jt)* **R** *vacant*

FOSTON (All Saints) *see* Harton *York*

FOSTON (St Bartholomew) *see* Four Saints *Leic*

FOSTON (St Peter) *see* Saxonwell *Linc*

FOSTON-ON-THE-WOLDS (St Andrew) *see* Beeford w Frodingham and Foston *York*

FOTHERBY (St Mary), North Thoresby and Grainsby w Waithe *Linc 15* **P** *Ld Chan (2 turns), R H C Haigh Esq, Trustees, and Exors Revd J M Ashley (1 turn), Dbp, G F Sleight Esq, MMCET, and Bp (2 turns), R H C Haigh Esq, Trustees and Mrs M F Davis (1 turn)* **V** *vacant*

FOTHERINGHAY (St Mary and All Saints) *see* Warmington, Tansor and Cotterstock etc *Pet*

FOULDEN (All Saints) *see* Oxborough w Foulden and Caldecote *Nor*

FOULRIDGE (St Michael and All Angels), Laneshawbridge and Trawden *Blackb 6* **P** *Bp and DBP* **R** J W KNOTT

FOULSHAM (Holy Innocents) *see* Heart of Norfolk *Nor*

FOUNTAINS Group, The, comprising Aldfield, Dallowgill, Grewelthorpe, Kirkby Malzeard, Mickley, Sawley, and Winksley *Leeds 23* **P** *D&C Ripon* **R** *vacant*

FOUR ELMS (St Paul) *see* Hever, Four Elms and Mark Beech *Roch*

FOUR MARKS (Good Shepherd) *Win 2* **P** *Bp*
V H J D WRIGHT

FOUR OAKS (All Saints) *Birm 7* **P** *Bp* **V** D A LEAHY

FOUR RIVERS, comprising Bedfield, Brundish, Cratfield, Laxfield, Monk Soham, Tannington, Wilby, and Worlingworth w Southolt *St E 13* **P** *Bp, Dr F H C Marriott, Simeon's Trustees, R C Rouse, and DBP (jt)* **R** D P BURRELL
NSM D J MULRENAN, R J ARTISS

FOUR SAINTS Benefice, The, comprising Countesthorpe, Foston, Peatling Magna, and Willoughby Waterleys *Leic 7*
P *Bp and DBP (jt)* **R** *vacant*

FOUR SAINTS Team, The *see* 4Saints Team *Liv*

FOURSTONES (St Aidan) *see* Warden w Newbrough *Newc*

FOVANT (St George), Sutton Mandeville and Teffont Evias w Teffont Magna and Compton Chamberlayne *Sarum 11*
P *Reformation Ch Trust, Bp, and Ch Soc Trust (jt)* **R** *vacant*

FOWEY (St Fimbarrus) *Truro 1* **P** *Ch Soc Trust*
V P DE GREY-WARTER

FOWLMERE (St Mary), Foxton, Shepreth and Thriplow *Ely 7* **P** *Bp* **R** A E MELANIPHY

FOWNHOPE (St Mary) w Mordiford, Brockhampton and Fawley and Woolhope *Heref 3* **P** *D&C (4 turns), and Major R J Hereford (1 turn)* **R** C K W MOORE

FOXCOTE (St James the Less) *see* Peasedown St John w Wellow and Foxcote etc *B & W*

FOXDALE (St Paul) *see* Marown, Foxdale and Baldwin *S & M*

FOXEARTH (St Peter and St Paul) *see* N Hinckford *Chelmsf*

FOXHAM (St John the Baptist) *see* Marden Vale *Sarum*

FOXHILL (Chapel) *see* Frodsham *Ches*

FOXHOLE (St Boniface) *see* Paignton St Jo *Ex*

FOXLEY (not known) *see* Gauzebrook *Bris*

FOXLEY (St Thomas) *see* Heart of Norfolk *Nor*

FOXT (St Mark the Evangelist) *see* Kingsley and Foxt-w-Whiston and Oakamoor etc *Lich*

FOXTON (St Andrew) w Gumley and Laughton *Leic 3* **P** *Bp Leic and D&C Linc (alt)* **P-in-c** P J OXLEY

FOXTON (St Laurence) *see* Fowlmere, Foxton, Shepreth and Thriplow *Ely*

FOY (St Mary) *see* StowCaple *Heref*

FRADLEY (St Stephen) *see* Alrewas *Lich*

FRADSWELL (St James the Less) *see* Mid Trent *Lich*

FRAMFIELD (St Thomas à Becket) *Chich 18* **P** *Mrs E R Wix*
V C D LAWRENCE

FRAMILODE (St Peter) *see* Stroudwater Team *Glouc*

FRAMINGHAM EARL (St Andrew) *see* Poringland *Nor*

FRAMINGHAM PIGOT (St Andrew) *see* Thurton w Ashby St Mary, Bergh Apton etc *Nor*

FRAMLAND Parishes, The HIGH, comprising Branston-by-Belvoir, Croxton Kerrial, Harston, Knipton, Saltby, and Sproxton *Leic 2* **P** *Duke of Rutland and Sir Lyonel Tollemache Bt (jt)* **P-in-c** D J COWIE **Hon C** J L HUTCHINSON

FRAMLAND, SOUTH, comprising Buckminster, Coston, Saxby w Stapleford and Wyfordby, and Wymondham *Leic 2* **P** *Ld Chan, Duke of Rutland, Lady Gretton, and Sir Lyonel Tollemache Bt (by turn)* **P-in-c** D J COWIE
Hon C J L HUTCHINSON

FRAMLINGHAM (St Michael) w Saxtead *St E 14* **P** *Pemb Coll Cam* **R** M SANDERS

FRAMPTON (St Mary) *see* Charminster, Stinsford and the Chalk Stream villages *Sarum*

FRAMPTON (St Mary) (St Michael) *Linc 21* **P** *Trustees*
V S SARVANANTHAN

FRAMPTON COTTERELL (St Peter) *see* Fromeside *Bris*

FRAMPTON MANSELL (St Luke) *see* Kemble, Poole Keynes, Somerford Keynes etc *Glouc*

FRAMPTON ON SEVERN (St Mary) *see* Stroudwater Team *Glouc*

FRAMSDEN (St Mary) *see* Debenham and Helmingham *St E*

FRAMWELLGATE MOOR (St Aidan) *see* Dur N *Dur*

FRANCE LYNCH (St John the Baptist) *see* Bisley, Chalford, France Lynch, and Oakridge etc *Glouc*

FRANCHE (St Barnabas) *see* Kidderminster Ismere *Worc*

FRANKBY (St John the Divine) w Greasby St Nicholas *Ches 8* **P** *D&C* **V** K P OWEN

FRANKLEY (St Leonard) *Birm 3* **P** *Bp* **P-in-c** J M PLATT

FRANKTON (St Nicholas) *see* Draycote Gp *Cov*

FRANSHAM, GREAT (All Saints) *see* Launditch and the Upper Nar *Nor*

FRANSHAM, LITTLE (St Mary) *as above*

FRANT (St Alban) w Eridge *Chich 16* **P** *Bp and Marquess of Abergavenny (jt)* **R** B J MARTIN **NSM** I A J TRASK

FREASLEY (St Mary) *see* Dordon *Birm*

FRECHEVILLE (St Cyprian) *Sheff 2* **P** *Bp* **R** *vacant*

FRECKENHAM (St Andrew) *see* Mildenhall *St E*

FRECKLETON (Holy Trinity) and Warton St Paul *Blackb 10*
P *Bp and Ch Ch Ox (jt)* **V** J GREENHALGH **NSM** F E HAINES

FREEBY (St Mary) *see* Melton Mowbray *Leic*

FREEHAY (St Chad) *see* Cheadle w Freehay *Lich*

FREELAND (St Mary the Virgin) *see* Hanborough and Freeland *Ox*

FREEMANTLE (Christ Church) *Win 13* **P** *Bp* **R** *vacant*

FREETHORPE (All Saints) *see* Acle and Bure to Yare *Nor*

FREISTON (St James), Butterwick w Bennington, and Leverton *Linc 21* **P** *Ld Chan and Bp (alt)*
P-in-c A J HIGGINSON

FREMINGTON (St Peter), Instow and Westleigh *Ex 14*
P *D&C, Christie Trustees, and MMCET (jt)*
C K J BRIMACOMBE, T W N SIMPSON

FRENCHAY (St John the Baptist) and Stapleton *Bris 5* **P** *Bp and St Jo Coll Ox (jt)* **R** C E SUGDEN **OLM** J M LEE

FRENSHAM (St Mary the Virgin) *Guildf 3* **P** *Ld Chan*
V J L WALKER

FRESHFORD (St Peter) w Limpley Stoke and Hinton Charterhouse *B & W 8* **P** *Simeon's Trustees and V Norton St Phil (jt)* **P-in-c** M S TAYLOR

FRESHWATER (All Saints) *see* W Wight *Portsm*

FRESHWATER BAY (St Agnes) *as above*

FRESSINGFIELD (St Peter and St Paul) *see* Sancroft *St E*

FRESTON (St Peter) *see* Holbrook, Stutton, Freston, Woolverstone etc *St E*

FRETHERNE (St Mary the Virgin) *see* Stroudwater Team *Glouc*

FRETTENHAM (St Swithin) *see* Coltishall w Gt Hautbois, Frettenham etc *Nor*

FRIAR PARK (St Francis of Assisi) *see* W Bromwich St Fran *Lich*

FRIARMERE (St Thomas) *see* Saddleworth *Man*

FRICKLEY (All Saints) *see* Bilham *Sheff*

FRIDAY BRIDGE (St Mark) *see* Fen Orchards *Ely*

FRIDAYTHORPE (St Mary) *see* Waggoners *York*

FRIERN BARNET (All Saints) *Lon 14* **P** *Bp* **V** G A D PLATTEN **C** R J WILKINSON **NSM** D J BOOKER, H LAMB

FRIERN BARNET (St James the Great) (St John the Evangelist) *Lon 14* **P** *D&C St Paul's*
R P A WALMSLEY-MCLEOD

FRIERN BARNET (St Peter le Poer) *Lon 14* **P** *D&C St Paul's*
P-in-c P H SUDELL

FRIESTHORPE (St Peter) *see* Middle Rasen Gp *Linc*

FRIETH (St John the Baptist) *see* Hambleden Valley *Ox*

FRIEZLAND (Christ Church) *see* Saddleworth *Man*

FRILSHAM (St Frideswide) *see* Hermitage *Ox*

FRIMLEY (St Francis) (St Peter) *Guildf 6* **P** *R Ash*
R S G THOMAS   **OLM** G E C SHORTLAND
FRIMLEY GREEN (St Andrew) and Mytchett *Guildf 6* **P** *Bp*
V vacant
FRINDSBURY (All Saints) w Upnor and Chattenden *Roch 6*
P *Bp* **V** N J COOPER **C** S F VALLENTE-KERR
FRING (All Saints) *see* Docking, The Birchams, Fring etc *Nor*
FRINGFORD (St Michael) *see* Shelswell *Ox*
FRINSTED (St Dunstan) *see* Tunstall and Bredgar *Cant*
**FRINTON (St Mary Magdalene) (St Mary the Virgin Old
Church)** *Chelmsf 23* **P** *CPAS* **R** D E SMITH
FRISBY-ON-THE-WREAKE (St Thomas of Canterbury) *see*
Upper Wreake *Leic*
FRISKNEY (All Saints) *Linc 21* **P** *Bp*
P-in-c F J M COTTON-BETTERIDGE
FRISTON (St Mary Magdalene) *see* Alde Sandlings *St E*
FRISTON (St Mary the Virgin) *see* E Dean w Friston and
Jevington *Chich*
FRITHELSTOCK (St Mary and St Gregory) *see* Gt and Lt
Torrington and Frithelstock *Ex*
FRITHVILLE (St Peter) *see* Sibsey w Frithville *Linc*
FRITTENDEN (St Mary) *see* Sissinghurst w Frittenden *Cant*
FRITTON (St Catherine) *see* Hempnall *Nor*
FRITTON (St Edmund) *see* Somerleyton, Ashby, Fritton,
Herringfleet etc *Nor*
FRITWELL (St Olave) *see* Cherwell Valley *Ox*
FRIZINGHALL (St Margaret) *Leeds 2* **P** *Bp*
P-in-c M E WATSON
FRIZINGTON (St Paul) *see* Crosslacon *Carl*
FROCESTER (St Andrew) *see* Stroudwater Team *Glouc*
FRODESLEY (St Mark) *see* Condover w Frodesley, Acton
Burnell etc *Heref*
FRODINGHAM (St Lawrence) and New Brumby *Linc 6*
P *Lord St Oswald* **V** P BRENT **C** L A E COCKRAM, S TIERNEY
FRODINGHAM, NORTH (St Elgin) *see* Beeford w Frodingham
and Foston *York*
FRODSHAM (St Lawrence) *Ches 3* **P** *Ch Ch Ox*
NSM A C ASKWITH
FROGMORE (Holy Trinity) *St Alb 5* **P** *CPAS* **V** N J WEIR
C M A SMITH **NSM** N A WARD
FROLESWORTH (St Nicholas) *see* Upper Soar *Leic*
FROME (Christ Church) (St Mary) *B & W 3* **P** *Bp* **V** vacant
FROME (Holy Trinity) *B & W 3* **P** *Bp* **V** G A OWEN
NSM C SHAW NOTICE
FROME (St John the Baptist) *B & W 3* **P** *DBP* **V** C ALSBURY
FROME ST QUINTON (St Mary) *see* Melbury *Sarum*
FROME VALLEY Group of Parishes, The, comprising Acton
Beauchamp, Bishops Frome, Castle Frome and Fromes Hill,
Evesbatch, Much Cowarne, Ocle Pychard, and Stanford
Bishop *Heref 2* **P** *Bp (6 turns), MMCET (2 turns), D&C (1
turn)* **V** S BAGGS **C** R J ALLAWAY
FROME VAUCHURCH (St Mary) *see* Melbury *Sarum*
FROMES HILL (St Matthew) *see* Frome Valley *Heref*
FROMESIDE, comprising Frampton Cotterell, Iron Acton,
Winterbourne, and Winterbourne Down *Bris 5* **P** *SMF, Ch
Ch Ox, and St Jo Coll Ox (jt)* **P-in-c** M STRANGE
C D G JONES, R B N LATHAM **OLM** H V SMITH, J C CHARD,
J L HODGE, R CONWAY
FROSTENDEN (All Saints) *see* Wrentham, Covehithe w
Benacre etc *St E*
FROXFIELD (All Saints) *see* Whitton *Sarum*
FROXFIELD (St Peter on the Green) *see* Steep and Froxfield w
Privett *Portsm*
FROXFIELD (St Peter) *as above*
FROYLE (Assumption of the Blessed Virgin Mary) *see* Bentley,
Binsted and Froyle *Win*
FRYERNING (St Mary the Virgin) *see* Ingatestone w Fryerning
Chelmsf
FUGGLESTONE (St Peter) *see* Wilton w Netherhampton and
Fugglestone *Sarum*
FULBECK (St Nicholas) *see* S Cliff Villages Gp *Linc*
FULBOURN (St Vigor w All Saints) *Ely 4* **P** *St Jo Coll Cam*
R A A GOODMAN **C** M T PATEMAN
FULBROOK (St James the Great) *see* Burford w Fulbrook,
Taynton, Asthall etc *Ox*
FULFORD (St Oswald) *York 7* **P** *Abp* **V** T MCDONOUGH
FULFORD-IN-STONE (St Nicholas) w Hilderstone *Lich 12*
P *D&C* **V** M REYNOLDS
FULHAM (All Saints) *Lon 9* **P** *Bp* **V** P A SEABROOK
C R GUNDERSON, W D LEVANWAY
FULHAM (Christ Church) *Lon 9* **P** *CPAS* **V** S C R LEES
FULHAM (St Alban) (St Augustine) *Lon 9* **P** *Bp and City
Corp (jt)* **V** M HOGG
FULHAM (St Andrew) Fulham Fields *Lon 9* **P** *Bp*
V L A BILINDA **NSM** J A COWLEY

FULHAM (St Dionis) Parson's Green *Lon 9* **P** *Bp*
V T J STILWELL **C** L M M CORBETT **NSM** C GIBBS
FULHAM (St Etheldreda) (St Clement) *Lon 9* **P** *Bp*
V R GUNDERSON
FULHAM (St Mary) North End *Lon 9* **P** *Ch Soc Trust*
V R W CURL
FULHAM (St Matthew) *Lon 9* **P** *Ch Patr Trust* **V** W J ROGERS
C K MILLER **Dss** V S PIERSON
FULHAM (St Peter) *Lon 9* **P** *Bp* **V** R B C STANDRING
C D A LEE
FULKING (Good Shepherd) *see* Poynings w Edburton,
Newtimber and Pyecombe *Chich*
FULL SUTTON (St Mary) *see* Garrowby Hill *York*
FULLBROOK (St Gabriel) *see* Walsall St Gabr Fulbrook *Lich*
FULLETBY (St Andrew) *see* Hemingby Gp *Linc*
FULMER (St James) *see* Gerrards Cross and Fulmer *Ox*
FULMODESTON (Christ Church) w Croxton *Nor 14* **P** *CCC
Cam* **P-in-c** F R A MASON
FULSHAW (St Anne) *see* Wilmslow *Ches*
FULSTOW (St Laurence) *see* Fotherby, N Thoresby and
Grainsby w Waithe *Linc*
FULWELL (St Michael and St George) *Lon 10* **P** *Bp*
V E J KENDALL
FULWOOD (Christ Church) *Blackb 13* **P** *V Lanc*
P-in-c C P BOLAND **C** E M MCLEAN
FULWOOD (Christ Church) *Sheff 4* **P** *CPAS*
V P A WILLIAMS **C** A A FEARNLEY, C K CONN, B C COOPER,
C E D TUFNELL, P F SCAMMAN
FULWOOD (St Cuthbert) *see* Preston St Cuth *Blackb*
FULWOOD Lodge Moor (St Luke) *see* Lodge Moor St Luke
Sheff
FUNDENHALL (St Nicholas) *see* Upper Tas Valley *Nor*
FUNTINGTON (St Mary) and West Stoke w Sennicotts
Chich 3 **P** *Bp* **R** C M B HUXTABLE
FUNTLEY (St Francis) *see* Fareham SS Pet and Paul *Portsm*
FURNACE GREEN (St Andrew) *Chich 6* **P** *CPAS*
V R E POOLE
FURNESS VALE (St John) *see* Disley *Ches*
FURNEUX PELHAM (St Mary the Virgin) *see* Braughing,
Furneux Pelham and Stocking Pelham *St Alb*
FURNHAM (Good Shepherd) *see* Chard Gd Shep Furnham
B & W
FURZE PLATT (St Peter) *Ox 5* **P** *Bp* **V** D K SHORT
C K P COLYER **NSM** J E ELLINGTON
FURZEBANK (Worship Centre) *see* Bentley Em and
Willenhall H Trin *Lich*
FURZEDOWN (St Paul) *S'wark 17* **P** *Patr Bd* **TR** R J POWELL
TV M S RICHEUX **Hon C** G M VEVERS **NSM** J ALLEN,
J CONNELL, S E M CLARKE
FURZTON (not known) *see* Watling Valley *Ox*
FYFIELD (St Nicholas) *see* Appleshaw, Kimpton, Thruxton,
Fyfield etc *Win*
FYFIELD (St Nicholas) *see* Upper Kennet *Sarum*
FYFIELD (St Nicholas) w Tubney and Kingston Bagpuize
Ox 19 **P** *St Jo Coll Ox* **V** D A A PICKERING
**FYFIELD (St Nicholas), Moreton w Bobbingworth and
Willingale w Shellow and Berners Roding** *Chelmsf 3*
P *Ld Chan, St Jo Coll Cam, MMCET, and Major G N
Capel-Cure (by turn)* **P-in-c** C A HAWKINS
FYLINGDALES (St Stephen) and Hawsker cum Stainsacre
York 21 **P** *Abp* **V** S J SMALE
G7 Benefice, comprising Charing, Charing Heath, Egerton,
Hothfield, Little Chart, Pluckley, and Westwell *Cant 6*
P *Abp, D&C, and Lord Hothfield (jt)* **C** J W BATESON
GADDESBY (St Luke) *see* S Croxton Gp *Leic*
GADDESDEN, GREAT (St John the Baptist) *see* Gt
Berkhamsted, Gt and Lt Gaddesden etc *St Alb*
GADDESDEN, LITTLE (St Peter and St Paul) *as above*
GAINFORD (St Mary) *Dur 6* **P** *Trin Coll Cam*
P-in-c E K G HARROP
GAINSBOROUGH (All Saints) (St George) and Morton
Linc 2 **P** *Bp* **TR** vacant
GALLEY COMMON (St Peter) *see* Hartshill and Galley
Common *Cov*
GALLEYWOOD (Junior School Worship Centre) *see*
Galleywood Common *Chelmsf*
GALLEYWOOD COMMON (St Michael and All Angels)
Chelmsf 10 **P** *CPAS* **V** D J CATTLE **C** G E FRASER,
S R GILLINGHAM
GALMINGTON (St Michael) *B & W 18* **P** *Bp*
V J C RICHARDS **C** T L POTTAGE
GALMPTON (Chapel of The Good Shepherd) *see* Brixham w
Churston Ferrers and Kingswear *Ex*
**GAMESLEY (Bishop Geoffrey Allen Church and County
Centre)** *see* Charlesworth and Gamesley *Derby*

GAMLINGAY (St Mary the Virgin) and Everton *Ely 13*
   P *Bp, Clare Coll Cam, and Down Coll Cam (by turn)*
   P-in-c H A F YOUNG
GAMSTON (St Luke) and Bridgford *S'well 6*   **P** *DBP*
   V M A FRASER   **C** J R MOLE
GANAREW (St Swithin)   *see* Wye Reaches Gp *Heref*
GANTON (St Nicholas)   *see* Hertford *York*
GARBOLDISHAM (St John the Baptist)   *see* Guiltcross *Nor*
GARFORD (St Luke)   *see* Marcham w Garford and Shippon
   Ox
GARFORTH (St Mary the Virgin) *Leeds 16*   **P** *DBP*
   R J C D BROWN
GARGRAVE (St Andrew) w Coniston Cold *Leeds 20*   **P** *Bp*
   V *vacant*
GARRETTS GREEN (St Thomas) and Lea Hall *Birm 8*   **P** *Bp*
   V P M BRACHER   **NSM** S J LARKIN, W H MARTIN
GARRIGILL (St John)   *see* Alston Moor *Newc*
GARROWBY HILL, comprising Bishop Wilton, Bugthorpe, Full
   Sutton, Kirby Underdale, and Skirpenbeck *York 5*   **P** *Ld*
   Chan (1 turn), Abp, D&C, and Earl of Halifax (3 turns)
   R L C MUNT   **NSM** M L KAVANAGH
GARSDALE (St John the Baptist)   *see* Sedbergh, Cautley and
   Garsdale *Carl*
GARSDON (All Saints)   *see* Woodbridge *Bris*
GARSINGTON (St Mary), Cuddesdon and Horspath *Ox 20*
   P *Ripon Coll Cuddesdon, Trin Coll Ox, and DBP (jt)*
   NSM M D CHAPMAN
GARSTANG (St Helen) Churchtown and St Michaels-on-
   Wyre *Blackb 9*   **P** *Dr I R H Jackson and R P Hornby Esq (jt)*
   V A W WILKINSON
GARSTANG (St Thomas) *Blackb 9*   **P** *V Churchtown St Helen*
   V J GRIFFITHS
GARSTON (St Michael) *Liv 2*   **P** *Trustees*   **V** R HARVEY
   C A M TUNSTALL
GARSTON, EAST (All Saints)   *see* Lambourn Valley *Ox*
GARSWOOD (St Andrew)   *see* Ashton-in-Makerfield H Trin
   Liv
GARTHORPE (St Mary)   *see* Crowle Gp *Linc*
GARTON IN HOLDERNESS (St Michael)   *see* S Holderness
   Coast *York*
GARTON ON THE WOLDS (St Michael and All Angels)   *see*
   Woldsburn *York*
GARVESTON (St Margaret)   *see* Barnham Broom and Upper
   Yare *Nor*
GARWAY (St Michael)   *see* St Weonards *Heref*
GASTARD (St John the Baptist)   *see* Gtr Corsham and Lacock
   Bris
GATCOMBE (St Olave) *Portsm 7*   **P** *Qu Coll Ox*   **R** M C BAGG
GATE BURTON (St Helen)   *see* Lea Gp *Linc*
GATE HELMSLEY (St Mary)   *see* Harton *York*
GATEACRE (St Stephen) *Liv 2*   **P** *Bp*   **TR** P H JANVIER
   TV S P DOORE   **NSM** K A CANTY
GATELEY (St Helen)   *see* Upper Wensum Village Gp *Nor*
GATESHEAD (St Chad)   *see* Bensham and Teams *Dur*
GATESHEAD (St Edmund's Chapel w Holy Trinity)
   (Venerable Bede) *Dur 11*   **P** *Bp and The Crown (alt)*
   P-in-c M MACKAY   **NSM** A PHILLIPS
GATESHEAD (St George) *Dur 11*   **P** *Trustees*   **P-in-c** R GRANT
GATESHEAD (St Helen) *Dur 11*   **P** *Bp*   **P-in-c** Y GREENER
   C A I G CRAWFORD
GATESHEAD (St Ninian) Harlow Green   *see* Harlow Green and
   Lamesley *Dur*
GATESHEAD FELL (St John) *Dur 11*   **P** *Bp*
   P-in-c D M LINDLEY   **NSM** K COULSON
GATESHEAD Lobley Hill (All Saints)   *see* Hillside *Dur*
GATLEY (St James) *Ches 17*   **P** *R Stockport St Thos*
   V M D CARLISLE
GATTEN (St Paul) *Portsm 7*   **P** *Ch Patr Trust*
   P-in-c M A WILLIAMS
GATTON (St Andrew)   *see* Merstham, S Merstham and
   Gatton *S'wark*
GAULBY (St Peter) *Leic 5*   **P** *Ch Soc Trust*   **P-in-c** B DAVIS
GAUTBY (All Saints)   *see* Bardney *Linc*
GAUZEBROOK, comprising Alderton, Easton Grey, Foxley w
   Bremilham, Hullavington, Luckington, Norton, Sherston
   Magna, and Stanton St Quintin *Bris 6*   **P** *Bp, D&C, Eton*
   Coll, and M Neeld Esq (jt)   **C** E MEAD   **OLM** S E HARVEY
GAWBER (St Thomas)   *see* Cen Barnsley *Leeds*
GAWCOTT (Holy Trinity)   *see* Lenborough *Ox*
GAWSWORTH (St James) w North Rode *Ches 13*   **P** T R R
   Richards Esq and Bp (jt)   **R** C E WILSON
GAYDON (St Giles) w Chadshunt *Cov 8*   **P** *Bp*
   P-in-c N M CHATTERTON
GAYHURST (St Peter) w Ravenstone, Stoke Goldington
   and Weston Underwood *Ox 16*   **P** *Bp and Lord Hesketh (jt)*
   R C E PUMFREY

GAYTON (St Mary)   *see* Pattishall w Cold Higham and
   Gayton w Tiffield *Pet*
GAYTON (St Nicholas)   *see* Ashwicken w Leziate, Bawsey etc
   Nor
GAYTON (St Peter)   *see* Mid Trent *Lich*
GAYTON LE WOLD (St Peter)   *see* Asterby Gp *Linc*
GAYTON THORPE (St Mary)   *see* Ashwicken w Leziate,
   Bawsey etc *Nor*
GAYWOOD (St Faith) King's Lynn *Nor 19*   **P** *Patr Bd*
   TR J M BOYD   **TV** K T K KERR   **C** L L PURNELL
GAZELEY (All Saints)   *see* Dalham, Gazeley, Higham, Kentford
   and Moulton *St E*
GEDDING (St Mary the Virgin)   *see* Bradfield St Clare,
   Bradfield St George etc *St E*
GEDDINGTON (St Mary Magdalene) w Weekley *Pet 9*
   P *Boughton Estates*   **P-in-c** G F GAMBLE
GEDLING (All Hallows) *S'well 7*   **P** *DBP*   **R** M D JOHNSON
   C J E LAMB
GEDNEY (St Mary Magdalene)   *see* Mid Elloe Gp *Linc*
GEDNEY Drove End (Christ Church)   *see* Long Sutton w
   Lutton etc *Linc*
GEDNEY HILL (Holy Trinity)   *see* Elloe Fen Gp *Linc*
GEDNEY HILL (St Polycarp) *as above*
GEE CROSS (Holy Trinity) (St Philip's Mission Room)
   Ches 14   **P** *V Werneth*   **P-in-c** H SCARISBRICK
GELDESTON (St Michael)   *see* Gillingham w Geldeston,
   Stockton, Ellingham etc *Nor*
GENTLESHAW (Christ Church) *Lich 1*   **P** *MMCET*
   P-in-c L M MCKEON
GEORGEHAM (St George) *Ex 14*   **P** *MMCET*
   R M C NEWBON
GERMAN (St John the Baptist) The Royal Chapel   *see* W Coast
   S & M
GERMANSWEEK (St German)   *see* Okehampton, Inwardleigh,
   Belstone, Sourton etc *Ex*
GERMOE (St Germoe)   *see* W Kerrier *Truro*
GERRANS (St Gerran) w St Anthony-in-Roseland and
   Philleigh *Truro 6*   **P** *Bp and MMCET (jt)*   **R** *vacant*
GERRARDS CROSS (St James) and Fulmer *Ox 9*   **P** *Bp and*
   Simeon's Trustees (jt)   **R** M D BEEBY   **C** B M CLARKE,
   B M TOPHAM, J R LEACH   **NSM** J M ROTH, M R L BEEBEE
GESTINGTHORPE (St Mary)   *see* Halstead Area *Chelmsf*
GIDDING, GREAT (St Michael)   *see* N Leightonstone *Ely*
GIDDING, LITTLE (St John) *as above*
GIDEA PARK (St Michael) *Chelmsf 2*   **P** *Bp*   **V** D J P KIRK
GIDLEIGH (Holy Trinity)   *see* Chagford, Gidleigh, Throwleigh
   etc *Ex*
GIGGETTY LANE (The Venerable Bede)   *see* Smestow Vale
   Lich
GIGGLESWICK (St Alkelda) and Rathmell w Wigglesworth
   Leeds 20   **P** *Bp and Ch Trust Fund Trust (jt)*   **C** S C DAWSON
GILCRUX (St Mary)   *see* Aspatria w Hayton and Gilcrux *Carl*
GILDERSOME (St Peter)   *see* Drighlington and Gildersome
   Leeds
GILLAMOOR (St Aidan)   *see* Kirkbymoorside w Gillamoor,
   Farndale etc *York*
GILLING (St Agatha)   *see* Holmedale *Leeds*
GILLING EAST (Holy Cross)   *see* Ampleforth w Oswaldkirk,
   Gilling E etc *York*
GILLINGHAM (Holy Trinity) *Roch 3*   **P** *Bp*   **V** A RICHARDSON
   NSM S A TAYLOR
GILLINGHAM (St Augustine) *Roch 3*   **P** *Bp*   **P-in-c** A K LANE
   NSM N J P RAWLINS
GILLINGHAM (St Barnabas) *Roch 3*   **P** *Bp*   **V** *vacant*
GILLINGHAM (St Luke)   *see* New Brompton St Luke *Roch*
GILLINGHAM (St Mark) *Roch 3*   **P** *Hyndman Trustees*
   V V M L MUTHALALY   **C** A J MASKELL
GILLINGHAM (St Mary Magdalene) *Roch 3*   **P** *DBP*
   V *vacant*
GILLINGHAM (St Mary the Virgin), Milton-on-Stour and
   Silton *Sarum 5*   **P** *Bp and DBP (jt)*   **R** J P GREENWOOD
   C E C PEGLER   **NSM** T F HEATON
GILLINGHAM (St Mary) w Geldeston w Stockton w
   Ellingham St Mary and Kirby Cane *Nor 8*   **P** *Ld Chan (1*
   turn), Bp, MMCET and Ch Trust Fund Trust (1 turn)   **R** *vacant*
GILLINGHAM, SOUTH (St Matthew) *Roch 3*   **P** *Patr Bd*
   TR B S SENIOR   **TV** P M LENTON DE DICKIN   **C** A MITRA
   NSM C A ALLEN, P M ALEXANDER
GILMORTON (All Saints)   *see* Avon-Swift *Leic*
GILSLAND (St Mary Magdalene)   *see* Lanercost, Walton,
   Gilsland and Nether Denton *Carl*
GILSTEAD (St Wilfrid)   *see* Bingley H Trin *Leeds*
GILSTON (St Mary)   *see* High Wych and Gilston w Eastwick
   St Alb
GIMINGHAM (All Saints)   *see* Trunch Group *Nor*

GIPPING (Chapel of St Nicholas) *see* Bacton w Wyverstone, Cotton and Old Newton etc *St E*

GIPSY HILL (Christ Church) *S'wark 12* **P** *CPAS* **V** J E CROUCHER **C** E P LOWTH

GIPTON (Church of the Epiphany) and Oakwood *Leeds 13* **P** *Bp and DBF (jt)* **V** K A FITZSIMONS **C** S A KASIBANTE

GIRLINGTON (St Philip), Heaton and Manningham *Leeds 2* **P** *Patr Bd* **R** C J W CHORLTON **C** S M JENNINGS Hon **C** D J POOLE

GIRTON (St Andrew) *Ely 6* **P** *Ld Chan* **C** D JOHNSON

GIRTON (St Cecilia) *see* E Trent *S'well*

GISBURN (St Mary the Virgin) *Blackb 7* **P** *Bp* **V** *vacant*

GISLEHAM (Holy Trinity) *see* Kessingland, Gisleham and Rushmere *Nor*

GISLINGHAM (St Mary) *see* S Hartismere *St E*

GISSING (St Mary the Virgin) *see* Winfarthing w Shelfanger w Burston w Gissing etc *Nor*

GITTISHAM (St Michael) *see* Honiton, Gittisham, Combe Raleigh, Monkton etc *Ex*

GIVENDALE, GREAT (St Ethelburga) *see* Pocklington Wold *York*

GLAISDALE (St Thomas) *see* Middle Esk Moor *York*

GLANDFORD (St Martin) *see* Blakeney w Cley, Wiveton, Glandford etc *Nor*

GLANVILLES WOOTTON (St Mary the Virgin) *see* Three Valleys *Sarum*

GLAPTHORN (St Leonard) *see* Oundle w Ashton and Benefield w Glapthorn *Pet*

GLAPWELL (St Andrew) *see* Ault Hucknall and Scarcliffe *Derby*

GLASCOTE (St George) and Stonydelph *Lich 4* **P** *Patr Bd* **TR** G D SIMMONS **C** S G BENNETT **NSM** M R LE-WORTHY **OLM** P D FAULTLESS

GLASCOTE HEATH (St Peter) *see* Glascote and Stonydelph *Lich*

GLASSHOUGHTON (St Paul) *see* Castleford *Leeds*

GLASSON (Christ Church) *see* Cockerham w Winmarleigh and Glasson *Blackb*

GLASTON (St Andrew) *see* Lyddington, Bisbrooke, Caldecott, Glaston etc *Pet*

GLASTONBURY (St John the Baptist) (St Benedict) w Meare *B & W 4* **P** *Bp* **V** D J L MACGEOCH **C** D M GREENFIELD

GLATTON (St Nicholas) *see* Sawtry and Glatton *Ely*

GLAVEN VALLEY Group *see* Blakeney w Cley, Wiveton, Glandford etc *Nor*

GLAZEBURY (All Saints) w Hollinfare *Liv 13* **P** *Bp and R Warrington (jt)* **Hon C** A COOPER **NSM** J HARNEY

GLAZELEY (St Bartholomew) *see* Highley w Billingsley, Glazeley etc *Heref*

GLEADLESS (Christ Church) *Sheff 1* **P** *DBP* **P-in-c** P R ALLEN **C** D L V WILKINSON **NSM** A RHODES, C D I REES

GLEADLESS VALLEY (Holy Cross) *Sheff 1* **P** *DBP* **V** D J MIDDLETON **C** S C DEERING

GLEM VALLEY *see* Glemsford, Hartest w Boxted, Somerton etc *St E*

GLEMHAM, GREAT (All Saints) *see* Alde River *St E*

GLEMHAM, LITTLE (St Andrew) *as above*

GLEMSFORD (St Mary the Virgin), Hartest w Boxted, Somerton and Stanstead (Glem Valley United Benefice) *St E 9* **P** *Bp, The Crown, and Ch Soc Trust (by turn)* **R** P J PRIGG

GLEN AULDYN (St Fingan) *see* Bride, Lezayre and N Ramsey *S & M*

GLEN GROUP, The, comprising Pinchbeck, Surfleet, and West Pinchbeck *Linc 19* **P** *Bp* **V** D C SWEETING

GLENEAGLES *Pet 6* **P** *Bp* **V** M C PEREIRA **C** A J MIDDLETON

GLENFIELD (St Peter) and Newtown Linford *Leic 9* **P** *Bp* **R** R J TRETHEWEY **NSM** S E ANDREWS

GLENHOLT (St Anne) *see* Bickleigh and Shaugh Prior *Ex*

GLENTHAM (St Peter) *see* Owmby Gp *Linc*

GLENTWORTH (St Michael) *see* Trentcliffe Gp *Linc*

GLINTON (St Benedict), Etton, Maxey, Peakirk and Northborough *Pet 11* **P** *D&C and Sir Philip Naylor-Leyland Bt (jt)* **V** M-A B TISDALE

GLODWICK (St Mark w Christ Church) *Man 15* **P** *Bp* **V** *vacant*

GLOOSTON (St John the Baptist) *see* Welham, Glooston and Cranoe and Stonton Wyville *Leic*

GLOSSOP (All Saints) *Derby 4* **P** *Patr Bd* **P-in-c** D H MUNDY **NSM** N M PEPPER **OLM** N W SHAW

GLOUCESTER (St Aldate) *see* Coney Hill *Glouc*

GLOUCESTER (St Catharine) *Glouc 2* **P** *Bp* **V** J F PESTELL

GLOUCESTER (St George) w Whaddon *Glouc 2* **P** *Bp* **V** B D CLIFFORD

GLOUCESTER (St James and All Saints) (Christ Church) *Glouc 2* **P** *Bp* **V** J H JENSEN **NSM** J M HOWARD

GLOUCESTER (St Paul) and St Stephen *Glouc 2* **P** *Bp* **V** R P FITTER **C** H L DE GRUYTHER

GLOUCESTER CITY St Mark (St Mary de Crypt) (St John the Baptist) (St Mary de Lode) (St Nicholas) and Hempsted *Glouc 2* **P** *D&C (1 turn), Bp (3 turns), Ld Chan (1 turn)* **R** N M ARTHY

GLOUCESTER DOCKS Mariners' Church Proprietary Chapel *Glouc 2* **Chapl** A M OSMOND

GLYMPTON (St Mary) *see* Wootton w Glympton and Kiddington *Ox*

GLYNDE (St Mary), West Firle and Beddingham *Chich 21* **P** *Bp and D&C Windsor (alt)* **P-in-c** P C OWEN-JONES

GNOSALL (St Lawrence) *see* Adbaston, High Offley, Knightley, Norbury etc *Lich*

GOADBY (St John the Baptist) *see* Coplow *Leic*

GOADBY MARWOOD (St Denys) *see* Ironstone Villages *Leic*

GOATHILL (St Peter) *see* Milborne Port w Goathill etc *B & W*

GOATHLAND (St Mary) *see* Middle Esk Moor *York*

GOATHURST (St Edward the King and Martyr) *see* Aisholt, Enmore, Goathurst, Nether Stowey etc *B & W*

GOBOWEN (All Saints) *see* Selattyn and Hengoed w Gobowen *Lich*

GODALMING (St Peter and St Paul) *Guildf 4* **P** *Bp* **TR** J E VLACH **C** S T SAMUELS **OLM** R HARVIE

GODINGTON (Holy Trinity) *see* Shelswell *Ox*

GODMANCHESTER (St Mary) and Hilton *Ely 10* **P** *D&C Westmr and Bp (jt)* **V** D W BUSK

GODMANSTONE (Holy Trinity) *see* Buckland Newton, Cerne Abbas, Godmanstone etc *Sarum*

GODMERSHAM (St Lawrence the Martyr) *see* King's Wood *Cant*

GODREVY, comprising Gwinear, Hayle, Phillack, and St Erth *Truro 5* **P** *Patr Bd* **TR** S CLIFTON **NSM** P M MURLEY, S A CHALCRAFT

GODSHILL (All Saints) *Portsm 7* **P** *Guild of All So* **V** J M RYDER **NSM** C A SMITH

GODSHILL (St Giles) *see* Fordingbridge and Hyde and Breamore etc *Win*

GODSTONE (St Nicholas) and Blindley Heath *S'wark 25* **P** *Bp and Ms Z Goad (jt)* **R** P D O'CONNELL

GOFF'S OAK (St James) *see* Cheshunt *St Alb*

GOLBORNE (St Thomas) *see* Lowton and Golborne *Liv*

GOLCAR (St John the Evangelist) and Longwood *Leeds 11* **P** *V Huddersfield* **V** S C CROOK

GOLDEN CAP TEAM (Team Ministry), comprising Bettiscombe and Pilsdon, Catherston Leweston, Charmouth, Chideock, Hawkchurch, Lyme Regis, Marshwood, Monkton Wyld, Whitchurch Canonicorum w Stanton St Gabriel and Fishpond, and Wootton Fitzpaine *Sarum 2* **P** *Patr Bd* **NSM** V LUCKETT

GOLDENHILL St John the Evangelist and Tunstall *Lich 11* **P** *Bp* **V** T W J STATHER

GOLDERS GREEN (St Alban the Martyr and St Michael) *Lon 15* **P** *Bp* **V** R G MORTON

GOLDHANGER (St Peter) *see* Gt Totham and Lt Totham w Goldhanger *Chelmsf*

GOLDINGTON (St Mary the Virgin) *St Alb 9* **P** *Bp* **P-in-c** S P DOMMETT

GOLDS HILL (St Paul) *see* W Bromwich St Jas w St Paul *Lich*

GOLDSBOROUGH (St Mary) *see* Knaresborough, Goldsborough, Nidd and Brearton *Leeds*

GOLDSWORTH PARK (St Andrew) *Guildf 12* **P** *Bp* **V** K E WYLES **NSM** J A M VICKERS

GOLDTHORPE (St John the Evangelist and St Mary Magdalene) w Hickleton *Sheff 12* **P** *CR (2 turns), Earl of Halifax (1 turn)* **V** C R SCHAEFER **Hon C** A BRISCOE

GOMERSAL (St Mary) *Leeds 6* **P** *Bp* **V** K NICHOLL

GONALSTON (St Laurence) *see* Epperstone, Gonalston, Oxton and Woodborough *S'well*

GONERBY, GREAT (St Sebastian) *see* Barrowby and Gt Gonerby *Linc*

GOOD EASTER (St Andrew) *see* High and Gd Easter w Margaret Roding *Chelmsf*

GOODERSTONE (St George) *see* Cockley Cley w Gooderstone *Nor*

GOODLEIGH (St Gregory) *see* Barnstaple H Trin and Goodleigh *Ex*

GOODMANHAM (All Saints) *York 5* **P** *Abp* **R** C R PINCHBECK

GOODMAYES (All Saints) *Chelmsf 6* **P** *Hyndman Trustees* **V** *vacant*

GOODMAYES (St Paul) *Chelmsf 6* **P** *Bp* **V** J E F BUCHAN

GOODNESTONE (Holy Cross) *see* Canonry *Cant*

GOODRINGTON (St George) and Collaton St Mary *Ex 11*
P *Bp* V G DEIGHTON C G M J VAN OMMEREN
GOODSHAW (St Mary and All Saints) and Crawshawbooth
Man 11 P *Bp and Wm Hulme Trustees (jt)* V *vacant*
GOODWORTH CLATFORD (St Peter) *see* Abbotts Ann and
Upper Clatford and Goodworth Clatford *Win*
**GOOLE (St John the Evangelist) (St Mary) (Mariners' Club
and Chapel)** *Sheff 10* P *Bp* P-in-c H PATTON
GOOSE GREEN (St Paul) *Liv 15* P *Bp* P-in-c N J COOK
C M J WADE
GOOSEY (All Saints) *see* Stanford in the Vale w Goosey and
Hatford *Ox*
GOOSNARGH (St Mary the Virgin) *see* Fellside Team *Blackb*
GOOSTREY (St Luke) *Ches 11* P V *Sandbach* V H E BUCKLEY
GORAN HAVEN (St Just) *see* St Goran w Caerhays *Truro*
GOREFIELD (St Paul) *see* Wisbech St Mary and Guyhirn w
Ring's End etc *Ely*
**GORING (St Thomas of Canterbury) and Streatley with
South Stoke** *Ox 24* P *Ch Ch Ox and Bp (jt)*
V B L M PHILLIPS C W J MIDDLETON NSM E J DOWDING
GORING-BY-SEA (St Mary) (St Laurence) *Chich 20* P *Bp*
V K D LITTLEJOHN
GORLESTON (St Andrew) *Nor 6* P *Ch Trust Fund Trust*
V B HALL C M K SIMM
GORLESTON (St Mary Magdalene) *Nor 6* P *Bp and Ch Trust
Fund Trust (jt)* V M J PRICE
GORNAL (St Peter) and Sedgley *Worc 10* P *Patr Bd*
TR G E HEWLETT TV C A MITCHELL
GORNAL, LOWER (St James the Great) *Worc 10* P *Bp*
V J W MOTT
GORSLEY (Christ Church) *see* Newent and Gorsley w
Cliffords Mesne *Glouc*
**GORTON (Emmanuel) (St James) (St Philip) and Abbey
Hey** *Man 1* P *Patr Bd and Prime-Min (alt)* TR C P SMITH
C C A HEWISON
GOSBECK (St Mary) *see* N Bosmere *St E*
**GOSBERTON (St Peter and St Paul), Gosberton Clough
and Quadring** *Linc 19* P *Bp and D&C (jt)* V I R WALTERS
GOSBERTON CLOUGH (St Gilbert and St Hugh) *see*
Gosberton, Gosberton Clough and Quadring *Linc*
GOSCOTE, EAST (St Hilda) *see* Fosse Team *Leic*
GOSFIELD (St Catherine) *see* Halstead Area *Chelmsf*
GOSFORTH (All Saints) *Newc 2* P *Bp* V A J SHIPTON
NSM B A DAVIES
GOSFORTH (St Hugh) *Newc 2* P *Bp* P-in-c A J SHIPTON
NSM B A DAVIES
GOSFORTH (St Mary) *see* Seatallan *Carl*
GOSFORTH (St Nicholas) *Newc 2* P *Bp* V *vacant*
GOSFORTH VALLEY (St Andrew) *see* Dronfield w Holmesfield
Derby
GOSFORTH, NORTH (St Columba) *see* Ch the King *Newc*
GOSPEL LANE (St Michael) *see* Hall Green St Mich *Birm*
GOSPORT (Christ Church) *Portsm 3* P *Bp* V A G DAVIS
GOSPORT (Holy Trinity) *Portsm 3* P *DBP* V A G DAVIS
GOSSOPS GREEN (St Alban) and Bewbush *Chich 6* P *Bp*
V A M ALEXANDER C E A GREEN
GOTHAM (St Lawrence) *see* A453 churches of S Notts *S'well*
GOUDHURST (St Mary the Virgin) w Kilndown *Cant 11*
P *Abp and The Crown (alt)* V H E NELSON
GOULCEBY (All Saints) *see* Asterby Gp *Linc*
GOXHILL (All Saints) *see* Barrow and Goxhill *Linc*
GOXHILL (St Giles) *see* Aldbrough, Mappleton w Goxhill
and Withernwick *York*
GRADE (St Grada and the Holy Cross) *see* St Keverne,
St Ruan w St Grade and Landewednack *Truro*
GRAFFHAM (St Giles) w Woolavington *Chich 10* P *Bp*
P-in-c V A E TURNER
GRAFFOE Group, comprising Boothby Graffoe, Coleby,
Harmston, Navenby, Temple Bruer, and Wellingore *Linc 12*
P *Ch Coll Cam, D&C and DBP, Oriel Coll Ox, and Mrs P N
Fullerton (by turn)* R M J GODBOLD NSM S G WILLIAMS,
S J DAVIES
GRAFHAM (All Saints) *see* E Leightonstone *Ely*
GRAFHAM (St Andrew) *see* Bramley and Grafham *Guildf*
GRAFTON FLYFORD (St John the Baptist) *see* Abberton, The
Flyfords, Naunton Beauchamp etc *Worc*
GRAFTON REGIS (St Mary) *see* Blisworth, Alderton, Grafton
Regis etc *Pet*
GRAFTON UNDERWOOD (St James the Apostle) *see*
Cranford w Grafton Underwood and Twywell *Pet*
GRAFTON, EAST (St Nicholas) *see* Savernake *Sarum*
GRAHAME PARK (St Augustine) Conventional District
Lon 15 Min B J GABOR
GRAIN (St James) w Stoke *Roch 6* P *DBP* V *vacant*
GRAINSBY (St Nicholas) *see* Fotherby, N Thoresby and
Grainsby w Waithe *Linc*

GRAINTHORPE (St Clement) *see* Marshchapel, Somercotes
and Grainthorpe w Conisholme *Linc*
GRAMPOUND (St Nun) *see* Probus, Ladock and Grampound
w Creed and St Erme *Truro*
GRANBOROUGH (St John the Baptist) *see* Schorne *Ox*
GRANBY (All Saints) *see* Wiverton in the Vale *S'well*
GRAND UNION Benefice *see* Blisworth, Alderton, Grafton
Regis etc *Pet*
GRANDBOROUGH (St Peter) *see* Leam Valley *Cov*
GRANGE (Holy Trinity) *see* Keswick St Jo w Borrowdale *Carl*
GRANGE (St Andrew) *Ches 3* P *Bp* V E L SPEAKE
GRANGE FELL (not known) *see* Cartmel Peninsula *Carl*
GRANGE MOOR (St Bartholomew) *see* Kirkheaton *Leeds*
GRANGE PARK (St Peter) *Lon 18* P *Bp* V S P L COLEMAN
C J R BELL
GRANGE-OVER-SANDS (St Paul) *see* Cartmel Peninsula *Carl*
GRANGETOWN (St Aidan) *Dur 14* P V *Ryhope* V D RAINE
GRANGETOWN (St Hilda of Whitby) *York 17* P *Abp*
V E L MATHIAS-JONES
**GRANSDEN, GREAT (St Bartholomew) and Abbotsley and
Lt Gransden and Waresley** *Ely 13* P *Pemb Coll Cam (1
turn), Clare Coll Cam (2 turns), and Ball Coll Ox (1 turn)*
P-in-c R E BLANCHFLOWER
GRANSDEN, LITTLE (St Peter and St Paul) *see* Gt Gransden
and Abbotsley and Lt Gransden etc *Ely*
GRANTA VALE Group, The, comprising Balsham, Great and
Little Abington, Hildersham, West Wickham, West Wratting,
and Weston Colville *Ely 5* P *Patr Bd* R I G MCCOLL
NSM K R BISHOP
GRANTCHESTER (St Andrew and St Mary) *Ely 3* P *CCC
Cam* P-in-c R C ROSBOROUGH
GRANTHAM (St Anne) *see* S Grantham *Linc*
GRANTHAM (St John the Evangelist) *see* Grantham,
Manthorpe *Linc*
GRANTHAM (St Wulfram) *Linc 20* P *Bp* R S W CRADDUCK
C J G TITLEY, M J PARKIN NSM J M ROWLAND, J T FARLEY
GRANTHAM (The Ascension) *see* Grantham, Harrowby w
Londonthorpe *Linc*
GRANTHAM (The Epiphany) Earlesfield *see* S Grantham *Linc*
GRANTHAM Harrowby (The Ascension) w Londonthorpe
Linc 20 P *Bp* V S J PARSONS OLM L BATTY
GRANTHAM Manthorpe (St John the Evangelist) *Linc 20*
P *Bp* P-in-c S W CRADDUCK C J G TITLEY, M J PARKIN
**GRANTHAM, SOUTH The Trinity (St Anne) (St John the
Evangelist)** *Linc 20* P *Bp and R Grantham (jt)*
V D SHENTON C J S PARKIN
GRAPPENHALL (St Wilfrid) *Ches 4* P P G *Greenall Esq*
R J E PROUDFOOT
GRASBY (All Saints) *see* Caistor *Linc*
GRASMERE (St Oswald) *Carl 11* P *Qu Coll Ox* R *vacant*
GRASSENDALE (St Mary) *Liv 2* P *Trustees* V P ELLIS
GRATELEY (St Leonard) *see* Portway and Danebury *Win*
GRATWICH (St Mary the Virgin) *see* Uttoxeter Area *Lich*
GRAVELEY (St Botolph) *see* Papworth *Ely*
GRAVELEY (St Mary) *see* Stevenage St Nic and Graveley
St Alb
GRAVELLY HILL (All Saints) *Birm 7* P *Bp* V R J WALKER-HILL
GRAVENEY (All Saints) *see* Boughton-under-Blean w Dunkirk
etc *Cant*
GRAVENHURST (no church), Shillington and Stondon
St Alb 8 P *Bp* V R C WINSLADE
GRAVESEND (Holy Family) w Ifield *Roch 4* P *Bp and Mrs S
Edmeades-Stearns (jt)* R R A MARTIN C K A SEGGIE
GRAVESEND (St Aidan) *Roch 4* P *Bp* V M J PAYNE
C K A SEGGIE NSM J P LITTLEWOOD
GRAVESEND (St George) *Roch 4* P *Bp* R J A FLETCHER
C M A K NELSON
GRAVESEND (St Mary) *Roch 4* P R *Gravesend* V T OLIVER
GRAYINGHAM (St Radegunda) *Linc 8* P *Bp*
P-in-c K E COLWELL OLM J WILSON
GRAYRIGG (St John) *see* Beacon *Carl*
GRAYS NORTH (St John the Evangelist) *Chelmsf 16* P *Bp*
V C P RUSSELL
GRAYS THURROCK (St Peter and St Paul) *Chelmsf 16*
P *DBP* TR D BARLOW TV C A KOSLA, D N N PETERSON
C S E FRYER Hon C A F BURFORD OLM C L HASLER
GRAYSHOTT (St Luke) *Guildf 3* P *Bp* V J W D HASWELL
Hon C G E KNIFTON NSM W A SUTTON
GRAYSWOOD (All Saints) *see* Haslemere and Grayswood
Guildf
GRAYTHWAITE (Mission Room) *see* Hawkshead and Low
Wray w Sawrey and Rusland etc *Carl*
GREASBROUGH (St Mary) *Sheff 6* P *Sir Philip Naylor-Leyland
Bt* P-in-c L S WORTLEY NSM D ETCHELL, N ELSOM
GREASBY (St Nicholas) *see* Frankby w Greasby *Ches*
GREASLEY (St Mary) *S'well 4* P *Bp* V *vacant*

GREAT *see also under substantive place name*

GREATER *see also under substantive place name*

GREAT CAMBRIDGE ROAD (St John the Baptist and St James) *Lon 19* **P** *D&C St Paul's* **V** *vacant*

GREAT GLEN (St Cuthbert) *see* Oadby Gt Glen *Leic*

GREAT MOOR (St Saviour) *see* Stockport St Sav *Ches*

GREATFORD (St Thomas à Becket) *see* Uffington Gp *Linc*

GREATHAM (not known) *see* Amberley w N Stoke and Parham, Wiggonholt etc *Chich*

GREATHAM (St John the Baptist) *Dur 3* **P** *Trustees* **P-in-c** P M BULLOCK

GREATHAM (St John the Baptist), Empshott and Hawkley w Priors Dean *Portsm 4* **P** *Bp and DBP (jt)* **V** P A SUTTON

GREATSTONE (St Peter) *see* Brookland, Fairfield, Brenzett w Snargate etc *Cant*

GREATWORTH (St Peter) *see* Chenderit *Pet*

GREEN HAMMERTON (St Thomas) *see* Gt and Lt Ouseburn w Marton cum Grafton etc *Leeds*

GREEN HEATH (St Saviour) *see* Hednesford *Lich*

GREEN STREET GREEN (St Mary) and Pratts Bottom *Roch 16* **P** *Bp* **C** J TRANTER

GREEN VALE (Holy Trinity) *see* Stockton H Trin w St Mark *Dur*

GREENFIELD (St Mary) *see* Saddleworth *Man*

GREENFIELDS (United Church) *see* Shrewsbury St Geo w Greenfields *Lich*

GREENFORD (Holy Cross) (St Edward the Confessor) *Lon 22* **P** K Coll Cam **R** G W MILLER

GREENFORD, NORTH (All Hallows) *Lon 22* **P** *Bp* **P-in-c** K M GREENIDGE

GREENGATES (St John the Evangelist) and Thorpe Edge *Leeds 3* **P** *D&C Bradf and Vs Bradf, Calverley and Idle (jt)* **V** M E WINTER **NSM** S O NUTTALL

GREENHAM (St Mary the Virgin) *Ox 6* **P** *Bp* **V** D L R MCLEOD **NSM** B R JONES, J BRAMHALL

GREENHAM (St Peter) *see* Wellington and Distr *B & W*

GREENHEAD (St Cuthbert) *see* Haltwhistle and Greenhead *Newc*

GREENHILL (St John the Baptist) *Lon 23* **P** *Bp, Adn, and V Harrow St Mary (jt)* **V** B D HINGSTON **C** A Y MORE **Hon C** D P BYRNE

GREENHILL (St Peter) *Sheff 2* **P** *Bp* **V** E J LUNN **C** G B WHITE, P M BROWN, T K HOLE

GREENHITHE (St Mary) *Roch 2* **P** *Ch Soc Trust and Personal Reps Canon T L Livermore (jt)* **R** *vacant*

GREENHOW HILL (St Mary) *see* Upper Nidderdale *Leeds*

GREENLANDS (St Anne) *Blackb 8* **P** *Bp and V Blackpool St Steph (jt)* **P-in-c** D A PREST

GREENLANDS (St John the Evangelist) *see* Ipsley *Worc*

GREEN'S NORTON (St Bartholomew) *see* Towcester w Caldecote and Easton Neston etc *Pet*

GREENSIDE (St John) *Dur 12* **P** R Ryton w Hedgefield **V** T I BRAZIER

GREENSTEAD (St Andrew) (St Edmund's Church Hall) (St Matthew) w Colchester St Anne *Chelmsf 21* **P** *Patr Bd and Ld Chan (alt)* **P-in-c** T C PLATTS **TV** S E HOWLETT

GREENSTEAD GREEN (St James Apostle) *see* Halstead Area *Chelmsf*

GREENSTED-JUXTA-ONGAR (St Andrew) *see* Chipping Ongar w Shelley etc *Chelmsf*

GREENWICH (St Alfege) *S'wark 1* **P** *The Crown* **C** C L RISDON, P A MANN **NSM** F G WAKELING, S K NSHIMYE

GREENWICH, EAST (Christ Church) St Andrew w St Michael) (St George) *S'wark 1* **P** *Patr Bd* **TR** M CAVE **NSM** J N PHILPOTT-HOWARD, R T YEAGER

GREETE (St James) *see* Tenbury *Heref*

GREETHAM (All Saints) *see* Horncastle Gp *Linc*

GREETHAM (St Mary the Virgin) *see* Cottesmore and Burley, Clipsham, Exton etc *Pet*

GREETLAND (St Thomas) and West Vale *Leeds 7* **P** V Halifax **C** D BURROWS

GREETWELL (All Saints) *see* S Lawres Gp *Linc*

GREINTON (St Michael and All Angels) *see* Middlezoy w Othery, Moorlinch and Greinton *B & W*

GRENDON (All Saints) *see* Baddesley Ensor w Grendon *Birm*

GRENDON (St Mary) *see* Yardley Hastings, Denton and Grendon etc *Pet*

GRENDON BISHOP (St John the Baptist) *see* Bredenbury *Heref*

GRENDON UNDERWOOD (St Leonard) *see* The Claydons and Swan *Ox*

GRENOSIDE (St Mark) *Sheff 3* **P** *Bp and V Ecclesfield (jt)* **NSM** C WILLIAMS

GRESHAM (All Saints) *see* Aylmerton, Runton, Beeston Regis and Gresham *Nor*

GRESLEY (St George and St Mary) *Derby 7* **P** *Simeon's Trustees* **V** M J FIRBANK

GRESSENHALL (Assumption of the Blessed Virgin Mary) *see* Launditch and the Upper Nar *Nor*

GRESSINGHAM (St John the Evangelist) *see* Hornby w Claughton and Whittington etc *Blackb*

GRETTON (Christ Church) *see* Winchcombe *Glouc*

GRETTON (St James the Great) w Rockingham and Cottingham w East Carlton *Pet 7* **P** *Bp, Comdr L M M Saunders Watson, Sir Geoffrey Palmer Bt, and BNC Ox (jt)* **V** *vacant*

GREWELTHORPE (St James) *see* Fountains Gp *Leeds*

GREYSTOKE (St Andrew) *see* Greystoke w Penruddock, Mungrisdale etc *Carl*

GREYSTOKE (St Andrew) w Penruddock, Mungrisdale and Matterdale *Carl 4* **P** *Patr Bd* **R** *vacant*

GREYSTONES (St Gabriel) *Sheff 2* **P** *Dean* **P-in-c** A P STEVENSON

GREYWELL (St Mary) *see* N Hants Downs *Win*

GRIMEHILLS (St Mary) *see* Darwen St Barn *Blackb*

GRIMETHORPE (St Luke) w Brierley *Leeds 17* **P** *Bp* **P-in-c** P CARTWRIGHT

GRIMLEY (St Bartholomew) *see* Hallow and Grimley w Holt *Worc*

GRIMOLDBY (St Edith) *see* Mid Marsh Gp *Linc*

GRIMSARGH (St Michael) *Blackb 13* **P** R Preston **V** N SALT

GRIMSBURY (St Leonard) *see* Banbury St Leon *Ox*

GRIMSBY (St Augustine of Hippo) *Linc 3* **P** TR Gt Grimsby SS Mary and Jas **V** *vacant*

GRIMSBY, GREAT (St Andrew w St Luke and All Saints) *Linc 3* **P** *Bp* **V** *vacant*

GRIMSBY, GREAT (St Mary and St James) (St Hugh) (St Mark) (St Martin) *Linc 3* **P** *Bp* **TR** A P DODD **TV** K L A FARRELL **NSM** J M VASEY, P M BARLOW

GRIMSBY, LITTLE (St Edith) *see* Fotherby, N Thoresby and Grainsby w Waithe *Linc*

GRIMSHOE, comprising Feltwell, Hockwold w Wilton, Northwold, Southery, and Weeting *Ely 9* **P** *Bp, G&C Coll Cam, Guild of All So (by turn)* **R** J A HORAN

GRIMSTEAD, EAST (Holy Trinity) *see* Clarendon *Sarum*

GRIMSTEAD, WEST (St John) *as above*

GRIMSTON (St Botolph) *see* Ashwicken w Leziate, Bawsey etc *Nor*

GRIMSTON (St John the Baptist) *see* Old Dalby, Nether Broughton, Saxelbye etc *Leic*

GRIMSTON, NORTH (St Nicholas) *see* W Buckrose *York*

GRINDALE (St Nicholas) *see* Rudston, Boynton, Carnaby etc *York*

GRINDLETON (St Ambrose) *see* Bolton by Bowland w Grindleton *Blackb*

GRINDON (All Saints) *see* Calton, Cauldon, Grindon, Waterfall etc *Lich*

GRINDON (St James) *see* Stockton Country Par *Dur*

GRINDON (St Oswald) *see* Sunderland St Mary, St Thos and St Oswald *Dur*

GRINGLEY-ON-THE-HILL (St Peter and St Paul) *see* Beckingham, Walkeringham, Misterton, etc *S'well*

GRINSHILL (All Saints) *see* Astley, Clive, Grinshill and Hadnall *Lich*

GRINSTEAD, EAST (St Mary the Virgin) *Chich 6* **P** *Bp* **V** A C WOGAN **NSM** D W HADFIELD, J GAYFORD

GRINSTEAD, EAST (St Swithun) *Chich 6* **P** *Bp* **V** A R HAWKEN **NSM** G M W PARRY, J K PEATY, K E HIGGS

GRINSTEAD, WEST (St George) *Chich 7* **P** *Bp* **P-in-c** A C LETSCHKA **NSM** S MITCHELL

GRINTON (St Andrew) *see* Swaledale *Leeds*

GRISTHORPE (St Thomas) *see* Filey *York*

GRISTON (St Peter and St Paul) *see* Caston, Griston, Merton, Thompson etc *Nor*

GRITTLETON (St Mary the Virgin) *see* By Brook *Bris*

GROBY (St Philip and St James) and Ratby *Leic 9* **P** *Bp and Baroness Mowbray, Segrave and Stourton (jt)* **R** E T W BAMPTON **NSM** L N COLLEY

GROOMBRIDGE (St John the Evangelist) *see* Speldhurst w Groombridge and Ashurst *Roch*

GROOMBRIDGE, NEW (St Thomas) *Chich 16* **P** R Withyham **V** S E FRANCIS

GROSMONT (St Matthew) *see* Middle Esk Moor *York*

GROSVENOR CHAPEL (no dedication) Chapel of Ease in the parish of Hanover Square St George w St Mark *Lon 3* **P-in-c** R M FERMER **Hon C** S D DEWEY **NSM** A R L PIGGOT

GROTON (St Bartholomew) *see* Boxford, Edwardstone, Groton etc *St E*

GROVE (St Helen) *see* Retford Area *S'well*

GROVE (St John the Baptist) *see* Vale *Ox*

GROVE PARK (St Augustine) *see* Lee St Aug *S'wark*

GROVEHILL (Resurrection) *see* Hemel Hempstead *St Alb*

GRUNDISBURGH (St Mary the Virgin) *see* Carlford *St E*

GUARLFORD (St Mary) *see* Powick and Guarlford and Madresfield w Newland *Worc*
GUERNSEY (Holy Trinity) *Win 14* **P** Trustees **V** J P HONOUR
GUERNSEY (St André de la Pommeraye) *Win 14* **P** *The Crown* **R** T R BARKER **NSM** J E C ROBILLIARD
GUERNSEY (St John the Evangelist) *Win 14* **P** Trustees **V** M E J BARRETT **C** P A GRAYSMITH
GUERNSEY (St Marguerite de la Foret) *Win 14* **P** *The Crown* **R** C M CLAXTON
GUERNSEY (St Martin) *Win 14* **P** *The Crown* **R** D J FOOT
GUERNSEY (St Matthew) Cobo *Win 14* **P** *R Ste Marie du Castel* **V** S I LAMB **NSM** B J HERVÉ
GUERNSEY (St Michel du Valle) *Win 14* **P** *The Crown* **R** S K TANSWELL
GUERNSEY (St Peter Port) *Win 14* **P** *The Crown* **R** M E J BARRETT **C** P A GRAYSMITH
GUERNSEY (St Philippe de Torteval) *Win 14* **P** *The Crown* **R** M R CHARMLEY **NSM** T B CHARMLEY
GUERNSEY (St Pierre du Bois) *Win 14* **P** *The Crown* **R** A DATTA
GUERNSEY (St Sampson) *Win 14* **P** *The Crown* **R** vacant
GUERNSEY (St Saviour) (Chapel of St Apolline) *Win 14* **P** *The Crown* **R** M R CHARMLEY **NSM** T B CHARMLEY
GUERNSEY (St Stephen) *Win 14* **P** *R St Peter Port* **V** J B MOORE
GUERNSEY (Ste Marie du Castel) *Win 14* **P** *The Crown* **R** S I LAMB **NSM** B J HERVÉ
GUERNSEY L'Islet (St Mary) *see* Guernsey St Sampson *Win*
GUESTLING (St Laurence) *see* Westfield and Guestling *Chich*
GUESTWICK (St Peter) *see* Heart of Norfolk *Nor*
GUILDEN MORDEN (St Mary) *see* Shingay Gp *Ely*
GUILDEN SUTTON (St John the Baptist) *see* Plemstall w Guilden Sutton *Ches*
GUILDFORD (All Saints) *Guildf 5* **P** *Bp* **V** B A WATSON
GUILDFORD (Christ Church) *Guildf 5* **P** *Simeon's Trustees* **V** N J WILLIAMS **C** J C TRICKEY **NSM** B G MCNAIR SCOTT
GUILDFORD (Holy Spirit) *see* Burpham *Guildf*
GUILDFORD (Holy Trinity) (St Mary the Virgin) (St Michael) *Guildf 5* **P** *Bp* **R** R L COTTON **C** T G E POTE **OLM** J J HEDGECOCK, R M PIERCE
GUILDFORD (St Luke) *see* Burpham *Guildf*
GUILDFORD (St Nicolas) *Guildf 5* **P** *Bp* **R** A H NORMAN
GUILDFORD (St Saviour) *Guildf 5* **P** *Simeon's Trustees* **R** M C L NORRIS **C** J CRONIN, L M WEBB **NSM** J MANKEL, P A FENNER
GUILSBOROUGH (St Ethelreda) and Hollowell and Cold Ashby and Cottesbrooke w Great Creaton and Thornby and Ravensthorpe and Spratton *Pet 2* **P** *Bp, DBP, A R MacDonald-Buchanan Esq, and J S McCall Esq (jt)* **R** C W PECK **C** A TWIGG, J H CRAIG PECK **NSM** C MOSS
GUILTCROSS, comprising Blo' Norton, Garboldisham, Kenninghall, and Riddlesworth *Nor 11* **P** *Bp, Mrs C Noel, Exors C P B Goldson, and DBP (jt)* **R** vacant
GUISBOROUGH (St Nicholas) *York 16* **P** *Abp* **R** A PHILLIPSON
GUISELEY (St Oswald King and Martyr) w Esholt *Leeds 15* **P** *Bp, Trin Coll Cam, and Mrs N A Gottlieb (jt)* **R** D PICKETT **NSM** J T RICHARDSON
GUIST (St Andrew) *see* Heart of Norfolk *Nor*
GUITING POWER (St Michael) *see* The Guitings, Cutsdean, Farmcote etc *Glouc*
GUITINGS, Cutsdean, Farmcote, Upper and Lower Slaughter w Eyford and Naunton, The *Glouc 8* **P** *Bp, Ch Ch Ox, Guiting Manor Amenity Trust, and F E B Witts Esq (jt)* **R** K R SCOTT **OLM** S B PESTELL
GULDEFORD, EAST (St Mary) *see* Rye *Chich*
GULVAL (St Gulval) and Madron *Truro 5* **P** *Ld Chan and Bp (jt)* **V** T ST J HAWKINS **NSM** J S THOMAS, P G BUTTERFIELD
GULWORTHY (St Paul) *see* Tavistock, Gulworthy and Brent Tor *Ex*
GUMLEY (St Helen) *see* Foxton w Gumley and Laughton *Leic*
GUNBY (St Nicholas) *see* Witham Gp *Linc*
GUNBY (St Peter) *see* Burgh Gp *Linc*
GUNHOUSE (St Barnabas) *see* Trentside E *Linc*
GUNN CHAPEL (Holy Name) *see* Swimbridge, W Buckland, Landkey, and E Buckland *Ex*
GUNNERTON (St Christopher) *see* Chollerton w Birtley and Thockrington *Newc*
GUNNESS (St Barnabas) *see* Trentside E *Linc*
GUNNISLAKE (St Anne) *see* Tamar Valley *Truro*
GUNTHORPE (St John the Baptist) *see* Burton Joyce, Bulcote and Stoke Bardolph etc *S'well*
GUNTHORPE (St Mary) *see* Stiffkey and Bale *Nor*
GUNTON St Peter (St Benedict) *Nor 9* **P** CPAS **R** vacant

GUNWALLOE (St Winwalloe) *see* Mullion and Cury w Gunwalloe *Truro*
GURNARD (All Saints) w Cowes St Faith *Portsm 7* **P** *Bp* **V** A COLLINSON **C** S A SUTCLIFFE **NSM** D M NETHERWAY
GUSSAGE (St Andrew) *see* Sixpenny Handley w Gussage St Andrew etc *Sarum*
GUSSAGE ALL SAINTS (All Saints) *see* Chase *Sarum*
GUSSAGE ST MICHAEL (St Michael) *as above*
GUSTARD WOOD (St Peter) *see* Wheathampstead *St Alb*
GUSTON (St Martin of Tours) *see* Dover Town *Cant*
GWEEK (Mission Church) *see* Constantine *Truro*
GWENNAP (St Weneppa) *see* St Stythians w Perranarworthal and Gwennap *Truro*
GWINEAR (St Winnear) *see* Godrevy *Truro*
GWITHIAN (St Gwithian) *as above*
HABBERLEY (St Mary) *see* Minsterley, Habberley and Hope w Shelve *Heref*
HABERGHAM (All Saints) *see* W Burnley All SS *Blackb*
HABERGHAM EAVES (St Matthew the Apostle) *see* Burnley St Matt w H Trin *Blackb*
HABROUGH (St Margaret) *see* Abbey Gp *Linc*
HABTON, GREAT (St Chad) *see* Kirby Misperton w Normanby and Salton *York*
HACCOMBE (St Blaise) *see* Shaldon, Stokeinteignhead, Combeinteignhead etc *Ex*
HACCONBY (St Andrew) *see* Ringstone in Aveland Gp *Linc*
HACHESTON (St Andrew) *see* Orebeck *St E*
HACKBRIDGE and Beddington Corner (All Saints) *S'wark 23* **P** *Bp* **V** S L BILLIN
HACKENTHORPE (Christ Church) *Sheff 2* **P** *Bp* **P-in-c** P R ALLEN **C** D L V WILKINSON **NSM** C D I REES
HACKFORD (St Mary the Virgin) *see* High Oak, Hingham and Scoulton w Wood Rising *Nor*
HACKINGTON (St Stephen) *Cant 3* **P** *Adn Cant* **P-in-c** K MADDY **Hon C** S C E LAIRD
HACKNESS (St Peter) w Harwood Dale *York 15* **P** *Lord Derwent* **V** L M HELLMUTH
HACKNEY (St James) *see* Clapton St Jas *Lon*
HACKNEY (St John) (St Luke) *Lon 5* **P** *Bp, Adn, Lord Amherst, and St Olave Hart Street Trustees (jt)* **R** A S GORDON **C** J OLADIPO, M D NELSON
HACKNEY (St Luke) Homerton Terrace *see* Hackney *Lon*
HACKNEY (St Michael and All Angels) *see* S Hackney St Mich w Haggerston St Paul *Lon*
HACKNEY (St Thomas) *see* Stamford Hill St Thos *Lon*
HACKNEY MARSH (All Souls) *Lon 5* **P** *Patr Bd* **TR** C T MAIN **C** S E PADDOCK **NSM** S P PLUMB
HACKNEY Mount Pleasant Lane (St Matthew) *see* Upper Clapton St Matt *Lon*
HACKNEY WICK (St Mary of Eton) *Lon 5* **P** *Eton Coll* **V** S MAKIN **NSM** D C GRAY
HACKNEY, OVER (Mission Room) *see* Darley, S Darley and Winster *Derby*
HACKNEY, SOUTH (St John of Jerusalem) *see* S Hackney St Jo w Ch Ch *Lon*
HACKNEY, SOUTH (St John of Jerusalem) w Christ Church *Lon 5* **P** *Lord Amherst* **R** A M W WILSON **NSM** G A NEWMAN
HACKNEY, SOUTH (St Michael and All Angels) London Fields w Haggerston St Paul *Lon 5* **P** *R S Hackney St Jo w Ch Ch* **V** D GERRANS **NSM** J H IRWIN
HACKNEY, WEST (St Paul) *Lon 5* **P** *Bp* **R** W D N WEIR **NSM** J C GAU
HACKTHORN (St Michael and All Angels) *see* Owmby Gp *Linc*
HACONBY (St Andrew) *see* Ringstone in Aveland Gp *Linc*
HADDENHAM (Holy Trinity) *Ely 8* **P** *Adn Ely* **V** F E G BRAMPTON
HADDENHAM (St Mary the Virgin) *see* Wychert Vale *Ox*
HADDISCOE (St Mary) *see* Raveningham Gp *Nor*
HADDLESEY (St John the Baptist) w Hambleton and Birkin *York 4* **P** *Abp and Simeon's Trustees (jt)* **P-in-c** A V BURR
HADDON (St Mary) *see* Stilton w Denton and Caldecote etc *Ely*
HADDON, EAST (St Mary the Virgin) *see* Brington w Whilton and Norton etc *Pet*
HADDON, OVER (St Anne) *see* Bakewell, Ashford w Sheldon and Rowsley *Derby*
HADDON, WEST (All Saints) *see* Long Buckby w Watford and W Haddon w Winwick *Pet*
HADFIELD (St Andrew) *Derby 4* **P** *Bp* **V** F A WALTERS
HADHAM, LITTLE (St Cecilia) *see* Albury, Lt Hadham and Much Hadham *St Alb*
HADHAM, MUCH (St Andrew) *as above*
HADLEIGH (St Barnabas) *Chelmsf 13* **P** *Bp* **P-in-c** R CARTWRIGHT **NSM** C ROBINSON, J E TURNER

HADLEIGH (St James the Less) *Chelmsf 13*   **P** *Dr P W M Copeman and A R C Copeman Esq (jt)*   **P-in-c** R CARTWRIGHT   **NSM** C ROBINSON, J E TURNER

HADLEIGH (St Mary), Layham and Shelley *St E 4*   **P** *St Jo Coll Cam and Abp (alt)*   **V** J H DELFGOU   **NSM** S J WHITE

HADLEY (Holy Trinity) and Wellington Christ Church *Lich 20*   **P** *Bp, Adn Salop, and V Wellington All SS w Eyton*   **C** P H J THORNEYCROFT

HADLEY WOOD (St Paul) Proprietary Chapel *Lon 18*   **Min** R MACKAY

HADLOW (St Mary) *Roch 8*   **P** *Exors Miss I N King*   **V** P J WHITE   **C** N J HARVEY

HADLOW DOWN (St Mark) *see* Buxted and Hadlow Down *Chich*

HADNALL (St Mary Magdalene) *see* Astley, Clive, Grinshill and Hadnall *Lich*

HADSTOCK (St Botolph) *see* Saffron Walden and Villages *Chelmsf*

HADZOR w Oddingley (St James) *see* Bowbrook S *Worc*

HAGBOURNE (St Andrew) *see* The Churn *Ox*

HAGGERSTON (St Chad) *Lon 5*   **P** *The Crown*   **V** J J WESTCOTT

HAGLEY (St John the Baptist) *Worc 12*   **P** *Exors Viscount Cobham*   **R** R J C NEWTON

HAGLEY, WEST (St Saviour) *see* Hagley *Worc*

HAGNABY (St Andrew) *see* Bolingbroke Deanery *Linc*

HAGWORTHINGHAM (Holy Trinity) *as above*

HAIGH (St David) *see* Wigan All SS *Liv*

HAIL WESTON (St Nicholas) *see* The Staughtons w Hail Weston *Ely*

HAILE (not known) *see* Egremont and Haile *Carl*

HAILES (Chapel) *see* Winchcombe *Glouc*

HAILEY (St John the Evangelist) *see* Witney *Ox*

HAILSHAM (St Mary) (Emmanuel) *Chich 13*   **P** *Ch Soc Trust*   **V** D J BOURNE   **C** R M GRAHAM

HAINAULT (St Paul) *Chelmsf 6*   **P** *Bp*   **V** K ASHTON   **NSM** S A CLARKE-MOISLEY

HAINFORD (All Saints) *see* Coltishall w Gt Hautbois, Frettenham etc *Nor*

HAINTON (St Mary) *see* Barkwith Gp *Linc*

HALA (St Paul's Centre) *see* Scotforth *Blackb*

HALAM (St Michael) *see* Edingley w Halam *S'well*

HALAS, comprising Cradley, Halesowen, Hasbury, Lapal, and Romsley *Worc 9*   **P** *Patr Bd*   **TR** R S HALL   **TV** D MELVILLE, H CHARLTON, M K LECLÉZIO

HALBERTON (St Andrew) *see* Sampford Peverell, Uplowman, Holcombe Rogus etc *Ex*

HALDEN, HIGH (St Mary the Virgin) *see* Bethersden w High Halden and Woodchurch *Cant*

HALDENS (Christ the King) *see* Digswell *St Alb*

HALDON *see* Teignmouth, Ideford w Luton, Ashcombe etc *Ex*

HALE (St David) *see* Timperley *Ches*

HALE (St John the Evangelist) *see* Badshot Lea and Hale *Guildf*

HALE (St Mary) *see* Fordingbridge and Hyde and Breamore etc *Win*

HALE (St Mary) *see* S Widnes *Liv*

HALE (St Peter) and Ashley *Ches 10*   **P** *V Bowdon*   **V** K J STANTON

HALE BARNS (All Saints) w Ringway *Ches 10*   **P** *Bp*   **V** G C JAQUISS

HALE, GREAT (St John the Baptist) *see* Heckington and Helpringham Gp *Linc*

HALE, UPPER (St Mark) *see* Badshot Lea and Hale *Guildf*

HALES (St Mary) *see* Cheswardine, Childs Ercall, Hales, Hinstock etc *Lich*

HALESOWEN (St John the Baptist) *see* Halas *Worc*

HALESWORTH (St Mary) *see* Blyth Valley *St E*

HALEWOOD (St Nicholas) (St Mary) and Hunts Cross Team, The *Liv 2*   **P** *Patr Bd*   **TR** M P WOODSFORD

HALEY HILL (All Souls) *see* Halifax w Siddal *Leeds*

HALFORD (Our Blessed Lady) *see* Stourdene Gp *Cov*

HALFORD (St Thomas) w Sibdon Carwood *Heref 10*   **P** *Bp and R Holden (alt)*   **NSM** M G WILLIAMS

HALFWAY (St Peter) *see* W Sheppey *Cant*

HALIFAX (St Hilda) *see* Warley and Halifax St Hilda *Leeds*

HALIFAX (All Saints) *Leeds 10*   **P** *Ch Trust Fund Trust*   **V** S LEES

HALIFAX (Holy Trinity) (St Jude) *Leeds 10*   **P** *Bp, V Halifax, and trustees (jt)*   **C** M D PETCH

HALIFAX (St Anne-in-the-Grove) *see* Southowram and Claremount *Leeds*

HALIFAX (St John the Baptist) (All Souls) w Siddal *Leeds 10*   **P** *The Crown and Ch Trust Fund Trust (alt)*   **V** H J BARBER   **C** J L FINN   **Hon C** D J CARPENTER   **NSM** S L SCOTT

HALIFAX MINSTER *see* Halifax w Siddal *Leeds*

HALIFAX St Augustine (School Hall) and Mount Pellon *Leeds 10*   **P** *Bp, Simeon's Trustees, and local trustees (jt)*   **V** J HELLEWELL

HALL GREEN (Church of the Ascension) *Birm 5*   **P** *Bp, V Yardley, and Vice-Chmn of PCC (jt)*   **V** N BOUMENJEL

HALL GREEN (St Michael) *Birm 5*   **P** *Bp*   **P-in-c** M W STEPHENSON

HALL GREEN (St Peter) *Birm 5*   **P** *Bp*   **V** M W STEPHENSON

HALL STREET (St Andrew) *see* Stockport and Brinnington *Ches*

HALLAM, WEST (St Wilfred) and Mapperley w Stanley *Derby 8*   **P** *Bp*   **R** G R TURNER-CALLIS   **OLM** J V HUTCHINSON

HALLATON (St Michael and All Angels) and Allexton, w Horninghold, Tugby, and East Norton, and Slawston *Leic 5*   **P** *Bp, DBP, and E Brudenell Esq (jt)*   **R** C M HEBDEN

HALLING (St John the Baptist) *see* Cuxton and Halling *Roch*

HALLINGBURY, GREAT (St Giles) (St Andrew) and LITTLE (St Mary the Virgin) *Chelmsf 4*   **P** *Bp and Charterhouse (jt)*   **P-in-c** D W HERRICK

HALLIWELL (St Luke) *see* W Bolton *Man*

HALLIWELL (St Margaret) *see* Heaton Ch Ch w Halliwell St Marg *Man*

HALLIWELL (St Peter) (Barrow Bridge Mission) (St Andrew's Mission Church) *Man 7*   **P** *Trustees*   **V** P D HARDINGHAM   **C** O R PRESTON   **NSM** C WATSON

HALLOUGHTON (St James) *see* W Trent *S'well*

HALLOW (St Philip and St James) and Grimley w Holt *Worc 3*   **P** *Bp*   **R** *vacant*

HALLWOOD Ecumenical Parish (St Mark) *Ches 3*   **P** *DBP*   **V** L J MACINNES

HALSALL (St Cuthbert), Lydiate and Downholland *Liv 14*   **P** *Bp and Brig D H Blundell-Hollinshead-Blundell (jt)*   **R** P L ROBINSON   **NSM** D L BAKER

HALSE (Mission Church) *see* Brackley St Pet w St Jas *Pet*

HALSE (St James the Less) *see* Milverton w Halse, Fitzhead and Ash Priors *B & W*

HALSETOWN (St John's in the Fields) *see* St Ives and Halsetown *Truro*

HALSHAM (All Saints) *see* Burstwick, Burton Pidsea etc *York*

HALSTEAD (St Margaret) *see* Knockholt w Halstead *Roch*

HALSTEAD AREA (St Andrew), including Colne Engaine, Earls Colne, Gestingthorpe, Gosfield, Great Maplestead, Greenstead Green, Little Maplestead, Pebmarsh, and White Colne *Chelmsf 19*   **P** *Patr Bd*   **P-in-c** K E DE BOURCIER   **TV** G W ELLIS, M D PAYNE   **C** J J PARROTT, R F BRAISBY   **NSM** B VINCENT

HALSTOCK (St Mary) *see* Melbury *Sarum*

HALSTOW, HIGH (St Margaret) (All Hallows) and Hoo St Mary *Roch 6*   **P** *MMCET and Ch Soc Trust (jt)*   **R** S G GWILT

HALSTOW, LOWER (St Margaret) *see* The Six *Cant*

HALTER DEVIL (Mission Room) *see* Mugginton and Kedleston *Derby*

HALTON (St Mary) *Ches 3*   **P** *Bp*   **P-in-c** A MITCHELL

HALTON (St Michael and All Angels) *see* Wendover and Halton *Ox*

HALTON (St Oswald and St Cuthbert and King Alfwald) *see* Corbridge w Halton and Newton Hall *Newc*

HALTON (St Wilfred) *see* Slyne w Hest and Halton w Aughton *Blackb*

HALTON (St Wilfrid) and Osmondthorpe St Philip *Leeds 16*   **P** *Bp*   **V** H J SMITH   **C** R G DENTON

HALTON HOLGATE (St Andrew) *see* Bolingbroke Deanery *Linc*

HALTON QUAY (St Indract's Chapel) *see* Tamar Valley *Truro*

HALTON WEST (Mission Church) *see* Hellifield and Long Preston *Leeds*

HALTON, EAST (St Peter) *see* Abbey Gp *Linc*

HALTON, WEST (St Etheldreda) *see* Alkborough *Linc*

HALTWHISTLE (Holy Cross) and Greenhead *Newc 10*   **P** *Bp*   **V** *vacant*

HALVERGATE (St Peter and St Paul) *see* Acle and Bure to Yare *Nor*

HALWELL (St Leonard) *see* Diptford w N Huish, Ermington, Halwell etc *Ex*

HALWILL (St Peter and St James) *see* Ashwater, Halwill, Beaworthy, Clawton etc *Ex*

HAM (All Saints) *see* Savernake *Sarum*

HAM (St Andrew) *S'wark 15*   **P** *K Coll Cam*   **P-in-c** A H L PETTIT

HAM (St Barnabas Mission Church) *see* Chard St Mary w Combe St Nicholas, Wambrook etc *B & W*

HAM (St James the Less) *see* Plymouth St Pet and H Apostles *Ex*

HAM (St Richard) *S'wark 16* P *Bp* P-in-c S C COUPLAND
NSM S E ATKINS
HAM HILL VILLAGES, comprising Chiselborough, Middle
Chinnock, Montacute, Norton-sub-Hamdon, Odcombe,
Stoke sub Hamdon, and West Chinnock *B & W 5* P *Bp, Ch
Patr Trust, and Ch Ch Ox (jt)* C M A GURNER
NSM G J W EDMUNDS
HAMBLE LE RICE (St Andrew) *Win 10* P *St Mary's Coll Win*
V G J WHITING C R W SANDAY
HAMBLEDEN (St Mary the Virgin) *see* Hambleden Valley *Ox*
HAMBLEDEN VALLEY, comprising Fawley, Fingest,
Hambleden w Frieth, Medmenham, and Turville *Ox 18*
P *Bp, Viscount Hambleden, and Miss M Mackenzie (jt)*
R S M SOUTHGATE NSM S A MORTON
HAMBLEDON (St Peter and St Paul) *see* Soberton, Newtown
and Hambledon *Portsm*
HAMBLEDON (St Peter) *see* Busbridge and Hambledon
Guildf
HAMBLETON (St Andrew) *see* Oakham, Ashwell, Braunston,
Brooke, Egleton etc *Pet*
HAMBLETON (St Mary) *see* Haddlesey w Hambleton and
Birkin *York*
HAMBLETON (The Blessed Virgin Mary) *see* Waterside Par
Blackb
HAMBRIDGE (St James the Less) *see* Isle Valley *B & W*
HAMER (All Saints) and Healey *Man 17* P *Bp*
P-in-c G BARNETT
HAMERINGHAM (All Saints) *see* Fen and Hill Gp *Linc*
HAMERTON (All Saints) *see* N Leightonstone *Ely*
HAMILTON Conventional District *Leic 1* Min E RAWLINGS
HAMILTON TERRACE (St Mark) *see* St Marylebone St Mark
Hamilton Terrace *Lon*
HAMMER (St Michael) *see* Fernhurst, Lynchmere and
Camelsdale *Chich*
HAMMERFIELD (St Francis of Assisi) *see* Boxmoor St Jo *St Alb*
HAMMERSMITH (Holy Innocents) (St John the Evangelist)
Lon 9 P *Bp* P-in-c D W G MATTHEWS
NSM P P Y MULLINGS
HAMMERSMITH (St Luke) *Lon 9* P *Bp* V R M BASTABLE
NSM W M HAMILTON-BOX
HAMMERSMITH (St Matthew) *Lon 9* P *Trustees*
V G H CHIPLIN
HAMMERSMITH (St Michael and St George) *see* White City
Lon
HAMMERSMITH (St Paul) *Lon 9* P *Bp* V S G DOWNHAM
C M F J RUOFF NSM V I THOMAS
HAMMERSMITH (St Peter) *Lon 9* P *Bp* V C C CLAPHAM
C H PRENTICE
HAMMERSMITH (St Saviour) *see* Cobbold Road St Sav w
St Mary *Lon*
HAMMERSMITH (St Simon) *Lon 9* P *Simeon's Trustees*
V C J COLLINGTON
HAMMERSMITH, NORTH (St Katherine) *Lon 9* P *Bp*
P-in-c J TATE NSM L C TATE
HAMMERWICH (St John the Baptist) *see* Burntwood, Chase
Terrace etc *Lich*
HAMMOON (St Paul) *see* Okeford *Sarum*
HAMNISH (St Dubricius and All Saints) *see* Leominster *Heref*
HAMPDEN PARK (St Mary) and The Hydnye *Chich 14* P *Bp*
P-in-c A J RANSOM NSM J MANN
HAMPDEN, GREAT (St Mary Magdalene) *see* Prestwood and
Gt Hampden *Ox*
HAMPDEN, LITTLE (not known) *see* Gt Missenden w
Ballinger and Lt Hampden *Ox*
HAMPNETT (St George) *see* Northleach w Hampnett and
Farmington etc *Glouc*
HAMPRESTON (All Saints) *Sarum 9* P *Patr Bd* TR S A L PIX
TV E W MCLEOD, P CHABALA
HAMPSTEAD (Christ Church) *Lon 16* P *Trustees*
V P D CONRAD
HAMPSTEAD (Emmanuel) West End *Lon 16* P *Bp*
V J G F KESTER NSM A ARNELL, A FRITZE-SHANKS
HAMPSTEAD (St Cuthbert) *see* W Hampstead St Cuth *Lon*
HAMPSTEAD (St James) *see* Kilburn St Mary w All So and W
Hampstead St Jas *Lon*
HAMPSTEAD (St John) *Lon 16* P *DBP* V J J FLETCHER
C A R LEPINE
HAMPSTEAD (St John) Downshire Hill Proprietary Chapel
Lon 16 C C J BRIXTON Min T A WATTS
HAMPSTEAD (St Jude on the Hill) *see* Hampstead Garden
Suburb *Lon*
HAMPSTEAD (St Luke) *see* W Hampstead St Luke *Lon*
HAMPSTEAD (St Saviour) *see* S Hampstead St Sav *Lon*
HAMPSTEAD (St Stephen w All Hallows) *Lon 16* P *DBP and
D&C Cant (jt)* V D N C HOULDING
HAMPSTEAD Belsize Park (St Peter) *see* Belsize Park *Lon*

HAMPSTEAD GARDEN SUBURB (St Jude on the Hill) *Lon 15*
P *Bp* V A R G WALKER
HAMPSTEAD NORREYS (St Mary) *see* Hermitage *Ox*
HAMPSTEAD, SOUTH (St Saviour) *Lon 16* P *V Hampstead
St Jo* P-in-c P S NICHOLSON
HAMPSTEAD, WEST (Holy Trinity) *Lon 16* P *MMCET*
V A K KEIGHLEY C K L BREUSS
HAMPSTEAD, WEST (St Cuthbert) *Lon 16* P *Ch Trust Fund
Trust* P-in-c J G F KESTER NSM H V THOMAS
HAMPSTEAD, WEST (St Luke) *Lon 16* P *CPAS*
V A C TRESIDDER C T I POUNTAIN
HAMPSTHWAITE (St Thomas à Becket) and Killinghall and
Birstwith *Leeds 21* P *Mrs S J Finn, Sir James Aykroyd Bt, Sir
Thomas Ingilby Bt, and Bp (jt)* V vacant
HAMPTON (All Saints) *Lon 10* P *Ld Chan* V G K WARDELL
HAMPTON (no dedication) *Ely 15* P *Bp* V S P KINDER
C R H HILDITCH
HAMPTON (St Andrew) *see* Herne Bay Ch Ch *Cant*
HAMPTON (St Mary the Virgin) *Lon 10* P *Ld Chan*
V B R LOVELL NSM C F LOVELL
HAMPTON BISHOP (St Andrew) *see* Tupsley w Hampton
Bishop *Heref*
HAMPTON GAY (St Giles) *see* Akeman *Ox*
HAMPTON HILL (St James) *Lon 10* P *V Hampton St Mary*
V D N WINTERBURN NSM J A CAMMIDGE
HAMPTON LOVETT (St Mary and All Saints) *see* Elmley
Lovett w Hampton Lovett and Elmbridge w Rushock and
Hartlebury and Ombersley w Doverdale *Worc*
HAMPTON LUCY (St Peter ad Vincula) w Charlecote and
Loxley *Cov 8* P *Sir Edmund Fairfax-Lucy Bt (3 turns),
Col A M H Gregory-Hood (1 turn)* R vacant
HAMPTON POYLE (St Mary the Virgin) *see* Kidlington w
Hampton Poyle *Ox*
HAMPTON WICK (St John the Baptist) *Lon 10* P *Bp*
V J M FIELD C A R EVANS
HAMPTON, GREAT AND LITTLE (St Andrew) *see* Bengeworth
and Hampton etc *Worc*
HAMPTON-IN-ARDEN (St Mary and St Bartholomew) w
Bickenhill St Peter *Birm 10* P *Birm Dioc Trustees and Guild
of All So (jt)* R S C L DIMES
HAMSEY (St Peter) *Chich 21* P *Bp* R vacant
HAMSTALL RIDWARE (St Michael and All Angels) *see* Kings
Bromley, The Ridwares and Yoxall *Lich*
HAMSTEAD (St Bernard) *Birm 2* P *Bp* P-in-c D G JONES
HAMSTEAD (St Paul) *Birm 2* P *Bp* V vacant
HAMSTEAD MARSHALL (St Mary) *see* Walbury Beacon *Ox*
HAMSTERLEY (St James) and Witton-le-Wear *Dur 5* P *Bp
and The Crown (alt)* P-in-c B E MECHANIC
HAMWORTHY (St Gabriel) (St Michael) *Sarum 7* P *MMCET*
R T J NISBET
HANBOROUGH (St Peter and St Paul) and Freeland *Ox 29*
P *St Jo Coll Ox* R D S TYLER C E K HOPEGOOD JONES
NSM M J MADDEN, S J SPANKIE
HANBURY (St Mary the Virgin) *see* Bowbrook N *Worc*
HANBURY (St Werburgh), Newborough and Rangemore
Lich 13 P *DBP and Personal Reps Lord Burton (jt)* V L REES
HANDBRIDGE (St Mary without the Walls) *see* Ches St Mary
Ches
HANDCROSS (All Saints) *see* Slaugham and Staplefield
Common *Chich*
HANDFORTH (St Chad) *Ches 17* P *R Cheadle*
V S J BURMESTER
HANDLEY (All Saints) *see* Tattenhall w Burwardsley and
Handley *Ches*
HANDLEY (St Mark) *see* N Wingfield, Clay Cross and Pilsley
Derby
HANDSWORTH (Good News Asian Church) Proprietary
Chapel *Birm 2* NSM J M CHAUDHARY
HANDSWORTH (St Andrew) *Birm 2* P *Bp*
V D T MACHIRIDZA
HANDSWORTH (St James) *Birm 2* P *Bp*
P-in-c D T MACHIRIDZA NSM W HAMILTON
HANDSWORTH (St Mary) *Sheff 1* P *DBP* R K H JOHNSON
HANDSWORTH (St Mary) Epiphany *Birm 2* P *Bp*
R R STEPHEN
HANDSWORTH (St Michael) (St Peter) *Birm 2* P *Bp*
NSM J M CHAUDHARY
HANDSWORTH WOODHOUSE (St James) *see* Woodhouse
St Jas *Sheff*
HANFORD (St Matthias) *Lich 12* P *Bp* P-in-c S A MORRIS
OLM D J AITKEN
HANGER HILL (Ascension) and West Twyford *Lon 22* P *Bp
and DBP (jt)* V S J REED NSM P D HARRIS
HANGER LANE (St Ann) *see* S Tottenham St Ann *Lon*
HANGING HEATON (St Paul) *see* Batley *Leeds*

HANGLETON (St Helen) (St Richard) *Chich 20* **P** *Bp*
V K G PERKINTON

HANHAM (Christ Church) (St George) *Bris 5* **P** *Bp*
V B M CHARLES　**NSM** C E EVANS, J F J GOODRIDGE

HANKERTON (Holy Cross) *see* Braydon Brook *Bris*

HANLEY (All Saints) *see* Stoke-upon-Trent and Fenton *Lich*

HANLEY CASTLE (St Mary), Hanley Swan and Welland
Worc 5 **P** *Ld Chan and Exors Sir Berwick Lechmere Bt (alt)*
P-in-c B UNWIN　**NSM** S M E ADENEY

HANLEY CHILD (St Michael and All Angels) *see* Teme Valley S
Worc

HANLEY Holy Evangelists (St Luke) *Lich 11* **P** *Bp*
TR P E JONES　**TV** S A SMITH　**C** P D SWAN, S L PENDUCK

HANLEY SWAN (St Gabriel) *see* Hanley Castle, Hanley Swan
and Welland *Worc*

HANLEY WILLIAM (All Saints) *see* Teme Valley S *Worc*

HANNAH (St Andrew) cum Hagnaby *see* Alford Gp *Linc*

HANNEY, WEST (St James the Great) *see* Vale *Ox*

HANNINGFIELD, EAST (All Saints) *Chelmsf 10* **P** *CPAS*
P-in-c T G A BROWN

HANNINGFIELD, SOUTH (St Peter) *see* Downham w S
Hanningfield and Ramsden Bellhouse *Chelmsf*

HANNINGFIELD, WEST (St Mary and St Edward) *Chelmsf 10*
P *DBP*　**P-in-c** S W NEED

HANNINGTON (All Saints) *see* Baughurst, Ramsdell,
Wolverton w Ewhurst etc *Win*

HANNINGTON (St John the Baptist) *see* Highworth w
Sevenhampton and Inglesham etc *Bris*

HANNINGTON (St Peter and St Paul) *see* Walgrave w
Hannington and Wold and Scaldwell *Pet*

HANOVER SQUARE (St George) *Lon 3* **P** *Bp*　**R** R N S LEECE
NSM A R L PIGGOT, A W MCCORMACK

HANSLOPE (St James the Great) w Castlethorpe *Ox 16*
P *Bp*　**V** G E ECCLESTONE

HANWELL (St Christopher) *Lon 22* **P** *Bp*
R S VERNON-YORKE

HANWELL (St Mary) *Lon 22* **P** *Bp*　**V** A J DAND

HANWELL (St Mellitus w St Mark) *Lon 22* **P** *Bp*
P-in-c M P MELLUISH　**C** S P PLUMB　**NSM** J R G HYDE

HANWELL (St Peter) *see* Ironstone *Ox*

HANWELL (St Thomas) *Lon 22* **P** *The Crown*
V R B CHAPMAN　**C** S E DAND

HANWOOD, GREAT (St Thomas) and Longden and
Annscroft w Pulverbatch *Heref 12* **P** *J A de Grey-Warter*
Esq, Bp, and MMCET (jt)　**R** G D PHILLIPS
OLM O S DAWSON-CAMPBELL

HANWORTH (All Saints) *Lon 11* **P** *Bp*　**C** S DIDUK

HANWORTH (St Bartholomew) *see* Roughton and Felbrigg,
Metton, Sustead etc *Nor*

HANWORTH (St George) *Lon 11* **P** *Bp*　**R** vacant

HANWORTH (St Richard of Chichester) *Lon 11* **P** *Bp*
V C W HOLMES　**C** C J KENNEDY, S DIDUK

HAPPISBURGH (St Mary) *see* Bacton, Happisburgh,
Hempstead w Eccles etc *Nor*

HAPTON (St Margaret) *see* Padiham w Hapton and Padiham
Green *Blackb*

HAPTON (St Margaret) *see* Upper Tas Valley *Nor*

HARBERTON (St Andrew) *see* Diptford w N Huish,
Ermington, Halwell etc *Ex*

HARBERTONFORD (St Peter) *as above*

HARBLEDOWN (St Michael and All Angels) *Cant 3* **P** *Abp*
R P J HARNDEN

HARBORNE (St Faith and St Laurence) *Birm 1* **P** *Bp*
V P A WHITE

HARBORNE (St Peter) *Birm 1* **P** *Bp*　**V** vacant

HARBORNE HEATH (St John the Baptist) *Birm 1* **P** *Ch Soc*
Trust　**V** L J BROWNE　**C** F J R GREGSON, J M TATTERSALL

HARBOROUGH MAGNA (All Saints) *see* Revel Gp *Cov*

HARBRIDGE (All Saints) *see* Ringwood w Ellingham and
Harbridge etc *Win*

HARBURY (All Saints) and Ladbroke *Cov 10* **P** *Bp*　**R** vacant

HARBY (All Saints) *see* E Trent *S'well*

HARBY (St Mary the Virgin) *see* Vale of Belvoir *Leic*

HARDEN (St Saviour) and Wilsden, Cullingworth and
Denholme *Leeds 1* **P** *Patr Bd*　**TR** E C R BURGE
TV S MCCARTER　**NSM** E MOY

HARDENHUISH (St Nicholas) *see* Chippenham St Paul w
Hardenhuish etc *Bris*

HARDHAM (St Botolph) *see* Bury w Houghton and
Coldwaltham and Hardham *Chich*

HARDINGHAM (St George) *see* Barnham Broom and Upper
Yare *Nor*

HARDINGSTONE (St Edmund), Piddington w Horton and
Quinton and Preston Deanery *Pet 4* **P** *Bp*　**V** B J HOLLINS

HARDINGTON MANDEVILLE (Blessed Virgin Mary) *see* Coker
Ridge *B & W*

HARDINGTON VALE, comprising Farleigh Hungerford,
Hemington, Laverton, Norton St Philip, Rode, and Tellisford
B & W 3 **P** *Bp and J B Owen-Jones Esq (jt)*　**R** C H WALKER

HARDLEY (St Margaret) *see* Loddon, Sisland, Chedgrave,
Hardley and Langley *Nor*

HARDRAW (St Mary and St John) *see* Upper Wensleydale
Leeds

HARDRES, LOWER (St Mary) *see* Bridge *Cant*

HARDRES, UPPER (St Peter and St Paul) *see* Chartham and
Upper Hardres w Stelling *Cant*

HARDWICK (St Leonard) *see* Mears Ashby and Hardwick and
Sywell etc *Pet*

HARDWICK (St Margaret) *see* Hempnall *Nor*

HARDWICK (St Mary) *see* Lordsbridge *Ely*

HARDWICK, EAST (St Stephen) *see* Carleton and E Hardwick
Leeds

HARDWICK-CUM-TUSMORE (St Mary) *see* Shelswell *Ox*

HARDWICKE (Holy Trinity) *see* Cusop w Blakemere,
Bredwardine w Brobury etc *Heref*

HARDWICKE (St Mary the Virgin) *see* Schorne *Ox*

HARDWICKE (St Nicholas) and Elmore w Longney *Glouc 2*
P *Adn Glouc and Ld Chan (alt)*　**NSM** G R W PARFITT

HAREBY (St Peter and St Paul) *see* Bolingbroke Deanery *Linc*

HAREFIELD (St Mary the Virgin) *Lon 24* **P** *The Hon J E F*
Newdegate　**V** W M DAVIES

HAREHILLS (St Aidan) *see* Leeds St Aid *Leeds*

HAREHILLS (St Cyprian and St James) *see* Burmantofts and
Harehills *Leeds*

HARELAW (St Thomas) and Annfield Plain *Dur 4* **P** *Bp and*
The Crown (alt)　**NSM** S U TENGE-HESLOP

HARESCOMBE (St John the Baptist) *see* Painswick,
Sheepscombe, Cranham, The Edge etc *Glouc*

HARESFIELD (St Peter) *see* Stroudwater Team *Glouc*

HAREWOOD (Methodist Chapel) *see* Collingham w
Harewood *Leeds*

HARFORD (St Petroc) *see* Ivybridge w Harford *Ex*

HARGRAVE (All Saints) *see* Raunds, Hargrave, Ringstead and
Stanwick *Pet*

HARGRAVE (St Edmund King and Martyr) *see* Chevington w
Hargrave, Chedburgh w Depden etc *St E*

HARGRAVE (St Peter) *Ches 5* **P** *Bp*　**V** C H DEAKIN

HARKSTEAD (St Mary) *see* Shoreline *St E*

HARLASTON (St Matthew) *see* Mease Valley *Lich*

HARLAXTON Group, The (St Mary and St Peter), including
Denton, Stroxton, Woolsthorpe, and Wyville *Linc 20* **P** *Bp,*
DBP, Sir Richard Welby Bt, D&C, and Duke of Rutland (jt)
R S D HARROP

HARLESCOTT (Holy Spirit) (Emmanuel) *Lich 19* **P** *Bp*
C M J HEATH　**NSM** G W SMALL

HARLESDEN (All Souls) *Lon 21* **P** *The Crown*
V M D MOORHEAD

HARLESDEN (St Mark) *see* Kensal Rise St Mark *Lon*

HARLESTON (St Augustine) *see* Combs and Finborough *St E*

HARLESTON (St John the Baptist) *see* Redenhall w Scole *Nor*

HARLESTONE (St Andrew) *see* Brington w Whilton and
Norton etc *Pet*

HARLEY (St Mary) *see* Wenlock *Heref*

HARLING, EAST (St Peter and St Paul) w West, Bridgham
w Roudham, Larling, Brettenham and Rushford *Nor 11*
P *Ld Chan (1 turn), DBP, Sir Robin Nugent Bt, C D F Musker*
Esq, Major E H C Garnier, and Exors Sir John Musker (3 turns)
P-in-c D R SMITH　**OLM** C D BROWN

HARLINGTON (Christ Church) *see* W Hayes *Lon*

HARLINGTON (St Mary the Virgin) *St Alb 8* **P** *Bp*
V S J WILLIAMS

HARLINGTON (St Peter and St Paul) *Lon 24* **P** *Bp*
R M E SMITH

HARLOW (St Mary and St Hugh w St John the Baptist)
Chelmsf 4 **P** *Simeon's Trustees and Bp (alt)*　**V** vacant

HARLOW (St Mary Magdalene) *Chelmsf 4* **P** *V Harlow*
St Mary and St Hugh etc　**V** J W E RODLEY　**NSM** G R NEAVE

HARLOW GREEN (St Ninian) and Lamesley *Dur 11* **P** *Bp*
V M WORTHINGTON　**NSM** G J LACKENBY

HARLOW Town Centre (St Paul) w Little Parndon *Chelmsf 4*
P *Patr Bd*　**TR** M J HARRIS　**TV** J G M POYNTZ
C N J JOSS-POTHEN　**NSM** B C AYLETT

HARLSEY (St Oswald) *see* Osmotherley w Harlsey and
Ingleby Arncliffe *York*

HARLTON (Assumption of the Blessed Virgin Mary) *see*
Lordsbridge *Ely*

HARMANSWATER (St Paul) *see* Bracknell *Ox*

HARMONDSWORTH (St Mary the Virgin) *Lon 24* **P** *DBP*
V A O CHRISTIAN-IWUAGWU　**NSM** C K OKPALA, T B I OLISA

HARMSTON (All Saints) *see* Graffoe Gp *Linc*

HARNHAM (St George) (All Saints) *Sarum 13* **P** *Bp (1 turn),*
V Britford (2 turns)　**V** R M ROBERTS　**NSM** J G POPPLETON

HARNHILL (St Michael and All Angels) *see* S Cotswolds *Glouc*
HAROLD HILL (St George) *Chelmsf 2* **P** *Bp* **V** S C MOORE
HAROLD HILL (St Paul) *Chelmsf 2* **P** *Bp* **V** R D MOUL
  C M T BAILEY
HAROLD WOOD (St Peter) *Chelmsf 2* **P** *New Coll Ox*
  V R A HUDSON **C** R V J POWER
HAROME (St Saviour) *see* Kirkdale w Harome, Nunnington
  and Pockley *York*
HARPENDEN (St John the Baptist) *St Alb 7* **P** *DBP*
  V B J ZYCH **C** J C BROWN
HARPENDEN (St Nicholas) (All Saints) *St Alb 7* **P** *Ld Chan*
  R D L STAMPS **C** J T HADLEY, S L GOODSON
HARPFORD (St Gregory the Great) *see* Ottery St Mary,
  Alfington, W Hill, Tipton etc *Ex*
HARPHAM (St John of Beverley) *see* The Beacon *York*
HARPLEY (St Lawrence) *see* Ashwicken w Leziate, Bawsey etc
  Nor
HARPOLE (All Saints) *see* Bugbrooke, Harpole, Kislingbury
  etc *Pet*
HARPSDEN (St Margaret) *see* Shiplake w Dunsden and
  Harpsden *Ox*
HARPSWELL (St Chad) *see* Trentcliffe Gp *Linc*
**HARPTREE, EAST (St Laurence) w WEST (Blessed Virgin
  Mary) and Hinton Blewett** *B & W 9* **P** *Duchy of Cornwall
  Hon* **C** K P SPRAY
HARPUR HILL (St James) *see* Buxton w Burbage and King
  Sterndale *Derby*
HARPURHEY (Christ Church) *Man 4* **P** *Bp and Trustees (jt)*
  P-in-c N R ELLIOTT
HARPURHEY (St Stephen) *see* Harpurhey *Man*
HARRABY (St Elisabeth) *Carl 3* **P** *Bp* **P-in-c** E M SMITH
HARRIETSHAM (St John the Baptist) *see* Len Valley *Cant*
HARRINGAY (St Paul) *Lon 19* **P** *Bp* **P-in-c** P R SNOW
  C P J HENDERSON
HARRINGTON (St Mary) *see* S Ormsby Gp *Linc*
HARRINGTON (St Mary) and Distington *Carl 7* **P** *The Hon J
  N Lowther and Mrs E H S Thornely (jt)* **R** J H POWLEY
HARRINGTON (St Peter and St Paul) *see* Arthingworth,
  Harrington w Oxendon and E Farndon *Pet*
HARRINGWORTH (St John the Baptist) *see* Lyddington,
  Bisbrooke, Caldecott, Glaston etc *Pet*
HARROGATE (St Luke's Church Centre) *see* Kirby-on-the-
  Moor, Cundall w Norton-le-Clay etc *Leeds*
HARROGATE (St Mark) *Leeds 21* **P** *Peache Trustees*
  C D J WATTS, K S MASON **NSM** J W HANDLEY
HARROGATE (St Wilfrid) *Leeds 21* **P** *Bp*
  TR G R WADDINGTON
HARROGATE, HIGH (Christ Church) *Leeds 21* **P** *Bp*
  V M S EVANS
HARROGATE, HIGH (St Peter) *Leeds 21* **P** *Ch Patr Trust*
  V A J P GARROW **C** C C CLAYTON **Hon C** T J HURREN
  NSM R T NOLAN
HARROLD (St Peter and All Saints) *see* Chellington *St Alb*
HARROW (All Saints) *see* Harrow Weald All SS *Lon*
HARROW (Christ Church) *see* Roxeth *Lon*
HARROW (Holy Trinity) *see* Wealdstone H Trin *Lon*
HARROW (St Alban) *see* N Harrow St Alb *Lon*
HARROW (St Mary) *see* Harrow St Mary *Lon*
HARROW (St Michael and All Angels) *see* Harrow Weald
  St Mich *Lon*
HARROW (St Paul) *see* S Harrow St Paul *Lon*
HARROW (St Peter) *see* W Harrow *Lon*
HARROW GREEN (Holy Trinity and St Augustine of Hippo)
  see Leytonstone H Trin and St Aug Harrow Green *Chelmsf*
HARROW ON THE HILL (St Mary) *Lon 23* **P** *Bp, Adn, and Hd
  Master Harrow Sch (jt)* **V** J E POWER
HARROW ROAD (Emmanuel) *see* W Kilburn St Luke and
  Harrow Road Em *Lon*
HARROW WEALD (All Saints) *Lon 23* **P** *Bp, Adn, V Harrow
  St Mary, and R Bushey (jt)* **V** J W BARKER **NSM** P M WARD
HARROW WEALD (St Michael and All Angels) *Lon 23* **P** *Bp*
  V J STOWELL
HARROW, NORTH (St Alban) *Lon 23* **P** *Bp* **V** K A TUCKETT
HARROW, SOUTH (St Paul) *Lon 23* **P** *R St Bride Fleet Street w
  Bridewell and Trin Gough Square* **V** I P DOWSETT
  C S B JOHNSON
HARROW, WEST (St Peter) *Lon 23* **P** *Bp and Ch Patr Trust
  (jt)* **V** R E A GREEN **C** R E CAMPBELL
HARROWBARROW (All Saints) *see* Tamar Valley *Truro*
HARROWBY (The Ascension) *see* Grantham, Harrowby w
  Londonthorpe *Linc*
**HARROWDEN, GREAT (All Saints) w LITTLE (St Mary the
  Virgin) and Orlingbury and Isham w Pytchley** *Pet 6*
  P *Bp and Sir Philip Naylor-Leyland Bt (jt)* **R** A SMITH
  NSM G ALDERSON

HARSTON (All Saints) w Hauxton and Newton *Ely 5* **P** *Bp
  (2 turns), D&C (1 turn)* **P-in-c** S J TALBOTT
  C S M BOWDEN-PICKSTOCK
HARSTON (St Michael and All Angels) *see* High Framland
  Par *Leic*
HARSWELL (St Peter) *see* Holme and Seaton Ross Gp *York*
HART (St Mary Magdalene) w Elwick Hall *Dur 3* **P** *Bp and
  DBP (alt)* **P-in-c** J BURBURY
HART PLAIN *see* Hartplain *Portsm*
HARTBURN (All Saints) *see* Stockton St Pet *Dur*
HARTBURN (St Andrew) *see* Bolam w Whalton and Hartburn
  w Meldon *Newc*
HARTCLIFFE (St Andrew) *see* Bris St Andr Hartcliffe *Bris*
HARTEST (All Saints) *see* Glemsford, Hartest w Boxted,
  Somerton etc *St E*
HARTFIELD (St Mary) w Coleman's Hatch *Chich 16* **P** *Bp
  and Earl De la Warr (jt)* **R** J A C SEAR
HARTFORD (All Saints) and Houghton w Wyton *Ely 10*
  P *Bp* **R** G J BOUCHER **C** K J BAKER **NSM** A O'NEILL,
  E J G STRICKLAND
HARTFORD (St John the Baptist) *Ches 6* **P** *Ch Soc Trust*
  V M I A SMITH **C** A G HAM, D ALLDRIDGE **NSM** G AGAR,
  P W HIGHTON
HARTHILL (All Hallows) and Thorpe Salvin *Sheff 5* **P** *Bp*
  P-in-c G SCHOFIELD
**HARTING (St Mary and St Gabriel) w Elsted and Treyford
  cum Didling** *Chich 9* **P** *Bp* **R** vacant
HARTINGTON (St Giles) *see* Taddington, Chelmorton and
  Monyash etc *Derby*
HARTISMERE, NORTH, comprising Brome, Burgate, Palgrave,
  Stuston, Thrandeston, and Wortham *St E 12* **P** *MMCET,
  K Coll Cam, Bp, and DBP (jt)* **R** A R WATKINS
HARTISMERE, SOUTH, comprising Gislingham, Mellis, Stoke
  Ash w Thwaite, Thorndon w Rishangles, Thornham Magna,
  Thornham Parva, Wetheringsett, and Yaxley *St E 12* **P** *Bp,
  Comdr F P Brooke-Popham, MMCET, Ch Soc Trust, SMF, and
  Lord Henniker (jt)* **R** J C LALL
HARTLAND (St Nectan) *see* Parkham, Alwington, Buckland
  Brewer etc *Ex*
HARTLAND COAST *see* Parkham, Alwington, Buckland
  Brewer etc *Ex*
HARTLEBURY (St James) *see* Elmley Lovett w Hampton
  Lovett and Elmbridge w Rushock and Hartlebury and
  Ombersley w Doverdale *Worc*
HARTLEPOOL (Holy Trinity) (St Mark's Centre) *Dur 3* **P** *Bp*
  V R HALL
HARTLEPOOL (St Aidan) (St Columba) *Dur 3* **P** *Bp*
  P-in-c G S M SAMPSON
HARTLEPOOL (St Hilda) *Dur 3* **P** *Bp* **P-in-c** V J BROWN
HARTLEPOOL (St Luke) *Dur 3* **P** *Bp* **P-in-c** N R SHAVE
HARTLEPOOL (St Oswald) *Dur 3* **P** *Bp* **V** G BUTTERY
HARTLEPOOL (St Paul) *Dur 3* **P** *Bp* **V** R E MASSHEDAR
HARTLEY (All Saints) *see* Fawkham and Hartley *Roch*
HARTLEY BROOK (Mission Hall) *see* Becontree St Mary
  Chelmsf
HARTLEY MAUDITT (St Leonard) *see* Northanger *Win*
HARTLEY WESPALL (St Mary) *see* Sherfield-on-Loddon and
  Stratfield Saye etc *Win*
**HARTLEY WINTNEY (St John the Evangelist), Elvetham,
  Winchfield and Dogmersfield** *Win 5* **P** *Bp and Sir Euan
  Anstruther-Gough-Calthorpe Bt (jt)* **P-in-c** A SMITH
  C M R BIANCHI
HARTLEY, NEW (St Michael and All Angels) *see* Delaval *Newc*
HARTLIP (St Michael and All Angels) *see* The Six *Cant*
HARTON (St Peter) (St Lawrence) *Dur 13* **P** *D&C*
  P-in-c K L BOARDMAN
HARTON, comprising Bossal, Crambe, Flaxton, Foston, Gate
  Helmsley, Sand Hutton, Upper Helmsley, and Whitwell
  York 6 **P** *Abp and D&C Dur (1 turn) Abp (1 turn)*
  R C L WINGFIELD **C** H L SUEKARRAN
HARTPLAIN (not known) *Portsm 5* **P** *DBP*
  Dn-in-c K A MACFARLANE
HARTPURY (St Mary the Virgin) *see* Ashleworth, Corse,
  Hartpury, Hasfield etc *Glouc*
**HARTSHEAD (St Peter), Hightown, Roberttown and
  Scholes** *Leeds 6* **P** *V Birstall, TR Dewsbury, and Bp (alt)*
  NSM S M HOLT, S P ROCHELL **OLM** J C LEE
HARTSHILL (Holy Trinity) and Galley Common *Cov 5* **P** *Ch
  Patr Trust and Bp (jt)* **V** H D BARNES **C** S L CROFTS
HARTSHILL (Holy Trinity), Penkhull and Trent Vale *Lich 11*
  P *Bp and R Stoke-upon-Trent (jt)* **R** C J RUSHTON
HARTSHORNE (St Peter) and Bretby *Derby 7* **P** *Bp and
  MMCET (jt)* **C** A J REDSHAW, G P RUTTER, P R BOSHER,
  S J GREENWOOD **NSM** F D STARTIN **OLM** C A BUCKLEY
HARTWELL (St John the Baptist) *see* Salcey *Pet*

HARTWITH (St Jude)   see Dacre w Hartwith and Darley w Thornthwaite *Leeds*

HARTY (St Thomas Apostle)   see Eastchurch w Leysdown and Harty *Cant*

HARVINGTON (St James)   see Church Lench w Rous Lench and Abbots Morton etc *Worc*

HARWELL (St Matthew) w Chilton *Ox 26*   P *DBP and CPAS (jt)*   R J L MOBEY   NSM J RADFORD   OLM P M ROLLS

HARWICH PENINSULA, The (St Nicholas), including Dovercourt and Ramsey *Chelmsf 22*   P *Patr Bd*   TR M A SHAW   C L R S CLARKE-MOISLEY, S J WINNEY

HARWOOD (Christ Church) *Man 12*   P *DBP*   V W L OLIVER   OLM A E MORGAN, H MOLLOY, J K GORDON

HARWOOD DALE (St Margaret)   see Hackness w Harwood Dale *York*

HARWOOD, GREAT (St Bartholomew) St John *Blackb 7*   P *Patr Bd*   V G J BIRCH

HARWORTH (All Saints) *S'well 1*   P *Sir John Whitaker Bt*   P-in-c N R SKIPWORTH

HASBURY (St Margaret)   see Halas *Worc*

HASCOMBE (St Peter)   see Dunsfold and Hascombe *Guildf*

HASELBECH (St Michael)   see Clipston, Haselbech, Kelmarsh, Marston Trussell etc *Pet*

HASELBURY PLUCKNETT (St Michael and All Angels)   see Wulfric Benefice *B & W*

HASELEY (St Mary)   see Hatton w Haseley, Rowington w Lowsonford etc *Cov*

HASELEY, GREAT (St Peter)   see Gt w Lt Milton and Gt Haseley *Ox*

HASELOR (St Mary and All Saints)   see Alcester Minster *Cov*

HASELTON (St Andrew)   see Northleach w Hampnett and Farmington etc *Glouc*

HASFIELD (St Mary)   see Ashleworth, Corse, Hartpury, Hasfield etc *Glouc*

HASKETON (St Andrew)   see Carlford *St E*

HASLAND (St Paul) *Derby 3*   P V *Chesterfield*   R G N BORROWDALE

HASLEMERE (St Bartholomew) (St Christopher) and Grayswood *Guildf 4*   P *Ld Chan*   OLM F J GWYNN, R J MANLEY-COOPER

HASLINGDEN (St James) w Grane and Stonefold *Blackb 1*   P *Bp and Hulme Trustees (jt)*   V D STEPHENSON   NSM D ALLSOP

HASLINGDEN (St Peter)   see Laneside *Blackb*

HASLINGDEN (St Thomas)   see Musbury *Blackb*

HASLINGFIELD (All Saints)   see Lordsbridge *Ely*

HASLINGTON (St Matthew) w Crewe Green St Michael *Ches 15*   P *Bp*   P-in-c P J LLOYD

HASSALL GREEN (St Philip)   see Sandbach Heath w Wheelock *Ches*

HASSINGHAM (St Mary)   see Burlingham St Edmund w Lingwood, Strumpshaw etc *Nor*

HASTINGS (Christ Church and St Andrew)   see Blacklands Hastings Ch Ch and St Andr *Chich*

HASTINGS (Emmanuel and St Mary in the Castle) *Chich 15*   P *MMCET and Hyndman Trustees (alt)*   V M G LANE   NSM R BROWNING

HASTINGS (Holy Trinity) *Chich 15*   P *Bp*   V S G D LARKIN   C T L BELL

HASTINGS (St Clement) (All Saints) *Chich 15*   P *Bp*   R *vacant*

HASTINGS (St Peter and St Paul)   see Hollington St Jo *Chich*

HASWELL (St Paul) and Shotton *Dur 2*   P *Bp*   NSM A STAINSBY, M PETERS

HATCH BEAUCHAMP (St John the Baptist)   see Beercrocombe w Curry Mallet, Hatch Beauchamp etc *B & W*

HATCH END (St Anselm) *Lon 23*   P *Bp*   V D M GREEN

HATCH WARREN AND BEGGARWOOD (Immanuel) *Win 4*   P *Bp*   P-in-c M W BARKER

HATCH, WEST (St Andrew)   see Beercrocombe w Curry Mallet, Hatch Beauchamp etc *B & W*

HATCHAM (St Catherine) *S'wark 2*   P *Haberdashers' Co*   V S A JAMES   NSM E B KORMI, J ELLIOTT

HATCHAM (St James) (St George) (St Michael) *S'wark 2*   P *Ch Patr Soc*   V *vacant*

HATCHAM PARK (All Saints) *S'wark 2*   P *Hyndman Trustees (2 turns), Haberdashers' Co (1 turn)*   OLM J FRANCIS

HATCLIFFE (St Mary)   see Wolds Gateway Group *Linc*

HATFIELD   see Bp's Hatfield, Lemsford and N Mymms *St Alb*

HATFIELD (St Lawrence) *Sheff 10*   P *Bp*   V E A TURNER-LOISEL

HATFIELD (St Leonard)   see Leominster *Heref*

HATFIELD BROAD OAK (St Mary the Virgin) and Bush End *Chelmsf 4*   P *Bp*   V N A WORMELL

HATFIELD HEATH (Holy Trinity) and Sheering *Chelmsf 4*   P *Ch Ch Ox and V Hatfield Broad Oak (alt)*   P-in-c D JEWSON

HATFIELD HYDE (St Mary Magdalene) *St Alb 18*   P *Marquess of Salisbury*   V A A LAUCKNER

HATFIELD PEVEREL (St Andrew) w Ulting *Chelmsf 24*   P *Bp*   V S R NORTHFIELD   NSM D R CLARK-MAYERS

HATFIELD REGIS   see Hatfield Broad Oak and Bush End *Chelmsf*

HATHERDEN (Christ Church)   see Pastrow *Win*

HATHERLEIGH (St John the Baptist)   see Okehampton, Inwardleigh, Belstone, Sourton etc *Ex*

HATHERN (St Peter and St Paul)   see Kegworth, Hathern, Long Whatton, Diseworth etc *Leic*

HATHEROP (St Nicholas)   see S Cotswolds *Glouc*

HATHERSAGE (St Michael and All Angels) w Bamford and Derwent, and Grindleford *Derby 4*   P *Duke of Devonshire, Earl Temple, and A C H Barnes Esq (jt)*   R *vacant*

HATHERTON (St Saviour) *Lich 3*   P A R W Littleton Esq   OLM G M JOYNSON

HATLEY ST GEORGE (St George)   see Gamlingay and Everton *Ely*

HATTERS LANE (St Andrew)   see High Wycombe *Ox*

HATTERSLEY (St Barnabas) *Ches 14*   P *Bp*   P-in-c D A HAYES

HATTON (All Saints) *Derby 6*   P *Bp and N J M Spurrier Esq (jt)*   V *vacant*

HATTON (Holy Trinity) w Haseley, Rowington w Lowsonford and Honiley and Wroxall *Cov 4*   P *Bp*   R K J MOBBERLEY   NSM S MOBBERLEY

HATTON (St Stephen)   see Hemingby Gp *Linc*

HAUGH (St Leonard)   see S Ormsby Gp *Linc*

HAUGHLEY (St Mary the Virgin) w Wetherden and Stowupland *St E 8*   P *Ld Chan, Bp, and DBP (by turn)*   P-in-c D B SINGLETON

HAUGHTON (St Anne) *Man 13*   P *DBP*   C K J MAMBU, M HOWARTH, P R DIXON

HAUGHTON (St Chad)   see Whittington and W Felton w Haughton *Lich*

HAUGHTON (St Giles)   see Bradeley, Church Eaton, Derrington and Haughton *Lich*

HAUGHTON (St Mary the Virgin) *Man 13*   P *Bp*   R M R GLEW

HAUGHTON LE SKERNE (St Andrew) *Dur 7*   P *Bp*   R M R EAST   NSM S CHEW

HAUTBOIS, GREAT (Holy Trinity)   see Coltishall w Gt Hautbois, Frettenham etc *Nor*

HAUXTON (St Edmund)   see Harston w Hauxton and Newton *Ely*

HAUXWELL (St Oswald)   see Lower Wensleydale *Leeds*

HAVANT (St Faith) *Portsm 5*   P *Bp*   P-in-c T P KENNAR

HAVEN Group, The, comprising Bicker, Donington, Sutterton, Swineshead, and Wigtoft *Linc 21*   P *Bp, D&C, Simeon's Trustees, and DBP (2 turns), Prime-Min (1 turn)*   V C P ROBERTSON   NSM S L HENTLEY

HAVEN, THE Conventional District *Chich 14*   Min J B P BROOK

HAVENSTREET (St Peter) *Portsm 7*   P *SMF*   V V M BROWN

HAVERHILL (St Mary the Virgin) w Withersfield *St E 3*   P *Bp*   V *vacant*

HAVERIGG (St Luke)   see Millom *Carl*

HAVERING-ATTE-BOWER (St John)   see Collier Row St Jas and Havering-atte-Bower *Chelmsf*

HAVERINGLAND (St Peter)   see Aylsham and Distr *Nor*

HAVERSHAM (St Mary)   see Lamp *Ox*

HAVERSTOCK HILL (Holy Trinity)   see Kentish Town St Silas and H Trin w St Barn *Lon*

HAVERTHWAITE (St Anne)   see Cartmel Peninsula *Carl*

HAWBUSH (St Paul)   see Brierley Hill *Worc*

HAWES (St Margaret)   see Upper Wensleydale *Leeds*

HAWES SIDE (St Christopher) and Marton Moss St Nicholas *Blackb 8*   P *Bp*   V L M DANIELS   OLM S TOMLINSON

HAWKCHURCH (St John the Baptist)   see Golden Cap Team *Sarum*

HAWKEDON (St Mary)   see Chevington w Hargrave, Chedburgh w Depden etc *St E*

HAWKESBURY (St Mary)   see Boxwell, Leighterton, Didmarton, Oldbury etc *Glouc*

HAWKHURST (St Laurance) *Cant 11*   P *Ch Ch Ox*   V R G DREYER

HAWKINGE (St Luke) *Cant 8*   P *Abp*   P-in-c R P GRINSELL

HAWKLEY (St Peter and St Paul)   see Greatham, Empshott and Hawkley w Priors Dean *Portsm*

HAWKRIDGE (St Giles)   see Exmoor *B & W*

HAWKSHAW (St Mary)   see Holcombe and Hawkshaw *Man*

HAWKSHEAD (St Michael and All Angels) and Low Wray w Sawrey and Rusland and Satterthwaite *Carl 11*   P *Bp*   V J S DIXON   NSM N F HALLAM

HAWKSWOOD (Emmanuel)   see Hailsham *Chich*

HAWKSWORTH (St Mary and All Saints) *see* Whatton w Aslockton, Hawksworth, Scarrington etc *S'well*
HAWKSWORTH WOOD (St Mary) *see* Abbeylands *Leeds*
HAWKWELL (Emmanuel) (St Mary the Virgin) *Chelmsf 14*
  P *CPAS* **P-in-c** N E ROWAN
HAWLEY (Holy Trinity) *Guildf 1* **P** *Keble Coll Ox*
  V W F P PERRY
HAWLEY, SOUTH (All Saints) *see* Hawley H Trin *Guildf*
HAWLING (St Edward) *see* Sevenhampton w Charlton Abbots, Hawling etc *Glouc*
HAWNBY (All Saints) *see* Upper Ryedale *York*
HAWORTH (St Michael and All Angels) and Cross Roads cum Lees *Leeds 1* **P** *Bp, V Bradf, and Haworth Ch Lands Trust (jt)* **R** P M MULLINS **C** A R BENNETT **NSM** J ROBERTS
HAWRIDGE (St Mary) w Cholesbury and St Leonard *Ox 17*
  P *Bp, Chpl Trust, and Neale's Charity (jt)* **R** D J BURGESS
  C D E BEESLEY
HAWSKER (All Saints) *see* Fylingdales and Hawsker cum Stainsacre *York*
HAWSTEAD (All Saints) *see* St Edm Way *St E*
HAWTHORN (St Michael and All Angels) and Murton *Dur 2* **P** *D&C and I Pemberton Esq (alt)* **NSM** P P PATERSON
HAWTON (All Saints) *see* Farndon w Thorpe, Hawton and Cotham *S'well*
HAXBY (St Mary) and Wigginton *York 7* **P** *Abp and Ld Chan (alt)* **R** K D JACKSON **NSM** N A S BENSON
HAXEY (St Nicholas) *Linc 1* **P** *Ld Chan* **V** *vacant*
HAY MILL (St Cyprian) *see* Yardley St Cypr Hay Mill *Birm*
HAYDOCK (St James) *Liv 13* **P** *R Ashton-in-Makerfield*
  V G A WELSBY **NSM** I C WYNNE
HAYDOCK (St Mark) *Liv 10* **P** *MMCET* **V** D B LEATHERS
HAYDON BRIDGE (St Cuthbert) and Beltingham w Henshaw *Newc 10* **P** *Bp and V Haltwhistle and Greenhead (jt)* **V** B H CARTER **NSM** G ALEXANDER
HAYDON WICK (St John) *Bris 7* **P** *CPAS* **V** R W ADAMS
HAYES (Christ Church) *see* W Hayes *Lon*
HAYES (St Anselm) *Lon 24* **P** *Bp* **V** *vacant*
HAYES (St Edmund of Canterbury) *Lon 24* **P** *Bp*
  V P S MACKENZIE
HAYES (St Jerome) *see* W Hayes *Lon*
HAYES (St Mary the Virgin) *Roch 13* **P** *D&C* **R** N JOHN
HAYES (St Mary) *Lon 24* **P** *Keble Coll Ox* **R** N G T WHEELER
HAYES, NORTH (St Nicholas) *Lon 24* **P** *Bp and Keble Coll Ox (jt)* **V** J A EVANS
HAYES, WEST (Christ Church) (St Jerome) *Lon 24* **P** *Bp and Hyndman Trustees (jt)* **V** I W JONES
HAYFIELD (St Matthew) and Chinley w Buxworth *Derby 4*
  P *Bp and Resident Freeholders (jt)* **V** J F HUDGHTON
HAYLE (St Elwyn) *see* Godrevy *Truro*
HAYLING ISLAND (St Andrew) Eastoke *Portsm 5* **P** *DBP*
  P-in-c J C GAFFIN **C** D A CURRAM
HAYLING, NORTH (St Peter) *Portsm 5* **P** *DBP*
  P-in-c J C GAFFIN
HAYLING, SOUTH (St Mary) *Portsm 5* **P** *DBP*
  P-in-c J C GAFFIN
HAYNES (Mission Room) *see* Campton, Clophill and Haynes *St Alb*
HAYNES (St Mary) *as above*
HAYTON (St James) *see* Aspatria w Hayton and Gilcrux *Carl*
HAYTON (St Martin) *see* Londesborough Wold *York*
HAYTON (St Mary Magdalene) *see* Eden, Gelt and Irthing *Carl*
HAYTON (St Peter) *see* Retford Area *S'well*
HAYWARDS HEATH (Church of the Ascension) *Chich 5*
  P *Bp* **P-in-c** M P JONES
HAYWARDS HEATH (Church of the Presentation) *see* Haywards Heath St Wilfrid *Chich*
HAYWARDS HEATH (St Richard) *Chich 5* **P** *Bp*
  V C BRADING **Hon C** L D POODHUN
HAYWARDS HEATH (St Wilfrid) (Church of the Presentation) *Chich 5* **P** *Bp* **V** R C W SMITH
  NSM D C YOUNG, J M ELLIOTT
HAYWOOD, GREAT (St Stephen) *see* Abbots Bromley, Blithfield, Colton, Colwich etc *Lich*
HAZELBURY BRYAN (St Mary and St James) and the Hillside Parishes *Sarum 5* **P** *Duke of Northumberland (2 turns), Bp, G A L-F Pitt-Rivers Esq, Exors F N Kent Esq, and Bp (1 turn each)* **NSM** D GINGELL
HAZELWELL (St Mary Magdalen) *Birm 4* **P** *Bp*
  V M R FORBES
HAZELWOOD (St John the Evangelist), Holbrook and Milford *Derby 6* **P** *Bp and DBP (jt)* **P-in-c** N J FENTON
HAZLEMERE (Holy Trinity) *Ox 18* **P** *Peache Trustees*
  V M J MEARDON **C** C L GERARD, D W E MEERING
HEACHAM (St Mary) and Snettisham *Nor 15* **P** *Patr Bd*
  TR V M WILSON **C** R C ALEXANDER

HEADBOURNE WORTHY (St Swithun) *Win 7* **P** *Univ Coll Ox and Lord Northbrook (alt)* **R** P E BRADISH **NSM** E CHASE
HEADCORN (St Peter and St Paul) and The Suttons *Cant 11*
  P *Abp* **V** F A HASKETT
HEADINGLEY Team Ministry (St Michael and All Angels) (St Chad) *Leeds 15* **P** *Patr Bd* **TR** M A WHATMOUGH
  TV H F LIEVESLEY **NSM** A E BIRKIN, K WARD
HEADINGTON (St Andrew) *Ox 1* **P** *Keble Coll Ox*
  V D W MCFARLAND **C** T D HOWLES **NSM** J R STRAWBRIDGE
HEADINGTON (St Mary) *Ox 1* **P** *Bp* **V** E P BOSSWARD
  C B A BAKER
HEADINGTON QUARRY (Holy Trinity) *Ox 1* **P** *Bp*
  V L R BIRON-SCOTT **NSM** R J C GILBERT
HEADLESS CROSS (St Luke) *see* Redditch Ch the K *Worc*
HEADLEY (All Saints) *Guildf 3* **P** *Qu Coll Ox* **R** A E BARTON
  NSM H E KEMPSTER
HEADLEY (St Mary the Virgin) and Box Hill w Walton on the Hill *Guildf 9* **P** *Bp* **R** H N L LATHAM
  NSM C M J HANCOCK
HEADLEY (St Peter) *see* Kingsclere and Ashford Hill w Headley *Win*
HEADON (St Peter) *see* Retford Area *S'well*
HEADSTONE (St George) *Lon 23* **P** *Bp* **V** S R KEEBLE
HEAGE (St Luke) *see* Ambergate and Heage *Derby*
HEALAUGH (St John the Baptist) *see* Rural Ainsty *York*
HEALD GREEN (St Catherine) *Ches 17* **P** *Bp*
  V J DEVADASON
HEALEY (Christ Church) *see* Hamer and Healey *Man*
HEALEY (St John) *see* Slaley, Healey and Whittonstall *Newc*
HEALEY (St Paul) *see* Masham and Healey *Leeds*
HEALING (St Peter and St Paul) *see* Wolds Gateway Group *Linc*
HEAMOOR (St Thomas) *see* Gulval and Madron *Truro*
HEANOR (St Laurence) *Derby 8* **P** *Wright Trustees*
  P-in-c K PADLEY **C** L SHEMILT
HEANTON PUNCHARDON (St Augustine), Marwood and West Down *Ex 14* **P** *Bp, CPAS, and St Jo Coll Cam (jt)*
  P-in-c S N PAINTING **C** C J RABY
HEAP BRIDGE (St Thomas and St George) *see* Heywood St Marg and Heap Bridge *Man*
HEAPEY (St Barnabas) and Withnell *Blackb 4* **P** *V Leyland*
  V A F HOGARTH **NSM** G K BULLOCK
HEAPHAM (All Saints) *see* Lea Gp *Linc*
HEART OF EDEN, The, comprising Appleby, Asby, Dufton, Kirkby Thore, Long Marton, Milburn, Newbiggin, Ormside, Temple Sowerby, and Warcop w Musgrave *Carl 1* **P** *Bp, Adn Carl, D&C, Lord Hothfield, and Major and Mrs Sawrey-Cookson (jt)* **C** P J BOYLES, S J FYFE
  NSM D J PATTIMORE, K PATTIMORE
HEART OF ENGLAND, The, comprising Bidford-on-Avon, Binton, Exhall w Wixford, Salford Priors, and Temple Grafton *Cov 7* **P** *Bp, Peache Trustees, and Dioc Trustees (jt)*
  R P A WALKER
HEART OF NORFOLK Team Ministry, The, comprising Bawdeswell, Billingford, Bintree, Foulsham, Foxley, Guestwick, Guist, North Elmham, Stibbard, Themelthorpe, Twyford, Wood Norton, and Worthing *Nor 18* **P** *Patr Bd*
  TR S E KIMMIS **TV** C J DAVIES, W M CARTWRIGHT
HEATH (Mission Church) *see* Uttoxeter Area *Lich*
HEATH AND REACH (St Leonard) *see* Ouzel Valley *St Alb*
HEATH HAYES (St John) *Lich 3* **P** *Bp and D&C (jt)*
  V D G WATKIN **NSM** D G WATKIN, R J HEATH
HEATH TOWN (Holy Trinity) *Lich 27* **P** *CPAS*
  V R C MERRICK **C** R E WILSHIRE **Hon C** P E V GOLDRING
HEATH, LITTLE (Christ Church) *see* Lt Heath *St Alb*
HEATH, THE (not known) *see* Bromfield *Heref*
HEATHCOTE *Cov 11* **P** *Bp and Ld Chan (alt)* **V** R J BUDD
HEATHER (St John the Baptist) *see* Ibstock w Heather *Leic*
HEATHERLANDS (St John the Evangelist) *Sarum 7*
  P *MMCET* **V** D G M PRICE **C** P D HOMDEN
HEATHERYCLEUGH (St Thomas) *see* Upper Weardale *Dur*
HEATHFIELD (All Saints) (St Richard) *Chich 13* **P** *Bp*
  V C S MITCHELL **C** T H FIKSEAUNET
HEATHFIELD (St Catherine) *see* Bovey Tracey St Jo w Heathfield *Ex*
HEATHFIELD (St John the Baptist) *see* Deane Vale *B & W*
HEATON (Christ Church) w Halliwell St Margaret *Man 7*
  P *Patr Bd* **V** J FRENCH **Hon C** P H BURMAN
HEATON (St Barnabas) *see* Girlington, Heaton and Manningham *Leeds*
HEATON (St Gabriel) *see* Newc St Gabr *Newc*
HEATON (St Martin) *see* Girlington, Heaton and Manningham *Leeds*
HEATON CHAPEL (St Thomas) *see* Heatons *Man*
HEATON MERSEY (St John the Baptist) *as above*
HEATON MOOR (St Paul) *as above*

HEATON NORRIS (Christ w All Saints) *as above*
HEATON REDDISH (St Mary) *Man 2* **P** *Trustees* **R** *vacant*
HEATON, HIGH (St Francis) *see* Newc St Fran *Newc*
HEATONS, comprising Heaton Mersey, Heaton Moor, Heaton
Norris, and Norris Bank *Man 2* **P** *Patr Bd (4 turns), The*
Crown (1 turn) **TR** M H MAXWELL **TV** D BROWNHILL,
H T SCANLAN **C** C F ALLISON, W E RUBIE **NSM** O MOLUDY
HEAVITREE (St Michael and All Angels) (St Lawrence) and
St Mary Steps *Ex 3* **P** *Patr Bd* **TR** R H S EASTOE
TV J F SEWARD **C** A HOBBS **NSM** A P JOHNSON
HEBBURN (St Cuthbert) (St Oswald) *Dur 13* **P** *The Crown*
and TR Jarrow (alt) **V** A MAXWELL
HEBBURN (St John) *Dur 13* **P** *Bp* **P-in-c** I M SOMASUNDRAM
HEBDEN (St Peter) *see* Linton in Craven *Leeds*
HEBDEN BRIDGE (St James) and Heptonstall *Leeds 8* **P** *V*
Halifax **P-in-c** K L MARSHALL
HEBRON (St Cuthbert) *see* Mitford and Hebron *Newc*
HECK (St John the Baptist) *see* Gt Snaith *Sheff*
HECKFIELD (St Michael) *see* Whitewater *Win*
HECKINGTON (St Andrew) and Helpringham Group of
Parishes, The, including Asgarby, Burton Pedwardine,
Great Hale and Little Hale, Scredington, and Swaton *Linc 14*
P *Bp, D&C, DBP, and the Rt Revd A C Foottit (1 turn), Ld Chan*
(1 turn) **R** C R HARRINGTON
HECKMONDWIKE (All Souls) (St James) (w Norristhorpe)
and Liversedge *Leeds 6* **P** *V Birstall* **V** K G YOUNG
NSM C H S SHEARD, S M HOLT **OLM** J C LEE
HEDDINGTON (St Andrew) *see* Oldbury *Sarum*
HEDDON-ON-THE-WALL (St Andrew) *Newc 9* **P** *Ld Chan*
P-in-c A D MCCARTAN
HEDENHAM (St Peter) *see* Ditchingham, Hedenham,
Broome, Earsham etc *Nor*
HEDGE END (St John the Evangelist) *Win 10* **P** *Bp*
V C M ROWBERRY **NSM** K ROWBERRY, S E LITJENS
HEDGE END (St Luke) *Win 10* **P** *Bp* **V** F C GIBBS
NSM H J RICHENS
HEDGERLEY (St Mary the Virgin) *see* Farnham Royal w
Hedgerley *Ox*
HEDINGHAMS and Upper Colne, The, comprising Castle
Hedingham, Great Yeldham, Little Yeldham, Sible
Hedingham, Stambourne, Tilbury juxta Clare, and
Toppesfield *Chelmsf 19* **P** *Duchy of Lanc (1 turn), The Crown*
(1 turn), Bp, J Lindsay Esq and Trustees (1 turn), Ld Chan
(1 turn) **R** E G PAXTON **C** J M TOMKINS
NSM M H M BURSELL
HEDNESFORD (St Peter) *Lich 3* **P** *Bp* **V** P KELLY
C A C T KELLY
HEDON (St Augustine), Paull, Sproatley and Preston in
Holderness *York 12* **P** *Abp* **P-in-c** S H PULKO
Hon C P W WEST
HEDSOR (St Nicholas) and Bourne End *Ox 18* **P** *Bp*
R J V BINNS
HEDWORTH (St Nicholas) *see* The Boldons *Dur*
HEELEY (Christ Church) *Sheff 1* **P** *The Crown* **V** S R EVANS
HEENE (St Botolph) *Chich 4* **P** *D&C* **P-in-c** P D C KANE
HEIGHAM (Holy Trinity) *Nor 3* **P** *Ch Trust Fund Trust*
R R D JAMES **C** J N PINTO
HEIGHAM (St Barnabas) *see* The Mitre Benefice *Nor*
HEIGHAM (St Thomas) *see* The Mitre Benefice *Nor*
HEIGHINGTON (St Michael) and Darlington St Matthew
and St Luke *Dur 7* **P** *D&C and Bp (alt)* **V** L M SCOTT
NSM R A DAWSON
HEIGHTINGTON (St Giles) *see* Mamble w Bayton, Rock w
Heightington etc *Worc*
HELHOUGHTON (All Saints) *see* E w W Rudham,
Helhoughton etc *Nor*
HELIONS BUMPSTEAD (St Andrew) *see* Two Rivers *Chelmsf*
HELLAND (St Helena) *see* Camelside *Truro*
HELLESDON (St Mary) (St Paul and St Michael) *Nor 2* **P** *Bp*
V A ALDER
HELLIDON (St John the Baptist) *see* Daventry *Pet*
HELLIFIELD (St Aidan) and Long Preston *Leeds 20* **P** *Ch Ch*
Ox **V** S M STOBART
HELLINGLY (St Peter and St Paul) and Upper Dicker
Chich 13 **P** *Abp and Bp (jt)* **V** *vacant*
HELMDON (St Mary Magdalene) *see* Astwell *Gp Pet*
HELME (Christ Church) *see* Meltham *Leeds*
HELMINGHAM (St Mary) *see* Debenham and Helmingham
St E
HELMSLEY (All Saints) *York 19* **P** *The Hon Jake Duncombe*
V T J ROBINSON **NSM** H RAWLINGS
HELMSLEY, UPPER (St Peter) *see* Harton *York*
HELPERTHORPE (St Peter) *see* Weaverthorpe w Helperthorpe,
Luttons Ambo etc *York*
HELPRINGHAM (St Andrew) *see* Heckington and
Helpringham *Gp Linc*

HELPSTON (St Botolph) *see* Barnack w Ufford, Bainton,
Helpston and Wittering *Pet*
HELSBY (St Paul) and Dunham-on-the-Hill *Ches 3* **P** *Bp*
V G H GREEN
HELSINGTON (St John) *see* Underbarrow w Helsington
Carl
HELSTON (St Michael) and Wendron *Truro 4* **P** *Patr Bd*
TR D G MILLER **OLM** D NOAKES
HEMBLINGTON (All Saints) *see* Blofield *Nor*
HEMEL HEMPSTEAD (Holy Trinity) Leverstock Green *see*
Langelei *St Alb*
HEMEL HEMPSTEAD (St Benedict) Bennetts End *as above*
HEMEL HEMPSTEAD (St Mary) *St Alb 2* **P** *Ld Chan*
TR J K WILLIAMS **TV** A S JANES, P J STEVENSON,
R W GRAHAM **C** C S E WAINMAN **NSM** H A KEMP,
L GEOGHEGAN, T J BARTON
HEMEL HEMPSTEAD (St Mary) Apsley End *see* Langelei
St Alb
HEMINGBROUGH (St Mary the Virgin) *see* Riccall, Barlby
and Hemingbrough *York*
HEMINGBY Group, The (St Margaret), including West
Ashby, Baumber, Belchford, Edlington, Fulletby, Hatton, and
Great Sturton *Linc 13* **P** *Bp, DBP, and Keble Coll Ox (*
2 turns), Ld Chan (1 turn) **OLM** P E SMITH
HEMINGFORD ABBOTS (St Margaret of Antioch) *Ely 10*
P *Lord Hemingford* **P-in-c** P H CUNLIFFE **C** E B ATLING
HEMINGFORD GREY (St James) *Ely 10* **P** *CPAS*
V P H CUNLIFFE **C** E B ATLING
HEMINGSTONE (St Gregory) *see* N Bosmere *St E*
HEMINGTON (Blessed Virgin Mary) *see* Hardington Vale
B & W
HEMINGTON (St Peter and St Paul) *see* Barnwell,
Hemington, Luddington in the Brook etc *Pet*
HEMLEY (All Saints) *see* Waldringfield w Hemley and
Newbourne *St E*
HEMLINGTON (St Timothy) *York 17* **P** *Abp* **V** R A DESICS
HEMPNALL (St Margaret) *Nor 5* **P** *Ld Chan (1 turn), Patr Bd*
(5 turns) **TR** M M KINGSTON **TV** E N BILLETT
HEMPSTEAD (All Saints) *see* Matlaske *Nor*
HEMPSTEAD (All Saints) *see* S Gillingham *Roch*
HEMPSTEAD (St Andrew) *see* Bacton, Happisburgh,
Hempstead w Eccles etc *Nor*
HEMPSTEAD (St Andrew) *see* Thaxted, The Sampfords,
Radwinter and Hempstead *Chelmsf*
HEMPSTED (St Swithun) *see* Glouc City and Hempsted
Glouc
HEMPTON (Holy Trinity) and Pudding Norton *Nor 14*
P *The Crown* **OLM** G D GOULD, P J NORWOOD
HEMPTON (St John the Evangelist) *see* Deddington w
Barford, Clifton and Hempton *Ox*
HEMSBY (St Mary) *see* Flegg Coastal Benefice *Nor*
HEMSWELL (All Saints) *see* Trentcliffe *Gp Linc*
HEMSWORTH (St Helen) *Leeds 18* **P** *Bp* **R** R W HART
HEMYOCK (St Mary) w Culm Davy, Clayhidon and
Culmstock *Ex 7* **P** *DBP, SMF, and D&C (jt)* **R** *vacant*
HENBURY (St Mary the Virgin) *Bris 2* **P** *Lord Middleton*
(1 turn), Bp (3 turns) **V** D P LLOYD
HENBURY (St Thomas) *see* Macclesfield St Jo w Henbury
Ches
HENDFORD (Holy Trinity) *see* Yeovil H Trin w Barwick *B & W*
HENDON (All Saints) Childs Hill *Lon 15* **P** *Bp*
P-in-c R J A SIMS-WILLIAMS
HENDON (St Alphage) *Lon 15* **P** *Bp* **V** H D MOORE
HENDON (St Ignatius) *Dur 14* **P** *Bp* **R** A C JONES
HENDON (St Mary) (Christ Church) *Lon 15* **P** *Bp*
V J A GITTOES
HENDON (St Paul) Mill Hill *Lon 15* **P** *Bp* **V** J E JAMES
C J E LOWE
HENDON, WEST (St John) and Cricklewood St Peter *Lon 15*
P *Bp* **V** J E CANDY **C** R W HUTCHINSON
HENDRED, EAST (St Augustine of Canterbury) *see* Wantage
Downs *Ox*
HENDRED, WEST (Holy Trinity) *as above*
HENFIELD (St Peter) w Shermanbury and Woodmancote
Chich 8 **P** *Bp* **R** P S J DOICK **C** H A NEALE-STEVENS
HENGROVE (Christ Church) *Bris 1* **P** *Bp and Simeon's*
Trustees (alt) **V** *vacant*
HENHAM (St Mary the Virgin) and Elsenham w Ugley
Chelmsf 20 **P** *Ch Hosp, Ch Soc Trust, and Bp (jt)*
V G TOWNSEND **C** G A TUBBS
HENLEAZE (St Peter) *Bris 2* **P** *Bp* **V** C M PILGRIM
HENLEY (St Peter) *see* Claydon *St E*
HENLEY IN ARDEN (St John the Baptist) *see* Beaudesert and
Henley-in-Arden w Ullenhall *Cov*
HENLEY-ON-THAMES (Holy Trinity) *Ox 24* **P** *R Rotherfield*
Greys St Nich **V** D R B CARTER **C** S P W BREWSTER

HENLEY-ON-THAMES (St Mary the Virgin) w Remenham *Ox 24* **P** *Bp and Jes Coll Ox (jt)* **R** J C TAYLER

HENLOW (St Mary the Virgin) and Langford *St Alb 8* **P** *Ld Chan* **V** S L SPELLER

HENNOCK (St Mary) *see Bovey Tracey SS Pet, Paul and Thos w Hennock Ex*

HENNY, GREAT (St Mary) *see N Hinckford Chelmsf*

HENSALL (St Paul) *see Gt Snaith Sheff*

HENSHAW (All Hallows) *see Haydon Bridge and Beltingham w Henshaw Newc*

HENSINGHAM (St John) (Keekle Mission) *Carl 5* **P** *Trustees* **V** F T PEARSON **C** S G N WALKER

HENSTEAD (St Mary) *see Wrentham, Covehithe w Benacre etc St E*

HENSTRIDGE (St Nicholas) *see Abbas and Templecombe, Henstridge and Horsington B & W*

HENTLAND (St Dubricius) *see St Weonards Heref*

HENTON (Christ Church) *see Coxley w Godney, Henton and Wookey B & W*

HEPPLE (Christ Church) *see Upper Coquetdale Newc*

HEPTONSTALL (St Thomas à Becket and St Thomas the Apostle) *see Hebden Bridge and Heptonstall Leeds*

HEPWORTH (Holy Trinity) *see Upper Holme Valley Leeds*

HEPWORTH (St Peter) *see Stanton St E*

HEREFORD (St Francis) *see Heref S Wye Heref*

HEREFORD (St Martin) *as above*

HEREFORD (St Peter w St Owen) (St James) *Heref 3* **P** *Simeon's Trustees* **V** A P MORGAN **C** E S T SWATTRIDGE **OLM** S A ELSON

HEREFORD SOUTH WYE (St Francis) (St Martin) *Heref 3* **P** *Bp* **TR** A M DOWDESWELL

HEREFORD, LITTLE (St Mary Magdalene) *see Tenbury Heref*

HEREFORD, WEST Team Ministry (All Saints) (Holy Trinity) (St Michael) (St Nicholas) *Heref 3* **P** *Patr Bd (3 turns) Ld Chan (1 turn)* **TR** R NORTH **TV** R C HULSE

HERMITAGE (Holy Trinity) *Ox 6* **P** *Patr Bd* **TR** E W LAUTENBACH **TV** S M WEBSTER **NSM** M KIRBY, S A THORN

HERMITAGE (St Mary) *see Three Valleys Sarum*

HERNE (St Martin) *Cant 4* **P** *Abp* **V** C SMITH **C** C DARKINS **NSM** S E RAND

HERNE BAY (Christ Church) (St Andrew's Church and Centre) *Cant 4* **P** *Simeon's Trustees* **V** A W EVERETT **C** D P HAZELL

HERNE BAY (St Bartholomew) *see Reculver and Herne Bay St Bart and Hoath Cant*

HERNE HILL (St Paul) (St Saviour) *S'wark 9* **P** *Bp and Simeon's Trustees (jt)* **V** B GOODYEAR **NSM** B J HUGHES, G S TAYLEUR, H PETERS

HERNER (Chapel) *see Newport and Bishops Tawton Ex*

HERNHILL (St Michael) *see Boughton-under-Blean w Dunkirk etc Cant*

HERODSFOOT (All Saints) *see Duloe and Herodsfoot Truro*

HERONSGATE (St John the Evangelist) *see Mill End and Heronsgate w W Hyde St Alb*

HERRIARD (St Mary) *see N Hants Downs Win*

HERRINGFLEET (St Margaret) *see Somerleyton, Ashby, Fritton, Herringfleet etc Nor*

HERRINGTHORPE (St Cuthbert) *Sheff 6* **P** *Bp* **V** K R SKIDMORE

HERRINGTON (St Aidan), Penshaw and Shiney Row *Dur 10* **P** *Bp and The Crown (alt)* **R** S W OSMAN **C** S GRUNDY

HERSHAM (St Peter) *Guildf 8* **P** *Bp* **V** J A RICHARDSON

HERSTMONCEUX (All Saints) and Wartling *Chich 13* **P** *Bp* **P-in-c** R J STEVEN

HERSTON (St Mark) *see Swanage and Studland Sarum*

HERTFORD (All Saints) (St Andrew) *St Alb 19* **P** *Ld Chan (1 turn), Duchy of Lanc (2 turns), Patr Bd (1 turn)* **TR** J M H LOVERIDGE **TV** H A STEWART, R C THOMPSON, S J DRYDEN **NSM** D R PEPPER, W SELLERS

HERTFORD HEATH (Holy Trinity) *see Hertford St Alb*

HERTFORD, comprising Folkton, Ganton, Hunmanby, Muston, and Willerby *York 15* **P** *MMCET (1 turn), Abp, N H T Wrigley Esq, and MMCET (1 turn)* **R** T P PARKER

HERTINGFORDBURY (St Mary) *see Hertford St Alb*

HESKETH (All Saints) w Becconsall *Blackb 5* **P** *Trustees* **R** D C DICKINSON

HESKET-IN-THE-FOREST (St Mary the Virgin) *see Inglewood Gp Carl*

HESLERTON, WEST (All Saints) *see Buckrose Carrs York*

HESLINGTON (St Paul) *York 2* **P** *Abp* **V** J NOBEL

HESSAY (St John the Baptist) *see Rural Ainsty York*

HESSENFORD (St Anne) *see St Germans w Antony and Sheviock Truro*

HESSETT (St Ethelbert) *see Rougham, Beyton w Hessett and Rushbrooke St E*

HESSLE (All Saints) *York 14* **P** *Ld Chan* **V** G D TURNER **NSM** C R TETLEY

HESTER WAY LANE (St Silas) *see W Cheltenham Glouc*

HESTON (All Saints) (St Leonard) *Lon 11* **P** *Bp* **V** S S MCCALLA **Hon C** J K KAOMA

HESWALL (Church of the Good Shepherd) (St Peter) *Ches 8* **P** *W A B Davenport Esq* **R** M S J CANNAM **C** J A CARLSON, J J WISE **NSM** E S WESTON

HETHE (St Edmund King and Martyr and St George) *see Shelswell Ox*

HETHEL (All Saints) *see Mulbarton w Bracon Ash, Hethel and Flordon Nor*

HETHERSETT (St Remigius) w Canteloff w Little Melton and Great Melton *Nor 7* **P** *G&C Coll Cam, E C Evans-Lombe Esq, and Em Coll Cam (by turn)* **R** D A MCCLEAN

HETHERSGILL (St Mary) *see Bewcastle, Stapleton and Kirklinton etc Carl*

HETTON, SOUTH (Holy Trinity) *Dur 2* **P** *Bp* **NSM** D W BOND

HETTON-LYONS (St Michael and St Nicholas) w Eppleton *Dur 10* **P** *Bp (1 turn), The Crown (2 turns)* **P-in-c** T WALL

HEVENINGHAM (St Margaret) w Ubbeston, Huntingfield and Cookley *St E 17* **P** *Capt the Revd J S Peel* **V** vacant

HEVER (St Peter), Four Elms and Mark Beech *Roch 11* **P** *Bp and C Talbot Esq (jt)* **R** vacant

HEVERSHAM (St Peter) and Milnthorpe *Carl 10* **P** *Trin Coll Cam* **P-in-c** B T KERR

HEVINGHAM (St Mary the Virgin and St Botolph) *see Horsford, Felthorpe and Hevingham Nor*

HEWELSFIELD (St Mary Magdalene) *see St Briavels w Hewelsfield and Brockweir Glouc*

HEWISH (Good Shepherd) *see Wulfric Benefice B & W*

HEWORTH (Christ Church) *York 7* **P** *Ch Trust Fund Trust* **V** P E DEO

HEWORTH (Holy Trinity) (St Wulstan) *York 7* **P** *Ch Trust Fund Trust* **R** M B WOODMANSEY

HEWORTH (St Alban) *see Windy Nook St Alb Dur*

HEWORTH (St Mary) *Dur 11* **P** *Bp* **V** K E JAMIE

HEXAGON, The: Arnesby w Shearsby, Bruntingthorpe, Husbands Bosworth, Mowsley and Knaptoft, and Theddingworth *Leic 7* **P** *Bp and DBP (jt)* **R** A E A BICKLEY **C** A H TARRY

HEXHAM (St Andrew) *Newc 10* **P** *Mercers' Co and Viscount Allendale (alt)* **NSM** C E ROBSON

HEXTABLE (St Peter) *see Swanley St Paul Roch*

HEXTHORPE (St Jude) *see Edlington and Hexthorpe Sheff*

HEXTON (St Faith) *see Barton-le-Cley w Higham Gobion and Hexton St Alb*

HEY (St John the Baptist) *Man 15* **P** *R Ashton-under-Lyne Gd Shep* **V** L E M WOODALL **C** S ROBINSON **NSM** C S STEEL

HEYBRIDGE (St Andrew) (St George) w Langford *Chelmsf 11* **P** *D&C St Paul's and Lord Byron (alt)* **P-in-c** A J HUMPHREYS

HEYDON (Holy Trinity) *see Icknield Way Villages Chelmsf*

HEYDON (St Peter and St Paul) *see Aylsham and Distr Nor*

HEYDOUR (St Michael and All Angels) *see E Loveden Linc*

HEYFORD (St Peter and St Paul) w Stowe Nine Churches and Flore w Brockhall *Pet 3* **P** *The Revd S Hope, Ch Ch Ox, DBP and Bp (by turn)* **R** S P BURROW

HEYFORD, LOWER (St Mary) *see Cherwell Valley Ox*

HEYFORD, UPPER (St Mary) *as above*

HEYHOUSES (St Nicholas) *see W Pendleside Blackb*

HEYHOUSES ON SEA (St Anne) *see St Annes St Anne Blackb*

HEYSHAM (St Peter) (St Andrew) (St James) *Blackb 11* **P** *C E C Royds Esq* **R** A T OSBORN

HEYSHOTT (St James) *see Cocking w W Lavington, Bepton and Heyshott Chich*

HEYSIDE (St Mark) and Royton *Man 16* **P** *Bp and Trustees (jt)* **V** J A READ

HEYTESBURY (St Peter and St Paul) *see Upper Wylye Valley Sarum*

HEYTHROP (St Nicholas) *see Gt w Lt Tew and Heythrop Ox*

HEYWOOD (St James) *Man 14* **P** *Bp* **V** vacant

HEYWOOD (St John) (St Luke) *Man 14* **P** *Patr Bd* **V** vacant

HEYWOOD (St Margaret) and Heap Bridge *Man 14* **P** *Patr Bd* **V** S J BANKS **OLM** I WARRINGTON

HIBALDSTOW (St Hybald) *see Scawby, Redbourne and Hibaldstow Linc*

HICKLETON (St Wilfrid) *see Goldthorpe w Hickleton Sheff*

HICKLING (St Luke) w Kinoulton and Broughton Sulney (Upper Broughton) *S'well 5* **P** *The Crown, Qu Coll Cam, and Bp (by turn)* **P-in-c** P D S MASSEY **NSM** M R WOODWARD

HICKLING (St Mary) *see Ludham, Potter Heigham, Hickling and Catfield Nor*

HIGH   *see also under substantive place name*
HIGH BROOMS (St Matthew) *Roch 12*   **P** *CPAS Patr Trust*
    V C B WICKS
HIGH CROSS (St John the Evangelist) *St Alb 19*   **P** *DBP*
    V A J DUNCAN
HIGH DOWNS *Cant 14*   **P** *Abp, D&C, and MMCET (jt)*
    P-in-c S H LILLICRAP
HIGH GREEN (St Saviour)   *see Mortomley St Sav High Green*
    Sheff
HIGH HAM (St Andrew)   *see Aller, High w Low Ham and*
    Huish Episcopi cum Langport B & W
HIGH LANE (St Thomas) *Ches 16*   **P** *R Stockport*
    V J E PARKER
HIGH LEGH (St John) *Ches 12*   **P** *R H Cornwall-Legh Esq*
    P-in-c P J ROBINSON   **NSM** P M COPE, P M ROBINSON
HIGH LEGH (St John)   *see High Legh Ches*
HIGH OAK, Hingham and Scoulton w Wood Rising,
    including Deopham, Hackford, Morley St Botolph, Morley
    St Peter, and Wicklewood *Nor 7*   **P** *Bp, Adn Humbleyard,*
    D&C, D&C Cant, Earl of Kimberley, Earl of Verulam, Sir A E H
    Heber-Percy, and Trustees   **R** C B REED   **C** S WALLACE-JONES
HIGHAM (St John the Evangelist)   *see Fence-in-Pendle and*
    Higham Blackb
HIGHAM (St John the Evangelist) and Merston *Roch 6*
    P *St Jo Coll Cam*   **V** J F SOUTHWARD
HIGHAM (St Mary), Holton St Mary, Raydon and Stratford
    St Mary *St E 4*   **P** *Duchy of Lanc, Reformation Ch Trust, and*
    Mrs S E F Holden   **NSM** M R CARR
HIGHAM FERRERS (St Mary the Virgin) w Chelveston *Pet 8*
    P *Bp*   **C** M A C DALLISTON, T P MCLEAN
HIGHAM GOBION (St Margaret)   *see Barton-le-Cley w*
    Higham Gobion and Hexton St Alb
HIGHAM GREEN (St Stephen)   *see Dalham, Gazeley, Higham,*
    Kentford and Moulton St E
HIGHAM-ON-THE-HILL (St Peter)   *see Fenn Lanes Gp Leic*
HIGHAMPTON (Holy Cross)   *see Black Torrington, Bradford*
    w Cookbury etc Ex
HIGHAMS PARK (All Saints) Hale End *Chelmsf 7*   **P** *Bp*
    V M D PORTER
HIGHBRIDGE (St John the Evangelist) *B & W 1*   **P** *Bp*
    C D D CROUCH
HIGHBROOK (All Saints) and West Hoathly *Chich 5*   **P** *Ld*
    Chan   **P-in-c** N W KINRADE
HIGHBURY (Christ Church) (St John) (St Saviour) *Lon 6*
    P *CPAS*   **V** A J CHRICH   **NSM** T J I WITTER
HIGHBURY NEW PARK (St Augustine) *Lon 6*   **P** *CPAS*
    V G A M ANSTIS
HIGHCLERE (St Michael and All Angels)   *see NW Hants Win*
HIGHCLIFFE (St Mark) *Win 9*   **P** *Bp*   **V** G M NOBES
HIGHER   *see under substantive place name*
HIGHERTOWN (All Saints) and Baldhu *Truro 6*   **P** *Bp and*
    Viscount Falmouth (alt)   **P-in-c** J J PUTNAM
    NSM H A PRESTON, J C MULLETT
HIGHFIELD (All Saints) *Ox 1*   **P** *Bp*   **V** J E COCKE
HIGHFIELD (Christ Church)   *see Portswood Ch Ch Win*
HIGHFIELD (St Catherine)   *see New Bury w Gt Lever Man*
HIGHFIELD (St Mary)   *see Sheff St Mary Bramall Lane Sheff*
HIGHFIELD (St Matthew) *Liv 15*   **P** *Trustees*   **V** *vacant*
HIGHFIELD (St Paul)   *see Hemel Hempstead St Alb*
HIGHGATE (All Saints) *Lon 20*   **P** *Bp*   **P-in-c** T I MILLER
    NSM A J M MCKAY, J H ROGERS
HIGHGATE (St Alban the Martyr and St Patrick) *Birm 2*
    P *Keble Coll Ox*   **V** G A SYKES
HIGHGATE (St Augustine) *Lon 20*   **P** *Bp*
    Hon C W A WHITCOMBE
HIGHGATE (St Michael) *Lon 20*   **P** *Bp*   **V** O AYODEJI
    C R M J GREAVES   **NSM** J H ROGERS
HIGHLEY (St Mary) w Billingsley, Glazeley and Deuxhill
    and Chelmarsh *Heref 8*   **P** *MMCET*   **V** M A HARRIS
    C T B KING   **NSM** D R POYNER, V R SMITH
HIGHNAM (Holy Innocents), Tibberton w Rudford and
    Taynton *Glouc 3*   **P** *D&C, T J Fenton Esq, and A E Woolley*
    (jt)   **P-in-c** H M K SAMMON
HIGHTERS HEATH (Immanuel) *Birm 4*   **P** *Bp*   **V** *vacant*
HIGHTOWN (All Saints)   *see Castleford Leeds*
HIGHTOWN (St Stephen) *Liv 8*   **P** *Bp*   **V** J H H ASHTON
HIGHWEEK (All Saints)   *see Newton Abbot Ex*
HIGHWORTH (St Michael) w Sevenhampton and
    Inglesham and Hannington *Bris 7*   **P** *Bp (4 turns), Mrs M G*
    Hussey-Freke (1 turn)   **V** G D SOWDEN   **C** E R M SWINERD
HILBOROUGH (All Saints) w Bodney *Nor 13*   **P** *DBP*
    P-in-c Z M FERGUSON   **Hon C** L M LUBBE
HILDENBOROUGH (St John the Evangelist) *Roch 11*   **P** *V*
    Tonbridge   **V** T R SAIET   **NSM** S BRAID
HILDERSHAM (Holy Trinity)   *see Granta Vale Gp Ely*

HILDERSTONE (Christ Church)   *see Fulford w Hilderstone*
    Lich
HILFIELD (St Nicholas)   *see Three Valleys Sarum*
HILGAY (All Saints) *Ely 9*   **P** *Hertf Coll Ox*   **R** *vacant*
HILL (St James) *Birm 7*   **P** *Bp*   **V** A D RAMBLE
    NSM J A RAMBLE
HILL (St Michael)   *see Berkeley w Wick, Breadstone, Newport,*
    Stone etc Glouc
HILL CROOME (St Mary)   *see Upton-on-Severn, Ripple, Earls*
    Croome etc Worc
HILL TOP (St James)   *see W Bromwich St Jas w St Paul Lich*
HILLESDEN (All Saints)   *see Lenborough Ox*
HILLESLEY (St Giles)   *see Charfield and Kingswood w*
    Wickwar etc Glouc
HILLFARRANCE (Holy Cross)   *see Deane Vale B & W*
HILLINGDON (All Saints) *Lon 24*   **P** *Bp*   **V** D P BANISTER
    NSM D CICILY ANTONY
HILLINGDON (St John the Baptist) *Lon 24*   **P** *Bp*
    V A BRADFORD   **NSM** J SHALLOE
HILLINGTON (St Mary the Virgin) *Nor 15*   **P** *E W Dawnay*
    Esq   **R** J B V RIVIERE
HILLMORTON (St John the Baptist) *Cov 6*   **P** *Bp*
    P-in-c S E GOLD   **Hon C** M I SIMMONS
HILLOCK (St Andrew) and Unsworth *Man 10*   **P** *Bp, R Stand*
    All SS, and R Prestwich St Mary (jt)   **V** D A WILLIAMS
    NSM A M WHITTLEWORTH   **OLM** M RYAN
HILLSBOROUGH and Wadsley Bridge (Christ Church)
    Sheff 4   **P** *Ch Patr Trust*   **P-in-c** P J GOODACRE
    NSM R R OTIENO
HILLSIDE Lobley Hill and Marley Hill *Dur 12*   **P** *Bp and The*
    Crown (alt)   **V** G MACKNIGHT   **C** R J BALFOUR
HILMARTON (St Lawrence)   *see Lyneham and Woodhill*
    Sarum
HILPERTON (St Michael and All Angels)   *see Canalside*
    Benefice Sarum
HILPERTON MARSH (St Mary Magdalen)   *as above*
HILSTON (St Margaret)   *see S Holderness Coast York*
HILTON (All Saints)   *see Piddle Valley, Hilton and Ansty,*
    Cheselbourne etc Sarum
HILTON (St Mary Magdalene)   *see Godmanchester and*
    Hilton Ely
HILTON (St Peter)   *see Stainton w Hilton York*
HILTON w Marston-on-Dove *Derby 6*   **P** *N J M Spurrier Esq*
    V *vacant*
HIMBLETON (St Mary Magdalene)   *see Bowbrook S Worc*
HIMLEY (St Michael and All Angels)   *see Smestow Vale Lich*
HINCASTER (Mission Room)   *see Heversham and Milnthorpe*
    Carl
HINCHLEY WOOD (St Christopher) *Guildf 8*   **P** *Bp*
    V P D JENNER   **NSM** C A MULLINS
HINCKFORD, NORTH, comprising Alphamstone, Belchamp,
    Belchamp Otten, Belchamp Walter, Bulmer, Foxearth, Great
    and Little Henny, Lamarsh, Liston and Borley, Middleton,
    Ovington, Pentlow, Twinstead, and Wickham *Chelmsf 19*
    P *Patr Bd (4 turns), Ld Chan (1 turn)*   **TR** M H KING
    TV G M MORGAN   **C** P A GROVER
HINCKLEY (Assumption of St Mary the Virgin) (St Francis)
    (St Paul) *Leic 10*   **P** *Bp*   **V** *vacant*
HINCKLEY (Holy Trinity) *Leic 10*   **P** *DBP*   **R** S J WEARN
    C M G A COOPER
HINCKLEY (St John the Evangelist) *Leic 10*   **P** *DBP*
    V G J WESTON   **C** D LUTSENKO, J M BERRY
HINDERCLAY (St Mary)   *see Stanton St E*
HINDERWELL (St Hilda), Roxby and Staithes w Lythe,
    Ugthorpe and Sandsend *York 21*   **P** *Abp*   **R** M JACKSON
HINDHEAD (St Alban)   *see Churt and Hindhead Guildf*
HINDLEY (All Saints)   *see Chapelfields Liv*
HINDLEY (St Peter)   *as above*
HINDLEY GREEN (St John)   *as above*
HINDOLVESTON (St George)   *see Briston, Burgh Parva,*
    Hindolveston etc Nor
HINDON (St John the Baptist)   *see Nadder Valley Sarum*
HINDRINGHAM (St Martin)   *see Barney, Hindringham,*
    Thursford, Great Snoring, Little Snoring and Kettlestone
    and Pensthorpe Nor
HINGHAM (St Andrew)   *see High Oak, Hingham and*
    Scoulton w Wood Rising Nor
HINKSEY, NEW (St John the Evangelist)   *see S Hinksey Ox*
HINKSEY, NORTH (St Lawrence)   *see Osney Ox*
HINKSEY, SOUTH (St Laurence) *Ox 2*   **P** *Bp*   **V** R ANGELICI
HINSTOCK (St Oswald)   *see Cheswardine, Childs Ercall,*
    Hales, Hinstock etc Lich
HINTLESHAM (St Nicholas)   *see Elmsett w Aldham,*
    Hintlesham, Chattisham etc St E
HINTON ADMIRAL (St Michael and All Angels)   *see Bransgore*
    and Hinton Admiral Win

HINTON AMPNER (All Saints) *see* Upper Itchen *Win*
HINTON BLEWETT (St Margaret) *see* E w W Harptree and
Hinton Blewett *B & W*
HINTON CHARTERHOUSE (St John the Baptist) *see*
Freshford, Limpley Stoke and Hinton Charterhouse *B & W*
HINTON MARTEL (St John the Evangelist) *see* Wimborne
Minster and the N Villages *Sarum*
HINTON PARVA (St Swithun) *see* Lyddington and
Wanborough and Bishopstone etc *Bris*
HINTON ST GEORGE (St George) *see* Merriott w Hinton,
Dinnington and Lopen *B & W*
HINTON ST MARY (St Mary) *see* Sturminster Newton,
Hinton St Mary and Lydlinch *Sarum*
HINTON WALDRIST (St Margaret) *see* Cherbury w Gainfield
Ox
HINTON-IN-THE-HEDGES (Holy Trinity) *see* Aynho and
Croughton w Evenley etc *Pet*
HINTON-ON-THE-GREEN (St Peter) *see* Bengeworth and
Hampton etc *Worc*
HINTS (St Bartholomew) *Lich 1* **P** *Personal Reps A E Jones
Esq* **V** *vacant*
HINXHILL (St Mary) *see* Wye *Cant*
HINXTON (St Mary and St John) *Ely 5* **P** *Jes Coll Cam*
P-in-c P M SHARKEY
HINXWORTH (St Nicholas) *see* Ashwell w Hinxworth and
Newnham *St Alb*
HIPSWELL (St John the Evangelist) *Leeds 22* **P** *Bp*
V A R M CROMARTY
HISTON (St Andrew) *Ely 6* **P** *MMCET*
V N J BLANDFORD-BAKER **C** K C DOUGLASS
HITCHAM (All Saints) *see* Rattlesden w Thorpe Morieux,
Brettenham etc *St E*
HITCHAM (St Mary) *Ox 12* **P** *Eton Coll* **V** S A SAMPSON
HITCHIN (Holy Saviour) (St Faith) (St Mark) (St Mary) and
St Paul's Walden *St Alb 3* **P** *Patr Bd* **TV** I C TODD,
J F MAINWARING, M CROWLEY **C** D A B DREW
NSM F S E GIBBS
HITHER GREEN (St Swithun) *see* Lewisham St Swithun *S'wark*
HITTISLEIGH (St Andrew) *see* Chagford, Gidleigh,
Throwleigh etc *Ex*
HIXON (St Peter) *see* Mid Trent *Lich*
HOAR CROSS (Holy Angels) w Newchurch *Lich 13* **P** *Bp
and Meynell Ch Trust* **P-in-c** G P BOTT
HOARWITHY (St Catherine) *see* St Weonards *Heref*
HOATH (Holy Cross) *see* Reculver and Herne Bay St Bart and
Hoath *Cant*
HOATHLY, EAST (not known) *see* Chiddingly w E Hoathly
Chich
HOATHLY, WEST (St Margaret) *see* Highbrook and W
Hoathly *Chich*
HOBS MOAT (St Mary) *Birm 10* **P** *Bp* **P-in-c** L GRANNER
HOBY (All Saints) *see* Upper Wreake *Leic*
HOCKERILL (All Saints) *St Alb 15* **P** *Bp Lon*
V S D MANSFIELD **NSM** S A TARRAN
HOCKERING (St Michael) *see* Mattishall and the Tudd Valley
Nor
HOCKHAM, GREAT (Holy Trinity) *see* Caston, Griston,
Merton, Thompson etc *Nor*
HOCKLEY (St Matthew) *see* Wilnecote *Lich*
HOCKLEY (St Peter and St Paul) *Chelmsf 14* **P** *Wadh Coll
Ox* **P-in-c** K R HAVEY **Hon C** S S STROEBEL
HOCKLIFFE (St Nicholas) *see* Ouzel Valley *St Alb*
HOCKWOLD w WILTON (St James) *see* Grimshoe *Ely*
HOCKWORTHY (St Simon and St Jude) *see* Sampford
Peverell, Uplowman, Holcombe Rogus etc *Ex*
HODDESDON (St Catherine and St Paul) *St Alb 17*
P *Peache Trustees* **V** R E B PENNANT **C** K E CARTER
HODDLESDEN (St Paul) *see* Over Darwen St Jas and
Hoddlesden *Blackb*
HODGE HILL (St Philip and St James) *Birm 8* **P** *Bp*
TR A D BARRETT **C** J R CREWES **NSM** S A NASH
HODNET (St Luke) *Lich 17* **P** *Sir Algernon Heber-Percy KCVO*
P-in-c E QUIREY
HOE (St Andrew) *see* Dereham and Distr *Nor*
HOGGESTON (Holy Cross) *see* Schorne *Ox*
HOGHTON (Holy Trinity) *Blackb 5* **P** V *Leyland* **V** *vacant*
HOGNASTON (St Bartholomew) *see* Hulland, Atlow,
Kniveton, Bradley and Hognaston *Derby*
HOGSTHORPE (St Mary) *see* Chapel St Leonards and
Hogsthorpe etc *Linc*
HOLBEACH (All Saints) *Linc 18* **P** *Bp* **V** R J SEAL
HOLBEACH FEN (St John) *see* Elloe Stone *Linc*
HOLBEACH HURN (St Luke) *see* Mid Elloe Gp *Linc*
HOLBEACH MARSH (St Mark) *as above*

HOLBECK (St Luke the Evangelist) *Leeds 14* **P** *Bp, V Leeds
St Pet, and Meynell Ch Trust (jt)* **C** J PÉCHÈR, P R MASON
NSM K G ELLIOTT
HOLBETON (All Saints) *Ex 20* **P** *The Crown*
P-in-c A C LEGGE
HOLBORN (St Alban the Martyr) w Saffron Hill St Peter
Lon 17 **P** *D&C St Paul's* **V** C M SMITH **NSM** R G CORP
HOLBORN (St George the Martyr) Queen Square (Holy
Trinity) (St Bartholomew) Grays Inn Road *Lon 17* **P** *Ch
Soc Trust* **R** J H VALENTINE **C** J R HAITH
NSM P B HOWARTH
HOLBORN (St Giles-in-the-Fields) *see* St Giles-in-the-Fields
Lon
HOLBROOK (All Saints), Stutton, Freston, Woolverstone
and Wherstead *St E 15* **P** *Patr Bd* **R** J M SEGGAR
HOLBROOK (St Mark) *Chich 7* **P** *Abp Cant, Bp, and Bp
Horsham (jt)* **V** R S COLDICOTT **NSM** E JINKS
HOLBROOK (St Michael) *see* Hazelwood, Holbrook and
Milford *Derby*
HOLBROOK ROAD (St Swithin) *see* Belper *Derby*
HOLBROOKS (St Luke) *Cov 2* **P** *Bp* **V** S P OAKES
HOLBURY (Good Shepherd) *see* Fawley *Win*
HOLCOMBE (Emmanuel) (Canon Lewis Hall) and
Hawkshaw *Man 8* **P** *R Bury St Mary and F Whowell Esq (jt)*
R P H SUMSION **OLM** R W AIREY, V J D FLETCHER
HOLCOMBE (St Andrew) *see* Holcombe *B & W*
HOLCOMBE (St George) *see* Dawlish w Holcombe, Cofton
and Starcross *Ex*
HOLCOMBE BURNELL (St John the Baptist) *see* Tedburn
St Mary, Cheriton Bishop, Whitestone etc *Ex*
HOLCOMBE ROGUS (All Saints) *see* Sampford Peverell,
Uplowman, Holcombe Rogus etc *Ex*
HOLCOT (St Mary and All Saints) *see* Brixworth w Holcot *Pet*
HOLDENHURST (St John the Evangelist) and Iford *Win 8*
P *Bp* **V** A L MCPHERSON **C** J M SEARE
HOLDERNESS COAST, SOUTH, comprising Garton-in-
Holderness w Grimston, Hilston, Hollym, Holmpton,
Owthorne, Roos, Tunstall and Withernsea *York 12* **P** *Abp,
SMF, and Ld Chan (by turn)* **V** M T FAULKNER
Hon C P W WEST **NSM** D J BERRY
HOLDGATE (Holy Trinity) *see* Corvedale Benefice *Heref*
HOLFORD (St Mary the Virgin) *see* Quantock Coast *B & W*
HOLKHAM (St Withiburga) w Egmere w Warham,
Wells-next-the-Sea and Wighton *Nor 14* **P** *Viscount Coke
(2 turns), M J Beddard Esq (2 turns), and D&C (1 turn)*
R B A STEWART
HOLLACOMBE (St Petroc) *see* Holsworthy, Hollacombe,
Pyworthy etc *Ex*
HOLLAND FEN (All Saints) *see* Brothertoft Gp *Linc*
HOLLAND PARK (St George the Martyr) (St John the
Baptist) *Lon 12* **P** *Trustees and Bp (jt)* **V** J B HEARD
C N O TRAYNOR, P WOLTON
HOLLAND, GREAT (All Saints) *see* Kirby-le-Soken w Gt
Holland *Chelmsf*
HOLLAND, NEW (Christ Church) *see* Barrow and Goxhill
Linc
HOLLAND-ON-SEA (St Bartholomew) *Chelmsf 23* **P** *Ch Patr
Trust* **C** D J LOWER **OLM** S E WIGGINS
HOLLESLEY (All Saints) *see* Wilford Peninsula *St E*
HOLLINFARE (St Helen) *see* Glazebury w Hollinfare *Liv*
HOLLINGBOURNE (All Saints) *see* N Downs *Cant*
HOLLINGTON (St John the Evangelist) *see* Rocester and
Croxden w Hollington *Lich*
HOLLINGTON (St John the Evangelist) (St Peter and
St Paul) *Chich 15* **P** *Ch Patr Trust* **V** L J W DEAN
NSM M HINKLEY
HOLLINGTON (St Leonard) (St Anne) *Chich 15* **P** *CPAS*
R R M M CREIGHTON
HOLLINGWORTH (St Hilda) *see* Milnrow and New Hey
Man
HOLLINGWORTH (St Mary) w Tintwistle *Ches 14* **P** *Patr Bd*
V B A PERRIN
HOLLINWOOD (St Margaret) and Limeside *Man 16* **P** *Bp
and V Prestwich (jt)* **V** *vacant*
HOLLOWAY (Emmanuel) *see* Tollington *Lon*
HOLLOWAY Hanley Road (St Saviour) *as above*
HOLLOWAY, UPPER (St John the Evangelist) *Lon 6* **P** *Ch
Patr Trust* **V** A COMFORT
HOLLOWAY, WEST (St Luke) *Lon 6* **P** *CPAS*
NSM M D E WROE
HOLLOWELL (St James) *see* Guilsborough and Hollowell and
Cold Ashby etc *Pet*
HOLLY HALL (St Augustine) *see* Dudley *Worc*
HOLLY HILL (Church Centre) *see* Frankley *Birm*
HOLLYBUSH (All Saints) *see* Berrow w Pendock, Eldersfield,
Hollybush etc *Worc*

HOLLYM (St Nicholas)   *see* S Holderness Coast *York*
HOLMBRIDGE (St David)   *see* Upper Holme Valley *Leeds*
HOLMBURY ST MARY (St Mary the Virgin)   *see* Abinger and
   Coldharbour and Wotton and Holmbury St Mary *Guildf*
HOLME (All Saints) and Seaton Ross Group, The, including
   Everingham and Harswell *York 5*   **P** *St Jo Coll Cam and Ld
   Chan (alt)*   **R** S V COPE
HOLME (Holy Trinity)   *see* Burton and Holme *Carl*
HOLME (St Giles)   *see* E Trent *S'well*
HOLME (St Giles)   *see* Yaxley and Holme w Conington *Ely*
HOLME CULTRAM (St Cuthbert)   *see* Solway Plain *Carl*
HOLME CULTRAM (St Mary) *as above*
HOLME EDEN (St Paul) and Wetheral w Warwick *Carl 2*
   P *D&C and DBP (jt)*   **P-in-c** G J SKINNER   **C** P G DIXON
HOLME HALE (St Andrew)   *see* Necton, Holme Hale w N and
   S Pickenham *Nor*
HOLME PIERREPONT (St Edmund King and Martyr)   *see* Lady
   Bay w Holme Pierrepont and Adbolton *S'well*
HOLME VALLEY, The UPPER, comprising Hepworth,
   Holmbridge, Holmfirth, Netherthong, New Mill,
   Thurstonland, and Upperthong *Leeds 12*   **P** *Patr Bd*
   TR J S ROBERTSHAW   **TV** K GRIFFIN, M D ELLERTON,
   N M HEATON   **NSM** A R BROOKE, E BARROW, S W DIXON
   OLM G B BAMFORD
HOLME WOOD (St Christopher)   *see* Tong and Laisterdyke
   Leeds
HOLME, EAST (St John the Evangelist)   *see* Wareham *Sarum*
HOLMEDALE, comprising Barningham, Gilling, Hutton
   Magna, Kirkby Ravensworth, and Wycliffe *Leeds 22*   **P** *Bp
   and A C P Wharton Esq (jt)*   **R** A P KIRBY
HOLME-IN-CLIVIGER (St John) w Worsthorne *Blackb 3*
   P *Patr Bd*   **V** *vacant*
HOLME-NEXT-THE-SEA (St Mary)   *see* Hunstanton St Mary w
   Ringstead Parva etc *Nor*
HOLME-ON-SPALDING-MOOR (All Saints)   *see* Holme and
   Seaton Ross Gp *York*
HOLME-ON-SPALDING-MOOR (Old School Mission Room) *as
   above*
HOLMER (St Bartholomew) (St Mary) w Huntington
   Heref 3   **P** *D&C*   **V** S M LEE   **C** R J ORAM
HOLMER GREEN (Christ Church)   *see* Penn Street *Ox*
HOLMES CHAPEL (St Luke)   *see* Church Hulme *Ches*
HOLMESDALE (St Philip)   *see* Dronfield w Holmesfield *Derby*
HOLMESFIELD (St Swithin) *as above*
HOLMEWOOD (St Alban Mission)   *see* Heath *Derby*
HOLMFIELD (St Andrew)   *see* Bradshaw and Holmfield *Leeds*
HOLMFIRTH (Holy Trinity)   *see* Upper Holme Valley *Leeds*
HOLMPTON (St Nicholas)   *see* S Holderness Coast *York*
HOLMSIDE (St John the Evangelist)   *see* Lanchester and
   Burnhope *Dur*
HOLMWOOD (St Mary Magdalene)   *see* Surrey Weald *Guildf*
HOLMWOOD, NORTH (St John the Evangelist) *Guildf 7*
   P *Bp*   **OLM** C LAZENBY, J E SCHOFIELD
HOLNE (St Mary the Virgin)   *see* Ashburton, Bickington,
   Buckland in the Moor etc *Ex*
HOLNEST (Church of the Assumption)   *see* Three Valleys
   Sarum
**HOLSWORTHY (St Peter and St Paul), Hollacombe,
   Pyworthy, Pancrasweek and Bridgerule** *Ex 16*   **P** *DBP*
   P-in-c E M A BURKE
HOLT (St Andrew) w High Kelling *Nor 17*   **P** *St Jo Coll Cam*
   R H C STOKER   **C** S A GRAHAM
HOLT (St James)   *see* Wimborne Minster and the N Villages
   Sarum
HOLT (St Katharine)   *see* Broughton Gifford, Gt Chalfield and
   Holt *Sarum*
HOLT (St Martin)   *see* Hallow and Grimley w Holt *Worc*
HOLTBY (Holy Trinity)   *see* Rural E York *York*
HOLTON (St Bartholomew)   *see* Albury w Tiddington etc *Ox*
HOLTON (St Nicholas)   *see* Camelot Par *B & W*
HOLTON (St Peter)   *see* Blyth Valley *St E*
HOLTON ST MARY (St Mary)   *see* Higham, Holton St Mary,
   Raydon and Stratford *St E*
HOLTON-CUM-BECKERING (All Saints)   *see* Wragby Gp *Linc*
HOLTON-LE-CLAY (St Peter), Tetney and North Cotes
   Linc 4   **P** *Ld Chan, Bp, and Duchy of Lancaster (by turn)*
   V C M WOADDEN   **NSM** J WEST
HOLTON-LE-MOOR (St Luke)   *see* Woldmoor Gp *Linc*
HOLTSPUR (St Thomas)   *see* Beaconsfield *Ox*
HOLWELL (St Laurence)   *see* Three Valleys *Sarum*
HOLWELL (St Leonard)   *see* Ab Kettleby and Holwell w
   Asfordby *Leic*
HOLWELL (St Mary the Virgin)   *see* Shill Valley and
   Broadshire *Ox*
HOLWELL (St Peter), Ickleford and Pirton *St Alb 3*   **P** *DBP
   and D&C Ely (jt)*   **R** M FANE DE SALIS   **NSM** M S HOLFORD

HOLWORTH (St Catherine by the Sea)   *see* Watercombe
   Sarum
HOLY ISLAND (St Mary the Virgin) *Newc 12*   **P** *Bp*
   V S A ST L HILLS
HOLYBOURNE (Holy Rood)   *see* Alton *Win*
HOLYMOORSIDE (St Peter)   *see* Brampton St Thos *Derby*
HOLYSTONE (St Mary the Virgin)   *see* Upper Coquetdale
   Newc
HOLYWELL (St John the Baptist)   *see* Bluntisham cum Earith
   w Colne and Holywell etc *Ely*
HOLYWELL (St Mary)   *see* Seghill *Newc*
HOMERSFIELD (St Mary)   *see* The Saints *St E*
HOMERTON (Christ Church on the Mead)   *see* Hackney
   Marsh *Lon*
HOMERTON (St Barnabas w St Paul) *as above*
HOMINGTON (St Mary the Virgin)   *see* Chalke Valley *Sarum*
HONEYCHURCH (St Mary)   *see* Chagford, Gidleigh,
   Throwleigh etc *Ex*
HONICKNOWLE (St Francis)   *see* Ernesettle, Whitleigh and
   Honicknowle *Ex*
HONILEY (St John the Baptist)   *see* Hatton w Haseley,
   Rowington w Lowsonford etc *Cov*
HONING (St Peter and St Paul)   *see* Smallburgh w Dilham w
   Honing and Crostwight *Nor*
HONINGHAM (St Andrew) *Nor 16*   **P** *DBP*   **V** *vacant*
HONINGTON (All Saints)   *see* Blackbourne *St E*
HONINGTON (All Saints)   *see* Shipston-on-Stour w
   Honington and Idlicote *Cov*
HONINGTON (St Wilfred)   *see* S Cliff Villages Gp *Linc*
**HONITON (St Michael) (St Paul), Gittisham, Combe
   Raleigh, Monkton, Awliscombe and Buckerell** *Ex 4*
   P *DBP*   **TR** S E ROBERTS
HONLEY (St Mary) *Leeds 5*   **P** R *Almondbury*   **V** M R SHORT
HONOR OAK PARK (St Augustine of Canterbury) *S'wark 5*
   P *Bp*   **P-in-c** C J L BOSWELL   **NSM** M BROOKS
HOO (All Hallows)   *see* High Halstow w All Hallows and Hoo
   St Mary *Roch*
HOO (St Andrew and St Eustachius)   *see* Mid Loes *St E*
HOO (St Werburgh) *Roch 6*   **P** *D&C*   **V** *vacant*
HOOBROOK (St Cecilia)   *see* Kidderminster E *Worc*
HOOE (St John the Evangelist)   *see* Plymstock and Hooe *Ex*
HOOE (St Oswald) *Chich 12*   **P** *Bp*   **P-in-c** P A FROSTICK
HOOK (St John the Evangelist)   *see* Whitewater *Win*
HOOK (St Mary the Virgin)   *see* Airmyn, Hook and Rawcliffe
   Sheff
HOOK (St Mary) w Warsash *Portsm 2*   **P** *Bp*
   P-in-c J M TERRY, N S TERRY
HOOK (St Paul)   *see* Tolworth, Hook and Surbiton *S'wark*
HOOK COMMON (Good Shepherd)   *see* Upton-on-Severn,
   Ripple, Earls Croome etc *Worc*
**HOOK NORTON (St Peter) w Great Rollright, Swerford
   and Wigginton** *Ox 22*   **P** *Bp, DBP, BNC Ox, and Jes Coll Ox
   (jt)*   **R** J D FAULL   **NSM** C G TURNER, M CUNNINGHAM
HOOKE (St Giles)   *see* Beaminster Area *Sarum*
HOOLE (All Saints) *Ches 2*   **P** *Simeon's Trustees*
   V R J KIRKLAND
HOOLE (St Michael) *Blackb 5*   **P** *Reps of Mrs E A Dunne and
   Mrs D Downes (jt)*   **R** A J TEMPLEMAN
HOOTON (St Paul) *Ches 9*   **P** *Trustees*   **V** K HOWARD
HOOTON PAGNELL (All Saints)   *see* Bilham *Sheff*
HOOTON ROBERTS (St John)   *see* Ravenfield, Hooton
   Roberts and Braithwell *Sheff*
HOP CHURCHES Benefice, The, comprising Bosbury, Canon
   Frome, Munsley, Stoke Edith, Stretton Grandison w
   Ashperton, Tarrington, and Yarkhill *Heref 5*   **P** *Bp (4 turns),
   D&C (2 turns), Exors A T Foley Esq (2 turns), R Hopton Esq
   (1 turn), H W Wiggin Esq (1 turn)*   **V** A J WILLIAMS
   NSM E N SEABRIGHT
HOPE (Holy Trinity)   *see* Minsterley, Habberley and Hope w
   Shelve *Heref*
HOPE (St James) and Pendlebury St John *Man 20*
   P *Trustees*   **V** G M THOMAS   **OLM** P M MANLEY
HOPE (St Peter), Castleton and Bradwell *Derby 4*   **P** *Bp and
   D&C Lich (jt)*   **OLM** J E BARNES
HOPE BAGOT (St John the Baptist)   *see* Tenbury *Heref*
HOPE BOWDLER (St Andrew)   *see* Apedale Gp *Heref*
**HOPE CHURCH ISLINGTON (St Mary Magdalene)
   (St David)** *Lon 6*   **P** *Bp and V Islington St Mary (jt)*
   V P V ZAPHIRIOU   **C** M P WAY, S J H MCDONALD
HOPE COVE (St Clements)   *see* Salcombe and Malborough w
   S Huish *Ex*
HOPE MANSEL (St Michael)   *see* Ariconium *Heref*
HOPESAY (St Mary the Virgin)   *see* Clun Valley *Heref*
HOPE-UNDER-DINMORE (St Mary the Virgin)   *see* Leominster
   Heref
HOPTON (All Saints)   *see* Stanton *St E*

HOPTON (St Margaret) w Corton *Nor 9*   **P** *Ld Chan and D&C (alt)*   **V** vacant

HOPTON (St Peter)   *see Mid Trent Lich*

HOPTON CASTLE (St Edward)   *see Middle Marches Heref*

HOPTON WAFERS (St Michael and All Angels)   *see Cleobury Mortimer w Hopton Wafers etc Heref*

HOPTON, UPPER (St John the Evangelist)   *see Mirfield Leeds*

HOPWAS (St Chad)   *see Tamworth Lich*

HOPWOOD (St John)   *see Heywood St Jo and St Luke Man*

HORAM (Christ Church) (St James) *Chich 13*   **P** *Bp*   **V** P-J GUY

HORBLING (St Andrew)   *see Billingborough Gp Linc*

HORBURY (St Peter and St Leonard) w Horbury Bridge (St John) *Leeds 19*   **P** *Dean*   **C** N R JOHNSON

HORBURY JUNCTION (St Mary) *Leeds 19*   **P** *DBP*   **P-in-c** K R M CAMPBELL   **NSM** D M WALKER

HORDEN (St Mary) *Dur 2*   **P** *Bp*   **P-in-c** K G MCNEIL

HORDLE (All Saints) *Win 11*   **P** *Bp*   **V** P J TAYLOR

HORDLEY (St Mary the Virgin)   *see Baschurch and Weston Lullingfield w Hordley Lich*

HORFIELD (Holy Trinity) *Bris 3*   **P** *Bp*   **R** D J MCGLADDERY

HORFIELD (St Gregory) *Bris 3*   **P** *Bp*   **P-in-c** J WILSON

HORHAM (St Mary)   *see Athelington, Denham, Horham, Hoxne etc St E*

HORKESLEY, GREAT (All Saints)   *see W Bergholt and Gt Horkesley Chelmsf*

HORKESLEY, GREAT (St John) *as above*

HORKESLEY, LITTLE (St Peter and St Paul)   *see Wormingford, Mt Bures and Lt Horkesley Chelmsf*

HORKSTOW (St Maurice) *Linc 8*   **P** *DBP*   **V** D P ROWETT   **NSM** R M JAGGS-FOWLER

HORLEY (St Bartholomew) (St Francis) (St Wilfrid) *S'wark 24*   **P** *Patr Bd*   **TR** L J WELLS   **TV** N NGURURI   **NSM** M T Z MUTIKANI

HORLEY (St Etheldreda)   *see Ironstone Ox*

HORLEY ROW (St Wilfrid)   *see Horley S'wark*

HORMEAD (St Nicholas), Wyddial, Anstey, Brent Pelham and Meesden *St Alb 16*   **P** *St Jo Coll Cam, Ch Coll Cam, and Bp (by turn)*   **V** J T L SAWYER

HORN HILL (St Paul)   *see Chalfont St Peter Ox*

HORNBLOTTON (St Peter)   *see Six Pilgrims B & W*

HORNBY (St Margaret) w Claughton and Whittington w Arkholme and Gressingham *Blackb 14*   **P** *Patr Bd*   **V** M J HAMPSON   **NSM** J L SMITH

HORNBY (St Mary)   *see Lower Wensleydale Leeds*

HORNCASTLE Group, The (St Mary the Virgin), including Ashby Puerorum, Greetham, High Toynton, Martin, Thimbleby, and Thornton *Linc 13*   **P** *Bp, Baroness Willoughby de Eresby and D&C (jt)*   **R** P C PATRICK   **NSM** J F PARKIN   **OLM** P E SMITH

HORNCHURCH (Holy Cross) *Chelmsf 2*   **P** *Bp and New Coll Ox (alt)*   **P-in-c** J F PATCHING

HORNCHURCH (St Andrew) (St George) (St Matthew) *Chelmsf 2*   **P** *New Coll Ox*   **V** B R HOBSON   **C** K A WYLIE, S M RYAN   **OLM** S E GROOMBRIDGE

HORNCHURCH Elm Park (St Nicholas)   *see Elm Park St Nic Hornchurch Chelmsf*

HORNCHURCH, SOUTH (St John and St Matthew) *Chelmsf 2*   **P** *MMCET*   **V** K J BROWNING

HORNDALE (St Francis)   *see Gt Aycliffe Dur*

HORNDON EAST (St Francis) and West Horndon w Little Warley and Childerditch *Chelmsf 8*   **P** *Sir Antony Browne's Sch, Bp and MMCET (jt)*   **V** vacant

HORNDON ON THE HILL (St Peter and St Paul)   *see Orsett and Bulphan and Horndon on the Hill Chelmsf*

HORNE (St Mary)   *see The Windmill S'wark*

HORNING (St Benedict)   *see Ashmanhaugh, Barton Turf etc Nor*

HORNINGHOLD (St Peter)   *see Hallaton and Allexton, w Horninghold, Tugby etc Leic*

HORNINGLOW (St John the Divine) *Lich 13*   **P** *Trustees*   **V** M R FREEMAN   **C** D B GORWOOD

HORNINGSEA (St Peter) *Ely 2*   **P** *St Jo Coll Cam*   **P-in-c** A J FORD

HORNINGSHAM (St John the Baptist)   *see Cley Hill Villages Sarum*

HORNINGTOFT (St Edmund)   *see Upper Wensum Village Gp Nor*

HORNSEA (St Nicholas), Atwick and Skipsea *York 11*   **P** *Ld Chan and Abp (alt)*   **V** C N MINETT STEVENS   **NSM** M M DESBOROUGH

HORNSEY (Christ Church) *Lon 20*   **P** *Bp*   **V** A O J PYMBLE

HORNSEY (Holy Innocents) *Lon 20*   **P** *Bp*   **V** B KERRIDGE   **C** P J HENDERSON

HORNSEY (St Mary) (St George) *Lon 20*   **P** *Bp*   **R** B BATSTONE   **C** A STUTTARD

HORNSEY RISE (St Mary) *Lon 6*   **P** *Ch Patr Trust*   **V** T L R MERCHANT   **NSM** R I MERCHANT

HORNTON (St John the Baptist)   *see Ironstone Ox*

HORRABRIDGE (St John the Baptist)   *see Yelverton, Meavy, Sheepstor, Walkhampton, Sampford Spiney and Horrabridge Ex*

HORRINGER (St Leonard) *St E 10*   **P** *Bp and DBP (jt)*   **R** C R GRIFFITHS

HORSEHEATH (All Saints)   *see Linton Ely*

HORSELL (St Mary the Virgin) *Guildf 12*   **P** *Bp*   **V** S E HAYES   **Hon C** P BROWN

HORSENDON (St Michael and All Angels)   *see Risborough Ox*

HORSEY (All Saints)   *see Flegg Coastal Benefice Nor*

HORSFORD (All Saints), Felthorpe and Hevingham *Nor 2*   **P** *Sir Thomas Agnew Beevor Bt and Bp (jt)*   **R** M T M MCPHEE

HORSFORTH (St Margaret)   *see Abbeylands Leeds*

HORSHAM (Holy Trinity) (St Leonard) (St Mary the Virgin) (St Mark) *Chich 7*   **P** *Patr Bd*   **TV** D W BOUSKILL, N L LOVELESS   **C** R J TUCK   **NSM** B P NEW, K A BAILEY

HORSHAM (St Mark)   *see Holbrook Chich*

HORSHAM ST FAITH (St Andrew and St Mary), Spixworth and Crostwick *Nor 2*   **P** *Bp and DBP (jt)*   **P-in-c** R H MASKELL

HORSINGTON (All Saints)   *see Woodhall Spa Gp Linc*

HORSINGTON (St John the Baptist)   *see Abbas and Templecombe, Henstridge and Horsington B & W*

HORSLEY (Holy Trinity)   *see N Tyne and Redesdale Newc*

HORSLEY (St Clement)   *see Denby Gp Derby*

HORSLEY (St Martin)   *see Nailsworth w Shortwood, Horsley etc Glouc*

HORSLEY HILL (St Lawrence the Martyr) South Shields *Dur 13*   **P** *D&C*   **P-in-c** P W D CHILD

HORSLEY WOODHOUSE (St Susanna)   *see Denby Gp Derby*

HORSLEY, EAST (St Martin) *Guildf 10*   **P** *D&C Cant*   **R** R PITTARIDES   **NSM** R DURWARD

HORSLEY, WEST (St Mary) *Guildf 10*   **P** *Col A R N Weston*   **R** P HERRINGTON

HORSMONDEN (St Margaret) *Roch 8*   **P** *Bp*   **R** T E FFRENCH   **C** J P FFRENCH

HORSPATH (St Giles)   *see Garsington, Cuddesdon and Horspath Ox*

HORSTEAD (All Saints)   *see Coltishall w Gt Hautbois, Frettenham etc Nor*

HORSTED KEYNES (St Giles) *Chich 5*   **P** *Bp*   **P-in-c** D J MURDOCH

HORSTED PARVA (St Michael and All Angels)   *see Lt Horsted Chich*

HORSTED, LITTLE (St Michael and All Angels) *Chich 18*   **P** *The Rt Revd P J Ball*   **R** vacant

HORTON (St James the Elder)   *see Sodbury Vale Glouc*

HORTON (St Mary the Virgin)   *see Newsham and Horton Newc*

HORTON (St Michael and All Angels) and Wraysbury *Ox 12*   **P** *Major J M Halford and D&C Windsor (jt)*   **V** C T GIBSON

HORTON (St Michael)   *see Cheddleton, Horton, Longsdon and Rushton Spencer Lich*

HORTON (St Peter)   *see Isle Valley B & W*

HORTON (St Wolfrida)   *see Wimborne Minster and the N Villages Sarum*

HORTON KIRBY (St Mary)   *see Darent Valley Roch*

HORTON, GREAT (St John the Evangelist) *Leeds 2*   **P** *V Bradf*   **V** J E BAVINGTON   **C** A A DICKSON

HORTON, LITTLE (All Saints) (St Oswald) *Leeds 2*   **P** *Bp and J F Bardsley Esq (jt)*   **V** A S TREASURE   **C** D A JONES, J M GREEN, J W HINTON   **NSM** M M MALEK

HORTON-CUM-STUDLEY (St Barnabas)   *see Beckley, Forest Hill, Horton-cum-Studley and Stanton St John Ox*

HORTON-IN-RIBBLESDALE (St Oswald)   *see Langcliffe w Stainforth and Horton Leeds*

HORWICH (Holy Trinity) (St Catherine) (St Elizabeth) and Rivington *Man 9*   **P** *Patr Bd*   **TR** S FLETCHER   **TV** M C BEHREND   **C** J S SMITH   **NSM** N J BUTTERWORTH   **OLM** C P TRACEY, G M SMART, P D HARLEY

HORWOOD (St Michael)   *see Newton Tracey, Horwood, Alverdiscott etc Ex*

HORWOOD, GREAT (St James)   *see Winslow w Gt Horwood and Addington Ox*

HORWOOD, LITTLE (St Nicholas)   *see Newton Longville, Mursley, Swanbourne etc Ox*

HOSE (St Michael)   *see Vale of Belvoir Leic*

HOTHAM (St Oswald) *York 13*   **P** *Ld Chan*   **P-in-c** B WORSDALE

HOTHFIELD (St Margaret)   *see G7 Benefice Cant*

HOUGH GREEN (St Basil and All Saints) *Liv 12*   **P** *Bp*   **V** P W DAWKIN

HOUGHAM (All Saints)   *see S Cliff Villages Gp Linc*

HOUGHAM (St Laurence)　*see* Alkham w Capel le Ferne and Hougham *Cant*

HOUGH-ON-THE-HILL (All Saints)　*see* S Cliff Villages Gp *Linc*

HOUGHTON (All Saints)　*see* Mid Test *Win*

HOUGHTON (St Giles)　*see* Walsingham, Houghton and Barsham *Nor*

HOUGHTON (St John the Evangelist) (St Peter) *Carl 3*　**P** *Trustees*　**P-in-c** A P J TOWNER

HOUGHTON (St Martin)　*see* E w W Rudham, Helhoughton etc *Nor*

HOUGHTON (St Nicholas)　*see* Bury w Houghton and Coldwaltham and Hardham *Chich*

HOUGHTON CONQUEST (All Saints)　*see* Wilshamstead and Houghton Conquest *St Alb*

HOUGHTON LE SPRING (St Michael and All Angels) *Dur 10*　**P** *Bp*　**P-in-c** J W BARRON

HOUGHTON REGIS (All Saints) (St Thomas) *St Alb 11*　**P** *DBP*　**P-in-c** D GALANZINO

HOUGHTON w WYTON (St Mary)　*see* Hartford and Houghton w Wyton *Ely*

HOUGHTON, GREAT (St Mary)　*see* Cogenhoe and Gt and Lt Houghton w Brafield *Pet*

HOUGHTON, LITTLE (St Mary the Blessed Virgin)　*as above*

HOUGHTON, NEW (Christ Church)　*see* E Scarsdale *Derby*

HOUGHTON-ON-THE-HILL (St Catharine)　*see* Cornerstone Team *Leic*

HOUND (St Edward the Confessor) (St Mary the Virgin) *Win 10*　**P** *St Mary's Coll Win*　**P-in-c** R W SANDAY

HOUNSLOW (Holy Trinity) *Lon 11*　**P** *Bp*　**V** S K WRIGHT　**C** D WILLIAMS

HOUNSLOW (St Paul) (Good Shepherd) *Lon 11*　**P** *Bp*　**V** C M A CLARKE　**C** D J THOMAS

HOUNSLOW (St Stephen) *Lon 11*　**P** *Bp*　**V** *vacant*

HOVE (All Saints) *Chich 20*　**P** *Bp*　**V** R A GREEN　**C** A D I REID

HOVE (Bishop Hannington Memorial Church) (Holy Cross) *Chich 20*　**P** *Trustees*　**V** P R MOON　**C** D A HOWARTH, T A J GAGE

HOVE (St Andrew Old Church) *Chich 20*　**P** *Bp*　**P-in-c** D T HENDERSON

HOVE (St John the Baptist) *Chich 20*　**P** *Bp*　**P-in-c** E M COLLINS　**NSM** J F GREENFIELD

HOVE (St Philip) *Chich 20*　**P** *Bp*　**V** *vacant*

HOVE EDGE (St Chad)　*see* Lightcliffe and Hove Edge *Leeds*

HOVERINGHAM (St Michael)　*see* W Trent *S'well*

HOVETON (St John)　*see* Wroxham w Hoveton, Belaugh and Tunstead etc *Nor*

HOVETON (St Peter)　*as above*

HOVINGHAM (All Saints)　*see* The Street Par *York*

HOW CAPLE (St Andrew and St Mary)　*see* StowCaple *Heref*

HOWARDIAN GROUP, The, comprising Bulmer, Dalby w Whenby, Huttons Ambo, Terrington, and Welburn *York 6*　**P** *Abp*　**R** *vacant*

HOWDEN Team Ministry, The (St Peter), comprising Blacktoft, Eastrington, Howden w Barmby on the Marsh, Laxton, Newport, and Wressle *York 13*　**P** *Abp (4 turns), Ld Chan (1 turn)*　**TR** J H LITTLE　**TV** L A KENNY

HOWE (St Mary the Virgin)　*see* Poringland *Nor*

HOWE BRIDGE (St Michael and All Angels)　*see* Atherton and Hindsford w Howe Bridge *Man*

HOWELL HILL (St Paul) *Guildf 9*　**P** *Bp*　**V** M J WAINWRIGHT　**C** P DEVER　**NSM** D N SENIOR, S HARRIS

HOWGILL (Holy Trinity)　*see* Firbank, Howgill and Killington *Carl*

HOWICK (St Michael and All Angels)　*see* Longhoughton w Howick *Newc*

HOWLE HILL (St John the Evangelist)　*see* Ross w Walford and Brampton Abbotts *Heref*

HOWSHAM (St John)　*see* Harton *York*

HOXNE (St Peter and St Paul)　*see* Athelington, Denham, Horham, Hoxne etc *St E*

HOXTON (Holy Trinity) (St Mary) *Lon 5*　**P** *Bp*　**V** A C NEWCOMBE

HOXTON (St Anne) (St Columba) *Lon 5*　**P** *The Crown*　**V** B L BELL　**C** A JONES, N J CHARLES

HOXTON (St John the Baptist) w Ch Ch *Lon 5*　**P** *Haberdashers' Co and Adn (jt)*　**V** G HUNTER　**C** C M TAYLOR

HOYLAKE (Holy Trinity and St Hildeburgh) *Ches 8*　**P** *Bp*　**V** P A ROSSITER　**NSM** J C HARRISON

HOYLAND (St Peter) (St Andrew) *Sheff 11*　**P** *Bp and Sir Philip Naylor-Leyland Bt (jt)*　**V** R B PARKER

HOYLAND, HIGH (All Saints), Scissett and Clayton West *Leeds 12*　**P** *Bp*　**R** S L FARRIMOND　**NSM** K B CURRIE

HOYLANDSWAINE (St John the Evangelist)　*see* W Barnsley *Leeds*

HUBBERHOLME (St Michael and All Angels)　*see* Upper Wharfedale w Littondale and Littondale *Leeds*

HUCCABY (St Raphael)　*see* Ashburton, Bickington, Buckland in the Moor etc *Ex*

HUCCLECOTE (St Philip and St James) *Glouc 2*　**P** *Bp*　**P-in-c** M W CLOSE

HUCKING (St Margaret)　*see* N Downs *Cant*

HUCKNALL (St Peter and St Paul)　*see* W Hucknall *S'well*

HUCKNALL, WEST (St Peter and St Paul) *S'well 4*　**P** *Bp*　**V** J L STEPHENS

HUDDERSFIELD (Holy Trinity) *Leeds 11*　**P** *Simeon's Trustees*　**V** M R WILKINS　**NSM** R C SWINDELL

HUDDERSFIELD (St Francis) Fixby　*see* Fixby and Cowcliffe *Leeds*

HUDDERSFIELD (St Hilda) Cowcliffe　*as above*

HUDDERSFIELD (St John the Evangelist)　*see* Birkby and Woodhouse *Leeds*

HUDDERSFIELD (St Peter) *Leeds 11*　**P** *DBP*　**NSM** C A HAWKINS

HUDDERSFIELD All Saints (St Thomas) *Leeds 11*　**P** *DBP*　**V** L A PINFIELD

HUDDERSFIELD Emmanuel　*see* Newsome and Armitage Bridge and S Crosland *Leeds*

HUDDERSFIELD, NORTH (St Cuthbert)　*see* Birkby and Birchencliffe *Leeds*

HUDDINGTON (St James)　*see* Bowbrook S *Worc*

HUDSWELL (St Michael and All Angels)　*see* Richmond w Hudswell and Downholme and Marske *Leeds*

HUGGATE (St Mary)　*see* Pocklington Wold *York*

HUGGLESCOTE (St John the Baptist) w Donington, Ellistown and Snibston *Leic 8*　**P** *Bp*　**TR** O S WOOLCOCK　**C** C J HAYWOOD

HUGHENDEN (St Michael) *Ox 18*　**P** *DBP*　**V** K M JOHNSON　**NSM** H E PETERS, T A JONES

HUGHLEY (St John the Baptist)　*see* Wenlock *Heref*

HUISH (St James the Less)　*see* Shebbear, Buckland Filleigh, Sheepwash etc *Ex*

HUISH (St Nicholas)　*see* Vale of Pewsey *Sarum*

HUISH CHAMPFLOWER (St Peter)　*see* Wiveliscombe and the Hills *B & W*

HUISH EPISCOPI (Blessed Virgin Mary)　*see* Aller, High w Low Ham and Huish Episcopi cum Langport *B & W*

HUISH, SOUTH (Holy Trinity)　*see* Salcombe and Malborough w S Huish *Ex*

HULCOTE (St Nicholas)　*see* Cranfield and Hulcote w Salford *St Alb*

HULCOTT (All Saints)　*see* Bierton and Hulcott *Ox*

HULL (Ascension)　*see* Derringham Bank *York*

HULL (Holy Apostles)　*see* Kingston upon Hull H Trin *York*

HULL (Most Holy and Undivided Trinity)　*as above*

HULL (St Aidan) Southcoates　*see* Kingston upon Hull St Aid Southcoates *York*

HULL (St Alban)　*see* Kingston upon Hull St Alb *York*

HULL (St Cuthbert) *York 14*　**P** *Abp*　**V** J C COWAN　**NSM** M L MEESAM

HULL (St John the Baptist)　*see* Newington w Hull St Andr *York*

HULL (St John) Newland *York 14*　**P** *Abp*　**V** M TINKER

HULL (St Martin) w The Transfiguration *York 14*　**P** *Abp*　**V** J C HILL

HULL (St Mary the Virgin) Lowgate　*see* Kingston upon Hull St Mary *York*

HULL (St Mary) Sculcoates *York 14*　**P** *V Sculcoates*　**V** P LAMB

HULL (St Nicholas)　*see* Kingston upon Hull St Nic *York*

HULL (St Paul)　*see* Sculcoates *York*

HULL (St Thomas)　*see* Derringham Bank *York*

HULL, NORTH (St Michael and All Angels) *York 14*　**P** *Abp*　**V** D A WALKER

HULLAND (Christ Church), Atlow, Kniveton, Bradley and Hognaston *Derby 1*　**P** *Patr Bd*　**R** P L MICHELL　**NSM** L WEBB

HULLAVINGTON (St Mary Magdalene)　*see* Gauzebrook *Bris*

HULLBRIDGE (St Thomas of Canterbury)　*see* Rettendon and Hullbridge *Chelmsf*

HULME (Ascension) *Man 3*　**P** *Trustees*　**P-in-c** F SHER　**NSM** P J HIBBERT

HULME WALFIELD (St Michael)　*see* Marton, Siddington w Capesthorne etc *Ches*

HULTON, LITTLE (St John the Baptist)　*see* Walkden and Lt Hulton *Man*

HULTON, OVER (St Andrew)　*see* Deane *Man*

HUMBER (St Mary the Virgin)　*see* Leominster *Heref*

HUMBERSTON (St Peter) *Linc 4*　**P** *Bp*　**C** L C VINCER　**OLM** P R SALMON

HUMBERSTONE (St Mary)　*see* Ascension TM *Leic*

HUMBLE, WEST (St Michael)   see Leatherhead and Mickleham *Guildf*

HUMBLETON (St Peter)   see Burstwick, Burton Pidsea etc *York*

HUMPHREY PARK (St Clement)   see Davyhulme Ch Ch and Urmston *Man*

HUMSHAUGH (St Peter) w Simonburn and Wark *Newc 8*
P *Bp*   P-in-c S G WILKINSON   NSM R E HARRISON

HUNCOAT (St Augustine)   see Accrington St Jo w Huncoat *Blackb*

HUNCOTE (St James the Greater)   see Narborough and Huncote *Leic*

HUNDLEBY (St Mary)   see Bolingbroke Deanery *Linc*

HUNDON (All Saints)   see Stour Valley *St E*

HUNDRED RIVER and Wainford, comprising Brampton, Ellough and Weston, Ilketshall St Andrew, Redisham, Ringsfield, Shadingfield, Sotterley w Willingham, Stoven, and Westhall *St E 17*   P *DBP, Shadingfield Property Ltd, Bp, F D L Barnes Esq, Miss to Seafarers, Magd Coll Cam, and Ch Soc Trust (jt)*   P-in-c P H O MILLER   NSM J M LOFTUS

HUNGARTON (St John the Baptist)   see Coplow *Leic*

HUNGERFORD (St Lawrence) and Denford *Ox 6*   P *D&C Windsor*   V M W SAUNDERS   NSM T R SHARPLES

HUNMANBY (All Saints)   see Hertford *York*

HUNNINGHAM (St Margaret)   see Offchurch Gp *Cov*

HUNSDON (St Dunstan) (St Francis) w Widford and Wareside *St Alb 19*   P *DBP*   R M P DUNSTAN

HUNSINGORE (St John the Baptist)   see Lower Nidderdale *Leeds*

HUNSTANTON (St Edmund) w Ringstead *Nor 15*
P *H Le Strange Esq*   NSM A J MONRO

HUNSTANTON (St Mary) w Ringstead Parva, Holme-next-the-Sea, Thornham, Brancaster, Burnham Deepdale and Titchwell *Nor 15*   P *Bp, Exors of the late H le Strange Esq, and Exors of the late H S N Simms-Adams Esq (jt)*   R vacant

HUNSTANWORTH (St James)   see Blanchland w Hunstanworth and Edmundbyers etc *Newc*

HUNSTON (St Leodegar)   see N Mundham w Hunston and Merston *Chich*

HUNSTON (St Michael)   see Pakenham w Norton, Tostock etc *St E*

HUNTINGDON (All Saints) (St Barnabas) (St Mary) *Ely 10*
P *Bp (2 turns), Ld Chan (1 turn)*   R J A RANDALL
C L M DAVIS

HUNTINGFIELD (St Mary)   see Heveningham *St E*

HUNTINGTON (All Saints) *York 7*   P *D&C*
R I G BIRKINSHAW   C C J PARK   NSM J J LINDSEY

HUNTINGTON (St Luke)   see Ches St Paul w St Luke *Ches*

HUNTINGTON (St Mary Magdalene)   see Holmer w Huntington *Heref*

HUNTINGTON (St Thomas à Becket)   see Kington w Huntington, Old Radnor, Kinnerton etc *Heref*

HUNTINGTON (St Thomas)   see Cannock and Huntington *Lich*

HUNTLEY (St John the Baptist) and Longhope, Churcham and Bulley *Glouc 3*   P *Bp and D&C (jt)*   P-in-c L S BLOOM
C D A GILL

HUNTON (St James)   see Upper Dever *Win*

HUNTON (St Mary)   see Coxheath, E Farleigh, Hunton, Linton etc *Roch*

HUNTS CROSS (St Hilda)   see Halewood and Hunts Cross *Liv*

HUNTSHAM (All Saints)   see Bampton, Morebath, Clayhanger, Petton etc *Ex*

HUNTSHAW (St Mary Magdalene)   see Newton Tracey, Horwood, Alverdiscott etc *Ex*

HUNTSPILL, The (All Saints) (St Peter and All Hallows) and Mark *B & W 1*   P *Bp and Ball Coll Ox (jt)*   R vacant

HUNWICK (St Paul)   see Hunwick and Willington *Dur*

HUNWICK (St Paul) and Willington *Dur 8*   P V *Bp Auckland and R Brancepeth (alt)*   V D L SPOKES

HUNWORTH (St Lawrence)   see Brinton, Briningham, Hunworth, Stody etc *Nor*

HURDSFIELD (Holy Trinity) *Ches 13*   P *Hyndman Trustees*
V J C R GIBSON

HURLEY (Resurrection)   see Baxterley w Hurley and Wood End and Merevale etc *Birm*

HURLEY (St Mary the Virgin)   see Burchetts Green *Ox*

HURSLEY (All Saints)   see Compton, Hursley, and Otterbourne *Win*

HURST (St John the Evangelist) *Man 13*   P *The Crown*
V E J DEVALL

HURST (St Nicholas)   see Ruscombe and Twyford w Hurst *Ox*

HURST GREEN (Holy Trinity)   see Salehurst, Hurst Green and Robertsbridge *Chich*

HURST GREEN (St John the Evangelist)   see Oxted *S'wark*

HURST GREEN (St John the Evangelist) and Mitton *Blackb 7*
P *Bp and J E R Aspinall Esq (jt)*   P-in-c B R MCCONKEY
C K J HERSCHELL

HURSTBOURNE PRIORS (St Andrew), Longparish, St Mary Bourne and Woodcott *Win 6*   P *Bp and J C Woodcock Esq (jt)*   V C L MARSHALL   NSM D M MARSDEN, R J SUTCLIFFE

HURSTBOURNE TARRANT (St Peter) and Faccombe and Vernham Dean and Linkenholt *Win 3*   P *Bp*   C T A LEWIS

HURSTPIERPOINT (Holy Trinity) (St George) *Chich 8*
P *Hurstpierpoint Coll*   R J E WILLIS   C J D NAUDÉ
NSM D M BEER

HURSTWOOD, HIGH (Holy Trinity) *Chich 18*   P *Abp*
P-in-c M S ASHWORTH

HURWORTH (All Saints) *Dur 7*   P *Ch Soc Trust*
P-in-c A THORP   NSM H M THORP

HUSBANDS BOSWORTH (All Saints)   see Hexagon *Leic*

HUSBORNE CRAWLEY (St Mary Magdalene or St James)   see Aspley Guise w Husborne Crawley and Ridgmont *St Alb*

HUSTHWAITE (St Nicholas)   see Coxwold and Husthwaite *York*

HUTHWAITE (All Saints) *S'well 4*   P V *Sutton-in-Ashfield*
V C A K MAIDEN

HUTTOFT (St Margaret)   see Sutton, Huttoft and Anderby *Linc*

HUTTON (All Saints) (St Peter) *Chelmsf 8*   P *D&C St Paul's*
P-in-c A G SMITH   NSM A BAXTER

HUTTON (Blessed Virgin Mary) and Locking *B & W 10*
P *DBP and MMCET (jt)*   R A L WILKINS

HUTTON BUSCEL (St Matthew)   see Upper Derwent *York*

HUTTON CRANSWICK (St Peter) w Skerne, Watton and Beswick *York 10*   P *Abp*   V S R J ELLIOTT

HUTTON HENRY (St Francis)   see Wheatley Hill, Thornley and Wingate w Hutton Henry *Dur*

HUTTON MAGNA (St Mary)   see Holmedale *Leeds*

HUTTON ROOF (St John the Divine)   see Kirkby Lonsdale *Carl*

HUTTON, OLD (St John the Baptist) and New Hutton (St Stephen) *Carl 10*   P V *Kendal*   P-in-c A WHITTAKER
C C A BENTLEY   NSM M MASHITER

HUTTON-IN-THE-FOREST (St James)   see Inglewood Gp *Carl*

HUTTON-LE-HOLE (St Chad)   see Lastingham w Appleton-le-Moors, Rosedale etc *York*

HUTTONS AMBO (St Margaret)   see Howardian Gp *York*

HUXHAM (St Mary the Virgin)   see Brampford Speke, Cadbury, Newton St Cyres etc *Ex*

HUXLEY (St Andrew)   see Hargrave *Ches*

HUYTON (St George)   see 4Saints Team *Liv*

HUYTON (St Michael) *Liv 7*   P *Earl of Derby*   V vacant

HUYTON QUARRY (St Gabriel) *Liv 7*   P V *Huyton St Mich*
V M K ROGERS   C J W FORSTER

HYDE (Holy Ascension)   see Fordingbridge and Hyde and Breamore etc *Win*

HYDE (St George) (St Thomas) *Ches 14*   P *Bp, R Cheadle, and R Stockport (jt)*   V J D BENTLIFF   C C BOOTHROYD

HYDE HEATH (Mission Church)   see Lt Missenden *Ox*

HYDE, WEST (St Thomas of Canterbury)   see Mill End and Heronsgate w W Hyde *St Alb*

HYDNEYE (St Peter)   see Hampden Park and The Hydnye *Chich*

HYKEHAM (All Saints) (St Hugh) (St Michael and All Angels) *Linc 12*   P *Ld Chan and Bp (alt)*   R P G COLLINS
NSM G F REID

HYLTON, SOUTH (St Mary) *Dur 14*   P *Bp*   V vacant

HYSON GREEN (St Stephen) and Forest Fields *S'well 9*
P *CPAS*   V C R BURROWS   C N BAHADUR
NSM D WATKINSON

HYSSINGTON (St Etheldreda)   see Churchstoke w Hyssington and Sarn *Heref*

HYTHE (St John the Baptist) *Win 11*   P *Bp*   V J ELVIDGE

HYTHE (St Leonard) (Holy Cross) *Cant 8*   P R *Saltwood*
P-in-c A J SWEENEY   C P M DULLEY   NSM L SEEAR

HYTHE Butts Ash (St Anne)   see Hythe *Win*

IBBERTON (St Eustace)   see Hazelbury Bryan and the Hillside Par *Sarum*

IBSTOCK (St Denys) w Heather *Leic 8*   P *Bp and MMCET (jt)*
R vacant

IBSTONE (St Nicholas)   see S Chilterns *Ox*

ICKBURGH (St Peter) w Langford *Nor 13*   P *Bp*   R vacant

ICKENHAM (St Giles) *Lon 24*   P *Eton Coll*   R F A DAVIES

ICKFORD (St Nicholas)   see Worminghall w Ickford, Oakley and Shabbington *Ox*

ICKHAM (St John the Evangelist)   see Littlebourne and Ickham w Wickhambreaux etc *Cant*

ICKLEFORD (St Katherine)   see Holwell, Ickleford and Pirton *St Alb*

ICKLESHAM (St Nicolas) *see* Winchelsea and Icklesham *Chich*

ICKLETON (St Mary Magdalene) *Ely 5* **P** *Ld Chan*
P-in-c P J SHAKESHAFT **NSM** P M SHARKEY

ICKLINGHAM (All Saints w St James) *see* Mildenhall *St E*

ICKNIELD WAY VILLAGES, comprising Great Chishill, Little Chishill, Chrishall, Duddenhoe End, Elmdon, Heydon, and Strethall *Chelmsf 20* **P** *Patr Bd* **R** D A R SODADASI

ICKNIELD, comprising Britwell Salome, Pyrton and Shirburn, Swyncombe, and Watlington *Ox 20* **P** *Ld Chan (1 turn)*, *Ch Ch Ox (1 turn)*, *Bp and Earl of Macclesfield (1 turn)* **R** D E J THOMPSON **NSM** A M PATERSON

ICOMB (St Mary) *see* Broadwell, Evenlode, Oddington, Adlestrop etc *Glouc*

IDBURY (St Nicholas) *see* Wychwood *Ox*

IDDESLEIGH (St James) *see* Dolton, Dowland, Iddesleigh etc *Ex*

IDE (St Ida) *see* Alphington, Shillingford St George and Ide *Ex*

IDE HILL (St Mary the Virgin) *see* Sundridge w Ide Hill and Toys Hill *Roch*

IDEFORD (St Mary the Virgin) *see* Teignmouth, Ideford w Luton, Ashcombe etc *Ex*

IDEN (All Saints) *see* Rye *Chich*

IDLE (Holy Trinity) *Leeds 3* **P** *V Calverley* **V** N J TAYLOR **C** A O LAOTAN

IDLICOTE (St James the Great) *see* Shipston-on-Stour w Honington and Idlicote *Cov*

IDRIDGEHAY (St James) *see* Wirksworth *Derby*

IDSWORTH (St Hubert) *see* Blendworth w Chalton w Idsworth *Portsm*

IFFLEY (St Mary the Virgin) *Ox 1* **P** *Ch Ch Ox*
V A R MCKEARNEY **C** N CHRISTENSEN **NSM** W C BEAVER

IFIELD (St Margaret) *Chich 6* **P** *Bp* **C** J GATER

IFIELD (St Margaret) *see* Gravesend H Family w Ifield *Roch*

IFORD (St Nicholas) w Kingston and Rodmell and Southease *Chich 21* **P** *Bp and Gorham Trustees (jt)* **V** G M DAW **NSM** M C BROWN

IFORD (St Saviour) *see* Holdenhurst and Iford *Win*

IGHTFIELD (St John the Baptist) *see* Adderley, Ash, Calverhall, Ightfield etc *Lich*

IGHTHAM (St Peter) *Roch 10* **P** *Mrs L K Ford*
R T R HATWELL

IKEN (St Botolph) *see* Wilford Peninsula *St E*

ILAM (Holy Cross) *see* Alstonfield, Ilam and Wetton *Lich*

ILCHESTER (St Mary Major) w Northover, Limington, Yeovilton and Podimore *B & W 5* **P** *Bp Lon (7 turns), Bp (1 turn), and Wadh Coll Ox (1 turn)* **R** B S FAULKNER

ILDERTON (St Michael) *see* Doddington, Ilderton, Kirknewton and Wooler *Newc*

ILFORD, GREAT (St Alban) *Chelmsf 6* **P** *Bp* **V** S HALSTEAD

ILFORD, GREAT (St Andrew) *Chelmsf 6* **P** *Bp* **V** M SEGAL **OLM** H J MORRIS

ILFORD, GREAT (St John the Evangelist) *Chelmsf 6* **P** *Bp* **P-in-c** K P B LOVESEY

ILFORD, GREAT (St Luke) *Chelmsf 6* **P** *Bp* **V** J BROWN

ILFORD, GREAT (St Margaret of Antioch) (St Clement) *Chelmsf 6* **P** *Patr Bd* **V** S G PUGH

ILFORD, GREAT (St Mary the Virgin) *Chelmsf 6* **P** *V Gt Ilford* **V** G E J P JONES

ILFORD, LITTLE (St Barnabas) *Chelmsf 5* **P** *Bp* **P-in-c** R L RYAN

ILFORD, LITTLE (St Michael and All Angels) *Chelmsf 5* **P** *Hertf Coll Ox* **C** N P MORROW

ILFRACOMBE (Holy Trinity) (St Peter), Lee, Woolacombe, Bittadon and Mortehoe *Ex 17* **P** *Patr Bd*
P-in-c J W ROLES **TV** G A B KING-SMITH **C** A E LEWIS, M A L ALDRIDGE-COLLINS **NSM** L WALTERS

ILFRACOMBE (St Philip and St James), Combe Martin and Berrynarbor *Ex 17* **P** *Bp and Ch Trust Fund Trust (jt)* **R** P CHURCHER **C** W COLE

ILKESTON (Holy Trinity) *Derby 8* **P** *Bp*
Hon C T F BARNFATHER **NSM** G A C ORTON

ILKESTON (St John the Evangelist) *Derby 8* **P** *V Ilkeston St Mary* **P-in-c** A J BAGULEY **C** C F R HEMMINGS, C FRENCH

ILKESTON (St Mary the Virgin) *Derby 8* **P** *Bp*
P-in-c A J BAGULEY

ILKETSHALL ST ANDREW (St Andrew) *see* Hundred River and Wainford *St E*

ILKETSHALL ST JOHN (St John the Baptist) *see* The Saints *St E*

ILKETSHALL ST LAWRENCE (St Lawrence) *as above*

ILKETSHALL ST MARGARET (St Margaret) *as above*

ILKLEY (All Saints) *Leeds 4* **P** *Hyndman Trustees* **V** M S COE **NSM** M P REID, R F WATSON

ILKLEY (St Margaret) *Leeds 4* **P** *CR* **V** P C GRAY

ILLOGAN (St Illogan) *see* St Illogan *Truro*

ILLSTON (St Michael and All Angels) *see* Gaulby *Leic*

ILMER (St Peter) *see* Risborough *Ox*

ILMINGTON (St Mary) and Stretton-on-Fosse and Ditchford w Preston-on-Stour w Whitchurch and Atherstone-on-Stour *Cov 9* **P** *Bp, MMCET, and Ms C A Alston-Roberts-West (jt)* **P-in-c** C GOBLE
Hon C S W FLETCHER

ILMINSTER (Blessed Virgin Mary) and Whitelackington *B & W 16* **P** *Bp* **V** J E STOBART **NSM** D PERREAU

ILSINGTON (St Michael) *Ex 8* **P** *D&C Windsor*
V D R HARRIS

ILSLEY, EAST (St Mary) *see* Hermitage *Ox*

ILSLEY, WEST (All Saints) *see* E Downland *Ox*

ILTON (St Peter) *see* Isle Valley *B & W*

IMMINGHAM (St Andrew) *Linc 4* **P** *Bp and DBP (jt)*
V J DONN

IMPINGTON (St Andrew) *Ely 6* **P** *Adn Cam*
V N J BLANDFORD-BAKER **C** K C DOUGLASS

INCE (St James) *see* Thornton-le-Moors w Ince and Elton *Ches*

INCE IN MAKERFIELD (Christ Church) *see* Wigan All SS *Liv*

INCE IN MAKERFIELD (St Mary) *as above*

INDIAN QUEEN (St Francis) *see* St Enoder *Truro*

INGATESTONE (St Edmund and St Mary) w Fryerning *Chelmsf 8* **P** *Bp and Wadh Coll Ox (jt)* **V** P SHERRING **C** M W HOUGHTON

INGESTRE (St Mary the Virgin) *see* Stafford St Jo and Tixall w Ingestre *Lich*

INGHAM (All Saints) *see* Spring Line Gp *Linc*

INGHAM (Holy Trinity) *see* Stalham, E Ruston, Brunstead, Sutton and Ingham *Nor*

INGHAM (St Bartholomew) *see* Blackbourne *St E*

INGLEBY ARNCLIFFE (All Saints) *see* Osmotherley w Harlsey and Ingleby Arncliffe *York*

INGLEBY BARWICK (St Francis) *York 20* **P** *Abp*
V J C ROUNDTREE **C** N J B STEVENSON
NSM T D CHARLTON

INGLEBY GREENHOW (St Andrew), Bilsdale Priory and Kildale w Kirkby-in-Cleveland *York 20* **P** *Abp, Adn Cleveland, Bp Whitby, Viscount De L'Isle, R G Beckett Esq, and A H W Sutcliffe Esq (jt)* **V** M A HEADING

INGLETON (St John the Evangelist) *Dur 7* **P** *Lord Barnard* **P-in-c** K STEVENTON

INGLETON (St Mary the Virgin) *see* Bentham, Burton-in-Lonsdale, Chapel-le-Dale etc *Leeds*

INGLEWOOD Group, The, comprising Ainstable, Armathwaite, Calthwaite, Hesket-in-the-Forest, Hutton-in-the-Forest, Ivegill, and Skelton *Carl 4* **P** *Bp, D&C, CCC Ox, and E P Ecroyd Esq (jt)* **R** *vacant*

INGOL (St Margaret) *Blackb 13* **P** *Bp* **P-in-c** C P WALKER

INGOLDISTHORPE (St Michael) *see* Dersingham, Anmer, Ingoldisthorpe etc *Nor*

INGOLDMELLS (St Peter and St Paul) *see* Skegness Gp *Linc*

INGOLDSBY (St Bartholomew) *see* N Beltisloe Gp *Linc*

INGRAM (St Michael) *see* Chatton w Chillingham, Eglingham and S Charlton and Ingram *Newc*

INGRAVE (St Nicholas) (St Stephen) *Chelmsf 8* **P** *Bp and Ch Patr Trust (jt)* **V** P S HAMILTON

INGRAVE (St Stephen) Conventional District *Chelmsf 8*
NSM J A SEDANO

INGROW (St John the Evangelist) with Hainworth *Leeds 1*
P *Bp* **P-in-c** T A RAISTRICK **NSM** J M INESON

INGS (St Anne) *see* Staveley, Ings and Kentmere *Carl*

INGWORTH (St Lawrence) *see* Erpingham w Calthorpe, Ingworth, Aldborough etc *Nor*

INHAM NOOK (St Barnabas) *see* Chilwell *S'well*

INKBERROW (St Peter) *see* Inkberrow w Cookhill and Kington w Dormston *Worc*

INKBERROW (St Peter) w Cookhill and Kington w Dormston *Worc 1* **P** *Bp* **R** B E RIENSTRA
NSM D HAYWARD-WRIGHT

INKERSALL (St Columba) *see* Staveley and Barrow Hill *Derby*

INKPEN (St Michael) *see* Walbury Beacon *Ox*

INNS COURT (Holy Cross) *see* Filwood Park *Bris*

INSKIP (St Peter) *see* Copp w Inskip *Blackb*

INSTOW (All Saints Chapel) *see* Fremington, Instow and Westleigh *Ex*

INSTOW (St John the Baptist) *as above*

INTWOOD (All Saints) *see* Swardeston w E Carleton, Intwood, Keswick etc *Nor*

INWARDLEIGH (St Petroc) *see* Okehampton, Inwardleigh, Belstone, Sourton etc *Ex*

INWORTH (All Saints) *see* Thurstable and Winstree *Chelmsf*

IPING (St Mary) *see* Linch w Iping Marsh, Milland and Rake etc *Chich*

IPPLEPEN (St Andrew) w Torbryan, Denbury, Broadhempston and Woodland *Ex 9* **P** *The Crown (1 turn), D&C Windsor and SMF (jt)* **R** A S DOWN

IPSDEN (St Mary the Virgin) *see* Langtree *Ox*

IPSLEY (St Peter) *Worc 7* **P** *Patr Bd* **TR** G E P NATHANIEL **TV** R W HARDING **NSM** I D EVANS

IPSWICH (All Hallows) *St E 1* **P** *Bp* **P-in-c** C MANSELL

IPSWICH (All Saints) *see* Triangle, St Matt and All SS *St E*

IPSWICH (St Augustine of Hippo) *St E 1* **P** *Bp* **NSM** I G DANIELS

IPSWICH (St Bartholomew) *St E 1* **P** *Bp* **V** P J CARTER

IPSWICH (St Helen) (Holy Trinity) (St Clement w St Luke) *St E 1* **P** *Ch Patr Trust* **P-in-c** T ROUT

IPSWICH (St John the Baptist) (St Andrew) *St E 1* **P** *Simeon's Trustees and Bp (jt)* **V** M N PRENTICE **NSM** J BACHU

IPSWICH (St Margaret) *St E 1* **P** *Simeon's Trustees* **V** D CUTTS

IPSWICH (St Mary at Stoke) (St Peter) (St Francis) (St Clare's Church Centre) *St E 1* **P** *Bp* **TR** R C HINSLEY **TV** J FENNELL C D L GIBBS **NSM** K PALMER, M J DYE

IPSWICH (St Mary at the Elms) *St E 1* **P** *Guild of All So* **P-in-c** J A THACKRAY

IPSWICH (St Mary-le-Tower) (St Nicholas) *St E 1* **P** *Bp (3 turns), Ch Patr Trust (1 turn)* **V** C A G JENKIN **NSM** J M GOSNEY

IPSWICH (St Matthew) *see* Triangle, St Matt and All SS *St E*

IPSWICH (St Thomas) *St E 1* **P** *Bp* **P-in-c** J BRUECK **C** C H V CONNOLLY

IPSWICH Triangle (Community Centre) *see* Triangle, St Matt and All SS *St E*

IPSWICH Waterfront Churches *see* Ipswich St Helen, H Trin, and St Luke *St E*

IPSWICH, SOUTH WEST *see* Ipswich St Mary at Stoke w St Pet and St Fran *St E*

IRBY (St Chad's Mission Church) *see* Thurstaston *Ches*

IRBY ON HUMBER (St Andrew) *see* Wolds Gateway Group *Linc*

IRBY-IN-THE-MARSH (All Saints) *see* Burgh Gp *Linc*

IRCHESTER (St Katharine) w Stanton Cross *Pet 6* **P** *Bp* **V** C M LOMAS

IREBY (St James) *see* Binsey *Carl*

IRELAND WOOD (St Paul) *Leeds 15* **P** *R Adel* **V** M J HARLOW **C** M D BROUGHTON

IRLAM (St John the Baptist) *Man 18* **P** *Trustees* **V** J E WARHURST

IRNHAM (St Andrew) *see* Corby Glen *Linc*

IRON ACTON (St James the Less) *see* Fromeside *Bris*

IRONBRIDGE (St Luke) *see* Coalbrookdale, Iron-Bridge and Lt Wenlock *Heref*

IRONSTONE VILLAGES Family of Churches, The, comprising Eastwell, Eaton, Goadby Marwood, Scalford, Stonesby, and Waltham-on-the-Wolds *Leic 2* **P** *Lady Gretton, Ld Chan, Duke of Rutland, Bp, and Sir Lyonel Tollemache Bt (by turn)* **R** M J A BARR

IRONSTONE: Drayton, Hanwell, Horley, Hornton, Shenington w Alkerton, and Wroxton w Balscote *Ox 23* **P** *Ld Chan (1 turn), Bp, Earl De la Warr, and DBP (1 turn)* **R** J READER

IRONVILLE (Christ Church) *see* Riddings and Ironville *Derby*

IRSTEAD (St Michael) *see* Ashmanhaugh, Barton Turf etc *Nor*

IRTHINGTON (St Kentigern) *see* Eden, Gelt and Irthing *Carl*

IRTHLINGBOROUGH (St Peter), Great Addington, Little Addington and Woodford *Pet 8* **P** *Bp, Sir Philip Naylor-Leyland Bt, and DBP (jt)* **R** J T P HALL **NSM** P M TATE

IRTON (St Paul) *see* Black Combe, Drigg, Eskdale etc *Carl*

ISEL (St Michael) *see* Binsey *Carl*

ISFIELD (St Margaret) *Chich 18* **P** *Abp* **Hon C** M D BLANCH

ISHAM (St Peter) *see* Gt w Lt Harrowden and Orlingbury and Isham etc *Pet*

ISLE ABBOTTS (Blessed Virgin Mary) *see* Isle Valley *B & W*

ISLE BREWERS (All Saints) *as above*

ISLE OF DOGS (Christ Church and St John) (St Luke) *Lon 7* **P** *Bp* **V** T F PYKE **C** E J DIX

ISLE VALLEY, comprising Ashill, Broadway, Donyatt, Hambridge w Earnshill, Horton, Ilton, Isle Abbotts, and Isle Brewers *B & W 16* **P** *Bp, D&C Bris, and Dr W P Palmer (jt)* **V** P DENISON

ISLEHAM (St Andrew) *see* Three Rivers Gp *Ely*

ISLES OF SCILLY: St Mary's, St Agnes, St Martin's, Bryher and Tresco *Truro 6* **P** *Duchy of Cornwall* **Chapl** P R GAY

ISLEWORTH (All Saints) *Lon 11* **P** *D&C Windsor* **V** A C WALTON **NSM** C I G M E O GISLESKOG

ISLEWORTH (St Francis of Assisi) *Lon 11* **P** *Bp* **V** P VANNOZZI

ISLEWORTH (St John the Baptist) (St Mary the Virgin) *Lon 11* **P** *Bp and V Isleworth All SS (jt)* **V** D S MACLURE **C** O A DOUGLAS-PENNANT

ISLEWORTH (St Luke) *see* Spring Grove St Mary *Lon*

ISLEWORTH (St Mary) Osterley Road *as above*

ISLEY WALTON (All Saints) *see* Ashby-de-la-Zouch and Breedon on the Hill *Leic*

ISLINGTON (St James the Apostle) (St Peter) *Lon 6* **P** *Bp* **V** A J BURNISTON

ISLINGTON (St Jude and St Paul) *see* Mildmay Grove St Jude and St Paul *Lon*

ISLINGTON (St Mark) *see* Clerkenwell St Mark *Lon*

ISLINGTON (St Mary Magdalene) *see* Hope Ch Islington *Lon*

ISLINGTON (St Mary) *Lon 6* **P** *CPAS* **C** C E SHUTTLEWORTH

ISLINGTON Hope Church *see* Hope Ch Islington *Lon*

ISLIP (St Nicholas) *see* Ray Valley *Ox*

ISLIP (St Nicholas) *see* Thrapston, Denford and Islip *Pet*

ISTEAD RISE (St Barnabas) *Roch 1* **P** *Bp* **V** A K VAUGHAN

ITCHEN ABBAS (St John the Baptist) *see* Itchen Valley *Win*

ITCHEN VALLEY, The, comprising Avington, Easton, Itchen Abbas, and Martyr Worthy *Win 1* **P** *Ld Chan* **P-in-c** A M PEASE

ITCHEN, UPPER, comprising Beauworth, Bramdean, Cheriton, Hinton Ampner, Kilmeston, and Tichborne *Win 1* **P** *The Crown (2 turns), D&C (1 turn)* **R** C W DURRANT **C** J C BROOKSHAW

ITCHENOR, WEST (St Nicholas) *see* W Wittering and Birdham w Itchenor *Chich*

ITCHINGFIELD (St Nicholas) w Slinfold *Chich 6* **P** *Bp* **R** S J HALL **NSM** R A CATTELL

ITTERINGHAM *see* Aylsham and Distr *Nor*

IVEGILL (Christ Church) *see* Inglewood Gp *Carl*

IVER (St Peter) *Ox 12* **P** *Trustees* **V** R H GOODING

IVER HEATH (St Margaret) *Ox 12* **P** *Trustees* **R** A S MONTGOMERIE

IVINGHOE (St Mary the Virgin) w Pitstone and Slapton and Marsworth *Ox 15* **P** *Bp and Ch Ch Ox (jt)* **V** A P MANNING

IVINGTON (St John) *see* Leominster *Heref*

IVYBRIDGE (St John the Evangelist) w Harford *Ex 20* **P** *Bp* **V** *vacant*

IVYCHURCH (St George) *see* Romney Marsh *Cant*

IWADE (All Saints) *see* The Six *Cant*

IWERNE COURTNEY (St Mary) *see* Iwerne Valley *Sarum*

IWERNE MINSTER (St Mary) *as above*

IWERNE VALLEY, comprising Ashmore, Fontmell Magna, Iwerne Courtney and Iwerne Steepleton, Iwerne Minster, and Sutton Waldron *Sarum 7* **P** *D&C Windsor, DBP, G A L F Pitt-Rivers Esq, and Mrs P Kelway-Bamber (jt)* **V** D W JOHN **Hon C** J E WARING

IXWORTH (St Mary) *see* Blackbourne *St E*

IXWORTH THORPE (All Saints) *as above*

JACKFIELD (St Mary) *see* Broseley w Benthall, Jackfield, Linley etc *Heref*

JACOBSTOW (St James) *see* Week St Mary Circle of Par *Truro*

JACOBSTOWE (St James) *see* Okehampton, Inwardleigh, Belstone, Sourton etc *Ex*

JARROW (St John the Baptist) (St Paul) (St Peter) and Simonside *Dur 13* **P** *The Crown and Bp (alt)* **R** G H MAUDE **C** S G HILL

JARROW GRANGE (Christ Church) *Dur 13* **P** *Lord Northbourne* **P-in-c** I M SOMASUNDRAM

JARVIS BROOK (St Michael and All Angels) *Chich 16* **P** *Bp* **V** A W WEAVER

JERSEY (All Saints) *Win 15* **P** *R St Helier, Bp, and The Crown (by turn)* **V** D G GRANTHAM

JERSEY (Holy Trinity) *Win 15* **P** *The Crown* **R** G J HOUGHTON

JERSEY (St Andrew) *Win 15* **P** *Dean of Jersey* **V** M H BARRETT

JERSEY (St Brelade) (Communicare Chapel) (St Aubin) *Win 15* **P** *The Crown* **R** M F W BOND

JERSEY (St Clement) *Win 15* **P** *The Crown* **R** D M SHAW **NSM** M J DRYDEN, T L C BROMLEY

JERSEY (St Helier) *Win 15* **P** *The Crown* **R** M R KEIRLE **NSM** A D WILLIAMS

JERSEY (St John) *Win 15* **P** *The Crown* **R** B L SPROATS

JERSEY (St Lawrence) *Win 15* **P** *The Crown* **R** P J WARREN

JERSEY (St Luke) St James *Win 15* **P** *Bp and The Crown (alt)* **V** N B P BARRY

JERSEY (St Mark) *Win 15* **P** *Bp* **V** M P L SHEA **C** G S J BARTLEMAN

JERSEY (St Martin) *Win 15* **P** *The Crown* **P-in-c** J A SCOTT

JERSEY (St Mary) *Win 15* **P** *The Crown* **R** T J NEILL

JERSEY (St Ouen) (St George) *Win 15* **P** *The Crown*
R I PALLENT   **NSM** H L GUNTON
JERSEY (St Paul) Proprietary Chapel *Win 15*
Min P J BROOKS
JERSEY (St Peter) *Win 15* **P** *The Crown*   **R** M J PHILLIPS
JERSEY (St Saviour) *Win 15* **P** P W DYSON
JERSEY (St Simon) *Win 15* **P** *R St Helier, Bp, and The Crown
(by turn)* **V** D G GRANTHAM
JERSEY DE GROUVILLE (St Martin) (St Peter la Roque)
Win 15 **P** *The Crown* **R** *vacant*
JERSEY Gouray (St Martin) *Win 15* **P** *Bp and The Crown (alt)*
V J R WATTLEY
JERSEY Greve d'Azette (St Nicholas) *see Jersey St Clem Win*
JERSEY Millbrook (St Matthew) *Win 15* **P** *The Crown*
V P J WARREN
JESMOND (Clayton Memorial Church) *Newc 2* **P** *Trustees*
V D R J HOLLOWAY   **C** J J S PRYKE   **Hon C** A F MUNDEN
JESMOND (Holy Trinity) *Newc 2* **P** *Patr Bd*   **C** T SANDERSON
JESMOND (St George) *see Newc St Geo and St Hilda Newc*
JESMOND (St Hilda) *as above*
JEVINGTON (St Andrew) *see E Dean w Friston and Jevington
Chich*
JOYDENS WOOD (St Barnabas) *see Bexley Roch*
JURBY (St Patrick) *see Andreas, Ballaugh, Jurby and Sulby
S & M*
KATE'S HILL (St John) *see Dudley St Jo Worc*
KEA (All Hallows) (Old Church) *Truro 6* **P** *V St Clement*
P-in-c M C BAKER   **C** W F HARWOOD
KEAL, EAST (St Helen) *see Bolingbroke Deanery Linc*
KEAL, WEST (St Helen) *as above*
KEARSLEY (St Stephen) *see Farnworth, Kearsley and
Stoneclough Man*
KEASDEN (St Matthew) *see Clapham-with-Keasden and
Austwick Leeds*
KEDINGTON (St Peter and St Paul) *see Stourhead St E*
KEEDWELL HILL (Ascension) *see Long Ashton w Barrow
Gurney and Flax Bourton B & W*
KEELBY (St Bartholomew) *see Wolds Gateway Group Linc*
KEELE (St John the Baptist) *Lich 9* **P** T H G Howard-Sneyd
Esq **V** P C JONES
KEEVIL (St Leonard) *see Trowbridge St Jas and Keevil Sarum*
**KEGWORTH (St Andrew), Hathern, Long Whatton,
Diseworth, Belton and Osgathorpe** *Leic 6* **P** *Patr Bd*
TR L J WILSON   **TV** L D CORKE
KEIGHLEY (All Saints) (St Andrew) *Leeds 1* **P** *Patr Bd*
TR M C CANSDALE   **TV** G A J POTTER, J L PRITCHARD
C T A RAISTRICK   **Hon C** M S FOY   **NSM** J LONG,
J M INESON, N C THOMAS
KEINTON MANDEVILLE (St Mary Magdalene) *see Wheathill
Priory Gp B & W*
KELBROOK (St Mary) *see Earby w Kelbrook Leeds*
KELBY (St Andrew) *see E Loveden Linc*
KELHAM (St Wilfrid) *see Averham w Kelham S'well*
KELLET, NETHER (St Mark) *see Bolton-le-Sands Blackb*
KELLET, OVER (St Cuthbert) *Blackb 14* **P** *Reformation Ch
Trust* **V** P R BOULTER
KELLING (St Mary) *see Weybourne Gp Nor*
KELLINGTON (St Edmund) *see Knottingley and Kellington
w Whitley Leeds*
KELLOE (St Helen) and Coxhoe *Dur 1* **P** *Bp* **V** *vacant*
KELLS (St Peter) *Carl 5* **P** *Bp* **NSM** A J BANKS
KELLY (St Mary the Virgin) *see Lifton, Broadwoodwidger,
Stowford etc Ex*
KELMARSH (St Denys) *see Clipston, Haselbech, Kelmarsh,
Marston Trussell etc Pet*
KELMSCOTT (St George) *see Shill Valley and Broadshire Ox*
KELSALE (St Peter) *see Saxmundham w Kelsale cum Carlton
St E*
KELSALL (St Philip) *Ches 2* **P** *V Tarvin* **NSM** K M ANDREWS
KELSEY, NORTH (All Hallows) *see Woldmoor Gp Linc*
KELSEY, SOUTH (St Mary) *as above*
KELSHALL (St Faith) *see Therfield w Kelshall St Alb*
KELSTERN (St Faith) *see Binbrook Gp Linc*
KELSTON (St Nicholas) *see Bath Weston St Jo w Kelston
B & W*
KELVEDON (St Mary the Virgin) and Feering *Chelmsf 24*
P *Bp* **P-in-c** S F GARWOOD
KELVEDON HATCH (St Nicholas) *see Bentley Common,
Kelvedon Hatch and Navestock Chelmsf*
KEMBERTON (St Andrew) *see Beckbury, Badger, Kemberton,
Ryton, Stockton etc Lich*
**KEMBLE (All Saints), Poole Keynes, Somerford Keynes w
Sharncote, Coates, Rodmarton and Sapperton w
Frampton Mansell** *Glouc 7* **P** *Bp, Lord Bathurst, Mrs L R
Rank, Guild of All So, and DBP (2 turns), Duchy of Lanc
(1 turn)* **R** T G KEMP   **NSM** D R E AUSTIN

KEMERTON (St Nicholas) *see Ashchurch and Kemerton
Glouc*
KEMP TOWN (St Mary) *Chich 19* **P** *Bp, Mrs R A Hinton,
A C R Elliott Esq, T J Elliott Esq, and the Revd Canon D H
McKittrick (jt)* **V** A J WOODWARD   **NSM** H M BENNETT
KEMPLEY (St Edward) *see Redmarley D'Abitot,
Bromesberrow, Pauntley etc Glouc*
**KEMPSEY (St Mary the Virgin) and Severn Stoke w
Croome d'Abitot** *Worc 5* **P** *D&C and Croome Estate
Trustees (alt)* **R** M BADGER
KEMPSFORD (St Mary) *see S Cotswolds Glouc*
KEMPSHOTT (St Mark) *Win 4* **P** *Bp* **V** N J SUCH
KEMPSTON (All Saints) *St Alb 9* **P** *Bp* **V** E J LOMAX
KEMPSTON (Transfiguration) *St Alb 9* **P** *Bp*
V S K C RICHARDSON
KEMSING (St Mary the Virgin) and Woodlands *Roch 10*
P *DBP* **P-in-c** J R OAKLEY
KENARDINGTON (St Mary) *see Saxon Shoreline Cant*
KENCHESTER (St Michael) *see Magnis Gp Heref*
KENCOT (St George) *see Shill Valley and Broadshire Ox*
KENDAL (Holy Trinity) (All Hallows Chapel) *Carl 10* **P** *Trin
Coll Cam* **P-in-c** R J SANER-HAIGH   **C** A F UNDERWOOD
NSM G SKILLING, P A HENDERSON
KENDAL (St George) *see Beacon Carl*
KENDAL (St Thomas) *Carl 10* **P** *CPAS* **P-in-c** G W BRIGGS
KENDAL (St Thomas) *see Beacon Carl*
KENDRAY (St Andrew) *Sheff 12* **P** *V Ardsley*
V P C W JACKSON
KENILWORTH (St John) *Cov 4* **P** *Simeon's Trustees*
V A M ATTWOOD   **Hon C** J E ARMSTRONG
KENILWORTH (St Nicholas) (St Barnabas) *Cov 4* **P** *Ld Chan*
V S BAILEY   **C** A G BAXTER, R B R MOORE
KENLEY (All Saints) *S'wark 22* **P** *Abp* **P-in-c** J MIDDLEMISS
NSM E J GOODRIDGE
KENLEY (St John the Baptist) *see Wenlock Heref*
KENN (St Andrew) *see Exminster, Kenn, Kenton w
Mamhead, and Powderham Ex*
KENN (St John the Evangelist) *see Yatton Moor B & W*
KENNERLEIGH (St John the Baptist) *see N Creedy Ex*
KENNET, EAST (Christ Church) *see Upper Kennet Sarum*
KENNETT (St Nicholas) *see Three Rivers Gp Ely*
KENNINGHALL (St Mary) *see Guiltcross Nor*
KENNINGTON (St John the Divine w St James the Apostle)
S'wark 11 **P** *Ripon Coll Cuddesdon and Bp (jt)*
V M WILLIAMS   **C** H HARKNETT, N J QUANRUD
NSM S D T HARRIES, S LABRAN
KENNINGTON (St Mark) *S'wark 11* **P** *Abp* **V** S H COULSON
KENNINGTON (St Mary) *see Ashford Town Cant*
KENNINGTON (St Swithun) *see Radley, Sunningwell and
Kennington Ox*
KENNINGTON CROSS (St Anselm) *see N Lambeth S'wark*
KENNINGTON PARK (St Agnes) *S'wark 10* **P** *SMF*
V P G ENSOR
KENSAL GREEN (St John) *Lon 2* **P** *Bp* **V** D M ACKERMAN
KENSAL RISE (St Mark) *Lon 21* **P** *Bp and Trustees (jt)*
V W P G LEAF   **C** A M CARMICHAEL, R J BEDFORD
KENSAL RISE (St Martin) *Lon 21* **P** *Bp and Trustees (jt)*
V G P NOYCE   **C** S V SCHUIL-BREWER   **Hon C** E J BARRATT
KENSAL TOWN (St Thomas) (St Andrew) (St Philip) *Lon 12*
P *Hyndman Trustees* **V** S J MCNALLY-CROSS
KENSINGTON (Christ Church) *Lon 12* **P** *Bp*
V M R O'DONOGHUE   **C** M HARRIS, R G POWELL
KENSINGTON (Holy Trinity w All Saints) *see S Kensington H
Trin w All SS Lon*
KENSINGTON (St Barnabas) *Lon 12* **P** *V Kensington St Mary
Abbots w St Geo and Ch Ch* **V** A J H BUCKLER   **C** J J SERGENT
KENSINGTON (St Clement) *see Notting Dale St Clem w
St Mark and St Jas Lon*
KENSINGTON (St George) *see Holland Park Lon*
KENSINGTON (St Helen) (Holy Trinity) *Lon 12* **P** *Bp*
V S R DIVALL   **C** A M HOLT
KENSINGTON (St James) *see Notting Dale St Clem w
St Mark and St Jas Lon*
KENSINGTON (St Luke) *see S Kensington St Luke Lon*
KENSINGTON (St Mary Abbots) *Lon 12* **P** *Bp*
V E R DINWIDDY SMITH   **C** J N A MACNEANEY
KENSINGTON (St Stephen) *see S Kensington St Steph Lon*
KENSINGTON All Saints *see Liv All SS Liv*
KENSINGTON, SOUTH (Holy Trinity w All Saints) *Lon 3*
P *D&C Westmr* **P-in-c** E M V RUSSELL   **NSM** P KETTLE
KENSINGTON, SOUTH (St Luke) *Lon 8* **P** *Ch Patr Trust*
V A N BEAVIS
KENSINGTON, SOUTH (St Stephen) *Lon 12* **P** *Guild of All
So* **P-in-c** P R BARNES
KENSINGTON, WEST (St Andrew) *see Fulham St Andr Lon*

KENSINGTON, WEST (St Mary)   *see* Fulham St Mary N End *Lon*

KENSINGTON, WEST (St Mary) The Boltons   *see* W Brompton St Mary w St Peter and St Jude *Lon*

KENSWORTH (St Mary the Virgin), Studham and Whipsnade *St Alb 11*   **P** *Ld Chan and D&C St Paul's (alt)*   **V** N Y LENTHALL

KENTCHURCH (St Mary)   *see* Ewyas Harold w Dulas, Kenderchurch etc *Heref*

KENTFORD (St Mary)   *see* Dalham, Gazeley, Higham, Kentford and Moulton *St E*

KENTISBEARE (St Mary)   *see* Willand, Uffculme, Kentisbeare etc *Ex*

KENTISBURY (St Thomas)   *see* Shirwell, Loxhore, Kentisbury, Arlington, etc *Ex*

KENTISH TOWN (St Benet and All Saints) *Lon 17*   **P** *The Crown and D&C St Paul's (alt)*   **V** P B ANTHONY   **NSM** N S PALMER

KENTISH TOWN (St Luke)   *see* Oseney Crescent St Luke *Lon*

KENTISH TOWN (St Martin) (St Andrew) *Lon 17*   **P** *Exors Dame Jewell Magnus-Allcroft*   **V** C M BARRETT FORD

KENTISH TOWN (St Silas) and (Holy Trinity) w St Barnabas *Lon 17*   **P** *Bp and D&C St Paul's (jt)*   **V** G C ROWLANDS

KENTMERE (St Cuthbert)   *see* Staveley, Ings and Kentmere *Carl*

KENTON (All Saints)   *see* Debenham and Helmingham *St E*

KENTON (All Saints)   *see* Exminster, Kenn, Kenton w Mamhead, and Powderham *Ex*

KENTON (Ascension) *Newc 2*   **P** *Bp*   **P-in-c** A A PLUMMER

KENTON (St Mary the Virgin) *Lon 23*   **P** *Bp*   **V** E J LEWIS   **C** M J CASHMORE   **NSM** M J STILL

KENTON, SOUTH (Annunciation) *Lon 21*   **P** *Bp*   **NSM** T P GODDARD

KENWYN (St Keyne) w St Allen *Truro 6*   **P** *Bp*   **R** C P PARSONS   **OLM** R W HUMPHRIES

KERESLEY (St Thomas) and Coundon *Cov 2*   **P** *Bp*   **V** M NORRIS

KERESLEY END (Church of the Ascension)   *see* Keresley and Coundon *Cov*

KERRIDGE (Holy Trinity)   *see* Bollington *Ches*

KERRIER, WEST, comprising Breage w Godolphin and Ashton, Porthleven, Sithney, and St Germoe *Truro 4*   **P** *Bp and The Crown (alt)*   **V** *vacant*

KERSAL MOOR (St Paul) *Man 20*   **P** *Trustees*   **R** L P LONGDEN   **C** O D EDWARDS   **OLM** H A SHEDLOCK, M J DYSON

KERSAL, LOWER (St Aidan)   *see* Salford All SS *Man*

KERSEY (St Mary)   *see* Elmsett w Aldham, Hintlesham, Chattisham etc *St E*

KERSWELL GREEN (St John the Baptist)   *see* Kempsey and Severn Stoke w Croome d'Abitot *Worc*

KESGRAVE (All Saints) *St E 1*   **P** *Bp*   **V** R SPITTLE   **NSM** G JONES

KESSINGLAND (St Edmund), Gisleham and Rushmere *Nor 9*   **P** *Ld Chan (1 turns) and Bp (2 turns)*   **R** M L BISHOP

KESTON (not known) (St Audrey) *Roch 16*   **P** *D&C*   **R** C F MORRISON

KESWICK (All Saints)   *see* Swardeston w E Carleton, Intwood, Keswick etc *Nor*

KESWICK (St John) w Borrowdale *Carl 6*   **P** *Trustees*   **V** C H HOPE

KESWICK, EAST (St Mary Magdalene)   *see* Bardsey *Leeds*

KETLEY (St Mary the Virgin)   *see* Cen Telford *Lich*

KETTERING (All Saints) *Pet 9*   **P** *SMF*   **V** *vacant*

KETTERING (Christ the King) *Pet 9*   **P** *R Barton Seagrave w Warkton*   **V** R J BEWLEY   **C** E R JEANS, P J KELLEHER

KETTERING (St Andrew) *Pet 9*   **P** *Bp*   **V** N R WILLS

KETTERING (St Mary the Virgin) (St John the Evangelist) *Pet 9*   **P** *SMF*   **P-in-c** J E MOWBRAY

KETTERING (St Peter and St Paul) (St Michael and All Angels) *Pet 9*   **P** *Comdr L M M Saunders Watson*   **R** D C WALSH   **C** A L J WATSON, C R WALSH

KETTERINGHAM (St Peter)   *see* Swardeston w E Carleton, Intwood, Keswick etc *Nor*

KETTLEBASTON (St Mary)   *see* Monks Eleigh w Chelsworth and Brent Eleigh etc *St E*

KETTLEBROOK (St Andrew)   *see* Tamworth *Lich*

KETTLEBURGH (St Andrew)   *see* Orebeck *St E*

KETTLESTONE (All Saints)   *see* Barney, Hindringham, Thursford, Great Snoring, Little Snoring and Kettlestone and Pensthorpe *Nor*

KETTLETHORPE (St Peter and St Paul)   *see* Saxilby Gp *Linc*

KETTLEWELL (St Mary)   *see* Upper Wharfedale and Littondale *Leeds*

KETTON (St Mary the Virgin) and Tinwell *Pet 12*   **P** *Bp and Burghley Ho Preservation Trust Ltd (jt)*   **V** *vacant*

KEW (St Anne) *S'wark 16*   **P** *The Crown*   **V** N J WORN

KEW (St Francis of Assisi) *Liv 9*   **P** *Bp, Adn Warrington, and V Southport All SS and All So (jt)*   **V** A P J GALBRAITH

KEW (St Philip and All Saints) (St Luke) *S'wark 16*   **P** *Bp*   **V** P W HART

KEWSTOKE (St Paul)   *see* Milton and Kewstoke *B & W*

KEYHAM, NORTH (St Thomas)   *see* Plymouth St Pet and H Apostles *Ex*

KEYINGHAM (St Nicholas)   *see* Easington w Skeffling, Keyingham, Ottringham etc *York*

KEYMER (St Cosmas and St Damian)   *see* Clayton w Keymer *Chich*

KEYMER (St Francis of Assisi)   *as above*

KEYNSHAM (St Francis) (St John the Baptist) *B & W 9*   **P** *Patr Bd*   **TR** S A M'CAW   **TV** M R BURKE   **C** N M WILLIAMS

KEYSOE (St Mary the Virgin)   *see* Bolnhurst w Keysoe *St Alb*

KEYSTON (St John the Baptist)   *see* W Leightonstone *Ely*

KEYWORTH (St Mary Magdalene) and Stanton-on-the-Wolds and Bunny w Bradmore *S'well 5*   **P** *Bp and Ld Chan (alt)*   **R** T H C MEYRICK

KIBWORTH (St Wilfrid) and Smeeton Westerby and Saddington *Leic 3*   **P** *Mert Coll Ox and Bp (jt)*   **R** L FREMMER

KIDBROOKE (St James) *S'wark 1*   **P** *Patr Bd*   **R** K W HITCH   **NSM** S R ASTON

KIDBROOKE (St Nicholas) *S'wark 1*   **P** *Bp and Simeon's Trustees (jt)*   **V** T M LINKENS

KIDDERMINSTER (St John the Baptist) (Holy Innocents) *Worc 11*   **P** *Patr Bd*   **TR** T J WILLIAMS   **TV** L C BETSON   **NSM** A VACCARO

KIDDERMINSTER (St Mary and All Saints) Ismere *Worc 11*   **P** *Patr Bd*   **TR** N R TAYLOR   **TV** B A WOODALL, S A ARCHER

KIDDERMINSTER EAST (St George) (St Chad) (St Cecilia) *Worc 11*   **P** *Ld Chan (1 turn), Patr Bd (2 turns)*   **TV** R J LEGGE

KIDDERMINSTER WEST   *see* Kidderminster St Jo and H Innocents *Worc*

KIDDINGTON (St Nicholas)   *see* Wootton w Glympton and Kiddington *Ox*

KIDLINGTON (St Mary the Virgin) w Hampton Poyle *Ox 2*   **P** *Patr Bd*   **TR** F M-L SCROGGIE   **TV** M J DAVIS

KIDLINGTON, SOUTH (St John the Baptist)   *see* Kidlington w Hampton Poyle *Ox*

KIDMORE END (St John the Baptist)   *see* Rotherfield Peppard and Kidmore End etc *Ox*

KIDSGROVE (St Thomas) *Lich 9*   **P** *MMCET*   **V** I BAKER

KILBURN (Mission Room)   *see* Denby Gp *Derby*

KILBURN (St Augustine) (St John) *Lon 2*   **P** *SMF*   **V** C J AMOS

KILBURN (St Mary)   *see* Thirkleby w Kilburn and Bagby *York*

KILBURN Priory Road (St Mary) w All Souls and W Hampstead St James *Lon 16*   **P** *Bp, Ch Patr Trust, and trustees (jt)*   **V** R G THOMPSON   **C** C N RINK   **NSM** D L YELDHAM, R HUTCHISON

KILBURN, WEST (St Luke) and Harrow Road Emmanuel *Lon 2*   **P** *CPAS and Hyndman Trustees (jt)*   **V** A G THOM   **C** E A J C WALFORD, J F BARRY

KILBY (St Mary Magdalene)   *see* Wistow *Leic*

KILDALE (St Cuthbert)   *see* Ingleby Greenhow, Bilsdale Priory etc *York*

KILDWICK (St Andrew) *Leeds 4*   **P** *Ch Ch Ox*   **P-in-c** J S BACON

KILHAM (All Saints)   *see* Rudston, Boynton, Carnaby etc *York*

KILKHAMPTON (St James the Great) w Morwenstow *Truro 8*   **P** *DBP and Bp (jt)*   **NSM** R WARD-SMITH

KILLAMARSH (St Giles) and Renishaw *Derby 3*   **P** *The Crown*   **R** H GUEST

KILLERTON (Holy Evangelist)   *see* Broadclyst, Clyst Honiton, Pinhoe, Rockbeare etc *Ex*

KILLINGHALL (St Thomas the Apostle)   *see* Hampsthwaite and Killinghall and Birstwith *Leeds*

KILLINGHOLME, NORTH (St Denys)   *see* Abbey Gp *Linc*

KILLINGTON (All Saints)   *see* Firbank, Howgill and Killington *Carl*

KILLINGWORTH (St John) *Newc 1*   **P** *V Longbenton St Bart*   **C** S A MOON   **NSM** A H MEIGHEN

KILMERSDON (St Peter and St Paul) w Babington *B & W 11*   **P** *Lord Hylton*   **R** D A IZZARD

KILMESTON (St Andrew)   *see* Upper Itchen *Win*

KILMINGTON (St Giles), Stockland, Dalwood, Yarcombe and Shute *Ex 4*   **P** *Bp and D&C (2 turns), The Crown (1 turn)*   **P-in-c** S A HOLLOWAY

KILMINGTON (St Mary the Virgin)   *see* Upper Stour *Sarum*

KILNDOWN (Christ Church)   *see* Goudhurst w Kilndown *Cant*

KILNGREEN (Diggle Mission Church)   *see* Saddleworth *Man*

KILNHURST (St Thomas) *Sheff 12*   **P** *Ld Chan*
V A R BREWERTON   **C** T A BROWN
KILNWICK (All Saints)   *see* Woldsburn *York*
KILPECK (St Mary and St David)   *see* Ewyas Harold w Dulas,
Kenderchurch etc *Heref*
KILSBY (St Faith)   *see* Daventry *Pet*
KILVE (Blessed Virgin Mary)   *see* Quantock Coast *B & W*
KILVERSTONE (St Andrew)   *see* Thetford *Nor*
KILVINGTON (St Mary) *S'well 3*   **P** E G Staunton Esq
P-in-c E I MURRAY
KILVINGTON, SOUTH (St Wilfrid)   *see* Thirsk *York*
KILWORTH, NORTH (St Andrew)   *see* Avon-Swift *Leic*
KILWORTH, SOUTH (St Nicholas) *as above*
KIMBERLEY (Holy Trinity) and Nuthall *S'well 8*   **P** *Bp*
R B M HOLBROOK   **NSM** G M HALL
KIMBERLEY (St Peter)   *see* Barnham Broom and Upper Yare
Nor
KIMBERWORTH (St Thomas) (St Mark) and Kimberworth
Park *Sheff 6*   **P** *Bp*   **C** L S WORTLEY
KIMBERWORTH PARK (St John)   *see* Kimberworth and
Kimberworth Park *Sheff*
KIMBLE, GREAT (St Nicholas)   *see* Ellesborough, The Kimbles
and Stoke Mandeville *Ox*
KIMBLE, LITTLE (All Saints) *as above*
KIMBLESWORTH (St Philip and St James)   *see* Dur N *Dur*
KIMBOLTON (St Andrew)   *see* S Leightonstone *Ely*
KIMBOLTON (St James the Great)   *see* Leominster *Heref*
KIMCOTE (All Saints)   *see* Avon-Swift *Leic*
KIMMERIDGE (St Nicholas of Myra)   *see* St Aldhelm *Sarum*
KIMPTON (St Peter and St Paul)   *see* Appleshaw, Kimpton,
Thruxton, Fyfield etc *Win*
KIMPTON (St Peter and St Paul) w Ayot St Lawrence
St Alb 7   **P** *Bp*   **P-in-c** L L P WILLIAMS
KINETON (St Peter)   *see* Edgehill Churches *Cov*
KING CROSS (St Paul) *Leeds 10*   **P** *Bp*   **V** K J BARNARD
KING STERNDALE (Christ Church)   *see* Buxton w Burbage
and King Sterndale *Derby*
KINGHAM (St Andrew)   *see* Chipping Norton *Ox*
KINGMOOR (St Peter)   *see* Houghton *Carl*
KING'S BECK, comprising Banningham, Colby, Felmingham,
Skeyton, Sloley, Suffield, Swanton Abbot, and Tuttington
Nor 12   **P** *Bp, D&C, P H C Barber Esq, S D Shaw Esq, and DBP
(jt)*   **R** K R DALLY
KINGS BROMLEY (All Saints), The Ridwares and Yoxall
Lich 1   **P** *Bp, D&C, and Personal Reps Lord Leigh (jt)*
R *vacant*
KING'S CAPLE (St John the Baptist)   *see* StowCaple *Heref*
KING'S CLIFFE (All Saints), Bulwick and Blatherwycke,
Collyweston, Easton-on-the-Hill and Laxton *Pet 10*   **P** *Bp,
Exors G T G Conant, F&A George Ltd, and Burghley Ho
Preservation Trust Ltd (2 turns), Ld Chan (1 turn)*
V P J DAVIES
KINGS HEATH (All Saints) *Birm 4*   **P** *V Moseley St Mary*
V Q D WARBRICK
KINGS HEATH (Church on the Heath) *Pet 4*   **P** *Bp*
V R A WOODS
KINGS LANGLEY (All Saints)   *see* Langelei *St Alb*
KING'S LYNN (All Saints)   *see* S Lynn *Nor*
KING'S LYNN (St John the Evangelist) *Nor 19*   **P** *Bp*
V R J ROGERS
KING'S LYNN (St Margaret) w St Nicholas *Nor 19*   **P** *D&C*
TR C J IVORY   **TV** R J ROGERS   **C** A C RAYNER
KING'S LYNN (St Peter)   *see* Clenchwarton and W Lynn *Ely*
KING'S NORTON (St John the Baptist)   *see* Gaulby *Leic*
KINGS NORTON (St Nicolas) *Birm 3*   **P** *Patr Bd*
TR L C WRIGHT   **C** C E MATLOCK   **NSM** E C IKECHUKWU
KING'S NYMPTON (St James)   *see* S Molton w Nymet
St George, Chittlehamholt etc *Ex*
KING'S PYON (St Mary the Virgin)   *see* Canon Pyon w King's
Pyon, Birley and Wellington *Heref*
KINGS RIPTON (St Peter)   *see* N Leightonstone *Ely*
KING'S STANLEY (St George)   *see* Stroudwater Team *Glouc*
KING'S SUTTON (St Peter and St Paul) and Newbottle and
Charlton *Pet 1*   **P** *SMF and Lady Townsend (jt)*
V M J ROBINSON
KING'S WALDEN (St Mary) and Offley w Lilley *St Alb 3*
P *Sir Thomas Pilkington Bt (2 turns), St Jo Coll Cam (1 turn),
D K C Salusbury-Hughes Esq and Mrs P A L McGrath (2 turns)*
V T J BELL
KING'S WOOD, comprising Challock and Molash, Chilham,
Crundale, and Godmersham *Cant 2*   **P** *Abp and J S Wheeler
Esq (jt)*   **R** *vacant*
KING'S WORTHY (St Mary) (St Mary's Chapel) *Win 7*
P *Univ Coll Ox and Lord Northbrook (alt)*   **R** P E BRADISH
NSM E CHASE

KINGSBRIDGE (St Edmund the King and Martyr),
Dodbrooke, and West Alvington *Ex 13*   **P** *Bp Ex and D&C
Sarum (jt)*   **R** J M TAYLOR
KINGSBURY (Holy Innocents) *Lon 21*   **P** *D&C St Paul's*
V N C WOODWARD   **NSM** S HAMEEM
KINGSBURY (St Andrew) *Lon 21*   **P** *The Crown*   **V** J RENDELL
KINGSBURY (St Peter and St Paul) *Birm 9*   **P** *Bp*
P-in-c J C WHITE   **NSM** C J YOUNG
KINGSBURY EPISCOPI (St Martin)   *see* Martock w Kingsbury
Episcopi and Ash *B & W*
KINGSCLERE (St Mary) and Ashford Hill w Headley *Win 6*
P *Bp*   **V** B S READ
KINGSCLERE WOODLANDS (St Paul)   *see* Kingsclere and
Ashford Hill w Headley *Win*
KINGSCOTE (St John the Baptist)   *see* Nailsworth w
Shortwood, Horsley etc *Glouc*
KINGSDON (All Saints)   *see* Somerton w The Charltons and
Kingsdon *B & W*
KINGSDOWN (St Edmund the King and Martyr) *Roch 10*
P *D&C*   **R** S CORRY   **NSM** H JOHNSON
KINGSDOWN (St John the Evangelist)   *see* Walmer and
Cornilo *Cant*
KINGSDOWN and Creekside *Cant 14*   **P** *Ld Chan (1 turn),
Abp, Adn Cant, D&C, and MMCET (1 turn)*   **V** S H LILLICRAP
KINGSEY (St Nicholas)   *see* Wychert Vale *Ox*
KINGSHURST (St Barnabas) *Birm 8*   **P** *Bp*   **V** F J JOHNSON
KINGSKERSWELL (St Mary), Abbotskerswell and
Coffinswell *Ex 9*   **P** *Ld Chan*   **V** *vacant*
KINGSLAND (St Michael and All Angels) w Eardisland,
Aymestrey and Leinthall Earles *Heref 6*   **P** *DBP (2 turns),
Ld Chan (1 turn)*   **P-in-c** J M READ
KINGSLEY (All Saints)   *see* Northanger *Win*
KINGSLEY (St John the Evangelist)   *see* Norley, Crowton and
Kingsley *Ches*
KINGSLEY (St Werburgh) and Foxt-w-Whiston and
Oakamoor w Cotton *Lich 6*   **P** *R Cheadle w Freehay and Mrs
N A Faulkner (jt)*   **R** S M SYMONS
KINGSNORTH (St Michael and All Angels)   *see* Ashford Town
Cant
KINGSNYMPTON   *see* S Molton w Nymet St George,
Chittlehamholt etc *Ex*
KINGSTAG (not known)   *see* Spire Hill *Sarum*
KINGSTANDING (St Luke) *Birm 2*   **P** *Bp*   **V** B A I SMART
KINGSTANDING (St Mark) *Birm 2*   **P** *Bp*   **V** P CALVERT
KINGSTEIGNTON (St Michael) and Teigngrace *Ex 9*   **P** *Bp*
V M P SMITH   **NSM** S J GILL
KINGSTHORPE (St John the Baptist) (St David) (St Mark)
Pet 4   **P** *Patr Bd*   **TR** L J BUTLER   **TV** R M HETHERINGTON
C D C MAUD
KINGSTON (All Saints and St Andrew)   *see* Papworth *Ely*
KINGSTON (All Saints) (St John the Evangelist) (St John
the Baptist) *S'wark 15*   **P** *Patr Bd*   **TR** J P WILKES
TV A R BECK   **NSM** D BELL
KINGSTON (St Giles)   *see* Barham Downs w Adisham *Cant*
KINGSTON (St James)   *see* Modbury, Bigbury, Ringmore etc
Ex
KINGSTON (St James)   *see* St Aldhelm *Sarum*
KINGSTON (St James)   *see* W Wight *Portsm*
KINGSTON (St Pancras)   *see* Iford w Kingston and Rodmell
and Southease *Chich*
KINGSTON BAGPUIZE (St John the Baptist) w Southmoor   *see*
Fyfield w Tubney and Kingston Bagpuize *Ox*
KINGSTON BUCI (St Giles)   *see* Old Shoreham and Kingston
Buci *Chich*
KINGSTON BUCI (St Julian) *as above*
KINGSTON DEVERILL (St Mary)   *see* Cley Hill Villages *Sarum*
KINGSTON HILL (St Paul) *S'wark 15*   **P** *DBP*   **V** A G RYLETT
NSM F M M DE QUIDT
KINGSTON LACY (St Stephen)   *see* Bridge Par *Sarum*
KINGSTON LISLE (St John the Baptist)   *see* Ridgeway *Ox*
KINGSTON PARK (not known) *Newc 2*   **P** *Bp*   **V** *vacant*
KINGSTON SEYMOUR (All Saints)   *see* Yatton Moor *B & W*
KINGSTON ST MARY (The Blessed Virgin Mary)   *see* S
Quantock *B & W*
KINGSTON UPON HULL (Most Holy and Undivided Trinity)
York 14   **P** *CPAS*   **P-in-c** F WHITE   **NSM** I M WILSON
KINGSTON UPON HULL (St Aidan) Southcoates *York 14*
P *Simeon's Trustees*   **V** R P PHILLIPS
KINGSTON UPON HULL (St Alban) *York 14*   **P** *Abp*
V G P THORNALLEY   **NSM** L A GILLARD
KINGSTON UPON HULL (St Cuthbert)   *see* Hull St Cuth *York*
KINGSTON UPON HULL (St John the Baptist)   *see* Newington
w Hull St Andr *York*
KINGSTON UPON HULL (St Martin)   *see* Hull St Martin w
Transfiguration *York*

KINGSTON UPON HULL (St Mary the Virgin) *York 14*
P *Abp* **P-in-c** J TALLANT
KINGSTON UPON HULL (St Matthew) *see* Newington w
Hull St Andr *York*
KINGSTON UPON HULL (St Nicholas) *York 14* **P** *Abp*
V P COPLEY **C** J R FOREMAN
KINGSTON UPON HULL (St Paul) *see* Sculcoates *York*
KINGSTON UPON HULL (St Stephen) *as above*
KINGSTON UPON THAMES (All Saints) *see* Kingston *S'wark*
KINGSTON UPON THAMES (St John the Evangelist) *as above*
KINGSTON UPON THAMES (St Luke) *S'wark 15* **P** *Bp*
V M G HISLOP
KINGSTON VALE (St John the Baptist) *see* Kingston *S'wark*
KINGSTONE (St John and All Saints) *see* Winsmoor *B & W*
KINGSTONE (St John the Baptist) *see* Uttoxeter Area *Lich*
KINGSTONE (St Michael and All Angels) *see* Cagebrook *Heref*
KINGSTON-ON-SOAR (St Winifred) *see* A453 churches of S
Notts *S'well*
KINGSWEAR (St Thomas of Canterbury) *see* Brixham w
Churston Ferrers and Kingswear *Ex*
KINGSWINFORD (St Mary) *Worc 10* **P** *Bp* **R** G KENDALL
KINGSWOOD (Church of the Ascension) (Holy Trinity)
Bris 5 **P** *Patr Bd* **TR** B M CHARLES **NSM** C E EVANS,
J F J GOODRIDGE
KINGSWOOD (St Andrew) *S'wark 24* **P** *Bp and R&S Ch Trust*
(jt) **P-in-c** C A COLTON
KINGSWOOD (St Mary the Virgin) *see* Charfield and
Kingswood w Wickwar etc *Glouc*
KINGSWOOD, LOWER (Wisdom of God) *see* Kingswood
S'wark
KINGTON (St James) *see* Inkberrow w Cookhill and Kington
w Dormston *Worc*
**KINGTON (St Mary) w Huntington, Old Radnor, Kinnerton
and Titley** *Heref 4* **P** *Patr Bd* **R** B L T GRIFFITH
C L K MACDERMOTT **NSM** P J BUCKINGHAM
KINGTON LANGLEY (St Peter) *see* Draycot *Bris*
KINGTON MAGNA (All Saints) *see* Stour Vale *Sarum*
KINGTON ST MICHAEL (St Michael) *Bris 4* **P** *Patr Bd*
OLM D J KILMISTER
KINGTON, WEST (St Mary the Virgin) *see* By Brook *Bris*
KINGWESTON (All Saints) *see* Wheathill Priory Gp *B & W*
KINLET (St John the Baptist) *see* Cleobury Mortimer w
Hopton Wafers etc *Heref*
**KINNERLEY (St Mary) w Melverley, Knockin w Maesbrook
and Maesbury** *Lich 18* **P** *Bp and Trustees (jt)*
R C PRECIOUS **C** A C J GOMPERTZ **OLM** P L WEST
KINNERSLEY (St James) *see* Eardisley w Bollingham,
Willersley, Brilley etc *Heref*
KINNERTON (St Mary the Virgin) *see* Kington w
Huntington, Old Radnor, Kinnerton etc *Heref*
KINNERTON, HIGHER (All Saints) *see* Dodleston *Ches*
KINNINVIE (Mission Room) *see* Barnard Castle w Whorlton
Dur
KINOULTON (St Luke) *see* Hickling w Kinoulton and
Broughton Sulney *S'well*
KINSBOURNE GREEN (St Mary) *see* Harpenden St Nic *St Alb*
KINSHAM (All Saints) *see* Presteigne w Discoed, Kinsham,
Lingen and Knill *Heref*
KINSLEY (Resurrection) w Wragby *Leeds 18* **P** *Bp and Lord
St Oswald (jt)* **V** J HADJIOANNOU
KINSON (St Andrew) (St Philip) and West Howe *Sarum 7*
P *Patr Bd* **TR** L SHIRVILL **TV** C A BROOKS **C** D D DALTON
KINTBURY (St Mary the Virgin) *see* Walbury Beacon *Ox*
KINVER (St Peter) and Enville *Lich 23* **P** *Bp, Mrs A D
Williams, and DBP (jt)* **C** D R WALTON **OLM** N M CAINES
KINWARTON (St Mary the Virgin) *see* Alcester Minster *Cov*
KIPPAX (St Mary the Virgin) *see* Allerton Bywater, Kippax
and Swillington *Leeds*
KIPPINGTON (St Mary) *Roch 9* **P** *DBP* **V** D B KITLEY
NSM L LEITHEAD
KIRBY BEDON (St Andrew) *see* Rockland St Mary w
Hellington, Bramerton etc *Nor*
KIRBY BELLARS (St Peter) *see* Upper Wreake *Leic*
KIRBY CANE (All Saints) *see* Gillingham w Geldeston,
Stockton, Ellingham etc *Nor*
KIRBY GRINDALYTHE (St Andrew) *see* Weaverthorpe w
Helperthorpe, Luttons Ambo etc *York*
KIRBY MISPERTON (St Laurence) w Normanby and Salton
York 19 **P** *Lady Clarissa Collin, Abp, and St Jo Coll Cam (by
turn)* **P-in-c** R G BARKER **C** M BROSNAN
KIRBY MUXLOE (St Bartholomew) *see* Desford and Kirby
Muxloe *Leic*
KIRBY SIGSTON (St Lawrence) *see* Northallerton w Kirby
Sigston *York*
KIRBY UNDERDALE (All Saints) *see* Garrowby Hill *York*
KIRBY WISKE (St John the Baptist) *see* Lower Swale *Leeds*

KIRBY, WEST (St Andrew) *Ches 8* **P** *D&C* **V** *vacant*
KIRBY, WEST (St Bridget) *Ches 8* **P** *D&C* **R** J G BLEAZARD
NSM D K CHESTER
KIRBY, WEST (St Michael and All Angels) *see* Newton *Ches*
KIRBY-LE-SOKEN (St Michael) w Great Holland *Chelmsf 23*
P *Bp and CPAS (jt)* **R** M D J HOLDAWAY
**KIRBY-ON-THE-MOOR (All Saints), Cundall w Norton-le-
Clay and Skelton-cum-Newby** *Leeds 23* **P** *Bp, Sir Arthur
Collins, and R E J Compton Esq (jt)* **V** A J ASKEW
KIRDFORD (St John the Baptist) *Chich 10* **P** *Lord Egremont*
V P A LUCAS
KIRK ANDREAS (St Andrew) *see* Andreas, Ballaugh, Jurby and
Sulby *S & M*
KIRK BRAMWITH (St Mary) *see* Fishlake w Sykehouse and
Kirk Bramwith etc *Sheff*
KIRK CHRIST RUSHEN (Holy Trinity) *see* Rushen *S & M*
KIRK DEIGHTON (All Saints) *see* Spofforth w Kirk Deighton
Leeds
KIRK ELLA (St Andrew) and Willerby *York 14* **P** *D&C*
R A S B CARTER **C** D R SPENCE
KIRK FENTON (St Mary) *see* Tadcaster *York*
KIRK HALLAM (All Saints) *Derby 8* **P** *Bp* **P-in-c** C FRENCH
C C F R HEMMINGS
KIRK HAMMERTON (St John the Baptist) *see* Lower
Nidderdale *Leeds*
KIRK IRETON (Holy Trinity) *see* Wirksworth *Derby*
KIRK LANGLEY (St Michael) *Derby 6* **P** *G Meynell Esq and
J M Clark-Maxwell Esq (alt)* **P-in-c** B J STOBER
KIRK MAROWN (St Runius) *see* Marown, Foxdale and
Baldwin *S & M*
KIRK MAUGHOLD (St Maughold) *see* Maughold and S
Ramsey *S & M*
KIRK ONCHAN (St Peter) *see* Onchan, Lonan and Laxey
S & M
KIRK PATRICK (Holy Trinity) *see* W Coast *S & M*
KIRK SANDALL and Edenthorpe (Good Shepherd) *Sheff 8*
P *Ld Chan* **R** S A BECK
KIRK SMEATON (St Peter) *see* Went Valley *Leeds*
KIRKANDREWS ON EDEN (St Mary) *see* Barony of Burgh
Carl
KIRKANDREWS ON ESK (St Andrew) *see* Arthuret w
Kirkandrews-on-Esk and Nicholforest *Carl*
KIRKBAMPTON (St Peter) *see* Barony of Burgh *Carl*
KIRKBRIDE (St Bride) *see* Bowness-on-Solway, Kirkbride and
Newton Arlosh *Carl*
KIRKBRIDE (St Bridget) *see* Bride, Lezayre and N Ramsey
S & M
KIRKBURN (St Mary) *see* Woldsburn *York*
KIRKBURTON (All Hallows) and Shelley *Leeds 12* **P** *Bp*
V A R A GRANT **OLM** J M CRAVEN
KIRKBY (St Andrew) *see* Woldmoor Gp *Linc*
KIRKBY (St Chad) (St Mark) (St Martin) (St Andrew) *Liv 7*
P *Patr Bd* **TR** J D FAGAN **TV** A L LAWLOR, P C LEA
KIRKBY FLEETHAM (St Mary) *see* Lower Swale *Leeds*
KIRKBY GREEN (Holy Cross) *see* Digby Gp *Linc*
KIRKBY IN ASHFIELD (St Thomas) *S'well 4* **P** *Bp*
NSM K CHARLES
KIRKBY IN ASHFIELD (St Wilfrid) *S'well 4* **P** *Bp* **R** *vacant*
KIRKBY IRELETH (St Cuthbert) *Carl 9* **P** *D&C York* **V** *vacant*
KIRKBY KNOWLE (St Wilfrid) *York 19* **P** *Abp*
P-in-c D E GAMBLE **NSM** W A DEWING
KIRKBY KNOWLE (St Wilfrid) *see* Kirkby Knowle *York*
KIRKBY LAYTHORPE (St Denys) *Linc 14* **P** *Bp and DBP (alt)*
OLM V GREENE
KIRKBY LONSDALE (St Mary the Virgin) Team Ministry,
including Barbon, Casterton, Hutton Roof, Lupton,
Mansergh, Middleton, and Preston Patrick *Carl 10* **P** *Patr
Bd* **TR** R J SNOW **TV** A E PETTIFOR **NSM** S M O'LOUGHLIN
KIRKBY MALHAM (St Michael the Archangel) *see*
Kirkby-in-Malhamdale *Leeds*
KIRKBY MALLORY (All Saints) *see* Newbold de Verdun,
Barlestone and Kirkby Mallory *Leic*
KIRKBY MALZEARD (St Andrew) *see* Fountains Gp *Leeds*
KIRKBY OVERBLOW (All Saints) *see* Lower Wharfedale *Leeds*
KIRKBY RAVENSWORTH (St Peter and St Felix) *see* Holmedale
Leeds
KIRKBY STEPHEN (not known) *see* Upper Eden *Carl*
KIRKBY THORE (St Michael) *see* Heart of Eden *Carl*
KIRKBY UNDERWOOD (St Mary and All Saints) *see* Ringstone
in Aveland Gp *Linc*
KIRKBY WHARFE (St John the Baptist) *see* Tadcaster *York*
KIRKBY WOODHOUSE (St John the Evangelist) *see* Annesley
w Newstead and Kirkby Woodhouse *S'well*
KIRKBY, SOUTH (All Saints) *Leeds 18* **P** *Guild of All So*
P-in-c P CARTWRIGHT

KIRKBY-IN-CLEVELAND (St Augustine)   *see* Ingleby Greenhow, Bilsdale Priory etc *York*

KIRKBY-IN-MALHAMDALE (St Michael the Archangel) *Leeds* 20   **P** *D&C Bradf*   **V** *vacant*

KIRKBYMOORSIDE (All Saints) w Gillamoor, Farndale, **Bransdale and Edstone** *York* 19   **P** *Lady Clarissa Collin and Abp (jt)*   **V** M BROSNAN   **NSM** B J GILLESPIE

KIRKBY-ON-BAIN (St Mary)   *see* Bain Valley Gp *Linc*

KIRKDALE (St Athanaseus with St Mary) *Liv* 1   **P** *Simeon's Trustees*   **V** *vacant*

KIRKDALE (St Gregory) w Harome, Nunnington and **Pockley** *York* 19   **P** *Abp, Adn Cleveland, and Lady Clarissa Collin (2 turns), Ox Univ (1 turn)*   **V** S J BINKS

KIRKDALE (St Lawrence) *Liv* 1   **P** *CPAS*   **V** M J GRIFFIN

KIRKDALE (St Paul)   *see* Kirkdale St Lawr *Liv*

KIRKHAM (St Michael) *Blackb* 10   **P** *Ch Ch Ox*   **V** R W BUNDAY   **NSM** K THORN

KIRKHARLE (St Wilfrid)   *see* Kirkwhelpington, Kirkharle, Kirkheaton and Cambo *Newc*

KIRKHAUGH (Holy Paraclete)   *see* Alston Moor *Newc*

KIRKHEATON (St Bartholomew)   *see* Kirkwhelpington, Kirkharle, Kirkheaton and Cambo *Newc*

KIRKHEATON (St John the Baptist) *Leeds* 5   **P** *Ch Trust Fund Trust*   **R** I R JONES

KIRKHOLT (St Thomas) *Man* 17   **P** *Bp*   **C** D W GRIFFITHS, F K B GRIFFITHS

KIRKLAND (Mission Church)   *see* Lamplugh w Ennerdale *Carl*

KIRKLAND (St Lawrence)   *see* Cross Fell Gp *Carl*

KIRKLEATHAM (St Cuthbert) (St Hilda) *York* 16   **P** *Abp*   **V** M D STRAND

KIRKLEES VALLEY, comprising Brandlesholme, Elton, and Woolfold *Man* 8   **P** *R Bury St Mary*   **V** S D J COOK   **C** L OSBALDESTON

KIRKLEVINGTON (St Martin and St Hilary) w Picton, and **High and Low Worsall** *York* 20   **P** *Abp (3 turns), V Northallerton w Kirby Sigston (1 turn)*   **P-in-c** W J FORD   **Hon C** A J HUTCHINSON   **NSM** R OPALA

KIRKLEY (St Peter and St John) *Nor* 9   **P** *Bp and DBP (jt)*   **P-in-c** H CHANDLER

KIRKLINGTON (St Michael) w Burneston and Wath and **Pickhill** *Leeds* 25   **P** *Ch Soc Trust, Mrs M St B Anderson, G W Prior-Wandesforde Esq, and DBP (jt)*   **R** S R GAMBLE

KIRKLINGTON (St Swithin) w Hockerton *S'well* 3   **P** *Bp*   **P-in-c** C G PEARSE   **NSM** M A GROVES

KIRKLINTON (St Cuthbert)   *see* Bewcastle, Stapleton and Kirklinton etc *Carl*

KIRKNEWTON (St Gregory)   *see* Doddington, Ilderton, Kirknewton and Wooler *Newc*

KIRKOSWALD (St Oswald), Renwick w Croglin, Great **Salkeld and Lazonby** *Carl* 4   **P** *Bp*   **R** K M BUTTERFIELD   **C** A S PYE

KIRKSTALL (St Stephen)   *see* Abbeylands *Leeds*

KIRKSTEAD (St Leonard)   *see* Woodhall Spa Gp *Linc*

KIRKTHORPE (St Peter)   *see* Warmfield *Leeds*

KIRKWHELPINGTON (St Bartholomew) w Kirkharle and **Kirkheaton, and Cambo** *Newc* 11   **P** *Ld Chan (2 turns), J P P Anderson Esq (1 turn), and Bp (1 turn)*   **P-in-c** J P MASON

KIRMINGTON (St Helen)   *see* Brocklesby Park, Croxton and North Wolds *Linc*

KIRMOND-LE-MIRE (St Martin)   *see* Walesby Gp *Linc*

KIRSTEAD (St Margaret)   *see* Brooke, Kirstead, Mundham w Seething and Thwaite *Nor*

KIRTLING (All Saints) *Ely* 4   **P** *Mrs D A Bowlby and Countess Ellesmere (alt)*   **V** *vacant*

KIRTLINGTON (St Mary the Virgin)   *see* Akeman *Ox*

KIRTON (Holy Trinity) *S'well* 3   **P** *SMF*   **P-in-c** Z BURTON   **C** A K ALLS   **NSM** M A GROVES

KIRTON (St Mary and St Martin)   *see* Nacton and Levington w Bucklesham etc *St E*

KIRTON HOLME (Christ Church)   *see* Brothertoft Gp *Linc*

KIRTON IN HOLLAND (St Peter and St Paul) w Algarkirk **and Fosdyke** *Linc* 21   **P** *Bp and Mercers' Co (1 turn), The Crown (1 turn)*   **V** P F BLANCH

KIRTON IN LINDSEY (St Andrew) w Manton *Linc* 8   **P** *Bp*   **P-in-c** K E COLWELL   **C** K M DARBY   **OLM** J WILSON

KISLINGBURY (St Luke)   *see* Bugbrooke, Harpole, Kislingbury etc *Pet*

KITT GREEN (St Francis of Assisi) and Marsh Green *Liv* 15   **P** *R Wigan, Bp, V Pemberton and Duke of Sutherland (jt)*   **C** R M SHEEHAN

KITTISFORD (St Nicholas)   *see* Wellington and Distr *B & W*

KNAITH (St Mary)   *see* Lea Gp *Linc*

KNAPHILL (Holy Trinity) w Brookwood *Guildf* 12   **P** *CPAS*   **V** N J HOPKINS   **OLM** J LEVETT

KNAPTON (St Peter)   *see* Trunch Group *Nor*

KNAPWELL (All Saints)   *see* Papworth *Ely*

KNARESBOROUGH (Holy Trinity) (St John the Baptist), **Goldsborough, Nidd and Brearton** *Leeds* 21   **P** *Patr Bd*   **TR** G A F HINCHCLIFFE   **TV** S G MCDERMOTT

KNARESDALE (St Jude)   *see* Alston Moor *Newc*

KNEBWORTH (St Martin) (St Mary the Virgin and **St Thomas of Canterbury)** *St Alb* 20   **P** *Hon D A Fromanteel*   **R** J T PYE

KNEESALL (St Bartholomew) w Laxton and Wellow *S'well* 3   **P** *DBP and Bp (jt)*   **P-in-c** Z BURTON   **C** A K ALLS   **NSM** M A GROVES

KNEETON (St Helen)   *see* E Bridgford and Kneeton *S'well*

KNIGHTLEY (Christ Church)   *see* Adbaston, High Offley, Knightley, Norbury etc *Lich*

KNIGHTLEY PARISHES   *see* Badby w Newham and Charwelton w Fawsley etc *Pet*

KNIGHTON (St Guthlac)   *see* Knighton *Leic*

KNIGHTON (St Mary Magdalene) *Leic* 1   **P** *Bp*   **V** M A JONES   **C** M J C GOUGH

KNIGHTON, WEST (St Peter)   *see* Watercombe *Sarum*

KNIGHTON-ON-TEME (St Michael and All Angels)   *see* Teme Valley N *Worc*

KNIGHT'S ENHAM (St Michael and All Angels) (St Paul's **Church Centre)** *Win* 3   **P** *Bp*   **P-in-c** L DAVIES

KNIGHTSBRIDGE (St Paul) Wilton Place   *see* Wilton Place St Paul *Lon*

KNILL (St Michael and All Angels)   *see* Presteigne w Discoed, Kinsham, Lingen and Knill *Heref*

KNIPTON (All Saints)   *see* High Framland Par *Leic*

KNIVETON (St Michael and All Angels)   *see* Hulland, Atlow, Kniveton, Bradley and Hognaston *Derby*

KNOCKHOLT (St Katharine) w Halstead *Roch* 9   **P** *D&C*   **R** T M EDWARDS

KNOCKIN (St Mary)   *see* Kinnerley w Melverley, Knockin w Maesbrook and Maesbury *Lich*

KNODISHALL (St Lawrence)   *see* Alde Sandlings *St E*

KNOOK (St Margaret)   *see* Upper Wylye Valley *Sarum*

KNOSSINGTON (St Peter)   *see* Whatborough Gp *Leic*

KNOTTINGLEY (St Botolph) and Kellington w Whitley *Leeds* 18   **P** *Patr Bd*   **TR** C A FLATTERS   **NSM** M J MARSH

KNOTTY ASH (St John) *Liv* 5   **P** *R W Derby*   **V** J M JESSON

KNOWBURY (St Paul)   *see* The Ashfords *Heref*

KNOWL HILL (St Peter)   *see* Wargrave w Knowl Hill *Ox*

KNOWLE (Holy Nativity) *Bris* 1   **P** *Bp*   **P-in-c** S A HAWKINS

KNOWLE (St Barnabas)   *see* Filwood Park *Bris*

KNOWLE (St John the Baptist) (St Lawrence and St Anne) *Birm* 10   **P** *Bp*   **V** G P LANHAM   **C** E A PEACHEY, M J SIMPSON

KNOWLE (St John)   *see* Budleigh Salterton, E Budleigh w Bicton etc *Ex*

KNOWLE (St Martin) *Bris* 1   **P** *Bp*   **V** R A WARING   **C** L J VERRALL-KELLY

KNOWLE, WEST (Holy Cross)   *see* Filwood Park *Bris*

KNOWSLEY (St Mary)   *see* 4Saints Team *Liv*

KNOWSTONE (St Peter)   *see* Bishopsnympton, Charles, E Anstey, High Bray etc *Ex*

KNOYLE, EAST (St Mary the Virgin)   *see* St Bartholomew *Sarum*

KNOYLE, WEST (St Mary the Virgin)   *see* Mere w W Knoyle and Maiden Bradley *Sarum*

KNUTSFORD (St Cross) Cross Town *Ches* 12   **P** *Mrs J Singer*   **V** P D DEAKIN   **NSM** S D L GOWLER

KNUTSFORD (St John the Baptist) and Toft *Ches* 12   **P** *Bp (3 turns), Mrs L M Anderson (1 turn)*   **V** N T ATKINSON   **C** D G H YOUNG

KNUTTON (St Mary) *Lich* 9   **P** *Sir Beville Stanier Bt and T H G Howard-Sneyd Esq (alt)*   **V** J WATKINS   **NSM** S M SIDEBOTTOM

KNUZDEN (St Oswald) *Blackb* 2   **P** *Bp*   **V** M A MORRIS

KNYPERSLEY (St John the Evangelist)   *see* Biddulph Moor and Knypersley *Lich*

KYME, NORTH (St Luke)   *see* Carr Dyke Gp *Linc*

KYME, SOUTH (St Mary and All Saints) *as above*

KYNNERSLEY (St Chad)   *see* Edgmond w Kynnersley and Preston Wealdmoors *Lich*

KYRE WYARD (St Mary)   *see* Teme Valley S *Worc*

LACEBY (St Margaret)   *see* Wolds Gateway Group *Linc*

LACEY GREEN (Church Hall)   *see* Wilmslow *Ches*

LACEY GREEN (St John the Evangelist)   *see* Risborough *Ox*

LACH DENNIS (All Saints)   *see* Lostock Gralam *Ches*

LACHE (St Mark) cum Saltney *Ches* 2   **P** *Bp*   **V** H E A JOHNSTON   **C** A J THOMAS, S CHESTERS

LACKFORD (St Lawrence)   *see* Lark Valley *St E*

LACOCK (St Cyriac)   *see* Gtr Corsham and Lacock *Bris*

LADBROKE (All Saints)   *see* Harbury and Ladbroke *Cov*

LADBROKE GROVE (St Michael and All Angels) *see* Notting Hill St Mich and Ch Ch *Lon*

LADDINGFORD (St Mary) *see* Yalding w Collier Street *Roch*

LADOCK (St Ladoca) *see* Probus, Ladock and Grampound w Creed and St Erme *Truro*

LADY BAY (All Hallows) w Holme Pierrepont and Adbolton *S'well* 6 **P** *Bp and DBP (jt)* **V** *vacant*

LADYBARN (St Chad) *Man* 6 **P** *Bp* **R** M R HEWERDINE **C** R MANN **NSM** A J SIMPSON

LADYBROOK (St Mary the Virgin) *see* Mansfield St Jo w St Mary *S'well*

LADYWOOD (St John the Evangelist) (St Peter) *Birm* 2 **P** Trustees **V** I HARPER **C** I D E LEWIS

LAFFORD Group, The NORTH, comprising Anwick, Cranwell, Evedon, Leasingham, and Ruskington *Linc* 14 **P** *Bp and DBP (jt)* **NSM** L M HUNTER, N R PANTING

LAFFORD, SOUTH, comprising Aswarby, Aunsby, Dembleby, Folkingham, Newton, Osbournby, Pickworth, Scott Willoughby, Swarby, Threekingham, and Walcot *Linc* 14 **P** *G Heathcote Esq, Bp, J Wilson Esq, D&C, DBP, N Playne Esq, Sir Bruno Welby Bt, and Lady Willoughby de Eresby (by turn)* **C** J C WATT

LAINDON (St Nicholas) w Dunton *Chelmsf* 12 **P** *Bp* **P-in-c** A A PETRINE

LAIRA (St Augustine) *see* Plymouth Em, St Paul Efford and St Aug *Ex*

LAIRA (St Mary the Virgin) *see* Sutton-on-Plym, Plymouth St Simon and St Mary *Ex*

LAISTERDYKE (St Mary) *see* Tong and Laisterdyke *Leeds*

LAITHKIRK (not known) *see* Lower Teesdale *Leeds*

LAKE (Good Shepherd) *Portsm* 7 **P** *Bp* **P-in-c** D L LAWRENCE-MARCH **NSM** C A SMITH

LAKENHAM (St Alban) *see* The Mitre Benefice *Nor*

LAKENHAM (St John the Baptist and All Saints) *see* Nor Lakenham St Jo and All SS and Tuckswood *Nor*

LAKENHAM (St Mark) *see* Nor Lakenham St Mark *Nor*

LAKENHEATH (St Mary), Santon Downham and Eveden *St E* 7 **P** *Bp, Earl of Iveagh, and D&C Ely (1 turn), Ld Chan (1 turn)* **NSM** P W TAMS

LALEHAM (All Saints) *Lon* 13 **P** *Earl of Lucan* **V** A SAVILLE **NSM** I C SMAILES

LAMARSH (Holy Innocents) *see* N Hinckford *Chelmsf*

LAMBERHURST (St Mary) and Matfield *Roch* 8 **P** *D&C and V Brenchley (jt)* **V** A J AXON

LAMBETH (St John the Evangelist) *see* Waterloo St Jo w St Andr *S'wark*

LAMBETH, NORTH (St Anselm) (St Mary's Mission) (St Peter) *S'wark* 11 **P** *The Crown (1 turn), Patr Bd (2 turns)* **TR** A R AAGAARD **C** J L MORGANS **NSM** M A K HILBORN, S E DAVIDSON

LAMBETH, SOUTH (St Anne and All Saints) *S'wark* 11 **P** *Abp and Bp* **V** F C DYER **C** V J ELSTON **NSM** M A K HILBORN

LAMBETH, SOUTH (St Margaret the Queen) *see* Streatham Hill St Marg *S'wark*

LAMBETH, SOUTH (St Stephen) *S'wark* 11 **P** CPAS **V** W A WILSON

LAMBFOLD Benefice, The, comprising Adstone, Blakesley, Farthingstone, Lichborough, and Maidford *Pet* 5 **P** *Bp, Hertf Coll Ox, Sons of Clergy Corp, and S R de C Grant-Rennick Esq (alt)* **R** T J E FERNYHOUGH

LAMBLEY (Holy Trinity) *S'well* 7 **P** *Revd W J Gull* **P-in-c** M D JOHNSON

LAMBLEY (St Mary and St Patrick) *see* Alston Moor *Newc*

LAMBOURN VALLEY, The (St Michael and All Angels) *Ox* 6 **P** *Bp and Ch Ch Ox (jt)* **V** J M MINTERN

LAMBOURNE (St Mary and All Saints) *see* Vale of Roding *Chelmsf*

LAMBROOK, EAST (St James) *see* S Petherton w The Seavingtons and The Lambrooks *B & W*

LAMERTON (St Peter) *see* Milton Abbot, Dunterton, Lamerton etc *Ex*

LAMESLEY (St Andrew) *see* Harlow Green and Lamesley *Dur*

LAMMAS (St Andrew) *see* Aylsham and Distr *Nor*

LAMORBEY (Holy Redeemer) *Roch* 17 **P** *Bp* **V** M J JEMMETT

LAMORBEY (Holy Trinity) *Roch* 17 **P** *Mrs H K L Whittow* **V** M F J BLAKELY

LAMORRAN (St Moran) *see* Tresillian and Lamorran w Merther *Truro*

LAMP, comprising Emberton, Haversham w Little Linford, and Tyringham w Filgrave *Ox* 16 **P** CPAS **R** R A CADDELL **OLM** H J LOWNDES

LAMPLUGH (St Michael) w Ennerdale *Carl* 5 **P** Trustees **R** *vacant*

LAMPORT (All Saints) *see* Maidwell w Draughton, Lamport w Faxton *Pet*

LAMYATT (St Mary and St John) *see* Alham Vale *B & W*

LANCASTER (Christ Church) (Christ Church Worship Centre) *Blackb* 11 **P** *V Lanc and Trustees (jt)* **V** *vacant*

LANCASTER (St Chad) *see* Skerton St Chad *Blackb*

LANCASTER (St Mary) w St John and St Anne *Blackb* 11 **P** Trustees **V** C W NEWLANDS

LANCASTER (St Paul) *see* Scotforth *Blackb*

LANCASTER (St Thomas) *Blackb* 11 **P** CPAS **V** J L SCAMMAN **C** C COOKE, H C SCAMMAN

LANCHESTER (All Saints) and Burnhope *Dur* 4 **P** *Ld Chan (2 turns), The Crown (1 turn)* **V** *vacant*

LANCING (St James the Less) w Coombes *Chich* 4 **P** *Bp Lon* **P-in-c** S J DATE

LANCING (St Michael and All Angels) *Chich* 4 **P** *Bp* **V** F A J SMITH **C** T K FINK-JENSEN

LANDBEACH (All Saints) *Ely* 6 **P** CCC *Cam* **P-in-c** D J CHAMBERLIN **C** P H BUTLER **NSM** S BRADFORD

LANDCROSS (Holy Trinity) *see* Bideford, Landcross, Littleham etc *Ex*

LANDEWEDNACK (St Wynwallow) *see* St Keverne, St Ruan w St Grade and Landewednack *Truro*

LANDFORD (St Andrew) *see* Forest and Avon *Sarum*

LANDKEY (St Paul) *see* Swimbridge, W Buckland, Landkey, and E Buckland *Ex*

LANDRAKE (St Michael) w St Erney and Botus Fleming *Truro* 11 **P** *Bp and MMCET (jt)* **P-in-c** C M SIGRIST

LANDSCOVE (St Matthew) *see* Buckfastleigh, Dean Prior, Littlehempston etc *Ex*

LANDULPH (St Leonard and St Dilpe) *see* Tamar Valley *Truro*

LANDYWOOD (St Andrew) *see* Gt Wyrley *Lich*

LANE END (Holy Trinity) *see* S Chilterns *Ox*

LANEAST (St Sidwell and St Gulvat) *see* Moorland Gp *Truro*

LANEHAM (St Peter) *see* Retford Area *S'well*

LANERCOST (St Mary Magdalene), Walton, Gilsland and Nether Denton *Carl* 2 **P** *Bp, Adn, and the Hon P C W Howard (jt)* **P-in-c** A M HUGHES

LANESIDE (St Peter) *Blackb* 1 **P** *V Haslingden St Jas* **V** S C BROWN **NSM** D ALLSOP

LANGAR (St Andrew) *see* Wiverton in the Vale *S'well*

LANGCLIFFE (St John the Evangelist) w Stainforth and Horton-in-Ribblesdale *Leeds* 20 **P** *Bp, Adn Craven, W R G Bell Esq, N Caton Esq, and Churchwardens of Horton-in-Ribblesdale (jt)* **P-in-c** S C DAWSON

LANGDALE (Holy Trinity) *see* Loughrigg *Carl*

LANGDALE END (St Peter) *see* Upper Derwent *York*

LANGDALE, LITTLE (Mission Chapel) *see* Loughrigg *Carl*

LANGDON HILLS (St Mary and All Saints) *Chelmsf* 12 **P** *D&C St Paul's* **R** C E HOPKINSON

LANGDON, EAST (St Augustine) *see* St Margarets-at-Cliffe w Westcliffe etc *Cant*

LANGDON, WEST (St Mary the Virgin) *as above*

LANGELEI, comprising Apsley End, Bennetts End, King's Langley, and Leverstock Green *St Alb* 2 **P** *Patr Bd* **TR** E M HOOD **TV** J A MCDONALD, R L HOWLETT **C** M HOWARTH

LANGFORD (Blessed Virgin Mary) *see* Churchill and Langford *B & W*

LANGFORD (St Andrew) *see* Henlow and Langford *St Alb*

LANGFORD (St Bartholomew) *see* E Trent *S'well*

LANGFORD (St Giles) *see* Heybridge w Langford *Chelmsf*

LANGFORD (St Matthew) *see* Shill Valley and Broadshire *Ox*

LANGFORD BUDVILLE (St Peter) *see* Wellington and Distr *B & W*

LANGFORD, LITTLE (St Nicholas of Mira) *see* Wylye and Till Valley *Sarum*

LANGHAM (St George) *see* Gillingham, Milton-on-Stour and Silton *Sarum*

LANGHAM (St Mary the Virgin) *see* Badwell and Walsham *St E*

LANGHAM (St Mary the Virgin) w Boxted *Chelmsf* 21 **P** *Bp and Duchy of Lanc (alt)* **P-in-c** A J ELMES **C** H R COOPER, R G GIBBS, S L HAYWARD **NSM** A L MASON, P W MANN

LANGHAM (St Peter and St Paul) *see* Oakham, Ashwell, Braunston, Brooke, Egleton etc *Pet*

LANGHAM EPISCOPI (St Andrew and St Mary) *see* Stiffkey and Bale *Nor*

LANGHAM PLACE (All Souls) *Lon* 4 **P** *The Crown* **R** H PALMER **C** J W DYER, L A IJAZ, M B JACKSON, P J NICHOLAS, R I TICE, S R C NICHOLS **Hon C** M J H MEYNELL

LANGHO BILLINGTON (St Leonard) *Blackb* 7 **P** *V Blackb* **V** T J SWINDELLS

LANGLEY (All Saints and Martyrs) *Man 14* **P** *Patr Bd*
V P H MILLER   **NSM** A M CLISSOLD, N R WHITAKER,
S D MORGAN

LANGLEY (St Francis) *see* Fawley *Win*

LANGLEY (St John the Evangelist) *see* Clavering w Langley,
Arkesden etc *Chelmsf*

LANGLEY (St John) *see* Oldbury, Langley and Londonderry
Birm

LANGLEY (St Mary the Virgin) *see* Arden Valley *Cov*

LANGLEY (St Mary) *see* N Downs *Cant*

LANGLEY (St Michael) *see* Loddon, Sisland, Chedgrave,
Hardley and Langley *Nor*

LANGLEY BURRELL (St Peter) *see* Chippenham St Paul w
Hardenhuish etc *Bris*

LANGLEY GREEN (St Leonard) *see* Ifield *Chich*

LANGLEY MARISH (St Mary the Virgin) *Ox 12* **P** *Patr Bd*
TR R J GRAYSON   **TV** O I AOKO   **C** S E LEPP

LANGLEY MARSH (St Luke's Mission Church) *see*
Wiveliscombe and the Hills *B & W*

LANGLEY MILL (St Andrew) and Aldercar *Derby 8* **P** *V*
Heanor **P-in-c** K PADLEY   **C** L SHEMILT, P M HALLSWORTH

LANGLEY PARK (All Saints) *Dur 1* **P** *The Crown* **V** M J PEERS
NSM T HOLDEN

LANGLEYBURY (St Paul) *St Alb 6* **P** *D W A Loyd Esq*
V R J C WEBSTER

LANGNEY (St Richard of Chichester) *Chich 14* **P** *Bp*
V T EZAT

LANGOLD (St Luke) *see* Carlton-in-Lindrick and Langold w
Oldcotes *S'well*

LANGRICK (St Margaret of Scotland) *see* Brothertoft Gp *Linc*

LANGRIDGE (St Mary Magdalene) *see* Bath Weston All SS w
N Stoke and Langridge *B & W*

LANGRISH (St John the Evangelist) *Portsm 4* **P** *Bp*
V J BALL

LANGSETT (St Bartholomew) *see* Sheffield Vine *Sheff*

LANGSTONE (St Nicholas) *see* Havant *Portsm*

LANGTOFT (St Michael) *see* Ness Gp *Linc*

**LANGTOFT (St Peter) w Foxholes, Butterwick, Cottam and
Thwing** *York 10* **P** *Abp and Keble Coll Ox (2 turns), Ld Chan
(1 turn)* **V** S P GRANT

LANGTON (St Andrew) *see* W Buckrose *York*

LANGTON (St Margaret) *see* Woodhall Spa Gp *Linc*

LANGTON (St Peter) *as above*

LANGTON BY PARTNEY (St Peter and St Paul) *see*
Bolingbroke Deanery *Linc*

LANGTON GREEN (All Saints) *Roch 12* **P** *R Speldhurst*
V L J TRAINOR

LANGTON HERRING (St Peter) *see* Abbotsbury, Portesham
and Langton Herring *Sarum*

LANGTON LONG (All Saints) *see* Blandford Forum and
Langton Long *Sarum*

LANGTON MATRAVERS (St George) *see* St Aldhelm *Sarum*

LANGTON ON SWALE (St Wilfrid) *see* Lower Swale *Leeds*

LANGTON, GREAT (St Wilfrid) *as above*

LANGTON-BY-WRAGBY (St Giles) *see* Wragby Gp *Linc*

LANGTONS and Shangton, The, comprising Church
Langton w Tur Langton, Shangton, and Thorpe Langton
Leic 5 **P** *Bp, E Brudenell Esq, and MMCET (jt)* **V** *vacant*

LANGTREE (All Saints) *see* Shebbear, Buckland Filleigh,
Sheepwash etc *Ex*

LANGTREE, comprising Checkendon, Ipsden, North Stoke,
Stoke Row, Whitchurch, and Woodcote *Ox 24* **P** *Patr Bd*
TR K G DAVIES   **TV** L J SMITH   **NSM** A M LINTON,
C L ALCOCK

LANGWATHBY (St Peter) *see* Cross Fell Gp *Carl*

LANGWITH, UPPER (Holy Cross) *see* E Scarsdale *Derby*

LANGWORTH (St Hugh) *see* Barlings *Linc*

LANHYDROCK (St Hydrock) *see* Bodmin *Truro*

LANIVET (not known) *as above*

LANLIVERY (St Brevita) *see* Lostwithiel Parishes *Truro*

LANLIVERY (St Brevita) *Truro 10* **P** *Bp (1 turn), Adn Bodmin
(1 turn), and DBP (2 turns)* **V** *vacant*

LANN PYDAR Benefice, The, comprising St Columb Major,
St Ervan, St Eval, and St Mawgan-in-Pydar *Truro 7* **P** *Bp and
D&C (jt)* **R** H C BABER   **C** T L LOWE

LANNER (Christ Church) *see* Redruth w Lanner and Treleigh
Truro

LANREATH (St Marnarck) *see* Trelawny *Truro*

LANSALLOS (St Ildierna) *as above*

LANSDOWN (St Stephen) *see* Charlcombe w Bath St Steph
B & W

LANTEGLOS BY FOWEY (St Wyllow) *see* Trelawny *Truro*

LAPAL (St Peter) *see* Halas *Worc*

LAPFORD (St Thomas of Canterbury) *see* N Creedy *Ex*

LAPLEY (All Saints) *see* Watershed *Lich*

LAPWORTH (St Mary the Virgin) *Birm 5* **P** *Mert Coll Ox*
R P H GERARD

LARK VALLEY Benefice, The, comprising Culford, Flempton,
Fornham, Lackford, and Timworth *St E 10* **P** *R W Gough
Esq (1 turn), Bp (2 turns)* **P-in-c** M N HAWORTH
C L M SELMAN, M R SELMAN   **Hon C** T L JONES
NSM J C MANN, M M WEBB, V E GAGEN

LARKFIELD (Holy Trinity) *Roch 7* **P** *DBP*
P-in-c N L WILLIAMS

LARLING (St Ethelbert) *see* E w W Harling, Bridgham w
Roudham, Larling etc *Nor*

LASBOROUGH (St Mary) *see* Boxwell, Leighterton,
Didmarton, Oldbury etc *Glouc*

LASHAM (St Mary) *see* Bentworth, Lasham, Medstead and
Shalden *Win*

LASHBROOK (Mission Room) *see* Shiplake w Dunsden and
Harpsden *Ox*

**LASTINGHAM (St Mary) w Appleton-le-Moors, Rosedale
and Cropton** *York 19* **P** *Abp (2 turns), Ld Chan (1 turn)*
V H W GODFREY   **NSM** D HADDON-REECE

LATCHFORD (Christ Church) *Ches 4* **P** *R Grappenhall*
V J L GOODE

LATCHFORD (St James) (St Hilda) *Ches 4* **P** *R Grappenhall*
P-in-c M L RIDLEY   **C** R J ICKE

LATCHINGDON (Christ Church) *see* Mayland and
Latchingdon *Chelmsf*

LATHBURY (All Saints) *see* Newport Pagnell w Lathbury and
Moulsoe *Ox*

LATHOM PARK (St John) *see* Ormskirk *Liv*

LATIMER (St Mary Magdalene) *see* Chenies and Lt Chalfont,
Latimer and Flaunden *Ox*

LATTON (St John the Baptist) *see* Upper Thames *Bris*

LATTON (St Mary the Virgin) *see* Mary-at-Latton *Chelmsf*

LAUGHTON (All Saints) *see* Trentcliffe Gp *Linc*

LAUGHTON (All Saints) w Ripe and Chalvington *Chich 21*
P *Bp (2 turns), Hertf Coll Ox (1 turn)* **R** G R SMITH

LAUGHTON (St Luke) *see* Foxton w Gumley and Laughton
Leic

LAUGHTON-EN-LE-MORTHEN (All Saints) and Throapham
Sheff 5 **P** *Bp* **P-in-c** M RAJKOVIC

LAUNCELLS (St Andrew and St Swithin) *see* N Kernow *Truro*

**LAUNCESTON (St Mary Magdalene) (St Thomas the
Apostle) (St Stephen)** *Truro 9* **P** *Patr Bd* **C** A J HARDY,
T L FOLLAND

LAUNDITCH AND THE UPPER NAR, comprising Beeston-
next-Mileham, Bittering Parva, East Lexham, Great
Dunham, Great and Little Fransham, Gressenhall, Litcham
w Kempston, Little Dunham, Longham, Mileham,
Rougham, Stanfield, Tittleshall w Godwick, Weasenham,
Wellingham, Wendling, and West Lexham *Nor 16* **P** *Ld
Chan (1 turn), Patr Bd (2 turns)* **TR** H D BUTCHER
TV J HEMP   **C** M A FIFE   **NSM** K D BLOGG

LAUNTON (Assumption of the Blessed Virgin Mary) *see*
Bicester w Bucknell, Caversfield and Launton *Ox*

LAVANT (St Mary) (St Nicholas) *Chich 2* **P** *Earl of March
and Kinrara* **R** D JARRATT

**LAVENDER HILL (The Ascension) and Battersea St Philip w
St Bartholomew** *S'wark 14* **P** *Bp and Keble Coll Ox (jt)*
V I C YOUNG

**LAVENDON (St Michael) w Cold Brayfield, Clifton Reynes
and Newton Blossomville** *Ox 16* **P** *T V Sutthery Esq, The
Revd S F Hamill-Stewart, Exors M E Farrer Esq, and Bp (jt)*
R C E PUMFREY

LAVENHAM (St Peter and St Paul) w Preston *St E 6* **P** *G&C
Coll Cam, and Em Coll Cam (by turn)* **R** S G F EARL
C C P TYLER   **NSM** E B E CATTERMOLE

**LAVER, HIGH (All Saints) w Magdalen Laver and Little
Laver and Matching** *Chelmsf 3* **P** *Bp* **P-in-c** C A HAWKINS

LAVER, LITTLE (St Mary the Virgin) *see* High Laver w
Magdalen Laver and Lt Laver etc *Chelmsf*

LAVERSTOCK (St Andrew) *see* Salisbury St Mark and
Laverstock *Sarum*

LAVERSTOKE (St Mary) *see* Overton w Laverstoke and
Freefolk *Win*

LAVERTON (Blessed Virgin Mary) *see* Hardington
Vale *B & W*

LAVINGTONS, Cheverells, and Easterton, The *Sarum 17*
P *Bp and Ch Ch Ox (jt)* **R** M J HARRISON

LAWFORD (St Mary), Little Bentley and The Bromleys
Chelmsf 22 **P** *St Jo Coll Cam, Community of the Resurr
Mirfield, and Em Coll Cam (jt)* **V** S A HERON
NSM S J MORRIS

LAWHITTON (St Michael) *see* Three Rivers *Truro*

LAWLEY (St John the Evangelist) *see* Cen Telford *Lich*

LAWRENCE WESTON (St Peter) and Avonmouth *Bris 2*
P *Bp* **P-in-c** A J MURRAY **C** S A LEIGHTON
NSM F E BREALEY

LAWRES Group, The SOUTH, comprising Cherry Willingham, Fiskerton, and Reepham *Linc 5* **P** *D&C Linc, D&C Pet, and Mercers' Co (jt)* **R** D P GREEN **OLM** C BASON, S K BRADLEY

LAWSHALL (All Saints) *see* St Edm Way *St E*

LAWTON (All Saints) *see* Church Lawton *Ches*

LAWTON MOOR (St Michael and All Angels) *Man 6* **P** *Bp*
P-in-c C D HEWITT

LAXEY (Christ Church) *see* Onchan, Lonan and Laxey *S & M*

LAXFIELD (All Saints) *see* Four Rivers *St E*

LAXTON (All Saints) *see* King's Cliffe, Bulwick and Blatherwycke, Collyweston etc *Pet*

LAXTON (St Michael) *see* Kneesall w Laxton and Wellow *S'well*

LAXTON (St Peter) *see* Howden *York*

LAYER BRETON (St Mary the Virgin) *see* Thurstable and Winstree *Chelmsf*

LAYER MARNEY (St Mary the Virgin) *as above*

LAYER-DE-LA-HAYE (St John the Baptist) *as above*

LAYHAM (St Andrew) *see* Hadleigh, Layham and Shelley *St E*

LAYSTON *see* Aspenden, Buntingford and Westmill *St Alb*

LAYTON (St Mark) and Staining St Luke *Blackb 8* **P** *CPAS*
V P A LILLICRAP **C** H R BOYD

LAYTON, EAST (Christ Church) *see* Forcett and Aldbrough and Melsonby *Leeds*

LAZONBY (St Nicholas) *see* Kirkoswald, Renwick w Croglin, Gt Salkeld etc *Carl*

LEA (St Christopher) (St Barnabas) *Blackb 13* **P** *Bp*
V P G HAMBORG

LEA (St Giles) *see* Woodbridge *Bris*

LEA CROSS (St Anne) *see* Pontesbury I and II *Heref*

LEA Group, The (St Helen), including Corringham, Gate Burton, Heapham, Knaith, Marton, Pilham, Springthorpe, and Upton w Kexby *Linc 2* **P** *DBP, Bp, and Exors Lt Col J E W G Sandars (1 turn), Ld Chan (1 turn)* **R** P WAIN
OLM D J COTTON

LEA HALL (St Richard) *see* Garretts Green and Lea Hall *Birm*

LEA MARSTON (St John the Baptist) *see* The Whitacres, Lea Marston, and Shustoke *Birm*

LEA, THE (St John the Baptist) *see* Ariconium *Heref*

LEADEN RODING (St Michael) *see* S Rodings *Chelmsf*

LEADENHAM (St Swithin) *Linc 22* **P** P R Reeve Esq
R C A GOLDSMITH

LEADGATE (St Ives) *Dur 4* **P** *Bp* **V** *vacant*

LEAFIELD (St Michael and All Angels) *see* Forest Edge *Ox*

LEAGRAVE (St Luke) *St Alb 12* **P** *Bp*
V G K N SENTAMU BAVERSTOCK **C** J J MCLAREN

LEAKE (St Mary) w Over and Nether Silton and Kepwick *York 18* **P** *Abp* **P-in-c** D E GAMBLE **NSM** W A DEWING

LEAKE, EAST (St Mary), WEST (St Helena), Stanford-on-Soar, Rempstone and Costock *S'well 6* **P** *Bp, DBP, Lord Belper, and SS Coll Cam (jt)* **P-in-c** T J PARKER
C M W M ALLEN

LEAKE, OLD (St Mary) w Wrangle *Linc 21* **P** *Bp and DBP (alt)* **P-in-c** F J M COTTON-BETTERIDGE

LEALHOLM (St James's Chapel) *see* Middle Esk Moor *York*

LEAM LANE (St Andrew) *Dur 11* **P** *Bp* **V** A RAINE

LEAM VALLEY, comprising Flecknoe, Grandborough, Leamington Hastings, and Willoughby *Cov 6* **P** *Bp (2 turns), Mrs H M O Lodder (1 turn)* **P-in-c** M A HINKS

LEAMINGTON HASTINGS (All Saints) *see* Leam Valley *Cov*

LEAMINGTON PRIORS (All Saints) *Cov 11* **P** *Bp*
V C H WILSON

LEAMINGTON PRIORS (St Mary) *Cov 11* **P** *Ch Patr Trust*
V R A JONES

LEAMINGTON PRIORS (St Paul) *Cov 11* **P** *Ch Patr Trust*
V J N JEE **C** A M TAMS, R M SMITH **Hon C** G L PRINGLE

LEAMINGTON SPA (Holy Trinity) *Cov 11* **P** *Bp and M Heber-Percy Esq (jt)* **V** C H WILSON **C** E L PEERS
NSM F A SMITH

LEAMINGTON SPA (St Mark) *see* New Milverton *Cov*

LEAMINGTON, SOUTH (St John the Baptist) *Cov 11* **P** *Bp*
V S PARKER

LEAMORE (St Aidan) *see* Blakenall Heath *Lich*

LEASINGHAM (St Andrew) *see* N Lafford Gp *Linc*

LEASOWE (St Chad) *Ches 7* **P** *Bp* **P-in-c** D S MARSHALL

LEATHERHEAD (All Saints) (St Mary and St Nicholas) and Mickleham *Guildf 10* **P** *Bp Guildf and D&C Roch (jt)*
R G D OSBORNE **C** I M STONEHOUSE **Hon C** J P HARKIN

LEATHLEY (St Oswald) *see* Washburn and Mid-Wharfe *Leeds*

LEATON (Holy Trinity) and Albrighton w Battlefield *Lich 19*
P *Mrs J M Jagger* **P-in-c** M TOOP **C** H M LINS

LEAVELAND (St Laurence) *see* Shepherds Lees *Cant*

LEAVENHEATH (St Matthew) *see* Stoke by Nayland w Leavenheath and Polstead *St E*

LEAVENING (not known) *see* W Buckrose *York*

LEAVESDEN (All Saints) *St Alb 6* **P** *Bp* **V** E B GREEN
NSM E P JAMES

LECHLADE (St Lawrence) *see* S Cotswolds *Glouc*

LECK (St Peter) *see* E. Lonsdale *Blackb*

LECKFORD (St Nicholas) *see* Mid Test *Win*

LECKHAMPSTEAD (Assumption of the Blessed Virgin Mary) *see* N Buckingham *Ox*

LECKHAMPSTEAD (St James) *see* W Downland *Ox*

LECKHAMPTON (St Christopher) *see* S Cheltenham *Glouc*

LECKHAMPTON (St Peter) *as above*

LECKHAMPTON (St Philip and St James) *as above*

LECONFIELD (St Catherine) *see* Lockington and Lund and Scorborough w Leconfield *York*

LEDBURY (St Michael and All Angels) w Eastnor *Heref 5*
P *Bp (2 turns), J F S Hervey-Bathhurst Esq (1 turn)*
V K G M HILTON-TURVEY **NSM** W F SIMMONDS

LEDGEMOOR (Mission Room) *see* Canon Pyon w King's Pyon, Birley and Wellington *Heref*

LEDSHAM (All Saints) w Fairburn *York 4* **P** *Lady Elizabeth Hastings Estate Charity* **P-in-c** A D ROBINSON

LEDSTON LUCK (Mission Church) *see* Ledsham w Fairburn *York*

LEE (Good Shepherd) (St Peter) *S'wark 4* **P** *R Lee St Marg*
V B C SHEPHERD **C** S J SIMPSON **NSM** T NDEGWA

LEE (St Augustine) Grove Park *S'wark 4* **P** *Bp*
V G A BERRIMAN

LEE (St John the Baptist) *see* The Lee *Ox*

LEE (St Margaret) *S'wark 4* **P** *Ld Chan* **R** T GOODE

LEE (St Matthew) *see* Ilfracombe, Lee, Woolacombe, Bittadon etc *Ex*

LEE (St Mildred) Burnt Ash Hill *S'wark 4* **P** *Bp*
V T W C LAKE **NSM** D S CLIFTON, M BARBER

LEE (St Oswald) *see* St Oswald in Lee w Bingfield *Newc*

LEE BROCKHURST (St Peter) *see* Wem, Lee Brockhurst etc *Lich*

LEE, The (St John the Baptist) *Ox 17* **P** *Bp* **V** D J BURGESS

LEEBOTWOOD (St Mary) *see* Dorrington w Leebotwood, Longnor, Stapleton etc *Heref*

LEEDS (All Hallows) *Leeds 15* **P** *Bp and DBP (jt)*
P-in-c H GROENEWALD

LEEDS (All Souls) *see* Potternewton w Lt London *Leeds*

LEEDS (Parish Church) *see* Leeds City *Leeds*

LEEDS (St Aidan) *Leeds 13* **P** *R Leeds City* **V** A M HOFBAUER

LEEDS (St Cyprian and St James) *see* Burmantofts and Harehills *Leeds*

LEEDS (St Edmund King and Martyr) *see* Roundhay St Edm *Leeds*

LEEDS (St George) *Leeds 15* **P** *Simeon's Trustees*
TR E L WOOLF **TV** A W C SMITH, J R SEABOURNE, J SWALES
C E R RIDGEWAY, J WILKINS **Hon C** J H WALKER

LEEDS (St Nicholas) *see* N Downs *Cant*

LEEDS (St Paul) *see* Ireland Wood *Leeds*

LEEDS (St Saviour) *see* Leeds Richmond Hill *Leeds*

LEEDS (St Wilfrid) *Leeds 13* **P** *Bp* **NSM** T J BUCKINGHAM

LEEDS (St Wilfrid) Halton *see* Halton and Osmondthorpe *Leeds*

LEEDS Belle Isle (St John and St Barnabas) and Hunslet *see* Belle Isle and Hunslet *Leeds*

LEEDS CITY (St Peter) (Holy Trinity) *Leeds 13* **P** *DBP*
R S J C CORLEY **C** J A CLARK **NSM** S J ROBINSON

LEEDS Gipton (Church of the Epiphany) *see* Gipton and Oakwood *Leeds*

LEEDS Richmond Hill (St Saviour) *Leeds 13* **P** *Bp and Keble Coll Ox (jt)* **V** *vacant*

LEEDSTOWN (St James's Mission Church) *see* Crowan and Treslothan *Truro*

LEEK (All Saints) (St Edward the Confessor) (St John the Evangelist) (St Luke) (St Paul) and Meerbrook *Lich 8*
P *Patr Bd* **TR** N R IRONS **TV** D C NICOL, M J MALINS

LEEK WOOTTON (All Saints) *Cov 4* **P** *Lord Leigh*
P-in-c J E PERRYMAN

LEEMING (St John the Baptist) *see* Bedale and Leeming and Thornton Watlass *Leeds*

LEEMING BAR (St Augustine) *as above*

LEE-ON-THE-SOLENT (St Faith) *Portsm 3* **P** *Bp*
V P M CHAMBERLAIN **C** M E KELLS **NSM** B T WILLIAMS, S E DENT

LEES HILL (Mission Hall) *see* Lanercost, Walton, Gilsland and Nether Denton *Carl*

LEESFIELD (St Thomas) *Man 15* **P** *Bp* **V** E J DISLEY
NSM D J HALFORD

LEESFIELD Knoll's Lane (St Agnes) *see* Leesfield *Man*

LEGBOURNE (All Saints) and Wold Marsh *Linc 15* **P** *Ld Chan (1 turn), Bp, Exors Viscountess Chaplin, Ch Trust Fund Trust, D&C, and DBP (1 turn), Duchy of Lanc (1 turn)*
V J E ROBINSON
LEGSBY (St Thomas) *Linc 7* **P** *Bp* **P-in-c** S W JOHNSON
LEICESTER (All Saints) *see* Scraptoft *Leic*
LEICESTER (Church of the Nativity) *see* Emmaus Par Team *Leic*
LEICESTER (Holy Apostles) (St Oswald) *Leic 1* **P** *DBP and Ridley Hall Cam (jt)* **P-in-c** J C MCGINLEY **C** J K RIDGE
NSM A R LEIGHTON
LEICESTER (Holy Spirit) (St Andrew) (St Nicholas) *Leic 1*
P *Bp* **TV** H F FADRIQUELA **C** K S F ROOMS, M M H SIMPSON
LEICESTER (Holy Trinity w St John the Divine) *Leic 1*
P *Peache Trustees* **V** J C MCGINLEY **C** C W SZEJNMANN,
D C HENDRA, E A SUTHERLAND, J K PATEL, J K RIDGE
LEICESTER (Martyrs) *Leic 1* **P** *Bp* **V** O B HERMO
C G K HUTCHINSON
LEICESTER (St Aidan) *Leic 1* **P** *Bp* **V** S LUMBY
LEICESTER (St Alban) *see* Leic Resurr *Leic*
LEICESTER (St Anne) (St Paul) w St Augustine *Leic 1* **P** *Bp*
V E A WILSON
LEICESTER (St Chad) *Leic 1* **P** *Bp* **P-in-c** M J COURT
C C M KING
LEICESTER (St Christopher) *Leic 1* **P** MMCET
V C P COLLINS
LEICESTER (St James the Greater) *Leic 1* **P** *Bp*
V A QUIGLEY **NSM** J M SHARP
LEICESTER (St John the Baptist) *see* Emmaus Par Team *Leic*
LEICESTER (St Margaret and All Saints) *see* The Abbey *Leic*
Leic
LEICESTER (St Mary de Castro) *Leic 1* **P** *Bp*
P-in-c D MAUDLIN **NSM** S P WARD
LEICESTER (St Peter) *see* Leic Presentation *Leic*
LEICESTER (St Philip) *Leic 1* **P** *Adn Leic, V Evington, V Leic H Trin, G A Cooling Esq, and A S Price Esq (jt)*
P-in-c J M SURRIDGE
LEICESTER (St Stephen) *see* N Evington *Leic*
LEICESTER (St Theodore of Canterbury) *Leic 1* **P** *Bp*
P-in-c S LEIGHTON
LEICESTER Emmaus *see* Emmaus Par Team *Leic*
LEICESTER FOREST EAST (St Andrew) *Leic 9* **P** *Bp*
P-in-c D J HOVER
LEICESTER Presentation of Christ (St Barnabas) (St Peter)
Leic 1 **P** *Bp* **P-in-c** J M SURRIDGE
LEICESTER Resurrection (St Alban) (All Saints) (St Peter)
Leic 1 **P** *Bp* **P-in-c** P CLEMENT **C** S GEORGE, S M STEVENS
LEICESTER, The Abbey (St Margaret and All Saints) *Leic 1*
P *Bp* **P-in-c** M R BATTISON
LEIGH (All Saints' Mission) *see* Bedford Leigh *Man*
LEIGH (All Saints) *see* Upper Thames *Bris*
LEIGH (All Saints) *see* Uttoxeter Area *Lich*
LEIGH (Holy Saviour) *see* White Horse *Sarum*
LEIGH (St Andrew) *see* Three Valleys *Sarum*
LEIGH (St Bartholomew) *see* Brockham Green and Leigh *S'wark*
LEIGH (St Catherine) *see* Twigworth, Down Hatherley, Norton, The Leigh etc *Glouc*
LEIGH (St Clement) *Chelmsf 13* **P** *Bp* **P-in-c** C R HILLMAN
C N M DALLEY **NSM** C E SANDOVER
LEIGH (St Edburga) *see* Worcs W Rural *Worc*
LEIGH (St Mary the Virgin) *Man 19* **P** *Bp* **V** K D CRINKS
NSM K E SLAYEN
LEIGH (St Mary) *Roch 11* **P** *Ch Trust Fund Trust*
V L W G KEVIS
LEIGH PARK (St Francis) *Portsm 5* **P** *Bp* **V** J G P JEFFERY
LEIGH UPON MENDIP (St Giles) w Stoke St Michael
B & W 3 **P** *DBP and V Doulting (jt)* **P-in-c** A E DICKSON
LEIGH WOODS (St Mary the Virgin) *see* Abbots Leigh w Leigh Woods *Bris*
LEIGH, LITTLE (St Michael and All Angels) *see* Aston by Sutton, Lt Leigh and Lower Whitley *Ches*
LEIGH, NORTH (St Mary) *Ox 28* **P** *Ld Chan* **V** M I G DIXON
NSM N K PIKE
LEIGH, SOUTH (St James the Great) *see* Cogges and S Leigh *Ox*
LEIGH, WEST (St Alban) *Portsm 5* **P** *Bp* **P-in-c** K B GREEN
LEIGHLAND (St Giles) *see* Old Cleeve, Leighland and Treborough *B & W*
LEIGH-ON-SEA (St Aidan) the Fairway *Chelmsf 13* **P** *Bp*
V G M TARRY
LEIGH-ON-SEA (St James) *Chelmsf 13* **P** *Bp*
V W G BULLOCH
LEIGH-ON-SEA (St Margaret of Antioch) *Chelmsf 13* **P** *Bp*
P-in-c D V WYLIE

LEIGHS, GREAT (St Mary the Virgin) and LITTLE (St John) and Little Waltham *Chelmsf 9* **P** *Linc Coll Ox, Reformation Ch Trust, and Ex Coll Ox (jt)* **C** D C PIERCE **NSM** S SYKES
LEIGHTERTON (St Andrew) *see* Boxwell, Leighterton, Didmarton, Oldbury etc *Glouc*
LEIGHTON (St Mary) *see* Wrockwardine Deanery *Lich*
LEIGHTON BROMSWOLD (St Mary) *see* W Leightonstone *Ely*
LEIGHTON BUZZARD (All Saints) *see* Ouzel Valley *St Alb*
LEIGHTON-CUM-MINSHULL VERNON (St Peter) and Warmingham *Ches 15* **P** *Bp and J C Crewe Esq (jt)*
V P F DE J GOGGIN
LEIGHTONSTONE, EAST, comprising Brampton, Ellington, and Grafham *Ely 10* **P** *Bp and Peterho Cam (jt)*
V J V TAYLOR **C** M D BIGG
LEIGHTONSTONE, NORTH, comprising Abbots Ripton, Alconbury, Buckworth, Great Gidding, Great and Little Stukeley, Hamerton, Kings Ripton, Upton, Winwick and Wood Walton *Ely 10* **P** *Patr Bd* **R** M C FLAHERTY
LEIGHTONSTONE, SOUTH, comprising Barham and Woolley, Covington, Easton, Kimbolton, Spaldwick, Stow Longa, and Tilbrook *Ely 10* **P** *Patr Bd* **V** P M HOWSON
LEIGHTONSTONE, WEST, comprising Brington, Catworth, Keyston, Leighton Bromswold, Molesworth, and Old Weston *Ely 10* **P** *Bp and Sir Philip Naylor-Leyland Bt (jt)*
P-in-c C M BRENNAND
LEINTHALL EARLES (St Andrew) *see* Kingsland w Eardisland, Aymestrey etc *Heref*
LEINTHALL STARKES (St Mary Magdalene) *see* Wigmore Abbey *Heref*
LEINTWARDINE (St Mary Magdalene) *as above*
LEIRE (St Peter) *see* Upper Soar *Leic*
LEISTON (St Margaret) *St E 16* **P** *Ch Hosp*
P-in-c R W FINCH **NSM** M A H FINCH
LELANT (St Uny) *see* Carbis Bay w Lelant *Truro*
LEMINGTON, LOWER (St Leonard) *see* Moreton-in-Marsh w Batsford, Todenham etc *Glouc*
LEMSFORD (St John the Evangelist) *see* Bp's Hatfield, Lemsford and N Mymms *St Alb*
LEN VALLEY, The, comprising Boughton Malherbe, Harrietsham, Lenham, and Ulcombe *Cant 13* **P** *Abp, All So Coll Ox, Viscount Chilston, and Lord Cornwallis (jt)*
P-in-c J P HUGGINS **NSM** M E HART
LENBOROUGH, comprising Adstock, Gawcott, Hillesden, and Padbury *Ox 11* **P** *Ch Ch Ox, Cam Univ, and New Coll Ox (2 turns), Ld Chan (1 turn)* **V** R M ROBERTS
LENHAM (St Mary) *see* Len Valley *Cant*
LENTON (Holy Trinity) (Priory Church of St Anthony)
S'well 9 **P** CPAS **V** M R SMITH **NSM** M E HAMPSON
LENTON (St Peter) *see* N Beltisloe Gp *Linc*
LENTON ABBEY (St Barnabas) *S'well 9* **P** CPAS
P-in-c R KELLETT **C** G T WHITE, J W L HUGHES,
L P B O'BOYLE
LENWADE (All Saints) *see* Reepham and Wensum Valley *Nor*
LEOMINSTER (St Peter and St Paul) *Heref 6* **P** *Patr Bd*
TR M J KNEEN **TV** M BURNS **NSM** W DUMMERT
OLM P SMITH
LEONARD STANLEY (St Swithun) *see* Stroudwater Team *Glouc*
LEPTON (St John the Evangelist), Emley and Flockton w Denby Grange *Leeds 12* **P** *Lord Savile, R Carter's Trustees, and R Kirkheaton (jt)* **R** V KEATING **C** D NOUWEN
LESBURY (St Mary) w Alnmouth *Newc 6* **P** *Dioc Soc*
V I D MACKARILL **NSM** B K COOPER
LESNEWTH (St Michael and All Angels) *see* Boscastle and Tintagel Gp *Truro*
LESSINGHAM (All Saints) *see* Bacton, Happisburgh, Hempstead w Eccles etc *Nor*
LETCHWORTH (St Mary the Virgin) (St Michael) *St Alb 3*
P *Guild of All So* **P-in-c** R J KOZAK
LETCHWORTH (St Paul) w Willian *St Alb 3* **P** *Bp*
V J C MCQUAID **NSM** A J FERRIS
LETCOMBE BASSETT (St Michael and All Angels) *see* Ridgeway *Ox*
LETCOMBE REGIS (St Andrew) *as above*
LETHERINGHAM (St Mary) *see* Mid Loes *St E*
LETHERINGSETT (St Andrew) *see* Blakeney w Cley, Wiveton, Glandford etc *Nor*
LETTON (St John the Baptist) w Staunton, Byford, Mansel Gamage and Monnington *Heref 4* **P** *Sir John Cotterell Bt (2 turns), Exors Mrs Dew (1 turn), Ch Ch Ox (3 turns), and DBP (1 turn)* **R** *vacant*
LETWELL (St Peter) *see* Firbeck w Letwell *Sheff*
LEUSDON (St John the Baptist) *see* Ashburton, Bickington, Buckland in the Moor etc *Ex*
LEVEDALE (Mission Church) *see* Penkridge *Lich*

LEVELS ARC Benefice, The, comprising Drayton, Long
Sutton and Long Load, Muchelney, and Pitney *B & W 5*
P *Bp, Adn Wells, D&C, D&C Bris, and V Martock (jt)*
V R J TWITTY

LEVEN (Holy Trinity)   see Brandesburton and Leven *York*

LEVENS (St John the Evangelist) *Carl 10*   P *Trustees*
P-in-c B T KERR

LEVENSHULME (St Andrew) (St Mark) (St Peter) *Man 2*
P *Bp and Trustees (jt)*   R G E C REEVES

LEVER BRIDGE (St Stephen and All Martyrs)   see Leverhulme
Man

LEVER, GREAT (St Michael w St Bartholomew)   see New Bury
w Gt Lever *Man*

LEVER, LITTLE (St Matthew) *Man 7*   P V Bolton-le-Moors
St Pet   V J WISEMAN   NSM I C ANTHONY

LEVERHULME, comprising Breightmet, Lever Bridge, Tonge
Fold, and Top o' th' Moss *Man 12*   P *The Crown*
TV V C MASTERS   OLM S P MCGREGOR

LEVERINGTON (St Leonard), Newton and Tydd St Giles
Ely 14   P *Bp*   R S K GARDNER

LEVERSTOCK GREEN (Holy Trinity)   see Langelei *St Alb*

LEVERTON (St Helena)   see Freiston, Butterwick w
Bennington, and Leverton *Linc*

LEVERTON, NORTH (St Martin)   see Retford Area *S'well*

LEVERTON, SOUTH (All Saints) *as above*

LEVINGTON (St Peter)   see Nacton and Levington w
Bucklesham etc *St E*

LEVISHAM (St John the Baptist)   see Pickering w Lockton and
Levisham *York*

LEWANNICK (St Martin)   see Three Rivers *Truro*

LEWES (St Anne) (St Michael) (St Thomas at Cliffe) w All
Saints *Chich 21*   P *Bp and SMF (1 turn), Ld Chan (1 turn)*
R R A MOATT   Hon C D N A BROAD   NSM J A EGAR,
P D YATES

LEWES (St John sub Castro)   see Trin in Lewes *Chich*

LEWES (St John sub Castro) and South Malling *Chich 21*
P *Bp and MMCET (jt)*   R *vacant*

LEWES (St Mary)   see Lewes St Anne and St Mich and St Thos
etc *Chich*

LEWISHAM (St Mary) *S'wark 4*   P *Earl of Dartmouth*
V S P HALL   C S I M MATHIAS

LEWISHAM (St Stephen) and St Mark *S'wark 4*   P *Keble Coll
Ox*   NSM P J HUDSON

LEWISHAM (St Swithun) Hither Green *S'wark 4*   P V
Lewisham St Mary   P-in-c J A EVANS

LEWKNOR (St Margaret)   see Thame *Ox*

LEWSEY (St Hugh)   see Luton Lewsey St Hugh *St Alb*

LEWTRENCHARD (St Peter)   see Lifton, Broadwoodwidger,
Stowford etc *Ex*

LEXDEN (St Leonard) *Chelmsf 21*   P *Bp*   P-in-c M J SIMPKINS
OLM J V MESSINGER, V E MENDHAM

LEXHAM, EAST (St Andrew)   see Launditch and the Upper
Nar *Nor*

LEXHAM, WEST (St Nicholas) *as above*

LEYBOURNE (St Peter and St Paul) *Roch 7*   P *Major Sir David
Hawley Bt*   R M A J BUCHAN

LEYBURN (St Matthew) w Bellerby *Leeds 25*   P *Lord Bolton
and Mrs M E Scragg (alt)*   V S J HANSCOMBE

LEYFIELDS (St Francis)   see Tamworth *Lich*

LEYLAND (St Ambrose) *Blackb 5*   P V *Leyland*
V D J E CLARKE   NSM C D F CROMBIE, G E ASHWORTH

LEYLAND (St Andrew) *Blackb 5*   P *CPAS*
V D G WHITEHOUSE   C D J BELL, M B COOK, M L SIMPSON,
P E HARVEY

LEYLAND (St James) *Blackb 5*   P *Sir Henry Farington Bt*
P-in-c M A M WOLVERSON

LEYLAND (St John) *Blackb 5*   P V *Leyland St Andr and CPAS
(jt)*   V A S MEESON   NSM B J WILSON

LEYTON (All Saints) *Chelmsf 7*   P V *St Mary's Leyton*
V M I HOLMDEN

LEYTON (Christ Church) *Chelmsf 7*   P *Ch Trust Fund Trust*
V M E BURKILL

LEYTON (Emmanuel) *Chelmsf 7*   P *Bp*   V A ADEMOLA
NSM E C ROSE

LEYTON (St Catherine) (St Paul) *Chelmsf 7*   P V *Leyton
St Mary w St Edw*   V W N DONOGHUE

LEYTON (St Mary w St Edward) and St Luke *Chelmsf 7*
P *Simeon's Trustees*   V *vacant*

LEYTONSTONE (Holy Trinity and St Augustine of Hippo)
Harrow Green *Chelmsf 7*   P *Bp*   P-in-c N WALSH

LEYTONSTONE (St Andrew) *Chelmsf 7*   P *Bp*
V J P KENNINGTON   NSM A D C MACKENNA

LEYTONSTONE (St John the Baptist) *Chelmsf 7*   P *Bp*
V D R BRITTON   C P R KERSYS-HULL   NSM P A KHAN

LEYTONSTONE (St Margaret w St Columba) *Chelmsf 7*
P *Bp*   P-in-c N WALSH   C R A B MACAULAY

LEZANT (St Briochus)   see Three Rivers *Truro*

LEZAYRE (Holy Trinity)   see Bride, Lezayre and N Ramsey
S & M

LICHBOROUGH (St Martin)   see Lambfold *Pet*

LICHFIELD (Christ Church) and Longdon *Lich 1*   P *Bp*
V J L WATERFIELD   C E COOKSEY

LICHFIELD (St Chad) *Lich 1*   P *D&C*   R P R CLARK

LICHFIELD (St John's Hospital) Proprietary Chapel *Lich 1*
P *Bp*   Master H M BARTON

LICHFIELD (St Michael) (St Mary) and Wall St John *Lich 1*
P *D&C*   R S N H BAKER   C M L CLARK   NSM D YOUNGS,
R L C BULL

LICKEY, The (Holy Trinity) *Birm 3*   P V *Bromsgrove*
V S L GIDNEY

LIDEN (St Timothy)   see Swindon Dorcan *Bris*

LIDGATE (St Mary)   see Bansfield *St E*

LIDGET GREEN (St Wilfrid)   see Bradf St Wilfrid w St Columba
Leeds

LIFTON (St Mary), Broadwoodwidger, Stowford,
Lewtrenchard, Thruselton and Kelly w Bradstone *Ex 22*
P *Bp, Mrs A M Baring-Gould Almond, W F Kelly Esq, and J B
Wollocombe Esq (jt)*   V *vacant*

LIGHTBOWNE (St Luke) *Man 4*   P *D&C*   R *vacant*

LIGHTCLIFFE (St Matthew) and Hove Edge *Leeds 7*   P *Bp
and V Halifax (jt)*   V K M BUCK

LIGHTHORNE (St Laurence) *Cov 8*   P *Lady Willoughby de
Broke*   R *vacant*

LIGHTHOUSE LONDON   see W Hampstead Trin *Lon*

LIGHTWATER (All Saints) *Guildf 6*   P *Ld Chan and Bp (alt)*
V D SIGSWORTH   OLM R KIDD

LILBOURNE (All Saints)   see Crick and Yelvertoft w Clay
Coton and Lilbourne *Pet*

LILLESHALL (St Michael and All Angels) and Muxton
Lich 15   P *Bp*   V M W LEFROY   OLM J EVANS

LILLEY (St Peter)   see King's Walden and Offley w Lilley *St Alb*

LILLINGSTONE DAYRELL (St Nicholas)   see N Buckingham *Ox*

LILLINGSTONE LOVELL (Assumption of the Blessed Virgin
Mary) *as above*

LILLINGTON (St Martin)   see Sherborne w Castleton,
Lillington and Longburton *Sarum*

LILLINGTON (St Mary Magdalene) and Old Milverton
Cov 11   P *Bp*   V W M SMITH   NSM R C PANTLING,
S M FAIRHURST

LILLIPUT (Holy Angels) *Sarum 7*   P *Bp*   V E L ELLIS
NSM A J SMITH

LIMBER, GREAT (St Peter)   see Brocklesby Park, Croxton and
North Wolds *Linc*

LIMEHOUSE (St Anne) (St Peter) *Lon 7*   P *BNC Ox*
R R A BRAY   C M C C NODDER

LIMESIDE (St Chad)   see Hollinwood and Limeside *Man*

LIMINGTON (The Blessed Virgin Mary)   see Ilchester w
Northover, Limington, Yeovilton etc *B & W*

LIMPENHOE (St Botolph)   see Acle and Bure to Yare *Nor*

LIMPLEY STOKE (St Mary)   see Freshford, Limpley Stoke and
Hinton Charterhouse *B & W*

LIMPSFIELD (St Peter) (St Andrew) and Tatsfield *S'wark 25*
P *Bp*   TR J F PERCIVAL   TV V C SHORT   NSM W M HARVEY

LINBY (St Michael) w Papplewick *S'well 4*   P T W A Cundy
Esq*   P-in-c T H RAAFF

LINCH (St Luke) w Iping Marsh, Milland and Rake and
Stedham w Iping *Chich 9*   P *Bp*   R P A BANCROFT

LINCHMERE (St Peter)   see Fernhurst, Lynchmere and
Camelsdale *Chich*

LINCOLN (All Saints) *Linc 11*   P *Bp*   V P V NOBLE

LINCOLN (St Botolph by Bargate) *Linc 11*   P *Bp*
P-in-c J S CULLIMORE   Hon C N BURGESS   NSM J L HART

LINCOLN (St Faith) (St Martin) (St Peter-at-Arches) *Linc 11*
P *Bp*   V J A WEARING

LINCOLN (St George) Swallowbeck *Linc 11*   P *Bp and
V Skellingthorpe (jt)*   V T J VOLTZENLOGEL

LINCOLN (St Giles) *Linc 11*   P *Bp*   V N J BUCK   C P BEATTIE,
R G BECK

LINCOLN (St John the Baptist) (St John the Evangelist)
Linc 11   P *Bp*   V *vacant*

LINCOLN (St Mary Magdalene w St Paul in the Bail)
(St Michael on the Mount) *Linc 11*   P *Bp, D&C, and Adn
Linc (jt)*   V A P SMITH   NSM J M HEPBURN

LINCOLN (St Mary-le-Wigford) (St Benedict) (St Mark)
Linc 11   P *Bp*   P-in-c J S CULLIMORE   Hon C N BURGESS
NSM J L HART

LINCOLN (St Nicholas) (St John) Newport *Linc 11*   P *Bp
and D&C (alt)*   V H W F JONES   C A E JOLLEY

LINCOLN (St Peter in Eastgate) *Linc 11*   P *Bp*
V E M C BOWES-SMITH   C A W M WARD, J S RADCLIFFE

LINCOLN (St Peter-at-Gowts) (St Andrew) *Linc 11*   P *Bp*
P-in-c J S CULLIMORE   Hon C N BURGESS   NSM J L HART

LINCOLN (St Swithin) *Linc 11* **P** *Bp* **V** J A PRESTWOOD **C** J D G SNELLING, M RODGERS **Hon C** N BURGESS
LINCOLN St Peter in Carlton *Linc 11* **P** *Bp* **V** E M C BOWES-SMITH
LINDAL AND MARTON (St Peter) *see* Pennington and Lindal w Marton and Bardsea *Carl*
LINDFIELD (All Saints) *Chich 5* **P** *Ch Soc Trust* **V** D J CLARKE **C** H E BOURNE, S C SILK
LINDLEY (St Stephen) *Leeds 11* **P** *V Huddersfield* **V** R N FIRTH
LINDOW (St John) *Ches 12* **P** *Bp* **V** S R GALES
LINDRIDGE (St Lawrence) *see* Teme Valley N *Worc*
LINDSELL (St Mary the Virgin) *see* Stebbing and Lindsell w Gt and Lt Saling *Chelmsf*
LINDSEY (St Peter) *see* Bildeston w Wattisham and Lindsey, Whatfield etc *St E*
LINFORD (St Francis) *see* E and W Tilbury and Linford *Chelmsf*
LINFORD, GREAT (St Andrew) *see* Stantonbury and Willen *Ox*
LINFORD, LITTLE (St Leonard) *see* Lamp *Ox*
LINGDALE (Mission Room) *see* Boosbeck and Lingdale *York*
LINGEN (St Michael and All Angels) *see* Presteigne w Discoed, Kinsham, Lingen and Knill *Heref*
LINGFIELD (St Peter and St Paul) and Dormansland *S'wark 25* **P** *Bp* **V** K J PERCIVAL **NSM** N K HINTON
LINGWOOD (St Peter) *see* Burlingham St Edmund w Lingwood, Strumpshaw etc *Nor*
LINKENHOLT (St Peter) *see* Hurstbourne Tarrant, Faccombe, Vernham Dean etc *Win*
LINKINHORNE (St Mellor) *see* Callington Cluster *Truro*
LINSLADE (St Barnabas) *see* Ouzel Valley *St Alb*
LINSLADE (St Mary) *as above*
LINSTEAD PARVA (St Margaret) *see* Blyth Valley *St E*
LINTHORPE (St Barnabas) *York 17* **P** *Abp* **V** D J GOODHEW **C** M N WALLEY **Hon C** L J E GOODHEW
LINTHWAITE (Christ Church) *see* Crosland Moor and Linthwaite *Leeds*
LINTON (Christ Church) *see* Walton-on-Trent w Croxall, Rosliston etc *Derby*
LINTON (St Mary the Virgin) *see* Ariconium *Heref*
LINTON (St Mary) *Ely 5* **P** *Patr Bd* **TR** M A GUITE **TV** I ST J FISHER **C** M L WILCOCKSON, N J BOWN
LINTON (St Nicholas) *see* Coxheath, E Farleigh, Hunton, Linton etc *Roch*
LINTON IN CRAVEN (St Michael) *Leeds 24* **P** *D&C Bradf* **R** D MACHA
LINWOOD (St Cornelius) *Linc 7* **P** *MMCET* **P-in-c** S W JOHNSON
LIPHOOK (Church Centre) *see* Bramshott and Liphook *Portsm*
LISCARD (St Thomas) *Ches 7* **P** *Bp* **V** R T NELSON
LISCARD Resurrection (St Mary w St Columba) *Ches 7* **P** *Bp* **P-in-c** P T COOPER **C** E WHITE
LISKEARD (St Martin) and St Keyne *Truro 12* **P** *Simeon's Trustees* **V** S J MORGAN **C** P T AINDOW
LISS (St Mary) (St Peter) (St Saviour) *Portsm 4* **P** *Bp* **R** C D WILLIAMS **C** R F HUTCHINS
LISSET (St James of Compostella) *see* Beeford w Frodingham and Foston *York*
LISSINGTON (St John the Baptist) *Linc 7* **P** *D&C York* **P-in-c** S W JOHNSON
LISSINGTON (St John the Baptist) *see* Lissington *Linc*
LISTON (not known) *see* N Hinckford *Chelmsf*
LITCHAM (All Saints) *see* Launditch and the Upper Nar *Nor*
LITCHFIELD (St James the Less) *see* Whitchurch w Tufton and Litchfield *Win*
LITHERLAND (St John and St James) (St Paul) (St Philip) and Orrell Hey Team Ministry *Liv 6* **P** *Patr Bd* **TR** A D STOTT **TV** R S SANGRA **NSM** A J FINCH
LITTLE *see also under substantive place name*
LITLINGTON (St Catherine) *see* Shingay Gp *Ely*
LITLINGTON (St Michael the Archangel) *see* Alfriston w Lullington, Litlington, W Dean and Folkington *Chich*
LITTLE BIRCH (St Mary) *see* Wormelow Hundred *Heref*
LITTLE DART Team Ministry *see* Burrington, Chawleigh, Cheldon, Chulmleigh etc *Ex*
LITTLE HEATH (Christ Church) *St Alb 14* **P** *Ch Patr Trust* **V** D G B NEWSTEAD **C** C D EDWARDS **NSM** R H WIKNER
LITTLE VENICE (St Mary) (St Saviour) *Lon 2* **P** *Bp* **V** G S BRADLEY
LITTLEBOROUGH (Holy Trinity) *Man 17* **P** *Bp, TR Rochdale, and D&C (jt)* **V** I BULLOCK **NSM** C D BINNS, D NEWTON **Dss** K J OLIVER
LITTLEBOURNE (St Vincent) and Ickham w Wickhambreaux and Stodmarsh *Cant 1* **P** *Abp, D&C, Ch Trust Fund Trust, and Adn Cant (jt)* **R** vacant

LITTLEBURY (Holy Trinity) *see* Saffron Walden and Villages *Chelmsf*
LITTLEBURY GREEN (St Peter) *as above*
LITTLEDEAN (St Ethelbert) *see* Cinderford w Littledean *Glouc*
LITTLEHAM (St Margaret) w Lympstone *Ex 1* **P** *Patr Bd* **TV** B H CAMBRIDGE **C** H D RYDEN **NSM** L A HOLMAN
LITTLEHAM (St Swithin) *see* Bideford, Landcross, Littleham etc *Ex*
LITTLEHAMPTON (St James) (St Mary) *Chich 1* **P** *Bp* **NSM** P P SEDLMAYR
LITTLEHEMPSTON (St John the Baptist) *see* Buckfastleigh, Dean Prior, Littlehempston etc *Ex*
LITTLEMOOR (St Francis of Assisi) *see* Weymouth Ridgeway *Sarum*
LITTLEMORE (St Mary the Virgin and St Nicholas) *Ox 1* **P** *Or Coll Ox* **P-in-c** M C M ARMITSTEAD **C** H R CARTWRIGHT **NSM** T J MORGAN
LITTLEOVER (St Peter) *Derby 5* **P** *PCC* **V** A C M DRING
LITTLEPORT (St George) *Ely 8* **P** *Bp* **V** J H ROBSON
LITTLETON (St Catherine of Alexandria) *see* The Downs *Win*
LITTLETON (St Mary Magdalene) *see* Shepperton and Littleton *Lon*
LITTLETON DREW (All Saints) *see* By Brook *Bris*
LITTLETON, HIGH (Holy Trinity) *see* Paulton w Farrington Gurney and High Littleton *B & W*
LITTLETON, NORTH (St Nicholas) *see* E Vale and Avon Villages *Worc*
LITTLETON, SOUTH (St Michael the Archangel) *as above*
LITTLETON, WEST (St James) *see* Marshfield w Cold Ashton and Tormarton etc *Bris*
LITTLETON-ON-SEVERN (St Mary of Malmesbury) *see* Alveston and Littleton-on-Severn w Elberton *Bris*
LITTLEWICK (St John the Evangelist) *see* Burchetts Green *Ox*
LITTLEWORTH (Holy Ascension) *see* Cherbury w Gainfield *Ox*
LITTON (Christ Church) *see* Tideswell *Derby*
LITTON (St Mary the Virgin) *see* Chewton Mendip w Ston Easton, Litton etc *B & W*
LITTON CHENEY (St Mary) *see* Bride Valley *Sarum*
LIVERMERE, GREAT (St Peter) *see* Blackbourne *St E*
LIVERPOOL (All Souls) Springwood *Liv 2* **P** *The Crown* **V** P ELLIS
LIVERPOOL (Christ Church) Norris Green *Liv 5* **P** *Bp* **V** H A EDWARDS **C** T R LANGDON-SMITH
LIVERPOOL (Our Lady and St Nicholas) *Liv 1* **P** *Sir William Gladstone Bt* **R** C A PAILING **C** F B BUTLER GALLIE **NSM** M A MONTROSE, W H ADDY
LIVERPOOL (St Anne) *see* Stanley and Stoneycroft St Paul *Liv*
LIVERPOOL (St Christopher) Norris Green *Liv 5* **P** *Bp* **NSM** B A SMITH
LIVERPOOL (St James in the City) *Liv 3* **P** *Bp* **P-in-c** J PADFIELD **C** E W DOWN
LIVERPOOL (St Luke in the City) (St Bride w St Saviour) (St Michael in the City) (St Stephen w St Catherine) *Liv 3* **P** *Patr Bd* **TR** M THRELFALL-HOLMES **NSM** G REEVE, S DOYLE
LIVERPOOL (St Philip w St David) *see* Liv All SS *Liv*
LIVERPOOL All Saints (St Mary) (St Philip w St David) St John the Divine *Liv 1* **P** *Patr Bd* **V** M D COATES **C** P SALTMARSH, R KISA **NSM** A MURRAY, I D CASSIDY
LIVERSEDGE (Christ Church) *see* Heckmondwike (w Norristhorpe) and Liversedge *Leeds*
LIVERTON (St Michael) *see* Easington w Liverton *York*
LIVERTON MINES (St Hilda) *as above*
LIVESEY (St Andrew) *Blackb 2* **P** *Trustees* **V** J P MILTON-THOMPSON
LIVING BROOK Benefice, The *see* Hardingstone, Piddington w Horton and Quinton and Preston Deanery *Pet*
LLANDINABO (St Junabius) *see* Wormelow Hundred *Heref*
LLANFAIR WATERDINE (St Mary) *see* Middle Marches *Heref*
LLANGARRON (St Deinst) *see* Wye Brooks Benefice *Heref*
LLANGROVE (Christ Church) *as above*
LLANGUA (St James) *see* Ewyas Harold w Dulas, Kenderchurch etc *Heref*
LLANVEYNOE (St Beuno and St Peter) *see* Black Mountains Gp *Heref*
LLANWARNE (Christ Church) *see* Wormelow Hundred *Heref*
LLANYBLODWEL (St Michael), Llanymynech, Morton and Trefonen *Lich 18* **P** *Ld Chan (1 turn), Bp and Earl of Powis (2 turns)* **R** K R TRIMBY
LLANYMYNECH (St Agatha) *see* Llanyblodwel, Llanymynech, Morton and Trefonen *Lich*
LOBLEY HILL (All Saints) *see* Hillside *Dur*

LOCKERLEY (St John) and East Dean w East and West Tytherley *Win 12* **P** *DBP (1 turn), H B G Dalgety Esq (2 turns)* **V** J M PITKIN

LOCKING (St Augustine) *see* Hutton and Locking *B & W*

LOCKINGE (All Saints) *see* Wantage Downs *Ox*

LOCKINGE, WEST (All Souls) *as above*

LOCKINGTON (St Mary) and Lund and Scorborough w Leconfield *York 8* **P** *Abp* **R** C FISHER-BAILEY

LOCKINGTON (St Nicholas) *see* Castle Donington and Lockington cum Hemington *Leic*

LOCKS HEATH (St John the Baptist) *Portsm 2* **P** *Bp* **V** G R FOSTER **C** M A P MORITZ

LOCKTON (St Giles) *see* Pickering w Lockton and Levisham *York*

LODDINGTON (St Leonard) *see* Rothwell w Orton and Rushton w Glendon etc *Pet*

LODDINGTON (St Michael and All Angels) *Leic 5* **P** *Bp* **V** *vacant*

LODDISWELL (St Michael and All Angels) *see* Thurlestone, S Milton, Churchstow etc *Ex*

LODDON (Holy Trinity), Sisland, Chedgrave, Hardley and Langley *Nor 8* **P** *Bp, E G Gilbert Esq, Gt Hosp, and Sir Christopher Beauchamp Bt (jt)* **V** D C OWEN **OLM** A M BALL, J C HAYLOCK, R M HOFFMANN

LODDON REACH, comprising Beech Hill, Shinfield, Spencers Wood and Grazeley, and Swallowfield *Ox 7* **P** *Patr Bd* **TR** P WILLIS **TV** D J LITTLE **NSM** C A SPENCE

LODE (St James) *see* Anglesey Gp *Ely*

LODERS (St Mary Magdalene) *see* Eggardon and Colmers *Sarum*

LODGE MOOR (St Luke) *Sheff 4* **P** *CPAS* **V** C H STEBBING **C** I N C LOTHIAN **NSM** G J SMALLMAN, T MORRIS

LODGE, THE (St John) *see* St Martins and Weston Rhyn *Lich*

LODSWORTH (St Peter) *see* Easebourne, Lodsworth and Selham *Chich*

LOFTHOUSE (Christ Church) *see* Rothwell, Lofthouse, Methley etc *Leeds*

LOFTUS-IN-CLEVELAND (St Leonard) and Carlin How w Skinningrove *York 16* **P** *Ld Chan (2 turns), Abp (1 turn)* **R** A GAUNT

LONAN (All Saints) *see* Onchan, Lonan and Laxey *S & M*

LONDESBOROUGH (All Saints) *see* Londesborough Wold *York*

LONDESBOROUGH WOLD (All Saints), including Burnby, Hayton, and Shiptonthorpe *York 5* **P** *Abp (1 turn), Abp and Mrs P R Rowlands (1 turn)* **NSM** D B BROADHURST

LONDON (St Bartholomew the Less) Smithfield Gate *see* Smithfield Gt St Bart *Lon*

LONDON (St Martin Ludgate) *see* St Andr-by-the-Wardrobe w St Ann, Blackfriars and St Martin Ludgate *Lon*

LONDON CITY CHURCHES:

All Hallows Berkynchirche-by-the-Tower w St Dunstan-in-the-East *Lon 1* **P** *Abp* **V** K HEDDERLY **NSM** S C A ACLAND

Great St Bartholomew, Smithfield *Lon 1* **P** *D&C Westmr* **R** M A WALKER

St Andrew-by-the-Wardrobe w St Ann, Blackfriars and St Martin Ludgate *Lon 1* **P** *PCC, Mercers' Co, and D&C St Paul's (jt)* **R** L J MILLER **C** C D FISHLOCK **Hon C** J A MILLER, J L OSBORNE

St Botolph Aldgate w Holy Trinity Minories *Lon 1* **P** *Bp* **V** L J JØRGENSEN **C** A E J RICHARDSON

St Botolph without Bishopsgate *Lon 1* **P** *D&C St Paul's* **P-in-c** D T ARMSTRONG

St Bride Fleet Street w Bridewell and Trinity Gough Square *Lon 1* **P** *D&C Westmr* **R** A J JOYCE **NSM** J R LAKE

St Edmund-the-King and St Mary Woolnoth w St Nicholas Acons, All Hallows Lombard Street, St Benet Gracechurch, St Leonard Eastcheap, St Dionis Backchurch and St Mary Woolchurch Haw and St Clement Eastcheap w St Martin Orgar *Lon 1* **P** *Patr Bd* **R** R C THORPE

St Giles Cripplegate w St Bartholomew Moor Lane and St Alphage London Wall and St Luke Old Street w St Mary Charterhouse and St Paul Clerkenwell *Lon 1* **P** *D&C St Paul's* **R** K M RUMENS **C** J HOGAN **NSM** A F NORRIS

St Helen, Bishopsgate w St Andrew Undershaft and St Ethelburga, Bishopsgate and St Martin Outwich and St Mary Axe *Lon 1* **P** *Merchant Taylors' Co* **R** W T TAYLOR **C** A GLYN, C W D SKRINE, H EATOCK-TAYLOR, J J CHILD, L CORNELIUS, M J FULLER, M MANTLE, P R SNOW **NSM** J H HOUGHTON

St James Garlickhythe w St Michael Queenhithe and Holy Trinity-the-Less *Lon 1* **P** *D&C St Paul's* **P-in-c** T J HANDLEY

St Magnus the Martyr w St Margaret New Fish Street and St Michael Crooked Lane *Lon 1* **P** *DBP* **R** J P WARNER

St Margaret Lothbury and St Stephen Coleman Street w St Christopher-le-Stocks, St Bartholomew-by-the-Exchange, St Olave Old Jewry, St Martin Pomeroy, St Mildred Poultry and St Mary Colechurch *Lon 1* **P** *Simeon's Trustees* **R** W J H CROSSLEY **NSM** D C WHITE, M FOX

St Mary at Hill w St Andrew Hubbard, St George Botolph Lane and St Botolph by Billingsgate *Lon 1* **P** *Ball Coll Ox (2 turns), PCC (1 turn), and Abp (1 turn)* **R** *vacant*

St Mary le Bow w St Pancras Soper Lane, All Hallows Honey Lane, All Hallows Bread Street, St John the Evangelist Watling Street, St Augustine w St Faith under St Paul's and St Mildred Bread Street w St Margaret Moyses *Lon 1* **P** *Grocers' Co (1 turn), Abp (2 turns)* **R** G R BUSH

St Michael Cornhill w St Peter le Poer and St Benet Fink *Lon 1* **P** *Drapers' Co* **C** H EATOCK-TAYLOR

St Olave Hart Street w All Hallows Staining and St Catherine Coleman *Lon 1* **P** *Trustees* **NSM** N J L MOTTERSHEAD

St Peter Cornhill *Lon 1* **P** *City Corp* **R** W T TAYLOR **C** L CORNELIUS **NSM** J H HOUGHTON

St Sepulchre w Christ Church Greyfriars and St Leonard Foster Lane *Lon 1* **P** *St Jo Coll Ox* **P-in-c** D L INGALL **C** S C BANNISTER

St Stephen Walbrook and St Swithun London Stone w St Benet Sherehog and St Mary Bothaw w St Laurence Pountney *Lon 1* **P** *Grocers' Co and Magd Coll Cam (alt)* **P-in-c** S R BAXTER

St Vedast w St Michael-le-Querne, St Matthew Friday Street, St Peter Cheap, St Alban Wood Street, St Olave Silver Street, St Michael Wood Street, St Mary Staining, St Anne and St Agnes and St John Zachary Gresham Street *Lon 1* **P** *D&C St Paul's* **P-in-c** P A KENNEDY

LONDON COLNEY (St Peter) *St Alb 5* **P** *Bp* **V** P A JONES **NSM** P S GREEN

LONDON DOCKS (St Peter) w Wapping St John *Lon 7* **P** *Bp* **R** J W BESWICK **Hon C** R S LADDS

LONDON GUILD CHURCHES:

All Hallows London Wall *Lon 1* **P** *Ld Chan* **V** *vacant*

St Andrew Holborn *Lon 1* **P** *Bp* **C** G R F WILLIS, M G C YOUNG

St Benet Paul's Wharf *Lon 1* **P** *Bp* **P-in-c** A GLYN

St Botolph without Aldersgate *Lon 1* **P** *Bp* **P-in-c** S M C DOWDY **C** P B BRENTFORD, P C MARTIN

St Dunstan in the West *Lon 1* **P** *Abp* **C** J D WILKINSON

St Katharine Cree *Lon 1* **P** *Bp* **V** *vacant*

St Lawrence Jewry *Lon 1* **P** *City Corp* **V** D W PARROTT

St Margaret Pattens *Lon 1* **P** *Ld Chan* **NSM** A J KEEP

St Mary Abchurch *Lon 1* **P** *CCC Cam* **V** *vacant*

St Mary Aldermary *Lon 1* **P** *The Crown and Ld Chan (alt)* **P-in-c** P A KENNEDY

St Michael Paternoster Royal *Lon 1* **P** *Bp* **Asst Chapl** A D G WRIGHT

LONDONDERRY (St Mark) *see* Oldbury, Langley and Londonderry *Birm*

LONDONTHORPE (St John the Baptist) *see* Grantham, Harrowby w Londonthorpe *Linc*

LONG ASHTON (All Saints) w Barrow Gurney and Flax Bourton *B & W 12* **P** *Bp and Lady Virginia Gibbs (jt)* **NSM** R Q GREATREX

LONG BENNINGTON (St Swithin) *see* Saxonwell *Linc*

LONG BENTON (St Bartholomew) *Newc 3* **P** *Ball Coll Ox* **V** M P LEE

LONG BENTON (St Mary Magdalene) *Newc 3* **P** *Ball Coll Ox* **V** P A CRAIGHEAD **NSM** J TERRY

LONG BREDY (St Peter) *see* Bride Valley *Sarum*

LONG BUCKBY (St Lawrence) w Watford and West Haddon w Winwick *Pet 2* **P** *Bp and DBP (1 turn), Ld Chan (1 turn)* **V** G I COLLINGRIDGE **C** A SMITH

LONG CLAWSON (St Remigius) *see* Vale of Belvoir *Leic*

LONG COMPTON (St Peter and St Paul) *see* S Warks Seven Gp *Cov*

LONG CRENDON (St Mary the Virgin) w Chearsley and Nether Winchendon *Ox 10* **P** *Bp and R V Spencer-Bernard Esq (jt)* **V** R M PHILLIPS

LONG DITTON (St Mary) *Guildf 8* **P** *Bp S'wark* **C** K SATKUNANAYAGAM

LONG EATON (St John) *Derby 8* **P** *Bp* **V** S J TREDWELL

LONG EATON (St Laurence) *Derby 8*   **P** *Bp*
   Hon C T F BARNFATHER   **NSM** G A C ORTON
LONG HANBOROUGH (Christ Church)   *see* Hanborough and
   Freeland *Ox*
LONG ITCHINGTON (Holy Trinity) and Marton *Cov 10*
   P *Bp*   **P-in-c** J EVERITT
LONG LANE (Christ Church)   *see* Boylestone, Church
   Broughton, Dalbury, etc *Derby*
LONG MARSTON (All Saints)   *see* Marston Moor *York*
LONG MARTON (St Margaret and St James)   *see* Heart of
   Eden *Carl*
LONG MELFORD (Holy Trinity)   *see* Chadbrook *St E*
LONG MELFORD (St Catherine)   *as above*
LONG NEWNTON (Holy Trinity)   *see* Tetbury, Beverston,
   Long Newnton etc *Glouc*
LONG PRESTON (St Mary the Virgin)   *see* Hellifield and Long
   Preston *Leeds*
LONG RISTON (St Margaret)   *see* Skirlaugh, Catwick, Long
   Riston, Rise, Swine w Ellerby *York*
LONG STANTON (All Saints) w St Michael *Ely 6*   **P** *Magd*
   Coll Cam and Bp (alt)   **P-in-c** S D GILL   **C** E R COPE
LONG STANTON (St Michael and All Angels)   *see* Wenlock
   Heref
LONG STRATTON and Pilgrim Team Ministry, The,
   comprising Aslacton, Bunwell, Carleton Rode, Great
   Moulton, Stratton St Mary, Stratton St Michael, Tibenham,
   and Wacton *Nor 5*   **P** *Patr Bd*   **TR** H Y WILCOX
   TV J Y MADINDA   **OLM** G M OSBORNE
LONG SUTTON (All Saints)   *see* N Hants Downs *Win*
LONG SUTTON (Holy Trinity)   *see* Levels Arc *B & W*
**LONG SUTTON (St Mary) w Lutton and Gedney Drove
   End, Dawsmere** *Linc 18*   **P** *The Crown, Bp, and Ld Chan (by
   turn)*   **V** J P E SIBLEY   **OLM** H M DEAN
LONG WHATTON (St Mary)   *see* Kegworth, Hathern, Long
   Whatton, Diseworth etc *Leic*
LONG WITTENHAM (St Mary the Virgin)   *see* Dorchester *Ox*
LONGBOROUGH (St James)   *see* Moreton-in-Marsh w
   Batsford, Todenham etc *Glouc*
LONGBRIDGE (St John the Baptist) *Birm 3*   **P** *Bp*
   V C J CORKE
LONGBRIDGE DEVERILL (St Peter and St Paul)   *see* Cley Hill
   Villages *Sarum*
LONGBURTON (St James)   *see* Sherborne w Castleton,
   Lillington and Longburton *Sarum*
LONGCOT (St Mary the Virgin)   *see* Shrivenham and
   Ashbury *Ox*
LONGDEN (St Ruthen)   *see* Gt Hanwood and Longden and
   Annscroft etc *Heref*
LONGDON (St James)   *see* Lichfield and Longdon *Lich*
**LONGDON (St Mary), Castlemorton, Bushley, Queenhill w
   Holdfast** *Worc 5*   **P** *Bp, D&C Westmr, and Soc of the Faith (jt)*
   V C A MOSS
LONGDON-UPON-TERN (St Bartholomew)   *see*
   Wrockwardine Deanery *Lich*
LONGFIELD (Mission Room) (St Mary Magdalene) *Roch 1*
   P *Ld Chan*   **P-in-c** D L TURNER
LONGFLEET (St Mary) *Sarum 7*   **P** MMCET   **V** A N PERRY
   C M A HAY
LONGFORD (St Chad)   *see* Boylestone, Church Broughton,
   Dalbury, etc *Derby*
LONGFORD (St Thomas) *Cov 2*   **P** *Bp*   **V** *vacant*
LONGFRAMLINGTON (St Mary the Virgin) w Brinkburn
   Newc 6   **P** *Bp*   **P-in-c** T J HARVEY   **NSM** C M A HEPPER
LONGHAM (St Andrew and St Peter)   *see* Launditch and the
   Upper Nar *Nor*
LONGHILL (St Margaret)   *see* Sutton St Mich *York*
LONGHIRST (St John the Evangelist)   *see* Bothal and
   Pegswood w Longhirst *Newc*
LONGHOPE (All Saints)   *see* Huntley and Longhope,
   Churcham and Bulley *Glouc*
LONGHORSLEY (St Helen) *Newc 11*   **P** *Ld Chan*   **V** *vacant*
**LONGHOUGHTON (St Peter and St Paul) (including
   Boulmer) w Howick** *Newc 6*   **P** *Duke of Northumberland and
   Bp (alt)*   **V** I D MACKARILL   **NSM** B K COOPER
LONGLEVENS (Holy Trinity)   *see* Wotton St Mary *Glouc*
LONGNEWTON (St Mary)   *see* Preston-on-Tees and
   Longnewton *Dur*
LONGNEY (St Lawrence)   *see* Hardwicke and Elmore w
   Longney *Glouc*
**LONGNOR (St Bartholomew), Quarnford, Sheen and
   Warslow w Elkstone** *Lich 5*   **P** *Bp, V Alstonfield, and DBP
   (jt)*   **V** J C BAINES   **C** D M GREEN
LONGNOR (St Mary)   *see* Dorrington w Leebotwood,
   Longnor, Stapleton etc *Heref*
LONGPARISH (St Nicholas)   *see* Hurstbourne Priors,
   Longparish etc *Win*

LONGRIDGE (St Lawrence) (St Paul) *Blackb 13*   **P** *Trustees*
   V M J BARTON
LONGSDON (St Chad)   *see* Cheddleton, Horton, Longsdon
   and Rushton Spencer *Lich*
LONGSIGHT (St Agnes)   *see* Birch-in-Rusholme St Agnes w
   Longsight St Jo etc *Man*
LONGSIGHT (St Luke) *Man 1*   **P** *D&C and Trustees (jt)*
   R E O ADOYO
LONGSLEDDALE (St Mary)   *see* Beacon *Carl*
LONGSOLE (Mission Room)   *see* Barming *Roch*
LONGSTOCK (St Mary)   *see* Mid Test *Win*
LONGSTONE (St Giles), Curbar and Stony Middleton
   Derby 4   **P** *V Bakewell etc and R Hathersage etc (jt)*
   V J S CROFT
LONGSTOWE (St Mary)   *see* Papworth *Ely*
LONGTHORPE (St Botolph) *Pet 11*   **P** *Sir Philip Naylor-
   Leyland Bt*   **V** J BULLEN
LONGTON (St Andrew) *Blackb 5*   **P** A F Rawstorne Esq
   V A PARKINSON
LONGTON (St James and St John) and Meir *Lich 11*   **P** *Bp*
   R P W BENNETT
LONGTON (St Mary and St Chad) *Lich 11*   **P** *Bp*
   V K A PALMER
LONGTON HALL (St Paul) *Lich 11*   **P** *The Crown*
   V J ALESSI
LONGTON, NEW (All Saints) *Blackb 5*   **P** *Bp*
   V D M ROGERS
LONGWELL GREEN (All Saints) *Bris 5*   **P** *Bp*
   P-in-c B W GOODWIN   **OLM** S P BRITTON
LONGWORTH (St Mary)   *see* Cherbury w Gainfield *Ox*
LONSDALE, EAST, comprising Tatham, Tatham Fells, Tunstall
   w Melling and Leck, and Wray *Blackb 14*   **P** *Patr Bd*
   V M H CANNON   **Hon C** S J WILLIAMS
LOOE (St Nicholas) and Morval *Truro 12*   **P** *Ld Chan
   (1 turn), Bp and D&C (1 turn)*   **R** P P C SHARP
LOOSE (All Saints) *Cant 12*   **P** *Abp*   **V** S A PRICE
   C C J WATSON LEE   **NSM** C H THOM
LOPEN (All Saints)   *see* Merriott w Hinton, Dinnington and
   Lopen *B & W*
LOPHAM NORTH (St Nicholas)   *see* Diss *Nor*
LOPHAM SOUTH (St Andrew)   *as above*
LOPPINGTON (St Michael and All Angels) w Newtown
   Lich 21   **P** *Bp and R Wem (jt)*   **P-in-c** A J B CLAYTON
LORD'S HILL   *see* Southampton Lord's Hill and Lord's Wood
   Win
LORDSBRIDGE Team, The, comprising Barton, Caldecote,
   Comberton, Coton, Dry Drayton, Great Eversden,
   Hardwick, Harlton, Haslingfield, Little Eversden, and Toft
   Ely 1   **P** *Ld Chan (1 turn), Patr Bd (2 turns)*   **TR** A M MYERS
   TV M D NEWTON, R GILBERT   **C** C M REDSELL, P O GARNELL
   NSM C I A FRASER, M J REISS
LORTON (St Cuthbert) and Loweswater w Buttermere
   Carl 6   **P** *Bp and Earl of Lonsdale (alt)*   **P-in-c** S E WARD
   Hon C R W BAILEY
LOSCOE (St Luke)   *see* Denby Gp *Derby*
LOSTOCK (St Thomas and St John) *Man 9*   **P** *Bp and TR
   Deane St Mary the Virgin (jt)*   **P-in-c** T P CLARK
   C B M WILKINSON
LOSTOCK GRALAM (St John the Evangelist) *Ches 6*
   P *V Witton*   **NSM** D A DALBY
LOSTOCK HALL (St James) and Farington Moss *Blackb 5*
   P *Bp and V Penwortham (jt)*   **V** M P MCMURRAY
LOSTWITHIEL (St Bartholomew) Parishes *Truro 10*   **P** *D&C,
   DBP, and A D G Fortescue Esq (jt)*   **P-in-c** P J BEYNON
   NSM S I BAWDEN
LOTHERSDALE (Christ Church)   *see* Sutton w Cowling and
   Lothersdale *Leeds*
LOTHERTON (St James)   *see* Aberford w Micklefield *York*
LOTTISHAM (The Blessed Virgin Mary)   *see* Baltonsborough
   w Butleigh, W Bradley etc *B & W*
LOUDWATER (St Peter) *Ox 10*   **P** MMCET   **V** *vacant*
LOUGHBOROUGH (All Saints) w Holy Trinity *Leic 6*   **P** *Bp
   and Em Coll Cam (jt)*   **R** W M DALRYMPLE   **C** E J SHARMAN
   NSM M CARROLL
LOUGHBOROUGH (Emmanuel) *Leic 6*   **P** *Bp and Em Coll
   Cam (jt)*   **P-in-c** M J BROADLEY   **C** B J GARDNER,
   S M HARVEY
LOUGHBOROUGH (Good Shepherd) *Leic 6*   **P** *Bp*
   V S WILLETTS
LOUGHRIGG Team Ministry, The, comprising Ambleside,
   Brathay, and Langdale *Carl 11*   **P** *Patr Bd*   **TR** B LOCK
   NSM G G WRIGLEY, N F HALLAM
LOUGHTON (All Saints)   *see* Watling Valley *Ox*
LOUGHTON (not known)   *see* Ditton Priors w Neenton,
   Burwarton etc *Heref*

LOUGHTON (St John the Baptist) (St Gabriel) (St Nicholas) *Chelmsf 3* **P** W W Maitland Esq **R** C M DAVIES **C** S B S PETERS, S R H MAGINNIS **OLM** B A READ

LOUGHTON (St Mary the Virgin) *Chelmsf 3* **P** *Bp* **V** M C MACDONALD **C** S P OPIE

LOUGHTON (St Michael and All Angels) *Chelmsf 3* **P** *Bp* **V** L A PETITT **NSM** M P PETITT **OLM** E A PRICE, L A SMART

LOUND (St John the Baptist) *see* Somerleyton, Ashby, Fritton, Herringfleet etc *Nor*

LOUNDSLEY GREEN (Church of the Ascension) *Derby 3* **P** *Bp* **P-in-c** P J GREEN **C** D P MOUNCER

LOUTH (Holy Trinity Church Centre) (St James) (St Michael) *Linc 15* **P** *Patr Bd* **TR** N J W BROWN **TV** J E TURVILLE **C** A M M ROBINSON **OLM** R W MANSFIELD

LOVEDEN, EAST, comprising Ancaster, Greylees, Heydour, Kelby, Rauceby, Welby, and Wilsford *Linc 22* **P** *Bp (2 turns), DBP (1 turn), and Mrs G V Hoare (1 turn)* **R** G MACHELL

LOVERSALL (St Katherine) *see* Wadworth w Loversall and Balby *Sheff*

LOVINGTON (St Thomas à Becket) *see* Six Pilgrims *B & W*

LOVINGTON (St Thomas à Becket) *see* Six Pilgrims *B & W*

LOW *see also under substantive place name*

LOW FELL (St Helen) *see* Gateshead St Helen *Dur*

LOW HILL (Good Shepherd) *see* Bushbury *Lich*

LOW MOOR (Holy Trinity) and Oakenshaw *Leeds 3* **P** *Bp and V Bradf (jt)* **V** I R JENNINGS **NSM** D P ELLIS

LOWDHAM (St Mary the Virgin) *see* Burton Joyce, Bulcote and Stoke Bardolph etc *S'well*

LOWER *see also under substantive place name*

LOWER MOOR (St Stephen and All Martyrs) *see* Coldhurst and Oldham St Steph *Man*

LOWESBY (All Saints) *see* Whatborough Gp *Leic*

LOWESTOFT (Christ Church) *Nor 9* **P** CPAS **V** M C PAYNE **C** J M CARTER

LOWESTOFT (Good Shepherd) *see* Lowestoft St Marg *Nor*

LOWESTOFT (St Andrew) *Nor 9* **P** *Ch Patr Tr* **V** D ROGERS

LOWESTOFT (St Margaret) *Nor 9* **P** *Bp, Adn Norfolk, and DBP (jt)* **R** M J ASQUITH

LOWESWATER (St Bartholomew) *see* Lorton and Loweswater w Buttermere *Carl*

LOWICK (St John the Baptist) and Kyloe w Ancroft *Newc 12* **P** *D&C Dur (2 turns), Bp (1 turn)* **V** *vacant*

LOWICK (St Luke) *see* Coniston and the Crake Valley *Carl*

LOWICK (St Peter) *see* Brigstock w Stanion and Lowick and Sudborough *Pet*

LOWSONFORD (St Luke) *see* Hatton w Haseley, Rowington w Lowsonford etc *Cov*

LOWTHER (St Michael) *see* N Westmorland *Carl*

LOWTHORPE (St Martin) *see* The Beacon *York*

LOWTON (St Luke) (St Mary) and Golborne *Liv 13* **P** *Patr Bd* **TR** J R STOTT **TV** T HODSON

LOXBEARE (St Michael and All Angels) *see* Washfield, Stoodleigh, Withleigh etc *Ex*

LOXHORE (St Michael and All Angels) *see* Shirwell, Loxhore, Kentisbury, Arlington, etc *Ex*

LOXLEY (St Nicholas) *see* Hampton Lucy w Charlecote and Loxley *Cov*

LOXTON (St Andrew) *see* Crook Peak *B & W*

LOXWOOD (St John the Baptist) *see* Alfold and Loxwood *Guildf*

LOZELLS (St Paul and St Silas) *Birm 2* **P** *Aston Patr Trust* **P-in-c** A J COZENS

LUBENHAM (All Saints) *see* Market Harborough and The Transfiguration etc *Leic*

LUCCOMBE (The Blessed Virgin Mary) *see* Porlock and Porlock Weir w Stoke Pero etc *B & W*

LUCKER (St Hilda) *see* Belford and Lucker *Newc*

LUCKINGTON (St Mary) *see* Gauzebrook *Bris*

LUDBOROUGH (St Mary) *see* Fotherby, N Thoresby and Grainsby w Waithe *Linc*

LUDDENDEN (St Mary) w Luddenden Foot *Leeds 8* **P** *Bp and V Halifax (alt)* **P-in-c** I SPARKS **NSM** M S H MACDONALD

LUDDESDOWN (St Peter and St Paul) *see* Cobham w Luddesdowne and Dode *Roch*

LUDDINGTON (All Saints) *see* Stratford-upon-Avon, Luddington etc *Cov*

LUDDINGTON (St Margaret) *see* Barnwell, Hemington, Luddington in the Brook etc *Pet*

LUDDINGTON (St Oswald) *see* Crowle Gp *Linc*

LUDFORD (St Giles) *see* The Ashfords *Heref*

LUDFORD MAGNA (St Mary) *see* Binbrook Gp *Linc*

LUDGERSHALL (St Mary the Virgin) *see* Bernwode *Ox*

LUDGERSHALL (St James) and Tidworth *Sarum 14* **P** *Ld Chan and DBP (alt)* **V** T J LAUNDON **C** J HOLDEN

LUDGVAN (St Ludgvan and St Paul), Marazion, St Hilary and Perranuthnoe *Truro 5* **P** *D&C, Lord St Levan, and H M Parker Esq (jt)* **R** N G MARNS **C** J E RISBRIDGER, K NORFOLK **NSM** L P GARTHWAITE

LUDHAM (St Catherine), Potter Heigham, Hickling and Catfield *Nor 12* **P** *Bp and G M H Mills Esq (jt)* **V** *vacant*

LUDLOW (St John) (St Laurence) *Heref 11* **P** *Bp and Earl of Plymouth (jt)* **R** K I PRICE

LUFFENHAM, NORTH (St John the Baptist) *see* Empingham, Edith Weston, Lyndon, Manton etc *Pet*

LUFFENHAM, SOUTH (St Mary the Virgin) *see* Barrowden and Wakerley w S Luffenham etc *Pet*

LUFTON (St Peter and St Paul) *see* Tintinhull w Chilthorne Domer, Yeovil Marsh etc *B & W*

LUGWARDINE (St Peter) *see* Bartestree Cross *Heref*

LULLINGSTONE (St Botolph) *see* Eynsford w Farningham and Lullingstone *Roch*

LULLINGTON (All Saints) *see* Beckington w Standerwick, Berkley, Rodden etc *B & W*

LULLINGTON (All Saints) *see* Seale and Lullington w Coton in the Elms *Derby*

LULLINGTON (Good Shepherd) *see* Alfriston w Lullington, Litlington, W Dean and Folkington *Chich*

LULWORTHS, (St Andrew) (Holy Trinity) Winfrith Newburgh and Chaldon, The *Sarum 8* **P** *Bp (3 turns), Col Sir Joseph Weld (1 turn)* **P-in-c** R J MARSDEN

LUMLEY (Christ Church) *Dur 10* **P** *Bp* **V** *vacant*

LUND (All Saints) *see* Lockington and Lund and Scorborough w Leconfield *York*

LUND (St John the Evangelist) *Blackb 10* **P** *Ch Ch Ox* **V** J L BANNISTER

LUNDWOOD (St Mary Magdalene) *Leeds 17* **P** *Bp* **V** *vacant*

LUNDY ISLAND (St Helen) *see* Parkham, Alwington, Buckland Brewer etc *Ex*

LUPPITT (St Mary) *see* Broadhembury, Dunkeswell, Luppitt, Plymtree, Sheldon, and Upottery *Ex*

LUPSET (St George) *Leeds 19* **P** *Bp* **P-in-c** M C CRABTREE **C** E C PEETERS

LUPTON (All Saints) *see* Kirkby Lonsdale *Carl*

LURGASHALL (St Lawrence) *Chich 10* **P** *Lord Egremont* **V** *vacant*

LUSBY (St Peter) *see* Bolingbroke Deanery *Linc*

LUSTLEIGH (St John the Baptist) *see* Moretonhampstead, Manaton, N Bovey and Lustleigh *Ex*

LUTON (All Saints) (St Peter) *St Alb 12* **P** *Bp* **V** D W KESTERTON **NSM** J M BURKE

LUTON (Christ Church) *Roch 5* **P** *R Chatham* **P-in-c** A S LEONARD

LUTON (Christ Church) *see* Bushmead *St Alb*

LUTON (Holy Cross) *see* Marsh Farm *St Alb*

LUTON (St Andrew) *St Alb 12* **P** *Bp* **V** G A FINLAYSON

LUTON (St Anne) (St Christopher) Round Green *St Alb 12* **P** *Bp, V Luton St Mary, and Peache Trustees* **V** A D CROSBY

LUTON (St Francis) *St Alb 12* **P** *Peache Trustees, Bp, and V Luton (jt)* **V** N D GREW **C** S HANCOCK

LUTON (St John) *see* Teignmouth, Ideford w Luton, Ashcombe etc *Ex*

LUTON (St Mary) *St Alb 12* **P** *Peache Trustees* **V** M C JONES **C** A N GARDNER, N K MWANDIA **NSM** C A MOSS

LUTON (St Matthew) High Town *St Alb 12* **P** *Ch Patr Trust* **P-in-c** M C JONES **C** N K MWANDIA

LUTON (St Paul) *St Alb 12* **P** *Peache Trustees* **V** *vacant*

LUTON (St Saviour) *St Alb 12* **P** *Bp* **P-in-c** Y M SMEJKAL

LUTON Lewsey (St Hugh) *St Alb 12* **P** *Bp* **V** J PIENAAR **C** A J GLIDDON

LUTON Limbury (St Augustine of Canterbury) *St Alb 12* **P** *Bp* **V** J O NYAONGO

LUTTERWORTH (St Mary) w Cotesbach and Bitteswell *Leic 7* **P** *The Crown (3 turns), Ld Chan (1 turn), and Ch Hosp (1 turn)* **R** C A M STYLES **C** T E BROWN

LUTTON (St Nicholas) *see* Long Sutton w Lutton etc *Linc*

LUTTON (St Peter) *see* Barnwell, Hemington, Luddington in the Brook etc *Pet*

LUTTONS AMBO (St Mary) *see* Weaverthorpe w Helperthorpe, Luttons Ambo etc *York*

LUXBOROUGH (Blessed Virgin Mary) *see* Exmoor *B & W*

LUXULYAN (St Cyrus and St Julietta) *Truro 1* **P** *Bp (1 turn), Adn Cornwall (1 turn), and DBP (2 turns)* **P-in-c** J S J WILLIAMS

LYDBROOK (Holy Jesus) *see* Drybrook, Lydbrook and Ruardean *Glouc*

LYDBURY NORTH (St Michael and All Angels) *see* Bishop's Castle w Mainstone, Lydbury N etc *Heref*

LYDD (All Saints) *see* Brookland, Fairfield, Brenzett w Snargate etc *Cant*

LYDDEN (St Mary the Virgin) *see* Temple Ewell w Lydden *Cant*

LYDDINGTON (All Saints) and Wanborough and Bishopstone w Hinton Parva *Bris 7* **P** *Bp and Ld Chan (alt)* **P-in-c** W A O'CONNELL

LYDDINGTON (St Andrew), Bisbrooke, Caldecott, Glaston, Harringworth, Seaton and Stoke Dry *Pet 12* **P** *Bp, G T G Conant Esq, Exors R E M Elborne Esq, Burghley Ho Preservation Trust Ltd, and Peterho Cam (jt)* **V** J E BAXTER

LYDEARD ST LAWRENCE (St Lawrence) *see* Bishop's Lydeard w Lydeard St Lawrence etc *B & W*

LYDFORD (St Petrock) *see* Okehampton, Inwardleigh, Belstone, Sourton etc *Ex*

LYDFORD ON FOSSE (St Peter) *see* Wheathill Priory Gp *B & W*

LYDGATE (St Anne) *see* Saddleworth *Man*

LYDHAM (Holy Trinity) *see* Wentnor w Ratlinghope, Myndtown, Norbury etc *Heref*

LYDIARD MILLICENT (All Saints) *see* NW Swindon and Lydiard Millicent *Bris*

LYDIARD TREGOZE (St Mary) *see* W Swindon and Lydiard Tregoze *Bris*

LYDIATE (St Thomas) *see* Halsall, Lydiate and Downholland *Liv*

LYDLINCH (St Thomas à Beckett) *see* Sturminster Newton, Hinton St Mary and Lydlinch *Sarum*

LYDNEY (St Mary the Virgin), Woolaston, Alvington and Aylburton *Glouc 1* **P** *Ld Chan (2 turns), DBP (1 turn)* **R** D A GARDINER **NSM** N M J SUMMERFIELD

LYE, The (Christchurch) and Stambermill *Worc 12* **P** *Bp and CPAS (alt)* **V** S M FALSHAW **NSM** C A KENT

LYFORD (St Mary) *see* Cherbury w Gainfield *Ox*

LYME REGIS (St Michael the Archangel) *see* Golden Cap Team *Sarum*

LYMINGE (St Mary and St Ethelburga) w Paddlesworth and Stanford w Postling and Radegund *Cant 8* **P** *Abp* **P-in-c** J A WEEKS **OLM** S G DOUGAL

LYMINGTON (St Thomas the Apostle) (All Saints) *Win 11* **P** *Bp* **V** P B C SALISBURY

LYMINSTER (St Mary Magdalene) and Wick *Chich 1* **P** *Bp and Eton Coll on nomination of BNC Ox (jt)* **V** T I ROBSON **C** V L BARON

LYMM (St Mary the Virgin) *Ches 4* **P** *Bp* **R** B J JAMESON

LYMPNE (St Stephen) and Saltwood *Cant 8* **P** *Abp* **NSM** P F HILL

LYMPSHAM (St Christopher) *see* Brent Knoll, E Brent and Lympsham *B & W*

LYMPSTONE (Nativity of the Blessed Virgin Mary) *see* Littleham-cum-Exmouth w Lympstone *Ex*

LYNDHURST (St Michael) and Emery Down and Minstead *Win 11* **P** *Bp and P J P Green Esq (jt)* **P-in-c** D S POTTERTON

LYNDON (St Martin) *see* Empingham, Edith Weston, Lyndon, Manton etc *Pet*

LYNEAL (St John the Evangelist) *see* Petton w Cockshutt, Welshampton and Lyneal etc *Lich*

LYNEHAM (St Michael) and Woodhill, including Bradenstoke, Broad Town, Clyffe Pypard, Hilmarton, and Tockenham *Sarum 16* **P** *The Crown (2 turns), DBP (1 turn), Ld Chan (1 turn)* **R** E R H ABBOTT

LYNESACK (St John the Evangelist) *Dur 6* **P** *Bp* **P-in-c** B WHITLEY

LYNG (St Bartholomew) *see* Athelney *B & W*

LYNG (St Margaret) *see* Reepham and Wensum Valley *Nor*

LYNGFORD (St Peter) *see* Taunton Lyngford *B & W*

LYNMOUTH (St John the Baptist) *see* Lynton, Brendon, Countisbury etc *Ex*

LYNN, SOUTH (All Saints) *Nor 19* **P** *Bp* **R** A R LING **C** J R E BELL

LYNN, WEST (St Peter) *see* Clenchwarton and W Lynn *Ely*

LYNSTED (St Peter and St Paul) *see* Kingsdown and Creekside *Cant*

LYNTON (St Mary the Virgin), Brendon, Countisbury, Parracombe, Martinhoe and Trentishoe *Ex 17* **P** *Bp* **R** S M STAYTE **NSM** J S LOVEDAY

LYONS (St Michael and All Angels) *see* Hetton-Lyons w Eppleton *Dur*

LYONSDOWN (Holy Trinity) *St Alb 14* **P** *Ch Patr Trust* **V** C W G DOBBIE

LYONSHALL (St Michael and All Angels) *see* Pembridge w Moor Court, Shobdon, Staunton etc *Heref*

LYTCHETTS, The (not known) (St Mary the Virgin) and Upton *Sarum 7* **P** *Patr Bd* **TV** S H PARTRIDGE **NSM** H R BOND **OLM** H D PAGE-CLARK

LYTHAM (St Cuthbert) *Blackb 10* **P** *DBP* **V** N A WELLS **C** A D THOMAS

LYTHAM (St John the Divine) *Blackb 10* **P** J C Hilton Esq **P-in-c** A R WOOD

LYTHAM ST ANNE (St Margaret of Antioch) *see* St Annes St Marg *Blackb*

LYTHAM ST ANNE (St Thomas) *see* St Annes St Thos *Blackb*

LYTHAM ST ANNES (St Paul) *see* Fairhaven *Blackb*

LYTHE (St Oswald) *see* Hinderwell, Roxby and Staithes etc *York*

MABE (St Laudus) *Truro 3* **P** *Bp* **P-in-c** S SMITH **C** A J EVANS

MABLETHORPE (St Mary) w Trusthorpe *Linc 10* **P** *Bp Lon (2 turns), Bp Linc (1 turn)* **R** P J LILEY **Hon C** C H LILLEY **OLM** J TOMPKINS

MACCLESFIELD (Holy Trinity) *see* Hurdsfield *Ches*

MACCLESFIELD (St John the Evangelist) w Henbury *Ches 13* **P** *Bp* **V** T ROBINSON **NSM** N G ROBINSON

MACCLESFIELD (St Paul) *Ches 13* **P** *Bp* **P-in-c** M F FOX

MACCLESFIELD Team Parish, The, (All Saints) (Christ Church) (St Michael and All Angels) (St Peter) (St Barnabas) *Ches 13* **P** *Patr Bd* **TR** M N STEPHENS **TV** A B WILLIAMS **C** K BRADY **NSM** R WARDLE

MACKWORTH (All Saints) *Derby 6* **P** J M Clark-Maxwell Esq **P-in-c** B J STOBER

MACKWORTH (St Francis) *Derby 5* **P** *Bp* **V** *vacant*

MADEHURST (St Mary Magdalene) *see* Slindon, Eartham and Madehurst *Chich*

MADELEY (All Saints) *Lich 9* **P** J C Crewe Esq **V** P T CHANTRY **C** J J BESWICK PALLISTER **NSM** G A BAILEY

MADELEY (St Michael) *Heref 13* **P** *Patr Bd* **P-in-c** L N CRONIN **TV** A H WALDEN **C** I R MCINTYRE **NSM** D A TAFFINDER

MADINGLEY (St Mary Magdalene) *Ely 6* **P** *Bp* **V** *vacant*

MADLEY (Nativity of the Blessed Virgin Mary) w Tyberton, Peterchurch, Vowchurch and Turnastone *Heref 1* **P** *Bp and D&C (jt)* **R** S D LOCKETT

MADRESFIELD (St Mary) *see* Powick and Guarlford and Madresfield w Newland *Worc*

MADRON (St Maddern) *see* Gulval and Madron *Truro*

MAER (St Peter) *see* Chapel Chorlton, Maer and Whitmore *Lich*

MAESBROOK (St John) *see* Kinnerley w Melverley, Knockin w Maesbrook and Maesbury *Lich*

MAESBURY (St John the Baptist) *as above*

MAGDALEN LAVER (St Mary Magdalen) *see* High Laver w Magdalen Laver and Lt Laver etc *Chelmsf*

MAGHULL (St Andrew) (St James) (St Peter) and Melling *Liv 8* **P** *Patr Bd* **TR** J HILL **TV** D HAMLETT **NSM** G ARDERN

MAGNIS Group Benefice, The, comprising Bishopstone, Bridge Sollars, Brinsop w Wormsley, Credenhill, Kenchester, and Mansel Lacy w Yazor *Heref 3* **P** R M Ecroyd Esq, Major D J C Davenport and Bp (3 turns), Ld Chan (1 turn) **P-in-c** R R D DAVIES-JAMES **NSM** A C DEANE

MAIDA VALE (St Peter) *see* Paddington St Mary Magd and St Pet *Lon*

MAIDA VALE (St Saviour) *see* Lt Venice *Lon*

MAIDEN BRADLEY (All Saints) *see* Mere w W Knoyle and Maiden Bradley *Sarum*

MAIDEN NEWTON (St Mary) *see* Melbury *Sarum*

MAIDENHEAD (St Andrew and St Mary Magdalene) *Ox 5* **P** *Peache Trustees* **V** W M C STILEMAN **C** D A ATALLAH, I D D MILLER, J C DRAKE, N WATKINSON **NSM** D N ANDREW

MAIDENHEAD (St Luke) *Ox 5* **P** *Bp* **V** S M LYNCH **NSM** T J ROBINSON

MAIDENHEAD (St Mark's Hospital Church) *see* Furze Platt *Ox*

MAIDENHEAD (St Peter) *see* Furze Platt *Ox*

MAIDFORD (St Peter and St Paul) *see* Lambfold *Pet*

MAIDS MORETON (St Edmund) *see* N Buckingham *Ox*

MAIDSTONE (All Saints) (St Philip) w St Stephen Tovil *Cant 12* **P** *Abp* **P-in-c** I R PARRISH

MAIDSTONE (St Faith) *Cant 12* **P** *Abp* **P-in-c** A J HOUSTON

MAIDSTONE (St Luke the Evangelist) *Cant 12* **P** *Abp and CPAS* **V** C H KEY

MAIDSTONE (St Martin) *Cant 12* **P** *Abp* **P-in-c** J H ADDISON

MAIDSTONE (St Michael and All Angels) *Cant 12* **P** *Abp* **C** N D BRYSON

MAIDSTONE (St Paul) *Cant 12* **P** *Abp* **P-in-c** A W SEWELL

MAIDSTONE Barming Heath (St Andrew) *see* Barming Heath *Cant*

MAIDWELL (St Mary) w Draughton and Lamport w Faxton *Pet 2* **P** *Bp (3 turns), Sir Ian Isham Bt (1 turn)* **C** J V J G WATSON

MAINSTONE (St John the Baptist) *see* Bishop's Castle w Mainstone, Lydbury N etc *Heref*

MAISEMORE (St Giles) *see* Ashleworth, Corse, Hartpury, Hasfield etc *Glouc*

MAKER (St Mary and St Julian) w Rame, Millbrook, St John and Torpoint *Truro 11* **P** *The Crown (1 turn), Bp, Earl of Mount Edgcumbe, and Sir John Carew Pole Bt (1 turn)* **R** M B BROWN

MALBOROUGH (All Saints) *see* Salcombe and Malborough w S Huish *Ex*

MALDEN (St James) *S'wark 15* **P** *Bp* **V** K J THOMAS

MALDEN (St John) *S'wark 15* **P** *Mert Coll Ox* **V** *vacant*

MALDEN, NEW (Christ Church) (St John the Divine) and Coombe *S'wark 15* **P** *CPAS* **V** S J KUHRT **C** E K OSGOOD

MALDON (All Saints w St Peter) *Chelmsf 11* **P** *Bp* **V** S CARTER

MALDON (St Mary) w Mundon *Chelmsf 11* **P** *D&C Westmr* **P-in-c** J F DICKENS **NSM** R J WIGGS

MALIN BRIDGE (St Polycarp) *Sheff 4* **P** *Bp* **V** G L KALSI **NSM** L A YAULL

MALINSLEE (St Leonard) *see* Cen Telford *Lich*

MALLERSTANG (St Mary) *see* Upper Eden *Carl*

MALLING, EAST (St James) and Teston *Roch 7* **P** *Peache Trustees and D&C (jt)* **V** N L WILLIAMS

MALLING, SOUTH (St Michael the Archangel) *see* Trin in Lewes *Chich*

MALLING, WEST (St Mary) w Offham *Roch 7* **P** *Ld Chan and DBP (alt)* **V** D R J GREEN **C** M MONTGOMERY

MALMESBURY (St Peter and St Paul) and Upper Avon *Bris 6* **P** *Ch Trust Fund Trust (2 turns), Ld Chan (1 turn)* **V** O C M ROSS **NSM** M CHURCHER **OLM** L M SULLIVAN

MALPAS (St Andrew) *see* St Clement *Truro*

MALPAS (St Oswald) and Threapwood and Bickerton *Ches 5* **P** *Patr Bd* **R** I A DAVENPORT **C** H J MOLESWORTH

MALTBY (St Bartholomew) (Ascension) (Venerable Bede) *Sheff 5* **P** *Bp* **TR** M RAJKOVIC

MALTON (St Michael) and Old Malton *York 6* **P** *Sir Philip Naylor-Leyland Bt* **V** G W DIGGINS

MALTON, OLD (St Mary the Virgin) *see* Malton and Old Malton *York*

MALVERN (Holy Trinity) (St James) *Worc 2* **P** *Bp and D&C Westmr (jt)* **V** W D NICHOL

MALVERN (St Andrew) *see* Malvern Chase *Worc*

MALVERN CHASE (St Andrew), including Pickersleigh and Wyche *Worc 2* **P** *Patr Bd* **TR** D C BRUCE **TV** L SPARKES **C** P J L MYRES

MALVERN LINK (Church of the Ascension) (St Matthias) w Cowleigh *Worc 2* **P** *Trustees of late Else Countess Beauchamp* **V** P T JOHNSON **NSM** S BEVERLY

MALVERN, GREAT (Christchurch) *Worc 2* **P** *Bp* **V** R G JONES **C** J GORDON **Hon C** H F GODDARD

MALVERN, GREAT (St Mary and St Michael) *Worc 2* **P** *Bp* **V** R G CORKE

MALVERN, LITTLE (St Giles) *Worc 2* **P** *Exors T M Berington Esq* **V** E G KNOWLES

MALVERN, WEST (St James) *see* Malvern H Trin and St Jas *Worc*

MAMBLE (St John the Baptist) w Bayton, Rock w Heightington w Far Forest *Worc 11* **P** *Ld Chan and R Ribbesford w Bewdley etc (alt)* **C** S E BUTCHER

MAMHEAD (St Thomas the Apostle) *see* Exminster, Kenn, Kenton w Mamhead, and Powderham *Ex*

MANACCAN (St Manaccus and St Dunstan) *see* Meneage *Truro*

MANATON (St Winifred) *see* Moretonhampstead, Manaton, N Bovey and Lustleigh *Ex*

MANBY (St Mary) *see* Mid Marsh Gp *Linc*

MANCETTER (St Peter) *Cov 5* **P** *Ch Patr Trust* **V** L A MUDD

MANCHESTER (Apostles) w Miles Platting *Man 1* **P** *DBP* **P-in-c** E L TRIMBLE **NSM** P M SCOTT

MANCHESTER (Church of the Resurrection) *see* Manchester Gd Shep and St Barn *Man*

MANCHESTER (St Ann) *Man 3* **P** *Bp* **R** J N ASHWORTH **C** P R HORLOCK, S N ISAAC

MANCHESTER (St John Chrysostom) Victoria Park *Man 1* **P** *Bp* **R** I D GOMERSALL **Hon C** K A C WASEY **OLM** C N HARTLEY

MANCHESTER Clayton (St Cross w St Paul) *Man 1* **P** *Bp* **R** C J MOORE

MANCHESTER Good Shepherd (St Barnabas) (Church of the Resurrection) *Man 1* **P** *The Crown and Trustees (alt)* **R** M H ONUIGBO

MANEA (St Nicholas) *see* Christchurch and Manea and Welney *Ely*

MANEY (St Peter) *Birm 7* **P** *Bp* **V** *vacant*

MANFIELD (All Saints) *see* E Dere Street *Leeds*

MANGOTSFIELD (St James) *Bris 5* **P** *Peache Trustees* **V** T M TAYLOR

MANLEY (St John the Evangelist) *see* Alvanley *Ches*

MANNINGFORD BRUCE (St Peter) *see* Vale of Pewsey *Sarum*

MANNINGHAM (St Paul and St Jude) *see* Girlington, Heaton and Manningham *Leeds*

MANNINGS HEATH (Church of the Good Shepherd) *see* Nuthurst and Mannings Heath *Chich*

MANOR PARK (St Barnabas) *see* Lt Ilford St Barn *Chelmsf*

MANOR PARK (St John the Baptist) and Whitby Road *Ox 12* **P** *Eton Coll* **V** G V R HOWARD

MANOR PARK (St Mary the Virgin) *see* Lt Ilford St Mich *Chelmsf*

MANOR PARK (St Michael and All Angels) *as above*

MANOR PARK (William Temple) *see* Sheff Manor *Sheff*

MANSEL LACY (St Michael) *see* Magnis Gp *Heref*

MANSERGH (St Peter) *see* Kirkby Lonsdale *Carl*

MANSFIELD (St Augustine) and Pleasley Hill St Barnabas *S'well 2* **P** *Bp* **V** *vacant*

MANSFIELD (St John the Evangelist) (St Mary) *S'well 2* **P** *Bp* **V** *vacant*

MANSFIELD (St Lawrence) *S'well 2* **P** *Bp* **P-in-c** P J STEAD

MANSFIELD (St Mark) *S'well 2* **P** *Bp* **V** C J PHILLIPS **C** J S CURRY

MANSFIELD (St Peter and St Paul) *S'well 2* **P** *Bp* **V** C J PHILLIPS **C** J S CURRY

MANSFIELD Oak Tree Lane *S'well 2* **P** *DBP* **P-in-c** P J STEAD

MANSFIELD WOODHOUSE (St Edmund King and Martyr) *S'well 2* **P** *Bp* **V** N J CARNALL

MANSTON (St Catherine) *see* St Laur in Thanet *Cant*

MANSTON (St James) *Leeds 16* **P** *R Barwick in Elmet* **V** C A JAMES

MANSTON (St Nicholas) *see* Okeford *Sarum*

MANTHORPE (St John the Evangelist) *see* Grantham, Manthorpe *Linc*

MANTON (St Mary the Virgin) *see* Empingham, Edith Weston, Lyndon, Manton etc *Pet*

MANUDEN (St Mary the Virgin) *see* Clavering w Langley, Arkesden etc *Chelmsf*

MAPERTON (St Peter and St Paul) *see* Camelot Par *B & W*

MAPLEBECK (St Radegund) *S'well 3* **P** *Sir Philip Naylor-Leyland Bt* **P-in-c** C G PEARSE **NSM** M A GROVES

MAPLEDURHAM (St Margaret) *see* Caversham Thameside and Mapledurham *Ox*

MAPLEDURWELL (St Mary) *see* N Hants Downs *Win*

MAPLESTEAD, GREAT (St Giles) *see* Halstead Area *Chelmsf*

MAPLESTEAD, LITTLE (St John) *as above*

MAPPERLEY (Holy Trinity) *see* W Hallam and Mapperley w Stanley *Derby*

MAPPLEBOROUGH GREEN (Holy Ascension) *see* Arden Marches *Cov*

MAPPLETON (All Saints) *see* Aldbrough, Mappleton w Goxhill and Withernwick *York*

MAPPOWDER (St Peter and St Paul) *see* Hazelbury Bryan and the Hillside Par *Sarum*

MARAZION (All Saints) *see* Ludgvan, Marazion, St Hilary and Perranuthnoe *Truro*

MARBURY (St Michael) w Tushingham and Whitewell *Ches 5* **P** *MMCET and Bp (jt)* **P-in-c** V G GURR

MARCH (St John) (St Mary) (St Peter) (St Wendreda) *Ely 11* **P** *Patr Bd* **TR** A J SMITH **TV** M J PURNELL **NSM** J E REES

MARCHAM (All Saints) w Garford and Shippon *Ox 19* **P** *Bp and Ch Ch Ox (jt)* **V** R G ZAIR **NSM** R C SIEBERT

MARCHINGTON (St Peter) *see* Uttoxeter Area *Lich*

MARCHINGTON WOODLANDS (St John) *as above*

MARCHWOOD (St John) *Win 11* **P** *Bp* **P-in-c** S A HONES

MARCLE, LITTLE (St Michael and All Angels) *see* Cider Churches *Heref*

MARCLE, MUCH (St Bartholomew) *as above*

MARDEN (All Saints) *see* Cannings and Redhorn *Sarum*

MARDEN (St Hilda) w Preston Grange *Newc 5* **P** *Bp* **V** P S BAGSHAW

MARDEN (St Mary the Virgin) *see* Maund Gp *Heref*

MARDEN (St Michael and All Angels) *Cant 11* **P** *Abp* **V** A A DUGUID

MARDEN ASH (St James) *see* High Ongar w Norton Mandeville *Chelmsf*

MARDEN VALE, comprising Bremhill, Calne and Blackland, Derry Hill, and Foxham *Sarum 16* **P** *The Crown and Patr Bd (alt)* **TR** R A KENWAY **TV** L S CARTER, T M MICHAUX

MARDEN, EAST (St Peter) *see* Octagon *Chich*

MARDEN, NORTH (St Mary) *as above*

MARDYKE Team, The, comprising Aveley, Belhus Park, Purfleet, and South Ockendon *Chelmsf 16* **P** *Patr Bd* **TR** A T FRANKLAND **TV** M J DRUMMOND, P D RABIN

MAREHAM ON THE HILL (All Saints) *see* Fen and Hill Gp *Linc*
MAREHAM-LE-FEN (St Helen) *as above*
MARESFIELD (St Bartholomew) *Chich 18* **P** *Ch Trust Fund Trust* **R** B W SEAR **NSM** P C INGRAM
MARFLEET (St Giles) (St George) (St Hilda) (St Philip)
York 14 **P** *Patr Bd* **TR** D A ROGERS **TV** A J MACPHERSON
MARGARET MARSH (St Margaret) *see* Shaftesbury *Sarum*
MARGARET RODING (St Margaret) *see* High and Gd Easter w Margaret Roding *Chelmsf*
MARGARET STREET (All Saints) *see* St Marylebone All SS *Lon*
MARGARETTING (St Margaret) w Mountnessing and Buttsbury *Chelmsf 8* **P** *Bp* **P-in-c** P SHERRING **C** M W HOUGHTON
MARGATE (All Saints) *Cant 5* **P** *Abp* **P-in-c** D L WATSON **C** D HARTLEY
MARGATE (Holy Trinity) *Cant 5* **P** *Ch Patr Trust* **V** C B STOCKING **C** J P HUFFMAN
MARGATE (St John the Baptist in Thanet) *Cant 5* **P** *Abp* **P-in-c** D L WATSON
MARGATE (St Paul) *see* Cliftonville *Cant*
MARGATE (St Philip) Northdown Park *Cant 5* **P** *Ch Patr Trust* **V** S GAY **C** M SAMADI
MARHAM (Holy Trinity) *see* W Norfolk Priory Gp *Ely*
MARHAMCHURCH (St Marwenne) *see* N Kernow *Truro*
MARHOLM (St Mary the Virgin) *see* Castor w Upton and Stibbington etc *Pet*
MARIANSLEIGH (St Mary) *see* Bishopsnympton, Charles, E Anstey, High Bray etc *Ex*
MARISHES, THE (St Francis) *see* Pickering w Lockton and Levisham *York*
MARK (Holy Cross) *see* The Huntspills and Mark *B & W*
MARK BEECH (Holy Trinity) *see* Hever, Four Elms and Mark Beech *Roch*
MARK CROSS (St Mark) *see* Rotherfield w Mark Cross *Chich*
MARKBY (St Peter) *see* Alford Gp *Linc*
MARKET BOSWORTH (St Peter) *see* Bosworth and Sheepy Gp *Leic*
MARKET DEEPING (St Guthlac) *Linc 19* **P** *Ld Chan* **R** *vacant*
MARKET DRAYTON (St Mary) *see* Drayton in Hales *Lich*
MARKET HARBOROUGH (St Dionysius) (The Transfiguration) - Little Bowden w Lubenham and Great Bowden *Leic 3* **P** *Patr Bd* **TR** B L HILL **TV** A J ILIFFE, B A WOOD **C** A W GILES, J R PICKERSGILL, S J HILL Hon **C** A T HELM, J WIXON **NSM** S M COOPER
MARKET LAVINGTON (St Mary of the Assumption) *see* The Lavingtons, Cheverells, and Easterton *Sarum*
MARKET OVERTON (St Peter and St Paul) *see* Oakham, Ashwell, Braunston, Brooke, Egleton etc *Pet*
MARKET RASEN (St Thomas the Apostle) *Linc 7* **P** *Ld Chan* **P-in-c** S W JOHNSON **C** C V WALKER
MARKET WEIGHTON (All Saints) *York 5* **P** *Abp* **V** C R PINCHBECK
MARKET WESTON (St Mary) *see* Stanton *St E*
MARKFIELD (St Michael), Thornton, Bagworth and Stanton under Bardon, and Copt Oak *Leic 9* **P** *MMCET* **R** S J NICHOLLS **NSM** P ASHBY
MARKHAM CLINTON (All Saints) *see* Tuxford w Weston, Markham Clinton etc *S'well*
MARKHAM, EAST (St John the Baptist) *see* Retford Area *S'well*
MARKINGTON (St Michael) *see* Bishop Thornton, Burnt Yates, Markington etc *Leeds*
MARKS GATE (St Mark) Chadwell Heath *Chelmsf 1* **P** *Bp* **V** *vacant*
MARKS TEY (St Andrew) and Aldham *Chelmsf 21* **P** *CPAS and MMCET (jt)* **P-in-c** I M SCOTT-THOMPSON **NSM** W J PAGDEN
MARKSBURY (St Peter) *see* Farmborough, Marksbury and Stanton Prior *B & W*
MARKYATE STREET (St John the Baptist) *see* Flamstead and Markyate Street *St Alb*
MARLBOROUGH (St Mary the Virgin) *Sarum 18* **P** *Patr Bd* **TR** C J SMITH **OLM** D P MAURICE
MARLBROOK (St Luke) *see* Bromsgrove *Worc*
MARLBROOK Team Ministry, The *see* Bath Twerton-on-Avon *B & W*
MARLDON (St John the Baptist) *see* Totnes w Bridgetown, Berry Pomeroy etc *Ex*
MARLESFORD (St Andrew) *see* Orebeck *St E*
MARLEY HILL (St Cuthbert) *see* Hillside *Dur*
MARLINGFORD (Assumption of the Blessed Virgin Mary) *see* Easton, Colton, Marlingford and Bawburgh *Nor*
MARLOW BOTTOM (St Mary the Virgin) *see* Gt Marlow w Marlow Bottom, Lt Marlow and Bisham *Ox*
MARLOW, GREAT (All Saints) w Marlow Bottom, Little Marlow and Bisham *Ox 18* **P** *Patr Bd* **TR** D T BULL

TV G H L WATTS, S A L WATTS, S FITZGERALD **C** R G SLADE **NSM** G L C SMITH, J R SMITH
MARLOW, LITTLE (St John the Baptist) *see* Gt Marlow w Marlow Bottom, Lt Marlow and Bisham *Ox*
MARLPIT HILL (St Paulinus) *see* Edenbridge *Roch*
MARLPOOL (All Saints) *Derby 8* **P** *V Heanor* **V** K PADLEY **C** L SHEMILT
MARLSTON (St Mary) *see* Bucklebury w Marlston *Ox*
MARNHULL (St Gregory) *Sarum 5* **P** *DBF* **P-in-c** P M SARGENT **C** G M HOCKEY **Hon C** A R WILDS
MAROWN (Old Parish Church) (St Runius), Foxdale and Baldwin *S & M* **P** *The Crown* **V** J A WARD
MARPLE (All Saints) *Ches 16* **P** *R Stockport St Mary* **V** D R CURRIE **C** J S BEATTY, P N HARRIS **NSM** L S CURRIE
MARPLE, LOW (St Martin) *Ches 16* **P** *Keble Coll Ox* **V** E P MCKENNA
MARR (St Helen) *see* Bilham *Sheff*
MARSDEN (St Bartholomew) and Slaithwaite w East Scammonden *Leeds 11* **P** *R Almondbury w Farnley Tyas and V Huddersfield (jt)* **V** *vacant*
MARSDEN, GREAT (St John's Church Centre) w Nelson St Philip *Blackb 6* **P** *The Crown and Bp (alt)* **V** L A HILLIARD **C** V SOHAIL
MARSDEN, LITTLE (St Paul) w Nelson St Mary and Nelson St Bede *Blackb 6* **P** *Bp* **V** G S JAMIESON
MARSH (St George) *see* Lancaster St Mary w St John and St Anne *Blackb*
MARSH BALDON (St Peter) *see* Dorchester *Ox*
MARSH FARM (Holy Cross) *St Alb 12* **P** *Bp* **P-in-c** R A H BROWN
MARSH GIBBON (St Mary the Virgin) *see* The Claydons and Swan *Ox*
MARSHALSWICK (St Mary) *see* St Alb St Mary Marshalswick *St Alb*
MARSHAM (All Saints) *see* Aylsham and Distr *Nor*
MARSHCHAPEL (St Mary the Virgin), Somercotes and Grainthorpe w Conisholme *Linc 15* **P** *Duchy of Lancaster (4 turns), Bp and Magd Coll Cam (2 turns), R H C Haigh Esq, Trustees and Exors Revd J M Ashley (1 turn), R H C Haigh Esq, Trustees, and Mrs M F Davis (1 turn)* **V** *vacant*
MARSHFIELD (St Mary the Virgin) w Cold Ashton and Tormarton w West Littleton *Bris 4* **P** *New Coll Ox and Bp (alt)* **V** S A V WHEELER **NSM** A M E KEMP **OLM** C L GODFREY
MARSHLAND, The, comprising Adlingfleet, Eastoft, Swinefleet, and Whitgift *Sheff 10* **P** *Ld Chan and Bp (alt)* **P-in-c** J L SMITH
MARSHWOOD (St Mary) *see* Golden Cap Team *Sarum*
MARSKE (St Edmund King and Martyr) *see* Richmond w Hudswell and Downholme and Marske *Leeds*
MARSKE IN CLEVELAND (St Mark) *York 16* **P** *Trustees* **V** D TEMBEY
MARSKE, NEW (St Thomas) *York 16* **P** *Abp* **V** A M F REED
MARSTON (St Leonard) *see* Stafford St Mary and Marston *Lich*
MARSTON (St Mary) *see* S Cliff Villages Gp *Linc*
MARSTON (St Nicholas) w Elsfield *Ox 1* **P** *Bp and D&C (jt)* **V** E K DENNO **NSM** A G G GOSLER
MARSTON BIGOT (St Leonard) *see* Nunney and Witham Friary, Marston Bigot etc *B & W*
MARSTON GREEN (St Leonard) *Birm 8* **P** *Birm Dioc Trustees* **V** P A HARRISON **C** J S ROBERTS
MARSTON MAGNA (Blessed Virgin Mary) *see* Chilton Cantelo, Ashington, Mudford, Rimpton etc *B & W*
MARSTON MEYSEY (St James) *see* S Cotswolds *Glouc*
MARSTON MONTGOMERY (St Giles) *see* S Dales *Derby*
MARSTON MOOR, comprising Askham Richard, Bilbrough, Long Marston, Rufforth, and Tockwith *York 1* **P** *MMCET, C York Esq, Abp, and N W Wailes-Fairbairn Esq (jt)* **V** M J OTTER
MARSTON MORTEYNE (St Mary the Virgin) w Lidlington *St Alb 9* **P** *Bp and St Jo Coll Cam (alt)* **R** Q D CHANDLER **NSM** C MCFARLANE
MARSTON ON DOVE (St Mary) *see* Hilton w Marston-on-Dove *Derby*
MARSTON SICCA (St James the Great) *see* Quinton, Welford, Weston and Marston Sicca *Glouc*
MARSTON ST LAWRENCE (St Lawrence) *see* Chenderit *Pet*
MARSTON TRUSSELL (St Nicholas) *see* Clipston, Haselbech, Kelmarsh, Marston Trussell etc *Pet*
MARSTON, NEW (St Michael and All Angels) *Ox 1* **P** *Bp* **V** E B BARDWELL
MARSTON, NORTH (Assumption of the Blessed Virgin Mary) *see* Schorne *Ox*
MARSTON, SOUTH (St Mary Magdalene) *see* Stratton St Margaret w S Marston etc *Bris*

MARSTOW (St Matthew) *see* Wye Brooks Benefice *Heref*

MARSWORTH (All Saints) *see* Ivinghoe w Pitstone and Slapton and Marsworth *Ox*

MARTHAM (St Mary) and Repps w Bastwick, Thurne and Clippesby *Nor 6* **P** *Bp, D&C, DBP and K Edw VI Gr Sch (jt)* **P-in-c** S R SIVYER

MARTIN (All Saints) *see* W Downland *Sarum*

MARTIN (Holy Trinity) *see* Carr Dyke Gp *Linc*

MARTIN (St Michael) *see* Horncastle Gp *Linc*

MARTIN HUSSINGTREE (St Michael) *see* Salwarpe and Hindlip w Martin Hussingtree *Worc*

MARTINDALE (Old Church) *see* Barton, Pooley Bridge, Martindale etc *Carl*

MARTINDALE (St Peter) *as above*

MARTINHOE (St Martin) *see* Lynton, Brendon, Countisbury etc *Ex*

MARTLESHAM (St Mary the Virgin) w Brightwell *St E 11* **P** *Bp* **P-in-c** T J TATE **NSM** C A PINDER, M RITTMAN

MARTLESHAM HEATH (St Michael and All Angels) *see* Martlesham w Brightwell *St E*

MARTLEY (St Peter) *see* Worcs W Rural *Worc*

MARTOCK (All Saints) w Kingsbury Episcopi and Ash *B & W 5* **P** *Bp and D&C (jt)* **V** *vacant*

MARTON (Room) *see* Middleton, Newton and Sinnington *York*

MARTON (St Esprit) *see* Long Itchington and Marton *Cov*

MARTON (St James), Siddington w Capesthorne, and Eaton w Hulme Walfield and Swettenham *Ches 11* **P** *Bp, MMCET, and Sir W A B Davenport (jt)* **V** I M ARCH **C** A NAYLOR

MARTON (St Margaret of Antioch) *see* Lea Gp *Linc*

MARTON (St Mary) *see* Forest of Galtres *York*

MARTON (St Paul) *Blackb 8* **P** *V Poulton-le-Fylde* **V** L A ATKINS

MARTON CUM GRAFTON (Christ Church) *see* Gt and Lt Ouseburn w Marton cum Grafton etc *Leeds*

MARTON IN CRAVEN (St Peter) *see* Broughton, Marton and Thornton *Leeds*

MARTON-IN-CHIRBURY (St Mark) *see* Chirbury, Marton, Middleton and Trelystan etc *Heref*

MARTON-IN-CLEVELAND (St Cuthbert) *York 17* **P** *Abp* **V** A J GRANT **C** C D TODD, S M TYNDALL

MARTYR WORTHY (St Swithun) *see* Itchen Valley *Win*

MARWOOD (St Michael and All Angels) *see* Heanton Punchardon, Marwood and W Down *Ex*

MARY TAVY (St Mary) *see* Peter Tavy and Mary Tavy *Ex*

MARYFIELD (St Philip and St James) *see* Maker w Rame, Millbrook, St John and Torpoint *Truro*

MARYLEBONE ROAD (St Marylebone) *see* St Marylebone w H Trin *Lon*

MARYPORT (St Mary) (Christ Church), Netherton, Flimby and Broughton Moor *Carl 7* **P** *Patr Bd* **TV** S M MCKENDREY **NSM** M T STILWELL

MARYSTOWE (St Mary the Virgin) *see* Milton Abbot, Dunterton, Lamerton etc *Ex*

MASBROUGH (St Paul) *Sheff 6* **P** *Bp and Ld Chan (alt)* **P-in-c** P J BATCHFORD

MASHAM (St Mary the Virgin) and Healey *Leeds 23* **P** *Trin Coll Cam* **V** D J CLEEVES **C** S L LAWTON

MASSINGHAM, GREAT (St Mary) *see* Ashwicken w Leziate, Bawsey etc *Nor*

MASSINGHAM, LITTLE (St Andrew) *as above*

MATCHBOROUGH (Christ Church) *see* Ipsley *Worc*

MATCHING (St Mary) *see* High Laver w Magdalen Laver and Lt Laver etc *Chelmsf*

MATCHING GREEN (St Edmund) *as above*

MATFEN (Holy Trinity) *see* Stamfordham w Matfen *Newc*

MATFIELD (St Luke) *see* Lamberhurst and Matfield *Roch*

MATHON (St John the Baptist) *see* Cradley w Mathon and Storridge *Heref*

MATLASKE (St Peter), including Baconsthorpe, Barningham, Edgefield, Hempstead, Plumstead, and Saxthorpe w Corpusty *Nor 17* **P** *Duchy of Lanc (1 turn), CPAS, D&C, T J R Courtauld Esq, SMF, and Pemb Coll Cam (2 turns)* **R** D J H LONGE

MATLOCK (St Giles) (St John the Baptist), Dethick, Lea and Holloway *Derby 1* **P** *Bp and DBF (jt)* **R** B M CROWTHER-ALWYN

MATLOCK BANK (All Saints) and Tansley *Derby 1* **P** *Bp* **V** R B READE **C** D J BATTISON **NSM** A J PHILLIPS

MATLOCK BATH (Holy Trinity) and Cromford *Derby 1* **P** *Ch Trust Fund Trust* **P-in-c** P N W GRAYSHON

MATSON (St Katharine) *Glouc 2* **P** *D&C* **R** *vacant*

MATTERDALE (not known) *see* Greystoke w Penruddock, Mungrisdale etc *Carl*

MATTERSEY (All Saints) *see* Bawtry w Austerfield, Misson, Everton and Mattersey *S'well*

MATTINGLEY (not known) *see* Whitewater *Win*

MATTISHALL (All Saints) and the Tudd Valley *Nor 16* **P** *Bp, G&C Coll Cam, DBP, and J V Berney Esq (jt)* **R** M A MCCAGHREY **C** A R WOODS **NSM** S E THURGILL

MATTISHALL BURGH (St Peter) *see* Mattishall and the Tudd Valley *Nor*

MAUGHOLD (St Maughold) and South Ramsey *S & M* **P** *The Crown* **V** C I LOWDON

MAULDEN (St Mary) *St Alb 8* **P** *Bp* **R** L KLIMAS

MAUNBY (St Michael) *see* Lower Swale *Leeds*

MAUND Group of Parishes, comprising Bodenham, Felton and Preston Wynne, Marden w Amberley and Wisteston, and Sutton St Nicholas and Sutton St Michael *Heref 3* **P** *Bp (2 turns), D&C (1 turn)* **R** P M ROBERTS

MAUTBY (St Peter and St Paul) *see* S Trin Broads *Nor*

MAVESYN RIDWARE (St Nicholas) *see* Kings Bromley, The Ridwares and Yoxall *Lich*

MAVIS ENDERBY (St Michael) *see* Bolingbroke Deanery *Linc*

MAWDESLEY (St Peter) *see* Croston, Bretherton and Mawdesley w Bispham *Blackb*

MAWNAN (St Mawnan) (St Michael) *Truro 3* **P** *Bp* **P-in-c** J H CLARE

MAXEY (St Peter) *see* Glinton, Etton, Maxey, Peakirk and Northborough *Pet*

MAXSTOKE (St Michael and All Angels) *Birm 8* **P** *Lord Leigh* **V** R N PARKER

MAY HILL (All Saints) *see* Huntley and Longhope, Churcham and Bulley *Glouc*

MAYBRIDGE (St Richard) and West Tarring *Chich 4* **P** *Abp Cant and Bp (jt)* **R** M J LYON **C** I H EDGAR **NSM** G T SPENCER

MAYBUSH (St Peter) and Southampton St Jude *Win 13* **P** *Bp* **P-in-c** J J BAKKER

MAYBUSH Redbridge (All Saints) *see* Maybush and Southampton St Jude *Win*

MAYFAIR (Christ Church) extra-parochial place *Lon 3* **C** N G ASHTON, S R FUREY, J O ROACH **NSM** P ALLCOCK

MAYFIELD (St Dunstan) *Chich 16* **P** *Keble Coll Ox* **V** N J PRIOR

MAYFIELD (St John the Baptist) *see* Alton w Bradley-le-Moors and Denstone etc *Lich*

MAYFORD (Emmanuel) *see* Woking St Jo *Guildf*

MAYLAND (St Barnabas) (St Barnabas Family Centre) and Latchingdon *Chelmsf 11* **P** *Bp and Abp (jt)* **V** *vacant*

MEANWOOD (Holy Trinity) *Leeds 15* **P** *Bp* **V** J ROGERS **NSM** M J BRADLEY

MEARE (Blessed Virgin Mary and All Saints) *see* Glastonbury w Meare *B & W*

MEARS ASHBY (All Saints) and Hardwick and Sywell w Overstone *Pet 6* **P** *Duchy of Cornwall (2 turns), Bracegirdle Trustees (1 turn), and Mrs C K Edmiston (1 turn)* **R** K M HUTCHINS

MEASE VALLEY, comprising Clifton Campville, Edingale, Elford, and Harlaston *Lich 4* **P** *Bp, Exors Major F C Pipe-Wolferstan, and Mrs E V G Inge-Innes-Lillingston (jt)* **R** J W R GRICE **OLM** C S TYLER, N J BUSBY

MEASHAM (St Laurence) *see* Woodfield *Leic*

MEAVY (St Peter) *see* Yelverton, Meavy, Sheepstor, Walkhampton, Sampford Spiney and Horrabridge *Ex*

MEDBOURNE (St Giles) *see* Six Saints circa Holt *Leic*

MEDMENHAM (St Peter and St Paul) *see* Hambleden Valley *Ox*

MEDOMSLEY (St Mary Magdalene) *Dur 4* **P** *Bp* **NSM** I W WAUGH

MEDSTEAD (St Andrew) *see* Bentworth, Lasham, Medstead and Shalden *Win*

MEERBROOK (St Matthew) *see* Leek and Meerbrook *Lich*

MEESDEN (St Mary) *see* Hormead, Wyddial, Anstey, Brent Pelham etc *St Alb*

MEETH (St Michael and All Angels) *see* Okehampton, Inwardleigh, Belstone, Sourton etc *Ex*

MEIR (Holy Trinity) *see* Longton and Meir *Lich*

MEIR HEATH (St Francis of Assisi) and Normacot *Lich 11* **P** *Bp and DBP (jt)* **V** D W MCHARDY

MEIR PARK (St Clare) *see* Meir Heath and Normacot *Lich*

MELBECKS (Holy Trinity) *see* Swaledale *Leeds*

MELBOURN (All Saints) *Ely 7* **P** *D&C* **P-in-c** E A SHIPP **NSM** M L PRICE

MELBOURNE (St Michael), Ticknall, Smisby and Stanton by Bridge *Derby 7* **P** *Bp* **V** S T SHORT

MELBURY (St Mary the Virgin) (St Osmund) *Sarum 3* **P** *Patr Bd* **TR** T J GREENSLADE **TV** D E INGLES, L J WILCOCK

MELBURY ABBAS (St Thomas) *see* Shaftesbury *Sarum*

MELBURY BUBB (St Mary the Virgin) *see* Melbury *Sarum*

MELBURY OSMUND (St Osmund) *as above*

MELCHBOURNE (St Mary Magdalene) *see* The Stodden Churches *St Alb*

MELCOMBE HORSEY (St Andrew) *see* Piddle Valley, Hilton and Ansty, Cheselbourne etc *Sarum*

MELDON (St John the Evangelist) *see* Bolam w Whalton and Hartburn w Meldon *Newc*

MELDRETH (Holy Trinity) *Ely 7*   **P** *D&C*   **P-in-c** E A SHIPP   **NSM** M L PRICE

MELKSHAM (St Barnabas) (St Michael and All Angels) *Sarum 15*   **P** *DBP*   **TR** B D BLACKFORD   **TV** A SOWTON   **NSM** H BEGLEY

MELKSHAM FOREST (St Andrew) *see* Melksham *Sarum*

MELLING (St Thomas) *see* Maghull and Melling *Liv*

MELLING (St Wilfrid) *see* E Lonsdale *Blackb*

MELLIS (St Mary the Virgin) *see* S Hartismere *St E*

MELLOR (St Mary) *see* Balderstone, Mellor and Samlesbury *Blackb*

MELLOR (St Thomas) *Ches 16*   **P** *Bp*   **V** T WARD

MELLS (St Andrew) w Buckland Dinham, Elm, Whatley, Vobster and Chantry *B & W 3*   **P** *DBP (2 turns), Bp (1 turn)*   **R** C A FAIRCLOUGH   **NSM** B L DAVIES

MELMERBY (St John the Baptist) *see* Cross Fell Gp *Carl*

MELPLASH (Christ Church) *see* Beaminster Area *Sarum*

MELSONBY (St James the Great) *see* Forcett and Aldbrough and Melsonby *Leeds*

MELTHAM (St Bartholomew) *see* Meltham *Leeds*

MELTHAM Christ the King (St Bartholomew) (St James) *Leeds 5*   **P** *Simeon's Trustees, R Almondbury w Farnley Tyas, and Bp (jt)*   **V** J S DRACUP   **NSM** D SHIELDS, P ROLLS   **OLM** J F RADCLIFFE

MELTHAM MILLS (St James) *see* Meltham *Leeds*

MELTON (St Andrew) and Ufford *St E 18*   **P** *D&C Ely (3 turns), and T R E Blois-Brooke Esq (1 turn)*   **R** P G HAMBLING   **Hon C** P J BROWN

MELTON CONSTABLE (St Peter) *see* Briston, Burgh Parva, Hindolveston etc *Nor*

MELTON MOWBRAY (St Mary) *Leic 2*   **P** *Patr Bd*   **TR** K P ASHBY   **TV** M E BARR

MELTON ROSS (Ascension) *see* Brocklesby Park, Croxton and North Wolds *Linc*

MELTON, GREAT (All Saints) *see* Hethersett w Canteloff w Lt and Gt Melton *Nor*

MELTON, HIGH (St James) *see* Barnburgh w Melton on the Hill etc *Sheff*

MELTON, LITTLE (All Saints) *see* Hethersett w Canteloff w Lt and Gt Melton *Nor*

MELVERLEY (St Peter) *see* Kinnerley w Melverley, Knockin w Maesbrook and Maesbury *Lich*

MEMBURY (St John the Baptist) *see* Axminster, Chardstock, All Saints etc *Ex*

MENDHAM (All Saints) *see* Sancroft *St E*

MENDLESHAM (St Mary) *St E 8*   **P** *SMF*   **V** P T GRAY

MENEAGE (St Anthony) (St Martin) (St Mawgan) *Truro 4*   **P** *Ld Chan and Bp (alt)*   **P-in-c** M H NORTH

MENHENIOT (St Lalluwy and St Antoninus) *Truro 12*   **P** *Ex Coll Ox*   **P-in-c** R M BELL

MENSTON (St John the Divine) w Woodhead *Leeds 4*   **P** *Bp*   **V** S PROUDLOVE   **NSM** A J HOWORTH

MENTMORE (St Mary the Virgin) *see* Cottesloe *Ox*

MEOLE BRACE (Holy Trinity) *Lich 19*   **P** *J K Bather Esq*   **V** P J CANSDALE   **C** C GOMPERTZ   **NSM** C RUXTON, V PITT

MEOLS, GREAT (St John the Baptist) *Ches 8*   **P** *Bp*   **V** G A ROSSITER

MEOLS, NORTH Team Ministry, The (St Cuthbert), including Banks and Crossens *Liv 9*   **P** *Patr Bd*   **TR** K J R CLARKE   **C** C P GREGORY

MEON BRIDGE, comprising Droxford, Exton, and Meonstoke w Corhampton *Portsm 1*   **P** *Bp*   **R** A W FORREST   **C** D B MORGAN, S T MARTELL

MEON, EAST (All Saints) *Portsm 4*   **P** *Ld Chan*   **V** J BALL

MEON, WEST (St John the Evangelist) and Warnford *Portsm 4*   **P** *Bp and DBP (alt)*   **C** J BALL

MEONSTOKE (St Andrew) *see* Meon Bridge *Portsm*

MEOPHAM (St John the Baptist) w Nurstead *Roch 1*   **P** *D&C and Mrs S Edmeades-Stearns (jt)*   **R** A E DAVIE

MEPAL (St Mary) *see* Witcham w Mepal *Ely*

MEPPERSHALL (St Mary the Virgin) and Shefford *St Alb 8*   **P** *Bp and St Jo Coll Cam (alt)*   **V** V M GOODMAN

MERE (St Michael the Archangel) w West Knoyle and Maiden Bradley *Sarum 12*   **P** *Bp*   **P-in-c** C A WILSON-BARKER

MERESIDE (St Wilfrid) *see* Blackpool St Wilfrid *Blackb*

MEREVALE (St Mary the Virgin) *see* Baxterley w Hurley and Wood End and Merevale etc *Birm*

MEREWORTH (St Lawrence), Wateringbury and West Peckham *Roch 7*   **P** *D&C and Viscount Falmouth (jt)*   **R** *vacant*

MERIDEN (St Laurence) *Cov 4*   **P** *Chapter Cov Cathl*   **P-in-c** L LILLEY

MERRINGTON (St John the Evangelist) *Dur 5*   **P** *D&C*   **P-in-c** B A HILTON   **NSM** D T ACKERLEY

MERRIOTT (All Saints) w Hinton, Dinnington and Lopen *B & W 14*   **P** *D&C Bris (2 turns), Bp (1 turn)*   **R** J R HICKS   **C** R B HICKS   **NSM** N J CLARKE

MERROW (St John the Evangelist) *Guildf 5*   **P** *Earl of Onslow*   **R** R STUART-BOURNE   **C** B J HANSON

MERRY HILL (St Joseph of Arimathea) *see* Penn Fields *Lich*

MERRYMEET (St Mary) *see* Menheniot *Truro*

MERSEA, WEST (St Peter and St Paul) w East (St Edmund), Peldon, Great and Little Wigborough *Chelmsf 24*   **P** *The Crown (1 turn), Patr Bd (2 turns)*   **C** T E WALKER

MERSHAM (St John the Baptist) *see* Stour Downs *Cant*

MERSTHAM (St Katharine), South Merstham and Gatton *S'wark 24*   **P** *Patr Bd*   **TR** P M PULLINGER   **TV** B B M BROWN   **NSM** L J ABRAMS   **OLM** V J WILLIAMS

MERSTHAM, SOUTH (All Saints) *see* Merstham, S Merstham and Gatton *S'wark*

MERTON (All Saints) *see* Shebbear, Buckland Filleigh, Sheepwash etc *Ex*

MERTON (St James) *S'wark 13*   **P** *Bp and V Merton St Mary (jt)*   **V** J M ROSENTHAL   **NSM** A M BUDDEN

MERTON (St John the Divine) *see* Merton Priory *S'wark*

MERTON (St Mary) *S'wark 13*   **P** *Bp*   **V** J A HAYWARD   **NSM** J A BERSWEDEN

MERTON (St Peter) *see* Caston, Griston, Merton, Thompson etc *Nor*

MERTON (St Swithun) *see* Ray Valley *Ox*

MERTON PRIORY *S'wark 13*   **P** *Patr Bd*   **TR** M F EMINSON   **TV** A G JUDGE   **Hon C** D J SWAN   **NSM** B S ALAGOA

MESHAW (St John) *see* Burrington, Chawleigh, Cheldon, Chulmleigh etc *Ex*

MESSING (All Saints) *see* Thurstable and Winstree *Chelmsf*

MESSINGHAM (Holy Trinity) w East Butterwick, Scotter w East Ferry and Scotton w Northorpe *Linc 6*   **P** *Bp (2 turns), Ld Chan (1 turn)*   **R** D J SWANNACK   **OLM** D L LANGFORD, W KEAST

MESTY CROFT (St Luke) *see* Wednesbury St Paul Wood Green *Lich*

METFIELD (St John the Baptist) *see* Sancroft *St E*

METHERINGHAM (St Wilfred) w Blankney and Dunston *Linc 12*   **P** *Bp (2 turns), Br Field Products Ltd (1 turn)*   **V** A T COATES

METHLEY (St Oswald) *see* Rothwell, Lofthouse, Methley etc *Leeds*

METHWOLD (St George) *see* Wissey Valley *Ely*

METTINGHAM (All Saints) *see* Bungay *St E*

METTON (St Andrew) *see* Roughton and Felbrigg, Metton, Sustead etc *Nor*

MEVAGISSEY (St Peter) *see* St Mewan w Mevagissey and St Ewe *Truro*

MEXBOROUGH (St John the Baptist) *Sheff 12*   **P** *Adn York*   **P-in-c** E J S MORRISON

MEYSEY HAMPTON (St Mary) *see* S Cotswolds *Glouc*

MICHAEL (St Michael and All Angels) *see* W Coast *S & M*

MICHAELCHURCH ESCLEY (St Michael) *see* Black Mountains Gp *Heref*

MICHAELSTOW (St Michael) *see* Camelside *Truro*

MICHELDEVER (St Mary) *see* Upper Dever *Win*

MICHELMERSH (Our Lady) and Awbridge and Braishfield and Farley Chamberlayne and Timsbury *Win 12*   **P** *Bp*   **R** S C PITTIS   **NSM** J E C THOMPSON

MICKLEFIELD (St Mary the Virgin) *see* Aberford w Micklefield *York*

MICKLEGATE (Holy Trinity) *see* York H Trin Micklegate *York*

MICKLEHAM (St Michael) *see* Leatherhead and Mickleham *Guildf*

MICKLEOVER (All Saints) (St John the Evangelist) *Derby 5*   **P** *Bp and MMCET (jt)*   **V** P F WALLEY   **NSM** A G ROWLANDS, M P STAUNTON   **OLM** I D GODLINGTON, P M PRITCHARD

MICKLETON (St Lawrence) *see* Vale and Cotswold Edge *Glouc*

MICKLEY (St George) *see* Bywell and Mickley *Newc*

MICKLEY (St John the Evangelist) *see* Fountains Gp *Leeds*

MID CHURNET *see* Kingsley and Foxt-w-Whiston and Oakamoor etc *Lich*

MID ELLOE Group, The, comprising Holbeach Hurn, Holbeach Marsh, Fleet, and Gedney *Linc 18*   **P** *V Holbeach and DBP (1 turn), The Crown (1 turn)*   **NSM** E D CRUST

MID LOES, comprising Ashfield-cum-Thorpe, Charsfield w Debach, Cretingham, Dallinghoo, Earl Soham, Hoo,

Letheringham, and Monewden *St E 14*   **P** *Ld Chan (1 turn),*
MMCET, CPAS, Bp, and Wadh Coll Ox (1 turn)   **R** S F BRIAN
C K L B MARTIN

MID MARSH Group, The, comprising Alvingham, Great
Carlton, Grimoldby, Manby, and South Cockerington
Linc 15   **P** A M D Hall Esq, Bp, D&C, and Lady Mowbray (by
turn)   **OLM** J R SELFE, L W CARROLL

MID TEST, The, comprising Broughton w Bossington,
Houghton, Leckford, Longstock, Mottisfont, and
Stockbridge *Win 12*   **P** *Ld Chan (1 turn), C M Brendish Esq*
(1 turn), Bp and St Jo Coll Ox (1 turn)   **R** P W BOWDEN

MID TRENT, comprising Fradswell, Gayton, Hixon, Milwich,
Salt, Sandon, Stowe-by-Chartley, and Weston-upon-Trent
Lich 17   **P** *Patr Bd*   **TV** M G CADWALLADER
OLM C V STARKIE

MIDDLE *see also under substantive place name*

MIDDLE MARCHES Benefice, The, comprising Bedstone,
Bucknell, Chapel Lawn, Clungunford, Hopton Castle,
Llanfair Waterdine, and Stowe *Heref 9*   **P** *Earl of Powis, J*
Coltman-Rogers Esq, Grocers' Co (1 turn), Mrs E B Rocke, Sir
Huw Ripley Bt, P J H Barnes Esq (1 turn)   **V** A C BALLARD

MIDDLE RASEN Group, The, comprising Faldingworth w
Buslingthorpe, Friesthorpe w Snarford, Middle Rasen Drax,
Newton and Toft, and West Rasen *Linc 7*   **P** *Bp,*
Charterhouse, and DBP (jt)   **R** B S DIXON

MIDDLEHAM (St Mary and St Alkelda) w Coverdale and
East Witton and Thornton Steward *Leeds 25*   **P** *Bp, R*
Craven-Smith-Milnes Esq, and W R Burdon Esq (jt)
R J M PAYNE   **C** E J MOODY

MIDDLESBROUGH (All Saints) *York 17*   **P** *Abp*
V G HOLLAND

MIDDLESBROUGH (Ascension) *York 17*   **P** *Abp*
P-in-c E NAZIR MASIH

MIDDLESBROUGH (St Agnes) *York 17*   **P** *Abp*
P-in-c A J GRANT

MIDDLESBROUGH (St Columba w St Paul) *York 17*   **P** *Abp*
V S COOPER   **NSM** P M KRONBERGS

MIDDLESBROUGH (St John the Evangelist) *York 17*   **P** *Abp*
V S COOPER

MIDDLESBROUGH (St Martin of Tours) (St Cuthbert)
York 17   **P** *Abp*   **V** *vacant*

MIDDLESBROUGH (St Oswald) (St Chad) *York 17*   **P** *Abp*
V S RICHARDSON   **NSM** K A DEAN

MIDDLESBROUGH (St Thomas) *York 17*   **P** *Abp*
V T M LEATHLEY

MIDDLESMOOR (St Chad) *see* Upper Nidderdale *Leeds*

MIDDLESTOWN (St Luke) *Leeds 19*   **P** R Thornhill
P-in-c J M GEARY

MIDDLETON (All Saints) *see* N Hinckford *Chelmsf*

MIDDLETON (Holy Ghost) *see* Kirkby Lonsdale *Carl*

MIDDLETON (Holy Trinity) *see* Bromfield *Heref*

MIDDLETON (Holy Trinity) *see* Yoxmere *St E*

MIDDLETON (St Andrew), Newton and Sinnington *York 19*
P *Abp (2 turns), Simeon's Trustees (1 turn)*   **P-in-c** R G BARKER

MIDDLETON (St John the Baptist) *see* Curdworth, Middleton
and Wishaw *Birm*

MIDDLETON (St Leonard) (St Margaret) and Thornham
Man 14   **P** *Bp*   **OLM** D E BROOKS, K HAMNETT, P J DEMAIN,
S L SPENCER

MIDDLETON (St Mary the Virgin) (St Cross) *Leeds 14*
P *V Rothwell and DBP (jt)*   **V** A T C MYERS

MIDDLETON (St Mary) *see* Middlewinch *Nor*

MIDDLETON (St Michael and All Angels) *see* Youlgreave,
Middleton, Stanton-in-Peak etc *Derby*

MIDDLETON (St Nicholas) *Chich 1*   **P** D&C
V W T MARSTON

MIDDLETON CHENEY (All Saints) *see* Chenderit *Pet*

MIDDLETON JUNCTION (St Gabriel) *see* Chadderton
St Mark *Man*

MIDDLETON ON LEVEN (St Cuthbert) *see* Rudby in
Cleveland w Middleton *York*

MIDDLETON ON THE WOLDS (St Andrew) *see* Woldsburn
York

MIDDLETON SCRIVEN (St John the Baptist) *see* Stottesdon w
Farlow, Cleeton St Mary etc *Heref*

MIDDLETON ST GEORGE (St George) (St Laurence) *Dur 7*
P *Bp*   **P-in-c** A THORP   **NSM** H M THORP

MIDDLETON STONEY (All Saints) *see* Akeman *Ox*

MIDDLETON TYAS (St Michael and All Angels) *see* E Dere
Street *Leeds*

MIDDLETON-BY-WIRKSWORTH (Holy Trinity) *see*
Wirksworth *Derby*

MIDDLETON-IN-CHIRBY (Holy Trinity) *see* Chirbury, Marton,
Middleton and Trelystan etc *Heref*

MIDDLETON-IN-TEESDALE (St Mary the Virgin) w Forest
and Frith *Dur 6*   **P** *Lord Barnard and The Crown (alt)*
P-in-c J BARKER   **NSM** A P WALLBANK

MIDDLEWICH (St Michael and All Angels) w Byley *Ches 6*
P *Bp*   **V** S M DREW   **NSM** A P BOULTON, C M HUGHES,
E WOODE, L V REED

MIDDLEWINCH, comprising East Winch w West Bilney,
Middleton, North Runcton, and West Winch *Nor 19*   **P** *Ld*
Chan (2 turns), Bp and W O Lancaster Esq (1 turn), Ms E J C
Bostock and Ms C M Mackay (1 turn)   **R** R MUBARAK

MIDDLEZOY (Holy Cross) w Othery, Moorlinch and
Greinton *B & W 4*   **P** *Bp*   **R** *vacant*

MIDGHAM (St Matthew) *see* Aldermaston and
Woolhampton *Ox*

MIDHURST (St Mary Magdalene and St Denis) *Chich 9*
P *Bp*   **V** D A WILLIS

MIDSOMER NORTON (St John the Baptist) w Clandown
B & W 11   **P** *Ch Ch Ox*   **V** C G CHIPLIN

MID-WYEDEAN CHURCHES *see* Coleford, Staunton,
Newland, Redbrook etc *Glouc*

MILBER (St Luke) *see* Newton Abbot *Ex*

MILBORNE (St Andrew) *see* Puddletown, Tolpuddle and
Milborne w Dewlish *Sarum*

MILBORNE PORT (St John the Evangelist) w Goathill and
Charlton Horethorne w Stowell *B & W 2*   **P** *Bp and J K*
Wingfield Digby Esq (jt)   **V** S J GODFREY

MILBORNE WICK (Mission Church) *see* Milborne Port w
Goathill etc *B & W*

MILBOURNE (Holy Saviour) *see* Ponteland *Newc*

MILBURN (St Cuthbert) *see* Heart of Eden *Carl*

MILCOMBE (St Laurence) *see* Bloxham w Milcombe and S
Newington *Ox*

MILDEN (St Peter) *see* Monks Eleigh w Chelsworth and
Brent Eleigh etc *St E*

MILDENHALL (St John the Baptist) *see* Marlborough *Sarum*

MILDENHALL (St Mary) *St E 7*   **P** *Patr Bd (2 turns), Ld Chan*
(1 turn)   **C** S BARTON, S M LEATHLEY   **NSM** C BUTCHER,
D A BUTCHER

MILDMAY GROVE (St Jude and St Paul) *Lon 6*   **P** *CPAS*
P-in-c J A S HILL

MILE CROSS (St Catherine) *Nor 2*   **P** *Dr J P English, Canon G*
F Bridger, the Revd K W Habershon, and the Revd H Palmer (jt)
V M J E HARTLEY   **OLM** R E LAMBERT

MILE OAK (The Good Shepherd) *see* Portslade St Nic and
St Andr and Mile Oak *Chich*

MILEHAM (St John the Baptist) *see* Launditch and the Upper
Nar *Nor*

MILES PLATTING (St Cuthbert) *see* Man Apostles w Miles
Platting *Man*

MILFORD (Holy Trinity) *see* Hazelwood, Holbrook and
Milford *Derby*

MILFORD (St John the Evangelist) *Guildf 4*   **P** *V Witley*
V C G POTTER

MILFORD, SOUTH (St Mary the Virgin) *see* Monk Fryston
and S Milford *York*

MILFORD-ON-SEA (All Saints) *Win 11*   **P** *Bp*   **V** *vacant*

MILL END (St Peter) and Heronsgate w West Hyde *St Alb 4*
P *Bp and V Rickmansworth*   **V** S G CUTMORE
C S F FRAMPTON

MILL HILL (John Keble Church) *Lon 15*   **P** *Bp*
P-in-c S M ROWBORY

MILL HILL (St Michael and All Angels) *Lon 15*   **P** *Bp*
V S P YOUNG   **NSM** H BETTS

MILL HILL (St Paul) *see* Hendon St Paul Mill Hill *Lon*

MILLAND (St Luke) *see* Linch w Iping Marsh, Milland and
Rake etc *Chich*

MILLBROOK (All Saints) *see* Maker w Rame, Millbrook,
St John and Torpoint *Truro*

MILLBROOK (Christ the King) *see* Kettering Ch the King *Pet*

MILLBROOK (Holy Trinity) *Win 13*   **P** *Bp*   **R** *vacant*

MILLBROOK (St James) *Ches 14*   **P** *Bp, V Stalybridge St Paul,*
and Mrs E Bissill (jt)   **P-in-c** T J HAYES   **C** C W VINEY

MILLBROOK (St Michael and All Angels) *see* Ampthill w
Millbrook and Steppingley *St Alb*

MILLERS DALE (St Anne) *see* Tideswell *Derby*

MILLFIELD (St Mark) and Pallion St Luke *Dur 14*   **P** *Bp*
V *vacant*

MILLFIELD (St Mary) *Dur 14*   **P** *The Crown*   **V** B SKELTON

MILLHOUSES (Holy Trinity) *see* Abbeydale and Millhouses
Sheff

MILLHOUSES (St Oswald) *see* Sheff St Pet and St Oswald
Sheff

MILLINGTON (St Margaret) *see* Pocklington Wold *York*

MILLOM (Holy Trinity) (St George) *Carl 9*   **P** *Bp and Trustees*
(jt)   **NSM** C CARTER

MILNROW (St James) and New Hey *Man 17*   **P** *Bp and R Rochdale*   **V** J E PITMAN   **NSM** S E WARD

MILNSHAW (St Mary Magdalen)   *see* Accrington St Andr, St Mary and St Pet and Church Kirk *Blackb*

MILNTHORPE (St Thomas)   *see* Heversham and Milnthorpe *Carl*

MILSON (St George)   *see* Cleobury Mortimer w Hopton Wafers etc *Heref*

MILSTEAD (St Mary and the Holy Cross)   *see* Tunstall and Bredgar *Cant*

MILSTON (St Mary)   *see* Avon River *Sarum*

MILTON (All Saints) *Ely 6*   **P** *K Coll Cam*   **R** D J CHAMBERLIN   **NSM** S BRADFORD

MILTON (St Blaise)   *see* DAMASCUS *Ox*

MILTON (St James) (St Andrew's Church Centre) (St Patrick) *Portsm 6*   **P** *V Portsea St Mary*   **P-in-c** P R ARMSTEAD   **C** H C DEADMAN

MILTON (St John the Evangelist)   *see* Adderbury w Milton *Ox*

MILTON (St Mary Magdalene) *Win 9*   **P** *V Milford*   **R** A H BAILEY

MILTON (St Peter) w St Jude and Kewstoke *B & W 10*   **P** *Ld Chan*   **V** G P EALES

MILTON (St Philip and St James) *Lich 8*   **P** *Bp*   **V** B E STATHAM   **OLM** J M COOPER

MILTON (St Simon and St Jude)   *see* Gillingham, Milton-on-Stour and Silton *Sarum*

MILTON ABBAS (St James the Great)   *see* Winterborne Valley and Milton Abbas *Sarum*

MILTON ABBOT (St Constantine), Dunterton, Lamerton, Sydenham Damerel, Marystowe and Coryton *Ex 22*   **P** *Bp, Bedford Estates, J W Tremayne Esq, Mrs E J Bullock, P T L Newman Esq (jt)*   **V** A J ATKINS

MILTON BRYAN (St Peter)   *see* Woburn w Eversholt, Milton Bryan, Battlesden etc *St Alb*

MILTON CLEVEDON (St James)   *see* Alham Vale *B & W*

MILTON COMBE (Holy Spirit)   *see* Buckland Monachorum *Ex*

MILTON DAMEREL (Holy Trinity)   *see* Bradworthy, Sutcombe etc *Ex*

MILTON ERNEST (All Saints), Pavenham and Thurleigh *St Alb 13*   **P** *Bp (2 turns), Lord Luke (1 turn)*   **P-in-c** P R KAY

MILTON KEYNES (Christ the Cornerstone) *Ox 14*   **P** *Bp*   **V** E LOZADA-UZURIAGA   **C** T NORWOOD   **NSM** K STRAUGHAN, P OXLEY

MILTON KEYNES VILLAGE (All Saints)   *see* Walton Milton Keynes *Ox*

MILTON LILBOURNE (St Peter)   *see* Vale of Pewsey *Sarum*

MILTON MALSOR (Holy Cross)   *see* Blisworth, Alderton, Grafton Regis etc *Pet*

MILTON NEXT GRAVESEND (Christ Church) *Roch 4*   **P** *Bp*   **V** S A WOMERSLEY   **C** K A SEGGIE   **NSM** J P LITTLEWOOD

MILTON NEXT GRAVESEND (St Peter and St Paul) w Denton *Roch 4*   **P** *Bp*   **R** G V HERBERT

MILTON REGIS (Holy Trinity) w Murston, Bapchild and Tonge *Cant 15*   **P** *Abp, D&C, and St Jo Coll Cam (jt)*   **V** G M A ROGERS   **C** S R YOUNG

MILTON REGIS (St Mary)   *see* Sittingbourne w Bobbing *Cant*

MILTON, GREAT (St Mary the Virgin) w Little (St James) and Great Haseley *Ox 20*   **P** *Bp and D&C Windsor (jt)*   **R** S N CRONK

MILTON, SOUTH (All Saints)   *see* Thurlestone, S Milton, Churchstow etc *Ex*

MILTON-UNDER-WYCHWOOD (St Simon and St Jude)   *see* Wychwood *Ox*

MILVERTON (St Michael) w Halse, Fitzhead and Ash Priors *B & W 19*   **P** *Bp, Adn, R Wiveliscombe and the Hills, and MMCET (jt)*   **R** H L STAINER

MILVERTON, NEW (St Mark) *Cov 11*   **P** *CPAS*   **V** J C PARKER

MILVERTON, OLD (St James)   *see* Lillington and Old Milverton *Cov*

MILWICH (All Saints)   *see* Mid Trent *Lich*

MIMMS *see also* MYMMS

MIMMS, SOUTH (Christ Church) *Lon 14*   **P** *Ch Patr Trust*   **V** A M RIMMER

MINCHINHAMPTON (Holy Trinity) w Box and Amberley *Glouc 4*   **P** *Bp and DBP (jt)*   **R** H N GILBERT   **NSM** P J SPIERS, S F EMERY

MINEHEAD (St Andrew) (St Michael) (St Peter) *B & W 15*   **P** *Lt Col G W F Luttrell and Bp (jt)*   **V** S J ROBINSON   **NSM** C M MACDONALD

MINETY (St Leonard)   *see* Braydon Brook *Bris*

MININGSBY WITH EAST KIRKBY (St Nicholas)   *see* Bolingbroke Deanery *Linc*

MINLEY (St Andrew) *Guildf 1*   **P** *Bp*   **V** W F P PERRY

MINNIS BAY (St Thomas)   *see* Birchington w Acol and Minnis Bay *Cant*

MINSKIP (Mission Room)   *see* Aldborough w Boroughbridge and Roecliffe *Leeds*

MINSTEAD (All Saints)   *see* Lyndhurst and Emery Down and Minstead *Win*

MINSTER (St Mary the Virgin)   *see* Wantsum Gp *Cant*

MINSTER (St Merteriana)   *see* Boscastle and Tintagel Gp *Truro*

MINSTER IN SHEPPEY (St Mary and St Sexburga)   *see* W Sheppey *Cant*

MINSTER LOVELL (St Kenelm)   *see* Witney *Ox*

MINSTERLEY (Holy Trinity), Habberley and Hope w Shelve *Heref 12*   **P** *Bp (3 turns), DBP (3 turns), New Coll Ox (2 turns), J J C Coldwell Esq (1 turn)*   **R** G D TULK

MINSTERWORTH (St Peter)   *see* Westbury-on-Severn w Flaxley, Blaisdon etc *Glouc*

MINTERNE MAGNA (St Andrew)   *see* Buckland Newton, Cerne Abbas, Godmanstone etc *Sarum*

MINTING (St Andrew)   *see* Bardney *Linc*

MIREHOUSE (St Andrew) *Carl 5*   **P** *Bp*   **C** F T PEARSON, P M KERRY

MIRFIELD (St Mary) *Leeds 9*   **P** *Bp*   **V** H C BAKER   **NSM** H C BUTLER

MISERDEN (St Andrew)   *see* Brimpsfield w Birdlip, Syde, Daglingworth etc *Glouc*

MISSENDEN, GREAT (St Peter and St Paul) w Ballinger and Little Hampden *Ox 17*   **P** *Bp*   **V** R E HARPER   **C** E M LOWSON

MISSENDEN, LITTLE (St John the Baptist) *Ox 17*   **P** *Earl Howe*   **P-in-c** J V SIMPSON

MISSON (St John the Baptist)   *see* Bawtry w Austerfield, Misson, Everton and Mattersey *S'well*

MISTERTON (All Saints)   *see* Beckingham, Walkeringham, Misterton, etc *S'well*

MISTERTON (St Leonard)   *see* Avon-Swift *Leic*

MISTERTON (St Leonard)   *see* Wulfric Benefice *B & W*

MISTLEY (St Mary and St Michael) w Manningtree and Bradfield *Chelmsf 22*   **P** *DBP and Bp (jt)*   **R** D TURNER   **NSM** J R BRIEN   **OLM** C F SCARGILL

MITCHAM (Ascension) Pollards Hill *S'wark 13*   **P** *Bp*   **V** J M THOMAS

MITCHAM (Christ Church)   *see* Merton Priory *S'wark*

MITCHAM (St Barnabas) *S'wark 13*   **P** *Bp*   **V** J G CAVALCANTI

MITCHAM (St Mark) *S'wark 13*   **P** *Bp*   **V** N J STONE

MITCHAM (St Olave) *S'wark 13*   **P** *The Crown*   **P-in-c** G PIPER

MITCHAM (St Peter and St Paul) *S'wark 13*   **P** *Keble Coll Ox*   **V** D M B PENNELLS   **NSM** M J COCKFIELD

MITCHELDEAN (St Michael and All Angels)   *see* Abenhall w Mitcheldean *Glouc*

MITFORD (St Mary Magdalene) and Hebron *Newc 11*   **P** *Ld Chan and the Revd B W J Mitford (alt)*   **P-in-c** A M LAMB

MITRE, The, comprising Heigham St Barnabas w St Bartholomew, Heigham St Thomas, and Lakenham St Alban *Nor 3*   **P** *Bp and D&C (jt)*   **V** I H DYBLE   **C** A C WOODMAN, D M ROWLANDSON, D Z LLOYD, E C LAND, J N PAYNE, M T LUSCOMBE, P J BROMBLEY   **NSM** M C A HUTTON

MIXBURY (All Saints)   *see* Shelswell *Ox*

MIXENDEN (Holy Nativity) and Illingworth *Leeds 10*   **P** *Bp and V Halifax (jt)*   **V** R SUTHERLAND   **NSM** Y J K HAGAN

MOBBERLEY (St Wilfrid) *Ches 12*   **P** *Bp*   **V** R I BLAY

MOCCAS (St Michael and All Angels)   *see* Cusop w Blakemere, Bredwardine w Brobury etc *Heref*

MODBURY (St George), Bigbury, Ringmore, Kingston, and Aveton Gifford *Ex 13*   **P** *Bp Ex, D&C Ex, DBP, MMCET, and P K M Ramm Esq*   **R** M J ROWLAND

MODDERSHALL (All Saints)   *see* Stone Ch Ch and Oulton *Lich*

MOGGERHANGER (St John the Evangelist)   *see* Cople, Moggerhanger and Willington *St Alb*

MOLASH (St Peter)   *see* King's Wood *Cant*

MOLDGREEN (Christ Church) and Rawthorpe St James *Leeds 5*   **P** *R Kirkheaton and DBP (jt)*   **P-in-c** C A CHESHIRE

MOLESCROFT (St Leonard)   *see* Beverley Minster *York*

MOLESEY, EAST (St Mary) *Guildf 8*   **P** *Bp*   **V** R G LLOYD   **C** N W KURZ

MOLESEY, EAST (St Paul) *Guildf 8*   **P** *Bp*   **V** A L FARMER

MOLESEY, WEST (St Peter) *Guildf 8*   **P** *Canon W K Perry-Gore*   **P-in-c** R G LLOYD   **C** A I MUNRO

MOLESWORTH (St Peter)   *see* W Leightonstone *Ely*

MOLLAND (St Mary)   *see* Bishopsnympton, Charles, E Anstey, High Bray etc *Ex*

MOLLINGTON (All Saints)   *see* Shires' Edge *Ox*

MOLTON, NORTH (All Saints)   *see* Bishopsnympton, Charles, E Anstey, High Bray etc *Ex*

MOLTON, SOUTH (St Mary Magdalene) w Nymet St George, Chittlehamholt, Chittlehampton w Umberleigh, Filleigh, Kingsnympton, and Warkleigh w Satterleigh *Ex 18*   **P** *Patr Bd*   **TR** F M GRANDEY

TV D K COLEMAN   **C** B J SANDERS   **NSM** C M G POUNCEY, L P FLATT
MONEWDEN (St Mary)   *see* Mid Loes *St E*
MONGEHAM, GREAT (St Martin)   *see* Deal St Leon w St Rich and Sholden etc *Cant*
MONK BRETTON (St Paul) Leeds 17   **P** V Royston
V B T B BELL   **C** B W RADFORD
MONK FRYSTON (St Wilfrid of Ripon) and South Milford York 4   **P** Ld Chan and Abp (alt)   **R** P F ROBERTS
MONK SHERBORNE (All Saints)   *see* The Sherbornes w Pamber *Win*
MONK SOHAM (St Peter)   *see* Four Rivers *St E*
MONKEN HADLEY (St Mary the Virgin) Lon 14   **P** Bp
R T RENZ
MONKHOPTON (St Peter)   *see* Bridgnorth and Morville Par *Heref*
MONKLAND (All Saints)   *see* Leominster *Heref*
MONKLEIGH (St George)   *see* Bideford, Landcross, Littleham etc *Ex*
MONKMOOR (St Peter)   *see* Shrewsbury H Cross *Lich*
MONKOKEHAMPTON (All Saints)   *see* Dolton, Dowland, Iddesleigh etc *Ex*
MONKS ELEIGH (St Peter) w Chelsworth and Brent Eleigh w Milden and Kettlebaston St E 6   **P** Bp, Guild of All So, Ld Chan (2 turns), and M J Hawkins Esq   **R** vacant
MONKS HORTON (St Peter)   *see* Stour Downs *Cant*
MONKS KIRBY (St Edith)   *see* Revel Gp *Cov*
MONKS RISBOROUGH (St Dunstan)   *see* Risborough *Ox*
MONKSEATON (St Mary) Newc 5   **P** Bp   **V** R A WOOD
C B J F JARVIS   **NSM** M C CONNORS
MONKSEATON (St Peter) Newc 5   **P** Bp   **V** vacant
MONKSILVER (All Saints)   *see* Quantock Towers *B & W*
MONKTON (St Mary Magdalene)   *see* Wantsum Gp *Cant*
MONKTON COMBE (St Michael)   *see* Combe Down w Monkton Combe and S Stoke *B & W*
MONKTON FARLEIGH (St Peter)   *see* N Bradford on Avon and Villages *Sarum*
MONKTON WYLD (St Andrew)   *see* Golden Cap Team *Sarum*
MONKTON, WEST (St Augustine)   *see* S Quantock *B & W*
MONKWEARMOUTH (All Saints) (St Andrew) (St Peter) Dur 14   **P** Bp   **TR** R G E BRADSHAW   **TV** A M WATSON
OLM P G A SMITHSON
MONKWOOD (Mission Church)   *see* Bishop's Sutton and Ropley and W Tisted *Win*
MONNINGTON-ON-WYE (St Mary)   *see* Letton w Staunton, Byford, Mansel Gamage etc *Heref*
MONTACUTE (St Catherine of Alexandria)   *see* Ham Hill Villages *B & W*
MONTFORD (St Chad)   *see* Bicton, Montford w Shrawardine and Fitz *Lich*
MONTON (St Paul)   *see* Eccles *Man*
MONXTON (St Mary)   *see* Portway and Danebury *Win*
MONYASH (St Leonard)   *see* Taddington, Chelmorton and Monyash etc *Derby*
MOOR (St Thomas)   *see* Fladbury, Hill and Moor, Wyre Piddle etc *Worc*
MOOR ALLERTON (St John the Evangelist) (St Stephen) and Shadwell Team Ministry, including Alwoodley and Moortown Leeds 13   **P** Patr Bd   **TR** J SMITH
TV D L M YOUNG, S V KAYE   **C** C R C BAXFIELD
MOOR COURT (St Mary)   *see* Pembridge w Moor Court, Shobdon, Staunton etc *Heref*
MOOR GRANGE (St Andrew)   *see* Abbeylands *Leeds*
MOOR MONKTON (All Saints)   *see* Rural Ainsty *York*
MOORCOURT (St Mary)   *see* Pembridge w Moor Court, Shobdon, Staunton etc *Heref*
MOORE MILNER (Church Institute)   *see* Daresbury *Ches*
MOORENDS (St Wilfrith) Sheff 10   **P** Bp   **V** vacant
MOORHOUSE (Chantry Chapel)   *see* Kneesall w Laxton and Wellow *S'well*
MOORHOUSES (St Lawrence)   *see* Fen and Hill Gp *Linc*
MOORLAND Group, The, comprising Altarnon, Davidstow, Laneast, and St Clether Truro 9   **P** Duchy of Cornwall (1 turn), Bp, D&C, and SMF (1 turn)   **C** H J WEST
MOORLAND TEAM   *see* Ashburton, Bickington, Buckland in the Moor etc *Ex*
MOORLINCH (Blessed Virgin Mary)   *see* Middlezoy w Othery, Moorlinch and Greinton *B & W*
MOORSHOLM (St Mary) York 21   **P** Abp   **V** vacant
MOORSIDE (St Thomas)   *see* Oldham Moorside *Man*
MOORTOWN (St Stephen)   *see* Moor Allerton and Shadwell *Leeds*
MORBORNE (All Saints)   *see* Stilton w Denton and Caldecote etc *Ely*
MORCHARD BISHOP (St Mary)   *see* N Creedy *Ex*

MORCOTT (St Mary the Virgin)   *see* Barrowden and Wakerley w S Luffenham etc *Pet*
MORDEN (St Lawrence) (St George) (St Martin) (Emmanuel Church Hall) S'wark 13   **P** Patr Bd
TR D R HEATH-WHYTE   **TV** A D WENHAM, D M RUDDICK, M S H DAVEY   **Hon C** P S OMUKU
MORDEN (St Mary)   *see* Red Post *Sarum*
MORDIFORD (Holy Rood)   *see* Fownhope w Mordiford, Brockhampton etc *Heref*
MORE (St Peter)   *see* Wentnor w Ratlinghope, Myndtown, Norbury etc *Heref*
MOREBATH (St George)   *see* Bampton, Morebath, Clayhanger, Petton etc *Ex*
MORECAMBE (Holy Trinity)   *see* Poulton-le-Sands w Morecambe St Laur *Blackb*
MORECAMBE (St Barnabas) Blackb 11   **P** R Poulton-le-Sands
V M T CHILDS
MORECAMBE (St Christopher)   *see* Bare *Blackb*
MORECAMBE (St James)   *see* Heysham *Blackb*
MORECAMBE (St John)   *see* Sandylands *Blackb*
MORECAMBE (St Peter)   *see* Heysham *Blackb*
MORECAMBE (The Ascension)   *see* Torrisholme *Blackb*
MORELEIGH (All Saints)   *see* Diptford w N Huish, Ermington, Halwell etc *Ex*
MORESBY (St Bridget) Carl 5   **P** Earl of Lonsdale
P-in-c P M KERRY
MORESBY PARKS (Mission Church)   *see* Moresby *Carl*
MORESTEAD (not known)   *see* S Downs Gateway Churches *Win*
MORETON (Christ Church) Ches 8   **P** Simeon's Trustees
R G J COUSINS   **NSM** B A TURNER, D A STOTT
MORETON (St Mary)   *see* Adbaston, High Offley, Knightley, Norbury etc *Lich*
MORETON (St Mary)   *see* Fyfield, Moreton w Bobbingworth etc *Chelmsf*
MORETON (St Nicholas), Woodsford and Crossways w Tincleton Sarum 1   **P** R Frampton-Hobb Esq   **R** J A BIRDSEYE
MORETON CORBET (St Bartholomew) Lich 21   **P** C C Corbet Esq   **R** R J CRESSWELL
MORETON HALL (Christ Church)   *see* Bury St Edmunds Ch Ch *St E*
MORETON MORRELL (Holy Cross)   *see* Newbold Pacey w Moreton Morrell *Cov*
MORETON PINKNEY (St Mary the Virgin)   *see* Culworth w Sulgrave and Thorpe Mandeville etc *Pet*
MORETON SAY (St Margaret of Antioch)   *see* Adderley, Ash, Calverhall, Ightfield etc *Lich*
MORETON VALENCE (St Stephen)   *see* Stroudwater Team *Glouc*
MORETON, NORTH (All Saints)   *see* The Churn *Ox*
MORETON, SOUTH (St John the Baptist) *as above*
MORETONHAMPSTEAD (St Andrew), Manaton, North Bovey and Lustleigh Ex 8   **P** Bp and DBP (jt)   **R** vacant
MORETON-IN-MARSH (St David) w Batsford, Todenham, Lower Lemington and Longborough w Sezincote Glouc 8   **P** Bp and Lord Dulverton (1 turn), and Bp, Lord Dulverton, Lord Leigh, and Mrs S Peake (1 turn)   **R** S M WOOKEY
NSM B J P THOMPSON
MORETON-ON-LUGG (St Andrew)   *see* Pipe-cum-Lyde and Moreton-on-Lugg *Heref*
MORGAN'S VALE (St Birinus)   *see* Forest and Avon *Sarum*
MORLAND (St Lawrence)   *see* N Westmorland *Carl*
MORLEY (St Matthew) and Smalley Derby 8   **P** Bp
P-in-c K J PLANT
MORLEY (St Peter) (St Paul) Leeds 14   **P** Patr Bd
TV S M FORREST-REDFERN   **OLM** K M DAVIS
MORLEY ST BOTOLPH (St Botolph)   *see* High Oak, Hingham and Scoulton w Wood Rising *Nor*
MORLEY ST PETER (St Peter) *as above*
MORNINGTHORPE (St John the Baptist)   *see* Hempnall *Nor*
MORPETH (St Aidan) (St James) (St Mary the Virgin) Newc 11   **P** Bp   **R** S J H WHITE
MORRIS GREEN (St Bede)   *see* Bolton St Bede *Man*
MORSTON (All Saints)   *see* Stiffkey and Bale *Nor*
MORTEHOE (St Mary Magdalene)   *see* Ilfracombe, Lee, Woolacombe, Bittadon etc *Ex*
MORTIMER COMMON (St John)   *see* Stratfield Mortimer and Mortimer W End etc *Ox*
MORTIMER WEST END (St Saviour) *as above*
MORTLAKE (St Mary) w East Sheen S'wark 16   **P** Patr Bd
TR A L NICKSON   **TV** D A GUEST, J A BARROW
MORTOMLEY (St Saviour) High Green Sheff 3   **P** Bp
V vacant
MORTON (Holy Cross) and Stonebroom w Shirland Derby 2   **P** Bp, St Jo Coll Cam, Adn Chesterfield, and trustees (by turn)   **NSM** C D WOOD, J A EPTON

MORTON (St Denis) *see* W Trent *S'well*
MORTON (St John the Baptist) *see* Ringstone in Aveland Gp *Linc*
MORTON (St Luke) and Riddlesden *Leeds 1* **P** *Bp*
V A C ST J WALKER C G H HOWLES NSM J RAMSDEN
MORTON (St Paul) *see* Gainsborough and Morton *Linc*
MORTON (St Philip and St James) *see* Llanyblodwel, Llanymynech, Morton and Trefonen *Lich*
MORTON BAGOT (Holy Trinity) *see* Arden Marches *Cov*
MORTON, EAST *see* Morton and Riddlesden *Leeds*
MORVAH (St Bridget of Sweden) *see* Pendeen w Morvah *Truro*
MORVAL (St Wenna) *see* Looe and Morval *Truro*
MORVILLE (St Gregory) *see* Bridgnorth and Morville Par *Heref*
MORWENSTOW (St John the Baptist) *see* Kilkhampton w Morwenstow *Truro*
MOSBOROUGH (St Mark) *Sheff 1* **P** *Bp* V S T STEWART
NSM L S CASTLE
MOSELEY (St Agnes) *Birm 4* **P** *V Moseley St Mary*
V P H ANSELL
MOSELEY (St Anne) (St Mary) *Birm 4* **P** *Bp* V D J STRATHIE
C H S WHITE
MOSLEY COMMON (St John) *see* Astley, Tyldesley and Mosley Common *Man*
MOSS BANK (Mission Church) *see* Carr Mill *Liv*
MOSS SIDE (Christ Church) *Man 3* **P** *Trustees*
R S D A KILLWICK
MOSS SIDE (St James w St Clement) *see* Whalley Range St Edm and Moss Side etc *Man*
MOSSER (St Michael's Chapel) *see* Brigham, Clifton, Dean and Mosser *Carl*
MOSSER (St Philip) *as above*
MOSSLEY (Holy Trinity) *see* Congleton *Ches*
MOSSLEY (St George) *Man 13* **P** *Bp and R Ashton-under-Lyne (jt)* V D WARNER NSM I C BROCKLEHURST
OLM D BRADWELL
MOSSLEY ESTATE (St Thomas Church) *see* Bloxwich *Lich*
MOSSLEY HILL (St Barnabas) (St Matthew and St James) *Liv 2* **P** *Patr Bd* TR A KENNEDY TV N C MILFORD
C M J RAFFAY NSM S-A MASON
MOSSWOOD (St Barnabas) *see* Cannock and Huntington *Lich*
MOSTERTON (St Mary) *see* Beaminster Area *Sarum*
MOSTON (St Chad) *Man 4* **P** *Bp* **P-in-c** P MAUDSLEY
MOSTON (St Luke) *see* Lightbowne *Man*
MOSTON (St Mary) *Man 4* **P** *D&C* **P-in-c** P MAUDSLEY
MOTCOMBE (St Mary) *see* Shaftesbury *Sarum*
MOTSPUR PARK (Holy Cross) *S'wark 13* **P** *Bp* V R S TAYLOR
MOTTINGHAM (St Andrew) (St Alban Mission Church) *S'wark 3* **P** *Bp* R I M WELCH
MOTTINGHAM (St Edward the Confessor) *S'wark 3* **P** *Bp* V C J SHELLEY
MOTTISFONT (St Andrew) *see* Mid Test *Win*
MOTTISTONE (St Peter and St Paul) *see* W Wight *Portsm*
MOTTRAM IN LONGDENDALE (St Michael) *Ches 14* **P** *Bp* V *vacant*
MOULSECOOMB (St Andrew) *Chich 19* **P** *Bp* **P-in-c** M POWELL TV B GRAY-HAMMOND
NSM J W M COLLINS
MOULSFORD (St John the Baptist) *see* Cholsey and Moulsford *Ox*
MOULSHAM (St John the Evangelist) *Chelmsf 10* **P** *Dean* **P-in-c** G E FRASER C D J CATTLE, S R GILLINGHAM
NSM E S MCALLISTER
MOULSHAM (St Luke) *Chelmsf 10* **P** *Bp* **P-in-c** G E FRASER
C D J CATTLE, S R GILLINGHAM
MOULSOE (The Assumption of the Blessed Virgin Mary) *see* Newport Pagnell w Lathbury and Moulsoe *Ox*
MOULTON (All Saints) *see* Elloe Stone *Linc*
MOULTON (Mission Church) *see* E Dere Street *Leeds*
MOULTON (St James) *see* Elloe Stone *Linc*
MOULTON (St Peter and St Paul) *Pet 4* **P** *Ch Soc Trust* V A T J BYFIELD C J J DEJA
MOULTON (St Peter) *see* Dalham, Gazeley, Higham, Kentford and Moulton *St E*
MOULTON (St Stephen the Martyr) *Ches 6* **P** *R Davenham* **P-in-c** M R GREEN
MOULTON, GREAT (St Michael) *see* Long Stratton and Pilgrim TM *Nor*
MOUNT BURES (St John) *see* Wormingford, Mt Bures and Lt Horkesley *Chelmsf*
MOUNT GOULD (St Simon) *see* Sutton-on-Plym, Plymouth St Simon and St Mary *Ex*
MOUNT HAWKE (St John the Baptist) *see* St Agnes and Mount Hawke w Mithian *Truro*

MOUNT PELLON (Christ Church) *see* Halifax St Aug and Mount Pellon *Leeds*
MOUNTFIELD (All Saints) *see* Brightling, Mountfield and Netherfield *Chich*
MOUNTNESSING (St Giles) *see* Margaretting w Mountnessing and Buttsbury *Chelmsf*
MOUNTSORREL (Christ Church) (St Peter) *Leic 6* **P** *CPAS and Bp* **P-in-c** C E RESCH C D B WALKER
MOW COP (St Luke's Mission Church) *see* Odd Rode *Ches*
MOW COP (St Thomas) *Lich 11* **P** *The Crown* V G C HUBBARD NSM P A JACKSON
MOWSLEY (St Nicholas) *see* Hexagon *Leic*
MOXLEY (All Saints) *see* Darlaston and Moxley *Lich*
MUCH *see also under substantive place name*
MUCH BIRCH (St Mary and St Thomas à Becket) *see* Wormelow Hundred *Heref*
MUCHELNEY (St Peter and St Paul) *see* Levels Arc *B & W*
MUCKLESTONE (St Mary) *see* Ashley and Mucklestone and Broughton and Croxton *Lich*
MUDEFORD (All Saints) *Win 9* **P** *Bp* **P-in-c** A P JABLONSKI
NSM A J JABLONSKI
MUDFORD (Blessed Virgin Mary) *see* Chilton Cantelo, Ashington, Mudford, Rimpton etc *B & W*
MUGGINTON (All Saints) and Kedleston *Derby 6* **P** *Major J W Chandos-Pole* **P-in-c** B J STOBER
MUGGLESWICK (All Saints) *see* Blanchland w Hunstanworth and Edmundbyers etc *Newc*
MUKER (St Mary) *see* Swaledale *Leeds*
MULBARTON (St Mary Magdalene) w Bracon Ash, Hethel and Flordon *Nor 7* **P** *R T Berney Esq (1 turn), Mrs R M Watkinson (2 turns), DBP (1 turn), and Ld Chan (1 turn)* R A D MILLER C A J NORTH
MULLION (St Mellanus) and Cury w Gunwalloe *Truro 4* **P** *Bp* V S O GRIFFITHS
MUMBY (St Thomas of Canterbury) *see* Chapel St Leonards and Hogsthorpe etc *Linc*
MUNCASTER (St Michael) *see* Black Combe, Drigg, Eskdale etc *Carl*
MUNDEN, LITTLE (All Saints) *see* Standon and The Mundens w Sacombe *St Alb*
MUNDESLEY (All Saints) *see* Trunch Group *Nor*
MUNDFORD (St Leonard) w Lynford *Nor 13* **P** *Ch Patr Trust* **P-in-c** Z M FERGUSON Hon C L M LUBBE
MUNDHAM (St Peter) *see* Brooke, Kirstead, Mundham w Seething and Thwaite *Nor*
MUNDHAM, NORTH (St Stephen) w Hunston and Merston *Chich 2* **P** *St Jo Coll Cam* **NSM** S R EVERARD
MUNGRISDALE (St Kentigern) *see* Greystoke w Penruddock, Mungrisdale etc *Carl*
MUNSLEY (St Bartholomew) *see* Hop Churches *Heref*
MUNSLOW (St Michael) *see* Corvedale Benefice *Heref*
MUNSTER SQUARE (Christ Church) (St Mary Magdalene) *Lon 17* **P** *Bp* **P-in-c** S J JONES
MURCOTT (Mission Room) *see* Ray Valley *Ox*
MURROW (Corpus Christi) *see* Wisbech St Mary and Guyhirn w Ring's End etc *Ely*
MURSLEY (St Mary the Virgin) *see* Newton Longville, Mursley, Swanbourne etc *Ox*
MURSTON (All Saints) *see* Milton Regis w Murston, Bapchild and Tonge *Cant*
MURTON (Holy Trinity) *see* Hawthorn and Murton *Dur*
MURTON (St James) *see* Osbaldwick w Murton *York*
MURTON (St John the Baptist) *see* Heart of Eden *Carl*
MUSBURY (St Michael) *see* Colyton, Musbury, Southleigh and Branscombe *Ex*
MUSBURY (St Thomas) *Blackb 1* **P** *The Crown* V D STEPHENSON NSM D ALLSOP, J A BALKWELL
MUSGRAVE (St Theobald) *see* Heart of Eden *Carl*
MUSKHAM, NORTH (St Wilfrid) and SOUTH (St Wilfrid) *S'well 3* **P** *Ld Chan* C G A L HADLEY
MUSTON (All Saints) *see* Hertford *York*
MUSTON (St John the Baptist) *see* Vale of Belvoir *Leic*
MUSWELL HILL (St James) (St Matthew) *Lon 20* **P** *Bp and CPAS (jt)* V C M GREEN C M A MURTHEN, P J MULLINS
NSM H C HENDRY
MUTFORD (St Andrew) *see* Carlton Colville and Mutford *Nor*
MUXTON (St John the Evangelist) *see* Lilleshall and Muxton *Lich*
MYDDELTON SQUARE (St Mark) *see* Clerkenwell St Mark *Lon*
MYDDLE (St Peter) *Lich 21* **P** *Bp* R A J B CLAYTON
MYLAND (St Michael) *see* Colchester St Mich Myland *Chelmsf*
MYLOR (St Mylor) w Flushing *Truro 3* **P** *Bp* NSM A J STEVENSON, J A JAMES
MYLOR BRIDGE (All Saints) *see* Mylor w Flushing *Truro*

MYMMS *see also* MIMMS

MYMMS, NORTH (St Mary)   *see* Bp's Hatfield, Lemsford and N Mymms *St Alb*

MYMMS, SOUTH (King Charles the Martyr)   *see* Potters Bar K Chas *St Alb*

MYMMS, SOUTH (St Giles) and Ridge *St Alb 14*   **P** *DBP* **V** *vacant*

MYNDTOWN (St John the Baptist)   *see* Wentnor w Ratlinghope, Myndtown, Norbury etc *Heref*

MYTHOLMROYD (St Michael)   *see* Erringden *Leeds*

MYTON ON SWALE (St Mary)   *see* Brafferton w Pilmoor, Myton-on-Swale etc *York*

NABURN (St Matthew)   *see* Escrick and Stillingfleet w Naburn *York*

NACKINGTON (St Mary)   *see* Bridge *Cant*

NACTON (St Martin) and Levington w Bucklesham and Foxhall w Kirton and Falkenham *St E 11*   **P** *Ld Chan and DBP (alt)*   **P-in-c** I A WILSON   **C** S J JENKINS

NADDER VALLEY, comprising Ansty, Barford St Martin and Burcombe, Baverstock, Chilmark, Compton Chamberlayne, Dinton, Fonthill Bishop w Berick St Leonard, Fonthill Gifford, Fovant, Hindon w Chicklade and Pertwood, Sutton Mandeville, Swallowcliffe, Teffont Evias w Teffont Magna, and Tisbury *Sarum 11*   **P** *Patr Bd (4 turns), Ld Chan (1 turn)* **TR** G SOUTHGATE   **TV** E BRIGHTWELL, J M HULME **C** M H G HAYTER   **NSM** J M NAISH, T FOX   **Dss** A R SYMES

NAFFERTON (All Saints) w Wansford *York 10*   **P** *Abp* **V** S R J ELLIOTT

NAILSEA (Christ Church) w Tickenham *B & W 12*   **P** *CPAS (3 turns), Ld Chan (1 turn)*   **R** *vacant*

NAILSEA (Holy Trinity) *B & W 12*   **P** *MMCET* **R** J M PACKMAN   **NSM** T S DEAN

NAILSTONE (All Saints) and Carlton w Shackerstone *Leic 10*   **P** *The Crown and DBP (alt)*   **C** J G HARGREAVES

NAILSWORTH (St George) w Shortwood, Horsley and Newington Bapath w Kingscote *Glouc 4*   **P** *Bp* **V** C A BLAND   **NSM** S J JARVIS

NANPANTAN (St Mary in Charnwood) *Leic 6*   **P** *Bp and Em Coll Cam (jt)*   **V** A E ADSHEAD

NANPEAN (St George)   *see* St Stephen in Brannel *Truro*

NANSTALLON (St Stephen's Mission Room)   *see* Bodmin *Truro*

NANTWICH (St Mary) *Ches 15*   **P** *Q H Crewe Esq and J C Crewe Esq (jt)*   **R** M HART   **C** P K WHEELER   **NSM** B R MOSS

NAPTON-ON-THE-HILL (St Lawrence), Lower Shuckburgh and Stockton *Cov 10*   **P** *Ld Chan (2 turns), Sir Rupert Shuckburgh Bt (1 turn), and New Coll Ox (2 turns)* **P-in-c** G S ROBERTS   **NSM** C A PARKES, C M NEWBORN

NAR VALLEY, The, comprising Castle Acre, Narborough, Newton-by-Castle Acre, Pentney, South Acre, and West Acre *Nor 13*   **P** *Bp (1 turn), Earl of Leicester, H C Birkbeck Esq, and Bp (1 turn)*   **R** S R NAIRN   **NSM** R G HOWELLS

NARBOROUGH (All Saints)   *see* Nar Valley *Nor*

NARBOROUGH (All Saints) and Huncote *Leic 7*   **P** *SMF* **R** *vacant*

NARFORD (St Mary)   *see* Nar Valley *Nor*

NASEBY (All Saints)   *see* Clipston, Haselbech, Kelmarsh, Marston Trussell etc *Pet*

NASH (All Saints)   *see* Buckingham *Ox*

NASH (St John the Baptist)   *see* Tenbury *Heref*

NASSINGTON (St Mary the Virgin and All Saints), Apethorpe, Thornhaugh and Wansford, Woodnewton and Yarwell (The Watersmete Benefice) *Pet 10*   **P** *Bp and Personal Reps Lord Brassey of Apethorpe (jt)*   **V** J D TAILBY

NATELY SCURES (St Swithun)   *see* N Hants Downs *Win*

NATLAND (St Mark) *Carl 10*   **P** *V Kendal H Trin* **P-in-c** A WHITTAKER   **C** C A BENTLEY   **NSM** M MASHITER, M P JAYNE

NAUGHTON (St Mary)   *see* Bildeston w Wattisham and Lindsey, Whatfield etc *St E*

NAUNTON (St Andrew)   *see* The Guitings, Cutsdean, Farmcote etc *Glouc*

NAUNTON BEAUCHAMP (St Bartholomew)   *see* Abberton, The Flyfords, Naunton Beauchamp etc *Worc*

NAVENBY (St Peter)   *see* Graffoe Gp *Linc*

NAVESTOCK (St Thomas)   *see* Bentley Common, Kelvedon Hatch and Navestock *Chelmsf*

NAWTON (St Hilda)   *see* Kirkdale w Harome, Nunnington and Pockley *York*

NAYLAND (St James) w Wiston *St E 4*   **P** *Ld Chan (2 turns) and DBP (1 turn)*   **P-in-c** M J WOODROW

NAZEING (All Saints) (St Giles) *Chelmsf 4*   **P** *Ld Chan* **P-in-c** H E-A GHEORGHIU GOULD

NEASDEN (St Catherine w St Paul) *Lon 21*   **P** *Bp and D&C St Paul's (jt)*   **V** R W HARRISON

NEATISHEAD (St Peter)   *see* Ashmanhaugh, Barton Turf etc *Nor*

NECHELLS (St Matthew)   *see* Aston and Nechells *Birm*

NECTON (All Saints), Holme Hale w Pickenham, North and South *Nor 13*   **P** *Major-Gen R S Broke, Ch Soc Trust, MMCET and S Pickenham Estate Co Ltd (jt)*   **R** S L THORP

NEDGING (St Mary)   *see* Bildeston w Wattisham and Lindsey, Whatfield etc *St E*

NEEDHAM (St Peter)   *see* Redenhall w Scole *Nor*

NEEDHAM MARKET (St John the Baptist) w Badley *St E 2* **P** *PCC*   **P-in-c** D R WILLIAMS **C** S E HOUSSEMAYNE DU BOULAY

NEEN SAVAGE (St Mary)   *see* Cleobury Mortimer w Hopton Wafers etc *Heref*

NEEN SOLLARS (All Saints)   *as above*

NEENTON (All Saints)   *see* Ditton Priors w Neenton, Burwarton etc *Heref*

NEITHROP (St Paul)   *see* Banbury St Paul *Ox*

NELSON (St John the Evangelist)   *see* Gt Marsden w Nelson St Phil *Blackb*

NELSON (St Mary)   *see* Lt Marsden w Nelson St Mary and Nelson St Bede *Blackb*

NELSON (St Paul)   *as above*

NEMPNETT THRUBWELL (Blessed Virgin Mary)   *see* Chew Stoke w Nempnett Thrubwell *B & W*

NENE CROSSINGS   *see* Irthlingborough, Gt Addington, Lt Addington etc *Pet*

NENTHEAD (St John)   *see* Alston Moor *Newc*

NESS Group, The, comprising Baston, Langtoft, and Thurlby *Linc 19*   **P** *Ld Chan (1 turn), Bp and DBP (2 turns)* **V** C BAILEY   **OLM** M J HOWARD

NESS, GREAT (St Andrew)   *see* Ruyton XI Towns w Gt and Lt Ness *Lich*

NESS, LITTLE (St Martin)   *as above*

NESTON (St Mary and St Helen) *Ches 9*   **P** *D&C* **V** A D H DAWSON   **C** J C ASKWITH   **NSM** J CALVERT

NESTON (St Phillip and St James)   *see* Gtr Corsham and Lacock *Bris*

NESTON, LITTLE (St Michael and All Angels)   *see* Neston *Ches*

NETHER *see under substantive place name*

NETHERAVON (All Saints)   *see* Avon River *Sarum*

NETHERBURY (St Mary)   *see* Beaminster Area *Sarum*

NETHEREXE (St John the Baptist)   *see* Brampford Speke, Cadbury, Newton St Cyres etc *Ex*

NETHERFIELD (St George) *S'well 7*   **P** *DBP*   **R** *vacant*

NETHERFIELD (St John the Baptist)   *see* Brightling, Mountfield and Netherfield *Chich*

NETHERHAMPTON (St Katherine)   *see* Wilton w Netherhampton and Fugglestone *Sarum*

NETHERLEY (Christ Church)   *see* Gateacre *Liv*

NETHERSEAL (St Peter)   *see* Seale and Lullington w Coton in the Elms *Derby*

NETHERTHONG (All Saints)   *see* Upper Holme Valley *Leeds*

NETHERTHORPE (St Stephen)   *see* Sheffield Vine *Sheff*

NETHERTON (All Souls)   *see* Maryport, Netherton, Flimby and Broughton Moor *Carl*

NETHERTON (St Andrew)   *see* Darby End and Netherton *Worc*

NETHERTON (St Andrew)   *see* Middlestown *Leeds*

NETHERTON (St Oswald) and Sefton *Liv 6*   **P** *Patr Bd* **TR** D H STATTER   **TV** S M ELLIOTT

NETHERWITTON (St Giles)   *see* Nether Witton *Newc*

NETLEY MARSH (St Matthew)   *see* Totton *Win*

NETTLEBED (St Bartholomew) w Bix, Highmoor, Pishill and Rotherfield Greys *Ox 24*   **P** *DBP, Earl of Macclesfield, Ch Patr Trust, and Trin Coll Ox (jt)*   **R** *vacant*

NETTLECOMBE (Blessed Virgin Mary)   *see* Quantock Towers *B & W*

NETTLEDEN (St Lawrence)   *see* Gt Berkhamsted, Gt and Lt Gaddesden etc *St Alb*

NETTLEHAM (All Saints) *Linc 5*   **P** *Bp*   **V** R H CROSSLAND **NSM** C A ZOTOV, J A SHAW

NETTLESTEAD (St Mary the Virgin)   *see* E Peckham and Nettlestead *Roch*

NETTLESTEAD (St Mary)   *see* Bramford w Lt Blakenham, Baylham and Nettlestead *St E*

NETTLETON (St John the Baptist)   *see* Woldmoor Gp *Linc*

NETTLETON (St Mary)   *see* By Brook *Bris*

NEVENDON (St Peter)   *see* Pitsea w Nevendon *Chelmsf*

NEVILLE'S CROSS (St John)   *see* Dur St Marg and Neville's Cross St Jo *Dur*

NEW *see under substantive place name*

NEW BOROUGH and Leigh (St John the Evangelist) *Sarum 9*   **P** *Ch Soc Trust*   **V** P H BRECKWOLDT   **C** M T LEE

NEW BUILDINGS (Beacon Church)   *see* Crediton, Shobrooke and Sandford etc *Ex*

NEW FERRY (St Mark) *Ches 8*   **P** *R Bebington* **V** A Q GREENOUGH   **C** P J CHAMBERLIN

NEW HAW (All Saints) *Guildf 11* **P** *Bp* **V** A K REID
OLM M L OLIVER
NEW MILL (Christ Church) *see* Upper Holme Valley *Leeds*
NEW MILLS (St George) *Derby 4* **P** V *Glossop* **V** *vacant*
NEW PARKS (St Aidan) *see* Leic St Aid *Leic*
NEWARK-ON-TRENT (Christ Church) *S'well 3* **P** *The Crown*
V P S FRANKLIN
NEWARK-ON-TRENT (St Mary Magdalene) (St Leonard)
S'well 3 **P** *The Crown* **P-in-c** D C PICKERSGILL **C** C M LEE
NEWBALD (St Nicholas) *York 13* **P** *Abp* **P-in-c** M R BUSHBY
NEWBIGGIN (St Edmund) *see* Heart of Eden *Carl*
NEWBIGGIN HALL (St Wilfrid) *Newc 4* **P** *Bp*
P-in-c A M PATERSON **C** W H M NION
NEWBIGGIN-BY-THE-SEA (St Bartholomew) *see* Woodhorn w
Newbiggin *Newc*
NEWBOLD (St John the Evangelist) w Dunston *Derby 3*
P R Chesterfield **V** B D GRIFFITHS **C** A R BLACKWELL
NEWBOLD (St Peter) *see* Deeplish and Newbold *Man*
NEWBOLD DE VERDUN (St James), Barlestone and Kirkby
Mallory *Leic 10* **P** *Bp and* Trin Coll Ox *(jt)*
P-in-c S M IVES-SMITH **C** H M AUCKEN **NSM** J A DOWNS
NEWBOLD ON AVON (St Botolph) *Cov 6* **P** H A F W
Boughton Leigh Esq **V** P M WILKINSON **NSM** D J BUSSEY
NEWBOLD ON STOUR (St David) *see* Stourdene Gp *Cov*
NEWBOLD PACEY (St George) w Moreton Morrell *Cov 8*
P *Qu Coll Ox and Lt Col J E Little (alt)* **C** R E SAUM
NEWBOROUGH (All Saints) *see* Hanbury, Newborough and
Rangemoor *Lich*
NEWBOROUGH (St Bartholomew) *see* Eye, Newborough and
Thorney *Pet*
NEWBOTTLE (St James) *see* King's Sutton and Newbottle and
Charlton *Pet*
NEWBOTTLE (St Matthew) *Dur 10* **P** *Bp* **V** E WILKINSON
NEWBOURNE (St Mary) *see* Waldringfield w Hemley and
Newbourne *St E*
NEWBROUGH (St Peter) *see* Warden w Newbrough *Newc*
NEWBURGH (Christ Church) w Westhead *Liv 14* **P** *Bp and*
V Ormskirk (jt) **P-in-c** J E MORGAN **OLM** C DRAPER,
J SEPHTON
NEWBURN (St Michael and All Angels) *Newc 4* **P** MMCET
V A J HARDING
NEWBURY (St George) (St John the Evangelist) *Ox 6* **P** *Bp*
V R A BEVAN **NSM** T WINROW
NEWBURY (St Nicolas and St Mary Speenhamland) *Ox 6*
P *Bp* **R** W D HUNTER SMART **C** J M MAWDESLEY
NSM J M MACDONALD
NEWBY (St Mark) *York 15* **P** *Abp* **V** M J LEIGH
C S A MORAY
NEWCASTLE (St John the Evangelist) *see* Clun Valley *Heref*
NEWCASTLE UNDER LYME (St George) *Lich 9* **P** R
Newcastle w Butterton **V** M F BALL
NEWCASTLE UNDER LYME (St Giles) w Butterton *Lich 9*
P *Simeon's Trustees* **C** J P J PENDUCK **NSM** P NISBECK
OLM J WALKER
NEWCASTLE UNDER LYME (St Paul) *Lich 9* **P** *Trustees*
V S C MADDISON
NEWCASTLE UPON TYNE (Christ Church) (St Ann) *Newc 2*
P *Bp* **V** A W MARKS
NEWCASTLE UPON TYNE (Holy Cross) *Newc 4* **P** *Bp*
V *vacant*
NEWCASTLE UPON TYNE (St Andrew) *Newc 2* **P** *Bp and*
V Newc St Nic (jt) **V** M J HILLS
NEWCASTLE UPON TYNE (St Francis) High Heaton *Newc 3*
P *Bp* **V** R W LAWRANCE **C** J C COOPER
NEWCASTLE UPON TYNE (St Gabriel) Heaton *Newc 3* **P** *Bp*
V J H LAWSON **C** T L USHER **NSM** F G CHARLTON
NEWCASTLE UPON TYNE (St George) (St Hilda) *Newc 2*
P *Bp* **V** B C HURST **C** S L KEATES **NSM** D A AVERY,
P H PEARSON
NEWCASTLE UPON TYNE (St John the Baptist) *Newc 2*
P V *Newc* **V** *vacant*
NEWCASTLE UPON TYNE (St Luke) *Newc 2* **P** *Bp and*
V Newcastle (jt) **NSM** A B WARD, R C I WARD
NEWCASTLE UPON TYNE (St Oswald) *see* Byker St Mark and
Walkergate St Oswald *Newc*
NEWCASTLE UPON TYNE (St Paul) *see* Elswick *Newc*
NEWCASTLE UPON TYNE (St Philip) and St Augustine and
(St Matthew w St Mary) *Newc 4* **P** *Bp* **V** R G S DEADMAN
NEWCASTLE UPON TYNE (St Thomas) Proprietary Chapel
Newc 2 **NSM** B DOOLAN
NEWCASTLE UPON TYNE Christ the King *see* Ch the King
Newc
NEWCHAPEL (St James the Apostle) *Lich 11* **P** CPAS
V J R ARNOLD
NEWCHURCH (All Saints) *Portsm 7* **P** *Bp*
V J F O'SHAUGHNESSY

NEWCHURCH (not known) w Croft *Liv 13* **P** *Bp*
OLM B ALLDRED
NEWCHURCH (St Nicholas w St John) *Man 11* **P** *Bp*
V P A KING
NEWCHURCH (St Peter and St Paul) *see* Romney Marsh *Cant*
NEWDIGATE (St Peter) *see* Surrey Weald *Guildf*
NEWENDEN (St Peter) *see* Tenterden, Rother and Oxney
Cant
NEWENT (St Mary the Virgin) and Gorsley w Cliffords
Mesne *Glouc 3* **P** *Bp* **R** S I V MASON **C** D M BROWNE
NSM R G CHIVERS
NEWHALL (St John) *Derby 7* **P** *Bp* **P-in-c** P J DOUGLAS
NEWHAVEN (St Michael) *Chich 21* **P** *Ch Patr Trust*
R M M MILLER
NEWHEY (St Thomas) *see* Milnrow and New Hey *Man*
NEWICK (St Mary) *Chich 18* **P** *Ch Soc Trust*
P-in-c J W HOLLINGSWORTH **C** P K MUNDY
NEWINGTON (St Christopher) *see* St Laur in Thanet *Cant*
NEWINGTON (St Giles) *see* Dorchester *Ox*
NEWINGTON (St John the Baptist) w Hull St Andrew
York 14 **P** *Abp and V Hull H Trin (jt)* **V** T A COTSON
NEWINGTON (St Martin) *see* Hull St Martin w
Transfiguration *York*
NEWINGTON (St Mary the Virgin) *see* The Six *Cant*
NEWINGTON (St Mary) *S'wark 10* **P** *Bp* **R** G A FRASER
Hon C M E TODD
NEWINGTON (St Nicholas) *see* Cheriton w Newington *Cant*
NEWINGTON (St Paul) *S'wark 10* **P** *Bp* **C** J A CARRUTHERS
NEWINGTON, SOUTH (St Peter ad Vincula) *see* Bloxham w
Milcombe and S Newington *Ox*
NEWLAND (All Saints) *see* Coleford, Staunton, Newland,
Redbrook etc *Glouc*
NEWLAND (St John) *see* Hull St Jo Newland *York*
NEWLAND (St Lawrence) *see* Bradwell on Sea and
St Lawrence *Chelmsf*
NEWLANDS (not known) *see* Upper Derwent *Carl*
NEWLAY LANE (St Margaret's Church Hall) *see* Bramley *Leeds*
NEWLYN (St Newlyn) *Truro 5* **P** *Bp* **V** *vacant*
NEWLYN (St Peter) *Truro 5* **P** *Bp* **P-in-c** K R OWEN
C A M YATES, S YATES
NEWMARKET (All Saints) *St E 7* **P** *Bp* **V** M E OSBORNE
C S M ALLISON **NSM** S P SHAW
NEWMARKET (St Mary the Virgin) w Exning St Agnes
St E 7 **P** *Bp and DBP (alt)* **R** J C HARDY
C M L D DRINKWATER **NSM** C P BELDING, J R LIND
NEWNHAM (St Mark) *see* Cambridge St Mark *Ely*
NEWNHAM (St Michael and All Angels) *see* Badby w
Newnham and Charwelton w Fawsley etc *Pet*
NEWNHAM (St Nicholas) *see* N Hants Downs *Win*
NEWNHAM (St Peter and St Paul) *see* Kingsdown and
Creekside *Cant*
NEWNHAM (St Peter) w Awre and Blakeney *Glouc 1*
P *Haberdashers' Co and Bp (alt)* **V** R W JAMES **C** J D KNIGHT
NEWNHAM (St Vincent) *see* Ashwell w Hinxworth and
Newnham *St Alb*
NEWNTON, NORTH (St James) *see* Vale of Pewsey *Sarum*
NEWPORT (St John the Baptist) *Portsm 7* **P** *Ch Patr Trust*
NSM J K HALLAM
NEWPORT (St John the Baptist) and Bishops Tawton *Ex 14*
P *Bp* **V** A DODWELL **NSM** C R SCOFFIELD
NEWPORT (St Mary the Virgin) w Widdington, Quendon
and Rickling *Chelmsf 21* **P** *Bp and DBP (jt)* **V** N R MCLEOD
NEWPORT (St Nicholas) w Longford, and Chetwynd
Lich 15 **P** *Bp* **R** M A SMITH
NEWPORT (St Stephen) *see* Howden *York*
NEWPORT (St Thomas) *Portsm 7* **P** *Bp* **V** K P ARKELL
NSM J K HALLAM
NEWPORT PAGNELL (St Luke) w Lathbury and Moulsoe
Ox 16 **P** *Bp, Ch Ch Ox, and Lord Carrington (jt)*
R N A P EVANS
NEWQUAY (St Michael) *Truro 7* **P** *Bp* **P-in-c** J S THOROLD
C L M G CHANTLER **NSM** P J KNEEBONE
NEWSHAM (St Bede) and Horton *Newc 1* **P** *Bp and*
V Woodhorn w Newbiggin (jt) **V** *vacant*
NEWSHOLME (St John) *see* Oakworth *Leeds*
NEWSOME (St John the Evangelist) and Armitage Bridge
and South Crosland *Leeds 5* **P** *DBP, TR Almondbury w*
Farnley Tyas, and R Kirkheaton (jt) **P-in-c** J ANDERSON
NSM D KENT **OLM** C A SYKES
NEWSTEAD (St Mary the Virgin) *see* Annesley w Newstead
and Kirkby Woodhouse *S'well*
NEWTIMBER (St John the Evangelist) *see* Poynings w
Edburton, Newtimber and Pyecombe *Chich*
NEWTON (Good Shepherd) *see* Clifton w Newton and
Brownsover *Cov*

NEWTON (Mission Church) *see* Embleton w Rennington and Rock *Newc*

NEWTON (St Botolph) *see* S Lafford *Linc*

NEWTON (St John the Baptist) *see* Black Mountains Gp *Heref*

NEWTON (St Luke) *see* Bp's Hatfield, Lemsford and N Mymms *St Alb*

NEWTON (St Margaret) *see* Harston w Hauxton and Newton *Ely*

NEWTON (St Mary) w Flowery Field *Ches 14* **P** *V Mottram* **P-in-c** S M O'FLAHERTY

NEWTON (St Michael and All Angels) *Ches 8* **P** *R W Kirby St Bridget* **V** C J COVERLEY **C** A C WHORTON

NEWTON (St Oswald) *see* Gt Ayton w Easby and Newton under Roseberry *York*

NEWTON (St Petrock) *see* Shebbear, Buckland Filleigh, Sheepwash etc *Ex*

NEWTON ABBOT (All Saints) (St Mary) (St Paul) *Ex 9* **P** *Patr Bd* **TR** E P PARKES **TV** G D REGAN, N J DEBNEY

NEWTON ARLOSH (St John the Evangelist) *see* Bowness-on-Solway, Kirkbride and Newton Arlosh *Carl*

NEWTON AYCLIFFE (St Clare) *see* Gt Aycliffe *Dur*

NEWTON BLOSSOMVILLE (St Nicolas) *see* Lavendon w Cold Brayfield, Clifton Reynes etc *Ox*

NEWTON BROMSWOLD (St Peter) *see* Rushden St Mary w Newton Bromswold *Pet*

NEWTON BY TOFT (St Michael) *see* Middle Rasen Gp *Linc*

NEWTON FERRERS (Holy Cross) w Revelstoke *Ex 20* **P** *Bp and Comdr P E Yonge* **P-in-c** A C LEGGE **C** J LANNON

NEWTON FLOTMAN (St Mary the Virgin), Swainsthorpe, Tasburgh, Tharston, Saxlingham Nethergate and Shotesham *Nor 5* **P** *Patr Bd* **TR** D M DAVIDSON **TV** A C UZOIGWE

NEWTON GREEN (All Saints) *see* Boxford, Edwardstone, Groton etc *St E*

NEWTON HALL (All Saints) *see* Dur N *Dur*

NEWTON HARCOURT (St Luke) *see* Wistow *Leic*

NEWTON HEATH (All Saints) *Man 4* **P** *The Crown and D&C (alt)* **R** A P WICKENS

NEWTON IN MAKERFIELD (Emmanuel) *see* Newton *Liv*

NEWTON IN MAKERFIELD (St Peter) *as above*

NEWTON IN THE ISLE (St James) *see* Leverington, Newton and Tydd St Giles *Ely*

NEWTON KYME (St Andrew) *see* Tadcaster *York*

NEWTON LONGVILLE (St Faith), Mursley, Swanbourne, Little Horwood and Drayton Parslow *Ox 15* **P** *New Coll Ox, Ch Soc Trust, Lord Cottesloe, Ch Patr Trust, and MMCET (jt)* **V** S G FAULKS **NSM** D TALKS **OLM** J K BROWN

NEWTON ON OUSE (All Saints) *see* Skelton w Shipton and Newton on Ouse *York*

NEWTON POPPLEFORD (St Luke) *see* Ottery St Mary, Alfington, W Hill, Tipton etc *Ex*

NEWTON PURCELL (St Michael) *see* Shelswell *Ox*

NEWTON REGIS (St Mary) *see* All So N Warks *Birm*

NEWTON REIGNY (St John) *see* Penrith w Newton Reigny and Plumpton Wall *Carl*

NEWTON SOLNEY (St Mary the Virgin) *see* Foremark and Repton w Newton Solney *Derby*

NEWTON ST CYRES (St Cyr and St Julitta) *see* Brampford Speke, Cadbury, Newton St Cyres etc *Ex*

NEWTON ST LOE (Holy Trinity) *see* Saltford w Corston and Newton St Loe *B & W*

NEWTON Team, The, (All Saints) (Emmanuel) (St John the Baptist) (St Peter) *Liv 13* **P** *Patr Bd* **TR** C J STAFFORD **TV** S B GREY **C** G R BANTON **NSM** C A CLOSE

NEWTON TONY (St Andrew) *see* Bourne Valley *Sarum*

NEWTON TRACEY (St Thomas à Becket), Horwood, Alverdiscott, Huntshaw, Yarnscombe, Tawstock, Atherington, High Bickington, Roborough, St Giles in the Wood and Beaford *Ex 19* **P** *Ld Chan (1 turn), Patr Bd (3 turns)* **TR** G J OWEN **TV** P G BYSOUTH **C** T E DOYLE **NSM** A B SPEED-ANDREWS

NEWTON VALENCE (St Mary) *see* Northanger *Win*

NEWTON, NORTH (St Peter) *see* Alfred Jewel *B & W*

NEWTON, OLD (St Mary) *see* Bacton w Wyverstone, Cotton and Old Newton etc *St E*

NEWTON, SOUTH (St Andrew) *see* Wylye and Till Valley *Sarum*

NEWTON, WEST (St Matthew) *see* Solway Plain *Carl*

NEWTON, WEST (St Peter and St Paul) *see* Sandringham w W Newton and Appleton etc *Nor*

NEWTON-BY-CASTLE-ACRE (All Saints) *see* Nar Valley *Nor*

NEWTON-IN-WIRRAL (St Michael and All Angels) *see* Newton *Ches*

NEWTON-LE-WILLOWS (All Saints) *as above*

NEWTON-ON-RAWCLIFFE (St John) *see* Middleton, Newton and Sinnington *York*

NEWTON-ON-TRENT (St Peter) *see* Saxilby Gp *Linc*

NEWTOWN (Holy Spirit) *see* W Wight *Portsm*

NEWTOWN (Holy Trinity) *see* Soberton, Newtown and Hambledon *Portsm*

NEWTOWN (King Charles the Martyr) *see* Loppington w Newtown *Lich*

NEWTOWN (St George) *see* Birm St Geo *Birm*

NEWTOWN (St Mark) *Liv 15* **P** *Bp, Duke of Sutherland, and V Pemberton (jt)* **P-in-c** W J GIBBONS **OLM** E TAULTY, M JENNINGS, S Y FULFORD

NEWTOWN (St Mary the Virgin and St John the Baptist) *see* Burghclere w Newtown and Ecchinswell w Sydmonton *Win*

NEWTOWN (St Paul) *see* Longnor, Quarnford, Sheen etc *Lich*

NEWTOWN LINFORD (All Saints) *see* Glenfield and Newtown Linford *Leic*

NIBLEY, NORTH (St Martin) *see* Tyndale *Glouc*

NICHOLFOREST (St Nicholas) *see* Arthuret w Kirkandrews-on-Esk and Nicholforest *Carl*

NIDD (St Paul and St Margaret) *see* Knaresborough, Goldsborough, Nidd and Brearton *Leeds*

NIDDERDALE, LOWER, comprising Hunsingore, Kirk Hammerton, and Nun Monkton *Leeds 23* **P** *Trustees K Bell Esq, DBP, and C J Dent Esq (jt)* **R** M P SPURGEON

NIDDERDALE, UPPER, comprising Bewerley Grange, Greenhow Hill, Middlesmoor, Pateley Bridge, Ramsgill, and Wilsill *Leeds 23* **P** *D&C Ripon and V Masham and Healey (jt)* **V** D C HALL

NINEBANKS (St Mark) *see* Allendale w Whitfield *Newc*

NINEFIELDS (St Lawrence School Worship Centre) *see* Waltham H Cross *Chelmsf*

NINFIELD (St Mary the Virgin) *Chich 12* **P** *D&C Cant* **P-in-c** P A FROSTICK

NITON (St John the Baptist) *Portsm 7* **P** *Qu Coll Ox* **R** N J PORTER

NOAK HILL (St Thomas) *see* Harold Hill St Paul *Chelmsf*

NOCTON (All Saints) *see* Branston w Nocton and Potterhanworth *Linc*

NOEL PARK (St Mark) *Lon 19* **P** *Bp* **V** S P J CLARK

NOKE (St Giles) *see* Ray Valley *Ox*

NONINGTON (St Mary the Virgin) *see* Canonry *Cant*

NORBITON (St Peter) *S'wark 15* **P** *V Kingston All SS* **V** P A HOLMES

NORBURY (All Saints) *see* Wentnor w Ratlinghope, Myndtown, Norbury etc *Heref*

NORBURY (St Mary and St Barlok) w Snelston *Derby 1* **P** *Mrs M F Stanton, L A Clowes Esq, and V Ashbourne (by turn)* **P-in-c** D C J BALLARD **C** A J MARSHALL, C E MCDONALD

NORBURY (St Oswald) *S'wark 21* **P** *Bp* **V** A BRUNT **C** A M FORSTER

NORBURY (St Peter) *see* Adbaston, High Offley, Knightley, Norbury etc *Lich*

NORBURY (St Philip) *S'wark 21* **P** *Bp* **V** Y FRANCIS **NSM** T DRUMMOND

NORBURY (St Stephen) and Thornton Heath *S'wark 21* **P** *Bp* **V** G P THOMPSON **OLM** J B FORBES

NORBURY (St Thomas) *Ches 16* **P** *Lord Newton* **NSM** V G HINDMARSH

NORDEN (St Paul) w Ashworth and Bamford *Man 17* **P** *Bp* **V** S C NOLAN

NORFOLK PARK (St Leonard) *see* Arbourthorne and Norfolk Park *Sheff*

NORFOLK, WEST Priory Group, The, comprising Fincham, Marham, Nordelph, Shouldham, Shouldham Thorpe, South Runcton, Stow Bardolph and Stow Bridge, Tottenhill, Watlington, Wimbotsham, and Wormegay *Ely 9* **P** *Bp, St Jo Coll Cam, and R T Townley Esq (jt)* **P-in-c** D KAROON

NORHAM (St Cuthbert) and Duddo *Newc 12* **P** *D&C (1 turn), D&C Dur (2 turns)* **V** G R J KELSEY

NORK (St Paul) w Burgh Heath *Guildf 9* **P** *The Crown and Bp (alt)* **V** A L WILLIAMS **OLM** F M ELLINGHAM

NORLAND (St Luke) *see* Ryburn *Leeds*

NORLANDS (St James) *see* Notting Dale St Clem w St Mark and St Jas *Lon*

NORLEY (St John the Evangelist), Crowton and Kingsley *Ches 3* **P** *Bp, V Frodsham, and V Weaverham (jt)* **NSM** H MERRINGTON

NORMACOT (Holy Evangelists) *see* Meir Heath and Normacot *Lich*

NORMANBY (St Andrew) *see* Kirby Misperton w Normanby and Salton *York*

NORMANBY (St George) *see* Eston w Normanby *York*

NORMANBY-LE-WOLD (St Peter) *see* Walesby Gp *Linc*

NORMANTON (All Saints) *Leeds 19* **P** *Trin Coll Cam* **V** A MURRAY

NORMANTON (St Giles) *Derby 5* **P** *CPAS* **V** N A A BARBER
  C S J BOSWELL, W A ELEY

NORMANTON, SOUTH (St Michael) *Derby 2* **P** *MMCET*
  R S M POTTER

NORMANTON-LE-HEATH (Holy Trinity) *see* Woodfield *Leic*

NORMANTON-ON-SOAR (St James) *see* Sutton Bonington w
  Normanton-on-Soar *S'well*

NORMANTON-ON-TRENT (St Matthew) *see* Tuxford w
  Weston, Markham Clinton etc *S'well*

NORRIS BANK (St Martin) *see* Heatons *Man*

NORRIS GREEN (St Christopher) *see* Liv St Chris Norris
  Green *Liv*

NORRISTHORPE (All Souls) *see* Heckmondwike (w
  Norristhorpe) and Liversedge *Leeds*

NORTH *see under substantive place name*

NORTH BURY Team Ministry *see* Bury St Edmunds All SS w
  St Jo and St Geo *St E*

NORTH CAVE (All Saints) w Cliffe *York 13* **P** *C H J Carver
  Esq* **P-in-c** B WORSDALE

NORTH CHAPEL (St Michael) w Ebernoe *Chich 10* **P** *Lord
  Egremont* **R** *vacant*

NORTH CORNWALL Cluster of Churches, comprising Port
  Isaac, St Endellion, St Kew, and St Minver w St Enodoc and
  St Michael Rock *Truro 10* **P** *Bp and DBP (jt)* **R** E J WILD
  C R H JONES **NSM** G ASHTON

NORTH COVE (St Botolph) *see* Worlingham w Barnby and N
  Cove *St E*

NORTH DOWNS, comprising Bearsted, Boxley, Detling,
  Hollingbourne, Hucking, Leeds and Broomfield, Otham w
  Langley, and Thurnham *Cant 13* **P** *Patr Bd* **TR** J CORBYN
  TV M A PAVEY, P A KITE

NORTH END (Ascension) *see* Portsea Ascension *Portsm*

NORTH END (Chapel of Ease) *see* Burton Dassett *Cov*

NORTH END (St Francis) *see* Portsea N End St Mark *Portsm*

NORTH END (St Mark) *as above*

NORTH END (St Nicholas) *as above*

NORTH HAMPSHIRE DOWNS Benefice, The, comprising
  Herriard w Winslade, Long Sutton, Newnham w Nately
  Scures w Mapledurwell w Up Nately w Greywell, Odiham,
  South Warnborough, Tunworth, Upton Grey, and Weston
  Patrick *Win 5* **P** *Bp, Qu Coll Ox, St Jo Coll Ox, N McNair
  Scott Esq, and J L Jervoise Esq (jt)* **R** S R BUTLER
  C A L BROWN, H O'SULLIVAN **NSM** C P DUDGEON,
  L J SCARD, M L L HAWRISH

NORTH HILL (St Torney) *see* Three Rivers *Truro*

NORTH KERNOW Benefice, The, comprising Bude Haven,
  Launcells, Marhamchurch, and Stratton *Truro 8* **P** *Duchy of
  Cornwall (1 turn), Bp, PCC Bude Haven, and CPAS (1 turn)*
  C D K BARNES **NSM** R WARD-SMITH

NORTH SHIELDS (St Augustine) (Christ Church) *Newc 5*
  P *Patr Bd* **TR** G EVANS **Hon C** P J KNIBBS
  NSM D A ROBINSON, M HALL

NORTH WEALD BASSETT (St Andrew) *Chelmsf 3* **P** *Bp*
  V *vacant*

NORTH WEST HAMPSHIRE Benefice, The, comprising
  Ashmansworth, Crux Easton, East Woodhay, Highclere, and
  Woolton Hill *Win 6* **P** *Bp and Earl of Carnarvon (jt)*
  R C DALE **Hon C** M J BAMFORTH

NORTHALLERTON (All Saints) w Kirby Sigston *York 18*
  P *D&C Dur* **V** F R MAYER-JONES **C** C L BACKHOUSE,
  D JOHNSON

NORTHAM (St Margaret) *see* Appledore, Northam and
  Westward Ho! *Ex*

NORTHAMPTON (All Saints w St Katharine) (St Peter) *Pet 4*
  P *Bp and R Foundn of St Kath (jt)* **R** O J COSS

NORTHAMPTON (Christ Church) *Pet 4* **P** *Bp*
  P-in-c A CUTHBERTSON **NSM** A M MARCH

NORTHAMPTON (Church on the Heath) *see* Kings Heath *Pet*

NORTHAMPTON (Emmanuel) *Pet 4* **P** *DBP*
  TR H DU G SPENCELEY **NSM** D SPENCELEY

**NORTHAMPTON (Holy Sepulchre w St Andrew and
  St Lawrence)** *Pet 4* **P** *Bp* **V** M W J HILLS
  NSM A M MARCH

NORTHAMPTON (Holy Trinity) (St Paul) *Pet 4* **P** *Bp*
  V A C MCGOWAN **NSM** A M MARCH

**NORTHAMPTON (St Alban the Martyr) (Glorious
  Ascension)** *Pet 4* **P** *Bp* **V** J A EVANS

NORTHAMPTON (St Benedict) *Pet 4* **P** *Bp* **V** M A DAVIS

NORTHAMPTON (St David) *see* Kingsthorpe *Pet*

NORTHAMPTON (St Giles) *Pet 4* **P** *Simeon's Trustees*
  V S A KELLY **C** T S SMITH

NORTHAMPTON (St James) *see* Dallington and St James *Pet*

NORTHAMPTON (St Mary the Virgin) *Pet 4* **P** *Bp* **V** *vacant*

NORTHAMPTON (St Matthew) *Pet 4* **P** *DBP*
  V N M SETTERFIELD

NORTHAMPTON (St Michael and All Angels w St Edmund)
  Pet 4 **P** *Bp* **V** M W J HILLS **NSM** A M MARCH, P D MUNCH

NORTHANGER Benefice, The, comprising Chawton, East
  Tisted w Colemore, East Worldham, Farringdon, Hartley
  Mauditt w West Worldham, Kingsley w Oakhanger, Newton
  Valence, and Selborne *Win 2* **P** *Bp (1 turn), D&C (1 turn),
  Bp and Sir James Scott Bt (1 turn)* **R** A J PEARS
  NSM L A LEON

NORTHAW (St Thomas of Canterbury) and Cuffley
  St Alb 17 **P** *Mrs S Peasley* **V** C R H KILGOUR

NORTHBOROUGH (St Andrew) *see* Glinton, Etton, Maxey,
  Peakirk and Northborough *Pet*

NORTHBOURNE (St Augustine) *see* Eastry and
  Woodnesborough *Cant*

NORTHCHURCH (St Mary) and Wigginton *St Alb 1*
  P *Duchy of Cornwall and Bp (alt)* **R** J A GORDON
  NSM M J EGGLETON

NORTHDOWN PARK (St Philip) *see* Margate St Phil *Cant*

NORTHEN PLAIN, The *see* Andreas, Ballaugh, Jurby and
  Sulby *S & M*

NORTHENDEN (St Wilfrid) *Man 6* **P** *Bp*
  P-in-c A R BRADLEY

NORTHFIELD (St Laurence) *Birm 3* **P** *Keble Coll Ox*
  R J E CHAPMAN **NSM** D PYCOCK

NORTHFLEET (All Saints) *see* Perry Street *Roch*

NORTHFLEET (St Botolph) and Rosherville *Roch 4* **P** *Patr
  Bd and The Crown (alt)* **P-in-c** G S COLVILLE
  NSM C R S SHOWERS

NORTHGATE (St Elizabeth) *see* Crawley *Chich*

NORTHIAM (St Mary) *Chich 17* **P** *MMCET* **R** R H WHITE

NORTHILL (St Mary the Virgin) *see* Caldecote, Northill and
  Old Warden *St Alb*

NORTHINGTON (St John the Evangelist) *see* Farleigh,
  Candover and Wield *Win*

**NORTHLEACH (St Peter and St Paul) w Hampnett and
  Farmington, Cold Aston w Notgrove and Turkdean, and
  Compton Abdale w Haselton** *Glouc 8* **P** *Bp (2 turns), Ld
  Chan (1 turn)* **R** *vacant*

NORTHLEIGH (St Giles) *see* Offwell, Northleigh, Farway,
  Cotleigh etc *Ex*

NORTHLEW (St Thomas of Canterbury) *see* Okehampton,
  Inwardleigh, Belstone, Sourton etc *Ex*

NORTHMOOR *see* Okehampton, Inwardleigh, Belstone,
  Sourton etc *Ex*

NORTHMOOR (St Denys) *see* Lower Windrush *Ox*

NORTHMOOR GREEN (St Peter and St John) *see* Alfred Jewel
  B & W

NORTHOLT (St Joseph the Worker) (St Hugh) West End
  Lon 22 **P** *DBP* **C** S F MELCHOR, S F METRY

NORTHOLT (St Mary) (St Richard) *Lon 22* **P** *BNC Ox*
  R C D HILL

NORTHOLT PARK (St Barnabas) *Lon 22* **P** *Bp*
  V E A J CARGILL THOMPSON **NSM** P A LINDERS

NORTHORPE (St John the Baptist) *see* Messingham w E
  Butterwick, Scotter w E Ferry and Scotton w Northorpe *Linc*

NORTHOWRAM (St Matthew) *Leeds 7* **P** *Bp*
  V C E BARNARD **C** J T ALLISON

NORTHREPPS (St Mary) *see* Poppyland *Nor*

NORTHUMBERLAND HEATH (St Paul) *see* Erith St Paul *Roch*

NORTHWICH (Holy Trinity) *Ches 6* **P** *Bp*
  P-in-c C S SEDDON

NORTHWICH (St Luke) *Ches 6* **P** *Bp* **P-in-c** D L MOCK
  C P J PRITCHARD

NORTHWOLD (St Andrew) *see* Grimshoe *Ely*

NORTHWOOD (Emmanuel) *Lon 23* **P** *Ch Trust Fund Trust*
  V T J MEATHREL **C** T D SCOTT

NORTHWOOD (Holy Trinity) *Lon 23* **P** *Trustees*
  V A L LYNES **NSM** J M BRIDGES

NORTHWOOD (Holy Trinity) *see* Hanley H Ev *Lich*

NORTHWOOD (St John the Baptist) *Portsm 7* **P** *Bp*
  R A COLLINSON **C** S A SUTCLIFFE **NSM** D M NETHERWAY

NORTHWOOD GREEN (Mission Church) *see* Westbury-on-
  Severn w Flaxley, Blaisdon etc *Glouc*

NORTHWOOD HILLS (St Edmund the King) *Lon 23* **P** *Bp*
  V M A MILLER

NORTHWOOD Pinner Road (St Edmund the King) *see*
  Northwood Hills St Edm *Lon*

NORTON (All Saints) *see* Brington w Whilton and Norton
  etc *Pet*

NORTON (All Saints) *see* Gauzebrook *Bris*

NORTON (St Andrew) *see* Pakenham w Norton, Tostock etc
  St E

NORTON (St Berteline and St Christopher) *Ches 3* **P** *DBP*
  P-in-c S C TORR

NORTON (St Egwin) *see* Evesham w Norton and Lenchwick
  Worc

NORTON (St George) (St Nicholas) *St Alb 3* **P** *Bp*
V T A SHARP **C** C L HARALD
NORTON (St James) *Sheff 2* **P** *CCC Cam* **R** G B WHITE
C E J LUNN, P M BROWN, T K HOLE
NORTON (St James) *see* Stoulton w Drake's Broughton and
Pirton etc *Worc*
NORTON (St Mary the Virgin) *Dur 9* **P** *Bp*
P-in-c M E ANDERSON **NSM** C WALTON, J L EASTERBY
NORTON (St Mary) *see* Kingsdown and Creekside *Cant*
NORTON (St Mary) *see* Twigworth, Down Hatherley,
Norton, The Leigh etc *Glouc*
NORTON (St Michael and All Angels) *Dur 9* **P** *V Norton*
St Mary **P-in-c** M E ANDERSON **NSM** C WALTON,
J L EASTERBY
NORTON (St Michael and All Angels) and Wollaston
Worc 12 **P** *Bp* **V** N G KALENIUK **Hon C** D M FARMER
NORTON (St Peter) *see* Norton juxta Malton *York*
NORTON BAVANT (All Saints) *see* Upper Wylye Valley *Sarum*
NORTON BRIDGE (St Luke) *see* Chebsey, Creswell, Ellenhall,
Ranton etc *Lich*
NORTON CANES (St James) *Lich 3* **P** *Bp* **R** N L HIBBINS
NORTON CANON (St Nicholas) *see* Weobley w Sarnesfield
and Norton Canon *Heref*
NORTON CUCKNEY (St Mary) *S'well 1* **P** *Lady Alexandra*
Cavendish Bentinck **P-in-c** D R GOUGH **C** R J HANFORD
NORTON DISNEY (St Peter) *see* Withamside *Linc*
NORTON FITZWARREN (All Saints) *see* Staplegrove w Norton
Fitzwarren *B & W*
NORTON IN HALES (St Chad) *see* Woore and Norton in
Hales *Lich*
NORTON IN THE MOORS (St Bartholomew) *Lich 8*
P *Walsingham Coll Trust Assn* **P-in-c** B E STATHAM
NORTON JUXTA MALTON (St Peter) *York 6* **P** *Abp*
V R A HIRST **C** B L W GUNTER
NORTON JUXTA TWYCROSS (Holy Trinity) *see* Woodfield
Leic
NORTON LEES (St Paul) *Sheff 2* **P** *R Norton* **V** P M BROWN
C E J LUNN, G B WHITE, T K HOLE
NORTON LINDSEY (Holy Trinity) *see* Arden Valley *Cov*
NORTON MALREWARD (Holy Trinity) *see* Chew Magna w
Dundry, Norton Malreward etc *B & W*
NORTON MANDEVILLE (All Saints) *see* High Ongar w
Norton Mandeville *Chelmsf*
NORTON ST PHILIP (St Philip and St James) *see* Hardington
Vale *B & W*
NORTON SUB HAMDON (The Blessed Virgin Mary) *see* Ham
Hill Villages *B & W*
NORTON SUBCOURSE (St Mary) *see* Raveningham Gp *Nor*
NORTON WOODSEATS (St Chad) *see* Woodseats St Chad
Sheff
NORTON, EAST (All Saints) *see* Hallaton and Allexton, w
Horninghold, Tugby etc *Leic*
NORTON, OVER (St James) *see* Chipping Norton *Ox*
NORWELL (St Laurence) w Ossington, Cromwell, Caunton,
and Sutton w Carlton on Trent *S'well 3* **P** *Bp and SMF (jt)*
V M ADAMS
NORWICH (Christ Church) *see* Eaton Ch Ch *Nor*
NORWICH (Christ Church) *see* New Catton Ch Ch *Nor*
NORWICH (Holy Trinity) *see* Heigham H Trin *Nor*
NORWICH (St Andrew) *Nor 1* **P** *PCC* **V** M J YOUNG
NORWICH (St Andrew) *see* Eaton St Andr *Nor*
NORWICH (St Anne) *see* Earlham *Nor*
NORWICH (St Barnabas) *see* The Mitre Benefice *Nor*
NORWICH (St Catherine) *see* Mile Cross *Nor*
NORWICH (St Elizabeth) *see* Earlham *Nor*
NORWICH (St Francis) *see* Nor Heartsease St Fran *Nor*
NORWICH (St Giles) *Nor 1* **P** *Ld Chan and Bp (alt)*
V D T THORNTON
NORWICH (St Helen) *Nor 1* **P** *Gt Hosp Nor* **V** E S LANGAN
NORWICH (St John the Baptist) Timberhill w Norwich
St Julian *Nor 1* **P** *Bp, Guild of All So, and D&C (jt)*
P-in-c R O STANTON
NORWICH (St Julian) *see* Nor St Jo w St Julian *Nor*
NORWICH (St Luke) *see* New Catton St Luke w St Aug *Nor*
NORWICH (St Mary Magdalene) w St James *Nor 2* **P** *D&C*
P-in-c L S TILLETT **OLM** J SPENCER
NORWICH (St Mary) *see* Earlham *Nor*
NORWICH (St Matthew) *see* Thorpe St Matt *Nor*
NORWICH (St Michael) *see* Bowthorpe *Nor*
NORWICH (St Peter Mancroft) (St John Maddermarket)
Nor 1 **P** *PCC* **R** E J CARTER **C** F H HAWORTH,
G V KIRK-SPRIGGS
NORWICH (St Stephen) *Nor 1* **P** *D&C* **V** M M LIGHT
C A J D IRVING
NORWICH (St Thomas) *see* The Mitre Benefice *Nor*

NORWICH Colegate and Tombland (St George) *Nor 1*
P *Bp and D&C* **V** A M E LEWIS
NORWICH Heartsease (St Francis) *Nor 1* **P** *Bp*
C P G JORDAN, T G WILLIAMS, T I SIBANDA
NORWICH Lakenham (St Mark) *Nor 1* **P** *D&C*
V S E WEST-LINDELL
NORWICH, Lakenham (St John the Baptist and All Saints)
and Tuckswood St Paul *Nor 1* **P** *Bp and D&C (jt)*
P-in-c P G RIDER **NSM** R J RAYNER
NORWOOD (All Saints) *see* Upper Norwood All SS *S'wark*
NORWOOD (Holy Innocents) *see* S Norwood H Innocents
and St Mark *S'wark*
NORWOOD (St Alban the Martyr) *see* S Norwood St Alb
S'wark
NORWOOD (St John) *see* Upper Norwood St Jo *S'wark*
NORWOOD (St Leonard) *see* Sheff St Leon Norwood *Sheff*
NORWOOD (St Luke) *see* W Norwood St Luke *S'wark*
NORWOOD (St Mark) *see* S Norwood H Innocents and
St Mark *S'wark*
NORWOOD (St Mary the Virgin) *Lon 22* **P** *SMF*
P-in-c D J C BOOKLESS **C** A K BOOKLESS
NORWOOD, SOUTH (Holy Innocents) (St Mark) *S'wark 21*
P *Bp* **V** R F HUNTE
NORWOOD, SOUTH (St Alban the Martyr) *S'wark 21* **P** *Bp*
V S W GILBERT
NORWOOD, UPPER (All Saints) *S'wark 21* **P** *V Croydon*
V L S A MARSH
NORWOOD, UPPER (St John) *S'wark 21* **P** *Bp*
V J A PRITCHARD **C** D M TROTT
NORWOOD, WEST (St Luke) *S'wark 12* **P** *Abp*
V D R DAVIS
NOTGROVE (St Bartholomew) *see* Northleach w Hampnett
and Farmington etc *Glouc*
NOTTING DALE (St Clement) (St Mark) and Norlands
St James *Lon 12* **P** *Bp* **V** *vacant*
NOTTING HILL (All Saints) (St Columb) *Lon 12* **P** *SMF*
P-in-c P P CORBETT
NOTTING HILL (St John) *Lon 12* **P** *Bp* **V** W H TAYLOR
Hon C L R GALON
NOTTING HILL (St Michael and All Angels) (Christ Church)
(St Francis) *Lon 12* **P** *Trustees* **P-in-c** P P CORBETT
NOTTING HILL (St Peter) *Lon 12* **P** *Bp* **V** P ALLERTON
NSM A MAY
NOTTINGHAM (St Andrew) *S'well 9* **P** *Peache Trustees*
V C E GOODE
NOTTINGHAM (St Ann w Emmanuel) *S'well 9* **P** *Trustees*
V A M COLLINS **C** N J HILL
NOTTINGHAM (St George w St John the Baptist) *S'well 9*
P *Bp* **P-in-c** I D MCCORMACK **C** J A FRANKLIN
NOTTINGHAM (St Jude) *S'well 7* **P** *CPAS* **V** J C ALLISTER
C A J DIXON
NOTTINGHAM (St Mary the Virgin) the Lace Market
S'well 9 **P** *Bp* **V** T A GILLUM
NOTTINGHAM (St Nicholas) *S'well 9* **P** *CPAS*
R S D SILVESTER **C** G E A FRANK, J M BLAKELEY
NSM I B PAUL
NOTTINGHAM (St Peter and St James) (All Saints) *S'well 9*
P *Bp* **R** C D HARRISON **C** R H DAVEY
NOTTINGHAM (St Saviour) *S'well 9* **P** *CPAS* **V** H L HALL
NOTTINGHAM (St Stephen) *see* Hyson Green and Forest
Fields *S'well*
NOWTON (St Peter) *see* St Edm Way *St E*
NUFFIELD (Holy Trinity) *Ox 24* **P** *MMCET* **R** *vacant*
NUN MONKTON (St Mary) *see* Lower Nidderdale *Leeds*
NUNBURNHOLME (St James) *see* Pocklington Wold *York*
NUNEATON (St Mary) *Cov 5* **P** *V Nuneaton* **V** T G WINTLE
NUNEATON (St Nicolas) *Cov 5* **P** *The Crown*
V K A BETTERIDGE
NUNHEAD (St Antony) (St Silas) *S'wark 8* **P** *Bp*
V D J OGUNYEMI **Hon C** M N A TORRY
NUNNEY (All Saints) and Witham Friary, Marston Bigot,
Wanstrow and Cloford *B & W 3* **P** *Bp, SMF, and C N*
Clarke Esq and Duke of Somerset (jt) **P-in-c** A E DICKSON
NUNNINGTON (All Saints) *see* Kirkdale w Harome,
Nunnington and Pockley *York*
NUNTHORPE (St Mary the Virgin) (St Mary's Church Hall)
York 20 **P** *Abp* **V** T STEPHENS **C** L R WILD
NUNTON (St Andrew) *see* Chalke Valley *Sarum*
NURSLING (St Boniface) and Rownhams *Win 12* **P** *Bp*
R G DIXON
NURSTEAD (St Mildred) *see* Meopham w Nurstead *Roch*
NUTBOURNE (St Wilfrid) *see* Chidham *Chich*
NUTFIELD (St Peter and St Paul) *see* Bletchingley and
Nutfield *S'wark*
NUTFIELD, SOUTH (Christ Church) *S'wark 25* **P** *Ch Patr*
Trust **V** A J WAY

NUTHALL (St Patrick) *see* Kimberley and Nuthall *S'well*
NUTHURST (St Andrew) and Mannings Heath *Chich 7*
  P *Bp Lon* **R** *vacant*
NUTHURST (St Thomas) *see* Packwood w Hockley Heath *Birm*
NUTLEY (St James the Less) *Chich 18* **P** *R Maresfield*
  V B W SEAR **NSM** P C INGRAM
NYMET (St George) *see* S Molton w Nymet St George,
  Chittlehamholt etc *Ex*
NYMET ROWLAND (St Bartholomew) *see* N Creedy *Ex*
NYMPSFIELD (St Bartholomew) *see* Dursley, Uley, Owlpen
  etc *Glouc*
NYNEHEAD (All Saints) *see* Wellington and Distr *B & W*
OADBY (St Paul) (St Peter) Great Glen, including Burton
  Overy, Carlton Curlieu, and Glen Magna *Leic 3* **P** *Patr Bd*
  TR S A BAILEY **TV** K K FORD **C** S J COLLINS
OAKAMOOR (Holy Trinity) *see* Kingsley and Foxt-w-Whiston
  and Oakamoor etc *Lich*
OAKDALE (St George) *Sarum 7* **P** *Bp* **V** P M DRAPER
OAKE (St Bartholomew) *see* Deane Vale *B & W*
OAKENGATES (Holy Trinity), Priors Lee and Wrockwardine
  Wood *Lich 20* **P** *Bp and V Shifnal (jt)* **R** D J LOUGHRAN
  C L R HARPER
OAKENSHAW CUM WOODLANDS (St Andrew) *see* Low
  Moor and Oakenshaw *Leeds*
OAKFORD (St Peter) *see* Washfield, Stoodleigh, Withleigh
  etc *Ex*
OAKHAM (All Saints), Ashwell, Braunston, Brooke,
  Egleton, Hambleton, Langham, Market Overton, Teigh
  and Whissendine *Pet 12* **P** *Patr Bd* **TR** S R GRIFFITHS
  TV D L MARSH **C** C E OSBORN, I G OSBORNE
OAKHANGER (St Luke's Mission Church) *see* Alsager Ch Ch
  Ches
OAKHANGER (St Mary Magdalene) *see* Northanger *Win*
OAKHILL (All Saints) *see* Beacon Trinity *B & W*
OAKINGTON (St Andrew) *Ely 6* **P** *Qu Coll Cam*
  V J C ALEXANDER
OAKLEY (St Leonard) w Wootton St Lawrence *Win 4* **P** *Qu*
  Coll Ox and D&C (alt) **R** B A KAUTZER
OAKLEY (St Mary) *see* Bromham w Oakley and Stagsden
  St Alb
OAKLEY (St Mary) *see* Worminghall w Ickford, Oakley and
  Shabbington *Ox*
OAKLEY (St Nicholas) *see* N Hartismere *St E*
OAKLEY (St Peter) *see* Henham and Elsenham w Ugley
  Chelmsf
OAKLEY SQUARE (St Matthew) *see* Old St Pancras *Lon*
OAKLEY, GREAT (All Saints), Wix, Wrabness, Tendring and
  Beaumont-cum-Moze *Chelmsf 22* **P** *Ld Chan (1 turn), Ch*
  Patr Trust, St Jo Coll Cam, DBP, and Ball Coll Ox (2 turns)
  V E BARNES **C** K D EMERSON **NSM** L F GARNHAM
OAKLEY, GREAT (St Michael), and LITTLE (St Peter) *Pet 7*
  P *H W G de Capell Brooke Esq and Boughton Estates Ltd (alt)*
  P-in-c A M SEARLE
OAKRIDGE (St Bartholomew) *see* Bisley, Chalford, France
  Lynch, and Oakridge etc *Glouc*
OAKS IN CHARNWOOD (St James the Greater) *see* Shepshed
  and Oaks in Charnwood *Leic*
OAKSEY (All Saints) *see* Braydon Brook *Bris*
OAKWOOD (no dedication) *Derby 5* **P** *Bp and MMCET (jt)*
  V *vacant*
OAKWOOD (St Thomas) *Lon 18* **P** *Bp* **V** R J L ALLDRITT
OAKWORTH (Christ Church) *Leeds 1* **P** *Bp*
  NSM B G PARTRIDGE
OARE (Blessed Virgin Mary) w Culbone *B & W 15* **P** *Bp*
  R *vacant*
OARE (Holy Trinity) *see* Vale of Pewsey *Sarum*
OARE (St Bartholomew) *see* E Downland *Ox*
OARE (St Peter) *see* Kingsdown and Creekside *Cant*
OATLANDS (St Mary) *Guildf 8* **P** *Bp* **V** F O OLOKOSE
OBORNE (St Cuthbert) *see* Queen Thorne *Sarum*
OCCOLD (St Michael) *see* Eye *St E*
OCKBROOK (All Saints) *Derby 8* **P** *Lt Col T H Pares*
  V T M SUMPTER
OCKENDON, NORTH (St Mary Magdalene) *Chelmsf 2* **P** *Bp*
  R *vacant*
OCKENDON, SOUTH (St Nicholas) *see* Mardyke *Chelmsf*
OCKER HILL (St Mark) *Lich 25* **P** *Bp* **V** M LIDDELL
  C G HARTILL
OCKFORD RIDGE (St Mark) *see* Godalming *Guildf*
OCKHAM (All Saints) w Hatchford and Downside *Guildf 10*
  P *Bp* **R** H M GREAR
OCKLEY (St Margaret) *see* Surrey Weald *Guildf*
OCLE PYCHARD (St James the Great) *see* Frome Valley *Heref*
OCTAGON, comprising Compton, East Marden,
  Forestside, North Marden, Racton, and Stoughton

  Chich 3 **P** *Bp, Bp Lon,and Stansted Park Foundation (jt)*
  R L A YATES
ODCOMBE (St Peter and St Paul) *see* Ham Hill Villages
  B & W
ODD RODE (All Saints) *Ches 11* **P** *R Astbury*
  R P S ATKINSON
ODDINGLEY (St James) *see* Bowbrook S *Worc*
ODDINGTON (Holy Ascension) *see* Broadwell, Evenlode,
  Oddington, Adlestrop etc *Glouc*
ODDINGTON (St Andrew) *see* Ray Valley *Ox*
ODDINGTON (St Nicholas) *see* Broadwell, Evenlode,
  Oddington, Adlestrop etc *Glouc*
ODELL (All Saints) *see* Chellington *St Alb*
ODIHAM (All Saints) *see* N Hants Downs *Win*
ODSTOCK (St Mary) *see* Chalke Valley *Sarum*
OFFCHURCH Group, The (St Gregory), including
  Hunningham, Wappenbury, and Weston under Wetherley
  Cov 10 **P** *Ld Chan (1 turn), Bp (3 turns)* **V** H PRIESTNER
OFFENHAM (St Mary and St Milburgh) *see* E Vale and Avon
  Villages *Worc*
OFFERTON (St Alban) (St John) *Ches 18* **P** *Bp*
  P-in-c C M RABLEN
OFFHAM (Old St Peter) *see* Hamsey *Chich*
OFFHAM (St Michael) *see* W Malling w Offham *Roch*
OFFLEY (St Mary Magdalene) *see* King's Walden and Offley
  w Lilley *St Alb*
OFFLEY, HIGH (St Mary the Virgin) *see* Adbaston, High
  Offley, Knightley, Norbury etc *Lich*
OFFORD D'ARCY w OFFORD CLUNY (All Saints) *see* Buckden
  w the Offords *Ely*
OFFTON (St Mary) *see* S Bosmere *St E*
OFFWELL (St Mary the Virgin), Northleigh, Farway,
  Cotleigh and Widworthy *Ex 4* **P** *Trustees, R T Marker Esq,*
  Cotleigh PCC, and Bp (jt) **V** *vacant*
OGBOURNE ST ANDREW (St Andrew) *see* Ridgeway *Sarum*
OGBOURNE ST GEORGE (St George) *as above*
OGLEY HAY (St James) *Lich 1* **P** *Bp* **V** *vacant*
OGWELL (St Bartholomew) *see* Newton Abbot *Ex*
OKEFORD Benefice, The, comprising Childe Okeford,
  Hammoon, Manston, Okeford Fitzpaine, and Shillingstone
  Sarum 5 **P** *G A L-F Pitt-Rivers Esq and DBP (alt)*
  R L M S COOK **C** K A F WILSON
OKEFORD FITZPAINE (St Andrew) *see* Okeford *Sarum*
OKEHAMPTON (All Saints) (St James), Inwardleigh,
  Belstone, Sourton, Bridestowe, Bratton Clovelly,
  Germansweek, Lydford, Hatherleigh, Northlew w
  Ashbury, Exbourne, Meeth and Jacobstowe *Ex 10* **P** *Patr*
  Bd (5 turns), Duchy of Cornwall (1 turn) **TR** S W COOK
  TV A J BROOK, L D WINSBURY **C** R A F BACHE
OKEWOOD (St John the Baptist) *see* Ewhurst w Okewood
  and Forest Green *Guildf*
OLD *see under substantive place name*
OLD FORD (St Paul) (St Mark) *Lon 7* **P** *Hyndman Trustees*
  and CPAS (jt) **V** J C HUGHESDON **C** D S PILKINGTON
  NSM A I KEECH
OLD HEATH (St Barnabas) *see* Colchester St Barn *Chelmsf*
OLD HILL (Holy Trinity) *Worc 9* **P** *Ch Soc Trust*
  V N S GOWERS **C** R A HACKETT
OLD KIRK BRADDAN (St Brendan) *see* Braddan *S & M*
OLD LANE (Mission Church) *see* Bloxwich *Lich*
OLDBERROW (St Mary) *see* Arden Marches *Cov*
OLDBURY (Christ Church), Langley, and Londonderry
  Birm 6 **P** *The Crown (1 turn), Bp (3 turns)* **V** K L EVANS
OLDBURY (St Nicholas) *see* Bridgnorth and Morville Par
  Heref
OLDBURY, comprising Calstone Wellington, Cherhill,
  Compton Bassett, Heddington, and Yatesbury *Sarum 16*
  P *Bp, CPAS, Marquess of Lansdowne, and C E R Money-Kyrle*
  Esq (jt) **R** M C EARWICKER
OLDBURY-ON-SEVERN (St Arilda) *see* Thornbury and
  Oldbury-on-Severn w Shepperdine *Glouc*
OLDCOTES (St Mark's Mission Church) *see* Carlton-in-
  Lindrick and Langold w Oldcotes *S'well*
OLDHAM (St Barnabas) *see* Clarksfield and Waterhead *Man*
OLDHAM (St Chad) *see* Hollinwood and Limeside *Man*
OLDHAM (St James) (St Ambrose) *Man 15* **P** *Bp and R*
  Prestwich (jt) **V** *vacant*
OLDHAM (St Mary w St Peter) *Man 16* **P** *Patr Bd*
  V D J PALMER **NSM** J M HURLSTON
OLDHAM (St Paul) and Werneth *Man 16* **P** *Bp*
  V N J ANDREWES **Hon C** D J QUARMBY
OLDHAM (St Stephen and All Martyrs) *see* Coldhurst and
  Oldham St Steph *Man*
OLDHAM Moorside (St Thomas) *Man 15* **P** *Trustees*
  V D OWEN **C** R A DASHWOOD

OLDHURST (St Peter) *see* Somersham w Pidley and Oldhurst and Woodhurst *Ely*

OLDLAND (St Anne) *Bris 5* P *Bp* V B W GOODWIN

OLDRIDGE (St Thomas) *see* Tedburn St Mary, Cheriton Bishop, Whitestone etc *Ex*

OLDSWINFORD (St Mary) *see* Old Swinford Stourbridge *Worc*

OLIVER'S BATTERY (St Mark) *see* Stanmore *Win*

OLLERTON (St Giles) (St Paulinus) w Boughton *S'well 3* P *Ld Chan and Bp (alt)* P-in-c Z BURTON C A K ALLS NSM M A GROVES

OLNEY (St Peter and St Paul) *Ox 16* P *Bp* R A J D PRITCHARD-KEENS

OLTON (St Margaret) *Birm 10* P *Bp and V Bickenhill (jt)* V D E WRIGHT NSM S M CHANDLER

OLVESTON (St Mary the Virgin) *see* Almondsbury and Olveston *Bris*

OMBERSLEY (St Andrew) *see* Elmley Lovett w Hampton Lovett and Elmbridge w Rushock and Hartlebury and Ombersley w Doverdale *Worc*

ONCHAN (St Peter), Lonan and Laxey *S & M* P *The Crown* TV J DUDLEY

ONECOTE (St Luke) *see* Butterton, Ipstones-w-Berkhamsytch etc *Lich*

ONEHOUSE (St John the Baptist) *see* Combs and Finborough *St E*

ONGAR, HIGH (St Mary the Virgin) w Norton Mandeville *Chelmsf 3* P *Ch Soc Trust* P-in-c S H GIBBS

ONIBURY (St Michael and All Angels) *see* Bromfield *Heref*

ONSLOW SQUARE (Holy Trinity) (St Paul) and South Kensington St Augustine *Lon 8* P *Bp, MMCET, and Keble Coll Ox (jt)* V N G P GUMBEL C A J WOOLDRIDGE, A L RAYMENT, B J WILLIS, B M BRYANT, D J MATTHEWS, H E ADAMS, J M LEES, J S WILLIS, M G THOMAS, M P LAYZELL, N K LEE, P J P WYNTER, P W COWLEY, R J BARSTOW, S FOSTER, S J FOLLETT, W R VAN DER HART Hon C J A K MILLAR NSM A J MORLEY, J A C RAY, M D ROPER, S COLMAN, T C JACKSON

OPENSHAW (St Barnabas) *see* Manchester Gd Shep and St Barn *Man*

OPENSHAW, HIGHER (St Clement) *Man 1* P *Trustees* P-in-c P G JUMP C D R J MULLANEY, T R HOLLINGSBEE

OPENWOODGATE (St Mark) *see* Belper *Derby*

ORBY (All Saints) *see* Burgh Gp *Linc*

ORCHARD (Community Centre) *see* Egglescliffe *Dur*

ORCHARD PORTMAN (St Michael) *see* Beercrocombe w Curry Mallet, Hatch Beauchamp etc *B & W*

ORCHARD WAY (St Barnabas) *see* W Cheltenham *Glouc*

ORCHARDLEIGH (Blessed Virgin Mary) *see* Beckington w Standerwick, Berkley, Rodden etc *B & W*

ORCHESTON (St Mary) *see* Salisbury Plain *Sarum*

ORCOP (St John the Baptist) *see* St Weonards *Heref*

ORDSALL (All Hallows) *see* Retford Area *S'well*

ORDSALL (St Clement) and Salford Quays *Man 20* P *Bp* R S KEARNEY

ORE (Christ Church) *Chich 15* P *Simeon's Trustees* V L C J DUCKETT NSM J R TUTTON

ORE (St Helen) (St Barnabas) *Chich 15* P *Simeon's Trustees* R P PARKS

OREBECK *St E 14* P *The Crown (1 turn), MMCET, J Austin Esq, Capt J L Round-Turner, Ch Soc Trust, and Lord Marlesford (1 turn)* P-in-c G HEDGER

ORESTON (Church of the Good Shepherd) *see* Plymstock and Hooe *Ex*

ORFORD (St Andrew) *Liv 11* P *Bp* V M RAYNOR

ORFORD (St Bartholomew) *see* Wilford Peninsula *St E*

ORFORD (St Margaret) *Liv 11* P *Bp* V D T HOWARD

ORLESTONE (St Mary) *see* Saxon Shoreline *Cant*

ORLETON (St George) *see* Leominster *Heref*

ORLINGBURY (St Mary) *see* Gt w Lt Harrowden and Orlingbury and Isham etc *Pet*

ORMESBY (St Cuthbert) *York 17* P *Abp* V J S CROFT NSM J E CALDWELL

ORMESBY ST MARGARET (St Margaret) w Scratby, Ormesby St Michael and Rollesby *Nor 6* P *Bp, D&C, DBP and R J H Tacon Esq (jt)* V *vacant*

ORMESBY ST MICHAEL (St Michael) *see* Ormesby St Marg w Scratby, Ormesby St Mich etc *Nor*

ORMESBY, NORTH (Holy Trinity) *York 17* P *Abp* V D P BLACK

ORMSBY Group, The South (St Leonard), including Bag Enderby, Brinkhill, Harrington, Haugh, Ruckland w Farforth, Maidenwell and Oxcombe, Somersby, and Tetford *Linc 9* P A J Massingberd-Mundy Esq, Sir Thomas Ingilby Bt, Mert Coll Ox, Bp, and DBP (jt) R *vacant*

ORMSGILL (St Francis) *see* N Barrow *Carl*

ORMSIDE (St James) *see* Heart of Eden *Carl*

ORMSKIRK (St Peter and St Paul) *Liv 14* P *Earl of Derby* P-in-c P A BICKNELL NSM S E HAYNES

ORPINGTON (All Saints) *Roch 16* P *D&C* V *vacant*

ORPINGTON (Christ Church) *Roch 16* P *Ch Trust Fund Trust, Bp, and V Orpington (jt)* V S SMITH

ORRELL (St Luke) *Liv 15* P *Bp* C R M SHEEHAN

ORRELL HEY (St John and St James) *see* Litherland and Orrell Hey *Liv*

ORSETT (St Giles and All Saints) and Bulphan and Horndon on the Hill *Chelmsf 16* P *Bp and D&C St Paul's (jt)* R S M MANN NSM S R BLAKE

ORSTON (St Mary) *see* Whatton w Aslockton, Hawksworth, Scarrington etc *S'well*

ORTON (All Saints) *see* High Westmorland *Carl*

ORTON GOLDHAY (St John) *see* The Ortons *Ely*

ORTON GOLDHAY (St John) Conventional District *Ely 13* Min S C GOWER

ORTON LONGUEVILLE (Holy Trinity) *see* The Ortons *Ely*

ORTON MALBORNE (not known) *as above*

ORTON WATERVILLE (St Mary) *as above*

ORTON, GREAT (St Giles) *see* Barony of Burgh *Carl*

ORTON-ON-THE-HILL (St Edith of Polesworth) *see* Bosworth and Sheepy Gp *Leic*

ORTONS, The (Holy Trinity) (St Mary) (St John) (not known) *Ely 15* P *Bp and Pemb Coll Cam (jt)* P-in-c I R FALVEY

ORWELL Group, The (St Andrew), including Arrington, Barrington, Croydon, and Wimpole *Ely 7* P *Bp, DBP, and Trin Coll Cam (jt)* R F A COUCH

OSBALDWICK (St Thomas) w Murton *York 2* P *Abp* V *vacant*

OSBOURNBY (St Peter and St Paul) *see* S Lafford *Linc*

OSENEY CRESCENT (St Luke) *Lon 17* P *Bp* V J MARCH C C S BROOKES, E R OSBORNE

OSGATHORPE (St Mary the Virgin) *see* Kegworth, Hathern, Long Whatton, Diseworth etc *Leic*

OSMASTON (St Martin) *see* Brailsford w Shirley, Osmaston w Edlaston etc *Derby*

OSMINGTON (St Osmond) *see* Weymouth Ridgeway *Sarum*

OSMONDTHORPE (St Philip) *see* Halton and Osmondthorpe *Leeds*

OSMOTHERLEY (St Peter) w Harlsey and Ingleby Arncliffe *York 18* P *J N Barnard Esq (1 turn), Ld Chan (2 turns)* P-in-c D E GAMBLE NSM W A DEWING

OSMOTHERLY (St John) *see* Ulverston St Mary w H Trin *Carl*

OSNEY (St Frideswide) *Ox 2* P *Bp and Ch Ch Ox (jt)* R C M SYKES C K V SEAGRAVE NSM J MOFFETT-LEVY

OSPRINGE (St Peter and St Paul) *see* Faversham *Cant*

OSSETT (Holy and Undivided Trinity) and Gawthorpe *Leeds 19* P *Bp and R Dewsbury (jt)* V C A HICKS OLM A SHACKLETON

OSSETT, SOUTH (Christ Church) *Leeds 19* P *Bp* V D J ROBERTSON

OSSINGTON (Holy Rood) *see* Norwell w Ossington, Cromwell etc *S'well*

OSWALDKIRK (St Oswald) *see* Ampleforth w Oswaldkirk, Gilling E etc *York*

OSWALDTWISTLE (Immanuel) (All Saints) (St Paul) *Blackb 1* P *Bp, DBP, R Church Kirk, The Ven C W D Carroll, G F Garnett Esq, and PCCs (jt)* V M J T JOSS NSM C GARNER

OSWESTRY (Holy Trinity) *Lich 18* P *Bp* V P T DARLINGTON

OSWESTRY (St Oswald) *Lich 18* P *Earl of Powis* V H L GIBBONS

OTFORD (St Bartholomew) *Roch 10* P *D&C Westmr* V *vacant*

OTHAM (St Nicholas) *see* N Downs *Cant*

OTHERY (St Michael) *see* Middlezoy w Othery, Moorlinch and Greinton *B & W*

OTLEY (All Saints) *Leeds 15* P *Bp* V G C BUTTANSHAW

OTLEY (St Mary) *see* Carlford *St E*

OTTER VALE *see* Ottery St Mary, Alfington, W Hill, Tipton etc *Ex*

OTTERBOURNE (St Matthew) *see* Compton, Hursley, and Otterbourne *Win*

OTTERBURN (St John the Evangelist) *see* N Tyne and Redesdale *Newc*

OTTERFORD (St Leonard) *see* Blackdown *B & W*

OTTERHAM (St Denis) *see* Boscastle and Tintagel Gp *Truro*

OTTERINGTON, NORTH (St Michael and All Angels) *see* The Thorntons and The Otteringtons *York*

OTTERINGTON, SOUTH (St Andrew) *as above*

OTTERSHAW (Christ Church) *Guildf 11* P *Bp* V S C FACCINI

OTTERTON (St Michael) *see* Budleigh Salterton, E Budleigh w Bicton etc *Ex*

OTTERY ST MARY (St Mary the Virgin), Alfington, West Hill, Tipton St John, Venn Ottery, Newton Poppleford, Harpford, Colaton Raleigh, Payhembury, Feniton and Escot *Ex 6* **P** *Patr Bd* **TR** S J A WESTON
TV D J CARRINGTON, M WARD **Hon C** A E H TURNER,
J G PANGBOURNE **NSM** M G DICK, R J ALLEN

OTTRINGHAM (St Wilfrid) *see* Easington w Skeffling, Keyingham, Ottringham etc *York*

OUGHTIBRIDGE (Ascension) *Sheff 3* **P** *Ch Patr Trust*
V J F E MANN

OUGHTRINGTON (St Peter) and Warburton *Ches 10* **P** *Bp and Viscount Ashbrook (jt)* **R** E M BURGESS

OULTON (St John the Evangelist) *see* Stone Ch Ch and Oulton *Lich*

OULTON (St John) *see* Rothwell, Lofthouse, Methley etc *Leeds*

OULTON (St Michael) *Nor 9* **P** *Ch Soc Trust* **R** *vacant*

OULTON (St Peter and St Paul) *see* Aylsham and Distr *Nor*

OULTON BROAD (St Mark) (St Luke the Evangelist) *Nor 9*
P *Simeon's Trustees* **OLM** M A BARNES

OUNDLE (St Peter) w Ashton and Benefield w Glapthorn
Pet 10 **P** *Bp and Mrs G S Watts-Russell (jt)* **R** S J WEBSTER
C J M BALL, N M DONNELLY

OUSBY (St Luke) *see* Cross Fell Gp *Carl*

OUSDEN (St Peter) *see* Bansfield *St E*

OUSEBURN, GREAT (St Mary) and LITTLE (Holy Trinity) w Marton cum Grafton and Whixley w Green Hammerton
Leeds 23 **P** *Bp, R Knaresborough and DBP (3 turns), St Jo Coll Cam (1 turn)* **V** S C FEASTER **NSM** J ROPER

OUT RAWCLIFFE (St John the Evangelist) *see* Waterside Par *Blackb*

OUTLANE (St Mary Magdalene) *see* Stainland and Outlane *Leeds*

OUTWELL (St Clement) *Ely 14* **P** *Bp* **R** *vacant*

OUTWOOD (St John the Baptist) *see* The Windmill *S'wark*

OUTWOOD (St Mary Magdalene), Stanley and Wrenthorpe *Leeds 19* **P** *Bp and D&C Wakef (jt)*
V G COGGINS **C** J J P BISH, J KERSHAW **NSM** D TEECE

OUTWOOD COMMON (St John the Divine) *see* Billericay and Lt Burstead *Chelmsf*

OUZEL VALLEY, The, comprising Billington, Egginton, Heath and Reach, Hockliffe, Leighton Buzzard, and Linslade
St Alb 11 **P** *Patr Bd* **TR** C F IRVINE **TV** B J MINTON,
N MCGEENEY, S P MARSH **OLM** W JONES

OVAL WAY (All Saints) *see* Chalfont St Peter *Ox*

OVENDEN (St George) *Leeds 10* **P** *V Halifax* **NSM** G ROPER

OVENDEN (St John the Evangelist) *see* Bradshaw and Holmfield *Leeds*

OVER *see also under substantive place name*

OVER (St Chad) *Ches 6* **P** *Bp* **V** C B MOORE **C** J P SMITH

OVER (St John the Evangelist) *Ches 6* **P** *Lord Delamere and W R Cullimore Esq (jt)* **V** G T CROWDER

OVER (St Mary) *Ely 6* **P** *Trin Coll Cam* **P-in-c** S D GILL
C E R COPE

OVER WALLOP (St Peter) *see* Portway and Danebury *Win*

OVERBURY (St Faith) w Teddington, Alstone and Little Washbourne w Beckford and Ashton under Hill *Worc 4*
P *D&C and MMCET (jt)* **C** D T LEWIS

OVERSEAL (St Matthew) *see* Seale and Lullington w Coton in the Elms *Derby*

OVERSTONE (St Nicholas) *see* Mears Ashby and Hardwick and Sywell etc *Pet*

OVERSTRAND (St Martin) *see* Poppyland *Nor*

OVERTON (St Helen) *Blackb 11* **P** *V Lanc* **V** L S MOFFATT

OVERTON (St Mary) w Laverstoke and Freefolk *Win 6*
P *Bp* **R** J A TOMKINS-RUSSELL

OVERTON (St Michael and All Angels) *see* Upper Kennet *Sarum*

OVING (All Saints) *see* Schorne *Ox*

OVING (St Andrew) *see* Tangmere and Oving *Chich*

OVINGDEAN (St Wulfran) *Chich 19* **P** *SMF*
R M C LLOYD WILLIAMS

OVINGHAM (St Mary the Virgin) and Wylam *Newc 9* **P** *Bp*
V T D K BIRCH

OVINGTON (St John the Evangelist) *see* Watton *Nor*

OVINGTON (St Mary) *see* N Hinckford *Chelmsf*

OVINGTON (St Peter) *see* Arle Valley *Win*

OWERMOIGNE (St Michael) *see* Watercombe *Sarum*

OWERSBY, NORTH (St Martin) *see* Woldmoor Gp *Linc*

OWLERTON (St John the Baptist) *Sheff 4* **P** *Ch Patr Trust*
V N A DAWSON **C** J E FRENCH

OWLPEN (Holy Cross) *see* Dursley, Uley, Owlpen etc *Glouc*

OWLSMOOR (St George) *Ox 8* **P** *Bp* **V** C M VAUGHAN

OWLSWICK (Chapel) *see* Risborough *Ox*

OWMBY Group, The (St Peter and St Paul), including Glentham w Caenby, Hackthorn, Saxby, and Spridlington
Linc 5 **P** *Duchy of Lanc, Bp and D&C, Bp and Mrs S Hutton, and C W A Cracroft-Eley (by turn)* **R** S E TURNBULL
OLM S DEACON

OWSLEBURY (St Andrew) *see* S Downs Gateway Churches *Win*

OWSTON (All Saints) *Sheff 7* **P** *DBP* **P-in-c** A B WALTON

OWSTON (St Andrew) *see* Whatborough Gp *Leic*

OWSTON (St Martin) *Linc 1* **P** *The Crown* **V** *vacant*

OWTHORNE (St Matthew) *see* S Holderness Coast *York*

OWTHORPE (St Margaret) *S'well 5* **P** *Trustees Sir Rupert Bromley Bt* **P-in-c** P D S MASSEY

OWTON MANOR (St James) *Dur 3* **P** *Bp* **V** S J LOCKE

OXBOROUGH (St John the Evangelist) w Foulden and Caldecote *Nor 13* **P** *G&C Coll Cam* **P-in-c** Z M FERGUSON
Hon C L M LUBBE

OXCLOSE (not known) *Dur 10* **P** *R Washington, TR Usworth, and V Fatfield (jt)* **P-in-c** G M RUSHTON

OXENDON (St Helen) *see* Arthingworth, Harrington w Oxendon and E Farndon *Pet*

OXENHALL (St Anne) *see* Redmarley D'Abitot, Bromesberrow, Pauntley etc *Glouc*

OXENHOPE (St Mary the Virgin) *Leeds 1* **P** *Bp*
V C M THATCHER **NSM** J ROBERTS

OXENTON (St John the Baptist) *see* Bishop's Cleeve and Woolstone w Gotherington etc *Glouc*

OXFORD (St Aldate) *Ox 2* **P** *Simeon's Trustees*
R C S G CLEVERLY **C** S C R PONSONBY, T W BATEMAN,
W R DONALDSON **NSM** C D LANDAU, L G HARRIS,
M BRICKMAN

OXFORD (St Andrew) *Ox 2* **P** *Trustees* **V** D J HEYWARD
C J R DWYER, P M WHITE, T C MURRAY **NSM** E J PITKETHLY,
T W HOWELL

OXFORD (St Barnabas and St Paul) (St Thomas the Martyr) *Ox 2* **P** *Keble Coll Ox and Ch Ch Ox (jt)*
V C M WOODS **C** S GILLINGHAM

OXFORD (St Clement) *Ox 1* **P** *Ox Ch Trust* **R** R E GIBSON
C P J LOCKLEY

OXFORD (St Ebbe w Holy Trinity and St Peter-le-Bailey)
Ox 2 **P** *Ox Ch Trust* **R** V E ROBERTS **C** B C G VANE,
J M KNIGHT, L P CATALLO, M J POPE, P D L WILKINSON,
T C DOSSOR **NSM** J C POOLE

OXFORD (St Frideswide) *see* Osney *Ox*

OXFORD (St Giles) St Philip and St James (St Margaret)
Ox 2 **P** *St Jo Coll Ox* **V** A W H BUNCH **C** D G T WALTERS

OXFORD (St Mary Magdalen) *Ox 2* **P** *Ch Ch Ox*
V P J GROVES **C** J A MERCER **NSM** J JONG

OXFORD (St Mary the Virgin) (St Cross or Holywell) (St Peter in the East) *Ox 2* **P** *Or Coll Ox and Mert Coll Ox (jt)* **V** W R S LAMB **C** J R W CROCKFORD
NSM A E RAMSEY, C BANNISTER-PARKER

OXFORD (St Matthew) *Ox 2* **P** *Ox Ch Trust* **R** J R WILLIAMS
C S G N TUCK **Hon C** J A WILLIAMS **NSM** J LEES,
M J RAYNER

OXFORD (St Michael at the North Gate w St Martin and All Saints) *Ox 2* **P** *Linc Coll Ox* **V** A G BUCKLEY

OXFORD Canning Crescent (St Luke) *see* Ox St Matt *Ox*

OXHEY (All Saints) *St Alb 6* **P** *Bp* **V** P M WISE **C** E J GUEST

OXHEY (St Matthew) *St Alb 6* **P** *DBP* **V** D M SHEPHERD

OXHILL (St Lawrence) *see* Tysoe w Oxhill and Whatcote *Cov*

OXLEY (Epiphany) and Wednesfield St Gregory *Lich 28*
P *Bp* **OLM** A E MARTIN

OXNEAD (St Michael & all Angels) *see* Aylsham and Distr *Nor*

OXSHOTT (St Andrew) *Guildf 10* **P** *Bp* **V** F A TRICKEY
Hon C C J TRICKEY

OXTED (St Mary) *S'wark 25* **P** *Bp* **TR** A ELTRINGHAM
C M S ANDERSON

OXTON (St Peter and St Paul) *see* Epperstone, Gonalston, Oxton and Woodborough *S'well*

OXTON (St Saviour) *Ches 1* **P** *DBP* **V** J KENNEDY
NSM T A DIXON

PACKINGTON (Holy Rood) *see* Woodfield *Leic*

PACKWOOD (St Giles) w Hockley Heath *Birm 5* **P** *Bp and M R Parkes Esq (alt)* **V** M CATLEY

PADBURY (St Mary the Virgin) *see* Lenborough *Ox*

PADDINGTON (St James) *Lon 2* **P** *Bp* **V** P R THOMAS
C O J DOBSON

PADDINGTON (St John the Evangelist) (St Michael and All Angels) *Lon 2* **P** *DBP* **V** S D MASON **C** D J WARNKE
NSM M LEGG

PADDINGTON (St Mary Magdalene) (St Peter) *Lon 2*
P *Keble Coll Ox and Ch Patr Trust* **V** R H EVERETT

PADDINGTON (St Saviour) *see* Lt Venice *Lon*

PADDINGTON (St Stephen w St Luke) *Lon 2*   **P** *Bp*
V R J DRYER   **NSM** M J LEE
PADDINGTON GREEN (St Mary)   *see* Lt Venice *Lon*
PADDLESWORTH (St Oswald)   *see* Lyminge w Paddlesworth,
Stanford w Paddlesworth etc *Cant*
PADDOCK WOOD (St Andrew) *Roch 8*   **P** *D&C Cant*
V B T KNAPP
PADGATE (Christ Church)   *see* Warrington E *Liv*
PADIHAM (St Leonard) w Hapton and Padiham Green
Blackb 3   **P** *Bp*   **V** M A JONES   **NSM** C S J WALKER
PADSTOW (St Petroc), St Merryn and St Issey w St Petroc
Minor *Truro 7*   **P** *Bp, Keble Coll Ox, and P J N Prideaux-Brune
Esq (jt)*   **R** S M HOLMES   **NSM** F GIORLA
PADWORTH (St John the Baptist)   *see* Stratfield Mortimer and
Mortimer W End etc *Ox*
PAGANHILL (Holy Spirit)   *see* Stroud Team *Glouc*
PAGHAM (St Thomas à Becket) *Chich 1*   **P** *Abp*   **V** *vacant*
PAGLESHAM (St Peter)   *see* Ashingdon w S Fambridge,
Canewdon and Paglesham *Chelmsf*
PAIGNTON (Christ Church) and Preston St Paul *Ex 11*
P *Bp and Peache Trustees (jt)*   **V** J R POUT
PAIGNTON (St John the Baptist) (St Andrew) (St Boniface)
Ex 11   **P** *DBP*   **V** R J CARLTON
PAILTON (St Denis)   *see* Revel Gp *Cov*
PAINSWICK (St Mary the Virgin), Sheepscombe, Cranham,
The Edge, Pitchcombe, Harescombe and Brookthorpe
Glouc 4   **P** *Bp, D&C, Mrs N Owen (1 turn), and Ld Chan (1
turn)*   **NSM** A J P LEACH   **OLM** D W NEWELL
PAKEFIELD (All Saints and St Margaret) *Nor 9*   **P** *Ch Patr
Trust*   **R** S R LORD
PAKENHAM (St Mary) w Norton, Tostock, Great Ashfield,
Hunston and Stowlangtoft *St E 5*   **P** *Bp, Peterho Coll Cam,
and DBP (jt)*   **R** K A VALENTINE   **NSM** J S G PRICE
PALGRAVE (St Peter)   *see* N Hartismere *St E*
PALLION (St Luke)   *see* Millfield St Mark and Pallion St Luke
Dur
PALMARSH (Holy Cross)   *see* Hythe *Cant*
PALMERS GREEN (St John the Evangelist) *Lon 18*
P *V Southgate Ch Ch*   **V** J V COLEMAN
PAMBER (St Mary and St John the Baptist)   *see* The
Sherbornes w Pamber *Win*
PAMPISFORD (St John the Baptist) *Ely 5*   **P** *Mrs B A
Killander*   **P-in-c** P J SHAKESHAFT
PANCRASWEEK (St Pancras)   *see* Holsworthy, Hollacombe,
Pyworthy etc *Ex*
PANFIELD (St Mary the Virgin)   *see* Bocking St Mary and
Panfield *Chelmsf*
PANGBOURNE (St James the Less) w Tidmarsh and
Sulham *Ox 4*   **P** *Bp, Ch Soc Trust, and Mrs I E Moon (jt)*
R H C W PARBURY
PANNAL (St Robert of Knaresborough) w Beckwithshaw
Leeds 21   **P** *Bp and Peache Trustees (jt)*   **V** J SMITH
C A L PALMER
PANSHANGER (United Church) *St Alb 18*   **P** *Bp*   **V** *vacant*
PAPPLEWICK (St James)   *see* Linby w Papplewick *S'well*
PAPWORTH (St Peter) *Ely 1*   **P** *Patr Bd*
TR N A DI CASTIGLIONE   **TV** S M DAY
PAR (St Mary the Virgin) (Good Shepherd) *Truro 1*   **P** *The
Crown*   **P-in-c** D J P ISIORHO
PARHAM (St Mary the Virgin)   *see* Orebeck *St E*
PARHAM (St Peter)   *see* Amberley w N Stoke and Parham,
Wiggonholt etc *Chich*
PARK BARN (St Clare)   *see* Westborough *Guildf*
PARKEND (St Paul) and Viney Hill *Glouc 1*   **P** *Bp and Univ
Coll Ox (jt)*   **V** S C NORTON
PARKGATE (St Thomas)   *see* Neston *Ches*
PARKHAM (St James), Alwington, Buckland Brewer,
Hartland, Welcombe, Clovelly, Woolfardisworthy West,
Bucks Mills and Lundy *Ex 15*   **P** *Patr Bd (4 turns), The
Crown (1 turn)*   **TR** J M SKINNER   **TV** M M E BRAY
NSM J HAYES, K L C BEER
PARKSTONE (Good Shepherd)   *see* Heatherlands St Jo *Sarum*
PARKSTONE (St John the Evangelist)   *as above*
PARKSTONE (St Luke) *Sarum 7*   **P** *Ch Trust Fund Trust*
V C M STRAIN
PARKSTONE (St Peter) and St Osmund w Branksea St Mary
Sarum 7   **P** *Patr Bd*   **C** S BEDBOROUGH
OLM P E SOUTHGATE
PARKWOOD (Christ Church) Conventional District *Cant 15*
Min A J HOUSTON
PARKWOOD (St Paul)   *see* S Gillingham *Roch*
PARLAUNT ROAD (Christ the Worker)   *see* Langley Marish *Ox*
PARLEY, WEST (All Saints) (St Mark) *Sarum 9*   **P** P E E
Prideaux-Brune Esq   **R** E C BOOTH   **NSM** S M W THOMAS
PARNDON, GREAT (St Mary) *Chelmsf 4*   **P** *Bp*
P-in-c R J ATTEW

PARNDON, LITTLE (St Mary)   *see* Harlow Town Cen w Lt
Parndon *Chelmsf*
PARR (St Peter) (St Paul) (St Philip) (Holy Trinity) *Liv 10*
P *Patr Bd*   **TR** C DORAN   **TV** P F ROWE   **C** G F H HITCHEN
OLM H MCCANN, M E TAYLOR
PARR MOUNT (Holy Trinity)   *see* Parr *Liv*
PARRACOMBE (Christ Church)   *see* Lynton, Brendon,
Countisbury etc *Ex*
PARSON'S GREEN (St Dionis)   *see* Fulham St Dionis *Lon*
PARTINGTON (St Mary) and Carrington *Ches 10*   **P** *Bp and
V Bowdon (alt)*   **P-in-c** A W KNIGHT   **C** L A M BREWSTER
PARTNEY (St Nicholas)   *see* Bolingbroke Deanery *Linc*
PARTRIDGE GREEN (St Michael and All Angels)
see W Grinstead *Chich*
PARWICH (St Peter)   *see* Fenny Bentley, Thorpe, Tissington,
Parwich etc *Derby*
PASSENHAM (St Guthlac) *Pet 5*   **P** *MMCET*
R J E PENNINGTON
PASTON (All Saints) *Pet 11*   **P** *Bp*   **R** M S BRIDGEN
PASTON (St Margaret)   *see* Trunch Group *Nor*
PASTROW, comprising Charlton w Foxcotte, Hatherden w
Tangley, Penton Mewsey, Smannell w Enham Alamein, and
Weyhill *Win 3*   **P** *Bp, Qu Coll Ox, and St Mary's Coll Win (jt)*
P-in-c A P RANDLE-BISSELL   **C** T C ETHERTON
PATCHAM (All Saints) *Chich 19*   **P** *MMCET*
V A L FLOWERDAY   **NSM** M PHILIP
PATCHING (St John the Divine)   *see* Findon w Clapham and
Patching *Chich*
PATCHWAY (St Chad) *Bris 5*   **P** *Trustees*   **P-in-c** H K JAMESON
C T J MEARDON   **NSM** S N HARRE-YOUNG
PATELEY BRIDGE (St Cuthbert)   *see* Upper Nidderdale *Leeds*
PATRICK BROMPTON (St Patrick)   *see* Lower Wensleydale
Leeds
PATRICROFT (Christ Church)   *see* Eccles *Man*
PATRINGTON (St Patrick)   *see* Easington w Skeffling,
Keyingham, Ottringham etc *York*
PATRIXBOURNE (St Mary)   *see* Bridge *Cant*
PATTERDALE (St Patrick) *Carl 4*   **P** *Bp and the Hon J N
Lowther (jt)*   **P-in-c** M RODHAM
PATTINGHAM (St Chad) w Patshull *Lich 23*   **P** *Bp and
M Kwiatkowska Esq (jt)*   **V** M P HOBBS
PATTISHALL (Holy Cross) w Cold Higham and Gayton w
Tiffield *Pet 5*   **P** *Bp, SS Coll Cam, and SMF (jt)*
R K A I JONGMAN
PAUL (St Pol de Lion) *Truro 5*   **P** *Ld Chan*   **P-in-c** A M YATES
C K R OWEN, S YATES
PAULERSPURY (St James the Apostle)   *see* Silverstone and
Abthorpe w Slapton etc *Pet*
PAULL (St Andrew and St Mary)   *see* Hedon, Paull, Sproatley
and Preston *York*
PAULSGROVE (St Michael and All Angels) *Portsm 6*   **P** *Bp*
V I NEWTON
PAULTON (Holy Trinity) w Farrington Gurney and High
Littleton *B & W 11*   **P** *Bp and Hyndman Trustees (jt)*
V *vacant*
PAUNTLEY (St John the Evangelist)   *see* Redmarley D'Abitot,
Bromesberrow, Pauntley etc *Glouc*
PAVENHAM (St Peter)   *see* Milton Ernest, Pavenham and
Thurleigh *St Alb*
PAWLETT (St John the Baptist)   *see* Puriton and Pawlett
B & W
PAXFORD (Mission Church)   *see* Vale and Cotswold Edge
Glouc
PAXTONS, The (Holy Trinity) (St James) w Diddington and
Southoe *Ely 13*   **P** *D&C Linc (2 turns), E G W Thornhill Esq
and Mert Coll Ox (1 turn each)*   **V** A S REED
PAYHEMBURY (St Mary the Virgin)   *see* Ottery St Mary,
Alfington, W Hill, Tipton etc *Ex*
PEACEHAVEN (Ascension) and Telscombe Cliffs w
Piddinghoe and Telscombe Village *Chich 21*   **P** *Bp and
Gorham Trustees (jt)*   **V** T J MILLS   **C** D M HAKE
PEAK DALE (Holy Trinity)   *see* Tideswell *Derby*
PEAK FOREST (Charles the King and Martyr)   *see* Fairfield,
Peak Forest and Dove Holes *Derby*
PEAKIRK (St Pega)   *see* Glinton, Etton, Maxey, Peakirk and
Northborough *Pet*
PEAR TREE (Jesus Chapel)   *see* Southampton St Mary Extra
Win
PEASEDOWN ST JOHN (St John the Baptist) w Wellow and
Foxcote w Shoscombe *B & W 11*   **P** *Bp*   **V** M G STREET
PEASEMORE (St Barnabas)   *see* E Downland *Ox*
PEASENHALL (St Michael)   *see* Yoxmere *St E*
PEASLAKE (St Mark)   *see* Shere, Albury and Chilworth *Guildf*
PEASMARSH (St Michael)   *see* Shalford *Guildf*
PEASMARSH (St Peter and St Paul)   *see* Brede w Udimore and
Beckley and Peasmarsh *Chich*

PEATLING MAGNA (All Saints) *see* Four Saints *Leic*

PEATLING PARVA (St Andrew) *see* Avon-Swift *Leic*

PEBMARSH (St John the Baptist) *see* Halstead Area *Chelmsf*

PEBWORTH (St Peter) *see* Vale and Cotswold Edge *Glouc*

PECKHAM (All Saints) Blenheim Grove *S'wark 8* **P** *Ch Trust Fund Trust* **V** J M MORTIMER **C** J C DAWKINS

PECKHAM (Christ Church) *see* Camberwell Ch Ch *S'wark*

PECKHAM (St John w St Andrew) *S'wark 8* **P** *Bp* **V** E O K ADELOYE

PECKHAM (St Mary Magdalene) (St Paul) *S'wark 8* **P** *Ch Patr Soc* **V** O A ADAMS

PECKHAM (St Saviour) *S'wark 9* **P** *Bp* **V** P E COLLIER

PECKHAM, EAST (Holy Trinity) and Nettlestead *Roch 8* **P** *St Pet Coll Ox and D&C Cant (jt)* **R** A H CARR **NSM** S M MORRELL

PECKHAM, WEST (St Dunstan) *see* Mereworth, Wateringbury and W Peckham *Roch*

PECKLETON (St Mary Magdalene) *Leic 9* **P** *Ld Chan* **P-in-c** S M IVES-SMITH **C** H M AUCKEN

PEDMORE (St Peter) *Worc 12* **P** *Oldswinford Hosp* **R** *vacant*

PEEL (St German's Cathedral) *see* W Coast *S & M*

PEEL (St Paul) *see* Walkden and Lt Hulton *Man*

PEEL GREEN (St Michael and All Angels) *see* Barton w Peel Green and Winton *Man*

PEEL Parishes, The *Lich 4* **P** *Bp* **R** J R IDDON **NSM** R G DAVIES

PEGSWOOD (St Margaret) *see* Bothal and Pegswood w Longhirst *Newc*

PELDON (St Mary) *see* W w E Mersea, Peldon, Gt and Lt Wigborough *Chelmsf*

PELSALL (St Michael and All Angels) *Lich 24* **P** *Bp* **V** C A ST A RAMSAY **NSM** A M MORRIS

PELTON (Holy Trinity) and West Pelton *Dur 10* **P** *Bp* **V** J LINTERN

PELTON, WEST (St Paul) *see* Pelton and W Pelton *Dur*

PELYNT (St Nun) *see* Trelawny *Truro*

PEMBERTON (St John) *Liv 15* **P** *R Wigan* **V** P G ANDERSON **NSM** A PARKINSON

PEMBERTON (St Mark) Newtown *see* Newtown *Liv*

PEMBRIDGE (St Mary the Virgin) w Moor Court, Shobdon, Staunton-on-Arrow, Byton and Lyonshall *Heref 4* **P** *Ld Chan (1 turn), Patr Bd (4 turns)* **R** A L BRANSTON

PEMBURY (St Peter) *Roch 8* **P** *Ch Ch Ox* **V** R M WORSSAM **NSM** C E WALSHAW

PEN SELWOOD (St Michael) *B & W 2* **P** *Bp* **R** *vacant*

PENCOMBE (St John) *see* Bredenbury *Heref*

PENCOYD (St Denys) *see* St Weonards *Heref*

PENCOYS (St Andrew) *see* Redruth w Lanner and Treleigh *Truro*

PENDEEN (St John the Baptist) w Morvah *Truro 5* **P** R A H Aitken Esq and C W M Aitken Esq (jt) **P-in-c** K E WEDGEWOOD

PENDEFORD (St Paul) *see* Tettenhall Regis *Lich*

PENDLEBURY (St Augustine) *see* Swinton and Pendlebury *Man*

PENDLESIDE, WEST, comprising Heyhouses, Pendleton, and Whalley *Blackb 7* **P** *Bp and J E R Aspinall (jt)* **V** R J CARMYLLIE **C** J LEE

PENDLETON (All Saints) *see* W Pendleside *Blackb*

PENDLETON (St Thomas) *see* Salford All SS *Man*

PENDLETON Claremont (Holy Angels) *as above*

PENDOCK CROSS (Holy Redeemer) *see* Berrow w Pendock, Eldersfield, Hollybush etc *Worc*

PENDOMER (St Roch) *see* Coker Ridge *B & W*

PENGE (Christ Church w Holy Trinity) *see* Anerley *Roch*

PENGE (St John the Evangelist) *Roch 13* **P** *Simeon's Trustees* **P-in-c** N J G POOLE

PENGE (St Paul) *see* Anerley *Roch*

PENGE LANE (Holy Trinity) *Roch 13* **P** *Bp* **V** N G READ **NSM** M A WILKINSON

PENHILL (St Peter) *Bris 7* **P** *Bp* **P-in-c** A L CHESWORTH **C** J A S HILLER, S D HALLS

PENHILL, comprising Aysgarth, Bolton cum Redmire, Preston-under-Scar cum Wensley, and West Witton *Leeds 25* **P** *Trin Coll Cam and Lord Bolton (jt)* **NSM** P S YEADON

PENHURST (St Michael the Archangel) *see* Ashburnham w Penhurst *Chich*

PENISTONE (St John the Baptist) and Thurlstone *Sheff 11* **P** *Bp* **TR** D J HOPKIN

PENKETH (St Paul) *see* Warrington W *Liv*

PENKEVIL (St Michael) *see* St Michael Penkevil *Truro*

PENKHULL (St Thomas) *see* Hartshill, Penkhull and Trent Vale *Lich*

PENKRIDGE Team, The (St Michael and All Angels), including Acton Trussell and Dunston *Lich 2* **P** *Patr Bd* **TR** G H YERBURY **TV** S MAYO **C** V E D HOWARTH

PENN (Holy Trinity) and Tylers Green *Ox 9* **P** *Earl Howe* **V** M D BISSET **C** G SUMMERS

PENN (St Bartholomew) (St Anne) *Lich 23* **P** *Bp* **V** B N WHITMORE **NSM** A STORER

PENN FIELDS (St Philip (St Aidan) *Lich 23* **P** *Ch Trust Fund Trust* **V** P H SMITH **C** T M LARKIN, T W EADY **NSM** J DALE

PENN STREET (Holy Trinity) *Ox 9* **P** *Earl Howe* **V** P M SIMMONS

PENNARD, EAST (All Saints) *see* Fosse Trinity *B & W*

PENNARD, WEST (St Nicholas) *see* Baltonsborough w Butleigh, W Bradley etc *B & W*

PENNINGTON (Christ Church) *Man 19* **P** *Trustees* **V** A W SAUNDERS **C** A C WHITTLE

PENNINGTON (St Mark) *Win 11* **P** *V Milford* **P-in-c** R N NOEL **NSM** E A ELLIOTT

PENNINGTON (St Michael and the Holy Angels) and Lindal w Marton and Bardsea *Carl 9* **P** *Bp and DBP (jt)* **V** *vacant*

PENNY LANE (St Barnabas) *see* Mossley Hill *Liv*

PENNYCROSS (St Pancras) *Ex 21* **P** *CPAS* **V** L BRASCHI

PENNYWELL (St Thomas) *see* Sunderland St Mary, St Thos and St Oswald *Dur*

PENPONDS (Holy Trinity) *see* Camborne, Tuckingmill and Penponds *Truro*

PENRITH (Christ Church) (St Andrew) w Newton Reigny and Plumpton Wall *Carl 4* **P** *Bp* **TR** D G SARGENT **TV** G M CREGEEN **C** A L JONES, M G EDWARDS

PENRUDDOCK (All Saints) *see* Greystoke w Penruddock, Mungrisdale etc *Carl*

PENSAX (St James the Great) *see* Teme Valley N *Worc*

PENSBY (St Michael and All Angels) *see* Barnston *Ches*

PENSHAW (All Saints) *see* Herrington, Penshaw and Shiney Row *Dur*

PENSHURST (St John the Baptist) and Fordcombe *Roch 12* **P** *Viscount De L'Isle* **R** T E HOLME **C** W D MACDOUGALL

PENSILVA (St John) *see* St Ive and Pensilva w Quethiock *Truro*

PENSNETT (St Mark) *Worc 10* **P** *Bp* **V** V J TOBIN **NSM** S M HALE

PENTEWAN (All Saints) *see* St Austell *Truro*

PENTLOW (St George and St Gregory) *see* N Hinckford *Chelmsf*

PENTNEY (St Mary Magdalene) *see* Nar Valley *Nor*

PENTON MEWSEY (Holy Trinity) *see* Pastrow *Win*

PENTONVILLE (St Silas w All Saints) (St James) *Lon 6* **P** *Bp* **V** R A WAKELING **C** A L MASON, J J CARTER, P W JAMES

PENTRICH (St Matthew) *see* Swanwick and Pentrich *Derby*

PENTRIDGE (St Rumbold) *see* Sixpenny Handley w Gussage St Andrew etc *Sarum*

PENWERRIS (St Michael and All Angels) (Holy Spirit) *Truro 3* **P** *V St Gluvias* **V** *vacant*

PENWORTHAM (St Leonard) *Blackb 5* **P** *Bp* **V** J N MANSFIELD

PENWORTHAM (St Mary) *Blackb 5* **P** *Miss A M Rawstorne* **V** C J NELSON

PENZANCE (St Mary) (St Paul) (St John the Baptist) *Truro 5* **P** *Bp* **TR** S YATES **C** A M YATES, K R OWEN

PEOPLETON (St Nicholas) and White Ladies Aston w Churchill and Spetchley and Upton Snodsbury and Broughton Hackett *Worc 4* **P** *Bp, Croom Estate Trustees, and Major R J G Berkley (1 turn), and Ld Chan (1 turn)* **P-in-c** G R NOYES **C** S A DANGERFIELD

PEOVER, OVER (St Lawrence) w Lower Peover (St Oswald) *Ches 12* **P** *DBP and Man Univ (jt)* **V** *vacant*

PEPER HAROW (St Nicholas) *see* Compton w Shackleford and Peper Harow *Guildf*

PEPLOW (The Epiphany) *see* Hodnet *Lich*

PERIVALE (St Nicholas) *Lon 22* **P** *Trustees* **P-in-c** A P JOHNSON

PERLETHORPE (St John the Evangelist) *S'well 2* **P** *Earl Manvers' Trustees* **P-in-c** I WEBB

PERRANARWORTHAL (St Piran) *see* St Stythians w Perranarworthal and Gwennap *Truro*

PERRANPORTH (St Michael's Mission Church) *see* Perranzabuloe and Crantock w Cubert *Truro*

PERRANUTHNOE (St Michael and St Piran) *see* Ludgvan, Marazion, St Hilary and Perranuthnoe *Truro*

PERRANZABULOE (St Piran) and Crantock w Cubert *Truro 7* **P** *Patr Bd* **P-in-c** A E BROWN **C** D J WILLOUGHBY, R J MONIE

PERROTT, NORTH (St Martin) *see* Wulfric Benefice *B & W*

PERROTT, SOUTH (St Mary)   *see* Beaminster Area *Sarum*
PERRY BARR (St John the Evangelist) *Birm 2*   **P** *Bp and trustees (jt)*   **V** B SCOTT   **C** S F L COOPER
PERRY BEECHES (St Matthew) *Birm 2*   **P** *St Martin's Trustees*
V A J A ROMANIS
PERRY COMMON (St Martin)   *see* Erdington Ch the K *Birm*
PERRY GREEN (St Thomas)   *see* Albury, Lt Hadham and Much Hadham *St Alb*
PERRY HILL (St George)   *see* Forest Hill w Lower Sydenham *S'wark*
PERRY STREET (All Saints) *Roch 4*   **P** *Bp*
P-in-c G S COLVILLE   **NSM** S J WALKER
PERSHORE (Holy Cross) w Pinvin, Wick and Birlingham *Worc 4*   **P** *Patr Bd*   **P-in-c** C A LORDING   **C** S DUNTON
PERTENHALL (St Peter)   *see* The Stodden Churches *St Alb*
PETER TAVY (St Peter) and Mary Tavy *Ex 22*   **P** *Guild of All So*   **R** *vacant*
PETERBOROUGH (All Saints) *Pet 11*   **P** *Bp*   **V** G S ROBERTS
PETERBOROUGH (Christ the Carpenter) *Pet 11*   **P** *Bp*
V S K KAYE
PETERBOROUGH (Holy Spirit) Bretton *Pet 11*   **P** *Bp*
P-in-c W S CROFT   **NSM** H M E DEL PINO
PETERBOROUGH (St John the Baptist) (Mission Church)
Pet 11   **P** *Bp*   **V** I C BLACK
PETERBOROUGH (St Jude) *Pet 11*   **P** *Bp*   **V** *vacant*
PETERBOROUGH (St Mark) *Pet 11*   **P** *Bp*   **V** A C HOLDSTOCK
C S D BERRY
PETERBOROUGH (St Mary) Boongate *Pet 11*   **P** *D&C*
V M P J MOORE   **NSM** K A MORROW
PETERBOROUGH (St Paul) *Pet 11*   **P** *Bp*   **V** R F WATKINSON
PETERCHURCH (St Peter)   *see* Madley w Tyberton, Peterchurch, Vowchurch etc *Heref*
PETERLEE (St Cuthbert) *Dur 2*   **P** *Bp*   **V** E E JONES
PETERSFIELD (St Peter) *Portsm 4*   **P** *Bp*   **V** W P M HUGHES
C S A CULLEN   **NSM** H M MITCHELL
PETERSHAM (All Saints) (St Peter) *S'wark 16*   **P** *Bp*
V T J E MARWOOD
PETERSMARLAND (St Peter)   *see* Shebbear, Buckland Filleigh, Sheepwash etc *Ex*
PETERSTOW (St Peter)   *see* StowCaple *Heref*
PETHAM (All Saints)   *see* Wye *Cant*
PETHERTON, NORTH (St Mary the Virgin)   *see* Alfred Jewel *B & W*
PETHERTON, SOUTH (St Peter and St Paul) w The Seavingtons and The Lambrooks *B & W 14*   **P** *Bp and D&C (jt)*   **R** T HANDY
PETHERWIN, NORTH (St Paternus)   *see* Egloskerry, N Petherwin, Tremaine, Tresmere etc *Truro*
PETHERWIN, SOUTH (St Paternus)   *see* Three Rivers *Truro*
PETROCKSTOWE (St Petrock)   *see* Shebbear, Buckland Filleigh, Sheepwash etc *Ex*
PETT (St Mary and St Peter)   *see* Fairlight and Pett *Chich*
PETT LEVEL (St Nicholas) *as above*
PETTAUGH (St Catherine)   *see* Debenham and Helmingham *St E*
PETTISTREE (St Peter and St Paul)   *see* Wickham Market w Pettistree *St E*
PETTON (not known) w Cockshutt, Welshampton and Lyneal w Colemere *Lich 16*   **P** *Bp and R K Mainwaring Esq (jt)*   **P-in-c** M E READ   **NSM** D BARNETT
PETTON (St Petrock)   *see* Bampton, Morebath, Clayhanger, Petton etc *Ex*
PETTS WOOD (St Francis) *Roch 16*   **P** *Bp*   **V** S A NIECHCIAL
PETWORTH (St Mary) *Chich 10*   **P** *Lord Egremont*
R P M GILBERT
PEVENSEY (St Nicolas) (St Wilfrid) *Chich 14*   **P** *Bp*
P-in-c A M WINDROSS
PEWSEY (St John the Baptist)   *see* Vale of Pewsey *Sarum*
PHEASEY (St Chad) *Lich 24*   **P** *DBP*   **V** *vacant*
PHILADELPHIA (St Thomas) Extra-Parochial Place *Sheff 4*
C L H HOWARTH, M J RUTTER, P FINDLEY
PHILLACK (St Felicitas)   *see* Godrevy *Truro*
PHILLEIGH (St Philleigh)   *see* Gerrans w St Anthony-in-Roseland and Philleigh *Truro*
PICCADILLY (St James)   *see* Westmr St Jas *Lon*
PICKENHAM, NORTH (St Andrew)   *see* Necton, Holme Hale w N and S Pickenham *Nor*
PICKENHAM, SOUTH (All Saints) *as above*
PICKERING (St Peter and St Paul) w Lockton and Levisham *York 19*   **P** *Abp*   **V** *vacant*
PICKHILL (All Saints)   *see* Kirklington w Burneston and Wath and Pickhill *Leeds*
PICKWELL (All Saints)   *see* Burrough Hill Pars *Leic*
PICKWORTH (All Saints)   *see* Gt and Lt Casterton w Pickworth and Tickencote *Pet*
PICKWORTH (St Andrew)   *see* S Lafford *Linc*

PIDDINGHOE (St John)   *see* Peacehaven and Telscombe Cliffs w Piddinghoe etc *Chich*
PIDDINGTON (St John the Baptist)   *see* Hardingstone, Piddington w Horton and Quinton and Preston Deanery *Pet*
PIDDINGTON (St Nicholas)   *see* Ray Valley *Ox*
PIDDLE VALLEY, Hilton and Ansty, Cheselbourne and Melcombe Horsey, The *Sarum 1*   **P** *Bp, Eton Coll, G A L-F Pitt-Rivers Esq, D&C Sarum, and D&C Win (by turn)*
V R J BUTCHER
PIDDLE, NORTH (St Michael)   *see* Abberton, The Flyfords, Naunton Beauchamp etc *Worc*
PIDDLEHINTON (St Mary the Virgin)   *see* Piddle Valley, Hilton and Ansty, Cheselbourne etc *Sarum*
PIDDLETRENTHIDE (All Saints) *as above*
PIDLEY CUM FENTON (All Saints)   *see* Somersham w Pidley and Oldhurst and Woodhurst *Ely*
PIERCEBRIDGE (St Mary)   *see* Coniscliffe *Dur*
PILHAM (All Saints)   *see* Lea Gp *Linc*
PILL (Christ Church), Portbury and Easton-in-Gordano
B & W 12   **P** *Bp*   **V** A L TIESEMA-SAMSOM
PILLATON (St Modwen)   *see* Penkridge *Lich*
PILLATON (St Odulph)   *see* Tamar Valley *Truro*
PILLERTON HERSEY (St Mary)   *see* Stourdene Gp *Cov*
PILLEY (Mission Church)   *see* Tankersley, Thurgoland and Wortley *Sheff*
PILLEY (St Nicholas)   *see* Boldre w S Baddesley *Win*
PILLING (St John the Baptist)   *see* Stalmine w Pilling *Blackb*
PILNING (St Peter) w Compton Greenfield *Bris 2*   **P** *Bp*
P-in-c P W ROWE   **OLM** A LLOYD
PILSLEY (St Mary the Virgin)   *see* N Wingfield, Clay Cross and Pilsley *Derby*
PILTON (All Saints)   *see* Aldwincle, Clopton, Pilton, Stoke Doyle etc *Pet*
PILTON (St John the Baptist) w Croscombe, North Wootton and Dinder *B & W 7*   **P** *Bp and Peache Trustees (jt)*
R C J BUTLER
PILTON (St Mary the Virgin) w Ashford *Ex 14*   **P** *Ld Chan*
V N B DILKES   **NSM** M SANDERS
PILTON (St Nicholas)   *see* Empingham, Edith Weston, Lyndon, Manton etc *Pet*
PIMLICO (St Barnabas) *Lon 3*   **P** *Bp*
P-in-c J M PEARSON-HICKS
PIMLICO (St Gabriel) *Lon 3*   **P** *Bp*   **V** O C G HIGGS
C M W DOBSON
PIMLICO (St James the Less)   *see* Westminster St Jas the Less *Lon*
PIMLICO (St Mary) Bourne Street *Lon 3*   **P** *Trustees*
V A S WALKER   **NSM** A D NORWOOD
PIMLICO (St Peter) w Westminster Christ Church *Lon 3*
P *Bp*   **V** R J WILLIAMSON   **C** J M KHOVACS
PIMLICO (St Saviour) *Lon 3*   **P** *Bp*   **V** M J CATTERICK
PIMLICO Bourne Street (St Mary)   *see* Pimlico St Mary Bourne Street *Lon*
PIMPERNE (St Peter), Stourpaine, Durweston and Bryanston *Sarum 6*   **P** *DBP (2 turns), D&C (1 turn)*
P-in-c B-J MARFLITT
PINCHBECK (St Mary)   *see* Glen Gp *Linc*
PINCHBECK, WEST (St Bartholomew) *as above*
PINHOE (Hall)   *see* Broadclyst, Clyst Honiton, Pinhoe, Rockbeare etc *Ex*
PINHOE (St Michael and All Angels) *as above*
PINNER (St Anselm)   *see* Hatch End St Anselm *Lon*
PINNER (St John the Baptist) *Lon 23*   **P** *V Harrow*
V P C HULLYER
PINNER VIEW (St George)   *see* Headstone St Geo *Lon*
PINVIN (St Nicholas)   *see* Pershore w Pinvin, Wick and Birlingham *Worc*
PINXTON (St Helen) (Church Hall) *Derby 2*   **P** *Bp*
C G MANLEY   **OLM** P F GOODCHILD
PIPE-CUM-LYDE (St Peter) and Moreton-on-Lugg *Heref 3*
P *Bp, Soc of the Faith, and D&C (by turn)*   **P-in-c** P J BROWN
NSM E S V VERWEY
PIRBRIGHT (St Michael and All Angels) *Guildf 12*   **P** *Ld Chan*   **V** *vacant*
PIRTON (St Mary)   *see* Holwell, Ickleford and Pirton *St Alb*
PIRTON (St Peter)   *see* Stoulton w Drake's Broughton and Pirton etc *Worc*
PISHILL (not known)   *see* Nettlebed w Bix, Highmoor, Pishill etc *Ox*
PITCHCOMBE (St John the Baptist)   *see* Painswick, Sheepscombe, Cranham, The Edge etc *Glouc*
PITCHFORD (St Michael and All Angels)   *see* Condover w Frodesley, Acton Burnell etc *Heref*
PITCOMBE (St Leonard)   *see* Bruton, Brewham, Pitcombe and Shepton Montague *B & W*

PITMINSTER (St Mary and St Andrew) *see* Blackdown *B & W*
PITNEY (St John the Baptist) *see* Levels Arc *B & W*
PITSEA (St Gabriel) w Nevendon *Chelmsf 12* **P** *Bp*
  R S A LAW
PITSFORD (All Saints) w Boughton *Pet 2* **P** *Bp* **R** S TROTT
PITSMOOR (Christ Church) *Sheff 3* **P** *Ch Patr Trust*
  P-in-c P J SALMON **NSM** S A GOODMAN, W H THOMAS
PITTINGTON (St Laurence) *see* Belmont and Pittington *Dur*
PITTON (St Peter) *see* Clarendon *Sarum*
PITTVILLE (All Saints) *see* N Cheltenham *Glouc*
PIXHAM (St Mary the Virgin) *see* Dorking w Ranmore *Guildf*
PIXLEY (St Andrew) *see* Cider Churches *Heref*
PLAISTOW (Holy Trinity) *see* Kirdford *Chich*
PLAISTOW (St Martin) *Chelmsf 5* **P** *Bp* **V** J V MEADWAY
  NSM C T OLADUJI
PLAISTOW (St Mary) *Roch 14* **P** *Bp* **V** A KEELER
PLAISTOW (St Philip and St James) (St Mary) *Chelmsf 5*
  P *Bp* **V** D A HOYTE **NSM** C T OLADUJI
PLAITFORD (St Peter) *see* Forest and Avon *Sarum*
PLAS NEWTON (St Michael) *Ches 2* **P** *Simeon's Trustees*
  V P RUGEN
PLATT (Holy Trinity) *see* Rusholme H Trin *Man*
PLATT (St Mary the Virgin) *Roch 10* **P** *Bp* **V** L E TURNER
PLATT BRIDGE (St Nathaniel) *see* Chapelfields *Liv*
PLAXTOL (not known) *see* Shipbourne w Plaxtol *Roch*
PLAYDEN (St Michael) *see* Rye *Chich*
PLAYFORD (St Mary) *see* Gt and Lt Bealings w Playford and
  Culpho *St E*
PLEASLEY (St Michael) *see* E Scarsdale *Derby*
PLEASLEY HILL (St Barnabas) *see* Mansfield St Aug and
  Pleasley Hill *S'well*
PLEASLEY VALE (St Chad) *see* Mansfield Woodhouse *S'well*
PLEMSTALL (St Peter) w Guilden Sutton *Ches 2* **P** *Capt P*
  Egerton Warburton **V** H S CARTY
PLESHEY (Holy Trinity) *Chelmsf 9* **P** *Bp* **P-in-c** M J ASTON
  C D C PIERCE
PLUCKLEY (St Nicholas) *see* G7 Benefice *Cant*
PLUMBLAND (St Cuthbert) *see* Binsey *Carl*
PLUMPTON (All Saints) (St Michael and All Angels) w East
  Chiltington cum Novington *Chich 21* **P** *Ld Chan*
  R G D BROSTER
PLUMPTON WALL (St John the Evangelist) *see* Penrith w
  Newton Reigny and Plumpton Wall *Carl*
PLUMSTEAD (All Saints) Shooters Hill *S'wark 6* **P** *CPAS*
  P-in-c H O APARANGA
PLUMSTEAD (St John the Baptist) w St James and St Paul
  S'wark 6 **P** *Simeon's Trustees and CPAS (alt)* **V** P J ROGERS
PLUMSTEAD (St Mark and St Margaret) *see* Plumstead
  Common *S'wark*
PLUMSTEAD (St Michael) *see* Matlaske *Nor*
PLUMSTEAD (St Nicholas) *S'wark 6* **P** *V Plumstead St Mark w*
  St Mary **V** A G STEVENS
PLUMSTEAD COMMON (St Mark and St Margaret)
  (Ascension) *S'wark 6* **P** *Bp and DBP (jt)* **V** C R WELHAM
  C B T ASMELASH
PLUMSTEAD, GREAT (St Mary) and LITTLE (St Gervase and
  Protase), Rackheath w Salhouse and Witton *Nor 4* **P** *Bp*
  and D&C (jt) **R** D J PLATTIN
PLUMTREE (St Mary) *S'well 5* **P** *DBP* **R** T H KIRKMAN
PLUNGAR (St Helen) *see* Vale of Belvoir *Leic*
PLYMOUTH (Emmanuel), St Paul Efford and St Augustine
  Ex 21 **P** *Patr Bd* **TR** K F FREEMAN **TV** A C WILLIAMS
  NSM B J CREE, D L CREE
PLYMOUTH (St Andrew) and St Paul Stonehouse *Ex 21*
  P *Patr Bd* **TR** J M DENT **TV** L P T SIM **C** T D PARTRIDGE
PLYMOUTH (St Gabriel) Peverell *Ex 21* **P** *Bp*
  P-in-c R T SILK **NSM** A OVERTON
PLYMOUTH (St John the Evangelist) *see* Sutton-on-Plym,
  Plymouth St Simon and St Mary *Ex*
PLYMOUTH (St Jude) *Ex 21* **P** *CPAS Patr Trust*
  P-in-c T SMITH **C** K R LOVELL
PLYMOUTH (St Mary the Virgin) *see* Plymouth Em, St Paul
  Efford and St Aug *Ex*
PLYMOUTH (St Mary the Virgin) *see* Sutton-on-Plym,
  Plymouth St Simon and St Mary *Ex*
PLYMOUTH (St Matthias) *see* Charles w Plymouth
  St Matthias *Ex*
PLYMOUTH (St Pancras) *see* Pennycross *Ex*
PLYMOUTH (St Peter) and the Holy Apostles *Ex 21* **P** *Bp*
  and Keble Coll Ox (jt) **P-in-c** D C WAY
PLYMOUTH (St Simon) *see* Sutton-on-Plym, Plymouth
  St Simon and St Mary *Ex*
PLYMOUTH Crownhill (Ascension) *Ex 21* **P** *Bp*
  P-in-c T THORP **C** C J ROUTLEDGE, R H WAKERELL,
  S P RUNDELL

PLYMPTON (St Mary the Blessed Virgin) (St Maurice)
  Ex 21 **P** *Patr Bd* **TR** R D HARRIS **TV** W D SWEENEY
  C S J SHARLAND
PLYMSTOCK (St Mary and All Saints) and Hooe *Ex 21*
  P *Patr Bd* **TR** J APPLEBY **TV** C J BUDDEN, D APPLEBY
PLYMTREE (St John the Baptist) *see* Broadhembury,
  Dunkeswell, Luppitt, Plymtree, Sheldon, and Upottery *Ex*
POCKLEY (St John the Baptist) *see* Kirkdale w Harome,
  Nunnington and Pockley *York*
POCKLINGTON (All Saints) *see* Pocklington Wold *York*
POCKLINGTON WOLD (All Saints), including Great
  Givendale, Huggate, Kilnwick Percy, Millington, and
  Nunburnholme *York 5* **P** *Abp* **NSM** D B BROADHURST
PODIMORE (St Peter) *see* Ilchester w Northover, Limington,
  Yeovilton etc *B & W*
PODINGTON (St Mary the Virgin) *see* Chellington *St Alb*
POINT CLEAR (Mission) *see* St Osyth and Great Bentley
  Chelmsf
POINTON (Christ Church) *see* Billingborough Gp *Linc*
POKESDOWN (All Saints) *Win 8* **P** *V Christchurch*
  V M R POWIS
POKESDOWN (St James) *Win 8* **P** *Bp* **P-in-c** J PARES
POLDEN WHEEL, The, comprising Ashcott, Burtle, Catcott,
  Chilton Polden, Edington, and Shapwick *B & W 4* **P** *Bp*
  V R W TWEEDY
POLEBROOK (All Saints) *see* Barnwell, Hemington,
  Luddington in the Brook etc *Pet*
POLEGATE (St John) (St Wilfrid) *Chich 14* **P** *Bp*
  V C G SPINKS **C** C J STYLES **NSM** R A HERKES
POLESWORTH (St Editha) *Birm 9* **P** *Ld Chan* **V** P A WELLS
POLING (St Nicholas) *Chich 1* **P** *Bp* **P-in-c** C M WOODRUFF
POLLARDS HILL (The Ascension) *see* Mitcham Ascension
  S'wark
POLLINGTON (St John the Baptist) *see* Gt Snaith *Sheff*
POLPERRO (St John the Baptist) *see* Trelawny *Truro*
POLRUAN (St Saviour) *as above*
POLSTEAD (St Mary) *see* Stoke by Nayland w Leavenheath
  and Polstead *St E*
POLTIMORE (St Mary the Virgin) *see* Brampford Speke,
  Cadbury, Newton St Cyres etc *Ex*
PONDERS END (St Matthew) *Lon 18* **P** *V Enfield*
  P-in-c S G BROWN
PONDERSBRIDGE (St Thomas) *see* Whittlesey, Pondersbridge
  and Coates *Ely*
PONSANOOTH (St Michael and All Angels) *see* Mabe *Truro*
PONSBOURNE (St Mary) *see* Lt Berkhamsted and Bayford,
  Essendon etc *St Alb*
PONSONBY (not known) *see* Seatallan *Carl*
PONTEFRACT (All Saints) (St Giles) *Leeds 18* **P** *Bp*
  V J M LAWSON **C** C M WATKINS **NSM** K B WARRENER,
  M J TAYLOR, R G WALKER, W D PHILLIPS **OLM** H MERRICK
PONTELAND (St Mary the Virgin) *Newc 4* **P** *Mert Coll Ox*
  V P T ALLINSON **NSM** C L BROWN
PONTESBURY First and Second Portions (St George)
  Heref 12 **P** *St Chad's Coll Dur* **R** *vacant*
PONTON, GREAT (Holy Cross) *see* Colsterworth Gp *Linc*
PONTON, LITTLE (St Guthlac) *as above*
POOL (St Wilfrid) *see* Lower Wharfedale *Leeds*
POOLBROOK (St Andrew) *see* Malvern Chase *Worc*
POOLE (St James w St Paul) *Sarum 7* **P** *Ch Soc Trust*
  R L J HOLT **C** L N PEARSON
POOLE KEYNES (St Michael and All Angels) *see* Kemble,
  Poole Keynes, Somerford Keynes etc *Glouc*
POOLEY BRIDGE (St Paul) *see* Barton, Pooley Bridge,
  Martindale etc *Carl*
POORTON, NORTH (St Mary Magdalene) *see* Eggardon and
  Colmers *Sarum*
POPLAR (All Saints) *Lon 7* **P** *Patr Bd* **TR** J A C HODGES
  TV M W WALL **NSM** J C SHELDON
POPLEY w Limes Park and Rooksdown (St Gabriel) *Win 4*
  P *Bp* **V** A BOTHAM
POPPLETON, NETHER (St Everilda) w Upper (All Saints)
  York 1 **P** *Abp* **V** J C E SYLVESTER **NSM** M C S FOSSETT
POPPYLAND, comprising Antingham, Northrepps,
  Overstrand, Sidestrand, Southrepps, Thorpe Market, and
  Trimingham *Nor 20* **P** *Duchy of Lancaster (2 turns), DBP,*
  MMCET, and Bp (4 turns) **R** S J M READING
PORCHESTER (St James) *S'well 7* **P** *Bp* **V** *vacant*
PORINGLAND (All Saints) *Nor 8* **P** *Bp, BNC Ox, J D Alston*
  Esq, and G H Hastings Esq (3 turns) and DBP (1 turn)
  R R H PARSONAGE **OLM** R M FOSTER
PORKELLIS (St Christopher) *see* Helston and Wendron *Truro*
PORLOCK (St Dubricius) and Porlock Weir w Stoke Pero,
  Selworthy and Luccombe *B & W 15* **P** *Ld Chan*
  R W H M LEMMEY **NSM** A M GIBBS, S R B HUMPHREYS

PORLOCK WEIR (St Nicholas)   *see* Porlock and Porlock Weir
w Stoke Pero etc *B & W*
PORT ERIN (St Catherine)   *see* Rushen *S & M*
PORT ISAAC (St Peter)   *see* N Cornwall Cluster *Truro*
PORT ST MARY (St Mary)   *see* Rushen *S & M*
PORTBURY (Blessed Virgin Mary)   *see* Pill, Portbury and
Easton-in-Gordano *B & W*
PORTCHESTER (St Mary) *Portsm 2*   **P** *J R Thistlethwaite Esq*
V I MEREDITH
PORTESHAM (St Peter)   *see* Abbotsbury, Portesham and
Langton Herring *Sarum*
PORTHILL (St Andrew)   *see* Bradwell and Porthill *Lich*
PORTHLEVEN (St Bartholomew)   *see* W Kerrier *Truro*
PORTHPEAN (St Levan)   *see* St Austell *Truro*
PORTISHEAD (St Peter) *B & W 12*   **P** *Patr Bd*
TR R M E DEWING   **TV** C A JUDSON, M J T FULLER
C L E DOWNS
PORTLAND Team Minstry (All Saints) (St Andrew)
(St John) *Sarum 4*   **P** *Patr Bd*   **TR** T F GOMM
TV J K MENZIES
PORTLEMOUTH, EAST (St Winwaloe Onocaus)   *see*
Stokenham, Slapton, Charleton w Buckland etc *Ex*
PORTLOE (All Saints)   *see* Veryan w Ruan Lanihorne *Truro*
PORTMAN SQUARE (St Paul)   *see* Langham Place All So *Lon*
PORTON (St Nicholas)   *see* Bourne Valley *Sarum*
PORTREATH (St Mary)   *see* St Illogan *Truro*
PORTSDOWN (Christ Church) *Portsm 5*   **P** *Simeon's Trustees*
V A M WILSON   **C** J E SMITH   **NSM** L B CAMERON, M JAMES
PORTSEA (All Saints) *Portsm 6*   **P** *V Portsea St Mary and Bp*
(jt)   **P-in-c** R C WHITE   **C** R J FOREY
PORTSEA (St Alban) *Portsm 6*   **P** *Bp*   **P-in-c** A J WOOD
PORTSEA (St Cuthbert) *Portsm 6*   **P** *Bp*   **V** A M KERR
NSM C G GULLY, K E MARLOW
PORTSEA (St George) *Portsm 6*   **P** *Bp*   **P-in-c** A J WOOD
C M R J BRAY
PORTSEA (St Luke)   *see* Southsea St Luke and St Pet *Portsm*
PORTSEA (St Mary) (St Faith and St Barnabas) (St Wilfrid)
Portsm 6   **P** *Win Coll*   **V** R C WHITE   **C** M C COLLIE
NSM S K WHITELOCK
PORTSEA (St Saviour) *Portsm 6*   **P** *Bp*
P-in-c B E A WEITZMANN
PORTSEA (The Ascension) *Portsm 6*   **P** *Bp*
C B E A WEITZMANN
PORTSEA North End (St Mark) *Portsm 6*   **P** *DBP*
P-in-c B M HACKETT   **TV** B E A WEITZMANN, S J DUDDLES
NSM R E WEEKS, R J WHARTON
PORTSLADE (St Nicolas) (St Andrew) and Mile Oak
Chich 20   **P** *Bp*   **P-in-c** D M SWYER   **NSM** P G PANNETT
PORTSWOOD (Christ Church) *Win 13*   **P** *Bp*
P-in-c M J ARCHER   **C** D A TORRANCE   **NSM** E J ROBERTS,
F M TYSON
PORTSWOOD (St Denys) *Win 13*   **P** *Bp*   **P-in-c** M J ARCHER
C D A TORRANCE, S V RUMBLE
PORTWAY AND DANEBURY Benefice, The, comprising
Amport, Grateley, Monxton, Nether Wallop, Over Wallop,
Quarley, and West Andover *Win 3*   **P** *Patr Bd*   **TV** V A COLE
Hon C M R GRAYSHON
POSBURY (St Francis Proprietary Chapel)   *see* Crediton,
Shobrooke and Sandford etc *Ex*
POSLINGFORD (St Mary)   *see* Stour Valley *St E*
POSTBRIDGE (St Gabriel)   *see* Ashburton, Bickington,
Buckland in the Moor etc *Ex*
POSTLING (St Mary and St Radegund)   *see* Lyminge w
Paddlesworth, Stanford w Postling etc *Cant*
POSTWICK (All Saints)   *see* Yare Valley *Nor*
POTT SHRIGLEY (St Christopher) *Chich 13*   **P** *MMCET*
P-in-c D J SWALES
POTTEN END (Holy Trinity)   *see* Gt Berkhamsted, Gt and Lt
Gaddesden etc *St Alb*
POTTER HEIGHAM (St Nicholas)   *see* Ludham, Potter
Heigham, Hickling and Catfield *Nor*
POTTERHANWORTH (St Andrew)   *see* Branston w Nocton
and Potterhanworth *Linc*
POTTERNE (St Mary the Virgin)   *see* Wellsprings *Sarum*
POTTERNEWTON (St Martin) w Little London *Leeds 13*
P *Simeon's Trustees, R Leeds City, DBP, and Trustees (jt)*
V N LO POLITO   **C** E T MAPFUMO   **NSM** G W W TURNBULL,
H BANKS, S J DE GAY
POTTERS BAR (King Charles the Martyr) *St Alb 14*   **P** *Bp*
Lon   **V** A C GAINES
POTTERS BAR (St Mary and All Saints) *St Alb 14*   **P** *Bp Lon*
V S CHRYSOSTOMOU
POTTERS GREEN (St Philip Deacon) *Cov 1*   **P** *Ld Chan*
V M L EAMAN
POTTERS MARSTON (St Mary)   *see* Barwell w Potters Marston
and Stapleton *Leic*

POTTERSPURY (St Nicholas) w Furtho and Yardley Gobion
w Cosgrove and Wicken *Pet 5*   **P** *D&C, Jes Coll Ox, and Soc*
Merchant Venturers Bris (jt)   **R** D C WHITTAKER
C S D M STANLEY
POTTO (St Mary)   *see* Whorlton w Carlton and Faceby *York*
POTTON (St Mary the Virgin) w Sutton and Cockayne
Hatley *St Alb 10*   **P** *The Crown (3 turns), St Jo Coll Ox (1 turn)*
R vacant
POUGHILL (St Michael and All Angels)   *see* N Creedy *Ex*
POUGHILL (St Olaf King and Martyr) *Truro 8*   **P** *Ch Soc Trust*
V vacant
POULNER (St John)   *see* Ringwood w Ellingham and
Harbridge etc *Win*
POULSHOT (St Peter)   *see* Wellsprings *Sarum*
POULTON (St Michael and All Angels)   *see* S Cotswolds *Glouc*
POULTON CARLETON (St Chad) and Singleton *Blackb 12*
P *DBP and Exors R Dumbreck Esq (jt)*   **V** M P KEIGHLEY
C L G WARD
POULTON LANCELYN (Holy Trinity) *Ches 8*   **P** *R Bebington*
V R K WILES
POULTON-LE-FYLDE (St Chad)   *see* Poulton Carleton and
Singleton *Blackb*
POULTON-LE-SANDS (Holy Trinity) w Morecambe
St Laurence *Blackb 11*   **P** *V Lanc*   **R** C J M KRAWIEC
POUND HILL (St Barnabas)   *see* Worth, Pound Hill and
Maidenbower *Chich*
POUNDSBRIDGE (Chapel)   *see* Penshurst and Fordcombe
Roch
POUNDSTOCK (St Winwaloe)   *see* Week St Mary Circle of Par
Truro
POWDERHAM (St Clement Bishop and Martyr)   *see*
Exminster, Kenn, Kenton w Mamhead, and Powderham *Ex*
POWERSTOCK (St Mary the Virgin)   *see* Eggardon and
Colmers *Sarum*
POWICK (St Peter) and Guarlford and Madresfield w
Newland *Worc 2*   **P** *Bp, Lady Rosalind Morrison, and Croome*
Estate Trustees (jt)   **R** G P CRELLIN
POYNINGS (Holy Trinity) w Edburton, Newtimber and
Pyecombe *Chich 8*   **P** *Ld Chan (1 turn), Bp and Abp (1 turn)*
R T W HARFORD
POYNTINGTON (All Saints)   *see* Queen Thorne *Sarum*
POYNTON (St George) *Ches 17*   **P** *Bp*   **V** R I MCLAREN
C A N SEAGO   **NSM** A S LIVINGSTON, C J BUCKLEY
POYNTON, HIGHER (St Martin)   *see* Poynton *Ches*
PRATTS BOTTOM (All Souls)   *see* Green Street Green and
Pratts Bottom *Roch*
PREES (St Chad)   *see* Edstaston, Fauls, Prees, Tilstock and
Whixall *Lich*
PREESALL (St Oswald)   *see* Waterside Par *Blackb*
PRENTON (St Stephen) *Ches 1*   **P** *Bp*   **V** M J GRAHAM
PRENTON DELL (St Alban)   *see* Prenton *Ches*
PRESCOT (St Mary) (St Paul) *Liv 7*   **P** *K Coll Cam*
V J A TAYLOR   **C** K MANNINGS   **NSM** P COWLEY
PRESHUTE (St George)   *see* Marlborough *Sarum*
PRESTBURY (St Mary)   *see* N Cheltenham *Glouc*
PRESTBURY (St Nicolas)   *as above*
PRESTBURY (St Peter) *Ches 13*   **P** *Ms C J C B Legh*
V P J M ANGIER   **NSM** A S RAVENSCROFT, S C J MURPHY
PRESTEIGNE (St Andrew) w Discoed, Kinsham, Lingen and
Knill *Heref 4*   **P** *Patr Bd*   **R** S HOLLINGHURST
NSM D VENABLES
PRESTON (All Saints)   *see* Hedon, Paull, Sproatley and
Preston *York*
PRESTON (All Saints) *Blackb 13*   **P** *Trustees*   **V** N J BUTTERY
PRESTON (All Saints)   *see* S Cerney w Cerney Wick,
Siddington and Preston *Glouc*
PRESTON (Church of the Ascension) *Lon 21*   **P** *Bp*
V O J FIELD
PRESTON (Emmanuel) *Blackb 13*   **P** *R Preston*
V P G HAMBORG
PRESTON (Good Shepherd)   *see* Brighton Gd Shep Preston
Chich
PRESTON (St Andrew)   *see* Weymouth Ridgeway *Sarum*
PRESTON (St Cuthbert) *Blackb 13*   **P** *Bp*   **V** M J BRADFORD
C K BHATTI, M T HUTCHINSON   **NSM** M R CLAYTON
PRESTON (St John the Baptist)   *see* Redmarley D'Abitot,
Bromesberrow, Pauntley etc *Glouc*
PRESTON (St John) (St George the Martyr) (Christ the
King Chapel) *Blackb 13*   **P** *DBP*   **R** S E HAIGH
C D A CRAVEN, J M GARDNER
PRESTON (St John) w Brighton St Augustine and
St Saviour *Chich 19*   **P** *Bp*   **V** A V BOWMAN
PRESTON (St Martin)   *see* Hitchin and St Paul's Walden *St Alb*
PRESTON (St Mary the Virgin)   *see* Lavenham w Preston *St E*
PRESTON (St Matthias)   *see* Brighton St Matthias *Chich*
PRESTON (St Mildred)   *see* Canonry *Cant*

PRESTON (St Paul) *see* Paignton Ch Ch and Preston St Paul *Ex*

PRESTON (St Peter and St Paul) *see* Empingham, Edith Weston, Lyndon, Manton etc *Pet*

PRESTON (St Stephen) *Blackb 13* **P** *Bp* **V** D J HANSON

PRESTON Acregate Lane (Mission) *see* Preston Risen Lord *Blackb*

PRESTON BAGOT (All Saints) *see* Claverdon w Preston Bagot *Cov*

PRESTON BISSET (St John the Baptist) *see* The Claydons and Swan *Ox*

PRESTON CANDOVER (St Mary the Virgin) *see* Farleigh, Candover and Wield *Win*

PRESTON CAPES (St Peter and St Paul) *see* Badby w Newham and Charwelton w Fawsley etc *Pet*

PRESTON NEXT FAVERSHAM (St Catherine) *see* Faversham *Cant*

PRESTON ON STOUR (St Mary) *see* Ilmington w Stretton-on-Fosse etc *Cov*

PRESTON PATRICK (St Patrick) *see* Kirkby Lonsdale *Carl*

PRESTON PLUCKNETT (St James the Great) (St Peter) *B & W 6* **P** *Bp* (2 turns), Mrs S W Rawlins (1 turn) **V** D M KEEN   **C** R E CHAPMAN

PRESTON The Risen Lord (St Matthew) (St Hilda) (St James's church hall) *Blackb 13* **P** *Patr Bd* **R** A MCHAFFIE

PRESTON UNDER SCARR (St Margaret) *see* Penhill *Leeds*

PRESTON WEALDMOORS (St Lawrence) *see* Edgmond w Kynnersley and Preston Wealdmoors *Lich*

PRESTON WYNNE (Holy Trinity) *see* Maund Gp *Heref*

PRESTON, EAST (St Mary) w Kingston *Chich 1* **P** *D&C* **V** A J PERRY   **C** E L HAM-RICHE

PRESTON-ON-TEES (All Saints) and Longnewton *Dur 9* **P** *Bp* **P-in-c** J C LAMBERT   **C** P A ARNOLD

PRESTON-ON-WYE (St Lawrence) *see* Cusop w Blakemere, Bredwardine w Brobury etc *Heref*

PRESTONVILLE (St Luke) *Chich 19* **P** *CPAS* **V** M B POOLE

PRESTWICH (St Gabriel) *Man 10* **P** *Bp* **V** S S WILLIAMS   **NSM** M TRIVASSE

PRESTWICH (St Hilda) *Man 10* **P** *Trustees* **V** *vacant*

PRESTWICH (St Margaret) (St George) *Man 10* **P** *R Prestwich St Mary* **V** D S A SANDERCOCK-PICKLES   **C** S S WILLIAMS   **NSM** S A WALKER

PRESTWICH (St Mary the Virgin) *Man 10* **P** *Trustees* **C** S S WILLIAMS   **OLM** C A BARNET, K A MCKIE

PRESTWOLD (St Andrew) *see* Wymeswold and Prestwold w Hoton *Leic*

PRESTWOOD (Holy Trinity) and Great Hampden *Ox 17* **P** *Bp and Hon I H Hope-Morley (jt)* **R** D J O KEARLEY-HEYWOOD   **C** K J LOVELL, N C O SPOOR

PRIDDY (St Lawrence) *B & W 1* **P** *Bp* **V** P M HOLLINGSWORTH

PRIDE PARK, Wilmorton, Allenton and Shelton Lock *Derby 5* **P** *Bp* **C** C A M HOLLYWELL

PRIESTWOOD (St Andrew) *see* Bracknell *Ox*

PRIMROSE HILL (Holy Trinity) *see* Lydney, Woolaston, Alvington and Aylburton *Glouc*

PRIMROSE HILL (St Mary the Virgin) w Avenue Road (St Paul) *Lon 16* **P** *Trustees* **V** M J BROWN   **C** N R WALTERS   **NSM** M J WAKEFIELD

PRINCE'S PARK (Christ the King) *Roch 5* **P** *Bp* **V** P J FILMER

PRINCES RISBOROUGH (St Mary) *see* Risborough *Ox*

PRIOR'S DEAN (not known) *see* Greatham, Empshott and Hawkley w Priors Dean *Portsm*

PRIORS HARDWICK (St Mary the Virgin) w Priors Marston and Wormleighton *Cov 10* **P** *Earl Spencer* **P-in-c** G S ROBERTS   **NSM** C A PARKES, C M NEWBORN

PRIORS LEE (St Peter) *see* Oakengates, Priors Lee and Wrockwardine Wood *Lich*

PRIORS MARSTON (St Leonard) *see* Priors Hardwick, Priors Marston and Wormleighton *Cov*

PRISTON (St Luke) *see* Timsbury w Priston, Camerton and Dunkerton *B & W*

PRITTLEWELL (St Luke) *Chelmsf 15* **P** *Bp* **P-in-c** B G DRURY

PRITTLEWELL (St Mary the Virgin) *Chelmsf 15* **P** *Bp* **P-in-c** P D MACKAY   **C** B NOGHIU, M J LINDOE

PRITTLEWELL (St Peter) w Westcliff St Cedd and the Saints of Essex *Chelmsf 15* **P** *Bp* **P-in-c** C S BALDWIN

PRITTLEWELL (St Stephen) *Chelmsf 15* **P** *Bp* **P-in-c** C S BALDWIN

PROBUS (St Probus and St Grace), Ladock and Grampound w Creed and St Erme *Truro 6* **P** *DBP* **TR** J P W FOOT   **Hon C** M E RICHARDS   **NSM** L C WHETTER

PRUDHOE (St Mary Magdalene) *Newc 9* **P** *Dioc Soc* **V** D J FREYHAN

PSALTER LANE (St Andrew) *Sheff 2* **P** *Trustees* **V** *vacant*

PUBLOW (All Saints) w Pensford, Compton Dando and Chelwood *B & W 9* **P** *Bp* **P-in-c** D M CALVERLEY

PUCKINGTON (St Andrew) *see* Winsmoor *B & W*

PUCKLECHURCH (St Thomas à Becket) and Abson *Bris 5* **P** *D&C* **V** S K YOUNG

PUDDINGTON (St Thomas à Becket) *see* N Creedy *Ex*

PUDDLETOWN (St Mary the Virgin), Tolpuddle and Milborne w Dewlish *Sarum 1* **P** *Bp, Ch Ch Ox, Viscount Rothermere, and trustees (jt)* **R** S C HILLMAN

PUDLESTON (St Peter) *see* Leominster *Heref*

PUDSEY (St James the Great) *see* Thornbury, Woodhall and Waterloo *Leeds*

PUDSEY (St Lawrence and St Paul) *Leeds 14* **P** *Bp and V Calverley (jt)* **V** R J DIMERY   **C** S M HARRISON

PULBOROUGH (St Mary) *Chich 11* **P** *Lord Egremont* **R** P R SEAMAN

PULFORD (St Mary the Virgin) *see* Eccleston and Pulford *Ches*

PULHAM (St Thomas à Beckett) *see* Three Valleys *Sarum*

PULHAM MARKET (St Mary Magdalene) *see* Dickleburgh and The Pulhams *Nor*

PULHAM ST MARY (St Mary the Virgin) *as above*

PULLOXHILL (St James the Apostle) *see* Silsoe, Pulloxhill and Flitton *St Alb*

PULVERBATCH (St Edith) *see* Gt Hanwood and Longden and Annscroft etc *Heref*

PUNCKNOWLE (St Mary the Blessed Virgin) *see* Bride Valley *Sarum*

PURBECK, WEST, comprising Affpuddle w Turnerspuddle, Bere Regis, and Wool and East Stoke *Sarum 8* **P** *Ball Coll Ox, Bp, and Keble Coll Ox (by turn)* **R** C M LANGFORD   **C** J M ALIDINA, S E WILLIAMS

PURBROOK (St John the Baptist) *Portsm 5* **P** *Bp* **P-in-c** A M WILSON   **C** J E SMITH   **NSM** L B CAMERON

PUREWELL (St John) *see* Christchurch *Win*

PURFLEET (St Stephen) *see* Mardyke *Chelmsf*

PURITON (St Michael and All Angels) and Pawlett *B & W 13* **P** *Ld Chan (1 turn), D&C Windsor (2 turns)* **P-in-c** D GODDARD

PURLEIGH (All Saints) *Chelmsf 11* **P** *Oriel Coll Ox* **P-in-c** J WILLMOT

PURLEY (Christ Church) *S'wark 22* **P** *Bp* **V** D J L MCHARDIE   **Hon C** S P STOCKS   **OLM** S P BISHOP

PURLEY (St Barnabas) *S'wark 22* **P** *Bp* **P-in-c** J MIDDLEMISS   **NSM** E J GOODRIDGE

PURLEY (St Mark) (St Swithun) *S'wark 22* **P** *Bp* **V** F M WEAVER

PURLEY (St Mary the Virgin) *Ox 4* **P** *Ld Chan* **R** D J ARCHER   **C** B J BAILEY

PURLWELL (St Andrew) *see* Batley *Leeds*

PURSE CAUNDLE (St Peter) *see* Spire Hill *Sarum*

PURTON (St John) *see* Sharpness, Purton, Brookend and Slimbridge *Glouc*

PURTON (St Mary) *Bris 7* **P** *Bp* **V** I D TWEEDIE-SMITH   **OLM** J M WELLS

PUSEY (All Saints) *see* Cherbury w Gainfield *Ox*

PUTFORD (St Stephen) *see* Bradworthy, Sutcombe etc *Ex*

PUTLEY (not known) *see* Cider Churches *Heref*

PUTNEY (St Margaret) *S'wark 18* **P** *Bp* **P-in-c** B Z GREEN

PUTNEY (St Mary) (All Saints) *S'wark 18* **P** *Patr Bd* **TR** J WHITTAKER   **C** J K HAYNES

PUTNEY, EAST (St Stephen) *see* Wandsworth St Mich w St Steph *S'wark*

PUTTENHAM (St John the Baptist) *see* Seale, Puttenham and Wanborough *Guildf*

PYECOMBE (Transfiguration) *see* Poynings w Edburton, Newtimber and Pyecombe *Chich*

PYLLE (St Thomas à Becket) *see* Fosse Trinity *B & W*

PYPE HAYES (St Mary the Virgin) *Birm 7* **P** *Bp and Aston Patr Trust (jt)* **V** *vacant*

PYRFORD (Church of the Good Shepherd) *see* Wisley w Pyrford *Guildf*

PYRFORD (St Nicholas) *as above*

PYRTON (St Mary) *see* Icknield *Ox*

PYTCHLEY (All Saints) *see* Gt w Lt Harrowden and Orlingbury and Isham etc *Pet*

PYWORTHY (St Swithun) *see* Holsworthy, Hollacombe, Pyworthy etc *Ex*

QUADRING (St Margaret) *see* Gosberton, Gosberton Clough and Quadring *Linc*

QUAINTON (Holy Cross and St Mary) *see* Schorne *Ox*

QUANTOCK COAST Benefice, The, comprising Dodington, East Quantoxhead, Fiddington, Holford w Dodington, Kilve w Kilton and Lilstock, Stogursey, and Stringston *B & W 17*

P *Bp, DBP, Eton Coll, and Lady Gass (jt)* R N MORGAN
Hon C A F TATHAM

QUANTOCK TOWERS, The, comprising Bicknoller,
Crowcombe, Monksilver, Nettlecombe, Sampford Brett,
and Stogumber *B & W 17* P *Bp, D&C Windsor, and D&C
Wells (jt)* R A V I BERNERS-WILSON Hon C B R G FLENLEY

QUANTOCK, SOUTH Benefice, The, comprising Broomfield,
Cheddon Fitzpaine, Kingston St Mary, and West Monkton
B & W 18 P *Bp and D&C (jt)* R M E STYLES C J D R COX,
T A HALLETT

QUANTOXHEAD, EAST (Blessed Virgin Mary) *see* Quantock
Coast *B & W*

QUANTOXHEAD, WEST (St Ethelreda) *as above*

QUARLEY (St Michael and All Angels) *see* Portway and
Danebury *Win*

QUARNDON (St Paul) *Derby 5* P *Exors Viscount Scarsdale*
P-in-c R C MATHEW C D M KNIGHT

QUARNFORD (St Paul) *see* Longnor, Quarnford, Sheen etc
Lich

QUARRENDON ESTATE (St Peter) *see* Aylesbury *Ox*

QUARRINGTON (St Botolph) w Old Sleaford *Linc 14* P *Bp*
R M S THOMSON C D A JENKINS

QUARRY BANK (Christ Church) *see* Brierley Hill *Worc*

QUATFORD (St Mary Magdalene) *see* Bridgnorth and
Morville Par *Heref*

QUATT (St Andrew) *see* Alveley and Quatt *Heref*

QUEDGELEY (St James) *Glouc 2* P *Bp* V J F WARD

QUEEN CAMEL (St Barnabas) *see* Cam Vale *B & W*

QUEEN CHARLTON (St Margaret) *see* Keynsham *B & W*

QUEEN THORNE, comprising Oborne, Over Compton and
Nether Compton, Poyntington, Sandford Orcas, and Trent
Sarum 3 P *Bp, The Revd J M P Goodden, K E Wingfield Digby
Esq, and MMCET (jt)* P D H T BOND

QUEENBOROUGH (Holy Trinity) *see* W Sheppey *Cant*

QUEENHILL (St Nicholas) *see* Longdon, Castlemorton,
Bushley, Queenhill etc *Worc*

QUEEN'S GATE (St Augustine) *see* Onslow Square and S
Kensington St Aug *Lon*

QUEEN'S PARK (St Barnabas) *see* Holdenhurst and Iford *Win*

QUEEN'S PARK (St Luke) *see* Brighton St Luke Queen's Park
Chich

QUEENSBURY (All Saints) *Lon 23* P *The Crown*
V K N BLAKE

QUEENSBURY (Holy Trinity) *Leeds 3* P *Bp* V S GOTT
NSM S A NEALE

QUENDON (St Simon and St Jude) *see* Newport w
Widdington, Quendon and Rickling *Chelmsf*

QUENIBOROUGH (St Mary) *see* Fosse Team *Leic*

QUENINGTON (St Swithun) *see* S Cotswolds *Glouc*

QUERNMORE (St Peter) *see* Dolphinholme w Quernmore
and Over Wyresdale *Blackb*

QUETHIOCK (St Hugh) *see* St Ive and Pensilva w Quethiock
Truro

QUIDENHAM Group, The (St Andrew), including Banham,
Eccles, New Buckenham, Old Buckenham, and Wilby *Nor 11*
P *Ld Chan (1 turn), Bp, Sir Thomas Beevor Bt, Major E H C
Garnier, Trustees, and New Buckenham PCC (3 turns)*
P-in-c S M WRIGHT

QUINTET GROUP *see* Aylmerton, Runton, Beeston Regis and
Gresham *Nor*

**QUINTON (St Swithun), Welford, Weston and Marston
Sicca** *Glouc 8* P *Bp, D&C Worc, and DBP (jt)*
V R GREENHALGH C J C K EDIE NSM A Y GRUNDY

QUINTON and PRESTON DEANERY (St John the Baptist) *see*
Hardingstone, Piddington w Horton and Quinton and
Preston Deanery *Pet*

QUINTON ROAD WEST (St Boniface) *Birm 1* P *Bp*
V R P YATES NSM J KNOX

QUINTON, The (Christ Church) *Birm 1* P *Bp*
C R J HEATHFIELD NSM A P WELLS

QUORN (St Bartholomew) *see* Quorndon *Leic*

QUORNDON (St Bartholomew) *Leic 6* P *Bp*
V D H BOWLER

QUY (St Mary) *see* Anglesey Gp *Ely*

RACKENFORD (All Saints) *see* Washfield, Stoodleigh,
Withleigh etc *Ex*

RACKHEATH (Holy Trinity) *see* Gt and Lt Plumstead,
Rackheath w Salhouse and Witton *Nor*

RACTON (St Peter) *see* Octagon *Chich*

RADBOURNE (St Andrew) *see* Boylestone, Church
Broughton, Dalbury, etc *Derby*

RADCLIFFE (St Andrew) Black Lane *Man 10* P *R Radcliffe
St Mary* V J E MCKEE

**RADCLIFFE (St Mary) (St Thomas and St John) (St Philip
Mission Church)** *Man 10* P *Patr Bd* TV E A BINNS

RADCLIFFE-ON-TRENT (St Mary) and Shelford *S'well 5*
P *DBP and Ld Chan (alt)* V M S TANNER C B R EVANS,
R E MITCHELL

RADCLIVE (St John the Evangelist) *see* Buckingham *Ox*

RADDESLEY Group of Parishes, The, comprising Brinkley,
Burrough Green, Carlton, Dullingham, Stetchworth, and
Westley Waterless *Ely 4* P *R J H Vestey Esq, Mrs B O
Killander, S F B Taylor Esq, Duke of Sutherland, Exors C
Thomas (5 turns), St Jo Coll Cam (1 turn)* P-in-c N A MANN

RADDINGTON (St Michael) *see* Wiveliscombe and the Hills
B & W

RADDON *see* Brampford Speke, Cadbury, Newton St Cyres
etc *Ex*

RADFORD (All Souls) (St Peter) *S'well 9* P *Bp* V *vacant*

RADFORD (St Nicholas) *Cov 2* P *Bp* P-in-c A D COLEMAN

RADFORD SEMELE (St Nicholas) *Cov 10* P *Bp*
P-in-c M C GREEN

RADFORD, NORTH (St Francis of Assisi) *see* Cov St Fran N
Radford *Cov*

**RADIPOLE (Emmanuel) (St Adhelm) (St Ann) and
Melcombe Regis** *Sarum 4* P *Patr Bd* TR N J CLARKE
TV J E HAINE, T P COOPEY C M J C RENYARD
NSM G A HEBBERN

RADLETT (Christ Church) *see* Aldenham, Radlett and
Shenley *St Alb*

RADLETT (St John) *as above*

**RADLEY (St James the Great), Sunningwell and
Kennington** *Ox 19* P *Bp, DBP, and Radley Coll (jt)*
R R M GLENNY C A K MATHEW OLM G J BECKETT

RADNAGE (St Mary) *see* W Wycombe w Bledlow Ridge,
Bradenham and Radnage *Ox*

RADNOR, OLD (St Stephen) *see* Kington w Huntington, Old
Radnor, Kinnerton etc *Heref*

RADSTOCK (St Nicholas) w Writhlington *B & W 11* P *Bp*
R D A IZZARD

RADSTONE (St Lawrence) *see* Astwell Gp *Pet*

RADWAY (St Peter) *see* Edgehill Churches *Cov*

RADWELL (All Saints) *see* Stotfold and Radwell *St Alb*

RADWINTER (St Mary the Virgin) *see* Thaxted, The
Sampfords, Radwinter and Hempstead *Chelmsf*

RAGDALE (All Saints) *see* Upper Wreake *Leic*

RAINBOW HILL (St Barnabas) *see* Worc St Barn w Ch Ch
Worc

RAINFORD (All Saints) *Liv 14* P *V Prescot* V J E HEIGHTON
NSM G M CARTER

RAINHAM (St Helen and St Giles) w Wennington *Chelmsf 2*
P *MMCET* NSM D J STAINER

RAINHAM (St Margaret) *Roch 3* P *Bp* V N J WARD
C J P JENNINGS

RAINHILL (St Ann) *Liv 10* P *Trustees* V A R CONANT
C L M JACKSON

RAINOW (Holy Trinity) w Saltersford and Forest *Ches 13*
P *Bp* V S D RATHBONE

RAINTON (not known) *see* Topcliffe, Baldersby w Dishforth,
Dalton etc *York*

RAINTON, EAST (St Cuthbert) *Dur 10* P *D&C* V *vacant*

RAINTON, WEST (St Mary) *Dur 10* P *Bp* R *vacant*

RAINWORTH (St Simon and St Jude) *see* Blidworth w
Rainworth *S'well*

RAITHBY (Holy Trinity) *see* Bolingbroke Deanery *Linc*

RAITHBY (St Peter) *see* Legbourne and Wold Marsh *Linc*

RAME (St Germanus) *see* Maker w Rame, Millbrook, St John
and Torpoint *Truro*

RAMPISHAM (St Michael and All Angels) *see* Melbury *Sarum*

RAMPSIDE (St Michael) *see* Aldingham, Dendron, Rampside
and Urswick *Carl*

RAMPTON (All Saints) *see* Cottenham w Rampton *Ely*

RAMPTON (All Saints) *see* Retford Area *S'well*

**RAMSBOTTOM (St Andrew) (St John) (St Paul) and
Edenfield** *Man 8* P *Patr Bd (3 turns), The Crown (1 turn)*
TR A J LINDOP C A HARPER OLM L HALLAM, S J WOOD

RAMSBURY (Holy Cross) *see* Whitton *Sarum*

RAMSDELL (Christ Church) *see* Baughurst, Ramsdell,
Wolverton w Ewhurst etc *Win*

RAMSDEN (St James) *see* Forest Edge *Ox*

RAMSDEN BELLHOUSE (St Mary the Virgin) *see* Downham w
S Hanningfield and Ramsden Bellhouse *Chelmsf*

RAMSDEN HEATH (St John) *as above*

RAMSEY (St Michael) *see* Harwich Peninsula *Chelmsf*

RAMSEY (St Thomas à Becket) *see* The Ramseys and Upwood
Ely

RAMSEY ST MARY'S (St Mary) *as above*

RAMSEY, NORTH (St Olave) *see* Bride, Lezayre and N Ramsey
S & M

RAMSEY, SOUTH (St Paul) *see* Maughold and S Ramsey
S & M

**RAMSEYS (St Thomas à Becket) (St Mary) and Upwood,
The** *Ely 12* **P** *Lord De Ramsey and Bp (jt)* **R** R A DARMODY
C R M DYBALL
RAMSGATE (St Mark) *see* St Laur in Thanet *Cant*
RAMSGATE (Christ Church) *Cant 5* **P** *Ch Patr Trust*
V P F TIZZARD
RAMSGATE (Holy Trinity) *Cant 5* **P** *Abp* **R** *vacant*
RAMSGATE (St George) *Cant 5* **P** *Abp* **R** *vacant*
RAMSGATE (St Luke) *Cant 5* **P** *CPAS* **V** P R WORLEDGE
RAMSGILL (St Mary) *see* Upper Nidderdale *Leeds*
RAMSHOLT (All Saints) *see* Wilford Peninsula *St E*
RANBY (St German) *see* Asterby Gp *Linc*
RANBY (St Martin) *see* Retford Area *S'well*
RAND (St Oswald) *see* Wragby Gp *Linc*
RANDWICK (St John the Baptist) *see* Stroud Team *Glouc*
RANGEMORE (All Saints) *see* Hanbury, Newborough and
Rangemoor *Lich*
RANGEWORTHY (Holy Trinity) *see* Charfield and Kingswood
w Wickwar etc *Glouc*
RANMOOR (St John the Evangelist) *Sheff 4* **P** *Trustees*
V M I RHODES
RANMORE (St Barnabas) *see* Dorking w Ranmore *Guildf*
RANSKILL (St Barnabas) *see* Blyth and Scrooby w Ranskill
S'well
RANTON (All Saints) *see* Chebsey, Creswell, Ellenhall,
Ranton etc *Lich*
RANWORTH (St Helen) *see* Broadside *Nor*
RASEN DRAX, MIDDLE (St Peter and St Paul) *see* Middle
Rasen Gp *Linc*
RASEN, WEST (All Saints) *as above*
RASKELF (St Mary) *see* Easingwold w Raskelf *York*
RASTRICK (St John the Divine) (St Matthew) *Leeds 7* **P** *Bp*
and V Halifax (jt) **V** M E RUSSELL **NSM** R S HANNAM
RATBY (St Philip and St James) *see* Groby and Ratby *Leic*
RATCLIFFE CULEY (All Saints) *see* Bosworth and Sheepy Gp
Leic
RATCLIFFE ON THE WREAKE (St Botolph) *see* Fosse Team *Leic*
RATCLIFFE-ON-SOAR (Holy Trinity) *see* A453 churches of S
Notts *S'well*
RATHMELL (Holy Trinity) *see* Giggleswick and Rathmell w
Wigglesworth *Leeds*
RATLEY (St Peter ad Vincula) *see* Edgehill Churches *Cov*
RATLINGHOPE (St Margaret) *see* Wentnor w Ratlinghope,
Myndtown, Norbury etc *Heref*
RATTERY (Blessed Virgin Mary) *see* Buckfastleigh, Dean Prior,
Littlehempston etc *Ex*
**RATTLESDEN (St Nicholas) w Thorpe Morieux, Brettenham
and Hitcham** *St E 6* **P** *Bp (3 turns), Ld Chan (1 turn)*
R C M S ROBINSON
RAUCEBY (St Peter) *see* E Loveden *Linc*
RAUGHTON HEAD (All Saints) *see* Dalston w Cumdivock,
Raughton Head and Wreay *Carl*
RAUNDS (St Peter), Hargrave, Ringstead and Stanwick
Pet 8 **P** *Ld Chan (1 turn), Bp and L G Stopford-Sackville Esq*
(2 turns) **R** J F ALDWINCKLE
RAVENDALE, EAST (St Martin) *see* Waltham Gp *Linc*
RAVENFIELD (St James), Hooton Roberts and Braithwell
Sheff 6 **P** *Bp and Sir Philip Naylor-Leyland Bt (jt)*
P-in-c P J HUGHES **Hon C** N BOWLER
RAVENGLASS (Mission Room) *see* Black Combe, Drigg,
Eskdale etc *Carl*
RAVENHEAD (St John the Evangelist) *see* Eccleston Team *Liv*
RAVENINGHAM Group, The (St Andrew), including Aldeby,
Burgh St Peter, Haddiscoe, Norton Subcourse, Thorpe-next-
Haddiscoe, Thurlton, Toft Monks, and Wheatacre *Nor 8*
P *Bp, Adn Nor, Sir Nicholas Bacon Bt, Major C A Boycott, D&C,
K Coll Cam, and DBP (jt)* **Hon C** A M R HOUSMAN
RAVENSBOURNE *see* Deptford St Jo w H Trin and Ascension
S'wark
RAVENSCAR (St Hilda) and Staintondale *York 15* **P** *Abp*
V L M HELLMUTH
RAVENSDEN (All Saints) *see* Wilden w Colmworth and
Ravensden *St Alb*
RAVENSHEAD (St Peter) *S'well 4* **P** *Bp* **V** C M BYROM
C C L MELLESS
RAVENSTHORPE (St Denys) *see* Guilsborough and Hollowell
and Cold Ashby etc *Pet*
**RAVENSTHORPE (St Saviour) and Thornhill Lees w Savile
Town** *Leeds 9* **P** *Bp and V Mirfield (jt)* **V** *vacant*
RAVENSTONE (All Saints) *see* Gayhurst w Ravenstone, Stoke
Goldington etc *Ox*
RAVENSTONE (St Michael and All Angels) *see* Coalville w
Bardon Hill and Ravenstone *Leic*
RAVENSTONEDALE (St Oswald) *see* High Westmorland *Carl*
RAWCLIFFE (St James) *see* Airmyn, Hook and Rawcliffe *Sheff*
RAWCLIFFE (St Mark) *see* Clifton *York*

RAWDON (St Peter) *Leeds 15* **P** *Trustees* **V** M G R D SMITH
RAWMARSH (St Mary the Virgin) w Parkgate *Sheff 6* **P** *Ld
Chan* **P-in-c** L S WORTLEY
RAWMARSH (St Nicolas) *see* Ryecroft St Nic *Sheff*
RAWNSLEY (St Michael) *see* Hednesford *Lich*
RAWRETH (St Nicholas) *Chelmsf 14* **P** *Pemb Coll Cam*
P-in-c R W JORDAN **Hon C** B C WALLACE, E A JORDAN
RAWTENSTALL (St Mary) and Constable Lee *Man 11*
P *CPAS* **C** N CASEY **NSM** J A BARRATT
RAWTHORPE (St James) *see* Moldgreen and Rawthorpe *Leeds*
RAY VALLEY, The, comprising Ambrosden, Charlton-on-
Otmoor, Islip, Merton, Noke, Oddington, Piddington, and
Woodeaton *Ox 21* **P** *Canon E G A W Page-Turner, Ex Coll
Ox, and Piddington PCC (1 Turn), D&C Westmr, Qu Coll Ox,
and Walsingham Coll (1 turn)* **R** S A HAYES
Hon C L R THIRTLE **NSM** L C HOLMES
RAYDON (St Mary) *see* Higham, Holton St Mary, Raydon
and Stratford *St E*
RAYLEIGH (Holy Trinity) (St Michael) *Chelmsf 14* **P** *Patr Bd*
TR D A OXTOBY **TV** T M MARLOW **NSM** T J NUTTER
RAYNE (All Saints) *see* Black Notley, Gt Notley and Rayne
Chelmsf
RAYNES PARK (St Saviour) *S'wark 13* **P** *Bp*
P-in-c P J KELLEY
RAYNHAM, EAST (St Mary) *see* E w W Rudham,
Helhoughton etc *Nor*
RAYNHAM, SOUTH (St Martin) *as above*
REACH (St Ethelreda and the Holy Trinity) *see* Burwell w
Reach *Ely*
READ (St John the Evangelist) and Simonstone St Peter
Blackb 7 **P** V *Whalley* **P-in-c** R D FIELDING
READ IN WHALLEY (St John the Evangelist) *see* Read and
Simonstone *Blackb*
READING (Christ Church) *Ox 7* **P** *Bp* **V** P A DAY
READING (Holy Trinity) *Ox 7* **P** *SMF* **P-in-c** R J SIMMONDS
READING (St Agnes w St Paul) (St Barnabas) *Ox 7* **P** *Bp*
C S J CADY
READING (St Giles w St Saviour) *Ox 7* **P** *Bp* **R** D A HARRIS
C K T KREJCI
READING (St John the Evangelist and St Stephen) *Ox 7*
P *Simeon's Trustees* **C** G S COLLINS
READING (St Laurence) *Ox 7* **P** *Bp* **V** C I RUSSELL
C C R JONES
READING (St Luke) (St Bartholomew) *Ox 7* **P** *Bp and V
Reading St Giles (alt)* **C** S TAJIMA **NSM** C F BLACKMAN
READING (St Mark) (All Saints) *Ox 7* **P** *Bp*
V J S E WILLIAMS **NSM** J R LEWIS
READING (St Mary the Virgin) *Ox 7* **P** *Bp* **V** S J PULLIN
C G FANCOURT **NSM** A T BOND, S A PULLIN
OLM J E SUMNER
READING (St Matthew) *Ox 7* **P** *Bp* **V** M P DOLPHIN
NSM K DOLPHIN
READING Greyfriars *Ox 7* **P** *Ch Trust Fund Trust*
V D G WALKER **C** A CAVENDER, J K ATKINS, J N FREEMAN,
S R EDEN-JONES
READING STREET (St Andrew) *Cant 5* **P** *Abp* **V** P MUSINDI
REAPSMOOR (St John) *see* Longnor, Quarnford, Sheen etc
Lich
REARSBY (St Michael and All Angels) *see* Fosse Team *Leic*
**RECULVER (St Mary the Virgin), St Bartholomew Herne
Bay and Holy Cross Hoath** *Cant 4* **P** *Abp*
P-in-c S J MARTIN **NSM** S PARRETT
RED HOUSE (St Cuthbert) *see* N Wearside *Dur*
RED POST, comprising Almer and Charborough, Bloxworth,
Morden, Winterbourne Kingston, and Winterbourne
Zelstone w Thomson and Anderson *Sarum 6* **P** *Mrs V M
Chattey, R G Plunkett-Ernle-Erle-Drax Esq, and Bp (by turn)*
V J C E POTTINGER **NSM** C M CHICHESTER
REDBOURN (St Mary) *St Alb 7* **P** *Earl of Verulam*
V W J M GIBBS **C** T H VICKERS
REDBROOK (St Saviour) *see* Coleford, Staunton, Newland,
Redbrook etc *Glouc*
REDCAR (St Peter) *York 16* **P** *Trustees* **V** R E HARRISON
NSM T BURGESS
REDCLIFFE BAY (St Nicholas) *see* Portishead *B & W*
REDCLIFFE WAY (St Mary the Virgin) *see* Bris St Mary
Redcliffe w Temple etc *Bris*
REDDISH (St Elisabeth) *Man 2* **P** *Bp* **R** A M STANTON
C K O'SULLIVAN **NSM** A J MITCHELL
REDDISH (St Mary) *see* Heaton Reddish *Man*
REDDISH, NORTH (St Agnes) *Man 2* **P** *The Crown* **R** *vacant*
REDDITCH (St Stephen) *see* Redditch H Trin *Worc*
REDDITCH Christ the King, comprising Astwood Bank,
Crabbs Cross, and Headless Cross- *Worc 7* **P** *Patr Bd*
TR M F BARTLETT **TV** G T READING **C** V L G BARLOW

REDDITCH Holy Trinity (St Stephen), including Beoley and Webheath *Worc 7* **P** *Patr Bd* **TR** R M CLARK
TV P J IRVING, P LAWLOR   **C** F D MOLONEY

REDE (All Saints)   *see* Chevington w Hargrave, Chedburgh w Depden etc *St E*

REDENHALL (Assumption of the Blessed Virgin Mary) w Scole *Nor 10*   **P** *Bp, Ex Coll Ox, MMCET, Adn Norfolk, and Sir Rupert Mann (jt)*   **R** N O TUFFNELL   **NSM** T H ROGERS
OLM S F AUCKLAND

REDGRAVE (St Mary) cum Botesdale St Mary w Rickinghall *St E 12*   **P** P J H Wilson Esq   **R** C R NORBURN

REDHILL (Christ Church)   *see* Wrington w Butcombe and Burrington *B & W*

REDHILL (Holy Trinity) *S'wark 24*   **P** *Simeon's Trustees*
V M J HOUGH   **C** S L ALEXANDER

REDHILL (St John the Evangelist) (Meadvale Hall) *S'wark 24* **P** *Bp*   **V** J S KRONENBERG   **C** S SRIKANTHA

REDHILL (St Matthew) *S'wark 24*   **P** *Bp*   **V** A T CUNNINGTON
NSM H J COOK

REDISHAM (St Peter)   *see* Hundred River and Wainford *St E*

REDLAND (not known) *Bris 3*   **P** *Ch Trust Fund Trust*
C J N WALFORD, S P FAUX   **NSM** N S CRAWLEY
OLM S A TRUSCOTT

REDLINGFIELD (St Andrew)   *see* Athelington, Denham, Horham, Hoxne etc *St E*

REDLYNCH (St Mary)   *see* Forest and Avon *Sarum*

REDLYNCH (St Peter)   *see* Bruton, Brewham, Pitcombe and Shepton Montague *B & W*

REDMARLEY D'ABITOT (St Bartholomew), Bromesberrow, Pauntley, Upleadon, Oxenhall, Dymock, Donnington, Kempley and Preston *Glouc 3*   **P** *Pemb Coll Ox, Bp, R D Marcon Esq, and Miss C Daniel (jt)*   **NSM** J M BOND
OLM V G CHESTER

REDMARSHALL (St Cuthbert)   *see* Stockton Country Par *Dur*

REDMILE (St Peter)   *see* Vale of Belvoir *Leic*

REDMIRE (St Mary)   *see* Penhill *Leeds*

REDNAL (St Stephen the Martyr) *Birm 3*   **P** *Bp*
V T B A SOTONWA   **NSM** S J JONES

REDRUTH (St Andrew) (St Euny) w Lanner and Treleigh *Truro 2*   **P** *DBP*   **TR** C J B BUSH   **TV** D A GRIGG
C G J ADAMSON

REED (St Mary)   *see* Barkway, Barley, Reed and Buckland *St Alb*

REEDHAM (St John the Baptist)   *see* Acle and Bure to Yare *Nor*

REEPHAM (St Mary) and Wensum Valley Team Ministry, The, including Alderford w Attlebridge, Bylaugh, Elsing, Great w Little Witchingham, Lyng, Reepham and Hackford w Whitwell and Kerdiston, Salle, Sparham, Swannington, Thurning, Wood Dalling, and Weston Longville w Morton-on-the-Hill *Nor 18*   **P** *Patr Bd*   **TR** K A F RENGERT
TV H C MCGUIRE

REEPHAM (St Peter and St Paul)   *see* S Lawres Gp *Linc*

REGENT'S PARK (St Mark) *Lon 16*   **P** *D&C St Paul's*
V W D F GULLIFORD   **C** M M HARBAGE

REGIL (St James Mission Church)   *see* Winford w Felton Common Hill *B & W*

REIGATE (St Luke) *S'wark 24*   **P** *Bp*   **V** A C COLPUS

REIGATE (St Mark) *S'wark 24*   **P** *Bp*   **V** M P COLTON
NSM R GRANT

REIGATE (St Mary Magdalene) *S'wark 24*   **P** *Trustees*
V R G WILSON   **C** E V GILMOUR, H J FRASER, K F CAPPER,
N T GRIFFITHS

REIGATE (St Philip) *S'wark 24*   **P** *Bp*   **V** J A PENN

REIGATE HEATH (not known)   *see* Reigate St Mary *S'wark*

REIGHTON (St Peter)   *see* Bempton w Flamborough, Reighton w Speeton *York*

REKENDYKE (St Jude) *Dur 13*   **P** *The Crown and D&C*
V *vacant*

REMENHAM (St Nicholas)   *see* Henley w Remenham *Ox*

REMPSTONE (All Saints)   *see* E and W Leake, Stanford-on-Soar, Rempstone etc *S'well*

RENDCOMB (St Peter)   *see* Churn Valley *Glouc*

RENDHAM (St Michael)   *see* Upper Alde *St E*

RENDLESHAM (St Gregory the Great)   *see* Wilford Peninsula *St E*

RENHOLD (All Saints) *St Alb 9*   **P** *MMCET*   **V** *vacant*

RENISHAW (St Matthew)   *see* Killamarsh and Renishaw *Derby*

RENNINGTON (All Saints)   *see* Embleton w Rennington and Rock *Newc*

RENWICK (All Saints)   *see* Kirkoswald, Renwick w Croglin, Gt Salkeld etc *Carl*

REPPS (St Peter)   *see* Martham and Repps w Bastwick, Thurne etc *Nor*

REPTON (St Wystan)   *see* Foremark and Repton w Newton Solney *Derby*

RESTON, NORTH (St Edith)   *see* Legbourne and Wold Marsh *Linc*

RETFORD AREA Team Ministry, The (St Michael the Archangel) (St Saviour) (St Swithin), including Askham, Babworth, Bole w Saundby, Bothamsall, Clarborough, East Drayton w Dunham-on-Trent, Darlton, Ragnall and Fledborough, East Markham, Eaton and Gamston, Elkesley, Grove, Hayton, Headon w Upton, Laneham, North Leverton, North Wheatley, Ordsall, Rampton, Scofton w Osberton, South Leverton, Stokeham, Sturton w Littleborough, Sutton-cum-Lound, Treswell w Cottam, and West Drayton *S'well 1*   **P** *Patr Bd*   **TV** M J CANTRILL,
S CADDY   **C** B C MARSTON, B T CLAYTON, C L YARRIEN,
E B GAMBLE   **NSM** D A BEAN, K BOTTLEY

RETTENDON (All Saints) and Hullbridge *Chelmsf 14*   **P** *Ld Chan and Bp (alt)*   **P-in-c** R W JORDAN   **Hon C** B C WALLACE
NSM S ADAMS

REVEL GROUP, The, comprising Brinklow, Churchover, Harborough Magna, Monks Kirkby, and Willey *Cov 6*   **P** *Bp, Trin Coll Cam, and H A F W Boughton-Leigh Esq (2 turns), Ld Chan (1 turn)*   **R** J A FOX

REVELSTOKE (St Peter)   *see* Newton Ferrers w Revelstoke *Ex*

REVESBY (St Lawrence)   *see* Fen and Hill Gp *Linc*

REWE (St Mary the Virgin)   *see* Brampford Speke, Cadbury, Newton St Cyres etc *Ex*

REYDON (St Margaret)   *see* Sole Bay *St E*

REYMERSTON (St Peter)   *see* Barnham Broom and Upper Yare *Nor*

RHODES (All Saints)   *see* Tonge, Rhodes and Alkrington *Man*

RHODES (All Saints) (St Thomas) *Man 14*   **P** *R Middleton*
V *vacant*

RHYDYCROESAU (Christ Church) *Lich 18*   **P** *Bp*
R H L GIBBONS

RIBBESFORD (St Leonard) w Bewdley and Dowles and Wribbenhall *Worc 11*   **P** *E J Winnington-Ingram Esq and R Kidderminster (alt)*   **R** M C GIBBINS

RIBBLETON (St Mary Magdalene) (Ascension) *Blackb 13* **P** *Bp, DBP, K Simpson Esq, D V Johnson Esq, and the Ven K Gibbons (jt)*   **R** K J FENTON

RIBBY CUM WREA (St Nicholas) and Weeton St Michael *Blackb 10*   **P** *V Kirkham*   **V** *vacant*

RIBCHESTER (St Wilfrid) w Stydd *Blackb 7*   **P** *Bp*
R B R MCCONKEY   **C** K J HERSCHELL

RIBSTON, LITTLE (St Helen)   *see* Spofforth w Kirk Deighton *Leeds*

RIBY (St Edmund)   *see* Wolds Gateway Group *Linc*

RICCALL (St Mary), Barlby and Hemingbrough *York 2* **P** *Abp*   **V** G HORNER   **NSM** D A LAMBETH

RICHARDS CASTLE (All Saints)   *see* The Ashfords *Heref*

RICHINGS PARK (St Leonard)   *see* Iver *Ox*

RICHMOND (Holy Trinity and Christ Church) *S'wark 16*
P *CPAS*   **V** D M WELLS

RICHMOND (St Luke)   *see* Kew St Phil and All SS w St Luke *S'wark*

RICHMOND (St Mary Magdalene) (St Matthias) (St John the Divine) *S'wark 16*   **P** *K Coll Cam*   **TR** W ROEST
TV A E CRAWFORD, N T SUMMERS   **NSM** A J WILLIAMS

RICHMOND (St Mary w Holy Trinity) w Hudswell and Downholme and Marske *Leeds 22*   **P** *Bp*   **R** M FLETCHER

RICHMOND HILL (St Saviour)   *see* Leeds Richmond Hill *Leeds*

RICKERSCOTE (St Peter) *Lich 10*   **P** *Bp and V Stafford St Paul (jt)*   **V** *vacant*

RICKLING (All Saints)   *see* Newport w Widdington, Quendon and Rickling *Chelmsf*

RICKMANSWORTH (St Mary the Virgin) *St Alb 4*   **P** *Bp*
V D J SNOWBALL   **NSM** S M TALBOT

RIDDINGS (Holy Spirit)   *see* Bottesford w Ashby *Linc*

RIDDINGS (St James) and Ironville *Derby 2*   **P** *Wright Trustees and V Alfreton (jt)*   **P-in-c** M J TAYLOR
NSM J O K PENFOLD

RIDDLESDEN (St Mary the Virgin)   *see* Morton and Riddlesden *Leeds*

RIDDLESDOWN (St James) *S'wark 22*   **P** *Bp*
P-in-c G G COHEN

RIDDLESWORTH (St Peter)   *see* Guiltcross *Nor*

RIDGE (St Margaret)   *see* S Mymms and Ridge *St Alb*

RIDGE, The   *see* Redditch H Trin *Worc*

RIDGEWAY (St John the Evangelist)   *see* Eckington and Ridgeway *Derby*

RIDGEWAY Churches, The   *see* Bishop's Castle w Mainstone, Lydbury N etc *Heref*

RIDGEWAY, comprising Childrey w West Challow, Letcombe Bassett, Letcombe Regis, and Sparsholt w Kingston Lisle *Ox 27*   **P** *DBP, CCC Ox, and Qu Coll Ox (jt)*   **R** L A HILL
C A D COLBROOK

RIDGEWAY, comprising Chiseldon w Draycot Folliat, Ogbourne St Andrew, and Ogbourne St George *Sarum 18* **P** *D&C Windsor and O H Langton Esq (jt)* **R** R R POWELL

RIDGEWELL (St Laurence) *see* Two Rivers *Chelmsf*

RIDGMONT (All Saints) *see* Aspley Guise w Husborne Crawley and Ridgmont *St Alb*

RIDING MILL (St James) *Newc 9* **P** *Viscount Allendale* **P-in-c** L CHAPMAN

RIDLEY (St Peter) *Roch 1* **P** *J R A B Scott Esq* **R** H M REEVES **NSM** E M ROBERTSON

RIDLINGTON (St Mary Magdalene and St Andrew) *see* Empingham, Edith Weston, Lyndon, Manton etc *Pet*

RIDLINGTON (St Peter) *see* Bacton, Happisburgh, Hempstead w Eccles etc *Nor*

RIEVAULX (St Mary) *see* Helmsley *York*

RIGSBY (St James) *see* Alford Gp *Linc*

RIGTON, NORTH (St John) *see* Lower Wharfedale *Leeds*

RILLINGTON (St Andrew) *see* Buckrose Carrs *York*

RIMPTON (Blessed Virgin Mary) *see* Chilton Cantelo, Ashington, Mudford, Rimpton etc *B & W*

RINGLAND (St Peter) *see* Taverham w Ringland *Nor*

RINGMER (St Mary the Virgin) *Chich 21* **P** *Abp* **V** E M MCCLEAVE

RINGMORE (All Hallows) *see* Modbury, Bigbury, Ringmore etc *Ex*

RINGSFIELD (All Saints) *see* Hundred River and Wainford *St E*

RINGSHALL (St Catherine) *see* S Bosmere *St E*

RINGSTEAD (Nativity of the Blessed Virgin Mary) *see* Raunds, Hargrave, Ringstead and Stanwick *Pet*

RINGSTEAD (St Andrew) *see* Hunstanton St Edm w Ringstead *Nor*

RINGSTONE IN AVELAND Group, The, comprising Dunsby, Haconby, Kirkby Underwood, Morton, and Rippingale *Linc 17* **P** *Bp (2 turns), Baroness Willoughby de Eresby and Charterhouse (1 turn)* **R** N G O BULLEN

RINGWAY Hale Barns (All Saints) *see* Hale Barns w Ringway *Ches*

RINGWOOD (St Peter and St Paul) w Ellingham and Harbridge and St Leonards and St Ives *Win 9* **P** *K Coll Cam, Earl of Normanton, and Bp (jt)* **V** M J H TRICK **C** I S WHITHAM

RINGWOULD (St Nicholas) *see* Walmer and Cornilo *Cant*

RIPE (St John the Baptist) *see* Laughton w Ripe and Chalvington *Chich*

RIPLEY (All Saints) *Derby 8* **P** *Wright Trustees* **V** J M WIGRAM **OLM** M BROOKES

RIPLEY (All Saints) *see* Bishop Thornton, Burnt Yates, Markington etc *Leeds*

RIPLEY (St Mary) *Guildf 12* **P** *Bp* **V** C J ELSON

RIPON (Holy Trinity) *Leeds 23* **P** *Simeon's Trustees* **V** C BUTLER **NSM** J A MONTGOMERY, H H GOWING

RIPPINGALE (St Andrew) *see* Ringstone in Aveland Gp *Linc*

RIPPLE (St Mary the Virgin) *see* Walmer and Cornilo *Cant*

RIPPLE (St Mary) *see* Upton-on-Severn, Ripple, Earls Croome etc *Worc*

RISBOROUGH, comprising Bledlow w Saunderton and Horsenden, Lacey Green, Monks Risborough, and Princes Risborough w Ilmer *Ox 10* **P** *Ld Chan (2 turns), Patr Bd (1 turn)* **TR** D G WILLIAMS **TV** A F BUNDOCK, J A TOMKINS **C** P K KERR **NSM** M D HUNT, N CHUMU MUTUKU

RISBY (St Giles) *see* Barrow *St E*

RISE (All Saints) *see* Skirlaugh, Catwick, Long Riston, Rise, Swine w Ellerby *York*

RISE PARK *see* Bestwood Em and St Mark w Rise Park *S'well*

RISEHOLME (St Mary) *see* Nettleham *Linc*

RISELEY (All Saints) w Bletsoe *St Alb 13* **P** *MMCET* **V** J A ISAACS

RISHTON (St Peter and St Paul) *Blackb 7* **P** *Trustees* **V** C G HOLDEN

RISHWORTH (St John) *see* Ripponden *Leeds*

RISLEY (All Saints) *see* Stanton-by-Dale w Dale Abbey and Risley *Derby*

RISSINGTON, GREAT (St John the Baptist) *see* Bourton-on-the-Water w Clapton etc *Glouc*

RISSINGTON, LITTLE (St Peter) *as above*

RIVENHALL (St Mary the Virgin and All Saints) *see* Witham and Villages *Chelmsf*

RIVER (St Peter and St Paul) *Cant 7* **P** *Abp* **P-in-c** A J BAWTREE

RIVER WERE Benefice, The, comprising Bishopstrow and Boreham, Warminster St Denys, and Upton Scudamore *Sarum 12* **P** *Bp, Qu Coll Ox, and DBP (jt)* **R** J T M DESROSIERS **C** S C HART

RIVERHEAD (St Mary) w Dunton Green *Roch 9* **P** *R Sevenoaks and Bp (jt)* **V** *vacant*

RIVERS Team Ministry, The, comprising Brinsworth, Catcliffe, Tinsley, and Treeton *Sheff 6* **P** *Patr Bd* **TV** M BAKER **NSM** P L BARRINGER

RIVERSMEET Benefice, The, comprising Blunham, Great Barford, Roxton, and Tempsford w Little Barford *St Alb 10* **P** *The Crown, Trin Coll Cam (2 turns), and Ball Coll Ox (by turn)* **P-in-c** G C BUCKLE

RIVINGTON (not known) *see* Horwich and Rivington *Man*

ROACH Parishes, comprising Barling Magna, Foulness, Little and Great Wakering, Rochford and Sutton w Shopland *Chelmsf 14* **P** *Patr Bd* **TR** K A LEPLEY **TV** S M GUEST

ROADE (St Mary the Virgin) *see* Salcey *Pet*

ROADWATER (St Luke) *see* Old Cleeve, Leighland and Treborough *B & W*

ROBERTSBRIDGE (Mission Room) *see* Salehurst, Hurst Green and Robertsbridge *Chich*

ROBERTTOWN (All Saints) *see* Hartshead, Hightown, Roberttown and Scholes *Leeds*

ROBOROUGH *see* Bickleigh and Shaugh Prior *Ex*

ROBOROUGH (St Peter) *see* Newton Tracey, Horwood, Alverdiscott etc *Ex*

ROBY (St Bartholomew) *Liv 7* **P** *Bp* **V** K E WHARTON **C** T M COATES

ROCESTER (St Michael) and Croxden w Hollington *Lich 14* **P** *Bp and Trustees (jt)* **P-in-c** E J JONES

ROCHDALE (St Aidan) *see* Sudden and Heywood All So *Man*

ROCHDALE (St Chad) St Edmund (St John the Divine) (St Mary) *Man 17* **P** *Bp* **R** J M COLEMAN

ROCHE (St Gomonda of the Rock) *Truro 1* **P** *Bp and DBP (jt)* **P-in-c** K P ARTHUR

ROCHESTER (St Justus) *Roch 5* **P** *Bp* **V** H M BURN **C** A L J PYRKE, B A A LAWAL

ROCHESTER (St Margaret) (St Peter's Parish Centre) *Roch 5* **P** *Bp and D&C (jt)* **V** J A LOVE **C** O O MAKANJUOLA

ROCHFORD (St Andrew) *see* Roach Par *Chelmsf*

ROCHFORD (St Michael) *see* Teme Valley S *Worc*

ROCK (St Peter and St Paul) *see* Mamble w Bayton, Rock w Heightington etc *Worc*

ROCK (St Philip and St James) *see* Embleton w Rennington and Rock *Newc*

ROCK FERRY (St Peter) *Ches 1* **P** *Bp* **V** C R SLATER **C** P J CHAMBERLIN

ROCKBEARE (St Mary w St Andrew) *see* Broadclyst, Clyst Honiton, Pinhoe, Rockbeare etc *Ex*

ROCKBOURNE (St Andrew) *see* W Downland *Sarum*

ROCKCLIFFE (St Mary the Virgin) and Blackford *Carl 2* **P** *D&C* **P-in-c** J J VAN DEN BERG

ROCKHAMPTON (St Oswald) *see* Cromhall, Tortworth, Tytherington, Falfield etc *Glouc*

ROCKINGHAM (St Leonard) *see* Gretton w Rockingham and Cottingham w E Carlton *Pet*

ROCKLAND (All Saints) *see* Gt and Lt Ellingham, Rockland and Shropham etc *Nor*

ROCKLAND (St Peter) *as above*

ROCKLAND ST MARY (St Mary) with Hellington, Bramerton, Surlingham, Claxton, Carleton St Peter and Kirby Bedon w Whitlingham *Nor 8* **P** *Bp, Adn Nor, MMCET, and BNC Ox (jt)* **OLM** M ANSELL

RODBOROUGH (St Mary Magdalene), Woodchester and Brimscombe *Glouc 4* **P** *Simeon's Trustees and Bp (jt)* **R** P A FRANCIS

RODBOURNE (Holy Rood) *see* Malmesbury and Upper Avon *Bris*

RODBOURNE CHENEY (St Mary) *Bris 7* **P** *CPAS* **R** N D J LINES

RODDEN (All Saints) *see* Beckington w Standerwick, Berkley, Rodden etc *B & W*

RODE (St Lawrence) *see* Hardington Vale *B & W*

RODE HEATH (Good Shepherd) *see* Odd Rode *Ches*

RODE, NORTH (St Michael) *see* Gawsworth w North Rode *Ches*

RODHUISH (St Bartholomew) *see* Dunster, Carhampton, Withycombe w Rodhuish etc *B & W*

RODING, HIGH (All Saints) *see* Gt Canfield w High Roding and Aythorpe Roding *Chelmsf*

RODINGS, SOUTH, comprising Abbess Roding, Beauchamp Roding, Leaden Roding, and White Roding *Chelmsf 18* **P** *Ld Chan, Bp, and Viscount Gough (by turn)* **R** *vacant*

RODINGTON (St George) *see* Wrockwardine Deanery *Lich*

RODLEY (Ecumenical Centre) *see* Farsley *Leeds*

RODLEY (Mission Church) *see* Westbury-on-Severn w Flaxley, Blaisdon etc *Glouc*

RODMELL (St Peter) *see* Iford w Kingston and Rodmell and Southease *Chich*

RODMERSHAM (St Nicholas) *see* Tunstall and Bredgar *Cant*

RODNEY STOKE (St Leonard) *see* Cheddar, Draycott and Rodney Stoke *B & W*
ROEHAMPTON (Holy Trinity) *S'wark 18* **P** *Bp* **V** *vacant*
ROFFEY (All Saints) *see* Colgate and Roffey *Chich*
ROGATE (St Bartholomew) w Terwick and Trotton w Chithurst *Chich 9* **P** *Ld Chan* **R** E M DOYLE
ROGERS LANE (St Andrew's Chapel) *see* Stoke Poges *Ox*
ROLLESBY (St George) *see* Ormesby St Marg w Scratby, Ormesby St Mich etc *Nor*
ROLLESTON (Holy Trinity) *see* W Trent *S'well*
ROLLESTON (St John the Baptist) *see* Coplow *Leic*
ROLLESTON (St Mary) *see* Anslow, Rolleston and Tutbury *Lich*
ROLLRIGHT, GREAT (St Andrew) *see* Hook Norton w Gt Rollright, Swerford etc *Ox*
ROLLRIGHT, LITTLE (St Phillip) *see* Chipping Norton *Ox*
ROLVENDEN (St Mary the Virgin) *see* Tenterden, Rother and Oxney *Cant*
ROMALDKIRK (St Romald) *see* Lower Teesdale *Leeds*
ROMANBY (St James) *see* Northallerton w Kirby Sigston *York*
ROMFORD (Ascension) Collier Row *Chelmsf 2* **P** *Trustees*
P-in-c M A POWER
ROMFORD (Good Shepherd) Collier Row *Chelmsf 2*
P *CPAS* **V** D H HAGUE **C** D M HARRIGAN
Hon C K S TURNER
ROMFORD (St Alban) *Chelmsf 2* **P** *Bp* **V** R S P HINGLEY
ROMFORD (St Andrew) (St Agnes) *Chelmsf 2* **P** *New Coll Ox* **P-in-c** L E DOSE
ROMFORD (St Augustine) Rush Green *see* Rush Green *Chelmsf*
ROMFORD (St Edward the Confessor) *Chelmsf 2* **P** *New Coll Ox* **V** M A POWER **C** D S BARNES-DAVIES
OLM R A CLARKE
ROMILEY (St Chad) *Ches 16* **P** *R Stockport St Mary*
V R L PENNYSTAN **C** W DRAIN
ROMNEY MARSH, The, comprising Burmarsh, Dymchurch, Ivychurch, New Romney, Newchurch, Old Romney and Midley, St Mary-in-the-Marsh, and St Mary's Bay *Cant 10*
P *Abp* **C** J S RICHARDSON
ROMNEY, NEW (St Nicholas) *see* Romney Marsh *Cant*
ROMNEY, OLD (St Clement) *as above*
ROMSEY (St Mary and St Ethelflaeda) *Win 12* **P** *Bp*
V T G WHARTON **C** N J GOWER **NSM** B G TAPHOUSE, D F WILLIAMS, P HOLLINGWORTH
ROMSLEY (Mission Room) *see* Halas *Worc*
ROMSLEY (St Kenelm) *as above*
ROOKERY, THE (St Saviour) *see* Mow Cop *Lich*
ROOS (All Saints) *see* S Holderness Coast *York*
ROOSE (St Perran) *see* S Barrow *Carl*
ROPLEY (St Peter) *see* Bishop's Sutton and Ropley and W Tisted *Win*
ROPSLEY (St Peter) *see* N Beltisloe Gp *Linc*
ROSE ASH (St Peter) *see* Bishopsnympton, Charles, E Anstey, High Bray etc *Ex*
ROSEDALE (St Lawrence) *see* Lastingham w Appleton-le-Moors, Rosedale etc *York*
ROSHERVILLE (St Mark) *see* Northfleet and Rosherville *Roch*
ROSLEY (Holy Trinity) *see* Westward, Rosley-w-Woodside and Welton *Carl*
ROSLISTON (St Mary) *see* Seale and Lullington w Coton in the Elms *Derby*
ROSS (St Mary the Virgin) w Walford and Brampton Abbotts *Heref 7* **P** *Bp (4 turns), Ld Chan (1 turn)*
R S A J SEMPLE **C** S J D TARLTON **Hon C** C J BLANCHARD
NSM C E A PASCOE
ROSSINGTON (St Michael) *Sheff 9* **P** *Bp* **R** *vacant*
ROSSINGTON, NEW (St Luke) *Sheff 9* **P** *Bp* **V** *vacant*
ROSTHERNE (St Mary) w Bollington *Ches 12* **P** C L S Cornwall-Legh Esq **V** P J ROBINSON **NSM** P M COPE, P M ROBINSON
ROTHAY (All Saints) *see* Upper Coquetdale *Newc*
ROTHERBY (All Saints) *see* Upper Wreake *Leic*
ROTHERFIELD (St Denys) w Mark Cross *Chich 16* **P** *Bp, Adn Lewes and Hastings, and Ch Patr Trust (jt)* **R** N F MASON
C S R WICKENS
ROTHERFIELD GREYS (Holy Trinity) *see* Henley H Trin *Ox*
ROTHERFIELD GREYS (St Nicholas) *see* Nettlebed w Bix, Highmoor, Pishill etc *Ox*
ROTHERFIELD PEPPARD (All Saints) and Kidmore End and Sonning Common *Ox 24* **P** *Bp and Jes Coll Ox (jt)*
R J E DE G STICKINGS **C** S H MORGAN **NSM** S WALKER
ROTHERHAM (All Saints) *Sheff 6* **P** *Bp* **V** P J BATCHFORD
ROTHERHITHE (Holy Trinity) *S'wark 7* **P** *R Rotherhithe St Mary* **V** A M DOYLE
ROTHERHITHE (St Katharine) *see* Bermondsey St Kath w St Bart *S'wark*

ROTHERHITHE (St Mary) w All Saints *S'wark 7* **P** *Clare Coll Cam* **R** M R NICHOLLS
ROTHERSTHORPE (St Peter and St Paul) *see* Bugbrooke, Harpole, Kislingbury etc *Pet*
ROTHERWICK (not known) *see* Whitewater *Win*
ROTHLEY (St Mary the Virgin and St John the Baptist) *Leic 4* **P** *MMCET* **V** R M GLADSTONE
ROTHWELL (Holy Trinity) w Orton and Rushton w Glendon and Pipewell and Loddington and Thorpe Malsor *Pet 9* **P** *Bp, J N Hipwell Esq, Mert Coll Ox, Hosp of Jes, and Keble Coll Ox (3 turns), Ld Chan (1 turn)*
R J R WESTWOOD
ROTHWELL (Holy Trinity), Lofthouse, Methley w Mickletown and Oulton w Woodlesford Team Ministry, The *Leeds 16* **P** *Duchy of Lancaster (1 turn), Patr Bd (3 turns)*
TR A A JOHN **TV** A L RHODES, S A HANCOX
ROTHWELL (St Mary the Virgin) *see* Caistor *Linc*
ROTTINGDEAN (St Margaret) *Chich 19* **P** *Bp*
V A M MOORE **C** L SULLIVAN
ROUGH CLOSE (St Matthew) *see* Meir Heath and Normacot *Lich*
ROUGH COMMON (St Gabriel) *see* Harbledown *Cant*
ROUGH HAY (St Christopher) *see* Darlaston and Moxley *Lich*
ROUGHAM (St Mary) *see* Launditch and the Upper Nar *Nor*
ROUGHAM (St Mary), Beyton w Hessett and Rushbrooke *St E 6* **P** *Bp, MMCET (2 turns), and Ld Chan* **R** N CUTLER
ROUGHTON (St Margaret) *see* Bain Valley Gp *Linc*
ROUGHTON (St Mary) and Felbrigg, Metton, Sustead, Bessingham and Gunton w Hanworth *Nor 20* **P** *Bp and Exors G Whately Esq (jt)* **R** J E FRYMANN
ROUGHTOWN (St John the Baptist) *Man 13* **P** *Bp*
NSM I C BROCKLEHURST
ROUGHTOWN (St John the Baptist) *see* Mossley *Man*
ROUNDHAY (St Edmund King and Martyr) *Leeds 13* **P** *Bp*
V N C J WRIGHT **C** C M CORLEY, C M N BALDING
NSM D L LOFTHOUSE
ROUNDS GREEN (St James) *Birm 6* **P** *V Langley*
P-in-c M J SERMON
ROUNDSHAW (St Paul) *see* S Beddington and Roundshaw *S'wark*
ROUNTON, WEST (St Oswald) and East (St Laurence) w Welbury *York 18* **P** *Ld Chan* **R** J M E COOPER
ROUS LENCH (St Peter) *see* Church Lench w Rous Lench and Abbots Morton etc *Worc*
ROUSHAM (St Leonard and St James) *Ox 21*
P C Cottrell-Dormer Esq **P-in-c** R C SMAIL
ROUTH (All Saints) *York 8* **P** *Ch Soc Trust and Reformation Ch Trust (jt)* **P-in-c** J W BAKER
ROWBERROW (St Michael and All Angels) *see* Axbridge w Shipham and Rowberrow *B & W*
ROWDE (St Matthew) and Bromham *Sarum 17* **P** *DBP and J A L Spicer Esq (jt)* **R** R E SCHOFIELD **NSM** A E WINTOUR
ROWINGTON (St Laurence) *see* Hatton w Haseley, Rowington w Lowsonford etc *Cov*
ROWLAND LUBBOCK (Memorial Hall) *see* E Horsley *Guildf*
ROWLANDS CASTLE (St John the Baptist) *Portsm 5* **P** *Bp*
P-in-c V I. MORGAN
ROWLANDS GILL (St Barnabas) *see* High Spen and Rowlands Gill *Dur*
ROWLEDGE (St James) *Guildf 3* **P** *Adn Surrey* **V** R W GANT
Hon C S J CRABTREE
ROWLESTONE (St Peter) *see* Ewyas Harold w Dulas, Kenderchurch etc *Heref*
ROWLEY (St Peter) *see* Walkington, Bishop Burton, Rowley etc *York*
ROWLEY REGIS (St Giles) *Birm 6* **P** *Ld Chan* **V** *vacant*
ROWNER (St Mary the Virgin) *Portsm 3* **P** *R J F Prideaux-Brune Esq* **R** J W DRAPER
ROWNEY GREEN (Mission Chapel) *see* Alvechurch *Worc*
ROWNHAMS (St John the Evangelist) *see* Nursling and Rownhams *Win*
ROWSLEY (St Katherine) *see* Bakewell, Ashford w Sheldon and Rowsley *Derby*
ROWSTON (St Clement) *see* Digby Gp *Linc*
ROWTON (All Hallows) *see* Wrockwardine Deanery *Lich*
ROXBOURNE (St Andrew) *Lon 23* **P** *Bp* **V** L P NORTH
ROXBY (St Mary) *see* Winterton Gp *Linc*
ROXBY (St Nicholas) *see* Hinderwell, Roxby and Staithes etc *York*
ROXETH (Christ Church) *Lon 23* **P** *Bp and Ch Patr Trust (jt)*
V S J DURRANT **NSM** E WEAVER
ROXHOLME *see* N Lafford Gp *Linc*
ROXTON (St Mary Magdalene) *see* Riversmeet *St Alb*
ROXWELL (St Michael and All Angels) *Chelmsf 9* **P** *New Coll Ox* **OLM** A MERCHANT

ROYAL WOOTTON BASSETT (St Bartholomew and All Saints) *Sarum 16* **P** *DBP* **V** J D CURTIS **C** O R BLEASE

ROYDON (All Saints) *see* Ashwicken w Leziate, Bawsey etc *Nor*

ROYDON (St Peter) *Chelmsf 4* **P** *Earl Cowley* **P-in-c** R J ATTEW

ROYDON (St Remigius) *see* Diss *Nor*

ROYSTON (St John the Baptist) *St Alb 16* **P** *Bp* **V** H A HUNTLEY **C** T T MUSIWACHO **NSM** J H FIDLER

ROYSTON (St John the Baptist) and Felkirk *Leeds 17* **P** *Bp* **V** M C TOMLINSON

ROYTON (St Paul) *Man 16* **P** *R Prestwich St Mary* **V** G HOLLOWOOD, **C** N R JOHNSON

ROYTON Longsight (St Anne) *see* Heyside and Royton *Man*

RUAN LANIHORNE (St Rumon) *see* Veryan w Ruan Lanihorne *Truro*

RUAN MINOR (St Rumon) *see* St Keverne, St Ruan w St Grade and Landewednack *Truro*

RUARDEAN (St John the Baptist) *see* Drybrook, Lydbrook and Ruardean *Glouc*

RUBERY (St Chad) *Birm 3* **P** *The Crown* **V** C E TURNER **C** S P CLANCY

RUCKINGE (St Mary Magdalene) *see* Saxon Shoreline *Cant*

RUCKLAND (St Olave) *see* S Ormsby Gp *Linc*

RUDBY IN CLEVELAND (All Saints) w Middleton *York 20* **P** *Abp* **P-in-c** W J FORD **Hon C** A J HUTCHINSON **NSM** D J SUDRON, R OPALA

RUDDINGTON (St Peter) *S'well 6* **P** *Simeon's Trustees* **V** A D BUCHANAN

RUDFORD (St Mary the Virgin) *see* Highnam, Tibberton w Rudford etc *Glouc*

RUDGWICK (Holy Trinity) *Chich 7* **P** *Ld Chan* **V** M P J KING **C** P DEAVES

RUDHAM, EAST and WEST (St Mary), Helhoughton, Houghton-next-Harpley, The Raynhams, Tatterford, and Tattersett *Nor 14* **P** *Bp, The Most Revd G D Hand, Marquess of Cholmondeley, and Marquess Townshend (jt)* **R** E L BUNDOCK

RUDHEATH (Licensed Room) *see* Witton *Ches*

RUDSTON (All Saints), Boynton, Carnaby, Kilham, Burton Fleming w Fordon, Grindale and Wold Newton *York 9* **P** *Abp (1 turn), Abp and MMCET (2 turns), Ld Chan (1 turn)* **V** G J OWEN **NSM** B E HODGSON

RUFFORD (St Mary the Virgin) and Tarleton *Blackb 5* **P** *Bp and St Pet Coll Ox (jt)* **R** vacant

RUFFORTH (All Saints) *see* Marston Moor *York*

RUGBY (St Andrew) *Cov 6* **P** *Bp* **NSM** R C ROGERS

RUGBY (St George) *Cov 6* **P** *Bp* **V** vacant

RUGBY (St Peter and St John) *Cov 6* **P** *Bp* **V** S M BRIDGE

RUGBY WEST (St Matthew and St Oswald) *Cov 6* **P** *Dioc Trustees and Ch Trust Fund Trust (jt)* **V** vacant

RUGELEY (St Augustine) *see* Brereton and Rugeley w Armitage *Lich*

RUGELEY (The Good Shepherd) *as above*

RUISHTON (St George) *see* Creech St Michael and Ruishton w Thornfalcon *B & W*

RUISLIP (St Martin) *Lon 24* **P** *D&C Windsor* **V** S EVANS **C** Y S WALKER **NSM** J R WHITE

RUISLIP (St Mary) *Lon 24* **P** *Bp* **V** E J LOBSINGER **NSM** A J BEATTIE

RUISLIP MANOR (St Paul) *Lon 24* **P** *Bp* **V** M E SELBY

RUMBURGH (St Michael and All Angels and St Felix) *see* The Saints *St E*

RUNCORN (All Saints) (Holy Trinity) *Ches 3* **P** *Bp and Ch Ch Ox (jt)* **V** D W GUEST

RUNCORN (St John the Evangelist) Weston *Ches 3* **P** *Bp* **V** V B GISBY

RUNCORN (St Michael and All Angels) *Ches 3* **P** *Bp* **NSM** H BROWNE

RUNCTON HOLME (St James) *see* W Norfolk Priory Gp *Ely*

RUNCTON, NORTH (All Saints) *see* Middlewinch *Nor*

RUNCTON, SOUTH (St Andrew) *see* W Norfolk Priory Gp *Ely*

RUNHALL (All Saints) *see* Barnham Broom and Upper Yare *Nor*

RUNHAM (St Peter and St Paul) *see* S Trin Broads *Nor*

RUNNINGTON (St Peter and St Paul) *see* Wellington and Distr *B & W*

RUNTON (Holy Trinity) *see* Aylmerton, Runton, Beeston Regis and Gresham *Nor*

RUNTON, EAST (St Andrew) *as above*

RUNWELL (St Mary) *see* Wickford and Runwell *Chelmsf*

RURAL EAST YORK, comprising Dunnington, Holtby, Stockton-on-Forest, and Warthill- *York 2* **P** *Abp* **R** N W R BIRD **NSM** T A JOYCE

RUSCOMBE (St James the Great) and Twyford w Hurst *Ox 8* **P** *Bp* **V** A C HARWOOD **Hon C** C SMITH, **G** F THEOBALD

RUSH GREEN (St Augustine) Romford *Chelmsf 2* **P** *Bp* **V** M D HOWSE

RUSHALL (Christ the King) (St Michael the Archangel) *Lich 24* **P** *Sir Andrew Buchanan Bt and H C S Buchanan Esq (jt)* **V** C R SUCH

RUSHALL (St Mary) *see* Dickleburgh and The Pulhams *Nor*

RUSHALL (St Matthew) *see* Vale of Pewsey *Sarum*

RUSHBROOKE (St Nicholas) *see* Rougham, Beyton w Hessett and Rushbrooke *St E*

RUSHBURY (St Peter) *see* Apedale Gp *Heref*

RUSHDEN (St Mary) *see* Clothall, Rushden, Sandon, Wallington and Weston *St Alb*

RUSHDEN (St Mary) w Newton Bromswold *Pet 8* **P** *CPAS* **R** S K PRIOR **C** P J NIGHTINGALE

RUSHDEN (St Peter) *Pet 8* **P** *CPAS* **V** R A HAWKINS **C** J ALLEN

RUSHEN Christ Church (Holy Trinity) *S & M* **P** *The Crown* **V** J A T HEATON **NSM** E S C HULL

RUSHEY MEAD (St Theodore of Canterbury) *see* Leic St Theodore *Leic*

RUSHFORD (St John the Evangelist) *see* E w W Harling, Bridgham w Roudham, Larling etc *Nor*

RUSHLAKE GREEN (Little St Mary) *see* Warbleton, Bodle Street Green and Dallington *Chich*

RUSHMERE (St Andrew) *St E 1* **P** *Bp* **V** S D FOSTER

RUSHMERE (St Michael) *see* Kessingland, Gisleham and Rushmere *Nor*

RUSHOCK (St Michael) *see* Elmley Lovett w Hampton Lovett and Elmbridge w Rushock and Hartlebury and Ombersley w Doverdale *Worc*

RUSHOLME (Holy Trinity) *Man 3* **P** *CPAS* **C** J A D SPENCE, P M MATHOLE, R B CRIDDLE, S R FOULDS, T J WICKHAM **NSM** P J GASKELL

RUSHTON (All Saints) *see* Rothwell w Orton and Rushton w Glendon etc *Pet*

RUSHTON SPENCER (St Lawrence) *see* Cheddleton, Horton, Longsdon and Rushton Spencer *Lich*

RUSKIN PARK (St Saviour) *see* Herne Hill *S'wark*

RUSKINGTON (All Saints) *see* N Lafford Gp *Linc*

RUSLAND (St Paul) *see* Hawkshead and Low Wray w Sawrey and Rusland etc *Carl*

RUSPER (St Mary Magdalene) *Chich 7* **P** *Bp* **R** N A FLINT

RUSTHALL (St Paul) (St Paul's Mission Church) *Roch 12* **P** *R Speldhurst* **V** R E N WILLIAMS

RUSTINGTON (St Peter and St Paul) *Chich 1* **P** *Bp* **V** vacant

RUSTON PARVA (St Nicholas) *see* The Beacon *York*

RUSWARP (St Bartholomew) *see* Whitby w Ruswarp *York*

RUTLAND WATER *see* Empingham, Edith Weston, Lyndon, Manton etc *Pet*

RUYTON XI TOWNS (St John the Baptist) w Great Ness and Little Ness *Lich 16* **P** *Bp and Guild of All So (jt) and Ld Chan (jt)* **P-in-c** L R BURNS

RYAL (All Saints) *see* Stamfordham w Matfen *Newc*

RYARSH (St Martin) *see* Birling, Addington, Ryarsh and Trottiscliffe *Roch*

RYBURGH, GREAT (St Andrew) *see* Upper Wensum Village Gp *Nor*

RYBURN Benefice, The (Cottonstones, Norland and Sowerby) *Leeds 8* **P** *Bp and DBP (jt)* **V** J ROBERTS **C** I SPARKS **NSM** L ENNIS

RYDAL (St Mary) *Carl 11* **P** *Bp* **V** vacant

RYDE (All Saints) *Portsm 7* **P** *Bp* **V** vacant

RYDE (St James) Proprietary Chapel *Portsm 7* **C-in-c** J H A LEGGETT

RYDE (St John the Baptist) Oakfield and Holy Trinity *Portsm 7* **P** *Bp and V St Helens (jt)* **P-in-c** S A THEOBALD **NSM** D K MABEY

RYE (St Mary the Virgin) *Chich 17* **P** *Patr Bd* **TR** D R FROST **TV** R J GOSTELOW **NSM** T F MUNRO

RYE HARBOUR (Holy Spirit) *see* Rye *Chich*

RYE PARK (St Cuthbert) *St Alb 17* **P** *DBP* **V** N L SHARP

RYECROFT (St Nicolas) Rawmarsh *Sheff 6* **P** *Bp* **P-in-c** S Y LEE

RYEDALE, UPPER, comprising Bilsdale Midcable, Old Byland, Cold Kirby, Hawnby, and Scawton *York 19* **P** *Abp and the Hon Jake Duncombe (jt)* **R** T J ROBINSON **NSM** H RAWLINGS

RYHALL (St John the Evangelist) w Essendine and Carlby *Pet 12* **P** *Burghley Ho Preservation Trust Ltd* **V** vacant

RYHILL (St James) *Leeds 19* **P** *Bp* **P-in-c** P CARTWRIGHT

RYHOPE (St Paul) *Dur 14* **P** *Bp* **V** D E CHADWICK

RYLSTONE (St Peter) *see* Burnsall w Rylstone *Leeds*

RYME INTRINSECA (St Hypolytus) *see* Three Valleys *Sarum*

RYSTON (St Michael)   *see* Denver and Ryston w Roxham etc *Ely*

RYTHER (All Saints)   *see* Cawood w Ryther and Wistow *York*

RYTON (Holy Cross) *Dur 12*   **P** *Bp*   **R** *vacant*

RYTON (Mission Chapel)   *see* Condover w Frodesley, Acton Burnell etc *Heref*

RYTON (St Andrew)   *see* Beckbury, Badger, Kemberton, Ryton, Stockton etc *Lich*

RYTON ON DUNSMORE (St Leonard)   *see* Baginton w Bubbenhall and Ryton-on-Dunsmore *Cov*

SACOMBE (St Catherine)   *see* Standon and The Mundens w Sacombe *St Alb*

SADBERGE (St Andrew) *Dur 7*   **P** *Bp*   **R** M R EAST   **NSM** S CHEW

SADDINGTON (St Helen)   *see* Kibworth and Smeeton Westerby and Saddington *Leic*

SADDLEWORTH (St Chad) *Man 15*   **P** *Patr Bd*   **TR** S A JONES   **TV** J R ROSEDALE, C A A JACKMAN, A E BRYAN   **Hon C** H A EDGERTON   **NSM** M C DONMALL, P H WILLIAMSON, R J LAMBERT   **OLM** B CHRISTOPHER, P J GILLIAN

SAFFRON WALDEN (St Mary) and Villages, including Ashdon, Debden, Great Chesterford, Hadstock, Little Chesterford, Littlebury, Wendens Ambo, and Wimbish w Thunderley *Chelmsf 20*   **P** *Ld Chan (1 turn), Patr Bd (2 turns)*   **TR** D R TOMLINSON   **TV** A JEEWAN, R D SPENCER   **C** R E PRIOR   **NSM** J SAXON, P W L GRIFFITHS, T K HARDINGHAM

SAHAM TONEY (St George)   *see* Ashill, Carbrooke, Ovington and Saham Toney *Nor*

ST AGNES (St Agnes)   *see* Is of Scilly *Truro*

ST AGNES (St Agnes) and Mount Hawke w Mithian *Truro 6*   **P** *Bp and D&C (alt)*   **P-in-c** A E BROWN   **C** D J WILLOUGHBY, R J MONIE

ST ALBANS (Christ Church) *St Alb 5*   **P** *Trustees*   **V** J M FOLLETT

ST ALBANS (St Luke) *St Alb 5*   **P** *DBP*   **V** M A SLATER   **NSM** D M HALSEY

ST ALBANS (St Mary) Marshalswick *St Alb 5*   **P** *Bp*   **V** G W HOLMES

ST ALBANS (St Michael) *St Alb 5*   **P** *Earl of Verulam*   **V** K P J PADLEY   **C** C E B KING

ST ALBANS (St Paul) *St Alb 5*   **P** *V St Alb St Pet*   **V** A R HURLE   **Hon C** G M ABBOTT   **NSM** A RADMALL, L M HURLE

ST ALBANS (St Peter) *St Alb 5*   **P** *The Crown*   **V** M C DEARNLEY   **C** A J HUZZEY

ST ALBANS (St Saviour) *St Alb 5*   **P** *Bp*   **V** R F WATSON   **NSM** A N FERRAR, T J HALTON

ST ALBANS (St Stephen) *St Alb 5*   **P** *J N W Dudley Esq*   **V** R M LEACH   **C** K A WAINWRIGHT   **NSM** P J MORIARTY

ST ALDHELM, comprising Church Knowle, Corfe Castle, Kimmeridge, Kingston, Langton Matravers, Steeple w Tyneham, and Worth Matravers *Sarum 8*   **P** *Major M J A Bond, Nat Trust, Exors D E Scott Esq, Bp, and R Swanage and Studland (jt)*   **R** I JACKSON   **C** J J MERCER

ST ALLEN (St Alleyne)   *see* Kenwyn w St Allen *Truro*

ST ANNES-ON-THE-SEA (St Anne) Heyhouses *Blackb 10*   **P** *J C Hilton Esq*   **V** A D LYON   **C** A J A EDWARDS

ST ANNES-ON-THE-SEA (St Margaret of Antioch) *Blackb 10*   **P** *Bp*   **V** A R HODGSON

ST ANNES-ON-THE-SEA (St Thomas) *Blackb 10*   **P** *J C Hilton Esq*   **V** C M SCARGILL

ST ANTHONY-IN-MENEAGE (St Anthony)   *see* Meneage *Truro*

ST AUSTELL (Holy Trinity) *Truro 1*   **P** *The Crown*   **V** H M FLINT   **C** I GULLAND

ST BARTHOLOMEW, comprising Donhead St Andrew, Donhead St Mary, East Knoyle, Sedgehill, and Semley *Sarum 11*   **P** *Ch Ch Ox, New Coll Ox, and DBP (by turn)*   **R** R WARHURST   **C** K MARTIN

ST BEES (St Mary and St Bega) *Carl 5*   **P** *Trustees*   **C** R A GIBBS

ST BLAZEY (St Blaise) *Truro 1*   **P** *Bp*   **P-in-c** J S J WILLIAMS

ST BREOKE (St Breoke) and Egloshayle in Wadebridge *Truro 10*   **P** *Bp and DBP (jt)*   **R** *vacant*

ST BREWARD (St Breward)   *see* Camelside *Truro*

ST BRIAVELS (St Mary the Virgin) w Hewelsfield and Brockweir *Glouc 1*   **P** *D&C Heref*   **P-in-c** D O TREHARNE   **C** R C SIMPSON   **OLM** D M REES

ST BURYAN (St Buriana), St Levan and Sennen *Truro 5*   **P** *Duchy of Cornwall*   **R** V S PERRETT

ST CLEER (St Clarus) *Truro 12*   **P** *Ld Chan*   **P-in-c** R M BELL   **Hon C** P J BIGGS

ST CLEMENT (St Clement) *Truro 6*   **P** *Bp*   **V** D J WILLOUGHBY

ST CLETHER (St Cliederus)   *see* Moorland Gp *Truro*

ST COLAN (St Colan)   *see* St Columb Minor and St Colan *Truro*

ST COLUMB MAJOR (St Columba)   *see* Lann Pydar *Truro*

ST COLUMB MINOR (St Columba) and St Colan *Truro 7*   **P** *Bp*   **P-in-c** C C MCQUILLEN-WRIGHT   **C** J S THOROLD, L M G CHANTLER

ST CROSS SOUTH ELMHAM (St George)   *see* The Saints *St E*

ST DECUMANS   *see* Watchet and Williton *B & W*

ST DENNIS (St Denys) *Truro 1*   **P** *Bp*   **P-in-c** K P ARTHUR

ST DEVEREUX (St Dubricius)   *see* Ewyas Harold w Dulas, Kenderchurch etc *Heref*

ST DOMINIC (St Dominica)   *see* Tamar Valley *Truro*

ST EDMUND WAY, comprising Bradfield Combust, Great Whelnetham, Hawstead, Lawshall, Nowton, and Stanningfield *St E 6*   **P** *Bp, Mrs J Oakes, and Lord de Saumarez*   **R** J D A PARSONS

ST ENDELLION (St Endelienta)   *see* N Cornwall Cluster *Truro*

ST ENODER (St Enoder) *Truro 7*   **P** *Bp*   **R** *vacant*

ST ENODOC (St Enodoc)   *see* N Cornwall Cluster *Truro*

ST ERME (St Hermes)   *see* Probus, Ladock and Grampound w Creed and St Erme *Truro*

ST ERNEY (St Erney)   *see* Landrake w St Erney and Botus Fleming *Truro*

ST ERTH (St Erth)   *see* Godrevy *Truro*

ST ERVAN (St Ervan)   *see* Lann Pydar *Truro*

ST EVAL (St Uvelas)   *as above*

ST EWE (All Saints)   *see* St Mewan w Mevagissey and St Ewe *Truro*

ST GENNYS (St Gennys)   *see* Week St Mary Circle of Par *Truro*

ST GEORGE-IN-THE-EAST (St Mary) *Lon 7*   **P** *Bp*   **V** P MCGEARY

ST GEORGE-IN-THE-EAST w St Paul *Lon 7*   **P** *Bp*   **R** R K SPRINGER   **C** A J HARRIS, V J E MCCARTHY   **Hon C** T CLAPTON   **NSM** A W M RITCHIE, J L HARRIS

ST GEORGES' (St George) *Lich 20*   **P** *Bp*   **C** K S EVANS

ST GERMANS (St Germans of Auxerre) w Antony and Sheviock *Truro 11*   **P** *Bp, Sir John Carew Pole Bt, and D&C Windsor (jt)*   **V** L PARKER

ST GILES IN THE WOOD (St Giles)   *see* Newton Tracey, Horwood, Alverdiscott etc *Ex*

ST GILES-IN-THE-FIELDS *Lon 3*   **P** *Bp*   **R** A C CARR

ST GILES-IN-THE-HEATH (St Giles)   *see* Boyton, N Tamerton, Werrington etc *Truro*

ST GLUVIAS (St Gluvias) *Truro 3*   **P** *Bp*   **V** S F WALES

ST GORAN (St Goranus) w Caerhays *Truro 1*   **P** *Bp*   **V** *vacant*

ST HELENS (St Catherine by the Green)   *see* Seaview, St Helens, Brading and Yaverland *Portsm*

ST HELENS (St Helen)   *as above*

ST HELENS Town Centre (St Helen) (Barton Street Mission) (St Andrew) (St Mark) (St Thomas) *Liv 10*   **P** *Patr Bd*   **TV** C J DANIEL-MCKEIGUE   **C** E A ANDERSON, N J WHITE, P M ATKINSON   **NSM** H WOOD

ST HELIER (St Peter) (Bishop Andrewes Church) *S'wark 23*   **P** *Bp*   **V** J M ITUMU   **NSM** A E DOERR

ST HILARY (St Hilary)   *see* Ludgvan, Marazion, St Hilary and Perranuthnoe *Truro*

ST ILLOGAN (St Illogan) *Truro 2*   **P** *Ch Soc Trust*   **R** S P ROBINSON   **C** A M SHARP   **NSM** M CARVETH

ST IPPOLYTS (St Ippolyts) w Great and Little Wymondley *St Alb 3*   **P** *Bp and MMCET (jt)*   **R** V A DEAR

ST ISSEY (St Issey)   *see* Padstow, St Merryn and St Issey w St Petroc Minor *Truro*

ST IVE (St Ive) and Pensilva w Quethiock *Truro 12*   **P** *Bp (1 turn), The Crown (2 turns)*   **P-in-c** R M BELL

ST IVES (All Saints) *Ely 12*   **P** *Guild of All So*   **V** J M AMEY   **C** A D J SHANNON

ST IVES (St Ia the Virgin) *Truro 5*   **P** *D&C and V Carbis Bay w Lelant (jt)*   **V** N J WIDDOWS   **NSM** K E MARWOOD

ST JAMES (St James)   *see* Shaftesbury *Sarum*

ST JOHN (St John the Baptist)   *see* Maker w Rame, Millbrook, St John and Torpoint *Truro*

ST JOHN IN BEDWARDINE (St John the Baptist) *Worc 3*   **P** *D&C*   **P-in-c** P J BRADFORD

ST JOHN IN WEARDALE (St John the Baptist)   *see* Upper Weardale *Dur*

ST JOHN LEE (St John of Beverley) *Newc 10*   **P** *Viscount Allendale*   **R** J J T THOMPSON

ST JOHN ON BETHNAL GREEN *Lon 7*   **P** *Patr Bd*   **TR** A J E GREEN   **NSM** C B HALL

ST JOHN'S WOOD (St John) *Lon 4*   **P** *Bp*   **V** A K BERGQUIST   **C** K T ANDRÉASSON

ST JOHN'S-IN-THE-VALE (St John), St Mary's Threlkeld and Wythburn *Carl 6*   **P** *Bp, Adn, V Crosthwaite, and Earl of Londsale (jt)*   **P-in-c** C H HOPE

ST JULIOT (St Julitta)   *see* Boscastle and Tintagel Gp *Truro*

ST JUST IN PENWITH (St Just) *Truro 5*   **P** *Ld Chan*
P-in-c K E WEDGEWOOD
ST JUST-IN-ROSELAND (St Just) and St Mawes *Truro 6*
P *A M J Galsworthy Esq*   **R** *vacant*
ST KEVERNE (St Keverne), St Ruan w St Grade and
Landewednack *Truro 4*   **P** *CPAS and P J Vyvyan-Robinson*
Esq (jt)   **R** P R SHARPE
ST KEW (St James the Great)   *see* N Cornwall Cluster *Truro*
ST KEYNE (St Keyna)   *see* Liskeard and St Keyne *Truro*
ST LAURENCE in the Isle of Thanet (St Laurence) *Cant 5*
P *Patr Bd*   **P-in-c** I A JACOBSON   **C** P J G BONE
NSM K I R COX
ST LAWRENCE (Old Church) (St Lawrence) *Portsm 7*   **P** *Bp*
R N J PORTER
ST LEONARD (St Leonard)   *see* Hawridge w Cholesbury and
St Leonard *Ox*
ST LEONARDS (Christ Church and St Mary Magdalen)
St Peter and St Paul *Chich 15*   **P** *Bp and SMF (jt)*
P-in-c P W WHEATLEY   **C** N W ARCHER   **NSM** R G RALPH
ST LEONARDS AND ST IVES (All Saints)   *see* Ringwood w
Ellingham and Harbridge etc *Win*
ST LEONARDS, UPPER (St John the Evangelist) *Chich 15*
P *Trustees*   **R** D R HILL   **NSM** J N HARTMAN, M P TURNBULL
ST LEONARDS-ON-SEA (St Matthew)   *see* Silverhill St Matt
Chich
ST LEONARDS-ON-SEA St Leonard (St Ethelburga) *Chich 15*
P *Hyndman Trustees*   **Hon C** E V WHEELER, W D BOULTON
ST LEVAN (St Levan)   *see* St Buryan, St Levan and Sennen
Truro
ST MABYN (St Mabena)   *see* Camelside *Truro*
ST MARGARET'S (St Margaret)   *see* Black Mountains Gp *Heref*
ST MARGARETS-AT-CLIFFE (St Margaret of Antioch) w
Westcliffe and East Langdon w West Langdon *Cant 7*
P *Abp*   **P-in-c** D E FAWCETT
ST MARGARET'S-ON-THAMES (All Souls) *Lon 11*   **P** *Bp*
V R S FRANK
ST MARTHA-ON-THE-HILL (St Martha)   *see* Shere, Albury and
Chilworth *Guildf*
ST MARTIN (St Martin)   *see* Looe and Morval *Truro*
ST MARTIN-IN-MENEAGE (St Martin)   *see* Meneage *Truro*
ST MARTIN-IN-THE-FIELDS *Lon 3*   **P** *Bp*   **V** S M B WELLS
C J A H EVENS, R A CARTER, S A HITCHINER
NSM W H MORRIS
ST MARTIN'S (St Martin)   *see* Is of Scilly *Truro*
ST MARTINS (St Martin) and Weston Rhyn *Lich 18*   **P** *Bp (2*
turns), Bp and Lord Trevor (1 turn)   **V** S J JERMY
ST MARY ABBOTS   *see* Kensington St Mary Abbots *Lon*
ST MARY BOURNE (St Peter)   *see* Hurstbourne Priors,
Longparish etc *Win*
ST MARY LE STRAND w St Clement Danes *Lon 3*   **P** *Ld Chan*
and Burghley Ho Preservation Trust Ltd (alt)
P-in-c P A E CHESTER   **NSM** C E BRADLEY, J O M CRAIG,
K G RIGLIN, R A BURRIDGE, T F DITCHFIELD
ST MARY-AT-LATTON Harlow (St Mary the Virgin)
Chelmsf 4   **P** J L H Arkwright Esq   **V** L S HURRY
C B D K JOSS-POTHEN   **NSM** M C R GREEN
ST MARYCHURCH (St Mary the Virgin) *Ex 11*   **P** *D&C*
P-in-c R A P WARD
ST MARY-IN-THE-MARSH (St Mary the Virgin)   *see* Romney
Marsh *Cant*
ST MARYLEBONE (All Saints) *Lon 4*   **P** *Bp*   **V** L A MOSES
C M N R BOWIE   **NSM** J BROWNING
ST MARYLEBONE (All Souls)   *see* Langham Place All So *Lon*
ST MARYLEBONE (Annunciation) Bryanston Street *Lon 4*
P *Bp*   **V** G C BEAUCHAMP
ST MARYLEBONE (St Cyprian) *Lon 4*   **P** *Bp*
P-in-c G C BEAUCHAMP   **Hon C** M G FULLER
ST MARYLEBONE (St Mark w St Luke)   *see* Bryanston Square
St Mary w St Marylebone St Mark *Lon*
ST MARYLEBONE (St Mark) Hamilton Terrace *Lon 4*   **P** *The*
Crown   **V** K M HARRISON
ST MARYLEBONE (St Marylebone) (Holy Trinity) *Lon 4*
P *The Crown*   **R** S J EVANS   **C** J M NOBLE,
K L HACKER HUGHES
ST MARYLEBONE (St Paul) *Lon 4*   **P** *The Crown*
R C A E DOWDING   **NSM** A J MULROY
ST MARYLEBONE (St Peter)   *see* Langham Place All So *Lon*
ST MARY'S (St Mary)   *see* Is of Scilly *Truro*
ST MARY'S BAY (All Saints)   *see* Romney Marsh *Cant*
ST MAWES (St Mawes)   *see* St Just-in-Roseland and St Mawes
Truro
ST MAWGAN (St Mawgan)   *see* Lann Pydar *Truro*
ST MAWGAN-IN-MENEAGE (St Mawgan)   *see* Meneage *Truro*
ST MELLION (St Melanus)   *see* Tamar Valley *Truro*
ST MERRYN (St Merryn)   *see* Padstow, St Merryn and St Issey
w St Petroc Minor *Truro*

ST MEWAN (St Mewan) w Mevagissey and St Ewe *Truro 1*
P *Bp, DBP, Penrice Ho (St Austell) Ltd, and A M J Galsworthy*
Esq (jt)   **R** M L BARRETT
ST MICHAEL PENKEVIL (St Michael) *Truro 6*   **P** *Viscount*
Falmouth   **P-in-c** L M BARLEY
ST MICHAEL ROCK (St Michael)   *see* N Cornwall Cluster
Truro
ST MICHAELCHURCH (St Michael)   *see* Alfred Jewel *B & W*
ST MICHAELS-ON-WYRE (St Michael)   *see* Garstang St Helen
and St Michaels-on-Wyre *Blackb*
ST MINVER (St Menefreda)   *see* N Cornwall Cluster *Truro*
ST NECTAN (St Nectan)   *see* Lostwithiel Parishes *Truro*
ST NEOT (St Neot) and Warleggan *Truro 12*   **P** *R G Grylls*
Esq (2 turns), DBP (1 turn)   **P-in-c** P J BIGGS
ST NEOTS (St Mary) *Ely 13*   **P** *P W Rowley Esq*   **C** H L TAME
ST NEWLYN EAST (St Newlina)   *see* Newlyn St Newlyn *Truro*
ST NICHOLAS (St Nicholas)   *see* Shaldon, Stokeinteignhead,
Combeinteignhead etc *Ex*
ST NICHOLAS AT WADE (St Nicholas)   *see* Wantsum Gp *Cant*
ST OSWALD IN LEE w Bingfield (St Mary) *Newc 8*   **P** *Bp*
P-in-c C F BULL, S A LUNN
ST OSYTH (St Peter and St Paul) and Great Bentley
Chelmsf 23   **P** *Bp*   **V** S E A MILES
ST PANCRAS (Holy Cross) (St Jude) (St Peter) *Lon 17*   **P** *Bp*
P-in-c C W CAWRSE
ST PANCRAS (Holy Trinity)   *see* Kentish Town St Silas and H
Trin w St Barn *Lon*
ST PANCRAS (Old Church) *Lon 17*   **P** *Patr Bd*   **TR** J I ELSTON
TV D R P WORTON, M R D THOMAS   **C** G R F WILLIS
ST PANCRAS (St Pancras) (St James) (Christ Church)
Lon 17   **P** *D&C St Paul's*   **V** A H STEVENS
ST PAUL'S CRAY (St Barnabas) *Roch 16*   **P** *CPAS*
V N G COLEMAN   **Hon C** J E RAWLING
ST PETER in the Isle of Thanet (St Peter the Apostle) *Cant 5*
P *Abp*   **V** J DURRANS
ST PETROC MINOR (St Petroc)   *see* Padstow, St Merryn and
St Issey w St Petroc Minor *Truro*
ST SAMPSON (St Sampson) *Truro 1*   **P** *Bp*
P-in-c P DE GREY-WARTER
ST STEPHEN IN BRANNEL (not known) *Truro 1*
P *Capt J D G Fortescue*   **P-in-c** E J WESTERMANN-CHILDS
ST STEPHENS (St Stephen)   *see* Saltash *Truro*
ST STYTHIANS (St Stythian) w Perranarworthal and
Gwennap *Truro 2*   **P** *Viscount Falmouth (2 turns),*
D&C (1 turn)   **P-in-c** S A BONE   **C** K E JONES, R D WALLIS
NSM J ROWE, S J C FLETCHER
ST TEATH (St Teatha)   *see* Camel-Allen *Truro*
ST TUDY (St Tudy)   *see* Camelside *Truro*
ST VEEP (St Cyricius)   *see* Lostwithiel Parishes *Truro*
ST WENN (St Wenna) and Withiel *Truro 7*   **P** *Bp and DBP*
P-in-c E C DEELEY
ST WEONARDS (St Weonard) *Heref 7*   **P** *Bp, D&C, and*
MMCET (jt)   **R** E J CATHIE   **NSM** F J PHILLIPS
ST WINNOW (St Winnow)   *see* Lostwithiel Parishes *Truro*
SAINTS, The, comprising South Elmham and Ilketshall *St E 17*
P *Bp (3 turns), Ld Chan (1 turn), and Duke of Norfolk (1 turn)*
C I B BYRNE   **NSM** L J COLLYER
SALCEY Benefice, The, comprising Ashton, Collingtree,
Courteenhall, Hartwell, and Roade *Pet 5*   **P** *Ld Chan and Bp*
(1 turn), N C Phipps Walker Esq and H C Wake Esq (1 turn)
V M J BURTON
SALCOMBE (Holy Trinity) and Malborough w South Huish
Ex 13   **P** *Keble Coll Ox and D&C Sarum (jt)*   **V** D A FRENCH
NSM P WHEELER, S J BALL
SALCOMBE REGIS (St Mary and St Peter)   *see* Sidmouth,
Woolbrook, Salcombe Regis, Sidbury etc *Ex*
SALCOTT VIRLEY (St Mary the Virgin)   *see* N Blackwater
Chelmsf
SALE (St Anne) (St Francis's Church Hall) *Ches 10*   **P** *DBP*
V A C COX
SALE (St Paul) *Ches 10*   **P** *Trustees*   **V** B E SHARP
SALEBY (St Margaret)   *see* Alford Gp *Linc*
SALEHURST (St Mary), Hurst Green and Robertsbridge
Chich 13   **P** *Bp*   **V** A M HAWKINS
SALESBURY (St Peter) *Blackb 7*   **P** *V Blackb*   **V** M J DUERDEN
NSM S G CHEESMAN
SALFORD (Sacred Trinity) *Man 20*   **P** *Sir Josslyn Gore-Booth*
Bt   **V** A I SALMON   **NSM** R C CRAVEN
SALFORD (St Clement) Ordsall   *see* Ordsall and Salford Quays
Man
SALFORD (St Mary)   *see* Chipping Norton *Ox*
SALFORD (St Mary)   *see* Cranfield and Hulcote w Salford
St Alb
SALFORD (St Paul w Christ Church) *Man 20*   **P** *The Crown*
and Trustees (alt)   **R** D S C WYATT

SALFORD (St Philip w St Stephen) *Man 20*   **P** *Bp and D&C (jt)*   **V** G J ROBINSON   **C** C T SAYBURN, H E J STODDART, S T WATKINSON

SALFORD All Saints, comprising Lower Kersal, Pendleton and Claremont, and Weaste, Seedley and Langworthy *Man 20*   **P** *Patr Bd*   **TR** D J A BURTON   **TV** I C J GORTON   **C** C P HAMILTON

SALFORD PRIORS (St Matthew) *see* Heart of England *Cov*

SALFORDS (Christ the King) *S'wark 24*   **P** *Bp*   **NSM** D ROSS

SALHOUSE (All Saints) *see* Gt and Lt Plumstead, Rackheath w Salhouse and Witton *Nor*

SALING, GREAT (St James) *see* Stebbing and Lindsell w Gt and Lt Saling *Chelmsf*

SALING, LITTLE (St Peter and St Paul) *as above*

SALISBURY (St Francis) and St Lawrence Stratford sub Castle *Sarum 13*   **P** *Bp (3 turns), D&C (1 turn)*   **V** J H T DE GARIS   **C** M J LEVINSOHN, P A OSTLI-EAST, S E WOOD-ROE

SALISBURY (St Mark) and Laverstock *Sarum 13*   **P** *D&C and Bp (alt)*   **V** A M BOUSFIELD

SALISBURY (St Martin) *Sarum 13*   **P** *Bp*   **V** D B FISHER

SALISBURY (St Thomas and St Edmund) *Sarum 13*   **P** *Bp and D&C (alt)*   **R** K J INGLIS   **Hon C** S F DEACON

SALISBURY PLAIN, comprising Chitterne, Orcheston, Shrewton, and Tilshead *Sarum 14*   **P** *Ld Chan (1 turn), Bp (2 turns), D&C (1 turn)*   **V** E J RANCE   **C** S J M JAVELLE

SALKELD, GREAT (St Cuthbert) *see* Kirkoswald, Renwick w Croglin, Gt Salkeld etc *Carl*

SALLE (St Peter and St Paul) *see* Reepham and Wensum Valley *Nor*

SALT (St James the Great) *see* Mid Trent *Lich*

SALTASH (St Nicholas and St Faith) *Truro 11*   **P** *Patr Bd*   **P-in-c** C M SIGRIST   **NSM** P M SELLIX

SALTBURN-BY-THE-SEA (Emmanuel) *York 16*   **P** *Abp, Adn Cleveland, Marquis of Zetland, Mrs M Brignall, and Mrs S L Vernon (jt)*   **V** A M F REED

SALTBY (St Peter) *see* High Framland Par *Leic*

SALTDEAN (St Nicholas) *Chich 19*   **P** *Bp*   **P-in-c** S J HORTON   **NSM** K E LAWSON

SALTER STREET (St Patrick) *Birm 5*   **P** *Bp and V Tamworth (jt)*   **V** *vacant*

SALTERHEBBLE (All Saints) *see* Halifax All SS *Leeds*

SALTERSFORD (St John the Baptist) *see* Rainow w Saltersford and Forest *Ches*

SALTFLEETBY (St Peter) *Linc 15*   **P** *Or Coll Ox, Bp, and MMCET (jt)*   **V** *vacant*

SALTFORD (Blessed Virgin Mary) w Corston and Newton St Loe *B & W 9*   **P** *DBP (2 turns), Duchy of Cornwall (1 turn)*   **R** D M WILSHERE

SALTHOUSE (St Nicholas) *see* Weybourne Gp *Nor*

SALTLEY (St Saviour) and Washwood Heath *Birm 11*   **P** *Bp and Trustees (jt)*   **V** A THOMPSON

SALTNEY FERRY (St Matthew) *see* Lache cum Saltney *Ches*

SALTON (St John of Beverley) *see* Kirby Misperton w Normanby and Salton *York*

SALTWOOD (St Peter and St Paul) *see* Lympne and Saltwood *Cant*

SALVINGTON (St Peter) *see* Findon Valley *Chich*

SALWARPE (St Michael) and Hindlip w Martin Hussingtree *Worc 8*   **P** *Bp, D&C, and Exors Lady Hindlip (by turn)*   **P-in-c** N G BYARD   **C** L J HANDY

SALWAY ASH (Holy Trinity) *see* Beaminster Area *Sarum*

SAMBOURNE (Mission Church) *see* Alcester Minster *Cov*

SAMBROOK (St Luke) *see* Cheswardine, Childs Ercall, Hales, Hinstock etc *Lich*

SAMFORD, NORTH *see* Sproughton w Burstall, Copdock w Washbrook etc *St E*

SAMLESBURY (St Leonard the Less) *see* Balderstone, Mellor and Samlesbury *Blackb*

SAMPFORD ARUNDEL (Holy Cross) *see* Wellington and Distr *B & W*

SAMPFORD BRETT (St George) *see* Quantock Towers *B & W*

SAMPFORD COURTENAY (St Andrew) *see* Chagford, Gidleigh, Throwleigh etc *Ex*

SAMPFORD PEVERELL (St John the Baptist), Uplowman, Holcombe Rogus, Hockworthy, Burlescombe and Halberton w Ash Thomas *Ex 7*   **P** *Patr Bd*   **TR** G H B LEWRY

SAMPFORD SPINEY (St Mary) *see* Yelverton, Meavy, Sheepstor, Walkhampton, Sampford Spiney and Horrabridge *Ex*

SAMPFORD, GREAT (St Michael) *see* Thaxted, The Sampfords, Radwinter and Hempstead *Chelmsf*

SAMPFORD, LITTLE (St Mary) *as above*

SANCREED (St Creden) *Truro 5*   **P** *D&C*   **P-in-c** K E WEDGEWOOD

SANCROFT, comprising Fressingfield, Mendham, Metfield, Stradbroke, Weybread, and Withersdale *St E 13*   **P** *Bp, Ch Soc Trust, Em Coll Cam, and SMF (jt)*   **R** S A LOXTON   **C** V G WILLIAMS   **NSM** P A SCHWIER

SANCTON (All Saints) *York 5*   **P** *Abp*   **V** C R PINCHBECK

SAND HILL (Church of the Good Shepherd) *see* Farnborough Gd Shep *Guildf*

SAND HUTTON (St Mary) *see* Harton *York*

SANDAL (St Catherine) *see* Wakefield St Andr and St Mary and Belle Vue *Leeds*

SANDAL MAGNA (St Helen) *Leeds 19*   **P** *Peache Trustees*   **V** R G MARTIN

SANDBACH (St Mary) *Ches 11*   **P** *DBP*   **V** *vacant*

SANDBACH HEATH (St John the Evangelist) w Wheelock *Ches 11*   **P** *V Sandbach*   **C** P J LLOYD   **Hon C** B J SWORD

SANDBANKS (St Nicolas) *see* Canford Cliffs and Sandbanks *Sarum*

SANDCROFT (St Cross) *see* The Saints *St E*

SANDCROFT (St George) *as above*

SANDERSTEAD (All Saints) (St Antony) (St Edmund the King and Martyr) *S'wark 22*   **P** *Bp*   **P-in-c** M R GREENFIELD   **TV** S F ATKINSON-JONES   **NSM** J C GROOMBRIDGE

SANDERSTEAD (St Mary) *S'wark 22*   **P** *Bp*   **V** G G COHEN   **Hon C** R J WHITELEY

SANDFORD (All Saints) *see* Winscombe and Sandford *B & W*

SANDFORD (St Martin) *see* Wareham *Sarum*

SANDFORD (St Swithin) *see* Crediton, Shobrooke and Sandford etc *Ex*

SANDFORD ORCAS (St Nicholas) *see* Queen Thorne *Sarum*

SANDFORD ST MARTIN (St Martin) *see* Westcote Barton w Steeple Barton, Duns Tew etc *Ox*

SANDFORD-ON-THAMES (St Andrew) *Ox 1*   **P** *DBP*   **P-in-c** R C MORGAN

SANDGATE (St Paul) *see* Folkestone Trin *Cant*

SANDHURST (Mission Church) *see* Benenden and Sandhurst *Cant*

SANDHURST (St Lawrence) *see* Twigworth, Down Hatherley, Norton, The Leigh etc *Glouc*

SANDHURST (St Michael and All Angels) *Ox 8*   **P** *Bp*   **R** J A CASTLE

SANDHURST (St Nicholas) *see* Benenden and Sandhurst *Cant*

SANDHURST, LOWER (St Mary) *see* Sandhurst *Ox*

SANDHUTTON (St Leonard) *see* Thirsk *York*

SANDIACRE (St Giles) *Derby 8*   **P** *Ld Chan*   **R** O TRELENBERG   **NSM** K W G JOHNSON

SANDIWAY (St John the Evangelist) *Ches 6*   **P** *Bp*   **V** *vacant*

SANDLEHEATH (St Aldhelm) *see* Fordingbridge and Hyde and Breamore etc *Win*

SANDON (All Saints) *see* Clothall, Rushden, Sandon, Wallington and Weston *St Alb*

SANDON (All Saints) *see* Mid Trent *Lich*

SANDON (St Andrew) *Chelmsf 10*   **P** *Qu Coll Cam*   **R** T G A BROWN

SANDOWN (Christ Church) *Portsm 7*   **P** *Ch Patr Trust*   **P-in-c** M A WILLIAMS   **NSM** T B RICHARDS

SANDOWN, LOWER (St John the Evangelist) *Portsm 7*   **P** *Bp*   **P-in-c** J HALL   **NSM** T B RICHARDS

SANDRIDGE (St Leonard) *St Alb 7*   **P** *Earl Spencer*   **V** *vacant*

SANDRINGHAM (St Mary Magdalene) w West Newton and Appleton, Wolferton w Babingley and Flitcham *Nor 15*   **P** *The Crown*   **R** J B V RIVIERE   **NSM** P A GISMONDI

SANDS (Church of the Good Shepherd) *see* Seale, Puttenham and Wanborough *Guildf*

SANDS (St Mary and St George) *see* High Wycombe *Ox*

SANDSEND (St Mary) *see* Hinderwell, Roxby and Staithes etc *York*

SANDWELL (St Philip) *see* W Bromwich St Phil *Lich*

SANDWICH (St Clement) and Worth *Cant 9*   **P** *Abp and Adn Cant (jt)*   **R** J M A ROBERTS   **NSM** R A BENDALL

SANDY (St Swithun) *St Alb 10*   **P** *Lord Pym*   **R** P H DAVIES

SANDY LANE (St Mary and St Nicholas) *see* Rowde and Bromham *Sarum*

SANDYLANDS (St John) *Blackb 11*   **P** *Bp*   **V** L MACLUSKIE

SANKEY, GREAT (St Mary) *see* Warrington W *Liv*

SANTON DOWNHAM (St Mary the Virgin) *see* Lakenheath, Santon Downham and Elveden *St E*

SAPCOTE (All Saints) and Sharnford w Wigston Parva *Leic 10*   **P** *Ld Chan and DBP (alt)*   **R** M J NORMAN

SAPEY, UPPER (St Michael) *see* Edvin Loach w Tedstone Delamere etc *Heref*

SAPPERTON (St Kenelm) *see* Kemble, Poole Keynes, Somerford Keynes etc *Glouc*

SAPPERTON (St Nicholas) *see* N Beltisloe Gp *Linc*

SARISBURY (St Paul) *Portsm 2*   **P** *V Titchfield*   **V** A J MATHESON

SARK (St Peter) *Win 14* **P** *Le Seigneur de Sercq*
P-in-c T R BARKER
SARN (Holy Trinity) *see* Churchstoke w Hyssington and Sarn
Heref
SARNESFIELD (St Mary) *see* Weobley w Sarnesfield and
Norton Canon *Heref*
SARRATT (Holy Cross) and Chipperfield *St Alb 4*
P *Churchwardens and DBP (jt)* **R** M M DU SAIRE
SATLEY (St Cuthbert), Stanley and Tow Law *Dur 8* **P** *Bp, Ld*
Chan, and R Brancepeth (by turn) **P-in-c** J P L WHALLEY
SATTERTHWAITE (All Saints) *see* Hawkshead and Low Wray
w Sawrey and Rusland etc *Carl*
SAUGHALL, GREAT (All Saints) *Ches 9* **P** *Bp*
P-in-c S M MANSFIELD **NSM** H M PANG
SAUL (St James the Great) *see* Stroudwater Team *Glouc*
SAUNDERTON (St Mary and St Nicholas) *see* Risborough *Ox*
SAUNTON (St Anne) *see* Braunton *Ex*
SAUSTHORPE (St Andrew) *see* Bolingbroke Deanery *Linc*
SAVERNAKE FOREST (St Katharine) *see* Savernake *Sarum*
SAVERNAKE, comprising Burbage, Chute w Chute Forest,
Collingbourne Ducis and Everleigh, Collingbourne
Kingston, East Grafton, Great Bedwyn, Ham, Little Bedwyn,
Savernake Forest, Shalbourne, and Tidcombe and Fosbury
Sarum 19 **P** *Patr Bd* **TR** M T MCHUGH **TV** J REID
NSM R A GRIST
SAW MILLS (St Mary) *see* Ambergate and Heage *Derby*
SAWBRIDGEWORTH (Great St Mary) *St Alb 15* **P** *Bp*
NSM D HORE
SAWLEY (All Saints) (St Mary) *Derby 8* **P** *D&C Lich*
R A J STREET **C** E JONES
SAWLEY (St Michael) *see* Fountains Gp *Leeds*
SAWREY (St Peter) *see* Hawkshead and Low Wray w Sawrey
and Rusland etc *Carl*
SAWSTON (St Mary) *Ely 5* **P** *SMF* **V** A C PARTRIDGE
SAWTRY (All Saints) and Glatton *Ely 15* **P** *Duke of*
Devonshire **R** *vacant*
SAXBY (St Helen) *see* Owmby Gp *Linc*
SAXBY ALL SAINTS (All Saints) *Linc 8* **P** F C H H Barton Esq
R D P ROWETT **NSM** R M JAGGS-FOWLER
SAXELBYE (St Peter) *see* Old Dalby, Nether Broughton,
Saxelbye etc *Leic*
SAXHAM, GREAT (St Andrew) *see* Barrow *St E*
SAXHAM, LITTLE (St Nicholas) *as above*
SAXILBY Group, The (St Botolph), including Kettlethorpe
and Newton-on-Trent *Linc 2* **P** *Bp and DBP (jt)*
P-in-c N A PENN-ALLISON **OLM** G STEVENS, J A VICKERS
SAXLINGHAM (St Margaret) *see* Stiffkey and Bale *Nor*
SAXLINGHAM NETHERGATE (St Mary) *see* Newton Flotman,
Swainsthorpe, Tasburgh, etc *Nor*
SAXMUNDHAM (St John the Baptist) w Kelsale cum
Carlton *St E 16* **P** *Patr Bd* **R** A J WOLTON
NSM N J STUCHFIELD
SAXON SHORE *see* Hunstanton St Mary w Ringstead Parva
etc *Nor*
SAXON SHORELINE, The, comprising Aldington, Bilsington,
Bonnington, Kenardington, Orlestone w Snave, Ruckinge,
and Warehorne *Cant 10* **P** *Abp and Ld Chan (alt)* **R** *vacant*
SAXONWELL, comprising Foston, Long Bennington,
Sedgebrook, and West Allington *Linc 22* **P** *Duchy of Lanc*
(2 turns), Ld Chan (1 turn) **P-in-c** H G ORRIDGE
SAXTEAD (All Saints) *see* Framlingham w Saxtead *St E*
SAXTHORPE (St Andrew) *see* Matlaske *Nor*
SAXTON (All Saints) *see* Sherburn in Elmet w Saxton *York*
SAYERS COMMON (Christ Church) *see* Albourne w Sayers
Common and Twineham *Chich*
SCACKLETON (St George the Martyr) *see* The Street Par *York*
SCALBY (St Laurence) *York 15* **P** *Abp* **V** L M HELLMUTH
SCALDWELL (St Peter and St Paul) *see* Walgrave w
Hannington and Wold and Scaldwell *Pet*
SCALEBY (All Saints) *see* Eden, Gelt and Irthing *Carl*
SCALFORD (St Egelwin) *see* Ironstone Villages *Leic*
SCAMBLESBY (St Martin) *see* Asterby Gp *Linc*
SCAMMONDEN, WEST (St Bartholomew) *see* Barkisland w
W Scammonden *Leeds*
SCAMPSTON (St Martin) *see* Buckrose Carrs *York*
SCAMPTON (St John the Baptist) *see* Spring Line Gp *Linc*
SCARBOROUGH (St Columba) *York 15* **P** *Abp*
P-in-c D J BELL
SCARBOROUGH (St James w Holy Trinity) *York 15* **P** *Abp*
and CPAS (jt) **P-in-c** D J BELL
SCARBOROUGH (St Luke) *York 15* **P** *Abp* **V** L M HELLMUTH
SCARBOROUGH (St Martin) *York 15* **P** *Trustees*
V D M DIXON
SCARBOROUGH (St Mary) w Christ Church and (Holy
Apostles) *York 15* **P** *Abp* **V** R J WALKER
NSM A M INGHAM, J C WELLS

SCARBOROUGH (St Saviour w All Saints) *York 15* **P** *Abp*
V D M DIXON
SCARCLIFFE (St Leonard) *see* Ault Hucknall and Scarcliffe
Derby
SCARISBRICK (St Mark) (Good Shepherd) *Liv 14*
P *V Ormskirk* **V** E HEANEY
SCARLE, NORTH (All Saints) *see* Swinderby *Linc*
SCARLE, SOUTH (St Helena) *see* E Trent *S'well*
SCARNING (St Peter and St Paul) *see* Dereham and Distr *Nor*
SCARRINGTON (St John of Beverley) *see* Whatton w
Aslockton, Hawksworth, Scarrington etc *S'well*
SCARSDALE, EAST, comprising Pleasley, Shirebrook, Upper
Langwith, and Whaley Thorns *Derby 2* **P** *Patr Bd*
TR J E DRAYCOTT **TV** K T BRADLEY **C** J C HANCOCK
OLM J A PALMER
SCARTHO (St Giles) St Matthew *Linc 3* **P** *Jes Coll Ox*
R S F CLEATON
SCAWBY (St Hybald), Redbourne and Hibaldstow *Linc 8*
P *T M S Nelthorpe Esq (2 turns), Bp (1 turn), and Duke of St Alb*
(1 turn) **P-in-c** D J EAMES
SCAWTHORPE (St Luke) *see* Doncaster St Leon and St Jude
Sheff
SCAWTON (St Mary) *see* Upper Ryedale *York*
SCAYNES HILL (St Augustine) *Chich 5* **P** *Bp* **V** L H BARNETT
NSM L J HOLLINGSWORTH
SCHOLES (St Philip and St James) *see* Hartshead, Hightown,
Roberttown and Scholes *Leeds*
SCHOLES (St Philip) *see* Elmete Trin *Leeds*
SCHORNE, comprising Dunton, Granborough, Hardwick,
Hoggeston, North Marston, Oving w Pitchcott, Quainton,
Waddesdon, Westcott, Over Winchendon and Fleet
Marston, and Whitchurch w Creslow *Ox 13* **P** *Patr Bd (2*
turns), Ld Chan (1 turn) **TR** D J MEAKIN **TV** P ELSMORE,
V M CRUDDAS **C** J M DOVE **NSM** S T FLASHMAN
SCISSETT (St Augustine) *see* High Hoyland, Scissett and
Clayton W *Leeds*
SCOFTON (St John the Evangelist) *see* Retford Area *S'well*
SCOLE (St Andrew) *see* Redenhall w Scole *Nor*
SCOPWICK (Holy Cross) *see* Digby Gp *Linc*
SCORBOROUGH (St Leonard) *see* Lockington and Lund and
Scorborough w Leconfield *York*
SCORTON (St Peter) and Barnacre All Saints and Calder
Vale St John the Evangelist *Blackb 9* **P** *Bp, V Lanc St Mary*
w St Jo and St Anne, and Mrs V O Shepherd-Cross (jt)
V A M MÜLLER
SCOTBY (All Saints) and Cotehill w Cumwhinton *Carl 2*
P *Trustees (2 turns), The Crown (1 turn)* **V** I S LAWRENCE
SCOTFORTH (St Paul) *Blackb 11* **P** *The Rt Revd J Nicholls*
V R B AECHTNER
SCOTHERN (St Germain) *see* Welton and Dunholme w
Scothern *Linc*
SCOTSWOOD (St Margaret) *see* Benwell and Scotswood
Newc
SCOTT WILLOUGHBY (St Andrew) *see* S Lafford *Linc*
SCOTTER (St Peter) *see* Messingham w E Butterwick, Scotter
w E Ferry and Scotton w Northorpe *Linc*
SCOTTON (St Genewys) *as above*
SCOTTON (St Thomas) *see* Walkingham Hill *Leeds*
SCOTTOW (All Saints) *Nor 18* **P** *Bp* **V** *vacant*
SCOULTON (Holy Trinity) *see* High Oak, Hingham and
Scoulton w Wood Rising *Nor*
SCRAPTOFT (All Saints) *Leic 1* **P** *Bp, Dr M J A Sharp, and*
DBP (jt) **V** M J COURT
SCRAYINGHAM (St Peter and St Paul) *see* Stamford Bridge
Gp *York*
SCREDINGTON (St Andrew) *see* Heckington and
Helpringham Gp *Linc*
SCREMBY (St Peter and St Paul) *see* Bolingbroke Deanery
Linc
SCREMERSTON (St Peter) *Newc 12* **P** *Bp*
Hon C D MACNAUGHTON
SCREVETON (St Wilfrid) *see* Car Colston w Screveton *S'well*
SCRIVELSBY (St Benedict) *see* Fen and Hill Gp *Linc*
SCROOBY (St Wilfrid) *see* Blyth and Scrooby w Ranskill
S'well
SCROPTON (St Paul) *see* S Dales *Derby*
SCRUTON (St Radegund) *see* Lower Swale *Leeds*
SCULCOATES (St Mary) *see* Hull St Mary Sculcoates *York*
SCULCOATES (St Paul) (St Stephen) *York 14* **P** *Abp and*
V Hull H Trin (1 turn), Ld Chan (1 turn) **V** P LAMB
SCULTHORPE (St Mary and All Saints) *see* N and S Creake w
Waterden, Syderstone etc *Nor*
SCUNTHORPE (All Saints) *see* Brumby *Linc*
SCUNTHORPE (The Resurrection) *see* Trentside E *Linc*
SEA MILLS (St Edyth) *Bris 2* **P** *Bp* **V** J E MONAGHAN

SEA PALLING (St Margaret)   *see* Bacton, Happisburgh, Hempstead w Eccles etc *Nor*

SEABOROUGH (St John)   *see* Beaminster Area *Sarum*

SEABROOK (Mission Hall)   *see* Cheriton w Newington *Cant*

SEACOMBE (St Paul) w Poulton *Ches 7*   **P** *Bp and trustees (jt)*   **V** P T COOPER   **C** E WHITE

SEACROFT (St James) (Church of the Ascension) (St Richard) (St Luke) (St Paul) *Leeds 16*   **P** *DBF*   **TR** M P BENWELL   **TV** D J MUGHAL

SEAFORD (St Leonard) w Sutton *Chich 21*   **P** *Ld Chan*   **V** P J OWEN   **C** A J LEE-PHILPOT

SEAGRAVE (All Saints)   *see* Sileby, Cossington and Seagrave *Leic*

SEAGRY (St Mary the Virgin)   *see* Draycot *Bris*

SEAHAM (St Mary the Virgin) and Dawdon *Dur 2*   **P** *Bp*   **V** P J A KENNEDY   **C** A M MAWHINNEY

SEAHAM HARBOUR (St John)   *see* Seaham and Dawdon *Dur*

SEAHAM, NEW (Christ Church)   *see* Dalton le Dale and New Seaham *Dur*

SEAL (St Peter and St Paul) *Roch 9*   **P** *DBP*   **V** J A LE BAS

SEAL CHART (St Lawrence) w Underriver *Roch 9*   **P** *Bp*   **V** S L WILLOUGHBY

SEALE (St Lawrence), Puttenham and Wanborough *Guildf 4*   **P** *Adn Surrey, C R I Perkins Esq, and Ld Chan (by turn)*   **R** S B THATCHER   **C** P E ROCHE

SEALE (St Peter) (St Matthew) and Lullington w Coton in the Elms *Derby 7*   **P** *Bp, R D Nielson Esq, and C W Worthington Esq (jt)*   **P-in-c** C D JEFFERSON   **OLM** C A BUCKLEY

SEAMER (St Martin), East Ayton and Cayton *York 15*   **P** *Abp*   **V** A J MORELAND   **NSM** J A DEAN

SEAMER IN CLEVELAND (St Martin)   *see* Stokesley w Seamer *York*

SEARBY (St Nicholas)   *see* Caistor *Linc*

SEASALTER (St Alphege)   *see* Whitstable *Cant*

SEASCALE (St Cuthbert)   *see* Seatallan *Carl*

SEATALLAN, comprising Beckermet St John, Beckermet w Ponsonby, Gosforth and Wasdale, and Seascale *Carl 5*   **P** *Bp, Adn W Cumberland, the Hon J N Lowther, P Stanley Esq, V St Bees, and DBP (jt)*   **R** J G RILEY

SEATHWAITE (Holy Trinity)   *see* Broughton and Duddon *Carl*

SEATON (All Hallows)   *see* Lyddington, Bisbrooke, Caldecott, Glaston etc *Pet*

SEATON (St Gregory) and Beer *Ex 4*   **P** *Lord Clinton and D&C (jt)*   **V** J C TREW   **NSM** S J HITCHCOCK

SEATON (St Paul)   *see* Camerton, Seaton and W Seaton *Carl*

SEATON CAREW (Holy Trinity) *Dur 3*   **P** *Bp*   **P-in-c** P M BULLOCK

SEATON HIRST (St John) (St Andrew) *Newc 11*   **P** *Bp*   **P-in-c** D J B TWOMEY   **C** J R SWINHOE

SEATON ROSS (St Edmund)   *see* Holme and Seaton Ross Gp *York*

SEATON SLUICE (St Paul)   *see* Delaval *Newc*

SEATON, WEST (Holy Trinity)   *see* Camerton, Seaton and W Seaton *Carl*

SEAVIEW (St Peter), St Helens, Brading and Yaverland *Portsm 7*   **P** *Bp and Trin Coll Cam (jt)*   **R** A R MORLEY

SEAVINGTON (St Michael and St Mary)   *see* S Petherton w The Seavingtons and The Lambrooks *B & W*

SEBERGHAM (St Mary)   *see* Caldbeck, Castle Sowerby and Sebergham *Carl*

SECKINGTON (All Saints)   *see* All So N Warks *Birm*

SEDBERGH (St Andrew), Cautley and Garsdale *Carl 10*   **P** *Trin Coll Cam*   **V** A B MCMULLON

SEDGEBERROW (St Mary the Virgin)   *see* Bengeworth and Hampton etc *Worc*

SEDGEBROOK (St Lawrence)   *see* Saxonwell *Linc*

SEDGEFIELD (St Edmund)   *see* Upper Skerne *Dur*

SEDGEFORD (St Mary)   *see* Docking, The Birchams, Fring etc *Nor*

SEDGEHILL (St Katherine)   *see* St Bartholomew *Sarum*

SEDGLEY (All Saints)   *see* Gornal and Sedgley *Worc*

SEDGLEY (St Mary the Virgin) *Worc 10*   **P** *Bp and V Sedgley All SS (jt)*   **P-in-c** E J STANFORD   **NSM** T WESTWOOD

SEDLESCOMBE (St John the Baptist) w Whatlington *Chich 12*   **P** *Ld Chan and Bp (alt)*   **P-in-c** K A MEPHAM

SEEND (Holy Cross)   *see* Wellsprings *Sarum*

SEER GREEN (Holy Trinity)   *see* Chalfont St Giles, Seer Green and Jordans *Ox*

SEETHING (St Margaret)   *see* Brooke, Kirstead, Mundham w Seething and Thwaite *Nor*

SEFTON PARK (Christ Church)   *see* Toxteth Park Ch Ch and St Mich w St Andr *Liv*

SEGHILL (Holy Trinity) *Newc 1*   **P** *The Crown*   **V** P G J HUGHES   **C** D M BELL

SEIGHFORD (St Chad)   *see* Chebsey, Creswell, Ellenhall, Ranton etc *Lich*

SELATTYN (St Mary) and Hengoed w Gobowen *Lich 18*   **P** *Bp and Mrs A F Hamilton-Hill (jt)*   **P-in-c** S J NICHOLSON

SELBORNE (St Mary)   *see* Northanger *Win*

SELBY (St James the Apostle) *York 4*   **P** *Simeon's Trustees*   **V** C J REID   **Hon C** D M REID

SELBY ABBEY (St Mary and St Germain) (St Richard) *York 4*   **P** *Abp*   **V** J C WEETMAN   **C** J J BELDER   **NSM** J S WATSON, N B WOODHALL

SELHAM (St James)   *see* Easebourne, Lodsworth and Selham *Chich*

SELLACK (St Tysilio)   *see* StowCaple *Heref*

SELLINDGE (St Mary the Virgin)   *see* Stour Downs *Cant*

SELLING (St Mary the Virgin)   *see* Shepherds Lees *Cant*

SELLY OAK (St Mary) *Birm 1*   **P** *Bp*   **NSM** D J PARKER, J M ADAMS

SELLY PARK (Christ Church) *Birm 4*   **P** *Trustees*   **V** *vacant*

SELLY PARK (St Stephen) (St Wulstan) *Birm 4*   **P** *Trustees*   **V** C B HOBBS   **C** A P MARTIN, B T WELLS

SELMESTON (St Mary)   *see* Arlington, Berwick, Selmeston w Alciston etc *Chich*

SELSDON (St Francis) Conventional District *S'wark 19*   **Min** P C WYATT

SELSDON (St John) (St Francis) *S'wark 19*   **P** *Bp*   **R** J J E ROWLEY

SELSEY (St Peter) *Chich 2*   **P** *Bp*   **R** A E WILKES

SELSIDE (St Thomas)   *see* Beacon *Carl*

SELSLEY (All Saints)   *see* Stroudwater Team *Glouc*

SELSTON (St Helen) *S'well 4*   **P** *Wright Trustees*   **V** M F SHOULER   **NSM** A DEMPSTER

SELWORTHY (All Saints)   *see* Porlock and Porlock Weir w Stoke Pero etc *B & W*

SELWORTHY (Lynch Chapel) *as above*

SEMER (All Saints)   *see* Bildeston w Wattisham and Lindsey, Whatfield etc *St E*

SEMINGTON (St George)   *see* Canalside Benefice *Sarum*

SEMLEY (St Leonard)   *see* St Bartholomew *Sarum*

SEMPRINGHAM (St Andrew)   *see* Billingborough Gp *Linc*

SEND (St Mary the Virgin) *Guildf 12*   **P** *Bp*   **P-in-c** A J SHUTT

SENNEN (St Sennen)   *see* St Buryan, St Levan and Sennen *Truro*

SENNICOTTS (St Mary)   *see* Funtington and W Stoke w Sennicotts *Chich*

SESSAY (St Cuthbert) *York 18*   **P** *Viscountess Downe*   **NSM** P PERCY

SETCHEY (St Mary)   *see* Middlewinch *Nor*

SETMURTHY (St Barnabas)   *see* Binsey *Carl*

SETTLE (Holy Ascension) *Leeds 20*   **P** *Trustees*   **C** S C DAWSON

SETTRINGTON (All Saints)   *see* W Buckrose *York*

SEVEN SAINTS   *see* New Bury w Gt Lever *Man*

SEVEN SOWERS   *see* Beercrocombe w Curry Mallet, Hatch Beauchamp etc *B & W*

SEVEN TOWERS   *see* Twigworth, Down Hatherley, Norton, The Leigh etc *Glouc*

SEVENHAMPTON (St Andrew) w Charlton Abbots, Hawling and Whittington, Dowdeswell and Andoversford w The Shiptons and Cold Salperton, and Withington *Glouc 8*   **P** *Bp, MMCET, T W Bailey Esq, E M Bailey Esq, and Mrs J A Stringer (1 turn); Bp, MMCET, and Mrs L E Evans (1 turn)*   **R** C A RANDALL

SEVENHAMPTON (St James)   *see* Highworth w Sevenhampton and Inglesham etc *Bris*

SEVENOAKS (St John the Baptist) *Roch 9*   **P** *Guild of All So*   **V** R D E JONES

SEVENOAKS (St Luke) *Roch 9*   **P** *Bp*   **C** A C BOURNE

SEVENOAKS (St Nicholas) *Roch 9*   **P** *Trustees*   **R** A M MACLEAY   **C** G J MCGRATH, M A TAYLOR, T J NASH   **Hon C** N N HENSHAW

SEVENOAKS WEALD (St George) *Roch 9*   **P** *R Sevenoaks*   **V** A H CARR

SEVERN STOKE (St Dennis)   *see* Kempsey and Severn Stoke w Croome d'Abitot *Worc*

SEVINGTON (St Mary)   *see* Ashford Town *Cant*

SEWARDS END (St James)   *see* Saffron Walden and Villages *Chelmsf*

SEWERBY (St John)   *see* Bridlington H Trin and Sewerby w Marton *York*

SEWSTERN (Holy Trinity)   *see* S Framland *Leic*

SHABBINGTON (St Mary Magdalene)   *see* Worminghall w Ickford, Oakley and Shabbington *Ox*

SHACKERSTONE (St Peter)   *see* Nailstone and Carlton w Shackerstone *Leic*

SHACKLEFORD (St Mary the Virgin)   *see* Compton w Shackleford and Peper Harow *Guildf*

SHADFORTH (St Cuthbert) and Sherburn *Dur 1* **P** *D&C*
P-in-c T E GLOVER **NSM** R S BRIGGS
SHADINGFIELD (St John the Baptist) *see* Hundred River and Wainford *St E*
SHADOXHURST (St Peter and St Paul) *see* Ashford Town *Cant*
SHADWELL (St Paul) *see* Moor Allerton and Shadwell *Leeds*
SHADWELL (St Paul) w Ratcliffe St James *Lon 7* **P** *Bp*
R P R WILLIAMS **C** C I ROGERS
SHAFTESBURY (St James) (St Peter) *Sarum 5* **P** *Patr Bd*
TR H E DAWES **TV** K A CLARKE, P R RINK
SHALBOURNE (St Michael and All Angels) *see* Savernake *Sarum*
SHALDEN (St Peter and St Paul) *see* Bentworth, Lasham, Medstead and Shalden *Win*
SHALDON (St Nicholas) (St Peter), Stokeinteignhead, Combeinteignhead and Haccombe *Ex 9* **P** *SMF and Col G P Arnold (jt)* **R** A M CHURCH
SHALFLEET (St Michael the Archangel) *see* W Wight *Portsm*
SHALFORD (St Andrew) *see* Finchingfield and Cornish Hall End etc *Chelmsf*
SHALFORD (St Mary the Virgin) *Guildf 5* **P** *Ld Chan*
V S J LLOYD
SHALSTONE (St Edward the Confessor) *see* W Buckingham *Ox*
SHAMLEY GREEN (Christ Church) *Guildf 2* **P** *Bp*
V S J DAVIES
SHANGTON (St Nicholas) *see* The Langtons and Shangton *Leic*
SHANKLIN (St Blasius) *Portsm 7* **P** *Bp* **P-in-c** J HALL
SHANKLIN (St Paul) *see* Gatten St Paul *Portsm*
SHANKLIN (St Saviour on the Cliff) *Portsm 7* **P** *Bp*
P-in-c D L LAWRENCE-MARCH **NSM** C A SMITH
SHAP (St Michael) *see* High Westmorland *Carl*
SHAPWICK (St Bartholomew) *see* Bridge Par *Sarum*
SHAPWICK (The Blessed Virgin Mary) *see* Polden Wheel *B & W*
SHARD END (All Saints) *Birm 8* **P** *Keble Coll Ox*
V A J CLUCAS
SHARDLOW (St James) *see* Aston on Trent, Elvaston, Weston on Trent etc *Derby*
SHARESHILL (St Luke and St Mary the Virgin) *see* Essington, Featherstone and Shareshill *Lich*
SHARLSTON (St Luke) *Leeds 19* **P** *Bp* **V** D C TEASDEL
SHARNBROOK (St Peter), Felmersham and Knotting w Souldrop *St Alb 13* **P** *Bp* **R** *vacant*
SHARNFORD (St Helen) *see* Sapcote and Sharnford w Wigston Parva *Leic*
SHARPNESS (St Andrew), Purton, Brookend and Slimbridge *Glouc 5* **P** *Magd Coll Ox and Bp (alt)*
R W J BOON **NSM** G M TUCKER
SHARRINGTON (All Saints) *see* Stiffkey and Bale *Nor*
SHAUGH PRIOR (St Edward) *see* Bickleigh and Shaugh Prior *Ex*
SHAVINGTON (St Mark) *see* Weston *Ches*
SHAW (Christchurch) *see* Atworth w Shaw and Whitley *Sarum*
SHAW (Holy Trinity) *Man 15* **P** *R Prestwich St Mary*
V K H CUNLIFFE
SHAW (Holy Trinity) *see* W Swindon and Lydiard Tregoze *Bris*
SHAW (St Mary) cum Donnington *Ox 6* **P** *DBP*
R M WOOD
SHAWBURY (St Mary the Virgin) *Lich 21* **P** *C C Corbet Esq*
V R J CRESSWELL
SHAWELL (All Saints) *see* Avon-Swift *Leic*
SHEARSBY (St Mary Magdalene) *see* Hexagon *Leic*
SHEBBEAR (St Michael), Buckland Filleigh, Sheepwash, Langtree, Newton St Petrock, Petrockstowe, Petersmarland, Merton and Huish *Ex 19* **P** *Ld Chan (1 turn), Patr Bd (2 turns)* **TR** M J WARREN **TV** S METZ
SHEDFIELD (St John the Baptist) and Wickham *Portsm 1* **P** *DBP and Sir Richard Rashleigh Bt (jt)* **R** P J ISAAC
C R M HOWLETT-SHIPLEY **Hon C** J MONTAGUE
NSM B R MCHUGH
SHEEN (St Luke) *see* Longnor, Quarnford, Sheen etc *Lich*
SHEEN, EAST (All Saints) *see* Mortlake w E Sheen *S'wark*
SHEEN, EAST (Christ Church) *as above*
SHEEPSTOR (St Leonard) *see* Yelverton, Meavy, Sheepstor, Walkhampton, Sampford Spiney and Horrabridge *Ex*
SHEEPWASH (St Lawrence) *see* Shebbear, Buckland Filleigh, Sheepwash etc *Ex*
SHEEPY (All Saints) *see* Bosworth and Sheepy Gp *Leic*
SHEERING (St Mary the Virgin) *see* Hatfield Heath and Sheering *Chelmsf*
SHEERNESS (Holy Trinity w St Paul) *see* W Sheppey *Cant*

SHEERWATER (St Michael and All Angels) *see* Woodham *Guildf*
SHEET (St Mary Magdalene) *Portsm 4* **P** *Bp*
V R G SAUNDERS **NSM** A J MARSH, P W MICKLETHWAITE
SHEFFIELD (St Aidan w St Luke) *see* Sheff Manor *Sheff*
SHEFFIELD (St Andrew) *see* Psalter Lane St Andr *Sheff*
SHEFFIELD (St Bartholomew) *see* Sheffield Vine *Sheff*
SHEFFIELD (St Catherine of Siena) Richmond Road *Sheff 1*
P *The Crown* **V** P A KNOWLES
SHEFFIELD (St Cuthbert) *Sheff 3* **P** *Ch Burgesses*
P-in-c M R SUTTON **C** P J SALMON
SHEFFIELD (St John the Evangelist) *Sheff 1* **P** *Ch Burgesses*
V *vacant*
SHEFFIELD (St Leonard) Norwood *Sheff 3* **P** *Bp*
P-in-c K RYDER-WEST **C** A T POULTNEY **NSM** J H DALEY
SHEFFIELD (St Mark) Broomhill *Sheff 4* **P** *Ch Burgesses*
V S HAMMERSLEY **C** C E THOMSON, S M COLVER
NSM S E RUSH
SHEFFIELD (St Mary) Bramall Lane *Sheff 2* **P** *Ch Burgesses and Dean (alt)* **V** C L DAWSON **NSM** G C D DUNCAN, K E CRIBB, L M N HALL
SHEFFIELD (St Matthew) Carver Street *Sheff 2* **P** *Bp and Sheff Ch Burgess Trust (jt)* **V** G L NAYLOR **Hon C** A WATSON
SHEFFIELD (St Oswald) St Peter *Sheff 2* **P** *Ch Burgesses*
V A NASCIMENTO COOK
SHEFFIELD (St Paul) Wordsworth Avenue *Sheff 3* **P** *DBP*
P-in-c A T POULTNEY
SHEFFIELD MANOR (St Swithun) *Sheff 1* **P** *Patr Bd*
TR J UPTON **NSM** K COLLEY, S BATTEN
SHEFFIELD PARK (St John the Evangelist) *see* Sheff St Jo *Sheff*
SHEFFIELD St Cecilia Parson Cross *Sheff 3* **P** *Bp*
V K RYDER-WEST **C** A T POULTNEY
SHEFFIELD The Vine, comprising Netherthorpe and Langsett *Sheff 4* **P** *Ch Burgesses and Ch Patr Trust (jt)* **V** W J BRIGGS
SHEFFORD (St Michael) *see* Meppershall and Shefford *St Alb*
SHEFFORD, GREAT (St Mary) *see* W Downland *Ox*
SHEINTON (St Peter and St Paul) *see* Wenlock *Heref*
SHELDON (St Giles) and Tile Cross *Birm 8* **P** *Bp and K E Wingfield Digby Esq (jt)* **V** A E LAVIN **C** M J HARRIS
SHELDON (St James the Greater) *see* Broadhembury, Dunkeswell, Luppitt, Plymtree, Sheldon, and Upottery *Ex*
SHELDON (St John) *see* Shirley St Jo *S'wark*
SHELDON (St Michael and All Angels) *see* Bakewell, Ashford w Sheldon and Rowsley *Derby*
SHELDWICH (St James) *see* Shepherds Lees *Cant*
SHELF (St Michael and All Saints) w Buttershaw St Aidan *Leeds 3* **P** *Bp* **TV** A J GREIFF **C** J L TRENHOLME
SHELFANGER (All Saints) *see* Winfarthing w Shelfanger w Burston w Gissing etc *Nor*
SHELFIELD (St Mark) and High Heath *Lich 24* **P** *R Walsall*
NSM A J MCCOSH
SHELFORD (St Peter and St Paul) *see* Radcliffe-on-Trent and Shelford *S'well*
SHELFORD, GREAT (St Mary) *Ely 5* **P** *Bp* **P-in-c** S J TALBOTT
SHELFORD, LITTLE (All Saints) *Ely 5* **P** *Bp* **R** S J SCOTT
SHELLAND (King Charles the Martyr) *see* Combs and Finborough *St E*
SHELLEY (All Saints) *see* Hadleigh, Layham and Shelley *St E*
SHELLEY (Emmanuel) *see* Kirkburton and Shelley *Leeds*
SHELLEY (St Peter) *see* Chipping Ongar w Shelley etc *Chelmsf*
SHELLINGFORD (St Faith) *see* Uffington, Shellingford, Woolstone and Baulking *Ox*
SHELROCK *see* Gt and Lt Ellingham, Rockland and Shropham etc *Nor*
SHELSLEY BEAUCHAMP (All Saints) *see* Worcs W Rural *Worc*
SHELSLEY WALSH (St Andrew) *as above*
SHELSWELL, comprising Cottisford and Hardwick-cum-Tusmore, Finmere, Fringford, Hethe, Mixbury, Newton Purcell w Shelswell, Stoke Lyne, and Stratton Audley and Godington *Ox 21* **P** *Ld Chan (1 turn) and Ch Ch Ox, CCC Ox, Baroness von Maltzahn, and R J Vallings Esq (1 turn)* **R** A E GOODALL **C** Y B MULLINS
SHELTON (Christ Church) and Oxon *Lich 19*
P *V Shrewsbury St Chad w St Mary* **V** *vacant*
SHELTON (St Mark) *see* Hanley H Ev *Lich*
SHELTON (St Mary and All Saints) *S'well 3* **P** *Bp*
P-in-c E I MURRAY
SHELTON (St Mary) *see* Hempnall *Nor*
SHELTON (St Mary) *see* The Stodden Churches *St Alb*
SHELVE (All Saints) *see* Minsterley, Habberley and Hope w Shelve *Heref*
SHENFIELD (St Mary the Virgin) *Chelmsf 8* **P** *Personal Reps R H Courage* **P-in-c** C J MANN
SHENINGTON (Holy Trinity) *see* Ironstone *Ox*
SHENLEY (St Mary) *see* Watling Valley *Ox*

SHENLEY GREEN (St David) *Birm 3*   **P** *Bp*   **V** M I BENNETT
SHENSTONE (St John the Baptist) and Stonnall *Lich 1*
P *MMCET*   **V** E A CHAMBERLAIN
SHENTON (St John the Evangelist)   *see Bosworth and Sheepy Gp* *Leic*
SHEPHERD'S BUSH (St Luke) Uxbridge Road   *see Hammersmith St Luke Lon*
SHEPHERD'S BUSH (St Stephen) (St Thomas) *Lon 9*   **P** *Bp*
V D ADIDE   **C** P J HOYLE
SHEPHERDS LEES, comprising Badlesmere w Leaveland, Selling, and Sheldwich *Cant 14*   **P** *Abp and D&C (jt)*
P-in-c P J NEWELL
SHEPLEY (St Paul)   *see Cumberworth, Denby, Denby Dale etc Leeds*
SHEPPERDINE (Chapel)   *see Thornbury and Oldbury-on-Severn w Shepperdine Glouc*
SHEPPERTON (St Nicholas) and Littleton *Lon 13*   **P** *Bp and C W L Barratt Esq (jt)*   **R** C J SWIFT   **C** T M ROSE
NSM P BARRIE
SHEPPEY, WEST, comprising Halfway, Minster in Sheppey, Queenborough, and Sheerness *Cant 15*   **P** *Abp and Ch Patr Trust (jt)*   **C** J M MCLAREN, P A RUSH
SHEPRETH (All Saints)   *see Fowlmere, Foxton, Shepreth and Thriplow Ely*
SHEPSHED (St Botolph) and Oaks in Charnwood *Leic 6*
P *DBP and Lord Crawshaw (jt)*   **V** L A HUMPHREYS
NSM J A BIRD
SHEPTON BEAUCHAMP (St Michael)   *see Winsmoor B & W*
SHEPTON MALLET (St Peter and St Paul) w Doulting
B & W 7   **P** *Duchy of Cornwall and Bp (alt)*
R J HUNTER DUNN   **C** R A PRIESTLEY
SHEPTON MONTAGUE (St Peter)   *see Bruton, Brewham, Pitcombe and Shepton Montague B & W*
SHERBORNE (Abbey Church of St Mary) (All Souls) (St Paul) w Castleton, Lillington and Longburton
Sarum 3   **P** *Patr Bd*   **TR** E J WOODS   **TV** J E TREGALE,
J M CRAW, L A MCCREADIE   **C** D R TREGALE, G R   BOKS,
H R L BONSEY, R C J R MARTIN
SHERBORNE (St Mary Magdalene), Windrush, the Barringtons and Aldsworth *Glouc 8*   **P** C T R Wingfield *Esq, Ch Ch Ox, and DBP (by turn)*   **V** vacant
SHERBORNES (St Andrew) (Vyne Chapel) w Pamber, The
Win 4   **P** *Bp and Qu Coll Ox (jt)*   **R** vacant
SHERBOURNE (All Saints)   *see Barford w Wasperton and Sherbourne Cov*
SHERBURN (St Hilda)   *see Buckrose Carrs York*
SHERBURN (St Mary)   *see Shadforth and Sherburn Dur*
SHERBURN IN ELMET (All Saints) w Saxton *York 4*   **P** *Abp*
V C WILTON   **NSM** W L J PLANT
SHERE (St James), Albury and Chilworth *Guildf 2*   **P** *Bp, Mrs H Bray, Duke of Northumberland, W F P Hugonin Esq, and the Hon M W Ridley (jt)*   **R** T D HEANEY   **C** M L CURRIER,
S M SOKOLOWSKI   **NSM** S F HUTTON   **OLM** D I OAKDEN
SHEREFORD (St Nicholas)   *see Upper Wensum Village Gp Nor*
SHERFIELD ENGLISH (St Leonard)   *see E w W Wellow and Sherfield English Win*
SHERFIELD-ON-LODDON (St Leonard) and Stratfield Saye w Hartley Wespall w Stratfield Turgis and Bramley *Win 5*
P *Bp, Duke of Wellington, D&C Windsor, and Qu Coll Ox (jt)*
R S A BALL   **NSM** J R LENTON
SHERFORD (St Martin)   *see Stokenham, Slapton, Charleton w Buckland etc Ex*
SHERIFF HUTTON (St Helen and the Holy Cross)   *see Forest of Galtres York*
SHERIFFHALES (St Mary)   *see Shifnal, Sheriffhales and Tong Lich*
SHERINGHAM (St Peter) *Nor 20*   **P** *Bp*   **V** C J HEYCOCKS
SHERINGHAM, UPPER (All Saints)   *see Weybourne Gp Nor*
SHERINGTON (St Laud) w Chicheley, North Crawley, Astwood and Hardmead *Ox 16*   **P** *Bp (2 turns), MMCET (1 turn), and Major J G B Chester (1 turn)*   **P-in-c** C P MANSFIELD
SHERMANBURY (St Giles)   *see Henfield w Shermanbury and Woodmancote Chich*
SHERNBOURNE (St Peter and St Paul)   *see Dersingham, Anmer, Ingoldisthorpe etc Nor*
SHERRARDS GREEN (St Mary the Virgin)   *see Malvern Chase Worc*
SHERRINGTON (St Cosmo and St Damian)   *see Upper Wylye Valley Sarum*
SHERSTON MAGNA (Holy Cross)   *see Gauzebrook Bris*
SHERWOOD (St Martin) *S'well 8*   **P** *Bp*   **V** B I BAGULEY
C S M PENDENQUE   **NSM** D M BAGULEY, J E WALKER
SHERWOOD PARK (St Philip)   *see Tunbridge Wells St Phil Roch*
SHEVINGTON (St Anne) *Blackb 4*   **P** R Standish   **V** A BROWN
C J BROWN

SHEVIOCK (Blessed Virgin Mary)   *see St Germans w Antony and Sheviock Truro*
SHIELDS, SOUTH (St Simon)   *see Jarrow and Simonside Dur*
SHIFFORD (St Mary)   *see Bampton w Clanfield Ox*
SHIFNAL (St Andrew), Sheriffhales and Tong *Lich 15*
P *R I Legge Esq and Bp (jt)*   **V** C D C THORPE
OLM M W SHAW
SHILBOTTLE (St James) *Newc 6*   **P** *Dioc Soc*
P-in-c H L O'SULLIVAN
SHILDON (St John) *Dur 5*   **P** *Bp*   **C** M J D HUDGHTON
Hon C P ROBSON
SHILL VALLEY and Broadshire, comprising Alvescot, Black Bourton, Broadwell w Kelmscott, Broughton Poggs w Filkins, Holwell, Kencot, Langford, Little Faringdon, Shilton, and Westwell *Ox 28*   **P** *J Heyworth Esq, Mrs P Allen, and Ch Ch Ox (1 turn), Ch Soc Tr, F R Goodenough Esq, and D F Goodenough Esq (1 turn)*   **R** H C MACINNES   **C** M R HODSON
SHILLING OKEFORD (Holy Rood)   *see Okeford Sarum*
SHILLINGFORD (St George)   *see Alphington, Shillingford St George and Ide Ex*
SHILLINGSTONE (Holy Rood)   *see Okeford Sarum*
SHILLINGTON (All Saints)   *see Gravenhurst, Shillington and Stondon St Alb*
SHILTON (Holy Rood)   *see Shill Valley and Broadshire Ox*
SHILTON (St Andrew)   *see Ansty and Shilton Cov*
SHIMPLINGTHORNE (St George)   *see Chadbrook St E*
SHINCLIFFE (St Mary the Virgin)   *see Dur St Oswald and Shincliffe Dur*
SHINEY ROW (St Oswald)   *see Herrington, Penshaw and Shiney Row Dur*
SHINFIELD (St Mary)   *see Loddon Reach Ox*
SHINGAY Group of Parishes, The, comprising Abington Pigotts, Guilden Morden, Litlington, Steeple Morden, Tadlow, and Wendy w Shingay *Ely 7*   **P** *Bp, Mrs E E Sclater, Ch Patr Trust, Down Coll Cam, New Coll Ox, and Jes Coll Cam (jt)*   **R** S F C WILLIAMS   **NSM** A K R BOL
SHIPBOURNE (St Giles) w Plaxtol *Roch 10*   **P** *Bp and F Read Esq (jt)*   **R** P J HAYLER
SHIPDHAM (All Saints)   *see Dereham and Distr Nor*
SHIPHAM (St Leonard)   *see Axbridge w Shipham and Rowberrow B & W*
SHIPHAY COLLATON (St John the Baptist) *Ex 11*   **P** *Bp*
P-in-c P IRETON
SHIPLAKE (St Peter and St Paul) w Dunsden and Harpsden
Ox 24   **P** *All So Coll Ox, D&C Windsor, and DBP (jt)*
R R S THEWSEY   **C** S J NESBITT
SHIPLEY (St Mary the Virgin) *Chich 7*   **P** *Sir Charles Burrell Bt*   **V** vacant
SHIPLEY (St Paul) *Leeds 1*   **P** *Simeon's Trustees*
V H HOWARTH   **NSM** J F BUTLER
SHIPLEY (St Peter) *Leeds 1*   **P** *V Shipley St Paul*   **V** J C RAINER
SHIPPON (St Mary Magdalene)   *see Marcham w Garford and Shippon Ox*
SHIPSTON-ON-STOUR (St Edmund) w Honington and Idlicote *Cov 9*   **P** *Jes Coll Ox, D&C Worc, Bp (jt)*
R S A EDMONDS   **NSM** J TUCKER
SHIPTON (Holy Evangelist)   *see Skelton w Shipton and Newton on Ouse York*
SHIPTON (St James)   *see Wenlock Heref*
SHIPTON BELLINGER (St Peter)   *see Appleshaw, Kimpton, Thruxton, Fyfield etc Win*
SHIPTON GORGE (St Martin)   *see Bride Valley Sarum*
SHIPTON MOYNE (St John the Baptist)   *see Tetbury, Beverston, Long Newnton etc Glouc*
SHIPTON OLIFFE (St Oswald)   *see Sevenhampton w Charlton Abbots, Hawling etc Glouc*
SHIPTON ON CHERWELL (Holy Cross)   *see Yarnton w Begbroke and Shipton-on-Cherwell Ox*
SHIPTONTHORPE (All Saints)   *see Londesborough Wold York*
SHIPTON-UNDER-WYCHWOOD (St Mary)   *see Wychwood Ox*
SHIREBROOK (Holy Trinity)   *see E Scarsdale Derby*
SHIREGREEN (St James and St Christopher) *Sheff 3*   **P** *Bp and Dean (alt)*   **P-in-c** D F DEAN-REVILL
SHIREHAMPTON (St Mary) *Bris 2*   **P** *Bp*
P-in-c H L JOHNSON
SHIREMOOR (St Mark) *Newc 5*   **P** *Bp*   **V** A G CURTIS
SHIREOAKS (St Luke)   *see Worksop Ch Ch and Shireoaks S'well*
SHIRES' EDGE, Claydon, Cropredy, Great Bourton, Mollington, and Wardington *Ox 23*   **P** *Bp*
V H A CAMPBELL
SHIRESHEAD (St James) *Blackb 11*   **P** *V Cockerham w Winmarleigh and Glasson*   **P-in-c** P J BALLARD

SHIRLAND (St Leonard)   *see* Morton and Stonebroom w Shirland *Derby*

SHIRLEY (St George) *S'wark 19*   **P** *Bp*   **V** B HENGIST   Hon **C** H A FIFE   **NSM** A M S DOVEY

SHIRLEY (St James the Great) *Birm 5*   **P** *Patr Bd*   **V** P D LAW-JONES   **C** P G DAY

SHIRLEY (St James) (St John) *Win 13*   **P** *Ch Patr Trust*   **P-in-c** D A CLARK   **NSM** L PHILLIPS

SHIRLEY (St John the Divine)   *see* Shirley *Birm*

SHIRLEY (St John) *S'wark 19*   **P** *Bp*   **V** L C GALE   **NSM** A M S DOVEY

SHIRLEY (St Michael)   *see* Brailsford w Shirley, Osmaston w Edlaston etc *Derby*

SHIRWELL (St Peter), Loxhore, Kentisbury, Arlington, East Down, Bratton Fleming, Challacombe and Stoke Rivers *Ex 17*   **P** *Patr Bd*   **TR** R E AUSTIN   **C** M C TYRRELL

SHOBDON (St John the Evangelist)   *see* Pembridge w Moor Court, Shobdon, Staunton etc *Heref*

SHOBROOKE (St Swithin)   *see* Crediton, Shobrooke and Sandford etc *Ex*

SHOCKLACH (St Edith)   *see* Tilston and Shocklach *Ches*

SHOEBURY, NORTH (St Mary the Virgin) *Chelmsf 15*   **P** *Ld Chan*   **V** *vacant*

SHOEBURY, SOUTH (St Andrew) (St Peter) *Chelmsf 15*   **P** *Hyndman Trustees*   **R** L M WILLIAMS

SHOLDEN (St Nicholas)   *see* Deal St Leon w St Rich and Sholden etc *Cant*

SHOLING (St Francis of Assisi) (St Mary) *Win 13*   **P** *Bp*   **C** H KHATUN, J A OLIVER, N J SMITH

SHOOTERS HILL (All Saints)   *see* Plumstead All SS *S'wark*

SHOOTERS HILL (Christ Church) *S'wark 6*   **P** *Bp*   **V** A R M VAN DEN HOF

SHORE (St Barnabas)   *see* Littleborough *Man*

SHOREDITCH (All Saints) Haggerston Road   *see* Dalston H Trin w St Phil and Haggerston All SS *Lon*

SHOREDITCH (St Anne) Hoxton Street   *see* Hoxton St Anne w St Columba *Lon*

SHOREDITCH (St Leonard) w St Michael *Lon 5*   **P** *Bp and Adn (jt)*   **P-in-c** E ADEKUNLE

SHOREHAM (St Peter and St Paul) *Roch 10*   **P** *D&C Westmr*   **V** D E REES

SHOREHAM, NEW (St Mary de Haura) and Shoreham Beach (Good Shepherd) *Chich 20*   **P** *Bp*   **V** A E WAIZENEKER   **C** J L BARTLETT   **NSM** J-J S AIDLEY

SHOREHAM, OLD (St Nicolas) and Kingston Buci *Chich 20*   **P** *Bp and Lord Egremont (jt)*   **R** J N GRANT   **NSM** B A WILSON

SHORELINE Benefice, The, comprising Chelmondiston, Erwarton, Harkstead, and Shotley *St E 15*   **P** *Ld Chan (1 turn), Bp (3 turns)*   **R** L OOSTERHOF

SHORNE (St Peter and St Paul) *Roch 4*   **P** *D&C*   **V** E HURST

SHORT HEATH (Holy Trinity)   *see* Bentley Em and Willenhall H Trin *Lich*

SHORT HEATH (St Margaret)   *see* Erdington Ch the K *Birm*

SHORTHAMPTON (All Saints)   *see* Charlbury w Shorthampton *Ox*

SHORTLANDS (St Mary) *Roch 13*   **P** *Bp*   **V** G J BEST   **NSM** J E PETERS

SHORWELL (St Peter)   *see* W Wight *Portsm*

SHOSCOMBE (St Julian)   *see* Peasedown St John w Wellow and Foxcote etc *B & W*

SHOTESHAM (All Saints w St Mary)   *see* Newton Flotman, Swainsthorpe, Tasburgh, etc *Nor*

SHOTLEY (St John) *Newc 9*   **P** *Lord Crewe's Trustees*   **P-in-c** G SMITH

SHOTLEY (St Mary)   *see* Shoreline *St E*

SHOTTERMILL (St Stephen) *Guildf 4*   **P** *Adn Surrey*   **V** J J RIDDLESTONE   **NSM** H R MITCHELL

SHOTTERY (St Andrew) *Cov 8*   **P** *Bp*   **V** C R GROOCOCK   **NSM** P EDMONDSON

SHOTTESBROOKE (St John the Baptist)   *see* White Waltham w Shottesbrooke *Ox*

SHOTTESWELL (St Lawrence)   *see* Edgehill Churches *Cov*

SHOTTISHAM (St Margaret)   *see* Wilford Peninsula *St E*

SHOTTLE (St Lawrence)   *see* Hazelwood, Holbrook and Milford *Derby*

SHOTTON (St Saviour)   *see* Haswell and Shotton *Dur*

SHOTWICK (St Michael)   *see* Burton and Shotwick *Ches*

SHOULDHAM (All Saints)   *see* W Norfolk Priory Gp *Ely*

SHOULDHAM THORPE (St Mary) *as above*

SHRAWARDINE (St Mary)   *see* Bicton, Montford w Shrawardine and Fitz *Lich*

SHRAWLEY (St Mary), Witley, Astley and Abberley *Worc 13*   **P** *Bp and Guild of All So (jt)*   **P-in-c** E G WHITTAKER   **C** M TURNER

SHRED (Mission Church)   *see* Marsden and Slaithwaite w E Scammonden *Leeds*

SHREWSBURY (All Saints and St Michael) *Lich 19*   **P** *Bp*   **P-in-c** P LOCKETT

SHREWSBURY (Christ Church)   *see* Shelton and Oxon *Lich*

SHREWSBURY (Holy Cross) (St Peter) *Lich 19*   **P** *Bp*   **V** T D ATFIELD

SHREWSBURY (Holy Trinity) (St Julian) *Lich 19*   **P** *Bp and Ch Patr Trust (jt)*   **P-in-c** C W DEVONISH

SHREWSBURY (St Chad) St Mary (St Alkmund) *Lich 19*   **P** *Bp*   **V** Y S PETERS

SHREWSBURY (St George of Cappadocia) w Greenfields United Church *Lich 19*   **P** *V Shrewsbury St Chad*   **V** T R VASBY-BURNIE   **C** F M H IDDON

SHREWSBURY (St Giles) w Sutton and Atcham *Lich 19*   **P** *Bp and R L Burton Esq (jt)*   **R** A R KNIGHT   **C** S J HOWES

SHREWTON (St Mary)   *see* Salisbury Plain *Sarum*

SHRIVENHAM (St Andrew) and Ashbury *Ox 25*   **P** *Ld Chan*   **V** N FERGUSSON

SHROPHAM (St Peter)   *see* Gt and Lt Ellingham, Rockland and Shropham etc *Nor*

SHROTON (St Mary)   *see* Iwerne Valley *Sarum*

SHRUB END (All Saints) (St Cedd) *Chelmsf 21*   **P** *Bp*   **V** *vacant*

SHUCKBURGH, LOWER (St John the Baptist)   *see* Napton-on-the-Hill, Lower Shuckburgh etc *Cov*

SHUDY CAMPS (St Mary)   *see* Linton *Ely*

SHURDINGTON (St Paul)   *see* Badgeworth, Shurdington and Witcombe w Bentham *Glouc*

SHUSTOKE (St Cuthbert)   *see* The Whitacres, Lea Marston, and Shustoke *Birm*

SHUTE (St Michael)   *see* Kilmington, Stockland, Dalwood, Yarcombe etc *Ex*

SHUTFORD (St Martin)   *see* Wykeham *Ox*

SHUTTINGTON (St Matthew)   *see* All So N Warks *Birm*

SIBBERTOFT (St Helen)   *see* Clipston, Haselbech, Kelmarsh, Marston Trussell etc *Pet*

SIBERTSWOLD (St Andrew)   *see* Bewsborough *Cant*

SIBFORD (Holy Trinity)   *see* Wykeham *Ox*

SIBLE HEDINGHAM (St Peter)   *see* The Hedinghams and Upper Colne *Chelmsf*

SIBSEY (St Margaret) w Frithville *Linc 21*   **P** *Ld Chan*   **V** *vacant*

SIBSON (St Botolph)   *see* Bosworth and Sheepy Gp *Leic*

SIBTHORPE (St Peter) *S'well 3*   **P** *Bp*   **P-in-c** E I MURRAY

SIBTON (St Peter)   *see* Yoxmere *St E*

SICKLINGHALL (St Peter)   *see* Lower Wharfedale *Leeds*

SID VALLEY   *see* Sidmouth, Woolbrook, Salcombe Regis, Sidbury etc *Ex*

SIDBURY (St Giles and St Peter)   *see* Sidmouth, Woolbrook, Salcombe Regis, Sidbury etc *Ex*

SIDCUP (Christ Church) Longland *Roch 17*   **P** *Ch Trust Fund Trust*   **V** T J PARSONS

SIDCUP (St Andrew) *Roch 17*   **P** *Bp*   **V** R C A HANKEY

SIDCUP (St John the Evangelist) w Footscray *Roch 17*   **P** *Ld Chan and D&C (alt)*   **V** C M KNIGHT-SCOTT   **NSM** A S J HEALY

SIDDAL (St Mark)   *see* Halifax w Siddal *Leeds*

SIDDINGTON (All Saints)   *see* Marton, Siddington w Capesthorne etc *Ches*

SIDDINGTON (St Peter)   *see* S Cerney w Cerney Wick, Siddington and Preston *Glouc*

SIDESTRAND (St Michael)   *see* Poppyland *Nor*

SIDFORD (St Peter)   *see* Sidmouth, Woolbrook, Salcombe Regis, Sidbury etc *Ex*

SIDLESHAM (St Mary Our Lady) *Chich 2*   **P** *Bp*   **P-in-c** S GUISE

SIDLEY (All Saints) *Chich 12*   **P** *R Bexhill*   **V** M J BAILEY   **C** A G J BIRKS

SIDLOW BRIDGE (Emmanuel) *S'wark 24*   **P** *DBP*   **P-in-c** S M WEAKLEY

SIDMOUTH (St Nicholas w St Giles), Woolbrook, Salcombe Regis, Sidbury w Sidford, and All Saints Sidmouth *Ex 6*   **P** *Patr Bd*   **TR** D R CAPORN   **NSM** A DENNY

SIGGLESTHORNE (St Lawrence) w Nunkeeling and Bewholme *York 11*   **P** *The Crown*   **P-in-c** A C SIMPSON   **NSM** M M DESBOROUGH

SILCHESTER (St Mary)   *see* Tadley w Pamber Heath and Silchester *Win*

SILCHESTER COMMON (Mission Church) *as above*

SILEBY (St Mary), Cossington and Seagrave *Leic 4*   **P** *Patr Bd*   **R** D C BEET

SILK WILLOUGHBY (St Denis) *Linc 14*   **P** *Sir Lyonel Tollemache Bt*   **R** *vacant*

SILKSTONE (All Saints)   *see* W Barnsley *Leeds*

SILKSTONE COMMON (Mission Room) *as above*

SILKSWORTH (St Matthew)   *see* Sunderland St Matt and St Wilfrid *Dur*

SILLOTH (Christ Church) *see* Solway Plain *Carl*
SILSDEN (St James) *Leeds 4* **P** *Bp, Adn Craven, and Trustees (jt)* **V** D J GRIFFITHS **C** S A GRIFFITHS
SILSOE (St James), Pulloxhill and Flitton *St Alb 8* **P** *Ball Coll Ox and Bp (alt)* **NSM** I M SMITH
SILTON (St Nicholas) *see* Gillingham, Milton-on-Stour and Silton *Sarum*
SILTON, NETHER (All Saints) *see* Leake w Over and Nether Silton and Kepwick *York*
SILTON, OVER (St Mary) *as above*
SILVER END (St Francis) *see* Witham and Villages *Chelmsf*
SILVERDALE (St John) *Blackb 14* **P** *V Warton* **V** *vacant*
SILVERDALE (St Luke) *Lich 9* **P** *T H G Howard-Sneyd Esq* **V** P C JONES
SILVERHILL (St Matthew) *Chich 15* **P** *Simeon's Trustees* **R** *vacant*
SILVERSTONE (St Michael) and Abthorpe w Slapton and Whittlebury and Paulerspury *Pet 5* **P** *T L Langton-Lockton Esq, Leeson's Trustees, and New Coll Ox (3 turns), The Crown (2 turns)* **R** P D MCLEOD
SILVERTON (St Mary), Butterleigh, Bickleigh and Cadeleigh *Ex 7* **P** *Bp and Sir Rivers Carew Bt* **NSM** C JENKINS, T M THOMPSON
SILVINGTON (St Michael) *see* Stottesdon w Farlow, Cleeton St Mary etc *Heref*
SIMONBURN (St Mungo) *see* Humshaugh w Simonburn and Wark *Newc*
SIMONSTONE (St Peter) *see* Read and Simonstone *Blackb*
SIMPSON (St Thomas) *see* Woughton *Ox*
SINFIN (St Stephen) *Derby 5* **P** *CPAS* **P-in-c** N H ELLIOTT
SINFIN MOOR (not known) *Derby 5* **P** *Bp* **V** *vacant*
SINGLETON (Blessed Virgin Mary) *see* E Dean, Singleton, and W Dean *Chich*
SINGLETON (St Anne) *see* Poulton Carleton and Singleton *Blackb*
SINNINGTON (All Saints) *see* Middleton, Newton and Sinnington *York*
SISLAND (St Mary) *see* Loddon, Sisland, Chedgrave, Hardley and Langley *Nor*
SISSINGHURST (Holy Trinity) w Frittenden *Cant 11* **P** *CPAS* **R** *vacant*
SITHNEY (St Sithney) *see* W Kerrier *Truro*
SITTINGBOURNE (Holy Trinity) (St Mary) (St Michael) w Bobbing *Cant 15* **P** *Patr Bd* **TR** M J RESCH **TV** L M JONES **C** C J PENFOLD, E B RESCH **OLM** S M SAMSON
SIX HILLS (Mission) *see* Old Dalby, Nether Broughton, Saxelbye etc *Leic*
SIX MILE BOTTOM (St George) *see* Lt Wilbraham *Ely*
SIX PILGRIMS, The, comprising Alford, Babcary, Hornblotton, Lovington, North Barrow, and South Barrow *B & W 2* **P** *Ch Soc Trust, D&C, DBF, and Bp (by turn)* **P-in-c** M I CLUTTERBUCK
SIX SAINTS circa Holt, comprising Blaston, Bringhurst, Great Easton, Medbourne cum Holt, and Stockerston *Leic 5* **P** *D&C Pet and Adn Leic (2 turns), St Jo Coll Cam (1 turn)* **R** S J BISHOP
SIX, The, comprising Hartlip, Iwade, Lower Halstow, Newington, Stockbury, and Upchurch *Cant 15* **P** *Abp, D&C, and Adn Maidstone (jt)* **V** J M STANIFORTH **C** S Z B NEVELL **NSM** A M LANE
SIXHILLS (All Saints) *see* Barkwith Gp *Linc*
SIXPENNY HANDLEY (St Mary) w Gussage St Andrew and Pentridge *Sarum 6* **P** *D&C Windsor and DBP (alt)* **P-in-c** R M A HANCOCK **C** M J FOSTER
SKEEBY (St Agatha's District Church) *see* Easby w Skeeby and Brompton on Swale etc *Leeds*
SKEFFINGTON (St Thomas à Beckett) *see* Coplow *Leic*
SKEFFLING (St Helen) *see* Easington w Skeffling, Keyingham, Ottringham etc *York*
SKEGBY (St Andrew) w Teversal *S'well 4* **P** *DBP and Ld Chan (alt)* **R** *vacant*
SKEGNESS Group, The, (St Clement) (St Matthew), including Addlethorpe and Ingoldmells *Linc 10* **P** *Bp and DBP (2 turns), and Ld Chan (1 turn)* **R** R G HOLDEN **C** M L HOULDERSHAW **OLM** C ANDERSON
SKELBROOKE (St Michael and All Angels) *see* Adwick-le-Street w Skelbrooke *Sheff*
SKELLINGTHORPE (St Lawrence) w Doddington *Linc 12* **P** *MMCET* **R** S J DURANT **OLM** F CLARKE
SKELLOW (St Michael and All Angels) *see* Owston *Sheff*
SKELMANTHORPE (St Aidan) *Leeds 12* **P** *Bp* **V** *vacant*
SKELMERSDALE (St Paul) *Liv 14* **P** *V Ormskirk* **P-in-c** C B SPITTLE **C** D M HARRISON, J E B SHEPHERD **NSM** A KAZICH **OLM** C JACKSON
SKELSMERGH (St John the Baptist) *see* Beacon *Carl*

SKELTON (All Saints) w Upleatham *York 16* **P** *Abp* **R** V E M-B HAYNES
SKELTON (St Giles) w Shipton and Newton on Ouse *York 3* **P** *Abp* **P-in-c** M H WAINWRIGHT **C** D M COYNE, E C HASSALL, M E YOUNG, M HARRISON, S WHITING **NSM** C C CRANFIELD, C C GITTENS, C J TOASE, S P POPE, T M GANT
SKELTON (St Michael) *see* Inglewood Gp *Carl*
SKELTON-CUM-NEWBY (St Helen's Old Church) *see* Kirby-on-the-Moor, Cundall w Norton-le-Clay etc *Leeds*
SKENDLEBY (St Peter and St Paul) *see* Bolingbroke Deanery *Linc*
SKERNE (St Leonard) *see* Hutton Cranswick w Skerne, Watton and Beswick *York*
SKERNE, UPPER, comprising Bishop Middleham, Fishburn, Sedgefield, Trimdon, and Trimdon Grange *Dur 9* **P** *Ld Chan (1 turn), Patr Bd (2 turns)* **TR** G M SHORT **TV** E A BLAND
SKERTON (St Chad) *Blackb 11* **P** *Bp* **V** *vacant*
SKERTON (St Luke) *Blackb 11* **P** *Trustees* **V** *vacant*
SKEYTON (All Saints) *see* King's Beck *Nor*
SKIDBY (St Michael) *see* Walkington, Bishop Burton, Rowley etc *York*
SKILGATE (St John the Baptist) *see* Dulverton w Brushford, Brompton Regis etc *B & W*
SKILLINGTON (St James) *see* Colsterworth Gp *Linc*
SKIPSEA (All Saints) *see* Hornsea, Atwick and Skipsea *York*
SKIPTON (Christ Church) w Carleton St Mary *Leeds 24* **P** *Ch Ch Ox and R Skipton H Trin (jt)* **V** R HARRIS **C** A WHEATLEY **NSM** T L CANTLOW
SKIPTON (Holy Trinity) *Leeds 24* **P** *Ch Ch Ox* **R** *vacant*
SKIPTON ON SWALE (St John) *see* Topcliffe, Baldersby w Dishforth, Dalton etc *York*
SKIPWITH (St Helen) *see* Bubwith w Skipwith *York*
SKIRBECK (Holy Trinity) *Linc 21* **P** *Trustees* **V** E WARD **C** I S WARD
SKIRBECK (St Nicholas) *Linc 21* **P** *DBP* **R** *vacant*
SKIRBECK QUARTER (St Thomas) *see* Boston *Linc*
SKIRLAUGH (St Augustine), Catwick, Long Riston, Rise, Swine w Ellerby *York 11* **P** *Abp, Abp and Baroness de Stempel, and Ld Chan (by turn)* **V** A C SIMPSON **NSM** M M DESBOROUGH
SKIRPENBECK (St Mary) *see* Garrowby Hill *York*
SKIRWITH (St John the Evangelist) *see* Cross Fell Gp *Carl*
SLAD (Holy Trinity) *see* Stroud Team *Glouc*
SLADE GREEN (St Augustine) *Roch 15* **P** *Bp* **P-in-c** J D BENNETT, P WRIGHT
SLAIDBURN (St Andrew) w Tosside *Leeds 20* **P** *Bp and Ch Soc Trust (jt)* **P-in-c** J T OLDFIELD
SLAITHWAITE (St James) *see* Marsden and Slaithwaite w E Scammonden *Leeds*
SLALEY (St Mary the Virgin), Healey and Whittonstall *Newc 9* **P** *Bp, V Bywell St Pet, and D&C (jt)* **V** H SAVAGE
SLAPTON (Holy Cross) *see* Ivinghoe w Pitstone and Slapton and Marsworth *Ox*
SLAPTON (St Botolph) *see* Silverstone and Abthorpe w Slapton etc *Pet*
SLAPTON (St James the Great) *see* Stokenham, Slapton, Charleton w Buckland etc *Ex*
SLAUGHAM (St Mary) and Staplefield Common *Chich 5* **P** *Mrs D M Irwin-Clark* **R** C A SMITH **Hon C** K W HABERSHON
SLAUGHTER, LOWER (St Mary) *see* The Guitings, Cutsdean, Farmcote etc *Glouc*
SLAUGHTER, UPPER (St Peter) *as above*
SLAUGHTERFORD (St Nicholas) *see* By Brook *Bris*
SLAWSTON (All Saints) *see* Hallaton and Allexton, w Horninghold, Tugby etc *Leic*
SLEAFORD (St Denys) *Linc 14* **P** *Bp* **V** P A JOHNSON **C** R A KNIGHT
SLEDMERE (St Mary) *see* Waggoners *York*
SLEEKBURN (St John) *see* Bedlington, Cambois and Sleekburn *Newc*
SLEIGHTS (St John) *see* Lower Esk *York*
SLIMBRIDGE (St John the Evangelist) *see* Sharpness, Purton, Brookend and Slimbridge *Glouc*
SLINDON (St Chad) *see* Eccleshall *Lich*
SLINDON (St Mary), Eartham and Madehurst *Chich 1* **P** *Bp, D&C, and Mrs J Izard (jt)* **P-in-c** P H JONES
SLINFOLD (St Peter) *see* Itchingfield w Slinfold *Chich*
SLINGSBY (All Saints) *see* The Street Par *York*
SLIPTON (St John the Baptist) *Pet 9* **P** *L G Stopford Sackville Esq* **V** *vacant*
SLITTING MILL (St John the Baptist) *see* Brereton and Rugeley w Armitage *Lich*

SLOANE STREET (Holy Trinity)   *see* Upper Chelsea H Trin and St Sav *Lon*
SLOLEY (St Bartholomew)   *see* King's Beck *Nor*
SLOUGH (St Paul) (Christ Church) *Ox 12*   P *Trustees*
V *vacant*
SLYNE WITH HEST (St Luke) and Halton St Wilfrid w Aughton St Saviour *Blackb 14*   P *Bp and Exors R T Sanderson (jt)*   R S M SEED
SMALL HEATH (All Saints) *Birm 11*   P *Patr Bd*
V J R A SAMPSON
SMALLBURGH (St Peter) w Dilham w Honing and Crostwight *Nor 12*   P *Bp, T R Cubitt Esq, and J C Wickman Esq (jt)*   R S P LAWRENCE   OLM A P BEVAN
SMALLEY (St John the Baptist)   *see* Morley and Smalley *Derby*
SMALLFIELD (Church Room)   *see* The Windmill *S'wark*
SMALLHYTHE (St John the Baptist)   *see* Tenterden, Rother and Oxney *Cant*
SMALLTHORNE (St Saviour) *Lich 11*   P *R Norton in the Moors*
P-in-c A C SWIFT
SMALLWOOD (St John the Baptist)   *see* Astbury and Smallwood *Ches*
SMANNELL (Christ Church)   *see* Pastrow *Win*
SMARDEN (St Michael)   *see* Biddenden and Smarden *Cant*
SMEATON, GREAT (St Eloy)   *see* Wiske Benefice *Leeds*
SMEETH (St Mary)   *see* Stour Downs *Cant*
SMEETON WESTERBY (Christ Church)   *see* Kibworth and Smeeton Westerby and Saddington *Leic*
SMESTOW VALE TEAM, comprising Bobbington, Himley, Swindon, Trysull, and Wombourne *Lich 23*   P *Patr Bd*
TR A P BROWN   TV C A HOST, R J FISHER   C S J WATSON
SMETHCOTT (St Michael)   *see* Dorrington w Leebotwood, Longnor, Stapleton w Heref
SMETHWICK (Old Church) *Birm 6*   P *Dorothy Parkes Trustees*
V D BUCKLEY   C C C SHEKERIE
SMETHWICK (Resurrection) (St Stephen and St Michael) *Birm 6*   P *Bp*   V D R GOULD   NSM N M ROSS
SMETHWICK (St Matthew w St Chad) *Birm 6*   P *Bp and V Smethwick (alt)*   P-in-c L M ARLIDGE
SMISBY (St James)   *see* Melbourne, Ticknall, Smisby and Stanton *Derby*
SMITHILLS HALL (Chapel)   *see* Halliwell St Pet *Man*
SMORRALL LANE (St Andrew)   *see* Bedworth *Cov*
SNAILWELL (St Peter)   *see* Three Rivers Gp *Ely*
SNAINTON (St Stephen)   *see* Upper Derwent *York*
SNAITH (St Laurence Priory)   *see* Gt Snaith *Sheff*
SNAITH, GREAT (Holy Trinity) (St John the Baptist) (St Paul) *Sheff 10*   P *Bp*   TR E E M ROBERTSHAW   C D T H RYAN   NSM P W HIBBS
SNAPE (St John the Baptist)   *see* Alde River *St E*
SNAPE CASTLE (Chapel of St Mary)   *see* W Tanfield and Well w Snape and N Stainley *Leeds*
SNARESTONE (St Bartholomew)   *see* Woodfield *Leic*
SNARGATE (St Dunstan)   *see* Brookland, Fairfield, Brenzett w Snargate etc *Cant*
SNEAD (St Mary the Virgin)   *see* Wentnor w Ratlinghope, Myndtown, Norbury etc *Heref*
SNEATON (St Hilda)   *see* Lower Esk *York*
SNEINTON (St Christopher) w St Philip *S'well 9*   P *CPAS and Trustees (alt)*   P-in-c N J HILL
SNEINTON (St Cyprian) *S'well 9*   P *Bp*   V *vacant*
SNEINTON (St Stephen) w St Matthias *S'well 9*   P *Bp and SMF (jt)*   V *vacant*
SNELLAND (All Saints)   *see* Wragby Gp *Linc*
SNELSTON (St Peter)   *see* Norbury w Snelston *Derby*
SNETTISHAM (St Mary)   *see* Heacham and Snettisham *Nor*
SNEYD (Holy Trinity) *Lich 11*   P *Bp*   V B L WILLIAMS
SNEYD GREEN (St Andrew) *Lich 11*   P *Bp*   V J N GANDON
SNIBSTON (St Mary)   *see* Hugglescote w Donington, Ellistown and Snibston *Leic*
SNITTERBY (St Nicholas)   *see* Bishop Norton, Waddingham and Snitterby *Linc*
SNITTERFIELD (St James the Great)   *see* Arden Valley *Cov*
SNODLAND (All Saints) (Christ Church) *Roch 7*   P *Bp and CPAS (jt)*   R D A PEARSON-SMITH   NSM S M BROOKS
SNORING, GREAT (St Mary)   *see* Barney, Hindringham, Thursford, Great Snoring, Little Snoring and Kettlestone and Pensthorpe *Nor*
SNORING, LITTLE (St Andrew) *as above*
SNOWSHILL (St Barnabas)   *see* Winchcombe *Glouc*
SOAR, UPPER, comprising Ashby Parva, Claybrooke, Dunton Bassett, Frolesworth, and Leire *Leic 7*   P *The Crown (1 turn), Mrs A M Finn, Adn Loughb, and Ball Coll Ox (1 turn)*
R *vacant*
SOBERTON (St Peter), Newtown and Hambledon *Portsm 1*   P *Ld Chan and Bp (jt)*   V D B MORGAN   C A W FORREST
SOCKBURN (All Saints)   *see* Dinsdale w Sockburn *Dur*

SODBURY VALE Benefice, The, comprising Chipping Sodbury, Horton, Little Sodbury, and Old Sodbury *Glouc 5*
P *D&C Worc, Duke of Beaufort, and CPAS (jt)*   R D BOWERS
NSM P T FEWINGS
SODBURY, LITTLE (St Adeline)   *see* Sodbury Vale *Glouc*
SODBURY, OLD (St John the Baptist) *as above*
SOHAM (St Andrew) *Ely 8*   P *Pemb Coll Cam*
R E J WHALLEY
SOHO (St Anne) (St Thomas) (St Peter) *Lon 3*   P *R Westmr St Jas*   P-in-c R S F BUCKLEY   NSM K G RIGLIN
SOLE BAY, comprising Blythburgh, Reydon, Sotherton, South Cove, Southwold, Uggeshall, Walberswick, and Wangford *St E 17*   P *Patr Bd*   TR S J PITCHER   TV A D PERRY
NSM J E A MILLER
SOLIHULL (Catherine de Barnes) (St Alphege) (St Helen) (St Michael) *Birm 10*   P *Patr Bd*   TR J E B KENCHINGTON
TV H T GREENHAM, S H MARSHALL   C S J GIBSON
SOLLERS HOPE (St Michael)   *see* StowCaple *Heref*
SOLWAY PLAIN, comprising Bromfield, Holme Cultram, Silloth, Waverton, and West Newton *Carl 7*   P *Patr Bd*
R B ROTHWELL   NSM M T STILWELL
SOMBORNE (St Peter and St Paul) w Ashley *Win 12*   P *Bp*
P-in-c J M PITKIN   Hon C R A BURNINGHAM
SOMERBY (All Saints)   *see* Burrough Hill Pars *Leic*
SOMERBY (St Margaret)   *see* Brocklesby Park, Croxton and North Wolds *Linc*
SOMERBY, NEW (St Anne)   *see* S Grantham *Linc*
SOMERBY, OLD (St Mary Magdalene)   *see* N Beltisloe Gp *Linc*
SOMERCOTES (St Thomas) *Derby 2*   P *Bp*
P-in-c I N L BLACK   C M J TAYLOR   NSM J O K PENFOLD
SOMERCOTES, NORTH (St Mary)   *see* Marshchapel, Somercotes and Grainthorpe w Conisholme *Linc*
SOMERFORD (All Saints)   *see* Astbury and Smallwood *Ches*
SOMERFORD KEYNES (All Saints)   *see* Kemble, Poole Keynes, Somerford Keynes etc *Glouc*
SOMERFORD, GREAT (St Peter and St Paul)   *see* Woodbridge *Bris*
SOMERFORD, LITTLE (St John the Baptist) *as above*
SOMERLEYTON (St Mary), Ashby, Fritton, Herringfleet, Blundeston and Lound *Nor 9*   P *Lord Somerleyton and SMF (jt)*   R G BROOKS
SOMERS TOWN (St Mary the Virgin)   *see* Old St Pancras *Lon*
SOMERSAL HERBERT (St Peter)   *see* S Dales *Derby*
SOMERSBY (St Margaret)   *see* S Ormsby Gp *Linc*
SOMERSHAM (St John the Baptist) w Pidley and Oldhurst and Wooodhurst *Ely 12*   P *Bp*   V S F SIMPSON
Hon C F J KILNER   NSM S G EVANS
SOMERSHAM (St Mary)   *see* Bosmere *St E*
SOMERTON (St James)   *see* Cherwell Valley *Ox*
SOMERTON (St Margaret)   *see* Glemsford, Hartest w Boxted, Somerton etc *St E*
SOMERTON (St Michael and All Angels) w The Charltons and Kingsdon *B & W 5*   P *Bp (2 turns), DBP (1 turn)*
P-in-c A J SYMONDS
SOMERTON, WEST (St Mary)   *see* Flegg Coastal Benefice *Nor*
SOMPTING (St Mary the Virgin) (St Peter) *Chich 4*   P *OStJ*
V *vacant*
SONNING (St Andrew) (St Patrick) *Ox 8*   P *Bp*
V J A F TAYLOR   NSM K L TOOGOOD
SONNING COMMON (Christ the King)   *see* Rotherfield Peppard and Kidmore End etc *Ox*
SOOKHOLME (St Augustine)   *see* Warsop *S'well*
SOPLEY (St Michael and All Angels)   *see* Burton and Sopley *Win*
SOPWORTH (St Mary the Virgin)   *see* Boxwell, Leighterton, Didmarton, Oldbury etc *Glouc*
SOTHERTON (St Andrew)   *see* Sole Bay *St E*
SOTWELL (St James)   *see* Wallingford *Ox*
SOUDLEY (St Michael)   *see* Cinderford w Littledean *Glouc*
SOULBURY (All Saints)   *see* Cottesloe *Ox*
SOULDERN (Annunciation of the Blessed Virgin Mary)   *see* Cherwell Valley *Ox*
SOULDROP (All Saints)   *see* Sharnbrook, Felmersham and Knotting w Souldrop *St Alb*
SOUNDWELL (St Stephen) *Bris 5*   P *Bp*   P-in-c L J WIGMORE
NSM A J G COOPER   OLM J M WILTSHIRE
SOURTON (St Thomas of Canterbury)   *see* Okehampton, Inwardleigh, Belstone, Sourton etc *Ex*
SOUTH   *see also under substantive place name*
SOUTH ACRE (St George)   *see* Nar Valley *Nor*
SOUTH BANK (St John) *York 17*   P *Abp*   V T M LEATHLEY
SOUTH CAVE (All Saints) and Ellerker w Broomfleet *York 13*   P *CPAS and D&C Dur (jt)*   V M J PROCTOR
NSM P R DRAPER
SOUTH COVE (St Lawrence)   *see* Sole Bay *St E*

SOUTH DALES, The, comprising Alkmonton, Cubley, Doveridge, Marston Montgomery, Scropton, Somersal Herbert, and Sudbury *Derby 6*   **P** *Bp and Duke of Devonshire (jt)*   **R** J J VICKERSTAFF   **NSM** J M LEGH, P R JONES

SOUTH DOWNS GATEWAY Churches, comprising Colden Common, Morestead, Owslebury, and Twyford *Win 7*   **P** *Bp and Em Coll Cam (jt)*   **V** D A DRAISEY

SOUTH HILL (St Sampson)   *see* Callington Cluster *Truro*

SOUTH MOOR (St George)   *see* Stanley and S Moor *Dur*

SOUTH PARK (St Luke)   *see* Reigate St Luke *S'wark*

SOUTH POOL (St Nicholas and St Cyriac)   *see* Stokenham, Slapton, Charleton w Buckland etc *Ex*

SOUTH SHIELDS (All Saints) (St Mary w St Martin) *Dur 13*   **P** *Patr Bd*   **TR** M P THOMPSON

SOUTH SHIELDS (St Hilda) w St Thomas *Dur 13*   **P** *D&C*   **V** *vacant*

SOUTH SHIELDS (St Lawrence the Martyr)   *see* Horsley Hill St Lawr *Dur*

SOUTH SHIELDS St Aidan (St Stephen) The Lawe *Dur 13*   **P** *Bp and D&C*   **R** *vacant*

SOUTH SHORE (Holy Trinity) *Blackb 8*   **P** J C Hilton Esq   **V** T CHARNOCK   **C** E J SWARBRICK

SOUTH SHORE (St Peter) *Blackb 8*   **P** *Bp*   **V** T CHARNOCK   **C** E J SWARBRICK

SOUTH TRINITY BROADS, The, comprising Billockby, Burgh St Margaret (Fleggburgh), Filby, Mautby, Runham, Stokesby, and Thrigby *Nor 6*   **P** *Bp, Adn Nor, DBP, Mrs Z K Cognetti, R T Daniel Esq, and I F M Lucas Esq (jt)*   **P-in-c** S M HEMSLEY HALLS

SOUTH WARWICKSHIRE SEVEN Group, The, comprising Barcheston, Barton-on-the-Heath, Burmington, Cherington, Long Compton, Whichford, and Wolford *Cov 9*   **P** *Bp, Mert Coll Ox, Ch Ch Ox, and Trin Coll Ox (jt)*   **R** S P ALLEN   **C** B H DYSON

SOUTHALL (Christ the Redeemer) *Lon 22*   **P** *Bp*   **V** N J ORCHARD   **NSM** W MASIH

SOUTHALL (Emmanuel) *Lon 22*   **P** *Bp and Ch Patr Trust (jt)*   **V** W E GILL

SOUTHALL (Holy Trinity) *Lon 22*   **P** *Ch Patr Trust*   **V** M F BOLLEY

SOUTHALL (St George) *Lon 22*   **P** *D&C St Paul's*   **V** C RAMSAY

SOUTHALL GREEN (St John) *Lon 22*   **P** *Ch Patr Trust*   **V** A L POULSON   **C** I M DUNMORE

SOUTHAM (Ascension)   *see* Bishop's Cleeve and Woolstone w Gotherington etc *Glouc*

SOUTHAM (St James) *Cov 10*   **P** *The Crown*   **P-in-c** V J BISIKER

SOUTHAMPTON (Christ Church) Portswood   *see* Portswood Ch Ch *Win*

SOUTHAMPTON (St Alban the Martyr)   *see* Swaythling *Win*

SOUTHAMPTON (St Barnabas) *Win 13*   **P** *Bp*   **V** *vacant*

SOUTHAMPTON (St Denys) Portswood   *see* Portswood St Denys *Win*

SOUTHAMPTON (St Jude)   *see* Maybush and Southampton St Jude *Win*

SOUTHAMPTON (St Mark) *Win 13*   **P** *Ch Patr Trust*   **P-in-c** K E HICKEN   **C** Y M NICHOLSON

SOUTHAMPTON (St Mary Extra) *Win 13*   **P** *Bp*   **P-in-c** M J A NEWTON

SOUTHAMPTON (St Mary) *Win 13*   **P** *Bp*   **P-in-c** J M FINCH   **C** A E HILL   **NSM** N D LEIGH

SOUTHAMPTON (St Michael the Archangel) *Win 13*   **P** *Bp*   **V** D G DEBOYS   **NSM** J M SELLIN, P R HAND

SOUTHAMPTON Lord's Hill and Lord's Wood *Win 13*   **P** *Bp*   **P-in-c** C H KNIGHTS

SOUTHAMPTON Thornhill (St Christopher) *Win 13*   **P** *Bp*   **P-in-c** D W JENNINGS   **NSM** M D J RENSHAW

SOUTHBERGH (St Andrew)   *see* Barnham Broom and Upper Yare *Nor*

SOUTHBOROUGH (Christ Church) *Roch 12*   **P** *CPAS Patr Trust*   **R** N S CORNELL

SOUTHBOROUGH (St Matthew)   *see* High Brooms *Roch*

SOUTHBOROUGH (St Peter)   *see* Bidborough St Lawr and Southborough St Pet *Roch*

SOUTHBOROUGH (St Thomas) *Roch 12*   **P** *Bp*   **P-in-c** R C WILSON   **C** D J DE MATTOS

SOUTHBOURNE (All Saints)   *see* Pokesdown All SS *Win*

SOUTHBOURNE (St Christopher) *Win 8*   **P** *Bp*   **P-in-c** A L MCPHERSON

SOUTHBOURNE (St John the Evangelist) w West Thorney *Chich 3*   **P** MMCET   **V** M J LUFF

SOUTHBOURNE (St Katharine) (St Nicholas) *Win 8*   **P** *Bp*   **V** K J CABLE

SOUTHBROOM (St James) *Sarum 17*   **P** *D&C*   **V** K J BRINDLE   **C** R J SAINT   **NSM** S A IBBETSON

SOUTHCHURCH (Christ Church) *Chelmsf 15*   **P** *Bp*   **V** S N ROSCOE

SOUTHCHURCH (Holy Trinity) *Chelmsf 15*   **P** *Abp Cant*   **P-in-c** R T HUMBLE

SOUTHCOURT (Good Shepherd) *Ox 10*   **P** *Ch Patr Trust*   **V** C R HARTLEY

SOUTHEA (Emmanuel)   *see* Wisbech St Mary and Guyhirn w Ring's End etc *Ely*

SOUTHEASE (St Peter)   *see* Iford w Kingston and Rodmell and Southease *Chich*

SOUTHEND (St John the Baptist) (St Mark) (All Saints) (St Alban) *Chelmsf 15*   **P** *Patr Bd*   **TV** W N PAXTON   **Hon C** M A BALLARD   **NSM** C E SANDOVER, P E OWEN

SOUTHEND (St Peter)   *see* Bradfield and Stanford Dingley *Ox*

SOUTHEND-ON-SEA (St Saviour) Westcliff *Chelmsf 15*   **P** *Bp, Adn Southend, and Churchwardens (jt)*   **V** L R MULLEN   **NSM** J F WILKINSON

SOUTHERY (St Mary)   *see* Grimshoe *Ely*

SOUTHFIELDS (St Barnabas) *S'wark 18*   **P** *Bp*   **V** I S TATTUM   **NSM** J G BOYCE

SOUTHFIELDS (St Michael and All Angels)   *see* Wandsworth St Mich w St Steph *S'wark*

SOUTHFLEET (St Nicholas) *Roch 1*   **P** *CPAS*   **P-in-c** J M YOUNG

SOUTHGATE (Christ Church) *Lon 18*   **P** *V Edmonton All SS*   **V** C LIMBERT   **NSM** H H MIALL

SOUTHGATE (St Andrew) *Lon 18*   **P** *Bp*   **V** E N TURNER   **C** E G BROWN

SOUTHGATE, NEW (St Paul) *Lon 14*   **P** *V Southgate Ch Ch*   **V** *vacant*

SOUTHILL (All Saints)   *see* Clifton and Southill *St Alb*

SOUTHLAKE (St James) *Ox 7*   **P** *DBP*   **V** L R SMITH

SOUTHLEIGH (St Lawrence)   *see* Colyton, Musbury, Southleigh and Branscombe *Ex*

SOUTHMEAD (St Stephen) *Bris 2*   **P** *Bp*   **V** *vacant*

SOUTHMINSTER (St Leonard) and Steeple *Chelmsf 11*   **P** *Govs Charterhouse and Lord Fitzwalter (jt)*   **P-in-c** P E C BEGLEY

SOUTHOE (St Leonard)   *see* The Paxtons w Diddington and Southoe *Ely*

SOUTHOVER (St John the Baptist)   *see* Trin in Lewes *Chich*

SOUTHOWRAM (St Anne-in-the-Grove) and Claremount *Leeds 10*   **P** *V Halifax*   **C** K A SHOESMITH, K J BARNARD   **NSM** E S KILPATRICK

SOUTHPORT (All Saints) *Liv 9*   **P** *Trustees*   **P-in-c** T D L CARPENTER   **C** S T MARSHALL

SOUTHPORT (Christ Church) *Liv 9*   **P** *Trustees*   **V** S MCGANITY   **C** S J RENISON   **NSM** R MILTON

SOUTHPORT (Emmanuel) *Liv 9*   **P** *PCC*   **V** *vacant*

SOUTHPORT (Holy Trinity) *Liv 9*   **P** *Trustees*   **V** T D L CARPENTER

SOUTHPORT (St Luke) *Liv 9*   **P** *V Southport H Trin*   **V** *vacant*

SOUTHPORT (St Philip) (St Paul) *Liv 9*   **P** *V Southport Ch Ch and Trustees (jt)*   **P-in-c** S MCGANITY

SOUTHPORT (St Simon and St Jude) All Souls *Liv 9*   **P** *Trustees*   **C** A D LIGGINS

SOUTHPORT, KEW (St Francis of Assisi)   *see* Kew *Liv*

SOUTHREPPS (St James)   *see* Poppyland *Nor*

SOUTHREY (St John the Divine)   *see* Bardney *Linc*

SOUTHROP (St Peter)   *see* S Cotswolds *Glouc*

SOUTHSEA (Holy Spirit) *Portsm 6*   **P** *Bp*   **P-in-c** R T LAWSON   **C** P R ARMSTEAD

SOUTHSEA (St Jude) *Portsm 6*   **P** *Trustees*   **C** A S DENLEY, N R SMART

SOUTHSEA (St Luke) (St Peter) *Portsm 6*   **P** *Bp and Ch Patr Trust (jt)*   **P-in-c** A-M MCCABE   **C** J A TWINE   **NSM** B W R STEPHENSON

SOUTHSEA (St Margaret of Scotland) *Portsm 6*   **P** *Bp*   **V** *vacant*

SOUTHSEA (St Simon) *Portsm 6*   **P** *Ch Patr Trust*   **P-in-c** A D FINN

SOUTHTOWN (St Mary)   *see* Gt Yarmouth *Nor*

SOUTHWARK (Christ Church) *S'wark 10*   **P** *Marshall's Charity*   **V** *vacant*

SOUTHWARK (Holy Trinity w St Matthew) *S'wark 10*   **P** *Bp*   **R** H F ADÁN FERNÁNDEZ   **C** A GARCIA FUERTE   **Hon C** G R KINGS

SOUTHWARK (St George the Martyr) (St Alphege) (St Jude) *S'wark 10*   **P** *Lon Corp (1 turn), Ld Chan (4 turns), Walsingham Coll Trust Assn (1 turn)*   **R** J M W SEDGWICK   **C** D W D ADAMSON, S R HOLE   **Hon C** F Y-C HUNG   **OLM** D PAPE

SOUTHWATER (Holy Innocents) *Chich 7*   **P** *V Horsham*   **V** K F GODFREY

SOUTHWAY (The Holy Spirit) *see* Tamerton Foliot and Southway *Ex*
SOUTHWELL (Holy Trinity) *S'well 3* **P** CPAS **V** A W PORTER
SOUTHWELL (St Andrew) *see* Portland *Sarum*
SOUTHWICK (Holy Trinity) *see* N Wearside *Dur*
SOUTHWICK (St James) w Boarhunt *Portsm 1*
  P R Thistlewayte Esq **P-in-c** S BROCKLEHURST
SOUTHWICK (St Mary the Virgin) *see* Warmington, Tansor and Cotterstock etc *Pet*
SOUTHWICK (St Michael and All Angels) (St Peter)
  Chich 20 **P** Bp and Ld Chan (alt) **R** J D S FRENCH
SOUTHWICK (St Thomas) *see* N Bradley, Southwick, Heywood and Steeple Ashton *Sarum*
SOUTHWOLD (St Edmund King and Martyr) *see* Sole Bay *St E*
SOWERBY (St Mary) *see* Ryburn *Leeds*
SOWERBY (St Oswald) *York 18* **V** Abp **NSM** P PERCY
SOWERBY (St Peter) *see* Ryburn *Leeds*
SOWERBY BRIDGE (Christ Church) *Leeds 10* **P** V Halifax
  V A DICK
SOWTON (St Michael and All Angels) *see* Broadclyst, Clyst Honiton, Pinhoe, Rockbeare etc *Ex*
SPALDING (St John the Baptist) w Deeping St Nicholas
  Linc 19 **P** Bp **V** vacant
SPALDING (St Mary and St Nicolas) *Linc 19* **P** Feoffees
  V J D BENNETT **C** A J WORKMAN, P E MCWILLIAMS
SPALDING (St Paul) *Linc 19* **P** Bp and V Spalding (jt)
  P-in-c J D BENNETT **C** P N WHITELEY
SPALDWICK (St James) *see* S Leightonstone *Ely*
SPARHAM (St Mary) *see* Reepham and Wensum Valley *Nor*
SPARKBROOK (Christ Church) *Birm 11* **P** Aston Trustees
  V vacant
SPARKBROOK (St Agatha) w Balsall Heath St Barnabas
  Birm 2 **P** Bp **P-in-c** J E D LUFF
SPARKFORD (St Mary Magdalene) *see* Cam Vale *B & W*
SPARKHILL (St John the Evangelist) *Birm 11* **P** Dioc Trustees
  and Aston Trustees (alt) **V** vacant
SPARKWELL (All Saints) *Ex 20* **P** D&C Windsor
  C D H ROBINSON
SPARROW HALL (St George) *see* Fazakerley Em *Liv*
SPARSHOLT (Holy Cross) *see* Ridgeway *Ox*
SPARSHOLT (St Stephen) *see* The Downs *Win*
SPAXTON (St Margaret) *see* Aisholt, Enmore, Goathurst, Nether Stowey etc *B & W*
SPEEN (St Mary the Virgin) *see* Newbury St Nic and Speen *Ox*
SPEETON (St Leonard) *see* Bempton w Flamborough, Reighton w Speeton *York*
SPEKE (St Aidan) (All Saints) *Liv 2* **P** Bp **R** vacant
SPELDHURST (St Mary the Virgin) w Groombridge and Ashurst *Roch 12* **P** DBP **R** D P WREN
SPELSBURY (All Saints) *see* Chase *Ox*
SPEN, HIGH (St Patrick) and Rowlands Gill *Dur 12* **P** Bp
  V vacant
SPENCER Beneface *see* Brington w Whilton and Norton etc *Pet*
SPENCERS WOOD (St Michael and All Angels) *see* Loddon Reach *Ox*
SPENNITHORNE (St Michael) *see* Lower Wensleydale *Leeds*
SPENNYMOOR (St Paul) and Whitworth *Dur 5* **P** D&C
  V M P TARLING **C** A J SMITH
SPETISBURY (St John the Baptist) w Charlton Marshall and Blandford St Mary *Sarum 6* **P** Worc Coll Ox (1 turn), Bp (2 turns) **R** vacant
SPEXHALL (St Peter) *see* Blyth Valley *St E*
SPILSBY (St James) *see* Bolingbroke Deanery *Linc*
SPIRE HILL, comprising Purse Caundle, Stalbridge, Stock Gaylard, and Stourton Caundle *Sarum 5* **P** Bp, CCC Cam, and Mrs J C M Langmead (jt) **R** vacant
SPITAL (St Agnes) *see* Clewer St Andr *Ox*
SPITAL (St Leonard's Mission Room) *see* Chesterfield St Mary and All SS *Derby*
SPITALFIELDS (Christ Church w All Saints) *Lon 7*
  P MMCET **R** A RIDER **C** D J WOLF
SPITALGATE (St John the Evangelist) *see* S Grantham *Linc*
SPITTAL (St John) *Newc 12* **P** Bp and Mercers' Co (alt)
  Hon C D MACNAUGHTON
SPIXWORTH (St Peter) *see* Horsham St Faith, Spixworth and Crostwick *Nor*
SPOFFORTH (All Saints) w Kirk Deighton *Leeds 21* **P** Bp
  P-in-c S EARLE **NSM** B RYAN
SPONDON (St Werburgh) *Derby 5* **P** Mrs L B Palmer
  V J F HOLLYWELL **C** W P WATERS
SPOTLAND (St Clement) and Oakenrod *Man 17* **P** Bp
  V K L SMEETON **NSM** R C FINDLOW, S BARRON

SPRATTON (St Andrew) *see* Guilsborough and Hollowell and Cold Ashby etc *Pet*
SPREYTON (St Michael) *see* Chagford, Gidleigh, Throwleigh etc *Ex*
SPRIDLINGTON (St Hilary) *see* Owmby Gp *Linc*
SPRING GROVE (St Mary) *Lon 11* **P** Ch Patr Trust
  V E A MATTHEWS **Hon C** M A WARMAN
SPRING LINE Group, The, comprising Aisthorpe, Brattleby, Burton by Lincoln, Cammeringham, North Carlton, South Carlton, Fillingham, Ingham, and Scampton *Linc 5* **P** Lady Monson, Ball Coll Ox, J M Wright Esq, Bp, and DBP (jt)
  R S T MATTAPALLY **OLM** S DEACON, W G WILLIAMS
SPRING PARK (All Saints) *S'wark 19* **P** Bp **V** Y V CLARKE
SPRINGFIELD (All Saints) *Chelmsf 9* **P** Air Cdre N S Paynter
  P-in-c S M M ISKANDER **C** D C PIERCE, S D PEARCE
SPRINGFIELD (Holy Trinity) *Chelmsf 9* **P** Simeon's Trustees
  V K A RODDY **OLM** I D FULLER
SPRINGFIELD (St Christopher) *Birm 11* **P** Trustees
  V T THOMAS
SPRINGFIELD, EAST (Church of Our Saviour) (not known)
  Chelmsf 9 **P** Bp **V** vacant
SPRINGFIELD, NORTH (St Augustine of Canterbury)
  Chelmsf 9 **P** Bp **P-in-c** C J BROWN **C** D C PIERCE
SPRINGFIELDS (St Stephen) *see* Wolverhampton St Martin and St Steph *Lich*
SPRINGTHORPE (St George and St Laurence) *see* Lea Gp *Linc*
SPRINGWELL (St Mary the Virgin) *see* Sunderland St Mary and St Pet *Dur*
SPRINGWOOD (All Souls) *see* Liv All So Springwood *Liv*
SPROATLEY (St Swithin) *see* Hedon, Paull, Sproatley and Preston *York*
SPROTBROUGH (St Mary the Virgin) *Sheff 7* **P** Bp
  R B A J BARRACLOUGH **C** R A HEATON
SPROUGHTON (All Saints) w Burstall, Copdock w Washbrook and Belstead and Bentley w Tattingstone
  St E 15 **P** Patr Bd **R** A D SHANNON
SPROWSTON (St Cuthbert) (St Mary and St Margaret) w Beeston *Nor 2* **P** D&C **R** S C STOKES **C** A S BUNTER,
  D AKRILL, P I HARVEY **NSM** M A HIDER
SPROXTON (St Bartholomew) *see* High Framland Par *Leic*
SPROXTON (St Chad) *see* Helmsley *York*
SQUIRRELS HEATH (All Saints) *Chelmsf 2* **P** Bp
  V C W WRAGG
STADHAMPTON (St John the Baptist) *see* Dorchester *Ox*
STAFFHURST WOOD (St Silvan) *see* Limpsfield and Tatsfield *S'wark*
STAFFORD (St Bertelin) and Whitgreave St John *Lich 10*
  P Bp and Earl of Harrowby (jt) **V** J E EVANS
STAFFORD (St Chad) *Lich 10* **P** Bp **V** R J S GRIGSON
STAFFORD (St John the Baptist) and Tixall w Ingestre
  Lich 10 **P** Bp and Earl of Shrewsbury and Talbot (jt)
  V C N RUDD
STAFFORD (St Mary) and Marston *Lich 10* **P** Bp and Earl of Harrowby (jt) **V** R J S GRIGSON
STAFFORD (St Paul) (St Thomas and St Andrew) *Lich 10*
  P V Castle Ch and Hyndman Trustees (jt) **V** M G STRANG
  C A M THOMAS
STAFFORD, WEST (St Andrew) *see* Dorchester and the Winterbournes *Sarum*
STAGSDEN (St Leonard) *see* Bromham w Oakley and Stagsden *St Alb*
STAGSHAW CHAPEL (St Aidan) *see* St John Lee *Newc*
STAINBY (St Peter) *see* Witham Gp *Linc*
STAINCLIFFE (Christ Church) and Carlinghow *Leeds 9*
  P V Brownhill and V Batley (jt) **V** G NEWTON
  Hon C M G INMAN
STAINCROSS (St John the Evangelist) *see* Darton w Staincross and Mapplewell *Leeds*
STAINDROP (St Mary) *Dur 6* **P** Lord Barnard
  P-in-c K STEVENTON
STAINES (Christ Church) *Lon 13* **P** Bp **V** M BURLEY
STAINES (St Mary) (St Peter) *Lon 13* **P** Ld Chan
  NSM C C HENLEY
STAINFIELD (St Andrew) *see* Bardney *Linc*
STAINFORTH (St Mary) *Sheff 10* **P** Bp **V** vacant
STAINFORTH (St Peter) *see* Langcliffe w Stainforth and Horton *Leeds*
STAINING (St Luke Mission Church) *see* Layton and Staining *Blackb*
STAINLAND (St Andrew) and Outlane *Leeds 7* **P** V Halifax
  V R A CHAPMAN **C** D BURROWS
STAINLEY, NORTH (St Mary the Virgin) *see* W Tanfield and Well w Snape and N Stainley *Leeds*
STAINLEY, SOUTH (St Wilfrid) *see* Bishop Thornton, Burnt Yates, Markington etc *Leeds*
STAINMORE (St Stephen) *see* Upper Eden *Carl*

STAINTON (St Peter w St Paul) w Hilton *York 20* **P** *Abp (2 turns), DBP (1 turn)* **V** V G HATTON
STAINTON (St Winifred) *see* Tickhill w Stainton *Sheff*
STAINTON BY LANGWORTH (St John the Baptist) *see* Barlings *Linc*
STAINTON LE VALE (St Andrew) *see* Walesby Gp *Linc*
STAINTON, GREAT (All Saints) *see* Stockton Country Par *Dur*
STAINTONDALE (St John the Baptist) *see* Ravenscar and Staintondale *York*
STAITHES (St Peter) *see* Hinderwell, Roxby and Staithes etc *York*
STAKEFORD (Holy Family) *see* Choppington *Newc*
STALBRIDGE (St Mary) *see* Spire Hill *Sarum*
STALHAM (St Mary), East Ruston, Brunstead, Sutton and Ingham *Nor 12* **P** *Bp, DBP and Mrs S F Baker (jt)* **R** S P LAWRENCE **OLM** A P BEVAN
STALISFIELD (St Mary) *see* High Downs *Cant*
STALLING BUSK (St Matthew) *see* Upper Wensleydale *Leeds*
STALLINGBOROUGH (St Peter and St Paul) *see* Wolds Gateway Group *Linc*
STALMINE (St James) w Pilling St John the Baptist *Blackb 9* **P** *Bp, V Lanc St Mary, Mrs C B Mason-Hornby, and H D H Elletson Esq (jt)* **V** A J SHAW **C** N H S BARRACLOUGH **OLM** J M KIRKHAM
STALYBRIDGE (Holy Trinity and Christ Church) *Ches 14* **P** *Trustees* **V** G KENNAUGH
STALYBRIDGE (St George) *Man 13* **P** *Lord Deramore and R Ashton-under-Lyne St Mich (jt)* **V** *vacant*
STALYBRIDGE (St Paul) *Ches 14* **P** *Trustees* **P-in-c** K E HANDLEY
STAMBOURNE (St Peter and St Thomas Becket) *see* The Hedinghams and Upper Colne *Chelmsf*
STAMBRIDGE (St Mary and All Saints) *Chelmsf 14* **P** *Ld Chan (1 turn), Charterhouse (3 turns)* **R** *vacant*
STAMFORD (All Saints) w St John the Baptist *Linc 16* **P** *Ld Chan and Burghley Ho Preservation Trust Ltd (alt)* **Hon C** D M BOND
STAMFORD (Christ Church) *Linc 16* **P** *Bp* **V** *vacant*
STAMFORD (St George) (St Paul) *Linc 16* **P** *Burghley Ho Preservation Trust Ltd* **R** M A N TAYLOR **C** S R SIMCOX
STAMFORD (St Mary) (St Martin) *Linc 16* **P** *Burghley Ho Preservation Trust Ltd* **R** G A COOPER
STAMFORD BRIDGE Group of Parishes, The (St John the Baptist), including Catton and Scrayingham *York 5* **P** *Lord Egremont (2 turns), The Crown (1 turn)* **R** S G PRITCHARD **NSM** M H ELLISON
STAMFORD HILL (St Bartholomew) *Lon 5* **P** *The Crown* **V** C L CARD-REYNOLDS
STAMFORD HILL (St Thomas) *Lon 5* **P** *R Hackney* **V** W G CAMPBELL-TAYLOR **NSM** M F E STEWART, S C EJIAKU
STAMFORDHAM (St Mary the Virgin) w Matfen *Newc 9* **P** *Ld Chan* **P-in-c** R L S SCHEFFER
STANBRIDGE (St John the Baptist) *see* Totternhoe, Stanbridge and Tilsworth *St Alb*
STANBURY (Mission Church) *see* Haworth and Cross Roads cum Lees *Leeds*
STAND (All Saints) *Man 10* **P** *Earl of Wilton* **R** T E MORRIS **C** D A WILLIAMS **NSM** A M WHITTLEWORTH
STANDISH (St Nicholas) *see* Stroudwater Team *Glouc*
STANDISH (St Wilfrid) *Blackb 4* **P** *Bp* **R** A HOLLIDAY **C** R A M FEENEY **NSM** C L MARTLEW
STANDLAKE (St Giles) *see* Lower Windrush *Ox*
STANDON (All Saints) *see* Cotes Heath and Standon and Swynnerton etc *Lich*
STANDON (St Mary) and The Mundens w Sacombe *St Alb 15* **P** *Ch Trust Fund Trust, K Coll Cam, and R Abel-Smith Esq (1 turn), Ch Trust Fund Trust (1 turn)* **R** E J CHITHAM
STANFIELD (St Margaret) *see* Launditch and the Upper Nar *Nor*
STANFORD (All Saints) *Nor 13* **P** *Bp* **V** *vacant*
STANFORD (All Saints) *see* Lyminge w Paddlesworth, Stanford w Postling etc *Cant*
STANFORD (St Nicholas) *see* Avon-Swift *Leic*
STANFORD BISHOP (St James) *see* Frome Valley *Heref*
STANFORD DINGLEY (St Denys) *see* Bradfield and Stanford Dingley *Ox*
STANFORD IN THE VALE (St Denys) w Goosey and Hatford *Ox 25* **P** *D&C Westmr (3 turns), Simeon's Trustees (2 turns)* **V** P A EDDY
STANFORD RIVERS (St Margaret) *see* Chipping Ongar w Shelley etc *Chelmsf*
STANFORD-LE-HOPE (St Margaret) w Mucking *Chelmsf 16* **P** *MMCET* **R** J A K GUEST
STANFORD-ON-AVON (St Nicholas) *see* Avon-Swift *Leic*

STANFORD-ON-SOAR (St John the Baptist) *see* E and W Leake, Stanford-on-Soar, Rempstone etc *S'well*
STANFORD-ON-TEME (St Mary) *see* Teme Valley S *Worc*
STANGROUND (St John the Baptist) (St Michael and All Angels) and Farcet *Ely 15* **P** *Em Coll Cam* **P-in-c** A J AVERY **C** C R AVERY
STANHOE (All Saints) *see* Docking, The Birchams, Fring etc *Nor*
STANHOPE (St Thomas) *see* Upper Weardale *Dur*
STANION (St Peter) *see* Brigstock w Stanion and Lowick and Sudborough *Pet*
STANLEY (All Saints) *see* W Hallam and Mapperley w Stanley *Derby*
STANLEY (St Andrew) *as above*
STANLEY (St Andrew) and South Moor *Dur 4* **P** *Bp (3 turns) and The Crown (1 turn)* **V** S CLARK
STANLEY (St Anne) and Stoneycroft St Paul *Liv 5* **P** *V W Derby St Mary and St Chad's Coll Dur (jt)* **V** E L WILLIAMS **C** G HUGHES **Hon C** C WARRILOW
STANLEY (St Thomas) *see* Satley, Stanley and Tow Law *Dur*
STANLEY PONTLARGE (Chapel) *see* Winchcombe *Glouc*
STANMER w Falmer *Chich 19* **P** *Bp* **V** *vacant*
STANMORE (St Luke) *Win 7* **P** *Bp* **P-in-c** E P A DINES **C** M R GARDNER
STANMORE, GREAT (St John the Evangelist) *Lon 23* **P** *R O Bernays Esq* **R** I M STONE **C** J D RAPSON
STANMORE, LITTLE (St Lawrence) *Lon 23* **P** *Bp* **R** P M REECE
STANNINGFIELD (St Nicholas) *see* St Edm Way *St E*
STANNINGLEY (St Thomas) *Leeds 14* **P** *V Leeds St Pet* **R** R I M COUTTS
STANNINGTON (Christ Church) *Sheff 4* **P** *Bp* **P-in-c** T J FLETCHER **C** J E COOPER **NSM** A M COOK
STANNINGTON (St Mary the Virgin) *Newc 11* **P** *Bp* **P-in-c** C R PICKFORD
STANSFIELD (All Saints) *see* Bansfield *St E*
STANSTEAD (St James) *see* Glemsford, Hartest w Boxted, Somerton etc *St E*
STANSTEAD ABBOTS (St Andrew) *see* Gt Amwell w St Margaret's and Stanstead Abbots *St Alb*
STANSTEAD ST MARGARET (St Mary the Virgin) *as above*
STANSTED (St Mary) w Fairseat and Vigo *Roch 10* **P** *Bp* **R** C J L NOBLE
STANSTED MOUNTFITCHET (St John) w Birchanger and Farnham *Chelmsf 18* **P** *Bp, New Coll Ox, and Mrs L A Murphy (jt)* **R** P J WILKIN **NSM** H M FLACK
STANTON (All Saints), including Barningham, Coney Weston, Hepworth, Hinderclay, Hopton, Market Weston, and Thelnetham *St E 5* **P** *K Coll Cam, MMCET, Exors S Holt-Wilson, and Bp (1 turn), The Crown (1 turn), Ld Chan (1 turn)* **R** C R BLADEN **NSM** A J BARCLAY
STANTON (St Gabriel) *see* Golden Cap Team *Sarum*
STANTON (St Mary and All Saints) *see* Markfield, Thornton, Bagworth and Stanton etc *Leic*
STANTON (St Mary) *see* Alton w Bradley-le-Moors and Denstone etc *Lich*
STANTON (St Michael and All Angels) *see* Winchcombe *Glouc*
STANTON BY BRIDGE (St Michael) *see* Melbourne, Ticknall, Smisby and Stanton *Derby*
STANTON DREW (St Mary the Virgin) *see* Chew Magna w Dundry, Norton Malreward etc *B & W*
STANTON FITZWARREN (St Leonard) *see* Stratton St Margaret w S Marston etc *Bris*
STANTON HARCOURT (St Michael) *see* Lower Windrush *Ox*
STANTON HILL (All Saints) *see* Skegby w Teversal *S'well*
STANTON LACY (St Peter) *see* Bromfield *Heref*
STANTON ON HINE HEATH (St Andrew) *Lich 21* **P** *Sir Beville Stanier Bt* **V** R J CRESSWELL
STANTON PRIOR (St Lawrence) *see* Farmborough, Marksbury and Stanton Prior *B & W*
STANTON ST BERNARD (All Saints) *see* Vale of Pewsey *Sarum*
STANTON ST JOHN (St John the Baptist) *see* Beckley, Forest Hill, Horton-cum-Studley and Stanton St John *Ox*
STANTON ST QUINTIN (St Giles) *see* Gauzebrook *Bris*
STANTONBURY (Christ Church) and Willen *Ox 14* **P** *Patr Bd* **TR** P A SMITH **TV** N A POPHAM **NSM** C O IWUAGWU **OLM** S R MUTHUVELOE
STANTON-BY-DALE (St Michael and All Angels) w Dale Abbey and Risley *Derby 8* **P** *Bp* **R** P J SELBY
STANTON-IN-PEAK (Holy Trinity) *see* Youlgreave, Middleton, Stanton-in-Peak etc *Derby*
STANTON-ON-THE-WOLDS (All Saints) *see* Keyworth and Stanton-on-the-Wolds and Bunny etc *S'well*
STANWAY (St Albright) (St Andrew) *Chelmsf 21* **P** *Magd Coll Ox* **P-in-c** A C BUSHELL

STANWAY (St Peter) *see* Winchcombe *Glouc*
STANWELL (St Mary the Virgin) *Lon 13* **P** *Ld Chan*
P-in-c S J KING **C** A D GARNER
STANWICK (St Laurence) *see* Raunds, Hargrave, Ringstead and Stanwick *Pet*
STANWIX (St Michael) *Carl 3* **P** *Bp* **V** N D BEER
C C J HARDING **NSM** J R LIBBY
STAPEHILL (All Saints) *see* Hampreston *Sarum*
STAPENHILL (Immanuel) *Derby 7* **P** *Ch Soc Trust*
P-in-c C D JEFFERSON **OLM** C A BUCKLEY
STAPENHILL (St Peter) w Cauldwell *Derby 7* **P** *Ch Soc Trust*
V M ANDREYEV
STAPLE (St James) *see* Eastry and Woodnesborough *Cant*
STAPLE FITZPAINE (St Peter) *see* Beercrocombe w Curry Mallet, Hatch Beauchamp etc *B & W*
STAPLE TYE (St James) *Chelmsf 4* **P** *Bp* **P-in-c** C C OKEKE
STAPLECROSS (St Mark) *see* Ewhurst *Chich*
STAPLEFIELD COMMON (St Mark) *see* Slaugham and Staplefield Common *Chich*
STAPLEFORD (All Saints) *see* Withamside *Linc*
STAPLEFORD (St Andrew) *Ely 5* **P** *D&C* **P-in-c** S J TALBOTT
C C L G COATES **NSM** S W TAYLOR
STAPLEFORD (St Helen) (St Luke) *S'well 8* **P** *CPAS*
V P A HUXTABLE **C** L CARTWRIGHT, S P FELLOWS
STAPLEFORD (St Mary) *see* Beane Valley *St Alb*
STAPLEFORD (St Mary) *see* Wylye and Till Valley *Sarum*
STAPLEFORD ABBOTTS (St Mary) *see* Vale of Roding *Chelmsf*
STAPLEFORD TAWNEY (St Mary the Virgin) *see* Theydon Par *Chelmsf*
STAPLEGROVE (St John the Evangelist) w Norton Fitzwarren *B & W 18* **P** *Bp and MMCET (jt)* **R** M S KIVETT
STAPLEHURST (All Saints) *Cant 11* **P** *St Jo Coll Cam*
R S TETZLAFF
STAPLETON (Holy Trinity) *see* Frenchay and Stapleton *Bris*
STAPLETON (St John) *see* Dorrington w Leebotwood, Longnor, Stapleton etc *Heref*
STAPLETON (St Martin) *see* Barwell w Potters Marston and Stapleton *Leic*
STAPLETON (St Mary) *see* Bewcastle, Stapleton and Kirklinton etc *Carl*
STARBECK (St Andrew) *Leeds 21* **P** *V Harrogate Ch Ch*
V P G CARMAN **C** S A PICKERING
STARCROSS (St Paul) *see* Dawlish w Holcombe, Cofton and Starcross *Ex*
STARSTON (St Margaret) *see* Dickleburgh and The Pulhams *Nor*
START BAY *see* Stokenham, Slapton, Charleton w Buckland etc *Ex*
STARTFORTH (Holy Trinity) *see* Lower Teesdale *Leeds*
STATFOLD (St Matthew) *see* Mease Valley *Lich*
STATHERN (St Guthlac) *see* Vale of Belvoir *Leic*
STAUGHTONS, The (St Andrew) (All Saints) w Hail Weston *Ely 13* **P** *Mert Coll Ox, St Jo Coll Ox, and CCC Ox (by turn)*
V L N BLAND
STAUNTON (All Saints) *see* Coleford, Staunton, Newland, Redbrook etc *Glouc*
STAUNTON (St James) *see* Ashleworth, Corse, Hartpury, Hasfield etc *Glouc*
STAUNTON (St Mary) w Flawborough *S'well 3*
P E G Staunton Esq **P-in-c** E I MURRAY
STAUNTON-ON-ARROW (St Peter) *see* Pembridge w Moor Court, Shobdon, Staunton etc *Heref*
STAUNTON-ON-WYE (St Mary the Virgin) *see* Letton w Staunton, Byford, Mansel Gamage etc *Heref*
STAVELEY (All Saints) *see* Walkingham Hill *Leeds*
STAVELEY (St James), Ings and Kentmere *Carl 11*
P V Kendal H Trin **P-in-c** S H P THOMPSON
STAVELEY (St John the Baptist) and Barrow Hill *Derby 3*
P *Bp, Adn Chesterfield, and Duke of Devonshire (jt)*
TR R S F JONES **TV** A P ARNOLD
STAVELEY IN CARTMEL (St Mary) *see* Cartmel Peninsula *Carl*
STAVERTON (St Catherine) *see* Twigworth, Down Hatherley, Norton, The Leigh etc *Glouc*
STAVERTON (St Mary the Virgin) *see* Daventry *Pet*
STAVERTON (St Paul de Leon) *see* Buckfastleigh, Dean Prior, Littlehempston etc *Ex*
STAWELL (St Francis) *see* Middlezoy w Othery, Moorlinch and Greinton *B & W*
STAWLEY (St Michael and All Angels) *see* Wellington and Distr *B & W*
STEANE (St Peter) *see* Aynho and Croughton w Evenley etc *Pet*
STEART BAY (St Andrew) *see* Cannington, Otterhampton, Combwich and Stockland *B & W*
STEBBING (St Mary the Virgin) and Lindsell w Great and Little (Bardfield) Saling *Chelmsf 18* **P** *Bp*

P-in-c T E GOODBODY **C** S E HURLEY **NSM** C M HAWKES
OLM M H PELLY
STECHFORD (All Saints) (St Andrew) *Birm 11* **P** *St Pet Coll Ox* **V** G S GAKURU
STEDHAM (St James) *see* Linch w Iping Marsh, Milland and Rake etc *Chich*
STEEP (All Saints) and Froxfield w Privett *Portsm 4* **P** *Ld Chan and Magd Coll Cam (alt)* **V** J E OWEN
NSM S R COLLINGRIDGE
STEEPING, GREAT (All Saints) *see* Bolingbroke Deanery *Linc*
STEEPING, LITTLE (St Andrew) *as above*
STEEPLE (St Lawrence and All Saints) *see* Southminster and Steeple *Chelmsf*
STEEPLE (St Michael and All Angels) *see* St Aldhelm *Sarum*
STEEPLE ASHTON (St Mary the Virgin) *see* N Bradley, Southwick, Heywood and Steeple Ashton *Sarum*
STEEPLE ASTON (St Peter and St Paul) w North Aston and Tackley *Ox 29* **P** *BNC Ox, St Jo Coll Ox, and J D Taylor Esq (jt)* **R** E M GREEN
STEEPLE BARTON (St Mary) *see* Westcote Barton w Steeple Barton, Duns Tew etc *Ox*
STEEPLE BUMPSTEAD (St Mary) *see* Two Rivers *Chelmsf*
STEEPLE CLAYDON (St Michael) *see* The Claydons and Swan *Ox*
STEEPLE LANGFORD (All Saints) *see* Wylye and Till Valley *Sarum*
STEEPLE MORDEN (St Peter and St Paul) *see* Shingay Gp *Ely*
STEETLEY (All Saints) *see* Elmton w Creswell and Whitwell w Steetley *Derby*
STEETON (St Stephen) *Leeds 1* **P** *V Kildwick* **V** D COLEMAN
STELLA (St Cuthbert) *see* Blaydon and Swalwell *Dur*
STELLING (St Mary) *see* Chartham and Upper Hardres w Stelling *Cant*
STENIGOT (St Nicholas) *see* Asterby Gp *Linc*
STEPNEY (St Dunstan and All Saints) *Lon 7* **P** *Bp*
R T F CRITCHLOW
STEPPINGLEY (St Lawrence) *see* Ampthill w Millbrook and Steppingley *St Alb*
STERNFIELD (St Mary Magdalene) *see* Alde River *St E*
STERT (St James) *see* Cannings and Redhorn *Sarum*
STETCHWORTH (St Peter) *see* Raddesley Gp *Ely*
STEVENAGE (All Saints) Pin Green *St Alb 20* **P** *Bp*
V P J ORTON
STEVENAGE (Holy Trinity) (Christ the King) *St Alb 20* **P** *Bp*
V R E CARROLL **NSM** A J THOMAS, F C SOUTER
STEVENAGE (St Andrew and St George) *St Alb 20* **P** *Bp*
R C E BUNCE **C** N P MULCOCK **NSM** J A PAGE
STEVENAGE (St Hugh) (St John) Chells *St Alb 20* **P** *Bp*
V C K PERERA
STEVENAGE (St Mary) Shephall *St Alb 20* **P** *Bp*
V V A HATHAWAY
STEVENAGE (St Nicholas) and Graveley *St Alb 20* **P** *Bp*
V D M BROWN
STEVENAGE (St Peter) Broadwater *St Alb 20* **P** *Bp*
V C R SHARPLES **C** P FOSTER
STEVENTON (St Michael and All Angels) *see* DAMASCUS *Ox*
STEVENTON (St Nicholas) *see* N Waltham and Steventon, Ashe and Deane *Win*
STEVINGTON (Church Room) *see* Chellington *St Alb*
STEVINGTON (St Mary the Virgin) *as above*
STEWKLEY (St Michael and All Angels) *see* Cottesloe *Ox*
STEWTON (St Andrew) *see* Louth *Linc*
STEYNING (St Andrew) *Chich 11* **P** *Bp* **V** M D G HEATHER
C S P MILLS
STIBBARD (All Saints) *see* Heart of Norfolk *Nor*
STIBBINGTON (St John the Baptist) *see* Castor w Upton and Stibbington etc *Pet*
STICKER (St Mark's Mission Church) *see* St Mewan w Mevagissey and St Ewe *Truro*
STICKFORD (St Helen) *see* Bolingbroke Deanery *Linc*
STICKLEPATH (St Mary) *see* Okehampton, Inwardleigh, Belstone, Sourton etc *Ex*
STICKLEPATH (St Paul) w Roundswell *Ex 14* **P** *Bp*
V G CHAVE-COX
STICKNEY (St Luke) *see* Bolingbroke Deanery *Linc*
STIFFKEY (St John and St Mary) and Bale *Nor 17*
P *MMCET, Bp, DBP, Keble Coll Ox, and Sir Euan Hamilton Anstruther-Gough-Calthorpe Bt (jt)* **R** I C WHITTLE
STIFFORD (St Cedd) (St Mary) *Chelmsf 16* **P** *Bp*
R A R B HIGGS
STILLINGFLEET (St Helen) *see* Escrick and Stillingfleet w Naburn *York*
STILLINGTON (St John) *see* Stockton Country Par *Dur*
STILLINGTON (St Nicholas) *see* Forest of Galtres *York*
STILTON (St Mary Magdalene) w Denton and Caldecote and Folkesworth w Morborne and Haddon *Ely 15*

P *MMCET and Bp, Ld Chan (alt)* **P-in-c** R J GIBBS
C M W PYBUS
STINCHCOMBE (St Cyr) *see* Cam w Stinchcombe *Glouc*
STINSFORD (St Michael) *see* Charminster, Stinsford and the Chalk Stream villages *Sarum*
STIPERSTONES Group, The *see* Minsterley, Habberley and Hope w Shelve *Heref*
STIRCHLEY (All Saints) *see* Cen Telford *Lich*
STIRCHLEY (Ascension) *Birm 4* **P** *R Kings Norton*
V C A GRYLLS
STISTED (All Saints) *see* Cressing w Stisted and Bradwell etc *Chelmsf*
STITHIANS (St Stythian) *see* St Stythians w Perranarworthal and Gwennap *Truro*
STIXWOULD (St Peter) *see* Woodhall Spa Gp *Linc*
STOAK (St Lawrence) *see* Ellesmere Port *Ches*
STOCK (St Barnabas) *see* Spire Hill *Sarum*
STOCK HARVARD (All Saints) *Chelmsf 10* **P** *Guild of All So*
P-in-c S W NEED
STOCKBRIDGE (Old St Peter) *see* Mid Test *Win*
STOCKBRIDGE (St Peter) *as above*
STOCKBRIDGE VILLAGE (St Jude) *see* 4Saints Team *Liv*
STOCKBURY (St Mary Magdalene) *see* The Six *Cant*
STOCKCROSS (St John) *see* E Downland *Ox*
STOCKERSTON (St Peter) *see* Six Saints circa Holt *Leic*
STOCKING FARM (St Luke) and Beaumont Leys *Leic 1* **P** *Bp*
V S R DELAFORCE
STOCKING PELHAM (St Mary) *see* Braughing, Furneux Pelham and Stocking Pelham *St Alb*
STOCKINGFORD (St Paul) *Cov 5* **P** *V Nuneaton*
V K I MASSEY **C** J L JOYCE
STOCKLAND (St Mary Magdalene) *see* Cannington, Otterhampton, Combwich and Stockland *B & W*
STOCKLAND (St Michael and All Angels) *see* Kilmington, Stockland, Dalwood, Yarcombe etc *Ex*
STOCKLAND GREEN (St Mark) *Birm 7* **P** *The Crown*
P-in-c R J WALKER-HILL
STOCKLEIGH ENGLISH (St Mary the Virgin) *see* N Creedy *Ex*
STOCKLEIGH POMEROY (St Mary the Virgin) *as above*
STOCKLINCH (St Mary Magdalene) *see* Winsmoor *B & W*
STOCKPORT (St George) *Ches 18* **P** *Trustees* **V** E C HALL
C J B ARNOTT
STOCKPORT (St Mark) *see* Edgeley and Cheadle Heath *Ches*
STOCKPORT (St Martin) *see* Heatons *Man*
STOCKPORT (St Mary) (St Thomas) (St Andrew) and Brinnington *Ches 18* **P** *Bp and G&C Coll Cam (jt)*
R L S CULLENS
STOCKPORT (St Matthew) *see* Edgeley and Cheadle Heath *Ches*
STOCKPORT (St Peter) *Ches 18* **P** *Ch Union* **R** *vacant*
STOCKPORT (St Saviour) *Ches 18* **P** *Trustees*
V D V COOKSON
STOCKSFIELD (St John) *see* Bywell and Mickley *Newc*
STOCKTON (Parish Church) *Dur 9* **P** *Bp*
P-in-c M G MILLER **C** E V HUDGHTON
STOCKTON (St Andrew) *see* Teme Valley N *Worc*
STOCKTON (St Chad) *see* Beckbury, Badger, Kemberton, Ryton, Stockton etc *Lich*
STOCKTON (St John the Baptist) *see* Wylye and Till Valley *Sarum*
STOCKTON (St Michael and All Angels) *see* Gillingham w Geldeston, Stockton, Ellingham etc *Nor*
STOCKTON (St Michael and All Angels) *see* Napton-on-the-Hill, Lower Shuckburgh etc *Cov*
STOCKTON CHRISTCHURCH (St Chad) (St James) (St John the Baptist) *Dur 9* **P** *Bp* **P-in-c** J L SHARPE
STOCKTON Country Parish, comprising Bishopton, Great Stainton, Grindon, Redmarshall, Stillington, and Wynyard Park *Dur 9* **P** *Bp, Ld Chan, The Crown, and D&C (by turn)*
P-in-c C A GIBBS
STOCKTON HEATH (St Thomas) *Ches 4* **P** *P G Greenall Esq*
V M L RIDLEY **C** R J ICKE
STOCKTON ON TEES (Holy Trinity) (St Mark) *Dur 9* **P** *Bp*
P-in-c P S D NEVILLE
STOCKTON-ON-TEES (St Paul) *Dur 9* **P** *The Crown*
V *vacant*
STOCKTON-ON-TEES (St Peter) *Dur 9* **P** *Bp*
P-in-c W E BRAVINER **C** P MURRAY
STOCKTON-ON-TEES (St Thomas) *see* Stockton Par Ch *Dur*
STOCKTON-ON-THE-FOREST (Holy Trinity) *see* Rural E York *York*
STOCKWELL (St Andrew) (St Michael) *S'wark 11* **P** *Bp*
V E M WOOFF **NSM** I S FAULKNER
STOCKWITH, EAST (St Peter) *see* Trentcliffe Gp *Linc*
STOCKWITH, WEST (St Mary the Virgin) *see* Beckingham, Walkeringham, Misterton, etc *S'well*

STOCKWOOD (Christ the Servant) *see* Bris Ch the Servant Stockwood *Bris*
STODDEN Churches, The, comprising Dean, Melchbourne, Pertenhall, Shelton, Swineshead, and Yelden *St Alb 13*
P *MMCET and DBP (alt)* **P-in-c** S C HOLROYD
STODMARSH (St Mary) *see* Littlebourne and Ickham w Wickhambreaux etc *Cant*
STODY (St Mary) *see* Brinton, Briningham, Hunworth, Stody etc *Nor*
STOGUMBER (Blessed Virgin Mary) *see* Quantock Towers *B & W*
STOGURSEY (St Andrew) *see* Quantock Coast *B & W*
STOKE (St Mary and St Andrew) *see* Colsterworth Gp *Linc*
STOKE (St Michael) Coventry *Cov 1* **P** *Bp and Ld Chan (alt)*
TR C MCARTHUR **C** N W PHILLIPS
NSM J S WATKINS-WOLLNER
STOKE (St Peter and St Paul) *see* Grain w Stoke *Roch*
STOKE ABBOTT (St Mary) *see* Beaminster Area *Sarum*
STOKE ALBANY (St Botolph) w Wilbarston and Ashley w Weston-by-Welland and Sutton Bassett *Pet 7*
P *Comdr L M M Saunders-Watson (2 turns), Bp (1 turn), DBP (1 turn)* **R** *vacant*
STOKE ALDERMOOR (St Catherine) and New Century Park *Cov 1* **P** *Ld Chan and Bp (alt)* **V** E K FORBES STONE
STOKE ASH (All Saints) *see* S Hartismere *St E*
STOKE BARDOLPH (St Luke) *see* Burton Joyce, Bulcote and Stoke Bardolph etc *S'well*
STOKE BISHOP (St Mary Magdalene) *Bris 2* **P** *Bp*
C J D WHITE, S J POTTER **OLM** A K CATTELL, H J TRAPNELL, M J HALL
STOKE BLISS (St Peter) *see* Teme Valley S *Worc*
STOKE BRUERNE (St Mary the Virgin) *see* Blisworth, Alderton, Grafton Regis etc *Pet*
STOKE BY CLARE (St John the Baptist) *see* Stour Valley *St E*
STOKE BY NAYLAND (St Mary) w Leavenheath and Polstead *St E 4* **P** *Mrs S E F Holden and St Jo Coll Ox (alt)*
P-in-c M J WOODROW
STOKE CANON (St Mary Magdalene) *see* Brampford Speke, Cadbury, Newton St Cyres etc *Ex*
STOKE CHARITY (St Mary and St Michael) *see* Upper Dever *Win*
STOKE CLIMSLAND (not known) *see* Callington Cluster *Truro*
STOKE D'ABERNON (St Mary the Virgin) *Guildf 10*
P *K Coll Cam* **R** R G HILLIARD
STOKE DAMEREL (St Andrew w St Luke) *Ex 21* **P** *The Crown* **R** K A ROBUS
STOKE DOYLE (St Rumbold) *see* Aldwincle, Clopton, Pilton, Stoke Doyle etc *Pet*
STOKE DRY (St Andrew) *see* Lyddington, Bisbrooke, Caldecott, Glaston etc *Pet*
STOKE EDITH (St Mary) *see* Hop Churches *Heref*
STOKE FLEMING (St Peter), Blackawton, Strete and East Allington *Ex 13* **P** *Bp and DBP (jt)* **V** A B SHAW
STOKE GABRIEL (St Gabriel) *see* Totnes w Bridgetown, Berry Pomeroy etc *Ex*
STOKE GIFFORD (St Michael) *Bris 5* **P** *Bp* **R** S JONES
C T Y BENYON **NSM** J C BRADLEY
STOKE GOLDING (St Margaret) *see* Fenn Lanes Gp *Leic*
STOKE GOLDINGTON (St Peter) *see* Gayhurst w Ravenstone, Stoke Goldington etc *Ox*
STOKE HAMMOND (St Luke) *see* Brickhills and Stoke Hammond *Ox*
STOKE HEATH (St Alban) *see* Cov St Alb *Cov*
STOKE HILL (St Peter) *Guildf 5* **P** *Bp* **V** K L ROSSLYN-SMITH
C R D C DRISCOLL
STOKE HOLY CROSS (Holy Cross) w Dunston, Arminghall and Caistor St Edmunds w Markshall *Nor 8* **P** *D&C and Mrs D Pott (jt)* **R** R J BAKER **NSM** L MARSH
STOKE LACY (St Peter and St Paul) *see* Bromyard and Stoke Lacy *Heref*
STOKE LYNE (St Peter) *see* Shelswell *Ox*
STOKE MANDEVILLE (St Mary the Virgin) *see* Ellesborough, The Kimbles and Stoke Mandeville *Ox*
STOKE NEWINGTON (St Andrew) *Lon 5* **P** *Bp*
P-in-c C A ENGA **NSM** C L J MORGAN
STOKE NEWINGTON (St John the Evangelist) *see* Brownswood Park *Lon*
STOKE NEWINGTON (St Mary) (Old Parish Church) *Lon 5*
P *Bp* **R** H M BAKER **C** R H LIDDELL **NSM** A SHEERAN
STOKE NEWINGTON (St Olave) *Lon 5* **P** *Ld Chan*
V V A ROBERTS
STOKE NEWINGTON COMMON (St Michael and All Angels) *Lon 5* **P** *Bp* **V** S A GAYLE
Hon C W G CAMPBELL-TAYLOR

STOKE NEWINGTON St Faith (St Matthias) and All Saints
Lon 5 **P** *City Corp* **V** D J LAMBERT
STOKE ORCHARD (St James the Great) *see* Deerhurst and
Apperley w Forthampton etc *Glouc*
STOKE PARK (St Peter) *see* Ipswich St Mary at Stoke w St Pet
and St Fran *St E*
STOKE PERO (not known) *see* Porlock and Porlock Weir w
Stoke Pero etc *B & W*
STOKE POGES (St Giles) *Ox 12* **P** *Ch Ch Ox* **V** N D BRADY
STOKE PRIOR (St Luke) *see* Leominster *Heref*
STOKE PRIOR (St Michael), Wychbold and Upton Warren
Worc 8 **P** *Bp and D&C (alt)* **P-in-c** V W BEYNON
NSM A D MORRIS
STOKE RIVERS (St Bartholomew) *see* Shirwell, Loxhore,
Kentisbury, Arlington, etc *Ex*
STOKE ROW (St John the Evangelist) *see* Langtree *Ox*
STOKE ST GREGORY (St Gregory) *see* Athelney *B & W*
STOKE ST MARY (St Mary) *see* Beercrocombe w Curry
Mallet, Hatch Beauchamp etc *B & W*
STOKE ST MICHAEL (St Michael) *see* Leigh upon Mendip w
Stoke St Michael *B & W*
STOKE ST MILBOROUGH (St Milburgha) *see* Bromfield *Heref*
STOKE SUB HAMDON (The Blessed Virgin Mary) *see* Ham
Hill Villages *B & W*
STOKE TALMAGE (St Mary Magdalene) *see* Thame *Ox*
STOKE TRISTER (St Andrew) *see* Charlton Musgrove,
Cucklington and Stoke Trister *B & W*
STOKE UPON TERN (St Peter) *see* Cheswardine, Childs
Ercall, Hales, Hinstock etc *Lich*
STOKE, EAST (St Oswald) w Syerston *S'well 3* **P** *Bp*
P-in-c E I MURRAY
STOKE, NORTH (St Martin) *see* Bath Weston All SS w N
Stoke and Langridge *B & W*
STOKE, NORTH (St Mary the Virgin) *see* Langtree *Ox*
STOKE, SOUTH (St Andrew) *see* Goring and Streatley w S
Stoke *Ox*
STOKE, SOUTH (St James the Great) *see* Combe Down w
Monkton Combe and S Stoke *B & W*
STOKE, SOUTH (St Leonard) *see* Arundel w Tortington and S
Stoke *Chich*
STOKE, WEST (St Andrew) *see* Funtington and W Stoke w
Sennicotts *Chich*
STOKEHAM (St Peter) *see* Retford Area *S'well*
STOKEINTEIGNHEAD (St Andrew) *see* Shaldon,
Stokeinteignhead, Combeinteignhead etc *Ex*
STOKENCHURCH (St Peter and St Paul) *see* S Chilterns *Ox*
STOKE-NEXT-GUILDFORD (St John the Evangelist) *Guildf 5*
P *Simeon's Trustees* **R** M C WOODWARD **C** N J HILL
OLM N S SHARPE
STOKENHAM (St Michael and All Angels), Slapton,
Charleton w Buckland-Tout-Saints, East Portlemouth,
South Pool, and Chivelstone *Ex 13* **P** *The Crown (1 turn),*
Bp, DBP, Sir Neil Jephcott Bt, and Ms S Tyler (1 turn), and Ld
Chan (1 turn) **NSM** M V BERRETT
STOKESAY (St Christopher) (St John the Baptist) *Heref 10*
P *T P D La Touche Esq* **NSM** M G WILLIAMS
STOKESBY (St Andrew) *see* S Trin Broads *Nor*
STOKESLEY (St Peter and St Paul) w Seamer *York 20* **P** *Abp*
R A P HUTCHINSON
STOKE-UPON-TRENT (St Peter-ad-Vincula) (St Paul) and
Fenton *Lich 11* **P** *Bp* **TR** A S L J WICKENS **TV** G E EZE,
T P MERRY **C** V L FLANAGAN **NSM** G HARRISON, J BIRKIN
OLM H W DUROSE
STOLFORD (St Peter) *see* Quantock Coast *B & W*
STON EASTON (Blessed Virgin Mary) *see* Chewton Mendip
w Ston Easton, Litton etc *B & W*
STONDON (All Saints) *see* Gravenhurst, Shillington and
Stondon *St Alb*
STONDON MASSEY (St Peter and St Paul) *see* Blackmore
and Stondon Massey *Chelmsf*
STONE (All Saints) *see* Berkeley w Wick, Breadstone,
Newport, Stone etc *Glouc*
STONE (Christ Church) and Oulton-with-Moddershall
Lich 12 **P** *Simeon's Trustees* **P** H C KINGMAN
STONE (St John the Baptist) *see* Wychert Vale *Ox*
STONE (St Mary the Virgin) *see* Kidderminster E *Worc*
STONE (St Michael and St Wulfad) w Aston (St Saviour)
Lich 12 **P** *Bp* **R** I R CARDINAL **NSM** A M HUDSON,
J G COTTERILL
STONE CROSS (St Luke) w Langney, North *Chich 14* **P** *Bp*
V J D VINE **C** D L PEGG
STONE near Dartford (St Mary) *Roch 2* **P** *Bp* **R** K W CLARK
NSM A B S HARRIS-FAULKNER
STONE QUARRY (St Luke) *see* E Grinstead St Swithun *Chich*
STONEBRIDGE (St Michael and All Angels) *Lon 21* **P** *Bp*
V S J LIEBERT

STONEBROOM (St Peter) *see* Morton and Stonebroom w
Shirland *Derby*
STONEGATE (St Peter) *Chich 16* **P** *E J B Hardcastle Esq and*
Mrs C J J Reid (jt) **P-in-c** P R RATCLIFF
STONEGRAVE (Holy Trinity) *see* Ampleforth w Oswaldkirk,
Gilling E etc *York*
STONEHAM, NORTH (St Nicholas) (All Saints) and Bassett
Win 10 **P** R H W Fleming Esq* **P-in-c** S J WILLIAMS
C C E PHILBRICK, J B HARVEY **Hon C** N BOAKES
NSM R PRIETO-DURAN
STONEHAM, SOUTH (St Mary) *see* Swaythling *Win*
STONEHOUSE (St Paul) *see* Plymouth St Andr and
Stonehouse *Ex*
STONE-IN-OXNEY (St Mary the Virgin) *see* Tenterden,
Rother and Oxney *Cant*
STONELEIGH (St John the Baptist) *Guildf 9* **P** *Bp*
P-in-c M L BORLEY
STONELEIGH (St Mary the Virgin) w Ashow *Cov 4* **P** *Lord*
Leigh and Bp (jt) **P-in-c** N J MOON
STONESBY (St Peter) *see* Ironstone Villages *Leic*
STONESFIELD (St James the Great) w Combe Longa *Ox 29*
P *Duke of Marlborough* **R** A R TURNER
STONEY MIDDLETON (St Martin) *see* Longstone, Curbar and
Stony Middleton *Derby*
STONEY STANTON (St Michael) *see* Broughton Astley and
Croft w Stoney Stanton *Leic*
STONEYCROFT (All Saints) *Liv 5* **P** *Bp*
P-in-c A J H LEATHERBARROW **NSM** D JEYARAJ
STONEYCROFT (St Paul) *see* Stanley and Stoneycroft St Paul
Liv
STONHAM ASPAL (St Mary and St Lambert) *see* N Bosmere
St E
STONNALL (St Peter) *see* Shenstone and Stonnall *Lich*
STONTON WYVILLE (St Denys) *see* Welham, Glooston and
Cranoe and Stonton Wyville *Leic*
STONY MIDDLETON (St Martin) *see* Longstone, Curbar and
Stony Middleton *Derby*
STONY STRATFORD (St Mary and St Giles) w Calverton
Ox 14 **P** *Bp and DBP (jt)* **R** R NORTHING
NSM O A ADEBIYI
STONYDELPH (St Martin in the Delph) *see* Glascote and
Stonydelph *Lich*
STOODLEIGH (St Margaret) *see* Washfield, Stoodleigh,
Withleigh etc *Ex*
STOPHAM (St Mary the Virgin) and Fittleworth *Chich 10*
P *D&C and Col Sir Brian Barttelot Bt (jt)* **P-in-c** D R CROOK
STOPSLEY (St Thomas) *St Alb 12* **P** *Bp* **V** D G ALEXANDER
C R BARR
STORRIDGE (St John the Baptist) *see* Cradley w Mathon and
Storridge *Heref*
STORRINGTON (St Mary) *Chich 11* **P** *Keble Coll Ox*
R K A WINDSLOW **Hon C** C A HADLEY **NSM** A R ROSS,
R W TOOVEY
STOTFOLD (St Mary the Virgin) and Radwell *St Alb 3* **P** *Bp*
V W T BRITT **NSM** G J CLARK
STOTTESDON (St Mary) w Farlow, Cleeton St Mary,
Silvington, Sidbury and Middleton Scriven *Heref 8* **P** *Bp*
R M H DABORN
STOUGHTON (Emmanuel) *Guildf 5* **P** *Simeon's Trustees*
V F SCAMMELL **C** S CHATTEN **OLM** R P F MASTERS
STOUGHTON (St Mary) *see* Octagon *Chich*
STOULTON (St Edmund) w Drake's Broughton and Pirton
and Norton *Worc 4* **P** *Croome Estate Trustees, D&C, and Bp*
(jt) **C** E L GOLDBY, G R NOYES, S A DANGERFIELD
STOUR DOWNS Benefice, The, comprising Brabourne,
Mersham, Monks Horton, Sellindge, Smeeth, and Stowting
Cant 6 **P** *Abp* **P-in-c** C R T DENYER
STOUR PROVOST (St Michael and All Angels) *see* Stour Vale
Sarum
STOUR VALE, comprising Buckhorn Weston, East Stour,
Fifehead Magdalen, Kington Magna, Stour Provost, Stour
Row, Todber, and West Stour *Sarum 5* **P** *Bp* **V** R P PRIEST
STOUR VALLEY, The, comprising Cavendish, Clare w
Poslingford, Hundon, Stoke-by-Clare, and Wixoe *St E 3*
P *DBP, Jes Coll Cam, Lady Loch, and Duchy of Lanc (by turn)*
R S MITCHELL **NSM** L A SEBBAGE
STOUR, EAST (Christ Church) *see* Stour Vale *Sarum*
STOUR, UPPER, comprising Bourton, Kilmington, Stourton,
and Zeals *Sarum 12* **P** H C Hoare Esq (1 turn), Bp (2 turns),
and Bourton Chpl Trustees (1 turn)* **R** vacant
STOUR, WEST (St Mary) *see* Stour Vale *Sarum*
STOURBRIDGE (St Thomas) *Worc 12* **P** *Bp* **V** A K SILLIS
C A R HADLEY
STOURDENE Group, The, comprising Alderminster, Butler's
Marston, Ettington, Halford, Newbold-on-Stour, and
Pillerton Hersey w Pillerton Priors *Cov 9* **P** *SMF, Bp, Major*

and Mrs J E Shirley, Miss M L P Shirley, P E Shirley Esq, Ch Ch Ox, Jes Coll Ox, and Mr and Mrs G Howell **R** S L GOBLE

STOURHEAD, comprising Barnardiston, Great Bradley, Great Thurlow, Great Wratting, Hundon, Kedington, Little Bradley, Little Thurlow, and Little Wratting *St E 3* **P** *E H Vestey Esq, St Chad's Coll Dur, Ridley Hall Cam, and Walsingham Coll Trust (jt)* **V** *vacant*

STOURPAINE (Holy Trinity) *see* Pimperne, Stourpaine, Durweston and Bryanston *Sarum*

STOURPORT-ON-SEVERN (St Michael and All Angels) and Wilden *Worc 13* **P** *Earl Baldwin of Bewdley and V Kidderminster St Mary and All SS (jt)* **V** C J SALEH **NSM** J M A QUINN

STOURTON (St Peter) *see* Upper Stour *Sarum*

STOURTON CAUNDLE (St Peter) *see* Spire Hill *Sarum*

STOVEN (St Margaret) *see* Hundred River and Wainford *St E*

STOW BARDOLPH (Holy Trinity) *see* W Norfolk Priory Gp *Ely*

STOW BEDON (St Botolph) *see* Caston, Griston, Merton, Thompson etc *Nor*

STOW BRIDGE Mission (St Peter) *see* W Norfolk Priory Gp *Ely*

STOW Group, The (St Mary the Virgin), including Coates, Torksey, and Willingham-by-Stow *Linc 2* **P** *Bp and DBP (jt)* **P-in-c** A N A PENN-ALLISON **OLM** J A VICKERS

STOW LONGA (St Botolph) *see* S Leightonstone *Ely*

STOW MARIES (St Mary and St Margaret) *see* Cold Norton w Stow Maries *Chelmsf*

STOW ON THE WOLD (St Edward), Condicote and The Swells *Glouc 8* **P** *DBP and Ch Ch Ox (jt)* **R** M P SHORT **Hon C** A WHITAKER

STOW, WEST (St Mary) *see* Lark Valley *St E*

STOWCAPLE *Heref 7* **P** *Bp (7 turns), D&C (2 turns), Exors Brig A F L Clive (1 turn)* **V** C M R PEMBERTON **C** T G J STARLING

STOWE (Assumption of St Mary the Virgin) *Ox 11* **P** *Stowe Sch* **V** *vacant*

STOWE (St Michael and All Angels) *see* Middle Marches *Heref*

STOWE BY CHARTLEY (St John the Baptist) *see* Mid Trent *Lich*

STOWE NINE CHURCHES (St Michael) *see* Heyford w Stowe Nine Churches and Flore etc *Pet*

STOWE, UPPER (St James) *as above*

STOWELL (St Leonard) *see* Chedworth, Yanworth and Stowell, Coln Rogers etc *Glouc*

STOWELL (St Mary Magdalene) *see* Milborne Port w Goathill etc *B & W*

STOWEY (St Nicholas and Blessed Virgin Mary) *see* Clutton w Cameley, Bishop Sutton and Stowey *B & W*

STOWEY, NETHER (Blessed Virgin Mary) *see* Aisholt, Enmore, Goathurst, Nether Stowey etc *B & W*

STOWEY, OVER (St Peter and St Paul) *as above*

STOWFORD (St John the Baptist) *see* Lifton, Broadwoodwidger, Stowford etc *Ex*

STOWLANGTOFT (St George) *see* Pakenham w Norton, Tostock etc *St E*

STOWMARKET (St Peter and St Mary) *St E 8* **P** *Ch Patr Trust* **V** M W EDEN **NSM** R M STRETCH

STOWTING (St Mary the Virgin) *see* Stour Downs *Cant*

STOWUPLAND (Holy Trinity) *see* Haughley w Wetherden and Stowupland *St E*

STRADBROKE (All Saints) *see* Sancroft *St E*

STRADISHALL (St Margaret) *see* Bansfield *St E*

STRADSETT (St Mary) *see* Downham Market and Stradsett *Ely*

STRAGGLETHORPE (St Michael) *see* Brant Broughton and Beckingham *Linc*

STRAITS, The (St Andrew) *see* Gornal and Sedgley *Worc*

STRAMSHALL (St Michael and All Angels) *see* Uttoxeter Area *Lich*

STRANTON (All Saints) *Dur 3* **P** *St Jo Coll Dur* **V** N R SHAVE **C** M M DELVES **NSM** C R HALL

STRATFIELD MORTIMER (St Mary) and Mortimer West End w Padworth *Ox 4* **P** *Eton Coll, Ld Chan, and Englefield Estate Trust Corp (by turn)* **V** P CHAPLIN

STRATFIELD SAYE (St Mary) *see* Sherfield-on-Loddon and Stratfield Saye etc *Win*

STRATFORD (St John the Evangelist w Christ Church) *Chelmsf 5* **P** V W Ham **V** D A RICHARDS **C** C C ASINUGO, D M SCOTT, R S OTULE **OLM** N BRYZAK

STRATFORD (St Paul) and St James *Chelmsf 5* **P** *Ch Patr Trust* **V** I B ANDERSON

STRATFORD ST MARY (St Mary) *see* Higham, Holton St Mary, Raydon and Stratford *St E*

STRATFORD SUB CASTLE (St Lawrence) *see* Salisbury St Fran and Stratford sub Castle *Sarum*

STRATFORD-UPON-AVON (Holy Trinity), Luddington and Clifford Chambers *Cov 8* **P** *Bp* **R** P J TAYLOR **C** S R JARVIS **NSM** K DYER

STRATTON (St Andrew) *see* N Kernow *Truro*

STRATTON (St Mary the Virgin) *see* Charminster, Stinsford and the Chalk Stream villages *Sarum*

STRATTON (St Peter) *see* Churn Valley *Glouc*

STRATTON AUDLEY (St Mary and St Edburga) *see* Shelswell *Ox*

STRATTON ON THE FOSSE (St Vigor) *see* Chilcompton w Downside and Stratton on the Fosse *B & W*

STRATTON ST MARGARET (St Margaret) w South Marston and Stanton Fitzwarren *Bris 7* **P** *Bp and Mert Coll Ox (jt)* **NSM** M J TIDEY

STRATTON ST MARY (St Mary) *see* Long Stratton and Pilgrim TM *Nor*

STRATTON ST MICHAEL (St Michael) *as above*

STRATTON STRAWLESS (St Margaret) *see* Coltishall w Gt Hautbois, Frettenham etc *Nor*

STRATTON, EAST (All Saints) *see* Upper Dever *Win*

STRATTON, UPPER (St Philip) *Bris 7* **P** *Bp* **P-in-c** A L CHESWORTH **C** J A S HILLER

STREAT (not known) *see* Ditchling, Streat and Westmeston *Chich*

STREATHAM (Christ Church) *S'wark 12* **P** *Bp and R Streatham St Leon (jt)* **V** S FIELDGATE

STREATHAM (Immanuel) (St Andrew) *S'wark 12* **P** *Bp, Hyndman Trustees, and R Streatham St Leon (jt)* **V** *vacant*

STREATHAM (St Leonard) *S'wark 12* **P** *Bp* **R** A E NORMAN-WALKER **C** H N ARGLES-GRANT

STREATHAM (St Peter) *S'wark 12* **P** *St Steph Ho Ox* **V** *vacant*

STREATHAM (St Thomas) *see* Telford Park *S'wark*

STREATHAM HILL (St Margaret the Queen) *S'wark 12* **P** *Bp* **P-in-c** G S A I GERMAIN-POWELL

STREATHAM PARK (St Alban) *see* Furzedown *S'wark*

STREATHAM VALE (Holy Redeemer) *S'wark 12* **P** *CPAS* **V** I H GILMOUR

STREATHAM, WEST (St James) *see* Furzedown *S'wark*

STREATLEY (St Margaret) *St Alb 12* **P** *Bp* **NSM** P DI LEO

STREATLEY (St Mary) *see* Goring and Streatley w S Stoke *Ox*

STREET (Holy Trinity) (Mission Church) w Walton and Compton Dundon *B & W 4* **P** *DBP and Bp Lon (jt)* **C** D M GREENFIELD

STREET Parishes, The, comprising Amotherby, Barton-le-Street, Hovingham, and Slingsby *York 6* **P** *Abp, SMF, Sir William Worsley Bt, and Mrs C Roberts (jt)* **R** M E ALLWOOD

STREETLY (All Saints) *Lich 24* **P** *Bp* **V** A F WALKER **C** C C M OKORONKWO

STRELLEY (All Saints) *see* Bilborough and Strelley *S'well*

STRENSALL (St Mary the Virgin) *York 3* **P** *Abp* **V** M HARRISON **C** D M COYNE, E C HASSALL, K A MCBRIDE, M E YOUNG, M H WAINWRIGHT, S WHITING **NSM** C C CRANFIELD, C C GITTENS, C J TOASE, D V HICKS, S P POPE, T M GANT

STRETE (St Michael) *see* Stoke Fleming, Blackawton, Strete and E Allington *Ex*

STRETFORD (All Saints) *Man 5* **P** *Bp* **R** L K MAGUIRE

STRETFORD (St Bride) *see* Old Trafford St Bride *Man*

STRETFORD (St Matthew) *Man 5* **P** *D&C* **R** K L BURGESS **NSM** S W SCHOFIELD

STRETHALL (St Mary the Virgin) *see* Icknield Way Villages *Chelmsf*

STRETHAM (St James) *see* Ely *Ely*

STRETTON (St John) *see* Penkridge *Lich*

STRETTON (St Mary) w Claymills *Lich 13* **P** *Baroness Gretton* **P-in-c** G J CROSSLEY **C** B L CARE

STRETTON (St Matthew) and Appleton Thorn *Ches 4* **P** *Mrs P F du Bois Grantham and Dr S P L du Bois Davidson (jt)* **V** A D J JEWELL **C** R E MOCK

STRETTON (St Nicholas) *see* Cottesmore and Burley, Clipsham, Exton etc *Pet*

STRETTON GRANDISON (St Lawrence) *see* Hop Churches *Heref*

STRETTON ON DUNSMORE (All Saints) *see* Draycote Gp *Cov*

STRETTON ON DUNSMORE (Mission Church) *as above*

STRETTON ON FOSSE (St Peter) *see* Ilmington w Stretton-on-Fosse etc *Cov*

STRETTON PARVA (St John the Baptist) *see* Gaulby *Leic*

STRETTON SUGWAS (St Mary Magdalene) *Heref 3* **P** *DBP* **P-in-c** P J BROWN **NSM** E S V VERWEY

STRETTON, LITTLE (All Saints) *see* Church Stretton *Heref*

STRICKLAND, GREAT (St Barnabas) *see* N Westmorland *Carl*

STRINES (St Paul) *see* Marple All SS *Ches*

STRINGSTON (St Mary the Virgin) *see* Quantock Coast *B & W*

STRIXTON (St Romwald) *see* Wollaston w Strixton and Bozeat etc *Pet*

STROOD (St Francis) *Roch 6* **P** *Bp* **V** S L COPESTAKE **C** J C SMITH, S F VALLENTE-KERR

STROOD (St Nicholas) w St Mary *Roch 6* **P** *Bp and D&C (jt)* **V** D W GREEN **C** S F VALLENTE-KERR

STROUD (Holy Trinity) *see* Stroud Team *Glouc*

STROUD (Mission Church) *see* Steep and Froxfield w Privett *Portsm*

STROUD (St Alban Mission Church) *see* Stroud Team *Glouc*

STROUD GREEN (Holy Trinity) *Lon 20* **P** *Bp* **V** P J HENDERSON

STROUD Team Ministry, The (St Laurence) (Holy Trinity) (St Alban Mission Church), including Cainscross, Randwick, Uplands, and Whiteshill *Glouc 4* **P** *Patr Bd* **TR** K E STACEY **TV** S G HOWELL **NSM** M J PAGE

STROUDWATER Team, The, comprising Arlingham, Eastington, Framilode, Frampton-on-Severn, Fretherne, Frocester, Haresfield, Kings Stanley, Leonard Stanley, Moreton Valence, Saul, Selsley, Standish, Stonehouse, and Whitminster *Glouc 4* **P** *Patr Bd* **TR** S G HARRISON **TV** D BISHOP, E PALIN **C** J R THOMPSON

STROXTON (All Saints) *see* Harlaxton Gp *Linc*

STRUBBY (St Oswald) *see* Legbourne and Wold Marsh *Linc*

STRUMPSHAW (St Peter) *see* Burlingham St Edmund w Lingwood, Strumpshaw etc *Nor*

STUBBINGS (St James the Less) *see* Burchetts Green *Ox*

STUBBINS (St Philip) *see* Ramsbottom and Edenfield *Man*

STUBBS CROSS (St Francis) *see* Ashford Town *Cant*

STUBSHAW CROSS (St Luke) *see* Ashton-in-Makerfield St Thos *Liv*

STUBTON (St Martin) *see* Claypole *Linc*

STUDHAM (St Mary the Virgin) *see* Kensworth, Studham and Whipsnade *St Alb*

STUDLAND (St Nicholas) *see* Swanage and Studland *Sarum*

STUDLEY (Nativity of the Blessed Virgin Mary) *see* Arden Marches *Cov*

STUDLEY (St John the Evangelist) *Sarum 15* **P** R Trowbridge St Jas **V** A P WOOD

STUKELEY, GREAT (St Bartholomew) *see* N Leightonstone *Ely*

STUKELEY, LITTLE (St Martin) *as above*

STUNTNEY (Holy Cross) *see* Ely *Ely*

STURMER (St Mary) *see* Two Rivers *Chelmsf*

STURMINSTER MARSHALL (St Mary) *see* Bridge Par *Sarum*

STURMINSTER NEWTON (St Mary), Hinton St Mary and Lydlinch *Sarum 5* **P** Col J L Yeatman (1 turn), G A L-F Pitt-Rivers Esq (3 turns), V Iwerne Valley (1 turn) **V** P M SARGENT **C** K J WELLS

STURRY (St Nicholas) w Fordwich and Westbere w Hersden *Cant 3* **P** *Abp, Ld Chan, and St Aug Foundn Cant (by turn)* **R** P A CORNISH

STURTON (St Hugh) *see* Stow Gp *Linc*

STURTON, GREAT (All Saints) *see* Hemingby Gp *Linc*

STURTON-LE-STEEPLE (St Peter and St Paul) *see* Retford Area *S'well*

STUSTON (All Saints) *see* N Hartismere *St E*

STUTTON (St Aidan) *see* Tadcaster *York*

STUTTON (St Peter) *see* Holbrook, Stutton, Freston, Woolverstone etc *St E*

STYDD (St Saviour) *see* Ribchester w Stydd *Blackb*

STYVECHALE (St James) *Cov 3* **P** Col A M H Gregory-Hood **V** J M MAYNARD **C** A C RICHARDSON

SUCKLEY (St John the Baptist) *see* Worcs W Rural *Worc*

SUDBOROUGH (All Saints) *see* Brigstock w Stanion and Lowick and Sudborough *Pet*

SUDBOURNE (All Saints) *see* Wilford Peninsula *St E*

SUDBROOKE (St Edward) *see* Barlings *Linc*

SUDBURY (All Saints) *see* S Dales *Derby*

SUDBURY (All Saints) w Ballingdon and Brundon *St E 9* **P** Simeon's Trustees **NSM** J A OFFORD

SUDBURY (St Andrew) *Lon 21* **P** *Bp* **V** G S THOMAS **NSM** M J ARNOLD

SUDBURY (St Gregory) St Peter and Chilton *St E 9* **P** *Bp (3 turns), Ch Soc Trust (1 turn)* **P-in-c** C A COLLINS **C** T J MUMFORD **NSM** J A OFFORD

SUDDEN (St Aidan) and Heywood All Souls *Man 14* **P** Patr Bd **V** M A READ **OLM** I TAYLOR

SUDELEY MANOR (St Mary) *see* Winchcombe *Glouc*

SUFFIELD (St Margaret) *see* King's Beck *Nor*

SUFFIELD PARK (St Martin) *see* Cromer *Nor*

SUFFOLK HEIGHTS *see* Chevington w Hargrave, Chedburgh w Depden etc *St E*

SUGLEY (Holy Saviour) *Newc 4* **P** *Bp* **P-in-c** N HESLOP

SULBY (St Stephen's Chapel) *see* Andreas, Ballaugh, Jurby and Sulby *S & M*

SULGRAVE (St James the Less) *see* Culworth w Sulgrave and Thorpe Mandeville etc *Pet*

SULHAM (St Nicholas) *see* Pangbourne w Tidmarsh and Sulham *Ox*

SULHAMSTEAD ABBOTS (St Mary) and Bannister w Ufton Nervet *Ox 4* **P** Qu Coll Ox and Or Coll Ox (alt) **P-in-c** J W S PATON

SULLINGTON (St Mary) and Thakeham w Warminghurst *Chich 11* **P** *Bp and DBP (alt)* **P-in-c** S STEVENS

SUMMERFIELD (Christ Church) (Cavendish Road Hall) *Birm 1* **P** R Birm St Martin w Bordesley **V** vacant

SUMMERSDALE (St Michael) *see* Chich St Paul and Westhampnett *Chich*

SUMMERSTOWN (St Mary) *S'wark 17* **P** Ch Soc Trust **V** J J G FLETCHER

SUMMERTOWN (St Michael and All Angels) *Ox 2* **P** St Jo Coll Ox **V** G R KNIGHT **NSM** C E LEAL, W L A PRYOR

SUNBURY, UPPER (St Saviour) *Lon 13* **P** V Sunbury **V** R CROSS

SUNBURY-ON-THAMES (St Mary) *Lon 13* **P** D&C St Paul's **V** A V J DOWNES **NSM** C GEORGE

SUNDERLAND (St Bede) Town End Farm *see* N Wearside *Dur*

SUNDERLAND (St Chad) *Dur 14* **P** *Bp* **V** J D CHADD **C** P BARKER

SUNDERLAND (St Cuthbert) Red House *see* N Wearside *Dur*

SUNDERLAND (St Ignatius) *see* Hendon *Dur*

SUNDERLAND (St Mary the Virgin) (St Peter) *Dur 14* **P** *Bp* **P-in-c** K J BAGNALL **C** G M YOUNG

SUNDERLAND (St Matthew) (St Wilfrid) *Dur 14* **P** *Bp* **V** D TOLHURST **C** P BISTRAN

SUNDERLAND MINSTER (St Michael and All Angels and St Benedict Biscop) *Dur 14* **P** *Bp* **V** J S BAIN **C** A C DOWSETT **Hon C** C S HOWSON **NSM** J TYSON

SUNDERLAND POINT (Mission Church) *see* Overton *Blackb*

SUNDERLAND St Mary (St Thomas) (St Oswald) *Dur 14* **P** *Bp* **V** vacant

SUNDERLAND, NORTH (St Paul) *Newc 7* **P** Lord Crewe's Trustees **P-in-c** A S MACPHERSON

SUNDON (St Mary) *St Alb 12* **P** *Bp* **P-in-c** Y M SMEJKAL

SUNDRIDGE (St Mary) w Ide Hill and Toys Hill *Roch 9* **P** *Abp* **R** P E DAVIES

SUNNINGDALE (Holy Trinity) *Ox 3* **P** *Bp* **V** J G HUTCHINSON

SUNNINGHILL (St Michael and All Angels) and South Ascot *Ox 3* **P** St Jo Coll Cam **V** S A JOHNSON

SUNNINGWELL (St Leonard) *see* Radley, Sunningwell and Kennington *Ox*

SUNNYSIDE (St Barnabas) *see* E Grinstead St Swithun *Chich*

SUNNYSIDE (St Michael and All Angels) w Bourne End *St Alb 1* **P** CPAS **V** R S FARDELL

SURBITON (St Andrew) (St Mark) *S'wark 15* **P** *Bp* **V** R S STANIER **C** M J JOHNS-PERRING

SURBITON (St Matthew) *see* Tolworth, Hook and Surbiton *S'wark*

SURBITON HILL (Christ Church) *S'wark 15* **P** Ch Soc Trust and Trustees (jt) **V** J D BIRCHALL **C** A N APPADOO, J B ERLEBACH **NSM** E O BAIKIE

SURFLEET (St Laurence) *see* Glen Gp *Linc*

SURLINGHAM (St Mary) *see* Rockland St Mary w Hellington, Bramerton etc *Nor*

SURREY WEALD, comprising Capel, Holmwood, Newdigate and Ockley *Guildf 7* **P** Patr Bd (1 turn), Ld Chan (2 turns) **TR** A D J COE **TV** B STEADMAN-ALLEN, E R RICHARDSON **NSM** N E COE **OLM** M L GILPIN

SUSTEAD (St Peter and St Paul) *see* Roughton and Felbrigg, Metton, Sustead etc *Nor*

SUTCOMBE (St Andrew) *see* Bradworthy, Sutcombe etc *Ex*

SUTTERTON (St Mary) *see* Haven Gp *Linc*

SUTTON (All Saints) *see* Potton w Sutton and Cockayne Hatley *St Alb*

SUTTON (All Saints) *see* Wilford Peninsula *St E*

SUTTON (Christ Church) (St Barnabas) (St Nicholas) *S'wark 23* **P** Patr Bd **P-in-c** F M ARNOLD **TV** P BROOKS **NSM** B FRASER, D R BILLIN

SUTTON (St Andrew) *Ely 8* **P** D&C **V** M HANCOCK

SUTTON (St Barnabas' Mission Church) *see* Macclesfield Team *Ches*

SUTTON (St Clement), Huttoft and Anderby *Linc 10* **P** *Bp (2 turns), Magd Coll Cam (1 turn)* **R** P J LILEY **Hon C** C H LILLEY **OLM** J TOMPKINS

SUTTON (St James) *York 14* **P** *Abp* **V** G NAYLOR

SUTTON (St James), Wincle, Wildboarclough and Bosley *Ches 13* **P** Patr Bd **V** J E HARRIES **NSM** S R MORRIS

SUTTON (St John the Baptist) *see* Barlavington, Burton w Coates, Sutton and Bignor *Chich*

SUTTON (St Mary)   *see* Calow and Sutton cum Duckmanton *Derby*

SUTTON (St Michael and All Angels)   *see* Castor w Upton and Stibbington etc *Pet*

SUTTON (St Michael)   *see* Stalham, E Ruston, Brunstead, Sutton and Ingham *Nor*

SUTTON (St Nicholas) (All Saints) (St Michael and All Angels) *Liv 10*   **P** *Patr Bd*   **TR** M L MOORE   **TV** G A MILFORD   **C** M G FERGUSON, S Q MOORE

SUTTON (St Thomas) w Cowling and Lothersdale *Leeds 4*   **P** *Ch Ch Ox and Bp (jt)*   **V** H M COLLINGS   **C** B J GREENFIELD

SUTTON AT HONE (St John the Baptist)   *see* Darent Valley *Roch*

SUTTON BASSETT (All Saints)   *see* Stoke Albany w Wilbarston and Ashley etc *Pet*

SUTTON BENGER (All Saints)   *see* Draycot *Bris*

SUTTON BINGHAM (All Saints)   *see* Coker Ridge *B & W*

SUTTON BRIDGE (St Matthew) and Tydd St Mary *Linc 18*   **P** *Bp and Ld Chan (alt)*   **V** *vacant*

SUTTON BY DOVER (St Peter and St Paul)   *see* Walmer and Cornilo *Cant*

SUTTON CHENEY (St James)   *see* Bosworth and Sheepy Gp *Leic*

SUTTON COLDFIELD (Holy Trinity) *Birm 7*   **P** *Bp*   **R** W J ROUTH   **C** L CARR

SUTTON COLDFIELD (St Chad) *Birm 7*   **P** *Bp*   **V** J NICHOLAS

SUTTON COLDFIELD (St Columba) *Birm 7*   **P** *Bp*   **V** R S ALLEN

SUTTON COURTENAY (All Saints)   *see* DAMASCUS *Ox*

SUTTON GREEN (All Souls)   *see* Woking St Pet *Guildf*

SUTTON HILL (Pastoral Centre)   *see* Madeley *Heref*

SUTTON IN ASHFIELD (St Mary Magdalene) *S'well 4*   **P** *Bp*   **V** A J NICOLLS

SUTTON IN ASHFIELD St Michael and All Angels *S'well 4*   **P** *Bp*   **C** J E COTTERILL

SUTTON IN HOLDERNESS (St Michael) *York 14*   **P** *Abp*   **C** P A WICK

SUTTON LE MARSH (St Clement)   *see* Sutton, Huttoft and Anderby *Linc*

SUTTON MADDOCK (St Mary)   *see* Beckbury, Badger, Kemberton, Ryton, Stockton etc *Lich*

SUTTON MANDEVILLE (All Saints)   *see* Nadder Valley *Sarum*

SUTTON MONTIS (Holy Trinity)   *see* Cam Vale *B & W*

SUTTON ON DERWENT (St Michael)   *see* Derwent Ings *York*

SUTTON ON THE FOREST (All Hallows)   *see* Forest of Galtres *York*

SUTTON ON THE HILL (St Michael)   *see* Boylestone, Church Broughton, Dalbury, etc *Derby*

SUTTON PARK (St Andrew) and Wawne *York 14*   **P** *Abp*   **V** C J VAN STRAATEN   **C** B J NORTON   **NSM** F ROBINSON

SUTTON ST EDMUND (St Edmund King and Martyr)   *see* Elloe Fen Gp *Linc*

SUTTON ST JAMES (St James) *as above*

SUTTON ST MICHAEL (St Michael)   *see* Maund Gp *Heref*

SUTTON ST NICHOLAS   *see* Long Sutton w Lutton etc *Linc*

SUTTON ST NICHOLAS (St Nicholas)   *see* Maund Gp *Heref*

SUTTON UNDER BRAILES (St Thomas à Becket) *Cov 9*   **P** *Bp*   **R** G HEIGHTON   **NSM** J W ROLFE

SUTTON VALENCE (St Mary the Virgin)   *see* Headcorn and The Suttons *Cant*

SUTTON VENY (St John the Evangelist)   *see* Upper Wylye Valley *Sarum*

SUTTON WALDRON (St Bartholomew)   *see* Iwerne Valley *Sarum*

SUTTON, EAST (St Peter and St Paul)   *see* Headcorn and The Suttons *Cant*

SUTTON, GREAT (St John the Evangelist) *Ches 9*   **P** *V Eastham*   **V** A J DUTTON

SUTTON, NORTH   *see* Plymouth Em, St Paul Efford and St Aug *Ex*

SUTTON-CUM-LOUND (St Bartholomew)   *see* Retford Area *S'well*

SUTTON-ON-PLYM (St John the Evangelist), Plymouth St Simon and St Mary Laira *Ex 21*   **P** *Bp, St Simon Trustees, and Keble Coll Ox (jt)*   **NSM** A OVERTON

SUTTON-ON-SEA (St Clement)   *see* Sutton, Huttoft and Anderby *Linc*

SUTTON-ON-TRENT (All Saints)   *see* Norwell w Ossington, Cromwell etc *S'well*

SWABY (St Nicholas)   *see* Legbourne and Wold Marsh *Linc*

SWADLINCOTE (Emmanuel) *Derby 7*   **P** *V Gresley*   **P-in-c** G P RUTTER   **C** A J REDSHAW, S J GREENWOOD   **OLM** C A BUCKLEY

SWAFFHAM (St Peter and St Paul) and Sporle *Nor 13*   **P** *Bp (2 turns), DBP (1 turn)*   **V** J R ALLAN   **NSM** H B DE LYON

SWAFFHAM BULBECK (St Mary)   *see* Anglesey Gp *Ely*

SWAFFHAM PRIOR (St Mary) *as above*

SWAFIELD (St Nicholas)   *see* Trunch Group *Nor*

SWAINSTHORPE (St Peter)   *see* Newton Flotman, Swainsthorpe, Tasburgh, etc *Nor*

SWAINSWICK (Blessed Virgin Mary)   *see* Bath St Sav w Swainswick and Woolley *B & W*

SWALCLIFFE (St Peter and St Paul)   *see* Wykeham *Ox*

SWALE, LOWER, comprising Ainderby Steeple w Yafforth and Kirby Wiske w Maunby, and Kirkby Fleetham w Langton on Swale and Scruton *Leeds 25*   **P** *D&C York, Duke of Northumberland, and Bp (jt)*   **R** J M LANE

SWALECLIFFE (St John the Baptist)   *see* Whitstable *Cant*

SWALEDALE, comprising Arkengarthdale, Grinton, Melbecks, and Muker *Leeds 22*   **P** *Bp*   **V** C J HEWLETT   **C** A M STEWART SMITH

SWALLOW (Holy Trinity)   *see* Caistor *Linc*

SWALLOWBECK (St George)   *see* Linc St Geo Swallowbeck *Linc*

SWALLOWCLIFFE (St Peter)   *see* Nadder Valley *Sarum*

SWALLOWFIELD (All Saints)   *see* Loddon Reach *Ox*

SWALWELL (Holy Trinity)   *see* Blaydon and Swalwell *Dur*

SWANAGE (All Saints) (St Mary the Virgin) and Studland *Sarum 8*   **P** *Patr Bd*   **TR** J O MANN   **TV** A J CORKE   **C** S S L SONET

SWANBOURNE (St Swithun)   *see* Newton Longville, Mursley, Swanbourne etc *Ox*

SWANLAND (St Barnabas) *York 14*   **P** *CPAS*   **V** F R SCOTT

SWANLEY (St Mary) *Roch 2*   **P** *Guild of All So*   **V** D C BATLEY-GLADDEN

SWANLEY (St Paul) *Roch 2*   **P** *Merchant Taylors' Co*   **V** J W D DOUGLAS

SWANMORE (St Barnabas) *Portsm 1*   **P** *DBP*   **V** C L TOWNS

SWANMORE (St Michael and All Angels) *Portsm 7*   **P** *SMF*   **V** *vacant*

SWANNINGTON (St George)   *see* Whitwick, Thringstone and Swannington *Leic*

SWANNINGTON (St Margaret)   *see* Reepham and Wensum Valley *Nor*

SWANSCOMBE (St Peter and St Paul) *Roch 4*   **P** *DBP*   **P-in-c** M T HURLEY

SWANTON ABBOT (St Michael)   *see* King's Beck *Nor*

SWANTON MORLEY (All Saints)   *see* Dereham and Distr *Nor*

SWANTON NOVERS (St Edmund)   *see* Brinton, Briningham, Hunworth, Stody etc *Nor*

SWANWICK (St Andrew) and Pentrich *Derby 8*   **P** *Wright Trustees and Duke of Devonshire (alt)*   **V** A B SIMPSON

SWARBY (St Mary and All Saints)   *see* S Lafford *Linc*

SWARCLIFFE (St Luke)   *see* Seacroft *Leeds*

SWARDESTON (St Mary the Virgin) w East Carleton, Intwood, Keswick and Ketteringham *Nor 7*   **P** *Bp, DBP, and Miss M B Unthank (jt)*   **R** P D BURR

SWARKESTONE (St James)   *see* Aston on Trent, Elvaston, Weston on Trent etc *Derby*

SWATON (St Michael)   *see* Heckington and Helpringham Gp *Linc*

SWAVESEY (St Andrew) *Ely 6*   **P** *Jes Coll Cam*   **P-in-c** S D GILL   **C** E R COPE

SWAY (St Luke) *Win 11*   **P** *Bp*   **V** E J MITCHELL

SWAYFIELD (St Nicholas)   *see* Corby Glen *Linc*

SWAYTHLING (St Mary) (St Alban the Martyr) *Win 13*   **P** *Bp and TR Southn City Cen (jt)*   **V** P M DOCKREE

SWEFFLING (St Mary)   *see* Upper Alde *St E*

SWELL (St Catherine)   *see* Curry Rivel w Fivehead and Swell *B & W*

SWELL, LOWER (St Mary)   *see* Stow on the Wold, Condicote and The Swells *Glouc*

SWELL, UPPER (St Mary) *as above*

SWEPSTONE (St Peter)   *see* Woodfield *Leic*

SWERFORD (St Mary)   *see* Hook Norton w Gt Rollright, Swerford etc *Ox*

SWETTENHAM (St Peter)   *see* Marton, Siddington w Capesthorne etc *Ches*

SWILLAND (St Mary)   *see* Carlford *St E*

SWILLINGTON (St Mary)   *see* Allerton Bywater, Kippax and Swillington *Leeds*

SWIMBRIDGE (St James the Apostle), West Buckland, Landkey, and East Buckland *Ex 17*   **P** *Bp and Trustees Earl Fortescue (jt)*   **P-in-c** S O'ROURKE   **NSM** G F SQUIRE

SWINBROOK (St Mary)   *see* Burford w Fulbrook, Taynton, Asthall etc *Ox*

SWINDERBY (All Saints) *Linc 12*   **P** *Bp, Ld Chan, E M K Kirk Esq, and D&C (by turn)*   **P-in-c** A C J VAUGHAN   **NSM** J T ROOKE   **OLM** P W WALKER

SWINDON (All Saints) (St Barnabas) *Bris 7*   **P** *Bp*   **OLM** B A SHEPPARD

SWINDON (Christ Church) (St Mary) *Bris 7* **P** *Ld Chan*
V S M STEVENETTE **OLM** D A HARDWICK
SWINDON (St Andrew) (St John the Baptist) *Bris 7* **P** *Ld Chan* **P-in-c** L E FLETCHER **NSM** L M MOREY
SWINDON (St Augustine) *Bris 7* **P** *Bp* **P-in-c** J P SALES **C** K E SMITH, P W FREELAND
SWINDON (St John the Evangelist) *see Smestow Vale Lich*
SWINDON (St Lawrence) *see N Cheltenham Glouc*
SWINDON (St Peter) *see Penhill Bris*
SWINDON Dorcan, comprising Covingham, Eldene, and Liden *Bris 7* **P** *Bp* **R** T A WIGLEY **C** R S J SMITH **OLM** S F FISHER
SWINDON New Town (St Mark) (St Adhelm) (St Luke) (St Saviour) *Bris 7* **P** *Bp* **R** vacant
SWINDON, NORTH (St Andrew) *Bris 7* **P** *Bp* **P-in-c** S A ROBERTSON **NSM** P C ASHBY, R E COOK
SWINDON, NORTH WEST and Lydiard Millicent *Bris 7* **P** *Bp* **V** T V ROBERTS **NSM** P F ROBERTS
SWINDON, WEST and Lydiard Tregoze *Bris 7* **P** *Bp* **V** C D DEVERELL **NSM** P C ASHBY, T L TOWNSEND, T M DAY
SWINE (St Mary) *see Skirlaugh, Catwick, Long Riston, Rise, Swine w Ellerby York*
SWINEFLEET (St Margaret) *see The Marshland Sheff*
SWINESHEAD (St Mary) *see Haven Gp Linc*
SWINESHEAD (St Nicholas) *see The Stodden Churches St Alb*
SWINFORD (All Saints) *see Avon-Swift Leic*
SWINFORD, OLD Stourbridge (St Mary) *Worc 12* **P** *Bp* **R** J F FLITCROFT **C** A J W FRENCH
SWINHOPE (St Helen) *see Binbrook Gp Linc*
SWINNOW (Christ the Saviour) *see Stanningley St Thos Leeds*
SWINSTEAD (St Mary) *see Edenham w Witham on the Hill and Swinstead Linc*
SWINTON (Holy Rood) *Man 18* **P** *TR Swinton and Pendlebury* **P-in-c** D E FAIR
SWINTON (St Margaret) *Sheff 12* **P** *Sir Philip Naylor-Leyland Bt* **V** C J BARLEY
SWINTON (St Peter) and Pendlebury *Man 18* **P** *Patr Bd* **TR** J P SHEEHY
SWISS COTTAGE (Holy Trinity) *see W Hampstead Trin Lon*
SWITHLAND (St Leonard) *see Woodhouse, Woodhouse Eaves and Swithland Leic*
SWYNCOMBE (St Botolph) *see Icknield Ox*
SWYNNERTON (St Mary) *see Cotes Heath and Standon and Swynnerton etc Lich*
SWYRE (Holy Trinity) *see Bride Valley Sarum*
SYDE (St Mary) *see Brimpsfield w Birdlip, Syde, Daglingworth etc Glouc*
SYDENHAM (All Saints) *S'wark 5* **P** *V Sydenham St Bart* **P-in-c** P H SMITH
SYDENHAM (Holy Trinity) and Forest Hill *S'wark 5* **P** *Simeon's Trustees* **P-in-c** E C J STOCK
SYDENHAM (St Bartholomew) *S'wark 5* **P** *Earl of Dartmouth* **V** J M PERRY
SYDENHAM (St Mary) *see Chinnor, Sydenham, Aston Rowant and Crowell Ox*
SYDENHAM (St Philip) *S'wark 5* **P** *V Sydenham St Bart* **V** P W TIERNAN
SYDENHAM DAMEREL (St Mary) *see Milton Abbot, Dunterton, Lamerton etc Ex*
SYDENHAM, LOWER (St Michael and All Angels) *see Forest Hill w Lower Sydenham S'wark*
SYDERSTONE (St Mary) *see N and S Creake w Waterden, Syderstone etc Nor*
SYDLING ST NICHOLAS (St Nicholas) *see Charminster, Stinsford and the Chalk Stream villages Sarum*
SYERSTON (All Saints) *see E Stoke w Syerston S'well*
SYKEHOUSE (Holy Trinity) *see Fishlake w Sykehouse and Kirk Bramwith etc Sheff*
SYLEHAM (St Mary) *see Athelington, Denham, Horham, Hoxne etc St E*
SYMONDS GREEN (Christ the King) *see Stevenage H Trin St Alb*
SYMONDSBURY (St John the Baptist) *see Eggardon and Colmers Sarum*
SYRESHAM (St James) *see Astwell Gp Pet*
SYSONBY (St Leonard) *see Melton Mowbray Leic*
SYSTON (St Anne) *see Warmley, Syston and Bitton Bris*
SYSTON (St Mary) *see S Cliff Villages Gp Linc*
SYSTON (St Peter and St Paul) *see Fosse Team Leic*
SYWELL (St Peter and St Paul) *see Mears Ashby and Hardwick and Sywell etc Pet*
TABLEY, OVER (St Paul) *Ches 12* **P** *Bp* **P-in-c** P J ROBINSON **NSM** P M COPE, P M ROBINSON
TACKLEY (St Nicholas) *see Steeple Aston w N Aston and Tackley Ox*

TACOLNESTON (All Saints) *see Upper Tas Valley Nor*
TADCASTER (St Mary the Virgin) *York 1* **P** *Abp, J Fielden Esq, and T E Fielden Esq (1 turn), Abp (1 turn)* **C** S C BIDDLESTONE
TADDINGTON (St Michael), Chelmorton and Monyash, Hartington, Biggin and Earl Sterndale *Derby 4* **P** *Duke of Devonshire and V Bakewell (jt)* **V** R J BENSON **NSM** J S FOUNTAIN
TADDIPORT (St Mary Magdalene) *see Gt and Lt Torrington and Frithelstock Ex*
TADLEY (St Mary) (St Peter) (St Paul) w Pamber Heath and Silchester *Win 4* **P** *Bp and Duke of Wellington (jt)* **R** R J S C HARLOW **C** G C SAKAKINI **NSM** R W YOUNG
TADLEY (St Paul) *see Tadley w Pamber Heath and Silchester Win*
TADLEY (St Peter) *as above*
TADLEY, NORTH (St Mary) *as above*
TADLOW (St Giles) *see Shingay Gp Ely*
TADMARTON (St Nicholas) *see Wykeham Ox*
TADWORTH (Good Shepherd) *S'wark 24* **P** *V Kingswood St Andr* **V** T R ASTIN
TAKELEY (Holy Trinity) w Little Canfield *Chelmsf 18* **P** *Bp and Ch Coll Cam* **P-in-c** R J BURLES
TALATON (St James the Apostle) *see Whimple, Talaton, Clyst St Lawr and Clyst Hydon Ex*
TALBOT VILLAGE (St Mark) *Sarum 7* **P** *Trustees* **V** R A HIGGINS
TALKE O' THE HILL (St Martin) *see Alsagers Bank, Audley and Talke Lich*
TALKIN (not known) *see Eden, Gelt and Irthing Carl*
TALLAND (St Tallan) *see Trelawny Truro*
TALLINGTON (St Lawrence) *see Uffington Gp Linc*
TAMAR VALLEY Benefice, The, comprising Calstock, Landulph, St Dominick, and St Mellion w Pillaton *Truro 11* **P** *Duchy of Cornwall (1 turn), SMF, D&C, and Trustees Major J Coryton (1 turn)* **R** C M PAINTER
TAMERTON FOLIOT (St Mary) and Southway *Ex 21* **P** *Ld Chan* **TR** D B M GILL **TV** I M ROBERTSON
TAMERTON, NORTH (St Denis) *see Boyton, N Tamerton, Werrington etc Truro*
TAMWORTH (St Editha) *Lich 4* **P** *Bp* **V** A W GORDON **C** V M C VAN DEN BERGH **NSM** B ROSTILL
TANDRIDGE (St Peter) *see Oxted S'wark*
TANFIELD (St Margaret of Antioch) w Burnopfield and Dipton *Dur 4* **P** *Bp* **V** A P MILLER
TANFIELD, WEST (St Nicholas) and Well w Snape and North Stainley *Leeds 23* **P** *Bp and Mrs M E Bourne-Arton (alt)* **C** S L LAWTON
TANGLEY (St Thomas of Canterbury) *see Pastrow Win*
TANGMERE (St Andrew) and Oving *Chich 2* **P** *Bp and Duke of Richmond (jt)* **P-in-c** T MARSHALL
TANHOUSE The Oaks (Conventional District) *Liv 14* **C** R SHUTTLEWORTH **Min** W D PETTY
TANKERSLEY (St Peter), Thurgoland and Wortley *Sheff 11* **P** *Dowager Countess of Wharncliffe, Sir Philip Naylor-Leyland Bt, and V Silkstone (jt)* **R** K J E HALE
TANNINGTON (St Ethelbert) *see Four Rivers St E*
TANSLEY (Holy Trinity) *see Matlock Bank and Tansley Derby*
TANSOR (St Mary) *see Warmington, Tansor and Cotterstock etc Pet*
TANWORTH (St Mary Magdalene) *Birm 5* **P** *F D Muntz Esq* **V** P E F CUDBY
TAPLOW (St Nicolas) and Dropmore *Ox 12* **P** *Eton Coll and DBP (jt)* **V** J S CRESSWELL **NSM** S J JOHNSON
TARDEBIGGE (St Bartholomew) *Worc 7* **P** *Earl of Plymouth* **V** R M CLARK
TARLETON (Holy Trinity) *see Rufford and Tarleton Blackb*
TARPORLEY (St Helen) *Ches 5* **P** *Bp (4 turns), D&C (1 turn), and Sir John Grey Regerton Bt (1 turn)* **R** G J A WATMORE **NSM** J M OSBORNE
TARRANT GUNVILLE (St Mary) *see Chase Sarum*
TARRANT HINTON (St Mary) *as above*
TARRANT KEYNSTON (All Saints) *as above*
TARRANT MONKTON (All Saints) *as above*
TARRANT RUSHTON (St Mary) *as above*
TARRING NEVILLE (St Mary) *see Denton w S Heighton and Tarring Neville Chich*
TARRING, WEST (St Andrew) *see Maybridge and W Tarring Chich*
TARRINGTON (St Philip and St James) *see Hop Churches Heref*
TARVIN (St Andrew) *Ches 2* **P** *Bp* **V** A L D FRIEND **NSM** B A KING
TAS VALLEY *see Newton Flotman, Swainsthorpe, Tasburgh, etc Nor*
TAS VALLEY, UPPER *see Upper Tas Valley Nor*

TASBURGH (St Mary) *see* Newton Flotman, Swainsthorpe, Tasburgh, etc *Nor*

TASLEY (St Peter and St Paul) *see* Bridgnorth and Morville Par *Heref*

TATENHILL (St Michael and All Angels) *see* Barton under Needwood w Dunstall and Tatenhill *Lich*

TATHAM (St James the Less) *see* E Lonsdale *Blackb*

TATHAM FELLS (Good Shepherd) *as above*

TATHWELL (St Vedast) *see* Legbourne and Wold Marsh *Linc*

TATSFIELD (St Mary) *see* Limpsfield and Tatsfield *S'wark*

TATTENHALL (St Alban) w Burwardsley and Handley *Ches 5*　**P** *Bp, Miss N C Barbour, and D&C (jt)*　**R** L MUTETE

TATTENHAM CORNER (St Mark) *Guildf 9*　**P** *Bp*
V D C WILLIAMSON

TATTENHOE (St Giles) *see* Watling Valley *Ox*

TATTERFORD (St Margaret) *see* E w W Rudham, Helhoughton etc *Nor*

TATTERSETT (All Saints and St Andrew) *as above*

TATTERSHALL (Holy Trinity) *see* Bain Valley Gp *Linc*

TATTINGSTONE (St Mary) *see* Sproughton w Burstall, Copdock w Washbrook etc *St E*

TATWORTH (St John the Evangelist) *see* Chaffcombe, Cricket Malherbie etc *B & W*

TAUNTON (All Saints) *B & W 18*　**P** *Bp*　**V** E M SHEARCROFT

TAUNTON (Holy Trinity) *B & W 18*　**P** *Bp*　**V** J B V LAURENCE
C A H BURNHAM

TAUNTON (St Andrew) *B & W 18*　**P** *Bp*　**V** R P LODGE
C K M GOUGH

TAUNTON (St James) *B & W 18*　**P** *Simeon's Trustees*
V F R M WUYTS

TAUNTON (St Mary Magdalene) (St John the Evangelist) *B & W 18*　**P** *Bp and Ch Patr Trust (jt)*　**Hon C** J R EASTELL

TAUNTON (St Peter) Lyngford *B & W 18*　**P** *Bp*　**V** D TURLEY
R P SEABROOK　**NSM** P CHARLESWORTH

TAVISTOCK (St Eustachius), Gulworthy and Brent Tor *Ex 22*　**P** *Bp*　**V** C G HARDWICK　**C** J A BLOWEY
NSM M J LOADER, S J TUCKER

TAWSTOCK (St Peter) *see* Newton Tracey, Horwood, Alverdiscott etc *Ex*

TAWTON, NORTH (St Peter) *see* Chagford, Gidleigh, Throwleigh etc *Ex*

TAWTON, SOUTH (St Andrew) *as above*

TAYNTON (St John the Evangelist) *see* Burford w Fulbrook, Taynton, Asthall etc *Ox*

TAYNTON (St Laurence) *see* Highnam, Tibberton w Rudford etc *Glouc*

TEALBY (All Saints) *see* Walesby Gp *Linc*

TEAN, UPPER (Christ Church) *see* Uttoxeter Area *Lich*

TEBAY (St James) *see* High Westmorland *Carl*

TEDBURN ST MARY (St Mary), Cheriton Bishop, Whitestone w Oldridge and Holcombe Burnell *Ex 5*
P *Bp, DBP, and Ch Patr Trust (jt)*　**V** M R WOOD

TEDDINGTON (St Mark) *Lon 11*　**P** *Bp*　**V** K A WELLMAN
C J M B KISSELL

TEDDINGTON (St Mary) (St Alban the Martyr) *Lon 10*
P *Bp*　**V** J B MOFFATT　**C** A D A FRANCE-WILLIAMS
NSM C E HALMSHAW, M E HAWES

TEDDINGTON (St Nicholas) *see* Overbury w Teddington, Alstone etc *Worc*

TEDDINGTON (St Peter and St Paul) *Lon 10*　**P** *Bp*
P-in-c J B MOFFATT　**C** A D A FRANCE-WILLIAMS, S D PEDLEY

TEDSTONE DELAMERE (St James) *see* Edvin Loach w Tedstone Delamere etc *Heref*

TEESDALE, LOWER, comprising Bowes, Laithkirk, Romaldkirk w Cotherstone, and Startforth and Rokeby w Brignall *Leeds 22*　**P** *Ld Chan (1 turn), Earl of Strathmore and Kinghorne (1 turn), Bp, Lords of the Manor of Bowes, and DBP (1 turn)*　**R** J BARKER　**NSM** A P WALLBANK

TEFFONT EVIAS (St Michael) *see* Nadder Valley *Sarum*

TEFFONT MAGNA (St Edward) *as above*

TEIGH (Holy Trinity) *see* Oakham, Ashwell, Braunston, Brooke, Egleton etc *Pet*

TEIGNGRACE (St Peter and St Paul) *see* Kingsteignton and Teigngrace *Ex*

TEIGNMOUTH (St James) (St Michael the Archangel), Ideford w Luton, Ashcombe and Bishopsteignton *Ex 5*
P *Patr Bd*　**TR** R D WITHNELL　**TV** J H FROST
NSM V ATKINSON

TELFORD PARK (St Stephen) (St Thomas) *S'wark 12*
P *V Streatham and CPAS (jt)*　**V** M L GORDON　**C** J P YEATES

TELFORD, CENTRAL (Christ the King): Dawley, Lawley, Malinslee, Stirchley, Brookside and Hollinswood *Lich 20*
P *Patr Bd (3 turns), The Crown (1 turn)*　**TR** T STOREY
TV J E HOLMES, L R PLUMMER　**NSM** H PAGE

TELLISFORD (All Saints) *see* Hardington Vale *B & W*

TELSCOMBE (St Laurence) *see* Peacehaven and Telscombe Cliffs w Piddinghoe etc *Chich*

TEME VALLEY NORTH: Knighton-on-Teme, Lindridge, Pensax, Menith Wood, and Stockton *Worc 13*　**P** *Bp and D&C (alt)*　**P-in-c** E G WHITTAKER

TEME VALLEY SOUTH: Eastham, Rochford, Stoke Bliss, Hanley Child, Hanley William, Kyre Wyard and Stanford-on-Teme *Worc 13*　**P** *Ld Chan, Bp, and Mrs M M Miles (by turn)*　**P-in-c** J CURTIS

TEME VALLEY, LOWER *see* Worcs W Rural *Worc*

TEMPLE (St Catherine) *see* Camelside *Truro*

TEMPLE BALSALL (St Mary) *Birm 10*　**P** *Lady Leveson Hosp*
V K A M LLOYD ROBERTS

TEMPLE BRUER (St John the Baptist) *see* Graffoe Gp *Linc*

TEMPLE CLOUD (St Barnabas) *see* Clutton w Cameley, Bishop Sutton and Stowey *B & W*

TEMPLE EWELL (St Peter and St Paul) w Lydden *Cant 7*
P *Abp*　**R** *vacant*

TEMPLE GRAFTON (St Andrew) *see* Heart of England *Cov*

TEMPLE GUITING (St Mary) *see* The Guitings, Cutsdean, Farmcote etc *Glouc*

TEMPLE HIRST (St John the Baptist) *see* Haddlesey w Hambleton and Birkin *York*

TEMPLE NORMANTON (St James the Apostle) *Derby 3*
P *Bp*　**V** G N BORROWDALE

TEMPLE SOWERBY (St James) *see* Heart of Eden *Carl*

TEMPLECOMBE (Blessed Virgin Mary) *see* Abbas and Templecombe, Henstridge and Horsington *B & W*

TEMPLETON (St Margaret) *see* Washfield, Stoodleigh, Withleigh etc *Ex*

TEMPSFORD (St Peter) *see* Riversmeet *St Alb*

TEN MILE BANK (St Mark) *see* Hilgay *Ely*

TENBURY Team Minstry, The (St Mary) (St Michael and All Angels), including Burford, Clee Hill, Coreley, Greete, Hope Bagot, Little Hereford, and Whitton *Heref 11*　**P** *Patr Bd*
TR S E HARRIS　**TV** M J INGLIS　**NSM** S FOSTER

TENDRING (St Edmund King and Martyr) *see* Gt Oakley, Wix, Wrabness etc *Chelmsf*

TENPENNY VILLAGES, The, comprising Alresford, Elmstead, and Frating w Thorrington *Chelmsf 23*　**P** *Bp, Jes Coll Cam, and St Jo Coll Cam (jt)*　**V** A I FORDYCE　**NSM** P J HART

TENTERDEN (St Mildred) (St Michael and All Angels), Rother and Oxney *Cant 10*　**P** *Patr Bd*　**TR** L J HAMMOND
TV J R DARKINS, P L M FOGDEN　**C** C T A HODGKINS,
J T KENNETT　**NSM** J A SHAW

TERLING (All Saints) *see* Witham and Villages *Chelmsf*

TERRIERS (St Francis) *see* High Wycombe *Ox*

TERRINGTON (All Saints) *see* Howardian Gp *York*

TERRINGTON ST CLEMENT (St Clement) *Ely 14*　**P** *The Crown*　**V** R J SLIPPER

TERRINGTON ST JOHN (St John) *see* E Marshland *Ely*

TERWICK (St Peter) *see* Rogate w Terwick and Trotton w Chithurst *Chich*

TESTON (St Peter and St Paul) *see* E Malling and Teston *Roch*

TESTWOOD (St Winfrid) *see* Totton *Win*

TETBURY (St Mary the Virgin and St Mary Magdalen), Beverston, Long Newnton and Shipton Moyne *Glouc 7*
P *DBP, R Boggis-Rolfe Esq, and Mrs J C B Joynson (4 turns), The Crown (1 turn)*　**R** V J HUGHES　**C** R H CHURCH

TETCOTT (Holy Cross) *see* Ashwater, Halwill, Beaworthy, Clawton etc *Ex*

TETFORD (St Mary) *see* S Ormsby Gp *Linc*

TETNEY (St Peter and St Paul) *see* Holton-le-Clay, Tetney and N Cotes *Linc*

TETSWORTH (St Giles) *see* Thame *Ox*

TETTENHALL REGIS (St Michael and All Angels) *Lich 23*
P *Patr Bd*　**TR** R M REEVE　**TV** S A DOUGLAS
C C M A LEIGHTON

TETTENHALL WOOD (Christ Church) and Perton *Lich 23*
P *Patr Bd*　**TR** P C WOOTTON　**TV** J M CODY
OLM C V TOUGH

TEVERSAL (St Katherine) *see* Skegby w Teversal *S'well*

TEVERSHAM (All Saints) *Ely 2*　**P** *Bp*　**P-in-c** A J FORD

TEW, GREAT (St Michael and All Angels) w Little (St John the Evangelist) and Heythrop *Ox 22*　**P** *Bp and J M Johnston Esq (jt)*　**V** V J THOMAS

TEWIN (St Peter) *see* Welwyn *St Alb*

TEWKESBURY (Holy Trinity) *Glouc 9*　**P** *Ch Soc Trust*
V S M M WALKER

TEWKESBURY (St Mary the Virgin) w Walton Cardiff and Twyning *Glouc 9*　**P** *Ld Chan (2 turns) and Ch Ch Ox (1 turn)*
V P R WILLIAMS　**C** E P SAUVEN, S J M HAMILTON,
W A RUFFLE

TEY, GREAT (St Barnabas) and LITTLE (St James the Less) w Wakes Colne and Chappel *Chelmsf 19*　**P** *Bp, DBP, PCC Chappel and Ch Patr Trust (jt)*　**R** J RICHARDSON

TEYNHAM (Primary School Worship Centre) *see* Kingsdown and Creekside *Cant*

TEYNHAM (St Mary) *as above*

THAKEHAM (St Mary) *see* Sullington and Thakeham w Warminghurst *Chich*

THAME (St Mary the Virgin) (Barley Hill Church) *Ox 20* **P** *Patr Bd* **TR** A W GARRATT **TV** R B CROSS **C** M D READING **Hon C** R COPPING, S H BAYNES **NSM** G C CHOLDCROFT, G P WATERSON

THAMES DITTON (St Nicholas) *Guildf 8* **P** *K Coll Cam* **V** A C COWIE **C** S S KLAIR

THAMES VIEW (Christ Church) *Chelmsf 1* **P** *Bp* **V** U A CHINDABATA

THAMES, UPPER, comprising Ashton Keynes, Cricklade, Latton, and Leigh *Bris 6* **P** *Bp, D&C, and Hon P N Eliot (jt)* **V** P J P BRADLEY **NSM** S E DANBY

THAMESHEAD *see* Kemble, Poole Keynes, Somerford Keynes etc *Glouc*

THAMESMEAD (Church of the Cross) (St Paul's Ecumenical Centre) (William Temple) *S'wark 6* **P** *Bp* **TR** H P EGGLESTON **TV** J E G MACY, V J YEADON

THANET (St Andrew) *see* Reading Street *Cant*

THANET (St Peter the Apostle) *see* St Peter-in-Thanet *Cant*

THANINGTON (St Nicholas) (St Faith's Mission Church) *Cant 3* **P** *Abp* **V** *vacant*

THARSTON (St Mary) *see* Newton Flotman, Swainsthorpe, Tasburgh, etc *Nor*

THATCHAM (St Mary) *Ox 6* **P** *Patr Bd* **TR** M D BENNET **TV** N A HULKS **C** L C ONUGHA **NSM** B HARLAND **OLM** M E FONTAINE

THATTO HEATH (St Matthew) *see* Eccleston Team *Liv*

THAXTED (St John the Baptist, Our Lady and St Laurence), The Sampfords, Radwinter and Hempstead *Chelmsf 20* **P** *Bp, Guild of All So, New Coll Ox, and Keble Coll Ox (jt)* **R** P G TARRIS **NSM** P D C BROWN **OLM** S M LACON

THEALE (Christ Church) *see* Isle of Wedmore *B & W*

THEALE (Holy Trinity) *Ox 4* **P** *Magd Coll Ox* **V** M E DAVY

THEBERTON (St Peter) *see* Yoxmere *St E*

THEDDINGWORTH (All Saints) *see* Hexagon *Leic*

THEDDLETHORPE (St Helen) *Linc 15* **P** *Baroness Willoughby de Eresby (2 turns), Bp (1 turn)* **R** *vacant*

THELBRIDGE (St David) *see* Burrington, Chawleigh, Cheldon, Chulmleigh etc *Ex*

THELNETHAM (St Nicholas) *see* Stanton *St E*

THELVETON (St Andrew) *see* Dickleburgh and The Pulhams *Nor*

THELWALL (All Saints) *Ches 4* **P** *Keble Coll Ox* **V** D J BLACK

THEMELTHORPE (St Andrew) *see* Heart of Norfolk *Nor*

THENFORD (St Mary the Virgin) *see* Chenderit *Pet*

THERFIELD (St Mary the Virgin) w Kelshall *St Alb 16* **P** *Ld Chan and D&C St Paul's (alt)* **R** *vacant*

THETFORD (St Cuthbert) St Peter *Nor 11* **P** *Patr Bd* **TR** P D HERBERT **TV** H L JARY, R A HEYWOOD

THETFORD, LITTLE (St George) *see* Ely *Ely*

THEYDON BOIS (St Mary) *see* Theydon Par *Chelmsf*

THEYDON GARNON (All Saints) *as above*

THEYDON MOUNT (St Michael) *as above*

THEYDON Parishes, The, including Stapleford Tawney w Theydon Mount, Theydon Bois, and Theydon Garnon *Chelmsf 3* **P** *Bp and DBP (jt)* **V** J E FRY **NSM** C A NEWNHAM

THIMBLEBY (St Margaret) *see* Horncastle Gp *Linc*

THIRKLEBY (All Saints) w Kilburn and Bagby *York 18* **P** *Abp* **NSM** P PERCY

THIRSK (St Mary) *York 18* **P** *Abp* **R** D J SIMPSON **C** D J BIGGS **NSM** J M GILLANDERS, R W SIDGWICK

THISTLETON (St Nicholas) *see* Cottesmore and Burley, Clipsham, Exton etc *Pet*

THIXENDALE (St Mary) *see* Waggoners *York*

THOCKRINGTON (St Aidan) *see* Chollerton w Birtley and Thockrington *Newc*

THOMPSON (St Martin) *see* Caston, Griston, Merton, Thompson etc *Nor*

THORESBY, NORTH (St Helen) *see* Fotherby, N Thoresby and Grainsby w Waithe *Linc*

THORESBY, SOUTH (St Andrew) *see* Legbourne and Wold Marsh *Linc*

THORESWAY (St Mary) *see* Walesby Gp *Linc*

THORGANBY (All Saints) *see* Binbrook Gp *Linc*

THORGANBY (St Helen) *see* Derwent Ings *York*

THORINGTON (St Peter) *see* Blyth Valley *St E*

THORLEY (St James the Great) *St Alb 15* **P** *Bp* **C** R ATKINSON

THORLEY (St Swithun) *see* W Wight *Portsm*

THORMANBY (St Mary Magdalene) *see* Brafferton w Pilmoor, Myton-on-Swale etc *York*

THORNABY, NORTH (St Luke) (St Paul) *York 17* **P** *Abp* **V** C H RAZZALL

THORNABY, SOUTH (St Mark) (St Peter ad Vincula) *York 17* **P** *Abp* **V** *vacant*

THORNAGE (All Saints) *see* Brinton, Briningham, Hunworth, Stody etc *Nor*

THORNBOROUGH (St Mary) *see* Buckingham *Ox*

THORNBURY (St Anna) *see* Bredenbury *Heref*

THORNBURY (St Margaret), Woodhall and Waterloo *Leeds 2* **P** *Bp* **V** N CLEWS **NSM** R A JOHNSON

THORNBURY (St Mary) (St Paul) and Oldbury-on-Severn w Shepperdine *Glouc 5* **P** *Ch Ch Ox* **C** J E LUDLOW

THORNBURY (St Peter) *see* Black Torrington, Bradford w Cookbury etc *Ex*

THORNBY (St Helen) *see* Guilsborough and Hollowell and Cold Ashby etc *Pet*

THORNCOMBE (The Blessed Virgin Mary) *see* Chaffcombe, Cricket Malherbie etc *B & W*

THORNDON (All Saints) *see* S Hartismere *St E*

THORNE (St Nicholas) *Sheff 10* **P** *Bp* **V** D A GREEN

THORNE COFFIN (St Andrew) *see* Tintinhull w Chilthorne Domer, Yeovil Marsh etc *B & W*

THORNE ST MARGARET (St Margaret) *see* Wellington and Distr *B & W*

THORNER (St Peter) *see* Elmete Trin *Leeds*

THORNES (St James) w Christ Church *Leeds 19* **P** *DBP* **P-in-c** M C CRABTREE **C** E C PEETERS

THORNEY (St Helen) *see* E Trent *S'well*

THORNEY HILL (All Saints) *see* Bransgore and Hinton Admiral *Win*

THORNEY, WEST (St Nicholas) *see* Southbourne w W Thorney *Chich*

THORNEYBURN (St Aidan) *see* N Tyne and Redesdale *Newc*

THORNFALCON (Holy Cross) *see* Creech St Michael and Ruishton w Thornfalcon *B & W*

THORNFORD (St Mary Magdalene) *see* Three Valleys *Sarum*

THORNGUMBALD (St Mary) *see* Burstwick, Burton Pidsea etc *York*

THORNHAM (All Saints) *see* Hunstanton St Mary w Ringstead Parva etc *Nor*

THORNHAM (St James) *see* High Crompton and Thornham *Man*

THORNHAM (St John) *see* Middleton and Thornham *Man*

THORNHAM MAGNA (St Mary Magdalene) *see* S Hartismere *St E*

THORNHAM PARVA (St Mary) *as above*

THORNHAUGH (St Andrew) *see* Nassington, Apethorpe, Thornhaugh etc *Pet*

THORNHILL (Mission Church) *see* Seatallan *Carl*

THORNHILL (St Christopher) *see* Southampton Thornhill St Chris *Win*

THORNHILL (St Michael and All Angels) and Whitley Lower *Leeds 9* **P** *Lord Savile* **R** D NASH

THORNHILL LEES (Holy Innocents w St Mary) *see* Ravensthorpe and Thornhill Lees w Savile Town *Leeds*

THORNLEY (St Bartholomew) *see* Wolsingham and Thornley *Dur*

THORNTHWAITE (St Mary the Virgin) *see* Upper Derwent *Carl*

THORNTHWAITE (St Saviour) *see* Dacre w Hartwith and Darley w Thornthwaite *Leeds*

THORNTON (St Frideswyde) and Crosby All Saints *Liv 8* **P** *Bp, CPAS, and V Gt Crosby St Luke (jt)* **V** K ROGERS

THORNTON (St James) *Leeds 3* **P** *V Bradf* **V** C H GWINNETT **NSM** G HARDISTY

THORNTON (St Michael) *see* Barmby Moor Gp *York*

THORNTON (St Peter) *see* Markfield, Thornton, Bagworth and Stanton etc *Leic*

THORNTON (St Wilfrid) *see* Horncastle Gp *Linc*

THORNTON CURTIS (St Lawrence) *see* Abbey Gp *Linc*

THORNTON DALE (All Saints) w Allerston, Ebberston, Ellerburn and Wilton *York 19* **P** *Abp* **NSM** S E GOUGH

THORNTON HEATH (St Jude w St Aidan) *S'wark 21* **P** *Bp* **V** N K NTEGE

THORNTON HEATH (St Paul) *S'wark 21* **P** *The Crown* **P-in-c** D L THOMPSON

THORNTON HOUGH (All Saints) *Ches 9* **P** *Simeon's Trustees* **V** V L BARRETT

THORNTON IN CRAVEN (St Mary) *see* Broughton, Marton and Thornton *Leeds*

THORNTON LE FEN (St Peter) *see* Brothertoft Gp *Linc*

THORNTON LE STREET (St Leonard) *see* The Thorntons and The Otteringtons *York*

THORNTON RUST (Mission Room) *see* Penhill *Leeds*

THORNTON STEWARD (St Oswald) *see* Middleham w Coverdale and E Witton etc *Leeds*

THORNTON WATLASS (St Mary the Virgin)   *see* Bedale and Leeming and Thornton Watlass *Leeds*
THORNTON, LITTLE (St John) *Blackb 12*   **P** *Bp*
V J L ATKINSON
THORNTON-IN-LONSDALE (St Oswald)   *see* Bentham, Burton-in-Lonsdale, Chapel-le-Dale etc *Leeds*
THORNTON-LE-FYLDE (Christ Church) *Blackb 12*   **P** *Trustees*
V D E PLATT
THORNTON-LE-MOOR (All Saints)   *see* Woldmoor Gp *Linc*
THORNTON-LE-MOORS (St Mary) w Ince and Elton *Ches 3*
P *Bp*   **V** *vacant*
THORNTONS (St Leonard) and The Otteringtons, The
York 18   **P** *Ch Ch Ox, Linc Coll Ox, and Abp (by turn)*
V R J WILLIAMSON
THOROTON (St Helena)   *see* Whatton w Aslockton, Hawksworth, Scarrington etc *S'well*
THORP ARCH (All Saints)   *see* Bramham *York*
THORPE (St Andrew) (Good Shepherd) *Nor 1*
P *Trustees W J Birkbeck Esq*   **R** J W STEWART
THORPE (St Laurence)   *see* Farndon w Thorpe, Hawton and Cotham *S'well*
THORPE (St Leonard)   *see* Fenny Bentley, Thorpe, Tissington, Parwich etc *Derby*
THORPE (St Mary) *Guildf 11*   **P** *Keble Coll Ox*   **V** D S MILES
NSM G H MEE, J E WINN-SMITH
THORPE (St Matthew) *Nor 1*   **P** R *Thorpe St Andr*
V P G JORDAN   **C** T G WILLIAMS, T I SIBANDA
THORPE (St Peter)   *see* The Wainfleet Gp *Linc*
THORPE ABBOTS (All Saints)   *see* Redenhall w Scole *Nor*
THORPE ACHURCH (St John the Baptist)   *see* Aldwincle, Clopton, Pilton, Stoke Doyle etc *Pet*
THORPE ACRE w Dishley (All Saints) *Leic 6*   **P** *Bp*
V K A ELLIOTT
THORPE ARNOLD (St Mary the Virgin)   *see* Melton Mowbray *Leic*
THORPE AUDIN (Mission Room)   *see* Woolley *Leeds*
THORPE BASSETT (All Saints)   *see* Buckrose Carrs *York*
THORPE BAY (St Augustine) *Chelmsf 15*   **P** *The Crown*
V J COLLIS   **C** C J GILES
THORPE CONSTANTINE (St Constantine)   *see* Mease Valley *Lich*
THORPE EDGE (St John the Divine)   *see* Greengates and Thorpe Edge *Leeds*
THORPE END (St David) *Nor 1*   **P** *Bp*   **V** T C DAWSON
THORPE EPISCOPI (St Andrew)   *see* Thorpe St Andr *Nor*
THORPE HESLEY (Holy Trinity) *Sheff 6*   **P** *Sir Philip Naylor-Leyland Bt*   **V** L BROADHEAD
THORPE LANGTON (St Leonard)   *see* The Langtons and Shangton *Leic*
THORPE MALSOR (All Saints)   *see* Rothwell w Orton and Rushton w Glendon etc *Pet*
THORPE MANDEVILLE (St John the Baptist)   *see* Culworth w Sulgrave and Thorpe Mandeville etc *Pet*
THORPE MARKET (St Margaret)   *see* Poppyland *Nor*
THORPE MORIEUX (St Mary the Virgin)   *see* Rattlesden w Thorpe Morieux, Brettenham etc *St E*
THORPE SALVIN (St Peter)   *see* Harthill and Thorpe Salvin *Sheff*
THORPE SATCHVILLE (St Michael and All Angels)
see S Croxton Gp *Leic*
THORPE WILLOUGHBY (St Francis of Assisi)   *see* Brayton *York*
THORPE-LE-SOKEN (St Michael) *Chelmsf 23*   **P** *Bp*   **V** *vacant*
THORPE-NEXT-HADDISCOE (St Matthias)   *see* Raveningham Gp *Nor*
THORPE-ON-THE-HILL (St Michael)   *see* Swinderby *Linc*
THORRINGTON (St Mary Magdalene)   *see* Tenpenny Villages *Chelmsf*
THORVERTON (St Thomas of Canterbury)   *see* Brampford Speke, Cadbury, Newton St Cyres etc *Ex*
THRANDESTON (St Margaret)   *see* N Hartismere *St E*
THRAPSTON (St James), Denford and Islip *Pet 10*   **P** *Ld Chan (2 turns), L G Stopford-Sackville Esq (1 turn)*
R N D R ROBSON
THREAPWOOD (St John)   *see* Malpas and Threapwood and Bickerton *Ches*
THRECKINGHAM (St Peter)   *see* S Lafford *Linc*
THREE BRIDGES (St Richard) *Chich 6*   **P** *Bp*
P-in-c C P SPENCER
THREE LEGGED CROSS (All Saints)   *see* Verwood *Sarum*
THREE RIVERS Group, The, comprising Chippenham, Fordham, Isleham, Kennett, and Snailwell *Ely 4*   **P** *Jes Coll Cam and Mrs D A Crawley (2 turns), Ld Chan (1 turn)*
R D R CLEUGH   **C** A H JONES   **NSM** S P POTTS
THREE RIVERS, The, comprising Lawhitton, Lewannick, Lezant, North Hill, and South Petherwin *Truro 9*   **P** *Ld Chan (1 turn), Ox Univ, Bp, and DBP (1 turn)*   **P-in-c** H J WEST

THREE VALLEYS, The, comprising Batcombe, Beer Hackett, Bishop's Caundle, Bradford Abbas w Clifton Maybank, Caundle Marsh, Chetnole, Folke, Glanvilles Wootton, Hermitage, Holnest, Holwell, Leigh, Pulham, Ryme Intrinseca, Thornford, and Yetminster and Hilfield *Sarum 3*
P *Patr Bd*   **TR** A J D GILBERT   **TV** G R MOODY, J R F KIRLEW
THREEKINGHAM (St Peter)   *see* S Lafford *Linc*
THRELKELD (St Mary)   *see* St John's-in-the-Vale, Threlkeld and Wythburn *Carl*
THREXTON (All Saints)   *see* Gt and Lt Cressingham w Threxton *Nor*
THRIGBY (St Mary)   *see* S Trin Broads *Nor*
THRIMBY (St Mary)   *see* N Westmorland *Carl*
THRINGSTONE (St Andrew)   *see* Whitwick, Thringstone and Swannington *Leic*
THRIPLOW (St George)   *see* Fowlmere, Foxton, Shepreth and Thriplow *Ely*
THROCKING (Holy Trinity)   *see* Ardeley, Benington, Cottered w Throcking etc *St Alb*
THROCKLEY (St Mary the Virgin)   *see* Newburn *Newc*
THROCKMORTON (Chapelry)   *see* Abberton, The Flyfords, Naunton Beauchamp etc *Worc*
THROOP (St Paul) *Win 8*   **P** *Ch Soc Trust*   **P-in-c** J FINDLAY
THROPTON (St Andrew)   *see* Upper Coquetdale *Newc*
THROWLEIGH (St Mary the Virgin)   *see* Chagford, Gidleigh, Throwleigh etc *Ex*
THROWLEY (St Michael and All Angels)   *see* High Downs *Cant*
THRUMPTON (All Saints)   *see* A453 churches of S Notts *S'well*
THRUSHELTON (St George)   *see* Lifton, Broadwoodwidger, Stowford etc *Ex*
THRUSSINGTON (Holy Trinity)   *see* Fosse Team *Leic*
THRUXTON (St Bartholomew)   *see* Cagebrook *Heref*
THRUXTON (St Peter and St Paul)   *see* Appleshaw, Kimpton, Thruxton, Fyfield etc *Win*
THRYBERGH (St Leonard) *Sheff 6*   **P** *Mrs P N Fullerton Hon C* N BOWLER
THUNDERSLEY (St Michael and All Angels) (St Peter)
Chelmsf 13   **P** *Bp*   **P-in-c** A J HUDSON   **OLM** S R CROUCHER
THUNDERSLEY, NEW (St George) *Chelmsf 13*   **P** *Bp*
C P HILLMAN
THUNDRIDGE (St Mary) *St Alb 19*   **P** *Bp*   **V** A J DUNCAN
THURCASTON (All Saints)   *see* Anstey and Thurcaston w Cropston *Leic*
THURCROFT (St Simon and St Jude) *Sheff 5*   **P** *Bp*
P-in-c M RAJKOVIC
THURGARTON (St Peter)   *see* W Trent *S'well*
THURGOLAND (Holy Trinity)   *see* Tankersley, Thurgoland and Wortley *Sheff*
THURLASTON (All Saints)   *see* Enderby w Lubbesthorpe and Thurlaston *Leic*
THURLASTON (St Edmund)   *see* Dunchurch *Cov*
THURLBY (St Firmin)   *see* Ness Gp *Linc*
THURLBY (St Germain)   *see* Withamside *Linc*
THURLEIGH (St Peter)   *see* Milton Ernest, Pavenham and Thurleigh *St Alb*
THURLESTONE (All Saints), South Milton, Churchstow, Woodleigh and Loddiswell *Ex 13*   **P** *Bp Ex, D&C Ex, D&C Sarum, and MMCET (jt)*   **R** D G HARTLEY
THURLOW, GREAT (All Saints)   *see* Stourhead *St E*
THURLOW, LITTLE (St Peter) *as above*
THURLOXTON (St Giles)   *see* Alfred Jewel *B & W*
THURLSTONE (St Saviour)   *see* Penistone and Thurlstone *Sheff*
THURLTON (All Saints)   *see* Raveningham Gp *Nor*
THURMASTON (St Michael and All Angels)   *see* Fosse Team *Leic*
THURNBY (St Luke)   *see* Cornerstone Team *Leic*
THURNBY LODGE (Christ Church)   *see* Ascension TM *Leic*
THURNE (St Edmund)   *see* Martham and Repps w Bastwick, Thurne etc *Nor*
THURNHAM (St Mary the Virgin)   *see* N Downs *Cant*
THURNING (St Andrew)   *see* Reepham and Wensum Valley *Nor*
THURNING (St James the Great)   *see* Barnwell, Hemington, Luddington in the Brook etc *Pet*
THURNSCOE (St Helen) (St Hilda) *Sheff 12*   **P** *Bp and Sir Philip Naylor-Leyland Bt (jt)*   **R** *vacant*
THURROCK, LITTLE (St John the Evangelist)   *see* Grays North *Chelmsf*
THURROCK, LITTLE (St Mary the Virgin)   *see* Grays Thurrock *Chelmsf*
THURROCK, WEST (Church Centre) *as above*
THURSBY (St Andrew) *Carl 3*   **P** *D&C*   **P-in-c** G P RAVALDE

THURSFORD (St Andrew) *see* Barney, Hindringham, Thursford, Great Snoring, Little Snoring and Kettlestone and Pensthorpe *Nor*

THURSLEY (St Michael and All Angels) *Guildf 4* **P** *V Witley* **NSM** D J ORME

THURSTABLE and Winstree, comprising Birch w Layer Breton, Copford, Easthorpe, Great Braxted, Inworth, Layer de la Haye, Layer Marney, Messing, and Tolleshunt Knights w Tiptree *Chelmsf 24* **P** *Duchy of Lanc (1 turn), Ld Chan (1 turn), Patr Bd (3 turns)* **TR** A-M L RENSHAW **TV** L J SMITH **NSM** C A GORRINGE

THURSTASTON (St Bartholomew) *Ches 8* **P** *D&C* **R** E J TURNER

THURSTON (St Peter) *see* Gt Barton and Thurston *St E*

THURSTONLAND (St Thomas) *see* Upper Holme Valley *Leeds*

THURTON (St Ethelbert) w Ashby St Mary, Bergh Apton w Yelverton and Framingham Pigot *Nor 8* **P** *Bp and Major J H Thursby, Bp and MMCET, and Ld Chan (by turn)* **R** C D ELLIS

THUXTON (St Paul) *see* Barnham Broom and Upper Yare *Nor*

THWAITE (All Saints) *see* Erpingham w Calthorpe, Ingworth, Aldborough etc *Nor*

THWAITE (St Mary) *see* Brooke, Kirstead, Mundham w Seething and Thwaite *Nor*

THWAITES (St Anne) *see* Millom *Carl*

THWAITES BROW (St Barnabas) *see* Keighley *Leeds*

THWING (All Saints) *see* Langtoft w Foxholes, Butterwick, Cottam etc *York*

TIBBERTON (All Saints) w Bolas Magna and Waters Upton *Lich 15* **P** *R Edgmond w Kynnersley etc, MMCET, and A B Davies Esq (jt)* **R** H M MORBY

TIBBERTON (Holy Trinity) *see* Highnam, Tibberton w Rudford etc *Glouc*

TIBBERTON (St Peter ad Vincula) *see* Bowbrook S *Worc*

TIBENHAM (All Saints) *see* Long Stratton and Pilgrim TM *Nor*

TIBSHELF (St John the Baptist) *see* Blackwell w Tibshelf *Derby*

TICEHURST (St Mary) and Flimwell *Chich 16* **P** *Bp, Mrs A Sellick, and J Pilcher Esq (jt)* **V** A F EVANS

TICHBORNE (St Andrew) *see* Upper Itchen *Win*

TICHMARSH (St Mary the Virgin) *see* Aldwincle, Clopton, Pilton, Stoke Doyle etc *Pet*

TICKENCOTE (St Peter) *see* Gt and Lt Casterton w Pickworth and Tickencote *Pet*

TICKENHAM (St Quiricus and St Julietta) *see* Nailsea Ch Ch w Tickenham *B & W*

TICKHILL (St Mary) w Stainton *Sheff 9* **P** *Bp* **V** A EARL

TICKNALL (St George) *see* Melbourne, Ticknall, Smisby and Stanton *Derby*

TICKTON (St Paul) *see* Beverley Minster *York*

TIDCOMBE (St Michael) *see* Savernake *Sarum*

TIDDINGTON *see* Albury w Tiddington etc *Ox*

TIDDINGTON (St Peter) *see* Alveston *Cov*

TIDEBROOK (St John the Baptist) *Chich 16* **P** *V Wadhurst and V Mayfield (alt)* **P-in-c** P R RATCLIFF

TIDEFORD (St Luke) *see* St Germans w Antony and Sheviock *Truro*

TIDENHAM (St Mary) w Beachley and Lancaut *Glouc 1* **P** *Bp* **V** D O TREHARNE **C** J P HAMILTON **OLM** D M REES

TIDENHAM CHASE (St Michael and All Angels) *see* Tidenham w Beachley and Lancaut *Glouc*

TIDESWELL (St John the Baptist) *Derby 4* **P** *D&C Lich* **V** S I D WHITE **NSM** G M WHITE

TIDMARSH (St Laurence) *see* Pangbourne w Tidmarsh and Sulham *Ox*

TIDMINGTON (not known) *see* Shipston-on-Stour w Honington and Idlicote *Cov*

TIDWORTH (Holy Trinity) *see* Ludgershall and Tidworth *Sarum*

TIFFIELD (St John the Baptist) *see* Pattishall w Cold Higham and Gayton w Tiffield *Pet*

TILBROOK (All Saints) *see* S Leightonstone *Ely*

TILBURY DOCKS (St John the Baptist) *Chelmsf 16* **P** *Bp* **V** T M CODLING

TILBURY, EAST (St Katherine) and West Tilbury and Linford *Chelmsf 16* **P** *Ld Chan* **P-in-c** M J MARSHALL

TILBURY-JUXTA-CLARE (St Margaret) *see* The Hedinghams and Upper Colne *Chelmsf*

TILE CROSS (St Peter) *see* Sheldon and Tile Cross *Birm*

TILE HILL (St Oswald) *Cov 3* **P** *Bp* **V** *vacant*

TILEHURST (St Catherine of Siena) and Calcot *Ox 7* **P** *Magd Coll Ox* **V** G M ROWELL

TILEHURST (St George) (St Mary Magdalen) *Ox 7* **P** *Bp* **V** A J CARLILL

TILEHURST (St Michael) *Ox 7* **P** *Magd Coll Ox* **R** E C RATCLIFFE

TILFORD (All Saints) *see* The Bourne and Tilford *Guildf*

TILGATE (Holy Trinity) *see* S Crawley *Chich*

TILLINGHAM (St Nicholas) *Chelmsf 11* **P** *D&C St Paul's* **P-in-c** S K POSS

TILLINGTON (All Hallows) *Chich 10* **P** *Lord Egremont* **P-in-c** D L SMITH

TILMANSTONE (St Andrew) *see* Eastry and Woodnesborough *Cant*

TILNEY ALL SAINTS (All Saints) *see* E Marshland *Ely*

TILNEY ST LAWRENCE (St Lawrence) *as above*

TILSHEAD (St Thomas à Becket) *see* Salisbury Plain *Sarum*

TILSTOCK (Christ Church) *see* Edstaston, Fauls, Prees, Tilstock and Whixall *Lich*

TILSTON (St Mary) and Shocklach *Ches 5* **P** *Bp* **R** *vacant*

TILSTONE FEARNALL (St Jude) *see* Bunbury and Tilstone Fearnall *Ches*

TILSWORTH (All Saints) *see* Totternhoe, Stanbridge and Tilsworth *St Alb*

TILTON ON THE HILL (St Peter) *see* Whatborough Gp *Leic*

TILTY (St Mary the Virgin) *see* Broxted w Chickney and Tilty etc *Chelmsf*

TIMBERHILL (St John the Baptist) *see* Nor St Jo w St Julian *Nor*

TIMBERLAND (St Andrew) *see* Carr Dyke Gp *Linc*

TIMBERSCOMBE (St Petroc) *see* Dunster, Carhampton, Withycombe w Rodhuish etc *B & W*

TIMPERLEY (Christ Church) (Holy Cross) *Ches 10* **P** *Trustees* **V** J W BRIDGMAN **C** A S EDDLESTON, J C BRIDGMAN

TIMSBURY (Blessed Virgin Mary) w Priston, Camerton and Dunkerton *B & W 11* **P** *Bp, Ball Coll Ox, and R W Lovegrove Esq (jt)* **P-in-c** M A BLEWETT **NSM** A R G ROAKE

TIMSBURY (St Andrew) *see* Michelmersh and Awbridge and Braishfield etc *Win*

TIMWORTH (St Andrew) *see* Lark Valley *St E*

TINCLETON (St John the Evangelist) *see* Moreton, Woodsford and Crossways w Tincleton *Sarum*

TINGEWICK (St Mary Magdalene) *see* W Buckingham *Ox*

TINGRITH (St Nicholas) *see* Westoning w Tingrith *St Alb*

TINSLEY (St Lawrence) *see* Rivers Team *Sheff*

TINTAGEL (St Materiana) *see* Boscastle and Tintagel Gp *Truro*

TINTINHULL (St Margaret) w Chilthorne Domer w Yeovil Marsh and Thorne Coffin and Lufton *B & W 6* **P** *Guild of All So* **P-in-c** P M DOWN **NSM** A J YOUNG

TINTWISTLE (Christ Church) *see* Hollingworth w Tintwistle *Ches*

TINWELL (All Saints) *see* Ketton and Tinwell *Pet*

TIPTOE (St Andrew) *see* Hordle *Win*

TIPTON (St John the Evangelist) *Lich 25* **P** *V W Bromwich St Jas* **V** S B SAYER

TIPTON (St John) *see* Ottery St Mary, Alfington, W Hill, Tipton etc *Ex*

TIPTON (St Mark) *see* Ocker Hill *Lich*

TIPTON (St Matthew) St Martin and St Paul *Lich 25* **P** *MMCET, and Simeon's Trustees (jt)* **V** A C BOWER **C** C D WATSON

TIPTREE (St Luke) *see* Thurstable and Winstree *Chelmsf*

TIRLEY (St Michael) *see* Ashleworth, Corse, Hartpury, Hasfield etc *Glouc*

TISBURY (St John the Baptist) *see* Nadder Valley *Sarum*

TISMANS COMMON (St John the Baptist) *see* Rudgwick *Chich*

TISSINGTON (St Mary) *see* Fenny Bentley, Thorpe, Tissington, Parwich etc *Derby*

TISTED, EAST w Colemore (St James) *see* Northanger *Win*

TISTED, WEST (St Mary Magdalene) *see* Bishop's Sutton and Ropley and W Tisted *Win*

TITCHFIELD (St Peter) *Portsm 2* **P** *D&C Win* **P-in-c** S ALLMAN **NSM** J A TREVITHICK

TITCHWELL (St Mary) *see* Hunstanton St Mary w Ringstead Parva etc *Nor*

TITLEY (St Peter) *see* Kington w Huntington, Old Radnor, Kinnerton etc *Heref*

TITTENSOR (St Luke) *see* Cotes Heath and Standon and Swynnerton etc *Lich*

TITTLESHALL (St Mary) *see* Launditch and the Upper Nar *Nor*

TIVERTON (St Andrew) *Ex 7* **P** *Bp* **P-in-c** R J GORDON **C** R L MAUDSLEY

TIVERTON (St George) (St Paul) *Ex 7* **P** *MMCET and Peache Trustees (jt)* **P-in-c** A J HUMM **C** J M MONTAGUE **NSM** D A LYDDON

TIVERTON (St Peter) and Chevithorne w Cove *Ex 7* **P** *Peache Trustees (3 turns), Ld Chan (1 turn)* **R** R J GORDON

TIVETSHALL (St Mary and St Margaret) *see* Winfarthing w Shelfanger w Burston w Gissing etc *Nor*

TIVIDALE (St Michael the Archangel) (Holy Cross) (St Augustine) *Lich 25* **P** *Bp* **V** M M ENNIS

TIVINGTON (St Leonard) *see* Porlock and Porlock Weir w Stoke Pero etc *B & W*

TIXALL (St John the Baptist) *see* Stafford St Jo and Tixall w Ingestre *Lich*

TIXOVER (St Luke) *see* Barrowden and Wakerley w S Luffenham etc *Pet*

TOCKENHAM (St Giles) *see* Lyneham and Woodhill *Sarum*

TOCKHOLES (St Stephen) *see* Darwen St Cuth w Tockholes St Steph *Blackb*

TOCKWITH (Epiphany) *see* Marston Moor *York*

TODBER (St Andrew) *see* Stour Vale *Sarum*

TODDINGTON (St Andrew) *see* Winchcombe *Glouc*

TODDINGTON (St George of England) and Chalgrave *St Alb 11* **P** *Bp and DBP (jt)* **P-in-c** L J WASHINGTON

TODENHAM (St Thomas of Canterbury) *see* Moreton-in-Marsh w Batsford, Todenham etc *Glouc*

TODMORDEN (St Mary) (Christ Church) w Cornholme and Walsden *Leeds 8* **P** *DBP and Bp (jt)* **P-in-c** J C JUKES **NSM** J L FLOOD, N K WHITE

TODWICK (St Peter and St Paul) *Sheff 5* **P** *Bp* **P-in-c** V C CAMBER

TOFT (St Andrew) *see* Lordsbridge *Ely*

TOFT (St John the Evangelist) *see* Knutsford St Jo and Toft *Ches*

TOFT MONKS (St Margaret) *see* Raveningham Gp *Nor*

TOFTREES (All Saints) *Nor 14* **P** *Marquess Townshend* **V** *vacant*

TOFTS, WEST and Buckenham Parva *Nor 13* **P** *Guild of All So* **R** *vacant*

TOKYNGTON (St Michael) *Lon 21* **P** *Bp* **V** *vacant*

TOLLADINE (Christ Church) *see* Worc St Barn w Ch Ch *Worc*

TOLLAND (St John the Baptist) *see* Wiveliscombe and the Hills *B & W*

TOLLARD ROYAL (St Peter ad Vincula) *see* Chase *Sarum*

TOLLER FRATRUM (St Basil) *see* Melbury *Sarum*

TOLLER LANE (St Chad) *Leeds 2* **P** *Keble Coll Ox* **P-in-c** L P BEADLE

TOLLER PORCORUM (St Andrew) *see* Beaminster Area *Sarum*

TOLLERTON (St Michael) *see* Alne *York*

TOLLERTON (St Peter) *S'well 5* **P** *Ld Chan* **P-in-c** A R HOWE

TOLLESBURY (St Mary) *see* N Blackwater *Chelmsf*

TOLLESHUNT D'ARCY (St Nicholas) *as above*

TOLLESHUNT MAJOR (St Nicholas) *as above*

TOLLINGTON (St Mark) *Lon 6* **P** *Patr Bd* **TR** E L CLUTTERBUCK **TV** T GOLDING

TOLPUDDLE (St John the Evangelist) *see* Puddletown, Tolpuddle and Milborne w Dewlish *Sarum*

TOLWORTH (Emmanuel) *see* Surbiton Hill Ch Ch *S'wark*

TOLWORTH (St George), Hook and Surbiton *S'wark 15* **P** *The Crown (1 turn), Patr Bd (2 turns)* **TR** H M HANCOCK **TV** D NYIRONGO, L I WICKINGS **NSM** C G LUCAS

TOMBLAND (St George) *see* Nor Colegate and Tombland *Nor*

TONBRIDGE (St Peter and St Paul) (St Andrew) (St Philip) (St Saviour) *Roch 11* **P** *Mabledon Trust* **V** M E BROWN **C** W D CARR

TONBRIDGE (St Stephen) (St Eanswythe Mission Church) *Roch 11* **P** *CPAS* **V** M BARKER **C** M S A BARKER **NSM** S B PERKINS

TONG (St Bartholomew) *see* Shifnal, Sheriffhales and Tong *Lich*

TONG (St James) and Laisterdyke *Leeds 3* **P** *Simeon's Trustees and CR (jt)* **R** G S HODGSON **C** H M HODGSON, P J SLINGSBY

TONGE (St Giles) *see* Milton Regis w Murston, Bapchild and Tonge *Cant*

TONGE (St Michael), Rhodes and Alkrington *Man 14* **P** *Patr Bd* **V** J CALOW

TONGE FOLD (St Chad) *see* Leverhulme *Man*

TONGE MOOR (St Augustine) (St Aidan) *Man 12* **P** *Keble Coll Ox* **V** D A DAVIES

TONGHAM (St Paul) *Guildf 1* **P** *Adn Surrey* **V** C F HOLT **C** R B VICCAJEE

TOOT BALDON (St Lawrence) *see* Dorchester *Ox*

TOOTING (All Saints) *S'wark 17* **P** *Bp* **V** M E CHRISTIE **NSM** S A WHITEHOUSE **OLM** G R WALLER

TOOTING GRAVENEY (St Nicholas) *S'wark 17* **P** *MMCET* **R** C J DAVIS

TOOTING, UPPER (Holy Trinity) (St Augustine) *S'wark 17* **P** *Bp and R Streatham St Leon (jt)* **V** A P DAVEY **NSM** S D JACKSON

TOP VALLEY (St Philip) *see* Bestwood St Matt w St Phil *S'well*

TOPCLIFFE (St Columba), Baldersby w Dishforth, Dalton and Skipton on Swale *York 18* **P** *Abp, Viscountess Downe, and D&C (jt)* **V** S JUKES

TOPCROFT (St Margaret) *see* Hempnall *Nor*

TOPPESFIELD (St Margaret) *see* The Hedinghams and Upper Colne *Chelmsf*

TOPSHAM (St Margaret) and Wear *Ex 3* **P** *D&C* **V** L S GRACE **C** P J INGERSLEV **NSM** J J HORWOOD

TORBRYAN (Holy Trinity) *see* Ipplepen w Torbryan, Denbury, Broadhempston and Woodland *Ex*

TORKSEY (St Peter) *see* Stow Gp *Linc*

TORMARTON (St Mary Magdalene) *see* Marshfield w Cold Ashton and Tormarton etc *Bris*

TORPENHOW (St Michael and all Angels) *see* Binsey *Carl*

TORPOINT (St James) *see* Maker w Rame, Millbrook, St John and Torpoint *Truro*

TORQUAY (St John) *see* Torre and Torquay St Jo *Ex*

TORQUAY (St Luke) *Ex 11* **P** *D&C* **V** P J MARCH

TORQUAY (St Martin) Barton *Ex 11* **P** *V St Marychurch* **V** G CHAPMAN

TORQUAY (St Matthias) (St Mark) (Holy Trinity) *Ex 11* **P** *Ch Patr Trust, Bp and Torwood Trustees (jt)* **R** J A BECKETT **C** S R YATES **NSM** P M B BARTON

TORRE (All Saints) and Torquay St John *Ex 11* **P** *Bp* **V** P J MARCH **Hon C** J S LEE

TORRIDGE *see* Shebbear, Buckland Filleigh, Sheepwash etc *Ex*

TORRINGTON, EAST (St Michael) *see* Barkwith Gp *Linc*

TORRINGTON, GREAT (St Michael), Little Torrington and Frithelstock *Ex 19* **P** *Ch Ch Ox (8 turns), Lord Clinton (1 turn), Prayer Book Soc (1 turn)* **V** P J BEVAN

TORRINGTON, LITTLE (St Giles) *see* Gt and Lt Torrington and Frithelstock *Ex*

TORRISHOLME (Ascension) *Blackb 11* **P** *Bp* **V** D M PORTER

TORTWORTH (St Leonard) *see* Cromhall, Tortworth, Tytherington, Falfield etc *Glouc*

TORVER (St Luke) *see* Coniston and the Crake Valley *Carl*

TOSELAND (St Michael) *see* Papworth *Ely*

TOSSIDE (St Bartholomew) *see* Slaidburn w Tosside *Leeds*

TOSTOCK (St Andrew) *see* Pakenham w Norton, Tostock etc *St E*

TOTHAM, GREAT (St Peter) and Little Totham w Goldhanger *Chelmsf 24* **P** *Bp and Ld Chan (alt)* **NSM** S M GODSMARK

TOTHAM, LITTLE (All Saints) *see* Gt Totham and Lt Totham w Goldhanger *Chelmsf*

TOTLAND BAY (Christ Church) *see* W Wight *Portsm*

TOTLEY (All Saints) *Sheff 2* **P** *Bp* **NSM** A F CREASEY

TOTNES (St Mary) w Bridgetown, Berry Pomeroy, Dartington, Marldon, Ashprington, Cornworthy and Stoke Gabriel *Ex 12* **P** *Patr Bd* **TR** J C OULD **TV** D A PARSONS **C** G STILL, S C JONES **NSM** A D SUMNER

TOTON (St Peter) *S'well 9* **P** *CPAS* **V** C D BOURNE

TOTTENHAM (All Hallows) *Lon 19* **P** *D&C St Paul's* **V** R B PEARSON

TOTTENHAM (Holy Trinity) *Lon 19* **P** *Bp* **V** O A FAGBEMI **C** A D WILLIAMS

TOTTENHAM (St Bartholomew) *see* Stamford Hill St Bart *Lon*

TOTTENHAM (St Benet Fink) *Lon 19* **P** *D&C St Paul's* **V** J A H HILL **NSM** M G BURRIDGE

TOTTENHAM (St Cuthbert) *see* Chitts Hill St Cuth *Lon*

TOTTENHAM (St Mary the Virgin) *Lon 19* **P** *Bp* **V** S J MORRIS **C** A H RIMMER

TOTTENHAM (St Paul) *Lon 19* **P** *V Tottenham All Hallows* **V** S A DAWKINS

TOTTENHAM (St Philip the Apostle) *Lon 19* **P** *Bp* **P-in-c** L R CLARK **NSM** M G BURRIDGE

TOTTENHAM, SOUTH (St Ann) *Lon 19* **P** *D&C St Paul's* **V** J S SWIFT

TOTTENHILL (St Botolph) *see* W Norfolk Priory Gp *Ely*

TOTTERIDGE (St Andrew) *St Alb 14* **P** *R Hatfield* **V** T P SEAGO

TOTTERNHOE (St Giles), Stanbridge and Tilsworth *St Alb 11* **P** *Bp* **V** K DAVID

TOTTINGTON (St Ann) *Man 8* **P** *R Bury St Mary* **V** H W BEARN **OLM** R B MOFFAT

TOTTON, comprising Calmore, Eling, Netley Marsh, and Testwood *Win 11* **P** *Bp* **TR** C D STEED **TV** J R REEVE, S M MARCHANT

TOVE *see* Towcester w Caldecote and Easton Neston etc *Pet*

TOW LAW (St Philip and St James) *see* Satley, Stanley and Tow Law *Dur*

TOWCESTER (St Lawrence) w Caldecote and Easton Neston and Greens Norton and Bradden (The Tove Benefice) *Pet 5* **P** *The Crown (1 turn), Bp, Lord Hesketh, and J E Grant-Ives Esq (1 turn)* **V** P E CHALLEN **C** E W PELLY

TOWEDNACK (St Tewinock) *Truro 5* **P** *Bp*
P-in-c E V A FOOT

TOWER CHAPEL (St Nicholas) *see* Whitehaven *Carl*

TOWERSEY (St Catherine) *see* Thame *Ox*

TOWN END FARM (St Bede) *see* N Wearside *Dur*

TOWNEND (St Paul) *see* Morley *Leeds*

TOWNSTAL (St Clement) *see* Dartmouth and Dittisham *Ex*

TOXTETH (St Bede) (St Clement) *Liv 3* **P** *Simeon's Trustees*
V E JONES **C** T G PRABHAKARA RAO

TOXTETH (St Gabriel) *see* Dingle *Liv*

TOXTETH (St Margaret) *Liv 3* **P** *St Chad's Coll Dur*
P-in-c R G LEWIS **NSM** J STEPHENSON

TOXTETH (St Philemon) *Liv 3* **P** *CPAS* **R** B R ELFICK

TOXTETH PARK (Christ Church) (St Michael-in-the-Hamlet) (St Andrew) *Liv 3* **P** *Simeon's Trustees and Trustees (jt)* **V** K J HITCHMAN

TOXTETH PARK (St Agnes and St Pancras) *Liv 3* **P** *St Chad's Coll Dur* **V** D J LLOYD

TOXTETH PARK (St Cleopas) *see* Dingle *Liv*

TOYNTON ALL SAINTS (All Saints) *see* Bolingbroke Deanery *Linc*

TOYNTON ST PETER (St Peter) *as above*

TOYNTON, HIGH (St John the Baptist) *see* Horncastle Gp *Linc*

TOYS HILL (Hall) *see* Hever, Four Elms and Mark Beech *Roch*

TRAFALGAR SQUARE (St Martin-in-the-Fields) *see* St Martin-in-the-Fields *Lon*

TRAFFORD, OLD (St Bride) *Man 5* **P** *Trustees*
R P J MATTHEWS **OLM** O H SAMUEL, V M ECCLES

TRAFFORD, OLD (St Hilda) *see* Firswood and Gorse Hill *Man*

TRAFFORD, OLD (St John the Evangelist) *Man 5* **P** *The Crown* **R** J D HUGHES **OLM** C J ASPINALL

TRANMERE (St Catherine) *Ches 1* **P** *R Bebington*
V J R TERRY

TRANMERE (St Paul w St Luke) *Ches 1* **P** *Bp* **V** P J PARRY

TRAWDEN (St Mary the Virgin) *see* Foulridge, Laneshawbridge and Trawden *Blackb*

TREALES (Christ Church) *Blackb 10* **P** *V Kirkham*
NSM C M MORTON

TREBOROUGH (St Peter) *see* Old Cleeve, Leighland and Treborough *B & W*

TREDINGTON (St Gregory) and Darlingscott *Cov 9* **P** *Jes Coll Ox* **P-in-c** C GOBLE **Hon C** S W FLETCHER

TREDINGTON (St John the Baptist) *see* Deerhurst and Apperley w Forthampton etc *Glouc*

TREETON (St Helen) *see* Rivers Team *Sheff*

TREFONEN (All Saints) *see* Llanyblodwel, Llanymynech, Morton and Trefonen *Lich*

TREGADILLET (St Mary's Mission) *see* Launceston *Truro*

TREGONY (not known) w St Cuby and Cornelly *Truro 6*
P *Bp* **P-in-c** E L WATSON

TREKNOW (Holy Family) *see* Boscastle and Tintagel Gp *Truro*

TRELAWNY, comprising Lanreath, Lansallos, Lanteglos by Fowey, and Pelynt *Truro 12* **P** *DBP, D&C, W G Mills Esq, J B Kitson Esq, and H M Parker Esq (jt)* **R** M E ELLIOTT

TRELEIGH (St Stephen) *see* Redruth w Lanner and Treleigh *Truro*

TRELYSTAN (St Mary the Virgin) *see* Chirbury, Marton, Middleton and Trelystan etc *Heref*

TREMAINE (St Winwalo) *see* Egloskerry, N Petherwin, Tremaine, Tresmere etc *Truro*

TRENDLEWOOD (Conventional District) *B & W 12*
C M D TAYLOR **Min** J S TILLEY

TRENEGLOS (St Gregory) *see* Week St Mary Circle of Par *Truro*

TRENT (St Andrew) *see* Queen Thorne *Sarum*

TRENT VALE (St John the Evangelist) *see* Hartshill, Penkhull and Trent Vale *Lich*

TRENT, WEST, comprising Bleasby, Halloughton, Hoveringham, Morton, Rolleston, Thurgarton, and Upton *S'well 3* **P** *Trin Coll Cam (1 turn), Ld Chan (2 turns)* **V** P W WHITE

TRENTCLIFFE Group, The, comprising Blyborough, Blyton, East Stockwith, Glentworth, Harpswell, Hemswell, Laughton, and Willoughton *Linc 2* **P** *Bp, Ch Soc Trust, MMCET, and SMF (1 turn), Ld Chan (1 turn)* **V** M BRISCOE **NSM** C A SULLY

TRENTHAM (St Mary and All Saints) *Lich 12* **P** *CPAS*
V A G STONE **NSM** D PAMMENT

TRENTISHOE (St Peter) *see* Lynton, Brendon, Countisbury etc *Ex*

TRENTSIDE EAST, comprising Gunness and Scunthorpe the Resurrection *Linc 6* **P** *Bp Linc (2 turns), Bp Lon (1 turn)*
R *vacant*

TRESCO (St Nicholas) *see* Is of Scilly *Truro*

TRESHAM (not known) *see* Tyndale *Glouc*

TRESILLIAN (Holy Trinity) and Lamorran w Merther *Truro 6*
P *Viscount Falmouth* **P-in-c** L M BARLEY

TRESLOTHAN (St John the Evangelist) *see* Crowan and Treslothan *Truro*

TRESMERE (St Nicholas) *see* Egloskerry, N Petherwin, Tremaine, Tresmere etc *Truro*

TRESWELL (St John the Baptist) *see* Retford Area *S'well*

TRETHEVY (St Piran) *see* Boscastle and Tintagel Gp *Truro*

TRETIRE (St Mary) *see* St Weonards *Heref*

TREVALGA (St Petroc) *see* Boscastle and Tintagel Gp *Truro*

TREVENSON (St Illogan) *see* St Illogan *Truro*

TREVERBYN (St Peter) *Truro 1* **P** *The Crown*
P-in-c K P ARTHUR

TREVONE (St Saviour) *see* Padstow, St Merryn and St Issey w St Petroc Minor *Truro*

TREWEN (St Michael) *see* Egloskerry, N Petherwin, Tremaine, Tresmere etc *Truro*

TREYFORD CUM DIDLING (St Andrew) *see* Harting w Elsted and Treyford cum Didling *Chich*

TRIANGLE (All Saints) (St Matthew) (Community Centre)
Ipswich *St E 1* **P** *Bp and Ld Chan (alt)* **R** N S ATKINS
C A K BUTTRESS, D F MORRISON **NSM** L A CAREY, R H BEST

TRIGG MAJOR Conventional District *Truro 9*
P-in-c P M KNIGHT

TRIMDON (St Mary Magdalene) *see* Upper Skerne *Dur*

TRIMDON GRANGE (St Alban) *as above*

TRIMINGHAM (St John the Baptist) *see* Poppyland *Nor*

TRIMLEY (St Martin) *see* Walton and Trimley *St E*

TRIMPLEY (Holy Trinity) *see* Kidderminster Ismere *Worc*

TRING (St Martha) (St Peter and St Paul) (St Mary) *St Alb 1*
P *Bp* **TR** H BELLIS **TV** J C BANISTER, M E GRACE
C S MARSHALL **NSM** D F JAQUET

TRINITY IN LEWES, including Lewes St John sub Castro, South Malling, and Southover *Chich 21* **P** *CPAS Patr Trust*
R S J DAUGHTERY **C** J J R MIDDLETON **NSM** J J BAMBER

TROSTON (St Mary the Virgin) *see* Blackbourne *St E*

TROTTISCLIFFE (St Peter and St Paul) *see* Birling, Addington, Ryarsh and Trottiscliffe *Roch*

TROTTON (St George) *see* Rogate w Terwick and Trotton w Chithurst *Chich*

TROUTBECK (Jesus Church) *see* Windermere St Mary and Troutbeck *Carl*

TROWBRIDGE (Holy Trinity) *see* Trowbridge St Thos and W Ashton *Sarum*

TROWBRIDGE (St James) and Keevil *Sarum 15* **P** *Ch Patr Trust and D&C (jt)* **R** R G THOMAS

TROWBRIDGE (St Thomas) and West Ashton *Sarum 15*
P *CPAS* **V** J A COUTTS

TROWELL (St Helen) *see* Trowell, Awsworth and Cossall *S'well*

TROWELL (St Helen), Awsworth and Cossall *S'well 8* **P** *Bp and Lord Middleton (jt)* **NSM** P C WHITEHEAD

TROWSE (St Andrew) *Nor 1* **P** *D&C* **P-in-c** R R BRABY

TRULL (All Saints) w Angersleigh *B & W 18* **P** *DBP and M V Spurway Esq (jt)* **R** A J WADSWORTH

TRUMPINGTON (St Mary and St Michael) *Ely 3* **P** *Trin Coll Cam* **V** M J MAXWELL **NSM** S M HARRIS

TRUNCH GROUP, The (St Botolph), comprising Gimingham, Knapton, Mundesley, Paston, and Trunch w Swafield and Bradfield *Nor 20* **P** *Duchy of Lancaster (3 turns), Bp, Adn, DBP, and Peterho Cam (1 turn)* **R** A E JONES

TRURO (St Mary's Cathedral and Parish Church) *Truro 6*
P *The Crown* **C** L M BARLEY **Hon C** A G BASHFORTH

TRURO St Paul (St George the Martyr) (St John the Evangelist) *Truro 6* **P** *The Crown (1 turn), Bp and V Kenwyn St Cuby (1 turn)* **V** *vacant*

TRUSHAM (St Michael and All Angels) *see* Chudleigh w Chudleigh Knighton and Trusham *Ex*

TRUSLEY (All Saints) *see* Boylestone, Church Broughton, Dalbury, etc *Derby*

TRUSTHORPE (St Peter) *see* Mablethorpe w Trusthorpe *Linc*

TRYSULL (All Saints) *see* Smestow Vale *Lich*

TUBNEY (St Lawrence) *see* Fyfield w Tubney and Kingston Bagpuize *Ox*

TUCKHILL (Holy Innocents) *see* Claverley w Tuckhill *Heref*

TUCKSWOOD (St Paul) *see* Nor Lakenham St Jo and All SS and Tuckswood *Nor*

TUDDENHAM (St Martin) *see* Westerfield and Tuddenham w Witnesham *St E*

TUDDENHAM (St Mary) *see* Mildenhall *St E*

TUDDENHAM, EAST (All Saints) *see* Mattishall and the Tudd Valley *Nor*

TUDDENHAM, NORTH (St Mary the Virgin) *as above*

TUDELEY (All Saints) *see* Capel United Ben *Roch*

TUDHOE (St David) *see* Croxdale and Tudhoe *Dur*

TUDHOE GRANGE (St Andrew) *see* Bowburn and Tudhoe Grange *Dur*

TUEBROOK (St John) *see* W Derby St Jo *Liv*

TUFFLEY (St Barnabas) *Glouc 2* **P** *Bp* **C** S J TODD

TUFNELL PARK (St George and All Saints) *Lon 6* **P** *Trustees and CPAS (jt)* **P-in-c** A M LILLEY **C** M D STONE

TUFTON (St Mary) *see* Whitchurch w Tufton and Litchfield *Win*

TUGBY (St Thomas à Becket) *see* Hallaton and Allexton, w Horninghold, Tugby etc *Leic*

TUGFORD (St Catherine) *see* Corvedale Benefice *Heref*

TULSE HILL (Holy Trinity and St Matthias) *S'wark 12* **P** *Simeon's Trustees and Peache Trustees (jt)* **V** R P DORMANDY **C** N W SMITH **NSM** W W SHARPE

TUNBRIDGE WELLS (Christ Church) *Roch 12* **P** *Mabledon Trust and CPAS (jt)* **V** T M HUMPHREY **C** G E J TAYLOR

TUNBRIDGE WELLS (King Charles the Martyr) *Roch 12* **P** *Trustees* **V** L J POWELL **NSM** C L ALLWOOD, S M PARTRIDGE

TUNBRIDGE WELLS (St Barnabas) *Roch 12* **P** *Guild of All So* **V** J F CASTER

TUNBRIDGE WELLS (St James) *Roch 12* **P** *Ch Trust Fund Trust* **V** J P STEWART **C** J A HAMMILL

TUNBRIDGE WELLS (St John) *Roch 12* **P** *CPAS and V Tunbridge Wells H Trin (jt)* **C** R W FARR

TUNBRIDGE WELLS (St Luke) *Roch 12* **P** *Five Trustees* **V** C M GLASS

TUNBRIDGE WELLS (St Mark) Broadwater Down *Roch 12* **P** *Bp* **P-in-c** L J POWELL

TUNBRIDGE WELLS (St Peter) Windmill Fields *Roch 12* **P** *Trustees and CPAS (jt)* **V** M P WARREN

TUNBRIDGE WELLS (St Philip) *Roch 12* **P** *Ch Trust Fund Trust* **V** R N THOMAS

TUNSTALL (All Saints) *see* S Holderness Coast *York*

TUNSTALL (Christ Church) *see* Goldenhill and Tunstall *Lich*

TUNSTALL (Holy Trinity) *see* Catterick *Leeds*

TUNSTALL (St John the Baptist) *see* E Lonsdale *Blackb*

TUNSTALL (St John the Baptist) and Bredgar *Cant 15* **P** *Abp, D&C, O P Doubleday Esq, S G McCandlish Esq, Lady Kingsdown, and J Nightingale Esq (jt)* **R** A E PINNEGAR **NSM** K D JACOBS

TUNSTALL (St Michael and All Angels) *see* Wilford Peninsula *St E*

TUNSTEAD (St Mary) *see* Wroxham w Hoveton, Belaugh and Tunstead etc *Nor*

TUNSTEAD (Holy Trinity) *see* Bacup and Stacksteads *Man*

TUNWORTH (All Saints) *see* N Hants Downs *Win*

TUPSLEY (St Paul) w Hampton Bishop *Heref 3* **P** *Bp* **V** N P ARMSTRONG **C** R H ROBERTSON

TUPTON (St John) *see* N Wingfield, Clay Cross and Pilsley *Derby*

TUR LANGTON (St Andrew) *see* The Langtons and Shangton *Leic*

TURKDEAN (All Saints) *see* Northleach w Hampnett and Farmington etc *Glouc*

TURNASTONE (St Mary Magdalene) *see* Madley w Tyberton, Peterchurch, Vowchurch etc *Heref*

TURNDITCH (All Saints) *see* Belper Ch Ch w Turnditch *Derby*

TURNERS HILL (St Leonard) *Chich 6* **P** *Bp* **P-in-c** D A TICKNER

TURNFORD (St Clement) *see* Cheshunt *St Alb*

TURNHAM GREEN (Christ Church) *Lon 11* **P** *Bp* **V** R J MOY **C** J M HOLDER, L J HOLDER, N L MOY

TURNWORTH (St Mary) *see* Winterborne Valley and Milton Abbas *Sarum*

TURTON MOORLAND MINISTRY (St Anne) (St James) *Man 12* **P** *Patr Bd* **TV** C T HAYDEN **NSM** J H M AINSWORTH **OLM** A M BULCOCK, C D JAMIESON

TURVEY (All Saints) *see* Chellington *St Alb*

TURVILLE (St Mary) *see* Hambleden Valley *Ox*

TURWESTON (Assumption of the Blessed Virgin Mary) *see* W Buckingham *Ox*

TUSHINGHAM (St Chad) *see* Marbury w Tushingham and Whitewell *Ches*

TUTBURY (St Mary the Virgin) *see* Anslow, Rolleston and Tutbury *Lich*

TUTSHILL (St Luke) *see* Tidenham w Beachley and Lancaut *Glouc*

TUTTINGTON (St Peter and St Paul) *see* King's Beck *Nor*

TUXFORD (St Nicholas) w Weston, Markham Clinton, Normanton upon Trent and Marnham *S'well 3* **P** *Bp and Ld Chan (alt)* **V** G P PRICE

TWEEDMOUTH (St Bartholomew) *Newc 12* **P** *D&C Dur* **Hon C** D MACNAUGHTON

TWERTON-ON-AVON *see* Bath Twerton-on-Avon *B & W*

TWICKENHAM (All Hallows) *Lon 10* **P** *D&C St Paul's* **V** K D BELL

TWICKENHAM (All Saints) *Lon 10* **P** *Bp* **V** A J LANE

TWICKENHAM (St Mary the Virgin) *Lon 10* **P** *D&C Windsor* **V** R J H WILLIAMS **C** P J ASHWIN-SIEJKOWSKI

TWICKENHAM COMMON (Holy Trinity) *Lon 10* **P** *Bp* **V** T M GARRETT **C** C L KEAR **Hon C** N R GARRETT

TWICKENHAM, EAST (St Stephen) (St Paul) *Lon 10* **P** *CPAS* **V** J P B BARNES **C** A G D WATKINS, H C A FOXWOOD

TWIGWORTH (St Matthew), Down Hatherley, Norton, The Leigh, Evington, Sandhurst and Staverton w Boddington *Glouc 3* **P** *Ld Chan (1 turn), Bp Glouc and D&C Bris (1 turn)* **V** J SKEPPER **NSM** P J DONALD

TWINEHAM (St Peter) *see* Albourne w Sayers Common and Twineham *Chich*

TWINSTEAD (St John the Evangelist) *see* N Hinckford *Chelmsf*

TWITCHEN (St Peter) *see* Bishopsnympton, Charles, E Anstey, High Bray etc *Ex*

TWO GATES (St Peter) *see* Wilnecote *Lich*

TWO MILE ASH (not known) *see* Watling Valley *Ox*

TWO MILE HILL (St Michael) *Bris 3* **P** *The Crown* **P-in-c** R J LING **C** M HOTCHKISS **NSM** M M CRITCHLOW **OLM** N G CALLEN

TWO RIVERS *see* Holbrook, Stutton, Freston, Woolverstone etc *St E*

TWO RIVERS *see* Newton Tracey, Horwood, Alverdiscott etc *Ex*

TWO RIVERS, The, comprising Ashen, Birdbrook, Helions Bumpstead, Ridgewell, Steeple Bumpstead, and Sturmer *Chelmsf 19* **P** *Duchy of Lancaster (1 turn), Bp and DBP (1 turn), Ld Chan (1 turn)* **R** J D LOWE **C** C M ROBERTSON **Hon C** S E CRUSE **NSM** T C LOWE

TWO SHIRES *see* Chaffcombe, Cricket Malherbie etc *B & W*

TWYCROSS (St James) *see* Bosworth and Sheepy Gp *Leic*

TWYFORD (Assumption of the Blessed Virgin Mary) *see* The Claydons and Swan *Ox*

TWYFORD (St Andrew) *see* Aston on Trent, Elvaston, Weston on Trent etc *Derby*

TWYFORD (St Andrew) *see* S Croxton Gp *Leic*

TWYFORD (St Mary the Virgin) *see* Ruscombe and Twyford w Hurst *Ox*

TWYFORD (St Nicholas) *see* Heart of Norfolk *Nor*

TWYNING (St Mary Magdalene) *see* Tewkesbury w Walton Cardiff and Twyning *Glouc*

TWYWELL (St Nicholas) *see* Cranford w Grafton Underwood and Twywell *Pet*

TYBERTON (St Mary) *see* Madley w Tyberton, Peterchurch, Vowchurch etc *Heref*

TYDD ST GILES (St Giles) *see* Leverington, Newton and Tydd St Giles *Ely*

TYDD ST MARY (St Mary) *see* Sutton Bridge and Tydd St Mary *Linc*

TYE GREEN (St Barnabas) *see* Cressing w Stisted and Bradwell etc *Chelmsf*

TYE GREEN (St Stephen) w St Andrew Netteswell *Chelmsf 4* **P** J L H Arkwright Esq **P-in-c** D L MCINDOE **Hon C** C C OKEKE **OLM** A T KEEBLE

TYLDESLEY (St George) *see* Astley, Tyldesley and Mosley Common *Man*

TYLERS GREEN (St Margaret) *see* Penn and Tylers Green *Ox*

TYLER'S HILL (St George) *see* Gt Chesham *Ox*

TYNDALE, comprising Alderley, North Nibley, and Wotton-under-Edge w Ozleworth *Glouc 5* **P** *Ch Ch Ox and Bp (jt)* **NSM** M E LANGLEY, P C E MARSH

TYNE, NORTH and Redesdale Team, comprising Bellingham, Corsenside, Elsdon, Falstone w Greystead and Thorneyburn, Horsley w Byrness, and Otterburn *Newc 8* **P** *Patr Bd* **TR** S M RAMSARAN **NSM** E L RYDER

TYNEMOUTH (St John Percy) *Newc 5* **P** *Dioc Soc* **C** L J CLEMINSON **Hon C** P INGHAM

TYNEMOUTH Balkwell (St Peter) *see* Balkwell *Newc*

TYNEMOUTH Cullercoats (St Paul) *Newc 5* **P** *Dioc Soc* **V** J VILASECA-BRUCH

TYNEMOUTH PRIORY (Holy Saviour) *Newc 5* **P** *Dioc Soc* **V** S DIXON **NSM** M RAILTON

TYNINGS LANE (St Mary's Mission Church) *see* Aldridge *Lich*

TYRINGHAM (St Peter) *see* Lamp *Ox*

TYRLEY (Mission Room) *see* Drayton in Hales *Lich*

TYSELEY (St Edmund) *Birm 11* **P** *The Crown* **V** *vacant*

TYSOE (Assumption of the Blessed Virgin Mary) w Oxhill and Whatcote *Cov 9* **P** *Marquess of Northampton and DBP (jt)* **P-in-c** G HEIGHTON

TYTHBY (Holy Trinity) *see* Wiverton in the Vale *S'well*

TYTHERINGTON (St James) *see* Cromhall, Tortworth, Tytherington, Falfield etc *Glouc*

TYTHERINGTON (St James)   *see* Upper Wylye Valley *Sarum*

TYTHERLEY, EAST (St Peter)   *see* Lockerley and E Dean w E and W Tytherley *Win*

TYTHERLEY, WEST (St Peter) *as above*

TYTHERTON KELLAWAYS (St Giles)   *see* Draycot *Bris*

TYTHERTON LUCAS (St Nicholas)   *see* Chippenham St Andr w Tytherton Lucas *Bris*

TYWARDREATH (St Andrew) w Tregaminion *Truro 1*
P *DBP*   **P-in-c** D J P ISIORHO

UBLEY (St Bartholomew)   *see* Blagdon w Compton Martin and Ubley *B & W*

UCKFIELD (Holy Cross) (St Saviour) *Chich 18*   **P** *Abp*
P-in-c J C WALL

UDIMORE (St Mary)   *see* Brede w Udimore and Beckley and Peasmarsh *Chich*

UFFCULME (St Mary the Virgin)   *see* Willand, Uffculme, Kentisbeare etc *Ex*

UFFINGTON (Holy Trinity)   *see* Wrockwardine Deanery *Lich*

UFFINGTON (St Mary), Shellingford, Woolstone and Baulking *Ox 25*   **P** *Bp (2 turns), J J Twynam Esq (1 turn)*
R J H GOULSTON

UFFINGTON Group, The (St Michael and All Angels), including Barholme, Braceborough, Greatford, Tallington, West Deeping, and Wilsthorpe *Linc 16*   **P** *Ld Chan (2 turns), Bp (2 turns), D&C (1 turn)*   **R** A P BEESLEY

UFFORD (Assumption of the Blessed Virgin Mary)   *see* Melton and Ufford *St E*

UFTON (St Michael and All Angels) *Cov 10*   **P** *Bp*   **V** *vacant*

UGBOROUGH (St Peter)   *see* Diptford w N Huish, Ermington, Halwell etc *Ex*

UGGESHALL (St Mary)   *see* Sole Bay *St E*

UGGLEBARNBY (All Saints)   *see* Lower Esk *York*

UGLEY (St Peter)   *see* Henham and Elsenham w Ugley *Chelmsf*

UGTHORPE (Christ Church)   *see* Hinderwell, Roxby and Staithes etc *York*

UKELEY (St Peter)   *see* Henham and Elsenham w Ugley *Chelmsf*

ULCEBY (All Saints)   *see* Alford Gp *Linc*

ULCEBY (St Nicholas)   *see* Abbey Gp *Linc*

ULCOMBE (All Saints)   *see* Len Valley *Cant*

ULDALE (St James)   *see* Binsey *Carl*

ULEY (St Giles)   *see* Dursley, Uley, Owlpen etc *Glouc*

ULGHAM (St John the Baptist) *Newc 11*   **P** *Bp*
P-in-c J J L DOBSON   **NSM** D M BAKER

ULLENHALL (St Mary the Virgin)   *see* Beaudesert and Henley-in-Arden w Ullenhall *Cov*

ULLESKELFE (St Saviour)   *see* Tadcaster *York*

ULLEY (Holy Trinity)   *see* Aston cum Aughton w Swallownest and Ulley *Sheff*

ULLINGSWICK (St Luke)   *see* Bredenbury *Heref*

ULPHA (St John)   *see* Broughton and Duddon *Carl*

ULROME (St Andrew)   *see* Bridlington Ch Ch w Bessingby and Ulrome *York*

ULTING (All Saints)   *see* Hatfield Peverel w Ulting *Chelmsf*

ULVERSTON (St Mary w Holy Trinity) (St Jude) *Carl 9*
P *Peache Trustees*   **R** A C BING   **C** M B SIMPSON

UMBERLEIGH (Church of the Good Shepherd)   *see* S Molton w Nymet St George, Chittlehamholt etc *Ex*

UNDERBARROW (All Saints) w Helsington *Carl 10*   **P** *V Kendal H Trin*   **V** *vacant*

UNDERRIVER (St Margaret)   *see* Seal Chart w Underriver *Roch*

UNDERSKIDDAW (Parish Room)   *see* Crosthwaite Keswick *Carl*

UNDERWOOD (St Michael and All Angels)   *see* Brinsley w Underwood *S'well*

UNSTONE (St Mary)   *see* Dronfield w Holmesfield *Derby*

UNSWORTH (St Andrew)   *see* Hillock and Unsworth *Man*

UNSWORTH (St George)   *see* Hillock and Unsworth *Man*

UP HATHERLEY (St Philip and St James) *Glouc 6*   **P** *Soc of the Faith*   **V** M L CATHERALL

UP MARDEN (St Michael)   *see* Octagon *Chich*

UP NATELY (St Stephen)   *see* N Hants Downs *Win*

UP WALTHAM   *see* Upwaltham *Chich*

UPAVON (St Mary the Virgin)   *see* Vale of Pewsey *Sarum*

UPCHURCH (St Mary the Virgin)   *see* The Six Cant

UPHAM (All Saints) (Blessed Mary of Upham) *Portsm 1*
P *Ld Chan*   **R** J C HUNT   **NSM** J BELOE, K F WICKERT

UPHILL (St Barnabas Mission Church)   *see* Weston-super-Mare St Nic w St Barn *B & W*

UPHILL (St Nicholas) *as above*

UPHOLLAND (St Thomas the Martyr) *Liv 14*   **P** *Patr Bd*
P-in-c P A LOCK

UPLANDS (All Saints)   *see* Stroud Team *Glouc*

UPLANDS GROUP   *see* Guilsborough and Hollowell and Cold Ashby etc *Pet*

UPLEADON (St Mary the Virgin)   *see* Redmarley D'Abitot, Bromesberrow, Pauntley etc *Glouc*

UPLOWMAN (St Peter)   *see* Sampford Peverell, Uplowman, Holcombe Rogus etc *Ex*

UPLYME (St Peter and St Paul) w Axmouth *Ex 4*   **P** *CPAS and Hyndman Trustees (jt)*   **NSM** A M STUCKEY

UPMINSTER (St Laurence) *Chelmsf 2*   **P** *W R Holden Esq*
R S M BRASIER   **NSM** R J MURRAY

UPNOR (St Philip and St James)   *see* Frindsbury w Upnor and Chattenden *Roch*

UPOTTERY (St Mary the Virgin)   *see* Broadhembury, Dunkeswell, Luppitt, Plymtree, Sheldon, and Upottery *Ex*

UPPER *also see under substantive place name*

UPPER KENNET, comprising Avebury, Broad Hinton, Overton and Fyfield w East Kennett, Winterbourne Bassett, and Winterbourne Monkton w Berwick Bassett *Sarum 18*   **P** *Bp*
R M T SHEPHERDSON

UPPER TAS VALLEY, comprising Ashwellthorpe, Forncett End, Forncett St Mary, Forncett St Peter, Fundenhall, Hapton, Tacolneston, and Wreningham *Nor 7*   **P** *Bp, Keble Coll Ox, Ch Coll Cam, and MMCET (by turn)*   **P-in-c** L D A AVERY

UPPERBY (St John the Baptist) *Carl 3*   **P** *D&C*   **R** *vacant*

UPPERBY (St John the Baptist)   *see* Upperby *Carl*

UPPERTHONG (St John the Evangelist)   *see* Upper Holme Valley *Leeds*

UPPINGHAM (St Peter and St Paul) w Ayston and Belton w Wardley *Pet 12*   **P** *Bp*   **R** R D WATTS

UPPINGTON (Holy Trinity)   *see* Wrockwardine Deanery *Lich*

UPSHIRE (St Thomas)   *see* Waltham H Cross *Chelmsf*

UPTON (All Saints)   *see* Lea Gp *Linc*

UPTON (Holy Ascension) *Ches 2*   **P** *Duke of Westmr*
V P NEWMAN   **NSM** D O'BRIEN

UPTON (St Dunstan)   *see* The Lytchetts and Upton *Sarum*

UPTON (St James)   *see* Dulverton w Brushford, Brompton Regis etc *B & W*

UPTON (St John the Baptist)   *see* Castor w Upton and Stibbington *Pet*

UPTON (St Laurence)   *see* Upton cum Chalvey *Ox*

UPTON (St Margaret)   *see* Broadside *Nor*

UPTON (St Margaret)   *see* N Leightonstone *Ely*

UPTON (St Mary Magdalene) *Ex 11*   **P** *Simeon's Trustees and Ch Patr Trust (alt)*   **R** S M LEACH   **C** R M DENSMORE
NSM I N KIYAGA, J H GARNER

UPTON (St Mary the Virgin)   *see* The Churn *Ox*

UPTON (St Mary) *Ches 8*   **P** *Simeon's Trustees*
V N J EASTWOOD   **C** S H WARRELL

UPTON (St Peter and St Paul)   *see* W Trent *S'well*

UPTON BISHOP (St John the Baptist)   *see* Ariconium *Heref*

UPTON CROSS (St Paul)   *see* Callington Cluster *Truro*

UPTON CUM CHALVEY (St Mary) *Ox 12*   **P** *Bp*
TR A S ALLEN   **TV** A C STEWART   **NSM** L R HILLIER

UPTON GREY (St Mary)   *see* N Hants Downs *Win*

UPTON HELLIONS (St Mary the Virgin)   *see* Crediton, Shobrooke and Sandford etc *Ex*

UPTON LOVELL (St Augustine of Canterbury)   *see* Upper Wylye Valley *Sarum*

UPTON MAGNA (St Lucia)   *see* Wrockwardine Deanery *Lich*

UPTON NOBLE (St Mary Magdalene)   *see* Alham Vale *B & W*

UPTON PARK (St Alban)   *see* E Ham H Trin *Chelmsf*

UPTON PRIORY (Church of the Resurrection) *Ches 13*   **P** *Bp*
NSM A S RAVENSCROFT

UPTON PYNE (Our Lady)   *see* Brampford Speke, Cadbury, Newton St Cyres etc *Ex*

UPTON SCUDAMORE (St Mary the Virgin)   *see* River Were *Sarum*

UPTON SNODSBURY (St Kenelm)   *see* Peopleton and White Ladies Aston w Churchill etc *Worc*

UPTON ST LEONARDS (St Leonard) *Glouc 2*   **P** *Bp*
P-in-c C M INGRAM   **C** J R TURK

UPTON WARREN (St Michael)   *see* Stoke Prior, Wychbold and Upton Warren *Worc*

UPTON-ON-SEVERN (St Peter and St Paul), Ripple, Earls Croome w Hill Croome and Strensham *Worc 5*   **P** *Bp (2 turns), Mrs A J Hyde-Smith and Mrs A L Wynne (1 turn)*
P-in-c B UNWIN   **NSM** G R MOORE, S M E ADENEY

UPWALTHAM (St Mary the Virgin) *Chich 10*   **P** *Lord Egremont*   **P-in-c** D L SMITH

UPWELL (St Peter) *Ely 14*   **P** *R T Townley Esq*   **R** *vacant*

UPWELL CHRISTCHURCH (Christ Church)   *see* Christchurch and Manea and Welney *Ely*

UPWEY (St Laurence)   *see* Weymouth Ridgeway *Sarum*

UPWOOD (St Peter)   *see* The Ramseys and Upwood *Ely*

URCHFONT (St Michael and All Angels)   *see* Cannings and Redhorn *Sarum*

URMSTON (St Clement)   *see* Davyhulme Ch Ch and Urmston *Man*

URSWICK (St Mary the Virgin and St Michael) *see* Aldingham, Dendron, Rampside and Urswick *Carl*

USHAW MOOR (St Luke) *see* Brandon and Ushaw Moor *Dur*

USSELBY (St Margaret) *see* Woldmoor Gp *Linc*

USWORTH (Holy Trinity) (St Michael and All Angels) *Dur 10* **P** *Bp* **R** J WING

UTKINTON (St Paul) *see* Tarporley *Ches*

UTLEY (St Mark) *see* Keighley *Leeds*

UTTERBY (St Andrew) *see* Fotherby, N Thoresby and Grainsby w Waithe *Linc*

UTTOXETER AREA (St Mary the Virgin), including Bramshall, Checkley, Gratwich, Kingstone, Leigh, Marchington Woodlands, Stramshall, and Upper Tean *Lich 14* **P** *Patr Bd* **TR** M J SHERWIN **TV** J C CANT **NSM** L J WRAY-WEAR **OLM** C H BROWN, C W DALE, J S LANDER

UXBRIDGE (St Andrew) (St Margaret) (St Peter) *Lon 24* **P** *Bp* **TR** A G STUDDERT-KENNEDY **C** J A HUGHMAN **Hon C** T D ATKINS **NSM** J JENKINS, T A RAPSON

UXBRIDGE ROAD (St Luke) *see* Hammersmith St Luke *Lon*

VALE and Cotswold Edge, comprising Blockley, Bourton-on-the-Hill, Chipping Campden, Church Honeybourne, Dorsington, Ebrington, Mickleton, Pebworth, Weston-sub-Edge w Aston-sub-Edge, and Willersey w Saintbury *Glouc 8* **P** *Patr Bd (3 turns) and Ld Chan (1 turn)* **TR** S C BISHOP **TV** D L DELAP, S A WATTS **NSM** K GRUMBALL

VALE OF BELVOIR Parishes, comprising Barkestone, Bottesford, Harby, Hose, Long Clawson, Muston, Plungar, Redmile, and Stathern *Leic 2* **P** *Patr Bd (2 turns), Ld Chan (1 turn)* **TV** D C PAYNE

VALE OF PEWSEY, comprising Alton Barnes w Alton Priors, Beechingstoke, Charlton, Easton Royal, Huish and Oare, Manningford Bruce and Manningford Abbots, Milton Lilbourne, North Newnton, Pewsey, Rushall, Stanton St Bernard, Upavon, Wilcot, and Woodborough w Manningford Bohune *Sarum 19* **P** *Patr Bd* **TR** D F LARKEY **TV** J C TOTNEY, M J WINDSOR **C** C M HEBER-PERCY **OLM** G E R OSBORNE

VALE OF RODING, comprising Chigwell, Chigwell Row, Lambourne w Abridge, and Stapleford Abbots *Chelmsf 3* **P** *The Crown (1 turn), Ld Chan (1 turn), Patr Bd (2 turns)* **TV** P A PRESTON, R K GAYLER **C** E M PETERSON

VALE, comprising Challow, Denchworth, Grove, and Hanney *Ox 27* **P** *Bp, D&C Windsor, and Worc Coll Ox (jt)* **V** W J N DURANT **C** A J GILL **NSM** P D B GOODING

VALLEY END (St Saviour) *see* Chobham w Valley End *Guildf*

VALLEY PARK (St Francis) *Win 10* **P** *Bp* **P-in-c** S P MCCLELLAND

VANGE (St Chad) *Chelmsf 12* **P** *MMCET* **R** D A O IBIAYO

VAUXHALL (St Peter) *see* N Lambeth *S'wark*

VENN OTTERY (St Gregory) *see* Ottery St Mary, Alfington, W Hill, Tipton etc *Ex*

VENTA GROUP *see* Belton and Burgh Castle *Nor*

VENTNOR (Holy Trinity) *Portsm 7* **P** *Bp* **V** H E WRIGHT

VENTNOR (St Alban) *see* Godshill *Portsm*

VENTNOR (St Catherine) *Portsm 7* **P** *Ch Patr Trust* **V** H E WRIGHT

VERNHAM DEAN (St Mary the Virgin) *see* Hurstbourne Tarrant, Faccombe, Vernham Dean etc *Win*

VERWOOD (St Michael and All Angels) *Sarum 9* **P** *Bp* **V** D L MATTHEWS **NSM** P E MILES

VERYAN (St Symphorian) w Ruan Lanihorne *Truro 6* **P** *D&C and DBP (jt)* **P-in-c** P A GREENHALGH

VICTORIA DOCKS (Ascension) *Chelmsf 5* **P** *Bp* **V** D V CHESNEY **C** A E STOTT

VICTORIA DOCKS (St Luke) *Chelmsf 5* **P** *Ld Chan* **Hon C** P E EJINKONYE

VICTORIA PARK (St Chrysostom) *see* Man Victoria Park *Man*

VICTORIA PARK (St Mark) *see* Old Ford St Paul and St Mark *Lon*

VIGO (Village Hall) *see* Stansted w Fairseat and Vigo *Roch*

VINEY HILL (All Saints) *see* Parkend and Viney Hill *Glouc*

VIRGINIA WATER (Christ Church) *Guildf 11* **P** *Simeon's Trustees* **V** S D N VIBERT **NSM** W C BISSETT

VIRGINSTOW (St Bridget) *see* Boyton, N Tamerton, Werrington etc *Truro*

VOWCHURCH (St Bartholomew) *see* Madley w Tyberton, Peterchurch, Vowchurch etc *Heref*

WABERTHWAITE (St John) *see* Black Combe, Drigg, Eskdale etc *Carl*

WACTON (All Saints) *see* Long Stratton and Pilgrim TM *Nor*

WADDESDON (St Michael and All Angels) *see* Schorne *Ox*

WADDINGHAM (St Mary and St Peter) *see* Bishop Norton, Waddingham and Snitterby *Linc*

WADDINGTON (St Helen) *Blackb 7* **P** *E C Parker Esq* **V** C D WOOD

WADDINGTON (St Michael) *Linc 12* **P** *Linc Coll Ox* **R** A R BARBER

WADDON (St George) *see* Croydon St Jo *S'wark*

WADEBRIDGE *see* St Breoke and Egloshayle *Truro*

WADENHOE (St Michael and All Angels) *see* Aldwincle, Clopton, Pilton, Stoke Doyle etc *Pet*

WADHURST (St Peter and St Paul) *Chich 16* **P** J M *Hardcastle Esq and M R Toynbee Esq (jt)* **P-in-c** P R RATCLIFF

WADSLEY (no dedication) *Sheff 4* **P** *Ch Patr Trust* **P-in-c** D J BROWN

WADWORTH (St John the Baptist) *see* Wadworth w Loversall and Balby *Sheff*

WADWORTH (St John the Baptist) w Loversall and Balby *Sheff 9* **P** *Bp (2 turns), V Doncaster (1 turn), DBP (1 turn)* **V** A PRICE **NSM** A TEASDALE, E G STRAFFORD

WAGGONERS, comprising Cowlam, Fimber, Fridaythorpe, Sledmere, Thixendale, and Wetwang *York 10* **P** *Abp and Sir Tatton Sykes Bt, and Ld Chan (alt)* **P-in-c** J A TONKIN

WAINCLIFFE (St David) *see* Beeston *Leeds*

WAINFLEET Group, The (All Saints) (St Mary) (St Michael), including Croft and Thorpe *Linc 10* **P** *Ld Chan, Bp and T E Pitts Esq (alt)* **R** G MORGAN

WAITHE (St Martin) *see* Fotherby, N Thoresby and Grainsby w Waithe *Linc*

WAKEFIELD (St Andrew) St Mary (St Swithun's Centre) and Belle Vue St Catherine *Leeds 19* **P** *Peache Trustees and V Sandal Magna (jt)* **V** D I GERRARD **C** A N GRIFFIN, K ROBERTSON **NSM** D DODGSON

WAKEFIELD (St John the Baptist) *Leeds 19* **P** *Dean* **V** S J BUCHANAN **NSM** P ELLIS

WAKEFIELD (St Michael the Archangel) *see* Westgate Common *Leeds*

WAKERING, GREAT (St Nicholas) *see* Roach Par *Chelmsf*

WAKERING, LITTLE (St Mary the Virgin) *as above*

WAKES COLNE (All Saints) *see* Gt and Lt Tey w Wakes Colne and Chappel *Chelmsf*

WALBERSWICK (St Andrew) *see* Sole Bay *St E*

WALBERTON (St Mary) w Binsted *Chich 1* **P** *Bp* **V** T J C WARD

WALBROOK Epiphany *Derby 5* **P** *Patr Bd* **TR** A J WARD **TV** S J CARTWRIGHT **C** S L WATSON **NSM** A R TILL

WALBURY BEACON Benefice, The, comprising Combe, Enborne, Hamstead Marshall, Inkpen, Kintbury, and West Woodhay *Ox 6* **P** *Bp, D&C Windsor, DBP, and H M Henderson Esq (jt)* **P-in-c** M A J WILSON **NSM** T R WOOD

WALCOT (St Nicholas) *see* S Lafford *Linc*

WALCOTT (All Saints) *see* Bacton, Happisburgh, Hempstead w Eccles etc *Nor*

WALCOTT (St Oswald) *see* Carr Dyke Gp *Linc*

WALDEN, LITTLE (St John) *see* Saffron Walden and Villages *Chelmsf*

WALDERSLADE (St William) *see* S Chatham H Trin *Roch*

WALDINGFIELD, GREAT (St Lawrence) *see* Acton w Gt Waldingfield *St E*

WALDINGFIELD, LITTLE (St Lawrence) *see* Boxford, Edwardstone, Groton etc *St E*

WALDITCH (St Mary) *see* Bridport *Sarum*

WALDRINGFIELD (All Saints) w Hemley and Newbourne *St E 11* **P** *The Revd Canon T Waller and the Revd A H N Waller, Ld Chan, and Mrs S E F Holden (by turn)* **P-in-c** I A WILSON **C** S J JENKINS

WALDRON (All Saints) *Chich 13* **P** *Ex Coll Ox* **P-in-c** G M PITCHER

WALES (St John the Baptist) *Sheff 5* **P** *Bp* **V** G SCHOFIELD

WALESBY (St Edmund) *S'well 3* **P** *DBP* **P-in-c** Z BURTON **C** A K ALLS **NSM** M A GROVES

WALESBY Group, The (St Mary and All Saints), including Claxby, Croxby, Kirmond-le-Mire, Normanby le Wold, North Willingham, Stainton-le-Vale, Tealby, and Thoresway *Linc 7* **P** *C Drakes Esq, DBP, and Bp (jt)* **V** C W HEWITT **OLM** E TURNER

WALFORD (St Michael and All Angels) *see* Ross w Walford and Brampton Abbotts *Heref*

WALGRAVE (St Peter) w Hannington and Wold and Scaldwell *Pet 2* **P** *Bp (2 turns), BNC Ox (1 turn)* **P-in-c** D M BENT **C** H M BENT

WALHAM GREEN (St John) (St James) *Lon 9* **P** *Bp* **V** *vacant*

WALKDEN (St Paul) and Little Hulton *Man 18* **P** *Patr Bd* **TR** D P COOPER **TV** G F PAGE **OLM** E HARTIGAN

WALKER (Christ Church) *Newc 3* **P** *Bp* **V** *vacant*

WALKERGATE (St Oswald) *see* Byker St Mark and Walkergate St Oswald *Newc*

WALKERINGHAM (St Mary Magdalene) *see* Beckingham, Walkeringham, Misterton, etc *S'well*

WALKERN (St Mary the Virgin) see Ardeley, Benington, Cottered w Throcking etc St Alb

WALKHAMPTON (St Mary the Virgin) see Yelverton, Meavy, Sheepstor, Walkhampton, Sampford Spiney and Horrabridge Ex

WALKINGHAM HILL, comprising Arkendale, Copgrove, Farnham, Scotton, and Staveley Leeds 21 P Bp, DBP, R Knaresborough, MMCET, and Major Sir Arthur Collins (jt) R C L RENSHAW

WALKINGTON (All Hallows), Bishop Burton, Rowley and Skidby York 8 P Abp and N A C Hildyard Esq (1 turn), Abp (1 turn) R D H MESSER

WALKLEY (St Mary) Sheff 4 P Bp V M A FITZGERALD

WALL (St George) see St Oswald in Lee w Bingfield Newc

WALL (St John the Baptist) see Lich St Mich w St Mary and Wall Lich

WALL HEATH (Ascension) see Kingswinford St Mary Worc

WALLASEY (St Hilary) Ches 7 P Bp R A W WARD NSM R H AVERY

WALLASEY (St Nicholas) All Saints Ches 7 P Bp and DBP (jt) V J J STAPLES

WALLINGFORD (St Mary le More w All Hallows) (St Leonard) Ox 26 P Bp TR D RICE TV K V BEER

WALLINGTON (Holy Trinity) S'wark 23 P Ch Soc Trust V J L HILLS

WALLINGTON (Springfield Church) Extra-Parochial Place S'wark 23 C J M PETRIE Min J M LINDSAY-SCOTT

WALLINGTON (St Mary) see Clothall, Rushden, Sandon, Wallington and Weston St Alb

WALLINGTON (St Michael and All Angels) see S Beddington and Roundshaw S'wark

WALLINGTON (St Patrick) S'wark 23 P Ch Soc Trust V D M KING

WALLISDOWN (St Saviour) see Talbot Village Sarum

WALLOP, NETHER (St Andrew) see Portway and Danebury Win

WALLSEND (St John the Evangelist) Newc 5 P Bp C E C DUFF

WALLSEND (St Peter) (St Luke) Newc 5 P Bp C E KORMOS

WALMER (St Mary) (St Saviour) (Blessed Virgin Mary) and Cornilo Cant 9 P Abp, Ch Patr Trust, and S Toynbee Esq (jt) R S W COOPER C C M T WOOD, S J O'CONNOR

WALMERSLEY ROAD (Christ Church) (St John w St Mark) Man 8 P R Bury St Mary and trustees (jt) V D J THOMPSON

WALMGATE (St Denys) see York St Denys York

WALMLEY (St John the Evangelist) Birm 7 P Trustees V A J EVANS C B W COOK

WALMSLEY (Christ Church) see Turton Moorland Man

WALNEY ISLAND (St Mary the Virgin) Carl 8 P V Dalton-in-Furness V A G BATCHELOR

WALPOLE (St Mary the Virgin) see Blyth Valley St E

WALPOLE ST PETER (St Peter and St Paul) w Walpole St Andrew Ely 14 P The Crown and DBP (alt) R B L BURTON

WALSALL (Annunciation of Our Lady) see Walsall St Gabr Fulbrook Lich

WALSALL (St Andrew) Lich 24 P Bp V I M TEMPLETON

WALSALL (St Gabriel) Fulbrook Lich 24 P Bp V R M MCINTYRE C R F HUME

WALSALL (St Luke) Lich 24 P Bp V M R KINDER

WALSALL (St Martin) Lich 24 P Bp V J E MAYO-LYTHALL

WALSALL (St Matthew) Lich 24 P Patr Bd R J W TROOD

WALSALL (St Paul) Lich 24 P R Walsall V M R KINDER

WALSALL (St Peter) Lich 24 P R Walsall V A G BURNAGE C C P LANE

WALSALL THE PLECK (St John) and Bescot Lich 24 P V Walsall V E J REYNOLDS C M R KINDER, Y J BECKETT

WALSALL WOOD (St John) Lich 24 P R Walsall P-in-c D P S BABBINGTON

WALSDEN (St Peter) see Todmorden w Cornholme and Walsden Leeds

WALSGRAVE ON SOWE (St Mary) Cov 1 P Ld Chan V M TYLER NSM F E TYLER

WALSHAM LE WILLOWS (St Mary) see Badwell and Walsham St E

WALSHAM, NORTH (St Nicholas), Edingthorpe, Worstead and Westwick Nor 12 P Duchy of Lancaster (1 turn), Bp and D&C (2 turns) V P CUBITT C R I E DINES OLM N J M PATERSON

WALSHAM, SOUTH (St Mary) see Broadside Nor

WALSHAW (Christ Church) Man 8 P Simeon's Trustees P-in-c S P OPENSHAW

WALSINGHAM (St Mary and All Saints) (St Peter), Houghton and Barsham Nor 14 P J Gurney Esq and Capt J D A Keith (jt) P-in-c H A M WILLIAMS OLM G D GOULD

WALSOKEN (All Saints) Ely 14 P DBP R A R LANDALL

WALTERSTONE (St Mary) see Ewyas Harold w Dulas, Kenderchurch etc Heref

WALTHAM (Holy Cross) Chelmsf 3 P Patr Bd TR P H SMITH C A J GUEST NSM J M SMITH, S A J BEGLEY, T I SCOTT

WALTHAM CROSS (Christ Church) see Cheshunt St Alb

WALTHAM Group, The (All Saints) (St Matthew), including Ashby, Barnoldby le Beck, Brigsley, and Ravendale Linc 4 P Parkinson Settled Estates and Bp (1 turn), The Crown (1 turn), Ld Chan (1 turn) R K BOHAN NSM A HUNDLEBY, R M FOWLER

WALTHAM ON THE WOLDS (St Mary Magdalene) see Ironstone Villages Leic

WALTHAM ST LAWRENCE (St Lawrence) Ox 5 P Lord Braybrooke P-in-c C O MASON

WALTHAM, GREAT (St Mary and St Lawrence) w Ford End Chelmsf 9 P Trin Coll Ox C D C PIERCE NSM S SYKES

WALTHAM, LITTLE (St Martin) see Gt and Lt Leighs and Lt Waltham Chelmsf

WALTHAM, NEW (St Matthew) see Waltham Gp Linc

WALTHAM, NORTH (St Michael) and Steventon, Ashe and Deane Win 6 P DBP P-in-c J A TOMKINS-RUSSELL NSM J FOSTER

WALTHAMSTOW (St Andrew) Chelmsf 7 P Bp P-in-c S G O O OLUKANMI NSM H GILBERT

WALTHAMSTOW (St Barnabas and St James the Great) Chelmsf 7 P Bp V S M P SAXBY

WALTHAMSTOW (St Gabriel) St Luke (St Mary) (St Stephen) Chelmsf 7 P Patr Bd TR V C CONANT TV A W ELEYAE C A R CHILDS, J V MOWBRAY

WALTHAMSTOW (St John) Chelmsf 7 P TR Walthamstow V K J C BUSH

WALTHAMSTOW (St Michael and All Angels) Chelmsf 7 P Bp V vacant

WALTHAMSTOW (St Peter-in-the-Forest) Chelmsf 7 P Bp V P K TRATHEN NSM S E DIPLOCK

WALTHAMSTOW (St Saviour) Chelmsf 7 P Bp V S R S TELEN

WALTON (Holy Trinity) Ox 10 P Ch Patr Trust V C R TREFUSIS NSM R J PENTLAND

WALTON (Holy Trinity) see Street w Walton and Compton Dundon B & W

WALTON (not known) see Avon-Swift Leic

WALTON (St John the Evangelist) Ches 4 P P G Greenall Esq P-in-c A J RAGGETT

WALTON (St John) Derby 3 P Bp V N GREEN NSM H J MOORE, R SMITH

WALTON (St Mary) see Lanercost, Walton, Gilsland and Nether Denton Carl

WALTON (St Mary) (St Philip) and Trimley St E 11 P Ld Chan (1 turn) Ch Trust Fund Trust and Bp (1 turn) C C A COOK NSM W P SMITH

WALTON (St Paul) see Sandal St Helen Leeds

WALTON (St Peter) see Bramham York

WALTON (St Thomas) see Baswich Lich

WALTON BRECK (Christ Church) (Holy Trinity) Liv 1 P Simeon's Trustees V D G GAVIN

WALTON CLEVEDON (St Mary) see E Clevedon w Clapton in Gordano etc B & W

WALTON D'EIVILLE (St James) Cov 4 P Sir Richard Hamilton Bt R G J BARTLEM NSM B COLEMAN, S W HOOD

WALTON IN GORDANO (St Paul) see E Clevedon w Clapton in Gordano etc B & W

WALTON LE SOKEN (All Saints) Chelmsf 23 P Bp P-in-c P D EDWARDS

WALTON LE WOLDS (St Mary) see Barrow upon Soar w Walton le Wolds Leic

WALTON Milton Keynes, comprising Milton Keynes Village and Wavendon Ox 14 P DBP R M J TRENDALL

WALTON ON THE HILL (St John) Liv 4 P Bp, Adn, and R Walton (jt) V F E MYATT

WALTON ON THE HILL (St Luke) Liv 4 P Bp V F R CAIN

WALTON STREET (St Saviour) see Upper Chelsea H Trin and St Sav Lon

WALTON, EAST (St Mary) see Ashwicken w Leziate, Bawsey etc Nor

WALTON, HIGHER (All Saints) Blackb 5 P V Blackb V vacant

WALTON, WEST (St Mary) Ely 14 P Ld Chan R B L BURTON

WALTON-LE-DALE (St Leonard) Blackb 5 P V Blackb St Mary and St Paul NSM N J PROCTER

WALTON-ON-THAMES (St Mary) Guildf 8 P Bp V C J BLAIR, J L BLAIR C A J OEHRING, C J MERRICK

WALTON-ON-THE-HILL (St Mary) (St Aidan) *Liv 8* **P** *Bp*
TV J A FLOOD
WALTON-ON-THE-HILL (St Peter) *see* Headley and Box Hill
w Walton on the Hill *Guildf*
WALTON-ON-TRENT (St Lawrence) w Croxall, Rosliston w
Linton and Castle Gresley *Derby 7* **P** *Bp and R D Nielson*
Esq (jt) **P-in-c** C D JEFFERSON **OLM** C A BUCKLEY
WALWORTH (St Christopher) *S'wark 10* **P** *Bp and Pemb Coll*
Miss **P-in-c** E L EAMES **NSM** D F WICKREMASINGHE
WALWORTH (St John w the Lady Margaret) *S'wark 10* **P** *Bp*
V J F WALKER **Hon C** G S ASKEY
WALWORTH (St Peter) *S'wark 10* **P** *Bp*
R A D P MOUGHTIN-MUMBY **C** M T E ROBINSON
Hon C S MOUGHTIN-MUMBY
WAMBROOK (Blessed Virgin Mary) *see* Chard St Mary w
Combe St Nicholas, Wambrook etc *B & W*
WANBOROUGH (St Andrew) *see* Lyddington and
Wanborough and Bishopstone etc *Bris*
WANBOROUGH (St Bartholomew) *see* Seale, Puttenham and
Wanborough *Guildf*
WANDSWORTH (All Saints) (Holy Trinity) *S'wark 18* **P** *Ch*
Soc Trust **V** G S PRIOR **C** B R GRAHAM
WANDSWORTH (St Anne) (St Faith) *S'wark 18* **P** *Bp*
V G P JEANES
WANDSWORTH (St Michael and All Angels) (St Stephen)
S'wark 18 **P** *CPAS and Ch Soc Trust (jt)* **V** S MELLUISH
C R BOOTHROYD, T S ARMSTRONG **NSM** P M TAYLOR
WANDSWORTH (St Paul) Wimbledon Park *S'wark 18* **P** *Bp*
P-in-c S M BOLEN **NSM** N A VON FRAUNHOFER
WANDSWORTH COMMON (St Mary Magdalene) *S'wark 17*
P *Bp* **V** P J BOARDMAN
WANDSWORTH COMMON (St Michael) *see* Battersea
St Mich *S'wark*
WANGFORD (St Peter) *see* Sole Bay *St E*
WANLIP (Our Lady and St Nicholas) *see* Birstall and Wanlip
Leic
WANSFORD (St Mary the Virgin) *see* Nassington, Apethorpe,
Thornhaugh etc *Pet*
WANSFORD (St Mary) *see* Nafferton w Wansford *York*
WANSTEAD (Holy Trinity) Hermon Hill *Chelmsf 6* **P** *Bp*
Hon C P J MOSSOP
WANSTEAD (St Mary) (Christ Church) *Chelmsf 6* **P** *Bp*
R N R DUNN **C** T A BRITT **Hon C** G A CLARKE
NSM R J WYBER
WANSTROW (Blessed Virgin Mary) *see* Nunney and Witham
Friary, Marston Bigot etc *B & W*
WANTAGE (St Peter and St Paul) *Ox 27* **P** *D&C Windsor*
V P A WELLS **C** C M ASHTON
WANTAGE DOWNS, comprising Ardington w Lockinge, East
Hendred, and West Hendred *Ox 27* **P** *Bp, CCC Ox, and C L*
Loyd Esq (jt) **R** O CAMAIONI
WANTISDEN (St John the Baptist) *see* Wilford Peninsula *St E*
WANTSUM Group, The, comprising Chislet, Minster,
Monkton, and St Nicholas-at-Wade *Cant 5* **P** *Abp*
V A R BRADDY **C** K A GOODING, M D W DARKINS,
V S CONEYS
WAPLEY (St Peter) *see* Yate *Bris*
WAPPENBURY (St John the Baptist) *see* Offchurch Gp *Cov*
WAPPENHAM (St Mary the Virgin) *see* Astwell Gp *Pet*
WARBLETON (St Mary), Bodle Street Green and
Dallington *Chich 13* **P** *Bp and The Revd E S Haviland (jt)*
R M A LLOYD
WARBLINGTON (St Thomas à Becket) w Emsworth
Portsm 5 **P** *Bp and J H Norris Esq (alt)* **R** A F SHEARD
C J E NORTHEY **NSM** J E PRICE
WARBOROUGH (St Lawrence) *Ox 20* **P** *CCC Ox*
V S E BOOYS
WARBOYS (St Mary Magdalene) w Broughton and Bury w
Wistow *Ely 12* **P** *Bp and Ch Soc Trust (jt)*
R G A DAWSON-JONES **NSM** J TIPLADY
WARBSTOW (St Werburgh) *see* Week St Mary Circle of Par
Truro
WARBURTON (St Werburgh) *see* Oughtrington and
Warburton *Ches*
WARCOP (St Columba) *see* Heart of Eden *Carl*
WARD END (Christ Church) *see* Ward End w Bordesley
Green *Birm*
WARD END Holy Trinity (St Margaret) w Bordesley Green
Birm 11 **P** *The Crown (1 turn), Bp and Aston Patr Trust (1*
turn) **C** S K BARTER
WARDEN (St Michael and All Angels) w Newbrough
Newc 10 **P** *Bp* **V** J J T THOMPSON
WARDEN, OLD (St Leonard) *see* Caldecote, Northill and Old
Warden *St Alb*
WARDINGTON (St Mary Magdalene) *see* Shires' Edge *Ox*
WARDLEWORTH (St Mary w St James) *see* Rochdale *Man*

WARDLEY (All Saints) *see* Swinton and Pendlebury *Man*
WARDLOW (Good Shepherd) *see* Longstone, Curbar and
Stony Middleton *Derby*
WARE (Christ Church) *St Alb 19* **P** *CPAS* **V** J L W HOOKWAY
C C L ROLLS
WARE (St Mary the Virgin) *St Alb 19* **P** *Trin Coll Cam*
V Y R PENTELOW **C** D O SHEPPARD
WAREHAM (Lady St Mary) (St Martin) *Sarum 8* **P** *Patr Bd*
TR S F EVERETT **TV** S J COCKSEDGE **NSM** M YOUNG
WAREHORNE (St Matthew) *see* Saxon Shoreline *Cant*
WARESIDE (Holy Trinity) *see* Hunsdon w Widford and
Wareside *St Alb*
WARESLEY (St James) *see* Gt Gransden and Abbotsley and Lt
Gransden etc *Ely*
WARFIELD (St Michael the Archangel) (All Saints)
(St Peter) *Ox 3* **P** *DBP* **V** C M MABUZA **C** D G BROWN,
M L PORTER-BABBAGE
WARGRAVE (St Mary the Virgin) w Knowl Hill *Ox 8* **P** *Lord*
Remnant **V** J R M COOK **C** H N BARNE, S W TURVILLE
WARHAM (All Saints) *see* Holkham w Egmere w Warham etc
Nor
WARK (St Michael) *see* Humshaugh w Simonburn and Wark
Newc
WARKLEIGH (St John) *see* S Molton w Nymet St George,
Chittlehamholt etc *Ex*
WARKTON (St Edmund King and Martyr) *see* Barton
Seagrave w Warkton *Pet*
WARKWORTH (St Lawrence) and Acklington *Newc 6* **P** *Bp*
and Duke of Northumberland (alt) **P-in-c** H L O'SULLIVAN
NSM C A SHIELD
WARKWORTH (St Mary the Virgin) *see* Chenderit *Pet*
WARLEGGAN (St Bartholomew) *see* St Neot and Warleggan
Truro
WARLEY (Christ Church) and Gt Warley St Mary *Chelmsf 8*
P *Bp and Hon G C D Jeffreys (jt)* **P-in-c** S J HULL
C A W MCCONNAUGHIE
WARLEY (St John the Evangelist) and Halifax St Hilda
Leeds 10 **P** *V Halifax and Bp* **V** C E GREENWOOD
WARLEY WOODS (St Hilda) *Birm 6* **P** *Bp* **V** *vacant*
WARLEY, GREAT (St Mary the Virgin) *see* Warley Ch Ch and
Gt Warley St Mary *Chelmsf*
WARLEY, LITTLE (St Peter) *see* E and W Horndon w Lt Warley
and Childerditch *Chelmsf*
WARLINGHAM (All Saints) w Chelsham and Farleigh
S'wark 25 **P** *Patr Bd* **TR** M K EDMONDS **TV** J P ASHTON
C R E CHAPMAN
WARMFIELD (St Peter) *Leeds 19* **P** *Oley Trustees Clare Coll*
Cam **V** L TINNISWOOD
WARMINGHAM (St Leonard) *see* Leighton-cum-Minshull
Vernon and Warmingham *Ches*
WARMINGTON (St Mary the Blessed Virgin), Tansor and
Cotterstock and Fotheringhay and Southwick *Pet 10*
P *Bp and D&C Linc (alt)* **V** *vacant*
WARMINGTON (St Michael) *see* Edgehill Churches *Cov*
WARMINSTER (Christ Church) *Sarum 12* **P** *R Warminster*
St Denys etc **V** L S DOBBINS **NSM** A J EDWARDS,
M R COLLINS
WARMINSTER (St Denys) *see* River Were *Sarum*
WARMLEY (St Barnabas), Syston and Bitton *Bris 5* **P** *Bp*
R J C E ANDREW **Hon C** J E NORMAN **NSM** S L BISHOP
OLM R A HUMPHREY
WARMSWORTH (St Peter) *Sheff 9* **P** *Bp* **R** I SMITH
NSM J M S JONES
WARMWELL (Holy Trinity) *see* Watercombe *Sarum*
WARNBOROUGH, SOUTH (St Andrew) *see* N Hants Downs
Win
WARNDON (St Nicholas) *Worc 6* **P** *Bp* **C** D M COOKSEY
WARNDON (St Wulstan) *see* Worc St Wulstan *Worc*
WARNERS END (St Alban) *see* Hemel Hempstead *St Alb*
WARNFORD (Our Lady) *see* W Meon and Warnford *Portsm*
WARNHAM (St Margaret) *Chich 7* **P** *J C Lucas Esq*
P-in-c J A BARNES
WARREN PARK (St Clare) *Portsm 5* **P** *Bp* **V** J G P JEFFERY
WARREN ROW (St Paul) *see* Wargrave w Knowl Hill *Ox*
WARRINGTON (Holy Trinity) (St Ann) *Liv 11* **P** *R*
Warrington and Simeon's Trustees (jt) **V** S COWAN
C J L WHEATLEY **OLM** C E BATEY, P LOVATT
WARRINGTON (St Barnabas) Bank Quay *Liv 11* **P** *R*
Warrington and Bp (jt) **V** K L F TIMMIS
WARRINGTON (St Elphin) (St John) *Liv 11* **P** *Lord Lilford*
C S MCTAGGART
WARRINGTON EAST (Christ Church) (Transfiguration)
(Resurrection) (Ascension) *Liv 11* **P** *Patr Bd*
TR N G SHAW **TV** R H ROBERTS, T MCLOUGHLIN

WARRINGTON WEST, comprising Great Sankey, Penketh, and Westbrook *Liv 11* **P** *Patr Bd* **TR** J C TEAR, S J BAKER **TV** M X THORPE, S F PEPPIATT

WARSLOW (St Lawrence) *see* Longnor, Quarnford, Sheen etc *Lich*

WARSOP (St Peter and St Paul) *S'well 2* **P** *Trustees* **R** A FLETCHER

WARTHILL (St Mary) *see* Rural E York *York*

WARTLING (St Mary Magdalene) *see* Herstmonceux and Wartling *Chich*

WARTNABY (St Michael) *see* Old Dalby, Nether Broughton, Saxelbye etc *Leic*

WARTON (Holy Trinity) *see* All So N Warks *Birm*

WARTON (St Oswald or Holy Trinity) w Yealand Conyers *Blackb 14* **P** *Bp* **V** R A R FIGG

WARTON (St Paul) *see* Freckleton and Warton St Paul *Blackb*

WARWICK SQUARE (St Gabriel) *see* Pimlico St Gabr *Lon*

WARWICK Team, The New (St Mary) (St Nicholas) (St Paul) *Cov 11* **P** *Ld Chan and Patr Bd (alt)* **TR** V S ROBERTS **TV** D THOMPSON, J HEARN, L J DUCKERS **C** V A M TIMMIS **NSM** A N C MORGAN

WARWICKSHIRE, NORTH *see* All So N Warks *Birm*

WARWICKSHIRE, SOUTH *see* S Warks Seven Gp *Cov*

WASDALE HEAD (St Olaf) *see* Seatallan *Carl*

WASDALE, NETHER (St Michael) *as above*

WASH COMMON (St George) *see* Newbury St Geo and St Jo *Ox*

WASHBOURNE, GREAT (St Mary) *see* Winchcombe *Glouc*

WASHBURN and Mid-Wharfe, comprising Blubberhouses, Denton, Farnley, Fewston, Leathley, and Weston *Leeds 21* **P** *Bp, G N le G Horton-Fawkes Esq, Lt Col H V Dawson and C Wyvill Esq (jt)* **P-in-c** S T J MCCAULAY **NSM** A J COLLINS

WASHFIELD (St Mary the Virgin), Stoodleigh, Withleigh, Calverleigh, Oakford, Templeton, Loxbeare, Rackenford, and Cruwys Morchard *Ex 7* **P** *Patr Bd* **TR** S K GORDON-JEFFS **NSM** J C W ROBERTS

WASHFORD (St Mary) *see* Old Cleeve, Leighland and Treborough *B & W*

WASHFORD PYNE (St Peter) *see* N Creedy *Ex*

WASHINGBOROUGH (St John) w Heighington and Canwick *Linc 12* **P** *DBP and Mercers' Co (jt)* **R** G C GOALBY

WASHINGTON (Holy Trinity) *Dur 10* **P** *Bp* **R** D C GLOVER **C** J W ESTALL **NSM** B R FORRESTER

WASHINGTON (St Mary) *see* Chanctonbury *Chich*

WASHWOOD HEATH (St Mark) *see* Saltley and Washwood Heath *Birm*

WASING (St Nicholas) *see* Aldermaston and Woolhampton *Ox*

WASKERLEY (St Andrew) *see* Blanchland w Hunstanworth and Edmundbyers etc *Newc*

WASPERTON (St John the Baptist) *see* Barford w Wasperton and Sherbourne *Cov*

WASS (St Thomas) *see* Coxwold and Husthwaite *York*

WATCHET (St Decuman) (Holy Cross Chapel) and Williton *B & W 17* **P** *Bp* **V** C F GILBERT **C** K A FLENLEY

WATCHFIELD (St Thomas's Chapel) *see* Shrivenham and Ashbury *Ox*

WATER EATON (St Frideswide) *Ox 14* **P** *Bp* **P-in-c** C BUTT **C** S J HALLETT

WATER NEWTON (St Remigius) *see* Castor w Upton and Stibbington etc *Pet*

WATER ORTON (St Peter and St Paul) *Birm 8* **P** *Patr Bd* **V** P B TULLETT

WATER STRATFORD (St Giles) *see* W Buckingham *Ox*

WATERBEACH (St John) *Ely 6* **P** *Bp* **P-in-c** D J CHAMBERLIN **C** P H BUTLER **NSM** S BRADFORD

WATERCOMBE, comprising Broadmayne, Owermoigne, Warmwell, and West Knighton *Sarum 1* **P** *M Cree Esq (1 turn), MMCET (2 turns), and Sir Robert Williams Bt (1 turn)* **R** D J A DOBLE

WATERDEN (All Saints) *see* N and S Creake w Waterden, Syderstone etc *Nor*

WATERFALL (St James and St Bartholomew) *see* Calton, Cauldon, Grindon, Waterfall etc *Lich*

WATERFORD (St Michael and All Angels) *see* Beane Valley *St Alb*

WATERHEAD (Holy Trinity) *see* Clarksfield and Waterhead *Man*

WATERHOUSES (St Paul) *Dur 1* **P** *R Brancepeth Esq* **V** M J PEERS **NSM** T HOLDEN

WATERINGBURY (St John the Baptist) *see* Mereworth, Wateringbury and W Peckham *Roch*

WATERLOO (Christ Church) *St John Liv 6* **P** *Trustees and Simeon's Trustees (jt)* **V** G J CUFF

WATERLOO (St John the Evangelist) (St Andrew) *S'wark 11* **P** *Abp and CPAS (jt)* **V** G W GODDARD

Hon C R M LAMPARD **NSM** G S N KAZIRO, L M BEWICK **OLM** D PAPE

WATERLOOVILLE (St George the Martyr) *Portsm 5* **P** *Bp* **V** C R LAWLOR

WATERMILLOCK (All Saints) *see* Barton, Pooley Bridge, Martindale etc *Carl*

WATERMOOR (Holy Trinity) *see* Cirencester *Glouc*

WATERPERRY (St Mary the Virgin) *see* Albury w Tiddington etc *Ox*

WATERS UPTON (St Michael) *see* Tibberton w Bolas Magna and Waters Upton *Lich*

WATERSHED, comprising Blymhill, Lapley, and Weston-under-Lizard *Lich 2* **P** *Keble Coll Ox and Earl of Bradford Trustees (jt)* **R** R E DALE **C** C BRUMFITT

WATERSIDE GROUP *see* Ludham, Potter Heigham, Hickling and Catfield *Nor*

WATERSIDE PARISHES of Hambleton, Out Rawcliffe and Preesall *Blackb 9* **P** *Bp, V Kirkham, and V Garstang St Helen etc (jt)* **V** A J SHAW **C** N H S BARRACLOUGH **NSM** D BANKS **OLM** J M KIRKHAM

WATERSTOCK (St Leonard) *see* Albury w Tiddington etc *Ox*

WATERTHORPE (Emmanuel) *see* Beighton *Sheff*

WATFORD (Christ Church) (St Mark) *St Alb 6* **P** *Bp, V Watford, and Churchwardens (jt)* **V** J D CAMPBELL

WATFORD (St Andrew) *St Alb 6* **P** *Bp and Churchwardens (jt)* **V** I C PANKHURST

WATFORD (St John) *St Alb 6* **P** *Bp* **V** D E STEVENSON

WATFORD (St Luke) *St Alb 6* **P** *Bp, Adn St Alb, V Watford, and Ch Trust Fund Trust (jt)* **V** *vacant*

WATFORD (St Mary) *St Alb 6* **P** *Ch Trust Fund Trust* **V** A W RINDL **C** J P BROCKLESBY

WATFORD (St Michael and All Angels) *St Alb 6* **P** *Bp* **V** G R CALVERT

WATFORD (St Peter and St Paul) *see* Long Buckby w Watford and W Haddon w Winwick *Pet*

WATFORD (St Peter) *St Alb 6* **P** *Bp* **NSM** A P PRIOR, M PILAVACHI

WATH (St Mary) *see* Kirklington w Burneston and Wath and Pickhill *Leeds*

WATH-UPON-DEARNE (All Saints) *Sheff 12* **P** *Ch Ch Ox* **V** J D PARKER **C** C E BURTON

WATLING VALLEY, Milton Keynes (not known) *Ox 14* **P** *Patr Bd* **TR** M J MORRIS **TV** S C GRENHAM-THOMPSON **NSM** A L ADEBIYI

WATLINGTON (St Leonard) *see* Icknield *Ox*

WATLINGTON (St Peter and St Paul) *see* W Norfolk Priory Gp *Ely*

WATTISFIELD (St Margaret) *see* Badwell and Walsham *St E*

WATTON (St Mary) *Nor 13* **P** *Ld Chan* **V** G FOSTER **C** M A SØRENSEN

WATTON (St Mary) *see* Hutton Cranswick w Skerne, Watton and Beswick *York*

WATTON AT STONE (St Mary and St Andrew) *see* Beane Valley *St Alb*

WAVENDON (Assumption of the Blessed Virgin Mary) *see* Walton Milton Keynes *Ox*

WAVERTON (St Peter) w Aldford and Bruera *Ches 5* **P** *Bp, D&C, and Duke of Westmr (jt)* **R** J T P BEAUCHAMP **NSM** K R B JONES

WAVERTREE (Holy Trinity) *Liv 3* **P** *Bp* **R** R J E CLACK

WAVERTREE (St Bridget) (St Thomas) *Liv 3* **P** *Simeon's Trustees and R Wavertree H Trin (jt)* **C** E JONES, R A GARLAND

WAVERTREE (St Mary) *Liv 3* **P** *Bp* **R** J P ASQUITH

WAWNE (St Peter) *see* Sutton Park and Wawne *York*

WAXHAM, GREAT (St John) *see* Bacton, Happisburgh, Hempstead w Eccles etc *Nor*

WAYFORD (St Michael and All Angels) *see* Wulfric Benefice *B & W*

WAYLAND Group, The *see* Caston, Griston, Merton, Thompson etc *Nor*

WEALD (St George) *see* Sevenoaks Weald *Roch*

WEALD, SOUTH (St Peter) *Chelmsf 8* **P** *Bp* **P-in-c** J BRADBURY

WEALDSTONE (Holy Trinity) *Lon 23* **P** *Bp* **V** T M MALONEY **NSM** F E MALONEY

WEARDALE, UPPER, comprising Eastgate, Frosterley, Heatherycleugh, St John's Chapel, Stanhope and Rookhope, and Westgate *Dur 8* **P** *Bp (5 turns), Duchy of Lancaster (1 turn), and Ld Chan (1 turn)* **R** *vacant*

WEARE (St Gregory) *see* Crook Peak *B & W*

WEARE GIFFARD (Holy Trinity) *see* Bideford, Landcross, Littleham etc *Ex*

WEARSIDE, NORTH, comprising Red House, Southwick, and Town End Farm *Dur 14* **P** *Patr Bd* **TR** S W ELSTOB **TV** C M NOPPEN, J A BRADSHAW

WEASENHAM (All Saints) *see* Launditch and the Upper Nar *Nor*

WEASENHAM (St Peter) *as above*

WEASTE (St Luke w All Saints) *see* Salford All SS *Man*

WEAVERHAM (St Mary the Virgin) *Ches 6* **P** *Bp*
V P M WITHINGTON

WEAVERTHORPE (St Andrew) w Helperthorpe, Luttons Ambo and Kirby Grindalythe w Wharram *York 6* **P** *Abp and D&C (jt)* **V** A D BOWDEN

WEBHEATH (St Philip) *see* Redditch H Trin *Worc*

WEDDINGTON (St James) and Caldecote *Cov 5* **P** *Bp*
P-in-c K A BETTERIDGE

WEDMORE, The Isle of (St Mary), including Allerton, Blackford and Theale *B & W 1* **P** *Bp and D&C (jt)*
V R W NEILL

WEDNESBURY (St Bartholomew) (St James) St John *Lich 25*
P *Bp and Trustees (jt)* **R** M J DANKS

WEDNESBURY (St Paul) Wood Green *Lich 25* **P** *Bp*
V D C NJUGUNA

WEDNESFIELD (St Gregory) *see* Oxley and Wednesfield St Greg *Lich*

WEDNESFIELD (St Thomas) (St Augustine and St Chad) (St Alban) *Lich 28* **P** *Patr Bd* **TR** N E WATSON
TV T R H FISH

WEEDON (School Chapel) *see* Schorne *Ox*

WEEDON BEC (St Peter and St Paul) w Everdon and Dodford *Pet 3* **P** *Bp* **P-in-c** B J GALLAGHER

WEEDON LOIS (St Mary and St Peter) *see* Astwell Gp *Pet*

WEEFORD (St Mary the Virgin) *see* Whittington w Weeford *Lich*

WEEK (St Barnabas) *see* Win St Barn *Win*

WEEK ST MARY Circle of Parishes (St Mary the Virgin)
Truro 8 **P** *Bp, Walsingham Coll, Guild of All So, SS Coll Cam, and Earl of St Germans (jt)* **C** D K BARNES, H J ASTON
NSM R J TERRY

WEEKLEY (St Mary the Virgin) *see* Geddington w Weekley *Pet*

WEELEY (St Andrew) and Little Clacton *Chelmsf 23* **P** *Bp and BNC Ox (alt)* **R** vacant

WEETHLEY (St James) *see* Alcester Minster *Cov*

WEETING (St Mary) *see* Grimshoe *Ely*

WEETON (St Barnabas) *see* Lower Wharfedale *Leeds*

WEETON (St Michael) *see* Ribby cum Wrea and Weeton *Blackb*

WEETSLADE (St Paul) *Newc 1* **P** *Bp* **V** A MAUGHAN
NSM S RENDALL

WELBORNE (All Saints) *see* Mattishall and the Tudd Valley *Nor*

WELBOURN (St Chad) *Linc 22* **P** *Hyndman Trustees*
R C A GOLDSMITH

WELBURN (St John the Evangelist) *see* Howardian Gp *York*

WELBURY (St Leonard) *see* Rounton w Welbury *York*

WELBY (St Bartholomew) *see* E Loveden *Linc*

WELBY (St Bartholomew) *see* Melton Mowbray *Leic*

WELCOMBE (St Nectan) *see* Parkham, Alwington, Buckland Brewer etc *Ex*

WELDON (St Mary the Virgin) w Deene *Pet 7* **P** *DBP and E Brudenell Esq (jt)* **R** K M TAYLOR **C** D R REITH

WELFORD (St Gregory) *see* W Downland *Ox*

WELFORD (St Peter) *see* Quinton, Welford, Weston and Marston Sicca *Glouc*

WELHAM (St Andrew), Glooston and Cranoe and Stonton Wyville *Leic 5* **P** *Bp, E Brudenell Esq, and MMCET (jt)*
R vacant

WELL (St Margaret) *see* Alford Gp *Linc*

WELL (St Michael) *see* W Tanfield and Well w Snape and N Stainley *Leeds*

WELL HILL (Mission) *see* Chelsfield *Roch*

WELLAND (St James) *see* Hanley Castle, Hanley Swan and Welland *Worc*

WELLESBOURNE (St Peter) *Cov 8* **P** *Ld Chan*
V G J BARTLEM **NSM** B COLEMAN, S W HOOD, W E BIDDINGTON

WELLING (St John the Evangelist) *Roch 15* **P** *Bp*
V A J D FOOT

WELLING (St Mary the Virgin) *S'wark 6* **P** *Bp*
P-in-c N D R NICHOLLS

WELLINGBOROUGH (All Hallows) *Pet 6* **P** *Exors Major E C S Byng-Maddick* **Hon C** C A OSTLER

WELLINGBOROUGH (All Saints) *Pet 6* **P** *V Wellingborough*
Hon C C A OSTLER

WELLINGBOROUGH (St Andrew) (St Barnabas) *Pet 6* **P** *Bp*
V M S COTTON **NSM** R RAILTON

WELLINGBOROUGH (St Mark) *Pet 6* **P** *Bp* **V** B W D LEWIS

WELLINGBOROUGH (St Mary the Virgin) *Pet 6* **P** *Guild of All So* **V** R J T FARMER

WELLINGHAM (St Andrew) *see* Launditch and the Upper Nar *Nor*

WELLINGORE (All Saints) *see* Graffoe Gp *Linc*

WELLINGTON (All Saints) (St John the Baptist) and District *B & W 16* **P** *Patr Bd* **TR** T L V TREANOR
TV A G ELLACOTT, S C GARNER **C** J E SCOTT
NSM M C HEARL

WELLINGTON (All Saints) w Eyton (St Catherine) *Lich 20*
P *Ch Trust Fund Trust* **V** T S CARTER **C** D J SIMS

WELLINGTON (Christ Church) *see* Hadley and Wellington Ch Ch *Lich*

WELLINGTON (St Margaret of Antioch) *see* Canon Pyon w King's Pyon, Birley and Wellington *Heref*

WELLINGTON HEATH (Christ Church) *see* Cider Churches *Heref*

WELLOW (St Julian the Hospitaller) *see* Peasedown St John w Wellow and Foxcote etc *B & W*

WELLOW (St Swithin) *see* Kneesall w Laxton and Wellow *S'well*

WELLOW, EAST w WEST (St Margaret) and Sherfield English *Win 12* **P** *Bp and CPAS (jt)* **V** C F PETTET

WELLS (St Cuthbert) w Wookey Hole *B & W 7* **P** *D&C*
V S DENYER **C** L C T JORDAN **NSM** C M COWLIN

WELLS (St Thomas) w Horrington *B & W 7* **P** *D&C*
V T C OSMOND **C** J E SHELLARD-JAMES **NSM** N T FRIDD

WELLS-NEXT-THE-SEA (St Nicholas) *see* Holkham w Egmere w Warham etc *Nor*

WELLSPRINGS Benefice, The, comprising Bulkington, Potterne, Poulshot, Seend, and Worton and Marston *Sarum 17* **P** *Bp and D&C (jt)* **R** A C BRIDEWELL
NSM J C J RAJA

WELNEY (St Mary) *see* Christchurch and Manea and Welney *Ely*

WELSH FRANKTON (St Andrew) *see* Criftins w Dudleston and Welsh Frankton *Lich*

WELSH NEWTON (St Mary the Virgin) *see* Wye Brooks Benefice *Heref*

WELSHAMPTON (St Michael) *see* Petton w Cockshutt, Welshampton and Lyneal etc *Lich*

WELTON (St Helen) w Melton *York 14* **P** *DBP* **V** E E BIELBY
C G R HOLDSWORTH

WELTON (St James) *see* Westward, Rosley-w-Woodside and Welton *Carl*

WELTON (St Martin) *see* Daventry *Pet*

WELTON (St Mary) and Dunholme w Scothern *Linc 5* **P** *Bp and DBP (jt)* **V** A S WATSON **C** R HESKINS
NSM P D MAPLE, P J IEVINS **OLM** C A JONES

WELTON-LE-MARSH (St Martin) *see* Burgh Gp *Linc*

WELTON-LE-WOLD (St Martin) *see* Louth *Linc*

WELWICK (St Mary) *see* Easington w Skeffling, Keyingham, Ottringham etc *York*

WELWYN GARDEN CITY (St Francis of Assisi) *St Alb 18*
P *Bp* **V** J E FENNELL **C** E M N LAVELLE

WELWYN Team Ministry (St Mary the Virgin) (St Michael), including Ayot St Peter, Codicote, Datchworth, and Tewin *St Alb 18* **P** *Patr Bd* **TR** D L MUNCHIN **TV** P T WALLER, S L UNDERWOOD **C** D J HOLROYD-THOMAS **NSM** S V BECK

WEM (St Peter and St Paul), Lee Brockhurst and Weston under Redcastle *Lich 21* **P** *Lord Barnard and Sir Algernon Heber-Percy KCVO (jt)* **R** N P HERON

WEMBDON (St George) *B & W 13* **P** *Ch Soc Trust*
V C D E MOLL **NSM** S P TAYLOR

WEMBLEY (Annunciation) *see* S Kenton *Lon*

WEMBLEY (Church of the Ascension) *see* Preston *Lon*

WEMBLEY (St Augustine) *see* Wembley Park *Lon*

WEMBLEY (St John the Evangelist) *Lon 21* **P** *Ch Patr Trust*
V vacant

WEMBLEY PARK (St Augustine) *Lon 21* **P** *Bp*
V H M ASKWITH

WEMBLEY, NORTH (St Cuthbert) *Lon 21* **P** *Bp*
V S R MORRIS

WEMBURY (St Werburgh) *Ex 20* **P** *D&C Windsor* **V** vacant

WEMBWORTHY (St Michael) *see* Burrington, Chawleigh, Cheldon, Chulmleigh etc *Ex*

WENDENS AMBO (St Mary the Virgin) *see* Saffron Walden and Villages *Chelmsf*

WENDLEBURY (St Giles) *see* Akeman *Ox*

WENDLING (St Peter and St Paul) *see* Launditch and the Upper Nar *Nor*

WENDOVER (St Mary) (St Agnes's Chapel) and Halton
Ox 17 **P** *Ld Chan* **R** S M MORING **NSM** S E PRENDERGAST

WENDRON(St Wendron) *see* Helston and Wendron *Truro*

WENDY (All Saints) *see* Shingay Gp *Ely*

WENHAM, GREAT (St John) *see* Capel St Mary w Lt and Gt Wenham *St E*

WENHASTON (St Peter) *see* Blyth Valley *St E*

WENLOCK, comprising Berrington w Betton Strange, Church Preen, Cound, Cressage, Easthope, Harley, Hughley, Kenley, Much Wenlock w Bourton, Sheinton, Shipton, and Stanton Long *Heref 10* **P** *Patr Bd* **TR** M C STAFFORD
  C A M WALKER **NSM** J A CUMBERLAND
WENLOCK, LITTLE (St Lawrence) *see* Coalbrookdale, Iron-Bridge and Lt Wenlock *Heref*
WENLOCK, MUCH (Holy Trinity) *see* Wenlock *Heref*
WENNINGTON (St Mary and St Peter) *see* Rainham w Wennington *Chelmsf*
WENSLEYDALE, LOWER, comprising Crakehall, Finghall, Hauxwell, Hornby, Patrick Brompton w Hunton, and Spennithorne *Leeds 25* **P** *Bp (1 turn), D&C York (1 turn), Sir Henry Beresford-Peirse Bt (1 turn), R J Dalton Esq and M C A Wyvill Esq (1 turn)* **R** R D C LAWTON
WENSLEYDALE, UPPER, comprising Askrigg, Hardraw, Hawes, and Stalling Busk *Leeds 25* **P** *Bp, R Penhill, G L Metcalfe, and E A Cherniavsky (jt)* **V** D J CLARK
WENSUM Village Group, UPPER, comprising Brisley, Colkirk w Oxwick w Pattesley, Gateley, Great Ryburgh, Horningtoft, Shereford w Dunton, and Whissonsett *Nor 14* **P** *Marquess Townshend, the Revd C S P Douglas Lane, Ch Coll Cam, and DBP (jt)* **R** R D STAPLEFORD
WENT VALLEY, comprising Darrington, Kirk Smeaton, and Wentbridge *Leeds 18* **P** *Bp, Earl of Rosse, and Sir Philip Naylor-Leyland Bt (jt)* **V** A T JUDD
WENTBRIDGE (St John) *see* Went Valley *Leeds*
WENTNOR (St Michael and All Angels) w Ratlinghope, Myndtown, Norbury, More, Lydham and Snead *Heref 9*
  P *Ch Ch Ox (4 turns) and J J C Coldwell Esq (1 turn)* **R** *vacant*
WENTWORTH (Harley Mission Church) (Holy Trinity) *Sheff 12* **P** *Sir Philip Naylor-Leyland Bt* **V** *vacant*
WENTWORTH (St Peter) *see* Witchford w Wentworth *Ely*
WEOBLEY (St Peter and St Paul) w Sarnesfield and Norton Canon *Heref 4* **P** *Bp (2 turns), R A Marshall Esq (1 turn)*
  V *vacant*
WEOLEY CASTLE (St Gabriel) *Birm 1* **P** *Bp*
  V F J HARRISON-SMITH
WEREHAM (St Margaret) *see* Wissey Valley *Ely*
WERNETH (St Paul) *Ches 16* **P** *DBP* **V** L BOYLE
  NSM W S ATKINSON
WERRINGTON (St John the Baptist w Emmanuel) *Pet 11*
  P *Bp* **V** G H ROGERS **C** S J FEAR **NSM** K C FEAR
WERRINGTON (St Martin of Tours) *see* Boyton, N Tamerton, Werrington etc *Truro*
WERRINGTON (St Philip) and Wetley Rocks *Lich 6* **P** *Bp and V Caverswall and Weston Coyney w Dilhorne (jt)*
  V M S FOLLIN **OLM** I T COPELAND, S J PARKER
WESHAM (Christ Church) *Blackb 10* **P** *V Kirkham*
  V A R BEVERLEY
WESSINGTON (Christ Church) *see* Ashover and Brackenfield w Wessington *Derby*
WEST *see also under substantive place name*
WEST ACRE (All Saints) *see* Nar Valley *Nor*
WEST BAY (St John) *see* Bridport *Sarum*
WEST COAST, comprising Dalby, German, Kirk Patrick, and Michael *S & M* **V** N P GODFREY **NSM** J E HAMER
WEST DEAN (All Saints) *see* Alfriston w Lullington, Litlington, W Dean and Folkington *Chich*
WEST DEAN (St Andrew) *see* E Dean, Singleton, and W Dean *Chich*
WEST DEAN (St Mary) *see* Clarendon *Sarum*
WEST DOWN (St Calixtus) *see* Heanton Punchardon, Marwood and W Down *Ex*
WEST DOWNLAND, comprising Brightwalton w Catmore, Chaddleworth, Fawley, Great Shefford, Leckhampstead, and Welford w Wickham *Ox 6* **P** *Bp, Sir Philip Wroughton, and D&C Westmr (jt)* **R** M F KEEN **C** J HOWELL
WEST END (Holy Trinity) *see* Bisley and W End *Guildf*
WEST END (St George) *see* Esher *Guildf*
WEST END (St James) *Win 10* **P** *Bp* **V** V A MAUNDER
  NSM L S GALVIN
WEST GREEN (Christ Church w St Peter) *Lon 19* **P** *Bp*
  NSM G D BOND
WEST GREEN (St Peter) *Chich 6* **P** *Bp* **V** P B WELCH
  C J M BALDWIN
WEST HAM (All Saints) *Chelmsf 5* **P** *The Crown*
  V A W M SUMMERS **NSM** D P WADE
WEST HAM (St Matthew) *Chelmsf 5* **P** *CPAS*
  V C C ASINUGO **C** D A RICHARDS **NSM** S M ELDRIDGE
WEST HEATH (St Anne) *Birm 3* **P** *Bp* **P-in-c** P H-S CHO
WEST HILL (St Michael the Archangel) *see* Ottery St Mary, Alfington, W Hill, Tipton etc *Ex*
WEST MOORS (St Mary the Virgin) *Sarum 9* **P** *Bp*
  V A P MUCKLE **C** R M WELLS **NSM** L MORRIS

WEST OF SEVERN *see* Ashleworth, Corse, Hartpury, Hasfield etc *Glouc*
WEST ORCHARD (St Luke) *see* Shaftesbury *Sarum*
WEST ROW (St Peter) *see* Mildenhall *St E*
WESTBERE (All Saints) *see* Sturry w Fordwich and Westbere w Hersden *Cant*
WESTBOROUGH (All Saints) *see* Claypole *Linc*
WESTBOROUGH (St Clare) (St Francis) *Guildf 5* **P** *Bp*
  TR S M HODGES **TV** S POWNALL **OLM** D R PETERS
WESTBOURNE (Christ Church) Chapel *Win 8*
  Min N R T HISCOCKS
WESTBOURNE (St John the Baptist) *Chich 3* **P** *Bp*
  R A P C DOYE
WESTBROOK (All Saints) *see* Margate All SS *Cant*
WESTBROOK (St James) *see* Warrington W *Liv*
WESTBROOK (St Philip) *as above*
WESTBURY (All Saints) *see* White Horse *Sarum*
WESTBURY (St Augustine) *see* W Buckingham *Ox*
WESTBURY (St Mary), Worthen and Yockleton *Heref 12*
  P *Bp (2 turns), New Coll Ox (1 turn)* **R** D MOSS
WESTBURY PARK (St Alban) *see* Westbury-on-Trym St Alb *Bris*
WESTBURY SUB MENDIP (St Lawrence) w Easton *B & W 1*
  P *Bp* **V** P M HOLLINGSWORTH
WESTBURY-ON-SEVERN (St Peter and St Paul) w Flaxley, Blaisdon and Minsterworth *Glouc 3* **P** *Bp, D&C Heref, and Sir Thomas Crawley-Boevey Bt (jt)* **P-in-c** S C TAYLOR
  C D A GILL
WESTBURY-ON-TRYM (Holy Trinity) *Bris 2* **P** *SMF*
  V A H HART
WESTBURY-ON-TRYM (St Alban) *Bris 2* **P** *Bp*
  V E L LANGLEY **OLM** J M DOYLE
WESTCLIFF (Church of Reconciliation) *see* Brumby *Linc*
WESTCLIFF (St Andrew) *Chelmsf 15* **P** *Bp*
  P-in-c P A GAMBLING **OLM** C LUCAS
WESTCLIFF (St Cedd and the Saints of Essex) *see* Prittlewell St Pet w Westcliff St Cedd *Chelmsf*
WESTCLIFF (St Michael and All Angels) *Chelmsf 15* **P** *Bp*
  P-in-c T LOH **C** M M WALKER, S P COLLIER **OLM** C LUCAS
WESTCLIFF (St Saviour) *see* Southend St Sav Westcliff *Chelmsf*
WESTCLIFFE (St Peter) *see* St Margarets-at-Cliffe w Westcliffe etc *Cant*
WESTCOMBE PARK (St George) *see* E Greenwich *S'wark*
WESTCOTE (St Mary the Virgin) *see* Broadwell, Evenlode, Oddington, Adlestrop etc *Glouc*
WESTCOTE BARTON (St Edward the Confessor) w Steeple Barton, Duns Tew and Sandford St Martin and Over w Nether Worton *Ox 29* **P** *Bp, DBP, Duke of Marlborough, Exors Mrs S C Rittson-Thomas, P J Schuster, and D C C Webb Esq (jt)* **R** J WRIGHT
WESTCOTT (Holy Trinity) *Guildf 7* **P** *Bp* **V** A C JONAS
WESTCOTT (St Mary) *see* Schorne *Ox*
WESTDENE (The Ascension) *see* Patcham *Chich*
WESTERDALE (Christ Church) *York 21* **P** *Abp* **V** *vacant*
WESTERFIELD (St Mary Magdalene) and Tuddenham w Witnesham *St E 1* **P** *Bp, Peterho Cam, and DBP (alt)*
  P-in-c A W FORSDIKE **NSM** C A FORSDIKE
WESTERHAM (St Mary the Virgin) *Roch 9* **P** *J St A Warde Esq* **V** K P BARNARD
WESTERLEIGH (St James the Great) *see* Yate *Bris*
WESTERN DOWNLAND, comprising Damerham, Martin, Rockbourne, and Whitsbury *Sarum 11* **P** *Hyndman Trustees, A N Hanbury Esq, and W J Purvis Esq (jt)* **R** L M PLAYER
WESTERN SHORE *see* Heacham and Snettisham *Nor*
WESTFIELD (St Andrew) *see* Barnham Broom and Upper Yare *Nor*
WESTFIELD (St John the Baptist) and Guestling *Chich 17* **P** *Bp and DBP (jt)* **NSM** J C COLLINS
WESTFIELD (St Mark) *see* Woking St Pet *Guildf*
WESTFIELD (St Mary) *Carl 7* **P** *Bp* **V** S G AXTELL
WESTFIELD (St Peter) *B & W 11* **P** *Bp* **P-in-c** I D ROUSELL
WESTGATE (St Andrew) *see* Upper Weardale *Dur*
WESTGATE (St James) *Cant 5* **P** *Abp* **V** S G RAE
WESTGATE (St Martin of Tours) *see* Torrisholme *Blackb*
WESTGATE COMMON (St Michael the Archangel) *Leeds 19*
  P *V Alverthorpe* **V** *vacant*
WESTGATE-ON-SEA (St Saviour) *Cant 5* **P** *Abp*
  P-in-c K A GOODING
WESTHALL (St Andrew) *see* Hundred River and Wainford *St E*
WESTHAM (St Mary the Virgin) *Chich 14* **P** *Duke of Devonshire* **NSM** F M BALDWIN
WESTHAMPNETT (St Peter) *see* Chich St Paul and Westhampnett *Chich*
WESTHEAD (St James) *see* Newburgh w Westhead *Liv*

WESTHIDE (St Bartholomew)   *see* Bartestree Cross *Heref*
WESTHOPE (Mission Room)   *see* Canon Pyon w King's Pyon, Birley and Wellington *Heref*
WESTHORPE (St Margaret)   *see* Badwell and Walsham *St E*
WESTHOUGHTON (St Bartholomew)   *see* Blackrod, Daisy Hill, Westhoughton and Wingates *Man*
WESTLANDS (St Andrew) *Lich 9*   **P** *Simeon's Trustees*
   V J A DAWSWELL
WESTLEIGH (St Peter)   *see* Fremington, Instow and Westleigh *Ex*
WESTLEIGH (St Peter) (St Paul) *Man 19*   **P** *Bp, V Leigh St Mary, and Dioc Chan (jt)*   **V** J M COOPER   **NSM** J AITKEN, K E SLAYEN
WESTLETON (St Peter)   *see* Yoxmere *St E*
WESTLEY (St Mary)   *see* Horringer *St E*
WESTLEY WATERLESS (St Mary the less)   *see* Raddesley Gp *Ely*
WESTMESTON (St Martin)   *see* Ditchling, Streat and Westmeston *Chich*
WESTMILL (St Mary the Virgin)   *see* Aspenden, Buntingford and Westmill *St Alb*
WESTMINSTER (St James the Less) *Lon 3*   **P** *D&C Westmr*   **V** E A GODDARD   **Hon C** A J GODDARD   **NSM** F M LAU
WESTMINSTER (St James) Piccadilly *Lon 3*   **P** *Bp (2 turns), Ld Chan (1 turn)*   **R** L C WINKETT   **C** J L MEADER   **NSM** D R NORRIS, H W J VALENTINE, I P KHOVACS
WESTMINSTER (St Mary le Strand)   *see* St Mary le Strand w St Clem Danes *Lon*
WESTMINSTER (St Matthew) *Lon 3*   **P** *D&C Westmr*   **V** P A E CHESTER   **NSM** J W P AITKEN, P L HANAWAY
WESTMINSTER (St Michael)   *see* Ches Square St Mich w St Phil *Lon*
WESTMINSTER (St Saviour)   *see* Pimlico St Sav *Lon*
WESTMINSTER (St Stephen) w St John *Lon 3*   **P** *The Crown*   **V** G M BUCKLE   **C** C V DUCE
WESTMINSTER Hanover Square (St George)   *see* Hanover Square St Geo *Lon*
WESTMORLAND, HIGH, comprising Bampton, Orton w Tebay, Ravenstonedale, and Shap w Swindale *Carl 1*   **P** *Bp, Adn Carl, Mrs A Browning, M Metcalfe-Gibson Esq, the Hon J N Lowther, and Resident Landowners (jt)*   **P-in-c** A J HURD   **NSM** F A PARKINSON
WESTMORLAND, NORTH comprising Askham and Lowther, Bolton, Cliburn, Clifton and Brougham, Crosby Ravensworth, Great Strickland, Morland, and Thrimby *Carl 1*   **P** *D&C, Lord Hothfield, DBP, and the Hon J N Lowther (jt)*   **R** S J FYFE   **NSM** S P CLARK, S R PEARL
WESTOE, SOUTH (St Michael and All Angels) *Dur 13*   **P** *Bp*   **V** vacant
WESTON (All Saints) *Ches 15*   **P** *Bp*   **V** R J GRIFFITHS
WESTON (All Saints) *Guildf 8*   **P** *Bp*   **V** S G L WOOD   **NSM** M WOOD
WESTON (All Saints)   *see* Bath Weston All SS w N Stoke and Langridge *B & W*
WESTON (All Saints)   *see* Quinton, Welford, Weston and Marston Sicca *Glouc*
WESTON (All Saints)   *see* Tuxford w Weston, Markham Clinton etc *S'well*
WESTON (All Saints)   *see* Washburn and Mid-Wharfe *Leeds*
WESTON (Emmanuel)   *see* Bath Weston St Jo w Kelston *B & W*
WESTON (Holy Trinity) *Win 13*   **P** *Bp*   **P-in-c** D MEDWAY
WESTON (Holy Trinity)   *see* Clothall, Rushden, Sandon, Wallington and Weston *St Alb*
WESTON (St John the Evangelist)   *see* Bath Weston St Jo w Kelston *B & W*
WESTON (St John the Evangelist)   *see* Runcorn St Jo Weston *Ches*
WESTON (St Mary)   *see* Cowbit *Linc*
WESTON (St Peter)   *see* Hundred River and Wainford *St E*
WESTON BAMPFYLDE (Holy Cross)   *see* Cam Vale *B & W*
WESTON BEGGARD (St John the Baptist)   *see* Bartestree Cross *Heref*
WESTON BY WELLAND (St Mary)   *see* Stoke Albany w Wilbarston and Ashley etc *Pet*
WESTON COLVILLE (St Mary)   *see* Granta Vale Gp *Ely*
WESTON COYNEY (St Andrew)   *see* Caverswall and Weston Coyney w Dilhorne *Lich*
WESTON FAVELL (St Peter) *Pet 4*   **P** *DBP*   **R** D G KIRBY   **C** M SMITH
WESTON HILLS (St John the Evangelist)   *see* Cowbit *Linc*
WESTON IN GORDANO (St Peter and St Paul)   *see* E Clevedon w Clapton in Gordano etc *B & W*
WESTON LONGVILLE (All Saints)   *see* Reepham and Wensum Valley *Nor*
WESTON LULLINGFIELD (Holy Trinity)   *see* Baschurch and Weston Lullingfield w Hordley *Lich*

WESTON MILL (St Philip) *Ex 21*   **P** *Bp*   **P-in-c** M C DOYLE
WESTON ON TRENT (St Mary the Virgin)   *see* Aston on Trent, Elvaston, Weston on Trent etc *Derby*
WESTON PATRICK (St Lawrence)   *see* N Hants Downs *Win*
WESTON RHYN (St John)   *see* St Martins and Weston Rhyn *Lich*
WESTON SUPER MARE (All Saints) and St Saviour *B & W 10*   **P** *Bp*   **P-in-c** A K W HUGHES   **NSM** S A BOYD
WESTON SUPER MARE (Christ Church) (Emmanuel) *B & W 10*   **P** *Trustees*   **V** T G E WEBBER   **C** R A CLARK
WESTON SUPER MARE (St John the Baptist) *B & W 10*   **P** *Bp and Trustees (jt)*   **R** P M ASHMAN   **NSM** J A BIRKETT
WESTON TURVILLE (St Mary the Virgin) *Ox 17*   **P** *All So Coll Ox*   **R** D N WALES   **NSM** S E FELLOWS
WESTON UNDER REDCASTLE (St Luke)   *see* Wem, Lee Brockhurst etc *Lich*
WESTON UNDER WETHERLEY (St Michael)   *see* Offchurch Gp *Cov*
WESTON UNDERWOOD (St Laurence)   *see* Gayhurst w Ravenstone, Stoke Goldington etc *Ox*
WESTON UPON TRENT (St Andrew)   *see* Mid Trent *Lich*
WESTON ZOYLAND (Blessed Virgin Mary) w Chedzoy *B & W 13*   **P** *Bp*   **V** C D KEYS
WESTON, OLD (St Swithun)   *see* W Leightonstone *Ely*
WESTON, SOUTH (St Lawrence)   *see* Thame *Ox*
WESTONING (St Mary Magdalene) w Tingrith *St Alb 8*   **P** *Ld Chan*   **V** N L WASHINGTON
WESTON-ON-THE-GREEN (St Mary)   *see* Akeman *Ox*
WESTON-SUB-EDGE (St Lawrence)   *see* Vale and Cotswold Edge *Glouc*
WESTON-SUPER-MARE (St Nicholas) (St Barnabas) *B & W 10*   **P** *Patr Bd*   **R** M K MADELEY
WESTON-SUPER-MARE (St Paul) *B & W 10*   **P** *Bp*   **V** A M ALDEN   **C** C P SINCLAIR
WESTON-UNDER-LIZARD (St Andrew)   *see* Watershed *Lich*
WESTON-UNDER-PENYARD (St Lawrence)   *see* Ariconium *Heref*
WESTOW (St Mary)   *see* W Buckrose *York*
WESTWARD (St Hilda), Rosley-with-Woodside and Welton *Carl 3*   **P** *D&C*   **P-in-c** E REID
WESTWARD HO! (Holy Trinity)   *see* Appledore, Northam and Westward Ho! *Ex*
WESTWAY (St Katherine)   *see* N Hammersmith St Kath *Lon*
WESTWELL (St Mary)   *see* G7 Benefice *Cant*
WESTWELL (St Mary)   *see* Shill Valley and Broadshire *Ox*
WESTWICK (St Botolph)   *see* N Walsham, Edingthorpe, Worstead and Westwick *Nor*
WESTWOOD (St John the Baptist) *Cov 3*   **P** *Bp*   **P-in-c** D G HAMMOND
WESTWOOD (St Mary the Virgin)   *see* Bradford on Avon H Trin, Westwood and Wingfield *Sarum*
WESTWOOD (St Mary) Jacksdale   *see* Selston *S'well*
WESTWOOD, LOW (Christ Church)   *see* Ebchester *Dur*
WETHERAL (Holy Trinity and St Constantine)   *see* Holme Eden and Wetheral w Warwick *Carl*
WETHERBY (St James) *Leeds 21*   **P** *Bp*   **P-in-c** B A GIBLIN
WETHERDEN (St Mary the Virgin)   *see* Haughley w Wetherden and Stowupland *St E*
WETHERINGSETT (All Saints)   *see* S Hartismere *St E*
WETHERSFIELD (St Mary Magdalene)   *see* Finchingfield and Cornish Hall End etc *Chelmsf*
WETLEY ROCKS (St John the Baptist)   *see* Werrington and Wetley Rocks *Lich*
WETTENHALL (St David)   *see* Acton and Worleston, Church Minshull etc *Ches*
WETTON (St Margaret)   *see* Alstonfield, Ilam and Wetton *Lich*
WETWANG (St Nicholas)   *see* Waggoners *York*
WEXHAM (St Mary) *Ox 12*   **P** *Ld Chan*   **P-in-c** A M PARRY
WEYBOURNE (All Saints), Upper Sheringham, Kelling, Salthouse, Bodham and East and West Beckham (The Weybourne Group) *Nor 17*   **P** *Bp (2 turns), Sir Charles Mott-Radclyffe (1 turn), D&C (1 turn), and Lord Walpole (1 turn)*   **R** vacant
WEYBREAD (St Andrew)   *see* Sancroft *St E*
WEYBRIDGE (St James) *Guildf 8*   **P** *Ld Chan*   **R** B D PROTHERO   **C** L S BISHOP
WEYHILL (St Michael and All Angels)   *see* Pastrow *Win*
WEYMOUTH (Holy Trinity) (St Nicholas) *Sarum 4*   **P** *Bp*   **V** A S GOUGH
WEYMOUTH (St Edmund)   *see* Wyke Regis *Sarum*
WEYMOUTH (St John)   *see* Radipole and Melcombe Regis *Sarum*
WEYMOUTH (St Mary) *as above*
WEYMOUTH (St Paul) *Sarum 4*   **P** *Bp*   **V** A LIPOVSKY

WEYMOUTH RIDGEWAY, comprising Bincombe and Broadwey, Buckland Ripers, Littlemoor, Osmington w Poxwell, Preston w Sutton Poyntz, and Upwey *Sarum 4* **P** *Patr Bd* **TR** T R WEST **TV** P ELLIOTT **NSM** B E J ELLIS

WHADDON (St Margaret) *see* Glouc St Geo w Whaddon *Glouc*

WHADDON (St Mary the Virgin) *see* Canalside Benefice *Sarum*

WHADDON (St Mary) *Ely 7* **P** *D&C Windsor* **V** C J YANDELL

WHADDON (St Mary) *see* Buckingham *Ox*

WHADDON (St Mary) *see* Clarendon *Sarum*

WHADDON (St Michael) *see* Cheltenham St Mich *Glouc*

WHALEY BRIDGE (St James) *Ches 16* **P** *Bp and Bp Derby (alt)* **P-in-c** M A JONES

WHALEY THORNS (St Luke) *see* E Scarsdale *Derby*

WHALLEY (St Mary and All Saints) *see* W Pendleside *Blackb*

WHALLEY RANGE (St Edmund) and Moss Side St James w St Clement *Man 3* **P** *Bp and Simeon's Trustees (jt)* **R** A W HARDY **C** G R E THOMAS **OLM** S AWALE

WHALLEY RANGE (St Margaret) *Man 3* **P** *Trustees* **P-in-c** R G BOULTER

WHALTON (St Mary Magdalene) *see* Bolam w Whalton and Hartburn w Meldon *Newc*

WHAPLODE (St Mary) *see* Elloe Stone *Linc*

WHAPLODE DROVE (St John the Baptist) *see* Elloe Fen Gp *Linc*

WHARFEDALE, LOWER, comprising Kirkby Overblow w Sicklinghall, Pool and Arthington, and Weeton w North Rigton and Stainburn *Leeds 21* **P** *Bp, V Otley, and W G C Sheepshanks Esq (jt)* **Hon C** D J WHEELER **NSM** R HUDSPETH

WHARFEDALE, UPPER and Littondale, comprising Arncliffe w Halton Gill, Hubberholme, and Kettlewell w Conistone *Leeds 24* **P** *Bp, Mrs J E Wright, and W R G Bell Esq (jt)* **P-in-c** J W F THEODOSIUS

WHARRAM (St Mary) *see* Weaverthorpe w Helperthorpe, Luttons Ambo etc *York*

WHARTON (Christ Church) *Ches 6* **P** *R Davenham* **V** T D HANSON

WHATBOROUGH Group of Parishes, The, comprising Cold Overton, Knossington, Lowesby, Owston and Withcote, and Tilton-on-the-Hill *Leic 5* **P** *Bp* **P-in-c** J L LEWIS

WHATCOTE (St Peter) *see* Tysoe w Oxhill and Whatcote *Cov*

WHATFIELD (St Margaret) *see* Bildeston w Wattisham and Lindsey, Whatfield etc *St E*

WHATLEY (St George) *see* Mells w Buckland Dinham, Elm, Whatley etc *B & W*

WHATLINGTON (St Mary Magdalene) *see* Sedlescombe w Whatlington *Chich*

WHATTON (St John of Beverley) w Aslockton, Hawksworth, Scarrington, Orston and Thoroton *S'well 5* **P** *Trustees* **V** *vacant*

WHEATACRE (All Saints) *see* Raveningham Gp *Nor*

WHEATCROFT (St Michael and All Angels) *see* Scarborough St Martin *York*

WHEATFIELD (St Andrew) *see* Thame *Ox*

WHEATHAMPSTEAD (St Helen) *St Alb 7* **P** *Bp* **R** R M BANHAM **NSM** K E DAYMOND

WHEATHILL (Holy Trinity) *see* Ditton Priors w Neenton, Burwarton etc *Heref*

WHEATHILL PRIORY Group of Parishes, The, comprising Barton St David, Keinton Mandeville w Kingweston, and Lydford on Fosse *B & W 2* **P** *Ch Soc Trust and J H Cordle Esq (1 turn), A J Whitehead Esq (2 turns), Bp (1 turn), and Mrs E J Burden (1 turn)* **P-in-c** E J DURHAM

WHEATLEY (St Mary the Virgin) *see* Albury w Tiddington etc *Ox*

WHEATLEY (St Mary) *see* Doncaster St Mary and St Paul *Sheff*

WHEATLEY HILL (All Saints), Thornley and Wingate w Hutton Henry *Dur 2* **P** *Bp* **P-in-c** F J GRIEVE **C** C HARRIS

WHEATLEY HILLS (St Aidan) w Intake *Sheff 8* **P** *Bp* **V** D J GOSS

WHEATLEY PARK (St Paul) *see* Doncaster St Mary and St Paul *Sheff*

WHEATLEY, NORTH (St Peter and St Paul) *see* Retford Area *S'well*

WHEATON ASTON (St Mary) *see* Watershed *Lich*

WHEELOCK (Christ Church) *see* Sandbach Heath w Wheelock *Ches*

WHELDRAKE (St Helen) *see* Derwent Ings *York*

WHELFORD (St Anne) *see* S Cotswolds *Glouc*

WHELLEY (St Stephen) *see* Wigan All SS *Liv*

WHELNETHAM, GREAT (St Thomas à Becket) *see* St Edm Way *St E*

WHELNETHAM, LITTLE (St Mary) *see* Bradfield St Clare, Bradfield St George etc *St E*

WHEPSTEAD (St Petronilla) *see* Horringer *St E*

WHERSTEAD (St Mary) *see* Holbrook, Stutton, Freston, Woolverstone etc *St E*

WHERWELL (St Peter and Holy Cross) *see* The Downs *Win*

WHETSTONE (St John the Apostle) *Lon 14* **P** *Bp* **P-in-c** L DAVIDSON

WHETSTONE (St Peter) *see* Cosby and Whetstone *Leic*

WHICHAM (St Mary) *see* Black Combe, Drigg, Eskdale etc *Carl*

WHICHFORD (St Michael) *see* S Warks Seven Gp *Cov*

WHICKHAM (St Mary the Virgin) *Dur 12* **P** *Ld Chan* **R** B J ABBOTT

WHIDDON Team Ministry, The *see* Chagford, Gidleigh, Throwleigh etc *Ex*

WHILTON (St Andrew) *see* Brington w Whilton and Norton etc *Pet*

WHIMPLE (St Mary), Talaton, Clyst St Lawrence and Clyst Hydon *Ex 6* **P** *DBP, D&C and MMCET (jt)* **R** C E MARTIN **C** M R KERSLAKE

WHINBURGH (St Mary) *see* Barnham Broom and Upper Yare *Nor*

WHINMOOR (St Paul) *see* Seacroft *Leeds*

WHINNEY HILL (St Peter) *see* Thrybergh *Sheff*

WHIPPINGHAM (St Mildred) w East Cowes *Portsm 7* **P** *Ld Chan* **R** S A PATERSON

WHIPSNADE (St Mary Magdalene) *see* Kensworth, Studham and Whipsnade *St Alb*

WHIPTON (St Boniface) *Ex 3* **P** *Bp* **P-in-c** J W BYATT

WHISSENDINE (St Andrew) *see* Oakham, Ashwell, Braunston, Brooke, Egleton etc *Pet*

WHISSONSETT (St Mary) *see* Upper Wensum Village Gp *Nor*

WHISTON (St Mary the Virgin) *see* Yardley Hastings, Denton and Grendon etc *Pet*

WHISTON (St Mildred) *see* Kingsley and Foxt-w-Whiston and Oakamoor etc *Lich*

WHISTON (St Nicholas) *Liv 7* **P** *V Prescot* **V** A J TELFER

WHITACRE, NETHER (St Giles) *see* The Whitacres, Lea Marston, and Shustoke *Birm*

WHITACRE, OVER (St Leonard) *as above*

WHITACRES, Lea Marston, and Shustoke, The *Birm 8* **P** K E Wingfield Digby Esq (1 turn), Bp (2 turns), and Ld Chan (1 turn) **R** R L STEPHENS

WHITBECK (St Mary) *see* Black Combe, Drigg, Eskdale etc *Carl*

WHITBOURNE (St John the Baptist) *see* Edvin Loach w Tedstone Delamere etc *Heref*

WHITBURN (no dedication) *Dur 14* **P** *Bp* **R** *vacant*

WHITBY (St Hilda) (St John) (St Mary) w Ruswarp *York 21* **P** *Abp* **TR** M G T GOBBETT

WHITBY (St Thomas) *see* Ellesmere Port *Ches*

WHITCHURCH (All Hallows) w Tufton and Litchfield *Win 6* **P** *Bp* **P-in-c** D M ROCHE **Hon C** M R CHRISTIAN

WHITCHURCH (St Alkmund) *Lich 21* **P** *Bp* **R** J M HUNT **C** E ATACK

WHITCHURCH (St Andrew) *Ex 22* **P** *Bp* **P-in-c** S A BRASSIL **NSM** M L DONNE

WHITCHURCH (St Augustine) *Bris 1* **P** *Bp* **C** J C KEAN, M L SOUTHCOMBE **NSM** P A HUNTER

WHITCHURCH (St Dubricius) *see* Wye Reaches Gp *Heref*

WHITCHURCH (St John the Evangelist) *see* Schorne *Ox*

WHITCHURCH (St Mary the Virgin) *see* Ilmington w Stretton-on-Fosse etc *Cov*

WHITCHURCH (St Mary the Virgin) *see* Langtree *Ox*

WHITCHURCH (St Nicholas) *Bris 1* **P** *Bp* **V** *vacant*

WHITCHURCH CANONICORUM (St Candida and Holy Cross) *see* Golden Cap Team *Sarum*

WHITCHURCH HILL (St John the Baptist) *see* Langtree *Ox*

WHITE CITY (St Michael and St George) *Lon 9* **P** *Bp* **V** B P HUMPHRIES **NSM** A J ROONEY

WHITE COLNE (St Andrew) *see* Halstead Area *Chelmsf*

WHITE HORSE, The, comprising Dilton Marsh and Westbury *Sarum 12* **P** *Bp* **TV** C E HUSBAND **C** M OTTO

WHITE LADIES ASTON (St John) *see* Peopleton and White Ladies Aston w Churchill etc *Worc*

WHITE NOTLEY (St Etheldreda) *see* Witham and Villages *Chelmsf*

WHITE RODING (St Martin) *see* S Rodings *Chelmsf*

WHITE WALTHAM (St Mary the Virgin) w Shottesbrooke *Ox 5* **P** *Sir John Smith* **P-in-c** D A ATALLAH **C** W M C STILEMAN

WHITECHAPEL (St James) *see* Fellside Team *Blackb*

WHITEFIELD (St Andrew) *see* Hillock and Unsworth *Man*

WHITEFRIARS (no dedication) Rushden *Pet 8* **P** *CPAS*
V C A YOUNGMAN
WHITEGATE (St Mary) w Little Budworth *Ches 6* **P** *Bp, Lord Delamere and W R Cullimore Esq (alt)* **V** P C O DAWSON
NSM J T STOPFORD
WHITEHALL (St Ambrose) *see* E Bris St Ambrose and St Leon *Bris*
WHITEHALL PARK (St Andrew) *Lon 6* **P** *Ch Patr Trust*
V S R CLARKE
WHITEHAVEN (St James) *Carl 5* **P** *Patr Bd*
P-in-c R JACKSON **C** A M RILEY
WHITEHAWK (St Cuthman) *Chich 19* **P** *Bp*
P-in-c R M COATES **C** S J TENNANT
WHITEHILLS (St Mark) *see* Kingsthorpe *Pet*
WHITELACKINGTON (Blessed Virgin Mary) *see* Ilminster and Whitelackington *B & W*
WHITELEAS (St Mary w St Martin) *see* S Shields All SS *Dur*
WHITELEY Conventional District *Portsm 2* **C-in-c** P J MILLS
Min A J MATHESON, A V ADENIRAN
WHITEPARISH (All Saints) *see* Clarendon *Sarum*
WHITESHILL (St Paul) *see* Stroud Team *Glouc*
WHITESTAUNTON (St Andrew) *see* Chard St Mary w Combe St Nicholas, Wambrook etc *B & W*
WHITESTONE (St Catherine) *see* Tedburn St Mary, Cheriton Bishop, Whitestone etc *Ex*
WHITESTONE (St John the Evangelist) *as above*
WHITEWATER Benefice, The, comprising Heckfield w Mattingley and Rotherwick, and Hook *Win 5* **P** *Bp and New Coll Ox (alt)* **R** M E DE QUIDT **C** M J LEWIS
NSM S M HOAD
WHITEWELL (St Mary) *see* Marbury w Tushingham and Whitewell *Ches*
WHITEWELL (St Michael) *Blackb 7* **P** *Bp* **V** *vacant*
WHITFIELD (Holy Trinity) *see* Allendale w Whitfield *Newc*
WHITFIELD (St James) (St Luke) *Derby 4* **P** *Bp* **V** T S MAY
WHITFIELD (St John the Evangelist) *see* Astwell Gp *Pet*
WHITFIELD (St John) *see* Allendale w Whitfield *Newc*
WHITFIELD (St Peter) *see* Bewsborough *Cant*
WHITFORD (St Mary at the Cross) *see* Kilmington, Stockland, Dalwood, Yarcombe etc *Ex*
WHITGIFT (St Mary Magdalene) *see* The Marshland *Sheff*
WHITGREAVE (St John the Evangelist) *see* Stafford St Bertelin and Whitgreave St Jo *Lich*
WHITKIRK (St Mary) *Leeds 16* **P** *Meynell Ch Trust* **V** M PEAT
WHITLEIGH (St Chad) *see* Ernesettle, Whitleigh and Honicknowle *Ex*
WHITLEY (Christ Church) *see* Reading Ch Ch *Ox*
WHITLEY (St Helen) *Newc 10* **P** *Bp* **V** A J PATTERSON
WHITLEY (St James) *Cov 1* **P** *Bp* **P-in-c** A M RICHARDS
WHITLEY BRIDGE (All Saints) *see* Knottingley and Kellington w Whitley *Leeds*
WHITLEY LOWER (St Mary and St Michael) *see* Thornhill and Whitley Lower *Leeds*
WHITLEY, LOWER or NETHER (St Luke) *see* Aston by Sutton, Lt Leigh and Lower Whitley *Ches*
WHITLINGHAM (St Andrew) *see* Rockland St Mary w Hellington, Bramerton etc *Nor*
WHITMINSTER (St Andrew) *see* Stroudwater Team *Glouc*
WHITMORE (St Mary and All Saints) *see* Chapel Chorlton, Maer and Whitmore *Lich*
WHITNASH (St Margaret) *Cov 11* **P** *Lord Leigh*
R R W S SUFFERN
WHITNEY (St Peter and St Paul) *see* Eardisley w Bollingham, Willersley, Brilley etc *Heref*
WHITSBURY (St Leonard) *see* W Downland *Sarum*
WHITSTABLE (All Saints) (St Alphage) (St Andrew) (St Peter) *Cant 4* **P** *DBP* **TR** R C WEBBLEY
TV D VAN K VANNERLEY, P J STUBBINGS, S C TILLOTSON
NSM R J TUGWELL
WHITSTONE (St Anne) *see* Week St Mary Circle of Par *Truro*
WHITTINGHAM (St Bartholomew) and Edlingham w Bolton Chapel *Newc 6* **P** *D&C Carl and D&C Dur (alt)*
V *vacant*
WHITTINGTON (Christ Church) *see* Wissey Valley *Ely*
WHITTINGTON (St Bartholomew) *Derby 3* **P** *Bp*
R J E MORRIS **OLM** J QUICK
WHITTINGTON (St Bartholomew) *see* Sevenhampton w Charlton Abbots, Hawling etc *Glouc*
WHITTINGTON (St Giles) w Weeford *Lich 1* **P** *Bp*
V J P B B PHILLIPS
WHITTINGTON (St John the Baptist) and West Felton w Haughton *Lich 18* **P** *Bp and Mrs A F Hamilton-Hill (jt)*
C J G CASTILLO-BURLEY
WHITTINGTON (St Michael the Archangel) *see* Hornby w Claughton and Whittington etc *Blackb*
WHITTINGTON (St Philip and St James) *see* Worc SE *Worc*

WHITTINGTON, NEW (St Barnabas) *see* Whittington *Derby*
WHITTLEBURY (St Mary) *see* Silverstone and Abthorpe w Slapton etc *Pet*
WHITTLE-LE-WOODS (St John the Evangelist) *Blackb 4*
P V *Leyland* **V** P R M VENABLES **C** P T DAVIES
WHITTLESEY (St Andrew) (St Mary), Pondersbridge and Coates *Ely 11* **P** *Ld Chan (2 turns), Patr Bd (1 turn)*
TR N A WHITEHOUSE
WHITTLESFORD (St Mary and St Andrew) *Ely 5* **P** *Jes Coll Cam* **P-in-c** P J SHAKESHAFT **NSM** O M K COLES
WHITTLEWOOD *see* Silverstone and Abthorpe w Slapton etc *Pet*
WHITTON (St Augustine of Canterbury) *Lon 10* **P** *Bp*
V *vacant*
WHITTON (St John the Baptist) *see* Alkborough *Linc*
WHITTON (St Mary and St Botolph) and Thurleston w Akenham *St E 1* **P** *Bp (2 turns), Exors G K Drury Esq (1 turn)* **P-in-c** M N C SOKANOVIC **NSM** E FALLA
WHITTON (St Mary) *see* Tenbury *Heref*
WHITTON (St Philip and St James) *Lon 10* **P** V *Twickenham St Mary* **V** D M CLOAKE
WHITTON, comprising Aldbourne, Axford, Baydon, Chilton Foliat, Froxfield, and Ramsbury *Sarum 18* **P** *Patr Bd*
TV R C FLOATE, S E RODD **C** K M RIZZELLO
WHITTONSTALL (St Philip and St James) *see* Slaley, Healey and Whittonstall *Newc*
WHITWELL (St John the Evangelist) *see* Harton *York*
WHITWELL (St Lawrence) *see* Elmton w Creswell and Whitwell w Steetley *Derby*
WHITWELL (St Mary and St Rhadegunde) *Portsm 7* **P** *Bp*
V N J PORTER
WHITWELL (St Michael and All Angels) *see* Empingham, Edith Weston, Lyndon, Manton etc *Pet*
WHITWELL (St Michael and All Angels) *see* Reepham and Wensum Valley *Nor*
WHITWICK (St John the Baptist), Thringstone and Swannington *Leic 8* **P** *Duchy of Lanc (2 turns), Bp (1 turn)*
R E P ANGELL
WHITWOOD (All Saints) *see* Castleford *Leeds*
WHITWORTH (not known) *see* Spennymoor and Whitworth *Dur*
WHITWORTH (St Bartholomew) w Facit *Man 11* **P** *Bp and Keble Coll Ox (jt)* **NSM** J M WATSON
WHIXALL (St Mary) *see* Edstaston, Fauls, Prees, Tilstock and Whixall *Lich*
WHIXLEY (Ascension) *see* Gt and Lt Ouseburn w Marton cum Grafton etc *Leeds*
WHORLTON (Holy Cross Old Church) w Carlton and Faceby *York 20* **P** *Mrs A P F Kynge* **P-in-c** W J FORD
Hon C A J HUTCHINSON **NSM** D J SUDRON, R OPALA
WHORLTON (St John the Evangelist) *Newc 4* **P** *Bp*
P-in-c M G HUNTER
WHORLTON (St Mary) *see* Barnard Castle w Whorlton *Dur*
WHYKE (St George) w Rumboldswhyke St Mary and Portfield All Saints *Chich 2* **P** *Bp* **R** T L PESKETT
C T J BOUTLE
WHYTELEAFE (St Luke) *see* Caterham *S'wark*
WIBSEY (St Paul) *Leeds 3* **P** *Bp* **V** T J-L GUILLEMIN
C J L TRENHOLME
WIBTOFT (Assumption of Our Lady) *see* Upper Soar *Leic*
WICHENFORD (St Lawrence) *see* Worcs W Rural *Worc*
WICK (All Saints) *see* Lyminster and Wick *Chich*
WICK (St Bartholomew) w Doynton and Dyrham *Bris 5*
P *Simeon's Trustees, Ld Chan, and M H W Blaythwayt Esq (by turn)* **P-in-c** T J K BELL
WICK (St Mary) *see* Pershore w Pinvin, Wick and Birlingham *Worc*
WICK ST LAWRENCE (St Lawrence) *see* Worle *B & W*
WICKEN (St John the Evangelist) *see* Potterspury w Furtho and Yardley Gobion etc *Pet*
WICKEN (St Laurence) *Ely 4* **P** *Ch Patr Trust* **R** *vacant*
WICKEN BONHUNT (St Margaret) *see* Clavering w Langley, Arkesden etc *Chelmsf*
WICKENBY (St Peter and St Lawrence) *see* Wragby Gp *Linc*
WICKERSLEY (St Alban) *Sheff 6* **P** *DBP* **R** P J HUGHES
Hon C N BOWLER
WICKFORD (St Andrew) (St Catherine) and Runwell *Chelmsf 12* **P** *Patr Bd* **TR** J FREEMAN **NSM** S J WISE
OLM S J LISSENDEN
WICKHAM (St Nicholas) *see* Shedfield and Wickham *Portsm*
WICKHAM (St Swithun) *see* W Downland *Ox*
WICKHAM BISHOPS (St Bartholomew) w Little Braxted *Chelmsf 24* **P** *Bp (3 turns), CCC Cam (1 turn)*
P-in-c J H LE SÈVE **NSM** D R CLARK-MAYERS
WICKHAM MARKET (All Saints) w Pettistree *St E 14* **P** *Ch Trust Fund Trust and Ld Chan (alt)* **V** L SIU

WICKHAM SKEITH (St Andrew)　*see* Bacton w Wyverstone, Cotton and Old Newton etc *St E*

WICKHAM ST PAUL (St Paul and All Saints)　*see* N Hinckford *Chelmsf*

WICKHAM, EAST (St Michael the Archangel) *S'wark 6*
　P *D&C*　**V** P ORGAN　**C** T M C BATES　**NSM** M W SMITH

WICKHAM, WEST (St Francis) (St Mary of Nazareth) *S'wark 19*　**P** *Bp*　**V** H M O'SULLIVAN

WICKHAM, WEST (St John) *S'wark 19*　**P** *Bp*　**V** J J H WARD

WICKHAM, WEST (St Mary)　*see* Granta Vale Gp *Ely*

WICKHAMBREAUX (St Andrew)　*see* Littlebourne and Ickham w Wickhambreaux etc *Cant*

WICKHAMBROOK (All Saints)　*see* Bansfield *St E*

WICKHAMFORD (St John the Baptist)　*see* Broadway w Wickhamford *Worc*

WICKHAMPTON (St Andrew)　*see* Acle and Bure to Yare *Nor*

WICKLEWOOD (All Saints)　*see* High Oak, Hingham and Scoulton w Wood Rising *Nor*

WICKMERE (St Andrew)　*see* Aylsham and Distr *Nor*

WICKWAR (Holy Trinity)　*see* Charfield and Kingswood w Wickwar etc *Glouc*

WIDDINGTON (St Mary)　*see* Newport w Widdington, Quendon and Rickling *Chelmsf*

WIDDRINGTON (Holy Trinity) *Newc 11*　**P** *Bp*
　P-in-c J J L DOBSON　**NSM** D M BAKER

WIDECOMBE-IN-THE-MOOR (St Pancras)　*see* Ashburton, Bickington, Buckland in the Moor etc *Ex*

WIDEMOUTH BAY (Our Lady and St Anne)　*see* Week St Mary Circle of Par *Truro*

WIDFORD (St John the Baptist)　*see* Hunsdon w Widford and Wareside *St Alb*

WIDFORD (St Mary) (Holy Spirit) *Chelmsf 10*　**P** *CPAS*
　R S R GILLINGHAM　**C** A P BROWN, D J CATTLE, G E FRASER

WIDFORD (St Oswald)　*see* Burford w Fulbrook, Taynton, Asthall etc *Ox*

WIDMER END (Good Shepherd)　*see* Hazlemere *Ox*

WIDMERPOOL (St Peter)　*see* Willoughby-on-the-Wolds w Wysall and Widmerpool *S'well*

WIDNES, EAST (St Ambrose) (St John) (St Luke) (Cronton Mission) *Liv 12*　**P** Patr Bd　**TV** L C MCIVER
　C R L PEARSON

WIDNES, SOUTH (St Mary) (St Paul) *Liv 12*　**P** Patr Bd
　TV G S SHARPLES　**C** B G NOBLE, C S GAUDION

WIDWORTHY (St Cuthbert)　*see* Offwell, Northleigh, Farway, Cotleigh etc *Ex*

WIELD (St James)　*see* Farleigh, Candover and Wield *Win*

WIGAN (All Saints) (St Andrew) (St Anne) (St Catharine) (St George) (St John the Baptist) (St Michael and All Angels) (St Stephen) *Liv 15*　**P** Patr Bd　**TR** W J GIBBONS
　TV C O NICHOLSON, J F SHOESMITH, S HIGGINSON,
　S L NICHOLSON　**C** J M MAGILL　**OLM** L M PERRIN

WIGAN (St James) (St Thomas) *Liv 15*　**P** R Wigan and Bp (jt)
　P-in-c C N J COOK

WIGBOROUGH, GREAT (St Stephen)　*see* W w E Mersea, Peldon, Gt and Lt Wigborough *Chelmsf*

WIGBOROUGH, LITTLE (St Nicholas)　*as above*

WIGGATON (St Edward the Confessor)　*see* Ottery St Mary, Alfington, W Hill, Tipton etc *Ex*

WIGGENHALL ST GERMANS (St Mary the Virgin)　*see* E Marshland *Ely*

WIGGENHALL ST MARY (St Mary Magdalene)　*as above*

WIGGINTON (St Bartholomew)　*see* Northchurch and Wigginton *St Alb*

WIGGINTON (St Giles)　*see* Hook Norton w Gt Rollright, Swerford etc *Ox*

WIGGINTON (St Leonard) (St James) *Lich 4*　**P** V Tamworth
　V D A DYSON　**NSM** E F M MILLS, R DAVIES
　OLM V B MORRIS

WIGGINTON (St Nicholas)　*see* Haxby and Wigginton *York*

WIGGONHOLT (not known)　*see* Amberley w N Stoke and Parham, Wiggonholt etc *Chich*

WIGHILL (All Saints)　*see* Rural Ainsty *York*

WIGHT, WEST, comprising Brighstone, Brook, Calbourne, Freshwater, Mottistone, Newtown, Shalfleet, Shorwell w Kingston, Thorley, Totland Bay, and Yarmouth *Portsm 7*　**P** Patr Bd　**TR** C TODD　**TV** L C POTTER　**NSM** L M BUSHELL, L M PORTER

WIGHTON (All Saints)　*see* Holkham w Egmere w Warham etc *Nor*

WIGMORE (St James the Apostle)　*see* Wigmore Abbey *Heref*

WIGMORE ABBEY, comprising Adforton, Aston, Brampton Bryan, Burrington, Downton, Elton, Leinthall Starkes, Leintwardine, and Wigmore *Heref 6*　**P** Trustees
　R M D CATLING

WIGSLEY　*see* E Trent *S'well*

WIGSTON (All Saints) (St Wistan) (St Thomas) *Leic 3*
　P *Haberdashers' Co*　**V** T THURSTON-SMITH　**C** C J JOHNSON

WIGSTON (St Wistan)　*see* Wigston *Leic*

WIGSTON MAGNA (All Saints)　*as above*

WIGSTON PARVA (St Mary the Virgin)　*see* Sapcote and Sharnford w Wigston Parva *Leic*

WIGSTON, SOUTH (St Thomas)　*see* Wigston *Leic*

WIGTOFT (St Peter and St Paul)　*see* Haven Gp *Linc*

WIGTON (St Mary) *Carl 3*　**P** *Bp*　**V** G P RAVALDE

WILBARSTON (All Saints)　*see* Stoke Albany w Wilbarston and Ashley etc *Pet*

WILBERFOSS (St John the Baptist) w Kexby *York 5*
　P *Viscount de Vesci and Lord Egremont (alt)*

WILBRAHAM, GREAT (St Nicholas) *Ely 4*　**P** DBP
　V A A GOODMAN　**C** M T PATEMAN

WILBRAHAM, LITTLE (St John) *Ely 4*　**P** CCC Cam
　R A A GOODMAN　**C** M T PATEMAN

WILBURTON (St Peter) *Ely 8*　**P** Adn Ely　**V** F E G BRAMPTON

WILBURY (St Thomas) *St Alb 3*　**P** *Bp*　**V** vacant

WILBY (All Saints)　*see* Quidenham Gp *Nor*

WILBY (St Mary the Virgin)　*see* Gt Doddington and Wilby and Ecton *Pet*

WILBY (St Mary)　*see* Four Rivers *St E*

WILCOT (Holy Cross)　*see* Vale of Pewsey *Sarum*

WILCOTE (St Peter)　*see* Forest Edge *Ox*

WILDBOARCLOUGH (St Saviour)　*see* Sutton, Wincle, Wildboarclough and Bosley *Ches*

WILDEN (All Saints)　*see* Stourport and Wilden *Worc*

WILDEN (St Nicholas) w Colmworth and Ravensden *St Alb 13*　**P** Ld Chan, Bp, and DBP (by turn)
　P-in-c T C WILSON

WILFORD (St Wilfrid) *S'well 6*　**P** Lt Col Peter Clifton
　R vacant

WILFORD HILL (St Paul) *S'well 6*　**P** DBP　**V** T P FOX

WILFORD PENINSULA, The, comprising Alderton, Bawdsey, Boyton, Bromeswell, Butley, Chillesford, Eyke, Hollesley, Iken, Orford, Ramsholt, Rendlesham, Shottisham, Sudbourne, Sutton, Tunstall, and Wantisden *St E 18*　**P** Patr Bd　**TV** M E REYNOLDS, R M HATCHETT

WILKSBY (All Saints)　*see* Fen and Hill Gp *Linc*

WILLAND (St Mary the Virgin), Uffculme, Kentisbeare and Blackborough *Ex 7*　**P** Bp, CPAS, and H Chandler Esq (jt)
　P-in-c S G G TALBOT　**C** J A DALE

WILLASTON (Christ Church) *Ches 9*　**P** DBF
　P-in-c S W BAZELY　**NSM** L R BANNON

WILLASTON (St Luke)　*see* Wistaston *Ches*

WILLEN (St Mary Magdalene)　*see* Stantonbury and Willen *Ox*

WILLENHALL (Holy Trinity)　*see* Bentley Em and Willenhall H Trin *Lich*

WILLENHALL (St Anne) *Lich 28*　**P** Mrs L Grant-Wilson
　V vacant

WILLENHALL (St Giles) *Lich 28*　**P** Trustees　**V** vacant

WILLENHALL (St John the Divine) *Cov 1*　**P** V Cov H Trin
　V P I A HOWELL　**C** C L JACKSON

WILLENHALL (St Stephen) *Lich 28*　**P** *Bp*
　OLM M P BATCHELOR

WILLERBY (St Luke)　*see* Kirk Ella and Willerby *York*

WILLERBY (St Peter)　*see* Hertford *York*

WILLERSEY (St Peter)　*see* Vale and Cotswold Edge *Glouc*

WILLESBOROUGH (St Mary the Virgin)　*see* Ashford Town *Cant*

WILLESDEN (St Mark)　*see* Kensal Rise St Mark *Lon*

WILLESDEN (St Martin)　*see* Kensal Rise St Martin *Lon*

WILLESDEN (St Mary) *Lon 21*　**P** D&C St Paul's
　V C P PHILLIPS

WILLESDEN (St Matthew) *Lon 21*　**P** *Bp*　**V** A J TEATHER

WILLESDEN GREEN (St Andrew) (St Francis of Assisi) *Lon 21*　**P** *Bp*　**V** C P M PATTERSON

WILLEY (St Leonard)　*see* Revel Gp *Cov*

WILLIAN (All Saints)　*see* Letchworth St Paul w Willian *St Alb*

WILLINGALE (St Christopher)　*see* Fyfield, Moreton w Bobbingworth etc *Chelmsf*

WILLINGDON (St Mary the Virgin) *Chich 14*　**P** D&C
　V K R C AGNEW　**NSM** M F WOODWARD, S A WILKINSON

WILLINGHAM (St Mary and All Saints) *Ely 6*　**P** *Bp*
　P-in-c S D GILL　**C** E R COPE

WILLINGHAM BY STOW (St Helen)　*see* Stow Gp *Linc*

WILLINGHAM, NORTH (St Thomas)　*see* Walesby Gp *Linc*

WILLINGHAM, SOUTH (St Martin)　*see* Barkwith Gp *Linc*

WILLINGTON (St Lawrence)　*see* Cople, Moggerhanger and Willington *St Alb*

WILLINGTON (St Michael) *Derby 7*　**P** CPAS　**V** S A STARKEY

WILLINGTON (St Stephen)　*see* Hunwick and Willington *Dur*

WILLINGTON QUAY (St Paul)　*see* Willington *Newc*

WILLINGTON Team, The (Good Shepherd) (St Mary the Virgin) (St Paul) *Newc 5*   **P** *The Crown*   **TR** S MCCORMACK   **TV** J MOONEY   **NSM** E M K WATSON

WILLISHAM (St Mary)   *see* S Bosmere *St E*

WILLITON (St Peter)   *see* Watchet and Williton *B & W*

WILLOUGHBY (St Helen)   *see* Alford Gp *Linc*

WILLOUGHBY (St Nicholas)   *see* Leam Valley *Cov*

WILLOUGHBY WATERLEYS (St Mary)   *see* Four Saints *Leic*

WILLOUGHBY-ON-THE-WOLDS (St Mary and All Saints) w Wysall and Widmerpool *S'well 5*   **P** *MMCET*   **R** S D HIPPISLEY-COX

WILLOUGHTON (St Andrew)   *see* Trentcliffe Gp *Linc*

WILMCOTE (St Andrew)   *see* Aston Cantlow and Wilmcote w Billesley *Cov*

WILMINGTON (St Mary and St Peter)   *see* Arlington, Berwick, Selmeston w Alciston etc *Chich*

WILMINGTON (St Michael) *Roch 2*   **P** *D&C*   **V** C M CHAMBERS

WILMSLOW (St Bartholomew) *Ches 12*   **P** *Bp*   **R** C E THROUP   **C** K E ALLAN   **NSM** R A YATES

WILNE (St Chad) and Draycott w Breaston *Derby 8*   **P** *Bp*   **R** C J SMEDLEY   **NSM** G W DUNDAS

WILNECOTE (Holy Trinity) *Lich 4*   **P** *V Tamworth*   **V** O HARRISON

WILSDEN (St Matthew)   *see* Harden and Wilsden, Cullingworth and Denholme *Leeds*

WILSFORD (St Mary)   *see* E Loveden *Linc*

WILSFORD (St Michael)   *see* Woodford Valley w Archers Gate *Sarum*

WILSFORD (St Nicholas)   *see* Cannings and Redhorn *Sarum*

WILSHAMSTEAD (All Saints) and Houghton Conquest *St Alb 9*   **P** *St Jo Coll Cam and Bp (alt)*   **V** S J TOZE

WILSHAW (St Mary)   *see* Meltham *Leeds*

WILSILL (St Michael and All Angels)   *see* Upper Nidderdale *Leeds*

WILSTHORPE (St Faith)   *see* Uffington Gp *Linc*

WILSTONE (St Cross)   *see* Tring *St Alb*

WILTON (St Cuthbert) *York 16*   **P** *Abp*   **V** *vacant*

WILTON (St George) *B & W 18*   **P** *Mrs E C Cutbush*   **V** G H J CLAPHAM

WILTON (St George)   *see* Thornton Dale w Allerston, Ebberston etc *York*

WILTON (St Mary and St Nicholas) w Netherhampton and Fugglestone *Sarum 11*   **P** *Earl of Pembroke*   **R** M R WOOD   **NSM** S C TITLEY, S M WOOD

WILTON PLACE (St Paul) *Lon 3*   **P** *Bp*   **V** A G GYLE   **Hon C** N S MERCER

WIMBISH (All Saints)   *see* Saffron Walden and Villages *Chelmsf*

WIMBLEDON (Emmanuel) Ridgway Proprietary Chapel *S'wark 13*   **C** J F ADAMS, J SKIDMORE   **Min** R A R WEEKES

WIMBLEDON (St Luke)   *see* Wimbledon Park St Luke *S'wark*

WIMBLEDON (St Mary) (St Matthew) (St Mark) (St John the Baptist) *S'wark 13*   **P** *Patr Bd*   **TR** A J HODGSON   **TV** C B GARDNER, H C ORCHARD, S P A EDMONDS   **C** Y KOH   **Hon C** N H S BERSWEDEN

WIMBLEDON PARK (St Luke) *S'wark 13*   **P** *Simeon's Trustees*   **V** R J R PAICE   **C** A P O'BRIEN

WIMBLEDON PARK (St Paul)   *see* Wandsworth St Paul *S'wark*

WIMBLEDON, SOUTH (All Saints) *S'wark 13*   **P** *Bp*   **P-in-c** C W NOKE

WIMBLEDON, SOUTH (Holy Trinity and St Peter)   *see* Merton Priory *S'wark*

WIMBLEDON, SOUTH (St Andrew) *S'wark 13*   **P** *Bp*   **P-in-c** C J D LAMONT   **C** B W RICKARDS

WIMBLEDON, WEST (Christ Church) *S'wark 13*   **P** *TR Wimbledon*   **V** M J BURNS

WIMBLINGTON (St Peter)   *see* Doddington w Benwick and Wimblington *Ely*

WIMBORNE (St John the Evangelist)   *see* New Borough and Leigh *Sarum*

WIMBORNE MINSTER (St Cuthberga) and the Northern Villages, including Hinton Martel, Holt, Horton and Chalbury, and Witchampton, Stanbridge and Long Crichel w More Crichel *Sarum 9*   **P** *Governors of Wimborne Minster (3 turns), DBP (1 turn)*   **R** A J W ROWLAND   **C** S C ALLEN   **NSM** H WALDSALL, W S FRENCH

WIMBORNE ST GILES (St Giles)   *see* Cranborne w Boveridge, Edmondsham etc *Sarum*

WIMBOTSHAM (St Mary)   *see* W Norfolk Priory Gp *Ely*

WIMPOLE (St Andrew)   *see* Orwell Gp *Ely*

WINCANTON (St Peter and St Paul) *B & W 2*   **P** *D&C*   **R** *vacant*

WINCH, WEST (St Mary)   *see* Middlewinch *Nor*

WINCHCOMBE (St Peter) *Glouc 9*   **P** *Patr Bd*   **P-in-c** J P HOSKINS   **TV** J A HOOK, J A NEWCOMBE   **C** R E MURRAY

WINCHELSEA (St Thomas) (St Richard) and Icklesham *Chich 17*   **P** *Bp and Guild of All So (jt)*   **R** J P MEYER

WINCHENDON, NETHER (St Nicholas)   *see* Long Crendon w Chearsley and Nether Winchendon *Ox*

WINCHENDON, OVER (St Mary Magdalene)   *see* Schorne *Ox*

WINCHESTER (All Saints)   *see* E Win *Win*

WINCHESTER (Christ Church) *Win 7*   **P** *Simeon's Trustees*   **V** S J L CANSDALE   **C** G A WATKINSON   **NSM** B R WAKELIN

WINCHESTER (Holy Trinity) *Win 7*   **P** *Bp*   **R** *vacant*

WINCHESTER (St Barnabas) *Win 7*   **P** *Bp*   **P-in-c** E P A DINES   **C** M R GARDNER

WINCHESTER (St Bartholomew) (St Lawrence) (St Swithun-upon-Kingsgate) *Win 7*   **P** *Ld Chan*   **P-in-c** K P KOUSSEFF   **NSM** A GOULDING

WINCHESTER (St Cross Hospital w St Faith) *Win 7*   **P** *Bp*   **P-in-c** P L KRINKS   **NSM** H L HEALEY

WINCHESTER (St John the Baptist w St Martin Winnall)   *see* E Win *Win*

WINCHESTER (St Luke)   *see* Stanmore *Win*

WINCHESTER (St Matthew) (St Paul's Mission Church) *Win 7*   **P** *Bp*   **R** N P SEAL   **NSM** E B STUART, M C COPPING

WINCHESTER, EAST (All Saints), including Chilcomb *Win 7*   **P** *Bp and Ld Chan (alt)*   **P-in-c** M J GRIFFITHS   **NSM** C M SMITH

WINCHFIELD (St Mary the Virgin)   *see* Hartley Wintney, Elvetham, Winchfield etc *Win*

WINCHMORE HILL (Holy Trinity) *Lon 18*   **P** *V Winchmore Hill St Paul*   **P-in-c** R D E BOLTON

WINCHMORE HILL (St Paul) *Lon 18*   **P** *V Edmonton*   **V** D P SANDHAM   **NSM** C B ZUCKERT

WINCLE (St Michael)   *see* Sutton, Wincle, Wildboarclough and Bosley *Ches*

WINCOBANK (St Thomas)   *see* Brightside w Wincobank *Sheff*

WINDERMERE (St Martin) and St John *Carl 11*   **P** *Bp and Trustees (jt)*   **R** J J RICHARDS

WINDERMERE (St Mary) Applethwaite and Troutbeck *Carl 11*   **P** *Bp*   **V** D M B WILMOT   **C** J C GILLESPIE

WINDHILL (Christ Church) *Leeds 1*   **P** *Bp*   **P-in-c** M E WATSON

WINDLESHAM (St John the Baptist) *Guildf 6*   **P** *Ld Chan*   **R** J HILLMAN

WINDMILL, The, comprising Burstow, Horne, and Outwood *S'wark 25*   **P** *Ld Chan (1 turn), Bp (2 turns)*   **R** N J CALVER   **NSM** C E SARGENT

WINDRUSH (St Peter)   *see* Sherborne, Windrush, the Barringtons etc *Glouc*

WINDRUSH, LOWER, comprising Northmoor, Standlake, Stanton Harcourt, and Yelford *Ox 28*   **P** *Bp, DBP, St Jo Coll Ox, D&C Ex, and B Babington-Smith Esq (jt)*   **R** *vacant*

WINDSOR, NEW (Holy Trinity) (St John the Baptist w All Saints) *Ox 5*   **P** *Ld Chan*   **TR** S N LODGE

WINDSOR, OLD (St Peter and St Andrew) (St Luke's Mission Room) *Ox 5*   **P** *Ld Chan*   **V** A S M SHOKRALLA

WINDY NOOK (St Alban) *Dur 11*   **P** *V Heworth St Mary*   **P-in-c** D M LINDLEY   **NSM** K COULSON

WINESTEAD (St German)   *see* Easington w Skeffling, Keyingham, Ottringham etc *York*

WINFARTHING (St Mary) w Shelfanger w Burston w Gissing and Tivetshall *Nor 10*   **P** *Ld Chan, Bp, and DBP (jt), Hertf Coll Ox (alt)*   **R** D F MILLS

WINFORD (Blessed Virgin Mary and St Peter) w Felton Common Hill *B & W 9*   **P** *Worc Coll Ox and Mrs H D Pullman (jt)*   **R** *vacant*

WINFORTON (St Michael and All Angels)   *see* Eardisley w Bollingham, Willersley, Brilley etc *Heref*

WINFRITH NEWBURGH (St Christopher)   *see* The Lulworths, Winfrith Newburgh and Chaldon *Sarum*

WING (St Peter and St Paul)   *see* Empingham, Edith Weston, Lyndon, Manton etc *Pet*

WING w Grove (All Saints)   *see* Cottesloe *Ox*

WINGATE GRANGE (Holy Trinity)   *see* Wheatley Hill, Thornley and Wingate w Hutton Henry *Dur*

WINGATES (St John the Evangelist)   *see* Blackrod, Daisy Hill, Westhoughton and Wingates *Man*

WINGERWORTH (All Saints) *Derby 3*   **P** *Bp*   **R** J D POSTON   **OLM** J A WILLIS

WINGFIELD (St Andrew)   *see* Athelington, Denham, Horham, Hoxne etc *St E*

WINGFIELD (St Mary)   *see* Bradford on Avon H Trin, Westwood and Wingfield *Sarum*

WINGFIELD, NORTH (St Lawrence), Clay Cross and Pilsley *Derby 2*   **P** *Bp*   **TR** C COOPER   **TV** L C HAYLER, R A K LAW   **C** A B ALLISON, M H BOWN, R G LAWRENCE

WINGFIELD, SOUTH (All Saints) *see* Crich and S Wingfield *Derby*

WINGHAM (St Mary the Virgin) *see* Canonry *Cant*

WINGRAVE (St Peter and St Paul) *see* Cottesloe *Ox*

WINKBURN (St John of Jerusalem) *S'well 3* **P** *Bp* **P-in-c** C G PEARSE **NSM** M A GROVES

WINKFIELD (St Mary the Virgin) and Cranbourne *Ox 3* **P** *Bp* **V** T H MORDECAI

WINKLEBURY (Good Shepherd) and Worting *Win 4* **P** *MMCET* **R** J A K WIGMORE **C** T W DENNIS

WINKLEIGH (All Saints) *Ex 19* **P** *D&C* **P-in-c** H S E BLAINE

WINKSLEY (St Cuthbert and St Oswald) *see* Fountains Gp *Leeds*

WINLATON (St Paul) *Dur 12* **P** *Bp* **R** *vacant*

WINMARLEIGH (St Luke) *see* Cockerham w Winmarleigh and Glasson *Blackb*

WINNERSH (St Mary the Virgin) *Ox 8* **P** *Bp* **P-in-c** J R WARREN

WINNINGTON (St Luke) *see* Northwich St Luke *Ches*

WINSCOMBE (St James) and Sandford *B & W 10* **P** *D&C* **C** A J HISCOX

WINSFORD (St Mary Magdalene) *see* Exmoor *B & W*

WINSHAM (St Stephen) *see* Chaffcombe, Cricket Malherbie etc *B & W*

WINSHILL (St Mark) *Derby 7* **P** *Lady H M Gretton and Baroness Gretton (jt)* **P-in-c** P R BOSHER, F D STARTIN

WINSLEY (St Nicholas) *see* N Bradford on Avon and Villages *Sarum*

WINSLOW (St Laurence) w Great Horwood and Addington *Ox 13* **P** *Ld Chan (3 turns), New Coll Ox (2 turns), and DBP (1 turn)* **R** R A LIGHTBOWN **C** M NELSON

WINSMOOR, comprising Barrington, Chillington, Cudworth, Dowlishwake, Kingstone, Puckington, Shepton Beauchamp, and Stocklinch *B & W 14* **P** *Bp, D&C, CR, and P G H Speke Esq (jt)* **V** G A WADE

WINSON (St Michael) *see* S Cotswolds *Glouc*

WINSTER (Holy Trinity) *Carl 10* **P** *V Kendal H Trin* **P-in-c** M D WOODCOCK

WINSTER (St John the Baptist) *see* Darley, S Darley and Winster *Derby*

WINSTON (St Andrew) *Dur 6* **P** *Bp* **P-in-c** E K G HARROP

WINSTON (St Andrew) *see* Debenham and Helmingham *St E*

WINSTONE (St Bartholomew) *see* Brimpsfield w Birdlip, Syde, Daglingworth etc *Glouc*

WINTERBORNE CLENSTON (St Nicholas) *see* Winterborne Valley and Milton Abbas *Sarum*

WINTERBORNE HOUGHTON (St Andrew) *as above*

WINTERBORNE KINGSTON (St Nicholas) *see* Red Post *Sarum*

WINTERBORNE STICKLAND (St Mary) *see* Winterborne Valley and Milton Abbas *Sarum*

WINTERBORNE VALLEY and Milton Abbas, The *Sarum 6* **P** *Bp (3 turns) and P D H Chichester Esq (1 turn)* **P-in-c** A J RYAN

WINTERBORNE WHITECHURCH (St Mary) *see* Winterborne Valley and Milton Abbas *Sarum*

WINTERBOURNE (St James) *see* E Downland *Ox*

WINTERBOURNE (St Michael the Archangel) *see* Fromeside *Bris*

WINTERBOURNE ABBAS (St Mary) *see* Dorchester and the Winterbournes *Sarum*

WINTERBOURNE BASSETT (St Katharine) *see* Upper Kennet *Sarum*

WINTERBOURNE DOWN (All Saints) *see* Fromeside *Bris*

WINTERBOURNE EARLS (St Michael and All Angels) *see* Bourne Valley *Sarum*

WINTERBOURNE GUNNER (St Mary) *as above*

WINTERBOURNE MONKTON (St Mary Magdalene) *see* Upper Kennet *Sarum*

WINTERBOURNE MONKTON (St Simon and St Jude) *see* Dorchester and the Winterbournes *Sarum*

WINTERBOURNE ST MARTIN (St Martin) *as above*

WINTERBOURNE STEEPLETON (St Michael) *as above*

WINTERBOURNE STOKE (St Peter) *see* Wylye and Till Valley *Sarum*

WINTERBOURNE ZELSTONE (St Mary) *see* Red Post *Sarum*

WINTERINGHAM (All Saints) *see* Winterton Gp *Linc*

WINTERSLOW (All Saints) *see* Clarendon *Sarum*

WINTERSLOW (St John) *as above*

WINTERTON (Holy Trinity and All Saints) *see* Flegg Coastal Benefice *Nor*

WINTERTON Group, The (All Saints), including Appleby, Roxby, and Winteringham *Linc 6* **P** *Bp, Lord St Oswald, Exors Capt J G G P Elwes, and Em Coll Cam (jt)* **V** A C NUNN **NSM** P A COOKE **OLM** J J WHITEHEAD

WINTHORPE (All Saints) *see* E Trent *S'well*

WINTHORPE (St Mary) *see* Skegness Gp *Linc*

WINTON (St Alban), Moordown and Charminster *Win 8* **P** *Bp* **V** M E SMITH **C** J M SHARP **NSM** J L WILLIAMS

WINTON (St Mary Magdalene) *see* Barton w Peel Green and Winton *Man*

WINWICK (All Saints) *see* N Leightonstone *Ely*

WINWICK (St Michael and All Angels) *see* Long Buckby w Watford and W Haddon w Winwick *Pet*

WINWICK (St Oswald) *Liv 13* **P** *Bp* **R** J L STEVENTON **NSM** V M HANCOCK

WIRKSWORTH (St Mary), including Bonsall, Bradbourne, Brassington, Carsington, Elton, Idridgehay, Kirk Ireton, Middleton, and Wirksworth *Derby 1* **P** *Bp* **TR** D C TRUBY **TV** C A T L VICENCIO PRIOR **NSM** K J ORFORD, R H PRINCE

WISBECH (St Augustine) *Ely 14* **P** *Bp* **V** *vacant*

WISBECH (St Peter and St Paul) *Ely 14* **P** *Bp* **P-in-c** M L BRADBURY **C** C J WILKINSON

WISBECH ST MARY (St Mary) and Guyhirn w Ring's End and Gorefield and Southea w Murrow and Parson Drove *Ely 14* **P** *Bp* **P-in-c** R D PARKINSON

WISBOROUGH GREEN (St Peter ad Vincula) *Chich 10* **P** *Bp Lon* **P-in-c** C R JENKINS

WISHAW (St Chad) *see* Curdworth, Middleton and Wishaw *Birm*

WISHFORD, GREAT (St Giles) *see* Wylye and Till Valley *Sarum*

WISKE Benefice, The, comprising Birkby, Danby Wiske w Hutton Bonville, Great Smeaton w Appleton Wiske, and the Cowtons *Leeds 22* **P** *MMCET and DBP (jt)* **P-in-c** L C THORIUS **Hon C** S J GOLDING

WISLEY (not known) w Pyrford *Guildf 12* **P** *Bp* **R** N J AIKEN **C** M R A POTTER

WISSETT (St Andrew) *see* Blyth Valley *St E*

WISSEY VALLEY Benefice, The, comprising Barton Bendish, Beachamwell w Shingham, Boughton, Methwold, Wereham, West Dereham, Whittington, and Wretton w Stoke Ferry *Ely 9* **P** *Ld Chan (1 turn), Bp, DBP and Ch Patr Trust (2 turns)* **R** K R WATERS **C** C NICHOLAS-LETCH

WISSINGTON (St Mary the Virgin) *see* Nayland w Wiston *St E*

WISTANSTOW (Holy Trinity) *Heref 10* **P** *Bp* **R** *vacant*

WISTASTON (St Mary) *Ches 15* **P** *Trustees* **R** M F TURNBULL **C** P A NORTH

WISTOW (All Saints) *see* Cawood w Ryther and Wistow *York*

WISTOW (St John the Baptist) *see* Warboys w Broughton and Bury w Wistow *Ely*

WISTOW (St Wistan) *Leic 3* **P** *Bp and The Hon Ann Brooks (jt)* **V** P J O'REILLY **C** S D MATTHEWS

WITCHAM (St Martin) w Mepal *Ely 8* **P** *D&C* **R** M HANCOCK

WITCHAMPTON (St Mary and St Cuthberga and All Saints) *see* Wimborne Minster and the N Villages *Sarum*

WITCHFORD (St Andrew) w Wentworth *Ely 8* **P** *D&C* **P-in-c** F E G BRAMPTON

WITCHINGHAM GREAT (St Mary) *see* Reepham and Wensum Valley *Nor*

WITCOMBE, GREAT (St Mary) *see* Badgeworth, Shurdington and Witcombe w Bentham *Glouc*

WITHAM (St Nicolas) and Villages, including Fairstead, Faulkbourne, Rivenhall and Silver End, Terling, and White Notley *Chelmsf 24* **P** *Patr Bd* **TV** P S G WATKIN **C** C A NEWMARCH, W ABBOTT **NSM** G P DOWLING, S M MALAM

WITHAM FRIARY (Blessed Virgin Mary and St John the Baptist and All Saints) *see* Nunney and Witham Friary, Marston Bigot etc *B & W*

WITHAM Group, The, comprising Gunby, North Witham, South Witham, and Stainby *Linc 17* **P** *Sir Lyonel Tollemache Bt, J R Thorold Esq, and Bp (jt)* **R** *vacant*

WITHAM, NORTH (St Mary) *see* Witham Gp *Linc*

WITHAM, SOUTH (St John the Baptist) *as above*

WITHAM-ON-THE-HILL (St Andrew) *see* Edenham w Witham on the Hill and Swinstead *Linc*

WITHAMSIDE, comprising Auborn, Bassingham, Carlton-le-Moorland, Norton Disney, Stapleford, and Thurlby *Linc 12* **P** *Lady Jean Nevile, CCC Ox, Lord Middleton, Bp, and W R S Brown Esq (jt)* **R** D L FREEMAN

WITHCALL (St Martin) *see* Legbourne and Wold Marsh *Linc*

WITHERIDGE (St John the Baptist) *see* Burrington, Chawleigh, Cheldon, Chulmleigh etc *Ex*

WITHERLEY (St Peter) *see* Fenn Lanes Gp *Leic*

WITHERNWICK (St Alban) *see* Aldbrough, Mappleton w Goxhill and Withernwick *York*

WITHERSDALE (St Mary Magdalene) *see* Sancroft *St E*

WITHERSFIELD (St Mary the Virgin) *see* Haverhill w Withersfield *St E*

WITHERSLACK (St Paul) *Carl 10* **P** *DBP*
 P-in-c M D WOODCOCK
WITHIEL (St Clement) *see* St Wenn and Withiel *Truro*
WITHIEL FLOREY (St Mary Magdalene) *see* Dulverton w
 Brushford, Brompton Regis etc *B & W*
WITHINGTON (St Christopher) *see* W Didsbury and
 Withington St Chris *Man*
WITHINGTON (St Crispin) *Man 3* **P** *Bp* **R** P C S DAVIES
WITHINGTON (St John the Baptist) *see* Wrockwardine
 Deanery *Lich*
WITHINGTON (St Michael and All Angels) *see*
 Sevenhampton w Charlton Abbots, Hawling etc *Glouc*
WITHINGTON (St Paul) *Man 6* **P** *Trustees*
 R H M CORCORAN **C** M P CORCORAN
WITHINGTON (St Peter) *see* Bartestree Cross *Heref*
WITHINGTON, LOWER (St Peter) *see* Chelford and Lower
 Withington w Marthall *Ches*
WITHLEIGH (St Catherine) *see* Washfield, Stoodleigh,
 Withleigh etc *Ex*
WITHNELL (St Paul) *see* Heapey and Withnell *Blackb*
WITHYBROOK (All Saints) *see* Wolvey, Copston Magna and
 Withybrook *Cov*
WITHYCOMBE (St Nicholas) *see* Dunster, Carhampton,
 Withycombe w Rodhuish etc *B & W*
**WITHYCOMBE RALEIGH (St John the Evangelist) (St John
 in the Wilderness) (All Saints)** *Ex 1* **P** *Patr Bd*
 TR R SELLERS **TV** O MURPHY, S J HOYLE
WITHYHAM (St John the Evangelist) *see* Crowborough St Jo
 Chich
WITHYHAM (St Michael and All Angels) *Chich 16* **P** *Earl De
 la Warr* **R** J M CAMPBELL
WITHYPOOL (St Andrew) *see* Exmoor *B & W*
WITHYWOOD (shared church) *Bris 1* **P** *Bp*
 P-in-c D A J MADDOX
WITLEY (All Saints) *Guildf 4* **P** *Bp* **V** J O MCKERAN
WITLEY, GREAT (St Michael) *see* Shrawley, Witley, Astley and
 Abberley *Worc*
WITLEY, LITTLE (St Michael) *as above*
WITNESHAM (St Mary) *see* Westerfield and Tuddenham w
 Witnesham *St E*
WITNEY (St Mary the Virgin) (Holy Trinity) *Ox 28* **P** *Patr
 Bd* **TR** T C WRIGHT **TV** V J WHIFFIN **C** H R B WHITE,
 J HANCE, R A MEIKLE **Hon C** M W THOMAS, S J WRIGHT
 NSM J R COLLICUTT MCGRATH
WITTENHAM, LITTLE (St Peter) *see* Dorchester *Ox*
WITTERING (All Saints) *see* Barnack w Ufford, Bainton,
 Helpston and Wittering *Pet*
WITTERING, EAST (St Anne) *see* Earnley and E Wittering
 Chich
**WITTERING, WEST (St Peter and St Paul) and Birdham w
 Itchenor** *Chich 2* **P** *Bp* **R** J R SWINDELLS
 Hon C C J HANKINS **NSM** B F HOLBEN, J M MOULD,
 S J MANOUCH
WITTERSHAM (St John the Baptist) *see* Tenterden, Rother
 and Oxney *Cant*
WITTON (St Helen) *Ches 6* **P** *Bp* **NSM** D A DALBY,
 S J MILLINCHIP
WITTON (St Margaret) *see* Bacton, Happisburgh, Hempstead
 w Eccles etc *Nor*
WITTON (St Margaret) *see* Gt and Lt Plumstead, Rackheath
 w Salhouse and Witton *Nor*
WITTON GILBERT (St Michael and All Angels) *see* Dur N *Dur*
WITTON LE WEAR (St Philip and St James) *see* Hamsterley
 and Witton-le-Wear *Dur*
WITTON PARK (St Paul) *Dur 5* **P** *Bp* **P-in-c** B E MECHANIC
WITTON, EAST (St John the Evangelist) *see* Middleham w
 Coverdale and E Witton etc *Leeds*
WITTON, NETHER (St Giles) *Newc 11* **P** *Ld Chan*
 P-in-c J P MASON **C** F J SAMPLE
WITTON, WEST (St Bartholomew) *see* Penhill *Leeds*
WIVELISCOMBE (St Andrew) and the Hills *B & W 19* **P** *Bp
 and A H Trollope-Bellew Esq (4 turns), Ld Chan (1 turn)*
 R M J WALKER
WIVELSFIELD (St Peter and St John the Baptist) *Chich 5*
 P *DBP* **V** C J POWELL **C** S D J SHOREY
WIVENHOE (St Mary) *Chelmsf 21* **P** *Bp* **R** E B E LAMMENS
WIVERTON IN THE VALE *S'well 5* **P** *CPAS and Bp, Ld Chan
 (alt)* **R** *vacant*
WIVETON (St Mary) *see* Blakeney w Cley, Wiveton,
 Glandford etc *Nor*
WIX (St Mary the Virgin) *see* Gt Oakley, Wix, Wrabness etc
 Chelmsf
WIXFORD (St Milburga) *see* Heart of England *Cov*
WIXOE (St Leonard) *see* Stour Valley *St E*

**WOBURN (St Mary) w Eversholt, Milton Bryan, Battlesden
 and Pottesgrove** *St Alb 8* **P** *Bedf Estates Trustees*
 V S W NUTH
WOBURN SANDS (St Michael) *St Alb 8* **P** *Bp* **V** D J YOUNG
WOKING (Christ Church) *Guildf 12* **P** *Ridley Hall Cam*
 V P J HARWOOD **C** D V SMITH, P FORD **NSM** M S SMITH,
 P A SIMPSON
WOKING (St John the Baptist) *Guildf 12* **P** *V Woking St Pet*
 V G A LUCAS **C** D NEWMAN
WOKING (St Mary of Bethany) *Guildf 12* **P** *V Woking Ch Ch*
 V M G WALLACE **C** S A TAPP
WOKING (St Paul) *Guildf 12* **P** *Ridley Hall Cam*
 V N P HUTCHINSON
WOKING (St Peter) *Guildf 12* **P** *Patr Bd*
 P-in-c J M G THOMAS **C** S WAAKO
WOKINGHAM (All Saints) *Ox 8* **P** *Bp* **R** D P HODGSON
 C H V HIGGINSON
WOKINGHAM (St Paul) *Ox 8* **P** *DBP* **R** R J LAMEY
 C P J E MUKHOLI **NSM** J H A HATTAWAY, R G HOLMES
WOKINGHAM (St Sebastian) *Ox 8* **P** *Bp* **V** A P MARSDEN
 NSM E C FUDGE
WOLBOROUGH (St Mary) *see* Newton Abbot *Ex*
WOLD (St Andrew) *see* Walgrave w Hannington and Wold
 and Scaldwell *Pet*
WOLD NEWTON (All Saints) *see* Binbrook Gp *Linc*
WOLD NEWTON (All Saints) *see* Rudston, Boynton, Carnaby
 etc *York*
WOLDINGHAM (St Agatha) *see* Caterham *S'wark*
WOLDINGHAM (St Paul) *as above*
WOLDMOOR Group of Parishes, The, comprising Holton le
 Moor, Kirkby w Kingerby, Nettleton, North and South
 Kelsey, North Owersby, Thornton le Moor, and Usselby
 Linc 7 **P** *Bp (3 turns), J M B Young Esq and S B Young Esq
 (1 turn)* **V** M E C TOYNE
WOLDS GATEWAY Group, The, Aylesby, Beelsby, Hatcliffe,
 Healing, Irby on Humber, Keelby, Laceby, Riby, and
 Stallingborough *Linc 4* **P** *DBP, Bp, Earl of Yarborough,
 J E Spilman Esq and Ridley Hall Cam (jt)* **V** P T STEVENS
 C M A HUTSON, P L REEVES **NSM** C MITCHELL
 OLM J M GLOSSOP
WOLDSBURN, comprising Bainton, Garton on the Wolds,
 Kilnwick, Kirkburn, Middleton on the Wolds, and North
 Dalton *York 10* **P** *Abp, St Jo Coll Ox, and A J Page Esq
 (1 turn), and Ld Chan (1 turn)* **P-in-c** J V ANDERSON
WOLFERTON (St Peter) *see* Sandringham w W Newton and
 Appleton etc *Nor*
WOLFORD (St Michael) *see* S Warks Seven Gp *Cov*
WOLLASTON (St James) *see* Norton and Wollaston *Worc*
**WOLLASTON (St Mary) w Strixton and Bozeat and Easton
 Maudit** *Pet 6* **P** *Bp and Marquess of Northn (jt)*
 V A I MORTON **C** D J AIREY
WOLLASTON, GREAT (All Saints) *see* Ford, Gt Wollaston and
 Alberbury w Cardeston *Heref*
WOLLASTON, GREAT (St John the Baptist) *as above*
WOLLATON (St Leonard) *S'well 8* **P** *Lord Middleton*
 R T J PULLEN **NSM** K A HANFORD
WOLLATON PARK (St Mary) *S'well 9* **P** *CPAS* **V** J H CURRAN
WOLLESCOTE (St Andrew) *Worc 12* **P** *Bp* **V** *vacant*
WOLSINGHAM (St Mary and St Stephen) and Thornley
 Dur 8 **P** *Bp* **P-in-c** J P L WHALLEY
WOLSTANTON (St Margaret) *Lich 9* **P** *Bp*
 P-in-c T B BLOOR **C** P M GRIFFIN
WOLSTON (St Margaret) and Church Lawford *Cov 6*
 P *DBP (2 turns), Bp (1 turn)* **V** K J FLANAGAN
 Hon C P A H SIMMONDS
WOLVERCOTE (St Peter) and Wytham *Ox 2* **P** *Ch Ch Ox
 and Mert Coll Ox (jt)* **V** C J DRAPER **C** S L FLASHMAN
 NSM S A CROWTHER, W H WHYTE
WOLVERHAMPTON (All Saints) *see* Cen Wolverhampton
 Lich
WOLVERHAMPTON (St Andrew) *Lich 27* **P** *Bp*
 V C L THOMAS
WOLVERHAMPTON (St Chad and St Mark) *see* Cen
 Wolverhampton *Lich*
WOLVERHAMPTON (St John) *as above*
WOLVERHAMPTON (St Jude) *Lich 27* **P** *CPAS*
 V P S ROBERTSON
WOLVERHAMPTON (St Luke) Blakenhall *Lich 27* **P** *Trustees*
 V R J ESPIN-BRADLEY
WOLVERHAMPTON (St Martin) (St Stephen) *Lich 27* **P** *Bp*
 NSM A H HUTCHINSON, R C GILBERT
WOLVERHAMPTON (St Matthew) *Lich 27* **P** *Baldwin Pugh
 Trustees* **V** M HIRD **C** G K GREENWAY **OLM** L M VAWER
WOLVERHAMPTON (St Peter) *see* Cen Wolverhampton *Lich*
WOLVERHAMPTON Pond Lane (Mission Hall) *see*
 Wolverhampton St Luke *Lich*

WOLVERHAMPTON, CENTRAL (All Saints) (St Chad and St Mark) (St John in the Square) (St Peter) *Lich 27* **P** *Patr Bd* **TR** D W WRIGHT **TV** R G GASTON **C** A K WALSH, H BABIY

WOLVERLEY (St John the Baptist) *see* Kidderminster Ismere *Worc*

WOLVERTON (Holy Trinity) (St George the Martyr) *Ox 14* **P** *Bp* **R** G S BARROW-JONES

WOLVERTON (St Catherine) *see* Baughurst, Ramsdell, Wolverton w Ewhurst etc *Win*

WOLVERTON (St Mary the Virgin) *see* Arden Valley *Cov*

WOLVEY (St John the Baptist), Copston Magna and Withybrook *Cov 5* **P** *Bp* **V** J M VAUGHAN

WOLVISTON (St Peter) *see* Billingham *Dur*

WOMBOURNE (St Benedict) *see* Smestow Vale *Lich*

WOMBRIDGE (St Mary and St Leonard) *Lich 20* **P** W J *Charlton Meyrick Esq* **P-in-c** K S EVANS

WOMBWELL (St Mary) (St George) *Sheff 12* **P** *Trin Coll Cam* **R** J G ARMSTRONG

WOMERSLEY (St Martin) *Leeds 18* **P** *Earl of Rosse* **V** A C MARTLEW

WONERSH (St John the Baptist) w Blackheath *Guildf 2* **P** *Selw Coll Cam* **NSM** D PETERS, K L PAKENHAM

WONSTON (Holy Trinity) *see* Upper Dever *Win*

WONSTON, SOUTH (St Margaret) *see* Lower Dever *Win*

WOOBURN (St Paul) *Ox 18* **P** *Bp* **V** M J WALLINGTON

WOOD DALLING (St Andrew) *see* Reepham and Wensum Valley *Nor*

WOOD DITTON (St Mary) w Saxon Street *Ely 4* **P** *Duke of Sutherland* **V** vacant

WOOD END (St Chad) *Cov 1* **P** *Ld Chan* **V** B J NASH

WOOD END (St Michael and All Angels) *see* Baxterley w Hurley and Wood End and Merevale etc *Birm*

WOOD GREEN (St Michael) w Bounds Green (St Gabriel) (St Michael-at-Bowes) *Lon 19* **P** *Patr Bd* **TR** I G BOOTH **TV** E YILDIRIM **C** A P R COATES

WOOD GREEN (St Paul) *see* Wednesbury St Paul Wood Green *Lich*

WOOD NORTON (All Saints) *see* Heart of Norfolk *Nor*

WOOD STREET (St Alban) *see* Worplesdon *Guildf*

WOODBASTWICK (St Fabian and St Sebastian) *see* Broadside *Nor*

WOODBOROUGH (St Mary Magdalene) *see* Vale of Pewsey *Sarum*

WOODBOROUGH (St Swithun) *see* Epperstone, Gonalston, Oxton and Woodborough *S'well*

WOODBRIDGE (St John the Evangelist) and Bredfield *St E 18* **P** *Ch Patr Trust (3 turns), and Ld Chan (1 turn)* **V** C E HOWARD **NSM** A WILLIAMS, M M E ROBERTS, W HERBERT

WOODBRIDGE (St Mary the Virgin) *St E 18* **P** *Bp* **R** K S MCCORMACK **NSM** M J HARE

WOODBRIDGE, comprising Brinkworth, Dauntsey, Garsdon, Great Somerford, Lea and Cleverton, and Little Somerford *Bris 6* **P** *Bp, Ch Soc Trust, and Ex Coll Ox (jt)* **R** S WILKINSON **OLM** M J GRAHAM

WOODBURY (Holy Cross) *see* Axminster, Chardstock, All Saints etc *Ex*

WOODBURY (St Swithun) *see* Aylesbeare, Clyst St George, Clyst St Mary etc *Ex*

WOODBURY SALTERTON (Holy Trinity) *as above*

WOODCHESTER (St Mary) *see* Rodborough, Woodchester and Brimscombe *Glouc*

WOODCHURCH (All Saints) *see* Bethersden w High Halden and Woodchurch *Cant*

WOODCHURCH (Holy Cross) *Ches 1* **P** *DBP* **R** C J BROAD **NSM** J TUPLIN

WOODCOTE (St Leonard) *see* Langtree *Ox*

WOODCOTE (St Mark) *see* Purley St Mark and St Swithun *S'wark*

WOODCOTT (St James) *see* Hurstbourne Priors, Longparish etc *Win*

WOODDITTON (St Mary) *see* Wood Ditton w Saxon Street *Ely*

WOODEATON (Holy Rood) *see* Ray Valley *Ox*

WOODFIELD Team Benefice, The, comprising Appleby Magna and Swepstone w Snarestone and Norton-juxta-Twycross, Donisthorpe, Measham, Normanton le Heath, and Packington *Leic 8* **P** *Patr Bd (6 turns), The Crown (1 turn), Ld Chan (1 turn)* **TR** V M ELPHICK **C** J DYER **NSM** W T COLLEY

WOODFORD (All Saints) *see* Woodford Valley w Archers Gate *Sarum*

WOODFORD (Christ Church) *Ches 12* **P** W A B *Davenport Esq* **V** D J T RUSSELL

WOODFORD (St Barnabas) *Chelmsf 6* **P** *Bp* **V** W OBEDOZA

WOODFORD (St Mary the Virgin) *see* Irthlingborough, Gt Addington, Lt Addington etc *Pet*

WOODFORD (St Mary w St Philip and St James) *Chelmsf 6* **P** *Bp* **R** I D TARRANT

WOODFORD BRIDGE (St Paul) *Chelmsf 6* **P** R *Woodford* **V** O FRANKLIN

WOODFORD HALSE (St Mary the Virgin) *see* Aston-le-Walls, Byfield, Boddington, Eydon etc *Pet*

WOODFORD VALLEY w Archers Gate, including the Durnfords and Wilsford cum Lake *Sarum 14* **P** *Bp* **V** M J M PERRY

WOODFORD WELLS (All Saints) (St Andrew) *Chelmsf 6* **P** *Trustees* **V** P G HARCOURT **C** A J TODD, G L WILSON, G R M DICKS, M P CASTLETON, S D POLLARD, T P JEE **NSM** D J BLACKLEDGE, D J MARTIN, M D PORTER

WOODFORD, SOUTH (Holy Trinity) *see* Wanstead H Trin Hermon Hill *Chelmsf*

WOODGATE VALLEY (St Francis) *see* Bartley Green *Birm*

WOODGREEN (St Boniface) *see* Fordingbridge and Hyde and Breamore etc *Win*

WOODHALL SPA Group, including Bucknall, Horsington, Kirkstead, Langton w Old Woodhall, and Stixwould *Linc 13* **P** *Bp and DBP (jt)* **R** R J E MAJOR

WOODHAM (All Saints) *Guildf 12* **P** *Bp* **V** I W FORBES **C** G HOLLAND

WOODHAM (St Elizabeth of Hungary) *see* Gt Aycliffe *Dur*

WOODHAM FERRERS (St Mary) and Bicknacre *Chelmsf 10* **P** *Lord Fitzwalter* **P-in-c** C M BALL

WOODHAM FERRERS, SOUTH (Holy Trinity) (St Mary) *Chelmsf 10* **P** *Bp* **V** C M BALL

WOODHAM MORTIMER (St Margaret) w Hazeleigh *Chelmsf 11* **P** *Bp* **P-in-c** J WILLMOT

WOODHAM WALTER (St Michael) *Chelmsf 11* **P** *Ch Soc Trust* **P-in-c** J WILLMOT

WOODHAY, EAST (St Martin) *see* NW Hants *Win*

WOODHAY, WEST (St Laurence) *see* Walbury Beacon *Ox*

WOODHORN (no church) w Newbiggin *Newc 11* **P** *Bp* **V** A D O'GRADY

WOODHOUSE (Christ Church) *see* Birkby and Woodhouse *Leeds*

WOODHOUSE (St James) *Sheff 1* **P** *Bp* **P-in-c** P R ALLEN **C** D L V WILKINSON **NSM** C D I REES, J K FOX

WOODHOUSE (St Mary in the Elms), Woodhouse Eaves and Swithland *Leic 6* **P** *Ld Chan and DBP (alt)* **R** L C TEMPERLEY-BARNES

WOODHOUSE EAVES (St Paul) *see* Woodhouse, Woodhouse Eaves and Swithland *Leic*

WOODHOUSE PARK (Wm Temple Church) *see* Wythenshawe *Man*

WOODHOUSE St Mark and Wrangthorn *Leeds 15* **P-in-c** A W C SMITH

WOODHOUSES (not known) *see* Bardsley *Man*

WOODHURST (St John the Baptist) *see* Somersham w Pidley and Oldhurst and Woodhurst *Ely*

WOODINGDEAN (Holy Cross) *Chich 19* **P** *Bp* **V** H A ROSE

WOODKIRK (St Mary) *see* W Ardsley *Leeds*

WOODLAND (St John the Baptist) *see* Ipplepen w Torbryan, Denbury, Broadhempston and Woodland *Ex*

WOODLAND (St John the Evangelist) *see* Broughton and Duddon *Carl*

WOODLAND (St Mary) *see* Lynesack *Dur*

WOODLANDS (All Saints) *Sheff 7* **P** *Bp* **V** S J GARDNER

WOODLANDS (Ascension) *see* Cranborne w Boveridge, Edmondsham etc *Sarum*

WOODLANDS (St Katherine) *B & W 3* **P** *DBP* **V** C ALSBURY

WOODLANDS (St Mary) *see* Kemsing and Woodlands *Roch*

WOODLEIGH (St Mary the Virgin) *see* Thurlestone, S Milton, Churchstow etc *Ex*

WOODLEY (Emmanuel) *Ox 7* **P** *DBP* **V** S C RIORDAN

WOODLEY (St James) *see* Southlake *Ox*

WOODLEY (St John the Evangelist) *Ox 7* **P** *DBP* **V** E MARQUEZ, L R SMITH **C** S P M TEMPLETON

WOODMANCOTE (Mission Church) *see* Westbourne *Chich*

WOODMANCOTE (St James) *see* Upper Dever *Win*

WOODMANCOTE (St Mark) *see* Dursley, Uley, Owlpen etc *Glouc*

WOODMANCOTE (St Peter) *see* Henfield w Shermanbury and Woodmancote *Chich*

WOODMANSEY (St Peter) *see* Beverley Minster *York*

WOODMANSTERNE (St Peter) *S'wark 24* **P** *Ld Chan* **R** vacant

WOODNESBOROUGH (St Mary the Blessed Virgin) *see* Eastry and Woodnesborough *Cant*

WOODNEWTON (St Mary) *see* Nassington, Apethorpe, Thornhaugh etc *Pet*

WOODPLUMPTON (St Anne) *Blackb 9* **P** *V St Michael's-on-Wyre* **V** vacant

WOODRISING (St Nicholas) *see* High Oak, Hingham and Scoulton w Wood Rising *Nor*

WOODSEATS (St Chad) *Sheff 2* **P** *Bp* **V** T K HOLE **C** E J LUNN, G B WHITE, J A A NORRIS, P M BROWN

WOODSETTS (St George) *Sheff 5* **P** *Bp* **V** vacant

WOODSFORD (St John the Baptist) *see* Moreton, Woodsford and Crossways w Tincleton *Sarum*

WOODSIDE (All Saints) *see* Lymington *Win*

WOODSIDE (St Andrew) *St Alb 12* **P** *D&C St Paul's* **V** C A PULLINGER

WOODSIDE (St James) *Leeds 15* **P** *Bp* **V** J M F CAIN

WOODSIDE (St Luke) *see* Croydon Woodside *S'wark*

WOODSIDE GREEN (St Andrew) *see* Gt Hallingbury and Lt Hallingbury *Chelmsf*

WOODSIDE PARK (St Barnabas) *Lon 14* **P** *Ch Patr Trust* **V** H D KENDAL **C** A M CLARKE, C A ALEXANDER, H L SHANNON, M PAVLOU

WOODSTOCK (St Mary Magdalene) and Bladon *Ox 29* **P** *Duke of Marlborough and Bp (jt)* **C** A H VENNING **NSM** S C HENSON

WOODSTON (St Augustine of Canterbury) (Mission Church) *Ely 15* **P** *Bp* **R** W P L GAMMON

WOODTHORPE (St Mark) *S'well 7* **P** *Bp* **V** M H ROBERTS **C** J A BULL

WOODTON (All Saints) *see* Hempnall *Nor*

WOODVILLE (St Stephen) *see* Blackfordby and Woodville *Leic*

WOOKEY (St Matthew) *see* Coxley w Godney, Henton and Wookey *B & W*

WOOKEY HOLE (St Mary Magdalene) *see* Wells St Cuth w Wookey Hole *B & W*

WOOL (Holy Rood) *see* W Purbeck *Sarum*

WOOLACOMBE (St Sabinus) *see* Ilfracombe, Lee, Woolacombe, Bittadon etc *Ex*

WOOLASTON (St Andrew) *see* Lydney, Woolaston, Alvington and Aylburton *Glouc*

WOOLAVINGTON (Blessed Virgin Mary) w Cossington and Bawdrip *B & W 13* **P** *D&C Windsor and J A Church Esq (alt)* **R** vacant

WOOLBEDING (All Hallows) *Chich 9* **P** *Bp* **R** D A WILLIS

WOOLBROOK (St Francis of Assisi) *see* Sidmouth, Woolbrook, Salcombe Regis, Sidbury etc *Ex*

WOOLER (St Mary) *see* Doddington, Ilderton, Kirknewton and Wooler *Newc*

WOOLFARDISWORTHY (Holy Trinity) *see* Parkham, Alwington, Buckland Brewer etc *Ex*

WOOLFARDISWORTHY EAST (St Mary) *see* N Creedy *Ex*

WOOLFOLD (St James) *see* Kirklees Valley *Man*

WOOLHAMPTON (St Peter) *see* Aldermaston and Woolhampton *Ox*

WOOLHOPE (St George) *see* Fownhope w Mordiford, Brockhampton etc *Heref*

WOOLLAND (not known) *see* Hazelbury Bryan and the Hillside Par *Sarum*

WOOLLEY (All Saints) *see* Bath St Sav w Swainswick and Woolley *B & W*

WOOLLEY (St Peter) *Leeds 19* **P** *Bp* **P-in-c** K A N GREAVES

WOOLPIT (Blessed Virgin Mary) w Drinkstone *St E 6* **P** *Bp and A Harvie-Clark Esq (alt)* **R** M R FARRELL **NSM** H M BIRT

WOOLSTASTON (St Michael and All Angels) *see* Dorrington w Leebotwood, Longnor, Stapleton etc *Heref*

WOOLSTHORPE (St James) *see* Harlaxton Gp *Linc*

WOOLSTON (Church of the Ascension) *see* Warrington E *Liv*

WOOLSTON (St Mark) *Win 13* **P** *Bp* **V** M J A NEWTON

WOOLSTONE (All Saints) *see* Uffington, Shellingford, Woolstone and Baulking *Ox*

WOOLSTONE (Holy Trinity) *see* Woughton *Ox*

WOOLSTONE (St Martin) *see* Bishop's Cleeve and Woolstone w Gotherington etc *Glouc*

WOOLTON HILL (St Thomas) *see* NW Hants *Win*

WOOLTON, MUCH (St Peter) *Liv 2* **P** *Bp* **R** C J CROOKS **C** A J RADFORD

WOOLVERSTONE (St Michael) *see* Holbrook, Stutton, Freston, Woolverstone etc *St E*

WOOLWICH (St Mary Magdalene and St Andrew) (St Michael and All Angels) *S'wark 1* **P** *Bp and Keble Coll Ox (jt)* **R** J VAN DER VALK

WOOLWICH (St Thomas) *see* Charlton *S'wark*

WOOLWICH, NORTH (St John) w Silvertown *Chelmsf 5* **P** *Bp and Lon Corp (alt)* **V** J S FRASER

WOORE (St Leonard) and Norton in Hales *Lich 17* **P** *Bp and CPAS (jt)* **P-in-c** D G ALCOCK

WOOSEHILL (Community Church) *see* Wokingham St Paul *Ox*

WOOTTON (St Andrew) *see* Abbey Gp *Linc*

WOOTTON (St Edmund) *Portsm 7* **P** *DBP* **R** V M BROWN

WOOTTON (St George the Martyr) *Pet 4* **P** *Ex Coll Ox* **V** L A JEFFREYS

WOOTTON (St Martin) *see* Elham w Denton and Wootton and Acrise *Cant*

WOOTTON (St Mary the Virgin) *St Alb 9* **P** *MMCET* **V** P M ACKROYD **C** P A YOUNG **Hon C** A S ATKINS

WOOTTON (St Mary) w Glympton and Kiddington *Ox 29* **P** *New Coll Ox (2 turns), Bp (1 turn), and Exors E W Towler Esq (1 turn)* **R** E E S JONES

WOOTTON (St Peter) *Ox 19* **P** *Bp* **V** vacant

WOOTTON BASSETT (St Bartholomew and All Saints) *see* R Wootton Bassett *Sarum*

WOOTTON BRIDGE (St Mark) *see* Wootton *Portsm*

WOOTTON COURTENAY (All Saints) *see* Dunster, Carhampton, Withycombe w Rodhuish etc *B & W*

WOOTTON FITZPAINE (not known) *see* Golden Cap Team *Sarum*

WOOTTON RIVERS (St Andrew) *see* Vale of Pewsey *Sarum*

WOOTTON ST LAWRENCE (St Lawrence) *see* Oakley w Wootton St Lawrence *Win*

WOOTTON WAWEN (St Peter) *Cov 7* **P** *K Coll Cam* **P-in-c** A B LARKIN

WOOTTON, NORTH (All Saints) *see* The Ch in the Woottons *Nor*

WOOTTON, NORTH (St Peter) *see* Pilton w Croscombe, N Wootton and Dinder *B & W*

WOOTTON, SOUTH (St Mary) *see* The Ch in the Woottons *Nor*

WORCESTER (All Saints) *see* Worc St Nic and All SS w St Helen *Worc*

WORCESTER (St Barnabas) (Christ Church) *Worc 6* **P** *Bp* **TR** J A WATSON **C** K K BREWIS

WORCESTER (St Clement) and Lower Broadheath *Worc 3* **P** *Bp and D&C (jt)* **C** S L COTTRILL

WORCESTER (St George w St Mary Magdalene) *Worc 6* **P** *Bp and V Claines (alt)* **P-in-c** J C MUSSON **NSM** D P DAVIES, P HONNIBALL, S E POLLARD

WORCESTER (St Helen) *see* Worc St Nic and All SS w St Helen *Worc*

WORCESTER (St John in Bedwardine) *see* St Jo in Bedwardine *Worc*

WORCESTER (St Martin in the Cornmarket) w St Swithun and St Paul *Worc 6* **P** *Patr Bd* **V** C S BUTLER **NSM** T J CLARKE

WORCESTER (St Nicholas) *see* Warndon St Nic *Worc*

WORCESTER (St Wulstan) *Worc 6* **P** *Bp* **V** S E NORTHALL

WORCESTER Dines Green (St Michael), and Crown East, Rushwick *Worc 3* **P** *Bp and D&C (jt)* **P-in-c** P J BRADFORD **C** A M POTTER

WORCESTER PARK (Christ Church w St Philip) *S'wark 23* **P** *R Cheam* **V** S A NADARAJAH

WORCESTER SOUTH EAST (St Martin w St Peter) (St Mark in the Cherry Orchard) (Holy Trinity w St Matthew) *Worc 6* **P** *Patr Bd* **TV** A G STAND, R J FARMER **NSM** R A PARRY

WORCESTER St Nicholas (All Saints) (St Helen) *Worc 6* **P** *Patr Bd* **V** R W JOHNSON **C** A K SMITH, O T GALLACHER

WORCESTERSHIRE WEST RURAL Team Ministry, The, comprising Alfrick and Lulsley, Broadwas, Clifton-upon-Teme, Cotheridge, Leigh and Bransford, Lower Sapey, Martley, Shelsley Beauchamp, Shelsley Marsh, Suckley, and Wichenford *Worc 3* **P** *Patr Bd (2 turns), The Crown (1 turn)* **TR** D R SHERWIN **TV** A M POTTER **C** R C ELLIOTT **NSM** J DENNISTON

WORDSLEY (Holy Trinity) *Worc 10* **P** *Patr Bd* **TR** C S JONES **C** R L ROWSON

WORFIELD (St Peter) *Heref 8* **P** *Trustees of the late J R S Greenshields Esq* **V** J H STOKES

WORKINGTON (St John) *Carl 7* **P** *R Workington* **NSM** M T STILWELL

WORKINGTON (St Michael) *Carl 7* **P** *Mrs E H S Thornely* **C** P J POWELL

WORKSOP (Christ Church) and Shireoaks *S'well 1* **P** *Bp and CPAS (jt)* **V** L H DE ANDRADE LIMA **C** A A T SHIELLS

WORKSOP (St Anne) *S'well 1* **P** *Bp* **P-in-c** D R GOUGH **C** R J HANFORD

WORKSOP (St John the Evangelist) *S'well 1* **P** *CPAS* **P-in-c** T C STANFORD

WORKSOP (St Paul) *S'well 1* **P** *Bp* **P-in-c** N SPICER

WORKSOP PRIORY (St Mary and St Cuthbert) *S'well 1* **P** *St Steph Ho Ox* **V** N SPICER **C** J M O VYSE

WORLABY (St Clement) *Linc 8* **P** *DBP* **V** G O MITCHELL

WORLDHAM, EAST (St Mary the Virgin)   *see* Northanger *Win*

WORLDHAM, WEST (St Nicholas) *as above*

WORLE (St Martin) (St Mark's Church Centre) *B & W 10*
P *Ld Chan*   **TR** E J FLEMING   **TV** C G ELMS, E C AMYES
NSM G C BUNCE

WORLESTON (St Oswald)   *see* Acton and Worleston, Church Minshull etc *Ches*

WORLINGHAM (All Saints) w Barnby and North Cove
St E 17   **P** *Ld Chan*   **P-in-c** J R PENN

WORLINGTON (All Saints)   *see* Mildenhall *St E*

WORLINGTON, EAST (St Mary)   *see* Burrington, Chawleigh, Cheldon, Chulmleigh etc *Ex*

WORLINGTON, WEST (St Mary) *as above*

WORLINGWORTH (St Mary)   *see* Four Rivers *St E*

WORMBRIDGE (St Peter)   *see* Ewyas Harold w Dulas, Kenderchurch etc *Heref*

WORMEGAY (St Michael and All Angels and Holy Cross)   *see* W Norfolk Priory Gp *Ely*

WORMELOW HUNDRED, comprising Dewsall w Callow, Little Birch, Llandinabo, Llanwarne, Much Birch, and Much Dewchurch *Heref 7*   **P** A W Twiston-Davies Esq (1 turn), Bp (3 turns), and Ld Chan (1 turn)   **R** M JOHNSON

WORMHILL (St Margaret)   *see* Tideswell *Derby*

WORMINGFORD (St Andrew), Mount Bures and Little Horkesley *Chelmsf 21*   **P** *Exors J J Tufnell Esq and Keble Coll Ox (jt)*   **C** A J ELMES, H R COOPER, R G GIBBS, S L HAYWARD
NSM P W MANN

WORMINGHALL (St Peter and St Paul) w Ickford, Oakley and Shabbington *Ox 10*   **P** Bp and Guild of All So (jt)
R D R KABOLEH

WORMINGTON (St Katharine)   *see* Winchcombe *Glouc*

WORMLEIGHTON (St Peter)   *see* Priors Hardwick, Priors Marston and Wormleighton *Cov*

WORMLEY (Church Room)   *see* Broxbourne w Wormley *St Alb*

WORMLEY (St Laurence) *as above*

WORMSHILL (St Giles)   *see* Tunstall and Bredgar *Cant*

WORPLESDON (St Mary the Virgin) *Guildf 5*   **P** Eton Coll
R A B RUSSELL   **NSM** R BROTHWELL, T J WEIL

WORSALL, HIGH AND LOW (All Saints)   *see* Kirklevington w Picton, and High and Low Worsall *York*

WORSBROUGH (St Mary) w Elsecar *Sheff 11*   **P** DBP and Sir Philip Naylor-Leyland Bt (alt)   **V** S G CHAPMAN

WORSBROUGH (St Thomas)   *see* Worsbrough Common w Worsbrough St Thos *Sheff*

WORSBROUGH COMMON (St Luke) w Worsbrough St Thomas and St James *Sheff 11*   **P** Bp (2 turns), The Crown (1 turn)   **V** A BATEMAN

WORSLEY (St Mark) *Man 18*   **P** Bp   **TR** M J WILLIAMS
TV K HOPWOOD OWEN   **NSM** D E FAIR   **OLM** D HAWKINS

WORSLEY MESNES (not known)   *see* Wigan St Jas w St Thos *Liv*

WORSTEAD (St Mary)   *see* N Walsham, Edingthorpe, Worstead and Westwick *Nor*

WORSTHORNE (St John the Evangelist)   *see* Holme-in-Cliviger w Worsthorne *Blackb*

WORTH (St Nicholas), Pound Hill and Maidenbower
Chich 6   **P** DBP   **R** M J BOAG   **C** S L UPCHURCH

WORTH (St Peter and St Paul)   *see* Sandwich and Worth *Cant*

WORTH MATRAVERS (St Aldhelm)   *see* St Aldhelm *Sarum*

WORTH MATRAVERS (St Nicholas) *as above*

WORTHAM (St Mary the Virgin)   *see* N Hartismere *St E*

WORTHEN (All Saints)   *see* Westbury, Worthen and Yockleton *Heref*

WORTHING (Christ Church) *Chich 4*   **P** R Broadwater, Bp and Bp Horsham, Ch Soc Trust, and CPAS (jt)
P-in-c D W RENSHAW

WORTHING (St Andrew) *Chich 4*   **P** Keble Coll Ox
P-in-c J K T ELDRIDGE

WORTHING (St George) (Emmanuel) *Chich 4*   **P** Ch Soc Trust   **V** vacant

WORTHING (St Margaret)   *see* Heart of Norfolk *Nor*

WORTHING (St Matthew) *Chich 4*   **P** R Broadwater, Bp and Bp Horsham, Ch Soc Trust, and CPAS (jt)   **V** P F D TAYLOR
C N D STANNARD

WORTHING, WEST (St John the Divine) *Chich 4*   **P** Bp
V J K T ELDRIDGE

WORTHINGTON (St Matthew)   *see* Ashby-de-la-Zouch and Breedon on the Hill *Leic*

WORTING (St Thomas of Canterbury)   *see* Winklebury and Worting *Win*

WORTLEY (St John the Evangelist) and Farnley *Leeds 14*
P Bp and Trustees (jt)   **R** vacant

WORTLEY (St Leonard)   *see* Tankersley, Thurgoland and Wortley *Sheff*

WORTON (Christ Church)   *see* Wellsprings *Sarum*

WORTON, NETHER (St James)   *see* Westcote Barton w Steeple Barton, Duns Tew etc *Ox*

WORTON, OVER (Holy Trinity) *as above*

WOTTON (St John the Evangelist)   *see* Abinger and Coldharbour and Wotton and Holmbury St Mary *Guildf*

WOTTON ST MARY WITHOUT (Holy Trinity) *Glouc 2*   **P** Bp
V G A GIBBENS

WOTTON UNDERWOOD (All Saints)   *see* Bernwode *Ox*

WOTTON-UNDER-EDGE (St Mary the Virgin)   *see* Tyndale *Glouc*

WOUGHTON, comprising Fishermead, Simpson, Woolstone, and Woughton-on-the-Green *Ox 14*   **P** Bp   **R** I C HERBERT
OLM P NORRIS

WOUGHTON-ON-THE-GREEN (St Mary)   *see* Woughton *Ox*

WOULDHAM (All Saints)   *see* Burham and Wouldham *Roch*

WRABNESS (All Saints)   *see* Gt Oakley, Wix, Wrabness etc *Chelmsf*

WRAGBY (St Michael and Our Lady)   *see* Kinsley w Wragby *Leeds*

WRAGBY Group, The (All Saints), including Holton cum Beckering, Langton by Wragby, Rand, Snelland, and Wickenby *Linc 13*   **P** Bp, MMCET, and DBP (jt)
R M N HOLDEN

WRAMPLINGHAM (St Peter and St Paul)   *see* Barnham Broom and Upper Yare *Nor*

WRANGLE (St Mary and St Nicholas)   *see* Old Leake w Wrangle *Linc*

WRANGTHORN (St Augustine of Hippo)   *see* Woodhouse and Wrangthorn *Leeds*

WRATTING, GREAT (St Mary)   *see* Stourhead *St E*

WRATTING, LITTLE (St Mary) *as above*

WRATTING, WEST (St Andrew)   *see* Granta Vale Gp *Ely*

WRAWBY (St Mary the Virgin)   *see* Brigg, Wrawby and Cadney cum Howsham *Linc*

WRAXALL (All Saints) *B & W 12*   **P** Trustees   **R** F M BINDING
NSM J C HARRIS

WRAXALL (St Mary)   *see* Melbury *Sarum*

WRAXALL, NORTH (St James)   *see* Colerne w N Wraxall *Bris*

WRAXALL, SOUTH (St James)   *see* N Bradford on Avon and Villages *Sarum*

WRAY (Holy Trinity)   *see* E Lonsdale *Blackb*

WRAYSBURY (St Andrew)   *see* Horton and Wraysbury *Ox*

WREAKE, UPPER, comprising Brooksby, Frisby-on-the-Wreake, Hoby, Kirby Bellars, Ragdale, and Rotherby *Leic 2*
P Bp and DBP (jt)   **P-in-c** D P HARKNETT

WREAY (St Mary)   *see* Dalston w Cumdivock, Raughton Head and Wreay *Carl*

WRECCLESHAM (St Peter) *Guildf 3*   **P** Bp
V J A DRAKE-SMITH

WRENBURY (St Margaret)   *see* Baddiley and Wrenbury w Burleydam *Ches*

WRENINGHAM (All Saints)   *see* Upper Tas Valley *Nor*

WRENTHAM (St Nicholas), Covehithe w Benacre, Henstead w Hulver and Frostenden *St E 17*   **P** Susan Lady Gooch   **V** vacant

WRENTHORPE (St Anne)   *see* Outwood, Stanley and Wrenthorpe *Leeds*

WRESSLE (St John of Beverly)   *see* Howden *York*

WRESTLINGWORTH (St Peter)   *see* Dunton w Wrestlingworth and Eyeworth *St Alb*

WRETHAM (St Ethelbert)   *see* Thetford *Nor*

WRETTON (All Saints)   *see* Wissey Valley *Ely*

WRIBBENHALL (All Saints)   *see* Ribbesford w Bewdley and Dowles and Wribbenhall *Worc*

WRIGHTINGTON (St James the Great) *Blackb 4*   **P** Bp
V S M DNISTRIANSKYJ

WRINGTON (All Saints) w Butcombe and Burrington
B & W 10   **P** Patr Bd   **R** D R GENT   **NSM** A M HEMMING

WRITTLE (All Saints) w Highwood *Chelmsf 9*   **P** New Coll Ox
OLM A MERCHANT

WROCKWARDINE WOOD (Holy Trinity)   *see* Oakengates, Priors Lee and Wrockwardine Wood *Lich*

WROCKWARDINE, The Deanery of (St Peter) *Lich 22*
P Patr Bd   **TR** D A ACKROYD   **TV** S WILLIAMS   **C** L A KNIGHT

WROOT (St Pancras)   *see* Epworth Gp *Linc*

WROSE (St Cuthbert) *Leeds 3*   **P** The Crown   **V** C D BLAKE
Hon C P B STOODLEY

WROTHAM (St George) *Roch 10*   **P** D&C   **R** E M A WRIGHT

WROUGHTON (St John the Baptist and St Helen) and Wichelstowe *Bris 7*   **P** Bp   **V** P R N HARRISON
OLM B M ABREY

WROXALL (St John the Evangelist) *Portsm 7*   **P** Bp   **V** vacant

WROXETER (St Mary)   *see* Wrockwardine Deanery *Lich*

WROXHAM (St Mary) w Hoveton St John w Hoveton St Peter, Belaugh and Tunstead w Sco' Ruston *Nor 12*
P Bp   **R** E A JUMP   **C** T J JESSOP

WROXTON (All Saints) *see* Ironstone *Ox*

WULFRIC Benefice, The, comprising Crewkerne, Haselbury Plucknett, Misterton, North Perrott, and Wayford *B & W 14* **P** *Ld Chan (4 turns), Bp and H W F Hoskyns Esq (1 turn)* **R** S M HUNTLEY **C** J R MORRIS

WYBERTON (St Leodegar) *Linc 21* **P** DBP **R** S SARVANANTHAN

WYBUNBURY (St Chad) and Audlem w Doddington *Ches 15* **P** *Bp and Lady Rona Delves Broughton (jt)* **V** H F CHANTRY

WYCH, HIGH (St James) and Gilston w Eastwick *St Alb 15* **P** *V Sawbridgeworth (2 turns), P T S Bowlby Esq (1 turn)* **P-in-c** W E G CARTER

WYCHBOLD (St Mary de Wyche) *see* Stoke Prior, Wychbold and Upton Warren *Worc*

WYCHE (All Saints) *see* Malvern Chase *Worc*

WYCHERT VALE, comprising Aston Sandford, Cuddington, Haddenham, Kingsey, and Stone w Dinton and Hartwell *Ox 10* **P** *Bp, D&C Roch, and Grocers' Co (jt)* **C** N J ROSE, P N GROVES **NSM** J D HAWKINS, P M MANDER **OLM** N H FEATHERSTON

WYCHLING (St Margaret) *see* Kingsdown and Creekside *Cant*

WYCHNOR (St Leonard) *Lich 1* **P** *Personal Reps W H Harrison Esq* **V** J W ALLAN **NSM** E A WALL

WYCHWOOD, comprising Fifield w Idbury, Milton-under-Wychwood, and Shipton-under-Wychwood *Ox 22* **P** *Bp* **V** G P CLEMENT

WYCK RISSINGTON (St Laurence) *see* Bourton-on-the-Water w Clapton etc *Glouc*

WYCLIFFE (St Mary) *see* Holmedale *Leeds*

WYCOMBE AND CHADWELL (St Mary) *see* Ironstone Villages *Leic*

WYCOMBE LANE (St Mary) *see* Wooburn *Ox*

WYCOMBE MARSH (St Anne and St Peter) *see* High Wycombe *Ox*

WYCOMBE, HIGH (All Saints) (St Andrew) (St Anne and St Peter) (Christ the Servant King) (St James) (St Mary and St George) *Ox 18* **P** *Patr Bd* **TR** H W ELLIS **TV** C D OWEN, H K GRAHAM, J-S S GALLANT, S P DUST, W J BULL **C** J J DADE, N K WORSFOLD **NSM** P VINEY **OLM** J LOCK

WYCOMBE, WEST (St Laurence) (St Paul) w Bledlow Ridge, Bradenham and Radnage *Ox 18* **P** *Bp, DBP, Peache Trustees, and Sir Francis Dashwood Bt (jt)* **R** A B BARTON **NSM** J S ELLIS, L J RICHARDSON, V J BEAUMONT

WYDDIAL (St Giles) *see* Hormead, Wyddial, Anstey, Brent Pelham etc *St Alb*

WYE (St Gregory and St Martin) *Cant 2* **P** *Abp* **V** R HOLY **C** L M LAWRENCE **OLM** L A CROSS

WYE BROOKS Benefice, The, comprising Goodrich, Llangarron, Llangrove, Marstow, Welsh Bicknor, and Welsh Newton w Llanrothal *Heref 7* **P** *Bp (2 turns), D&C and DBP (2 turns)* **V** P J BENTHAM **NSM** R C B JONES

WYE REACHES Group, The, comprising Bishopswood, Dixton Newton, Ganarew, and Whitchurch *Heref 7* **P** *Bp (5 turns), Ld Chan (1 turn)* **V** K V CECIL

WYE, SOUTH Rural Parishes, including Ballingham, Dinedor, Holme Lacy, and Little Dewchurch *Heref 3* **P** *Bp (1 turn), D&C (1 turn), Worc Coll Ox (1 turn)* **V** vacant

WYESHAM (St James) *see* Wye Reaches Gp *Heref*

WYFORDBY (St Mary) *see* S Framland *Leic*

WYKE (Holy Trinity) *see* Bruton, Brewham, Pitcombe and Shepton Montague *B & W*

WYKE (St Barnabas) *see* Win St Barn *Win*

WYKE (St Mark) *Guildf 5* **P** *Bp* **V** A R M CRAVEN

WYKE (St Mary the Virgin) *Leeds 3* **P** *Bp* **V** L J WORMSLEY **Hon C** M R M LYONS

WYKE REGIS (All Saints) (St Edmund) *Sarum 4* **P** D&C **R** A S KAY **NSM** B A PORT

WYKEHAM (All Saints) *see* Upper Derwent *York*

WYKEHAM: Broughton w North Newington, Epwell w Sibford, Shutford, Swalcliffe, and Tadmarton *Ox 23* **P** *New Coll, Worc Coll, and Lord Saye and Sele (jt)* **R** R L HAWKES **NSM** E A HAWKES, J H TATTERSALL

WYKEN (Holy Cross) *see* Caludon H Cross Cov *Cov*

WYKEN (St Mary Magdalene) (Church of the Risen Christ) *Cov 1* **P** *Ld Chan and Bp (alt)* **V** vacant

WYLAM (St Oswin) *see* Ovingham and Wylam *Newc*

WYLDE GREEN (Emmanuel) *Birm 7* **P** *Bp* **P-in-c** J J BRIDGE

WYLYE (St Mary the Virgin) *see* Wylye and Till Valley *Sarum*

WYLYE AND TILL VALLEY, comprising Berwick St James, Great Wishford, Little Langford, South Newton, Stapleford, Steeple Langford, Stockton, Winterbourne Stoke, and Wylye *Sarum 14* **P** *D&C Windsor, Bp, D&C, and DBP (jt)* **P-in-c** J PLOWS

WYLYE VALLEY TEAM, UPPER, comprising Boyton, Codford St Mary, Codford St Peter, Heytesbury w Tytherington and Knook, Norton Bavant, Sherrington, Sutton Veny, and Upton Lovell *Sarum 12* **P** *Patr Bd (5 turns), Ld Chan (1 turn)* **P-in-c** T HOBSON **TV** C G STRIDE

WYMERING (St Peter and St Paul) *Portsm 6* **P** *Nugee Foundn* **V** A L WEBB

WYMESWOLD (St Mary) and Prestwold w Hoton *Leic 6* **P** *S J Packe-Drury-Lowe Esq and Bp (by turn)* **P-in-c** C R WATTS

WYMINGTON (St Lawrence) *see* Chellington *St Alb*

WYMONDHAM (St Mary and St Thomas) *Nor 7* **P** *Bp* **V** C P RELF-PENNINGTON **C** S SEALY

WYMONDHAM (St Peter) *see* S Framland *Leic*

WYMONDLEY, GREAT (St Mary the Virgin) *see* St Ippolyts w Gt and Lt Wymondley *St Alb*

WYMONDLEY, LITTLE (St Mary the Virgin) *as above*

WYMYNSWOLD (St Margaret) *see* Barham Downs w Adisham *Cant*

WYNYARD PARK (Chapel) *see* Stockton Country Par *Dur*

WYRE PIDDLE (St Anne) *see* Fladbury, Hill and Moor, Wyre Piddle etc *Worc*

WYRESDALE, OVER (Christ Church) *see* Dolphinholme w Quernmore and Over Wyresdale *Blackb*

WYRLEY, GREAT (St Mark) *Lich 3* **P** *R Cannock* **V** M ARNOLD

WYSALL (Holy Trinity) *see* Willoughby-on-the-Wolds w Wysall and Widmerpool *S'well*

WYTHALL (St Mary) *Birm 5* **P** *R Kings Norton* **V** A J FEATHERSTONE **C** M E PARTON

WYTHAM (All Saints) *see* Wolvercote and Wytham *Ox*

WYTHBURN (not known) *see* St John's-in-the-Vale, Threlkeld and Wythburn *Carl*

WYTHENSHAWE (St Francis of Assisi) (St Luke) (St Martin) (St Richard of Chichester) (William Temple Church) *Man 6* **P** *Patr Bd* **TV** C D HEWITT, I C FELLOWS, M J APPLEBY **C** C A SCHOFIELD **OLM** G R MILLER

WYTHENSHAWE Lawton Moor (St Michael and All Angels) *see* Lawton Moor *Man*

WYTHER (Venerable Bede) *Leeds 14* **P** *Bp* **P-in-c** A J PEARSON

WYTHOP (St Margaret) *see* Binsey *Carl*

WYVERSTONE (St George) *see* Bacton w Wyverstone, Cotton and Old Newton etc *St E*

WYVILLE (St Catherine) *see* Harlaxton Gp *Linc*

YAFFORTH (All Saints) *see* Lower Swale *Leeds*

YALDING (St Peter and St Paul) w Collier Street *Roch 8* **P** *Ld Chan* **V** P A KISH **C** L C CORNELL

YANWORTH (St Michael) *see* Chedworth, Yanworth and Stowell, Coln Rogers etc *Glouc*

YAPHAM (St Martin) *see* Barmby Moor Gp *York*

YAPTON (St Mary) *see* Clymping and Yapton w Ford *Chich*

YARCOMBE (St John the Baptist) *see* Kilmington, Stockland, Dalwood, Yarcombe etc *Ex*

YARDLEY (St Cyprian) Hay Mill *Birm 11* **P** *Bp* **V** vacant

YARDLEY (St Edburgha) *Birm 11* **P** *St Pet Coll Ox* **V** W J SANDS

YARDLEY (St Lawrence) *see* Ardeley, Benington, Cottered w Throcking etc *St Alb*

YARDLEY GOBION (St Leonard) *see* Potterspury w Furtho and Yardley Gobion etc *Pet*

YARDLEY HASTINGS (St Andrew), Denton and Grendon w Castle Ashby and Whiston *Pet 6* **P** *Marquess of Northampton and Bp (alt)* **R** P YORK **C** A J OLIVER **Hon C** J E TEBBY

YARDLEY WOOD (Christ Church) *Birm 4* **P** *Bp* **V** L M GASTON

YARDLEY, SOUTH (St Michael and All Angels) *Birm 11* **P** *Bp* **V** vacant

YARE VALLEY Churches, The, comprising Braydeston, Brundall, and Postwick *Nor 4* **P** *Bp and MMCET (jt)* **R** P-J B LEECH

YARKHILL (St John the Baptist) *see* Hop Churches *Heref*

YARLINGTON (Blessed Virgin Mary) *see* Camelot Par *B & W*

YARM (St Mary Magdalene) *York 20* **P** *Abp* **R** W J FORD

YARMOUTH (St James) *see* W Wight *Portsm*

YARMOUTH, GREAT (St Nicholas) (St Paul) (St Mary) *Nor 6* **P** *Patr Bd* **TR** S W J WARD **TV** J J SANDER-HEYS **C** H LYNCH **NSM** F W CLIFF **OLM** S R ANDREWS

YARNFIELD (Mission Room St Barnabas) *see* Cotes Heath and Standon and Swynnerton etc *Lich*

YARNSCOMBE (St Andrew) *see* Newton Tracey, Horwood, Alverdiscott etc *Ex*

YARNTON (St Batholomew) w Begbroke and Shipton-on-Cherwell *Ox 29* **P** *Duke of Marlborough, Bp, and Brasenose Coll Ox (jt)* **V** O R H PETTER

YARWELL (St Mary Magdalene) *see* Nassington, Apethorpe, Thornhaugh etc *Pet*

YATE (St Mary) *Bris 5*   P *Bp*   TR I M WALLACE
TV I P MACFARLANE   C G L THOMAS, H G SNOOK
OLM J L HODGE

YATELEY (St Peter) *Win 5*   P *Bp*   R *vacant*

YATESBURY (All Saints) *see* Oldbury *Sarum*

YATTENDON (St Peter and St Paul) *see* Hermitage *Ox*

YATTON (All Saints) *see* Cider Churches *Heref*

YATTON KEYNELL (St Margaret) *see* By Brook *Bris*

YATTON MOOR (St Mary the Virgin) *B & W 12*   P *DBF*
TR T C N SCOTT   TV N B THOMAS

YAVERLAND (St John the Baptist) *see* Seaview, St Helens, Brading and Yaverland *Portsm*

YAXHAM (St Peter) *see* Mattishall and the Tudd Valley *Nor*

YAXLEY (St Mary the Virgin) *see* S Hartismere *St E*

YAXLEY (St Peter) and Holme w Conington *Ely 15*   P *Ld Chan (2 turns), J H B Heathcote Esq (1 turn)*   V S L HARE

YEADON (St John the Evangelist) *Leeds 15*   P *Bp and R Guiseley w Esholt (jt)*   V R M WALKER

YEALAND CONYERS (St John the Evangelist) *see* Warton St Oswald w Yealand Conyers *Blackb*

YEALMPTON (St Bartholomew) and Brixton *Ex 20*   P *D&C Windsor and Bp (jt)*   V *vacant*

YEARSLEY (Holy Trinity) *see* Crayke w Brandsby and Yearsley *York*

YEAVELEY (Holy Trinity) *see* Brailsford w Shirley, Osmaston w Edlaston etc *Derby*

YEDINGHAM (St John the Baptist) *see* Buckrose Carrs *York*

YELDEN (St Mary) *see* The Stodden Churches *St Alb*

YELDHAM, GREAT (St Andrew) *see* The Hedinghams and Upper Colne *Chelmsf*

YELDHAM, LITTLE (St John the Baptist) *as above*

YELFORD (St Nicholas and St Swithin) *see* Lower Windrush *Ox*

YELLING (Holy Cross) *see* Papworth *Ely*

YELVERTOFT (All Saints) *see* Crick and Yelvertoft w Clay Coton and Lilbourne *Pet*

YELVERTON (St Mary) *see* Thurton w Ashby St Mary, Bergh Apton etc *Nor*

YELVERTON (St Paul), Meavy, Sheepstor, Walkhampton, Sampford Spiney and Horrabridge *Ex 22*   P *Bp, D&C Windsor and Lord Roborough (1 turn), Duchy of Cornwall (1 turn), Ld Chan (1 turn)*   C D A CAINE

YEOFORD CHAPEL (Holy Trinity) *see* Crediton, Shobrooke and Sandford etc *Ex*

YEOVIL (Holy Trinity) w Barwick *B & W 6*   P *Ms Y L Bennett and Ms R S Mullen (1 turn), The Crown (3 turns)*
C D R YOUNG

YEOVIL (St Andrew) (St John the Baptist) w Kingston Pitney *B & W 6*   P *DBP*   R J DUDLEY-SMITH

YEOVIL (St James the Great) *see* Preston Plucknett *B & W*

YEOVIL (St Michael and All Angels) *B & W 6*   P *Bp*
V D R ANDERSON   C E ISTED   NSM J E HAWES

YEOVIL (St Peter) *see* Preston Plucknett *B & W*

YEOVIL MARSH (All Saints) *see* Tintinhull w Chilthorne Domer, Yeovil Marsh etc *B & W*

YETMINSTER (St Andrew) *see* Three Valleys *Sarum*

YIEWSLEY (St Matthew) *Lon 24*   P *V Hillingdon*
V R C YOUNG   C A V BASTIDAS

YOCKLETON (Holy Trinity) *see* Westbury, Worthen and Yockleton *Heref*

YORK (All Saints) North Street *York 7*   P *D&C*
NSM J M HANKS

YORK (All Saints) Pavement w St Crux and St Michael Spurriergate *York 7*   P *Abp*   P-in-c E J NATTRASS
C S D EARIS   NSM D C E SIMPSON, D J HOBMAN, K G BOULTON

YORK (Christ Church) *see* Heworth Ch Ch *York*

YORK (Holy Redeemer) *see* Acomb H Redeemer *York*

YORK (Holy Trinity) Micklegate *York 7*   P *D&C*
P-in-c E J NATTRASS   NSM D J HOBMAN, K G BOULTON

YORK (James the Deacon) *see* Acomb Moor *York*

YORK (St Barnabas) *York 7*   P *CPAS*   P-in-c J M A LEE
C M R WOODCOCK

YORK (St Chad) *York 7*   P *Abp*   P-in-c J K DAY
C T F GIBBONS   NSM M N M SENTAMU

YORK (St Clement w St Mary) Bishophill *York 7*   P *Abp and D&C (jt)*   R A STOKER   NSM D H EFIRD, G J PETERS

YORK (St Denys) *York 7*   P *Abp*   P-in-c E J NATTRASS
C S D EARIS   NSM D C E SIMPSON, D J HOBMAN, K G BOULTON

YORK (St Helen) Stonegate w (St Martin) Coney Street *York 7*   P *Abp*   P-in-c E J NATTRASS   C S D EARIS
NSM D C E SIMPSON, D J HOBMAN, K G BOULTON

YORK (St Hilda) *York 7*   P *Abp*   P-in-c A F WAKEFIELD
C J L MADIN

YORK (St Lawrence w St Nicholas) *York 7*   P *D&C*
P-in-c E J NATTRASS   NSM D J HOBMAN, K G BOULTON

YORK (St Luke) *York 7*   P *Abp*   V J M DOYLE-BRETT
NSM N F SYKES

YORK (St Michael-le-Belfrey) (St Cuthbert) *York 7*   P *Abp*
V M J PORTER   C A J BAKER, M J PERKINS
NSM C N SELVARATNAM, E A RANSFORD, M G SWAFFIELD, W J ROBERTS

YORK (St Olave w St Giles) *York 7*   P *Abp*
P-in-c E J NATTRASS   C S D EARIS   NSM D C E SIMPSON, D J HOBMAN, K G BOULTON

YORK (St Paul) Holgate Road *York 7*   P *CPAS*   C H A MADIN, M R WOODCOCK

YORK (St Stephen) *see* Acomb St Steph and St Aid *York*

YORK (St Thomas w St Maurice) *York 7*   P *Abp*
P-in-c A J RYCROFT

YORK Acomb (St Aidan) *see* Acomb St Steph and St Aid *York*

YORK, Rural East *see* Rural E York *York*

YOULGREAVE (All Saints), Middleton, Stanton-in-Peak and Birchover *Derby 4*   P *Duke of Devonshire and N B B Davie-Thornhill Esq (jt)*   P-in-c L A M PETHERAM

YOXALL (St Peter) *see* Kings Bromley, The Ridwares and Yoxall *Lich*

YOXFORD (St Peter) *see* Yoxmere *St E*

YOXMERE Benefice, The, comprising Darsham, Dunwich, Middleton cum Fordley, Peasenhall, Sibton, Theberton w Eastbridge, Westleton, and Yoxford *St E 16*   P *The Crown (1 turn), Ch Patr Trust, Lady Penelope Gilbey, Shadingfield Property, J K A Brooke Esq, CPAS, and Bp (2 turns)*
V C H REDGRAVE   NSM B E R JOLLEY

ZEAL MONACHORUM (St Peter) *Ex 2*   P *DBP*   R *vacant*

ZEALS (St Martin) *see* Upper Stour *Sarum*

ZENNOR (St Senera) *Truro 5*   P *Bp*   P-in-c E V A FOOT

WELSH BENEFICES AND CHURCHES

An index of benefices of the Church in Wales (shown in bold type), together with entries for churches and other licensed places of worship. Where the church name is the same as the benefice (or the first place name in the benefice), the church entry is omitted. Church dedications are indicated in brackets.

The benefice entry gives the full legal name, followed by the diocese, its deanery number (p. 915), and the name(s) and appointment(s) of the clergy serving there. The following are the main abbreviations used; for others see the full list of abbreviations.

C	Curate	P-in-c	Priest-in-charge
C-in-c	Curate-in-charge	Par Dn	Parish Deacon
Hon C	Honorary Curate	R	Rector
Hon Par Dn	Honorary Parish Deacon	TR	Team Rector
I	Incumbent	TV	Team Vicar
NSM	Non-stipendiary Minister	V	Vicar

ABBEY CWMHIR (St Mary the Virgin) *see* Ithon Valley *S & B*
ABERAERON (Holy Trinity) *see* Henfynyw w Aberaeron and Llanddewi Aberarth etc *St D*
ABERAMAN (St Margaret) and Cwmaman *Llan 8*
  P-in-c M GIBBON
ABERAVON (St Mary) (Holy Trinity) (St Agnes) *Llan 5*
  TR N CAHILL **TV** R G AP ROBERT **NSM** J A SLENNETT
ABERBARGOED (St Peter) *see* Upper Islwyn *Mon*
ABERCANAID (St Peter) *see* Merthyr Tydfil St Dav and Abercanaid *Llan*
ABERCONWY Mission Area, comprising Bryn Pydew, Craigydon, Deganwy, Eglwysbach, Glan Conwy, Llanddoget, Llandudno Junction, Llangystenin, Llanrhos, Llanrwst, and Penrhyn Bay *St As 5* **I** N W CARTER
  TV S F HILDRETH **C** E PARRY, G CHIGUMIRA, J FRASER
ABERCRAF (St David) *see* Cwmtawe Uchaf *S & B*
ABERCYNON (St Donat) (St Gwynno) *Llan 8* **V** *vacant*
ABERDARE (St Fagan) *Llan 8* **V** R A GREEN
  NSM P GODSALL
ABERDARE (St John the Baptist) (St Elvan) (St Matthew) (St John the Evangelist) *Llan 8* **V** R E DAVIES
ABERDARON (St Hywyn) *see* Bro Enlli *Ban*
ABERDYFI (St Peter) *see* Bro Ystumanner *Ban*
ABEREDW (St Cewydd) *see* Erwood Gp w Painscastle Gp *S & B*
ABERERCH (St Cawrdaf) *see* Bro Eifionydd *Ban*
ABERFFRAW (St Beuno) *see* Bro Cadwaladr *Ban*
ABERGAVENNY (Holy Trinity) (Christ Church) *Mon 1*
  P-in-c M SOADY **C** J A PEARSE, T H R S J BATES
ABERGAVENNY (St Mary) (Christchurch) w Llanwenarth Citra *Mon 1* **I** M SOADY **C** J A PEARSE, T H R S J BATES
ABERGELE (St Michael) *see* Aled Miss Area *St As*
ABERGORLECH (St David) *see* Cynwyl Gaeo w Llansawel and Talley etc *St D*
ABERGWILI (St David) *see* Carmarthen St Pet and Abergwili etc *St D*
ABERGWYNGREGYN (St Bodfan) *see* Dwylan *Ban*
ABERGYNOLWYN *see* Bro Ystumanner *Ban*
ABERHAFESP (St Gwynog) *see* Cedewain Miss Area *St As*
ABERKENFIG (St John) *see* Llansantffraid, Bettws and Aberkenfig *Llan*
ABER-MORFA Mission Area, comprising Bodelwyddan, Rhuddlan, Rhyl, Rhyl St Ann, and Towyn *St As 1*
  I G R MANSFIELD **TV** C M FEAK **C** C S SPENCER, J COXALL
ABERNANT (St Lucia) *see* Bro Sancler *St D*
ABERNANT (St Matthew) *see* Aberdare *Llan*
ABERPERGWM (St Cadoc) *see* Vale of Neath *Llan*
ABER-PORTH (St Cynwyl) *see* Bro Teifi *St D*
ABERTILLERY (St Michael) w Cwmtillery w Llanhilleth w Six Bells *Mon 8* **P-in-c** M PARKER
ABERTYSSWG (St Paul) *see* Rhymney *Mon*
ABERYSKIR (St Mary and St Cynidr) *see* Dan yr Eppynt *S & B*
ABERYSTWYTH (St Michael) (Holy Trinity) (St Mary) (St Anne) *St D 9* **TV** J-D LAURENCE, M S ANSELL
  NSM D C JONES, L F MORGAN
AFAN VALE *see* Glyncorrwg and the Upper Afan Valley etc *Llan*
ALED Mission Area, comprising Abergele, Betws-yn-Rhos w Trofarth, Brynymaen, Colwyn, Colwyn Bay, Llanddulas, Llandrillo-yn-Rhos, Llanelian, Llysfaen, Petryal, and St George *St As 5* **I** D T B LEWIS **P-in-c** G COOPER
  TV C R OWEN, D Q BELLAMY, K A JOHNSON
  Hon C R M WATTS **NSM** J SEARL, S STOREY
ALLTMAWR (St Mauritius) *see* Buallt *S & B*

ALLTWEN (St John the Baptist) *see* Cilybebyll *Llan*
ALYN Mission Area, comprising Broughton w Berse, Brymbo, Bwlchgwyn, Gresford, Gwersyllt, Holt, Isycoed, Llay, Minera w Coedpoeth, Rossett, and Southsea *St As 11*
  I P R-M DE G GOWER **TV** H BUTLER, J P HARRIS, J T HUGHES, W R MARSHALL **C** D A CAWDELL **NSM** S PIERCY, Y PRYCE
AMBLESTON (St Mary) *see* Spittal w Trefgarn and Ambleston w St Dogwells *St D*
AMLWCH (St Eleth) *see* Bro Eleth *Ban*
AMMANFORD (All Saints) *see* Betws w Ammanford *St D*
AMMANFORD (St Michael) *as above*
AMROTH (St Elidyr) *see* St Issell's and Amroth w Crunwere and Marros *St D*
ANGLE (St Mary) *see* Monkton *St D*
ARTHOG (St Catherine) *see* Bro Cymer *Ban*
BAGILLT (St Mary and St Peter) *see* Estuary and Mountain Miss Area *St As*
BAGLAN (St Catherine) (St Baglan) *Llan 5*
  P-in-c S JENKYNS **C** E JENKYNS
BALA (Christ Church) *see* Penedeyrn Miss Area *St As*
BANGOR (Eglwys y Groes) *see* Bro Deiniol *Ban*
BANGOR (St David) *as above*
BANGOR (St Mary) *as above*
BANGOR (St Peter) *as above*
BANGOR MONACHORUM (St Dunawd) *see* Maelor Miss Area *St As*
BANGOR TEIFI (St David) *see* Llandysul w Bangor Teifi and Llanfairollwyn etc *St D*
BARGOED (St Gwladys) and Deri w Brithdir *Llan 9*
  P-in-c R A D LINDSAY
BARMOUTH *see* Bro Ardudwy *Ban*
BARRY (All Saints) (St Baruc) (St Dyfan and St Teilo) *Llan 3*
  TR B ANDREWS **TV** K W LAKE, R C PARRISH **C** C C SEATON
BASSALEG (St Basil) *Mon 5* **TR** C M L STONE
BEACON HILL *S & B 2* **V** *vacant*
BEACONS, THE *S & B 1* **P-in-c** K RICHARDS **C** A N JEVONS
  OLM E BRAMLEY
BEAUFORT (St David) *see* Upper Ebbw Valleys *Mon*
BEAUMARIS (St Catherine) *see* Bro Seiriol *Ban*
BEAUMARIS (St Cawrdaf) *as above*
BEAUMARIS (St Mary and St Nicholas) *as above*
BEAUMARIS (St Michael) *as above*
BEAUMARIS (St Seiriol) *as above*
BEDDGELERT (St Mary) *see* Bro Eifionydd *Ban*
BEDWAS (St Barrwg) w Machen w Michaelston-y-Fedw w Rudry *Mon 5* **R** P D CROCKER **C** D A ROBERTS
  NSM A B PARKES, R P MULCAHY
BEDWELLTY (St Sannan) *see* Upper Islwyn *Mon*
BEGELLY (St Mary) w Ludchurch and East Williamston *St D 3* **R** *vacant*
BERRIEW (St Beuno) *see* Pool Miss Area *St As*
BERSHAM (St Mary) *see* Wrexham *St As*
BETTISFIELD (St John the Baptist) *see* Maelor Miss Area *St As*
BETTWS *see* Dan yr Eppynt *S & B*
BETTWS (St David) *Mon 6* **P-in-c** H J DAVIES
BETTWS (St David) *see* Llansantffraid, Bettws and Aberkenfig *Llan*
BETTWS CHAPEL *see* Llantilio Pertholey w Bettws Chpl etc *Mon*
BETTWS DISSERTH (St Mary) *see* Colwyn *S & B*
BETTWS NEWYDD (not known) *see* Raglan Gp *Mon*
BETWS (Holy Trinity) *see* Glasbury and Llowes w Clyro and Betws *S & B*

BETWS (St David) w Ammanford *St D 12*   **P-in-c** S BALE
  NSM L REES
BETWS BLEDRWS (St Bledrws or St Michael) *see* Lampeter w
  Maestir and Silian and Llangybi and Betws Bledrws *St D*
BETWS CEDEWAIN (St Beuno) *see* Cedewain Miss Area *St As*
BETWS GARMON (St Garmon) *see* Llanbeblig w Caernarfon
  and Betws Garmon etc *Ban*
BETWS LEUCU (St Lucia) *see* Llanddewi Brefi and Llangeitho
  St D
BETWS-Y-COED (St Mary) *see* Bro Gwydyr *Ban*
BETWS-YN-RHOS (St Michael) *see* Aled Miss Area *St As*
BEULAH *see* Blaenau Irfon *S & B*
BIRCHGROVE (St John) *see* Llansamlet *S & B*
BISHOPSTON (St Teilo) *see* Three Cliffs *S & B*
BISHTON (St Cadwaladr) *see* Magor *Mon*
BISTRE (All Saints) *see* Borderlands Miss Area *St As*
BISTRE (Emmanuel) *as above*
BISTRE (St Cecilia) *as above*
BLACKWOOD (St Margaret) *see* Upper Islwyn *Mon*
BLAENAU FFESTINIOG (St David) *see* Bro Moelwyn *Ban*
BLAENAU IRFON *S & B 2*   **P-in-c** P M E B BERESFORD-WEBB
BLAENAVON (St Peter) *see* Upper Torfaen *Mon*
BLAENGWRACH (St Mary) *see* Vale of Neath *Llan*
BLAENPENNAL (St David) *see* Tregaron Gp *St D*
BLAENPORTH (St David) *see* Bro Teifi *St D*
BLAENWYSG *S & B 1*   **V** M P WILDING
BLAINA (St Peter) *see* Upper Ebbw Valleys *Mon*
BLEDDFA (St Mary Magdalene) *see* Beacon Hill *S & B*
BLETHERSTON (St Mary) *see* Llawhaden w Bletherston and
  Uzmaston *St D*
BODEDERN (St Edern) *see* Bro Cwyfan *Ban*
BODELWYDDAN (St Margaret) *see* Aber-Morfa Miss Area
  St As
BODEWRYD (St Mary) *see* Bro Padrig *Ban*
BODFARI (St Stephen) *see* Denbigh Miss Area *St As*
BODWROG (St Twrog) *see* Bro Cyngar *Ban*
BONTDDU *see* Bro Ardudwy *Ban*
BONVILSTON (St Mary) *see* St Nicholas w Bonvilston and
  St George-super-Ely *Llan*
BONYMAEN (St Margaret) *see* Glantawe *S & B*
BORDERLANDS Mission Area, comprising Bistre,
  Broughton, Buckley, Connah's Quay, Ewloe, Hawarden,
  Hope, Llanfynydd, Pentrobin, Sandycroft, Sealand, and
  Shotton *St As 13*   **I** M J BATCHELOR   **P-in-c** A O MAYES,
  P POWELL   **TV** A R PAWLEY, A S JONES, D B EVANS, N A KELLY,
  S D GREEN   **C** G K STANNING, G L ERLANDSON
  NSM A CRONIN, S BAIRD
BORTH (St Matthew) and Eglwys-fach and Llangynfelyn
  St D 9   **V** vacant
BOSHERSTON (St Michael) *see* Monkton *St D*
BOTWNNOG (St Beuno) *see* Bro Madryn *Ban*
BOUGHROOD (St Cynog) *see* Llandefalle and Llyswen w
  Boughrood etc *S & B*
BRACKLA (St Mary) *see* Coity, Nolton and Brackla w
  Coychurch *Llan*
BRAWDY (St David) *see* Gtr Dewisland *St D*
BRECHFA (St Teilo) and Llanfihangel Rhos-y-corn *St D 13*
  P-in-c L CHAMBERS   **NSM** R NOCK
BRECON (Cathedral of St John the Evangelist) *S & B 1*
  V vacant
BRECON (St David) w Llanspyddid and Llanilltyd *S & B 1*
  V vacant
BRECON (St Mary) *S & B 1*   **P-in-c** S E GRIFFITH
  NSM J M DAY   **OLM** G TODD
BRIDELL (St David) *see* Bro Teifi *St D*
BRIDGEND (St Illtud) *see* Newcastle *Llan*
BRIDGEND (St Mary) *see* Coity, Nolton and Brackla w
  Coychurch *Llan*
BRIGHTON, NEW (St James) *see* Mold Miss Area *St As*
BRITHDIR (St David) *see* Bargoed and Deri w Brithdir *Llan*
BRITHDIR (St Mary) *see* Tanat Valley Miss Area *St As*
BRO ARDUDWY, including Caerdeon, Harlech, Llanaber,
  Llanddwywe, Llandecwyn, Llanfair-juxta-Harlech, and
  Llanfihangel-y-Traethau *Ban 3*   **V** T HODGES
  NSM L R BAILY
BRO ARWYSTLI, including Llangurig, Llanidloes, Trefeglwys,
  and Camo *Ban 3*   **V** L B COWAN   **C** J PRICE
  NSM A C GWALCHMAI
BRO CADWALADR *Ban 1*   **V** E C WILLIAMS   **NSM** A HUGHES,
  E R ROBERTS, N WEBB
BRO CELYNNIN *Ban 2*   **V** D A PARRY   **C** E PARRY
BRO CWYFAN *Ban 1*   **R** P N BARRATT   **C** R L MOULES-JONES
BRO CYBI *Ban 1*   **V** A F HERRICK   **C** J R BAILEY, N A RIDINGS
BRO CYFEILIOG and Mawddwy, including Machynlleth and
  Mallwyd *Ban 3*   **V** M J BEECROFT   **NSM** J M EVANS,
  P N WARD

BRO CYMER, including Arthog, Brithdir, Bryncoedifor,
  Dolgellau, Fairbourne, Llanelltud, Llanfachreth,
  Llangelynnin, and Rhoslefain *Ban 3*   **R** T R WEBB
  NSM R L FORD
BRO CYNGAR *Ban 1*   **R** S R LEYLAND
BRO DEINIOL, including Conwy and Caerhun *Ban 2*
  TR K L JONES   **C** C V JOHN, T J JONES
BRO DWYNWEN *Ban 1*   **P-in-c** E ROBERTS   **C** N E STARKEY
BRO EIFIONYDD, including Abererch, Beddgelert, Criccieth,
  Denio, Dolbenmaen, Llanarmon, Llangybi, Llanystymdwy,
  Porthmadog, and Treflys *Ban 3*   **V** D J WILLIAMS
  TV K V WILLIAMS   **NSM** N GOLDING
BRO ELETH *Ban 1*   **R** K S ELLIS   **NSM** P E JONES
BRO ENLLI, including Pwllheli, Llanbedrog, and Aberdaron
  Ban 3   **V** A JONES   **C** H A BRYANT, J FLETCHER
BRO ERYRI, including Llanberis, Penisarwaun, and Deiniolen
  Ban 2   **C** R W TOWNSEND   **NSM** A F C WILCOX
BRO GWYDYR *Ban 2*   **P-in-c** S ELLIOTT   **C** S T A FREEMAN
BRO LLIEDI, comprising Dafen, Felin-Foel, Hendy, Llanelli,
  Llangennech, and Llwynhendy *St D 16*
  P-in-c D H E MOSFORD   **C** E L WHITTICK, S MILNE
  NSM H NICHOLLS, P C A MANSEL LEWIS, R C LOWE
BRO MADRYN, including Botwnnog, Bryncroes, Edern,
  Llandudwen, Llangwnnadl, Llaniestyn, Nefyn, Pistyll, and
  Tudweiliog *Ban 3*   **V** R S WOOD   **C** S L ROBERTS
BRO MOELWYN, including Blaenau Ffestiniog, Ffestiniog,
  Maentwrog, Penrhyndeudraeth, and Trawsfynydd *Ban 3*
  V R P BARNES
BRO OGWEN (Christ Church) *Ban 2*   **V** J G MATTHEWS
  NSM C E MCCREA
BRO PADRIG *Ban 1*   **R** vacant
BRO SANCLER *St D 10*   **P-in-c** C R LEWIS-JENKINS,
  E A HOWELLS   **NSM** C COURT, H A F BRUCE
BRO SEIRIOL *Ban 1*   **V** vacant
BRO TEIFI *St D 5*   **V** J S BENNETT   **P-in-c** C D FROST,
  P G B RATCLIFFE   **NSM** A G KENT, C HAMILTON
BRO TYSILIO, including Menai Bridge, Pentraeth, and
  Benllech *Ban 1*   **V** A WILLIAMS   **C** V S MORRIS
  Hon C G T JONES   **NSM** H JONES, L J RENDLE, T AP SION
BRO YSTUMANNER, including Aberdyfi, Bryn-Cruf,
  Llanegryn, Llanfihangel-y-Pennant, Tal-y-Llyn, and Tywyn
  Ban 3   **V** R P HANSFORD   **NSM** C C TEN WOLDE, S J ROLLINS
BRONINGTON (Holy Trinity) *see* Maelor Miss Area *St As*
BRONLLYS (St Mary) *see* Talgarth w Bronllys w Llanfilo *S & B*
BRONWYDD (St Celynnin) *see* Llanpumsaint w
  Llanllawddog *St D*
BROUGHTON (St Mary) *see* Borderlands Miss Area *St As*
BROUGHTON (St Paul) *see* Alyn Miss Area *St As*
BRYMBO (St Mary) *as above*
BRYN (St Tydfil) *see* Llangynwyd w Maesteg *Llan*
BRYN A MOR Mission Area, comprising Cwm, Dyserth,
  Ffynnongroyw, Gwaenysgor, Llanasa, Meliden, Prestatyn,
  and Trelawnyd *St As 1*   **P-in-c** J C HARVEY
BRYN PYDEW (St Katherine) *see* Aberconwy Miss Area *St As*
BRYNAMAN (St Catherine) w Cwmllynfell *St D 12*
  V A TEALE
BRYNCETHIN *see* Llansantffraid, Bettws and Aberkenfig *Llan*
BRYNCOEDIFOR (St Paul) *see* Bro Cymer *Ban*
BRYNCROES (St Mary) *see* Bro Madryn *Ban*
BRYNEGLWYS (St Tysilio) *see* Valle Crucis Miss Area *St As*
BRYNFORD (St Michael) *see* Estuary and Mountain Miss
  Area *St As*
BRYNGLAS (All Saints) *see* Newport All SS *Mon*
BRYNGWRAN *see* Bro Cwyfan *Ban*
BRYNGWYN (St Mary) *see* Newcastle Emlyn and Llandyfriog
  etc *St D*
BRYNGWYN (St Michael) *see* Erwood Gp w Painscastle Gp
  S & B
BRYNGWYN (St Peter) *see* Raglan Gp *Mon*
BRYNMAWR (St Mary the Virgin) *S & B 1*   **V** vacant
BRYNNA *see* Llanharan w Peterston-super-Montem *Llan*
BRYNMAEN (Christ Church) *see* Aled Miss Area *St As*
BUALLT (St Mary) *S & B 2*   **V** N HOOK   **OLM** J DAY
BUCKHOLT (St John the Baptist) *see* Monmouth w
  Overmonnow etc *Mon*
BUCKLEY (Good Shepherd) *see* Borderlands Miss Area *St As*
BUCKLEY (St Matthew) *as above*
BUILTH WELLS (St Mary) *see* Buallt *S & B*
BULWARK (St Christopher) *see* Chepstow *Mon*
BURRY PORT (St Mary) and Pwll *St D 11*   **P-in-c** N P JONES
BURTON (St Mary) *see* Llanstadwell and Burton and
  Rosemarket *St D*
BUTE TOWN (St Aidan) *see* Pontlottyn and Fochriw *Llan*
BUTTINGTON (All Saints) *see* Pool Miss Area *St As*
BWLCH (All Saints) *see* Llyn Safaddan *S & B*
BWLCHGWYN (Christ Church) *see* Alyn Miss Area *St As*

BWLCHYCIBAU (Christ Church)   *see* Vyrnwy Miss Area *St As*

BYLCHAU (St Thomas)   *see* Denbigh Miss Area *St As*

CADOXTON-JUXTA-BARRY (St Cadoc)   *see* Barry *Llan*

CADOXTON-JUXTA-BARRY (St Mary)   *as above*

CADOXTON-JUXTA-NEATH (St Catwg) and Tonna *Llan 6*
P-in-c A J M MEREDITH

CAERAU (St Cynfelin)   *see* Glyncorrwg and the Upper Afan
Valley etc *Llan*

CAERAU w Ely (St David) (St Timothy) *Llan 2*   **V** J L SMITH
NSM C J LEE

CAERDEON (St Philip)   *see* Bro Ardudwy *Ban*

CAEREINION Mission Area, comprising Garthbeibio,
Llanerfyl, Llanfair Caereinion, Llangadfan, Llangynyw,
Llanllugan, Manafon, Meifod, Pont Dolanog, and Pont
Robert *St As 7*   **I** J E JAMES   **P-in-c** Y KHUSHI
NSM E G JONES, J G HAWKINS

CAEREITHIN (St Teilo) *S & B 3*   **V** vacant

CAERFALLWCH (St Paul)   *see* Estuary and Mountain Miss
Area *St As*

CAERGEILIOG   *see* Bro Cwyfan *Ban*

CAERGYBI   *see* Bro Cybi *Ban*

CAERHUN (St Mary)   *see* Bro Celynnin *Ban*

CAERLEON (St Cadoc) and Llanfrechfa Group, The *Mon 6*
V S A PRATTEN   **C** W C TAYLER

CAERNARFON (Feed My Lambs)   *see* Llanbeblig w
Caernarfon and Betws Garmon etc *Ban*

CAERNARFON (St Mary)   *as above*

CAERPHILLY (St Andrew)   *see* Eglwysilan and Caerphilly *Llan*

CAERPHILLY (St Catherine)   *as above*

CAERPHILLY (St Martin)   *as above*

CAERWENT (St Stephen and St Tathan)   *see* Wentwood *Mon*

CAERWYS (St Michael)   *see* Denbigh Miss Area *St As*

CALDICOT (St Mary) *Mon 3*   **TR** R M REARDON

CALLWEN (St John the Baptist)   *see* Cwmtawe Uchaf *S & B*

CAMROSE (St Ishmael) *St D 1*   **V** vacant

CANTON (St Catherine) *Llan 1*   **V** vacant

CANTON (St John) *Llan 1*   **R** vacant

CANTON Cardiff (St Luke) *Llan 1*   **TR** M R PREECE
TV E L REES-KENNY   **NSM** J R JENKINS

CANTREF (St Mary)   *see* The Beacons *S & B*

CAPEL (Dewi Sant)   *see* Llansadwrn w Llanwrda and
Manordeilo *St D*

CAPEL BANGOR (St David)   *see* Llanbadarn Fawr and Elerch
and Penrhyncoch etc *St D*

CAPEL COELBREN (Capel Coelbren)   *see* Cwmtawe Uchaf
S & B

CAPEL COLMAN (St Colman)   *see* Bro Teifi *St D*

CAPEL CYNON (St Cynon)   *see* Llanarth and Capel Cynon w
Talgarreg etc *St D*

CAPEL DEWI (St David)   *see* Llanfihangel-ar-arth w Capel
Dewi *St D*

CAPEL IFAN (St John the Baptist)   *see* Gwendraeth Fawr *St D*

CAPEL LLANILLTERNE (St Ellteyrn)   *see* Pentyrch and Capel
Llanillterne *Llan*

CAPEL MAIR   *see* Llangeler w Pen-Boyr *St D*

CAPEL NEWYDD (St Paul)   *see* Upper Torfaen *Mon*

CAPEL Y GROES   *see* Carmarthen St Pet and Abergwili etc
St D

CAPEL-Y-FFIN (St Mary)   *see* Hay w Llanigon and Capel-y-Ffin
S & B

CARDIFF (Christ Church) Roath Park *Llan 1*
P-in-c T O HUGHES   **NSM** J HILLEBERT

CARDIFF (Dewi Sant) *Llan 1*   **V** D C LLOYD
NSM R W LINECAR

CARDIFF (St Andrew and St Teilo)   *see* Cathays *Llan*

CARDIFF (St German) (St Saviour) *Llan 1*   **P-in-c** P S O'HARE

CARDIFF (St Luke)   *see* Canton Cardiff *Llan*

CARDIFF (St Mary) *Llan 1*   **P-in-c** D J ATKINS

CARDIFF (St Michael and All Angels)   *see* Cathays *Llan*

CARDIFF City Parish (St John the Baptist) *Llan 1*
P-in-c S J JONES   **C** L M HANNEY   **NSM** R W LINECAR

CARDIGAN (St Mary)   *see* Bro Teifi *St D*

CAREW (St Mary) and Cosheston and Nash and Redberth
St D 3   **V** vacant

CARMARTHEN (St Peter) (St John the Evangelist) and
Abergwili and Capel y Groes *St D 10*   **P-in-c** M A R HILL
NSM J M BRITTON, M WEBSTER, R MOORE

CARMARTHEN St David (Christ Church) *St D 10*
V P H B THOMAS   **C** D A RICHARDS   **NSM** R W MASKELL

CARMEL (Eglwys Fair)   *see* Catheiniog *St D*

CARNO (St John)   *see* Bro Arwystli *Ban*

CARROG (St Ffraid)   *see* Valle Crucis Miss Area *St As*

CASCOB (St Michael)   *see* E Radnor *S & B*

CASTELLAN   *see* Bro Teifi *St D*

CASTLE BYTHE   *see* W Cemaes *St D*

CASTLE CAEREINION (St Garmon)   *see* Pool Miss Area *St As*

CATHAYS (St Andrew and St Teilo) (St Michael and All
Angels) *Llan 1*   **P-in-c** C R DOWNS   **NSM** M J UNDERDOWN

CATHEDINE (St Michael)   *see* Llyn Safaddan *S & B*

CATHEINIOG *St D 13*   **P-in-c** S E JONES   **NSM** V A HOPE-BELL

CEDEWAIN Mission Area, comprising Aberhafesp, Betws
Cedewain, Dolfor, Kerry, Llanllwchaiarn and Newtown,
Llanmerewig, Llanwyddelan, Mochdre, and Tregynon
St As 6   **I** N W MORRIS   **TV** N F M MORRIS

CEFN (St Mary)   *see* Denbigh Miss Area *St As*

CEFN COED (St John the Baptist) w Vaynor *S & B 1*
P-in-c T J WILLIAMS

CEFN FOREST (St Thomas)   *see* Upper Islwyn *Mon*

CEFNLLYS (St Michael)   *see* Glan Ithon *S & B*

CELLAN (All Saints)   *see* Llanddewi Brefi and Llangeitho *St D*

CEMAES   *see* Bro Padrig *Ban*

CEMAES, WEST *St D 2*   **P-in-c** A T FURSE, C C BROWN,
N A LLEWELLYN   **C** J E PARKER   **NSM** J M ANNIS, R DAVIES,
S BARNETT

CEMAIS (St Tydecho)   *see* Bro Cyfeiliog and Mawddwy *Ban*

CENARTH (St Llawddog)   *see* Newcastle Emlyn and
Llandyfriog etc *St D*

CERRIGYDRUDION (St Mary Magdalene)   *see* Penedeyrn Miss
Area *St As*

CHEPSTOW (St Mary) *Mon 3*   **V** P R AVERAY   **C** L RYDER

CHERITON   *see* Monkton *St D*

CHERITON (St Cadoc)   *see* Llangennith w Llanmadoc and
Cheriton *S & B*

CHIRK (St Mary)   *see* Offa Miss Area *St As*

CILCAIN (St Mary)   *see* Mold Miss Area *St As*

CILCENNIN (Holy Trinity)   *see* Llanfihangel Ystrad and
Cilcennin w Trefilan etc *St D*

CILFYNYDD (St Luke)   *see* Pontypridd *Llan*

CILGERRAN (St Llawddog)   *see* Bro Teifi *St D*

CILIAU AERON (St Michael)   *see* Llanerch Aeron w Ciliau
Aeron and Dihewyd etc *St D*

CILRHEDYN *St D 5*   **V** vacant

CILYBEBYLL (St John the Evangelist) *Llan 6*   **P-in-c** J SHAW

CIL-Y-CWM (St Michael) and Ystrad-ffin w Rhandirmwyn
Llanfair-ar-y-Bryn *St D 14*   **P-in-c** E A MCKNIGHT

CLOCAENOG (St Foddhyd)   *see* Dyffryn Clwyd Miss Area *St As*

CLUNDERWEN (St David)   *see* Whitland w Cyffig and
Henllan Amgoed etc *St D*

CLYDACH (St Mary) (St Michael) *S & B 3*
C-in-c D T MARTIN

CLYDACH VALE (St Thomas)   *see* Tonypandy w Clydach Vale
w Williamstown *Llan*

CLYDAU (St Clydai)   *see* Crymych Gp *St D*

CLYNNOG FAWR (St Beuno)   *see* Uwch Gwyrfai Beuno Sant
Ban

CLYRO (St Michael and All Angels)   *see* Glasbury and Llowes
w Clyro and Betws *S & B*

CLYTHA   *see* Llanarth w Clytha and Llansantffraed etc *Mon*

COCKETT (St Peter)   *see* Swansea St Pet *S & B*

COEDKERNEW   *see* Marshfield w St Bride's Wentloog *Mon*

COEDYPAEN (Christchurch)   *see* Usk Min Area *Mon*

COETMOR (Christ Church)   *see* Bro Ogwen *Ban*

COITY (St Mary), Nolton and Brackla w Coychurch *Llan 4*
R M KOMOR, M R C THORNE   **C** M P BROADWAY

COLVA (St David)   *see* New Radnor and Llanfihangel
Nantmelan etc *S & B*

COLWINSTON (St Michael), Llandow and Llysworney
Llan 7   **P-in-c** A M KETTLE

COLWYN *S & B 2*   **C** L M WATSON

COLWYN (St John the Baptist)   *see* Aled Miss Area *St As*

COLWYN BAY (St David)   *as above*

COLWYN BAY (St Paul)   *as above*

COMINS COCH   *see* Llanbadarn Fawr and Elerch and
Penrhyncoch etc *St D*

CONNAH'S QUAY (St David's Mission Church)   *see*
Borderlands Miss Area *St As*

CONNAH'S QUAY (St Mark)   *as above*

CONWY (St Mary and All Saints)   *see* Bro Celynnin *Ban*

CORRIS (Holy Trinity)   *see* Bro Cyfeiliog and Mawddwy *Ban*

CORWEN (St Mael and St Sulien)   *see* Valle Crucis Miss Area
St As

COSHESTON (St Michael)   *see* Carew and Cosheston and
Nash and Redberth *St D*

COWBRIDGE (Holy Cross) *Llan 7*   **TR** S P ADAMS
TV V L ASHLEY

COYCHURCH (St Crallo)   *see* Coity, Nolton and Brackla w
Coychurch *Llan*

CRAI (St Ilid)   *see* Blaenwysg *S & B*

CRAIGYDON (St Paul)   *see* Aberconwy Miss Area *St As*

CREGRINA (St David)   *see* Colwyn *S & B*

CRIBYN (St Silin)   *see* Llanfihangel Ystrad and Cilcennin w
Trefilan etc *St D*

CRICCIETH (St Catherine) *see* Bro Eifionydd *Ban*

CRICKADARN (St Mary) *see* Erwood Gp w Painscastle Gp *S & B*

CRICKHOWELL (St Edmund) w Cwmdu and Tretower
S & B 1 **V** R Y KHAN

CRIGGION (St Michael) *see* Pool Miss Area *St As*

CRINDAU (All Saints) *see* Newport All SS *Mon*

CRINOW (St Teilo) *see* Narberth w Mounton w Robeston Wathen etc *St D*

CROESCEILIOG (St Mary) *see* Cwmbran *Mon*

CROSS HANDS (St Anne) *see* Gors-las *St D*

CROSS INN (Holy Trinity) *see* Llanllwchaearn and Llanina *St D*

CROSS KEYS (St Catherine) *see* Lower Islwyn Min Area *Mon*

CROSSGATES *see* Ithon Valley *S & B*

CRUGYBYDDAR (St Peter) *see* Beacon Hill *S & B*

CRYMYCH Group, The *St D 1* **P-in-c** J H L COPUS

CRYNANT (St Margaret) *see* Dulais Valley *Llan*

CWM (St Mael and St Sulien) *see* Bryn a Mor Miss Area *St As*

CWM (St Paul) *see* Upper Ebbw Valleys *Mon*

CWMAFAN (St Michael) *Llan 5* **P-in-c** E JENKYNS
C S JENKYNS

CWMAMAN (Christ Church) *St D 12* **C** C E JONES

CWMAMAN (St Joseph) *see* Aberaman and Cwmaman *Llan*

CWMANN (St James) *see* Pencarreg and Llanycrwys *St D*

CWMAVON (St Michael) *see* Cwmafan *Llan*

CWMBACH (St Mary Magdalene) *Llan 8*
P-in-c C B W SMITH

CWMBACH LLECHRYD (St John the Divine) *see* Upper Wye *S & B*

CWMBRAN (St Gabriel) *Mon 8* **V** N C PERRY **TV** E E KERL
C B SUMMERS **NSM** F M A EVANS, H D THOMAS, S M HOBBS

CWMCARN (St John the Evangelist) *see* Lower Islwyn Min Area *Mon*

CWMCARVAN (St Clement) *see* Rockfield and Dingestow Gp *Mon*

CWM-COCH (St Mark) *see* Llandybie *St D*

CWMDARE (St Luke) *see* Aberdare St Fagan *Llan*

CWMDDAUDDWR (St Bride) *see* Gwastedyn *S & B*

CWMDDAUDDWR (St Winifred) *as above*

CWMDU (St Michael the Archangel) *see* Crickhowell w Cwmdu and Tretower *S & B*

CWMDUAD (St Alban) *see* Cynwyl Elfed *St D*

CWMFFRWD (St Anne) *see* Llangunnor w Cwmffrwd *St D*

CWMLLYNFELL (St Margaret) *see* Brynaman w Cwmllynfell *St D*

CWMPARC (St George) *see* Pen Rhondda Fawr *Llan*

CWMTAWE UCHAF *S & B 3* **V** *vacant*

CWMTILLERY (St Paul) *see* Abertillery w Cwmtillery w Llanhilleth etc *Mon*

CWMYOY (St Martin) *see* Llanfihangel Crucorney w Oldcastle etc *Mon*

CWRT-HENRI (St Mary) *see* Catheiniog *St D*

CYDWELI (St Mary) (St Teilo) and Llandyfaelog *St D 11*
P-in-c T COPELAND

CYFFIG (St Cyffig) *see* Whitland w Cyffig and Henllan Amgoed etc *St D*

CYMAU (All Saints) *see* Borderlands Miss Area *St As*

CYMMER (St John the Evangelist) *see* Porth Newydd *Llan*

CYNCOED (All Saints) (St Edeyrn) *Mon 5* **TR** J A HENLEY
C J THORNE, M DAVIS **NSM** B A SMITH

CYNWYL ELFED (St Cynwyl) *St D 10* **V** *vacant*

CYNWYL GAEO (St Cynwyl) w Llansawel and Talley and Abergorlech *St D 14* **P-in-c** D A WILSON

DAFEN (St Michael and All Angels) *see* Bro Lliedi *St D*

DALE (St James) and St Brides w Marloes and Hasguard w St Ishmael's *St D 4* **P-in-c** A P JOHNSON **NSM** G FORD

DAN YR EPPYNT *S & B 1* **P-in-c** M A BAILEY

DAROWEN (St Tudur) *see* Bro Cyfeiliog and Mawddwy *Ban*

DEFYNNOG (St Cynog) *see* Blaenwysg *S & B*

DEGANWY (All Saints) *see* Aberconwy Miss Area *St As*

DENBIGH (St Marcella) *see* Denbigh Miss Area *St As*

DENBIGH (St Mary) *as above*

DENBIGH Mission Area, comprising Bodfari, Bylchau, Caerwys, Cefn, Henllan, Llandyrnog, Llangwyfan, Llannefydd, Llanrhaeadr-yng-Nghinmeirch, Nantglyn, Sinan, Trefnant, and Tremeirchion *St As 2* **P-in-c** G SPENCER
TV P A WALKER, V C ROWLANDS **NSM** C THOMAS

DENIO (St Peter) *see* Bro Eifionydd *Ban*

DERI (St Peter) *see* Bargoed and Deri w Brithdir *Llan*

DEVAUDEN (St James) *see* Itton and St Arvans w Penterry and Kilgwrrwg w Devauden *Mon*

DEWISLAND, GREATER *St D 2* **P-in-c** D C HOARE,
M H ROWLANDS **NSM** M I PLANT

DIHEWYD (St Vitalis) *see* Llanerch Aeron w Ciliau Aeron and Dihewyd etc *St D*

DINAS (Misson) w Penygraig *Llan 11* **P-in-c** J M THOMAS

DINAS (St Brynach) *see* W Cemaes *St D*

DINGESTOW (St Dingad) *see* Rockfield and Dingestow Gp *Mon*

DINHAM *see* Wentwood *Mon*

DINMAEL (St Catherine) *see* Penedeyrn Miss Area *St As*

DISERTH (St Cewydd) *see* Glan Ithon *S & B*

DOLBENMAEN (St Mary) *see* Bro Eifionydd *Ban*

DOLFOR (St Paul) *see* Cedewain Miss Area *St As*

DOLGARROG (St Mary) *see* Bro Celynnin *Ban*

DOLGELLAU (St Mary) *see* Bro Cymer *Ban*

DOLWYDDELAN (St Gwyddelan) *see* Bro Gwydyr *Ban*

DOWLAIS (All Saints) (Christ Church) and Penydarren
Llan 9 **P-in-c** C A OWEN

DULAIS VALLEY *Llan 6* **P-in-c** E M REES

DWYGYFYLCHI (St David) *see* Dwylan *Ban*

DWYGYFYLCHI (St Gwynin) *as above*

DWYGYFYLCHI (St Seiriol) *as above*

DWYLAN *Ban 2* **V** J E BROWN

DYFFRYN *see* Bro Ardudwy *Ban*

DYFFRYN (St Matthew) *Llan 6* **V** S J BODYCOMBE

DYFFRYN CLWYD Mission Area, comprising Clocaenog, Derwen, Efenechtyd, Gyffylliog, Llanarmon yn Ial, Llanbedr Dyffryn Clwyd, Llanelidan, Llanfair Dyffryn Clwyd, Llanfwrog, Llangynhafal, and Llanychan w Llanynys *St As 3*
TV J S EVANS, R W CARTER **C** D C PARRY JONES

DYFFRYN HONDDU (St Cynog) *see* Dan yr Eppynt *S & B*

DYSERTH (St Bridget) *see* Bryn a Mor Miss Area *St As*

DYSERTH (St Mael and St Sulien) *as above*

DYSERTH (St Michael) *as above*

EBBW VALE (Christchurch) *see* Upper Ebbw Valleys *Mon*

EDERN (St Edern) *see* Bro Madryn *Ban*

EFENECHTYD (St Michael) *see* Dyffryn Clwyd Miss Area *St As*

EGLWYS FAIR A CURIG *St D 10* *vacant*

EGLWYS FAIR GLYN-TAF *see* Whitland w Cyffig and Henllan Amgoed etc *St D*

EGLWYS GYMYN (St Margaret) *see* Lampeter Velfrey and Llanddewi Velfrey etc *St D*

EGLWYS NEWYDD (St Michael) *see* Grwp Bro Ystwyth a Mynach *St D*

EGLWYS OEN DUW *see* Blaenau Irfon *S & B*

EGLWYS-FACH (St Michael) *see* Borth and Eglwys-fach and Llangynfelyn *St D*

EGLWYSILAN (St Ilan) and Caerphilly *Llan 9*
TR M GREENAWAY-ROBBINS **TV** P P SMITH
C A D C HIGHWAY, E L LE BRUN POWELL

EGLWYSRHOS (St Eleri and St Mary) *see* Aberconwy Miss Area *St As*

EGLWYSWRW (St Cristiolus) *see* Bro Teifi *St D*

ELERCH (St Peter) *see* Llanbadarn Fawr and Elerch and Penrhyncoch etc *St D*

ELY (St David) *see* Caerau w Ely *Llan*

ELY (St Timothy) *as above*

ERBISTOCK (St Hilary) *see* Maelor Miss Area *St As*

ERWOOD Group w The Painscastle Group, The *S & B 2*
P-in-c P G KEOWN

ESCLUSHAM (Holy Trinity) *see* Wrexham *St As*

ESGAIRGEILIOG *see* Bro Cyfeiliog and Mawddwy *Ban*

ESTUARY AND MOUNTAIN Mission Area, comprising Bagillt, Brynford, Caerfallwch, Flint, Gorsedd, Halkyn, Holywell, Mostyn, Rhesycae, Whitford, and Ysgeifiog *St As 4*
TV A W COLEMAN, B HARVEY, H N BURGESS
C L C S STROUD, R BATEMAN **NSM** A HOOPER

EVANCOYD (St Peter) *see* New Radnor and Llanfihangel Nantmelan etc *S & B*

EWENNY (St Michael) *see* Glamorgan Heritage Coast *Llan*

EWLOE (Holy Spirit) *see* Borderlands Miss Area *St As*

EYTON (St Deiniol) *see* Maelor Miss Area *St As*

FAIRBOURNE (St Cynon) *see* Bro Cymer *Ban*

FAIRWATER (St Peter) *Llan 2* **V** C P SUTTON

FAWR *see* Llandeilo Fawr and Taliaris *St D*

FELINDRE (St Barnabas) *see* Llangeler w Pen-Boyr *St D*

FELIN-FOEL (Holy Trinity) *see* Bro Lliedi *St D*

FELIN-GWM (St John) *see* Llanegwad w Llanfihangel Uwch Gwili *St D*

FERNDALE (St Dunstan) *see* Rhondda Fach Uchaf *Llan*

FERRYSIDE (St Thomas) *see* St Ishmael's w Llan-saint and Ferryside *St D*

FFESTINIOG (St Michael) *see* Bro Moelwyn *Ban*

FFYNNONGROYW (All Saints) *see* Bryn a Mor Miss Area *St As*

FISHGUARD (St Mary) *see* W Cemaes *St D*

FLEMINGSTON (St Michael) *see* Cowbridge *Llan*

FLEUR-DE-LIS (St David) *see* Upper Islwyn *Mon*

FLINT (St Mary and St David) *see* Estuary and Mountain Miss Area *St As*

FLINT (St Thomas) *as above*

FOCHRIW (St Mary and St Andrew)   *see* Pontlottyn and Fochriw *Llan*
FORDEN (St Michael)   *see* Pool Miss Area *St As*
FREYSTROP (St Justinian)   *see* Llangwm w Freystrop and Johnston *St D*
FRON (Mission Church)   *see* Pool Miss Area *St As*
FRONCYSYLLTE (St David)   *see* Offa Miss Area *St As*
FRONGOCH   *see* Penedeyrn Miss Area *St As*
GABALFA (St Mark) *Llan 1*   **V** M J R NELSON
GAERWEN   *see* Bro Cadwaladr *Ban*
GARTHBEIBIO (St Tydecho)   *see* Caereinion Miss Area *St As*
GARTHELI (St Gartheli)   *see* Llanddewi Brefi and Llangeitho *St D*
GELLIGAER (St Catwg) (St Margaret) *Llan 9*
   P-in-c G C POWELL
GILESTON (St Giles)   *see* Glamorgan Heritage Coast *Llan*
GILFACH GOCH (St Barnabas)   *see* Tonyrefail w Gilfach Goch *Llan*
GILVACH (St Margaret)   *see* Gelligaer *Llan*
GLADWESTRY (St Mary)   *see* New Radnor and Llanfihangel Nantmelan etc *S & B*
GLAIS (St Paul)   *see* Llansamlet *S & B*
GLAMORGAN Heritage Coast *Llan 7*   **TR** E C R COUNSELL
   TV C A VAUGHAN, K R PRIME   **C** M WALFORD
   NSM J D PETERS
GLAN ELY (Resurrection) *Llan 2*   **P-in-c** J GOULD
   C D JONES
GLAN ITHON *S & B 2*   **R** A PERRIN   **C** B E CURNOW, P LETSON
GLANGRWYNEY (Mission Church)   *see* Vale of Gwrynne *S & B*
GLANOGWEN (Christ Church)   *see* Bro Ogwen *Ban*
GLANTAWE (St Margaret) (St Peter) *S & B 3*   **V** *vacant*
GLASBURY (St Peter) (All Saints) and Llowes w Clyro and Betws *S & B 1*   **V** D E THOMAS
GLASCOED (St Michael)   *see* Mamhilad w Monkswood and Glascoed Chapel *Mon*
GLASCOMBE (St David)   *see* Colwyn *S & B*
GLYN   *see* Brecon St David w Llanspyddid and Llanilltyd *S & B*
GLYNCORRWG (St John the Baptist) and the Upper Afan Valley w Caerau St Cynfelyn *Llan 5*   **P-in-c** B J REANEY
GLYNDYFRDWY (St Thomas)   *see* Valle Crucis Miss Area *St As*
GLYNTAFF (St Mary)   *see* Pontypridd *Llan*
GOETRE (St Peter) w Llanover *Mon 4*   **R** J A COLLIER
GOLDCLIFFE (St Mary Magdalen)   *see* Magor *Mon*
GORSEDD (St Paul)   *see* Estuary and Mountain Miss Area *St As*
GORSEINON (St Catherine) *S & B 4*   **P-in-c** A MORGAN
GORS-LAS (St Lleian) *St D 12*   **P-in-c** V K JONES
   NSM J B JONES
GOVILON (Christchurch) w Llanfoist w Llanelen *Mon 1*
   P-in-c C R WALTERS
GOWER, SOUTH WEST *S & B 4*   **C** J W DAVIES
GOWERTON (St John the Evangelist) *S & B 4*   **P-in-c** A F PYE
   C S RUMBELOW
GRAIG (St John)   *see* Pontypridd *Llan*
GRANDSTON (St Catherine)   *see* Gtr Dewisland *St D*
GRANGETOWN (St Paul) w Cardiff St Dyfrig and St Samson *Llan 1*   **V** *vacant*
GRESFORD (All Saints)   *see* Alyn Miss Area *St As*
GRIFFITHSTOWN (St Hilda)   *see* Panteg and Griffithstown *Mon*
GROESWEN (St David)   *see* Pentyrch and Capel Llanillterne *Llan*
GRONANT (St Winifred)   *see* Bryn a Mor Miss Area *St As*
GROSMONT (St Nicholas) and Skenfrith and Llangattock Lingoed and Llanfair Chapel *Mon 1*   **P-in-c** L E BURRETT
GRWP BRO YSTWYTH A MYNACH: Llanfihangel-y-Creuddyn w Llanafan-y-Trawscoed w Llanwnnws w Ysbyty Ystwyth w Ysbyty Cynfyn w Lantrisant w Eglwys Newydd *St D 9*   **NSM** R G MORRIS
GUILSFIELD (St Aelhaiarn)   *see* Pool Miss Area *St As*
GUMFRESTON (St Lawrence)   *see* Tenby *St D*
GWAENYSGOR   *see* Bryn a Mor Miss Area *St As*
GWASTEDYN *S & B 2*   **P-in-c** L R SHARPE   **NSM** E RONICLE
GWEHELOG   *see* Usk Min Area *Mon*
GWENDDWR (St Dubricius)   *see* Erwood Gp w Painscastle Gp *S & B*
GWENDRAETH FAWR *St D 11*   **P-in-c** M C CHARLES
GWENLLI (St Mark)   *see* Llanarth and Capel Cynon w Talgarreg etc *St D*
GWERNAFFIELD (Holy Trinity)   *see* Mold Miss Area *St As*
GWERNFFRWD (St David)   *see* Llanrhidian w Llanyrnewydd *S & B*
GWERSYLLT (Holy Trinity)   *see* Alyn Miss Area *St As*
GWRYNNE   *see* Vale of Gwrynne *S & B*
GWYDDELWERN (St Beuno)   *see* Valle Crucis Miss Area *St As*

GWYNFE (All Saints)   *see* Llangadog and Gwynfe w Llanddeusant *St D*
GYFFIN (St Benedict)   *see* Bro Celynnin *Ban*
GYFFYLLIOG (St Mary)   *see* Dyffryn Clwyd Miss Area *St As*
HAFOD (St John)   *see* Cen Swansea *S & B*
HAKIN (St Mary)   *see* Hubberston and Herbrandston *St D*
HALKYN (St Mary the Virgin)   *see* Estuary and Mountain Miss Area *St As*
HANMER (St Chad)   *see* Maelor Miss Area *St As*
HARLECH (St Tanwg)   *see* Bro Ardudwy *Ban*
HAROLDSTON ST ISSELLS (St Issell)   *see* Haverfordwest *St D*
HAROLDSTON WEST (St Madog)   *see* Walton W w Talbenny and Haroldston W *St D*
HAVERFORDWEST (St Martin) *St D 1*   **V** *vacant*
HAWARDEN (St Deiniol)   *see* Borderlands Miss Area *St As*
HAY (St Mary) (St John) w Llanigon and Capel-y-Ffin *S & B 1*   **V** R D WILLIAMS
HAYSCASTLE (St Mary)   *see* Gtr Dewisland *St D*
HENDY (St David)   *see* Bro Lliedi *St D*
HENEGLWYS (St Llwydian)   *see* Bro Cyngar *Ban*
HENFYNYW (St David) w Aberaeron and Llanddewi Aberarth w Llanbadarn Trefeglwys *St D 7*   **V** J P LEWIS
HENLLAN (St Sadwrn)   *see* Denbigh Miss Area *St As*
HENLLYS (St Peter)   *see* Cwmbran *Mon*
HENRYD (St Celynin Old Parish Church)   *see* Bro Celynnin *Ban*
HENRY'S MOAT (St Bernard)   *see* W Cemaes *St D*
HEOL-Y-CYW (St Paul)   *see* Llanilid w Pencoed *Llan*
HERBRANDSTON (St Mary)   *see* Hubberston and Herbrandston *St D*
HEYOPE (St David)   *see* Beacon Hill *S & B*
HIGH CROSS (St Anne)   *see* Bassaleg *Mon*
HIRWAUN (St Lleurwg) (St Winifred) *Llan 8*   **P-in-c** C J REES
HOLT (St Chad)   *see* Alyn Miss Area *St As*
HOLY ISLAND   *see* Bro Cybi *Ban*
HOLYHEAD (Morawelon)   *see* Bro Cybi *Ban*
HOLYHEAD (St Cybi)   *as above*
HOLYHEAD (St Ffraid)   *as above*
HOLYHEAD (St Gwenfaen)   *as above*
HOLYWELL (Holy Trinity)   *see* Estuary and Mountain Miss Area *St As*
HOLYWELL (St James)   *as above*
HOLYWELL (St Peter)   *as above*
HOPE (St Cynfarch)   *see* Borderlands Miss Area *St As*
HOWEY (St David)   *see* Glan Ithon *S & B*
HUBBERSTON (St David) (Holy Spirit) and Herbrandston *St D 4*   **I** A P BOOKLESS
HUNDLETON (St David)   *see* Monkton *St D*
ILSTON (St Illtyd)   *see* Three Cliffs *S & B*
IRFON VALLEY *S & B 2*   **P-in-c** P M E B BERESFORD-WEBB
ISLWYN, LOWER Ministry Area *Mon 7*   **Hon C** M J JEFFORD
   NSM M REDWOOD, S T SMITH, V I HODGES
ISLWYN, UPPER *Mon 7*   **TR** M OWEN   **TV** N S ADAMS,
   V J BUTLER   **C** H REES, L K PHILBRICK, L TAYLOR
   Hon C T MORGAN   **NSM** B JONES
ISYCOED (St Paul)   *see* Alyn Miss Area *St As*
ITHON VALLEY, The *S & B 2*   **C** R STORER
ITTON (St Deiniol) and St Arvans w Penterry and Kilgwrrwg w Devauden *Mon 3*   **V** M J GOLLOP
   NSM M E ZORAB
JEFFREYSTON (St Jeffrey) w Reynoldston and Loveston and Martletwy w Lawrenny and Yerbeston *St D 3*
   P-in-c P R MACKNESS   **NSM** B H ROBERTS
JOHNSTON (St Peter)   *see* Llangwm w Freystrop and Johnston *St D*
JORDANSTON (St Cawrda)   *see* Gtr Dewisland *St D*
KEMEYS COMMANDER (All Saints)   *see* Raglan Gp *Mon*
KENFIG   *see* Pyle w Kenfig *Llan*
KENFIG HILL (St Theodore) *Llan 5*   **P-in-c** J R H DURLEY
KERRY (St Michael)   *see* Cedewain Miss Area *St As*
KILGETTY   *see* Begelly w Ludchurch and E Williamston *St D*
KILGWRRWG (Holy Cross)   *see* Itton and St Arvans w Penterry and Kilgwrrwg w Devauden *Mon*
KILLAY (St Hilary) (St Martin) *S & B 4*   **V** P J GWYNN
KILVEY (All Saints)   *see* Swansea St Thos and Kilvey *S & B*
KNELSTON   *see* SW Gower *S & B*
KNIGHTON (St Edward)   *see* E Radnor *S & B*
LALESTON (St David) and Merthyr Mawr w Penyfai *Llan 4*
   P-in-c A M BEER
LAMPETER (St Peter) w Maestir and Silian and Llangybi and Betws Bledrws *St D 8*   **P-in-c** M A ROWLANDS
   NSM E ARNOLD-DAVIES, J C M KIMBER
LAMPETER VELFREY (St Peter) and Llanddewi Velfrey and Eglwys Gymyn *St D 3*   **P-in-c** P H DAVIES
LAMPHEY (St Faith and St Tyfei)   *see* Monkton *St D*
LANDORE and Treboeth *S & B 3*   **V** D JONES

LANGSTONE (not known)   *see* Magor *Mon*
LAUGHARNE (St Martin)   *see* Bro Sancler *St D*
LAWRENNY (St Caradog)   *see* Jeffreyston w Reynoldston and Loveston etc *St D*
LECKWITH   *see* Penarth and Llandough *Llan*
LETTERSTON (St Giles)   *see* W Cemaes *St D*
LISVANE (St Denys) *Llan 1*   **V** J B GRIFFITHS
LITTLE NEWCASTLE (St Peter)   *see* W Cemaes *St D*
LLANABER (St David)   *see* Bro Ardudwy *Ban*
LLANABER (St John) *as above*
LLANABER (St Mary) *as above*
LLANAELHAEARN (St Aelhaiarn)   *see* Uwch Gwyrfai Beuno Sant *Ban*
LLANAFAN FAWR (St Afan)   *see* Upper Wye *S & B*
LLANAFAN-Y-TRAWSCOED (St Afan)   *see* Grwp Bro Ystwyth a Mynach *St D*
LLANALLGO (St Gallo)   *see* Bro Eleth *Ban*
LLANANNO (St Anno)   *see* Ithon Valley *S & B*
LLANARMON (St Garmon)   *see* Bro Eifionydd *Ban*
LLANARMON DYFFRYN CEIRIOG (St Garmon)   *see* Valle Crucis Miss Area *St As*
LLANARMON MYNYD (St Garmon)   *see* Tanat Valley Miss Area *St As*
LLANARMON YN IAL (St Garmon)   *see* Dyffryn Clwyd Miss Area *St As*
LLANARTH (St David) (St Teilo) and Capel Cynon w Talgarreg and (St Mark) *St D 7*   **V** C L BOLTON
LLANARTH w Clytha and Llansantffraed St Bride w Llanddewi Rhyderch and Llangattock-juxta-Usk *Mon 1*   **P-in-c** J HUMPHRIES
LLANARTHNE (St David) and Llanddarog *St D 10*   **P-in-c** B D WITT
LLANASA (St Asaph and St Cyndeyrn)   *see* Bryn a Mor Miss Area *St As*
LLANBABO (St Pabo)   *see* Bro Cwyfan *Ban*
LLANBADARN FAWR (St Padarn)   *see* Ithon Valley *S & B*
LLANBADARN FAWR (St Padarn) and Elerch and Penrhyncoch and Capel Bangor *St D 9*   **P-in-c** A G LOAT   **C** A J EVANS, L L DAFIS   **NSM** H R EVANS, R EVANS
LLANBADARN FYNYDD (St Padarn)   *see* Ithon Valley *S & B*
LLANBADARN ODWYN (St Padarn)   *see* Llanddewi Brefi and Llangeitho *St D*
LLANBADARN TREFEGLWYS (St Padarn)   *see* Henfynyw w Aberaeron and Llanddewi Aberarth etc *St D*
LLANBADARN-Y-GARREG (St Padarn)   *see* Erwood Gp w Painscastle Gp *S & B*
LLANBADOC (St Madog)   *see* Usk Min Area *Mon*
LLANBADRIG (St Padrig)   *see* Bro Padrig *Ban*
LLANBEBLIG (St Peblig) w Caernarfon and Betws Garmon w Waunfawr *Ban 2*   **TR** R F DONALDSON
LLANBEDR (St Peter)   *see* Bro Ardudwy *Ban*
LLANBEDR DYFFRYN CLWYD (St Peter)   *see* Dyffryn Clwyd Miss Area *St As*
LLANBEDR PAINSCASTLE (St Peter)   *see* Erwood Gp w Painscastle Gp *S & B*
LLANBEDR PONT STEFFAN   *see* Lampeter w Maestir and Silian and Llangybi and Betws Bledrws *St D*
LLANBEDR YSTRAD YW (St Peter)   *see* Vale of Gwrynne *S & B*
LLANBEDR, UPPER (St Peter)   *see* Bro Gwydyr *Ban*
LLANBEDRGOCH (St Peter)   *see* Bro Tysilio *Ban*
LLANBEDROG (St Pedrog)   *see* Bro Enlli *Ban*
LLANBERIS (St Padarn)   *see* Bro Eryri *Ban*
LLANBERIS (St Peris) *as above*
LLANBISTER (St Cynllo)   *see* Ithon Valley *S & B*
LLANBLETHIAN (St Blethian)   *see* Cowbridge *Llan*
LLANBOIDY (St Brynach)   *see* Meidrim and Llanboidy and Merthyr *St D*
LLANBRYN-MAIR (St Mary)   *see* Bro Cyfeiliog and Mawddwy *Ban*
LLANCARFAN (St Cadoc)   *see* Penmark w Llancarfan w Llantrithyd *Llan*
LLANDAFF (Cathedral of St Peter and St Paul w St Dyfrig, St Teilo and St Euddogwy) *Llan 2*   **V** G H CAPON
LLANDAFF NORTH (All Saints)   *see* Whitchurch *Llan*
LLANDANWG   *see* Bro Ardudwy *Ban*
LLANDAVENNY   *see* Wentwood *Mon*
LLANDDAROG (St Twrog)   *see* Llanarthne and Llanddarog *St D*
LLANDDEINIOL (St Deiniol)   *see* Llansantffraed w Llanrhystud and Llanddeiniol *St D*
LLANDDEINIOLEN (St Deiniol)   *see* Bro Eryri *Ban*
LLANDDERFEL (St Derfel)   *see* Penedeyrn Miss Area *St As*
LLANDDEW (St David) *S & B 1*   **OLM** G TODD
LLANDDEWI   *see* Blaenau Irfon *S & B*
LLANDDEWI (St David)   *see* SW Gower *S & B*
LLANDDEWI ABERARTH (St David)   *see* Henfynyw w Aberaeron and Llanddewi Aberarth etc *St D*

LLANDDEWI BREFI (St David) and Llangeitho *St D 8*   **P-in-c** W D JONES
LLANDDEWI FACH (St David)   *see* Erwood Gp w Painscastle Gp *S & B*
LLANDDEWI RHONDDA (St David)   *see* Pontypridd *Llan*
LLANDDEWI RHYDDERCH (St David)   *see* Llanarth w Clytha and Llansantffraed etc *Mon*
LLANDDEWI VELFREY (St David)   *see* Lampeter Velfrey and Llanddewi Velfrey etc *St D*
LLANDDEWI YSTRADENNI (St David)   *see* Ithon Valley *S & B*
LLANDDEWI'R CWM (St David)   *see* Buallt *S & B*
LLANDDOGET (St Doged)   *see* Aberconwy Miss Area *St As*
LLANDDONA (St Dona)   *see* Bro Seiriol *Ban*
LLANDDOWROR (St Teilo)   *see* Bro Sancler *St D*
LLANDDULAS (St Cynfryd)   *see* Aled Miss Area *St As*
LLANDDWYWE (St Ddwywe)   *see* Bro Ardudwy *Ban*
LLANDECWYN (St Tecwyn) *as above*
LLANDEFAELOG-FACH (St Maelog)   *see* Dan yr Eppynt *S & B*
LLANDEFALLE (St Matthew) and Llyswen w Boughrood and Llanstephen w Talachddu *S & B 1*   **R** I P CHARLESWORTH
LLANDEGFAN (St Tegfan)   *see* Bro Tysilio *Ban*
LLANDEGLA (St Tecla)   *see* Valle Crucis Miss Area *St As*
LLANDEGLEY (St Tecla)   *see* Ithon Valley *S & B*
LLANDEGVETH (St Tegfeth)   *see* Caerleon and Llanfrechfa *Mon*
LLANDEILO FAWR (St Teilo) and Taliaris *St D 13*   **V** M S SADLER
LLANDEILO GRABAN (St Teilo)   *see* Erwood Gp w Painscastle Gp *S & B*
LLANDEILO TAL-Y-BONT (St Teilo) (St Michael) *S & B 4*   **V** J N GILLIBRAND
LLANDENNY (St John the Apostle)   *see* Raglan Gp *Mon*
LLANDEUSSANT (St Simon and St Jude)   *see* Llangadog and Gwynfe w Llanddeusant *St D*
LLANDEVAUD (St Peter)   *see* Wentwood *Mon*
LLANDEWI FACH   *see* Caerleon and Llanfrechfa *Mon*
LLANDEWI SKIRRID (St David)   *see* Llantilio Pertholey w Bettws Chpl etc *Mon*
LLANDILO'R FAN (St Teilo)   *see* Blaenwysg *S & B*
LLANDINAM (St Llonio)   *see* Bro Arwystli *Ban*
LLANDINGAT (St Dingad) w Myddfai *St D 14*   **NSM** T B NELSON
LLANDINORWIG (Christ Church)   *see* Bro Eryri *Ban*
LLANDOGO (St Oudoceus) w Whitebrook Chapel and Tintern Parva *Mon 2*   **P-in-c** N P JUCKES   **OLM** J F AVERY, R A DAGGER
LLANDOUGH (St Dochdwy)   *see* Cowbridge *Llan*
LLANDOUGH (St Dochdwy)   *see* Penarth and Llandough *Llan*
LLANDOVERY   *see* Llandingat w Myddfai *St D*
LLANDOW (Holy Trinity)   *see* Colwinston, Llandow and Llysworney *Llan*
LLANDRE (St Michael)   *see* Llanfihangel Genau'r Glyn and Llangorwen *St D*
LLANDRILLO (St Trilio)   *see* Penedeyrn Miss Area *St As*
LLANDRILLO-YN-RHOS (St George)   *see* Aled Miss Area *St As*
LLANDRILLO-YN-RHOS (St Trillo) *as above*
LLANDRINDOD (Holy Trinity)   *see* Glan Ithon *S & B*
LLANDRINDOD (Old Parish Church) *as above*
LLANDRINIO (St Trinio, St Peter and St Paul)   *see* Pool Miss Area *St As*
LLANDRYGARN (St Trygarn)   *see* Bro Cyngar *Ban*
LLANDUDNO (St Tudno) (Holy Trinity) *Ban 2*   **V** A C SULLY   **C** M D PRITCHARD, M K R STALLARD   **NSM** S RHYS EVANS
LLANDUDNO JUNCTION (St Michael)   *see* Aberconwy Miss Area *St As*
LLANDUDWEN (St Tudwen)   *see* Bro Madryn *Ban*
LLANDULAIS IN TIR ABAD (St David)   *see* Blaenau Irfon *S & B*
LLANDWROG (St Twrog)   *see* Uwch Gwyrfai Beuno Sant *Ban*
LLANDYBIE (St Tybie) *St D 12*   **P-in-c** H M OWEN
LLANDYFAELOG (St Maelog)   *see* Cydweli and Llandyfaelog *St D*
LLANDYFAN (Church)   *see* Llandybie *St D*
LLANDYFODWG (St Tyfodwg) and Cwm Ogwr *Llan 4*   **P-in-c** J J JENKINS
LLANDYFRIOG (St Tyfriog)   *see* Newcastle Emlyn and Llandyfriog etc *St D*
LLANDYFRYDOG (St Tyfrydog)   *see* Bro Eleth *Ban*
LLANDYGAI (St Ann)   *see* Bro Ogwen *Ban*
LLANDYGAI (St Tegai) *as above*
LLANDYGWYDD (St Tygwydd)   *see* Bro Teifi *St D*
LLANDYRNOG (St Cwyfan)   *see* Denbigh Miss Area *St As*
LLANDYRNOG (St Tyrnog) *as above*
LLANDYRY (Church)   *see* Pen-bre *St D*
LLANDYSILIO (St Mary)   *see* Pool Miss Area *St As*

LLANDYSILIO (St Tysilio)   *see* Bro Tysilio *Ban*
LLANDYSILIO (St Tysilio)   *see* Pool Miss Area *St As*
LLANDYSILIO (St Tysilio)   *see* Whitland w Cyffig and Henllan Amgoed etc *St D*
LLANDYSILIOGOGO (St Tysilio)   *see* Llangrannog w Llandysiliogogo w Penbryn *St D*
LLANDYSSIL (St Tyssil)   *see* Pool Miss Area *St As*
LLANDYSUL (St Tysul) w Bangor Teifi and Llanfairollwyn w Llangynllo *St D 6*   P-in-c G M REID   NSM E DAVIES
LLANEDEYRN (All Saints)   *see* Cyncoed *Mon*
LLANEDI (St Edith) w Tycroes and Saron *St D 12*   P-in-c V K JONES
LLANEDWEN (St Edwen)   *see* Bro Dwynwen *Ban*
LLANEGRYN (St Mary and St Egryn)   *see* Bro Ystumanner *Ban*
LLANEGWAD (St Egwad) w Llanfihangel Uwch Gwili *St D 13*   V R J PATTINSON
LLANEILIAN (St Eilian)   *see* Bro Eleth *Ban*
LLANELEN (St Helen)   *see* Govilon w Llanfoist w Llanelen *Mon*
LLANELIAN (St Elian)   *see* Aled Miss Area *St As*
LLANELIDAN (St Elidan)   *see* Dyffryn Clwyd Miss Area *St As*
LLANELLI (St Elli) *S & B 1*   P-in-c C J BEVAN
LLANELLI (St Elli)   *see* Bro Lliedi *St D*
LLANELLI (St Peter)   *see* Bro Lliedi *St D*
LLANELLTUD (St Illtyd)   *see* Bro Cymer *Ban*
LLANELWEDD (St Matthew)   *see* Colwyn *S & B*
LLANENDDWYN (St Enddwyn)   *see* Bro Ardudwy *Ban*
LLANENGAN (St Engan)   *see* Bro Enlli *Ban*
LLANERCH AERON (St Non) w Ciliau Aeron and Dihewyd and Mydroilyn *St D 7*   I vacant
LLANERCH-Y-MEDD (St Mair)   *see* Bro Eleth *Ban*
LLANERFYL (St Erfyl)   *see* Caereinion Miss Area *St As*
LLANEUGRAD (St Eugrad)   *see* Bro Eleth *Ban*
LLANFABON (St Mabon)   *see* Treharris, Trelewis, Bedlinog and Llanfabon *Llan*
LLANFACHRAETH (St Machraeth)   *see* Bro Cwyfan *Ban*
LLANFACHRETH (St Machreth)   *see* Bro Cymer *Ban*
LLANFAELOG (St Maelog)   *see* Bro Cwyfan *Ban*
LLANFAELRHYS (St Maelrhys)   *see* Bro Enlli *Ban*
LLANFAES   *see* Brecon St David w Llanspyddid and Llanilltyd *S & B*
LLANFAETHLU (St Maethlu)   *see* Bro Padrig *Ban*
LLANFAIR (St Mary)   *see* Grosmont and Skenfrith and Llangattock etc *Mon*
LLANFAIR (St Mary)   *see* Llandingat w Myddfai *St D*
LLANFAIR CAEREINION (St Mary)   *see* Caereinion Miss Area *St As*
LLANFAIR CLYDOGAU (St Mary)   *see* Llanddewi Brefi and Llangeitho *St D*
LLANFAIR DISCOED (St Mary)   *see* Wentwood *Mon*
LLANFAIR DYFFRYN CLWYD (St Cynfarch and St Mary)   *see* Dyffryn Clwyd Miss Area *St As*
LLANFAIR KILGEDDIN   *see* Raglan Gp *Mon*
LLANFAIR MATHAFARN EITHAF (St Mary)   *see* Bro Tysilio *Ban*
LLANFAIR NANT-GWYN (St Mary)   *see* Bro Teifi *St D*
LLANFAIR NANT-Y-GOF (St Mary)   *see* W Cemaes *St D*
LLANFAIR TALHAEARN (St Mary)   *see* Aled Miss Area *St As*
LLANFAIR-AR-Y-BRYN (St Mary)   *see* Cil-y-Cwm and Ystrad-ffin w Rhandir-mwyn etc *St D*
LLANFAIRFECHAN (Christ Church)   *see* Dwylan *Ban*
LLANFAIR-IS-GAER (St Mary) (Old Parish Church) *Ban 2*   I vacant
LLANFAIR-JUXTA-HARLECH (St Mary)   *see* Bro Ardudwy *Ban*
LLANFAIRPWLLGWYNGYLLGOGERYCHWYRNDROBW LL-LLANTISILIOGOGOGOCH (St Mary)   *see* Bro Dwynwen *Ban*
LLANFAIR-YNG-NGHORNWY (St Mary)   *see* Bro Padrig *Ban*
LLANFAIR-YN-NEUBWLL   *see* Bro Cwyfan *Ban*
LLANFAIR-YN-Y-CWMWD (St Mary)   *see* Bro Dwynwen *Ban*
LLANFALLTEG w Castell Dwyran *St D 15*   V vacant
LLANFAREDD (St Mary)   *see* Colwyn *S & B*
LLANFECHAIN (St Garmon)   *see* Vyrnwy Miss Area *St As*
LLANFECHAN (St Afan)   *see* Irfon Valley *S & B*
LLANFECHELL (St Mechell)   *see* Bro Padrig *Ban*
LLANFERRES (St Berres)   *see* Mold Miss Area *St As*
LLANFEUGAN (St Meugan)   *see* The Beacons *S & B*
LLANFFINAN (St Ffinan)   *see* Bro Cadwaladr *Ban*
LLANFFLEWIN (St Fflewin)   *see* Bro Padrig *Ban*
LLANFIHANGEL ABERCYWYN (St Michael)   *see* Bro Sancler *St D*
LLANFIHANGEL ABERGWESSIN   *see* Blaenau Irfon *S & B*
LLANFIHANGEL ABERYTHYCH (St Michael)   *see* Catheiniog *St D*
LLANFIHANGEL BRYNPABUAN (St Michael and All Angels)   *see* Upper Wye *S & B*
LLANFIHANGEL CILFARGEN   *see* Catheiniog *St D*

LLANFIHANGEL CRUCORNEY (St Michael) w Oldcastle and Cwmyoy and Llanthony *Mon 1*   P-in-c D J YOUNG
LLANFIHANGEL FECHAN (St Michael)   *see* Dan yr Eppynt *S & B*
LLANFIHANGEL GENAU'R GLYN (St Michael) and Llangorwen *St D 9*   V vacant
LLANFIHANGEL GLYN MYFYR (St Michael)   *see* Penedeyrn Miss Area *St As*
LLANFIHANGEL GOBION (St Michael)   *see* Raglan Gp *Mon*
LLANFIHANGEL HELYGEN (St Michael)   *see* Glan Ithon *S & B*
LLANFIHANGEL LLEDROD (St Michael)   *see* Llanilar w Rhostie and Llangwyryfon etc *St D*
LLANFIHANGEL NANTBRAN (St Michael)   *see* Dan yr Eppynt *S & B*
LLANFIHANGEL NANTMELAN (St Michael)   *see* New Radnor and Llanfihangel Nantmelan etc *S & B*
LLANFIHANGEL PENBEDW   *see* Bro Teifi *St D*
LLANFIHANGEL PONTYMOILE (St Michael)   *see* Panteg and Griffithstown *Mon*
LLANFIHANGEL RHOS-Y-CORN (St Michael)   *see* Brechfa and Llanfihangel Rhos-y-corn *St D*
LLANFIHANGEL RHYDITHON (St Michael)   *see* Ithon Valley *S & B*
LLANFIHANGEL ROGIET   *see* Caldicot *Mon*
LLANFIHANGEL TALYLLYN (St Michael)   *see* Llyn Safaddan *S & B*
LLANFIHANGEL TRE'R BEIRDD (St Mihangel)   *see* Bro Eleth *Ban*
LLANFIHANGEL YSGEIFIOG (St Michael)   *see* Bro Cadwaladr *Ban*
LLANFIHANGEL YSTRAD (St Michael) and Cilcennin w Trefilan and Nantcwnlle *St D 7*   V vacant
LLANFIHANGEL-AR-ARTH (St Michael) w Capel Dewi *St D 6*   V B D TIMOTHY
LLANFIHANGEL-TOR-Y-MYNYDD (St Michael)   *see* Llanishen w Trellech Grange and Llanfihangel etc *Mon*
LLANFIHANGEL-UWCH-GWILI (St Michael)   *see* Llanegwad w Llanfihangel Uwch Gwili *St D*
LLANFIHANGEL-Y-CREUDDYN (St Michael)   *see* Grwp Bro Ystwyth a Mynach *St D*
LLANFIHANGEL-YNG-NGHWYNFA (St Michael)   *see* Vyrnwy Miss Area *St As*
LLANFIHANGEL-YN-NHYWYN   *see* Bro Cwyfan *Ban*
LLANFIHANGEL-Y-PENNANT (St Michael)   *see* Bro Ystumanner *Ban*
LLANFIHANGEL-YSTERN-LLEWERN (St Michael)   *see* Rockfield and Dingestow Gp *Mon*
LLANFIHANGEL-Y-TRAETHAU (St Michael)   *see* Bro Ardudwy *Ban*
LLANFILO (St Bilo)   *see* Talgarth w Bronllys w Llanfilo *S & B*
LLANFOIST (St Ffwyst)   *see* Govilon w Llanfoist w Llanelen *Mon*
LLANFRECHFA (All Saints)   *see* Caerleon and Llanfrechfa *Mon*
LLANFRYNACH (St Brynach)   *see* Cowbridge *Llan*
LLANFRYNACH (St Brynach)   *see* The Beacons *S & B*
LLANFWROG (St Mwrog and St Mary)   *see* Dyffryn Clwyd Miss Area *St As*
LLANFYLLIN (St Myllin)   *see* Vyrnwy Miss Area *St As*
LLANFYNYDD (St Egwad)   *see* Catheiniog *St D*
LLANFYNYDD (St Michael)   *see* Borderlands Miss Area *St As*
LLANFYRNACH (St Brynach)   *see* Crymych Gp *St D*
LLANGADFAN (St Cadfan)   *see* Caereinion Miss Area *St As*
LLANGADOG (St Cadog) and Gwynfe w Llanddeusant *St D 13*   V vacant
LLANGADWALADR (St Cadwaladr)   *see* Bro Cadwaladr *Ban*
LLANGADWALADR (St Cadwaladr)   *see* Tanat Valley Miss Area *St As*
LLANGAFFO (St Caffo)   *see* Bro Cadwaladr *Ban*
LLANGAMMARCH (St Cadmarch)   *see* Irfon Valley *S & B*
LLAN-GAN   *see* Whitland w Cyffig and Henllan Amgoed etc *St D*
LLANGAN (St Canna)   *see* Cowbridge *Llan*
LLANGANTEN (St Cannen)   *see* Irfon Valley *S & B*
LLANGAR (St John the Evangelist)   *see* Valle Crucis Miss Area *St As*
LLANGASTY TALYLLYN (St Gastyn)   *see* Llyn Safaddan *S & B*
LLANGATHEN (St Cathen)   *see* Catheiniog *St D*
LLANGATTOCK (St Cattwg) and Llangyndir *S & B 1*   R vacant
LLANGATTOCK LINGOED (St Cadoc)   *see* Grosmont and Skenfrith and Llangattock etc *Mon*
LLANGATTOCK-JUXTA-USK (St Cadoc)   *see* Llanarth w Clytha and Llansantffraed etc *Mon*
LLANGATTOCK-VIBON-AVEL (St Cadoc)   *see* Rockfield and Dingestow Gp *Mon*
LLANGEDWYN (St Cedwyn)   *see* Tanat Valley Miss Area *St As*

LLANGEFNI (St Cyngar)   *see* Bro Cyngar *Ban*
LLANGEINOR (St Ceinor) and the Garw Valley *Llan 4*
P-in-c R T PITMAN
LLANGEINWEN (St Ceinwen)   *see* Bro Dwynwen *Ban*
LLANGEITHO (St Ceitho)   *see* Llanddewi Brefi and Llangeitho
St D
LLANGELER (St Celer) w Pen-Boyr *St D 6*   **V** *vacant*
LLANGELYNNIN (St Celynin)   *see* Bro Cymer *Ban*
LLANGENNECH (St Gwynog)   *see* Bro Lliedi *St D*
LLANGENNI (St Cenau)   *see* Vale of Gwrynne *S & B*
LLANGENNITH (St Cenydd) w Llanmadoc and Cheriton
S & B 4   **Hon C** R G AUSTIN
LLANGERNYW (St Digain)   *see* Aled Miss Area *St As*
LLANGIAN (St Gian)   *see* Bro Enlli *Ban*
LLANGIWG *S & B 3*   **V** G H GREEN   **C** D T MARTIN
LLANGLYDWEN (St Cledwyn)   *see* Crymych Gp *St D*
LLANGOEDMOR (St Cynllo)   *see* Bro Teifi *St D*
LLANGOLLEN (St Collen)   *see* Valle Crucis Miss Area *St As*
LLANGOLLEN (St John)   *as above*
LLANGOLMAN (St Colman)   *see* W Cemaes *St D*
LLANGORSE (St Paulinus)   *see* Llyn Safaddan *S & B*
LLANGORWEN (All Saints)   *see* Llanfihangel Genau'r Glyn
and Llangorwen *St D*
LLANGRANNOG (St Carannog) w Llandysiliogogo w
Penbryn *St D 7*   **V** *vacant*
LLANGRISTIOLUS (St Cristiolus)   *see* Bro Cadwaladr *Ban*
LLANGUNNOG   *see* Llanishen w Trellech Grange and
Llanfihangel etc *Mon*
LLANGUNNOR (St Ceinwr) w Cwmffrwd *St D 10*   **V** *vacant*
LLANGURIG (St Curig)   *see* Bro Arwystli *Ban*
LLANGWLLONG (St Anau)   *see* Bro Cyngar *Ban*
LLANGWM (St Catherine)   *see* Penedeyrn Miss Area *St As*
LLANGWM (St Jerome) w Freystrop and Johnston *St D 4*
P-in-c J M ZIPPERLEN
LLANGWM ISAF (St John)   *see* Usk Min Area *Mon*
LLANGWNNADL (St Gwynhoedl)   *see* Bro Madryn *Ban*
LLANGWYFAN   *see* Denbigh Miss Area *St As*
LLANGWYFAN (St Cwyfan Old Church)   *see* Bro Cwyfan *Ban*
LLANGWYFAN (St Cwyfan)   *as above*
LLANGWYLLOG (St Cwyllog)   *see* Bro Cyngar *Ban*
LLANGWYRYFON (St Ursula)   *see* Llanilar w Rhostie and
Llangwyryfon etc *St D*
LLANGYBI (St Cybi)   *see* Bro Eifionydd *Ban*
LLANGYBI (St Cybi)   *see* Lampeter w Maestir and Silian and
Llangybi and Betws Bledrws *St D*
LLANGYBI (St Cybi)   *see* Usk Min Area *Mon*
LLANGYFELACH (St David and St Cyfelach) (St Teilo-on-
the-Clase) *S & B 3*   **C** A D PORTER
LLANGYNDEYRN (St Cyndeyrn)   *see* Trisant *St D*
LLANGYNDIR (St Cynidr and St Mary)   *see* Llangattock and
Llangynidr *S & B*
LLANGYNHAFAL (St Cynhafal)   *see* Dyffryn Clwyd Miss Area
St As
LLANGYNIN (St Cynin)   *see* Bro Sancler *St D*
LLANGYNLLO (St Cynllo)   *see* Beacon Hill *S & B*
LLANGYNLLO (St Cynllo)   *see* Llandysul w Bangor Teifi and
Llanfairollwyn etc *St D*
LLANGYNOG   *see* Buallt *S & B*
LLANGYNOG (St Cynog)   *see* Bro Sancler *St D*
LLANGYNOG (St Cynog)   *see* Tanat Valley Miss Area *St As*
LLANGYNWYD (St Cynwyd) (St Tydfil) w Maesteg *Llan 4*
V M H EVANS
LLANGYNYW (St Cynyw)   *see* Caereinion Miss Area *St As*
LLANGYSTENNIN (St Cystenin)   *see* Aberconwy Miss Area
St As
LLANHAMLACH (St Peter and St Illtyd)   *see* The Beacons
S & B
LLANHARAN (St Julius and St Aaron) w Peterston-super-
Montem *Llan 4*   **P-in-c** B A WOOD
LLANHARRY (St Illtud) *Llan 7*   **V** *vacant*
LLANHENNOCK (St John)   *see* Caerleon and Llanfrechfa *Mon*
LLANHILLETH (St Mark)   *see* Abertillery w Cwmtillery w
Llanhilleth etc *Mon*
LLANHYWEL (St Hywel)   *see* Gtr Dewisland *St D*
LLANIDAN (St Nidan)   *see* Bro Dwynwen *Ban*
LLANIDLOES (St Idloes)   *see* Bro Arwystli *Ban*
LLANIESTYN (St Iestyn)   *see* Bro Madryn *Ban*
LLANIESTYN (St Iestyn)   *see* Bro Seiriol *Ban*
LLANIGON (St Eigon)   *see* Hay w Llanigon and Capel-y-Ffin
S & B
LLANILAR (St Hilary) w Rhostie and Llangwyryfon w
Llanfihangel Lledrod and Llanwnnws *St D 9*
P-in-c S D EDWARDS   **NSM** T L DAVIS
LLANILID (St Illid and St Curig) w Pencoed *Llan 4*
R I M HODGES
LLANINA (St Ina)   *see* Llanllwchaearn and Llanina *St D*

LLANISHEN (Christ Church)   *see* Cardiff Ch Ch Roath Park
Llan
LLANISHEN (St Dennis) w Trellech Grange and
Llanfihangel Tor-y-Mynydd w Llangunnog and Llansoy
Mon 2   **V** *vacant*
LLANISHEN (St Isan) (St Faith) *Llan 1*   **V** *vacant*
LLANLLAWDDOG (St Llawddog)   *see* Llanpumsaint w
Llanllawddog *St D*
LLANLLAWER   *see* W Cemaes *St D*
LLANLLECHID (St Cross)   *see* Bro Ogwen *Ban*
LLANLLEONFEL (Parish Church)   *see* Irfon Valley *S & B*
LLANLLOWELL (St Llywel)   *see* Usk Min Area *Mon*
LLANLLUGAN (St Mary)   *see* Caereinion Miss Area *St As*
LLAN-LLWCH (St Mary)   *see* Bro Sancler *St D*
LLANLLWCHAEARN (St Llwchaiarn) and Llanina *St D 7*
P-in-c M F BAYNHAM   **NSM** J A MORTON
LLANLLWCHAIARN (All Saints)   *see* Cedewain Miss Area *St As*
LLANLLWCHAIARN (St Llwchaiarn)   *as above*
LLANLLWNI (St Luke or St Llonio)   *see* Llanybydder and
Llanwenog w Llanllwni etc *St D*
LLANLLYFNI (Christ Church)   *see* Uwch Gwyrfai Beuno Sant
Ban
LLANLLYFNI (St John)   *as above*
LLANLLYFNI (St Rhedyw)   *as above*
LLANLLYR-YN-RHOS (St Llyr)   *see* Glan Ithon *S & B*
LLANMADOC (St Madoc)   *see* Llangennith w Llanmadoc and
Cheriton *S & B*
LLANMAES (St Catwg)   *see* Glamorgan Heritage Coast *Llan*
LLANMARTIN (St Martin)   *see* Magor *Mon*
LLANMEREWIG (St Llwchaiarn)   *see* Cedewain Miss Area *St As*
LLANMIHANGEL (St Michael)   *see* Glamorgan Heritage Coast
Llan
LLANNEFYDD (St Nefydd and St Mary)   *see* Denbigh Miss
Area *St As*
LLAN-NON (St Non)   *see* Trisant *St D*
LLANNOR (Holy Cross)   *see* Bro Enlli *Ban*
LLANOVER (St Bartholomew)   *see* Goetre w Llanover *Mon*
LLANPUMSAINT (Five Saints) w Llanllawddog *St D 10*
C G JONES-HIGGS
LLANRHAEADR-YM-MOCHNANT (St Dogfan)   *see* Tanat
Valley Miss Area *St As*
LLANRHAEADR-YNG-NGHINMEIRCH (St Dyfnog)   *see*
Denbigh Miss Area *St As*
LLANRHIAN (St Rhian)   *see* Gtr Dewisland *St D*
LLANRHIDIAN (St Rhidian and St Illtyd) w Llanyrnewydd
S & B 4   **P-in-c** T D P ARDOUIN
LLANRHUDDLAD (St Rhuddlad)   *see* Bro Padrig *Ban*
LLANRHWYDRUS   *as above*
LLANRHYCHWYN (St Rhychwyn)   *see* Bro Gwydyr *Ban*
LLANRHYDD (St Meugan)   *see* Dyffryn Clwyd Miss Area *St As*
LLANRHYSTUD (St Restitutis)   *see* Llansantffraed w
Llanrhystud and Llanddeiniol *St D*
LLANRUG (St Michael)   *see* Bro Eryri *Ban*
LLANRUMNEY (St Dyfrig) *Mon 5*   **P-in-c** M I R DOWSETT
NSM A J JENKINS
LLANRWST (St Grwst)   *see* Aberconwy Miss Area *St As*
LLANSADWRN (St Sadwrn)   *see* Bro Tysilio *Ban*
LLANSADWRN (St Sadwrn) w Llanwrda and Manordeilo
St D 14   **P-in-c** V R SAYER   **NSM** D J THOMAS
LLANSADWRNEN (St Sadwrnen)   *see* Bro Sancler *St D*
LLAN-SAINT (All Saints)   *see* St Ishmael's w Llan-saint and
Ferryside *St D*
LLANSAMLET (St Samlet) (St John) (St Paul) *S & B 3*
V G D WATHAN
LLANSANNAN (St Sannan)   *see* Aled Miss Area *St As*
LLANSANNOR (St Senwyr)   *see* Cowbridge *Llan*
LLANSANTFFRAED (St Bridget)   *see* Llanarth w Clytha and
Llansantffraed etc *Mon*
LLANSANTFFRAED (St Bridget) w Llanrhystud and
Llanddeiniol *St D 7*   **V** J W SMITH
LLANSANTFFRAED-IN-ELWELL (St Bridget)   *see* Colwyn *S & B*
LLANSANTFFRAED-JUXTA-USK (St Bride)   *see* The Beacons
S & B
LLANSANTFFRAID GLAN CONWAY (St Ffraid)   *see* Aberconwy
Miss Area *St As*
LLANSANTFFRAID GLYN CEIRIOG (St Ffraid)   *see* Valle Crucis
Miss Area *St As*
LLANSANTFFRAID, Bettws and Aberkenfig *Llan 4*
V S BRUMWELL   **C** M KOMOR
LLANSANTFFRAID-YN-MECHAIN (St Ffraid)   *see* Vyrnwy Miss
Area *St As*
LLANSANTFRAID GLYN DYFRDWY (St Ffraid)   *see* Valle Crucis
Miss Area *St As*
LLANSAWEL (St Mary), Briton Ferry *Llan 6*   **V** S BIRDSALL
LLANSAWEL (St Sawyl)   *see* Cynwyl Gaeo w Llansawel and
Talley etc *St D*

LLANSILIN (St Silin)   *see* Tanat Valley Miss Area *St As*
LLANSOY (St Tysoi)   *see* Llanishen w Trellech Grange and
  Llanfihangel etc *Mon*
LLANSPYDDID (St Cattwg)   *see* Brecon St David w
  Llanspyddid and Llanilltyd *S & B*
LLANSTADWEL (St Tudwal) and Burton and Rosemarket
  St D 4   **P-in-c** A M CHADWICK   **NSM** J L HANCOCK,
  S M BESSANT
LLANSTEFFAN (St Ystyffan)   *see* Bro Sancler *St D*
LLANSTEPHEN (St Steffan)   *see* Llandefalle and Llyswen w
  Boughrood etc *S & B*
LLANTARNAM (St Michael)   *see* Cwmbran *Mon*
LLANTHETTY (St Tetti)   *see* The Beacons *S & B*
LLANTHONY (St David)   *see* Llanfihangel Crucorney w
  Oldcastle etc *Mon*
LLANTILIO CROSSENNY (St Teilo) and Penrhos w
  Llanvetherine and Llanvapley *Mon 1*   **P-in-c** C H A PRINCE
  NSM A DAWSON
LLANTILIO PERTHOLEY (St Teilo) w Bettws Chapel and
  Llanddewi Skirrid *Mon 1*   **P-in-c** J F GRAY
  NSM J L HUGHES
LLANTRISANT (Church)   *see* Grwp Bro Ystwyth a Mynach
  St D
LLANTRISANT (St Afran, St Ieuan and St Sanan)   *see* Bro
  Cwyfan *Ban*
LLANTRISANT (St Illtyd, St Gwynno and St Dyfodwg)
  (St Michael) (St David) *Llan 10*   **V** V L PARKINSON
  C S A BRETT
LLANTRISANT (St Peter, St Paul and St John)   *see* Usk Min
  Area *Mon*
LLANTRITHYD (St Illtyd)   *see* Penmark w Llancarfan w
  Llantrithyd *Llan*
LLANTWIT FARDRE (St Illtyd) *Llan 10*   **V** P M N GULLIDGE
LLANTWIT MAJOR (St Illtud)   *see* Glamorgan Heritage Coast
  Llan
LLANTYSILIO (St Tysilio)   *see* Valle Crucis Miss Area *St As*
LLANULID (St Ilid)   *see* Blaenwysg *S & B*
LLANVACHES (St Dyfrig)   *see* Wentwood *Mon*
LLANVAPLEY (St Mable)   *see* Llantilio Crossenny w Penrhos,
  Llanvetherine etc *Mon*
LLANVETHERINE (St James the Elder)   *as above*
LLANWDDYN (St Wyddyn)   *see* Vyrnwy Miss Area *St As*
LLANWELLWYFO (St Gwenllwyfo)   *see* Bro Eleth *Ban*
LLANWENARTH CITRA (St Peter)   *see* Abergavenny St Mary w
  Llanwenarth Citra *Mon*
LLANWENOG (St Gwenog)   *see* Llanybydder and Llanwenog
  w Llanllwni etc *St D*
LLANWERN (St Mary)   *see* Magor *Mon*
LLANWINIO (St Gwynio)   *see* Crymych Gp *St D*
LLANWNDA (St Gwyndaf)   *see* Uwch Gwyrfai Beuno Sant
  Ban
LLANWNDA (St Gwyndaf)   *see* W Cemaes *St D*
LLANWNNEN (St Lucia)   *see* Llanybydder and Llanwenog w
  Llanllwni etc *St D*
LLANWNNOG (St Gwynog)   *see* Bro Arwystli *Ban*
LLANWNNWS (St Gwnnws)   *see* Llanilar w Rhostie and
  Llangwyryfon etc *St D*
LLANWRDA (St Cwrdaf)   *see* Llansadwrn w Llanwrda and
  Manordeilo *St D*
LLANWRIN (St Ust and St Dyfrig)   *see* Bro Cyfeiliog and
  Mawddwy *Ban*
LLANWRTHWL (St Gwrthwl)   *see* Gwastedyn *S & B*
LLANWRTYD (St David)   *see* Blaenau Irfon *S & B*
LLANWRTYD WELLS (St James)   *as above*
LLANWYDDELAN (St Gwyddelan)   *see* Cedewain Miss Area
  St As
LLANWYNNO (Christ Church)   *see* Pontypridd *Llan*
LLANWYNNO (St Gwynno)   *as above*
LLANYBYDDER (St Peter) and Llanwenog w Llanllwni w
  Llanwnnen *St D 8*   **V** *vacant*
LLANYCHAEARN (St Llwchaiarn)   *see* Aberystwyth *St D*
LLANYCHAN (St Hychan)   *see* Dyffryn Clwyd Miss Area *St As*
LLANYCHAR (St David)   *see* W Cemaes *St D*
LLANYCHLWYDOG   *as above*
LLANYCRWYS (St David)   *see* Pencarreg and Llanycrwys *St D*
LLANYNGHENEDL VALLEY (St Michael)   *see* Bro Cwyfan *Ban*
LLANYNYS   *see* Buallt *S & B*
LLANYNYS (St Saeran)   *see* Dyffryn Clwyd Miss Area *St As*
LLANYRE   *see* Glan Ithon *S & B*
LLANYRNEWYDD (St Gwynour)   *see* Llanrhidian w
  Llanyrnewydd *S & B*
LLANYSTYMDWY (St John the Baptist)   *see* Bro Eifionydd *Ban*
LLANYWERN (St Mary the Virgin)   *see* Llyn Safaddan *S & B*
LLAWHADEN (St Aidan) w Bletherston and Uzmaston
  St D 1   **V** *vacant*
LLAWRYBETWS (St James)   *see* Penedeyrn Miss Area *St As*

LLAY (St Martin)   *see* Alyn Miss Area *St As*
LLECHRYD (St Tydfil)   *see* Bro Teifi *St D*
LLECHYLCHED (Holy Trinity)   *see* Bro Cwyfan *Ban*
LLISWERRY   *see* Newport Maindee and Lliswerry *Mon*
LLOWES (St Meilig)   *see* Glasbury and Llowes w Clyro and
  Betws *S & B*
LLWYDCOED (St James)   *see* Aberdare St Fagan *Llan*
LLWYDIARTH (St Mary)   *see* Vyrnwy Miss Area *St As*
LLWYNDERW (Holy Cross) (Clyne Chapel) *S & B 4*
  V J B DAVIES   **C** H D GRIFFITHS
LLWYNGWRIL   *see* Bro Cymer *Ban*
LLWYNHENDY (St David)   *see* Bro Lliedi *St D*
LLWYNYPIA   *see* Pont Rhondda *Llan*
LLYN SAFADDAN *S & B 1*   **P-in-c** K RICHARDS   **C** A N JEVONS,
  P LODGE   **OLM** E BRAMLEY
LLYSFAEN (St Cynfran)   *see* Aled Miss Area *St As*
LLYSWEN (St Gwendoline)   *see* Llandefalle and Llyswen w
  Boughrood etc *S & B*
LLYSWORNEY (St Tydfil)   *see* Colwinston, Llandow and
  Llysworney *Llan*
LLYS-Y-FRAN (St Meilyr)   *see* W Cemaes *St D*
LLYWEL (St David)   *see* Blaenwysg *S & B*
LOUGHOR (St Michael) (St David) *S & B 4*   **V** *vacant*
LOVESTON (St Leonard)   *see* Jeffreyston w Reynoldston and
  Loveston etc *St D*
LUDCHURCH (St Elidyr)   *see* Begelly w Ludchurch and E
  Williamston *St D*
MACHEN (St John the Baptist)   *see* Bedwas w Machen w
  Michaelston-y-Fedw w Rudry *Mon*
MACHEN (St Michael)   *as above*
MACHYNLLETH (St Peter)   *see* Bro Cyfeiliog and Mawddwy
  Ban
MAELOR Mission Area, comprising Bangor Monachorum,
  Bettisfield, Bronington, Erbistock, Hanmer and Tallarn
  Green, Marchwiel, Overton, Penley, and Worthenbury
  St As 12   **I** S M HUYTON   **P-in-c** P J MACKRIELL
  TV C HUGHES
MAENCLOCHOG (St Mary)   *see* W Cemaes *St D*
MAENORDEIFI (St David)   *see* Bro Teifi *St D*
MAENTWROG (St Twrog)   *see* Bro Moelwyn *Ban*
MAESGLAS (St Thomas)   *see* Newport Maesglas St Paul w
  St Steph and H Trin *Mon*
MAESMYNIS AND LLANYNYS (St David)   *see* Buallt *S & B*
MAESTEG (St David)   *see* Llangynwyd w Maesteg *Llan*
MAESTEG (St Michael)   *as above*
MAESTEILO (St John)   *see* Llandeilo Fawr and Taliaris *St D*
MAESTIR (St Mary)   *see* Lampeter w Maestir and Silian and
  Llangybi and Betws Bledrws *St D*
MAGOR (St Mary) *Mon 3*   **TR** J D HARRIS   **TV** C L JONES
  C S PATTERSON   **NSM** A R DAVIES, H I PREST
MAINDEE NEWPORT   *see* Newport Maindee and Lliswerry
  Mon
MALLWYD (St Tydecho)   *see* Bro Cyfeiliog and Mawddwy
  Ban
MALPAS (St Mary) *Mon 6*   **P-in-c** R C STEVENS   **C** M SELLERS
  NSM J A SIMS
MAMHILAD (St Illtud) w Monkswood and Glascoed
  Chapel *Mon 4*   **R** J A COLLIER
MANAFON (St Michael)   *see* Caereinion Miss Area *St As*
MANORBIER (St James) and St Florence *St D 3*   **V** *vacant*
MANORDEILO (St Paul)   *see* Llansadwrn w Llanwrda and
  Manordeilo *St D*
MANOROWEN (St Mary)   *see* W Cemaes *St D*
MANSELTON (St Michael and All Angels) and Cwmbwrla
  S & B 3   **P-in-c** I DREW-JONES
MARCHWIEL (St Marcella)   *see* Maelor Miss Area *St As*
MARCROSS (Holy Trinity)   *see* Glamorgan Heritage Coast
  Llan
MARGAM (St Mary) (St David)   *Llan 5*   **P-in-c** E F OWEN
MARLOES (St Peter)   *see* Dale and St Brides w Marloes and
  Hasguard w St Ishmael's *St D*
MARROS (St Lawrence)   *see* St Issell's and Amroth w
  Crunwere and Marros *St D*
MARSHFIELD (St Mary) w St Bride's Wentloog *Mon 5*
  P-in-c D E COLLINGBOURNE, S L COLLINGBOURNE
MATHERN (St Tewdric) *Mon 3*   **V** J E L WHITE   **NSM** R HAYES
MATHRY (Holy Martyrs)   *see* Gtr Dewisland *St D*
MATTHEWSTOWN (All Saints)   *see* Penrhiwceiber,
  Matthewstown and Ynysboeth *Llan*
MAUDLAM (St Mary Magdalene)   *see* Pyle w Kenfig *Llan*
MEIDRIM (St David) and Llanboidy and Merthyr *St D 10*
  V J GAINER
MEIFOD (St Tysilio and St Mary)   *see* Caereinion Miss Area
  St As
MELIDEN (St Mary Magdalene)   *see* Bryn a Mor Miss Area
  St As

MELIDEN (St Melyd) *as above*
MENAI BRIDGE (St Mary)   *see* Bro Tysilio *Ban*
MERTHYR (St Martin)   *see* Meidrim and Llanboidy and Merthyr *St D*
MERTHYR CYNOG (St Cynog)   *see* Dan yr Eppynt *S & B*
MERTHYR DYFAN (St Dyfan and St Teilo)   *see* Barry *Llan*
MERTHYR MAWR (St Teilo)   *see* Laleston and Merthyr Mawr w Penyfai *Llan*
MERTHYR TYDFIL (Christ Church) (St Luke) *Llan 9*
P-in-c M N PREVETT
MERTHYR TYDFIL (St David) (St Tydfil's Well) and Abercanaid *Llan 9*   **P-in-c** M N PREVETT   **C** C L RUSHTON
MERTHYR VALE (St Mary and Holy Innocents)   *see* Troedyrhiw w Merthyr Vale *Llan*
MICHAELSTON-LE-PIT (St Michael and All Angels)   *see* St Andrews Major w Michaelston-le-Pit *Llan*
MICHAELSTON-SUPER-AVON   *see* Cwmafan *Llan*
MICHAELSTON-Y-FEDW (St Michael)   *see* Bedwas w Machen w Michaelston-y-Fedw w Rudry *Mon*
MICHEL TROY (St Michael)   *see* Monmouth w Overmonnow etc *Mon*
MILFORD HAVEN (St Katherine) (St Peter) *St D 4*   **V** *vacant*
MINERA (St Mary)   *see* Alyn Miss Area *St As*
MINERA (St Tudfil) *as above*
MINWEAR (St Womar)   *see* Jeffreyston w Reynoldston and Loveston etc *St D*
MOCHDRE (All Saints)   *see* Cedewain Miss Area *St As*
MOLD (St Mary) Mission Area, comprising Cilcain, Gwernaffield, Llanferres, Mold, Nannerch, Nercwys, Northop, Pontblyddyn, Rhyd-y-mwyn, and Treuddyn   *St As 14*   **I** C M POOLMAN   **TV** D J S STROUD, K G HORSWELL   **NSM** K S STEWART
MONINGTON (St Nicholas)   *see* Bro Teifi *St D*
MONKNASH (St Mary)   *see* Glamorgan Heritage Coast *Llan*
MONKSWOOD (St Matthew)   *see* Mamhilad w Monkswood and Glascoed Chapel *Mon*
MONKTON (St Nicholas and St John) *St D 3*
P-in-c P O JONES   **TV** J P MAYNARD   **NSM** J ALLEN
MONMOUTH (St Mary the Virgin) w Overmonnow w Wonastow w Michel Troy *Mon 2*   **C** C M HAYNES   **NSM** J M BONE
MONTGOMERY (St Nicholas)   *see* Pool Miss Area *St As*
MORFIL   *see* W Cemaes *St D*
MORRISTON (St David) *S & B 3*   **V** H M LERVY
MOSTYN (Christ Church)   *see* Estuary and Mountain Miss Area *St As*
MOUNTAIN ASH (St Margaret) and Miskin *Llan 8*
V M K JONES
MOUNTON   *see* Narberth w Mounton w Robeston Wathen etc *St D*
MOUNTON (St Andoenus)   *see* Mathern *Mon*
MWNT (Holy Cross)   *see* Bro Teifi *St D*
MYDDFAI (St Michael)   *see* Llandingat w Myddfai *St D*
MYDROILYN (Holy Trinity)   *see* Llanerch Aeron w Ciliau Aeron and Dihewyd etc *St D*
MYNACHLOGDDU (St Dogmael)   *see* Crymych Gp *St D*
MYNYDD ISA   *see* Borderlands Miss Area *St As*
MYNYDDISLWYN (St Tudor)   *see* Upper Islwyn *Mon*
NANNERCH (St Michael)   *see* Mold Miss Area *St As*
NANTGLYN (St James)   *see* Denbigh Miss Area *St As*
NANTMEL (St Cynllo)   *see* Gwastedyn *S & B*
NANTYGLO (Holy Trinity and St Anne)   *see* Upper Ebbw Valleys *Mon*
NARBERTH (St Andrew) w Mounton w Robeston Wathen and Crinow and Minwear w Templeton *St D 3*
P-in-c M L COX   **C** S MURPHY
NASH (St Mary)   *see* Carew and Cosheston and Nash and Redberth *St D*
NASH (St Mary)   *see* Magor *Mon*
NEATH (St Thomas) (St David) (St Catherine) (St Peter and St Paul) *Llan 6*   **TR** L E NEWMAN   **C** E STREET, S GHEZZI
NEBO (Dewi Sant)   *see* Llansantffraed w Llanrhystud and Llanddeiniol *St D*
NEFYN (St David)   *see* Bro Madryn *Ban*
NELSON (St John the Baptist)   *see* Treharris, Trelewis, Bedlinog and Llanfabon *Llan*
NERCWYS (St Mary)   *see* Mold Miss Area *St As*
NEVERN (St Brynach)   *see* Bro Teifi *St D*
NEW HEDGES (St Anne)   *see* Tenby *St D*
NEW MOAT (St Nicholas)   *see* W Cemaes *St D*
NEW RADNOR (St Mary) and Llanfihangel Nantmelan and Evancoyd w Gladwestry and Colva *S & B 2*   **R** M T BEATON
NEW TREDEGAR (St Dingat)   *see* Upper Islwyn *Mon*
NEWBOROUGH (St Peter)   *see* Bro Dwynwen *Ban*
NEWBRIDGE (St Paul)   *see* Lower Islwyn Min Area *Mon*
NEWBRIDGE (St Peter) *as above*

NEWBRIDGE-ON-WYE (All Saints)   *see* Upper Wye *S & B*
NEWCASTLE (St Illtud) *Llan 4*   **V** D E C LLOYD
NEWCASTLE EMLYN (Holy Trinity) and Llandyfriog and Troedyraur and Cenarth and Henllan *St D 6*
V D J L ROBERTS
NEWCHURCH (St Mary)   *see* Erwood Gp w Painscastle Gp *S & B*
NEWCHURCH (St Michael) *St D 10*   **V** *vacant*
NEWCHURCH (St Peter)   *see* Wentwood *Mon*
NEWMARKET   *see* Bryn a Mor Miss Area *St As*
NEWPORT (All Saints) *Mon 6*   **P-in-c** C WATKINS   **NSM** E F JONES
NEWPORT (Cathedral of St Woolos) (St Martin) (St Mark) *Mon 6*   **V** L TONGE
NEWPORT (St John Baptist) *Mon 6*   **V** *vacant*
NEWPORT (St Mark)   *see* Newport St Woolos w St Mark *Mon*
NEWPORT (St Mary)   *see* W Cemaes *St D*
NEWPORT Christ Church *Mon 6*   **NSM** S BLEWETT
NEWPORT Maesglas (St Paul) (St Stephen) and Holy Trinity (St Thomas) *Mon 6*   **P-in-c** J S J GROVES
NEWPORT Maindee and Lliswerry (St Andrew) (St John the Evangelist) (St Mary) (St Philip) *Mon 6*
V W C INGLE-GILLIS   **NSM** J K BEARDMORE, L BATT
NEWPORT St Julian (St Julius and St Aaron) (St Teilo) *Mon 6*   **P-in-c** D C MATTHEWS   **NSM** S J HELKVIST
NEWQUAY (St Llwchaiarn)   *see* Llanllwchaearn and Llanina *St D*
NEWTON (St Peter) *S & B 4*   **V** C M DARVILL
NEWTON NOTTAGE (St John the Baptist) (All Saints) (St David) *Llan 5*   **R** P R MASSON   **NSM** G LUNN
NEYLAND (St Clement)   *see* Llanstadwel and Burton and Rosemarket *St D*
NICHOLASTON (St Nicholas)   *see* Three Cliffs *S & B*
NOLTON (St Madog)   *see* Gtr Dewisland *St D*
NOLTON (St Mary)   *see* Coity, Nolton and Brackla w Coychurch *Llan*
NORTHOP (St Eurgain and St Peter)   *see* Mold Miss Area *St As*
NORTHOP (St Mary) *as above*
NORTON (Mission Church)   *see* Oystermouth *S & B*
NORTON (St Andrew)   *see* E Radnor *S & B*
NOTTAGE (St David)   *see* Newton Nottage *Llan*
OFFA Mission Area, comprising Chirk, Penycae, Rhosllanerchrugog, Ruabon, and Rhosymedre *St As 12*
I K J TILTMAN   **TV** M J G WILKINSON, P K BETTINSON   **NSM** P M OWENS
OGMORE VALE (St David)   *see* Llandyfodwg and Cwm Ogwr *Llan*
OVERMONNOW (St Thomas)   *see* Monmouth w Overmonnow etc *Mon*
OVERTON (St Mary the Virgin)   *see* Maelor Miss Area *St As*
OXWICH (St Illtyd)   *see* SW Gower *S & B*
OYSTERMOUTH (All Saints) *S & B 4*   **V** K EVANS
PAINSCASTLE (St Peter)   *see* Erwood Gp w Painscastle Gp *S & B*
PANTEG (St Mary) and Griffithstown *Mon 8*
R P A GOLLEDGE   **NSM** A S LITTLER
PANTYFFRID (Mission Church)   *see* Pool Miss Area *St As*
PATRICIO (St Issui the Martyr)   *see* Vale of Gwrynne *S & B*
PEMBROKE (St Mary)   *see* Monkton *St D*
PEMBROKE DOCK (St John) (St Patrick) (St Teilo) *St D 3*
P-in-c A GRACE   **NSM** M A EVANS
PEN RHONDDA FAWR *Llan 11*   **P-in-c** P A LEYSHON
PENALLT (Old Church)   *see* Trellech and Penallt *Mon*
PENALLY (St Nicholas)   *see* Tenby *St D*
PENARTH (All Saints) (St Peter) *Llan 3*   **V** P A COX   **C** A REEVES
PENARTH (St Augustine) (Holy Nativity) and Llandough *Llan 3*   **P-in-c** M JONES   **C** R HILL   **NSM** R M GRIFFITHS
PEN-BOYR (St Llawddog)   *see* Llangeler w Pen-Boyr *St D*
PEN-BRE (St Illtud) *St D 11*   **V** D G DAVIES   **C** J FLANAGAN
PENBRYN (St Michael)   *see* Llangrannog w Llandysiliogogo w Penbryn *St D*
PENCADER (St Mary)   *see* Llanfihangel-ar-arth w Capel Dewi *St D*
PENCARREG (St Patrick) and Llanycrwys *St D 8*   **V** *vacant*
PENCLAWDD   *see* Llanrhidian w Llanyrnewydd *S & B*
PENCOED (St David)   *see* Llanilid w Pencoed *Llan*
PENCOED (St Paul) *as above*
PENDERYN MELLTE (St Cynog) *S & B 1*   **P-in-c** T J WILLIAMS
PENDINE (St Margaret) and Llanmiloe *St D 10*   **V** *vacant*
PENDOYLAN (St Cadoc) w Welsh St Donats *Llan 7*
C D T MORRIS, M J DAVIES   **NSM** A COOPER
PENEDEYRN Mission Area, comprising Bala, Betws Gwerful Goch, Cerrigydrudion, Llandderfel, Llandrillo-yn-Edeirnion, Llanfihangel Glyn Myfyr, Llangar, Llangwm, Llawrybetws,

and Ysbyty Ifan w Pentrefoelas *St As* 8 **P-in-c** C S B ROBERTS
TV S J ROBERTS

PENEGOES (St Cadfarch) *see* Bro Cyfeiliog and Mawddwy
Ban

PENHOW (St John the Baptist) *see* Wentwood *Mon*

PENISARWAEN (St Helen) *see* Bro Eryri *Ban*

PENLEY (St Mary Magdalene) *see* Maelor Miss Area *St As*

PENLLECH *see* Bro Madryn *Ban*

PENLLERGAER (St David) S & B 4 **V** *vacant*

PENLLYN (St John the Evangelist) *see* Cowbridge *Llan*

PENMACHNO (St Tudclud) *see* Bro Gwydyr *Ban*

PENMAEN (St David) *see* Upper Islwyn *Mon*

PENMAEN (St John the Baptist) *see* Three Cliffs *S & B*

PENMAENMAWR *see* Dwylan *Ban*

PENMARK (St Mary) w Llancarfan w Llantrithyd *Llan* 3
P-in-c D G BELCHER

PENNANT MELANGELL (St Melangel) *see* Tanat Valley Miss
Area *St As*

PENNARD (St Mary) *see* Three Cliffs *S & B*

PENPONT (no dedication) *see* Dan yr Eppynt *S & B*

**PENRHIWCEIBER (St Winifred), Matthewstown and
Ynysboeth** *Llan* 8 **P-in-c** B T RABJOHNS

PENRHOS (Holy Trinity) *see* Pool Miss Area *St As*

PENRHOS (St Cadoc) *see* Llantilio Crossenny w Penrhos,
Llanvetherine etc *Mon*

PENRHOSLLUGWY (St Michael) *see* Bro Eleth *Ban*

PENRHYDD *see* Bro Teifi *St D*

PENRHYNCOCH (St John) *see* Llanbadarn Fawr and Elerch
and Penrhyncoch etc *St D*

PENRHYNDEUDRAETH (Holy Trinity) *see* Bro Moelwyn *Ban*

PENRHYNSIDE BAY (St David) *see* Aberconwy Miss Area *St As*

PENRHYS (no dedication) *see* Rhondda Fach Uchaf *Llan*

PENRICE (St Andrew) *see* SW Gower *S & B*

PENSARN (St David) *see* Aled Miss Area *St As*

PENSTROWED (St Gwrhai) *see* Bro Arwystli *Ban*

PENTERRY (St Mary) *see* Itton and St Arvans w Penterry and
Kilgwrrwg w Devauden *Mon*

PENTIR (St Cedol) *see* Bro Ogwen *Ban*

PENTRAETH (St Mary) *see* Bro Tysilio *Ban*

PENTRE (St Peter) *see* Ystradyfodwg *Llan*

PENTRECHWYTH (St Peter) *see* Glantawe *S & B*

PENTROBIN (St John) *see* Borderlands Miss Area *St As*

PENTWYN (St David) *see* Cyncoed *Mon*

PENTYRCH (St Cadwg) and Capel Llanilltterne *Llan* 2
V S M JOHN

PENYBONTFAWR (St Thomas) *see* Tanat Valley Miss Area
St As

PENYCAE (St Thomas) *see* Offa Miss Area *St As*

PENYCLAWDD (St Martin) *see* Rockfield and Dingestow Gp
Mon

PENYFAI (All Saints) *see* Laleston and Merthyr Mawr w
Penyfai *Llan*

PENYFFORDD (Emmanuel) *see* Borderlands Miss Area *St As*

PENYGRAIG (St Barnabas) *see* Dinas w Penygraig *Llan*

PENYWAUN (St Winifred) *see* Hirwaun *Llan*

PETERSTON-SUPER-ELY (St Peter) w St Brides-super-Ely
Llan 7 **R** M J DAVIES **C** D T MORRIS **NSM** A COOPER

PETERSTON-SUPER-MONTEM (St Peter) *see* Llanharan w
Peterston-super-Montem *Llan*

PILLETH (Our Lady of Pilleth) *see* E Radnor *S & B*

PISTYLL (St Beuno) *see* Bro Madryn *Ban*

PONT AMAN (St Thomas) *see* Betws w Ammanford *St D*

PONT DOLANOG (St John the Evangelist) *see* Caereinion
Miss Area *St As*

PONT RHONDDA *Llan* 11 **V** P S GALE

PONT ROBERT (St John the Evangelist) *see* Caereinion Miss
Area *St As*

PONTARDAWE (St Peter) *see* Llangiwg *S & B*

PONTARDDULAIS *see* Llandeilo Tal-y-bont *S & B*

PONTARFYNACH *see* Grwp Bro Ystwyth a Mynach *St D*

PONTARGOTHI (Holy Trinity) *see* Llanegwad w Llanfihangel
Uwch Gwili *St D*

PONTBLYDDYN (Christ Church) *see* Mold Miss Area *St As*

PONTERWYD *see* Grwp Bro Ystwyth a Mynach *St D*

PONTFADOG (St John) *see* Valle Crucis Miss Area *St As*

PONTFAEN (St Brynach) *see* W Cemaes *St D*

PONT-IETS (St Mary) *see* Gwendraeth Fawr *St D*

PONTLLANFRAITH (St Augustine) *see* Upper Islwyn *Mon*

PONTLLIW (St Anne) *see* Penllergaer *S & B*

PONTLOTTYN (St Tyfaelog) (St Aidan) and Fochriw *Llan* 9
P-in-c R A D LINDSAY

PONTNEATHVAUGHAN (St John) *see* Penderyn Mellte *S & B*

PONTNEWYDD (Holy Trinity) *see* Cwmbran *Mon*

PONTPRENNAU (no dedication) *see* Cyncoed *Mon*

PONTRHYDFENDIGAID (St David) *see* Tregaron Gp *St D*

PONTSIAN (St John) *see* Llandysul w Bangor Teifi and
Llanfairollwyn etc *St D*

PONTYATES (St Mary) *see* Gwendraeth Fawr *St D*

PONTYBEREM (St John) *as above*

PONTYCLUN (St Paul) w Talygarn *Llan* 7 **V** *vacant*

PONTYCYMMER (St David) *see* Llangeinor and the Garw
Valley *Llan*

PONTYMISTER (St Margaret) *see* Lower Islwyn Min Area *Mon*

PONTYPOOL (St Matthew) *see* Upper Torfaen *Mon*

PONTYPRIDD (St Catherine) *Llan* 10 **TV** J A MITSON,
M D GABLE, P A LEWIS

POOL Mission Area, comprising Berriew, Buttington, Castle
Caereinion, Criggion, Forden, Guilsfield, Llandrinio,
Llandysilio, Llandyssil, Montgomery, Penrhos, Pool Quay,
and Welshpool *St As* 9 **R** I S G WILLSON **P-in-c** A E J SMITH,
C L RHODES **C** J M WILKES **NSM** E C YATES

POOL QUAY (St John the Evangelist) *see* Pool Miss Area *St As*

PORT EYNON (St Cattwg) *see* SW Gower *S & B*

PORT TALBOT (St Agnes) *see* Aberavon *Llan*

PORT TALBOT (St David) *see* Margam *Llan*

PORT TALBOT (St Theodore) (St Peter) *Llan* 5 **V** *vacant*

PORTH NEWYDD *Llan* 11 **P-in-c** J M THOMAS

PORTHCAWL (All Saints) *see* Newton Nottage *Llan*

PORTHKERRY (St Curig) and Rhoose *Llan* 3
P-in-c M A PRINCE

PORTHMADOG (St John) *see* Bro Eifionydd *Ban*

PORTMADOC (St Cyngar) *as above*

PORTSKEWETT (St Mary) *see* Caldicot *Mon*

PRENDERGAST (St David) w Rudbaxton *St D* 1
P-in-c M L OSBORNE

PRESELI, WEST *St D* 1 **V** *vacant*

PRESTATYN (Christ Church) *see* Bryn a Mor Miss Area *St As*

PRESTATYN (Church of Holy Spirit) *as above*

PRINCES GATE (St Catherine) *see* Lampeter Velfrey and
Llanddewi Velfrey etc *St D*

PUNCHESTON (St Mary) *see* W Cemaes *St D*

PWLL (Holy Trinity) *see* Burry Port and Pwll *St D*

PWLLCROCHAN (St Mary) *see* Monkton *St D*

PWLLHELI *see* Bro Enlli *Ban*

PYLE (St James) (St Mary Magdalene) w Kenfig *Llan* 5
V D A WALKER

QUAR, THE (St Tydfil's Well) *see* Merthyr Tydfil St Dav and
Abercanaid *Llan*

QUEENSFERRY (St Andrew) *see* Borderlands Miss Area *St As*

RADNOR (St Mary) *see* New Radnor and Llanfihangel
Nantmelan etc *S & B*

RADNOR, EAST *S & B* 2 **V** M L COPE

RADNOR, WEST *see* Ithon Valley *S & B*

RADYR (St John the Baptist) (Christ Church) *Llan* 2
P-in-c V E BURROWS

RAGLAN GROUP (St Cadoc) *Mon* 4 **R** T G CLEMENT

REDBERTH (Church) *see* Carew and Cosheston and Nash
and Redberth *St D*

REDWICK (St Thomas) *see* Magor *Mon*

RESOLVEN (St David) *see* Vale of Neath *Llan*

REYNOLDSTON (St George) *see* SW Gower *S & B*

REYNOLDSTON (St James) *see* Jeffreyston w Reynoldston
and Loveston etc *St D*

RHANDIRMWYN (St Barnabas) *see* Cil-y-Cwm and
Ystrad-ffin w Rhandir-mwyn etc *St D*

RHAYADER (St Clement) *see* Gwastedyn *S & B*

RHESYCAE (Christ Church) *see* Estuary and Mountain Miss
Area *St As*

RHEWL (Church) *see* Dyffryn Clwyd Miss Area *St As*

RHIWLAS (Mission Church) *see* Tanat Valley Miss Area *St As*

RHONDDA FACH UCHAF *Llan* 11 **P-in-c** D M JONES

RHOOSE (St Peter) *see* Porthkerry and Rhoose *Llan*

RHOS (St James) *see* Llangeler w Pen-Boyr *St D*

RHOSBEIRIO *see* Bro Padrig *Ban*

RHOSCOLYN *see* Bro Cybi *Ban*

RHOSDDU *see* Wrexham *St As*

RHOSESEMOR *see* Estuary and Mountain Miss Area *St As*

RHOSILI (St Mary the Virgin) *see* SW Gower *S & B*

RHOSLLANNERCHRUGOG (St David) *see* Offa Miss Area *St As*

RHOSLLANNERCHRUGOG (St Mary) *as above*

RHOSTIE *see* Llanilar w Rhostie and Llangwyryfon etc *St D*

RHOSYMEDRE (St John the Evangelist) *see* Offa Miss Area
St As

RHUDDLAN (St Mary) *see* Aber-Morfa Miss Area *St As*

RHULEN (St David) *see* Colwyn *S & B*

RHYDYBRIW (Capel Rhydybriw) *see* Blaenwysg *S & B*

RHYDYFELIN (St Luke) *see* Pontypridd *Llan*

RHYD-Y-MWYN (St John the Evangelist) *see* Mold Miss Area
St As

RHYL (Holy Trinity) *see* Aber-Morfa Miss Area *St As*

RHYL (St Ann) *as above*

RHYL (St John) *as above*
RHYL (St Thomas) *as above*
RHYMNEY (St David) *Mon 7* **V** *vacant*
RISCA (St Mary) *see Lower Islwyn Min Area Mon*
ROATH (St German) *see Cardiff St German w St Sav Llan*
ROATH (St Margaret) (St Anne) (St Edward) *Llan 1*
  V S LISK **NSM** R COOMBS
ROATH (St Martin) *Llan 1* **V** I D HAMER **NSM** T G WATKIN
ROATH (St Saviour) *see Cardiff St German w St Sav Llan*
ROATH PARK (Christ Church) *see Cardiff Ch Ch Roath Park Llan*
ROBESTON WATHEN (Church) *see Narberth w Mounton w Robeston Wathen etc St D*
ROBESTON WEST (St Andrew) *see Walwyn's Castle and Robeston W St D*
ROCH (St Mary) *see Gtr Dewisland St D*
ROCKFIELD (St Cenedlon) w St Maughans w Llangattock-vibon-Avel w Llanfihangel-ystern-Llewern w Dingestow w Llangovan and Penyclawdd w Tregaer w Cwmcarvan *Mon 2* **V** *vacant*
ROGERSTONE (St John the Baptist) *see Bassaleg Mon*
ROGIET (St Mary) *see Caldicot Mon*
ROSEMARKET (St Ishmael) *see Llanstadwel and Burton and Rosemarket St D*
ROSSETT (Christ Church) *see Alyn Miss Area St As*
RUABON (All Saints) *see Offa Miss Area St As*
RUABON (St Mary) *as above*
RUDBAXTON (St Michael) *see Prendergast w Rudbaxton St D*
RUDRY (St James) *see Bedwas w Machen w Michaelston-y-Fedw w Rudry Mon*
RUMNEY (St Augustine) *Mon 5* **P-in-c** J R CONNELL
  C R J MAIDMENT
RUTHIN (St Peter) *see Dyffryn Clwyd Miss Area St As*
ST ANDREWS MAJOR (St Andrew) (St Peter) w Michaelston-le-Pit *Llan 3* **P-in-c** A P JAMES
  C J R ORMROD
ST ASAPH (Cathedral of St Asaph and St Cyndeyrn) *St As 1*
  TR N H WILLIAMS **C** S E HARPER
ST ATHAN (St Tathan) *see Glamorgan Heritage Coast Llan*
ST BRIDES (St Bridget) *see Dale and St Brides w Marloes and Hasguard w St Ishmael's St D*
ST BRIDES MAJOR (St Bridget) *see Glamorgan Heritage Coast Llan*
ST BRIDES MINOR (St Bride) *see Llansantffraid, Bettws and Aberkenfig Llan*
ST BRIDES NETHERWENT (St Bridget) *see Wentwood Mon*
ST BRIDE'S WENTLOOG (St Bride) *see Marshfield w St Bride's Wentloog Mon*
ST BRIDES-SUPER-ELY (St Bride) *see Peterston-super-Ely w St Brides-super-Ely Llan*
ST CLEARS (St Mary Magdalene) *see Bro Sancler St D*
ST DAVIDS (Cathedral of St David and St Andrew) *St D 2*
  C S WHITMARSH **NSM** G BUTCHER
ST DOGMAEL'S (St Thomas) *see Bro Teifi St D*
ST DOGWELLS (St Dogfael) *see Spittal w Trefgarn and Ambleston w St Dogwells St D*
ST DONATS (St Donat) *see Glamorgan Heritage Coast Llan*
ST FAGANS (St Mary) and Michaelston-super-Ely *Llan 2*
  P-in-c F A JACKSON
ST FLORENCE (St Florentius) *see Manorbier and St Florence St D*
ST GEORGE (St George) *see Aled Miss Area St As*
ST GEORGE-SUPER-ELY (St George) *see St Nicholas w Bonvilston and St George-super-Ely Llan*
ST HARMON (St Garmon) *see Gwastedyn S & B*
ST HILARY (St Hilary) *see Cowbridge Llan*
ST ISHMAEL'S (St Ishmael) *see Dale and St Brides w Marloes and Hasguard w St Ishmael's St D*
ST ISHMAEL'S (St Ishmael) w Llan-saint and Ferryside
  St D 11 **P-in-c** W J LAMBERT **C** H DE GRUCHY
ST ISSELL'S (St Issell) and Amroth w Crunwere and Marros
  St D 3 **V** *vacant*
ST LAWRENCE (St Lawrence) *see Gtr Dewisland St D*
ST LYTHANS (St Bleiddian) *see Wenvoe and St Lythans Llan*
ST MARY CHURCH (St Mary) *see Cowbridge Llan*
ST MARY HILL (St Mary) *as above*
ST MAUGHEN'S (St Meugan) *see Rockfield and Dingestow Gp Mon*
ST MELLONS (St Mellon) (Resurrection) *Mon 5* **V** D KELLEN
ST NICHOLAS (St Nicholas) *see Gtr Dewisland St D*
ST NICHOLAS (St Nicholas) w Bonvilston and St George-super-Ely *Llan 7* **P-in-c** M J DAVIES **C** D T MORRIS
  NSM A COOPER
ST PETROX (St Pedrog) *see Monkton St D*
ST PIERRE (St Peter) *see Mathern Mon*

ST THOMAS *see Haverfordwest St D*
ST TWYNNELLS (St Gwynog) *see Monkton St D*
SANDFIELDS *see Aberavon Llan*
SANDYCROFT (St Francis) *see Borderlands Miss Area St As*
SARON (St David) *see Llanedi w Tycroes and Saron St D*
SAUNDERSFOOT *see St Issell's and Amroth w Crunwere and Marros St D*
SEALAND (St Bartholomew) *see Borderlands Miss Area St As*
SEBASTOPOL (St Oswald) *see Panteg and Griffithstown Mon*
SENGHENYDD (St Peter) *see Eglwysilan and Caerphilly Llan*
SEVEN SISTERS (St David) *see Dulais Valley Llan*
SEVEN SISTERS (St Mary) *as above*
SHIRENEWTON (St Thomas à Becket) *see Mathern Mon*
SHOTTON (St Ethelwold) *see Borderlands Miss Area St As*
SILIAN (St Sulien) *see Lampeter w Maestir and Silian and Llangybi and Betws Bledrws St D*
SINAN (All Saints) *see Denbigh Miss Area St As*
SIX BELLS (St John) *see Abertillery w Cwmtillery w Llanhilleth etc Mon*
SKENFRITH (St Bride) *see Grosmont and Skenfrith and Llangattock etc Mon*
SKETTY (St Paul) (Holy Trinity) *S & B 4*
  V R J DAVIES-HANNEN **OLM** M THOMAS
SKEWEN (St John) (St Mary) *Llan 6* **P-in-c** C W COLES
SOLVA (St Aidan) *see Gtr Dewisland St D*
SOUTHERNDOWN (All Saints) *see Glamorgan Heritage Coast Llan*
SOUTHSEA (All Saints) *see Alyn Miss Area St As*
SPITTAL (St Mary) w Trefgarn and Ambleston w St Dogwells *St D 1* **V** R REES
STACKPOLE ELIDOR (St James and St Elidyr) *see Monkton St D*
STEYNTON (St Cewydd and St Peter) *St D 4*
  P-in-c J R CECIL
STRATA FLORIDA (St Mary) *see Tregaron Gp St D*
SULLY (St John the Baptist) *Llan 3* **P-in-c** J R ORMROD
SWANSEA (Christ Church) *see Cen Swansea S & B*
SWANSEA (Holy Trinity) *as above*
SWANSEA (St Barnabas) *S & B 3* **P-in-c** D M GRIFFITHS
SWANSEA (St Gabriel) *S & B 3* **V** D M GRIFFITHS
SWANSEA (St James) *S & B 3* **V** H M WILLIAMS
SWANSEA (St Luke) *see Manselton and Cwmbwrla S & B*
SWANSEA (St Mary) *see Cen Swansea S & B*
SWANSEA (St Nicholas-on-the-Hill) and St Jude *S & B 3*
  V A JONES
SWANSEA (St Peter) *S & B 3* **P-in-c** J S WRIGHT
SWANSEA (St Thomas) (St Stephen) and Kilvey *S & B 3*
  P-in-c S L BUNTING
SWANSEA, CENTRAL (Christ Church) (St John) (St Mary and Holy Trinity) *S & B 3* **V** I K REES **C** H REES, I M FOLKS,
  S ALDRED **NSM** J T ANTHONY
TAI'RGWAITH (St David) *see Cwmaman St D*
TALACHDDU (St Mary) *see Llandefalle and Llyswen w Boughrood etc S & B*
TALBENNY (St Mary) *see Walton W w Talbenny and Haroldston W St D*
TALGARREG (St David) *see Llanarth and Capel Cynon w Talgarreg etc St D*
TALGARTH (St Gwendoline) w Bronllys w Llanfilo *S & B 1*
  V R T EDWARDS
TALIARIS (Holy Trinity) *see Llandeilo Fawr and Taliaris St D*
TALLEY (St Michael) *see Cynwyl Gaeo w Llansawel and Talley etc St D*
TALYBONT (St Cross) *see Bro Ogwen Ban*
TALYBONT (St David) *see Llanfihangel Genau'r Glyn and Llangorwen St D*
TALYGARN (St Anne) *see Pontyclun w Talygarn Llan*
TAL-Y-LLYN (St David) *see Bro Ystumanner Ban*
TANAT VALLEY Mission Area, comprising Hirnant, Llangadwaladr, Llangedwyn, Llangynog, Llanrhaeadr-ym-Mochnant w Llanarmon Mynydd Mawr, Llansilin, and Pennant *As 7* **I** L D NORMAN **C** C M BROWNE
  NSM P W HEANEY
TEMPLETON (St John) *see Narberth w Mounton w Robeston Wathen etc St D*
TENBY (St Mary) (St Julian's Chapel) *St D 3* **TR** A J GRACE
  TV R N WAINWRIGHT **C** J A C R BARDER
  NSM J W MORGAN
THREE CLIFFS *S & B 4* **V** P BROOKS **NSM** N E KING
TINTERN (St Michael) *see Llandogo w Whitebrook Chpl and Tintern Parva Mon*
TON PENTRE *see Ystradyfodwg Llan*
TONDU (St John) *see Llansantffraid, Bettws and Aberkenfig Llan*
TONGWYNLAIS (St Michael) (St James) *Llan 2*
  P-in-c Z E KING
TONMAWR (St Teilo) *see Neath Llan*

TONNA (St Anne)   *see* Cadoxton-juxta-Neath and Tonna *Llan*

TONYPANDY (St Andrew) w Clydach Vale w Williamstown *Llan 11*   **P-in-c** T J COX   **C** J M THOMAS

TONYREFAIL (St David) (St Alban) w Gilfach Goch *Llan 11* **V** R E MOVERLEY

TON-YR-YWEN (School)   *see* Llanishen *Llan*

TORFAEN, UPPER, comprising Blaenavon, Capel Newydd, and Pontypool *Mon 8*   **P-in-c** R W NOY   **C** P W GODSELL

TOWNHILL   *see* Swansea St Nic and St Jude *S & B*

TOWYN (St Mary)   *see* Aber-Morfa Miss Area *St As*

TRAEAN-GLAS (St Mary)   *see* Blaenwysg *S & B*

TRALLWNG (St David)   *see* Dan yr Eppynt *S & B*

TRAWSFYNYDD (St Madryn)   *see* Bro Moelwyn *Ban*

TREALAW (All Saints)   *see* Pont Rhondda *Llan*

TREBANOS (St Michael)   *see* Clydach *S & B*

TREBOETH (St Alban)   *see* Landore and Treboeth *S & B*

TREDEGAR (St George) (St James) *Mon 7*   **NSM** E JONES

TREDUNNOC (St Andrew)   *see* Usk Min Area *Mon*

TREFDRAETH (Eglwys Crist y Brenin)   *see* Bro Cadwaladr *Ban*

TREFDRAETH (St Beuno)   *as above*

TREFEGLWYS (St Michael)   *see* Bro Arwystli *Ban*

TREFGARN (St Michael)   *see* Spittal w Trefgarn and Ambleston w St Dogwells *St D*

TREFILAN (St Hilary)   *see* Llanfihangel Ystrad and Cilcennin w Trefilan etc *St D*

TREFLYS (St Michael)   *see* Bro Eifionydd *Ban*

TREFNANT (Holy Trinity)   *see* Denbigh Miss Area *St As*

TREFRIW (St Mary)   *see* Bro Gwydyr *Ban*

TREGAEAN (St Caian)   *see* Bro Cyngar *Ban*

TREGAER (St Mary)   *see* Rockfield and Dingestow Gp *Mon*

TREGARON GROUP (St Caron) *St D 8*   **V** P W DAVIES **NSM** A W LEWIS

TREGARTH (St Mair)   *see* Bro Ogwen *Ban*

TRE-GROES (St Ffraid)   *see* Llandysul w Bangor Teifi and Llanfairollwyn etc *St D*

TREGYNON (St Cynon)   *see* Cedewain Miss Area *St As*

TREHARRIS (St Matthias), Trelewis, Bedlinog and Llanfabon *Llan 9*   **P-in-c** G J COOMBES

TREHERBERT (St Mary Communion Centre)   *see* Pen Rhondda Fawr *Llan*

TRELAWNYD (St Michael)   *see* Bryn a Mor Miss Area *St As*

TRE-LECH A'R BETWS (St Teilo)   *see* Bro Sancler *St D*

TRELLECH (St Nicholas) and Penallt *Mon 2*   **V** *vacant*

TRELLECH GRANGE (not known)   *see* Llanishen w Trellech Grange and Llanfihangel etc *Mon*

TREMEIRCHION (Corpus Christi)   *see* Denbigh Miss Area *St As*

TREMORFA (St Philip) Conventional District *Llan 1* **P-in-c** M J R NELSON

TREORCHY (St Matthew)   *see* Pen Rhondda Fawr *Llan*

TRETHOMAS (St Thomas)   *see* Bedwas w Machen w Michaelston-y-Fedw w Rudry *Mon*

TRETOWER (St John the Evangelist)   *see* Crickhowell w Cwmdu and Tretower *S & B*

TREUDDYN (St Mary)   *see* Mold Miss Area *St As*

TREVETHIN (St Cadoc)   *see* Upper Torfaen *Mon*

TREVETHIN (St John the Divine)   *as above*

TREVOR (Church)   *see* Valle Crucis Miss Area *St As*

TREWALCHMAI (St Morhaiarn)   *see* Bro Cyngar *Ban*

TRISANT *St D 11*   **TR** *vacant*

TROEDRHIWGARTH (St Mary the Virgin) *Llan 4* **V** C T REANEY

TROED-YR-AUR (St Michael)   *see* Newcastle Emlyn and Llandyfriog etc *St D*

TROEDYRHIW (St John) w Merthyr Vale *Llan 9* **V** S J BARNES

TROSTEY (St David)   *see* Raglan Gp *Mon*

TROWBRIDGE MAWR (St Hilary)   *see* Rumney *Mon*

TUDWEILIOG (St Cwyfan)   *see* Bro Madryn *Ban*

TUMBLE (Dewi Sant)   *see* Trisant *St D*

TY SIGN (St David)   *see* Lower Islwyn Min Area *Mon*

TYCOCH (All Souls) *S & B 4*   **V** P J GWYNN

TYCROES (St Edmund)   *see* Llanedi w Tycroes and Saron *St D*

TYLORSTOWN (Holy Trinity)   *see* Rhondda Fach Uchaf *Llan*

TYWYN (St Cadfan)   *see* Bro Ystumanner *Ban*

UNDY (St Mary)   *see* Magor *Mon*

UPPER EBBW VALLEYS *Mon 8*   **NSM** C I LEWIS, P V GRIFFITHS

USK (St Mary) Ministry Area *Mon 4*   **V** K J HASLER **Hon C** G W OPPERMAN   **NSM** P E LOVE, R J W GREENLAND

UWCH GWYRFAI Beuno Sant *Ban 2*   **V** J L JONES **Hon C** D HOLLINGS

UZMASTON (St Ismael)   *see* Llawhaden w Bletherston and Uzmaston *St D*

VALE OF GWRYNNE, The *S & B 1*   **P-in-c** C P BOWLER

VALE OF NEATH *Llan 6*   **V** A J DAVIES

VALLE CRUCIS Mission Area, comprising Bryneglwys, Corwen, Glyndyfrdwy, Gwyddelwern, Llanarmon Dyffryn Ceiriog, Llandegla, Llangollen and Trevor, Llantysilio, Llansantffraid Glyn Ceiriog, Llansantffraid Glyn Dyfrdwy, and Portfadog *St As 10*   **I** M K SNELLGROVE   **C** L A TAYLOR **NSM** D M P EVANS, P J CAREY

VALLEY (St Michael)   *see* Bro Cwyfan *Ban*

VAYNOR (St Gwynno)   *see* Cefn Coed w Vaynor *S & B*

VYRNWY Mission Area, comprising Bwlchycibau, Llanfechain, Llanfihangel-yng-Nghwynfa, Llanfyllin w Llanwddyn, Llansantffraid-yn-Mechain, and Llwydiarth *St As 7*   **I** H J MORRIS   **P-in-c** S E BURTON

WALTON EAST (St Mary)   *see* Wiston w Walton E and Clarbeston *St D*

WALTON WEST (All Saints) w Talbenny and Haroldston West *St D 4*   **R** *vacant*

WALWYN'S CASTLE (St James the Great) and Robeston West *St D 4*   **P-in-c** R M M JOHNSON

WAUNARLLWYDD (St Barnabas) *S & B 4*   **V** I DAVIES

WAUNFELIN (St John the Divine)   *see* Upper Torfaen *Mon*

WELSH ST DONATS (St Donat)   *see* Pendoylan w Welsh St Donats *Llan*

WELSHPOOL (St Mary)   *see* Pool Miss Area *St As*

WENTWOOD *Mon 3*   **C** S INGLE-GILLIS   **NSM** J S WATERS

WENVOE (St Mary) and St Lythans *Llan 3* **P-in-c** J R ORMROD

WHITCHURCH (St David)   *see* Gtr Dewisland *St D*

WHITCHURCH (St Mary) (St Thomas) (All Saints) *Llan 2* **TR** J G DAVIS   **TV** A M FLIPSE, P A MORTIMER   **C** N GILL **Hon C** H G LEWIS

WHITFORD (St Mary and St Beuno)   *see* Estuary and Mountain Miss Area *St As*

WHITLAND (St Mary) w Cyffig and Henllan Amgoed and Llan-gan w Llandysilio and Clunderwen *St D 3* **V** K G TAYLOR

WHITTON (St David)   *see* E Radnor *S & B*

WICK (St James)   *see* Glamorgan Heritage Coast *Llan*

WILCRICK (St Mary)   *see* Magor *Mon*

WILLIAMSTON, EAST (Church)   *see* Begelly w Ludchurch and E Williamston *St D*

WILLIAMSTOWN (St Illtud)   *see* Tonypandy w Clydach Vale w Williamstown *Llan*

WISTON (St Mary Magdalene) w Walton East and Clarbeston *St D 1*   **V** *vacant*

WOLVESNEWTON (St Thomas à Becket)   *see* Usk Min Area *Mon*

WONASTOW (St Wonnow)   *see* Monmouth w Overmonnow etc *Mon*

WORTHENBURY (St Deiniol)   *see* Maelor Miss Area *St As*

WREXHAM (St Giles's Parish Church) (St Mark) (St Mary) (All Saints) (St Margaret) (St James) (St John) *St As 15* **P-in-c** S B ERLANDSON   **TV** J P SMITH, J S BRAY, S ERRINGTON **C** R E SPAREY-TAYLOR   **NSM** H M E SHOTTON, J TOUT

WYE, UPPER *S & B 2*   **P-in-c** P M E BERESFORD-WEBB

WYNDHAM (St David)   *see* Llandyfodwg and Cwm Ogwr *Llan*

Y FERWIG (St Pedrog)   *see* Bro Teifi *St D*

YERBESTON   *see* Jeffreyston w Reynoldston and Loveston etc *St D*

YNYSBOETH   *see* Penrhiwceiber, Matthewstown and Ynysboeth *Llan*

YNYSCYNON (St Cynon)   *see* Pont Rhondda *Llan*

YNYSDDU (St Theodore)   *see* Upper Islwyn *Mon*

YNYSHIR (St Anne) *Llan 11*   **V** *vacant*

YSBYTY CYNFYN (St John the Baptist)   *see* Grwp Bro Ystwyth a Mynach *St D*

YSBYTY IFAN (St John the Baptist)   *see* Penedeyrn Miss Area *St As*

YSBYTY YSTWYTH (St John the Baptist)   *see* Grwp Bro Ystwyth a Mynach *St D*

YSFA (St Mark)   *see* Gwastedyn *S & B*

YSGEIFIOG (St Mary)   *see* Estuary and Mountain Miss Area *St As*

YSTALYFERA (St David) *S & B 3*   **V** T J HEWITT

YSTRAD MEURIG (St John the Baptist)   *see* Tregaron Gp *St D*

YSTRAD MYNACH (Holy Trinity) w Llanbradach *Llan 9* **V** S P KIRK

YSTRAD RHONDDA (St Stephen)   *see* Pont Rhondda *Llan*

YSTRAD ROAD (St Illtyd)   *see* Swansea St Pet *S & B*

YSTRADFELLTE (St Mary)   *see* Penderyn Mellte *S & B*

YSTRAD-FFIN (St Paulinus)   *see* Cil-y-Cwm and Ystrad-ffin w Rhandir-mwyn etc *St D*

YSTRADGYNLAIS (St Cynog) *S & B 3*   **R** D ROBERTS **OLM** D OWEN

YSTRADOWEN (St Owain)   *see* Cowbridge *Llan*

YSTRADYFODWG (St John the Baptist) *Llan 11* **V** H H ENGLAND-SIMON

SCOTTISH INCUMBENCIES

An index of incumbencies of the Scottish Episcopal Church. The incumbency entry gives the full legal name, followed by the diocese and the name(s) and appointment(s) of the clergy serving there. Church dedications are indicated in brackets. The following are the main abbreviations used; for others see the full list of abbreviations.

C	Curate	**NSM**	Non-stipendiary Minister
Dss	Deaconess	**P-in-c**	Priest-in-charge
Hon C	Honorary Curate	**R**	Rector

ABERCHIRDER (St Marnan) *Mor* **P-in-c** M L E LAST
ABERDEEN (Cathedral of St Andrew) *Ab* **R** I M POOBALAN
ABERDEEN (St Clement) *Ab* **C** N J BOWRY
ABERDEEN (St Devenick) *see* Bieldside *Ab*
ABERDEEN (St James) *Ab* **P-in-c** R GREEN
  NSM R B EDWARDS
ABERDEEN (St John the Evangelist) *Ab* **Hon C** C S GIBSON
ABERDEEN (St Margaret of Scotland) *Ab* **R** A E NIMMO
  Hon C D H WRIGHT, J DUTHIE
ABERDEEN (St Mary) *Ab* **R** T TAGGART **C** J M HOBBS
ABERDEEN (St Ninian) *Ab* **P-in-c** J B LYON **C** N J BOWRY
  NSM J J TSUKADA
ABERDOUR (St Columba) - All Souls Fife *St And*
  P-in-c D L NORBY **NSM** C LATIMER
ABERFOYLE (St Mary) *St And* **R** R W GROSSE
ABERLOUR (St Margaret of Scotland) **R** *vacant*
ABOYNE (St Peter) *Ab* **P-in-c** V R HANCOCK
AIRDRIE (St Paul) *Glas* **R** P J O'MAOIL MHEANA
ALEXANDRIA (St Mungo) **R** *vacant*
ALFORD (St Andrew) **R** *vacant*
ALL SOULS FIFE *see* ABERDOUR; BURNTISLAND; and
  INVERKEITHING
ALLOA (St John the Evangelist) **R** *vacant*
ALYTH (St Ninian) *St And* **NSM** D A CAMERON
ANNAN (St John the Evangelist) *Glas*
  P-in-c M P CALLAGHAN
APPIN *see* W Highland Region *Arg*
ARBROATH (St Mary) *Bre* **R** P T MEAD
ARDBRECKNISH (St James) *Arg* **R** M R CAMPBELL
ARDROSSAN (St Andrew) *Glas* **NSM** A MONTGOMERIE
ARPAFEELIE (St John the Evangelist) *Mor* **R** M O LANGILLE
ARRAN, ISLE OF *Arg* **P-in-c** S P M MACKENZIE
AUCHENBLAE *see* Drumtochty *Bre*
AUCHINDOIR (St Mary) *Ab* **R** J B WALKER
  NSM D ATKINSON
AUCHMITHIE (St Peter) *Bre* **R** P T MEAD
AUCHTERARDER (St Kessog) *St And* **P-in-c** T A DOWLING
AYR (Holy Trinity) *Glas* **R** A R BALDOCK
BAILLIESTON (St John) *see* Glas E End *Glas*
BALERNO (St Mungo) *Edin* **R** M J H ROUND **C** O CLEGG
BALLACHULISH (St John) **R** *vacant*
BALLATER (St Kentigern) *Ab* **P-in-c** V R HANCOCK
BANCHORY (St Ternan) *Ab* **R** L M DOWNS
BANFF (St Andrew) *Ab* **P-in-c** J M PAISEY
BARROWFIELD (St John the Baptist) **R** *vacant*
BATHGATE (St Columba) *Edin* **R** C A BARCLAY
BEARSDEN (All Saints) *Glas* **R** K H FREEMAN
BIELDSIDE (St Devenick) *Ab* **R** G BOWYER
  Dss J E MACCORMACK
BIRNAM *see* Dunkeld *St And*
BISHOPBRIGGS (St James-the-Less) *Glas* **R** P R WATSON
BLAIR ATHOLL *see* Kilmaveonaig *St And*
BLAIRGOWRIE (St Catherine) *St And* **NSM** D A CAMERON
BO'NESS (St Catharine) *Edin* **R** W J SHAW
BRAEMAR (St Margaret) **R** *vacant*
BRECHIN (St Andrew) **R** *vacant*
BRIDGE OF ALLAN (St Saviour) *St And* **R** E F J MULLINER
BRIDGE OF WEIR (St Mary) *Glas* **R** D C GIFFORD
  C H GONZALEZ PENA
BRIDGEND *see* Islay *Arg*
BRORA (St Columba) *Mor* **R** J E P CURRALL **NSM** S L SCOTT
BROUGHTY FERRY (St Mary) *Bre* **R** F W BRIDGER
  C H R BRIDGER
BUCKIE (All Saints) *Ab* **P-in-c** J M PAISEY
BUCKSBURN (St Machar) *Ab* **P-in-c** D HEDDLE
BUCKSTONE (St Fillan) *see* Edin St Fillan *Edin*
BURNSIDE *see* Moffat *Glas*
BURNTISLAND (St Serf) - All Souls Fife *St And*
  P-in-c D L NORBY **NSM** C LATIMER
BURRAVOE (St Colman) *Ab* **P-in-c** N A BRICE
  NSM E H MCNAB, G R BOOTH

CALLANDER (St Andrew) *St And* **R** R W GROSSE
CAMBUSLANG (St Cuthbert) **R** *vacant*
CAMPBELTOWN (St Kiaran) **R** *vacant*
CARNOUSTIE (Holy Rood) *Bre* **P-in-c** D D S DE VERNY
CASTLE DOUGLAS (St Ninian) *Glas* **R** C G KETLEY
CATHEDRAL OF THE ISLES *see* Cumbrae (or Millport) *Arg*
CATTERLINE (St Philip) **R** *vacant*
CHALLOCH (All Saints) **R** *vacant*
CHAPELHILL *see* Cruden Bay *Ab*
CHOIR Chapl St Ninian's Cathl Perth **I** *vacant*
CLARKSTON (St Aidan) *Glas* **R** N H TAYLOR
CLERMISTON *see* Edin Clermiston Em *Edin*
CLYDEBANK (St Columba) **R** *vacant*
COATBRIDGE (St John the Evangelist) **R** *vacant*
COLDSTREAM (St Mary and All Souls) *Edin* **R** J B SMITH
COLINTON *see* Edin St Cuth *Edin*
COMRIE (St Serf) *St And* **R** G S EVANS
COUPAR ANGUS (St Anne) *St And* **NSM** D A CAMERON
COURTHILL Chapel *see* Kishorn *Mor*
COVE BAY (St Mary) **R** *vacant*
CRAIGHALL *see* Ellon *Ab*
CRIEFF (St Columba) *St And* **R** G S EVANS
CROACHY *see* Strathnairn St Paul *Mor*
CROMARTY (St Regulus) *Mor* **R** M O LANGILLE
CRUDEN BAY (St James the Less) *Ab* **R** D B A BERK
  NSM G P WHALLEY
CULLODEN (St Mary-in-the-Fields) **R** *vacant*
CUMBERNAULD (Holy Name) **R** *vacant*
CUMBRAE (Cathedral of The Isles and Collegiate Church
  of the Holy Spirit) **R** *vacant*
CUMINESTOWN (St Luke) **R** *vacant*
CUPAR (St James the Great) *St And* **R** R ANETTS
  Hon C J B BLACK
DALBEATTIE (Christ Church) *Glas* **R** C G KETLEY
  NSM B M SCOTT
DALKEITH (St Mary) *Edin* **R** P S HARRIS **C** J DU ROCHER
  NSM E S JONES, J O GODFREY, M E JONES
DALMAHOY (St Mary) *Edin* **R** C DOWNEY
DALRY (St Peter)** **R** *vacant*
DENNISTOUN (St Kentigern) *see* Glas E End *Glas*
DINGWALL (St James the Great) *Mor* **P-in-c** J BOOTHBY
  NSM R FLOCKHART, V S SAUNDERS
Dioc Chapl **I** *vacant*
DIOCESAN AIDS Officer **I** *vacant*
DOLLAR (St James the Great) *St And* **R** C I LOWDON
DORNOCH (St Finnbarr) *Mor* **P-in-c** J E P CURRALL
DOUNE (St Modoc) *St And* **R** A M PEDEN
DOWNFIELD (St Luke) *see* Dundee St Luke *Bre*
DRUMLITHIE (St John the Baptist) *Bre* **R** M J R TURNER
DRUMTOCHTY (St Palladius) *Bre* **R** M J R TURNER
DUFFTOWN (St Michael and All Angels) *Mor*
  P-in-c M L E LAST
DUMBARTON (St Augustine) **R** *vacant*
DUMFRIES (St John the Evangelist) *Glas* **R** J H AITON
  Hon C A M SHUKMAN, G J SIMMONS, G M WARWICK,
    S P BALLARD **NSM** J M G CLARK MAXWELL
DUNBAR (St Anne) *Edin* **R** D M HALL
DUNBLANE (St Mary) *St And* **R** N A BROWN
DUNDEE (Cathedral of St Paul) **R** *vacant*
DUNDEE (St John the Baptist) *Bre* **C** H R BRIDGER
DUNDEE (St Luke) *Bre* **P-in-c** K J DIXON
DUNDEE (St Margaret) **R** *vacant*
DUNDEE (St Martin) *Bre* **P-in-c** F W BRIDGER
  C H R BRIDGER
DUNDEE (St Mary Magdalene) *Bre* **R** D SHEPHERD
DUNDEE (St Ninian) *Bre* **P-in-c** E M LAMONT
DUNDEE (St Salvador) *Bre* **R** C H CLAPSON
DUNFERMLINE (Holy Trinity) *St And* **R** K W RATHBAND
DUNKELD (St Mary) w Birnam **R** *vacant*
DUNOON (Holy Trinity) *Arg* **R** D J RAILTON
DUNS (Christ Church) **R** *vacant*

DUROR (St Adamnan)   *see* W Highland Region *Arg*
EAST END   *see* Glas E End *Glas*
EAST KILBRIDE (St Mark) *Glas*   R P G M FLETCHER
EASTGATE (St Peter)   *see* Peebles *Edin*
EASTRIGGS (St John the Evangelist) *Glas*
   P-in-c M P CALLAGHAN
EDINBURGH (Cathedral of St Mary) *Edin*   R J A CONWAY
   C A PHILIP   NSM G P FOSTER
EDINBURGH (Christ Church) *Edin*   R S E MACDONALD
   C J A GREEN, J A WRIGHT, L G GRAHAM
EDINBURGH (Emmanuel)   R *vacant*
EDINBURGH (Good Shepherd) *Edin*   R D J B FOSTEKEW
EDINBURGH (Holy Cross)   R *vacant*
EDINBURGH (Old St Paul)   R *vacant*
EDINBURGH (St Barnabas) *Edin*   P-in-c P D DIXON
   NSM A C ANDERSON
EDINBURGH (St Columba) *Edin*   R D G PATON-WILLIAMS
   TV R O GOULD   C A C W WAGSTAFF
EDINBURGH (St Cuthbert) *Edin*   R N MCNELLY
EDINBURGH (St David of Scotland)   R *vacant*
EDINBURGH (St Fillan) *Edin*   R R INNES
EDINBURGH (St James the Less) *Edin*   R S I BUTLER
   NSM J L MACLAREN, J P MITCHELL
EDINBURGH (St John the Evangelist) *Edin*   R M DÜNZKOFER
   C D COOPER, R A ADDIS   NSM C A HUME, P J BRAND,
   S KILBEY
EDINBURGH (St Margaret of Scotland) *Edin*
   P-in-c M C REED
EDINBURGH (St Mark) *Edin*   R S B MARRIAGE
EDINBURGH (St Martin of Tours) *Edin*   R Y A GOOLJARY
EDINBURGH (St Michael and All Saints) *Edin*
   R M D ROBSON   C J B PENMAN
EDINBURGH (St Ninian) *Edin*   R F S BURBERRY
   C O T BREWER-LENNON
EDINBURGH (St Paul and St George) *Edin*   R D G RICHARDS
   C E L TALBOT, P A SAWREY
EDINBURGH (St Peter)   R *vacant*
EDINBURGH (St Philip and St James)   R *vacant*
EDINBURGH (St Salvador) *Edin*   P-in-c A J BAIN
   C M WOJCIECHOWSKI
EDINBURGH (St Thomas) Private Chapel *Edin*
   I D W MCCARTHY
EDINBURGH (St Vincent) *Edin*   P-in-c A M MACLEAN
   C W L F MOUNSEY
ELGIN (Holy Trinity) w Lossiemouth (St Margaret) *Mor*
   R T N RONGONG   NSM J SCLATER
ELIE AND EARLSFERRY (St Michael and All Angels)
   R *vacant*
ELLON (St Mary on the Rock) *Ab*   R D B A BERK
   NSM C A FOX, G P WHALLEY, R SPENCER, S SPENCER
EOROPAIDH (St Moluag) *Arg*   P-in-c P J MOGER
   NSM C P A LOCKHART
ERSKINE   *see* Renfrew *Glas*
EYEMOUTH (St Ebba)   R *vacant*
FALKIRK (Christ Church) *Edin*   R S L K SHAW
FASQUE (St Andrew) *Bre*   R M J R TURNER
FETTERCAIRN   *see* Fasque *Bre*
FOCHABERS Gordon Chapel *Mor*   P-in-c M L E LAST
FORFAR (St John the Evangelist) *St And*   R E C GARMAN
FORRES (St John the Evangelist) *Mor*   P-in-c H INBADAS
FORT WILLIAM (St Andrew) *Arg*   R G A GUINNESS
FORTROSE (St Andrew) *Mor*   R M O LANGILLE
FRASERBURGH (St Peter) *Ab*   P-in-c K E SUCKLING
FYVIE (All Saints) *Ab*   P-in-c A R MACDONALD
GALASHIELS (St Peter) *Edin*   C S C E CAKE
GALLOWGATE   *see* Aberdeen St Marg *Ab*
GARTCOSH (St Andrew)   R *vacant*
GATEHOUSE OF FLEET (St Mary) *Glas*   R S D HAZLETT
GLASGOW (All Saints) *Glas*   P-in-c S M P MAITLAND
GLASGOW (Cathedral of St Mary the Virgin) *Glas*
   R K HOLDSWORTH   NSM M LITTLE
GLASGOW (Good Shepherd)   R *vacant*
GLASGOW (St Bride) *Glas*   R K FRANCIS
GLASGOW (St George)   R *vacant*
GLASGOW (St Margaret) *Glas*   R S ROBERTSON
   C M S MCTERNAN
GLASGOW (St Matthew) *Glas*   R D K WOSTENHOLM
GLASGOW (St Ninian) *Glas*   R P ROMANO
GLASGOW (St Oswald)   R *vacant*
GLASGOW (St Silas) Private Chapel *Glas*   R M J AYERS
   C J D LAPPING
GLASGOW East End (St John) (St Kentigern) (St Serf) *Glas*
   P-in-c M J W BENTON-EVANS   NSM L A IRELAND
GLENCARSE (All Saints)   R *vacant*
GLENCOE (St Mary)   R *vacant*

GLENROTHES (St Luke the Evangelist) - Central Fife Team
   Ministry *Var*   C G F DILLON
GLENURQUHART (St Ninian)   R *vacant*
GOUROCK (St Bartholomew)   R *vacant*
GRANGEMOUTH (St Mary) *Edin*   R W J SHAW
GRANTOWN-ON-SPEY (St Columba) *Mor*
   Hon C A G SPARHAM, R J GILLINGS
GREENOCK (St John the Evangelist) *Glas*   R W NESBITT
GRETNA (All Saints) *Glas*   P-in-c M P CALLAGHAN
GREYFRIARS   *see* Kirkcudbright *Glas*
GRULINE (St Columba)   *see* W Highland Region *Arg*
GULLANE (St Adrian) *Edin*   R S D METZNER
HADDINGTON (Holy Trinity) *Edin*   R E A O'RYAN
   NSM J WOOD
HAMILTON (St Mary the Virgin) *Glas*   C J D LIVINGSTONE
   NSM D JASPER
HARRIS, ISLE OF (Christ Church) *Arg*   P-in-c J D L DAVIES
HAWICK (St Cuthbert) *Edin*   C S C E CAKE
HELENSBURGH (St Michael and All Angels) *Glas*
   R D M IND   C P J SMITH
HILLINGTON (Good Shepherd)   *see* Glas Gd Shep *Glas*
HUNTLY (Christ Church) *Mor*   P-in-c M L E LAST
HYNDLAND (St Bride)   *see* Glas St Bride *Glas*
INNERLEITHEN (St Andrew) *Edin*   NSM C B AITCHISON,
   C CHAPLIN
INSCH (St Drostan) *Ab*   P-in-c A R MACDONALD
INVERARAY (All Saints) *Arg*   P-in-c S P M MACKENZIE
INVERBERVIE (St David of Scotland)   R *vacant*
INVERGORDON (St Ninian) *Mor*   P-in-c J BOOTHBY
INVERGOWRIE (All Souls) *Bre*   P-in-c A W CUMMINS
INVERKEITHING (St Peter) - All Souls Fife *St And*
   P-in-c D L NORBY   NSM C LATIMER
INVERNESS (Cathedral of St Andrew) *Mor*   C N A J HIGGOTT
INVERNESS (St John the Evangelist) *Mor*   P-in-c J CUTHBERT
   C C Y CALEY
INVERNESS (St Michael and All Angels) *Mor*
   P-in-c J CUTHBERT   C C Y CALEY
   Hon C G H STRANRAER-MULL
INVERURIE (St Mary) *Ab*   R J B WALKER   NSM D ATKINSON
IONA (St Columba)   R *vacant*
IRVINE (St Andrew) Local Ecumenical Partnership *Glas*
   NSM A MONTGOMERIE
ISLAY (St Columba)   R *vacant*
ISLE OF HARRIS   *see* Harris Ch Ch *Arg*
JEDBURGH (St John the Evangelist) *Edin*   P-in-c A J COOPER
JOHNSTONE (St John) *Glas*   R R J PRESTON
JORDANHILL (All Saints)   *see* Glas All SS *Glas*
KEITH (Holy Trinity) *Mor*   P-in-c M L E LAST
KELSO (St Andrew) *Edin*   R R D KING   C G REDPATH
   Hon C I D L CLARK
KEMNAY (St Anne) *Ab*   P-in-c J B WALKER
   NSM D ATKINSON
KENTALLEN (St Moluag)   *see* W Highland Region *Arg*
KESSOCK-TORE   *see* Arpafeelie *Mor*
KILLIN (St Fillan) *St And*   R G S EVANS
KILMACOLM (St Fillan) *Glas*   R D C GIFFORD
   C H GONZALEZ PENA
KILMARNOCK (Holy Trinity) *Glas*   R M P JEPP
KILMARTIN (St Columba) *Arg*   P-in-c S P M MACKENZIE
KILMAVEONAIG (St Adamnan) *St And*   R E M J M BAKER
KINCARDINE O'NEIL (Christ Church)   R *vacant*
KINGHORN (St Mary and St Leonard) *St And*   R C N FRASER
KINLOCH RANNOCH (All Saints) *St And*   R E M J M BAKER
KINLOCHLEVEN (St Paul)   *see* W Highland Region *Arg*
KINLOCHMOIDART (St Finian)   R *vacant*
KINROSS (St Paul) *St And*   R D G MACKENZIE MILLS
KIRKCALDY (St Peter) *St And*   R C N FRASER
KIRKCUDBRIGHT (St Francis of Assisi) *Glas*   R S D HAZLETT
KIRKWALL (St Olaf) *Ab*   R D DAWSON
KIRRIEMUIR (St Mary) *St And*   P-in-c R P HARLEY
KISHORN Chapel *Mor*   NSM H S WIDDOWS
LADYBANK (St Mary) *St And*   R R ANETTS
LADYCROFT   *see* Balerno *Edin*
LANARK (Christ Church) *Glas*   R A R SHERIDAN
   C L JOHNSTON
LANGHOLM (All Saints)   R *vacant*
LARGS (St Columba) *Glas*   R G B FYFE
LASSWADE (St Leonard) *Edin*   R P S HARRIS
   C J DU ROCHER   NSM E S JONES, J O GODFREY, M E JONES
LAURENCEKIRK (St Laurence) *Bre*   R M J R TURNER
LEITH (St James the Less)   *see* Edin St Jas *Edin*
LENZIE (St Cyprian) *Glas*   R L S IRELAND
LERWICK (St Magnus) *Ab*   R N A BRICE   NSM E H MCNAB,
   G R BOOTH
LEVEN (St Margaret) - Central Fife Team Ministry   R *vacant*
LEWIS, ISLE OF   *see* Stornoway *Arg*

LINLITHGOW (St Peter) *Edin*   **R** C A BARCLAY
LOCHALSH (St Donnan)   **R** *vacant*
LOCHEARNHEAD (St Angus) *St And*   **R** G S EVANS
LOCHEE (St Margaret)   *see* Dundee St Marg *Bre*
LOCHGELLY (St Finnian) - Central Fife Team Ministry
   St And   **NSM** M A DINELEY
LOCHGILPHEAD (Christ Church) *Arg*
   P-in-c S P M MACKENZIE
LOCHINVER (St Gilbert)   **R** *vacant*
LOCKERBIE (All Saints) *Glas*   **R** PS JOB RETNASELVAM
   P-in-c M P CALLAGHAN
LONGSIDE (St John) *Ab*   **R** R N O'SULLIVAN
LOSSIEMOUTH (St Margaret)   *see* Elgin w Lossiemouth *Mor*
LUNAN HEAD (St Margaret) *St And*   **R** K W RATHBAND
MARYGATE   *see* Pittenweem *St And*
MASTRICK (St Clement)   *see* Aberdeen St Clem *Ab*
MAYBOLE (St Oswald) *Glas*   **C** J W GEEN
MELROSE (Holy Trinity) *Edin*   **R** P V P BLACKLEDGE
   C M PEDERSEN   **NSM** D W WOOD
MILLPORT   *see* Cumbrae (or Millport) *Arg*
MILNGAVIE (St Andrew) *Glas*   **R** A HAGENBUCH
MOFFAT (St John the Evangelist) *Glas*
   R PS JOB RETNASELVAM   **P-in-c** M P CALLAGHAN
MONIFIETH (Holy Trinity) *Bre*   **P-in-c** K G G GIBSON
   NSM W J MCAUSLAND
MONKLANDS   *see* Airdrie *Glas*
MONKSTOWN   *see* Ladybank *St And*
MONTROSE (St Mary and St Peter)   **R** *vacant*
MORNINGSIDE (Christ Church)   *see* Edin Ch Ch *Edin*
MOTHERWELL (Holy Trinity) *Glas*   **R** R E KILGOUR
MUCHALLS (St Ternan)   **R** *vacant*
MULL, ISLE OF   *see* W Highland Region *Arg*
MURRAYFIELD (Good Shepherd)   *see* Edin Gd Shep *Edin*
MUSSELBURGH (St Peter) *Edin*   **R** A J REID
MUTHILL (St James) *St And*   **P-in-c** T A DOWLING
NAIRN (St Columba) *Mor*   **R** A J SIMPSON
NETHER LOCHABER (St Bride)   **R** *vacant*
NEW GALLOWAY (St Margaret of Scotland)   **R** *vacant*
NEW PITSLIGO (St John the Evangelist)   **R** *vacant*
NEWBURGH (St Katherine)   **R** *vacant*
NEWLANDS (St Margaret)   *see* Glas St Marg *Glas*
NEWPORT-ON-TAY (St Mary)   **R** *vacant*
NEWTON STEWART   *see* Challoch *Glas*
NORTH BALLACHULISH   *see* Onich *Arg*
NORTH BERWICK (St Baldred) *Edin*   **R** S D METZNER
NORTH MEARNS   *see* Stonehaven *Bre*
OBAN (Cathedral of St John) *Arg*   **Hon C** I E WALTER
OLD DEER (St Drostan) *Ab*   **R** R N O'SULLIVAN
OLDMELDRUM (St Matthew) *Ab*   **P-in-c** R SPENCER
ONICH (St Bride)   **R** *vacant*
PAISLEY (Holy Trinity and St Barnabas) *Glas*
   R D K M DAVISON
PEEBLES (St Peter) *Edin*   **NSM** C B AITCHISON, C CHAPLIN
PENICUIK (St James the Less) *Edin*   **NSM** N F SUTTLE
PERTH (Cathedral of St Ninian) *St And*
   R H B FARQUHARSON
PERTH (St John the Baptist) *St And*   **R** G S TAYLOR
PETERHEAD (St Peter) *Ab*   **R** R N O'SULLIVAN
PILTON (St David)   *see* Edin St Dav *Edin*
PITLOCHRY (Holy Trinity) *St And*   **R** E M J M BAKER
PITTENWEEM (St John the Evangelist)   **R** *vacant*
POLLOCKSHIELDS (St Ninian)   *see* Glas St Ninian *Glas*
POLTALLOCH   *see* Kilmartin *Arg*

POOLEWE (St Maelrubha) *Mor*   **NSM** H S WIDDOWS
PORT GLASGOW (St Mary the Virgin) *Glas*   **R** D C GIFFORD
   C H GONZALEZ PENA
PORTNACROIS (Holy Cross)   *see* W Highland Region *Arg*
PORTPATRICK (St Ninian)   **R** *vacant*
PORTREE (St Columba) *Arg*   **P-in-c** R F BUNGARD
POSSILPARK (St Matthew)   *see* Glas St Matt *Glas*
PRESTONPANS (St Andrew)   **R** *vacant*
PRESTWICK (St Ninian) *Glas*   **R** H J ROSS
RENFREW (St Margaret) *Glas*   **R** R J PRESTON
ROSLIN (Collegiate Church of St Matthew) *Edin*
   P-in-c J E ROULSTON
ROTHESAY (St Paul) *Arg*   **R** D J RAILTON
ROTHIEMURCHUS (St John the Baptist) *Mor*
   Hon C A G SPARHAM, R J GILLINGS   **NSM** J M JONES
ST ANDREWS (All Saints) *St And*   **R** A C COLES
   Hon C D W DAY, G J M SAUNDERS, M C ALDCROFT
   NSM I M MICHAEL
ST ANDREWS (St Andrew) *St And*   **R** T A HART
   NSM R T EVANS
ST FILLANS (Church of the Holy Spirit)   **R** *vacant*
SANDYLOAN   *see* Gullane *Edin*
SELKIRK (St John the Evangelist) *Edin*   **C** S C E CAKE
   Hon C D D SCEATS
SHETTLESTON (St Serf)   *see* Glas E End *Glas*
SKYE, ISLE OF   *see* Portree *Arg*
SOUTH QUEENSFERRY (Priory Church St Mary of Mount
   Carmel) *Edin*   **P-in-c** T J HARKIN   **NSM** I MACROBERT
STANLEY (St Columba)   **R** *vacant*
STIRLING (Holy Trinity) *St And*   **R** C J WUTSCHER
   Hon C G J WILLEY
STONEHAVEN (St James)   **R** *vacant*
STORNOWAY (St Peter) *Arg*   **P-in-c** P J MOGER
STRANRAER (St John the Evangelist)   **R** *vacant*
STRATHNAIRN (St Paul) *Mor*   **P-in-c** K B COLLINS
   Hon C R F BURKITT
STRATHPEFFER (St Anne) *Mor*   **P-in-c** J BOOTHBY
   NSM R FLOCKHART, V C SAUNDERS
STRATHTAY (St Andrew) *St And*   **R** E M J M BAKER
STRICHEN (All Saints)   **R** *vacant*
STROMNESS (St Mary) *Ab*   **P-in-c** T P MILLER
STRONTIAN   **R** *vacant*
TAIN (St Andrew) *Mor*   **P-in-c** J E P CURRALL
   NSM S L SCOTT
TARFSIDE (St Drostan) *Bre*   **P-in-c** J NELSON
TAYPORT (St Margaret of Scotland)   **R** *vacant*
TEINDHILLGREEN   *see* Duns *Edin*
THURSO (St Peter and Holy Rood) *Mor*   **C** E CHARMAN
TOFTS   *see* Dalry *Glas*
TROON (St Ninian) *Glas*   **R** T C O MONTGOMERY
TURRIFF (St Congan)   **R** *vacant*
UDDINGSTON (St Andrew) *Glas*   **C** J D LIVINGSTONE
ULLAPOOL (St Mary the Virgin)   **R** *vacant*
WEST HIGHLAND Region *Arg*   **P-in-c** A A C FAIRCLOUGH
WEST LINTON (St Mungo)   **R** *vacant*
WESTGATE   *see* Dunbar *Edin*
WESTHILL Community Church *Ab*   **R** I J FERGUSON
WHITERASHES (All Saints) *Ab*   **R** J B WALKER
WHITING BAY   *see* Is of Arran *Arg*
WICK (St John the Evangelist) *Mor*   **C** E CHARMAN
WISHAW (St Andrew) *Glas*   **R** R E KILGOUR
WOODHEAD OF FETTERLETTER   *see* Fyvie *Ab*
YELL   *see* Burravoe *Ab*

IRISH BENEFICES AND CHURCHES

An index of benefices of the Church of Ireland (shown in bold type), together with entries for churches and other licensed places of worship. Where the church name is the same as that of the benefice (or the first place name in the benefice), the church entry is omitted. Church dedications are indicated in brackets.

The benefice entry gives the full legal name, together with the diocese and the name(s) and appointment(s) of clergy serving there. The following are the main abbreviations used; for others see the full list of abbreviations.

Bp's C	Bishop's Curate	I	Incumbent (includes Rector or Vicar)
C	Curate	NSM	Non-stipendiary Minister
C-in-c	Curate-in-charge	P-in-c	Priest-in-charge
Hon C	Honorary Curate		

AASLEAGH (St John the Baptist) *see* Tuam w Cong and Aasleagh *T, K & A*

ABBEYLEIX (St Michael and All Angels) w Ballyroan, Ballinakill, Killermogh, Aughmacart, Durrow and Attanagh *C & O* I *vacant*

ABBEYSTREWRY (no dedication) w Creagh, Tullagh, Castlehaven and Caheragh *C, C & R* I J K ARDIS

ABINGDON (no dedication) *see* Killaloe w Stradbally *L & K*

ACHILL (Holy Trinity) *see* Aughaval w Achill, Knappagh, Dugort etc *T, K & A*

ACTON (no dedication) and Drumbanagher *Arm* I G B SPENCE **Bp's C** D W R DUNN

ADARE (St Nicholas) and Kilmallock w Kilpeacon, Croom, Kilflynn, Kilfinane, Knockaney, Bruff and Caherconlish *L & K* I E P BEASLEY

AGHABOG (no dedication) *see* Ematris w Rockcorry, Aghabog and Aughnamullan *Clogh*

AGHADERG (St Mellan) w Donaghmore and Scarva *D & D* **P-in-c** T J TEGGARTY

AGHADOE *see* Killarney w Aghadoe and Muckross *L & K*

AGHADOWEY (St Guaire) *D & R* I L D A CRAWFORD-MCCAFFERTY

AGHADOWN (Church Cross) *see* Ballydehob w Aghadown *C, C & R*

AGHADOWN (St Matthew) *as above*

AGHADRUMSEE (no dedication) w Clogh and Drumsnatt *Clogh* I *vacant*

AGHALEE (Holy Trinity) *D & D* I G P MCADAM

AGHALURCHER (no dedication) w Tattykeeran, Cooneen and Mullaghfad *Clogh* I J M MCCLENAGHAN

AGHANAGH (no dedication) *see* Boyle and Elphin w Aghanagh, Kilbryan etc *K, E & A*

AGHANCON (no dedication) *see* Shinrone w Aghancon etc *L & K*

AGHANLOO (St Lugha) *see* Tamlaghtard w Aghanloo *D & R*

AGHAVEA (no dedication) *Clogh* I J R MCLOUGHLIN

AGHAVILLY (St Mary) *see* Tynan w Middletown and Aghavilly *Arm*

AGHER (no dedication) *see* Dunboyne and Rathmolyon *M & K*

AGHERTON (St John the Baptist) *Conn* I M R K FERRY

AHASCRAGH *see* Aughrim w Ballinasloe etc *L & K*

AHERLA *see* Moviddy Union *C, C & R*

AHOGHILL (St Colmanell) w Portglenone *Conn* I D C CHRISTIE

ALDERGROVE *see* Killead w Gartree *Conn*

ALMORITIA (St Nicholas) *see* Mullingar, Portnashangan, Moyliscar, Kilbixy etc *M & K*

ALTEDESERT (no dedication) *see* Kildress w Altedesert *Arm*

ANNACLONE (Christ Church) *see* Magherally w Annaclone *D & D*

ANNADUFF (St Ann) *see* Kiltoghart w Drumshambo, Annaduff and Kilronan *K, E & A*

ANNAGH (St Andrew) w Drumaloor, Cloverhill and Drumlane *K, E & A* I T J WOODS

ANNAGHMORE (St Francis) *Arm* I D S MCVEIGH

ANNAHILT (Ascension) w Magherahamlet *D & D* I J R HOWARD

ANNALONG (no dedication) *D & D* **C** R C SMYTH

ANTRIM (All Saints) *Conn* I S R MCBRIDE **C** A D G MCALISTER

ANTRIM (St Patrick) *see* Connor w Antrim St Patr *Conn*

ARBOE (no dedication) *see* Ballinderry, Tamlaght and Arboe *Arm*

ARDAGH (St Patrick) w Tashinny, Shrule and Kilcommick *K, E & A* I *vacant*

ARDAMINE (St John the Evangelist) w Kiltennel, Glascarrig, Kilnamanagh, Kilmuckridge and Monamolin *C & O* I *vacant*

ARDARA (St Connall) w Glencolumbkille, Inniskeel, Glenties and Lettermacaward *D & R* **C** R WRAY

ARDCARNE (no dedication) *see* Boyle and Elphin w Aghanagh, Kilbryan etc *K, E & A*

ARDCLINIS (St Mary) and Tickmacrevan w Layde and Cushendun *Conn* **P-in-c** H A MACARTHUR

ARDEE (St Mary) *see* Drogheda w Ardee, Collon and Termonfeckin *Arm*

ARDGLASS (St Nicholas) *see* Lecale Gp *D & D*

ARDKEEN (Christ Church) *see* Ballyhalbert w Ardkeen *D & D*

ARDMORE (no dedication) w Craigavon *D & D* **Bp's C** T J CADDEN

ARDMORE (St Paul) *see* Youghal Union *C, C & R*

ARDNAGEEHY (no dedication) *see* Fermoy Union *C, C & R*

ARDOYNE (Immanuel) *see* Belfast H Trin and St Silas *Conn*

ARDQUIN (no dedication) *see* Ballyphilip w Ardquin *D & D*

ARDRAHAN *see* Aughrim w Ballinasloe etc *L & K*

ARDSTRAW (St Eugene) w Baronscourt, Badoney Lower and Badoney Upper and Greenan *D & R* I I E DINSMORE

ARDTREA (St Andrew) w Desertcreat *Arm* I D J BELL

ARKLOW (St Saviour) w Inch and Kilbride *D & G* I N J W SHERWOOD

ARMAGH (St Mark) *Arm* I M T KINGSTON

ARMAGHBREAGUE (no dedication) *see* Keady w Armaghbreague and Derrynoose *Arm*

ARMOY (St Patrick) w Loughguile and Drumtullagh *Conn* I C R A EASTON **NSM** D J STEELE, G H NEVIN

ARVAGH (no dedication) w Carrigallen, Gowna and Columbkille *K, E & A* **P-in-c** H R HICKS

ASHFIELD (no dedication) *see* Drumgoon *K, E & A*

ASKEATON (St Mary) *see* Rathkeale w Askeaton, Kilcornan and Kilnaughtin *L & K*

ATHBOY (St James) *see* Trim and Athboy Gp *M & K*

ATHLONE (St Mary) w Benown, Kiltoom and Forgney *M & K* I W L STEACY

ATHY (St Michael) w Kilberry, Fontstown and Kilkea *D & G* I O M R DONOHOE

AUGHANUNSHIN *see* Conwal Union w Gartan *D & R*

AUGHAVAL (no dedication) w Achill, Knappagh, Dugort, Castlebar and Turlough *T, K & A* I V H ROGERS

AUGHAVAS (no dedication) *see* Mohill w Farnaught, Aughavas, Oughteragh etc *K, E & A*

AUGHER (no dedication) w Newtownsaville and Eskrahoole *Clogh* I *vacant*

AUGHNACLIFFE *see* Arvagh w Carrigallen, Gowna and Columbkille *K, E & A*

AUGHNACLOY *see* Carnteel and Crilly *Arm*

AUGHNAMULLAN (Christ Church) *see* Ematris w Rockcorry, Aghabog and Aughnamullan *Clogh*

AUGHRIM (Holy Trinity) w Ballinasloe, Clontuskert, Ahascragh, Woodlawn, Kilmacduagh and Ardrahan *L & K* I J M GODFREY

AUGHRIM (St John the Evangelist) *see* Castlemacadam w Ballinaclash, Aughrim etc *D & G*

BADONEY LOWER (St Patrick) *see* Ardstraw w Baronscourt, Badoney Lower etc *D & R*

BADONEY UPPER (St Aichen) *as above*

BAILIEBOROUGH (no dedication) w Knockbride, Shercock and Mullagh *K, E & A* I I HORNER

BALBRIGGAN (St George) *see* Holmpatrick w Balbriggan and Kenure *D & G*

BALGRIFFIN (St Doulagh) *see* Malahide w Balgriffin *D & G*

BALLEE (no dedication) *see* Bright w Ballee and Killough *D & D*

BALLIGAN   *see* Ballywalter w Inishargie *D & D*

BALLINA   *see* Killala w Dunfeeny, Crossmolina, Kilmoremoy etc *T, K & A*

BALLINACLASH (no dedication)   *see* Castlemacadam w Ballinaclash, Aughrim etc *D & G*

BALLINADEE (no dedication)   *see* Bandon Union *C, C & R*

BALLINAFAD   *see* Boyle and Elphin w Aghanagh, Kilbryan etc *K, E & A*

BALLINALEA   *see* Mostrim w Granard, Clonbroney, Killoe etc *K, E & A*

BALLINALECK   *see* Cleenish w Mullaghdun *Clogh*

BALLINAMALLARD   *see* Magheracross *Clogh*

BALLINAMORE   *see* Mohill w Farnaught, Aughavas, Oughteragh etc *K, E & A*

BALLINASLOE (St John the Evangelist)   *see* Aughrim w Ballinasloe etc *L & K*

BALLINATONE   *see* Castlemacadam w Ballinaclash, Aughrim etc *D & G*

BALLINDERRY (no dedication) *Conn*   I T CLELAND

BALLINDERRY (St John), Tamlaght and Arboe *Arm*
I W B PAINE

BALLINEEN   *see* Kinneigh Union *C, C & R*

BALLINGARRY (no dedication)   *see* Cloughjordan w Borrisokane etc *L & K*

BALLINLOUGH   *see* Roscommon w Donamon, Rathcline, Kilkeevin etc *K, E & A*

BALLINROBE (St Mary)   *see* Tuam w Cong and Aasleagh *T, K & A*

BALLINTEMPLE (no dedication)   *see* Kilmore w Ballintemple *K, E & A*

BALLINTOGHER   *see* Taunagh w Kilmactranny, Ballysumaghan etc *K, E & A*

BALLINTOY (no dedication) w Rathlin and Dunseverick *Conn*   I P M BARTON

BALLISODARE (Holy Trinity) w Collooney and Emlaghfad *T, K & A*   I A P ISON

BALLIVOR   *see* Trim and Athboy Gp *M & K*

BALLNACARGY   *see* Mullingar, Portnashangan, Moyliscar, Kilbixy etc *M & K*

BALLYBAY (Christ Church) w Mucknoe and Clontibret *Clogh*   I vacant

BALLYBEEN (St Mary) *D & D*   I J W CHESHIRE
NSM N GORDON

BALLYBRACK (St Matthias)   *see* Killiney Ballybrack *D & G*

BALLYBUNNION   *see* Tralee w Kilmoyley, Ballymacelligott etc *L & K*

BALLYCARRY   *see* Kilroot and Templecorran *Conn*

BALLYCASTLE (Holy Trinity)   *see* Ramoan w Ballycastle and Culfeightrin *Conn*

BALLYCLARE   *see* Ballynure and Ballyeaston *Conn*

BALLYCLOG (St Patrick)   *see* Brackaville w Donaghendry and Ballyclog *Arm*

BALLYCLUG (St Patrick)   *see* Ballymena w Ballyclug *Conn*

BALLYCOMMON   *see* Geashill w Killeigh and Ballycommon *M & K*

BALLYCONNELL   *see* Kildallon and Swanlinbar *K, E & A*

BALLYCOTTON   *see* Youghal Union *C, C & R*

BALLYCULTER (Christ Church)   *see* Lecale Gp *D & D*

BALLYDEHOB (St Matthias) w Aghadown *C, C & R*
I S T MCCANN

BALLYEASTON (St John the Evangelist)   *see* Ballynure and Ballyeaston *Conn*

BALLYEGLISH (St Matthias)   *see* Desertlyn w Ballyeglish *Arm*

BALLYGAWLEY (no dedication)   *see* Errigle Keerogue w Ballygawley and Killeshil *Arm*

BALLYHAISE   *see* Drung w Castleterra, Larah and Lavey etc *K, E & A*

BALLYHALBERT (St Andrew) w Ardkeen *D & D*
I J J HEMPHILL

BALLYHOLME (St Columbanus) *D & D*   I S E DOOGAN
C M A FLANAGAN

BALLYHOOLEY (no dedication)   *see* Fermoy Union *C, C & R*

BALLYJAMESDUFF (no dedication)   *see* Kildrumferton w Ballymachugh and Ballyjamesduff *K, E & A*

BALLYKELLY   *see* Tamlaghtfinlagan w Myroe *D & R*

BALLYLESSON   *see* Drumbo *D & D*

BALLYMACARRETT (St Patrick) (St Christopher) (St Martin) *D & D*   I J J CUNNINGHAM

BALLYMACASH (St Mark) *Conn*   I L M GIBSON   C W K JEFFREY

BALLYMACELLIGOTT (no dedication)   *see* Tralee w Kilmoyley, Ballymacelligott etc *L & K*

BALLYMACHUGH (St Paul)   *see* Kildrumferton w Ballymachugh and Ballyjamesduff *K, E & A*

BALLYMACKEY (St Michael)   *see* Nenagh *L & K*

BALLYMACORMACK (no dedication)   *see* Templemichael w Clongish, Clooncumber etc *K, E & A*

BALLYMAGLASSON   *see* Dunboyne and Rathmolyon *M & K*

BALLYMAHON   *see* Ardagh w Tashinny, Shrule and Kilcommick *K, E & A*

BALLYMARTLE (no dedication)   *see* Kinsale Union *C, C & R*

BALLYMASCANLAN (St Mary) w Creggan and Rathcor *Arm*
C G G WALMSLEY   NSM R W R MOORE

BALLYMENA (St Patrick) w Ballyclug *Conn*
I R M MCCONNELL

BALLYMONEY   *see* Kinneigh Union *C, C & R*

BALLYMONEY (St Patrick) w Finvoy and Rasharkin *Conn*
I A J SWEENEY   NSM B M HOWE

BALLYMORE   *see* Clondehorkey w Cashel *D & R*

BALLYMORE (St Mark) *Arm*   I T S FORSTER

BALLYMORE EUSTACE (St John)   *see* Blessington w Kilbride, Ballymore Eustace etc *D & G*

BALLYMOTE   *see* Ballisodare w Collooney and Emlaghfad *T, K & A*

BALLYMOYER (St Luke)   *see* Newtownhamilton w Ballymoyer and Belleck *Arm*

BALLYNAFEIGH (St Jude) *D & D*   I P C BOURKE

BALLYNAHINCH   *see* Magheradroll *D & D*

BALLYNAKILL (St Thomas)   *see* Omey w Ballynakill, Errislannan and Roundstone *T, K & A*

BALLYNASCREEN   *see* Kilcronaghan w Draperstown and Sixtowns *D & R*

BALLYNURE (Christ Church) and Ballyeaston *Conn*
I J D CAMPBELL-SMYTH

BALLYPHILIP (no dedication) w Ardquin *D & D*   I vacant

BALLYRASHANE (St John the Baptist) w Kildollagh *Conn*
I A E ADAMS

BALLYSALLY (St Andrew)   *see* Coleraine *Conn*

BALLYSCULLION (no dedication)   *see* Drummaul w Duneane and Ballyscullion *Conn*

BALLYSCULLION (St Tida) *D & R*   P-in-c E R LAVERY

BALLYSEEDY (no dedication)   *see* Tralee w Kilmoyley, Ballymacelligott etc *L & K*

BALLYSHANNON   *see* Kilbarron w Rossnowlagh and Drumholm *D & R*

BALLYSILLAN   *see* Belfast St Mark *Conn*

BALLYSUMAGHAN (no dedication)   *see* Taunagh w Kilmactranny, Ballysumaghan etc *K, E & A*

BALLYWALTER (Holy Trinity) w Inishargie *D & D*   I S C BELL

BALLYWARD   *see* Drumgath w Drumgooland and Clonduff *D & D*

BALLYWILLAN (Holy Trinity) *Conn*   I P K MCDOWELL
NSM R J SIMPSON

BALRATHBOYNE   *see* Kells Union *M & K*

BALTEAGH (St Canice) w Carrick *D & R*   I D H J FERRY

BALTIMORE   *see* Abbeystrewry Union *C, C & R*

BALTINGLASS (St Mary) w Ballynure, Stratford-on-Slaney and Rathvilly *C & O*   I vacant

BANAGHER (St Moresuis)   *see* Cumber Lower w Banagher *D & R*

BANAGHER (St Paul)   *see* Clonfert Gp *L & K*

BANBRIDGE   *see* Seapatrick *D & D*

BANDON (St Peter) w Rathclaren, Innishannon, Ballinadee and Brinny *C, C & R*   I D F A MACCARTHY
NSM E C M FERGUSON

BANGOR (St Columbanus)   *see* Ballyholme *D & D*

BANGOR (St Comgall) *D & D*   I N H PARKER

BANGOR ABBEY (Bangor Abbey) *D & D*   I R NESBITT
C M GALLAGHER

BANGOR Primacy (Christ Church) *D & D*
Bp's C F G RUTLEDGE

BANTRY   *see* Kilmocomogue *C, C & R*

BARONSCOURT (no dedication)   *see* Ardstraw w Baronscourt, Badoney Lower etc *D & R*

BARR (no dedication)   *see* Donacavey w Barr *Clogh*

BEARA (St Peter)   *see* Kilmocomogue *C, C & R*

BECTIVE   *see* Trim and Athboy Gp *M & K*

BELFAST (All Saints) *Conn*   I T S JOHNSTON

BELFAST (Cathedral of St Anne) *Conn*   NSM J M ELSDON

BELFAST (Christ Church) *Conn*   I vacant

BELFAST (Holy Trinity) (St Silas) *Conn*   P-in-c D M ACHESON

BELFAST (St Aidan) *Conn*   P-in-c R MOORE

BELFAST (St Andrew) *Conn*   I vacant

BELFAST (St Bartholomew) *Conn*   I T K D GRAHAM

BELFAST (St Brendan) *D & D*   C J HARRIS

BELFAST (St Christopher)   *see* Ballymacarrett *D & D*

BELFAST (St Clement) *D & D*   I vacant

BELFAST (St Donard) *D & D*   I K H HIGGINS

BELFAST (St George) *Conn*   I B STEWART   NSM I M FRAZER

BELFAST (St Jude)   *see* Ballynafeigh St Jude *D & D*

BELFAST (St Katharine) *Conn*   I W J TAGGART

BELFAST (St Mark) *Conn*   I R H MOORE   P-in-c C B DIXON

BELFAST (St Martin)   *see* Ballymacarrett *D & D*

BELFAST (St Mary Magdalene) *Conn*   **NSM** R E COTTER
BELFAST (St Mary) (Holy Redeemer) *Conn*
   P-in-c R H MOORE
BELFAST (St Matthew) *Conn*   **I** T MCROBERTS
BELFAST (St Michael) *Conn*   **I** *vacant*
BELFAST (St Nicholas) *Conn*   **I** *vacant*
BELFAST (St Ninian) *Conn*   **I** *vacant*
BELFAST (St Patrick)   *see* Ballymacarrett *D & D*
BELFAST (St Paul) (St Barnabas) *Conn*
   C I HAWTHORNE-STEELE
BELFAST (St Peter) (St James) *Conn*   **I** C B LACEY
BELFAST (St Simon) (St Philip) *Conn*   **P-in-c** R MOORE
BELFAST (St Stephen) (St Luke) *Conn*   **P-in-c** J I CARSON
BELFAST (St Thomas) *Conn*   **I** P JACK
BELFAST Malone (St John) *Conn*   **I** S A FIELDING
BELFAST Titanic Quarter *D & D*   **Bp's C** C I BENNETT
BELFAST Upper Falls (St John the Baptist) *Conn*
   NSM M A REID
BELFAST Upper Malone (Epiphany) *Conn*   **I** *vacant*
BELFAST Whiterock (St Columba) *Conn*   **P** S BLAKE
BELLAGHY   *see* Ballyscullion *D & R*
BELLEEK (no dedication)   *see* Garrison w Slavin and Belleek
   Clogh
BELLEEK (St Luke)   *see* Newtownhamilton w Ballymoyer and
   Belleck *Arm*
BELLERENA   *see* Tamlaghtard w Aghanloo *D & R*
BELMONT (St Peter)   *see* Londonderry Ch Ch, Culmore,
   Muff and Belmont *D & R*
BELTURBET   *see* Annagh w Drumaloor, Cloverhill and
   Drumlane *K, E & A*
BELVOIR (Transfiguration) *D & D*   **I** A A MCCARTNEY   **C** J MOULD
BENOWN (no dedication)   *see* Athlone w Benown, Kiltoom
   and Forgney *M & K*
BILLIS (no dedication)   *see* Lurgan w Billis, Killinkere and
   Munterconnaught *K, E & A*
BILLY (no dedication) w Derrykeighan *Conn*
   I J R ANDERSON
BIRR (St Brendan) w Eglish, Lorrha, Dorrha and Lockeen
   L & K   **I** R W CARNEY   **NSM** R M GILL
BLACKLION   *see* Killinagh w Kiltyclogher and Innismagrath
   K, E & A
BLACKROCK (All Saints)   *see* Stillorgan w Blackrock *D & G*
BLACKROCK (St Michael)   *see* Douglas Union w Frankfield
   C, C & R
BLARNEY   *see* Carrigrohane Union *C, C & R*
BLESSINGTON (St Mary) w Kilbride, Ballymore Eustace
   and Holywood *D & G*   **I** L W RUDDOCK
BOHO (no dedication)   *see* Devenish w Boho *Clogh*
BOOTERSTOWN (St Philip and St James)   *see* Dublin
   Booterstown *D & G*
BORNACOOLA   *see* Templemichael w Clongish,
   Clooncumber etc *K, E & A*
BORRISNAFARNEY (no dedication)   *see* Cloughjordan w
   Borrisokane etc *L & K*
BORRISOKANE (no dedication)   *as above*
BOURNEY (St Burchin)   *see* Roscrea w Kyle, Bourney and
   Corbally *L & K*
BOVEVAGH (St Eugenius)   *see* Dungiven w Bovevagh *D & R*
BOYLE (no dedication) and Elphin w Aghanagh, Kilbryan,
   Ardcarne and Croghan *K, E & A*   **I** J E T YENDALL
BRACKAVILLE (Holy Trinity) w Donaghendry and Ballyclog
   Arm   **I** A RAWDING
BRANTRY (Holy Trinity)   *see* Caledon w Brantry *Arm*
BRAY (Christ Church) *D & G*   **I** B T STANLEY
BRIGHT (no dedication) w Ballee and Killough *D & D*
   I *vacant*
BRIGOWN (St George)   *see* Fermoy Union *C, C & R*
BRINNY (no dedication)   *see* Bandon Union *C, C & R*
BROOKEBOROUGH   *see* Aghavea *Clogh*
BROOMHEDGE (St Matthew) *Conn*   **I** P J GALBRAITH
BROUGHSHANE   *see* Skerry w Rathcavan and
   Newtowncrommelin *Conn*
BRYANSFORD   *see* Castlewellan w Kilcoo *D & D*
BUNBEG   *see* Gweedore, Carrickfin and Templecrone *D & R*
BUNCLODY (St Mary) w Kildavin, Clonegal and Kilrush
   C & O   **I** *vacant*
BUNCRANA   *see* Fahan Lower and Upper *D & R*
BUNDORAN   *see* Cloonclare w Killasnett, Lurganboy and
   Drumlease *K, E & A*
BUSH   *see* Ballymascanlan w Creggan and Rathcor *Arm*
BUSHMILLS   *see* Dunluce *Conn*
CAHERAGH (St Mary)   *see* Abbeystrewry Union *C, C & R*
CAHERCONLISH (St Ailbe)   *see* Adare and Kilmallock w
   Kilpeacon, Croom etc *L & K*
CAIRNCASTLE (St Patrick)   *see* Kilwaughter and Cairncastle w
   Craigy Hill *Conn*

CALARY (no dedication)   *see* Newcastle w
   Newtownmountkennedy and Calary *D & G*
CALEDON (St John) w Brantry *Arm*   **I** *vacant*
CALRY (no dedication) *K, E & A*   **I** P H BAMBER
CAMLOUGH (Christ the Redeemer) w Mullaglass *Arm*
   I A P S SYNNOTT   **C** W J MCCRACKEN
CAMP   *see* Dingle w Killiney and Kilgobbin *L & K*
CAMUS-JUXTA-BANN (St Mary) *D & R*   **I** P LYONS
CAMUS-JUXTA-MOURNE (Christ Church) *D & R*   **I** *vacant*
CAPPAGH (St Eugene) w Lislimnaghan *D & R*   **I** D J QUINN
CARBURY (no dedication)   *see* Clonsast w Rathangan,
   Thomastown etc *M & K*
CARLOW (St Mary) w Urglin and Staplestown *C & O*
   I *vacant*
CARNALEA (St Gall) *D & D*   **I** M A PARKER
CARNALWAY (St Patrick)   *see* Newbridge w Carnalway and
   Kilcullen *M & K*
CARNDONAGH   *see* Moville w Greencastle, Donagh,
   Cloncha etc *D & R*
CARNLOUGH   *see* Ardclinis and Tickmacrevan w Layde and
   Cushendun *Conn*
CARNMONEY (Holy Evangelists) *Conn*   **I** A J HEBER
   NSM C R HARVEY
CARNTEEL (St James) and Crilly *Arm*   **I** E R G WEST
CARRICK (no dedication)   *see* Balteagh w Carrick *D & R*
CARRICKFERGUS (St Nicholas) *Conn*   **I** G T W DAVISON
   C C C W JONES
CARRICKFIN (St Andrew)   *see* Gweedore, Carrickfin and
   Templecrone *D & R*
CARRICKMACROSS (St Fin Barre) w Magheracloone *Clogh*
   I C A MCCONAGHIE
CARRICK-ON-SHANNON   *see* Kiltoghart w Drumshambo,
   Annaduff and Kilronan *K, E & A*
CARRIGALINE (St Mary) w Killanully and Monkstown
   C, C & R   **I** E M E MURRAY   **NSM** A M MURPHY,
   H E A MINION
CARRIGALLEN (no dedication)   *see* Arvagh w Carrigallen,
   Gowna and Columbkille *K, E & A*
CARRIGANS   *see* Taughboyne, Craigadooish,
   Newtowncunningham etc *D & R*
CARRIGART   *see* Mevagh w Glenalla *D & R*
CARRIGROHANE (St Peter) w Garrycloyne, Inniscarra and
   Magourney *C, C & R*   **I** R JONAS   **C** R J FERRIS
CARROWDORE (Christ Church) w Millisle *D & D*
   I C A J DAVIS
CARRYDUFF (St Ignatius)   *see* Killaney w Carryduff *D & D*
CASHEL (Cathedral of St John the Baptist) w Magorban,
   Tipperary, Clonbeg and Ballintemple *C & O*   **I** *vacant*
CASHEL (no dedication)   *see* Clondehorkey w Cashel *D & R*
CASTLEARCHDALE (St Patrick)   *see* Derryvullen N w
   Castlearchdale *Clogh*
CASTLEBAR (Christ Church)   *see* Aughaval w Achill,
   Knappagh, Dugort etc *T, K & A*
CASTLEBLAYNEY   *see* Ballybay w Mucknoe and Clontibret
   Clogh
CASTLECOMER (St Mary) w the Colliery Church, Mothel
   and Bilboa *C & O*   **I** *vacant*
CASTLECONNELL   *see* Killaloe w Stradbally *L & K*
CASTLECONNOR (no dedication)   *see* Killala w Dunfeeny,
   Crossmolina, Kilmoremoy etc *T, K & A*
CASTLEDAWSON (Christ Church) *D & R*   **I** C R J WELSH
CASTLEDERG   *see* Derg w Termonamongan *D & R*
CASTLEDERMOT (St James)   *see* Narraghmore and Timolin w
   Castledermot etc *D & G*
CASTLEGREGORY   *see* Dingle w Killiney and Kilgobbin *L & K*
CASTLEHAVEN (no dedication)   *see* Abbeystrewry Union
   C, C & R
CASTLEKNOCK (St Brigid) and Mulhuddart w Clonsilla
   D & G   **I** W P HOUSTON
CASTLELOST   *see* Mullingar, Portnashangan, Moyliscar,
   Kilbixy etc *M & K*
CASTLEMACADAM (Holy Trinity) w Ballinaclash, Aughrim
   and Macreddin *D & G*   **I** *vacant*
CASTLEMAINE   *see* Kilcolman w Kiltallagh, Killorglin,
   Knockane etc *L & K*
CASTLEMARTYR (St Anne)   *see* Youghal Union *C, C & R*
CASTLEPOLLARD (St Michael) and Oldcastle w
   Loughcrew, Mount Nugent, Mayne and Drumcree *M & K*
   I D G O'CATHAIN
CASTLEREA   *see* Roscommon w Donamon, Rathcline,
   Kilkeevin etc *K, E & A*
CASTLERICKARD   *see* Dunboyne and Rathmolyon *M & K*
CASTLEROCK (Christ Church) w Dunboe and Fermoyle
   D & R   **I** C MAC BRUITHIN   **NSM** A QUIGLEY
CASTLETERRA (no dedication)   *see* Drung w Castleterra,
   Larah and Lavey etc *K, E & A*

CASTLETOWN   *see* Kells Union *M & K*
CASTLETOWN   *see* Rathkeale w Askeaton, Kilcornan and Kilnaughtin *L & K*
CASTLETOWNBERE (St Peter)   *see* Kilmocomogue *C, C & R*
CASTLETOWNROCHE (no dedication)   *see* Mallow Union *C, C & R*
CASTLETOWNSEND   *see* Abbeystrewry Union *C, C & R*
CASTLEVENTRY (no dedication)   *see* Ross Union *C, C & R*
CASTLEWELLAN (St Paul) w Kilcoo *D & D*   **I** B S CADDEN
CAVAN   *see* Urney w Denn and Derryheen *K, E & A*
CELBRIDGE (Christ Church) w Straffan and Newcastle-Lyons *D & G*   **I** S M NEILL
CHAPELIZOD (St Laurence)   *see* Dublin Crumlin w Chapelizod *D & G*
CHARLEMONT (no dedication)   *see* Moy w Charlemont *Arm*
CLABBY (St Margaret)   *see* Tempo and Clabby *Clogh*
CLANABOGAN (no dedication)   *see* Edenderry w Clanabogan *D & R*
CLANE (St Michael and All Angels) w Donadea and Coolcarrigan *M & K*   **I** *vacant*
CLARA (St Brigid) w Liss, Moate and Clonmacnoise *M & K*   **I** *vacant*
CLARE (no dedication)   *see* Loughgilly w Clare *Arm*
CLAUDY   *see* Cumber Upper w Learmount *D & R*
CLEENISH (no dedication) w Mullaghdun *Clogh*   **I** G P BRIDLE
CLIFDEN   *see* Omey w Ballynakill, Errislannan and Roundstone *T, K & A*
CLOGH (Holy Trinity)   *see* Aghadrumsee w Clogh and Drumsnatt *Clogh*
CLOGHER (Cathedral of St Macartan) w Errigal Portclare *Clogh*   **I** O M G DOWNEY
CLOGHERNY (St Patrick) w Seskinore and Drumnakilly *Arm*   **R** *vacant*
CLONAKILTY   *see* Kilgariffe Union *C, C & R*
CLONALLON (no dedication) and Warrenpoint w Kilbroney *D & D*   **I** C J MCCORMACK, D J MCCARTNEY
CLONARD   *see* Mullingar, Portnashangan, Moyliscar, Kilbixy etc *M & K*
CLONASLEE   *see* Mountmellick w Coolbanagher, Rosenallis etc *M & K*
CLONBRONEY (St John)   *see* Mostrim w Granard, Clonbroney, Killoe etc *K, E & A*
CLONBULLOGUE   *see* Clonsast w Rathangan, Thomastown etc *M & K*
CLONCHA (no dedication)   *see* Moville w Greencastle, Donagh, Cloncha etc *D & R*
CLONDALKIN (St John) w Rathcoole *D & G*   **I** A J RUFLI
   NSM A A SHINE
CLONDEHORKEY (St John) w Cashel *D & R*   **I** C D PIERCE
CLONDEVADDOCK (Christ the Redeemer) w Portsalon and Leatbeg *D & R*   **Hon C** D GRISCOME
CLONDUFF (St John)   *see* Drumgath w Drumgooland and Clonduff *D & D*
CLONENAGH (no dedication) w Offerlane, Borris-in-Ossory, Seirkieran and Roskelton *C & O*   **I** *vacant*
CLONES (St Tighernach) w Killeevan *Clogh*   **I** R TAYLOR
CLONEYHURKE (no dedication)   *see* Portarlington w Cloneyhurke, Lea etc *M & K*
CLONFADFORAN   *see* Tullamore w Durrow, Newtownfertullagh, Rahan etc *M & K*
CLONFEACLE (St Patrick) w Derrygortreavy *Arm*   **I** S J COUSINS
CLONFERT (Cathedral of St Brendan) w Donanaughta, Banagher and Lickmolassy *L & K*   **P-in-c** R C MCCARTNEY
CLONGISH (St Paul)   *see* Templemichael w Clongish, Clooncumber etc *K, E & A*
CLONLARA   *see* Killaloe w Stradbally *L & K*
CLONLEIGH (St Lugadius)   *see* Raphoe w Raymochy and Clonleigh *D & R*
CLONMACNOISE (St Kieran)   *see* Clara w Liss, Moate and Clonmacnoise *M & K*
CLONMEL (St Mary) w Innislounagh, Tullaghmelan, Fethard, Kilvemnon and Cahir *C & O*   **I** *vacant*
CLONMELLON   *see* Trim and Athboy Gp *M & K*
CLONOE (St Michael)   *see* Tullaniskin w Clonoe *Arm*
CLONSAST (no dedication) w Rathangan, Thomastown, Monasteroris, Carbury and Rahan *M & K*   **I** S L MARRY
CLONSILLA (St Mary)   *see* Castleknock and Mulhuddart w Clonsilla *D & G*
CLONTARF   *see* Dublin Clontarf *D & G*
CLONTIBRET (St Colman)   *see* Ballybay w Mucknoe and Clontibret *Clogh*
CLONTUSKERT (St Matthew)   *see* Aughrim w Ballinasloe etc *L & K*

CLOONCLARE (no dedication) w Killasnett, Lurganboy and Drumlease *K, E & A*   **P-in-c** B M MCCARTHY
   C R A BEADLE
CLOONCUMBER (no dedication)   *see* Templemichael w Clongish, Clooncumber etc *K, E & A*
CLOONEY (All Saints) w Strathfoyle *D & R*   **I** D R MCBETH
   C R JONES   **NSM** M T E PEOPLES
CLOUGH   *see* Craigs w Dunaghy and Killagan *Conn*
CLOUGHFERN (Ascension) *Conn*   **C** A E STEWART
CLOUGHJORDAN (St Kieran) w Borrisokane, Ballingary, Borrisnafarney and Templeharry *L & K*   **I** T I MITCHELL
CLOUGHMILLS   *see* Craigs w Dunaghy and Killagan *Conn*
CLOVERHILL (St John)   *see* Annagh w Drumaloor, Cloverhill and Drumlane *K, E & A*
CLOYNE (Cathedral of St Colman) w Inch, Corkbeg, Midleton and Gurranekennefeake *C, C & R*   **I** S D GREEN
COACHFORD   *see* Carrigrohane Union *C, C & R*
COALISLAND   *see* Brackaville w Donaghendry and Ballyclog *Arm*
COLAGHTY   *see* Lack *Clogh*
COLEBROOK   *see* Aghalurcher w Tattykeeran, Cooneen etc *Clogh*
COLERAINE   *see* Killowen *D & R*
COLERAINE (St Patrick) *Conn*   **I** R COOKE
COLIN (St Andrew)   *see* Derriaghy w Colin *Conn*
COLLON (no dedication)   *see* Drogheda w Ardee, Collon and Termonfeckin *Arm*
COLLOONEY (St Paul)   *see* Ballisodare w Collooney and Emlaghfad *T, K & A*
COLPE (St Columba)   *see* Julianstown and Colpe w Drogheda and Duleek *M & K*
COLUMBKILLE (St Thomas)   *see* Arvagh w Carrigallen, Gowna and Columbkille *K, E & A*
COMBER (St Mary) *D & D*   **I** *vacant*
CONARY (St Bartholomew)   *see* Dunganstown w Redcross and Conary *D & G*
CONG (St Mary)   *see* Tuam w Cong and Aasleagh *T, K & A*
CONNOR (St Saviour) w Antrim St Patrick *Conn*   **I** I W MAGOWAN
CONVOY (St Ninian) w Monellan and Donaghmore *D & R*   **I** W T LONG
CONWAL (no dedication) w Aughanunshin and Gartan *D & R*   **I** D A HOULTON
COOKSTOWN   *see* Derryloran *Arm*
COOLBANAGHER (St John)   *see* Mountmellick w Coolbanagher, Rosenallis etc *M & K*
COOLCARRIGAN (no dedication)   *see* Clane w Donadea and Coolcarrigan *M & K*
COOLKELLURE (St Edmund)   *see* Fanlobbus Union *C, C & R*
COOLOCK (St John)   *see* Raheny w Coolock *D & G*
COONEEN (no dedication)   *see* Aghalurcher w Tattykeeran, Cooneen etc *Clogh*
COOTEHILL   *see* Drumgoon *K, E & A*
CORBALLY (Christ Church)   *see* Roscrea w Kyle, Bourney and Corbally *L & K*
CORK (Cathedral of St Fin Barre) (St Nicholas) *C, C & R*   **I** N K DUNNE
CORK (St Ann) Shandon w St Mary *C, C & R*   **NSM** P J GEARY
CORKBEG (St Michael and All Angels)   *see* Cloyne Union *C, C & R*
CORRAWALLEN (no dedication)   *see* Kildallon and Swanlinbar *K, E & A*
COURTMACSHERRY (St John the Evangelist)   *see* Kilgariffe Union *C, C & R*
CRAIGADOOISH (no dedication)   *see* Taughboyne, Craigadooish, Newtowncunningham etc *D & R*
CRAIGAVAD   *see* Glencraig *D & D*
CRAIGAVON (St Saviour)   *see* Ardmore w Craigavon *D & D*
CRAIGS (no dedication) w Dunaghy and Killagan *Conn*   **NSM** A R HALLIGAN, T S KELLY
CRAIGY HILL (All Saints)   *see* Kilwaughter and Cairncastle w Craigy Hill *Conn*
CREAGH   *see* Abbeystrewry Union *C, C & R*
CREAGH   *see* Aughrim w Ballinasloe etc *L & K*
CRECORA   *see* Adare and Kilmallock w Kilpeacon, Croom etc *L & K*
CREGAGH (St Finnian) *D & D*   **I** J D M PIERCE
   NSM R J C KETTYLE
CREGGAN (no dedication)   *see* Ballymascanlan w Creggan and Rathcor *Arm*
CRILLY (St George)   *see* Carnteel and Crilly *Arm*
CRINKEN (St James) *D & G*   **I** T D STEVENSON
CROGHAN (Holy Trinity)   *see* Boyle and Elphin w Aghanagh, Kilbryan etc *K, E & A*
CROM (Holy Trinity)   *see* Kinawley w H Trin *K, E & A*

CROOKHAVEN (St Brendan) *see* Kilmoe Union *C, C & R*

CROOM (no dedication) *see* Adare and Kilmallock w Kilpeacon, Croom etc *L & K*

CROSSGAR *see* Kilmore and Inch *D & D*

CROSSHAVEN *see* Templebreedy w Tracton and Nohoval *C, C & R*

CROSSMOLINA (no dedication) *see* Killala w Dunfeeny, Crossmolina, Kilmoremoy etc *T, K & A*

CROSSPATRICK Group (no dedication) w Kilcommon, Kilpipe, Preban and Carnew, The *C & O* **I** vacant

CRUMLIN *see* Dublin Crumlin w Chapelizod *D & G*

CRUMLIN (St John) *see* Glenavy w Tunny and Crumlin *Conn*

CRUMLIN ROAD *see* Belfast St Mary w H Redeemer *Conn*

CULDAFF (no dedication) *see* Moville w Greencastle, Donagh, Cloncha etc *D & R*

CULFEIGHTRIN (no dedication) *see* Ramoan w Ballycastle and Culfeightrin *Conn*

CULLYBACKEY *see* Craigs w Dunaghy and Killagan *Conn*

CULMORE (Holy Trinity) *see* Londonderry Ch Ch, Culmore, Muff and Belmont *D & R*

CUMBER LOWER (Holy Trinity) w Banagher *D & R* **I** vacant

CUMBER UPPER (no dedication) w Learmount *D & R* **I** J R D SLATER

CURRAGH (Garrison Church of St Paul) *see* Kildare w Kilmeague and Curragh *M & K*

CURRIN (St Andrew) w Drum and Newbliss *Clogh* **I** vacant

CUSHENDALL *see* Ardclinis and Tickmacrevan w Layde and Cushendun *Conn*

CUSHENDUN (no dedication) *as above*

DALKEY (St Patrick) *D & G* **I** B J HAYES **NSM** K P CONROY

DARTREY *see* Ematris w Rockcorry, Aghabog and Aughnamullan *Clogh*

DELGANY (Christ Church) *D & G* **I** N J W WAUGH **NSM** H E A LEW

DENN (no dedication) *see* Urney w Denn and Derryheen *K, E & A*

DERG (no dedication) w Termonamongan *D & R* **I** P A FERGUSON **C** N C QUINN

DERNAKESH (Chapel of Ease) *see* Drumgoon *K, E & A*

DERRALOSSARY *see* Rathdrum w Glenealy, Derralossary and Laragh *D & G*

DERRIAGHY (Christ Church) w Colin *Conn* **NSM** K W GAMBLE

DERRYBRUSK (St Michael) *see* Maguiresbridge w Derrybrusk *Clogh*

DERRYGONNELLY *see* Inishmacsaint *Clogh*

DERRYGORTREAVY (St Columba) *see* Clonfeacle w Derrygortreavy *Arm*

DERRYHEEN (no dedication) *see* Urney w Denn and Derryheen *K, E & A*

DERRYKIGHAN (St Colman) *see* Billy w Derrykeighan *Conn*

DERRYLANE (no dedication) *see* Killeshandra w Killegar and Derrylane *K, E & A*

DERRYLIN *see* Kinawley w H Trin *K, E & A*

DERRYLORAN (St Luran) *Arm* **I** R J N PORTEUS **NSM** W J A DAWSON

DERRYNOOSE (St John) *see* Keady w Armaghbreague and Derrynoose *Arm*

DERRYVOLGIE (St Columba) *Conn* **I** W J BOYD

DERRYVULLEN NORTH (St Tighernach) w Castlearchdale *Clogh* **I** P THOMPSON

DERRYVULLEN SOUTH (St Tighernach) w Garvary *Clogh* **NSM** E G M THOMPSON

DERVOCK *see* Billy w Derrykeighan *Conn*

DESERTCREAT (no dedication) *see* Ardtrea w Desertcreat *Arm*

DESERTLYN (St John) w Ballyeglish *Arm* **I** A N STRINGER

DESERTMARTIN (St Conghall) w Termoneeny *D & R* **I** M P DORNAN

DESERTOGHILL (no dedication) *see* Errigal w Garvagh *D & R*

DESERTSERGES (no dedication) *see* Kinneigh Union *C, C & R*

DEVENISH (St Molaise) w Boho *Clogh* **Bp's C** S C AJUKA

DIAMOND (St Paul) *see* Tartaraghan w Diamond *Arm*

DINGLE (St James) w Killiney and Kilgobbin *L & K* **I** vacant

DOAGH *see* Kilbride *Conn*

DOLLINGSTOWN (St Saviour) *see* Magheralin w Dollingstown *D & D*

DONABATE (St Patrick) *see* Swords w Donabate and Kilsallaghan *D & G*

DONACAVEY (no dedication) w Barr *Clogh* **I** J WOODS

DONADEA (St Peter) *see* Clane w Donadea and Coolcarrigan *M & K*

DONAGH (no dedication) *see* Moville w Greencastle, Donagh, Cloncha etc *D & R*

DONAGH (St Salvator) w Tyholland and Errigal Truagh *Clogh* **C** L A CAPPER

DONAGHADEE (no dedication) *D & D* **R** I R GAMBLE

DONAGHCLONEY (St Patrick) w Waringstown *D & D* **I** B R MARTIN

DONAGHEADY (St James) *D & R* **I** R P STOCKITT

DONAGHENDRY (St Patrick) *see* Brackaville w Donaghendry and Ballyclog *Arm*

DONAGHMORE (St Bartholomew) *see* Aghaderg w Donaghmore and Scarva *D & D*

DONAGHMORE (St Michael) w Upper Donaghmore *Arm* **I** P A THOMPSON

DONAGHMORE (St Patrick) *see* Convoy w Monellan and Donaghmore *D & R*

DONAGHMORE, UPPER (St Patrick) *see* Donaghmore w Upper Donaghmore *Arm*

DONAGHPATRICK (St Patrick) *see* Kells Union *M & K*

DONAMON (no dedication) *see* Roscommon w Donamon, Rathcline, Kilkeevin etc *K, E & A*

DONANAUGHTA (St John the Baptist) *see* Clonfert Gp *L & K*

DONARD (no dedication) *see* Donoughmore and Donard w Dunlavin *D & G*

DONEGAL (no dedication) w Killymard, Lough Eske and Laghey *D & R* **I** D I HUSS

DONEGORE (St John) *see* Templepatrick w Donegore *Conn*

DONEMANA *see* Donagheady *D & R*

DONERAILE (St Mary) *see* Mallow Union *C, C & R*

DONNYBROOK (St Mary) *see* Dublin Irishtown w Donnybrook *D & G*

DONOUGHMORE (no dedication) and Donard w Dunlavin *D & G* **I** N J O'RAW

DORRHA (no dedication) *see* Birr w Lorrha, Dorrha and Lockeen *L & K*

DOUGLAS (St Luke) w Blackrock, Frankfield and Marmullane *C, C & R* **I** A M WILKINSON **C** D G D BOWLES **NSM** P T HANNA

DOWN (Cathedral of the Holy and Undivided Trinity) *D & D* **C** S J MCDONALD

DOWN (St Margaret) w Hollymount *D & D* **I** vacant

DOWNPATRICK *see* Down Cathl *D & D*

DOWNPATRICK *see* Down H Trin w Hollymount *D & D*

DRAPERSTOWN (St Columb) *see* Kilcronaghan w Draperstown and Sixtowns *D & R*

DREW MEMORIAL *see* Belfast St Simon w St Phil *Conn*

DRIMOLEAGUE (St Matthew) *see* Fanlobbus Union *C, C & R*

DRINAGH (Christ Church) *as above*

DROGHEDA (St Mary) *see* Julianstown and Colpe w Drogheda and Duleek *M & K*

DROGHEDA (St Peter) w Ardee, Collon and Termonfeckin *Arm* **I** I B JAMIESON **NSM** J MOORE

DROMAHAIR *see* Cloonclare w Killasnett, Lurganboy and Drumlease *K, E & A*

DROMARA (St John) w Garvaghy *D & D* **I** C TAYLOR

DROMARD (Christ Church) *see* Skreen w Kilmacshalgan and Dromard *T, K & A*

DROMOD (St Michael and All Angels) *see* Kenmare w Sneem, Waterville etc *L & K*

DROMORE (Cathedral of Christ the Redeemer) *D & D* **I** S G WILSON **NSM** T J MCKEOWN

DROMORE (Holy Trinity) *Clogh* **I** A T E QUILL

DRUM (no dedication) *see* Currin w Drum and Newbliss *Clogh*

DRUMACHOSE (Christ Church) *D & R* **I** S MCVEIGH

DRUMALOOR (St Andrew) *see* Annagh w Drumaloor, Cloverhill and Drumlane *K, E & A*

DRUMANY (Christ Church) *see* Kinawley w H Trin *K, E & A*

DRUMBANAGHER (St Mary) *see* Acton and Drumbanagher *Arm*

DRUMBEG (St Patrick) *D & D* **I** W S NIXON

DRUMBO (Holy Trinity) *D & D* **P-in-c** W M N JAMISON

DRUMCAR *see* Kilsaran w Drumcar, Dunleer and Dunany *Arm*

DRUMCLAMPH (no dedication) w Lower Langfield and Upper Langfield *D & R* **I** R G KEOGH

DRUMCLIFFE (St Columba) w Kilrush, Kilfenora, Kilfarboy, Kilnasoolagh, Shannon and Kilferagh *L & K* **NSM** P E MCKEE HANNA

DRUMCLIFFE (St Columba) w Lissadell and Munninane *K, E & A* **I** I J HANNA

DRUMCONDRA *see* Dublin Drumcondra w N Strand *D & G*

DRUMCONRATH (St Peter) *see* Kingscourt w Syddan *M & K*

DRUMCREE (Ascension) *Arm* **I** G F GALWAY

DRUMCREE (St John) *see* Castlepollard and Oldcastle w Loughcrew etc *M & K*

DRUMGATH (St John) w Drumgooland and Clonduff *D & D* **I** G W MACARTNEY

DRUMGLASS (St Anne) w Moygashel *Arm* **I** A J FORSTER **C** G HARE **NSM** M E M STEVENSON

DRUMGOOLAND (no dedication) *see* Drumgath w Drumgooland and Clonduff *D & D*

DRUMGOON (All Saints) *see* Drumgoon *K, E & A*

DRUMGOON (All Saints) w Ashfield, Killesherdoney and Dernakesh *K, E & A* **P-in-c** A J LINDSAY **Bp's** C D T MOSES

DRUMHOLM (no dedication) *see* Kilbarron w Rossnowlagh and Drumholm *D & R*

DRUMINISKILL (Chapel of Ease) *see* Killesher *K, E & A*

DRUMKEERAN *see* Killinagh w Kiltyclogher and Innismagrath *K, E & A*

DRUMKEERAN (no dedication) w Templecarne and Muckross *Clogh* **NSM** C G EAMES

DRUMLANE (no dedication) *see* Annagh w Drumaloor, Cloverhill and Drumlane *K, E & A*

DRUMLEASE (no dedication) *see* Cloonclare w Killasnett, Lurganboy and Drumlease *K, E & A*

DRUMMAUL (St Brigid) w Duneane and Ballyscullion *Conn* **I** D P KERR

DRUMMULLY (no dedication) *see* Galloon w Drummully and Sallaghy *Clogh*

DRUMNAKILLY (Holy Trinity) *see* Clogherny w Seskinore and Drumnakilly *Arm*

DRUMQUIN *see* Drumclamph w Lower and Upper Langfield *D & R*

DRUMRAGH (St Columba) w Mountfield *D & R* **I** B I LINTON **C** R J ROBINSON, S J K HANILY

DRUMREILLY (no dedication) *see* Mohill w Farnaught, Aughavas, Oughteragh etc *K, E & A*

DRUMSHAMBO (St John) *see* Kiltoghart w Drumshambo, Annaduff and Kilronan *K, E & A*

DRUMSNATT (St Molua) *see* Aghadrumsee w Clogh and Drumsnatt *Clogh*

DRUMTALLAGH (no dedication) *see* Armoy w Loughguile and Drumtullagh *Conn*

DRUNG (no dedication) w Castleterra, Larah and Lavey and Killoughter *K, E & A* **I** N T JONES

DUBLIN (Christ Church Cathedral) Group: (St Andrew) (St Werburgh) (St Michan) and Grangegorman *D & G* **V** D A PIERPOINT

DUBLIN (Irish Church Missions) and St Thomas *D & G* **I** *vacant*

DUBLIN (St Ann) (St Stephen) *D & G* **I** D I GILLESPIE **NSM** M J O'CONNOR, Y A GINNELLY

DUBLIN (St Bartholomew) w Leeson Park *D & G* **I** A MCCROSKERY

DUBLIN (St Catherine and St James) (St Audoen) *D & G* **I** M D GARDNER **C** E HEASLIP **NSM** C E BAKER, M M WALLER

DUBLIN (St George and St Thomas) *D & G* **I** *vacant*

DUBLIN (Zion Church) *D & G* **I** S A FARRELL

DUBLIN Booterstown (St Philip and St James) *D & G* **I** G V WHARTON **NSM** S S HARRIS

DUBLIN Clontarf (St John the Baptist) *D & G* **I** E C L ROBINSON **NSM** A E LODGE

DUBLIN Crumlin (St Mary) w Chapelizod *D & G* **I** R E JACKSON

DUBLIN Drumcondra (no dedication) w North Strand *D & G* **I** E G BUNTING

DUBLIN Irishtown (St Matthew) w Donnybrook *D & G* **Bp's** C J B MARCHANT

DUBLIN Mount Merrion (St Thomas) *D & G* **I** G V WHARTON

DUBLIN Rathfarnham (no dedication) *D & G* **I** A GALLIGAN **C** R J O'KELLY

DUBLIN Rathmines (Holy Trinity) w Harold's Cross *D & G* **I** R D JONES

DUBLIN Sandford (no dedication) w Milltown *D & G* **I** S GYLES **NSM** A M O'FARRELL

DUBLIN Sandymount (St John the Evangelist) *D & G* **P-in-c** P A BARLOW

DUBLIN Santry (St Pappan) w Glasnevin and Finglas *D & G* **I** D W OXLEY

DUBLIN Whitechurch (no dedication) *D & G* **I** A H N MCKINLEY

DUGORT (St Thomas) *see* Aughaval w Achill, Knappagh, Dugort etc *T, K & A*

DULEEK *see* Julianstown and Colpe w Drogheda and Duleek *M & K*

DUN LAOGHAIRE (Christ Church) *D & G* **I** Á B ÓLAFSDÓTTIR O'HANLON

DUNAGHY (St James) *see* Craigs w Dunaghy and Killagan *Conn*

DUNANY *see* Kilsaran w Drumcar, Dunleer and Dunany *Arm*

DUNBOE (St Paul) *see* Castlerock w Dunboe and Fermoyle *D & R*

DUNBOYNE (St Peter and St Paul) w Rathmolyon, Dunshaughlin, Maynooth, Agher and Rathcore *M & K* **I** E T GRIFFIN **C** A E G IRVINE **NSM** A V STEWART

DUNDALK (St Nicholas) w Heynestown *Arm* **C** G G WALMSLEY **NSM** R W R MOORE

DUNDELA (St Mark) *D & D* **I** H STEED **C** C G ST JOHN

DUNDONALD (St Elizabeth) *D & D* **I** T G ANDERSON

DUNDRUM (St Donard) *see* Kilmegan w Maghera *D & D*

DUNEANE (no dedication) *see* Drummaul w Duneane and Ballyscullion *Conn*

DUNFANAGHY (Holy Trinity), Raymunterdoney and Tullaghbegley *D & R* **I** D SKUCE

DUNFEENY (no dedication) *see* Killala w Dunfeeny, Crossmolina, Kilmoremoy etc *T, K & A*

DUNGANNON *see* Drumglass w Moygashel *Arm*

DUNGANSTOWN (St Kevin) w Redcross and Conary *D & G* **I** J R HEANEY

DUNGIVEN (no dedication) w Bovevagh *D & R* **I** M W J LONEY

DUNGLOE *see* Gweedore, Carrickfin and Templecrone *D & R*

DUNKERRIN (no dedication) *see* Shinrone w Aghancon etc *L & K*

DUNLAVIN (St Nicholas) *see* Donoughmore and Donard w Dunlavin *D & G*

DUNLECKNEY (St Mary) w Nurney, Lorum and Kiltennel *C & O* **I** *vacant*

DUNLEER (no dedication) *see* Kilsaran w Drumcar, Dunleer and Dunany *Arm*

DUNLUCE (St John the Baptist) *Conn* **I** G E GRAHAM

DUNMANWAY *see* Fanlobbus Union *C, C & R*

DUNMURRY (St Colman) *Conn* **I** A R MCLAUGHLIN

DUNNALONG (St John) *see* Leckpatrick w Dunnalong *D & R*

DUNSEVERICK (no dedication) *see* Ballintoy w Rathlin and Dunseverick *Conn*

DUNSFORD (St Mary) *see* Lecale Gp *D & D*

DUNSHAUGHLIN (St Seachnal) *see* Dunboyne and Rathmolyon *M & K*

DURROW (St Columba) *see* Tullamore w Durrow, Newtownfertullagh, Rahan etc *M & K*

DURRUS (St James the Apostle) *see* Kilmocomogue *C, C & R*

EASKEY (St Anne) *see* Killala w Dunfeeny, Crossmolina, Kilmoremoy etc *T, K & A*

EDENDERRY *see* Clonsast w Rathangan, Thomastown etc *M & K*

EDENDERRY (no dedication) w Clanabogan *D & R* **I** R W CLARKE

EDGEWORTHSTOWN *see* Mostrim w Granard, Clonbroney, Killoe etc *K, E & A*

EGLANTINE (All Saints) *Conn* **I** J W KERNOHAN

EGLINTON *see* Faughanvale *D & R*

EGLISH (Holy Trinity) w Killylea *Arm* **I** F W ATKINS

ELPHIN (no dedication) *see* Boyle and Elphin w Aghanagh, Kilbryan etc *K, E & A*

EMATRIS (St John the Evangelist) w Rockcorry, Aghabog and Aughnamullan *Clogh* **NSM** M B PRINGLE

EMLAGHFAD (no dedication) *see* Ballisodare w Collooney and Emlaghfad *T, K & A*

ENNIS *see* Drumcliffe w Kilnasoolagh *L & K*

ENNISCORTHY (St Mary) w Clone, Clonmore, Monart and Templescobin *C & O* **I** *vacant*

ENNISKEEN *see* Kingscourt w Syddan *M & K*

ENNISKERRY *see* Powerscourt w Kilbride *D & G*

ENNISKILLEN *see* Rossorry *Clogh*

ENNISKILLEN (Cathedral of St Macartin) *Clogh* **I** K R J HALL

ERRIGAL (St Paul) w Garvagh *D & R* **I** C M HAYES

ERRIGAL PORTCLARE (no dedication) *see* Clogh w Errigal Portclare *Clogh*

ERRIGAL TRUAGH (St Muadhan) *see* Donagh w Tyholland and Errigal Truagh *Clogh*

ERRIGLE KEEROGUE (no dedication) w Ballygawley and Killeshil *Arm* **I** *vacant*

ERRISLANNAN (no dedication) *see* Omey w Ballynakill, Errislannan and Roundstone *T, K & A*

ESKRAHOOLE (no dedication) *see* Augher w Newtownsaville and Eskrahoole *Clogh*

EYRECOURT *see* Clonfert Gp *L & K*

FAHAN LOWER (Christ Church) and UPPER (St Mura) *D & R* **C** J H MCGAFFIN

FALLS, LOWER (St Luke) *see* Belfast St Steph w St Luke *Conn*

FALLS, UPPER *see* Belfast Upper Falls *Conn*

FANLOBBUS (St Mary) w Drimoleague, Drinagh and Coolkellure *C, C & R* **I** C P JEFFERS

FARNAUGHT (no dedication) *see* Mohill w Farnaught, Aughavas, Oughteragh etc *K, E & A*

FAUGHANVALE (St Canice) *D & R* **I** D P HOEY **NSM** B J HASSAN

FENAGH (All Saints) w Myshall, Aghade and Ardoyne
C & O I *vacant*
FERMOY (Christ Church) w Ballyhooley, Knockmourne,
Ardnageehy and Brigown *C, C & R* I G A PAULSEN
NSM W H HILL
FERMOYLE (no dedication) *see* Castlerock w Dunboe and
Fermoyle *D & R*
FERNS (Cathedral of St Edan) w Kilbride, Toombe,
Kilcormack and Ballycarney *C & O* I *vacant*
FERRY, EAST *see* Cloyne Union *C, C & R*
FIDDOWN (no dedication) w Clonegam, Guilcagh and
Kilmeaden *C & O* I *vacant*
FINAGHY (St Polycarp) *Conn* I A L STEWART
FINGLAS (St Canice) *see* Dublin Santry w Glasnevin and
Finglas *D & G*
FINNER (Christ Church) *see* Killinagh w Kiltyclogher and
Innismagrath *K, E & A*
FINTONA *see* Donacavey w Barr *Clogh*
FINVOY (no dedication) *see* Ballymoney w Finvoy and
Rasharkin *Conn*
FIVEMILETOWN (St John) *Clogh* I T K HANLON
FLORENCECOURT *see* Killesher *K, E & A*
FONTSTOWN (St John the Evangelist) *see* Athy w Kilberry,
Fontstown and Kilkea *D & G*
FORGNEY (St Munis) *see* Athlone w Benown, Kiltoom and
Forgney *M & K*
FOXFORD *see* Straid *T, K & A*
FOYNES *see* Rathkeale w Askeaton, Kilcornan and
Kilnaughtin *L & K*
FRANKFIELD (Holy Trinity) *see* Douglas Union w Frankfield
C, C & R
FRENCH CHURCH *see* Portarlington w Cloneyhurke, Lea etc
M & K
FRENCHPARK *see* Roscommon w Donamon, Rathcline,
Kilkeevin etc *K, E & A*
GALLOON (St Comgall) w Drummully and Sallaghy *Clogh*
I A D C KERR
GALWAY (St Nicholas) w Kilcummin *T, K & A*
I L E A PEILOW
GARRISON (no dedication) w Slavin and Belleek *Clogh*
I C N NJOKU
GARRYCLOYNE (no dedication) *see* Carrigrohane Union
C, C & R
GARTAN (St Columba) *see* Conwal Union w Gartan *D & R*
GARTREE (no dedication) *see* Killead w Gartree *Conn*
GARVAGH *see* Errigal w Garvagh *D & R*
GARVAGHY (no dedication) *see* Dromara w Garvaghy
D & D
GARVARY (Holy Trinity) *see* Derryvullen S w Garvary *Clogh*
GEASHILL (St Mary) w Killeigh and Ballycommon *M & K*
I *vacant*
GILFORD *see* Tullylish *D & D*
GILFORD (St Paul) *D & D* I D I CADDOO
GILNAHIRK (St Dorothea) *D & D* **NSM** M S WALSHE
GLANDORE *see* Ross Union *C, C & R*
GLASLOUGH *see* Donagh w Tyholland and Errigal Truagh
Clogh
GLASNEVIN (St Mobhi) *see* Dublin Santry w Glasnevin and
Finglas *D & G*
GLENAGEARY (St Paul) *D & G* I G G DOWD
GLENALLA (St Columbkille) *see* Mevagh w Glenalla *D & R*
GLENARM *see* Ardclinis and Tickmacrevan w Layde and
Cushendun *Conn*
GLENAVY (St Aidan) w Tunny and Crumlin *Conn*
I J E C RUTTER
GLENBEIGH (St John) *see* Kilcolman w Kiltallagh, Killorglin,
Knockane etc *L & K*
GLENCAIRN *see* Belfast St Andr *Conn*
GLENCAR *see* Clooncare w Killasnett, Lurganboy and
Drumlease *K, E & A*
GLENCOLUMBKILLE (St Columba) *see* Ardara w
Glencolumbkille, Inniskeel etc *D & R*
GLENCRAIG (Holy Trinity) *D & D* I C J SIMPSON
GLENDERMOTT (no dedication) *D & R* I S R T BOYD
C N J CAIRNS **NSM** W A BURNS
GLENEALY (no dedication) *see* Rathdrum w Glenealy,
Derralossary and Laragh *D & G*
GLENOE *see* Glynn w Raloo *Conn*
GLENTIES (no dedication) *see* Ardara w Glencolumbkille,
Inniskeel etc *D & R*
GLENVILLE *see* Fermoy Union *C, C & R*
GLYNN (St John) w Raloo *Conn* I D LOCKHART
GOREY (Christ Church) w Kilnahue, Leskinfere and
Ballycanew *C & O* I *vacant*
GORTIN *see* Ardstraw w Baronscourt, Badoney Lower etc
D & R

GOWNA (no dedication) *see* Arvagh w Carrigallen, Gowna
and Columbkille *K, E & A*
GRACEFIELD (no dedication) *see* Woodschapel w Gracefield
Arm
GRANARD (St Patrick) *see* Mostrim w Granard, Clonbroney,
Killoe etc *K, E & A*
GRANGE (St Aidan) *see* Loughgall w Grange *Arm*
GRANGEGORMAN (All Saints) *see* Dublin Ch Ch Cathl Gp
D & G
GREENAN (no dedication) *see* Ardstraw w Baronscourt,
Badoney Lower etc *D & R*
GREENCASTLE (St Finian) *see* Moville w Greencastle,
Donagh, Cloncha etc *D & R*
GREENISLAND (Holy Name) *Conn* I *vacant*
GREY ABBEY (St Saviour) w Kircubbin *D & D* I G WITHERS
GREYSTONES (St Patrick) *D & G* I D S MUNGAVIN
NSM R G GUILDEA
GROOMSPORT (no dedication) *D & D* I D J M POLLOCK
GURRANEKENNEFEAKE (no dedication) *see* Cloyne Union
C, C & R
GWEEDORE (St Patrick), Carrickfin and Templecrone
D & R **P-in-c** T D ALLEN C E A FITZGERALD
HAROLD'S CROSS (no dedication) *see* Dublin Rathmines w
Harold's Cross *D & G*
HELEN'S BAY (St John the Baptist) *D & D* I T C KINAHAN
HEYNESTOWN (St Paul) *see* Dundalk w Heynestown *Arm*
HIGHFIELD *see* Belfast Whiterock *Conn*
HILLSBOROUGH (St Malachi) *D & D* I B A FOLLIS
HILLTOWN *see* Drumgath w Drumgooland and Clonduff
D & D
HOLLYMOUNT (no dedication) *see* Down H Trin w
Hollymount *D & D*
HOLMPATRICK (St Patrick) w Balbriggan and Kenure
D & G I A KELLY **NSM** T A O'BRIEN
HOLYWOOD (St Kevin) *see* Blessington w Kilbride,
Ballymore Eustace etc *D & G*
HOLYWOOD (St Philip and St James) *D & D* I G A HARRON
C K D MCGRATH
HORSELEAP *see* Clara w Liss, Moate and Clonmacnoise
M & K
HOWTH (St Mary) *D & G* I W K M BREW
INCH *see* Cloyne Union *C, C & R*
INCH (no dedication) *see* Arklow w Inch and Kilbride *D & G*
INCH (no dedication) *see* Kilmore and Inch *D & D*
INISHARGIE (St Andrew) *see* Ballywalter w Inishargie *D & D*
INISHMACSAINT (St Ninnidh) *Clogh* I *vacant*
INNISCALTRA (St Caimin) *see* Killaloe w Stradbally *L & K*
INNISCARRA (no dedication) *see* Carrigrohane Union
C, C & R
INNISHANNON (Christ Church) *see* Bandon Union *C, C & R*
INNISKEEL (no dedication) *see* Ardara w Glencolumbkille,
Inniskeel etc *D & R*
INNISMAGRATH (no dedication) *see* Killinagh w
Kiltyclogher and Innismagrath *K, E & A*
INVER *see* Larne and Inver *Conn*
INVER (St John the Evangelist) w Mountcharles, Killaghtee
and Killybegs *D & R* **Bp's C** L E FARRELL
IRISHTOWN *see* Dublin Irishtown w Donnybrook *D & G*
IRVINESTOWN *see* Derryvullen N w Castlearchdale *Clogh*
ISLANDMAGEE (St John) *see* Whitehead and Islandmagee
Conn
JOANMOUNT *see* Belfast H Trin and St Silas *Conn*
JORDANSTOWN (St Patrick) *Conn* I N P BAYLOR
JULIANSTOWN (St Mary) and Colpe w Drogheda and
Duleek *M & K* I K M POULTON
KEADY (St Matthew) w Armaghbreague and Derrynoose
Arm I *vacant*
KELLS (St Columba) w Balrathboyne, Moynalty,
Donaghpatrick and Castletown *M & K* I W A SEALE
KELLS (St Mary) w Ballaghtobin, Kilmogany, Ennisnag,
Inistioge and Kilfane *C & O* I *vacant*
KENAGH *see* Ardagh w Tashinny, Shrule and Kilcommick
K, E & A
KENMARE (St Patrick) w Sneem, Dromod and Valentia
L & K **P-in-c** M R CAVANAGH
KENTSTOWN (St Mary) *see* Navan w Kentstown, Tara, Slane,
Painestown etc *M & K*
KENURE (no dedication) *see* Holmpatrick w Balbriggan and
Kenure *D & G*
KESH *see* Magheraculmoney *Clogh*
KILBARRON (St Anne) w Rossnowlagh and Drumholm
D & R I B R RUSSELL
KILBERRY (no dedication) *see* Athy w Kilberry, Fontstown
and Kilkea *D & G*
KILBIXY (St Bigseach) *see* Mullingar, Portnashangan,
Moyliscar, Kilbixy etc *M & K*

KILBONANE (St Mark)   *see* Moviddy Union *C, C & R*

KILBRIDE (no dedication)   *see* Blessington w Kilbride, Ballymore Eustace etc *D & G*

KILBRIDE (St Bride) *Conn*   **I** W D HUMPHRIES

KILBRIDE (St Brigid)   *see* Arklow w Inch and Kilbride *D & G*

KILBRIDE BRAY (no dedication)   *see* Powerscourt w Kilbride *D & G*

KILBRONEY (no dedication)   *see* Clonallon and Warrenpoint w Kilbroney *D & D*

KILBRYAN (no dedication)   *see* Boyle and Elphin w Aghanagh, Kilbryan etc *K, E & A*

KILCLEAGH   *see* Clara w Liss, Moate and Clonmacnoise *M & K*

KILCLIEF (no dedication)   *see* Lecale Gp *D & D*

KILCLUNEY (St John)   *see* Mullabrack w Markethill and Kilcluney *Arm*

KILCOCK   *see* Dunboyne and Rathmolyon *M & K*

KILCOLMAN (no dedication) w Kiltallagh, Killorglin, Knockane and Glenbeigh *L & K*   **P-in-c** F A KEEGAN **C** A-M L STUART

KILCOMMICK (no dedication)   *see* Ardagh w Tashinny, Shrule and Kilcommick *K, E & A*

KILCOO (no dedication)   *see* Castlewellan w Kilcoo *D & D*

KILCOOLEY (no dedication) w Littleton, Crohane and Fertagh *C & O*   **I** *vacant*

KILCOOLEY (St Columba)   *see* Bangor Abbey *D & D*

KILCORNAN (no dedication)   *see* Rathkeale w Askeaton, Kilcornan and Kilnaughtin *L & K*

KILCROHANE   *see* Kenmare w Sneem, Waterville etc *L & K*

KILCRONAGHAN (no dedication) w Draperstown and Sixtowns *D & R*   **I** *vacant*

KILCULLEN (St John)   *see* Newbridge w Carnalway and Kilcullen *M & K*

KILCUMMIN (no dedication)   *see* Galway w Kilcummin *T, K & A*

KILDALLON (no dedication) w Newtowngore and Corrawallen and Swanlinbar w Kinawley, Templeport and Tomregan *K, E & A*   **P-in-c** S J DONOHOE **C** R L WALLER

KILDARE (Cathedral of St Brigid) w Kilmeague and Curragh Garrison Church *M & K*   **I** T WRIGHT

KILDARTON (no dedication)   *see* Lisnadill w Kildarton *Arm*

KILDOLLAGH (St Paul)   *see* Ballyrashane w Kildollagh *Conn*

KILDRESS (St Patrick) w Altedesert *Arm*   **I** D M MATCHETT

KILDRUMFERTON (St Patrick) w Ballymachugh and Ballyjamesduff *K, E & A*   **C** S M SCOTT

KILFARBOY (Christ Church)   *see* Drumcliffe w Kilnasoolagh *L & K*

KILFAUGHNABEG (Christ Church)   *see* Ross Union *C, C & R*

KILFENORA (Cathedral of St Fachan)   *see* Drumcliffe w Kilnasoolagh *L & K*

KILFERAGH (no dedication) *as above*

KILFINANE (St Andrew)   *see* Adare and Kilmallock w Kilpeacon, Croom etc *L & K*

KILFLYNN (no dedication) *as above*

KILGARIFFE (no dedication) w Kilmalooda, Kilnagross, Timoleague and Courtmacsherry *C, C & R*   **I** K E SUTTON

KILGLASS (no dedication)   *see* Killala w Dunfeeny, Crossmolina, Kilmoremoy etc *T, K & A*

KILGLASS (St Anne)   *see* Mostrim w Granard, Clonbroney, Killoe etc *K, E & A*

KILGOBBIN (no dedication)   *see* Dingle w Killiney and Kilgobbin *L & K*

KILHORNE   *see* Annalong *D & D*

KILKEA (no dedication)   *see* Athy w Kilberry, Fontstown and Kilkea *D & G*

KILKEE   *see* Drumcliffe w Kilnasoolagh *L & K*

KILKEEL (Christ Church) *D & D*   **I** *vacant*

KILKEEVIN (Holy Trinity)   *see* Roscommon w Donamon, Rathcline, Kilkeevin etc *K, E & A*

KILKENNY (Cathedral of St Canice) (St John), Aghour and Kilmanagh *C & O*   **I** *vacant*

KILKENNY WEST   *see* Athlone w Benown, Kiltoom and Forgney *M & K*

KILL (no dedication) *D & G*   **I** A T BREEN

KILL (St John)   *see* Naas w Kill and Rathmore *M & K*

KILL O' THE GRANGE   *see* Kill *D & G*

KILLADEAS (Priory Church)   *see* Trory w Killadeas *Clogh*

KILLAGAN (no dedication)   *see* Craigs w Dunaghy and Killagan *Conn*

KILLAGHTEE (St Peter)   *see* Inver w Mountcharles, Killaghtee and Killybegs *D & R*

KILLALA (Cathedral of St Patrick) w Dunfeeny, Crossmolina, Kilmoremoy, Castleconnor, Easkey and Kilglass *T, K & A*   **I** S J MCWHIRTER   **P-in-c** J K MCWHIRTER

KILLALLON (St John)   *see* Trim and Athboy Gp *M & K*

KILLALOE (Cathedral of St Flannan) w Stradbally, Clonlara, Mountshannon, Abingdon and Tuomgraney *L & K*   **NSM** L J GREEN

KILLANEY (St Andrew) w Carryduff *D & D*   **I** S H LOWRY

KILLANNE (St Anne) w Killegney, Rossdroit and Templeshanbo *C & O*   **I** *vacant*

KILLANULLY   *see* Carrigaline Union *C, C & R*

KILLARGUE (no dedication)   *see* Killinagh w Kiltyclogher and Innismagrath *K, E & A*

KILLARNEY (St Mary) w Aghadoe and Muckross *L & K*   **P-in-c** S J LUMBY

KILLASHEE (St Paul)   *see* Templemichael w Clongish, Clooncumber etc *K, E & A*

KILLASNETT (no dedication)   *see* Cloonclare w Killasnett, Lurganboy and Drumlease *K, E & A*

KILLCONNELL   *see* Aughrim w Ballinasloe etc *L & K*

KILLEA (St Fiach)   *see* Taughboyne, Craigadooish, Newtowncunningham etc *D & R*

KILLEAD (St Catherine) w Gartree *Conn*   **I** *vacant*

KILLEEVAN (no dedication)   *see* Clones w Killeevan *Clogh*

KILLEGAR (no dedication)   *see* Killeshandra w Killegar and Derrylane *K, E & A*

KILLEIGH (no dedication)   *see* Geashill w Killeigh and Ballycommon *M & K*

KILLELAGH (no dedication)   *see* Maghera w Killelagh *D & R*

KILLERY   *see* Taunagh w Kilmactranny, Ballysumaghan etc *K, E & A*

KILLESHANDRA (no dedication) w Killegar and Derrylane *K, E & A*   **I** A N CALVIN

KILLESHER (St John) *K, E & A*   **I** R J WEST

KILLESHERDONEY (St Mark)   *see* Drumgoon *K, E & A*

KILLESHIL (St Paul)   *see* Errigle Keerogue w Ballygawley and Killeshil *Arm*

KILLESHIN (no dedication) w Cloydagh and Killabban *C & O*   **I** *vacant*

KILLETER   *see* Derg w Termonamongan *D & R*

KILLINAGH (no dedication) w Kiltyclogher and Innismagrath *K, E & A*   **I** *vacant*

KILLINCHY (no dedication) w Kilmood and Tullynakill *D & D*   **I** S T R GAMBLE

KILLINEY (Holy Trinity) *D & G*   **I** G L HASTINGS

KILLINEY (St Brendan)   *see* Dingle w Killiney and Kilgobbin *L & K*

KILLINEY Ballybrack (St Matthias) *D & G*   **I** W P OLHAUSEN **NSM** N R STRATFORD

KILLINKERE (no dedication)   *see* Lurgan w Billis, Killinkere and Munterconnaught *K, E & A*

KILLISKEY (no dedication)   *see* Wicklow w Killiskey *D & G*

KILLODIERNAN (no dedication)   *see* Nenagh *L & K*

KILLOE (St Catherine)   *see* Mostrim w Granard, Clonbroney, Killoe etc *K, E & A*

KILLORAN (no dedication)   *see* Tubbercurry w Killoran *T, K & A*

KILLORGLIN (no dedication)   *see* Kilcolman w Kiltallagh, Killorglin, Knockane etc *L & K*

KILLOUGH (St Anne)   *see* Bright w Ballee and Killough *D & D*

KILLOUGHTER (no dedication)   *see* Drung w Castleterra, Larah and Lavey etc *K, E & A*

KILLOUGHY   *see* Tullamore w Durrow, Newtownfertullagh, Rahan etc *M & K*

KILLOWEN   *see* Kinneigh Union *C, C & R*

KILLOWEN (St John) *D & R*   **I** D M COLLINS **NSM** W J HOLMES

KILLSALLAGHAN (St David)   *see* Swords w Donabate and Kilsallaghan *D & G*

KILLUCAN (St Etchen)   *see* Mullingar, Portnashangan, Moyliscar, Kilbixy etc *M & K*

KILLYBEGS (no dedication)   *see* Inver w Mountcharles, Killaghtee and Killybegs *D & R*

KILLYGARVAN (St Columb)   *see* Tullyaughnish w Kilmacrennan and Killygarvan *D & R*

KILLYLEA (St Mark)   *see* Eglish w Killylea *Arm*

KILLYLEAGH (St John the Evangelist) *D & D*   **I** C P DARLING

KILLYMAN (St Andrew) *Arm*   **I** M R W LENNOX

KILLYMARD (no dedication)   *see* Donegal w Killymard, Lough Eske and Laghey *D & R*

KILMACABEA (no dedication)   *see* Ross Union *C, C & R*

KILMACDUAGH (no dedication)   *see* Aughrim w Ballinasloe etc *L & K*

KILMACRENNAN (St Finnian and St Mark)   *see* Tullyaughnish w Kilmacrennan and Killygarvan *D & R*

KILMACSHALGAN (St Mary)   *see* Skreen w Kilmacshalgan and Dromard *T, K & A*

KILMACTRANNY (no dedication)   *see* Taunagh w Kilmactranny, Ballysumaghan etc *K, E & A*

KILMAINHAMWOOD   *see* Kingscourt w Syddan *M & K*

LONDONDERRY (Christ Church), Culmore, Muff and Belmont *D & R* I R S MILLER **NSM** K M MCATEER
LONDONDERRY (St Augustine) *D & R* I vacant
LONGFORD *see* Templemichael w Clongish, Clooncumber etc *K, E & A*
LORRHA (St Ruadhan) *see* Birr w Lorrha, Dorrha and Lockeen *L & K*
LOUGH ESKE (Christ Church) *see* Donegal w Killymard, Lough Eske and Laghey *D & R*
LOUGHBRICKLAND *see* Aghaderg w Donaghmore and Scarva *D & R*
LOUGHCREW *see* Castlepollard and Oldcastle w Loughcrew etc *M & K*
LOUGHGALL (St Luke) w Grange *Arm* I P R SMITH
LOUGHGILLY (St Patrick) w Clare *Arm* I vacant
LOUGHGUILE (All Saints) *see* Armoy w Loughguile and Drumtullagh *Conn*
LOUGHINISLAND (no dedication) *D & D* I vacant
LUCAN (St Andrew) w Leixlip *D & G* I J S PEOPLES
LURGAN (Christ the Redeemer) (St Andrew) *D & D*
  I J M HARVEY   C G GIMPEL, S H JOHNSTON
LURGAN (no dedication) w Billis, Killinkere and Munterconnaught *K, E & A* I C W L MCCAULEY
LURGAN (St John the Evangelist) *D & D* I J M WHITE
LURGANBOY (Chapel of Ease) *see* Cloonclare w Killasnett, Lurganboy and Drumlease *K, E & A*
MACOSQUIN *see* Camus-juxta-Bann *D & R*
MACREDDIN *see* Castlemacadam w Ballinaclash, Aughrim etc *D & G*
MACROOM *see* Moviddy Union *C, C & R*
MAGHABERRY (Methodist church) *D & D*
  P-in-c C P E KAKURU
MAGHERA (no dedication) *see* Kilmegan w Maghera *D & D*
MAGHERA (St Lurach) w Killelagh *D & R* I T P KERR
MAGHERACLOONE (St Molua) *see* Carrickmacross w Magheracloone *Clogh*
MAGHERACROSS (no dedication) *Clogh* I B J HARPER
MAGHERACULMONEY (St Mary) *Clogh* C P J BRYSON
MAGHERADROLL (no dedication) *D & D* I W W RUSSELL
MAGHERAFELT (St Swithin) *Arm* I T SCOTT
MAGHERAGALL (no dedication) *Conn* I N J DARK
MAGHERAHAMLET (no dedication) *see* Annahilt w Magherahamlet *D & D*
MAGHERALIN (Holy and Undivided Trinity) w Dollingstown *D & D* I S A GENOE   C C E BAXTER
MAGHERALLY (St John the Evangelist) w Annaclone *D & D*
  I D M PALMER
MAGOURNEY *see* Carrigrohane Union *C, C & R*
MAGUIRESBRIDGE (Christ Church) w Derrybrusk *Clogh*
  I G M S WATSON
MALAHIDE (St Andrew) w Balgriffin *D & G* I N E C GAMBLE
MALIN *see* Moville w Greencastle, Donagh, Cloncha etc *D & R*
MALLOW (St James) w Doneraile and Castletownroche
  C, C & R I E E M LYNCH
MALLUSK (St Brigid) *Conn* I W A BOYCE
MALONE *see* Belfast Malone St Jo *Conn*
MALONE, UPPER *see* Belfast Upper Malone (Epiphany) *Conn*
MANORCUNNINGHAM *see* Raphoe w Raymochy and Clonleigh *D & R*
MANORHAMILTON *see* Cloonclare w Killasnett, Lurganboy and Drumlease *K, E & A*
MARKETHILL (no dedication) *see* Mullabrack w Markethill and Kilcluney *Arm*
MARMULLANE (St Mary) *see* Douglas Union w Frankfield *C, C & R*
MARYBOROUGH (St Peter) w Dysart Enos and Ballyfin
  C & O I vacant
MAYNE *see* Castlepollard and Oldcastle w Loughcrew etc *M & K*
MAYNOOTH (St Mary) *see* Dunboyne and Rathmolyon *M & K*
MEENGLASS (Ascension) *see* Stranorlar w Meenglas and Kilteevogue *D & R*
MEVAGH (Holy Trinity) w Glenalla *D & R* I vacant
MIDDLE CHURCH (no dedication) *see* Ballinderry *Conn*
MIDDLETOWN (St John) *see* Tynan w Middletown and Aghavilly *Arm*
MIDLETON (St John the Baptist) *see* Cloyne Union *C, C & R*
MILLISLE (St Patrick) *see* Carrowdore w Millisle *D & D*
MILLTOWN *see* Kilcolman w Kiltallagh, Killorglin, Knockane etc *L & K*
MILLTOWN (St Andrew) *Arm* I M H T MILLIKEN
MILLTOWN (St Philip) *see* Dublin Sandford w Milltown *D & G*
MILLTOWN MALBAY *see* Drumcliffe w Kilnasoolagh *L & K*

MITCHELSTOWN *see* Fermoy Union *C, C & R*
MOATE (St Mary) *see* Clara w Liss, Moate and Clonmacnoise *M & K*
MOHILL (St Mary) w Farnaught, Aughavas, Oughteragh, Kiltubride and Drumreilly *K, E & A* I L M FROST
MOIRA (St John) *D & D* I J M MEGARRELL   C P D MUNCE
MONAGHAN (St Patrick) w Tydavnet and Kilmore *Clogh*
  I I T H BERRY
MONASTEREVAN (St John the Evangelist) *see* Portarlington w Cloneyhurke, Lea etc *M & K*
MONASTERORIS (no dedication) *see* Clonsast w Rathangan, Thomastown etc *M & K*
MONELLAN (St Anne) *see* Convoy w Monellan and Donaghmore *D & R*
MONEYMORE *see* Desertlyn w Ballyeglish *Arm*
MONEYREAGH (no dedication) *see* Orangefield w Moneyreagh *D & D*
MONKSTOWN (Good Shepherd) *Conn* I vacant
MONKSTOWN (no dedication) *D & G* I R H BYRNE
MONKSTOWN (St John) *see* Carrigaline Union *C, C & R*
MOSSLEY (Holy Spirit) *Conn* I P B JONES
MOSTRIM (St John) w Granard, Clonbroney, Killoe, Rathaspeck and Streete *K, E & A* **P-in-c** C S SNELL
MOUNT MERRION (Pentecost) *D & D* I A P GREEN
  P-in-c D A MCCLAY
MOUNT MERRION (St Thomas) *see* Dublin Mt Merrion *D & G*
MOUNT NUGENT (St Bride) *see* Castlepollard and Oldcastle w Loughcrew etc *M & K*
MOUNTCHARLES (Christ Church) *see* Inver w Mountcharles, Killaghtee and Killybegs *D & R*
MOUNTFIELD (no dedication) *see* Drumragh w Mountfield *D & R*
MOUNTMELLICK (St Paul) w Coolbanagher, Rosenallis and Clonaslee *M & K* I S T IRVINE
MOUNTSHANNON *see* Killaloe w Stradbally *L & K*
MOVIDDY (no dedication), Kilbonane, Kilmurry, Templemartin and Macroom *C, C & R* I vacant
MOVILLA (no dedication) *D & D* I A N PEEK
MOVILLE (St Columb) w Greencastle, Donagh, Cloncha and Culdaff *D & R* I vacant
MOY (St James) w Charlemont *Arm* I A W A MAYES
MOYBOLOGUE *see* Kingscourt w Syddan *M & K*
MOYDOW (no dedication) *see* Ardagh w Tashinny, Shrule and Kilcommick *K, E & A*
MOYGASHEL (no dedication) *see* Drumglass w Moygashel *Arm*
MOYGLARE (All Saints) *see* Dunboyne and Rathmolyon *M & K*
MOYLISCAR *see* Mullingar, Portnashangan, Moyliscar, Kilbixy etc *M & K*
MOYNALTY (St Mary) *see* Kells Union *M & K*
MOYNTAGHS *see* Ardmore w Craigavon *D & D*
MOYRUS *see* Omey w Ballynakill, Errislannan and Roundstone *T, K & A*
MUCKAMORE (St Jude) (St Matthias) *Conn* I J MCCLURE
MUCKNOE (St Maeldoid) *see* Ballybay w Mucknoe and Clontibret *Clogh*
MUCKROSS (Holy Trinity) *see* Killarney w Aghadoe and Muckross *L & K*
MUCKROSS (St John) *see* Drumkeeran w Templecarne and Muckross *Clogh*
MUFF (no dedication) *see* Londonderry Ch Ch, Culmore, Muff and Belmont *D & R*
MULHUDDART (St Thomas) *see* Castleknock and Mulhuddart w Clonsilla *D & G*
MULLABRACK (no dedication) w Markethill and Kilcluney *Arm* I vacant
MULLAGH (no dedication) *see* Bailieborough w Knockbride, Shercock and Mullagh *K, E & A*
MULLAGHDUN (no dedication) *see* Cleenish w Mullaghdun *Clogh*
MULLAGHFAD (All Saints) *see* Aghalurcher w Tattykeeran, Cooneen etc *Clogh*
MULLAGLASS (St Luke) *see* Camlough w Mullaglass *Arm*
MULLAVILLY (no dedication) *Arm* I D E CAIRNS
MULLINGAR (All Saints) w Portnashangan, Moyliscar, Kilbixy, Almoritia, Killucan, Clonard and Castlelost *M & K* I M A GRAHAM   **NSM** H M SCULLY, T N HOLMES
MUNNINANE (St Kevin) *see* Drumcliffe w Lissadell and Munninane *K, E & A*
MUNTERCONNAUGHT (no dedication) *see* Lurgan w Billis, Killinkere and Munterconnaught *K, E & A*
MURRAGH (no dedication) *see* Kinneigh Union *C, C & R*
MYROE (St John) *see* Tamlaghtfinlagan w Myroe *D & R*
MYROSS *see* Ross Union *C, C & R*

NAAS (St David) w Kill and Rathmore *M & K*   I P G HEAK
NARRAGHMORE (Holy Saviour) and Timolin w Castledermot and Kinneagh *D & G*   I *vacant*
NAVAN (St Mary) w Kentstown, Tara, Slane, Painestown and Stackallen *M & K*   I J D M CLARKE   **NSM** E ARMSTRONG
NENAGH (St Mary) w Ballymackey, Templederry and Killodiernan *L & K*   I R L SMYTH   **NSM** P E MCKEE HANNA
NEWBLISS (no dedication) *see* Currin w Drum and Newbliss *Clogh*
NEWBRIDGE (St Patrick) w Carnalway and Kilcullen *M & K*   I T WRIGHT   **NSM** F M GRASHAM
NEWCASTLE (no dedication) w Newtownmountkennedy and Calary *D & G*   I W L BENNETT
NEWCASTLE (St John) *D & D*   I I M ELLIS
NEWCASTLE-LYONS (no dedication) *see* Celbridge w Straffan and Newcastle-Lyons *D & G*
NEWCESTOWN *see* Kinneigh Union *C, C & R*
NEWMARKET-ON-FERGUS *see* Drumcliffe w Kilnasoolagh *L & K*
NEWRY (St Mary) (St Patrick) *D & D*   I *vacant*
NEWTOWNARDS (St Mark) *D & D*   I C J MATCHETT
NEWTOWNBUTLER *see* Galloon w Drummully and Sallaghy *Clogh*
NEWTOWNCROMMELIN (no dedication) *see* Skerry w Rathcavan and Newtowncrommelin *Conn*
NEWTOWNCUNNINGHAM (All Saints) *see* Taughboyne, Craigadooish, Newtowncunningham etc *D & R*
NEWTOWNFERTULLAGH *see* Tullamore w Durrow, Newtownfertullagh, Rahan etc *M & K*
NEWTOWNFORBES *see* Templemichael w Clongish, Clooncumber etc *K, E & A*
NEWTOWNGORE (no dedication) *see* Kildallon and Swanlinbar *K, E & A*
NEWTOWNHAMILTON (St John) w Ballymoyer and Belleck *Arm*   I *vacant*
NEWTOWNMOUNTKENNEDY (St Matthew) *see* Newcastle w Newtownmountkennedy and Calary *D & G*
NEWTOWNSAVILLE (no dedication) *see* Augher w Newtownsaville and Eskrahoole *Clogh*
NEWTOWNSTEWART *see* Ardstraw w Baronscourt, Badoney Lower etc *D & R*
NOHOVAL (no dedication) *see* Templebreedy w Tracton and Nohoval *C, C & R*
NURNEY (no dedication) *see* Portarlington w Cloneyhurke, Lea etc *M & K*
OLDCASTLE (St Bride) *see* Castlepollard and Oldcastle w Loughcrew etc *M & K*
OMAGH *see* Drumragh w Mountfield *D & R*
OMEY (Christ Church) w Ballynakill, Errislannan and Roundstone *T, K & A*   I *vacant*
ORANGEFIELD (St John the Evangelist) w Moneyreagh *D & D*   I R R WILSON   **NSM** R A B MOLLAN
OUGHTERAGH (no dedication) *see* Mohill w Farnaught, Aughavas, Oughteragh etc *K, E & A*
OUGHTERARD *see* Galway w Kilcummin *T, K & A*
PACKANE *see* Nenagh *L & K*
PAINESTOWN *see* Navan w Kentstown, Tara, Slane, Painestown etc *M & K*
PALLASKENRY *see* Rathkeale w Askeaton, Kilcornan and Kilnaughtin *L & K*
PASSAGE WEST *see* Douglas Union w Frankfield *C, C & R*
PETTIGO *see* Drumkeeran w Templecarne and Muckross *Clogh*
POMEROY (no dedication) *Arm*   I *vacant*
PORTADOWN (St Columba) *Arm*   I W M ADAIR   **C** G HAMILTON
PORTADOWN (St Gobhan) *see* Seagoe *D & D*
PORTADOWN (St Mark) *Arm*   I W J C ORR   **C** K W MARSHALL, L A M BURDEN   **NSM** A MCWILLIAMS
PORTAFERRY *see* Ballyphilip w Ardquin *D & D*
PORTARLINGTON (St Paul) w Cloneyhurke, Lea, Monasterevin, Nurney and Rathdaire *M & K*   I L T C STEVENSON
PORTGLENONE (no dedication) *see* Ahoghill w Portglenone *Conn*
PORTNASHANGAN *see* Mullingar, Portnashangan, Moyliscar, Kilbixy etc *M & K*
PORTRUSH *see* Ballywillan *Conn*
PORTSALON (All Saints) *see* Clondevaddock w Portsalon and Leatbeg *D & R*
PORTSTEWART *see* Agherton *Conn*
PORTUMNA (Christ Church) *see* Clonfert Gp *L & K*
POWERSCOURT (St Patrick) w Kilbride *D & G*   I C J HALLISSEY   **NSM** R I T LILBURN
RAHAN *see* Clonsast w Rathangan, Thomastown etc *M & K*

RAHAN (St Carthach) *see* Tullamore w Durrow, Newtownfertullagh, Rahan etc *M & K*
RAHENY (All Saints) w Coolock *D & G*   I N MCCAUSLAND
RALOO (no dedication) *see* Glynn w Raloo *Conn*
RAMELTON *see* Tullyaughnish w Kilmacrennan and Killygarvan *D & R*
RAMOAN (St James) w Ballycastle and Culfeightrin *Conn*   I D E FERGUSON
RANDALSTOWN *see* Drummaul w Duneane and Ballyscullion *Conn*
RAPHOE (Cathedral of St Eunan) w Raymochy and Clonleigh *D & R*   I K A L BARRETT
RASHARKIN (St Andrew) *see* Ballymoney w Finvoy and Rasharkin *Conn*
RATHANGAN (no dedication) *see* Clonsast w Rathangan, Thomastown etc *M & K*
RATHASPECK (St Thomas) *see* Mostrim w Granard, Clonbroney, Killoe etc *K, E & A*
RATHBARRON *see* Tubbercurry w Killoran *T, K & A*
RATHCAVAN (no dedication) *see* Skerry w Rathcavan and Newtowncrommelin *Conn*
RATHCLAREN (Holy Trinity) *see* Bandon Union *C, C & R*
RATHCLINE (no dedication) *see* Roscommon w Donamon, Rathcline, Kilkeevin etc *K, E & A*
RATHCOOLE (no dedication) *see* Clondalkin w Rathcoole *D & G*
RATHCOOLE (St Comgall) *Conn*   **P-in-c** A MOORE
RATHCOR (no dedication) *see* Ballymascanlan w Creggan and Rathcor *Arm*
RATHCORE (St Ultan) *see* Dunboyne and Rathmolyon *M & K*
RATHDAIRE (Ascension) *see* Portarlington w Cloneyhurke, Lea etc *M & K*
RATHDOWNEY (no dedication) w Castlefleming, Donaghmore, Rathsaran and Aghavoe *C & O*   I *vacant*
RATHDRUM (St Saviour) w Glenealy, Derralossary and Laragh *D & G*   I B M O'REILLY
RATHFARNHAM *see* Dublin Rathfarnham *D & G*
RATHFRILAND *see* Drumgath w Drumgooland and Clonduff *D & D*
RATHGAR *see* Dublin Zion Ch *D & G*
RATHKEALE (Holy Trinity) w Askeaton, Foynes, Kilcornan and Kilnaughtin *L & K*   **P-in-c** P COMERFORD
RATHLIN (St Thomas) *see* Ballintoy w Rathlin and Dunseverick *Conn*
RATHMICHAEL (no dedication) *D & G*   I *vacant*
RATHMINES *see* Dublin Rathmines w Harold's Cross *D & G*
RATHMOLYON (St Michael and All Angels) *see* Dunboyne and Rathmolyon *M & K*
RATHMORE (St Columbkille) *see* Naas w Kill and Rathmore *M & K*
RATHMULLAN *see* Tullyaughnish w Kilmacrennan and Killygarvan *D & R*
RATHMULLAN (no dedication) w Tyrella *D & D*   I *vacant*
RATHOWEN *see* Mostrim w Granard, Clonbroney, Killoe etc *K, E & A*
RAYMOCHY (no dedication) *see* Raphoe w Raymochy and Clonleigh *D & R*
RAYMUNTERDONEY (St Paul) *see* Dunfanaghy, Raymunterdoney and Tullaghbegley *D & R*
REDCROSS (Holy Trinity) *see* Dunganstown w Redcross and Conary *D & G*
REDHILLS *see* Drung w Castleterra, Larah and Lavey etc *K, E & A*
RICHHILL (St Matthew) *Arm*   I G MCMURRAY
RIVERSTOWN *see* Taunagh w Kilmactranny, Ballysumaghan etc *K, E & A*
ROCHFORT BRIDGE *see* Mullingar, Portnashangan, Moyliscar, Kilbixy etc *M & K*
ROCKCORRY (no dedication) *see* Ematris w Rockcorry, Aghabog and Aughnamullan *Clogh*
ROSCOMMON (St Colman) w Donamon, Rathcline, Kilkeevin, Kiltullagh and Tybohine *K, E & A*   I *vacant*
ROSCREA (St Cronan) w Kyle, Bourney and Corbally *L & K*   I J A GALBRAITH
ROSENALLIS (St Brigid) *see* Mountmellick w Coolbanagher, Rosenallis etc *M & K*
ROSS (Cathedral of St Fachtna) w Kilmacabea, Myross, Kilfaughnabeg and Castleventry *C, C & R*   I C L PETERS
ROSS, NEW (St Mary) w OLD (St Mary), Whitechurch, Fethard, Killesk and Tintern *C & O*   I *vacant*
ROSSCARBERY *see* Ross Union *C, C & R*
ROSSES POINT (no dedication) *see* Sligo w Knocknarea and Rosses Pt *K, E & A*
ROSSINVER (no dedication) *see* Killinagh w Kiltyclogher and Innismagrath *K, E & A*

ROSSNAKILL   *see* Clondevaddock w Portsalon and Leatbeg *D & R*

ROSSNOWLAGH (St John)   *see* Kilbarron w Rossnowlagh and Drumholm *D & R*

ROSSORRY (no dedication) *Clogh*   **I** I W ELLIS   **NSM** F I NIXON

ROSTREVOR   *see* Clonallon and Warrenpoint w Kilbroney *D & D*

ROUNDSTONE (no dedication)   *see* Omey w Ballynakill, Errislannan and Roundstone *T, K & A*

RUNCURRAN   *see* Kinsale Union *C, C & R*

RYNAGH   *see* Clonfert Gp *L & K*

SAINTFIELD (no dedication) *D & D*   **I** C J POLLOCK

SALLAGHY (no dedication)   *see* Galloon w Drummully and Sallaghy *Clogh*

SANDFORD   *see* Dublin Sandford w Milltown *D & G*

SANDHILL   *see* Sligo w Knocknarea and Rosses Pt *K, E & A*

SANDYMOUNT   *see* Dublin Sandymount *D & G*

SANTRY   *see* Dublin Santry w Glasnevin and Finglas *D & G*

SAUL (St Patrick)   *see* Lecale Gp *D & D*

SCARVA (St Matthew)   *see* Aghaderg w Donaghmore and Scarva *D & D*

SCHULL (Holy Trinity)   *see* Kilmoe Union *C, C & R*

SCOTSHOUSE   *see* Currin w Drum and Newbliss *Clogh*

SEAFORDE   *see* Lecale Gp *D & D*

SEAGOE (St Gobhan) *D & D*   **I** T J CADDEN   **C** S W MOLES

SEAPATRICK (Holy Trinity) (St Patrick) *D & D*   **I** T R WEST   **C** A T R IRWIN   **NSM** J R CORBETT

SESKINORE (no dedication)   *see* Clogherny w Seskinore and Drumnakilly *Arm*

SEYMOUR HILL   *see* Kilmakee *Conn*

SHANDON (St Ann)   *see* Cork St Ann's Union *C, C & R*

SHANKILL   *see* Belfast St Matt *Conn*

SHANKILL   *see* Lurgan Ch the Redeemer *D & D*

SHANNON (Christ Church)   *see* Drumcliffe w Kilnasoolagh *L & K*

SHERCOCK (no dedication)   *see* Bailieborough w Knockbride, Shercock and Mullagh *K, E & A*

SHINRONE (St Mary) w Aghancon, Dunkerrin and Kinnitty *L & K*   **I** *vacant*

SHRULE (no dedication)   *see* Ardagh w Tashinny, Shrule and Kilcommick *K, E & A*

SION MILLS (Good Shepherd)   *see* Urney w Sion Mills *D & R*

SIXMILECROSS (St Michael) w Termonmaguirke *Arm*   **I** A BARR

SIXTOWNS (St Anne)   *see* Kilcronaghan w Draperstown and Sixtowns *D & R*

SKERRIES   *see* Holmpatrick w Balbriggan and Kenure *D & G*

SKERRY (St Patrick) w Rathcavan and Newtowncrommelin *Conn*   **I** A P CAMPBELL

SKIBBEREEN   *see* Abbeystrewry Union *C, C & R*

SKREEN (no dedication) w Kilmacshalgan and Dromard *T, K & A*   **P-in-c** N H L REGAN

SLANE (St Patrick)   *see* Navan w Kentstown, Tara, Slane, Painestown etc *M & K*

SLAVIN (no dedication)   *see* Garrison w Slavin and Belleek *Clogh*

SLIGO (Cathedral of St Mary and St John the Baptist) w Knocknarea and Rosses Point *K, E & A*   **I** A WILLIAMS

SNEEM (Transfiguration)   *see* Kenmare w Sneem, Waterville etc *L & K*

SPANISH POINT   *see* Drumcliffe w Kilnasoolagh *L & K*

STACKALLEN   *see* Navan w Kentstown, Tara, Slane, Painestown etc *M & K*

STEWARTSTOWN   *see* Brackaville w Donaghendry and Ballyclog *Arm*

STILLORGAN (St Brigid) w Blackrock *D & G*   **I** I GALLAGHER   **NSM** R D MARSHALL

STONEYFORD (St John) *Conn*   **P-in-c** W J FARR

STORMONT (St Molua) *D & D*   **I** E C RUTHERFORD

STRABANE   *see* Camus-juxta-Mourne *D & R*

STRADBALLY (All Saints)   *see* Killaloe w Stradbally *L & K*

STRADBALLY (St Patrick) w Ballintubbert, Coraclone, Timogue and Luggacurren *C & O*   **I** *vacant*

STRAFFAN (no dedication)   *see* Celbridge w Straffan and Newcastle-Lyons *D & G*

STRAID (no dedication) *T, K & A*   **P-in-c** A J WILLS

STRAND, NORTH (no dedication)   *see* Dublin Drumcondra w N Strand *D & G*

STRANGFORD   *see* Lecale Gp *D & D*

STRANMILLIS (St Bartholomew)   *see* Belfast St Bart *Conn*

STRANORLAR (no dedication) w Meenglas and Kilteevogue *D & R*   **I** A W PULLEN

STRATHFOYLE (no dedication)   *see* Clooney w Strathfoyle *D & R*

STREETE (no dedication)   *see* Mostrim w Granard, Clonbroney, Killoe etc *K, E & A*

SUMMER COVE   *see* Kinsale Union *C, C & R*

SWANLINBAR (St Augustine)   *see* Kildallon and Swanlinbar *K, E & A*

SWATRAGH   *see* Maghera w Killelagh *D & R*

SWORDS (St Columba) w Donabate and Kilsallaghan *D & G*   **I** N D S PHAIR   **NSM** K E LONG, K H SHERWOOD

SYDDAN (St David)   *see* Kingscourt w Syddan *M & K*

SYDENHAM   *see* Belfast St Brendan *D & D*

TAGHMON (St Munn) w Horetown and Bannow *C & O*   **I** *vacant*

TALLAGHT (St Maelruain) *D & G*   **I** W R H DEVERELL   **NSM** A E J BENNETT

TAMLAGHT   *see* Derryvullen S w Garvary *Clogh*

TAMLAGHT (St Luke)   *see* Ballinderry, Tamlaght and Arboe *Arm*

TAMLAGHTARD (St Gedanus) w Aghanloo *D & R*   **I** D H J FERRY

TAMLAGHTFINLAGAN (St Findlunganus) w Myroe *D & R*   **I** H R GIVEN

TANEY (Christ Church) (St Nahi) *D & G*   **I** R WARREN   **C** N J PIERPOINT

TARA   *see* Navan w Kentstown, Tara, Slane, Painestown etc *M & K*

TARBERT   *see* Tralee w Kilmoyley, Ballymacelligott etc *L & K*

TARTARAGHAN (St Paul) w Diamond *Arm*   **I** D HILLIARD

TASHINNY (no dedication)   *see* Ardagh w Tashinny, Shrule and Kilcommick *K, E & A*

TATTYKEERAN (no dedication)   *see* Aghalurcher w Tattykeeran, Cooneen etc *Clogh*

TAUGHBOYNE (St Baithan) w Craigadooish, Newtowncunningham and Killea *D & R*   **I** D W T CROOKS

TAUNAGH (no dedication) w Kilmactranny, Ballysumaghan and Killery *K, E & A*   **I** *vacant*

TEAMPOL-NA-MBOCHT (Altar)   *see* Kilmoe Union *C, C & R*

TEMPLEBREEDY (Holy Trinity) w Tracton and Nohoval *C, C & R*   **I** M JACKSON

TEMPLECARNE (no dedication)   *see* Drumkeeran w Templecarne and Muckross *Clogh*

TEMPLECORRAN (St John)   *see* Kilroot and Templecorran *Conn*

TEMPLECRONE (St Crone)   *see* Gweedore, Carrickfin and Templecrone *D & R*

TEMPLEDERRY (no dedication)   *see* Nenagh *L & K*

TEMPLEHARRY (no dedication)   *see* Cloughjordan w Borrisokane etc *L & K*

TEMPLEMARTIN (St Martin)   *see* Moviddy Union *C, C & R*

TEMPLEMICHAEL (St John) w Clongish, Clooncumber, Killashee and Ballymacormack *K, E & A*   **I** *vacant*

TEMPLEMORE (St Mary) w Thurles and Kilfithmone *C & O*   **I** *vacant*

TEMPLEMORE Londonderry (Cathedral of St Columb) *D & R*   **I** R J STEWART

TEMPLEPATRICK (St Patrick) w Donegore *Conn*   **I** J J MOULD

TEMPLEPORT (St Peter)   *see* Kildallon and Swanlinbar *K, E & A*

TEMPLETRINE (no dedication)   *see* Kinsale Union *C, C & R*

TEMPO (no dedication) and Clabby *Clogh*   **I** M A ARMSTRONG

TERENURE   *see* Dublin Rathfarnham *D & G*

TERMONAMONGAN (St Bestius)   *see* Derg w Termonamongan *D & R*

TERMONEENY (no dedication)   *see* Desertmartin w Termoneeny *D & R*

TERMONFECKIN (St Feckin)   *see* Drogheda w Ardee, Collon and Termonfeckin *Arm*

TERMONMAGUIRKE (St Columbkille)   *see* Sixmilecross w Termonmaguirke *Arm*

THOMASTOWN (no dedication)   *see* Clonsast w Rathangan, Thomastown etc *M & K*

TICKMACREVAN (St Patrick)   *see* Ardclinis and Tickmacrevan w Layde and Cushendun *Conn*

TIMOLEAGUE (Ascension)   *see* Kilgariffe Union *C, C & R*

TIMOLIN (St Mullin)   *see* Narraghmore and Timolin w Castledermot etc *D & G*

TOBERMORE   *see* Kilcronaghan w Draperstown and Sixtowns *D & R*

TOMREGAN (no dedication)   *see* Kildallon and Swanlinbar *K, E & A*

TOOMNA (no dedication)   *see* Kiltoghart w Drumshambo, Annaduff and Kilronan *K, E & A*

TOORMORE   *see* Kilmoe Union *C, C & R*

TRACTON   *see* Templebreedy w Tracton and Nohoval *C, C & R*

TRALEE (St John the Evangelist) w Kilmoyley, Ballymacelligott, Ballyseedy, Listowel and Ballybunnion *L & K* **I** J C STEPHENS **Hon C** P G C JONES
TRILLICK (Christ Church) *see* Kilskeery w Trillick *Clogh*
TRIM (Cathedral of St Patrick) and Athboy Group, The *M & K* **I** P D BOGLE
TRORY (St Michael) w Killadeas *Clogh* **I** *vacant*
TUAM (Cathedral of St Mary) w Cong and Aasleagh *T, K & A* **I** A J GRIMASON
TUAMGRANEY (St Cronan) *see* Killaloe w Stradbally *L & K*
TUBBERCURRY (St George) w Killoran *T, K & A* **P-in-c** P J NORMAN
TUBRID *see* Drumkeeran w Templecarne and Muckross *Clogh*
TULLAGH (no dedication) *see* Abbeystrewry Union *C, C & R*
TULLAGHBEGLEY (St Ann) *see* Dunfanaghy, Raymunterdoney and Tullaghbegley *D & R*
TULLAMORE (St Catherine) w Durrow, Newtownfertullagh, Rahan, Tyrellspass and Killoughy *M & K* **I** I G DELAMERE
TULLANISKIN (Holy Trinity) w Clonoe *Arm* **I** W H BLAIR
TULLOW (no dedication) *D & G* **I** L J TANNER
TULLOW (St Columba) w Shillelagh, Aghold and Mullinacuff *C & O* **I** *vacant*
TULLYAUGHNISH (St Paul) w Kilmacrennan and Killygarvan *D & R* **I** H GILMORE
TULLYLISH (All Saints) *D & D* **I** B J A CRUISE
TULLYNAKILL (no dedication) *see* Killinchy w Kilmood and Tullynakill *D & D*
TUNNY (St Andrew) *see* Glenavy w Tunny and Crumlin *Conn*
TURLOUGH (no dedication) *see* Aughaval w Achill, Knappagh, Dugort etc *T, K & A*
TYBOHINE (no dedication) *see* Roscommon w Donamon, Rathcline, Kilkeevin etc *K, E & A*
TYDAVNET (St Davnet) *see* Monaghan w Tydavnet and Kilmore *Clogh*
TYHOLLAND (St Sillian) *see* Donagh w Tyholland and Errigal Truagh *Clogh*
TYNAN (St Vindic) w Middletown and Aghavilly *Arm* **I** M H HAGAN

TYRELLA (St John) *see* Rathmullan w Tyrella *D & D*
TYRELLSPASS (St Sinian) *see* Tullamore w Durrow, Newtownfertullagh, Rahan etc *M & K*
UPPER DONAGHMORE (St Patrick) *see* Donaghmore w Upper Donaghmore *Arm*
URNEY (Christ Church) w Sion Mills *D & R* **C** J H MCFARLAND
URNEY (no dedication) w Denn and Derryheen *K, E & A* **I** M R LIDWILL
VALENTIA (St John the Baptist) *see* Kenmare w Sneem, Waterville etc *L & K*
VIRGINIA *see* Lurgan w Billis, Killinkere and Munterconnaught *K, E & A*
WARINGSTOWN (Holy Trinity) *see* Donaghcloney w Waringstown *D & D*
WARRENPOINT (no dedication) *see* Clonallon and Warrenpoint w Kilbroney *D & D*
WATERFORD (Christ Church Cathedral) w Killea, Drumcannon and Dunhill *C & O* **I** *vacant*
WATERVILLE *see* Kenmare w Sneem, Waterville etc *L & K*
WESTPORT *see* Aughaval w Achill, Knappagh, Dugort etc *T, K & A*
WEXFORD (St Iberius) and Kilscoran Union *C & O* **I** *vacant*
WHITECHURCH *see* Dublin Whitechurch *D & G*
WHITEGATE *see* Cloyne Union *C, C & R*
WHITEHEAD (St Patrick) and Islandmagee *Conn* **I** M F TAYLOR
WHITEHOUSE (St John) *Conn* **I** E O'BRIEN
WHITEROCK *see* Belfast Whiterock *Conn*
WICKLOW (no dedication) w Killiskey *D & G* **I** J A H KINKEAD **NSM** K G RUE
WILLOWFIELD (no dedication) *D & D* **I** D A MCCLAY
WOODBURN (Holy Trinity) *Conn* **I** T A G MCCANN
WOODLAWN (no dedication) *see* Aughrim w Ballinasloe etc *L & K*
WOODSCHAPEL (St John) w Gracefield *Arm* **I** E R MURRAY
YOUGHAL (St Mary's Collegiate) w Ardmore, Castlemartyr and Ballycotton *C, C & R* **P-in-c** A D H ORR
ZION *see* Dublin Zion Ch *D & G*

THE DIOCESE IN EUROPE

Diocesan Office, 14 Tufton Street, London SW1P 3QZ
T: (020) 7898 1155
E: bron.panter@churchofengland.org
W: www.europe.anglican.org

ARCHDEACONS
1. Eastern   L S NATHANIEL
2. France   M L WILLIAMS
3. Gibraltar   vacant
4. Italy and Malta   vacant
5. North West Europe   P D VROLIJK
6. Germany and Northern Europe   L S NATHANIEL
7. Switzerland   A KELHAM

Further information may be obtained from the appropriate archdeacon (the archdeaconry number is given after the name of each country). Mission to Seafarers chaplaincies are listed separately at the end of the section.

Andorra 3

Served from Barcelona

Austria 1

VIENNA (Christ Church)   Chapl P M S CURRAN,
C M WALTNER

Azerbaijan 1

BAKU   vacant

Belgium 5

ANTWERP (St Boniface)   Chapl A R WAGSTAFF
BRUGES (St Peter)   P-in-c A U NWAEKWE
BRUSSELS (Pro-Cathedral of the Holy Trinity)
Sen Chapl P D VROLIJK, Asst Chapl F E SIMON,
Assoc Chapl J A WILKINSON
GHENT (St John)   P-in-c S M MURRAY
KNOKKE (St George)   P-in-c A U NWAEKWE
LEUVEN   P-in-c J D MCDONALD
LIÈGE   vacant
OSTEND   Chapl A U NWAEKWE
TERVUREN   Asst Chapl N J GREGORY
YPRES (St George)   vacant

Bosnia and Herzegovina 1

SARAJEVO (St Anthony)   vacant

Bulgaria 1

Served from Bucharest (Romania)

Croatia 1

Served from Vienna (Austria)

Czech Republic 1

PRAGUE   Chapl NATHANIAL

Denmark 6

COPENHAGEN (St Alban) w Aarhus   Chapl M S PRASADAM

Estonia 6

TALLINN (St Timothy and St Titus)   P-in-c G P PIIR

Finland 6

HELSINKI w Kerava, Kuopio, Mikkeli, Oulu, Pori, Tampere,
Turku and White Nile   Chapl T MÄKIPÄÄ

France 2

AIX-EN-PROVENCE   see Marseille w Aix-en-Provence
AMBERNAC   see Poitou-Charentes

AQUITAINE (Bertric Burée, Bordeaux, Limeuil, Monteton,
Périgueux-Chancelade, Sorges, Ste Nathalène and
Doudrac)   Chapl A D LOMAS, Asst Chapl E A MORRIS,
C C L SULLIVAN
ARRAS   see Lille
BARBEZIEUX ST HILAIRE   see Poitou-Charentes
BEAULIEU-SUR-MER (St Michael)   P-in-c A W INGHAM
BORDEAUX   see Aquitaine
BOULOGNE-SUR-MER   see Pas de Calais
BRITTANY (Ploërmel, Huelgoat and Rostrene)
Chapl R T ADAMS
CAEN   see Paris St George
CAHORS   see Midi-Pyrénées and Aude
CALAIS   see Pas de Calais
CANNES (Holy Trinity)   Chapl G P WILLIAMS
CAYLUS   see Midi-Pyrénées and Aude
CHANTILLY (St Peter)   Chapl S L TILLETT
CHEF BOUTONNE   see Poitou-Charentes
CIVRAY   see Poitou-Charentes
DINARD (St Bartholomew)   Chapl G I WILTON
FONTAINEBLEAU   vacant
GIF SUR YVETTE   see Versailles
GRATOT HOMÉEL (Christ Church)   see La Manche
GRENOBLE   vacant
HESDIN   see Pas de Calais
HUELGOAT   see Brittany
JARNAC   see Poitou-Charentes
LA MANCHE w Gratot Hommëel and Virey   vacant
LA ROCHEFOUCAULD   see Poitou-Charentes
LE GARD   vacant
LILLE (Christ Church)   P-in-c D M R FLACH
LIMEUIL   see Aquitaine
LORGUES w Fayence   vacant
LYON   Chapl B L HARDING
MAGNÉ   see Poitou-Charentes
MAISONS-LAFFITTE (Holy Trinity)   vacant
MARSEILLE (All Saints) w Aix-en-Provence
Chapl C J A JOHNSTON
MENTON (St John)   vacant
MIDI-PYRÉNÉES and Aude (Cahors, Caylus, Tarn, Toulouse
and Valence d'Agen)   Chapl D S LANGDON-GRIFFITHS,
Asst Chapl A H JEWISS
MONTETON   see Aquitaine
NANTES   see Vendée
NICE (Holy Trinity) w Vence   Chapl P J E JACKSON
NORD PAS DE CALAIS (Boulogne-sur-Mer, Calais and
Hesdin)   Chapl K A REID
PARIS (St George) Chapl M W OSBORNE,
C N RAZAFINDRATSIMA
PARIS (St Michael)   Chapl J J CLARK
PAS DE CALAIS   vacant
PARTHENAY   see Poitou-Charentes
PAU (St Andrew)   Chapl R F DENNIS
PÉRIGUEUX-CHANCELADE   see Aquitaine
PLOËRMEL   see Brittany
POITOU-CHARENTES (Christ the Good Shepherd) w
Ambernac, Barbézieux St Hilaire, Chef Boutonne,
Civray, Jarnac, La Rochefoucauld, Magné, Parthenay,
St Jean d'Angély, Verteuil and Villejésus
Asst Chapl P J J KNIGHT
PORT GRIMAUD see St Raphaël
ROSTRENEN   see Brittany

ST JEAN D'ANGÉLY *see* Poitou-Charentes
ST RAPHAËL (St John the Evangelist) w Port Grimaud
  Chapl T D WILSON
STE NATHALÈNE *see* Aquitaine
SORGES *see* Aquitaine
STRASBOURG Chapl L M BARWICK
TARN *see* Midi-Pyrénées and Aude
TOULOUSE *see* Midi-Pyrénées and Aude
VALENCE D'AGEN *see* Midi-Pyrénées and Aude
VENCE (St Hugh) *see* Nice w Vence
VENDÉE (Puy de Serre, La Chapelle Archard and La
  Chapelle Palluau) Chapl H L DOOR
VERNET-LES-BAINS (St George) P-in-c D T PHILLIPS
VERSAILLES (St Mark) Chapl D R HANSON
VERTEUIL *see* Poitou-Charentes
VILLEJÉSUS *see* Poitou-Charentes
VIREY *see* La Manche

Georgia 1

TBILISI *vacant*

Germany 6

BERLIN (St George) Chapl C W JAGE-BOWLER
BONN w Cologne Chapl M BULLOCK,
  Asst Chapl R A GARDINER
DRESDEN *see* Berlin
DÜSSELDORF (Christ Church) Chapl S J WALTON
FREIBURG-IM-BREISGAU P-in-c C K PARSONS
HAMBURG (St Thomas à Becket) *vacant*
HEIDELBERG *vacant*
LEIPZIG Chapl G M REAKES-WILLIAMS
STUTTGART (St Catherine) Chapl K K WERNER

Gibraltar 3

GIBRALTAR (Cathedral of the Holy Trinity) (Dean) *vacant*

Greece 1

ATHENS, GREATER Chapl L W DOOLAN,
  Asst Chapl D B BRYANT-SCOTT, **C** C R SACCALI
  C JULIA BRADSHAW
CORFU (Holy Trinity) P-in-c J J WILSON
CRETE (St Thomas, the Apostle)

Hungary 1

BUDAPEST P-in-c F M HEGEDUS

Italy 4

AVIANO *see* Venice
BARI *see* Naples
BOLOGNA *see* Florence
BORDIGHERA *see* Menton
CADENABBIA *see* Milan
CAPRI *see* Naples
FLORENCE (St Mark) w Siena (St Peter) and Bologna
  Chapl W B LISTER, **Asst Chapl** G PANCETTI
GENOVA (The Holy Ghost) *vacant*
MACERATA *see* Rome
MILAN (All Saints) *vacant*
NAPLES (Christ Church) w Sorrento, Capri and Bari
  vacant
PADOVA Chapl A OSAROMPKE
PALERMO (Holy Cross) *vacant*
ROME (All Saints) w Macerata Chapl R J WARREN
SIENA *see* Florence
SORRENTO *see* Naples
TAORMINA (St George) *vacant*
TRIESTE *see* Venice
VARESE Served from Lugano (Switzerland)
VENICE (St George) w Trieste Chapl M M BRADSHAW
VINCENZA Served by US Army Base

Latvia 6

RIGA (St Saviour) *vacant*

Luxembourg 5

LUXEMBOURG Chapl G P READ

Malta and Gozo 4

VALLETTA (Pro-Cathedral of St Paul)
  Sen Chapl S H M GODFREY
Sliema (Holy Trinity) Chapl C M UPTON

Monaco 2

MONTE CARLO (St Paul) Chapl L A C MACLEAN

Morocco 3

CASABLANCA (St John the Evangelist)
  P-in-c M S EL KISS MIHANNY
TANGIER (St Andrew) Chapl D C OBIDIEGWU

The Netherlands 5

AMSTERDAM (Christ Church) w Heiloo
  Chapl A M STRANGE
ARNHEM (St Willibrord) *vacant*
EINDHOVEN Chapl F P NOORDANUS
HAARLEM *vacant*
HAGUE, THE (St John and St Philip) C G D MATUMONA
NIJMEGEN *vacant*
ROTTERDAM (St Mary) Chapl J L C PRIDMORE,
  C A ROBINSON-MULLER, H SUNIL
TWENTE (St Mary) Chapl B G RODFORD
UTRECHT (Holy Trinity) w Zwolle Chapl D G PHILLIPS,
  Asst Chapl G N CROWE, **C** C A NICHOLLS,
  Hon Asst Chapl S W VAN LEER
VOORSCHOTEN Chapl R J CREW
ZWOLLE *see* Utrecht

Norway 6

OSLO (St Edmund) w Bergen, Trondheim , Stavanger,
  Drammen, Moss, Sandefjord, Tromsö and Kristiansand
  Sen Chapl D M MCCALLIG

Poland 1

WARSAW w Gdansk P-in-c D V A BROWN

Portugal 3

ALGARVE (St Vincent) Chapl R J KEAN, R H HAMILTON
ALMANCIL *see* Algarve
ESTORIL *see* Lisbon
GORJÕES *see* Algarve
LISBON (St George) w Estoril (St Paul) *vacant*
MADEIRA (Holy Trinity) Chapl M R JARMAN
PORTO (or OPORTO) (St James) Chapl P J BOURNE
PRAIA DA LUZ *see* Algarve
TAVIRA *see* Algarve

Romania 1

BUCHAREST (The Resurrection) *vacant*

Russian Federation 1

MOSCOW (St Andrew) w Vladivostock Chapl M D ROGERS
ST PETERSBURG *vacant*

Serbia 1

BELGRADE Chapl J R FOX

Slovakia

Served from Vienna (Austria)

Slovenia

Served from Vienna (Austria)

Spain 3

ALCOCEBRE *see* Costa Azahar
ALBOX *see* Costa Almeria and Costa Calida
ALHAURÍN EL GRANDE *see* Costa del Sol East
ALMUÑÉCAR *see* Nerja and Almuñécar
BARCELONA (St George) Chapl J B CHAPMAN
BENALMADENA COSTA *see* Costa del Sol East
CALA D'OR *see* Palma de Mallorca

CALAHONDA   *see* Costa del Sol East
CALPE   *see* Costa Blanca
CAMPOVERDE   *see* Torrevieja
COIN   *see* Costa del Sol East
COSTA ALMERIA   Chapl V C ORAM,
  Asst Chapl A W BENNETT
COSTA AZAHAR (St Christopher)   Chapl L P DARRANT
COSTA BLANCA   Sen Chapl Q M RONCHETTI,
  Asst Chapl J H BOOKER, R MIDDLETON, D R WITTS
COSTA BRAVA   Chapl R A SHOCK
COSTA CALIDA   *see* Costa Almeria
COSTA DEL SOL EAST   Chapl N L STIMPSON
COSTA DEL SOL WEST   P-in-c A A LOW
COSTACABANA   *see* Costa Almeria and Costa Calida
DENIA   *see* Costa Blanca
EL CAMPELLO   *see* Costa Blanca
FORMENTERA   *see* Ibiza
FUENGIROLA (St Andrew)   *see* Costa del Sol East
FUERTEVENTURA   P-in-c R J HORROCKS
GANDIA   *see* Costa Blanca
IBIZA *vacant*
JÁVEA *see* Costa Blanca
LA MANGA   *see* Torrevieja
LA MARINA   *see* Torrevieja
LA PALMA *vacant*
LA SIESTA   *see* Torrevieja
LAGO JARDIN   *see* Torrevieja
LANZAROTE   Chapl S G EVANS
LAS PALMAS (Holy Trinity)   Chapl P G WIGNALL
LOS BALCONES   *see* Torrevieja
LOS GIGANTES   *see* Tenerife Sur
MADRID (St George) *vacant*
MÁLAGA (St George)   Chapl R J FROST,
  Asst Chapl D A CAGE
MALLORCA   *see* Palma de Mallorca
MENORCA   P-in-c P STRUDWICK
MOJÁCAR   *see* Costa Almeria
NAZARET   *see* Lanzarote
NERJA and Almuñécar   Chapl N C THOMAS
PALMA DE MALLORCA (St Philip and St James)
  Chapl D J WALLER
PLAYA BLANCA   *see* Lanzarote
PLAYA DE LAS AMERICAS   *see* Tenerife Sur
PLAYA DEL INGLES   *see* Las Palmas
PUERTO DE LA CRUZ Tenerife (All Saints)
  Chapl P M CLIFFORD
PUERTO DEL CARMEN   *see* Lanzarote
PUERTO POLLENSA   *see* Palma de Mallorca
PUERTO SOLLER   *see* Palma de Mallorca
ROQUETAS DE MAR   *see* Costa Almeria and Costa Calida
SAN PEDRO   *see* Costa del Sol West

SAN RAFAEL   *see* Ibiza
SANTA EULALIA   *see* Ibiza
SOTOGRANDE   *see* Costa del Sol West
TENERIFE SUR (St Eugenio)   P-in-c E J POOLE
TORREVIEJA   P-in-c R A SEABROOK
VINAROS   *see* Costa Azahar

Sweden 6

GOTHENBURG (St Andrew) w Halmstad, Jönköping and
  Uddevalla   P-in-c D A BRUCE
STOCKHOLM (St Peter and St Sigfrid) w Gävle and
  Västerås   Chapl N S HOWE

Switzerland 7

ANZERE   *see* Montreux
BADEN   *see* Zürich
BASLE   Chapl H C JONES, **Asst Chapl** R B HILLIARD,
  A L LOWEN, M D POGSON
BERNE (St Ursula)   Asst Chapl SH J MARSHALL
CHÂTEAU D'OEX   *see* Vevey
GENEVA (Holy Trinity) v*acant*
GSTAAD   *see* Montreux
LA CÔTE   P-in-c C J COOKE, **Asst Chapl** J CHAMBEYRON
LAUSANNE (Christ Church) w Neuchâtel
  Chapl C L BLOOMFIELD
LUGANO (St Edward the Confessor)   P-in-c N S D GIBSON
MONTHEY   *see* Montreux
MONTREUX (St John) w Anzere, Gstaad and Monthey
  Chapl P W ORMROD
NEUCHÂTEL   *see* Lausanne
ST GALLEN   *see* Zürich
VEVEY (All Saints) w Château d'Oex   Chapl C J ATKINSON,
  Asst Chapl M E BUSSMANN
VILLARS   *see* Montreux
ZUG   *see* Zürich
ZÜRICH (St Andrew) w Baden, St Gallen and Zug   *vacant*

Turkey 1

ANKARA (St Nicholas)   Hon C E E AHMADINIA
ISTANBUL (Christ Church) (Chapel of St Helena) w Moda
  (All Saints)   Chapl I W L SHERWOOD
ISTANBUL, Pera *vacant*
IZMIR (SMYRNA) (St John the Evangelist) w Bornova
  (St Mary Magdalene)   Chapl J A D BUXTON

Ukraine 1

KIEV (Christ Church) *vacant*

MISSION TO SEAFARERS CHAPLAINCIES

Belgium 5

ANTWERP   *Lay Chapl*
GHENT   Chapl S M MURRAY

France 2

DUNKERQUE   Chapl P S EDELLt

The Netherlands 5

ROTTERDAM and Schiedam   Chapl D A WOODWARD
VLISSINGEN *vacant*

CHAPLAINS TO HER MAJESTY'S SERVICES

ROYAL NAVY

Chaplain of the Fleet and Archdeacon for the Royal Navy
Director General Naval Chaplaincy Service
The Ven M J GOUGH QHC
Royal Naval Chaplaincy Service, Mail Point 1–2, Leach Building, Whale Island, Portsmouth PO2 8BY
Tel (023) 9262 5055   Fax 9262 5134

Chaplains RN

M D ALLSOPP	R T M J DUCKETT	D J JEAL
P M AMEY	M L EVANS	A J F MANSFIELD
P R ANDREW	J S FRANCIS	J C MONEY
O J BALOGUN	P F GARVIE	E A A NORTHEY
R W BARBER	M F GODFREY	S P RASON
N A BEARDSLEY	A HILLIER	D J SIMPSON
A J P BLAINE	S T HORNE	N THORNHILL
P R BRYCE	M H JACKSON	M WAGSTAFF
A S CORNESS	T M ST J JAMES	E R WILLS

ARMY

Chaplain General HM Land Forces and Archdeacon for the Army
The Ven C M LANGSTON QHC
Ministry of Defence, Chaplains (Army), HQ Land Forces, 2nd Floor Zone 6,
Ramillies Building, Marlborough Lines, Monxton Road, Andover SP11 8HJ
Tel (01264) 381841   Fax 381824

Chaplains to the Forces

D J ADAMS	S J H DUNWOODY	A J NICOLLS
N J D ADLEY	J DURBIN	A J NORTH
G D ALLEN	A J EARL	T R PLACE
J M AMEY	H D EVANS	R PLUCK
P B ARCHIBALD	S J FARMER	S S PRATT
D A BANTING	A J FELTHAM-WHITE	I M R PRICE
K G BARRY	P T FRANCIS	R M PRIEST
A R F BATTEY	L F GANDIYA	S A RICHARDS
C D BELL	C A GILLHAM	R J RICHARDSON
A S F BENNETT	E G A GORRINGE	P A ROBINSON
S F BLOXAM-ROSE	R A B HALL	I C ROGERS
J R G BRADBURY	A B HARDING	C L ROTERS
P G BURROWS	J A HARDING	M RUTTER
J W CALDWELL	L T J HILLARY	A SCOTT
M W A CHADWICK	T R C HINEY	G C SMITH
J S CLARKE	P C HULLYER	M W B SPEEKS
M S R COLES	I A KEMP	A C STEELE
G L COLLINGWOOD	C D KINCH	J J E SUTTON
I R COLSON	P W S KING	N S TODD
D P CONNING	N P KINSELLA	C A TOME DA SILVA
D P CREES	A M LATIFA	A J TOTTEN
D D CRITCHLOW	S H LODWICK	J L VINCENT
A I DALTON	T J MATHEWS	N C WILLIAMS
D S DEMPSEY	K D MENTZEL	S G WILSON
P DIXON	P J MILLS	
R J DOWNES	D T MORGAN	

ROYAL AIR FORCE

Chaplain-in-Chief and Archdeacon for the RAF
The Ven J R ELLIS QHC
Chaplaincy Services, Valiant Block, HQ Air Command, RAF High Wycombe HP14 4UE
Tel (01494) 496800   Fax 496343

Chaplains RAF

K N AKWASI-YEBOAH	J A HOBSON	P A RENNIE
K S BRUCE	C J HODDER	D RICHARDSON
R L CANNON	J M S HOLLAND	S J SHAW
K S CAPELIN-JONES	I A JONES	M D SHELDON
A J CHAPMAN	S P LAMOND	P J STEPHENS
M F CHATFIELD	C D LAWRENCE	M STEVENS
R P CLEMENT	G L LEGOOD	A M TUCKER
A L DYER	C A MITCHELL	A W WAKEHAM-DAWSON
G D FIRTH	D J NORFIELD	G E WITHERS
R V HAKE	C J O'DELL	E L WYNN
C J HARRISON	D T OSBORN	
A D HEWETT	M C PERRY	

PRISON CHAPLAINS

HM PRISON SERVICE (England and Wales)

Chaplain General to HM Prisons
The Ven J S RIDGE

Chaplaincy HQ, Post Point 3.08, 3rd Floor Red Zone, Clive House, 70 Petty France, London SW1H 9HD
T: 03000-475186   F: 476822/3

Prisons

Altcourse   G A O JESSON
Ashfield   E A PERRY, A THOMSON
Belmarsh   T G JACQUET
Berwyn   A PIERCE-JONES
Birmingham   P GILLON
Brixton   I G THOMPSON
Bronzefield   M J MCCARRON
Buckley Hall   H A EDGERTON, R W A REECE
Bure   I COOPER
Cardiff   N R SANDFORD
Channings Wood   P F HARTOPP, N R MARTIN
Coldingley   R D S SANDERS
Dartmoor   L H COOPER
Dorchester   R A BETTS, E W D TILDESLEY
Dovegate   N J KELLY
Drake Hall   S J MORRIS, E K WYKES
Durham   M D TETLEY, R L TOBIN
East Sutton Park   S A SIMPSON
Eastwood Park   A J WILLIAMS
Elmley   J K M NJOROGE
Erlestoke   S G ASCOUGH, S A IBBETSON
Exeter   M D MILLER
Ford   A C OEHRING
Forest Bank   A C MCMULLEN, D R OTTLEY
Frankland   A V WEST
Full Sutton   G R HOCKEN, B MERRINGTON
Garth   D W GOODWIN, G C TURNER
Gartree   E V HIGGINS
Grendon and Spring Hill   P G HILL, S P Z SMITH,
   M B WHITAKER
Guys Marsh   P C BROWNE
Haverigg   G JONES, R P SPRATT
Hewell   M A SCHUTTE
High Down   B FRASER, E J F GBONDA
Hindley   L J SWEET
Hollesley Bay   M R RENNARD
Holme House   S BELL, K M BROOKE
Hull   N J WHETTON
Huntercombe   I D THACKER

Isle of Wight   J A SWAINE
Kirkham   D NOBLET
Kirklevington Grange   A J HUTCHINSON
Leyhill   B E DAVIS, L G HEWISH
Lindholme   C L SMITH
Littlehey   D J KINDER, M C LAWSON, T MCFADDEN
Liverpool   P N TYERS
Long Lartin   S BLAKE, S W NEWNES
Low Newton   S K R PARKINSON
Lowdham Grange   J M SAVAGE
Maidstone   G L BURN
Manchester   J E CALLADINE, H R F MARTIN
Mount, The   P J ABREY
New Hall   L K GREENWOOD-HAIGH
Northumberland   T J K CONLIN
Norwich   O O SOTONWA
Nottingham   M TYACK
Oakwood   O T OLUMUYIWA
Onley   S K GILLARD-FAULKNER
Parc (Bridgend)   D C TILT
Pentonville   A A ADAMOLEKUN, J W P AITKEN, J DAVIES
Peterborough   J A C WIEGMAN
Preston   B A EATON, G MILLER
Risley   L J SWEET
Send   L J MASON, M A STIRLING TROY
Stafford   J C HONOUR
Stocken   T S WRIGHT
Styal   Y L YATES
Sudbury   H THAKE
Swinfen Hall   S NTOYIMONDO
Thameside   G R HARPER
Verne, The   G A HEBBERN
Wandsworth   A A ADAMOLEKUN, T CLAPTON
Warren Hill   W J SALMON
Winchester   D J HINKS, C S MCCLELLAND
Wolds, The   B WORSDALE
Wormwood Scrubs   J C STEPHENSON
Wymott   C D F CROMBIE

Young Offender Institutions

Deerbolt   R L TOBIN
Feltham   M J BOYES, P FOSTER
Lancaster Farms   D NOBLET
Rochester   R W MAYO, B N B MUSINDI

Thorn Cross   S G VERHEY
Werrington House   J C CUTTELL
Wetherby   D E HERTH, A R ROWE

Immigration Centres

Colnbrook   J W GEEN

CHANNEL ISLANDS PRISON SERVICE

Guernsey   P J GRAYSMITH

NORTHERN IRELAND PRISON SERVICE

Maghaberry   J R HOWARD

HOSPITAL CHAPLAINS

2GETHER NHS FOUNDATION TRUST   H CLARKE, J A RHODES
5 BOROUGHS PARTNERSHIP NHS FOUNDATION
TRUST   P LOVATT
ABERDEEN MATERNITY   *see* NHS Grampian
ABERDEEN ROYAL INFIRMARY   *see* NHS Grampian
ABRAHAM COWLEY UNIT Chertsey   *see* Surrey and Borders
Partnership NHS Foundn Trust
ADDENBROOKE'S Cambridge   *see* Cam Univ Hosps NHS
Foundn Trust
AIREDALE GENERAL   *see* Airedale NHS Foundn Trust
AIREDALE NHS FOUNDATION TRUST   D J GRIFFITHS,
J P SMITH, R L MULLIGAN
ALDEBURGH AND DISTRICT COMMUNITY   *see* Suffolk
Coastal Primary Care Trust
ALDER HEY CHILDREN'S NHS FOUNDATION
TRUST   A R BROCKBANK, D J WILLIAMS
ALEXANDRA Redditch   *see* Worcs Acute Hosps NHS Trust
ALNWICK INFIRMARY   *see* Northumbria Healthcare NHS
Foundn Trust
ALTRINCHAM GENERAL   *see* Trafford Healthcare NHS Trust
AMBERSTONE Hailsham   *see* E Sussex Healthcare NHS Trust
AMERSHAM   *see* Bucks Healthcare NHS Trust
ARCHERY HOUSE Dartford   *see* Kent & Medway NHS and Soc
Care Partnership Trust
ASHFORD   *see* E Kent Hosps Univ NHS Foundn Trust
and Surrey and Borders Partnership NHS Foundn Trust
ASHFORD AND ST PETER'S HOSPITALS NHS FOUNDATION
TRUST   L W GAMLEN
ASHINGTON   *see* Northumbria Healthcare NHS Foundn
Trust
ATKINSON MORLEY   *see* SW Lon and St George's Mental
Health NHS Trust
BARKING, HAVERING AND REDBRIDGE UNIVERSITY
HOSPITALS NHS TRUST   P J WRIGHT, S M HARTLEY,
T COLEMAN
BARNES   *see* SW Lon and St George's Mental Health NHS
Trust
BARNET, ENFIELD AND HARINGEY MENTAL HEALTH NHS
TRUST   T M BARON
BARTLET Felixstowe   *see* Suffolk Coastal Primary Care Trust
BASILDON AND THURROCK UNIVERSITY HOSPITALS NHS
FOUNDATION TRUST   D F BATES, L G PEALL
BATH AND WEST COMMUNITY NHS TRUST   M JOYCE
BATTLE Reading   *see* R Berks NHS Foundn Trust
BEDFORD HOSPITAL NHS TRUST   N A MCINTOSH
BELFAST HEALTH AND SOCIAL CARE TRUST   D W GAMBLE
BENNION CENTRE Leicester   *see* Leics Partnership NHS Trust
BENSHAM Gateshead   *see* Gateshead Health NHS Foundn
Trust
BERKSHIRE HEALTHCARE NHS FOUNDATION
TRUST   C J STOTT
BERWICK INFIRMARY   *see* Northumbria Healthcare NHS
Foundn Trust
BETHLEM ROYAL Beckenham   *see* S Lon and Maudsley NHS
Foundn Trust
BEXHILL   *see* E Sussex Healthcare NHS Trust
BIDEFORD   *see* N Devon Healthcare NHS Trust
BILLINGE   *see* Wrightington, Wigan and Leigh NHS Foundn
Trust
BIRCH HILL   *see* Pennine Acute Hosps NHS Trust
BIRMINGHAM CHILDREN'S HOSPITAL NHS FOUNDATION
TRUST   E BLAIR-CHAPPELL, M A ROBINSON
BIRMINGHAM CITY   *see* Sandwell and W Birm Hosps NHS
Trust
BIRMINGHAM SKIN   *see* Sandwell and W Birm Hosps NHS
Trust
BIRMINGHAM WOMEN'S NHS FOUNDATION
TRUST   D G JONES, P NASH
BISHOP AUCKLAND GENERAL   *see* Co Durham and
Darlington NHS Foundn Trust
BLACK COUNTRY PARTNERSHIP NHS FOUNDATION
TRUST   E C LOUIS
BLACKBERRY HILL Bristol   *see* N Bris NHS Trust
BLACKBURN ROYAL INFIRMARY   *see* E Lancs Hosps NHS Trust
BLACKPOOL TEACHING HOSPITALS NHS FOUNDATION
TRUST   H S HOUSTON
BLACKPOOL, FYLDE AND WYRE HOSPITALS NHS
TRUST   C G LORD

BLYTH COMMUNITY   *see* Northumbria Healthcare NHS
Foundn Trust
BODMIN   *see* Cornwall Partnership NHS Foundn Trust
BOLTON GENERAL   *see* Bolton NHS Foundn Trust
BOLTON NHS FOUNDATION TRUST   B S GASKELL,
C D BINNS, J NICHOLLS, P THORN, S FOSTER
BOOTHAM PARK   *see* York Teaching Hosp NHS Foundn Trust
BOURNEMOUTH, ROYAL GENERAL   *see* R Bournemouth and
Christchurch Hosps NHS Foundn Trust
BOWNESS UNIT Prestwich   *see* Gtr Man W Mental Health
NHS Foundn Trust
BRADFORD TEACHING HOSPITALS NHS FOUNDATION
TRUST   J N FIELDER
BRADGATE MENTAL HEALTH UNIT Leicester   *see* Leics
Partnership NHS Trust
BRANDON MENTAL HEALTH UNIT Leicester   *see* Leics
Partnership NHS Trust
BRIDGWATER   D GODDARD
BRIDLINGTON AND DISTRICT   *see* York Teaching Hosp NHS
Foundn Trust
BRIDPORT COMMUNITY   *see* SW Dorset Primary Care Trust
BRIGHTON AND SUSSEX UNIVERSITY HOSPITALS NHS
TRUST   J M ELLIOTT
BRISTOL GENERAL   *see* Univ Hosps Bris NHS Foundn Trust
BRISTOL ROYAL HOSPITAL FOR CHILDREN   *see* Univ Hosps
Bris NHS Foundn Trust
BRISTOL ROYAL INFIRMARY   *see* Univ Hosps Bris NHS
Foundn Trust
BROADGREEN Liverpool   *see* R Liverpool and Broadgreen
Univ Hosps NHS Trust
BROADOAK Mental Health Unit   *see* Mersey Care NHS
Foundn Trust
BRONGLAIS GENERAL   *see* Hywel Dda Health Bd
BROOMFIELD Chelmsford   *see* Mid-Essex Hosp Services NHS
Trust
BRYN Y NEUADD Llanfairfechan   *see* NW Wales NHS Trust
BUCKINGHAMSHIRE HEALTHCARE NHS TRUST   C E HOUGH
BUCKLAND Dover   *see* E Kent Hosps Univ NHS Foundn Trust
BUCKNALL Stoke-on-Trent   *see* N Staffs Combined
Healthcare NHS Trust
BURNLEY GENERAL   *see* E Lancs Hosps NHS Trust
BURTON HOSPITALS NHS FOUNDATION TRUST   A C THORP,
A J HINES, H J BAKER
CAERPHILLY DISTRICT MINERS'   *see* Gwent Healthcare NHS
Trust
CALDERDALE AND HUDDERSFIELD NHS FOUNDATION
TRUST   G SPENCER, M D ELLERTON
CAMBRIDGE UNIVERSITY HOSPITALS NHS FOUNDATION
TRUST   D P FORD, P M SHARKEY, V A WESTON
CAMBRIDGESHIRE AND PETERBOROUGH NHS FOUNDATION
TRUST   J P NICHOLSON
CANTERBURY St Martin's   *see* Kent & Medway NHS and Soc
Care Partnership Trust
CARDIFF AND VALE NHS TRUST   E J BURKE, R V C LEWIS
CARE FOR VETERANS Worthing   B A MILES
CASTLE HILL Cottingham   *see* Hull and E Yorks Hosps NHS
Trust
CASTLEFORD NORMANTON AND DISTRICT   *see* Mid Yorks
Hosps NHS Trust
CATERHAM   *see* Surrey and Sussex Healthcare NHS Trust
CAVELL CENTRE Peterborough   *see* Cambs and Pet NHS
Foundn Trust
CEFN COED Swansea   *see* Swansea NHS Trust
CENTRAL MIDDLESEX NHS TRUST   M D MOORHEAD
CHAPEL ALLERTON Leeds   *see* Leeds Teaching Hosps NHS
Trust
CHARLTON LANE CENTRE Leckhampton   *see* Glos Hosps
NHS Foundn Trust
CHELMSFORD Broomfield   *see* Mid-Essex Hosp Services NHS
Trust
CHELSEA AND WESTMINSTER HOSPITAL NHS FOUNDATION
TRUST   M J LEE
CHELTENHAM GENERAL   *see* Glos Hosps NHS Foundn Trust
CHEPSTOW COMMUNITY   *see* Gwent Healthcare NHS Trust
CHERRY KNOWLE Sunderland   *see* Northumberland, Tyne
and Wear NHS Foundn Trust
CHESTERTON Cambridge   *see* Cam Univ Hosps NHS Foundn
Trust

CHICHESTER St Richard's   *see* W Sussex Hosps NHS Foundn Trust

CHRISTCHURCH   *see* R Bournemouth and Christchurch Hosps NHS Foundn Trust

CHRISTIE NHS FOUNDATION TRUST
Manchester   A R BRADLEY, F A JENKINSON, K L DUNN

CHURCHILL, THE Oxford   *see* Ox Univ Hosps NHS Foundn Trust

CIRENCESTER   *see* Glos Hosps NHS Foundn Trust

CITY Birmingham   *see* Sandwell and W Birm Hosps NHS Trust

CITY GENERAL Stoke-on-Trent   *see* Univ Hosp of N Staffs NHS Trust

CITY HOSPITALS SUNDERLAND NHS FOUNDATION TRUST   O R OMOLE, P H WEBB

CLAYBURY Woodford Bridge   *see* Forest Healthcare NHS Trust Lon

CLAYTON Wakefield   *see* Mid Yorks Hosps NHS Trust

CLIFTON Lytham St Annes   *see* Blackpool, Fylde and Wyre Hosps NHS Trust

COLINDALE   *see* Enfield Primary Care Trust

COLMAN Norwich   *see* Norfolk Primary Care Trust

CONQUEST Hastings   *see* E Sussex Healthcare NHS Trust

COOKRIDGE Leeds   *see* Leeds Teaching Hosps NHS Trust

CORK UNIVERSITY   D R NUZUM

CORNWALL PARTNERSHIP NHS FOUNDATION TRUST   E C DEELEY, M E PINNOCK

COUNTESS MOUNTBATTEN   I S MCFARLANE

COUNTESS MOUNTBATTEN HOSPICE Southampton   *see* Univ Hosp Southn NHS Foundn Trust

COUNTESS OF CHESTER HOSPITAL NHS FOUNDATION TRUST   E M GARDNER, G M HIBBERT

COUNTY DURHAM AND DARLINGTON NHS FOUNDATION TRUST   K S TROMANS

COVENTRY AND WARWICKSHIRE   *see* Univ Hosps Cov and Warks NHS Trust

COVENTRY AND WARWICKSHIRE PARTNERSHIP NHS TRUST   S P MOULT

CROMER   *see* Norfolk and Nor Univ Hosps NHS Foundn Trust

CROMER AND DISTRICT   *see* Norfolk Primary Care Trust

CROYDON HEALTH SERVICES NHS TRUST   A M S DOVEY

CROYDON MENTAL HEALTH SERVICES Warlingham
see S Lon and Maudsley NHS Foundn Trust

CUMBERLAND INFIRMARY   *see* N Cumbria Univ Hosps NHS Trust

DARLINGTON MEMORIAL   *see* Co Durham and Darlington NHS Foundn Trust

DELANCEY Leckhampton   *see* Glos Hosps NHS Foundn Trust

DELLWOOD Reading   *see* R Berks NHS Foundn Trust

DERBY TEACHING HOSPITALS NHS FOUNDATION TRUST   M HARGREAVES, P A SHORT, S C NEAL, T ROBINSON

DERBYSHIRE CHILDREN'S   *see* Derby Teaching Hosps NHS Foundn Trust

DERBYSHIRE ROYAL INFIRMARY   *see* Derby Teaching Hosps NHS Foundn Trust

DEREHAM   *see* Norfolk Primary Care Trust

DERRIFORD   *see* Plymouth Hosps NHS Trust

DEVONSHIRE ROAD Blackpool   *see* Blackpool, Fylde and Wyre Hosps NHS Trust

DEWSBURY AND DISTRICT   *see* Mid Yorks Hosps NHS Trust

DIANA, PRINCESS OF WALES Grimsby   *see* N Lincs and Goole NHS Foundn Trust

DORKING   *see* Surrey and Sussex Healthcare NHS Trust

DORSET COUNTY HOSPITAL NHS FOUNDATION TRUST   R A BETTS, R C J R MARTIN

DORSET HEALTHCARE UNIVERSITY NHS FOUNDATION TRUST   M G OATES

DR GRAY'S Elgin   *see* NHS Grampian

DUNSTON HILL Gateshead   *see* Gateshead Health NHS Foundn Trust

DURHAM AND DARLINGTON NHS FOUNDATION TRUST   *see* Co Durham and Darlington NHS Foundn Trust

EAST HAM MEMORIAL   *see* E Lon NHS Foundation Trust

EAST KENT HOSPITALS UNIVERSITY NHS FOUNDATION TRUST   P F HILL

EAST LANCASHIRE HOSPITALS NHS TRUST   A S HORSFALL, D L ANDERSON

EAST LONDON NHS FOUNDATION TRUST   N J COPSEY

EAST SUFFOLK AND NORTH ESSEX NHS FOUNDATION TRUST   C J COOK, H A N PLATTS, M K LING

EAST SURREY PRIORITY CARE NHS TRUST   N J COPSEY

EAST SUSSEX HEALTHCARE NHS TRUST   F M BALDWIN, G J A COOK, G R ATFIELD, M P TURNBULL

EASTBOURNE GENERAL   *see* E Sussex Healthcare NHS Trust

EDEN VALLEY Carlisle   J HURST

ENFIELD PRIMARY CARE TRUST   T M BARON

EPSOM AND ST HELIER UNIVERSITY HOSPITALS NHS TRUST   K S REEVES

EPSOM St Ebba's   *see* Surrey and Borders Partnership NHS Foundn Trust

EVELINA CHILDREN'S London   S M TAYLOR

FAIRFIELD GENERAL   *see* Pennine Acute Hosps NHS Trust

FARNHAM   *see* Surrey and Borders Partnership NHS Foundn Trust

FARNHAM ROAD Guildford   *see* Surrey and Borders Partnership NHS Foundn Trust

FIELDHEAD Wakefield   *see* SW Yorks Partnership NHS Foundn Trust

FINCHLEY MEMORIAL   *see* Enfield Primary Care Trust

FIVE BOROUGHS PARTNERSHIP NHS FOUNDATION TRUST   *see* 5 Boroughs Partnership NHS Foundn Trust

FOREST HEALTHCARE NHS TRUST
London   S BEURKLIAN-CARTER

FORSTER GREEN   *see* Belfast Health and Soc Care Trust

FORTH VALLEY NHS TRUST   T NJUGUNA

FREEMAN Newcastle   *see* Newcastle upon Tyne Hosps NHS Foundn Trust

FRENCHAY Bristol   *see* N Bris NHS Trust

FRIMLEY HEALTH NHS FOUNDATION TRUST   B D BURBIDGE, C E L SMITH, E J TOMS, J J SISTIG

FULBOURN Cambridge   *see* Cam Univ Hosps NHS Foundn Trust

FURNESS GENERAL Barrow-in-Furness   *see* Univ Hosps of Morecambe Bay NHS Foundn Trust

GATESHEAD HEALTH NHS FOUNDATION TRUST   G R ROWLANDS, J ROBINSON

GEORGE ELIOT HOSPITAL NHS TRUST
Nuneaton   M J HAMMOND, R J WITCOMBE, S P MOULT

GLANGWILI GENERAL   *see* Hywel Dda Health Bd

GLENFIELD Bennion Centre   *see* Leics Partnership NHS Trust

GLENFIELD Bradgate Mental Health Unit   *see* Leics Partnership NHS Trust

GLENFIELD Leicester   *see* Univ Hosps Leic NHS Trust

GLOUCESTERSHIRE HOSPITALS NHS FOUNDATION TRUST   C A MCCLURE, J R THOMPSON

GOOLE AND DISTRICT   *see* N Lincs and Goole NHS Foundn Trust

GORSE HILL Leicester   *see* Leics Partnership NHS Trust

GREAT ORMOND STREET HOSPITAL FOR CHILDREN NHS FOUNDATION TRUST   D A MOORE BROOKS, J D LINTHICUM, P J SHERRINGTON

GREAT WESTERN HOSPITALS NHS FOUNDATION TRUST   A GOSDEN, C J OWEN, D R E AUSTIN, J A COUTTS

GREATER GLASGOW AND CLYDE NHS   R F JONES

GREATER MANCHESTER WEST MENTAL HEALTH NHS FOUNDATION TRUST   B S GASKELL, G M BERESFORD JONES

GREENACRES Dartford   *see* Kent and Medway NHS and Soc Care Partnership Trust

GRIMSBY   *see* N Lincs and Goole NHS Foundn Trust

GUY'S AND ST THOMAS' NHS FOUNDATION TRUST
London   C B HALL, G A NEWMAN, J M WATTS, M A K HILBORN, N O TRAYNOR, R A SHAW, S BEURKLIAN-CARTER, S M TAYLOR, W W SHARPE

GWENT HEALTHCARE NHS TRUST   A W TYLER, M J MARSDEN

HALTON GENERAL   *see* Warrington and Halton Hosps NHS Foundn Trust

HAM GREEN Bristol   *see* N Bris NHS Trust

HAMPSHIRE HOSPITALS NHS FOUNDATION TRUST   C S WHITEHEAD, J L WILLIAMS, V J PERRICONE

HAROLD WOOD   *see* Barking Havering and Redbridge Hosps NHS Trust

HARPLANDS Stoke-on-Trent   *see* N Staffs Combined Healthcare NHS Trust

HARTSHILL ORTHOPAEDIC   *see* Univ Hosp of N Staffs NHS Trust

HASLAR   *see* Portsm Hosps NHS Trust

HEART OF ENGLAND NHS FOUNDATION TRUST   L M BUSFIELD, M MACLACHLAN

HEMEL HEMPSTEAD GENERAL   *see* W Herts Hosps NHS Trust

HERGEST UNIT Ysbyty Gwynedd   *see* NW Wales NHS Trust

HERTFORDSHIRE PARTNERSHIP UNIVERSITY NHS FOUNDATION TRUST   R J S ALLEN, V M HARVEY

HEXHAM   *see* Northumbria Healthcare NHS Foundn Trust

HIGHBURY Bulwell   *see* Notts Healthcare NHS Foundn Trust

HILL HOUSE Swansea   *see* Swansea NHS Trust

HINCHINGBROOKE HEALTH CARE NHS TRUST   S GRIFFITH

HOPE Salford   *see* Salford R NHS Foundn Trust

HUDDERSFIELD ROYAL INFIRMARY   *see* Calderdale and Huddersfield NHS Foundn Trust

HULL AND EAST YORKSHIRE HOSPITALS NHS TRUST   A M LAIRD, C R TETLEY

HULTON Bolton *see* Bolton Hosp NHS Trust
HUMBER NHS FOUNDATION TRUST E ROSE
HURSTWOOD PARK Haywards Heath *see* Brighton and Sussex Univ Hosps NHS Trust
HYWEL DDA HEALTH BOARD E HOWELLS
IDA DARWIN Cambridge *see* Cam Univ Hosps NHS Foundn Trust
IMPERIAL COLLEGE HEALTHCARE NHS TRUST M J LEE, R RATCLIFFE
ISLE OF WIGHT NHS TRUST D M NETHERWAY, J K HALLAM, K S BURKE, L J TROMBETTI, S H HOLT
JAMES PAGET UNIVERSITY HOSPITALS NHS FOUNDATION TRUST S R ANDREWS
JERSEY GROUP J A DAVY, M TURNER, T L C BROMLEY
JESSOP WOMEN'S Sheffield *see* Sheff Teaching Hosps NHS Foundn Trust
JOHN RADCLIFFE Oxford *see* Ox Univ Hosps NHS Foundn Trust
KELLING Holt *see* Norfolk Primary Care Trust
KENT AND CANTERBURY *see* E Kent Hosps Univ NHS Foundn Trust
KENT AND MEDWAY NHS AND SOCIAL CARE PARTNERSHIP TRUST E HURST, M CLEEVE, P R BECKINSALE, R A BIERBAUM, S A J MITCHELL
KENT AND SUSSEX Tunbridge Wells *see* Maidstone and Tunbridge Wells NHS Trust
KETTERING GENERAL HOSPITAL NHS FOUNDATION TRUST N PURVEY-TYRER, R G BROWN
KIDDERMINSTER *see* Worcs Acute Hosps NHS Trust
KING EDWARD VII Midhurst D B WELSMAN
KING GEORGE Redbridge *see* Barking, Havering and Redbridge Hosps NHS Trust
KING'S COLLEGE HOSPITAL NHS FOUNDATION TRUST K A CARPANI, S L SUTHERLAND
KINGSTON HOSPITAL NHS FOUNDATION TRUST Surrey S M VAN BEVEREN
LANSDOWNE *see* Cardiff and Vale NHS Trust
LEEDS AND YORK PARTNERSHIP NHS FOUNDATION TRUST B M KIMARU
LEEDS GENERAL INFIRMARY *see* Leeds Teaching Hosps NHS Trust
LEEDS TEACHING HOSPITALS NHS TRUST A CLAYTON, B RHODES, D J MCCLINTOCK, I WILLIAMS
LEICESTER GENERAL *see* Univ Hosps Leic NHS Trust
LEICESTER GENERAL Brandon Mental Health Unit *see* Leics Partnership NHS Trust
LEICESTER ROYAL INFIRMARY *see* Univ Hosps Leic NHS Trust
LEICESTERSHIRE PARTNERSHIP NHS TRUST T H GIRLING
LEIGH INFIRMARY *see* Wrightington, Wigan and Leigh NHS Foundn Trust
LEIGHTON Crewe *see* Mid Cheshire Hosps NHS Foundn Trust
LEWISHAM AND GREENWICH NHS TRUST E B KORMI, K PARKES, L SEEAR, R EMMANUEL, W J DAVID
LIFECARE Caterham *see* Surrey and Borders Partnership NHS Foundn Trust
LINCOLN COUNTY *see* United Lincs Hosps NHS Trust
LINCOLN DISTRICT HEALTH SERVICES NHS TRUST AND LINCOLN HOSPITALS NHS TRUST W G WILLIAMS
LINCOLN St Barnabas' Hospice *see* Linc Distr Health Services and Hosps NHS Trust
LINCOLN St George's *see* Linc Distr Health Services and Hosps NHS Trust
LINCOLNSHIRE PARTNERSHIP NHS FOUNDATION TRUST A M PAVEY
LITTLE PLUMSTEAD *see* Norfolk Primary Care Trust
LITTLEMORE Oxford *see* Ox Health NHS Foundn Trust
LIVERPOOL CARDIOTHORACIC CENTRE *see* R Liverpool and Broadgreen Univ Hosps NHS Trust
LIVERPOOL WOMEN'S NHS FOUNDATION TRUST L J N PARRY
LLANDOUGH *see* Cardiff and Vale NHS Trust
LLANDUDNO GENERAL *see* NW Wales NHS Trust
LLANFRECHFA GRANGE Cwmbran *see* Gwent Healthcare NHS Trust
LONDON AND SURREY *see* R Marsden NHS Foundn Trust
LONDON NORTH WEST HEALTHCARE NHS TRUST J M BEVIS-KNOWLES
LOUTH COUNTY *see* United Lincs Hosps NHS Trust
LUTON AND DUNSTABLE UNIVERSITY HOSPITAL NHS FOUNDATION TRUST E A BRADLEY, M A TREMBATH
MAIDSTONE AND TUNBRIDGE WELLS NHS TRUST N J MITRA
MAINDIFF COURT Abergavenny *see* Gwent Healthcare NHS Trust

MANCHESTER *see* Gtr Man W Mental Health NHS Foundn Trust
MANCHESTER AND SALFORD SKIN *see* Salford R NHS Foundn Trust
MANCHESTER MENTAL HEALTH AND SOCIAL CARE TRUST A G RUSTED
MANCHESTER UNIVERSITY NHS FOUNDATION TRUST M P CORCORAN
MANOR Walsall *see* Walsall Healthcare NHS Trust
MATER *see* Belfast Health and Soc Care Trust
MATTHEW HAY BUILDING Aberdeen *see* NHS Grampian
MAUDSLEY Denmark Hill *see* S Lon and Maudsley NHS Foundn Trust
MEADOWBROOK UNIT Salford *see* Gtr Man W Mental Health NHS Foundn Trust
MEDWAY MARITIME Gillingham *see* Kent and Medway NHS and Soc Care Partnership Trust
MEDWAY NHS FOUNDATION TRUST D V GOWER, L COOKE, S C SPENCER
MERSEY CARE NHS FOUNDATION TRUST J P RAFFAY
MID CHESHIRE HOSPITALS NHS FOUNDATION TRUST C J SANDERSON
MID YORKSHIRE HOSPITALS NHS TRUST D T HAYES, S HULME
MID-ESSEX HOSPITAL SERVICES NHS TRUST K M SALA, S M MALAM
MILLBROOK MENTAL HEALTH UNIT Sutton-in-Ashfield *see* Notts Healthcare NHS Foundn Trust
MILTON KEYNES UNIVERSITY HOSPITAL NHS FOUNDATION TRUST A J FERRIS
MONKWEARMOUTH Sunderland *see* Northumberland, Tyne and Wear NHS Foundn Trust
MORAY Hospitals A L WILLIS
MORPETH COTTAGE *see* Northumbria Healthcare NHS Foundn Trust
MORRISTON Swansea *see* Swansea NHS Trust
MOSSLEY HILL Liverpool *see* Mersey Care NHS Foundn Trust
MOUNT, THE Bishopstoke *see* Hants Hosps NHS Foundn Trust
MUSGRAVE PARK *see* Belfast Health and Soc Care Trust
MUSGROVE PARK Taunton *see* Taunton and Somerset NHS Foundn Trust
NAPSBURY St Albans *see* Enfield Primary Care Trust
NEVILL HALL Abergavenny *see* Gwent Healthcare NHS Trust
NEW CROSS Wolverhampton *see* R Wolv NHS Trust
NEWCASTLE Freeman *see* Newcastle upon Tyne Hosps NHS Foundn Trust
NEWCASTLE GENERAL *see* Newcastle upon Tyne Hosps NHS Foundn Trust
NEWCASTLE Royal Victoria Infirmary *see* Newcastle upon Tyne Hosps NHS Foundn Trust
NEWCASTLE St Nicholas *see* Northumberland, Tyne and Wear NHS Foundn Trust
NEWCASTLE UPON TYNE HOSPITALS NHS FOUNDATION TRUST F M COLLIN, J A ANDERSON
NEWHAM PRIMARY CARE TRUST N J COPSEY
NEWTON ABBOT *see* S Devon Healthcare NHS Foundn Trust
NHS GRAMPIAN I N PALLETT, J DUTHIE, N C MILNE, S SPENCER
NHS TAYSIDE D SHEPHERD, D J GORDON, P T MEAD
NINEWELLS Dundee *see* NHS Tayside
NORFOLK AND NORWICH UNIVERSITY HOSPITALS NHS FOUNDATION TRUST A V WOODROW, J L NURSEY, J M STEWART
NORFOLK COMMUNITY HEALTH AND CARE NHS TRUST E H GARRARD, J M STEWART
NORFOLK PRIMARY CARE TRUST P A ATKINSON
NORTH BRISTOL NHS TRUST A J PARKER, A M BUCKNALL, A R GOOD, N A HECTOR, R CONWAY, W B M DOWIE
NORTH CUMBRIA UNIVERSITY HOSPITALS NHS TRUST A GRAY, M C DANKS-FLOWER
NORTH DEVON DISTRICT Barnstaple *see* N Devon Healthcare NHS Trust
NORTH HAMPSHIRE *see* Hants Hosps NHS Foundn Trust
NORTH MANCHESTER GENERAL *see* Pennine Acute Hosps NHS Trust
NORTH MIDDLESEX UNIVERSITY HOSPITAL NHS TRUST J G S MORGAN
NORTH STAFFORDSHIRE COMBINED HEALTHCARE NHS TRUST L P LUCKING
NORTH STAFFORDSHIRE ROYAL INFIRMARY *see* Univ Hosp of N Staffs NHS Trust
NORTH SURREY PRIMARY CARE TRUST J C L RUNNACLES
NORTH TYNESIDE GENERAL North Shields *see* Northumbria Healthcare NHS Foundn Trust

NORTH WEST ANGLIA NHS FOUNDATION TRUST J J CHAMBERLIN, J M THOMSON, P M DUFFETT-SMITH
NORTH WEST WALES NHS TRUST W ROBERTS
NORTHAMPTON GENERAL HOSPITAL NHS TRUST G A SARMEZEY
NORTHAMPTONSHIRE HEALTHCARE NHS FOUNDATION TRUST R J T FARMER
NORTHERN DEVON HEALTHCARE NHS TRUST J A CARTWRIGHT
NORTHERN GENERAL Sheffield see Sheff Teaching Hosps NHS Foundn Trust
NORTHERN LINCOLNSHIRE AND GOOLE NHS FOUNDATION TRUST C M J THODY
NORTHUMBERLAND, TYNE AND WEAR NHS FOUNDATION TRUST C J WORSFOLD, J GOODE, M C CONNORS, S D MASON
NORTHUMBRIA HEALTHCARE NHS FOUNDATION TRUST C J CLINCH, E A M G BROWN, J L J COOPER, N WILSON
NORWICH COMMUNITY see Norfolk Primary Care Trust
NORWICH, WEST see Norfolk and Nor Univ Hosps NHS Foundn Trust
NOTTINGHAM UNIVERSITY HOSPITAL NHS TRUST City Hospital Campus L M RAYNOR, P KEY
NOTTINGHAM UNIVERSITY HOSPITAL NHS TRUST Queen's Medical Centre Campus A M BROOKS, C T DOLBY, G SPENCER, J HEMSTOCK
NOTTINGHAMSHIRE HEALTHCARE NHS FOUNDATION TRUST T W POWNALL-JONES
NUNNERY FIELDS Canterbury see E Kent Hosps Univ NHS Foundn Trust
OAKS, THE Moray see NHS Grampian
ORSETT see Basildon and Thurrock Univ Hosps NHS Foundn Trust
OVERDALE St Helier see Jersey Gp of Hosps
OXFORD HEALTH NHS FOUNDATION TRUST G P HARRISON, S J HORNER, S L BUSHELL
OXFORD UNIVERSITY HOSPITALS NHS FOUNDATION TRUST F M G HALL, J RADFORD, J E COCKE, S F SEWELL
OXTED see Surrey and Sussex Healthcare NHS Trust
PAIGNTON see S Devon Healthcare NHS Foundn Trust
PEACE HOSPICE Watford M J CARTER
PEMBURY Tunbridge Wells see Maidstone and Tunbridge Wells NHS Trust and Kent and Medway NHS and Soc Care Partnership Trust
PENDERED CENTRE Northampton see Northants Healthcare NHS Foundn Trust
PENDLE COMMUNITY Nelson see E Lancs Hosps NHS Trust
PENNINE ACUTE HOSPITALS NHS TRUST, THE G KENNEDY, K R CARMYLLIE, N ALEXANDER
PENNINE CARE NHS FOUNDATION TRUST A G RUSTED
PETERBOROUGH AND STAMFORD HOSPITALS NHS FOUNDATION TRUST J J PRICE, M B JONES, R E HIGGINS
PILGRIM Boston see United Lincs Hosps NHS Trust
PINDERFIELDS GENERAL Wakefield see Mid Yorks Hosps NHS Trust
PLAISTOW see Newham Primary Care Trust
PLYMOUTH HOSPITALS NHS TRUST A P BARTON, J M COLLIS, S J T PEARCE
PONTEFRACT GENERAL INFIRMARY see Mid Yorks Hosps NHS Trust
POOLE HOSPITAL NHS FOUNDATION TRUST E J LLOYD, I R PEARCE
POOLE St Ann's see Dorset HealthCare University NHS Foundn Trust
PORTSMOUTH HOSPITALS NHS TRUST B R SMITH, D A BANTING, J POWER
PRINCE PHILIP Llanelli see Hywel Dda Health Bd
PRINCESS ALEXANDRA HOSPITAL NHS TRUST Harlow C C OKEKE, G A NEWMAN, T R WEEKS
PRINCESS ANNE Southampton see Univ Hosp Southn NHS Foundn Trust
PRINCESS ELIZABETH Guernsey L S LE VASSEUR
PRINCESS MARINA Northampton see Northants Healthcare NHS Foundn Trust
PRINCESS ROYAL Haywards Heath see Brighton and Sussex Univ Hosps NHS Trust
PRINCESS ROYAL Hull see Hull and E Yorks Hosps NHS Trust
PRIORITY HOUSE Maidstone see Kent and Medway NHS and Soc Care Partnership Trust
PRIORY Birmingham J A GRIFFIN
QUEEN ALEXANDRA Portsmouth see Portsm Hosps NHS Trust J A JONES
QUEEN ELIZABETH Birmingham see Univ Hosp Birm NHS Foundn Trust
QUEEN ELIZABETH Gateshead see Gateshead Health NHS Foundn Trust

QUEEN ELIZABETH HOSPITAL KING'S LYNN NHS FOUNDATION TRUST S L GREEN
QUEEN ELIZABETH THE QUEEN MOTHER Margate see E Kent Hosps Univ NHS Foundn Trust
QUEEN VICTORIA HOSPITAL NHS FOUNDATION TRUST East Grinstead M E TRASK
QUEEN VICTORIA Morecambe see Univ Hosps of Morecambe Bay NHS Foundn Trust
QUEEN'S Burton-on-Trent see Burton Hosps NHS Foundn Trust
QUEEN'S MEDICAL CENTRE UNIVERSITY HOSPITAL Nottingham, Department of Psychiatry and Psychiatric Medicine see Notts Healthcare NHS Foundn Trust
QUEEN'S PARK Blackburn see E Lancs Hosps NHS Trust
QUEEN'S Romford see Barking, Havering and Redbridge Hosps NHS Trust
RAIGMORE HOSPITAL NHS TRUST Inverness A A SINCLAIR
RAMPTON Retford see Notts Healthcare NHS Foundn Trust
RAMSGATE GENERAL see E Kent Hosps Univ NHS Foundn Trust
RATHBONE Liverpool see Mersey Care NHS Foundn Trust
REDBRIDGE King George see Barking, Havering and Redbridge Hosps NHS Trust
RIBCHESTER A D HINDLEY
RIDGEWOOD CENTRE Frimley see Surrey and Borders Partnership NHS Foundn Trust
ROCHDALE INFIRMARY see Pennine Acute Hosps NHS Trust
ROOKWOOD Llandaff see Cardiff and Vale NHS Trust
ROWLEY REGIS Warley see Sandwell and W Birm Hosps NHS Trust
ROXBURGHE HOUSE Aberdeen see NHS Grampian
ROYAL ABERDEEN CHILDREN'S see NHS Grampian
ROYAL ALBERT EDWARD INFIRMARY see Wrightington, Wigan and Leigh NHS Foundn Trust
ROYAL ALEXANDRA CHILDREN'S Brighton see Brighton and Sussex Univ Hosps NHS Trust
ROYAL BELFAST HOSPITAL FOR SICK CHILDREN see Belfast Health and Soc Care Trust
ROYAL BERKSHIRE NHS FOUNDATION TRUST R J SIMMONDS
ROYAL BOURNEMOUTH AND CHRISTCHURCH HOSPITALS NHS FOUNDATION TRUST A SESSFORD, A M NEWTON
ROYAL BROMPTON AND HAREFIELD NHS FOUNDATION TRUST B MAHILUM, C T BARKER, N K LEE
ROYAL CORNHILL Aberdeen see NHS Grampian
ROYAL CORNWALL HOSPITALS TRUST D P WHITTING, J K P S ROBERTSHAW
ROYAL DERBY see Derby Teaching Hosps NHS Foundn Trust
ROYAL DEVON AND EXETER NHS FOUNDATION TRUST J J HORWOOD, S R SWARBRICK, S W COOK
ROYAL FREE LONDON NHS FOUNDATION TRUST C CARSON, P D CONRAD
ROYAL GWENT Newport see Gwent Healthcare NHS Trust
ROYAL HALLAMSHIRE Sheffield see Sheff Teaching Hosps NHS Foundn Trust
ROYAL HAMPSHIRE COUNTY Winchester see Hants Hosps NHS Foundn Trust
ROYAL HOSPITAL HASLAR see Portsm Hosps NHS Trust
ROYAL JUBILEE MATERNITY SERVICE see Belfast Health and Soc Care Trust
ROYAL LANCASTER INFIRMARY see Univ Hosps of Morecambe Bay NHS Foundn Trust
ROYAL LIVERPOOL AND BROADGREEN UNIVERSITY HOSPITALS NHS TRUST C J PETER, G A PERERA
ROYAL MARSDEN NHS FOUNDATION TRUST London and Surrey A E DOERR, A J MCCULLOCH
ROYAL NATIONAL ORTHOPAEDIC HOSPITAL NHS TRUST W A BROOKER
ROYAL OLDHAM see Pennine Acute Hosps NHS Trust
ROYAL SHREWSBURY see Shrewsbury and Telford Hosp NHS Trust
ROYAL SOUTH HAMPSHIRE see Univ Hosp Southn NHS Foundn Trust
ROYAL SUSSEX COUNTY Brighton see Brighton and Sussex Univ Hosps NHS Trust
ROYAL UNITED HOSPITALS BATH NHS FOUNDATION TRUST C L DICKSON, N J K TEGALLY
ROYAL VICTORIA Belfast see Belfast Health and Soc Care Trust
ROYAL VICTORIA Folkestone see E Kent Hosps Univ NHS Foundn Trust
ROYAL VICTORIA INFIRMARY Newcastle see Newcastle upon Tyne Hosps NHS Foundn Trust
ROYAL WOLVERHAMPTON NHS TRUST C W FULLARD, S PETTY
ST ALBANS CITY see W Herts Hosps NHS Trust
ST ALBANS Napsbury see Enfield Primary Care Trust

ST ANDREW'S HEALTHCARE Birmingham, Essex, Northampton, Nottinghamshire   M J MARSHALL, P R EVANS, R M HETHERINGTON

ST ANNE'S CENTRE St Leonards-on-Sea   *see* E Sussex Healthcare NHS Trust

ST ANN'S Poole   *see* Dorset HealthCare University NHS Foundn Trust

ST ANN'S Tottenham   *see* Barnet, Enfield and Haringey Mental Health NHS Trust

ST BARNABAS' HOSPICE Lincoln   *see* Linc Distr Health Services and Hosps NHS Trust

ST CADOC'S Caerleon   *see* Gwent Healthcare NHS Trust

ST CLEMENT'S London   *see* E Lon NHS Foundation Trust

ST CROSS Rugby   *see* Univ Hosps Cov and Warks NHS Trust

ST EBBA'S Epsom   *see* Surrey and Borders Partnership NHS Foundn Trust

ST EDMUND'S Northampton   *see* Northn Gen Hosp NHS Trust

ST GEORGE'S HEALTHCARE NHS TRUST London   R B REYNOLDS

ST GEORGE'S Lincoln   *see* Linc Distr Health Services and Hosps NHS Trust

ST GEORGE'S Stafford   *see* S Staffs and Shropshire Healthcare NHS Foundn Trust

ST GEORGE'S UNIVERSITY HOSPITALS NHS FOUNDATION TRUST   C S W VAN D'ARQUE, J S MCARTHUR-EDWARDS

ST HELENS AND KNOWSLEY HOSPITALS NHS TRUST   P TAYLOR

ST HELIER Carshalton   *see* Epsom and St Helier Univ Hosps NHS Trust

ST JAMES'S UNIVERSITY Leeds   *see* Leeds Teaching Hosps NHS Trust

ST LUKE'S Bradford   *see* Bradf Teaching Hosps NHS Foundn Trust

ST MARTIN'S Bath   *see* Bath and West Community NHS Trust

ST MARTIN'S Canterbury   *see* Kent and Medway NHS and Soc Care Partnership Trust

ST MARY'S Kettering   *see* Northants Healthcare NHS Foundn Trust

ST MARY'S Portsmouth   *see* Portsm Hosps NHS Trust

ST MICHAEL'S Aylsham   *see* Norfolk Primary Care Trust

ST MICHAEL'S Bristol   *see* Univ Hosps Bris NHS Foundn Trust

ST NICHOLAS Newcastle   *see* Northumberland, Tyne and Wear NHS Foundn Trust

ST PETER'S Chertsey   *see* Ashford and St Pet Hosps NHS Foundn Trust   *see* N Surrey Primary Care Trust

ST RICHARD'S Chichester   *see* W Sussex Hosps NHS Foundn Trust

ST SAVIOUR   *see* Jersey Gp of Hosps

ST THOMAS' London   *see* Guy's and St Thos' NHS Foundn Trust

ST WOOLOS Newport   *see* Gwent Healthcare NHS Trust

SALFORD ROYAL NHS FOUNDATION TRUST   A J HESLOP, J I HULSE, J L HOOD

SALISBURY NHS FOUNDATION TRUST   A R SYMES, F E CANHAM, K S M STEPHENS

SALKELD DAY Chepstow   *see* Gwent Healthcare NHS Trust

SANDWELL AND WEST BIRMINGHAM HOSPITALS NHS TRUST   D H GARNER

SCARBOROUGH GENERAL   *see* York Teaching Hosp NHS Foundn Trust

SCUNTHORPE GENERAL   *see* N Lincs and Goole NHS Foundn Trust

SEACROFT Leeds   *see* Leeds Teaching Hosps NHS Trust

SELBY WAR MEMORIAL   *see* York Teaching Hosp NHS Foundn Trust

SELLY OAK   *see* Univ Hosp Birm NHS Foundn Trust

SHEFFIELD HEALTH AND SOCIAL CARE NHS FOUNDATION TRUST   S H ROSS

SHEFFIELD TEACHING HOSPITALS NHS FOUNDATION TRUST   H C BLACKBURN, J H DALEY, M J NEWITT, M R COBB, R A E LAMBERT

SHOTLEY BRIDGE GENERAL Consett   *see* Co Durham and Darlington NHS Foundn Trust

SHREWSBURY AND TELFORD HOSPITAL NHS TRUST   M G WILLIAMS, M I FEARNSIDE, P HRYZIUK

SINGLETON Swansea   *see* Swansea NHS Trust

SIR ROBERT PEEL Tamworth   *see* S Staffs and Shropshire Healthcare NHS Foundn Trust

SOBELL HOUSE Oxford   *see* Ox Univ Hosps NHS Foundn Trust

SOMERSET PARTNERSHIP NHS FOUNDATION TRUST   B E PRIORY

SOUTH LONDON AND MAUDSLEY NHS FOUNDATION TRUST   I N FISHWICK

SOUTH SHORE Blackpool   *see* Blackpool, Fylde and Wyre Hosps NHS Trust

SOUTH STAFFORDSHIRE AND SHROPSHIRE HEALTHCARE NHS FOUNDATION TRUST   K A SHAW

SOUTH TYNESIDE NHS FOUNDATION TRUST   P R BEALING

SOUTH WARWICKSHIRE GENERAL HOSPITALS NHS TRUST   F E TYLER, H F COCKELL, R C PANTLING, S S MILES

SOUTH WEST DORSET PRIMARY CARE TRUST   E J WOODS, P J RINGER

SOUTH WEST LONDON AND ST GEORGE'S MENTAL HEALTH NHS TRUST   A R BECK, T MATIKAINEN-CASTLEDINE

SOUTH WEST YORKSHIRE PARTNERSHIP NHS FOUNDATION TRUST   B M KIMARU, C M GARTLAND

SOUTHAMPTON GENERAL   *see* Univ Hosp Southn NHS Foundn Trust

SOUTHEND UNIVERSITY HOSPITAL NHS FOUNDATION TRUST   D R CHILDS

SOUTHERN HEALTH NHS FOUNDATION TRUST   C E FENNEMORE, E L A D'AETH, N P FENNEMORE, V J LAWRENCE

SOUTHLANDS Shoreham-by-Sea   *see* W Sussex Hosps NHS Foundn Trust

SOUTHMEAD Bristol   *see* N Bris NHS Trust

SPRINGFIELD UNIVERSITY   *see* SW Lon and St George's Mental Health NHS Trust

STANDISH Stonehouse   *see* Glos Hosps NHS Foundn Trust

STOKE MANDEVILLE Aylesbury   *see* Bucks Healthcare NHS Trust

STOKE-ON-TRENT CITY GENERAL   *see* Univ Hosp of N Staffs NHS Trust

SUFFOLK COASTAL PRIMARY CARE TRUST   N J WINTER

SUNDERLAND ROYAL   *see* City Hosps Sunderland NHS Foundn Trust

SURREY AND BORDERS PARTNERSHIP NHS FOUNDATION TRUST   N J COPSEY

SURREY AND SUSSEX HEALTHCARE NHS TRUST   S NJOKA

SUSSEX COMMUNITY NHS FOUNDATION TRUST   D A KNIGHT

SUSSEX PARTNERSHIP NHS FOUNDATION TRUST   G REEVES, S J HOBBS

SWANSEA NHS TRUST   D M GRIFFITHS, N R GRIFFIN, P J GWYNN

TAMESIDE AND GLOSSOP INTEGRATED CARE NHS FOUNDATION TRUST   J M HURLSTON

TAMESIDE GENERAL   *see* Pennine Acute Hosps NHS Trust

TAUNTON AND SOMERSET NHS FOUNDATION TRUST   G J W EDMUNDS, J M FRENCH

TEES, ESK AND WEAR VALLEYS NHS FOUNDATION TRUST   B O OMOBUDE, C JAY, P L WALKER

TEIGNMOUTH   *see* S Devon Healthcare NHS Foundn Trust

TELFORD Princess Royal   *see* Shrewsbury and Telford Hosp NHS Trust

TEWKESBURY   *see* Glos Hosps NHS Foundn Trust

THANET MENTAL HEALTH UNIT Margate   *see* Kent & Medway NHS and Soc Care Partnership Trust

TOGETHER NHS FOUNDATION TRUST   *see* 2gether NHS Foundn Trust

TORBAY AND SOUTH DEVON NHS FOUNDATION TRUST   A D SUMNER

TRAFFORD HEALTHCARE NHS TRUST   C J BROWN

TRANWELL UNIT Gateshead   *see* Northumberland, Tyne and Wear NHS Foundn Trust

TREDEGAR GENERAL   *see* Gwent Healthcare NHS Trust

ULVERSTON   *see* Univ Hosps of Morecambe Bay NHS Foundn Trust

UNITED LINCOLNSHIRE HOSPITALS NHS TRUST   A AMELIA, B A HUTCHINSON, B M S CHAMBERS, C M BONNEYWELL, J FRESHNEY, J M ROWLAND, K M TOMLIN, P BEATTIE

UNIVERSITY Aintree   *see* Mersey Care NHS Foundn Trust

UNIVERSITY Durham   *see* Co Durham and Darlington NHS Foundn Trust

UNIVERSITY HOSPITAL BIRMINGHAM NHS FOUNDATION TRUST   R J HILL-BROWN, R M WHARTON

UNIVERSITY HOSPITAL OF NORTH STAFFORDSHIRE NHS TRUST   L B VARQUEZ

UNIVERSITY HOSPITAL OF WALES   *see* Cardiff and Vale NHS Trust

UNIVERSITY HOSPITAL SOUTHAMPTON NHS FOUNDATION TRUST   K A MACKINNON, P A BOGGUST, S A TAUSON, S M PITKIN

UNIVERSITY HOSPITALS BRISTOL NHS FOUNDATION TRUST   J E NORMAN, M A SNOOK, N J ARCHER

UNIVERSITY HOSPITALS COVENTRY AND WARWICKSHIRE NHS TRUST   E A JONES, S F BETTERIDGE, S R TASH

UNIVERSITY HOSPITALS OF LEICESTER NHS TRUST   S H J WRATTEN, S J WRIGHT

UNIVERSITY HOSPITALS OF MORECAMBE BAY NHS FOUNDATION TRUST   I J J DEWAR, J L TYRER

UNIVERSITY HOSPITALS OF NORTH MIDLANDS NHS TRUST C S B ROUTLEDGE, V L FLANAGAN
VICTORIA Blackpool *see* Blackpool, Fylde and Wyre Hosps NHS Trust
WALKERGATE Newcastle *see* Newcastle upon Tyne Hosps NHS Foundn Trust
WALSALL HEALTHCARE NHS TRUST A E COLES, K A DUCKETT, L A W SWABY
WALSGRAVE GENERAL Coventry *see* Univ Hosps Cov and Warks NHS Trust
WALTON COMMUNITY *see* N Surrey Primary Care Trust
WANSBECK GENERAL Ashington *see* Northumbria Healthcare NHS Foundn Trust
WARNEFORD Leamington Spa *see* S Warks Gen Hosps NHS Trust
WARRINGTON AND HALTON HOSPITALS NHS FOUNDATION TRUST J E DUFFIELD, P J TURNER
WARWICKSHIRE, SOUTH *see* S Warks Gen Hosps NHS Trust
WATFORD GENERAL *see* W Herts Hosps NHS Trust
WELLINGTON C F E ROWLEY
WELLS ROAD CENTRE Mapperley *see* Notts Healthcare NHS Foundn Trust
WEST CORNWALL *see* R Cornwall Hosps Trust
WEST CUMBERLAND *see* N Cumbria Univ Hosps NHS Trust
WEST HERTFORDSHIRE HOSPITALS NHS TRUST G O OCHOLA
WEST MIDDLESEX UNIVERSITY HOSPITAL NHS TRUST M W SSERUNKUMA
WEST SUFFOLK NHS FOUNDATION TRUST D WEBB, S D GRIFFITHS
WESTERN SUSSEX HOSPITALS NHS FOUNDATION TRUST R E BENNETT
WESTMORLAND GENERAL *see* Univ Hosps of Morecambe Bay NHS Foundn Trust
WESTON AREA HEALTH NHS TRUST D L GRACE
WESTON PARK Sheffield *see* Sheff Teaching Hosps NHS Foundn Trust
WEYMOUTH COMMUNITY *see* Dorset Co Hosp NHS Foundn Trust
WHARFEDALE GENERAL Otley *see* Leeds Teaching Hosps NHS Trust

WHELLEY *see* Wrightington, Wigan and Leigh NHS Foundn Trust
WHIPPS CROSS *see* Forest Healthcare NHS Trust Lon
WHISTON Prescot *see* St Helens and Knowsley Hosps NHS Trust
WHITBY *see* York Teaching Hosp NHS Foundn Trust
WHITCHURCH *see* Cardiff and Vale NHS Trust
WHITTINGTON HOSPITAL NHS TRUST A O BADEJO
WILLIAM HARVEY Arundel Unit *see* Kent & Medway NHS and Soc Care Partnership Trust
WILLIAM HARVEY Ashford *see* E Kent Hosps Univ NHS Foundn Trust
WINWICK Warrington *see* 5 Boroughs Partnership NHS Foundn Trust
WIRRAL UNIVERSITY TEACHING HOSPITAL NHS FOUNDATION TRUST L J N PARRY, M COWAN
WOKING COMMUNITY *see* Surrey and Borders Partnership NHS Foundn Trust
WOODEND Aberdeen *see* NHS Grampian
WOODLANDS Worsley *see* Gtr Man W Mental Health NHS Foundn Trust
WOOLMANHILL Aberdeen *see* NHS Grampian
WORCESTER ROYAL *see* Worcs Acute Hosps NHS Trust
WORCESTERSHIRE ACUTE HOSPITALS NHS TRUST D P RYAN
WORCESTERSHIRE HEALTH AND CARE NHS TRUST S ROSENTHAL
WRIGHTINGTON, WIGAN AND LEIGH NHS FOUNDATION TRUST A J EDWARDS, C JACKSON, C P TRACEY, M RYAN
WYCOMBE *see* Bucks Healthcare NHS Trust
WYE VALLEY NHS TRUST L C RHODES
YEOVIL DISTRICT HOSPITAL NHS FOUNDATION TRUST J M CUMMINGS, L A SCOTT, R M BURT
YORK Teaching Hospital NHS Foundation Trust C J HAYES, D M COX, G M WEBB, L M HOLLIS, R J BAILES
YSBYTY GWYNEDD Penrhosgarnedd *see* NW Wales NHS Trust
YSBYTY PENRHOS STANLEY Holyhead *see* NW Wales NHS Trust
YSTRAD MYNACH Hengoed *see* Gwent Healthcare NHS Trust

HOSPICE CHAPLAINS

ACORNS Wolverhampton   P H SMITH
ARTHUR RANK Cambridge   K C MORRISON
BLYTHE HOUSE Chapel-en-le-Frith   S H COCKSEDGE
CHESTNUT TREE HOUSE Arundel   S J GURR
CHILDREN'S SOUTH WEST Fremington   G C PHILLIPS
COMPTON Wolverhampton   E I DE JONGE
DOUGLAS MACMILLAN Blurton   M L T MCGONIGLE
EARL MOUNTBATTEN Newport   R A DEEDES
EDEN HALL MARIE CURIE Hampstead   D L YELDHAM
EXETER HOSPISCARE   D J WALFORD
GARDEN HOUSE Letchworth   A J FERRIS
GREENWICH AND BEXLEY COTTAGE   H O APARANGA
ISABEL Welwyn Garden City   R S ALLEN
JERSEY   G J HOUGHTON
JOSPICE Liverpool   A R BROCKBANK
KATHARINE HOUSE Banbury   J P JONES
KEMP Kidderminster   P J L CODY, S FOSTER
LECKHAMPTON COURT   R C PESTELL
LOROS Leicester   B DAVIES, C A LACEY
MARIE CURIE CENTRE Newcastle upon Tyne   K J FRANCIS
MARIE CURIE Edinburgh   M F CHATTERLEY
MARIE CURIE Liverpool   R E PRYCE
MARY ANN EVANS Nuneaton   G HANCOCK, P DODDS
MYTON HAMLET Warwick   W S GRAHAM
NAOMI HOUSE Sutton Scotney   M R CHRISTIAN
NORFOLK, THE Snettisham   S M MARTIN
NORTH LONDON   S P YOUNG
OAKHAVEN TRUST   J E L ALEXANDER
OVERGATE Elland   D BURROWS
PHYLLIS TUCKWELL Farnham   J L WALKER,
   S M R CUMMING-LATTEY
PILGRIMS Thanet   K I R COX
PRIMROSE Bromsgrove   D R L WHITE

RICHARD HOUSE   T N ALEXANDER-WATTS
ROWANS, THE Purbrook   C G GULLY
ROWCROFT Torquay   G STILL
SAM BEARE Weybridge   B D PROTHERO
SEVERN Shrewsbury   E C PHILLIPS, H J EDWARDS, J E HOLMES,
   P M FREEMAN
SOBELL HOUSE Oxford   G T G SYKES
SPRINGHILL Rochdale   A L OXBORROW
ST ANDREW'S Airdrie   M LITTLE
ST ANN'S Manchester   I C ANTHONY
ST BARNABAS HOUSE Worthing   S J GURR
ST ELIZABETH Ipswich   A J OAKEY-JONES, M A H FINCH
ST GEMMA'S Moortown   D L LOFTHOUSE
ST JOHN'S Wirral   P B PRITCHARD
ST JOSEPH'S Hackney   J A ALTY
ST LEONARD'S York   D B WILLIAMSON, S A WHITTINGTON
ST LUKE'S CHESHIRE Winsford   J T STOPFORD, R J GATES
ST LUKE'S Sheffield   M W P REEDER
ST MARGARET'S Taunton   A E FULTON
ST MICHAEL'S Harrogate (Crimple House)   K COUCHMAN
ST MICHAEL'S Hereford   J GROVES
ST MICHAEL'S St Leonards-on-Sea   G L DRIVER
ST NICHOLAS Bury St Edmunds   S M CONNELL, S M NUTT
ST OSWALD'S Newcastle upon Tyne   C L BROWN
ST PETER AND ST JAMES North Chailey   S C M MCLARNON
ST RICHARD'S Worcester   S ROSENTHAL, C E GRIFFITHS
ST WILFRID'S Chichester   J P COOPER
STRATHCARRON Denny   S M COATES
SUSSEX BEACON Brighton   J K T ELDRIDGE
TRINITY IN THE FYLDE Blackpool   P E BERRY
TYNEDALE Hexham   J L JACKSON
WEALD Tunbridge Wells   P C STEPHENS
WHEATFIELDS Leeds   D A BUCK

EDUCATIONAL CHAPLAINS

UNIVERSITIES

ABERDEEN   D HEDDLE
ABERTAY   D SHEPHERD
ABERYSTWYTH   S R BELL
ANGLIA RUSKIN   N S COOPER, J THORNTON
ASHRIDGE EXECUTIVE EDUCATION   L GEOGHEGAN
BANGOR   N J JARVIS
BATH   J N RAWLINSON
BATH SPA   J P KNOTT
BEDFORDSHIRE   A F M GOODMAN
BIRMINGHAM   S JONES
BISHOP GROSSETESTE
   Lincoln   P G GREEN, M J S JACKSON
BOLTON   G M SMART
BRADFORD   A J HOWORTH
BRISTOL   E G A DAVIS
CAMBRIDGE
   Churchill   J RAWLINSON
   Corpus Christi   A P DAVISON
   Downing   K J EYEONS
   Fitzwilliam   G STEVENSON
   Girton   A M GUITE
   Gonville and Caius   C J-B HAMMOND, D H JONES
   King's   A C R HAMMOND
   Magdalene   S C ATKINS, S BARRINGTON-WARD
   Newnham   H D SHILSON-THOMAS
   Queens'   M T BAYLISS, T C HARLING
   Selwyn   H D SHILSON-THOMAS
   Trinity   J E SUMMERS
   Trinity Hall   S J PLANT
   Wolfson   R C ROSBOROUGH
CARDIFF   D K SHEEN
CARDIFF METROPOLITAN   P K FITZPATRICK
CENTRAL LANCASHIRE   A CLITHEROW
CHESTER   E M BURGESS, P J JENNER, L C RHODES
COVENTRY   A M RICHARDS
CUMBRIA   C J KENNEDY, A J LOGAN
DE MONTFORT   J ARENS, H A SURRIDGE
DERBY   A P DICKENS
DUBLIN CITY   J B MARCHANT
DUNDEE   J R AULD, A WALLER
DURHAM   G WORT
   Collingwood   G WORT
   Grey   G WORT
   Hatfield   A BASH
   St Chad's   D W RUSHTON
   St Hild and St Bede   T M FERGUSON
   Trevelyan   G WORT
   Van Mildert   G WORT
EAST ANGLIA   D T THORNTON
EDINBURGH   F S BURBERRY, H A HARRIS
EXETER   H S J ALDERSON, C M MASON
GLASGOW   K FRANCIS
GLOUCESTERSHIRE   N D DAVIES, S C WITCOMBE
GREENWICH   S COOK
HERIOT-WATT   M J H ROUND
HERTFORDSHIRE   F C SOUTER
HUDDERSFIELD   C A CHESHIRE, C J TRUMAN
HULL   J C COWAN
IMPERIAL COLLEGE LONDON   A W WILLSON
KEELE   S J COUVELA
KENT   S C E LAIRD
KINGSTON   D BUCKLEY
LANCASTER   K J HUGGETT
LEEDS   A J COLLEDGE
LEICESTER   L S BRIGGS
LIVERPOOL   R G LEWIS
LIVERPOOL JOHN MOORES   R G LEWIS

LONDON
   Central Chaplaincies   A W WILLSON
   Goldsmiths' College   A J CLARKE
   King's   J O M CRAIG, K G RIGLIN
   London School of Economics and Political Science   J A WALTERS
   Queen Mary   A SHARPLES
   Queen Mary and Westfield   N J GOULDING
   Royal Holloway and Bedford New   O B EDGAR
   Royal Veterinary College   A S MARSHALL
   University   C E BRADLEY
LOUGHBOROUGH   C D TAYLOR
MANCHESTER   J B EDSON
MANCHESTER METROPOLITAN   J B EDSON
NORTHAMPTON   S N MOUSIR-HARRISON
NORTHUMBRIA AT NEWCASTLE   A P BOWSHER
NOTTINGHAM   M R SMITH
NOTTINGHAM TRENT   R H DAVEY
OXFORD
   All Souls   J H DRURY
   Balliol   B R L KINSEY
   Brasenose   J C BALDWIN
   Christ Church   C J Y HAYNS
   Exeter   A M ALLEN
   Hertford   M A SMITH
   Keble   N J EVERETT
   Lincoln   M K MARSHALL
   Magdalen   S M ALKIRE, A D BOWYER
   Merton   S M JONES, J A MERCER, M STAFFORD
   New   S BRIDGE, E D LONGFELLOW
   Oriel   R J D WAINWRIGHT
   Pembroke   A R TEAL
   Queen's   K A M PRICE
   St Hugh's   S C HENSON
   St John's   E C MACFARLANE
   St Peter's   E J PITKETHLY
   Trinity   E M PERCY
   University   A F GREGORY
   Wadham   J R BAUN
   Worcester   T KUIN LAWTON
OXFORD BROOKES   S MATHEW
PORTSMOUTH   C SHERMAN
READING   M D LAYNESMITH
ROBERT GORDON   I M POOBALAN
ROEHAMPTON   D J ESHUN
ROYAL COLLEGE OF ART   A W WILLSON
ROYAL NORTHERN COLLEGE OF MUSIC   J B EDSON
SALFORD   H TOMLINSON, K A C WASEY
SHEFFIELD   J M S CLINES, D L V WILKINSON
SHEFFIELD HALLAM   H R L ROULSTON
ST ANDREWS   S J FERGUSON
ST MARK AND ST JOHN   M J PARKMAN, I N KIYAGA, C M^cILROY
ST MELLITUS
   College   P J SWITHINBANK
STAFFORDSHIRE   M WILLIAMS
STIRLING   E F J MULLINER
SUNDERLAND   C S HOWSON
SUSSEX   C F P MCDERMOTT
UNIVERSITY COLLEGE CORK   A G MARLEY
UNIVERSITY OF THE ARTS
   London   M W J DEAN, W A WHITCOMBE
WALES TRINITY ST DAVID   E L WHITTICK
WARWICK   K E PEARSON
WEST LONDON   E C FRANCE
WEST OF ENGLAND, BRISTOL   J K NICHOLSON
WESTMINSTER   J M NOBLE
WINCHESTER   C A DAY
WOLVERHAMPTON   S SCHOFIELD
YORK ST JOHN   A C ROWLEY, J E SPECK

COLLEGES OF HIGHER EDUCATION

CITY COLLEGE *Norwich*   D Z LLOYD

HARINGEY, ENFIELD AND NORTH EAST LONDON   S P J CLARK

COLLEGES OF FURTHER EDUCATION

BISHOP BURTON COLLEGE OF AGRICULTURE
   York   R F PARKINSON
DUCHY COLLEGE *Stoke Climsland*   A W STEPHENS
GOWER COLLEGE SWANSEA   A MORGAN
FARNBOROUGH COLLEGE OF
   TECHNOLOGY   G P H NEWTON

SOMERSET COLLEGE OF ARTS AND
   TECHNOLOGY   P J HUGHES
LEICESTER   J M SHARP
SUFFOLK NEW   T ROUT
SWINDON   S F FISHER

SCHOOLS

ABBOTS BROMLEY   G P BOTT
ABINGDON   P D B GOODING, S M STEER
ALDENHAM *Hertfordshire*   P S GREEN, J C PERRIS
ALL SAINTS' ACADEMY *Cheltenham*   K J SAMUEL
ALL SAINTS ACADEMY *Dunstable*   T A DAVIS
ALL SAINTS' CHURCH OF ENGLAND PRIMARY
   Peterborough   M R MATTHEWS
ALLEYN'S *Dulwich*   E A LANDER
ALTON   W MATTHEWS
ARCHBISHOP SENTAMU ACADEMY *Hull*   A RICHARDS
ARCHBISHOP'S *Canterbury*   K MADDY
ARDINGLY COLLEGE *Haywards Heath*   A J STARK-ORDISH
ARK ALL SAINTS ACADEMY *Camberwell*   J G A ROBERTS
ARK BURLINGTON DANES ACADEMY *London*   H J WHITTAKER
ASHFORD   R W BELLAMY
BABLAKE *Coventry*   J SLAVIC
BACON'S COLLEGE *Rotherhithe*   R J HALL
BANCROFT'S *Woodford Green*   I MOORE
BAPCHILD AND TONGE CHURCH OF ENGLAND
   PRIMARY   S R YOUNG
BARNARD CASTLE   D R MOORE
BENNETT MEMORIAL DIOCESAN *Tunbridge Wells*   R A KNAPP
BERKHAMSTED *Herts*   J E MARKBY
BETHANY *Goudhurst*   S L WILLOUGHBY
BIRKENHEAD *Merseyside*   M R J TURNER
BISHOP HENDERSON *Taunton*   J A JEFFERY
BISHOP WORDSWORTH'S *Salisbury*   A W GOUGH
BLOXHAM   D C WEAVER
BLUE COAT *Reading*   K L TOOGOOD
BLUNDELL'S *Tiverton*   T C HUNT
BRADFIELD COLLEGE *Berkshire*   P M HANSELL
BRADFORD ACADEMY   R I TAYLOR
BRENTWOOD *Essex*   A W MCCONNAUGHIE
BRIGHTON COLLEGE   R C AMESS
BROMSGROVE   P S J HEDWORTH
CANFORD *Wimborne*   P A JACK
CANON SLADE *Bolton*   T R LILLEY
CANTERBURY CHRIST CHURCH   J T LAW, D A STROUD
CHARTERHOUSE *Godalming*   C A CASE, A J M WATKINSON
CHELTENHAM COLLEGE   A J DUNNING, A F G SAMUEL,
   K J SAMUEL
CHELTENHAM LADIES' COLLEGE   J A GOODWIN, H R WOOD
CHICHESTER   A I GREEN, K J ROBINSON
CHIGWELL *Essex*   G J SCOTT
CHRIST'S HOSPITAL *Horsham*   C J HUXLEY-JONES
CITY OF LONDON FREEMEN'S *Ashtead*   J R L PRIOR
CLIFTON COLLEGE *Bristol*   S J CHAPMAN
COKETHORPE *Witney*   I B HOWARD
COLFE'S *London*   S P HALL
COTHILL HOUSE *Abingdon*   T R PERRY
COTTESMORE *Crawley*   M C PERRY
COVENTRY BLUE COAT CHURCH OF
   ENGLAND   C M VICKERS
CRANLEIGH PREPARATORY *Surrey*   N H GREEN
CRANLEIGH *Surrey*   T M P LEWIS
DAME ALLAN'S *Newcastle*   J MCGOWAN
DAUNTSEY'S *Devizes*   D R JOHNSON
DEAN CLOSE *Cheltenham*   J C G ASH
DOWNE HOUSE *Berkshire*   A K H PLATT
DULWICH COLLEGE   T BUCKLER
DULWICH PREPARATORY *Cranbrook*   D F P RUTHERFORD
DURHAM   S A MCMURTARY
DURHAM HIGH   B P S VALLIS

EAST GLENDALOUGH   S M ZIETSMAN
EASTBOURNE COLLEGE   D J MERCERON
ELIZABETH COLLEGE *Guernsey*   P A GRAYSMITH
ELLESMERE COLLEGE *Shropshire*   P J GRATION
EMANUEL *Wandsworth*   S LABRAN
EPSOM COLLEGE   A M J HAVILAND
ETON COLLEGE *Berkshire*   D M BOND, R E R DEMERY,
   S J N GRAY, P A HESS, C M JONES
EXETER   T P CARSON
FELSTED *Essex*   N J LITTLE
FETTES COLLEGE *Edinburgh*   A CLARK
FOREST *Snaresbrook*   P K TRATHEN
FRAMLINGHAM COLLEGE *Woodbridge*   B A BAYMAN
GIGGLESWICK   A J LADDS
GODOLPHIN *Salisbury*   S M WOOD
GORDON'S *Woking*   S J NORBRON
GREIG CITY ACADEMY   P J HENDERSON
GRESHAM'S *Holt*   B R ROBERTS
GREYCOAT HOSPITAL   M R OWEN, G D SWINTON
GRYPHON *Sherborne*   D R TREGALE
GUILDFORD   M C WOODWARD
HABERDASHERS' ASKE'S *Elstree*   M BRANDON
HABERDASHERS' MONMOUTH SCHOOL FOR
   GIRLS   C M HAYNES, C R SWARTZ
HARROW   J E POWER, N TIVEY
HARTFORD CHURCH OF ENGLAND HIGH   P W HIGHTON
HARTPURY *Gloucester*   R M C WHEELER
HEATHFIELD *Ascot*   D C CLUES
HIGHGATE *London*   R P S EASTON
HURSTPIERPOINT COLLEGE *Hassocks*   J J N SYKES
IMMANUEL COLLEGE CHURCH OF ENGLAND
   Bradford   S P HACKING
IPSWICH   H J CROMPTON-BATTERSBY
JAMES ALLEN'S GIRLS' *Dulwich*   C SCHNYDER
JCB ACADEMY   E J JONES
KING EDWARD VI *Southampton*   J G POPPLETON
KING EDWARD'S *Bath*   C L O'NEILL
KING EDWARD'S *Witley*   D C STANDEN
KING HENRY VIII *Coventry*   A HOGGER-GADSBY
KING WILLIAM'S COLLEGE *Isle of Man*   E J SCOTT
KINGHAM HILL *Oxfordshire*   A M SAVAGE
KING'S COLLEGE SCHOOL *Wimbledon*   J W CROSSLEY
KING'S COLLEGE *Taunton*   M A SMITH
KING'S *Dublin*   P R CAMPION
KING'S ELY   R A LANE
KING'S *Rochester*   S J PADFIELD
KING'S *Worcester*   M R DORSETT
KING'S, THE *Canterbury*   L R F COLLINS, M C ROBBINS
KOINONIA FEDERATION OF ST MARY MAGDALENE CHURCH
   OF ENGLAND SCHOOL AND CHRIST CHURCH CHURCH
   OF ENGLAND PRIMARY SCHOOL   D G HUBBUCK
LADY MARGARET *Fulham*   C S NEWBOLD
LANCING COLLEGE   R K HARRISON
LICENSED VICTUALLERS' *Ascot*   N J JARVIS
LICHFIELD CATHEDRAL   T R PLANT
LIVERPOOL HOPE   S SHAKESPEARE
LLANDAFF CATHEDRAL   W A DAVID
LONDON DESIGN AND ENGINEERING UNIVERSITY
   TECHNICAL COLLEGE   V J E MCCARTHY
LORETTO *Musselburgh*   P V PARKER
LOUGHBOROUGH SCHOOLS FOUNDATION   E J YORK
MAGDALEN COLLEGE SCHOOL *Oxford*   W W BELL
MAIDWELL HALL   J V J G WATSON

MALVERN COLLEGE D P IBBOTSON
MALVERN ST JAMES GIRLS' SCHOOL K TAPLIN
MANOR *York* M A HAND
MANSHEAD ACADEMY *Luton* T A DAVIS
MARLBOROUGH COLLEGE J H BLOKLAND, D CAMPBELL,
   T W G NOVIS
MERCHANT TAYLORS' *Crosby* D A SMITH
MILL HILL *London* R J WARDEN
MILLFIELD *Somerset* P C A HARBRIDGE
MILTON ABBEY *Dorset* J H DAVIS
MONKTON COMBE *Bath* A G P HUTCHINSON
MONMOUTH C R SWARTZ
MORETON HALL A B STRATFORD
NORTHBOURNE PARK *Deal* D N J HALE
NORWICH C J CHILD
NORWICH UNIVERSITY OF THE ARTS M J YOUNG
OAKHAM T F TREGUNNO
OSWESTRY A D CRANSTON
OUNDLE *Peterborough* M E A COULTER, B J CUNNINGHAM
PANGBOURNE COLLEGE *Berkshire* N G T JEFFERS
PETER SYMONDS COLLEGE *Winchester* N P SEAL
PETERBOROUGH T B SHERRING
PIPERS CORNER M J MEARDON
PITSFORD *Northamptonshire* S TROTT
POCKLINGTON *York* J GOODAIR, W J ROBERTS
PORTSMOUTH GRAMMAR S C HUNT
PREBENDAL *Chichester* I E SMALE
PRESTFELDE *Shrewsbury* A C V ALDOUS
QUAINTON HALL *Harrow* M J STILL
QUEEN ANNE'S *Caversham* R A ROSS
QUEEN MARGARET'S *York* R L OWEN
QUEEN MARY'S *Baldersby Park* P PERCY, G J A WRIGHT
RADLEY COLLEGE *Oxfordshire* P J TAYLOR, D WILSON
REED'S *Cobham* A C WINTER
REIGATE GRAMMAR P M JACKSON
RENDCOMB COLLEGE *Cirencester* R J EDY
REPTON *Derby* N C ROBERTS
RIDDLESWORTH HALL *Norwich* K A HAWKES
RIPLEY ST THOMAS CHURCH OF ENGLAND HIGH
   Lancaster A K WOLTON
RISHWORTH *Ripponden* J S BRADBERRY
ROEDEAN *Brighton* G N RAINEY
ROSSHALL ACADEMY *Glasgow* J F LYON
ROYAL MASONIC FOR GIRLS *Rickmansworth* J S QUILL
ROYAL RUSSELL *Croydon* H L KIRK
ROYAL WOLVERHAMPTON R MAXFIELD
RUGBY R M HORNER
SALFORD CITY ACADEMY A E KAY
SANDWELL *West Bromwich* J A LEACH
SEAFORD COLLEGE *Petworth* C N DATCHLER
SEDBERGH P L SWEETING
SEVENOAKS N N HENSHAW
SHERBORNE GIRLS C E WINDLE
SHIPLAKE *Henley-on-Thames* C R BRIGGS
SHREWSBURY A C V ALDOUS, A F C KEULEMANS
SIR ROBERT WOODARD ACADEMY *Lancing* H J HUGHES
SOLIHULL A C HUTCHINSON
ST ALBANS C D PINES
ST ALBAN'S ACADEMY *Birmingham* G A SYKES
ST ALBANS HIGH SCHOOL FOR
   GIRLS D C FITZGERALD CLARK
ST ANTONY'S LEWESTON *Sherborne* L A MCCREADIE
ST BEDE'S *Cambridge* A N M CLARKE
ST BEDE'S *Reigate* J A PENN
ST CATHERINE'S *Bramley* B G MCNAIR SCOTT
ST CATHERINE'S *Eastbourne* D J GARRATT

ST CECILIA'S WANDSWORTH CHURCH OF
   ENGLAND P A KURK
ST CHAD'S CATHOLIC AND CHURCH OF ENGLAND HIGH
   Runcorn E L SPEAKE
ST COLUMBA'S *Dublin* D J OWEN
ST DAVID'S COLLEGE *Llandudno* T R HALL
ST DUNSTAN'S COLLEGE *Catford* C J L BOSWELL
ST EDMUND'S *Canterbury* M S BENNETT
ST EDWARD'S *Oxford* E A LENNON
ST GABRIEL'S COLLEGE *Camberwell* S D T HARRIES
ST GEORGE'S *Ascot* S A L WATTS
ST GEORGE'S *Gravesend* T OLIVER
ST GEORGE'S *Windsor* J COORE
ST HELEN'S AND ST KATHARINE'S *Abingdon* E A M BIRCH
ST JOHN'S *Leatherhead* C M S MOLONEY
ST LAWRENCE COLLEGE *Ramsgate* A J P GOODWIN-HUDSON
ST MARGARET'S CHURCH OF ENGLAND HIGH *Aigburth,*
   Liverpool K L MILLER
ST MARK'S CHURCH OF ENGLAND ACADEMY
   Mitcham R A BURGE-THOMAS
ST MARY MAGDALENE ACADEMY *London* A I KEECH,
   S C KORN
ST MARYLEBONE CHURCH OF ENGLAND J M NOBLE
ST MARY'S *Calne* J M BEACH
ST MARY'S HALL *Brighton* A H MANSON-BRAILSFORD
ST MARY'S *Shaftesbury* L J LANE
ST MICHAEL'S *Otford* D E REES
ST OLAVE'S GRAMMAR *Orpington* J E BOWEN
ST PAUL'S *Barnes* P L F ALLSOP
ST PAUL'S GIRLS' *Hammersmith* M S KNOX
ST PAUL'S *Hammersmith* M S KNOX
ST PETER'S *Cambridge* C N TWEDDELL
ST PETER'S *York* D A JONES
ST SAVIOUR'S AND ST OLAVE'S *Newington* I E VIBERT
ST SWITHUN'S *Winchester* P WALLINGTON
ST VINCENT *Gosport* C J L J THOMPSON
STAMFORD M A S GOODMAN
STOCKPORT GRAMMAR L E J LEAVER
STOWE *Buckingham* T D MULLINS
TONBRIDGE D A PETERS
TRELOAR COLLEGE *Alton* S GOLDING
TRENT COLLEGE *Nottingham* B C RANDALL
TRINITY AND ALL SAINTS COLLEGE *Leeds* R G BOULTER
TRINITY *Belvedere* A S J HEALY
TRINITY *Carlisle* C J KENNEDY
TRINITY *Lewisham* J A EVANS
TUDOR HALL *Banbury* S M BOURNE, A M RICHARDSON
TWYFORD CHURCH OF ENGLAND HIGH
   Acton D J BRAMMER
UPPINGHAM *Leicestershire* J B J SAUNDERS
WARMINSTER R T AYERS-HARRIS
WARWICK V A M TIMMIS
WELLS CATHEDRAL J E JEPSON
WESTMINSTER G J WILLIAMS
WESTMINSTER CITY G D SWINTON
WESTONBIRT H A MONAGHAN
WHITGIFT *School and House Croydon* F A BAYES
WILLIAM PERKIN CHURCH OF ENGLAND HIGH
   Greenford D J BRAMMER
WILSON'S HOSPITAL *Multyfarnham* H M SCULLY
WINCHESTER COLLEGE S A THORN, J M WHITE
WORKSOP COLLEGE *Nottinghamshire* M R ASKEY
WREKIN COLLEGE *Telford* M J HORTON
WYCLIFFE COLLEGE *Gloucestershire* D A PRESCOTT
WYCOMBE ABBEY *High Wycombe* P J NASH
WYMONDHAM COLLEGE I JONES

THEOLOGICAL EDUCATION INSTITUTIONS

All Saints Centre for Mission and Ministry
113 Aiken Hall, University of Chester, Crab Lane,
Warrington WA2 0BD
T: (01925) 534373 E: info@allsaintscentre.org
W: www.allsaintscentre.org
Prin THE VEN J APPLEGATE

Church of Ireland Theological Institute
Braemor Park, Dublin 14, Republic of Ireland
T: (00353) (1) 492 3506 E: admin@theologicalinstitute.ie
W: www.theologicalinstitute.ie
Dir M J ELLIOTT

College of the Resurrection
Stocks Bank Road, Mirfield WF14 0BW
T: (01924) 490441 E: gjohnson@mirfield.org.uk
W: www.college.mirfield.org.uk
Prin M C R SOWERBY

Cranmer Hall
St John's College, 3 South Bailey, Durham DH1 3RJ
T: 0191-334 3894 E: enquiries@cranmerhall.com
W: www.community.dur.ac.uk/cranmer.hall
Warden P J J PLYMING

Cumbria Christian Learning
Church House, 19-24 Friargate, Penrith CA11 7XR
T: (01768) 807765
E: admin@cumbriachristianlearning.org.uk
W: www.cumbriachristianlearning.org.uk
Dir R HANNAFORD

Eastern Region Ministry Course
1A The Bounds, Lady Margaret Road, Cambridge CB3 0BJ
T: (01223) 760444 E: admin@ermc.cam.ac.uk
W: www.ermc.cam.ac.uk
Prin A S JENSEN

Guildford Local Ministry Programme
Church House, 20 Alan Turing Road, Guildford GU2 7YF
T: (01483) 790319 E: steve.summers@cofeguildford.org.uk
W: www.cofeguildford.org.uk/about/dvm/go-lmp
Prin S B SUMMERS

Lincoln School of Theology
Edward King House, Minster Yard, Lincoln LN2 1PU
T: (01522) 504050 E: sally.myers@lincoln.anglican.org
W: www.lincoln.anglican.org/lincoln-school-of-theology
Prin S A MYERS

Lindisfarne College of Theology
Church House, St John's Terrace, North Shields NE29 6HS
T: 0191-270 4144 E: enquiries@lindisfarnect.org
W: www.lindisfarnect.org
Prin D J BRYAN

Oak Hill College
Chase Side, London N14 4PS
T: (020) 8449 0467 F: 8441 5996 E: reception@oakhill.ac.uk
W: www.oakhill.ac.uk
Pres J S JUCKES

Oxford Local Ministry Programme
Church House Oxford, Langford Locks, Kidlington
OX5 1GF
T: (01865) 208282 E: phil.cooke@oxford.anglican.org
W: www.oxford.anglican.org
Prin P N TOVEY

**The Queen's Foundation for Ecumenical Theological
Education**
Somerset Road, Edgbaston, Birmingham B15 2QH
T: 0121-454 1527 E: enquire@queens.ac.uk
W: www.queens.ac.uk
Prin D J P HEWLETT

Ridley Hall
Ridley Hall Road, Cambridge CB3 9HG
T: (01223) 746580 E: info@ridley.cam.ac.uk
W: www.ridley.cam.ac.uk
Prin M J VOLLAND

Ripon College Cuddesdon, including Cuddesdon,
Portsmouth Pathway, and Cuddesdon: Gloucester and
Hereford
Cuddesdon, Oxford OX44 9EX
T: (01865) 877404 F: 875431 E: enquiries@rcc.ac.uk
W: www.rcc.ac.uk
Prin THE RT REVD H I J SOUTHERN

St Augustine's College of Theology
52 Swan Street, West Malling ME19 6JX
T: (01732) 252656 E: office@staugustinescollege.ac.uk
W: www.staugustinescollege.ac.uk
Prin A P R GREGORY

St Hild College
Stocks Bank Road, Mirfield WF14 0BW
T: (01924) 481925 E: enquiries@sthild.org
W: www.sthild.org
Prin M T POWLEY

St John's College
Chilwell Lane, Bramcote, Nottingham NG9 3DS
T: 0115-925 1114 E: enquiries@stjohns-nottm.ac.uk
W: www.stjohns-nottm.ac.uk
Team Ldr S A NASH

St Mellitus College
St Jude's Church, 24 Collingham Road, London SW5 0LX
T: (020) 7052 0573 E: info@stmellitus.ac.uk
W: www.stmellitus.ac.uk
Dean A N EMERTON

St Padarn's Institute
St Michael's Conference Centre, 54 Cardiff Road, Llandaff,
Cardiff CF5 2YJ
T: (029) 2056 3379 E: info@stmichaels.ac.uk
W: www.stpadarns.ac.uk
Prin J DUFF

St Stephen's House
16 Marston Street, Oxford OX4 1JX
T: (01865) 613500 F: 613513 E: enquiries@ssho.ox.ac.uk
W: www.ssho.ox.ac.uk
Prin R WARD

Sarum College
19 The Close, Salisbury SP1 2EE
T: (01722) 424800 E: info@sarum.ac.uk
W: www.sarum.ac.uk
Prin J W WOODWARD

Scottish Episcopal Institute
21 Grosvenor Crescent, Edinburgh EH12 5EE
T: 0131-243 1347 E: pdo@scotland.anglican.org
W: www.scotland.anglican.org
Prin A L TOMLINSON

South West Ministry Training Course
Riverside Church and Conference Centre,
13–14 Okehampton Street, Exeter EX4 1DU
T: (01392) 272544 E: admin@swmtc.org.uk
W: www.swmtc.org.uk
Jt-Prin J ROWE[1], P J SOURBUT

Trinity College
Stoke Hill, Bristol BS9 1JP
T: 0117-968 2803 E: info@trinitycollegebristol.ac.uk
W: www.trinitycollegebristol.ac.uk
Prin S W DOHERTY

1   Dr Rowe is a lay person.

Westcott House
Jesus Lane, Cambridge CB5 8BP
T: (01223) 741000 E: info@westcott.cam.ac.uk
W: www.westcott.cam.ac.uk
Prin C M CHIVERS

Wycliffe Hall
54 Banbury Road, Oxford OX2 6PW
T: (01865) 274200 F: 274215 E: enquiries@wycliffe.ox.ac.uk
W: www.wycliffe.ox.ac.uk
Prin M F LLOYD

BISHOPS OF ANGLICAN DIOCESES OVERSEAS

AUSTRALIA

PROVINCE OF NEW SOUTH WALES

Armidale	Richard Alexander Lewers PO Box 198, Armidale NSW 2350 T: (0061) (2) 6772 4491 F: (0061) (2) 6772 9261 E: office@armidaleanglicandiocese.com
Bathurst	Ian Stanley Palmer PO Box 23, Bathurst NSW 2795 T: (0061) (2) 6331 1722 F: (0061) (2) 6332 2772 E: registrar@bathurstanglican.org
Canberra and Goulburn	Stuart Peter Robinson GPO Box 1981, Canberra ACT 2601 T: (0061) (2) 6232 3600 F: (0061) (2) 6245 7199 E: trevor.ament@anglicands.org.au
(Assistant)	Matthew Peter Brain address etc as above T: (0061) (2) 6245 7101 E: matt.brain@anglicands.org.au
(Assistant)	Trevor Willam Edwards address etc as above F: (0061) (2) 6232 3650 E: trevor.edwards@anglicancg.org.au
(Assistant)	Stephen Kim Pickard 15 Blackall Street, Barton ACT 2600 T as above E: spickard@csu.edu.au
Grafton	Sarah Anne Macneil PO Box 4, Grafton NSW 2460 T: (0061) (2) 6642 4122 F: (0061) (2) 6643 1814 E: admin@graftondiocese.org.au
Newcastle	Gregory Edwin Thompson PO Box 817, Newcastle NSW 2300 T: (0061) (2) 4926 3733 F: (0061) (2) 4926 1968 E: reception@newcatleanglican.org.au
(Assistant)	Peter Derrick James Stuart address etc as above E: bishoppeter@newcastleanglican.org.au
Riverina	Alan Robert Gillion PO Box 10, Narrandera NSW 2700 T: (0061) (2) 6959 1648 F: (0061) (2) 6959 2903 E: rivdio@bigpond.com
Sydney (Archbishop and Metropolitan)	Glenn Naunton Davies PO Box Q190, QVB Post Office NSW 1230 T: (0061) (2) 9265 1555 F: (0061) (2) 9265 1543 E: archbishop@sydney.anglican.asn.au
(Liverpool)	Peter Robert Lin address as above T/F: (0061) (2) 9823 4244
(North Sydney)	Christopher Edwards address as above T: (0061) (2) 9265 1527 F: (0061) (2) 9265 1543
(South Sydney)	Michael Rennie Stead address etc as above T: (0061) (2) 9265 1530 E: mstead@sydney.anglican.asn.au
(Western Sydney formerly Parramatta)	Ivan Yin Lee PO Box Q190, QVB Post Office NSW 1230 T: (0061) (2) 9265 1574 F: (0061) (2) 9633 3636 E: ilee@sydney.anglican.asn.au

(Wollongong)	Peter Lindsay Hayward 74 Church Street, Wollongong NSW 2500 T: (0061) (2) 4201 1800 F: (0061) (2) 4228 4296 E: phayward@wollongong.anglican.asn.au

PROVINCE OF QUEENSLAND

Brisbane (Archbishop and Metropolitan)	Phillip John Aspinall GPO Box 421, Brisbane QLD 4001 T: (0061) (7) 3835 2218 F: (0061) (7) 3832 5030 E: archbishop@anglicansq.org.au
(Northern Region)	Jonathan Charles Holland address etc as above E: jholland@anglicanchurchsq.org.au
(Southern Region)	Alison Menzies Taylor address etc as above T: (0061) (7) 3835 2213 E: amtaylor@anglicanchurchsq.org.au
(Western Region)	Cameron David Venables Box 2600, Toowoomba QLD 4350 T: (0061) (7) 4639 1875 F: (0061) (7) 4632 6882 E: cvenables@anglicanchurchsq.org.au
North Queensland	William James Ray PO Box 1244, Townsville QLD 4810 T: (0061) (7) 4771 4175 F: (0061) (7) 4721 1756 E: bishopnq@anglicannq.org
Northern Territory, The	Gregory David Anderson PO Box 2950, Darwin NT 0801 T: (0061) (8) 8941 7440 F: (0061) (8) 8941 7446 E: bishop@ntanglican.org.au
Rockhampton	David Alan Robinson PO Box 710, Rockhampton QLD 4702 T/F: (0061) (7) 4927 3188 E: drobinson@anglicanchurchcq.org.au

PROVINCE OF SOUTH AUSTRALIA

Adelaide (Archbishop and Metropolitan)	Geoffrey Martyn Smith 18 King William Road, North Adelaide SA 5006 T: (0061) (8) 8305 9350 F: (0061) (8) 8305 9399
(Assistant)	Timothy Harris address etc as above E: tharris@adelaideanglicans.com
(Assistant)	Christopher William McLeod PO Box 70, Brighton SA 5048 T as above E: cmcleod@adelaideanglicans.com
The Murray	John Frank Ford PO Box 394, Murray Bridge SA 5253 T: (0061) (8) 8532 2270 F: (0061) (8) 8532 5760 E: bishop@murray.anglican.org
Willochra	John Stead PO Box 96, Gladstone SA 5473 T: (0061) (8) 8662 2249 F: (0061) (8) 8662 2027 E: bishop@diowillochra.org.au

PROVINCE OF VICTORIA

Ballarat	Garry John Weatherill PO Box 89, Ballarat VIC 3350 T: (0061) (3) 5331 1183 F: (0061) (3) 5333 2982 E: bishop@ballaratanglican.org.au

Bendigo	Andrew William Curnow AM PO Box 2, Bendigo VIC 3552 T: (0061) (3) 5443 4711 F: (0061) (3) 5441 2173 E: bishop@bendigoanglican.org.au
Gippsland	Kay Maree Goldsworthy PO Box 928, Sale VIC 3853 T: (0061) (3) 5144 2044 F: (0061) (3) 5144 7183 E: bishopkay@gippsanglican.org.au
Melbourne (Archbishop and Primate)	Philip Leslie Freier The Anglican Centre, 209 Flinders Lane, Melbourne VIC 3000 T: (0061) (3) 9653 4220 F: (0061) (3) 9653 4268 E: archbishop@melbourneanglican.org.au
(Eastern Region)	Genieve Mary Blackwell *address etc as above* E: gblackwell@melbourneanglican.org.au
(North-Western Region)	Philip James Huggins *address etc as above* E: bishopphiliphuggins@ melbourneanglican.org.au
(Southern Region)	*vacant* *address etc as above* E: sthregbishop@melbourneanglican.org.au
Wangaratta	Anthony John Parkes PO Box 457, Wangaratta VIC 3676 T: (0061) (3) 5721 3484 F: (0061) (3) 5722 1427 E: bishop@wangaratta-anglican.org.au

PROVINCE OF WESTERN AUSTRALIA

Bunbury	Allan Bowers Ewing PO Box 15, Bunbury WA 6231 T: (0061) (8) 9721 2100 F: (0061) (8) 9791 2300 E: bishop@bunbury.org.au
North West Australia	Gary Neville Nelson PO Box 2783, Geraldton WA 6531 T: (0061) (8) 9921 7277 F: (0061) (8) 9964 2220 E: bishop@anglicandnwa.org
Perth (Archbishop and Metropolitan)	Roger Adrian Herft AM GPO Box W2067, Perth WA 6846 T: (0061) (8) 9325 7455 F: (0061) (8) 9221 4118 E: archbishop@perth.anglican.org
(Assistant)	Katherine Ann Wilmot *address etc as above* E: kwilmot@perth.anglican.org
(Assistant)	Jeremy Noel Robert James *address etc as above* E: jjames@perth.anglican.org

EXTRA-PROVINCIAL DIOCESES

Defence Force (and Bishop Assistant to the Primate)	Ian Keese Lambert Department of Defence, DSG-Duntroon ACT 2600 T: (0061) (2) 9265 9202 F: (0061) (2) 9265 9959 E: ian.lambert1@defence.gov.au
Tasmania	Richard James Condie GPO 748, Hobart TAS 7001 T: (0061) (3) 6220 2015 F: (0061) (3) 6223 8968 E: rcondie@anglicantas.org.au

BRAZIL

Amazon	Marinez Rosa dos Santos Bassotto Avenida Sezerdelo Correia, 514, Batista Campos, Belem - PA, 66025–240 T/F: (0055) (91) 9841 98497 E: marinez.bassotto@gmail.com

Brasília	Maurício José Araújo de Andrade EQS 309/310, sala 1 – Asa Sul, Caixa Postal 093, Brasília - DF, 70359–970 T: (0055) (61) 3443 4305 F: (0055) (61) 3443 4337 E: brasilia2003@gmail.com *or* mandrade@ ieab.org.br
Paraná (formerly Curitiba) (Primate)	Naudal Alves Gomes Rua Sete de Setembro 3927, Centro, Curitiba - PR, 80250-010 T: (0055) (41) 3232 0917 M: (41) 99682-7459 E: naudal@yahoo.com.br *or* naudal321@ gmail.com
Pelotas	Renato da Cruz Raatz Rua Felix da Cunha 425, Centro, Caixa Postal 791, Pelotas - RS, 96001–970 T/F: (0055) (53) 3227 7120 E: renatoraatz@terra.com.br *or* renatoraatz@ bol.com.br *or* rcraatz@ieab.org.br
Recife	João Câncio Peixoto Rua Alfredo de Medeiros 60, Espinheiro, Recife - PE, 52021–030 T: (0055) (81) 3421 1684 E: joao.peixoto1@uol.com.br
Rio De Janeiro	Eduardo Coelho Grillo Rua Fonseca Guimarães 12, Santa Teresa, Rio de Janeiro - RJ, 20240–260 T: (0055) (21) 2220 2148 F: (0055) (21) 2252 9686 M: (21) 99368-0094 E: bispodarj@gmail.com
São Paulo	Flávio Borges Irala Rua Borges Lagoa 172, Vila Clementino, São Paulo - SP, 04038–030 T: (0055) (11) 5549 9086 *or* 5579 9011 F: (0055) (11) 5083 2619 E: flavioirala@ieab.org.br *or* flavioirala@ gmail.com
South Western Brazil	Francisco de Assis da Silva Avenida Rio Branco 880/Sub-solo, Centro, Caixa Postal 116, Santa Maria - RS, 97010–970 T/F: (0055) (55) 3221 4328 E: fassis@ieab.org.bs *or* xicoasilva@gmail. com
Southern Brazil	Humberto Maiztegui Avenida Ludolfo Boehl 278, Baairro Teresópolis, Porto Alegre - RS, 91720–150 T/F: (0055) (51) 3318 6199 E: dmsec@terra.com.br *or* bispohumberto@ ieab.org.br

BURMA see MYANMAR

BURUNDI

Bujumbura	Eraste Bigirimana BP 1300, Bujumbura T: (00257) (22) 249104 E: bigirimanaeraste@yahoo.fr
Buye	Sixbert Macumi BP 94, Ngozi T: (00257) (22) 302210 F: (00257) (22) 302 317 E: buyedioc@yahoo.fr
Gitega	Aimé Joseph Kimararungu BP 23, Gitega T: (00257) (22) 402247 E: eab.diogitega@gmail.com *or* aimejosephk@yahoo.com
Makamba (Archbishop of Burundi)	Martin Blaise Nyaboho BP 96, Makamba T: (00257) (22) 508080 E: eabdiocmak@yahoo.fr
Matana	Seth Ndayirukiye BP 30, Bujumbura T: (00257) (79) 923832 E: canonseth@gmail.com *or* iranezereza14@ gmail.com

Muyinga — Paisible Ndacayisaba
BP 55, Muyinga, Burundi
T: (00257) (79) 700043
E: ndacp@yahoo.com

Rumonge — Pedaculi Birakengana
T: (00257) (79) 970926
E: birakepeda@yahoo.fr

Rutana — Pontien Ribakare
T: (00257) (79) 979619 or (61) 742395
E: diocrutana@gmail.com

CANADA

Primate of Canada — Linda Carol Nicholls
80 Hayden Street, Toronto ON M4Y 3G2
T: (001) (416) 924 9192
F: (001) (416) 924 0211
E: primate@national.anglican.ca

National Indigenous Anglican Bishop — Mark Lawrence MacDonald
address etc as above
E: mmacdonald@national.anglican.ca

British Columbia — Logan McMenamie
900 Vancouver Street, Victoria BC V8V 3V7
T: (001) (250) 386 7781
F: (001) (250) 386 4013
E: bishop@bc.anglican.ca or synod@
bc.anglican.ca

Caledonia — 201–4716 Lazelle Avenue, Terrace BC V8G 1T2
T: (001) (250) 635 6016
F: (001) (250) 635 6026
E: bishopbill@telus.net or caledonia@telus.net

Territory of the People — Barbara J Andrews
360 Nicola Street, Kamloops BC V2C 2P5
T: (001) (778) 471 5573
F: (001) (778) 471 5586
E: apcibishop@shaw.ca or apci@shaw.ca

Kootenay — John Elswood Privett
201–380 Leathead Road, Kelowna BC V1X 2H8
T: (001) (778) 478 8310
F: (001) (778) 478 8314
E: bishop@kootenay.info or admin@
kootenay.info

New Westminster (Archbishop and Metropolitan) — Melissa Maxine Skelton
580–410 West Georgia Street, Vancouver BC V6B 5A1
T: (001) (604) 684 6309
F: (001) (604) 684 7017
E: bishop@vancouver.anglican.ca

Yukon — Larry D Robertson
PO Box 31136, Whitehorse YT Y1A 5P7
T: (001) (867) 667 7746
F: (001) (867) 667 6125
E: synodoffice@klondiker.com

Central Newfoundland — John Watton
34 Fraser Road, Gander NL A1V 2E8
T: (001) (709) 256 2372
F: (001) (709) 256 2396
E: bishopwatton@icloud.com

Eastern Newfoundland and Labrador — Geoffrey Curtis Ralph Peddle
19 King's Bridge Road, St John's NL A1C 3K4
T: (001) (709) 576 6697
F: (001) (709) 576 7122
E: geoffpeddle48@gmail.com or ecrisby@
anglicanenl.net

Fredericton — David Edwards
115 Church Street, Fredericton NB E3B 4C8
T: (001) (506) 459 1801
F: (001) (506) 460 0520
E: edwardsdavid300@gmail.com or
diocese@anglican.nb.ca

Montreal — Mary Irwin-Gibson
1444 Union Avenue, Montreal QC H3A 2B8
T: (001) (514) 843 9443
F: (001) (514) 843 3221
E: bishops.office@montreal.anglican.ca

Nova Scotia and Prince Edward Island (Archbishop and Metropolitan) — Ronald Wayne Cutler
1340 Martello Street, Halifax NS B3H 1X3
T: (001) (902) 420 0717
F: (001) (902) 425 0717
E: rcutler@nspeidiocese.ca or office@
nspeidiocese.ca

Quebec — Bruce Joseph Andrew Myers
31 rue des Jardins, Quebec QC G1R 4L6
T: (001) (418) 692 3858
F: (001) (418) 692 3876
E: bmyers@quebec.anglican.ca

Western Newfoundland — John Organ
25 Main Street, Corner Brook NL A2H 1C2
T: (001) (709) 639 8712
F: (001) (709) 639 1636
E: bishop dsown@nf.aibn.com

Algoma (Archbishop and Metropolitan) — Anne Germond
PO Box 1168, Sault Ste Marie ON P6A 5N7
T: (001) (705) 256 5061
F: (001) (705) 946 1860
E: bishop@dioceseofalgoma.com or
secretary@dioceseofalgoma.com

Huron — Linda Carol Nicholls
190 Queens Avenue, London ON N6A 6H7
T: (001) (519) 434 6893
F: (001) (519) 673 4151
E: bishops@huron.anglican.ca

Moosonee (Moosonee Mission Area) — Anne Germond
135 Adelaide Street East, Toronto ON M5C 1L8
T: (001) (416) 363 6021 ext 250
F: (001) (416) 363 3683
E: cjohnson@toronto.anglican.ca

Niagara — Susan J A Bell
Cathedral Place 252 James Street North, Hamilton ON L8R 2L3
T: (001) (905) 527 1316 ext 129
F: (001) (905) 527 1281
E: bishop@niagara.anglican.ca

Ontario — Michael Douglas Oulton
90 Johnson Street, Kingston ON K7L 1X7
T: (001) (613) 544 4774 ext 129
F: (001) (613) 547 3745
E: moulton@ontario.anglican.ca or synod@
ontario.anglican.ca

Ottawa — John Holland Chapman
71 Bronson Avenue, Ottawa ON K1R 6G6
T: (001) (613) 233 7741
F: (001) (613) 232 3995
E: bishopsoffice@ottawa.anglican.ca

Toronto — Andrew Asbil
135 Adelaide Street East, Toronto ON M5C 1L8
T: (001) (416) 363 6021 ext 250
F: (001) (416) 363 3683

(York-Simcoe) — Peter Decourcy Fenty
PO Box 233, King City ON L3B 1A5
T: (001) (905) 833 8327
F: (001) (905) 833 8329
E: pfenty@toronto.anglican.ca

(Trent-Durham) — Riscylla Walsh Shaw
207–965 Dundas Street West, Whitby ON L1P 1G8
T: (001) (905) 668 1558
F: (001) (905) 668 8216
E: rshaw@toronto.anglican.ca

(York-Scarborough) — Kevin Robertson
135 Adelaide Street East, Toronto ON M5C 1L8
T: (001) (416) 363 6021 ext 253
F: (001) (416) 363 3683
E: krobertson@toronto.anglican.ca

(York-Credit Valley) — Jenny Andison
address etc as above
T: (001) (416) 363 6021 ext 223
F: (001) (416) 363 3683
E: jandison@toronto.anglican.ca

The Arctic	David W Parsons PO Box 190, 4910 51st Street, Yellowknife NT X1A 2N2 T: (001) (867) 873 5432 F: (001) (867) 873 8478 E: arctic@arcticnet.org
(Suffragans)	Joey Royal *address etc as above* Annie Ittoshat *address etc as above* Lucy Netser *address etc as above*
Athabasca	Fraser W Lawton PO Box 6868, Peace River AB T8S 1S6 T: (001) (780) 624 2767 F: (001) (780) 624 2365 E: bpath@telusplanet.net *or* dioath@ telusplanet.net
Brandon	William Cliff 403 13th Street, Brandon MB R7A 4P9 T: (001) (204) 727 7550 F: (001) (204) 727 4135 E: bishop@brandon.anglican.ca *or* info@ brandon.anglican.ca
Calgary (Archbishop and Metropolitan)	Gregory Kerr-Wilson 180, 1209–59th Avenue South-East, Calgary AB T2H 2P6 T: (001) (403) 243 3673 F: (001) (403) 243 2182 E: gkerrwilson@calgary.anglican.ca *or* diocese@calgary.anglican.ca
Indigenous Bishop for Treaty 7 Territory	Sidney Black *address etc as above* E: sidblack@telusplanet.net
Edmonton	Jane Alexander 1035 Street, Edmonton AB T5J 0X5 T: (001) (780) 439 7344 F: (001) (780) 439 6549 E: bishop@edmonton.anglican.ca *or* churched@edmonton.anglican.ca
Keewatin	Diocese exists but has no parishes under its jurisdiction
Mishamikoweesh (Indigenous Spiritual Ministry of)	Lydia Mamakwa PO Box 65, Kingfisher Lake ON P0V 1Z0 T: (001) (807) 532 2085 F: (001) (807) 532 2344 E: lydiam@kingfisherlake.ca
Qu'Appelle	Robert Hardwick 1501 College Avenue, Regina SK S4P 1B8 T: (001) (306) 522 1608 F: (001) (306) 352 6808 E: bishop.rob@sasktel.net
Rupert's Land	Geoffrey Woodcroft 935 Nesbitt Bay, Winnipeg MB R3T 1W6 T: (001) (204) 992 4212 F: (001) (204) 992 4219 E: bishop@rupertsland.ca *or* general@ rupertsland.ca
Saskatchewan	Michael W Hawkins 1308 5th Avenue East, Prince Albert SK S6V 2H7 T: (001) (306) 763 2455 F: (001) (306) 764 5172 E: bishopmichael@sasktel.net *or* synod@ sasktel.net
(Diocesan Indigenous Bishop)	Adam Halkett *address etc as above* E: bishopadam@sasktel.net
Saskatoon	Chris Harper 1403 9th Avenue North, Saskatoon SK S7K 2Z6 T: (001) (306) 244 5651 F: (001) (306) 244 4606

CENTRAL AFRICA

Botswana	Metlhayotlhe Rawlings Beleme PO Box 769, Gaborone, Botswana T: (00267) 395 3779 F: (00267) 395 3015 E: angli diocese@info.bw
Central Zambia	Derek Gary Kamukwamba PO Box 70172, Ndola, Zambia T: (00260) (2) 612431 E: adcznla@zamnet.zm
Central Zimbabwe	Ignatius Makumbe PO Box 25, Gweru, Zimbabwe T: (00263) (54) 221030 F: (00263) (54) 221097 E: diocent@telconet.co.zw
Eastern Zambia	William Muchombo PO Box 510154, Chipata, Zambia T/F: (00260) 21-622 1294 E: dioeastzm@zamnet.zm
Harare	Farai Mutamiri PO Box 981, Harare, Zimbabwe E: mutamiri68@gmail.com
Lake Malawi	Francis Kaulanda PO Box 30349, Lilongwe 3, Malawi T: (00265) (1) 797858 F: (00265) (1) 797548 E: franciskaulanda@yahoo.com
Luapula	Robert Mumbi PO Box 710210, Mansa, Luapula, Zambia T: (00260) (2) 821680 E: diopula@zamtel.zm
Lusaka	David Njovu PO Box 30183, Lusaka, Zambia T: (00260) (1) 254789 F: (00260) (1) 252449 E: bishop@lusakadiocese.org *or* davidnjovu1961@zamnet.zm *or* davidnjovu1961@gmail.com
Manicaland	Erick Ruwona 113 Herbert Chitepo Street, Mutare, Zimbabwe T: (00263) (20) 68418 E: ruwonaerick@gmail.com
Masvingo	Godfrey Tawonezwi PO Box 1421, Masvingo, Zimbabwe T: (00263) (39) 362536 E: bishopgodfreytawonezvi@gmail.com
Matabeleland	Cleophas Lunga PO Box 2422, Bulaweyo, Zimbabwe T: (00263) (9) 61370 F: (00263) (9) 68353 E: clunga@aol.com
Northern Malawi	Fanuel Emmanuel Magangani PO Box 120, Mzuzu, Malawi T: (00265) (1) 312858 E: magangani@sdup.org.mw
Northern Zambia (Archbishop)	Albert Chama PO Box 22137, Kitwe, Zambia T: (00260) (2) 223264 F: (00260) (2) 224778 E: chama albert@yahoo.ca
Southern Malawi	Alinafe Kalemba PO Box 30220, Chichiri, Blantyre, 3, Malawi T: (00265) (1) 641218 F: (00265) (1) 641235 E: dean@sdup.org.mw
Upper Shire	Brighton Vitta Malasa Private Bag 1, Chilema, Zomba, Malawi T: (00265) (1) 539203 E: malasab@yahoo.com.uk

CENTRAL AMERICA

Costa Rica	Orlando Gomez Apartado 2773-1000, San José, Costa Rica T: (00506) 225 0209 E: iarca@me.com

El Salvador — Juan David Alvarado Melgar
47 Avenida Sur, 723 Col Flor Blanca, Apt
Postal (01), 274 San Salvador, El Salvador
T: (00503) 2223 2252
E: anglican.es@gmail.com

Guatemala — Armando Román Guerra-Soria
Apt 58A, Avenida La Castellana 40–06,
Guatemala City, Zona 8, Guatemala
T: (00502) 2472 0852
F: (00502) 2472 0764
E: agepiscopal@yahoo.com

Nicaragua — Sturdie Downs
Apt 1207, Managua, Nicaragua
T: (00505) (2) 222 5174
F: (00505) (2) 254 5248
E: secretaria diocesana@hotmail.com

Panama
(Primate) — Julio Murray Thompson
Box R, Balboa, Republic of Panama
T: (00507) 212 0062 or 507 262 2051
E: bpjuliomurray@hotmail.com

CHILE

Concepción — Enrique Lago Zugadi
Juez Waldo Seguel 560, dept 74, Punta
Arenas, Región de Magallanes y de la
Antártica Chilena, 6200732
T: (0056) (2) 638 3009
E: elago@iach.cl

Santiago
(Primate) — Hector Zavala Muñoz
Victoria Subercaseaux 41, RM Casilla
50675, Correo Central, Santiago, 6200732
T: (0056) (2) 638 3009
F: (0056) (2) 639 4581
E: tzavala@iach.cl

Temuco — Abelino Apeleo Puel
Lazcano 232 Chol Chol, Región Araucanía,
5040156
T: (0056) (2) 638 3009
E: aapeleo@gmail.com

Valparaiso — Samuel Morrison Munro
Los Benedictinos 63, Viña del Mar, Región
de Valparaíso, 2562120
T: (0056) (32) 248 3657
E: smorrison@iach.cl

CONGO (formerly ZAÏRE)

Aru — Georges Titre Ande
PO Box 226, Arua, Uganda
M: (00243) 81-039 3071
E: revdande@yahoo.co.uk

Boga — Mugenyi William Bahemuka
PO Box 25586, Kampala, Uganda
M: (00243) 99-066 8639
E: mugenyiwilliam@yahoo.com

Brazzaville — Molanga Jean Botola
address temp unknown
E: molangab@gmail.com

Bukavu — Sylvestre Bahati
Avenue Pagni No 2, Q/Nyalukemba, C/
Ibanda, Bukavu, Democratic Republic of
the Congo
M: (00243) 99-401 3647
E: bahati bali@yahoo.fr

Goma — Kadhoro Desire Makanirwa
address temp unknown
M: (00243) 99-704 6544
E: rvmukanirwa@yahoo.fr

Kamango — Sabiti Tibafa Daniel
PO Box 25586, Kampala, Uganda
M: (00243) 99-779 1013
E: sabititibafa@gmail.com

Kasai — Marcel Kapinga
No 05 Avenue Makenga, District Bonzola,
Common Dibindi, Mbuji-Mayi, Kasai
Oriental, Democratic Republic of Congo
M: (00243) 81-606 1423
E: anglicanekasai2@gmail.com

Katanga
(formerly Shaba) — Bertin Subi
c/o UMM, PO Box 22037, Kitwe, Zambia
M: (00243) 84-450 0288
E: peacbertinsubi@yahoo.fr

(Assistant) — Lawrence Elisha Tendwa
address as above
M: (00243) 82-462 1849
E: bishopetcongo@gmail.com

Kindu
(Archbishop) — Zacharie Masimango Katanda
Avenue Penemisenga No 4, C/ Kasuku,
Kindu Maniema, Rwanda
M: (00243) 81-328 6255
E: angkindu@yahoo.fr

Kinshasa — Achille Mutshindu
PO Box 16482, Kinshasa 1, Democratic
Republic of Congo
M: (00243) 81-017 6596
E: revasmutsh1@gmail.com

Kisangani — Lambert Funga Botolome
Avenue Bowane No 10, Quartier des
Musiciens, C/Makiso, PO Box 86,
Kisangani, DR Congo or c/o PO Box 25586,
Kampala, Uganda
M: (00243) 99-725 2868
E: lambertfunga@hotmail.com

Nord Kivu — Adolphe Muhindo Isesomo
PO Box 322, Butembo, DR Congo, or PO
Box 25586 Kampala, Uganda
M: (00243) 99-854 8601
E: bishopisesomo@hotmail.com

CEYLON (SRI LANKA)

Colombo — Dhiloraj Ranjit Canagasabey
368/3A Bauddhaloka Mawatha, Colombo
07700, Sri Lanka
T: (0094) (1) 684811
E: anglican@slttalk.net

Kurunegala — Keerthisiri Fernando
Bishop's House, 31 Kandy Road,
Kurunegala, 60000, Sri Lanka
T: (0094) (37) 222 2191
E: bishopkg@sltnet.lk

HONG KONG

Hong Kong
Island
(Archbishop) — Paul Kwong
71 Bonham Road, Hong Kong, China
T: (00852) 2526 5366
F: (00852) 2523 3344
E: do.dhk@hkskh.org

Eastern Kowloon — Timothy Kwok
Diocesan Office, 4/F Holy Trinity Bradbury
Centre, 139 Ma Tau Chung Road, Kowloon
City, Kowloon, Hong Kong, China
T: (00852) 2713 9983
F: (00852) 2711 1609
E: office.dek@hkskh.org

Western
Kowloon — Andrew Chan
Diocesan Office, 11 Pak Po Street,
Mongkok, Kowloon, Hong Kong, China
T: (00852) 2783 0811
F: (00852) 2783 0799
E: dwk@hkskh.org

INDIAN OCEAN

Antananarivo — Samoela Jaona Ranarivelo
Évêché Anglican, Lot VK57 ter,
Ambohimanoro, 101 Antananarivo,
Madagascar
T: (00261) (20) 222 0827
F: (00261) (20) 226 1331
E: eemdanta@yahoo.com

Antsiranana — Théophile Botomazava
Évêché Anglican, BP 278, 4 rue Grandidier,
201 Antsiranana, Madagascar
T: (00261) (20) 822 2776

Fianarantsoa	Gilbert Rateloson Rakotondravelo Évêché due Diocese Fianarantsoa, BP 1418 301 Fianarantsoa, Madagascar T: (00261) (20) 755 1583 M: (00261) (33) 73 06781 E: eemdiofianara@yahoo.fr
Mahajanga	*vacant* Évêché Anglican, BP 570, 401 Mahajanga, Madagascar T: (00261) (62) 23611
Mauritius	Gérald James Ian Ernest Bishop's House, Nallatamby Road, Phoenix, Mauritius T: (00230) 686 5158 F: (00230) 697 1096 E: dioang@intnet.mu
Seychelles (Archbishop)	James Richard Wong Yin Song PO Box 44, Victoria, Mahé, Seychelles T: (00248) 321 977 *or* 323 879 F: (00248) 224 043 M: (00248) (52) 7770 E: angdio@seychelles.net
Toamasina	Jean Paul Solo Évêché Anglican, Lot VK57 ter, Ambohimanoro, 101 Antananarivo, Madagascar T: (00261) (20) 533 1663 F: (00261) (20) 533 1689 M: (00261) (32) 04 55143 E: eemtoam@moov.mg
Toliara	Todd MacGregor Eklesia Episkopaly, Malagasy, BP 408601, Toliara, Madagascar T: (00261) (33) 374 2745

JAPAN

Chubu	Peter Ichiro Shibusawa 28–1 Meigetsu-cho, 2-chome, Showa-ku, Nagoya 466–0034 T: (0081 (52) 858 1007 F: (0081 (52) 858 1008 E: office.chubu@nskk.org
Hokkaido (Primate)	Nathaniel Makoto Uematsu Kita 15 jo, Nishi 5-20, Kita-Ku, Sapporo 001-0015 T: (0081 (11) 717 8181 F: (0081 (11) 736 8377 E: hokkaido@nskk.org
Kita Kanto	Zerubbabel Katsuichi Hirota 2–172 Sakuragi-cho, Omiya-ku, Saitama-shi 331–0852 T: (0081 (48) 642 2680 F: (0081 (48) 648 0358 E: kitakanto@nskk.org
Kobe	Augustine Naoaki Kobayashi 5–11–1 Yamatedori, Chuo-ku, Kobe-shi 650–0011 T: (0081 (78) 351 5469 F: (0081 (78) 382 1095 E: aao52850@syd.odn.ne.jp
Kyoto	Stephen Takashi Kochi 380 Okakuencho, Shimotachiuri-agaru, Karasumadori, Kamikyo-ku, Kyoto 602–8011 T: (0081 (75) 431 7204 F: (0081 (75) 441 4238 E: nskk-kyoto@kvp.biglobe.ne.jp
Kyushu	Luke Ken-ichi Muto 2–9–22 Kusakae, Chuo-ku, Fukuoka 810–0045 T: (0081 (92) 771 2050 F: (0081 (92) 771 9857 E: d-kyushu@ymt.bbiq.jp
Okinawa	David Eisho Uehara 3–5–5 Meada, Urasoe-shi, Okinawa 910-2102 T: (0081 (98) 942 1101 F: (0081 (98) 942 1102 E: office.okinawa@nskk.org

Osaka	Andrew Haruhisa Iso 2–1–8 Matsuzaki-cho, Abeno-ku, Osaka 545–0053 T: (0081 (6) 6621 2179 F: (0081 (6) 6621 3097 E: office.osaka@nskk.org
Tohoku	John Masato Yoshida 2–13–15 Kokubun-cho, Aoba-ku, Sendai 980-0803 T: (0081 (22) 223 2349 F: (0081 (22) 223 2387 E: sec.tohoku@nskk.org
Tokyo	Francis Xavier Hiroyuki Takahashi 3–6–18 Shiba Koen, Minato-ku, Tokyo 105-0011 T: (0081 (3) 3433 0987 F: (0081 (3) 3433 8678 E: general-sec.tko@nskk.org
Yokohama	Ignatius Osamu Irie 14–57 Mitsuzawa Shimo-cho, Kanagawa-ku, Yokohama 221-0852 T: (0081 (45) 321 4988 F: (0081 (45) 321 4978 E: g-sec.yokohama@anglican.jp

JERUSALEM AND THE MIDDLE EAST

Cyprus and the Gulf (Bishop in)	Michael Augustine Owen Lewis PO Box 22075, Nicosia 1517, Cyprus T: (00357) (22) 671220 F: (00357) (22) 674553 E: bishop@spidernet.com.cy
Egypt With North Africa and the Horn of Africa (Bishop in) (Primate)	Mouneer Hanna Anis Diocesan Office, PO Box 87, Zamalek Distribution, 11211, Cairo, Egypt T: (0020) (2) 738 0829 F: (0020) (2) 735 8941 E: bishopmouneer@gmail.com
(Suffragan) (Horn of Africa)	Grant Lemarquand *address etc as above*
Iran (Bishop in)	Azad Marshall St Thomas Center, Raiwind Road, PO Box 688, Lohore, Punjab, 54000, Pakistan T: (0092) (42) 542 0452 E: bishop@saintthomascenter.org
Jerusalem (Bishop in) (Archbishop)	Suheil Dawani St George's Close, PO Box 1278, Jerusalem 91 019, Israel T: (00972) (2) 627 1670 F: (00972) (2) 627 3847 E: bishop@j-diocese.com

KENYA

All Saints Cathedral (Primate)	Jackson Nasoore Ole Sapit PO Box 40502, 00100 Nairobi T: (00254) (20) 714755 F: (00254) (20) 718442 *or* 714750 M: (00254) 734-916358 E: archoffice@ackenya.org
Bondo	David Kodia PO Box 240, 40601 Bondo T: (00254) (33) 520415 E: bishop.kodia@bondoanglican.org
Bungoma	George Wafula Mechumo PO Box 2392, 50200 Bungoma T: (00254) (337) 30481 M: (00254) 726-400718 *or* 733-680921 E: georgemechumo@yahoo.com *or* ackbungomadiocese@yahoo.com
Butere	Timothy Wambunya PO Box 54, 50101 Butere T: (00254) (20) 2447585 F: (00254) (53) 2062785 E: tlwambunya@gmail.combuterediocese@ gmail.com
Eldoret	Chrisopher K Ruto PO Box 3404, 30100 Eldoret T: (00254) (53) 2062785 M: (00254) 710-577545 E: ackeldoret@africaonline.co.ke

Embu
David Muriithi Ireri
PO Box 189, 60100 Embu
T: (00254) (68) 30614
F: (00254) (68) 30468
M: (00254) 728-787403 or 737-126276
E: ackembu@yahoo.com

Kajiado
Gadiel Katanga Lenini
PO Box 203, 01100 Kajiado
T: (00254 (203) 513911
M: (00254) 716-392564 or 715-216610
E: ackajiado@gmail.com

Kapsabet
Paul Korir
PO Box 643, 30300 Kapsabet
M: (00254) 792-711277 or 732-961710
E: info@ackkapsabetdiocese.org

Katakwa
John Okude Omuse
PO Box 68, 50244 Amagoro
T: (00254) (55) 54079
F: (00254) (33) 754017
E: ackatakwa@swiftkenya.com

Kericho
Ernest Kiprotich Ng'eno
PO Box 678, 20200 Kericho
T: (00254) (52) 20112
M: (00254) 717-267442
E: ackkcodioc@yahoo.com

Kirinyaga
Joseph Kibichwa
PO Box 95, 10304 Kutus
T: (00254) (163) 44221
F: (00254) (163) 44020
E: info@ackirinyaga.org

Kitale
Stephen Kewasis Nyorsok
PO Box 4176, 30200 Kitale
T: (00254) (54) 31631
E: ack.ktl@gmail.com

Kitui
Josephat Mule
PO Box 1054, 90200 Kitui
T: (00254) (141) 22682
F: (00254) (41) 22119
E: ac.kitui09@yahoo.com

Machakos
Joseph Mutungi
PO Box 282, 90100 Machakos
T: (00254) (44) 21379
F: (00254) (044) 20178
M: (00254) 704-521061 or 738-981942
E: ackmachakos@gmail.com

Makueni
Francis Mboya Matui
PO Box 532, 90300 Wote
T: (00254) (44) 21379
E: ackmakueni@gmail.com

Malindi
Lawrence Dena
PO Box 6110, 80200 Malindi
M: (00254) 722-536743 or 735-953635
E: dena_larry@yahoo.com or
ackmalindidiocese@gmail.com

Maralal
Jacob A Lesuuda
PO Box 42, 20600 Maralal
M: (00254) 722-693168
E: bishopjlesuuda@gmail.com

Marsabit
Daniel Qampicha
PO Box 51, 60500 Marsabit or c/o MAF
Kenya, PO Box 21123, 00505 Nairobi
M: (00254) 700-319730
E: ackbishopmarsabit@gmail.com

Maseno East
Joshua Owiti
PO Box 31, 40101 Ahero
M: (00254) 714-890166
E: ackmasenoeast@gmail.com

Maseno North
Charles Kaskan Asilutwa
PO Box 416, 50100 Kakemega
E: ackmnorth@jambo.co.ke

Maseno South
Francis Mwayi Abiero
PO Box 114, 40100 Kisumu
T: (00254) (57) 202 5148
F: (00254) (35) 21009
M: (00254) 733-709378 or 722-601110
E: bpfabiero@yahoo.com

Maseno West
Joseph Otieno Wasonga
PO Box 793, 40600 Siaya
M: (00254) 722-280648
E: ack.masenowest@gmail.com

Mbeere
Moses Masamba Nthukah
PO Box 122, 60104 Siakago
M: (00254) 721-423840
E: bishopmbeere@gmail.com or
bishopmbeere@ackdiocesembeere.org

Meru
Charles Mwendwa
PO Box 427, 60200 Meru
M: (00254) 721-270460 or 725-558948
E: ackdmeru@yahoo.com

Mombasa
Alphonce Mwaro Baya
PO Box 80072, 80100 Mombasa
T: (00254) (11) 311105
T: (00254) (11) 227837
E: thinga5153@gmail.com

Mount Kenya Central
Timothy Gichere
PO Box 121, 10200 Murang'a
T: (00254) (60) 203560 or 203559
E: ackmkcentral@wananchi.com

Mount Kenya South
Timothy Ranji
PO Box 886, 00900 Kiambu
T: (00254) (66) 22521
M: (00254) 724-583596 or 735-212414
E: info@ack.mtkenya.org or
ackdiocesemtkenyasouth@gmail.com

Mount Kenya West
Joseph Wasonga
PO Box 793, 40600 Siaya
E: ack.masenowest@gmail.com

Mumias
Joseph Wandera
PO Box 213, 50102 Mumias
T: (00254) (33) 341232
E: ackmumiasdiocese@yahoo.com

Murang'a South
Julius Karanu Wa Gicheru
PO Box 414, 01020 Kenol
M: (00254) 737-436466 or 733-263547
E: ackmurangasouth@gmail.com or
juliuskaranu@yahoo.com

Nairobi
Joel Waweru Mwangi
PO Box 72846, 00200 Nairobi
T: (00254) (20) 444 0524
F: (00254) (20) 226259
M: (00254) 726-610520 or 733-226337
E: bishop@acknairobidiocese.org

Nakuru
Joseph Muchai
PO Box 56, 20100 Nakuru
T: (00254) (37) 212155
F: (00254) (37) 44379
M: (00254) 707-681686 or 729-558423
E: acknkudioc@africaonline.co.ke

(Suffragan - Baringo Area)
Musa Kamuren
address etc as above
E: musakamuren@gmail.com

Nambale
Robert Magina Barasa
PO Box 4, 50409 Nambale
T: (00254) (33) 624040
F: (00254) (33) 624071
M: (00254) 726-592257
E: acknambale@swiftkenya.com or
magina12@yahoo.co.uk

Nyahururu
Stephen Kabora
PO Box 926, 20300 Nyahururu
T: (00254) (65) 2032179
E: nyahudc@gmail.com

Southern Nyanza
James Kenneth Ochiel
PO Box 65, 40300 Homa Bay
T: (00254) (385) 22127
F: (00254) (385) 22056
M: (00254) 721-794968
E: jkochiel@yahoo.com or acksnyanza@
swiftkenya.com

(Suffragan - Kisii Area)
John Orina Omangi
PO Box 121, 40200 Kisii
M: (00254) 725-534047
E: jowamboi@yahoo.com

Taita-Taveta	Liverson Mng'onda PO Box 75, 80300 Voi T: (00254) (43) 203 0096 E: mngodaliv@gmail.com *or* acktaita@ ackenya.org
Thika	Julius Wanyoike PO Box 214, 01000 Thika T: (00254) (15) 121735 F: (00254) (15) 131544 E: info@ackthikadiocese.org

KOREA

Busan	Onesimus Dongsin Park Bishop's Office, 18 Daecheng-dong 2Ga, Jung-Ku, Busan 600-092 T: (0082) (51) 463 5742 F: (0082) (51) 463 5957 E: onesimus63@hanmail.net
Daejeon (Primate)	Moses Nagjun Yoo Bishop's Office, 87-6 Sunhwa 2-dong, Jung-gu, Daejeon 301-823 T: (0082) (42) 256 9988 F: (0082) (42) 255 8918 E: primate.ack@gmail.com
Seoul	Peter Lee Bishop's Office, 16 Sejong-daero 19-gil, Jung-gu, Seoul 100-120 T: (0082) (2) 735 6157 F: (0082) (2) 723 2640

MELANESIA

Banks and Torres	Alfred Patterson Worek PO Box 19, Sola, Vanualava, Torba Province, Vanuatu T: (00678) 540 3401 F: (00678) 38520 E: dobtbishop@gmail.com
Central Melanesia (Primate)	George Takeli PO Box 19, Honiara, Solomon Islands T: (00677) 744 0313 E: g.takeli@comphq.org.sb
Central Solomons	Ben Seka PO Box 52, Tulagia, CIP, Solomon Islands T: (00677) 32042 E: bishopseka@gmail.com
Guadalcanal	Nathan Tome PO Box 19, Honiara, Solomon Islands T: (00677) 23337 E: dbishop@dog.com.sb
Hanuato'o	Alfred Karibongi PO Box 20, Kira Kira, Makira/Ulawa Province, Solomon Islands T: (00677) 747 3816 E: bishophanuatoo@solomon.com.sb
Malaita	Samuel Sahu Bishop's House, PO Box 7, Auki, Malaita Province, Solomon Islands T: (00677) 745 8686 F: (00677) 21098 E: sam.malaita@gmail.com
Temotu	Leonard Dawea PO Box 50, Lata, Santa Cruz, Temotu Province, Solomon Islands T: (00677) 53080 F: (00677) 53092 E: bjdawea@gmail.com
Vanuatu	James Tama Bishop's House, PO Box 238, Luganville, Santo, Vanuatu T: (00678) 37065 F: (00678) 36331 E: tamajames63@gmail.com
Ysabel	Ellison Quity Bishop's House, PO Box 6, Buala, Jejevo, Ysabel Province, Solomon Islands T: (00677) 35034 F: (00677) 35071 E: ellison.jejevo@gmail.com

MEXICO

Cuernavaca	Enrique Treviño Cruz Calle Minerva #1, Fracc Delicias, CP 62330 Cuernavaca, Morelos T: (0052) (777) 315 2870 E: diocesisdecuernavaca@hotmail.com
Mexico	Carlos Touché-Porter San Jerónimo #117, Col San Ángel, Delegación Álvaro Obregón, Mexico City DF 1000 T: (0052) (33) 5616 2205 E: diocesisdemexico@gmail.com
Northern Mexico (Archbishop)	Francisco Manuel Moreno Acatlán 102 Oriente, Col Mitras Centro, Monterrey, Nuevo Leon 64460 T: (0052) (81) 8333 0992 F: (0052) (81) 8348 7362 E: primado@anglicanmx.org
Southeastern Mexico	Benito Juárez-Martínez Avenida de Las Américas #73, Col Aguacatal, Xalapa, Veracruz 91130 T: (0052) (228) 814 6951 E: obispobenito.49@gmail.com
Western Mexico	Ricardo Joel Gómez Osnaya Torres Quintero #15, Col Seattle, Zapopan, Jalisco 45150 T: (0052) (33) 3560 4727 F: (0052) (33) 3560 4726

MYANMAR (BURMA)

Hpa-an	Saw Mark Maung Doe Bishop Kone: Ward 4, Hpa-an, Kayin State M: (0095) 9-3235 2242 E: markmgdoe@gmail.com
Mandalay	David Nyi Nyi Naing Diocesan Office, 22 Pinya Road, Mandalay T: (0095) (2) 34110 M: (0095) 9-4027 84402 E: davidnaing@gmail.com
Myitkyina	John Zau Li 147 Thankin Net Pe Road, Thinda Quarters, Mytikyina, Kachin State M: (0095) 9-4202 76183 E: johnzauli@gmail.com
Sittwe	James Min Dein May Yu Street, Sittwe, Rakhine State M: (0095) 9-4563 82049 E: bishopjamesmindein@gmail.com
Toungoo	Saw John Wilme Diocesan Office, Nat-shin Naung Street, Ward 20, Toungoo M: (0095) 9-566 1187 E: auntysan54@gmail.com
Yangon (Archbishop)	Stephen Than Myint Oo 140, Pyidaungsu Yeiktha Street, PO Box 11191, Yangon F: (0095) (1) 395314 M: (0095) 9-506 3735 E: stephenthan777@gmail.com
(Assistant)	Samuel Htan Oak 44 Bishop Home, Pyay Road, Yangon M: (0095) 97-323 0770 E: sthangoak40@gmail.com

NEW ZEALAND (AOTEAROA, NEW ZEALAND AND POLYNESIA)

Aotearoa (Primate/ Archbishop)	Donald Steven Tamihere PO Box 568, Gisborne 4040, New Zealand T: (0064) (6) 867 8856 F: (0064) (6) 867 8859 M: (0064) 21-240 7527 E: bishop@tairawhiti.org.nz
Auckland	Ross Graham Bay PO Box 37242, Parnell, Auckland 1151, New Zealand T: (0064) (9) 302 7201 F: (0064) (9) 302 7217 E: bishop.office@auckanglican.org.nz

(Assistant)	James Andrew White *address as above* T: (0064) (9) 302 7288 E: jwhite@auckanglican.org.nz
Christchurch	Peter Ruane Carrell PO Box 4438, Christchurch 8140, New Zealand T: (0064) (3) 341 3399 F: (0064) (3) 379 5954 M: (0064) 27-477 2975 E: bishop@anglicanlife.org.nz
Dunedin	Steven Benford PO Box 13170, Green Island, Dunedin 9052, New Zealand T: (0064) (3) 488 0820 F: (0064) (3) 488 2038 E: bishop.steven@calledsouth.org.nz
Nelson	Stephen Maina Mwangi PO Box 100, Nelson 7040, New Zealand T: (0064) (3) 548 3124 F: (0064) (3) 548 2125 M: (0064) 21-242 4737 E: bishopelect@nelsonanglican.nz
Polynesia (Primate/ Archbishop)	Fereimi Cama PO Box 35, Suva, Fiji T: (00679) 330 4716 M: (00679) 976 8766 E: archbishop@dioceseofpolynesia.org
(Suffragan - Tonga)	Afa Vaka *address as above* E: afavaka@yahoo.co.nz
(Suffragan - Viti Levu West)	Gabriel Mahesh Prasad Sharma PO Box 300, Nadi Airport, Nadi, Fiji T: (00679) 670 0582 M: (00679) 927 4829 E: gabsharma@yahoo.com
(Suffragan - Vanua Levu and Taveuni)	Henry Raymond Bull PO Box 61, Dreketi, Macuata, Fiji T: (00679) 731 2043 M: (00679) 931 5573 E: henryrbull@hotmail.com
Te Manawa o Te Wheke	Ngarahu Katene 42B Carter Drive, Rotorua 3015, New Zealand T: (0064) (7) 345 7800 E: bishop@motw.org.nz
Te Tai Tokerau	Te Kitohi Wiremu Pikaahu PO Box 59103, Mangere Bridge, Auckland 2151 T: (0064) (9) 275 7520 M: (0064) 27-473 8931 E: tkwp@xtra.co.nz
Te Tairawhiti	Donald Steven Tamihere (see above)
Te Upoko o Te Ika	Waitohiariki Quayle E: quaylew@xtra.co.nz
Te Waipounamu	Richard Rangi Wallace PO Box 10086, Phillipstown, Christchurch 8145, New Zealand T: (0064) (3) 389 1683 F: (0064) (3) 389 0912 E: reception@waipounamu.org.nz
Waiapu	Andrew William Lindsay Hedge PO Box 227, Napier 4140, New Zealand T: (0064) (6) 835 8230 F: (0064) (6) 835 0680 E: bishopandrew@waiapu.com
Waikato and Taranaki (Primate/ Archbishop)	Philip Richardson PO Box 547, Taranaki Mail Centre, New Plymouth 4340, New Zealand T: (0064) (6) 759 1178 F: (0064) (6) 759 1180 E: bishop@taranakianglican.org.nz
(Suffragan - Waikato)	*vacant* PO Box 21, Hamilton 3240, New Zealand T: (0064) (7) 857 0020 F: (0064) (7) 836 9975 E: bishopspa@waikatoanglican.org.nz

Wellington	Justin Charles Hopkins Duckworth PO Box 12046, Wellington 6144, New Zealand T: (0064) (4) 472 1057 M: (0064) 27-562 5765 E: bishops@wn.ang.org.nz
(Assistant)	Eleanor Ruth Sanderson *address etc as above*

NIGERIA

PROVINCE OF ABA

Arochukwu- Ohafia	Johnson Chibueze Onuoha Bishopscourt, PO Box 193, Arochukwa, Abia State M: (00234) 802-538 6407 E: aroohafia@anglican.ng.org
Ikwuano	Chigozirim U Onyegbule Bishopscourt, PO Box 5, Ahaba-Oloko, Abia State M: (00234) 803-085 9319 E: ikwuano@anglican-nig.org
Isiala Ngwa	Owen Nwankujiobi Azubuike Bishopscourt, St George's Cathedral Compound, PNB 2033, Mbawsi, Abia State M: (00234) 805-467 0528 E: bpowenazubuike@yahoo.com
Isiala Ngwa South (Archbishop elect)	Isaac Nwaobia St Peter's Cathedral Compound, PO Box 15, Owerrinta, Abia State M: (00234) 803-711 9317 E: isialangwasouth@anglican-nig.org
Isiukwuato	Manasses Chijiokem Okere Bishopscourt, PO Box 350, Ovim, Abia State M: (00234) 803-338 6221 E: isiukwuato@anglican-nig.org
Ukwa	Samuel Kelechi Eze PO Box 20468, Aba, Abia State M: (00234) 803-789 2431 E: kelerem53787@yahoo.com
Umuahia (Archbishop)	Ikechi Nwachukwu Nwosu St Stephen's Cathedral Compound, PO Box 96, Umuahia, Abia State T: (00234) (88) 221037 F: (00234) 803-549 9066 E: ik nwosu01@yahoo.com

PROVINCE OF ABUJA

Abuja (Metropolitan and Primate)	Nicholas Dikeriehi Orogodo Okoh Episcopal House, 24 Douala Street, Wuse District, Zone 5, PO Box 212, Abuja, ADCP Garki T: (00234) (56) 580682 E: nickorogodo@yahoo.com
Bida (Missionary diocese)	Jonah Kolo Bishop's House, St John's Mission Compound, PO Box 14, Bida T: (00234) (66) 461694 E: bida@anglican-nig.org
Gboko	Emmanuel Nyitsse
Gwagwalada	Moses Tabwaye Diocesan Headquarters, Secretariat Road, PO Box 287, Gwagwalada, Abuja T: (00234) (9) 882 2083 E: mosestabwaye@yahoo.com
Idah	Joseph N Musa Bishopscourt's, PO Box 25, Idah, Kogi State E: idah@anglican-nig.org
Kafanchan	Marcus M Dogo PO Box 29, Kafanchan, Kaduna State T: (00234) (61) 20634
Kubwa	Duke Timothy Akamisoko Bishop's House, PO Box 67, Kubwa, Abuja FCT, Nigeria M: (00234) 803-451 9437 E: dukesoko@yahoo.com

Kwoi   Paul Samuel Zamani
              Bishop's Residence, Cathedral Compound,
              Samban Gide, PO Box 173, Kwoi, Kaduna
              State
              T: (00234) (80) 651 8160
              E: paulzamani@yahoo.com

Lafia   Godwin A Robinson
              PO Box 560, Lafia, Nasarawa State
              E: gadeyirobins@gmail.com

Makurdi   Nathan Nyitar Inyom
              Bishopscourt, PO Box 1, Makurdi, Benue
              State
              T: (00234) (44) 533349
              F: (00234) 803-614 5319
              E: makurdi@anglican.skannet.com.ng

Otukpo   David K Bello
              Bishopscourt, PO Box 360, Otukpo, Benue
              State
              T: (00234) (803) 309 1778
              E: bishopdkbello@yahoo.com

Zaki-Biam   Benjamin A Vager
              Bishopscourt, PO Box 600, Yam Market
              Road, Zaki-Biam, Benue State
              T: (00234) (803) 676 0018
              E: rubavia@yahoo.com

Zonkwa   Jacob W Kwashi
              Bishop's Residence, PO Box 26, Zonkwa,
              Kaduna State 802002
              T: (00234) (803) 311 0252
              E: zonkwa@anglican-nig.org

PROVINCE OF BENDEL

Akoko Edo   Jolly Oyekpen
              Bishopscourt, PO Box 10, Igarra, Edo State
              M: (00234) 803-470 5941
              E: venjollye@yahoo.com

Asaba   Justus Nnaemeka Mogekwu
              Bishopscourt, PO Box 216, Cable Point,
              Asaba, Delta State
              M: (00234) 802-819 2980
              E: justusmogekwu@yahoo.com

Benin   Peter O J Imasuen
              Bishopscourt, PO Box 82, Benin City, Edo
              State
              T: (00234) (52) 250552

Esan   Friday John Imakhai
(Archbishop) Bishopscourt, Ojoelen, PO Box 921,
              Ekpoma, Edo State
              T: (00234) (55) 981079
              E: bishopimaekhai@hotmail.com

Etsako   Jacob O B Bada
              Bishopscourt, PO Box 11, Jattu, Auchi,
              Edo State

Ikka   Peter Onekpe
              St John's Cathedral, PO Box 1063, Agbor,
              Delta State
              T: (00234) (55) 25014

Ndokwa   David Obiosa
              Bishopscourt, 151 Old Sapele Road,
              Obiaruka, Delta Square
              M: (00234) 803-776 9464
              E: dfao1963@yahoo.com

Oleh   John Usiwoma Aruakpor
              Bishopscourt, PO Box 8, Oleh, Delta State
              T: (00234) (53) 701062
              F: (00234) 802-307 4008
              E: angoleh2000@yahoo.com

Sabongidda-Ora Augustine Ehijimetor Ohilebo
              Bishopscourt, PO Box 13, Sabongidda-Ora,
              Edo State
              T: (00234) (57) 54132
              E: ohileboaugustine143@gmail.com

Sapele   Blessing Erifeta
              Bishopscourt, PO Box 52, Sapele, Delta
              State
              M: (00234) 803-662 4282
              E: dioceseofsapele@yahoo.com

Ughelli   Cyril Odutemu
              Bishopscourt, Ovurodawanre, PO Box 760,
              Ughelli, Delta State
              T: (00234) (53) 600403
              F: (00234) 803-530 7114
              E: ughellianglican@yahoo.com

Warri   Christian Esezi Ideh
              Bishopscourt, 17 Mabiaku Road, GRA, PO
              Box 4571, Warri, Delta State
              T: (00234) (53) 255857
              F: (00234) 805-102 2680
              E: angdioceseofwarri@yahoo.com

Western Izon Edafe Emamezi
              Bishopscourt, PO Box 5, Patani, Delta State
              T: (00234) (822) 056228
              E: anglizon@yahoo.co.uk

PROVINCE OF ENUGU

Abakaliki   Monday C Nkwoagu
              All Saints' Cathedral, PO Box 112,
              Abakaliki, Ebonyi State
              T: (00234) (43) 220762
              E: abakaliki@anglican-nig.org

Afikpo   A Paul Udogu
              Bishop's House, Uwana, PO Box 699,
              Afikpo, Ebonyi State
              E: udogupaul@yahoo.com

Awgu-Aninri   Emmanuel Ugwu
              Bishopscourt, PO Box 305, Awgu, Enugu
              State
              M: (00234) 803-334 9360
              E: afamnonye@yahoo.com

Eha-Amufu   Daniel Olinya
              St Andrew's Cathedral, Bishopscourt, PO
              Box 85, Eh-Amufu, Enugu State
              M: (00234) 803-089 2131
              E: dankol@yahoo.com

Ikwo   Kenneth Ifemene
              Bishop's Residence, Agubia Ikwo, PO Box
              998, Abakaliki, Ebonyi State
              M: (00234) 805-853 4849
              E: bishopikwoanglican.@yahoo.com

Ngbo   Christian I Ebisike
              Bishop's House, PO Box 93, Abakaliki,
              Ebonyi State
              M: (00234) 806-779 4899
              E: vendchris@yahoo.com

Nike   Evans Jonathan Ibeagha
              Bishopscourt, Trans-Ekulu, PO Box 2416,
              Enugu, Enugu State
              M: (00234) 803-324 1387
              E: pnibeagha@yahoo.com

Nsukka   Aloysius Agbo
              St Cypran's Compound, PO Box 516,
              Nsukka, Enugu State
              M: (00234) 803-932 7840
              E: nsukka@anglican-nig.org

Oji River   Amos Amankechinelo Madu
(Archbishop) PO Box 123, Oji River, Enugu State
              M: (00234) 803-670 4888
              E: amosmadu@yahoo.com

Udi   Chioke Augustine Aneke
              Bishopscourt, PO Box 30, Udi, Enugu State
              M: (00234) 806-908 9690
              E: bpchijiokeudi@yahoo.com

PROVINCE OF IBADAN

Ajayi Crowther Olugbenga Oduntan
              Bishopscourt, Iseyin, PO Box 430, Iseyin,
              Oyo State
              M: (00234) 803-719 8182
              E: ajayicrowtherdiocese@yahoo.com

Etiki Kwara   Andrew Ajayi
              M: (00234) 803-470 3522
              E: andajayi@yahoo.com

Ibadan   Joseph O Akinfenwa
(Archbishop) PO Box 3075, Mapo, Ibadan
              T: (00234) (2) 810 1400
              F: (00234) (2) 810 1413
              E: ibadan@anglican.skannet.com.ng

Ibadan North
Segun Okubadejo
Bishopscourt, Moyede, PO Box 28961,
Agodi, Ibadan
T: (00234) (2) 810 7482
E: angibn@skannet.com

Ibadan South
Akintunde Popoola
Bishopscourt, PO Box 166, St David's
Compound, Kudeti, Ibadan
T/F: (00234) (2) 231 9141
E: tpopoola@anglican-nig.org

Ife
Olubunmi A Akinlade
Bishopscourt, PO Box 312, Ife-Ife, Osun
State
T: (00234) (36) 230046
E: olubunmiakinlade@gmail.com

Ife East
Oluseyi Oyelade
Bishop's House, PMB 505, Modakeke-Ife,
Osun State
M: (00234) 802-322 4962
E: seyioyelade@yahoo.com

Ijesa North East
Joseph Alaba Olusola
PO Box 40, Ipetu Ijesha, Ogun State
M: (00234) 803-942 8275
E: bpafsola@gmail.com

Ijesa North
Isaac Oluyamo
Bishopscourt, PO Box 4, Ijebu-Ijesha, Osun
State
M: (00234) 802-344 0333

Ilesa
Samuel Olubayu Sowale
Diocesan Headquarters, Muroko Road, PO
Box 237, Iesha, Osun State
T: (00234) (36) 460138
E: ilesha@anglican-nig.org

Ilesa South West
Samuel Egbebunmi
Bishopscourt, Cathedral of the Holy Trinity,
Imo Ilesa, Osun State
M: (00234) 803-307 1876
E: segbebunmi@yahoo.com

Ogbomoso
vacant
Bishopscourt, St David's Anglican
Cathedral, PO Box 1909, Ogbomosho,
Osun State

Oke-Ogun
Cornelius Adagbada
Bishopscourt, PO Box 30, Saki, Oyo State
M: (00234) 802-323 3365
E: solomonamusan@yahoo.com

Oke-Osun
Abraham Akinlalu
Bishopscourt, PO Box 251, Gbongan, Osun
State
M: (00234) 803-771 7194
E: abrahamakinlalu@yahoo.com

Osun
James Afolabi Popoola
PO Box 285, Osogbo, Osun State
T: (00234) (35) 240325
F: (00232) 803-356 1628
E: folapool@yahoo.com

Osun North East
vacant
Bishopscourt, PO Box 32, Otan Ayegbaju,
Osun State
M: (00234) 803-388 2678
E: bamisebi2002@yahoo.co.uk

Oyo
Williams Oluwarotimi Aladekugbe
Ojogbodu Housing Estate, PO Bos 1020,
Oyo, Oyo State
T: (00234) (38) 240225
F: (00234) 803-857 2120
E: aladewilly2007@gmail.com

PROVINCE OF JOS

Bauchi
Musa Tula
Bishop's House, 2 Hospital Road, PO Box
2450, Bauchi
T: (00234) (77) 546460
E: bauchi@anglican-nig.org

Bukuru
Jwan Zhumbes
Bishopscourt, Plot 31, Citrus Estate,New
Abuja, Plateau State
M: (00234) 803-397 9906
E: jwanbyfaith@yahoo.com

Damaturu
Yohannah A Audu
PO Box 312, Damaturu, Yobe State
E: rt.revdyohaanahaaudu@gmail.com

Gombe
(Primate elect)
Henry C Ndukuba
Cathedral Church of St Peter, PO Box 39,
Gombe
T: (00234) (72) 221212
F: (00234) (72) 221 141
E: gombe@anglican-nig.org

Jalingo
Foreman Nedison
PO Box 4, Magami, Jalingo, Taraba State
E: foremannedison@ymail.com

Jos
(Archbishop)
Benjamin A Kwashi
Bishopscourt, PO Box 6283, Jos, 930001,
Plateau State
T: (00234) (73) 612 2215
E: benkwashi@gmail.com

Langtang
Stanley Fube
87 Solomon Lar Road, PO Box 38,
Langtang, Plateau State
M: (00234) 803-605 8767
E: stanleyfube@gmail.com

Maiduguri
Emmanuel Morris
Bishopscourt, PO Box 1693, Maiduguri,
Borno State
T/F: (00234) (76) 234010
E: bishope-45@yahoo.com

Pankshin
Olumuyiwa Ajayi
Diocesan Secretariat, PO Box 24, Pankshin,
Plateau State
M: (00234) 803-344 7318
E: olumijayi@yahoo.com

Yola
Markus A Ibrahim
PO Box 601, Jimeta-Yola, Adamawa State
T: (00234) (75) 624303
F: (00234) 803-045 7576
E: marcusibrahim2002@yahoo.com

PROVINCE OF KADUNA

Bari
Idris Zubairu
Bishopscourt, Gidan Mato Bari, Kano State
M: (00234) 808-559 7183

Dutse
Markus Yohanna Danbinta
PO Box 67, Yadi, Dutse, Jigawa State
E: danbinta@gmail.com

Gusau
John Garba Danbinta
PO Box 64, Gusau, Zamfara State
T: (00234) (63) 204747
E: gusau@anglican.skannet.com

Ikara
Yusuf Ishaya Janfalan
Bishopscourt, PO Box 23, Ikara, Kaduna
State
M: (00234) 803-679 3865
E: ikara@anglican-nig.org

Kaduna
Timothy Yahaya
PO Box 72, Kaduna
T/F: (00234) 806-594 4694
E: timothyyahaya@yahoo.com

Kano
Zakka Lalle Nyam
Bishopscourt, PO Box 362, Kano
T/F: (00234) (64) 647816
E: kano@anglican.skannet.com.ng

Katsina
Jonathan Bamaiyi
Bishop's Lodge, PO Box 904, Katsina
T: (00234) (65) 432718
M: (00234) 803-601 5584
E: bpjonathanbamaiyi@yahoo.co.uk

Kebbi
(Archbishop)
Edmund E Akanya
Bishop's Residence, PO Box 701, Birnin
Kebbi, Kebbi State
T: (00234) (68) 321179
F: (00234) 803-586 1060
E: eekanya@yahoo.com

Sokoto
Augustine Omole
Bishop's Lodge, 68 Shuni Road, PO Box
3489, Sokoto
T: (00234) (60) 234639
F: (00234) 803-542 3765
E: akin sok@yahoo.com

Wusasa   Ali Buba Lamido
PO Box 28, Wusasa, Zaria, Kaduna State
T: (00234) (69) 334 594
E: lamido2sl@aol.co.uk

Zaria   Abiodun Ogunyemi
Bishopscourt, PO Box 507, Zaria, Kaduna State
T: (00234) (74) 522142
E: abidup2000@yahoo.com

PROVINCE OF KWARA

Igbomina   Emmanuel Adekola
Bishopscourt, PO Box 102, Oro, Kwara State
M: (00234) 803-669 1940
E: adekola4christ@yahoo.com

Igbomina West   Olajide Adebayo
Bishop's House, PO Box 32, Oke Osin,
Kwara State
E: jideadebayo@yahoo.com

Jebba   Timothy Adewole
Bishopscourt, PO Box 2, Jebba, Kwara State
M: (00234) 803-572 5298
E: bishopadewole@yahoo.com

Kwara
(Archbishop)   Olusegun Adeyemi
Bishopscourt, Fate Road, PO Box 1884,
Ilorin, Kwara State
T: (00234) (31) 220879
F: (00234) 803-325 8068
E: bishopolusegun@yahoo.com

New Busa   Israel Amoo
Bishopscourt, PO Box 208, New Bussa,
Niger State
M: (00234) 803-677 3839
E: bishopamoo@yahoo.com

Offa   Akintunde Popoola
Bishop's House, 78–80 Ibrahim Road, PO
Box 21, Offa, Kwara State
M: (00234) 805-925 0011
E: tpopoola@anglican-nig.org

Omu-Aran   Philip Adeyemo
Bishop's House, PO Box 244, Omu-Aran,
Kwara State
M: (00234) 806-592 4891
E: rtrevadeyemo@yahoo.com

PROVINCE OF LAGOS

Awori   Johnson Akinwamide Atere
Bishopscourt, PO Box 10, Ota, Ogun State
M: (00234) 803-553 7284
E: dioceseofawori@yahoo.com

Badagry   Joseph Babatunde Adeyemi
Bishopscourt, PO Box 7, Badagry, Lagos
State
T: (00234) (1) 773 5546
M: (00234) 803-306 4601
E: badagry@anglican-nig.org

Egba   Emmanuel O Adekunle
Bishopscourt, Cathedral of St Peter, PO Box
46, Ile-oluji, Ondo State
E: egba@anglican-nig.org or mowadayo@
yahoo.com

Egba West   Samuel Ajani
Bishopscourt, Oke-Ata Housing Estate, PO
Box 6204, Sapon, Abeokuta
M: (00234) 805-518 4822
E: samuelajani@yahoo.com

Ifo   Nathaniel Oladejo Ogundipe
Bishopscourt, Trinity House KM1, Ibogun
Road, PO Box 104, Ifo, Ogun State
M: (00234) 802-778 4377
E: jaodejide@yahoo.com

Ijebu   Ezekiel Awosoga
Bishopscourt, Ejinrin Road, PO Box 112,
Ijebu-Ode
T: (00234) (37) 432 886
E: ijebu@anglican-nig.org or bishop@
ang-ijebudiocese.com

Ijebu North   Solomon Kuponu
Bishopscourt, Oke-Sopen, Ijebu-Igbo, Ogun
State
M: (00234) 803-741 9372
E: dioceseofijebunorth@yahoo.com

Lagos   Humphery Olumakaiye
29 Marina, PO Box 13, Lagos
T: (00234) (1) 263 6026
E: bamisebi2002@yahoo.co.uk

Lagos Mainland   Babatunde Colenso Akinpelu Johnson
Bishop's House, PO Box 849, Ebute, Lagos
M: (00234) 802-312 7244
E: bcajohnson@yahoo.com

Lagos West   James Olusola Odedeji
Vining House, 3rd Floor, Archbishop
Vining Memorial Cathedral, Oba Akinjobi
Road, GRA Ikeja
T: (00234) (1) 493 7333
F: (00234) (2) 493 7337
E: dioceseoflagoswest@yahoo.com

Remo
(Archbishop)   Michael Olusina Fape
Bishopscourt, Ewusi Street, PO Box 522,
Sagamu, Ogun State
T: (00234) (37) 640598
E: remo@anglican-nig.org

Yewa   Michael Adebayo Oluwarohunbi
Bishopscourt, PO Box 484, Ilaro, Ogun
State
T: (00234) (39) 440695

PROVINCE OF LOKOJA

Doko   Uriah Kolo
PO Box 1513, Bida, Niger State
M: (00234) 803-590 6327
E: uriahkolo@gmail.com

Ijumu   Paul Olarewaju Ojo
Bishopscourt, PO Box 90, Iyara-Ijumi Kogi
State
M: (00234) 807-500 8780
E: efikupolati@yahoo.com

Kabba   Steven Akobe
Bishopscourt, Obara Way, PO Box 62,
Kabba, Kogi State
T: (00234) (58) 300633
F: (00234) 803-471 4759

Kontagora   Jonah Ibrahim
Bishop's House, GPA PO Box 1, Kontagora,
Niger State
M: (00234) 803-625 2032
E: jonahibrahim@yahoo.co.uk

Kutigi   Jeremiah Ndana Kolo
Bishop's House, St John's Mission
Compound, PO Box 14, Bida
M: (00234) 803-625 2032
E: bishopkolo@yahoo.com

Lokoja
(Archbishop)   Emmanuel Sokowamju Egbunu
(Archbishop of the Province of Lokoja)
Bishopscourt
PO Box 11, Bethany, Lokoja, Koji State
T: (00234) (58) 220588
E: emmanuelegbunu@yahoo.co.uk

Minna   Daniel Abu Yisa
Bishopscourt, Dutsen Kura, PO Box 2469,
Minna
M: (00234) 803-588 6552
E: danyisa2007@yahoo.com

Ogori-Magongo   Festus Davies
Bishop's House, St Peter's Cathedral, Ogori,
Kogi State
M: (00234) 803-451 0378
E: fessyoladiran@yahoo.com

Okene   Emmanuel Onsachi
Bishopscourt, PO Box 43, Okene, Kogi State
M: (00234) 803-700 0016
E: okenediocese@yahoo.com

PROVINCE OF THE NIGER

Aguata
(Archbishop)
Christian Ogochukwu Efobi
Bishopscourt, PO Box 1128, Ekwulobia,
Anambra State
M: (00234) 803-750 1077
E: christianefobi@yahoo.com

Amichi
Ephraim Ikeakor
Bishopscourt, PO Box 13, Amichi, Anambra
State
M: (00234) 803-317 0916
E: eoikeakor@yahoo.com

Awka
Alexander Ibezim
Bishopscourt, PO Box 130, Awka, Anambra
State
T: (00234) (48) 550058
E: chioma1560@aol.com

Enugu
(Archbishop)
Emmanuel O Chukwuma
Bishop's House, PO Box 418, Enugu, Enugu
State
T: (00234) (42) 453804
F: (00234) (42) 259 808
E: enugu@anglican-nig.org

Ihiala
Ralph Okafor
Bishopscourt, St Silas Cathedral, PO Box 11,
Ihiala, Anambra State
M: (00234) 803-711 2408
E: raphoka@yahoo.com

Mbamili
Henry Okeke
Bishopscourt, PO Box 2653, Onitsha,
Anambra State
M: (00234) 803-644 9780
E: bishopokeke@yahoo.com

Niger West
Johnson Ekwe
Bishop's House, Anambra, Anambra State
M: (00234) 803-384 3339

Nnewi
Godwin Izundu Nmezinwa Okpala
Bishopscourt, PO Box 2630, Uruagu-Nnewi,
Anambra State
F: (00234) (46) 462676
M: (00234) 803-348 5714
E: okpalagodwin@yahoo.co.uk

Ogbaru
vacant
Bishopscourt, PO Box 46, Atani, Anambra
State
M: (00234) 803-721 7876
E: info@ogbaruanglicandiocese.org

On the Niger
Owen Chidozie Nwokolo
Bishopscourt, Ozala Road, Onitsha,
Anambra State
M: (00234) 803-726 0548
E: owenelsie@yahoo.com

PROVINCE OF NIGER DELTA

Aba
Bishopscourt, 70–72 St Michael's Road, PO
Box 212, Aba, Abia State
T: (00234) (82) 227666
E: aba@anglican-nig.org

Aba Ngwa North
Nathan C Kanu
Bishopscourt, All Saints Cathedral,
Abayi-Umuocham 1610165, Owerri Road,
PO Box 43, Aba, Abia State
M: (00234) 803-822 4623
E: odinathnfe@sbcglobal.net

Ahoada
Clement Nathan Ekpeye
Bishopscourt, St Paul's Cathedral, PO Box 4,
Ahoada East L.G.A., Rivers State
M: (00234) 806-356 6242
E: ahoada@anglican-nig.org

Calabar
Tunde Adeleye
Bishopscourt, PO Box 74, Calabar, Cross
River State
T: (00234) (87) 232812
F: (00234) (88) 220835
E: calabar@anglican-nig.org

Enugu North
Sosthenes Eze
Bishopscourt, St Mary's Cathedral,
Ngwo-Enugu
M: (00234) 803-870 9362
E: bishopsieze@yahoo.com

Etche
Precious Nwala
Bishopscourt, PO Box 89, Okehi, Etche
Rivers State
M: (00234) 807-525 2842
E: etchediocese@yahoo.com *or*
precious model5@yahoo.com

Evo
Innocent Ordu
Bishopscourt, PO Box 3576, Port Harcourt,
Rivers State
M: (00234) 803-715 2706
E: innocent-ordu@yahoo.com

Ikwerre
Blessing Enyindah
Bishopscourt, St Peter's Cathedral, PO Box
14229, Port Harcourt, Rivers State
M: (00234) 802-321 2824
E: blessingenyindah@yahoo.com

Niger Delta
Ralph Ebirien
PO Box 115, Port Harcourt, Rivers State
M: (00234) 708-427 9095
E: revpalph ebirien@yahoo.com

**Niger Delta
North**
(Archbishop)
Ignatius Crosby Ogborun Kattey
PO Box 53, Diobu, Port Harcourt, Rivers
State
M: (00234) 803-309 4331
E: bishopicokattey@yahoo.com

Niger Delta West
Emmanuel O Oko-Jaja
Bishopscourt, PO Box 10, Yenagoa, Bayelsa
State
M: (00234) 803-870 2099
E: niger-delta-west@anglican-nig.org

Northern Izon
Victor Agberam
Bishopscourt, PO Box 705, Yenagoa,
Bayelsa State
M: (00234) 803-316 0938
E: fred nyanabo@yahoo.co.uk

Ogbia
James Oruwori
Bishop's House, 10 Queens Street, Ogbia
Town, Bayelsea State
E: jaoruwori@yahoo.com

Ogoni
Solomon S Gberegbara
Bishopscourt, PO Box 73, Bori-Ogoni,
Rivers State
M: (00234) 803-339 2545
E: ogoni@anglican-nig.org

Okrika
Tubokosemie Atere
Bishopscourt, PO Box 11, Okrika, Rivers
State
M: (00234) 803-312 5226
E: dioceseofokrika@yahoo.com

Uyo
Prince Asuko Antai
Bishopscourt, PO Box 70, Uyo, Akwa Ibom
State
M: (00234) 802-916 2305
E: uyo@anglican-nig.org

PROVINCE OF ONDO

Akoko
(Archbishop)
Gabriel Akinbiyi
PO Box 572, Ikare-Akoko, Ondo State
T: (0031) (31) 801011
E: bishopgabrielakinbiyi@yahoo.com

Akure
Simeon O Borokini
Bishopscourt, PO Box 1622, Akure, Ondo
State
T/F: (00234) (34) 241572

**Diocese on the
Coast** (formerly
Ikale-Ilaje)
Joshua Ebunoluwa Ogunele
Bishopscourt, Ikoya Road, PMB 3,
Ilutitun-Osooro, Ondo State
M: (00234) 803-467 1879
E: joshuaonthecoast@yahoo.ca

Ekiti
(Archbishop
elect)
Christopher Omotunde
Bishopscourt, PO Box 12, Okesa St,
Ado-Ekiti, Ekiti State
T: (00234) (30) 250305
E: adedayoekiti@yahoo.com

Ekiti-Oke
Isaac O Olubowale
Bishopscourt, PO Box 207, Usi-Ekiti, Ekiti
State
M: (00234) 803-600 9582
E: ekitioke@anglican-nig.org

Ekiti West

Rufus Adepoju
Bishop's Residence, 6 Ifaki St, PO Box 477,
Ijero-Ekiti
T: (00234) (30) 850314
E: ekitiwest@anglican-nig.org

Idoani

Ezekiel Dahunsi
Bishopscourt, PO Box 100 Idoani, Ondo
State
M: (00234) 803-384 4029
E: bolaezek@yahoo.com

Ilaje

Fredrick Olugbemi
Bishopscourt, PO Box 146, Igbokoda, Ondo
State
M: (00234) 806-624 8662
E: forogbemi@yahoo.com

Ile-Oluji

Samson Adekunle
Bishopscourt, Cathedral of St Peter, PO Box
46, Ile-Oluji, Ondo State
M: (00234) 803-454 1236
E: adkulesamson86@yahoo.co.uk

Irele-Eseodo

Felix O Akinbuluma
Bishopscourt, Sabomi Road, Ode Irele,
Ondo State
F: (00234) 803-472 1813
M: (00234) 805-671 2653
E: felixgoke@yahoo.com

Ondo

Stephen Oni
Bishopscourt, College Rd, PO Box 265,
Ondo
T: (00234) (34) 610718
E: ondoanglican@yahoo.co.uk

Owo

Stephen Ayodeji Akinwale Fagbemi
Bishopscourt, PO Box 472, Owo, Ondo
State
F: (00234) 803-475 4291
M: (00234) 803-695 6811
E: saaf95@hotmail.com

PROVINCE OF OWERRI

Egbu

Geoffrey E Okorafor
All Saints' Cathedral, PO Box 1967, Owerri,
Imo State
T: (00234) (83) 231797
E: egbu@anglican-nig.org

Ideato
(Archbishop)

Caleb A Maduomo
Bishopscourt, PO Box 2, Ndizuogu, Imo
State
M: (00234) 803-745 4503
E: bpomacal@hotmail.com

Ikeduru

Emmanuel C Maduwike
Bishop's House, PO Box 56, Atta, Imo State
M: (00234) 803-704 4686
E: emmamaduwike@yahoo.com

Mbaise

Chamberlain Chinedu Ogunedo
Bishopscourt, PO Box 10, Ife, Ezinihitte
Mbaise, Imo State
M: (00234) 803-336 9836
E: ogunedochi@yahoo.com

Ohaji-Egbema

Chidi Collins Oparaojiaku
Bishop's House, PO box 8026, New Owerri,
Imo State
M: (00234) 803-312 1063
E: chidioparachiaku@yahoo.com

Okigwe

Edward Osuegbu
Bishopscourt, PO Box 156, Okigwe, Imo
State
M: (00234) 803-724 6374
E: edchuc@justice.com

Okigwe North

Godson Udochukwu Ukanwa
PO Box 127, Anara, Imo State
M: (00234) 803-672 4314
E: venukanwa@yahoo.com

Okigwe South

David Onuoha
Bishopscourt, Ezeoke Nsu, PO Box 235,
Nsu, Ehime Mbano LGA, Imo State
M: (00234) 803-672 4314
E: okisouth@yahoo.com

On the Lake

Chijioke Oti
Bishopscourt, PO Box 36, Oguta, Imo State,
Nigeria
M: (00234) 802-788 8738
E: chijiokeoti72@yahoo.com

Orlu

Bennett C I Okoro
Bishopscourt, PO Box 260, Nkwerre, Imo
State
T: (00234) (82) 440538
E: anglicannaorlu@yahoo.com

Oru

Geoffrey Chukwunenye
PO Box 91, Mgbidi, Imo State
M: (00234) 803-308 1270
E: geoinlagos@yahoo.com

Owerri

Cyril C Chukwunonyerem Okorocha
Bishop's Bourne, PMB 1063, Owerri, Imo
State
T: (00234) (83) 230784
F: (00234) 803-338 9344
E: owerri anglican@yahoo.com

PAPUA NEW GUINEA

Archbishop

Allan Rirme Migi
PO Box 673, Lae, Morobe Province, 411
E: archbishopmigi95@gmail.com

Aipo Rongo

Nathan Ingen
PO Box 893, Mt Hagen, Western Highlands
Province
T: (00675) 542 1131
F: (00675) 542 1181
E: bishopnathan2@gmail.com

Dogura

Tennyson Bogar
PO Box 19, Dogura via Alotau, Milne Bay
Province
T: (00675) 641 1530
F: (00675) 983 5120
E: tennysonbogar.tb@gmail.com

New Guinea
Islands

vacant
Bishop's House, PO Box 806, Kimbe, West
New Britain Province
T/F: (00675) 983 5120
E: AllanRirmeMigi@gmail.com

Popondota

Lindsley Ihove
Bishop's House, PO Box 26, Popondetta,
Oro Province
T: (00675) 629 7194
F: (00675) 629 7476
E: bplindsleyihove@gmail.com

Port Moresby

Denny Bray Guka
PO Box 6491, Boroko, NCD
T: (00675) 323 2489
F: (00675) 323 2493
E: acpngpom@global.net.pg

THE PHILIPPINES

Prime Bishop

Joel Atiwag Pachao
PO Box 10321, Broadway Centrum, 1112
Quezon City
T: (0063) (2) 722 8481
F: (0063) (2) 721 1923
E: ecpnational@yahoo.com.ph

Central
Philippines

Dixie Copanut Taclobao
281 E. Rodriguez Sr Ave, 1102 Quezon City
T: (0063) (2) 412 8561
F: (0063) (2) 724 2143
E: taclobaodixie@yahoo.com.ph

Davao

Jonathan Labasan Casimina
Km. 3 McArthur Highway, Matina, Davao
City 8000
T: (0063) (82) 299 1511
F: (0063) (82) 296 9629
E: episcopaldioceseofdavao@yahoo.com

North Central
Philippines

Nestor Dagas Poltic
358 Magsaysay Ave, 2600 Baguio City
T: (0063) (74) 443 7705
E: wanding43@yahoo.com

Northern Luzon	Hilary Ayban Pasikan Bulanao, 3800 Tabuk City, Kalinga M: (0063) (29) 083 345503 E: junpasikan@yahoo.com
Northern Philippines	Brent Harry W Alawas 2616 Bontoc, Mountain Province T/F: (0063) (74) 602 1026 E: ednpbrent@yahoo.com
Santiago	Alexander A Wandag Maharlika Highway, 3311 Divisoria Santiago City, Isabela T: (0063) (78) 662 1561 E: alexanderwandag@rocketmail.com
Southern Philippines	Danilo Labacanacruz Bustamante 186 Sinsuat Ave, 9600 Cotabato City T: (0063) (64) 421 2960 F: (0063) (64) 421 1703 E: edsp_ecp@yahoo.com

RWANDA

Butare	Nathan Gasatura BP 225, Butare T: (00250) 30710 F: (00250) 30504 E: nathangasatura@gmail.com
Byumba	Emmanuel Ngendahayo BP 17, Byumba T/F: (00250) 64242 E: engendahayo@gmail.com
Cyangugu	Nathan Amooti Rusengo BP 52, Cyangugu T: (00250) 788 409 061 E: nathanamooti@gmail.com
Gahini	Alexis Bilindabagabo BP 22, Kigali T: (00250) 67422 F: (00250) 77831 E: abilindabagabo@gmail.com
Gasabo	Onesphore Rwaje PO Box 2487, Kigali, Rwanda T/F: (00250) 64242 E: onesphorerwaje@yahoo.fr
Kibungo	Emmanuel Ntazinda EER Kibungo Diocese, BP 719, Kibungo T/F: (00250) 566194 E: emmanuelntazinda@ymail.com
Kigali	Louis A Muvunyi EER/DK, BP 61, Kigali T: (00250) 576340 E: louismuvunyi@hotmail.com
Kigeme	Assiel Musabyimana BP 67, Gikongoro T: (00250) 535086 E: dkigemeear@yahoo.fr
Kivu	Augustin Ahimana BP 166 Gisenyi T: (00250) 788 350 119 E: aamurekezi@gmail.com
Shyira (Archbishop)	Laurent Mbanda EER Shyira Diocese, BP 52, Ruhengeri T: (00250) 46602 F: (00250) 546449 E: mbandalaurent@gmail.com
Shyogwe	Jéred Kalimba BP 27, Gitarama T: (00250) 62372 F: (00250) 62460 E: kalimbaj60@yahoo.fr

SOUTH AMERICA

Argentina (Presiding Bishop)	Gregory James Venables 25 de Mayo 282, Capital Federal, Buenos Aires 1001, Argentina T: (0054) (11) 4342 4618 F: (0054) (11) 4784 1277 E: diocesisanglicue@fibertel.cam.ar

Bolivia	Raphael Samuel Iglesia Anglicana Episcopal de Bolivia, Casilla 848 Cochabamba, Bolivia T/F: (00591) (4) 440 1168 E: raphaelsamuel@gmail.com
Northern Argentina	Nicholas James Quested Drayson Iglesia Anglicana, Casilla 187, Salta 4400, Argentina T: (0054) (387) 431 1718 F: (0054) (371) 142 0100 E: nicobispo@gmail.com
Paraguay	Peter John Henry Bartlett Iglesia Anglicana de Paraguaya, Casilla de Correo 1124, Asunción, Paraguay T: (00595) (21) 200933 F: (00595) (21) 214 328 E: peterparaguay@gmail.com
Peru	Jorge Luis Aguilar Calle Doña María 141, Los Rosales, Surco, Lima 33, Peru T: (0051) (1) 449 0600 E: cocosac59@hotmail.com
(Suffragan)	*vacant* *address etc as above*
Uruguay	*vacant* Reconquista 522, Montevideo 11000, Uruguay 11300 T: (00598) (2) 915 9627 F: (00598) (2) 916 2519 E: iglesiaau@gmail.com

SOUTH EAST ASIA

Kuching	Danald Jute Bishop's House, PO Box 347, 93704 Kuching, Sarawak, Malaysia T: (0060) (82) 240187 F: (0060) (82) 426488 E: bpofkuching@gmail.com
(Assistant)	Nelson Ugas Bulang *address etc as above*
Sabah	Melter Jiki Tais PO Box 10811, 88809 Kota Kinabalu, Sabah, Malaysia T: (0060) (88) 245846 F: (0060) (88) 261422 E: uskupmjtais@gmail.com
(Assistant)	John Yeo 201, Jalan Dunlop, 91000 Tawau T: (0060) (89) 772212 F: (0060) (89) 761451 E: ad.johnyeo@gmail.com
Singapore	Rennis Ponniah St Andrew's Village, No 1, Francis Thomas Drive, #01–01, Singapore 359340 T: (0065) (62) 887585 F: (0065) (62) 885574 E: rennis@anglican.org.sg
(Assistant)	Low Jee King St Andrew's Village, No 1, Francis Thomas Drive, #01–01, Singapore 359340 T: (0065) (62) 888944 *F as above* E: lowjeeking@gmail.com
West Malaysia (Archbishop and Primate)	Datuk Ng Moon Hing No 214 Jalan Pahang, 53000 Kuala Lumpur, Malaysia T: (0060) (3) 4024 3213 F: (0060) (3) 4032 3225 E: canonmoon@gmail.com
(Suffragan)	Jason Selvaraj Christ Church, 48, Jalan Gereja, 75000 Melaka, Malaysia T/F: (0060) (62) 848804 E: jasondaphne101@gmail.com

(Suffragan)   Charles K Samuel
St George's Church, 1 Lebuh Farquhar,
10200 Penang, Malaysia
T: (0060) (64) 261 2739
F: (0060) (64) 264 2292
E: vencan.cs@gmail.com

SOUTH SUDAN

PROVINCE OF AMADI

Lui
(Archbishop)   Stephen Dokolo Ismail Mbalah
PO Box 110, Juba, South Sudan
E: stephen.dokolo@gmail.com

Mundri   Bismark Monday Avokaya Azumu
PO Box 110, Juba, South Sudan
T: (00211) 621 974 812
E: bismarkavokaya@gmail.com

Wandi   Yohanas Benjamin Dirar
PO Box 110, Juba, South Sudan
T: (00211) 922 367 367
E: bishopyohana@gmail.com

Yeri   John Abraham Nyari
PO Box 110, Juba, South Sudan
E: yeridioceses@gmail.com

PROVINCE OF CENTRAL EQUATORIA

Kajo Keji   Emmanuel Murye Modi
PO Box 110, Juba, South Sudan
E: bishopkk@gmail.com

Lainya   Eliaba Lako Obede
PO Box 110, Juba, South Sudan
E: eliabalakoobed@gmail.com

Liwolo Area   Joseph Aba Nicanor
PO Box 110, Juba, South Sudan
T: (00256) 779 018 110
E: josephabaduduka@yahoo.co.uk

Lomega
(Archbishop)   Paul Benjamin Yugusuk
PO Box 110, Juba, South Sudan
E: ce archbishop@southsudan.anglican.org

Morobo   James Kenyi Elia
PO Box 110, Juba, South Sudan
T: (00211) 924 302 412
E: lonjorokonimejames@gmail.com

Mundu Area
(Suffragan)   Samuel Lomue Eluzai
PO Box 110, Juba, South Sudan
T: (00211) 927 506 419
E: samuellomude2017@gmail.com

Panyana Area
(Suffragan)   Seme Nigo Abinda
PO Box 110, Juba, South Sudan
T: (00211) 922 198 181
E: bp.nigoabiuda@gmail.com

Rejaf   Edward Oliver Mathew Tombe
PO Box 110, Juba, South Sudan
T: (00249) (811) 20040
F: (00249) (183) 20065
E: bishop@rejaf.anglican.org

Rokon   Francis Loyo Mori
PO Box 110, Juba, South Sudan
T: (00211) 928 122 065
E: bployo@yahoo.co.uk

Terekeka   Paul Modi Farjala
PO Box 110, Juba, South Sudan
E: modipaul5@gmail.com

Wondurba   Matthew Taban Peter
PO Box 110, Juba, South Sudan
E: bplmatthewpeter@gmail.com

Yei   Hilary Adeba Luate
PO Box 110, Juba, South Sudan
E: hill shepherd@yahoo.com

PROVINCE OF EASTERN BAHR EL GHAZAL

Akot   Isaac Dhieu Ater
PO Box 110, Juba, South Sudan
T: (00211) 928 122 065
E: cholk2002@yahoo.com

Aluakluak   Isaac Nyaryiel Aleth
c/o ECS, PO Box 110, Lakes State, South
Sudan
T: (00211) 923 045 451
E: aluakluakdiocese@gmail.com

Awerial   David Akau Kuol Mayom
PO Box 110, Juba, South Sudan
T: (00211) 955 526 396
E: bpkuol2@gmail.com

Cueibet   Elijah Matueny Awet
PO Box 110, Juba, South Sudan
T: (00211) 926 572 471
E: elijahawet@yahoo.com

Malek Rup   Peter Marial Agok
PO Box 110, Juba, South Sudan
E: petermarial@gmail.com

Maper   William Mading Machar
PO Box 110, Juba, South Sudan
T: (00211) 926 164 875
E: williammading@hotmail.com

Nyang   Paul Tokmach Lual
PO Box 110, Juba, South Sudan
T: (0011) 927 285 141
E: nyangdiocese@gmail.com

Pacong   Joseph Maker Atot
PO Box 110, Juba, South Sudan
E: ecs.pacongdiocese@yahoo.com

Rumbek
(Archbishop)   Alapayo Manyang Kuctiel
PO Box 110, Juba, South Sudan
E: alapayo.kuctiel@gmail.com

(Assistant)   Elizabeth Awut Ngor
address etc as above

Wulu   Zacharia Mangar Apeti
PO Box 110, Juba, South Sudan
T: (00211) 922 214 010
E: zecheriamangar@gmail.com

Yirol   David Akau
c/o ECS, PO Box 110, Lakes State, South
Sudan
E: ecsyiroldiocese@yahoo.com

PROVINCE OF EASTERN EQUATORIA

Kapoeta   Isaac Deu Chol
PO Box 110, Juba, South Sudan
T: (00211) 928 263 770
E: isaacdue@gmail.com

Magwi   Ogeno Charles Opoka
PO Box 110, Juba, South Sudan
T: (00211) 925 852 729
E: charles.ogeno@yahoo.com

Nimule Area   Martin Abuni
PO Box 110, Juba, South Sudan
T: (00211) 921 230 455
E: lowiraa@gmail.com

Torit
(Archbishop)   Bernard Oringa Balmoi
PO Box 110, Juba, South Sudan
T: (00211) 927 542 597
E: bishop@torit.anglican.org

(Assistant -
Kapoeta Area)   Isaac Deu Chon

PROVINCE OF JONGLEI

Akobo   John Jock Chol
PO Box 110, Juba, South Sudan
T: (00211) 923 226 583
E: johnchol45@gmail.com

Attooch   Moses Anur Ayom
PO Box 110, Juba, South Sudan
T: (00211) 91 489 017
E: mosesanurayom@yahoo.com

Ayod   Thomas Tut Gany
PO Box 110, Juba, South Sudan
T: (00211) 915 888 555
E: tutgany@gmail.com

Bor
(Archbishop)   Ruben Akurdid Ngong
PO Box 110, Juba, South Sudan
T: (00211) 926 572 471
E: archjip2008@gmail.com

Duk   Daniel Deng Abot
PO Box 110, Juba, South Sudan
E: danieldengabot@gmail.com

Kongor   Gabriel Thuch Agot
PO Box 110, Juba, South Sudan
T: (00211) 955 225 139
E: agothgabriel@gmail.com

Malek   Peter Joh Abraham Mayom
PO Box 110, Juba, South Sudan
E: malekdiocese@gmail.com

Twik East   Ezekiel Diing Ajang Malangdit
PO Box 110, Juba, South Sudan
T: (00211) 955 682 118
E: malangajang@gmail.com

Wanglei Area   Zechariah Mayok Biar
(Suffragan)   PO Box 110, Juba, South Sudan
T: (00211) 915 616 361
E: manyok34@gmail.com

Wernyol   Gabriel Kuol Garang
PO Box 110, Juba, South Sudan
T: (00211) 916 071 671
E: bishopk2016@gmail.com

PROVINCE OF JUBA

Juba   Justin Badi Arama
(Primate)   c/o ECS, PO Box 7576, Kampala, Uganda
T: (00211) 920 010 066
E: archbishop@southsudan.anglican.org

(Assistant)   Fraser Yugu Elias
PO Box 110, Juba, South Sudan
T: (00211) 956 143 577
E: bishopyugu@gmail.com

PROVINCE OF NORTHERN BAHR EL GHAZAL

Abyei   Michael Deng K Bol
PO Box 110, Juba, South Sudan
T: (00211) 924 444 810
E: abyeianglicanchurch@hotmail.com

Aweil   Abraham Yel Nhial
PO Box 110, Juba, South Sudan
T: (00211) 955 621 584
E: yelnhial@gmail.com

Gogrial   Abraham Ngor Mangong
PO Box 110, Juba, South Sudan
T: (00211) 912 777 077
E: abrahamngor4@gmail.com

Tonj   Peter Yuol Gur
PO Box 110, Juba, South Sudan
T: (00211) 925 788 054
E: tonjmission2@gmail.com

Wau   Moses Deng Bol
(Archbishop of   PO Box 110, Juba, South Sudan
Northern Bahr El   E: mosesdengbol@gmail.com
Ghazal)

PROVINCE OF UPPER NILE

Maiwut Area   Peter Gatbel Kunen Lual
PO Box 110, Juba, South Sudan
T: (00211) 916 287 184
E: pgkunen2014@gmail.com

Malakal   Hilary Garang Deng
(Archbishop)   PO Box 110, Juba, South Sudan
T: (00211) 913 333 333
E: hdengawer@gmail.com

(Assistant -   John Gattek
Bentiu Area)   PO Box 114, Malakal, South Sudan
T: (00211) 921 023 690
E: bishop@bentiu.anglican.org

(Assistant - Nasir   Peter Gatbel Kunen
Area)   *address as above*
E: pgkunen2014@gmail.com

Nasir   Simon Lual Bang Jal
PO Box 110, Juba, South Sudan
T: (00211) 954 173 739
E: mothernyaod@gmail.com

Panrieng   David Kiir Mayath
PO Box 110, Juba, South Sudan
T: (00211) 911 167 362
E: dkiir12@gmail.com

Renk   Joseph Garang Atem
PO Box 110, Juba, South Sudan
E: josephatem@gmail.com

PROVINCE OF WESTERN EQUATORIA

Ezo   John Kereboro Zawo
PO Box 110, Juba, South Sudan
T: (00211) 818 593 217
E: bishop@ezo.anglican.org

Maridi   Wilson Elias Kamani
PO Box 110, Juba, South Sudan
T: (00211) 926 102 922
E: bishopkamani@gmail.com

Nzara   Samuel Peni Enosa
(Archbishop)   PO Box 110, Juba, South Sudan
E: sam.enosa@gmail.com

Olo   Tandema Obede
PO Box 110, Juba, South Sudan
E: bishop.olo@maridi.anglican.org

Yambio   Peter Munde Yacoub
PO Box 110, Juba, South Sudan
T: (00211) 925 567 704
E: bishop@yambio.anglican.org

SOUTHERN AFRICA

Angola   Andre Soares
(Missionary   Av Lenini, Travessa D Antonia Saldanha N
Diocese)   134, CP 10 341, Luanda, Angola
T: (00244) (2) 395 792
F: (00244) (2) 396 794
E: anglicanangola@yahoo.com *or*
bispo-Soares@hotmail.com

Cape Town   Thabo Makgoba
(Archbishop and   20 Bishopscourt Drive, Bishopscourt,
Primate)   Claremont, Cape Town, 7708 South Africa
T: (0027) (21) 763 1300
F: (0027) (21) 797 1298 *or* 761 4193
E: archpa@anglicanchurchsa.org.za

(Suffragan -   Garth Counsell
Table Bay)   PO Box 1932, Cape Town, 8000 South
Africa
T: (0027) (21) 469 3760
F: (0027) (21) 465 1571
E: tablebay@ctdiocese.org.za *or*
bishopsuffragan@ctdiocese.org.za

Christ the King   William Mostert
PO Box 1653, Rosettenville, 2130 South
Africa
T: (0027) (11) 435 0097
F: (0027) (11) 435 2868
E: bishop@ctkdiocese.co.za

False Bay   Margaret Brenda Vertue
PO Box 2804, Somerset West, 7129 South
Africa
T: (0027) (21) 852 5243
F: (0027) (21) 852 9430
E: bishopm@falsebaydiocese.org.za

Free State   Dintoe Stephen Letloenyane
(formerly   PO Box 411, Bloemfontein, 9300 South
Bloemfontein)   Africa
T: (0027) (51) 447 6053
F: (0027) (51) 447 5874
E: bishopdintoe@dsc.co.za

George   Brian Melvyn Marajh
PO Box 227, George, 6530 South Africa
T/F: (0027) (44) 873 5680
E: bishopbrian@georgediocese.org.za

Grahamstown   Ebenezer St Mark Ntlali
PO Box 181, Grahamstown, 6140 South
Africa
T: (0027) (46) 636 1996
F: (0027) (46) 622 5231
E: bishop@grahamstowndiocese.org.za

Highveld   Mthetheleli Charles May
PO Box 17462, Benoni West, 1503 South
Africa
T: (0027) (11) 422 2231
F: (0027) (11) 420 1336
E: bishophveld@iafrica.com

Johannesburg	Stephen Mosimanegape Moreo PO Box 39, Westhoven, Gauteng, 2142South Africa T: (0027) (11) 375 2700 F: (0027) (11) 486 1015 E: steve.moreo@anglicanjoburg.org.za	Pretoria	Allan John Kannemeyer 802 Pretorius Street, Arcadia 0083, PO Box 1032, Pretoria, 0001 South Africa T: (0027) (12) 430 2345 F: (0027) (12) 430 2224 E: ptabish@dioceseofpretoria.org
Kimberley and Kuruman	Oswald Peter Patrick Swartz PO Box 45, Kimberley, 8300 South Africa T: (0027) (53) 833 2433 F: (0027) (53) 831 2730 E: oppswartz@onetel.com or Kkdiocese. bishop@telkomsa.net	Saldanha Bay	Raphael Bernard Viburt Hess PO Box 420, Malmesbury, 7299 South Africa T: (0027) (22) 487 3885 F: (0027) (22) 487 3886 E: bishop@dioceseofsaldanhabay.org.za or lizel@dioceseofsaldanhabay.org.za
Lebombo	Carlos Simão Matsinhe CP 120, Maputo, Mozambique T: (00258) (1) 405 885 F: (00258) (1) 401 093 E: carlosmatsinhe@rocketmail.com	St Helena	*vacant* PO Box 62, Island of St Helena, South Atlantic T: (00290) 4471 F: (00290) 4728
Lesotho	Adam Andrease Mallane Taaso PO Box 87, Maseru 100, Lesotho T: (00266) (22) 311 974 F: (00266) (22) 310 161 E: dioceselesotho@ecoweb.co.ls	St Mark the Evangelist	Martin Andre Breytenbach PO Box 643, Polokwane, 0700 South Africa T: (0027) (15) 297 3297 F: (0027) (15) 297 0408 E: martin@stmark.org.za
Matlosane (formerly Klerksdorp)	Stephen Molopi Diseko PO Box 11417, Klerksdorp, 2570 South Africa T: (0027) (18) 464 2260 F: (0027) (18) 462 4939 E: bishopstephen@diocesematlosane.co.za or mikeomoipinmoye@yahoo.com	Swaziland	Ellinah Ntfombi Wamukoya Bishop's House, Muir Street, Mbabane, Swaziland T: (00268) 404 3624 F: (00268) 404 6759 E: bishopen@swazilanddiocese.org.sz
Mbashe	Elliot Sebenzile Williams PO Box 1184, Butterworth, 4960 South Africa T: (0027) (47) 491 8030 F: (0027) (43) 740 4766 E: dioceseofmbhashe@telkomsa.net	Ukhahlamba	Moses Madywabe PO Box 1673, Queenstown, Eastern Cape, 116 South Africa T: (0027) (45) 838 3261 F: (0027) (45) 838 2874
Mpumalanga	Daniel Malasela Kgomosotho PO Box 4327, White River, 1240 South Africa T: (0027) (13) 751 1960 F: (0027) (13) 751 3638 E: diompu@telkomsa.net	Umzimvubu	Sitembele Mzamane PO Box 25, Umtata, Transkei, 5100 South Africa T: (0027) (47) 532 4450 F: (0027) (47) 532 4191 E: anglicbspmthatha@intekom.co.za
Mthatha (formerly St John's)	Hummingfield Charles Nkosinathi Ndwandwe PO Box 25, Umtata, Transkei, 5100 South Africa T: (0027) (47) 532 4450 F: (0027) (47) 532 4191 E: anglicbspmthatha@intekom.co.za	Zululand	*vacant* PO Box 147, Eshowe, 3815 South Africa T/F: (0027) 354 742 047 E: bishopsec@netactive.co.za
			SUDAN
Namibia	Luke Lungile Pato PO Box 57, Windhoek, Namibia T: (00264) (61) 238 920 F: (00264) (61) 225 903 E: bishop@anglicanchurchnamibia.com	El-Obeid	Ismail Gabriel Abudigin PO Box 211, El Obeid, Sudan T: (00211) 967 247 262 E: bishop@elobeid.anglican.org
Nampula	Manuel Ernesto CP 264, Lichinga, Niassa, Mozambique T/F: (00258) 712 0735 E: mernesto.diocese.niassa@gmail.com	Kadugli and Nuba Mountains	Andudu Adam Einail PO Box 35, Kadugli, Sudan T/F: (00249) (63) 182 2898 E: bishop@kadugli.anglican.org
Natal	*vacant* PO Box 47439, Greyville, 4023 South Africa T: (0027) (31) 309 2066 F: (0027) (31) 308 9316 E: bishop@dionatal.org.za	(Assistant)	Hassan Osman *address etc as above* E: hassan.ojamis@gmail.com
(North West)	Tsietse Edward Seleoane PO Box 463, Ladysmith, 3370 South Africa T: (0027) (36) 631 4650 F: (0027) 86 547 1882 E: bishopseleoane@dionatal.org.za	Khartoum (Archbishop)	Ezekiel Kondo PO Box 65, Omdurman, 35 Khartoum, Sudan T: (00249) 912 359 768 E: bishop@khartoum.anglican.org
Niassa	Vicente Msossa CP 264, Lichinga, Niassa, Mozambique T/F: (00258) 712 0735 E: bishop.niassa@gmail.com	Port Sudan	Abdu Elnur Kodi PO Box 278, Red Sea State, Sudan T: (00249) (31) 21224 E: bunukaa@live.com
		Wad Medani	Saman Farajalla Mahdi awaiting details E: bishop@wadmedani.anglican.org
Port Elizabeth	Edward Ronald Daniels PO Box 7109, Newton Park, 6055 South Africa E: bishop@pediocese.org.za		**TANZANIA**
		Biharamulo	Yusuph Vithalis PO Box 15, Biharamulo, Kagera E: vithalisyusuph@yahoo.com

Central Tanganyika
Dickson Chilongani
PO Box 15, Dodoma
T: (00255) (26) 232 1714
F: (00255) (26) 232 4518
E: chilongani@anglican.or.tz

Dar Es Salaam
Valentino Mokiwa
PO Box 25016, Ilala, Dar-es-Salaam
T: (00255) (22) 286 4426
E: mokiwa–valentine@hotmail.com

Kagera
Aaron Kijanjali
PO Box 18, Ngara
T: (00255) (28) 222 3624
F: (00255) (28) 222 2518
E: dkagera@googlemail.com

Kibondo
Sospeter Ndenza
PO Box 15, Kibondo
T: (00255) (75) 469 6846
E: sndenzas@yahoo.co.uk

Kiteto
Isaiah Chambala
PO Box 74, Kibaya, Kiteto
T: (00255) (27) 255 2106
E: bishopofkiteto@yahoo.com

Kondoa
Given Gaula
PO Box 7, Kondoa
T: (00255) (26) 236 0312
F: (00255) (26) 236 0304 or 0324
E: givenmgaula@gmail.com

Lake Rukwa
Mathayo Kasagara
PO Box 14, Mpanda
E: kasagarajr@gmail.com

Lweru
Jackton Yeremiah Lugumira
PO Box 12, Muleba
T: (00255) (713) 274 085
E: jact@bukobaonline.com

Mara
George Okoth
PO Box 131, Musoma
T: (00255) (28) 262 2376
F: (00255) (28) 262 2414

Masasi
James Almasi
Private Bag, PO Masasi, Mtwara
T: (00255) (23) 251 0016
F: (00255) (23) 251 0351
E: jamesalmasi@yahoo.com

Morogoro
Godfrey Sehaba
PO Box 320, Morogoro
T/F: (00255) (23) 260 4602
E: bishopgsehaba@gmail.com

Mount Kilimanjaro
Stanley Elilekia Hotay
PO Box 1057, Arusha
T: (00255) (27) 254 8396
F: (00255) (27) 254 4187
E: hotaystanley@yahoo.com

Mpwapwa (Archbishop)
Jacob Erasto Chimeledya
PO Box 2, Mpwapwa
T: (00255) (26) 232 0017 or 0825
F: (00255) (26) 232 0063
E: jacobchimeledya@hotmail.com

Newala
Oscar Mnung'a
PO Box 92, Newala
T: (00255) (78) 233 8822
E: rtrevonewala@gmail.com

Rift Valley
John Lupaa
PO Box 16, Manyoni
T: (00255) (26) 254 0013
F: (00255) (26) 250 3014
E: act-drv@maf.or.tz

Rorya
John Adiema
PO Box 38, Musoma
T: (00255) (75) 289 3957

Ruaha
Joseph Mgomi
PO Box 1028, Iringa
T: (00255) (26) 270 1211
F: (00255) (26) 270 2479
E: actruaha@gmail.com

Ruvuma
Raphael Haule
PO Box 1357, Songea, Ruvuma
T: (00255) (25) 260 0090
F: (00255) (25) 260 2987
bishopactruvuma@gmail.com

Shinyanga
Charles Kija Ngusa
PO Box 421, Shinyanga
T: (00255) (25) 276 3584
E: cknqusa@yahoo.com

South West Tanganyika
Matthew Mhagama
PO Box 32, Njombe
T: (00255) (26) 278 2010
F: (00255) (26) 278 2403
E: dswt@africaonline.co.tz

Southern Highlands
John Mwela
PO Box 198, Mbeya
M: (00255) 754 266 668
E: mwelajohn@yahoo.co.uk

Tabora
Elias Chakupewa
PO Box 1408, Tabora
T: (00255) (26) 260 4124
F: (00255) (26) 260 4899
E: chakupewalucy@yahoo.com

Tanga
Maimbo Mndolwa
PO Box 35, Korogwe, Tanga
T: (00255) (27) 264 0631
F: (00255) (27) 264 0568
E: imba612@yahoo.com

Tarime
Mwita Akiri
PO Box 410, Tarime
T: (00255) (78) 817 7400
E: bishop.tarime@gmail.com

Victoria Nyanza
Boniface Kwangu
PO Box 278, Mwanza
T: (00255) (28) 250 0627
F: (00255) (28) 250 0676
E: bandmkwangu@yahoo.co.uk

Western Tanganyika
Sadock Makaya
PO Box 13, Kasulu
T: (00255) (28) 281 0321
F: (00255) (28) 281 0706
E: smakaya1@yahoo.co.uk

Zanzibar
Michael Hafidh
PO Box 5, Mkunazini, Zanzibar
T: (00255) (24) 223 5348
F: (00255) (24) 223 6772
E: mhhafidh@gmail.com or anglicanrorya@yahoo.com

UGANDA

Ankole
Sheldon Mwesigwa
PO Box 14, Mbarara, Ankole
T: (00256) 787 084 301
E: ruharu@utiouline.co.ug

Bukedi
Samuel Egesa
PO Box 170, Tororo
M: (00256) 772 542 164
E: bukedidiocese@yahoo.com

Bunyoro-Kitara
Nathan Kyamanywa
PO Box 20, Hoima
T: (00256) 464 40128
M: (00256) 776 648 232
E: nathan.kyamanywa@gmail.com

Busoga
Michael Kyomya
PO Box 1568, Jinja
F: (00256) 432 0547
M: (00256) 752 649 102
E: busogadiocese@gmail.com

Central Buganda
Jackson Matovu
PO Box 1200, Kinoni-Gomba, Mpigi
F: (00256) 772 242 742
M: (00256) 772 475 640
E: mapetoruvusi@yahoo.com

Central Busoga
Patrick Wakula
awaiting details
T: (00256) 782 510 482

East Ruwenzori	Edward Bamucwanira PO Box 1439, Kamwenge T: (00256) 772 906 236 E: edward_bamu@yahoo.com
Kampala (Archbishop)	Stanley Ntagali PO Box 335, Kampala T: (00256) 414 279 218 F: (00256) 414 251 925 E: abpcou@gmail.com
(Assistant)	Hannington Mutebi *address as above* T: (00256) 414 290 231 F: (00256) 414 342 601 E: mutebihanning@yahoo.com
Karamoja	Joseph Abura PO Box 44, Moroto T: (00256) 782 658 502 E: loukomoru@gmail.com
Kigezi	George Bagamuhunda PO Box 3, Kabale T: (00256) 772 450 019 F: (00256) 486 22802 E: bishopkigezi@infocom.co.ug
Kinkizi	Dan Zoreka PO Box 77, Kanungu M: (00256) 772 507 163 E: zorekadan@yahoo.com
Kitgum	Stanley Ntagali PO Box 187, Kitgum M: (00256) 772 959 924 E: abpcou@gmail.com
Kumi	Thomas Edison Irigei PO Box 18, Kumi M: (00256) 772 659 460 E: kumimothersunion@yahoo.com
Lango	John Charles Odurkami PO Box 6, Lira M: (00256) 772 614 000 E: bishoplango@yahoo.com
Luwero	Eridard Kironde Nsubuga PO Box 125, Luwero M: (00256) 772 349 669 E: eridard.nsugua@gmail.com
Madi and West Nile	Charles Collins Andaku PO Box 370, Arua M: (00256) 772 382 324 E: andakucollins@gmail.com
Masindi-Kitara	George Kasangaki PO Box 515, Masindi T: (00256) 772 618 822 E: georgewakasa@gmail.com
Mbale	Patrick Gidudu Bishop's House, PO Box 473, Mbale T: (00256) 453 3533 M: (00256) 782 625 619 E: patrickhgidudu@yahoo.com
Mityana	Stephen Samuel Kaziimba PO Box 102, Mityana T: (00256) 772 512 175 E: sakazimba@yahoo.com
Muhabura	Cranmer Mugisha PO Box 22, Kisoro F: (00256) 486 30059 M: (00256) 712 195 891 E: cranhopmu@yahoo.co.uk
Mukono	William James Ssebaggala PO Box 39, Mukono T: (00256) 41 290 229 M: (00256) 712 860 742 E: Jamesebagala@yahoo.co.uk
Namirembe	Wilberforce Kityo Luwalira PO Box 14297, Kampala T: (00256) 414 271 682 M: (00256) 712 942 161 E: omulabirizi@gmail.com

Nebbi	Alphonse Watho-kudi PO Box 27, Nebbi M: (00256) 772 650 032 E: bpalphonse@ekk.org
North Ankole	Stephen Namanya c/o PO Box 14, Rushere-Kiruhura M: (00256) 772 622 116 E: nadsrushere@yahoo.com
North Karamoja	James Nasak PO Box 26, Kotido T: (00256) 772 660 228 E: jnasak@yahoo.com
North Kigezi	Patrick Tugume-Tusingwire PO Box 23, Rukungiri T: (00256) 777 912 010 E: earfchairman@yahoo.com
North Mbale	Samuel Gidudu PO Box 2357, Mbale T: (00256) 782 853 094 F: (00256) 752 655 225 E: revsamgidudu@yahoo.com
Northern Uganda	Johnson Gakumba PO Box 232, Gulu M: (00256) 772 601 421 E: johnson.gakumba@gmail.com
Northwest Ankole	Amos Magezi awaiting details T: (00256) 772 525 856 E: amosmagezi@gmail.com
Ruwenzori	Reuben Kisembo Bishop's House, PO Box 37, Fort Portal T: (00256) 772 838 193 E: reubenkisembo@gmail.com
Sebei	Paul Kiptoo Masaba PO Box 23, Kapchorwa M: (00256) 772 312 502 E: repkmasaba@yahoo.co.uk
Soroti	George Erwau PO Box 107, Soroti M: (00256) 772 565 607 E: georgeerwau@yahoo.com
South Ankole	Nathan Ahimbisibwe PO Box 39, Ntungamo T: (00256) 772 660 636 E: revnathan2000@yahoo.com
South Rwenzori	Jackson Nzerebende Tembo PO Box 142, Kasese F: (00256) 483 44450 M: (00256) 772 713 736 E: srdiocese@gmail.com
West Ankole	Yona Katoneene PO Box 140, Bushenyi M: (00256) 752 377 192 E: yona.katoneene@yahoo.com
West Buganda	Jackson Matovu PO Box 242, Masaka M: (00256) 772 475 640 E: mapetoruvusi@yahoo.com
West Lango	Alfred Acur Okodi awaiting details T: (00256) 772 523 153

UNITED STATES OF AMERICA

Presiding Bishop	Michael Bruce Curry Episcopal Church Center, 815 Second Avenue, New York NY 10017, USA T: (001) (212) 716 6000 E: sjones@episcopalchurch.org
(Office of Pastoral Development)	Frank Clayton Matthews 2857 Trent Road, New Bern NC 28562, USA T: (001) (252) 635 5004
(Bishop Suffragan for Armed Services and Federal Ministries)	Carl Walter Wright 3504 Woodley Road NW, Washington DC 20016, USA T: (001) (646) 434 0275

Alabama (IV)
John McKee Sloan
Carpenter House, 521 N 20th Street,
Birmingham AL 35203–2611, USA
T: (001) (205) 715 2060
F: (001) (205) 715 2066
E: ksloan@dioala.org

Alaska (VIII)
Mark A Lattime
1205 Denali Way, Fairbanks, Alaska
99701–4137, USA
T: (001) (907) 452 3040
F: (001) (907) 456 6552
E: mlattime@gci.net

Albany (II)
William Howard Love
580 Burton Road, Greenwich NY 12834,
USA
T: (001) (518) 962 3350
F: (001) (518) 692 3352
E: bishoplove@albanydiocese.org

Arizona (VIII)
Jennifer Reddall
114 West Roosevelt Street, Phoenix AZ
85003–1406, USA
T: (001) (602) 254 0976
F: (001) (602) 495 6603
E: bishopelect@azdiocese.org

Arkansas (VII)
Larry R Benfield
310 West 17th Street, Little Rock AR
72216–4668, USA
T: (001) (501) 372 2168
F: (001) (501) 372 2147
E: bishopbenfield@mac.com

Atlanta (IV)
Robert Christopher Wright
2744 Peachtree Road, Atlanta GA 30305,
USA
T: (001) (404) 601 5320
F: (001) (404) 601 5330
E: bishopwright@episcopalatlanta.org

Bethlehem (III)
Kevin Donnelly Nichols
333 Wyandotte Street, Bethlehem PA
18015–1527, USA
T: (001) (610) 691 5655
F: (001) (610) 691 1682
E: kevin@diobeth.org

California (VIII)
Marc Handley Andrus
1055 Taylor Street, San Francisco CA 94108,
USA
T: (001) (415) 673 5015
F: (001) (415) 673 9268
E: bishopmarc@diocal.org

Central Ecuador (IX)
Victor Alfonso Scantlebury
Diocesan Office, Calle El tiempo no
37-189y, El Comercio El Batan, Quito,
Ecuador
T: (00593) (2) 245 6948
F: (00593) (02) 227 1627
E: obispo846vas@aol.com

Central Florida (IV)
Gregory Orrin Brewer
Diocesan Office, 1017 E Robinson Street,
Orlando FL 32801, USA
T: (001) (407) 423 3567
F: (001) (407) 872 0006
E: bpbrewer@cfdiocese.org

Central Gulf Coast (IV)
James Russell Kendrick
201 North Baylen Street, Pensacola FL
32502, USA
T: (001) (850) 434 7337
F: (001) (850) 434 8577
E: bishopkendrick@diocgc.org

Central New York (II)
DeDe Duncan-Probe
1020 7th North Street, Suite 200, Liverpool,
NY, 13088-6192
T: (001) (315) 474 6596
F: (001) (315) 478 1632
E: bishop@cnyepiscopal.org

Central Pennsylvania (III)
Audrey Scanlan
101 Pine Street, Harrisburg PA 17101, USA
T: (001) (717) 236 5959
F: (001) (717) 236 6448
E: ascanlan@diocesecpa.org

Chicago (V)
Jeffrey Dean Lee
65 East Huron Street, Chicago IL 60611,
USA
T: (001) (312) 751 4200
F: (001) (312) 787 4534
E: bishop@episcopalchicago.org

Colombia (IX)
Francisco José Duque-Gomez
Cra 6 no 49–85 Piso 2, Bogotá DC,
Colombia
T: (0057) (1) 288 3167
F: (0057) (1) 288 3248
E: obispoduque@hotmail.com

Colorado (VI)
Kimberly Danielle Lucas
1300 Washington Street, Denver CO 80203,
USA
T: (001) (303) 837 1173
F: (001) (303) 837 1311
E: bishopkym@episcopalcolorado.org

Connecticut (I)
Ian Theodore Douglas
290 Pratt Street, Meriden CT 061450, USA
T: (001) (203) 639 3501
F: (001) (203) 235 1008
E: itdouglas@episcopalct.org

(Suffragan)
Laura Ahrens
address etc as above
E: lahrens@episcopalct.org

Dallas (VII)
George R Sumner Jr
1630 North Garrett Avenue, Dallas TX
75206, USA
T: (001) (214) 826 8310
F: (001) (214) 826 5968
E: gsumner@edod.org

Delaware (III)
Kevin S Brown
913 Wilson Road, Wilmington DE
19803-4012, USA
T: (001) (302) 256 0374
F: (001) (302) 543 8084
E: bishop@delaware.church

Dominican Republic (IX)
Moisés Quezada Mota
DMG 30046 Agape Flights, 100 Airport
Avenue, Venice FL 34285, USA
T: (001) (809) 688 6016
F: (001) (809) 688 6364
E: mquezada@iglepidom.org

East Carolina (IV)
Robert Stuart Skirving
705 Doctors Drive, Kinston NC 28501, USA
T: (001) (252) 522 0885
F: (001) (252) 523 5272
E: rskirving@diocese-eastcarolina.org

East Tennessee (IV)
Brian Lee Cole
814 Episcopal School Way, Knoxville TN
37932, USA
T: (001) (865) 966 2110
E: bcole@dioet.org

Eastern Michigan (V)
Steven Todd Ousley
1821 Avalon, Saginaw MI 48638 USA
T: (001) (989) 752 6020
F: (001) (989) 752 6628
E: tousley@eastmich.org

Eastern Oregon (VIII)
Patrick William Bell
1104 Church Stret, Cove OR 97824, USA
T: (001) (541) 568 4514
E: pbell@episdioeo.org

Easton (III)
Santosh Kumar Marray
314 North Street, Easton MD 21601, USA
T: (001) (410) 822 1919
F: (001) (410) 763 8259
E: bishop@dioceseofeaston.org

Eau Claire (V)
William Jay Lambert
510 South Farwell Street, Eau Claire WI
54701, USA
T: (001) (715) 835 3331
F: (001) (715) 835 9212
E: bishop1075@icloud.com

El Camino Real (VIII)
Mary Gray-Reeves
154 Central Avenue, Salinas CA 93901, USA
T: (001) (831) 394 4465
F: (001) (831) 394 7133
E: info@realepiscopal.org

Europe, Convocation of Episcopal Churches in	Pierre Welté Whalen American Cathedral of the Holy Trinity, 23 Avenue George V, F-75008 Paris, France T: (0033) (1) 53 23 84 06 F: (0033) (1) 49 52 96 85 E: bishop@tec-europe.org
Florida (IV)	Samuel Johnson Howard 325 North Market Street, Jacksonville FL 32202-2796, USA T: (001) (904) 356 1328 F: (001) (904) 355 1934 E: jhoward@diocesefl.org
Fond Du Lac (V)	Matthew Alan Gunter 1051 North Lynndale Drive, Suite 1B, Appleton WI 54914–3094, USA T: (001) (920) 830 8866 F: (001) (920) 830 8761 E: mgunter@diofdl.org
Fort Worth (VII)	James Scott Mayer 4301 Meadowbank Drive, Fort Worth TX 76103, USA T: (001) (817) 534 9000 F: (001) (817) 534 1904 E: contact@edfw.org
Georgia (IV)	Scott Anson Benhase 611 East Bay Street, Savannah GA 31401, USA T: (001) (912) 236 4279 F: (001) (912) 236 2007 E: bishop@gaepiscopal.org
Haiti (II)	Jean Zaché Duracin BP 1309, Port-au-Prince, Haiti T: (00509) 257 1624 E: epihaiti@egliseepiscopaledhaiti.org
Hawaii (VIII)	Robert LeRoy Fitzpatrick Diocesan Office, 229 Queen Emma Square, Honolulu HI 96813–2304, USA T: (001) (808) 536 7776 F: (001) (808) 538 7194 E: rlfitzpatrick@episcopalhawaii.org
Honduras (IX)	Lloyd Emmanuel Allen 23 Ave C 21 St Colony Trejo, San Pedro Sula, Honduras 21105 T: (00504) 556 6155 F: (00504) 566 6467
Idaho (VIII)	Brian James Thom 1858 Judith Lane, Boise ID 83705, USA T: (001) (208) 345 4440 F: (001) (208) 345 9735 E: bthom@idahodiocese.org
Indianapolis (V)	Jennifer Lynn Baskerville-Burrows 1100 West 42nd Street, Indianapolis IN 46208, USA T: (001) (317) 926 5454 F: (001) (317) 926 5456 E: bishop@indydio.org
Iowa (VI)	Alan Scarfe 225 37th Street, Des Moines IA 50312–4305, USA T: (001) (515) 277 6165 F: (001) (515) 277 0273 E: ascarfe@iowaepiscopal.org
Kansas (VII)	Cathleen Bascom 835 South-West Polk Street, Topeka KS 66612–1688, USA T: (001) (785) 235 9255 F: (001) (785) 235 2449
Kentucky (IV)	Terry Allen White 425 South 2nd Street, Louisville KY 40202, USA T: (001) (502) 584 7148 F: (001) (502) 587 8123 E: bishopwhite@episopalky.org
Lexington (IV)	Mark van Koevering 203 East 4th Street, Lexington KY 40588-0610, USA T: (001) (859) 252 6527 F: (001) (859) 231 9077
Litoral Ecuador (IX)	Alfredo Morante Box 0901–5250, Calle Amarilis Fuentes 603 entre Avenida José Vincento Trujillo y la Calle 'D', Barrio Centenario, Guayaquil, Ecuador T: (00593) (4) 244 6699 F: (00593) (4) 244 3088 E: info@litoralepiscopal.org
Long Island (II)	Lawrence C Provenzano 36 Cathedral Avenue, Garden City NY 11530–0510, USA T: (001) (516) 248 4800 F: (001) (516) 248 1616 E: lprovenzano@dioceseli.org
Los Angeles (VIII)	*vacant* 840 Echo Park Avenue, Box 512164, Los Angeles CA 90051, USA T: (001) (213) 482 2040 F: (001) (213) 482 5304 E: bishop@ladiocese.org
(Coadjutor)	John Harvey Taylor *address etc as above*
(Suffragan)	Diane M Jardine Bruce *address etc as above* E: djbsuffragan@ladiocese.org
Louisiana (IV)	Morris King Thompson 1623 7th Street, New Orleans LA 70115, USA T: (001) (504) 895 6634 F: (001) (504) 895 6637 E: mthompson@edola.org
Maine (I)	Stephen Taylor Lane Loring House, 143 State Street, Portland ME 04101–3799, USA T: (001) (207) 772 1953 F: (001) (207) 773 0095 E: slane@episcopalmaine.org
Maryland (III)	Eugene Taylor Sutton 4 East University Parkway, Baltimore MD 21218, USA T: (001) (410) 467 1399 F: (001) (617) 482 8431 E: esutton@episcopalmaryland.org
Massachusetts (I)	Alan McIntosh Gates 138 Tremont Street, Boston MA 02111–1318, USA T: (001) (617) 482 5800 E: agates@diomass.org
(Suffragan)	Gayle Elizabeth Harris *address etc as above* E: gharris@diomass.org
Michigan (V)	Wendell Nathaniel Gibbs Jr 4800 Woodward Avenue, Detroit MI 48201, USA T: (001) (313) 833 4000 F: (001) (313) 831 0259 E: bishop@edomi.org
Milwaukee (V)	Steven Andrew Miller 804 E Juneau Avenue, Milwaukee WI 53202–2798, USA T: (001) (414) 272 3028 E: bishop@diomil.org
Minnesota (VI)	Brian N Prior 1730 Clifton Place, Suite 201, Minneapolis MN 55403-3242, USA T: (001) (612) 871 5311 F: (001) (612) 871 0552 E: info@episcopalmn.org
Mississippi (IV)	Brian Richard Seage 118 North Congress Street, Jackson MS 39225-3107, USA T: (001) (601) 948 5954 F: (001) (601) 354 3401 E: brseage@dioms.org

Missouri (V)	George Wayne Smith 1210 Locust Street, St Louis MO 63103, USA T: (001) (314) 231 1220 F: (001) (314) 231 3373 E: bishop@diocesemo.org
Montana (VI)	Charles Franklin Brookhart Jr 515 North Park Avenue, Helena MT 59601–8135, USA T: (001) (406) 442 2230 F: (001) (406) 442 2238 E: cfbmt@qwestoffice.net
Navajoland Area Mission (VIII)	David Earle Bailey 1227 Mission Avenue, Farmington NM 87499–0720, USA T: (001) (505) 326 7194 F: (001) (505) 327 6904
Nebraska (VI)	J Scott Barker 109 North 18th Street, Omaha NE 68102–4903, USA T: (001) (402) 341 5373 F: (001) (402) 341 8683 E: sbarker@episcopal-ne.org
Nevada (VIII)	Dan Thomas Edwards 9480 South Eastern Avenue, Suite 236, Las Vegas NV 89123–8037, USA T: (001) (702) 737 9190 F: (001) (702) 737 6488 E: dan@episcopalnevada.org
New Hampshire (I)	Alfred Robert Hirschfeld 63 Green Street, Concord NH 03301, USA T: (001) (603) 224 1914 F: (001) (603) 225 7884 E: arh@nhepiscopal.org
New Jersey (II)	William H (Chip) Stokes 808 West State Street, Trenton NJ 08618–5326, USA T: (001) (609) 394 5281 F: (001) (609) 394 9546 E: wstokes@dioceseofnj.org
New York (II)	Andrew Marion Lenow Dietsche Synod House, 1047 Amsterdam Avenue, New York NY 10025, USA T: (001) (212) 316 7400 F: (001) (212) 316 7405 E: bpdietsche@dioceseny.org
(Suffragan)	Allen Kunho Shin address as above T: (001) (212) 316 7465 E: bpshin@dioceseny.org
(Assistant)	Mary Douglas Glasspool address as above T: (001) (212) 316 7442 E: bpglasspool@dioceseny.org
Newark (II)	Carlye Juanita Hughes 31 Mulberry Street, Newark NJ 07102, USA T: (001) (973) 430 9976 F: (001) (923) 622 3503 E: chughes@dioceseofnewark.org
North Carolina (IV)	Samuel Sewall Rodman III 200 West Morgan Street, Suite 300, Raleigh NC 27601, USA T: (001) (919) 834 7474 F: (001) (919) 834 7546 E: sam.rodman@episdionc.org
North Dakota (VI)	Michael Gene Smith 3600 South 25th Street, Fargo ND 58104–6861, USA T: (001) (701) 235 6688 F: (001) (701) 232 3077 E: bpnodak@aol.com
Northern California (VIII)	Barry Leigh Beisner 350 University Avenue, Suite 280, Sacramento CA 95816, USA T: (001) (916) 442 6918 F: (001) (916) 442 6927 E: barry@norcalepiscopal.org
Northern Indiana (V)	Douglas Everett Sparks 117 North Lafayette Boulevard, South Bend IN 46601, USA T: (001) (574) 233 6489 F: (001) (574) 287 7914 E: bishop@ednin.org
Northern Michigan (V)	Rayford Jeffrey Ray 131 East Ridge Street, Marquette MI 49855, USA T: (001) (906) 228 7160 F: (001) (906) 228 7171 E: rayfordray@upepiscopal.org
Northwest Texas (VII)	James Scott Mayer 1802 Broadway Avenue, Lubbock TX 79401, USA T: (001) (806) 763 1370 F: (001) (806) 472 0641 E: bishopmayer@nwtdiocese.org
Northwestern Pennsylvania (III)	Sean Walter Rowe 145 West 6th Street, Erie, PA 16501, USA T: (001) (814) 456 4203 F: (001) (814) 454 8703 E: seanrowe@dionwpa.org
Ohio (V)	Mark Hollingsworth Jr 2230 Euclid Avenue, Cleveland OH 44115–2499, USA T: (001) (216) 774 0457 F: (001) (216) 771 9252 E: mh@dohio.org
Oklahoma (VII)	vacant 924 North Robinson, Oklahoma City OK 73102, USA T: (001) (405) 232 4820 F: (001) (405) 232 4912
Olympia (VIII)	Gregory Harold Rickel 1551 10th Avenue, Seattle WA 98102, USA T: (001) (206) 325 4200 F: (001) (206) 325 4631 E: grickel@ecww.org
Oregon (VIII)	Michael Joseph Hanley 11800 South-West Military Lane, Portland OR 97219, USA T: (001) (503) 636 5613 F: (001) (503) 636 5616 E: bishop@episcopaldioceseoregon.org
Pennsylvania (III)	Daniel George Polycarpio Gutierrez 3717 Chestnut Street, Suite 300, Philadelphia PA 19104, USA T: (001) (215) 627 6434 F: (001) (215) 900 2928 E: dgutierrez@diopa.org
Pittsburgh (III)	Dorsey Winter Marsden McConnell 325 Oliver Avenue, Suite 300, Pittsburgh PA 15222-2406, USA T: (001) (412) 721 0853 F: (001) (412) 471 5591 E: dmcconnell@episcopalpgh.org
Puerto Rico (IX)	Rafael Morales Maldonado PO Box 902, St Just, PR 00978-0902, Puerto Rico T: (001) (787) 761 9800 F: (001) (787) 761 0320
Rhode Island (I)	William Nicholas Knisely 275 North Main Street, Providence RI 02903–1298, USA T: (001) (401) 274 4500 F: (001) (401) 274 9430 E: nicholas@episcopalri.org
Rio Grande (VII)	Michael Louis Vono 6400 Coors Boulevard North West, Albuquerque NM 87107–4811, USA T: (001) (505) 881 0636 F: (001) (505) 883 9048 E: bp.michael@dioceserg.org
Rochester (II)	Prince Grenville Singh 935 East Avenue, Rochester NY 14607, USA T: (001) (585) 473 2977 F: (001) (585) 473 3195 E: prince@episcopaldioceseofrochester.org

San Diego (VIII)   Susan Brown Snook
2083 Sunset Cliffs Boulevard, San Diego CA
92107, USA
T: (001) (619) 291 5947
F: (001) (619) 291 8362

San Joaquin
(VIII)   David C Rice
1528 Oakdale Road, Modesto CA 95355,
USA
T: (001) (209) 576 0104
F: (001) (209) 576 0114
E: bishopdavid@diosanjoaquin.org

South Dakota
(VI)   John Thomas Tarrant
500 S Main Avenue, Sioux Falls SD
57104–6814, USA
T: (001) (605) 338 9751
F: (001) (605) 336 6243
E: bishop.diocese@midconetwork.com

Southeast Florida
(IV)   Peter David Eaton
525 North-East 15 Street, Miami FL 33132,
USA
T: (001) (305) 373 0881
F: (001) (305) 375 8054
E: info@diosef.org

Southern Ohio
(V)   Thomas Edward Breidenthal
412 Sycamore Street, Cincinnati OH 45202,
USA
T: (001) (513) 421 0311
F: (001) (513) 421 0315
E: tbreidenthal@diosohio.org

Southern
Virginia (III)   Herman (Holly) Hollerith IV
11827 Canon Boulevard, Suite 101,
Newport News VA 23606, USA
T: (001) (757) 423 8287
F: (001) (757) 440 5354
E: bishop@diosova.org

Southwest
Florida (IV)   Dabney Tyler Smith
8005 25th Street East, Parrish FL
34219–9405, USA
T: (001) (941) 556 0315
F: (001) (941) 556 0321
E: dsmith@episcopalswfl.org

Southwestern
Virginia (III)   Mark Allen Bourlakas
1002 1st Street, Roanoke VA 24016, USA
T: (001) (757) 423 8287
F: (001) (757) 440 5354
E: bishopmark@dioswva.org

Spokane (VIII)   Gretchen Rehberg
245 East 13th Avenue, Spokane WA
99202–1114, USA
T: (001) (509) 624 3191
F: (001) (509) 747 0049
E: gretchenr@spokanediocese.org

Springfield (V)   Daniel Hayden Martins
821 South 2nd Street, Springfield IL 62704,
USA
T: (001) (217) 525 1876
F: (001) (217) 525 1877
E: bishop@episcopalspringfield.org

Taiwan (VIII)   David Jung-Hsin Lai
10060 Hangzhou South Road, Taipei City,
Taiwan, Republic of China
T: (00886) (2) 2341 1265
F: (00886) (2) 2396 2014
E: skh.tpe@msa.hinet.net

Tennessee (IV)   John Crawford Bauerschmidt
3700 Woodmont Boulevard, Nashville TN
37215, USA
T: (001) (615) 251 3322
F: (001) (615) 251 8010
E: info@edtn.org

Texas (VII)   Charles Andrew Doyle
1225 Texas Avenue, Houston TX
77002–3504, USA
T: (001) (713) 353 2100
F: (001) (713) 520 5723
E: adoyle@epicenter.org

(Suffragan)   Dena Arnall Harrison
510 Rathervue Place, PO Box 2247, Austin
TX 78768–2247, USA
T: (001) (512) 478 0580
F: (001) (512) 478 5615
E: dharrison@epicenter.org

(Suffragan)   Jeff Wright Fisher
2695 S Southwest Loop 323, Tyler, TX
75701, USA
T: (001) (888) 579 6012
E: jfisher@epicenter.org

(Assistant)   Hector Monterroso
Diocesan Center, 1225 Texas Avenue,
Houston, TX 77002-3504, USA
T: (001) (713) 520 6444
F: (001) (866) 645 5245
E: hmonterroso@epicenter.org

Upper South
Carolina (IV)   William Andrew Waldo
1115 Marion Street, Columbia SC 29201,
USA
T: (001) (803) 771 7800
F: (001) (803) 799 5119
E: bishopwaldo@edusc.org

Utah (VIII)   Scott Byron Hayashi
75 South 200 East Street, Salt Lake City UT
84110–2147, USA
T: (001) (801) 322 4131
F: (001) (801) 322 5096
E: shayashi@episcopal-ut.org

Venezuela (IX)   *vacant*
Centro Diocesano, Avenue Caroní No 100,
Colinas de Bello Monte, Caracas, Venezuela

Vermont (I)   Thomas Clark Ely
5 Rock Point Road, Burlington VT 05401,
USA
T: (001) (802) 863 3431
F: (001) (802) 860 1562
E: tely@dioceseofvermont.org

Virgin Islands
(II)   Edward Ambrose Gumbs
13 Commandant Gade, Charlotte Amaille,
St Thomas VI 00801, USA
T: (001) (340) 776 1797
F: (001) (340) 777 8485
E: bpambrosegumbs@yahoo.com

Virginia (III)   Shannon Sherwood Johnston
110 West Franklin Street, Richmond VA
23220, USA
T: (001) (804) 643 8451
F: (001) (804) 644 6928
E: sjohnston@thediocese.net

(Suffragan)   Susan Ellyn Goff
address etc as above
E: sgoff@thediocese.net

Washington DC
(III)   Mariann Edgar Budde
Mount St Alban, Washington DC
20016–5094, USA
T: (001) (202) 537 6555
F: (001) (202) 364 6605
E: mebudde@edow.org

West Missouri
(VII)   Martin Scott Field
420 West 14th Street, Kansas City MO
64105–3227, USA
T: (001) (816) 471 6161
F: (001) (816) 471 0379
E: bishopfield@diowestmo.org

West Tennessee
(IV)   Don Edward Johnson
692 Poplar Avenue, Memphis TN 38105,
USA
T: (001) (901) 526 0023
F: (001) (901) 526 1555
E: bishopjohnson@episwtn.org

West Texas (VII)   David Mitchell Reed
Bishop Jones Center, PO Box 6885, 111
Torcido Drive, San Antonio TX 78209, USA
T: (001) (210) 824 5387
F: (001) (210) 824 2164
E: david.reed@dwtx.org

(Suffragan) Jennifer Brooke-Davidson
address etc as above
E: jennifer.brooke-davidson@dwtx.org

West Virginia William Michie Klusmeyer
(III) 1608 Virginia Street East, Charleston WV
25311, USA
T: (001) (304) 344 3597
F: (001) (304) 343 3295
E: mklusmeyer@wvdiocese.org

Western Kansas Michael Pierce Milliken
(VII) 2 Hyde Park, Hutchinson KS 67502, USA
T: (001) (620) 662 0011
F: (001) (620) 662 2930
E: tec.wks2011@gmail.com

Western Jacob W Owensby
Louisiana (VII) 335 Main Street, Pineville LA 71360, USA
T: (001) (318) 422 1304
F: (001) (318) 442 8712
E: bishopjake@diocesewla.org

Western Douglas John Fisher
Massachusetts (I) 37 Chestnut Street, Springfield MA 01103,
USA
T: (001) (413) 737 4786
F: (001) (413) 746 9873
E: communications@diocesewma.org

Western Whayne Miller Hougland
Michigan (V) 535 South Burdick Street, Suite 1,
Kalamazoo MI 49007, USA
T: (001) (269) 381 2710
F: (001) (269) 381 7067
E: wmhougland@edwm.org

Western New Ralph William Franklin
York (II) 1064 Brighton Road, Tonawanda NY 14150,
USA
T: (001) (716) 881 0660
F: (001) (716) 881 1724
E: rwfranklin@episcopalwny.org

Western North José Antonio McLoughlin
Carolina (IV) 900-B Center Park Drive, Asheville NC
28805, USA
T: (001) (828) 225 6656
F: (001) (828) 225 6657
E: bishopjose@diocesewnc.org

Wyoming (VI) John Sheridan Smylie
123 South Durbin Street, Casper WY 82601,
USA
T: (001) (307) 265 5200
F: (001) (307) 577 9939
E: bishopsmylie@wyomingdiocese.org

WEST AFRICA

Accra Daniel Sylvanus Mensah Torto
Bishopscourt, PO Box 8, Accra, Ghana
T: (00233) 302 662 292
M: (00233) 27-749 6479
E: dantorto@yahoo.com

Asante Cyril Kobina Ben-Smith
Mampong Anglican Diocese of Asante Mampong,
Mampong, Ashanti Region, Ghana
M: (00233) 24-774308
E: bishop.mampong@yahoo.co.uk

Bo Emmanuel Josie Samuel Tucker
PO Box 21, Bo, Southern Province, Sierra
Leone
M: (00232) 76-677862
E: ejstucker@gmail.com

Cameroon Dibo Thomas-Babyngton Elango
BP 15705, New Bell, Douala, Cameroon
T: (00237) 7555 8276
E: revdibo2@yahoo.com

Cape Coast Victor R Atta-Baffoe
Bishopscourt, PO Box A 233, Adisadel
Estates, Cape Coast, Ghana
T: (00233) (33) 212 3502
F: (00233) (42) 32637
M: (00233) 20-652319
E: victorattabaffoe@yahoo.com

Dunkwa-on- Edmund K Dawson Ahmoah
Offin PO Box DW42, Dunkwa-on-Offin
M: (00233) 24-464 4764
E: papacy11@yahoo.co.uk

Freetown Thomas Arnold Ikunika Wilson
Bishop's Court, PO Box 537, Freetown,
Sierra Leone
M: (00232) 22-251307
E: vicnold2003@gmail.com

The Gambia James Allen Yaw Odico
Bishopscourt, PO Box 51, Banjul, The
Gambia, West Africa
T: (00220) 770 5915
E: jayawodico@gmail.com

Guinea Jacques Boston
BP 187, Conakry, Guinea
T: (00224) (632) 204660
M: (00224) 63-587938
E: bostonjacques@yahoo.com

Ho Matthias K Mededues-Badohu
Bishopslodge, PO Box MA 300, Ho, Volta
Region, Ghana
T: (00233) 3620 26644 *or* 28606
M: (00233) 20-816 2246
E: matthiaskwab@googlemail.com

Koforidua Felix Odei Annancy
PO Box 980, Koforidua, Ghana
M: (00233) 26-681 9414

Kumasi Daniel Yinka Sarfo
(Primate and Bishop's House, PO Box 144, Kumasi,
Metropolitan) Ghana
T/F: (00233) (51) 24 117
M: (00233) 27-789 0411
E: anglicandioceseofkumasi@yahoo.com *or*
dysarfo2000@yahoo.co.uk

Liberia Jonathan Bau-Bau Bonaparte Hart
(Archbishop) PO Box 10–0277, 1000 Monrovia 10,
Liberia
T: (00231) 777 070 418
M: (00231) 88-651 6343
E: jbbhart@yahoo.com *or* bishopecl12@
yahoo.com

Sekondi Alexander Kobina Asmah
PO Box 85, Sekondi, Ghana
T: (00233) (208) 378 295
M: (00233) 20-837 8295
E: alexasmah@yahoo.com

Sunyani Festus Yeboah-Asuamah
PO Box 23, Sunyani, Ghana
T: (00233) (35) 202 3213
M: (00233) 20-812 1670
E: fyasuamah@yahoo.com

Tamale *vacant*
PO Box 110, Tamale, Ghana
T: (00233) (24) 341 9864

Wiawso Abraham Kobina Ackah
PO Box 4, Sefwi, Wiawso, Ghana
M: (00233) 274 005 952
E: bishopackah@yahoo.com

WEST INDIES

Bahamas and the Laish Zane Boyd
Turks and Caicos Church House, PO Box N-7107, Nassau,
Islands Bahamas
T: (001) (242) 322 3015
F: (001) (242) 322 7943
E: bishopboyd@bahamasanglican.org

Barbados Michael Maxwell
Mandeville House, Collymore Rock,
St Michael, Barbados
T: (001) (246) 426 2761
F: (001) (246) 426 0871
E: jwdh@outlook.com

Belize Philip Silvin Wright
Diocesan Office, 25 Southern Foreshore, PO
Box 535, Belize City, Belize
T: (00501) (2) 273029
F: (00501) (2) 276898
E: bzediocese@btl.net

Guyana	Charles Alexander Davidson The Diocesan Office, PO Box 10949, 49 Barrack Street, Georgetown, Guyana, West Indies T: (00592) (226) 3862 F: (00592) (227) 6091 E: dioofguy@networksgy.com
Jamaica and the Cayman Islands (Archbishop)	Howard Kingsley Ainsworth Gregory Church House, 2 Caledonia Ave, Kingston 5, Jamaica T: (001) (876) 920 2712 F: (001) (876) 960 1774 E: bishop.jamaica@anglicandiocese.com *or* hkagregory@hotmail.com
(Kingston)	Robert McLean Thompson 3 Duke Street, Kingston, Jamaica, West Indies T: (001) (876) 924 9044 F: (001) (876) 948 5362 E: bishop.kingston@anglicandiocese.com
(Mandeville)	*vacant* Bishop's Residence, 3 Cotton Tree Road, PO Box 84, Mandeville, Jamaica, West Indies T: (001) (876) 625 6818 F: (001) (876) 625 6819
(Montego Bay)	Leon Paul Golding PO Box 346, Montego Bay, Jamaica, West Indies T: (001) (876) 952 4963 F: (001) (876) 971 8838
North Eastern Caribbean and Aruba	Leroy Errol Brooks St Mary's Rectory, PO Box 180, The Valley, Anguilla T: (001) (264) 497 2235 F: (001) (264) 497 8555 E: brookx@anguillanet.com
Trinidad and Tobago	Claude Berkley Hayes Court, 21 Maraval Road, Port of Spain, Trinidad, Trinidad and Tobago, West Indies T: (001) (868) 622 7387 F: (001) (868) 628 1319 E: diocesett@tstt.net.tt

Windward Islands	Calvert Leopold Friday Bishop's Court, Montrose, PO Box 502, St Vincent, West Indies T: (001) (784) 456 1895 F: (001) (784) 456 2591 E: diocesewi@vincysurf.com

EXTRA-PROVINCIAL DIOCESES

Bermuda	Nicholas Bayard Botolf Dill Diocesan Office, PO Box HM 769, Hamilton HM CX, Bermuda T: (001) (441) 292 6987 F: (001) (441) 292 5421 E: diocese@anglican.bm
Cuba	Maria Griselda Delgado del Carpio Calle 6 No 273, Vedado, Plaza de la revolucion, Ciudad de La Habana, CP 10400, Cuba T: (0053) (7) 833 5760 E: griselda@enet.cu
Falkland Islands	Timothy Martin Thornton Lambeth Palace, London SE1 7JU T: (020) 7898 1200
Lusitanian Church (Canterbury)	José Jorge Tavares de Pina Cabral Diocesan Centre, Rua Afonso de Albuquerque, 86 Mafamude 4430–003 Vila Nova de Gaia, Portugal T: (00351) (22) 375 4018 F: (00351) (22) 375 2016 E: bispopinacabral@igreja-lusitana.org
The Spanish Reformed Episcopal Church (Canterbury)	Carlos López-Lozano Spanish Reformed Episcopal Church, Calle Beneficencia 18, 28004 Madrid T: (0034) (91) 445 2560 F: (0034) (91) 594 4572 E: eclesiae@arrakis.es

BISHOPS OF CHURCHES WHERE ANGLICANS HAVE UNITED WITH CHRISTIANS OF OTHER TRADITIONS

NORTH INDIA

Agra
Prem Prakash Habil
Bishop's House, 4/116-B Church Road, Civil Lines, Agra 282 002, Uttar Pradesh
T: (0091) (562) 285 4845 or 285 1481
F: (0091) (562) 252 0074
M: (0091) (941) 272 2501
E: doacni@gmail.com or bishopofagra@gmail.com

Amritsar
(Moderator)
Pradeep Kumar Samantaroy
26 R B Prakash Chand Road, Opp Police Ground, Amritsar 143 001, Punjab
T/F: (0091) (183) 222 2910 or 256 2010
M: (0091) (981) 546 2121
E: bunu13@rediffmail.com

Andaman and Nicobar Islands
Christopher Paul
Cathedral Church Compound, MUS, Car Nicobar 744301 or Post Box No 19, Port Blair 744 101, Andaman and Nicobar Islands
M: (0091) (947) 601 6030
E: cniportblair@yahoo.co.in

Barrackpore
(Moderator's Episcopal Comissary)
vacant
Bishop's Lodge, 86 Middle Road, Barrackpore, Kolkata 700120, West Bengal
T: (0091) (332) 593 1852
F: (0091) (332) 592 0147

Bhopal
Manoj Charan
Masihi Kanya Hr. Sec. School Campus, 9 Boundary Road, Indore 452 001 Madhya Pradesh
T: (0091) (731) 249 2789
M: (0091) (942) 515 5379
E: charan manoj@yahoo.com

Calcutta
Paritosh Canning
Bishop's House, 51 Chowringhee Rd, Calcutta 700 071, West Bengal
T: (0091) (336) 534 7770
F: (0091) (332) 822 6340

Chandigarh
Younas Massey
Bishop's House, Mission Compound, Brown Road, Ludhiana 141 001, Punjab
T/F: (0091) (161) 222 5706
M: (0091) (991) 564 1109
E: bishopdoc2000@yahoo.com

Chhattisharh
(Moderator's Episcopal Comissary)
Robert Ali
Opp. Raj Bhavan, Gate No. 1, Civil Lines, Raipur 492 001, Chhattisgarh
T/F: (0091) (771) 221 0015
M: (0091) (992) 618 6636
E: bishop.robertali@gmail.com

Chotanagpur
B B Baskey
Bishop's Lodge, PO Box 1, Church Road, Ranchi 834 001, Jharkhand
T: (0091) (651) 235 0281
F: (0091) (651) 235 1184
M: (0091) (947) 019 3053 or 754 911 3206
E: rch cndta@sancharnet.in or chotanagpurdiocese@gmail.com

Cuttack
(Moderator's Episcopal Comissary)
Surendra Kumar Nanda
Bishop's House, Mission Road, Cuttack 753 001, Orissa
T: (0091) (671) 230 0102
M: (0091) (943) 732 3975
E: sknanda62@gmail.com

Delhi
(Moderator's Episcopal Comissary)
Warris Masih
Bishop's House, 1 Church Lane, Off North Avenue, New Delhi 110 004
T: (0091) (112) 371 7471 or 335 8006 or 010 3520
M: (0091) (800) 360 2000
E: wkmasih@yahoo.co.in

Durgapur
Probal Kanto Dutta
Diocesan Bhavan, Aldrin Path, Bidhan Nagar, Dugapur 713 212, Dist. Burdwan, West Bengal
T/F: (0091) (343) 253 4552 or 253 6220
E: probaldutta@ymail.com

Eastern Himalaya
(Moderator's Episcopal Comissary)
vacant
CNI Diocesan Centre, Gandhi Road, PO Box 4, Darjeeling 734 101, West Bengal
E: easternhimalaya2010@yahoo.co.in

Gujarat
Silvans S Christian
Bishop's House, I.P. Mission Compound, Ellisbridge, Ahmedabad 380 006, Gujarat
T/F: (0091) (792) 656 1950
M: (0091) (740) 522 7086
E: gujdio@yahoo.co.in or christiansilvans@yahoo.com

Jabalpur
Prem Chand Singh
Bishop's House, 2131 Napier Town, Jabalpur 482 001, Madhya Pradesh
T: (0091) (761) 262 2109 or 262 2692
M: (0091) (942) 515 5379
E: bishoppcsingh@yahoo.co.in

Kolhapur
Sandeep Suresh Vibhute
Bishop's House, EP School Compound, Nagala Park, Kolhapur 416 001, Maharashtra
T/F: (0091) (231) 265 4832
M: (0091) (983) 348 0299
E: bishopprakashpatole@gmail.com

Lucknow
Peter Baldev
25/11 Mahatma Gandhi Marg, Allahabad 211 011, Uttar Pradesh
T: (0091) (989) 790 8072
E: peterbaldev@yahoo.com or bishopoflucknow@rediffmail.com

Marathwada
Madhukar U Kasab
Bungalow 28/A, Mission Compound, Cantonment, Aurangabad 431 002, Maharashtra
T: (0091) (240) 237 3136
M: (0091) (976) 482 2888
E: revmukasab@yahoo.co.in or bishopofmarathwada@rediffmail.com

Mumbai
Prakash Dinkar Patole
19 Hazarimal Somani Marg Fort, Mumbai 400 001
T: (0091) (222) 207 3904
F: (0091) (222) 206 0248
M: (0091) (983) 348 0299
E: cnibombaydiocese@yahoo.com or bishopprakashpatole@gmail.com

Nagpur
Paul Dupare
Cathedral House, Opp. Indian Coffee House, Sadar, Nagpur 440 001, Maharashtra
T/F: (0091) (712) 255 3351
M: (0091) (982) 335 4614
E: nagpurdiocese@rediffmail.com

Nasik | Pradip Lemuel Kamble
Bishop's House, 1 Outram Road, Tarakpur,
Ahmednagar 414 001, Maharashtra
T: (0091) (241) 241 1806
F: (0091) (241) 242 2314
M: (0091) (942) 109 9721
E: bishopofnasik@rediffmail.com

North East India | Michael Herenz
Bishop's Kuti, Shillong, Meghalaya 793 003
T: (0091) (364) 222 3155
M: (0091) (943) 554 6652
E: michaelherenz@gmail.com

Patna | Philip Phembuar Marandih
Bishop's House, Christ Church Compound,
Bhagalpur 812 001, Bihar
T: (0091) (641) 240 0033 or 230 0714
M: (0091) (943) 121 3138
E: cnipatna@rediffmail.com

Phulbani | Bijay Kumar Nayak
Bishop's House, Mission Compound,
Gudripori, Gudaigiri, Phulbani 762 100,
Kandhamal, Odisha 762 004
T: (0091) (684) 726 0569
M: (0091) (943) 796 5389
E: bp.bkn@rediffmail.com

Pune | Sharad Yuvraj Gaikwad
1A, General Bhagat Marg (Stevely Road),
Red Bungalow, Pune 411 001, Maharashtra
T: (0091) (202) 633 4374
M: (0091) (976) 482 2888
E: bishopofpune@gmail.com

Rajasthan | Darbara Singh
2/10 CNI Social Centre, Civil Lines, Opp.
Bus Stand, Jaipur Road, Ajmer 305 002
T: (0091) (145) 242 0633
F: (0091) (145) 262 1627
M: (0091) (800) 360 2000
E: darbarasingh0145@gmail.com

Sambalpur | Pinuel Dip
Bishop's House, Mission Compound,
Bolangir 767 001, Odisha
T: (0091) (665) 223 0625
M: (0091) (943) 833 6476
E: bishoppinueldip@gmail.com

SOUTH INDIA

Cochin
(formerly North
Kerala) | Baker Ninan Fenn
CSI Diocesan Office, PO Box 104, Shoranur
679 121, Palakkad District, Kerala
T: (0091) (46) 6222 2545 or 6222 2426
F: (0091) (46) 6222 2545
E: csicochindiocese@gmail.com or
revbnfenn@gmail.com

Coimbatore
(Bishop in) | Timothy Ravinder
Diocesan Office, 256 Race Course Road,
Coimbatore 641 018, Tamil Nadu
T: (0091) (42) 222 3605 or 222 1655
F: (0091) (42) 222 3369
E: csi.bpcbe@gmail.com

Dornakal
(Bishop in) | Vadapalli Prasada Rao
Diocesan Office, Epiphany Cathedral
Compound, Dornakal 506 381, Warangal
Dist., Telangana
E: dkbpoff@hotmail.com

East Kerala
(Bishop in) | Kayalakkakathu George Daniel
CSI Diocesan Office, Melukavumattom,
Kottayam 686 652, Kerala State
F: (0091) (4822) 219 044
E: csiekd@gmail.com or bishopkgdaniel@
rediffmail.com

Jaffna | Daniel Selvaratnam Thiagarajah
Bishop's office in Colombo, 17, Frances
Road, Colombo 6, Sri Lanka
T: (0094) (21) 225 0827 or 0826
F: (0094) (11) 258 2015
E: bishopthiagarajah@gmail.com

Kanyakumari
(Bishop in) | *vacant*
CSI Diocesan Office, 71A Dennis Street,
Nagercoil 629 001, Kanyakumari District,
Tamil Nadu
F: (0091) (4652) 226 560
E: csikkd@bsnl.in

Karimnagar
(Bishop in) | K Reuben Mark
CSI Diocesan Office, 2-8-95 CVRN Road,
PO Box 40, Mukarampura Post, Karimnagar
505 001,Telangana
F: (0091) (878) 226 2971
E: reubenmark@hotmail.com

Karnataka
Central
(Bishop in) | Prasanna Kumar Samuel
CSI Diocesan Office, 20 Third Cross, CSI
Compound, Bangalore 560 027, Karnataka
T: (0091) (80) 2222 3766 or 2222 4941
E: bishop@csikcd.in or revpksamuel@gmail.
com

Karnataka North
(Bishop in) | Ravikumar J Niranjan
CSI Diocesan Office, All Saints' Church
Compound, Haliyal Road, Dharwad 580
008, Karnataka
F: (0091) (836) 274 5461
E: haradoni.rn@gmail.com

Karnataka South
(Bishop in) | Mohan Manoraj
CSI Diocesan Office, Balmatta, Mangalore
575 002, Karnataka
F: (0091) (824) 243 2363
E: csiksd2014@gmail.com or mohhanrraj@
gmail.com

Kollam
Kottarakara
(Bishop in) | Oommen George
Diocesan Office, Kollam Kottarakara, N H
208, Chinnakada, Kollam 691 001, Kerala
T: (0091) (474) 274 3403
E: revoommengeorge@gmail.com

Krishna-
Godavari
(Moderator) | George Cornelius Tantepudi
CSI Diocesan Office, CSI TA Bass Complex,
Gopala Reddy Road, Governorpet,
Vijayawada 520 002, Andhra Pradesh
F: (0091) (866) 2573673
E: revcornelius@gmail.com

Madhya Kerala
(Deputy
Moderator) | Thomas Kanjirappally Oommen
CSI Bishop's office, Cathedral Road,
Kottayam 686 001, Kerala
F: (0091) (481) 256 6536
E: csimkdbishopsoffice@gmail.com

Madras | George Stephen Jeyaraj
Diocesan Office, PO Box 4914, 226
Cathedral Road, Chennai 600 086, Tamil
Nadu
T: (0091) (44) 2811 3929 or 3933 or 7629
F: (0091) (44) 2811 0608
E: bishopgeorgestephen@gmail.com

Madurai-
Ramnad
(Bishop in) | Marialouis Joseph
'Rev. Grub's Garden', No.5 Bhulabai Desai
Road, Chokkikulam, Madurai 625 002,
Tamil Nadu
T: (0091) (452) 2338222
F: (0091) (452) 2339888
E: bishopmjoseph@gmail.com

Malabar
(formerly within
North Kerala) | Royce Manoj Kumar Victor
CSI Diocesan Office, Bank Road, Calicut
673 001, Kerala
T: (0091) (495) 272 1748
E: csimalabardiocese@gmail.com

Medak | A C Solomon Raj
Diocesan Office, 10-3-65, Church House,
Golden Jubilee Bhavan, Old Lancer Lane,
Secunderabad 500 025, Telangana
T: (0091) (40) 2783 3151 or 2782 2189
F: (0091) (40) 27820543

Nandyal | Eggoni Pushpalalitha
CSI Diocesan Office, Nandyal RS 518 502,
Kurnool Dist., Andhra Pradesh
T: (0091) (8514) 222 477
E: csibishopnandyal@gmail.com or rt.rev.
pushpalalitha@gmail.com

Rayalaseema (Bishop in)	B D Prasada Rao CSI Diocesan Office, R.S.Road, Kadapa, Andhra Pradesh T: (0091) (8562) 325 320 *or* 275 200 F: (0091) (8562) 275 200 E: lbd prasad@yahoo.co.in
South Kerala (Bishop in)	A Dharmaraj Rasalam CSI Diocesan office, LMS Compound, Trivandrum 695 033, Kerala State T: (0091) (471) 231 8662 *or* 231 5490 F: (0091) (471) 231 6439 E: bishoprasalam@yahoo.com
Thoothukudi-Nazareth (Moderator's Episcopal Comissary)	Samuel Devasahayam Ebenezer Clement Diocesan Office, Caldwell Higher Secondary School Campus, Beach Road, Thoothukudi 628 004 T: (0091) (461) 232 9408 F: (0091) (461) 232 8408 E: csitnd@bsnl.in
Tirunelveli (Bishop in)	Jayaraj J Christdoss CSI Diocesan Office, PO Box 116, 16, No. 5 Punithavathiyar Street, Palayamkottai, North High Ground Road, Tirunelveli 627 002, Tamil Nadu T: (0091) (462) 257 8744 F: (0091) (462) 257 4525 E: bishopcsitirunelveli@gmail.com
Trichy-Tanjore	Gnanamuthu Paul Vasanthakumar CSI Diocesan Office, Allithurai Road, Puthur, Tiruchiarapalli 620 017, Tamil Nadu T: (0091) (431) 241 1102 *or* 277 0172 *or* 277 1254 F: (0091) (431) 241 8485 *or* 277 0172 E: csittd@rediffmail.com
Vellore (Bishop in)	*vacant* CSI Diocesan Office, 3/1, Anna Salai, Vellore 632 001, Tamil Nadu T: (0091) (416) 223 2160 *or* 221 6324 F: (0091) (416) 222 3835 E: csi.vlrdiocese@gmail.com

BANGLADESH

Barisal	Shourabh Pholia Oxford Mission, Bogra Road, Barisal 8200 E: spholia72@gmail.com
Dhaka (Moderator)	Paul Shishir Saker Church of Bangladesh, 54/1 Barobag, Mirpur 2, Dhaka 1216 T: (00880) (2) 902 4761 E: pssaker19@gmail.com
Kushtia	Samuel Sunil Mankhin 94 N S Road, Thanapara, Kushtia 7000 T/F: (00880) (71) 54618 E: bishop mankhin@yahoo.com

PAKISTAN

Faisalabad	John Samuel Bishop's House, PO Box 27, Mission Road, Gojra, Distt Toba Tek Sing T: (0092) (46) 351 4689 M: (0092) (300) 655 0074 E: jsamuel@brain.net.pk
Hyderabad	Kaleem John 27 Liaquat Road, Civil Lines, Hyderabad 71000, Sindh T: (0092) (22) 278 0221 M: (0092) (301) 244 5690 E: kaleemjohn@aol.com
Karachi	Sadiq Daniel Holy Trinity Cathedral, Fatima Jinnah Road, Karachi 75533 T: (0092) (21) 521 6843 M: (0092) (301) 822 2003 E: sadiqdaniel@hotmail.com
Lahore	Irfan Jamil Bishopsbourne, Cathedral Close, The Mall, Lahore 54005 T: (0092) (42) 723 3560 *or* 7120 766 F: (0092) (42) 722 1270 M: (0092) (333) 475 6730 E: 9thbishopoflahore@gmail.com
Multan	Leo Rodrick Paul 113 Qasim Road, PO Box 204, Multan Cantt T: (0092) (61) 458 3694 M: (0092) (300) 630 2101 E: bishop mdcop@bain.net.pk
Peshawar	Humphrey Sarfaraz Peters Diocesan Centre, 1 Sir Syed Road, Peshawar Cantt 2504 T: (0092) (91) 527 9094 F: (0092) (91) 527 7499 M: (0092) (300) 858 0325 E: bishopdop@hotmail.com
Raiwind (Moderator)	Azad Marshall 17 Waris Road, PO Box 2319, Lahore 3 T: (0092) (42) 758 8950 F: (0092) (42) 757 7255 E: bishop@saintthomascenter.org
Sialkot	Alwin Samuel Lal Kothi, Barah Patthar, Sialkot 2, Punjab F: (0092) (432) 264 828 M: (0092) (305) 730 2201 E: chs sialkot@yahoo.com

PROVINCIAL OFFICES

From which further information may be sought.

Anglican Communion Office   St Andrew's House, 16 Tavistock Crescent, Westbourne Park, London W11 1AP, UK
   T: (020) 7313 3900   F: (020) 7313 3999   E: aco@anglicancommunion.org

Australia   Suite 4, Level 5, 189 Kent Street, Sydney NSW 2000, Australia
   T: (0061) (2) 8267 2700   F: (0061) (2) 8267 2727   E: gsoffice@anglican.org.au

Bangladesh   Church of Bangladesh, 54/1 Barobag, Mirpur 2, Dhaka 1216, Bangladesh
   T: (00880) (2) 902 5876   F: (00880) (2) 805 3729   E: cobsynod@churchofbangladesh.org

Brazil   Praça Olavo Bilac 63, Campos Elíseos, CEP 01201–050, São Paulo, Brazil
   T/F: (0055) (11) 3667 8161   E: acavalcante@ieab.org.br

Burundi   BP 2098, Bujumbura, Burundi
   T: (00257) (2) 222 4389   E: peab@cbinf.com

Canada   80 Hayden Street, Toronto ON M4Y 3G2, Canada
   T: (001) (416) 924 9192   F: (001) (416) 968 7983   E: mthompson@national.anglican.ca

Central Africa   Central Africa PO Box 22317, Kitwe, Zambia
   T: (00260) (2) 223 264   F: (00260) (2) 224 778

Central America   Apartado 1207, Managua, Nicaragua
   T: (00505) (2) 222 5174   F: (00505) 222 452 48   E: secretaria_diocesana@hotmail.com

Ceylon   Bishop's House, 368/3A Bauddhaloka Mawatha, Colombo 7, Sri Lanka
   T: (0094) (1) 684810   F: (0094) (1) 684811   E: sec.diocese.tr@gmail.com

Congo   11 Av Basalakala, Commune de Kalamu, Kinshasa 1, DR Congo
   T: (00243) (99) 541 2138   E: anglican.congo@yahoo.com

England   Church House, Great Smith Street, London SW1P 3NZ, UK
   T: (020) 7898 1000   E: enquiry@churchofengland.org

Hong Kong   16/F Tung Wai Commercial Building, 109–111 Gloucester Road, Wanchai, Hong Kong SAR
   T: (00852) 2526 5355   F: (00852) 2521 2199   E: office1@hkskh.org

Indian Ocean   Diocesan Church House, 37th St Paul Rd, Vacoas, Mauritius
   T: (00230) 686 5158   E: psec.acio@gmail.com

Ireland   Church of Ireland House, Church Avenue, Rathmines, Dublin 6, DO6 CF67, Republic of Ireland
   T: (00353) (1) 4978 422   F: (00353) (1) 497 8792   E: chiefofficer@rcbdub.org

Japan   65–3 Yarai-cho, Shinjuku-ku, Tokyo 162–0805, Japan
   T: (0081) (35) 228 3171   F: (0081) (3) 5228 3175   E: general-sec.po@nskk.org

Jerusalem and the Middle East   2 Grigori Afxentiou, Nicosia 1515, PO Box 22075, Cyprus
   E: georgia@spidernet.com.cy

Kenya   PO Box 40502, 00100 Nairobi, Kenya
   T: (00254) (20) 714 755   F: (00254) (2) 718 442   E: archoffice@ackenya.org

Korea   16 Sejong-daero 19-gil, Jung-gu, Seoul 100–120, Korea
   T: (0082) (2) 738 8952   F: (0082) (2) 737 4210   E: anglicankorea@gmail.com

Melanesia   Provincial Headquarters, PO Box 19, Honiara, Solomon Islands
   T: (0067) 20470   E: hauriasi_A@comphq.org.sb

Mexico   Acatlán 102 Oriente, Col Mitras Centro, Monterrey, Nuevo Leon, 64460, Mexico
   T: (0052) (81) 8333 0992   F: (0052) (81) 8348 7362   E: awalls@anglicanmx.org

Myanmar (Burma)   PO Box 11191, 140 Pyidaungsu Yeiktha Road, Dagon, Yangon, Myanmar
   T: (0095) (1) 395 279   F: (0095) (1) 39 5350   E: myinthtet@gmail.com

New Zealand (Aotearoa, New Zealand and Polynesia)   PO Box 87188, Meadowbank, Auckland 1742, New Zealand
   T: (0064) (9) 521 4439   E: gensecm@anglicanchurch.org.nz

Nigeria   24 Douala Street, Wuse Zone 5, Abuja, Nigeria
   T: (00234) (95) 236 950   E: communicator1@anglican-nig.org

North India   CNI, 16 Pandit Pant Marg, New Delhi 110001, India
   T: (0091) (11) 4231 4000   E: alwanmasih@cnisynod.org

Pakistan   St John's Cathedral, 1 Sir Syed Road, Peshawar Cantt 25000, Pakistan
   T: (0092) (91) 527 6519

Papua New Guinea   Box 673, Lae 411, Morobe Province, Papua New Guinea
   T: (00675) 472 4262   F: (00675) 472 1852   E: dpk07jan@gmail.com

Philippines   PO Box 10321, Broadway Centrum, 1112 Quezon City, Philippines
   F: (0063) (2) 721 1923   E: flaw997@gmail.com

Rwanda   BP 2487, Kigali, Rwanda
   F: (00250) 516 162   E: frkaremera@yahoo.co.uk

Scotland   21 Grosvenor Crescent, Edinburgh EH12 5EE, UK
   T: (0131) 255 6357   F: (0131) 346 7247   E: *via website* www.scotland.anglican.org

South America   Cro. Gral. Belgrano 946, Hurlingham, Buenos Aires 1686, Argentina
   T: (0053) (114) 452 7555   E: danielgenovesi@gmail.com

South East Asia   PO Box 10811, 88809 Kota Kinablu, Sabah, Malaysia
   E: kenneththien@gmail.com

South India   CSI Centre, 5 Whites Road, Royapettah, Chennai 600 041, India
T: (0091) (44) 2852 1566   F: (0091) (44) 2852 3258   E: synodcsi@gmail.com

South Sudan   PO Box 110, Juba, South Sudan
E: provincialsecretary@sudan.anglican.org

Southern Africa   20 Bishopscourt Drive, Bishopscourt, Claremont, 7708 South Africa
T: (0027) (21) 763 1300   F: (0027) (21) 797 1329   E: peo@anglicanchurchsa.org.za

Sudan   *See Anglican Communion website for contact details*

Tanzania   PO Box 899, Dodoma, Tanzania
T: (00255) (26) 232 4574   F: (00255) (26) 232 4565   E: chinyongole@gmail.com

Uganda   PO Box 14123, Kampala, Uganda
F: (00256) (414) 251 925   E: COUOffice@gmail.com

USA   Episcopal Church Center, 815 Second Avenue, New York NY 10017, USA
T: (001) (212) 716 6000   F: (001) (212) 490 3298   E: *via website* www.episcopalchurch.org

Wales   The Church in Wales, 2 Callaghan Square, Cardiff CF10 5BT, UK
T: (029) 2034 8200   E: *via website* wwwchurchinwales.org.uk

West Africa   PO Box KN 2023, Kaneshie, Accra, Ghana
T: (00233) (302) 257 370   E: cpwa2014@gmail.com

West Indies   Provincial Secretariat, Bamford House, Society Hill, St John, Barbados, West Indies
T: (001) (246) 423 0842   F: (001) (246) 423 0855   E: cpwi@caribsurf.com

ADDRESSES UNKNOWN

ALDIS, John Arnold. b 43. d 69. rtd 08; PtO *Glouc* from 14.

ANDREW, Donald. b 35. d 66. rtd 00.

APPELBE, Canon Frederick Charles. b 52. d 87. rtd 19.

ARTISS, Rebecca Jane. b 72. d 18. NSM Four Rivers *St E* from 18.

ASH, David Nicholas. b 61. d 03. V Prestatyn *St As* 15–17.

ASHTON, Canon William *Grant*. b 57. d 85. rtd 19; PtO *Blackb* from 19.

BAILY, Linda Rosemary. d 06. NSM Bro Ardudwy *Ban* from 15.

BAIN-DOODU, Canon Joseph Justice. b 56. d 86. PtO *Portsm* 09–12.

BARCLAY, Adam John. b 61. d 18. NSM Stanton *St E* from 18.

BARLING, Michael Keith. b 38. d 66. rtd 03.

BARTON, Trevor James. b 50. d 87. NSM Hemel Hempstead *St Alb* from 87.

BAXTER, Terence Hugh. b 48. d 92. PtO *Eur* from 11.

BAYLEY, Anne Christine. b 34. d 91. PtO *Heref* 05–19.

BENSON, Richard John. b 55. d 94. rtd 19.

BINKS, Robert Peter. b 73. d 10. P-in-c Warley Ch Ch and Gt Warley St Mary *Chelmsf* 14–18.

BLAIR, William *Henry*. b 66. d 04. Tullaniskin w Clonoe *Arm* from 19.

BOWDEN, Mrs Mary Eiluned. d 07. rtd 19.

BRUNT, Canon Philippa Ann. b 53. d 98. rtd 17.

BUTLER, Edward Daniel. b 42. d 68. PtO *Chich* 74–99.

CAPLE, Stephen Malcolm. b 55. d 88. rtd 19.

CARSON-FEATHAM, Canon Lawrence William. b 53. d 78. SSM from 77; rtd 19.

CHALKLEY, Andrew William Guy. b 64. d 95. R Beckington w Standerwick, Berkley, Rodden etc *B & W* 10–18.

CLARK, Canon Caroline Robbins (*Robbin*). b 45. d 81. rtd 16.

CLARK, Michael James. b 71. d 02. Miss Community Development Adv *Ex* from 19.

✠CLARKE, The Rt Revd Kenneth Herbert. b 49. d 72. Chmn SAMS (Ireland) from 94; Miss Dir from 13.

CLEMENTS, Andrew. b 48. d 73. rtd 19.

CLITHEROW, Canon Andrew. b 50. d 79. Hon Can Blackb Cathl from 07; Chapl Cen Lancs Univ from 12; Chapl to The Queen from 08.

COLMAN, Susan. b 59. d 12. NSM Onslow Square and S Kensington St Aug *Lon* from 12; PtO *Win* from 14.

CONWAY, Philip James. b 66. d 95. Chapl Abbots Bromley Sch 16–19.

COOPER, Mrs Jennifer Ann Lisbeth. b 45. d 04. rtd 13.

COOPER, Mrs Margaret *Anne*. b 54. d 14. PtO *Guildf* 18–19.

COX, Canon Sheila Margaret. b 54. d 03. rtd 19.

CRACKNELL, Heather Louise. b 76. d 11. V Nor Heartsease St Fran 17–19.

CRAIG, Gillean Weston. b 49. d 77. rtd 18; PtO *Cant* from 19.

CROOS, Sebastian John *Princely*. b 59. d 04. rtd 19.

DIETZ, Matthew Paul Richard. b 70. d 07. Chapl Taunton Sch 14–18.

DIXON, Charles William. b 41. d 81. rtd 06.

DOWMAN, Canon Jonathan Robert. b 76. d 07. Pioneer Development Worker *Leic* from 14; PtO from 15; Hon Can Leic Cathl from 19.

DREW, Daniel Alexander Blair. b 86. d 16. Australia from 19.

DUFF, Michael Ian. b 63. d 99. V Southsea St Jude *Portsm* 07–19; Hon Can Portsm Cathl 17–19.

DUNN, Derek William Robert. b 48. d 89. Bp's C Acton and Drumbanagher *Arm* from 09; V Choral Arm Cathl from 14.

EDMUNDS, Andrew Charles. b 57. d 89. rtd 19.

ELLERY, Ian Martyn William. b 56. d 82. rtd 16.

ELLIS, John Roland. b 32. d 69. rtd 99; PtO *Mon* from 12.

ENNION, Peter. b 56. d 89. rtd 19; PtO *Blackb* from 19.

EVANS, Daniel Barri. b 50. d 03. TV Hawarden *St As* from 15; TV Borderlands Miss Area from 17.

EVANS, Mrs Jennifer. b 41. d 88. Hon C Chaffcombe, Cricket Malherbie etc *B & W* 10–19.

EVANS, Nigel William Reid. b 70. d 01. TR Bucknall *Lich* 10–18; RD Stoke-on-Trent 17–18.

FAULKNER, Iain Stuart. d 12. NSM Stockwell St Andr and St Mich *S'wark* from 18.

FERRY, Malcolm Ronald Keith. b 66. d 96. I Agherton *Conn* from 19.

FINCH, Mrs Alison. b 59. d 92. rtd 18.

FINLINSON, Paul. b 58. d 89. PtO *Blackb* from 95; *Eur* from 19.

FLEMING, Miss Clare Margaret. b 55. d 87. PtO *St E* from 12.

FOOT, Daniel Henry Paris. b 46. d 79. rtd 16.

FREARSON, Andrew Richard. b 57. d 83. R Dollar *St And* 10–18.

GILMORE, David Samuel. b 70. d 03. R Soho St Anne w St Thos and St Pet *Lon* 08–10.

✠GOOD, The Rt Revd Kenneth Raymond. b 52. d 77. rtd 19.

GOODMAN, Brother Kevin Charles. b 54. d 06. C Cant St Dunstan, St Mildred and St Pet from 17.

GOODRIDGE, Paul Charles. b 54. d 04. Chapl Bucharest w Sofia *Eur* 16–19.

GREENWOOD, David Neal. b 70. d 14. P-in-c Kincardine O'Neil *Ab* 17–18.

GREENWOOD, Sharon. b 44. d 07. NSM Welling *S'wark* 07–18.

GRETTON-DANN, Judith Adrienne. b 75. d 14. NSM Chesterton Gd Shep *Ely* 14–19.

HALLETT, Howard *Adrian*. b 43. d 81. rtd 05.

HALLISSEY, Catherine Jane. d 14. I Powerscourt w Kilbride *D & G* from 19.

HARDY, Christopher Richard. b 52. d 90. rtd 19.

HARMER, Timothy James. b 47. d 95. rtd 12; PtO *Carl* from 16.

HARREX, David Brian. b 54. d 89. rtd 17; PtO *Bris* from 19.

HARRIS, John. b 54. d 86. rtd 13.

HARRIS, William Edric Mackenzie. b 46. d 75. rtd 16.

HART, David John. b 58. d 85. PtO *Lich* from 17.

HEWLETT, David Bryan. b 49. d 79. rtd 17; PtO *Heref* from 17.

HINDLE, Anne Margaret. b 57. d 99. rtd 19.

HINTON, Michael George. b 27. d 83. PtO *Cant* 95–19.

HOLDING, Kenneth George Frank. b 27. d 77. rtd 92.

HORTON, John. b 49. d 07. rtd 19.

HUGHES, Canon David Michael. b 41. d 68. rtd 09; PtO *Ches* from 09.

INCH, Vivian Ann. b 57. d 13. OLM High Wycombe *Ox* 13–16.

JAMES, Andrew Nicholas. b 54. d 80. rtd 19.

✠JAMES, The Rt Revd Graham Richard. b 51. d 75. Hon Can Dallas from 89; rtd 19.

JEFFORD, Peter Ernest. b 29. d 54. rtd 92.

JESSETT, David Charles. b 55. d 79. rtd 19.

KENNEDY, Brother Philip Bartholomew. b 47. d 98. SSF from 77; PtO *Chelmsf* from 17.

KIRBY, Mrs Elizabeth. b 56. d 10. rtd 19.

LAMB, Nicholas Henry. b 52. d 79. rtd 16.

LAVARELLO-SMITH, Mrs Lorna Mary. b 64. d 13. S Africa from 16.

LENTON de DICKIN, Mrs Patricia Margarita. b 72. d 08. TV S Gillingham *Roch* from 19.

LEONARD, John Francis. b 48. d 72. rtd 18.

McKEE, Patrick Joseph. b 49. d 94. rtd 19.

MANN, Julian Farrer Edgar. b 64. d 96. V Oughtibridge *Sheff* 00–19.

MASSIAH, Amrela Celeste. b 60. d 07. P-in-c St Phil St Martin Barbados from 16.

MAXTED, Neil Andrew. b 58. d 92. rtd 19.

MITCHELL, Alec Silas. b 52. d 99. rtd 18.

MOODY, Canon Christopher John Everard. b 51. d 75. rtd 19.

MORRIS, William Hazlitt. b 62. d 09. NSM St Martin-in-the-Fields *Lon* 09–19.

MORROW, David. b 63. d 89. rtd 11.

MURPHY, Mrs Deborah Ann. b 67. d 93. PtO *Lich* 14–18.

MUSSER, Ms Christine. b 55. d 00. rtd 19.

NENER, Canon Thomas *Paul* Edgar. b 42. d 80. rtd 10; PtO *Liv* from 16.

✠NTAHOTURI, The Most Revd Bernard. b 48. d 73. Dir Angl Cen Rome 17–18.

NWOGU, Okwunna Nketa. b 66. d 94. Adn Nigeria from 08; USA from 17.

NYATSANZA, Petros Hamutendi. b 69. d 95. Kenya from 18.

✠PAIN, The Rt Revd Richard Edward. b 56. d 84. rtd 19.

PARKER, Mrs Ann Jacqueline. b 41. d 95. Asst Chapl N Bris NHS Trust from 98; PtO *Bris* from 11.

PARSONS, George Horace Norman. b 19. d 68. rtd 85.

PARSONS, Stephen Drury. b 54. d 82. rtd 19.

PATTERSON, Anthony. b 43. d 83. rtd 11.

PAYNE, Mrs Anne Margaret. b 52. d 14. PtO *Guildf* from 18.

PENNIE, Mrs Fiona Clare. b 64. d 15. PtO *Liv* from 19.

PETERS, Malcolm John. b 71. d 03. PtO *Chelmsf* 18–19.

PRIME, David Alan. b 54. d 12. PtO *Mon* 15–17.

PRITCHETT, Antony Milner. b 63. d 98. rtd 19.

RAMSEY, Victoria Claire. b 71. d 11. C Ex St Mark, St Sidwell and St Matt 11–18.

RAYMENT, Andrew David. b 45. d 80. rtd 11.

REES, Miss Susan Mary. b 61. d 02. P-in-c Pontyclun w Talygarn *Llan* 14–19; P-in-c Llanharry 14–19.

REES-JONES, Mrs Diana Mary. b 58. **d** 07. rtd 19.

REEVES, Kenneth William. b 38. **d** 69. rtd 92; PtO *Nor* from 05.

REID, Donald. b 58. **d** 85. PtO *Edin* 15–17.

ROSS, Ashley Dawn. b 85. **d** 14. PtO *Liv* from 17.

RUITERS, Ivan John. b 61. **d** 96. S Africa from 18.

RUSSELL, Eric Watson. b 39. **d** 69. rtd 09.

SACRE, Phillip Daniel. b 83. **d** 14. C Gt Clacton *Chelmsf* 14–19.

SAWYER, Frank Denzil. b 71. **d** 97. Chapl Gtr Lisbon *Eur* 16–19.

SELLERS, George William. b 35. **d** 89. rtd 05.

SHORTER, Mrs Anne Roberta. b 56. **d** 09. rtd 19.

SKINNER, Stephen John. b 52. **d** 83. rtd 18.

SMALLWOOD, Simon Laurence. b 58. **d** 92. V Becontree St Geo *Chelmsf* 03–19.

SMART, Harry Gavin. b 67. **d** 94. Lead Mental Health Chapl Lincs Partnership NHS Foundn Trust 07–13.

SMITH, Mrs Denise. b 46. **d** 08. rtd 16; PtO *Man* from 18.

SOWDEN, Charles William Bartholomew. b 47. **d** 97. rtd 17.

STANLEY, Canon John Alexander. b 31. **d** 56. rtd 18; PtO *Ches* from 19.

STARTIN, Nicola Gail. b 57. **d** 90. Chapl Haslar Immigration Removal Cen 02–18.

STEPHENSON, James Alexander. b 77. **d** 11. Zambia from 19.

THOMSON, Sydney Bruce. b 49. **d** 07. rtd 19.

TRINDER, Miss Gillian Joyce. b 68. **d** 11. Chapl Ypres *Eur* 17–19.

WAKELIN, Alan Frank. b 32. **d** 60. rtd 97.

WALKER, Canon Lesley Ann. b 53. **d** 88. Hon Can Truro Cathl from 15; rtd 19.

WALLACE, James Marchant. **d** 11. C Waterford w Killea, Drumcannon and Dunhill *C & O* 11–17.

WALTNER, Moise (Mike). b 75. **d** 15. C Vienna *Eur* from 15.

WATSON, Timothy Daniel. b 71. **d** 11. R Hackett H Cross Australia from 18.

WATTS, David Henry. b 27. **d** 53. rtd 89.

WEDGE, Christopher Graham. b 67. **d** 06. PtO *Man* from 19.

WHITE, Canon Vernon Philip. b 53. **d** 77. Can Th Westmr Abbey 11–18; Sub-Dean 16–18; Visiting Prof K Coll Lon 11–18.

WHITMARSH, Mrs Pauline. b 45. **d** 04. rtd 14; PtO *Sarum* from 14.

WILKIE, Mrs Donna Louise. b 81. **d** 15. C Bris St Matt and St Nath from 18.

WILLIAMS, Julian Thomas. b 65. **d** 91. R Nursling and Rownhams *Win* 00–19.

WILTON, Mrs Gillian Linda. b 57. **d** 87. PtO *Eur* from 19.

WITCOMBE, Michael David. b 53. **d** 78. V Llanishen *Llan* 02–19.

WOOD, Brian Richard. b 49. **d** 07. rtd 19.

WOOD, Roger Graham. b 49. **d** 76. rtd 19.

WOODSFORD, Canon Andrew Norman. b 43. **d** 67. rtd 08; PtO *S'well* from 08.

YATES, Christopher David. **d** 10. V Eastbourne St Sav and St Pet *Chich* 16–17.

CLERGY WHO HAVE DIED SINCE THE LAST EDITION

A list of clergy who have died since 14 August 2019 when the compilation of the 2020–2021 edition was completed. The month and year of death (if known) are recorded with each entry.

ABEL, David John. 09/17
ABELL, Peter John. 01/19
ABLEWHITE, Stanley Edward. 05/19
ACKLAM, Leslie Charles. 12/18
ADAMS, Charles Alexander. 02/19
ADEY, John Douglas. 08/18
ADLINGTON, David John. 01/18
AHRENS, Irene Karla Elisabeth. 05/19
AINSWORTH, Peter. 01/19
AITKEN, Leslie St John Robert. 01/18
ALFORD, John. 07/18
ALLARD, John Ambrose. 12/17
ALLEN, Peter John Douglas. 12/18
ALLRED, Frank. 08/18
ALLSO, Michael Neal. 03/19
ANCRUM, John. 02/19
ANDERSON, David Graham. 01/19
ANDERSON, Michael. 04/19
APPLEFORD, Patrick Robert Norman. 12/18
ARCHER, Stanley Edwin. 09/17
ARNOLD, Sonja Marie. 05/18
ASKEW, Richard George. 01/19
ASTON, Glyn. 07/18
ATKINSON, Samuel Charles Donald. 02/18
ATTAWAY, Elizabeth Ann. 11/17
ATTFIELD, David George. 05/19
AUSTIN, George Bernard. 01/19
AUSTIN, Michael Ridgwell. 12/17
AYLING, John Michael. 12/17
AYLWARD, James Gareth. 10/17
BABINGTON, Gervase Hamilton. 11/17
BACHELL, Kenneth George. 05/18
BADDELEY, Martin James. 06/18
BAGULEY, Paul. 11/17
BAILLIE, Frederick Alexander. 03/18
BAILLIE, Frederick Alexander. 03/18
BAINBRIDGE, John Richard. 11/17
BAINES, Noel Edward (Ted). 09/17
BALDOCK, Norman. 12/18
✠BALL, Peter John. 06/19
BANGAY, Edward Newman. 01/19
BANKS, Brian William Eric. 05/19
BANKS, John Alan. 02/18
BANKS, Michael Lawrence. 07/18
BARBER, Margaret Ann. 09/18
BARHAM, Jennifer Mary. 07/18
BARLOW, Edward Burnley. 10/17
✠BARNES, Edwin Ronald. 02/19
BARRELL, Adrian Edward. 03/19
BARRETT, Gary John. 01/18
BARRETT, Kenneth Sydney. 08/18
BARTLE, David Colin. 12/18
BATCHELOR, Alan Harold. 12/18
BATES, William Hugh. 09/17
BATESON, Geoffrey Frederick. 08/18
BATTMAN, John Brian. 01/19
BATTY, Stephen Roy. 05/18
BAXTER, David Norman. 08/19
BAYLDON, Roger. 12/17
BAYNES, Matthew Thomas Crispin. 09/18
✠BEAK, Robert Michael Cawthorn. 01/18
BEARE, William. 03/19
BECK, Alan. 05/19
BECKERLEG, Barzillai. 04/18
BECKWITH, John Douglas. 11/18
BEESLEY, Ramon John. 10/17
BEGGS, Norman Lindell. 02/18
BELING, David Gibson. 03/19
BELL, Antony Fancourt. 04/18
BELL, John Christopher. 12/17
BELLAMY, Mervyn Roger Hunter. 06/18
BELLINGER, Denys Gordon. 07/18

BELOE, Robert Francis. 04/18
BENNETT, Ian Frederick. 12/17
BENNETT, Osmond Shirley. 08/18
BENNETT, Roy Donald. 07/18
BENTHAM, John William. 08/19
BENTLEY, Frank Richard. 04/19
BENTLEY, Graham John. 04/19
BERESFORD, Florence. 06/18
BERRY, Peter Austin. 05/18
BEVAN, Gareth Edward. 11/17
BEVAN, Richard Justin William. 03/18
BEWES, Richard Thomas. 05/19
BIBBY, Paul Benington. 02/19
✠BICKERSTETH, John Monier. 01/18
BIGGIN, Ronald. 03/18
BILLINGS, Derek Donald. 12/18
BIRCH, Thomas Reginald. 02/19
BIRD, Norman David. 02/18
BIRT, David Edward. 12/18
BISH, Donald. 04/18
BISHOP, David Henry Ryder. 05/19
BLACK, Robert John Edward Francis Butler. 09/18
BLACK, Robert John Edward Francis Butler. 09/18
BLACKBURN, Peter James Whittaker. 01/18
BLACKMAN, Brian David Eric. 01/18
BLACKSHAW, Trevor Roland. 07/18
BLACKTOP, Graham Leonard. 11/17
BLAKE, Philip Charles. 09/18
BLANKENSHIP, Charles Everett. 08/18
BLANKLEY, Roger Henry. 02/18
BLOOMFIELD, Susan Marie. 06/18
BLOXHAM, Oliver. 08/18
BLYTH, Bryan Edward Perceval. 02/18
✠BOND, Charles Derek. 07/18
BONNER, David Robert. 09/17
BONSALL, Charles Henry Brash. 04/19
BOOKER, Gerald Dennis. 09/19
BOTT, Theodore Reginald. 11/18
BOTT, Theodore Reginald. 11/18
BOTTING, Michael Hugh. 04/18
BOUGHTON, Paul Henry. 01/18
BOULD, Arthur Roger. 06/19
BOURNE, Henry. 08/18
BOWEN, David John. 04/19
BOX, Reginald Gilbert (Brother Reginald). 02/19
BOXALL, Keith Michael. 12/17
BOYCE, John Frederick. 01/18
BOYLAND, Henry Hubert. 01/19
BRADLEY, Brian Hugh Granville. 02/18
BRAE, Yvonne Rosetta. 03/18
BRAY, Kenneth John. 09/19
BREWER, Christina Anne. 02/19
BRINDLEY, Stuart Geoffrey Noel. 06/18
BROADBENT, Edward Ronald. 08/17
BROUGH, Gerald William. 12/17
BROWN, Bernard Herbert Vincent. 09/18
BROWN, Clive Lindsey. 02/18
BROWN, Colin. 05/19
BROWN, Elizabeth Charlotte. 02/18
BROWN, James Philip. 03/18
BROWN, Nicholas Francis Palgrave. 02/18
BROWN, Philip Roy. 01/18
✠BROWN, Ronald. 06/19
BROWNE, Aubrey Robert Caulfeild. 09/18
BRUCE, Francis Bernard. 12/17
BRYAN, William Terence. 11/17
BUCKLER, George Anthony (Tony). 07/18
BUCKMAN, Rossly David. 10/18

BUGG, Peter Richard. 04/18
BUNCE, Raymond Frederick. 10/18
BURDEN, Michael Henry. 05/18
BURGESS, Henry Percival. 01/19
BURGESS, John Edward. 03/19
BURGESS, Michael Anglin. 02/18
BURMAN, William Guest. 01/19
BURTON, Antony William James. 08/18
BURTON, Norman George. 08/17
BUSSEY, Norman. 11/17
BUTLER, Alan. 04/19
BUTT, Rowland Donald. 04/19
BYWORTH, Christopher Henry Briault. 08/17
CADDICK, Lloyd Reginald. 03/19
CADMAN, Margaret Elizabeth. 01/18
CAESAR, Anthony Douglass. 07/18
CALDWELL, Alan. 03/19
CALLIS, Stephen Harby. 12/18
CALVERT, John Stephen. 03/19
CANDELAND, Thomas Blyde. 02/18
CANHAM, John Graham. 07/19
CARMAN, Jill Youde. 05/19
CARRUTHERS, Arthur Christopher (Kester). 09/18
CAWTE, David John. 03/19
CAYTON, John. 09/17
CHALLICE, John Richard. 10/18
CHAMBERLAIN, Allen Charles William. 01/18
✠CHAMBERLAIN, Neville. 10/18
CHAMBERS, Christine. 10/17
CHAMPION, John Oswald Cecil. 04/19
CHANDA, Daniel Khazan. 04/19
CHAPMAN, Carl Lewis. 07/18
CHAPMAN, Michael Robin. 03/19
CHARLEY, Julian Whittard. 09/17
CHING, Derek. 06/19
CHITTENDEN, John Bertram d'Encer. 07/18
CHITTENDEN, Roy Norman. 10/17
CIANCHI, Dalbert Peter. 01/18
CLARKE, Douglas Charles. 04/18
CLARKE, Eric Samuel. 12/18
CLARKE, Harold George. 03/18
CLARKE, Ronald George. 10/18
CLARKSON, Eric George. 01/18
CLASPER, John. 05/19
CLAYTON, John. 04/18
CLYDE, John. 03/19
COBB, Marjorie Alice. 01/18
COE, John Norris. 12/18
COFFIN, Stephen. 03/19
COGGINS, Richard James. 11/17
COHEN, Clive Ronald Franklin. 04/19
COLBY, David Allan. 02/18
COLE, Michael Berkeley. 11/17
COLEMAN, Michael. 03/18
COLLETT, George Ernest. 07/18
COLLIE, Bertie Harold Guy. 01/19
COLLIS, Michael Alan. 01/18
COLMAN, Geoffrey Hugh. 09/17
CONLEY, James Alan. 12/17
CONWAY, Alfred Sydney. 06/18
COOK, Judith Mary. 06/19
COOK, Robert Bond. 01/19
COOMBE, James Anthony. 11/17
COOMBE, Michael Thomas. 12/18
COOPER, Brian Hamilton. 03/19
COOPER, Cecil Clive. 01/19
COOPER, Herbert William. 10/18
COOPER, Jeremy John. 01/18
COOPER, John Edward. 01/19
COPPING, John Frank Walter Victor. 08/18
CORBETT, John David. 03/19

1170

CORDY, Gordon Donald. 01/18
CORNISH, Anthony. 09/18
CORNISH, Dennis Henry Ronald. 04/19
COTTON, Richard William. 08/18
COURTNEY, Avril Marilyn. 10/17
COUSSMAKER, Colin Richard Chad. 08/18
COWLING, John Francis. 12/17
COX, Paul Graham. 11/17
COX, Susan Margaret. 06/19
CRADDOCK, Jeremy Graham. 08/17
CRAIG, Eric. 01/18
CRAIG-WILD, Dorothy Elsie (Dhoe). 06/19
CRANIDGE, Wendy Ann. 05/19
CRASTON, Richard Colin. 01/18
CREASEY, David John. 12/18
CROCKER, Keith Gwillam. 11/17
CROSS, John Henry Laidlaw. 11/18
CROSSLEY, George Alan. 04/19
CROWE, Eric Anthony. 11/18
CROWTHER, Frank. 01/19
CROWTHER-GREEN, Michael Leonard. 09/18
CRUICKSHANKS, Arlene Elizabeth Henderson. 02/19
CRUMP, Stephen Thomas. 07/19
CUMMINS, James Ernest. 10/18
CURRIE, Alan Richard. 09/17
CURTIS, Peter Bernard. 07/19
CURWEN, David. 03/19
CURWEN, James Gilbert. 03/18
DAGLISH, John David. 08/19
DAKIN, Reginald James Blanchard. 10/17
DALE, Barbara. 09/18
DARBY, Michael Barwick. 01/18
DAVENPORT, Sybil Ann. 03/19
DAVEY, John. 01/19
DAVIDSON, Ian George. 07/19
DAVIES, Bernard. 11/18
DAVIES, Clifford Thomas. 01/18
DAVIES, Dillwyn. 02/19
DAVIES, Evelyn Dorothy. 12/18
✠DAVIES, Francis James Saunders. 03/18
DAVIES, John Melvyn George. 03/18
DAVIES, John Oswell. 05/18
DAVIES, Mervyn Morgan. 10/17
DAVIES, Raymond Emlyn Peter. 04/18
DAVIES, Roy Basil. 07/19
DAVIS, John Brian. 11/18
DAWES, Julian Edward. 05/19
DAY, Audrey. 03/18
de BOWEN, Alfred William. 12/17
DE WIT, John. 06/18
DE WOLF, Mark Anthony. 04/18
DEACON, Donald (Brother Angelo). 02/19
DEACON, Timothy Randall. 07/18
DEAKIN, John Hartley. 07/19
DEAN, Alan. 12/18
DEAN, Andrew James. 07/18
DEAN, Arthur. 07/18
DEAN, John Milner. 09/17
DESMOND, Margaret Elspeth. 07/18
DEVINE, Maureen Mary. 05/18
DEVONSHIRE, Roger George. 12/17
DICKERSON, Richard Keith. 04/18
DICKINSON, Henry. 03/19
DICKINSON, Simon Braithwaite Vincent. 02/19
DIXON, David. 09/17
DIXON, Roger John. 04/18
DOBBS, George Christopher. 03/19
DODSWORTH, George Brian Knowles. 07/19
DOGGETT, Margaret Ann. 10/18
DOHERTY, Deana Rosina Mercy. 01/18
DOWNER, Cuthbert John. 10/17
DRIVER, Deborah Jane. 04/18
DROWN, Richard. 11/18
DRUMMOND, Christopher John Vaughan. 12/18
DUFF, Garden Ian. 03/18
DUFFETT, Paul Stanton. 09/17

DUGUID, Reginald Erskine. 01/19
DUNCAN, William Albert. 02/19
DUNKERLEY, James Hobson. 08/18
DUNN, Anne. 12/17
DUNN, Christopher George Hunter. 09/19
DURELL, Jane Vavasor. 01/18
DUTFIELD, Alan. 03/19
DUXBURY, Margaret Joan. 04/18
EADES, Jonathan Peter. 12/18
EARNSHAW, Robert Richard. 06/18
EARP, John William. 04/18
EDGELL, Hugh Anthony Richard. 06/18
EDWARDS, David Lawrence. 04/18
EDWARDS, Peter Clive. 05/18
EDWARDS, Steven Charles. 03/19
EDWARDSON, Joseph Philip. 02/19
ELLENS, Gordon Frederick Stewart. 04/18
ELLIOTT, Peter. 03/19
ELLIOTT, Peter Wolstenholme. 03/19
ELLIOTT, William. 12/17
ELLIS, Malcolm Railton. 02/19
✠ELLISON, John Alexander. 08/19
ELSON, John Frederick. 02/18
ELVY, Peter David. 08/19
EMM, Robert Kenneth. 01/19
ENEVER, John William. 12/18
ENGLISH, Peter Gordon. 12/17
ETTERLEY, Peter Anthony Gordon. 10/18
EUSTICE, Peter Lafevre. 09/19
EVANS, David Frederick Francis. 12/17
EVANS, David Leslie Bowen. 04/19
EVANS, Desmond. 02/18
EVANS, Gareth Rae. 12/18
EVANS, John Griffiths. 12/17
EVANS, Madeleine Thelma Bodenham. 07/18
EVERSON, Owen Neville. 03/18
FACER, Rosemary Jane. 05/18
FAIRBROTHER, Robin Harry. 09/18
FAIRWEATHER, David James. 04/18
FARRANT, David Stuart. 01/18
FARRAR, James Albert. 03/18
FARRAR, Roy Alfred. 07/18
FARRER, Michael Robert Wedlake. 05/18
FAULKNER, Roger Kearton. 01/18
FAURE WALKER, Edward William. 06/18
FAWCETT, Pamela Margaret. 03/19
FEATHERSTONE, John. 08/18
FEREDAY, Harold James Rodney. 06/19
FERGUSSON, Catherine Margaret. 11/18
FIELDING, John Joseph. 02/19
FILLINGHAM, Richard James. 11/17
FINCH, Thomas. 05/19
FISHER, Humphrey John. 05/19
FISHLOCK, Margaret Winifred (Peggy). 03/18
FITZHARRIS, Barry. 10/17
FLEMING, Ronald Thorpe. 12/18
FLETCHER, Douglas. 09/17
FOOT, Paul. 03/19
FORBES, John Francis. 08/18
FORBES ADAM, Sir Stephen Timothy Beilby Bt. 03/19
FORD, David George. 07/18
FORGAN, Eleanor. 10/17
FORSTER, David John. 04/19
FORWARD, Ronald George. 12/17
FOSBUARY, David Frank. 04/18
FOSTER, Albert Edward John. 02/19
FOX, Harvey Harold. 03/18
FOX, Maurice Henry George. 05/18
FRANCE, John Andrew. 11/17
FRANCIS, Annette. 03/19
FRAY, Roger William. 07/19
FREE, James Michael. 07/19
FREEBAIRN-SMITH, Jane. 04/19
FRENCH, Dendle Charles. 11/18
FRESTON, John Samuel Kern. 09/18
FROST, Julian. 01/18

FROST, Ronald Andrew. 01/18
FROSTICK, John George. 04/19
FRYER, George. 05/19
GALES, Alan. 11/17
GALT, Ian Ross. 06/18
GAMBLE, David Lawrence. 05/19
GARDINER, Kenneth Ashton. 05/18
GARDNER, Anthony Brian. 11/18
GARRISH, Elaine Joan. 11/17
GASH, Christopher Alan Ronald. 04/18
GASH, Wilfred John. 01/18
GATES, John Michael. 02/18
GAY, Colin James. 06/18
GEACH, Sarah Jane. 01/19
✠GEAR, Michael Frederick. 01/18
GERRISH, David Victor. 02/18
GIBBARD, Roger. 04/18
GIBBS, William Gilbert. 09/18
GIBSON, Brenda. 02/19
GIBSON, David Innes. 07/19
GIBSON, Thomas Thomson. 02/19
GILCHRIST, Lawrence Edward. 12/17
GILL, Gary George. 05/19
GILLIONS, Michael George. 12/17
GIRARD, William Nicholas Charles. 02/18
GODDARD, David. 11/18
GODDARD, John David. 02/18
GOMPERTZ, Helen Morey. 10/18
GOODCHILD, John McKillip. 12/18
GOODER, Martin Lee. 06/19
GOODHEW, Roy William. 12/18
GOODMAN, Derek George. 06/18
GOODSELL, Patrick. 03/18
GORDON, Edward John. 04/18
GORDON, Robert Andrew. 12/17
GORDON CLARK, Charles Philip. 06/18
GORICK, Janet Margaret. 12/17
GOUGH, David Kenneth. 11/18
GRAHAM, Anthony Stanley David. 12/18
GRAINGER, Bruce. 09/19
GRAINGER, Horace. 12/18
GRANT, Rodney Arthur. 07/19
GREEN, Edward John. 01/19
GREEN, Edward Michael Bankes. 02/19
GREEN, Richard Charles. 03/19
GREGORY, Graham. 04/19
GRETTON, Tony Butler. 11/18
GRICE, Charles. 08/19
GRIFFIN, Gerald Albert Francis. 11/18
GRIFFITH, Frank Michael. 01/18
GRIFFITH, John Laurence Powell. 03/18
GRIFFITHS, David Percy Douglas. 03/18
GRIFFITHS, Roger. 01/19
GROVER, Wilfrid John. 02/18
GUEST, David. 06/19
GUNSTONE, John Thomas Arthur. 07/18
✠HABGOOD, John Stapylton. 03/19
HAGGAN, David Anthony. 10/17
HAINES, Anne Elizabeth. 01/19
HAINES, Anne Elizabeth Colton. 01/19
HALAHAN, Maxwell Crosby. 01/19
HALL, Ann Addington. 05/19
HALL, Ronald Cecil. 03/18
HALLAM, Peter Hubert. 05/19
HALLETT, Raymond. 12/18
HALLOWS, John Martin. 06/18
HALSEY, Anthony Michael James. 01/18
HAMLETT, Leslie. 11/17
HAMMOND, Brian Leonard. 01/18
HAMPSON, Robert Edward. 05/18
HANCOCK, Ivor Michael. 06/19
HARDMAN, Bryan Edwin. 12/18
HARDWICK, John Audley. 09/18
HARDY, Michael Frederick Bryan. 01/18
HARGREAVES-STEAD, Terence Desmond. 08/17
HARRIS, Derrick William. 09/17
HARRIS, Kenneth. 06/18
HARRISON, Brian John. 07/18
HARRISON, Philip Hubert. 03/19

HARTRIDGE, James Bernard Robertson. 07/19
HARVEY, Anthony Ernest. 01/18
HARVEY, John. 02/19
HASLAM, James Robert. 04/18
HASTEY, Erle. 03/18
HASTROP, Paul. 03/18
HATHAWAY, John Albert. 08/18
HAWKINS, Andrew Robert. 11/18
HAWTHORNE, William James (Jim). 07/18
HAYES, Brian Richard Walker. 12/17
HAYES, David Roland Payton. 01/19
HAYNES, John Stanley. 03/18
HAYNES, Peter. 03/18
HAZELL, Frederick Roy. 07/19
HAZELL, Thomas Jeremy. 06/19
HAZLEHURST, David John Benedict (Benny). 12/18
HEAD, Derek Leonard Hamilton. 07/18
HEADLAND, James Frederick. 02/18
HEALD, William Roland. 04/18
HEBDEN, John Percy. 02/18
HEFFER, William John Gambrell. 03/19
HEMINGWAY, Peter. 08/17
HENDERSON, Alastair Roy. 04/19
HENLEY, David Edward. 12/18
HETHERINGTON, Glynis Catherine. 04/19
HEWITT, William Patrick. 09/18
HIGHAM, Jack. 06/18
HILLS, Richard Leslie. 05/19
HINKSMAN, Adrian James Terence. 10/18
HIRST, Carol Anne. 06/19
HITCHMOUGH, William. 06/18
HODGE, Albert. 12/18
HODGKINSON, John. 06/19
HOEY, Thomas Kenneth (Augustine). 09/17
HOLDEN, Jack Crawford (Simon). 02/19
HOLMES, Anthony David Robert. 10/18
HOLMES, Clive Horace. 04/18
HOLMES, Frank. 04/19
HOLYER, Vincent Alfred Douglas. 07/18
HOPE, Edith. 02/18
HOWARD JONES, Raymond Vernon. 11/17
HOWE, David Randall. 11/17
HOWE, Frances Ruth. 09/17
HOWE, John. 03/18
HOWELL, David. 11/17
HOWES, Kathleen Valerie. 11/18
HOWITT, John Leslie. 12/17
HUBBARD, David Harris. 03/19
HUGHES, Steven Philip. 02/19
HULETT, Peter. 05/19
HULME, Norman. 03/18
HUMPHREY, Heather Mary. 02/18
HUMPHRYES, Garry James. 06/19
HUNT, Alan. 05/19
HUNTER, Frank Geoffrey. 06/19
HUNTER, Ian Paton. 10/17
HURLEY, Daniel Timothy. 08/18
HURLOCK, Ronald James. 03/19
HURT, Grenda Mary. 11/18
HUTCHINSON, Hugh Edward. 04/18
HUXHAM, Hector Hubert. 03/19
HUXLEY, William Thomas. 03/19
HYDE, Anthony Arthur. 02/19
✠INWOOD, Richard Neil. 04/19
ISAACS, John Kenneth. 09/17
ISAM, Margaret Myra Elizabeth (Wendy). 12/18
ISBISTER, Charles. 10/18
JACKSON, David. 03/18
JACSON, Edward Shallcross Owen. 09/19
JAMES, Joshua John Gerwyn. 05/19
JARMAN, John Geoffrey. 04/18
JASPER, Jonathan Ernest Farley. 08/18
JEFFERSON, Michael William. 05/18
JEFFERY, Peter Noel. 01/19

JENNER, Michael Albert. 08/19
JENNINGS, Peter James. 01/19
JENNINGS, Thomas Robert. 09/18
JEPPS, Philip Anthony. 10/17
JOB, Evan Roger Gould. 08/18
JOHNSON, Beverley Charles. 07/18
JOHNSON, Christopher Dudley. 07/18
JOHNSON, Colin Gawman. 07/18
JOHNSON, Peter Colin. 12/18
JONES, Alan John. 01/18
JONES, Alwyn Humphrey Griffith. 01/18
JONES, David Roy. 02/18
JONES, Gareth. 10/17
JONES, Margaret. 01/19
JONES, William Douglas. 11/18
JONES, William Douglas. 11/18
JORDAN, Robert Brian. 09/18
KASOZI, Jackson Nsamba. 08/18
KAYE-BESLEY, Lesley Kathleen. 11/18
KEENAN, Leslie Herbert (Bertie). 02/19
KELLY, Dennis Charles. 07/19
KELLY, Edward William Moncrieff. 04/19
KELLY, William. 10/18
KELLY, William Edward. 11/18
KENNY, Frederick William Bouvier. 12/17
KERR, Arthur Henry. 08/18
KERR, Charles Alexander Gray. 04/18
KERRIN, Albert Eric. 08/18
KING, Brian Henry. 07/19
KING, Dennis. 12/18
KING, John. 06/19
KING, Michael Charles. 01/19
KINGHAM, Derek Henry. 12/17
KIRBY, David Anthony. 02/19
KIRKPATRICK, William John Ashley. 01/18
LAMBERT, Ian Anderson. 09/17
LANE, Anthony James. 05/19
LAPAGE, Michael Clement. 07/18
LARNER, Gordon Edward Stanley. 01/19
LAW, Richard Lindsey. 01/18
LAW, Robert James. 03/18
LAWRENCE, Leonard Roy. 04/18
LAWSON, David William. 11/17
LAWSON, Robert William. 01/19
LEA, Richard John Rutland. 02/18
LEACH, Gerald. 09/17
LEAK, John Michael. 04/18
LEES, Allan Garside. 11/18
LEGG, Peter Ellis. 01/19
LEIGH, Dennis Herbert. 03/19
LEIGH, Roy Stephen. 10/18
LENDRUM, William Henry. 08/18
LENNARD, Elizabeth Jemima Mary Patricia (Mary Pat). 11/17
LEONARD, Peter Michael. 10/18
LEWIS, David Tudor. 09/19
LEWIS, John Thomas. 02/19
LEWIS, Norman Eric. 02/18
LEWIS LLOYD, Timothy David. 08/18
LINFORD, John Kenneth. 10/17
LLOYD, Simon David. 08/19
LONG, Edward Percy Eades (Bill). 02/18
LONG, Michael David Barnby. 08/18
LOUGHTON, Michael. 12/18
LOVEJOY, John Geoffrey. 03/19
LOWE, John Forrester. 01/19
LOWEN, John Michael. 12/17
LUBKOWSKI, Richard Jan. 02/19
LUCAS, Paul de Neufville. 11/18
LYON, Dennis. 06/18
MACE, David Sinclair. 03/19
MacGREGOR, Alan John. 02/19
McINTOSH, David Henry. 07/19
MacINTOSH, George Grant. 10/18
MACKAY, Hedley Neill. 05/18
McKEEMAN, David Christopher. 09/18
MACKEY, John. 05/18
MACKIE, Ian William. 09/17
McKINNEY, James Alexander. 01/19
MACLEAN, Kenneth John Forbes. 01/18

McLEAN, Michael Stuart. 11/17
MACNAUGHTON, James Alastair. 10/17
MAGEE, Frederick Hugh. 04/19
MAGOR, Robert Jolyon. 09/18
MAHONEY, William Denis. 03/19
MAHONY, Conal Martin. 09/17
MANLEY, Gordon Russell Delpratt. 09/17
MANN, Donald Leonard. 12/17
MANN, Gillian Mary. 01/18
MAPSON, John Victor. 11/17
MARKHAM, Deryck O'Leary. 06/18
MARRIOTT, Frank Lewis. 05/19
MARRISON, Geoffrey Edward. 11/17
MARSDEN-JONES, Watkin David. 12/17
MARSHALL, Basil Eustace Edwin. 03/19
MARSHALL, Rodney Henry. 12/18
MARTIN, David Alfred. 03/19
MARTIN, Richard Hugh. 04/18
MARTIN, Vicky. 04/19
MASON, William Frederick. 11/18
MASON, William Hugh Owen. 10/17
MATTHEWS, Francilla Lacey. 03/19
MATTHEWS, Terence Leslie. 08/17
MATTY, Horace Anthony (Tony). 02/18
MAY, Donald Charles Leonard. 03/19
MAY, George Louis. 04/19
MEAD, John Harold. 09/18
MEDHURST, Leslie John. 02/19
MELBOURNE, Brian Kenneth. 01/18
MELINSKY, Michael Arthur Hugh. 10/18
MELINSKY, Michael Arthur Hugh. 10/18
MELLOR, David John. 09/17
MILLER, Geoffrey Edward. 04/19
MILLER, Paul Richard. 08/18
MILLS, Alan Francis. 04/18
MILTON, Claudius James Barton. 11/17
MINCHEW, Donald Patrick. 08/18
MINORS, Graham Glyndwr Cavil. 01/19
MOORE, Edward James. 03/18
MOORE, John. 11/18
MOORE, Terry Chapple. 01/19
MOORE, William Morris. 04/18
MORAN, Adrian Peter. 11/17
MORGAN, Anthony Paul George. 02/19
MORGAN, Christopher John. 04/19
MORGAN, Clive. 01/18
MORGAN, Michael John. 09/17
MORPHY, Michael John. 08/19
MORRIS, Bernard Lyn. 06/19
MORRIS, Brian Michael Charles. 07/19
MORRIS, John. 07/18
MORTON, Mark Paul. 05/19
MOSS, Kenneth Charles. 03/18
MOTH, Susan. 07/18
MOXON, Michael Anthony. 07/19
MULKERN, Richard Neville. 07/19
MUNRO, Terence George. 07/18
MUNT, Cyril. 12/18
MURNANE, Terence Francis. 04/18
MURRIE, Clive Robert. 02/18
MUST, Albert Henry. 08/19
MYATT, Philip Bryan. 07/19
NANCARROW, Caroline Elisabeth. 12/17
NAYLOR, Robert James. 12/19
NEAL, Christopher Charles. 02/19
NEAL, Frances Mary. 05/19
NEUDEGG, Joan Mary. 01/18
NEWELL, Samuel James. 08/19
✠NEWING, Dom Kenneth Albert. 05/19
NEWTH, Barry Wilfred. 04/18
NICHOLL, John Hawdon. 01/18
NICHOLLS, Brian Albert. 11/17
NICHOLSON, Harold Sydney Leonard. 11/17
NICHOLSON, Trevor Parry. 06/19
NOBBS, Edward Frank Leslie. 05/19
NOBLE, Alexander Frederick Innes (Sandy). 04/18
NORBURN, Richard Henry. 11/17

NORRIS, Barry John. 01/18
NORRIS, Eric Richard. 10/17
✠NOTT, Peter John. 08/18
NUGENT, Eric William. 12/17
NUNN, Peter Michael. 07/18
OAKES, Graham. 08/19
OAKES, Melvin. 09/18
ODDY, Frederick Brian. 05/18
OLDHAM, Dale Raymond. 11/17
OLDNALL, Frederick Herbert. 10/17
OLDROYD, Trevor. 09/17
OLPHIN, Maureen Rose. 09/18
ORCHARD, Tryphena Jane. 05/19
ORME, John. 05/18
OSBORN, John Geoffrey Rowland. 07/19
OSBORNE, Robin Orbell. 05/18
OTTER, Anthony Frank. 10/18
OWEN, Graham Wynne. 05/19
PAGE, Dorothy Jean. 06/19
PAGET, Alfred Ivor. 12/17
PAIN, Michael Broughton George. 09/18
PAINTER, John. 10/17
PAKENHAM, Charles Wilfrid. 01/18
PALMER, Peter Parsons. 06/18
PALMER, Robert William. 03/18
PARKER, John Bristo. 09/17
PARKIN, Trevor Kinross. 08/17
PARRY, Nicholas John Sinclair. 07/18
PARTRIDGE, David John Fabian. 01/18
PATEMAN, Edward Brian. 02/19
PATERSON, David. 06/19
PATERSON, Rex Douglas Trevor. 12/18
PATTERSON, John. 07/18
PATTERSON, Trevor Harold. 10/17
PATTISON, Graham Bentley. 11/17
PEACOCK, John. 07/19
PEAKE, Sue. 04/19
PEARCE, John Frederick Dilke. 09/17
PEARSON, Brian Robert. 08/19
PEARSON, Christian David John (Brother Christian). 07/18
PEARSON, George Michael. 12/17
PEARSON, George Michael. 12/17
PEARSON, John Graham. 03/18
PEAT, Lawrence Joseph. 03/18
PEDDER, Brian. 12/17
PELL, Charles Andrew. 04/19
PELLEY, John Lawless. 05/19
PELLING, Nicholas Philip. 08/18
PERCIVAL, Richard Thomas. 11/18
PERDUE, Ernon Cope Todd. 12/18
PERKS, David Leonard Irving. 08/19
PERRY, David William. 06/18
PETERSON, Dennis. 05/19
PETTY, John Fitzmaurice. 08/17
PHILLIPS, Horace George. 02/18
PHILLIPS, Kenneth John. 10/17
PHILLIPS, Peter. 03/18
PHILLIPS, Thomas Wynford. 06/18
PICKERING, John Michael Staunton. 12/18
PILKINGTON, John Rowan. 04/19
PITCHER, Ronald Charles Frederick. 06/19
PLATT, John Dendy. 06/19
PLAXTON, Edmund John Swithun. 12/18
PONT, Gordon John Harper. 03/19
POOLE, David. 08/18
PORTEOUS, Michael Stanley. 07/18
POTHEN, Simon John. 11/17
POTIPHER, John Malcolm Barry. 04/18
POULTON, Arthur Leslie. 09/18
POWELL, Colin Arthur. 07/19
PRAGNELL, John William. 08/17
PRATT, William Ralph. 03/18
PREECE, Ronald Alexander. 05/18
PRESTON, Donald George. 06/19
PRICE, Richard Philip. 09/18
PRINS, Stanley Vernon. 06/18
PRIOR, Kenneth Francis William. 02/18
PUGH, Ronald Keith. 10/18
PULFORD, Stephen Ian. 06/18
PYNE, Robert Leslie. 06/19

RAMSAY, Eric Nicolson. 05/18
RAMSDEN, Arthur Stuart. 01/18
RANDALL, Gareth John. 08/18
RANDELL, David Peter. 10/17
RAVENS, David Arthur Stanley. 08/18
RAWLING, Stephen Charles. 02/18
RAYMENT, Helen Elizabeth. 10/18
RAYNER, Karen June. 09/18
READ, Andrew Gordon. 05/19
READ, John Samuel. 09/17
RECORD, Marion Eva. 03/18
REDWOOD, David Leigh. 07/19
REED, Alan Ronald. 12/18
REES, Percival Antony Everard. 08/19
REES, Richard Michael. 03/18
REEVES, Christopher. 09/17
REVELL, Patrick Walter Millard. 10/18
REYNOLDS, David Hammerton. 08/17
RICE, Peter Langford. 11/18
RICHARDS, David. 02/18
RICHARDS, John William. 01/19
RICHARDSON, Michael Arkley. 03/19
RICHMOND, Gordon Hazlewood. 11/18
RIDDELSDELL, John Creffield. 03/18
RIDLEY, Michael Edward. 12/17
RIDLEY, Simon. 07/18
RILEY, John Martin. 02/18
RIMMER, Paul Nathanael. 07/18
ROBBINS, Peter Tyndall. 12/17
ROBERTS, Joseph Aelwyn. 01/18
ROBINSON, Raymonde Robin. 08/19
ROBSON, Gilbert Alan. 04/18
RODGERS, John Terence Roche. 01/18
ROGERS, Kenneth. 02/19
ROGERS, William Arthur. 09/17
ROGERSON, John William. 09/18
ROLSTON, Cyril Willis Matthias. 09/17
ROOKE, John George Michael. 12/18
ROSS, Frederick Kenneth Wilson. 01/18
ROSS, Henry Ernest. 06/19
ROSSITER, Donald William Frank. 02/19
ROWE, John Goring. 12/17
ROWSELL, John Bishop. 11/17
ROYLE, Stanley Michael. 09/18
RUDIGER, David John. 12/18
RUMENS, John Henry. 05/18
RUSK, Frederick John. 02/19
RUTHERFORD, John Bilton. 02/18
RYALL, John Francis Robert. 01/18
SALMON, Mark Harold. 07/19
SALMON, Mark Harold. 07/19
SANDERSON, Scott. 04/18
SAUNDERS, David. 12/17
SAUNDERS, Malcolm Walter Mackenzie. 07/19
SCAIFE, Andrew. 04/18
SCHARIAH, Zechariah. 01/19
SCHOFIELD, John Verity. 11/17
SCOTT, Gordon. 01/18
SCOTT, Helen Ruth. 02/19
SCREECH, Michael. 06/18
SCREECH, Michael Andrew. 06/18
SCRINE, Ralph. 10/17
SEAL, Philip Trevor. 09/18
SEAR, Terence Frank. 11/18
SEATON, James Bradbury. 03/18
SENIOR, George. 07/19
SENNITT, Nicholas David. 06/19
SERJEANT, John Frederick. 12/18
SEYMOUR, David. 12/17
SHACKLETON, Ian Roderick. 03/19
SHARPLES, Derek. 03/18
SHARPLEY, Roger Ernest Dion. 02/18
SHAW, David Parlane. 12/18
SHAW, Peter Haslewood. 09/18
SHEARER, John Frank. 09/18
SHEPHERD, Frederick John. 03/19
SHEPPARD, Derrick Richard Adam. 06/19
SHIELDS, Michael Penton. 12/18
SHINER, Michael Joseph. 02/18
SHOTTER, Edward Frank. 07/19
SIMMONDS, David Brian. 06/18
SIMMONDS, Edward Alan. 08/19

SIMMONS, Maurice Samuel. 11/17
SIMPSON, Geoffrey Sedgwick. 02/18
SIMPSON, Janet Mary. 10/17
SIMPSON, John Arthur. 04/19
SITCH, Keith Frank. 10/17
SKELLEY, Janice Ann. 10/17
SKLIROS, Michael Peter. 10/18
SKUBLICS, Ernest. 04/19
SLATER, Philip David. 10/17
SMALL, David Binney. 08/19
SMITH, David Watson. 09/18
SMITH, Derek Arthur. 09/17
SMITH, Derek Arthur Byott. 01/18
✠SMITH, Donald Westwood. 04/18
SMITH, Elizabeth Ann. 08/19
SMITH, Geoffrey Cobley. 09/17
SMITH, James. 10/17
SMITH, James Edward. 07/19
SMITH, James Henry. 09/18
SMITH, John William. 09/19
SMITH, Kenneth Victor George. 10/18
SMITH, Penelope Rawling. 03/18
SMITH, Peter Michael. 11/17
SMITH, Raymond Frederick. 06/19
SMITH, Ronald William. 03/18
SMITH, Rowan Quentin. 05/18
SMITH, Wendy Hamlyn. 04/18
SMITS, Eric. 01/18
SMOUT, Michael John. 03/18
SNOW, Campbell Martin Spencer. 03/18
SOUPER, Patrick Charles. 04/18
SOUTHWARD, Douglas Ambrose. 05/19
SPEAKMAN, Joseph Frederick. 01/19
SPENCE, James Knox. 08/18
SPRAY, Charles Alan Francis Thomas. 07/19
SPRENT, Michael Francis (Brother Giles). 08/18
SPURIN, Richard Mark. 02/19
STAINES, Michael John. 11/18
STEDMAN, Robert Alfred. 01/19
STEPHENSON, John Joseph. 06/19
STEWART, William Jones. 04/19
STOKES, Donald Roy. 08/19
STOKES, Terence Walter. 03/19
STONE, Michael Graham. 09/17
STOTT, Antony. 06/19
STOTT, Antony John. 06/19
STOTT, Eric. 08/18
STRATTON, John Jefferies. 09/17
STREVENS, Richard Ernest Noel. 01/18
STUART, Herbert James. 02/19
SURTEES, Brian Lawrence. 02/18
SWABY, Keith Graham. 09/17
SWAIN, David Noel. 10/18
SWANBOROUGH, Robert Charles. 09/19
SWANN, Antony Keith. 11/17
SWEET, Margaret Adelaide. 01/18
TALBOT, Alan John. 08/18
TAMPLIN, Roger Ian. 12/17
TAPLIN, John. 01/18
TAYLOR, Brian. 12/17
TAYLOR, Norman. 04/18
TAYLOR, Roy Partington. 11/17
TEED, John Michael. 10/18
TEGGIN, John. 12/17
TELLINI, Gianfranco. 11/17
THOMAS, Bryan. 05/18
THOMAS, David Glynne. 07/19
THOMAS, Edward Walter Dennis. 08/17
THOMAS, Richard Frederick. 11/18
THOMAS, Simon Jonathan Francklin. 03/19
THOMAS, Thomas John Samuel. 07/19
THOMAS, William George. 04/19
THOMAS, William Phillip. 09/17
THOMPSON, Eric John. 03/18
THOMPSON, Gordon Henry Moorhouse. 02/19
THOMSON, Richard Irving. 03/19
TILLEY, Peter Robert. 02/18
TODD, Joy Gertrude. 09/18
TODD, Norman Henry. 04/18
TOLL, Brian Arthur. 01/18

TONGE, Malcolm. 09/17
TOOGOOD, Noel Hare. 12/18
TOOLEY, Norman Oliver. 07/18
TOOMBS, Ian Melvyn. 12/18
TOWNROE, Edward John. 07/18
TOWNSEND, Peter. 03/19
TOWNSHEND, Edward George Hume. 09/17
TREANOR, Terence Gerald. 04/18
TREASURE, Joy Elvira. 03/18
TRILL, Victor Alfred Mansfield. 10/17
TUCKER, Desmond Robert. 06/19
TUCKER, John Yorke Raffles. 11/17
TURNER, Donald. 12/18
TURNER, Lawrence John. 08/19
TURNER, Thomas Francis. 12/17
TWYFORD, Arthur Russell. 09/17
USHER, George. 11/17
VALENTINE, Jeremy Wilfred. 08/19
VERSCHOYLE, Dermot Henry. 02/19
VETTERS, Shirley Jacqueline Margaret. 01/18
VINER, Leonard Edwin. 07/19
VOGT, Robert Anthony. 12/18
WADE, Walter. 07/18
WADSWORTH, Roy. 09/17
WAIYAKI, Jennie. 09/19
WAKEFIELD, David Geoffrey. 07/18
WALKER, David Grant. 12/17
WALKER, Edward Charles. 09/18
WALKER, Margaret (Sister Lucy Clare). 09/18
WALKER, Walter Stanley. 10/18
WALSH, John Alan. 07/19
WARD, Geoffrey Edward. 04/18
WARD, Michael Henry. 12/18
WARD, William Francis. 10/18
WARDEN, John Michael. 06/18
WAREHAM, Sheila. 10/17
WARING, John Valentine. 07/19
WARREN, Norman Leonard. 06/19
WARREN, Robert Irving. 04/18
WATERS, Jill Christine. 05/19
WATKINS, Hilary Odette. 02/19
WATKINS, William Hywel. 07/18

WATLING, Brian. 11/18
WATLING, David Brian. 11/18
WATLING, Rosemary Dawn. 09/18
WATSON, John Lionel. 03/19
WATSON, John Walter. 09/17
WATSON, Kenneth Roy. 10/18
WATSON, Laurence Leslie. 01/19
WATSON, Leonard Alexander David. 08/19
WATSON, Richard Rydill. 04/18
WATTS, Frank Walter. 06/18
WATTS, John Stanley. 03/19
WATTS, Paul George. 08/19
WEBB, Harold William. 10/17
WELLS, Robert Crosby. 08/18
WELLS, William David Sandford. 10/17
WEYMAN PACK-BERESFORD, John Derek Henry. 05/18
WHALLEY, Michael Thomas. 06/19
WHEATLEY, Gordon Howard. 08/18
WHEATON, David Harry. 04/18
WHEELER, Leonie Marjorie. 05/18
WHEELER, Richard Anthony (Tony). 08/18
WHITE, Christopher Norman Hessler. 06/19
WHITE, Teresa Joan. 04/19
WHITEHEAD, Michael Hutton. 05/18
WHITESIDE, Peter George. 10/17
WHITTLE, Glen Charles. 04/18
WHITTY, Gordon William. 03/18
WICKHAM, Lionel Ralph. 12/17
WICKS, Susan Lynn. 10/17
WIDDOWSON, Charles Leonard. 01/18
WIGFIELD, Thomas Henry Paul. 06/18
WIGHTMAN, David William Lyle. 01/18
WILCOX, Jeffry Reed. 02/18
WILKINSON, David Edward Paul. 09/18
WILKINSON, John Donald. 01/18
WILKINSON, Michael Alan. 05/18
WILKS, Ernest Howard. 10/17
WILLCOX, Pauline. 08/19
WILLIAMS, David Humphrey. 03/18
WILLIAMS, David Leslie. 03/19

WILLIAMS, George Maxwell Frazer. 12/18
WILLIAMS, Hugh Marshall. 03/18
WILLIAMS, Ifan. 06/18
WILLIAMS, Thomas Bruce. 02/18
WILLIAMSON, Anthony William. 02/19
✠WILLIAMSON, Robert Kerr (Roy). 09/19
WILSON, Arthur Guy Ross. 11/18
WILSON, Charles Roy. 02/19
WILSON, Frederick John. 06/19
WILSON, Harold Marcus. 02/19
WILSON, Hilary Anne. 12/18
WILSON, John Clifford. 11/17
WODEHOUSE, Armine Boyle. 08/17
WOOD, Keith. 04/19
WOOD, Michael Edmund. 12/18
WOODHEAD, Bernice. 09/17
WOODS, David Edward. 07/19
WOODS, Philip Raymond. 04/18
WOODWARD, Arthur Robert Harry (Bob). 06/19
WORDSWORTH, Jeremy Nathaniel. 08/19
WORRALL, Frederick Rowland. 02/18
WORRALL, Frederick Rowland. 02/18
WORSDALL, John Robin. 10/18
WRAIGHT, John Radford. 03/19
WRAKE, John. 09/18
WRIGHT, John Douglas. 01/19
WRIGHT, Philip. 02/19
WRIGHT, Phillip. 09/17
WRIGHT, William Hutchinson. 03/19
WYATT, Richard Norman. 04/19
WYNN, Richard David. 10/18
YATES, Anthony Hugh. 12/18
YEOMAN, Douglas. 05/18
YEWDALL, Mary Doreen. 05/19
YIEND, Paul Martin. 09/19
YORKE, Michael Leslie. 04/19
YOULD, Guy Martin. 06/18
YOUNG, David. 02/19
YOUNG, Janette. 12/17
YOUNG, Jonathan Frederick. 01/18

MAPS

ENGLAND AND WALES

50miles
80km

Provincial Boundary
Diocesan Boundary
Cathedral City

LINCOLN

YORK

NOTTINGHAM
SOUTHWELL &

SHEFFIELD

DERBY

Ripon
DURHAM

Wakefield
Bradford

LEEDS
NEWCASTLE

MANCHESTER

CHESTER

CARLISLE

BLACKBURN
LIVERPOOL

ST ASAPH

SCOTLAND

SODOR
AND MAN

IRELAND

NORWICH

ST EDMUNDSBURY
AND IPSWICH

ELY

CHELMSFORD

CANTERBURY

ROCHESTER

ST ALBANS

LONDON

SOUTHWARK

CHICHESTER

GUILDFORD

PETERBOROUGH

LEICESTER

COVENTRY

OXFORD

WINCHESTER

PORTSMOUTH

BIRMINGHAM

LICHFIELD

WORCESTER

GLOUCESTER

BRISTOL

SALISBURY

HEREFORD

MONMOUTH

BATH AND WELLS

BANGOR

SWANSEA
AND
BRECON

LLANDAFF

EXETER

ST DAVIDS

TRURO

The Channel Islands are annexed
to the Diocese of Winchester

The Isles of Scilly are included
in the Diocese of Truro

1177

SCOTLAND

| 0 | 10 | 20 | 30 | 40 | 50 miles |
| 0 | 20 | 40 | 60 | 80 km |

Provincial Boundary

Diocesan Boundary

● Location of Cathedral

ABERDEEN AND ORKNEY

ABERDEEN AND ORKNEY

SHETLAND ISLANDS

MORAY,

ROSS

AND

CAITHNESS

● Inverness

ARGYLL

AND

THE ISLES

● Oban

ST ANDREWS,

DUNKELD

AND

DUNBLANE

Perth ●

ABERDEEN

AND

ORKNEY

Aberdeen ●

BRECHIN

● Dundee

● Glasgow

Edinburgh ●

GLASGOW

AND

GALLOWAY

EDINBURGH

IRELAND

ENGLAND

IRELAND

0 10 20 30 40 50miles

0 20 40 60 80km

〰 Provincial Boundary

⌒ Diocesan Boundary

⌒ National Boundary

• Location of Cathedral

Londonderry

CONNOR

Raphoe

DERRY AND RAPHOE

Belfast

Lisburn

ARMAGH

Dromore

Clogher

Downpatrick

Enniskillen

Armagh

DOWN
AND
DROMORE

CLOGHER

Sligo

Killala

Kilmore

KILMORE, ELPHIN
AND ARDAGH

Trim

TUAM, KILLALA
AND ACHONRY

Dublin

Tuam

MEATH AND KILDARE

Clonfert

Kildare

DUBLIN AND
GLENDALOUGH

LIMERICK, ARDFERT, AGHADOE,
KILLALOE, KILFENORA, CLONFERT,
KILMACDUAGH AND EMLY

Leighlin

Kilkenny

Ferns

Killaloe

Limerick

CASHEL, WATERFORD, LISMORE,
OSSORY, FERNS AND LEIGHLIN

Cashel

Waterford

Lismore

CORK, CLOYNE
AND ROSS

Cork

Cloyne

Ross